DIRECTORY
OF
AMERICAN
SCHOLARS

DIRECTORY
OF
AMERICAN
SCHOLARS

NINTH EDITION

VOLUME IV

PHILOSOPHY, RELIGION, & LAW

Rita C. Velázquez, Editor

FAIRFIELD UNIV. LIBRARY

JUN 1 7 1999

The Gale Group

DETROIT • SAN FRANCISCO • LONDON • BOSTON • WOODBRIDGE, CT

Rita C. Velázquez, Editor

Project Associates and Contributing Editors: Michelle
Eads, Amanda Quick

Contributing Staff: Mary Alampi, Caryn Anders, Katy Balcer, Anja
Barnard, Donna Batten, Donna Craft, Andrea DeJong, Sarah DeMar, Sheila Dow, Kim
Forster, William Harmer, Kelly Hill, LySandra Hill, Sonya Hill, Crystal Holombo, Theresa
MacFarlane, Christine Maurer, Matthew Miskelly, Jacqueline Mueckenheim, Erin Nagel,
Lynn Pearce, Terry Peck, Maureen Puhl, Donna Wood.

Contributors: Chapter House, IMPS; The Electronic
Scriptorium, Ltd.

Managing Editor: Keith Jones

Manager, Technical Support Services: Theresa Rocklin
Programmer/Analyst: Jim Edwards

Manufacturing Manager: Dorothy Maki
Senior Buyer: Wendy Blurton

Product Design Manager: Cindy Baldwin
Art Director: Eric Johnson
Graphic Artist: Gary Leach

While every effort has been made to ensure the reliability of the information presented in this publication, The Gale Group does not guarantee the accuracy of the data contained herein. Gale
accepts no payment for listing; and inclusion in the publication of any organization, agency, institution, publication, service, or individual does not imply endorsement of the editors or
publisher.

Errors brought to the attention of the publisher and verified to the satisfaction of the publisher will be
corrected in future editions.

This publication is a creative work fully protected by all applicable copyright laws, as well as by
misappropriation, trade secret, unfair competition, and other applicable laws. The authors and editors
of this work have added value to the underlying factual material herein through one or more of the
following: unique and original selection, coordination, expression, arrangement, and classification of
the information.

All rights to this publication will be vigorously defended.

Copyright (c)1999
The Gale Group
27500 Drake Rd.
Farmington Hills, MI 48331-3535

All rights reserved including the right of reproduction in whole or in part in any form.

ISBN: 0-7876-3165-5 (Volume 1)
ISBN: 0-7876-3166-3 (Volume 2)
ISBN: 0-7876-3167-1 (Volume 3)
ISBN: 0-7876-3168-X (Volume 4)
ISBN: 0-7876-3859-5 (Volume 5)
ISBN: 0-7876-3164-7 (set)
ISSN: 0070-5101
Printed in the United States of America
Published in the United States by The Gale Group

CONTENTS

PREFACE

First published in 1942 under the auspices of the American Council of Learned Societies, The Directory of American Scholars remains the foremost biographical reference to American humanities scholars. With the ninth edition, The Gale Group is continuing the tradition.

The directory is arranged for convenient use in four subject volumes: Volume I: History; Volume II: English, Speech, and Drama; Volume III: Foreign Languages, Linguistics, and Philology; Volume IV: Philosophy, Religion, and Law. Each volume of biographical listings contains a geographic index. Volume V contains an alphabetical index, a discipline index, an institutional index and a cumulative geographic index of scholars listed in the first four volumes.

The ninth edition of the Directory of American Scholars profiles more than 24,000 United States and Canadian scholars currently active in teaching, research, and publishing. The names of entrants were obtained from a variety of sources, including former entrants, academic deans, or citations in professional journals. In most cases, nominees received a questionnaire to complete, and selection for inclusion was made based on the following criteria:

1. Achievement, by reason of experience and training, of a stature in scholarly work equivalent to that associated with the doctoral degree, coupled with current activity in such work;

or

2. Achievement as evidenced by publication of scholarly works;

or

3. Attainment of a position of substantial responsibility by reason of achievement as outlined in (1) and (2).

Enhancements to the ninth edition include an index volume, simplifying the search for a particular scholar or a particular group of scholars. Indexing by discipline is sorted by primary and secondary majors, in some cases including majors that are not traditionally considered as humanities. Those individuals involved in several fields are cross-referenced into appropriate volumes.

The ninth edition of The Directory of American Scholars is produced by fully automated methods. Limitations in the printing method have made it necessary to omit most diacritics.

Individual entries can include place and year of birth, *primary discipline(s), vital statistics, education, honorary degrees, past and present professional experience, concurrent positions, *membership in international, national and regional societies, honors and awards, *research interest, *publications, and mailing address. Elements preceded by an asterisk are limited as to the number of items included. If an entrant exceeded these limitations, the editors selected the most recent information. Biographies received in the offices of The Gale Group after the editorial deadline were included in an abbreviated manner.

The editors have made every effort to include material as accurately and completely as possible within the confines of format and scope. However, the publishers do not assume and hereby disclaim any liability to any party for any loss or damage caused by errors or omissions in the Directory of American Scholars, whether such errors or omissions result from negligence, accident, or any other cause.

Thanks are expressed to those who contributed information and submitted nominations for the new edition. Many societies provided membership lists for the research process and published announcements in their journals or newsletters, and their help is appreciated.

Comments and suggestions regarding any aspect of the ninth edition are invited and should be addressed to The Editors, Directory of American Scholars, The Gale Group, 27500 Drake Road, Farmington Hills, MI 48333-3535.

ADVISORS

David M. Fahey
Professor of History
Miami University
Miami, Ohio

Patricia Hardesty
Humanities Reference/Liaison Libraran
George Mason University
Fairfax, Virginia

Stephen Karetzky
Library Director, Associate Professor
Felician College
Lodi, New Jersey

ABBREVIATIONS

AAAS American Association for the Advancement of Science
AAUP American Association of University Professors
abnorm abnormal
acad academia, academic, academica, academie, academique, academy
accad accademia
acct account, accountant, accounting
acoust acoustical, accounstic(s)
adj adjunct, adjutant
actg acting
activ activities, activity
addn addition(s), additional
AID Agency for International Development
adjust adjust
admin administration, administrative
adminr administrator(s)
admis admissions
adv advisor(s), advisory
advan advance(d), advancement
advert advertisement, advertising
aerodyn aerodynamic(s)
aeronaut aeronautic(s), aeronautical
aesthet aesthetics
affil affiliate(s), affiliation
agr agricultural, agriculture
agt agent
AFB Air Force Base
AHA American Historical Association
akad akademi, akademia
Ala Alabama
Algem algemeen, algemen
allergol allergological, allergology
allgem allgemein, allgemeine, allgemeinen
Alta Alberta
Am America, Americain, American, Americana, Americano, Amerika, Amerikaansch, Amerikaner, Amerikanisch, Amerikansk
anal analysis, analytic, analytical
analog analogue
anat anatomic, anatomical, anatomy
ann annal(s)
anthrop anthropological, anthropology
anthropom anthropometric, anthropometrical, anthropometry
antiq antiquaire(s), antiquarian, antiquary(ies), antiquities
app appoint, appointed, appointment
appl applied
appln application
approx approximate, approximately
Apr April

apt apartment(s)
arbit arbitration
arch archiv, archiva, archive(s), archivio, archivo
archaeol archaeological, archaeology
archaol archaologie, archaologisch
archeol archeological, archeologie, archeologique, archeology
archit architectural, architecture
Arg Argentina, Argentine
Ariz Arizona
Ark Arkansas
asn association
asoc asociacion
assoc(s) associate(s), associated
asst assistant
Assyriol Assyriology
astrodyn astrodynamics
astron astronomical, astronomy
astronaut astronautical, astronautics
astronr astronomer
attend attendant, attending
atty attorney
audiol audiology
Aug August
auth author(s)
AV audiovisual
ave avenue

b born
BC British Columbia
bd board
behav behavior, behavioral, behaviour, behavioural
Bibl Biblical, Biblique
bibliog bibliografia, bibliographic, bibligraphical, bibliography(ies)
bibliogr bibliographer
bibliot biblioteca, bibliotec, bibliotek, bibliotheca, bibliothek, bibliothequeca
biog biographical, biography
biol biological, biology
bk(s) books
bldg building
blvd boulevard
bol boletim, boletin
boll bollettino
bor borough
bot botanical, botany
br branch
Brit Britain, British
Bro(s) Brother(s)
bull bulletin

bur bureau
bus business
BWI British West Indies

c children
Calif California
Can Canada, Canadian, Canadien, Canadienne
cand candidate
cartog cartografic, cartographical, cartography
cartogra cartographer
Cath Catholic, Catholique
CBS Columbia Broadcasting System
cent central
Cent Am Central America
cert certificat, certificate, certified
chap chapter
chem chermical, chemistry
chg charge
chemn chairman
Cie Compagnie
cient cientifica, cientifico
class classical
clin(s) clinic(s)
Co Companies, Company, County
coauth coauth
co-dir co-director
co-ed co-editor
co-educ co-educational
col(s) colegio, college(s), collegiate
collab collaboration, collaborative, collaborating, collaborator
Colo Colorado
Comdr Commander
com commerce, commercial
commun communication(s)
comn(s) commission(s)
comnr commissioner
comp comparative, comparee
compos composition(s)
comput computer, computing
comt committee
conf conference
cong congress
Conn Connecticut
conserv conservacion, conservation, conservatoire, conservatory
consol consolidated, consolidation
const constitution, constitutional
construct construction
consult consultant, consulting
contemp contemporary
contrib contribute, contribution

contribur contributor
conv convention
coop cooperation, cooperative
coord coordinating, coordination
coordr coordinator
corresp corresponding
Corp Corporation
coun council, counsel, counseling
counr councillor, counselor
criminol criminology
Ct Court
ctr center
cult cultra, cultural, culturale, culture
cur curator
curric curriculum
cybernet cybernetics
CZ Canal Zone
Czeck Czechoslovakia

DC District of Columbia
Dec December
Del Delaware
deleg delegate, delegations
demog demographic, demography
demonstr demonstrator
dent dental, dentistry
dep deputy
dept department
Deut Deutsch, Deutschland
develop development
diag diagnosis, diagnostic
dialectol dialectology
dig digest
dipl diploma, diploma, diplomate, diplome
dir director(s), directory
   directory
Diss Abstr Dissertation Abstracts
dist district
distrib distributive
distribr distributors
div division, divorced
doc document, documentation
Dom Dominion
Dr Doctor, Drive
Drs Doctroandus

e east
ecol ecological, ecology
econ economic(s), economical, economy
ed edicion, edition, editor, editorial, edizione
educ education, educational
educr educator(s)
Egyptol Egyptology
elec electric, electrical, electricity
   electrical
elem elementary
emer emeriti, emeritus
encour encouragement
encycl encyclopedia
employ employment
Eng England
environ environment, environmental
EPDA Education Professions Development Act
equip equipment
ERIC Educational Resources Information Center
ESEA Elementary & Secondary Education Act
espec especially
estab established, establishment
estud estudante, estudas, estudianet, estudio(s), estudo(s)
ethnog ethnographical, ethnography
ethnol ethnological, ethnology
Europ European
eval evaluation
evangel evangelical
eve evening
exam examination

examr examiner
except exceptional
exec executive(s)
exeg exegesis(es), exegetic, exegetical, exegetics
exhib exhibition(s)
exp experiment, experimental, experimentation
exped expedition(s)
explor exploration(s)
expos exposition
exten extension

fac faculties, faculty
facil facilities, facility
Feb February
fed federal
fedn federation
fel(s) fellow(s), fellowship(s)
filol filologia, filologico
filos filosofia, filosofico
Fla Florida
FLES Foreign Languages in the Elementary Schools
for foreign
forsch forschung, forschungen
found foundation
Fr Francais(s), French
Ft Fort

Ga Georgia
gen general, generale
geneal genealogical, genealogy
genoot genootschap
geod geodesy, geodetic
geog geografia, geografico, geographer(s), geographic, geographie, geographical, geography
geogr geographer
geol geologic, geological, geology
geophys geophysical
Ger German, Germanic, Germanisch, Germany
Ges gesellschaft
gov governing, governors
govt government
grad graduate
Gr Brit Great Britain
guid guidance
gym gymnasium

handbk(s) handbooks
Hawaii
Hisp Hispanic, Hispanico, Hispano
hist historie, historia, historial, historic, historica, historical, historique, historische, history
histol histology, histological
Hoshsch Hoshschule
hon honorable, honorary
hosp(s) hospital(s)
hq headquarters
HumRRO Human Resources Research Office
hwy highway

Ill Illinois
illum illuminating, illumination
illus illustrate, illustration
illusr illustrator
imp imperial
improv improvement
Inc Incorporated
incl include, included, includes, including
Ind Indiana
indust(s) industrial, industry(ies)
infor information
inst institut, institute(s), institution(s), instituto
instnl institutional, institutionalized

instr instruction, instructor(s)
instruct instructional
int internacional, international, internazionale
intel intelligence
introd introduction
invest investigacion, investiganda, investigation, investigative
investr investigator
ist istituto
Ital Italia, Italian, Italiana, Italiano, Italica, Italien, Italienisch, Italienne, Italy

J Journal
Jan January
jour journal, journalism
jr junior
jurisp jurisprudence
juv juvenile(s)

Kans Kansas
Koninki koninklijk
Ky Kentucky

La Louisiana
lab laboratorie, laboratorio, laboratorium, laboratory(ies)
lang language(s)
lect lecture(s)
lectr lecturer
legis legislacion, legislatief, legislation, legislative, legislativo, legislature, legislazione
lett letter(s), lettera, letteraria, letterature, lettere
lib liberal
libr libary(ies), librerio
librn librarian(s)
lic license, lecencia
ling linguistic(s), linguistica, linguistique
lit liteary, literatur, literatura, literature, littera, literature
Ltd Limited

m married
mach machine(s), machinery
mag magazine
Man Manitoba
Mar March
Mariol Mariological, Mariology
Mass Massachusetts
mat matematica, matematiche, matematico, matematik
math mathematics, mathematical, mathematics, mathematik, mathematique(s), mathematisch
Md Maryland
mech mechanical
med medical, medicine
Mediter Mediterranean
mem member, memoirs, memorial
ment mental, mentally
metrop metropolitan
Mex Mexican, Mexicano, Mexico
mfg manufacturing
mfr manufacture, manufacturer
mgr manager(s)
mgt management
Mich Michigan
mid middle
mil military
Minn Minnesota
Miss Mississippi
mitt mitteilung
mkt market, marketing
MLA Modern Language Association of America

Mo Missouri
mod modern,moderna, moderne, moderno
monatsh monatsheft(e)
monatsschr monatsschrift
monogr monograph
Mont Montana
morphol morphologica, morphologie, morphology
mt mount, mountain(s)
munic municipal
mus museum(s)
musicol musicological, musicology

n north
nac nacional
NASA National Aeronautics & Space Administration
nat nationaal, national, nationale, nationalis, naturalized
NATO North Atlantic Treaty Organization
naz nazionale
NB New Brunswick
NC North Carolina
MCTE National Council of Teachers of English
NDak North Dakota
NDEA National Defense Education Act
NEA National Education Association
Nebr Nebraska
Ned Nederland, Nederlandsch
Nev Nevada
Neth Netherlands
Nfld Newfoundland
NH New Hampshire
NJ New Jersey
NMex New Mexico
no number
nonres nonresident
norm normal, normale
Norweg Norwegian
Nov November
NS Nova Scotia
NSW New South Wales
NT Northwest Territories
numis numismatic, numismatico, numismatique
NY New York
NZ New Zealand

occas occasional
occup occupation, occupational
Oct October
Ohio
OEEC Organization for European Economic Cooperation
off office, officer(s), official(s)
Okla Oklahoma
Ont Ontario
oper operation(s), operational, operative
ord ordnance
Ore Oregon
orgn organization, organizational
orient oriental, orientale, orientalist, orientalia
ornithol ornithological, ornithology

Pa Pennsylvania
Pac Pacific
paleontol paleontological, paleontology
PanAm Pan American
pedag pedagogia, pedagogic, pedagogical, pedagogico, pedagogoie, pedagogik, pedagogique, pedagogy
Pei Prince Edward Island
penol penological, penology
phenomenol phenomenological, phenomenologie, phenomenology
philol philologica, philological, philologie, philologisch,

philology
philos philosophia, philosophic, philosophical, philosophie, philosophique, philosophisch, philosophical, philosohpy, philosozophia
photog photographic, photography
photogr photographer(s)
phys physical
pkwy parkway
pl place
polit politica, political, politicas, politico, politics,
politek, politike, politique, politsch, politisk
polytech polytechnic
pop population
Pontif Pontifical
Port Portugal, Portuguese
postgrad postgraduate
PR Puerto Rico
pract practice
prehist prehistoric
prep preparation, preparatory
pres president
Presby Presbyterian
preserv preservation
prev prevention, preventive
prin principal(s)
prob problem(s)
probtn probation
proc proceeding
prod production
prof professional, professor, professorial
prog program(s), programmed, programming
proj project, projective
prom promotion
prov province, provincial
psychiat psychiatria, psychiatric, psychiatrica, psychiatrie, psychiatrique, psychiatrisch, psychiatry
psychol psychological
pt point
pub pub, publique
publ publication(s), published, publisher(s), publishing
pvt private

qm quartermaster
quad quaderni
qual qualitative, quality
quart quarterly
Que Quebec

rd road
RD Rural Delivery, Rural Free Delivery Rural Free Delivery
rec record(s), recording
rech recherche
redevelop redevelopment
ref reference
regist register, registered, registration
registr registrar
rehabil rehabilitation
rel(s) relacion, relation(s), relative, relazione
relig religion, religious
rep representative
repub republic
req requirement(s)
res research, reserve
rev review, revised, revista, revue
rhet rhetoric, rhetorical
RI Rhode Island
Rt Right
Rte Route
Russ Russian
rwy railway

s south
SAfrica South Africa

SAm South America, South American
Sask Saskatchewan
SC South Carolina
Scand Scandinavian
sch(s) school(s)
scholar scholarship
sci science(s), scientia, scientific, scientifico, scientifique, scienza
SDak South Dakota
SEATO Southeast Asia Treaty Organization
sec secondary
sect section
secy secretary
sem seminaire, seminar, seminario, seminary
sen senator, sneatorial
Sept September
ser serial, series
serv service(s)
soc social, sociedad, sociedade, societa, societas, societate, societe, societet, society(ies)
soc sci social science(s)
sociol sociological, sociology
Span Spanish
spec special
sq square
sr senior
sr sister
St Saint, Street
sta station
statist statistical, statistics
Ste Sainte, Suite
struct structural, structure(s)
subcomt subcommittee
subj subject
substa substa
super superieur, superior, superiore
suppl supplement, supplementary
supt superintendent
supv supervising, supervision
supvr supervisor
supvry supervisory
surg surgical, surgery
surv survey
Swed Swedish
Switz Switzerland
symp symposium
syst system, systematic

tech technic(s), technica, technical, technicky, techniczny, techniek, technik, technika, technikum, technique, technisch
technol technologic, technological, technologicke, technologico, technologiczny, technologie, technologika, technologique, technologisch, technology
tecnol tecnologia, tecnologica, technologico
tel telegraph(s), telephone
temp temporary
Tenn Tennessee
Terr Terrace
teol teologia, teologico
Tex Texas
textbk textbook(s)
theol theological, theologie, theologique, theologisch, theology
theoret theoretic(al)
ther therapy
trans transactions
transp transportation
transl translation, translator(s)
treas treasurer, treasury
trop tropical
TV television

twp township

u und
UAR United Arab Republic
UK United Kingdom
UN United Nations
unemploy unemployment
UNESCO United Nations Educational,
Scientific & Cultural
Organization
UNICEF United Nations Children's Fund
univ(s) universidad, universite,
university(ies)
UNRRA United Nations Relief &
Rehabilitation Administration
UNRWA United Nations Relief & Works
Agency
USA United States of America
US United States

USPHS United States Public Health
Service
USSR Union of Soviet Socialist Republics
Utah

Va Virginia
var various
veg vegetable(s), vegetation
ver vereeniging, verein, vereingt,
vereinigung
vet veteran, veterinarian, veterinary
VI Virgin Islands
vis visiting
voc vocational
vocab vocabulary
vol(s) volume(s), voluntary, volunteer(s)
vchmn vice chairman
vpres vice president
Vt Vermont

w west
Wash Washington
wetensch wetenschappelijk, wetenschappen
WHO World Health Organization
WI West Indies
wid widow, widowed, widower
Wis Wisconsin
wiss wissenschaft(en), wissenschaftliche(e)
WVa West Virginia
Wyo Wyoming

yearbk yearbook(s)
YMCA Young Men's Christian Association
YMHA Young Men's Hebrew Association
YWCA Young Women's Christian Associa-
tion
YWHA Young Women's Hebrew Association

z zeitschrift

Biographies

A

AAGAARD-MOGENSEN, LARS
PERSONAL Born 03/30/1944, Randers, Denmark, m, 1967, 1 child **DISCIPLINE** PHILOSOPHY **EDUCATION** Temple Univ, 72-74; State Univ of NY Bockport, MA, philos, 71; Aarhos Univ, Mag art, philos, 72, PhD, philos aesthetics, 76. **CAREER** Aarhus Univ, 65-70; Copenhagen Univ, 78; Hellenic Intl Sch, Athens, 78-79; Gent State Univ, 79-80; Wash Univ, St. Louis, 80-82; Harvard Univ Summer Sch, 81; St. Cloud State Univ, 82-83; Rochester Inst of Tech, 83-87; Wassard Co, 87-; FIT, 93; Sch of Visual Arts, NY, 94-; Univ Antioch, 98-. **HONORS AND AWARDS** Younger Creative and Sci Writers' Award, Ministry of Culture, Copenhagen, 77/78; Danish Res Coun for the Humanities; Humanistic Facul, Aarhus Univ; dir, Project Art in Culture, Belgium, 78-80; Phi Kappa Phi, 83; Rector's Medal, Helsinki Univ, 85. **SELECTED PUBLICATIONS** Auth, Hartnack's Hegel's Logic, Indianapolis, 98; auth, Real Art, Gent, 94; auth, The Idea of the Museum, NY, 88; auth, Worldmakings' Ways, Gent, 87; auth, Text, Literature and Aesthetics, Amsterdam, 86; auth, Art in Culture I-III, Gent, 85; auth, Our Art, Gent, 83; auth, Contemporary Aesthetics in Scandinavia, Lund, 80; auth, Aestetisk kultur, Copenhagen, 79; auth, The JAAC 35 year Index, ASA Cleveland, 79; auth, Om Tolerance, Humanistica, 78; auth, Culture and Art, Humanities Press Inc, 76. **CONTACT ADDRESS** 3757 Main St., Burdett, NY, 14818-9631.

AAGESON, JAMES W.
PERSONAL Born 11/24/1947, Havre, MT, m, 1970, 3 children **DISCIPLINE** NEW TESTAMENT STUDIES; HISTORY OF EARLY CHRISTIANITY **EDUCATION** MDiv, 76, MTh, 77, PhD, 84. **CAREER** Prof Relig, Concordia,Col. **MEMBERSHIPS** Soc Bibl Lit; Cath Bibl Asn **RESEARCH** Pauline Studies; New Testament Socio-linguistics; Jewish-Christian relations. **SELECTED PUBLICATIONS** Auth, Written Also for Our Sake: Paul and the Art of Biblical Interpretation, John Knox Press, 93; Paul's Gospel and the Language of Control: A Summary, Teaching at Concordia, 93; Judaizing and Lectionary, Early Jewish, Anchor Bible Dictionary; Typology, Correspondence, and the Application of Scripture in Romans 9-11, The Pauline Writings: A Sheffield Reader, Sheffield Acad Press, 95; Control in Pauline Language and Culture: A Study of Rom 6; New Testament Studies, 96; A Theoretical Context for Understanding I Cor 1:18-2:16, Teaching at Concordia, 96; 2 Timothy and Its Theology: In Search of a Theological Pattern, Soc of Bibl Lit Sem Papers, 97. **CONTACT ADDRESS** 901 S Eight St., Moorhead, MN, 56562. **EMAIL** aageson@cord.edu

AARONS, LESLIE ANN
PERSONAL Born 06/18/1964, New York, NY **DISCIPLINE** PHILOSOPHY **EDUCATION** Duquesne Univ, MA, 87, PhD, 95. **CAREER** Lectr, Calif State Univ, Bakersfield, 97-98. **HONORS AND AWARDS** NEH summer grant, 96. **MEMBERSHIPS** APA; SWIP. **RESEARCH** Gender studies; history of Western civilization. **CONTACT ADDRESS** Dept of Philosophy, California State Univ, Bakersfield, 8117 Willowglen Dr, Bakersfield, CA, 93311. **EMAIL** dr_aarons@yahoo.com

ABBOTT, W.R.
DISCIPLINE PHILOSOPHY **EDUCATION** Ohio State Univ, PhD, 66. **SELECTED PUBLICATIONS** Auth, pub(s) on epistemology, philosophy of mind, Spinoza, rationalists, and philosophy of language. **CONTACT ADDRESS** Dept of Philosophy, Waterloo Univ, 200 University Ave W, Waterloo, ON, N2L 3G1. **EMAIL** wrabbott@uwaterloo.ca

ABDUL-MASIH, MARGUERITE
PERSONAL Born 11/14/1956, Kuwait **DISCIPLINE** THEOLOGY **EDUCATION** Bryn Mawr Coll, BA, 78; Johns Hopkins Univ, MA, 81, PhD, 85; Univ St Michael's Coll, Mdiv, 89, PhD, 95; Regis Coll, STL, 95. **CAREER** Asst Prof, 96-, St Mary's Univ. **MEMBERSHIPS** CTSA, AAR, Sabul ecumenical center for peace & justice in Palestine. **RESEARCH** Religion & science, inter-regional dialogue, peace in middle east. **SELECTED PUBLICATIONS** Auth, Experience and Christology in the Thoughts of Haus Frie and Edward Schillebeecks, Can Corp for the Study of Relig, forthcoming. **CONTACT ADDRESS** 2074 Robie St, #2205, Halifax, NS, B3K 5L3. **EMAIL** magi.abdul-masih@stmarys.ca

ABE, NOBUHIKO
PERSONAL Born 10/26/1941, Utsunomiya, Japan, m, 1978, 1 child **DISCIPLINE** THEOLOGY **EDUCATION** Northwst Univ, PhD, 72; Harvard Univ, ThD, 93 **CAREER** Res Assoc, 93-97, Harvard Div Sch **MEMBERSHIPS** Am Acad of Relig; Assoc of Asian Studies **RESEARCH** Constructive Theology; Comparative Theology **SELECTED PUBLICATIONS** Rev, The Social Self in Zen and American Pragmatism, The Eastern Budhist, 97 **CONTACT ADDRESS** 25 Grozier Rd, Cambridge, MA, 02138.

ABEGG G., MARTIN
PERSONAL Born 03/06/1950, Peoria, IL, m, 1975, 2 children **DISCIPLINE** RELIGIOUS STUDIES **EDUCATION** Bradley Univ, BS, 72; Northwestern Baptist Sem, MDiv, 83; Hebrew Univ, Jerusalem, MA Studies, 84-87; Hebrew Union Coll, MA, 90, PhD, 92. **CAREER** Instr, 82-84, Northwestern Bap Sem; res Fel, 88-91, Hebrew Union Coll; vis Lectr, 90-91, Univ of Cincinnati; co-Dir Dead Sea Scrolls Project, 91-96, Institute of Mediterranean Studies & Biblical Arch Stud; Assoc Prof, 92-95, Grace Theo Sem, IL; co-Dir, 95-, Dead Sea Scrolls Institute, Trinity Western Univ; Asst Prof, Religious Studies, 95-, Trinity Western Univ, Langley BC. **HONORS AND AWARDS** Who's Who in Biblical Studies & Archaeology. **MEMBERSHIPS** BAS **RESEARCH** Dead Sea Scrolls **SELECTED PUBLICATIONS** Co-auth, The Fragmentary Remains of 11QTorah Temple Scroll, 11QTb, 11QTc and 4QparaTorah, in: Hebrew Union College Annual, 91; auth, Messianic Hope and 4Q285, A Reassessment, in: J of Bib Lit, 94; The Messiah at Qumran, Are We Still Seeing Double? in: Dead Sea Discoveries 2, 95; co-auth, The Dead Sea Scrolls, A New Translation, San Fran, HarperCollins, 96; Qumran and Exile, in: Exile Old Testament, Jewish and Christian Conceptions, ed, J Scott, Leiden, E J Brill, 97; review, The Complete Dead Sea Scrolls in English, by Geza Vermes, in: J of Semitic Studies, forthcoming. **CONTACT ADDRESS** 2277 Olympic Place, Abbotsford, BC, V2Y 1Y1. **EMAIL** abegg@twu.ca

ABEL, DONALD C.
PERSONAL Born 06/26/1948, Pomeroy, WA, m, 1988 **DISCIPLINE** PHILOSOPHY **EDUCATION** Gonzaga Univ, BA, 71; Tulane Univ, MA, 73; St Michael's Inst, PhL, 75; Loyola Univ Chicago, MD, 79; Northwest Univ, PhD, 83. **CAREER** Instr, Gonzaga Univ, 73-75; instr, Northwest Univ, 81-83; ed, Great Books Found, 83-84; asst prof, St Norbert Coll, 84-91; assoc prof, Norbert Coll, 91-. **HONORS AND AWARDS** Univ Fel, Northwest Univ, 78-79; Diss Year Fel, Northwest Univ, 81; Sasser Young prof Award, 86; Ledvna Award for Excellence in Teaching, 88; King Distinguished Scholar Award, 93. **MEMBERSHIPS** Am Philos Asn; Am Cath Philos Asn; Soc for Ancient Greek Philos; Soc for Philos and Psychol. **RESEARCH** Philosophy of human nature; Ethics; Medieval Philos. **SELECTED PUBLICATIONS** Auth, Freud on Instinct and Morality, 89; ed, Theories of Human Nature, 93; Fifty Readings in Philosophy, 94; Discourses: A Database of Philosophy Read-

ings. 94; Human Nature, Philos of educ, An Encycl, 96; Aquinas and Freud on the Human Soul, Aquinas on Mind and Intellect, 96. **CONTACT ADDRESS** St Norbert Col, 100 Grant St, De Pere, WI, 54115. **EMAIL** abeldc@sncac.snc.edu

ABELA, PAUL R.
DISCIPLINE PHILOSOPHY **EDUCATION** Univ Toronto, BA; Queen's Univ, Ont; Oxford Univ, Balliol Col, PhD. **CAREER** Asst prof, Loyola Univ, 96-; 2yr postdr res fel, Univ Toronto. **RESEARCH** Kant; early modern philosophy; metaphysics; epistemology. **SELECTED PUBLICATIONS** Articles in, Idealistic Stud & Philos Quart. **CONTACT ADDRESS** Dept of Philosophy, Loyola Univ, Chicago, 820 N. Michigan Ave., Chicago, IL, 60611.

ABELE, ROBERT P.
PERSONAL Born 03/20/1955, Dayton, OH **DISCIPLINE** PHILOSOPHY **EDUCATION** Univ Dayton, BA, 76; Mt St Mary, MDiv, 83; Athenaeum of Ohio, MA, 85; Marquette Univ, PhD, 95. **CAREER** Lectr, philos, 88-90, 91-94, adj fac, 95, Marquette Univ; lectr philos, Carthage Col, 91; adj fac, Milwaukee Area Tech Col, 95; adj fac, Oakton Col, 96; adj fac, Col of DuPage, 96; asst prof, Silver Lake Col, 96-. **HONORS AND AWARDS** Scholar, Archdiocese of Cincinnati, 79-82, Marquette Univ, 85-92; fac development award, 97-98. **MEMBERSHIPS** C G Jung Inst; Concerned Philos for Peace; APA; Joseph Campbell Found; Greenpeace. **SELECTED PUBLICATIONS** Auth, Moral Questions on the Bombing of Libya, Milwaukee Sentinel, 96; auth, The Just War Theory and the Persian Gulf War, Milwaukee J, 91. **CONTACT ADDRESS** 3912 Memorial Dr, Two Rivers, WI, 54212.

ABELL, JENNIE
DISCIPLINE LAW **EDUCATION** Queen's Univ, BA; Univ Saskatchewan, LLB; York Univ, LLM. **CAREER** Assoc prof, 88-. **RESEARCH** Criminal law and procedure; law, poverty and social change; feminist theory and law; women and human rights: international perspectives. **SELECTED PUBLICATIONS** Auth, Criminal Law and Procedure: Cases, Context and Critique and Criminal Law; Procedure: Proof, Defences and Beyond; pubs on legal aid, feminist theory, women and violence, and human rights. **CONTACT ADDRESS** Fac Common Law, Univ Ottawa, 550 Cumberland St, PO Box 450, Ottawa, ON, K1N 6N5.

ABRAHAM, GERALD
DISCIPLINE CRIMINAL LAW, CRIMINAL PROCEDURE, FAMILY LAW, CHILDREN AND THE LAW **EDUCATION** NY Univ, AB, 51; NY Univ Sch Law, JD, 53 **CAREER** Prof; fac, Villanova Univ, 62-; aasoc dean acad aff, 77-92; clerked for, Honorable Charles Froessel, NY Ct Appeals; past tchg fel, Harvard Univ Law Sch; taught at, Duquesne Law Sch, Univ Gottingen, Ger. **MEMBERSHIPS** Past pres, Mental Health Asn Southwestern Pa; chem, Chester Co Mental Health Retardation Bd & chp, Haverford State Hosp Patients Rights Rev Comt. **RESEARCH** Family law, children and the law. **SELECTED PUBLICATIONS** Coauth, Amram's Pennsylvania Practice, 96. **CONTACT ADDRESS** Law School, Villanova Univ, 800 Lancaster Ave, Villanova, PA, 19085-1692. **EMAIL** abraham@law.vill.edu

ABRAHAMSEN, VALERIE
PERSONAL Born 10/05/1954, Norwood, MA **DISCIPLINE** RELIGION **EDUCATION** Univ S Carolina, BA, 75; Harvard Div Sch, MTS, 79, ThD, 86. **CAREER** Inst, 98-; Lasell College; Registrar, 93-98 MGH Inst Hlth Professions; adj fac, 95-, Bunker Hill Comm College; Ethics/Prof admin, 86-89, Harvard Univ. **HONORS AND AWARDS** Who's Who in

Biblical Studies and Archaeol; Who's Who of Amer Women. **MEMBERSHIPS** SBL; AAR; AIA; AACRAO. **RESEARCH** Women in Early Christianity; Women in Greco-Roman antiquity; New Testament archaeology; Philippi. **SELECTED PUBLICATIONS** Auth, Jesus According to Barbara Walker, J Higher Criticism, in press; Women in the Proseuche at Philippi, Women in Scripture: A Dictionary of Named and Unnamed Women in the Hebrew Bible, Apocrypha, and New Testament, Houghton-Mifflin Co, in press; Burials from Greek Macedonia: Possible Evidence for Same-Sex Committed Relationships in Early Christianity, J Higher Criticism, 97; Art Ancient, Historical Encyc of World Slavery, ed, Junius P Rodriguez, Santa Barbara, ABC-CLIO, 97; Essays in Honor of Marija Gimbutas: A Response, J Feminist studies in Religion, 97; The Goddess and Healing: Nursing's Heritage from Antiquity, J Holistic Nursing, 97; Women and Worship at Philippi: Diana/Artemis and Other Cults in the Early Christian Era, Portland ME, Astarte Shell Press, 95. **CONTACT ADDRESS** 47 Seaverns Ave #1R, Jamaica Plain, MA, 02130. **EMAIL** vabrahamse@aol.com

ABRAMSON, HAROLD I.
DISCIPLINE LAW **EDUCATION** Univ MI, BBA, 71; Syracuse Univ, JD, 74; Harvard Univ, MPA, 82, LLM, 83. **CAREER** Prof Law, Touro Col; spec coun and dir, Utility Intervention Off of the NY State Consumer Protection Bd; staff atty, Monroe County Legal Assistance Corp; arbitrator, Compulsory Arbitration Prog, Rochester, NY; dir, summer law prog, Moscow State Univ. **MEMBERSHIPS** Ch, NY State Bar Asn Comt on Alternative Dispute Resolution. **SELECTED PUBLICATIONS** Written a number of articles on administrative law, government regulation, and dispute resolution. **CONTACT ADDRESS** Touro Col, Brooklyn, NY, 11230. **EMAIL** HalA@tourolaw.edu

ABU-NIMER, MOHAMMED
DISCIPLINE PEACE AND CONFLICT RESOLUTION **EDUCATION** George Mason Univ, PhD. **CAREER** Prof, Am Univ. **RESEARCH** Research on conflict resolution and dialogue for peace among Palestinians and Jews in Israel; Israeli-Palestinian conflict **SELECTED PUBLICATIONS** Articles, Jour Peace & Changes, Am Jour Econ & Sociol. **CONTACT ADDRESS** American Univ, 4400 Massachusetts Ave, Washington, DC, 20016.

ACAMPORA, CHRISTA DAVIS
DISCIPLINE PHILOSOPHY **EDUCATION** Emory Univ, PhD, 97; MA, 95; Hollins Col, BA, 90. **CAREER** Asst prof Philos, Univ Maine, present. **MEMBERSHIPS** Amer Philos Assoc; Soc for Philos Sport; N Amer Niezsche Soc; Soc of Women in Philos. **RESEARCH** 19th & 20th Century Continental Philosophy. **SELECTED PUBLICATIONS** Re/Introducting Nietzsche's Homer's Contest: A New Translation with Notes and Commentary, in Nietzscheana, 95. **CONTACT ADDRESS** Dept of Philosophy, Maine Univ, Orono, ME, 04469-5776. **EMAIL** christa.acampora@umit.maine.edu

ACHINSTEIN, PETER
PERSONAL Born 06/30/1935, New York, NY, 3 children **DISCIPLINE** PHILOSOPHY **EDUCATION** Harvard Univ, AB, 56, AM, 58, PhD, 61. **CAREER** Asst prof, Univ Iowa, 61-62; from asst prof to assoc prof, 62-68, prof philos, Johns Hopkins Univ, 68; vis prof, Mass Inst Technol, 65-66; Guggenheim fel, 66; mem US nat comt, Int Union Hist & Philos Sci, 68-72; adv panel, div hist & philos sci, Nat Sci Found, 68-69 & 79-81; vis prof grad center, City Univ New York, 73; mem Steering Comt of Prog Comt 6th Int Cong Logic, Methodology, & Philos of Sci, 76-; Lady Davis vis prof, Hebrew Univ, Jerusalem, 76. **HONORS AND AWARDS** Lakatos Award, 93. **MEMBERSHIPS** Am Philos Assn; Philos Sci Assn. **RESEARCH** Philosophy of science. **SELECTED PUBLICATIONS** Auth, The Problem of Theoretical Terms, 65; auth, Concepts of Science, 68; coed, The Legacy of Logical Positivism, Johns Hopkins Univ, 69; auth, Law and Explanation, Oxford Univ, 71; art, What is an Explanation?, Am Philos Quart, 1/77; art, Concepts of Evidence, Mind, 1/78; auth, The Nature of Explanation, Oxford Univ Press, 82; auth, Particles and Waves, Oxford University Press, 91. **CONTACT ADDRESS** Dept of Philosophy, Johns Hopkins Univ, 3400 N Charles St, Baltimore, MD, 21218-2680. **EMAIL** peter.achinstein@jhr.edu

ACHTEMEIER, PAUL JOHN
PERSONAL Born 09/03/1927, Lincoln, NE, m, 1952, 2 children **DISCIPLINE** NEW TESTAMENT **EDUCATION** Elmhurst Col, AB, 49; Union Theol Sem(NY), BD, 52, ThD(New Testament), 58. **CAREER** Instr Greek & Bibl lit, Elmhurst Col, 56-57; asst prof New Testament, Lancaster Theol Sem, 57-59, assoc prof, 59-61, prof, 61-73; Prof New Testament, Union Theol Sem, Va, 73, Bk rev ed, Theol & Life, 58-65; recording secy, NAm Area Coun, World Alliance Reformed & Presby Churches, 63-70; tutor, grad sch ecumenical studies, World Coun Churches, Univ Geneva, 63-64; vis prof, Pittsburgh Theol Sem, 67-68; participant, Int Greek New Testament Proj, 68-69; vis prof New Testament, Lutheran Theol Sem, Gettysburg, 70-72; sem assoc, Columbia Univ, 72-; mem, Roman Cath-Reformed & Presbyterian Bilateral Consult, 72-80; assoc ed, Interpretation, Cath Bibl Quart. **MEMBERSHIPS** Soc Bibl Lit (exec secy, 77-80); Cath Bibl Asn; Soc Studies New Testament; Am Theol Soc; Am Coun Learned Soc. **RESEARCH** Gospel of Mark; interpretation of the New Testament; form and function of miracle stories in hellenistic world. **SELECTED PUBLICATIONS** Coauth, To save all people, United Church, 67; auth, An Introduction to the New Hermeneutic, Westminster, 69; Toward the isolation of Pre-Markan Miracle Catenae, 72, J Bibl Lit; Gospel miracle tradition and the Divine Man, interpretation, 72; coauth & ed, Epiphany, Fortress, 73; Mark, Fortress, 75; An Invitation to Mark, Doubleday, 78; The Inspiration of Scripture, Westminster, 80; A Rereading of Romans, Justice, Jews, and Gentiles, Interpretation, A Journal of Bible and Theology, Vol 0050, 96. **CONTACT ADDRESS** Union Theol Sem, 3401 Brook Rd, Richmond, VA, 23227.

ACHTENBERG, DEBORAH
DISCIPLINE HISTORY OF PHILOSOPHY, ANCIENT PHILOSOPHY **EDUCATION** New Schl for Soc Res, PhD, 82. **CAREER** Assoc prof, Univ Nev, Reno. **RESEARCH** Aristotle; ethics; political philosophy. **SELECTED PUBLICATIONS** Essays on Aristotle's ethics were recently published in Crossroads of Norm and Nature: Essays on Aristotle's 'Ethics' and 'Metaphysics' (Rowman & Littlefield Press), Essays in Ancient Greek Philosophy IV (SUNY) and Feminism and Ancient Philosophy (Routledge). **CONTACT ADDRESS** Univ Nev, Reno, Reno, NV, 89557. **EMAIL** achten@scs.unr.edu

ACKERMAN, FELICIA
DISCIPLINE PHILOSOPHY **EDUCATION** Cornell Univ, AB 68; Univ Michigan, PhD 76. **CAREER** Brown Univ, asst to full prof, 74 to 98-; UCLA, vis asst prof 76; Univ St. Andrews, vis hon lectr, 81; Hebrew Univ Jerusalem, sr Fulbright lecrt, 85. **HONORS AND AWARDS** Fulbright fel; NEH fel; O.Henry Awd **MEMBERSHIPS** APA; MLA; NCTE; IAS **RESEARCH** Philo lit, lang; methodology of analytic philo; med ethics. **SELECTED PUBLICATIONS** Auth, Flourish Your Heart in this World, in: M. Nussbaum and C. Sunstein, eds, Clones and Clones: Facts and Fantasies About Human Cloning, Norton, 98; Flourish Your Heart in this World: Action Emotion and Reason in: Malory's Le Morte D'Arthur, Midwest Stud Philo, 98; Assisted Suicide, Terminal Illness, Severe Disability and the Double Standard, in: M P Baffin et al, eds, Physician Assisted Suicide: Expanding the Debate, Routledge, 98; Buddies, Commentary, 94. **CONTACT ADDRESS** Dept of Philosophy, Brown Univ, Providence, RI, 02912.

ACKERMAN, JAMES S.
DISCIPLINE RELIGIOUS STUDIES **EDUCATION** Harvard Univ, PhD, 66. **CAREER** Prof emer. **RESEARCH** Religion and literature of Israel and the Ancient Near East; Bible as literature. **SELECTED PUBLICATIONS** Auth, pubs on monograph on the wilderness narratives in the Pentateuch. **CONTACT ADDRESS** Dept of Religious Studies, Indiana Univ, Bloomington, 300 N Jordan Ave, Bloomington, IN, 47405.

ACKERMAN, ROBERT M.
DISCIPLINE ALTERNATIVE DISPUTE RESOLUTION, LEGAL HISTORY, LEGAL PROFESSION **EDUCATION** Colgate Univ, BA, 73; Harvard Univ, JD, 76. **CAREER** Assoc, Holme, Roberts & Owen, Denver, Colo, 76-80; asst profr, Dickinson Univ, 80- 83; assoc prof, 83-85; prof, 85; vis lectr, Leicester Polytechnic Sch Law, Eng, 87; vis prof, Pa State Univ, 89; vis prof, Univ Vienna, 94; dean-. **MEMBERSHIPS** Mem, Phi Beta Kappa; Soc Prof(s) in Dispute Resolution. **SELECTED PUBLICATIONS** Auth, Instructor's Manual with Simulation and Problem Materials to Accompany Riskin Westbrook's Dispute Resolution and Lawyers. **CONTACT ADDRESS** Sch of Law, Willamette Univ, 900 State St, Salem, OR, 97301. **EMAIL** rackerma@willamette.edu

ACKLEY, JOHN B.
PERSONAL Born 09/24/1948, Dayton, OH, m, 1974 **DISCIPLINE** SYSTEMATIC THEOLOGY **EDUCATION** Wittenberg Univ, BA, 71; Lutheran Theol Sem, MDiv, 75; Catholic Univ Amer, PhD, 88. **CAREER** St Timothy's Episcopal Church VA, Assoc Mus Dir, 88-; Hospice N VA, Chaplain's Asst, 87-90; Church Good Shep VA, Dir music organ, 81-85; Emanuel Lutheran Church, Dir mus organ, 75-81. **HONORS AND AWARDS** Lutheran Honor Awd; Eliza-Catherine Smith Fel; AGO, Exceptional Ser Awd; Who's Who in the South and SW; Intl Who's Who. **MEMBERSHIPS** AAR; Hymn Soc; AGO; Study of Ministry Comm. **RESEARCH** Ecclesiology; Clergy-Musician relations. **SELECTED PUBLICATIONS** Auth, The Church of the Word: A Comparative Study of Word, Church and Office of the Thought of Karl Rahner and Gerhard Ebeling, NY, Peter Lang Pub, 93; auth, Professionally Speaking: Clergy-Musician Relations II, Amer Organist, 91, 92. **CONTACT ADDRESS** 8658 Liberia Ave, Manassas, VA, 20110.

ADAMEK, WENDI
PERSONAL Born 11/25/1959, Honolulu, HI, m, 1998 **DISCIPLINE** RELIGION **EDUCATION** Stanford Univ, PhD, 98. **CAREER** Asst Prof, 98-, Univ of IA. **HONORS AND AWARDS** Fulbright Fel, Javits Fel, Bukkyo Dendo Kyokai. **MEMBERSHIPS** AAR, AAS. **RESEARCH** Tang Buddhism, Dunhuang Studies. **CONTACT ADDRESS** School of Religion, Univ of Iowa, 314 Gilmore Hall, Iowa City, IA, 52242. **EMAIL** wendi-adamek@uiowa.edu

ADAMO, DAVID TUESDAY
PERSONAL Born 01/05/1949, Irunda-Isanlu, Yagba Lga, Kogi, Nigeria, m **DISCIPLINE** THEOLOGY **EDUCATION** ECWA Theol Seminary Nigeria, BTh 1977; Southern Methodist University Dallas, MTh 1980; University of the State of New York, BS 1982; Indiana Christian University, RelD 1983; Baylor University, PhD 1986. **CAREER** Titcombe College, Nigeria, instructor 1977-78; Paul Quinn College, prof, 1983-86; University of Ilorin, senior lecturer, 1986-91; Moi University, Kenya, prof, 1991-93; Delta State University, professor, 1993-. **HONORS AND AWARDS** Paul Quinn College, nominated most distinguished prof/scholar for Sigma Theta Award, 1985, award for teaching excellence and general services, 1986; Outstanding Contribution to Black History Month, Federal Housing Authority, 1986. **MEMBERSHIPS** American Academy of Religion, 1985-; Nigerian Assn for Biblical Studies, 1986-91; Society of Biblical Literature, 1985-; Natl Assn for Professors of Hebrew, 1985-. **SELECTED PUBLICATIONS** Publications "The Problem of Translating the Hebrew Old Testament Book Titles into Yoruba Language of Nigeria," The Bible Translator 1984; "Black American Heritage," Texian Press 1985; "The Black Prophet in the Old Testament," Journal of Arabic and Religion 1987. **CONTACT ADDRESS** Professor of Religion, Delta State Univ, Abraka, ..

ADAMS, DOUGLAS GLENN
PERSONAL Born 04/12/1945, DeKalb, IL, m, 1968 **DISCIPLINE** THEOLOGY & ARTS **EDUCATION** Duke Univ, BA, 67; Pac Sch Relig, MDiv & MA, 70; Grad Theol Union, ThD, 74. **CAREER** Asst prof Am relig & art, Univ Mont, 75-76; asst prof liturgy & arts, 76-79, assoc prof to prof Christianity & Arts, Pac Sch Relig, 79-84; Smithsonian fel art hist, 74-75; doctoral fac relig & arts, Grad Theol Union, 77-. **MEMBERSHIPS** Int Sacred Dance Guild; Am Acad Relig; fel N Am Acad Liturgy; Polanyi Soc; Col Art Assn; Soc for the Arts, Rel, and Contemporary Culture. **RESEARCH** Early American liturgy; American art history; theology and dance. **SELECTED PUBLICATIONS** Auth, Transcendence with the Human body in Art: Segal, De Staebler, Johns, and Christo, Crossroads, 91; auth, Eyes To See Wholeness: Visual Arts as Biblical and Theological Studies, EMI Press, 95; auth, The Prostitute in the Family Tree: Discovering Humor and Irony in the Bible, Westminster, John Knox, 97. **CONTACT ADDRESS** Pac Sch of Religion, 1798 Scenic Ave, Berkeley, CA, 94709-1323. **EMAIL** dadams@psr.edu

ADAMS, FREDERICK R., JR.
PERSONAL Born 07/20/1950, Belleville, IL, m, 1972, 1 child **DISCIPLINE** PHILOSOPHY **EDUCATION** Southern IL Univ, Edwardsville, BA, 72, MA , 74; Univ Wis, PhD, 82. **CAREER** Instr, , 80-81, Lawrence Univ, Appleton, WI; lect,82, Univ WI-Madison; asst prof, 82-86, Augustina Col, Rock Island, IL; asst prof, 86-88, chr, dept of philos, 88-97, Cent Mich Univ; chr, dept of philos, Univ Del, 97-. **HONORS AND AWARDS** Fulbright Res fel, Univ Bristol, UK, 78; Dean's Fel, Univ WI, 79-80; NEH fel, Univ NE, 83, 84, Rutgers Univ, 92; vis scholar, Stanford Univ, Ctr for Stud of Lang & Info, 92; 20th Fritz Marti Lect, Southern Ill Univ, Edwardsville, 95; Univ Tchng Excel Award, Cent Mich Univ, 95. **MEMBERSHIPS** Aristotelian Soc; Fulbright Alumni Asn; Am Philos Asn; Soc for Philos and Psychol; Southern Soc for Philos and Psychol; Phi Sigma Tau Nat Honor Soc; Phi Kappa Phi Nat Honor Soc. **RESEARCH** Cognitive science; epistemology; philos of mind. **SELECTED PUBLICATIONS** Auth, Goal-Directed Systems, Univ Microfilms Int, 92; coauth, Reflections on Philosophy, St Martin's, 93; auth, Simon Says, Stanford Hum Rev Sup, 94; auth, Trying: You've Got to Believe, Philos Res, 95; coauth, Rock Beats Scissors: Historicalism Fights back, Analysis, 97; auth, Cognitive Trying, Contemp Action Theory, vol 1, Kluwer, 97; coauth, The Semantics of Fictional Names, Pacific Philos Quart, 97;coauth, Fodor's Asymmetric Causal Dependency Theory and Proximal Projections, So J of Philos, 97;coauth, Functions and Goal-Directedness, Nature's Purposes, MIT/Adams, 98; coauth, Object Dependent Thoughts, Perspectival Thoughts, and Psychological Generalizations, Dialectica, forthcoming. **CONTACT ADDRESS** Dept Philosophy, Univ of Delaware, Newark, DE, 19716. **EMAIL** Fa@udel.edu

ADAMS, GEORGE
DISCIPLINE LAW **EDUCATION** McMaster Univ, BA; Osgoode Hall Law Sch, LLB; Harvard Univ, LLM. **CAREER** Prof, 71- **HONORS AND AWARDS** Walter Owen Bk Prize, 87. **SELECTED PUBLICATIONS** Auth, Canadian Labour Law; pubs on labour law treatise. **CONTACT ADDRESS** Fac of Law, Univ Toronto, 78 Queen's Park, Toronto, ON.

ADAMS, GREGORY B.
DISCIPLINE ANTITRUST, CONTRACTS AND CORPORATE LAW, AND PROFESSIONAL RESPONSIBILITY **EDUCATION** La State Univ, BS, 77, JD, 73; Columbia Univ, LLM, 79, JSD, 86. **CAREER** Assoc prof, Univ of SC. **SELECTED PUBLICATIONS** Coauth, SC Corporate Practice Manual; co-reporter, SC Bus Corp Act. **CONTACT ADDRESS** School of Law, Univ of S. Carolina, Law Center, Columbia, SC, 29208. **EMAIL** Greg@law.law.sc.edu

ADAMS, JOHN OSCAR
PERSONAL Born 04/03/1937, Chatanooga, TN **DISCIPLINE** LAW **EDUCATION** Wayne State Univ, BS 1962; Loyola Univ, JD 1970. **CAREER** Detroit Publ School, instr 1962-64; Pasadena City Coll, lecturer 1964-65; IBM LA, mgr, sys engr, instr 1964-70; IBM Corp Hdqtr, attny antitrust 1970-72; US Senate Small bus Comm, minor coun 1972-75; City of Los Angeles, dep city attny 1975-76; Wallace & Wallace, special counsel 1975-80; Adams Industries Inc of CA, president, bd chmn 1978-82; Attorney at law 1982-; art dealer 1985-. **HONORS AND AWARDS** Special Achievement Awd Los Angeles Urban League 1970; Saturday Review Commen Issue 1975; Men of Achievement; "Future Hope for the US"; **MEMBERSHIPS** Former chairman and mem of bd of dirs Hollywood Chamber of Commerce; bd dirs Hollywood Arts Council; mem Supreme Court, CA, NY, Washington DC Bar Assns; former mem Hollywood Kiwanis. **SELECTED PUBLICATIONS** "Notes of an Afro-Saxon." **CONTACT ADDRESS** Adams & Alexander, 8383 Wilshire Blvd #528, Beverly Hills, CA, 90211.

ADAMS, MARILYN M.
DISCIPLINE HISTORICAL THEOLOGY **EDUCATION** Univ Ill, AB, 64; Cornell Univ, PhD, 67; Princeton Theol Sem, ThM, 84; ThM, 85. **HONORS AND AWARDS** NEH, Younger Humanist fel, 74-75; Am Coun Learned Soc fel, 88-89; UC Pres Coun Hum fel, 88-89; Guggenheim fel, 89-90. **SELECTED PUBLICATIONS** Auth, Ockham's Treatise on Predestination, God's Foreknowledge, and Future Contingents, Century-Crofts, 69; Paul of Venice: On the Truth and Falsity of Propositions and On the Significatum of a Proposition, Oxford Univ Press, 77; William Ockham, Notre Dame Univ Press, 87; Ed, The Philosophical Theology of John Duns Scotus: A Collection of Essays by Allan B. Wolter, Oxford Univ Press, 90; Couth, The Problem of Evil, Oxford Univ Press, 90. **CONTACT ADDRESS** Yale Univ, 409 Prospect St., New Haven, CT, 06511-2167.

ADAMS, MICHELLE
DISCIPLINE LAW **EDUCATION** Brown Univ, BA; CUNY, JD; Harvard Univ, LLM: **CAREER** Prof, Seton Hall Univ, 95-; staff atty, Legal Aid Soc, NY. **HONORS AND AWARDS** Charles Hamilton Houston fel, Harvard Univ, 93. **SELECTED PUBLICATIONS** Publ in the areas of housing, race and sex discrimination. **CONTACT ADDRESS** Seton Hall Univ, South Orange, NJ. **EMAIL** adamsmch@shu.edu

ADDAMS, ROBERT DAVID
PERSONAL Born 02/12/1957, Chicago, IL **DISCIPLINE** LAW **EDUCATION** Princeton University, AB, 1978; Columbia University Graduate School of Journalism, MSJ, 1980; Columbia University School of Law, JD, 1982. **CAREER** Goodman, Eden, Millender & Bedrosian, associate attorney, 1982-86; National Conference of Black Lawyers, associate director, 1986; City Coll of NY, Revson Prof, 1986-87; Association of Legal Aid Attorneys, executive director, 1986-92; Institute for Mediation and Conflict Resolution, president/chief executive officer, currently; Brooklyn Coll, visiting prof, currently. **HONORS AND AWARDS** Princeton University Department of Afro-American Studies, Sr Thesis Prize, 1978; Revson Fellowship City College of New York Center for Legal Education, 1986-87; Brooklyn Coll, Belle Zeller, Visiting Distinguished Professorship, 1994-. **MEMBERSHIPS** National Conference of Black Lawyers, board of directors, 1985-87; Metropolitan Black Bar Association, 1992; State Bar of Michigan, 1982-92; National Lawyers Guild, 1982-86; American Bar Association, 1982-84; National Bar Association, 1982-84; Wolverine Bar Association, 1982-86; NY State Mediation Assn, bd of dirs, 1993-94. **CONTACT ADDRESS** President/CEO, Institute for Mediation and Conflict Resolution, PO Box 15, New York, NY, 10031.

ADDIS, LAIRD CLARK
PERSONAL Born 03/25/1937, Dath, NY, m, 1962, 2 children **DISCIPLINE** PHILOSOPHY **EDUCATION** Univ Iowa, BA, 59, PhD, 64 Brown Univ, MA, 60. **CAREER** Instr, 63-64, from asst prof to prof, 64-74, PROF PHILOS, UNIV IOWA, 74-, Chmn Dept, 77-85; Sr Fulbright lectr, Univ Groningen, 70-71. **MEMBERSHIPS** Am Philos Asn; Philos Sci Asn; Am Soc for Aesthetics, and others. **RESEARCH** Philosophy of mind; philosophy of the human sciences; metaphysics; aesthetics. **SELECTED PUBLICATIONS** Auth, The Logic of Society: A Philosophical Study, Univ Minn, 75; Natural Signs: A Theory of Intentionality, Temple Univ, 89; Of Mind and Music, Cornell Univ Press, 99. **CONTACT ADDRESS** Dept of Philos, Univ Iowa, 269 English Phil Bld, Iowa City, IA, 52242-1408. **EMAIL** laird-addis@uiowa.edu

ADELMAN, HOWARD
PERSONAL Born 01/07/1938, Toronto, ON, Canada **DISCIPLINE** PHILOSOPHY **EDUCATION** Univ Toronto, BA, 60, MA, 63, PhD, 71. **CAREER** Lectr, Univ Toronto, 63-64; asst prof, 66-70, assoc prof, 70-80, PROF PHILOSOPHY, YORK UNIV, 80-, assoc & acting dean, Atkinson Col, 69-71, ch philos dept, 74-77, dir grad prog philos, 80-83, 95-96. **SELECTED PUBLICATIONS** Auth, The Beds of Academe, 70; auth, The Holiversity, 73; auth, Canada and the Indochinese Refugees, 82; coauth, Early Warnings and Conflict Management: Genocide in Rwanda, 96; ed, The Indochinese Refugee Movement in Canada, 80; ed, Refugee Policy: Canada and the United States, 91; ed, Hungarian Refugees, 93; ed, Legitimate and Illegitimate Discrimination, 95; co-ed, The University Game, 68; co-ed, Refuge or Asylum? A Choice for Canada, 90; co-ed, African Refugees, 93; co-ed, Multiculturalism, Jews and Canadian Identity, 96. **CONTACT ADDRESS** Dept of Philosophy, York Univ, 4700 Keele St, Downsview, ON, M3J 1P3. **EMAIL** hadelman@yorku.ca

ADELMAN, MARTIN JEROME
PERSONAL Born 02/22/1937, Detroit, MI, m, 1961 **DISCIPLINE** LAW **EDUCATION** Univ Mich, AB, 58, MS, 59, JD, 62. **CAREER** Actg dean, 74-75, PROF LAW, SCH OF LAW, WAYNE STATE UNIV, 73-; Law clerk, Fed Dist Ct, Mich, 62-63; assoc, Honigman, Miller, Schwartz & Cohn, 63-64; patent atty, Burroughs Corp, 64-65; assoc, Barnard, McGlynn & Reising, 65-68, partner, 68-73; book rev ed, The Antitrust Bull, 47-79; vis prof law, Sch of Law, Univ Mich, 82. **RESEARCH** Patent law; antitrust law; law and economics. **SELECTED PUBLICATIONS** Auth, Territorial restraints in international technology agreements after Topco, Antitrust Bull, 72 & Patent Law Rev, 73; The integrity of the administrative process, Sherman Section 2 and Per Se Rules-Lessons of fraud on the Patent Office, Wayne Law Rev, 72, J Patent Off Soc, 73 & Patent Law Rev, 73; Secrecy and patenting: Some proposals for resolving the conflict, Am Patent Law Asn Quart, 73 & Patent Law Rev, 73; Patent-antitrust: Patent dynamics and field of use licensing, NY Univ Law Rev, 75, Patent Law Rev, 495 & J of Reprints for Antitrust Law & Econ 429; Property rights theory and patent-antitrust: The role of compulsory licensing, NY Univ Law Rev, 77, Intellectual Property Law Rev 77 & J of Reprints for Antitrust Law & Econ 287; The relevant market paradox - attempted and completed patent fraud monopolization, Ohio State Law J, 77, Intellectual Property Law Rev 115 & J of Reprints for Antitrust Law & Econ 709; Use of industrial property as a Clandestine Cartel, Am J Comp Law, 82; The Supreme Court, market structure and innovation: Chakrabarty, Rohm & Haas, Antitrust Bull, 82; Patent Law Perspectives, 8 vol, updated continuously; co-auth, Cases and materials on Patent Law, West Group, 98. **CONTACT ADDRESS** Sch of Law, Wayne State Univ, 468 Ferry Mall, Detroit, MI, 48202-3698. **EMAIL** m-adelman@wayne.edu

ADKINS, ARTHUR WILLIAM HOPE
PERSONAL Born 10/17/1929, Leicester, England, m, 1961, 2 children **DISCIPLINE** CLASSICS; PHILOSOPHY **EDUCATION** Oxford Univ, BA, 52, MA, 55, DPhil, 57. **CAREER** Asst lectr Latin humanities, Univ Glasgow, 54-56; lectr Greek, Bedford Col, Univ London, 56-61; fel class lang & lit, Exeter Col, Oxford, 61-65; prof classics, Univ Reading, 66-74; chmn, Dept Classics, 75-80, PROF GREEK, PHILOS & EARLY CHRISTIAN LIT, UNIV CHICAGO, 74- ; Vis sr fel classics Soc Humanities, Cornell Univ, 69-70. **MEMBERSHIPS** Soc Promotion Hellenic Studies; Class Asn Gt Brit; Am Philol Asn; Am Philos Asn; Asn Ancient Historians. **RESEARCH** Greek philosophy; Greek thought and religion; Greek literature. **SELECTED PUBLICATIONS** Auth, Merit and Responsibility: A Study in Greek Values, Clarendon, Oxford, 60; contribr, Greek religion, In: Historia Religionum Handbook for the History of Religions, Leiden, Brill, 69; auth, From the Many to the One: A Study of Personality and Views of Human Nature in the Context of Ancient Greek Society, Values and Beliefs, Constable, London & Cornell Univ, 70; Moral Values and Political Behavior in Ancient Greece, Chatto & Windus, London & Clark Irwin, Toronto, 72; Paralysis and Akrasia in Eth Nic 1102b16 ff, Am J Philos, Vol 97, 62-64; Polupragmosune and minding one's own business: A study in Greek social and political values, CP, 76; Callinus 1 and Tyrtaeus 10 as poetry, HSCP, 77; Lucretius I, 137 ff and the problems of writing Versus Latini, Phoenix, 77; Ethics with Aristotle, Classical Philol, Vol 0088, 93; Hybris- A Study in the Values of Honor and Shame in Ancient Greece, Class Jour, Vol 0090, 95; Aidos - The Psychology and Ethics of Honor and Shame in Ancient Greek Literature, Class Jour, Vol 0090, 95. **CONTACT ADDRESS** Dept of Classics, Univ of Chicago, 1050 E 59th St, Chicago, IL, 60637.

ADLER, JACOB
DISCIPLINE SOCIAL AND POLITICAL PHILOSOPHY **EDUCATION** Harvard Univ, PhD. **CAREER** Philos, Univ Ark **SELECTED PUBLICATIONS** Auth, The Urgings of Conscience, Temple Univ Press, 92. **CONTACT ADDRESS** Univ Ark, Fayetteville, AR, 72701. **EMAIL** jadler@comp.uark.edu

ADLER, JOSEPH
PERSONAL Born 03/14/1948, Suffern, NY, m, 1982, 1 child **DISCIPLINE** RELIGIOUS STUDIES **EDUCATION** Univ Rochester, BA, 70; Univ Calif Santa Barbara, MA, 77, PhD, 84. **CAREER** Vis asst prof, Univ S Calif, 86-87; asst prof, 87-94, assoc prof, 94-, Kenyon Col. **MEMBERSHIPS** Amer acad Rel; Soc Study of Chinese Rel; Asn Asian stud (s); Soc Asian and Comparative Philos. **RESEARCH** Neo-Confucian religious thought and practice in Sung dynasty China. **CONTACT ADDRESS** Dept of Religion, Kenyon Col, Gambier, OH, 43022. **EMAIL** adlerj@kenyon.edu

AGICH, GEORGE J.
PERSONAL Born 05/27/1947, Rochester, PA, m, 1980, 1 child **DISCIPLINE** PHILOSOPHY **EDUCATION** Duquesne Univ, BA, eng & philos, 69; Univ Tex Austin, MA, philos, 71, PhD, philos, 76. **CAREER** Asst prof to prof, med humanities and psychiat, Southern Ill Univ Sch of Med, 76-96; F. J. O'Neill chair, clinical bioethics, chair, dept of bioethics, Cleveland Clinic Found, 97-. **RESEARCH** Bioethics; Philosophy of medicine; Philosophy of psychiatry. **SELECTED PUBLICATIONS** Article, Ethical Issues in Managed Care, Oncology Issues, 13, no 3, 25-27, May/Jun, 98; article, Can the Patient Make Treatment Decisions? Evaluating Decisional Capacity, Cleveland Clinic Jour of Med, 64, 461-464, Oct, 97; article, Ethics Expert Testimony: Against the Skeptics, Jour of Med and Philos, 22, 381-403, 97; article, Consent in Patients with Mental Illness, Current Opinion in Psychiat, 10, 423-26, 97; article, Maladie Chronique et Autonomie: Des Lecons pour Comprehension Schizophrenie, L'Evolution Psychiatrique, 62, 401-409, 97; article, Ethics Committees and Consultants in the United States, Gesundheits-Oeconomica, 89-100, 95; article, Disease, Functions, Values, and Psychiatric Classification, Philos, Psychiat, and Psychol, 2, 219-231, 95; article, Authority in Ethics Consultation, Jour of Law, Med and Ethics, 23, 273-283, 95; article, Key Concepts: Autonomy, Philos, Psychiat, and Psychol, I, 267-269, Dec, 94; article, Expertise in Ethics Consultation: Reaction to Fox and Stocking, HEC Forum 6, 379-383, Nov, 94; article, Consent in Children and at the End of Life, Current Opinion in Psychiat, 7, 426-429, 94; article, On Values in Recent American Psychiatric Classification, Jour of Med and Philos, 19, 261-277, 94; article, Privacy and Medical Record Information, Jour of the Amer Med Info Asn, 1, 323-324, Jul-Aug, 94. **CONTACT ADDRESS** Dept. of Bioethics, Cleveland Clinic Foundation, 9500 Euclid Av., Cleveland, OH, 44195. **EMAIL** agichg@desmtp.ccf.org

AHLERS, ROLF
PERSONAL Born 06/22/1936, Hamburg, Germany, m, 1966, 2 children **DISCIPLINE** PHILOSOPHY OF RELIGION **EDUCATION** Drew, Princeton Univ, Univ Hamburg, PhD. **CAREER** Asst prof, theol, Hamburg Univ, 61-66; asst prof, philos & relig, Ill Col, 66-72; prof, philos, Russell Sage Col, 73-. **HONORS AND AWARDS** NEH grant for younger Humanists, 72-73; Who's Who in Amer. **MEMBERSHIPS** Amer Acad of Relig; Hegel Soc of Amer. **RESEARCH** German idealism; Early German idealism; Early romanticism; German. **SELECTED PUBLICATIONS** Auth, The Community of Freedom, Barth and Presuppositionless Theology, Peter Lang Publ Inc, Bern/NY, 89; auth, The Barmen Theological Declaration of 1934, Archeology of a Confessional Text, Edwin Mellon Press, Toronto, NY, 86; rev, Beyond All Reason: The Radical Assault on Truth in American Law, Zeitschrift fur Philos Forschung, 98; rev, Die Rolle des Einflusses von J. J. Rousseau auf die Herausbildung von Hegels Jugendideal, Owl of Minerva, 98; rev, Das Angfangsproblem bei Karl Leonhard Reinhold, Eine Systematische und entwicklungsgeschichliche Untersuchung zur Philosophie Reinholds in der Zeit von 1789 bis 1803, Owl of Minerva, 98; rev, Religionsphilosophie und Spekulative Theologie vols. 3 and 3.1 of Philosophisch-literarische Streitsachen, The Jour of Relig, 97. **CONTACT ADDRESS** 3 Academy Rd., Albany, NY, 12208-3102. **EMAIL** ahlerr@sage.edu

AHLSTROM, GOSTA WERNER
PERSONAL Born 08/27/1918, Sandviken, Sweden, m, 1952, 2 children **DISCIPLINE** OLD TESTAMENT **EDUCATION** Univ Uppsala, Teol Lic, 54, Teol Dr, 59, Fil Kand, 61. **CAREER** From instr to asst prof Old Testament, Univ Uppsala, 54-63; vis assoc prof, 62-63, assoc prof, 63-76, PROF OLD TESTAMENT & ANCIENT PALESTINIAN STUDIES, UNIV CHICAGO, 76- ; Ann prof, W F Albright Inst Archaeol Res, Jerusalem, 69-70, staff mem, Am excavations in Israel, Cyprus & Tuninsia, 69-77; trustee, 70-74. **MEMBERSHIPS** Am Orient Soc; Am Schs Orient Res; Archaeol Inst Am; Soc Bibl Lit; Der Deutsche Verein zur Erforschung Palastinas (pres, 76-78). **RESEARCH** Syro-Palestinian history and religions; Palestinian archaeology. **SELECTED PUBLICATIONS** Auth, Psalm 89 Eine Liturgie aus dem Ritual des leidenden Konigs, 59 & Aspects of Syncretism in Israelite Religion, 63, CWK Gleerup, Lund; Joel and the Temple Cult of Jerusalem, Brill, Leiden, 71; An Israelite God figurine from Hazor, Orient Suecana, 72; Prophecy, In: Encyclopedia Britannica, 74; Winepresses and cup-marks of the Jenin-Megiddo survey, Bull Am Schs Oreint Res, No 231, 78; Another Moses tradition, J Near Eastern Studies, No 39, 80; Royal administration and national religion in ancient Palestine, Brill Leiden, 81; Palestine in Prehellenic Time, Jour of Near Eastern Studies, Vol 0053, 94. **CONTACT ADDRESS** Univ of Chicago, Swift Hall, Chicago, IL, 60637.

AHN, TIMOTHY MYUNGHOON
PERSONAL Born 05/21/1953, Korea, m, 1978, 2 children **DISCIPLINE** CHRISTIAN EDUCATION **EDUCATION** Boston Univ, PhD, 94. **CAREER** Sr Pastor, Arcola Korean United Methodist Church. **CONTACT ADDRESS** S-62 Paramus Rd, Paramus, NJ, 07652.

AICHELE, GEORGE
PERSONAL Born 06/12/1944, Washington, DC, m, 1968, 2 children **DISCIPLINE** THEOLOGY **EDUCATION** Univ Ill, BA, 65; Garrett Theol Sem, BD, 69; Northwest Univ, PhD, 74. **CAREER** Chaplain, Northwest Univ, 74-75; instr, N Iowa Community Coll, 76-77; instr Upper Iowa Univ, 77-78; Adrian Coll Mich, 78-; prof Adrian Coll Mich, 90-. **MEMBERSHIPS** Am Acad Rel; Soc Bibl Lit; Cath Bibl Asn; Int Asn For Fantasy in Art and Lit; Internet discussions gropus. **SELECTED PUBLICATIONS** Auth, Jesus Framed, 96; Sign, Text, Scripture: Semiotics and the Bible, 97; co-ed, Semeia:69/70: Intertextuality and the Bible, 95; The Bible and fantasy. Journal for the Fantastic in the Arts, 97; The Monstrous and the Unspeakable: the Bible as Fantastic Literature, 97; Violence, Utopia, and the Kingdom of God, 98. **CONTACT ADDRESS** Dept of Philosophy and Religion, Adrian Col, Adrian, MI, 49221.

AIRHART, PHYLLIS
PERSONAL Born 06/24/1953, Moncton, NB, Canada, m, 1979 **DISCIPLINE** RELIGION **EDUCATION** Univ Manitoba, BA, 77; Univ Chicago, MA, 81, PhD, 85. **CAREER** Asst prof, 85-90, assoc prof, 90-, hist of christianity, Emmanuel College, Victoria Univ, cross-appointed to religion, 94-, Univ of Toronto. **HONORS AND AWARDS** Victoria Univ Award for Excellence in Tchng, 91. **MEMBERSHIPS** Amer Hist Soc; Amer Soc of Church history; Can Catholic Hist Soc; Can Methodist Hist Soc; Can Soc of Church History. **RESEARCH** Religion in N America; gender & religion; religion and social reform; revivalism. **SELECTED PUBLICATIONS** Auth, Serving the Present Age Revivalism Progressivism and the Methodist Tradition in Canada, McGill-Queen Univ Press, 92; coed, Faith Traditions and the Family, Westminster John Knox Press, 96; coed, Christianizing the Social Order a Founding Vision of the United Church of Canada, Toronto J of Theology, 96; art, Art, Christianizing the Social Order and Founding Myths Double Vision, Christianizing the Social Order A Founding Vision of the United Church of Canada, Toronto Jour of Theology, 96; art, Condensation and Heart Religion Canadian Methodists as Evangelicals 1884-1925, Aspects of the Canadian Evangelical Exper, McGill-Queen Univ Press, 97; art, As Canadian as Possible under the Circumstances Reflections on the Study of North American Protestantism, New Directions in Amer Rel History, Oxford Univ Press, 97; art, Ecumenical Theological Education and Denominational Relationships The Emmanuel College Case 1960-1985, Theological Ed in Canada, United Church Pub House, 98. **CONTACT ADDRESS** Victoria Univ, 75 Queens Park Cr, Toronto, ON, M5S 1K7. **EMAIL** pairhart@chass.utoronto.ca

AKIN, DANIEL L.
DISCIPLINE THEOLOGY **EDUCATION** Criswell Col, BA; Southwestern Baptist Theol Sem, MDiv; Univ Tex, PhD. **CAREER** Assoc prof, Southeastern Baptist Theol Sem; dean, Sch of Theol, S Baptist Theol Sem. **MEMBERSHIPS** Mem, S Baptist Hist Soc; Soc Sci Stud of Rel; Evangel Theol Soc. **SELECTED PUBLICATIONS** Ed, Believer's Study Bible. **CONTACT ADDRESS** Sch Theol, Southern Baptist Theol Sem, 2825 Lexington Rd, Louisville, KY, 40280. **EMAIL** dakin@sbts.edu

AL'UQDAH, WILLIAM MUJAHID
PERSONAL Born 10/29/1953, Cincinnati, OH, m, 1976 **DISCIPLINE** LAW **EDUCATION** University of Cincinnati, BS, 1982; Salmon P Chase College of Law, JD, 1987. **CAREER** Hamilton County Prosecutors Office, asst district Attorney, 1988-94; WCIN 1480 AM Radio, sports dir and on air personality, 1992-; Harmon, Davis and Keys Co, LPA, senior assoc, 1994-96; Lawson and Gaines, Attorney, 1996-. **HONORS AND AWARDS** Black Professionals, Scholarship, 1986. **MEMBERSHIPS** Black Male Coalition, first exec dir, 1988-89; Black Law Student Assn of America, president, 1985-86. **SELECTED PUBLICATIONS** The Good, The Bad, and The Ugly, Criminal Justice State of Cincinnati, sponsored by Cincinnati Urban League, 1995; When Going Gets Tough, Central State University Symposium, Welfare Reform, 1982. **CONTACT ADDRESS** Harmon, Davis & Keys Co LPA, 1014 Vine Street, Cincinnati, OH, 45202.

ALBERS, ROBERT H.
DISCIPLINE PASTORAL CARE **EDUCATION** Wartburg Sem, MDiv, 66; S Calif Sch Theol, PhD, 82. **CAREER** Vis lectr, Dana Col, 76-78; grad res asst, S Calif Sch, 79-81; vis lectr, S Calif Sch of Theol, 80-81; asst prof, 81; dir, Ministry in Pastoral Care and Soc Change prog, 85; act dean of students, 82-83; prof, 91-. **HONORS AND AWARDS** Ed, Jour of Ministry in Addiction and Recovery. **MEMBERSHIPS** Mem, Minn Chem Dependency Assn; Interfaith Network for Chem Dependency. **SELECTED PUBLICATIONS** Auth, A Life of Prayer, ALC confirmation material, 84; Healing the Hurts: Separation and Loss, 91; Why Do People Suffer?, Responding to Evil and Suffering, 92; Shame: A Faith Perspective, 95. **CONTACT ADDRESS** Dept of PastoralCare, Luther Sem, 2481 Como Ave, St. Paul, MN, 55108. **EMAIL** ralbers@luthersem.edu

ALBIN, THOMAS R.
PERSONAL Born 05/10/1951, Wakeeney, KS, m, 1971, 3 children **DISCIPLINE** CHURCH HISTORY **EDUCATION** Oral Roberts Univ, BA, 73, MA, 76; Fuller Theol Sem, MA, 77; Univ Cambridge, PhD 99. **CAREER** Vis lect, 87-88, Boston Univ School of Theol, adj fac, 89; asst prof, 88-92, Univ Dubuque Theol Sem, dir, contextual ed & instr in spiritual formation, 92-, Univ Dubuque Theol Sem. **HONORS AND AWARDS** BA, magna cum laude, 73; MA, 78; G. Lemuel Fenn Ministerial Scholar; John Wesley Fel, a Fund for Theol Ed, ATFE, 78-82; Bethune-Baker grant, fac of Div, Cambridge Univ; Pasadena Methodist Found Scholar; Charis Award for Excel in Tchng, UDTS, 90-91, 92-93. **MEMBERSHIPS** Am Academy of Relig; Charles Wesley Found; Oxford Inst for Methodist Theol Stud: Spiritual Dirs Int; Wesley Hist Soc, Eng. **SELECTED PUBLICATIONS** Auth, Spiritual Formation and Contextual Education, in the Report of the Proceedings of the Asn of Theol Field Ed, 93; auth, John and Charles Wesley, The Dict of Christian Ethics & Pastoral Theol, IVP, 95; auth, What We Believe and Why We Believe It: Understanding Our Doctrinal Standards and Our Theological Task, a 6 wk stud, pvtly printed, local United Methodist Churches, 96; rev, Of Laughter in the Amen Corner: The Life of Evangelist Sam Jones by Kathleen Minnix, 93, pub in Missiology: An Int Rev, vol XXV, no 2, 97; auth, One week of devotions in Disciplines 1999, Upper Room, 98; auth, The Charles Wesley Family in Bristol, Proceed of the Charles Wesley Soc, vol 4, 97, 98; auth, The Role of Small Groups in Early Methodist Spiritual Formation, in The Role of the Heart in N Amer Methodism, Scarecrow Press. **CONTACT ADDRESS** 1925 Carter Rd, Dubuque, IA, 52001. **EMAIL** talbin@univ.dbq.edu

ALBRECHT, GLORIA H.
DISCIPLINE RELIGION AND ETHICS **EDUCATION** Univ Md, BA; Johns Hopkins Univ, MLA; St Mary's Sem, STM; Temple Univ, PhD. **CAREER** Assoc prof; Univ Detroit Mercy, 92-. **RESEARCH** Business and economic ethics, feminist ethics and theology, and women's studies. **CONTACT ADDRESS** Dept of Religious Studies, Univ of Detroit Mercy, 4001 W McNichols Rd, PO Box 19900, Detroit, MI, 48219-0900. **EMAIL** ALBRECGH@udmercy.edu

ALDER, JOSEPH A.
PERSONAL Born 03/14/1948, Suffern, NY, m, 1982, 1 child **DISCIPLINE** RELIGION **EDUCATION** Univ Rochester, BA, 70; Univ Calif, Santa Barbara, MA, 77, PhD, 84. **CAREER** Vis asst prof, Univ S Calif, 86-87; from asst prof to assoc prof, 87-, Kenyon Col. **MEMBERSHIPS** Am Acad Religion; Asn Asian Stud; Society Stud Chinese Religions. **RESEARCH** Neo-Confucianism **SELECTED PUBLICATIONS** Auth, Descriptive and Normative Principle(li) in Confucian Moral Metaphysics: Is/Ought from the Chinese Perspective, 81; coauth, Sung Dynasty Uses of the I Ching, 90; auth, art, Response and Responsibility: Chow Tun-I and Neo-Confucian Resources for Environmental Ethics, 98; auth, art, Zhou Dunyi: The Metaphysics and Practice of Sagehood, 98. **CONTACT ADDRESS** Dept of Religion, Kenyon Col, Gambier, OH, 43022. **EMAIL** adlerj@kenyon.edu

ALEXAKIS, ALEXANDER
DISCIPLINE RELIGION **EDUCATION** Oxford Univ, PhD, 92. **CAREER** Asst prof. **RESEARCH** History of the Byzantine church and theology; relations between Constantinople and Rome; patristics; hagiography; Byzantine literature and epistolography; Byzantine ecclesicastic procedural law; paleography. **SELECTED PUBLICATIONS** Auth, Codex Parisinus Graecus 1115 and its Archetype, pubs on iconoclasm and Byzantine hagiography. **CONTACT ADDRESS** Dept of Religion, Columbia Col, New York, 2960 Broadway, New York, NY, 10027-6902. **EMAIL** aa177@columbia.edu

ALEXAKOS, PANOS D.
DISCIPLINE PHILOSOPHY **EDUCATION** Villanova Univ, MA, 85; Pa State Univ, PhD, 95. **CAREER** Instr. **RESEARCH** Contemporary continental philosophy; history of philosophy. **SELECTED PUBLICATIONS** Auth, Metamorphoses: On the Limits of Thought, 91; A Case of Mistaken Identity: The Censorship of American Psycho, 91; The Power of Consciousness and the Force of Circumstance in Sartre's Philosophy (rev), 91; Nietzsche on Truth and Philosophy (rev), Int Philos Quart, 93. **CONTACT ADDRESS** Dept of Philosophy, Knoxville, TN, 37996. **EMAIL** palexakos@aol.com

ALEXANDER, GEORGE J.
PERSONAL Born 03/08/1931, Berlin, Germany, m, 1958, 2 children **DISCIPLINE** LAW **EDUCATION** Univ PA, AB, 53, JD, 59; Yale Univ, LLM, 65, JSD, 69. **CAREER** Instr law, Univ Chicago, 59-60; from asst prof to prof, Syracuse Univ, 60-67, prof & assoc dean, 67-70; dean sch law and prof law, 70-85, Sutro Prof Law, 96-, Univ Santa Clara, 70-; consult, US Comn Civil Rights, 62-63, Educ Policies Res Ctr, 68- & Syracuse Res Corp Policy Inst, 69-; mem, Int Inst Space Law; consult, US Comptroller Gen, 77- **HONORS AND AWARDS** Order of the Coif, Justinian Hon Soc, Ralph E Kharas Civil Liberty Award. **MEMBERSHIPS** Am Bar Asn; Soc Am Law Teachers; Int Inst Space Law; Int Comt Human Rights. **RESEARCH** Antitrust and trade regulation law; constitutional law; psychiatry and law. **SELECTED PUBLICATIONS** Auth, Civil Rights, USA, Public Schools . . . Buffalo, New York, US Govt Printing Off, 63; chaps, In: World Unfair Competition Law, M Nijoff, The Hague, 65; Jury Instructions on Medical Issues, Allen Smith, 66; Honesty and Competition: False Advertising Law and Policy Under FTC Administration, Syracuse Univ, 67; chap, In: Changing Aspects of Business Law, Heath, 67; coauth, The Aged and the Need for Surrogate Management, Syracuse Univ, 72; auth, Commercial Torts, Allen Smith, 73; Ed Int Perspectives on Aging; auth Law and Mental Disorder, Carolina Acad, 98. **CONTACT ADDRESS** Sch Law, Univ Santa Clara, 500 El Camino Real, Santa Clara, CA, 95053-0001. **EMAIL** GJAlexander@scu.edu

ALEXANDER, HARRY TOUSSAINT
PERSONAL Born 07/22/1924, New Orleans, LA, m **DISCIPLINE** LAW **EDUCATION** Georgetown Univ School of Law, JD 1952; Xavier Univ, BS 1949. **CAREER** Georgetown Univ, rsch asst Cmdr Langdon P Marvin 1951-52; Office of Price Stabilization, atty adv 1952-53; Private practice, attny 1953; US Attny DC, asst 1953-61, spec attny 1961-64, staff asst criminal div 1964-65; US Dept of Justice, attny 1961-66; Superior Ct DC, assoc judge 1966-76; HOWARD UNIV SCHOOL OF LAW, ADJ PROF 1970-. **HONORS AND AWARDS** Dr Cruezot Awd; Frederick W Shea Awd; Wm H Hastie Awd Natl Conf of Black Lawyers 1976; Outstanding Comm Serv Awd 1975; Outstanding Serv DC C of C;Cert of Degree Strategic Air Command 1973; Martin Luther King Jr Outstanding Serv Awd Howard Univ School of Law 1977; Harry Toussaint Alexander Day DC Council; TV appearances The Admin of Juv Criminal Justice; radioappearances The Admin of Cinal Juv Justice. **MEMBERSHIPS** Mem Judicial Conf DC; comm Abolition of Mandatory Capital Punishment DC 1959-62; mem Prob Connected with Mental Exams of the Accused in Criminal Cases Before Trial 1960-63, Cardoza Comm on Judicial Conf, Amer Bar Assoc; mem 1961-65, recording sec 1955-60, WA Bar Assoc; mem Phi Delta Phi Intl Legal Frat, PAlpha Delta Intl Legal Frat; pres NAACP DC 1977, United Natl Bank of WA 1977, Family & Child Serv of WA 1971, Natl Conf of Christians & Jews 1965-70; vchmn BSA 1966, Interreligious Comm on Race Rels 1963-66, Scouters Intl Rep St Gabriels Cath Church 1963-65; mem, 1st natl vice pres 1960-62 Xavier Univ Alumni Assoc; pres NW Boundary Civic Assoc 1958-60; vice pres Natl Fed of Cath Coll Students LA Reg; mem US Natl Students Assoc; pres, vice pres LA-MS-AR Reg1947-48,48-49; treas NAACP YouCouncil New Orleans LA. **SELECTED PUBLICATIONS** "Appeals in Fed Jurisdiction" NBA 1960, "Curbing Juvenile Delinquency with Adequate Playground Facilities" 1957, "The Nature of Our Heritage" 1950-51, "The Unconstitutionality of Segregation in Ed" 1950-51, "Due Process Required in Revocation of a Conditional Pardon" 1950-51, "The Antislavery Origins of the Fourteenth Amendment", "Convention Coverage" Assoc Negro Press Inc 1947, Xavier Herald 1946-49.

ALEXANDER, LARRY
PERSONAL Born 09/23/1943, Fort Worth, TX, m, 3 children **DISCIPLINE** PHILOSOPHY **EDUCATION** Williams Col, BA, 65; Yale Univ, LLB, 68. **CAREER** Res Atty, Calif Court Appeal, 68-70; Asst Prof to Prof, 70-95, Warren Distinguished Prof Law, Univ San Diego, 95-; Vis Prof, Univ Calif, 89; Vis Prof, Univ Pa, 95. **HONORS AND AWARDS** Summer Stipend, NEH, 73; Summer Fel, Inst Humane Studies, 79. **MEMBERSHIPS** Am Soc Polit & Legal Philos; Am Philos Asn. **RESEARCH** Constitutional law; criminal law; legal and moral philosophy. **SELECTED PUBLICATIONS** Coauth, Whom Does the Constitution Command?, Greenwood Press, 88; auth, Contract Law, Dartmouth Publ Co, 91; Constitutionalism: Philosophical Foundations, Cambridge Univ Press, 98; coauth, Past Imperfect: Rules, Principles, and the Dilemnas of Law, Duke Univ Press (forthcoming); auth, Legal Rules and Legal Reasoning, Dartmouth Publ Co (forthcoming); Freedom of Speech, Dartmouth Publ Co (forthcoming); author of numerous articles. **CONTACT ADDRESS** School of Law, Univ San Diego, 5998 Alcala Rd., San Diego, CA, 92110.

ALEXANDER, LAURENCE BENEDICT
PERSONAL Born 10/31/1959, New Orleans, LA, m, 1988 **DISCIPLINE** LAW **EDUCATION** University of New Orleans, BA, 1981; University of Florida, MA, 1983; Tulane University, School of Law, JD, 1987. **CAREER** The Times-Picayune, New Orleans, staff writer, 1981; The Houma Courier, staff writer, 1982; The Times Picayune, staff writer, 1982-85; University of New Orleans, director of journalism program, assistant professor of journalism, 1987-88; Temple University, director of news editorial sequence, assistant professor of communications, 1988-91; The Philadelphia Inquirer, summer copy editor, 1989-92; University of Florida, assistant professor of journalism, 1991-94, chair of journalism, 1994-98, associate professor, 1994-. **HONORS AND AWARDS** AEJMC/ACEJMC Baskett Mosse Award, 1994; AEJMC, AHANA Research Grant, 1990; The Poynter Institute, Selected Teaching Fellow, 1989; Press Club of New Orleans, Deadline News Writing Award, 1985. **MEMBERSHIPS** Assn for Education in Journalism and Mass Communication, 1989-; International Communications Association, 1992-; Society of Professional Journalists, 1989-; Natl Assn of Black Journalists, 1989-; American Bar Association, 1987-; Louisiana State Bar Associa-

tion, 1987-. **SELECTED PUBLICATIONS** Major works published in: The Tulane Maritime Lawyer, 1987; The Black Law Journal, 1989; Newspaper Research Journal, 1992, 1994, 1995, 1996; Western Journal of Black Studies, 1992; Communications and the Law, 1993, 1996; Journalism Educator, 1994, Notre Dame Journal of Legislation, 1997; Editor and Publisher, 1990, 1993, 1996. **CONTACT ADDRESS** Dept of Journalism, Univ of Florida, 3052 Weimer Hall, Gainesville, FL, 32611.

ALEXANDER, RALPH H.
PERSONAL Born 09/03/1936, Tyler, TX, m, 1964, 3 children **DISCIPLINE** SEMITICS AND OLD TESTAMENT; ARCHAEOLOGY **EDUCATION** Rice Univ, AB, 59; Dallas Theol Sem, ThM, 63, ThD, 68. **CAREER** Instr, S Bible Training School, 63-64, 65-66; asst prof of Bible and Archaeology, Wheaton Col, 66-72; prof Hebrew Scripture, dir summer quart Israel Prog, 74 & 78, W Baptist Sem, 73-87; assoc archaeologist, Albright Inst Archaeology, 77-78; dir, Advan Trng Studies Coordr Old Testament Concentration Bibl Educ Exten Int Austria, 87-95; dir, educ develop & advan trng studies, cis, bibl educ exten int, Moscow, 95-. **HONORS AND AWARDS** US Govt Fulbright grant, Israel, 64-65; Henry Thiessen Award New Testament; Outstanding Young Men Amer, 70; Outstanding Educ Amer; Who's Who Relig. **MEMBERSHIPS** Amer Schools Oriental Res; Archeol Inst Amer; Evangel Theol Soc; Fel Evangel Europ Tchrs; Inst Bibl Res; Israel Explor Soc; Nat Asn Hebrew Prof; Near East Archeol Soc; Soc Bibl Lit. **RESEARCH** Psalms; Old Testament Archaeology; Old Testament Law & Prophets. **SELECTED PUBLICATIONS** Contribur, New Commentary on the Whole Bible, Tyndale, 94; auth, Marriage and Divorce, Dictionary of Old Testament Ethics, Baker, 96; A New Covenant and An Eternal People, Israel: The Land and the People, Kregel, 98. **CONTACT ADDRESS** Box 3366, Gresham, OR, 97030. **EMAIL** ralphmyrna@earthlink.net

ALEXANDER, SCOTT C.
DISCIPLINE RELIGIOUS STUDIES **EDUCATION** Columbia Univ, PhD, 93. **CAREER** Asst prof. **RESEARCH** History and comparative study of religions; Islamic religion and society; medieval studies. **SELECTED PUBLICATIONS** Auth, Islamic heresiography, Jour Mid E Studies, 87. **CONTACT ADDRESS** Dept of Religious Studies, Indiana Univ, Bloomington, 300 N Jordan Ave, Bloomington, IN, 47405.

ALEXANDER, THOMAS
PERSONAL Born 09/08/1952, Albuquerque, NM, m, 1983, 2 children **DISCIPLINE** PHILOSOPHY **EDUCATION** Univ New Mexico, BA, 74; Emory Univ, MA, 76, PhD, 84. **CAREER** Asst prof, assoc prof, prof S Ill Univ, Carbondale, 85-. **MEMBERSHIPS** APA; Soc for the Advanc Am Philos. **RESEARCH** American philosophy; John Dewey. **SELECTED PUBLICATIONS** Auth, John Dewey's Theory of Art Experience and Nature, SUNY, 87. **CONTACT ADDRESS** Dept of Philosophy, Southern Illinois Univ, Carbondale, IL, 62901.

ALEXANDER, W.M.
PERSONAL Born 12/05/1928, Jacksonville, FL, m, 1953, 3 children **DISCIPLINE** PHILOSOPHY OF RELIGION **EDUCATION** Davidson Col, AB, 50; Louisville Presbyterian Sem, BD, 53; Harvard Univ, STM, 57; Princeton Theological Sem, PhD, 61. **CAREER** From asst prof to prof, St Andrews Col, 61-83, distinguished prof, St Andrews Col, 83-. **HONORS AND AWARDS** ACLS res grant; Coun for Philos Studies sem; NEH grants, Ohio State, Yale. **MEMBERSHIPS** Am Philos Asn; Metaphys Soc of Am; Am Acad of Relig. **RESEARCH** 18th century, incl Hamann and Kant; John Philoponos, 6th century scientist & philosopher. **SELECTED PUBLICATIONS** Auth, Johann Georg Hamann: Philosophy and Faith, various articles, incl one in the Encyclopedia of Philosophy. **CONTACT ADDRESS** Dept of Religion and Philosophy, St Andrews Col, Laurinburg, NC, 28352.

ALEXANDRAKIS, APHRODITE
PERSONAL Born 02/09/1945, Alexandria, Egypt, m, 1964, 3 children **DISCIPLINE** PHILOSOPHY **EDUCATION** Rutgers Univ-Douglas Col, BA, 68; Univ Miami, MA, 76, PhD, 86. **CAREER** Adjunct lect, Barry Univ, 81-92, asst prof of philos and humanities, 92-94, assoc prof, 94-98, PROF OF PHILOS AND HUMANITIES, BARRY UNIV, 98-. **HONORS AND AWARDS** Barry Univ Professional Award, 91-98; Outstanding Faculty Award, Barry Univ, 96-97. **MEMBERSHIPS** Am Philos Asn; Am Cath Philos Asn; Int Soc for Neoplatonic Studies; Soc for Ancient Philos. **RESEARCH** Platonic and Neoplatonic theories of beauty. **SELECTED PUBLICATIONS** Auth, Plotinus' Notion of Beauty: Its Significance and Application in Renaissance Painting, Annales D'esthetique, 92-93; The Notion of Beauty in Plotinus and Hegel, Philosophia, 91-92; The Notion of Beauty in Space in Light of Greek Aesthetics, Skepsis: A J for Philos and Inter-Disciplinary Res, 92; The Classical Notion of Beauty in Byzantine Art, Diotima 23, 95; Plotinian Influence on Psellus' Dialectic, Soc for Ancient Greek Philos, Univ NY, SUNY Press, Jan 95; Sensual Beauty Ideal Beauty and Works of Art, Alexandria The J of the Western Cosmological Traditions, April 97; Animal Images in Greek Thought and Art, Prima Philosophia, July 98; Plotinus' Aesthetic Approach to the One, Philosophia, The Academy of Athens, April 98; Neopythagoreanizing Influences on Plotinus Mystical Notion of Numbers, Philos Inquiry, April 98; Does Modern Art Reflect Plotinus' Notion of Beauty?, J of Neoplatonic Studies, May 98. **CONTACT ADDRESS** 6647 Tarrega St., Coral Gables, FL, 33146. **EMAIL** alexandr@catherine.barry.edu

ALEXANIAN, JOSEPH M.
DISCIPLINE NEW TESTAMENT TEXTUAL CRITICISM **EDUCATION** Wheaton Col , AB, 52; Fuller Theol Sem, Mdiv, 55; Univ Chicago, PhD, 82. **CAREER** Relig, Trinity Int Univ. **SELECTED PUBLICATIONS** Area: Armenian text of Acts and Luke. **CONTACT ADDRESS** Trinity Int Univ, 2065 Half Day Road, Deerfield, IL, 60015.

ALFORD, HAILE LORRAINE
PERSONAL Born 07/00/1949, Brooklyn, NY **DISCIPLINE** LAW **EDUCATION** Herbert H Lehman, BA 1971; Rutgers Univ School of Law Camden, JD 1976. **CAREER** Jr HS, teacher 1971; Wiltwyck School for Boys, teacher 1972-73; Lincoln Univ, adj lecturer 1981-; Hercules Inc, attny 1976-. **MEMBERSHIPS** Mem ABA Labor Law Sect 1976-, NBA Corp Sect 1976-, PA Bar Assoc 1976-, DE Bar Assoc 1981-. **CONTACT ADDRESS** Hercules Inc, Hercules Plaza, Wilmington, DE, 19894.

ALI-JACKSON, KAMIL
PERSONAL Born 03/04/1959, El Paso, TX, m, 1985 **DISCIPLINE** LAW **EDUCATION** Princeton Univ, AB, 1981; Harvard Law School, JD, 1984. **CAREER** McCarter & English, associate, 1984-86; Pepper, Hamilton & Scheetz, associate, 1986-90; Merck & Co Inc, director, Corporate Licensing, 1990-. **HONORS AND AWARDS** Princeton Univ, Ralph G Treen Memorial Scholarship, 1980. **MEMBERSHIPS** National Bar Association, 1986-92; Philadelphia Bar Association, 1986-92; Pennsylvania Bar Association, 1986-. **SELECTED PUBLICATIONS** The Experienced Hand, How to Make the Most of an Internship, 1980. **CONTACT ADDRESS** Merck & Co Inc, One Merck Dr, Whitehouse Station, NJ, 08889-0100.

ALISTAIR, MACLEOD
DISCIPLINE PHILOSOPHY **EDUCATION** Univ Glasgow, MA; Queen's Univ, PhD. **CAREER** Dept Philos, Queen's Univ **RESEARCH** Ethics; social and political philosophy; philosophy of law. **SELECTED PUBLICATIONS** Auth, Paul Tillich: An Essay on the Role of Ontology in his Philosophical Theology, Allen and Unwin, 73; Freedom and Equality: A False Antithesis, Univ Kans, 97. **CONTACT ADDRESS** Philosophy Dept, Queen's Univ, Kingston, ON, K7L 3N6.

ALLEN, ANITA
DISCIPLINE PHILOSOPHY **EDUCATION** Harvard Univ, BA; Univ Mich, PhD, 79. **CAREER** Asst prof, Carnegie Mellon Univ, 78-80; asst prof, Univ Pittsburgh, 85-87, adj prof, 87-. **RESEARCH** Race relations policy; law and literature **SELECTED PUBLICATIONS** Auth, Uneasy Access: Privacy for Women in a Free Society, 88; co-auth, Cases and Materials on Privacy Law, 92. **CONTACT ADDRESS** Dept of Philosophy, Georgetown Univ, 37th and O St, Washington, DC, 20057.

ALLEN, BERNARD LEE
PERSONAL Born 07/19/1937, Weston, WV, m, 1964, 2 children **DISCIPLINE** HISTORY, PHILOSOPHY **EDUCATION** WVa Univ, BS, 59; Southern Ill Univ, MA, 64; WVa Univ, PhD(hist), 71. **CAREER** Instr hist & philos, WVa Univ, Parkersburg, 66-68 & WVa Univ, 70-71; asst prof hist & philos, 71-74, actg asst dean arts & sci, 75-76; assoc prof, 74-81, dean arts & sci & actg dean occup tech, 76, asst dean instr, 79-80, PROF HIST & PHILOS, PARKERSBURG COMMUNITY COL, 81-;adj instr, Wheeling Jesuit Univ, 93-98; adj instr, Washington St Comm Coll, 93-98. **HONORS AND AWARDS** Bd of Dir, WV Hum Fnd, Outstand Svc to Higher Edu, WV Prof of the Yr. **MEMBERSHIPS** Appalachian Stud Assn, WV Hist Assn of Col and Univ Tchrs of Hist; Oil, Gas, and Indus Hist Assn. **RESEARCH** John Dewey's philosophy of history; mid-Ohio valley; women of the Ohio valley; U.S. social and ideological history; the Virginias and the Carolinas. **SELECTED PUBLICATIONS** Auth, John Dewey's Views on History, 1859-1971, Univ Microfilms, 71; Oarkersburg: A Bicentennial History, Parkersburg Bicentennial Commission, 85; Lessons, Data Day, 90; Compassion: A History of the Harry Logan Children's Home, Harry Logan Children's Home Fnd, 92; co-auth, Where It All Began, 94. **CONTACT ADDRESS** Parkersburg Community Col, 300 Campus Dr, Box 167-A, Parkersburg, WV, 26101-8647. **EMAIL** ballen@alha.wuup.wvnet.edu

ALLEN, COLIN
DISCIPLINE PHILOSOPHY **EDUCATION** Univ Calif, Los Angeles, PhD. **CAREER** Assoc prof, Texas A&M Univ. **SELECTED PUBLICATIONS** Auth, Belief and Concept Attribution in Non-human Animals, Philos Sci, 91; Mental Content, Brit J for the Philos Sci, 92; It Isn't What You Think: A New Idea About Intentional Causation, Nous, 95 & Function, Adaptation, and Design, Philos Sci, 95; coauth, Intentionality, Social Play, and Definition, Biology and Philosophy, 94. **CONTACT ADDRESS** Dept of Philosophy, Texas A&M Univ, 314 Bolton Hall, College Station, TX, 77843-4237.

ALLEN, DIOGENES
PERSONAL Born 10/17/1932, Lexington, KY, m, 1958, 4 children **DISCIPLINE** PHILOSOPHICAL THEOLOGY **EDUCATION** Univ Ky, BA, 54; Oxford Univ, BA, 57, MA, 61; Yale Univ, BD, 59, MA, 61, PhD, 65. **CAREER** Asst prof to assoc prof, York Univ, 64-67; assoc prof, prof, Stuart prof of philos, Princeton Theol Sem, 67-. **HONORS AND AWARDS** Rhodes scholar, Rockefeller fel; res fel ATS; PEW scholarship; Templeton award in science & theol; Center of Theol Inquiry fel. **MEMBERSHIPS** Am Phil Assn; Am Theol Soc; Am Weil Soc; Leibniz Gesellschaft; Am Acad Relig. **RESEARCH** Science & relig, spirituality, Simone Weil, 17th cen philos. **SELECTED PUBLICATIONS** Auth, Mechanical Explanations and the Ultimate Origin of the Universe According to Leibniz, 83, Steiner; auth, Philosophy for Understanding Theology, 85, John Knox Press, and German translation Philosophie fuer das Theologiestudium, 95, Chr. Kaiser; auth, Christian Belief in a Postmodern World: The Full Wealth of Conviction, 89, John Knox Press; coauth, Nature, Spirit, and Community: Issues in the Thought of Simone Weil, 94, SUNY; auth, Spiritual Theology: the Theology of Yesterday for Help Today, 97, Cowley Publications; auth, "Intellectual Inquiry and Spiritual Formation," in Essentials of Christian Community, 96, T & T Clark; auth, "Christian Spirituality and Psychology," in Linning to the Psyche: Explorations into Christian Psychology, 97, Eerdmans; auth, "Jesus and Human Experience," in The Truth about Jesus, 98, Eerdmans; auth, "Natural Evil and the Love of God," Relig Studies, Dec 80; auth, "George Herbert and Simone Weil," Relig and Lit, Aug 85; auth, "Mozart's Don Giovanni and Love of Neighbor," Theol Today, Oct 88; auth, "The Issues Posed by the Order of the Universe," Proceedings of the V Leibniz Kongress, 88; auth, "Incarnation in the Gospels and the Bhagavad-Gita," Faith and Philos, Jan 89; auth, "The End of the Modern World," Christian Scholars Rev, July 83; auth, "Manifestations of the Supernatural according to Simone Weil: An Essay in Theological Reasoning," Cahiers Simone Weil, Sept 94. **CONTACT ADDRESS** Princeton Theol Sem, Princeton, NJ, 08542. **EMAIL** diogenes.allen@ptsem.edu

ALLEN, O. WESLEY, JR.
PERSONAL Born 06/16/1965, Sylacavoa, AL, m, 1995, 1 child **DISCIPLINE** NEW TESTAMENT **EDUCATION** Yale Divinity School, Mdiv, 90; Birmingham, Southern Coll, BA, 87; Emory Univ, PhD, 96. **CAREER** Dean of the Chapel, 98-, DePauw Univ. **MEMBERSHIPS** Soc Biblical Lit. **RESEARCH** Synoptic Gospels. **SELECTED PUBLICATIONS** Auth, The Death of Herod: The narrative and theological function of retribution in Like-Acts, 97; Good News from Thinville: Stories of heart and hope, spring, 99; Interpreting the Synoptic Gospels, Fall, 99. **CONTACT ADDRESS** DePauw Univ, 209 E Seminary St, Greencastle, IN, 46135. **EMAIL** wallen@depauw.edu

ALLEN, ROBERT F.
PERSONAL Born 02/09/1959, Detroit, MI, m, 1990, 2 children **DISCIPLINE** PHILOSOPHY **EDUCATION** Univ Michigan, BA, Wayne State Univ, PhD. **CAREER** Central Michigan Univ Detroit, adj prof, 94-. **MEMBERSHIPS** APA **RESEARCH** Metaphysics **CONTACT ADDRESS** Dept of Philosophy, Central Michigan Univ, 9300 Salem, Redford, MI, 48239-1508. **EMAIL** RAllen2322@aol.com

ALLEN, RONALD J.
PERSONAL Born 04/26/1949, Poplar Bluff, MO, m, 1975, 5 children **DISCIPLINE** NEW TESTAMENT, HOMILETICS **EDUCATION** Phillips Univ, AB, 71; Union Theol Sem, MDiv, 74; Drew Univ, PhD, 77. **CAREER** Co-pastor, First Christian Church, Grand Is, Nebr, 77-82; asst and assoc prof of Preaching and New Test, Christian Theol Sem, Indianapolis, 82- . **MEMBERSHIPS** SBL; Acad Homiletics; Relig Speech Commun Asn. **RESEARCH** Preaching **SELECTED PUBLICATIONS** Auth, The Teaching Sermon, Abingdon, 95; coauth, Holy Root, Holy Branches, Abingdon, 96; coauth, Theology for Preaching, Abingdon, 97; Interpreting the Gospel, Chalice, 98; Patterns for Preaching, Chalice, 98; coauth, The Vital Church, Chalice 98. **CONTACT ADDRESS** Dept of New Testament, Christian Theol Sem, 1000 W 42nd St, Indianaplois, IN, 46208. **EMAIL** rallen@cts.edu

ALLISON, DALE C., JR.
PERSONAL Born 11/25/1955, Wichita, KS, m, 1982, 3 children **DISCIPLINE** BIBLICAL STUDIES **EDUCATION** Whichita State Univ, BA, 77; Duke Univ, MA, 79, PhD, 82. **CAREER** Res assoc, TX Christian Academy, 82-86; res scholar, Saint Paul School of Theology, 86-89; res fel, Friends Univ, 89-97; assoc prof of New Testament and Early Christianity, Pittsburgh Theol Sem, 97-. **HONORS AND AWARDS** Recipient of Pew Charitable Trust grant, 97-98. **MEMBERSHIPS** Studiorum Novi Testamenti Societas; Soc of Biblical Lit. **RESEARCH** Ancient Judaism and early Christianity. **SELECTED PUBLICATIONS** Auth, The End of the Ages has Come: An Early Interpretation of the Passion and Resurrection of Jesus, Fortress, 85, T & T Clark, 87; with W D Davies, An Exegetical and Critical Commentary on the Gospel according to St Matthew, T & T Clark, 88, vol 2, T & T Clark, 91, vol 3, T & T Clark, 97; with W D Davies, The New Moses: A Matthean Typology, Fortress and T & T Clark, 93; The Silence of Angels,

Trinity Press Int, 95; The Jesus Tradition in Q, Trinity Press Int, 97; Jesus of Nazareth: Millenarian Prophet, Fortress, 98; The Sermon on the Mount: Inspiring the Moral Imagination, Crossroad, forthcoming 99. **CONTACT ADDRESS** Pittsburgh Theol Sem, 616 N Highland Ave, Pittsburgh, PA, 15206.

ALMEDER, ROBERT F.
DISCIPLINE THEORY OF KNOWLEDGE, PHILOSOPHY OF SCIENCE, ETHICAL THEORY, AMERICAN PHILOS **EDUCATION** Univ Pa, PhD, 69. **CAREER** Prof, Ga State Univ; ed, Am Philos Quart. **SELECTED PUBLICATIONS** Auth, Blind Realism: An Essay on Human Knowledge and Natural Science; Death and Personal Survival; The Philosophy of Charles S. Peirce; Harmless Naturalism. **CONTACT ADDRESS** Georgia State Univ, Atlanta, GA, 30303. **EMAIL** phlrra@panther.gsu.edu

ALMEIDA, ONESIMO
PERSONAL Born 12/18/1946, Azores, Portugal, m, 1992, 3 children **DISCIPLINE** PHILOSOPHY **EDUCATION** Portuguese Cath Univ, Lisbon, BA, 72; Brown Univ, MA, 77, PhD, 80. **CAREER** Prof and chemn Dept of Portuguese and Brazilian Stud, Brown Univ, 91- . **HONORS AND AWARDS** Srec Essay Prize, 86; officer, Order of Prince Henry, Pres of Portugal. **MEMBERSHIPS** APA; Soc for the Study of European Ideas; Am Portuguese Stud Asn. **RESEARCH** Sixteenth century Portugal; world views, values and ideologies. **SELECTED PUBLICATIONS** Auth, Que Nome e Esse, O Nezimo? 94; ed, Y.R. Migueis, Aforismos Edesaforismos De Aparicio, 96; auth, Rio Atlantico, 97. **CONTACT ADDRESS** Brown Univ, PO Box 0, Providence, RI, 02912. **EMAIL** onesimo_almeida@brown.edu

ALPERSON, PHILIP A.
DISCIPLINE PHILOSOPHY **EDUCATION** Univ Toronto, PhD. **CAREER** Dept Philos, Univ Louisville **HONORS AND AWARDS** Ed, The Jour of Aesthet and Art Criticism. **RESEARCH** Aesthetics. **SELECTED PUBLICATIONS** Auth, articles on musical performance and improvisation, the philos of art and mus edu, value theory, and the aesthet theories of Hegel and Schopenhauer; ed, The Philosophy of the Visual Arts, Oxford, 92; What Is Music?, An Introduction to the Aesthetics of Music, Penn State UP, 94; Musical Worlds: New Directions in the Philosophy of Music, Penn State UP, 98. **CONTACT ADDRESS** Dept of Philos, Univ Louisville, 2301 S 3rd St, Louisville, KY, 40292. **EMAIL** paalpe01@homer.louisville.edu

ALPERT, REBECCA T.
PERSONAL Born 04/12/1950, Brooklyn, NY, 2 children **DISCIPLINE** RELIGION **EDUCATION** Temple Univ, PhD, 78. **CAREER** Dean of Students, Reconstructionist Rabbinical Col, 79-88; Dir of Adult Progs, Temple Univ, 89-92, co-dir, Women's Studies Prog, 92-, asst prof, Religion, Temple Univ, 96-. **HONORS AND AWARDS** Lambda Literary Award for Religion/Spirituality, 98. **MEMBERSHIPS** Am Academy of Relig; Nat Women's Studies Asn; Reconstructionist Rabbinical Asn. **RESEARCH** Relig and sexuality; women in Judaism. **SELECTED PUBLICATIONS** Auth, Joshua Loth Liebman: The Peace of Mind Rabbi, in Faith and Freedom: Essays in Honor of Franklin Littell, ed R Libowitz, Pergamon Press, 87; The Quest for Economic Justice: Kaplan's Response to the Challenge of Communism 1929-1940, in The American Judaism of Mordecai Kaplan, ed M Scult, E Goldsmith and R Seltzer, NY Univ Press, 90; Challenging Male/Female Complementarity: Jewish Lesbians and the Jewish Tradition, in People of the Body: Jews and Judaism from an Embodied Perspective, ed Howard Eilberg-Schwartz, SUNY Press, 92; Sometimes the Law is Cruel: the Construction of a Jewish Anti-Abortion Position in the Writings of Immanuel Jakobovits in J of Feminist Studies in Relig, fall 95; with Goldie Milgram, Women in the Reconstructionist Rabbinate in Religious Institutions and Women's Leadership: New Roles Inside the Mainstream, ed Catherine Wessinger, Univ SC Press, 96; On Seams and Seamlessness, in Judaism Since Gender, eds Laura Levitt and Miriam Peskowitz, Routledge, 96, reprinted from Shofar: An Interdisciplinary Journal of Jewish Studies, fall 95; Like Bread on the Seder Plate: Jewish Lesbians and the Transformation of Tradition, Columbia Univ Press, 97, Lambda Literary Award, 98; with J Staub, Exploring Judaism: A Reconstructionist Approach, Reconstructionist Press, 85, rev ed, 99. **CONTACT ADDRESS** 6817 Milton St, Philadelphia, PA, 19119. **EMAIL** ralpert@nimbus.temple.edu

ALTER, TORIN
DISCIPLINE PHILOSOPHY OF MIND **EDUCATION** UCLA, PhD, 95. **CAREER** Philos, Col NJ. **SELECTED PUBLICATIONS** Auth, Mary's New Perspective, Australian Jour Philos, 95. **CONTACT ADDRESS** Col of New Jersey, PO Box 7718, Ewing, NJ, 08628-0718.

ALTMAN, IRA
PERSONAL Born 03/17/1944, Russia, m, 1969, 1 child **DISCIPLINE** PHILOSOPHY **EDUCATION** CUNY Grad Sch and Univ Ctr. **CAREER** Stevens Inst Technol, 74-78; Pace Univ, 85-92; Yeshiva Univ, 90-92; Touro Col, 91- ; Suffolk County Comm Col, SUNY, 90- ; Queensborough Comm Col CUNY, 95- ; **HONORS AND AWARDS** Univ fel; Marc Showitz Memorial Scholar; contribur World Congress of Philos; Philos Educ Delegation: Citizens Embassador Prog of People to People Int; Who's Who in Am Educ. **MEMBERSHIPS** APA; LIPS. **RESEARCH** Cognitive science; philosophy of mind; epistemology. **SELECTED PUBLICATIONS** Auth, The Concept of Intelligence, Univ Press of Am; auth, Lectures in Critical Thinking, Copley Press; auth, Lectures in Philosophy, American Heritage; auth, Readings in Philosophy, McGraw-Hill. **CONTACT ADDRESS** 43-43 Kissena Blvd, Flushing, NY, 11355. **EMAIL** altmanh@voyager.bxscience.edu

ALTMAN, SCOTT A.
DISCIPLINE FAMILY LAW **EDUCATION** Univ Wis, BA, 83; Harvard Univ, JD,87. **CAREER** Virginia S.& Fred H. Bice prof & assoc dean, Univ Southern Calif;clerked, Honorable Dorothy Nelson, Judge US Ct Appeals 9th Circuit. **RESEARCH** Jurisprudence & family law. **SELECTED PUBLICATIONS** Auth, Should Child Custody Rules Be Fair; Divorcing Threats and Offers; Child Custody and Justice,; Beyond Candor & A Patchwork Theory of Blackmail. **CONTACT ADDRESS** School of Law, Univ Southern Calif, University Park Campus, Los Angeles, CA, 90089. **EMAIL** saltman@law.usc.edu

ALWARD, LORI L.
PERSONAL Born 12/31/1957, Tacoma, WA, s **DISCIPLINE** PHILOSOPHY **EDUCATION** Univ North Carolina, Chapel Hill, MA, 87, PhD, 97. **CAREER** Vis asst prof, Univ Puget Sound, 96- . **HONORS AND AWARDS** Javits fel, 86-90; Kennan fel, 85-86. **MEMBERSHIPS** APA; Soc for the Study of Women Philos. **RESEARCH** Ethics; social and political philosophy; feminst theory; Kant. **CONTACT ADDRESS** 2911 N 12 St, Tacoma, WA, 98406. **EMAIL** lalward@ups.edu

AMAKER, NORMAN CAREY
PERSONAL Born 01/15/1935, New York, NY, m, 1962 **DISCIPLINE** LAW **EDUCATION** Amherst Clg, BA (cum laude) 1956; Columbia U, JD 1959. **CAREER** NAACP Legal Def Fund NYC, atty 1960-68, first asst cnsl 1968-71; Nbrh Legal Serv Prog Wash DC, exec dir 1971-73; Natl Comm Agnst Dscrmntn in Housing, gen cnsl; 1973; Rutgers Univ, prof of law 1973-76; Loyola Univ of Chicago Law Sch, prof of law 1976-. **HONORS AND AWARDS** IBPOE of W Awd 1965; BALSA Awd 1973. **MEMBERSHIPS** Sch bd mem Dist 202 Evanston Twnshp H S 1980-87, pres pro-tem 1983-84; pres Chicago Forum Chicago 1982-83; bd of gov Soc of Am Law Tchrs 1979-87. **SELECTED PUBLICATIONS** Auth, Civil Liberties & Civil Rghts Oceana 1967; Civil Rights and the Reagan Adm, Urban Inst Wash DC, 988. **CONTACT ADDRESS** Loyola Univ, Chicago, 1 E Pearson St, 526, Chicago, IL, 60611.

AMAN, ALFRED C., JR.
PERSONAL Born 07/07/1945, Rochester, NY, m, 1976 **DISCIPLINE** POLITICAL SCIENCE, LAW **EDUCATION** Univ Rochester, AB, 67; Univ Chicago, JD, 70. **CAREER** Intern, 67, exec comm Econ devel, NY St Constitutional Convention; assoc, 69, Covington & Burling, Wash, DC, and Sullivan & Cromwell, NY; law clerk, 70-72, Hon Elbert P. Tuttle, US Court of Appeals, Fifth Circuit; adj prof, 71-75, Law, Emory Univ; assoc, 72-75, Sutherland, Asbill & Brennan, Atlanta, Wash, DC, 75-77; vis fel, 83-84, 90-91, Wolfson Col, Cambridge Univ; assoc prof, 77-83, prof of Law, 83-91, Cornell Law School; res fel, 93, Bellagio Study & Conf Ctr, Rockefeller Found; vis prof Law, 97, Univ Paris (II), Inst of Comparative Law, 98, 99; Fulbright Dist Chr in Comparative Constitutional and Administrative Law, Trento Univ School of Law, Italy, 98; dean, prof, Ind Univ School of Law, 91-. **HONORS AND AWARDS** Phi Beta Kappa; Univ Scholar; William E. Townsend fel Award for Achievement in Polit Sci; Exec ed, Univ Chicago Law Rev; Nat Honor Scholar. **MEMBERSHIPS** DC Bar; GA Bar; NY Bar; IN Bar; Am Bar Asn; IN State Bar Asn; Federal Bar Asn. **RESEARCH** Globalization; administrative law; comparative constitutional law. **SELECTED PUBLICATIONS** Auth, Administrative Law In A Global Era, Cornell Univ Press, 93; coauth, Administrative Law Treatise, West Pub Co, 93; auth, Administrative Law and Process, Matthew-Bender Corp, 93, supp, 97, 2nd ed; ed, The Globalization of Law, Politics and Markets, 1 Indiana J. Global Legal Stud, 93; auth, Preserving the Eggshell Planet: A Global Perspective on Domestic Regulation, 102 Yale Law J, 2107, 93; auth, Administrative Law for a New Century, The Province of Administrative Law, Hart Pub, Oxford, 97; auth, The Globalizing State: A Future-Oriented Perspective on the Public/Private Distinction, Federalism and Democracy, 32 Vand J trans L, 98. **CONTACT ADDRESS** School of Law, Indiana Univ, Bloomington, 211 S Indiana Ave, Bloomington, IN, 47405. **EMAIL** Fredaman@law.indiana.edu

AMARU-HALPERN, BETSY
PERSONAL Born 09/07/1939, Ahoona, PA, d, 4 children **DISCIPLINE** RELIGION **EDUCATION** Barnard BA, 61; Brandeis Univ, MA, 63; Harvard Univ, MAT 63; Univ MA, PhD, 69. **CAREER** Prof 81-, Vassar College. **MEMBERSHIPS** SBL **RESEARCH** Judaism. **SELECTED PUBLICATIONS** Auth, Empowered Women: Wives and Mothers in the Book of Jubilees, Leiden, EJ Brill, forthcoming; Rewriting the Bible: Land and Covenant in Post-Biblical Jewish Literature, Philadelphia, Trinity Press Intl, 94; The Empowerment of Rachel in the Book of Jubilees, proceedings of the 12th World Congress of Jewish Studies, forthcoming; The Renaming of Levi, Pseudepigraphic Perspectives: The Apocrypha and the Pseudepigrapha in Light of the Dead Sea Scrolls, eds M Stone, E Chazon, Leiden, EJ Brill, forthcoming; The Portrait of Sarah in Jubilees, Jewish Studies in a New Europe, eds U Haxen, H Trautner-Kromann, K Goldschmidt Salamon, Copenhagen Reitzel A/S, 98; Exile and Return in the Book of Jubilees, Exile: Old Testament Jewish Christian Conceptions, ed James M Scott, Leiden, EJ Brill, 97; Jewish Civilization in Christian Academic Settings, Teaching Jewish Civilization, ed, Moshe Davis, Jerusalem, Magnes 96, Hebrew Edition; rev, Christopher Wright's God's People in God's Land, Hebrew Studies, 95; The First Women Wives and Mothers in Jubilees, J Biblical Lit, 94; Teaching Judaism in a Christian Academic Setting, in: A Global Approach to Higher Education, ed, Moshe Davis, NY, NY U Press, 94; rev, The Land of Israel in Judaism, W D Davies's, The Territorial Dimension of Judaism, Midstream, 93. **CONTACT ADDRESS** Vassar Col, Box 55, Poughkeepsie, NY, 12604.

AMBROSIO, FRANCIS J.
PERSONAL New York, NY **DISCIPLINE** PHILOSOPHY **EDUCATION** Fordham Univ, BA, PhD. **CAREER** Asst prof, St Joseph's Univ, 76-79; assoc prof, 81-. **RESEARCH** Existentialism; Christian philosophy. **SELECTED PUBLICATIONS** Auth, Fra Angelico at San Marco: The Place of Art; co-ed, Text and Teaching, Georgetown; The Question of Christian Philosophy Today, Fordham Univ. **CONTACT ADDRESS** Dept of Philosophy, Georgetown Univ, 37th and O St, Washington, DC, 20057.

AMBROSIO, MICHAEL P.
DISCIPLINE LAW **EDUCATION** Montclair State Col, BA; Cath Univ, JD. **CAREER** Prof, 70-, dir, Seton Hall Law Schl Clin Prog, Seton Hall Univ; vis prof, Southwestern Univ; vis scholar, Univ Florence; assoc, grad sem, Columbia Univ. **HONORS AND AWARDS** Prof of the Yr, Delta Theta Phi Int Legal Fraternity, 88., Founder, Seton Hall Law Schl Clin Prog, Seton Hall Univ. **MEMBERSHIPS** NJ Bar Asn. **SELECTED PUBLICATIONS** Publ in the areas of legal ethics and professional malpractice. **CONTACT ADDRESS** Seton Hall Univ, South Orange, NJ. **EMAIL** ambrosmi@lanmail.shu.edu

AMBROZIC, ALOYSIUS M.
PERSONAL Born 01/27/1930, Gabrje, Slovenia **DISCIPLINE** THEOLOGY **EDUCATION** St Augustine's Sem; Univ San Tommaso, STL, 58; Pontificio Inst Biblico, SSL, 60; Univ Wurzburg, ThD, 70. **CAREER** Prof, 60-67, dean stud, St Augustine's Sem, 71-76; prof, Toronto Sch Theol, 70-76; aux bishop, Roman Cath Archdiocese Toronto, 76-86; Coadjutor Archbishop Toronto, 86-90; ARCHBISHOP, ROMAN CATHOLIC ARCHDIOCESE OF TORONTO, 90-. **MEMBERSHIPS** Cath Bibl Asn Am; ACEBAC. **SELECTED PUBLICATIONS** Auth, The Hidden Kingdom, 72; auth,Remarks on the Canadian Catechism, 74; auth, Oce, posveceno bodi tvoje ime, 80; auth, Oce, zgodi se tvoja volja, 96. **CONTACT ADDRESS** Roman Catholic Archdiocese of Toronto, 1155 Yonge St, Toronto, ON, M4T 1W2.

AMERIKS, KARL
DISCIPLINE PHILOSOPHY **EDUCATION** Yale Univ, PhD. **CAREER** Prof. **RESEARCH** European philosophy fron the 17th century to the present. **SELECTED PUBLICATIONS** Auth, Kant's Theory of Mind, 82; Understanding Apperception Today, Kant Cont Epistemol, 94; The Ineliminable Subject: From Kant to Frank, 95; Kant's Lectures on Metaphysics, 96; Probleme der Moralitat bei Kant und Hegel, 95; New Views on Kant's Judgment of Taste, 97. **CONTACT ADDRESS** Philosophy Dept, Univ of Notre Dame, 336/7 O'Shaughnessy, Notre Dame, IN, 46556. **EMAIL** ameriks.2@nd.edu

AMICO, ROBERT P.
PERSONAL Born 04/03/1947, Dorchester, MA, m, 1982, 1 child **DISCIPLINE** PHILOSOPHY **EDUCATION** Univ Rochester, PhD, 86. **CAREER** Prof philos, St. Bonaventure Univ. **MEMBERSHIPS** APA; AAUP. **RESEARCH** Epistemology. **SELECTED PUBLICATIONS** Auth, The Problem of the Criterion, Rowman & Littlefield, 93. **CONTACT ADDRESS** St. Bonaventure Univ, PO Box 101, St. Bonaventure, NY, 14778. **EMAIL** ramico@sbu.edu

AMIN RAZAVI, MEHDI
PERSONAL Born 09/22/1957, Mashhad, Iran, m, 1982, 2 children **DISCIPLINE** RELIGION **EDUCATION** Temple Univ, PhD 89; Univ Washington, MA 81, BA 79. **CAREER** Mary Washington College, assoc prof, dir, 90-; Prince George's Comm Coll, adj prof, 87-90; George Washington Univ, teach asst, 85-87. **HONORS AND AWARDS** Kabbani Awd; Mahvi Foun Awd; Outstanding Yng Fac Awd; Kut F Leidecker Ch. **MEMBERSHIPS** APA; AAR. **RESEARCH** Islamic philo; medieval philo; philo religion. **SELECTED PUBLICATIONS**

Auth, An Anthology of Philosophy In Persia, co-ed, vol 2, OUP, 2000; An Anthology of Philosophy of Persia, co-ed, vol 1, OUP, 1999; Philosophy Religion and the Question of Intolerance, co-ed, NY, SUNY Press, 97; The Islamic Intellectual tradition in Persia, ed, London, Curzon Press, 96; Suhrawardi and the School of Illumination, London, Curzon Press, 96; The Complete Bibliography of the Works of Seyyed Hossein Nasr: From 1958-1993, coauth, Malaysia, Islamic Acad of Sci Press, 94; Ibn Sina's Theory Knowledge by Presence, in: Synthesis Philosphica Croatia, forthcoming; Avicenna and Suhrawardi on Knowledge, Jour of Islamic Sci and Philo, forthcoming; Ontological and Metaphysical Perspectives of SH Nasr, in Living Lib of Philosophers, ed L.E. Hahn, forthcoming; Mystical and Philosophical Poetry of Suhrawardi, in: Treatises on Islamic philosophy, ed, Z Morris, Kazi Press, 99. **CONTACT ADDRESS** Dept of Classics Philosophy and Religion, Mary Washington Col, Fredericksburg, VA, 22401. **EMAIL** maminraz@mwc.edu

AMMON, THEODORE G.

DISCIPLINE HISTORY OF PHILOSOPHY, EPISTEMOLOGY, PHILOSOPHY AND LITERATURE **EDUCATION** Miss State Univ, BA; Wash Univ, MA, PhD. **CAREER** Dept Philos, Millsaps Col **SELECTED PUBLICATIONS** Publ on, ethical duties of teachers; philos underpinnings of lit of Jorge Luis Borges; teaching strategies for moral develop. **CONTACT ADDRESS** Dept of Philosophy, Millsaps Col, 1701 N State St, Jackson, MS, 39210. **EMAIL** ammontg@okra.millsaps.edu

AMORE, ROY C.

PERSONAL Born 09/10/1942, Newark, OH **DISCIPLINE** RELIGIOUS STUDIES **EDUCATION** Ohio Univ, BA, 64; Drew Univ (NJ), BD, 67; Columbia Univ, PhD, 70. **CAREER** Lectr, Drew Univ, 68-69; vis lectr, Upsala Univ (NJ), 69; instr, Bard Col, 69-70; asst to assoc prof, 70-81, coordr Asian stud prog, 80-81, 82-86, PROF RELIGIOUS STUDIES, UNIV WINDSOR, 81-, dept head, 86-88; Wilson-Craven prof, Southwestern Univ, 78-79. **MEMBERSHIPS** Can Coun Southeast Asian stud (pres, 80-82); Can Asian Stud Asn (vice pres 80-82); Can Soc Stud Relig. **SELECTED PUBLICATIONS** Auth, Two Masters, One Message, 78, Asian ed 85; coauth, Lustful Maidens and Ascetic Kings: Buddhist and Hindu Stories of Life, 81; coauth, Buddhism, in World Religions: Eastern Traditions, 96; ed, Developments in Buddhist Thought: Canadian Contributions to Buddhist Studies, 79; co-ed, Culture and Development in Southeast Asia, 87. **CONTACT ADDRESS** Dept of Political Science, Univ of Windsor, 401 Sunset Ave, Windsor, ON, N9B 3P4. **EMAIL** amore@uwindsor.ca

ANCHUSTEGUI, ANN-MARIE

PERSONAL Born 08/28/1962, Twin Falls, ID **DISCIPLINE** PHILOSOPHY **EDUCATION** Univ Wisconsin Madison, MA, 88; Wayne State Univ, PhD, 97. **CAREER** ADJ FAC, 94-98. **HONORS AND AWARDS** Grad tchg assistantship, 88-89. **MEMBERSHIPS** APA. **RESEARCH** Aesthetics; Philosophy of Mind. **CONTACT ADDRESS** Philosophy Dept, Wayne State Univ, Detroit, MI, 48201. **EMAIL** ad5846@wayne.edu

ANDERSEN, ROGER WILLIAM

PERSONAL Born 10/20/1948, Chicago, IL, m, 1975, 2 children **DISCIPLINE** LAW **EDUCATION** Knox Col, BA, 70; Univ Iowa, JD, 73; Univ Ill, LLM, 78. **CAREER** Legal Writing instr, Col of Law, Univ Ill, 76-77; asst prof, Sch of Law, Oklahoma City Univ, 77-79; from assoc prof to prof Law, Col of Law, Univ Toledo, 79-83; vis prof, Univ Richmond, 83-84; vis scholar, Wolfson College, Cambridge, England, 90. **HONORS AND AWARDS** Phi Beta Kappa. **SELECTED PUBLICATIONS** Coauth (with Dr LeRoy Rogers), Time-limited water rights: Legal and economic considerations, Gonz Law Rev, 77; auth, The resource conservation and Recovery Act of 1976: Closing the gap, Wis Law Rev, 78 & Solid & Hazardous Waste Management in Wis, Clew, 4/79; Stating objectives for a legal writing course, J Legal Educ, 79; Some lessons learned in two legal writing programs, Newsletter of the Asn Am Law Sch Sect on Legal Writing, Reasoning and Res, 8/80; Accessible private housing: A suggested agenda, Notre Dame Law, 80; Understanding Trusts and Estates, Matthew Bender, 94; Fundamentals of Trusts and Estates, Matthew Bender, 96, with John Gaubatz, Ira Bloom, Lewis Solomon, with Teachers Guide. **CONTACT ADDRESS** Col of Law, Univ of Toledo, 2801 W Bancroft St, Toledo, OH, 43606-3391. **EMAIL** randers3@utoledo.edu

ANDERSON, CHARLES SAMUEL

PERSONAL Born 03/04/1930, Madison, WI, m, 1951, 2 children **DISCIPLINE** HISTORICAL THEOLOGY **EDUCATION** St Olaf Col, BA, 51; Univ Wis, MA, 54; Luther Theol Sem, BD, 57; Union Theol Sem, NY, PhD (Hist Theol & Reformation Studies), 62. **CAREER** Teaching asst English, Univ Wis, 53-54; from asst prof to prof Hist Theol, Luther Theol Sem, 61-77, dir Grad Studies, 68-72, vpres Acad Affairs & dean, 77-80, pres, Augsburg Col, 80-97, clergyman, Am Lutheran Church, 57-; mem, Rockefeller Scholar Area Selection Comt, 63, 69; comn Inter Church Affairs, Am Lutheran Church, 64; vis lectr, Northwestern Lutheran Theol Sem, 64; Am Asn Theol Sch sabbatical studies grant, 67-68; vis lectr, Concordia Theol Sem, 68; Bush Found fel, 71-; chmn div Theol Studies, Lutheran Coun USA, 72-. **HONORS AND AWARDS** Phi Betta Kappa, Rockefeller & Martin Luther fell; Bush Leadership fell. **MEMBERSHIPS** Am Soc Church Hist; Renaissance Soc Am; Soc Reformation Res. **RESEARCH** Reformation theology; the military aspects of the Reformation; improvement of education for ministry. **SELECTED PUBLICATIONS** Auth, International Luther studies, Ecumenist, 66; Will the real Luther please stand up, Dialog, 67; The Reformation Then and Now, 67; The Augsburg Historical Atlas of Christianity in the Middle Ages and Reformation, 67, 72 & ed, Readings in Luther for Laymen, 67, Augsburg; auth, Robert Barnes, In: Interpretors of Luther, 68 & ed, Facet Books Reformation Series, 69-, Fortress; auth, Faith and Freedom: The Christian Faith According to the Lutheran Confessions, Augsburg, 78. **CONTACT ADDRESS** 1377 Grantham St, St. Paul, MN, 55108. **EMAIL** andersoc@visi.com

ANDERSON, DAVID LEECH

DISCIPLINE PHILOSOPHY **EDUCATION** Whitman Col, BA; Regent Col, DCS; Harvard Univ, MTS, PhD. **CAREER** Assoc prof. **SELECTED PUBLICATIONS** Auth, A Dogma of Metaphysical Realism, Am Philos Quarterly, 95. **CONTACT ADDRESS** Dept of Philosophy, Illinois State Univ, Normal, IL, 61761. **EMAIL** dlanders@ilstu.edu

ANDERSON, DAVID M.

PERSONAL Born 12/15/1958, Atlantic City, NJ **DISCIPLINE** PHILOSOPHY **EDUCATION** George Wash Univ, BA, 81; Univ MI, PhD, 90. **CAREER** Asst prof lect, 96-98, Philos, George Wash Univ, Univ Cincinnati & Col of Charleston; assoc prof lect, 96-97, adj assoc prof, grad sch of polit management, 97-98, George Wash Univ. **HONORS AND AWARDS** Charlotte Newcombe Found fel, 87-88; Phi Beta Kappa, 82. **MEMBERSHIPS** APA; Soc for the Advancement of Socio-Economics; Commentaria Network. **RESEARCH** Ethics; social and political philos; business ethics; ethics and political management. **SELECTED PUBLICATIONS** Auth, False Stability and Defensive Justification in Rawlsian Liberalism: A Feminist Critique, in The Ethics of Liberal Democracy: Morality and Democracy in Theory and Practice, Berg Pubs, 94, Contemporary Philos, vol XIV, no 5, 92; auth, Scholars Roundtable: Remarks on Dr. Martin Luther King Jr's Concept of the Beloved Community, Inst for Conflict Analysis and Resolution Newsl, vol 7, no 3, 95, & The First Annual Scholars Roundtable on Peace & Conflict Stud: A Report to the Wash Area Consortium of Univ, 96; auth, A Few Questions for Communitarians, The Responsive Community, vol 6, no 2, 96; auth, Communitarian Approaches to the Economy, Merits ands Limits of Markets, Springer-Verlag, 98; A Viable Strategy for Women's Progress, Women's Progress: Perspectives on the Past: Blueprint for the Future, Conf Proceed, Inst for Women's Policy Res 98; auth, Part of the Project of Building a Progressive Coalition: Uniting Working Mothers and Welfare Mothers Behind a National Family Policy, Inherent and Instrumental Value: An Excursion of Value Inquiry, Intentional Scholars Pubs, 99. **CONTACT ADDRESS** Graduate Sch of Political Management, George Washington Univ, 2147 F St NW, Washington, DC, 20052. **EMAIL** davidand@gwa.edu

ANDERSON, DENNIS A.

DISCIPLINE CHURCH ADMINISTRATION **EDUCATION** Gustavus Adolphus Col, BA, 59; Augustana Theol Sem, MDiv, 63; Austin Presbyterian Sem, Grad Stud, 64-65; Gustavus Adolphus Col, DD, 78; Midland Lutheran Col, DHL, 80; Wittenberg Univ, DD, 90. **CAREER** Sec Interpretation/Regional dir Amer Missions, Lutheran Church Am, 71-73; Bishop, Nebraska Synod, Lutheran Church Am, 78-87; Bishop, Nebraska Synod, Evangel Lutheran Church Am, 88-90; president, 90-. **SELECTED PUBLICATIONS** Auth, Mission90 Bible Study/Witness, Augsburg, 91; co-auth, The Many Faces of Pastoral Ministry, Augsburg, 89; contrib, Sacraments and Daily Life - Homiletical Helps, Div Parish Svc, Lutheran Church Am, 87. **CONTACT ADDRESS** Ministry Dept, Trinity Lutheran Sem, 2199 E Main St, Columbus, OH, 43209-2334. **EMAIL** danderso@trinity.capital.edu

ANDERSON, DOUGLAS R.

PERSONAL Born 05/17/1953, Keene, NH, m, 1976, 2 children **DISCIPLINE** PHILOSOPHY **EDUCATION** Penn State Univ, PhD, 84. **CAREER** Wittenburg Univ, 84-90; Penn State Univ, 90-. **RESEARCH** Am philos; hist of philos. **SELECTED PUBLICATIONS** Auth, Creativity and the Philosophy of C. S. Pierce, Martinus Nijhoff Pubs, The Hague, 87; auth, Strands of System: The Philosophy of Charles Pierce, Purdue Univ Press, 95; co-ed, Philosophy in Experience: American Philosophy in Transition, Fordham Univ Press, 97; chap, intros, & 1 chap auth, "Pierce and Representative Persons". **CONTACT ADDRESS** Dept of Philosophy, Pennsylvania State Univ, University Park, PA, 16802. **EMAIL** dra3@psu.edu

ANDERSON, ELIZABETH S.

PERSONAL Born 12/05/1959, Boston, MA, m, 1992, 2 children **DISCIPLINE** PHILOSOPHY **EDUCATION** Swarthmore Col, BA, 81; Harvard Univ, MA, 87, PhD, 87. **CAREER** Tchg fel, Harvard Univ, 83-85; vis instr philos, Swarthmore Col, 85-86; asst prof philos, 87-93, assoc prof philos and women's stud, 93-, Univ Michigan. **HONORS AND AWARDS** Humanities Inst Fel, Univ Michigan, 89-90; Univ Mich Col of LS&A excellence in educ award, 91; selected by The Philos Asn, one of ten best philos papers in 91; Arthur F. Thurnau prof, awarded for excellence in undergrad tchg, 94. **MEMBERSHIPS** APA; Soc for Analytic Feminism. **RESEARCH** Ethics; social and political philosophy; philosophy of the social sciences; feminist theory; epistemology. **SELECTED PUBLICATIONS** Auth, Value in Ethics and in Economics, Harvard, 93; auth, The Democratic University: The Role of Justice in The Production of Knowledge, Social Philos and Policy, 95; auth, Feminist Epistemology: An Interpretation and Defense, Hypatia, 95; auth, Knowledge, Human Interests, and Objectivity in Feminist Epistemology, Philos Topics, 95; auth, Reasons, Attitudes, and Values: Replies to Sturgeon and Piper, Ethics, 96; auth, Comment on Dawson's Exit, Voice, and Values in Economic Institutions, Econom and Philos, 97; auth, Practical Reason and Incommensurable Goods, in Chang, ed, Incommensurability, Incomparability, and Practical Reason, Harvard, 97; auth, Pragmatism, Science, and Moral Inquiry, in Fox, ed, In Face of the Facts: Moral Inquiry in American Scholarship, Cambridge, 98; auth, John Stuart Mill on Democracy as Sentimental Education, in Rorty, ed, Philosophy of Education, Chicago, 98; auth, What Is The Point of Equality? Ethics, 99. **CONTACT ADDRESS** Dept of Philosophy, Univ of Michigan, 435 South State St, Angell Hal, Ann Arbor, MI, 48109-1003. **EMAIL** eandersn@umich.edu

ANDERSON, JAMI L.

DISCIPLINE PHILOSOPHY **EDUCATION** Ariz State Univ, BA, 89; Univ Southern Calif, PhD, 95. **CAREER** Tchg Asst, Univ Southern Calif, 95; Instr, Otis Liberal Arts Col, 95; Asst prof, Univ Central Ark, 95-. **MEMBERSHIPS** Am Philos Asn; Ark Philos Asn; North Am Socy Soc Philos; Hegel Soc Am; Soc Study Women Philos. **RESEARCH** History of political philosophy; contemporary politcal philosophy; moral philosophy; Rawls; critical reasoning. **SELECTED PUBLICATIONS** Auth, Book review of State Punishment, Philos Today, 96; Reciprocity as a Justification for Retribution, Criminal Justice Ethics, 97; Understanding Punishment as Annulment, Soc Philos Today, 97. **CONTACT ADDRESS** Univ Central Ark, 201 Donaghey Ave, Conway, AR, 72035-0001. **EMAIL** jamia@mail.uca.edu

ANDERSON, MARVIN W.

PERSONAL Born 01/12/1933, Montevideo, MN, m, 1961, 2 children **DISCIPLINE** THEOLOGY, HISTORY **EDUCATION** Univ Wash, BA, 55; Bethel Sem, BD, 59; Aberdeen Univ, PhD(Reformation hist), 64. **CAREER** Instr hist, Bethel Col, Minn, 60-61; instr hist & Greek, Northwestern Col, Minn, 61-62; from asst prof to assoc prof, 64-73, prof hist theol, Bethel Sem, 73-93, Am Coun Learned Socs grant-in-aid, 69-70; Am Asn Theol Schs fel, 70-71, res fel, 77-78; prof church hist, Southern Baptist Seminary, 94-. **MEMBERSHIPS** Am Soc Church Hist; Am Soc Reformation Res; Renaissance Soc Am; Ecclesiastical Hist Soc, England. **RESEARCH** Renaissance Europe from 1300 to 1500; Reformation studies from 1500 to 1563; Italian Reformation from 1519 to 1563. **SELECTED PUBLICATIONS** Auth, Luther's Sola Fide in Italy 1542-1551, Church Hist, 3/69; Gregorio Cortese and Roman Catholic Reform, 16th Century Essays & Studies, 70; Gospel and Authority, Augsburg, 71; Peter Martyr, Reformed Theologian (1542-1562): His Letters to Bullinger and Calvin, 16th Century J, 4/73; Peter Martyr: A Reformer in Exile (1542-1562), Degraaf, 75; The Battle for the Gospel: Bible and Reformation 1444-1589, Baker, 78; Royal Idolatry, Arch Reformations-Geschichte, 78; Evangelical Foundations: Religion in England, 1378-1683, Peter Lang, 87. **CONTACT ADDRESS** Southern Baptist Sem, 2825 Lexington Rd, Louisville, KY, 40280.

ANDERSON, MICHELLE J.

DISCIPLINE FEMINIST LEGAL THEORY, CRIMINAL LAW, CRIMINAL PROCEDURE **EDUCATION** Univ Calif at Santa Cruz, BA, 89; Yale Law Sch, JD, 94; Georgetown Univ Law Ctr, LLM, 97. **CAREER** Asst prof; clerked to, Honorable William A. Norris, US Ct Appeals 9th Circuit; past tchg fel and Adjuadj prof in Appellate Litigation Prog, Georgetown Univ Law Ctr; past vis prof, Georgetown's Ins for Public Repr. **HONORS AND AWARDS** Orville H. Schell Ctr, Int Human Rights fel; Ford Found fel in Public Int Law. **RESEARCH** Feminist legal theory. **SELECTED PUBLICATIONS** Auth, Silencing Women's Speech, in The Price We Pay: The Case Against Racist Speech, Hate Propaganda, and Pornography 122, 95 & A License To Abuse: The Impact of Conditional Status on Female Immigrants, 102 Yale L.J. 1401, 93. **CONTACT ADDRESS** Law School, Villanova Univ, 800 Lancaster Ave, Villanova, PA, 19085-1692. **EMAIL** anderson@law.vill.edu

ANDERSON, MYRON GEORGE

PERSONAL Born 05/05/1930, Minneapolis, MN, m, 1957 **DISCIPLINE** PHILOSOPHY **EDUCATION** Univ Minn, BA, 51, MA, 54; Brown Univ, PhD, 59. **CAREER** Instr, Trinity Col, Conn, 56-60, asst prof, 60-65; assoc prof, 65-70, Prof Philos, St Cloud State Univ, 70-, Chairperson Dept, 73-. **MEMBERSHIPS** Am Philos Asn. **RESEARCH** Epistemology; history of modern philosophy; social and political philosophy. **CONTACT ADDRESS** Dept of Philosophy, St. Cloud State Univ, 720 4th Ave S, St. Cloud, MN, 56301-4498. **EMAIL** manderson@stcloudstate.edu

ANDERSON, NEIL D.
PERSONAL Born 04/19/1952, Newcastle, PA, m, 1975, 3 children **DISCIPLINE** THEOLOGY **EDUCATION** Asbury Col, BA, 88; Asbury Theol Sem, MDiv, 91; Drew Univ, MA, 94, PhD, candidate, 98-. **CAREER** Zarephath Bible Inst, 94-96; Asbury Col, asst prof, 96-. **MEMBERSHIPS** AAR, WHS, WTS, NAPS. **RESEARCH** Patristics, John Wesley; new testament. **CONTACT ADDRESS** Dept of Bible and Theology, Asbury Col, 1 Macklem Dr, Wilmore, KY, 40390. **EMAIL** neil.anderson@asbury.edu

ANDERSON, STANLEY DANIEL
PERSONAL Born 06/27/1937, Gary, Ind, m, 1963, 3 children **DISCIPLINE** PHILOSOPHY **EDUCATION** Wheaton Col, Ill, BA, 59, MA, 62; Gordon Divinity Sch, BD, 62; Boston Univ, MA, 72; Univ Minn, PhD, 80. **CAREER** Instr, 68-70, asst prof, 72-76, assoc prof, 76-80, Prof Philos, Bethel Col, 80- **MEMBERSHIPS** Am Philos Asn; Soc Christian Philosophers. **RESEARCH** Ethical theory; social philosophy; philosophy of higher education. **CONTACT ADDRESS** Dept of Philos, Bethel Col, 3900 Bethel Dr, Saint Paul, MN, 55112-6999. **EMAIL** andsta@bethel.edu

ANDERSON, SUSAN L.
PERSONAL Born 11/13/1944, Portland, OR, m, 1974, 1 child **DISCIPLINE** PHILOSOPHY **EDUCATION** Vassar Col, BA, 66; UCLA, PhD, 74. **CAREER** UCLA, tchg assoc, 68-70; Calif State, inst, 70-71; Univ Connecticut, inst, asst prof, assoc prof, prof, 72-, Mount Holyoke Col, vis asst prof, 77. **HONORS AND AWARDS** Three NEH fel, two Yale fel, listed in: WWWWomen, Int WWE, WWE, DAS, Int WWPBW, IntlW-WI, WWH. **MEMBERSHIPS** APA **RESEARCH** The Self; applied ethics. **SELECTED PUBLICATIONS** Auth, Being Held Morally Responsible for an Action versus Acting Responsibly/ Irresponsibly, Jour Philos Res, 95; auth, Natural Rights and the Individualism vs. Collectivism Debate, Jour Value Inquiry, 95; auth, Problems in Developing a Practical Theory of Moral Responsibility, Jour Value Inquiry, 96; auth, Of Butterflies and Frogs, Falling in Love with Wisdom, eds., D. D. Karnos & R. G. Shoemaker, Oxford Univ Pr, 93; Nelly's Dark Day, in: Myriads, U Conn Lit Jour, 98. **CONTACT ADDRESS** Dept of Philosophy, Univ of Connecticut, 1 University Place, Stamford, CT, 06901-2315. **EMAIL** slanders@uconnvm.uconn.edu

ANDERSON, SUSAN LEIGH
PERSONAL Born 11/13/1944, Portland, OR, m, 1974, 1 child **DISCIPLINE** PHILOSOPHY **EDUCATION** Vassar Col, AB, 66; Univ Calif, Los Angeles, PhD(philos), 74. **CAREER** Teaching assoc philos, Univ Calif, Los Angeles, 68-70; instr, Calif State Univ, Northridge, 70-71; asst prof, 72-80, Assoc Prof Philos, 80-91, PROF, UNIV CONN, 91-; Nat Endowment for Humanities fel, Princeton Univ, 75 & Brown Univ, 78; Univ Calif, Santa Cruz, 92; Lilly fel, Yale Univ, 76; Yale vis fac fel, 90- 91; reviewer & panelist, Nat Endowment for Humanities; vis asst Prof, Mt Holyoke Col, 77. **MEMBERSHIPS** Am Philos Asn. **RESEARCH** The Self; applied ethics; 19th century philosophy; philosophy in literature. **SELECTED PUBLICATIONS** Auth, Coconsciousness and numerical identity of the person, Philos Studies, 76; The substantive center theory versus the bundle theory, Monist, 78; Chisholm's argument that a person cannot be an Ens Successivum, Philos Studies, 80; The Libertarian conception of freedom, Int Philos Quart, 81; Plantinga and the Free Will Defense, 81; auth, Criticism of Liberal/ Feminist Views on Abortion, Public Affairs Q, 87; auth, Evil, J Value Inquiry, 90; auth, The Status of Frozen Embryos, Public Affairs Q, 90; auth, A Picture of the Self which Supports Moral Responsibility, The Monist, 91; auth, Equal Opportunity, Freedom and Sex- Stereotyping, J Philos Res, 91; auth, Philosophy and Fiction, Metaphilosophy, 92; auth, Being Held Morally Responsible for an Actions versus Acting Responsibly/ Irresponsibly, J Philos Res, 95; auth, Natural Rights and the Individualism vs Collectivism Debate, J Value Inquiry, 95; auth, Problems in Developing a Practical Theory of Moral Responsibility, J Value Inquiry, 96. **CONTACT ADDRESS** Dept of Philos, Univ of Conn, 1 University Pl, Stamford, CT, 06901-2315. **EMAIL** slanders@uconnvm.uconn.edu

ANDERSON, VINTON RANDOLPH
PERSONAL Born 07/11/1927, Somerset, Bermuda, m, 1952 **DISCIPLINE** THEOLOGY **EDUCATION** Wilberforce University, BA (with honors); Payne Theological Seminary, MDiv, 1952; Kansas University, MA, philosophy; Yale University Divinity School, continuing education; Urban Training Center for Christian Missions. **CAREER** St Mark AME Church, pastor, 1952-53; Brown Chapel AME Church, pastor, 1953-55; St Luke AME Church, Lawrence, pastor, 1955-59; St Paul AME Church, Wichita, pastor, 1959-64; St Paul AME Church, St Louis, pastor, 1964-72; presiding bishop, chief pastor: 9th Episcopal District, Alabama, 1972-76; 3rd Episcopal District, Ohio, West Virginia, West Pennsylvania, 1976-84; Office of Ecumenical Relations and Development, 1984-88; 5th Episcopal District, 14 states including 255 Churches west of the Mississippi River, 1988-. **HONORS AND AWARDS** Ebony Magazine, Religion Award, 1988, 1991; American Black Achievement Awards, 1991; National Association for Equal Opportunity in Higher Education, Distinguished Alumni Honoree, 1988; Honorary Doctorate Degrees: Eden Theological Seminary; Paul Quinn College; Wilberforce University; Payne Theological Seminary; Temple Bible College; Morris Brown College. **MEMBERSHIPS** World Council of Churches, numerous committees and delegations; World Methodist Council, North American Region, first vice pres, executive committee; World Methodist Council and Conference, delegate, 1961-; National Council of Churches, governing board, Faith & Order Commission, chairperson; Congress of National Black Churches, vice pres, charter member; Consultation on Church Union, vice pres; United Methodist Church, General Commission of Christian Unity and Interreligious Concern; Schomburg Center for Research in Black Culture, national advisory board; NAACP, life member; Urban League, St Louis dialogue group. **SELECTED PUBLICATIONS** Developed: church hymnal, The Bicentennial Edition; first AME Book of Worship; established, edited: The Connector; produced, edited: A Syllabus For Celebrating The Bicentennial; numerous articles in publications of the AME Church. **CONTACT ADDRESS** African Methodist Episcopal Church, 4144 Lindell Blvd, Suite 222, St. Louis, MO, 63108.

ANDERSON, WILLIAM P.
DISCIPLINE RELIGIOUS STUDIES **EDUCATION** Princeton Univ, PhD. **CAREER** Res scholar, Inst d'histoire de la Reformatiabout Univ de Geneve; vis, prof, Inst Oecumenique, Univ de Geneve, World Coun Churches and The United Theolog Sem; past vis lect, Grad Sch for Religion and Philosophy, St Petersburg Asn of Scholars, St. Petersburg, Russ; prof, Univ Dayton.. **RESEARCH** Historical theology, early Christian church, Protestant Christianity. **SELECTED PUBLICATIONS** Auth, Aspects of the Theology of Karl Barth and Basic Issues in Christian Philosophy. **CONTACT ADDRESS** Dept of Religious Studies, Univ of Dayton, 300 College Park, 321 Humanities, Dayton, OH, 45469-1679. **EMAIL** anderson@checkov.hm.udayton.edu

ANDERSON-GOLD, SHARON
DISCIPLINE SOCIAL-POLITICAL PHILOSOPHY, HISTORY OF PHILOSOPHY **CAREER** Assoc prof, Rensselaer Polytech Inst. **RESEARCH** The philos of Kant. **SELECTED PUBLICATIONS** Publ many articles on law, ethics, hist, cult and relig in Kant's philos. **CONTACT ADDRESS** Rensselaer Polytech Inst, Troy, NY, 12180. **EMAIL** selmer@rpi.edu

ANDREASEN, NANCY C.
DISCIPLINE PSYCHIATRY **EDUCATION** Univ Nebr, BA (summa cum laude), 58; Radcliffe Col, MA, 59; Univ Nebr, PhD, 63; Univ Iowa, MD, 70. **CAREER** Instr, English, Nebr Wesleyan, 60-61; instr, English, Univ Nebr, 62-63; asst prof English, 63-66, from asst prof to assoc prof psychiat, 73-81, prof psychiat, 81-, dir, Mental Health Clinical Res Ctr, 87-, Andrew H. Woods Prof Psychiat, 92-97, Andrew H. Woods Chair Psychiat, 97-, Univ Iowa; sr consult, Northwick Park Hospital, London, 83; Acad Vis, Maudsley Hospital, London, 86; Ed, Am J Psychiat; Assoc Ed, Schizophrenia Bull. **HONORS AND AWARDS** Dean Award, Am Col Psychiat; Distinguished Service Award, Am Col Psychiat; Fac Schol Award, Univ Iowa; Fel, Royal Col Physicians and Surgeons of Canada; Fogarty Sr. Int Fel; Foundations' Fund Prize, Am Psychiat Asn; Fulbright Fel; Hall-Mercer Award, Pa Hospital; Hibbs Award, Am Psychiat Asn; Nelson Urban Res Award, Iowa Mental Health Asn; Kempf Award, Am Psychiat Asn; Kolb Award, Columbia Univ; Marion Faye Spencer Award; Menninger Award for Psychiat Res; Merit Award, Nat Inst Mental Health; Phi Kappa Phi; recipient of numerous other awards and grants. **MEMBERSHIPS** Am Med Asn; Acad Psychiat Consortium, Ctr Advanced Study Behavioral Sci; Am Psychopathol Asn (secy 81-87, vpres 87-88, pres 89-90); Am Psychiat Asn; Am Asn Advancement Sci; Am Col Neuropsychopharmacology; Am Col Psychiat; Inst Med; Int Soc Neuroimaging in Psychiat; Int Col Neuropsychopharmacol; Johnson County Med Soc; Nat Advisory Comt Med; Org Human Brain Mapping; Psychiat Res Soc (pres 85-86); Soc Biological Psychiat; Soc Neuroscience; World Psychiat Asn (Chair, Neuroimaging Section). **RESEARCH** Neuroimaging; cognitive and behavioral neuroscience; diagnosis, instrument development, and clinical assessment; schizophrenia. **SELECTED PUBLICATIONS** Coauth, Introductory Textbook of Psychiatry, Am Psychiat Press, 90, 2nd ed, 94; co-ed, Positive versus Negative Schizophrenia, Springer-Verlag, 90; ed, Schizophrenia: From Mind to Molecule, Am Psychiatric Press, 94; co-ed, Psychotic Continuum, Springer-Verlag, 94; author and editor of numerous articles and other publications. **CONTACT ADDRESS** Dept Psychiat, Univ Iowa, MHCRC, 2911 JPP, Iowa City, IA, 52242.

ANDREEN, WILLIAM L.
DISCIPLINE LAW **EDUCATION** Col Wooster, BA, 75; Columbia Univ Sch Law, JD, 77. **CAREER** Prof, Univ Ala . **HONORS AND AWARDS** Col Wooster prize in hist. **MEMBERSHIPS** Phi Beta Kappa; Exec comt, Env Law Sec Asn Amer Law Schools. **CONTACT ADDRESS** Law Dept, Univ of Alabama, Box 870000, Tuscaloosa, AL, 35487-0383. **EMAIL** wandreen@law.ua.edu

ANDRESEN, JENSINE
PERSONAL Born 02/06/1964, Flint, MI **DISCIPLINE** RELIGION **EDUCATION** Princeton Univ, BSE, 86; Columbia Univ, MA, 89; Harvard Univ, MA, 92, PhD, 97. **CAREER** Vis asst prof, 97-98, Univ Vermont; asst prof, 98- , Boston Univ. **MEMBERSHIPS** Am Acad Relig; Inst of Relig in an Age of Sci. **RESEARCH** Religion and sciences; social ethics. **CONTACT ADDRESS** 745 Commonwealth Ave, Boston, MA, 02215. **EMAIL** jensine@bu.edu

ANDREW, SCOTT
PERSONAL Born 10/23/1950, CT, m, 1973 **DISCIPLINE** PHILOSOPHY **EDUCATION** Southwestern Baptist Theol Sem, PhD, 92. **MEMBERSHIPS** APA **RESEARCH** War theory. **CONTACT ADDRESS** 4016 32nd St, Mt. Rainier, WA, 20712.

ANDREWS, KRISTIN
PERSONAL Born 03/16/1971, Nashville, TN **DISCIPLINE** PHILOSOPHY **EDUCATION** Antioch Coll, BA, 92; Western Mich Univ, MA, 95. **HONORS AND AWARDS** Phi Kappa Phi. **MEMBERSHIPS** Am Philos Asn; Europ Soc of Philos and Psychol; Southern Soc of Philos and Psychol. **RESEARCH** Philosophy and Psychology; Philosophy and Language. **SELECTED PUBLICATIONS** Auth, The First Step, the case for Great Ape equality: The Argument for Other Minds, Etica and Animali: The Great Ape Project, 96. **CONTACT ADDRESS** Philosophy Dept, Univ of Minn, 224 Church SE, 355 Ford Hall, Minneapolis, MN, 55455. **EMAIL** andre029@tc.umn.edu

ANDRUS, KAY L.
DISCIPLINE LEGAL RESEARCH **EDUCATION** Brigham Young Univ, BA, MLS, JD. **CAREER** Prof & dir, Law Libr; Creighton Univ, 90-; past assoc law lib dir, Northwestern Univ Sch Law; Reader Sevc(s) libn, asst prof, Southern Ill Univ; past sr ref libn, Southern Methodist Univ; past asst law lib dir, Okla City Univ. **SELECTED PUBLICATIONS** Pub(s) in, J Air Law and Commerce; Syllabus; Libr J & Southern Ill Univ Law J. **CONTACT ADDRESS** School of Law, Creighton Univ, 2500 California Plaza, Omaha, NE, 68178. **EMAIL** andrus@culaw.creighton.edu

ANGELELLI, IGNAZIO ALFREDO
PERSONAL Born 04/03/1933, Rome, Italy, m, 1959, 3 children **DISCIPLINE** PHILOSOPHY **EDUCATION** Univ Fribourg, PhD(philos), 65. **CAREER** Instr, Univ Notre Dame, 66-67; from asst prof to assoc prof, 67-72, Prof Philos, Univ Tex, Austin, 72-. **RESEARCH** History of logic; logic; history of philosophy, 1500-1900. **SELECTED PUBLICATIONS** Auth, Studies on G Frege and traditional philosophy, Reidel, Holland, 67. **CONTACT ADDRESS** Dept of Philosophy, Univ of Texas, Austin, Austin, TX, 78712-1026. **EMAIL** plac565@utxvms.cc.utexas.edu

ANGELL, RICHARD B.
PERSONAL Born 10/14/1918, Scarsdale, NY, m, 1949, 5 children **DISCIPLINE** PHILOSOPHY **EDUCATION** Swarthmore, BA, 40; Univ PA, MGA , 48; Harvard, MA, 48, PhD, 54. **CAREER** Asst prof to full prof, 54-68, Ohio Wesleyan; prof, 68-89, chmn philos dept, 68-73, 76-78, emeritus prof, 89-, Wayne State Univ. **MEMBERSHIPS** APA. **RESEARCH** Logic. **SELECTED PUBLICATIONS** Auth, Reasoning and Logic, 64; auth, Analytic Logic, forthcoming. **CONTACT ADDRESS** 150 Kendal Dr, Kennett Square, PA, 19348. **EMAIL** AngelRB@aol.com

ANKERSEN, THOMAS T.
DISCIPLINE LAW **EDUCATION** Univ S Fla, BA, MA; Univ Fla, JD. **CAREER** Atty, asst in Law, Ctr for Govt Responsibility, Univ Fla Col Law; dir, Center's Mesoamerican Env Law Prog; aff fac mem, Univ Florida's Ctr for Latin Amer Stud; guest ed, Span lang jour Mesoamerica; Fla Law Rev; past atty, Denver and Tallahassee off,; past sr litigation assoc, Peeples, Earl and Blank, Miami. **HONORS AND AWARDS** Dean Frank Maloney env law writing awd. **MEMBERSHIPS** Pres bd Dir, Env and Natural Resources Law Ctr; Tropical Ecosystems Directorate US Dept of State Man and the Biosphere Prog; bd dir, Forest Mgt Trust; bd adv, Fla Defenders of the Env. **RESEARCH** Coastal law and policy, water law, and legal issues associated with protection of biological diversity. **SELECTED PUBLICATIONS** Auth, Law, Sci and Little Old Ladies: The Many Hands That Made a Movement, J Fla Humanities Coun, 95; coauth, The Environmental Impacts of Intl Finance Corporation Lending and Proposals for Reform: A Case Study of Conservation and Oil Development in the Guatemalan Peten, J Env Law, 99; Ecosystem Management and the Everglades: A Legal and Institutional Analysis, J Land Use and Env Law 473, 96. **CONTACT ADDRESS** School of Law, Univ of Florida, PO Box 117629, Gainesville, FL, 32611-7629. **EMAIL** ankersen@law.ufl.edu

ANSBRO, JOHN J.
PERSONAL Born 11/16/1932, New York, NY **DISCIPLINE** PHILOSOPHY **EDUCATION** St. Joseph's Sem, BA, 55; Fordham Univ, MA, 57, PhD, 64. **CAREER** Lectr, Manhattan Col, 58-59, instr, 59-63, asst prof, 63-68, assoc prof, 68-79, full prof, 79-93, chmn dept of philos, 77-81. **HONORS AND AWARDS** Ford Found grant, 73; Samuel Rubin Found grant,

85. **MEMBERSHIPS** Am Asn of Univ Prof; Am Philos Asn; Soc for Ancient Greek Philos; Hegel Soc of Am; Soren Kierkegaard Soc; Soc for the Advan of Am Philos. **RESEARCH** History of philosophy; philosophy of nonviolence; African-American studies. **SELECTED PUBLICATIONS** Auth, Martin Luther King, Jr.: The Making of a Mind, 93; "Martin Luther King's Debt to Hegel," 94; "The Credo of Marcus Garvey," 94; "The Credo of Malcolm X," 95; "The Credo of W.E.B. DuBois," 95; "President Nelson Mandela's Appreciation of the Power of the Negative," 97; "Martin Luther King's Appreciation of the Power of the Negative," 97; "Frederick Douglass's Appreciation of the Power of the Negative," 97; "Malcolm X's Appreciation of the Power of the Negative," 98; "Marcus Garvey's Appreciation of the Power of the Negative," 98. **CONTACT ADDRESS** 65 Greenvale Ave, Yonkers, NY, 10703.

ANTOCI, PETER
PERSONAL Born 05/06/1963, NY **DISCIPLINE** RELIGIOUS STUDIES **EDUCATION** Catholic Univ of Am, PhD 95. **CAREER** UMBC Shriver Peaceworker Prog, assoc dir; George Mason Univ, adj prof. **HONORS AND AWARDS** Leadershp Washington. **MEMBERSHIPS** AAR **RESEARCH** Religion and Culture Hermeneutics. **SELECTED PUBLICATIONS** Auth, Scandal and Marginality in the Vitae of Holy Fools, in: Christianity and Lit, 95. **CONTACT ADDRESS** 1810 Calvert St NW #3, Washington, DC, 20009.

ANTON, JOHN P.
PERSONAL Born 11/02/1920, Canton, OH, m, 1955, 3 children **DISCIPLINE** PHILOSOPHY **EDUCATION** Columbia Univ, BS, 49, MA, 50, PhD, 54. **CAREER** Asst prof Philos, Univ NE, 55-58; assoc prof Philos, Ohio Wesleyan Univ, 58-62; prof Philos, State Univ NY/Buffalo, 62-69; Calloway Prof Philos, Emory Univ, 69-82; DISTINGUISHED PROF PHILOS, UNIV SOUTH FL, 82-. **HONORS AND AWARDS** Honorary member, Phi Beta Kappa; honorary doctorate of Philos, Univ of Athens; Cozzesp member, Academy of Athens; honorary member, Parnassus Literary Soc; honorary citizen of Olympia; honorary pres, Int Assoc Greek Philos. **MEMBERSHIPS** Amer Philos Assoc; Soc Ancient Greek Philos; Amer Soc Aesthetics; Int Soc Neoplatonic Studies. **RESEARCH** Ancient Greek philos and culture; Aristotle; Plato; Plotinus; Metaphysics; philos of art; classical political theories; modern Greek poetry. **SELECTED PUBLICATIONS** Ed and intro & notes, Upward Panic: The Autobiography of Eva Palmer Sikelianos, London: Gordon and Breach Science Pubs, Harwood Academic Pubs, 93; auth, The Poetry and Poetics of Constantine P. Cavafy, London: Harwood Academic Pubs, 95; Categories and Experience: Essays on Aristotelian Themes, Dowling Col Press, 96; Aristotle's On the Nature of Logos, in The Philos of Logos, ed K. Boudouris, vol I, Athens, 96, reissued with additions in Philos Inquiry, vol XVIII, nos 1-2, winter/spring 96; Plotinus and Augustine on Cosmic Alienation: Proodos and Epistrophe, in J of Neoplatonic Studies, vol IV/2, spring 96; ed and intro, Twenty Letters on the Ancient Drama by Eva Palmer-Sikelianos, bylingual ed, trans into Greek by Loukia Tsokopoulou, Athens: Nea Synora: A Livanisn Pub, 97; auth, Arcadia in the Poetry of Kostis Palamas, in Nea Estia, vol 141, no 1672, 3/1/97; Neoplatonic Elements in Arethas' Scholia on Aristotle and Porphyry, in Neoplatonisme et Philosophie Medieval, Actes du Colloque international, Societe Int pour l'Etude de la Philosophie Medieval (Oct 95), ed Linos G. Benakis, Brepols, 97; Plato as Critic of Democracy: Ancient and Modern, in Platonic Political Philos, proceedings of the VIII Conference of the Int Assoc Greek Philos, vol I, ed K. Boudouris, Athens, 97. **CONTACT ADDRESS** Dept Philos, Univ South FL, Tampa, FL, 33620. **EMAIL** anton@chuma.cas.usf.edu

ANTONELLI, GIAN ALDO
PERSONAL Born 02/10/1962, Torino, Italy, m, 1987, 2 children **DISCIPLINE** PHILOSOPHY **EDUCATION** Univ Torino, Laurea, 86; Univ Pittsburgh, PhD, 92. **CAREER** Lectr, Yale Univ, 93 96; vis asst prof, Stanford Univ, 96-97; asst prof, Mich State Univ, 97-98; asst prof, Univ Calif Irvine, 98-. **HONORS AND AWARDS** Fulbrigth Scholar, 87; Rotary Int Scholar, 87. **MEMBERSHIPS** Asn for Symbolic Logic; Am Philos Asn. **RESEARCH** Pure and Applied Logic; Philosophy of Mathematics. **SELECTED PUBLICATIONS** Auth, The Complexity of Revision, Notre Dame J of Formal Logic, 94; Non-Well-Founded Sets via Revision Rules, J of Philos Logic, 94; A Revision-Theoretic Analysis of the Arithmetical Hierarchy, Notre Dame J of Formal Logic, 94; What's in a Function?, Synthese, 96; Defeasible Inheritance on Cyclic Networks, Artificial Intelligence, 97; Godel, Penrose, e I fondamenti dell'intelligenza artificiale, Sistemi Intelligenti, 97; Extensional Quotients for Type Theory and the Consistency Problem for NF, J of Symbolic Logic, 98; coauth, Backwards Forward Induction, TARK, 94; Games Servers Play: A Procedural Approach, Intelligent Agents II, 96; Game-Theoretic Axioms for Local Rationality and Bounded Knowledge, J of Logic, Lang, and Information, 95. **CONTACT ADDRESS** Dept of Philosophy, Univ of Calif, Irvine, CA, 92697-4555. **EMAIL** aldo@uci.edu

APOSTOLOS-CAPPADONA, DIANE
PERSONAL Born 05/10/1948, Trenton, NJ **DISCIPLINE** AMERICAN CULTURAL HISTORY; RELIGION AND CULTURE **EDUCATION** Cath Univ of Amer, MA, 79; George Wash Univ, BA, 70, MA, 73, PhD, 88. **CAREER** Lectr, relig, Mt Vernon Col, 80-85; lectr, relig, George Wash Univ, 81-86; adj facul, christ and art, Pacific Sch of Relig, 85-86, 88-92; adj prof, art and culture, Liberal Studies prog, Georgetown Univ, 85-; res prof, Ctr for Muslim-Christian understanding, Georgetown Univ, 96-. **HONORS AND AWARDS** Sr fel, Ctr for the Study of World Relig, Harvard Univ, 96-97; res grant, Amer Acad of Relig; res grant, Amer Coun of Learned Soc; NEH grant. **MEMBERSHIPS** Amer Acad of Relig; Amer Asn of Mus; Amer Asn of Univ Women; Amer Studies Asn; Col Art Asn; Col Theol Soc; Congress on Res in Dance; Soc for Art, Relig, and Contemporary Culture. **RESEARCH** Images of women in religious art; Iconography of the Black Madonna; Relationship between art, gender, religion and culture; Iconography of Mary Magdalene. **SELECTED PUBLICATIONS** Auth, Dictionary of Women in Religious Art, Oxford Univ Press, 98; auth, Dictionary of Christian Art, Continuum Publ, 98; auth, Beyond Belief: The Artistic Journey and two entries in Beyond Belief: Modern Art and the Religious Imagination, The Nat Gallery of Victoria, Melbourne, 98; entries, Encycl of Comparative Iconography, 98; auth, Picturing Devotion: Rogier's Saint Luke Drawing the Virgin and Child, Saint Luke Drawing the Virgin and Child: Essays in Context, Brepols, 97; auth, Encyclopedia of Women in Religious Art, Continuum Publ, 96; auth, Picasso's Guernica as Mythic Iconoclasm: An Eliadean Reading of Modern Art, Myth and Method, Univ Va Press, 96; entries, The Dictionary of Art and The New Catholic Encyclopedia, vol 19: suppl, 96; auth, The Spirit and the Vision: The Influence of Christian Romanticism on the Development of 19th-century American Art, Scholar's Press, 95; co-ed, Women, Creativity and the Arts, Contiuum Publ, 95; ed, Art, Creativity, and the Sacred, Continuum Publ, 95; entries, Harper's Dictionary of Religion, 95; auth, Dictionary of Christian Art, Continuum Publ, 94; co-ed, Isamu Noguchi: Essays and Conversations, 94; auth, Noguchi at the Dance! Dance Collection, NY Publ Libr for the Performing Arts, 94. **CONTACT ADDRESS** Center for Muslim-Christian Understanding, Georgetown Univ, ICC #260, Washington, DC, 20057-1052. **EMAIL** apostold@gusun.georgetown.edu

APPEL, FREDERICK
PERSONAL Canada **DISCIPLINE** POLITICAL SCIENCE; POLITICAL PHILOSOPHY **EDUCATION** McGill Univ, PhD, 95. **CAREER** Postdoctoral fel, Ctr for Europ Studies, 96-98; lectr, Prog for Degrees in Social Studies, Harvard Univ, 98-99; **HONORS AND AWARDS** Les Fords FCAR Postdoctoral Fel, 96-98. **MEMBERSHIPS** Amer Philos Asn; Amer Polit Sci Asn **RESEARCH** History of social and political thought (esp 19th Century); Contemporary political philosophy. **SELECTED PUBLICATIONS** Auth, Nietzsche contra Democracy, Cornell Univ Press, 98. **CONTACT ADDRESS** Social Studies Program, Harvard Univ, 59 Shepard St, Hilles Lib, Cambridge, MA, 02138. **EMAIL** appel@fas.harvard.edu

APPELBAUM, PAUL S.
PERSONAL Born 11/30/1951, New York, NY, m, 1974, 3 children **DISCIPLINE** BIOLOGY, MEDICINE AND PSYCHIATRY **EDUCATION** Columbia Col, AB, 72; Harvard Med Sch, MD, 76. **CAREER** Asst to assoc prof, psychiat and law, Univ Pittsburgh, 80-84; assoc prof, psychiat, Harvard Med Sch, 84-85; A.F. Zeleznik distinguished prof, psychiat, Univ Mass Med Sch, 85-; chair, dept of psychiat, Univ Mass Med Sch, 92-; fel, Ctr for Advan Study in the Behavioral Sci, 96-97. **HONORS AND AWARDS** Pfizer vis prof, Md Pscyhiat Res Ctr, Univ Md, 98; Edward J. Strecker, MD award, Inst of Pa Hospital and Jefferson Med Col, 97; Fritz Redlich fel, Ctr for Advan Study in the Behavioral Sci, 96-97; Manfred S. Guttmacher award, Amer Psychiat Asn and Amer Acad of Psychiat, 96; Will Solimene award, Amer Med Writers Asn, 95; Pfizer vis prof, dept of psychiat, Univ Calif Davis, 95; Saleem Shah Mem award, State Mental Health Forensic Dir Asn, 93. **MEMBERSHIPS** Amer Med Asn; Intl Acad of Law and Mental Health; Mass Psychiat Soc; Amer Soc of Law, Med and Ethics; Amer Acad of Psychiat and the Law; Pa Psychiat Soc; Mass Psychiat Soc; Amer Psychiat Asn. **RESEARCH** Violence, its prediction and control; Ethical issues in general medical and psychiatric practice; Legal regulation of medical practice; Phenomenology of delusions. **SELECTED PUBLICATIONS** Co-auth, Assessing Competence To Consent To Treatment: A Guide for Physicians and Other Health Professionals, Oxford Univ Press, 98; co-ed, Trauma & Memory: Clinical & Legal Controversies, Oxford Univ Press, 97; auth, Almost a Revolution: Mental Health Law and the Limits of Change, Oxford Univ Press, 94; co-auth, Violence by people discharged from acute psychiatric inpatient facilities and by others in the same neighborhoods, Arch Gen Psychiat, 98; co-auth, C: The MacCAT-T: A clinical tool to assess patients' capacities to make treatment decisions, Psychiat Svc, 97; auth, A theory of ethics for forensic psychiatry, Jour Amer Acad Psychiat Law, 97; auth, Almost a revolution: an international perspective on the law of involuntary commitment, Jour Amer Acad Psychiat Law, 97; co-auth, Capacities of hospitalized, medically ill patients to consent to treatment, Psychosomatics, 97; co-auth, Twenty years after Tarasoff: reviewing the duty to protect, Harvard Rev Psychiat, 96; co-auth, Constructing competence: formulating standards of legal competence to make medical decisions, Rutgers Law Rev, 96; co-auth, Psychotherapists' duties to third parties: Ramona and beyond, Amer Jour Psychiat, 95; co-auth, Moral stage of reasoning & the misperceived duty to report past crimes (misprision), Intl Jour Law Psychiat, 95; co-auth, Boundaries in psychotherapy: model guidelines, Psychiat: Interpersonal and Bio Processes, 95. **CONTACT ADDRESS** 55 Lake Ave. N, Worcester, MA, 01655. **EMAIL** paul.appelbaum@banyan.ummed.edu

APPELL, ANNETTE RUTH
DISCIPLINE INDIVIDUAL LIBERTIES, JUVENILE AND FAMILY LAW AND TRIAL PRACTICE **EDUCATION** Northwestern Univ JD, 86. **CAREER** Ed bd, Northwestern J of Int Law and Bus; atty, Sonnenschein Nath & Rosenthal, Meites, Frackman, Mulder & Burgerin, Off of the Pub Guardian of Cook County, Chicago; clin instr, atty, Northwestern Univ, 92-96; asst prof, Univ SC, Columbia, 96-98; assoc prof, mem, clin fac, Univ Nev, Las Vegas. **SELECTED PUBLICATIONS** Published extensively in the area of children's rights and family law. **CONTACT ADDRESS** Univ Nev, Las Vegas, Las Vegas, NV, 89154.

APPIAH, KWAME ANTHONY
DISCIPLINE AFRO-AMERICAN STUDIES AND PHILOSOPHY **EDUCATION** Cambridge Univ, England, BA, PhD. **CAREER** Prof. **MEMBERSHIPS** Past pres, Socr African Philos in NAm & is an ed of Transition. **RESEARCH** Epistemology and philosophy of language; African philosophy; philosophical problems of race and racism; Afro-American and African literature and literary theory. **SELECTED PUBLICATIONS** Auth, My Father's House: Africa in the Philosophy of Culture, 92 & Color Conscious: The Political Morality of Race, 96. **CONTACT ADDRESS** Dept of Philosophy, Harvard Univ, 8 Garden St, Cambridge, MA, 02138. **EMAIL** appiah@fas.harvard.edu

APPLEGATE, JUDITH K.
PERSONAL Born 10/01/1948, KS, s, 3 children **DISCIPLINE** THEOLOGY **EDUCATION** Portland State Univ, BA, 71; Western Evangel Sem, MA, 81; Earlham Sch Relig, MDiv, 82; Vanderbilt Univ, PhD, 89. **CAREER** Western Evangel Sem, adj fac, 79-81; George Fox Col, adj fac, 83; Earlham Sch of Relig, asst prof, 87-96; Center for the Prevention of Sexual and Violence, prog specialist, 96-. **HONORS AND AWARDS** Ordained Quaker Minister. **RESEARCH** New Testament; feminist Studies; justice issues for women; spirituality; domestic violence; Ministerial ethics. **SELECTED PUBLICATIONS** Auth, And she wet his feet with her tears: A Feminist Interpretation of Luke 7:36-50, Marking Boundaries, Sheffield: Sheffield Acad Press, 98; auth, The Bible as Friend, Foe and Elder, Pendle Hill Study Center, Wallingford, PA, 96; auth, Women in the Gospels, Ohio Northern Univ, Ada, OH, 93; auth, The Co-Elect Woman of 1 Peter, in: New Testament Studies, 92. **CONTACT ADDRESS** PO Box 21641, Seattle, WA, 98111. **EMAIL** 76677.1403@compuserve.com

AQUILA, RICHARD E.
DISCIPLINE PHILOSOPHY **EDUCATION** Harvard Univ, BA, 65; Northwestern Univ, MA, 67, PhD, 68. **CAREER** Prof. **RESEARCH** History of modern philosophy; philosophy of mind. **SELECTED PUBLICATIONS** Auth, Intentionality: A Study of Mental Acts, Pa State Univ, 77; Rhyme or Reason: A Limerick History of Philosophy, Univ Am, 81; Representational Mind: A Study of Kant's Theory of Knowledge, Univ Ind, 83; Matter in Mind: A Study of Kant's Transcendental Deduction, Univ ind, 89; The Holistic Character of Kantian Intuition, Kluwer Acad, 94; Intentionality, Basil Blackwell, 95; The Content of Cartesian Sensation and the Intermingling of Mind and Body, Hist Philos Quart, 95; Unity of Apperception as a Quasi-Object in the first Critique, Marquette Univ, 95; Self as Matter and Form: Some Reflections on Kant's View of the Soul, SUNY, 97. **CONTACT ADDRESS** Dept of Philosophy, Knoxville, TN, 37996. **EMAIL** raquila@utk.edu

AQUINO, MARIA PILAR
DISCIPLINE LIBERATION THEOLOGY AND CHRISTIAN SOCIAL ETHICS **EDUCATION** Pontifical Cath Univ of Salamanca, Spain, STD. **CAREER** Dept Theo, Univ San Diego **RESEARCH** Cath soc thought; Cath theology; feminist theologies. **SELECTED PUBLICATIONS** Ed 1 bk & auth, 2 bks and numerous articles on, the contrib of women to theol, soc, and the Church. **CONTACT ADDRESS** Dept of Theological and Relig Studies, Univ of San Diego, 5998 Alcal Park, Maher 297, San Diego, CA, 92110-2492. **EMAIL** aquino@acusd.edu

ARAIZA, WILLIAM
DISCIPLINE LAW **EDUCATION** Columbia Univ, BA, 83; Georgetown Univ, MS, 85; Yale Univ, JD, 90. **CAREER** Clerk, hon William Norris, US Ct of Appeals, 9th Circuit; clerk, hon David Souter, US Supreme Ct; adj, Univ Calif, LA Law Sch; vis prof, Univ Calif, Hastings Col Law, 97. **SELECTED PUBLICATIONS** Auth & coauth texts on, administrative and international law. **CONTACT ADDRESS** Law School, Loyola Marymount Univ, 7900 Loyola Blvd, Burns 310, Los Angeles, CA, 90045. **EMAIL** waraiza@lmulaw.lmu.edu

ARAND, CHARLES P.
PERSONAL Born 04/27/1957, Amarillo, TX, m, 1980, 2 children **DISCIPLINE** THEOLOGY **EDUCATION** Concordia Col, BA, 80; Concordia Sem, MDiv, 84, STM, 87, ThD, 89. **CAREER** Pastor, St. John, New Minden & St. Luke, Covington, Ill, 84-87; asst prof, 89-95, assoc prof, systematic theol, 95-, chemn dept, 95- , asst dean fac, 96-98, fac marshall, 97- , actg dean of fac, 97, Concordia Sem; assoc vpres for acad aff, 98-. **MEMBERSHIPS** Am Acad Relig; Sixteenth-Century Stud Conf; Soc for Reformation Res. **RESEARCH** Catechisms, Luther's and Lutheran; creeds and Reformation confessions; trinitarian studies; Christology. **SELECTED PUBLICATIONS** Auth, Testing the Boundaries: Windows to Lutheran Identity, Concordia, 95; auth, Apology as Polemical Commentary, in Wengert, ed, Philip Melanchthon (1497-1560) and the Commentary, Sheffield, 97; auth, The Small Catechism within the Catechumenate, Lutheran Forum, 98; auth, The Life of Faith: A Theological Overview of the Small Catechism, in, Arkkila, ed, The Gospel is the Power of God: The Third International Confessional Lutheran Conference, Sley-Kirjat, 98. **CONTACT ADDRESS** Concordia Sem, 801 DeMun Ave, St. Louis, MO, 63105. **EMAIL** arandc@csl.edu

ARBAUGH, GEORGE E.
PERSONAL Born 10/31/1933, Hartford, WI, m, 1955, 3 children **DISCIPLINE** PHILOSOPHY **EDUCATION** Augustana Col, BA, 55; State Univ Iowa, MA, 58, PhD, 59. **CAREER** From asst prof to assoc prof, 59-67, prof philos, 59-, Pac Lutheran Univ. **MEMBERSHIPS** Am Philos Assn; Soren Kierkegaard Soc. **RESEARCH** Ethics and theory of value; metaphysics and epistemology; Kierkegaard and existentialism. **SELECTED PUBLICATIONS** Coauth, Kierkegaard's Authorship, Allen & Unwin, 68. **CONTACT ADDRESS** Dept of Philosophy, Pac Lutheran Univ, 12180 Park Ave S, Tacoma, WA, 98447-0014. **EMAIL** arbaugge@netscape.net

ARBINO, GARY P.
PERSONAL m **DISCIPLINE** ARCHAEOLOGY, OLD TESTAMENT INTERPRETATION **EDUCATION** Humboldt State Univ, BA; Golden Gate Baptist Theol Sem, MDiv, PhD. **CAREER** Asst curator, design dir, Marian Eakins Archaeol Coll, 91; adj prof, 92-96; guest asst prof, 96-98; curator, Marian Eakins Archaeol Coll, 98; asst prof, Golden Gate Baptist Theol Sem-. **HONORS AND AWARDS** Will Edd Langford Memorial scholar, 92; Who's Who Among Students In Amer Univ(s) and Col(s), 89, 92; Broadman Seminarian Award, 89; National Dean's List, 87, 92., Supvr, Sem library's audio-visual dept and video production studio, 90-96; Lib Circulation Svc, 94-96. **MEMBERSHIPS** Mem, Amer Sch(s) of Oriental Res; Soc Biblical Lit; member adv bd, Nat Assn prof(s)of Hebrew. **SELECTED PUBLICATIONS** Pub(s), Biblical Illustrator. **CONTACT ADDRESS** Golden Gate Baptist Theol Sem, 201 Sem Dr, Mill Valley, CA, 94941-3197. **EMAIL** GaryArbino@ggbts.edu

ARCHIE, LEE C.
PERSONAL Born 06/20/1944, Houston, TX, d, 1 child **DISCIPLINE** PHILOSOPHY **EDUCATION** Austin Col, BS, 67; Univ Arkansas, MA, 72, PhD, 77. **CAREER** Lectr, Univ Arkansas, 77-78; prof, Lander Univ, 78-. **HONORS AND AWARDS** Redia essay prize, 78; prof of the year, 84. **MEMBERSHIPS** APA; Philos of Sci Assn. **RESEARCH** Philosophy of science. **SELECTED PUBLICATIONS** Auth, The No-Alternative Paradox and the Possibility of Metaphysics, Contemp Philos, 95; auth, An Analysis of the Hobbes' Game, Tchg Philos, 95. **CONTACT ADDRESS** Dept of Philosophy, Lander Univ, PO Box 6031, Greenwood, SC, 29649. **EMAIL** larchie@lander.edu

ARGALL, RANDALL A.
DISCIPLINE RELIGION **EDUCATION** Univ Iowa, PhD, 92. **CAREER** Asst prof, chaplain, Jamestown Col, 98- . **MEMBERSHIPS** Soc Bibl Lit. **CONTACT ADDRESS** 808 19th St NE, Jamestown, ND, 58401. **EMAIL** argall@acc.jc.edu

ARGEN, RALPH J., III
PERSONAL Born 07/26/1958, Buffalo, NY, m, 1983, 3 children **DISCIPLINE** GEOLOGY; LAW; PHILOSOPHY **EDUCATION** Syracuse Univ, BS, 81; State Univ NY Buffalo, MS, 88, MA, 89, JD, 93, PhD, 94. **CAREER** Construction mgt, Corp Couns. **MEMBERSHIPS** PA Bar Asn; Wash DC Bar Asn. **RESEARCH** Construction law; Ethics; Environmental Ethics and Value Theory. **SELECTED PUBLICATIONS** Auth, The Commensurability of Environmental Geology and Petroleum Geology, AAPG Bulletin, vol 74, 600, May 90. **CONTACT ADDRESS** 17711 Crystal Cove Pl, Tampa, FL, 33549. **EMAIL** murphy2093@aol.com

ARGRETT, LORETTA COLLINS
PERSONAL m **DISCIPLINE** LAW **EDUCATION** Howard Univ, BS, 1958; Institute Fur Organische Chemie, Technische Hochschule; Harvard Law School, JD, 1976. **CAREER** US Congress, Joint Committee on Taxation, attorney; Wald, Harkrader and Ross, attorney, partner; Howard Univ School of Law, professor; US Justice Dept, Tax Div, asst attorney general, 1993-. **HONORS AND AWARDS** Greenwood Voters League, Outstanding Service and Achievement in the Field of Law, 1994. **MEMBERSHIPS** Harvard Law School, visiting committee mem, 1987-93; American Bar Foundation, fellow, 1993-; District of Columbia Bar, legal ethics committee mem, 1993-97; Univ of Baltimore Law School, Graduate Tax Program, advisory committee mem, 1986-; American Bar Assn, standing comm on ethics and professional responsibility, 1998-. **SELECTED PUBLICATIONS** Auth, Tax treatment of higher education expenditures: an unfair investment disincentive, 41 Syracuse Law Rev 621, 90 & Proposed tax incentives for education - a critique and counterproposal, 41 Tax Notes 461, 88; coauth, Settlement Reference Manual, Wash, DC, US Dept Justice, Tax Div, 96. **CONTACT ADDRESS** Assistant Attorney General, US Justice Department Tax Division, 950 Pennsylvania Ave NW, Rm 4143, Washington, DC, 20530.

ARKWAY, ANGELA
DISCIPLINE PHILOSOPHY **EDUCATION** Graduate Center, City Univ NY, PhD, 95. **CAREER** Adj asst prof, 95-96, Pace Univ NY; vis asst prof, 96-97, Univ Cincinnati; adj asst prof, 97- NY Univ. **MEMBERSHIPS** APA; Soc for Phil & Psychl. **RESEARCH** Philosophy of mind; the simulation theory; the theory theory of our folk psychological practices. **SELECTED PUBLICATIONS** Art, The Simulation Theory the Theory Theory and Folk Psychological Exploration, Phil Stud, 99. **CONTACT ADDRESS** 54 Riverside Dr, Apt 7C, New York, NY, 10024. **EMAIL** ajarkway@pipeline.com

ARLEN, JENNIFER H.
DISCIPLINE LAW **EDUCATION** Harvard Univ, BA,82; NY Univ, JD, PhD,86. **CAREER** Ivadelle & Theodore Johnson prof Law & Bus, Univ Southern Calif; dir, Olin Prog in Law and Rational Choice; clerked, Honorable Phyllis Kravitch, Judge US Ct Appeals 11th Circuit; past ch, Torts Section & past ch, Law and Econ Sect Asn Amer Law Sch. **MEMBERSHIPS** Amer Law Inst. **RESEARCH** Corporate civil & criminal liability, particularly securities fraud; tort liability for death & injury; law & economics. **SELECTED PUBLICATIONS** Auth, The Potentially Perverse Effects of Corporate Criminal Liability; Vicarious Liability for Fraud in Securities Markets: Theory and Evidence; A Political Theory of Corporate Taxation. **CONTACT ADDRESS** School of Law, Univ Southern Calif, University Park Campus, Los Angeles, CA, 90089. **EMAIL** jarlen@law.usc.edu

ARMENTROUT, DONAL SMITH
DISCIPLINE THEOLOGY **EDUCATION** Roanoke Col, BA, 61; Lutheran Theol Sem, BD, 64; Vanderbilt Univ, PhD, 70. **CAREER** Asst prof, 70-75, assoc prof, 75-81, dir, Vanderbilt/Sewanee Jt DMin prog, 74-84, DIR ADV DEGR PROGM 84-, ASSOC DEAN, PROF, 81-, SCH THEOL, SEWANEE. **CONTACT ADDRESS** Sch Theol, Univ of the South, 335 Tennessee Ave, Sewanee, TN, 37383-0001. **EMAIL** darmentr@seraphl.sewanee.edu

ARMOUR, JODY D.
DISCIPLINE LAW **EDUCATION** Harvard Univ, AB,82; Univ Calif, Berkeley,86, JD. **CAREER** Prof; Univ Southern Calif; private practice; taught at, Univ Calif, Berkeley; Ind Univ & Univ Pittsburgh. **RESEARCH** Race issues in legal decisionmaking. **SELECTED PUBLICATIONS** Auth, Just Desserts: Narrative, Perspective, Choice & Blame; Stereotypes & Prejudice: Helping Legal Decisionmakers Break the Prejudice Habit & Negrophobia & Reasonable Racism: The Hidden Costs of Being Black in America. **CONTACT ADDRESS** School of Law, Univ Southern Calif, University Park Campus, Los Angeles, CA, 90089. **EMAIL** jarmour@law.usc.edu

ARMSTRONG, JOHN M.
PERSONAL Born 10/29/1967, Washington, DC, m, 1989, 2 children **DISCIPLINE** PHILOSOPHY **EDUCATION** Brigham Young Univ, BA, 92; Univ Ariz, MA, 95, PhD, 98. **CAREER** Asst prof, S Va Col, 98-. **HONORS AND AWARDS** William H Fink Prize for Outstanding PhD student, Dept of Philos, Univ Ariz, 96-97. **MEMBERSHIPS** Amer Philos Assoc. **RESEARCH** Ancient Greek philos; ethics. **SELECTED PUBLICATIONS** Auth, Epicurean Justice, Phronesis, 97; art, Aristotle on the Philosophical Nature of Poetry, Classical Quarterly, 98. **CONTACT ADDRESS** Div of Arts & Humanities, Southern Virg Col, Buena Vista, VA, 24416. **EMAIL** jarmstrong@southernvirginia.edu

ARMSTRONG, SUSAN JEAN
PERSONAL Born 05/23/1941, Minneapolis, MN, 4 children **DISCIPLINE** PHILOSOPHY **EDUCATION** Bryn Mawr Col, AB, 63, PhD(philos), 76. **CAREER** Asst prof philos, Univ the Pac, 69-70; asst prof Philos, 72-76, chemn dept, 73-75, 77, assoc prof, 76-80, prof philos, Humboldt State Univ, 81-. **MEMBERSHIPS** Am Philos Asn. **RESEARCH** Ethics; metaphysics; philosophy psychology. **SELECTED PUBLICATIONS** Ed, with Richard Butzler, Environmental Ethics, McGraw-Hill, 93, 98. **CONTACT ADDRESS** Dept Philos, Humboldt State Univ, 1 Harps St, Arcata, CA, 95521-8299. **EMAIL** sja@axe.humboldt.edu

ARNELLE, HUGH JESSE
PERSONAL Born 12/30/1933, New Rochelle, NY, m **DISCIPLINE** LAW **EDUCATION** PA State Univ, BA 1955; Dickinson School of Law, JD 1962; admitted to practice CA, PA, United States Supreme Court. **CAREER** AU State Univ All-Amer Basketball, 1952-54; PA State Univ, honorable mention All-Amer Football 1953-54; NBA Ft Wayne Piston, 1955-56; NFL Baltimore Colts, 1957-58; Dept of Labor, atty 1962-63; Peace Corps, assoc dir 1963-65, dir 1965-66, staff 1966-67; FPC, asst to gen counsel 1967-68; IDEA Inc Chas F Kettering Found 1968-69; Morrison Foerster Holloway, atty 1971-73; US Dist Ct, asst federal public defender, sr partner, 1985-; private practice 1973-85; Arnelle & Hastie, civil litigation & public finance atty, senior partner, 1985-. **MEMBERSHIPS** Mem Coll of Civil Trial Advocacy 1976; faculty Hastings Law School Criminal Trial Advocacy 1977; mem Hall of Fame NY 1977; commissioner San Francisco Redevelopment Agency 1981-; bd of dir SF Boys Club 1981-; mem Amer Bd of Criminal Trial Lawyers 1982-; exec commissioner, bd of trustees San Francisco World Affairs Council 1983-; bd of trust PA State Univ; PA State Board of Trustees, vice chairman, 1993-; PA State Univ; dir Renaissance Fund PA State Univ; mem Charles Houston Bar Assn; life mem Natl Bar Assn, Bar of PA, CA, Bar of US Supreme Court; diplomate Hastings Law School; mem Natl Panel of Arbit, Amer Trial Lawyers Assn, Westchester County Hall of Fame; National Football Foundation Hall of Fame, 1993; adj prof Hastings Law School Coll of Advocacy; former pres Afro-American Hist Society; board of directors San Francisco Op; bd of dir Bay Area UNICEF; Corporate BoardS, Wells Fargo Bank and Wells Fargo & Co, director, 1991, FPL Groups Inc, director, 1990, Waste Management, Inc, director, 1992, University Governance, Pennsylvania State University Board of Trustees, vice-chairman, 1993. **CONTACT ADDRESS** Arnelle & Hastie, 455 Market St, San Francisco, CA, 94105.

ARNESON, RICHARD J.
DISCIPLINE POLITICAL AND SOCIAL PHILOSOPHY **EDUCATION** Univ Calif-Berkeley, PhD, 75. **CAREER** PROF, PHILOS, UNIV CALIF, SAN DIEGO. **RESEARCH** Polit and social philos; Applied philos. **SELECTED PUBLICATIONS** Auth, "Democratic Rights at National and Workplace Levels," The Idea of Democracy, Cambridge Univ Press, 93; "Autonomy and Preference Formation," In Harm's Way, Cambridge Univ Press, 94; "Cracked Foundations of Liberal Equality," Dworkin and His Critics, Basil Blackwell, 95; "Against 'Complex Equality', Pluralism, Justice, and Equality," Oxford Univ Press, 95. **CONTACT ADDRESS** Dept of Philos, Univ Calif, San Diego, 9500 Gilman Dr, La Jolla, CA, 92093.

ARNOLD, BARRY
PERSONAL Born 09/29/1951, Mooresville, NC, m, 1984 **DISCIPLINE** PHILOSOPHY **EDUCATION** Davidson Col, AB, 73; Rice Univ, Grad Fel, 73-75; Emory Univ, M.Div, 76, PhD, 86; Univ Glasgow, Postgraduate Fel, 76. **CAREER** Prof, Andrew Col, 83-84; from asst to assoc to acting chemn, 86-, Univ W Fla; Private Practice Counseling, Pace, 96-. **HONORS AND AWARDS** Phi Beta Kappa; Phi Kappa Phi; Who's Who Among Am Tchrs; Who's Who in Am., Dist Tchg Award, Univ W Fla, 88, 90,95. **MEMBERSHIPS** Am Conseling Asn; Nat Asn Cognitive Behavorial Therapists; Am Acad Rel; Am Col Counselors. **RESEARCH** Psychoanalysis and religion; bioethics; alternative medicine. **SELECTED PUBLICATIONS** Auth, The Pursuit of Virtue, 88; coauth, Essays in American Ethics, 91; ed, The Reshaping of Psychoanalysis, 88-89. **CONTACT ADDRESS** Dept of Philosophy, Univ of West Florida, 11000 University Pky, Pensacola, FL, 32514.

ARNOLD, BILL T.
PERSONAL Born 09/01/1955, Lancaster, KY, m, 1977, 3 children **DISCIPLINE** OLD TESTAMENT AND ANCIENT NEAR EASTERN STUDIES **EDUCATION** Asbury Col, BA, 77; Asbury Theol Sem, M Div, 80; Hebrew Union Col, PhD, 85. **CAREER** Assoc prof, old testament and bibl lang, Wesley Bibl Sem, 85-89; prof, old testament and bibl lang, Wesley Bible Sem, 89-91; assoc prof, old testament and semitic lang, Ashland Theol Sem, 91-93; prof, old testament and semitic lang, Ashland Theol Sem, 93-95; prof, old testament and semitic lang, Asbury Theol Sem, 95-. **HONORS AND AWARDS** Lykins Found Scholar, 77-78; Magee Christ Educ Found Scholar, 73-79; Intl Hon Soc of Theta Phi, 79; Joseph and Helen Regenstein Found fel, 80-81; S. H. and Helen R. Scheuer grad fel, 82-84; Nat Endow for the Humanities, summer stipend, 88; Eta Beta Rho, Nat Hon Soc of Students of Hebrew Lang and Culture, 92. **MEMBERSHIPS** Amer Oriental Soc; Amer Sch of Orient Res; Inst for Bibl Res; Nat Asn of the Prof of Hebrew; Soc of Bibl Lit; Wesleyan Theol Soc. **RESEARCH** Genesis; History of Israelite religion; Israelite historiography. **SELECTED PUBLICATIONS** Auth, What Has Nebuchadnezzar to do with David? On the Neo-Babylonian Period and Early Israel, Syria-Mesopotamia and the Bible, Sheffield Acad Press, 98; articles, The New Intl Dict of Old Testament Theol and Exegesis, Zondervan Publ House, 97; auth, The Use of Aramaic in the Hebrew Bible: Another Look at Bilingualism in Ezra and Daniel, Jour of Northwest Semitic Lang, 22, 2, 1-16, 96; auth, Luke's Characterizing Use of the Old Testament in the Book of Acts, 300-323, Hist, Lit, and Soc in the Book of Acts, Cambridge Univ Press, 96; auth, Age, Old (the Aged), Daniel, Theology of

Manna Vision, Evang Dict of Bibl Theol, Baker Book House, 96; auth, Forms of Prophetic Speech in the Old Testament: A Summary of Claus Westermann's Contributions, Ashland Theol Jour, 27, 30-40, 95; auth, Babylonians, 43-75, Peoples of the Old Testament World, Baker Book House, 94; auth, The Weidner Chronicle and the Idea of History is Israel and Mespotamia, 129-148, Faith, Tradition, and History: Old Testament Historiography in Its Near Eastern Context, Eisenbrauns, 94. **CONTACT ADDRESS** Asbury Theol Sem, 204 N Lexington Ave, Wilmore, KY, 40390-1199. **EMAIL** Bill_Arnold@ats.wilmore.ky.us

ARNOLD, LIONEL A.
PERSONAL Born 08/30/1921, Greenville, PA, s **DISCIPLINE** RELIGIOUS STUDIES **EDUCATION** Thiel Coll, AB (Cum Laude) 1943; Anderson Coll, BTh 1943-44; Oberlin Grad Sch, MA BD 1947; Harvard Univ, STM 1955; Drew Univ, PhD 1969. **CAREER** LeMoyne-Owen Coll, college pastor, 1947-64, dean, 1964-71; OK State Univ, prof 1971-86, prof emeritus. **HONORS AND AWARDS** Hon Doc Humane Letters, Thiel Coll Greenville, PA 1964. **CONTACT ADDRESS** Religious Stds, Oklahoma State Univ.

ARNOLD, PHILIP P.
DISCIPLINE RELIGION **EDUCATION** Univ Colo, BA, 85; Univ London, Inst Archaeol, MA, 86; Univ Chicago, PhD, 92. **CAREER** Asst prof, Univ Mo, Columbia, 92-95; ASST PROF AM RELIGS, SYRACUSE UNIV, 96-. **CONTACT ADDRESS** Dept of Relig, Syracuse Univ, 501 Hall Langs, Syracuse, NY, 13244. **EMAIL** pparnold@syr.edu

ARNOLD, RUDOLPH P.
PERSONAL Born 05/24/1948, Harlem, NY, m **DISCIPLINE** LAW **EDUCATION** Howard Univ, BA 1970; Univ of CT, JD 1975; NY Univ, LLM 1976. **CAREER** Aetna Life & Casualty 1971-72; Legal Aid Soc of Hartford Cty, attny 1976-81; Arnold & Hershinson, attny 1982-84; Arnold & Assoc, atty 1985-; Society for Savings Bancorp Inc, chmn, 1991-93. **HONORS AND AWARDS** Natl Bar Assn, 1980-; Hartford County Bar, Pro Bond Award, 1991. **MEMBERSHIPS** CT Bar Assn, Hartford Bar Assn; bd of dir, Urban League 1977-79; deputy mayor Hartford City Council 1979-83; bd of dir World Affairs Ctr 1983-88; chmn, Hartford Comm TV 1986-89; bd dir Soc for Savings 1987-93; Natl Bar Assn; Amer Bar Assn; lifetime mem, NAACP; dir, Natl Council for Intl Visitors 1989-92; Hartford Public Library, board of directors, 1994-; National Association Bond Lawyer; Natl Assn Securities Prof. **SELECTED PUBLICATIONS** What You Should Know About Evictions, 1981 **CONTACT ADDRESS** Arnold & Assoc, 80 Cedar Street, Hartford, CT, 06106.

ARNOLD, SCOTT
DISCIPLINE PHILOSOPHY **EDUCATION** Univ Penn, BA, 73; Univ Mass at Amherst, PhD, 79. **CAREER** Prof, Univ Ala at Birmingham, 82-; vis scholar, Social Philos and Policy Ctr, Bowling Green State Univ, 87-88; Title VIII fel, US State Dept, Hoover Inst at Stanford Univ, 90-91; vis scholar, Social Philos and Policy Ctr at Bowling Green State Univ, 92. **RESEARCH** History of philosophy; contemporary political philosophy. **SELECTED PUBLICATIONS** Auth, Marx's Radical Critique of Capitalist Society, Oxford UP, 90; The Philosophy and Economic of Market Socialism, Oxford UP, 94; co-ed, Philosophy Then and Now, Basil Blackwell; Affirmative Action and the Demands of Justice, Social Philosophy & Policy 16, 1998; The Monitoring Problem for Market Socialist Firms, in Advances in Austrian Economics, JAI Press, 1996; Capitalism, Socialism, and Equity Ownership, in Liberty for the 21st Century, Rowman & Littlefield, 1995; Market Socialism, Critical Review 6, 1993. **CONTACT ADDRESS** Dept of Philosophy, Univ of Alabama, Birmingham, 1400 University Blvd, Birmingham, AL, 35294-1150. **EMAIL** sarnold@uab.edu

ARONOWICZ, ANNETTE
PERSONAL Born 03/09/1952, Poland **DISCIPLINE** RELIGIOUS STUDIES **EDUCATION** UCLA, PhD, 82. **CAREER** ASSOC PROF, DEPT OF REL STUDIES, FRANKLIN AND MARSHALL COL. **HONORS AND AWARDS** Jerusalem Fellows. **MEMBERSHIPS** AAR; ASSR; AJS. **RESEARCH** Post-war Jewish thought in France; modern religious thought. **SELECTED PUBLICATIONS** Auth, Nine Talmudic Readings by Emmanuel Uvinas, IN Univ Press, 91; Jews and Christians on Time and Eternity, Stanford, 98. **CONTACT ADDRESS** Religious Studies Dept., Franklin and Marshall Col, Box 3003, Lancaster, PA, 17604. **EMAIL** A_Aronowicz@ACAD.FandM.edu

ARP, KRISTANA
PERSONAL Born 08/12/1951, CA, d, 1 child **DISCIPLINE** PHILOSOPHY **EDUCATION** Univ Chicago, BA, 75; Univ Calif, PhD, 87. **CAREER** Asst prof, Long Island Univ, 90-96; assoc prof, Long Island Univ, 96-; chair Philos Dept, Long Island Univ, 97-. **HONORS AND AWARDS** Univ Calif Dissertation Fel, 86-86; Univ Calif Regents' Fel, 80-81. **MEMBERSHIPS** Beauvor Circle, Ed of Newsletter, 95-97; Soc Phenomenol & Existential Philos; Amer Philos Assoc **RESEARCH** Simone de Beauvoir; Edmund Husserl; Existentialist Ethics; Phenomenology; Feminism. **SELECTED PUBLICATIONS** An Eye for an Eye, by Simone de Beauvoir, Writings on Ethics, Politics and Sexuality of The Beauvoir Series, Ind Univ Pr, forthcoming; Beauvoir as Situated Subject: The Ambiguities of Life in World War II France, The Existential Phenomenolgy of Simone de Beauvoir, Kluwer Acad Publ, forthcoming; A Different Voice in the Phenomenological Tradition: Simone de Beauvoir and the Ethics of Care, Feminist Phenomenology, Kluwer Acad Publ, forthcoming; book note, Rousseau and the Politics of Ambiguity, by Mira Morgenstern, Ethics, forthcoming. **CONTACT ADDRESS** Dept of Philosophy, Long Island Univ, Brooklyn, NY, 11201. **EMAIL** karp@phoenix.liv.edu

ARRINGTON, ROBERT LEE
PERSONAL Born 10/19/1938, Bainbridge, GA, m, 1961, 2 children **DISCIPLINE** PHILOSOPHY **EDUCATION** Vanderbilt Univ, BA, 60; Tulane Univ, MA, 62, PhD(philos), 66. **CAREER** Asst prof philos, Univ Southern Miss, 63-66; asst prof, 66-69, assoc prof, 69-79, prof philos & chmn dept, Ga State Univ, 79-, Am Coun Learned Socs fel, 74-75. **MEMBERSHIPS** Am Philos Asn; Southern Soc Philos & Psychol. **RESEARCH** Wittgenstein; philosophy of psychology; ethics. **SELECTED PUBLICATIONS** Can there be a linguistic phenomenology?, Philos Quart, 75; Rationalism, Realism, and Relativisim, Cornell Univ Press, 89; Western Ethics, Blackwell, 97; A Companion to the Philosophers, Blackwell, 98; ed, Wittgenstein ans Quine, co-ed, Routledge, 96; Criteria and entailment, Ratio, 6/79; Mechanism and calculus, Wittgenstein: Sources & Perspectives, 79; Practical reason, responsibility, and the psychopath, J Theory Social Behav, 3/79; Advertising and behavior control, J Bus Ethics, 2/82. **CONTACT ADDRESS** Dept of Philosophy, Georgia State Univ, 33 Gilmer St S E, Atlanta, GA, 30303-3080. **EMAIL** phlrla@panther.gsu.edu

ARROW, DENNIS WAYNE
PERSONAL Born 07/27/1949, Chicago, IL **DISCIPLINE** CONSTITUTIONAL & AMERICAN INDIAN LAW **EDUCATION** George Washington Univ, BA, 70; CA Western Sch Law, JD, 74; Harvard Law Sch, LLM, 75. **CAREER** PROF LAW, OKLA CITY UNIV, 75-. **MEMBERSHIPS** OK Constitutional Rev Study Commission, 88-91; Assoc Justice, Supreme Court of the Cheyenne-Arapaho Tribes, 95-.. **RESEARCH** Constitutional and Am Indian law. **SELECTED PUBLICATIONS** Auth, The Propsed Regime for the Unilateral Exploitation of the Deep Seabed, Harvard Int Law J, 80; The Customary Norm Process and the Deep Seabed, Ocean Develop & Int Law J, 81; The Dimensions of the Newly-Emergent Quasi-fundamental Right to Ballot Access, OK City Univ Law Rev, 81; The Alternative Seabed Mining Regime: 1981, Fordham Int Law J, 81 & 82; Prospective Impacts of the Draft Sea Convention, Int Property Invest J, 83; Seabeds, Sovereignty, and Objective Regimes, Fordham Inst Law J, 84; Contemporary Tensions in Constitutional Indian Law, OK City Univ Law Rev, 87; Federal Question Jurisdiction and American Indian Law, OK City Univ Law Rev, 89; The Indian Free Exercise Clause, Sovereignty Symposium, 91; Representative Government and Popular Distrust, OK City Univ Law Rev, 92; Bankruptcy Relief Against Governmental Entities, Consumer Finance Law Quart Report, 93; Oklahoma's Tribal Courts: A Prologue, The First Fifteen Years of the Modern Era, and a Glimpse of the Road Ahead, OK City Univ Law Rev, 94; Oklahoma Tribal Court Reports, vols 1-3, Native Am Legal Resource Center, 94-96; Pomobabble: Postmodern Newspeak and Constitutional Meaning for the Uninitiated, MI Law Rev, 97. **CONTACT ADDRESS** Sch Law, Oklahoma City Univ, 2501 N Blackwelder, Oklahoma City, OK, 73106-1493.

ASCOUGH, RICHARD S.
PERSONAL Born 08/27/1962, Darlington, United Kingdom, m, 1985, 1 child **DISCIPLINE** THEOLOGY **EDUCATION** Univ of St. Michael's Col, Toronto Sch of Theol, PhD, 97. **CAREER** Asst prof, Inst of Pastoral Stud, Loyola Univ, 97- . **HONORS AND AWARDS** John M Kelly Award, Toronto Sch of Theol, 96; Gov Gen Acad Gold Medal, Univ of St Michael's Col, 97. **MEMBERSHIPS** Chicago Soc of Bibl Res; Am Soc of Greek and Latin Epigraphy; Catholic Bibl Asn; Can Soc of Bibl Stud; Soc of Bibl Lit. **RESEARCH** New Testament; early Christianity and its social context; voluntary associations in antiquity. **SELECTED PUBLICATIONS** Auth, Rejection and Repentance: Peter and the Crowds in Luke's Passion Narrative, Biblica, 93; auth, An Analysis of the Baptismal Ritual of the Didache, Studia Liturgica, 94; auth, Narrative Technique and Generic Designation: Crowd Scenes in Luke-Acts and in Chariton, Catholic Bibl Q, 96; auth, The Completion of a Religious Duty: The Background of 2 Cor 8.1-15, New Testament Stud, 96; auth, Translocal Relationships Among Voluntary Associations and Early Christianity, J of Early Christian Stud, 97; auth, Civic Pride at Philippi: The Text-Critical Problem of Acts 16. 12, New Testament Stud, 98; auth, What Are They Saying About the Formation of Pauline Churches? Paulist, 98. **CONTACT ADDRESS** Inst of Pastoral Studies, Loyola Univ, 6525 N Sheridan Rd, Chicago, IL, 60626. **EMAIL** rascoug@luc.edu

ASHANIN, CHARLES B.
PERSONAL Born 11/15/1920, Montenegro, Yugoslavia, m, 1953, 4 children **DISCIPLINE** RELIGION HISTORY **EDUCATION** Church Col, Yugoslavia, AB, 43; Univ Glasgow, BD, 52, PhD, 55. **CAREER** Asst prof relig, Univ Col Ghana, 55-60; from assoc prof to prof relig & philos, Allen Univ, 60-65; prof, Claflin Univ, 65-67; assoc prof early church hist, 67-76, PROF EARLY CHURCH HIST, CHRISTIAN THEOL SEM, 76-; Guest scholar, Princeton Theol Sem, 57; vis scholar & Lilly fel, Harvard Divinity Sch, 64-65; assoc ed, The Logas, 68-; fel, Woodbrooke Col, Eng, 73-74; mem, Patristic Cong Am Acad Relig. **MEMBERSHIPS** Am Soc Church Hist; Orthodox Theol Soc Am. **RESEARCH** Roman Empire and Christian Church in the IV century; history of Christian humanism from the beginning until AD 1536; philosophy of religion; religion and culture; Emperor Constantine and his age. **SELECTED PUBLICATIONS** Auth, Cultural and Existential Aspects of Religious Language, J Relig Thought, 65-66; Ethics of Eastern Orthodox Church, In: Dictionary of Christian Ethics, Westminster, 67; The Church Historian in Dialogue, Encounter, winter 68; The Black Heroes of the Philadelphia Plague in 1793, In: Religion in Pluralistic Society, E J Brill, Leiden, 76; Theology of Liberation: European Frontier, Encounter, winter 77; Backgrounds of Early Christianity, with E. Ferguson, Church History, Vol 64, 95. **CONTACT ADDRESS** Christian Theol Sem, 1000 W 42nd St, Indianapolis, IN, 46208.

ASHBROOK, JAMES BARBOUR
PERSONAL Born 11/01/1925, Adrian, MI, m, 1948, 4 children **DISCIPLINE** RELIGION PSYCHOLOGY **EDUCATION** Denison Univ, AB, 47; Colgate Rochester Divinity Sch, BD, 50; OH State Univ, MA, 62, PhD(psychol), 64; Am Bd Prof Psychol, dipl clin psychol; Am Asn Pastoral Coun, dipl. **CAREER** Pastor, S Congregational Church, Rochester, NY, 50-54 & First Baptist Church, Granville, OH, 55-60; from assoc prof to prof pastoral theol, Colgate Rochester Divinity Sch, 60-69; prof psychol & theol, Colgate Rochester Divinity Sch, Bexley Hall, Crozer Sem, 69-81; PROF RELIG & PERSONALITY, GARRETT-EVANGELICAL THEOL SEM, 81-, Am Asn Theol Schs fel, 71-72 & Univ Rochester, 71-73; consult, Primary Ment Health Proj, 71-77 & Family Ctr, Monroe County, NY, 71-75; CLIN CONSULT, ST ANN'S HOME FOR ELDERLY, 73-. **HONORS AND AWARDS** LLD, Denison Univ, OH, 76. **RESEARCH** Ministerial leadership; the working brain; theological expressions. **SELECTED PUBLICATIONS** Auth, From Biogenetic Structuralism to Mature Contemplation to Prophetic Consciousness, Zygon, vol 28, 93; The Cry For the Other-The Biocultural Womb of Human-Development, vol 29, Zygon, 94; Toward a New Creation of Being, vol 31, Zygon, 96; Making Sense of God-How I Got to the Brain, reprinted from the Seminary-Times, fall 88, Aygon, vol 31, 96; Interfacing Religion and the Neurosciences--A Review of 25 Years of Exploration and Reflection, vol 31, Zygon, 96; A Rippling Relatableness in Reality, vol 31, Zygon, 96; Mind As Humanizing the Brain--Toward a Neurotheology of Meaning, Zygon, vol 32, 97. **CONTACT ADDRESS** Garrett-Evangelical Theol Sem, 2121 Sheridan Rd, Evanston, IL, 60201.

ASHBY, WILLIAM JAMES
PERSONAL Born 09/27/1943, Detroit, MI, m, 1969, 2 children **DISCIPLINE** ROMANCE LINGUISTICS, FRENCH LANGUAGE AND LITERATURE **EDUCATION** Alma Col, BA, 65; Univ MI, MA, 66, PhD(Romance ling), 73. **CAREER** Asst prof, 71-80, ASSOC PROF FRENCH, UNIV CA, SANTA BARBARA, 80-, Am Coun Learned Socs res fel, 76. **MEMBERSHIPS** Ling Soc Am; MLA; Am Asn Teachers Fr. **RESEARCH** Sociolinguistics; French language. **SELECTED PUBLICATIONS** Auth, Sociolinguistics and Contemporary French, with D. Ager, Can J of Ling, vol 39, 94; French-From Dialect to Standard, with R. Anthony, Language in Society, vol 23, 94; Linguistic Consequences of Language Contact and Restriction--The Case of French in Ontario, Canada, with R. Mougeon and E. Beniak, Can J of Ling, vol 39, 94; A Grammar of the Norman French of the Channel Islands-The Dialects of Jersey and Sark, with A. Liddicoat, French Rev, vol 69, 96; The French Conditional Tense in Journalistic Discourse--An Essay in Discriptive Linguistics--French, with P. Haillet, French Rev, vol 70, 97. **CONTACT ADDRESS** Dept of French, Univ CA, 552 University Rd, Santa Barbara, CA, 93106-0001.

ASHE, MARIE
DISCIPLINE LAW **EDUCATION** Clark Univ, BA, 66; Tufts Univ, MA, 71; Univ Nebr, 79. **CAREER** Law Sch, Suffolk Univ **RESEARCH** Constitutional law; criminal law; jurisprudence. **SELECTED PUBLICATIONS** Auth, Mind's Opportunity: Birthing a Poststructuralist Feminist Jurisprudence, 95; The Bell Jar and the Ghost of Ethel Rosenberg, Routlege, 95; Postmodernism, Legal Ethics, and Representation of 'Bad Mothers', Routlege, 95; Poststructuralist Feminist Jurisprudence, Univ Ca, 95; co-auth, Child Abuse: A Problem for Feminist Theory, 94. **CONTACT ADDRESS** Law School, Suffolk Univ, Beacon Hill, Boston, MA, 02114. **EMAIL** mashe@acad.suffolk.edu

ASHLEY, BENEDICT M
PERSONAL Born 05/03/1915, Neodesha, KS **DISCIPLINE** PHILOSOPHY, THEOLOGY **EDUCATION** Univ Chicago,

MA, 38; Univ Notre Dame, PhD(polit sci), 41; Aquinas Inst, PhD(philos), 50. **CAREER** Pres, Aquinas Inst, IL, 62-69; prof moral theol, Inst Relig & Human Develop, Univ TX Med Sch, Houston, 69-72; PROF MORAL THEOL, AQUINAS INST THEOL, 73-, DIR, ALBERTUS MAGNUS LYCEUM, 62-; regent of studies, St Albert Great Prov, Dominican Fathers, 72-. **RESEARCH** Philosophy of nature and education; moral theology; medical ethics. **SELECTED PUBLICATIONS** Auth, Catholicism as a Sign System, 3 Religious Languages, Am J of Semiotics, vol 10, 93. **CONTACT ADDRESS** Aquinas Inst of Theol, 2570 Asbury Rd, Dubuque, IA, 52001.

ASHLEY, JAMES MATTHEW
DISCIPLINE PHILOSOPHY OF SCIENCE **EDUCATION** St. Louis Univ, BS 82; Weston Sch of Theol, MTS, 88; Univ Chicago, PhD, 93. **CAREER** Asst prof, 93-. **RESEARCH** Science and theology; liberation theology. **SELECTED PUBLICATIONS** Auth, Interruptions: Mysticism, Theology and Politics in the Work of Johannes Baptist Metz, 98; The Turn to Spirituality? The Relationship Between Theology and Spirituality, 95; A Post-Einsteinian Settlement? On Spirituality as a Possible Border-Crossing Between Religion and the New Science, 98; ed, A Passion for God: The Mystical-Political Dimension of Christianity, 98. **CONTACT ADDRESS** History and Philosophy of Science Dept, Univ of Notre Dame, Notre Dame, IN, 46556. **EMAIL** James.M.Ashley.2@nd.edu

ASHTON, DIANNE C.
PERSONAL Born 06/21/1949, Buffalo, NY, m, 1988 **DISCIPLINE** RELIGIOUS STUDIES **EDUCATION** Adelphi Univ, BA, 71; Univ MA, graduate studies, 74; Temple Univ, PhD, 86. **CAREER** Instr/grad asst, Temple Univ, 82-83, 86; instr, Col of Gen Studies, Univ PA, 87; instr, LaSalle Univ, 86-88; instr, Netyzky Inst, Gratz Col, 86-88; instr, Rutgers Univ, 88; PROF RELIG (early tenure), ROWAN UNIV, 86-. **HONORS AND AWARDS** Nat Merit Scholarship, 67; Scholarship Awards, Temple Univ Relig Dept, 78-85; America-Holy Land Studies Int Conference, Nat Archives, Washington, DC, full stipend, 83; Franklin fel for extended res, Amer Jewish Archives, 84; PhD awarded with distinction, Temple Univ, 87; Rapoport Post Doctoral fel, Amer Jewish Archives, 88; Separately Budgeted Res Grants, Rowan Univ, 91, 92, 93, 94, 95, 96, 98; Margerite R. Jacobs Post Doctoral fel, Amer Jewish Archives, 98. **MEMBERSHIPS** Philadelphia Consort on the Study of Relig, 88-95; Nat Assoc for Multicultural Ed, 91-94; Amer Academy Relig; Amer Studies Assoc; Assoc for Jewish Studies; Israeli Anthropology Assoc; Org of Amer Hist; Soc for the Scientific Study of Relig; Relig Res Assoc. **RESEARCH** Women in Amer Judaism and in Amer Jewish history. **SELECTED PUBLICATIONS** Auth, Four Centuries of Jewish Women's Spirituality: A Sourcebook , ed and intros with Ellen M. Umansky: Beacon Press, 92; The Feminization of Jewish Education, Transformations, v 3, no 2, fall 92; Souls Have No Sex: Philadelphia Women Who Shaped American Jewish Life, in Murray Friedman, ed When Philadelphia Was the Capital of Jewish America, Assoc Univ Presses, 93; The Philadelphia Group: A Guide to Archival and Bibliographic Collections, compiled for the Center for Amer Jewish Hist: Temple Univ, 93; Grace Aguilar and the Matriarchal Theme in Jewish Women's Spirituality, in Maurie Sacks, ed, Active Voices: Women in Jewish Culture, Univ IL Press, 95; Crossing Boundaries: The Career of Mary M. Cohen, in Amer Jewish Hist, vol 83, no 2, June 95; Recent Scholarship on American Jewry, Relig Studies Rev, vol 21, no 2, April 95; Rebecca Gratz, Amer Nat Biography, Amer Council of Learned Socs and Oxford Univ Press, 96; Rebecca Gratz, Jewish Women in America: An Historical Encyclopedia, Carlson Pubs, 97; Jewish Life in Pennsylvania, PA Hist Assoc, Ethnic Hist Series, 98; Rebecca Gratz: Women and Judaism in Antebellum America, Detroit: Wayne State Univ Press, 98. **CONTACT ADDRESS** Dept of Philos and Relig, Rowan Univ, Bruce Hall, Glassboro, NJ, 08028. **EMAIL** ashton@jupiter.rowan.edu

ASHWORTH, EARLINE JENNIFER
PERSONAL Born 10/06/1939, Sevenoaks, England **DISCIPLINE** PHILOSOPHY **EDUCATION** Cambridge Univ, BA, 60, MA, 64; Bryn Mawr Col, PhD(philos), 65. **CAREER** From lectr to asst prof philos, Univ Man, 64-69; from asst prof to assoc prof, 69-75, PROF PHILOS, UNIV WATERLOO, 75-. **MEMBERSHIPS** Can Philos Asn; Mediaeval Acad Am; Soc Int Etude Philos Medievale. **RESEARCH** History of logic in 15th and 16th centuries. **SELECTED PUBLICATIONS** Auth, Language and Logic in the Post-Medieval Period, D Reidel, Holland, 74; The Tradition of Medieval Logic and Speculative Grammar From Anselm to the End of the Seventeenth Century: A Bibliography From 1836 Onward, Pontifical Inst Mediaeval Studies, Toronto, 78; Renaissance Argument-Valla and Agricola in the Traditions of Rhetoric and Dialectic, with P. Mack, Renaissance Quart, vol 48, 95; "Destructiones Modorum Significandi,' Latin and English, L. Kacmarek, ed, Speculum-A J of Medieval Studies, vol 71, 96. **CONTACT ADDRESS** Dept of Philos, Univ of Waterloo, Waterloo, ON, N2L 3G1.

ASHWORTH, JENNIFER E.
DISCIPLINE PHILOSOPHY **EDUCATION** Bryn Mawr Col, PhD, 65. **HONORS AND AWARDS** Fel, Royal Soc Can. **RESEARCH** Medieval and post-medieval logic; medieval philosophy; Aquinas. **SELECTED PUBLICATIONS** Auth, Language and Logic in the Post-Medieval Period, D. Reidel, 74; The Tradition of Medieval Logic and Speculative Grammar from Anselm to the End of the Seventeenth Century: A Bibliography from 1836 Onwards, PIMS, 78; Studies in Post-Medieval Semantics, Variorum, 85; ed, Paul of Venice, Logica Magna Part II, Fascicule 8, Oxford, 88; The Routledge Encycl of Philos, 98. **CONTACT ADDRESS** Dept of Philosophy, Waterloo Univ, 200 University Ave W, Waterloo, ON, N2L 3G1. **EMAIL** ejashwor@uwaterloo.ca

ASKIN, FRANK
PERSONAL Born 01/08/1932, Baltimore, MD, m, 1960, 4 children **DISCIPLINE** LAW **EDUCATION** City Col New York, BA, 66; Rutgers Univ, JD, 66. **CAREER** From asst prof to assoc prof, 66-71, prof law, Rutgers Univ, Newark, 71-, gen coun & Mem, nat bd, Am Civil Liberties Union, 69-; mem, bd gov, Soc Am Law Teachers, 73-76; spec counsel, Comt Educ & Labor, US House Rep, 76-77, special counsel, Cout Ops Comm, U.S. House Rep, 87-92 78-. **MEMBERSHIPS** Soc Am Law Teachers; Am Civil Liberties Union. **RESEARCH** Constitutional litigation; federal courts and procedure; law and social science. **SELECTED PUBLICATIONS** Auth, The Case for Compensatory Treatment, Rutgers Law Rev, 69; Police Dossiers and Emerging Principles of First Amendment Adjudication, Stanford Law Rev, 70; Surveillance: The Social Science Perspective, Columbia Human Rights Law Rev, 72; ;Defending Rights: A Life in Law and Politics, Humanities Press, 97. **CONTACT ADDRESS** Sch of Law, Rutgers Univ, 15 Washington St, Newark, NJ, 07102-3192. **EMAIL** faskin@uinoy.rutgers.edu

ASKLAND, ANDREW
PERSONAL Born 08/16/1951, New York, NY **DISCIPLINE** PHILOSOPHY **EDUCATION** Univ of Maryland, JD, 98; Univ of Col-Boulder, PhD, 95. **CAREER** Instr, Univ Colorado. **MEMBERSHIPS** Am Philos Asn; CO Bar Asn; MD Bar Asn; DC Bar Asn. **RESEARCH** Philosophy of law; Philosophy of economics; Professional ethics; Environmental philosophy. **SELECTED PUBLICATIONS** Auth The Tardy Berry Picker: A Criticism of the Market Metaphor for Civil Society, Publ Affairs Quart, 94; Conflicting Accounts of Equal Opportunity, Int Jour Appl Philos, 96; Fostering Market Competence, Jour of Thought, 97; The Sin of Inequality, Jour Philos Res, 98; A Justification of Compensation to the Descendants of Wrong Parties: An Intended Analogy, Pub Affairs Quart, 98. **CONTACT ADDRESS** 1561 S Foothills Hwy, Boulder, CO, 80303. **EMAIL** andrew_askland@yahoo.com

ASPELL, PATRICK JOSEPH
PERSONAL Born 06/21/1930, Boston, MA, 1 child **DISCIPLINE** PHILOSOPHY, PSYCHOLOGY **EDUCATION** Oblate Col, BA, 56; Cath Univ Am, STL & MA, 57, PhD(philos), 59; Univ Redlands, MA, 79; US Int Univ, PhD(psychol), 82. **CAREER** From instr to assoc prof philos, Oblate Col, 59-70, chmn dept, 68-81, prof, 70-81; Lectr philos, Cath Univ Am, 61-63; vis asst prof, Univ Tex, San Antonio, 80-81; publisher, Lfewings, Ltd.; vice pres, Aspell Empowerment Enter, Inc. **MEMBERSHIPS** Christian Asn Psychol Stud. **RESEARCH** History of philosophy; theories of knowledge; metapsychol; psychol. **SELECTED PUBLICATIONS** Auth, A critique of Santayana's epistemology, Mod Schoolman, 61; Objective knowledge according to Ralph Barton Perry, New Scholasticism, 62; Plato and Anaxagoras, In: The New Cath Encycl, McGraw, 67; History of Philosophy, coauth, Readings in Ancient Western Philosophy, 70, Ancient Western Philosophy, 71, auth, Medieval Western Philosophy, 78 & Readings in Medieval Western Philosophy, 78, Appleton; auth, The Enneagram Personality Portraits: Enhancing Professional Relationships; The Enneagram Inventory and Profile, Enhancing Team Performance, Improving Problem-Solving Skills, Leadership Styles and the Enneagram, Jossey Bass; auth, What Drives You Crazy?, Human Resource Dev Press. **CONTACT ADDRESS** 247 Barbara Dr, San Antonio, TX, 78216. **EMAIL** info@aspell.com

ATKINS, ROBERT
DISCIPLINE PHILOSOPHY **EDUCATION** City Col NY, BS; Univ Calif Berkeley, MA; JD; PhD. **CAREER** Prof. **SELECTED PUBLICATIONS** Auth, pubs on philosophical and legal issues. **CONTACT ADDRESS** Philosophy Dept, Union Inst, 440 E McMillan St, Cincinnati, OH, 45206-1925.

ATKINS, ROBERT A., JR.
PERSONAL Born 10/07/1949, Dallas, TX, m, 1971, 2 children **DISCIPLINE** BIBLICAL STUDIES **EDUCATION** Elmhurst Col, BA; Northwestern Univ, MDiv, PhD. **CAREER** Instr, Northwestern Univ, 73-76; Lectr, Loyola Univ, 76-78; pastor, 80-. **MEMBERSHIPS** SBL; AAR; AACC. **RESEARCH** Psychology; Biblical studies. **SELECTED PUBLICATIONS** Auth, Egalitarian Community, Alabama, 91. **CONTACT ADDRESS** First United Methodist Church, 100 W Cossitt Ave, La Grange, IL, 60525. **EMAIL** bobatkins@iname.com

ATLAS, JAY DAVID
PERSONAL Born 02/01/1945, Houston, TX **DISCIPLINE** PHILOSOPHY & LINGUISTICS **EDUCATION** Amherst Col, AB, 66; Princeton Univ, PhD, 76. **CAREER** Asst prof, 76-80, assoc prof Philos, 81-88, prof philos, Pomona Col, 89-, Mem common rm, Wolfson Col, Oxford, 78 & 80; vis fel, Princeton Univ, 79; sr assoc, JurEcon, Inc, 81-; res assoc, Inst Advan Study School Hist, Princeton, NJ, 82-84, 86; vis lectr, Dept Philos, Univ Hong Kong, 86; vis prof, Dept Philos, UCLA, 89-95; vis prof, Dept Dutch Ling, Univ Groningen, The Netherlands, spring 95; vis scholar, Max Planck Inst for Psycolinguistics, nijmegen, The Netherlands, 97. **MEMBERSHIPS** Am Philos Asn; Asn Symbolic Logic. **RESEARCH** Philos of lang; metaphysics; linguistics and lit theory. **SELECTED PUBLICATIONS** Auth, Frege's polymorphous concept of presupposition and its role in theory of meaning, Semantikos, 1: 29-44; Presupposition: A sematico-pragmatic account, Pragmatics Microfiche, 1.4, D13-G9, 75; Negation, ambiguity, and presupposition, Ling & Philos, 1: 321-336; On presupposing, Mind, 87: 396-411; Reference, meaning, and translation, Philos Books, 21: 129-140; coauth, It-clefts, informativeness, and logical form: Radical pragmatics, In: Radical Pragmatics, Acad Press, 81; auth, Is not logical?, Proc 11th Int Symposium on Multiple-Valued Logic, Inst Elec & Electronics Engrs, 81; Comparative adjectives and adverbials of degree, Ling & Philos, 84; Whate are negative existence statements about?, Ling & Philos, 88; Philosophy without Ambiguity: A Logico-Linguistic Essay, Clarendon Press, Oxford, 89; Only noun phrases, pseudo-negative generalized quantitatives, negative plarity items, and monotanacity, J Semantics, 96. **CONTACT ADDRESS** Dept Philos, Pomona Col, 333 N College Way, Claremont, CA, 91711-6319. **EMAIL** jatlas@pomona.edu

ATLESON, JAMES B.
PERSONAL Born 09/24/1938, Akron, OH, m, 1961, 2 children **DISCIPLINE** LAW **EDUCATION** Ohio State Univ, BA, 60, JD, 62; Stanford Univ, LLM, 64. **CAREER** Asst prof, 64-69, Prof Law, Fac Law, State Univ NY Buffalo, 69-, NY Fac fels, State Univ NY, 68 & 70; Baldy fel, 74. **MEMBERSHIPS** Labor Law Group; Indust Rel Res Asn; Am Arbitration Asn; Union Dem Asn; Law & Soc Asn. **RESEARCH** Labor law; internal union democracy. **SELECTED PUBLICATIONS** Auth, NLRB & Jurisdictional Disputes, Georgetown Law Rev, 64; Union Members Right to Free Speech and Assembly, Minn Law Rev, 67; Workmen's Compensation: Third Party Actions and Apportionment of Attorneys Fees, Buffalo Law Rev, 70; Union Fines & Picket Lines, Univ Calif, Los Angeles Law Rev, 70; Disciplinary Discharges, Arbitration and NLRB Deference, Buffalo Law Rev, 71; Work Group Behavior and Wildcat Strikes, Ohio State Law J, 73; Threats to Health and Safety, Minn Law Rev, 75; coauth, & Collective Bargaining in Private Employment, Bur Not Affairs, spring 78, 2nd ed, Est Pub, 84; The Law of Collective Bargaining and Wartime Labor Regulation, in Miller & Cornford, eds, American Labor in the Era of World War II, Praeger, 95; Labor and the Wartime State, University of Illinois, 98. **CONTACT ADDRESS** Fac of Law, SUNY, Buffalo, J L O Hall, Buffalo, NY, 14260-0001. **EMAIL** atleson@acsu.buffalo.edu

ATTERTON, PETER C.
PERSONAL Born 06/22/1961, London, England **DISCIPLINE** PHILOSOPHY **EDUCATION** Univ Essex, Colchester Eng, PhD, 86-90. **CAREER** San Diego State Univ Cal, lectr, 95-. **HONORS AND AWARDS** Brit Acad Award **MEMBERSHIPS** APA **RESEARCH** Cont philo; Kantian ethics; hist ethics. **SELECTED PUBLICATIONS** Auth, Levinas's Skeptical Critique of Metaphysics and Anti-humanism, Philo Today, 1997, Power's Blind Struggle for Existence: Foucault, Genealogy and Darwinism, Hist of the Human Sciences Jour, 1994, Levinas and the Language of Peace: A Response to Derrida, Philo Today, 1992. **CONTACT ADDRESS** Dept of Philosophy, San Diego State Univ, 1566 Missouri St, San Diego, CA, 92109-3038. **EMAIL** atterton@rohan.sdsu.edu

ATTRIDGE, HAROLD WILLIAM
PERSONAL Born 11/24/1946, New Bedford, MA, m, 1968, 2 children **DISCIPLINE** NEW TESTAMENT, PATRISTICS **EDUCATION** Boston Col, BA, 67; Cambridge Univ, BA, 69, MA, 73; Harvard Univ, PhD(New Testament), 75. **CAREER** Asst prof, 77-80, assoc Prof New Teatament, Perkins Sch Theol, SOUTHERN METHODIST UNIV, 80-, Harvard Univ jr fel, 74-77. **MEMBERSHIPS** Soc Bibl Lit; Cath Bibl Asn; Int Asn Coptic Studies; Am Philol Asn. **SELECTED PUBLICATIONS** Auth, P Oxy 1081 and the Sophia Jesu Christi, Enchoria, 75; co-ed, The Syrian Goddess (De Dea Syria) attributed to Lucian, 76, auth, The Interpretation of Biblical History in the Antiquitates Judaicae of Josephus, 76 & First-Century Cynicism in the Epistles of Heraclitus, 76, Scholars; contribr, Translations of the Tripartite Tractate and the Dialogue of the Savior in the Nag Hammadi Library in English, Harper, 77; co-ed, Philo of Byblos, The Phoenician History, Cath Bibl Asn, 81; The Apocalypse of Elijah, Scholars, 81; A Key to the Peshita Gospels, Vol 1-Alpha-Dalath, with T C. Falla, Cath Biblical Quart, Vol 55, 93; Cynics and Christian Origins, with F. G. Downing, Catholic Hist Rev, Vol 80, 94; Cracking the Gnostic Code-The Powers in Gnosticism, with W. Wink, J of Relig, Vol 75, 95; The Rise of Normative Christianity, with A. J. Hultgren, Vol 75, 95; The Orthodox Corruption of Scripture-The Effect

of Early Christological Controversies on the Text of the New-Testamnet, with B. D. Ehrman, Cath Biblical Quart, Vol 57, 95; Philo in Early-Christian Literature- A Survey, with D. T. Runia, J of the Am Oriental Soc, Vol 115, 95; The Understanding of the Diaspora by Jews of the Hellenistic and Early Roman Periods, German, with W. C. Vanunnik, J of the Am Oriental Soc, Vol 115, 95; Rewriting the Bible-Land and Covenant in Post-Biblical Jewish Literature, with B. Halpernamaru, J of the Am Oriental Soc, Vol 116, 96; Gnosticism and the New Testament, with P. Perkins, Interpretation-A J of Bible and Theology, Vol 50, 96; The Rise and Fall of Jewish Nationalism-Jewish and Christian Ethnicity in Acient Palestine, with D. Mendels, J of the Am Oriental Soc, Vol 116, 96; Resurrection Reconsidered-Thomas and John in Controversy, with G. J. Riley, Cath Biblical Quart, Vol 58, 96; Paul and Philodemus-Adaptability in Epicurean and Early-Christian Psychagogy, with C. E. Glad, J of Biblical Lit, Vol 116, 97; On the Origins of Christian Homiletics-The 'Epistle to the Hebrews'-A Note on Rhetorical Analysis (Italian), with P. Garuti, Biblica, Vol 78, 97. **CONTACT ADDRESS** Univ Notre Dame, Notre Dame, IN, 46556.

ATWOOD, CRAIG D.
PERSONAL Born 12/02/1960, NC, m, 3 children **DISCIPLINE** RELIGION **EDUCATION** Univ NC Chapel Hill, BA, 83; Moravian Sem, M Div, 87; Princeton Sem, PhD, 95. **CAREER** Chaplain, Moravian Col, 86-88; asst dean, Moravian Sem, 88-89; prof, relig, Salem Col, 95-. **HONORS AND AWARDS** Salem Col Summer Sabbatical grant, 97; Aldridge fel grant, Jan, 97; PTS merit scholar, 89-93; Lilly Endow grant, 88-89; David Bishop award, MTS, 87; Streetman award, 94; Magna Cum Laude grad, MTS, 87; Rotary scholar, Univ NC, 79. **MEMBERSHIPS** Amer Acad of Relig; Amer Soc of Church Hist. **RESEARCH** Moravian history; Zinzendorf. **SELECTED PUBLICATIONS** Article, The Joyfulness of Death in Eighteenth Century Moravian Communities, Communal Soc, Fall, 97; article, Sleeping in the Arms of Christ: Sanctifying Sexuality in the Eighteen Century Moravian Church, Jour of the Hist of Sex, 8, no 2, Summer, 97; article, Zinzendorf's Litany of the Wounds of the Husband, Lutheran Quart, Spring, 97; article, Moravian Community and American Discommunity, The Hinge, Fall, 97; article, Zinzendorf's 1749 Reprimand to the Brudergemeine, Transactions of the Moravian Hist Soc, 29, Fall, 96; article, Mother of All Souls: Zinzendorf's Doctrine of the Holy Spirit, Koinonia, 4, no 2, Fall, 92; article, Deconstruction and the Destruction of Meaning, Koinonia, 3, no 2; rev, Der Pentateuch: Die Geschichte Seiner Erforshung Neben Einer Auswertung, Jour of the Amer Acad of Relig, 64, no 4, Winter, 96; rev, Die grosse Zinzendorf-Trilogie, Koinonia, 6, no 1, Spring, 94; rev, The Heliand, Koinonia, 5, no 2, Fall, 93; rev, Awash in a Sea of Faith, Koinonia, 4, no 1, Spring, 92; rev, Herrnhaag: Eine Religiose Kommunitat im 18th Jahrhundert, Koinonia, 5, no 2, Fall, 93; rev, The Transformation of Moravian Bethlehem: From Communal Mission to Family Economy, Church Hist, 60, no 3, 91; rev, Religion, Society, and Utopia in Nineteenth Century America, Koinonia, 3, no 1, 91. **CONTACT ADDRESS** PO Box 10548, Winston-Salem, NC, 27108. **EMAIL** atwood@salem.edu

AUBLE, JOEL
DISCIPLINE PHILOSOPHY **EDUCATION** Northwestern Univ, PhD. **CAREER** Assoc prof. **RESEARCH** Critical thinking; world religions; philosophy and literature; existentialism. **SELECTED PUBLICATIONS** Auth, pubs on obligation theory and critical thinking. **CONTACT ADDRESS** Philosophy Dept, State Univ of West Georgia, Carrollton, GA, 30118. **EMAIL** jauble@westga.edu

AUDET, LEONARD
PERSONAL Born 11/26/1932, Maria, PQ, Canada **DISCIPLINE** RELIGION **EDUCATION** Univ Montreal, BA, 54, DTh, 62; Ponitificum Institutum Biblicum Rome, LSS, 64. **CAREER** Prof Holy Scripture, Sch Theol, Joliette, 65-67; priest, 71-74, SUPERIOR GENERAL, CONGREGATION OF THE CLERICS OF SAINT VIATOR, 88-; Prof New testament lit, Univ Montreal, 67-88, dir bible dept, 73-77, dean theol, 77-85 **MEMBERSHIPS** Societe Canadienne de theologie; Asn Catholique des etudes Bibliques au Can. **SELECTED PUBLICATIONS** Coauth, Resurrection. Esperance humaine et don de Dieu, 71; coauth, Jesus? De l'histoire a la foi, 74; coauth, Neuve est ta Parole, 74; coauth, A Companion to Paul, 75; coauth, Vivante est ta parole, 75; coauth, Apres Jesus. Autorite et liberte dans le peuple de Dieu, 77; coauth, Je crois en Dieu, 89 **CONTACT ADDRESS** Chierici di San Viatore, CP 10793, Rome, ., 00144.

AUDI, ROBERT
DISCIPLINE ETHICS, EPISTEMOLOGY, AND PHILOSOPHY OF MIND **EDUCATION** Univ Mich, PhD, 67. **CAREER** Charles J Mach Distinguished Prof, Univ Nebr, Lincoln. **MEMBERSHIPS** Past pres, Ctr Div, Am Philos Asn. **SELECTED PUBLICATIONS** Auth, The Structure of Justification, Cambridge, 93; Acting from Virtue, Mind 104, 95; Perceptual Experience, Doxastic Practice, and the Rationality of Religious Commitment, J of Philos Res XX, 95; Ed-in-Ch, The Cambridge Dictionary of Philosophy, 95. **CONTACT ADDRESS** Univ Nebr, Lincoln, Lincoln, NE, 68588-0417.

AUNE, BRUCE ARTHUR
PERSONAL Born 11/07/1933, Minneapolis, MN, m, 1955, 1 child **DISCIPLINE** PHILOSOPHY **EDUCATION** Univ Minn, BA, 55, MA, 57, PhD, 60. **CAREER** Instr philos, Oberlin Col, 60-62; from asst prof to assoc prof, Univ Pittsburgh, 62-66; head dept, 66-70, Prof Philos, Univ Mass, Amherst, 66-, Res fel, Minn Ctr Philos Sci, 60; Guggenheim fel, 63-64; resident fel, Ctr Advan Study in Behav Sci, 74-75. **HONORS AND AWARDS** Fulbright lectr, 82. **MEMBERSHIPS** Am Philos Asn; Mind Asn. **RESEARCH** Epistemology; metaphysics; history of philosophy. **SELECTED PUBLICATIONS** Auth, On the complexity of avowals, Philos in Am, 66; Statements and propositions, Nous, 67; Knowledge, Mind, and Nature, 67 & Rationalism, Empiricism, and Pragmatism, 70, Random; Reason and Action, Reidel, 77; Kant's theory of morals, Princeton, 80; auth, Metaphysics, Minnesota, 85; auth, Knowledge of External World, 90. **CONTACT ADDRESS** Dept of Philosophy, Univ of Mass, Amherst, MA, 01002. **EMAIL** aune@philos.umass.edu

AUNE, JAMES ARNT
DISCIPLINE PHILOSOPHY **EDUCATION** Northwestern Univ, PhD. **CAREER** Assoc prof, Texas A&M Univ. **SELECTED PUBLICATIONS** Auth, Rhetoric and Marxism; contribur, At the Intersection: Rhetoricand Cultural Studies; Refiguring Realism: International Relations and Rhetorical Practices; Argumentation and the Rhetoric of Assent; Rhetoric and Philosophy; Texts in Context; assoc ed, Commun Stud; ed, Argumentation and Advocacy. **CONTACT ADDRESS** Dept of Speech Communication, Texas A&M Univ, College Station, TX, 77843-4234. **EMAIL** csnidow@tamu.edu

AUNE, MICHAEL
DISCIPLINE WORSHIP **EDUCATION** St. Olaf Col, AB; Luther Theol Sem, MDiv; Univ Notre Dame, MA, PhD. **CAREER** Vis scholar, Linguistic Soc Am Summer Inst; instr, Cook Training Sch for Ministry, 83; prof, 78-; PLTS Dean of the Chapel. **HONORS AND AWARDS** GTU Core Doctoral fac; Dean's soc of Doctoral fel(s), GTU, 89-90; co-org, GTU Interdisciplinary Workshop on Ritual; adv coun, Word and World; exec comm, Ctr for Hermeneutical Stud, GTU. **SELECTED PUBLICATIONS** Auth, Religious and Social Ritual, State U of New York P, 96; To Move the Heart: Rhetoric and Ritual in the Theology of Philip Melanchthon, Christian UP, 94; rev, To Move the Heart: Rhetoric and Ritual, Theol of Philip Melanchthon. **CONTACT ADDRESS** Dept of Worship, Pacific Lutheran Theol Sem, 2770 Marin Ave, Berkeley, CA, 94708-1597. **EMAIL** mbaune@sirius.com

AVERILL, EDWARD W.
DISCIPLINE PHILOSOPHY **EDUCATION** Harvard Univ, BA; UCLA, Santa Barbara, MS, PhD. **CAREER** Prof, TX Tech Univ, 80-. **RESEARCH** Philosophical psychol; philos of lang. **SELECTED PUBLICATIONS** Auth, Are Physical Properties Dispositions?, The Philos of Sci; Color and the Anthropocentric Problem, The J of Philos; The Primary-Secondary Quality Distinction, The Philos Rev; The Relational Nature of Color, The Philos Rev. **CONTACT ADDRESS** Texas Tech Univ, Lubbock, TX, 79409-5015. **EMAIL** avewa@ttacs.ttu.edu

AVERY-PECK, ALAN J.
PERSONAL Born 06/26/1953, Chicago, IL, m, 1981, 2 children **DISCIPLINE** HISTORY OF RELIGION; JUDAISM **EDUCATION** Brown Univ, PhD, 81. **CAREER** Dir, Jewish studies, Tulane Univ, 81-93; KRAFT-HIATT PROF IN JUDAIC STUDIES, COL OF THE HOLY CROSS, 93-. **MEMBERSHIPS** AAR/SBL **RESEARCH** Rabbinic Judaism. **SELECTED PUBLICATIONS** Auth, Rhetorical Argumentation in Early Rabbinic Pronouncement Stories, in Vernon K. Robins, ed, The Rhetoric of Pronouncement, Semia: An Experimental Journal for Biblical Criticism, vol 64, 93; Judaism, with Jacob Neusner, in The Reader's Adviser, 14th ed, vol 4: The Best of Philosophy and Religion, R. R. Bowker, NJ, 94; The Mishnah, Tosefta, and the Talmuds: The Problem of Text and Context, in Jacob Neusner, ed, Handbuch der Orientalistik Judaistik: Judaism in Late Antiquity, Part One, The Literary and Archaeological Sources, E. J. Brill, Leided, 94; The Talmud of Babylonia, An American Translation, vol V, Tractatae Rosh Hashanah, Brown Judaic Studies: Scholars Press, Atlanta, 95; The Politics of the Mishnah in its Contemporary Context, in J. Neusner, ed, Religion and Political Order: Politics in Classical and Contemporary Christianity, Islam and Judaism, Atlanta, Scholars Press, 96; The Exodus in Jewish Faith: The Problem of God's Intervention in History, in the Annual of Rabbinic Judaism, vol 1, Brill, 98; ed, with Jacob Neusner, Where We Stand: Issues and Debates in the Study of Ancient Judaism, vol 1, Handbuch der Orientalistik, E. J. Brill, Leiden, 98; ed, The Annual of Rabbinic Judaism: Ancient, Medieval, and Modern, vol 1, E. J. Brill, Leiden, 98. **CONTACT ADDRESS** Dept of Relig Studies, Col of the Holy Cross, Box 17, Worchester, MA, 01610-2395. **EMAIL** AAvery@Holycross.edu

AWN, PETER
DISCIPLINE RELIGION **EDUCATION** Harvard Univ, PhD, 78. **CAREER** Prof. **HONORS AND AWARDS** Phillip and Ruth Hettleman Awd. **MEMBERSHIPS** Am Council Learned Soc. **SELECTED PUBLICATIONS** Auth, Satan's Tragedy and Redemption: Ibls in Sufi Psychology. **CONTACT ADDRESS** Dept of Religion, Columbia Col, New York, 2960 Broadway, New York, NY, 10027-6902. **EMAIL** awn@columbia.edu

AXINN, SIDNEY
PERSONAL Born 01/30/1923, New York, NY, m, 1947, 2 children **DISCIPLINE** PHILOSOPHY **EDUCATION** Univ PA, AB, 47, PhD(philos), 55. **CAREER** From instr to assoc prof, 49-63, chmn dept, 52-67, PROF PHILOS, TEMPLE UNIV, 63-, ADJ PROF PSYCHIAT PHILOS, SCH MED, TEMPLE UNIV, 65-. **MEMBERSHIPS** Am Philos Asn; Asn Polit & Legal Philos; Asn Philos Law & Soc Philos. **RESEARCH** Philosophy of science; social ethics; history of philosophy. **SELECTED PUBLICATIONS** Auth, Two Concepts of Optimism, Philos Sci, 54; Kant, Logic, and the Concept of Mankind, Ethics, 58; Fallacy of the Single Risk, Philos Sci, 66; Kant and the Moral Antinomy, Ottawa Kant Cong, Ottawa Univ, 76; coauth, On the Logic of the Ignorance Relations, Am Philos Quart, 76; auth, Kant and Goodman on Possible Individuals, Monist, 78; Philip P. Wiener, 1905-1992-Obituary, J of the History of Ideas, Vol 54, 93. **CONTACT ADDRESS** Dept of Philos, Temple Univ, Philadelphia, PA, 19122.

AXTELL, G.S.
PERSONAL Born 06/05/1957, Oakland, CA, m, 1994 **DISCIPLINE** PHILOSOPHY **EDUCATION** Univ Hawaii, PhD, 91 **CAREER** Univ Nevada, 92- **HONORS AND AWARDS** NEH Fel; Board of Ed Consultants, Amer Philos Quarterly, 1997-2000; Certificate Merit, Ntl Judicial Col, 93 **MEMBERSHIPS** Amer Philos Assoc; Soc Advancement Amer Philos; Philos Sci Assoc; 4S Soc; Hist Sci Soc; Amer Soc Value Inquiry; N Amer Soc Social Philos; Int Soc Chinese Philos; Soc Asian Comparative Philos **RESEARCH** American Philosophy; Dewey; James: Epistemology; Philosophy of Religion; Asian Traditions of India; China & Japan; Social & Political Thought **SELECTED PUBLICATIONS** Auth, "The Role of the Intellectual Virtues in the Reunification of Epistemology," Monist, 98; auth, "Recent Work on Virtue Epistemology," Amer Philos Quarterly, 97; auth, "Epistemic Virtue-Talk: The Reemergence of American Axiology?," Jrnl Speculative Philos, 96 **CONTACT ADDRESS** Dept Philos/102, Univ Nevada, Reno, Reno, NV, 89557-0056. **EMAIL** axtell@scs.unr.edu

AYALA, FRANCISCO J.
PERSONAL Born 03/12/1934, Madrid, Spain, m, 1985, 2 children **DISCIPLINE** GENETICS **EDUCATION** Univ Madrid, Spain, BS, 55; Columbia Univ, NY, MS, 63, PhD, 64. **CAREER** Asst prof, Rockefeller Univ, NY, 67-71; assoc prof-prof, Univ CA, Davis, 71-87; Distinguished Prof, Bilogical Sciences, Univ CA, Irvine, 87-89; Donald Bren prof, Biological Sciences, Univ CA, Irvine, 89-. **HONORS AND AWARDS** Dr Honoris Causa: Univ Leon, Spain, 82, Univ Madrid, 86, Univ Barcelona, 86, Univ Athens, Greece, 91, Univ Vigo, Spain, 96; Prof Honoris Causa: Univ Islas Baleares, Spain, 98; Medal, Col of France, 79; Gold Mendel Medal, Czech Republic Academy of Sciences, 94. **MEMBERSHIPS** US Nat Academy of Sciences; Am Academy of Arts and Sciences; Am Philos Asn; Pres-elect, pres, chmn, Am Asn for the Advancement of Science, 93-96; President's Committee of Advisors on Science and Technology, 94-. **RESEARCH** Population and evolutionary genetics; philos of biology; bioethics. **SELECTED PUBLICATIONS** Auth, Is Esterase-P Encoded by a Cryptic Pseudogene in Drosophila melanogaster?, with E S Balakirev, Genetics, 96; Erratic Evoltution of Glydcerol-3-Phosphate Dehydrogenase in Drosophila, Chymomyza, and Ceratitus, with J Kwiatowski, M Krawczyk, M Jaworski, and D Skarecky, J Mol Evol, 97; Evolution of the Drosophila obscura Species Group Inferred from the Gpdh and Sod Genes, Molecular Phylogenetics and Evolution, with E Barrio, 97; DNA Variation at the Sod Locus of Drosophila melanogaster: An Unfolding Story of Natural Selection, with R R Hudson and A G Saez, Proc Nat Academy Sci, USA, 97; Vagaries of the Molecular Clock, Proc Nat Academy Sci USA, 97; Plasmodium falciparum Antigenic Diversity: Evidence of Clonal Population Structure, with S M Rich and R R Hudson, Proc Nat Academy Sci USA, 97; Origin of the Metazoan phlya: Molecular Clocks Confirm Paleontological Estimates, with A Rzhetsky and F Jose Ayala, Proc Nat Academy Sci USA, 98; New Drosophila Introns Originate by Duplication, R Tarrio and F Rodriguez-Trelles, 98; Interspecific Laboratory Competition of the Recently Sympatric Species Drosophila subobscura and Drosophila pseudoobscura, with M Pascual and L Serra, Evolution, 98; Is Sex Better? Parasites Say "No," Proc Nat Academy Sci USA, 98; Malaria's Eve: Evidence of a Recent Population Bottlenack Throughout the World Populations of Plasmodium falciparum, with S M Rich, M C Licht, and R R Hudson, Proc Nat Academy Sci USA, 98; Genetic Polymorphism and Natural Selection in the Malaria Parasite Plasmodium falciparum, with A A Escalente and A A Lal, Genetics, 98; author of over 650 articles and publications. **CONTACT ADDRESS** Dept Ecol & Evolutionary Biol, Univ of California, Irvine, Irvine, CA, 92697-2525. **EMAIL** FJAyala@uci.edu

AYDEDE, MURAT
PERSONAL Born 08/18/1961, Ankara, Turkey, m, 1982, 1 child **DISCIPLINE** PHILOSOPHY **EDUCATION** Bogazici

Univ, BA, 86; Univ MD Col Park, PhD, 93. **CAREER** Stanford Univ, vis Scholar, 93-94; Xerox PARC Consult, 93-94; Univ Chicago, asst prof 94-. **MEMBERSHIPS** APA, SPP, SSPP **RESEARCH** Philo of Mind; Psych; Philo Lang. **SELECTED PUBLICATIONS** Auth, Language of Thought Hypothesis, in: Stanford Encycl of Philo, ed E. Zalta, Stanford: CSLI Pub, 98; Aristotle on Episteme and Nous: The Posterior Analytics, South Jour of Philo 98; Has Fodor Really Changed His Mind on Narrow Content, Mind and Lang, 97; Pure Informational Semantics and the Broad; Narrow Dichotomy, in Maribor Papers in Nat Sem, ed Dunja Jutronic, Maribor Univ Press, 97; Language of Thought: The Connectionist Contribution, Mind and Lang, 97; On the Relation Between Phenomenal and Representational Properties, Brain and Behav Sciences, 97. **CONTACT ADDRESS** Dept of Philosophy, Univ of Chicago, 1050 E 59th St, Chicago, IL, 60637. **EMAIL** m-aydede@uchicago.edu

AYERS, JAMES R.
PERSONAL Born 01/06/1953, Hanover, PA, m, 1972, 3 children **DISCIPLINE** RELIGION **EDUCATION** Lancaster Bible Col, BS, 80; Rider Col, MA, 85; Oxford Grad Sch, MLitt, 91, Dphil, 92. **CAREER** Dir, Phila Col of Bible, 80-86; sen pastor, Easton Union Church, 86-93; chemn, 93-, dir, 94-, Lancaster Bible Col. **HONORS AND AWARDS** Oxford Chalice Award, 92; Who's Who Among Am Tchrs, 95. **MEMBERSHIPS** Evangelical Theol Society **RESEARCH** AIDS; church ministries **SELECTED PUBLICATIONS** Auth, Confronting the Youth Crisis, 85; auth, The Quagmire of HIV/AIDS Related Issues Which Haunt the Church, 95; auth, Focus on Fatherhood, 95; auth, Revitalizing the Church, 96. **CONTACT ADDRESS** 5842 Clarkson Dr, East Petersburg, PA, 17520. **EMAIL** jayers@lbc.edu

B

BAADE, HANS WOLFGANG
PERSONAL Born 12/16/1929, Berlin, Germany, m, 1957, 2 children **DISCIPLINE** LAW **EDUCATION** Syracuse Univ, AB, 49; Univ Kiel, Dr iur, 51; Duke Univ, LLB & LLM, 55; Hague Acad Int Law, dipl, 56. **CAREER** Res assoc int law, Univ Kiel, 55-60; from assoc prof to prof law, Duke Univ, 60-70; prof, Univ Toronto, 70-71; Albert Sidney Burleson prof, 71-75, Hugh Lamar Stone Chair Civil Law, Univ TX, Austin, 75-, Ed secy, Jahrbuch Int Recht, 56-60; Privatdozent, Univ Kiel, 60; ed, Law & Contemp Problems, 61-65; dir, Am Asn Comp Studies Law, 61-; chmn, comt regional affairs, Am Soc Int Law, 67-68; consult, proj group on govt reform, WGer Fed Ministry of Interior, 69; consult, Spanish & Mexican water law, State of TX, 80. **MEMBERSHIPS** Am Asn Comp Studies Law; Am Foreign Law Asn; Am Soc Int Law. **RESEARCH** Public international and comparative law; Southwestern legal history; conflict of laws; Roman Law in the Water, Mineral and Public Land Law of the Southwestern United-States, Am J of Comparative Law, Vol 40, 92; Time and Meaning-Notes on the Intertemporal La of Statutory Construction and Constitutional Interpretation, Am J of Comparative Law, Vol 43, 95. **CONTACT ADDRESS** School of Law, Univ of TX, Austin, TX, 78712.

BABBITT, SUSAN
DISCIPLINE PHILOSOPHY **EDUCATION** Univ Ottawa, BA; Cornell Univ, MA; PhD. **CAREER** Dept Philos, Queen's Univ **RESEARCH** Contemporary moral philosophy; philosophy of science. **SELECTED PUBLICATIONS** Auth, Impossible Dreams: Rationality, Integrity and Moral Imagination, Westview, 96. **CONTACT ADDRESS** Philosophy Dept, Queen's Univ, Kingston, ON, K7L 3N6. **EMAIL** babbitts@post.queensu.ca

BABCOCK, BARBARA ALLEN
PERSONAL Born 07/06/1938, Washington, DC, m, 1979 **DISCIPLINE** LAW **EDUCATION** Univ PA, AB, 60; Yale Law Sch, LLB, 63. **CAREER** Law clerk to Judge Henry W Edgerton, US Ct Appeals, Washington, DC, 63-64; assoc, Edward Bennet Williams, Washington, DC, 64-66; staff atty, Legal Aid Agency, Washington, DC, 66-68; dir, Pub Defender Serv, Washington, DC, 68-72; assoc prof law, 72-77, PROF LAW, STANFORD LAW SCH, 79-, Asst atty gen, Civil Div, Dept Justice, Washington, DC, 77-79. **SELECTED PUBLICATIONS** Coauth, Sex Discrimination and the Law: Causes and Remedies, 75 & A Civil Procedure: Cases and Comments on the Process of Adjudication, 77, Little, Brown & Co; auth, Voir dire: Preserving its Wonderful Power, 27: 545 & Evidence Favorable to an Accused and Effective Assistance of Counsel, Stanford Law Rev; Gender Bias in the Courts and Civic and Legal Education-Introduction, Stanford Law Rev, Vol 45, 93; Western Women Lawyers, Stanford Law Rev, Vol 45, 93; Remarks on the Occasion of the Publication of 'Called From Within', Women Lawyers of Hawaii March 12, 1993, Biography-An Interdisciplinary Quart, Vol 16, 93; A Place in the Palladium-Womens Rights and Jury Service, Univ of Cincinnati Law Rev, Vol 61, 93; Contracted Biographies and Other Obstacles to Truth-Commentary, NY Univ Law Rev, Vol 70, 95; A Unanimous Jury is Fundamental to Our Democracy, Harvard J of Law and Public Policy, Vol 20, 97. **CONTACT ADDRESS** Stanford Law Sch, Stanford Univ, Stanford, CA, 94305-1926.

BABCOCK, WILLIAM SUMMER
PERSONAL Born 06/18/1939, Boston, MA, m, 1960, 2 children **DISCIPLINE** CHURCH HISTORY **EDUCATION** Brown Univ, AB, 61; Yale Univ, MA, 65, PhD(relig studies), 71. **CAREER** From instr to asst prof, 67-77, ASSOC PROF CHURCH HIST, PERKINS SCH THEOL, SOUTHERN METHODIST UNIV, 77-, Am Coun Learned Socs studies fel, 73-74. **MEMBERSHIPS** Am Soc Church Hist; Mediaeval Acad Am; NAm Patristics Soc; Am Cath Hist Asn. **RESEARCH** Augustine; Latin Patristics; history of Christian theology. **SELECTED PUBLICATIONS** Auth, Grace, Freedom and Justice: Augustine and the Christian Tradition, summer 73 & Patterns of Roman Selfbood: Marcus Aurelius and Augustine of Hippo, fall 74, Perkins Sch Theol J; Augustine's Interpretation of Romans (AD 394-396), Augustinian Studies 19, 79; Agustin y Ticonio: sobre la appropriacion latina de Pablo, Augustinus, 7-12/81; Art and Architecture, Christian, In: Abingdon Dict of Living Religions, 81; Is There Only One True Religion or Are There Many, with S. M. Ogden, Theology Today, Vol 50, 94. **CONTACT ADDRESS** Perkins Sch of Theol, Southern Methodist Univ, Dallas, TX, 75275.

BABER, HARRIET ERICA
PERSONAL Born 01/06/1950, Paterson, NJ, m, 1972, 3 children **DISCIPLINE** PHILOSOPHY **EDUCATION** Lake Forest Col, BA, 71; Johns Hopkins Univ, MA, 76, PhD, 80. **CAREER** Instr philos, Northern IL Univ, 80-81; from asst prof to assoc prof, 81-92, prof philos, Univ San Diego, 92. **MEMBERSHIPS** Am Philos Asn; Soc Christian Philosophers. **RESEARCH** Metaphysics; philos of mind; philosophical theol. **SELECTED PUBLICATIONS** Auth, The lifetime language, Philos Studies. **CONTACT ADDRESS** Dept of Philos, Univ San Diego, 5998 Alcala Park, San Diego, CA, 92110-2492. **EMAIL** barber@acusd.edu

BABICH, BABETTE E.
PERSONAL Born 11/14/1956, New York, NY, s **DISCIPLINE** PHILOSOPHY **EDUCATION** SUNY - Stonybrook, BA; Boston Col, PhD, 87. **CAREER** Vis Asst Prof, Denison Univ, 87-88; Asst Prof, Marquette Univ, 88-89; Assoc Prof, Fordham Univ, 89-; Adj Res Prof, Georgetown Univ, 97-. **HONORS AND AWARDS** Fulbright Fel, 83-85; Fulbright Prof, 91-91. **MEMBERSHIPS** Am Philos Asn; Soc Philos and Eng. **RESEARCH** Philosophy of science and technology; aesthetics; antiquity. **SELECTED PUBLICATIONS** Auth, Nietzsche's Philosophy of Science: Reflecting Science on the Ground of Art and Life, SUNY Press, 94; ed, From Phenomenology to Thought, Errancy, and Desire: Essays in Honor of William J. Richardson, S.J., Dordrecht, 95; co-ed, Continental and Postmodern Perspectives in the Philosophy of Science, Avebury, 95; Nietzsche and the Sciences, Boston Studies in the Philosophy of Science, Kluwer (forthcoming 97); Heidegger's Philosophy of Science (in prep); author of numerous articles. **CONTACT ADDRESS** Dept Philosophy, Fordham Univ, 113 W. 60th St., New York, NY, 10023. **EMAIL** babich@mary.fordham.edu

BABLER, JOHN
PERSONAL m, 6 children **DISCIPLINE** SOCIAL WORK AND MINISTRY-BASED EVANGELISM **EDUCATION** UT Dallas, BGS, 83; Southwestern Baptist Theol Sem, MACSS, 89, PhD, 95; UTA, MSSW, 89. **CAREER** Adj prof, 92-95; asst prof, Southwestern Baptist Theol Sem, 95-. **HONORS AND AWARDS** Soc work coord, Huguley Hospice; prog dir, Childrens's Home. **SELECTED PUBLICATIONS** Auth, Hospice: An Opportunity for Truly Wholistic Social Work, Christianity and Soc Work, NACSW, 98; A Comparison of Spiritual Care Provided by Hospice Social Workers, Nurses, and Spiritual Care Professionals, Hospice Jour, 97. **CONTACT ADDRESS** Sch Edu Ministries, Southwestern Baptist Theol Sem, PO Box 22000, Fort Worth, TX, 76122-0418. **EMAIL** jeb@swbts.swbts.edu

BACCHIOCCHI, SAMUELE
PERSONAL Rome, Italy **DISCIPLINE** THEOLOGY AND CHURCH HISTORY **EDUCATION** Newbold Col, Eng, BA; Andrews Univ, BD, MA; Pontifical Gregorian Univ, Ital, PhD, summa cum laude, 74. **CAREER** Prof, Andrews Univ. **HONORS AND AWARDS** Gold medal, Pope Paul VI. **SELECTED PUBLICATIONS** Auth, Immortality or Resurrection? A Biblical Study on Human Nature and Destiny; From Sabbath to Sunday: A Historical Investigation of the Rise of Sunday Observance in Early Christianity; Divine Rest for Human Restlessness: A Theological Study of the Good News of the Sabbath for Today; The Sabbath in the New Testament. Answers to Questions; God's Festivals in Scripture and History, Vol I: The Spring Festivals; God's Festivals in Scripture and History, Vol 2: The Fall Festivals; Wine in the Bible: A Biblical Study on the Use of Alcoholic Beverages; The Advent Hope for Human Hopelessness. A Theological Study of the Meaning of the Second Advent for Today; Women in the Church: A Biblical Study on the Role of Women in the Church; Christian Dress and Adornment; Hal Lindsey's Prophetic Jigsaw Puzzle: Five Predictions that Failed!; The Time of the Crucifixion and the Resurrection; The Marriage Covenant: A Biblical Study on Marriage, Divorce, and Remarriage. **CONTACT ADDRESS** Andrews Univ, Berrien Springs, MI, 49104-0180.

BACH, KENT
PERSONAL Born 07/10/1943, San Francisco, CA, m, 1984, 2 children **DISCIPLINE** PHILOSOPHY **EDUCATION** Harvard, AB, 64; UC-Berkeley, PhD, 68. **CAREER** Tchg asst, UC-Berkeley, 64-67; asst prof, Univ Nebraska, 68-69; asst to assoc to full prof, San Francisco State Univ, 69-. **MEMBERSHIPS** Am Philos Asn; Soc Philos & Psychol; AAUP. **RESEARCH** Philosophy of language; Theory of knowledge, Philosophy of mind. **SELECTED PUBLICATIONS** Auth Meaning, speech acts, and communication, Basic Topics in the Philosophy of Language, Prentice-Hall, 94; Emotional disorder and attention, Philosophical Psychopathy, MIT Press, 94; Semantic slack: What is said and more, Foundations of Speech Act Theory, Routledge, 94; Conversational impliciture, Mind & Language, 94; Terms of agreement, Ethics, 95; Standardization and conventionalization, Linguistics and Philosophy, 96; Do belief reports report beliefs?, Pac Philos Quart, 97; The semantics-pregmatics distinction: What it is and why it matters, Linguistisch e Berichte, 97; assorted entries Cambridge Dictionary of Philos, Oxford Companion to Philoso, Routledge Encyclo of Philos, MIT Encyclo of Cognitive Sci. **CONTACT ADDRESS** Dept of Philosophy, San Francisco State Univ, San Francisco, CA, 94132. **EMAIL** kbach@sfsu.edu

BACH, SHIRLEY
DISCIPLINE BIOMEDICAL ETHICS **EDUCATION** Univ Wis, PhD. **CAREER** Prof, W Mich Univ. **SELECTED PUBLICATIONS** Auth, Social Biology, Kendall/Hunt. **CONTACT ADDRESS** Kalamazoo, MI, 49008. **EMAIL** bach@wmich.edu

BACHE, CHRISTOPHER MARTIN
PERSONAL Born 07/04/1949, Vicksburg, MS, m, 1976 **DISCIPLINE** PSYCHOLOGY & PHILOSOPHY OF RELIGION **EDUCATION** Univ Notre Dame, AB, 71; Cambridge Univ, MA, 73; Brown Univ, PhD(philos relig), 78. **CAREER** Asst Prof Relig Studies, Youngstown State Univ, 78-. **HONORS AND AWARDS** Distinguished Prof, Youngstown State Univ, 82. **MEMBERSHIPS** Am Acad Relig; Asn Transpersonal Psychol; Soc Sci Study Relig; Am Philos Asn. **RESEARCH** LSD psychotherapy and the critical study of mysticism; the psychology of mysticism; metaphor theory. **SELECTED PUBLICATIONS** Auth, Lifecycles: Reincarnation & the Web of Life, 90. **CONTACT ADDRESS** Dept of Philos & Relig Studies, Youngstown State Univ, One University Plz, Youngstown, OH, 44555-0002. **EMAIL** cmbache@cc.ysv.edu

BACHMAN, JAMES V.
PERSONAL Born 06/14/1946, Council Bluffs, IA **DISCIPLINE** PHILOSOPHY AND THEOLOGY **EDUCATION** Math and philos, Valparaiso Univ, BS, 64-68; Fulbright grantee, BA, theol, Cambridge Univ, 68-70; Concordia Sem, ministry, M Div, 70-72; theol, Cambridge Univ, England, MA, 74; philos, Fla State Univ Tallahassee, PhD, 86. **CAREER** Pastor, Our Redeemer Luth Church, Lake City, Fla, 71-81; full-time facul, philos and world relig, Lake City Community Col, 71-81; dept chair, comp educ, Lake City Community Col, 79-81; pastor/dir, Univ Luth Ctr, Tallahassee, 81-89; asst prof, philos, Fla State Univ Tallahassee, 86-89; occasional visiting prof, Concordia Theol Sem, Ft Wayne, Ind, 95-96; occasional visiting prof, Concordia Sem, St Louis, Mo, 92-; coord of curric and prog planning, dept of philos, Valparaiso Univ, 89-92, 94-95; John R. Eckrich chair, relig and the healing arts, prof of philos, Valparaiso Univ, 89-. **HONORS AND AWARDS** Fulbright grantee, Cambridge Univ, England, 68-70; col teaching fel, Fla State Univ, 82-83; univ fel, Fla State Univ Tallahassee, 83-86; Phi Kappa Phi, 84-; Fla State Univ Coun of Instr grant, 89; visiting scholar, The Hastings Ctr, mar, 89; Who's Who in Relig, 85 & 91; Dict of Intl Bio, 93; grant for supporting and mentoring Health Ethics Fellows, 95-97. **MEMBERSHIPS** Amer Philos Asn; Chicago Clinical Ethics Prog; The Park Ridge Ctr; The Fla-Ga District; Luth Church- Mo Synod. **SELECTED PUBLICATIONS** Auth, Christians and Procreative Choices: How Do God's Chosen Choose?, CTCR, 97; auth, Witnessing in a Culture of Choice, GEM Module Course, Luth Church Mo Synod, 96; auth, Christian Care at Life's End, CTCR doc, 93; co-auth, What If....? Toward Excellence in Reasoning, 91; auth Teacher's Manual for What If....? Toward Excellence in Reasoning, 91; auth, chap, The Appeal to Authority, Fallacies: Classical and Contemporary Readings, The Penn State Univ Press, 95; article, Religious Voices in Secular Settings, Invited Papers of the Austrian Ludwig Wittgenstein Society, aug, 98; article, Two Sermon Studies, Concordia Jour, apr, 98; article, The Ten Suggestions: Putting Theology into Practice, Concordia Jour, apr, 98; article, Putting Theories into Practice, Proceedings of the Austrian Ludwig Wittgenstein Society, aug, 97; article, Ministry in a Culture of Choice, Concordia Jour, jan, 97; article, Ethics at VU, Valpo, 96; article, Here I Stand, a Reformation Homily, The Cresset, nov, 95; article, Compassion, Maximal vs. Minimal Ethics, Ready Reference: Ethics, Salem Press, 175-176, 536-537, 94. **CONTACT ADDRESS** Dept. of Philosophy, Valparaiso Univ, Valparaiso, IN, 46383.

BACK, ALLAN
DISCIPLINE PHILOSOPHY **EDUCATION** Univ Tex Austin, PhD, 79. **CAREER** Asst prof, Rice Univ, 83-84; asst prof, Wayne State Univ, 84-85; asst prof, Dickinson Coll, 85-86;

Prof, Kutztown Univ, 87-. **HONORS AND AWARDS** Phi Beta Kappa. **MEMBERSHIPS** Am Philos Asn, Soc for Greek Philos. **RESEARCH** History and Philosophy of Logic; Ancient Philosophy; Medieval Philosophy; Comparative Philosophy. **SELECTED PUBLICATIONS** Auth, Avicena and Averroes: The Islamic Background, Individuation in Scholasticism, 94; Aristotelian Necessities, Hist and Philos of Logic, 95; On Reduplication, 96; The Triplex Status Naturae and its Justification, Studies in the Hist of Logic, 96; rev, Geneerische Kennzeichungen, Nous, 96; Avicenna and Descartes on the Wax Example, Proceedings of the SIEPM Conference, 96. **CONTACT ADDRESS** Dept of Philosophy, Kutztown Univ, Pennsylvania, Kutztown, PA, 19530. **EMAIL** Back@kutztown.edu

BACKHOUSE, CONSTANCE B.
DISCIPLINE LAW **EDUCATION** Osgoode Hall Law Sch, LLB, 75; Harvard Univ, LLM, 79. **CAREER** Prof. **HONORS AND AWARDS** Willard Hurst Prize, 92; Outstanding Bk Human Rights, 93. **RESEARCH** Sex discrimination; human rights; labour law; criminal law. **SELECTED PUBLICATIONS** Auth, Petticoats and Prejudice: Women and Law in Nineteenth Century Canada, 92; The Secret Oppression: Sexual Harassment of Working Women and Challenging Times: The Women's Movement in Canada and the United States, 93. **CONTACT ADDRESS** Fac of Law, Univ Western Ontario, London, ON, N6A 3K7.

BAEHR, AMY R.
PERSONAL Born 04/15/1966, Livingston, NJ, m, 1998 **DISCIPLINE** PHILOSOPHY **EDUCATION** State Univ of New York at Stony Brook, PhD. **CAREER** Asst Prof and Chr Dept of Philosophy, 97-, Moravian Col. **MEMBERSHIPS** Amer Phil Assoc; Soc for Women in Phil. **RESEARCH** Contemporary political philosophy; liberalism; feminist philosophy **SELECTED PUBLICATIONS** Auth, Towards a New Feminist Liberalism: Okin, Rawls, and Habermas, Hyapatia 11, 96, and The Philosophy of Rawls, 98; Feminists Reconsider the Self and Families, Constellations, 97. **CONTACT ADDRESS** Dept of Philosophy, Moravian Col, 1200 Main St., Bethlehem, PA, 18018. **EMAIL** mearb01@moravian.edu

BAER, EUGEN SILAS
PERSONAL Born 08/19/1937, Klosters, Switzerland, m, 1967, 1 child **DISCIPLINE** PHILOSOPHY, PSYCHOLOGY **EDUCATION** Univ Fribourg, Lic, 65; Yale Univ, PhD(Philos), 71. **CAREER** Asst prof, 71-77, chmn dept, 73-74, assoc prof Philos, Hobart & William Smith Cols, 77-, semi-sabbatical leave, Univ Aix-en-Provence, France, 74-75; fel, Nat Humanities Inst, Univ Chicago, 76-77. **MEMBERSHIPS** Am Philos Asn; AAUP; Semiotic Soc Am; Int Asn Semiotic Studies. **RESEARCH** Semiotics; psychiatry; psychoanalysis. **SELECTED PUBLICATIONS** Auth, The language of the unconscious according to Jacques Lacan, 71, Semiotic approaches to psychiatry, 72 & Semiotic approaches to human behavior, 73, Semiotica; Semiotic Approaches to Psychotherapy, Ind Univ, Bloomington, 75; Ideas and archetypes--a synopsis of Kant and Jung, Philosophy Today, 76; Myth and illness: Identity and difference, Contemp Psychoanal, 76; Semiotic model theory in psychoanalysis, 77 & Things are stories--a manifesto for a reflexive semiotics, 78, Semiotica. **CONTACT ADDRESS** Dept of Philosophy, Hobart & William Smith Cols, 300 Pulteney St, Geneva, NY, 14456-3382. **EMAIL** baer@hws.edu

BAERGEN, RALPH
DISCIPLINE PHILOSOPHY **EDUCATION** Syracuse Univ, PhD, 90. **CAREER** Assoc prof. **RESEARCH** Medical ethics; epistemology. **SELECTED PUBLICATIONS** Auth, Contemporary Epistemology. **CONTACT ADDRESS** Dept of English and Philosophy, Idaho State Univ, Pocatello, ID, 83209. **EMAIL** baerralp@isu.edu

BAGLEY, STANLEY B.
PERSONAL Born 09/07/1935, Trenton, NJ, m **DISCIPLINE** THEOLOGY **EDUCATION** Morehouse Coll, BA 1958; Crozer Theol Sem, BD 1961; Ashland Theol Sem, MDiv 1973; Univ of OK, grad study, 1967; Century University, PhD, 1994; Association Mental Health Clergy, certified professional mental health clergy, 1976; Department of VA National Black Chaplin Association, certified clinical chaplain, 1996. **CAREER** Galilee Bapt Ch Trenton NJ, asst pastor 1961-65; Calvary Bapt Ch, pastor 1965-67; Bapt Campus Ministry Langston Univ, dir 1967-70; Hough Ch, minister of educ comm 1970-71; VA Medical Center Brecksville OH, chaplain 1971-; Lakeside Bapt Ch E Cleveland OH, pastor 1972-1979. **HONORS AND AWARDS** Christian Leadership Citation Bapt Student Union Langston Univ 1969; Outstanding Young Man, Outstanding Amer Found, 1970; 33 Degree Free Mason; United Supreme Council 33 Degree Ancient and Accepted Scottish Rite of Freemasonry Prince Hall Affiliation; loaned executive from VAMC to the Combined Federal Campaign, 1988; Crozer Theological Seminary, Crozer Scholar, 1989, 1995. **MEMBERSHIPS** E Cleveland Ministerial Alliance 1975; Assn of Mental Health Clergy, bd certified chaplain, 1974; Ohio Health Care Chaplains; Amer Protestant Hosp Assn; College of Chaplains; chmn, Evangelism Com Bapt Minister's Conf Cleveland OH; Dept of Metropolitan Ministry Cleveland Baptist Assn; life mem and golden heritage life mem, NAACP; Omega Psi Phi Fraternity Inc; American Association of Christian Counselors; Associations of Christian Marriage Counselors; Dept of Veterans Affairs, Natl Black Chaplains Assn, certified clinical chaplain, 1996. **CONTACT ADDRESS** VA Medical Ctr, 10000 Brecksville Rd, Brecksville, OH, 44141.

BAILEY, ALISON
DISCIPLINE PHILOSOPHY **EDUCATION** Dickinson Col, BA, 83; Colo State Univ, MA, 86; Univ Cincinnati, PhD, 93. **CAREER** Asst prof. **SELECTED PUBLICATIONS** Auth, Posterity and Strategic Policy: A Moral Assessment of Nuclear Policy Options, Univ Am, 89; Mothering, Diversity and Peace: Comments on Sara Ruddick's Feminist Maternal Peace Politics, Jour Soc Philos, 95; Mothers, Birthgivers and Peacemakers: A Critical Reflection on Maternal Peace Politics, 97. **CONTACT ADDRESS** Dept of Philosophy, Illinois State Univ, Normal, IL, 61761.

BAILEY, JAMES L.
PERSONAL Born 03/16/1938, Columbus, OH, m, 1963, 2 children **DISCIPLINE** THEOLOGY **EDUCATION** Capital Univ, BA, 60; Trinity Lutheran Sem, BD, 64; Univ of St Andrews, PhD, 67. **CAREER** Pastor, 67-70, Hope Lutheran Church Cincinnati; Asst Prof, 70-74, Trinity Lutheran Sem; Asst Prof, Assoc Prof, 75-85, Concordia Coll; Assoc Prof, Prof, 85-, Wartburg Theo Sem. **HONORS AND AWARDS** Trinity Luth Sem, dist alumnus Awd. **MEMBERSHIPS** SBL. **RESEARCH** New Testament, sermon on the mount. **SELECTED PUBLICATIONS** Co-auth, Literary Texts in the New Testament A Handbook, Louisville John Knox/Westminster Press, 92; co-auth, The Sermon on the Mount, Model for Contrast Community, forthcoming; Mark, Men's Bible Study Series, Augsburg, 87; auth, Experiencing the Kingdom as a Little Child, A Rereading of Mark 10:13-16, in: Word and World, 95; auth, A Pattern for Interpreting Biblical Texts, in: Currents in Theology and Mission, 95; The Bible, As We Become Open to God's Word, We Shall Be Changed, in: Parish Teacher, 90. **CONTACT ADDRESS** Wartburg Theological Sem, 333 Wartburg Pl, Dubuque, IA, 52004-5004. **EMAIL** jjbailey@mwci.net

BAILEY, LEE
PERSONAL Born 11/21/1943, West Palm Beach, FL, m, 1974, 2 children **DISCIPLINE** RELIGION & CULTURE **EDUCATION** Univ IL, BFA, 65; Union Theol Sem, Columbia Univ, M Div, 70; Syracuse Univ, PhD (Humanities), 83. **CAREER** Assoc prof, Dept of Philos & Relig, Ithaca Col, NY, 83-. **HONORS AND AWARDS** Res grants, Syracuse Univ, Ithaca Col; listed in Who's Who in the East, 95, 96, 97. **MEMBERSHIPS** Am Academy of Relig. **RESEARCH** Near-death experiences; technology and culture, mythology. **SELECTED PUBLICATIONS** Auth, Preface to Religious Projection by Fokke Sierksma, the English trans from the Dutch by Jacob Faber, UMI, 90; Preface to Envisioning the Invisible by Han Fortmann, the English trans from the Dutch by Jacob Faber, UMI, 91; The No-Thing-ness of Near-Death Experiences & Unknown Well-Known Near-Death Experiences, articles in The Near-Death Experience: A Reader, Routledge, 96; co-auth with Jenny Yates, The Near-Death Experience: A Reader, Routledge, 96; The Titanic Enchantment and Education, Voice of the Liberal Arts at Ithaca Col, 1:1, spring 98; A Little Death: Tibetan Delogs and the Near-Death Experience, J of Near-Death Studies, in press; numerous other articles and publications. **CONTACT ADDRESS** Dept of Philos and Relig, Ithaca Col, Ithaca, NY, 14850. **EMAIL** Bailey@ic4.ithaca.edu

BAILEY, RANDALL CHARLES
PERSONAL Born 05/26/1947, Malden, MA, m, 1973 **DISCIPLINE** RELIGION **EDUCATION** Brandeis Univ, Waltham, MA, BA (cum laude), 1969; Univ of Chicago, IL, AM, Social Serv Admin, 1972; Candler School of Theology, Atlanta, GA, MDiv (cum laude), 1979; Emory Univ, Atlanta, GA, PhD, Religion, 1987. **CAREER** PCSAP Loop College, Chicago, IL, dir of educ prog, 1972-1973; Shelby Co Devel Coord Dept, Memphis, TN, assoc dir, 1973; Atlanta Univ School of Social Work, Atlanta, GA, asst prof, 1973-81; First Cong Church, UCC, Atlanta, GA, asst minister, 1980-81; INTERDENOMINATIONAL THEOLOGICAL CENTER, ATLANTA, GA, instructor 1981-87, asst prof 1987-90, ASSOC PROF 1990-; ANDREW W MELLON, ASSOC PROF, 1998-. **HONORS AND AWARDS** Distinguished Serv Award, Atlanta Natl Assn of Black Social Workers, 1978; Fellow, Black Doctoral Prog/FTE, 1979-81, 1984-85; "Litany for Beginning," Inauguration of Mayor Andrew Young, 1981; Fellow, United Negro Coll Fund, 1984-85. **MEMBERSHIPS** Mem, Black Theology Project, 1986-; co-chair, Afro-Amer Theology & Biblical Hermeneutics Soc of Biblical Lit, 1987-94; co-chair, Unity/Renewal Study, COFO/NCCCUSA, 1988-92; mem, Div Educ & Min/NCCCUSA, 1988-91, Bible Translation & Utilization Comm DEM/NCCCUSA, 1988-, Soc for the Study of Black Religion, 1988-; mem exec bd, NCCCUSA. **SELECTED PUBLICATIONS** Author: "Wash Me White as Snow: When Bad is Turned to Good, Race, Class and the Politics of Bible Translation," Seneia 76, 1996; "The Redemption of Yhwh: A Literary Critical Function of the Songs of Hannah and David," Biblical Interpretation, 1995; "'Is That Any Name for a Nice Hebrew Boy?' - Exodus 2:1-10: The De-Africanization of an Israelite Hero," The Recover of Black Presence: An Interdisciplinary Exploration, Abingdon, 1995; "They're Nothing but Incestuous Bastards: The Polemical Use of Sex and Sexuality in Hebrew Canon Narrative," Reading From This Place: Social Location and Biblical Interpretation in the United States, Fortress, 1994; "And Then They Will Know That I Am YHWH: The P Recasting of the Plague Narratives," JITC, 1994; "What Price Inclusivity?: An Afrocentric Reading of Dangerous Biblical Texts," Voices from the Third World, 1994; "Cobb Clergy's Gay Stance Loses Punch in Biblical Debate," Atlanta Journal/Constitution, p F2, June 26, 1994; "A De-politicized Gospel: Reflections on Galatians 5:22-23," Ecumenical Trends, 22 No 1, Jan 1993; "Doing the Wrong Thing: Male-Female Relationships in the Hebrew Canon," We Belong Together: The Churches in Solidarity with Women, Friendship Press, 1992; David in Love and War: The Pursuit of Power in a Samuel 10-12, Sheffield, 1990; numerous other publications. **CONTACT ADDRESS** Old Testament and Hebrew, Interdenominational Theol Ctr, 700 MLK Jr Dr, SW, Atlanta, GA, 30314.

BAILEY, STORM M.
PERSONAL Columbia, SC, m, 1981, 5 children **DISCIPLINE** PHILOSOPHY **EDUCATION** Wheaton Col, Ba, 87; Univ Wisc, Madison, MA, PhD, 97. **CAREER** Asst prof philos, Luther Col. **CONTACT ADDRESS** Luther Col, 700 College Dr, Decorah, IA, 52101. **EMAIL** baileyst@luther.edu

BAILIFF, JOHN
PERSONAL Born 03/24/1936, San Pedro, CA, d, 3 children **DISCIPLINE** PHILOSOPHY **EDUCATION** Stanford Univ, AB, 58; Penn State Univ, MA, 61, PhD, 66. **CAREER** Instr, Penn State Univ, 61-63; instr, Univ Nev Las Vegas, 63-66; asst prof, 66-69, assoc prof, 69-74, prof, philos, 74-94, prof emer, philos, 94-, Univ Wisc Stevens Point. **HONORS AND AWARDS** Stanford Club scholar, 54-56; Crossett scholar in philos, Stanford Univ, 56-58; NDEA fel, philos, Penn State Univ, 60-63; Phi Kappa Phi, Penn State Univ, 63. **MEMBERSHIPS** Amer Philos Asn; Heidegger Conf; Soc for Phenomenol & Existential Philos; Intl Asn for Philos & Lit. **RESEARCH** Heidegger studies; Philosophy and fiction. **SELECTED PUBLICATIONS** Rev, Gibt es auf Erden ein Mass? and Ethos und Lebenswelt, Man and World, 88; auth, Truth and Power, Man and World, 87; auth, The Essence of Teaching, Teaching Forum, 87; auth, Elementary Logics, 2nd ed, Univ Wisc, 73; auth, Elementary Logics, Univ Wisc, 69; auth, Religious Discourse and Existence, Philos Forum, 67; auth, On the Ideal Observer, Philos and Phenomenol Res, 64. **CONTACT ADDRESS** 932 Bukolt Ave., Stevens Point, WI, 54481-1733. **EMAIL** jbailiff@uwsp.edu

BAIRD, DAVIS
PERSONAL Born 04/12/1954, Boston, MA, m, 1994, 1 child **DISCIPLINE** PHILOSOPHY **EDUCATION** Brandeis, BA, 76; MA, 81, PhD, 81, Stanford Univ. **CAREER** Visiting Asst Prof, Univ AZ, 81-82; Asst Prof, 82-88, Assoc Prof, 88-, Chair, 92-, Univ S. Carolina **MEMBERSHIPS** Amer Phil Assoc; Phil of Science Assoc; British Assoc for Phil of Science; Intl Soc for Phil of Chemistry; Soc for Phil and Tech. **RESEARCH** Philosophy of scientific instrumentation; philosophy of analytical chemistry, instructive logic. **SELECTED PUBLICATIONS** Coauth, Scientific Instruments, Scientific Progress and the Cyclotron, British Journal for the Philosophy of Science, 90; Auth, Baird Associate's Commercial Three-Meter Grating Spectograph and the Tranformation of Analytical Chemistry, Rittenhouse, 91; Analytical Chemistry and the Big Scientific Instrumentation Revolution, Annals of Science, 93; Coauth, Facts Well Put, British Journal for the Philosophy of Science, 94; Auth, Meaning in a Material Medium, PSA, 95; Scientific Instrument Making, Epistemology and the Conflict Between Gift and Commodity Economies, Techne: Electronic Journal of the Society for Philosophy and Technology, 97; The Thing-y-ness of Things: Materiality and and Design, Lessons from Spectrochemical Instrumentation, Studies in the Philosophy of Technology, forthcoming; Scientific Instrumentation and Instrumental Objectivity, The Philosophy of Chemistry, forthcoming; Encapsulating Knowledge: The Direct Reading Spectrometer, Foundations of Chemistry, forthcoming. **CONTACT ADDRESS** Dept of Philosophy, Univ of S. Carolina, Columbia, SC, 29208. **EMAIL** bairdd@garnet.cla.sc.edu

BAIRD, FORREST
DISCIPLINE PHILOSOPHY **EDUCATION** Westmont, BA; Fuller, Mdiv; Claremont Grad Sch, MA, PhD. **CAREER** Instr, Fuller Theol Sem; prof, 78-. **HONORS AND AWARDS** Res fel, Inst Ecumenical and Cult Res, St John's Univ., Selected, three graduating classes, Most Influential Prof; voted, Tch Yr (3). **RESEARCH** Chinese philosophy; the problem of evil. **SELECTED PUBLICATIONS** Ed, Human Thought and Action: Readings in Western Intellectual History; co-auth, Introduction to philosophy: A Case Study Approach, HarperCollins. **CONTACT ADDRESS** Dept of Rel/Philos, Whitworth Col, 300 West Hawthorne Rd, Spokane, WA, 99251. **EMAIL** fbaird@whitworth.edu

BAIRD, ROBERT DAHLEN
PERSONAL Born 06/29/1933, Philadelphia, PA, m, 1954, 4 children **DISCIPLINE** RELIGION **EDUCATION** Houghton

Col, BA, 54; Fuller Theol Sem, BD, 57; Southern Methodist Univ, STM, 59; Univ Iowa, PhD(Relig), 64. **CAREER** From instr to asst prof Philos & Relig, Univ Omaha, 62-65; from asst prof to assoc prof Hist Relig, 66-73, prof Hist Relig, Univ Iowa, 74-; dir School of Relg, Univ Iowa, 95-; Soc Relig Higher Educ fel, 65-66; Am Inst Indian Studies fac fel, India, 71-72; book rev ed, J Am Acad Relig, 80-. **MEMBERSHIPS** Am Acad Relig; Asn Asian Studies. **RESEARCH** History of religious methodology; religion in India. **SELECTED PUBLICATIONS** Auth, Category Formation and the History of Religions, Mouton, The Hague, 71; coauth, Indian and Far Eastern Religious Traditions, Harper, 72; auth, The Symbol of Emptiness and the Emptiness of Symbols, Humanitas, Spring 72; Mr Justice Gajendragadkar and the Religion of the Indian Secular State, J Const & Parliamentary Studies, 12/72; ed, Methodological Issues in Religious Studies, New Horizons, 75; auth, Religion and the Secular: Categories for Religious Conflict and Religious Change in Independent India, In: Religion and Social Conflict in South Asia, 76 & Religion and the Legitimation of Nehru's Concept of the Secular State, In: Religion and the Legitimation of Power in South Asia, 78, Brill; ed & contribr, Religion in Modern India, Manohar, New Delhi, 81. **CONTACT ADDRESS** Sch of Relig, Univ of Iowa, 308 Gilmore Hall, Iowa City, IA, 52242-1376. **EMAIL** robert-baird@uiowwa.eud

BAIRD, ROBERT MALCOLM
PERSONAL Born 05/30/1937, Memphis, TN, m, 1959, 3 children **DISCIPLINE** PHILOSOPHY **EDUCATION** Baylor Univ, BA, MA, 61; Southern Baptist Theol Sem, BD, 64; Emory Univ, PhD(philos), 67. **CAREER** Instr philos, Baylor Univ, 60-61; asst prof, Oglethorpe Col, 66-67 & NE Wesleyan Univ, 67-68; asst prof, 68-70, assoc prof, 70-78, PROF PHILOS, BAYLOR UNIV, 79-. **MEMBERSHIPS** Am Philos Asn; AAUP. **RESEARCH** Existentialism; history of modern philosophy; contemporary ethics. **SELECTED PUBLICATIONS** Auth, John Dewey's Two Meta-ethical Views, Southwestern J Philos, fall 70; Philosophy, Southern Baptist Convention Press, spring 71; Existentialism, Death, and Caring, J Relig & Health, 4/76; The Sixties, the Students, the Conflict with Authority: Lessons in Retrospect, J Thought, 4/77; coauth, Thomas Reid's Criticisms of Adam Smith's Theory of the Moral Sentiments, J Hist Ideas, 9/77; Leibniz and Locke: On the Relationship Between Metaphysics and Science, Sci, Faith, & Revelation: An Approach Christian Philos, 79; The Creative Role of Doubt in Religion, J Relig Health, fall 80; Reasoned Commitment in the Face of Uncertainty, Contemp Philos: Philos Res Anal, fall, 81. **CONTACT ADDRESS** Dept of Philos Col of Arts & Sci, Baylor Univ, Waco, TX, 76703.

BAKAN, JOEL
DISCIPLINE LAW **EDUCATION** Simon Fraser Univ, BA, 81; Oxford Univ, BA, 83; Dalhousie Univ, LLB, 84; Harvard Univ, LLM, 87. **CAREER** Law Clerk, Justice Brian Dickson, Supreme Court Can, 85; asst prof, Osgoode Hall Law, 87-90; Assoc prof, 90-. **HONORS AND AWARDS** Tchg Excellence Awd; UBC Killam Res Prize. **RESEARCH** Constitutional law; legal theory; socio legal studies. **SELECTED PUBLICATIONS** Co-auth, Developments in Constitutional Law, Court Law Rev, 95; Rights, Nationalism and Social Movements in Canadian Constitutional Politics, 95. **CONTACT ADDRESS** Fac of Law, Univ British Columbia, 1822 East Mall, Vancouver, BC, V6T 1Z1. **EMAIL** bakan@law.ubc.ca

BAKER, BEVERLY POOLE
PERSONAL Born 01/14/1944, Birmingham, AL, m, 1968 **DISCIPLINE** LAW **EDUCATION** Univ of Alabama at Birmingham, BA (summa cum laude), 1982; Cumberland School of Law, Birmingham AL, JD, 1985. **CAREER** McMillan & Spratling, Birmingham, AL, atty, 1985-86; Haskell Slaughter & Young, Birmingham, AL, atty, 1986-. **HONORS AND AWARDS** Dean's Award, Univ of Alabama at Birmingham, 1981, 1982; Fellow, Amer Assn of Univ Women, 1984. **MEMBERSHIPS** American Bar Assn, Standing Committee on Lawyers' Public Service Responsibility; co-chair, Equal Opportunity Committee of the Litigation Section; Natl Bar Assn; Natl Assn of Bond Lawyers; Magic City Bar Assn; Birmingham Bar Assn; Leadership Alabama, board of directors, alumni council; Leadership Birmingham; Jefferson County Medical Examiners Comm; Research Council of Alabama; Cumberland School of Law, advisory board; University of Alabama in Birmingham Leadership Council. **SELECTED PUBLICATIONS** "Perceptions and Propinquity on Police Patrol," SE Sociological Assn, 1982; "Privacy in a High-Tech World," seminar, 1985; "The Age Discrimination in Employment Act and Termination of the Public Sector Employee," Alabama Bar Inst Seminar, 1989; "Basic Wage and Hour Law in AL," NBI, 1996. **CONTACT ADDRESS** 1901 Sixth Ave N, Ste 1200, Birmingham, AL, 35203.

BAKER, C. EDWIN
PERSONAL Born 05/28/1947, Nashville, TN **DISCIPLINE** CONSTITUTIONAL LAW, LEGAL PHILOSOPHY, MASS MEDIA **EDUCATION** Stanford Univ, BA, 69; Yale Univ, JD, 72. **CAREER** Asst prof, Univ Toledo, 72-75; asst prof, Univ Ore, 75-79, assoc prof, 79-81 & prof, 81-82; Prof Law, Univ Pa, 82-, Fel, Harvard Univ, 74-75; vis prof law, Univ Tex, 80 & Univ Pa, 81-82; Staff Atty, ACLU, NY, 87-88; Fel, Shorentein Barone Ctr, Kennedy Sch Govt, Harvard, 92; vis prof, Cornell Univ, 93; Vis Lombard Prof, Kennedy Sch Govt, Harvard Univ, 93. **RESEARCH** Mass media; constitutional law. **SELECTED PUBLICATIONS** Auth, Human Liberty and Freedom of Speech, Oxford Univ 89; Advertising and a Democratic Press, Princeton, 94; author of numerous journal articles. **CONTACT ADDRESS** Law Sch, Univ of Pa, 3400 Chestnut St, Philadelphia, PA, 19104-6204. **EMAIL** ebaker@oyez.law.upenn.edu

BAKER, DONALD W.
DISCIPLINE LAW **EDUCATION** Southern Methodist Univ, BA, 67; Univ Tex, JD 70. **CAREER** Ira Drayton Pruitt sr prof, Univ Ala. **RESEARCH** Commercial transactions,.bankruptcy, and contracts. **SELECTED PUBLICATIONS** Auth, A Lawyer's Basic Guide to Secured Transactions, Amer Law Inst. **CONTACT ADDRESS** Law Dept, Univ of Alabama, Box 870000, Tuscaloosa, AL, 35487-0000. **EMAIL** dbaker@law.ua.edu

BAKER, JOHN ARTHUR
PERSONAL Born 01/15/1937, Liverpool, England, m, 1964, 2 children **DISCIPLINE** PHILOSOPHY, ETHICS **EDUCATION** Oxford Univ, BA, 61, MA, 63, BPhil, 63, DPhil, 69. **CAREER** Lectr. Balliol Col, Oxford Univ, 63-64, Exeter & Trinity Col, 64-67; asst prof, 67-72, ASSOC PROF PHILOS, UNIV CALGARY, 72-, Vis lectr, Trinity Col, Oxford Univ, 76. **MEMBERSHIPS** Can Philos Asn; Humanities Asn Can. **RESEARCH** Decision theory; philosophy of language; classical Greek philosophy. **SELECTED PUBLICATIONS** Auth, A Select Bibliography of Moral Philosophy: Oxford Study Aids in Philosophy Series, Vol IX, Oxford Univ, 77. **CONTACT ADDRESS** Dept of Philos, Univ of Calgary, Calgary, AB, T2L 1B4.

BAKER, JOHN M.
PERSONAL m, 1975, 1 child **DISCIPLINE** PHILOSOPHY **EDUCATION** Oxford Univ, BA, 71; Univ Toronto, MA, 72, Oxford Univ, PhD, 74. **CAREER** Bradford Univ, lectr, 76-77; Nat Univ Ireland Dublin, lectr 77-. **HONORS AND AWARDS** Birkbeck Col, Hon Res fel, SUNY Stony Brook, res assoc, Yale, vis fel. **MEMBERSHIPS** APA, APSA, PSA, PSAI. **RESEARCH** Equarity; egalitarian theory and democratic theory. **SELECTED PUBLICATIONS** Auth, Utilitarianism and Secondary Principles, Philos Quart, 71; auth, An Egalitarian Case for Basic Income, Arguing for Basic Income, ed., P. Van Parijs, Verso, 92; auth, Fair Representation and the Concept of Proportionality Political Studies, 96; auth, Studying Equality, Imprints, 97; auth, Equality, Social Policy in Ireland: Principles, Practice and Problems, ed., S. Healy & B. Reynolds, Dublin: Oak Tree Pr, 98; coauth, Responsibility for Needs, Necessary Goods: Our Responsibilities to Meet Others Needs, ed., G. Brock, Lanham, MD: Rowman and Littlefield, 98. **CONTACT ADDRESS** Dept of Politics, Univ Col Dublin, PO Box 208343, New Haven, CT, 06520-8343. **EMAIL** john.baker@ucd.ie

BAKER, JOHN R.
DISCIPLINE LOGIC, PHILOSOPHY OF RELIGION **EDUCATION** Hardin-Simmons Univ, BA, 61; Southwestern Baptist Theol Sem, BD, PhD, 69; Vanderbilt Univ, MA, PhD, 73. **CAREER** Assoc prof, La State Univ. **RESEARCH** Metaphysical areas related to identity and to Christian theology. **SELECTED PUBLICATIONS** Published in the areas of analytic metaphysics, theistic proofs, and Whiteheadian studies. **CONTACT ADDRESS** Dept of Philos and Relig Stud, Louisiana State Univ, 106 Coates Hall, Baton Rouge, LA, 70803.

BAKER, LYNNE R.
DISCIPLINE PHILOSOPHY **EDUCATION** Vanderbilt Univ, PhD, 72. **CAREER** Asst prof, Mary Baldwin Coll, 72-76; asst prof, assoc prof, prof, Middlebury Coll, 76-94; prof, Univ Mass Amherst, 89-. **HONORS AND AWARDS** Phi Beta Kappa; Fel Nat Humanities Center; Fel Woodrow Wilson Int Center for Scholars. **MEMBERSHIPS** Am Philos Asn; Soc for Philos and Psychol; Soc of Christian Philos. **RESEARCH** Philosophy of Mind; Metaphysics. **SELECTED PUBLICATIONS** Auth, Attitudes as Nonentities, Philos Studies, 95; Content Meets Consciousness, Philos Topics, 94; Need a Christian be a Mind-Body Dualist?, Faith and Philos, 95; Science and the Attitudes: A Replay to Sanford, Behavior and Philos, 96; Why Constitution is Not Identity, J of Philos, 97. **CONTACT ADDRESS** Univ of Mass, Bartlett Hall 352, PO Box 30525, Amherst, MA, 01003-0525. **EMAIL** lrbarker@philos.umass.edu

BAKER, ROBERT B.
PERSONAL Born 12/05/1937, New York, NY, m, 1958, 2 children **DISCIPLINE** PHILOSOPHY **EDUCATION** CUNY, BA, 59; Univ Minn, PhD, 67. **CAREER** Instr, 64-65, Univ Minn; from instr to asst prof, 65-69, Univ Iowa; asst prof, 69-73, adj prof biomed ethics, 73-74,, Wayne St Univ Med Sch, Wayne State Univ; asst prof, 73-80, coord, Med Term Abroad, 76-, co-dir, Health & Human Values, 79-, assoc prof, 80-88, chmn, 82-95, Human Subj Res Comm, dir, 84-88, CHUC, prof, 89-, chmn, 91-96, phil dept, Union Col, NY; vis assoc prof, 81, NYU Med Ctr; vis prof, 96-, Ctr Bioethics, Univ Penn. **HONORS AND AWARDS** NEH jr res fel, 69; Coun of Philos Stud Sum Stud Grant, Rochefeller Bros Fund, 74; Natl Endow for Humanities Sel Fields Fel, 74-75; Melon Fel, 76-77; Inst of Health & Human Values Fel, 77-78; Ethical Values in Sci & Tech, NEH-NSF, 81-82; Computers in Humanities Undergrad Curriculum, CHUC, 84-86; Amer Philos Soc travel grant, 94-95; Wood Inst Fel, 96-97. **RESEARCH** Bioethics, hist of medical ethics, social and political philosophy; philosophy of medicine; philosophy of sex. **SELECTED PUBLICATIONS** Art, Resistance to Medical Ethics Reform in the Nineteenth Century, Malloch Rm Newsl of NY Acad of Med, 96; art, The Impact of Legislation Requiring DNR Orders: New York State Compared to Neighboring States, J of Intensive Care Med 11, 96; art, Recent Works in the History of Medical Ethics and Its Relevance to Bioethics, APA Newsl, 96; art, The Kappa Lambda Society of Hippocrates: The Secret Origins of the American Medical Association, Fugitive Leaves, Col of Phys of Phil, 97; coauth, Crisis, Ethics and the American Medical Association: 1847 and 1997, J of Amer Med Assn, 97; art, Multiculturalism, Postmodernism and the Bankruptcy of Fundamentalism, Kennedy Inst Ethics J, 98; art, A Theory of International Bioethics, Kennedy Inst Ethics J, 98; coauth, The American Medical Ethics Revolution, John Hopkins, 99. **CONTACT ADDRESS** Dept of Philosophy, Union Col, 807 Union St, Schenectady, NY, 12308-3107. **EMAIL** bakerr@union.edu

BAKER, THOMAS EUGENE
PERSONAL Born 02/25/1953, Youngstown, OH, m, 1977, 1 child **DISCIPLINE** CONSTITUTIONAL LAW **EDUCATION** Fla State Univ, BS, 74; Univ Fla, JD, 77. **CAREER** James Madison Chair & Dir Constitutional Law Resource Ctr, Drake Univ Law Sch, 98-; law clerk to Hon J C Hill, US Ct Appeals, 5th Circuit, 77-79; from asst prof to prof Constitutional Law, Tex Tech Univ, 79-98; acting admin asst, Chief Justice William H. Rehnquist, 86; Fulbright Prof, Univ Athens, Greece, 92. **RESEARCH** Constitutional law; federal courts. **SELECTED PUBLICATIONS** Auth, Rationing Justice on Appeal - The Problems of the U.S. Courts of Appeals, West Publ Co, 94; "The Most Wonderful Work...", in Our Constitution Interpreted, West Publ Co, 96; Can a Good Christian Be a Good Lawyer?, Univ Notre Dame Press, 98. **CONTACT ADDRESS** School of Law, Drake Univ, Des Moines, IA, 50311. **EMAIL** tbaker@acad.drake.edu

BAKER-KELLY, BEVERLY
PERSONAL Born 11/02/1942, Detroit, MI, m, 1966 **DISCIPLINE** LAW **EDUCATION** Howard Univ, 1961-62; Univ of Mich, BA, 1964; Columbia Univ, MA, 1966, MEd, 1970, School of International Affairs, Certificate of African Studies, 1970, EdD, 1973; Univ of California, Berkeley, JD, 1976; Harvard Univ, MA, 1977, PhD, 1978; Johns Hopkins Univ, 1984-86; London School of Economics, 1991-92. **CAREER** Columbia Univ, co-dir of African-American Summer Studies Program, 1970; Univ of Windsor, sociology instructor, 1971-73; Greenberg and Glusker, law clerk, 1974; Dunn and Cruthcer, law clerk, 1975; Legal Aid Society, law clerk, 1976; California State Univ, assoc prof, 1976-82; Mayr, Galle, Weiss-Tessback, und Ben Ibler, Attorneys at Law, stagiaire, 1978-79; UNESCO, stagiaire, 1979-80; Univ of Maryland, US Army Bases, lecturer and facilitator, 1980; Southern Poverty Law Cent, assoc, 1981; Univ of Calif, dir of Academic Support Program, lecturer, 1982-84; Research Management Services, partner and director of Intl Law Div, 1984-86; Focus Intl Consultancy, dir, 1986-93; Private Immigration Law Practice, 1991-93; Howard Univ, visiting assoc prof, 1993-; Golden Gate University, School of Law, 1996, 1997. **HONORS AND AWARDS** Natl Bar Assn, Presidential Award for Outstanding Service, 1992, 1993, 1995. **MEMBERSHIPS** Natl Bar Assn, Intl Law Section, Chair, 1994-96; Union Internationale Des Avocats; Boalt Hall Fund for Diversity, VP/Bd of Dir, 1988-91. **SELECTED PUBLICATIONS** Assoc Ed, California Law Review; Articles Editor, Black Law Journal; Co-author, The African-American Encyclopedia of Education, 1994; A Study of the Degree of Transnationalization of College and Non-College Educated Blacks, Columbia Univ; Housing Conceptions and Satisfactions of Residents in Federally Subsidized Lower-Middle Income Housing, Harvard Univ; "US Immigration: A Wake up Call," Howard Law Journal, 1995. **CONTACT ADDRESS** Attorney, 2983 Burdeck Dr, Oakland, CA, 94602.

BAKHURST, DAVID J.
DISCIPLINE PHILOSOPHY **EDUCATION** Keele Univ, BA; Oxon, MA; DPhil. **CAREER** Dept Philos, Queen's Univ **RESEARCH** Russian philosophy; metaethics. **SELECTED PUBLICATIONS** Auth, Consciousness and Revolution in Soviet Philosophy, Cambridge, 91. **CONTACT ADDRESS** Philosophy Dept, Queen's Univ, Kingston, ON, K7L 3N6. **EMAIL** bakhurst@post.queensu.ca

BALAS, DAVID L.
PERSONAL Born 08/06/1929, Kispest, Hungary **DISCIPLINE** THEOLOGY, PHILOSOPHY **EDUCATION** Pontif Univ St Anselm, Rome, LicTheol, 56, LicPhilos, 58, STD, 63. **CAREER** From instr to assoc prof, 59-72, chmn dept theol, 67-74 & 79-80, PROF THEOL, UNIV DALLAS, 77-, Grad Dean & Dir, Inst Philos Studies, 80-, Pres, Coun Southwestern Theol Schs, 72-74; prof extraordinarius theol fundamentalis et dogmaticae, Pontif Athenaeum Anselmianum, Rome, 75-77.

MEMBERSHIPS Am Acad Relig; Am Cath Philos Asn; Cath Theol Soc Am; NAm Patristic Soc (vpres, 75 & 81-83); Int Asn Patristic Studies. **RESEARCH** Hellenistic philosophy and patristic thought, especially Gregory of Nyssa; philosophy of religion; theological anthropology. **SELECTED PUBLICATIONS** Auth, Metousia Theou: Man's Participation in God's Perfections According to St Gregory of Nyssa, Herder, Rome, 66; Christian Transformation of Greek Philosophy, Proc Am Cath Philos Asn, 66; The Encounter Between Christianity and Contemporary Philosophy in the Second Century, Anglican Theol Rev, 66 & 68; Recent Surveys of the History in the Early Church and the Tasks of the Historiography of Early Christianity, Church Hist, 72; Theology as Interpretation of Tradition, Proc Cath Theol Soc Am, 73; The Idea of Participation in the Structure of Origen's Thought, In: Origeniana: Premier colloque international des etudes origeniennes, Instituto di Lettaratura Christiana Antica, Barl, 75; Eternity and Time in Gregory of Nyssa's Contra Eunomium, In: Gregor von Nyssa und die Philosophie Sweites internationales Kolloquium, uber Gregor von Nyssa, Brill, Leiden, 76; Marcion Revisited: A Post-Harnack Perspective, In: Texts and Testaments, Trinity Univ Press, 80; Christianity and Classical Culture-The Metamorphosis of Natural Theology in the Christian Encounter with Hellenism, with J. Pelikan, J of Relig, Vol 75, 95; The Spirit of God-The Exegesis of '1-Corinthians' and '2-Corinthians' in the Pneumatomachian Controversy of the 4th-Century, with M. A. G. Haykin, Church History, Vol 66, 97. **CONTACT ADDRESS** Univ Dallas, Irving, TX, 75060.

BALCOMB, RAYMOND
PERSONAL Born 02/08/1923, San Bernardino, CA, m, 1944, 5 children **DISCIPLINE** NEW TESTAMENT **EDUCATION** San Jose St Col, AB, 44; Boston Univ Sch of Theol, STB, 47; Boston Univ Grad Sch, PhD, 51 **CAREER** Ordain Meth Clergy, 48; Adj Faculty, 98-pres, Claremont Sch of Theol **HONORS AND AWARDS** Lucinda Bidwell Beebe Fel, 47 **RESEARCH** Church History; Archaeology of Middle East **SELECTED PUBLICATIONS** Auth, Stir What You've Got, Abingdon Press; Auth, Try Reading the Bible This Way, Westminster **CONTACT ADDRESS** 868 SW Troy, Portland, OR, 97219. **EMAIL** rbalcomb@uswest.net

BALDNER, KENT
DISCIPLINE MODERN PHILOSOPHY **EDUCATION** Univ Calif, PhD. **CAREER** Assoc prof, W Mich Univ. **RESEARCH** Emmanuel Kant **SELECTED PUBLICATIONS** Articles, Philos Quart; Electronic Jour Analytic Philos. **CONTACT ADDRESS** Kalamazoo, MI, 49008. **EMAIL** baldner@wmich.edu

BALDWIN, CYNTHIA A.
PERSONAL Born 02/08/1945, McKeesport, PA, m, 1967 **DISCIPLINE** LAW **EDUCATION** Pennsylvania State Univ, University Park PA, BA, English, 1966, MA, English, 1974; Duquesne Univ School of Law, Pittsburgh PA, JD, 1980. **CAREER** Pennsylvania State Univ, McKeesport PA, asst dean student affairs, 1976-77; Neighborhood Legal Serv, McKeesport PA, staff atty, 1980-81; Office of Attorney Gen, PA, deputy atty gen, 1981-83, atty-in-charge, 1983-86; Palkovitz and Palkovitz, McKeesport PA, atty; DUQUESNE UNIV OF LAW, PITTSBURGH PA, adjunct professor, 1984-86, visiting professor, 1986-87, ADJUNCT PROFESSOR, 1989-; ALLEGHENY COUNTY, COURT OF COMMON PLEAS, ADULT/FAMILY DIVISION, AND CIVIL DIVISION JUDGE, 1990-. **HONORS AND AWARDS** Susan B Anthony Award, Women's Bar Assoc 1998; Distinguished Daughters of Pennsylvania Award, Governor Tom Ridge, 1996; Tribute to Women Award in the Professions, YWCA, 1987; Humanitarian Service Award, Penn State Forum on Black Affairs, 1989; Whitney M Young Jr Service Award, Boy Scouts of America, 1991; Women's Equality Day Recognition Plaque, Greater Pittsburgh Comm on Women, 1990; Inducted into MCK School Hall of Fame, 1990; first black woman elected to the Allegheny County, PA, bench for a ten-year term; first black woman installed as president of Penn State Alumni Assn. **MEMBERSHIPS** Penn State, bd of trustees, Gubernational Appointee, 1995-97; exec comm, Homer S Brown Law Assn, 1980-97; vice pres, bd of dir, Neighborhood Legal Serv Assn, 1986-88; pres-elect, 1987-88, Penn State Alumni Assn; president 1989-91; bd of dir, Greater Pittsburgh YMCA, 1987-; mem, Allegheny County Bar Assn, 1980-, Greater Pittsburgh Commn on Women, 1987-, Pennsylvania Bar Assn, 1988-, Pennsylvania Bar Assn House of Delegates, 1988-; member, Pennsylvania Commission on Crime and Delinquency. **CONTACT ADDRESS** 820 City-County Bldg, Pittsburgh, PA, 15219.

BALDWIN, DONALD E.
PERSONAL Born 07/24/1936, Hardin, MT, m, 1960, 5 children **DISCIPLINE** THEOLOGY **EDUCATION** Univ Calif, BA, 62; Fuller Theology Sem, M.Div, 66; Univ Colo, MA, 72; Univ Mo, PhD, 78. **CAREER** Asst prof, Evangel Univ, 66-77; teaching fel, Univ Mo, 71-73; adj prof, Fuller Sem, 82; adj prof, Center Theological Studies, 85; vis prof, Continental Sem, 90. **HONORS AND AWARDS** Nat Teaching Fel, Univ Mo; Teaching Award, Nat Science Found; Fuller Sem Auxillary Award; Prof of the Year. **MEMBERSHIPS** APA; Int Berkley Society; Society of Christian Philos. **RESEARCH** Philosophy of religion; ethics. **SELECTED PUBLICATIONS** Auth, Introduction to Philosophy; coauth, The Complete Biblical Library; auth, Power, Ethics and Team Building; auth, Leadership and Team Building. **CONTACT ADDRESS** Vanguard Univ of Southern Calif, 55 Fair Dr, Costa Mesa, CA, 92626. **EMAIL** dbaldwin@sccu.edu

BALDWIN, FLETCHER N., JR.
DISCIPLINE LAW **EDUCATION** Univ Ga, AB, JD; Univ Ill, LLM; Yale Univ, LLM. **CAREER** Prof, Univ Fla, 62-. **HONORS AND AWARDS** Cofounder and lect, Human Rights Peace Inst, Makerere Univ; Cofounder and dir, Ctr Intl Financial Crimes Stud. **MEMBERSHIPS** Ga Bar; Amer Law Inst; Order of the Coif; Phi Beta Kappa; Phi Kappa Phi. **RESEARCH** Constitutional law, political and civil rights, criminal procedure, international financial crimes. **SELECTED PUBLICATIONS** Coauth, Money Laundering, Asset Forfeiture and Intl Financial Crimes. **CONTACT ADDRESS** School of Law, Univ of Florida, PO Box 117625, Gainesville, FL, 32611-7625. **EMAIL** baldwin.f@law.ufl.edu

BALDWIN, GORDON BREWSTER
PERSONAL Born 09/03/1929, Binghamton, NY, m, 1958, 2 children **DISCIPLINE** LAW **EDUCATION** Haverford Col, BA, 50; Cornell Univ, LLB, 53. **CAREER** Pvt pract law, Rochester, NY, 53; lawyer int law, Judge Advocate Gen Sch, US Army, 54-57; from asst prof to assoc prof law, 57-64, assoc dean law sch, 60-63 & 68-70, Prof Law, Univ Wis-Madison, 64-, Consult, US Naval War Col, 60-65, vis prof int law, 63-64; vis prof law, Ain Shams Univ, Cairo, 66-67 & Tehran Univ, Iran, 70-71; lectr, US Dept State Cult Affairs Prog, Cyprus & Iran, 69; dir, Off Educ Prog, Univ Wis, 71-; mem adv screening comt law, Fulbright-Hays Prog, 72-75. **MEMBERSHIPS** Am Bar Asn; Am Law Sch Asn; Am Soc Int Law. **RESEARCH** Constitutional, international and military law. **SELECTED PUBLICATIONS** Auth, Justice Fortas on dissent, Wis Law Rev, 69; Administration of justice by laymen in Iran, World Asn Judges, 72; The Iranian legal system, Int Lawyer, 73; The foreign affairs advice privilege, Wis Law Rev, 76. **CONTACT ADDRESS** Law Sch, Univ of Wis, 975 Bascom Mall, Madison, WI, 53706-1301. **EMAIL** gbaldwin@facstaff.wisc.edu

BALDWIN, JOHN R.
DISCIPLINE COMMUNICATION; RELIGIOUS STUDIES **EDUCATION** Abilene Christian Univ, Masters, 91; Ariz State Univ, PhD, 94. **CAREER** Asst prof, Ill State Univ, 94-. **HONORS AND AWARDS** Ralph E. Cooley Award, top intercultural paper, nat conf of the Speech Commun Assn. **MEMBERSHIPS** Nat Commun Assn, Cent States Commun Assn, Int Network on Personal Rels, Soc for Int Educ, Training and Res. **RESEARCH** Intergroup/Intercultural commun; relationships; issues of tolerance. **SELECTED PUBLICATIONS** Co-auth, An African American communication perspective, Intercultural communication: A reader, Wadsworth, 7th ed, 140-147, 94; co-auth, Definitions of culture: Conceptualizations from five disciplines, Urban Studies Ctr, Ariz State Univ, 94; auth, Lost and Found: Ethics in intercultural/interethnic communication studies, Seeking understanding of communication, language and gender, CyberSpace, 94; co-auth, The layered perspective of cultural (in)tolerance(s): The roots of a multidisciplinary approach, Intercultural Communication Theory, Sage, 59-90, 95; Book review, Understudied relationships: Off the beaten track, ISSPR Bulletin: Official News Journal of the International Society for the Study of Personal Relationships, 16-18, 96; co-auth, An African American Communication Perspective, Intercultural communication: A reader, Wadsworth, 8th ed, 147-154, 97; co-auth, Family culture and relationship differences as a source of intercultural communication, Readings in cultural contexts, Mayfield, 335-344, 98; co-auth, Layers and holograms: A new look at prejudice, Communication of Prejudice, Sage, 57-84, 98; Auth, Tolerancee/intolerance: A historical and multidisciplinary view of prejudice, Communication of Prejudice, Sage, 24-56, 98. **CONTACT ADDRESS** Dept of Commun, Illinois State Univ, Ill State Univ, PO Box 4480, Normal, IL, 61790-4480. **EMAIL** jrbaldw@ilstu.edu

BALDWIN, LEWIS V.
PERSONAL Born 09/17/1949, Camden, Alabama, m, 1979 **DISCIPLINE** THEOLOGY **EDUCATION** Talladega College, BA, history, 1971; Colgate-Rochester, Bexley Hall, Crozer Seminary, MA, black church studies, 1973, MDiv, theology, 1975; Northwestern University, PhD, history of Christianity, 1980. **CAREER** Wooster College, visiting assistant professor of religion, 1981-92; Colgate University, assistant professor of philosophy and religion, 1982-84, visiting assistant professor of church history, 1983-84, Colgate-Rochester Divinity School; Vanderbilt University, assistant professor of religious studies, 1984-90, associate professor, 1991-. **HONORS AND AWARDS** US Jaycees, Outstanding Young Man of America, 1975, 1980, 1985, 1990; American Theological Library Association, Book Award, 1981; Mid-West Publishers' Association, MBA Book Award, 1992. **MEMBERSHIPS** Society for the Study of Black Religion, 1981-; American Academy of Religion, 1981-; American Society of Church History, 1981-; NAACP, 1980-; Southern Christian Leadership Conference, financial supporter, 1986-. **SELECTED PUBLICATIONS** Books published: Freedom is Never Free: A Biographical Profile of E D Nixon Sr, 1992; To Make the Wounded Whole: The Cultural Legacy of M L King Jr, 1992; There is a Balm in Gilead: The Cultural Roots of M L King Jr, 1991; The Mark of a Man: Peter Spencer and the African Union Methodist Tradition, 1987; Invisible Strands in African Methodism: The AUMP and UAME Churches, 1805-1980, 1983; Toward the Beloved Community: Martin Luther King Jr and South Africa, 1995. **CONTACT ADDRESS** Vanderbilt Univ, Garland Hall, Rm 305, 21st Ave S, Nashville, TN, 37235.

BALESTRA, DOMINIC JOSEPH
PERSONAL Born 05/21/1947, Philadelphia, PA, m, 1974, 3 children **DISCIPLINE** PHILOSOPHY OF SCIENCE, CLASSICAL MODERN PHILOSOPHY **EDUCATION** Saint Francis Col, BS, 68; Saint Louis Univ, PhD, 77. **CAREER** Instr, 75-76, asst prof, 76-82, asst chmn, 79-82, assoc prof philos, ch dept philos, 89-95, pres fac sen, 92-94, prof philos, 98, Fordham Univ, 82-, asst dir honors prog, Saint Louis Univ, 73-75, lectr philos, 73-75; bd gov, Manchester Col, Oxford Univ, 93-96; ed consult, Thought. **HONORS AND AWARDS** Phi Beta Kappa; Sigma Xi. **MEMBERSHIPS** Am Cath Philos Asn, Treas; Am Philos Asn. **RESEARCH** Rationality and historicity of the scientific enterprise; classical modern philosophy; Piaget's genetic epistemology. **SELECTED PUBLICATIONS** Auth, The centrality of perception: A phenomenol'l perspective in Leibniz, Dialogue, 10/76; Non-falsifiability: An inductivist perspective, Int Logic Rev, 12/79; The mind of Piaget: Its philosophical roots, Thought, 12/80; Dueling Ambitions, Franklin Bacon: The Temper of a Man, Fordham Univ, 93; Galileo's Unfinished Case and Its Cartesian Product: Method, History, and Rationality, Intl Philos Quart, 94; Rev of F Wormald, Francis Bacon: History, Politics, and Science, 1561-1626, Sixteenth Century J, 95; Rev of L Lampert, Nietzsche and Modern Times: A Study of Bacon, Descartes, and Nietzsche, Intl Philos Quart, 97; Science and Religion, Philosophy of Religion: A Guide to the Subject, O P London, 98; At the Origins of Modern Science: Demythologizing Pythagoreanism, The Modern Schoolman, 98. **CONTACT ADDRESS** Dept of Philosophy, Fordham Univ, 501 E Fordham Rd, Bronx, NY, 10458-5191. **EMAIL** Balestra@murray.fordham.edu

BALL, WILLIAM BATTEN
PERSONAL Born 08/28/1928, San Antonio, TX, m, 1956 **DISCIPLINE** LAW **EDUCATION** Woodrow Wilson Jr Coll, Chicago IL, 1944-45; Roosevelt Univ, Chicago IL, BS, Commerce, 1955, MBA, 1960; Chicago Kent Coll of Law of IL Inst of Technology, Chicago IL, JD, 1968. **CAREER** IRS, revenue officer 1955-57; Supreme Life Insurance Co, accountant, jr exec 1957-59; State of IL Dept of Labor, auditor 1959; IRS, agent 1959-67, appellate appeals officer 1967-86; management coordinator, 1972-73; Attorney, private practice, 1986-. **HONORS AND AWARDS** Various Awards & Honors, BSA; Outstanding Performance Award, IRS; master's thesis, "Insurance Co Annual Statement Preparation/Instructions," Roosevelt Univ, 1960. **MEMBERSHIPS** Member, Chicago & Cook Co Bar Assoc, IL State Bar Assn, Amer Bar Assn, Natl Bar Assn; chmn admin bd St Mark United Meth Ch 1973-77; troop committeeman BSA; member Order of the Arrow Natl Fraternity of Scout Honor Campers; member Order of Brotherhood; life member, Kappa Alpha Psi Fraternity Inc; member, bd of dir, Community Mental Health Council, 1982-87; Chicago Board of Education, mem of: Westcott Local School Council, 1989-93, chairman, Bylaws Committee, Subdistrict 8 Council Representative, 1989-93. **CONTACT ADDRESS** 8355 S Perry Ave, Chicago, IL, 60620.

BALLARD, HAROLD WAYNE, JR.
PERSONAL Born 09/16/1963, Wooster, OH, m, 1985, 2 children **DISCIPLINE** THEOLOGY **EDUCATION** Okla Baptist Univ, BA, 85; Golden Gate Baptist Theol Sem, MDiv, 90; S Baptist Theol Sem, PhD, 95. **CAREER** Instr, S Baptist Theol Sem, 94; instr, Boyce Bible Col, 95-97; asst prof Relig, Campbell Univ, 97-. **HONORS AND AWARDS** Outstanding Young Men of Am, 96, 98. **MEMBERSHIPS** Soc Bibl Lit; Nat Asn Baptist Prof Relig; Am Acad Relig. **RESEARCH** Psalms and wisdom literature; Hebrew Bible. **SELECTED PUBLICATIONS** Auth, The Divine Warrior Motif in the Psalms, 98. **CONTACT ADDRESS** PO Box 603, Buies Creek, NC, 27506. **EMAIL** ballard@mailcenter.campbell.edu

BALLENTINE, KRIM M.
PERSONAL Born 10/22/1936, St. Louis, MO, m, 1979, 1 child **DISCIPLINE** CRIMINAL LAW **EDUCATION** Wayne State Univ **CAREER** US Marshals Serv, Chief Deputy, 66-95; Icop Investigations, O/O, 95-98; Virgin Is Police Dept, Asst Commish, 98-. **HONORS AND AWARDS** Rotary Paul Harris Fel, Mark Twain Society, Hon Member **MEMBERSHIPS** GSA, DAV, ROA, NOBLE, IACP, IALEIA, FBI-NA, MOPOA, APA. **RESEARCH** Racism; Philosophy **SELECTED PUBLICATIONS** Auth, Krim's Simplistic Philosophies, Vantage Press NY, 88; Virgin Is Bus Jour, columnist, 88-89; WVWI Radio, host Niteline, 85-87. **CONTACT ADDRESS** Virgin Islands Police Dept, PO Box 305396, St Thomas, VI, 00803. **EMAIL** krimicop@islands.vi

BALMER, RANDALL
PERSONAL Born 10/22/1954, Chicago, IL, m, 1998, 3 children **DISCIPLINE** RELIGION **EDUCATION** Princeton

Univ, PhD 85. **CAREER** Columbia Univ, asst prof, assoc prof, assoc prof Barnard, prof Barnard, 85 to 94- **HONORS AND AWARDS** Sidney E Mead Prize; Nominated for Emmy Awd Acad Tele Arts and Sciences, 93-94. **MEMBERSHIPS** AAR; ATAS; ASCH. **RESEARCH** Evangelicalism; Acadian History and Culture. **SELECTED PUBLICATIONS** Auth, Grant Us Courage: Travels Along the Mainland of American Protestantism, NY Oxford Univ Press, 96; The Presbyterians, coauth, Denominations in Amer Series, ed Henry Warner Bowden, NY and Westport CT, Greenwood Press, 93, pbk 94; Mine Eyes Have Seen the Glory: A Journey into the Evangelical Subculture in America, NY, Oxford Univ Press, 89, expanded 93, 3rd ed 99; Modern Christian Revivals, coed, Urbana and Chicago, Univ IL Press, 93; In the Beginning: The Creationist Controversy, writer and presenter for PBS, produced by WTTW-Television, Chicago, produced by Kay Weibel, dir by Jack Ginay; Crusade: The Life of Billy Graham, exec prod, writer and presenter for PBS, produced by WTTW-Television, Chicago and Cutting Edge Prod, London, dir by Julian Norridge, recut for broadcast in A&E Biography Series, 95; Mine Eyes Have Seen the Glory, writer and presenter for PBS, Prod by WTTW-Television, Chicago and Isis Prod, London, dir by Julie Norridge. **CONTACT ADDRESS** Dept of Religion, Columbia Univ, 3009 Broadway, New York, NY, 10027-6598. **EMAIL** rb281@columbia.edu

BANCHETTI-ROBINO, MARINA P.
PERSONAL Born 11/07/1963, Montevideo, Uruguay **DISCIPLINE** PHILOSOPHY **EDUCATION** Univ Miami, BA, 85; MA, 90; PhD, 91. **CAREER** Adj prof, Fla A&M Univ, 91-93; vis asst prof, 93-95; asst prof, 95-, Fla Atlantic Univ. **HONORS AND AWARDS** NSF travel grant 10th Intl Cong of Logic, Methodology and Philos of Sci, presentation of lect; Col Res Yr, 97-98, asst prof. **MEMBERSHIPS** Intl Asn Philos & Lit; Philos of Sci Asn; Husserl Cir; Am Philos Asn; So Soc Philos and Psych, Fla Philos Asn. **RESEARCH** Phenomenology; philosophy of science; philosophy of language, philosophy of mind. **SELECTED PUBLICATIONS** "Follesdal on the Notion of the Noema," in Husserl Stud, 93; "On the Use of Fictional Works in Eng Ethics Courses," APA Newsl on Tchg Philos, 96; "Husserl's Theory of Language as Calculus Ratiocinator," Synthese, 97; author, "A Wittgensteinian Approach to Scientific Instrumentalism," Role of Pragmatics in Contemporary Philosophy, Austrian Ludwig Wittgenstein Society, 97. **CONTACT ADDRESS** Dept of Philosophy, Florida Atlantic Univ, PO Box 3091, Boca Raton, FL, 33431-0991. **EMAIL** banchett@fau.edu

BANDMAN, BERTRAM
PERSONAL m **DISCIPLINE** BIOETHICS, PHILOSOPHY OF LAW, PHILOSOPHY OF RELIGION **EDUCATION** Columbia Univ, BS, MA, PhD. **CAREER** Prof, Long Island Univ; exec comt, Conf on Methods in Philos and the Sci. **HONORS AND AWARDS** Trustee Award, Long Island Univ; Human Rights fel, Columbia Univ. **RESEARCH** Children's rights; the moral development of health care providers. **SELECTED PUBLICATIONS** Auth, The Child's Right to Inquire, in Thinking Children and Education, Kendall/Hunt, 93; The Adolescent's Right to Freedom, Care and Enlightenment, in Thinking Children and Education, Kendall/Hunt, 93; coauth, Nursing Ethics Through The Life Span, Appelton-Lange, 95; Critical Thinking, Appelton-Lange, 95; coed, Philosophical Essays on Teaching, Lippincott, 69; Philosophical Essays on Curriculum, Lippincott, 69; Bioethics and Human Rights: A Reader for Health Professionals, Little Brown, 78. **CONTACT ADDRESS** Long Island Univ, Brooklyn, NY, 11201-8423. **EMAIL** sferguso@hornet.liunet.edu

BANDSTRA, BARRY L.
PERSONAL Born 04/05/1951, Chicago, IL, m, 1971, 3 children **DISCIPLINE** RELIGIOUS STUDIES **EDUCATION** Yale Univ, PhD, 82. **CAREER** Prof, 83-. **HONORS AND AWARDS** Mellon Fel, 85-86. **MEMBERSHIPS** Soc of Bibl Lit; Chicago Soc for Bibl Res. **RESEARCH** Hebrew grammar and syntax. **SELECTED PUBLICATIONS** Auth, Reading the Old Testament, 95. **CONTACT ADDRESS** Dept of Religion, Hope Col, 125 E 10th St, Holland, MI, 49423. **EMAIL** bandstra@hope.edu

BANGERT, MARK PAUL
DISCIPLINE PASTORAL THEOLOGY; WORSHIP AND MUSIC **EDUCATION** Concordia Sem; Univ Minn, PhD. **CAREER** John H. Tietjen prof; dir, Pub events at LSTC; dir, LSTC Chorus, 83-93; dir, Adult Mus, St. Luke Lutheran Church. **HONORS AND AWARDS** Bd mem, Paul Manz Inst. **MEMBERSHIPS** Mem, intl study group on Bach res. **SELECTED PUBLICATIONS** Pub(s), widely in the area of church music. **CONTACT ADDRESS** Dept of Pastoral Theology, Worship and Music, Lutheran Sch of Theol, 1100 E 55th St, Chicago, IL, 60615. **EMAIL** mbangert@lstc.edu

BANGS, CARL
PERSONAL Born 04/05/1922, Seattle, WA, m, 1942, 3 children **DISCIPLINE** THEOLOGY **EDUCATION** Pasadena Col, AB, 45; Nazarene Theol Sem, BD, 49; Univ Chicago, PhD(theol), 58. **CAREER** From asst prof to assoc prof relig & philos, Olivet Nazarene Col, 53-61; assoc prof, 61-66, PROF HIST OF THEOL, ST PAUL SCH THEOL, 66-, Kansas City Coun Higher Educ res grant, 63; Fulbright prof theol, State Univ Leiden, 68-69, guest prof, 75. **HONORS AND AWARDS** Christian Res Found Prize, 62. **MEMBERSHIPS** Am Soc Church Hist (pres, 72); Am Theol Soc (pres Midwest Div, 66-67); Am Soc Reformation Res; Dutch Church Hist Soc. **RESEARCH** Dutch Reformation; Arminianism; Mennonite history. **SELECTED PUBLICATIONS** Auth, The Communist Encounter, Beacon Hill, 63; De herstructering van de theologische opleiding, Theol en Praktijk, 7/69; Arminius: A Study in the Dutch Reformation, 71; All the Best Bishoprics and Deaneries: The Enigma of Arminian politics, Church Hist, 3/73; God, Creation, and Providence in the Thought of Jacob Arminius-Sources and Directions of Scholastic Protestantism in the Era of Early Orthodoxy, with R. A. Muller, Church History, Vol 66, 97. **CONTACT ADDRESS** St Paul Sch of Theol, 5123 Truman Rd, Kansas City, MO, 63127.

BANKS, SHARON P.
PERSONAL Born 09/21/1942, Washington, DC **DISCIPLINE** LAW **EDUCATION** Morgan State Coll, BA 1964; Howard Univ Law Sch, JD 1967. **CAREER** Neighborhood Legal Serv Program, 1967-72; Private Practice, attorney 1972-; Howard Univ, part-time teacher 1969-72, full-time teacher 1972-. **MEMBERSHIPS** Mem Natl, Amer, DC Bar Assns; Howard Univ Law Alumni Assn; bd dir DC ACIU; Kappa Beta Pi Legal Sor. **CONTACT ADDRESS** Dept of Pol Sci, Howard Univ, 112 Douglass Hall, Washington, DC, 20001.

BANNAN, JOHN F.
DISCIPLINE PHILOSOPHY **EDUCATION** Catholic Univ America, AB, MA; Univ Louvain, Belgium, PhD. **CAREER** Prof, Loyola Univ Chicago, 57-; chp & dir, grad Stud; fac, New Rochelle Col, NY. **RESEARCH** Descartes; French phenomenology; Merleau-Ponty; Sartre; Levi-Strauss. **SELECTED PUBLICATIONS** Auth, Among his publications are The Philosophy of Merleau-Ponty,Harcourt, Brace, & World, 67; coauth, Law, Morality, and Vietnam: The Peace Militants and the Courts, Ind UP, 74. **CONTACT ADDRESS** Dept of Philosophy, Loyola Univ, Chicago, 820 N. Michigan Ave., Chicago, IL, 60611.

BAR-ON, DORIT
PERSONAL Tel Aviv, Israel, m, 1988, 1 child **DISCIPLINE** PHILOSOPHY **EDUCATION** Tel Aviv Univ, BA, 79; UCLA, MA, 80, PhD, 87. **CAREER** Asst prof, Univ Rochester, 87-89; vis prof, 88, asst prof, 89-94, assoc prf, 94-, Univ North Carolina, Chapel Hill; vis scholar, Tel Aviv Univ, 93. **HONORS AND AWARDS** Cum Laude, 79; NEH stipend, 92; Tanner Award for Excellence in Undergrad Tchg, 94; Max Chapman Fac Fel, 95; ACLS Grant, 96; Cognitive Sci Course Dev grant, 97; res and study assignment, 97. **MEMBERSHIPS** APA. **RESEARCH** Philosophy of mind; philosophy of language and of linguistics; twentieth-century analytic philosophy, especially Quine, Davidson, Dummett and Wittgenstein. **SELECTED PUBLICATIONS** Auth, Conceptual Relativism and Translation, in Preyer, ed, Language, Mind, and Epistemology, Kluwer, 94; auth, Indeterminacy of Translation: Theory and Practice, Philos and Phenomenol Res, 95; auth, Reconstructing Meaning: Grice and the Naturalization of Semantics, Pacific Philos Quart, 95; auth, Anti-Realism and Speaker Knowledge, Synthese, 96; auth, Natural Semantic Facts--Between Eliminativism and Hyper-Realism, in Jutronic, ed, The Maribor Papers in Naturalized Semantics, 97. **CONTACT ADDRESS** Philosophy Dept, Univ of No Carolina, Caldwell Hall CB 3125, Chapel Hill, NC, 27599-3125. **EMAIL** dbaron@email.unc.edu

BARAD, JUDITH
PERSONAL Born 02/09/1949, Chicago, IL, m, 1995, 1 child **DISCIPLINE** PHILOSOPHY **EDUCATION** Oakton Community Col, AA, 78; Loyola Univ of Chicago, BA, 80; Northwestern Univ, MA, 82; Northwestern Univ, PhD, 84. **CAREER** Part-time adjunct prof, Oakton Community Col, 84-85; part-time instr, Barat Col, 84-85; asst prof, 85-89, assoc prof, fall 89-94, full prof, 94, acting chair, fall 93-spring 94, chair, 94-, Ind State Univ. **HONORS AND AWARDS** John B. Lavezzorio Scholar, 78-80; nominee for Danforth fel, 79; Northwestern Scholar, 80; Teaching asst, 81-84; Nat Endow for the Humanities grant, Univ Notre Dame, 85; Ind State Univ res grant, 88; Excellence in educ award, Blue Key Nat Honor Fraternity, apr, 96; individual facul develop grant, Ind State Univ, may, 96; proposal incentive fund award, 96. **MEMBERSHIPS** Amer Cath Philos Asn; Amer Philos Asn; Intl Thomas Aquinas Soc; Soc for Medieval and Renaissance Philos; Ind Philos Asn; Intl Soc for Neoplatonic Studies. **RESEARCH** Thomas Aquinas; Medieval Philosophy; Philosophy of Relion; Ethics; Metaphysics **SELECTED PUBLICATIONS** Auth, Aquinas on the Role of Emotion in Moral Judgment and Activity, Moral and Polit Philos in the Middle Ages, NY, LEGAS, 95; auth, Tension in Aquinas Accounts Between the Ethical and Ontological Status of Animals, Greek and Medieval Studies in Honor of Leo Sweeney, NY, Peter Lang Publ Co, 94; auth, Aquinas and Evolution: A Compatible Duo, Medievalia, no 13, 1-11, apr, 93. **CONTACT ADDRESS** Philosophy Dept., Indiana State Univ, Terre Haute, IN, 47809. **EMAIL** pibarad@root.indstate.edu

BARANOWSKI, SHELLEY
PERSONAL Born 06/14/1946, Columbus, OH, m, 1969 **DISCIPLINE** RELIGION **EDUCATION** Wells Col, BA, 68; Princeton Univ, MA, 78; Princeton Univ, PhD, 80. **CAREER** Part-time positions, Princeton Univ, Douglass Col, Ohio State Univ, 80-84; vis asst prof, Kenyon Col, 85-89; asst prof hist, Univ Akron, 89-91; assoc prof hist, Univ Akron, 91-95; prof hist, Univ Akron, 95-. **HONORS AND AWARDS** ACLS Grant-in-Aid; Fel for Independent Study and Res, Nat Endowment for the Humanities; Fulbright-Hays Fel; DAAD Fel. **MEMBERSHIPS** AHA; German Studies Asn; Conf Group on Central European Hist; German Hist Soc; Ohio Acad of Hist. **RESEARCH** Twentieth century Germany; social and religious history. **SELECTED PUBLICATIONS** Auth, The Confessing Church, Conservative Elites and the Nazi State, Edwin Mellen Press, 86; auth, "Consent and Dissent: The Confessing Church and Conservative Oppositions to National Socialism", in Journal of Modern History 59 no.1, 87; auth, "Continuity and Contingency: Agrarian Elites, Conservative Institutions and East Elbia in Modern German History", in Social History 12 no. 3, 97; auth, "The Sanctity of Rural Life: Protestantism, Agrarian Politics and the Rise of Nazism in Pomerania during the Weimar Republic", in German History 9 no. 1, 91; auth, "Convergence on the Right: Agrarian Elite Radicalism and Nazi Populism in Pomerania, 1928-33", in Between Reform, Reaction, and Resistance: Essays in the History of German Conservatism, 1789-1945, Berg Publishers, 93; auth, The Sanctity of Rural Life. Nobility, Protestantism, and Nazism in Weimar Prussia, Oxford Univ Press, 95; auth, "East Elbian Landed Elites and Germany's Turn to Fascism: The Sonderweg Controversy Revisited", in European History Quart 26 no. 2, 96; auth, "Conservative Antisemitism from Weimar to the Third Reich", in German Studies Review 19 no. 3, 96. **CONTACT ADDRESS** Department of Akron, Univ of Akron, Akron, OH, 44325-1902. **EMAIL** savant@ibm.net

BARASH, CAROL ISAACSON
PERSONAL Born 10/22/1955, Detroit, MI, m, 1986, 2 children **DISCIPLINE** PHILOSOPHY **EDUCATION** Univ of Chicago, PhD. **CAREER** Founder, prin, Genetics, Ethics & Policy Consulting, 94- . **HONORS AND AWARDS** MCHB grant; SPRANS grant, Triggering Need to Know: Barriers to Learning Genetics, 97- . **MEMBERSHIPS** APA. **RESEARCH** Medical genetics; education. **SELECTED PUBLICATIONS** Auth, Consultation on Human Rights and Bioethics, Genetic Resource, 94; auth, Genetic Discrimination and What Consumers Can Do to Protect Themselves, Genetic Connections, Sonters Publ INK, 95; auth, Facing History and Ourselves Teaches ELSI Issues as Civics, Genetic Resource, 95; auth, Commentary: Genetic Testing in Children and Adolescents: Parental Authority, The Rights of Children and the Duties of Geneticists, Univ Chicago Law School Roundtable J, 96; auth,Genetic Privacy or Piracy, Global Insights, 96; auth, What is a Cost? What is a Benefit? Genetic Resource, 97; auth, The Need for Moral Leadership in Applying HGP Advances, 97; auth, Genetic Screening Under Ethically Defensible Conditions, conf proc, Int Bioethics Assn, 97. **CONTACT ADDRESS** 317 Lamartine St, Boston, MA, 02130. **EMAIL** cbarash@tiac.net

BARBEE, LLOYD AUGUSTUS
PERSONAL Born 08/17/1925, Memphis, TN, d **DISCIPLINE** LAW **EDUCATION** LeMoyne Coll, BA 1949; Univ of WI Madison, JD 1956. **CAREER** Industrial Commn of WI UC Dept, law examiner I 1957-62; Gov's Comm on Human Rights, legal consul 1959; NAACP, pres 1962-64; Milwaukee United Sch Integration Comm, chmn 1964; WI Legislature, state representative 1965-77; Univ of Wisconsin, Law Sch, teacher 1968-69, 1972; Univ of Wisconsin at Milwaukee, adjunct prof 1976-88; Bronx Community Coll, adjunct prof, 1990-92; private practice, Attorney, 1956-. **HONORS AND AWARDS** Milwaukee Man of the Yr Alpha Phi Alpha Frat Inc 1965; Medgar Evers Awd Milwaukee Br NAACP 1969; Outstanding & Continuing Contrib to Milwaukee Black Business Comm 1976; Disting Civil Serv Milwaukee Frontiers 1978; Lawyer Scholar Pub Serv Milwaukee Theological Inst 1978; Serv in Education Law & Govern St Mark AME Church 1979; Outstanding Serv as Law Sch Tchr Univ WI Madison Law Sch 1984; Univ of WI at Milwaukee, Coll of Letters & Sci Amer Studies Dept Faculty Award; Madison West HS, award for outstanding services toward improving civil rights in WI 1986; Wisconsin Black Political and Economic Development Council Award, 1987; Rufus King Education Award, 1989; Wisconsin Assn of Minority Attorneys Award, 1993; Milwaukee Homeless Project Inc, Award, 1993; Milwaukee Times, Black Excellence Award, 1994; Amer Civil Liberties Union, Wisconsin, Lifetime Civil Liberties Achievement Award, 1995; Annual James H Baker Award, 1996; Malcolm X Commemoration Mount Freedom Award, 1997; Dedication of West Barbee St, Milwaukee, WI; Mayor John Norquist Proclamation of Lloyd A Barbee Day, Sept 6, 1997. **MEMBERSHIPS** Mem State Bar of WI 1956-; chmn Enrolled Bills comm 1965-66; mem Comm on Joint Finance 1965-73; chmn Assembly Judiciary Comm 1973-77; mem Comm on Transportation 1969-77; pres/pres emeritus WI Black Lawyers Assn 1965-80; chmn WI Black Elected & Apptd Officials 1972-76; minister Political Empowerment Comm Natl Black Assembly 1973-75; Milwaukee Symphony Orchestra, bd of dirs, 1994-96; Natl Bar Assn; Wisconsin

Bar Assn; American Bar Assn. **CONTACT ADDRESS** 231 W Wisconsin Ave, Milwaukee, WI, 53203.

BARBIERI, WILLIAM A., JR.
PERSONAL Born 06/30/1965, Concord, MA, m **DISCIPLINE** ETHICS; RELIGIOUS STUDIES **EDUCATION** Yale Grad Sch, PhD, 92. **CAREER** Vis Assoc Prof, Holy Cross, 92-93; Vis Prof, Hebrew Univ of Jerusalem, 93-94; Asst Prof, Cath Univ Am, 94-. **HONORS AND AWARDS** Humboldt Fel, 99. **MEMBERSHIPS** Am Acad Relig. **RESEARCH** Ethics & political theory; comparative ethics. **SELECTED PUBLICATIONS** Auth, Ethics of Community: Citizenship & Group Rights in Germany, Duke, 98; Ethics and the Narrated Life, J Relig, 7/98. **CONTACT ADDRESS** School of Religious Studies, Catholic Univ of America, Washington, DC, 20064. **EMAIL** barbieri@cua.edu

BARBONE, STEVEN
PERSONAL Born 08/17/1960 **DISCIPLINE** PHILOSOPHY **EDUCATION** Marquette Univ, PhD, 97. **CAREER** Asst prof philos, San Diego State Univ, 97-. **HONORS AND AWARDS** Res grant, Marquette Univ, 92; Fulbright nominee, 93-94, 94-95; travel fel, 94-95, 95-96; NEH publ award, 95; Charles M Ross Trust fel award, 96. **MEMBERSHIPS** APA; Phi Sigma Tau; Soc for Philos of Sex and Love, N Am Spinoza Soc; AAUP; Soc for Lesbian and Gay Philos; Am Soc of Aesthet; Int Soc of Aesthet. **SELECTED PUBLICATIONS** Auth, Virtue and Sociality in Spinoza, Ivyun, 93; auth, Plato on the Beautiful, Lyceum V, 93; auth, Frugalitas in St. Augustine, Augustiniana, 94; coauth, Spinoza and the Problem of Suicide, Int Philos Quart, 94; coauth, Coming Out, Being Out, and Acts of Virtue, Jour of Homosexuality, 94; auth, Nothingness and Sartre's Fundamental Project, Philos Today, 94; auth, The Is/Ought Question in Hume, Indian Philos Quart, 94; auth, Infinity in Descartes, Philos Inquiry, 95; introd and notes in, Spinoza, Baruch. The Letters, Hackett, 95; coauth, Spinoza and Human Sexuality, and, Hatching Your Genes Before They're Counted, in Soble, ed, Sex, Love, & Friendship, Rodopi, 96; auth, Natural Law in William Ockham, Int Stud in Philos, 96; auth, Schlick on Aesthetics, Indian Philos Quart, 97. **CONTACT ADDRESS** Dept of Philosophy, San Diego State Univ, 5500 Campanile Dr, San Diego, CA, 92182. **EMAIL** barbone@rohan.edsu.edu

BARBOUR, HUGH
PERSONAL Born 08/07/1921, Peking, China, m, 1959, 3 children **DISCIPLINE** CHURCH HISTORY **EDUCATION** Harbard Univ, AB, 42; Union Theol Sem, NY, BD, 45; Yale Univ, PhD(relig), 52. **CAREER** Pastor, Congregational Church, Coventry, CT, 45-47; instr Bible & relig, Syracuse Univ, 47-49; instr Bible, Wellesley Col, 50-53; from asst prof to assoc prof relig, 53-67, PROF RELIG, EARLHAM COL, 67-, Mem gov bd, Nat Coun Churches, 72-. **MEMBERSHIPS** Soc Bibl Theol; Soc Bibl Lit. **RESEARCH** Theological writings of William Penn. **SELECTED PUBLICATIONS** Auth, The Quakers in Puritan England, Yale Univ, 64; Step by Step in Reading the Old Testament, Asn Press, 64; Programmed teaching for Old Testament, Relig Educ, 11-12/67; Protestant Quakerism, 71 & The God of peace, 72, Quaker Relig Thought; co-ed, Early Quaker Writings, 1650-1700, Eerdmans, 73; Margaret Fell and the Rise of Quakerism, with B. Y. Kunze, J of Relig, Vol 76, 96; Gentle Invaders-Quaker Women Educators and Racial Issues During the Civil-War and Reconstrution, with L. B. Selleck, Church History, Vol 66, 97. **CONTACT ADDRESS** 1840 SW E St., Richmond, IN, 47374.

BARBOUR, IAN GRAEME
PERSONAL Born 11/05/1923, Peking, China, m, 1947, 4 children **DISCIPLINE** RELIGION, PHYSICS **EDUCATION** Swarthmore Col, BA, 43; Duke Univ, MA, 46; Univ Chicago, PhD(physics), 49; Yale Univ, BD, 56. **CAREER** Asst prof physics, Kalamazoo Col, 49-51, assoc prof & chmn dept, 51-53; Ford fel, Yale Univ, 53-54; from asst prof to assoc prof relig, 55-65, PROF RELIG & PHYSICS, CARLETON COL, 65-, Fels, Am Coun Learned Socs, 63-64, Guggenheim & Fulbright, 67-68, Nat Endowment Humanities, 76 77 & Nat Humanities Ctr, 80-81; Lilly vis prof, Purdue Univ, 73-74. **MEMBERSHIPS** Am Acad Relig; AAAS. **RESEARCH** Contemporary theology; philosophy of science. **SELECTED PUBLICATIONS** Auth, Issues in Science and Religion, Prentice-Hall, 66; ed, Science and Religion, 68 & auth, Science and Secularity: The Ethics of Technology, 70, Harper; ed, Earth Might be Fair, Prentice-Hall, 72; Western Man and Environmental Ethics, Addison-Wesley, 73; auth, Myths, models and paradigms, SCM, 73; Technology, Environment and Human Values, Praeger, 80; Experiencing and Interpreting Nature in Science and Religion, Zygon, Vol 29, 94; Response to Critiques of Religion in an Age of Science, Zygon, Vol 31, 96; Response to Critiques of Ethics in an Age of Technology, Zygon, Vol 31, 96. **CONTACT ADDRESS** Dept of Relig, Carleton Col, Northfield, MN, 55057.

BARBOUR, JOHN D.
PERSONAL Born 08/08/1951, Kalamazoo, MI, m, 1978, 2 children **DISCIPLINE** RELIGION **EDUCATION** Oberlin Coll, BA 73; Univ Chicago, PhD 81. **CAREER** St Olaf Col, asst prof, assoc prof, prof, dept ch, 82-98. **RESEARCH** Relig and Lit, autobiography, ethics. **SELECTED PUBLICATIONS** Tragedy as a Critique of Virtue: The Novel and Ethical Reflection, Chico CA, Scholars press, 84; The Conscience of the Autobiographer; Ethical and Religious Dimensions of Autobiography, London, Macmillan and NY, ST Martins Press, 92; Versions of Deconversion: Autobiography and the Loss of Faith, Charlottesville, Univ VA Press, 94. **CONTACT ADDRESS** Dept of Relig, St Olaf Col, Northfield, MN, 55057. **EMAIL** barbourj@stolaf.edu

BARKER, EVELYN M.
PERSONAL Born 02/16/1927, Franklin, MA, m, 1951, 2 children **DISCIPLINE** PHILOSOPHY **EDUCATION** Wheaton Coll, BA, 48; Vassar Coll, MA, 49; Harvard Univ, PhD, 56. **CAREER** Instr, Wells Coll, 50-51; lect, asst prof, Mount Holyoke Coll, 56-61; vis prof, Ohio Wesleyan Univ, 62-63; vis prof, McCoy Coll, Johns Hopkins, 64-65; vis prof, Univ Md Evening Coll, 65-66; lect, assoc prof, Emerita, Univ MD, Baltimore County, 66-. **HONORS AND AWARDS** Phi Beta Kappa. **MEMBERSHIPS** Am Philos Asn; Soc for Ancient Greek Philos. **RESEARCH** Aristotle; Personal Relations, Bioethics, Phenomenology. **SELECTED PUBLICATIONS** Auth, Aristotle's Logic: Techne of Episteme?, The Philos of Logos, 96; Socratic Intolerance and Aristotelian Toleration, Philos, Rel and the Question of Intolerance, 97. **CONTACT ADDRESS** 4003 Keswick Rd, Baltimore, MD, 21211. **EMAIL** Kesbarkers@aol.com

BARKER, JEFFREY
DISCIPLINE PHILOSOPHY **EDUCATION** CA St Univ, BA, 78; Purdue Univ, MA, 80, PhD 83 **CAREER** Chair & Prof, Albright Col **CONTACT ADDRESS** Dept of Philos, Albright Col, Reading, PA, 19612-5234.

BARKER, PETER
PERSONAL Born 11/27/1949 **DISCIPLINE** PHILOSOPHY **EDUCATION** Univ Oxford, Eng, BA, 71; SUNY, Buffalo, PhD, 75. **CAREER** Instr, 72-75, SUNY-Buf; asst prof, 75-81, assoc prof, 81-84, Memphis St Univ; dir, grad prog, sci & tech, 85-87, assoc prof, 84-95, Va Polytechnic Inst & St Univ; prof, 95-, chmn, 97-, hist of sci dept, Univ Okla. **HONORS AND AWARDS** NEH: Sum Sem Col Tchrs, 84, Div Res Conf Grants, 84 & 89, Interpretive Res, Hum, Sci & Tech, Res Grant 92-94; Natl Sci Found, res grant, 92-94; vis fel, 92-93 Centrum Phil und Wissenschaftstheorie, Univ Konstanz Germany; vis scholar, Ctr Appl Psychol, Memphis St Univ, 90. **MEMBERSHIPS** Hist of Sci Soc; Phil Sci Assn; APA; So Soc for Phil & Psych. **SELECTED PUBLICATIONS** Co-ed, After Einstein: Proceedings of the Memphis State Einstein Centenary Conference, Mem St Press, 81; coauth, Pierre Duhem: Historian and Philosopher of Science, Synthese 83; 90; co-ed, Revolution and Continuity: Essays in the History and Philosophy of Early Modern Science, Cath Univ Amer Press, 91; coauth, Distance and Velocity in Kepler's Astronomy, Annals of Sci 51, 94; coauth, The Role of Rothmann in the Dissolution of the Celestial Spheres, British J Hist of Sci 28, 95; auth, Understanding Change and Continuity: Transmission and Appropriation in Sixteenth Century Natural Philosophy, Tradition, Transmission, Transformation, Brill, 96; coauth, Kuhn's Mature Philosophy of Science and Cognitive Science, Phil Psych 9, 96; auth, Kepler's Epistemology, Method & Order in Renaissance Natural Phil, Kluwer, 97; auth, Kuhn and the Sociological Revolution, Configurations 6:21, 98; coauth, Kuhn's Theory of Scientific Revolutions and Cognitive Psychology, Phil Psych 11:5, 98; coauth Realism and Instrumentalism in Sixteenth Century Astronomy: A Reappraisal, Persp on Sci, 98; co-trs, Pierre Duhem: Essays in History and Philosophy of Science, 96. **CONTACT ADDRESS** Dept of History of Science, Univ of Oklahoma, 601 Elm, Rm 622, Norman, OK, 73019-0315. **EMAIL** BarkerP@ou.edu

BARKER, WILLIAM SHIRMER, II
DISCIPLINE CHURCH HISTORY **EDUCATION** Princeton Univ, BA, 56; Cornell Univ, MA, 59; Covenant Theol Sem, BD, 60; Vanderbilt Univ, PhD, 70. **CAREER** Instr, Covenant Col, 58-64; asst prof, 64-70; assoc prof, dean of fac, 70-72; assoc prof, dean of fac, Covenant Theol Sem, 72-77; assoc prof, pres, 77-84; prof, Westminster Theol Sem, 87-. **SELECTED PUBLICATIONS** Ed, Presbyterian Jour, 84-87; auth, Puritan Profiles: 54 Influential Puritans at the Time When the Westminster Confession of Faith Was Written; The Hemphill Case, Benjamin Franklin, and Subscription to the Westminster Confession, Amer Presbyterians, 91. **CONTACT ADDRESS** Westminister Theol Sem, PO Box 27009, Philadelphia, PA, 19118.

BARKSDALE, LEONARD N., III
PERSONAL Born 11/11/1948, Galveston, TX, m, 1974 **DISCIPLINE** LAW **EDUCATION** University of Houston, BA, 1971; Thurgood Marshall School of Law, JD, 1974. **CAREER** Legal Aid Society of Louisville, attorney, 1974; Houston Legal Foundation, attorney, 1975; Houston Community College, law instructor, 1975-85; private practice of law, senior attorney, 1976-; Fifth Ward Missionary Baptist Church, minister, 1992-; Fifth Ward Missionary Baptist Church, pastor, currently. **HONORS AND AWARDS** Boys Scouts of America, Eagle Scout, 1964; Reginald Heber Smith Fellow, 1974-75; legal intern, United States Judge Advocate Gen, Pentagon, Washington, DC, 1972; Boy Scouts of America, Leadership Award, 1987; Sigma Gamma Rho Sorority, Men on the Move in the 90's, 1992. **MEMBERSHIPS** State Bar of Texas, 1974-; The National Bar Association, 1975-; Houston Lawyers Association, secretary, 1975-; Omega Psi Phi, 1970-; Central High School Alumni Association, vice pres, 1988-; Phi Alpha Delta, 1974; NAACP, 1990-; Houston Habitat for Humanity, board of directors, 1988-92. **CONTACT ADDRESS** Senior Attorney, Barksdale, Ray, Elmore, Robinson-Wallace, Fitzgerald, 2626 S Loop W, Ste 330, Houston, TX, 77054.

BARLOW, BRIAN C.
PERSONAL Born 09/24/1956, Bedford, IN, m, 1978, 1 child **DISCIPLINE** RELIGION; THEOLOGY AND PERSONALITY; DIVINITY; THEOLOGY; ETHICS; PSYCHOLOGY; **EDUCATION** Emory Univ, PhD, 92; Anderson Univ, MDiv, MA, AB, 84, 83, 78 **CAREER** Asst prof Philos Relig, Brenau Univ; visiting instr relig, Emory Univ **HONORS AND AWARDS** Robert T Jones Scholar, 89-90; Hodges Award, 83 **MEMBERSHIPS** Amer Acad Relig; Amer Philos Assoc; Soren Kierkegaard Soc; Karl Barth Soc **RESEARCH** Soren Kierkegaard; Psychoanaysis; Karl Barth **SELECTED PUBLICATIONS** "Christian Conversion: A Developmental Interpretation of Autonomy and Surrender." Pastoral Psychol, 88 **CONTACT ADDRESS** 1634 Ponce De Leon Ave NE #101, Atlanta, GA, 30307. **EMAIL** bbarlow@lib.brenan.edu

BARLOW, J. STANLEY
PERSONAL Born 08/25/1924, Johnson City, TN, m, 1951, 4 children **DISCIPLINE** PHILOSOPHY, RELIGION AND PSYCHOLOGY **EDUCATION** Wheaton, AB, 47; Princeton Theol Sem, BD, 50; Univ of St. Andrews, Scotland, PhD, 61; Vanderbilt, 43, 44, Harvard, 59-60; Univ Mich, 62-64. **CAREER** Admin, 64-66, Univ Minn; relig, admin, 66-71, Columbia Univ; Phil, CUNY-Col Staten Island, 72-95. **HONORS AND AWARDS** Robinson fel, 50; Danforth CCW grant, 59; Mich Scholar in Higher Ed Admin, 62-64; Columbia Univ. Sem Assoc, Higher Ed, 73-. **MEMBERSHIPS** APA. **RESEARCH** Mythopoeia and rationality, religion and culture. **SELECTED PUBLICATIONS** Auth, The Fall into Consciousness, Fortress, 73. **CONTACT ADDRESS** 107 Gladwin Ave, Leonia, NJ, 07605. **EMAIL** JBarlow31Z@aol.com

BARLOW, PHILIP L.
DISCIPLINE THEOLOGY **EDUCATION** Weber State Col, BA, 75; MTS, 80, ThD, 88, Harvard Univ. **CAREER** Assoc Ed, Journ for the Scientific Study of Religion, 88-90; Asst Prof, 90-94, Assoc Prof, 94-, Chair, 97-, Hanover Col; Co-editor, Religion in North America, Electronic Cultural Atlas Initiative, 98-. **CONTACT ADDRESS** Dept of Theological Studies, Hanover Col, Box 108, Hanover, IN, 47243-0108. **EMAIL** barlow@hanover.edu

BARMORE, FRANK E.
PERSONAL Born 06/20/1938, Manhattan, KS, m, 1967, 2 children **DISCIPLINE** PHYSICS **EDUCATION** Washington State Univ, BS honors, 60; Univ Wisconsin Madison, PhD, 73. **CAREER** Assoc Prof, 78-, Univ Wisconsin La Crosse; Sp Sci, scientist, 77-78, York Univ Cen Research Experimental; Research Assoc, 76-77, Univ Calgary; Asst Prof, 74-76, Mid East Tech Univ Turkey; Proj Assoc, 73-74, Univ Wis Madison; Asst Prof, 70-73, Milton College; Teach Asst, 66, Univ Wis; Sr Tech, 61-62, Amer Geo Soc Greenland. **HONORS AND AWARDS** Phi Beta Kappa. **MEMBERSHIPS** AAAS; AAPT; AGU; HSS; NASS; OSA; SAH; WASAL; Sigma Xi. **RESEARCH** Astronomical and atmospheric spectroscopes, meteorological optics, archaeoastronomy & geography. **SELECTED PUBLICATIONS** Auth, Spatial Analysis, The Wisconsin Idea and the UW-System: The Use and Abuse of Dispersion Statistics, Wis Geographer, 96; auth, Center Here Center There Center Center Everywhere, The Geographic Center of Wisconsin and the USA: Concepts Comments and Misconceptions, Wis Geographer, 93, reprinted in Solstice: An Electronic J Geog and Mathematics, Inst Math Geog, Ann Arbor, MI, 94; auth, The Earth isn't Flat, And it isn't Round Either! Some Significant and Little Known Effects of the Earth's Ellipsoidal Shape. Wis Geog, 92, reprinted, Solstice, 93; Where are We? Comments on the Concept on the Center of Population, Wis Geog 91. **CONTACT ADDRESS** Physics Dept, Univ Wis La Crosse, Cowley Hall, La Crosse, WI, 54601. **EMAIL** barmore@mail.uwla.edu

BARNBAUM, DEBORAH
PERSONAL Born 04/22/1967, Los Angeles, CA **DISCIPLINE** PHILOSOPHY **EDUCATION** UCLA, BA; Univ of Mass, MA, PhD. **CAREER** Asst Prof, 96-, Kent State Univ. **MEMBERSHIPS** APA, BENO, Hastings Center. **RESEARCH** Biomedical ethics, research ethics, moral theory. **SELECTED PUBLICATIONS** Auth, The Harm of Disease and Disability, Bio Qtly; Why Taniogotehis are not Pets, Thinking, J of Philo for Children; Immortality, Early-Onset and Late-Onset Diseases, The Proceedings of the Ohio Philosophical Association. **CONTACT ADDRESS** Kent State Univ, 320 Bowman Hall, Kent, OH, 44224. **EMAIL** dbarnbau@kent.edu

BARNES, GERALD
DISCIPLINE PHILOSOPHY OF MIND **EDUCATION** Harvard Univ, PhD, 68. **CAREER** Philos, Col NJ. **SELECTED PUBLICATIONS** Auth, Some Remarks on Belief and Desire, Philos Rev, 77; The Conclusion of Practical Reasoning, Analysis, 83. **CONTACT ADDRESS** Col of New Jersey, PO Box 7718, Ewing, NJ, 08628-0718.

BARNES, JOSEPH NATHAN
PERSONAL Born 11/29/1950, Hermondale, MO **DISCIPLINE** LAW **EDUCATION** Ibadan Univ Nigeria, Certificate in Intl Economics 1971; Antioch Coll, BA Finance & Commerce 1973; Univ of PA, MBA 1977; Univ of PA Sch of Law, JD1977. **CAREER** Spearman & Sterling, assoc atty 1977-81; Zimet Haines Moss & Friedman, assoc atty 1981-82; Barnes & Williams, partner 1982-85; Barnes & Darby, partner, beginning 1985; Barnes, McGhee, Neal, Poston & Segue, founding partner, currently. **HONORS AND AWARDS** Rockefeller Grant 1968,73; Natl Fellowship Foundation Fellow 1973,74; First Black NY Law firm listed in Dir of Municipal Bond Dealers 1987. **MEMBERSHIPS** Mem Natl Bar Assoc 1981-87; dir Black Entertainment & Sports Lawyers Assoc 1983-88; bd mem Urban League Manhattan Branch 1985-87; mem Metro Black Bar Assoc 1986-87, Natl Assoc of Securities Profls 1986-87; NY chmn telethon United Negro Coll Fund 1986, 1987, 1988; mem NAACP. **CONTACT ADDRESS** Barnes, McGhee, Neal, Poston & Segue, 888 7th Ave #1809, New York, NY, 10019-3201.

BARNES, MICHAEL H.
DISCIPLINE RELIGIOUS STUDIES **EDUCATION** Marquette Univ, PhD, Religious Studies, 76. **CAREER** PROF OF RELIGIOUS STUDIES, ALUMNI CHAIR IN HUMANITIES, UNIV OF DAYTON. **HONORS AND AWARDS** Teacher of the Year, 92; Templeton Award for course in Religion & Science, 97. **MEMBERSHIPS** AAR; CTS; CTSA; SSSR. **RESEARCH** Evolution of religious thought; science & religion. **SELECTED PUBLICATIONS** Auth, In the Presence of Mystery, Twenty-Third Pub, 84 & 90; Rationality in Religion, Religion, 97; Community, Clannishness, and the Common Good, Vol 41 of The Annual Pub of the Col Theology Soc, XXIII Publications, 96; The Presence and Absence of God, Praying, 96; Parallels in Cultural and Individual Development, Ethnicity, Nationality, and Religious Experience, Vol 37, Univ Press of Am, 95; A Reply to Michael Raschko, Theological Studies, 95; The Evolution of the Soul from Matter and the Role of Science in the Theology of Karl Rahner, Horizons, 94; Demythologization in the Theology of Karl Rahner, Theological Studies, 94; Having Faith, Being Critical, and Seeking Truth: A Response to Dale W. Cannon, Method and Theory in the Study of Religion, 94. **CONTACT ADDRESS** Univ Dayton, Dayton, OH, 45469-1549.

BARNES, WILLIE R.
PERSONAL Born 12/09/1931, Dallas, TX, m **DISCIPLINE** LAW **EDUCATION** UCLA, BA, political science, 1953; UCLA School of Law, JD, 1959. **CAREER** State of California, Dept of Corps, various Attorney positions, 1960-68, supvr corps counsel 1968-70, asst commr, 1970-75, commr of corps, 1975-79; UCLA Alumni Assn, general counsel, dir, 1983-86; Manatt Phelps Rothenberg & Phillips, sr partner, 1979-88; Wyman Bautzer, Kuchel & Silbert, sr partner, 1989-91; Katten, Muchin, Zavis & Weitzman, sr partner, 1991-92; Musick, Peeler & Garrett, sr partner, 1992-. **HONORS AND AWARDS** Practicing Law Institute, Certificate of Appreciation, 1973; UCLA Law School, Alumnus of the Year, 1976; California State Senate & Assembly, Resolutions of Commendation, 1979. **MEMBERSHIPS** Exec comm, Business & Corps Sec 1970-86; vp, dir UCLA Law Alumni Assn 1973; Comm Real Estate Franchises Mutual Funds; chmn SEC Liaison Comm 1974-78; chmn Real Estate Investment Comm 1974-78; president Midwest Securities Commission Assn 1978-79; 1st vice pres N Amer Securities Administration Assn 1978-79; co-managing ed, CA Bus Law Reporter 1983; exec comm Corp & Commercial Law Sec, Beverly Hills Bar Assn; board of governors Century City Bar Assn, 1982-84; vice chmn, Comm on Corp; vice chmn, Oil Investment Comm; active leadership in directing the Securities Reg Prog of CA; vice chair, exec committee Business Law Sec, California State Bar, 1983-86; Corp Banking & Bus Law, Fed Regulation of Securities, Commodities, Franchises & State Regulation Committees, Amer Bar Assn; chmn, bd of trustees, Wilshire United Methodist Church986-91; chmn Knox Keene Health Care Service Plan Comm 1976-79; chmn Leveraged Real Estate Task Force 1985-86; CA Senate Commission on Corporate Governance; Independent Commission to Review the Los Angeles Police Dept; advsry bd Institute of Corporate Counsel. **SELECTED PUBLICATIONS** Major role in developing uniform standards for real estate progs on nationwide basis; Acknowledged expert in real estate & oil & gas securities. **CONTACT ADDRESS** Musick, Peeler & Garrett, 1 Wilshire Blvd, Ste 200, Los Angeles, CA, 90017.

BARNETT LIDSKY, LYRISSA C.
DISCIPLINE LAW **EDUCATION** Tex A&M Univ, BA; Univ Tex, JD. **CAREER** Assoc prof; Univ Fla, 94-; clerk, Judge Joseph Sneed, US Ct of Appeals, 9th Circuit; articles ed, Tex Law Rev. **HONORS AND AWARDS** Ful sch, Cambridge Univ. **MEMBERSHIPS** Order of the Coif; Phi Kappa Phi; Fla Bar; Professionalism Comt Fla Bar, 95-; 8th Judicial Circuit Bar Asn; 8th Circuit Professionalism Comt; Fla Bar Media and Comm Law Comt, 97-. **RESEARCH** Torts, professional responsibility, jurisprudence, media law. **SELECTED PUBLICATIONS** Coauth, Torts: The Civil Law of Reparation for Harm Done by Wrongful Act. **CONTACT ADDRESS** School of Law, Univ of Florida, PO Box 117625, Gainesville, FL, 32611-7625. **EMAIL** barnett@law.ufl.edu

BARNETTE, HENLEE HULIX
PERSONAL Born 08/14/1911, Taylorsville, NC, m, 1956, 4 children **DISCIPLINE** ETHICS **EDUCATION** Wake Forest Col, BA, 40, DD, 98; Southern Baptist Theol Sem, ThM, 43, ThD, 46, PhD, 75. **CAREER** Asst prof sociol, Howard Col, 46-47; prof relig & sociol, Stetson Univ, 47-51; prof ethics, Southern Baptist Theol Sem, 51-77; Clin Prof Psychiat, Univ Louisville Sch Med, 77-, Carnegie grant, 49-50; Am Asn Theol Schs fel, Harvard Univ, 59-60; vis prof, dept environeng, Univ Fla, 72; consult, Christian Life Comn Southern Baptist Convention, 77-; mem bd dirs, DeLand Convalescent Ctr Inc, 77- **MEMBERSHIPS** Inst Soc, Ethics & Life Sci. **RESEARCH** Biomedical ethics; ethical conflicts of psychiatric patients; Martin Luther King Jr; Religious fundamentalism. **SELECTED PUBLICATIONS** Auth, Introducing Christian Ethics, Broadman, 61; Introduction to Communism, Baker Bk, 64; The New Theology and Morality, 67, Crucial Problems in Christian Perspective, 70, The Drug Crisis and the Church, 71 & The Church and the Ecological Crisis, 72, Westminster Col; Bioethics, Stetson Univ Press, 81; Exploring Medical Ethics, Mercer Univ Press, 82; Clarence Jordan: Turning Dreams into Deeds, Smyth and Helwys, 92. **CONTACT ADDRESS** 2909 Meadowlark Ave, Louisville, KY, 40206.

BARNHART, JOE EDWARD
PERSONAL Born 11/01/1931, Knoxville, TN, m, 1953, 2 children **DISCIPLINE** PHILOSOPHY **EDUCATION** Carson-Newman Col, BA, 53; Southern Baptist Theol Sem, BD, 56; Boston Univ, PhD(philos), 64. **CAREER** Asst prof philos, Carson-Newman Col, 57-58; instr, Western Carolina Univ, 61-64; asst prof, Univ Redlands, 64-66; assoc prof, Parsons Col, 66-67; assoc prof, 67-74, Prof Philos, N Tex State Univ, 74-. **MEMBERSHIPS** SWestern Philos Soc; Am Philos Asn; Southern Soc Philos & Psychol; Am Acad Relig; Soc Sci Study Relig. **RESEARCH** Philosophy of religion; philosophy of literature. **SELECTED PUBLICATIONS** Auth, Anthropological Nature in Feuerbach and Marx, Philos Today, winter 67; Human Rights as Absolute Claims and Reasonable Expectations, Am Philos Quart, 10/69; The Billy Graham Religion, United Church, 72; Religion and the Challenge of Philosophy, Littlefield, 75; The Study of Religion and Its Meaning, Mouton, 77; Egoism and Altruism, Southwestern J Philos, winter 76; The Free Will Defence: Responses to Flew and Plantinga, Relig Studies, 12/77; coauth, The Myth of the Complete Person, In: Feminism and Philosophy, Littlefield, 77; The New Birth: A Naturalistic View of Religious Conversion, Mercer Univ, 81; Sworn on the Altar of God-A Religious Biography of Thomas Jefferson, with E. S. Gaustad, J of Church and State, Vol 39, 97. **CONTACT ADDRESS** Univ N TX, Denton, TX, 76203.

BARNHART, MICHAEL G.
PERSONAL Born 03/22/1956, Sewanee, TN, m, 1983, 2 children **DISCIPLINE** PHILOSOPHY **EDUCATION** Haverford Col, BA, 79; Temple Univ, PhD, 91. **CAREER** Assoc prof, 92-, Kingsborough Comm Col, CUNY. **HONORS AND AWARDS** Phi Beta Kappa, hon phil, Haverford; Univ fel, Temple; 2 NEH sum sem; PSC-CUNY res fel. **MEMBERSHIPS** APA, Soc for Asian & Comp Phil; AAR, Assn for Asian Stud. **RESEARCH** Comparative phil; ethics; epistemology; metaphysics **CONTACT ADDRESS** Kingsborough Comm Col, CUNY, 2001 Oriental Blvd, Brooklyn, NY, 11235. **EMAIL** mbarnhart@ubcc.cuny.edu

BARON, CHARLES HILLEL
PERSONAL Born 08/18/1936, Philadelphia, PA, m, 1958, 3 children **DISCIPLINE** LEGAL MEDICINE & PHILOSOPHY **EDUCATION** Univ PA, AB, 58, PhD(philos), 72; Harvard Univ, LLB, 61. **CAREER** Teaching fel philos, Univ PA, 62-64, instr law, 64-65, asst prof, 65-66; assoc prof, 70-74, Prof Law, Boston Col, 74-, Vis prof, Cath Univ Am, 77; adj prof, Antioch Univ, 77; instr, Univ Southern CA, summer, 78 & Univ OR, summer, 79; scholar in residence, Hebrew Univ Jerusalem, 81. **MEMBERSHIPS** Am Soc Law & Med. **RESEARCH** Medical decision making for incompetent patients; blame as deterrent to effective use of legal sanction; human responsibility as a function of distinction between acts and omissions to act. **SELECTED PUBLICATIONS** Coauth, Real Freedom of Choice for the Consumer of Legal Services: Mr Dooley and the Closed Panel Option, Mass Law Quart, 73; Live Organ and Tissue Transplants from Minor Donors in Massachusetts, Boston Univ Law Rev, 75; auth, Voluntary Sterilization of the Mentally Retarded, Genetics and the Law, 76; Assuring Detached but Passionate Investigation and Decision Making, 78 & Medical Paternalism and the Rule of Law, 79, Am J Law & Med; The Open Society and its Enemies: Growing Professional Secrecy in Massachusetts, Medicolegal News, 80; co-ed, Use/Nonuse/Misuse of Applied Social Research in the Courts, ABT Books, 80; State Constitutional Law-Cases and Materials, 2nd Ed, with R. F. Williams, Temple Law Rev, Vol 67, 94; A Model State Act to Authorize and Regulate Physician-Assisted Suicide, Harvard J on Legislation, Vol 33, 96. **CONTACT ADDRESS** Law Sch, Boston Col, 885 Centre St, Newton, MA, 02159-1100.

BARON, MARCIE
PERSONAL Born 09/10/1955, Akron, OH, m, 1981, 1 child **DISCIPLINE** PHILOSOPHY **EDUCATION** Oberlin Col, BA, 76; MA, 78, PhD, 82, UNC-Chapel Hill. **CAREER** Instr, 81-82, Asst Prof, 82-83, Virginia Polytech Inst and State Univ; Visiting Asst Prof, 85, Stanford Univ; Visiting Asst Prof, 87, Univ Michigan; Visiting Assoc Prof, 90, Univ Chicago; Visting Asst Prof, 82-83, Asst Prof, 83-89, Assoc Prof, 89-96, Prof, 96-, Univ Illinois at Urbana-Champaign. **MEMBERSHIPS** Amer Phil Assoc; Illinois Phil Assoc; Intl Hume Soc; North Amer Kant Soc. **RESEARCH** Ethics and the philosophy of criminal law **SELECTED PUBLICATIONS** Auth, Freedom, Frailty and Impurity, Inquiry 36, 93; Kantian Ethics Almost Without Apology, 95; Kantian Ethics and Claims of Detachment, Feminist Interpretations of Immanuel Kant, 97; Coauth, Three Methods of Ethics: A Debate, 97; Auth, Love and Respect in the Doctrine of Virtue, The Southern Journal of Philosophy, forthcoming; Crimes, Genes, and Responsibility, Genetics and Criminal Behavior: Methods, Meanings and Morals, forthcoming; Supererogatory Acts and Imperfect Duties, Jahrbuch fur Recht und Ethik, forthcoming. **CONTACT ADDRESS** Dept of Philosophy, Univ of Illinois, 810 S. Wright St., 105 Greg H, Urbana, IL, 61801. **EMAIL** m-barron@uiuc.edu

BARR, DAVID LAWRENCE
PERSONAL Born 04/24/1942, Belding, MI, m, 1966, 3 children **DISCIPLINE** BIBLICAL STUDIES, HISTORY OF RELIGIONS **EDUCATION** Ft Wayne Bible Col, BA, 65; FL State Univ, MA, 69, PhD, 74. **CAREER** Consult relig pub educ, Relig Instr Asn, 67-71; instr relig, FL A&M Univ, 72-74; asst prof, Univ Northern IA, 74-75; asst prof, 75-80, assoc prof, 80-88, prof relig, Wright State Univ, 88, Chmn, Relig Dept, Wright State Univ, 80-86, Dir, Honors Prog 87-94. **HONORS AND AWARDS** Pres, Eastern Grt Lakes Bible Soc; Pres, Mideast Honors Asn; Phi Kappa Phi; Pres Fac. **MEMBERSHIPS** Soc Bibl Lit; Cath Bibl Asn, Am Acad Relig. **RESEARCH** Apocalypse of John; Narrative analysis; Soc world of early Christianity. **SELECTED PUBLICATIONS** Co-ed (with Nicholas Piediscalzi), The Bible in American Education, a centennial volume prepared for the Soc of Bibl Lit, Fortress Press and Scholars Press, 82; New Testament Story: An Introduction, Wadsworth Publ Co, 87, 2nd ed, 95; Co-ed (with Linda Bennett Elder and Elizabeth Struthers Malbon), Biblical and Humane: A Festschrift for John Priest; Tales of the End: A Narrative Commentary on the Book of Revelation, Polebridge Press, 98. **CONTACT ADDRESS** Dept of Relig, Wright State Univ, 3640 Colonel Glenn, Dayton, OH, 45435-0002. **EMAIL** dbarr@wright.edu

BARRETT, J. EDWARD
PERSONAL Born 12/18/1932, Philadelphia, PA, m, 1959, 2 children **DISCIPLINE** RELIGION, PHILOSOPHY **EDUCATION** Susquehanna Univ, AB, 55; Princeton Theol Sem, BD, 58, ThM, 60; Univ St Andrews, PhD(philos theol), 65. **CAREER** Pastor, Presby church, Glassboro, NJ, 58-62; from asst prof to prof philos & relig, 64-77, PROF RELIG, MUSKINGUM COL, 77-, Prof humanities, Tunghai Univ, Taiwan, 72-73. **MEMBERSHIPS** Am Acad Relig. **RESEARCH** Religious experience; philosophical theology. **SELECTED PUBLICATIONS** Auth, Tragedy, God and Thanksgiving, Presby Life, 11/67; The Christian Conspiracy, Christian Century, 2/68; A Theology of the Meaning of Life, Zygon, J Sci & Relig, 6/68; How Are You Programmed?, John Knox, 71; Pilgrims Progress, From Catechism to Pantheism, Religious Humanism, Vol 29, 95. **CONTACT ADDRESS** Dept of Relig & Philos, Muskingum Col, New Concord, OH, 43762.

BARRETT, JOHN A.
DISCIPLINE LAW **EDUCATION** Amherst Col, BA; Harvard Univ, JD. **CAREER** Assoc prof. **SELECTED PUBLICATIONS** Auth, The U.S. Approach to Resolving the Tension Between Environmental Liabilities and Bankruptcy Debt Forgiveness, Kluwer, 98; International Legal Education in the United States: Being Educated for Domestic Practice While Living in a Global Society, Am Univ J Int Law Policy, 97; The Status of International Legal Education in U.S. Law Schools: Plenty of Offerings but Too Few Students, Int Lawyer, 97; Crimes Involving Art, J Criminal Law Criminology, 96; Mexican Insolvency Law, Pace Int Law Rev, 95; The Effect of NAFTA on the Energy Industry of Third-Party Countries, Oil & Gas Law Tax Rev, 94; co-auth, International Sales Agreements: An Annotated Drafting and Negotiating Guide, Kluwer, 98. **CONTACT ADDRESS** Col Law, Univ of Toledo, Toledo, OH, 43606. **EMAIL** jbarret@pop3.utoledo.edu

BARRICK, WILLIAM D.
PERSONAL Born 01/05/1946, Hayden, CO, m, 1966, 4 children **DISCIPLINE** OLD TESTAMENT, HEBREW **EDUCATION** Denver Baptist Bible Col, Ba, 68; San Francisco Baptist Theol Sem, MDiv 71, ThM, 72; Grace Theol Sem, ThD, 81. **CAREER** Prof, Denver Baptist Theol Sem, 72-78; exegetical

consult for Bible transl, Chittagong, Bangladesh, 81-96; assoc prof, 97-98, prof, 98- , The Master's Sem, Sun Valley, Calif. **HONORS AND AWARDS** Denver Baptist Bible Col alumnus of the year, 80. **MEMBERSHIPS** Evangel Theol Soc; Soc of Bibl Lit; Natl Asn of Profs of Hebrew. **RESEARCH** Hebrew; Old Testament textual criticism; Leviticus; Job; Bible translation. **SELECTED PUBLICATIONS** Auth, William Carey: Memorable Man, Respected Personality, in Weber, ed, Mahan Sadhak William Carey, Bangladesh: Literature Division, 93, in Bengali; auth, the FACTS of Witnessing to People Outside Our Culture, Gospel Herald and the Sunday Sch Times, 94; auth, In the Folds of God's Garment, in 100 Meditations for Advent and Christmas, Upper Room Books, 94; consult, Holy New Testament, Bangladesh Bible Soc, 96; auth, 1 Samuel 1-17 Introduction and Mesages, Living Life, 97; auth, 1 Samuel 18-31 Messages, Living Life, 97; auth, 2 Samuel 1-14 Introduction and Messages, Living Life, 97; auth, 2 Samuel 14-24 Messages, Living Life, 97; auth, Hosea Introduction and Messages, Living Life, 97; auth, 1 Kings 1-4.28 Introduction and Messages and Proverbs 3:21-4:27 Messages, Living Life, 98; auth, Ancient Manuscripts and Biblical exposition, Master's Sem J, 98; auth, Isaiah 53 and 1 Kings 4:29-10:29 and Proverbs 5:1-23 Messages, Living Life, 98; auth, 1 Kings 19:1-22:53 and Proverbs 8:1-36 Messages, Living Life, 98; auth, Daniel 1:1-4:27 Introduction and Messages and Proverbs 10:22-12:8 Messages, Living Life, 98; auth, Daniel 4:28-12:13 and Proverbs 12:9-13:16 Messages, Living Life, 98; consult, Book of Psalms, Bangladesh Bible Soc, 98; consult, Pentateuch, Bangladesh Bible Soc, 98; consult, Holy Bible, Bangladesh Bible Soc, 98. **CONTACT ADDRESS** The Master's Sem, 13248 Roscoe Blvd, Sun Valley, CA, 91352. **EMAIL** bbarrick@mastersem.edu

BARRY, ROBERT M.
DISCIPLINE PHILOSOPHY **EDUCATION** Iona Col, BA; Fordham Univ, MA, PhD. **CAREER** Prof, Loyola Univ, 63-. **RESEARCH** American pragmatism, especially James and Dewey; philosophy of soc science. **SELECTED PUBLICATIONS** Auth, The Medieval: New Dimensions, 74. **CONTACT ADDRESS** Dept of Philosophy, Loyola Univ, Chicago, 820 N. Michigan Ave., Chicago, IL, 60611.

BARRY, WILLIAM ANTHONY
PERSONAL Born 11/22/1930, Worcester, MA **DISCIPLINE** PASTORAL THEOLOGY, CLINICAL PSYCHOLOGY **EDUCATION** Boston Col, AB, 56; Fordham Univ, MA, 60; Weston Col, STL, 63; Univ Mich, Ann Arbor, PhD(psychol), 68. **CAREER** Teacher Latin, English & Ger, Fairfield Prep Sch, Conn, 56-58; lectr psychol & staff psychologist, Univ Mich, Ann Arbor, 68-69; asst prof pastoral theol, Weston Sch Theol, 69-73, assoc prof, 73-78, dir, Ctr Relig Develop, 71-75, mem staff, 75-78; VProvincial, 78-84, asst nov dir, 85-88, Provincial, 91-97, CO-DIR, TERTIANSHIP, 97-, SOC JESUS NEW ENGLAND; Rector, Boston Col, 88-91; Staff psychologist, Ecumenical Career Coun Serv, Melrose, Mass, 70-71; consult, New Eng Prov Soc Jesus, 72-78; adj prof, Boston col, 88-91. **MEMBERSHIPS** Am Psychol Asn; Soc Sci Study Relig; Soc Psychol Study Social Issues. **RESEARCH** Personality and religious development; prayer and religious experience; pastoral counseling. **SELECTED PUBLICATIONS** Coauth, Personality development and the vocational choice of the ministry, J Coun Psychol, 67; auth, Marriage research and conflict: An integrative review, Psychol Bull, 70; The experience of the first and second weeks of the spiritual exercises, Rev Relig, 73; coauth, Communication, Conflict, and Marriage: Explorations in the Theory and Study of Relationships, Jossey-Bass, 74; Prayer in pastoral care, J Pastoral Care, 77; Spiritual direction and pastoral counseling, Pastoral Psychol, 77; The Practice of Spiritual Direction, Seabury, 82; auth, God's Passionate Desire and Our Response, Ave Maria, 93; auth, Allowing the Creator to Deal with the Creature: An Approach to the Spiritual Exercises of Ignatius of Loyola, Paulist, 94; auth, What Do I Want in Prayer? Paulist, 94; auth, Who Do You Say I Am? Meeting the Historical Jesus in Prayer, Ave Maria, 96; auth, Our Way of Proceeding: To Make the Constitutions of the Society of Jesus and Their Complementary Norms Our Own; Institute of Jesuit Sources, 97; auth, With an Everlasting Love: Developing an Intimate Relationship with God, Paulist, forthcoming. **CONTACT ADDRESS** Campion Center, 319 Concord Rd, Weston, MA, 02493-1398. **EMAIL** frbarry@bc.edu

BARTELT, ANDREW H.
PERSONAL Born 08/04/1949, Milwaukee, WI, m, 1979, 3 children **DISCIPLINE** THEOLOGY **EDUCATION** Concordia Sr Col, BA, 71; Cambridge Univ, England, Hon Degree, 73, MA, 77; Concordia Sem, MDiv, 76; Univ Mich, PhD, 91. **CAREER** From instr to assoc prof, 78-97, prof exegetical theol, 97- , asst acad advisor, 84-95, chemn dept, 94-98, Concordia Sem, dean of admin, 95-98, exec asst to pres, 95- , acting pres, 96, Vpres for Acad Affairs, 98- . **MEMBERSHIPS** Soc of Bibl Lit; Cath Bibl Soc; Bibl Archaeol Soc. **RESEARCH** Old Testament interpretation; preaching on Old Testament texts; Isaiah. **SELECTED PUBLICATIONS** Auth, Isaiah, Concordia, 94; auth, Isaiah Five and Nine: In-or Interdependence? in, Fortunate the Eyes That See: Essays in Honor of David Noel Freedman in Celebration of His 70th Birthday, Eerdmans, 95; auth, The Book Around Immanuel: Style and Structure of Isaiah 1-12, Eisenbrauns, 96; auth, Fundamental Biblical Hebrew, Concordia, forthcoming. **CONTACT ADDRESS** Concordia Sem, 801 DeMun Ave, St Louis, MO, 63105. **EMAIL** bartelta@csl.edu

BARTHOLET, ELIZABETH
PERSONAL Born 09/09/1940, New York, NY, 3 children **DISCIPLINE** LAW **EDUCATION** Radcliffe Col, BA, 62; Harvard Univ, LLB, 65. **CAREER** Atty, 65-77; prof of Law, Harvard Univ, 77- . **HONORS AND AWARDS** Mass Appleseed Ctr, Awd for Advocacy on Behalf of Foster Children; Radcliffe Col Alumnae Recognition Awd, 97; Morris Wasserstein Public Interest Ch at Harvard Law Sch, 96; Open Door Soc, Friends of Adoption Awd, 94; Catholic Adoptive Parents Asn, Media Achievement Awd, 94; Adoptive Parents Comm, Friends of Adoption Awd for Adoption Literature, 93. **MEMBERSHIPS** NAACP Legal Defense & Ed Fund, Inc. Am Acad Adoption Attys; US State Dept Advisory Com on Intercountry Adoption; Legal Action Ctr; Int Concerns Comt for Children; Appleseed Found Adv Coun; Brigham and Women's Hosp. **RESEARCH** Child welfare; adoption; reproductive technology. **SELECTED PUBLICATIONS** Auth, International Adoption: Current Status and Future Prospects, in The Future of Children, No. 1, 93; auth, Blood Knots, in American Prospect, 93; auth, Family Matters, in Vogue, 93; auth, What's Wrong with Adoption Law, in Trial, 94; auth, Family Bonds: Adoption & the Politics of Parenting, Houghton Mifflin, 94; auth, Adoption Rights and Reproductive Wrongs, in Power & Decision: the social Control of Reproduction, 94; auth, Race Separatism in the Family: More on the Transracial Adoption Debate, in 2 Duke J. Gender L. & Pol'y, 95; auth, Beyond Biology: The Politics of Adoption & Reproduction, in 2 Duke J. Gender L. & Pol'y, 95; coauth, Debate: Best Interests of the Child?, in Prospect, no. 11, 96; auth, What's Wrong with Adoption Law?, in The International Journal of Children's Rights, 96; auth, International Adoption: Propriety, Prospects and Pragmatics, J. Am. Acad. Matrim. Law, 96; auth, Pribate Race Preferences in Family Formation, Yale L.J., 98. **CONTACT ADDRESS** Law Sch, Harvard Univ, 1575 Mass Ave, Cambridge, MA, 02138. **EMAIL** ebarthol@law.harvard.edu

BARTKOWIAK, JULIA
PERSONAL Born 10/12/1957, Detroit, MI, m, 1978, 1 child **DISCIPLINE** PHILOSOPHY **EDUCATION** Wayne State Univ, BA, 83; Univ Rochester, MA, 86, PhD, 90. **CAREER** Kent State Univ, temp asst prof, 89-92; Clarion Univ, asst prof, 92-95, assoc prof, 95-. **HONORS AND AWARDS** Univ Rochester, Rush Rhees Fel, 84-87, Univ Fel, 84-88 **MEMBERSHIPS** APA, NASSP **RESEARCH** Ethics; social philo. **SELECTED PUBLICATIONS** Auth, The Role of Internalism in Moral Theory, in: Auslegung, 93; Trends Toward Part-Time Employment: Ethical Issues, in: Jour of Business Ethics, 93; Intellectual Walls, in: Frauen und Wissenschaftspolitik, Zurich: Philosophisches Institut, 94; The U.S. Media and the Liberal Tradition, in: Jour of Social Philo, 94; Contingent Work, in: The Blackwell Encycl Dictionary of Business Ethics, ed by Patricia H. Werhane, and R. Edward Freeman, Oxford: Blackwell Pub, 97; Religious Education in the Public Schools, Proceedings of the Twentieth World Congress of Philosophy, Philo Doc Center, 98. **CONTACT ADDRESS** Dept of Philosophy, Clarion Univ of Pennsylvania, Clarion, PA, 16214-1232. **EMAIL** bartkowi@clarion.edu

BARTKY, SANDRA
DISCIPLINE PHILOSOPHY **EDUCATION** Univ of Ill, PhD, 63. **CAREER** PROF OF PHILOS & WOMEN'S STUDIES, UNIV OF ILL, 65-. **HONORS AND AWARDS** Honorary doctorate in Humanities, New England Col, 97. **MEMBERSHIPS** APA; SWIP; RPA; SPEP. **RESEARCH** Social and political philosophy; feminist theory; phenomenology. **SELECTED PUBLICATIONS** Auth, Feminicity and Domination: Studies in the Phenomenology of Oppression, Routledge, 90. **CONTACT ADDRESS** 3520 Lake Shore Dr, Apt 7E, Chicago, IL, 60657.

BARTLETT, BETH
PERSONAL Born 05/21/1952, Akron, OH, m, 1988, 1 child **DISCIPLINE** PHILOSOPHY **EDUCATION** Col Wooster, BA, 74; Kent St, MA, 75; Univ Minn, PhD, 81. **CAREER** Instr, 80-81, asst prof, 81-87, assoc prof, 87-, Univ Minn - Duluth. **RESEARCH** Feminist theory, spirituality. **CONTACT ADDRESS** Univ of Minnesota, Duluth, 304 Cina Hall, Duluth, MN, 55812. **EMAIL** bbartlet@d.umn.edu

BARTLETT, STEVEN J.
PERSONAL Born 05/15/1945, Mexico, m **DISCIPLINE** PHILOSOPHY **EDUCATION** Raymond Col, BA, 65; Univ Calif, Santa Barbara, MA, 68; Univ Paris, PhD, 71. **CAREER** Res fel, Ctr for Stud of Democratic Inst, 69-70; vis asst prof, Univ Fla, 71-72; asst prof, Univ Hartford, 72-74; res fel, Max Planck Inst, 74-75; prof St Louis Univ, 75-84; res prof, Oregon State Univ, 89- ; vis scholar, Willamette Univ, 89- . **HONORS AND AWARDS** NSFR grant; AAAS grant; Lilly Found grant; Max Planck Gesellschaft fel; Alliance Francaise fel. **MEMBERSHIPS** APA. **RESEARCH** Epistemology; reflexivity. **SELECTED PUBLICATIONS** Auth, Metalogic of Reference: A Study in the Foundations of Possibility, Max Planck Inst, 75; auth, Conceptual Therapy: An Introduction to Framework-Relative Epistemology, Studies in Theory and Behavior, 83; coauth, Self-Reference: Reflections on Reflexivity, Martinus Nijhoff, 87; auth, Reflexivity: A Source Book in Self-Reference, Elsevier Science, 92. **CONTACT ADDRESS** 5550 Bethel Heights NW, Salem, OR, 97304.

BARTON, JOHN HAYS
PERSONAL Born 10/27/1936, Chicago, IL, m, 1959, 5 children **DISCIPLINE** INTERNATIONAL LAW **EDUCATION** Marquette Univ, BS, 58; Stanford Univ, JD, 68. **CAREER** Engr, Sylvania, 61-68; assoc, Wilmer, Cutler & Pickering, Washington, DC, 68-69; Prof Law, Law Sch, Stanford Univ, 69-, Res assoc, Int Inst Strategic Studies, London, 76-77; Vis Prof law, Univ MI, fall, 81. **MEMBERSHIPS** Am Soc Int Law. **RESEARCH** International organization; international technology flow; arms control. **SELECTED PUBLICATIONS** Auth, The Economic Basis of Damages for Breach of Contract, J Legal Studies, 72; Behind the Legal Explosion, Stanford Law Rev, 75; The Developing Nations and Arms Control, Studies in Comp Int Develop, 75; co-ed, International Arms Control: Issues and Agreements, Stanford Univ Press, 76; contribr, Nuclear Weapons and World Politics, McGraw Hill, 77; The Politics of Human Rights, NY Univ Press, 80; auth, The Politics of Peace, Stanford Univ Press, 81; The International Breeder's Rights System and Crop Plant Innovation, Science, 6/4/82; International- Law and Institutions For a New Age, Georgetown Law J, Vol 81, 93; Patent Scope in Biotechnology, IIC-International Review of Industrial Property and Copyright Law, Vol 26, 95; Patents and Antitrust-A Rethinking in Light of Patent Breadth and Sequential Innovation, Antitrust Law J, Vol 65, 97. **CONTACT ADDRESS** Law Sch, Stanford Univ, Stanford, CA, 94027.

BARTON, PETER G.
DISCIPLINE LAW **EDUCATION** Univ Toronto, BS, 63; Queen's Univ, LLB, 67; Harvard Univ, LLM, 68. **CAREER** Prof. **HONORS AND AWARDS** Co-ed, Can Jour Law. **RESEARCH** Civil and criminal procedure; criminal law. **SELECTED PUBLICATIONS** Auth, pubs on criminal procedure. **CONTACT ADDRESS** Fac of Law, Univ Western Ontario, London, ON, N6A 3K7.

BARWICK, DANIEL
PERSONAL Born 06/21/1968, Utica, NY, m, 1997 **DISCIPLINE** PHILOSOPHY **EDUCATION** SUNY Buffalo, PhD, 97. **CAREER** Alfred Stal. **MEMBERSHIPS** APA; Nat Asn of Scholars. **RESEARCH** Philosophy of education. **CONTACT ADDRESS** 49 Chestnut Ave, Dansville, NY, 14437.

BASCOM, ROBERT
PERSONAL Born 09/25/1951, Glendale, CA, m, 1976, 1 child **DISCIPLINE** RELIGIOUS STUDIES **EDUCATION** Claremont Grad Sch, PhD, 86. **CAREER** Transl consult, United Bible Soc, 86- . **MEMBERSHIPS** SBL. **RESEARCH** Anthropology; linguistics; Biblical studies. **SELECTED PUBLICATIONS** Auth, Adaptable for Translation, in Weis, ed, A Gift of God in Due Season, Sheffield, 96. **CONTACT ADDRESS** 2448 N Mar Vista Ave, Altadena, CA, 91001-2510. **EMAIL** bascom@sprynet.com

BASHIR, SHAHZAD
PERSONAL Born 03/12/1968, Bahawalpur, Pakistan, m, 1994 **DISCIPLINE** RELIGIOUS STUDIES **EDUCATION** Amherst Col, BA, 91; Yale Univ, PhD, 97. **CAREER** Instr, 96-97; Asst prof, 97- , Holy Cross Coll.. **MEMBERSHIPS** Am Acad Relig; Mid E Studies Asn; Soc Iranian Studies; Mid E Medievalists **RESEARCH** Islamic studies; Shi ism; Sufism; history of religions. **SELECTED PUBLICATIONS** Auth, Between Mysticism and Messianism: The Life and Thought of Mohammad NurbaLhsh (d.1464), Yale Univ, 97. **CONTACT ADDRESS** 28 Westfield St., Worcester, MA, 01602. **EMAIL** sbashir@holycross.edu

BASKIN, JUDITH R.
PERSONAL Born 07/03/1950, Hamilton, ON, Canada, m, 1973, 2 children **DISCIPLINE** JUDAIC STUDIES **EDUCATION** Antioch College, BA, 71; Yale Univ, PhD, 76. **CAREER** Assoc Prof, Prof, Ch, 88-, SUNY Albany; vis Asst Prof, 81-83, Yale Univ; Asst, Assoc Prof, 76-88, Univ Mass. **HONORS AND AWARDS** Danforth Fel; Woodrow Wilson; ACLS Gnt; Dist Teach Awd. **MEMBERSHIPS** AJS; AAR; MA. **RESEARCH** Rabbinic and Medieval Judaism; History of Jewish Women; Comparative Jewish and Christian Exegesis in Late Antiquity. **SELECTED PUBLICATIONS** Ed, Jewish Women in Historical Perspective, Wayne State Univ, forthcoming; ed, Women of the World: Jewish Women and Jewish Writing, Wayne State Univ Press, 94; coed, Gender and Jewish Studies: A Curriculum Guide, Biblio Press, 94; ed, Jewish Women in Historical Perspective, Wayne State Univ Press, 91; auth, Woman as Other in Rabbinic Literature: Where We Stand: Issues and Debates in Ancient Judaism, ed, Jacob Neusner, Alan J Avery-Peck, Brill, 99; auth, Women Saints in Judaism: Dolce of Worms, in: Women Saints in World Religions, ed, Arvind Sharma, State Univ NY Press, 99; Rabbinic Judaism and the Creation of Woman, in: Judaism Since Gender, ed, Miriam Peskowitz, Laura Levitt, Routledge, 97; Silent Partners: Women as Wives in Rabbinic Lit, in: Active Voices: Women in Jewish Culture, ed, Maurie Sacks, Univ IL Press, 95. **CONTACT ADDRESS** 33 Dover Dr, Delmar, NY, 12054. **EMAIL** baskin@cas.albany.edu

BASS, DOROTHY C.
PERSONAL Born 05/02/1949, m, 2 children **DISCIPLINE** RELIGION AND AMERICAN CIVILIZATION **EDUCATION** Wellesley Col, BA, 70; Union Theol Sem and Columbia Univ, MA, 72; Brown Univ, PhD, 80. **CAREER** William Rainey Harper instr, humanities, Univ Chicago, 80-82; asst prof to assoc prof, church hist, Chicago Theol Sem, 82-95; dir, Valparaiso Project on Educ and Formation of People in Faith, Valparaiso Univ, 91-. **HONORS AND AWARDS** Union Theol Sem Distinguished Alum Award, 96. **MEMBERSHIPS** Amer Acad of Relig; Amer Soc for Church Hist. **RESEARCH** Practical theology; Spirituality; Church history. **SELECTED PUBLICATIONS** Auth, Practicing Our Faith: A Way of Life for a Searching People, San Francisco, Jossy-Bass, 97; co-auth, Protestant, Catholic, Jew: The Transformative Possibilities of Educating across Religious Boundaries, Relig Educ, 90, 255-276, spring, 95; co-auth, Academic Soul-Searching: Christians and the University, Christ Century, 112, 9, 292-295, mar 15, 95; auth, Ministries in Higher Education: Context and Commitment, Faith and Learning Series, Cleveland, United Church of Christ, issue 5, 95; auth, Congregations and the Bearing of Traditions, Amer Congregations, vol 2, Chicago, Univ of Chicago Press, 94. **CONTACT ADDRESS** Valparaiso Univ, Linwood House, Valparaiso, IN, 46383.

BASSETT, WILLIAM W.
PERSONAL Born 12/18/1932, Peoria, IL, m, 1973, 3 children **DISCIPLINE** LAW; LEGAL HISTORY **EDUCATION** S. T.L. St. Mary of the Lake (IL), MA, 58; Gregorian Univ (Rome), JCD, 65; Cath Univ Am (Wash), JD, 72. **CAREER** Asst to assoc prof, 67-73, Cath Univ Am, 67-73; scholar in res, 73-74, Ludwig-Maximilians Universitat (Munich); vis prof 82-83, Univ Calif; PROF LAW, 74-, UNIV SAN FRANCISCO, 74-. **MEMBERSHIPS** Seldom Soc; Canon Law Soc Am; Asn Iuris Cononici Int; Am Soc Legal Hist **RESEARCH** Law of Religious Organizations; Legal History. **SELECTED PUBLICATIONS** California Commmunity Property Law, Bancroft Witness, 95; Religious Organizations and the Law, West, 98. **CONTACT ADDRESS** School of Law, Univ of San Francisco, 2150 Fulton St., San Francisco, CA, 94117. **EMAIL** Bassettw@usfca.edu

BASU, ANANYO
PERSONAL Born 04/04/1966, Calcutta, India, m, 1991, 1 child **DISCIPLINE** PHILOSOPHY **EDUCATION** Dartmouth Col, BA, 89; Duke Univ, PhD, 95. **CAREER** Vis asst prof, Mt Holyoke Col, 94-95; vis asst prof, philos, West Virginia Univ, 96, 97; asst prof philos, Univ Mass, Boston, 95-. **HONORS AND AWARDS** Francis Gramlich philos prize, Dartmouth Univ; Katherine Gilbert fel, Duke Univ. **MEMBERSHIPS** APA; Assoc for Asian Stud. **RESEARCH** Political theory; philosophy of science; Asian and African philosophy. **SELECTED PUBLICATIONS** Auth, Reducing Concern with Self: Parfit and the Ancient Buddhist Schools, in Allen, ed, Culture and Self: Philosophical and Religious Perspectives, East and West, Westview, 97; auth, Communitarianism and Individualism in African Thought, Int Stud in Philos, 98; auth, Response to Prof Huey-Li Li's Paper: Multicultural Foundations for Philosophy of Education: A Propaedeutic, Philos of Educ Proc, 98; auth, The Violence Initiative: Race, Class and Reductionist Biology, Race, Gender and Class, 99. **CONTACT ADDRESS** Dept of Philosophy, Univ of Massachusetts, 761 Northwest Dr, Morgantown, WV, 26505. **EMAIL** abasu@wvu.edu

BATEMAN, HERBERT W.
PERSONAL Born 05/06/1955, Camden, NJ, m, 1979, 1 child **DISCIPLINE** THEOLOGY AND THE NEW TESTAMENT **EDUCATION** Philadelphia Col of Bible, BS, 82; Dallas Theol Sem, ThM, 87, PhD, 93. **CAREER** Prof, new testament, Grace Theol Sem, 95-. **HONORS AND AWARDS** Outstanding Young Men of Amer, 88; Gold Heart Awards, Med City Hospital, 93; William M. Anderson Scholar Award, Dallas Theol Sem, apr, 93; Who's Who among America's Teachers, 88. **MEMBERSHIPS** Soc of Bibl Lit; Evang Theol Sem. **RESEARCH** The use of the Old Testament in the New Testament; Intertestamental history; The book of Hebrews. **SELECTED PUBLICATIONS** Book rev, A Guide to the Study of Greco-Roman and Jewish and Christian History and Literature, Bibliotheca Sacra, 152, 242-43, apr-jun, 95; book rev, Colossians & Philemon, Bibliotheca Sacra, 152, 118-19, jan-mar, 95; jour article, Were The Opponents at Philippi Necessarily Jewish, Bibliotheca Sacra, 155, 39-62, jan-mar, 98; jour article, World Missions, Bible Expositor and Illuminator, 69, dec 96-feb 97; jour article, Two First Century Messianic Uses of the Old Testament: Hebrews 1:5-13 and 4qflorilegium 1:1-19, Jour of the Evang Theol Soc, 38, 11-27, 95; jour article, The Use of Psalm 110:1 in the New Testament, Bibliotheca Sacra 149, 438-53, oct-dec 92; auth, Early Jewish Hermeneutics and Hebrews 1:5-13: The Impact of Early Jewish Exegesis on the Interpretation of a Significant New Testament Passage, New York: Peter Lang Publishing Company, 97. **CONTACT ADDRESS** 200 Seminary Dr., Winona Lake, IN, 46590. **EMAIL** hwbiv@aol.com

BATEMAN, PAUL E.
PERSONAL Born 02/28/1956, Highland Park, IL, m, 1978 **DISCIPLINE** LAW **EDUCATION** Illinois State University, BS, 1976; University of Michigan, JD, 1980. **CAREER** National Labor Relations Board, trial Attorney, 1980-84; Friedman & Koven, associate, 1984-86; Sachnoff & Weaver, shareholder, 1986-93; Burke, Warren & MacKay, shareholder, 1993-. **MEMBERSHIPS** American Bar Association, 1980-; University of Michigan Black Law Alumni, regional liasion, 1991-; Civic Federation of Chicago, advisory board, 1989-; Boy Scouts of America, cubmaster, 1992-. **SELECTED PUBLICATIONS** Illinois Institute of Continuing Legal Education, Age Discrimination, 1996; Investigations, Testing & Privacy, 1990. **CONTACT ADDRESS** Burke, Warren & MacKay, PC, 330 N Wabash, 22nd Fl, Chicago, IL, 60611.

BATES, GEORGE ALBERT
PERSONAL Born 05/30/1954, Charolttesville, VI **DISCIPLINE** LAW **EDUCATION** Princeton Univ, BA, 1976; Univ of VA, JD, 1980; Mediate Tech, Inc, General Mediation Cert, 1994. **CAREER** Princeton Univ Food Service, asst mgr, 1972-76; Univ of VA, grad asst track coach, 1976-80; State Farm Ins Co, automobile liability underwriter, 1976-77; US Dept of Labor, law clerk-judge Roy P Smith, 1980-81; Univ of VA, assoc dean/off afro-amer affairs, 1987; General Counsel North Amer Van Lines, norcross trans, 1990-94; Law Office of George A Bates, sole proprietor, 1983-; EEO/Diversity consultant, mediator. **HONORS AND AWARDS** Princeton Univ, Co-Captain Track Team, 1976; Track Team Keene-Fitzpatrick Award, 1975; Heptagonal Track Meet All-Ivy, Triple Jump, 1975; NJ State College Champion Triple Jump Winner, 1973-76; Univ of VA Office of Afro-Amer, Affairs Warrior Award, 1987; Saint Paul's College, Humanitarian Service Award, 1988; VA State Univ, Cooperative Extension Service, Humanitarian Service Award, 1987. **MEMBERSHIPS** Alpha Phi Alpha Fraternity, 1977-; Central VA Minority Bus Assn, 1987-; Old Dominion Bar Assn, past bd mem, 1985-; Cooperative Extension Srvc Bd VA State Univ, 1985-; Albemarle Co, NAACP, 1981-; UVA Black Law Alumni Assn, president, 1985-96. **SELECTED PUBLICATIONS** Co-editor w/Prof Kenneth R Redden, "Punitive Damages" Michie Co, 1980; Journalist for five local newspapers & manuscript in progress on "The History of Bid Whist"; mem of the Ministerial Training Program, Charlottesville Church of Christ-Worldwide Bible Way, 1997. **CONTACT ADDRESS** 644 Maxfield Rd, Keswick, VA, 22947.

BATES, JENNIFER
DISCIPLINE PHILOSOPHY **EDUCATION** Univ Toronto, BA, MA, PhD. **CAREER** Vis asst prof. **RESEARCH** Hegel and post-Kantian idealism; philosophy of the imagination and Aristotle. **SELECTED PUBLICATIONS** Pub(s), Bulletin of Hegel Soc of Great Brit; Philos in Rev. **CONTACT ADDRESS** Dept of Philosophy, Victoria Univ, PO Box 3045, Victoria, BC, V8W 3P4.

BATES, STANLEY P.
PERSONAL Los Angeles, CA, m, 2 children **DISCIPLINE** PHILOSOPHY **EDUCATION** Dartmouth Col, BA, 61; Oxford Univ, BA, 63, MA, 69; Harvard Univ, PhD, 77. **CAREER** Asst prof, Univ Chicago, 66-71; from asst to prof, Middlebury Col, 71-. **HONORS AND AWARDS** Marshall Scholar, Oxford Univ; Phi Beta Kappa; Walter Cerf Distinguished Coll Prof, Middlebury Col, 96. **MEMBERSHIPS** Am Philos Asn; Am Soc for Aesthetics; Int Asn for Philos and Lit. **RESEARCH** Philosophy; Aesthetics. **SELECTED PUBLICATIONS** Co-ed, The Way to Reason, 82; auth, "Skepticism and the Interpretation of Wittgenstein," 93; "The Mind's Horizon," 96, "Leo Tolstoy," 99. **CONTACT ADDRESS** Dept of Philosophy, Middlebury Col, Middlebury, VT, 05753. **EMAIL** bates@mail.middlebury.edu

BATEY, RICHARD A.
PERSONAL Born 01/19/1933, TN, m, 1953, 3 children **DISCIPLINE** RELIGION **EDUCATION** David Lipscomb Col, BA, 55; Vanderbilt Univ, BD, 58, PhD, 61. **CAREER** Asst prof New Testament theol, Harding Grad Sch Bible & Relig, 60-65; from asst prof to assoc prof Bible & relig, 65-72 , Prof Relig, Southwestern at Memphis, 72-; Fulbright res scholar, Univ Tubingen, 63-64; jr fel humanities, Memphis Acad Arts, 68-71; vis prof, St Mary's Col, Univ St Andrews, Scotland; W J Millard Chair Relig, 76- . **MEMBERSHIPS** Soc Bibl Lit; Am Acad Relig; Soc Study New Testament. **RESEARCH** New Testament theology; linguistic philosophy. **SELECTED PUBLICATIONS** Auth, So all Israel Will be Saved, Interpretation, 4/66; The One Flesh Union of Christ and the Church, New Testament Studies, 4/67; The Letter of Paul to the Romans, Sweet, 69; ed, New Testament Issues, SCM, England & Harper, 70; auth, New Testament Nuptial Imagery, Brill, Holland, 71; Jesus and the Poor, Harper, 72 & Ed Morcelliana, Italy, 73; Guidelines for Professional Ethics, J Am Col Dentists, 10/74; Thank God I'm OK, Abingdon. **CONTACT ADDRESS** 4327 Rhodes Ave, Memphis, TN, 38112.

BATHURST GILSON, ANNE
PERSONAL Born 08/11/1958, Warren, PA, m, 1995 **DISCIPLINE** THEOLOGY; ETHICS **EDUCATION** Chatham Col, BA, 82; Episcopal Divinity School, MDiv, 86; Union Theol Sem NYC, MPhil & PhD, 93. **CAREER** Vis scholar, Episcopal Divinity School, 95-96; Consult, Denominational NAT Agencies, 94-; independent scholar. **HONORS AND AWARDS** Fel, Soc Values Higher Educ. **MEMBERSHIPS** AAR; Soc Values Higher Educ **RESEARCH** Religious right; Economic policy; Christology. **SELECTED PUBLICATIONS** Auth, Eros Breaking Free: Interpreting Sexual Theo-Ethics, Pilgrim, 95; Deep in My Heart: Justice, Family, & the Religious Right, Pilgrim, 99. **CONTACT ADDRESS** 620 G St SE, Washington, DC, 20003. **EMAIL** abgilson@aol.com

BATTAGLIA, JACK M.
DISCIPLINE LAW **EDUCATION** Fordham Univ, BA, 68; Columbia Univ, JD, 71. **CAREER** Staff atty, Legis Drafting Res Fund, Columbia Univ, 71-73; pvt pract, NYC, 73-82; assoc prof Law, Touro Col, 82-84; pvt pract, San Francisco Bay Area, Calif, 84-92. **HONORS AND AWARDS** Harlan Fiske Stone scholar and tchg fel; Robert Noxan Toppan Prize in Const Law. **SELECTED PUBLICATIONS** Auth, Regulation of Hate Speech By Educational Institutions: A Proposed Policy, Santa Clara Law Rev. **CONTACT ADDRESS** Touro Col, Brooklyn, NY, 11230.

BATTENFIELD, JAMES R.
PERSONAL Born 12/13/1935, Lexington, KY **DISCIPLINE** RELIGIOUS STUDIES **EDUCATION** San Diego State Univ, BA, 58; Talbot Theol Sem, BD, 67, ThM, 69; Grace Theol Sem, ThD, 76; **CAREER** Instr, Talbot Theol Sem, 67-70; asst prof, prof, Grace Theol Sem, 70-90; lectr, Calif State Univ, Long Beach, 90-92; expeditions and study tours Near East, 93-94. **HONORS AND AWARDS** Magna Cum Laude, 69; Zion res travel grant, 74; Univ Calif Los Angeles Syriac Dict project grant, 78. **MEMBERSHIPS** Am School of Oriental Res; Bibl Archaeol Soc. **RESEARCH** Old Testament Pentateuch; ancient Near Eastern language and archaeology; Bible and science issues. **SELECTED PUBLICATIONS** Coauth, Madaba Plains Project: A Preliminary Report of the 1987 Season at Tell el-Umeiri and Vicinity, Bul of Am Schools Orient Res, 90; auth, Field C: The Northern Suburb, and, Field E: The Water System, in Madaba Plains Project 2, Andrews Univ, 91; auth, Archaeology, in LaSor, ed, Old Testament Survey, Eerdmans, 96; auth, Some Onomastic Considerations Concerning Sites in the Tall al- Umayri Region, Central Jordan, 1989, in Herr, ed, Madaba Plains Project 3: The 1989 Season at Tell el-Umeiri and Vicinity and Subsequent Studies, Andrews Univ, 97; contrib, Ancient Ammonites and Modern Arabs, Am Ctr of Orient Res, Jordan, 98. **CONTACT ADDRESS** 3356 Elm Ave, Long Beach, CA, 90807-4435. **EMAIL** jjbat@msn.com

BATTIN, MARGARET PABST
PERSONAL Born 11/29/1940, New Orleans, LA, 2 children **DISCIPLINE** PHILOSOPHY **EDUCATION** Bryn Mawr Col, BA, 63; Univ Calif, Irvine, MFA, 73, PhD(philos), 76. **CAREER** Asst prof, 75-80, assoc prof, 80-88, PROF PHILOS, UNIV UTAH, 88-; Nat Endowment Humanities fel independent study & res philos issues in suicide, 77-78. **HONORS AND AWARDS** Distinguished res award, Univ Utah, 97. **MEMBERSHIPS** Am Philos Asn; Am Soc Aesthet; Am Soc Bioethics and Humanities; Int Asn Bioethics **RESEARCH** Philosophical issues in suicide; fiction and philosophy; aesthetics. **SELECTED PUBLICATIONS** Auth, Aristotle's definition of tragedy in the Poetics, Parts I & II, J Aesthet & Art Criticism, winter 74 & spring 75; Terminal procedure (fiction), Am Rev, 75, reprinted, In: The Best American Short Stories 1976, Houghton Mifflin, 76; The sisters (fiction), In: Bitches and Sad Ladies, Harper's Mag Press, 75; Plato on true and false poetry, J Aesthet & Art Criticism, winter 77; co-ed, Suicide: The philosophical issues, St Martin's Press, 81; John Donne's Biathanatos, Garland Publ Co, 82; auth, Ethical Issues in Suicide, Prentice-Hall, 82; co-ed, Puzzles about Art, St Martin's Press, 89; co-ed, Ethical Issues in the Professions, Prentice-Hall, 89; auth, Ethics in the Sanctuary, Yale Univ Press, 90; auth, The Least Worst Death, Oxford Univ Press, 94; co-ed, Physician-Assisted Suicide: Expanding the Debate, Routledge, 98. **CONTACT ADDRESS** Dept of Philos, Univ of Utah, Orson Spencer Hall, Salt Lake City, UT, 84112-8916. **EMAIL** mp.battin@m.cc.utah.edu

BATTLE, MICHAEL
PERSONAL Born 12/12/1963, New Orleans, LA, m, 1996 **DISCIPLINE** RELIGIOUS STUDIES **EDUCATION** Duke Univ, BA, PhD; Princeton Sem, MDiv. **CAREER** Asst prof, Univ of the South, current; asst prof, Duke Divinity School, 99-. **MEMBERSHIPS** AAR. **RESEARCH** Spirituality; Theology; Ethics; South Africa. **SELECTED PUBLICATIONS** Auth, Reconciliation. **CONTACT ADDRESS** School of Theology, Univ of the South, 335 Tennessee Ave, Sewanee, TN, 37383-1000. **EMAIL** mbattle@sewanee.edu

BAUDER, MARK
PERSONAL Born 12/31/1958, Albuquerque, NM **DISCIPLINE** PHILOSOPHY **EDUCATION** Univ Wisc, PhD, 91. **MEMBERSHIPS** Am Philos Asn. **RESEARCH** Realism; Philosophy of science; Philosophy of mind; Philosophy of language; Philosophy of mathematics. **CONTACT ADDRESS** 108 W 45th, #110, Austin, TX, 78751. **EMAIL** mbauder@math.utexas.edu

BAUDUIT, HAROLD S.
PERSONAL Born 08/27/1930, New Orleans, LA **DISCIPLINE** LAW **EDUCATION** US Naval Acad, BS Engrg 1956; Univ of CO, MA Economics, MS Mgmt, JD Law. **CAREER** Univ of CO, atty faculty, 1972-76, instr bus law 1969-76, Economics & Black Studies, assistant professor law practice, 1983-. **HONORS AND AWARDS** Sigma Iota Epsilon Hon Mgmt Frat Univ CO 1969-72; Martin Luther King Jr Fellow; Woodrow Wilson Natl Fellowship Found 1969-71.

BAUER, NANCY
PERSONAL Born 06/12/1960, Phildadelphia, PA, m, 1989, 2 children **DISCIPLINE** PHILOSOPHY AND RELIGION **EDUCATION** Harvard and Radcliffe Col, AB, 82; Harvard Divinity Sch, Master of Theol Studies, 86; Harvard Univ, PhD, 97. **CAREER** Teacher, epistemol, 93, hist of philos, fall, 93, Commonwealth Sch; teaching fel, prob in med ethics, 86, Harvard Divinity Sch; tutorial leader, lit and relig, 87, sr thesis adviser, 94, teaching fel, 87-94, grp tutorial leader, spring, 91, 92, 96, Harvard Univ; asst prof, 97, Bentley Col; lectr, 98, 97, 95, vis asst prof, 98, Tufts Univ. **HONORS AND AWARDS** Cert of Distinction in Teaching, deductive logic, 88, facts and ethics, 89, intro to the prob of philos, 89, moral perfectionism, 90, autonomy and alienation, 93, moral perfectionism, 94, Harvard Univ; dissertation fel, Harvard Grad Soc, 94-95. **RESEARCH** Feminism and feminist philosophy; Continental philosophy, especially 19th century German and 20th century French; history of philosophy, especially Descarts and Kant; Social and political philosophy; Moral philosophy; Ancient philosophy; Aesthetics; Introductory logic. **SELECTED PUBLICATIONS** Rev, Feminist Interpretations of Simone de Beauvoir, Hypatia, 96; auth, Advaita Vedanta and Contemporary Western Ethics, Philos East and West, 87. **CONTACT ADDRESS** Dept. of Philosophy, Tufts Univ, Miner Hall, Medford, MA, 02155. **EMAIL** nbauer01@tufts.edu

BAUERSCHMIDT, FREDERICK CHRISTIAN
PERSONAL Born 09/21/1961 **DISCIPLINE** THEOLOGY AND ETHICS **EDUCATION** Univ South, BA, 84; Yale Divinity Sch, MAR, 89; Duke Univ, PhD, 96. **CAREER** Asst prof, Loyola Col, 94-; lectr, Duke Univ, 93. **HONORS AND AWARDS** Jr fac Sabbatical, Loyola Col Center Humanities, 97; Summer res grant, dean of Arts and Sci, Loyola Col, 95; dept fel, Duke Univ, 89-94; Dept Honors in Rel, Univ South, 84. **MEMBERSHIPS** Amer Acad Rel; Col Theol Soc; Soc Catholic Liturgy. **RESEARCH** Theology and Ethics. **SELECTED PUBLICATIONS** Essays in Refereed Journals, auth, Seeing Jesus: Julian of Norwich and the Text of Christ's Body, J Medieval and Early Modern Studies 27:2, 97; Julian of Norwich C Incorporated, Modern Theol 13:1, 97; Walking in the Pilgrim City, New Blackfriars 77:909, 96; The Abrahamic Voyage: Michel de Certeau and Theology, Modern Theol 12:1, 96; coauth, Eruditio without Religio The Dilemma of Catholics in the Academy, Communio: Int Catholic Rev 22:2, 95; essays in books, The Politics of the Little Way: Dorothy Day Reads Therese of Lisieux, In American Catholic Traditions: Resources for Renewal, Orbis Books, 97; unrefereed publ, Liturgical Rites and Wrongs: The Temptation to be Relevant, Commonweal, 95; Liturgy of the World C Liturgy of the Church, Publ of the Soc for Catholic Liturgy 2:2, 97; rev, P J Fitzpatrick, In Breaking of Bread, in Pro Ecclesia, 95; Grace Jantzen, Power, Gender and Christian Mysticism in Modern Theol 13:3, 97; papers presented, Not Without: Michel de Certeau and a Future for Christian Theology, Amer Acad Rel, Critical Theory section, Washington DC, 93; The Politics of the Little Way: Dorothy Day Reads Therese of Lisieux, The Col Theol Soc, Consultation on Mysticism and Politics, Dayton OH, 96; Neoplatonic Elements in the Christology of Julian of Norwich, Amer Acad Rel, Platonism and Neoplatonism section, New Orleans LA, 96; The Threefold Body: Theology After Suspicion, Christian Theol Res Fel, San Francisco, CA, 97. **CONTACT ADDRESS** Dept of Theology, Loyola Col, 4501 N Charles St, Baltimore, MD, 21210. **EMAIL** fcb@loyola.edu

BAUM, GREGORY G.
PERSONAL Born 06/20/1923, Berlin, Germany **DISCIPLINE** THEOLOGY **EDUCATION** McMaster Univ, BA, 46; Ohio State Univ, MA, 47; Univ Fribourg (Switzerland), ThD, 56. **CAREER** PROF EMER RELIGIOUS STUDIES, McGILL UNIV. **HONORS AND AWARDS** Off, Order Can, 90; hon doct, Huron Col; hon doct, St. Francis Xavier Univ; hon doct, Ohio Wesleyan Univ; hon doct, Lafayette Univ; hon doct, Waterloo Lutheran Univ; hon doct, McMaster Univ. **MEMBERSHIPS** Can Theol Soc; Can Soc Stud Relig; Cath Theol Soc Am. **SELECTED PUBLICATIONS** Auth, That They May Be One, 58; auth, The Jews and the Gospel, 61; auth, Progress and Perspective, 62; auth, Ecumenical Theology Today, 65; auth, Ecumenical Theology No.2, 67; auth, The Credibility of the Church Today, 68; auth, Faith and Doctrine, 69; auth, Man Becoming, 70; auth, New Horizon, 72; auth, Religion and Alienation, 75; auth, The Social Imperative, 78; auth, Catholics and Canadian Socialism, 80; auth, The Priority of Labour, 82; auth, Ethics and Economics, 84; auth, Theology and Society, 87; auth, Compassion and Solidarity, 88; auth, The Church in Quebec, 91; auth, Essays in Critical Theology, 94; auth, Karl Polyani on Ethics and Economics, 96; auth, The Church for Others: Protestant Theology in Communist East Germany, 96. **CONTACT ADDRESS** Dept of Religious Studies, McGill Univ, Montreal, PQ, H3A 2A7.

BAUM, ROBERT J.
PERSONAL Born 10/19/1941, Chicago, IL **DISCIPLINE** PHILOSOPHY **EDUCATION** Northwestern Univ, BA, 63; Ohio State Univ, PhD(philos), 69. **CAREER** From asst to prof philos, Rensselaer Polytech Inst, 69-82; prog dir, Nat Sci Found, 74-76; Prof Philos, Univ Fla, 81-, Dir, Ctr Study Human Dimensions Sci Technol, 76-81 & Ctr Appl Philos & Ethics in Professions, 81-; ed, Bus Prof Ethics J, 81-; ed, Prof Ethics: A Multidisciplinary J, 91-. **MEMBERSHIPS** Am Philos Asn; Soc for Bus Ethics; Asn for Practical and Prof Ethics. **RESEARCH** Theory of knowledge; ethics; applied philosophy. **SELECTED PUBLICATIONS** Auth & ed Philosophy and Mathematics, Freeman, Cooper & Co, 73; ed, Ethical Arguments for Analysis, 73, 2nd ed, 77 & auth, Logic, 74, 2nd ed 80, 3rd ed 89, 4th ed 96, Harcourt Brace & Co; ed, Ethical Problems in Engineering, RPI, 78, 2nd ed, 80; auth, Ethics and Engineering Curricula, Hastings Ctr, 80. **CONTACT ADDRESS** Dept of Philosophy, Univ of Florida, P O Box 118545, Gainesville, FL, 32611-8545. **EMAIL** rbaum@phil.ufl.edu

BAUMBACH, GERARD
PERSONAL Born 03/29/1946, Jackson Heights, NY, m, 1968, 3 children **DISCIPLINE** THEOLOGY **EDUCATION** St Michael's Coll, BA, 68; Univ Md MD, 75; NY Univ, PhD, 89. **CAREER** US Air Force Officer, 68-72; Dir Rel Educ, Church of Saint Clare NY, 72-78; William H Sadlier Inc, 78-; Executive Vice Pres, William H Sadlier Inc, 95-. **MEMBERSHIPS** Asn of Prof and Res in Rel Educ; Rel Educ Asn; Rel Edu Fel NY Univ; Albany Suburban Rel Educ Coord Asn; Coom for Adult and Home Educ; Phi Delta Kappa; kappa Delta Pi, Boy Scouts Of Am. **SELECTED PUBLICATIONS** Auth, Symposium Examines Catechetical Empowerment By Perish Prietss, Momentum, 94; Symposium Examines Priests' Empowering Role in Catechesis, Caravan, 94; The Priest as Empowerer of Catec hetical Ministry, 95; Experiencing Mystagogy: The sacred Pause of Easter, 96; A Never-Ending Relationship: Catechesis and Catholic Social Teaching, Catechetical Leadearship, 97; Spirituality for Lent and Easter: A Guide for Bridging the Mysteries, forthcoming. **CONTACT ADDRESS** William H. Sadlier Inc, Pine St, New York, NY, 10005.

BAUMEL JOSEPH, NORMA
PERSONAL m, 4 children **DISCIPLINE** JUDAISM, JEWISH LAW AND ETHICS **EDUCATION** Brooklyn Col, BA, 66; CUNY, MA, 68; Concordia Univ, PhD, 95. **CAREER** Asst prof; assoc of the ch, Quebec and Can Jewish Stud. **HONORS AND AWARDS** Grants, Heritage Can; FRDP., Pres, Intl Coalition for Agunah Rights (ICAR); consult, Can coalition of Jewish Women for the Get; founder, Montreal Women's Prayer group. **RESEARCH** Modern Jewish feminism, feminist readings of Biblical women. **SELECTED PUBLICATIONS** Auth, "A Feminist Scenario of the Jewish Future, Creating the Jewish Future," Ctr for Jewish Stud, 97; "Celebrating Women: A Jewish Profile, The Feminization of Ritual," Ctr for Stud in Rel and Soc, 97; You don't know me because you can label me: Self-identity of an Orthodox Feminist, A Jewish Sampler: Pattenrs in the Lives of Jewish Women, 96; "Zakhor: Memory, Ritual and Gender," Can Women Stud, 96; Rosh Hodesh Reflections, Celebrating the New Moon: Rosh Hodesh Anthology, Jason Aronson Publ, 96; The Feminist Challenge to Judaism: Critique and Transformation, Gender, Genre and Religion: Feminist Reflections, Wilfred Laurier UP, 95; "Jewish Education for Women: Rabbi Moshe Feinstein's Map of America," Amer Jewish Hist, 95. **CONTACT ADDRESS** Dept of Rel, Concordia Univ, Montreal, 1455 de Maisonneuve W, Montreal, PQ, H3G 1M8. **EMAIL** NOJO@VAX2.CONCORDIA.CA

BAUMGARTEN, ELIAS
PERSONAL Born 07/15/1945, New York, NY **DISCIPLINE** PHILOSOPHY **EDUCATION** Brandeis Univ, AB, 67; Northwestern Univ, MA, 71, PhD, 75. **CAREER** Instr, 72-75, asst prof, 75-80, Assoc Prof Philos, Univ Mich-Dearborn, 80-, Vis fel, Ctr Study Values & Social Policy, Univ Colo, fall, 81 & summer, 82 & vis assoc prof philos, spring, 82; bioethecist comm, Univ MI Med Center, 85-; res assoc, Center for Mid Eastern Nafrican Studies, Univ MI, 89-; Clinical Med Ethics consult, Univ MI Med Center, 93-; Board Adv, Med Updates on Theory diag & prevention, 96-; Board Adv, Jewish Peace Lobby, 96. **HONORS AND AWARDS** Distinguished Tchg Award, Univ MI-Dearborn, 77. **MEMBERSHIPS** Am Philos Asn; Am Asn Philos Tchr(s). **RESEARCH** Ethics and soc policy; bioethics; philos war peace and nationalism. **SELECTED PUBLICATIONS** Auth, The Ethical and Social Responsibilities of Philosophy Teachers, Metaphilos, 4/80; Wittgenstein's Conception of the Willing Subject, Man & World, 81; Ethics in the Academic Profession-A Socratic View, J Higher Educ, 5-6/82; The Right of Psychiatric Patients to Refuse Psychotropic Medication, Ethics, Humanism and Med. **CONTACT ADDRESS** Dept of Hum, Univ MI-Dearborn, 4901 Evergreen Rd, Dearborn, MI, 48128-1491. **EMAIL** elias@umich.edu

BAUMRIN, BERNARD HERBERT
PERSONAL Born 01/07/1934, New York, NY, m, 1953, 3 children **DISCIPLINE** PHILOSOPHY **EDUCATION** Ohio State Univ, AB, 56; Johns Hopkins Univ, PhD, 60; Columbia Univ, JD, 70. **CAREER** Dir forensics, Johns Hopkins Univ, 57-59; vis asst prof philos, Butler Univ, 60-61 & Antioch Col, 61; asst prof philos & chm Del sem philos sci, Univ Del, 61-64; asst prof philos, Wash Univ, 64-67; assoc prof, Hunter Col, 67-68; assoc prof, 68-73, prof Philos, Lehman Col & Grad Sch, City Univ New York, 73- ; adj prof med educ, Mt Sinai Sch of Med, 90- . **HONORS AND AWARDS** AEC; CUNY; Mellon; ACLS; NEH. **MEMBERSHIPS** Am Philos Asn; Am Bar Asn; Mind Asn; AAAS; AAUP. **RESEARCH** Philosophy of science; ethical theory; medical ethics jurisprudence. **SELECTED PUBLICATIONS** Auth, Preventive Detention, In: Dismantling the Criminal Law System: Decriminalization and Divestment, Wayne Law Rev, 3/73; Is There a Freedom Not to Speak?, Metaphilosophy, 1/75; Sexual Immorality Delineated, In: Philosophy and Sex, Prometheus, 75; Autonomy in Rawls and Kant, 76 & Autonomy Interest and the Kantian Interpretation, 77, Midwest Studies Philos; Towards Unravelling the Abortion Problem, In: Bioethics and Human Rights, Little, 78; Foundations of Academic Freedom and Tenure, Annals Scholar, fall 81; Two Concepts of Justice, Midwest Studies Philos, Vol VII, spring 82; auth, Moral Blindnes, in Metaphilosophy, 86; auth, Hobbes' Egalitarianiam, Nantes, 89; auth, The Ethics of Pandemics, APA Newsl, 89; auth, Chronic Illness, J of Med and Philos, 91; auth, Waste, J of Social Philos, 93; auth, Immorality, Midwest Stud, 96; auth, Divorce, In: Encyclopedia of Applied Ethics, 98. **CONTACT ADDRESS** 590 West End Ave, New York, NY, 10024.

BAUR, MICHAEL
PERSONAL Born 11/13/1963, Los Angeles, CA **DISCIPLINE** PHILOSOPHY, LAW **EDUCATION** Loyola Univ, BA, 85; Univ Toronto, MA, 86, PhD, 91; Harvard Law School, JD, 98. **CAREER** Asst prof, Catholic Univ, 91-95; asst prof, Fordham Univ, 98- . **HONORS AND AWARDS** Fulbright Scholar, Heidelberg, Ger, 88-89. **RESEARCH** German, Kant and Idealism, Epistemology, legal Philosophy. **CONTACT ADDRESS** Dept of Philosophy, Fordham Univ, Bronx, NY, 10458. **EMAIL** mbaur@murray.fordham.edu

BAXTER, DONALD L.
DISCIPLINE PHILOSOPHY AND SOCIAL ETHICS **EDUCATION** Oberlin Col, BA, 76; Univ Pittsburgh, MA, 80, PhD, 84. **CAREER** Dept Philos, Univ Conn **HONORS AND AWARDS** Co-winner, Leibniz Soc Essay Competition, 94. **RESEARCH** Metaphysics, Hume, Berkeley, Leibniz, Bradley. **SELECTED PUBLICATIONS** Auth, Abstraction, Inseparability, and Identity, Philos and Phenomenological Res, 97; Bradley on Substantive and Adjective: The ComplexUnity Problem, Perspectives on the Logic and Metaphysics of F H Bradley, Thoemmes Press, 96; Corporeal Substances and True Unities, Studia Leibnitiana, 95; Continuity and Common Sense, Intl Stud in Philos, 92. **CONTACT ADDRESS** Dept of Philos, Univ Conn, 1266 Storrs Rd, Storrs, CT, 06269. **EMAIL** baxter@uconnvm.uconn.edu

BAYCROFT, JOHN A.
PERSONAL Born 06/02/1933, Redcar, England **DISCIPLINE** RELIGION **EDUCATION** Christ Col, Cambridge (Synge sch), BA, 54, MA, 58; Ripon Hall, Oxford (GOE), 55; Trinity Col, Toronto, BD, 59; DD(hon), Montreal Diocesan Theol Col; DSLitt(jur dig), Thornloe Univ; DD(hon), Huron Col. **CAREER** Rector, Loughborough, 55-57; asst rector, St. Matthew's Church, Ottawa, 57-62; rector, Perth, Ont, 62-67; rector, St. Matthias Church, Ottawa, 67-84; rector, Christchurch Cathedral, dean, Ottawa, 84-86; suffragan bishop, Ottawa, 85-93; BISHOP OF OTTAWA, ANGLICAN CHURCH OF CANADA, 93-; lectr, Carleton Univ; mem fac theol, St. Paul Univ. **MEMBERSHIPS** Anglican/Roman Cath Int Comm; Anglican/Roman Cath Dialogue Can; Am Acad Relig; Soc Bible Lit; Can Church Hist. **SELECTED PUBLICATIONS** Auth, The Anglican Way, 80; auth, The Eucharistic Way, 82; auth, The Way of Prayer, 83. **CONTACT ADDRESS** Anglican Church of Canada, 71 Bronson Ave, Ottawa, ON, K1R 6G6.

BAYER, GREG
PERSONAL Born 06/03/1954, PA **DISCIPLINE** PHILOSOPHY **EDUCATION** St John's Coll, BA, 78; Univ Toronto, MA, 81; Univ Tex, PhD, 95. **CAREER** Teaching asst, Univ Toronto, 80-81; teaching asst, Univ Tex Austin, 91-94; asst instr, Univ Tex Austin, 95; asst prof, SMU, 95-06; asst prof, William and Mary, 96-97; asst prof, College of Wooster, 97-98. **MEMBERSHIPS** Am Philos Asn. **RESEARCH** Philosophy; Ancient Philosophy; Aristotle. **SELECTED PUBLICATIONS** Auth, Definition through Demonstration: Aristotle's two Syllogisms in Posterior Analytics II.8, Phronesis, 95; Mackie, Kripke and Causal Necessity, Southwest Philos Rev, 96; Coming to Know Principles in Posterior Analytics II.19, Aperion, 97; Aristotelian Inquiry in the Posterior Anal ytics: The What-IS-X? Question, Ancient Philos, 97; Classification and Explanation in Aristotle's Theory of Definition, J of the Hist of Philos, forthcoming; rev, of Analysis and Science in Aristotle, 97. **CONTACT ADDRESS** Institute for Advanced Studies, School of Historical Studies, Orden Ln, Princeton, NJ, 08540. **EMAIL** gbayer@ias.edu

BAYER, HANS F.
PERSONAL Born 10/27/1954, Stuttgart, Germany, m, 1976, 3 children **DISCIPLINE** NEW TESTAMENT EXEGESIS

EDUCATION Ashland Theol Sem, MA, 77, MDiv, 79; Univ Aberdeen, Scotland, PhD, 84. **CAREER** Dozent, German Theol Sem, Giessen, Ger, 84-94; assoc prof Covenant Theol Sem, 94- ; Dir ThM program, 96- . **HONORS AND AWARDS** Tyndale fel scholar, Cambridge, 83; AfeT Scholar, Germany, 82. **MEMBERSHIPS** Soc Bibl Lit; Evangelical Theol soc; Tyndale fel; AfeT/FEET. **RESEARCH** The Gospel of Mark; Acts. **SELECTED PUBLICATIONS** Auth, Jesus' Predictions of Vindication and Resurrection, Their Provenance, Meaning and Correlation, WUNT, 2/20, O. Hofius, M. Hengel, Tubingen, JCB Mohr (Paul Siebeck), 86, X + 289 S, (monograph); Rober Yarbrough, O. Cullmanns Progressiv-heilsgeschichtliche Konzeption, in Glaube und Geschichte, ed, Helge Stadelmann, TVG, GieBen/Wuppertal: Brunnen/Brockhaus, 88, 86, 319-347; Verstockung, Weissagen/Weissagung, Verziehen/ Verzogerung, in Das Grosse Bibellexikon, Bd 3, ed (s), H. Burkhardt, G. Maier, F. Grunzweig, F. Laubach, Wuppertal/ Giessen: Brockhaus/Brunnen, 89, 1641, 1645, 1681, 1682; Jesus-Interpretationen in der Sachliteratur: Franz Alts Jesus-der erste neue Mann, in Christlicher Glaube und Literatur, 5, ed (s) C.P. Thiede, Wuppertal: R. Brockhaus, 1991, 55-71; Predictions of Jesus' Passion and Resurrection, in Dictionary of Jesus and the Gospels, ed (s), J.B. Green, S. McKnight, Downers Grove, IL/Leicester, IVP, 92, 630-633; Christ-Centered Eschatology in Acts 3:17-26, in J.B. Green/M. Turner's Jesus of Nazareth, Lord and Christ, Essays on the Historical Jesus and New Testament Christology, Grand Rapids/Carlisle, Eerdmans/ Paternoster, 96, 236-250; The Preaching of Peter in Acts in I.H. Marshall/ E. Peterson's, Witness to the Gospel: The Theology of Acts, Grand Rapids/Cambridge, W.B. Eerdmans/The Paternoster Press, 98, 257-274. **CONTACT ADDRESS** Dept of Theology, Covenant Theol Sem, 12330 Conway Rd, St. Louis, MO, 63141.

BAYER, RICHARD C.
PERSONAL Born 07/13/1956, Philadelphia, PA **DISCIPLINE** SOCIAL ETHICS **EDUCATION** Univ TX AT Arlington, BA, 77, MA, 79; Univ Dallas, MA, 84; Graduate Theological Union, PhD, 90. **MEMBERSHIPS** Soc of Christian Ethics; Amer Acad of Religion; Catholic Theological Soc of Amer; Gabriel Marcel Soc. **RESEARCH** Ethics and economics; political theory **SELECTED PUBLICATIONS** Auth, Ryan's Living Wage: A Reinterpretation and Constructive Proposal, Journal for Peace and Justice Studies, 94; auth, Christian Personalism and Democratic Capitalism, Horizons, 94; auth, Christian Perspectives on A theory of Justice by John Rawls, Journal **CONTACT ADDRESS** 275 Hoym S, #4F, Fort Lee, NJ, 07024-5615.

BAYLIS, FRANCOISE
DISCIPLINE MEDICAL PHILOSOPHY **EDUCATION** McGill Univ, BA, 83; W Ontario Univ, MA, 84, PhD, 89. **CAREER** Prof. **RESEARCH** Medical ethics. **SELECTED PUBLICATIONS** Co-ed, Health Care Ethics in Canada, 95; "Errors in Medicine: Nurturing Truthfulness," Jour of Clinical Ethics, 97; "Health Care Ethics Consultation: Training in Virtue," Hum Stud, 98; Codes of Ethics, 98; auth, Informed Consent-New Reproductive Techniologies, Encycl of Reproductive Tech, 98; co-auth, Nat Coun on Bioethics in Human Res, Facilitating Ethical Research: Promoting Informed Choice, Discussion Document, NCBHR Communique, 96; "Women and Health Research: Working for Change," Jour of Clinical Ethics, 96; Child Abuse and Neglect: Cross-Cultural Considerations, Feminism and Families, 97; Medical Ethics and the Pediatric Surgeon, Surgery of Infants and Children, 97; "Bioethics for Clinicians: Ethical Dilemmas that Arise in the Care of Pregnant Women Can," Med Assoc Jour, 97; "Bioethics for Clinicians: Confidentiality," Can Med Assoc Jour, 97; Moral Residue: The Problem of Moral Compromise, Margin of Error, 98; Women and Health Research, Embodying Bioethics: Feminist Advances, 98; Reframing Research Involving Humans, The Politics of Women's Health: Exploring Agency and Autonomy, 98. **CONTACT ADDRESS** Dept of Philos, Dalhousie Univ, Halifax, NS, B3H 3J5. **EMAIL** fbaylis@tupdean1.med.dal.ca

BAZAN, BERNARDO C.
PERSONAL Born 10/26/1939, Mendoza, Argentina **DISCIPLINE** PHILOSOPHY **EDUCATION** Univ Cuyo (Arg), MA, 62; Univ Louvain (Belgium), LPhil, 65, PhD Phil, 67, PhD Medieval Stud, 72. **CAREER** Prof, Univ Cuyo (Arg), 69; assoc prof, 77, prof, 79-97, ch dept philos, 89-91, dean arts, 91-95, PROF EMER, UNIV OTTAWA, 97-; vis prof, Catholic Univ Am, 83-84. **HONORS AND AWARDS** Fel, Royal Soc Can. **SELECTED PUBLICATIONS** Auth, Siger de Brabant: Quaestiones in tertium De Anima, De Anima intellectiva, De aeternitate mundi, 72; auth, Siger de Brabant: ecrits de logique, de morale et de physique, 74; auth, S. Thomas Quaestiones disputatae de anima, 96; coauth, Trois commentaires anonymes sur le Traite de l'ame d'Aristote, 71; coauth, Les questions disputees dans les Facultes de theologie, de droit et de medecine, 85; co-ed, Political Philosophies in the Middle Ages, 95. **CONTACT ADDRESS** 8 Birch Ave, Toronto, ON, K1K 3G6.

BAZAN, CARLOS
DISCIPLINE PHILOSOPHY **EDUCATION** Univ Mendoza, BA, MA; Univ Louvain, MA, Dipl Sc Mediev, PhD. **CAREER** Prof, Univ Ottawa. **RESEARCH** Medieval and moral philosophy. **SELECTED PUBLICATIONS** Co-auth, Trois commentaires anonymes sur le Traite de l'ame d'Aristote, Paris, 71; Les Questions disputees et les questions quodlibetiques dans les Facultes de Theologie, de droit et de Medicine, Turnhout, Belgique, 85; auth, Siger de Brabant: Quaestiones in tertium De anima; De anima intellectiva; De aeternitate mundi, edition critique, Louvain-Paris, 72; Siger de Brabant: ecrits de logique, de morale et de physique, edition critique, Louvain-Paris, 74; S. Thomae de Aquino Quaes tinones disputatae de anima, dans Opera Omnia iussu Leonis XII P.M. edita, Rome-Paris, 96; ed, Moral and Political Philosophies in the Middle Ages, Actes du IXe Congres international de Philosophie medievale, Ottawa, 96. **CONTACT ADDRESS** Dept of Philosophy, Univ Ottawa, 70 Laurier Ave, PO Box 450, Ottawa, ON, K1N 6N5.

BEAL, TIMOTHY K.
DISCIPLINE RELIGIOUS STUDIES **EDUCATION** Emory Univ, PhD. **CAREER** Asst prof. **RESEARCH** Biblical studies. **SELECTED PUBLICATIONS** Auth, The Book of Hiding: Gender, Ethnicity, Annihilation, and Esther; co-auth, Reading Bibles, Writing Bodies: Identity and The Book; God in the Fray: Divine Ambivalence in the Hebrew Bible. **CONTACT ADDRESS** Religious Studies Dept, Eckerd Col, 54th Ave S, PO Box 4200, St Petersburg, FL, 33711. **EMAIL** bealtk@eckerd.edu

BEALE, DAVID OTIS
PERSONAL VA, m, 3 children **DISCIPLINE** CHURCH HISTORY, THEOLOGY **EDUCATION** Bob Jones Univ, BA, 73, MA, 75, PhD(church hist), 80. **CAREER** Grad asst hist & church hist, 73-78, prof Church Hist, Theology & Bible, Bob Jones Univ, 78-. **HONORS AND AWARDS** Certificate of Award, Society for the Advancement and Preservation of Fundamental Studies of the Christian Faith, 95. **MEMBERSHIPS** Society for the Advancement and Preservation of Fundamental Studies. **RESEARCH** Historical Theology; Church Fathers; Colonial American churches; American Christianity since 1800; Baptist History; continued on-site research in British Isles and Holland tracing roots of Puritans, Pilgrims, Methodists, and Baptists. **SELECTED PUBLICATIONS** Auth, A Pictorial History of Our English Bible, Bob Jones Univ Press, 82; In Pursuit of Purity: American Fundamentalism Since 1950, Bob Jones Univ Press, 86; Ancient Attitudes towards Abortion, 1/82; A Family Travel and Tour Guide: Role of Protestant Churches in Early American History, 7-8/82; Fundamentalism: Past and Present, 10/82; The Purgatory Myth, 1/83; Francis Makemie: Champion of Religious Liberty, 5-6/83; Peter Muhlenberg: from the Pulpit to the Battlefield, 7-8/83; Lessons from the Catacombs, 12/83; The Pilgroms and God's Providence, 11/84; The Log College, 3/85; Faith for Family; The Revelation of Jesus Christ, Rev 19:1-21, Bibl Viewpoint, 11/82. **CONTACT ADDRESS** Relig Dept, Bob Jones Univ, 1700 Wade Hampton, Greenville, SC, 29614-0001. **EMAIL** Beale_BookSearch@compuserve.com

BEALE, GREGORY
PERSONAL m, 3 children **DISCIPLINE** NEW TESTAMENT **EDUCATION** Southern Methodist Univ Dallas, BA, 71, MA, 76; Dallas Theol Sem, ThM, 76; Univ Cambridge, PhD, 80. **CAREER** Guest asst, asst prof, Grove City Col, 80-84; prof, Gordon-Conwell Theol Sem, 84 -; dir, ThM Prog in Biblical Theol. **MEMBERSHIPS** Mem, Evangel Theol Soc; Soc Biblical Lit; Inst Biblical Res; Tyndale Fel for Biblical and Theol Res. **RESEARCH** New Testament interpretative methodology, eschatology. **SELECTED PUBLICATIONS** Auth, The Use of Daniel in Jewish Apocalyptic Literature and in the Revelation of St John; ed, The Right Doctrine From the Wrong Text?, Essays on the Use of the Old Testament in the New, 94. **CONTACT ADDRESS** Gordon-Conwell Theol Sem, 130 Essex St, South Hamilton, MA, 01982.

BEAN, HEATHER ANN ACKLEY
PERSONAL Born 01/22/1966, Massillon, OH, m, 1993, 1 child **DISCIPLINE** RELIGION **EDUCATION** Claremont Grad Univ, PhD, 97. **CAREER** Prof, Scholars Bibl Col, 97-98; lectr, 98-. **HONORS AND AWARDS** Nat Merit Scholar, 84. **MEMBERSHIPS** Am Acad of Relig; Am Studies Asn; Appalachian Studies Asn. **RESEARCH** Religion; Philosophy of religion and theology. **CONTACT ADDRESS** Dept of Philosophy and Religion, Azusa Pacific Univ, 901 E. Alosta, Azusa, CA, 91702. **EMAIL** hbean@apu.edu

BEANBLOSSOM, RONALD EDWIN
PERSONAL Born 11/24/1941, Des Moines, IA, m, 1965, 2 children **DISCIPLINE** HISTORY OF MODERN PHILOSOPHY **EDUCATION** Morningside Col, BA, 64; Union Theol Sem, NY, BD, 67; Univ Rochester, PhD(philos), 71. **CAREER** Asst prof philos, Northern Ill Univ, 70-77; Univ Chaplain, Ohio Northern Univ, 79-; assoc prof Philos & relig, Ohio Northern Univ, 82-87; chemn dept Philos & relig, 88-91; prof Philos & relig, 87-. **HONORS AND AWARDS** Sara A Ridenour Endowed Chair for Humanities, 89-90. **MEMBERSHIPS** Am Philos Asn. **RESEARCH** British empiricism; theories of perception; problems of knowledge; Quarterly, 88; Natural Reason: Essays in Honor of Joseph Norio Uemura, Hamline, 92; Reid and Hume, On the Nature of Belief, Reid Studies, 98. **SELECTED PUBLICATIONS** Auth, Walton on rational action, Mind, 71; Thomas Reid's Inquiry & Essays, LLA, 75; Russel's indebtedness to Reid, Monist, 78; A new foundation for human scepticism, Philos Studies, 76. **CONTACT ADDRESS** Dept of Philos & Relig, Ohio Northern Univ, 525 S Main St, Ada, OH, 45810-1555.

BEANE, DOROTHEA ANNETTE
PERSONAL Born 03/30/1952, Plainfield, New Jersey, s **DISCIPLINE** LAW **EDUCATION** Spelman College, 1971-72; Drew University, BA, 1974; Rutgers-Newark College of Law, JD, 1977. **CAREER** US Department of Justice, Civil Division, Torts Branch, trial attorney, 1977-81; Law Firm of Robinson and Geraldo, associate attorney, 1981-82; US Department of Justice, assistant US attorney; Stetson University College of Law, assistant professor, 1990-. **HONORS AND AWARDS** US Department of Justice, Attorney General's Special Achievement Award, 1986; Women's Singles Table Tennis Championship of Jacksonville, FL, 1988-89; US Marshal's Service Letter of Appreciation, 1990; US Postal Service Letter of Appreciation, 1990. **MEMBERSHIPS** American Bar Association, 1990-; Black Law Students Association, faculty advisor, 1990-; Sarasota County American Inns of Court, academic master, 1990-; Association of American Law School, house of representatives, 1991; Stetson University Senate, representative, 1992-; American College of Legal Medicine, 1992-. **CONTACT ADDRESS** Professor, Stetson Col of Law, 1401-61st St South, Rm 211, St Petersburg, FL, 33707.

BEARD, JAMES WILLIAM, JR.
PERSONAL Born 09/16/1941, Chillicothe, OH, m **DISCIPLINE** LAW **EDUCATION** Hardin-Simmons Univ, BS 1967; TX So Univ, JD 1973; Univ of TX, LLM 1976. **CAREER** Thurgood Marshall Law School, TX Southern Univ, assoc prof of law, assoc dean for academic affairs & programs, dir fed tax clinic. **HONORS AND AWARDS** Outstanding Young Amer for 1977. **MEMBERSHIPS** Mem Amer Bar Assn, State Bar of TX; bd of govs Natl Bar Assn; chmn Sect of Taxation NBA; mem NAACP; past trust Houston Legal Found. **CONTACT ADDRESS** Thurgood Marshall Law Sch, Texas So Univ, 3100 Cleburne, Houston, TX, 77004.

BEARDSLEY, RUTH E.
PERSONAL Born 06/14/1936, El Paso, TX, d, 2 children **DISCIPLINE** PHILOSOPHY **EDUCATION** Univ Utah, BSN, 53; Univ Colorado, MA, 75, PhD, 85. **CAREER** Univ So Col, 83-86; adj instr, 82-92, chemn, philos dept, 92 -, Pikes Peak Commun Col; adj instr, Univ Col, 82-92. **HONORS AND AWARDS** NEH co-grantee, 82; Fulbright-Hays fel, 93; Fulbright-Hays, NEH, East-West Ctr field study, 94; NEH workshop, 96. **MEMBERSHIPS** APA; Soc Int Universalism. **RESEARCH** Problems with loyalty; undergraduate education; Asian philosophy. **SELECTED PUBLICATIONS** Auth, Don't Let Tactics Trip You Up, Am Jour of Nurs, 83; auth, dir, producer, video, Language Distortion and Propaganda Techniques, 83; auth, Meta-ethics of Commitment, Dialectics and Humanism, 90; auth, Meta-ethics of Commitment II, Conf notes, Western Social Sci Asn, 92; Loyalty and Commitment With Special Emphasis on China, Univ Chicago, 95. **CONTACT ADDRESS** Dept of Communications, Humanities and Social Scie, Pikes Peak Comm Col, 5675 S Academy Blvd, Colorado Springs, CO, 80906-5498. **EMAIL** ruth.beardsley@ppcc.cccoes.edu

BEASLEY, ALICE MARGARET
PERSONAL Born 04/27/1945, Tuskegee, AL **DISCIPLINE** LAW **EDUCATION** Marygrove Coll Detroit, MI, BA 1966; Univ of CA Berkeley, JD 1973. **CAREER** San Francisco Chronicle, writer 1970; Howard Prim Rice Nemerovski et al, atty 1973-74; Legal Aid Soc of Alameda Co, atty 1974-76; NAACP Legal Def & Educ Fund Inc, atty 1977-78; Erickson Beasley & Hewitt, atty/partner 1978-. **MEMBERSHIPS** Bd mem San Francisco Lawyer's Com for Urban Affairs 1978-; bd mem Legal Aid Soc of Alameda Co 1978-; mem Litigation com Equal rights Adv; mem CA State & Fed Bar Assns 1973-; bd mem Stiles Hall Univ YMCA 1978-; mem Black Women Lawyers Assn; mem Charles Houston Bar Assn; mem & assoc editor CA Law Review 1972-73; lectr Civil Rights Practice for Pract Law Inst/Equal Oppty Employment Commn/CA Continuing Educ of the Bar. **CONTACT ADDRESS** Erickson Beasley & Hewitt, 12 Geary St, San Francisco, CA, 94108.

BEATCH, B. RICHARD
DISCIPLINE PHILOSOPHY **EDUCATION** Univ Calgary, Can, BA, 89; SUNY at Buffalo, PhD, 94. **CAREER** Asst prof, Weber State Univ. **RESEARCH** Theory of knowledge, theories of truth, metaphysics, and philosophy of science. **SELECTED PUBLICATIONS** Auth, The Radical Nature of Margolis' Relativism, J Philos Res, Vol xxi, 96. **CONTACT ADDRESS** Dept of Political Science, Weber State Univ, 1403 University Cir, Ogden, UT, 84408-1403. **EMAIL** rbeatch@weber.edu

BEATTIE, GEOFFREY W.
DISCIPLINE LAW **EDUCATION** Univ Western Ontario, LLB, 84. **CAREER** Adj fac; partner, Tory Tory DesLauriers & Binnington **HONORS AND AWARDS** VP, Investment Banking Wood Gundy Inc, 87-90. **SELECTED PUBLICATIONS** Auth, pubs on corporate law. **CONTACT ADDRESS** Fac of Law, Univ Toronto, 78 Queen's Park, Toronto, ON.

BEATTY, JOHN
DISCIPLINE PHILOSOPHY **CAREER** Univ Ind, PhD. **RESEARCH** Philosophy of science; science and society. **SELECTED PUBLICATIONS** Auth, Dobzhansky and the Biology of Democracy: The Moral and Political Significance of Genetic Variation, Princeton, 94; Speaking of Species: Darwin's Strategy, MIT, 92; co-auth, The Propensity Interpretation of Fitness, MIT, 93. **CONTACT ADDRESS** Philosophy Dept, Univ of Minnesota, Twin Cities, 355 Ford Hall, 224 Church St SE, Minneapolis, MN, 55455. **EMAIL** jbeatty@tc.umn.edu

BEATTY, JOSEPH
DISCIPLINE PHILOSOPHY **EDUCATION** LaSalle Col, BA(English), 63; Johns Hopkins Univ, MA(Writing), 64; Haverford Col, MA(Philosophy), 66; Northwestern Univ, PhD(Philosophy), 72. **CAREER** Lectr, asst prof, Williams Col, 70-78; vis assoc prof, Duke Univ, 79-81; assoc prof, Davidson Col, 81-83; assoc prof, 83-, PROF, PHILOS, 88-, RANDOLPH-MACON COL; Kent fel, Danforth, 70; Nat Hum Ctr fel, 78-79; NEG summer sem, 89. **CONTACT ADDRESS** Dept of Philosophy, Randolph-Macon Col, Ashland, VA, 23005. **EMAIL** jbeatty@rmc.edu

BEATTY, OTTO, JR.
PERSONAL Born 01/26/1940, Columbus, OH, d **DISCIPLINE** LAW **EDUCATION** Howard University, Washington, DC, BA, business administration, 1961; Ohio State University, Columbus, OH, JD, 1965. **CAREER** Ohio House of Representatives, state representative, 1980-; Beatty & Roseboro, Columbus, OH, founder/senior partner, currently. **HONORS AND AWARDS** Citizens for Jesse Jackson Special Achievement Award; Outstanding Leadership Award, Columbus State Community College; Outstanding Service, Family Missionary Baptist Church; Outstanding Services Award, Franklin County Children's Services; 10 Outstanding Young Men Award, Junior Chamber of Commerce of Ohio; Meritorious Service Award, The Ohio Academy of Trial Lawyers; Community Service Award, Ohio Minority Businesses; Certificate of Appreciation for Dedicated Services, Upward Bound Program; Outstanding Legislator Award; Outstanding Local Trial Bar Association, Continuing Legal Education; Outstanding Worksites Award. "Damages in Soft Tissue Cases," Ohio Academy of Trial Lawyers; "Judgments under Ohio Tort Reform Law," "Proving Damages after Tort Reform," Ohio Legal Center. **MEMBERSHIPS** American Arbitration Assn; American Bar Assn; American Trial Lawyers Assn; Black Elected Democrats of Ohio; Columbus Area Black Elected Officials; Ohio State Consumer Education Assn; Natl Bar Assn; NAACP; Operation PUSH; Natl Conference of Black Lawyers, Columbus Chapter; Columbus Apartment Assn; Chamber of Commerce; Hunger Task Force of Ohio; Ohio Alliance of Black School Educators; Natl Black Programming Consortium; Black Chamber of Commerce; Columbus Assn of Black Journalists; Ohio Assn of Real Estate Brokers; Eastern Union Missionary Baptist Assn. **SELECTED PUBLICATIONS** "Damages in Soft Tissue Cases," Ohio Academy of Trial Lawyers; "Judgments under Ohio Tort Reform Law," "Proving Damages after Tort Reform," Ohio Legal Center. **CONTACT ADDRESS** Beatty & Roseboro Co., LPA, 233 S High St, Suite 300, Columbus, OH, 43205.

BEAUCHAMP, RICHARD A.
PERSONAL Born 09/29/1938, Richmond, VA, m, 1977, 2 children **DISCIPLINE** PHILOSOPHY **EDUCATION** Randolph-Macon Col, BA, 61; Yale Divinity Sch, Mdiv, 64; Duke Univ, PhD, 70. **CAREER** Instr, Duke Univ, 68-69; lectr, Mary Baldwin Col, 71-73; adjunct prof, Christopher Newport Col/St. Leo Col, 73-76; assoc prof, Thomas Nelson Community Col, 76-81; vis prof, Col of William and Mary, 89; asst prof, Christopher Newport Col, 89-92; asst prof, Col of William and Mary, 89-92; assoc prof, Christopher Newport Univ, 92-98. **MEMBERSHIPS** Am Philos Asn, Va Philos Asn; Am Acad of Relig; Am Asn of Col and Univ; Asn of General and Liberal Studies. **RESEARCH** Philosophy; Theology. **SELECTED PUBLICATIONS** Auth, "Peirce, Thirdness, and Pedagogy: Reforming the Paideia," 99; "A Naturalist in Spite of Himself: A Dialogue with E.S. Brightman," 99; "Ethics and Metaethics in Bowne's Philosphy," 97; "Persons and Time: A Habermasian Corrective to Heidegger," 99; "Essay Questions Without Essays: Relief for Bleary-Eyed Professors," 96; "Moral Theory and Moral Education: The Neglected Connection," 95. **CONTACT ADDRESS** Dept of Philosophy & Religious Studies, Christopher Newport Univ, 1 University Pl, Newport News, VA, 23606. **EMAIL** Beaucham@cnu.edu

BEAUCHAMP, TOM
PERSONAL Austin, TX **DISCIPLINE** PHILOSOPHY **EDUCATION** Yale Univ, BA; Johns Hopkins Univ, PhD, 70. **CAREER** Prof. **RESEARCH** History of modern philosophy and practical ethics; biomedical ethics; business ethics. **SELECTED PUBLICATIONS** Auth, Hume and the Problem of Causation, Oxford, 81; Principles of Biomedical Ethics, Oxford, 79; A History and Theory of Informed Consent, Oxford, 86; Philosophical Ethics, McGraw-Hill, 82. **CONTACT ADDRESS** Dept of Philosophy, Georgetown Univ, 37th and O St, Washington, DC, 20057.

BEAUCHESNE, RICHARD J.
DISCIPLINE RELIGIOUS STUDIES **EDUCATION** Oblate Col & Sem, BA, MA; Boston Univ, PhD. **CAREER** Relig, Emmanuel Col. **SELECTED PUBLICATIONS** Coauth, The Eucharist as Sacrifice: Ethics that Enlightens Doctrine and Cult (An Ecumenical Praxis), 91; The Supernatural Existential as Desire: Karl Rahner & Emmanuel Levinas Revisited, Eglise et Theologie, 92; Attention in Simone Weil and Dying as Supreme Attention, Univ St Paul, 95; Scriptural; Theological Arguments Against Women's Ordination (Simply Stated) and Responses in Journal of Ecumenical Studies, 95; Yves Congar Leaves Rich Legacy, Nat Catholic Reporter, 95; Simone Weil: Judaism, Christianity, and Islam, and Today's Feminist Critique of Patriarchy, The Religions of the Book, Univ Press Am, 96. **CONTACT ADDRESS** Emmanuel Col, Massachusetts, 400 The Fenway, Boston, MA, 02115.

BEAUDOIN, JOHN M.
PERSONAL Born 07/18/1968, Chicago, IL **DISCIPLINE** PHILOSOPHY **EDUCATION** Univ IA, PhD , 97. **CAREER** Adj asst prof, 97-., Univ Iowa **MEMBERSHIPS** APA; Philos of Sci Asn. **RESEARCH** Philos of relig, of science, and of mind. **SELECTED PUBLICATIONS** Auth, Evil, The Human Cognitive Condition, and Natural Theology, Relig Studes 34, 98. **CONTACT ADDRESS** Dept of Philosophy, Univ of Iowa, Iowa City, IA, 52240. **EMAIL** beaudoin@blue.weeg.uiowa.edu

BECHTEL, CAROL M.
PERSONAL Born 05/23/1959, Savannah, IL, d, 2 children **DISCIPLINE** THEOLOGY **EDUCATION** Yale Univ, PhD, 93. **CAREER** Presbyterian Sch of Christian Ed, assoc prof, 91-94; Western Theol Sem, assoc prof, 94-. **HONORS AND AWARDS** Reformed Church of Am, GSPT Award. **MEMBERSHIPS** SBL **RESEARCH** Psalms; Esther; intersection of Bible and music. **SELECTED PUBLICATIONS** Auth, Glimpses of Glory, Westminster John Knox Press, 98; auth, Sowing Tears Reaping Joy: The Bible and Brahms's Requiem, Kerygma, 97; auth, Hallelujah!: The Bible and Handel's Messiah, Kerygma, 95. **CONTACT ADDRESS** Dept of Old Testament, Western Theol Sem, 101 E. 13th St, Holland, MI, 49423-3622. **EMAIL** carol@westernsem.org

BECHTEL, LYN
PERSONAL Born 09/01/1939, NJ, m, 1990, 2 children **DISCIPLINE** BIBLICAL STUDIES **EDUCATION** Drew Univ Grad Sch, PhD, 83. **CAREER** Assoc prof of Hebrew Bible, Moravian Theol Sem, 89-98; vis assoc prof of Hebrew Bible, Drew Theol Sem, 98- . **MEMBERSHIPS** SBL. **RESEARCH** Feminist hermeneutics; Genesis; Deuteronomic theology; postmodern Biblical interpretation. **SELECTED PUBLICATIONS** Auth, The Perception of Shame Within the Divine/Human Relationship in Biblical Israel, in Hopfe, ed, Uncovering Ancient Stones: Essays in Memory of H. Neil Richardson, Eisenbrauns, 94; auth, What If Dinah Is Not Raped? (Genesis 34), J of the Stud of the Old Testament, 94; auth, Adam and Eve: A Myth about Human Maturation, 1994 Annual of Hermeneutics and Social Concern, Continuum, 94; auth, Genesis 2.4b-3.24: A Myth about Human Maturation, J for the Study of Old Testament, 95; auth, A Feminist Approach to the Book of Job, in Brenner, ed, Feminist Companion to Wisdom Literature, Sheffield, 95; auth, A Symbolic Level of Meaning of the Mariage in Cana Story, in Brenner, Feminist Companion to the Hebrew Scriptures in the new Testament, Sheffield, 95; auth, Shame, in Russell, ed, Dictionary of Feminist Theologies, 96; auth, Genesis 34 Revisited, in Rogerson, ed, Pentateuch, Sheffield, 97; auth, The Sanction of Shame in Biblical Israel, in Social-Scientific Old Testament Criticism, Sheffield, 97; auth, Sex, in Freedman, ed, Eerdmans Dictionary of the Bible, Eerdmans, 97; auth, A Feminist Reading of Genesis 19, in Brenner, ed, Feminist Companion to Genesis II, Sheffield, 98; auth, Dinah, Daughters and Wife of Lot, Woman Who Miscarries or Is Barren, Fruitful Wife, Daughters of the Region, Daughters of Jacob, in Meyers, ed, Women in Scripture: A Dictionary of Named and Unnamed Women in the Hebrew Bible, Apocrypha, and New Testament, Houghton Mifflin, 98; auth, Boundary Issues in Genesis 19, in Graham, ed, Marking Boundaries: Essays on/in Feminist Theological Hermeneutics, Sheffield, forthcoming. **CONTACT ADDRESS** 480 Raubsville Rd, Easton, PA, 18042. **EMAIL** lkdey@aol.com

BECHTEL, WILL
PERSONAL Born 12/01/1951, Detroit, MI **DISCIPLINE** PHILOSOPHY, PHILOSOPHY OF SCIENCE **EDUCATION** Kenyon Coll, AB, 73; Univ Chicago, PhD, 77. **CAREER** Asst prof, Northern Ky Univ, 77-80; Asst prof; Univ Ill Med Center, 80-83; asst prof and full prof, Ga State Univ, 83-94; PROF, Wash Univ St Louis, 94-. **MEMBERSHIPS** Philos of Sci Asn; Soc for Philos and Psychol; Southern Soc for Philos and Psychol; Cognitive Sci Soc; Cognitive Neuroscience Soc; Am Philos Asn. **RESEARCH** Philosophy of neuroscience and cognitive science; history and philosophy of biology. **SELECTED PUBLICATIONS** Auth, pubs on philosophy of neuroscience and cognitive science, history and philosophy of biology; coauth, Discovering Complexity: decomposition and localization as strategies in scientific research, 93; How to do things with logic, 94; A companion to cognitive science, 98; Connectionism and the mind II: Parallel processing, dynamics, and evolution, in press. **CONTACT ADDRESS** Dept of Philosophy, Wash Univ, St. Louis, MO, 63124. **EMAIL** bechtel@twinearth.wustl.edu

BECK, GUY
PERSONAL Born 08/03/1948, New York, NY, m, 1979 **DISCIPLINE** HISTORY OF RELIGION **EDUCATION** Syracuse Univ, PhD, MA; Univ FL, MA. **CAREER** Vis Asst Prof, 97-99, College of Charleston; Asst Prof, 95-97, Loyola Univ; act Asst Prof, 90-95, LSU. **HONORS AND AWARDS** Fulbright Schshp; AIIS SR Res Fel. **MEMBERSHIPS** AAR; SE. **RESEARCH** Sacred sound, Hindu Music; Phenomenology of Ethno musicology. **SELECTED PUBLICATIONS** Auth, Seven invited entries for Encarta Encyclopedia on CD-ROM by Microsoft Inc, including, Om, Bhagavata Purana, Sutra, Mudra, Prayer Wheel, Satori, Ahura Mazda, forthcoming; auth, Religious Music of Northern Areas, in: Garland Encyc of World Music: South Asia Volume, Alison Arnold, ed, forthcoming; Bhajan/Devotional Music, Music Festivals and Music Academies, for the Encyc of Hinduism, forthcoming; auth, Devotional Hymns from Sanskrit, in: Religions In India, DS Lopez Jr ed, Princeton Univ Press, 95; Fire in the Atman: Repentance in Hinduism, in: Repentance: A Comparative Perspective, Amitai Etzioni, David Carney, ed, Lanham MD, Rowman and Littlefield, 97. **CONTACT ADDRESS** Col of Charleston, 14 Glebe St, Charleston, SC, 29424. **EMAIL** beckg@cofc.edu

BECK, JOHN A.
DISCIPLINE OLD TESTAMENT **EDUCATION** Nortwest Coll Wis, BA, 78; Wis Lutheran Sem, MD, 82; Trinity Ev Divinity School Ill, ThM, 93; PhD, 97. **CAREER** Pastor of St Paul's Ev Lutheran Church Wis, 82-87; Chief flight Instr Northstar Aviation Wis, 87-91; Bible Transl Rev, God's Word to the Nat Bibl Soc Ohio, 92-94; Dir, Freshman Year Experience; Asst Prof; Concordia Univ Wis, 90-. **RESEARCH** The Rhetorical Function of Geography in Hebrew Narrative of the Old Testament. **SELECTED PUBLICATIONS** Auth, numerous presentations on freshman year experience conferences; contribur, The New International Dictionary of Old Testament Theology and Exegesis, 95. **CONTACT ADDRESS** 11637 Sunnyview Ave, Germantown, WI, 53022. **EMAIL** Jbeck@bach.cuw.edu

BECK, LEWIS WHITE
PERSONAL Born 09/26/1913, Griffin, GA, m, 1939, 2 children **DISCIPLINE** PHILOSOPHY **EDUCATION** Emory Univ, AB, 34; Duke Univ, AM, 35, PhD, 37. **CAREER** Instr philos, Emory Univ, 38-41; from asst prof to assoc prof, Univ DE, 41-48; prof, Lehigh Univ, 48-49; prof, 49-52, chmn dept philos, 49-66, from assoc dean to dean, grad sch, 52-57, Buhbank prof, 62-79, Emer Prof Intellectual & Moral Philos, Univ Rochester, 79-, Vis lectr, Columbia Univ, 50, Univ MN, 53 & Sir George Williams Univ, 69; Guggenheim fel, 57-58; Am Coun Learned Socs fel, 65-66, mem, bd dir, 70-78; vis prof philos, Univ Western Ont, 67-68; mem, counc Nat Endowment Humanities, 70-76, Mills prof, Univ CA, Berkeley, 73; Cassirer lectr, Yale Univ, 74; mem, counc, Am Acad Arts & Sci, 76-; Caroline Gannett prof humanities, Rochester Inst Technology, 82-83. **HONORS AND AWARDS** DLitt, Hamilton Col, 74; LHD, Emory Univ, 77; PhilDr, Univ Tubingen, Ger, 77. **MEMBERSHIPS** Am Philos Asn; Kant Ges; fel, Am Acad Arts & Sci; North East Am Soc Eighteenth Century Studies (pres, 77-78). **RESEARCH** Kant; Hume; Nietzsche. **SELECTED PUBLICATIONS** Auth, Philosophic Inquiry, Prentice-Hall, 53, 2nd ed, 68; Commentary on Kant's Critique of Practical Reason, Univ Chicago, 61; Studies in the Philosophy of Kant, Bobbs, 64; Early German Philosophy, Harvard Univ, 69; ed, Kant Studies Today, Open Ct Publ, 69; Proceedings of the Third International Kant Congress, Reidel, 72; auth, The Actor and the Spectator, 76 & Essays on Kant and Hume, 78, Yale Univ; The Genesis of Kant 'Critique of Judgement', with J. H. Zammito, Eighteenth-Century Studies,Vol 27, 93. **CONTACT ADDRESS** Dept of Philos, Univ of Rochester, Rochester, NY, 14627.

BECK, MARTHA CATHERINE
DISCIPLINE PHILOSOPHY **EDUCATION** Hamline Univ, BA; Bryn Mawr Col, MA, PhD. **CAREER** Asst prof, Lyon Col. **RESEARCH** Plato; Aristotle; Ethics; polit philos. **SELECTED PUBLICATIONS** Auth, Purdah and Human Rights. **CONTACT ADDRESS** Dept of Philos, Lyon Col, 300 Highland Rd, PO Box 2317, Batesville, AR, 72503. **EMAIL** mbeck@lyon.edu

BECK, NORMAN ARTHUR
PERSONAL Born 02/27/1933, Oak Harbor, OH, m, 1959, 3 children **DISCIPLINE** BIBLICAL THEOLOGY **EDUCATION** Capital Univ, BA, 58; Lutheran Theol Sem, BD, 62; Princeton Theol Sem, PhD, 67; Trinity Lutheran Sem, DD, 90. **CAREER** Instr New Testament, Princeton Theol Sem, 65-66; pastor, Good Shepherd Lutheran Church, 66-70 & King of Kings Lutheran Church, Ann Arbor, 70-75; asst prof, 75-80, assoc Prof theol, 80-85, prof theology and classical lang, 85- , TX Lutheran Univ, 80-. **MEMBERSHIPS** Soc Bibl Lit; Am Acad Relig; Am Schs Orient Res. **RESEARCH** The anti-Jewish polemic of the New Testament; Anti-Roman cryptograms in the New Testament. **SELECTED PUBLICATIONS**

Auth, The Last Supper as an efficacious symbolic act, J Bibl Lit, 70; Letters to Yound Churches (teacher's guide & student's bk), 74 & Hope in Disguise (teacher's guide & student's bk), 78 Augsburg; Four kinds of learning, Parish Teacher, 2/78; Why should we have church schools?, Church Teachers 8, 80; A new statement of faith for a new church, Dialog 20, 81; Reclaiming a Biblical text: The Mark 8:14-21 discussion about bread in the boat, Catholic Bibl Quart 43, 81; Scripture Notes A; Scripture Notes B; Scripture Notes C; Mature Christianity in the 21st Century; Anti-Roman Cryptograms in the New Testament. **CONTACT ADDRESS** Texas Lutheran Univ, 1000 W Court St, Seguin, TX, 78155-5999. **EMAIL** beck_n@txlutheran.edu

BECK, W. DAVID
PERSONAL Born 07/08/1947, Lancaster, PA, m, 1969, 4 children **DISCIPLINE** PHILOSOPHY **EDUCATION** Houghton Col, BA, 69; Trinity Evangelical Divinity School, MA, 71; Boston Univ, PhD, 80. **CAREER** Teaching Asst, 71-72, Univ Rhode Island; Instr, 73-74, Rhode Island Jr Col; Instr, 74-75, Boston Univ; Instr, 76-78, Bridgewater State Col; Asst/Assoc/Prof, 78-, Chr, Philosophy Dept, 81-88, Asst Dean, Graduate School of Religion, 87-89, Assoc VP for Faculty Devel, 88-97, Dean of Graduate Studies, 89-97, Assoc VP for Academic Affairs and Dean of Graduate School, 97-, Liberty Univ. **HONORS AND AWARDS** Pres, Evangelical Phil Soc. **MEMBERSHIPS** Amer Phil Assoc; Evangelical Phil Soc; Virginia Phil Assoc; Soc of Christian Philosophers; Assoc of Virginia Graduate Deans **RESEARCH** Cosmological argument for God's existence; faculty evaluation and development **SELECTED PUBLICATIONS** Auth, Designing a Christian University, Opening the American Mind, 91; God's Existence, Miracles: Has God Acted in History, 97. **CONTACT ADDRESS** School of Religion, Liberty Univ, Lynchburg, VA, 24506. **EMAIL** dbeck@liberty.edu

BECKER, EDWARD
DISCIPLINE ANALYTIC PHILOSOPHY AND PHILOSOPHY OF LANGUAGE **EDUCATION** Johns Hopkins Univ, PhD, 70. **CAREER** Assoc prof, Univ Nebr, Lincoln. **RESEARCH** Quine. **SELECTED PUBLICATIONS** Quine and the Problem of Significance, Proc of the 7th Int Wittgenstein Symp, 83; Holistic Behaviorism, Proc of the 9th Int Wittgenstein Symp, 85. **CONTACT ADDRESS** Univ Nebr, Lincoln, Lincoln, NE, 68588-0417.

BECKER, LAWRENCE C.
PERSONAL Born 04/26/1939, Lincoln, NB, Canada, m, 1967 **DISCIPLINE** PHILOSOPHY **EDUCATION** Midland Col, BA, 61; Univ Chicago, MA, 63, PhD, 65. **CAREER** Instr, 65-67, asst prof, 67-71, assoc prof, 71-78, prof, 78-79, fel, 89- , Hollins Col; prof, Col of William and Mary, 89- . **HONORS AND AWARDS** Nat Endowment Hum Fel, 71-72, 93-94; Rockefeller Found Hum Fel, 82-83; Ctr for Advanced Stud in the Behavioral Sci, 83-84. **RESEARCH** Ethics. **SELECTED PUBLICATIONS** Ed, "Freedom of Expression," Ethics, 93; "Citizenship, Democracy and Education," Ethics, 95; auth, "Trust as Noncognitive Security about Motives," Ethics, 96; "Stoic Children, The Philosopher's Child," Univ Rochester, 98; A New Stoicism, Princeton, 98. **CONTACT ADDRESS** Dept of Philosophy, Col of William and Mary, PO Box 8795, Williamsburg, VA, 23187. **EMAIL** lcbeck@facstaff.wm.edu

BECKER, LEWIS
DISCIPLINE FEDERAL SECURITIES REGULATION, SALES, CONSUMER TRANSACTIONS, FAMILY LAW **EDUCATION** Temple Univ, BS, 58; Univ Pa Sch Law, LLB, 61. **CAREER** Prof; Villanova Univ, 72-. **MEMBERSHIPS** ABA Family Law Section's Marital Property Comt, Alimony Committee, Ethics Comt. **RESEARCH** Family law, securities regulation. **SELECTED PUBLICATIONS** Contrib auth, Alimony, Child Support and Counsel Fees--awd, Modification and Enforcement, 88; Valuation and Distribution of Marital Property, 90, 91 and 94 ed; co-ed and contrib auth, Premarital and Marital Contracts: A Lawyer's Guide to Drafting and Negotiating Enforceable Marital and Cohabitation Agreements, 93. **CONTACT ADDRESS** Law School, Villanova Univ, 800 Lancaster Ave, Villanova, PA, 19085-1692. **EMAIL** becker@law.vill.edu

BECKETT, STEVEN J.
DISCIPLINE LAW **EDUCATION** Univ Ill, BA, JD. **CAREER** Founder, Beckett & Assoc; adj prof, Univ Ill Urbana Champaign **HONORS AND AWARDS** Awd, Ill pub defender asn, Champaign Co ACLU. **SELECTED PUBLICATIONS** Auth, Whatever Happened to the Bill of Rights? A Criminal Defense Lawyer's Perspective, Univ Ill Law Rev, 92; co-auth, Preparing For Your Deposition. **CONTACT ADDRESS** Law Dept, Univ Ill Urbana-Champaign, 52 E Gregory Dr, Champaign, IL, 61820. **EMAIL** sbeckett@law.uiuc.edu

BECKWITH, FRANK
DISCIPLINE APOLOGETICS **EDUCATION** Univ Nev, BA; Fordham Univ, MA, PhD; Simon Greenleaf Univ, MA. **CAREER** Adj prof. **SELECTED PUBLICATIONS** Co-auth, Relativism, Feet Firmly Planted in Mid Air, Baker Bk House, 98; See The Gods Fall: Four Rivals To Christianity, Col Press, 97; co-ed, The Abortion Controversy 25 Years After Roe V. Wade: A Reader, Wadsworth, 98; Affirmative Action: Social Justice Or Reverse Discrimination, Prometheus Bk(s), 97. **CONTACT ADDRESS** Southern Evangel Sem, 4298 McKee Rd, Charlotte, NC, 28270. **EMAIL** ses@perigee.net

BEDAU, HUGO ADAM
PERSONAL Born 09/23/1926, Portland, OR, m, 1990, 4 children **DISCIPLINE** PHILOSOPHY **EDUCATION** Univ Redlands, BA, 49; Boston Univ, MA, 51; Harvard Univ, MA, 53, PhD, 61. **CAREER** Instr philos, Dartmouth Col, 53-54; instr, Princeton Univ, 54-57, lectr, 58-61; Danforth teacher, Danforth Found, 57-58; Carnegie fel law & philos, Harvard Law Sch, 61-62; assoc prof philos, Reed Col, 62-66; prof, 66-70, chmn dept, 66-76, Austin Fletcher Prof Philos, Tufts Univ, 70-, Grant-in-aid, Soc Sci Res Coun, 62; Russell Sage Found res grant, 73; dir, Nat Endowment for Humanities summer sem, 75 & 80; Nat Endowment for Humanities summer res, 77; vis fel, Cambridge Univ, 80. **MEMBERSHIPS** Am Philos Asn; Am Soc Polit & Legal Philos; Soc Philos & Pub Affairs; Am Asn Advan Humanities. **RESEARCH** Ethics; social, legal and political philosophy. **SELECTED PUBLICATIONS** Ed, The Death Penalty in America, Doubleday, 64, rev ed, 67, 3rd ed, 82; Civil Disobedience, Pegasus, 68; Justice and Equality, Prentice-Hall, 71; coauth, Victimless Crimes, Prentice-Hall, 74; co-ed, Capital Punishment in the US, AMS, 76; auth, The Courts, the Constitution, and Capital Punishment, D C Heath, 77; Social Justice and Social Institutions, Midwest Studies Philos, 78; How to Argue about Prisoners' Rights, Rutgers Law Rev, 81; Rituals of Retribution-Capital Punishment in Germany 1600-1987, with R. J. Evans, J of Interdisciplinary Hist, Vol 28, 97. **CONTACT ADDRESS** Dept of Philos, Tufts Univ, Medford, MA, 02155-5555.

BEDELL, GEORGE CHESTER
PERSONAL Born 05/13/1928, Jacksonville, FL, m, 1952, 3 children **DISCIPLINE** RELIGION **EDUCATION** Univ of the South, BA, 50; Va Theol Sem, BD, 53; Univ NC, Chapel Hill, MA, 66; Duke Univ, PhD(relig), 69. **CAREER** Rector, Episcopal parishes, FL, 53-64; asst prof, 67-73, COURTESY ASSOC PROF RELIG, FL STATE UNIV, 73-, MEM STAFF, BD REGENTS, 71-; exec vice chancellor, 81. **MEMBERSHIPS** Am Acad Relig; Soc Sci Studies Relig; MLA; S Atlantic Mod Lang Asn. **SELECTED PUBLICATIONS** Auth, The Technique of Fiction Revisited, 7/68 & The Prayer Scene in Hamlet, 4/69, Anglican Theol Rev; Kierkegaard's Conception of Time, J Am Acad Relig, 9/69; Kierkegaard and Faulkner: Modalities of Existence, LA State Univ, 73; Religion in America, Macmillan, 75, 2nd ed, 82; Florida-Now, A Kinder, Gentler Press, Scholarly Pub, Vol 25, 93. **CONTACT ADDRESS** Bd of Regents, Florida State Univ, 107 W Gaines St, Tallahassee, FL, 32304.

BEESON, P.B.
PERSONAL Born 10/18/1908, Livingston, MT, m, 1942, 3 children **DISCIPLINE** MEDICINE **EDUCATION** McGill Univ, Montreal CA, MD, CM. **CAREER** Oxford Univ, Nuffield prof 65-74; Yale Univ, prof 52-65; Emory Univ GA, asst, assoc, prof, 42-52; P. B. Brigham Hosp, MA chf res; Rockefeller Univ, asst 37-39. **HONORS AND AWARDS** Hon Doc of Science at Emory, McGill and Yale Univ's; Hon Knighthood, British Empire **MEMBERSHIPS** AAP; IM; NM **RESEARCH** Infectious Diseases **SELECTED PUBLICATIONS** Auth, Fever of Unexplained Origin, Med, 61. **CONTACT ADDRESS** 21013 NE 122nd St, Redmond, WA, 98053.

BELFIORE, ELIZABETH STAFFORD
PERSONAL Born 06/21/1944, Austin, TX **DISCIPLINE** CLASSICAL LANGUAGE, PHILOSOPHY **EDUCATION** Barnard Col, AB, 66; Univ Calif, Los Angeles, MA, 74, PhD(classics), 78. **CAREER** Asst prof, Scripps Col, 79-80, asst prof to assoc prof 80-93, PROF CLASSICS UNIV MINN, 93-. **HONORS AND AWARDS** ACLU 85-86. **MEMBERSHIPS** Am Philol Asn; Class Asn MidWest & South; Women's Class Caucus; Soc Ancient Greek Philos **RESEARCH** Ancient philosophy; Greek tragedy. **SELECTED PUBLICATIONS** Auth, A Theory of Imitation in Plato's Republic, TAPA, 84; Wine and Catharsis of the Emotions in Plato's Laws, CQ, 86; Tragic Pleasures: Aristotlean Plot and Emotion, Princeton, 92; Xenia in Sophocles' Philoctetes, CJ, 94; Harming Friends: Problematic Reciprocity in Greek Tragedy, In: Reciprocity in Ancient Greece, Oxford, 98. **CONTACT ADDRESS** Dept of Classical & Near East Studies, Univ of Minn, 9 Pleasant St SE, Minneapolis, MN, 55455-0194. **EMAIL** esb@maroon.tc.umn.edu

BELL, DERRICK ALBERT, JR.
PERSONAL Born 11/06/1930, Pittsburgh, PA, m, 1992, 3 children **DISCIPLINE** LAW **EDUCATION** Duquesne Univ, AB, LLB, 52; Univ Pittsburgh Law School, 57 (Assoc ed-in-chief, Pittsburgh Law Rev). **CAREER** Staff Attorney, US Dept of Justice, 57-59; Exe Secretary, Pitts Branch of NAACP, 59-60; First Asst Counsel, NAACP Legal Defense and Ed Found, Inc, 60-66; Depury Dir, Office for Civil Rights, Dept of Health, Education, and Welfare, 66-67; Exe Dir, Western Center on Law and Poverty, Univ Southern CA Law School, 67-69; lect of Law, 69-71, Prof of Law, Harvard Univ, 71-80; Dean and Law Prof, Univ OR Law School, 81-85; Weld Prof of Law, Harvard Univ, 86-92; vis prof, NYU Law School, 91-93; Scholar-in-residence, NY Univ Law School, 93-94; vis prof, New York Univ Law School, 94-98. **HONORS AND AWARDS** Honorary degrees from Pace Law School, 66; Northeastern Law School, 84; Tougalso Col, 83; Mercy Col, 88; Allegheny Col, 89; Teacher of the Year Award presented by Am Law Schools, 85. **MEMBERSHIPS** Admitted to bars by examination in District of Columbia, 57; PA, 60; NY, 66; CA, 69; admitted to practice in US Supreme Court and in Federal Courts of Appeal in the Fourth, Fifth, Sixth, Eighth, and Tenth Circuits. **SELECTED PUBLICATIONS** Auth, Confronting Authority: Reflections of an Ardent Protester, 94; Constitutional Conflicts, 97; Gospel Choirs: Psalms of Survival in an Alien Land Called Home, 96; Afrolantica Legacies, 98. **CONTACT ADDRESS** 444 Central Park W, Apt 14B, New York, NY, 10025-4358. **EMAIL** dbell1930@aol.com

BELL, JOHN L.
DISCIPLINE PHILOSOPHY **EDUCATION** Exeter Col Oxford, BA, 65; Christ Church Oxford, DPhil, 69. **CAREER** Prof **RESEARCH** Mathematical logic; philosophy of mathematics; set theory; Boolean algebras; lattice theory; category theory. **SELECTED PUBLICATIONS** Auth, A Primer of Infinitesimal Analysis, Cambridge, 98; Zorn's Lemma and Complete Boolean Algebras in Intuitionistic Type Theories, Jour Symbolic Logic, 97; Polymodal Lattices and Polymodal Logic, Math Logic Quart, 96; Logical Reflections on the Kochen-Specker Theorem, Kluwer, 96; Infinitesimals and the Continuum, Math Intelligencer, 95; Type-Reducing Correspondences and Well-Orderings: Frege's and Zermelo's Constructions Re-examined, Jour Symbolic Logic, 95; Frege's Theorem and the Zermelo-Bourbaki Lemma Appendix to Frege's Philosophy of Mathematics, Harvard, 95; Fregean Extensions of First-Order Theories, Math Logic Quart, 94; Toposes & Local Set Theories: An Introduction, Oxford, 88; Boolean-Valued Models and Independence Proofs in Set Theory, Clarendon, 77; co-auth, Precovers, Modalities, and Universal Closure Operators in a Topos, Math Logic Quart, 96; Elementary Propositions and Independence, Notre Dame Jour Formal Logic, 96; Quasi Boolean Algebras and Simultaneously Definite Properties in Quantum Mechanics, Int Jour Theoretical Physics, 95. **CONTACT ADDRESS** Dept of Philosophy, Western Ontario Univ, London, ON, N6A 5B8.

BELL, LINDA A.
DISCIPLINE FEMINIST THEORY, EXISTENTIALISM, ETHICS, CONTINENTAL PHILOSOPHY **EDUCATION** Emory Univ, PhD, 73. **CAREER** Prof, Ga State Univ. **SELECTED PUBLICATIONS** Auth, Visions of Women; Sartre's Ethics of Authenticity; Rethinking Ethics in the Midst of Violence: A Feminist Approach to Freedom. **CONTACT ADDRESS** Georgia State Univ, Atlanta, GA, 30303. **EMAIL** phllab@panther.gsu.edu

BELL, NORA KIZER
PERSONAL Charleston, WV, m, 3 children **DISCIPLINE** PHILOSOPHY, BIOETHICS **EDUCATION** Randolph-Macon Woman's Col, BA; Univ So Carolina, MA; Univ N Carolina, PhD. **CAREER** Mem fac, 77- , chemn Dept Philos, 87-92, dir, Ctr for Bioethics, 92-93, Univ So Carolina; Dean, Col of Arts & Sci, Univ N Texas, 93-97; pres, Wesleyan Col, 97- . **HONORS AND AWARDS** Phi Beta Kappa; Omicron Delta Kappa; Mortar Board Woman of the Year, 88; J. Marion Sims Award, So Carolina Public Health Asn for advancing public health, 88; gubernatorial appointee, Comnr, So Carolina Comn on Aging, 89-93; So Carolina Woman of Achievement Award, 92; order of the Palmetto, So Carolina, 93; elected vis res fel, Inst for Adv Stud in Hum, Univ Edinburgh, 94; Tau Alpha Pi. **MEMBERSHIPS** Nat Acad Academic Leadership; Coun of Col of Arts and Sci. **SELECTED PUBLICATIONS** Ed and contribur, Who Decides? Conflicts of Rights in Health Care, Humana, 82; auth, Ethical Issues Involving Nutrition in the Critically Ill, in, Zaloga, ed, Nutrition in Critical Care, Mosby, 94; auth, Women and Children with AIDS: A Public Health Challenge for Metropolitan Universities, Metropolitan Univ, 95; auth, Responsibilities and Rights in the Promotion of Health: The Individual and the State, Social Sci and Medicine, 96; auth, Protocol 076: A New Look at Women and Children with AIDS, in Umeh, ed, Cross-Cultural Perspectives on HIV/AIDS Education, Africa World Press, forthcoming. **CONTACT ADDRESS** Office of the President, Wesleyan Col, 4760 Forsyth Rd, Macon, GA, 31210-4462. **EMAIL** nora_bell@post.wesleyan-college.edu

BELL, RICHARD H.
DISCIPLINE PHILOSOPHY **EDUCATION** Vanderbilt Col, BA, 60; Yale Univ, BD, 64, MA, 66, PhD, 68. **CAREER** Frank Halliday Ferris prof. **SELECTED PUBLICATIONS** Auth, Sensing the Spirit, The Westminster Press, 84; ed, The Grammar of the Heart: New Essays in Moral Philosophy and Theology, Harper & Row, 88; Simone Weil's Philosophy of Culture, Cambridge UP, 93. **CONTACT ADDRESS** Dept of Philos, Col of Wooster, Wooster, OH, 44691.

BELL, SHEILA TRICE
PERSONAL Born 08/25/1949, Pittsburgh, PA, m, 1971 **DISCIPLINE** LAW **EDUCATION** Wellesley Coll, BA 1971; Harvard Law Sch, JD 1974. **CAREER** Pine Manor Jr Coll, fac-

ulty mem 1972-74; Hutchins & Wheeler, assoc lawyer 1973-77; Private Legal Practice, Attorney 1977-79; Fisk Univ, univ counsel 1979-83; Northern KY Univ, acting univ counsel/ affirmative action officer 1984-85, univ legal counsel 1985-. **HONORS AND AWARDS** Equal Rights Amendment Commn for the Commonwealth of MA 1976; editorial bd The Journal of College and University Law 1982-83; Mayor's Special Task Force on Union Station Nashville TN 1982-83; **MEMBERSHIPS** Bd mem Family and Children's Services Nashville TN 1981-83; The Links Inc Cincinnati Chap, mem 1984-, vp 1986-89; mem Jack and Jill Inc Cincinnati Chap 1984-90; mem MA, TN, KY Bars, Amer Bar Assns; mem US Dist Courts of MA, the Middle Dist of TN and the Eastern Dist of KY, US Court of Appeals for the Sixth Circuit; bd mem Natl Assn of Coll and Univ Attys 1985-88; bd mem The Program for Cincinnati 1986-88; bd mem, Bethesda Hospital, Inc, 1990-. **SELECTED PUBLICATIONS** "Protection and Enforcement of College and University Trademarks" co-author w/Martin F Majestic in the Journal of College and Univ Law, Vol 10, No 1 1983-84. **CONTACT ADDRESS** Univ Legal Counsel, No Kentucky Univ, 834 Administrative Ctr, Highland Heights, KY, 41076.

BELLINZONI, ARTHUR J.
PERSONAL Brooklyn, NY **DISCIPLINE** HISTORY AND PHILOSOPHY OF RELIGION **EDUCATION** Princeton Univ, AB; Harvard Univ, MA, PhD. **CAREER** PROF RELIG, DIR PLANNED AND LEADERSHIP GIVING, WELLS COL **HONORS AND AWARDS** Exxon Educational Found Travel Grant for study in Israel; Ruth and Albert Koch Prof of Humanities, Wells Coll **MEMBERSHIPS** Soc Bibl Lit; Am Acad Relig; Am School Orient Res; Novi Testamenti Studiorum Soc. **RESEARCH** Old Testament; New Testament; Second Century; Middle East; Major Gift Fund Development. **SELECTED PUBLICATIONS** The Sayings of Jesus in the Writings of Justin Martyr, Brill; Intellectual Honesty and Religious Commitment, Fortress Press; The Two Source Hupothesis: A Critical Appraisal, Mercer University Press; The Influence of the Gospel of Matthew on Christian Literature Before Saint Irenaeus, Mercer Univ Press; "The Source of the Agraphon in Justin Martyr's Dialogue with Trypho 47:5," in Virgilae Christianae. **CONTACT ADDRESS** PO Box 5, Aurora, NY, 13026.

BELLIOTTI, RAYMOND A.
PERSONAL Born 06/17/1948, Dansville, NY, m, 1986, 2 children **DISCIPLINE** PHILOSOPHY; LAW **EDUCATION** Union Col, BA (cum laude), 70; Univ Miami, MA, 76, PhD, 77; Harvard Univ, JD (cum laude), 82. **CAREER** Attorney, Barrett Smith Schapiro Simon and Armstrong, NY City, 82-84; PROF PHILOSOPHY, SUNY FREDONIA, 84-. **HONORS AND AWARDS** Kasling Award for Excellence in Scholarship; Hagan Young Scholar Award for Excellence in Scholarship. **MEMBERSHIPS** SUNY Chancellor's Board for Excellence in Teaching. **SELECTED PUBLICATIONS** Auth, Justifying Law, Temple Univ Press, 92; Good Sex, Univ Press KS, 93; Seeking Identity, Univ Press KS, 95; Stacking Nietzsche, Greenwood Press, 99. **CONTACT ADDRESS** Philosophy, SUNY-Fredonia, 2109 Fenton Hall, Fredonia, NY, 14063. **EMAIL** belliotti@fredonia.edu

BELTON, ROBERT
PERSONAL Born 09/19/1935, High Point, NC, m **DISCIPLINE** LAW **EDUCATION** Univ of CT, BA 1961; Boston Univ, JD 1965. **CAREER** NAACP, Legal Defense & Educ Fund Inc, civil rights atty asst counsel; 1965-70; Chambers Stein & Ferguson Charlotte NC, atty 1970-75; Vanderbilt Univ School of Law, dir fair employment clinical law program 1975-77, assoc prof of law 1977-82; prof of law, 1982-; visiting prof of law, Harvard Law School, 1986-87; UNC School of Law, Chapel Hill NC, visiting prof of law 1990-91; NCCU Law School, Charles Hamilton Houston Distinguished Visiting Professor, 1997. **HONORS AND AWARDS** Awarded NC Legal Defense Fund Dinner Comm Plaque for successful litigation in area of employment discrimination 1973; counsel for plaintiffs in Harris v Forklift Sys, 1993; Griggs v. Duke Power Co., 401 US 424 (1971); Albemarle Paper Co vs. Moody, 422 US 405 (1975); **MEMBERSHIPS** American Association of Law Schools, executive committee, 1991-1994; Consultant TN Commn for Human Devel 1976-; editoral bd Class Action Reports 1978-89; consult Equal Employment Opportunity Commn Trial Advocacy Training Programs 1979-; consultant Pres Reorganization Proj Civil Rights 1978; consultant Office of Fed Contracts Compliance Programs Dept of Labor 1979-80; NC Assn of Black Lawyers; Amer Bar Assn; TN Bar Assn, NBA; Amer Law Institute, 1996-. **SELECTED PUBLICATIONS** Auth, Remedies in Employment Discirmination Law, Wiley, 1992; Discrimination in Employment , West, 1986; "Mr Justice Marshall and the Sociology of Affirmative Action" 1989; Reflections on Affirmative Action after Johnson and Paradise, 1988. **CONTACT ADDRESS** Sch of Law, Vanderbilt Univ, Nashville, TN, 37240.

BENCE, CLARENCE
DISCIPLINE RELIGIOUS STUDIES **EDUCATION** Houghton Col, BA, 66; Emory Univ, PhD, 81. **CAREER** Prof, 92-. **RESEARCH** Church history. **SELECTED PUBLICATIONS** Auth, Romans, Wesley. **CONTACT ADDRESS** Dept of Religion and Philosophy, Indiana Wesleyan Univ, 4201 S Wash St, Marion, IN, 46953. **EMAIL** bbence@indwes.edu

BENDER, ROSS THOMAS
PERSONAL Born 06/25/1929, Tavistock, ON, Canada, m, 1950, 5 children **DISCIPLINE** RELIGION **EDUCATION** Goshen Col, BA, 54, BD, & MRE, 56; Yale Univ, MA, 61, PhD(relig), 62. **CAREER** Asst prof, 62-64, dean, 64-69, Prof Christian Educ, Bibl Sem, Goshen Col, 64-, Dean, Mennonite Bibl Sem, 64-79; Nat Inst Mental Health fel, Div Family Stud, Univ Pa, 79-71; studies in religion & educ, Univ Geneva, Switzerland, 79-80; clin mem, Am Asn Marriage & Family Therapy, 71- **MEMBERSHIPS** Relig Educ Asn. **SELECTED PUBLICATIONS** Auth, The Knowledge of God in Primitive, Partial, or Profound--Essays on the Theory of Christian Education in Honor of Langdon,Alan, Relig Educ, Vol 0089, 94. **CONTACT ADDRESS** Associated Mennonite Biblical Sem, 3003 Benham Ave, Elkhart, IN, 46514.

BENDITT, THEODORE MATTHEW
PERSONAL Born 10/23/1940, Philadelphia, PA, m, 1968, 1 child **DISCIPLINE** PHILOSOPHY **EDUCATION** Univ of Penn, BA, 62, JD, 65, MA, 67; Univ of Pittsburgh, PhD, 71. **CAREER** Instr, 70-72, Asst Prof, 72-75, Duke Univ; Asst Prof, 75-78, USC; vis Assoc Prof, 79, Univ of Pittsburgh; Assoc Prof, 78-83, Prof, 83-, dean arts & humanities, 84-98, Univ of Alabama, Birmingham. **MEMBERSHIPS** APA, AAP&LP, Amintaphil. **RESEARCH** Political, legal & moral philosophy. **SELECTED PUBLICATIONS** Auth, Law as Rule and Principle, Stanford Univ Press, 78; Rights, Rowman & Littlefield, 82; The Research Demands of Teaching in Modern Higher Education, in: Morality Responsibility and the University, Studies in Academic Ethics, ed, S.M. Cahn, Temple Univ Press, 90; Rights, Civil and Economic, Rechtstheorie, 98; co-ed & contrib, Philosophy Them and Now, Basil Blackwell, 98. **CONTACT ADDRESS** Dept of Philosophy, Univ of Alabama, 407E Humanities Bldg, Birmingham, AL, 35294-1260. **EMAIL** tbenditt@uab.edu

BENFIELD, DAVID WILLIAM
PERSONAL Born 01/12/1941, Des Moines, IA, m, 1980, 1 child **DISCIPLINE** PHILOSOPHY **EDUCATION** St John's Col, Md, BA, 62; Brown Univ, BA, 66, PhD, 73. **CAREER** Asst prof philos, State Univ NY Stony Brook, 67-73; asst prof, 73-80, assoc prof, 80-91, Prof Philos, Montclair State Univ, 92-, Consult, Nat Endowment for Humanities, 75-77; Nat Endowment for Hum, summer, 74, 77 & 81; vis prof, Univ MI, summer, 76 & 80; mem, Am Philos Asn Comt Tchg, 81-84; vch, Conf Methods Philos & Sci, 82-83. **MEMBERSHIPS** Am Philos Asn; Soc Advan Am Philos; Soc Phenomenol & Existential Philos; Soc Philos & Pub Policy; Leibniz Soc. **RESEARCH** Metaphysics; epistemology; professional ethics. **SELECTED PUBLICATIONS** Auth, Johnstone on the truth of philosophical statements, Philos & Phenomenol Res, 9/71, Kant and uncaused events, Proc 4th Int Kant Cong, Part 2, 1: 179-185; The a priori a posteriori distinction, Philos & Phenomenol Res, 12/74; coauth, Identity, schmidentity--it's not all the same, Philos Studies, 2/75; auth, The a priori and the self-evident: A reply to Mr Casullo, Philos & Phenomenol Res, 12/77; Roderick M Chisholm, In: Routledge Encyclopedia of Philosophy, Routledge, 98. **CONTACT ADDRESS** Dept of Philos & Relig, Montclair State Univ, 1 Normal Ave, Upper Montclair, NJ, 07043-1699. **EMAIL** benfield@saturn.montclair.edu

BENHABIB, SEYLA
PERSONAL Born 09/09/1950, Istanbul, Turkey, d, 1 child **DISCIPLINE** PHILOSOPHY **EDUCATION** Yale, MPhil, 72, PhD, 72. **CAREER** Prof, 93, Harvard Univ. **HONORS AND AWARDS** AAUW, Humboldt & Fel; Lauss Mem Lectr. **MEMBERSHIPS** APSA; APAP. **RESEARCH** 19th & 20th century continental political triumph; feminist theory/social theory. **SELECTED PUBLICATIONS** Auth, Critique, Norm and Utopia: A Study of the Foundations of Critica Theory, Columbia Univ Press, 86; auth, Situating the Self: Gender, Community and Post-Modernism in Contemporary Ethics, Polity Press, Routledge, 93; coauth, Der Streit um Differenz, Fischer Verlag, 93; coauth, Feminist Contentions: A Philosophical Exchange; Routledge, 96; auth, The Reluctant Modernism of Hannah Arendt, Sage Pub, 96; auth, Kulturelle Vielfelt und Demokratische Gleichheit, Fischer Verlag, 98; auth, Hannah Arendt: Die Melancholische Denkerin der Moderne, Rotbuch Verlag, 98. **CONTACT ADDRESS** European Studies, Harvard Univ, 27 Kirkland St, Cambridge, MA, 02138. **EMAIL** benhabib@jss.harvard.edu

BENHAM, PRISCILLA
PERSONAL Born 01/30/1950, Berkeley, CA, m, 1986, 1 child **DISCIPLINE** THEOLOGY **EDUCATION** Patten Col, BS, 69; Holy Names, BA, 70; Wheaton Col, MA, 72; Drew Univ, PhD, 76. **CAREER** Prof, 75-, Pres, 83-, Patten Col. **SELECTED PUBLICATIONS** Coauth, The World of the Early Church, 90; Auth, A Comparison of the Counseling Techniques of Christ and Carl Rogers, 91; The Secret of the Parables in Mark Light of Apocalyptic Literature, 92. **CONTACT ADDRESS** Patten Col, 2433 Coolidge Rd., Oakland, CA, 94601.

BENIDICKSON, JAMIE
DISCIPLINE LAW **EDUCATION** Trent Univ, BA; Univ Toronto, LLB; Harvard Univ, LLM. **CAREER** Assoc prof. **RESEARCH** Legal history; administrative and environmental law. **SELECTED PUBLICATIONS** Auth, The Temagami Experience; Idleness, Water and a Canoe and the Environmental Law. **CONTACT ADDRESS** Fac Common Law, Univ Ottawa, 550 Cumberland St, PO Box 450, Ottawa, ON, K1N 6N5.

BENJAMIN, DON C., JR.
DISCIPLINE RELIGION **EDUCATION** St. Bonaventure Univ, BA, 64; Wash Theol Union, MDiv, Ordained, Order of CAR melites, 67; Catholic Univ of Amer, MA, 69; Claremont Grad Univ, PhD, 81. **CAREER** Rice Univ, lectr, 78-81; Univ of Houston, vis scholar, 86,88; Univ of S. Thomas, vis scholar, 80-83,94; Rice Univ, Scholar in Res, 81-96; Kino Institute of Theol, exec dir, 97-. **RESEARCH** OT; Hebrew bible; ancient near east hist. **SELECTED PUBLICATIONS** Co-ed, Old Testament Parallels: Laws and Stories from the Ancient Near East, Mahwah: Paulist, 97; Honor and Shame in the World of the Bible, in: Semeia: an Experimental Jour for Bib Crit, Atlanta; Scholars, 96; The Social World of Ancient Israel, 1250 - 587 BCE, Peabody: Hendrickson, 93; Deuteronomy and City Life: a Form Criticism of Texts with the Word City Hebrew: ir, in Deuteronomy 4:41-26:19, Univ Press of Amer, 93. **CONTACT ADDRESS** Kino Inst of Theol, 1224 E Northern Ave, Phoenix, AZ, 85020-4295. **EMAIL** dcben@worldnet.att.net

BENJAMIN, PAUL
PERSONAL Born 04/20/1940, Murunkan, Sri Lanka, m, 1968, 2 children **DISCIPLINE** OLD TESTAMENT **EDUCATION** Lutheran Sch of Theol, Chicago, PhD, 86. **CAREER** Prof, Pres and Prof, 86-91, Theol Coll of Lanka, Sri Lanka; Vis Intl Prof, 91-92, Wartburg Theol Sem, Bubuave, IA; Pastor, 93-98, Iowa Annual Conf of the United Methodist Church. **HONORS AND AWARDS** Confessor of Christ Award for Distinguished Ministry Lutheran Sch of Theol Stud. **MEMBERSHIPS** SBL. **RESEARCH** Old Testament Theology. **SELECTED PUBLICATIONS** Auth, articles to The Anchor Bible Dictionary, 92. **CONTACT ADDRESS** 905 Easy St, Burlington, IA, 52601. **EMAIL** PSRBEnjoz@aol.com

BENKO, STEPHEN
PERSONAL Born 06/13/1924, Budapest, Hungary, m, 1952, 4 children **DISCIPLINE** RELIGION, ANCIENT HISTORY **EDUCATION** Reformed Theol Sem Budapest, BD, 47; Univ Basel, PhD(relig), 51. **CAREER** Res fel, Divinity Sch, Yale Univ, 53-54; instr, Sch Theol, Temple Univ, 57-59 & lectr, Grad Sch Philos & Relig, 59-61; prof Bibl studies & patristics, Conwell Sch Theol, 60-69; PROF ANCIENT HIST, CALIF STATE UNIV, FRESNO, 69-. **MEMBERSHIPS** Am Hist Asn; Am Philol Asn; Am Soc Church Hist; Soc Bibl Lit. **RESEARCH** Ancient church history; ecumenical relations. **SELECTED PUBLICATIONS** Auth, Education, Culture and the Arts Transylvanian Cultural Hist, Hungarian Quart, Vol 0035, 94. **CONTACT ADDRESS** Dept of Hist, California State Univ, Fresno, Fresno, CA, 93740.

BENNETT, GERALD T.
DISCIPLINE LAW **EDUCATION** St Bernard's Col, BA; Barry Col, MA; Univ Fla, JD. **CAREER** Prof emer,Univ Fla, 68-. **HONORS AND AWARDS** Fla Bar Selig Goldin awd; L. Clayton Nance awd, Fla Public Defender's Asn., Drafted in Fla, ABA Standards on Trial by Jury, Discovery and Incompetency to Stand Trial. **MEMBERSHIPS** Fla Criminal Rules Comt, 74-; Fla Bar; Order of the Coif; Phi Kappa Phi. **RESEARCH** Criminal law, procedure and litigation skills. **CONTACT ADDRESS** School of Law, Univ of Florida, PO Box 117625, Gainesville, FL, 32611-7625. **EMAIL** bennett@law.ufl.edu

BENNETT, JAMES O.
DISCIPLINE PHILOSOPHY **EDUCATION** Univ La, BA, 66; Tulane Univ, MA, 69, PhD, 72. **CAREER** Assoc prof. **RESEARCH** Existentialism, with a secondary interest in American Pragmatism, and a tertiary interest in process philosophy. **SELECTED PUBLICATIONS** Auth, A Venn-Euler Hybrid Test for Categorical Syllogisms, Tchg Philos, 94; coauth, Karl Jaspers and Scientific Philosophy, Jour Hist Philos, 93. **CONTACT ADDRESS** Dept of Philosophy, Tennessee Univ, Knoxville, TN, 37996. **EMAIL** jobennet@utk.edu

BENNETT, PATRICIA W.
PERSONAL Born 08/31/1953, Forest, Mississippi, s **DISCIPLINE** LAW **EDUCATION** Tougaloo College, BA, 1975; Mississippi College School of Law, JD, 1979. **CAREER** Small Business Administration, attorney, 1979-80; Mississippi Attorney General, special asst attorney general, 1980-82; District Attorney of Hinds County, asst district attorney, 1982-87; US Attorney, asst US attorney, 1987-89; Mississippi College School of Law, professor, currently. **HONORS AND AWARDS** Women for Progress, Woman Achiever, 1988. **MEMBERSHIPS** Smith Robertson Museum Board, 1992; Central Mississippi Legal Services Corp Board, secretary, 1989-; YMCA Board of Directors, 1991-; Mississippi Board of Bar Commissioners, commissioner, 1992. **CONTACT ADDRESS** Professor, Mississippi Col School of Law, 151 E Griffith St, Jackson, MS, 39201.

BENNETT, PHILIP W.
DISCIPLINE PHILOSOPHY **EDUCATION** Rutgers Univ, BA, 64; NY Univ, MA, 66, PhD, 72. **CAREER** Assoc prof, State Univ NY, Cortland, 70-87; Instr, La State Univ, 92-. **CONTACT ADDRESS** 1601 Letitia St, Baton Rouge, LA, 70808. **EMAIL** p.bennett@worldnet.att.net

BENNETT, ROBERT A.
PERSONAL Born 01/11/1933, Baltimore, MD, m **DISCIPLINE** THEOLOGY **EDUCATION** Kenyon Coll, AB (magna cum laude) 1954; Gen Theo Seminary NYC, STB 1958, STM 1966; Harvard Univ, PhD 1974. **CAREER** Episcopal Diocese of Maryland, ordained priest, 1959; Episcopal Theo School/ Divinity School, instructor/asst prof, 1965-74, prof, 1974-94; Interdnmntnl Theo Center, Atlanta, visiting prof, 1973-77; Boston Univ School of Theology, visiting prof, 1975, 1982; Princeton Theo Seminary, visiting prof, 1975, 1983, 1986; Harvard Divinity School, visiting prof, 1976; Hebrew Univ, Jerusalem, Israel, fld arch stf supr, 1984; Episcopal Divinity Sch, prof Old Tstmt, 1974-94. **HONORS AND AWARDS** Phi Beta Kappa Kenyon Coll 1953; Fulbright Schlr Univ Copenhagen, Denmark 1954-55; Vstng Rsrch Schlr Am Rsrch Ctr Cairo, Egypt 1979-80; Rsrch Schlr Univ Khartoum, Sudan 1980; Fld Stf Tel Dor, Israel Hebrew Univ 1984. **MEMBERSHIPS** Trustee bd mem Interdenmntnl Theo Ctr, Atlanta 1973-77; vice-chr Stndng Litrgcl Commsn Episcopal Chrch 1982-; mem lctnry comm Natl Cncl Churchs of Chrst1982-; mem fnl slctn comm Fund for Theo Educ 1984-. **SELECTED PUBLICATIONS** Auth, "The Book of Zephaniah," The New Interpreter's Bible, vol 7, Abington Press, 1996; "Africa," Oxford Companion to the Bible, Oxford U Press, 1993; "Black Experience and the Bible," African American Religious Studies, Duke U Press, 1989; "The Bible for Today's Church," Seabury Press, 1979; "Black Episcopalians," The Episcopal Diocese of Massachusetts 1784-1984, 1984.

BENNETT-ALEXANDER, DAWN DEJUANA
PERSONAL Born 01/02/1951, Washington, DC, d **DISCIPLINE** LAW **EDUCATION** The Defiance College, 1968-70; Federal City College, BA, 1972; Howard University, School of Law, JD, 1975. **CAREER** The DC Court of Appeals, law clerk to Honorable Julia Cooper Mack, 1975-76; The White House Domestic Council, assistant to associate director & counsel, 1976-77; US Federal Trade Commission, law clerk, 1977-78; Antioch School of Law, instructor, 1979-80; Federal Labor Relations Authority, attorney, advisor, 1981-82; University of North Florida, associate professor of business & employment law, 1982-87; UNIV OF GA, ASSOC PROF LEGAL STUDIES, 1988-. **HONORS AND AWARDS** Selig Foundation, Selig Fellowship for Excellence in Research & Teaching, 1992; Terry Foundation, Terry Fellowship for Excellence in Research & Teaching, 1991; Consortium on Multi-Party Dispute Resolution, Seed Grant Award, 1992; Beta Gamma Sigma National Honor Society, selection to membership, 1992; McKnight Foundation, Florida Endowment Fund, McKnight Jr Faculty Award, Fellowship, 1984. **MEMBERSHIPS** Southeastern Academy of Legal Studies in Business, president, 1992-93; American Academy of Legal Studies in Business, co-chair, Employment Law Section, 1992-94; Georgia Political Action Committee PAC, 1993-94; National Council of Negro Women, 1983-; National Organization for Women, 1985-; treasurer, GA Now, 1993-95; DC Bar, 1979-; Friends of Athens Creative Theater, board member, 1990; Consumer Credit Counseling Services of NE Florida, board member, 1983-84; Girls Clubs of Jacksonville, Inc, board member, 1983-85. **SELECTED PUBLICATIONS** Employment Law for Business, Irwin Pub, 1995; The Legal, Ethical & Regulatory Environment of Business, South-Western Pub, 1996; "Hostile Environment Sexual Harassment: A Clearer View," Labor Law Journal, vol 42, no 3, p 131-143, March 1991; "The State of Affirmative Action in Employment: A Post Stotts Retrospective," American Business Law Journal, vol 27/4, p 565-597, winter 1990; "Sexual Harassment in the Office," Personnel Administrator, vol 33, no 6, p 174-88, June 1988. **CONTACT ADDRESS** Terry Col of Business, Univ of Georgia, 202 Brooks Hall, Athens, GA, 30602-6255.

BENSMAN, MARVIN ROBERT
PERSONAL Born 09/18/1937, Two Rivers, WI, m, 1965, 2 children **DISCIPLINE** MASS COMMUNICATIONS, LAW **EDUCATION** Univ WI, Madison, BA, 60, MS, 64, PhD, 69; Memphis State Univ, JD, 81. **CAREER** Teacher speech, West High Sch, Green Bay, WI, 60-62 & North High Sch, Sheboygan, WI, 62-63; instr mass commun, Univ VT, 67-69; asst prof, 69-73, assoc prof Mass Commun, Memphis State Univ , 73-85; FULL PROF, UNIV OF MEMPHIS, 85-. **MEMBERSHIPS** Broadcast Educ Asn; Southern Speech Commun Asn; Radio Hist Soc Am. **RESEARCH** History of broadcasting; archival audio materials; survey research. **SELECTED PUBLICATIONS** Auth, WJAZ-Zenith Case and the Chaos of 1926, fall 70 & coauth, Broadcasting-film Academic Budgets 1971-1972, summer 71, J Broadcasting; co-ed, History of Radio-Television Collection, Arno, 71; coauth, Broadcasting-film Academic Budgets-Updated 1973-74, J Broadcasting, summer 74; Sources of Broadcast Audio Programming (microfiche), ERIC/RCS Clearinghouse, 75; contribr, Regulation of broadcasting by the Department of Commerce, 1921-1927, In: Source Book on History of Radio-Television, 75; Obtaining Old Radio Programs, J Popular Cult, 79; co-auth, Radio Themes Recognition Test, on long-term memory, with Dr Thomas Crook, Head, Center for Aging, Nat Institute of Mental Health, Bethesda, MD, 80; auth, Selected Legal Decisions of 1981, J of Broadcasting, Vol 26:2, spring 82; Broadcast Regulation: Selected Cases and Decisions, Univ Press of Am, DC, 1st ed, 83, 2nd ed, 85 (designated Best Seller by Univ Press); Victor H. Laughter: Radio Pioneer, Tn Speech Commun J, fall 85; The Differences Between Broadcast and Journalism Law, Feedback, Broadcast Education Asn, Vol 27:2, 85; Book of Days, sections on Radio and Television technology and regulation, Pierus Pubs, Ann Arbor, MI, 87; Broadcast/Cable Regulation, Univ Press of Am, DC, 90; The Preservation of Electronic Media Archives, forward of book, Re-runs On File: A Guide to Electronic Media Archives, Lawrence Erlbaum & Assoc, fall 91; Radio Broadcast Programming for Research and Teaching, J of Radio Studies, spring 93; Encyclopedia of Popular Culture, ed Frank Chorba, three articles on Broadcast Archives and Programming, Greenwood Press, forthcoming 98; Historical Dictionary of American Radio, ed Donald G. Godfrey and Frederic A. Leigh, ten articles on early radio regulation and personalities, Greenwood Press, forthcoming 98. **CONTACT ADDRESS** Dept Commun, Univ of Memphis, Campus box 5265, Memphis, TN, 38152-0001. **EMAIL** mbensman@memphis.edu

BENSON, LEGRACE
PERSONAL Born 02/23/1930, Richmond, VA, w, 1952, 3 children **DISCIPLINE** ART; PHILOSOPHY; PERCEPTUAL PSYCHOLOGY **EDUCATION** Meredith Coll, AB, 51; Univ Georgia Athens, MFA, 56; Cornell Univ, PhD, 74. **CAREER** Asst prof, Cornell Univ, 68-71; assoc prof/assoc dean for special programs, Wells Coll, 71-77; assoc dean, SUNY-Empire State Coll, 77-80; coordinator of arts, humanities and communications study, center for distance learning, SUNY-Empire State Coll, 81-92. **HONORS AND AWARDS** Empire State Coll Excellence in Scholarship, 92. **MEMBERSHIPS** Natl Coalition of Independent Scholars; Haitian Studies Assn; Coll Art Assn; Latin Amer Studies Assn; Arts Council African Studies Assn; African Studies Assn; Canadian Assn Latin Amer and Caribbean Studies. **RESEARCH** Arts and Culture of Haiti; adult distance learning **SELECTED PUBLICATIONS** Auth, The Utopian Vision in Haitian Painting, Callaloo, Spring 92; Journal of Caribbean Studies, Observations on Islamic Motifs in Haitian Visual Arts, Winter 92/Spring 93; The Arts of Haiti Considered Ecologically, Paper for Culture Change and Technology in the Americas conference, Nov 95; Three Presentations of the Arts of Haiti, Journal of Haitian Studies, Autumn 96; Habits of Attention: Persistence of Lan Ginee in Haiti, in The African Diaspora African Origins and New-world Self-fashioning, 98; How Houngans Use the Light from Distant Stars; Muslim and Breton Survivals in Haitian Voudou Arts, 99; The Artists and the Arts of Haiti in Their Geographical and Conversational Domains, 99. **CONTACT ADDRESS** 314 E. Buffalo St., Ithaca, NY, 14850-4227. **EMAIL** LeGraceBenson@clarityconnect.com

BENSON, P. JANN
DISCIPLINE PHILOSOPHY **EDUCATION** Univ Colo, PhD, 71. **CAREER** Assoc prof. **RESEARCH** Ethics; history of philosophy. **SELECTED PUBLICATIONS** Co-auth, Strutting and Fretting. **CONTACT ADDRESS** Philosophy Dept, Colorado State Univ, Fort Collins, CO, 80523.

BENSON, PAUL H.
DISCIPLINE ETHICS **EDUCATION** Princeton Univ, PhD, 84. **CAREER** Dept Philos, Univ Dayton **RESEARCH** Action theory, philosophy of mind. **SELECTED PUBLICATIONS** Auth, Freedom and Value, Jour Philos, 87; Moral Worth, Philos Stud, 87; Free Agency and Self-worth, Jour Philos, 94. **CONTACT ADDRESS** Dept of Philos, Univ Dayton, 300 Col Park, Dayton, OH, 75062. **EMAIL** benson@checkov.hm.udayton.edu

BENSON, ROBERT W.
DISCIPLINE LAW **EDUCATION** Columbia Univ, AB, 64; Univ Calif, Berkeley, JD, 68. **CAREER** Prof Loyola, 73-; dir, Loyola summer prog Cent Am; Boalt Hall-Ford Found Int Legal Stud(s) fel, Brazil; worked in, Conn dept commun aff; private practice, Washington DC. **SELECTED PUBLICATIONS** Auth, City of Los Angeles' plain English law. **CONTACT ADDRESS** Law School, Loyola Marymount Univ, 7900 Loyola Blvd, Burns 416, Los Angeles, CA, 90045. **EMAIL** rbenson@lmulaw.lmu.edu

BENTON, CATHERINE
DISCIPLINE HISTORY OF RELIGION **EDUCATION** Columbia Univ, PhD, 91. **CAREER** LECTR, RELIG, LAKE FOREST COL, 87-. **CONTACT ADDRESS** Dept of Relig, Lake Forest Col, 555 N Sheridan Rd, Lake Forest, IL, 60045. **EMAIL** benton@lfc.edu

BEOUGHER, TIMOTHY K.
DISCIPLINE EVANGELISM **EDUCATION** Kans State Univ, BS; Southwestern Baptist Theol Sem, MDiv; Trinity Evangel Divinity Sch, ThM, PhD. **CAREER** Asst prof, Wheaton Col Grad Sch; assoc dir, Billy Graham assoc prof, 96, assoc dean, Billy Graham Sch Missions, Evangel and Church Growth, S Baptist Theol Sem. **SELECTED PUBLICATIONS** Auth, Overcoming Walls to Witnessing; Disciplemaking: Training Leaders to Make Disciples; Evangelism for a Changing World; and Accounts of a Campus Revival: Wheaton Col 95. **CONTACT ADDRESS** Southern Baptist Theol Sem, 2825 Lexington Rd, Louisville, KY, 40280. **EMAIL** tbeougher@sbts.edu

BEPKO, GERALD L.
PERSONAL Born 04/21/1940, Chicago, IL, m, 1968, 2 children **DISCIPLINE** LAW **EDUCATION** Northern Ill Univ, BS, 62; Chicago-Kent Col Law, JD, 65; Yale Univ, LLM, 72. **CAREER** Spec agent, Fed Bur Invest, 65-69; asst prof corp legal writing, Chicago-Kent Col Law, 69-72; assoc prof, 72-75, Prof Law, Ind Univ, Indianapolis, 75-, Dean, 81-86; vpres, Ind Univ, Chancellor, Ind Univ-Purdue Univ, Indianapolis (IUPUI), 86-94; VPRES LONG RANGE PLANNING, IND UNIV, CHANCELLOR, IUPUI, 94-; Consult & reporter, Fed Judicial Ctr, Washington, DC, 73-74; vis prof Univ Ill, 76-77, Ohio State Univ, 78-79 & Ind-Bloomington, summers 76-80. **HONORS AND AWARDS** Ford Fdn fel **MEMBERSHIPS** Perm Editorial Bd, Uniform Commercial Code **RESEARCH** Contract, commercial and related consumer law. **CONTACT ADDRESS** Indiana Univ-Purdue Univ, Indianapolis, 355 N Lansing St, Indianapolis, IN, 46202-2815. **EMAIL** gbecko@iupui.edu

BERENBAUM, MICHAEL
PERSONAL Born 07/31/1945, Newark, NJ, m, 1995, 2 children **DISCIPLINE** RELIGION **EDUCATION** Queens Col, BA, 67; Jewish Theol Sem, 63-67; Heb Univ, 65-66; Boston Univ, MA, 69; FL State Univ, PhD, 75. **CAREER** Colby-Sawyer Col, instr, 69-71; Wesleyan Univ, adj asst prof and chaplain 73-80; Zachor: The Holocaust Resource Cent, 78; Pres Comm on the Holocaust, 79-80; George Wash Univ, assoc prof, 81-83; Jew Comm Coun of Great Wash, exec dir, 80-83; Univ Maryland, vis prof, 83; Amer Univ, adj prof 87; Relig Act Center, sen scholar 86-88; Georgetown Univ, adj prof, 83-97; US Holocaust Mem Museum, research fel 87-88, proj dir, 88-93, dir, 93-97; Univ of Judaism, adj prof, 98-, Survivors of the Shoah Visual Hist Foundation, pres & CEO, 97-. **HONORS AND AWARDS** Nazareth Col Rochester, PhD (Honoris Causa), 95; Emmy, Cableace and Academy Awards for One Survivor Remembers: The Gerda Weissman Klein Story, 95-96, FL State Univ, Charles E. Merrill Fel, 72-73; Yale Univ, Ezera Styles Fel, 79; Amer Jew Press Assoc, Simon Rockower Award, 86- 87. **MEMBERSHIPS** SSVHF **SELECTED PUBLICATIONS** Auth, The Vision of the Void: Theological Reflections on the Works of Elie Wiesel, Wesleyan Univ Press, 79; After Tragedy and Triumph: Modern Jewish Thought and the American Experience, Cambridge Univ Press, 90; The World Must Know: The History of the Holocaust, Little Brown and Co, 93; Witness to the Holocaust: An Illustrated Documentary History of the Holocaust in the Words of Its Victims, Perpetrators and Bystanders, Harper Collins, 97, The Holocaust and History: The Known, the Unknown, the Disputed and the Reexamined, Indiana Univ Press, 98; articles, Women, Blacks and Jews: Theologians of Survival, Relig in Life, 76; What We Should Tell Our Children About the Holocaust, Sh'ma, 81; The Paradox of Prayer, Reform Judaism, 86; American Jews Opt Out, New Outlook, 88; ed, Reflections on the Uniqueness of the Holocaust, in: A Mosaic of Victims: Non-Jews Persecuted and Murdered by the Nazis, New York Univ Press, 90; The Mystifying Burden of Goodness, in: Dimensions, 90; Questions for the Unredeemed, Tikkun, 93; The Holocaust, World Book Encycl, 96; Eleanor Roosevelt and the Holocaust, in: The Eleanor Roosevelt Encycl, ed. Maurine H. Beasley and Holly Shulman, Greenwood Pub Group, Inc, 98. **CONTACT ADDRESS** Survivors of the Shoah Visual Hist Foundation, PO Box 3168, Los Angeles, CA, 90078-3168. **EMAIL** berenbaum@vhf.org

BERGANT, DIANNE
PERSONAL Born 08/07/1936, Milwaukee, WI **DISCIPLINE** BIBLE; FIRST TESTAMENT **EDUCATION** St Louis Univ, PhD, 75. **CAREER** Teach, St Louis Univ, 72; Marian College of Fond du Lac, WI, 72-78; Catholic Theological Union, 78-; Regional Seminary, Trindad, West Indies, 86; Regional Seminary, Trindad, West Indies, 98. **HONORS AND AWARDS** Gamma Pi Epsilon (Natl Jesuit Women's Honor Soc), 72; Who's Who in Biblical Studies and Archaeology, 86-87; While editor of The Bible Today, won Natl Catholic Press 1st place award in bible & devotion category, 87, 88, 90. **MEMBERSHIPS** Catholic Biblical Assn, 70; General Council of Congregation of Saint Agnes, 73-77; Soc of Biblical lit, 75; Chicago Soc of Biblical research, 79-; North Amer Conf on Relig and ecology, 85-95. **RESEARCH** Biblical interpretation; Integrity of creation; Feminism; Justice works in progress include commentaries on Song of Songs; Lamentations; Three-volume commentary on lectionary readings using a liturgical interpretive method. **SELECTED PUBLICATIONS** Auth, II Cantico Dei Cantici, 98; The Earth is the Lord's: The Bible, Ecology, and Worship, Liturgical, 98; auth, Song of Songs: The Love Poetry of Scripture, New City, 98; auth, Response to Vincent L. Wimbush, Black and Catholic: The Challenge and the Gift of Black Folk, Marquette Univ, 98; auth, Biblical Foundation for Christian Ministry, Together in God's Service: Toward a Theology of Ecclesial Ministry, US Cath Conf, 98. **CONTACT ADDRESS** Catholic Theol Union at Chicago, 5401 S Cornell Ave, Chicago, IL, 60615. **EMAIL** dbergant@ctu.edu

BERGE, PAUL S.
DISCIPLINE NEW TESTAMENT **EDUCATION** Luther Sem, BD, 63; Union Theol Sem, ThM, ThD. **CAREER** Instr, 73; tchg fel, Union Theol Sem, 72-73; dir the master of arts degree prog, 84; vis prof, Lutheran Theol Sem, Madagascar, 86-87; res fel, Yale Divinity Sch, 79-80; prof, 84-. **HONORS AND AWARDS** Pres, Como Park Lutheran Church; pastor, Our Savior's Lutheran Church, Montevideo, Minn, 64. **SELECTED PUBLICATIONS** Auth, Servants and Stewards of the Gospel: A Stewardship Bible Study from Paul's Letter to the Philippians, 83; Now You Are God's People: A Study in I Peter, 80; contrib, Toward Full Communion and Concordat of Agreement, 91; Implications of the Gospel, 88; The Hist Episcopate, 85. **CONTACT ADDRESS** Dept of New Testament, Luther Sem, 2481 Como Ave, St. Paul, MN, 55108. **EMAIL** pberge@luthersem.edu

BERGEN, ROBERT D.
PERSONAL Born 05/18/1954, Lawrence, KS, m, 1979, 1 child **DISCIPLINE** OLD TESTAMENT, BIBLICAL HEBREW **EDUCATION** Hardin Simmons Univ, BA, 76; Southwestern Baptist Theol Sem, Mdiv, 79, PhD, 86. **CAREER** Assoc Prof of OT and Biblical Lang, 86-98, Hannibal-LaGrange Coll. **MEMBERSHIPS** SBL, ETS, Inst of Biblical Res. **RESEARCH** Discourse Linguistics. **SELECTED PUBLICATIONS** Auth, 1,2 Samuel, New American Commentary, vol 7, 96; 1,2, Samuel, Shepherd's Notes, 98; Ed of Biblical Hebrew and Discourse Linguistics, 94. **CONTACT ADDRESS** Hannibal-LaGrange Col, 2800 Palmyra Rd, Hannibal, MO, 63401. **EMAIL** bbergen@hlg.edu

BERGER, ALAN L.
PERSONAL Born 11/16/1939, New Brunswick, NJ, m, 1971, 3 children **DISCIPLINE** RELIGIOUS STUDIES **EDUCATION** Univ Chicago, MA, 70; Syracuse Univ, PhD, 76. **CAREER** Prof, Syracuse Univ, 73-95; Chm Holocaust Studies, 95-. **MEMBERSHIPS** Am Acad of Relig; Am Jewish Hist Soc; Asn of Jewish Studies; Inst of the Int Conf on the Holocause and Genocide. **RESEARCH** Jewish literature and theology. **SELECTED PUBLICATIONS** Auth, Children of Job: Second-Generation Witnesses to the Holocause, 97; Judaism in the Modern World, 94; "Holocaust Denial: Tempest in a Teapot of Storm on the Horizon?," 98; "Bearing Witness: Theological Implications of Second-Generation Literature in America," 97; "How My Mind Has Changed," 97. **CONTACT ADDRESS** Florida Atlantic Univ, 777 Glades Rd, Boca Raton, FL, 33434. **EMAIL** Aberger@acc.fau.edu

BERGER, LAWRENCE
DISCIPLINE LAW **EDUCATION** Univ Pa, BS; Rutgers Univ, JD. **CAREER** Prof **RESEARCH** Property; real estate transactions; accounting. **SELECTED PUBLICATIONS** Auth, pubs on real property. **CONTACT ADDRESS** Law Dept, Univ of Nebraska, Lincoln, 103 Ross McCollum Hall, PO Box 830902, Lincoln, NE, 68588-0420. **EMAIL** lberger@unlinfo.unl.edu

BERGER, MARK
DISCIPLINE LAW **EDUCATION** Columbia Univ, BA; Yale Univ, JD. **CAREER** Prof **RESEARCH** Criminal law; criminal procedure; labor law. **SELECTED PUBLICATIONS** Auth, Taking the Fifth: The Supreme Court and the Privilege Against Self-Incrimination, 80; co-auth, Missouri Criminal Practice and Procedure, 86. **CONTACT ADDRESS** Law Dept, Univ of Missouri, Kansas City, 5100 Rockhill Rd, Kansas City, MO, 64110-2499. **EMAIL** bergerm@umkc.edu

BERGER, MORRIS I.
PERSONAL Born 08/05/1928, New York, NY, d, 1 child **DISCIPLINE** PHILOSOPHY OF EDUCATION, PHILOSOPHY **EDUCATION** NY State Col Teachers, BA, 50, MA, 52; Columbia Univ, PhD, 56. **CAREER** Assoc prof, 56-63, prof philos of educ, State Univ NY Albany, 63-, chemn dept found, 69-; Res fels, State Univ NY Res Found, 62, State Univ NY, 69-70. **MEMBERSHIPS** Philos Educ Soc; Am Philos Asn. **RESEARCH** Immigration and social settlements; existentialism; conceptual analysis. **SELECTED PUBLICATIONS** Coauth, Public Education in America, Harper, 58; John Dewey: Master Educator, Soc Advan Educ, 59; auth, Doing things with the concept of teaching, Proc Philos Educ Soc, 68; Teaching as Act & Enterprise: Some Reconsiderations, Studies Philos & Educ, fall 68; The Settlement, the Imigrant and the Public School, Arno Press, 80. **CONTACT ADDRESS** Dept of Ed Admin & Policy Studies, Univ at Albany, SUNY, 1400 Washington Ave, Albany, NY, 12222. **EMAIL** m.berger@albany.edu

BERGMANN, GUSTAV
PERSONAL Born 05/04/1906, Vienna, Austria, m, 1943, 1 child **DISCIPLINE** PHILOSOPHY **EDUCATION** Univ Vienna, PhD (math), 28, JD, 35. **CAREER** From lectr to prof, 39-74, Carver distinguished prof philos, 72-74, Emer PROF PHILOS AND PSYCHOL, UNIV IOWA, 74-, Co-ed, Philos Sci Asn J, 48-76; vis prof, Swedish Univs, 61-62. **HONORS AND AWARDS** PhD , Gothenburg Univ, 62. **MEMBERSHIPS** Am Philos Asn; Philos Sci Asn. **SELECTED PUBLICATIONS** Auth, Complete Dialects of Lower Saxony, Zeitschrift fur Germ, Vol 0006, 96; Complete Catalog of Recordings in the Deutsches Spracharchiv, Zeitschrift fur Germ, Vol 0004, 94; A Linguistic Atlas of the Czech Language--Zeitschrift fur Dialektologie und Linguistik, Vol 0061, 94; The Palatinate--Introduction to Linguistic Landscape, Zeitschrift fur Dialektologie und Linguistik, Vol 0060, 93; Complete Dialects of Lower Saxony, Zeitschrift fur Germ, Vol 0006, 96. **CONTACT ADDRESS** Dept of Philos, Univ of Iowa, Iowa City, IA, 52240.

BERGMANN, MICHAEL
PERSONAL Born 09/08/1964, Revelstoke, Canada, m, 1986, 2 children **DISCIPLINE** PHILOSOPHY **EDUCATION** Univ Notre Dame, PhD, 97. **CAREER** Asst prof, Perdue Univ, 97-. **HONORS AND AWARDS** Doc fel, Soc Sci hum res coun of Canada, 93-96. **MEMBERSHIPS** Amer Philos Asn; Soc Christian Philos. **RESEARCH** Epistemology; Metaphysics; Philosophy of Religion. **SELECTED PUBLICATIONS** Auth, A New Argument from Actualism to Serious Actualism, Nous 30, 96, 366-359; Review of R. Douglas Geivett's Evil and the Evidence for God, Faith and Philos 13, 436-441, 96; Internalism, Externalism and the No-Defeater Condition, Synthese 110, 97, 399-417. **CONTACT ADDRESS** Dept of Philosophy-1360 LAEB, Purdue Univ, West Lafayette, IN, 47906. **EMAIL** bergmann@omni.cc.purdue.edu

BERKEY, ROBERT FRED
PERSONAL Born 06/30/1930, Barberton, OH, m, 1957, 2 children **DISCIPLINE** RELIGION **EDUCATION** Otterbein Col, AB, 52; Oberlin Grad Sch Theol, BD, 55, STM, 56; Hartford Sem Found, PhD, 58. **CAREER** From instr to assoc prof, 58-72, prof relig, Mt Holyokde Col, 72-, lectr, Hartford Sem Found, 57-58; vis lectr, Smith Col, 62-63; vis lectr, Trinity Col, 63-64; Eli Lilly Found res fel & sr assoc, Westminster & Cheshunt Cols, Eng, 71-72; vis lectr, Smith Col, spring semester, 87; lectr, Ecumenical Christian Centre, Bongalore, India, July 94; vis scholar, member, Senior Common Room, St Cross Col, Oxford, and also Oxford Centre for Hebrew and Christian Studies, fall and spring semester, 94; vis scholar, Univ of Tubingen, fall and spring, 90-91. **MEMBERSHIPS** Soc Bibl Lit; Am Acad Relig. **RESEARCH** New and Old Testament. **SELECTED PUBLICATIONS** Auth, Eggidzein, Phthanein and Realized Eschatology, J Bibl Lit, 6/63; co-reviser, Essentials of Bible History, Ronald, 66; Realized Eschatology and the post-Bultmannians, Expository Times, 12/72; co-ed & contribr, Christological Perspectives, Pilgrim Press, 82; co-ed and contributor, Christology in Dialogue, 93; forthcoming, with Harvey R. McArthur, The Quest of the Historical Jesus, in Dictionary of Biblical Interpretation, Abingdon Press, summer/fall 98. **CONTACT ADDRESS** Dept of Relig, Mount Holyoke Col, 50 College St, South Hadley, MA, 01075-1461. **EMAIL** rberkey@mtholyoke.edu

BERKMAN, JOHN
DISCIPLINE RELIGIOUS STUDIES **EDUCATION** Duke Univ, PhD, 94 **CAREER** Dir, Hersher Inst Applied Ethics, 93-97; asst prof, Sacred Heart Univ, 93-97; ASST PROF, DEPT THEOL, CATHOLIC UNIV AM, 97-. **RESEARCH** Catholic moral theology; biomedical ethics. **SELECTED PUBLICATIONS** various **CONTACT ADDRESS** Dept Theol, Catholic Univ of America, Washington, DC, 20064. **EMAIL** berkman@cua.edu

BERLEANT, ARNOLD
PERSONAL Born 03/04/1932, Buffalo, NY, m, 1959, 3 children **DISCIPLINE** PHILOSOPHY **EDUCATION** Eastman Sch Music, Univ Rochester, BMus, 53, MA, 55; Univ Buffalo, PhD (philos), 62. **CAREER** From instr to lectr philos, Univ Buffalo, 60-62; from asst profto assoc prof, 62-70, PROF PHILOS, C W POST CTR, LONG ISLAND UNIV, 70-, Vis prof, Sarah Lawrence Col, 66-68; Am Coun Learned Soc travel grant, 72, 76. **MEMBERSHIPS** Am Soc Aesthet (secy-treas, 78-); Am Soc Value Inquiry; AAUP; AAAS. **RESEARCH** Aesthetics; existentialism and phenomenology; ethics. **SELECTED PUBLICATIONS** Auth, The Aesthetic of Landscape, J Aesthet Educ, Vol 0028, 94. **CONTACT ADDRESS** Dept of Philos, Long Island Univ, C.W. Post, Greenvale, NY, 11548.

BERLING, JUDITH
PERSONAL Born 09/08/1945, Jacksonville, FL **DISCIPLINE** THEOLOGY **EDUCATION** Carleton Col, BA, 67; MPhil, 74, PhD, 75, Columbia Univ. **CAREER** Asst/Assoc Prof, 74-87, Indiana Univ; Dean and VP for Academic Affairs, 87-95, Prof, 95-, Graduate Theological Union, Berkeley. **HONORS AND AWARDS** Phi Beta Kappa; Kent Fel; NDFL Fel; Woodrow Wilson Fel, NEH Summer Fellowship. **MEMBERSHIPS** Amer Acad of Religion; Amer Soc for the Study of Religion **RESEARCH** East Asian languages and cultures **SELECTED PUBLICATIONS** Auth, A Pilgrim in Chinese Culture: Understanding Religious Neighbors, 97. **CONTACT ADDRESS** Graduate Theol Union, 2400 Ridge Rd., Berkeley, CA, 94709.

BERMAN, HAROLD J.
PERSONAL Born 02/13/1918, Hartford, CT, m, 1941, 4 children **DISCIPLINE** LAW **EDUCATION** Dartmouth Col, BA 38; London Sch Economics, Certificate of Grad Studies, 39; Yale Univ, MA 42, LLB 47. **CAREER** Stanford Law Sch, asst prof, 47-48; Harvard Law Sch, asst prof, Storey Prof, Ames Prof, 48-85; Emory Law Sch, Woodruff Prof, 85-. **HONORS AND AWARDS** LLD Cath Univ of Am 91; DHL VA Theol Sem 95; Doctor honoris causa U of Ghent 97. **MEMBERSHIPS** AAAS; ASCL; ASLH; AAASS. **RESEARCH** Western legal tradition 1500-1700; esp Germany and England; History; Theology; Philosophy. **SELECTED PUBLICATIONS** Auth, Freedom of Religion in Russia: An Amicus Brief for the Defendant, Emory Intl L Rev, 98; auth, Interaction of Spiritual and Secular Law: The Sixteenth Century and Today, Univ Chicago, 97; auth, H. Jefferson Powell on the American Constitutional Tradition: A Conversation, Notre Dame L Rev 96; auth, The Legacy of the Past: Russian Law as the Foundation for Change, E/W Exec Guide, 97; auth, World Law and the Holy Spirit, The Living Pulpit, 96; auth, Max Weber as Legal Historian, coauth, The Cambridge Companion to Max Weber, ed, Stephen Turner, Cambridge Univ Press, forthcoming; The Transformation of English Legal Science: From Hale to Blackstone, coauth, Emory L Jour, 96; Religious Freedom and the Rights of Foreign Missionaries Under Russian Law, The Parker Sch Jour of E European Law, 95; auth, World Law, Fordham Intl L Jour , 95; auth, Faith and Order: The Reconciliation of Law and Religion, Scholars Press 93, auth, The Nature and Functions Of Law, 5th ed rev, with William R. Greiner, Samir N. Saliba, Foundation Press, 96. **CONTACT ADDRESS** School of Law, Emory Univ, 1301 Clifton Rd, Atlanta, GA, 30322. **EMAIL** hberman@law.emory.edu

BERMAN, JEFFREY B.
DISCIPLINE LAW **EDUCATION** City Univ NY, BS; Univ Denver, MS; Brooklyn Law Sch, JD. **CAREER** Prof **RESEARCH** Trial advocacy. **SELECTED PUBLICATIONS** Auth, Trial Advocacy Teacher's Manual; co-auth, Missouri Civil Procedure Form Book; The Story of a Civil Suit: Dominquez v. Scott's Food Stores Inc. **CONTACT ADDRESS** Law Dept, Univ of Missouri, Kansas City, 5100 Rockhill Rd, Kansas City, MO, 64110-2499. **EMAIL** bermanj@umkc.edu

BERMAN, SCOTT
PERSONAL Born 09/19/1962, Baltimore, MD, m, 1985, 2 children **DISCIPLINE** PHILOSOPHY **EDUCATION** Tulane Univ, BA, 84; Univ Wisc, Madison, MA, 87, PhD, 90. **CAREER** Vis asst prof, philos, Univ Neb, Lincoln, 90-91; asst prof, 91-97, assoc prof, 97- , philos, Saint Louis Univ. **HONORS AND AWARDS** Mellon Fac Development Grant, 92, 93, 94, 95, 96; Teacher of the Month, 93. **MEMBERSHIPS** Soc for Ancient Greek Philos; Int Asn for Greek Philos; Int Plato Soc; APA. **RESEARCH** Ancient Greek philosophy; contemporary analytic metaphysics. **SELECTED PUBLICATIONS** Auth, How Polus Was Refuted: Reconsidering Plato's Gorgias 474c-465c, Ancient Philos, 91; auth, Socrates and Callicles on Pleasure, Phronesis, 91; auth, Plato's Refutation of Constructivism in the Cratylus, J of Neoplatonic Stud, 94; auth, Plato's Explanation of False Belief in the Sophist, Apeiron, 96. **CONTACT ADDRESS** Dept of Philosophy, Saint Louis Univ, 3800 Lindell Blvd, PO Box 56907, St Louis, MO, 63156-0907. **EMAIL** bermansj@slu.edu

BERNIER, PAUL
DISCIPLINE COGNITIVE SCIENCE AND PHILOSOPHY OF MIND **EDUCATION** Univ Montreal, PhD. **CAREER** Prof. **RESEARCH** Philosophy of language. **SELECTED PUBLICATIONS** Pub(s), in Mind and Lang; Quebec Stud; Philos of Sci. **CONTACT ADDRESS** Dept of Philos, Concordia Univ, Montreal, 1455 de Maisonneuve W, Montreal, PQ, H3G 1M8. **EMAIL** pbernie@vax2.concordia.ca

BERNSTEIN, JERRY
DISCIPLINE PHILOSOPHY **EDUCATION** Univ Cambridge, UK, MPh, 91. **CAREER** Investment advisor, 20 years. **MEMBERSHIPS** Am Soc for Aesthetics; APA. **RESEARCH** Aesthetics; value theory. **CONTACT ADDRESS** 432 S Curson Ave, #6-H, Los Angeles, CA, 90036.

BERNSTEIN, MARK
PERSONAL Born 03/19/1948, Bronx, NY, m **DISCIPLINE** PHILOSOPHY **EDUCATION** Univ Calif Santa Barbara, PhD, philos, 82. **CAREER** Assoc prof, Univ Tex San Antonio. **HONORS AND AWARDS** NEH fel. **MEMBERSHIPS** APA; SSPP. **RESEARCH** Animal ethics; Metaphysics. **SELECTED PUBLICATIONS** Auth, Fatalism, Univ Neb; auth, On Moral Considerability, Oxford Univ Press; auth, Contractualism and Animals, Philos Studies; auth, Well-Being, Amer Philos Quart. **CONTACT ADDRESS** Dept. of Philosophy, Univ of Texas, San Antonio, TX, 78249. **EMAIL** mbernste@lonestar.utsa.edu

BERNSTEIN, RICHARD J.
PERSONAL Born 05/14/1932, Brooklyn, NY, m, 1955, 4 children **DISCIPLINE** PHILOSOPHY **EDUCATION** Univ Chicago, BA, 51; Columbia Univ, BS, 53; Yale Univ, MA, 55, PhD, 58. **CAREER** Instr, 54-57, asst prof, 58-63, assoc prof philos, 63-65, Yale Univ; Fulbright lectr, Hebrew Univ, 57-58; vis prof philos, Hebrew Univ, 65-66; prof philos, 66-78, chemn dept, 66-78, T. Wistar Brown Prof of Philos, 79-89, Haverford Col; vis adj prof, 81-83, Vera List Prof, Grad Fac, chemn Dept

of Philos, 89- , New School for Social Res; pres, Adirondack Work/Study Inc., 90- . **HONORS AND AWARDS** Summa cum Laude, 53; Phi Beta Kappa, 53; Tew Prize, 54; Pres, Charles S. Peirce Soc, 69; exec comm E Div APA, 68-70; ed, Rev of Metaphysics, 64-71; Harbison Award for Gifted Tchg, 70; sr fel NEH, 72-73; ACLS fel, 78-79; ed, Praxis Int, 80-84; NEH fel, 85-86; vpres & pres APA, E Div, & Metaphysical Soc of Am, 87-88; Robert Foster Cherry Award for Great Tchrs, 91; John Dewey Soc Award for Outstanding Achievement, 95. **MEMBERSHIPS** APA; Metaphysical Soc of Am. **SELECTED PUBLICATIONS** Auth, An Allegory of Modernity/Postmodernity: Habermas and Derrida, in Madison, ed, Working Through Derrida, Northwestern Univ, 93; auth, Hans Jonas: Rethinking Responsibility, Soc Res, 94; auth, American Pragmatism: The Conflict of Narratives, in Saatkamp, ed, Rorty and Pragmatism, Vanderbilt Univ, 95; auth, Are We Beyond the Enlightenment Horizon? in Shea, ed, Knowledge and Belief in America, Cambridge Univ, 95; auth, Hannah Arendt and the Jewish Question, MIT, 96; auth, The Banality of Evil Reconsidered, in Calhoun, ed, Hannah Arendt and the Meaning of Politics, Univ Minn, 96; auth, The Hermeneutics of Cross-Cultural Understanding, in Balslev, ed, Cross-Cultural Conversation, Scholars, 96; auth, Hans Jonas' Mortality and Morality, Grad Fac Philos J, 97; auth, Provocation and Appropriation: Hannah Arendt's Response to Martin Heidegger, Constellations, 97; auth, Freud & The Legacy of Moses, Cambridge Univ, 98. **CONTACT ADDRESS** Philosophy/Graduate Faculty, New Sch for Social Research, 85 Fifth Ave, New York, NY, 10003.

BERNSTEIN-NAHAR, AVI K.
PERSONAL Born 10/24/1963, Orlando, FL, m, 1993, 2 children **DISCIPLINE** RELIGION; PHILOSOPHY **EDUCATION** Brown Univ BA; Stanford Univ PhD. **CAREER** Univ of Toronto Ray D Wolfe fel, 97-98. **HONORS AND AWARDS** Ray D Wolfe Fel; Mem Foun Jewish Culture Fel; Ntl Foun Jewish Fel; Lady Davis Trust Fell **MEMBERSHIPS** AAR; AJS **RESEARCH** Modern Jewish Thought. **SELECTED PUBLICATIONS** Auth, Das einzige Herz der Sache: Hermann Cohen's Teaching Concerning Modern Jewish Identity, Yearbook of the Leo Blaeck Inst, 98. **CONTACT ADDRESS** Dept of Religion and Philosophy, Toronto Univ, 6 Preston St, Rye, NY, 10580. **EMAIL** avi.bernstein.nahar@utoronto.ca

BERNSTINE, DANIEL O.
PERSONAL Born 09/07/1947, Berkeley, CA, s **DISCIPLINE** LAW **EDUCATION** Univ of CA, BA 1969; NW Univ Sch of Law, JD 1972; Univ of WI Law Sch, LLM 1975. **CAREER** US Dept of Labor, staff atty 1972-73; Univ of WI Law Sch, teaching fellow 1974-75; Howard Univ Law Sch, asst prof 1975-78; Howard Univ, asst vice pres for legal affairs, 1984-87, general counsel, 1987-1990; Univ of WI Law Sch, prof, 1978-97, dean, 1990-97; Portland State University, president, currently. **SELECTED PUBLICATIONS** Various publications. **CONTACT ADDRESS** Portland State Univ, PO Box 751, Portland, OR, 97207.

BEROFSKY, BERNARD A.
PERSONAL Born 07/05/1935, Jersey City, NJ, m, 1962, 2 children **DISCIPLINE** PHILOSOPHY **EDUCATION** NY Univ, BA, 56; Columbia Univ, MA, 59, PhD, 63. **CAREER** Instr philos, Vassar Col, 63-64; asst prof, Univ MI, 64-67; from asst to assoc prof, 67-69, Prof Philos, Columbia Univ, 69-, Am Philos Soc grant, 67-; Am Coun Learned Soc fel, 72-73; Fulbright research fel, 87-88. **MEMBERSHIPS** Am Philos Asn. **RESEARCH** Determinism; autonomy; views on free will. **SELECTED PUBLICATIONS** Auth, Causality and general laws, J Philos, 3/66; The regularity theory, Nous, 11/68; Purposive action, Am Philos Quart, 10/70; Determinism, Princeton Univ, 71; co-ed, Introductory Philosophy, Harper, 2nd ed, 71; auth, Freedom from necessity, RKP, 87; Liberation from self, Cambridge, 95. **CONTACT ADDRESS** Dept of Philos, Columbia Univ, 2960 Broadway, New York, NY, 10027-6900. **EMAIL** beberofsky@aol.com

BERQUIST, JON L.
PERSONAL Born 12/19/1963, s **DISCIPLINE** RELIGION **EDUCATION** Northwest Christian Col, BA, 85; Vanderbilt Univ, MA, 88, PhD, 89. **CAREER** Phillips Grad Sem, asst prof, assoc prof, 89-94; Westminster John Knox Press, Acquisitions ed, 94-97; Chalis Press, Acad ed, 97-. **HONORS AND AWARDS** Vanderbilt Grad Fel, SCRS jr scholar. **MEMBERSHIPS** CBA, SBL, SSSR. **RESEARCH** Social world of ancient Israel; Persian Period Judah; Achaemenid Dynasty. **SELECTED PUBLICATIONS** Auth, Ancient Wine, New Wineskins: The Lord's Supper in Old Testament Perspective, St. Louis: Chalice Press, 91; auth, Reclaiming Her Story: The Witness of Women in the Old Testament, St. Louis, Chalice Press, 92; Surprises by the River: The Prophecy of Ezekiel, St. Louis Press, 93; auth, Judaism in Persia's Shadow: A Social and Historical Approach, Minneapolis: Fortress Press, 95; auth, Who Do You Say That I Am? Biblical Images and Ministerial Identity, Lexington Theol Quart, 94; auth, The Shifting Frontier: The Achaemenid Empire's Treatment of Western Colonies, Jour World Sys Res, 95; Postcolonization and Imperial Motives for Canonization, Semeia, 96. **CONTACT ADDRESS** 7012 Tholozan Ave, St. Louis, MO, 63109-1131.

BERRIDGE, JOHN MACLENNAN
PERSONAL Born 05/23/1938, Bridgewater, NS, Canada, m, 1966 **DISCIPLINE** THEOLOGY **EDUCATION** Mt Allison Univ, BA, 59; Pine Hill Divinity Hall, BD, 63; Univ Basel, DTheol, 67. **CAREER** Asst prof, 68-73, ASSOC PROF THEOL, ST FRANCIS XAVIER UNIV, 73-, Can Coun leave fel, 75-76. **MEMBERSHIPS** Soc Bibl Lit; Am Acad Relig. **RESEARCH** Old Testament; prophecy in the Old Testament; religion in modern India. **SELECTED PUBLICATIONS** Auth, A Redaction History of Jeremiah Ii,1 Iv,2, Cath Bibl Quart, Vol 0055, 93. **CONTACT ADDRESS** Francis Xavier Univ, Campus PO St, Box 86, Antigonish, NS, B2G 1C0.

BERSHAD, LAWRENCE
DISCIPLINE LAW **EDUCATION** Univ CT, AB; Georgetown Univ, JD. **CAREER** Prof, 72-, ch, Seton Hall Univ Athletic Coun, Seton Hall Univ; legal adv, Dept of Corrections of the DC; vice-ch, NJ Adv Coun of Corrections; mem, NJ Boxing Comn. **HONORS AND AWARDS** Criminal justice fel, Harvard Univ. **SELECTED PUBLICATIONS** Publ in the areas of criminal justice and sports law. **CONTACT ADDRESS** Seton Hall Univ, South Orange, NJ. **EMAIL** bershadla@lanmail.shu.edu

BERSOFF, DONALD N.
DISCIPLINE CRIMINAL LAW **EDUCATION** NY Univ, BS, 58, MA, 60, PhD, 65; Yale Univ Law Sch, JD, 76. **CAREER** Prof & dir, Law/Psychology Prog; Villanova Univ, 90-. **HONORS AND AWARDS** Distinguished alumni awd, NY Univ Sch Educ, Health, Nursing, and Arts Prof, 81; Who's Who in Am, 82-; **MEMBERSHIPS** Bd dir, Amer Psychol Asn, 94-97, and a Comn mem on, 3rd Circuit Task Force for Equal Treatment in the Courts, Commission on Race and Ethnicity, 95-97; Past ch, Educ and Training in Law and Psychology, 94-95; ed bd(s), J Legal Educ, Behavioral Sci and the Law & Ethics and Behavior; assoc ed, Law and Human Behavior. **RESEARCH** Mental health, social science and the law. **SELECTED PUBLICATIONS** Auth, Ethical Conflicts in Psychology, 95; sr coauth, Legal Issues in Computerized Psychological Testing, The Computer and the Decision-Making Process, 91; Explicit Ambiguity: The 1992 Ethics Code as an Oxymoron, 25 Prof Psychology: Res and Practice 382, 94 & Legal Issues in the Assessment and Treatment of Individuals with Dual Diagnoses, 62 J Consulting and Clinical Psychology 55, 94. **CONTACT ADDRESS** Law School, Villanova Univ, 800 Lancaster Ave, Villanova, PA, 19085-1692. **EMAIL** bersoffd@law.vill.edu

BERTHOLD, GEORGE CHARLES
PERSONAL Born 03/01/1935, Lawrence, MA **DISCIPLINE** THEOLOGY, BYZANTINE STUDIES **EDUCATION** St John's Sem, BA, 59, MA, 63; Cath Inst, Paris, STD, 75; Villanova Univ, BA, 77. **CAREER** Asst prof, 76-80, ASSOC PROF THEOL, ST ANSELM'S COL, 80- **MEMBERSHIPS** Cath Theol Soc Am; Col Theol Soc. **RESEARCH** Patristic studies, chiefly of the later Greek period; ecumenics. **SELECTED PUBLICATIONS** Auth, Maximus the Confessor--Divine Essence and Energies, Theol Stud, Vol 0057, 96; Gregory of Nyssa and the Christianity of Late Antiquity, J Early Christian Stud, Vol 0003, 95. **CONTACT ADDRESS** Dept of Theol, St Anselm's Col, Manchester, NH, 03102.

BERTOLET, ROD
PERSONAL Born 03/22/1949, Allentown, PA **DISCIPLINE** PHILOSOPHY **EDUCATION** Franklin & Marshall Col, BA, 71; Univ Wi Madison, PhD, 77. **CAREER** Asst prof to assoc prof to prof, dept head, Purdue Univ, 77- . **HONORS AND AWARDS** Fel, Center for Humanistic Stud, Purdue Univ, 87, 91. **MEMBERSHIPS** Amer Philos Assoc, Ind Philos Assoc. **RESEARCH** Philos of lang, philos of mind. **SELECTED PUBLICATIONS** Auth, What is Said: A Theory of Indirect Speech Reports, Philos Stud Series, Kluwer Acad Publ, 90; Demonstratives and Intentions, Ten Years Later, Commun & Cognition, 93; Hasker on Middle Knowledge, Faith & Psychol, 94; Saving Eliminativism, Philos Psychol, 94; Conventions and Coreferentiality, J of Philos Res, 94. **CONTACT ADDRESS** Dept of Philosophy, Purdue Univ, West Lafayette, IN, 47907. **EMAIL** bertolet@purdue.edu

BESANCON SPENCER, AIDA
PERSONAL Santo Domingo, Dominican Republic, m, 1 child **DISCIPLINE** NEW TESTAMENT **EDUCATION** Douglass Col, Rutgers State Univ, BA; Princeton Theol Sem, MDiv, ThM; S Baptist Sem, PhD. **CAREER** Instr, Trenton State Col; NY Theol Sem; Alpha-Omega Community Theol Sch; vis scholar, Harvard Divinity Sch; prof, Gordon-Conwell Theol Sem, 82-. **HONORS AND AWARDS** Christianity Today Bk Award, 96., Ch, Evangel Theol Soc(s); Presbyterian minister. **SELECTED PUBLICATIONS** Auth, Joy through the Night: Biblical Resources for Suffering People, InterVarsity, 94; The Goddess Revival, Baker, 95; The Gloabal God, Baker, 98; contrib, Shaped by God's Love, World Wide, 90; The New Testament Criticism and Interpretation, Zondervan, 91; Through No Fault of Their Own?, Baker, 91; Study Bible for Women, Baker, 96. **CONTACT ADDRESS** Gordon-Conwell Theol Sem, 130 Essex St, South Hamilton, MA, 01982.

BESCHLE, D. L.
PERSONAL Born 10/15/1957, CT, s **DISCIPLINE** LAW **EDUCATION** Fordham Univ, BA, 73; New York Univ School of Law, JD, 76; Temple Univ School of Law, LLM, 83. **CAREER** Teaching fel, Temple Univ School of Law, 79-81; ASST PROF, 81-85, ASSOC PROF, 85-97, PROF, 98-, JOHN MARSHALL LAW SCHOOL. **MEMBERSHIPS** Order of the Coif. **RESEARCH** Constitutional law; law and religion; antitrust law. **SELECTED PUBLICATIONS** Auth, What's Guilt (Or Deterrence) Got To Do With It?: The Death Penalty, Ritual, and Mimetic Violence, William & Mary Law Rev, 97; auth, You've Got To Be Carefully Taught: Justifying Affirmative Action After Croson and Adarand, NC Law Rev, 96; auth, The Role of Courts in the Debate On Assisted Suicide: A Communitarian Approach, Ethics & Public Politics, 95; auth, Defining the Scope of the Constitutional Right to Marry: More Than Tradition, Less Than Unlimited Autonomy, Notre Dame Law Rev, 94; auth, The Use of Religion as Part of the Best Interests Test in Child Custody Disputes, Child, Family & State: Law and Policy Reader, Temple Univ Press, 94; auth, Catechism or Imagination: Is Justice Scalia's Judicial Style Typically Catholic, Villanova Law Rev, 92; auth, Conditional Spending and the First Amendment: Maintaining the Commitment to Rational Liberal Dialogue, Mo Law Rev, 92. **CONTACT ADDRESS** John Marshall Law Sch, 315 S Plymouth Ct, Chicago, IL, 60604. **EMAIL** 7beschle@jmls.edu

BESSNER, RONDA
DISCIPLINE LAW **EDUCATION** McGill Univ, BA, 77, BCL, 81, LLB, 81; Harvard Univ, LLM, 86. **CAREER** Adj fac; Senior Legal Analyst, Commission of Inquiry on the Blood System in Canada **SELECTED PUBLICATIONS** Auth, pubs on criminal law, evidence, constitutional law and family law. **CONTACT ADDRESS** Fac of Law, Univ Toronto, 78 Queen's Park, Toronto, ON.

BESSON, PAUL SMITH
PERSONAL Born 05/11/1953, New York, NY, s **DISCIPLINE** LAW **EDUCATION** Cornell Univ, BS labor relations 1975, MBA marketing/finance 1976; Northwestern Univ, JD 1980; Georgetown University Law Center, LLM, 1995. **CAREER** Cummins Engine Co, market planning analyst 1976-77; Jewel Companies, Inc, labor relations counsel 1980-82, mgr personnel/labor relations 1982-83; NBC, Inc, mgr labor relations, 1984-88, dir employee relations, 1988-1998; Director, Talent Negotiations and Labor Relations; American Commercial Lines, LLC, Sr VP Human Resources 1998-. **MEMBERSHIPS** Mem Amer, IL, Chicago, DC Bar Assn; mem IL, NY, & DC Bars; bd of dir Cornell Club Assn 1982; pres Cornell Black Alumni Assn Chicago 1982-83; Amer Arbitration Assn panel commercial arbitrations; hearing officer, Civil Serv Commn IL; bd of dir ABE Credit Union; pres, Cornell Black Alumni Assn, Washington, DC, 1989-91; Capital Press Club; Washington Association of Black Journalists; mediator, US District Court, Dist of Columbia; Advisor Council GE African American Forum. **SELECTED PUBLICATIONS** Contributing writer Black Enterprise Magazine; **CONTACT ADDRESS** 1710 E. Market St., Jeffersonville, IN, 47130.

BEST, ERNEST E
PERSONAL Born 12/26/1919, Toronto, ON, Canada, m, 1945, 3 children **DISCIPLINE** RELIGION, PHILOSOPHY **EDUCATION** Univ Toronto, BA, 40, MA, 42, BD, 49; Drew Univ, PhD, 58. **CAREER** Assoc prof hist relig and soc ethics, Lafayette Col, 60-65; prof soc ethics, Methodist Theol Sch, Ohio, 65-70; PROF RELIG STUDIES, VICTORIA COL, UNIV TORONTO, 70-, Am Asn Theol Schs fel, 68-69; Am Philos Soc res grant, 68-69. **MEMBERSHIPS** Can Soc Studies Relig; Can Soc Asian Studies; Asn Asian Studies; Am Soc Christian Ethics. **RESEARCH** Contemporary Japanese society since 1859; history and sociology of religions; social value theory. **SELECTED PUBLICATIONS** Auth, The Largest Amount of Good--Quaker Relief in Ireland, Stud Rel Sci Rel, Vol 0024,95; Seeds of Peace--A Buddhist Vision for Renewing Society, Stud Rel Sci Rel, Vol 0023, 94. **CONTACT ADDRESS** 9 Killer Deer Cres, Toronto, ON, M4G 2W7.

BEST, STEVEN
DISCIPLINE PHILOSOPHY **EDUCATION** Univ Ill, Urbana-Champaign, BA; Univ Chicago, MA; Univ Tex, Austin, PhD. **CAREER** Asst prof **RESEARCH** Cultural criticism; mass media; social theory; postmodern theory. **SELECTED PUBLICATIONS** Auth, The Politics of Historical Vision: Marx, Foucault, and Habermas, Guilford Press, NY; Murray Bookchin: Philosopher of Freedom, Guilford Press, NY, 99; coauth, Postmodern Theory: Critical Interrogations, Guilford Press, NY; The Postmodern Turn: Paradigm Shifts in Art, Theory, and Science, Guilford Press, NY; The Postmodern Adventure: Science, Technology, and Cultural Studies, Guilford Press, NY. **CONTACT ADDRESS** Dept of Philosophy, Univ of Texas, El Paso, 500 W University Ave, El Paso, TX, 79968. **EMAIL** best@utep.edu

BETHEL, ARTHUR CHARLES WALTER
PERSONAL Born 12/13/1940, Los Angeles, CA, m, 1970, 1 child **DISCIPLINE** ETHICS, ACTION THEORY **EDUCATION** Univ Calif, Santa Barbara, BA, 64, MA, 68, PhD(-

philos), 74. **CAREER** Prof Philos, Calif Polytech State Univ, 68- **MEMBERSHIPS** Am Philos Asn. **RESEARCH** Action and responsibility. **SELECTED PUBLICATIONS** Auth, Traditional Logic, Univ Press of Am, 82; Wanting to want, Philos Res Archives ; Logic: A Traditional Approach, Kendall-Hunt, 90. **CONTACT ADDRESS** Philos Dept, California Polytech State Univ, 1 Grand Ave, San Luis Obispo, CA, 93407-0001. **EMAIL** abethel@calpoly.edu

BETHEL, LEONARD LESLIE
PERSONAL Born 02/05/1939, Philadelphia, Pennsylvania, m **DISCIPLINE** THEOLOGY **EDUCATION** Lincoln Univ, BA 1961; Johnson C Smith Univ Sch of Theology, MDiv 1964; New Brunswick Theological Sem, MA 1971; Rutgers Univ, DEd 1975. **CAREER** Washington United Presbyterian Church, pastor 1964-67; Lincoln Univ, asst chaplain & dir counseling 1967-79; Bethel Presbyterian Church, pastor 1982-92; Rutgers Univ Dept Africana Studies, faculty & staff 1969-, assoc prof 1980-. **HONORS AND AWARDS** Phi Delta Kappa Rutgers Univ 1975; Paul Robeson Faculty Awd Rutgers Univ 1978; NAFEO Pres Citation Lincoln Univ 1981; Woodrow Wilson Fellow Princeton Univ 1984. **MEMBERSHIPS** Mem Bd of Trustees Rutgers Prep Sch 1971-84; fellow Rutgers Coll Rutgers Univ 1980-; mem Amer Assn Univ Profs Rutgers Univ 1980-; mem board of directors Plainfield Branch, Union County Coll, 1980-86; mem Frontiers Intl 1980-; mem Presbytery of Elizabeth 1982-; bd of trustees, Bloomfield Coll, 1980-86; bd of trustees, Lincoln Univ, 1996-; bd of dirs, VCC, 1980-87. **SELECTED PUBLICATIONS** Co-author, Advancement Through Service: A History of The Frontiers International, Lanham, University Press of America, 1991, Plainfield's African American: Northern Slavery to Church Freedom, University Press of America, 1997; author, Educating African Leaders: Missionism in America, Edwin Mellon Press, 1997. **CONTACT ADDRESS** Rutgers Univ, Beck Hall #112, New Brunswick, NJ, 08903.

BETT, RICHARD
PERSONAL Born 07/10/1957, London, England, m, 1986 **DISCIPLINE** CLASSICS AND PHILOSOPHY **EDUCATION** Oxford Univ, BA, 80; UC Berkley, PhD, 86. **CAREER** Asst Prof, Univ TX, 86-91; Asst Prof, 91-94; Assoc Prof, 94-, Sec Appt in Classics, 96-. **HONORS AND AWARDS** Fel Center for Hellenic Stud, Washington DC 94-95. **MEMBERSHIPS** APA; Soc for Ancient Greek Phil; North Amer Nietzsche Soc **RESEARCH** Ancient Greek philosophy, especially Greek skepticism. **SELECTED PUBLICATIONS** Art, Scepticism and Everyday Attitudes in Ancient and Modern Philosophy, Metaphilosophy, 93; art, What Did Pyrrho Think about the Nature of the Divine and the Good, Phronesis, 94; art, Aristocleson Timon on Pyrrho the Text it Logic and its Credibility, Oxford Stud in Ancient Phil, 94; auth, Sextus Against the Ethicists Scepticism, Relativisim or Both, Apeiron, 94; art, Hellenistic Essays Translated, Papers in Hellenistic Phil, 96; Entries in Encyl of Class Philos, 97. **CONTACT ADDRESS** Dept of Philosophy, Johns Hopkins Univ, Gilman Hall, Baltimore, MD, 21218-2890. **EMAIL** bett_r@jhunix.hcf.jhu.edu

BETZ, HANS DIETER
PERSONAL Born 05/21/1931, Lemgo, Germany, m, 1957, 3 children **DISCIPLINE** RELIGION **EDUCATION** Gymnasium Leopoldinum in Detmold, BA, 51; Theologische Hochschule Bethel, 51-52; Johannes Gutenberg, Univ Mainz, PhD, 57. **CAREER** Prof, Claremont Grad Sch, 63-78; Univ Chicago, 78-. **HONORS AND AWARDS** Johannes Gutenberg Stipendium, Univ Mainz, 53-55; Fel, World Coun of Churches, 55-56. **MEMBERSHIPS** Int Soc for New Testament Studies; Soc of Bibl Lit; Chicago Soc of Bibl Res; Inst for Antiquity and Christianity; Int Plutarch Soc; Alexander von Humboldt Asn of Am. **RESEARCH** Religion; New Testament Studies; Greco-Roman Religions. **SELECTED PUBLICATIONS** Auth, Antike und Christentum: Gesammlte Aufsatze IV, 98; The Sermon on the Mount, 95; Paulinische Studien: Gesammelte Aufsatze III, 94. **CONTACT ADDRESS** Divinity School, Univ of Chicago, 1025 E 58th St, Chicago, IL, 60637. **EMAIL** hansbetz@midway.uchicago.edu

BETZ, JOSEPH M.
PERSONAL Born 02/13/1940, Philadelphia, PA, m, 1963, 4 children **DISCIPLINE** PHILOSOPHY **EDUCATION** St Joseph's Col, BS, 61; Univ Chicago, MA, 64; Villanova Univ, MA, 66; Univ Chicago, PhD(ideas & methods), 73. **CAREER** Assoc Prof Philos, Villanova Univ, 66-. **MEMBERSHIPS** Soc Advan Am Philos; N Am Society for Soc Philosophy; Charles S Peirce Soc; Am Philos Asn. **RESEARCH** Ethics; social philosophy; American philosophy. **SELECTED PUBLICATIONS** Auth, Can civil disobedience be justified?, Social Theory & Pract, fall 70; The relation between love and justice, J Value Inquiry, fall 70; George Herbert Mead on human rights, Trans Charles S Peirce Soc, fall 74; John Dewey on natural rights, Bicentennial Sym Philos: Contrib Papers, 76; Violence: Garver's definition and a Deweyan correction, Ethics, 7/77; John Dewey on human rights, Trans Charles S Peirce Soc, winter 78. **CONTACT ADDRESS** Dept of Philosophy, Villanova Univ, 845 E Lancaster Ave, Villanova, PA, 19085. **EMAIL** jbetz@email.vill.edu

BEVANS, STEPHEN
PERSONAL Born 04/14/1944, Baltimore, MD **DISCIPLINE** THEOLOGY **EDUCATION** Divine Word Col, BA, 67; Univ Notre Dame, PhD, 86. **CAREER** Prof, Immaculate Conception Sch Theol, Philippines, 73-81; Luzbetak Prof Mission & Culture, Cath Theol Union, 86-. **MEMBERSHIPS** AAR, ASM, CTSA. **RESEARCH** Inculturation; mission; ecclesiology. **SELECTED PUBLICATIONS** Auth, John Oman and his Doctrine of God, Cambridge Univ Press, 92; auth, Models of Contextual Theology, Orbis Books, 92; auth, Cultural Expressions of Our Faith: Church Teachings and Pastoral Responses, USCC, 93; ed, New Directions in Mission and Evangelization, Orbis Books, Vol 1, 92, Vol 2, 94, Vol 3, forthcoming; ed, Dictionary of Mission: Theology, History, Perspectives, Orbis Books, 97; ed, Word Remembered, Word Proclaimed: Selected Papers from the SVD Centennial in North America, Steyler Verlag. **CONTACT ADDRESS** 5401 S Cornell, Chicago, IL, 60615. **EMAIL** sbevans@ctu.edu

BEYER, BRYAN E.
DISCIPLINE BIBLE **EDUCATION** Hebrew Union Col, 78; Denver Sem, 80; CO St Univ, 76 **CAREER** Academic Dean of Colum Bibl Col, 94-pres; Asst Dean of Colum Bibl Col 93-94; Assoc Prof of Bibl , Colum Int Univ, 1985-pres **MEMBERSHIPS** Natl Assoc of Profs of Hebrew **RESEARCH** Bible **SELECTED PUBLICATIONS** Coauth, Encountering the Old Testament, Baker Book House, 97; Coauth, New American Standard Study Bible, Lockman Foundation **CONTACT ADDRESS** Columbia Bible Col, PO Box 3122, Columbia, SC, 29230-3122. **EMAIL** bryan@ciu.edu

BEYER, BRYAN E.
DISCIPLINE BIBLE **EDUCATION** Hebrew Union Col, 78; Denver Sem, 80; CO St Univ, 76 **CAREER** Academic Dean of Colum Bibl Col, 94-pres; Asst Dean of Colum Bibl Col 93-94; Assoc Prof of Bibl , Colum Int Univ, 1985-pres **MEMBERSHIPS** Natl Assoc of Profs of Hebrew **RESEARCH** Bible **SELECTED PUBLICATIONS** Coauth, Encountering the Old Testament, Baker Book House, 97; Coauth, New American Standard Study Bible, Lockman Foundation **CONTACT ADDRESS** Columbia Bible Col, PO Box 3122, Columbia, SC, 29230-3122. **EMAIL** bryan@ciu.edu

BIALLAS, LEONARD JOHN
PERSONAL Born 05/03/1939, Pontiac, MI, m, 1974 **DISCIPLINE** THEOLOGY, RELIGIOUS STUDIES **EDUCATION** Univ Notre Dame, AB, 61; Holy Cross Col, MA, 65; Inst Cath, Paris, STD, 70. **CAREER** Asst prof relig, Am Col Paris, 67-70; asst prof theol, Univ Notre Dame, 70-73; assoc prof, 73-80, Prof Theol & Relig Studies, Quincy Univ, 80-, Consult relig studies, Nat Endowment Humanities, 77-79; ed, Bull Coun Study Relig, 77-85. **HONORS AND AWARDS** NEH Grant, Yale Univ, 79, Univ Calif, 76; Fac Development Fel Award, Quincy Univ (6 different years); Award for Outstanding Teaching and Nominee for the Council For Advancement and Support of Education, Quincy Univ, 78, 85, 86; Excellence in Teaching Award, Quincy Univ, 94; Trustees Award for Scholarly Achievement, Quincy Univ, 98. **MEMBERSHIPS** Coun Study Relig; Am Acad Relig; Cath Theol Soc Am; Col Theol Soc (vpres, 80-82). **RESEARCH** Christology; North American Indian religions; mythology. **SELECTED PUBLICATIONS** Auth, The psychological origins of violence and revolution, in Liberation, Revolution and Freedom, Seabury, 75; America: The myth of the Hunter, in America in Theological Perspective, Seabury, 76; Myths: Gods, Heroes, and Saviors, XXIII Publ, 86; World Religions: A Story Approach, XXIII Publ, 91; Dogmatic Theology, in The New Handbook of Christian Theology, 92; author of other articles and book chapters. **CONTACT ADDRESS** Quincy Univ, 1800 College Ave, Quincy, IL, 62301-2670. **EMAIL** biallas@quincy.edu

BIANCHI, EUGENE CARL
PERSONAL Born 05/05/1930, Oakland, CA **DISCIPLINE** RELIGION **EDUCATION** Gonzaga Univ, BA, 54, MA, 55; Col St Albert, Louvain, STL, 62; Columbia Univ, PhD, 66. **CAREER** Asst ed, Am Magazine, NY, 63-66; asst prof theol, Univ Santa Clara, 66-68; asst prof relig, 68-72, assoc prof relig, 72-82, prof relig, 82-, Emory Univ, 72-, pres, Soc Priests for Free Ministry, 69-71; Danforth Found Underwood fel, 72-73; distinguished vis prof, Calif State Univ, Sacramento, 75. **MEMBERSHIPS** Am Acad Relig. **RESEARCH** Spirituality of aging; religion and ecology; study of American Jesuits. **SELECTED PUBLICATIONS** Auth, John XXiii and American Protestants, Corpus, 68; Reconciliation: The function of the Church, Sheed, 69; The Religious Experience of Revolutionaries, Doubleday, 72; Aging as a Spiritual Journey, Crossroad, 82; On Growing Older, Crossroad, 85; Elder Wisdom, Crossroad, 94; coauth, From Machismo to Mutuality, Paulist, 75; ed, A Democratic Catholic Church, Crossroad, 91. **CONTACT ADDRESS** Dept of Religion, Emory Univ, 1364 Clifton Rd NE, Atlanta, GA, 30322-0001. **EMAIL** releb@emory.edu

BICA, CAMILLO C.
PERSONAL Born 01/07/1947, New York, NY, m, 1980, 2 children **DISCIPLINE** PHILOSOPHY **EDUCATION** NY Univ, MA, 88, CUNY, PhD, 95. **CAREER** Prof, 9 yrs, School of Visual Arts; advisor, Ethics Committee, 7 yrs, Dept of Veterans Affairs. **MEMBERSHIPS** APA **RESEARCH** Ethics & war, art & social responsibility. **SELECTED PUBLICATIONS** Auth, Interpreting Just War Theory's Jus in Bello Criterion of Discrimination, in: Pub Affairs Qtly, 98; Establishing Liability in War, Pub Affairs Qtly, 97; Collateral Violence and the Doctrine of Double Effect, in: Pub Affairs Qtly, 97; Social Responsibility and the Artist, in: Art & Academe, 95; Through a Philosopher's Eyes, The Observations and Cynical Rantings of a Vietnam Survivor, in: Words, 94. **CONTACT ADDRESS** 10 Belmont Dr, Smithtown, NY, 11787. **EMAIL** DrMiloB@aol.com

BICE, SCOTT H.
DISCIPLINE CONSTITUTIONAL LAW **EDUCATION** Univ Southern Calif, BS,65; JD,68. **CAREER** Carl Mason Franklin prof & dean, Univ Southern Calif; clerked, Honorable Earl Warren, Ch Justice US; app by, Ch Justice Calif Supreme Ct to serve on the Calif Judicial Council's Comn on the Future of the Courts; **HONORS AND AWARDS** Amer Bar Found, fel. **MEMBERSHIPS** Pres and dir, Asn Amer Law Deans; Amer Law Inst. **RESEARCH** Constitutional theory; federal jurisdiction. **SELECTED PUBLICATIONS** Auth, Standards of Judicial Review in Constitutional Law & Rationality Analysis in Constitutional Law. **CONTACT ADDRESS** School of Law, Univ Southern Calif, University Park Campus, Los Angeles, CA, 90089. **EMAIL** sbice@law.usc.edu

BIEGANOWSKI, RONALD
PERSONAL Born 05/23/1941, Milwaukee, WI **DISCIPLINE** ENGLISH, THEOLOGY **EDUCATION** St Louis Univ, BA, 65, MA, 66, PhL, 66; Jesuit Sch Theol, Berkeley, STM, 72; Fordham Univ, PhD (English), 77. **CAREER** Instr English, Marquette High Sch, Milwaukee, 66-69; ASST PROF ENGLISH, MARQUETTE UNIV, 76-, ASST CHMN, 80- **MEMBERSHIPS** MLA; Robert Frost Soc (treas, 78-). **RESEARCH** Robert Frost; modern American poetry; modern American fiction. **SELECTED PUBLICATIONS** Auth, Frost, Robert Star in a Stone Boat--A Grammar of Belief, Theol Stud, Vol 0057, 96. **CONTACT ADDRESS** Dept of English, Marquette Univ, Milwaukee, WI, 53233.

BIEN, JOSEPH J.
PERSONAL Born 05/22/1936, Cincinnati, OH, m, 1965 **DISCIPLINE** PHILOSOPHY **EDUCATION** Xavier Univ, BS & MA, 58; Univ Paris, DTC, 68. **CAREER** Lectr, Ecole des Arts et Manufacteurs, 65-68; asst prof. Univ Texas-Austin, 68-73; assoc prof & Prof, Univ Missouri-Columbia, 73- ; Dir Social Philos Course, Dubrovnik, 90- . **MEMBERSHIPS** Am Philos Asn; Soc Soc & Polit Philos; Cent States Philos Asn, SW Philos Soc. **RESEARCH** Political philosophy; post-war French thought; 19th Century philosophy. **SELECTED PUBLICATIONS** Ed, Political and Social Essays by Paul Ricoeur, Ohio Univ Press, 74; Phenomenology and the Social Sciences: A Dialogue, The Hague, 78; auth, History, Revolution, and Human Nature: Marx's Philosophical Anthropology, B R Gruner Publ Co, 84; ed, Leviathan, Klare Ltd, 86; Contemporary Social Thought, Klare Ltd, 89; Ethics and Politics, Klare Ltd, 92; Philosophical Issues and Problems, Simon & Schuster, 98. **CONTACT ADDRESS** 100 W Brandon Rd., Colombia, MO, 65203. **EMAIL** philjjb@showme.missouri.edu

BIJLEFELD, WILLEM A.
PERSONAL Born 05/08/1925, Tobelo, Indonesia, m, 1950, 4 children **DISCIPLINE** ISLAMIC STUDIES, HISTORY OF RELIGIONS **EDUCATION** Univ Groningen, BD, 46, Drs Theol, 50; Univ Utrecht, Dr Theol, 59. **CAREER** Chaplain to overseas studies, Univ Leiden, 50-55; consult, Islam in Africa Proj, Northern Nigeria, 59-64; asst prof Arabic and Islamic studies, Univ Ibadan, 64-66; assoc prof, 66-68, acad dean, 69-74, PROF ISLAMICS, HARTFORD SEM FOUND, 68-, Dir, Duncan Black Macdonald Ctr, 74-, Dir, Pierre Benignus Studies Ctr, Islam in Africa Proj, Ibadan, 64-66; ed, Muslim World, 67- **MEMBERSHIPS** Deut Ges Relig-u Missionswiss; fel Mid E Studies Asn. **RESEARCH** Qur'anic studies; history of the discipline of history of religions; Muslim-Christian relations, past and present. **SELECTED PUBLICATIONS** Auth, A Century of Arabic and Islamic Studies at Hartford Seminary, Muslim World, Vol 0083, 93. **CONTACT ADDRESS** D B Macdonald Ctr, Hartford Sem, 110 Sherman St, Hartford, CT, 06105.

BILANIUK, PETRO BORYS T.
PERSONAL Born 08/04/1932, Zalishyky, Ukraine, m, 1960, 4 children **DISCIPLINE** THEOLOGY, RELIGION **EDUCATION** Univ Montreal, BTh, 55; Univ Munich, Dr Theol, 61; Ukrainian Free Univ, PhD (hist, philos), 72. **CAREER** Lectr relig knowledge and theol, 62-65, from asst prof to assoc prof theol and relig studies, 65-74, PROF THEOL AND RELIG STUDIES, UNIV ST MICHAEL'S COL, UNIV TORONTO, 74-, Can Coun leave fel, 71-72, 78-79; vis prof Ukrainian theol, Ukrainian Free Univ, 72-, vis prof Church history, 73-; consultor, J Ecumenical Studies; mem, Nat Exec and Head Publ Comt, Shevchenko Sci Soc Can, 74-; vis prof Eastern Christian Theol, John XXIII Inst Eastern Christian Studies, 78- **HONORS AND AWARDS** Gold Commenorative Medal of St Peter and Paul from Pope Paul VI in private audience, 66; Diploma for Distinguished Achievement, Men of Achievement, Cambridge, Eng, 76; Certificate in recognization of distinguished achievements,

Int Who's Who of Intellectuals, Cambridge, Eng, 76. **MEMBERSHIPS** Can Theol Soc; Theol Soc Am; Col Theol Soc; N Am Acad Ecumenists; Soc Sci Study Relig. **RESEARCH** Systematic theology; Eastern Christianity; Teilhard de Chardin. **SELECTED PUBLICATIONS** Auth, Imperial Unity and Christian Divisions, Cath Hist Rev, Vol 0079, 93; Orientalis Varietas --The Roman Church and the Eastern Churches, J Ecumenical Stud, Vol 0033, 96; Eros and Transformation--Sexuality and Marriage--An Eastern Orthodox Perspective, Stud Rel Sci Religieuses, Vol 0023, 94; One Orthodoxy, J Ecumenical Stud, Vol 0033, 96. **CONTACT ADDRESS** Fac of Theol Univ, St Michael's Col, Toronto, ON, M5S 1J4.

BILLINGS, JOHN R.
PERSONAL m **DISCIPLINE** PHILOSOPHY **EDUCATION** Syracuse Univ, PhD, 67. **CAREER** Assoc prof; Univ Wis-SP, 66-; ordained presby clergy, McCormick Theol Sem, 84; McCormick Theol Sem; Fac Senate, 74-76, 87-88, 95-; ch, Stud Conduct Hearing bd, 91-92; ch, NCent Accreditation Study, 86-89; Salary Subcomt Fac Aff, 85-86; L & S Adv Comt, 83-87. **SELECTED PUBLICATIONS** Auth, The Empty Universe, Int Logic Rev, 77. **CONTACT ADDRESS** Dept of Religious Studies, Univ Wis-SP, Stevens Point, WI, 54481.

BILODEAU, LORRAINE
PERSONAL Born 12/09/1935, Holyoke, MA **DISCIPLINE** ELEMENTARY EDUCATION; RELIGIOUS EDUCATION; LIBRARY SCIENCE AND INFORMATION **EDUCATION** Catholic Teachers Col; BS, 69; Fairfield Univ, MA, 75; Dominican Univ, MLS, 88. **CAREER** Tchr, Rhode Island Catholic Sch; DRE dir, St. Leo the Great; librn, dir, Anna Maria Col. **MEMBERSHIPS** ALA; NEACRL; CLA; NECLA. **RESEARCH** Geneology and icons. **CONTACT ADDRESS** Mondor-Eagen Library, Anna Maria Col, Paxton, MA, 01612-1198. **EMAIL** lbilodeau@annamaria.edu

BILSKER, RICHARD L.
PERSONAL Born 04/02/1965, New Brunswick, NJ, m, 1995 **DISCIPLINE** PHILOSOPHY **EDUCATION** Florida Atlantic Univ, BA, 89, PhD 94. **CAREER** Tchg asst, 90-93, instr, 93-94, Fl State Univ Dept of Philos; instr, Univ Fl Div of Continuing Educ, 92-94; adj prof Community Col RI Dept Social Sci, 94-95; adj prof, Prince George's Community Col Dept of Philos, 96-97; asst prof philos, Charles County Community Col, 95- ; vis asst prof of philos, St. Mary's Col of Maryland, 97- . **HONORS AND AWARDS** Outstanding Service and Contribution Award, 97. **MEMBERSHIPS** APA; N Am Div Schopenhauer Soc; Asn for Advan of Community Col Tchg; E Sociol Soc; Asn for Humanist Soc. **RESEARCH** History of modern philosophy; nineteenth-century philosophy; Schopenhauer. **SELECTED PUBLICATIONS** Auth, Freud and Schopenhauer: Consciousness, the Unconscious, and the Drive Towards Death, Idealistic Stud, v 27; auth, rev of Peter Worsley's Knowledges: Culture, Counterculture, Subculture, in Humanity and Soc, v 22; auth, Crossing Disciplines: A Philosopher Teaches Sociology, Tchg Soc in Two-Year Col, 99. **CONTACT ADDRESS** Dept of Fine Arts and Humanities, Charles County Comm Col, 8730 Mitchell Rd, PO Box 910, La Plata, MD, 20646-0910. **EMAIL** richardb@charles.cc.md.us

BILSON, BETH
DISCIPLINE LAW **EDUCATION** Univ Saskatchewan, BA, 67, MA, 70, LLB, 77; Univ London, PhD, 82. **CAREER** Prof, 79-. **RESEARCH** Labour law; administrative law; Canadian legal history. **SELECTED PUBLICATIONS** Auth, The Canadian Law of Nuisance, Butterworths, 91; Workplace Equity: A Seat at the Policy Picnic, Good Jobs Bad Jobs No Jobs, 95. **CONTACT ADDRESS** Col of Law, Univ Saskatchewan, 15 Campus Dr, Saskatoon, SK, S7N 5A6. **EMAIL** Bilson@law.usask.ca

BINAU, BRAD A.
DISCIPLINE PASTORAL THEOLOGY **EDUCATION** Capital Univ, BA, 77; Trinity Lutheran Sem, MDiv, 81; Princeton Theol Sem, ThM, 82, PhD, 87. **CAREER** Assoc staff, Trinity Couns Svc, Princeton, 85-86; asst prof, 93-96; dir, Ministry in Context Prog, 93-; assoc prof, Trinity Lutheran Sem, 96-. **HONORS AND AWARDS** Bk rev ed, Pastoral Psychol. **MEMBERSHIPS** Soc Pastoral Theol; Amer Acad Rel. **SELECTED PUBLICATIONS** Rev(s), Review of The Child's Son, by Donald Capps, Pastoral Psychol, 96; Review of The Helper's Journey, by Dale Larson, Jour Pastoral Care, 95; auth, Trusting our Way to Blessedness, Selected Sermons, 91-92. **CONTACT ADDRESS** Ministry Dept, Trinity Lutheran Sem, 2199 E Main St, Columbus, OH, 43209-2334. **EMAIL** bbinau@trinity.capital.edu

BING, ROBERT
DISCIPLINE CRIMINOLOGY AND CRIMINAL JUSTICE **EDUCATION** FL State Univ, PhD. **CAREER** Assoc prof & dir, Criminol & Criminal Justice prog; serves as, Interim Grad Adv; bd, several criminal justice agencies within, Dallas-Fort Worth metroplex. **MEMBERSHIPS** Acad Criminal Justice Serv; Am Soc Criminol. **RESEARCH** Corrections; plea-bargaining; sentencing; criminal justice educ. **SELECTED PUBLICATIONS** Auth, Recreational Programs in Prison, in McShane and Williams' Encycl of Prisons, Garland Press, 95; coauth, Race, Delinquency and Discrimination: A Look at the Literature for Unanswered Questions Challenge, 6 2, 95; The Experiences of African-Americans and Whites in Criminal Justice Education: Do Race and Gender Differences Exist, J Criminal Justice Educ, 6 1, 95; Race and Homicide: The Routine Treatment of Blacks, J Commun and Minority Issues, 2 1, 95. **CONTACT ADDRESS** Criminology and Criminal Justice Prog, Univ of Texas at Arlington, 301 Univ Hall, PO Box 19595, Arlington, TX, 76019-0595. **EMAIL** rbing@uta.edu

BINKLEY, OLIN TRIVETTE
PERSONAL Born 08/04/1908, Harmony, NC, m, 1933, 2 children **DISCIPLINE** SOCIOLOGY OF RELIGION **EDUCATION** Wake Forest Col, BA, 28; Southern Baptist Theol Sem, ThB, 30; Yale Univ, BD, 31, PhD, 33. **CAREER** Assoc pastor, 31-33, Calvary Baptist Church, Conn; pastor, 33-38 Chapel Hill Baptist Church, NC; head dept relig, 38-44, Wake Forest Col; prof, 44-52, Christian sociol & ethics, Southern Baptist Theol Sem; prof, 52-74, dean fac, 58-63, pres, 63-74, emer pres, 74, Southeastern Baptist Theol Sem; lectr sociol, 37-38, Univ NC, Chapel Hill; vis fel, 51, Yale Univ; pres, 64-66, Am Assn Theol Schs in US & Can; trustee, Ministry Studies Bd in US; trustee, Keesee Educ Fund, 73-. **HONORS AND AWARDS** DD, Wake Forest Col, 51, Univ NC, Chapel Hill, 64; HHD, Campbell Col, NC, 73. **MEMBERSHIPS** Fel Am Sociol Assn. **RESEARCH** Ethical theory; family sociology. **SELECTED PUBLICATIONS** Auth, Effects of Church Relationship On Seminary Governance: A Southern Baptist Perspective, Theological Education, Assn Theol Schs, 75; auth, Revelation and the Christian Faith, Approaches to the Understanding of God, Wake Forest Univ, 77. **CONTACT ADDRESS** Box 311, Wake Forest, NC, 27587.

BIRCH, ADOLPHO A., JR.
DISCIPLINE LAW **EDUCATION** Lincoln Univ, 1950-52; Howard Univ, BA, 1956, JD, 1956. **CAREER** Private law practice, 1958-69; Meharry Medical Coll, adjunct prof of legal medicine, 1959-69; Davidson County, asst public defender, 1964-66, asst district attorney general, 1966-69; Davidson County Part 1, Court of General Sessions, judge, 1969-78; Fisk Univ, lecturer in law, 1970-72; Tennessee State Univ, lecturer in law, 1970-72; Criminal Court of Davidson County, Div III, judge, 1978-87; Tennessee Court of Criminal Appeals, assoc judge, 1987-93; Supreme Court of Tennessee, justice, chief justice, currently; Nashville School of Law, instructor in law, currently. **CONTACT ADDRESS** Chief Justice, Tennessee Supreme Court, 304 Supreme Court Bldg, Nashville, TN, 37219.

BIRCH, BRUCE CHARLES
PERSONAL Born 12/03/1941, Wichita, KS, m, 1962, 2 children **DISCIPLINE** OLD TESTAMENT, ANCIENT NEAR EASTERN STUDIES **EDUCATION** Southwestern Col, BA, 62; Southern Methodist Univ, BD, 65; Yale Univ, MA, 67, MPhil, 68, PhD, 70. **CAREER** Asst prof relig, Iowa Wesleyan Col, 68-70; asst prof Bible & relig, 70-71, Erskine Col; assoc prof Old Testament, 71-77, prof Old Testament, 77-, dean, 98-, Wesley Theol Sem; Chmn Nat Intersem Coun, 64-67; mem bd dir, Washington Int Col, 71-74; dir & chmn bd, Int Prog Human Resources Develop, 75-; res fel, Asn Theol Schs, 77-78; vis prof, Sch Theol, summer 82, Claremont. **MEMBERSHIPS** Soc Bibl Lit: Am Acad Relig. **RESEARCH** Deuteronomic history; Biblical theology; Biblical ethics. **SELECTED PUBLICATIONS** Auth, Let Justice Roll Down: Old Testament, Ethics, and Christian Life, Westminster, 91; auth, Hosea, Joel, Amos: Westminster Bible Companion, Westminster, 97; auth, 1 and 2 Samuel: The New Interpreter's Bible, v.2, Abingdon, 98. **CONTACT ADDRESS** Wesley Theol Sem, 4500 Mass Ave N W, Washington, DC, 20016-5632. **EMAIL** otbruce@aol.com

BIRD, FREDERICK
DISCIPLINE RELIGION **EDUCATION** Grad Theol Union, PhD, 73. **CAREER** Prof. **HONORS AND AWARDS** Ch, Concordia Univ Consultative Comm on a Proposed Univ Code of Ethics, 93-94. **RESEARCH** Comparative ethics, business ethics, sociology of religion. **SELECTED PUBLICATIONS** Auth, How Do Religions Affect Moralities, Soc Compass, 90; Religious Leadership, Rel and Cult, 92; Leadership and Charisma in New Religious Movements, The Handbook of Cults and Sects, 93; The Muted Conscience: Moral Silence And The Practice of Ethics in Business, Quorum Books, Greenwood Press, 96; Good Conversations: A Practical Role for Ethics in Business, Boston Col, 96; coauth, The Pursuit of the Therapeutic in New Religious Movements, The Rajneesh Papers, 92; Religion, Introduction to Sociology, 94; Power and Ethical Action, Managing Strategic Action, by C. Hardy, 94; The Ethics of Empowerment, Jour of Bus Ethics, 96; co-auth, co-ed, Ritual and Ethnic Identity: A Comparative Study of the Social Meaning of Liturgical Ritual in Synagogues, 94. **CONTACT ADDRESS** Dept of Rel, Concordia Univ, Montreal, 1455 de Maisonneuve W, Montreal, PQ, H3G 1M8.

BISHOP, MICHAEL
PERSONAL Born 01/09/1961, Washington, DC **DISCIPLINE** PHILOSOPHY **EDUCATION** UCSD, PhD, 90. **CAREER** Asst Prof, 90-96, Assoc Prof, 96-, Iowa State Univ. **HONORS AND AWARDS** Who's Who Among Amer Tchr, NEH Summer Seminar, Methodological Debates in 19th c Physics. **MEMBERSHIPS** APA, PSA, SPP. **RESEARCH** Philosophy of science, Epistemology. **SELECTED PUBLICATIONS** Auth, Why the Semantic Incommensurability Thesis is Self-Defeating. Philosophical Studies, 91; The Possibility of Conceptual Clarity in Philosophy, American Philosophical Quarterly, 92; Theory-Ladenness of Perception Arguments, eds, M Forbes & D Hull, PSA, 92; The Nature and Evolution of Human Language, A Response to Maxine Sheets-Johnstone, Between the Species. 92; Conceptual Change in Science: The Newton-Hooke Controversy, Scientific Methods: Conceptual and Historical Problems, Krieger Press, 94. **CONTACT ADDRESS** Iowa State Univ of Science and Tech, 402 Catt Hall, Ames, IA, 50011. **EMAIL** mikebish@iastate.edu

BITTNER, THOMAS
PERSONAL Born 11/09/1952, Pasadena, CA, s **DISCIPLINE** PHILOSOPHY **EDUCATION** Univ California-Berkeley, BA, 86; MA, 89, PhD, 94, Univ Washington. **CAREER** Lectr, Pacific Lutheran Univ, 95-96; Visiting Lectr, Univ Nevada, Las Vegas, 96-97; Lectr, visiting Asst Prof, Univ Maryland Baltimore County, 97-. **MEMBERSHIPS** Amer Phil Assoc **RESEARCH** Philosophy of the mind **SELECTED PUBLICATIONS** Auth, Probability and Infinite Sets, Cogito, 93; Consciousness and the Act of Will, Philosophical Studies, 96. **CONTACT ADDRESS** Dept of Philosophy, UMBC, 1000 Hilltop Circle, Baltimore, MD, 21250. **EMAIL** bittner@umbc.edu

BITTNER WISEMAN, MARY
PERSONAL Born 08/21/1936, Philadelphia, PA, m, 1989, 1 child **DISCIPLINE** PHILOSOPHY **EDUCATION** St Johns Col, AB, 59; Harvard Univ, AM, 63; Columbia Univ, PhD, 74 **CAREER** Prof, City Univ of NY **MEMBERSHIPS** Am Philos Assoc; Am Soc for Aesthetics; Col Art Assoc **RESEARCH** Feminism; Theory of Criticism **SELECTED PUBLICATIONS** "Gendered Symbols," Jrnl of Aesthetics & Art Criticism, 98 **CONTACT ADDRESS** 4936 Curley Hill Rd, Doylestown, PA, 18901. **EMAIL** lagold@aol.com

BIX, BRIAN
PERSONAL Born 09/01/1962, Minneapolis, MN, s **DISCIPLINE** PHILOSOPHY; LAW **EDUCATION** Washington Univ, BA, 83; Harvard Univ, JD, 86; Balliol Col, Oxford Univ, DPhil, 91. **CAREER** Lect, jurisprudence and legal reasoning, Kings Col, Univ of London, 91-93; assoc prof law, 95-98, PROF LAW, QUINNIPIAC LAW SCHOOL, 98-. **RESEARCH** Jurisprudence; family law; contract law; philos of language; Wittgenstein. **SELECTED PUBLICATIONS** Auth, Law, Language, and Legal Determinacy, Oxford Univ Press, 93; Physician Assisted Suicide and the American Constitution, 58 Modern Law Review 404, 95; Questions in Legal Interpretation, in Law and Interpretation 137, A. Marmor, ed, Oxford Univ Press, 95; Conceptual Questions and Jurisprudence, 1 Legal Theory 415, 95; Jules Coleman, Legal Postivism, and Legal Authority, 16 Quinnipiac Law Review 241, 96; Natural Law Theory, in A Companion to the Philosophy of Law and Legal Theory 223-240, D. Patterson, ed, Blackwell Press, 96; Jurisprudence: Theory and Context, Westview Press, 96; Consent, Sado-Masochism and the English Common Law, 17 Quinnipiac Law Review 157, 97; Dealing with Incommensurability for Dessert and Desert: Comments on Chapman and Katz, 146 Univ PA Law Review 1651, 98; H. L. A. Hart and the Hermeneutic Turn in Legal Theory, 52 SMU Law Review, forthcoming, 98; On Description and Legal Reasoning, in Rules and Reasoning, L. Meyer, ed, Hart Pub, forthcoming, 98; Bargaining in the Shadow of Love: Premarital Agreements and How We Think About Marriage, 40 William and Mary Law Review, forthcoming, 98; ed, Analyzing Law: New Essays in Legal Theory, Oxford Univ Press, 98; Patrolling the Boundaries: Inclusive Legal Postivism and the Nature of Jurisprudential Debate, 12 Canadian J of Law and Jurisprudence, forthcoming, 99. **CONTACT ADDRESS** Law Sch, Quinnipiac Col, 275 Mt Carmel Ave, Hamden, CT, 06518. **EMAIL** bix@quinnipiac.edu

BLACHOWICZ, JAMES
DISCIPLINE PHILOSOPHY **EDUCATION** Loyola Univ, BS, 66; Northwestern Univ, MA, 70 PhD, 70. **CAREER** Philos, Loyola Univ. **HONORS AND AWARDS** Prof, Loyola Univ, 71-. **RESEARCH** Philosophy of science; history of metaphysics; Hegel's Logic; contemporary epistemology; theories of discovery and inquiry. **SELECTED PUBLICATIONS** Auth, Of Two Minds: The Nature of Inquiry, SUNY Press, 98; essays in, Philos Sci, J Philos, Int Stud in the Philos Sci, Synthese, Idealistic Stud, Erkenntnis, Southern J Philos. **CONTACT ADDRESS** Dept of Philosophy, Loyola Univ, Chicago, 820 N. Michigan Ave., Chicago, IL, 60611.

BLACKBURN, SIMON
PERSONAL Born 07/12/1944, United Kingdom, m, 1968, 2 children **DISCIPLINE** PHILOSOPHY **EDUCATION** Cambridge Univ, BA, 65, PhD, 70. **CAREER** Fel, tutor, Pembroke Col, Oxford, 70-90; Edna J. Koury distinguished prof, philos, Univ North Carolina, Chapel Hill, 90-. **HONORS AND AWARDS** Hon LLD, Univ Sunderland. **MEMBERSHIPS** APA; Mind Assoc. **RESEARCH** Philosophy. **SELECTED**

PUBLICATIONS Auth, Spreading the Word, Oxford, 84; ed, Essays in Quasi-Realism, Oxford, 93; ed, The Oxford Dictionary of Philosophy, Oxford, 94; auth, Practical Tortoise Raising, Mind, 95; auth, Ruling Passions, Oxford, 98. **CONTACT ADDRESS** Dept of Philosophy, Univ of No Carolina, 3152 Caldwell Hall, Chapel Hill, NC, 27599. **EMAIL** simon_blackburn@unc.edu

BLACKBURN, TERENCE L.
DISCIPLINE BUSINESS ASSOCIATIONS, CORPORATE FINANCE, BUSINESS PLANNING, CLOSE CORPORAT **EDUCATION** Duquesne Univ, BA; Columbia Univ, JD. **CAREER** Prof; adj prof, 81-, full-time fac, 88-, Seton Hall Univ; Charles Evans Hughes fel; law clk, Judge Motley, Southern Dist NY; practiced corporate law, 2 law firms; gen couns, small investment gp. **SELECTED PUBLICATIONS** Publ on, corporate securities law and tender offer areas. **CONTACT ADDRESS** School of Law, Seton Hall Univ, Bayley Hall, 400 S. Ora, South Orange, NJ, 07079. **EMAIL** blackbte@lanmail.shu.edu

BLACKSTONE, THOMAS L.
PERSONAL Born 08/03/1962, Bangor, ME, m, 1986, 3 children **DISCIPLINE** NEW TESTAMENT **EDUCATION** Emory Univ, PhD, 95. **CAREER** Adj faculty, 96- , Bungor Theolog Seminary. **MEMBERSHIPS** Soc of Biblical Lit **RESEARCH** Interpretation; Intertextuality; New Testament models for homiletics **CONTACT ADDRESS** 7 Epworth St, Presque Isle, ME, 04769. **EMAIL** thomb@bangornews.infi.net

BLACKWELL, RICHARD JOSEPH
PERSONAL Born 07/31/1929, Cleveland, OH, m, 1954 **DISCIPLINE** PHILOSOPHY **EDUCATION** John Carroll Univ AB 50; St Louis Univ, MA, 52, PhD, 54. **CAREER** Instr philos, John Carroll Univ, 54-61; assoc prof, 61-66, PROF PHILOS, ST LOUIS UNIV, 66-. **MEMBERSHIPS** Am Cath Philos Asn; Philos Sci Asn. **RESEARCH** Philosophy of Aristotle; modern philosophy; philosophy of science. **SELECTED PUBLICATIONS** Auth, Galileo - for Copernicanism and for the Church, Vol 3, Stud in Hist and Philos of Sci, Vol 0027, 96. **CONTACT ADDRESS** Dept of Philos, St Louis Univ, 221 N Grand Blvd, Saint Louis, MO, 63103-2097.

BLAIR, GEORGE ALFRED
PERSONAL Born 01/13/1934, Watertown, MA, m, 1963, 2 children **DISCIPLINE** PHILOSOPHY **EDUCATION** Boston Col, AB, 58, MA, 59; Weston Col, PhL, 59: Fordham Univ, PhD(philos), 64. **CAREER** From instr to asst prof philos, Xavier Univ, 63-65; from asst prof to assoc prof, 65-75, PROF PHILOS, THOMAS MORE COL, 75-, CHMN DEPT, 68-, Fulbright exchange lectr, Argentina, 64. **MEMBERSHIPS** Am Cath Philos Asn. **RESEARCH** Aristotle; ethics; philosophy of science. **SELECTED PUBLICATIONS** Auth, Aristotle on Entelecheia - A Reply to Graham,Daniel, Am J of Philol, Vol 0114, 93. **CONTACT ADDRESS** Dept of Philos, Thomas More Col, 333 Thomas More Pky, Covington, KY, 41017-3495.

BLAISING, CRAIG A.
DISCIPLINE SYSTEMATIC THEOLOGY **EDUCATION** B.S., University of Texas, Austin; Th.M., Dallas Theological Seminary; Th.D., Dallas Theological Seminary; Ph.D., University of Aberdeen, Scotland **CAREER** Act dept ch, Dallas Theol Sem; act assoc dean-. **SELECTED PUBLICATIONS** Auth, Progressive Dispensationalism. **CONTACT ADDRESS** Sch Theol, Southern Baptist Theol Sem, 2825 Lexington Rd, Louisville, KY, 40280. **EMAIL** cblaising@sbts.edu

BLAKE, DEBORAH
DISCIPLINE RELIGIOUS STUDIES, CHRISTIAN ETHICS, HEALTHCARE ETHICS **EDUCATION** Univ Calif, Santa Barbara, BA, 74; Franciscan Sch of Theol, MA, 81; Grad Theol Un, PhD, 89. **CAREER** Assoc prof Relig Stud, Regis Col, 88-. **MEMBERSHIPS** Catholic Theol Soc of Am; Colo Health Care Ethics Comt Network; Soc of Christian Ethics; Soc of Health and Human Values. **RESEARCH** Cultural diversity and health care ethics; environmental issues in the context of culture. **SELECTED PUBLICATIONS** Auth, bk rev of Genetics, Creation and Creationism, by Lloyd Bailey, in The Catholic World, 237, 94; Revolution, Revision, or Reversal: Genetics-Ethics Curriculum, Sci and Educ, 3, 94; Voices, Values and Healthcare Reform in Colorado,Voices (Rocky Mountain Ctr for Healthcare Ethics), 1(1), 94; 'I Don't Speak Principles Only': The Language of Ethics Committees and the Language of Communities, Healthcare Ethics Comt Forum 7(5), 95; Toward a Sustainable Ethic: Virtue and the Environment, in And God Saw it was Good: Catholic Theology and the Environment, Drew Christiansen, S.J. and Walt Grazerm eds, US Catholic Conf, 96; coauth, Safe Sex or Love Lost, in Christian Perspectives on Sexuality and Gender, Adrian Thatcher and Elizabeth Stuart, eds, Gracewing and WB Eerdmans Publ Co, 96. **CONTACT ADDRESS** Dept of Relig Stud, Regis Col, 3333 Regis Blvd, Denver, CO, 80221. **EMAIL** ddblake@regis.edu

BLAKESLEY, CHRISTOPHER L.
PERSONAL Born 02/28/1945, Torrance, CA, m, 1968, 3 children **DISCIPLINE** CRIMINAL LAW, INTERNATIONAL LAW, FAMILY LAW, COMPARATIVE LAW **EDUCATION** Univ Utah, BA, 69; Tufts Univ, 70; Fletcher Sch Law & Dipl, MA, 70; Univ Utah, JD, 73; Columbia Univ, LLM, 76, JSD, 85. **CAREER** Prof, McGeorge Sch Law, Univ Pacific; US Dept State, Off Legal Adviser; PROF & CH, LAW, PAUL M HERBERT LAW CENTRE, LA STATE UNIV. **MEMBERSHIPS** Am Law Inst; Utah Bar Asn; Wash DC Bar Asn; Am Jour Compar Law; Asn Int de Droit Penal; Revue Int de Droit Penal; Am Bar Asn; Am Soc Int Law **RESEARCH** Comparative law; International law; Family law; Foreign law; Comparative criminal law & procedure. **SELECTED PUBLICATIONS** Terrorism, Drugs, International Law and the Protection of Human Liberty, "Innovations in International Law" series, Princeton Univ; Louisiana (and Comparative) Family Law, Lexis Law Publ, 97; The International Legal system: Documentary Supplement, 5th Ed., 99; The International Legal System, 5th ed, Blakesley, Firmage, Scott & Williams, 99. **CONTACT ADDRESS** Paul M Herbert Law Center, Louisiana State Univ, Baton Rouge, LA, 70803. **EMAIL** cblake@slu.edu

BLANCHETTE, OLIVA
PERSONAL Born 05/06/1929, Berlin, NH, 2 children **DISCIPLINE** PHILOSOPHY **EDUCATION** Boston Col, AB, 53, MA, 58; Col St Albert, Louvain, PhL, 54; Weston Col, STL, 61; Laval Univ, PhD(philos), 66. **CAREER** From instr to assoc prof, 64-74, dean sch philos, 68-73, Prof Philos, Boston Col, 74-, Dir, Inst Social Thought, 72-. **HONORS AND AWARDS** Am Cath Who's Who, 79; Int Authors and Writers Who's Who, 79, 86; Contemporary Authors, 80; Directory of Am Scholars, 82; Community Leaders of Am, 82; Who's Who Among Authors and Journalists, 83; Who's Who in Am, 85, 89, 91, 95, 96; Who's Who in the East, 85; Who's Who in Society, 88; Men of Achievement, 78, 88; Dictionary of Int Biography, 81, 89; Int Who's Who of Intellectuals, 88. **MEMBERSHIPS** Am Philos Asn; Hegel Soc Am; Metaphys Soc Am; Int Soc Metaphysics. **RESEARCH** Philosophy of history and religion; metaphysics; ethics; Aquinas;Hegel; Blondel. **SELECTED PUBLICATIONS** Auth, The Order of Generation and Time in the Philosophy of St Thomas Aquinas, Laval Theol Philos, 66; Initiative in History: A Christian-Marxist Exchange, an occaisonal paper published by the Church Soc for College Work, 67; The Four Causes as Texture of the Universe, Laval Theol Philos, 69; For a Fundamental Social Ethic: A Philosophy of Social Change, NY: Philos Libr, 73; Language, the Primordial Labor of History, Cult Hermeneutics, 74; Philosophy and Theology in Aquinas, Sci et Esprit, 76; Freedom & Determinism, BC Studies Phil, 77; Praxis and Labor in Hegel, Studies in Soviet Thought, 79; The Philosophic Beginning Thought, 81; Action (18930 by Maurice Blondel, trans with intro, Univ of Notre Dame Press, 84; Are There Two Questions of Being?, The Rev of Metaphysics, 45, 91; The Perfection of the Universe According to Aquinas: A Teleological Cosmology, Col Park: PA State Univ, 92; The Silencing of Philosophy, Fear and Trembling and Repetition, Int Kierkegaard Commentary, vol 6, ed Robert Perkins, Mrecer Univ Press, 93; Blondel's Original Philosophy of the Supernatural, Revista Portuguesa de Filosofia, XLIX, 93; The Logic of Perfection According to Aquinas, Thomas Aquinas and His Legacy, Studies in Philosophy and the History of Philosophy, vol 28, ed David Gallagher, The Cath Univ of Am Press, 94; Philosophy of Being: A Reconstructive Essay in Metaphysics, under review at E. J. Brill Pubs; Ethical Judgement in Health Care: Overcoming the Technological Bias, forthcoming; numerous other articles and book reviews. **CONTACT ADDRESS** Dept of Philos, Boston Col, 140 Commonwealth Ave, Chestnut Hill, MA, 02167-3800. **EMAIL** oliva.blanchette@bc.edu

BLANCHETTE, PATRICIA
DISCIPLINE PHILOSOPHY **EDUCATION** Univ, Calif, BA, 83; Stanford Univ, PhD, 90. **CAREER** Asst prof. **RESEARCH** Philosophy of logic; philosophy of language; philosophy of mathematics. **SELECTED PUBLICATIONS** Auth, Frege's Reduction, Hist Philos Logic, 94; Frege and Hilbert on Consistency, J Philos, 96; Realism in the Philosophy of Mathematics, Routledge, 98. **CONTACT ADDRESS** Philosophy Dept, Univ of Notre Dame, 336/7 O'Shaughnessy, Notre Dame, IN, 46556. **EMAIL** blanchette.1@nd.edu

BLAND, KALMAN PERRY
PERSONAL Born 03/04/1942, Chicago, IL, m, 1964, 2 children **DISCIPLINE** JEWISH PHILOSOPHY **EDUCATION** Columbia Univ, BS, 64; Jewish Theol Sem Am, BRE, 64, MHL, 67; Brandeis Univ, PhD(Medieval Jewish-Islamic philos), 72. **CAREER** Asst prof Judaic relig, Ind Univ, Bloomington, 72-73; asst prof relig and Jewish studies, 73-76, ASSOC PROF RELIG AND JEWISH STUDIES, DUKE UNIV, 76-, CHMN DEPT OF RELIG, 81-. **MEMBERSHIPS** Am Acad Relig; Asn Jewish Studies; Int Asn Neo-Platonic Studies; Am Oriental Soc. **RESEARCH** Medieval Jewish philosophy; Jewish mysticism; Medieval Jewish-Christian polemics. **SELECTED PUBLICATIONS** Auth, Medieval Jewish Aesthetics - Maimonides, Body, and Scripture in Profiat Duran, J of the Hist of Ideas, Vol 0054, 93; People of the Body - Jews and Judaism From An Embodied Perspective, J of Relig, Vol 0074, 94; Beauty, Maimonides, and Cultural Relativism in Medieval Jewish Thought, J of Medieval and Early Mod Stud, Vol 0026, 96. **CONTACT ADDRESS** Dept of Relig, Duke Univ, PO Box 4735, Durham, NC, 27706.

BLANKEMEYER, KENNETH JOSEPH
PERSONAL Born 08/07/1946, Cincinnati, OH, m, 1976 **DISCIPLINE** PHILOSOPHY, LOGIC **EDUCATION** Xavier Univ, BS, 68; Southern IL Univ, MA, 71, PhD, 74. **CAREER** INSTR TO PROF PHILOS, TULSA COM COL, 76-. **MEMBERSHIPS** Am Philos Asn; Southwestern Philos Soc. **RESEARCH** Ethics; religion. **SELECTED PUBLICATIONS** Auth, Can reliance on quasi-dependent meaning save Stevenson's ethics, J Thought, 1/77. **CONTACT ADDRESS** Liberal Arts Division, Tulsa Community Col, 909 S Boston Ave, Tulsa, OK, 74119-2011.

BLATTNER, WILLIAM
DISCIPLINE PHILOSOPHY **EDUCATION** Univ Pittsburgh, PhD, 89. **CAREER** Prof. **RESEARCH** Modern German philosophy; American pragmatism. **SELECTED PUBLICATIONS** Auth, The Concept of Death in Being and Time, Man and World, 94; Is Heidegger a Kantian Idealist?, Inquiry, 94; Existence and Self-Understanding in Being and Time, Philos Phenomenological Res, 96. **CONTACT ADDRESS** Dept of Philosophy, Georgetown Univ, 37th and O St, Washington, DC, 20057.

BLEICH, J. DAVID
DISCIPLINE PHILOSOPHY **EDUCATION** Brooklyn Col, BA, 60; Columbia Univ, MA, 68; NY Uni v, PhD, 74. **CAREER** Instr, Rutgers Univ, 62-63; Instr, Hunter Col, 62-69; Instr, Bar Ilan Univ, 70; Instr, Stern Col Women, 65-72; Adj Prof, Univ Haifa, 74-75; Assoc Prof, Yeshiva Univ, 78-79; Vis Assoc Prof, 79-83, Assoc Prof, 83-86, Prof Law, Benjamin N. Cardozo Sch Law, 86-; Vis Gruss Prof Ta Talmudic Civil Law, Univ Pa, 91-93; Dir Inst Advanced Study Jurisprudence & Family Law, 69-, Rosh Yeshivah, 69-, Herbert & Florence Tenzer Prof Jewish Law & Ethics, Rabbi Isaac Elchanan Theol Seminary, 81-. **HONORS AND AWARDS** Woodrow Wilson Nat Fel, 60-61; NY Regents Col Teaching Fel, 60-61; Nat Found Jewish Cult, 61-62; Post-Doctoral Fel, Hastings Inst Soc, Ethics, & Life Sci, 74-75; Founders Day Award, NY Univ, 74; Vis Schol, Oxford Ctr for Postgraduate Hebrew Studies, 80; Fel, Acad Jewish Philos, 80-; Irving M. Bunim Memorial Award for Schol Publ, 81. **SELECTED PUBLICATIONS** Auth, Judaism and Healing, Ktav Publ, 80; Birkas ha-Chammah, Mesorah Publ, 80; ed, With Perfect Faith: Foundations of Jewish Belief, Ktav Publ House, 83; auth, Contemporary Halakhic Problems, Ktav Publ House and Yeshiva Univ Press, Vol I, 77, Vol II, 83, Vol III, 89, Vol IV, 95; Time of Death in Jewish Law, Z. Berman Publ Co, 91; Be-Netivot ha-Halakhah, Yeshiva Univ Press, 96; author of numerous articles and other publications. **CONTACT ADDRESS** 400 E. 77th St., New York, NY, 10021.

BLENKINSOPP, JOSEPH
PERSONAL Born 04/03/1927, Durham, England, m, 2 children **DISCIPLINE** BIBLICAL STUDIES **EDUCATION** London Univ, BA, 48; Oxford Univ, PhD, 67. **CAREER** Prof, bibl stud, then John A O'Brien Prof Bibl Stud, Univ Notre Dame, 72- . **HONORS AND AWARDS** NEH res grant, 82-83; rector of Ecumenical Inst, Israel; pres, Catholic Bibl Asn, 89-90. **MEMBERSHIPS** Soc of Bibl Lit; Am Acad of Relig; Soc of Old Testament Stud (UK); Asn of Jewish Stud. **RESEARCH** Biblical literature and theology; history of Israel. **SELECTED PUBLICATIONS** Auth, Ezra-Nehemiah: A Commentary, Westminster, 88; auth, A Jewish Sect of the Persian Period, Catholic Bibl Q, 90; auth, The Judge of All the Earth: Theodicy in the Midrash on Genesis 18:22-33, J of Jewish Stud, 90; auth, The Social Context of the Outsider Woman in Proverbs 1-9, Biblica, 91; auth, The Pentateuch: An Introduction to the First Five Books of the Bible, Doubleday, 92; auth, Ecclesiastes 3.1-15: Another Interpretation, J for the Stud of the Old Testament, 95; auth, Deuteronomy and the Politics of Post-Mortem Existence, Vetus Testamentum, 95; auth, Sage, Priest, Prophet: Religious and Intelectual Leadership in Ancient Israel, Westminster, 95; auth, Wisdom and Law in the Old Testament: The Ordering of Life in Israel and Early Judaism, Oxford, 2d ed, 95; coauth, The Family in Ancient Israel, Westminster, 96; auth, A History of Prophecy in Israel, rev ed, Westminster, 96; auth, Th Judean Priesthood during the Neo-Babylonian and Early Achemenid Period: A Hypothesis, Cath Bibl Q, forthcoming; auth, An Assessment of the Alleged Pre-Exilic Date of the Priestly Material in the Pentateuch, in Zeitschrift fur die Alttestamentliche Wissenschaft, forthcoming. **CONTACT ADDRESS** Dept of Theology, Univ of Notre Dame, Notre Dame, IN, 46556.

BLESSING, KAMILA
PERSONAL Born 12/12/1948, Pittsburgh, PA, s **DISCIPLINE** RELIGION **EDUCATION** Carnegie-Mellon Univ, BS, 71; Univ Pitts, MSIS, 76, PhD, 77; Pitts Theol Sem, MA, 84; Duke Univ, PhD, 96. **CAREER** Campus Min, Carnigie-Mellon Univ, 78-83; Pastoral Min, Church of Ascension, 83-85; Rector, St Andrews Church, 85-86; Vicar, St Peters Church, 86-89; Int Rector, St. Pauls Church, 89-90; Priest Assoc, St Philips Church, 90-93; Priest in charge, Christ Church, 93-98; priest in charge, St Johns, 93-; Adj instr, Hermeneutics, Grace Sem, 85; res asst, 92-93, tchg asst, 94-96, Divinity School, Duke Univ.

HONORS AND AWARDS Am Soc Infor Sci Doctoral Forum Award, 77. **MEMBERSHIPS** Soc Bibl Lit; Amer Acad Relig; Asn Jewish Studies **RESEARCH** Techniques of interpretation; Paul and the Covenant; Paul's conceptuality of Covenant and the ways in which it relates to Gentiles and Jews; Communities of understanding and the way they define truth, scripture, and covenant as reflected in the New Testament text; Christian-Jewish relations; Impact of authoritative religious texts on the roles of women. **SELECTED PUBLICATIONS** Auth, Luke's Unjust Steward Viewed from the Window of Psychiatrist Milton Erickson, Soc Bibl Lit, 93; Isaac and Ishmael in Galatians: a Pro-Jewish View of Covenant, Asn Jewish Studies, 94; Murray Bowen's Systems Psychodynamics as Hermeneutic, Soc Bibl Lit, 95; Yet Without Sin: The Meaning of the Barren Woman at Galatians 4:27, Soc Bibl Lit, 96. **CONTACT ADDRESS** 109 S Windmere Ct., Rocky Mount, NC, 27803. **EMAIL** ixts@msn.com

BLEVINS, JAMES LOWELL
PERSONAL Born 08/25/1936, m, 1961, 3 children **DISCIPLINE** RELIGION **EDUCATION** Duke Univ, AB, 58; Eastern Baptist, MDV, 61; Southeastern Bap Sem, THN, 62; Southern Bap, Louisville, PhD, 65. **CAREER** Southern Bap Sem, prof new test, 76-; Mars Hill Col, prof Rel, 68-76. **MEMBERSHIPS** SNTS; SBL **RESEARCH** New Testament **SELECTED PUBLICATIONS** Revelation as Drama, 80; Greek Hymn Book; Revelation; 83; Messianic Secret, 1901-1965. **CONTACT ADDRESS** Dept New Testament, Southern Baptist Theol Sem, 2825 Lexington Rd, Louisville, KY, 40241.

BLEVINS, KENT
PERSONAL Born 11/01/1954, Columbia, SC, m, 1975, 3 children **DISCIPLINE** THEOLOGY **EDUCATION** Wake Forest Univ, BA, 75; Southern Baptist Theol Sem, MDiv, 78, PhD, 82. **CAREER** Assoc prof relig, Gardner-Webb Univ, 98-; assoc prof ethics practical theol, 94-98, asst prof systematic practical theol, 91-94, Int Baptist Theol Sem, Prague, Czech Rep; lectr, Portuguese Baptist Theol Sem, Portugal, 84-91. **RESEARCH** Ethics. **CONTACT ADDRESS** Dept of Theology, Gardner-Webb Univ, PO Box 7252, Boiling Springs, NC, 28017. **EMAIL** kblevins@gardner-webb.edu

BLIZEK, WILLIAM L.
PERSONAL Chicago, IL **DISCIPLINE** ETHICS, SOCIAL PHILOSOPHY, THE PHILOSOPHY OF RELIGION **EDUCATION** Southern Ill Univ, BA, 65, MA, 66; Univ Mo, Columbia, PhD, 70. **CAREER** Prof, Univ Nebr, Omaha, 70-; ed, Hum and Pub Life; coed, J of Relig and Film. **SELECTED PUBLICATIONS** Published articles in such journals as Brit J of Aesthet, Philos Exchange, Southern J of Philos, Metaphilosophy, Nebr Med J, Urban Rev, Criminal Justice and Ethics, and J of Commun Develop soc. **CONTACT ADDRESS** Univ Nebr, Omaha, Omaha, NE, 68182.

BLOCK, JOHN MARTIN
PERSONAL Born 01/23/1940, Chicago Heights, IL, m, 1963, 2 children **DISCIPLINE** LAW **EDUCATION** Furman Univ, BA, 63; Univ Wis-Madison, MA, 65, PhD, 69. **CAREER** Asst prof, 68-75, ASSOC PROF, FURMAN UNIV, 75-. **MEMBERSHIPS** AHA; Conf Group Cent Europ Hist; AAUP. **RESEARCH** Nineteenth and twentieth century European diplomatic history, British press history, modern Germany. **SELECTED PUBLICATIONS** Auth, Limiting The Use Of Heightened Scrutiny To Land-Use Exactions, NY Univ Law Rev, Vol 0071, 96. **CONTACT ADDRESS** Dept of Hist, Furman Univ, 3300 Poinsett Hwy, Greenville, SC, 29613-0002.

BLOCKER, H. GENE
PERSONAL Born 11/29/1937, Dallas, TX, m, 1962, 1 child **DISCIPLINE** AESTHETICS **EDUCATION** Univ Chicago, BA, 60; Univ Calif, Berkeley, PhD(philos), 66. **CAREER** Lectr moral philos, Univ Aberdeen, 65-68; lectr philos, Univ Sierra Leone, W Africa, 68-70; asst prof, Ill State Univ, Bloomington-Normal, 70 72; assoc prof, 72-77, PROF PHILOS, OHIO UNIV, 77-; vis prof, Univ Ibadau, Nigeria, 80-81. **HONORS AND AWARDS** Am Coun Learned Soc fel, 75-76. **RESEARCH** Philosophy of primitive art. **SELECTED PUBLICATIONS** Auth, Normative Cultures, Jour Chinese Philos, Vol 0023, 96; The Path Of Beauty, A Study Of Chinese Aesthetics, Jour Aesthetic Edu, Vol 0030, 96; Reply To Critics, Jour Aesthetic Edu, Vol 0029, 95. **CONTACT ADDRESS** Dept of Philos, Ohio Univ, Athens, OH, 45701.

BLODGETT, BARBARA
DISCIPLINE RELIGION **EDUCATION** Yale Univ, PhD, 99. **CAREER** Vis instr Relig, Oberlin Col, 96-98. **MEMBERSHIPS** Am Acad Relig; Soc Christian Ethics; Asn Practical & Professional Ethics; Feminist Approaches Bioethics. **RESEARCH** Feminist theological ethics. **CONTACT ADDRESS** Dept of Religion, Oberlin Col, 60 Canner St, New Haven, CT, 06511.

BLOESCH, DONALD G.
PERSONAL Born 05/03/1928, Bremen, IN, m **DISCIPLINE** THEOLOGY **EDUCATION** Elmhurst Col, BA, 50; Chicago Theological Seminary, BD, 53; Univ of Chicago, PhD, 56; Doane Col, Dr Div, 83; Oxford Univ, post-doctoral studies, 56-67; Basel Univ, post-doctoral studies, 63-64; Tubingen Univ, post-doctoral studies, 63-64. **CAREER** PROF OF THEOLOGY, 57-93, PROF OF THEOLOGY EMERITUS, UNIV OF DUBUQUE THEOLOGICAL SEMINARY, 93-. **HONORS AND AWARDS** Alumni Merit Awd, Elmhurst Col, 79. **MEMBERSHIPS** Am Theological Soc; Karl Barth Soc. **RESEARCH** Theology; spirituality. **SELECTED PUBLICATIONS** Auth, Freedom for Obedience, Harper & Row, 87; A Theology of Word & Spirit, InterVarsity Press, 92; Holy Scripture, InterVarsity Press, 94; God the Almighty, InterVarsity Press, 95; Jesus Christ: Savior & Lord, InterVarsity Press, 97. **CONTACT ADDRESS** 2185 St John Dr, Dubuque, IA, 52002.

BLOM, JOOST
DISCIPLINE LAW **EDUCATION** Univ British Columbia, BA, 67; LLB, 70; Oxford Univ, BCL, 72. **CAREER** Asst prof, 72-76; assoc prof, 76-81; prof, 81-; assoc dean, 82-85; vis prof, Osgoode Hall Law Sch, 81; lectr, Univ Victoria, 79-81. **RESEARCH** Contracts; torts; conflict of law; intellectual property; comparative law. **SELECTED PUBLICATIONS** Auth, pubs about contracts, torts, and conflict of laws and taxation. **CONTACT ADDRESS** Fac of Law, Univ British Columbia, 1822 East Mall, Vancouver, BC, V6T 1Z1. **EMAIL** blom@law.ubc.ca

BLOMBERG, CRAIG L.
PERSONAL Born 08/03/1955, Rock Island, IL, m, 2 children **DISCIPLINE** RELIGION **EDUCATION** Augustana Col, BA, 77; Trinity Evangel Divinity Sch, MA, 79; Univ Aberdeen, PhD, 82. **CAREER** Asst prof relig, Palm Beach Atlantic Col, 82-85; sr res fel, Tyndale House, Cambridge Univ, 85-86; from asst prof to assoc prof to prof, Denver Sem, 86-. **HONORS AND AWARDS** Paul Harris Rotary Fel. **MEMBERSHIPS** Evangel Theol Soc; Inst Bibl Res; Soc Bibl Lit; Studiorum Novi Testamenti Societas. **RESEARCH** New Testament; Greek. **SELECTED PUBLICATIONS** Coauth, The Image of God in Humanity: A Biblical-Psychological Perspective, Themelios, 93; auth, To What Extent is John Historically Reliable?, Perspective on John: Method and Interpretation in the Fourth Gospel, 93; coauth, Introduction to Biblical Interpretation, 93; auth, The Implications of Globalization for Biblical Understanding, The Globalization of Bibl Educ, 93; auth, Your Faith Has Made You Whole: The Evangelical Liberation Theology of Jesus, Jesus of Nazareth, Lord and Christ, 94; auth, the Parables of Jesus: Current Trends in Needs and Research, Studying the Historical Jesus: Evaluation of the State of Current Research, 94; auth, Dream Job, Jour Case Tchg, 93; auth, Historical Criticism of the New Testament, Found Bibl Interpretation, 94; auth, The Historical Reliability of the New Testament, Reasonable Faith, 94; auth, The Seventy-Four Scholars: Who Does the Jesus Seminar Really Speak For?, Christian Res Jour, 94; auth, Critical Issues in New Testament Studies for Evangelicals Today, Pathway into Holy Scripture, 94; auth, Where Do We Start Studying Jesus?, Jesus Under Fire, 95; auth, 1 Corinthians, 94; auth, Interpreting the Synoptic Gospels for Preaching, Faith & Mission, 94; auth, The Kingdom of God and Evangelical Theological Education, Didaskalia, 95; auth, The Globalization of Biblical Hermeneutics, Evangel Hermeneutics, 95; auth, Poetic Fiction, Subversive Speech, and Proportional Analogy in the Parables, Horizons Bibl Theol, 96; coauth, How Wide the Divide? A Mormon and Evangelical in Conversation, 97; auth, Jesus and the Gospels: An Introduction and Survey, 97; auth, When God's Word Comes to Me, What Happens Next?, Decision, Jan, 98. **CONTACT ADDRESS** Dept of Religion, Denver Conservative Baptist Sem, PO Box 10000, Denver, CO, 80250-0100. **EMAIL** craig@densem.edu

BLOOM, ALFRED
PERSONAL Born 11/09/1926, Philadelphia, PA, m, 1951, 2 children **DISCIPLINE** RELIGION **EDUCATION** Eastern Baptist Sem, AB & ThB, 51; Andover-Newton Theol Sch, BD & STM, 53; Harvard Univ, PhD, 63. **CAREER** Assoc prof relig, Univ Ore, 61-70; PROF RELIG, UNIV HAWAII, MANOA, 80-. **MEMBERSHIPS** Assn Asian Stud; Soc Sci Stud Rel; Amer Acad Rel. **RESEARCH** Old Testament, Japanese Buddhism. **SELECTED PUBLICATIONS** Auth, Sights On The Sixties, Jour Amer Hist, Vol 0080, 93; The New-York Intellectuals--From Vanguard To Institution, Amer Hist Rev, Vol 0102, 97. **CONTACT ADDRESS** Dept of Rel, Univ of Hawaii Manoa, Honolulu, HI, 96822.

BLOOM, JOHN A.
PERSONAL Born 05/25/1952, WI, m, 1977, 1 child **DISCIPLINE** BIBLICAL STUDIES **EDUCATION** Grinnell Col, BA, 74; Cornell Univ, MS, 77, PhD, 80; Biblical Theol Sem, MA, 83, MDiv, 83; Dropsie Col, MA, 86, PhD, 92. **CAREER** Postdoctoral res assoc, Cornell Univ, 81-82; vice-chemn of bd, 84-91, chemn, 91-93, North Penn Pregnancy Counseling Ctr; fel, Interdisciplinary Bibl Res Inst, Hatfield Penn, 88- ; lectr physics, Ursinus Col, 84-89, 92; consult, computer software and hardware, 86- ; asst prof, 93-95, assoc prof, physics, 95- , Biola Univ. **HONORS AND AWARDS** Grinnell Col Honors Scholar, 70-74; Chem Sr Honors Award, 74; Honors scholar, 80-83; Honors prog, Bibl Theol Sem, 82-83; Honors scholar, Dropsie Col, 83-86; Elise Bohstedt Scholar, 86-91; John Templeton Found, Sci and Relig Course Prog, 97; Provost Award for Excellence in Bibl Integration, Biola Univ, 98. **MEMBERSHIPS** Am Assoc Physics Tchrs; Am Soc for Engg Educ; Am Sci Affil; Biophysical Soc; Evangel Theol Soc; Sigma Xi; Soc of Bibl Lit. **RESEARCH** Cross cultural comparative study of creation accounts and of prophetic material; exegetical/historical problems in Israelite prehistory and history through the First Temple period; membrane biology; evolution; ancient technologies and science (medicine and mathematics); ancient document preservation via optical disc technology; use of computer image enhancement techniques in the study of ancient cuneiform and papyrus documents. **SELECTED PUBLICATIONS** Auth, Hosea's Adulterous Wife: A Portrayal of Israel, in Newman, ed, The Evidence of Prophecy: Fulfilled Prediction as a Testimony to the Truth of Christianity, Interdisciplinary Biblical Research Inst, 90; auth, Truth Via Prophecy, and, Why Isn't the Evidence Clearer, in Montgomery, ed, Evidence for Faith: Deciding the God Question, Word, 91; auth, Ancient Near Eastern Temple Assemblies: A Survey and Prolegomena, Annenberg Research Inst, 92 (PhD thesis); auth, On Human Origins : A Survey, Christian Scholar's Review, 97. **CONTACT ADDRESS** 12631 Biola Ave, La Mirada, CA, 90638. **EMAIL** john_bloom@peter.biola.edu

BLOWERS, LAVERNE P.
PERSONAL Born 05/16/1940, Rochester, NY, m, 1967, 2 children **DISCIPLINE** THEOLOGY **EDUCATION** Seattle Pacific Univ, BA, 62; Asbury Theolog Sem, Mdiv, 67; Fuller Theolog Sem, ThM, 71; Trinity Evangelical Divinity Sch, Dmiss, 89. **CAREER** Prof, dean, Faculdade de Teologia da lgreja Metodista Lirre, 72-80; asst prof, dir, Seattle Pacific Univ, 80-82; asst prof, dir, Roberts Wesleyan Col, 82-86; assoc prof, chemn, Bethel Col, 86-. **HONORS AND AWARDS** Missionary educator; Who's Who in Relig; Who's Who in the Midwest; Fac Stud Grant, Seattle Pacific, Roberts Wesleyan, Bethel Col. **MEMBERSHIPS** AAR; Am Society Missiology; Wesleyan Theolog Society; Evangelical Missiological Society. **RESEARCH** Theology and history of mission; systematic theology. **CONTACT ADDRESS** 1001 W McKinley Ave, Mishawaka, IN, 46545. **EMAIL** blowerl1@bethel-in.edu

BLUM, JOHN D.
PERSONAL Born 12/12/1948, Buffalo, NY, m, 1981, 2 children **DISCIPLINE** LAW **EDUCATION** Camsius Col, BA, 70; Notre Dame Law Sch, JD, 73; Harvard Univ, MHS, 74. **CAREER** Res Atty, Boston Univ Health Policy Ctr, 74-82; assoc prof, Penn State Univ Dept Health Policy Admin, 82-86; prof, dir, Loyala Univ Chicago Inst for Health Law, 86-. **HONORS AND AWARDS** Governance Found Fel, Modern Healthcare; U.S./Canada Fulbright Scholar; Malaysia/U.S. Fulbright Scholar. **MEMBERSHIPS** Am Health Lawyers Asn; Am Soc of Law Medicine and Ethics; Am Public Health Assn. **RESEARCH** Health policy and law. **SELECTED PUBLICATIONS** Auth, Evaluation of Medical Staff Using Fiscal Factors: Economic Credentialing, Jour of Health and Hospital Law Vol 26 No 3, 93; auth, Ontario Health Care: A Model To Be Emulated or Avoided?, National Forum, 93; auth, Universality, Quality & Economics: Finding a Balance in Ontario and British Colombia, Am Jour of Law and Med, Vol 20 No 1&2, 94; auth, Economic Credentialing Moves From the Hospital to Managed Care, Jour of Health Care Finance, 95; auth, The Evolution of Physician Credentialing into Managed Care Selective Contracting, Am Jour of Law and Med, Vol 22, No 2&3, 96; auth Legal Assessment: When Credentialing Becomes Selective Contracting, Cost & Quality Jour, Vol 3 No 3, 97; coauth, Credentialing Mandates and the Telemedical Doctor, New Medicine, Vol 1 No 4, 97; auth, North American Perspectives on Balancing Regional Government Health Mandates in Nova Scotia and Illinois with Federal Economic Imperatives, Dalhousie Law Jour, Vol 20 No 2, 97; auth, Safeguarding the Interests of People with AIDS in Managed Care Settings, Albany Law Review, Vol 61 No 3, 98. **CONTACT ADDRESS** Inst for Health Law, Loyola Univ, Chicago, 1 E Pearson St, Chicago, IL, 60611. **EMAIL** jblum@luc.edu

BLUM, KAREN M.
DISCIPLINE LAW **EDUCATION** Wells Col, BA, 74; Suffolk, JD, 76; Harvard Univ, LLM. **CAREER** Instr, 74-76; asst prof, 76-78; assoc prof, 78-83; prof, 83-. **RESEARCH** Affirmative action; civil procedure; civil rights; complex litigation; federal courts; police misconduct litigation. **SELECTED PUBLICATIONS** Auth, Section 1983 Hot Topics, Boston, 98; Justices Revisit Issue of Imposing Municipal Liability Under Section 1983 for Single Decision of Final Policymaker, 96; Local Government Liability Under Section 1983, 96; Qualified Immunity: Interlocutory Appeals, 96. **CONTACT ADDRESS** Law School, Suffolk Univ, Beacon Hill, Boston, MA, 02114. **EMAIL** kblum@acad.suffolk.edu

BLUM, LAWRENCE A.
PERSONAL Born 04/16/1943, Baltimore, MD, m, 1975, 3 children **DISCIPLINE** PHILOSOPHY; EDUCATION **EDUCATION** Princeton Univ, BA, 64; Harvard Univ, PhD, 74. **CAREER** Prof, Univ of Mass at Boston, 73- ; vis assoc prof, Univ of Calif, 84; vis prof, Stanford School of Educ, 90; vis prof, Columbia Univ, 90. **HONORS AND AWARDS** Chancellor's Distinguished Scho Award, Univ of Mass, 81, 94; NEH

fel for Col Tchrs, 86-87; Fel in Harvard Prog in Ethics and the Professions, 92-93. **MEMBERSHIPS** Am Philos Asn; Asn for Moral Educ; Philos of Educ Soc; Am Soc for Polit & Legal Philos. **RESEARCH** Moral philos; Multicult educ; Race studies; Moral educ. **SELECTED PUBLICATIONS** Auth, Friendship, Altruism, and Morality, 80; Moral Perception and Particularity, 94; Community and Virtue, How Should One Live?, ed R. Crisp, 96; Altruism and Egoism, Dictionnaire de philosophie morale, 96; Community, Philos of Educ: An Encyclopedia, ed J.J. Chambliss, 96; Race, Racism, and Pan-African Identity: Thoughts on K. Anthony Appiah's In My Father's House, New Polit Sci, double issue 38/39, 97; Multicultural Education as Values Education, Harvard Proj on Schooling and Children Working Paper, 97; Altruism and Benevolence, Encyclopedic Dictionary of Bus Ethics, eds P. Werhane and R.E. Freeman, 97; Schindler's Motives, Psychoculture: Rev of Psychology and Cult Studies, vol 1, no 2, 97; Recognition, Value, and Equality: A Critique of Charles Taylor's and Nancy Fraser's Accounts of Multiculturalism, Theorizing Multiculturalism: A Guide to the Current Debate, ed C. Willett, 98; Racial Integration Revisited, Norms and Values: Essays In Honor of Virginia Held, eds J. Graf Habera and M. Halfon, 98; coauth, A Truer Liberty: Simone Weil and Marxism, 89. **CONTACT ADDRESS** Dept of Philosophy, Boston Univ, 100 Morrissey Blvd., Boston, MA, 02125. **EMAIL** blum@umbsky.cc.umb.edu

BLUMBERG, GRACE GANZ
PERSONAL Born 02/16/1940, New York, NY, m, 1959, 1 child **DISCIPLINE** LAW **EDUCATION** Univ Colo, BA, 60; State Univ NY, Buffalo, JD, 71; Harvard Univ, Llm, 74. **CAREER** Law clerk, NY State Appelate Div, 71-72; teaching fel law, Harvard Law Sch, 72-74; asst prof, Sch Law, State Univ NY Buffalo, 74-77, assoc prof, 77-79, prof, 79-81; PROF, LAW SCH, UNIV CALIF, LOS ANGELES, 81-. **MEMBERSHIPS** Asn Am Law Sch. **RESEARCH** Social legislation; family law; women and the law. **SELECTED PUBLICATIONS** Auth, Who Should Do The Work Of Family-Law, Family Law Quart, Vol 0027, 93; Identifying and Valuing Goodwill At Divorce, Law And Contemp Problems, Vol 0056, 93. **CONTACT ADDRESS** Law Sch, Univ Calif, 405 Hilgard Ave, Los Angeles, CA, 90024.

BLUMBERG, PHILLIP IRVIN
PERSONAL Born 09/06/1919, Baltimore, MD, m, 1945, 4 children **DISCIPLINE** LAW **EDUCATION** Harvard Univ, AB, 39, JD, 42. **CAREER** Assoc, Willkie, Owen, Otis, Farr & Gallagher, 42-43; partner & assoc, Szold, Brandwen, Meyers & Blumberg, NY, 46-62; pres, Federated Develop Co, 62-68; prof law, Sch Law, Boston Univ, 68-74; DEAN & PROF LAW & BUS, SCH LAW, UNIV CONN, 74-, Mem, White House Conf Indust World Ahead, 72; Gov O'Neill's Comt Adv Judicial Nominations; trustee, Conn Bar Found. **MEMBERSHIPS** Am Bar Asn; Am Law Inst. **RESEARCH** Corporate social responsibility; corporate power and institutional investors; corporate power and worker participation in corporate ownership and management. **SELECTED PUBLICATIONS** Auth, Regulating Corporate Groups In Europe, Amer Jour of Comparative Law, Vol 0040, 92. **CONTACT ADDRESS** Sch of Law, Univ of Conn, West Hartford, CT, 06117.

BLUMENFELD, DAVID
DISCIPLINE HISTORY OF MODERN PHILOSOPHY, METAPHYSICS, ETHICS, ANALYTIC PHILOSOPHY **EDUCATION** Univ Calif, Berkeley, PhD, 66. **CAREER** Prof, assoc dean, Hum, Ga State Univ. **SELECTED PUBLICATIONS** Author of over twenty-five articles, including two recent ones in The Cambridge Companion to Leibniz, and an article on free will in Am Philos Quart. Editor of Proceedings from Ga State Univ Conference on Human Freedom. **CONTACT ADDRESS** Georgia State Univ, Atlanta, GA, 30303. **EMAIL** phlddb@panther.gsu.edu

BLUMENSON, ERIC D.
DISCIPLINE LAW **EDUCATION** Wesleyan Univ, BA, 68; Harvard Univ, JD, 72. **CAREER** Prof. **RESEARCH** Criminal law; criminal procedure; evidence; trial and appellate advocacy, clinical teaching. **SELECTED PUBLICATIONS** Auth, Policing for Profit: The Drug War's Hidden Economic Agenda, Univ Chicago, 98; The Drug War's Hidden Economic Agenda, Nation, 98; Mapping the Limits of Skepticism in Law and Morals, Tex Law Rev, 96. **CONTACT ADDRESS** Law School, Suffolk Univ, Beacon Hill, Boston, MA, 02114. **EMAIL** eblumens@acad.suffolk.edu

BLUMENTHAL, DAVID REUBEN
PERSONAL Born 12/28/1938, Houston, TX, m, 1967, 3 children **DISCIPLINE** RELIGION, JUDAIC STUDIES **EDUCATION** Univ Pa, BA, 60; Jewish Theol Sem, MA, 61; Columbia Univ, PhD, 72. **CAREER** Vis asst prof Mid Eastern lang, Univ Minn, 72-73; vis asst prof relig, Brown Univ, 73-74, asst prof, 74-76; ASSOC PROF RELIG & JAY & LESLIE COHEN CHMN PROG JUDAIC STUDIES, EMORY UNIV, 76-; NEH fel independent study, 78. **MEMBERSHIPS** Asn Jewish Studies; Am Acad Relig; Mediaeval Acad Am; Am Acad Jewish Res. **RESEARCH** Medieval Jewish philosophy; modern Judaism; Jewish mysticism. **SELECTED PUBLICATIONS** Auth, The Commentary of Hoter ben Shelomo to the Thirteen Principles of Maimonides, Brill, 74; A comparative table of the Bombay, Cairo & Beirut editions of the Rasa'il Ikhwan al-Safa, Arabica, 74; Maimonides' intellectualist mysticism and the superiority of the prophecy of Moses, Studies Medieval Cult, 76; Revelation: A modern dilemma, Conserv Judaism, 77; Understanding Jewish Mysticism, Ktav, 78; Some methodological reflections on the field of Jewish mysticism, Religion, 78; The Philosophic Questions and Answers of Hoter ben Shelomo, Brill, 79; co-ed & contribr, History, Religion & Spiritual Democracy: Essays in Honor of Joseph C Blau, Columbia Univ, 79. **CONTACT ADDRESS** Dept of Relig, Emory Univ, 537 Kilgo Circle, Atlanta, GA, 30322-0001. **EMAIL** reldrb@emory.edu

BLUMM, MICAHEL C.
PERSONAL Born 03/03/1950, Detroit, MI, m, 1982 **DISCIPLINE** ENVIRONMENTAL AND ENERGY LAW **EDUCATION** Williams Col, BA, 72; George Washington Univ, JD, 76, LLM, 79. **CAREER** Teaching fel Coastal law, Nat Resources Law Inst, 78-79; ASSOC PROF ENVIRON, PROPERTY, ENERGY AND FISHERIES LAW, SCH LAW, LEWIS AND CLARK COL, 79-, Prin investr, Sea Grant Col Prog, Ore State Univ, 79-; ed, Anadromous Fish Law Memo, Nat Resources Law Inst, 79-; vis prof, Univ San Francisco, 83. **RESEARCH** Hydropower development and anadromous fish protection; Pacific Northwest energy law; aquatic resources protection. **SELECTED PUBLICATIONS** Auth, Renouncing the Public Trust Doctrine--An Assessment Of The Validity Of Idaho House Bill-794, Ecology Law Quart, Vol 0024, 97; Public Choice Theory And The Public Lands--Why Multiple-Use Failed, Harvard Environ Law Rev, Vol 0018, 94. **CONTACT ADDRESS** Law Sch, Lewis & Clark Col, 10015 SW Terwilliger, Portland, OR, 97219-7768.

BLUMROSEN, ALFRED W.
PERSONAL Born 12/14/1928, Detroit, MI, m, 1952, 2 children **DISCIPLINE** LAW **EDUCATION** Univ MI, AB, 50, JD, 53. **CAREER** From asst prof to assoc prof labor law, 55-61, actg dean, 74-75, Prof Law, Rutgers Univ, Newark, 61-, Thomas A. Cowan Prof, 86, Mem panel arbitrators, NJ Mediation Bd, 57-; vis prof, Law Sch, La State Univ, 61-; consult, NJ State Civil Rights Comn, 63-65; mem panel arbitrators, Fed Mediation & Conciliation Serv, 64-; chief conciliations, US Equal Employment Opportunity Comn, 65-67, chief liaison & consult, 65-; vis prof, Law Sch, Howard Univ, 65-; mem panel arbitrators, Am Arbit Asn, 65-; spec atty, US Dept Justice, 68-; consult, US Dept Labor, 69-71, chmn, Inter-Agency Staff Coordr Comt Civil Rights, 69-70; consult, US Dept Housing & Urban Develop, 69; exec consult, MI Civil Rights Comn, 72-73; consult to chairperson, US Equal Employment Opportunity Comt, 77-79; couns, Kaye, Scholer, Fierman, Hays & Handler, 79-, adv US Dept of Labor, 95. **HONORS AND AWARDS** Am Bar Asn Ross Prize, 83 **MEMBERSHIPS** Am Bar Asn; Int Soc Labor Law & Soc Legis; Indust Rels Res Asn. **RESEARCH** Discrimination in employment; admin process. **SELECTED PUBLICATIONS** Coauth, Labor Relations and the Law, Little, 3rd ed, 65; auth, Black Employment and the Law, Rutgers Univ, 71; Strangers in paradise: Griggs v Duke Power Co and the concept of employment discrimination, Mich Law Rev, 72; Toward effective administration of new regulatory statutes, Admin Law Rev, 77; Affirmative Action in employment after Weber, Rutgers Law Rev, 81; Modern Law: The Law Transmission System and Equal Employment Opportunity, Univ of Wis Press, 93. **CONTACT ADDRESS** Sch of Law, Rutgers Univ, 15 Washington St, Newark, NJ, 07102-3192.

BLUMSTEIN, JAMES FRANKLIN
PERSONAL Born 04/24/1945, Brooklyn, NY, m, 1971 **DISCIPLINE** LAW **EDUCATION** Yale Univ, BA, 66, MA, 70, LLB, 70. **CAREER** From asst prof to assoc prof, 70-76, PROF LAW, VANDERBILT LAW SCH, 76-, Vis assoc prof law & policy sci, Duke Law Sch, 74-75; consult health policy, Dartmouth Med Sch, 75- & US Dept Health, Educ & Welfare, 76-, Nat Ctr Health Care Technol, 81 & Pres Comn Study Ethical Problems in Med & Biomed & Behav Res, 81. **MEMBERSHIPS** Am Bar Asn; Hastings Ctr; Inst Soc, Ethics & Life Sci. **RESEARCH** Constitutional law; health policy; civil rights. **SELECTED PUBLICATIONS** Auth, Federalism and Civil-Rights--Complementary And Competing Paradigms, Vanderbilt Law Rev, Vol 0047, 94; The Fraud and Abuse Statute in an Evolving Health-Care Marketplace--Life In The Health-Care Speakeasy, Amer Jour of Law & Medicine, Vol 0022, 96; Health-Care Reform and Competing Visions of Medical-Care--Antitrust and State Provider Cooperation Legislation, Cornell Law Rev, Vol 0079, 94. **CONTACT ADDRESS** Vanderbilt Law Sch, 2201 W End Ave S, Nashville, TN, 37240-0001.

BLUSTEIN, JEFFREY
PERSONAL Born 05/30/1947, Minneapolis, MN, m, 1970, 2 children **DISCIPLINE** PHILOSOPHY **EDUCATION** Univ of Minnesota, BA, 68; Harvard Univ, PhD, 74. **CAREER** Barnard Col, 74-82; Mercy Col, 82-94; Albert Einstein Col of Medicine Mountefiore Medical Ctr, 92- . **HONORS AND AWARDS** Phi Beta Kappa; Harvard Univ grad prize fel. **MEMBERSHIPS** APA; Hastings Ctr; Soc for Philos and Pub Aff; Inst for Criminal Justice Ethics. **RESEARCH** Ethics; moral psychology; medical ethics; family ethics. **SELECTED PUBLICATIONS** Auth, Ethical Issues in Anesthesiology, Anesthesiology Alert, 93; auth, Doing What the Patient Orders: Maintaining Integrity in the Doctor-Patient Relationship, Bioethics, 93; auth, The Family in Medical Decisionmaking, Hastings Center Report, 93, repr in Thomasma, ed, Clinical Medical Ethics Cases and Readings, Univ Pr of Am, 95; coauth, The Pro-Life Maternal-Fetal Medicine Physician: A Problem of Integrity, Hastings Center Report, 95; coauth, Reproductive Responsibility and Long-Acting Contraceptives, Hastings Center Report, 95; auth, Should Physicians With Strong Pro-Life Views Avoid Specializing in Perinatology? Physicians Weekly, 95; coauth, Abortion and the Maternal-Fetal Medicine Physician: A Reply, Hastings Center Report, 95; auth, Confidentiality and the Adolescent: An Ethical Analysis, in Cassidy, ed, Pediatric Ethics: From Principles to Practice, Harwood Academic, 96; auth, Intervention with Excessively Aggressive Children: Conceptual and Ethical Issues, in Ferris, ed, Understanding Aggressive Behavior in Children, New York Academy of Sciences, 96; coauth, Reproductive Responsibility and Long-Term Contraceptives, in Moskowitz, ed, Coerced Contraception?, Georgetown, 96; auth, A More Equitable Health Care System for Children: The Moral Argument, in Stein, ed, Health Care for Children: What's Right, What's Wrong, What's Next, United Hospital Fund of New York, 97; auth, Character-Principlism and the Particularity Objection, Metaphilosophy, 97; auth, Procreation and Parental Responsibility, J of Social Philos, 97; auth, What Bioethics Needs to Learn about Families, Theoretical Medicine and Bioethics, 98; ed, The Adolescent Alone, Cambridge, 99. **CONTACT ADDRESS** 425 7th St, Brooklyn, NY, 11215. **EMAIL** blustein@accom.yu.edu

BOADT, LAWRENCE E.
PERSONAL Born 10/26/1942, Los Angeles, CA, s **DISCIPLINE** BIBLICAL STUDIES (HEBREW SCRIPTURES) **EDUCATION** St. Paul's Col, MA, 67; Cath Univ of Amer, STL, 71, MA, 73; Pontifical Bibl Inst Rome, SSL, 74, SSD, 76. **CAREER** Roman Cath priest, 69-; adjunct asst prof, theol, Forham Univ, 74-76; prof to prof emer, Wash Theol Union, 76-97; publ, Paulist Press, 97- **HONORS AND AWARDS** Best Book of the Year, Bibl Archaeol Soc, 85. **MEMBERSHIPS** Soc of Bibl Lit; Amer Acad of Relig; Amer Sch of Orient Res; Cath Bibl Asn; Col Theol Soc; Cath Theol Soc of Amer. **RESEARCH** Ancient near eastern poetry; Prophetic phenomena. **SELECTED PUBLICATIONS** Auth, Preaching Biblical Texts, 95; auth, Anchor Bible Dictionary, 92; auth, Oxford Catholic Study Bible of the New American Bible, 92, auth, New Jerome Biblical Commentary, 90; auth, Shaping English Liturgy, 90; auth, Old Testament Reading Guide, 88; auth, Wisdom Literature and Book of Proverbs, 88; auth, Ezekiel and His Book, 86; auth, Reading the Old Testament: An Introduction, 85; auth, Jeremiah 26-52, Habakkuk, Zephaniah and Nahum, 83; auth, Jeremiah 1-25, 82; auth, Old Testament Message, 82; auth, Ezekiel's Oracles Against Egypt, 80. **CONTACT ADDRESS** Paulist Press, 997 Macarthur Blvd., Mahwah, NJ, 07430.

BOARDMAN, WILLIAM SMITH
PERSONAL Born 11/20/1939, Springfield, IL, 1 child **DISCIPLINE** PHILOSOPHY **EDUCATION** DePauw Univ, BA, 61; Univ Minn, PhD(philos), 67. **CAREER** Instr, 65-68, asst prof, 68-80, assoc, 80-90, PROF PHILOS, LAWRENCE UNIV, 90-, Nat Endowment for Humanities younger humanist fel, 71-72. **MEMBERSHIPS** Am Philos Asn. **SELECTED PUBLICATIONS** Auth, The Relativity of Perceptual Knowledge, Synthese, Vol 0094, 93; auth, Coordination and the Moral Obligation to Obey the Law, Ethics, 4-87. **CONTACT ADDRESS** Dept of Philos, Lawrence Univ, 115 S Drew St, Appleton, WI, 54911-5798. **EMAIL** william.s.boardman@Lawrence.edu

BOBIK, JOSEPH
PERSONAL Born 07/21/1927, Binghamton, NY, m, 1948, 5 children **DISCIPLINE** METAPHYSICS; PHILOSOPHY OF RELIGION **EDUCATION** St Bernard's Col, BA, 47; Univ Notre Dame, MA, 51, PhD, 53. **CAREER** Instr philos, Marymount Col, Calif, 53-54; instr, Marquette Univ, 54-55; asst prof, 55-61; asst chmn dept, 67-72, assoc prof Philos, Univ Notre Dame, 61-98; prof Philos, 98-; Notre Dame scholar on leave grant, 66; O'Brien Fund res grant, 68-69. **MEMBERSHIPS** Am Cath Philos Asn. **RESEARCH** Philosophy of religion. **SELECTED PUBLICATIONS** Auth, Aquinas on Being and Essence, Univ Notre Dame, 65; Matter and individuation, In: The Concept of Matter, 66; Intuition and God and some new metaphysicians, In: New Themes in Christian Philosophy, 68; ed, The Nature of Philosophical Inquiry, Univ Notre Dame, 70; auth, The Commentary of Conrad of Prussia on the De Ente et Essentia of Aquinas, Nijhoff, 74; The sixth way, Mod Schoolman, 74; A seventh way, New Scholasticism, 76. **CONTACT ADDRESS** Dept of Philosophy, Univ of Notre Dame, 336 Oshaugnessy Hall, Notre Dame, IN, 46556. **EMAIL** Joseph.Bodik.1@nd.edu

BOCHNOWSKI, MICHAEL
PERSONAL Born 08/04/1938, Brooklyn, NY **DISCIPLINE** RELIGIOUS EDUCATION **EDUCATION** New York Univ, PhD, 93. **CAREER** Dir relig educ, Ft Belvoir, Va, 86- . **HONORS AND AWARDS** Res fel, Yale Divinity Sch; U.S. Army Chief of Chaplains Writing Award Competition, 96. **MEMBERSHIPS** Am Asn Christian Counr; Relig Educ Asn. **RE-**

SEARCH Religion and worship. CONTACT ADDRESS 8637 Beerman Pl, Alexandria, VA, 22309-1616. EMAIL smbphd@aol.com

BOCK, DARRELL L.
PERSONAL Born 12/18/1953, Calgary, AB, Canada, m, 1975, 3 children **DISCIPLINE** NEW TESTAMENT **EDUCATION** Tx Univ, BA, 75; Dallas Theolog Sem, ThM, 79; Aberdeen Univ, PhD, 83. **CAREER** Prof Spiritual Develop & Culture, Center Christian Leadership, Dallas Theolog Sem, present; vis prof, Seminario Centro Americano, 98; adjunct prof New Testament, Southern Theolog Sem, 98; Evangelical Bibl Sem Lctr, Osaka, Japan, 98; Consultant, SEARCH Ministries, 97; Coord, IBR Jesus Studies Proj, 96; Plenary Speaker, Far West Regional Evangel Theolog Soc, 95; vis lctr, Wstminister West, Escondido, Calif, 95; vis prof, Seminario Teologico Centroamericano, Guatemala City, 94. **HONORS AND AWARDS** Fac Tchg Award, 87; Alexander Hamilton Scholar, 95-96. **MEMBERSHIPS** Studiorum Novi Testament Studies; Inst Bibl Res Treasurer; Amer Col Bibl Theologians; Bulletin for Bibl Res Ed Advisory Brd; Christianity Today Ed; Soc of Bibl Lit; Inst Bibl Res; Evangel Theolog Soc; Tyndale Soc. **RESEARCH** Historical Jesus; Use of Old Testament in New Testament. **SELECTED PUBLICATIONS** Ed, Three Views of the Millennium and Beyond, Zondervan, forthcoming; Blasphemy and Exaltation in Judaism and the Final Examination of Jesus, Mahr/Siebeck, forthcoming; Jesus vs. Sanhedrin: Why Jesus Lost His Trial, CT, 98; The Parable of the Rich Man in Lazarus, Southwestern Jour of Theology, 97. **CONTACT ADDRESS** Dept of Theology, Dallas Theol Sem, 3909 Swiss Ave, Dallas, TX, 75204. **EMAIL** dbockdts@aol.com

BODEUS, RICHARD-CLEMENT
PERSONAL Born 03/03/1948, Hermee, Belgium **DISCIPLINE** PHILOSOPHY **EDUCATION** Univ Liege, lic en phil classique, 70, lic en hist et litt orientales, 72, doct en phil et lettres, 81. **CAREER** Prof, l'Ecole Normale des Rivageois Liege, 70-71; aspirant du fonds de la res sci Belge, 72-76; prof titulaire, petit seminaire Saint-Roch, Ferrieres, 76-85; collaborateur sci a la section de philos et au centre d'hist des religions de l'Univ Liege, 81-85; prof agrege, 85-90, PROF TITULAIRE PHILOSOPHIE, UNIV MONTREAL, 90-, dir du dept, 92-96, vice doyen de la Fac des Etudes Superieures, 96-. **HONORS AND AWARDS** L'Academie des lettres, Soc Royale du Can. **MEMBERSHIPS** Soc philos du Que; Asn can de philos. **SELECTED PUBLICATIONS** Auth, Le philosophie et la cite, 82; auth, Lettres d'un affranchi, 86; auth, Politique et philosophie chez Aristote, 91; auth, Soljenitsyne, 91; auth, Aristote et la theologie des vivants immortels, 92; auth, Leibnitz-Thomasius, 93; auth, Aristote, de l'ame, 93; auth, The Political Dimensions of Aristotle's Ethics, 93; auth, Aristote, la justice et la Cite, 96. **CONTACT ADDRESS** Dept de philosophie, Univ of Montreal, CP 6128, Succ Centre Ville, Montreal, PQ, H3C 3J7.

BODLING, KURT A.
DISCIPLINE HISTORICAL THEOLOGY, LIBRARY SCIENCE **EDUCATION** Concordia Col, AA, 74; Concordia Sen Col, BA, 76; Concordia Sem, MDiv, 80, MST, 86; Univ Ill, MS; Fordham Univ, PhD cand. **CAREER** Ref, res asst, 81-86; asst dir, ref svcs, 86-87, Concordia Hist Inst; free-lance ed, Concordia Pub, 88-89; assoc lib, Winterthur Mus, 90-91; dean, spiritual life, 95-96, COL ARCH, 93- , asst prof, 91-98, ASSOC PROF, RELIG, 98-, DIR LIBR SVCS, 91-, CONCORDIA COL. **CONTACT ADDRESS** 214 Midland Ave, Tuchahoe, NY, 10707-4308.

BOEDEKER, EDGAR
PERSONAL Born 10/03/1968, St. Louis, MO **DISCIPLINE** PHILOSOPHY **EDUCATION** Northwestern Univ, PhD, 98. **HONORS AND AWARDS** Phi Betta Kappa, 90. **MEMBERSHIPS** Am Philos Assoc. **RESEARCH** Phenomenology, Wittgenstein. **CONTACT ADDRESS** 3100 Whitehaven St NW, Washington, DC, 20008. **EMAIL** boedeker@nwu.edu

BOETZKES, ELIZABETH
DISCIPLINE PHILOSOPHY **EDUCATION** Univ Calgary, PhD. **CAREER** Assoc prof. **RESEARCH** Health care ethics; philos of law; philos of religion; environmental philos. **CONTACT ADDRESS** Philosophy Dept, McMaster Univ, 1280 Main St W, Hamilton, ON, L8S 4L9.

BOGDAN, RADU J.
DISCIPLINE PHILOSOPHY **EDUCATION** Stanford Univ, PhD, 80. **CAREER** Prof, Tulane Univ: dir, Cognitive Stud Prog. **SELECTED PUBLICATIONS** Auth, Grounds for Cognition, Lawrence Erlbaum; Interpreting Minds, MIT Press, 97. **CONTACT ADDRESS** Dept of Philosophy, Tulane Univ, 6823 St Charles Ave, New Orleans, LA, 70118. **EMAIL** bogdan@mailhost.tcs.tulane.edu

BOGHOSSIAN, PAUL
PERSONAL Born 06/04/1957, Haifa, Israel **DISCIPLINE** PHILOSOPHY **EDUCATION** Trent Univ, BS, 78; Princeton Univ, MA, PhD, 86. **CAREER** Vis assoc prof, 91-, Princeton Univ; asst, assoc, prof, 84-92, Univ Mich; prof, chmn, phil, 92-, NY Univ. **HONORS AND AWARDS** NEH; Magdalen Col, Oxford; Univ J Landon; Australian Natl Univ. **MEMBERSHIPS** APA **RESEARCH** Phil of mind; phil of lang; epistemology **SELECTED PUBLICATIONS** Art, The Rule - Following Conversations, Mind, 89; art, The Transparency of Mental Content, Phil Persp, 94; art, What the Sokal Hoax Ought to Teach Us, Times Lit Suppl, 96; art, Analyticity Reconsidered, Nois, 96. **CONTACT ADDRESS** Dept of Philosophy, New York Univ, 100 Washington Sq, New York, NY, 10003. **EMAIL** paul.boghossian@nyu.edu

BOGUS, CARL T.
PERSONAL Born 05/14/1948, Fall River, MA, m, 1988, 3 children **DISCIPLINE** LAW **EDUCATION** Syracuse Univ, AB, 70; JD, 72. **CAREER** From assoc to partner, Steinberg, Greenstein, Gorelick & Price, Philadelphia, PA, 73-83; from assoc to partner, Mesirov Gelman Jaffe Cramer & Jamieson, Philadelphia, PA, 83-91; vis prof, Rutgers Univ Sch of Law-Camden, 92-96; assoc prof, Roger Williams Univ Sch of Law, 96-. **HONORS AND AWARDS** Ross Essay Award, Am Bar Asn, 91. **RESEARCH** Products liability; torts; gun control; legal profession. **SELECTED PUBLICATIONS** Auth, Pistols, Politics and Products Liability, in 59 Univ of Cincinatti Law Rev 1103, 91; The Invasion of Panama and the Rule of Law, in 26 The Int Lawyer 781, 92; The Strong Case for Gun Control, in The Am Prospect, summer, 92; Excessive Executive Compensation and The Failure of Corporate Democracy, in 41 Buffalo Law Rev 1, 93; Race, Riots and Guns, in 66 Southern Calif Law Rev 1365, 93; How Not To Be the NRA, in Tikkun, Jan./Feb., 94; The Contract and the Consumer, in The Am Prospect, spring, 95; War on the Common Law: The Struggle at the Center of Products Liability, in 60 Missouri Law Rev 1, 95; The Death of an Honorable Profession, in 71 Indiana Law J 911, 96; The Third Revolution in Procucts Liability, in 72 Chicago-Kent Law Rev 3, 96; The Hidden History of the Second Amendment, in 31 U.C. Davis Law Rev 309, 98; rev, Prozac on Trial, in The Nation, Jan. 6, 97; Ronald McDonald is a Bully, in The Nation, Nov. 24, 97; ed, Symposium on Generic Products Liability, in 72 Chicago-Kent Law Rev No.1, 96. **CONTACT ADDRESS** Sch of Law, Roger Williams Univ, Ten Metacom Ave, Bristol, RI, 02806. **EMAIL** ctb@rwulaw.rwu.edu

BOH, IVAN
PERSONAL Born 12/13/1930, Dolenji Lazi, Yugoslavia, m, 1957, 2 children **DISCIPLINE** PHILOSOPHY **EDUCATION** Ohio Univ, BA, 54; Fordham Univ, MA, 56; Univ Ottawa, PhD, 58. **CAREER** From instr to assoc prof philos, Clarke Col, 57-66; assoc prof, Mich State Univ, 66-69; PROF PHILOS, OHIO STATE UNIV, 69-, Instr Russ, Dubuque Community Sch Dist Eve Div, 59-60; vis asst prof, State Univ Iowa, 62-63; Fulbright res fel, Univ Munich, 64-65; mem adv bd, Notre Dame J Formal Logic, 70-; ed consult, New Scholasticism, 70-; consult ed, Franciscan Studies, 73- **MEMBERSHIPS** Am Philos Asn; Am Cath Philos Asn; Int Soc Study Philos. **RESEARCH** Translations from medieval logicians; history of medieval logic; Bergmann's ontology. **SELECTED PUBLICATIONS** Auth, Paul-Of-Venice, Logica Magna, Vol 1,--Tractatus De Necessitate Et Contingentia Futurorum--Latin And English, Speculum- Jour Medieval Stud, Vol 0068, 93; Nicholas-of-autrecourt--speculum- jourl medieval stud, vol 0071, 96. **CONTACT ADDRESS** Dept of Philos, Ohio State Univ, Columbus, OH, 43210.

BOHMBACH, KARLA G.
PERSONAL Born 09/02/1961, Alexandria, MN **DISCIPLINE** RELIGION **EDUCATION** Duke Univ, PhD, 96 **CAREER** Asst prof, Susquehanna Univ, 94- . **MEMBERSHIPS** Amer Acad Relig; Soc Bibl Lit. **RESEARCH** Feminist Biblical Scholarship. **CONTACT ADDRESS** Dept of Philosophy, Religion and Classical Studies, Susquehanna Univ, 514 University Ave, Selinsgrove, PA, 17870. **EMAIL** bohmbach@susqu.edu

BOISVERT, MATHIEU
DISCIPLINE RELIGION **CAREER** Prof, 92, Universite du Quebec a Montreal, department de sciences religieuses; dir of graduate studies, departement de sciences religieuses, 95. **HONORS AND AWARDS** John McGill Award, 86. **MEMBERSHIPS** Amer Acad of Relig; Canadian Soc for the study of relig; Societe Quebecoise pour 1 etude de la religion. **RESEARCH** Indian Buddhism; monasticism; asceticism. **SELECTED PUBLICATIONS** Ed and auth, Un Monde de religions, LesPresses, 97-98; auth, Pelerinage et tourisme, activites semblables, orientations distinctes, Teoros, Revue de recherche en tourisme, 97; The Method of interactive writing and university pedagogy, Blackwell, 98. **CONTACT ADDRESS** Dept des sciences religieuses, Univ du Quebec a Montreal, CP 8888 succursale centre-vill, Montreal, PQ, H3C 3P8. **EMAIL** boisvert.mathieu@uqam.ca

BOISVERT, RAYMOND
PERSONAL Born 10/04/1947, Lewiston, ME, m, 1970, 2 children **DISCIPLINE** PHILOSOPHY **EDUCATION** Providence Coll, BA. 69; Univ of Toronto, MA, 74; Emory Univ, PhD, 80. **CAREER** Instr, 78-84, Clark Coll; Asst, Assoc, Full Prof, 84-, Sienna Coll. **HONORS AND AWARDS** Fulbright Lectr, France, 91-92. **MEMBERSHIPS** Amer Philos Assoc; Soc for the Advancement of Amer Philos; Soc for Values in Higher Edu; Soc for Phenomenal and Existential Philos. **RESEARCH** Philosophy of ritual & food, interpretation theory, American Philosophy. **SELECTED PUBLICATIONS** Auth, John Dewey, Rethinking Our Time, SUNY Press, 97; Dewey's Metaphysics, Fordham Univ Press, 88; Dewey's Metaphysics, Reading Dewey, His Basic Ideas in Context, ed, Larry Hickman, Bloomington, Indiana Univ Press, 98; Beyond the Spectator Theory of Art, The Challenge of Pragmatism, Soundings, 95; John Dewey, An Old-Fashioned Reformer, Studies in Philosophy and Education, 94; From the Biological to the Logical in Classical American Pragmatism, Its Contemporary Vitality, Univ of Illinois Press, forthcoming. **CONTACT ADDRESS** Dept of Philosophy, Siena Col, Loudonville, NY, 12211. **EMAIL** Boisvert@Siena.edu

BOK, DEREK CURTIS
PERSONAL Born 03/22/1930, Bryn Mawr, PA, m, 1955, 3 children **DISCIPLINE** LAW **EDUCATION** Stanford Univ, BA, 51; Harvard Univ, JD, 54; George Washington Univ, MA, 58. **CAREER** Asst prof, 58-61, dean law sch, 68-71, PROF LAW, HARVARD UNIV, 61-, Pres, 71-, Chmn, Am Coun Educ, 81-82. **HONORS AND AWARDS** AB, Harvard Col, 71; LLD, Univ Ill, Princeton Univ & Yale Univ, 71. **MEMBERSHIPS** Am Philos Soc; Inst Med; fel Am Acad Arts & Sci. **RESEARCH** Labor law. **SELECTED PUBLICATIONS** Auth, In-Memoriam, Harvard Law Rev, Vol 0109, 96. **CONTACT ADDRESS** Office of the Pres, Harvard Univ, 79 John F Kennedy St, Cambridge, MA, 02138-5801.

BOKENKAMP, STEPHEN R.
DISCIPLINE RELIGIOUS STUDIES **EDUCATION** Univ Ca, PhD, 86. **CAREER** Assoc prof. **RESEARCH** Taoist studies; Mutual borrowing between Buddhism and Taoism; concepts of self and transcendence; meditation practice; messianism; views of script and scripture in Chinese religions. **SELECTED PUBLICATIONS** Auth, Sources of the Ling-pao Scriptures, Brussels, 83; Taoist Literature through the T'ang Dynasty, Univ Ind, 86; Stages of Transcendence: the Bh-mi Concept in Taoist Scripture, Univ Hawaii, 90. **CONTACT ADDRESS** Dept of Religious Studies, Indiana Univ, Bloomington, 300 N Jordan Ave, Bloomington, IN, 47405.

BOLCHAZY, LADISLAUS J.
PERSONAL Born 06/07/1937, Slovakia, m, 1965, 1 child **DISCIPLINE** CLASSICS AND PHILOSOPHY **EDUCATION** St. Joseph's Col & Sem, NY, BA, philos, 63; NY Univ, MS, classics, 67; SUNY Albany, PhD, classics, 73. **CAREER** Latin/eng, Iona Prep, 64-65; Latin/eng, Sacred Heart High Sch, 62-64; instr, Siena Col, 66-67; asst prof, La Salette Col and Sem, 71-75; visiting asst prof, Millersville State Univ, 75-76; visiting asst prof, Loyola Univ of Chicago, 76-77; adjunct prof, Loyola Univ of Chicago, 79-; pres, Bolchazy-Carducci Publ Inc. **HONORS AND AWARDS** NEH summer inst, ancient hist, Univ Mich, 77; NEH summer sem, Sophocles and Thucydides, Cornell Univ, 76; teaching fel, State Univ of NY Albany, 67-71; res grants, Loyola Univ, spring and summer, 77. **MEMBERSHIPS** Amer Philol Asn. **RESEARCH** History of ethical & theological concepts; Stylometric analysis of language. **SELECTED PUBLICATIONS** Auth, Hospitality in Antiquity, Ares Publ, Chicago, 96; auth, A Concordance to Ausonius, George Olms, Hildesheim, 83; auth, The Coin-Iscriptions and Epigraphical Abbreviations of Imperial Rome, Ares Publ, 78; auth, A Concordance to the Utopia of St. Thomas More, Georg Olms, Hildesheim, 78; auth, Hospitality in Early Rome, Ares Publ, Chicago, 77. **CONTACT ADDRESS** Ladislaus J. Bolchazy, PhD, Bolchazy-Carducci Publishers, Inc., 1000 Brown St., No 101, Unit 101, Wauconda, IL, 60084. **EMAIL** classics@bolchazy.com

BOLING, ROBERT GORDON
PERSONAL Born 11/24/1930, Terre Haute, IN, m, 1955, 2 children **DISCIPLINE** RELIGION **EDUCATION** Ind State Col, BS, 52; McCormick Theol Sem, BD, 56; Johns Hopkins Univ, Phd, 59. **CAREER** From instr to asst prof relig, Col Wooster, 59-64; assoc prof, 64-67, PROF OLD TESTAMENT, MCCORMICK THEOL SEM, 67-, Fels Fund grant, 58; Thayer fel, Am Schs Orient Res, 68-69; ed, Bibl Res. **MEMBERSHIPS** Am Schs Orient Res; Am Orient Soc; Soc Bibl Lit; Am Acad Relig. **RESEARCH** Old Testament language and literature; textual criticism; Ugaritica. **SELECTED PUBLICATIONS** Auth, Synonymous parallelism in the Psalms, J Semitic Studies, 7/60; Judges, The Elders in Ancient-Israel--A Study of a Biblical Institution, Jour Amer Oriental Soc, Vol 0112, 92; Prologue to History--The Yahwist as Historian in Genesis, Interpretation-Jour Bible and Theol, Vol 0048, 94. **CONTACT ADDRESS** McCormick Theol Sem, 5555 S Woodlawn Ave, Chicago, IL, 60637.

BOLTON, MARTHA BRANDT
DISCIPLINE PHILOSOPHY **EDUCATION** Ohio Wesleyan Univ, BA, 65; Univ Mich, PhD(philos), 73. **CAREER** Asst prof, 71-77, assoc prof philos, Rutgers Univ, 77-95. **HONORS AND AWARDS** Dilworth Fel, Inst for Advanced Study, 86-87; Fel, Center for Philos of Science, Univ Pittsburgh, 78; Council of Philo Studies Stipend, 74. **MEMBERSHIPS** Am Philos Asn; Soc for Women Philos; AAUP. **RESEARCH** Early mod-

ern philosophy; philosophy of feminism. **SELECTED PUBLICATIONS** Auth, Substances, substrata and names of substances in Locke's Essay, Philos Rev, 76; Some Aspects of the Philosophy of Catharine Trotter, J Hist of Philos, 93; The Nominalist Argument of the New essays, Leibnig Soc Rev, 96; Universals, Abstractions, and Essences of Kinds, Cambridge His of Seventeenth Century Philos, Cambridge Univ Press, 97. **CONTACT ADDRESS** Dept of Philos Livingston Col, Rutgers Univ, PO Box 270, New Brunswick, NJ, 08903-0270. **EMAIL** mbolton@rci.rutgers.edu

BOLTUC, PIOTR
PERSONAL Warsaw, Poland **DISCIPLINE** PHILOSOPHY, APPLIED ETHICS **EDUCATION** Bowling Green State Univ, PhD, 98. **CAREER** St Olaf Col, 96-98; asst prof, Univ Ill, Springfield, 98- . **HONORS AND AWARDS** Fulbright fel; Sr Common Room Mem, St Johns Col, Oxford. **MEMBERSHIPS** APA. **RESEARCH** Meta-ethics; East European studies; philosophy of mind. **SELECTED PUBLICATIONS** Transl, Jaki, Stanley: God and the Cosmologists, Wroclaw, Poland, 95; auth, Does Equality Have an Independent Moral Value? Dialogue and Universalism, 95; coauth, Understanding Action, rev of book by Frederick Schick, Econ and Philos, 95; auth, Reductionism and Qualia, Epistemologia, 98; auth, Why Russia is Needed for Regional Stability: An Application of Institutional Economics for Security Issues, in Kanet, ed, Post-Communist States in the World Community, Macmillan, 98; auth, Is There an Inherent Moral Value in the Second-Person Relationships? in Abbarno, ed, Inherent and Instrumental Value, Rodolpi, 99. **CONTACT ADDRESS** Dept of Philosophy, Univ of Illinois, PO Box 19243, Springfield, IL, 62794-9243. **EMAIL** pboltl@urs.edu

BOMBARDI, RONALD JUDE
DISCIPLINE PHILOSOPHY **EDUCATION** Le Moyne Col, BA, 75; Marquette Univ, PhD, 84. **CAREER** Assoc prof, 91-; asst prof, 84-91 & instr, 85, Middle Tenn State Univ; instr, Marquette Univ, 79-84; Arthur J. Schmitt fel, 78-79; Marquette Univ fel, 77-78. **HONORS AND AWARDS** Commencement Hon in Philos awd, 75. **MEMBERSHIPS** Amer Philos Asn; Philos Sci Asn & Tenn Philos Asn. **RESEARCH** Philosophies of Language and Logic; Philosophy of Science,History of Early Modern Philosophy. **SELECTED PUBLICATIONS** Auth, The Education of Searle's Demon, Idealistic Stud, Vol 23, 93. **CONTACT ADDRESS** Dept of Philosophy, Middle Tennessee State Univ, 1301 E Main St, Murfreesboro, TN, 37132-0001.

BOND, EDWARD J.
DISCIPLINE PHILOSOPHY **EDUCATION** Queen's Univ, BA; MA; Cornell Univ, PhD. **CAREER** Dept Philos, Queen's Univ **RESEARCH** Ethics and value theory; aesthetics; epistemology. **SELECTED PUBLICATIONS** Auth, Reason and Value, 93; Ethics and Human Well-being: an Introduction to Moral Philosophy, Garland, 96. **CONTACT ADDRESS** Philosophy Dept, Queen's Univ, Kingston, ON, K7L 3N6. **EMAIL** ejb@post.queensu.ca

BOND, GILBERT I.
DISCIPLINE THEOLOGY AND BLACK STUDIES **EDUCATION** Lawrence Univ, BA, 78; Bethany Theol Sem, MDiv, 88; Emory Univ, PhD, 94. **CAREER** Fac, Holy Rosary High Sch, 79-82; fac, St. Thomas More High Sch, 84-85; Adj prof, Bethany Theol Sem, 87-88; Vis prof, Bethany Theol Sem, 90; Asst instr, Emory Col, 93-94; Asst prof, Emory Col & Grad Inst Lib Arts; 94-96; Asst prof, Yale Univ, 96-. **HONORS AND AWARDS** Martin Luther King, Jr., Award for Leadership, 78; Fund Theol Educ Doc Fel, 88-90; Patricia Harris Fel, 88-92; Ass instr Award Tchg, 92-93; Dissertation Year Sch, 93. **SELECTED PUBLICATIONS** Auth, In Christos as Creolization; Anabaptist Liturgy and German Mysticism; Blues as Profane Performance. **CONTACT ADDRESS** Yale Univ, 409 Prospect St., New Haven, CT, 0651-2167.

BONDESON, WILLIAM B.
PERSONAL Born 03/30/1938 **DISCIPLINE** PHILOSOPHY **EDUCATION** Augustana Col, BA, 58; Univ Ill, MA, 62; Univ Chicago, PhD, 65. **CAREER** Prof; Curators' Distinguished tchg prof Family and Commun Med, 92-; adj clin prof Nursing; staff mem, Chicago Coun For Rel, 62-64; instr, Univ Mo-Columbia, 64-; ch, Dept Philos, 67-69; dir, Honors Col, 69-72; Col Gen Stud, 73-79 & Univ Concert Ser, 76-92; co-dir, Prog Hea Care and Human Values, 79-85; spec asst to deen and dir of develop, Col Arts and Sci, 85-87; fac liaison to the Alumni Asn, 87-91; prof Family and Commun Med, 88-; fac assoc to the Provost, 91-94; dir, Chamber Music Ser, 92-94; ACE fel to, Univ Nebr & VP Acad Aff, Univ Mid-Am; univ and publ serv, founding pres, Mus Associates; pres, Friends of the Libr; founding exec VP, Friends of Music;pres, Mo Citizens for the Arts; ch, Campus United Way; ch, City of Columbia Commn on the Arts; ch, Mo Dept of Mental Hea Prof Rev Comt; Dance Adv Comt of the Mo Arts Coun; Touring Adv Comt of the Mo Arts Coun; pres, Columbia Art League; ch, Med Ethics Prog Dir Nat Gp; ch, MU Hos and Clin Ethics Comt; V.A. Hosp Bioethics Comt; Lenoir Home Ethics Comt; pres, Fac/Staff Golf League; Co-founder, Wakonse Foundation for College Teaching; Co-dir, Wakonse Nat Conf on Col Tchg; Amer Mirror Lectr, Mo Humanities Coun, 92, 93, 94, 95, 96 & 97; pres, Univ Club; Amer Cancer Soc, Columbia Chap, Relay for Life Comt; pres, Search Comt, Univ Mo Sys; Chancellor Search and Screening Task Force, Univ Mo Sys. **HONORS AND AWARDS** Danforth Found fel, 58-65; Univ Chicago fel, 58-60; Summer Res fel, 67 & 71; Dean Fac fel, 69 & 70; fel to Harvard Inst for Educ Mgt, 78; ACLS fel, 78; Soc for Values in Higher Educ fel, 82 & Wakonse fel, 89; Phi Beta Kappa, 58; Omicron Delta Kappa, 82; Phi Kappa Phi, 84; Fac Alumni awd, 68; Amoco Tchg awd, 77; Purple Chalk awd, 79 & 84; Union Electric awd, 84; Panhellenic Outstanding Fac awd, 85; Beta Theta Pi Teaching Excellence awd, 86; Maxine Christopher Shutz awd and Lectureship, 89; Coun Advancement and Support Educ, Mo prof Yr, 89; CASE Nat Gold Medalist awd, 89; Coun of Chiefs, Amer Youth Found, 90; Mo Arts Coun awd, 93; MU Friends of the Library Distinguished Friend awd, 93; MU Alumni Asn Distinguished Fac awd, 93; Mo Stud Asn Distinguished Tchg awd, 93; Jefferson Club Distinguished Scholar, 94; Gamma Sigma Delta Outstanding Tchr awd, 94; Outstanding Tchr awd, Sigma Kappa, 95; Tapped for hon mem, Omicron Delta Kappa, 95; Who's Who Among Amer Teachers, 96; MU Excellence in Educ awd, 96; Beta Theta Pi Outstanding Tchr awd, 96; William T. Kemper fel, 97 & Outstanding Greek Fac awd, 97; $3.5 million for res and prog in, med ethics, arts, higher educ., Cofounder & co-ed, Wakonse J for Col Tchg and Learning, 96. **SELECTED PUBLICATIONS** Auth, Higher Education, the Research University, and the Re-affirmation of Excellence in Teaching, Univ Mo Spectrum, 90; The Cruzan Case and Some Issues of Public Policy, Governmental Affairs Newsletter, Governmental Affairs Program, Univ Mo, vol xxv, 91; Faculty Development and the New American Scholar, in To Improve the Acad, vol 11, 92; The Student Learning Imperative: Possibilities and Problems from a Faculty Point of View, J Col Stud Develop, 95 & Some Reflections on Teaching and Tenure, Wakonse J Col Tchg and Learning, 96; coauth, The Wakonse Conferences on College Teaching, J Counseling and Develop, vol 72, 94; co-ed, issue of Nat Forum, Pi Kappa Phi jour on health care issues, 93; contribur, Reidel Philosophy and Medicine Series: New Knowledge in the Biomedical Sciences, 82; Abortion and the Status of the Fetus, 83; Rights to Health Care, 90 & Reproductive Rights and Responsibilities, 87. **CONTACT ADDRESS** Dept of Philosophy, Univ of Missouri-Columbia, 309 University Hall, Columbia, MO, 65211. **EMAIL** philwb@showme.missouri.edu

BONEVAC, DANIEL ALBERT
PERSONAL Born 01/20/1955, Pittsburgh, PA, m, 1976, 2 children **DISCIPLINE** PHILOSOPHY **EDUCATION** Haverford Col, BA, 75; Univ Pittsburgh, MA, 77, PhD(philos), 80. **CAREER** Asst prof Philos, Univ Tex, Austin, 80-85, Ctr Cognitive Sci fel, Univ Tex, 82-83; from assoc prof to prof Philosophy, 85-92; dept chmn, 91. **HONORS AND AWARDS** Johnsonian Prize, J Philos, 80. **MEMBERSHIPS** Am Philos Asn. **RESEARCH** Metaphysics; philosophy of mathematics; philosophy of language. **SELECTED PUBLICATIONS** Auth, Reduction in the Abstract Sciences, Hackett Publ Co, 82; ed, Today's Moral Issues, Mayfild, 92, 96, 99. **CONTACT ADDRESS** Dept Philos, Univ of Texas, Austin, TX, 78712-1026. **EMAIL** dbonevac@la.utexas.edu

BONGMBA, ELIAS KIFON
PERSONAL Born 12/15/1953, Ntumbaw, Cameroon **DISCIPLINE** RELIGIOUS STUDIES **EDUCATION** Univ Denver, PhD. **CAREER** Adj fac, Red Rocks Commun Col, 94-95; asst prof relig stud, Rice Univ, 95- . **MEMBERSHIPS** Soc for African Philos of N Am; Bonhoeffer Soc; African Stud Asn; African Am Acad of Relig. **RESEARCH** African religions; contemporary postmodern thought, **CONTACT ADDRESS** MS 15 Religious Studies, Rice Univ, 6100 S Main St, Houston, TX, 77005. **EMAIL** bongmba@rice.edu

BONI, SYLVAIN
PERSONAL Born 11/12/1931, Paris, France, m, 1972, 2 children **DISCIPLINE** PHILOSOPHY **EDUCATION** Bryn Mawr Col, PhD, 81. **CAREER** Mentor, mentally gifted program, Central High Sch, Philadelphia, 12 yrs; adj prof, philos, Beaver Col, 6 yrs, adj prof, philos, LaSalle Univ, 17 years. **MEMBERSHIPS** APA. **RESEARCH** Philosophy of mind. **SELECTED PUBLICATIONS** Auth, The Self and the Other in the Ontologies of Sartre and Buber. **CONTACT ADDRESS** 1370 Lindsay Ln, Meadowbrook, PA, 19046. **EMAIL** sylBoni@aol.com

BONISTEEL, ROY
PERSONAL Born 05/29/1930, Ameliasburgh, ON, Canada **DISCIPLINE** RELIGION **EDUCATION** Laurentian Univ, DLitt, 79; Queen's Univ, DD, 80; Univ Windsor, LLD, 82; Mt St Vincent Univ, DHumLitt, 83; St. Francis Xavier Univ, LLD, 85; Univ PEI, LLD, 87. **CAREER** Reporter, Belleville Intelligencer, 48; reporter, Trenton Courier-Advocate, 49-59; announcer, CJBQ Belleville, 51-52; prog dir, CTKB St. Catharines, 53-64; dir broadcasting, United Church Can, 65-66; nat radio coordr, Anglican, Roman Cath & United Churches, 69-70; host, CBC-TV, Man Alive, 67-89. **HONORS AND AWARDS** ACTRA Award, 79; Christian Cult Award, Assumption Univ, 82; Gordon Sinclair Award Excellence Broadcast Jour, 85; Commemorative Medal, 125th Anniversary Can Confed, 92; Distinguished Can, Univ Regina, 94; mem, Order Can, 95. **SELECTED PUBLICATIONS** Auth, In Search of Man Alive, 80; auth, Man Alive: The Human Journey, 83; auth, There was a Time, 90; auth, All Things Considered, 97. **CONTACT ADDRESS** RR 5, Trenton, ON, K8V 5P8.

BONNEAU, NORMAND
PERSONAL Born 10/05/1948, Lewiston, ME, s **DISCIPLINE** BIBLICAL STUDIES **EDUCATION** Institut Catholique de Paris, STD, 83. **CAREER** Vis prof, 83-84, asst prof New Testament stud, 84-93, assoc prof, 93- , St Paul Univ. **MEMBERSHIPS** Catholic Bibl Asn of Am; Soc of Bibl Lit. **RESEARCH** Letters of Paul; the Roman Catholic Sunday lectionary; Synoptic Gospels. **SELECTED PUBLICATIONS** Auth, Images of God(s) in the New Testament World, in Abromaitis, ed, Roots: Finding Strength in Biblical Tradition, CCCB, 93; auth, Reflections on the Mystery of God and the AIDS Crisis, in Bonneau, ed, AIDS and Faith, Novalis, 93; auth, Fulfilled in Our Hearing: The Dynamism of Scripture in Liturgical Proclamation, in Gasslein, ed, Shaping a Priestly People: A Collection in Honour of Archbishop Hayes, Novalis, 94; auth, Preparing the Table of the Word, Liturgical, 97; auth, Bible and Liturgy, in Farmer, ed, The International Bible Commentary, Liturgical, 98; auth, The Sunday Lectionary: Ritual Word, Paschal Shape, Liturgical, 98. **CONTACT ADDRESS** St Paul Univ, 223 Main St, Ottawa, ON, K1S 1C4. **EMAIL** nbonneau@ustpaul.uottawa.ca

BONNETTE, DENNIS
PERSONAL Born 02/26/1939, Gardner, MA, m, 1962, 7 children **DISCIPLINE** PHILOSOPHY **EDUCATION** Univ Detroit, AB, 60; Univ Notre Dame, MA, 62, PhD, 70. **CAREER** Instr philos, Univ San Diego, 63-64; asst prof, Loyola Univ, La, 64-65 & Univ Dayton, 65-67; from Asst Prof to Assoc Prof, 67-90, Prof Philos, Niagara Univ, 90-, Dept Chmn, 93. **MEMBERSHIPS** Am Cath Philos Asn. **RESEARCH** Metaphysics; natural theology; ethics; evolution. **SELECTED PUBLICATIONS** Auth, The doctrinal crisis in Catholic higher education, Social Justice Rev, 11/67; Effects of secularism on higher education, Cath Educ Rev, 3/68; Ex umbris in veritatem, Triumph, 12/70; Aquinas' Proofs for God's Existence, Martinus Nijhoff, 73; Is the United States becoming the Fourth Reich?, 7-8/80 & When human life begins, 3-4/81, Social Justice Rev; The infinite being as sole adequate explanation of the phenomenon of inertia: A variation on the First Way of St Thomas Aquinas, Faith & Reason, summer 82; How Creation Implies God, Faith & Reason, 3-4, 85; A Philosophical Critical Analysis of Recent Ape-Language Studies, Faith & Reason 2-3, Fall 93. **CONTACT ADDRESS** Dept of Philos, Niagara Univ, Niagara Univ, NY, 14109-9999. **EMAIL** bonnette@niagara.edu

BONTEKOE, RON
PERSONAL Born 05/31/1954, Toronto, ON, Canada, d **DISCIPLINE** PHILOSOPHY **EDUCATION** Univ Toronto, BA, 77, B Ed, 78, PhD, 88; Queen's Univ, MA, 82; **CAREER** Lectr, Ryerson Polytech Univ, 88-90; asst prof, 90-95, assoc prof, 95-, Univ Hawaii Manoa; liberal arts fel, Harvard Law Sch, 97-98. **MEMBERSHIPS** Amer Philos Asn; Can Philos Asn. **RESEARCH** Hermeneutics; Epistemology; Philosophy of law. **SELECTED PUBLICATIONS** Auth, Paul Ricoeur, Encycl of Aesthetics, Oxford Univ Press, 98; auth, Friedrich Schleiermacher, Encycl of Aesthetics, Oxford Univ Press, 98; auth, Grounding a Theory of Rights in Fallibilist Epistemology, Justice and Democracy: Cross-Cultural Perspectives, Univ Hawaii Press, 97; co-ed, Justice and Democracy: Cross-Cultural Perspectives, Univ Hawaii Press, 97; co-ed, A Companion to World Philosophies, Blackwell Publ, 97; auth, Dimension of the Hermeneutic Circle, Humanities Press, 96; co-auth, The Interrelationship of Moral and Aesthetic Excellence, The Brit Jour of Aesthetics, 92; auth, Metaphysics: Should It Be Revisionary or Descriptive? Intl Philos Quart, 92; auth, Rorty's Pragmatism and the Pursuit of Truth, Intl Philos Quart, 90; auth, The Function of Metaphor, Philos and Rhetoric, 87; auth, A Fusion of Horizons: Gadamer and Schleiermacher, Intl Philos Quart, 87. **CONTACT ADDRESS** Philosophy Dept., Univ of Hawaii, 2530 Dole St., #D304, Honolulu, HI, 96822. **EMAIL** bontekoe@hawaii.edu

BOOMER, DENNIS
PERSONAL Born 10/30/1951, Hobbs, NM, m, 1983 **DISCIPLINE** RELIGION **EDUCATION** Hardin-Simmons Univ, BA, 74; Southwestern Baptist Theol Sem, MDiv, 77; Baylor Univ, PhD, 89. **CAREER** Univ of Mary Hardin-Baylor, 81-86; West Virginia Univ, vis assoc prof, 89-92; Reli Res Serv, founder & dir, 92-. **MEMBERSHIPS** AAR, SBL **RESEARCH** Apologetics; cults and new religions. **CONTACT ADDRESS** Religious Research Service, 2316 N MacArthur Blvd. #1177, Irving, TX, 75062. **EMAIL** dbommer300@aol.com

BOOZANG, KATHLEEN M.
DISCIPLINE LAW **EDUCATION** Boston Col, BS; WA Univ, JD; Yale Univ, LLM. **CAREER** Assoc prof, 90-, dir, Hea Law & Policy prog, Seton Hall Univ; ed, Law Rev, WA Univ. **MEMBERSHIPS** Order of the Coif, WA Univ. **SELECTED PUBLICATIONS** Writes frequently on health law issues. **CONTACT ADDRESS** Seton Hall Univ, South Orange, NJ. **EMAIL** boozanka@lanmail.shu.edu

BORAAS, ROGER STUART
PERSONAL Born 02/04/1926, Stillwater, MN, m, 1948, 3 children **DISCIPLINE** BIBLICAL STUDIES; OLD TESTAMENT **EDUCATION** Gustavus Adolphus Col, BA, 48; Augustana Theol Sem, BD, 52; Drew Univ, PhD, 65. **CAREER** From instr to assoc prof, 58-69, Prof Relig, Upsala Col, 69-91, Dir Area Studies Prog Ancient Near East, 67-84, Mem, Drew-McCormich exped, Balatah, 62, 64, 66 & 68; chief archaeologist, Andrews Univ exped, Heshbon, 68, 71, 73, 74, 76. **MEMBERSHIPS** Soc Bibl Lit; Am Schs Orient Res. **RESEARCH** Palestinian archaeology. **SELECTED PUBLICATIONS** Coauth, Heshbon, 1968, Andrews Univ Monogr, 69; auth, Rejm ed- Malfuf, Am Schs Orient Res Newslett, 69; coauth, Heshbon, 1971, Andrews Univ Monogr, 73; assoc ed Harpers Bible Dictionary, 85 & 96. **CONTACT ADDRESS** 50 Fernwood Rd, East Orange, NJ, 07017.

BORCHERT, GERALD LEO
PERSONAL Born 03/20/1932, Edmonton, AB, Canada, m, 1959, 2 children **DISCIPLINE** RELIGION, LAW **EDUCATION** Univ Alta, BA, 55, LLB, 56; Eastern Baptist Theol Sem, BD, 59; Princeton Theol Sem, ThM, 61, PhD, 67. **CAREER** Lawyer, Calgary, Alta, 56; part-time teaching fel Greek, Princeton Theol Sem, 60-62; from Assoc Prof to Prof, 63-77, acad dean & vpres, 70-77; prof & dean New Testament, Northern Baptist Sem, 77-80; from prof to Coleman Prof New Testament, Southern Baptist Seminary, 80-98; dir Doctoral Studies and Prof New Testament, Northern Baptist Seminary, 98-; Mem bd abstractors, Relig & Theol Abstr, 67-75, 96; civilian retreat master for US Army, 68; bibl lectr, N Am Continental Cong Crusade of Americas, 68-69; comnr, Int Comn Coop Christianity, Baptist World Alliance, 68-95, secy, 69-80, chair, 90-95, chair study and res div, 95-00; consult law & Christianity, Baptist Joint Comt Pub Affairs Can & US, 69-71, mem comt, 71-77, secy, 73-75, vchair, 75-77; dir-trustee, Am Inst Holy Land Studies, Jerusalem, 71-77, vis prof, 74; trustee, Tabor Col, 70-77; co-teacher, Hidden Treasures of the Bible, TV series of Chicago Sunday Evening Club, 78-79; numerous other visiting professorships. **MEMBERSHIPS** Soc Bibl Lit; Am Acad Relig; Am Schs Orient Res; Soc Study New Testament. **RESEARCH** New Testament, particulary studies in Paul, John and history of interpretation; gnosticism including Coptic studies; law, the relationship between justice and order. **SELECTED PUBLICATIONS** Auth, Form criticism, Foundations, 4/65; Great Themes from John, Baptist Life Asn, 66; The Dynamics of Pauline Evangelism, Roger Williams & NAm Baptist Sem, 69; Law, the Christian and the Contemporary Scene, in Emerging Patterns of Rights and Responsibilities Affecting Church and State, Baptist Joint Comt Pub Affairs, 69; Forum, Monthly Column in Baptist Herald, 70-77; Today's Model Church, Roger Williams, 71; Dynamics of Evangelism, Word Books, 76; Discovering Thessalonians, Guideposts, 86; Assurance and Warning, Broadman, 87; coauth, The Crisis of Fear, Broadman, 88; auth, John I-II (New American Commentary), Broadman, 96. **CONTACT ADDRESS** No Baptist Theol Sem, 660 E Butterfield Rd, Lombard, IL, 60148-5698. **EMAIL** gborchert@northern.seminary.edu

BORELLI, JOHN
PERSONAL Born 07/19/1946, Oklahoma City, OK, m, 1970, 3 children **DISCIPLINE** HISTORY OF RELIGIONS, THEOLOGY **EDUCATION** Fordham Univ, PhD, 76. **CAREER** Instr, Dept Theology, Fordham Univ, Bronx, NY, 75-76; Prof Religious Studies, Col Mount St Vincent, Riverdale, NY, 76-87; dir, Interreligous Relations, Nat Conference of Catholic Bishops, 87-. **HONORS AND AWARDS** Phi Beta Kappa, St. Louis Univ, 68. **MEMBERSHIPS** Consultor, Pontifical Coun for Interreligous Dialogue, Vatican; Int Buddhist-Christian Theological Encounter Group; Exec Coun, World Conference on Religion and Peace, USA; adv bd, Monastic Interreligous Dialogue; Am Academy of Religion; Soc for Buddhist-Christian Studies; Soc for Hindu-Christian Studies. **RESEARCH** Interreligous relations; theology of religions; the Hindu tradition; Yoga and meditation. **SELECTED PUBLICATIONS** Auth, Children of Abraham: Muslim-Christian-Jewish Relations, Mid-Stream 34, 2, April 95; The 1994 International Buddhist-Christian Theological Encounter, with Judith Simmer-Brown, Buddhist-Christian Studies, 15, 95; Interreligous Relations, Annual report, 1994, Pro Dialogo, Bul of the Pontifical Coun for Interreligous Dialogue, 89, 95; The Goal and Fruit of Catholic-Muslim Dialogue, The Living Light, Dept of Ed, US Cath Conference, 32, 2, winter 95; Talking With Muslims, Faith Alive, Cath News Service, Feb 96; Indispensable Resources on the Christian East and Other Important Books, Ecumenical Trends, 25, 6, June 96; Jesus Christ's Challenge to World Religions: A Response, The Continuing Challenge of Jesus Christ to the World, a Symposium on the Coming of the Third Millenium and the Jubilee Year 2000, sponsored by the NCCB Subcommittee on the Millenium, Sept 7-8, 96, Proceedings; The Virgin Mary in the Breadth and Scope of Interreligious Dialogue, Marian Spirituality and Interreligous Dialogue, Marian Studies, 47, 96; Introductory Address for Imam Warith Deen Mohammed, Living City, Oct, 97; The Catholic Church and Interreligous Dialogue, in Vatican II: The Continuing Agenda, ed by Anthony J Cernera, Sacred Heart Univ Press, 97; Religious Pluralism in India and the Mission of the Church, Periodic Paper #4, US Cath Mission Asn, in Mission Update 6, 4, Dec 97; Interreligous Relations, 1996, Annual Report, Pro Dialogo, Bul of the Pontifical Coun for Interreligious Dialogue, 96, 97; Islamic-Catholic Relations in the USA: Activities of the National Conference of Catholic Bishops (1996) and Recent Developments, Islamochristiana 23, 97; ed with John H Erickson, The Quest for Unity, Orthodox and Catholics in Dialogue, St Vladimir's Seminary Press/US Cath Conf, 96. **CONTACT ADDRESS** Interreligious Relations, 3211 Fourth St NE, Washington, DC, 20017. **EMAIL** seiamail@nccbuscc.org

BORG, DOROTHY
PERSONAL Born 09/04/1902, Elberon **DISCIPLINE** HISTORY, PUBLIC LAW **EDUCATION** Wellesley Col, AB, 23; Columbia Univ, MA, 31, PhD (pub law and govt), 46. **CAREER** Res assoc Am-Chinese rels, Inst Pac Rels, 38-59; res assoc, EAsian Res Ctr, Harvard Univ, 59-61; SR RES ASSOC, AM FAR EAST POLICY, EAST ASIAN INST, COLUMBIA UNIV, 62-, Lectr, Peking Univ, 47-48. **HONORS AND AWARDS** Bancroft Prize Hist, 65. **MEMBERSHIPS** AHA; Asn Asian Studies, Acad Polit Sci.. **SELECTED PUBLICATIONS** Auth, Social Protestantism in the 20th Century--History of the Inner Mission 1914-1945, J Mod Hist, Vol 0064, 92. **CONTACT ADDRESS** 22 Riverside Dr, New York, NY, 10023.

BORG, MARCUS J.
PERSONAL Born 03/11/1942, MN, m, 1985, 2 children **DISCIPLINE** THEOLOGY **EDUCATION** Concordia Col, BA, 64; Oxford, PhD, 72; **CAREER** Instr, 66-69, ast prof, 72-74, Concordia Col; ast prof, Carleton Col, 76-79; prof, Oregon St Univ, 79- **HONORS AND AWARDS** Rockefeller Fel; Danforth Fel; NEH Fel; Hundere Dist Prof of Relig and Cult. **MEMBERSHIPS** Soc Bibl Lit; Am Acad Relig. **RESEARCH** Historian of Jesus and Christian origins; religious studies, theology. **SELECTED PUBLICATIONS** Auth, Meeting Jesus again for the First Time, 94; Jesus in Contemporary Scholarship, 94; Jesus at 2000, 96; The God We Never Knew, 97; Conflict, Holiness, and Politics in the Teachings of Jesus, rev., 98; coauth, The Meaning of Jesus, 98. **CONTACT ADDRESS** 4137 SW Stephenson, Portland, OR, 97219.

BORJESSON, GARY
DISCIPLINE PHILOSOPHY **EDUCATION** Whitman Col, BA, 87; Emory Univ, MA, 94, PhD, 97. **CAREER** Asst prof, philos, Univ Central Ark, 98- . **HONORS AND AWARDS** Winner, Rev of Metaphysics dissertation essay competition, 98. **MEMBERSHIPS** APA; Metaphysics Soc of Am. **RESEARCH** Metaphysics; ancient philosophy; history of philosophy. **SELECTED PUBLICATIONS** Auth, A Sounding of Walden's Philosophical Dept, Philos and Lit, 94; auth, Not for Their Own Sake: Species and the Riddle of Individualiy, Rev of Metaphysics, forthcoming. **CONTACT ADDRESS** Dept of Philosophy, Univ of Central Arkansas, Conway, AR, 72035. **EMAIL** garyb@mail.uca.edu

BORK, ROBERT HERON
PERSONAL Born 03/01/1927, Pittsburgh, PA, m, 1952, 3 children **DISCIPLINE** LAW **EDUCATION** Univ Chicago, BA, 48, JD, 53. **CAREER** Managing ed, Chicago Law Rev, 53; res assoc, Univ Chicago, 53-54; private practice, New York, 54-55 and Chicago, 55-62; from assoc prof to prof, Yale Univ, 62-75; Solicitor Gen of US, 73-77; res scholar, Am Enterprise Inst, Wash, 77; Chancellor Kent Prof, Law Sch, Yale Univ, 77-79; Alexander M Bickel prof pub law, 79-81. Actg Atty Gen of the US, 73-74; Solicitor Gen of US, Dept Justice, Washington, DC, 73-77; trustee, Woodrow Wilson Int Ctr for Scholars, 73-78; resident scholar, Am Enterprise Inst, Washington, DC, 77; partner, Kirkland and Ellis, Washington, DC, 81-82; CIRCUIT JUDGE, US CT APPEALS FOR DC CIRCUIT, 82- **HONORS AND AWARDS** LLD, Creighton Univ Sch Law, 75; LHD, Wilkes-Barre Col, 76 and LLD, Notre Dame Law Sch, 82. **MEMBERSHIPS** Fel Am Acad Arts and Sci. **RESEARCH** Constitutional law; antitrust. **SELECTED PUBLICATIONS** Auth, Yes--The Passion for Equality Denigrates American Life, Aba J, Vol 0082, 96. **CONTACT ADDRESS** Law Sch, Yale Univ, 127 Wall St, New Haven, CT, 06520.

BOROWSKI, ODED
PERSONAL Born 08/26/1939, Israel, m, 1964, 2 children **DISCIPLINE** BIBLICAL ARCHAEOLOGY; BIBLICAL STUDIES **EDUCATION** Wayne State Univ, BA, 70; Univ Mich, PhD, 79. **CAREER** Ch, Dept of Near Eastern and Judaic Lang and Lit, Emory Univ, 88-91; INSTRUCT, ASST PROF, ASSOC PROF, EMORY UNIV, 77- . **HONORS AND AWARDS** Annual Professor, AIAR in Jerusalem, 95-96; Memorial Foundation for Jewish Culture, 94-95. **MEMBERSHIPS** Israel Explor Soc; Am Sch of Oriental Res; Soc for Bibl Lit; Nat Asoc of Prof of Hebrew. **RESEARCH** Ancient agriculture; ancient animal use; remote sensing and GPS in araeology; the Iron Age in Syria-Palestine. **SELECTED PUBLICATIONS** auth, The Pomegranate Bowl from Tell Halif, Israel Explor Jour, 95; Viticulture, Dictionary of Judaism in the Biblical Period, 96; auth, A Penetrating Look: An Experiment in Remote Sensing at Tell Halif, Retrieving the Past: Essays on Archaeological Research and Methodology in Honor of Gus W. Van Beek, 96; Food Storage, Granaries and Silos, Irrigation, The Oxford Encyclopedia of Near Eastern Archaeology, 96; auth, Every Living Thing: The Daily Use of Animals in Ancient Israel, 98. **CONTACT ADDRESS** Dept of MES, Emory Univ, S310 Callaway Center, Atlanta, GA, 30322. **EMAIL** oborows@emory.edu

BORRADORI, GIOVANNA
PERSONAL Born 07/24/1963, Milan, Italy, m, 1990, 2 children **DISCIPLINE** PHILOSOPHY **EDUCATION** Dottorato Univ, Milan Italy, 85; Diplome d'Etudes Approfondis, Univ Paris VIII, 87. **CAREER** Asst prof, philos, Vassar Col, 95-. **HONORS AND AWARDS** Fel, Ital Acad for Advan Studies, Columbia Univ, 98-99. **MEMBERSHIPS** Amer Philos Asn; Soc of Phenomenol and Existential Philos. **RESEARCH** Continental philosophy; Aesthetics; Philosophy of architecture. **SELECTED PUBLICATIONS** Auth, The American Philosopher, Chicago Univ Pres, 94; auth, Recoding Metaphysics: The New Italian Philosophy, Northwestern Univ Press, 89. **CONTACT ADDRESS** 455 E. 57th St., New York, NY, 10022. **EMAIL** giborradori@vassar.edu

BORROWS, JOHN
DISCIPLINE LAW **EDUCATION** British Columbia Univ, BA, 87; Univ Toronto, MA, 96; LLB, 90; LLM, 91; Osgoode Univ, JD, 94. **CAREER** Assoc prof, Osgoode Hall Sch; asst prof, Univ British Columbia, 92-94; assoc prof, 96-. **MEMBERSHIPS** Can Asn Law; Chippewas Nawash First Nation. **RESEARCH** First Nations and the law; natural resources law; environmental law. **SELECTED PUBLICATIONS** Auth, pubs about Chippewas Nawash First Nation legal rights and history. **CONTACT ADDRESS** Fac of Law, Univ British Columbia, 1822 East Mall, Vancouver, BC, V6T 1Z1. **EMAIL** borrows@law.ubc.ca

BORSCH, FREDERICK HOUK
PERSONAL Born 09/13/1935, Chicago, IL, m, 1960, 3 children **DISCIPLINE** ENGLISH LITERATURE, THEOLOGY **EDUCATION** Princeton Univ, AB, 57; Oxford Univ, MA, 63; Univ Birmingham (UK), PhD, 66. **CAREER** Tutor, Queens Coll, Birmingham (UK), 63-66; assoc prof, Seabury-Western Theol Sem, 66-71; prof, General Theol Sem, 71-72; dean, prof, Church Div Sch of the Pacific, 72-81; dean of chapel, prof, Princeton Univ, 81-88. **MEMBERSHIPS** Am Acad Rel; Soc Bib Lit; Studiorum Novi Testamenti Soc; Phi Beta Kappa. **RESEARCH** New Testament theology and literature; early church history. **SELECTED PUBLICATIONS** Auth, The Son of Man in Myth and History, Westminster Press, 67; auth, The Christian and Gnostic Son of Man, SCM Press, 70; auth, God's Parable, Westminster Press, 77; auth, Introducing the Lessons of the Church Year, Seabury Press, 78; auth, Power in Weakness, Fortress Press, 83; ed, Anglicanism and the Bible, Morehouse-Barlow, 84; auth, Many Things in Parables, Fortress Press, 88; auth, Outrage and Hope, Trinity Press Int, 96. **CONTACT ADDRESS** Box 512164, Los Angeles, CA, 90051-0164. **EMAIL** bishop@ladiocese.org

BOSS, JUDITH A.
PERSONAL Born 11/11/1942, Rochester, NY, d, 2 children **DISCIPLINE** SOCIAL ETHICS **EDUCATION** Boston Univ, PhD, 90. **CAREER** INDEPENDENT SCHOLAR, CENTER FOR THE STUDY OF HUMAN DEVELOPEMENT, BROWN UNIV, 96-. **MEMBERSHIPS** Am Philos Asn. **RESEARCH** Ethics; moral development. **SELECTED PUBLICATIONS** Auth, The Birth Lottery, Loyola Univ Press, 93; The Alien Abduction: a Case Study for Bioethics, Soc for the Study of Ethics and Animals Newsletter, no 7, March 95; The Morality of Prenatal Diagnosis, in Life and Learning, vol 5, ed Joseph W. Koterski, Georgetown Univ, 95; Circumcision, Free Inquiry, fall 97; Paradigm Shifts, Scientific Revolutions, and the Moral Justification of Experimentation on Non-Human Animals, Between the Species: A J of Ethics, summer/fall 95; Francine: A Fairy Tale for Philosophers Young and Old (fiction), Thinking: The J of Philos for Children, vol 12, no 2, 95; Teaching Ethics Through Community Service, The J of Experiential Ed, vol 18, May 95; Treading on Harrowed Ground: The Violence of Agriculture, in Institutional Violence, eds Deane Curtin and Robert Litke, Rodolphi Press, 96; Ethics for Life, Mayfield Pub Co, 97; Throwing Pearls to the Swine: Women, Forgiveness and the Unrepentant Abuser, in Perspectives on Power and Dominance, eds Laurence Bove and Laura D. Kaplan, Rodolphi Press, 97; Adopting an Aristotelian Approach to Teaching College Ethics, in Philos and Community Service Learning, Asn for the Advancement of Higher Ed, spring 98; Perspectives in Ethics, Mayfield Pub Co, 98; Outdoor Education and the Development of Civic Responsibility, ERIC Clearinghouse on Rural Education and Small Schools, forthcoming summer 98; Analyzing Moral Issues, Mayfield Pub Co, forthcoming 99. **CONTACT ADDRESS** 90 Robinson St., Narragansett, RI, 02882. **EMAIL** judyboss@uriacc.acc.uri

BOTHAM, THAD M.
PERSONAL Grand Junction, CO, m, 1997 **DISCIPLINE** PHILOSOPHY **EDUCATION** Texas A&M Univ, MA. **CAREER** Tchg asst, Texas A&M, 98-99. **HONORS AND AWARDS** Fel, Interdisciplinary Group for Hum; Texas A&M Regents Fel. **MEMBERSHIPS** APA. **RESEARCH** Counterfactual conditional semantics; metaphysics; philosophy of religion; logic. **CONTACT ADDRESS** 4110 College Main, Ste. 57, Bryan, TX, 77801. **EMAIL** socrates@tamu.edu

BOTKIN, DANIEL B.
DISCIPLINE BIOLOGY **EDUCATION** Univ Rochester, BA, 59; Univ Wisc, MA, 62; Rutgers Univ, PhD, 68. **CAREER** Asst prof to adj fac mem, School of Forestry and Environ Stud, Yale Univ, 68-78; assoc sci, Ecosystems Ctr, Marine Biol Lab, Woods Hole, 76-78; chemn Environ Stud Prog, 78-85, prof, biolog and environ, 78-92, Univ Calif, Santa Barbara; pres, Ctr for Study of Environ, Santa Barbara, 92- ; prof biol, George Mason Univ, 92- . **HONORS AND AWARDS** NSF predoctoral fel, 66-67; fel, Woodrow Wilson Int Ctr for Scholars; Sigma Xi natl lectr, 81-82, 82-83; fel, AAAS; Mitchell Int Prize for Sustainable Dev, 91; elected Environ Hall of Fame; Bernhard Eduard Fernow Award for Outstanding Contributions to Int Forestry, 95. **RESEARCH** Biology; ecology; the idea of nature; history of the idea of nature; early trends in America related to the conservation of natural resources. **SELECTED PUBLICATIONS** Auth, Our Natural History: The Lessons of Lewis and Clark, Putnam, 96; auth, Environmental Sciences: The Earth as a Living Planet, 1st through 3d ed, Wiley, 95, 97, 99; auth, The Blue Planet, Wiley, forthcoming; auth, Passages Voyage of Discovery: American Rivers Travel Companion to The Missouri River of Lewis and Clark, Putnam, 99; auth, Nobody's Garden: Thoreau and Nature, Island, forthcoming. **CONTACT ADDRESS** 332 B West Alamar Ave, Santa Barbara, CA, 93105.

BOULAD-AYOUB, JOSIANE
PERSONAL Born 02/22/1941, Alexandria, Egypt **DISCIPLINE** PHILOSOPHIE POLITIQUE **EDUCATION** Lyon III (France) LL, 63, DL, 79; Univ Montreal, MS, 78, PhD, 76. **CAREER** Dir, dp de philos, 92, PROF TITULAIRE DE PHILOSOPHIE POLITIQUE, UNIV QUEBEC MONTREAL, 92-. **HONORS AND AWARDS** Soc royale du Can. **MEMBERSHIPS** Centre de rech en sci cognitives; Soc philos Que; Asn can philos; Soc d'etudes du dix-huitieme siecle; Soc Nord-Am etudes JJ Rousseau. **SELECTED PUBLICATIONS** Auth, Contre nous de la tyrannie, 90; auth, Mimes et parades, 95; auth, Former un nouveau peuple?, 95; contribur & co-ed, Les Comites d'instruction publique de l'Assemblee Legislative et de la Convention, 97; ed, L'Esprit de la Revolution, 89; ed, Philosophie et Droit, 89; ed, Le Systeme de la nature (Baron d'Holbach), 93; ed, Le Systeme social (Baron d'Holbach), 94; L'Amour des lois, 96. **CONTACT ADDRESS** Dep de philosophie, Univ Quebec, Montreal, CP 8888, Succ Centre-Ville, Montreal, PQ, H3C 3P8.

BOUMAN, WALTER R.
DISCIPLINE SYSTEMATIC THEOLOGY **EDUCATION** Concordia Sem, BA, 52, MDiv, 54; Univ Heidelberg, ThD, 63; Gen Theol Sem, DD, 93. **CAREER** Assoc prof, Concordia Teachers Col, 63-71; vis prof, ELTS, 71-75; joint prof, ELTS/Hamma, 75-78; prof, 78-83; guest prof, Theol Hochschule Leipzig, 85; vis prof, Gen Theol Sem, 94-95; Edward C. Fendt prof, Trinity Lutheran Sem, 83-. **HONORS AND AWARDS** Pres, Lutheran Acad Scholar, 75-77. **MEMBERSHIPS** Amer Acad Rel. **SELECTED PUBLICATIONS** Co-auth, What Shall I Say?, Discerning God's Call to Ministry, Division for Ministry, Evangel Lutheran Church Am, 95;, Like Wheat Arising Green, Valparaiso, Indiana, 91. **CONTACT ADDRESS** Hist, Theol, Soc Dept, Trinity Lutheran Sem, 2199 E Main St, Columbus, OH, 43209-2334. **EMAIL** wbouman@trinity.capital.edu

BOURGEOIS, PATRICK LYALL
PERSONAL Born 03/17/1940, Baton Rouge, LA, m, 1968, 2 children **DISCIPLINE** PHILOSOPHY, RELIGION **EDUCATION** Notre Dame Sem, BA, 62, MA, 64; Notre Dame Univ, MA, 65; Duquesne Univ, PhD(philos), 70. **CAREER** Instr relig, Duquesne Univ, 65-67; from instr to asst prof philos, 68-78, Prof Philos, Loyola Univ of The South, 78-, Fac res grants, Loyola Univ, 72 & 73; La Endowment Humanities fels, State of La, 74 & 76-77. **HONORS AND AWARDS** Dux Academicus, 93. **MEMBERSHIPS** Soc Phenomenol & Existential Philos; Am Acad Relig; Southern Soc Philos & Psychol; Soc Advan Am Philos; Int Husserl & Phenomenol Res Soc. **SELECTED PUBLICATIONS** Auth, Existential phenomenology and phenomenology, Paul Ricoeur's Hermeneutical Phenomenology, Philos Today, 72; Extension of Ricoeur's Hermeneutic, Martinus Nijhoff, 75; Kierkegaard: Ethical marriage or aesthetic pleasure, Personalist, 76; coauth, Pragmatism, scientific methodology and phenomenological return to lived experience, Philos & Phenomenol Res, 77; Mead, Merleau-Ponty and the lived perceptual world, Philos Today, 77; auth, From the hermeneutics of symbols to the interpretation of texts, in an anthology, Ohio Univ, 78; coauth, Pragmatism and Phenomenology: A philosophic encounter, Grunner, 80; Fundamental ontology and epistemic foundations, In: New Scholasticism, Vol LX, 81; The Religious Within Experience & Existance, Duequesne Univ Press, 90. **CONTACT ADDRESS** Loyola Univ, 6363 St Charles Ave, New Orleans, LA, 70118-6195. **EMAIL** PBB31740@aol.com

BOURGUIGNON, HENRY J.
PERSONAL Born 08/19/1931, Lakewood, OH, m, 1971, 2 children **DISCIPLINE** LEGAL HISTORY; LAW **EDUCATION** Loyola Univ Chicago, AB, 54, MA, 58; Univ Mich, PhD(legal hist), 68, JD, 71. **CAREER** Trial atty, Dept Justice, 71-74; from Assoc Prof to Distinguished Univ Prof Law, Col Law, Univ Toledo, 74-. **HONORS AND AWARDS** Am Coun Learned Soc fel, England, 80-81. **MEMBERSHIPS** Am Soc Legal Hist (secy, 78-83). **RESEARCH** History of international law; constitutional law. **SELECTED PUBLICATIONS** Auth, The First Federal Court: The Federal Appellate Prize Court of the American Revolution, 1775-1787, Am Philos Soc, 77; Incorporation of the law of Nations during the American Revolution -- the case of the San Antonio, Am J of Int Law 71, 77; The Second Justice Harlan - His Principles of Judicial Decision Making, Supreme Ct Rev, 79; A Revisionist Revises Himself - A Review Essay, Tex Law Rev 64, 85; The Articles of Confederation, In: Encyclopedia of the American Judicial System, Charles Scribner's Sons, 87; Sir William Scott, Lord Stowell, Judge of the High Court of Admiralty, 1798-1828, Cambridge Univ Press, 87; The Belilos Case - New Light on Reservations to Multilateral Treaties, Va J of Int Law 29, 89; coauth, Coming to Terms with Death -- The Cruzan Case, Hast L.J. 42, 91; auth, Human Rights Decisions by the United Supreme Court - October Term 1990, Human Rights L.J. 13, 92; Human Rights Decisions by the United Supreme Court - October Term 1991, Human Rights L.J. 13, 92; The United States Supreme Court and Freedom of Expression - October Term 92, Human Rights L.J. 15, 94; Persons with Mental Retardation - The Reality Behind the Label, Cambridge Quart of Healthcare Ethics 3, 94; The Federal Key to the Judiciary Act of 1789, SC Law Rev 46, 95. **CONTACT ADDRESS** Col of Law, Univ of Toledo, 2801 W Bancroft St, Toledo, OH, 43606-3391.

BOURKE, VERNON JOSEPH
PERSONAL Born 02/17/1907, North Bay, ON, Canada, m, 1932, 3 children **DISCIPLINE** PHILOSOPHY **EDUCATION** Univ Toronto, BA, 28, MA, 29, PhD, 37. **CAREER** Lectr Greek philos, St Michael's Col, Univ Toronto, 28-31; from instr to prof, 31-75, EMER PROF PHILOS, ST LOUIS UNIV, 75-, Aquinas lectr, Marquette Univ, 47; assoc ed, Mod Schoolman, Speculum and Am J Jurisp; adv ed, Augustinian Studies, 70-; dir, Ctr Thomistic Studies, Univ St Thomas, 78-80; Fagothey chair philos, Univ Santa Clara, 81-82. **HONORS AND AWARDS** LLD, Bellarmine Col, Ky, 74; LitD, Univ St Thomas, 81. **MEMBERSHIPS** Am Philos Asn; Cath Comn Intellectual and Cult Affairs; Mediaeval Acad Am; Am Cath Philos Asn (pres, 48); Nat Cath Educ Asn; World Union Cath Philos Soc (pres, 63). **RESEARCH** Philosphy of St thomas Aquinas; history of mediaeval thought; contemporary ethics. **SELECTED PUBLICATIONS** Auth, Goodness and Rightness in Aquinas, Thomas--Summa Theologiae, Speculum J Medieval Stud, Vol 0069, 94. **CONTACT ADDRESS** Dept of Philos, St Louis Univ, St Louis, MO, 63103.

BOVON, FRANCOIS
PERSONAL Born 03/13/1938, Lausanne, Switzerland **DISCIPLINE** THEOLOGY **EDUCATION** Gymnase Classique Cantonal, Lausanne, BA, 56; Univ Lausanne, Licence en Theologie, 61; Univ Basel, ThD, 65. **CAREER** Prof, 67-93, dean theol, 76-79, Univ Geneva; Frothingham Prof of the Hist of Relig, Harvard Univ Div Sch, 93- . **HONORS AND AWARDS** Summa cum laude, 65; Dr Honoris Causa, Uppsala, Sweden, 93. **MEMBERSHIPS** SNTS; SBL; AELAC. **RESEARCH** New Testament; Luke-Acts; Christian apocryphal literature; early church. **SELECTED PUBLICATIONS** L'Evangile et l'Apotre: Le Christ Inseparable de ses Temoins, Le Moulin, 93; auth, The Role of the Scriptures in the Composition of the Gospel Accounts: The Temptations of Jesus (Lk 4:1-13 par.) and the Multiplication of the Loaves (Lk 9:10-17 par.) in O'Collins, ed, Luke and Acts, Paulist, 93; auth, The Gospel and the Apostle, Harvard Divinity Bull, 94; auth, The Words of Life in the Acts of the Apostle Andrew, Harvard Theol Rev, 94; auth, The Church in the New Testament, Ex Auditu, 94; auth, New Testament Traditions and Apocryphal Narratives, Pickwick, 95; auth, Ces chretiens qui revent: L'autorite du reve dans les premiers siecles du christianisme, in Hengel, ed, Geschichte-Tradition-Reflexion, Mohn, 96; auth, After Paul after Paul, Harvard Theol Rev, 97; auth, Apocalyptic Traditions in the Lukan Special Material: Reading Luke 18: 1-8, Harvard Theol Rev, 97; auth, The Child and the Beast: Fighting Violence in Ancient Christianity, Harvard Divinity Bull, 98; auth, The Canonical Structure of the New Testament: The Gospel and the Apostle, in Farmer, ed, International Bible Commentary, Liturgical, 98; auth, Luke: Portrait and Project in Farmer, ed, International Bible Commentary, Liturgical, 98. **CONTACT ADDRESS** The Divinity School, Harvard Univ, 45 Francis Ave, Cambridge, MA, 02138.

BOWDEN, HENRY WARNER
PERSONAL Born 04/01/1939, Memphis, TN, m, 1962, 2 children **DISCIPLINE** HISTORY, RELIGION **EDUCATION** Baylor Univ, AB, 61; Princeton Univ, AM, 64, PhD (relig), 66. **CAREER** From instr to asst prof, 64-71, asst dean col, 69-71, assoc prof, 71-79, PROF RELIG, DOUGLASS COL, RUTGERS UNIV, 79- **MEMBERSHIPS** Am Soc Church Hist; Orgn Am Historians. **RESEARCH** Historiographical studies, chiefly in the United States; religion of American Indians and missionary activities by Europeans. **SELECTED PUBLICATIONS** Auth, Native and Christian--Indigenous Voices on Religious Identity in the United States and Canada, Am Indian Cult Res J, Vol 0021, 97; Historians of the Christian Tradition--Their Methodology and Influence on Western Thought, Church Hist, Vol 0066, 97; Missionary Conquest--The Gospel and Native American Cultural Genocide, Church Hist, Vol 0064, 95; Historians of the Christian Tradition--Their Methodology and Influence on Western Thought, Church Hist, Vol 0066, 97 Choctaws and Missionaries in Mississippi, 1818-1918, Am Hist Rev, Vol 0102, 97; Converting the West--A Biography of Whitman, Narcissa, Pac Hist Rev, Vol 0061, 92. **CONTACT ADDRESS** Dept of Relig Douglass Col, Rutgers Univ, P O Box 270, New Brunswick, NJ, 08903-0270.

BOWDEN, JAMES HENRY
PERSONAL Born 10/28/1934, Louisville, KY, d, 3 children **DISCIPLINE** AMERICAN STUDIES, RELIGION **EDUCATION** Univ Louisville, MA, 59; Univ MN, Minneapolis, PhD, 70; Louisville Presbyterian Theol Sem, MA, 87. **CAREER** Instr Eng, Univ KY, 60-61, Univ MT, 62-64 & Colgate Univ, 65-66; from Instr to Assoc Prof, 66-80, Prof English, 80-98, Prof Emeritus, Ind Univ SE, 98-, Chmn Hum Div, 80-85; Assoc Dir, Am Studies Ctr, Warsaw, 85-86; Prof, Institut Teknologi Mari, Malaysia, 89-91. **HONORS AND AWARDS** Nat Endowment for the Humanities summer fel, Univ MI, 77; fel, Bread Loaf Writers Conf, 80. **RESEARCH** Relig in Am life; imaginative writing; theories of humor. **SELECTED PUBLICATIONS** Auth, The bland leading the bland, New Oxford Rev, 77; Go purple, West Branch, 77; The grief of Terry Magoo, Great River Rev, 77; The Bible and other Novels, Cresset, 78; Don't Lose This, It's My Only Copy, Col English, 79; ICU, Thornleigh Rev, 82; Conwell Lives, New Oxford Rev, 82; Peter DeVries, A Critical Study, G K Hall, 83. **CONTACT ADDRESS** Dept of Hum, Indiana Univ, Southeast, 4201 Grant Line Rd, New Albany, IN, 47150-2158. **EMAIL** jhbowden@iusmail.ius.indiana.edu

BOWDEN, MARIE ANN
DISCIPLINE LAW **EDUCATION** Mt. Allison Univ, BA, 76; Queen's Univ, LLB, 79; Osgoode Hall Law Sch, LLM, 81. **CAREER** Assoc prof, 81-. **HONORS AND AWARDS** Ed, Can Jour Environ Law Policy. **SELECTED PUBLICATIONS** Co-auth, Understanding Property: A Guide to Canada's Property Law. **CONTACT ADDRESS** Col of Law, Univ Saskatchewan, 15 Campus Dr, Saskatoon, SK, S7N 5A6. **EMAIL** Bowden@law.usask.ca

BOWDLE, DONALD N.
PERSONAL Born 02/02/1935, Easton, MD, m, 1994, 3 children **DISCIPLINE** THEOLOGY **EDUCATION** Lee College, BA 53; Bob Jones Univ, MA 59, PhD 61; Princeton Theol Seminary, ThM 62; Union Theol Seminary, ThD 70. **CAREER** Lee Univ, fac, teach admin, 62-; Georgia State Univ, adj fac, 93-97; Yale Univ Div Sch, vis lect, 85; VA Commonwealth Univ, adj fac, 67-69. **HONORS AND AWARDS** Post Doc Fel Yale Univ and Univ Edinburgh. **MEMBERSHIPS** ASCH; ETS; Karl Barth Soc NA. **RESEARCH** John Calvin; Karl Barth; Non-Wesleyan origins of Amer Pentecostalism. **SELECTED PUBLICATIONS** Auth, Holiness in the Highlands: A Profile of the Church of God, in: Christianity in Appalachia: Profiles In Regional Pluralism, ed Bill J. Leonard, Univ Tenn Press, forthcoming 98. **CONTACT ADDRESS** School of Religion, Lee Univ, Cleveland, TN, 37311. **EMAIL** dbowdle@leeuniversity.edu

BOWEN, DAVID H.
PERSONAL Born 10/28/1964, Virginia, MN **DISCIPLINE** PHILOSOPHY **EDUCATION** Univ Leuven, Belgium, drs, 98. **CAREER** Instr, 97-98, asst prof, 98-, Univ N Fla. **MEMBERSHIPS** APA; Int Asn of Philos & Lit; Soc for the Philos of Love and Sex. **RESEARCH** 19th century German philos; 20th century French philos; aesthetics; psychoanalysis. **SELECTED PUBLICATIONS** Auth, La pensee de Jacques Lacan, 1994-Louvain-Paris: Editions Peeters, 94. **CONTACT ADDRESS** Dept of History and Philosophy, Univ North Florida, Jacksonville, FL, 32224. **EMAIL** Elagabalus@compuserve.com

BOWERS, J.W.
PERSONAL Born 01/09/1942, Billings, MT, m, 1980, 7 children **DISCIPLINE** LAW AND ECONOMICS **EDUCATION** Yale Univ, BA, 64, Law Sch, LLB, 67. **CAREER** Assoc prof; Prof, Byron R Kantrow Prof, 82-, Louisiana State Univ Law Cen; Texas Tech Univ Law Sch, Assoc Prof, 78-81; Assoc and shhldr, 69-77, Briggs and Morgan MN; USAR, Cpt, 67-69. **MEMBERSHIPS** ABA; ALEA; CLC LA Law Inst. **RESEARCH** Bankruptcy and Commercial Law. **SELECTED PUBLICATIONS** Auth, Security Interests Creditor Priorities and Bankruptcy, title number 1500, in: the Encyclopedia of Law and Economics, De Geest et al, eds, Elgar, forthcoming 98, also pub on the internet by the Univ of Ghent; coauth, Bonds Liens and Insurance, Washington DC, Federal Pub Inc, 78, 79, 80, 81; Rev, Of Bureaucrats' Brothers-in-Law and Bankruptcy Taxes: Article Nine Filing Systems and the Market for Information, Minn L 95; auth, Rehabilitation Redistribution or Dissipation: The Evidence for Choosing Among Bankruptcy Hypotheses, Wash U L Qtly, 94; Kissing Off Economics and Misunderstanding Murphy's Law: Carlson's On the Efficiency Of Secured Lending, A Commentary, VA L Rev, 94; The Fantastic Wisconsylvania Zero-Bureaucratic-Cost School of Bankruptcy Theory: A Comment, Mich L Rev, 93. **CONTACT ADDRESS** Law Center, Louisiana State Univ, Baton Rouge, LA, 70803. **EMAIL** lmbowe@unix1.sncl.lsu.edu

BOWIE, NORMAN
DISCIPLINE PHILOSOPHY **EDUCATION** Univ Rochester, PhD. **RESEARCH** Ethics and political philosophy; corporate responsibility; ethical issues in management; ethical foundations of capitalism. **SELECTED PUBLICATIONS** Auth, New Direction in Corporate Responsibility, Bus Horizons, 91; Challenging the Egoistic Paradigm, Bus Ethics Quarterly, 91; co-auth, Business Ethics, Prentice-Hall, 90; co-ed, Ethics and Agency Theory, Oxford, 92. **CONTACT ADDRESS** Philosophy Dept, Univ of Minnesota, Twin Cities, 355 Ford Hall, 224 Church St SE, Minneapolis, MN, 55455. **EMAIL** nbowie@csom.umn.edu

BOWKER, WILBUR F.
PERSONAL Born 02/18/1910, Ponoka, AB, Canada **DISCIPLINE** LAW (HISTORY) **EDUCATION** Univ Alta, BA, 30, LLB, 32, LLD, 72; Sterling Fel, Yal Law Sch, 52-53; Univ Minn, LLM, 53. **CAREER** Law pract, Edmonton, 32-42; Can Army, 42-45; prof law, Univ Alta, 45-75(RETIRED), dean law, 48-68; dir, Alta Law Reform Inst, 68-75. **HONORS AND AWARDS** KC, 51; hon bencher, Law Soc Alta, 76; hon prof law, Univ Calgary, 77; hon mem, Can Bar Asn, 79 (pres award, 89); Justice Medal, Can Inst Admin Justice, 89; OC, 90. **MEMBERSHIPS** Can Asn Law Tchrs (pres, 56). **SELECTED PUBLICATIONS** Auth, Consolidation of Fifty Years of Legal Writings 1938-1988, 89. **CONTACT ADDRESS** 10925 85 Ave, Edmonton, AB, T6G 0W3.

BOWMAN, LEONARD JOSEPH
PERSONAL Born 02/04/1941, Detroit, MI, m, 2 children **DISCIPLINE** RELIGION; LITERATURE **EDUCATION** Duns Scotus Col MI, BA 63; Univ Detroit, MA 67; Fordham Univ, PhD 73. **CAREER** Marycrest Intl Univ, prof 73-94, vpres acad dean 94-97; Col Notre Dame MD, vpres acd affs, 97-. **MEMBERSHIPS** AAUP **RESEARCH** Medieval Franciscan Spirituality; St. Bonaventure. **SELECTED PUBLICATIONS** Auth, A Retreat With St. Bonaventure, Element Books Ltd, 93. **CONTACT ADDRESS** Dept of Academic Affairs, Notre Dame Col, 4003 Roundtop Rd, Baltimore, MD, 21218. **EMAIL** lbowman@udm.edu

BOWNE, DALE RUSSELL
PERSONAL Born 08/19/1934, Pickaway Co, OH, m, 1956, 2 children **DISCIPLINE** RELIGION, PHILOSOPHY **EDUCATION** Washington & Jefferson Col, BA, 56; Pittsburgh Theol Sem, MDiv, 59; Union theol Sem, NY, ThD, 63. **CAREER** From asst prof to assoc prof, 63-71, Prof Relig, Grove City Col, 71. **HONORS AND AWARDS** DD, Washington & Jefferson Col, 81. **MEMBERSHIPS** Am Acad Relig; Soc Bibl Lit. **RESEARCH** New Testament studies; general Bibl studies; philosophical ethics. **SELECTED PUBLICATIONS** Auth, How to Choose a Bible, Griggs Educ Serv, 79; Paradigms and Principal Parts for the Greek New Testament, 87; Harbison Heritage, 89. **CONTACT ADDRESS** Dept Relig, Grove City Col, 100 Campus Dr, Box 2623, Grove City, PA, 16127-2104. **EMAIL** drbowne@gcc.edu

BOYARIN, DANIEL
PERSONAL Born 12/06/1946, Asbury Park, NJ, m, 1967, 2 children **DISCIPLINE** TALMUD **EDUCATION** Goddard Col, BA, 68; Jewish Theolog Seminary, Master Hebrew Lit, 71; Columbia Univ, MA, 72; Jewish Theolog Seminary, PhD, 75 **CAREER** Hermann P. and Sophia Taubman prof, Univ California Berkeley, current; visiting prof, Talmud, Jewish Theolog Seminary, 92, 96; adjunct prof, Graduate Theolog Unio, 91; senior lctr, Bar-Ilan Univ, 90; visiting prof, Yeshiva Univ, 88; visiting assoc prof, Yale Univ, 85; **HONORS AND AWARDS** David Baumgardt Memorial Fel, 95; Crompton-Noll Award, 95; John Simon Guggenheim Found Fel, 93; President's Res Fel, Univ Calif, 93; Res Fel, Ntl Endowment Humanities, 92; Res Grant, Littauer Found, 91; Fel Institute for Advanced Studies of Shalom Hartman Inst, 88-94 **RESEARCH** Women's Studies; Gay and Lesbian Studies; Talmudic Culture **SELECTED PUBLICATIONS** Co-ed, Studies in Rabbinic Literature, Judah Magnes; auth, co-ed, Queer Theory and the Jewish Question, Columbia Univ, 98; auth, "Goyim Naches; or, Modernity and the Manliness of the Mentsh," Modernity, Culture and "the Jew," 98; auth, "The Colonial Masqued Ball," Theory and Crit, 97; **CONTACT ADDRESS** Univ Calif Berkeley, Berkeley, CA, 94720.

BOYCE, JAMES
DISCIPLINE NEW TESTAMENT **EDUCATION** Luther Sem, MDiv, 71; Univ NC, PhD, 74. **CAREER** Instr, Univ NC, 68-70; prof, 87-. **HONORS AND AWARDS** Minister of edu, Prince of Peace Lutheran Church, 74-77. **MEMBERSHIPS** Mem, Soc of Biblical Lit; Amer Philol Assn. **SELECTED PUBLICATIONS** Act ed, Word & World, 90-91; assoc ed, 93-94; cotransl, Mark the Evangelist by Willi Marxsen. **CONTACT ADDRESS** Dept of New Testament, Luther Sem, 2481 Como Ave, St. Paul, MN, 55108.

BOYD, JAMES W.
DISCIPLINE PHILOSOPHY **EDUCATION** Northwestern Univ, PhD, 70. **CAREER** Prof. **RESEARCH** Asian studies. **SELECTED PUBLICATIONS** Auth, Satan and Mara, 75; The Lion and the Dragon, 79; Guide to Zoroastrian Religion, 82; A Persian Offering, 91; co-auth, Ritual Art and Knowledge, 93. **CONTACT ADDRESS** Philosophy Dept, Colorado State Univ, Fort Collins, CO, 80523.

BOYD, ROBERT
PERSONAL Born 02/10/1952, Hillsdale, MI, m, 1974, 2 children **DISCIPLINE** PHILOSOPHY **EDUCATION** Tex Christian Univ, MA, 79. **CAREER** Adj assoc prof, philos, Tex Christ Univ, 93-96; instr, philos, Fresno City Col, 96-. **HONORS AND AWARDS** Who's Who Among Amer Teachers, 98; Who's Who in the South and Southwest, 97. **MEMBERSHIPS** Amer Asn of Philos Teachers; Amer Philos Asn; Soc of Christ Philos. **RESEARCH** Critical reasoning and logic. **SELECTED PUBLICATIONS** Auth, Strawson On Induction, The Philosophy of P.F. Strawson, Open Court Press, 98; auth, Inductive Reasoning and Rhetoric, Korean Jour of Thinking and Problem Solving, 98; auth, Teaching Writing with Logic, Col Teaching, 43, 95; auth, Writing With Logic in Mind, Harcourt Brace Col Publ, 94; auth, Argument Analysis and Critical Thinking, Korean Jour of Thinking and Problem Solving, 93; auth, Critical Reasoning: The Fixation of Belief, Colonial Press, 92; co-auth, Probability and Lycan's Paradox, Southwest Philos 88; co-auth, Semantic Trees and Philosophical Logics, Southwest Philos Studies, 83. **CONTACT ADDRESS** Philosophy, Fresno City Col, 1101 E. University, Fresno, CA, 93741. **EMAIL** bb045@merlin.fresno.com

BOYD, TOM WESLEY
PERSONAL Born 07/04/1933, Nashville, TN, d, 2 children **DISCIPLINE** THEOLOGY, PHILOSOPHY **EDUCATION** Bethany Nazarene Col, BA, 56; Univ Okla, MA, 62; Vanderbilt Univ, BD, 63, PhD(relig), 72. **CAREER** Instr theol, Vanderbilt Divinity Sch, 67-69; asst prof, 69-75, ASSOC PROF PHILOS, UNIV OKLA, 75-, Baldwing travel award, 79. **HONORS AND AWARDS** AMACO Outstanding Teaching Award, 76; Teacher of the Year Award, Univ Okla, 80. **MEMBERSHIPS** Southwestern Philos Asn; Am Acad Relig. **RESEARCH** Constructive theology; reinterpretation of traditional religious themes and symbols in light of contemporary insight; ethics of ecology with special attention to technology. **SELECTED PUBLICATIONS** Auth, Libri-Confusi--The So-Called Peisistratus Recension of Homer, Class Jour, Vol 0091, 95; A Regular Illustrated Book--Allingham, William and His Pre-Raphaelite Friends Make The Music Master, 1854-55, Publ Hist, Vol 0037, 95. **CONTACT ADDRESS** Dept of Philos, Univ of Okla, Norman, OK, 73069.

BOYLE, ASHBY D., II
DISCIPLINE RELIGIOUS STUDIES; LAW **EDUCATION** Princeton Univ, BA, 80; Univ Cambridge, M.Phil, 83; Columbia Univ, MA, 84; Yale Univ, MA, M.Phil, PhD, 90. **CAREER** Partner, McConnell Valdes LLP; law clerk, Chambers of Justice Sandra Day O'Connor, US Supreme Ct, 90-91. **HONORS AND AWARDS** Charles Evans Hughes Fel; Columbia Law School. **MEMBERSHIPS** AAR **RESEARCH** Religion and Constitution; Religious Ethics; International Law. **SELECTED PUBLICATIONS** Fear and Trembling at the Court: Dimensions of Understanding in the Supreme Court's Religion Jurisprudence, 3 Const.L.J., 93. **CONTACT ADDRESS** 15 Ballad Ln, New York, NY, 11790. **EMAIL** aboyle@compuserve.com

BOYLE, CHRISTINE
DISCIPLINE LAW **EDUCATION** Queen's, LLB; 71, LLM, 72. **CAREER** Owen vis prof, 90-92; prof, 92-. **HONORS AND AWARDS** Tchr Awd Acad Excellence, 95. **MEMBERSHIPS** Can Asn Law. **RESEARCH** Criminal law; feminist perpectives as law. **SELECTED PUBLICATIONS** Auth, The Law of Homicide, Thomson, 94; pubs about criminal law. **CONTACT ADDRESS** Fac of Law, Univ British Columbia, 1822 East Mall, Vancouver, BC, V6T 1Z1. **EMAIL** boyle@law.ubc.ca

BOYLE, F. LADSON
DISCIPLINE TAXATION **EDUCATION** Col Charleston, BS, 69; Univ SC, JD, 74; NY Univ, LM, 75. **CAREER** Prof, Univ of SC. **SELECTED PUBLICATIONS** Co-ed, Probate Practice Reporter. **CONTACT ADDRESS** School of Law, Univ of S. Carolina, Law Center, Columbia, SC, 29208. **EMAIL** Lad@law.law.sc.edu

BOYLE, FRANCIS
DISCIPLINE POLITICAL SCIENCE, LAW **EDUCATION** Univ Chicago, BA, 71; Harvard Law School, JD, 76; Harvard Grad Sch of Arts and Sci, MA, 78; PhD, 83. **CAREER** Tchg fel, Harvard Univ Dept of Govt, 76-78; ast prof, assoc prof, prof, Univ Ill, Champaign, Col of Law, 78- ; **HONORS AND AWARDS** Phi Beta Kappa; Sigma Xi Certificate of Merit; Magna Cum Laude, 76; Jerusalem Fund Award, 97; Dare to Speak Out Award, Coun for Natl Interest, 97. **SELECTED PUBLICATIONS** Auth, The Right of Citizen Resistance to State Crimes, in Mahoney, ed, Human Rights in the Twenty-First Century: A Global Challenge,, 93; auth, the Decolonization of Northern ireland, Asian Yearbook Int L, 94; auth, The Restoration of the Independent Nation State of Hawaii under International Law, St Thoms L Rev, 95; auth, The Bosnian People Charge Genocide, Aletheia, 96; auth, Is Bosnia the End of the Road for the United Nations? Periodica Islamica, 96; auth, Foundations of World Order: The Legalist Approach to International Relations, 1898-1921, Duke, 98. **CONTACT ADDRESS** 504 E Pennsylvania Ave, Champaign, IL, 61820. **EMAIL** fboyle@law.uiuc.edu

BOYLE, JOHN PHILLIPS
PERSONAL Born 08/23/1931, Iowa City, IA **DISCIPLINE** CATHOLIC THEOLOGY, BIOETHICS **EDUCATION** Ambrose Col, BA, 53; Pontif Gregorian Univ, STB, 55, STL, 57; Fordham Univ, PhD(theol), 72. **CAREER** Asst prof, 72-77, Assoc Prof Relig, Univ Iowa, 77-, Dir, Sch Relig, 79- **MEMBERSHIPS** Cath Theol Soc Am; Am Acad Relig; Soc Health & Human Values; Soc Christian Ethics. **RESEARCH** Church role in moral decisions; religion in public education; fundamental moral theology. **SELECTED PUBLICATIONS** Auth, Quality of Life--The New Medical Dilemma--Walter, Horizons, vol 0020, 93. **CONTACT ADDRESS** Sch of Relig, Univ of Iowa, 308 Gilmore Hall, Iowa City, IA, 52242-1376.

BOYS, SAMUEL A.
PERSONAL Born 07/07/1961, Plymouth, IN **DISCIPLINE** RELIGION, PSYCHOLOGY, ETHICS **EDUCATION** DePauw Univ, Greencastle, IN, BA, 84; Eden Theol Sem, St Louis, MDiv, 88. **CAREER** Ordained Minister, United Methodist Church; Chaplain: Bashor Children's Home; Prof of Ethics and Biblical Stud, Ancilla Coll. **HONORS AND AWARDS** Edu of the Ys, Ancilla Coll, 98. **MEMBERSHIPS** SBL, AAR. **RESEARCH** Biblical Ethics. **SELECTED PUBLICATIONS** Auth, The Messenger of the United Church, Where Have All the Morals Gone?, Biblical Ethics for the Next Generation. **CONTACT ADDRESS** 303 Colorado Dr, Goshen, IN, 46526.

BOZEMAN, THEODORE DWIGHT
PERSONAL Born 01/27/1942, Gainesville, FL, m, 1974 **DISCIPLINE** RELIGION, HISTORY **EDUCATION** Fla Presby Col, BA, 64; Union Theol Sem, New York, BD, 68; Union Theol Sem, Richmond, ThM, 70; Duke Univ, PhD, 74. **CAREER** From instr to asst prof, 74-78, from assoc prof to prof Am Relig Hist, Univ Iowa, 78-88; sr assoc mem, St. Antony's Coll, Oxford, 83-84. **MEMBERSHIPS** Am Soc Church Hist; Orgn Am Historians; Am Acad Relig; Southern Hist Assn. **RESEARCH** American religious history; history American religious thought; English and American Puritonism. **SELECTED PUBLICATIONS** Auth To Live Ancient Lives, The Primitivist Dimension in Puritonism, University of North Carolina, 88. **CONTACT ADDRESS** Sch of Relig, Univ of Iowa, 308 Gilmore Hall, Iowa City, IA, 52242-1376. **EMAIL** d-bozeman@uiowa.edu

BRAATEN, LAURIE
DISCIPLINE OLD TESTAMENT **EDUCATION** Eastern Nazarene Col, BA; Nazarene Theol Sem, Mdiv; Boston Univ, PhD. **CAREER** Ch, dept hist, Eastern Nazarene Col. **SELECTED PUBLICATIONS** Area: Old Testament. **CONTACT ADDRESS** Eastern Nazarene Col, 23 East Elm Ave, Quincy, MA, 02170-2999.

BRACEY, WILLIE EARL
PERSONAL Born 12/21/1950, Jackson, MS, m, 1987 **DISCIPLINE** LAW **EDUCATION** Wright Jr Coll, AA 1970; Mt Senario Coll, BS 1973; Eastern IL Univ, MS 1976; Southern IL Univ, JD 1979. **CAREER** Southern IL Univ, law clerk 1978-79; Southern IL Univ Ctr for Basic Skill, instr 1977-78; Southern IL Univ Law School, rsch asst 1977-78; Notre Dame Law School, teaching asst 1977; Western IL Univ, dir, student legal serv, 1979-87, asst vice pres for student affairs support servs; adj prof, college student personnel grad program, 1987-. **MEMBERSHIPS** Mem NAACP, 1979-, ATLA 1979-90, ABA 1979-90, IBA 1979-, McDonough City Bar Assn 1979-, Natl Assn of Student Personnel Admin 1987-; faculty mem Blue Key Honor Soc; Housing Commissoner, McDonough County Housing Authority, appointment ends 1998; Illinois Attorney General Date Rape Drugs Steering Committee, 1999. **CONTACT ADDRESS** Western Illinois Univ, One University Cir, Macomb, IL, 61455.

BRACKEN, JOSEPH A.
PERSONAL Born 03/22/1930, Chicago, IL **DISCIPLINE** PHILOSOPHY **EDUCATION** Xavier Univ, BA, 53; Loyola Univ, MA, 60; Univ of Freiburg, Germany, PhD, 68. **CAREER** St Mary's on the Lake Sem, asst prof, 68-74; Marquette Univ, assoc prof, 74-82; Xavier Univ, prof, 82-. **HONORS AND AWARDS** Col Theol Soc, Outstanding Book Award, 95 **MEMBERSHIPS** AAR, CTSA CTS MSA **RESEARCH** Trinitarian theo and process philo; comparative theol of relig; relig and science. **CONTACT ADDRESS** Dept of Theology, Xavier Univ, 3844 Victoria Parkway, Cincinnati, OH, 45207-1049. **EMAIL** bracken@xavier.xu.edu

BRACKEN, W. JEROME
PERSONAL Born 04/13/1940, Baltimore, MD **DISCIPLINE** THEOLOGY **EDUCATION** St Michael's Sem, MA, 68; Fordham Univ, PhD, 78. **CAREER** Assoc prof, St. Charles Bor-

romeo Sem, 89. **MEMBERSHIPS** Cath Theol Soc of Am; Fel of Cath Scholars. **RESEARCH** Sexual ethics; health care ethics; Christology; cognitive and affective learning. **SELECTED PUBLICATIONS** Auth, Roman Catholic Case Study, J of Ecumenical Stud, 90; auth, Roman Catholic Deliberations, J of Ecumenical Stud, 90; auth, Is the Early Embryo A Person?, Linacre Q, forthcoming. **CONTACT ADDRESS** Seton Hall Univ, South Orange, NJ, 07079. **EMAIL** brackeje@shu.edu

BRACKENRIDGE, ROBERT DOUGLAS
PERSONAL Born 08/06/1932, Youngstown, OH, m, 1954, 5 children **DISCIPLINE** HISTORY, CHURCH HISTORY **EDUCATION** Muskingum Col, BA, 54; Pittsburgh Theol Sem, BD, 57, ThM, 59; Glasgow Univ, PhD(church hist), 62. **CAREER** Pastor, Cross Rd United Presby Church, 58-60; from asst prof to assoc prof, 62-72, Prof Relig, Trinity Univ, Tex, 72-, Assoc, Danforth Found, 72- **HONORS AND AWARDS** Thornwell Award, 68; Piper Prof, Minnie Stevens Piper Found, 73; Distinguished Serv Award, Presby Hist Soc, 81. **MEMBERSHIPS** Presby Hist Soc (pres, 76-); Am Soc Church Hist; Am Acad Relig; Scottish Church Hist Soc. **SELECTED PUBLICATIONS** Auth, Power From on High--The Development of Mormon Priesthood--Prince, Rev Relig Res, vol 0037, 96; Dictionary of Scottish Church History and Theology--Cameron, Church Hist, vol 0064, 95; Dictionary of Scottish Church History and Theology--Cameron, Church Hist, vol 0064, 95; A History of Memphis-Theological-Seminary of the Cumberland-Presbyterian-Church, 1852-1990--Ingram, Am Presbyterians J, vol 0071, 93; A Contest of Faiths, Missionary Women and Pluralism in the American Southwest--Yohn, Am Presbyterians J, 96. **CONTACT ADDRESS** Dept of Relig, Trinity Univ, San Antonio, TX, 78287.

BRADEN, HENRY E., IV
PERSONAL Born 08/24/1944, New Orleans, LA, m **DISCIPLINE** LAW **EDUCATION** Le Moyne Coll, BS 1965; Loyola Univ Sch of Law, JD 1975. **CAREER** New Orleans Hometown Plan Urban League of New Orleans, author & dir 1974; Labor Educ & Advancement Prog, Total Community Action Inc, dir On-the-Job Training & Prog; Neighborhood Youth Corps Out of Sch Prog TCA Inc, dir 1966; LA Div of Employment Security, coord Hurricane Betsy Disaster Relief Proj 1965; City of New Orleans, past dir Ofc of Manpower & Economic Devel ; Murray, Murray, Ellis & Braden, atty private practice. **MEMBERSHIPS** Dem Nat Committeeman St of LA; Mem exec com Dem Natl Com Mem Met Area Com; LA Manpower Adv Com; columnist Op-ed; Page New Orleans States; exec vice pres Community Orgn for Urban Politics; New Orleans Industrial Devel Bd one of 3 blacks on LA Dem State Central Com; former pres St Augustines HS Alumni Assn; dir Building Dr St Augustines HS.

BRADIE, MICHAEL
PERSONAL Born 08/02/1940, Detroit, MI, m, 1969 **DISCIPLINE** PHILOSOPHY **EDUCATION** Mass Inst Technol, BS, 62; Boston Univ, MA, 65; Univ Hawaii, PhD(philos), 70. **CAREER** From instr to asst prof, 68-76, assoc prof, 76-81, Prof Philos, Bowling Green State Univ, 81-, Nat Endowment Humanities fel-in-residence philos, 76-77. **MEMBERSHIPS** Philos Sci Asn; AAAS; Am Philos Asn; Brit Soc Philos Sci. **RESEARCH** Philosophy of science; epistemology; analytic philosophy. **SELECTED PUBLICATIONS** Auth, Biology, Ethics and Animals--Rodd, Biology & Philosophy, vol 0012, 97; Created From Animals--The Moral Implications of Darwinism--Rachels, Biology & Philos, vol 0012, 97; Metaphor and Religious Language--Soskice, Zygon, Vol 0030, 95; Ontic Realism and Scientific Explanation, Philos Sci, vol 0063, 96; What Does Evolutionary Biology Tell Us About Philosophy and Religion, Zygon, vol 0029, 94; Philosophical Darwinism--On the Origin of Knowledge By Means of Natural Selection--Munz, Biology & Philos, vol 0011, 96. **CONTACT ADDRESS** Bowling Green State Univ, 1001 E Wooster St, Bowling Green, OH, 43403-0001.

BRADLEY, CRAIG M.
PERSONAL Born 12/05/1945, Downers Grove, IL, m, 1978, 2 children **DISCIPLINE** LAW **EDUCATION** Univ NC, AB, 67; Univ Va, JD, 70. **CAREER** Asst US Atty, Washington DC, 72-75; Law Clerk, Justice Rehnquist, US Supreme Court, 75-76; Sr Trial Atty, Public Integrity, US Dept Justice, 76-78; Vis Assoc Prof, Univ NC Law Sch, 78-79; James Louis Calamaras Prof Law, Ind Univ Sch Law, 79-; Vis Schol, Stanford Univ Law Sch, 85; Vis Lectr, Inst Int Law, 92. **HONORS AND AWARDS** Fulbright Sr Schol, Australian Nat Univ, 88-89; Alexander von Humboldt Schol, 82, 92. **MEMBERSHIPS** Am Bar Asn; AALS; Am Soc Comp Law. **RESEARCH** Criminal procedure; federal criminal law; comparative criminal law and procedure. **SELECTED PUBLICATIONS** Auth, The Failure of the Criminal Procedure Revolution, Univ Pa Press, 93; The Supreme Court's Two Models of the Fourth Amendment: Carpe Diem!, J Criminal Law and Criminol, 93; N.O.W. v Scheidler: When RICO Meets the First Amendment, Supreme Court Rev, 95; coauth, Public Perception, Justice, and The Search for Truth in Criminal Cases, Southern Calif Law Rev, 96; auth, The Rule of Law in an Unruly Age, Ind Law J, 96; ed and contribr, Criminal Procedure: A Worldwide View, Carolina Acad Press, 98; author of numerous other articles. **CONTACT ADDRESS** School of Law, Indiana Univ, Bloomington, Bloomington, IN, 47405. **EMAIL** bradley@law.indiana.edu

BRADLEY, DENIS J. M.
DISCIPLINE PHILOSOPHY **EDUCATION** Assumption Univ Windsor, BA; Univ Toronto. **CAREER** Prof. **SELECTED PUBLICATIONS** Auth, pubs on history of the faith-reason problematic in the Middle Ages, Aquinas's metaphysics and its relationship to post-Kantian transcendental philosophy, and Thomistic implications of philosophical pluralism. **CONTACT ADDRESS** Dept of Philosophy, Georgetown Univ, 37th and O St, Washington, DC, 20057.

BRADSHAW, DENNY
PERSONAL Born 04/05/1960, Estherville, IA **DISCIPLINE** PHILOSOPHY **EDUCATION** Mankato State Univ, BA, 82; Univ of Iowa, PhD, 88. **CAREER** Vis asst prof, Memphis State univ, 88-91; vis asst prof, Univ Ky, 91-92; asst prof, 92-98, assoc prof, 98- , Univ Texas, Arlington. **HONORS AND AWARDS** Summa Cum Laude, 82; fel, Phi Kappa Phi, 82-83; tchg-res fel, 82-83; grad col fel, 83-84; res grant, 96. **MEMBERSHIPS** AAUP; Texas Fac Asn; APA; Soc for Philos and Psych; Soc for Philos and Psych; Metroplex Inst for Neural Dynamics; N Texas Philos Asn. **RESEARCH** Metaphysics; epistemology; philosophy of mind; philosophy of language. **SELECTED PUBLICATIONS** Auth, Connectionism and the Specter of Representationalism, in Horgan, ed, Connectionism and the Philosophy of Mind, Kluwer, 91; auth, On the Need for A Metaphysics of Justification, Metaphilosophy, 92; auth, The Nature of Concepts, Philos Papers, 92; auth, The Non-Logical Basis of Metaphysics, Idealistic Stud, 96; auth, Meaning, Cognition, and the Philosophy of Thought: Vindicating Traditional Ontology, Jour of Philos Res, 98; auth, Patterns and Descriptions, Philos papers, forthcoming. **CONTACT ADDRESS** Dept of Philosophy and Humanities, Texas Univ, Arlington, TX, 76019-0527.

BRADY, JAMES B.
PERSONAL Born 08/30/1939, Harlingen, TX, m **DISCIPLINE** PHILOSOPHY, LAW **EDUCATION** Southern Methodist Univ, BA, 61; Univ Tex, JD, 64, PhD, 70. **CAREER** From lectr to asst prof, 67-73, assoc chmn, Dept Philos & dir undergrad studies, 70-72, assoc provost fac soc sci & admin, 72-75, co-dir, Baldy Ctr Law & Social Policy, 78-81, Assoc Prof Philos, State Univ NY Buffalo, 73-, Assoc ed, Tex Law Rev; res asst, State Bar Tex Comt Penal Code Rev, 66-67; vis mem, Linacre Col, Oxford Univ, 75. **SELECTED PUBLICATIONS** Auth, Recklessness, Law Philos, vol 0015, 96. **CONTACT ADDRESS** Dept of Philos, State Univ of NY, Buffalo, NY, 14222.

BRADY, JULES M.
PERSONAL Born 02/17/1919, St. Louis, MO **DISCIPLINE** PHILOSOPHY **EDUCATION** St Louis Univ, PhD, 49. **CAREER** Instr, 55-58, assoc prof, 68-70, Prof Philos, Rockhurst Col, 70. **MEMBERSHIPS** Am Cath Philos Asn. **SELECTED PUBLICATIONS** Auth, St Augustine's theory of seminal reasons, New Scholasticism, 4/64; Seminal reasons, In: New Catholic Encyclopedia, McGraw, 67; Note on the Fourth Way, spring, 74 & A contemporary approach to God's existence, winter, 77, New Scholasticism; An Augustine Treasury, Daughters of St Paul Press, 81; A Philospher's Search for the Infinite, Philos Libr, 82; An Aquinas Treasury, Publ Assoc, 88; New Approaches to God, Genesis Publ Co, 92; Newman for Everyone, Alba House, 96. **CONTACT ADDRESS** Dept of Philos, Rockhurst Col, 1100 Rockhurst Rd, Kansas City, MO, 64110-2561.

BRADY, MICHELLE E.
PERSONAL Born 01/15/1970, Lawrence, KS, s **DISCIPLINE** PHILOSOPHY **EDUCATION** BA, Haverford Col, 91; MA, 95, PhD, 98, Emory Univ. **CAREER** Teaching Instr, Emory Univ, 95-96, 98; Part-time Instr, 95-98, Georgia State Univ; Adjunct Faculty, Oglethorpe Univ, 98-. **HONORS AND AWARDS** Phi Betta Kappa, 91 **MEMBERSHIPS** Amer Phil Assoc **RESEARCH** Moral and Political Philosophy, Philosophical Antropology, Ancient Philosophy **CONTACT ADDRESS** Philosophy Dept, Emory Univ, Atlanta, GA, 30322. **EMAIL** mbrady@emory.edu

BRAITHWAITE, JOHN
DISCIPLINE LAW **CAREER** Vis prof. **SELECTED PUBLICATIONS** Auth, pubs on business regulation and criminal justice. **CONTACT ADDRESS** Fac of Law, Univ Toronto, 78 Queen's Park, Toronto, ON.

BRAITHWAITE, WILLIAM
DISCIPLINE LAW **EDUCATION** Windsor Univ, BA, 73; Univ Western Ontario, LLB, 76, LLM, 77. **CAREER** Law clerk, Justice Bora Laskin, Supreme Court Can; assoc dean, Osgoode Hall Law Sch, 82-83; prof. **MEMBERSHIPS** Chairman, Ontario Securities Commission Advisory Committee, 91-93 **SELECTED PUBLICATIONS** Auth, pubs on securities law. **CONTACT ADDRESS** Fac of Law, Univ Toronto, 78 Queen's Park, Toronto, ON.

BRAKAS, JURGIS
PERSONAL Born 11/14/1944, Copenhagen, Denmark, m, 1996 **DISCIPLINE** PHILOSOPHY **EDUCATION** Princeton Univ, AB, 68; Columbia Univ, PhD, 84. **CAREER** Part-time Asst Prof, Barnard Col (Columbia Univ), Queens Col & Baruch Col (CUNY), NYU, 88-90; Asst Prof, Marist Col, 90-. **HONORS AND AWARDS** Columbia Univ President's Fel, 72-73, 73-74. **MEMBERSHIPS** Amer Phil Assoc; Soc for Ancient Greek Phil; Ayn Rand Soc. **RESEARCH** Aristotle; logic; philosphy of logic **SELECTED PUBLICATIONS** Auth, Aristotle's Concept of the Universal, 88. **CONTACT ADDRESS** Dept of Philsophy, Marist Col, Poughkeepsie, NY, 12601. **EMAIL** jurgis.brakas@marist.edu

BRAKKE, DAVID
PERSONAL Born 05/10/1961, Long Beach, CA, s **DISCIPLINE** RELIGIOUS STUDIES **EDUCATION** Univ Va, BA, 83; Harvard Univ, M Div, 86; Yale Univ, MA, 87, M Phil, 89, PhD, 92. **CAREER** Visiting asst prof, relig, Concordia Col, 92-93; asst prof, relig, Ind Univ, 93-. **HONORS AND AWARDS** Mellon Fel in the Humanities; Ind Univ Outstanding Jr Facul. **MEMBERSHIPS** North Amer Patristic Soc; Amer Acad of Relig; Amer Soc of Church Hist; Intl Asn of Coptic Studies; Soc of Bibl Lit; Chicago Soc of Bibl Res. **RESEARCH** Early Christianity. **SELECTED PUBLICATIONS** Auth, Outside the Places, Within the Truth, Athanasius of Alexandria and the Localization of the Holy, Pilgrimage and Holy Space in Late Antique Egypt, Relig in the Graeco-Roman World, Leiden, Brill, 457-93, 98; co-reviser, Introduction to Christianity, 3rd ed, Belmont, Calif, Wadsworth, 97; auth, Athanasius of Alexandria and the Cult of the Holy Dead, Studia Patristica,32, 12-18, 97; auth, The Problematization of Nocturnal Emissions in Early Christian Syria, Egypt, and Gaul, Jour of Early Christ Studies, 3, 419-60, 95; auth, Athanasius and the Politics o Asceticism, Oxford Early Christian Studies, Clarendon Press, NY, Oxford Univ Press, 95; auth, The Greek and Syriac Versions of the Life of Antony, Le Museon, 107, 29-53, 94; auth, Canon Formation and Social Conflict in Fourth-Century Egypt: Athanasius of Alexandria's Thirty-Ninth Festal Letter, Harvard Theol Rev, 87, 395-419, 94; auth, The Authenticity of the Ascetic Athanasiana, Orientalia, 63, 17-56, 94. **CONTACT ADDRESS** Dept. of Religious Studies, Indiana Univ, Bloomington, Sycamore Hall 230, Bloomington, IN, 47405-2601. **EMAIL** dbrakke@indiana.edu

BRAKMAN, SARAH-VAUGHAN
DISCIPLINE PHILOSOPHY **EDUCATION** Mt Holyoke Col, BA, 86; Rice Univ, MA, 90, PhD, 94. **CAREER** Asst prof; ethics consult & voting mem, Ethics Comt, The Devereux Found, Devon, Pa, Jan 95-; Ethics Comt, The Grad Hosp, Philadelphia, Pa, Jan 94-; invited lect(s), papers & grand rounds; Ethical Traditions and Contemporary Life (joint), Nat Conf on Ethics and Popular Cult, The Ethics Ctr, Univ South Fa, Apr 96; Integenerational Responsibilities in Families: Who Owes What to Whom, Luncheon Lecture Series, The Ctr for Bioethics, Univ Pa, Apr 96; Moderator, Bioethics Symposium, Ethical Issues in Scientific Research, The Grad Hosp, Philadelphia, Pa, Mar 96; Filial Responsibilities and Gender: Who Owes What to Whom, Humanities Grand Rounds, Med Humanities Div, Med Col Pa and Hahnemann Univ, Sept 95; Intergeneraltional Responsibilities in Families: Who Owes What to Whom, Grand Rounds of the Dept Psychiat and Human Behavior, Jefferson Med Col, Thomas Jefferson Univ, June 95; Moderator Bioethics Symposium, Genetic Engineering: an Ethical Perspective, Grad Hosp, Philadelphia, Pa, Mar 95. **SELECTED PUBLICATIONS** Auth, The Case of the Golden Years: An Ethicist's Perspecitive, Bioethics Bul, 96; Adult Daughter Caregivers: Philosophical Analysis and Implications for Health Care Policy, A World Growing Old: The Coming Health Care Challenges, Washington, DC: Georgetown Univ Press, 95; Filial Responsibility and Long-Term Care Decision Making, Long-Term Care Decisions: Ethical and Conceptual Dimensions, Johns Hopkins Univ Press, 95: Daughter Caregivers: Philosophical Analysis and Implications for Health Care Policy, A World Growing Old: The Coming Health Care Challenges, Georgetown Univ Press, 95; Adult Daughter Caregivers, Hastings Ctr Report 24, 94; rev, Life and Death: Philosophical Essays in Biomedical Ethics, Cambridge Quart of Healthcare Ethics, 94; Teaching Tips, SHHV Stud Bul, 91. **CONTACT ADDRESS** Dept of Philosophy, Villanova Univ, 800 Lancaster Ave., Villanova, PA, 19085-1692.

BRAMANN, JORN KARL
PERSONAL Born 12/21/1938, Wuppertal, Germany **DISCIPLINE** PHILOSOPHY **EDUCATION** Univ Oregon, PhD, 71. **CAREER** Assoc Prof Philos, Frostburg State Univ. **RESEARCH** Theory of Culture, Motion Pictures. **SELECTED PUBLICATIONS** Capitol as Power, 84; Wittgenstein's Tractaties and the Modern Arts, 85; Traveling Light: An Introduction to Philosophy, 92, 98; Phantom Doors: A Mystery, 98. **CONTACT ADDRESS** Frostburg State Univ, Dept Philosophy, Frostburg, MD, 21532. **EMAIL** jornFsu@hotmail.com

BRAME, GRACE ADOLPHSEN
PERSONAL m **DISCIPLINE** THEOLOGY; SPIRITUALITY **EDUCATION** Wittenberg Univ, Bmus; Union Theol Sem, MSM; Temple Univ, MA, PhD 88. **CAREER** Villanova Univ, lectr 86-92; LaSalle Univ, grad, und grad 92-98. **HONORS AND AWARDS** Ezcell Ach Awd; Rep to APATS Conf; Delaware Women Rem; Legacy frm Del Women; Friends Cen Comm Res Gnt. **MEMBERSHIPS** CTSA; LSA; SSCS; CTS.

RESEARCH Contemplation and action; Lutheran spirituality; Comparative spirituality between Catholics Orthodox and Protestants; comparative spirituality between religions........ **SELECTED PUBLICATIONS** Auth, Faith: The Yes of the Heart, a response to Luther's Theology of the Heart, Augsburg, Fortress Press, forthcoming; Capacity for God: Evelyn Underhill's Theology of Spirituality, in progress; We have Tasted Eternity, The Lutheran, 98; Growing in Grace, The Lutheran, 97; Abide in Us, The Lutheran, 96. **CONTACT ADDRESS** Dept of Theology, La Salle Univ, 13 North Cliffe Dr, Wilmington, DE, 19809-1623.

BRAND, EUGENE L.
DISCIPLINE THEOLOGY **EDUCATION** Capital Univ, BA, 53; Lutheran Theol Sem, BD, 57; Heidelberg Univ, ThD; Lutheran Theol Sem, DD, 78; Christ Sem-Seminex, DHL, 81. **CAREER** Prof, Lutheran Theol Sem, 60-71; dir, Commn on Worship, Lutheran Church Am, 71-73; coord, Worship, LCA, 73-75; proj dir, Inter-Lutheran Commn on Worship, 75-78; dir, Office of Stud, Lutheran World Ministries, 77-81; Sec for Worship, Lutheran World Fed, 82-83; assoc dir, Dept Stud, sec, Interconfessional Dialogue and Ecclesiological Res, LWF, 84-90; asst gen sec, Ecumenical Aff, LWF, 90-96; distinguished intl prof in residence, 97-98. **HONORS AND AWARDS** Berakah Award, N Amer Acad Liturgy, 84; J. Sittler Award, Trinity Lutheran Sem, 91. **SELECTED PUBLICATIONS** Auth, Living Water and Sealing Spirit, Collegeville, 95; The Episcopal Office in the Nordic Lutheran Churches Seen from the Worldwide Perspective, Biskopsambetet, Nordisk Ekumenisk Skriftserie 23, Uppsala, 94; The Lutheran Common Service: Heritage and Challenge, Studia Liturgica 19, 89. **CONTACT ADDRESS** Hist, Theol, Soc Dept, Trinity Lutheran Sem, 2199 E Main St, Columbus, OH, 43209-2334. **EMAIL** ebrand@trinity.capital.edu

BRAND, MYLES
PERSONAL Born 05/17/1942, New York, NY, m, 1964, 1 child **DISCIPLINE** PHILOSOPHY **EDUCATION** Rensselaer Polytech Inst, BS, 64; Univ Rochester, PhD(philos), 67. **CAREER** From asst prof to assoc prof, Univ Ill, Chicago Circle, 67-76, prof, 76-81, chmn dept, 72-81; Prof Philos & Head Dept, Univ Ariz, 81- **MEMBERSHIPS** Am Philos Asn; Philos Sci Asn; Soc Philos & Psyhchol. **RESEARCH** Analytical metaphysics; philosophy of mind. **SELECTED PUBLICATIONS** Auth, Singing Guns, Am Hist, vol 0032, 97. **CONTACT ADDRESS** Dept of Philos, Univ of Ariz, Tucson, AZ, 85721.

BRANDOM, ROBERT D.
PERSONAL Born 03/13/1950, m, 1998, 2 children **DISCIPLINE** PHILOSOPHY **EDUCATION** Yale Univ, BA, 72; Princeton Univ, PhD, 77. **CAREER** Distinguished Service Prof, 76-, Univ of Pittsburgh. **SELECTED PUBLICATIONS** Auth, Making It Explicit: Reasoning, Representing and Discursive Commitment, Harvard Univ Press, 74; Study Guide to Sellars, Empiricism and the Philosophy of Mind, in: Empiricism and the Philosophy of Mind, Harvard Univ Press, 97; The Significance of Complex Numbers for Frege's Philosophy of Mathematics, Proceedings of the Aristotelian Society, 96; Knowledge and the Social Articulation of the Space of Reasons, Philosophy and Phenomenological Research, 95; Unsuccessful Semantics, Analysis, 94. **CONTACT ADDRESS** Dept of Philosophy, Univ of Pittsburgh, Pittsburgh, PA, 15260. **EMAIL** rbrandom@pitt.edu

BRANDON, ROBERT N.
DISCIPLINE PHILOSOPHY **EDUCATION** Harvard Univ, PhD, 77. **CAREER** Prof, Duke Univ. **RESEARCH** Logic. **SELECTED PUBLICATIONS** Auth, Adaptation and Environment, Princeton Univ, 90; co-ed, Genes, Organisms, Populations: Controversies over the Units of Selection, MIT, 84; publ(s) on philos sci. **CONTACT ADDRESS** Philos Dept, Duke Univ, West Duke Bldg, Durham, NC, 27706. **EMAIL** rbrandon@acpub.duke.edu

BRANDT, ERIC A.
PERSONAL Bloomington, IL **DISCIPLINE** RELIGIOUS STUDIES **EDUCATION** Univ Chicago, MA, 80; Columbia Univ, PhD, 90. **HONORS AND AWARDS** Res Grant from Amer Acad of Religion, 98. **MEMBERSHIPS** Amer Acad of Religion; Amer Phil Asn. **RESEARCH** Christianity and indigenous religions. **SELECTED PUBLICATIONS** Auth, Dangerous Liaisons Minorities in Conflict, NY New Press, 99. **CONTACT ADDRESS** 3856 19th St, No 4, San Francisco, CA, 94114. **EMAIL** brandtesf@aol.com

BRANDT, GREGORY J.
DISCIPLINE LAW **EDUCATION** Univ Saskatchewan, BA, 59; LLB, 61; Oxford Univ, BA, 64, MA, 68. **CAREER** Adj prof. **RESEARCH** Public law. **SELECTED PUBLICATIONS** Auth, pubs on constitutional law and labour law; coauth, Evidence and Procedure in Canadian Labour Arbitration. **CONTACT ADDRESS** Fac of Law, Univ Western Ontario, London, ON, N6A 3K7.

BRANDT, RICHARD BOOKER
PERSONAL Born 10/17/1910, Wilmington, OH, d, 2 children **DISCIPLINE** PHILOSOPHY **EDUCATION** Denison Univ, AB, 30; Cambridge Univ, BA, 33; Yale Univ, PhD, 36. **CAREER** From instr to prof philos, Swarthmore Col, 37-64; prof philos, Univ Mich, Ann Arbor, 64-81; Vis Prof, Law Ctr, Georgetown Univ, 82-, Guggenheim fel, 45-46; Fund Advan Educ fel, 53-54; fel, Inst Advan Studies Behav Sii, 69-70; Nat Endowment Humanities, 71-72; John Locke lectr, Oxford Univ, 74; assoc, Ctr Philos & Pub Policy, Univ Maryland, 80-81; vis prof, Fla State Univ, 81-82. **HONORS AND AWARDS** LittD, Denison Univ, 79. **MEMBERSHIPS** Am Philos Asn (vpres Eastern div, 64, Western div, 68, pres, 69); Am Soc Polit & Legal Philos (pres, 65-67); Soc Philos & Psychol (pres, 79-80). **RESEARCH** Ethics; epistemology; philosophy of mind. **SELECTED PUBLICATIONS** Auth, Conscience Rule Utilitarianism and the Criminal Law, Law Philos, vol 0014, 95. **CONTACT ADDRESS** Dept of Philos, Univ of Mich, Ann Arbor, MI, 48109.

BRANICK, VINCENT P.
PERSONAL Born 04/26/1941, San Francisco, CA, m, 1996, 3 children **DISCIPLINE** THEOLOGY, SCRIPTURE, BUSINESS ETHICS **EDUCATION** Pontifical Bibl Inst, SSD, 75; Univ Freiburg, PhilD, 71. **CAREER** Assoc prof of Relig & Philos, Chaminade Col of Honolulu, 73-78; prof Relig Studies, Univ Dayton, 77-; Woodrow Wilson fel. **MEMBERSHIPS** Cath Bibl Asn; Soc Bibl Lit. **RESEARCH** Biblical theology; Business ethics. **SELECTED PUBLICATIONS** Auth Wonder in a Technical World, An Introduction to Method and Writers of Philosophy, Univ Press Am, 80; The House Church in the Writing of Paul, Michael Glazier, 89; Understanding the New Testament and its Message, Paulist Press, 98. **CONTACT ADDRESS** Dept of Relig Studies, Univ of Dayton, Dayton, OH, 45469-1530. **EMAIL** branick@checkov.hm.udayton.edu

BRANSFORD WILSON, JR, JOE
DISCIPLINE SOUTH ASIAN STUDIES, RELIGIOUS STUDIES **EDUCATION** Univ Wis, Madison, BA, MA; Univ Va, PhD. **CAREER** Assoc prof Philos and Relig, asst ch and chair-elect, dept Philos and Relig, Univ NC, Wilmington. **RESEARCH** Yogacara School of Buddhism. **SELECTED PUBLICATIONS** Auth, Translating Buddhism from Tibetan: An Introduction to the Language of Literary Tibetan and the Study of Philosophy in Tibetan, Snow Lion, 92; Problems and Methods in the Translation of Buddhist Texts from Tibetan, in Buddhist Translations: Problems and Perspectives, Tibet House, 95; Tibetan Commentaries on Indian Shastras, in Jose Cabezon and Roger Jackson, eds, Tibetan Literature: Studies in Genre, Snow Lion, 96; Persons, Minds, and Actions: Indo-Tibetan Analyses of the Person in Anglo-American Perspective, in Ninian Smart and B Srinivasa Murthy, eds, East-West Encounters in Philosophy and Religion, Popular Prakashan, 96; The Monk as Bodhisattva: a Tibetan Integration of Buddhist Moral Points of View, J of Relig Ethics 24.2, 96. **CONTACT ADDRESS** Univ N. Carolina, Wilmington, Bear Hall, Wilmington, NC, 28403-3297. **EMAIL** wilsonj@uncwil.edu

BRANT, DALE
DISCIPLINE PHILOSOPHY **EDUCATION** Univ CA Irvine, BS, 86; BA, 86; MA, 91; PhD, 96. **CAREER** Philos, Valparaiso Univ. **HONORS AND AWARDS** Outstanding Hum tchg asst, Univ CA, 95; Regents Irvine Fel, Univ CA, 86-89; grad res fel, Univ CA, 86. **MEMBERSHIPS** Am Philos Asn. **RESEARCH** Metaphysics and epistemology; medieval philos; philos of relig; formal and informal logic, philos of lang; ancient philos and mod philos; ethics and soc/polit philos; philos of mind. **SELECTED PUBLICATIONS** Auth, On Plantinga's Way Out, Faith and Philos, 97. **CONTACT ADDRESS** Valparaiso Univ, 1500 E Lincoln Way, Valparaiso, IN, 46383-6493.

BRASSARD, FRANCIS
PERSONAL Born 02/16/1961, St. Hyacinthe, Canada, m, 1992, 1 child **DISCIPLINE** RELIGIOUS STUDIES **EDUCATION** McGill Univ, Phd, 97. **CAREER** Lectr, McGill Univ **HONORS AND AWARDS** Deans Honour List **RESEARCH** Mahayana Buddhism; South Asian religions. **SELECTED PUBLICATIONS** Forthcoming, The Concept of Bodhicitta in Shantidevas Bodhicarjauatara **CONTACT ADDRESS** 3355 ch Queen Mary, Apt 714, Montreal, PQ, H3V 1A5. **EMAIL** CYFB@musica.mcgill.CA

BRATTSTROM, BAYARD H.
PERSONAL Born 07/03/1929, Chicago, IL, m, 2 children **DISCIPLINE** BIOLOGY **EDUCATION** San Diego State Univ, BS, 51; Univ Calif, Los Angeles, MA, 53, PhD, 59. **CAREER** Asst to cur, 48-51, dir of ed, 49-51, Natural Hist Mus, San Diego; tchg asst, 51-56, assoc zool, 54-56, assoc prof zool, 62-63, Univ Calif, Los Angeles; instr biol, 56-60, Adelphi Univ; asst prof, assoc prof, prof, and prof emer, 60- , Calif State Univ, Fullerton. **HONORS AND AWARDS** Hon res assoc, Los Angeles County Mus of Natural Hist, 61-; mem council, AASS, 65-66, 69-72; NSF postdoc fel, 66-67; vis prof zool, Univ Queensland, 84; vis res, James Cook Univ, Queensland; res assoc Hubbs-Sea World Marine Res Inst, 81- ; fel, AAAS; fel, Herpetologists League. **MEMBERSHIPS** AAAS; Am Soc Zool; Ecol Soc Am; Soc Stud Evolution; Herpetologists League; Soc Systematic Zool; Soc Vertibrate Paleontol; Cooper Ornithological Soc; Am Ornithologists Union; Sigma Xi; Soc Stud Amphibians and Reptiles. **RESEARCH** Behavior; ecology; morphology and physiology of vertebrates, especially amphibians and reptiles; fossil reptiles; ecology; paleoecology; zoogeography; volcanoes; islands; deserts; tropics; urban ecology; habitat destruction. **SELECTED PUBLICATIONS** Auth, Wildlife Mortalities in PVC Claim Posts, Wildlife Soc Bull, 95; auth, Women in Science: Do We Ignore Female Role Models? Bull Ecol Soc Am, 95; auth, Super Skink Scooper: A Device for Catching Leaf Litter Skinks, Herpetology Rev, 96; auth, Developer's Devious Digressions; Environ Conserv, 96; auth, Evolution Is Not A Belief System, Daily Titan, 96; coauth, Surface Activity of the San Diego Horned Lizard, Phrynosoma coronatum blainvillei, Southwest Nat, 97; auth, Comments on Evolution and Religion, in Shermer, Why People Believe in Wierd Things, Freeman, 97; auth, The Circular Aesculepian Temple Tholos at Epidairos, Greece: An Early Snake Pit? Herpetology Rev, 98; auth, Strategies of Predator Attacks on The Schooling Fish, Selar crumenophthalmus, In Academy Bay, Socorro Island, Islas Revillagigedo, Mexico. Bull S Calif Acad Sci, 98; auth, coauth, Microhabitat Utilization by Some Queensland Australia Geckos, Dactylus, 98; auth, Seasonal and Microhabitat Partitioning of Calling Sites of Australian Frogs, Herpetofauna, 98; auth, Forensic Herpetology I: The Rattlesnake in the Mailbox Attempted Murder Case, Bull Chicago Herpetological Soc, 98; auth, Forensic Herpetology II: The McMartin Preschool Child Molestation Case and Alledged Animal Sacrifice and Torture, Including Reptiles. Bull Chicago Herpetological Soc, 98. **CONTACT ADDRESS** Dept of Biology, California State Univ, Fullerton, PO Box 6850, Fullerton, CA, 92834-6850. **EMAIL** bbrattstrom@fullerton.edu

BRAUCH, MANFRED T.
PERSONAL m, 3 children **DISCIPLINE** BIBLICAL THEOLOGY **EDUCATION** Houghton Col, BA; N Amer Baptist Sem, BD; Univ Hamburg, grad stud; Princeton Theol Sem, ThM; McMaster Univ, PhD. **CAREER** Prof, E Baptist Theol Sem. **MEMBERSHIPS** Mem, Inst for Biblical Res and Evangelicals for Soc Action. **SELECTED PUBLICATIONS** Auth, Hard Sayings of Paul, IVP, 89. **CONTACT ADDRESS** Eastern Baptist Theol Sem, 6 Lancaster Ave, Wynnewood, PA, 19096.

BRAUDE, BENJAMIN
DISCIPLINE HISTORY; RELIGION **EDUCATION** Harvard Univ, hist, BA, 67, MA, 75, PhD, 78. **CAREER** Affil, Ctr for Middle Eastern Studies, Harvard Univ, 67-; assoc dir and res assoc, Intl Sem-Conf on Minorities in the Middle East, Prog in Near Eastern Studies, Princeton Univ, 77-78; asst prof, dept of hist, Boston Col, 78-84; adjunct lectr, dept of theol, Boston Col, 79-; assoc prof, dept of hist, Boston Col, 84-; book rev ed, Mod Arab, Turkish, and Ottoman Hist and Polit Sci, Middle East Studies Asn Bull, 84-87; dir, Comt on Middle Eastern Studies, Boston Col, 86-; res assoc, dept of relig, Smith Col, 89-; **HONORS AND AWARDS** George W. Dillaway fel, 67-68; Sinclair Kennedy fel, 68; NDFL fel, 67-68, 68-69; Smith fel, 69-74; Bowdoin prize competition hon mention, 76-77; fel, Res Gp on Jewish World after 1492, Inst for Adv Studies, Hebrew Univ, Jerusalem, 91-92; res grant, Sassoon Intl Ctr for the Study of Antisemitism, 94-97; res grant, Lucius N. Littauer Found, 97. **MEMBERSHIPS** AHA; MESA; AJS. **RESEARCH** Middle Eastern, European, American and Jewish history, particularly issues of race and ethnicity. **SELECTED PUBLICATIONS** Article, Les Contours Indecis d'Une Nouvelle Geographie, Cahiers de Sci et Vie, no 44, 45-53, Apr, 98; article, The Sons of Noah and the Construction of Ethnic and Geographical Identities in the Medieval and Early Modern Periods, William and Mary Quart, 3rd series, vol 54, 103-142, Jan, 97; article, Burckhardt, Jean Louis, I, 427, Burton, Richard, I, 430, Canning, Stratford, I, 442-443, Dickson, Harold Richard Patrick, II, 569-570, Donme, II, 577-578, Doughty, Charles, II, 579, Lawrence, Thomas Edward, III, 1082, Millet System, III, 1224-1226, Minorities, III, 1229-1231, Palgrave, William Gifford, III, 1425, Pelly, Lewis, III, 1440, Philby, Harry St. John Bridger, III, 1461-1462, Thesiger, Wilfrid, IV, 1767, Encycl of the Mod Middle East, NY, 96; article, Mandeville's Jews among Others, Pilgrims and Travellers to the Holy Land, Proceedings of the Seventh Annual Symposium of the Philip M. and Ethel Klutznick Chair in Jewish Civilization, Omaha, 141-168, 96; article, Les Contes Persans de Menasseh Ben Israel: Polemique, Apologetique et Dissimulation a Amsterdam au xvii Siecle, Annales Hist, Sci Sociales, 49, 1107-1138, Sept-Oct, 94. **CONTACT ADDRESS** Dept. of History, Boston Col, Chestnut Hill, MA, 02467. **EMAIL** braude@bc.edu

BRAUER, JAMES L.
PERSONAL Born 09/29/1938, Julesburg, CO, m, 1964, 2 children **DISCIPLINE** THEOLOGY, MUSIC **EDUCATION** Concordia Col, AA, 58; Concordia Sr Col, BA, 60; Concordia Sem, MDiv, 64, STM, 67; Union Theol Sem, SMM, 72; CUNY, PhD, 83. **CAREER** Instr, Concordia Col, 65-71; from asst prof to prof, 71-87, exec dir, 87-91, Commission on Worship, Lutheran Church, Missouri Synod; guest instr, 90, assof prof practical theol, 91-98, prof, 98- chaplain, 91-92, dean of the chapel, 92- , Concordia Seminary. **MEMBERSHIPS** No Am Acad of Liturgy; Asn of Lutheran Musicians; Am Guild of Organists; Hymn Soc of N Am; Am Musicology Soc; Societas Liturgica;

Sixteenth Century Music Soc; Int Heinrich Schulz Soc. **RESEARCH** Music in the church; liturgy; the adult catechumenate. **SELECTED PUBLICATIONS** Composer, Trios on Four Advent/Christmas Carols for Strings, Winds or Organ, Concordia, 91; composer, When He Returns, SATB and Organ, Morning Star Music, 91; auth, The Church Year, in Lutheran Worship: History and Practice, Concordia, 91; auth, Does the Church Really Need the Adult Catechumenate Process, Lutheran Forum, 98; auth, Musica Contrafacta; Can Secular Music be Recycled for New Hymn Texts? Missio Apostolica, 98. **CONTACT ADDRESS** Concordia Sem, 801 DeMun Ave, St. Louis, MO, 63105. **EMAIL** brauerj@csl.edu

BRAUER, JERALD
PERSONAL Born 09/16/1921, Fond du Lac, WI, m, 1945, 3 children **DISCIPLINE** HISTORY OF CHRISTIANITY **EDUCATION** Carthage Col, AB, 43; Northwestern Lutheran Theol Sem, BD, 45; Univ Chicago, PhD, 48. **CAREER** Instr church hist & hist Christian thought, Union Theol Sem, NY, 48-50; from asst prof to prof church hist, 50-69, dean federated theol fac, 55-60, dean divinity sch, 60-70, Prof Hist Christianity, Univ Chicago, 69-, Naomi Shenstone Donnelley Prof, 69-, Kessler lectr, Hamma Divinity Sch & Wittenberg Col, 54; Merrick lectr, Ohio Wesleyan, 58; mem bd dirs, Rockefeller Theol Fel Prog & Inst Advan Pastoral Studies; trustee, Carthage Col; pres bd theol educ, Lutheran Church in Am, 62-68; deleg observer, Vatican Coun II, session 3, 64, session 4, 65; vis lectr, Univ Tokoyo & Kokagokuin Univ, 66; consult, NY State Dept Educ, 70-; vis fel, Ctr Studies Democratic Insts, 72 & 74; pres bd gov, Int House, 73-; Am Asn Theol Schs grant; fel, Ctr Policy Study, 74-79; Nat Endowment for Humanities fel, 77-78; chmn bd, Coun Relig & Int Affairs, 79- **HONORS AND AWARDS** DD, Miami Univ, 56; LLD, Carthage Col, 57; STD, Ripon Col, 61; LHD, Gettysburg Col, 63. **MEMBERSHIPS** Am Soc Church Hist (pres, 60). **RESEARCH** Puritanism influence in the United States and England; revivalism; religion in America. **SELECTED PUBLICATIONS** Auth, Paying the Words Extra--Religious Discourse in The Supreme-Court of the United-States--Sullivan, Int Rev Hist Relig, vol 0043, 96; Paying the Words Extra--Religious Discourse in the Supreme Court of the United States--Sullivan, Numen Int Rev Hist Relig, vol 0043, 96. **CONTACT ADDRESS** Divinity Sch, Univ of Chicago, 207 Swift Hall, Chicago, IL, 60637.

BRAUNGARDT, JURGEN
PERSONAL Born 03/02/1959, Coburg, Germany **DISCIPLINE** PHILOSOPHY **EDUCATION** Univ Munich, BA, 86; Jesuit Univ of Munich, MA, 87; Prof Sch of Psych, MA, 95; Grad Theol Union, Berkeley, PhD candidate. **CAREER** Author **MEMBERSHIPS** APA; Am Psych Assoc. **RESEARCH** Psychoanalysis, Frankfurt School. **CONTACT ADDRESS** 271 Vernon St, #303, Oakland, CA, 94610. **EMAIL** jurgen@autobahn.org

BRAXTON, EDWARD KENNETH
PERSONAL Born 06/28/1944, Chicago, IL, s **DISCIPLINE** THEOLOGY **EDUCATION** BA, 1966; MA, 1968; M, Div, 1969; STB, 1968; PhD, 1975; STD, 1976; Univ of Chicago, Postdoctoral Fellowship. **CAREER** Harvard Univ, 1976-77; Notre Dame Univ, visiting prof, 1977-78; Diocese of Cleveland, chancellor for theological affairs & personal theology; Archdiocese ofWashington, DC, chancellor for theological affairs, 1978-81; Rome North Amer Coll, scholar in residence, 1982-83; Univ of Chicago, Catholic Student Center, dir; William H Sadlier Inc, official theological cons; 1988 winter school lecturer, South Africa. **MEMBERSHIPS** Mem, Amer Acad of Religion; Catholic Theological Soc of Amer; Black Catholic Clergy Caucus; Catholic Bishop's Committee on Liturgy & Doctrine; bd of dir, St Mary of the Lake Seminary, Chicago; keynote speaker, 43 Intl Eucharistic Congress, Nairobi, Kenya; theological advisor to bishops of Africa & Madagascan, 1984; del, writer & speaker for Historic Natl Black Catholic Congress, Washington, DC 1987. **SELECTED PUBLICATIONS** Auth, The Wisdom Comm; numerous articles on Catholic Theological Religion; One Holy Catholic and Apostolic: Essays for the Community of Faith. **CONTACT ADDRESS** William H Sadlier Inc, 11 Park Place, New York, NY, 10007.

BRAYBROOKE, DAVID
PERSONAL Born 10/18/1924, Hackettstown, NJ, m, 1994, 7 children **DISCIPLINE** PHILOSOPHY **EDUCATION** Harvard Univ, BA, 48; Cornell Univ, MA, 51, PhD, 53. **CAREER** Prof philos and polit sci, 63-90, McCulloch Prof Emer Philos and Polit, Dalhousie Univ; prof govt, prof philos, Centennial Comn Chair Liberal Arts, Univ Texas, Austin, 90- . **HONORS AND AWARDS** Guggenheim fel, 62-63; fel Royal Soc of Can, 80- . **MEMBERSHIPS** Can Philos Asn; Can Polit Sci Asn; Am Philos Asn; Am Polit Sci Asn. **RESEARCH** Ethical theory, especially utilitarianism; deliberation in democracy; logic of rules. **SELECTED PUBLICATIONS** Coauth, Logic on the Track of Social Change, Oxford, 95; auth, Y-a-t-il une connaissance philosophique de la societe? in Proust, ed, La Connaissance Philosophique, Prassis Universitaires de France, 95; ed and contribur, Social Rules: Origin; Character; Logic; Change, Westview, 96; auth, Moral Objectives, Rules, and the Forms of Social Change, Univ Toronto, 98; auth, The Concept of Needs, with a Heartwarming Offer of Aid to Utilitarianism, in Brock, ed, Necessary Goods, Rowman & Littlefield, 98; contribur, Routledge Encyclopedia of Philosophy, Routledge, 98. **CONTACT ADDRESS** Dept of Government, Univ of Texas at Austin, Austin, TX, 78712-1087. **EMAIL** braeburn@jeeves.la.utexas.edu

BRECHT, ALBERT O.
DISCIPLINE LAW **EDUCATION** North Tex State Univ, BA,69 ; Univ Houston, JD,72; Univ Wash, MLL,73.. **CAREER** John Stauffer prof Univ Southern California , assoc dean & Ch inf off. **MEMBERSHIPS** Past pres, Amer Asn Law Libraries. **RESEARCH** Computerized legal research and the expanding role of law librarians in the scholarly mission of the faculty. **SELECTED PUBLICATIONS** Auth, The Impact of Automation on Academic Libraries & Changes in Legal Scholarship and Their Impact on Law School Library Reference Service. **CONTACT ADDRESS** School of Law, Univ Southern Calif, University Park Campus, Los Angeles, CA, 90089. **EMAIL** abrecht@law.usc.edu

BRECKENRIDGE, JAMES
PERSONAL Born 06/30/1935, St. Louis, MO, m, 1969, 2 children **DISCIPLINE** HISTORY OF RELIGIONS, CHURCH HISTORY **EDUCATION** Biola Col, BA, 57; Calif Baptist theol Sem, BD, 60; Univ Southern Calif, MA, 65, PhD(relig), 68. **CAREER** Lectr church hist & world relig hist, Am Baptist Sem the West, 67-74; ASSOC PROF HIST RELIG, BAYLOR UNIV, 74-, Lectr philos, Calif State Polytech Univ, 69-74. **MEMBERSHIPS** Am Acad Relig. **SELECTED PUBLICATIONS** Auth, Pelagius, Evangel Quart,70; Julian and Athanasius, theology, 73; Augustine and the Donatists, Foundations, 76; Religion and the problem of death, J Dharma, 79. **CONTACT ADDRESS** Dept of Relig, Baylor Univ, Waco, TX, 76703.

BREDECK, MARTIN JAMES
PERSONAL Born 11/05/1933, St. Louis, MO **DISCIPLINE** RELIGIOUS STUDIES, AMERICAN CATHOLICISM **EDUCATION** St Louis Univ, AB, 57, PhL, 58, MA, 58, STB, 66; Cath Univ Am, PhD(relig studies), 77. **CAREER** Instr class lang, St Louis Univ High Sch, 58-61; instr theol, St Joseph's Col, Pa, 71-74; lectr, Rockhurst Col, 74-76; asst prof relig studies, Mount St Mary's Col, Los Angeles, 76-78; asst prof, 78-81, assoc prof, 81-89; prof Theol & Relig Studies, Rockhurst Col, 89-. **HONORS AND AWARDS** Disting Serv Award 95; Exec Com MO St Conf AAUP; Who's Who Midwest, 26th Ed; Who's Who Wrld, 16th Ed. **MEMBERSHIPS** Am Acad Relig; Col Theol Soc; Am Assoc of Univ Profs. **RESEARCH** Cultural impact on Christianity; American pluralistic thought and Catholicism; space-age religious thought. **SELECTED PUBLICATIONS** The Question of Survival Revisited, Explorations, winter, 87; Imperfect Apostles, 88, Garland; Jesuit Theater in Italy: A Bibliography, AHSI, 97; **CONTACT ADDRESS** Rockhurst Col, 1100 Rockhurst Rd, Kansas City, MO, 64110-2561. **EMAIL** bredeck@vaxl.rockhurst.edu

BREEDEN, JAMES PLEASANT
PERSONAL Born 10/14/1934, Minneapolis, Minnesota **DISCIPLINE** THEOLOGY **EDUCATION** Dartmouth Coll, BA 1956; Union Theological Seminary NYC, MDiv 1960; Harvard Grad Sch of Educ, EdD 1972. **CAREER** Canon St Paul's Cathedral Episc Diocese of MA, 1963-65; Comm on Religion & Race Natl Council of Churches, asst dir, 1965-67; Comm on Church & Race MA Council of Churches, dir 1967-69; Harvard Grad Sch of Educ, assoc prof 1972-76; Univ of Das Salaam Tanzania, prof in ed 1973-75; Boston Public Schs, sr officer planning policy 1978-82; Ctr for Law & Ed, dir 1983-84; Dartmouth Coll, dean Wm Jewett Tucker Found 1984-. **HONORS AND AWARDS** Annual Award MA Soc Worker Assn 1964; The Young Men of Boston Boston Jr Chamber of Commerce 1965; Alper Award Civil Liberties Union MA 1978. **CONTACT ADDRESS** Wm Jewett Tucker Foundation, Dartmouth Col, Hanover, NH, 03755.

BREGMAN, LUCY
PERSONAL Born 12/18/1944, New York, NY **DISCIPLINE** RELIGIOUS STUDIES **EDUCATION** Brown Univ, BA, 66; Univ Chicago, MA, 70, PhD, 73. **CAREER** Asst prof, IN Univ, Bloomington, 72-74; asst prof, 74-80, assoc prof, 80-98, prof, Dept of Religion, Temple Univ, Philadelphia, PA, 98-. **HONORS AND AWARDS** Finch Symposium Lect, Fuller Theol Sem, 89. **MEMBERSHIPS** Am Academy of Relig; Soc for the Scientific Study of Relig; Asn for Death Ed & Counseling. **RESEARCH** Religion & psychology; death & dying. **SELECTED PUBLICATIONS** Auth, The Rediscovery of Inner Experience, Nelson-Hall, 82; Through the Landscape of Faith, Westminster, 86; Death in the Midst of Life, Baker Book House, 92; with Sara Thieimann, First Person Mortal: Autobiographies of Illness, Death & Grief, Paragon House, 95. **CONTACT ADDRESS** 238 McClellan St, Philadelphia, PA, 19148. **EMAIL** bregman@vm.temple.edu

BREHM, H. ALAN
PERSONAL m, 3 children **DISCIPLINE** NEW TESTAMENT **EDUCATION** Howard Payne Univ, BA, 83; Southwestern Baptist Theol Sem, MDiv, 86; PhD, 92. **CAREER** Adj tchr, 90-92; asst prof, 92-. **HONORS AND AWARDS** President's Scholar, Southwestern Sem, 83-84; Fulbright Scholar, Univ Tuebingen, 89-90., Pastor, Naruna Baptist Church, 81-83; Vaughan Baptist Church, 86-89. **MEMBERSHIPS** Soc Biblical Lit; Inst Biblical Res. **SELECTED PUBLICATIONS** Auth, Will the Real Jesus Please Stand? Evaluating the 'Third Quest of the Historical Jesus', Southwestern Jour Theol, 96; The Meaning of Hellenistes in Acts in Light of a Diachronic Analysis of Hellenizein, JSOT Press, 95; Paul's Relationship with the Jerusalem Apostles in Galatians 1 and 2, Southwestern Jour Theol, 94; The Significance of the Summaries for Interpreting Acts, Southwestern Jour Theol, 90. **CONTACT ADDRESS** Sch Theol, Southwestern Baptist Theol Sem, PO Box 22000, Fort Worth, TX, 76122-0418. **EMAIL** hab@swbts.swbts.edu

BRENNAN, JAMES FRANKLIN
PERSONAL Born 07/05/1932, Peoria, IL **DISCIPLINE** LAW **EDUCATION** Georgetown Univ, BS, 55; Univ Calif, Berkeley, MA, 60, PhD(hist), 63. **CAREER** Teaching asst Europ hist, Univ Calif, Berkeley, 60-62; asst prof, Ripon Col, 63-66; asst prof, 66-67, ASSOC PROF EUROP HIST, CENT WASH UNIV, 67- **MEMBERSHIPS** AHA; Am Asn Advan Slavic Studies. **RESEARCH** History of the labor and socialist movements in Russia; eighteenth century Russia. **SELECTED PUBLICATIONS** Auth, Between Hope and History in Meeting America Challenges For the 21st Century, Harvard J on Legislation, Vol 0034, 97; To Renew America, Harvard J on Legislation, Vol 0034, 97. **CONTACT ADDRESS** Dept of Hist, Central Washington Univ, Ellensburg, WA, 98926.

BRENNAN, MARY ALETHEA
PERSONAL Born 06/11/1909, Larksville, PA **DISCIPLINE** PHILOSOPHY CLASSICS **EDUCATION** Col Mt St Vincent, BA, 30; Cath Univ Am, MA, 44, PhL, 48, PhD(philos), 50; Univ Freiburg & Univ Dublin, 62. **CAREER** Instr chem & math, Cathedral High Sch, New York, NY, 34-35, chem, 35-41, head dept, 41-43; instr chem & Latin, 44-45, asst prof Latin, 45-47, from instr to assoc prof philos, 50-76, ADJ ASSOC PROF PHILOS, COL MT ST VINCENT, 76- **MEMBERSHIPS** Am Philos Soc; Am Cath Philos Asn; Metaphys Soc Am; Cath Class Asn (pres, 43-44). **RESEARCH** Science, especially chemistry. **SELECTED PUBLICATIONS** Auth, Religion, Law, and Power, the Making of Protestant Ireland, 1660-1760, Albion, Vol 0025, 93; Neither Kingdom Nor Nation in the Irish Quest For Constitutional-Rights, 1698-1800, Albion, Vol 0027, 95. **CONTACT ADDRESS** Dept of Philos, St Josephs Coll, Mt View, CA, 94039.

BRENNEMAN, WALTER L.
PERSONAL Born 12/05/1936, Harrisburg, PA, m, 1963, 6 children **DISCIPLINE** HISTORY OF RELIGION **EDUCATION** Gettysburg Col, BA; Univ Chicago, BA; Union Inst, PhD. **CAREER** Prof relig, Univ Ver, 68- . **MEMBERSHIPS** Am Acad Relig; Am Comt Irish Stud. **RESEARCH** Irish Celtic religion; Irish Celtic Christianity; phenomenological method. **SELECTED PUBLICATIONS** Auth, Spirals: A study in Symbol, Myth and Ritual, Univ Press Am, 78; coauth, The Seeing Eye: Hermeneutical Phenomenology in the Study of Religion, Penn State, 82; coauth, Crossing the Circle at the Holy Walls of Ireland, Univ Press of Vir, 95. **CONTACT ADDRESS** HLR32, PO Box 760, Montpelier, VT, 05602. **EMAIL** wbrennem@zoo.uvm.edu

BRENNEN, BONNIE
DISCIPLINE MEDIA ETHICS **EDUCATION** Calif State Univ, BA; Univ Iowa, PhD. **CAREER** Asst prof, 96-; **RESEARCH** Mass communications, communications history, media, society and popular culture. **SELECTED PUBLICATIONS** Co-ed, Newsworkers: Toward a History of the Rank and File, Univ Minn Press, 95; contribu, Jour Am Hist; Comm Theory; Comm Quart; Studies Popular Cult; Jour Comm Inquiry. **CONTACT ADDRESS** Va Commonwealth Univ, 600 W Franklin Street, Richmond, VA, 23220.

BRENNER, WILLIAM H.
DISCIPLINE PHILOSOPHY OF RELIGION **EDUCATION** Univ Va, PhD, 70. **CAREER** Philos, Old Dominion Univ. **RESEARCH** Wittgenstein, logic. **SELECTED PUBLICATIONS** Auth, Logic and Philosophy ;Elements of Modern Philosophy. **CONTACT ADDRESS** Old Dominion Univ, 4100 Powhatan Ave, Norfolk, VA, 23058. **EMAIL** WBrenner@odu.edu

BREST, PAUL
PERSONAL Born 08/09/1940, Jacksonville, FL, m, 1962, 2 children **DISCIPLINE** LAW **EDUCATION** Swarthmore Col, AB, 62; Harvard Univ, LLB, 65. **CAREER** PROF LAW, STANFORD UNIV, 69-, Vis prof law, Yale Univ, 77-78. **HONORS AND AWARDS** DL, Northeastern Univ, 80. **MEMBERSHIPS** Am Acad Arts & Sci. **RESEARCH** Legal theory; legal education. **SELECTED PUBLICATIONS** Auth, Plus Ca Change, Mich Law Rev, Vol 0091, 93; The Impact of information Technology on Judicial Administration in A Research Agenda For the Future, Southern Calif Law Rev, Vol 0066, 93; Legal Pedagogy in Discussion, Stanford Law Rev,

Vol 0045, 93; Ethics, Values, and Diversity in the Legal Academy in Discussion, Stanford Law Rev, Vol 0045, 93; On Teaching Professional Judgment, Wash Law Rev, Vol 0069, 94; Affirmative-Action For Whom, Stanford Law Rev, Vol 0047, 95; The Responsibility of Law-Schools in Educating Lawyers As Counselors and Problem Solvers, Law and Contemp Problems, Vol 0058, 95; Transformation in South-Africa in Cause and Effect--introductory Remarks, Stanford J Int Law, Vol 0032, 96. **CONTACT ADDRESS** Law Sch, Stanford Univ, Stanford, CA, 94305-1926.

BRETT, NATHAN C.
DISCIPLINE PHILOSOPHY OF LAW **EDUCATION** Univ New Hampshire, BA, 64; Univ Waterloo, MA, 68, PhD, 72. **CAREER** Assoc prof. **RESEARCH** Ethics, theories of justice, modern philosophy. **SELECTED PUBLICATIONS** Auth, "Hume on Personal Identity," Phil Quart, 72; Human Habits, CJP, 81; Property Rights and Justice, Man and Nature, 87; "Language Laws and Group Rights," Can Jour of Law and Jurisprudence, 91; "Mercy and Criminal Justice," Can Jour of Law and Jurisprudence, 92. **CONTACT ADDRESS** Dept of Philos, Dalhousie Univ, Halifax, NS, B3H 3J5. **EMAIL** nathan.brett@dal.ca

BRETZKE, JAMES T.
PERSONAL Born 02/22/1952, Milwaukee, WI, s **DISCIPLINE** MORAL THEOLOGY **EDUCATION** Pontifical Gregorian Univ, STD, 89 **CAREER** Asst Prof, 90-93, Pont Greg Univ; Asst Prof, 93-pres, Jesuit Sch of Theol **MEMBERSHIPS** SCE, CTSA, CTS, AAR, PCTS **RESEARCH** Cross Cultural Ethics, Scripture and Ethics; Korean Confucianism & Christianity **SELECTED PUBLICATIONS** Auth, Bibliography on Scripture and Christian Ethics, Edwin Mellen Press, 97; Auth, Consecrated Phrases, A Latin Dictionary of Theological Terms, Liturgical Press, 98 **CONTACT ADDRESS** Grad Theolog Union, Jesuit Sch of Theol, Berkeley, 1735 LeRoy Ave, Berkeley, CA, 94709-1193. **EMAIL** jbretzke@jstb.edu

BREWBAKER, WILLIAM S., III
DISCIPLINE LAW **EDUCATION** Vanderbilt Univ, 81; Univ Va, 86; Duke Univ, LLM, 93. **CAREER** Asst prof, 93; assoc prof, Univ Ala, 96-. **RESEARCH** Health care law, antitrust law, and property. **CONTACT ADDRESS** Law Dept, Univ of Alabama, Box 870000, Tuscaloosa, AL, 35487-0383. **EMAIL** wbrewbak@law.ua.edu

BREYER, STEPHEN GERALD
PERSONAL Born 08/15/1938, San Francisco, CA, m, 1967, 2 children **DISCIPLINE** LAW **EDUCATION** Stanford Univ, AB, 59; Oxford Univ, BA, 61; Harvard Univ, LLB, 64. **CAREER** Law clerk to Justice Goldberg, US Supreme Court, 64-65; spec asst to Asst US Atty Gen for Antitrust, US Dept Justice, 65-67; from asst prof to assoc prof, 67-75, PROF LAW, LAW SCH, HARVARD UNIV, 75-, Consult, Econ Coun of Can, 68-; mem, White House Task Force on Common Policy, 68-; Senate Commerce Comt, 70-; mem, Kennedy inst Polit, 71-; asst spec prosecutor, Watergate Spec Prosecution Force, 73; mem, Spec Coun, US Senate Judiciary Comn, 74-75, chief coun, 79-81; prof govt, J F Kennedy Sch, 78-81; judge, US Court Appeals for Ist Circuit, 81-; judicial rep, Admin Conf of US. **RESEARCH** Economic regulation; antitrust. **SELECTED PUBLICATIONS** Auth, The Federal Judicial Law Clerk Hiring Problem and the Modest March One Solution, Yale Law J, Vol 0104, 94. **CONTACT ADDRESS** Law Sch, Yale Univ, New Haven, CT, 06520-8306.

BRICKER, DANIEL P.
PERSONAL Born 08/15/1954, Little Rock, AR, s **DISCIPLINE** RELIGION **EDUCATION** Moody Bib Inst, BA, 77; Talbot Theol Sem, MDiv, 80; Fuller Theol Sem, PhD, 98. **CAREER** Azusa Pacific Univ, adj prof, 98-. **MEMBERSHIPS** ETS, SBL **RESEARCH** OT wisdom lit; Hebrew poetry; ancient near east studies and languages; Hebrew prophets; archaeology. **SELECTED PUBLICATIONS** Auth, The Doctrine of the Tow Ways in the Book of Proverb, Jour of the Evan Theo Society, 95; rev, The Book of Proverbs: A Survey of Modern Study, by R.N. Whybray, in: Jour of the Evan Theol Society, 97. **CONTACT ADDRESS** 1725 N Sierra Bonita, Pasadena, CA, 91104. **EMAIL** db21@aol.com

BRICKMAN, LESTER
PERSONAL Born 09/04/1940, New York, NY **DISCIPLINE** LAW **EDUCATION** Carnegie inst Technol, BS, 61; Univ Fla, LLB, 64; Yale Univ, LLM, 65. **CAREER** From asst prof to prof law, Univ Toledo, 65-76; actg dean, 80-82, PROF LAW, CARDOZO SCH LAW, YESHIVA UNIV, 76-, Dep dir, Asn Am Law Schs Study Wave Surv, 66-67; vis res prof, Coun Legal Educ for Prof Responsibility, 69-70, consult, 69-78; consult, Legal Serv, 67-75, hearing examr, Ohio Civil Rights Comn, 67-70; consult, Toledo Model Cities Prog, 68-69, Ford Found, 70-71, NCent Asn, 72, Law Enforcement Assistance Admin, 74, Nat Sci Found, 75-, Am Bar Asn Spec Comt on Specialization, 75 & US office Educ, 78. **MEMBERSHIPS** Law & Society Asn. **RESEARCH** Legal services delivery systems; legal paraprofessionals. **SELECTED PUBLICATIONS** Auth, Nonrefundable Retainers in A Response to Critics of the Absolute Ban, Univ Cincinnati Law Rev, Vol 0064, 95; Aba Regulation of Contingency Fees in Money Talks, Ethics Walks, Fordham Law Rev, Vol 0065, 96; Contingency Fees--Should Plaintiffs Lawyers in the Tobacco Settlement Receive Billions of Dollars--No--Congress Should Set the Fees For this Unique Case, Aba J, Vol 0083, 97. **CONTACT ADDRESS** Benjamin N Cardozo Sch of Law, Yeshiva Univ, 55 5th Ave, New York, NY, 10033-4301.

BRIER, BOB
PERSONAL Born 12/13/1943, New York, NY **DISCIPLINE** PHILOSOPHY **EDUCATION** Hunter Col, BA, 64; Univ NC, Chapel Hill, PhD(philos), 70. **CAREER** From asst prof to assoc prof, 71-80, PROF PHILOS, C W POST COL, LONG ISLAND UNIV, 80-. **MEMBERSHIPS** Am Philos Asn; Philos Sci Asn; Australasian Philos Sci Asn; AAAS; Parapsychol Asn. **RESEARCH** Ancient Egyptian philosophy. **SELECTED PUBLICATIONS** Auth, The use of Natron in Human Mummification in a Modern Experiment--Zeitschrift fur Agyptische Sprache und Altertumskunde, Vol 0124, 97. **CONTACT ADDRESS** CW Post Campus, Long Island Univ, Coll Arts & Sci, GREENVALE, NY, 11548.

BRIETZKE, PAUL H.
PERSONAL Born 07/30/1944, Chicago, IL, m, 1970, 1 child **DISCIPLINE** LAW **EDUCATION** Lake Forest Col, BA, 66; Univ Wis, JD, 69; Univ London, PhD(law), 79. **CAREER** Lectr law, Univ Malawi, 70-73; asst prof, Addis Abeba Univ, 73-75; lectr, Brunel Univ, England, 75-78; prof law, Valparaiso Univ, 78-, Nat Endowment for the Humanities fel, 80. **HONORS AND AWARDS** Phi Beta Kappa. **MEMBERSHIPS** Int Third World Legal Studies Asn; Soc Pub Teachers Law; Am Soc Political & Legal Philos. **RESEARCH** Comparative law; antitrust law; law and economics. **SELECTED PUBLICATIONS** Coauth, Traditional Courts Manual, Malawi Govt Printer, 72; auth, Murder & Manslaughter in Malawi's Traditional Courts, J African Law, 74; The Childbwe Murders Trials, African Studies Rev, 74; co-ed, Legal Analysis Teaching Materials, Addis Abeba Univ Press, 74; coauth, Ethiopia, Weltforum-Verlag, Munich, 76; auth, The Rightness of the Rightness of Things, Valparaiso Univ Law Rev, 79; Socialism & Law in the Ethopian Revolution, Rev Socialist Law, 81; Law, Development & the Ethiopian Revolution, Bucknell Univ Press, 82. **CONTACT ADDRESS** Dept of Law, Valparaiso Univ, 651 College Ave, Valparaiso, IN, 46383-6493. **EMAIL** Paul.Brietzke@valpu.edu

BRIGGS, JOHN
PERSONAL Born 01/08/1945, Detroit, MI, m, 1968 **DISCIPLINE** AESTHETICS AND PSYCHOLOGY, JOURNALISM **EDUCATION** Wesleyan Univ, college of Letters, Honors, BA, 68; NY Univ, MA, 72; The Union Inst, PhD, 81. **CAREER** English teacher, Patchogue High School, 68-71; Humanities fac, 73-87; adjunct fac, Brooklyn Col, 74; adjunct English dept fac, Mercy Col, 74-87; freelance sci writer, 81-; assoc prof, journalism coordr, WCSU, 87-95; prof, journalism coordr, WCSU, 95-; adjunct fac, Union Inst, 95-. **HONORS AND AWARDS** Listed in: Who's Who in the World; Who's Who in the East; Who's Who in Am Educ; Int Authors and Writers Who's Who; Contemporary Authors. **MEMBERSHIPS** Am Asn of Univ Profs; The National Writers' Union; The Sci and Medical Network; The Am Soc for Aesthetics. **RESEARCH** New science; aesthetics, creativity, war. **SELECTED PUBLICATIONS** Coauth, Looking Glass Universe, Simon and Schuster, 84; auth, Fire in the Crucible: The Alchemy of Creative Genius, St. Martin's Press, 88; coauth, Turbulent Mirror: an Illustrated Guide to Chaos Theory and the Science of Wholeness, Harper and Row, 89; coauth, Fractals: The Patterns of Chaos, Simon & Schuster, Touchstone, 92; auth, "Nuance, Metaphore and the Rhythm of the Mood Wave in Virginia Woolf", in Virginia Woolf Miscellanies: Proceedings of the First Annual Conference on Virginia Woolf, Pace Univ, 92; auth, "The Balm of Irony", in Voices on the Threshold of Tomorrow, Quest Books, 93; auth, "Dialogue between John Briggs and Morris Berman on the Possibility of Social Creativity and Its Attendant Dangers in Mass Society", in Troisiome Millionaire, 94; auth, "Exploring the Potentials of Creative Dialogue", ICIS Forum, 94; auth, "Chaos, Fractals, Aesthetics and the Environment", The Network, 94; auth, "Nuance and Omnivalence in the Creative Mind" in Advanced Development, A Journal of Adult Giftedness, 97. **CONTACT ADDRESS** Western Connecticut State Univ, White Street, Danbury, CT, 06810. **EMAIL** briggsjp@wcsu.ctstateu.edu

BRIGHOUSE, M.H.
PERSONAL Born 06/14/1963, Stockport, OK, m, 1991, 1 child **DISCIPLINE** PHILOSOPHY **EDUCATION** USC, PhD, 92 **CAREER** Asst Prof, 91-92, UC Davis; Assoc Prof, 98-pres, UW Madison **HONORS AND AWARDS** Cornell Univ, Inst for Ethics and Pub Life, Young Scholar, 98 **MEMBERSHIPS** APA **RESEARCH** Political Philosophy; Philosophy of Education **SELECTED PUBLICATIONS** Auth, School Choice: Some Theoretical Considerations, Verso, 98; Auth, Civic Education and Liberal Legitimacy, Ethics vol 108 no 4, 98, 719-745; Auth, Why Should States Fund Schools, British Journal of Educational Studies, 98 **CONTACT ADDRESS** Dept of Philos, 5119, UWisconsin Madison, 500 N Park St, Madison, WI, 53706. **EMAIL** brigthous@macc.wisc.edu

BRINK, DAVID O.
PERSONAL Born 01/16/1958, Minneapolis, MN, m, 2 children **DISCIPLINE** PHILOSOPHY **EDUCATION** Univ Minn, BA, 80; Cornell Univ, MA, 83; PhD, 85. **CAREER** Instr, Cornell Univ, 84; vis asst prof, Stanford Univ, 86; asst prof, Case W Res Univ, 85-87; asst prof, Mass Inst Technol, 87-91; asn prof, Mass Inst Technol, 91-94; Univ Calif, San Diego, asn prof, 94-96; Univ Calif, San Diego, full prof, 96-. **HONORS AND AWARDS** Old Dominion Fel, 90; Nat Endowment Humanities, 90-91; Andrew W Mellon, 90-91; Fel Center Advan Study Behav Scis, 90-91; Univ Calif Pres Fel, 98. **MEMBERSHIPS** Am Philos Asn. **RESEARCH** Ethical Theory; History of Ethics; Political Philosophy; Jurisprudence. **SELECTED PUBLICATIONS** Auth, Moral Realism and the Foundations of Ethics, 89; The Separateness of Persons, Distributive Norms, and Moral Theory, Value, Welfare and Morality, 93; Common Sense and First Principles, Sidgwick's Methods, Social Philosphy & Policy and Cultural Pluralism and Moral Knowledge, 94; A Reasonable Morality, Ethics, 94; Moral Conflict and Its Structure, The Philos Rev, 94,, Moral Dilemmas and Moral Theory, 95; Le Realisme Moral, Dictionaire de Philosphie Morale, 96; Rational Egoism and the Separateness of Persons, Reading Parfit, 97; Kantian Rationalism: Inescapability, Authority, and Supremacy, Ethics and Practical Reasons, 97; Self-love and Altruism, Soc Philos and Policy, 97; Moral Motivation, Ethics, 97; Eudaimonism, Love and Friendship, and Political Community, Soc Philos and Policy, 99; Legal Interpretation, Objectivity, and Morality, Objectivity in LAward and Morals, 99. **CONTACT ADDRESS** Philosophy Dept, Univ Calif San Diego, 9500 Gilman Dr, La Jolla, CA, 92093-0119.

BRINKMAN, JOHN T.
DISCIPLINE HISTORY OF RELIGION **EDUCATION** Fordham Univ, PhD, 88. **CAREER** Inst of Asian Stud, St John's Univ, 89-97. **MEMBERSHIPS** AAAS; AAR. **RESEARCH** Ecological dimension of world religion; East Asian thought; history of religions with refined focus in the sequence; Japan; Chiina; India; **SELECTED PUBLICATIONS** Auth, The Simplicity of Dogen, Eastern Buddhist, 94; auth, Harmony, Attribute of the Sacred and Phenomenal in Aquinas and Kukai, Buddhist-Christian Stud, 95; auth, The Simplicity of Nichiren, Eastern Buddhist, 95; auth, Simplicity: A Distinctive Quality of Japanese Spirituality, Peter Land, 96; auth, Cosmology and Consciousness, Buddhist-Christian Studies, 98; auth, The Kyoto Protocol and Exigent Ecological Vision, Int Shinto Found Symp Proc, 98-99. **CONTACT ADDRESS** 2 Darthouth Rd, Shoreham, NY, 11786.

BRINKMANN, KLAUS
PERSONAL Born 09/21/1944, Germany, m, 1974, 2 children **DISCIPLINE** PHILOSOPHY **EDUCATION** Univ Tubingen, PhD. **CAREER** Lectr, Univ Bonn, 79-82 & 84-88; Asst Prof, Philosophy, Boston Univ, 82-83; Asst Prof, Univ Tubingen, 84-89; assoc prof, philosophy, Boston Univ. **MEMBERSHIPS** Allgerneine Gesellsdraft fur Philos; Amer Philos Asn; Hegel Soc N Amer; N Amer Fichte Soc; Soc Ancient Greek Philos. **RESEARCH** Aristotle; German idealism; Hegel. **SELECTED PUBLICATIONS** Auth, Jaspers and Heidegger on Platos Idea of the Good, Heidegger and Jaspers, Temple Univ Press, 94; Tugendhat on Fichte and Self-Consciousness, Fichte: Historical Contexts/Contemporary Problems, Hum Press, 94; Hegels Critique of Kant and Pre-Kantian Metaphysics; Hegel and Transcendental Philosophy, Kluwer Acad Publ, 94; Kurswissen Politische Philosophie: Staat-Recht-Politik, Stuttgart-Dresden, 95; The Consistency of Aristotles Thought on Substance, Aristotles Philosophical Development, Problems and Prospects, Rowman & Littlefield, 95; Le platonisme de l Eudeme reexamine, L Aristote perdu, Roma-Atene, 95; Hegel on the Animal Organism, Laval theologique et philosophique, 96; Zenon fut-il meterialiste et nominaliste?, Diotima, 97; Hegel sur le cogito cartesien, Laval theologique et philosophique, 98; Egalite politique et inegalite factuelle: La reponse aristotelicienne a un dilemme politique, La Societa Civile et la Societa Politica nel Pensiero di Aristotele, Roma, 98; Jaspers and Arendt on Communication and Politics, Jahrbuch der Osterreichischen Karl-Jaspers-Gesellschaft, 98. **CONTACT ADDRESS** Philosophy Dept, Boston Univ, 745 Commonwealth Ave., Boston, MA, 02215. **EMAIL** brinkman@bu.edu

BRISCO, THOMAS V.
PERSONAL m, 2 children **DISCIPLINE** BIBLICAL BACKGROUNDS AND ARCHAELOLOGY **EDUCATION** Ouachita Baptist Univ, BA, 69; Southwestern Baptist Theol Sem, MDiv, 73; Southwestern Baptist Theol Sem, PhD, 81; advan stud, Cambridge Univ, 86. **CAREER** Tchg fel, Southwestern Baptist Theol Sem, 75-76; instr, Ouachita Baptist Univ, 77-80; instr, 80-82; asst prof, 82-90; assoc prof, 90-; assoc dean, Spec Masters Degrees. **HONORS AND AWARDS** David Meier Intl Stud League Award, Southwestern Baptist Theol Sem, 74; Outstanding Young Men of Am, 78, 79; Who's Who Among Students in Amer Univ(s) and Col(s), 76; Who's Who Among Biblical Archaeol., Interim pastor, Kingsland Baptist Church, 96-97; First Baptist Church, 95-96; First Baptist Church, Humble, 94-95; Intl Baptist Church, 93; First Baptist Church, Arkadelphia, 92-93; VP, Amer Sch(s) Oriental Res, 82-83; president, 83-84; VP, Nat Assn Baptist Prof(s) Rel, 91; pres, 92. **SELECTED PUBLICATIONS** Auth, Biblical Illustrator, Baptist Sunday Sch Bd, 79; Intl Standard Bible Encycl, Eerdmans, 88;

contrib, Holman Bible Dictionary, Broadman & Holman, 91. **CONTACT ADDRESS** Sch Theol, Southwestern Baptist Theol Sem, PO Box 22000, Fort Worth, TX, 76122-0418. **EMAIL** tvb@swbts.swbts.edu

BRISTER, C.W.
PERSONAL LA, m, 1 child **DISCIPLINE** THEOLOGY **EDUCATION** La Col, BA, 47; New Orleans Baptist Sem, BD, 52, M.Div, 73; Southwestern Baptist Theolog Sem, Th.D, 57, PhD, 74. **CAREER** Hultgren Distinguished prof, Southwestern Baptist Theolog Sem, 57-. **HONORS AND AWARDS** Who's Who Soc; Who's Who Rel; Directory Am Scholar; Who's Who South and Southwest., Toward MBA Fel Economics, 48-49, La State; NC Baptist Sch Pastoral Care, 60; Res Fel, 69-70, Southwestern Medical Sch. **MEMBERSHIPS** Baptist World Alliance; Am Asn Marriage & Family Therapy; Asn Clinical Pastoral Educ; Soc Pastoral Theolog; Family Systems Ministries Int. **RESEARCH** Clergy and missionary care. **SELECTED PUBLICATIONS** Auth, Pastoral Care in the Church, 92; auth, Change Happens: Finding Your Way Through Life's Transitions, 97. **CONTACT ADDRESS** Box 22036, Fort Worth, TX, 76122-0036. **EMAIL** cwb@swbts.swbts.edu

BRISTOW, CLINTON, JR.
PERSONAL Born 03/15/1949, Montgomery, Alabama, m, 1975 **DISCIPLINE** LAW **EDUCATION** Northwestern University, Evanston, IL, BS, 1971, JD, 1974, PhD, 1977; Governors State University, University Park, IL, MBA, 1984 **CAREER** Roosevelt University, Chicago, IL, professor, 1976-79; Olive-Harvey College, Chicago, IL, vice-president, 1979-81; Chicago State University, Chicago, IL, professor, chairperson, dean, 1981-; Alcorn State Univ, pres, 1981-95, 1995-. **HONORS AND AWARDS** Legal Opportunity Scholarship Awardee, Northwestern Univ, 1971; Urban Affairs Fellow, Northwestern Univ, 1976; Top Ladies of Distinction Role Model, TLOD Inc, 1987; Outstanding Educator Award, City of Chicago, Department of Human Services, 1991. **MEMBERSHIPS** President, Chicago Bd of Education, 1990-92. **CONTACT ADDRESS** President, Alcorn State Univ, 1000 ASU Dr, #359, Lorman, MS, 39096.

BRITT, BRIAN M.
PERSONAL Born 08/28/1964, Omaha, NE, m, 1989, 2 children **DISCIPLINE** RELIGION **EDUCATION** Oberlin Col, BA, 86; Univ Chicago, MA, 87, PhD, 92. **CAREER** Asst prof, relig & phil, 92-96, Wesleyan Col; asst prof, relig, 96-, Virginia Tech. **HONORS AND AWARDS** Dean's Grant, Ed Tech, 97; Vulcan Co Tchng Award, Wesleyan Col, 96; Phi Kappa Phi, 96; Natl Found Jew Culture Res Grant, 91; Inst Advan Stud of Relig, Jr Fel, 91-92; Divinity Schl Fel, 89-91; Divinity Schl Milo Jewett Prize, 89, 91; Phi Beta Kappa, Zeta of OH, 86. **MEMBERSHIPS** AAR; Soc of Bibl Lit; SE Conf Stud of Relig; Intl Walter Benjamin Assn. **SELECTED PUBLICATIONS** Art, The Aura of Benjamin's Untimely Death: An Interview With Lisa Fittko, Continuum 2, 93; art, Archive of Pure Language: Language and Scared Text in Benjamin's Philosophy, Continuum 3, 91; auth, Georgia Rallies 'Round the Flag', The Nation, 93; auth, Religious Right Runs Rampant: State of the Arts in Cobb County, The Nation, 94; auth, Walter Benjamin and the Bible, Continuum, 96; art, The Veil of Allegory in Hawthorne's The Blithedale Romance, Lit & Theol 10, 96; auth, Neo-Confederate Culture, Z Mag, 96; art, Snapshots of Belief: Apparitions of the Virgin Mary in Conyers, Georgia, Nova Religio, 98. **CONTACT ADDRESS** Religious Studies Program, Virginia Tech, Blacksburg, VA, 24061-0135. **EMAIL** bbritt@vt.edu

BROADIE, SARAH
DISCIPLINE PHILOSOPHY **EDUCATION** Oxford Univ, MA, 64; Edinburgh Univ, PhD, 78. **CAREER** Lectr, Univ Edinburgh, 67-84; prof, Univ Tex Austin, 84-86; prof, Yale Univ, 86-91; prof, Rutgers Univ, 91-93; prof, 93-. **HONORS AND AWARDS** Guggenheim Found fel; Fel of the Acad of Arts and Sci. **MEMBERSHIPS** Am Philos Asn; Am Asn for Univ Prof; Soc for Ancient Greek Philos. **SELECTED PUBLICATIONS** Auth, Ethics with Aristotle, 93. **CONTACT ADDRESS** Dept of Philosophy, Princeton Univ, 1879 Hall, Princeton, NJ, 08540.

BROCK, DAN W.
PERSONAL Born 12/05/1937, Mineola, NY, m, 1969, 1 child **DISCIPLINE** PHILOSOPHY **EDUCATION** Cornell Univ, BA, 60; Columbia Univ, PhD(philos), 70. **CAREER** Asst prof, 69-75, assoc prof, 75-79, PROF PHILOS, BROWN UNIV, 80-, Chmn Prog Bio-Med Ethics, 74-. **MEMBERSHIPS** Am Philos Asn; Am Soc Polit & Legal Philos. **RESEARCH** Ethics; political philosophy; biomedical ethics. **SELECTED PUBLICATIONS** Auth, Children of Choice in Freedom and the New Reproductive Technologies, Tex Law Rev, Vol 0074, 95; A Model State Act to Authorize and Regulate Physician Assisted Suicide, Harvard J on Legislation, Vol 0033, 96. **CONTACT ADDRESS** Ctr Biomed Eth, Brown Univ, Providence, RI, 02912.

BROCKELMAN, PAUL
DISCIPLINE PHILOSOPHY **EDUCATION** Northwestern Univ, PhD, 68. **CAREER** Prof, Univ NH, 63-. **RESEARCH** Existential phenomenology; phenomenology of religion; philosophy of religion; environmental theology; cosmology. **SELECTED PUBLICATIONS** Auth, The Inside Story: A Narrative Approach to Religious Understanding and Truth, SUNY, 92. **CONTACT ADDRESS** Philosophy Dept, Univ of New Hampshire, Hamilton Smith Hall, Durham, NH, 03824. **EMAIL** ptb@hopper.unh.edu

BROCKOPP, JONATHAN E.
DISCIPLINE RELIGIOUS STUDIES **EDUCATION** Valparaiso Univ, BA, 84; Yale Univ, MPhil, 92, PhD, 95; Am Univ in Cairo; Bourguiba Inst (Tunisia); Tubingen Univ (Germany). **CAREER** Adj asst prof, Fairfield Univ, 91; teach asst, Yale Univ, 91-92; vis lect, Amherst Col, 92-93; teach asst, Yale Univ, 94; Asst Prof Rel, Bard Coll. **HONORS AND AWARDS** Fulbright fel, 90-91; Yale Univ fel, 82-83, 88-93; Am Res Ctr in Egypt grant, 95; Bard Col Fac Res Travel grant, 96. **MEMBERSHIPS** Am Acad Rel; Am Inst Maghrib Stud; Am Oriental Soc; Am Res Ctr Egypt; Middle East Stud Asn. **RESEARCH** Islamic law; women and Islam; Arabic lang and lit; rel ethics. **SELECTED PUBLICATIONS** Auth, Early Islamic Jursiprudence in Egypt: Two Scholars and their Mukhtasars, Int J Middle East Studies, 98; auth, Re-reading the History of Early Maliki jurisprudence, J Am Oriental Soc, 98; auth, Islam, in The Pilgrim Library of World Religions, Pilgrim Press, 97; auth, Sources for Studying Islam, in The Pilgrim Library of World Religions, Pilgrim Press, 97. **CONTACT ADDRESS** Dept of Religion, Bard Col, Annandale, NY, 12504. **EMAIL** brockopp@bard.edu

BROD, HARRY
PERSONAL Born 02/01/1951, Berlin, Germany, m, 1980, 2 children **DISCIPLINE** PHILOSOPHY **EDUCATION** Univ Cal SD, PhD 81, MA 75; Ruhr Univ Germany, Fulbright Gnt, 76-77; NY Univ, BA 68-72. **CAREER** Temple Univ, asst prof; Univ Delaware, asst prof 94; Mount St Mary's College LA lecrt, Univ Cal LA lectr, Antioch Univ LA adj fac, Los Angeles Pasadena Sch Dist inst/edu, 92-94; Kenyon College, vis assoc prof 88-92; Harvard Law Sch, fel 87-88; Univ S Cal, lectr, sr lect, asst prof, 82-87; Cal State SB, lect 81-82; Palomar College, inst 78-80; Univ Cal SD, tch asst 73-78. **HONORS AND AWARDS** Fulbright Fel; Choice Outstanding Acad Book. **RESEARCH** Gender studies; political philosophy; Hegal. **SELECTED PUBLICATIONS** Auth, Theorizing Masculinity's, coed, Sage Pub, 94; Hegal's Philosophy of Politics: Idealism Identity and Modernity, Westview Press, 92; Who's Afraid of Lorena Bobbitt?, Second Thoughts: Critical Thinking from a Multicultural Perspective, ed Wanda Teays, Mayfield, 96; Of Mice and Supermen: Images of the Jewish Masculinity, gender and Judaism, ed, Tamar M. Rudavsky, NY Univ Press, 95, reprint, in: Redeeming Men: Essays on Men Masculinity's and Religion, eds, Stephen B Boyd, Merle Longwood, Mark W Muesse, Westminster; John Knox Press, 96; Gender Violence: Interdisciplinary Perspectives, eds, Laura O'Toole, Jessica R. Schiffman, reprinted, NYU Press, 96. **CONTACT ADDRESS** Dept of Philosophy, Temple Univ, 215 Pelman Rd, Philadelphia, PA, 19119.

BRODSKY, GARRY
DISCIPLINE ETHICS, SOCIAL AND POLITICAL PHILOSOPHY **EDUCATION** Brooklyn Col, BA, 54; Yale Univ, MA, 58; PhD, 61. **CAREER** Dept Philos, Univ Conn **HONORS AND AWARDS** BA with hon(s), 54. **RESEARCH** Nietzsche, Modernity and Postmodernity; ethics; social and politcal philosophy. **SELECTED PUBLICATIONS** Co-auth, Contemporary Readings in Social and Political Ethics, Prometheus Bk(s), 84; auth, A Way Of Being A Jew, A Way Of Being A Person, Goldberg and Krausz, Culture and Jewish Identity, Temple Univ Press, 93; West's Evasion of Pragmatism, Praxis Intl, 94. **CONTACT ADDRESS** Dept of Philos, Univ Conn, 344 Mansfield Rd, Storrs, CT, 06269.

BRODY, BORUCH ALTER
PERSONAL Born 04/21/1943, New York, NY, m, 1965 **DISCIPLINE** PHILOSOPHY **EDUCATION** Brooklyn Col, BA, 62; Princeton Univ, MA, 65, PhD(philos), 67. **CAREER** Lectr philos, Hunter Col, 66-67; from asst prof to assoc prof, Mass inst Technol, 67-75; Prof Philos, Rice Univ, 75-, PROF MEDICINE & DIR, CTR ETHICS, MED, PUB ISSUES, BAYLOR COL MED, 82-. **RESEARCH** Metaphysics; philosophy of law, philosophy & medicine. **SELECTED PUBLICATIONS** Auth, The Ends of Human Life in Medical Ethics in a Liberal Policy, Law and Soc inquiry--J Amer Bar Found, Vol 0018, 93; Just Doctoring in Medical Ethics in the Liberal State, Law and Soc inquiry--J Amer Bar Found, Vol 0018, 93. **CONTACT ADDRESS** Baylor Col of Med, Houston, TX, 77030.

BROGAN, DORIS DELTOSTO
DISCIPLINE LAW **EDUCATION** Rowan/Glassboro State Col, BA, 74; Villanova Univ Sch Law, JD, 81. **CAREER** Prof; Villanova Univ, 83-; assoc dean, Acad Aff, 92-. **HONORS AND AWARDS** Distinguished Alumna awd, Rowan/Glassboro St Col, 87. **MEMBERSHIPS** Amer Bar Asn; Pa and Philadelphia Bar Asn; bd dir, Del Co Legal Asst Asn. **RESEARCH** Ethics, domestic relations, abuse; conflict of laws. **SELECTED PUBLICATIONS** Auth, Attorney Client Privilege and Conflicts of Interest & Legal Ethics for Trial Lawyers, Pa Trial Lawyers Ass'n Course Text, 92; Lawyers' Responses to Client Perjury Under the New Pennsylvania Rules of Professional Conduct-What Judges Can Expect, 34 Vill L. Rev 63, 89; Divorce Settlement Agreements: The Problem of Merger or Incorporation and the Status of the Agreement in Relation to the Decree, 67 Neb L. Rev 235, 88 & The Domestic Relations Exceptions to Fed Diversity Jurisdiction, Matrimonial Litigation: Across State Lines, PBI Program Course Text, 85. **CONTACT ADDRESS** Law School, Villanova Univ, 800 Lancaster Ave, Villanova, PA, 19085-1692. **EMAIL** brogan@law.vill.edu

BROGAN, WALTER A.
DISCIPLINE PHILOSOPHY **EDUCATION** Catholic Univ, BA, 68; Northern Ill Univ, MA; Duquesne Univ, PhD, 81. **CAREER** Prof. **SELECTED PUBLICATIONS** Auth, Is Plato's Drama the Death of Tragedy, Int Stud in philos, 91; The Decentered Self: Nietzsche's Transgression of Metaphysical Subjectivity, The Southern J of Philos, 91; Haunting Resonances at the Threshold of Contemporary Philosophy, a rev article on Echoes After Heidegger by John Sallis, Research in Phenomenology, XXIII, 93; Twisting out of Metaphysics in John Sallis and the Path of Archaic Thinking, SUNY Press, 95; The Place of Aristotle in the Development of Heidegger's Phenomenology, Reading Heidegger from the Start SUNY Press, 94; The Tragic Figure of the Last Philosopher, Res in Phenomenol, 94; Heidegger's Aristotelian Reading of Plato: The Discovery of the Philosopher, Res in Phenomenol, 95; coauth, The Socratic Method: A Philosophical Assessment of Outcome-Based Education, Educ Forum, 95; co transl, Martin Heidegger, Aristotle's Metaphysics IX, 1-3: On the Essence and Actuality of Force, Ind Univ Press, 94. **CONTACT ADDRESS** Dept of Philosophy, Villanova Univ, 800 Lancaster Ave., Villanova, PA, 19085-1692.

BRONIAK, CHRISTOPHER
PERSONAL Born 04/05/1957, Detroit, MI, s **DISCIPLINE** PHILOSOPHY **EDUCATION** Loyla Univ, PhD, 97. **CAREER** Sr lectr, Loyola Univ, 89-94; adjunct, Roosevelt Univ, 97. **HONORS AND AWARDS** Summer fel, Loyola Univ, 89; tchg fel, Loyola Univ, 88-89, 90-91. **MEMBERSHIPS** APA; Am Cath Philos Asn; SAAP; SPEP; IAPL. **RESEARCH** Phenomenology; American pragmatism. **SELECTED PUBLICATIONS** auth, "Duty or Virtue as a Metaethical Question," Dialogos, 90; rev, Eugene Taylor's "William James on Consciousness Beyond the Margin," Trans of the Charles S. Peirce Soc, 96; auth, "James' Theory of Fringes," Trans of the Charles S. Peirce Soc, 96. **CONTACT ADDRESS** 6807 N Sherican Rd, Apt 612, Chicago, IL, 60626. **EMAIL** cbroniak@aon.com

BROOK, ANDREW
DISCIPLINE PHILOSOPHY **EDUCATION** Univ of Alberta and Oxford, PhD, 73. **CAREER** Vis scholar, Queen's Univ, 95; vis tutor, Univ Oxford, 95; fac, Toronto Inst of Contemp Psychoanalysis, 92-; assoc dean of grad stud, 79-80; Wexler vis prof, Bryn Mawr Col, 98-99; dir, Inst Interdisciplinary Stud, 91-; ch, Cognitive Sci Mgt Comm; prof-. **HONORS AND AWARDS** Lorne J Calhoun scholar for extra-curricular act, Univ Alberta, 65; Francis J Reeves grad scholar, Univ Alberta, 65-66; Woodrow Wilson fel, 65; Rhodes scholar, Alberta, 66; Carleton Univ Merit award, 77-78; SSHRC Leave fel and res grant, 79-80; Carleton Univ Scholarly Achievement award, 86; Levin prize, Can Psychoanalytic Soc, 91; Marston Lafrance res fel, Carleton Univ, 91-92; Prado Prize (joint winner), Can Psychoanalytic Soc, 94., Treasurer, Can Philos Assn; ch, Ed Comm, Can Lib Philos, 77-79; assoc ed, Intl Jour/Rev of Psychoanalysis, 90-92; ed bd, Can Jour of Psychoanalysis, 94-. **MEMBERSHIPS** Clinical mem, Can Psychoanalytic Soc. **RESEARCH** The project of interdisciplinary cognitive research, Kant. **SELECTED PUBLICATIONS** Auth, Kant and the Mind, Cambridge UP, 94, 2nd ed, 96, pb, 97; coauth, "Schopenhauer and Freud," Intl Jour of Psychoanalysis, 75, 94; "Fodor's New Theory of Content and Computation," Proc of the 18th Annual Conf of the Cognitive Sci Soc, Ablex, 96; auth, "Charles Taylor's Reconciling the Solitudes," Bulletin of the Soc of Socialist Stud, 94; "Kant and Cognitive Science," Proc of the 16th Annual Conf of the Cognitive Sci Soc, Ablex, 94; "Explanation in the Hermeneutic Science," Intl Jour of Psychoanalysis 76, 95; "Realism in the Refutation of Idealism," Proc of the 8th Intl Kant Cong, Marquette UP, 95; "Cognitive Science and Two Images of the Person," Proc of the 17th Annual Conf of the Cognitive Sci Soc, Ablex, 95; 0. Jackendoff and Consciousness, Pragmatics and Cognition 4, 96; Also Mind and Language 12, 97; Waste Management: Examples from the Nuclear Fuel Cycle, Contemp Moral Issues, McGraw Hill Ryerson, 97; Also in Canadian Issues in Applied Environmental Ethics, Broadview Press, 97; Reconciling the Two Images, in: Two Sciences of Mind, J. Benjamin, 97; "Approaches to Abstraction: A commentary," Intl Jour of Edu Res, 97; "Unity of Consciousness and Other Mental Unities," Proc of the 19th Annual Conf of the Cognitive Sci Soc, Ablex Press, 97. **CONTACT ADDRESS** Dept of Philos, Carleton Univ, 1125 Colonel By Dr, Ottawa, ON, K1S 5B6.

BROOKS, CATHERINE M.
DISCIPLINE LAW **EDUCATION** Thomas More Col Fordham Univ, BA; Fordham Univ, MA; Univ Va, JD. **CAREER** Prof Creighton Univ; past vis asst prof, Seton Hall Univ Sch

Law; served pvt pract; asst dep Public Defender, NJ Dept Pub Advocate, 83-88; app, Nebr Gov Comn on Juv Justice, 97. **HONORS AND AWARDS** Named 1 of 10 Outstanding Young Omahans, 94., Dir and co-founder, Ctr for the Study Childrens Issues, Creighton Univ. **MEMBERSHIPS** Nebr Permanency Plan Task Force; bd dir, Big Brothers Big Sisters Omaha. **SELECTED PUBLICATIONS** Auth, The Law's Response to Child Abuse and Neglect, Law, Mental Health, and Mental Disorder; ed & coauth, Nebr Juvenile Ct Procedures Manual; publ in, Lawyers for Children; Behavioral Sci and the Law; Criminal Behavior and Mental Health & Creighton Law Rev. **CONTACT ADDRESS** School of Law, Creighton Univ, 2500 California Plaza, Omaha, NE, 68178. **EMAIL** brooks@culaw.creighton.edu

BROOKS, ROY LAVON
PERSONAL Born 03/07/1950, New Haven, Connecticut, m **DISCIPLINE** LAW **EDUCATION** University of Connecticut, BA (magna cum laude), 1972; Yale University, JD, 1975. **CAREER** United States District Court, law clerk, 1975-77; Yale Law Journal, editor, 1975; Cravath, Swaine, & Moore, corporate attorney, 1977-79; University of San Diego, School of Law, professor, starting 1979; University of Minnesota, School of Law, professor, currently. **MEMBERSHIPS** Heartland Human Relations Assn, board of directors, 1984-86; NAACP San Diego Chapter, board of directors, 1987. **SELECTED PUBLICATIONS** Author of numerous publications including: Foreign Currency Translations, 1980; Small Business Financing, 1981; Affirmative Action in Law Teaching, 1982. **CONTACT ADDRESS** School of Law, Univ of Minnesota, 285 Law Center, Minneapolis, MN, 55455-0100.

BROSS, JAMES BEVERLEY
PERSONAL Born 11/21/1938, Knoxville, TN, m, 1959, 4 children **DISCIPLINE** RELIGION; HISTORY **EDUCATION** Cent Wesleyan Col, AB, 59; Univ Ill, MA, 65; Univ Iowa, PhD(relig), 72. **CAREER** Teacher math, Tenn Pub Schs, 59-60, 62-63 & All Tribes Indian Mission Sch, 60-62; instr, Southern Wesleyan Univ, 63-64; asst prof, Iowa Wesleyan Col, 65-68; teacher, Iowa Publ Schs, 72-73; Prof Relig, Southern Wesleyan Univ, 73-. **MEMBERSHIPS** Wesleyan Theol Soc; Am Soc Church Hist; Conf Faith & Hist; Evangelical Theol Soc. **RESEARCH** Puritanism in England; American religion. **CONTACT ADDRESS** Southern Wesleyan Univ, P O Box 1020, Central, SC, 29630-1020. **EMAIL** jbbross@hotmail.com

BROUDY, HARRY S.
PERSONAL Born 07/27/1905, Filipowa, Poland, m, 1947, 1 child **DISCIPLINE** PHILOSOPHY OF EDUCATION **EDUCATION** Boston Univ, AB, 29; Harvard Univ, MA, 33, PhD, 35. **CAREER** Supvr adult educ, Mass Dept Educ, 36-37; prof philos educ, Mass State Col North Adams, 37-49, Framingham, 39-57; PROF PHILOS, UNIV ILL, URBANA, 57-, Lectr, Cornell Univ, 62; Boyd H Bode lectr, Ohio State Univ, 63; ed, Educ Forum, 64-73; fel Ctr Advan Study Behav Sci, 67-68; consult, Educ Res Coun Am, Cleveland, 66-80; distinguished vis prof, Mem Univ, St John's Nfld, 74, Calif State Univ, Los Angeles, 78; Emens distinguished prof, Ball State Univ, 82. **HONORS AND AWARDS** DH, Oakland Univ, 69, Mass State Col, 81; DHL, Eastern Ky State Univ, 79. **MEMBERSHIPS** Philos Educ Soc (pres, 54); Asn Realistic Philos (pres, 55-56); Am Philos Asn; Metaphys Soc; Am Soc Aesthet. **RESEARCH** Aesthetic education; uses of schooling in nonschool situations; Polanyi's tacit knowing. **SELECTED PUBLICATIONS** Auth, Thoughts on Art Education, J Aesthetic Educ, Vol 0027, 93. **CONTACT ADDRESS** Col of Educ, Univ Illinois, Chicago, IL, 60680.

BROUGHTON, JANET SETZER
PERSONAL Born 08/23/1948, New York, NY, m, 1972 **DISCIPLINE** PHILOSOPHY **EDUCATION** Univ Calif, Davis, AB, 72; Princeton Univ, PhD(philos), 77. **CAREER** Instr Philos, Harvard Univ, 76-77, asst prof, 77-79; asst prof Philos, Univ Calif, Berkeley, 79-83; dept chmn, 89-94. **MEMBERSHIPS** Am Philos Asn. **RESEARCH** History of seventeenth and eighteenth century philosophy. **CONTACT ADDRESS** Dept of Philosophy, Univ of California, Berekely, 314 Moses Hall, Berkeley, CA, 94720-2391. **EMAIL** broughtn@socrates.berkeley.edu

BROWER, BRUCE W.
DISCIPLINE PHILOSOPHY **EDUCATION** Univ Pittsburgh, PhD, 85. **CAREER** Assoc prof, Tulane Univ. **SELECTED PUBLICATIONS** Auth, The Limits of Public Reason, J Philos; pub(s) in, Ethics; J Philos. **CONTACT ADDRESS** Dept of Philosophy, Tulane Univ, 6823 St Charles Ave, New Orleans, LA, 70118. **EMAIL** bbrower@mailhost.tcs.tulane.edu

BROWN, ALEXANDRA
PERSONAL Born 08/01/1955, Erwin, TN, s **DISCIPLINE** RELIGION/BIBLICAL STUDIES/NEW TESTAMENT **EDUCATION** Duke Univ, AB, 77; Yale Divinity Sch, MDIV, 80; Columbia Univ, Union Theol Seminary, PhD, 90. **CAREER** Assoc prof of relig, dept head, Washington & Lee Univ. **MEMBERSHIPS** Soc of Biblical Lit **RESEARCH** Pauline letters; early christianity **SELECTED PUBLICATIONS** Auth, The Cross and Human Transformation: Paul's Apocalyptic word in 1 Corinthians, 95; Putting Body and Soul Together: Essays in Honor of robin Scrogg, 97; The Word of the Cross: Pattern for Moral Discernment, Doctrine and Life, 97; The Gospel Takes Place: Paul's Theology of Power-in-Weakness in 2 Corinthians, Interpretation, July 98; Essays on Regeneration, Latter Days, and Judgement for the Eerdman's Dictionary of the Bible, forthcoming 98; Review of Joost Holleman, Resurrection and Parousia: A Traditio-Historical Study of Paul's Eschatology in 1 Corinthians 15, for the Journal of Biblical Literature, forthcoming 98. **CONTACT ADDRESS** Dept of Relig, Washington & Lee Univ, Newcomb Hall, Lexington, VA, 24450. **EMAIL** brown.a@wlu.edy

BROWN, ALISON L.
PERSONAL Born 01/28/1959, Champagne, IL, s, 1 child **DISCIPLINE** PHILOSOPHY **EDUCATION** Univ Utah, BA, 81, MA, 84; Univ Mass Amherst, PhD, 89. **CAREER** Author **HONORS AND AWARDS** Honorary mem, Iota Iota Iota, 96; Northern Ariz Univ res grants, 95, 94, 91, 90; Northern Ariz Univ Assoc Women Students Outstanding Woman Facul of the Year, 91; NEH summer inst, Univ Calif Santa Cruz, 90. **MEMBERSHIPS** Amer Philos Asn. **SELECTED PUBLICATIONS** Auth, Subjects of Deceit: A Phenomenology of Lying, State Univ of NY Press, 98; auth, Foucault's Play, Symploke, 96; auth, Hegelian Silences and the Politics of Communication: A Feminist Appropriation, Rethinking the Canon: Hegel, Pa State Press, 96; auth, Anxiety, God and the Feminine Divine, Kierkegaard in Post/Modernity, Studies in Continental Thought series, Univ Ind Press, 95; auth, Truth, Fear, and Writing: From Paper Village to Electronic Community, Postmodern Culture Series, State Univ of NY Press, 95; auth, Grave Voices: A Discussion about Praxis, Man and World, 25, 5-19, 92; co-auth, On the Rational Rejection of Utilitarianism and the Limitations of Moral Principles, Jour of Value Inquiry, 84. **CONTACT ADDRESS** 523 N. Agassiz, Flagstaff, AZ, 86001. **EMAIL** alison.brown@nau.edu

BROWN, AMOS CLEOPHILUS
PERSONAL Born 02/20/1941, Jackson, MS, m **DISCIPLINE** THEOLOGY **EDUCATION** Morehouse Coll, BA 1964; Crozer Seminary, MDiv 1968; VA Seminary & Coll, DD 1984; United Theological Seminary; Doctor of Ministry, 1990. **CAREER** NAACP, field sec 1960-62; St Paul Bapt Church Westchester PA, pastor 1965-70; Pilgrim Baptist St Paul MN, pastor 1970-76; Third Baptist San Francisco CA, pastor 1976-. **HONORS AND AWARDS** Outstanding Young Man of Amer Jr Chamber of Commerce 1974-76; Martin Luther King Jr Ministerial Awd Colgate-Rochester Div School 1984; Man of the Yr San Francisco Business & Professional Women Inc 1985. **MEMBERSHIPS** Pres MS Youth Council NAACP 1956-59, Hi-Y Clubs MS 1958-59; natl chmn NAACP Youth Dept 1960-62; chmn Amer Baptist Black Caucus 1972-80, chmn, Natl Baptist Civil Rights Comm 1982-; mem Comm Coll Gov Bd 1982-88; founding mem bd Black Amer Resp to African Crisis 1984; life member, NAACP; mem San Francisco City County Board of Supervisors, 1996-. **CONTACT ADDRESS** Third Baptist Church, 1399 McAllister, San Francisco, CA, 94115.

BROWN, BARRY
DISCIPLINE LAW **EDUCATION** Harvard Univ, BA, 68, EdM, 69; JD, 72. **CAREER** Prof. **RESEARCH** Bioethics; land transfer and finance; legal profession; real property. **SELECTED PUBLICATIONS** Auth, Reconciling Property Law with Advances in Reproductive Science, 95; When a Disposition is Not a Disposition, 90; co-auth, Massachusetts Condominium Law, 92. **CONTACT ADDRESS** Law School, Suffolk Univ, Beacon Hill, Boston, MA, 02114. **EMAIL** bbrown@acad.suffolk.edu

BROWN, BRYSON
DISCIPLINE PHILOSOPHY **EDUCATION** Trent Univ, BA; MA; Univ Pittsburgh, PhD, 85. **SELECTED PUBLICATIONS** Auth, pubs on logic and philosophy. **CONTACT ADDRESS** Dept of Philosophy, Lethbridge Univ, 4401 University Dr W, Lethbridge, AB, T1K 3M4. **EMAIL** brown@uleth.ca

BROWN, COLIN
PERSONAL Born 02/26/1932, Bradford, United Kingdom, m, 1958, 3 children **DISCIPLINE** RELIGION **EDUCATION** Univ Liverpool, BA, 53; Univ London, BD, 58; Univ Nottingham, MA, 61; Univ Bristol, PhD, 70; Univ Nottingham, DD, 94. **CAREER** Anglican / Episcopal Church, ordained min, 58-; Tyndale Hall / Trinity Col, Bristol, fac, 61-78; Univ Bristol, rec tchr, 61-72; Fuller Theol Sem, prof, 78-, assoc dean 88-97. **HONORS AND AWARDS** ECBPA, Gold Medallion, 85; C. Davis Weyerhaeuser Award for Excellence, 88 **MEMBERSHIPS** Tyndale Fel, AAR, SBL, SCP, IBR **RESEARCH** Quest of the hist Jesus. **SELECTED PUBLICATIONS** Auth, Karl Barth and the Christian Message, InterVarsity Press, 67; Philosophy and the Christian Faith, InterVarsity Press, ¤69l, 19th printing, 98; ed, History, Criticism and Faith, InterVarsity Press, 76, Fr trans, 82; Miracles and the Critical Mind, Paternoster Press, 85; Jesus in European Protestant Thought, 1778-1860, Labyrinth Press, 85, pbk ed Baker Book House, 88; That You May Believe, Paternoster Press, 85; History and Faith, InterVarsity Press, 87; Christianity and Western Thought, vol 1, From the Ancient World to the Age of Enlightenment, Downer Grove: InterVarsity Press, Apollos Press, 90. **CONTACT ADDRESS** Dept of Systematic Theology, Fuller Theol Sem, 135 N Oakland Ave, Pasadena, CA, 91182. **EMAIL** colbrn@fuller.edu

BROWN, CRAIG
DISCIPLINE LAW **EDUCATION** Otago Univ, LLB, 73; Univ Ill, LLM, 77; Otago Univ, LLD, 94. **CAREER** Prof. **RESEARCH** Insurance; torts; public international law. **SELECTED PUBLICATIONS** Auth, Insurance Law in Canada; No Fault Automobile Insurance in Canada, the Encyclopedia of Insurance Law; Canadian Insurance Contract Law in a Nutshell. **CONTACT ADDRESS** Fac of Law, Univ Western Ontario, London, ON, N6A 3K7.

BROWN, DALE W.
PERSONAL Born 01/12/1926, Wichita, KS, m, 1947, 3 children **DISCIPLINE** THEOLOGY **EDUCATION** McPherson Col, AB, 46; Bethany Bibl Sem, BD, 49; Northwestern Univ, PhD(church hist), 62. **CAREER** Asst prof philos & relig & dir relig life, McPherson Col, 58-62; assoc prof, 62-70, Prof theol, Bethany theol Sem, 70- **MEMBERSHIPS** Am theol Soc; Am Soc Church Hist. **RESEARCH** German pietism; theology of revolution; Brethren beliefs and practices. **SELECTED PUBLICATIONS** Auth, Four Words for World, 68 & Brethren and Pacifism, 70, Brethren; So Send I You, Faith & Life, 69; The Christian Revolutionary, 71 & Understanding Pietism, 78, Eerdmans; Flamed by the Spirit, Brethren, 78. **CONTACT ADDRESS** Dept of theol, Bethany Theol Sem, Butterfield & Meyers Rds, Oak Brook, IL, 60521.

BROWN, DANIEL ALOYSIUS
PERSONAL Born 07/13/1940, Chicago, IL **DISCIPLINE** RELIGIOUS STUDIES **EDUCATION** Marianum, Rome, STB, 63, STL, 65; Vatican Libr, dipl libr sci, 63; Cath Univ, PhD(relig & relig educ), 73. **CAREER** Teacher relig, Notre Dame High Sch, 65-66; chaplain, the Claremont Cols, 69-71 & Univ Southern Calif, 71-72; assoc prof, 72-78, PROF RELIG, CALIF STATE UNIV, FULLERTON, 78-, Vis lectr relig, Marianum Pontifical Fac theol, 74; Nat Endowment for Humanities fel, Univ Calif, Los Angeles-African Humanities inst, 78 & summer fel, Dumbarton Oaks, 78; Henry Luce fel, Univ Southern Calif, 79; Fulbright res fel, Italy, 82-83. **MEMBERSHIPS** Col theol Soc; Am Acad Relig; Soc Sci Study Relig. **RESEARCH** Religion and social issues; Medieval religious movements; religions in America. **SELECTED PUBLICATIONS** Auth, Maria Luisa Maurizei, la venerabile dalla morte ad oggi 183-1966, Moniales Ordinis Servorum, 66; Teaching the Old Testament to American students, Living Light, 68-69; The Need For a Sane Public Ritual, Worship, 73; Prayer, fasting and almsgiving, Communio, 74, reprinted Relig Teacher's J, 76; coauth, Is Mary a sign of unity among Christians? An empirical study, Mirianum, 75; auth, the clothes people wear, Way, 76; the mythical Shaman of Ames, Iowa as religious educator, Living Light, 77; Brothers and Service, Berwyn, 81. **CONTACT ADDRESS** Dept of Relig, California State Univ, Fullerton, Fullerton, CA, 92634.

BROWN, ERIC
PERSONAL Born 02/26/1970, Cincinnati, OH, m, 1994 **DISCIPLINE** PHILOSOPHY; CLASSICS **EDUCATION** Univ Chicago, AB, 91, AM, 93, PhD, 97; Univ Cambridge, Jan 96-May 96, visitor. **CAREER** Teaching Asst, Fall 93-95, instr, Fall 95, Univ Chicago; Asst prof, 97-present, Washington Univ. **HONORS AND AWARDS** Univ Chicago Century Fel, 91-95; Univ Chicago Mrs. Giles Whiting Doctoral Dissertation Fel, 96-97; nominated for a Jr. Fel in the Soc of Fels, Harvard Univ, 96. **RESEARCH** Ancient philosophy; ethics; metaethics; normative moral theory; social and political philosophy. **SELECTED PUBLICATIONS** Auth, A Defense of Plato's Argument for the Immortality of the Soul at Republic, 97; auth, Justice and Compulsion for Plato's Philsopher-Rulers, under review; review, Lawrence C. Becker, A New Stoicism, Journal of the History of Philosophy, forthcoming. **CONTACT ADDRESS** Washington Univ, St Louis, MO, 63130. **EMAIL** eabrown@twinearth.wustl.edu

BROWN, GEORGE, JR.
PERSONAL Born 12/19/1942, Philadelphia, PA, m, 1965, 3 children **DISCIPLINE** THEOLOGY **EDUCATION** Central Col, Pella IA, BA, 65; Western Theol Sem, BD, ordained, 69; Princeton Theol Sem, MTh, 71; Michigan State Univ, PhD, 89. **CAREER** Pottersville Reformed Church, minr, 69-73; Cent Reformed Church Grand Rapids, min, 73-88; Western Theol Sem Holland, MI, Dean of Fac, 88-96; assoc dean, prof, 96-. **HONORS AND AWARDS** RC in Am, Educator of the Yr, 96; Humanitarian Svc Award, 85. **MEMBERSHIPS** APRRE, ASCD. **RESEARCH** Religious Education Cirriculum. **SELECTED PUBLICATIONS** Coauth, Religious Education, 1960-1993: An Annotated Bibliography, Greenwood Press, 95; auth, Reformed Education in: Harper's Encycl of Relig Edu, ed, I.V. Cully and K.B. Cully, Harper & Row, 90; Selected Resources on Mentoring, CERCA RCA Educator, 95; Gospel and Culture Themes in Christian Religious Educational Literature, The Gospel and Our Culture, 90; Resource of Highest Value: Tapping the Experience of Adult Learners, Options MAACE

Scholarly Jour, 90. **CONTACT ADDRESS** Dept of Christian Education, Western Theol Sem, 101 E 13th St, Holland, MI, 49423-3622. **EMAIL** georgeb@westernsem.org

BROWN, HAROLD IRWIN
PERSONAL Born 12/04/1940, Brooklyn, NY, 2 children **DISCIPLINE** PHILOSOPHY **EDUCATION** Cooper Union, BCE, 62; City Col New York, MA, 65; Northwestern Univ, Evanston, PhD(philos), 70. **CAREER** Asst prof philos, Simpson Col, 68-69; asst prof, 69-75, assoc prof, 75-81, Prof Philos, Northern Ill Univ 81-, Nat Endowment for Humanities Younger Humanist fel, 72-73. **HONORS AND AWARDS** Winner 1978 Essay Competition, Am Philos Quart, 78; Presidential Res Prof at Northern Ill Univ, 96. **MEMBERSHIPS** Am Philos Asn; Philos Sci Asn; AAAS. **RESEARCH** Philosophy of science; theory of knowledge; philosophy of mind. **SELECTED PUBLICATIONS** Auth, Problem changes in science and philosophy, Metaphilosophy, 75; Paradigmatic proposition, Am Philos Quart, 75; Galileo, the elements and the tides, Studies Hist & Philos Sci, 76; Perception, Theory and Commitment, Precedent Publ, 77; On Being Rational, Am Philos Quart, 78; For a Modest Historicism, 78 & Observation and the Foundations of Objectivity, 79, Monist; The Paradigm Paradigm and Related Notions, Diogenes, 80; Incommensurability, Inquiry, 83; Being Rational, Philos of Sci, 83; Response to Siegel, Synthese, 83; Assimilation and Discovery, New Ideas in Psych, 83; Galileo on the Telescope and the Eye, J Hist of Ideas, 85; Sellars, Concepts and Conceptual Change, Synthese, 86; Naturalizing Observation, In: The Process of Science, Nijhoff, 87; Observation and Objectivity, Oxford, 87; Rationality, Routledge, 88; Normal Epistemology and Naturalized Epistemology, Inquiry, 88; Prospective Realism, Studies in Hist and Philos of Sci, 90; Cherniak on Scientific Realism, Brit J for the Philos of Sci, 90; Epistemic Concepts, Inquiry, 91; Direct Realism, Indirect Realism, and Epistemology, Philos and Phenomenol Res, 92; A Theory-Laden Observation Can Test the Theory, Brit J for the Philos of Sci, 93; Reason, Judgement, and Baye's Law, Philos of Sci, 94; Circular Justifications, In: PSA 1994, Philos of Sci Asn, 94; Empirical Testing, Inquiry, 95; The Methodological Roles of Theory in Science, In: The Scientific Basis of Geomorphology, Wiley, 96; Psychology, Naturalized Epistemology and Rationality, In: Philosophy and Psychology, Sage, 96. **CONTACT ADDRESS** Dept of Philosophy, No Illinois Univ, De Kalb, IL, 60115-2825. **EMAIL** hibrown@niu.edu

BROWN, HAROLD O.J.
PERSONAL m, 2 children **DISCIPLINE** SYSTEMATIC THEOLOGY **EDUCATION** Harvard Univ, BA; Harvard Divinity Sch, BDiv, ThM, PhD. **CAREER** Vis prof, Trinity Univ, 71-75; assoc prof, Trinity Univ, 76-83, 87; prof. **HONORS AND AWARDS** Fullbright, Danforth awards., Co-founder, ch, Christian Action Coun,; dir, Ctr Rel and Soc, Rockford Inst; instr, Intl Sem on Jurisprudence and Human Rights, Strasbourg; **MEMBERSHIPS** Mem, Stewards' Enclosure of the Henley Royal Regatta; Harvard Club NYC; Amer Theol Soc; Turnerschaft Saxonia Marburg. **RESEARCH** Right-to-life issues, ethics, especially medical and family values. **SELECTED PUBLICATIONS** Ed, Religion and Society Report; auth, Protest of a Troubled Protestant, Zondervan, 69; Christianity and the Class Struggle, Arlington House, 70; Death Before Birth, Thomas Nelson, 77; Reconstruction of the Republic, Arlington House, 77; Before the crash: a Biblical basis for economics, Christian Stud Ctr, 78; War: Four Christian Views, BMH Bk(s), 81; Heresies: The Image of Christ in the Mirror of Heresy and Orthodoxy from the Apostles to the Present, Doubleday 84; Christian Vision: Man & State: Religion, Society & the Constitution, Hillsdale Col Press, 89; Sensate Culture, Word, 96. **CONTACT ADDRESS** Dept of Systematic Theology, Reformed Theol Sem, 2101 Carmel Rd, Charlotte, NC, 28226.

BROWN, J. DANIEL
PERSONAL Born 01/27/1934, Cabarrus Co, NC, m, 1957, 2 children **DISCIPLINE** RELIGION, PHILOSOPHY **EDUCATION** Lenoir-Rhyne Col, BA, 56; Lutheran Southern Sem, MDiv, 59; Princeton Theol Sem, ThM, 60; Drew Univ PhD(theol & cult), 70. **CAREER** Instr relig, Converse Col, 65-67; from asst prof to assoc prof, 67-74, PROF RELIG & PHILOS, CATAWBA COL, 74-, Vis mem grad fac relig, Wake Forest Univ, 69-70. **MEMBERSHIPS** Am Acad Relig. **RESEARCH** Religion and literature; language. **SELECTED PUBLICATIONS** Auth, The absurd drama of Eugene Ionesco as religious ritual, Drew Gateway, 70; The comic, In: Echoes of the Wordless Word, Univ Mont, 73; Notes on Philosophy, Hunter, 76. **CONTACT ADDRESS** Catawba Col, Salisbury, NC, 28144.

BROWN, JAMES J.
PERSONAL Born 12/22/1937, Cleveland, OH, m, 1963, 3 children **DISCIPLINE** LAW **EDUCATION** Univ Pa, BS, 60; Cleveland State Univ, JD, 64; Washington Univ, LLM, 70. **CAREER** Asst prof, Sch Law, Univ Mo-Kansas City, 70-73, assoc prof, 74-76; assoc prof, Nova Univ Law Ctr, Ft Lauderdale, 76-78, prof, 78-81; vis prof, 81-82, PROF, COL LAW, STETSON UNIV, 82-, Assoc ed, Urban Lawyer, 70-74; consult & proj dir, Mo Dept Community Affairs, 72-74; vis prof, Col Law, Univ Ky, spring, 73; dir, Scribes, Am Soc Writers Legal Subj, 75-80; appointee, Governor Robert Grahams Adv Comt, 80-81. **MEMBERSHIPS** Am Planning Asn; Real Estate Educr Asn; Am Real Estate & Urban Econ Asn; Scribes, Am Soc Writers Legal Subj (pres, 74-75). **RESEARCH** Land use planning and zoning; environmental law; real property. **SELECTED PUBLICATIONS** Auth, New methods to overcome zoning restrictions against transportable housing, Proc 2nd Int Symp Lower-Cost Housing, No 251, 72; State Low-Rise Residential Building Code Model Enabling Legislation, Mo Dept Community Affairs, 73; Building Codes and Construction Statutes: Missouri's Experience, Univ Mo Press, 74; Building codes and construction statutes in Missouri, Urban Law Annual, 13: 81; Subdivision Law and Growth Management - Kushner, Ja/, Urban Lawyer, Vol 27, 1995. **CONTACT ADDRESS** Col of Law, Stetson Univ, 1401 61st St S, Saint Petersburg, FL, 33707-3299.

BROWN, JAMES R.
PERSONAL Montreal, PQ, Canada **DISCIPLINE** PHILOSOPHY **EDUCATION** Univ Guelph, BA, 73, MA, 75; Univ W Ont, PhD, 81. **CAREER** PROF PHILOSOPHY, UNIV TORONTO, 81- **SELECTED PUBLICATIONS** Auth, The Laboratory of the Mind, 91; auth, Smoke and Mirrors, 94; auth, Proofs and Pictures, 98; auth, A Guide to the Science of Wars, 99. **CONTACT ADDRESS** Dept of Philosophy, Univ of Toronto, 215 Huron St, Toronto, ON, M5S 1A1. **EMAIL** jrbrown@chass.utoronto.ca

BROWN, JERRY WAYNE
PERSONAL Born 02/24/1936, Frederick, OK, m, 1958, 1 child **DISCIPLINE** RELIGION, HISTORY **EDUCATION** Harvard Univ, AB, 58; Eastern Baptist Theol Sem, BD, 61; Univ Pa, MA, 61; Princeton Univ, MA, 63, PhD(relig), 64. **CAREER** Teaching fel relig, Princeton Univ, 63-64; asst prof, Bowdoin Col, 64-69, actg chmn dept, 64-65, resident prof, Sr Ctr, 65-66, dean students, 66-69; ASSOC PROF HIST, RIDER COL 69-, VPRES ACAD AFFAIRS, 70-;, PROVOST, 75-. **RESEARCH** Religion in America. **SELECTED PUBLICATIONS** The Rise of Biblical Criticism in American, 1800-1870, Wesleyan Univ, 69. **CONTACT ADDRESS** Dept of Hist, Rider Col, Lawrenceville, NJ, 08648.

BROWN, KENNETH
PERSONAL Born 03/05/1943, Chicago, IL, 2 children **DISCIPLINE** BIBLE, THEOLOGY, HISTORY **EDUCATION** Asbury Theol Sem, BA Theol, 66; Mdiv 76; Drew Univ, PhD, 88. **CAREER** Pastor/Minister, 66-; Prof, Vennard Coll, 76-79. **MEMBERSHIPS** Amer Acad Rel; ATLA; Wesleyan Theol Soc; Christian Holiness Partnership. **RESEARCH** Camp Meeting History; History of the Holiness Movement; Biographical Studies. **SELECTED PUBLICATIONS** Auth, Holy Ground, Too, The Camp Meeting Family Tree, Hazleton, Holiness Archives, 98. **CONTACT ADDRESS** 243 S Pine St, Hazleton, PA, 18201. **EMAIL** cmbooks@ptdprolog.net

BROWN, KENNETH LEE
PERSONAL Born 06/15/1933, Wichita, KS, m, 1960, 3 children **DISCIPLINE** PEACE STUDIES, RELIGION **EDUCATION** McPherson Col, AB, 55; Bethany Theol Sem, BD, 58; Duke Univ, PhD, 65. **CAREER** From instr to assoc prof, 61-73, Prof Relig & Philos, Manchester Col, 73-, Lilly Endowment Open Fel, Fel of Reconciliation, Inst for World Order, NYC, 78-79; dir, Peace Studies Inst & Prog in Conflict Resolution, 80. **MEMBERSHIPS** Am Acad Relig; Am Soc Christian Ethics. **RESEARCH** Soc ethics; polit philos; pacifism. **SELECTED PUBLICATIONS** Ed, Bull of the Peace Studies Inst, 80-; Auth, Christian's relationship to the state, In: Six Papers on Peace, Brethren, 69; The flow children, In: Life Styles, Scott, 71. **CONTACT ADDRESS** Peace Studies Inst, Manchester Col, 601 E College Ave, N Manchester, IN, 46962-1226. **EMAIL** klbrown@manchester.edu

BROWN, KRISTEN M.
DISCIPLINE 19TH CENTURY GERMAN PHILOSOPHY, ANCIENT PHILOSOPHY **EDUCATION** Stanford Univ, BA; Vanderbilt Univ, MA, PhD. **CAREER** Dept Philos, Millsaps Col **SELECTED PUBLICATIONS** Publ on, Embodiment and Feminine Other in Nietzsche & Form as Logos in Aristotle's Metaphysics Z and Politics. **CONTACT ADDRESS** Dept of Philosophy, Millsaps Col, 1701 N State St, Jackson, MS, 39210. **EMAIL** brownkm@okra.millsaps.edu

BROWN, LEE BATEMAN
PERSONAL Born 01/14/1932, Milton, IA, 1 child **DISCIPLINE** PHILOSOPHY **EDUCATION** Univ Utah, BA, 56; Northwestern Univ, MA, 58, PhD(philos), 66. **CAREER** Instr Philos, Northwestern & Roosevelt Univs, 60-61; from instr to asst prof, 61-71, ASSOC PROF PHILOS, OHIO STATE UNIV, 71-. **MEMBERSHIPS** Am Philos Asn; AAUP; Hegel Soc Am. **RESEARCH** Aesthetics; metaphysics. **SELECTED PUBLICATIONS** Auth, Definitions in art theory & Traditional aesthetics revisited, J Aesthet & Art Criticism; World interpretations and lived experience, Monist, Vol 55, No 2; Adorno Aesthetic Theory - The Redemption of Illusion - Zuidervaart,l/, J Aesthet Educ, Vol 27, 1993; Notes to Literature, Vol 1 - Adorno,TW/, J Aesthet Educ, Vol 27, 1993; Notes to Literature, Vol 2 - Adorno,TW/, J Aesthet Educ, Vol 28, 1994; American-Indians Knowledge about Fetal Alcohol Syndrome - An Exploratory-Study/, Am Indian Cult Res J, Vol 19, 1995. **CONTACT ADDRESS** Dept of Philos, Ohio State Univ, 230 N Oval Mall, Columbus, OH, 43210-1335.

BROWN, PAUL LLEWELLYN
PERSONAL Born 11/19/1920, Sutersville, PA, m, 1944, 1 child **DISCIPLINE** PHILOSOPHY, RELIGION **EDUCATION** Maryville Col, BA, 41; Western Theol Sem, STB, 44; Victoria Univ, Ont, ThD(philos relig), 53. **CAREER** Asst minister, First Presby Church, Wilkinsburg, Pa, 44-45; minister, Artesia, NMex, 45-47; from asst prof to assoc prof relig & philos, 49-68, PROF PHILOS, UNIV TULSA, 68-. **MEMBERSHIPS** Am Philos Asn; Asn Symbolic Logic; Charles S Peirce Soc; Southwestern Philos Asn; AAUP. **SELECTED PUBLICATIONS** Coauth, Elementary Modern Logic, Ronald, 65; auth, Omnicredulity and Religious Beliefs, Crane Rev, spring 61; Religion and Truth, Perspective, fall 72; Is God a person or personal being, Personalist. **CONTACT ADDRESS** Dept of Philos, Univ of Tulsa, Tulsa, OK, 74104.

BROWN, PETER G.
PERSONAL Born 01/15/1940, 3 children **DISCIPLINE** PHILOSOPHY **EDUCATION** Haverford Col, BA, 61; Columbia Univ, MA, Union Theological Seminary, 64, PhD(philos), 69. **CAREER** Teacher social & polit philos, Univ Md, College Park, 69-70; reseacher, Urban Inst, 70-73; prof philos, Univ Wash, 73-74; fel, Off Acad Contemp Prob, 74-76; founder & dir, Ctr Philos & Pub Policy, 76-81, actg dean, 80-81, Assoc Dean, Sch Pub Affairs, Univ Md, College Park, 81-, Vis fel, Battelle Seattle Res Ctr, 73-74. **HONORS AND AWARDS** Founded, the Inst for Philos and Pub policy, the School of Pub Affairs, Eastern Shore Land Conservancy; Established, the Environmental Policy Programs, Univ of Maryland's School of Public Affairs; Tree Farmer of the Year, Garrett County, Md, 95; Steward of Walker Pond, Hancock County Ma; Chair of the Rural Legacy Advisory Committee, Md. **MEMBERSHIPS** Fellow of the Hastings Center, member of the Cosmos Club. **RESEARCH** Governance and Protection of the Environment. **SELECTED PUBLICATIONS** Urban Inst, 75; The place of informed consent in social experiments: Some cautionary notes, In: Ethical and Legal Issues of Social Experimentation, Brookings Inst, 75; ed, Food Policy: The Responsibility of the United States in the Life and Death Choices, Free Press, 77 & 79; co-ed, Human Rights and US Foreign Policy: Principles and Applications, Lexington Bks, 79 & 80; Income Support: Conceptual and Policy Issues & Boundaries: National Autonomy and its Limits, Rowman & Littlefield, 81; auth, Ethics and policy research, Policy Anal, spring 76, Restoring the Public Trust: A Fresh Vision for Progressive Govt in Am, Beacon Press, 94; Ethics economics and international relations, for Edinburgh Univ Press; Assessing the behavior of public officials from a moral point of view, In: Public Duties: The Moral Obligations of Public Officials, Harvard Univ Press (in press). **CONTACT ADDRESS** Sch Pub Affairs, Univ Md, College Park, MD, 20742-0001. **EMAIL** pbrown@puafmail.umd.edu

BROWN, R.L.
PERSONAL Baltimore, MD, m, 1995, 3 children **DISCIPLINE** CONSTITUTIONAL LAW; CONSTITUTIONAL THEORY; EVIDENCE **EDUCATION** St Johns Col, BA, 78; Georgetown Univ Law Ctr, JD, 82. **CAREER** Judicial clerk, Hon Spottswood W Robinson, III Chief Justice, US Court Appeals District of Columbia Circle, 82-83 & Chambers of Hon Thurgood Marshall, Assoc Justice, US Supreme Court, 85 Term; atty adv, Off Legal Coun US Dept Justice, 83-85; assoc atty, Onek, Klein, & Farr, Wash DC, 86-88; asst prof, 88-91, assoc prof, 91-94, PROF, 94- , Vanderbilt Univ School of Law, 88- . **HONORS AND AWARDS** Asn Am Law Schools Scholar Papers Award, 93 **MEMBERSHIPS** Dist Columbia, US Court Appeals, 83; US Supreme Court, 86; ALI, 96. **RESEARCH** Separation of powers; Judicial review; Constitutional interpretation. **SELECTED PUBLICATIONS** Auth, Separated Powers and Ordered Liberty, Univ Penn Law Rev, 91; A Tribute to Justice Thurgood Marshall, or: How I Learned to Stop Worrying and Love Formalism, Temple Polit & Civil Rights Law Rev, 92; Tradition and Insight, Yale Law Jour, 93; When Political Questions Affect Individual Rights: The Other Nixon v. United States, Supreme Court Rev, 93; rev, The Interpretable Constitution, Constitutional Commentary, 94-95; Formal Neutrality in the Warren and Rehnquist Courts: Illusions of Similarity, Vanderbilt Law Rev, 97; Constitutional Tragedies: The Dark Side of Judgement, Constitutional Stupidities, Constitutional Tragedies, 98; Accountability, Liberty, and the Constitution, Columbia Law Rev, 98. **CONTACT ADDRESS** Vanderbilt Univ Law School, 21st Avenue South @ Grand, Suite 205, Nashville, TN, 37240. **EMAIL** rbrown@law.vanderbilt.edu

BROWN, ROBERT FATH
PERSONAL Born 06/06/1941, St. Louis, MO, m, 1963, 3 children **DISCIPLINE** PHILOSOPHY OF RELIGION **EDUCATION** DePauw Univ, BA, 63; Columbia Univ, MA, 67, PhD(relig), 71. **CAREER** From instr to asst prof, 70-75, ASSOC PROF PHILOS, UNIV DEL, 75-, Vis lectr philos, Hull Univ, England, 80-81. **MEMBERSHIPS** Am Acad Relig; Am Philos Asn; Soc Values Higher Educ; Hegel Soc Am. **RESEARCH** German idealism; history of western religious thought; problem of evil. **SELECTED PUBLICATIONS** Auth, The Later Philosophy of Schelling: The Influence of Boehme on the Works of 1809-1815, Bucknell Univ, 77; Schelling's Treatise on The Deities of Samothrace: A Translation and an Interpretation, Am Acad Relig, 77. **CONTACT ADDRESS** Dept of Philos, Univ Del, Newark, DE, 19711.

BROWN, SCOTT KENT
PERSONAL Born 10/01/1940, Murray, UT, m, 1966, 4 children **DISCIPLINE** EARLY CHRISTIAN HISTORY & LITERATURE **EDUCATION** Univ Calif, Berkeley, BA, 67; Brown Univ, PhD (Bibl studies), 72. **CAREER** Asst prof, 71-76, ASSOC PROF ANCIENT SCRIPTURE, BRIGHAM YOUNG UNIV, 76-, Mem, Inst Ancient Studies, Brigham Young Univ, 73-; corresp mem, Inst Antiquity & Christianity, Calif, 73-. **MEMBERSHIPS** Soc Bibl Lit. **RESEARCH** New Testament; New Testament apocrypha. **SELECTED PUBLICATIONS** Auth, James the Just and the question of Peter's leadership in the light of new sources, In: Sperry Lectr Series, Brigham Young Univ, 73; The book of Lehi: A lost record?, spring 74 & The Apocalypse of Peter (CG VII, 3): A translation, spring 74, Brigham Young Univ Studies; Masada + Excavations and Discoveries from the World of the New-Testament - Herod Fortress and the Zealots Last Stand - a Brigham-Young-University forum address, Brigham Young Univ Studies, Vol 36, 1997. **CONTACT ADDRESS** Dept of Ancient Scripture, Brigham Young Univ, Joseph Smith Bldg, Provo, UT, 84602-0002.

BROWN, STEPHEN G.
PERSONAL Born 12/04/1943, Glendale, CA, m, 1966, 4 children **DISCIPLINE** THEOLOGY **EDUCATION** Brandeis Univ, PhD, 74 **CAREER** Biola Univ, asst prof, 73-76; The Masters Col, assoc prof, 76-84; Shasta Bible Col, acad dean, 91-, Simpson Col, adj inst, 92-. **MEMBERSHIPS** SBL, IBR, ETS. **RESEARCH** Biblical Hebrew; Hebrew Bible; ancient near east. **CONTACT ADDRESS** Dept of Biblical Studies, Simpson Col, 10000 Tilton Mine Rd, Redding, CA, 96001.

BROWN, WILLIAM H., III
PERSONAL Born 01/19/1928, Philadelphia, PA, m, 1975 **DISCIPLINE** LAW **EDUCATION** Temple Univ, BS, 1952; Univ of PA Law School, JD, 1955. **CAREER** Schnader, Harrison, Segal & Lewis, partner, Attorney, 1974-; Norris, Brown & Hall, partner, 1964-68; Norris, Green, Harris & Brown, partner, 1962-64; Norris, Schmidt, Green, Harris & Higginbotham, assoc, 1956-62; EEOC, chmn, 1969-73; EEOC, commr, 1968-69; Deputy Dist Attorney, chief of frauds, 1968; chmn, Philadelphia Special Investigation Commn, 1985-86. **HONORS AND AWARDS** Award of Recognition, Alpha Phi Alpha, 1969; Handbook of Modern Personnel Admin, 1972; Philadelphia NAACP President's Award; Fidelity Award, Philadelphia Bar Assn, 1990; Legal Defense & Education Fund, Judge William H Haste Award, 1992; American Heart Association, Dr Edward S Cooper Award, 1995; The Urban League of Philadelphia, Whitney M Young Jr, Leadership Award, 1996; Lawyers' Committee for Civil Rights Under Law, The Whitney North Seymoure Award, 1996. **MEMBERSHIPS** Bd of dir, United Parcel Serv, 1983-; mem, Regional Bd of Dir, First PA Banking & Trust Co, 1968-73; co-chair, bd dir, mem exec comm, Lawyers Comm for Civil Rights Under Law; founding mem, World Association of Lawyers; permanent mem, 3rd Cir Judicial Conference; mem, Alpha Phi Alpha; Philadelphia, Am Fed & PA Bar Assn; life member, Nat Bar Assn; Am Arbitration Association; Am Law Inst; Inter-Am Bar Assn; mem, Commn on Higher Educ, Middle States Association of Coll; mem, National Sr Citizen's Law Center; faculty mem, Natl Inst Trial Advocacy, 1980-; faculty mem, Practicing Law Inst, 1970-85; pres, mem, bd of dir, National Black Child Devel Institute, 1986-; mem, bd of dir, Community Legal Services; board of directors, NAACP Legal Defense & Educ Fund; fellow, American Bar Foundation; member, board of directors, Philadelphia Diagnostic and Rehabilitation Center; National Senior Citizens Law Center, board of directors, 1988-94. **SELECTED PUBLICATIONS** numerous articles **CONTACT ADDRESS** Schnader Harrison Segal Lewis, 1600 Market St, Ste 3600, Philadelphia, PA, 19103.

BROWN, WILLIAM P.
PERSONAL Born 10/19/1958, Washington, DC, m, 1990, 2 children **DISCIPLINE** BIBLE STUDIES **EDUCATION** Emory Univ, PhD 91; Princeton Theol Sem, MDiv, honors, 85; Whitman Col, BA 81. **CAREER** Union Theol Sem, asst prof, assoc prof, 91 to 95-. **MEMBERSHIPS** SBL; ASOR; AAR. **RESEARCH** Wisdom Lit of Hebrew Bible; Creation Theology; Ethics. **SELECTED PUBLICATIONS** Auth, The Ethos of the Cosmos: The Genesis of Moral Imagination in the Bible, Grand Rapids, Eerdmans, forthcoming; Character in Crisis: A Fresh Approach to the Wisdom Literature of the Old Testament, Grand Rapids, Eerdmans, 96; auth, Obadiah-Malachi: Westminster Bible Companion, Louisville, Westminster/John Knox, 96; auth, A Royal Performance: Critical Notes on Psalm 110: 3ag-b, Jour of Biblical Lit, 98; auth, The Character of Covenant in the Old Testament: A Theocentric Probe, The Annual of the Soc of Christian Ethics, 96; auth, Psalm 139: The Pathos of Praise, Interpretation, 96; auth, Creation, in: The Eerdmans Dictionary of the Bible, ed DN Freedman, Grand Rapids, Eerdmans, forthcoming; Job The Book of, in: Dict of Biblical Interpretation, ed JH Hayes, Nashville, Abingdon, forthcoming; Genesis The Book Of, in: Harper's Bible Dictionary, 2nd ed, San Francisco, Harper and Row, 96. **CONTACT ADDRESS** Dept of Old Testament, Union Theology Sem, 3401 Brook Rd, Richmond, VA, 23227. **EMAIL** wbrown@utsva.edu

BROWNE, GREGORY M.
PERSONAL Born 07/05/1957, Bluffion, OH, s **DISCIPLINE** PHILOSOPHY **EDUCATION** Mich State Univ, MA, 84, PhD, 94. **CAREER** Adj Instr, Macomb Commun Col, 94-97, 98- . **MEMBERSHIPS** Am Philos Asn **RESEARCH** Necessary truth; A Prior knowledge; Philosophy of language; Causality; Natural kinds; Freewill; Theories of justice. **SELECTED PUBLICATIONS** Auth, Necessary Factual Truth, forthcoming. **CONTACT ADDRESS** 4667 Crow's Nest Ct., Brighton, MI, 48114.

BROWNE, STANLEY M.
DISCIPLINE PHILOSOPHY **EDUCATION** Howard Univ, BA, 69, MA, 74; Univ Ottawa, PhD, 83. **CAREER** Mellon fel, 81; asst prof, Howard Univ, 86-89; asst rpof, Tuskegee Univ, 78-83; Talladega Col, 77-78; asst prof, Youngstown Univ, 89-95; PROF, ALA A&M UNIV, 95-. **CONTACT ADDRESS** Dept of Hist, Pol Sci, Alabama A&M Univ, Normal, AL, 35762. **EMAIL** SBrowne@aamu.edu

BROWNING, DANIEL C.
PERSONAL Born 10/26/1956, Albany, GA, m, 1982, 2 children **DISCIPLINE** ARCHAEOLOGY; BIBLICAL BACKGROUNDS **EDUCATION** Univ Alabama Huntsville, BSE, 80; MDiv, 84, PhD, 88, Southwestern Baptist Theological Seminary. **CAREER** Instr, Texas Christian Univ, 87-89; Teaching Fel, 85-87, Adjunct Instr, 87-89, Southwestern Baptist Theological Seminary; Instr, 88-90, Tarrant County Jr. Col; Asst Prof, 90-93, Assoc Prof, 93-, William Carey Col. **HONORS AND AWARDS** Endowment for Biblical Research/American Schools of Oriental Research Travel Grant, 84; Research Fel, Albright Inst of Archaeological Research, Jerusalem, 88; Outstanding Faculty Member 95/96, William Carey Col (Student Govt Assoc Award), 96; Teaching Excellence Grants William Carey Col, 93-97. **MEMBERSHIPS** Amer Schools of Oriental Research; Israel Exploration Soc; Soc of Biblical Lit. **RESEARCH** Biblical backgrounds; culture of New Testament times; archaeological field work **SELECTED PUBLICATIONS** Auth, Land of Goshen, Biblical Illustrator 19, 93; The Other Side of the Sea of Galilee, Biblical Illustrator, 20, 94; Standards of Greatness in the First Century, Biblical Illustrator 21, 95; Coauth, Of Seals and Scrolls, Biblical Illustrator 22, 96; Auth, The Strange Search for the Ashes of the Red Hefer, Biblical Archaeologist, 96; The Hill Country is not Enough for Us: Recent Arcaheology and the Book of Joshua, Southwestern Journal of Theology, 98; Jesus as Carpenter, Biblical Illustrator, 98; Iron Age Loom Weights from Timnah, Tell Batash (Timnah) II: The Finds from the Iron Age II, forthcoming. **CONTACT ADDRESS** William Carey Col, Hattiesburg, MS, 39401. **EMAIL** browning@wmcarey.edu

BROWNING, DON S.
PERSONAL Born 01/13/1934, Trenton, MO, m, 1958, 2 children **DISCIPLINE** THEOLOGY & SOCIAL SCIENCES, PSYCHOLOGY OF RELIGION **EDUCATION** Univ Chicago, BD, 59, MA, 62, PhD, 64. **CAREER** Asst prof theol & pastoral care, Grad Sem, Phillips Univ, 63-65; from instr to assoc prof relig & psychol studies, 65-77, prof & dean, Disciples Divinity House, 77-80, Alexander Campbell Prof Relig & Psychol Studies, Divinity Sch, Univ Chicago, 80-, Asn Theol Sch res grant relig & psychol, 69-70 & 82; Guggenheim fel, 75-76. **HONORS AND AWARDS** Hon Dr of Divinity, Univ Glasgow, 98. **MEMBERSHIPS** Am Acad Relig; Soc Sci Study Relig; Am Asn of Practical Theol; Int Acad of Practical Theol. **RESEARCH** The relation of theology to the social sciences; practical theology; religious ethics. **SELECTED PUBLICATIONS** Auth, Atonement and Psychotheraphy, Westminster, 66; Generative man, Westminster, 73; Moral Context of Care, Westminster, 76; Pluralism and Personality, Bucknell Univ, 80; Religious Ethics and Pastoral Care, Fortress, 83; Religious Thought and the Modern Psychologies, Fortress, 87; A Fundamental Practical Theology, 91; coauth, From Culture Wars to Common Ground: Religion and the American Family Debate, Westminster, 97. **CONTACT ADDRESS** Divinity Sch, Univ of Chicago, 1025-35 E 58th St., Chicago, IL, 60637-1577. **EMAIL** dsbrowni@midwat.uchicago.edu

BROWNING, PETER
DISCIPLINE PHILOSOPHY **EDUCATION** Univ Chicago, PhD. **CAREER** Prof, Drury Col. **RESEARCH** Med ethics; relig(s) studies; feminist theology. **SELECTED PUBLICATIONS** Auth, Review of A Matter of Principles? Ferment in U.S. Bioethics, Trinity Intl, 95; Review of The Craft of Theology by Avery Dulles, Crossroad, 92; Homosexuality, Ordination and Polity, Quarterly Review, 94; ed, Proceedings of the Ethics, Higher Education and Church Relations Conference, 94. **CONTACT ADDRESS** Relig and Philos Dept, Drury Col, N Benton, PO Box 900, Springfield, MO, 65802.

BROWNSON, JAMES
PERSONAL Born 02/06/1955, Hackensack, NJ, m, 1979, 3 children **DISCIPLINE** NEW TESTAMENT STUDIES **EDUCATION** Univ Michigan, BA, 77; Western Theol Sem, MDiv, 80; Princeton Theol Sem, PhD, 90. **CAREER** Asst prof, Calvin Col, 89-90; James and Jean Cook prof of New Testament, 90- , acad dean, 96- , Western Theol Sem. **MEMBERSHIPS** Soc Bibl Lit. **RESEARCH** Gospel of John; hermeneutics; gospel studies. **SELECTED PUBLICATIONS** Auth, The Odes of Solomon and the Johannine Tradition, J for the Stud of the Pseudepigrapha 2, 88; auth, Pastor, Which Bible? Reformed Rev, 90; auth, Selecting a Translation of the Bible for Public Reading, Reformed Liturgy and Music, 90; auth, How to Read a Parable, the Church Herald, 91; auth, The Virtuous Interpreter, Perspectives, 91; auth, What is The Gospel? Reformed Rev, 91; auth, Thoughts on God-Language, Perspectives, 93; auth, Reflections on El Salvador, Perspectives, 93; auth, Speaking the Truth in Love: Elements of a Missional Hermeneutic, Int Rev of Mission, 94; auth, Narrow Gate, Wide Horizons, Perspectives, 94; auth, Only Grace, Perspectives, 95; auth, Speaking the Truth in Love: New Testament Resources for a Missional Hermeneutic, Trinity Press. **CONTACT ADDRESS** 101 E 13th St, Holland, MI, 49423. **EMAIL** Jim@westernsem.org

BROYLES, JAMES EARL
PERSONAL Born 12/24/1931, Spokane, WA, m, 1956, 4 children **DISCIPLINE** PHILOSOPHY **EDUCATION** Univ Idaho, BS, 54; Univ Wash, MA, 59, DPhil, 64. **CAREER** Teaching asst philos, Univ Wash, 59-61; from instr to asst prof, 61-72, chmn dept, 70-75, assoc prof, 72-77, prof philosophy, Wash State Univ, 77-; Vis prof, Univ Guam, 73-74. **MEMBERSHIPS** Northwestern Conf Philos (pres, 67); Am Philos Asn. **RESEARCH** British analytic philosophy; appraisal of argument; philosophical psychology. **SELECTED PUBLICATIONS** Auth, Logical and Empirical Factors in Conceptual Change, Proc Seventh Inter-Am Cong Philos, 68; Knowledge and mistake, Mind, 4/69; Language and common sense, Am Philos Quart, 7/69; An observation on Wittgenstein's use of fantasy, Metaphilos, 10/74; The fallacies of composition and division, Philos & Rhet, 75; The intellectural respectability of religion, Relig Humanist, autumn 77; Ryle: The category and location of mind, Personalist, 4/78; Talk about space: Wittgestein and Newton, Philos Invest, 81. **CONTACT ADDRESS** Dept of Philosophy, Washington State Univ, PO Box 645130, Pullman, WA, 99164-5130.

BRUCH, C.S.
PERSONAL Born 06/11/1941, d, 2 children **DISCIPLINE** LAW **EDUCATION** Shimer Col, BA, 60; Univ Calif Sch of Law, JD, 72. **CAREER** Actg prof, 73-78, prof of Law, 78- , Univ Calif, Davis School of Law; mem, Grad Gp in Human Develop, 79- . **HONORS AND AWARDS** Univ Calif, Davis, Academic Senate: First Annual Distinguished Public Service Award, 90; West Europ Reg Fulbright, 90; sr res fel, Humboldt Found, 92. **MEMBERSHIPS** Am Law Inst; U.S. Supreme Court Bar; Calif State Bar. **SELECTED PUBLICATIONS** Auth, When to Use and When to Avoid Mediation: An Attorney's Guide, Family and Conciliation Courts Rev, 93; auth, Child Abduction and the English Courts, in Bainham, ed, Frontiers of Family Law and Policy, Wylie, 93; auth, The Hague Convention on the Law Applicable to Succession to the Estates of Deceased Persons: Do Quasi-Community Property and Mandatory Survivorship Laws Need Protection? Law and Contemp Prob, 93; auth, International Child Abduction Cases: Experience Under the 1980 Hague Convention, in Eekelaar, ed, Parenthood in Modern Society, Martinus Nijhoff, 93; auth, The Central Authority's Role Under the Hague Child Abduction Convention: A Friend in Deed, Family Law Q, 94; auth, Statutory Reform of Constitutional Doctrine: Fitting International Shoe to Family Law, UC Davis L Rev, 95; auth, Family Support Across Frontiers--New Ideas from the Americas, in, Families Across Frontiers, Martinus Nijhoff, 95; auth, How to Draft a Successful Family Law Convention: Lessons from the Chikld Abduction Conventions, in, Children on the Move, Martinus Nijhoff, 95. **CONTACT ADDRESS** 1013 Stanford Dr, Davis, CA, 95616. **EMAIL** csbruch@ucdavis.edu

BRULAND, ESTHER
DISCIPLINE RELIGION **EDUCATION** Drew Univ, PhD, 90. **CAREER** Adj prof, Col of Wooster, 87; adj prof, Fuller Theol Sem, 88; vis asst prof, Oberlin Col, 90; adj prof, Youngstown State Univ, 93-95; adj prof, William Tyndale Col, 96- ; adj prof, Eastern Mich Univ, 96- . **HONORS AND AWARDS** Phi Beta Kappa, 90. **MEMBERSHIPS** AAR; Soc of Christian Ethics. **RESEARCH** Social change; women and religion; nineteenth century reform movements; ecumenism. **SELECTED PUBLICATIONS** Coauth, A Passion for Jesus, A Passion for Justice, Judson, 83; auth, Evangelical and Feminist Ethics: Complex Solidarities, J of Relig Ethics, 89; auth, Regathering, Eerdmans, 95. **CONTACT ADDRESS** 420 W Caledonia, Howell, MI, 48843-1118.

BRUMBAUGH, JOHN MAYNARD
PERSONAL Born 02/09/1927, Annapolis, MD **DISCIPLINE** LAW **EDUCATION** Swarthmore Col, BA, 48; Harvard Univ, LLB, 51. **CAREER** Teaching fel law sch, Harvard Univ, 55-56; from asst prof to assoc prof, 56-63, PROF LAW, SCH LAW, UNIV MD, BALTIMORE, 63-, Reporter, Comn Md Criminal Law, 65-81. **MEMBERSHIPS** Am Law Inst. **SELECTED PUBLICATIONS** Auth, The Straight-Line Method of Determining Personal Jurisdiction/, J Legal Educ, Vol 44, 1994. **CONTACT ADDRESS** Sch of Law, Univ of Md, 500 W Baltimore St, Baltimore, MD, 21201.

BRUNK, CONRAD
DISCIPLINE PHILOSOPHY **EDUCATION** Wheaton Col, BA, 67; Northwestern Univ, MA, 68; PhD, 74. **CAREER** Prof **RESEARCH** Social ethics; applied professional ethics. **SELECTED PUBLICATIONS** Auth, pub(s) on philos of religion, ethics and pub policy, peace and conflict, and soc and technology. **CONTACT ADDRESS** Dept of Philosophy, Waterloo Univ, 200 University Ave W, Waterloo, ON, N2L 3G1. **EMAIL** cbrunk@uwaterloo.ca

BRUNNEE, JUTTA
DISCIPLINE LAW **EDUCATION** Dalhousie Univ, LLM; Johannes Gutenberg Univ, JD. **CAREER** Asst prof, McGill Univ, 90-95; assoc prof, 95-. **HONORS AND AWARDS** Ed, Yearbook Int Environ Law. **MEMBERSHIPS** World Conserv Union's. **RESEARCH** International environmental law; European and Canadian environmental law; comparative law. **SELECTED PUBLICATIONS** Auth, Acid Rain and Ozone Layer Depletion: International Law and Regulation; pubs about international environmental law. **CONTACT ADDRESS** Fac of Law, Univ British Columbia, 1822 East Mall, Vancouver, BC, V6T 1Z1. **EMAIL** brunnee@law.ubc.ca

BRUNS, JAMES EDGAR
PERSONAL Born 08/02/1923, Islip, NY **DISCIPLINE** THEOLOGY **EDUCATION** St Joseph's Col & Sem, NY, AB, 45, MA, 53; Gregorian Univ, STD, 51; Ontif Bibl Inst, Rome, SSL, 53. **CAREER** Lectr theol, St John's Univ, NY, 55-59, asst prof, 59-62; from assoc prof to prof & chmn dept, 62-75; PRES, NOTRE DAME SEM SCH THEOL, 75-, Dir grad theol & relig studies, Inst Christian Thought, Univ St Michael's Col, 69-74, acad secy, 74-; Can Coun leave fel, 73-74; hist, Archdiocese New Orleans, 77- Mem; Soc Bibl Lit; Cath Bibl Asn Am; Am Acad Relig; Cath Theol Soc. **RESEARCH** Gnosticism; world of late antiqutiy; history of the church in Louisiana. **SELECTED PUBLICATIONS** Auth, Hear His Voice Today (Bible guide), Kenedy, 63; Old Testament history and the development of a sexual ethic, New Morality, 67; The Art and Thought of John, Herder, 69; The Christian Buddhism of St John, Paulist-Newman, 71; The altercation Jasonis et Papisci, Philos and Anastasius the Sinaite, Theol Studies, 6/73; God As Woman, Woman As God, Paulist Press, 73; The Forbidden Gospel, Harper, 76; The Agreement of Moses and Jesus in the Demonstratio Evangelica of Eusebius, Vigiliae Christianae, 77; John Gospel in New Perspective - Christology and the Realities of Roman Power - Cassidy,RS/, Cath Bibl Quart, Vol 56, 1994; John - Stibbe,MWG/, Cath Bibl Quart, Vol 56, 1994; Prologue and Gospel - The Theology of the 4th Evangelist - Harris,E/, Cath Bibl Quart, Vol 57, 1995; Philos, a Designation for the Jesus-Disciple Relationship - An Exegetico-Theological Investigation of the Term in the 4th-Gospel - Puthenkandathil,E/, Cath Bibl Quart, Vol 57, 1995; Angelus-Interpres - Angelic Explanations of the Text of the 'Apocalypse of John' - Structure, Substance and Background - German - Reichelt,H/, Cath Bibl Quart, Vol 58, 1996. **CONTACT ADDRESS** 2901 S Carrollton Ave, New Orleans, LA, 70118.

BRYANT, ALAN W.
DISCIPLINE LAW **EDUCATION** McGill, BC, 65; Univ Toronto, LLB, 68. **CAREER** Prof. **HONORS AND AWARDS** Tchg Awd, 76; Owen Bk Prize, 95. **SELECTED PUBLICATIONS** Auth, pubs on criminal law, evidence and advocacy; co-auth, The Law of Evidence in Canada, 94. **CONTACT ADDRESS** Fac of Law, Univ Western Ontario, London, ON, N6A 3K7.

BRYANT, DAVID J.
DISCIPLINE RELIGIOUS STUDIES **EDUCATION** Princeton Univ, PhD. **CAREER** Assoc prof. **RESEARCH** Christian thought; interaction of religion and Western culture; influence of religion on our treatment of the natural environment; religion and the arts. **SELECTED PUBLICATIONS** Auth, Faith and the Play of Imagination: On the Role of Imagination in Religion. **CONTACT ADDRESS** Religious Studies Dept, Eckerd Col, 54th Ave S, PO Box 4200, St Petersburg, FL, 33711. **EMAIL** bryantdj@eckerd.edu

BRYDEN, PHILIP
DISCIPLINE LAW **EDUCATION** Dalhousie Univ, BA, 75; Oxford Univ, BA; 78, BCL, 79; Harvard Univ, LLM, 85. **CAREER** Law Clerk, Justice Bertha Wilson, Supreme Court Can; asst prof, 85-91; assoc prof, 91-. **HONORS AND AWARDS** Pres, Can Asn Law; pres, Civil Liberties Asn. **MEMBERSHIPS** Can Asn Law; Civil Liberties Asn; Former Pres, Can Assoc Law Teachers; Former Pres B.C. Civil Liberties Assoc **SELECTED PUBLICATIONS** Auth, pubs about administrative law and constitutional law. **CONTACT ADDRESS** Fac of Law, Univ British Columbia, 1822 East Mall, Vancouver, BC, V6T 1Z1. **EMAIL** bryden@law.ubc.ca

BUB, JEFFREY
PERSONAL Born 02/12/1942, Cape Town, South Africa, m, 1990, 2 children **DISCIPLINE** PHYSICS **EDUCATION** Univ of Cape Town, BSc, 61, 62; London Univ, PhD, 66. **CAREER** Asst prof, philos, phys, Yale Univ, 69-71; asst prof, assoc prof, prof, philos, Univ Western Ontario, 71-86; prof, philos, Univ Maryland, 86- . **MEMBERSHIPS** Philos Sci Asn; APA; Int Quantum Structures Asn. **RESEARCH** Philosophy of physics, especially foundational problems of quantum mechanics; philosophy of science, especially methodological issues in cognitive neuropsychology. **SELECTED PUBLICATIONS** Auth, Triosthegonal Uniqueness Theorem and Its Relevance to the Interpretation of Quantum Mechanics, Physical Rev, 94; auth, Testing Models of Cognition Through the Analysis of Brain-Damaged Performance, Br J for the Philos of Sci, 94; auth, A Uniqueness Theorem for Interpretations of Quantum Mechanics, Stud in the Hist and Philos of Mod Phys, 96; auth, Schutte's Tautology and the Kochen-Specker Theorem, Found of Physics, 96; auth, Interpreting the Quantum World, Cambridge, 97. **CONTACT ADDRESS** Philosophy Dept, Univ of Maryland, College Park, NE, 20742. **EMAIL** jbub@carnap.umd.edu

BUBANY, CHARLES PHILLIP
PERSONAL Born 12/20/1940, Kirksville, MO, m, 1969, 2 children **DISCIPLINE** LAW **EDUCATION** St Ambrose Univ, BA, 62; Washington Univ, St Louis, JD, 65. **CAREER** Grad teaching asst law, Col Law, Univ Ill, 65-66; asst prof, Col Law, WVa Univ, 66-67; asst prof, 71-73, assoc prof, 73-75, prof law, Sch Law, Tex Tech Univ, 75-. **HONORS AND AWARDS** Nat Univ Continuing Educ Assoc, 91, Service to the Professions Award; George Herman Mahon Prof; Outstanding Law Prof, 94, 97, 98. **RESEARCH** Criminal justice; juvenile process; domestic relations law. **SELECTED PUBLICATIONS** Auth, The Texas Penal Code of 1974 in Annual Survey of Texas Law, Southwestern Law J, 28: 292; Constitutional Question Appellate Jurisdiction of the Missouri Supreme Court: The Albatross Hangs Heavy Still, Mo Law Rev, 39- 299; coauth (with Frank F Skillern), Taming the Dragon: An Adminstrative Law for Prosecutor Decisionmaking, Am Criminal Law Rev, 13: 473; auth, The Texas Confession Statute: Some New Wine in the Same Old Bottle, Tex Tech Law Rev, 10-67; contribr, Preparation and Trial of Criminal Cases, In: Texas Methods of Practice, West Publ Co, Vol 15, 79 & Vol 16, 80; coauth (with Perry Cockerell), Excluding Texas-style: Can Private Searches Poison the Fruit?, Tex Tech Law Rev, 12: 611; auth, Class C Misdemeanor Probation in Texas, South Tex Law J, 22: 249; Commentary to Chapter 21: Uniform Reciprocal Enforcement of Support Act, Tex Tech Law Rev, Vol 13, No 3; auth, Criminal Procedure: Trial and Appeal, Annual Survey of Texas Law, 45 SW Law L 91; Fifth Circuit Survey - Criminal Law, 27 Tex Tech Law Rev, 96; Counseling Clients to Do the Right Thing in Child Custody Cases, Children's Legal Rights J, winter 96; coauth, The Anatomy of a Client Interview, The Practical Lawyer, Dec 96; coauth, Texas Vehicle and Traffic Laws, 2nd ed, 97. **CONTACT ADDRESS** Sch of Law, Tex Tech Univ, Lubbock, TX, 79409-0004.

BUCHANAN, GEORGE WESLEY
PERSONAL Born 12/25/1921, Denison, IA, m, 1947, 3 children **DISCIPLINE** NEW TESTAMENT **EDUCATION** Simpson Col, BA, 47; Garrett Theol Sem, MDiv, 51; Northwestern Univ, MA, 52; Drew Univ, PhD, 59. **CAREER** Teacher high sch, Iowa, 43-44; pastor, Methodist church, Shelby, Iowa, 44-45, Wenona, Ill, 47-48, Kaukauna, Wis, 52-54, Towaco, NJ, 54-57 & Cincinnati, Ohio, 59-60; from asst prof to assoc prof, 60-66, prof New Testament, 66-92, prof emeritus, 92-, Wesley Theol Sem. **HONORS AND AWARDS** S H Scheuer Interfaith fel, 59-60; Am Asn Theol Schs fel, 66; Hebrew Union Col Bibl & Archaeol Sch fel, 66-67; Rosenstiel fel, Univ Notre Dame, 73; Claremont-Soc Bibl Lit fel, 80-81; LittD, Simpson Col, 73; DSL, Mellen Univ, 95., LittD, Simpson Col, 73. **MEMBERSHIPS** Soc Bibl Lit; Stud Novi Testamenti Soc; Cath Bibl Soc; AAUP; ed bd, Bibl Archaeol Rev; ed bd, Gospel Stud; adv bd, Arts and Hum Index; adv bd, Int Soc of Poetry. **RESEARCH** Christian origins; the historical Jesus; Jewish, Samaritan, and Christian literature; intertextuality. **SELECTED PUBLICATIONS** Auth, New Testament Eschatology: Historical and Cultural Background, Edwin Mellen, 93; auth, The Book of Revelation: Its Introduction and Prophecy, Edwin Mellen, 93; auth, Introduction to Intertextuality, Edwin Mellen, 95; auth, The Gospel According to Matthew, 2 v, Edwin Mellen, 96. **CONTACT ADDRESS** Wesley Theol Sem, 4400 Massachusetts Ave NW, Washington, DC, 20016-2415. **EMAIL** gweb@cpcug.org

BUCHER, GLENN R.
PERSONAL Born 05/20/1940, Mechanicsburg, PA, m, 1963, 2 children **DISCIPLINE** RELIGION, HIGHER EDUCATION **EDUCATION** Elizabethtown Col, AB, 62; Union Theol Sem, NY, MDiv, 65; Boston Univ, PhD(ethics), 68. **CAREER** Asst, Boston Univ, 66-67; instr philos, Emerson Col, 67-68; instr ethics & soc, Howard Univ, 68-70; asst prof, 70-75, assoc prof, 75-80, chmn dept, 78-80, actg dir, Ctr Prog Inst Renewal, 80-82, LINCOLN PROF RELIG, COL WOOSTER, 82-. **HONORS AND AWARDS** Distinguished Alumnus Award for Prof Achievement, Elizabethtown Col, Pa, 77. **MEMBERSHIPS** AAUP; Soc Sci Study Relig; Am Acad Relig; Am Soc Christian Ethics. **RESEARCH** American religious history; liberation theology and ethics; secuality and religion. **SELECTED PUBLICATIONS** Auth, Confusion and Hope: Clergy, Laity, and the Church in Transition, 74 & Straight, White, Male, 76, Fortress Press; The era of the trustees, Presby Surv, Vol 70, 12/80; Seventy futures for Presbyterianism: The Colleges of the Church, Presby Outlook, Vol 163, 4/20/81; The deferred maintenance of the faculty, The Chronicle of Higher Educ, Vol 22, 4/27/81; Worlds of total meaning: An interpretation of cult religion, Soundings, fall 81; Fourteen cases: The study of religion in church-related higher education, Coun Study of Relig Bull, 10/81; Church-related higher education: A review & assessment, Educ Rec, winter 82; Political Incorrectness and Theological Education/, Theol Today, Vol 49, 1993. **CONTACT ADDRESS** Dept of Relig, Col of Wooster, Beall Ave, Wooster, OH, 44691.

BUCK, HARRY MERWYN
PERSONAL Born 11/18/1921, Enola, PA, m, 1943, 2 children **DISCIPLINE** HISTORY OF RELIGIONS **EDUCATION** Albright Col, AB, 42; Evangel Sch Theol, MDiv, 45; Univ Chicago, PhD, 54. **CAREER** Pastor, Evangel United Brethren Church, Md, 42-46, Pa, 46-49; from instr to asst prof Bibl hist, 51-59, assoc prof Bible & relig, 59-68, prof Relig Studies, Wilson Col, 68-; consult, New Testament Greek Text Proj, Am Bible Soc, 55; mem, East-West Philosophers Conf, Honolulu, Hawaii, 59; comt lectionary study, Int Greek New Testament Proj, 59-; seminar Indian Civilization, Hyderabad, India, 61; managing ed, J Am Acad Relig, 61-73; chmn, Am Textual Criticism Sem, 60-62; fac training fel, Am Inst Indian Studies & hist relig fel, Soc Relig Higher Educ, 65-66; partic fel, Int Conf-Sem on Tamil Studies, Univ Malaya, 66; ed, Anima, 74-. **MEMBERSHIPS** Am Acad Relig; Soc Bibl Lit; Soc Study New Testament; Asn Asian Studies; Int Soc Study Relig. **RESEARCH** Epic literature of South Asia; function of sacred tradition; methodology in the history of religions. **SELECTED PUBLICATIONS** Co-ed, Religious Traditions and the Limits of Tolerance, Anima, 88; auth, Rama in Buddhist Cultures, 95; art, Beyond Walls, Fences, and Interreligious Dialogue, J of Ecumenical Studies, 97; auth, Beware the Self Evident, Dharma World, 98. **CONTACT ADDRESS** 1053 Wilson Ave, Chambersburg, PA, 17201.

BUCKINGHAM, DON
DISCIPLINE LAW **EDUCATION** Univ Saskatchewan, BA; Liege Univ, LLB, 86. **CAREER** Law clerk, Justice Heald, Federal Court Appeal; assoc prof. **HONORS AND AWARDS** Dir, Westminster Inst Ethics Human Values. **RESEARCH** International trade law; agricultural law. **SELECTED PUBLICATIONS** Auth, Does the WTO Care About Ecosystem Health: The Case of Trade in Agricultural Products, Ecosystem Health; A Recipe for Change: Towards an Integrated Approach to Food in International Law, 94; co-auth, Counting Our Chickens Before They Hatch: New Hope or No Hope for Discipline in Agricultural Trade under the new GATT and the NAFTA?, 94; Understanding the Law and Learning About Law, McGraw-Hill Ryers; co-ed, Law, Agriculture and the Farm Crisis, Purich, 92. **CONTACT ADDRESS** Col of Law, Univ Saskatchewan, 15 Campus Dr, Saskatoon, SK, S7N 5A6. **EMAIL** Buckingham@abyss.usask.ca

BUCKLEY, FRANCIS J.
PERSONAL Born 08/31/1928, Los Angeles, CA **DISCIPLINE** DOGMATIC THEOLOGY **EDUCATION** Gonzaga Univ, AB, 51, MA, 52; Alma Col, STL, 59; Univ Santa Clara, MA, 59; Gregorian Univ, STD, 64. **CAREER** Mem staff Latin & relig, Bellarmine Col Prep, 52-55; instr New Testament, 60-61, church hist, 61, from asst prof to assoc prof, 63-72, dir, grad prog relig educ, 74-75, actg chemn, dept theol, 71-73, chemn, dept theol & relig studies, 78-79, chemn, dept relig educ & pastoral ministries, 79-82, prof dogmatic theol, Univ San Francisco, 72-; mem, Catechetical Forum, 64-71, co-ed, Nat Catechetical Dir, 74-78; assoc ed, Theol Studies, 68-76; bd trustees, Jesuit Community Univ of San Francisco, 69-76 & 77-82; bd dirs, Coun Study of Relig, 72-75; dir proj renewal sacrament of penance, comt Pastoral Res & Practice, Nat Conf Cath Bishops, 73-76; bd trustees, Loyola Marymount Univ, 74; theol adv, US Bishops at Synod on Catechesis, 77; bd of trustees, Pacific Grad School of Psychology, 84-86, chemn, 86; bd of trustees, School of Applied Theology, 93-; consult, US Cath Conference, Dept of Ed, evaluation of catechetical texts, 97-; consult, Hispanic Telecommunications Network, 88-; consult, State of CA Coun for private postsecondary and vocational education, 93-. **HONORS AND AWARDS** Doctor of Humane Letters, Pacific Graduate School of Psychology, 88. **MEMBERSHIPS** Am Soc Church Hist; Cath Bibl Asn; Cath Theol Soc Am; Int Soc Jesuit Ecumenists; Asn Prof & Res Relig Educ; Col Theology Soc (pres, 72-74, bd, 69-76, regional chemn, 66-72). **RESEARCH** Pastoral theology; scripture; catechetics. **SELECTED PUBLICATIONS** Auth, Principles of Intercommunion, Proc Cath Theol Soc Am, 69 & Theol Dig, 69; Children and God: Communion, Confession, Confirmation, Corpus, 70, 2nd ed, Dimension Bks, 73; I confess--the Sacrament of Penance today, Ave Maria, 72; Religious Content for Children from Six to Twelve, Catechesis: Realities and Visions, US Cath Conf, 77; Punishment and Penance in a Changing Church and Society, Theology Confronts a Changing World, Twenty-Third Publ, 77; coauth, Lord of life Series, Sadlier, 78; auth, Right to the Sacraments of Initiation, Origins, 78 & Catholic Mind, 79; Reconciling, Ave Maria Press, 81; Team Teaching: What, Why, How, Sage, 98. **CONTACT ADDRESS** Dept Relig, Univ San Francisco, 2130 Fulton St, San Francisco, CA, 94117-1050. **EMAIL** buckley@usfca.edu

BUCKLEY, THOMAS W.
PERSONAL Born 06/11/1929, Abington, MA **DISCIPLINE** BIBLICAL STUDIES **EDUCATION** Harvard Col, BA, 49; Fordham Univ, MA, 52; Catholic Univ Am, STL, 58; Pontifical Bibl Inst, Rome, SSL, 60; Univ St Thomas Aquinas, Rome, STD, 62. **CAREER** Lectr theol, Regis Col, 60-61; prof New Testament, Bibl Greek, St. John's Sem, 63-81; lectr New Testament, St. Paul's House of Studies, 77-87; lectr in New Testament, St Scholastica Priory, 81-84; pastor St John's parish, Essex, MA, 81- . **MEMBERSHIPS** Catholic Bibl Asn; Soc of Bibl Lit. **RESEARCH** New Testament. **SELECTED PUBLICATIONS** Auth, Apostle to the Nations: The Life and Letters of St Paul: A Biblical Course, Daughters of St Paul, 81; auth, Seventy Times Seven: Sin, Judgment, and Forgiveness in Matthew, Liturgical, 91. **CONTACT ADDRESS** PO Box 986, Essex, MA, 01929.

BUCKWOLD, TAMARA
DISCIPLINE LAW **EDUCATION** Univ Saskatchewan, LLB, 80, LLM, 95. **CAREER** Asst prof, 87-. **MEMBERSHIPS** Law Soc Saskatchewan. **RESEARCH** Contracts and secured transactions. **SELECTED PUBLICATIONS** Auth, The Rights of Account and Inventory Financers Under the P.P.S.A.: Transamerica Commercial Finance Corp. v. Royal Bank of Canada, Sask Rev, 95; The Treatment of Receiver-Managers in the P.P. S.A.: Conceptual and Practical Implications, Can Bus Law Jour, 97; co-auth, The Personal Property Security Act and the Bankruptcy and Insolvency Act: Two Solitudes or Complementary Systems?, Banking and Finance Rev, 97. **CONTACT ADDRESS** Col of Law, Univ Saskatchewan, 15 Campus Dr, Saskatoon, SK, S7N 5A6. **EMAIL** Buckwold@law.usask.ca

BUCY, PAMELA H.
DISCIPLINE LAW **EDUCATION** Austin Col, BA, 75; Wash Univ Sch Law, JD, 78. **CAREER** Frank M. Bainbridge prof, Univ Ala. **MEMBERSHIPS** Order of the Coif. **RESEARCH** Criminal law, criminal procedure, white-collar crime. **SELECTED PUBLICATIONS** Auth, White Collar Crime, Cases and Materials, West, 91, 2d ed 97; Health Care Fraud, LJSP, 96; coauth, Federal Criminal Law, 97. **CONTACT ADDRESS** Law Dept, Univ of Alabama, Box 870000, Tuscaloosa, AL, 35487-0383. **EMAIL** pbucy@law.ua.edu

BUEHLER, ARTHUR
DISCIPLINE FUNDAMENTALISM, NATIONALISM, RELIGION **EDUCATION** Harvard Univ, PhD, 93. **CAREER** Asst prof, Colgate Univ. **RESEARCH** Study of Islam. **SELECTED PUBLICATIONS** Auth, Sufi Heirs of the Prophet: The Indian Naqshbandiyya and the Rise of the Sufi Mediating Shaykh, Univ SC Press, 98; The Naqshbandiyya in Timurid India: The Central Asian Legacy, Jour of Islamic Studies 7: 2,96; Currents of Sufism in Nineteenth- and Twentieth-Century Indo-Pakistan: An Overview, in Muslim World 87/3-4, 97; guest ed, new acad jour on Sufism, Sufi Illuminations 1:1, 97. **CONTACT ADDRESS** Dept of Philos and Relig, Colgate Univ, 13 Oak Drive, Hamilton, NY, 13346. **EMAIL** abuehler@mail.colgate.edu

BUEHLER, ARTHUR F.
DISCIPLINE JUDIASM, CHRISTIANITY, ISLAM **EDUCATION** Harvard Univ, PhD, 93. **CAREER** Asst prof, La State Univ, 98-. **RESEARCH** Sufi Shaykh. **SELECTED PUBLICATIONS** Auth, The Naqshbandiyya in Timurid India: The Central Asian Legacy, in J of Islamic Stud 7, 96; Currents of Sufism in Nineteenth-and Twentieth-Century Indo-Pakistan: An Overview, in Muslim World, 97. **CONTACT ADDRESS** Dept of Philos and Relig Stud, Louisiana State Univ, 106 Coates Hall, Baton Rouge, LA, 70803.

BUFFORD, EDWARD EUGENE
PERSONAL Born 07/15/1935, Birmingham, AL, m **DISCIPLINE** THEOLOGY **EDUCATION** Miles Coll, BA 1970; M Div Gammon Theol Sem, 1973; D Div Union Bapt Theol Sem, 1974. **CAREER** Centenary Un Meth Ch, minister; St Johns Un Meth Ch LA, 1972-74; Morning Star Un Meth Ch AL, 1969-72; Mt Moriah Un Meth Ch, 1967-69; Powell Chapel Lafayette AL, 1963-67; St Paul Jasper AL, 1962-63; St James, 1959-61; Watts Comm Ministries, dir 1972-74. **HONORS AND AWARDS** Crusade Scholar 1971. **MEMBERSHIPS** Mem NAACP; Masons; Alpha Phi Alpha Frat Inc. **CONTACT ADDRESS** 584 E Mc Lemore Ave, Memphis, TN, 38106.

BUFORD, THOMAS O.
PERSONAL Born 11/17/1932, Overton, TX, m, 1954, 3 children **DISCIPLINE** PHILOSOPHY **EDUCATION** NTex State Univ, BA, 55; Southwestern Baptist Theol Sem, BD, 58; Boston Univ, PhD, 63. **CAREER** Coordr of assistants, Dept Philos, Boston Univ, 59-60; asst prof philos, Ky Southern Col, 62-68 & NTex State Univ, 68-69; assoc prof, 69-76, Prof Philos, Furman Univ, 76-, Chmn Dept 80- **MEMBERSHIPS** Am Philos Asn; Southern Soc Philos & Psychol; Philos Educ Soc; SAtlantic Philos Educ Soc (pres, 80-82). **RESEARCH** Epistemology; philosophy of education, Ancient Greek philosophy. **SELECTED PUBLICATIONS** Ed, We Pass This Way But Once, Southern Press, 62; auth, Toward a philosophy of general education, Personalist, fall 67; Some random thoughts on curriculum building for today's students, South Baptist Educator, 12/68; Toward a Philosophy of Education, Holt, 69; Essays on Other Minds, Univ Ill, 70; coauth, Contemporary Studies in Philosophical Idealism, Claude Stark, 75; ed, Philosophy for Adults, Univ Press Am, 81; auth, In Search of a Calling, Mercer Univ Press; ed, Personalism Revisited, Rodopi, 98. **CONTACT ADDRESS** Dept of Philosophy, Furman Univ, Greenville, SC, 26913. **EMAIL** Tom.Buford@Furman.edu

BUHNEMANN, GULDRUN
DISCIPLINE INDIAN AND BUDDHIST STUDIES **EDUCATION** Vienna Univ, PhD, 80. **CAREER** Assoc prof, Univ Wisc Madison, 94-. **HONORS AND AWARDS** Nat Endow for the Humanities; Amer Coun of Learned Soc; Japan Soc for the Promotion of Sci. **MEMBERSHIPS** Amer Acad of Relig; Amer Orient Soc; Amer Coun of Southern Asian Art. **RESEARCH** Classical Indian studies; Religions of India. **SELECTED PUBLICATIONS** Auth, Sadhanasataka and Sadhanasatapancasika. Two Buddhist Sadhana Collections in Sanskrit Manuscript, Wien, Univ Wien, 94; auth, Nispannayogavali. Two Sanskrit Manuscripts from Nepal, Tokyo, The Ctr for East Asian Cultural Studies, 91; auth, The Hindu Deities Illustrated according to the Pratisthalaksanasarasamuccaya, Tokyo, The Ctr for East Asian Cultural Studies, 90; auth, Forms of Ganesa. A Study based on the Vidyarnavatantra, Wichtrach, Inst fur Indologie, 89; auth, The Worship of Mahaganapati according to the Nityotsava, Wichtrach, inst fur Indologie, 88; auth, Puja. A Study in Smarta Ritual, Vienna, Inst fur Indologie, Univ Wien, 88. **CONTACT ADDRESS** Dept. of Languages and Cultures of Asia, Univ of Wisconsin - Madison, 1242 Van Hise Hall, Madison, WI, 53706. **EMAIL** gbuhnema@facstaff.wisc.edu

BUICKEROOD, JAMES G.
PERSONAL Born 10/23/1951, Syracuse, NY, m, 1981 **DISCIPLINE** PHILOSOPHY **EDUCATION** Harper Col, BA, 81; Rutgers Univ, PhD, 88. **CAREER** Instr, philos, Rutgers Univ, 81-87; asst prof, San Jose State Univ, 88-89; vis asst prof, philos, College of William & Mary, 89-90; vis asst prof, philos, Washington Univ, 90-92; adj assoc prof, philos, Univ Delaware, 92-93. **MEMBERSHIPS** APA; Am Soc for Eighteenth-Century Stud; Soc for the Hist of Philos. **RESEARCH** Early Medieval philosophy; Locke; British materialism. **SELECTED PUBLICATIONS** Auth, Logic, in Black, ed, Dictionary of Eighteenth-Century World History, Blackwell, 94; auth, Pursuing the Science of Man: Some Difficulties in Understanding Eighteenth-Century Maps of the Mind, Eighteenth-Century Life, 95; ed, introd, A Philosophick Essay Concerning Ideas, According to Dr. Sherlock's Principles, AMS, 96; ed, introd, annotations, Smith, A Philosophical Discourse of the Nature of Rational and Irrational Souls, AMS, 98. **CONTACT ADDRESS** 3771 Lake Rd, Williamson, NY, 14589.

BULBULIA, AHMED I.
DISCIPLINE CONFLICT OF LAWS, CONTRACTS, CRIMINAL LAW, BUSINESS ASSOCIATIONS, INTERNATI **EDUCATION** London Sch Econ, LLB; Univ MI, LLM. **CAREER** Prof; Seton Hall Univ, 72-; barrister at law, Middle Temple & advocate before, Supreme Ct Safrica; taught at, Univ New Brunswick, Can & adj prof, Rutgers and NY Law Sch; dir, Legal Educ Opportunity, LEO, prog. **SELECTED PUBLICATIONS** Publ on, corporations and professional responsibility. **CONTACT ADDRESS** School of Law, Seton Hall Univ, Bayley Hall, 400 S. Ora, South Orange, NJ, 07079. **EMAIL** bulbulah@lanmail.shu.edu

BULL, ROBERT JEHU
PERSONAL Born 10/21/1920, Harrington, DE, m, 1959 **DISCIPLINE** CHURCH HISTORY, ARCHAEOLOGY **EDUCATION** Randolph-Macon Col, BA, 43; Duke Univ, BD, 46; Yale Univ, MA, 51, PhD, 56. **CAREER** Instr philos, Colgate Univ, 54-55; from instr to assoc prof, 55-70, field supvr, Drew Univ-McCormick Archaeol Exped, Jordan, 56-57, 60-62, 64, PROF CHURCH HIST, DREW UNIV, 70-, DIR, INST ARCHAEOL RES, 68-, Mem, Hazen Theol Discussion Group; Am Asn Theol Sch fel, Univ Utrecht, 59-60; Am Sch Orient Res, Jordan, 66-67; field supvr, Wooster Exped, Pella, 66; dir, Tell er Ras Exped, 66, 68; vpres, Comm Arch & Hist, United Methodist Church, 68; dir, Am Sch Orient Res, Jerusalem, 70-71, Joint Exped Khirbet Shemac, 1970 & Joint Exped Caesarea, 71; res prof, William Foxwell Albright Inst Archaeol Res, 74. **MEMBERSHIPS** Am Soc Church Hist; Am Sch Orient Res; Albright Inst Archaeol Res; Nat Lectr Archaeol Inst Am. **RESEARCH** Patristics; Palestinian archaeology; early American Methodist history. **SELECTED PUBLICATIONS** Auth, The Making of Our Tradition, Westminster, 67; coauth, The sixth campaign at Balatah, Bull Am Sch Orient Res, 4/68; The excavation of Tell er Ras, Bull Am Sch Orient Res, 4/68; The excavation of Tell er Ras on Mt Gerigim, Bibl Archaeologist, 5/68; Towards a Corpus Inscriptonum Latinarum Britannecarum in Palestina, Blestine Exploration Quart, 70; Tell er Ras, The Pottery, 71 & Tell er Ras, The Coins, 71, Smithsonian; co-ed, Eaesarea, The Preliminary Reports, Vol I, Harvard Univ, 74; auth, The Gold Coin Hoard at Caesarea + Ancient Numismatic Studies/, Bibl Archaeol, Vol 56, 1993; Caesarea and King Herod Magnificent City Plan/, Am J Archaeol, Vol 100, 1996. **CONTACT ADDRESS** Dept of Hist, Drew Univ, Madison, NJ, 07940.

BULLARD, EDWARD A., JR.
PERSONAL Born 04/02/1947, Syracuse, New York, m **DISCIPLINE** LAW **EDUCATION** Southern Univ, BS 1969; Syracuse Univ, MBA 1972; Univ of Detroit Law School, JD 1978. **CAREER** Carrier Corp, analyst 1969; Ernst & Young, accountant 1969-72; Univ of MI Flint, prof, 1972-93; GMI, assoc prof acctg 1972-1993; Detroit College of Business-Flint, prof, currently. **HONORS AND AWARDS** CPA NY 1977-; Outstanding Prof Univ of MI Flint 1979; mem Univ of Detroit Law Schl Moot Court Tax Team 1977. **MEMBERSHIPS** Bd mem Urban League Flint 1984, Flint Comm Devel Corp 1984; mem AICPA, Amer Acctg Assoc; adv Flint City Schools Bus Prog 1985; mem City of Flint Cable TV Advisory Panel; Small business consultant and urban analyst; mem Amer Business Law Assoc; board of directors, Urban League of Flint; board of directors, Flint Community Development Coordination; legal regress committee, executive committee, NAACP of Flint; advisory panel, Flint Cable TV; consultant, Junior Achievement, Beecher High School; mem, Congressional Black Caucus-Flint; numerous others. **CONTACT ADDRESS** Professor, Detroit Col of Business, Flint, 3488 N Jennings Rd, Flint, MI, 48504. **EMAIL** flebullaro@dcb.edu

BULLARD, JOHN MOORE
PERSONAL Born 05/06/1932, Winston-Salem, NC **DISCIPLINE** BIBLICAL STUDIES; ENGLISH LANGUAGE AND LITERATURE **EDUCATION** AB, 53, AM, 55, UNC- Chapel Hill; Mdiv, 57, PhD, 62, Yale Univ. **CAREER** Asst in Instruction, Yale Univ, 57-62; Asst Prof, 61-65, Assoc Prof, 65-70, Albert C. Outler Prof, 70-, Chmn, Dept of Religion, 63-, Wofford Col. **HONORS AND AWARDS** James Graduate Fel at Yale, 57-62; Dana Fel, Emory Univ, 89-90. **MEMBERSHIPS** Amer Acad of Religion; Soc of Biblical Lit; South Carolina Acad of Religion; New Bach Soc; Moravian Music Fdn. **RESEARCH** The Hymn as Literary form from ancient Sumerians to the Hebrew Psalter and beyond. **CONTACT ADDRESS** Dept of Religion, Wofford Col, 429 N. Church St., Spartanburg, SC, 29303. **EMAIL** bullardjm@wofford.edu

BULLOCK, ALICE G.
DISCIPLINE TAX LAW **EDUCATION** Howard Univ, BA, 72, JD, 75. **CAREER** Asst prof, 79; assoc dean, 88-90, and actg dean, 90; assoc dean, Acad Aff, 91-92 & interim dean, 96, Howard Univ. **MEMBERSHIPS** Dep dir, Asn Amer Law Sch, 92-94; Amer Law Inst; ABA Comt on Teaching Taxation; bd dir, Coun Legal Educ Opportunity; bd visitors, Brigham Young Univ Law Sch & bd trustees, Inst Independent Educ. **SELECTED PUBLICATIONS** Auth, Taxes, social policy and philanthropy: the untapped potential of low and middle income generosity, Cornell J Law and Public Policy, 97; A dean's role in supporting recruitment of minority faculty, Minority Law Teachers Conf 90, 10 St Louis Univ Public Law Rev 347, 91 & Is there life after safe harbor leasing, 19 New Eng Law Rev 1, 84; bk chap, Legal Issues in Mental Health, in Mental Health and Mental Illness in the Black Community, 90 & Taxes in Horowitz and Davidson, Legal Rights of Children, 84. **CONTACT ADDRESS** Dept of Law, Howard Univ, 2400 Sixth St NW, Washington, DC, 20059.

BULLOCK, JAMES
PERSONAL Born 08/22/1926, Charleston, MS, m **DISCIPLINE** LAW **EDUCATION** Texas Southern Univ, BA, JD, 1970. **CAREER** US Postal Service, supvr; TX Southern Univ, assoc dean law, assoc prof law, currently. **HONORS AND AWARDS** Phi Alpha Delta Outstanding Alumnus. **MEMBERSHIPS** Justice Greener Chap Phi Alpha Delta Legal Frat; TX Black Caucus; mem Am Bar Assn; Nat Bar Assn; State Bar TX; Houston Bar Assn; Houston Lawyers Assn; Phi Alpha Delta Legal Frat; mem S & Central YMCA; NAACP; Harris Co Cncl Orgn; TX Assn Coll Tchrs. **CONTACT ADDRESS** Sch of Law, Texas So Univ, 3100 Cleburne Avenue, Houston, TX, 77004.

BULLOCK, JOAN R.
DISCIPLINE LAW **EDUCATION** Mich State Univ, BA; Univ Toledo, JD; Univ Mich, MBA. **CAREER** Assoc prof. **SELECTED PUBLICATIONS** Auth, The Pebble in the Shoe: Making the Case for the Government Employee, 93; Abortion Rights in America, 94. **CONTACT ADDRESS** Col Law, Univ of Toledo, Toledo, OH, 43606. **EMAIL** joan.bullock@utoledo.edu

BUNGE, MARIO
DISCIPLINE PHILOSOPHY **EDUCATION** Univ Nat de La Plata, PhD. **RESEARCH** Theoretical physics; ontology; epistemology; philosophy of science. **SELECTED PUBLICATIONS** Auth, Treatise on Basic Philosophy, 89; co-auth, Philosophy of psychology, 87. **CONTACT ADDRESS** Philosophy Dept, McGill Univ, 845 Sherbrooke St, Montreal, PQ, H3A 2T5.

BUNGE, WILFRED F.
PERSONAL Born 11/21/1931, Caledonia, MN, m, 1963, 2 children **DISCIPLINE** RELIGION, CLASSICAL LANGUAGES **EDUCATION** Luther Col, BA, 53; Luther Theol Sem, BTh, 58; State Univ Iowa, MA, 55; Harvard Univ, ThD(-

New Testament), 66. **CAREER** Instr Relig & Classics, Luther Col, 56-57; instr Greek, Luther Theol Sem, 57-58; asst prof Relig & Classics & actg head Dept Relig, 62-69, assoc prof Relig, 69-74, registrar, 72-79, prof Relig, Luther Col, 74-, head dept, 79-87; Bk ed, Dialog, 66-70, asst prof, St John's Univ, Minn, 67-68. **MEMBERSHIPS** Soc Bibl Lit; Am Asn Col Registr & Admin Off; corresp mem Inst Antiq & Christianity. **RESEARCH** Ecumenical Christian dialogue; Greco-Roman religions; Apuleius. **SELECTED PUBLICATIONS** Auth, Critical method and the New Testament, In: Theological Perspectives, Luther Col, 64; transl, God's righteousness in Paul, the Bultmann School of Biblical interpretation: New directions?, 65 & Paul and Nascent Catholicism, Distinctive Protestant and Catholic themes reconsidered, 67, J Theol & Church, Harper Torchbk; coauth (with John Bale), The word and words: Liberal education of the clergy, Dialog, Spring 80; Warmly Weston: A Luther College Life, Decorah: Luther College Press, 98. **CONTACT ADDRESS** Dept of Classics & Relig, Luther Col, 700 College Dr, Decorah, IA, 52101-1045. **EMAIL** bungewil@luther.edu

BUNZL, MARTIN
DISCIPLINE PHILOSOPHY OF SCIENCE **EDUCATION** Univ Minn, BA, PhD. **CAREER** Instr, Rutgers, State Univ NJ, Livingston Col. **SELECTED PUBLICATIONS** Auth, The Context of Explanation, Kluwer, 93; Real History, Routledge, 97. **CONTACT ADDRESS** Dept of Philos, Rutgers, State Univ NJ, Livingston Col, 113 Davison Hall, Douglass, NJ, 28342. **EMAIL** bunzl@rci.rutgers.edu

BURBIDGE, JOHN WILLIAM
PERSONAL Born 02/29/1936, Hoiryung, Korea, m, 1958, 3 children **DISCIPLINE** PHILOSOPHY **EDUCATION** Univ Toronto, BA, 57, PhD(philos), 71; Yale Univ, MA, 58; Victoria Col, Ont, BD, 62. **CAREER** Lectr philos, Victoria Col, Ont, 58-59; minster in charge, Lakeview United Church, Port Credit, Ont, 63-68; from asst prof to assoc prof philos, 70-80, master, 77-82, PROF PHILOS, CHAMPLAIN COL, TRENT UNIV, 80-. **MEMBERSHIPS** Can Philos Asn; Can Soc Study Relig; Hegel Soc Am; Metaphysical Soc Am; Soc Philos & Relig. **RESEARCH** Hegel and Schelling; logic of religious belief; logic and syntax. **SELECTED PUBLICATIONS** Auth, One in Hope and Doctrine, Ryerson, 68; Concept and time in Hegel, Dialogue, 73; Being and Will, Paulist Press, 77; contribr, The necessity of contingency, In: Art and Logic in Hegel's Philosophy, Humanities, 80; contribr, Peirce on Historical Explanation, In: Pragmatism and Purpose, Univ Toronto Press, 81; auth, On Hegel's Logic, Humanities, 81; Man, God and death in Hegel's Phenomenology, Philos & Phenomenol Res, 81; Religion in Callaghan,Morley 'Such is my Beloved'/, J Can Dtudies-Revue d Etudes Canadiennes, Vol 27, 1992; **CONTACT ADDRESS** Dept of Philos, Trent Univ, Peterborough, ON, K9J 7B8.

BURCH, FRANCIS FLOYD
PERSONAL Born 05/15/1932, Baltimore, MD **DISCIPLINE** COMPARATIVE LITERATURE, THEOLOGY **EDUCATION** Fordham Univ, AB, 56, MA, 58; Woodstock Col, PhL, 57, STL, 64; Univ Paris, Dr, 67. **CAREER** Teacher English & French, Gonzaga High Sch, Washington, DC, 57-60; ordained priest, Roman Catholic, 63; from asst prof to assoc prof, 67-76, trustee, 71-76, asst acad dean, 72-74, prof English, St Joseph's Univ, PA, 76-, Scholar-in-residence English, Millersville State Col, 78. **HONORS AND AWARDS** Alpha Epsilon Delta; Alpha Sigma Nu; Merit Awards for teaching SJU, 80, 83. **MEMBERSHIPS** Int Soc Neoplatonic Studies; MLA; AAUP; Renaissance English Text Soc. **RESEARCH** Ironic, Conversational poetry 1850 to the present, French and Anglo-American; the neoplatonic tradition in literature and religion; Tristan Corbiere. **SELECTED PUBLICATIONS** Auth, Corbiere and Verlaine's Romances sans paroles, Mod Lang Rev, 58; Clement Mansfield Ingleby on Poe's Raven, Am Lit, 63; Soirees bretonnes: The first published verse of Alexis and Edouard Corbiere, Romance Notes, 70; Tristan Corbiere: L'originalite des amours jaunes et leur influence sur T S Eliot, Nizet, Paris, 70; co-ed, Tristan Corbiere: Oeuvres completes, Gallimard, Paris, 70; auth, Sur Tristan Corbiere: Lettres inedites adressees au poete et premieres critiques le concernant, Nizet, Paris, 75; Introd & transl, The Path to Transcendence: From Philosophy to Mysticism in Saint Augustine, Pittsburgh Theol Monogr Series, No 37, 81; The Iconography of Tristan Corbiere: A Manifold or Miscellaneous Self, Studies in Comparative Literature, 91; A Letter from Laurence Housman concerning A E Housman's Poetry, Notes and Queries, 92; RH Benson, Dictionary of Literary Biography, 95. **CONTACT ADDRESS** St. Joseph's Col, 5600 City Ave, Philadelphia, PA, 19131-1376.

BURCH, ROBERT W.
PERSONAL Born 03/31/1943, m, 1 child **DISCIPLINE** PHILOSOPHY **EDUCATION** Rice Univ, BA, 65, PhD, 69. **CAREER** Prof, Tex A&M Univ, 80-. **HONORS AND AWARDS** Phi Beta Kappa, 65; James A. and Alice G. Baker Scholar, 63-64; Thomas R. and Julia H. Franklin Scholar, 64-65; National Defense Educ Act Fel, 65-69; Tex A&M Univ Asn Former Students; Distinguished Tchg Awd, 83; Tex A&M Univ Col Liberal Arts Fifth Annual Humanities Lectr, 89. **RESEARCH** Logic and the history of logic, American philosophy. **SELECTED PUBLICATIONS** Auth, Study Guide for Hurley/Logic, 5th ed, Belmont, Calif: Wadsworth Publ Co, 94. **CONTACT ADDRESS** Dept of Philosophy, Texas A&M Univ, 314 Bolton Hall, College Station, TX, 77843-4237.

BURCH, SHARON PEEBLES
PERSONAL Monterey, CA, m, 1983 **DISCIPLINE** SYSTEMATIC THEOLOGY; PHILOSOPHY OF RELIGION **EDUCATION** Grad Theolog Union, PhD, 92. **CAREER** Asst prof, Boston Univ, 93-98 **HONORS AND AWARDS** N Amer Paul Tillich Soc Pres, 96 **MEMBERSHIPS** Amer Acad Relig; N Amer Paul Tillich Soc; Assoc Practical Theolog; Assoc of Professors & Researchers in Relig Educ; United Meth Assoc of Christian Educators; Pacific Coast & Theolog Soc; Boston Theolog Soc; Soc of Buddhist-Christian Studies. **RESEARCH** Practical Theology; Religious Education; Congregational Studies; Tillich Studies; Feminism; Postmodern Theology. **SELECTED PUBLICATIONS** Collective Absolute Presupposition, Peter Lang, forthcoming **CONTACT ADDRESS** Dept of Theology, Boston Univ, 745 Commonwealth Ave, Boston, MA, 02215. **EMAIL** spburch@bu.edu

BURGDORF JR., ROBERT L.
DISCIPLINE CONSTITUTIONAL LAW, CIVIL PROCEDURE **EDUCATION** Univ Notre Dame, AB, 70, JD, 73. **CAREER** Prof; co-dir, Legis Clin; past mem, Proj Action, Accessible Commun Transp in Our Nation, Nat Coun Handicapped & Nat Ctr for Law and the Handicapped; co-dir, Univ MD Sch of Law's Develop Disabilities Law Proj, 76-81. **HONORS AND AWARDS** Securing equal rights for persons with disabilities, fed Am(s) with Disabilities Act of 91; completed a legal treatise on disability discrimination in employ law for the Bureau of Nat Aff. **SELECTED PUBLICATIONS** Pub, a casebk & articles and reports in his field. **CONTACT ADDRESS** School of Law, Univ of District of Columbia, 4200 Connecticut Ave Northwest, Washington, DC, 20008.

BURGER, RONNA C.
DISCIPLINE PHILOSOPHY **EDUCATION** New Sch Soc Res, PhD, 73. **CAREER** Prof, Tulane Univ. **SELECTED PUBLICATIONS** Auth, The Phaedo, Yale; Plato's Phaedrus, Ala; pub(s) in, Rev Metaphysics; Interpretation; Essays in Ancient Greek Philos. **CONTACT ADDRESS** Dept of Philosophy, Tulane Univ, 6823 St Charles Ave, New Orleans, LA, 70118. **EMAIL** rburger@mailhost.tcs.tulane.edu

BURGER, WARREN EARL
PERSONAL Born 09/17/1907, St. Paul, MN, m, 1933, 2 children **DISCIPLINE** LAW **EDUCATION** William Mitchell Col Law, LLB, 31, LLD, 64. **CAREER** Assoc, Boyesen, Otis & Faricy and later partner, Faricy, Burger, Moore & Costello, 31-53; asst atty gen US, 53-56; judge, US Court of Appeals, 56-69; CHIEF JUSTICE, US SUPREME COURT, 69-, Mem fac, William Mitchell Col Law, 31-46, trustee; hon master bench, Middle Temple, Inns of Court, England, 69; chancellor, Bd Regents, Smithsonian Inst; chmn bd trustees, Nat Gallery Art; emer trustee, Macalester Col & Mayo Found. **MEMBERSHIPS** Am Bar Asn. **SELECTED PUBLICATIONS** Auth, The Decline of Professionalism, Proceedings of the Am Philos Soc, Vol 137, 1993; The Decline of Professionalism, Fordham Law Rev, Vol 63, 1995. **CONTACT ADDRESS** US Supreme Court, One First St NE, Washington, DC, 20543.

BURGESS, ANDREW J
PERSONAL Born 06/16/1936, m, 1994 **DISCIPLINE** RELIGIOUS STUDIES **EDUCATION** St Olaf Col, BA, 58; Yale Univ, PhD, 69; Univ Minn, MA, 94; Luther Theol Sem, MDiv, 95. **CAREER** Asst prof, religion, 69-76, Case Western Reserve Univ; vis assoc prof, religious stud, 76-78, Cleveland St Univ; assoc prof, philosophy, chmn, religious studies prog, 78-, Univ of New Mexico. **MEMBERSHIPS** Amer Acad of Religion; Amer Phil Asn; Soren Kierkegaard Soc. **RESEARCH** Philosophy of religion; history of Christian thought; Kierkegaard. **SELECTED PUBLICATIONS** Auth, Passion Knowing How and Understanding An Essay on the Concept of Faith, Amer Acad of Rel Acad Series 9, Scholars Press, 75; art, Repetition A Story of Suffering, Repetition Intl Kierkegaard Comm Vol VI, 93; art, Forstand in the Swenson-Lowrie Correspondence and in the Metaphysical Caprice, Phil Fragments and Johannes Climacus, Intl Kierkegaard Comm Vol VII, Mercer Univ Press, 94; art, Kierkegaard on Homiletics and the Genre of the Sermon, Jour of Comm and Religion, 94; art, The Bilateral Symmetry of Kierkegaards Postscript, Concluding Unscientific Postscript, Intl Kierkegaard Comm Vol XII, Mercer Univ Press, 97; art, Kierkegaard and Kenneth Burke on the Rhetoric of the Comic, Kierkegaard and Ethics Kierkegaard on the Language of Existence, Nakanishiya, 98. **CONTACT ADDRESS** Religious Studies Prog, Univ of New Mexico, Albuquerque, NM, 87131-1151. **EMAIL** aburgess@unm.edu

BURGESS, STANLEY M.
PERSONAL Born 11/27/1934, India, m, 1960, 5 children **DISCIPLINE** RELIGIOUS STUDIES **EDUCATION** Univ Michi, BA, 58, MA, 59; Univ Missouri, Columbia, PhD, 71. **CAREER** Tchr, hist, Emerson Jr High Sch, Flint, Mich, 57-58; fac memb, Evangelical Univ, 59-76; prof, relig stud, Southwest Missouri State Univ, 76- . **HONORS AND AWARDS** Burlington Northern Found fac achievement award, 89; Christianity Today Critics Choice award, 90; Tantur Scholar, 86. **MEMBERSHIPS** Am Acad Relig. **RESEARCH** Historical pneumatology. **SELECTED PUBLICATIONS** Auth, The Spirit and the Church: Antiquity, Hendrickson, 84, rereleased as The Holy Spirit: Ancient Christian Traditions, 94; auth, Reaching Beyond: Chapters in the History of Perfectionism, Hendrickson, 86; auth, Dictionary of Pentecostal and Charismatic Movements, Zondervan, 88; auth, The Holy Spirit: Eastern Christian Traditions, Hendrickson, 89; auth, The Holy Spirit: Medieval Roman Catholic and Reformation Traditions, Hendrickson, 97. **CONTACT ADDRESS** Dept of Religious Studies, Southwest Missouri State Univ, 901 S National, Springfield, MO, 65804. **EMAIL** StanleyBurgess@mail.smsu.edu

BURGH, RICHARD
DISCIPLINE PHILOSOPHY **EDUCATION** Rider Univ, BA cum laude; Univ Wis MA, PhD. **CAREER** Dept ch; instr, Rider Univ, 75-; Westminister, 92-. **HONORS AND AWARDS** NEH fel. **RESEARCH** Medical ethics. **SELECTED PUBLICATIONS** Extensive publ(s) on the moral foundation of the law. **CONTACT ADDRESS** Westminister Choir Col, Rider Univ, 101 Walnut, Princeton, NJ, 08540.

BURIAN, RICHARD M.
PERSONAL Born 09/14/1941, Hanover, NH, m, 3 children **DISCIPLINE** PHILOSOPHY **EDUCATION** Reed Col, BA, 63; Univ Pittsburgh, PhD, 71. **CAREER** Instr, asst prof, lectr, Brandeis Univ, 67-76; asst prof of philos, Fla A&M Univ, 68-69; assoc dean of col, Brandeis Univ, 73-76; assoc prof, Drexel Univ, 77-83; res assoc, Mus of Camparative Zoology, Harvard Univ, 76-77; vis assoc prof, Dept Hist and Philos of Sci, Univ Pittsburgh, 78-79; vis assoc prof, Dept of Philos and Hist, Div of Biol Sci, Univ Calif, 81-82; prof philos, Va Polytechnic Inst and State Univ 83-92; adjunct prof, Ctr for the Study of Sci in Society, Va Polytechnic Inst and State Univ, 83-92; head, Dept of Philos, Va Polytechnic Inst and State Univ, 83-92; resident fel, Nat Humanities Ctr, Research Triangle Park, 91-92; vis prof, Univ de Bourgogne, 92; dir, Ctr for the Study of Sci in Society, and the Grad Prog in Sci and Tech Studies, Va Polytechnic Inst and State Univ, 92-97; prof sci studies and philos, Va Polytechnic Inst and State Univ, 92-present. **HONORS AND AWARDS** Res grant, Nat Endowment for the Humanities for work on a Conceptual History of the Gene; Nat Sci Foun Conf Grant, Santa Fe Inst; resident fel, Nat Humanities Ctr; pres elect, Int Soc for Hist, Philos, and Soc Studies of Biology. **MEMBERSHIPS** Soc for Integrative and Comparative Biology; Am Asn for the Advan of Sci; Int Soc for Hist, Philos, and Soc Studies of Biology; Am Philos Asn; British Soc for the Hist of Sci; British Soc for the Philos of Sci; Federation of Am Scientists; Genetics Soc of Am; Hist of Sci Soc; Philos of Sci Asn; Sigma Xi, Soc de d'Histoire et d'Epistemologie des Sciences de la Vie; Soc for Integrative and Comparative Biology; Soc for the Study of Evolution; Soc for Social Studies of Sci; Soc of Systematic Biology; Union of Concerned Scientists. **RESEARCH** Philosophy of biology; philosophy of science; history of 19th and 20th century biology. **SELECTED PUBLICATIONS** Co-ed, Integration in Biology, in Biology and Philosophy, 8(3), 93; co-ed, The Right Organism for the Job, in Jour of the Hist of Biology, 26(2), 93; co-ed, PSA 1994, vol. 1, Philos of Sci Asn, 94; auth, Jean Brachet's Cytochemical Embryology: Connections with the Renovation of Biology in France?, in Les sciences biologiques et medicales en France 1920-1950, vol. 2, CNRS Editions, 94; auth, Dobzhansky on Evoluionary Dynamics, in The Evolution of Theodosius Dobzhansky, Princeton Univ Press, 94; auth, Comments on Hans-Jorg Rheinberger's 'From Experimental Systems to Cultures of Experimentation', in Concepts, Theories, and Rationality in the Biological Sciences: The Second Pittsburgh-Konstanz Colloquium in the Philosophy of Science, Univ Konstanz and Univ Pittsburgh Press, 95; co-ed, PSA 1994, vol. 2, Philos of Sci Asn, 95; auth, Some Epistemological Reflections on Polistes as a Model Organism, in Natural History and Evolution of an Animal Society: The Paper Wasp Case, Oxford Univ Press, 96; auth, Underappreciated Pathways Toward Molecular Genetics as illustrated by Jean Brachet's Chemical Embryology, in The Philosophy and History of Molecular Biology: New Perspectives, Dordrecht: Kluwer, 96; auth, On Conflicts Between Genetic and Developmental Viewpoints - and their Resolution in Molecular Biology, in Structure and Norms in Science, vol. 2 of the 10th Int Congress of Logic, Methodology, and Philosophy of Science, Dordrecht: Kluwer, 95; co-ed, Research Programs of the Rouge Cloitre, in History and Philosophy of the Life Sciences, 19(1), 97. **CONTACT ADDRESS** Dept of Philosophy, Virginia Polytech Inst and State Univ, Blacksburg, VA, 24061-0126. **EMAIL** rmburian@vt.edu

BURK, DAN L.
DISCIPLINE LAW **EDUCATION** Brigham Young Univ, BS, 85; Northwestern Univ, MS, 87; Stanford Univ, JSM; AZ State Univ, JD, cum laude, 90. **CAREER** Asst prof, Seton Hall Univ; vis asst prof, George Mason Univ; tchg fel, Stanford Univ; exec comt, ACS Div Chem Law; adv bd, AAAS Sci + Lit Prog; acad adv, Am Comt Interoperable Sys; policy adv, Coun Sci Soc Pres. **MEMBERSHIPS** Order of the Coif; Am Chem Soc; AAAS. **SELECTED PUBLICATIONS** Auth, Trademarks Along the Infobahn: A First Look at the Emerging Law of Cybermarks, Univ Richmond J of Law and Technol.

CONTACT ADDRESS Seton Hall Univ, South Orange, NJ. **EMAIL** burkdanl@shu.edu

BURKE, ALBIE

PERSONAL Born 03/21/1932, Rugby, ND, m, 1960, 2 children **DISCIPLINE** AMERICAN CONSTITUTIONAL & LEGAL HISTORY **EDUCATION** Univ Chicago, BA, 58, MA, 65, PhD, 68. **CAREER** Assoc prof, 72-77, prof hist, Calif State Univ, Long Beach, 77-. **MEMBERSHIPS** Am Civil Liberties Union; Orgn Am Historians; Am Soc Legal Hist. **SELECTED PUBLICATIONS** Auth, Federal regulation of congressional elections in Northern cities 1871-94, Am J Legal Hist, 1/70; ed, The Hist Teacher, 79-85. **CONTACT ADDRESS** Dept Hist, California State Univ, Long Beach, 1250 N Bellflower, Long Beach, CA, 90840-0001.

BURKE, MICHAEL B.

PERSONAL Born 02/16/1943, Quincy, MA **DISCIPLINE** PHILOSOPHY **EDUCATION** Univ Va, BA, 64; Univ Wis-Madison, PhD, 76. **CAREER** Asst prof, Bosphorus Univ, Istanbul, 76-79; Prof, Ind Univ, 80- . **HONORS AND AWARDS** Outstanding Mem Sch Liberal Arts, Ind Univ-Indpls, 97; IU Tchg Excellence Award, 97. **MEMBERSHIPS** Am Philos Asn; Philos Time Soc; Asn for Informal Logic and Critical Thinking. **RESEARCH** Metaphysics; Informal Logic. **SELECTED PUBLICATIONS** Auth, Cohabitation, Stuff, and Intermittent Existence, Mind, vol 355, no 355, July 80, 391-405; The Infinitistic Thesis, The S Jour Philos, vol 22, no 3, Fall 84, 295-305; Hume and Edwards on Why is There Something Rather Than Nothing?, The Australasian Jour Philos, vol 62, no 4, Dec 84, 355-362; Spatial Analogues of 'Annihilation and Recreation, Analysis, vol 45, no 1, Jan 85, 24-29; Unstated Premises, Informal Logic, vol 7, no 2-3, Spring and Fall 85, 107-118; Copper Statues and Pieces of Copper: A Challenge to the Standard Account, Analysis, vol 52, no 1, Jan 92, 12-17; Dion and theon: An Essentialist Solution to an Ancient Puzzle, the Jour Philos, vol 91, no 3, March 94, 129-139; Preserving the Principle of One Object to a Place: A Novel Account of the Relations Among Objects, Sorts, Sortals, and Persistence Conditions, Philos and Phenomenological Res, vol 54, no 3, Sept 94, 591-624; Denying the Antecedent: A Common Fallacy? Informal Logic, vol 16, no1, Winter 94, 23-30; Sortal Essentialism and the Potentiality Principle, Rev of Metaphysics, vol 49, no 3, March 96, 491-514; Tibbles the Cat: a Modern Sophisma, Philos Stud (s), vol 84, no 1, Oct 96, 63-74; Coinciding Objects: Reply to Lowe and Denkel, Analysis, vol 57, no 1, Jan 97, 11-18; Preserving the Principle of One Object to a Place: A Novel Account of the Relations Among Objects, Sorts, Sortals, and Persistence Conditions, reprinted in Material Constitution: A Reader, Lanham, MD, Rowman, 97, 236-269; Persons and Bodies: How to Avoid the New Dualism, Amer Philos Quart, vol 34, no 4, Oct 97, 457-467. **CONTACT ADDRESS** Dept of Philosophy, Indiana Univ-Purdue Univ, Indianapolis, 425 University Blvd, Indianapolis, IN, 46202. **EMAIL** mburke@iupui.edu

BURKE, RONALD R.

PERSONAL Harlan, IA, m, 1971, 2 children **DISCIPLINE** RELIGIOUS STUDIES **EDUCATION** Univ Notre Dame, BA, 66, MA, 68; Yale Univ, MPhil, 70, PhD, 74. **CAREER** Instr, Univ Nebr, Omaha, 71-; coed, J of Relig and Film. **HONORS AND AWARDS** NEH grant, Univ Calif, Santa Barbara, 78-79; NEH grant, Univ Calif, Berkeley, 92., Founder, Roman Cath Modernism Gp, Am Acad of Relig, 76. **MEMBERSHIPS** Bd dir, Roman Cath Modernism Gp, Am Acad of Relig. **SELECTED PUBLICATIONS** Ed, John Henry Newman: Theology and Reform, Garland, 92; conribur, Personality and Belief, Lanham, 94. **CONTACT ADDRESS** Univ Nebr, Omaha, Omaha, NE, 68182.

BURKE, WILLIAM THOMAS

PERSONAL Born 08/17/1926, Brazil, IN, m, 1959, 3 children **DISCIPLINE** LAW **EDUCATION** Ind State Univ, BS, 49; Ind Univ, JD, 53; Yale Univ, JSD, 59. **CAREER** Res assoc & lectr law, law sch, Yale Univ, 56-62; prof, Ohio State Univ, 62-68; fac chmn, Inst Marine Studies, 73, PROF LAW, UNIV WASH, 68-, PROF MARINE STUDIES, 76-. **MEMBERSHIPS** Marine Technol Soc (vpres, 72-74). **RESEARCH** International law of the sea. **SELECTED PUBLICATIONS** Coauth, The Public Order of the Oceans, Yale Univ, 62; auth, Ocean sciences technology and the future international law of the sea, Mershon Ctr Pamphlet, Ohio State Univ, 66; Contemporary legal problems in ocean development, In: Toward a Better Use of the Ocean, SIPRI, Stockholm, Sweden, 69; Straight Base-lines in International Maritime Boundary Delimitation - Reisman,MW, Westerman,GS/, Ocean Development and Int Law, Vol 25, 1994; United-Nations Resolutions on Driftnet Fishing - An Unsustainable Precedent for High Seas and Coastal Fisheries Management/, Ocean Development and Int Law, Vol 25, 1994; Implications for Fisheries Management of US Acceptance of the 1982 Convention on the Law of the Sea/, Am J Int Law, Vol 89, 1995; Importance of the 1982 UN Convention on the Law of the Sea and its Future-Development/, Ocean Development and International Law, Vol 27, 1996; Memorandum of Opinion on the Legality of the Designation of the Southern-Ocean Sanctuary by the IWC/, Ocean Development and Int Law, Vol 27, 1996; Legal-Aspects of the IWC Decision on the Southern-Ocean Sanctuary/, Ocean Development and Int Law, Vol 28, 1997; The International Regime of Fisheries - From UNCLOS 1982 to thc Presential Sea - Deyturriaga,JA/, Am J Int Law, Vol 91, 1997. **CONTACT ADDRESS** Sch of Law, Univ of Wash, Seattle, WA, 98195.

BURKETT, DELBERT ROYCE

PERSONAL Born 08/22/1949, Lamesa, TX, s **DISCIPLINE** NEW TESTAMENT; CHRISTIAN ORIGINS **EDUCATION** Duke Univ, Phd, 89. **CAREER** Vis asst prof, W Ky Univ, 89-90; vis asst prof, Appalachian St Univ, 90-93; asst prof, Lebanon Valley Col, 93-96; asst prof, La St Univ, 96-. **MEMBERSHIPS** Soc Bibl Lit **RESEARCH** Literary Sources of Early Christian Gospels; History of Apocalyptic Thought and Movements. **SELECTED PUBLICATIONS** The Son of Man Debate: A History and Evaluation, Society for New Testament Studies Monograph Series, Cambridge Univ, forthcoming; Two Accounts of Lazarus' Resurrection in John 11, Novum Testamentum 36, 94; The Nontitular Son of Man: A History and Critique, New Testament Studies 40, 94. **CONTACT ADDRESS** Dept Philos and Relig Studies, Louisiana State Univ, Baton Rouge, LA, 70803. **EMAIL** dburket@unix1.sncc.lsu.edu

BURKETT, RANDALL KEITH

PERSONAL Born 10/23/1943, Union City, IN, m, 1965 **DISCIPLINE** RELIGION, HISTORY **EDUCATION** Am Univ, AB, 65; Harvard Divinity Sch, MTS, 69; Univ Southern Calif, PhD(social ethics), 75. **CAREER** Admin asst curric develop, Univ Southern Calif, 72-73; assoc dir spec studies, 73-77, assoc coordr grants & res, 76-79, DIR SPEC STUDIES, COL OF HOLY CROSS, 77-, COORDR GRANTS & RES, 79-, Lectr, Ctr Exp Studies; ed, Afro-Am Relig Hist Group Newsletter, Am Acad of Relig, 76-; Nat Endowment for the Humanities fel, 79-80. **MEMBERSHIPS** Am Acad Relig; Am Soc Church Hist; Asn for Study Afro-Am Life & Hist. **RESEARCH** Afro-American religious history. **SELECTED PUBLICATIONS** Auth, Black Redemption: Churchmen Speak for the Garvey Movement, Temple Univ, 78; co-ed, Black Apostles: Afro-American Clergy Confront the Twentieth Century, G K Hall, 78; auth, Garveyism as a Religious Movement: The Institutionalization of a Black Civil Religion, Scarecrow, 78. **CONTACT ADDRESS** Off of Spec Studies, Col of the Holy Cross, Worcester, MA, 01610.

BURKEY, JOHN

PERSONAL Born 07/02/1953, Reading, PA, m, 1982, 2 children **DISCIPLINE** PHILOSOPHY **EDUCATION** Villanova, MA, 78; Duquesne, PhD, 85. **CAREER** Assoc Prof, Siena Col, 85-. **RESEARCH** Phenomenology; history of philosophy **CONTACT ADDRESS** Dept of Philosophy, Siena Col, Louisville, NY, 12211. **EMAIL** burkey@siena.edu

BURKHARDT, FREDERICK

PERSONAL Born 09/13/1912, New York, NY, m, 1973, 3 children **DISCIPLINE** PHILOSOPHY **EDUCATION** Columbia Univ, PhD, 40. **CAREER** Instr to assoc prof, 36-47, pres, 47-57, Bennington Col; pres, Am Coun of Learned Soc, 57-74; ed, The Works of William James, 75- ; ed, The Correspondence of Charles Darwin, 74- . **HONORS AND AWARDS** LLD, Columbia Univ and Univ Michigan. **MEMBERSHIPS** Phi Beta Kappa; HSS; AAAS; APA; APS; Am Antiq Soc; Mass Hist Soc. **RESEARCH** History and philosophy of science. **SELECTED PUBLICATIONS** Ed, The Works of William James, 18 v, Harvard, 75-88; ed, The Correspondence of Charles Darwin, 11 v, Cambridge Univ, 85-99; ed, The Letters of Charles Darwin: A Selection, Cambridge Univ, 96. **CONTACT ADDRESS** PO Box 1037, Bennington, VT, 05201. **EMAIL** fhb@gover.net

BURKHART, JOHN E.

PERSONAL Born 10/25/1927, Riverside, CA, m, 1951, 3 children **DISCIPLINE** THEOLOGY **EDUCATION** Occidental Col, BA, 49; Union Theol Sem, NY, BD, 52; Univ Southern Calif, PhD(relig), 59. **CAREER** From instr to assoc prof, 59-68, prof syst theol, 68-81, PROF THEOL, MCCORMICK THEOL SEM, 81-, Roblee lectr, Stephens Col, 63; vis prof theol, Garrett Theol Sem, 66 & DePaul Univ, 70; consult, US Cath Conf, 70; mem coun theol sems, United Presby Church, 73-79. **HONORS AND AWARDS** DD, Occidental Col, 64. **MEMBERSHIPS** Am Theol Soc (pres, 69-70); Am Acad Relig; Cath Theol Soc Am; Soc Values Higher Educ; Royal Anthrop Inst. **RESEARCH** Ecclesiology; liturgies; social anthropology. **SELECTED PUBLICATIONS** Auth, Understanding the Word of God, Bd Christian Educ, 64; Thinking from the table, 11/69 & Theology in an affluent society, 5/70, McCormick Quart; Authority, candor, and ecumenism: No famine in the land, 75; Levi-Strauss: Social anthropologist, Listening, 75; Understanding Worship, 81 & Have All the Seas Gone Dry?, 81, Reformed Liturgy & Music; Worship, Westminster, 82; The Oil-of-Gladness - Anointing in the Christian Tradition - Dudley,M, Rowell,G, Eds/, J Ecumenical Studies, Vol 31, 1994; Reshaping Table-Blessings + Observations on the So-Called Etiquette-of-Life Among Early Christians and Jews - Blessing and Thanksgiving to our God Revelation-vii,12, Interpretation, Vol 48, 1994; Through the Tempest - Theological Voyages in a Pluralistic Culture - Gilkey,L/, J Relig, Vol 74, 1994; The Eucharistic Mystery - Revitalizing the Tradition - Power,DN/, J Ecumenical Studies, Vol 31, 1994; So We Believe, So We Pray - Towards Koinonia in Worship - Best,TF, Heller,D/, J Ecumenical Studies, Vol 34, 1997. **CONTACT ADDRESS** Dept of Theol, McCormick Theol Sem, 5555 S Woodlawn Ave, Chicago, IL, 60637.

BURKLE, HOWARD R.

PERSONAL Born 07/15/1925, Monticello, AR, m, 1948, 3 children **DISCIPLINE** PHILOSOPHY, RELIGION **EDUCATION** Cent Mo State Col, AB, 45; Yale Univ, BD, 48, STM, 49, PhD(philos theol), 54. **CAREER** Asst prof relig, Colo Col, 51-54, philos, Dickinson Col, 54-58; assoc prof philos & relig, 58-66, prof philos, 66-68 PROF PHILOS & RELIG STUDIES & CHMN DEPT RELIG STUDIES, GRINNELL COL, 68-, Vis prof Christian ethics, Int Christian Univ, Tokyo, 61-62. **MEMBERSHIPS** Soc Phenomenol & Existential Philos; Am Acad Relig; Japanese Asn Studies Am Philos. **RESEARCH** Contemporary Philosophy of religion; social philosophy of Jean Paul Sartre. **SELECTED PUBLICATIONS** Auth, Counting against and counting decisively against, J Relig, 7/64; Schaff and Sartre on the grounds of individual freedom, Int Philos Quart, 12/65; Social freedom in Sartre's Critique de la raison dialectique, Rev Metaphysics, 6/66; The Non-existence of God, Herder & Herder, 69; Patching Gods Garment - Environment and Mission in the 21st-Century - Roberts,WD/, J Ecumenical Studies, Vol 33, 1996; What Kind of God - Essays in Honor of Rubenstein,Richard,L. - Rubenstein,BR, Berenbaum,M/, J Ecumenical Studies, Vol 34, 1997. **CONTACT ADDRESS** Dept of Relig, Grinnell Col, Grinnell, IA, 50112.

BURKS, ARTHUR WALTER

PERSONAL Born 10/13/1915, Duluth, MN, m, 1943, 3 children **DISCIPLINE** PHILOSOPHY **EDUCATION** DePauw Univ, BA, 36; Univ Mich, MA, 37, PhD(philos), 41. **CAREER** Teacher, high sch, Mich, 37-38; instr electrical engineering, Univ Pa, 41-46; from asst prof to assoc prof philos, 46-54, chmn dept computer & commun sci, 67-71, PROF PHILOS, UNIV MICH, ANN ARBOR, 54-, PROF COMPUTER & COMMUN SCI, 67-, DIR LOGIC OF COMPUTERS GROUP, 56-, Instr, Swarthmore Col, 45-46; consult MANIAC, Inst Advan Studies, Princeton, 46-48; digital computers, Burroughs Corp, 48-54; res assoc philos, Univ Chicago, 50-51; consult ORACLE, Argonne Nat Lab, 50-51; Guggenheim Mem fel, 53-54; res assoc philos, Harvard, 55; mem ed bd, Philos Sci, 55-; res prof applied mathematics, Univ Ill, Urbana, fall 60; mem comt to advise dir res, Atomic Energy Comn Digital Computers, 60-62; Am Coun Learned Soc fel, 62-63; vis prof, Indian Inst Technol, Kanpur, 65-66; consult ed, Synthese, an Int J Epistemology, Methodology & Philos Sci, 66-; fel, Ctr Advan Studies Behav Sci, Stanford Univ, 71-72. **HONORS AND AWARDS** ScD, DePauw Univ, 73. **MEMBERSHIPS** Am Philos Asn; Asn Computing Machinery; Mind Asn; Charles S Peirce Soc (pres, 54-55); Philos Sci Asn. **RESEARCH** Philosophy of science; inductive logic; computer organization. **SELECTED PUBLICATIONS** Logic, Computers and Men, Proceedings & Addresses Am Philos Asn, 72-73; Chance, Cause, Reason--An Inquiry into the Nature of Scientific Evidence, Univ Chicago Press, 77; Peirces Evolutionary Pragmatic Idealism/, Synthese, Vol 106, 1996; Who Invented the Computer - A Memoir of the 1940s/, Mich Quart Rev, Vol 36, 1997. **CONTACT ADDRESS** 3445 Vintage Valley, Ann Arbor, MI, 48105.

BURNEKO, GUY

DISCIPLINE LITERATURE, PHILOSOPHY OF SCIENCE, EVOLUTION OF CONSCIOUSNESS **EDUCATION** Fordham Univ, BA; Univ AK, MA; Emory Univ, PhD. **CAREER** Assoc prof, dir, Grad Liberal Stud, Golden Gate Univ. **HONORS AND AWARDS** NEH fel, Claremont Grad Sch & Stanford Univ. **MEMBERSHIPS** Acad of Consciousness Stud, Princeton Univ. **SELECTED PUBLICATIONS** Auth of articles on intercultural and philosophical interpretation, philosophical hermeneutics, interdisciplinary and transdisciplinary educ, intuition and cult develop, and other topics. **CONTACT ADDRESS** Golden Gate Univ, San Francisco, CA, 94105-2968.

BURNETT, FREDRICK WAYNE

PERSONAL Born 12/18/1944, Birmingham, AL, m, 1995, 2 children **DISCIPLINE** RELIGION **EDUCATION** Anderson Col, Ind, BA, 67, Anderson Theol Sem, MDiv, 70; Vanderbilt Divinity Sch, DMin, 73, Vanderbilt Univ, MA, 76, PhD, 79. **CAREER** From assoc prof to Prof Relig Studies, Anderson Univ, IN, 76. **MEMBERSHIPS** Soc Bibl Lit; Cath Bibl Asn Am; Am Acad Relig. **RESEARCH** The Gospel of Matthew and its community setting; lit criticism and New Testament studies; soc sci methodologies and New Testament studies. **SELECTED PUBLICATIONS** Auth, The Testament of Jesus-Sophia: A Redaction-Critical Study of the Eschatological Discourse in Matthew, Univ Press Am, 81; co-auth, The Postmodern Bible, Yale Univ Press, 95. **CONTACT ADDRESS** Anderson Univ, 1100 E 5th St, Anderson, IN, 46012-3495. **EMAIL** fburnett@kirk.anderson.edu

BURNOR, RICHARD N.

PERSONAL Born 08/26/1952, Cleveland, OH, m, 1979, 4 children **DISCIPLINE** PHILOSOPHY **EDUCATION** Bucknell Univ, BS, 74; MA, 78, PhD, 85, Univ Arizona. **CAREER** Lectr, Univ Arizona, 83-84; Supply Lectr, 84-85, Asst Visiting

Prof, 85-86, Univ Wyoming; Asst Prof, Towson State Univ, 86-93; Visiting Asst Prof, 93-96, Univ Toledo; Part time Instr, 96, Washtenaw Comm Col; Visiting Scholar, 96, Part time Instr, 97, Univ Toledo; Asst Prof, 97-, Felician Col. **HONORS AND AWARDS** Riesen Prize for Best Philosophy Paper, Univ Arizona, 83; Teaching Fel, Univ Wyoming Summer High School Inst, 86; Fel NEH Summer Seminar for College Teachers, 91; Felician Col Summer Research Stipend, 98. **MEMBERSHIPS** Amer Phil Assoc; Philosophy of Time Soc; The Soc of Christian Philosophers **RESEARCH** Philosophical interpretations of probability; theory acceptance; philosophy of time; philosophy of technology; new technologies in teaching **SELECTED PUBLICATIONS** Auth, Rethinking Objective Homogeneity: Statistical Versus Ontic Approaches, Philosophical Studies, 93; Review of Le Poidevin and MacBeath, Philosophy of Time, 93, Teaching Philosophy, 94; A Structural Model for Temporal Passage, The Southern Journal of Philosophy, 94; Outlines for Success: Outline Processors and Teaching Philosophy, Teaching Philosophy, 95. **CONTACT ADDRESS** Dept of Philosophy, Felician Col, 262 S Main St, Lodi, NJ, 07644. **EMAIL** RNVBURNOR@AOL.COM

BURNS, J. LANIER
PERSONAL m, 4 children **DISCIPLINE** HUMANITIES; THEOLOGY **EDUCATION** Davidson Col, AB, 65; Dallas Theolog Sem, ThM, 72, ThD, 79; Univ Tex, Dallas, PhD, 93. **CAREER** Pres, Am Council Asian Christian Acad, Evangelical Theolog Sem, 73-; Bd Adv, The Providence Sch, 91-; consult, The Damares Project, 98-; Bd Dir, K-Life Ministries, 91-98; Bd Dir, Pine Cove Ministries, 93-; ed consult, Zondervan Publ House, 88-; relig consult, The Los Angeles Times, 98. **HONORS AND AWARDS** Who's Who in Am, 85, Who's Who in Religion, 85; Sr Class Award for Faculty Excellence, 86; Who's Who in Leadership Society, 86; Who's Who in Science and Theol, 95; Who's Who among Am tchrs: The Best Tchrs in Am Selected by the Best Stud, 96. **MEMBERSHIPS** Am Acad Rel; Am Philolog Asn, Evangelical Theolog Society; Renaissance Society Am; Society Biblical Lit; Society Christian Philos; Dist Leadership Society. **CONTACT ADDRESS** Dept of Theology, Dallas Theol Sem, 3909 Swiss Ave, Dallas, TX, 75204-6411.

BURNS, J. PATOUT, JR.
PERSONAL Born 10/14/1939, New Orleans, LA, d **DISCIPLINE** THEOLOGY **EDUCATION** Spring Hill Col, BA, 63, MA, 64; Regis Col Toronto, MDiv, 70; Univ of St Michael's Col Toronto, 71; Yale Univ, PhD, 74. **CAREER** Jesuit Sch of Theol, asst prof, assoc prof, 74-80; Loyola Univ of Chicago, 80-86; Univ of Fla, prof, 86-90; Washington Univ St Louis, prof, 90-. **MEMBERSHIPS** AAR, NAPS. **RESEARCH** Christianity in Roman Africa. **SELECTED PUBLICATIONS** Auth, The Development of Augustine's Doctrine of Operative Grace, Paris: Etudes Augustiennes, 80; auth, War and its Discontents: Pacifism and Quietism in the Abrahamic Traditions, contrib ed., Washington: Georgetown Univ Pr, 96; auth, The Ethics of Warfare: Muslim, Jewish and Christian Religious Traditions: Conference Report, Jour Relig Pluralism, 93; auth, The Atmosphere of Election: Augustinianism as Common Sense, Jour Early Christian Studies, 93; auth, Delighting the Spirit: Augustine's Practice of Figurative Interpretation, De doctoria christiana: A Classic of Western Culture, ed. D. W. H. Arnold and P. Bright, Notre Dame: Univ Notre Dame Press, 95; auth, The Holiness of the Churches, The Unbounded Community, ed. W. Caferro and D. Fisher, NY: Garland Pub, 96. **CONTACT ADDRESS** Dept of Theology, Washington Univ, PO Box 1050, St. Louis, MO, 63130. **EMAIL** jpburns@artsci.wustl.edu

BURNS, STEVEN A.M.
DISCIPLINE PHILOSOPHY **EDUCATION** Acadia Univ, BA, 62; Alberta Univ, MA, 66; Univ London, PhD, 70. **CAREER** Prof. **RESEARCH** Wittgenstein, Plato, aesthetics, political philosophy. **SELECTED PUBLICATIONS** Auth, "Reason, Love and Laughter," Dialogue, 89; The Place of Art in a Reasonable Education, Reason in Tchg and Edu, 89; "Otto Weininger's Metaphysics," Jour Philos Res, 90; "If a Lion Could Talk," Wittgenstein Stud, 94; "Ethics and Socialism: Tensions in the Political Philosophy of J. G. Schurman," Jour Can Stud, 96. **CONTACT ADDRESS** Dept of Philos, Dalhousie Univ, Halifax, NS, B3H 3J5.

BURR, JOHN ROY
PERSONAL Born 07/18/1933, Oshkosh, WI, m, 1963, 3 children **DISCIPLINE** PHILOSOPHY **EDUCATION** Univ Wis, Madison, BA, 55; Columbia Univ, MA, 56, Phd, 59. **CAREER** Instr philos, Franklin & Marshall Col, 59-61; asst prof, Hood Col, 61-64; from asst prof to assoc prof, 64-68, chemn dept philos & div humanities, 66-76, prof philos, Univ Wis, Oshkosh, 68-, asst dean Col Lett & Sci, 76-79, pres fac senate, 83-84, 87-88; chemn univ acad policies com, 96-; mem fac senate, 81-96, 97-99; Partic, Hood Col Sem Prog on India, Ford Found, 63-64; Wis State Univ Oshkosh study grant int educ & Wis State Univ curric, 67; Wis State Univ Regents res grant, 71-72. **HONORS AND AWARDS** John McNRosebush Univ prof, 84; Phi Beta Kappa, Univ Wis, Madison, 54; Phi Kappa Phi, Univ Wis, Madison, 54. **MEMBERSHIPS** Am Philos Asn; Metaphys Soc Am; Asn Asian Studies; AAUP. **RESEARCH** Aesthetics; Indian philosophy; American Philos, William James. **SELECTED PUBLICATIONS** Co-ed, Philosophy and Contemporary Issues, Macmillan, 72, 2nd ed, 76 & 3rd ed, 80; auth, H L Mencken: Scientific skeptic, Menckeniana, summer 75; H L Mencken: American scientific skeptic, Bicentennial Symp Philos, CUNY Grad Ctr, 76; ed, Handbook of World Philosophy: Contemporary Developments Since 1945, 80 & auth, articles on Clarence Darrow, Joseph McCabe, and H L Mencken, In: Dict of Unbelief (in press), Greenwood Press; co-ed, Philosophy and Contemporary Issues, Macmillan, 72, 76, 80, 84, 88, 92, Prentice Hall, 96; ed, World Philosophy: A Contemporary Bibliography, Greenwood, 93. **CONTACT ADDRESS** Dept of Philosophy, Univ Wisconsin, Oshkosh, 800 Algoma Blvd, Oshkosh, WI, 54901-8617. **EMAIL** burr@vaxa.cis.uwosh.edu

BURRELL, DAVID
DISCIPLINE PHILOSOPHY **EDUCATION** Univ Notre Dame, AB, 54; Gregorian Univ, STL, 60; Yale Univ, PhD, 65. **CAREER** Prof. **RESEARCH** Medieval philosophy; philosophical theology; metaphysics. **SELECTED PUBLICATIONS** Auth, Creation or Emanation: Two Paradigms of Reason, 90; Al-Ghazali on Ninety-nine Beautiful Names of God, 92; Freedom and Creation in Three Traditions, 93; Aquinas and Islamic and Jewish Thinkers, 93; Islamicist as Interpreter, 97. **CONTACT ADDRESS** Philosophy Dept, Univ of Notre Dame, 336/7 O'Shaughnessy, Notre Dame, IN, 46556. **EMAIL** david.b.burrell.1@nd.edu

BURRES, KENNETH LEE
PERSONAL Born 08/12/1934, Topeka, KS, m, 1956, 3 children **DISCIPLINE** BIBLICAL STUDIES, LINGUISTICS **EDUCATION** Baker Univ, AB, 56; Garrett Theol Sem, BD, 60; Northwestern Univ, MA, 61, PhD, 70. **CAREER** Pastor, United Methodist Church, Gary, IN, 64-67; asst prof, 67-71, assoc prof Relig, 71-93, PROF, CENT METHODIST COL, 93-, CHAIR, DEPT OF PHILOS & RELIG, 97-. **MEMBERSHIPS** Soc Bibl Lit; Am Academy of Relig. **RESEARCH** Linguistic analysis of New Testament Greek; New Testament theology; early Christian history. **SELECTED PUBLICATIONS** Auth, Prolegomena to a new biblical lexicography, Soc Bibl Lit Sem Papers, 71. **CONTACT ADDRESS** Dept of Relig, Central Methodist Col, 411 Central Methodist Sq, Fayette, MO, 65248-1198. **EMAIL** ckburres@mcmsys.com

BURRINGTON, DALE E.
PERSONAL Born 03/27/1930, St. Louis, MO, m, 1976, 5 children **DISCIPLINE** PHILOSOPHY **EDUCATION** Johns Hopkins Univ, PhD, 64. **CAREER** Hartwick Col, prof, 62-96 **MEMBERSHIPS** APA, ALSC **RESEARCH** Philos of mind; moral responsibility; free will. **SELECTED PUBLICATIONS** Auth, The Command and the Orders in Brunner's Ethic, Scottish Jour of Theol, 67; auth, Blameworthiness, Jour Philos Res, 99. **CONTACT ADDRESS** 52 Dietz St, Oneonta, NY, 13820. **EMAIL** burringtond@hartwick.edu

BURRIS, JOHN, JR.
PERSONAL Born 02/06/1956, m, 1985 **DISCIPLINE** RELIGION **CAREER** Vist asst prof, 98, Wesleyan Univ; sr lectr, 98-99, Suffolk Univ. **HONORS AND AWARDS** Diss of Year, 96, Univ Calif, Santa Barbara **MEMBERSHIPS** Amer Acad of Religion. **RESEARCH** Amer religion; religion & colonialism **SELECTED PUBLICATIONS** Ed, Reflections in the Mirror of Religion, Macmillan Press, 97. **CONTACT ADDRESS** 79 B Broadmeadow #11, Marlborough, MA, 01752-5419. **EMAIL** kathjohn@gte.net

BURRIS, JOHN L.
PERSONAL Born 05/05/1945, Vallejo, CA, m **DISCIPLINE** LAW **EDUCATION** Vallejo Jr Coll, AA 1965; Golden Gate Coll San Francisco, BS 1967; Univ of CA Grad Sch of Bus Berkeley, MBA 1970; Univ of CA Sch of Law, JD 1973. **CAREER** Haskins & Sells San Francisco, acct/auditor 1967-69; Jenner & Block Chicago, assoc atty 1973-74; State Atty Office Cook Co Chicago, asst state atty 1975-76; Alameda Co DA Office Oakland, dep dist atty 1976-79; Harris, Alexander & Burris, atty; Law Office of John L Burris, atty, currently. **HONORS AND AWARDS** Outstanding Leadership Awd CA Assn of Black Lawyers 1980; Omegas Continental Boys Club, Outstanding Leadership Award, 1986; Second Baptist Church, Martin Luther King Leadership Award Vallejo, 1985; Clinton White, Outstanding Trial Lawyers, Charles Houston Bar Association, 1987; Loren Miller, Outstanding Civil Rights Lawyer, 1989; Alameda County's Peace Officer for Better Committee Relationship, Outstanding Merit Award, 1991; NAACP Legal Defense Fund, Bay Area Chapter, Pro Bono Award, 1992; Special investigation into fatal shooting of 15-year-old youth, & entry into NAACP offices by Oakland police officers. **MEMBERSHIPS** Past pres CA Assn of Black Lawyers; past president Charles Houston Bar Assn; spec consultant to president Natl Bar Assn; American Trial Lawyers Association; Alameda Co Bar Association; Kappa Alpha Psi Fraternity; Lawyers Committee for Urban Affairs - (SF); African-American Lawyers Against Apartheid; 100 Black Men, San Francisco Bay Chapter; Lawyer Delegate to Ninth Circuit, 1992. **CONTACT ADDRESS** Law Office of John L Burris, 1212 Broadway, 12th Floor, Oakland, CA, 94612.

BURT, DONALD X.
DISCIPLINE THEOLOGY **EDUCATION** Villanova Univ, AB, 52; Catholic Univ Am, MA, 55; PhD, 60. **CAREER** Prof. **SELECTED PUBLICATIONS** Auth, The Rush to Resurrection, Liturgical Press: Collegeville, Minn, 85; Emmanuel: Reflections on God with Us, Liturgical Press, 88; But When You Are Older Reflections on Coming to Age, Liturgical Press, 92; The Pilgrim God, Liturgical Press, 95; Augustine's World: an Introduction to his Speculative Philosophy, Univ Press Am, 96; Augustine On Divine Voluntarism, Angelicum, Angelicum Univ, Rome, Italy, 87; Augustine On The Morality Of Violence: Theoretical Issues And Applications, Atti: Congresso Internazionale Su S. Agostinio Nel XVI Centenario Della Conversion, Stud Ephemeridis Augustinianum, 26, Inst Patristicum Augustinianum, Rome, 87; Facts, Fables, and Moral Rules: An Analysis of the Abortion Debate, New Scholasticism, 88; Augustine on the Authentic Approach to Death, Augustinianum, Inst Patristicum Augustinianum, Rome, 88; Augustine On the State as a Natural Society, Augustiniana, 90; Augustine On The Authentic Approach To Death: A Summary of Research, Stud Patristica, 90; Courageous Optimism: Augustine on the good of Creation, Augustinian Studies, 90; Friendship and Subordination in Earthly Societies, Augustinian Stud(s), 92; Friendship and the State: A Summary of Research, Collectanea Augustiniana II: Presbyter Factus Sum, Peter Lang, 93. **CONTACT ADDRESS** Dept of Philosophy, Villanova Univ, 800 Lancaster Ave., Villanova, PA, 19085-1692.

BURT, ROBERT AMSTERDAM
PERSONAL Born 02/03/1939, Philadelphia, PA, m, 1964, 2 children **DISCIPLINE** LAW & PSYCHIATRY **EDUCATION** Princeton Univ, BA, 60; Oxford Univ, MA, 62; Yale Univ, JD, 64. **CAREER** Law clerk, chief judge David L Bazelon, US Court of Appeals, DC, 64-65; asst gen counsel, Off Spec Rep Trade Negotiations, Exec Off of President, 65-66; legis asst, Sen Joseph D Tydings, 66-68; assoc prof law, Univ Chicago, 68-70; from assoc prof to prof law, Univ Mich, Ann Arbor, 70-76, law in psychiat, 74-76; Prof Law, Yale Univ, 76-. **HONORS AND AWARDS** Mem Inst of Med, Nat Res Coun & Nat Acad Sci, 76; Rockefeller Found fel humanities, 76; Guggenheim fel, 97. **RESEARCH** Law and psychological disciplines, especially psychiatry, in regulating family relations and anti-social conduct; constitutional law. **SELECTED PUBLICATIONS** Auth, Taking Care of Strangers: The Rule of Law in Doctor-Patient Relations, Free Press, 79; The constitution of the family, Supreme Ct Rev, 79; auth, Two Jewish Justices, Univ Calif Press, 88; auth, The Constitution in Conflict, Harvard Univ Press, 92. **CONTACT ADDRESS** Law Sch, Yale Univ, PO Box 208215, New Haven, CT, 06520-8215. **EMAIL** robert.burt@yale.edu

BURTCHAELL, JAMES T.
DISCIPLINE THEOLOGY **CAREER** Prof Theol, Univ Notre Dame, 75-. **SELECTED PUBLICATIONS** Auth, The Dying of the Light: The Disengagement of Colleges and Universities from Their Christian Churches, Eerdmans, 98; Philemon's Problem: A Theology of Grace, Eerdmans, 98. **CONTACT ADDRESS** Univ of Notre Dame, Corby Hall, Notre Dame, IN, 46556. **EMAIL** jtbcsc@worldnet.att.net

BURTNESS, JAMES H.
DISCIPLINE SYSTEMATIC THEOLOGY **EDUCATION** St. Olaf Col, BA, 49; Luther Sem, BTh, 53; Princeton Sem, ThD, 58. **CAREER** Instr, 55; vis prof, Gurukul Theol Col, Madras, India, 63-64; ATS fel, Free Univ Berlin, 66-67; Lutheran tutor, Mansfield Col, Oxford, Eng, 73-74; prof, 72; prof emeri. **HONORS AND AWARDS** Ch, Aus Memorial Lectures Comm; pastor, Faith Lutheran Church, Albany, 58-60. **MEMBERSHIPS** Mem, Task Force on Church and Soc of the Commn for the New Lutheran Church. **RESEARCH** Christian ethics. **SELECTED PUBLICATIONS** Ed, Word & World, 79-81; auth, Shaping the Future: The Ethics of Dietrich Bonhoeffer, 84; Whatever You Do, 67; co-ed, The New Community in Christ; All Things Are Yours, 62. **CONTACT ADDRESS** Dept of Systematic Theology, Luther Sem, 2481 Como Ave, St. Paul, MN, 55108. **EMAIL** jburtnes@luthersem.edu

BURTON, KEITH
PERSONAL Born 08/01/1963, m, 1998, 2 children **DISCIPLINE** NEW TESTAMENT INTERPRETATION **EDUCATION** Northwst Univ, PhD, 94; Oakwood Col, BA, 87 **CAREER** Asst Prof of Relig, Oakwood Col; Res Asst, Garrett Evangel Theol Sem **HONORS AND AWARDS** Whos Who Among Teachers; Amer Bible Soc Greek & Hebrew Award **MEMBERSHIPS** Am Acad of Relig; Soc Bibl Lit; Cath Bibl Assoc **RESEARCH** Origins of Christianity in Africa; Blacks in Society; Rhetorical Understanding of New Testament **SELECTED PUBLICATIONS** Auth, So That You May be With Another, UMI, 95; We've Come This Far by Faith, A Voice in the Wilderness Publications, 96 **CONTACT ADDRESS** Dept of Relig, Oakwood Col, Huntsville, AL, 35896. **EMAIL** burton@oakwood.edu

BUSBY, KAREN
DISCIPLINE LAW **EDUCATION** Univ Manitoba, LLB, 81; Univ Columbia, LLM, 88. **CAREER** Asst prof, 88-93; assoc prof, 93-. **HONORS AND AWARDS** Ed, Can Jour Women

Law, 89-. **RESEARCH** Gender and the law; administrative law; civil procedure; research and writing. **SELECTED PUBLICATIONS** Auth, Penner and Lisa Fainstein, LRI, 89; pubs on obscenity law; co-ed, Equality Issues in Family Law: Considerations for Test-Case Litigation. **CONTACT ADDRESS** Fac of Law, Univ Manitoba, Robson Hall, Winnipeg, MB, R3T 2N2. **EMAIL** busby@cc.umanitoba.ca

BUSCH, THOMAS W.
PERSONAL Born 06/18/1937, Cleveland, OH, m, 1963, 3 children **DISCIPLINE** PHILOSOPHY **EDUCATION** St Joseph Col, BA, 60; Marquette Univ, MA, 62, PhD, 67. **CAREER** From instr to assoc prof, 64-77, PROF PHILOS, VILLANOVA UNIV, 77-. **MEMBERSHIPS** Soc Phenomenol & Existential Philos; Merleau-Ponty Circle. **RESEARCH** Contemporary French philosophy; phenomenology; philosophical anthropology. **SELECTED PUBLICATIONS** Auth, Being and Nothingness: Ontology vs Phenomenology, Southern J Philos, 65; Merleau-Ponty and the problem of origins, Philos Today, 67; From phenomenology to Marxism, Res Phenomenol, 72; Sartre: The phenomenological reduction and human relationships, J Brit Soc Phenomenol, 75; Sartre and the senses of alienation, Southern J Philos, 77; Phenomenology as humanism: The case of Husserl and Sartre, Res Phenomenol, 80; Sartre's use of the reduction: Being and Nothingness revisited, in Existence & Dialectic: Contemporary approaches to the philosophy of Jean-Paul Sartre, Duquesne Univ Press, 80; Coming to terms with Jean-Paul Sartre, Philos Today, fall 80; La Nausee: A lover's quarrel with Husserl, Res Phenomenol, 82; Beyond the cogito: The question of the continuity of Sartre's thought, Mod Schoolman, 3/83; Shifting paradigms: Sartre on critique, language and the role of the intellectual, in Critical and Dialectical Phenomenology, SUNY Press, 87; Gabriel Marcel on the death of man, in Contributions of Gabriel Marcel to Philosophy, Edwin Mellon, 89; The Power of Consciousness and the Force of Circumstances in Sartre's Philosophy, Ind Univ Press, 90; Sartre on surpassing the given, Philos Today, spring 91; Merleau-Ponty, Hermeneutics and Postmodernism, SUNY Press, 92; Ethics and ontology: Levinas and Merleau-Ponty, Man and World, 92; Secondary reflection as interpretation, Bull de la Societe Francaise de Philosophy de Langue Francaise, fall 95; Sartre and Ricoeur on imagination, Am Cath Philos Quart, autumn 96; Merleau-Ponty and Derrida on the phenomenon, in Ecart and Difference: Merleau-Ponty and Derrida on Seeing and Writing, Humanities, Press, 97. **CONTACT ADDRESS** Dept of Philos, Villanova Univ, 845 E Lancaster Ave, Villanova, PA, 19085. **EMAIL** tbusch@vill.edu

BUSCHART, DAVID
DISCIPLINE THEOLOGY **EDUCATION** Wheaton Col, BA; Trinity Evangel Divinity Sch, ThM, MDiv; Drew Univ, MPhil, PhD. **CAREER** Prof, Denver Sem, 98-. **HONORS AND AWARDS** Founding mem, Res Sci and Ethics Adv Comm, Wascana Rehabilitation Ctr, Regina, Saskatchewan. **MEMBERSHIPS** Mem, Amer Acad of Rel; Can Evangel Theol Assn; Evangel Theol Soc; Soc for the Stud of E Orthodoxy and Evangelicalism. **SELECTED PUBLICATIONS** Auth, Traditions of Protestant Theology. **CONTACT ADDRESS** Denver Conservative Baptist Sem, PO Box 10000, Denver, CO, 80250. **EMAIL** davidb@densem.edu

BUSH, L. RUSS
DISCIPLINE RELIGION **EDUCATION** Miss Col, BA, 67; Southwestern Sem, MDiv, 70, PhD, 75. **CAREER** Prof, 72-89, Southwestern Sem; dean, 89-, Southeastern Sem. **MEMBERSHIPS** Am Acad Religion; Society Biblical Lit; Evangelical Theol Society; Evangelical Philos Society; Society Christian Philos. **CONTACT ADDRESS** SEBTS, PO Box 1889, Wake Forest, NC, 27588. **EMAIL** lrbush@msn.com

BUSH, LUTHOR RUSSELL, III
DISCIPLINE PHILOSOPHY OF RELIGION **EDUCATION** Miss Col, BA, 67; Southwestern Baptist Theological Seminary, MDiv, 70, PhD, 75. **CAREER** Asst to assoc Prof of Philos of Religion, Southwestern Seminary, 72-89; Acad vp, Dean of fac, Prof of philos of religionN, Southeastern Baptist Theological Seminary, 89-. **MEMBERSHIPS** Am Acad of Rel; Soc of Christian Philos; Soc of Biblical Lit; Evangelical Theological Soc; Evangelical Philos Soc. **RESEARCH** Christian faith; arts and sciences. **SELECTED PUBLICATIONS** Auth, Psalms, 99; Baptists and the Bible, revised edition, 99. **CONTACT ADDRESS** Southeastern Baptist Theological Sem, Box 1889, Wake Forest, NC, 27588. **EMAIL** lrbush@msn.com

BUSH, NATHANIEL
PERSONAL Born 01/19/1949, Washington, DC, m **DISCIPLINE** LAW **EDUCATION** Ripon Coll, BA 1973; Cleveland Marshall Coll of Law, JD 1977; Wharton Sch of Business, certificate 1984. **CAREER** Distinguished visiting Prof of Law Cambridge Univ, grad asst 1976-77; Bureau of ATF Dept of Treas, Attorney 1979-81; Univ of the District of Columbia, adjunct prof criminology 1982-84; DC State Campaign Jesse Jackson for Pres, general counsel 1983-84; DC Bd of Educ, vice pres; Ward VII rep. **HONORS AND AWARDS** Moot Court Bd of Govs Cleveland Marshall Coll of Law; 1st place Third Annual Douglas Moot Court Competition 1975; Jessup Intl Moot Court Competition 1976; Outstanding Young Men of America, 1984. **MEMBERSHIPS** Bd of dir Southeast Neighbors Citizens Assoc; bd of dirs Far East Comm Serv Inc; chmn bd of dirs Concerned Citizens on Alcohol & Drug Abuse; mem Bar of the State of OH 1977; mem Bar of the District of Columbia 1979. **CONTACT ADDRESS** DC Bd of Education, 415 12th St NW, Washington, DC, 20019.

BUSS, MARTIN JOHN
PERSONAL Born 11/04/1930, Hunan, China, m, 1954, 4 children **DISCIPLINE** RELIGION **EDUCATION** Bloomfield Col, BA, 51; Princeton Theol Sem, BD, 54, ThM, 55; Yale Univ, PhD, 58. **CAREER** Vis asst prof relig, Macalester Col, 57-58; vis instr, Coe Col, 58-59; from asst prof to assoc prof, 59-77, PROF RELIG, EMORY UNIV, 77-; Am Coun Learned Soc fel, 64-65; assoc ed, J Bibl Lit, 70-74. **MEMBERSHIPS** Soc Bibl Lit; World Union Jewish Studies **RESEARCH** Israelite law; hermeneutics; comparative scriptures **SELECTED PUBLICATIONS** Auth, The language of the Divine I, J Bible & Relig, 61; The Psalms of Asaph and Korah, J Bibl Lit, 12/63; The beginning of human life as an ethical problem, J Relig, 7/67; The Prophetic Word of Hosea, Topelmann, Berlin, 69; The Distinction Between Civil and Criminal Law in Ancient Israel, Proc Sixth World Cong Jewish Studies, 77; Understanding communication, In: Encounter With the Text, Fortress Press, 79; Selfhood and biblical eschatology, Zeitschrift fur die alttestamentliche Wissenschaft, 88; Logic and Israelite law, Semeia, 89; Biblical Form Criticism in its Context, Sheffield Acad Press, 98. **CONTACT ADDRESS** Dept of Relig, Emory Univ, 1364 Clifton Rd N E, Atlanta, GA, 30322-0001. **EMAIL** relmjb@emory.edu

BUSSANICH, JOHN
DISCIPLINE GREEK PHILOSOPHY, MEDIEVAL PHILOSOPHY, PHILOSOPHY OF RELIGION, COMPARATIVE **EDUCATION** Stanford Univ, BA, 72, PhD, 82. **CAREER** Assoc prof, Univ NMex. **SELECTED PUBLICATIONS** Auth, The One and its Relation to Intellect in Plotinus: A Commentary on Selected Texts, Brill, 88; Plotinus' Metaphysics of the One, in The Cambridge Companion to Plotinus, ed, Lloyd P Gerson, Cambridge UP, 96; coed, Ancient Philosophy. **CONTACT ADDRESS** Univ NMex, Albuquerque, NM, 87131.

BUTCHVAROV, PANAYOT K.
PERSONAL Born 04/02/1933, Sofia, Bulgaria **DISCIPLINE** PHILOSOPHY **EDUCATION** Robert Coll, BA, 52; Univ of VA, MA, 54, PhD, 55. **CAREER** Instr, 55-57, Univ of Baltimore; Asst Prof, 57-59, Univ of SC; Asst Prof, 59-61, Assoc Prof, 61-66, Prof, 66-68, Syracuse Univ; Prof, 68-, Univ of IA. **HONORS AND AWARDS** Pres, APA. **MEMBERSHIPS** APA **RESEARCH** Epistemology, metaphysics, existentialism. **SELECTED PUBLICATIONS** Auth, Resemblance and Identity, IN Univ Press, 66; The Concept of Knowledge, Northwestern Univ Press, 70; Being Qua Being, IN Univ Press, 79; Skepticism in Ethics, IN Univ Press, 89; Skepticism About the External World, Oxford Univ Press, 98. **CONTACT ADDRESS** Dept of Philosophy, Univ of Iowa, 269 EPB, Iowa City, IA, 52242-1408. **EMAIL** panayot-butchvarov@uiowa.edu

BUTLER, CLARK WADE
PERSONAL Born 07/29/1944, Los Angeles, CA, m, 1971, 1 child **DISCIPLINE** PHILOSOPHY **EDUCATION** Univ Southern Calif, BA, 66, PhD(philos), 70. **CAREER** From instr to asst prof, 69-75, assoc prof, 75-80, actg chmn dept, 77-79, Prof Philos, Ind Univ-Purdue Univ, Ft Wayne, 80-, Chmn Dept, 79-83; Co-ed, Clio, 76- & Clio Hegel Studies, 81-. **HONORS AND AWARDS** Phi Beta Kappa **MEMBERSHIPS** Hegel Soc Am; Am Philos Soc; Int Hegel Vereinigung; Int Hegel Gesellschaft; Brit Hegel Soc. **RESEARCH** Hegel; metaphysics; social philosophy. **SELECTED PUBLICATIONS** Auth, G W F Hegel, G K Hall, 77; co-transl, Hegel: The Letters, Ind Univ Press, 84; auth, Hegelian Panentheism as Joachimite Christianity, In: Hegel's Philosophy of Religion, SUNY Press, 92; Empirical vs. Rational Order in the History of Philosophy, Owl of Minerva, Fall 94; The Reducibility of Ethics to Human Rights, Dialogue and Universalism, Univ Warsaw, vol 5, no 7, 95; Hegel's Logic: Between Dialectic and History, Northwestern Univ Press, 96; History as the Story of Freedom, Editions Rodopi (Amsterdam), 97; author of numerous other journal articles. **CONTACT ADDRESS** Dept of Philos Ind, Univ-Purdue Univ, 2101 Coliseum Blvd E, Fort Wayne, IN, 46805-1445. **EMAIL** butler@tpfw.edu

BUTLER, J. RAY
PERSONAL Born 08/05/1923, Roseboro, NC, m, 1943 **DISCIPLINE** THEOLOGY **EDUCATION** Shaw U, BA, BD, MDiv, 1974, DD, 1973; Friendship Coll, DD, 1966; Southeastern Theol Sem 1966-67; McKinley Theol Sem LLD 1976; Southeastern Theol Seminary DTh 1969. **CAREER** Ebenezer Bapt Ch Wilmington, pastor 1954-70; First Bapt Ch Creeddmoor, pastor; Mt Olive Bapt Ch Fayeteville, pastor; New Christian Chapel Bapt Ch RoseHill, pastor; Shiloh Bapt Church Winston-Salem, pastor 1970-90; United Cornerstone Baptist Church, Winston-Salem, NC, founder, pastor, 1990-. **HONORS AND AWARDS** Various tours in foreign countries; Pastor of Yr Award Midwestern Bapt Laymen's Fellowship Chicago 1975, 1976; elected Contbng Writer Nat Bapt Sunday Sch Publ Bd. **MEMBERSHIPS** Past pres Interdenom Ministerial All; past pres Interracieal Minist Assn; past pres Wilmington Civic League; past pres PTA; 1st vice pres NAACP; bd of dirARC; mem Man Power Delvel; mem Citizens Coalition Bd; pres-at-large Gen Bapt State Conv; pres Bapt Ministers Conf & Asso; mem Forsyth Clergy Assn Chmn of Gen Bapt St Conv of NC Inc; mem extension tchg staff of Shaw U; exec bd of Lott Carey Bapt Foreign Missions & Conv; appointed bd of licensed gen contractors Gov Jim Hunt of NC; founder, Shilohian/St Peters Day Care; moderator, Rowan Baptist Missionary Association, 1989-. **SELECTED PUBLICATIONS** Auth, The Christian Communion as Related to the Jewish Passover and Monetary Commitment, 1985. **CONTACT ADDRESS** United Cornerstone Missionary Baptist Church, 2745 Patria St, Winston-Salem, NC, 27127.

BUTLER, TRENT C.
PERSONAL Born 02/16/1941, Wichita Falls, TX, w, 1966, 2 children **DISCIPLINE** BIBLICAL STUDIES **EDUCATION** Hardin-Simmons Univ, BA, 63; Southern Baptist Theol Sem, BD, 66; Vanderbilt Univ, PhD, 71. **CAREER** Asst prof relig, Atlanta Baptist Col, 70-71; asst prof Old Testament, Int Baptist Theol Sem, Switzerland, 71-81; curric design ed, Baptist Sunday School Bd, 81-83; ed, Holmam Bible Pub, 83- . **MEMBERSHIPS** ETS; IBR; SBL; SSOT; ASOR. **RESEARCH** Old Testament language; Old Testament theology; Book of Joshua and historical Books. **SELECTED PUBLICATIONS** Ed, Holman Student Bible Dictionary, Holman, 93; ed, Holman Book of Maps, Charts and Reconstructions, Holman, 93; auth, Points for Emphasis, Broadman & Holman, 94, 95, 96, 97, 98; auth, Experiencing God Study Bible, Broadman & Holman, 95; auth, Cracking Old Testament Codes, Broadman & Holman, 95; auth, Experiencing God Calendar, Broadman & Holman, 95; auth, Narrative Form Criticism: Dead or Alive, in A Biblical Itinerary, Sheffield, 97; ed, Holman Bible Atlas, Holman, 98; auth, The Theology of Joshua, Rev and Expositor, 98. **CONTACT ADDRESS** 127 North Ave North, Nashville, TN, 37234-0064. **EMAIL** TButler@lifeway.com

BUXBAUM, RICHARD MANFRED
PERSONAL Born 04/16/1930, Friedberg, Germany, 2 children **DISCIPLINE** LAW **EDUCATION** Cornell Univ, AB, 50, LLB, 52; Univ Calif, Berkeley, LLM, 53. **CAREER** Atty, 53-61; dir Earl Warren Legal Inst, 70-75, Prof Law, Univ Calif, Berkeley, 61-; dean Int & Area Studies, Univ Calif Berkeley, 93-; ed in chief, Am Journal of Comparative Law, 87-. **HONORS AND AWARDS** Humboldt Research Prize, 92; Order of Merit, FedRepGermany, 93; Dr iur hc Univ Osnabruck, 93, Dr iur hc and Hon prof, Eotvos Lorand Univ, 93; Hon prof Peking Univ, 98. **MEMBERSHIPS** Am Bar Asn. **RESEARCH** Corporation law; government regulation of business; law and economic development; Int Assn Comparative Law; German Soc of Comparative Law. **SELECTED PUBLICATIONS** Auth, Restrictions inherent in the patent monopoly: A comparative critique, Univ Pa Law Rev, 65; Antitrust policy in modern society: Dilemmas and needs, In: Das Unternehmen in der Rechtsordnung, C F Muller, Karlsruhe, 67; co-ed, Corporations--Cases and Materials, Callaghan, 4th ed, 68 & West, 5th ed, 79; auth, Public participation in the enforcement of the antitrust laws, Calif Law Rev, 71; Die Private Klage als Mittel zur Durchsetzung Wirtschaftspolitischer Rechtsnormen, C F Muller, Karlsruhe, 72; The dissenter's appraisal remedy, Univ Calif, Los Angeles Law Rev, 76; The demand on boards of directors in derivative litigation, Calif Law Rev, 80; European Economic and Business Law with Hertig, Hirsch & Hopt, eds, 96; Responsibilities of Transnational Corporations to Host Nations, in Current Legal Issues in the Internationalization of Business Enterprises, Heng et al, eds, 96; Die Rechtsvergleichung zwischen nationalem Staat und internationaler Wirtschaft, in Rabels Zeitschrift, 96; Corporate Governance and Corporate Monitoring -- The Whys and Hows, in Australian Journal of Corporate Law, 96. **CONTACT ADDRESS** Sch of Law, Univ of California, Berkeley, 220 Boalt Hall, Berkeley, CA, 94720-7201. **EMAIL** bux@uclink.berkeley.edu

BYBEE, JAY S.
DISCIPLINE CONSTITUTIONAL LAW **EDUCATION** Brigham Young Univ, JD, cum laude, 80. **CAREER** Bus mngr, Brigham Young Univ Law Rev; assoc, Sidley & Austin, 81-84; atty, US Dept of Justice Off of Legal Policy and Civil Div, 84-89; assoc coun to the Pres, White House, 89-91; instr, La State Univ; prof, Univ Nev, Las Vegas. **SELECTED PUBLICATIONS** Published articles in various journals, including the Yale Law Journal, Northwestern University Law Review, Vanderbilt Law Review, and George Washington Law Review. **CONTACT ADDRESS** Univ Nev, Las Vegas, Las Vegas, NV, 89154.

BYER, INEZ
PERSONAL Born 03/22/1927, Kansas City, MO, m, 1949, 2 children **DISCIPLINE** PHILOSOPHY, RELIGION **EDUCATION** Univ Mo, Columbia, BA, 48, MA, 49, PhD(Philos), 68. **CAREER** Asst Philos, Univ Mo-Columbia, 63-65; asst prof, 65-73, prof Philos, Cottey Col, 73-. **MEMBERSHIPS** Am Philos Asn. **RESEARCH** Aesthetics. **CONTACT ADDRESS** Div of Humanities, Cottey Col, 1000 W Austin, Nevada, MO, 64772-2790. **EMAIL** IByer@Cottey.edu

BYMAN, SEYMOUR DAVID
PERSONAL Born 10/26/1934, Chicago, IL, m, 1956, 3 children **DISCIPLINE** RELIGIOUS HISTORY **EDUCATION** Univ Ill, Urbana, BA, 56; Roosevelt Univ, MA, 67; Northwestern Univ, PhD(hist), 71. **CAREER** Asst prof, 70-75, assoc prof, 75-78, PROF HIST, WINONA STATE UNIV, 78-, Assoc, Inst Psychohistory, 77-78. **MEMBERSHIPS** AHA. **RESEARCH** Martyrology. **SELECTED PUBLICATIONS** Auth, Tudor death stands, Moreana, 73; Suicide and alienation: Martyrdom in Tudor England, Psychoanal Rev, 74; Guilt and martyrdom: The case of John Bradford, Harvard Theol Rev, 75; A defense of psychohistory, 78 & Child raising and melancholia in Tudor England, 78, J Psychohistory; Ritualistic acts and compulsive behavior: The pattern of sixteenth century martyrdom, Am Hist Rev, 78; Humanities and the Law School Experience, J of Legal Educ, 85; The Perils of Psychohistory, J of Psychohistory, 88. **CONTACT ADDRESS** Dept of History, Winona State Univ, P O Box 5838, Winona, MN, 55987-0838. **EMAIL** sbyman@vax2.winona.msus.edu

BYNAGLE, HANS EDWARD
PERSONAL Born 02/24/1946, Ruurlo, Netherlands, m, 2 children **DISCIPLINE** LIBRARY SCIENCE, PHILOSOPHY **EDUCATION** Calvin Col, BA, 68; Kent State Univ, MLS, 76; Columbia Univ, PhD, 73. **CAREER** Friends Univ, 76-82; Eckerd Col, 82-83; libr dir, Whitworth Col, 83-. **MEMBERSHIPS** Am Libr Asn; Asn Col & Res Libr. **RESEARCH** Philosophical bibliography; Philosophy of history; Philosophy of mind; Idea of progress. **SELECTED PUBLICATIONS** Auth A Friends University Bibliography: Books by Alumni and Faculty, 1898-1979, Friends Univ, 79; Introduction: A Map ofTwentieth-Century Philosophy, Twentieth-Century Philosophy, Prentice-Hall, 96; Philosophy: A Guide to the Reference Literature, Libraries Unlimited, 86. **CONTACT ADDRESS** Cowles Libr, Whitworth Col, 300 W Hawthorne Road, Spokane, WA, 99251. **EMAIL** hbynagle@whitworth.edu

BYRD, JAMES DAVID, JR.
PERSONAL Born 06/05/1972, Fort Campbell, KY, s **DISCIPLINE** PHILOSOPHY **EDUCATION** Univ Central Fla, BA, 96; Univ Calif, Davis, PhD candidate. **CAREER** Tchg asst, Univ Calif, Davis, 97- . **HONORS AND AWARDS** Phi Theta Kappa. **MEMBERSHIPS** APA. **RESEARCH** Philosophy of mind; cognitive science. **CONTACT ADDRESS** 1111 J St, #152, Davis, CA, 95616. **EMAIL** jdbyrd@ucdavis.edu

BYRD, JERRY STEWART
PERSONAL Born 12/11/1935, Greenville, SC, m **DISCIPLINE** LAW **EDUCATION** Fisk Univ, BA 1961; Howard Univ, JD 1964; Southeastern Univ, ASBA 1975. **CAREER** Natl Labor Relations Bd Regional Adv Branch, atty 1964-65; Neighborhood Legal Serv, managing atty 1965-69 and 1974-81, dep dir 1970-71; Howard Univ, pol sci instructor 1971-72; Superior Ct of DC, hearing commissioner 1981-. **MEMBERSHIPS** Mem Hearing Comm Bd of Professional Responsibility 1982-85; Special Judges Division of the American Bar Association; Washington and National Bar Association; general secretary, Washington Buddhist Vihara Society, Inc; mem bd dir, Hospitality Comm Fed Credit Union; mem DC Consumer Goods Repair Bd 1974-77. **SELECTED PUBLICATIONS** parental Immunity in Negligence Actions Abolished, 9 How L J 183 (1963); Courts, Slums and Feasibility of Adopting the Warranty of Fitness, The DC Housing Research Comm Report 1967; Nix vs Watson, RS-650-80R; 18 Family Law Reporter (Nov 12, 1991). **CONTACT ADDRESS** Hearing Commissioner, Superior Court of DC, 500 Indiana Ave NW, Washington, DC, 20001.

BYRNE, EDMUND F.
PERSONAL Born 05/30/1933, Kansas City, Mo, 2 children **DISCIPLINE** PHILOSOPHY, LAW **EDUCATION** Saint Joseph's Col Ind, BA, 55; Loyola Univ Chicago, MA, 56; Univ Louvain, Belg, PhD(philos), 66; Ind Univ, JD, 78. **CAREER** Asst prof philos, Mich State Univ, 66-69; from asst prof to assoc prof, 69-76, Prof Philos, Ind Univ, Indianapolis, 76-, Chmn Dept, 79-, Prog coordr, Soc Study Philos & Technol, 76-, treas, 81- **MEMBERSHIPS** Am Philos Asn; Am Legal Studies Asn; Popular Cult Asn; Am Bar Asn; Am Legal Studies Asn; Popular Cult Asn; Soc Philos & Technol (treas, 81-). **RESEARCH** Philosophy of technology; philosophy of public policy; philosophy of law. **SELECTED PUBLICATIONS** Auth, Probability and Opinion, Nijhoff, The Hague, 68; coauth, Human Being and Being Human: Man's Philosophies of Man, Appleton-Century-Crofts, 69; auth, The depersonalization of violence, J Value Inquiry, fall 73; contribr, Philosophy and Technology: An Annual Compilation of Research, Vols I & II, JAI Press, 78 & 79; auth, After mental illness what?, In: Action and Responsibility, Bowling Green Univ, 80; Death and aging in technopolis, In: Philosophical Foundations of Gerontology, Human Sci Press, 81; US Domsat policy, In: Papers on Science of Science and Forecasting 1-2, Wroclaw, Poland, 81; The adversary system: Who needs it?, In: Ethics and the Legal Profession, Prometheus (in prep). **CONTACT ADDRESS** Dept of Philos, Indiana Univ-Purdue Univ, Indianapolis, 1100 W Michigan St, Indianapolis, IN, 46202-5140. **EMAIL** ebyrne@iupui.edu

BYRNE, PATRICK HUGH
PERSONAL Born 05/16/1947, Syracuse, NY, m, 1971, 1 child **DISCIPLINE** PHILOSOPHY **EDUCATION** Boston Col BS, 69, MA, 73; State Univ NY, Stony Brook, PhD(philos), 78. **CAREER** Asst prof, 75-80, ASSOC PROF PHILOS, BOSTON COL, 80-. **RESEARCH** Philosophy of 20th century science; philosophy of logic and mathematics; axiological ethical theory. **SELECTED PUBLICATIONS** Ed, Philosophy and Social Theory, Stony Brook Studies in Philosophy, Vol 1, 74; Resentment and the Preferential Option for the Poor/, Theol Studies, Vol 54, 1993. **CONTACT ADDRESS** Dept of Philos, Boston Col, 140 Commonwealth Ave, Chestnut Hill, MA, 02167-3800.

BYRNES, JOHN
PERSONAL Born 04/06/1970, Valparaiso, IN, m, 1998 **DISCIPLINE** PHILOSOPHY **EDUCATION** Carnegie Mellon Univ, PhD, 99. **MEMBERSHIPS** Asn of Symbolic Logic. **RESEARCH** Automated theorem proofs; Proof theory; Philosophy of mathematics. **SELECTED PUBLICATIONS** Auth, "Peirce's First-Order of Logic of 1885" in Transactions of the Charles S. Peirce Soc, 98; co-auth, "An Abstract Model for Parallel Computations: Gandy's Thesis," in The Monist, 98; co-auth, "Godel, Turing, and K-Graph Machines," in Logic in Florence, 98; co-auth, "Normal Natural Deduction Proofs (in Classical Logic)," in Studiea Logica, 98; auth, "Normal Forms Resulting From Proof Search Strategies," in Bull of Symbolic Logic, 97; co-auth, K-Graph Machines: Generalizing Turing's Machines and Arguments," in Godel, 96; co-auth, "A Graphical Presentation of Gandy's Parallel Machines," in Bul of Symbolic Logic, 96; co-auth, "A Mathematical Explication of Turing's Argument," in Bull of Symbolic Logic, 95. **CONTACT ADDRESS** Dept of Philosophy, Carnegie Mellon Univ, Pittsburgh, PA, 15217. **EMAIL** byrnes@cmu.edu

C

CABAL, TED
PERSONAL Born 12/24/1952, Whittier, CA, m, 1977, 3 children **DISCIPLINE** PHILOSOPHY OF RELIGION **EDUCATION** Swstrn Baptist Theol Sem, PhD, 95 **CAREER** Asst Prof, 93-95, Dallas Baptist Univ; Asst Prof, 95-98, Swstrn Baptist Theol Sem; Dean, 98-pres **HONORS AND AWARDS** Dallas Baptist Univ Religion Student of Year, 88; President's Scholar Award, 89; Who's Who Among Students in Amer **MEMBERSHIPS** Am Acad of Relig; Am Philos Assoc; Baptist Assoc of Philos Teachers; Evangelical Philos Soc; Evangelical Theological Soc; Ntl Assoc of Baptist Professors of Relig; Soc of Christian Philosophers **RESEARCH** Philosophy of Religion; Philosophy of Science **SELECTED PUBLICATIONS** Coauth, Rockamnia, SBC Life, 96; Auth, Shapers of Modern Evangelical Thought, Bullentine, 94 **CONTACT ADDRESS** 2825 Lexington Rd, Louisville, KY, 40280. **EMAIL** tcabal@sbts.edu

CADORETTE, CURT R.
PERSONAL Born 12/03/1948, Holyoke, MA **DISCIPLINE** RELIGIOUS STUDIES **EDUCATION** Univ Chicago, BA, 70, MA, 71; Regis Col, Toronto, STD, 85; Univ of St Michael's Col, Toronto, PhD, 85. **CAREER** Mary Knoll School of Theology, 86-94; Marxist Col, 87-88; Thiel Col, 89-91; assoc prof, Univ Rochester, 94-. **HONORS AND AWARDS** Adraham Karp Award for Teaching Excellence; Golden Key Honor Soc. **MEMBERSHIPS** Am Academy of Religion; Cath Theol Soc; Asn of Relig and Intellectual Life. **RESEARCH** Relig and society in Latin Am; Andean culture and relig. **SELECTED PUBLICATIONS** Auth, From the Heart of the People: The Theology of Gustavo Cutierrez, MeyerStone/Crossroad/Continuum, 88; Liberation from Violence: The Contemporary Catholic Challenge, in The Grail: An Ecumenical J, Sept 95; The Church in Peru, in The New Catholic Encyclopedia, vol 19, Dec 95; Liberating Catholicism: Living the Incarnation in a Post-Modern World, in The Month: A Review of Christian Thought and World Affairs, Aug 95; Catholicism in the Social Order of a New Era in Review for Religios, Sept-Oct 95; Liberating Mission: David Bosch and Latin American Christianity, in Mission in Bold Humility: David Bosch's Work Considered, Willem Saayman and Klippies Kritzinger, eds, Orbis Books, 96; Searching for Easter in Peru: Class, Culture and Evangelization, in Cross Currents: A Journal of the Asn for Relig and Intellectual Life, vol 46, no 2, 96; Christs in the Night: The Missiological Challenge of Andean Catholicism, in Missiology: An International Review, vol 25, no 1, Jan 97; Uncanny Grace: Christian Communities and the Survival of Hope, in Small Christian Communities: Imagining Future Church, Robert S Pelton, CSC, ed, Notre Dame Univ Press, 97; Liberation Theology: A Reader, Orbis Books, 92, 6th ed, 98; Legion and the Believing Community: Discipleship in an Imperial Age, in Paths That Lead to Life: The Church as Counterculture, SUNY Press, forthcoming 98; numerous other articles and publications. **CONTACT ADDRESS** Univ of Rochester, 430 Rush Rhees Library, Rochester, NY, 14627. **EMAIL** ccrt@troi.cc.rochester.eu

CADY, DUANE LYNN
PERSONAL Born 08/01/1946, Milwaukee, WI, m, 1969, 2 children **DISCIPLINE** PHILOSOPHY **EDUCATION** Hamline Univ, BA, 68; Brown Univ, Am, 70, PhD(Philos), 71. **CAREER** Asst prof Philos, Gustavus Adolphus Col, 71-74; assoc prof Philos, Hamline Univ, 74-, ed, Hamline Rev, 80-. **HONORS AND AWARDS** Conger Prize, Humanities Scholarship, 89; Sears-Roebuck Foundation Teaching Excellence & Campus Leadership Award, 90; Hamline Univ Com Social Action Award, 98. **MEMBERSHIPS** Am Philos Asn; Concerned Philos for Peace, Pres, 91; Fel of Reconciliation, natl council, 96-99. **RESEARCH** History of philosophy; ethics; soc & polit theory. **SELECTED PUBLICATIONS** Co-ed, Just War, Nonviolence & Nuclear Deterrence, 91; co-auth: Humanitarian Intervention: Just War vs Pacifism, 96; Bringing Peace Home: Feminism, Violence & Nature, 96. **CONTACT ADDRESS** Dept of Philosophy, Hamline Univ, 1536 Hewitt Ave, St. Paul, MN, 55104-1284.

CAFARO, PHILIP
PERSONAL Born 02/27/1962, New York, NY **DISCIPLINE** ETHICS, APPLIED ETHICS **EDUCATION** Univ Chicago, BA, 84; Univ Ga, MA, 88; Boston Univ, PhD, 97 **CAREER** Adj inst, 94, res ed, Boston Univ, 96; adj inst, Philos, 93-94, Col publ commun svc, 94-97, Univ Mass-Boston; adj inst, Emerson col, 96-97; asst prof, Southwest State Univ, 97- . **HONORS AND AWARDS** Univ fel for acad excellence, 86-88; hon, masters thesis, 88; Pres fel, 90-93; jr vis fel, 95. **RESEARCH** Logic; History of philosophy; Philosophy of science; Philosophy and literature. **SELECTED PUBLICATIONS** Auth, Thoreauvian Patriotism as an Environmental Virtue, Philos in the Contemp World, 2, 95, 1-9; Economic Consumption and the Quarrel Between Ethics and Economics, Acad Inquiry, 1, 95, 39-52; A Philosopher Gone Wild, rev of Conserving Natural Value, Conserv Biol, 9, 95, 965-966; To Market, to Market, to Buy...? rev of Dealing in Diversity, Conserv Biol, 10, 96, 687-688; Who Cares About Life? rev of The Value of Life, Conserv Bio, 11, 97, 580-581; Beating Back the Brownlash, rev of Betrayal of Science and Reason, Conserv Biol, 11, 97, 821-822; Runes of the North, rev of The Singing Wilderness and Listening Point, Conserv Biol, 12(1), 98, 255-257; Science Provides Meaning, rev of Green Space, Green Time: The Way of Science, Conserv Biol, 12(4), 98, 934-935; coauth, For Indian Wilderness, Terra Nova, 3(3), 98, 53-58; Virtue Ethics (Not Too) Simplified, Auslegung: A Jour Philos, 22, 98, 49-67; Less is More: Economic Consumption and the Good Life, Philos Today, 22, 98, 49-67. **CONTACT ADDRESS** Dept of Humanities, Southwest State Univ, Marshall, MN, 56258. **EMAIL** cafaro@ssu.southwest.msus.edu

CAFFENTZIS, C. GEORGE
DISCIPLINE PHILOSOPHY **EDUCATION** Princeton Univ, PhD, 78. **CAREER** Assoc prof; coordr, Comt for Acad, Freedom in Africa. **SELECTED PUBLICATIONS** Auth, Clipped Coins, Abused Words and Civil Government: John Locke's Philosophy of Money, 88; coaut, Anti-Samuelson: A Critique of a Representative Textbook of Bourgeois Economics, vols 1-4, 73-75; Midnight Oil: Work, Energy, War 1973-1992, 92. **CONTACT ADDRESS** Dept of Philosophy, Univ of Southern Maine, 96 Falmouth St, PO Box 9300, Portland, ME, 04104-9300. **EMAIL** Caffentz@usm.maine.edu

CAHAN, JEAN
DISCIPLINE JUDAIC STUDIES **EDUCATION** Johns Hopkins Univ, PhD, 83. **CAREER** Asst prof Judaic Stud, Univ Nebr, Lincoln. **RESEARCH** Philosophy of religion; philosophy of history. **SELECTED PUBLICATIONS** Published on Spinoza, modern Jewish philosophy and Marx. **CONTACT ADDRESS** Univ Nebr, Lincoln, Lincoln, NE, 68588-0417.

CAHILL, ANN J.
PERSONAL Born 08/30/1969, Gloucester, MA, m, 1998 **DISCIPLINE** PHILOSOPHY **EDUCATION** Col Holy Cross, BA, 1991; State Univ NY, PhD, 98. **CAREER** Asst prof, Elon Col, 98-99. **HONORS AND AWARDS** Am Fel Diss Fel, Am Asn Univ Women, 97. **MEMBERSHIPS** Soc Phenomenol Existential Philos; Am Philos Asn. **RESEARCH** Feminist theory; theory of the body; social and political philosophy. **CONTACT ADDRESS** Dept of Philosophy, Elon Col, 222 S. Mendenhall St., Apt. C, Greensboro, NC, 27403. **EMAIL** cahilla@elon.edu

CAHILL, LISA SOWLE
PERSONAL Born 03/27/1948, Philadelphia, PA, m, 1972, 5 children **DISCIPLINE** CHRISTIAN THEOLOGICAL ETHICS **EDUCATION** Univ Santa Clara, BA, 70; Univ Chicago, MA, 73, PhD(theol), 76. **CAREER** Assoc prof to J. DONALD MONAN, S. J. PROF THEOL, BOSTON COL, 76-; assoc ed, J Relig Ethics; ethics ed, Relig Studies Rev; advisory bd, J of Med and Philos; bd of dirs, Concilium. **HONORS AND AWARDS** Pres, Cath Theological Soc of Am, 92-93; pres, Soc of Christian Ethics, 97-98; Honorary degrees from: Santa Clara Univ, St Peter's Col, St Mary's Col, Nioraga, CA, Graduate Theological Univ, Lasell Col. **MEMBERSHIPS** Am Acad Relig; Soc Christian Ethics; Cath Theol Soc Am;Am Academy of Arts and Sciences; Nat Advisory bd on Ethics and Reproduction; March of Dimes advisory comm; Cath Comm Ground Initiative. **RESEARCH** The morality of care for the terminally ill; Christian theory of human rights; methodology in Christian ethics. **SELECTED PUBLICATIONS** Auth, Between the Sexes: Toward a Christian Ethics of sexuality, Fortress and Paulist Presses, 85, 7th printing, 97, Fortress Books; Religion and Arti-

ficial Reproduction: Inquiry into the Vatican Instruction on Human Life, with Thomas A. Shannon, Crossroad Press, 88; Women and Sexuality, Paulist Press, 92; Love Your Enemies: Discipleship, Pacifism, and Just War Theory, Fortress Press, 94; Embodiment, Morality, and Medicine, ed with Margaret A. Farley, Kluwer Academic Pubs, 95; Sex, Gender, and Christian Ethics, Cambridge Univ Press, 96; Christian Ethics: Problems and Prospects, in honor of James M. Gustafson, ed with James Childress, Pilgrim Press, 96. **CONTACT ADDRESS** Dept of Theol, Boston Col, 140 Commonwealth Ave, Chestnut Hill, MA, 02167-3800.

CAHILL, P. JOSEPH
PERSONAL Born 10/29/1923, Chicago, IL **DISCIPLINE** RELIGIOUS STUDIES **EDUCATION** Xavier Univ, Ohio, LittB, 47; Loyola Univ, Ill, MA, 55; Pontif Gregorian Univ, STD, 60. **CAREER** Asst prof theol, Bellarmine Sch Theol, 60-66; assoc dean sch theol, Loyola Univ, Ill, 66-67; assoc prof theol, Univ Notre Dame, 66-70; acting chmn dept relig studies, 70-74, PROF RELIG STUDIES, UNIV ALTA, 70-, Vis lectr, Beloit Col, 66; mem Jesuit Comn Probs of Belief & Unbelief, 66-; consult, Encycl Britannica, 68-; bd mem, Corp Publ of Acad Studies, Can, 73-; Can Coun leave & res fel, 76-77. **MEMBERSHIPS** Cath Theol Asn; Soc Sci Studies Relig; Soc Bibl Lit. **RESEARCH** Secularization and religious values; theology of Rudolf Bultmann; existentialism and Christian apologetics. **SELECTED PUBLICATIONS** Auth, The Narrative Jesus--A Semiotic Reading of Mark Gospel, Cath Biblical Quart, Vol 0057, 95. **CONTACT ADDRESS** Dept of Relig Stud, Univ of Alta, Edmonton, AB, T6G 0X7.

CAHN, EDGAR S.
DISCIPLINE EDUCATION LAW AND PROPERTY **EDUCATION** Swarthmore Col, BA, 56; Yale Univ, MA, 57, PhD, 60, JD, 63. **CAREER** Prof; tchs in, Publ Entitlements Clin; codean, Antioch Sch Law, 71-80; a vis scholar, Columbia Univ(s) Ctr, Study of Human Rights; sr res fel, Southeast FL Ctr on Aging, FL Int Univ; distinguished vis scholar, London Sch Econ, 86. **HONORS AND AWARDS** Co-founder, Nat Legal Serv prog; innovative concept of, ser credits or time dollars, as an economic strategy for addressing soc prob(s) is being implemented in 36 states and in Sweden, Japan & Can. **SELECTED PUBLICATIONS** Auth, Hunger; USA; Time Dollars; Our Brothers' Keeper: The Indian in White America; articles on, zoning, int law, public interest law, legal educ. **CONTACT ADDRESS** School of Law, Univ of District of Columbia, 4200 Connecticut Ave Northwest, Washington, DC, 20008.

CAHOONE, LAWRENCE
PERSONAL Born 08/31/1954, Providence, RI, m, 1985, 2 children **DISCIPLINE** PHILOSOPHY **EDUCATION** Clark Univ, BA, 76; St Univ of NY at Stony Brook, PhD, 85. **CAREER** Asst prof Philos, Boston Univ, 87-96; assoc prof Philos, Boston Univ, 96-. **HONORS AND AWARDS** Eugene McKayden Ntl Univ Pr Bk Award in Humanities, 89. **MEMBERSHIPS** Amer Philos Assoc **RESEARCH** Modernism; Postmodernism; Social and Political Theory; American Philosophy; European Philosophy; Liberalism; Civil Society. **SELECTED PUBLICATIONS** Dilemma of Modernity: Philosophy, Culture, and Anti-Culture, St Univ NY, 88; The Ends of Philosophy, St Univ of NY, 95; From Modernism to Postmodernism: An Anthology, Blackwell Publ, 96. **CONTACT ADDRESS** Dept of Philosophy, Boston Univ, 27 Euclid Ave, Lynn, MA, 01904. **EMAIL** lcahoone@bu.edu

CAIN, JAMES
PERSONAL Born 04/21/1951, d, 1 child **DISCIPLINE** PHILOSOPHY **EDUCATION** Univ Penn, PhD, 85. **CAREER** Lectr, res assoc, Princeton Univ, 86-89; vis asst prof, Virginia Tech, 89-90; vis asst prof, Univ Cincinnati, 90-91; vis asst prof, Univ Rochester, 91-92; vis asst prof, Univ Louisville, 92-96; vis lectr, Georgia State Univ, 96-97; asst prof, Oklahoma State Univ, 97- . **MEMBERSHIPS** APA; Soc of Christian Philos. **RESEARCH** Logic; philosophy of religion; metaphysics; ethics. **SELECTED PUBLICATIONS** Auth, Arithmetic with Satisfaction, Notre Dame J of Formal Logic, 95; auth, Infinite Utility, Australasian J of Philos, 95; auth, The Hume-Edwards Principle, Relig Stud, 95. **CONTACT ADDRESS** Dept of Philosophy, Oklahoma State Univ, Stillwater, OK, 74078-5064.

CAIRNS, ALAN
DISCIPLINE LAW **EDUCATION** Univ Toronto, BA, 53, MA, 57, Univ Oxford, DPhill, 63. **CAREER** Prof, 53- **HONORS AND AWARDS** Molson Prize, 82, Governor General's Int Awd, 94. **MEMBERSHIPS** Royal Soc Can **RESEARCH** Canadian federalism; Charter and the constitution. **SELECTED PUBLICATIONS** Auth, Constitution, Government and Society in Canada, 98, Disruptions: Constitutional Struggles from the Charter to Meech Lake, 91, Reconfigurations: Canadian Citizenship and Constitutional Change, 95, The Charter Versus Federalism, 92. **CONTACT ADDRESS** Col of Law, Univ Saskatchewan, 15 Campus Dr, Saskatoon, SK, S7N 5A6. **EMAIL** Cairns@law.usask.ca

CAIRNS, HUGH A.C.
PERSONAL Born 03/02/1930, Galt, ON, Canada **DISCIPLINE** LAW/POLITICAL SCIENCE/HISTORY **EDUCATION** Univ Toronto, BA, 53, MA, 57; St. Antony's Col, Oxford Univ, Dphil, 63. **CAREER** Instr to prof, polit sci, 60-95, chmn, 73-80, PROF EMER, UNIV BC, 95-; vis prof, Memorial Univ Nfld, 70-71; vis prof, Can stud, Univ Edinburgh, 77-78; vis prof, Can stud, Harvard Univ 82-83; Brenda and David McLean ch Can stud, 93-95; John Willis vis prof law, Univ Toronto, 95-96; PROF AND LAW FOUNDATION OF SASK CHAIR, COLLEGE OF LAW, UNIV OF SASKATCHEWAN, 97-. **HONORS AND AWARDS** Gold Medal Polit Sci & Econ, 53; Queen's Silver Jubilee Medal, 77; Pres Medal Univ Western Ont, 77; Molson Prize Can Coun, 82; Killam res fel, 89-91; Gov Gen Int Award Can Stud, 94; DLaws(hon), Carleton Univ, 94; DLaws(hon), Univ Toronto, 96; DLaws(hon), Univ BC, 98. **MEMBERSHIPS** Can Polit Sci Asn (pres, 76-77); Int Polit Sci Asn (mem coun, 76-79). **SELECTED PUBLICATIONS** Auth, Prelude to Imperialism: British Reactions to Central African Society 1840-1890, 65; coauth, A Survey of the Contemporary Indians of Canada: Economic, Political and Educational Needs and Policies, vol 1, 66; coauth, Constitution, Government and Society in Canada: Selected Essays by Alan C. Cairns, 88; coauth, Disruptions: Constitutional Struggles from the Charter to Meech Lake, 91; coauth, Charter versus Federalism: The Dilemmas of Constitutional Reform, 92; coauth, Reconfigurations: Canadian Citizenship and Constitutional Change, 95. **CONTACT ADDRESS** 1866 Main Mall, Vancouver, BC, V6T 1Z1.

CAIRNS WAY, ROSEMARY
DISCIPLINE LAW **EDUCATION** Queen's Univ, BM, LLB, LLM; Univ Western Ontario, MM. **CAREER** Assoc prof. **RESEARCH** Criminal law; constitutional law; legal theory. **SELECTED PUBLICATIONS** Auth, pubs on criminal law theory and impact of the Charter of Right; co-auth, Dimensions of Criminal Law. **CONTACT ADDRESS** Fac Common Law, Univ Ottawa, 550 Cumberland St, PO Box 450, Ottawa, ON, K1N 6N5.

CALABRESI, GUIDO
PERSONAL Born 10/18/1932, Milan, Italy, m, 1961, 3 children **DISCIPLINE** LAW **EDUCATION** Yale Coll, BS, analytical econ, 53; Oxford Univ, Magdalen Coll, BA, politics, philos, econ, 55, MA, politics, philos, econ, 59; Yale Univ Law School, LLB, 58. **CAREER** Asst instr, Dept Econ, Yale Coll, 55-56; Simpson, Thacher & Bartlett (law firm), summer 57; law clerk to Justice Hugo Black, U.S. Supreme Court, 58-59; asst prof law, 59-61, assoc prof law, 61-62, prof law, 62-70, John Thomas Smith Prof Law, 70-78, Sterling Prof Law, 78-95, dean, law school, 85-94, Sterling Prof Law Emeritus, professional lecturer, 95-, Yale Univ; consult, Dept Trans, Auto Insurance Study, 68-70; consult, Insurance Dept, Auto Insurance Report, State of New York, 69-70; judge, U.S. Court Appeals, Second Circuit, 94-. **HONORS AND AWARDS** Fellow, Timothy Dwight Coll, Yale Univ, 60-; Rhodes Scholar, 53; one of the Ten Outstanding Young Men in Am, U.S. Jr. Chamber of Commerce, 62; Laetare Medal, Univ Notre Dame, 85; named commendatore (honorary knight commander), Republic of Italy, 94; Fellows of Amer Bar Found Award for Outstanding Research in Law and Government, 98. **MEMBERSHIPS** Pres, bd trustees, St. Thomas Moore Chapel, Yale Univ, 97-; advisory bd, Meiklejohn Inst Legal Studies, 94-; bd mem, Natl Inst Social Sci Info, 94-; bd mem, Commn Women Professions, Amer Bar Assn, 95-; Order of Coif, Triennial Book Award Comt, 93-; Amer Philos Soc. **RESEARCH** Law **SELECTED PUBLICATIONS** Auth, "Faith in Law, Faith in People," Brooklyn Law Review, vol 61, 95; auth, "Altruism and Not for Profits: Ends as Well as Means," in Le Organizzazioni Senza Fini di Lucro (non-profit organizations), 96; coauth, "New Directions in Tort Law," Valparaiso Univ Law Review, 30, 96; auth, "Remarks: The Simple Virtues of The Cathedral, in Symposium, Property Rules, Liability Rules, and Inalienability: A Twenty-Five Year Retrospective," Yale Law Journ, vol 106, no 2201, 97; auth, "In Honor of Professor Lawrence Iannotti," Amer Journ Trial Advocacy, vol 20, no ix, 97. **CONTACT ADDRESS** 157 Church St., New Haven, CT, 06510.

CALDWELL, HARRY M.
DISCIPLINE CRIMINAL PROCEDURE **EDUCATION** CA State Univ, BA, 72; Pepperdine Univ, JD, 76. **CAREER** Prof; student wrtg ed, Pepperdine Law Rev; dep dist atty, County Riverside, 76-79; dep dist atty, County Santa Barbara, 79-80. **HONORS AND AWARDS** Harriet and Charles Luckman distinguished tchr fel, 91-96. **MEMBERSHIPS** Mem, State Bar CA; Am Bar Assn; Am Trial Lawyers Assn. **SELECTED PUBLICATIONS** Co-auth, California Criminal Trial Book, West, 90. **CONTACT ADDRESS** Sch of Law, Pepperdine Univ, 24255 Pacific Coast Hwy, Malibu, CA, 90263.

CALFEE, DENNIS A.
DISCIPLINE LAW **EDUCATION** Gonzaga Univ, BBA, JD; Univ Fla, LLM. **CAREER** Prof; cert public accountant; fac, Acad Int Taxation Rep China, 86, 88-96; past vis prof, Leiden Univ, The Neth; Peking Univ in Beijing, China; Acad Int Tax, Taipei, Taiwan; prof, Univ Fla, 75- ,assoc dean, 88-93; pat law clerk, Div III, Wash State Ct Appeals. **MEMBERSHIPS** Wash Bar. **RESEARCH** Taxation. **SELECTED PUBLICATIONS** Coauth, Federal Estate and Gift Taxation 6th ed. **CONTACT ADDRESS** School of Law, Univ of Florida, PO Box 117625, Gainesville, FL, 32611-7625. **EMAIL** calfee@law.ufl.edu

CALIAN, CARNEGIE SAMUEL
PERSONAL Born 07/01/1933, New York, NY, m, 1959, 3 children **DISCIPLINE** THEOLOGY, EASTERN ORTHODOX STUDIES **EDUCATION** Occidental Col, BA, 55; Princeton Theol Sem, BD, 58; Univ Basel, ThD, 62. **CAREER** Asst pastor, Calvary Presby Church, 58-60; vis prof theol, Dubuque Theol Sem, Univ Dubuque, 63-67, assoc prof, 67-72, prof, 72-81; pres & prof theol, Pittsburgh Theol Sem, 81-, consult, Eastern Orthrox affairs, United Presby Church Comn Ecumenical Mission & Rel, 63-; mem nat faith & order colloquium, Nat Coun Churches, 65-; Comt Five Rep the World Alliance N Am Area in Off Schs, 72; J Omar Good distinguished vis prof, Juniata Col, 75-77. **HONORS AND AWARDS** LLD, Westminster Col, 82. **MEMBERSHIPS** Am Theol Soc; Am Acad Relig; Soc Sci Studies Relig; AAUP; fel Soc Human Values Higher Educ. **RESEARCH** Eastern Christianity; reformed theology; Christian ethics. **SELECTED PUBLICATIONS** Auth, Where's the Passion for Excellence in the Church?, Morehouse Publishing, 89; auth, Theology Without Boundaries: Encounters of Eastern Orthodoxy and Western Tradition, Westminster/John Knox Press, 92. **CONTACT ADDRESS** Pittsburgh Theol Sem, 616 N Highland Ave, Pittsburgh, PA, 15206-2525.

CALKINS, MARTIN S.J.
PERSONAL Born 12/01/1952, Cleveland, OH **DISCIPLINE** BUSINESS ADMINISTRATION/BUSINESS ETHICS **EDUCATION** Xavier Univ, BS, 78; Am Grad School Int Mgt, MIM, 79; Weston School Theol, MD, 94; ThM, 94; Univ Va, PhD, 98. **CAREER** Int Admin Coordr, Luria Brothers & Co/Ogden Corp, 80-82; Int Sales Mgr, Perry Div/Affiliated Hospital Products, 83-84; instr, Univ Detroit Mercy, 89-91; instr, Univ Va, 94-98. **HONORS AND AWARDS** Who's Who in Am Univ and Coll, 93-94. **MEMBERSHIPS** Soc for Bus Ethics; Am Philos Asn; Acad of Mgt; Soc of Christian Ethics. **RESEARCH** Casuistry; Virtue ethics; Self-deception. **SELECTED PUBLICATIONS** Auth, The Christian Manager: Dilemmas in the Workplace, Cath World, 94; Tom Moeller, Univ Va, 96; Religion and Business Ethics, Blackwell Encycl Dictionary of Bus Ethics, 97; Post-industrial Fitness, Am Fitness Mag, 98; coauth, A Profile of Richard T De George, Bus Ethics, 96; Adam Smith, Aristotle, and the Virtues of Commerce, J of Value Inquiry, 98. **CONTACT ADDRESS** Santa Clara Univ, St Joseph's Hall Rm, Santa Clara, CA, 95053-0390. **EMAIL** mcalkins@scu.edu

CALLAHAN, DANIEL FRANCIS
PERSONAL Born 11/28/1939, Boston, MA **DISCIPLINE** MEDIEVAL & CHURCH HISTORY **EDUCATION** St John's Sem, Mass, BA, 62; Boston Col, MA, 66; Univ Wis-Madison, PhD(hist), 68. **CAREER** Asst prof, 68-77, ASSOC PROF MEDIEVAL HIST, UNIV DEL, 77-, Am Coun Learned Soc grant, 82. **MEMBERSHIPS** Mediaeval Acad Am; AHA; Am Cath Hist Asn. **RESEARCH** The church in France, 750-1050; Medieval pilgrimages. **SELECTED PUBLICATIONS** Auth, The Diocese of Arras From Ad1093 Up to the 14th-Century--Research on Religious Life in the North of France During the Middle-Ages, Cath Hist Rev, Vol 0082, 96; Ademar-of-Chabannes, Millennial Fears and the Development of Western Anti-Judaism-An Examination of the Role of the Apocalypse in Late 10th-Century European Communities andIts Effect on Jewish-Christian Relations, Jour Ecclesiastical Hist; The Archive and Possessions of the Abbey-of-Saint-Victor in Paris, Speculum-Jour Medieval Stud, Vol 0068, 93. **CONTACT ADDRESS** Dept of Hist, Univ of Del, Newark, DE, 19711.

CALLAHAN, JAMES
PERSONAL Born 03/03/1960, Hinsdale, IL, m, 1982, 4 children **DISCIPLINE** THEOLOGY **EDUCATION** Marquette Univ, PhD, 94. **CAREER** Asst prof theol, Wheaton Col, 94-. **MEMBERSHIPS** Am Acad Relig; Soc of Bibl Lit. **RESEARCH** Hermeneutics; narrative and theology. **SELECTED PUBLICATIONS** Auth, The Convergence of Narrative and Christology: Hans W. Frei on the Uniqueness of Jesus Christ, Jour of Evangel Theol Soc, 95; auth, Claritas Scripturae: The Role of Perspicuity in Protestant Hermeneutics, Jour of Evangel Theol Soc, 96; auth, Reforming Dispensationalism: The Battle for Dispensationalism's History, Fides et Historia, 96; auth, Primitivist Piety: The Ecclesiology of the Early Plymouth Brethren, in Dayton, ed, Studies in Evangelicalism, Scarecrow, 96; auth, The Bible Says: Evangelical and Postliberal Biblicism, Theol Today, 97; auth, articles in Elwell, ed, Evangelical Dictionary of Theology, rev ed, forthcoming. **CONTACT ADDRESS** Dept of Theology, Wheaton Col, Wheaton, IL, 60187. **EMAIL** james.p.callahan@wheaton.edu

CALLAN, T.
PERSONAL Born 02/06/1947, Helena, MT, m, 1981, 2 children **DISCIPLINE** RELIGION **EDUCATION** Gonzaga Univ, BA 69; Yale Univ, MPhil 72, PhD 76. **CAREER** Xavier Univ, asst prof 75-80; St Clement Parish, dir 80-83; Athenaeum of Ohio, asst prof 83-86, assoc prof, 86-92, prof, 92-, acad dean, 89-. **HONORS AND AWARDS** Woodrow Wilson Fel **MEM-**

BERSHIPS SBL; CBA; EGLBS **RESEARCH** Paul; New Testament Christology; Luke, Acts; Christianity and Judaism. **SELECTED PUBLICATIONS** Auth, The Origins of Christian Faith, Paulist, 94; The Background of the Apostolic Decree, Catholic Biblical Quart, 93; Paul the Law and the Jewish People, in:" Essays on Jews and Judaism in the New Testament, ed, D P Efroymson, E. J. Fisher, L. Klenicki, Collvi MN, Liturgical Press, 93. **CONTACT ADDRESS** Dept of Biblical Studies, Athenaeum of Ohio, 6616 Beechmont Ave, Cincinnati, OH, 45230. **EMAIL** tcallan@mtsm.org

CALLENDER, CARL O.
PERSONAL Born 11/16/1936, New York, NY, m **DISCIPLINE** LAW **EDUCATION** Brooklyn Comm Coll Brooklyn NY, 1960-61; Hunter Coll Bronx NY, AB 1961-64; Howard Univ Sch Law Washington DC, JD. **CAREER** Housing Litigation Bur NYC, dir 1975-76; Comm Law Ofcs Prgm, dir 1972-75; Comm Law Ofcs, deputy dir 1971-72; Comm Law & Ofcs, assoc dir 1971; CALS Reginald Heber Smith Fellow Prgm NYC, COORD 1970-71; Reginald Heber Smith fellow Harlem Assertion of Rights Inc, 1969-70; Harlem Assertion of Rights Inc, staff atty 1968-69; Palystreet NYC, dir 1967; Hunter Coll NYC, asst librn aide 1966; Ebenezer Gospel Tabernacle, ordained minister 1972. **HONORS AND AWARDS** "Student who made most & significant progress in senior year" 1967; Am Jurisprudence Award for Insurance 1967; half hour film on channel 2 "Eye On New York". **MEMBERSHIPS** Chmn & pres Natl Young People's Christian Assn Inc; chmn & pres Christian Leaders United Inc; mem elec com of Student Bar Assn administrative asst; Housing Research Com; Phi Alpha Delta Legal Fraternity. **SELECTED PUBLICATIONS** Prentice-Hall's Federal Tax Service Bulletins NJ, legal edit; "Attorney For The Defenseless" 1970. **CONTACT ADDRESS** 415 Louis Ave, Floral Park, NY, 11001.

CALLENDER, WILFRED A.
PERSONAL Born 03/23/1929, Colon, Panama, m **DISCIPLINE** LAW **EDUCATION** Brooklyn Coll, BA 1954; Brooklyn Coll, MA 1963; Brooklyn Law Sch, JD 1969. **CAREER** Boys High School Brooklyn, educator 1957-69; Dept Real Estate Commerce Labor Industry Corp Kings, asst dir 1969-70; Wade & Callender, atty 1972-; Hostos Community College, prof 1970-91; Wade & Callender ESQS Practice of Law. **MEMBERSHIPS** Mem Brooklyn Bar Assn; Bedford Stuyvesant Lawyers Assn; Natl Conf Black Lawyers; bd Trustees Encampment for Citizenship 1971-; pres Black Caucus Hostos 1972-; mem bd trustees Social Serv; bd NY Soc Ethical Culture. **CONTACT ADDRESS** 1501 No Strand Ave, Brooklyn, NY, 11226.

CALLIES, DAVID LEE
PERSONAL Born 04/21/1943, Chicago, IL, m, 1966, 1 child **DISCIPLINE** LAW **EDUCATION** DePauw Univ, AB, 65; Univ Mich, JD, 68; Univ Nottingham, LLM, 69. **CAREER** Adj assoc prof, Sch Archit & Urban Planning, Univ Wis-Milwaukee, 73-78; adj assoc prof, Col Urban Sci, Univ Ill, 76; PROF LAW, SCH LAW, UNIV HAWAII, 78-, Assoc & partner, Attorney at Law, Ross, Hardies, O'heefe, Babcock & Parsons, 69-78; coun, The Conservation Found, 74-76; reporter, Land Use Law & Zoning Digest, 79-; columnist, Sun edition, Honolulu Advertise, 81- **MEMBERSHIPS** Nat Acad Sci. **RESEARCH** Land use management; real property; state and local government. **SELECTED PUBLICATIONS** Auth, The Quiet Revolution Revisited--A Quarter-Century Of Progress, Urban Lawyer, Vol 0026, 94. **CONTACT ADDRESS** 4621 Aukai Ave, Honolulu, HI, 96816.

CALLOWAY, MARY CHILTON
PERSONAL Born 12/21/1945, RI, m, 1972, 2 children **DISCIPLINE** BIBLICAL STUDIES **EDUCATION** St John's Col, BA, 68; Columbia Univ, PhD, 79. **CAREER** Asst prof, 80-90, chemn theol dept, 95-99, assoc prof, Fordham Univ, 91- . **MEMBERSHIPS** Soc of Bibl Lit; Catholic Bibl Asn; Am Acad Relig. **RESEARCH** Hebrew Bible; Jeremiah; Biblical hermeneutics; literary criticism and the Bible. **SELECTED PUBLICATIONS** Auth, Sing, O Barren One: A Study in Comparative Midrash, Scholars, 86; auth, A Hammer that Breaks Rock in Pieces: prophetic Critique in Ancient Israel, in Evans, ed, Studies in Anti-Semitism and Early Christianity: Polemic and Faith, Augsburg Fortress, 93; auth, Canonical Criticism, in Haynes, ed, To Each its Own Meaning, John Knox, 93; auth, Exegesis as Banquet: Reading Jeremiah with the Rabbis, in Weis, ed, A Gift of God in Due Season, Academic, 96; auth, The Apocryphal/Deuterocanonical Books: An Anglican/Episcopal View, in Kohlenberger, ed, The Parallel Apocrypha, Oxford, 97; auth, Black Fire on White Fire: Historical Context and Literary Subtext in Jeremiah 37-38, in Papers from the Consultation on the Study of Jeremiah at the Society of Biblical Literature, Sheffield, forthcoming. **CONTACT ADDRESS** Theology Dept, Fordham Univ, Bronx, NY, 10458. **EMAIL** callaway@emedia.net

CALVERT-KOYZIS, NANCY
PERSONAL Born 12/14/1959, New York, NY, m, 1996 **DISCIPLINE** BIBLICAL STUDIES; NEW TESTAMENT **EDUCATION** Wheaton Col, BA, 82; Gordon-Conwell Theol Sem, M Div, 86; Univ Sheffield, PhD, 93. **CAREER** Teaching asst, new testament, Univ Sheffield, 89-90; asst prof, new testament, Wheaton Col, 90-96; prof, new testament, Tyndale Sem, Toronto, 96-. **HONORS AND AWARDS** Aldeen Fund Publ grant, Wheaton Col, spring, 96; Overseas res scholar, British govt, 87-89; grant, Tyndale House, Cambridge, 87-89, Parsonage Grad fel, Gordon-Conwell Theol Sem, 86-87. **MEMBERSHIPS** Soc of Bibl Lit; Inst of Bibl Res; Cath Bibl Asn. **RESEARCH** Pauline studies; Women in new testament world; Sociology of new testament world. **SELECTED PUBLICATIONS** Auth, On My Mind, Wheaton Alumni, 15, Spring, 96; auth, Abraham and Ancestors, Dict of the Later New Testament, vol 3, IVP, 97; auth, Galatians: Introduction and Notes, Women's Study New Testament, Harper/Baker, 95; auth, Philo's Use of Jewish Traditions About Abraham, SBL Seminar Papers, Scholar's Press, 94; auth, Abraham and Idolatry: Paul's Comparison of Obedience to the Law to Idolatry in Galatians 4:1-10, Paul and the Scriptures of Israel, Sheffield Acad Press, 93; auth, Abraham, Dict of Paul and his Letters, IVP, 93; auth, Abraham, Dict of Jesus and the Gospels, InterVarsity, 3-7, 92. **CONTACT ADDRESS** Ontario Theol Sem, 25 Ballyconnor Ct., North York, ON, M2M4B3. **EMAIL** ncalkoy@aol.com

CAMERON, DAVID L.
DISCIPLINE FEDERAL TAXATION, INTERNATIONAL TAXATION, STATE AND LOCAL TAXATION, PROPERT **EDUCATION** Mass Inst Tech, BS, 80; Northwestern Univ, JD, 86. **CAREER** Clk, Hon Edward F Hennessey, Chief Justice, Supreme Judicial Court of Mass, 86-87; assoc, Goodwin, Procter & Hoar, Boston, 87-90; asst prof, Willamette Univ, 90-94; assoc prof, 94-97; prof, 97-. **MEMBERSHIPS** Mem, Northwestern Univ Law Rev; Order of the Coif. **SELECTED PUBLICATIONS** Co-auth, Taxation of Intangible Assets, 97. **CONTACT ADDRESS** Sch of Law, Willamette Univ, 900 State St, Salem, OR, 97301. **EMAIL** dcameron@willamette.edu

CAMERON, DONALD M.
DISCIPLINE LAW **EDUCATION** Univ Toronto, BA, 75, MA, 76, LLB, 79. **CAREER** Partner, Smith Lyons **MEMBERSHIPS** Can Bar Asn; Comput Law Asn; Am Intellectual Property Law Asn; NY Intellectual Property Law Asn; Advocates' Soc; Am Bar Asn; Am Inst Aeronaut Astronaut; Can Aeronaut Space Inst; Licensing Exec Soc. **SELECTED PUBLICATIONS** Co-auth, Computer Contracts, Butterworth's Canadian Forms and Precedents and Eureka! Now What?, CCH. **CONTACT ADDRESS** Fac of Law, Univ Toronto, 78 Queen's Park, Toronto, ON.

CAMERY HOGGATT, JERRY
DISCIPLINE NEW TESTAMENT **EDUCATION** Boston Univ, PhD. **CAREER** Assoc prof, Southern CA Col. **SELECTED PUBLICATIONS** Auth, Speaking of God; Irony in the Mark's Gospel: Text and Subtext. **CONTACT ADDRESS** Dept of Relig, Southern California Col, 55 Fair Dr., Costa Mesa, CA, 92626.

CAMPANY, ROBERT F.
PERSONAL Born 04/04/1959, Columbus, MS **DISCIPLINE** RELIGIOUS STUDIES **EDUCATION** BA, Davidson Col, 81; Univ Chicago, MA, 83, PhD, 88, Univ Chicago. **CAREER** Assoc prof, Indiana Univ, 88-. **RESEARCH** Chinese religious history; History and methods of the study of religion. **SELECTED PUBLICATIONS** Auth, Strange Writing: Anomaly Accounts in Early medieval China, SUNY, 95; pubs on Confucian, Buddhist, and Taoist texts dating from the third century B.C.E. to the sixteenth century C.E. **CONTACT ADDRESS** Dept. of Religious Studies, Indiana Univ, Bloomington, 300 N Jordan Ave, Bloomington, IN, 47405. **EMAIL** campanyr@indian.edu

CAMPBELL, COURTNEY S.
DISCIPLINE BIOMEDICAL ETHICS **EDUCATION** Yale Univ, BA; Univ Va, MA, PhD. **CAREER** Philos, Oregon St Univ. **HONORS AND AWARDS** Dir, Prog Ethics, Sci, Environment. **SELECTED PUBLICATIONS** Ed, Duties to Others; What Price Parenthood?. **CONTACT ADDRESS** Dept Philos, Oregon State Univ, Corvallis, OR, 97331-4501.

CAMPBELL, GERRY
DISCIPLINE PHILOSOPHY **EDUCATION** University Western Ontario, BL, 64; Univ Laval, PhL, 66; PhD, 72. **HONORS AND AWARDS** Distinguished Tchr Awd, 80. **SELECTED PUBLICATIONS** Auth, Sartre's Absolute Freedom; Taking Issue: With the Case for Ordination. **CONTACT ADDRESS** Dept of Philosophy, St. Jerome's Univ, Waterloo, ON, N2L 3G3.

CAMPBELL, JOSEPH GORDON
PERSONAL Born 06/02/1934, Nashville, TN, m, 1958, 2 children **DISCIPLINE** RELIGION PHILOSOPHY **EDUCATION** Vanderbilt Univ, BA, 56; McCormick Theol Sem, BD, 62; Duke Univ, PhD(relig). **CAREER** Instr theol, 65-66, asst prof, 66-71, assoc prof, 71-82, PROF THEOL, HANOVER COL, 82- **MEMBERSHIPS** Am Acad Relig. **SELECTED PUBLICATIONS** Auth, Under Every Green Tree--Popular Religion In 6th-Century Judah, Jour Theol Stud, Vol 0044, 93; Scripture in the Damascus-Document--The Use of Explicit Old-Testament Quotations in Qumran Literature, Jour Jewish Stud, Vol 0044, 93. **CONTACT ADDRESS** Dept of Theol, Hanover Col, P O Box 108, Hanover, IN, 47243-0108.

CAMPBELL, LEE W.
DISCIPLINE LAW **EDUCATION** Westminster Col, BA,66; Univ Southern Calif, JD,74.. **CAREER** Clinical prof Univ Southern California; practd law in Los Angeles. **MEMBERSHIPS** Past dir, Calif Inst Trial Advocacy Skills; Los Angeles City Task Force on Family Diversity. **SELECTED PUBLICATIONS** Publ on, clinical education; lawyers' skills training; children's rights & evidence. **CONTACT ADDRESS** School of Law, Univ Southern Calif, University Park Campus, Los Angeles, CA, 90089.

CAMPBELL, RICHMOND M.
DISCIPLINE MORAL AND POLITICAL PHILOSOPHY **EDUCATION** Harvard Univ, BA, 64; Cornell Univ, PhD, 70. **CAREER** Prof. **RESEARCH** Philosophy of mind, philosophy of biology, feminism. **SELECTED PUBLICATIONS** Auth, The Virtues of Feminist Empiricism, Hypatia, 94; "Can Biology Make Ethics Objective?," Biol and Philos, 96; Illusions of Paradox: A Feminist Epistemology Naturalized, Roman & Littlefield, 98. **CONTACT ADDRESS** Dept of Philos, Dalhousie Univ, Halifax, NS, B3H 3J5. **EMAIL** richmond.campbell@dal.ca

CAMPBELL, SUSAN
DISCIPLINE PHILOSOPHY **EDUCATION** Univ Alberta, BA, 78, MA, 83; Univ Toronto, PhD, 92. **CAREER** Asst prof. **RESEARCH** Philosophical psychology, feminist theory, aesthetics, ethics. **SELECTED PUBLICATIONS** Auth, "Elegy and Identity," Daimon, 92; "Being Dismissed: The Politics of Emotional Expression," Hypatia, 94; Interpreting the Personal: Expression and the Formation of Feelings, Cornell UP, 97. **CONTACT ADDRESS** Dept of Philos, Dalhousie Univ, Halifax, NS, B3H 3J5. **EMAIL** susan.campbell@dal.ca

CAMPBELL, TED A.
PERSONAL Born 09/03/1953, Beaumont, TX, m, 1975, 2 children **DISCIPLINE** CHURCH HISTORY **EDUCATION** Univ N Tex, BA, 76; Oxford Univ, BA/MA, 79; SMU, PhD, 84 **CAREER** Visiting lctr, Methodist Thelog School, 84-85; asst prof, Duke Divinity, 85-93; prof, Wesley Theolog Seminary, 93 **MEMBERSHIPS** AAR; ASCH; World Methodist Hist Soc **RESEARCH** Wesleyan Studies; History of Christian Doctrine **SELECTED PUBLICATIONS** Auth, Christian Confessions, Westminister John Knox Press, 96; auth, John Wesley and Christian Antiquity, Kingsword Bks, 91; **CONTACT ADDRESS** Wesley Theol Sem, 4500 Massachussettes, Washington, DC, 20016. **EMAIL** tcamp@clark.net

CANEDAY, ARDEL B.
PERSONAL Born 01/16/1950, Minneapolis, MN, m, 1972, 2 children **DISCIPLINE** BIBLICAL STUDIES **EDUCATION** Trinity Evangelical Divinity School, PhD, 91. **CAREER** Assoc Prof Northwestern Col, 92- . **MEMBERSHIPS** Soc Bibl Lit; Inst Bibl Studies; Evangelical Theol Soc; Ctr of Am Exp **RESEARCH** Social & cultural issues; New Testament use of the Old Testament. **SELECTED PUBLICATIONS** Contrib, Eerdmans Bible Dictionary; Evangelical Inclusivism and the Exclusivity of the Gospel SBJT, 97. **CONTACT ADDRESS** Northwestern Col, 3003 Snelling Ave. N, St. Paul, MN, 55113. **EMAIL** abc@nwc.edu

CANNON, DALE W.
PERSONAL Born 03/22/1942, Sedro-Woolley, WA, m, 1966, 3 children **DISCIPLINE** RELIGIOUS STUDIES **EDUCATION** Seattle Pacific Col, BA, 65; Duke Univ, PhD, 69. **CAREER** Skidmore Col, 68-70; Univ Va, 70-73; Western Oregon Univ, 79- . **HONORS AND AWARDS** Magna cum laude, 65; NDEA Title IV fel, 65-66; Duke Scholar, 66-67; Kearns Fel, 67-68; Kent Fellow, 67-69; NEH summer sem, 78; NEH Inst, 88; East-West Center Inst on Infusing Asian Studies into the Curric, 92, res fel, Inst for Ecumenical and Cultural Res, 93 **MEMBERSHIPS** APA; Northwest Conf on Philos; Am Acad Relig; Polanyi Soc. **RESEARCH** Philosophical foundations of the comparative study of religion; phenomenology of religion; the idea of religious common sense; Michael Polanyi; Soren Kierkegaard;the concept of truth in all of its dimensions; the concepts of objectivity, empathy and personal judgment; children's philosophy. **SELECTED PUBLICATIONS** Auth, Reasoning Skills: An Overview, in Lipman, ed, Thinking Children and Education, Kendall/Hunt, 93; auth, Having Faith, Being Neutral, and Doing Justice: Toward a Paradigm of Responsibility in the Comparative Study of Religion, Method and Theory in the Stud of Relig, 93; auth, Different Ways of Christian Prayer, Different Ways of Being Christian: A Rationale for Some of the Differences Between Christians, Mid-Stream, 94; auth, Haven't You Noticed that Modernity is Bankrupt, Tradition and Discovery, 94-95; auth, Six Ways of Being Religious: A Framework for Comparative Studies of Religion, Wadsworth, 96; auth, Sanders' Analytic Rebuttal to Polanyi's Critics, With Some Musings on Polanyi's Idea of Truth, Tradition and

Discovery, 96-97; auth, An Existential Theory of Truth, Personalist Forum, 96; auth, Religious Taxonomy, Academia, and Interreligious Dialogue, Buddhist Christian Stud, 98. **CONTACT ADDRESS** Dept of Philosophy and Religious Studies, Western Oregon Univ, Monmouth, OR, 97361. **EMAIL** cannodw@wou.edu

CANNON, JOHN J.
DISCIPLINE LABOR LAW **EDUCATION** Villanova Univ, AB, 59; Villanova Univ Sch Law, JD, 62; Grad Stud, Georgetown Univ Law Ctr, 63-64. **CAREER** Prof, Villanova Univ.. **MEMBERSHIPS** Order of the Coif; Amer Bar Asn. **RESEARCH** Employment and labor law. **CONTACT ADDRESS** Law School, Villanova Univ, 800 Lancaster Ave, Villanova, PA, 19085-1692. **EMAIL** cannon@law.vill.edu

CANNON, KATIE GENEVA
PERSONAL Born 01/03/1950, Concord, NC, s **DISCIPLINE** THEOLOGY **EDUCATION** Barber-Scotia Coll, BS, Elementary Education (magna cum laude), 1971; Johnson C Smith Seminary, Atlanta, MDiv, 1974; Union Theological Seminary, New York, NY, MPhil, 1983, PhD, Christian Ethics, 1983. **CAREER** Episcopal Divinity School, asst prof; New York Theological Seminary, admin faculty, 1977-80; Ascension Presbyterian Church, first African-American female pastor, 1975-77; Yale Divinity School, visiting lecturer, 1987; Harvard Divinity School, visiting scholar, 1983-84; Wellesley College, visiting professor, 1991; Temple University, Department of Religion, associate professor of Christian ethics, currently. **HONORS AND AWARDS** Isaac R Clark Preaching Award, Interdenominational Theological Center, 1973; Rockfeller Prostestant Fellow Fund for Theological Educ, 1972-74; Rockefeller Doctoral Fellow Fund for Theological Educ, 1974-76; Ford Found Fellow Natl Fellowships Fund, 1976-77; Roothbert Fellow, 1981-83; Harvard Divinity School, woman research assoc, Ethics, 1983-84; Radcliffe Coll Bunting Inst, 1987-88; Episcopal Church's Conant Grant, 1987-88; Assn of Theological School Young Scholar Award, 1987-88; **MEMBERSHIPS** Ecumenical dialogue, Third World theologians, 1976-80; Middle East travel guide, NY Theological Seminary, 1978-80; editor, Que Pasa, 1982-; member, Amer Acad of Religion, 1983-, Assn of Black Women in Higher Educ, 1984-; bd of dir, Women's Theological Center 1984-; member bd dir, Soc of Christian Ethics, 1986-90; member, Soc for the Study of Black Religion 1986-; World Alliance of Reformed Churches Presbyterian & Congregational, 1986-91. **SELECTED PUBLICATIONS** Auth, Black Womanist Ethics, Scholars Press, 1988; co-ed, Inheriting Our Mothers' Garden, Westminster Press, 1988; Katie's Canon: Womanism and the Soul of the Black Community, 1995. **CONTACT ADDRESS** Department of Religion, Temple Univ, 646 Anderson Hall, Philadelphia, PA, 19122-2228.

CAPIZZI, JOSEPH E.
PERSONAL Born 07/24/1967, Staten Island, NY, m, 1995, 2 children **DISCIPLINE** THEOLOGY **EDUCATION** Univ Vir, BA, 89; Emory Univ, MTS, 93; Univ Notre Dame, PhD, 98. **CAREER** Asst Prof, Cath Univ Am, 97-. **MEMBERSHIPS** AAR; SCE. **RESEARCH** Political and social thought. **CONTACT ADDRESS** Theology Dept, Catholic Univ of America, Religious Studies School, Washington, DC, 20064. **EMAIL** mcapizzi@aol.com

CAPLAN, ARTHUR L.
PERSONAL Born 03/31/1950, Boston, MA, m, 1971, 1 child **DISCIPLINE** BIOETHICS **EDUCATION** Brandeis Univ, BA, 71; Columbia Univ, MA, 73; Columbia Univ, M.Phil, 75; Columbia Univ, PhD, 79. **CAREER** Dir, Center Bioethics, Univ Penn, 94-; Trustee Prof Bioethics, Univ Penn, 94-; Chief, Div Bioethics, Univ Penn, 96-; Dir, Center Biomedical Ethics, Univ Minn, 87-94; Prof Philos & Prof Surgery, Univ Minn, 87-94; assoc dir, Hastings Center, 85-87; vis assoc prof Philos, Univ Pitt, 86; assoc Humanities, Hastings Center, 77-84; assoc Social Medicine, Columbia Col of Physicians and Surgeons, 78-81; instr, Columbia Univ Col of Physicians and Surgeons, 77-78. **HONORS AND AWARDS** Hero of Public Health, Columbia Univ; Doctor of Laws, Elizabethtown Col, 98; Commencement Speech, Elizabethtown Col, 98; Univ S Carolina Convocation Address, 97; Beaver Col Doctor Laws, 97; Univ Minn School Medicine Commencement Speaker, 96; Philadelphia Col of Textiles & Design Convocation Speaker, 96; Philadelphia Col of Textiles & Sci Centennial Medal, 95; Brandeis Univ Alumni Achievement Award, 95; UTNE 100 Visionaries, 95; Col of Physicians of Philadelphia Fel, 94-; Amer Assoc Advancement Sci Fel, 94-; John Morgan Soc, 94-; Omicron Delta Kappa Honor Soc, 94-; Amer Assoc Bioethics Pres, 93-95; Univ Minn Commencement Speaker, 93. **MEMBERSHIPS** AIDS Med Found; Allina Health System; Amer Acad Pediatrics & Child Neurological Soc; Amer Assoc Advancement Sci; Amer Col Cardiology; Battelle Memorial Inst; Carnegie Found; Committee on Sci & Tech, US House of Reps; Consumers' Union; Heinz Fam Found; Labor Resources Committee, US Senate; Amer Acad Neurology Med Task Force; Amer Cancer Soc, Minn Cancer Council; Center for Disease Control; Ntl Inst of Health; Ntl Endowment for Humanities; NY Acad of Medicine; NY Acad of Sci; Dept Health & Human Services; US Congress Office of Tech Assessmet; President's Commission for the Study of Ethical Problems in Medicine and Biomedical and Behavioral Res; United Health Care. **RESEARCH** Medical Ethics; Health Policy; Ethical Issues in Science and Technology; History and Philosophy of Medicine and the Life Sciences. **SELECTED PUBLICATIONS** Ed, The American Medical Ethics Revolution: Sesquicentennial Reflections on the AMA's Code of Medical Ethics, Johns Hopkins Univ Pr, 98; Due Consideration: Controversy in the Age of Medical Miracles, John Wiley & Sons, 98; Am I My Brother's Keeper? The Ethical Frontiers of Biomedicine, Ind Univ Pr, 98; "Paradigms for clinical ethics consultation practice," Cambridge Quarterly of Healthcare Ethics, 98; "Dealing with Dolly: inside the national bioethics advisory commission," Health Affairs, 98. **CONTACT ADDRESS** Dept of Bioethnics, Univ of Pennsylvania, 60 W Mermaid Ln, Philadelphia, PA, 19118-4024. **EMAIL** caplan@mail.med.upenn.edu

CAPPS, DONALD E.
PERSONAL Born 01/30/1939, Omaha, NE, m, 1964, 1 child **DISCIPLINE** RELIGION **EDUCATION** Lewis and Clark Col, BA 60; Yale Div Sch, BD 63, STM 65; Univ Chicago, MA 66, PhD 70. **CAREER** Oregon State Univ, inst 69; Univ Chicago Div Sch, inst, asst prof, 69-74; Univ N Carolina, assoc prof, 74-76; Phillips Univ Grad Sem, assoc prof, prof, 76-81; Princeton Theo Seminary, William Harte Felmeth prof of pastoral theol, 81-. **HONORS AND AWARDS** SSSR pres; ThD honors Univ Uppsala. **MEMBERSHIPS** SSSR; SPT; AAR. **RESEARCH** Psychology of religion; psychology of art and selected genres; psychobiography; theory and practice of pastoral counseling; social scientific study of religion. **SELECTED PUBLICATIONS** Auth, Living Stories: Pastoral Counseling in Congregational Context, Fortress Press, 98; Men religion and Melancholia, Yale Univ Press, 97; The Child's Song: The Religious Abuse of Children, Westminster John Knox Press, 95; Agents of Hope: A Pastoral Psychology, Fortress Press, 95; The Poet's Gift: Toward the Renewal of Pastoral care, Westminster/John Knox Press, 93; The Depleted Self: Sin in a Narcissistic Age, Fortress Press, 93; Reframing: A New Method in Pastoral care, Fortress Press, 90. **CONTACT ADDRESS** Dept of Theology, Princeton Theol Sem, 64 Mercer St, PO Box 821, Princeton, NJ, 08542-0803.

CAPRA, DANIEL J.
DISCIPLINE CONSTITUTIONAL CRIMINAL PROCEDURE **EDUCATION** Rockhurst, AB, 74; Berkeley, JD, 77. **CAREER** Pvt practice, Lord, Day & Lord, 77-79; asst prof, Tulane Law Sch, 79-81; Philip D Reed prof, 81-; ch, Comm prof resp, Assn Bar NYC, 90-93; ch, Comm fed legis, Assn Bar NYC, 93-96. **MEMBERSHIPS** Mem, exec comm, Assn Bar NYC, 97-. **SELECTED PUBLICATIONS** Auth, Cases and Commentary on American Criminal Procedure, Columns on Evidence, NY Law Jour, 96; co-auth, Basic Criminal Procedure, Evidence: The Objection Method, 97; Federal Rules of Evidence Manual, NY Evidence Handbk, 97. **CONTACT ADDRESS** Law Sch, Fordham Univ, 113 W 60th St, New York, NY, 10023. **EMAIL** dcapra@mail.lawnet.fordham.edu

CAPRIOTTI, EMILE
PERSONAL Born 06/28/1950, Chicago Heights, IL **DISCIPLINE** LAW, PHILOSOPHY **EDUCATION** Univ of Southern Calif, PhD, 88; Ind Univ Law School, JD, 90; De Paul Univ College of Law, LLM, 98. **CAREER** Asst State's Attorney, Kankakee County State's Attorney Office. **HONORS AND AWARDS** Claude R Lambe Fellow, 88-89; 89-90. **MEMBERSHIPS** Am Bar Asn; Ill Bar Asn; Chicago Bar Asn; Kankakee County Bar Asn; Justinian Soc; Am Philos Asn; Federalist Soc. **RESEARCH** Medical ethics; Legal philosophy; Political Philosophy: Ethics. **SELECTED PUBLICATIONS** Auth, The Grounds and Limits of Political Obligation, 92. **CONTACT ADDRESS** Box 136, St. Anne, IL, 60964.

CAPUTO, JOHN D.
PERSONAL Born 10/26/1940, Philadelphia, PA, m, 1968, 3 children **DISCIPLINE** PHILOSOPHY **EDUCATION** LaSalle Univ, BA, 62; Villanova Univ, MA, 64; Bryn Mawr Col, PhD, 68. **CAREER** Villanova Univ, David R Cook prof, 92-; prof, 76-; assoc prof, 72-76; asst prof, 68-72; vis prof, New Sch for Soc Res, 94; distinguished adj prof, Fordham Univ Grad Prog, 85-88; vis prof, Fordham Univ, 80 & Duquesne Univ, 78; instr, St Joseph's Univ, 65-68; pres, Phi Kappa Phi, Villanova Univ Chap, 79-80; Univ Rank and Tenure Comt, 81-;Search Comt, VP for Acad Aff, 94-95; ch, Bd of Publ, 89-; chp, Dept Grad Prog, 85-91; dept chp, Bd of Trustees Liason Comt, Acad Aff, 72-80; Search Comt for Grad Dean, 86-87; Search Comt for Dir of Res, 85-86; Search Comt for Dean of Arts & Sci(s), 80-81; chp, Fac Coun, 76-78; exec co-dir, Soc for Phenomenol and Existential Philos, 92-95; ch, Comt on Career Opportunities, Amer Philos Asn, 90-93; mem, ex officio, Nat Bd of Off, Amer Philos Asn, 90-93; pres, Amer Catholic Philos Asn, 87-88; exec comt, Amer Philos Asn, Eastern Div, 86-89; exec co-dir, Greater Philadelphia Philos Consortium, 83-87; ser ed, Perspectives in Continental Philos, Fordham Univ Press; mem bd(s): Heidegger Stud, Man & World, Amer Catholic Philos Quart, Hist of Philos Quart, Stud in Contl Philos-Ind Univ Press; Joyful Wisdom, The J Postmodern Thought, Epoche & Int Adv Bd Handbk for the Philos of Relig in the 20th century; bd trustees, Radnor Township Mem Libr,86-89; Dem Cand for Radnor Township Sch Bd, 91, 93; dir educ, Radnor Township Dem Comt, 91-94. **HONORS AND AWARDS** NEH fel, Col Tchr(s), 91-91; NEHs, Summer stipend, 85; Amer Coun of Learned Soc(s), fel, 83-84; Outstanding Fac Schol Awd, Villanova Univ, 82; Summer Res Grant, Villanova Univ, 82; Distinguished Alumnus, Villanova Univ Grad Sch, 81; Amer Coun of Learned Soc(s), grant, 72. **MEMBERSHIPS** Hon mem, Phi Beta Kappa, Villanova Chap, 89. **SELECTED PUBLICATIONS** Auth, Deconstruction in a Nutshell: A Conversation with Jacques Derrida, Fordham Univ Press, 97; The Prayers and Tears of Jacques Derrida: Religion without Religion, Ind Univ Press, 97; Againsts Ethics: Contributions to a Poetics of Obligation with Constant Reference to Deconstruction, Studies in Continental Thought, Ind Univ Press, 93; Demythologizing Heidegger, Studies in the Philosophy of Religion, Ind Univ Press, 93; Radical Hermeneutics: Repetition, Deconstruction and the Hermeneutic Project, Studies in Phenomenology and Existential Philosophy, Ind Univ Press, 87; Soll die Philosophie das letzte Wort haben, Levinas und der junge Heidegger uber Philosophie und Glauben, Festschrift, Hermann Schafer, Haus der Geschichte, 1996; Instants, Secrets, Singularities: Dealing Death in Kierkegaard and Derrida, Kierkegaard in Post/Modernity, Ind Univ Press, 95; Dark Hearts: Heidegger, Richardson, and Evil., From Phenomenol to Thought, Errancy, and Desire, Kluwer, 96; Infestations: The Religion of the Death of God and Scott's Ascetic Ideal, Res in Phenomenol, 95; Bedevilling the Tradition: Deconstruction and Catholicism, (Dis)continuity and (De)construction: Reflections on the Meaning of the Past in Crisis Situations, Pharos, 95; coaut, Modernity and Its Discontents, Fordham Univ Press, 92; guest ed, J Amer Catholic Philos Quart, 64, 95; Heidegger Issue, Presenting Heidegger, Philos Today, 96; Phenomenology and Beyond, Selected Stud ies in Phenomenol & Existential Philososphy, vol 21; co-ed, Foucault and the Critique of Institutions, Pa State Univ Press, 93. **CONTACT ADDRESS** Dept of Philosophy, Villanova Univ, 800 Lancaster Ave., Villanova, PA, 19085-1692.

CARABALLO, WILFREDO
DISCIPLINE LAW **EDUCATION** St Joseph's Col, BA; NY Univ, JD. **CAREER** Prof, 75-, assoc dean, Seton Hall Univ, 88-90; distinguished vis prof, NY Univ, 86; pub advocate of NY, 90-92. **SELECTED PUBLICATIONS** Publ in the area of commercial law. **CONTACT ADDRESS** Seton Hall Univ, South Orange, NJ. **EMAIL** carabawi@lanmail.shu.edu

CARANFA, ANGELO
PERSONAL Born 05/24/1942, Rotello, Italy, s **DISCIPLINE** LETTERS; HUMANITIES; PHILOSOPHY EDUCATOR **EDUCATION** Stonehill Col, BS, 66; Boston Col, MA, 71; Univ Florence, PhD, 72. **CAREER** Adj instr, Newbury Jr Col, 75-76, Boston State Col, 76-78, Bridgeceplor State Col, 85-87, Stonehill Col, 78-85, 90-. **MEMBERSHIPS** Am Philos Asn **RESEARCH** 20th Century French aesthetics. **SELECTED PUBLICATIONS** Auth, II Tachisvelli Rekroucephll, 78; Clseepol: Beauty One Grace, 89; Proust: The Crestica Silence, 90; coed, Western Heritage: Man's Encounter with World, 84. **CONTACT ADDRESS** 27 Sprague Ave., Brockton, MA, 02302. **EMAIL** acaranfa@stonehill.edu

CARD, CLAUDIA F.
PERSONAL Born 09/30/1940, Madison, WI **DISCIPLINE** PHILOSOPHY **EDUCATION** Univ Wis-Madison, BA, 62; Harvard Univ, Am, 64, PhD, 69. **CAREER** Instr, 66-69, asst prof, 69-72, Assoc Prof Philos, Univ Wis-Madison, 72-, Vis assoc prof philos, Dartmouth Col, 78-79 & Univ Pittsburgh, 80. **HONORS AND AWARDS** Phi Kappa Phi, 61; Phi Beta Kappa, 62; NEH Fel, 74-75; Vilas Assoc, Univ Wis, 89-91; Distinguished Woman Philos of the Year, Soc Women Philos, 96. **MEMBERSHIPS** Am Philos Asn; Soc Women Philos; Nat Women's Study Asn; Soc for Lesbian & Gay Philos; N Am Nietzsche Soc; Soc Philosophic Study of Sport; Int Soc for the Study of Environmental Ethics. **RESEARCH** Ethics; feminist philosophy; social philosophy. **SELECTED PUBLICATIONS** Auth, On mercy, Philos Rev, 72; co-ed, Religious Commitment and Salvation, Charles E Merrill Co, 74; ed, Feminist Ethics, 91; Adventures in Lesbian Philosophy, 94; auth, Lesbian Choices, 95; The Unnatural Lottery, 96; editor of book series, Feminist Ethics, for Univ Press Kans; ed, Philos Book Reviews, J Homosexuality. **CONTACT ADDRESS** Dept of Philos, Univ of Wis, 600 North Park St, Madison, WI, 53706-1403. **EMAIL** cfcard@facstaff.wisc.edu

CARDOZO, MICHAEL H.
PERSONAL Born 09/15/1910, New York, NY, m, 1937, 3 children **DISCIPLINE** LAW **EDUCATION** Dartmouth Col, AB, 32; Yale Univ, LLB, 35. **CAREER** Atty, US Securities & Exchange Comn, 39-40; atty tax div, US Dept Justice, 40-42; atty Lend Lease Admin & Foreign Econ Admin, 42-45; mem legal adv off, US Dept State, 45-52, asst legal adv for econ affairs, 50-52; FROM ASSOC PROF TO PROF LAW, SCH LAW, CORNELL UNIV, 52-64; exec dir, Asn Am Law Schs, 63-73; Consult, 73-; pvt law pract, washington, dc, 73-, Guggenheim & Fulbright fels, Belg, 58-59; vis prof, Northwestern Univ, 61-62, Univ Pa, 63-64, Howard Univ, 64-65 & Georgetown Univ, 66-68; mem, fel rev panel, Nat Sci Found & Dept Health, Educ & Welfare, 66-73; vis prof, George Washington Univ, 80 & American Univ, 81 & 82. **MEMBERSHIPS** Am

Soc Int Law; Am Law Inst. **RESEARCH** Public and private international law; accreditation. **SELECTED PUBLICATIONS** Auth, Women Not in the Law-Schools, 1950 to 1963, Jour Legal Edu, Vol 0042, 92; Racial-Discrimination in Legal-Education, 1950 to 1963, Jour Legal Edu, Vol 0043, 93. **CONTACT ADDRESS** Suite 1004 1001 Connecticut Ave NW, Washington, DC, 20036.

CAREY, PATRICK W.
PERSONAL Born 07/02/1940, m, 2 children **DISCIPLINE** RELIGIOUS STUDIES; HISTORY OF AMERICAN RELIGION **EDUCATION** St John's Univ, BA, 62; St John's Sem, M Div, 66; Union Theol Sem, STM, 71; Fordham Univ, PhD, 75. **CAREER** Asst prof, St Peter's Col, 75-76; Elisabeth Seton Col, 76; Carleton Col, 76-77; Gustavus Adolphus, 77-78; from asst prof to assoc prof, Marquette Univ, 78-. **MEMBERSHIPS** Am Acad of Rel; Am Soc of Church Hist; U.S. Cath. Hist Soc; Am Cath. Hist Asn; Am Cath. Hist Soc of Philadelphia; Col Theol Soc; Cath. Theol Soc of Am. **RESEARCH** Hist of Am Rel. **SELECTED PUBLICATIONS** Auth, Orestes A. Brownson: Selected Writings, 91; The Roman Catholics, 93; The Roman Catholics in America, 96; Orestes A. Brownson: A Bibliography, 1826-1876, 96; Ontologism in American Catholic Thought, 1840-1900, Revue d'Histoire Ecclesiastique 91/3-4, 96; Catholicism, Encycl of the United States in the Twentieth Century, ed S. I. Kutler et al, 96; After Testem Benevolentiae and Pascendi, Catholic Southwest: A Jour of History and Culture 7, 96; ed, The Pastoral Letters of the United States Catholic Bishops, vol 6, 1989-1997, 98; coed, Theological Education in the Catholic Tradition: Contemporary Challenges, 97. **CONTACT ADDRESS** Dept of Theology, Marquette Univ, 100 Coughlin Hall, PO Box 1881, Milwaukee, WI, 53233-2295. **EMAIL** careyp@csd.mu.edu

CARGAS, HARRY JAMES
PERSONAL Born 06/18/1932, Hamtramck, MI, m, 1957, 6 children **DISCIPLINE** WORLD & AMERICAN LITERATURE AND RELIGION **EDUCATION** Univ Mich, Ann Arbor, BA, 57, MA, 58; St Louis Univ, PhD(English), 68. **CAREER** Teacher English, St David's Sch, NY, 58-60 & Montclair Acad, NJ, 60-61; ed-in-chief, Cath Bk Reporter, New York, 61-62 & Queen's Work Mag, St Louis, Mo, 63-64; dir, Orientation English Foreign Students, St Louis Univ, 64-69; assoc prof & chmn dept, 69-80, PROF LIT, LANG & RELIG, WEBSTER COL, 80-, Mem bk rev prog, Mo Pub Radio, 75-. **MEMBERSHIPS** PEN; Amnesty Int; Nat Inst on Holocaust. **RESEARCH** The Holocaust; contemporary world literature; process theology. **SELECTED PUBLICATIONS** Auth, Ace of Freedoms--Merton, Thomas Christ, Cithara-Essays Judeo-Christian Tradition, Vol 0033, 93. **CONTACT ADDRESS** Dept of English, Webster Col, 470 E Lockwood Ave, Saint Louis, MO, 63119-3194.

CARL, HAROLD F.
PERSONAL Born 11/18/1958, Marion, IL, m, 1980, 1 child **DISCIPLINE** SYSTEMATIC THEOLOGY **EDUCATION** Westminster Theol Sem, PhD. **CAREER** Assoc prof theol, Houston Grad Sch of Theol, 92-97; chaplain, Berry Col, 97-. **MEMBERSHIPS** Evang Theol Soc; Soc of Bibl Lit. **RESEARCH** Theology; Christology; Historical Theology. **SELECTED PUBLICATIONS** Auth, User Friendly Faith, full text reprint, SirS Renaissance Database, Mar, 98; User Friendly Faith: What liberals believed and why fundamentalists made such a fuss, Christ Hist, 55, vol 16, no 3, Aug, 97; Integrative Theology, vol 3, Lewis and Demarest, Book Rev, JETS, vol 40, no 2, Jun, 97; Jesus's Relational Language in John 14-16: Implications for the Doctrine of the Trinity, paper presented to the Annual Mtg of the Evangel Theol Soc, Nov, 96; Ministry in the Age of Technology, Gospel Monthly Mag, Feb, 96; The NIV and Homosexuality (Part 1 & 2), Gospel Monthly Mag, Dec 95, Jan 96; The Biblical Perspective on the Personhood of the Unborn, http://www.sehlat.com/lifelink/multi/real.html, Dec, 95; The Atonement, Gospel Monthly Mag, Oct, 95; What is the Atonement?, Houston Church Mag, Aug, 95; Imitating the Incarnation (Christ-like Self-sacrifice), Gospel Monthly Mag, Oct, 94. **CONTACT ADDRESS** PO Box 490460, Mt. Berry, GA, 30149-0460. **EMAIL** hcarl@berry.edu

CARLSTON, CHARLES E.
PERSONAL Born 11/14/1923, Lewistown, MT, m, 1945, 5 children **DISCIPLINE** RELIGION **EDUCATION** Harvard Univ, AB, 47, AM, 51, PhD, 58; Fuller Theol Sem, BD, 50. **CAREER** Vis prof church hist, theol sem, Univ Dubuque, 55-56; vis prof New Testament, 56-58, from assoc prof to prof New Testament lit & exeg, 58-64; assoc prof relig, Univ Iowa, 64-69; PROF NEW TESTAMENT, 69-71, NORRIS PROF NEW TESTAMENT, ANDOVER NEWTON THEOL SCH, 71-, Sealantic fel, Tubingen, 59-60; ed Bibl res, Chicago Soc Bibl Res J, 66-68; Fulbright res grant, Tubingen, 73; Asn Theol Schs & Soc Bibl Lit fel, Claremont, 77-78; ed, Sources Bibl Study, Soc Bibl Lit, 80- **MEMBERSHIPS** Soc Bibl Lit; Studiorum Novi Testamenti Soc; Cath Bibl Asn. **RESEARCH** New Testament. **SELECTED PUBLICATIONS** Auth, The Past of Jesus in the Gospels, Jour Biblical Lit, Vol 0112, 93; Heresy and Criticism--The Search for Authenticity in Early-Christian Lit, Jour Amer Acad Rel, Vol 0064, 96. **CONTACT ADDRESS** Andover Newton Theol Sch, Newton Centre, MA, 02159.

CARMAN, TAYLOR
DISCIPLINE PHILOSOPHY **EDUCATION** Stanford Univ, PhD, 93 **CAREER** Asst prof, Barnard Col. **MEMBERSHIPS** APA **RESEARCH** 19th and 20th century European philosophy. **SELECTED PUBLICATIONS** Auth, Heidegger's Concept of Presence, Inquiry, 95. **CONTACT ADDRESS** Dept of Philosophy, Barnard Col, 3009 Broadway, New York, NY, 10027. **EMAIL** tc113@columbia.edu

CARMELLA, ANGELA C.
DISCIPLINE LAW **EDUCATION** Princeton Univ, AB, summa cum laude; Harvard Univ, Master of Theol Stud, JD, cum laude. **CAREER** Prof, Seton Hall Univ, 88-; vis lectr Relig and Soc, fel, Ctr for the Std of Values in Pub Life, Harvard Univ; ed coun,J of Church and State; legal scholars bd, De Paul Law Sch Ctr for Church-State Stud; atty, Csaplar & Bok, Boston, MA. **MEMBERSHIPS** Nat Coun Churches. **SELECTED PUBLICATIONS** Publ widely on issues of church-state relationships. **CONTACT ADDRESS** Seton Hall Univ, South Orange, NJ. **EMAIL** carmelan@lanmail.shu.edu

CARMICHAEL, CALUM MACNEILL
PERSONAL Born 04/01/1938, Glasgow, Scotland, m, 1959, 3 children **DISCIPLINE** BIBLICAL AND SEMITIC STUDIES **EDUCATION** Glasgow Univ, BSc, 59; Edinburgh Univ, BD, 62; Oxford Univ, BLitt, 64. **CAREER** Sr res fel Jewish-non-Jewish rel, Univ Southampton, 66-67; asst prof Bibl & Semitic studies, 67-70, assoc prof Semitic lang & lit, 70-75, PROF COMP LIT & BIBL STUDIES, CORNELL UNIV, 75-, Am Coun Learned Soc grant-in-aid, 72 & 79; vis fel, Oxford Ctr Postgrad Hebrew Studies, 72, 72 & 82; fel, St Cross Col, Oxford, 82; Guggenheim fel, 82. **MEMBERSHIPS** Soc Bibl Lit; Jewish Law Asn. **RESEARCH** Biblical and ancient Near Eastern legal and wisdom literature; New Testament and Rabbinic Judaism. **SELECTED PUBLICATIONS** Auth, Laws of Leviticus-Xix--An Examination of Biblical Narrative in the Creation of Legal Texts in the Literary-Deuteronomistic History Of Ancient-Israel, Harvard Theol Rev, Vol 0087, 94; Forbidden Mixtures in Deuteronomy-Xxii,9-11 and Leviticus-Xix,9 --An Analysis of Encoded Historical Messages Shaping an Israelite National Identity, Vetus Testamentum, Vol 0045, 95. **CONTACT ADDRESS** Dept of Comp Lit, Cornell Univ, 143 Goldwin Smith, Ithaca, NY, 14853-0001.

CARNEY, JAMES DONALD
PERSONAL Born 12/27/1930, Evanston, IL, m, 1961, 2 children **DISCIPLINE** PHILOSOPHY **EDUCATION** Northern Baptist Theol Sem, BA, 53; Roosevelt Univ, MA, 53; Univ Nebr-Lincoln, PhD(philos), 59. **CAREER** From instr to asst prof philos, Kenyon Col, 59-63; lectr, Univ Otago, NZ, 63-64, sr lectr, 64-66; assoc prof, 66-67, PROF PHILOS, ARIZ STATE UNIV, 67-. **MEMBERSHIPS** Am Philos Asn. **RESEARCH** Linguistic analysis; logic. **SELECTED PUBLICATIONS** Auth, A Historical Theory of Art Criticism, Jour Aesthetic Edu, Vol 0028, 94. **CONTACT ADDRESS** Dept of Philos, Arizona State Univ, Tempe, Tempe, AZ, 85281.

CARNEY, WILLIAM J.
PERSONAL Born 05/10/1937, Chicago, IL, m, 1973, 3 children **DISCIPLINE** LAW, ECONOMICS **EDUCATION** Yale Univ, BA, 59, Llb, 62. **CAREER** Assoc, Holland & Hart, Denver, 62-68, partner, 68-70; pvt pract law, Aspen, CO, 70-73; assoc prof law, Col Law, Univ WY, 73-76, prof, 76-78; PROF LAW, SCH LAW, EMORY UNIV, 78-; Sr Mem Acad Staff, Law & Econ Ctr, 81-85. **MEMBERSHIPS** Am Law Inst. **RESEARCH** Law and Economic Analysis; Shareholder Conflicts; the Political Economy of Corporate Law. **SELECTED PUBLICATIONS** Auth, Exemptions from securities registration for small issues: Shifting from full disclosure, Land & Water Law Rev, 76; The Perils of Rule 146, Univ Toledo Law J, 77; Securities Practice: The Law in Georgia, Harrison Co, 80; Fundamental Corporate Changes, Minority Shareholders & Business Purposes, Am Bar Found Res J, 80; coauth, Defining a Security: Georgia's Struggle with the Risk Capital Test, Emory Law J, 81; ed, The Changing Role of the Corporate Attorney, Lexington Books, 82; auth, Shareholder Coordination Costs, Shark Repellants and Takeout Mergers, Am Bar Found Res J, 83; Toward a More Perfect Market for Corporate Control, Del J Corp L, 84; Takeover Tussles: The Courts' Tug-of-war with Corporate Boards, Business & Soc Rev, 85; Two-Tier Tender Offers and Shark Repellants, Midland J Corporate Finance, 86; Signalling and Causation in Insider Trading, Catholic U L Rev, 87; Controlling Management Opportunism in the Market for Corporate Control: An Agency Cost Model, WI L Rev, 88; The Limits of the Fraud on the Market Doctrine, Business Lawyer, 89; Does Defining Constituencies Matter?, Cinn L Rev, 90; coauth, The Theft of Time, Inc? Efficient Law and Efficient Markets, Regulation, 91; coauth, Vicarious Liability for Fraud on the Market: Theory and Evidence, 92; auth, The ALI's Corporate Governance Project: The Death of Property Rights?, Geo Wash L Rev, 93; Limited Liability Companies: Origins and Antecedents, Univ CO L Rev, 95; The Political Economy of Competition for Corporate Charters, J Legal Studies, 97; Large Bank Shareholders: Saviors or Substitutes?, J Applied Corp Finance, 97; The Production of Corporate Law, S CA Law Rev, 98; Explaining the Shape of Corporate Law, Managerial and Decision Econ, 98. **CONTACT ADDRESS** Sch Law, Emory Univ, 1364 Clifton Rd N E, Atlanta, GA, 30322-0001.

CARPENTER, ELIZABETH S.
PERSONAL Born 04/24/1944, Chicago, IL, m, 1967, 3 children **DISCIPLINE** RELIGIOUS STUDIES, PHILOSOPHY **EDUCATION** Randolph Macon Woman's Col, AB, 66; Univ IL, Chicago, AM (philos), 69; Univ VA, MA, 97, PhD (religious studies), 97. **HONORS AND AWARDS** AB with Honors in Philos. **MEMBERSHIPS** Am Academy Relig; Soc Biblical Lit; Soc Christian Ethics. **RESEARCH** Religious ethics; political theory; theology; philosophy. **CONTACT ADDRESS** 5345 Celt Rd, Stanardsville, VA, 22973.

CARPENTER, JAMES ANDERSON
PERSONAL Born 04/02/1928, King's Mountain, NC, m, 1954, 2 children **DISCIPLINE** THEOLOGY, PHILOSOPHY **EDUCATION** Wofford Col, BA, 48; Duke Univ, BD, 51; Cambridge Univ, PhD(theol), 59. **CAREER** Asst prof, 63-65, PROF DOGMATIC THEOL, GEN THEOL SEM, 65-, SUBDEAN, 74-, Am Philos Soc res grant, 68. **MEMBERSHIPS** Am Theol Soc; Soc Arts, Relig & Cult; Anglican Theol Soc. **RESEARCH** Nineteenth century theology and philosophy; liberal Catholic movement in England; the religious thought of Samuel Taylor Coleridge. **SELECTED PUBLICATIONS** Auth, The Scent of Eternity--A Life of Kirk, Harris, Elliot of Baltimore, Church Hist, Vol 0063, 94. **CONTACT ADDRESS** General Theol Sem, 3 Chelsea Sq, New York, NY, 10011.

CARR, ANNE E.
PERSONAL Born 11/11/1934, Chicago, IL **DISCIPLINE** THEOLOGY, RELIGIOUS STUDIES **EDUCATION** Mundelein Col, BA, 56; Marquette Univ, MA, 63; Univ Chicago, PhD(theol), 71. **CAREER** Asst prof relig studies, Mundelein Col, 63-73 & Ind Univ, Bloomington, 73-75; asst prof theol, 75-77, assoc dean, 77-81, Assoc Prof Theol, Divinity Sch, Univ Chicago, 77-. **HONORS AND AWARDS** Hon Degree, Doctor of Divinity, Jesuit Sch of Theol, 83; Honorary Degree, Doctor of Humane Letters, Loyola Univ, 95; John Courtney Murray Award for Excellence in Theology, Cath Theol Soc of Am, 97. **MEMBERSHIPS** Am Acad Relig; Cath Theol Soc Am; Col Theol Soc; Am Theol Soc. **RESEARCH** Contemporary Christology; women's studies; Rahner. **SELECTED PUBLICATIONS** Auth, Theology and experience in Karl Rahner, J Relig, summer 73; The church in process, In: Women and Catholic Priesthood, Paulist, 76; The Theological Method of Karl Rahner, Scholars, 77; contribr, Authentic theology in service of the church, In: Women Priests, Paulist, 77; auth, Seminar on Christology: Hans Kung's On Being a Christian, Proc Cath Theol Soc Am, 77; Women's ordination and Christian thought, Listening, spring 78; contribur, Research Report: Women in church and society, Cath Theol Soc Am, 78; auth, Is a Christian feminist theology possible, Theol Studies, 6/82. **CONTACT ADDRESS** Divinity Sch, Univ of Chicago, 1025-35 E 58th St., Chicago, IL, 60637-1577.

CARR, DAVID
DISCIPLINE RECENT CONTINENTAL EUROPEAN PHILOSOPHY **EDUCATION** Yale Univ, PhD, 66. **CAREER** Philos, Emory Univ. **HONORS AND AWARDS** Alexander von Humboldt Found; Soc Sci & Hum Res Coun, Canada. **SELECTED PUBLICATIONS** Auth, Phenomenology and the Problem of History; Time, Narrative and History; Interpreting Husserl; Transl, Husserl's The Crisis of European Sciences. **CONTACT ADDRESS** Emory Univ, Atlanta, GA, 30322-1950.

CARR, DAVIS
PERSONAL Born 02/01/1940, Parkersburg, WV, m, 1995, 3 children **DISCIPLINE** PHILOSOPHY **EDUCATION** Yale Univ, BA, 61; MA, 64; PhD, 66. **HONORS AND AWARDS** Woodrwow Wilson Fel, 61-62; US Gov Grant, 62-63; Morse fel, 69-70; Yale Sr Fac Fel, 75-76; Alexander von Humboldt Fel, 75-76, 79; Soc Sci and Humanities Res Council of Can, Res Grant, 83-84, 90., CAR Acting instr, Yale Univ, 64-66; asst prof, 66-72; assoc prof, 72-76; vis asst prof, New School for the Soc Res, 68; vis asst prof, Wash Univ, 71; assoc prof, Univ Okla, 76-78; assoc prof, Univ Ottawa, 78-79; vis prof, ,New School for the Soc Res, 90; prof, Univ Ottawa, 79-91; Prof, Emory Univ, 91-. **SELECTED PUBLICATIONS** Auth, Modernity, Postmodernity and the Philosophy of History, Am Cath Philos Quart, 94; Alfred Schutz and The Project of Phenomenological Social Theory, Phenomenol of the Cultural Disciplines, 94; getting the Story Straight: Narrative and Historical Knowledge, Historiography Between Modernism and Postmodernism, 94; The Question of the Subject: Heidegger and the TranscendentalTradition, Huma n Studies, 95; Kant's Theory of the Subject; Transcendental Philos Everyday Experience, 97; White und Ricoeur: Die Narrative Erzahloform und das Alltagliche, Metageschichte: hayden White und Paul Ricoeur, 97; Die Realitat der Geschichte, Historische Sinnbilding, 97; Margolis and Philosphy of History, 97. **CONTACT ADDRESS** Dept of Philosophy, Emory Univ, Atlanta, GA, 30322. **EMAIL** dcarr@emors.edu

CARR, THOMAS
PERSONAL Born 04/21/1962, Washington, DC, m, 1996, 1 child **DISCIPLINE** THEOLOGY AND RELIGION **EDUCATION** Princeton Theological Sem, M Div, 90; Oxford Univ, M Phil (theol & philos), 92, D Phil (theol), 98. **CAREER** Junior

dean, Oriel Col, Oxford, 93-96; adjunct lect, Westminster Col, Oxford, 94-96; ASST PROF, MOUNT UNION COL, 94-. **MEMBERSHIPS** Am Academy of Relig. **RESEARCH** Hermeneutics; Nietzsche; near death experiences; death & dying. **SELECTED PUBLICATIONS** Auth, A Man for Our Time?: Isaiah Berlin's Magus of the North, in Jof Relig and Public Life, June/July 94; Only a God Can Save Us: a review essay of John Macquarrie's Heidegger and Christianity, in J of Relig and Public Life, Aug/Sept 95; Heidegger and Jaspers, J of the Am Academy of Religion, vol LXIV, no 2, summer 96; Let Being Be (a review of Joanna Hodges' Heidegger and Ethics, Routledge Press, 95), Times Literary Supplement, Jan 16, 96; Newman and Gadamer: Toward a Hermeneutics of Religious Knowledge, Scholars Press, 96; Review of the Cambridge Companion to Nietzsche, in Times Higher Education Supplement, Sept 5, 97; Death and Dying: An Introduction, Simon & Schuster, forthcoming 99; The Truth that We Are: Gadamerian Ethics and the Theological Task, under consideration by Routledge Press; Zarathustra or Zossima: amor fati and the affirmation of life in Nietzsche and Dostoevski, J of the Am Academy of Religion, forthcoming. **CONTACT ADDRESS** Dept Relig & Philos, Mount Union Col, Alliance, OH, 44601. **EMAIL** carrtk@muc.edu

CARRIER, DAVID
DISCIPLINE PHILOSOPHY **EDUCATION** Columbia Univ, PhD. **CAREER** Philos, Carnegie Mellon Univ. **SELECTED PUBLICATIONS** Auth, Panofsky, Leo Steinberg, David Carrier. The Problem of Objectivity in Art History, Jour Aesthetics & Art Criticism, 89; Art History in the Mirror Stage. Interpreting Un Bar aux Folies-Bergre, History & Theory, 90; Poussin's Paintings, Pa State Press, 93. **CONTACT ADDRESS** Carnegie Mellon Univ, 5000 Forbes Ave, Pittsburgh, PA, 15213.

CARRINGTON, PAUL
PERSONAL Born 06/12/1931, Dallas, TX, m, 1952, 4 children **DISCIPLINE** LAW **EDUCATION** Univ TX, BA, 52; Harvard, LLB, 55 **SELECTED PUBLICATIONS** Co-ed, The Hague Conference on Private International Law, Law and Contemp. Prob., 94; coauth, Reflections on the Interface of Treaties and Rules of Procedure: Time for Federal Long-Arm Jurisdiction, Law and Contemp. Prob. 153; co-ed, Appeals, Michie & Co. 94; auth, How We Got Here and Where We are Headed: Revolutionary Changes, Practice Under the New Federal Rules of Civil Procedure, 94; auth, Our Courts Need Friends: How Rule 26 Came to Be, 94; auth, Legal Education for the People: Populism and Civic Virtue, 94; auth, The Missionary Diocese of Chicago, 94; auth, Good Sense and 21, 95; auth, The Twenty-First Wisdom, 95; auth, Der Einschluss kontinentalen Recht und Juritsen und Rechtskultur de USA, 95; auth, Hail!Langdell!, 95; auth, William Gardiner Hammond ad the Lieber Revival, 95; auth, Maurice Rosenberg, 95; auth, Federal Use of State Institutions, the Administration of Justice, 96; auth, ADR and Future Adjudication: A Primer of Dispute Resolution, 96; auth, A New Confederacy? Disunionism in the Federal Courts, 96; auth, A Tale of Two Lawyers, 97; coauth, Contract and Jurisdiction, 1996 Supreme Court Rev, 97; auth, Law as "The Common Thoughts of Men:" The Law-Teaching and Judging of Thomas McIntyre Cooley, 97; auth, The War on Drugs: Time for A Reality Check?, 97; coauth, The Constitutional Limits of Judicial Rulemaking: The Illegitimacy of Mass Tort Settlements Under Federal Rules 23,39, 97; coauth, Reluctant Experts, 97; coauth, Law and The Wisconsin Idea, 97; auth, Renovating Discovery, 97; auth, Law and Economics, the Creation of Federal Administrative Law, 97; auth, The Constitutional Law Scholarship of Thomas McIntyre Cooley, 97; auth, On Law and Science, 98; auth, O! Miss Larsen!, 98; auth, The New Social Darwinism, 98; auth, The Future of Civil Justice, North Carolina, 98; auth, Ernst Freund, 98; Auth, Remarks on Discovery Reform, 98; auth, Regulating Dispute Resolution Provisions, Adhesion Contracts, 98; auth, Moths to the Light: The Dubious Attractions of American Civil Procedure, Festschrift for Bernhard Grossfeld, 98; auth, Virtual Civil Litigation: A Visit to John Bunyan's Celestial City, 98. **CONTACT ADDRESS** Law Sch, Duke Univ, Durham, NC, 27708. **EMAIL** pdc@duke.law.edu

CARROLL, BEVERLEE JILL
PERSONAL Born 07/25/1963, Shreveport, LA **DISCIPLINE** RELIGIOUS STUDIES **EDUCATION** Rice Univ, PhD, 94. **CAREER** Lectr, 92- , Univ Houston; lectr, 96- , Rice Univ. **HONORS AND AWARDS** Charlotte Newcombe Dissertation Grant, 93-94; Research grant, Amer Acad of Relig, 97-98. **MEMBERSHIPS** Amer Acad of Relig **RESEARCH** Philosophy and religion; Religion and world politics. **CONTACT ADDRESS** 1518 Washington Ave, Apt E, Houston, TX, 77007-0775. **EMAIL** bjillc@aol.com

CARROLL, JOHN T.
PERSONAL Born 04/22/1954, Buffalo, NY, m, 1977, 2 children **DISCIPLINE** BIBLICAL STUDIES/NEW TESTAMENT **EDUCATION** Univ Tulsa, BA, 76; Oxford Univ, Dipl Theol, 78; Princeton Theol Sem, M Div, 79; PhD, 86. **CAREER** Asst prof, Louisiana State Univ, 86-91; assoc prof, 91-92; assoc prof, Union Theol Sem, 92-97; prof, 97- ; co-ed, Interpretation: A Jal of Bible and Theology, 96- . **HONORS AND AWARDS** ODK Graduate Fel; HS Gehman Prize. **MEMBERSHIPS** Soc of Bibl Lit; Catholic Bibl Asoc; Studiorum Novi Testamenti Soc. **RESEARCH** Luke - Acts; Gospel interpretation; early Christian eschatology. **SELECTED PUBLICATIONS** Auth, The End in the Synoptics, The Bible Today, 92; auth, Sickness and Healing in the New Testament Gospels, Interpretation, 95; co-auth with Joel B. Green, The Death of Jesus in Early Christianity, 95; co-auth with James R. Carroll, Preaching the Hard Sayings of Jesus, 96; Luke-Acts, Reading New Testament Today, 99. **CONTACT ADDRESS** Union Theological Sem and Presbyterian School, 3401 Brook Rd., Richmond, VA, 23227. **EMAIL** jcarroll@utsva.edu

CARROLL, RAOUL LORD
PERSONAL Born 03/16/1950, Washington, DC, m, 1979 **DISCIPLINE** LAW **EDUCATION** Morgan State Coll, BS 1972; St John's Univ Sch of Law, JD 1975; Georgetown Univ Law Center, 1980-81. **CAREER** Dept of Justice, asst US atty 1979-80; US Bd of Veterans Appeals, assoc mem 1980-81; Hart Carroll & Chavers, partner 1981-86; Bishop Cook Purcell & Reynolds, partner 1986-89; US Dept of Veterans Affairs, Washington, DC, general counsel 1989-91; US Dept of Housing and Urban Development, pres, Government National Mortgage Assn 1991-92; chief operating officer, M.R. Beal & Company, New York, NY, 1992-95; Christalex Partners, partner, currently. **MEMBERSHIPS** Washington Bar Assn, 1976-, District of Columbia Bar, 1979-; New York Bar, 1976-; Natl Bar Assn, 1977-; pres Black Asst US Attorney Assoc 1981-83; trustee, Christian Brothers Investment Services, Inc; chmn Amer Ctr for Intl Leadership 1985; trustee, The Enterprise Foundation. **SELECTED PUBLICATIONS** "After the Dust Settles, Other Modes of Relief," The Advocate Vol 10 No 6 1978. **CONTACT ADDRESS** 1420 N St NW, Washington, DC, 20005.

CARROLL, WARREN HASTY
PERSONAL Born 03/24/1932, Minneapolis, MN, m, 1967 **DISCIPLINE** CATHOLIC HISTORY **EDUCATION** Bates Col, BA, 53; Columbia Univ, MA, 54, PhD(hist), 59. **CAREER** Instr hist, Ind Univ, 57-58; asst command historian, Sec Air Force, US Strategic Air Command, 60-61; admin asst, Calif State Senator John G Schmitz, 67-70, legis asst, 70-72; dir, Christian Commonwealth Inst, 73-75; Pres, Christendom Col, 77-85, Contrib ed, Triumph Mag, 73-75; trustee, Seton Sch, Manassas, 76-. **MEMBERSHIPS** Fel Catholic Scholars. **RESEARCH** Church history in the broadest sense; history of the Spanish-speaking peoples; history of modern revolutionary movements, since 1789. **SELECTED PUBLICATIONS** Auth, Law: The Quest for Certainty, Am Bar Asn J, 1/63; The West come to Judgment, Triumph, 5/72; Philip II versus William Cecil: The Cleaving of Christendom, Faith & Reason, winter 75-76; coauth, Reasons for Hope, Christendom Col Press, 78; auth, The dispersion of the Apostles: Overview, Peter, spring 81, The Dispersion of the Apostles: Thomas, summer 81 & The Dispersion of the Apostles: St Jude and the Shroud, fall 81, Faith & Reason; 1917: Red Banners, White Mantle, Christendom Publ, 81; Our Lady of Guadalupe and the Conquest of Darkness, 83; The Founding of Christendom , 85; The Guillotine and the Cross, 86; The Building of Christendom, 87; Isabel of Spain, the Catholic Queen, 91; The Glory of Christendom, 93; The Rise and Fall of the Communist Revolution, 95; The Last Crusade, 96. **CONTACT ADDRESS** Christendom Col, 134 Christendom Dr, Box 87, Front Royal, VA, 22630-6534. **EMAIL** Warren.h.carroll@trincomm.org

CARSON, JAMES
DISCIPLINE PHILOSOPHY **EDUCATION** Univ Ky, PhD. **CAREER** Dept Philos, Queen's Univ **RESEARCH** Native American ethnohistory; intercultural contact in North America; antebellum Southern United States; political culture of the late 18th and early 19th century United States. **SELECTED PUBLICATIONS** Auth, pubs on state rights ideology in the American South, Native American cultural change and persistence, and Native American women in the American South. **CONTACT ADDRESS** Philosophy Dept, Queen's Univ, Kingston, ON, K7L 3N6. **EMAIL** jc35@qsilver.queensu.ca

CARSON, LOGAN
PERSONAL Born 07/12/1932, Marion, NC, m, 1960, 2 children **DISCIPLINE** THEOLOGY **EDUCATION** Shaw Univ, BA, 57; Hartford Sem, BD, 60; Louisville Presby, ThM, 61; Drew Univ, PhD, 80. **CAREER** Bible knowledge master, Waka Tchrs Col, 65-68; instr Relig, Mt. Claire State, 69-73; prof Relig, Garner-Webb, 73-94; prof theol, Southeastern Baptist Theol Sem, 94-. **HONORS AND AWARDS** Distinguished Service Award, 95; Outstanding Relig Tchr, Garner-Webb; Hebrew Prize, Hartford Sem, 59. **MEMBERSHIPS** SBL, ETS, ABPR. **RESEARCH** Books for lay people. **CONTACT ADDRESS** Dept of Theology, Southeastern Baptist Theological Sem, PO Box 1889, Wake Forest, NC, 27588-1889.

CARSON, THOMAS L.
PERSONAL Chicago, IL, m, 1982, 2 children **DISCIPLINE** PHILOSOPHY **EDUCATION** St Olaf Col, BA, 72; Brown Univ, PhD, 77. **CAREER** Vis lectr, Univ Calif Los Angeles, 76; asst prof, Va Tech, 77-85; assoc prof, 85-94, prof, 94-, Loyola Univ Chicago. **HONORS AND AWARDS** Phi Beta Kappa, 72; NEH fel for col teachers, 80-81. **MEMBERSHIPS** Amer Philos Asn. **RESEARCH** Ethics; Metaethics; Business ethics; Utilitarianism. **SELECTED PUBLICATIONS** Auth, Morality and the Good Life, Oxford Univ Press, 97; co-auth, Relativism and Normative Nonrealism: Basing Morality on Rationality, Metaphilos, 96; auth, Second Thoughts on Bluffing, Bus Ethics Quart, 93; auth, Friedman's Theory of Corporate Social Responsibility, Bus and Prof Ethics Jour, 93; auth, A Note on Hooker's Rule-Consequentialism, Mind, Vol C, 91; auth, Could Ideal Observers Disagree?, Philos and Phenomenol Res, 89; auth, Perpetual Peace: What Kant Should Have Said, Soc Theory and Practice, 88; auth, Who are We to Judge?, Teaching Philos, 88; auth, Hare's Defense of Utilitarianism, Philos Studies, 86; auth, Relativism and Nihilism, Philosophia, 85; auth, Bribery, Extortion, and The Foreign Corrupt Practices Act, Philos & Public Affairs, 85; auth, The Status of Morality, Philosophical Studies Series in Philosophy, 84; auth, Happiness, Contentment, and the Good Life, Pacific Philos Quart, 81. **CONTACT ADDRESS** Philosophy Dept., Loyola Univ, Chicago, IL, 60626. **EMAIL** tcarson@luc.edu

CARTER, BARRY EDWARD
PERSONAL Born 10/14/1942, Los Angeles, CA **DISCIPLINE** INTERNATIONAL AND PROPERTY LAW **EDUCATION** Stanford Univ, AB, 64; Princeton Univ, MPA, 66; Yale Univ, JD, 69. **CAREER** Prog analyst systems, Off Asst Secy Defense, 69-70 & Nat Security Coun Staff, 70-72; res fel, Inst Polit, Harvard Univ, 72; assoc, Wilmer, Cutler & Pickering, 73-75; sr coun, US Sen Select Comt Intelligence Activities, 75; assoc, Morrison & Foerster, 76-79; ASSOC PROF LAW, GEORGETOWN UNIV, 79-, Int affairs fel, Coun Foreign Rels, 72; mem, Soviet-Am Parallel Studies Prog, UN, 77. **MEMBERSHIPS** Coun Foreign Rels; Am Asn Law Schs. **RESEARCH** International economic sanctions; international business law; national security policies. **SELECTED PUBLICATIONS** Auth, International-Law and Institutions aor a New Age, Georgetown Law Jour, Vol 0081, 93. **CONTACT ADDRESS** Law Ctr, Georgetown Univ, 600 New Jersey N W, Washington, DC, 20001-2022.

CARTER, CHARLES EDWARD
PERSONAL Born 06/20/1925, Springfield, OH, d **DISCIPLINE** LAW **EDUCATION** Miami Univ OH, AB 1950; OH State Univ, LLB 1957, JD 1967. **CAREER** City of Springfield, OH, law dir 1960-69; Mahoming Co Legal Serv Youngstown, OH, 1969-71; NAACP, assoc gen counsel 1971-86; Corporate Counsel 1986-. **SELECTED PUBLICATIONS** "Civil Rights Handbook" NAACP 1979. **CONTACT ADDRESS** Corporate Counsel, NAACP, 4805 Mt Hope Dr, Baltimore, MD, 21215.

CARTER, CHARLES MICHAEL
PERSONAL Born 04/18/1943, Boston, MA **DISCIPLINE** LAW **EDUCATION** Univ of CA Berkeley, BS 1967; George Washington Univ Schl of Law, JD 1973. **CAREER** Winthrop, Stimson, Putnam, and Roberts, assc 1973-81; The Singer Comp, div counsel & finance staff and investment counsel 1981-83; RJR Nabisco Inc, sr corporate counsel 1983-87; Concurrent Computer Corporation, vice pres, general counsel & secretary of Corporate Development 1987-. **MEMBERSHIPS** Mem Amer Bar Assn, Natl Bar Assn. **CONTACT ADDRESS** Vice Pres, General Counsel, and Secretary, Concurrent Computer Corp., 2 Crescent Pl, Oceanport, NJ, 07757.

CARTER, DAVID K.
PERSONAL Born 06/20/1938, Portland, OR **DISCIPLINE** PHILOSOPHY **EDUCATION** Grinnell Coll, AB, 60; Yale Univ, MA, 65; PhD, 82. **CAREER** Asst prof, Univ Denver, 67-69; asst prof, Calif State Univ, 70-78; asst prof, Univ Tex Pan AM, 78-. **MEMBERSHIPS** Am Philos Asn. **RESEARCH** Ethics; American Philosophy. **CONTACT ADDRESS** 1108 Cardinal, McAllen, TX, 7854. **EMAIL** dcarter@panam.edu

CARTER, GUY C.
PERSONAL Born 02/21/1951, Austin, TX, m, 1994, 2 children **DISCIPLINE** HISTORICAL THEOLOGY **EDUCATION** Univ St. Thomas, BA, 73; Marquette Univ, MA, 80; Lutheran Sch Theol, MDiv, 86; Marquette Univ, PhD, 87. **CAREER** Pastor, Evangel Lutheran Abbey of St. Boniface, hamelin, Ger, 89-91; pastor, Grace Evangel Lutheran Church, NJ, 92-94; pastor, Trinity Evangel Lutheran Church, NJ, 94-89; adj lectr, St. Peter's Col, 92-98, asst prof, 98- . **HONORS AND AWARDS** Magna cum Laude, 73; Arthur J. Schmitt Doctoral Fel, 81-82, 82-83. **MEMBERSHIPS** Am Acad Relig; Soc of Bibl Lit; Int Bonhoeffer Soc for Arch & Res. **RESEARCH** Historical theology of the German Church struggle, 1933-45; Holocaust studies. **SELECTED PUBLICATIONS** Auth, "Walter A. Maier," Twentieth Century Shapers of American Ppular Religion, Greenwood, 89; co-ed, "Bonhoeffer's Ethics," Kok Pharos, 91; auth, "Evangelische Theologie und ihre Didaktik," Damit wir einander mahe sind, Haensel-Hohenhausen, 98. **CONTACT ADDRESS** Theology Dept, St. Peter's Col, 2641 Kennedy Blvd, Jersey City, NJ, 07306. **EMAIL** gcemc@earthlink.net

CARTER, JEFFREY D.R.
PERSONAL Born 04/18/1963, Boston, MA, m, 1996 **DISCIPLINE** THE HISTORY OF RELIGIONS; THE RELIGIONS

OF AFRICA **EDUCATION** Univ of Chicago, PhD, 97 **CAREER** Vis asst prof, Davidson Col, 97-98; vis asst prof, Univ S Carolina, 98-99. **HONORS AND AWARDS** Fulbright Dissertation Fel Nigeria; Pre-dissertation Fel Soc Sci Res Coun Nigeria; Inst Advan Study Relig Chicago. **MEMBERSHIPS** Amer Acad Relig **RESEARCH** Comparative religions; Indigenous religious traditions; Religions of Africa; Methods & theories in the study of religion. **SELECTED PUBLICATIONS** rev, Prey into Hunter: The Politics of Religious Experience, Jour Relig, 93; rev, The Social Control of Religious Zeal: A Study of Organizational Contradictions, Jour Relig, 95; rev, A History of Christianity in Africa: From Antiquity to the Present, Jour Relig, 97; Religion and Politics in Nigeria: A Study of Middle Belt Christianity, Jour Relig, 97; auth, Description is not Explanation: A Methodology of Comparison, Method & Theory in the Study of Religion, 98. **CONTACT ADDRESS** Dept of Religious Studies, Univ S Carolina, Columbia, SC, 29208. **EMAIL** carterj@garnet.cla.sc.edu

CARTER, JOHN ROSS
PERSONAL Born 06/22/1938, Baytown, TX, m, 1960 **DISCIPLINE** HISTORY OF RELIGIONS, BUDDHIST STUDIES **EDUCATION** Baylor Univ, BA, 60; Southern Baptist Theol Sem, BD, 63; Univ London, MTh, 65; Harvard Univ, PhD(hist relig), 72. **CAREER** Asst prof, 72-80, assoc prof relig, Colgate Univ, 80-, Dir, Fund Study Great Relig & Chapel House, Colgate Univ, 74-. **MEMBERSHIPS** Am Acad Relig; Asn Asian Studes. **RESEARCH** History of religion; Buddhist studies. **SELECTED PUBLICATIONS** Auth, Dhamma: Western Academic and Sinhalese Buddhist Interpretations, Hokuseido Press, Tokyo, 78; ed, Religiousness in Sri Lanka, Marga Inst, Colombo, 79; co-ed, Religiousness in Yoga by T K V Desikachar, Univ Press Am, 80. **CONTACT ADDRESS** Colgate Univ, 13 Oak Dr, Hamilton, NY, 13346-1379.

CARTER, LAWRENCE E., SR.
PERSONAL Born 09/23/1941, Dawson, GA, m **DISCIPLINE** RELIGION **EDUCATION** VA Univ of Lynchburg, BA Soc Studies 1964; Boston Univ, MDiv Theol 1968, STM Pastoral Care 1970, PhD Pastoral Care & Counseling 1978; Andover Newton Theol School, OH State Univ, New York University, Harvard University, Georgia State University, attended; Univ of Wisconsin, George Washington Univ, attended. **CAREER** Roxbury United Presbyterian Church, minister to youth 1965-67; Boston Public Schools, sub teacher 1966-77; Twelfth Baptists Church, minister of counseling 1968-71; Boston Univ Warren Residence Hall, resident counselor & asst dir 1968-71; Boston University MLK Jr African-American Cultural Center, director, 1971-73; People's Baptist Church, assoc minister 1971-78; Harvard Univ Divinity School, clergy teaching advisor 1976-77; Marsh Chapel Boston Univ, assoc dean 1978-79; MOREHOUSE COLL, PROF, DEPT OF PHILOSOPHY & RELIGION 1979-; MARTIN LUTHER KING JR INTL CHAPEL MOREHOUSE COLL, DEAN 1979-, archivist/curator, 1982-97. **HONORS AND AWARDS** Fulbright Scholar, Brazil, 1994; Citizenship Medal of the Year VA Coll 1964; Recognition of Outstanding Achievement in the field of Religion & Humanitarianism Omega Scroll of Honor Morehouse Coll 1979; Natl Black Christian Student Leadership Consultation Awd in Appreciation for Support & Commitment to Devel of Black Christian Leadership 1980; Delegate to United Nations Spec Committee Against Apartheid 1984; numerous radio & TV appearances including Ebenezer Church Serv WAGA Channel 5 Atlanta GA, "The Role of the Black Church" WAOK Interview Atlanta GA, WCNN Radio Anthony Johnson Commentary 1984, CNN Roy Patterson Interview 1984; Voted Faculty Mem of the Year Morehouse Coll Student Newspaper; Del to the 6th Assembly of the World Council of Churches 1983; Del to the World Baptist Youth Conf in Argentina, 1984; Del to 4thtl Council of Churches Dialogue between the Soviety Union Clergy & Amer Clergy in Moscow; Senate Concurrent Resolution by the State of MI in Honor of Dr Carter, 32nd Degree Mason Prince Hall Lodge, 1985. **MEMBERSHIPS** Mem Atlanta United Nations Assoc; board of directors Natl Council of Chuches of Christ 1983-90; mem Natl Assoc of Coll & Univ Chaplains, ACLU, Amer Acad of Religion, Assoc of Black Prof of Religion, Ministries to Blacks in Higher Ed, NAACP; coord Afro-Amer Studies Prog Simmons Coll, coord 1977-78; mem Soc for the Study of Black Religion, Class of Leadership Atlanta 1986; American Academy of Religion, 1979-. **CONTACT ADDRESS** Dept of Phil and Relig, Morehouse Col, 830 Westview Dr, PO Box 24, Atlanta, GA, 30314.

CARTER, MICHELE A.
PERSONAL Born 04/24/1949, Okinawa, Japan **DISCIPLINE** PHILOSOPHY, APPLIED ETHICS, BIOETHICS **EDUCATION** Univ Hawaii, BS, 72; Texas Womens Univ, MS, 82; Univ Tenn, PhD, 89. **CAREER** Postdr fel, Nat Inst Health Clin & Res Ethics Clin Ctr, 89-91; bioethics consult, Wash Hosp, 91-93; MEM INST MED HUM, ASST PROF, DEPT PREVENTIVE MED & COMMUN HEALTH, SCHOOL MED, UNIV TEX MED BRANCH, 93-; DIR, UNIV TEX MED BRANCH ETHICS CONSULT SERV, 93-; Univ Tenn Nat Alumni Asn Grad fel, 88-89; Bacon-Bearc Scholar Philos, 88-89; Rolf-Deiter Hermann Scholar Philos, 83. **MEMBERSHIPS** Am Soc Bioethics and Hum; Am Philos Asn; Kennedy Inst Ethics; Hasting's Ctr. **RESEARCH** Philosophy of trust; Clinical and research ethics; Ethics of health care practice. **SELECTED PUBLICATIONS** Auth Ethical Framework for Care of the Chronically Ill, Holistic Nursing Practice, 93; Patient-Provider Relationship in the Context of Genetic Testing for Hereditary Cancers, Jour Nat Cancer Inst, 95; Mental Health Services: Ethical Issues, Encyclo of Bioethics, Simon & Schuster MacMillan, 95; coauth Experiences of a Nursing Ethics Forum: Case Studies and Outcomes, Critical Care Nursing Clinics of N Am: Ethical Decision Making in the Critical Care Patient, 97; Optimizing Ethics Services and Education in a Teaching Hospital: Rounds vs Consultation, Jour of Clinical Ethics, 97. **CONTACT ADDRESS** 301 University Blvd, Galveston, TX, 77555-1311. **EMAIL** mcarter@utmb.edu

CARTER, PERCY A., JR.
PERSONAL Born 07/04/1929, Hampton, VI, m **DISCIPLINE** THEOLOGY **EDUCATION** VA Union U, AB 1949; Harvard Sch of Bus Adminstrn, 1951-52; M Div Andover-Newton, 1953; Boston Univ Sch of Theology, MST 1953; Harvard Divinity Sch, 1953-55; Brown U, 1958-59. **CAREER** Olney St Bapt Ch Providence RI, formerly pastored; Mt Calvary Bapt Ch Mansfield OH; Hosack St Bapt Ch Columbus OH, pastor, currently; Eastern Union Bible College of Columbus, OH, instructor, currently. **MEMBERSHIPS** Mem Bapt Pastor's Conf; mem Ministerial Alliance; mem Interdenom of Ministerial Alliance of Columbus OH; Met Area Church Bd Affiliate; broadcasts on radio weekly; previously served as substitue tchr on secondary level in pub sch; past chmn Mansfield Alliance for Progress; past chmn & founder Opport Indusl Cntr of Mansfield OH. **SELECTED PUBLICATIONS** Contrib "What Jesus Means to Me", "Seven Black Preachers" 1971. **CONTACT ADDRESS** Hosack Street Baptist Church, 1160 Watkins Rd, Columbus, OH, 43207.

CARTER, ROBERT EDGAR
PERSONAL Born 07/04/1937, Lawrence, MA, m, 1960, 2 children **DISCIPLINE** PHILOSOPHY **EDUCATION** Tufts Univ, AB, 59; Harvard Univ, MDiv, 62; Univ Toronto, MA, 63, PhD, 69. **CAREER** Asst philos, Tufts Univ, 60-62; instr, Univ Toronto, 62-65; lectr, Mem Univ Nfld, 65-66; assoc prof & chmn dept, Prince of Wales Col, 66-68; spec lectr found educ, McArthur Col, Queen's Univ, 68-69; assoc prof philos, Sir George Williams Univ, 69-73; assoc prof philos & master, Otonabee Col, 73-77, PROF PHILOS, TRENT UNIV, 78-, CHMN DEPT, 82- **HONORS AND AWARDS** Billings prize, Harvard Univ, 62. **MEMBERSHIPS** Am Philos Asn; Can Philos Asn; Am Soc Value Inquiry(pres, 76-77); Metaphys Soc; Soc Creative Philos. **RESEARCH** Value theory and ethics; ancient philosophy, phenomenology and existentialism; oriental philosophy. **SELECTED PUBLICATIONS** Auth, Indian Philosophy of Religion, Intl Jour Philos Rel, Vol 0034, 93; Zen Awakening and Society, Monumenta Nipponica, Vol 0048, 93; The Moral and Political Naturalism of Baron Kato, Hiroyuki, Monumenta Nipponica, Vol 0052, 97. **CONTACT ADDRESS** Trent Univ, 429 Downie St, Peterborough, ON, K9H 4J5.

CARTER, THEODORE ULYSSES
PERSONAL Born 10/16/1931, Birmingham, AL, m **DISCIPLINE** LAW **EDUCATION** Howard U, BA 1955; JD 1958; NY U, postgrad 1962-63. **CAREER** PA NJ bars, atty; IRS Phila, atty 1961-; Glassboro NJ State Coll, adj prof justice. **MEMBERSHIPS** Vol counsel Camden Legal Servs 1970-; mem Am Jud & Soc; Am Nat PA NJ Bar Assns; Howard Univ Alumni Assn. **CONTACT ADDRESS** Carter & Berry, 1400-02 Mt Ephraim Ave, Camden, NJ, 08104.

CARTER, WARREN
PERSONAL Born 01/06/1955, New Zealand, m, 1977, 2 children **DISCIPLINE** BIBLICAL STUDIES OF THE NEW TESTAMENT **EDUCATION** Victoria Univ of Wellington, BA; Melbourne Col of Divinity; Th M, BD; Princeton Theol Sem, PhD. **CAREER** Instr, new testament, 90-91, asst prof, new testament, 91-95, assoc prof, new testament, 95-, St Paul Sch of Theol, Ks City, Mo. **HONORS AND AWARDS** ATS Facul Fel, 98-99; SBL Reg Scholar Award, 95; ATS Globalization Award, 92. **MEMBERSHIPS** Soc of Bibl Lit; Cath Bibl Asn. **RESEARCH** History and literature of early Christian movement, espec Gospel of Matthew. **SELECTED PUBLICATIONS** Coauth, with J. P. Heil, Matthew's Parables: Audience-Oriented Perspectives, CBQMS, 30, Wash, CBA, 98; auth, Matthew: Storyteller, Interpreter, Evangelist, Peabody, Mass, Hendrickson, 96; auth, Discipleship and Households: A Study of Matthew 19-20, JSNTSS, 103, Sheffield, Sheffield Acad, JSOT, 94; auth, What are They Saying About Matthew's Sermon on the Mount?, Mahwah, NJ, Paulist Press, 94; articles, Towards an Imperial-Critical Reading of Matthew, SBL 1998 Sem Papers, Atlanta, Scholars, 98; Jesus I Have come Statements in Matthew's Gospel, Cath Bibl Quart, 60, 44-62, 98; Narrative/Literary Approaches to Matthean Theology: The Reign of the Heavens as an Example, Matthew 4:17-5:12, Jour for the Study of the New Testament, 67, 3-27, 97; Matthew 4: 18-22 and Matthean Discipleship: An Audience-Oriented Perspective, Cath Bibl Quart, 59, 58-75, 97; Community Definition and Matthew's Gospel, ed E. Lovering, SBL 1997 Sem Papers, Atlanta, Scholars, 637-63, 97. **CONTACT ADDRESS** St. Paul School of Theology, 5123 Truman Rd., Kansas City, MO, 64127. **EMAIL** wcarter@spst.edu

CARTWRIGHT, HELEN MORRIS
PERSONAL Born 07/18/1931, Ferndale, MI, m, 1959 **DISCIPLINE** PHILOSOPHY **EDUCATION** Univ Mich, AB, 54, MA, 57, PhD, 63. **CAREER** Asst prof, 68-73; assoc prof 73-85, PROF PHILOS, TUFTS UNIV, 85-98, PROF EMER, 98-. **MEMBERSHIPS** Am Philos Asn; Clare Hall, Univ Cambridge, life mem. **RESEARCH** Metaphysics; philosophy of language. **SELECTED PUBLICATIONS** Auth, Heraclitus and the Bath Water, Philos Rev, 10/65; Quantities, Philos Rev, 1/70; Amounts and Measure of Amount, Nous, 5/75; Parts and Partitives, Synthese, 84; Parts and Places in Being and Saying, MIT Press, 87; Underterminacy of Personal Identity, Synthese, 93; Some of a Plurality in Philosophical Perspectives, 96; A Note on Plural Pronouns, Synthese, 98. **CONTACT ADDRESS** Dept of Philos, Tufts Univ, Medford, MA, 02155-5555.

CARTY-BENNIA, DENISE S.
PERSONAL Born 06/28/1947, Reed City, MI **DISCIPLINE** LAW **EDUCATION** Barnard Coll Columbia U, BA 1969; Sch of Law Columbia U, JD 1973. **CAREER** Northeastern Univ School of Law, prof of law; Wayne State Univ Law School, pres, assoc prof of law 1975-77; Kaye/Scholer/Fierman/Hays & Handler, assoc atty 1973-75. **HONORS AND AWARDS** Outstandint serv award Nat Black Am Law Students Assn 1979; presidents award, Nat Bar Assn 1979; revson fellow, Greenburg Center for Law & Soc Policy City Coll NY 1979-80; appreciation award, NE Region Black Am Law Students As, 1980; summer humanities seminar award, Nat Endowment for the Humanities, 1980. **MEMBERSHIPS** Mem Am Bar Assn, NY State Bar Assn, mem Nat Bar & Assn 1974; mem bd of dir Affirmative Action Coordinating Center, 1978-; co-chmn bd of dir NCBL 1979-; Minority Group Sec Assn of Am Law Sch 1975-; Faculty & Legal Advisor Nat Black Am Law Students Assn 1977-; Cooperating Atty Cntr For Constitutional Rights Research Fellow Inst for the Stury of Educ Policy Howard Univ 1978. **CONTACT ADDRESS** Sch of Law, Northeastern Univ, 400 Huntington Ave, Boston, MA, 02115.

CARVALHO, JOHN
DISCIPLINE PHILOSOPHY **EDUCATION** Univ Calif, Santa Cruz, BA, 76; Duquesne Univ, MA, 79; PhD, 87. **CAREER** Asst prof, philos, 87-94, assoc prof, 95- , Villanova Univ; vis lectr, Bryn Mawr Col, 94-95; vis assoc prof, Haverford Col, 97. **HONORS AND AWARDS** Fel NEH Summer Inst, 88, 91, 94, 97; hon mention, Lindback Award for Teaching Excellence, 91, 93, 94; sum res grant, 93. **MEMBERSHIPS** APA; Am Soc for Aesthetics; Soc for Phenomenology and Existential Philos; Soc for Ancient Greek Philos; Soc for the Philos Study of the Contemp Visual Arts; Greater Phila Philos Consortium. **RESEARCH** Critical and cultural theory; ancient philosophy; nineteenth century philosophy; aesthetics. **SELECTED PUBLICATIONS** Auth, The Visible and Invisible in Merleau-Ponty and Foucault, Int Stud in Philos, XXV/3; Repetitions: Appropriating Representation in Contemporary Art, Philos Today, 91. **CONTACT ADDRESS** Dept of Philosophy, Villanova Univ, 800 Lancaster Ave., Villanova, PA, 19085-1692. **EMAIL** Carvalho@ucis.vill.edu

CARVER, FRANK G.
PERSONAL Born 05/27/1928, Crookston, NE, m, 1949, 2 children **DISCIPLINE** RELIGION **EDUCATION** Taylor Univ, BA, 50; Nazarene Theol Sem, BD, 54; Princeton Theol Sem, MTh, 58; Univ Edinburgh, PhD, 64. **CAREER** Pastor, Nazarene churches Nebr, NJ, & Scot, 49-59; Olivet Nazarene Col, 72; pastor, Nazarene Theol Col, Johannesburg, RSA, 79; prof Bibl lit & theol, dept ch, dir grad relig stud, Pasadena/Pt Loma Nazarene Col, 61-96; lectr Europ Nazarene Bibl Col, 96-98; prof emer relig, Pt Loma Nazarene Col, 97-. **MEMBERSHIPS** SBL, WTS. **RESEARCH** Classic spirituality. **SELECTED PUBLICATIONS** Auth, Nature of Biblical Prophecy, The Second Coming, Beacon Hill Pr of Ks Cty, 95; When Jesus Said Goodbye, Beacon Hill Pr of Ks Cty, 96; The Essence of Wesleyanism, The Preacher's Mag, 96; Growth in Sanctification, Festschrift for H. Ray Dunning, 99. **CONTACT ADDRESS** 4037 95 Porte De Palmas, San Diego, CA, 92122. **EMAIL** fgcarver@ptluma.edu

CARVER, MARC
DISCIPLINE POST-MODERN ETHICS **EDUCATION** Inst Christian Studies, BA, 79; Austin Presbyterian theol sem, Mdiv, 92; Princeton sem, ThM, 93; Claremont Sch Theol, PhD; cont edu, Seton hosp, 91; Princeton sem, 93; Austin Presbyterian sem, 94; Loyola Marymont, 96; Mount St Mary's Col, 96-98. **CAREER** Chaplain, Brackenridge State hosp, 91; adjunct fac, Inst Christian Studies, 93-95; assoc min, Univ Ave Church of Christ, 88-95; therapist, Pepperdine Couns Ctr, 96-97; pastoral couns, 97-; adjunct fac, 96-. **HONORS AND AWARDS** Silver Stallion Award, Annawakkee Residential Treatment, 85; scholarc awards, Inst Christian Studies, 87-89; Austin Presbyterian theol sem, 89-91; outstanding young man of Am award, 90; scolar awards, Claremont Sch Theol, 95-. **MEMBERSHIPS** Mem, Am Assn Pastoral Counselors; Am Acad Rel Soc Biblical Lit; Soc Pastoral Theol; Soc Sci Relig. **RESEARCH** Interaction of theol and personality theory, psychol of relig. **SELECTED PUBLICATIONS** Auth, Lessons of Job for Ministry: Are We Aiding or Afflicting?, Leaven 4/4, 96. **CONTACT ADDRESS** Dept of Relig, Pepperdine Univ, 24255 Pacific Coast Hwy, Malibu, CA, 90263. **EMAIL** mcarver@pepperdine.edu

CARY, PHILLIP
DISCIPLINE PHILOSOPHY & RELIG STUD **EDUCATION** Wash Univ, St. Louis, BA, 80; Yale Univ, MA, 89, PhD, 94. **CAREER** Adj fac, philos dept,93, Univ CT, Stamford; adj fac, 93-94, Hillier Col, Univ Hartford; Arthur J. Ennis Postdoct Fel, 94-97, Villanova Univ Core Hum Prog; Rocco A. and Gloria C. Postdoct Fel, Villanova Univ Core Hum Prog, 97-98; asst prof, Eastern Col, St. Davids, 98-. **HONORS AND AWARDS** Wash Univ: Mylonas Scholar, Phi Beta Kappa; Yale Univ: Univ Fel, Special Diss Fel. **MEMBERSHIPS** APA; Soc of Christian Philos;AAR. **RESEARCH** Augustine; hist of Christian thought. **SELECTED PUBLICATIONS** Auth, On Behalf of Classical Trinitarianism: an Historical and Systematic Critique of Rahner on the Trinity, The Thomist, 92; auth, God in the Soul: Or, the Residue of Augustine's Manichaean Optimism, Univ of Dayton Rev, 94; auth, The Logic of Trinitarian Doctrine, Relig and Theol Stud Fel Bul, 95; auth, Historical Perspectives on Trinitarian Doctrine, Relig and Theol Stud Fel Bul, 95; auth, Believing the Word: a Proposal about Knowing Other Persons, Faith & Philosophy, 13/1, 96; auth, Augustine: Philosopher and Saint, lect ser, Tchng Co, 97; auth, Philosophy and Religion in the West, lect ser, Tchng Co, 97; auth, What Licentius Learned: A Narrative Reading of the Cassiciacum Dialogues, Augustinian Stud, 29/1, 98; auth, Interiority in St. Augustine Through the Ages: an Encyclopedia, Eerdmans, forthcoming. **CONTACT ADDRESS** Philosophy Dept, Eastern Col, 1300 Eagle Rd, St. Davids, PA, 19087-3696. **EMAIL** pcary@eastern.edu

CASEBIER, ALLAN
PERSONAL Born 10/01/1934, Los Angeles, CA, m, 1994 **DISCIPLINE** PHILOSOPHY; HISTORY **EDUCATION** UCLA, MA, 64; Michigan, PhD, 69. **CAREER** Philos Prof, USC, IL; CINEMA/TELEVISION, USC, MIAMI, FL. **HONORS AND AWARDS** Fulbright, India, 82. **MEMBERSHIPS** Amer Philos Assoc; Amer Soc for Aesthetics; Soc for Cinema Studies. **RESEARCH** Aesthetics; ethics; ontology; film hist. **SELECTED PUBLICATIONS** Auth, Film Appreciation, NY: Harcourt Brace Jovanovich, 76; Social Responsibilities of the Mass Media, Washington, DC: Univ Press Amer, 78; The Phenomenology of Japanese Cinema, Quart Rev Film & Video, 90; Film and Phenomenology, NY: Cambridge Univ Press, 91; Phenomenology and Aesthetics, Encyclopedia of Aesthetics, Oxford Univ Press, 97; A Phenomenology of Motion Picture Experience, Film and Philosophy, vol 4, 98; The Japanese Aesthetic, Journal of Comparative Lit and Art, fall 98; Theorizing the Moving Image, Film and Philos, vol 5, 99; Representation: Cultural Representations and Signifying Practices, World Communication, winter 99; Critical Communication, manuscript in progress. **CONTACT ADDRESS** 5825 SW 35th St., Miami, FL, 33155. **EMAIL** casebier@umiami.ir.miami.edu

CASEY, EDWARD S.
PERSONAL Born 02/24/1939, Topeka, KS, m, 1962, 2 children **DISCIPLINE** PHILOSOPHY **EDUCATION** Yale Univ, BA, 61; Northwestern Univ, PhD, 67. **CAREER** Univ Calif, Santa Barbara, 67-68; Yale Univ, 68-78; State Univ New York, Stony Brook, 78- . **HONORS AND AWARDS** Phi Beta Kappa, Magna cum Laude, Yale Univ, 61; Woodrow Wilson fel, 62-63, 66-67; Fulbright fel, Paris, 64-66; Morse fel, Yale Univ, 72-73; ALLS fel, 78; NEH fel, 87-88; Rockefeller fel, Wesleyan Univ, 90. **MEMBERSHIPS** APA; Soc for Phenomenology and Existential Philos. **RESEARCH** Aesthetics; phenomenology; structuralism; poststructuralism; philosophy of psychoanalysis; philosophy of mind; philosophy of perception. **SELECTED PUBLICATIONS** Auth, Spirit and Soul: Essays in Philosophical Psychology, 91; auth, Getting Back into Place: Toward a Renewed Understanding of the Place-World, Indiana, 93; auth, The Fate of Place: A Philosophical History, California, 97. **CONTACT ADDRESS** Dept of Philosophy, SUNY, Stony Brook, Stony Brook, NY, 11794.

CASEY, JOHN DUDLEY
PERSONAL Born 01/18/1939, Worcester, MA, m, 1982, 4 children **DISCIPLINE** HISTORY, LAW, AND LITERATURE **EDUCATION** Harvard Coll, BA; Harvard Law School, LLB; Univ of Iowa, MFA. **CAREER** Prof of English, Univ of Va, 72-92. **HONORS AND AWARDS** Nat Board Award for Fiction, 89. **MEMBERSHIPS** P.E.N. **SELECTED PUBLICATIONS** Auth, The Half-life of Happiness, 98; auth, Supper at the Black Pearl, 95; auth, Spartina, 89; auth, Testimony & Demeanor, 79; auth, An American Romance, 77. **CONTACT ADDRESS** Dept of English, Univ of Virginia, Bryant Hall, Charlottesville, VA, 22904.

CASEY, KENNETH
PERSONAL Born 10/26/1956, Waco, TX, m, 1987, 3 children **DISCIPLINE** PHILOSOPHY **EDUCATION** Univ of Florida, BA; Southern Bapt Sem, MDiv, Vanderbilt, PhD. **CAREER** Author **MEMBERSHIPS** APA **RESEARCH** Ancient and medieval philo; hist of ethics; rhetoric and lit. **CONTACT ADDRESS** 5017 Ridgeview Dr, Bowling Green, KY, 42101.

CASEY, TIMOTHY
PERSONAL Born 10/08/1950, Cleveland, OH, m, 1972, 4 children **DISCIPLINE** PHILOSOPHY **EDUCATION** Loras Coll, BA, 72; Duquesne Univ, PhD, 86. **CAREER** Prof, Philos Dept, 87-, Univ of Scranton. **HONORS AND AWARDS** BA Magna Cum Laude; PhD, Honors. **MEMBERSHIPS** Amer Philos Assoc. **RESEARCH** Philosophy of Technology, Philosophy of Architecture, 20th Century Continental Philosophy. **SELECTED PUBLICATIONS** Coed, Lifeworld and Technology, Center for Advanced Research in Phenomenology and Univ Press of America, 90; auth, Architecture as Environmental Philosophy, Research in Philosophy and Technology, forthcoming in 99; Medieval Technology and the Husserlian Critique of Galilean Science, American Catholic Philosophical Quarterly, 97; Technology and Science as Philosophical Problems, CCICA Annual, pub by Catholic Commission on Intellectual and Cultural Affairs, 97; Technology and the Metaphysics of Technique, Research in Philosophy and Technology, 97; Architecture, in: The Encyclopedia of Phenomenology, Kluwer Academic Publishers, 97. **CONTACT ADDRESS** Dept of Philosophy, Univ of Scranton, Scranton, PA, 18510. **EMAIL** caseyt1@tiger.us.edu

CASS, RONALD ANDREW
PERSONAL Born 08/12/1949, Washington, DC, m, 1969, 2 children **DISCIPLINE** LAW **EDUCATION** Univ VA, BA, 70; Univ Chicago, JD, 73. **CAREER** Law clerk, US Court Appeals 3rd Circuit, 73-74; assoc, Arent, Fox, Kintner, Plotkin & Kahn, 74-76; asst prof, Univ VA, 76-81; asoc prof Law, 81-83, Prof Law, 83-, Dean, Boston Univ School of Law, 90-, Bigelas Prof, 95-; comm'r, vice-chair, US Int Trade Commn, 88-90. **HONORS AND AWARDS** Sr fel, Int Center Econ Res, 96-97; Distinguished Lecturer, Univ Francisco Marroquinn, 96. **MEMBERSHIPS** Am Enterprise Instr (adj scholar); Am Law Inst; Asn Am Law Deans; Mont Pelerin; New England Coun; New England Legal Found; Trans-Atlantic Policy Network. **RESEARCH** Administrative law; communications law; First Amendment. **SELECTED PUBLICATIONS** Coauth, Cable-satellite networking: Problems and Prospects, Cath Univ Law Rev, 75; auth, Ignorance of Law: A Maxim Re-examined, William & Mary Law Rev, 76; First Amendment Access to Government Facilities, Va Law Rev, 79; Damage Suits Against Public Officers, Univ PA Law Rev, 81; Revolution in the Wasteland: Value and Diversity in Television, Univ Press VA, 81; Administrative Law: Cases and Materials, with Colin S. Driver, Little, Brown, & Co, Boston, MA, 87 (teacher's manual, 87; Supplement, 90; Supplement, 93, with Colin S. Diver & Jack Beermann); Throwing Stones at the Mudbank: The Effect of Scholarship on Administrative Law, with Jack M. Beermann, 45 Administrative Law Rev 1, 93; Price Discrimination and Predation Analysis in Antitrust and International Trade: A Comment, 61, Univ of Cincinnati Law Rev 877, 93; Adminitrative Law: Cases and Materials, with Colin S. Diver & Jack Beermann, Little, Brown & Co, Boston, MA, 94, 2nd ed (teacher's manual 94; Teacher's Update, 96); The How and Why of Law School Accreditation, 45 J of Legal Ed 418, 95; The Optimal Pace of Privatization, 13 Boston Univ Int Law J 413, 95; Judging: Norms and Incentives of Retrospective Decision-making, 75 Boston Univ Law Rev, 95;Economics and International Law, 29 NY Univ J of Int Law & Politics 473, 97; Money, Power, and Politics: Governance Models and Campaign Finance Regulation, 6 Supreme Court Economic Rev 1, 98; International Trade in Telecommunications, with John Haring, MIT Press, Cambridge, MA & AEI Press, Washington, DC, 98; Administrative Law: Cases and Materials, with Colin S. Diver & Jack Beermann, Aspen Pubs, NY, NY, 98, 3rd ed (teacher's manual, 98); and many other articles, book chapters, reviews, reports, and essays. **CONTACT ADDRESS** Sch Law, Boston Univ, 765 Commonwealth Ave, Boston, MA, 02215-1401. **EMAIL** roncass@bu.edu

CASSEL, J. DAVID
PERSONAL Born 02/16/1950 **DISCIPLINE** THEOLOGY **EDUCATION** Grinnell Coll, BA, 72; Princeton Theo Sem, MDiv, 75; Univ of VA, PhD, 92. **CAREER** Asst Prof, 92-97, Assoc Prof, 98-, Hanover Coll. **MEMBERSHIPS** AAR, NAPS. **RESEARCH** History of Biblical interpretation, Cyril of Alexandria. **SELECTED PUBLICATIONS** Auth, Stewardship, Experiencing and Expressing God's Nurturing Love, in: Amer Bap Qtly, 98; Defending the Cannibals, in: Christian Hist, 98; Cyril of Alexandria, Champion of Christology, in: Covenant Companion, 94; Athanasius, Advocate for Equality within the Godhead, in: Covenant Companion, 94; Origin of Alexandria, Saint or Heretic, in: Covenant Companion, 94; Justin Martyr, Defending the Faith until Death, in: Covenant Companion, 94. **CONTACT ADDRESS** Dept of Theological Studies, Hanover Col, Hanover, IN, 47243. **EMAIL** cassel@hanover.edu

CASSELS, JAMIE
DISCIPLINE LAW **EDUCATION** Carleton Univ, BA, 76; Western Ontario Univ, LLB, 80; Columbia Univ, LLM, 81. **CAREER** Asst prof, 81-93; prof, 93-; assoc dean, 95-98. **RESEARCH** Environmental issues; law and society in India. **SELECTED PUBLICATIONS** Auth, The Uncertain Promise of Law: Lessons from Bhopal; pubs on contracts, legal theory, and remedies; co-auth, Remedies: Cases and Materials. **CONTACT ADDRESS** Fac of Law, Univ Victoria, PO Box 2400, Victoria, BC, V8W 3H7. **EMAIL** jcassels@uvic.ca

CASSIDY, LAURENCE LAVELLE
PERSONAL Born 06/09/1929, New York, NY **DISCIPLINE** PHILOSOPHY, THEOLOGY **EDUCATION** Bellarmine Col, AB, 54; Woodstock Col, STL, 62; Fordham Univ, MA, 64, PhD(philos), 68. **CAREER** Asst prof philos, Fordham Univ, 67-68; assoc prof, 69-81, prof Philos, St Peter's Col, 81-; chmn Philos Dept, 87-94; pres Chapter AAUP, 97-73; sec, 73-85. **MEMBERSHIPS** Am Philos Asn; Am Cath Philos Asn; AAUP; Soc Christian Philosophers; Astrologers Guild Am (vpres, 80-83); Jesuit Philo Assn, 69-. **RESEARCH** Rational theology; phenomenology and idealism; philosophy and parascience. **SELECTED PUBLICATIONS** Auth, Truth as immediacy, Jesuit Philos Asn, 72; The flat earth fallacy, Astrological Rev, Summer 73; The believing Christian as a dedicated astrologer, Astrological J, UK, Spring 79; Astrology and science, Astrological Rev, Winter 80; Existence and Presence, Univ Press Am, 81; Creationism and academic freedom, Academe, 3/82; The Spiritual World of Astrology, The Astrological Journal, 96; The Thinking Self, Univ Press Am, 97. **CONTACT ADDRESS** Dept of Philosophy, St. Peter's Col, 2641 Kennedy Blvd, Jersey City, NJ, 07306-5997.

CASSWELL, DONALD G.
DISCIPLINE LAW **EDUCATION** Univ Toronto, BS, 72, LLM, 80; York Univ, LLB, 76. **CAREER** Asst prof, 80-83; assoc prof, 83-92; prof, 92-; assoc dean, 90-93. **MEMBERSHIPS** Can Bar Asn. **RESEARCH** Evidence; torts; medical law; trial and appellate advocacy; immigration and refugee law; lesbian and gay rights law. **SELECTED PUBLICATIONS** Auth, pubs on AIDS, ethics and law, lesbians, gay men, and canadian law; co-auth, Fundamentals of Trial Techniques. **CONTACT ADDRESS** Fac of Law, Univ Victoria, PO Box 2400, Victoria, BC, V8W 3H7. **EMAIL** casswell@uvic.ca

CASTE, NICHOLAS J.
DISCIPLINE POLITICAL PHILOSOPHY, BUSINESS ETHICS **EDUCATION** SUNY, Stony Brook, BA, 72; Emory Univ, MA, 74, PhD, 80. **CAREER** Adj prof, Univ NC, Charlotte. **RESEARCH** The ethics of soc interaction in groups such as corporations and in polit syst such as democracies. **SELECTED PUBLICATIONS** Auth, Corporations and Rights, J of Value Inquiry 26, 92; Drug Testing in the Workplace, J of Bus Ethics 11, 92; Thinking Critically: Techniques for Logical Reasoning, West Publ Co, 95. **CONTACT ADDRESS** Univ N. Carolina, Charlotte, Charlotte, NC, 28223-0001. **EMAIL** njcaste@uncc.edu

CASTELLI, ELIZABETH
DISCIPLINE RELIGION **EDUCATION** Brown Univ, BA, 79; Claremont Grad Sch, MA, PhD, 78. **CAREER** Asst prof. **RESEARCH** Feminist interpretation of the Bible; early Christian martyrdom and asceticism; women's history in late antiquity; Bible and contemporary culture. **SELECTED PUBLICATIONS** Auth, Imitating Paul: A Discourse of Power, Westminster John Knox, 91; co-ed, Reimagining Christian Origins, Trinity, 96. **CONTACT ADDRESS** Dept of Religion, Columbia Col, New York, 2960 Broadway, New York, NY, 10027-6902. **EMAIL** ec225@columbia.edu

CASULLO, ALBERT
DISCIPLINE EPISTEMOLOGY AND METAPHYSICS **EDUCATION** Univ Iowa, PhD, 75. **CAREER** Prof, Univ Nebr, Lincoln. **RESEARCH** A priori knowledge. **SELECTED PUBLICATIONS** Auth, Revisability, Reliabilism, and A Priori Knowledge, Philos and Phenomenol Res 49, 88; Causality, Reliabilism, and Mathematical Knowledge, Philos and Phenomenol Res 52, 92; Analyticity and the A Priori, Can J of Philos, Suppl Vol 18, 93. **CONTACT ADDRESS** Univ Nebr, Lincoln, Lincoln, NE, 68588-0417.

CATALANO, JOSEPH STELLARIO
PERSONAL Born 10/16/1928, Brooklyn, NY **DISCIPLINE** PHILOSOPHY **EDUCATION** St John's Univ, BA, 50, MA, 56, PhD(philos), 62. **CAREER** From instr to asst prof philos, St John's Univ, 59-65; assoc prof, 65-73, PROF PHILOS, KEAN COL, NJ, 73-, St John's Univ res grant, 64; adj assoc prof, C W Post Col, Long Island Univ, 65 & New Sch Social Res, 68- **MEMBERSHIPS** Am Philos Asn; Asn Symbolic Logic. **RESEARCH** Existentialism. **SELECTED PUBLICATIONS** Auth, Crafting Marks Into Meanings, Philos and Lit, Vol 0020, 96; The Script Rose, Philos and Lit, Vol 0019, 95. **CONTACT ADDRESS** Dept of Philos, Kean Col of New Jersey, Union, NJ, 07083.

CATANIA, ANDREA
DISCIPLINE LAW **EDUCATION** Goucher Col, BA; Wesleyan Univ, MAT; St John's Univ, JD. **CAREER** Prof, Seton Hall Univ, 80-; instr, NY Law Schl; instr, Brooklyn Law Schl; pvt pract, NYC. **SELECTED PUBLICATIONS** Publ in the areas of fed jurisdiction and employ discrimination. **CONTACT ADDRESS** Seton Hall Univ, South Orange, NJ. **EMAIL** catanian@lanmail.shu.edu

CAUCHY, VENANT
PERSONAL Born 05/18/1924, North Bay, Canada, m, 1949, 10 children **DISCIPLINE** PHILOSOPHY **EDUCATION** Col Bourget, Can, BA, 44; Univ Montreal, PhB, 45, PhL, 46, PhD(-philos), 47. **CAREER** From instr to asst prof philos, St Louis Univ, 47-51; asst prof, Our Lady of the Lake Col, 51-53 & Fordham Univ, 53-57; from asst prof to assoc prof, 57-63, PROF PHILOS, UNIV MONTREAL, 63-, Can Coun fel, 68-69; co-ed, Rev Cirpho, 73- **MEMBERSHIPS** Can Philos Asn (pres, 78-79); Soc Philos Fr Lang (vpres). **RESEARCH** Post-Aristotelian Greek philosophy; philosophy of religion. **SELECTED PUBLICATIONS** Auth, Meaning and Knowledge--Proposals for Responsibility and Solidarity in The Modern World, Laval Theol et Philos, Vol 0052, 96; Chinese and Oriental Approaches to Philosophy and Culture, Jour Chinese Philos, Vol 0021, 94; Violence--Biology, History and Christian Morality, Laval Theol et Philos, Vol 0053, 97. **CONTACT ADDRESS** Dept of Philos, Univ of Montreal, Montreal, PQ, H3C 3J7.

CAUSEY, ROBERT LOUIS
PERSONAL Born 04/13/1941, Los Angeles, CA, m, 1964, 2 children **DISCIPLINE** LOGIC, COGNITIVE SCIENCE **EDUCATION** Calif Inst Technol, BS, 63; Univ Calif, Berkeley, PhD(logic & methodology of sci), 67. **CAREER** Asst prof, 67-73, assoc prof, 73-79, prof philos, Univ Tex, Austin, 79-, chmn dept, 80-88, assoc dir, Univ Tx Artificial Intelligence Lab, 84-97, Nat Sci Found res fel, 73-74 & 79-81, consult, 79-81. **MEMBERSHIPS** ACM; AAAI; AAAS; Philos Sci Asn; Am Philos Asn; Am Asn Advan Humanities. **RESEARCH** Cognitive Science; unity of science; applied logic. **SELECTED PUBLICATIONS** Auth, Derived Measurement, Dimensions and Dimensional Analysis, Philos Sci, 69; Attribute--Identities in Microreductions, J Philos, 72; Uniform Microreductions, Synthese, 72; contribr, Formal Methods in Methodology of Empirical Sciences, 76 & auth, Unity of Science, 77, Reidel; contribr, Current Research in Philosophy of Science, 79; Scientific Discovery, Logic, and Rationality, 80; auth, The Use of Microcomputers for Classroom Demonstrations, Issues in Higher Educ, 82; Logic, Sets, and Recursion, Jones & Bartlett, 94. **CONTACT ADDRESS** Dept of Philos, Univ of Tex, Austin, TX, 78712-1180. **EMAIL** RLC@cs.utexas.edu

CAVADINI, JOHN C.
PERSONAL Born 11/09/1953, New Haven, CT, m, 1979, 7 children **DISCIPLINE** THEOLOGY **EDUCATION** Wesleyan Univ, BA, 75; Marquette Univ, MA, 79; Yale, MA, 81, MPhil, 83, PhD, 88. **CAREER** Instr, 90-present, U of Notre Dame, Dept of Theology; chair, 97-present. **HONORS AND AWARDS** Phi Beta Kappa **MEMBERSHIPS** AAR; NAPS. **RESEARCH** History of Christian Theology; The early church; Medieval theology. **SELECTED PUBLICATIONS** Auth, Augustine's De Trinitate and the Quest for Truth, Theological Studies, 97; auth, Ambrose and Augustine de bono mortis, in The Limits of Ancient Christianity, Univ Mich, 98; auth, A Note on Gregory's Theology of the Miraculous in The Life and Miracles of St. Benedict, American Benedictine Review, forthcoming. **CONTACT ADDRESS** Dept of Theology, Notre Dame, IN, 46556. **EMAIL** cavadini.1@nd.edu

CAVALIER, ROBERT
DISCIPLINE ADVANCEMENT OF APPLIED ETHICS **EDUCATION** Duquesne Univ, PhD. **CAREER** Philos, Carnegie Mellon Univ. **SELECTED PUBLICATIONS** Auth, Making MOSAIC Webs Work on the Course Level, Syllabus Magazine, 95; Computers, Philosophy of Education: An Encyclopedia, Garland Publ, 96; Feminism and Pornography: A Dialogical Perspective, Computer-Mediated Communication, 96; Evaluating Evaluation in Light of Discipline-Specific Computational Turns Jour Computing Higher Educ, 96; Multimedia in Philosophy Teaching and Research in The Digital Phoenix: How Computers are Changing Philosophy, Blackwell, 97. **CONTACT ADDRESS** Carnegie Mellon Univ, 5000 Forbes Ave, Pittsburgh, PA, 15213.

CAVALLARO, ROSANNA
DISCIPLINE LAW **EDUCATION** Harvard Univ, BA, 83; JD, 86. **CAREER** Prof. **RESEARCH** Criminal law; evidence; legal profession. **SELECTED PUBLICATIONS** Auth, Police & Thieves (rev), Mich Law Rev, 98; A Big Mistake: Eroding the Defense of Mistake of Fact About Consent in Rape, Jour Criminal Law, 96. **CONTACT ADDRESS** Law School, Suffolk Univ, Beacon Hill, Boston, MA, 02114. **EMAIL** rcavalla@acad.suffolk.edu

CAVANAUGH, THOMAS A.
PERSONAL Born 05/24/1963, Erie, PA, m, 1994, 1 child **DISCIPLINE** PHILOSOPHY **EDUCATION** Univ of notre Dame, PhD, 95 **CAREER** Asst Prof, 94-, Univ of San Fran **HONORS AND AWARDS** RM Weaver Fel **MEMBERSHIPS** Am Philos Assoc; Int Assoc of Bioethics **RESEARCH** Bioethics; Ethics; Moral psychology **SELECTED PUBLICATIONS** Auth, Currently Accepted Practices that are Known to Lead to Death and PAS: Is There an Ethically relevant Difference? , Cambridge Quarterly of Healthcare Ethics 7, pp 373-379, 98; Act-Evaluation, Willing, and Double Effect, American Catholic Philosophical Quarterly, pp 243-253, 97 **CONTACT ADDRESS** Dept of Philosophy, Univ of San Francisco, San Francisco, CA, 94117-1080. **EMAIL** cavanaught@usfca.edu

CAVE, ERIC M.
PERSONAL Born 11/12/1965, Lund, Sweden **DISCIPLINE** PHILOSOPHY **EDUCATION** Trinity Univ, BA, 88; Univ Calif Irvine, MA, 90; PhD, 94. **CAREER** Vis asst prof, Union Coll, 94-95; asst prof Ark State Univ, 95-. **HONORS AND AWARDS** NEH Summer Res Sem Participant, 97. **MEMBERSHIPS** Am Philos Asn; Soc for the Philos of Sex and Love; Phi Beta Kappa. **RESEARCH** Ethics; Political Philosophy. **SELECTED PUBLICATIONS** Auth, A Leibnizian Account of Why Belief in the Christian Mysteries Is Justified, Rel Studies, 95; Would Pluralist Angels (Really) Need Government?, Philos Studies, 96; The Individual Rationality of Maintaining a Sense of Justice, Theory and Decision, 96; Habituation and Rational Preference Revision, Dialogue: Can Philos Rev, 98; Prefering Justice: Rationality, Self-Transformation, and the Sense of Justice, 98. **CONTACT ADDRESS** English and Philosophy, Box 1890, State University, AR, 72467-1890. **EMAIL** ecave@toltec.astate.edu

CAWS, PETER JAMES
PERSONAL Born 05/25/1931, Southall, England, m, 1987, 3 children **DISCIPLINE** PHILOSOPHY OF THE SCIENCES **EDUCATION** Univ London, BSc, 52; Yale Univ, MA, 54, PhD, 56. **CAREER** Instr natural sci, Mich State Univ, 56-57; from asst prof to assoc prof philos & chmn dept, Univ Kans, 57-62; exec assoc, Carnegie Corp, New York, 62-65, consult, 65-67; chmn dept philos, Hunter Col, 65-67, prof philos, 65-82; Univ Prof Philos, George Washington Univ, 82-; mem, Coun Philos Studies, 65-; mem, Nat Res Coun, 67-; exec officer, PhD prog philos, City Univ New York, 67-70; Am Coun Learned Soc fel, 72-73; mem, Bd Dir (Comn Int Coop), Am Philos Asn, 74-84; nat lectr, Soc Signma Xi, 75-77; Rockefeller Found fel, 79-80; vis prof, Fr NY Univ, spring, 82; Phi Beta Kappa vis schol, 83-84; vis prof, comp lit Univ Maryland, 85. **HONORS AND AWARDS** Pres medal, CUNY Grad Sch, 78; First Dist Lectr Business and Society Baruch Col, 86; hon mem Phi Beta Kappa, 92. **MEMBERSHIPS** Fel AAAS (vpres, 67-68); Am Philos Asn; Philos Sci Asn; Soc Gen Syst Res (pres, 66-67); Soc Am de Phil de Langue Francaise (pres, 92-94). **RESEARCH** Structure and development of theory and praxis; philosophy and politics; recent European philosophy. **SELECTED PUBLICATIONS** Ed, Two Centuries of Philosophy in America, Blackwell, 80; auth, Structuralism, Humanities, 88; auth, Yorick's World: Science and the Knowing Subject, California, 93; auth, Ethics from Experience, Wadsworth, 96. **CONTACT ADDRESS** Dept of Philosophy, George Washington Univ, 2035 H St NW, Washington, DC, 20052-0001. **EMAIL** pcaws@gwu.edu

CAYARD, W.W.
PERSONAL Born 04/05/1921, Port Arthur, TX, m, 1952, 4 children **DISCIPLINE** RELIGION **EDUCATION** Univ of S CA, PhD, 56 **CAREER** Inst, 56-86, Prof, 66-96; Chair, 69-86; W Liberty St Col **MEMBERSHIPS** Am Philos Assoc **RESEARCH** Quaker Topics; Historical Jesus **SELECTED PUBLICATIONS** Auth, Berdyaev's Philosophy of Freedom, University of Southern California Press, 56; Auth, A Quaker View of the Bible, Pittsburgh Friends Meeting Newsletter, 98, 10-11 **CONTACT ADDRESS** 100 Norman Dr, Cranberry Twp, PA, 16066-4232. **EMAIL** cayard@fyi.net

CECIRE, ROBERT C.
DISCIPLINE CHURCH HISTORY **EDUCATION** Wheaton Col, BA; Gordon Divinity Sch, BD; Univ Kans, MA, PhD. **CAREER** Adj prof, Bethel Col; Anoka-Ramsey Community Col; vis lectr, Univ Kans; lectr, Gordon Col; asst prof, Wiinebrenner Theol Sem, 97-; dir, Theol Stud. **MEMBERSHIPS** Mem, Soc Biblical Lit; Conf on Faith and History; Nat Hist Honor Soc. **SELECTED PUBLICATIONS** Rev(s), Jour Evangel Theol Soc; Res Publica Litterarum; pub, article on Encratism, Res Publica Litterarum. **CONTACT ADDRESS** Winebrenner Theol Sem, 701 E Melrose Ave, PO Box 478, Findlay, OH, 45839.

CEDERBLOM, JERRY
PERSONAL m, 1 child **DISCIPLINE** MORAL AND POLITICAL PHILOSOPHY, EPISTEMOLOGY, HISTORY OF PHILOSOPHY, CRITIC **EDUCATION** Whitman Col, BA, 67; Claremont Grad Sch, PhD, 72. **CAREER** Instr, Univ Nebr, Omaha; vis prof, Evergreen State Col. **HONORS AND AWARDS** Excellence in Tchg award, Univ Nebr, Omaha, 91. **SELECTED PUBLICATIONS** Coauth, Critical Reasoning; Ethics at Work; coed, Justice and Punishment. **CONTACT ADDRESS** Univ Nebr, Omaha, Omaha, NE, 68182.

CENKNER, WILLIAM
PERSONAL Born 10/25/1930, Cleveland, OH **DISCIPLINE** HISTORY OF RELIGIONS **EDUCATION** Providence Col, AB, 54; Pontif Fac Theol, STL, 59; Fordham Univ, PhD(hist relig), 69. **CAREER** Assoc prof hist, 69-80, ASSOC PROF HISTRELIG & RELIG EDUC, CATH UNIV AM, 80-, Chauncey Stillman Found res grant, 69; mem, Nat Coun Relig & Pub Educ, 72-; assoc ed, Col Theol Soc, 73- **MEMBERSHIPS** Col Theol Soc (pres, 78-80); Am Acad Relig; Asn Asian Studies. **RESEARCH** Encounter of world religions; religion and education; Sankaracarya's. **SELECTED PUBLICATIONS** Auth, Theology After Vedanta--An Experiment in Comparative Theology, Theol Stud, Vol 0054, 93; The Asrama System--The History and Hermeneutics of a Religious Institution, Theol Stud, Vol 0056, 95; World Religions in America--An Introduction, Horizons, Vol 0023, 96. **CONTACT ADDRESS** Sch of Relig Studies, Catholic Univ of America, 620 Michigan Ave NE, Washington, DC, 20064-0002.

CENTORE, FLOYD
DISCIPLINE PHILOSOPHY **EDUCATION** Canisius Col Buffalo, BA, 59; Univ Md, MA, 62; St John's Univ, PhD, 68. **CAREER** Prof **SELECTED PUBLICATIONS** Auth, A Note on Diversity and Difference; A Note on T.G. Smith's The Theory of Forms, Relations and Infinite Regress, A Note on W.J. Hill's The Doctrine of God After Vatican II; A Note on Wittgenstein as an Unwilling Nominalist; Aquinas on Inner Space; Atomism and Plato's Theaetetus; Camus, Pascal, and the Absurd; Classical Christian Philosophy and Temporality: Correcting a Misunderstanding; Copernicus, Hooke, and Simplicity; Don't Question My Catholicism! When Debate Is Legitimate, and When It Isn't; Evolution (some Philosophical Dimensions); Evolution After Darwin. **CONTACT ADDRESS** Dept of Philosophy, St. Jerome's Univ, Waterloo, ON, N2L 3G3.

CESARZ, GARY
PERSONAL Born 10/01/1950, Albuquerque, NM, m, 1998, 2 children **DISCIPLINE** PHILOSOPHY **EDUCATION** Univ of N Mex, BA, 74, MA, 78, PhD, 88. **CAREER** Instr, Chapman Univ, 78-97; from Tchg asst to tchg assoc to adj asst prof, 80-93, Univ N Mex; asst prof, Col Santa Fe, 86-89; instr, Auburn Univ, 97-. **HONORS AND AWARDS** Nat Hon Soc in Philos; Popejoy Dissertation Prize Nominee **MEMBERSHIPS** Am Philos Assoc; Soc for the Advancement of Am Philos; Leibniz Soc; Marcel Soc **RESEARCH** Early Modern Philosophy; Stoics; History of Philosophy; Descartes; Leibniz; Kant; Metaphysics; Idealism; Ancient Greek Philosophy **SELECTED PUBLICATIONS** Review, Stoics, Epicureans, and Sceptics, in Southwest Philos Studies, 98; **CONTACT ADDRESS** Dept of Philos, Auburn Univ, Auburn, AL, 36849-5210. **EMAIL** cesargl@mail.auburn.edu

CHALFANT, WILLIAM Y.
PERSONAL Born 10/03/1928, Hutchinson, KS, m, 1956, 2 children **DISCIPLINE** HISTORY; LAW **EDUCATION** Univ Kans, AB, 50; Univ Mich, Juris Dr, 56. **CAREER** Atty at Law, Branwe, Chalfant, & Hill, 56-. **HONORS AND AWARDS** Various. **MEMBERSHIPS** Kans Bar Asn; Am Bar Asn; SW Bar Asn; W Hist Asn; Santa Fe Trail Asn. **RESEARCH** Spanish Entrada on Western Plains; military history of Southern Plains; Plains Indians. **SELECTED PUBLICATIONS** Auth, Cheyennes and Horse Soldiers, Univ Okla Press, 89; auth, Without Quarter, Univ Okla Press, 91; Dangerous Passage, Univ Okla Press, 94; Cheyennes at Darkwater Creek, Univ Okla Press, 97. **CONTACT ADDRESS** Branwe, Chalfant & Hill, 411 First Nat Ctr, PO Box 2027, Hutchinson, KS, 67504-2027.

CHALMERS, DAVID
DISCIPLINE PHILOSOPHY **EDUCATION** Univ Adelaide, Australia, BS, MATH, COMP SCI; Ind Univ, PhD, Philos. **CAREER** PROF, PHILOS, UNIV CALIF, SANTA CRUZ. **HONORS AND AWARDS** McDonnell fel, Wash Univ. **MEMBERSHIPS** Asn Sci Stud Consciousness; Soc Philos Psychol. **RESEARCH** Philosophy of mind, related areas of cognitive science and metaphysics. **SELECTED PUBLICATIONS** Auth, The Conscious Mind: In Search of a Fundamental Theory, Oxford Univ Press, 96; Explaining Consciousness: The Hard Problem, MIT Press, 97. **CONTACT ADDRESS** Dept of Philos, Univ Calif, 1156 High St, Santa Cruz, CA, 95064. **EMAIL** chalmers@paradox.ucsc.edu

CHAMBERLAIN, GARY L.
PERSONAL Born 08/21/1938, Denver, CO, m, 1968, 2 children **DISCIPLINE** RELIGIOUS STUDIES **EDUCATION** St Louis Univ, BA, 62; Univ Chicago, MA, 67; Grad Theol Union, PhD, 73. **CAREER** Assoc prof, Webster Univ St Louis, 71-79; assoc prof; chair, 87-91; prof, Seattle Univ, 79-. **HONORS AND AWARDS** NEH Fel, 75-76; Summa cum laude, 62; Gaffney Endowed Chair, 91-94. **MEMBERSHIPS** Am Acad of Rel; Soc of Christian Ethics; Assoc Prof and Res in Rel Educ; Pax Christi; Amnesty Int; Sierra Club. **RESEARCH** Population, Consumption, and the Environment; Human Sexuality; Peace and Justice; Faith Development. **SELECTED PUBLICATIONS** Auth, Learning from the Japanese on Abortion, Am, 94; Catholics as Remnant in Japan, Nat Cath Reporter, 94; Kamagasaki: the Underside of Japan's economic Miracle, Japan Christian Rev, 94; Abortion, Family Life, and Economic Development in Belize, Belize Studies, 95. **CONTACT ADDRESS** Theology and Religious Studies, Seattle Univ, Seattle, WA, 98122. **EMAIL** gchamber@seattleu.edu

CHAMBERLAIN, PAUL
PERSONAL Born 12/24/1954, Alberta, BC, Canada, m, 1979, 2 children **DISCIPLINE** ETHICS **EDUCATION** Marquette Univ, PhD, 90 **CAREER** Asst Prof, 90-pres, Trinity Western Univ **MEMBERSHIPS** Can Philos Assoc; Soc of Christian Philos **RESEARCH** Physician Assisted Suicide; Ethical Foundations **CONTACT ADDRESS** Dept of Philosophy, Trinity Western Univ, 7600 Glover Rd, Langley, BC, V2Y 1Y1. **EMAIL** chamberl@twu.ca

CHAMBERLIN, BILL F.
DISCIPLINE LAW **EDUCATION** Univ Wash, BA, PhD; Univ Wis, Madison, MA. **CAREER** Prof, Univ Fla, 87-. **RESEARCH** Mass media law, first amendment theory, media law research. **CONTACT ADDRESS** School of Law, Univ of Florida, PO Box 117625, Gainesville, FL, 32611-7625. **EMAIL** chamberlin@law.ufl.edu

CHAMBERS, ALEX A.
PERSONAL Born 12/10/1934, Lorman, MS, m, 1960 **DISCIPLINE** RELIGION **EDUCATION** Stillman College, AB, 1960; Duke Univ, MDiv, 1968; Southeastern Univ, STD, 1971. **CAREER** Hayes Tabernacle Christian Methodist Church, minister; Vermont Avenue Presbyterian Church, minister to youth; St Joseph Christian Methodist Episcopal Church, minister; JC Penny, auditor; Kittrel College, visiting professor, 1966-67; FURMAN UNIV, PROFESSOR OF RELIGION, 1972-; Williams CME Church, Memphis, TN, minister; Mount Olive CME Church, Memphis, TN, minister, 1982-86; LANE COLLEGE, JACKSON, TN, PRESIDENT, 1986-. **HONORS AND AWARDS** Honorary Degrees: Kittrell Coll, DD; Natl Theological Seminary, LittD; Stillman Coll, LHD; Alumni of the Year, 1968, Distinguished Alumni Award, Stillman Coll, 1970. **MEMBERSHIPS** United Fund; editor, Eastern Index; exec vice pres/general, Van Hoose Mortuary. **SELECTED PUBLICATIONS** Author, "The Negro in the United States," Journal of Negro History, 1961. **CONTACT ADDRESS** Lane Col, 545 Lane Ave, Jackson, TN, 38301-4598.

CHAMBERS, JOHN CURRY, JR.
PERSONAL Born 05/22/1956, Newark, NJ, m, 1981 **DISCIPLINE** LAW **EDUCATION** Univ of Pennsylvania, BA; The Washington College of Law, American Univ, JD. **CAREER** American Petroleum Institute, principal RCRA Attorney, 1981-84; CONOCO, in-house counsel, 1985; McKenna & Cuneo, partner, 1986-97; Arent Fox, mem, 1997-. **MEMBERSHIPS** DC Bar; ABA, National Bar Assn; Environmental Law Editorial Institute, advisory bd, Journal of Environmental Permitting; advisory committee, ABA Conference on Minority Partners; committee, National Institute for the Environment; vice chair, ABA Teleconference & Video Programs Sonreel; vice chair, ABA Sonreel Diversity Committee; guest commentator, Natl Public Radio; founder, Brownfields Business Information Network; co-chair, ABA Video Teleconferences Committee; mem, EPA NACEPT Title VI Federal Advisory Committee on Implementation of Environmental Justice. **SELECTED PUBLICATIONS** Numerous publications. **CONTACT ADDRESS** Arent Fox, 1050 Connecticut Ave, Washington, DC, 20036.

CHAMBERS, JULIUS LEVONNE
PERSONAL Born 10/06/1936, Montgomery Co, NC, m **DISCIPLINE** LAW **EDUCATION** NC Central Univ Durham, BA History (summa cum laude) 1958; Univ of MI, MA 1959; Univ of NC Sch of Law, JD 1962; Columbia Univ Sch of Law ML 1963. **CAREER** Columbia Univ Sch of Law, assoc in law 1962-63; NAACP Legal Def & Educ Fund Inc, legal intern 1963-64; Chambers Stein Ferguson & Becton PA, pres 1964-84; Harvard Univ Law Sch, lecturer 1965; Univ of VA Law Sch, guest lecturer 1971-72; Univ of PA Sch of Law, lecturer 1972-90; Columbia University School of Law, adjunct 1978-91; NAACP Legal & Educ Fund Inc, dir counsel 1984-92; University of Michigan Law School, adjunct 1989-92; North Carolina Central University, chancellor 1993-. **HONORS AND AWARDS** WEB DuBois Awd Scotland Co 1973; Hall of Fame Awd NAACP 1975; numerous hon LLD degrees; various distinguished serv awds, frats & Assns. **MEMBERSHIPS** Mem numerous cts of practice 1962-; mem Amer, Natl, 26th Judicial Dist NC Bar Assns; NC Assn of Black Lawyers; mem Amer Bar Assn Section on Indiv Rights & Responsibilities; adv com Natl Bar Assn Equal Employment Oppor; mem NC Bar Assn Com on Rules of Appellate Procedure; mem NC State Bar Assn Const Study Com; mem various NAACP brs; mem various legal assns; bd of dirs Epilepsy Assn of NC; mem various Univ bds; mem various alumni assns; mem various frats; mem Friendship Baptist Church Charlotte. **CONTACT ADDRESS** No Carolina Central Univ, Durham, NC, 27707.

CHAMBERS, TIMOTHY
PERSONAL Born 05/04/1971, Milwaukee, WI **DISCIPLINE** PHILOSOPHY **EDUCATION** Univ CT, BS, 93, BA , 93; Tufts Univ, MA, 95; Brown Univ, ABD, 98. **MEMBERSHIPS** APA **RESEARCH** Epistemology; metaphysics; philosophical logic. **SELECTED PUBLICATIONS** Co-auth, Identification of Coumarin in Vanilla Extracts by TLC and HPLC, 65 J of Chem Ed, 88; auth, Quest for Truth Remains an Uncertain Pursuit, Hartford Courant, 90; co-auth, Evidence for Changes in the Alzheimer's Disease Brain Cortical Membrane Structure Mediated by Cholesterol, 13 Neurobiology of Aging, 92; auth, Note On a Contentious Conditional, 6 Lyceum, 94; auth, On Vagueness, Sorites, and Putnam's Intuitionistic Strategy, 81 The Monist, 98; auth, Time Travel: How Not to Defuse The Principle Paradox, 12 Ratio, forthcoming 99. **CONTACT ADDRESS** Dept of Philosophy, Brown Univ, Box 1918, Providence, RI, 02912. **EMAIL** Timothy_Chambers@brown.edu

CHAMBLISS, PRINCE C., JR.
PERSONAL Born 10/03/1948, Birmingham, AL, m, 1971 **DISCIPLINE** LAW **EDUCATION** Wesleyan Univ, 1966-68; Univ of Alabama, Birmingham, BA, 1971; Harvard Univ School of Law, JD, 1974. **CAREER** Univ of Alabama-Birmingham, special asst to pres, 1974-75; Judge Sam C Pointer Jr, law clerk, 1975-76; Armstrong Allen, et al, LAW, 1976-. **HONORS AND AWARDS** National Bar Assn, Judicial Conference Community Service Award, 1986; Memphis Legal Secretaries Assn, Boss of the Year, 1983. **MEMBERSHIPS** Tennessee Bd of Law Examiners, vp, 1988-; Tennessee Bar Assn, scy, 1994-97; Memphis Bar Assn, bd of dirs, 1994-, president, 1997-98; Ben F Jones Chapter of the National Bar Assn, chairman, judicial recommendations committee, 1978-; Grant Information Ctr Inc, chairman-elect, 1994-; Memphis Mid-South Chapter, bd of dirs American Red Cross, bd of dirs, 1987-. **SELECTED PUBLICATIONS** "Legal Ethics for Trial Lawyers," The Litigator; "Inconsistent Verdicts: How to Recognize & Cope With," The Litigator. **CONTACT ADDRESS** Armstrong, Allen, Prewitt, Gentry, Johnston & Holmes, 80 Monroe Ave, Ste 700, Memphis, TN, 38103.

CHANCE, J. BRADLEY
DISCIPLINE THEOLOGY **EDUCATION** Univ NC, Chapel Hill, AB, 75; Southwestern Baptist Theol Sem, MD, 78; Duke Univ, PhD, 84. **CAREER** PROF, WM JEWELL COL, 82-. **CONTACT ADDRESS** 969 Northwyck Dr, Liberty, MO, 64068.

CHANCELLOR, JAMES D.
PERSONAL Born 11/23/1944, St. Louis, MO, m, 1969, 2 children **DISCIPLINE** HISTORY OF RELIGION, ISLAM **EDUCATION** Duke Univ, PhD, 88. **CAREER** Assoc prof Relig, 85-89, Col Baptist Univ; dean, prof Rel, Col Christian Univ, 89-92; assoc prof Rel, S Bapt Theol Sem, 92- . **MEMBERSHIPS** AAR **RESEARCH** New Religious Movements; The Family **SELECTED PUBLICATIONS** Auth, The Night of the Cross, The Dividing Edge, Fall, 91; Christ and Religious Pluralism, Rev and Expositor, vol 91, no 4, Fall, 94; Religion in the Middle East, in Introduction to Missions, Broadman and Holman Publ, 98. **CONTACT ADDRESS** Dept of Religion, S Baptist Theological Sem, 2825 Lexington Rd, Louisville, KY, 40280. **EMAIL** jchancellor@sbts.edu

CHANDLER, EVERETT A.
PERSONAL Born 09/21/1926, Columbus, OH, d **DISCIPLINE** LAW **EDUCATION** Ohio State Univ, BSc in Educ 1955; Howard Univ Law School, JD 1958. **CAREER** Juvenile Ct Cuyahoga County, referee, support dept 1959; City of Cleveland OH, house insp 1960; Cuyahoga County Welfare Dept, legal inv 1960-64; Cuyahoga County OH, asst cty pros 1968-71; City of Cleveland OH, chief police prosecutor 1971-75; private practice, Attorney 1975-. **HONORS AND AWARDS** Main speaker banquet Frontiers Intl Columbus OH 1972; Cleveland Bar Association, Meritorious Service Award, 1972. **MEMBERSHIPS** Bd mem, Cedar Branch YMCA, 1965; Comm Action Against Addiction, 1975-80, bd chrmn, 1980-87; bd mem, Legal Aid Soc of Cleveland, 1980; polemarch and bd chmn, Kappa Alpha Psi Inc, Cleveland Alumni Chapter, 1976, 1980-83; NAACP; Urban League; bd mem, past bd pres, CIT Mental Health; Excelsior Lodge #11 F&AM; Mt Olive Missionary Baptist Church, 1958-. **SELECTED PUBLICATIONS** Book review vol 21 #2 Cleveland State Law School Law Review. **CONTACT ADDRESS** PO Box 28459, Cleveland, OH, 44128-0459.

CHANDLER, HUGH
DISCIPLINE PHILOSOPHY **EDUCATION** Cornell Univ, PhD, 64. **CAREER** Assoc prof, Univ Ill Urbana Champaign. **RESEARCH** Metaphysics; philosophy of mind; philosophy of religion; ethics. **SELECTED PUBLICATIONS** Auth, Theseus' Clothes-Pin; Indeterminate People; Sources of Essence; Some Ontological Arguments. **CONTACT ADDRESS** Philosophy Dept, Univ Ill Urbana Champaign, 52 E Gregory Dr, Champaign, IL, 61820. **EMAIL** hchandle@uiuc.edu

CHANDLER, JAMES P.
PERSONAL Born 08/15/1938, Bakersfield, CA, m **DISCIPLINE** LAW **EDUCATION** Univ CA, AB, JD; Havard U, LLM. **CAREER** THE NATL LAW CENTER, GEORGE WASHINGTON UNIV, PROF OF LAW 1977-; Univ CA, research asst; Boston Univ Law School, instructor 1970-71; Univ of MD Law School, asst assoc prof 1971-75; Univ of MS Law Center, distinguished visiting prof of law 1976; Univ CO Law School, visiting prof of law 1977. **MEMBERSHIPS** DC Bar; Am Soc Intl Law 1969-; Am Assn Univ Profs 1971-; Am Soc Law Profs 1974-; Alpha Phi Alpha Frat 1961-; bd dirs Ch God Evening Light Saints 1972-; Computer Law Assn 1974-; Woodbourne Ctr Inc 1974-76; sect council mem Am Bar Assn; consult Adminstrn Officer Cts St MD 1974-76; US Gen Acctng Office 1973-81. **CONTACT ADDRESS** School of Law, George Washington Univ, 2000 Pennsylvania Ave, Ste 185, Washington, DC, 20006-4211.

CHANDLER, MARTHE ATWATER
PERSONAL Chestertown, MD, m, 1982, 2 children **DISCIPLINE** PHILOSOPHY **EDUCATION** Vassar col, AB, magna cum laude, 62; Univ Chicago, MA, 64; Univ Ill-Chicago Cir, PhD, 80. **CAREER** Inst Philos, Central YMCA Commun Col, 71-80; vis asst prof, Philos, Univ Ky, 80-81; asst prof, Philos, DePauw Univ, 81-86; vis scholar, Univ Mich, Inter-Univ Consortium for Polit and Soc res, Summer, 88; vis prof Philos, Northwestern univ, 88-89; assoc prof, Philos, 86-94, prof, 94-, DePauw Univ. **MEMBERSHIPS** Amer Philos Asn; Soc Asian Compar Philos; Philos Sci Asn; Ind Philos Asn; Soc Women Philos. **RESEARCH** Philosophy of Social Science; Chinese Philosophy; Metaphysics of Time. **SELECTED PUBLICATIONS** Auth, Abortion Politics in the United States and Canada: Studies in Public Opinion, Praeger, 94; Coauth, Abortion in the United States and Canada: A Comparative Study of Public Opinion, in Abortion Politics in the United States and Canada: Studies in Public Opinion, Praeger, 94; Coauth, Two Faces of Feminism, in Perspectives on the Politics of Abortion, Paragon House, 95. **CONTACT ADDRESS** Dept of Philosophy, DePauw Univ, Greencastle, IN, 46135. **EMAIL** chandler@depauw.edu

CHANG, HOWARD F.
DISCIPLINE LAW **EDUCATION** Harvard Univ, AB, 82; Princeton Univ, MPA,85; Harvard Univ, JD,87; Mass Inst Technol, PhD,92.. **CAREER** Prof Univ Southern California; clerked for, Honorable Ruth Bader Ginsburg, Judge US Ct Appeals DC Circuit. **MEMBERSHIPS** Amer Law & Econ Asn. **RESEARCH** International trade regulation; intellectual property; immigration; law & economics. **SELECTED PUBLICATIONS** Auth, Liberalized Immigration as Free Trade: Economic Welfare & the Optimal Immigration Policy; An Economic Analysis of Trade Measures to Protect the Global Environment & Patent Scope, Antitrust Policy, and Cumulative Innovation; coauth, Bargaining & the Division of Value in Corporate Reorganization. **CONTACT ADDRESS** School of Law, Univ Southern Calif, University Park Campus, Los Angeles, CA, 90089. **EMAIL** hchang@law.usc.edu

CHAPMAN, DOUGLAS K.
DISCIPLINE LAW **EDUCATION** Ohio State Univ, BA; Ohio Northern Univ, JD. **CAREER** Prof. **SELECTED PUBLICATIONS** Auth, Enforceability of Settlement Agreement Allocations, Baylor, 95; Ohio's College Savings Plan: Buyer Beware, Univ Toledo, 89; Below Market Loans: From Abuse to Misuse-A Sports Illustration, 87. **CONTACT ADDRESS** Col Law, Univ of Toledo, Toledo, OH, 43606. **EMAIL** dchapma@utnet.utoledo.edu

CHAPPELL, DAVID WELLINGTON
PERSONAL Born 02/03/1940, St. John, NB, Canada, 2 children **DISCIPLINE** HISTORY OF RELIGIONS **EDUCATION** Mt Allison Univ, BA, 61; McGill Univ, BD, 65; Yale Univ, PhD(Chinese Buddhism), 76. **CAREER** Teaching asst world relig, Yale Univ, 70-71; actg asst prof Chinese relig, Univ Hawaii, 71-77; asst prof, Univ Toronto, 77-78; asst prof, 78-80, Prof Chinese Relig, Univ Hawaii, Manoa, 85- **MEMBERSHIPS** Asn for Asian Studies; Am Acad Relig; Soc Study Chinese Relig; NAm Soc Buddhist Studies; Soc for Buddhist-Christian Stu. **RESEARCH** Formation of Chinese Buddhism; Buddhist-Christian comparisons. **SELECTED PUBLICATIONS** Auth, Introduction to the T'ien-t'ai ssu-chiao-i, Eastern Buddhist, 5/76; A perspective on the Pure Land Doctrine of T'ien-t'ai Chih-i (538-597), (in Japanese), Taisho Daigaku Bukkyo gaku, 76; coed & contribr article, In: Buddhist and Taoist Studies (Vol I), Univ Hawaii, 77; contribr, Early Ch'an in China and Tibet, 82; ed, T'ien-t'ai Buddhism, Dai-ichi-Shobo, 83; auth, Pure Land Buddhism: History, Culture and Doctrine, Univ Calif, 97.Pure Land Buddhism: History, Culture and Doctrine, Univ Calif, 97. **CONTACT ADDRESS** Dept of Relig, Univ of Hawaii, 2530 Dole St, Honolulu, HI, 96822-2303. **EMAIL** dwchap@hawaii.edu

CHAPPELL, VERE CLAIBORNE
PERSONAL Born 03/22/1930, Rochester, NY, m, 1951, 8 children **DISCIPLINE** PHILOSOPHY **EDUCATION** Yale Univ, BA, 51, MA, 53, PhD, 58. **CAREER** Instr philos, Yale Univ, 54-57; from instr to prof, Univ Chicago, 57-70; head dept, 70-74, acting assoc provost & dean grad sch, 74-76, assoc provost, 77-78, Prof Philos, Univ Mass, Amherst, 78-, Managing ed, Rev Metaphysics, 54-56; asst ed, Ethics, 58-61; asst treas, Philos Quart, 59-69; consult ed, Random House, Inc-Alfred A Knopf Inc, 63-74; vis prof, Ind Univ, 67, Univ Ill, 68, Univ Notre Dame, 69 & Univ Southern Calif, 69; Nat Endowment for Humanities fel, 70; vis prof, Smith Col, 73-74; mem, Coun Philos Studies, 73-78; Mass Found for Humanities & Pub Policy grant, 81; Univ Mass Inst Advan Study fel, 81-82; vis prof, Mount Holyoke Col, 82. **MEMBERSHIPS** Am Philos Asn; Aristotelian Soc; Royal Inst Philos; Asn Computing Humanities; Soc Bus Ethics. **RESEARCH** History of philosophy, especially 17th and 18th century; metaphysics; theory of knowledge. **SELECTED PUBLICATIONS** Ed, The Philosophy of Mind, Prentice-Hall, 62; The Philosophy of David Hume, Random, 63; auth, Stuff and things, Aristotelian Soc Proc, 70-71; Selected articles on Locke, Philos Res Arch, 81; Locke, Berkeley and Hume, New Trends Philos, Tel Aviv, 82; auth, The Theory of

Ideas, Essays on Descartes Meditations, Univ of Calif, 86; coauth, Twenty-five Years of Descartes Scholarships, 1960-1984: A Bibliography, Garland, 87; auth, The Theory of Sensations, The Philosophy of Thomas Reid, Kluwer, 89; auth, Locke and Relative Identity, Hist of Philos Qrt 6, 89; auth, Locke on the Ontology of Matter, Living Things and Persons, Philos Stu 60, 90; auth, Essays on Early Modern Philosophers: From Descartes and Hobbes to Newton and Leibniz, 12 vols, Garland, 92; auth, The Cambridge Companion to Locke, Cambridge Univ, 94; ed, Locke's Theory of Ideas, The Cambridge Companion to Locke, Cambridge Univ, 94; auth, L'homme cartesien, Descartes. Ojecter et repondre, Univ France, 94; auth, Descartes' Compatibilism, Reason, Will, and Sensation: Studies in Cartesian Metaphysics, Oxford Univ, 94; auth, Locke on the Freedom of the Will, Locke's Philodophy: Content and Context, Oxford Univ, 94; auth, Descartes's Ontology, Topoi 16, 97; auth, Locke, Oxford Univ, 98; auth, Hobbes and Bramhall on Libertyand Necessity, Cambridge, 99. **CONTACT ADDRESS** Dept of Philos, Univ of Mass, Bartlett Hall, Amherst, MA, 01003-0002. **EMAIL** chappell@philos.umass.edu

CHAPPLE, C.K.
PERSONAL Born 09/04/1954, Medina, NY, m, 1974, 2 children **DISCIPLINE** HISTORY OF RELIGION **EDUCATION** SUNY Stony Brook, BA, 76; Fordham Univ, MA, 78, PhD, 80. **CAREER** Prof, 85-, Loyola Marymont Univ; Lectr, 80-85, SUNY Stony Brook; Asst Dir, 80-85, Inst Adv Stud Wld Rel. **HONORS AND AWARDS** 2 NEH Fels; Lily Gnt; College Fel; Chilton Ch Awd; Gannett Schlshp; IAAPEA Res Awd; CWHE Appre Certif; Grant Devel Gnt. **MEMBERSHIPS** AAR; AA; AIIS. **RESEARCH** Yoga Traditions; Jainism; Hinduism; Buddhism. **SELECTED PUBLICATIONS** Ed, Ecological Prospects: Scientific Religious and Aesthetic Perspectives, Albany, SUNY Press, 94, Intl edition, Delhi, Indian Books Cen, 95; auth, Nonviolence to Animals Earth and Self in Asian Traditions, Albany, NY, SUNY Press, 93, Intl edition, Delhi, Indian Books Cen, 95; ed, Jesuit Tradition in Education and Missions, Scranton, U of Scranton Press, 93; Haribhadra's Analysis of Patanjala and Kula Yoga in the Yogadrstisamuccaya, in: Open Boundaries: Jain Communities and Cultures in Indian History, ed, John E Cort, Albany, SUNY Press, 98; India: The Land of Plentitude, Satya, 98; Animals in the Buddhist Birth Stories, in: Buddhism and Ecology: The Interconnection of Dharma, and Deeds, ed, Mary Evelyn Tucker, Duncan Ryuken Williams, Cambridge MA, Harv Univ Cen Stud Of World Rel, 97; Renouncer Traditions Of India: Jainism and Buddhism, in: Ananya: A Portrait of India, ed, S Sn Sridhar, Nirmal K Mattoo, NY, Assoc of Indians in Amer, 97. **CONTACT ADDRESS** Dept Theol Studies, Loyola Marymount Univ, 7900 Loyola Blvd, Los Angeles, CA, 90045. **EMAIL** cchapple@lmumail.lmu.edu

CHARETTE, BLAINE
PERSONAL Ponoka, AB, Canada, m, 1980, 2 children **DISCIPLINE** NEW TESTAMENT **EDUCATION** Gordon-Conwell Theol Sem, MA, 82; Univ of Sheffield, PhD, 92. **CAREER** Asst prof, Emmanuel Col, Franklin Springs, GA, 91-95; ASSOC PROF, NORTHWEST COL, KIRKLAND, WA, 95-. **HONORS AND AWARDS** Phi Alpha Chi Honor Soc (Gordon-Conwell). **MEMBERSHIPS** Soc of Bib Lit; Inst for Biblical Res; Soc for Pentecostal Studies. **RESEARCH** Gospel of Matthew. **SELECTED PUBLICATIONS** Auth, The Theme of Recompense in Matthew's Gospel, JSNT Sup 79, Sheffield, JSOT Press,92; A Harvest for the People? An Interpretation of Matthew 9.37f, J for the Study of the New Testament 38, 90; To Proclaim Liberty to the Captives: Matthew 11.28-30 in the Light of OT Prophetic Expectation, New Testament Studies 38, 92; Speaking Against the Holy Spirit: The Correlation Between Messianic Task and National Fortunes in the Gospel of Matthew, J of Pentecostal Theol 3, 93; Never Has Anything Like This Been Seen in Israel: The Spirit as Eschatological Sign in Matthew's Gospel, J of Pentecostal Theol 8, 96. **CONTACT ADDRESS** 5811 110 Ave NE, Kirkland, WA, 98033. **EMAIL** blaine.charette@ncag.edu

CHARITY, RUTH HARVEY
PERSONAL Pittsylvania Count, VI, m **DISCIPLINE** LAW **EDUCATION** Howard Univ, BA, JD. **CAREER** Formerly asst to dir President's Cncl on Consumer Affairs; Indust Rel Analyst Wage Stabil Bd; law prof; former Dem Natl Committeewoman. **HONORS AND AWARDS** Founder/President Black Women for Political Action; Charter Mem natl Women's Chamber of Commerce; Natl Fedn of Dem Women Mid-Atlantic Region; Alpha Kappa Alpha Sor; NAACP; listed in Biography of Charlotte Hawkins Brown, Rights on Trial; Lecturer & consultant to political & civil rights & educational groups. **MEMBERSHIPS** Mem Pres's Comm on Civil Rights under the Law; past pres Old Dominion Bar Assn (1st woman to serve this capacity); mem Natl Bar Assn; formerly vice pres of Natl Bar Assn(1st woman to serve as vice pres of NBA at time of election); organiz Women's Sect Natl Bar Assn (1st natl orgn of Black women lawyers); mem Intl Fedn of Women Lawyers; past pres of Natl Assn of Black Women Lawyers; founder/pres VA Assn of Black Women Lawyers; past mem trustee bd Howard Univ;past mem trustee bd Palmer Meml Inst; mem bd of VA Seminary; past chrpsn VA State Adv Com US Civil Rights Comm (1st woman in VA to serve as chrpsn); mem Amer Assn of Univ Women; League of Women Voters; NOW; past mem Legal Staff State Conf NAACP; past natl parliamentarian Natl Cncl of Negro Women; pastgrand legal advisor Grand Templeughters IBPOE of W; past pres Chums Inc. **CONTACT ADDRESS** 514 S Main St, Danville, VA, 24543.

CHARLES, J. DARYL
PERSONAL Born 12 09/1950, Lancaster, PA, m, 1980, 3 children **DISCIPLINE** HERMENEUTICS **EDUCATION** Catholic Univ Amer and Westminster Theol Sem, PhD. **CAREER** Lectr, 88-95, Chesapeake Theol Sem; schl in res, 90-95, The Wilberforce Forum; aff fel, 96-97, Princeton Univ CSAR; Asst Prof, 97-, Taylor Univ. **MEMBERSHIPS** SRS; NAS; IBR; SBL; ETS. **RESEARCH** Religion and Culture; Criminal Justice; New Testament; Ethics. **SELECTED PUBLICATIONS** Auth, 2 Peter, Jude, BCBC, Herald Press, 98; Virtue Amidst Vice, JSNTSS, Sheffield Academic Press, 97; Literary Strategy in the Epistle of Jude, Assoc Univ Press, 93; translated, Roots of Wisdom, by Claus Westerman, Westminster/John Knox, 94; Blame it on the Beta-Boosters, in T Demy, G Stewart, eds, Genetic Engineering: A Christian Reader, Kregel, 98; auth, The Language and Logic of Virtue in 2 Peter 1:5-7, Bulletin for Biblical Res, 98; A Feisty Fundamentalism, Doing Theology in the Great Tradition, Regeneration Qtly, 98; Wordsmiths as Warriors: The Intellectual Honesty of GK Chesterton and CS Lewis, Parnassus, 98; Crime and the New Consensus, Soc Justice Rev, 98; Suicidal Thought in a Culture of Death, in: T Demy, G Stewart, eds, Suicide and the Christian Community: An Ethical Dilemma, Kregel, 97; Rights and Mass Murderers, Soc Justice Rev, 96; Evangelicals and Catholics Together: One Year Later, Pro Ecclesial, 96; Crime the Christian and Capitol Justice, J the Evangelical Theol Soc, 95; Outrageous Atrocity of Moral Imperative?: The Ethics of Capitol Punishment, Stud in Christian Ethics, 93; Reflections on Some Theologico-Ethnical Norms for Prison Ministry: A Response, Asbury Theol J, 93. **CONTACT ADDRESS** Dept of Philosophy, Taylor Univ, Upland, IN, 46989. **EMAIL** drcharles@tayloru.edu

CHARLTON, CHARLES HAYES
PERSONAL Born 12/22/1940, Radford, VI, m **DISCIPLINE** THEOLOGY **EDUCATION** Christiansburg Inst, 1959; VA Seminary, attended; E TN State Univ, attended; ETSU, BS 1982, M Ed 1984; Emmaus Bible Institute of Seminary, Elizabeth, TN, ThD, 1986; Cornerstone Univ, PhD Temperament Therapy. **CAREER** Radford City School Bd, 1972-74; City of Radford VA, mayor 1974-76; Friendship Bapt Church, pastor; CASA Northeast, Johnson City, TN, coordinator, 1987-; CASA, 1987-92; ETSU, Johnson City, TN, career counselor, 1991-92; City of Johnson City, planning commission, 1990-; NORTHEAST STATE TECH COMM COLL, instructor, beginning 1992, counselor & advisor, 1994, ASST PROF, currently; Emmaus Bible Inst & Seminary, Elizabethton, TN, dean of educ, 1984-89; Johnson City Board of Directors. **HONORS AND AWARDS** Radfords Outstanding Young Men Radford Jaycees 1973; VA Historical Society, honors for contributions to the State of VA **MEMBERSHIPS** Moderator Schaetter Meml Assoc of SW VA 1974-77; treas Bethel Dist Assoc; vice pres Radford Jaycees; moderator Bethel Dist Assoc of TN 1982-; dean ed Emmaus Bible Inst & Seminary Elizabethton TN 1984-; dir Pastors Conf of the TN BM&E Convention 1984-; pres, Black Ministers Alliance, 1990-91; zone chairman, Washington County Democratic Party, 1994-; City of Johnson City, TN, Board of Education, 1996-. **SELECTED PUBLICATIONS** Published Agony & Ecstasy of the Ministry, Making The Fundamentals Fun, 1993; Love is the Key, To Love And Be Loved, How To Really Love Your Pastor, This We Believe, Meditations on Love, 1994; author of religious columns published in Radford News Journal and Johnson City Press. **CONTACT ADDRESS** PO Box 246, Blountville, TN, 37617-0246.

CHARNEY, JONATHAN ISA
PERSONAL Born 10/29/1943, New York, NY, m, 1966, 3 children **DISCIPLINE** PUBLIC INTERNATIONAL LAW **EDUCATION** NY Univ, BA, 65; Univ Wis-Madison, JD, 68. **CAREER** Atty, US Dept Justice, Land & Nat Resources Div, 68-71, sect chief, 72; asst proflaw, 72-75, assoc prof, 75-78, PROF LAW, SCH LAW, VANDERBILT UNIV, 78-, Mem, US Adv Comt, Law of Sea, 73-; sr res assoc, Vanderbilt Inst Pub Policy Studies, 76-; consult, US Dept Commerce, 78-79, US Dept State, 81 - & Atty Gen, SC, 82- **MEMBERSHIPS** Am Soc Int Law. **RESEARCH** Law of the sea. **SELECTED PUBLICATIONS** Auth, Universal International-Law, Amer Jour Intl Law, Vol 0087, 93; 3rd-Party Dispute Settlement and International-Law, Columbia Jour Transnational Law, Vol 0036, 97; Central East-Asian Maritime Boundaries and the Law of the Sea, Amer Jour Intl Law, Vol 0089, 95; The Implications of Expanding International Dispute Settlement Systems--The 1982 Convention on the Law of The Sea, Amer Jour Intl Law, Vol 0090, 96; United-States Provisional Application of the 1994 Deep Seabed Agreement, Amer Jour Intl Law, Vol 0088, 94; Progress in International Maritime Boundary Delimitation Law, Amer Jour Intl Law, Vol 0088, 94; Equity and International-Law--A Legal Realist Approach to International Decision-Making, Amer Jour Intl Law, Vol 0089, 95; Politics, Values and Functions--International-Law in the 21st-Century, Columbia Jour Transnational Law, Vol 0036, 97; International-Law Decisions in National Courts, Amer Jour Intl Law, Vol 0091, 97; The United-States and the Revision of the 1982 Convention on the Law of the Sea, Ocean Development and Intl Law, Vol 0023, 92. **CONTACT ADDRESS** Sch of Law, Vanderbilt Univ, 2201 W End Ave S, Nashville, TN, 37240-0001.

CHARRON, WILLIAM C.
PERSONAL Born 02/25/1938, Denver, CO, m, 1962 **DISCIPLINE** PHILOSOPHY **EDUCATION** St Benedict's Col, KS, BA, 59; Univ Detroit, MA, 61; Marquette Univ, PhD, 66. **CAREER** Asst prof philos, St Benedict's Col, KS, 64-67; asst prof, 67-73, assoc prof, 73-80, Prof Philos, St Louis Univ, 80-, Ed, Mod Scholman, 89-. **MEMBERSHIPS** Am Philos Asn; Hume Soc; T S Eliot Society. **RESEARCH** Class mod philos; ethics; philos of mind. **SELECTED PUBLICATIONS** Auth, The simplicity of conscious experiences: A problem for neural identity theory, Mod Schollman, 5/74; Death: A philosophical perspective on the legal definitions, Wash Univ Law Quart, 12/75; Convention, games of strategy, and Hume's philosophy of law and government, Am Philos Quart, 10/80; Some legal definitions and semiotic: Toward a general theory, Semiotica, 12/80; The Prescriptives of the New Hobbesian Contractarian, In: Law and Semiotics, I, Plenum Press, 87; Mediation and Morality Conflicts, In: Law and Semiotics, II, Plenum Press, 88; On the Self-Refuting Statement There Is No Truth., Vivarium, 93; T S Eliot: Aristotelian Arbiter of Bradleyan Antinomies, The Modern Schoolman, 95; Public Reason, Mediation and Marakets: Kant against Rauls, In: Critic of Institutions: Horizons of Justice, Peter Lang, 96. **CONTACT ADDRESS** Dept of Philos, St Louis Univ, 3800 Lindell Blvd, Saint Louis, MO, 63156-0907.

CHASTAIN, CHARLES
DISCIPLINE PHILOSOPHY **EDUCATION** Princeton Univ, PhD. **CAREER** Assoc prof, Univ IL at Chicago. **RESEARCH** Epistemology and philos of lang; ethics. **SELECTED PUBLICATIONS** Auth, Reference and Context, MN Univ, 75. **CONTACT ADDRESS** Philos Dept, Univ Illinois Chicago, S Halsted St, PO Box 705, Chicago, IL, 60607. **EMAIL** cpcronin@uic.edu

CHAUSSE, GILLES
PERSONAL Born 06/06/1931, Montreal, PQ, Canada **DISCIPLINE** THEOLOGY/CHURCH HISTORY **EDUCATION** Univ Montreal, MA, 58, PhD, 73. **CAREER** Prof hist, Col Jean-de-Brebeuf Montreal, 69-85; PROF D'HISTOIRE DE L'EGLISE, FACULTE DE THEOLOGIE, UNIV MONTREAL, 86-. **HONORS AND AWARDS** Collaborateur a l'Institut historique de la Compagnie de Jesus a Rome; recipiendaire du Merite Diocesain 'Monseigneur Ignace Bourger', 86. **MEMBERSHIPS** Societe Canadienne d'Histoire de l'Eglise catholique **SELECTED PUBLICATIONS** Auth, Jean-Jacques Lartigue, premier eveque de Montreal, 80; coauth, Les Ultramontains canadiens-francais, 85; coauth, Le Christianisme d'ici a-t-il un avenir?, 88; coauth, L'Image de la Revolution francaise au Quebec 1789-1989, 89; coauth, Quebec, terre d'Evangile: les defis de l'evangelisation dans la culture contemporaine, 91; coauth, Montreal 1642-1992, 92; coauth, Dictionnaire Biographique du Canada, tomes 4-8; coauth, A Concise History of Christianity in Canada, 96. **CONTACT ADDRESS** Fac de Theologie, Univ Montreal, CP 6128, Succ Centre Ville, Montreal, PQ, H3C 3J7. **EMAIL** chausseg@magellan.umontreal.ca

CHEATHAM, CARL W.
PERSONAL Born 08/04/1940, Lincoln, AR, m, 1961, 4 children **DISCIPLINE** MODERN CHURCH HISTORY **EDUCATION** Harding Univ, BA, 62; Harding Graduate Sch, MTh, 65; Vanderbilt, MA, 79, PhD, 82. **CAREER** Prof, Faulkner Univ, 81-. **MEMBERSHIPS** Am Soc Church Hist; AAR; SBL; ETS. **RESEARCH** Restoration History **CONTACT ADDRESS** Faulkner Univ, 5345 Atlanta Hwy, Box 110, Montgomery, AL, 36109. **EMAIL** ccheatha@faulkner.edu

CHEEK, KING VIRGIL, JR.
PERSONAL Born 05/26/1937, Weldon, NC, m **DISCIPLINE** LAW **EDUCATION** Bates Coll ME, BA 1959; Univ of Chicago, MA 1960; Univ of Chicago Law School, JD 1964. **CAREER** Shaw Univ Raleigh, NC, asst econ prof 1964-65, acting dean 1956-66, dean 1966-67; private practice law Raleigh 1965-69; Shaw Univ, vice pres acad affairs 1965-69; Citizenship Lab, lectr 1968-69; Shaw Univ, pres 1969-71; Morgan State Coll, pres 1971-74; Union for Experimenting Colls & Univs, vice pres for planning & devel 1974-76, pres, 1976-78; New York Inst of Tech, exec dir ctr for leadership and career develop 1978-85; New York Inst of Tech, Ctr for Leadership and Career Develop, vice pres, dean of grad studies, exec dir 1985-89, vice pres institutional advancement, 1989-91, vice pres academic affairs, 1991-96. **HONORS AND AWARDS** Grand Commdr of Order of Star Africa 1971; Top Young Leaders in Amer Acad Change Magazine 1978; Disting Civilian Award AUS 1973; LLD DE State Coll 1970, Bates Coll, Univ of MD 1972; LHD Shaw Coll at Detroit 1983. **MEMBERSHIPS** Bd of dir Baltimore Contractors 1974-; bd of dir Inst for Econ Devel 1978-; bd of trustees Martin Center Coll; bd of trustees Shaw Coll Detroit; bd of visitors Univ of Chicago Law Sch; bd of trustees Warnborough Coll Oxford England. **CONTACT ADDRESS** 409 3rd St SW, Ste 202, Washington, DC, 20024.

CHEEVER, FRED
PERSONAL Born 03/09/1957, Rome, Italy, m, 1982, 2 children **DISCIPLINE** ENVIRONMENTAL LAW **EDUCATION** Stanford Univ, BA/MA, 89; UCLA, JD, 86. **CAREER** Judicial Clerk, US Court Appeals, 86-87; Assoc Atty, Sierra Club Legal Defense Fund, 87-89; Res Fel, Natural Resources Law Ctr, 90, Assoc Prof, 90-93, Prof Law, Univ Colo, 93-. **RESEARCH** Environmental law; endangered species law; public land law; property law. **SELECTED PUBLICATIONS** Auth, The Road to Recovery: A New Way of Thinking About the Endangered Species Act, Ecol Law Quart 1, 96; Human Population and the Loss of Biological Diversity -- Two Aspects of the Same Problem, Int J Environment & Pollution 62, 97; Public Good and Private Magic in the Law of Land Trusts and Conservation Easements: A Happy Present and a Troubled Future, Univ Denver Law Rev, 96; The Failure of the National Forest Management Act's Substantive Forest Practice Requirements: A Lesson in the Limits of Legislative Power, Oregon Law Rev, 98. **CONTACT ADDRESS** College of Law, Univ Denver, 1900 Olive St., Denver, CO, 80220. **EMAIL** fcheever@mail.law.du.edu

CHEMERINSKY, ERWIN
DISCIPLINE ADMINISTRATIVE LAW **EDUCATION** Northwestern Univ, BS, 75; Harvard Univ, JD,78. **CAREER** Sydney M. Irmas prof Public Interest Law, Legal Ethics and Polit Sci, Univ Southern California; lect, Fed Judicial Ctr; National Judicial Col; Ctr for Civic Educ & Constitutional Rights Found; testified before, US Senate Judiciary Comt; participated in, US Atty General's Prog for Honor Law Graduates;private practice,Wash, DC. **MEMBERSHIPS** Los Angeles City Charter Comn. **RESEARCH** Constitutional law; civil rights. **SELECTED PUBLICATIONS** Auth, Constitutional Law: Principles & Policies; Interpreting the Constitution; Fed Jurisdiction; The Values of Fedism & The First Amendment: When the Government Must Make Content Based Choices. **CONTACT ADDRESS** School of Law, Univ Southern Calif, University Park Campus, Los Angeles, CA, 90089.

CHEN, J.
PERSONAL Born 12/17/1966, Taipei, Taiwan, w **DISCIPLINE** LAW **EDUCATION** Harvard Univ, JD 91; Emory Univ, BA summa cum laude, MA 87; Univ Iceland, Fulbright Sch, 87-88. **CAREER** Univ Minnesota, assoc prof, 93-; Univ de Nantes, vis prof, 95; Justice Clarence Thomas, DC, law clerk, 92-93; Judge J. Michael Luttig, VA, law clerk, 91-92. **SELECTED PUBLICATIONS** Auth, Public Choice, forthcoming, 98, rev Econ and the Law: from Posner to Post-Modernism, Nicholas Mercuro, Steven G. Medema, 97; The Potable Constitution, Const Commentary, 98; Telric in Turmoil Telecommunications in transition: A Note on The Iowa Utilities Bd Litigation, Wake Forest L Rev 98; Filburn's Forgotten Footnote-Of Farm Team Federalism and Its Fate, Minn L Rev, 97; Embryonic Thoughts on Racial Identity as New Property, Colo L Rev 97; The Legal Process and Political Economy of Telecommunications Reform, Colum L Rev, 97; Feudalism Unmodified: Discourse on Farms and Firms, coauth, Drake L Rev, 97; The Most Dangerous Justice: The Supreme Court at the Bar of Mathematics, coauth, Cal L Rev, 96; Titanic Telecommunications, U L Rev, 96. **CONTACT ADDRESS** Dept of Law, Univ of Minnesota, 229 19th Ave S, Minneapolis, MN, 55455. **EMAIL** chenxo64@maroon.tc.umn.edu

CHEN, JOHN C.
PERSONAL Born 04/30/1949, Augusta, GA **DISCIPLINE** PSYCHIATRY **EDUCATION** Loma Linda Univ, MA 74; Claremont Grat Univ, PhD, 84; Univ Calif Law School, 87. **CAREER** Adj instr, philos, Fullerton Col, 89-90; adj asst prof, psychiat, Charles Drew Univ, 98- ; clinical asst prof, psychiat, Univ Calif, Los Angeles, 98- . **MEMBERSHIPS** APA; ABA; Soc for the Exploration of Psychothepy Integration; Chinese Hist Soc of Am; Calif Hist Soc. **RESEARCH** Philosophy of psychotherapy; Chinese American history; pediatric psychopharmacology. **SELECTED PUBLICATIONS** Auth, Refersal of Fortune: Images of America's Chinese, 1937-1944: The Dominance of California in DeWitt, ed, Readings in California Civilization, 4th ed. **CONTACT ADDRESS** 745 E Valley Blvd, #120, San Gabriel, CA, 91776.

CHENG, CHUNG-YING
PERSONAL Born 09/29/1935, Nanking, China, m, 1964, 4 children **DISCIPLINE** PHILOSOPHY; LINGUISTICS **EDUCATION** Nat Taiwan Univ, BA, 56; Univ Wash, MA, 58; Harvard Univ, PhD, 64. **CAREER** From asst prof to assoc prof, 63-74, prof philos, Univ Hawaii, Manoa, 74-, vis assoc prof, ch dept phil, 70-72, dir grad inst philos, 70-72, Nat Taiwan Univ, fall 65, vis prof, spring 68; prin investigator inquiries into class Chinese logic, Nat Sci Found grant, 65-67; fellow-participant, Summer Inst Ling, Univ Calif, Los Angeles, 66, Summer Inst Philos Sci, Stanford Univ, 67; vis assoc prof, Yale Univ, 68-69; E/W Ctr Commun Inst Sr. Fel, 78-79; pres Far E Inst Advan Studies, 85-92. **HONORS AND AWARDS** Pac Cult Found Grant, 87-88; Jiuli Zhouyi Award Best Essay Philos, 94; Honoris Doctoris Excellence Study Devel Chinese Philos Inst Far East Stud, 95; guest prof ceremony Wuhan Univ, 96, Jejiang Univ, 96, & Anhui Univ, 96. **MEMBERSHIPS** Eastern Div Am Philos Asn; Am Asn Asian Studies; Am Orient Soc; Soc Asian & Comp Philos (treas-secy, 68-); Charles S Pierce Soc; Int Soc Chinese Philos; Int Soc I Ching; Ctr Advan Studies Chinese Philos; Far E Inst Advanced Studies; Int Found Chines Mgt Contemp Ethics; Int Fed Confucian Studies. **RESEARCH** Chinese philosophy and logic; philosophy of language and logic; contemporary American philosophy and ethics. **SELECTED PUBLICATIONS** Coauth, Ontic commitment and the empty universe, J Philos, 7/65; auth, Classical Chinese logic: A preliminary description, Philos E & W, 65; Requirements for the validity of induction, Philos & Phenomenol Res, 3/68; Peirce's and Lewis' Theories of Induction, Martinus Nijihof, Hague, 69; Tai Chen's Inquiry into Goodness, Orient Soc, Hanover, 69; Chinese Philosophy and Chinese Civilization, 74 & Scientific Knowledge and Human Value, 75, San Min Publ Co, Taipei; The Philosophical Aspects of the Mind-Body Problem, Univ Hawaii, 75; auth C Theory: Yijing Philosophy of Kuanli, Dongda Book, 95; On the Spirits of Philosophy in China and West, E. Publ Ctr, 96; Study on Zhuxi and Neo-Confucianism, Lienking Press; ed Journal of Chinese Philosophy. **CONTACT ADDRESS** Dept Philos, Univ Hawaii, 2530 Dole St, Honolulu, HI, 96822-2303. **EMAIL** ccheng@hawaii.edu

CHERNUS, IRA
DISCIPLINE RELIGIOUS STUDIES **EDUCATION** Temple Univ, PhD. **CAREER** Prof. **SELECTED PUBLICATIONS** Auth, Nuclear Madness: Religion and Psychology of the Nuclear Age; Order and Disorder in the Definition of Peace; pubs on religious dimensions of nuclear weapons issues. **CONTACT ADDRESS** Religious Studies Dept, Univ of Colorado, Boulder, Boulder, CO, 80309. **EMAIL** Ira.Chernus@Colorado.edu

CHESNUTT, RANDALL D.
PERSONAL Born 07/30/1951, m, 1973, 2 children **DISCIPLINE** NEW TESTAMENT AND CHRISTIAN ORIGINS **EDUCATION** Alabama Christian Col, BA, 73; Harding Univ, MTh, 76, MA, 80; Duke Divinity Sch, ThM, 80; Duke Univ, PhD, 86. **CAREER** Res asst, Duke Univ, 81-83; tchg asst, Duke Univ, 80-84; vis instr, Abilene Christian Univ, 81-83; instr, asst prof, Seaver Col, Pepperdine Univ, 84-88; assoc prof, 88-94 ch, Soc Bibl Lit, 94; prof, 94-. **HONORS AND AWARDS** Edu tech grant, Pepperdine Univ, 94 **MEMBERSHIPS** Mem, ed b Sheffield Acad Press; Cath Bibl Assn, 92-93. **SELECTED PUBLICATIONS** Auth, Prayer from Alexander to Constantine: A Critical Anthology, Routledge, 96; From Death to Life: Conversion in Joseph and Aseneth, Journal for the Study of the Pseudepigrapha Supplement Series 16, Sheffield Acad Press, 95; From Text to Context: The Social Matrix of Joseph and Aseneth,, Society of Biblical Literature 96, Scholars Press, 96; co-auth, Prayer from Alexander to Constantine: A Critical Anthology, Routledge, 96; Prayers in the Old Testament Apocrypha and Pseudepigrapha, Prayer of a Convert to Judaism: Joseph and Aseneth 12-13, Apologetics and Missionary Propaganda in Alexandrian Judaism: Tcherikover Revisited, Proselytism in Early Judaism, Approaches to Ancient Judaism 7. Scholars Press/Brown Judaic Studies, 96; Jewish Women in the Greco-Roman Era, Essays on Women in Earliest Christianity, vol 1, Col Press, 93. **CONTACT ADDRESS** Dept of Relig, Pepperdine Univ, 24255 Pacific Coast Hwy, Malibu, CA, 90263. **EMAIL** chesnutt@pepperdine.edu

CHETHIMATTAM, JOHN BRITTO
PERSONAL Born 10/26/1922, Thottakad, India **DISCIPLINE** PHILOSOPHY, COMPARATIVE RELIGION **EDUCATION** Pontif Gregorian Univ, Rome, Lic, 53, MA, 54, ThD, 56; Fordham Univ, PhD(philos), 68. **CAREER** Lectr theol, Dharmaram Col, Bangalore, 56-62, prof philos & theol, 62-65; vis scholar, Harvard Univ, 66-67; from instr to asst prof, 67-70, assoc prof, 70-79, PROF PHILOS, FORDHAM UNIV, 79-, Rector, Dharmaram Col, Bangalore, 72-75; dir, Dharmanivas Res, Ctr, NJ. **MEMBERSHIPS** Indian Philos Cong; Am Orient Soc; Asn Asian Studies. **RESEARCH** Comparative ethics. **SELECTED PUBLICATIONS** Auth, Secular Humanism in Catholic Theology, Jour Dharma, Vol 0020, 95; The Future of Interreligious Dialog, Threats and Promises, Jour Dharma, Vol 0019, 94; A Philosophical Approach to the Ecological Crisis, Jour Dharma, Vol 0020, 95; Perceptions of Salvation, Jour Dharma, Vol 0022, 97; Freedom, Transcendence and Identity--Essays in Memory of Bhattacharya, Kalidas, Jour Dharma, Vol 0017, 92; Faith Seeking Understanding--An Introduction to Christian Theology, Jour Dharma, Vol 0017, 92; Where Does Our Dialog Go From Here, Jour Dharma, Vol 0019, 94; Modern Faith and Thought, Jour Dharma, Vol 0017, 92; Secular Humanism in Catholic Theology, Jour Dharma, Vol 0020, 95. **CONTACT ADDRESS** 89 Warrington Pl, East Orange, NJ, 07017.

CHILDRESS, JAMES FRANKLIN
PERSONAL Born 10/04/1940, Mt Airy, NC, m, 1958, 2 children **DISCIPLINE** RELIGIOUS, ETHICS **EDUCATION** Guilford Col, BM, 62; Yale Univ, BD, 65, MA, 67, PhD(Christian ethics), 68. **CAREER** From asst prof to prof relig studies, Univ Va, 68-75, chmn dept, 72-75; J P Kennedy Sr prof Christian ethics, Kennedy Inst, Georgetown Univ, 75-79; prof relig studies, 79-81, PROF RELIG STUDIES & MED EDUC, UNIV VA, 81-, Fel, Am Coun Learned Soc & Harvard Law Sch, 72-73; vis prof, Univ Chicago Div Sch, 77 & Princeton Univ, 78; co-ed, J of Relig Ethics, 78. **MEMBERSHIPS** Am Soc Christian Ethics; Am Acad Relig; Soc for Values Higher Educ; Am Soc Social & Polit Philos; fel Inst Soc, Ethics & Life Sci. **RESEARCH** Biomedical ethics; political ethics, including just war theory and laws of war; history of Christian ethics. **SELECTED PUBLICATIONS** Auth, Nonviolent Resistance, Trust and Risk-Taking 25 Years Later, Jour Rel Ethics, Vol 0025, 97. **CONTACT ADDRESS** Dept Relig Studies, Univ of Vs, 1 Cocke Hall, Charlottesville, VA, 22903-3248.

CHILDS, BREVARD SPRINGS
PERSONAL Born 09/02/1923, Columbia, SC, m, 1954, 2 children **DISCIPLINE** THEOLOGY **EDUCATION** Univ MI, AB, 47, MA, 48; Princeton Univ, BD, 50; Univ Basel, ThD, 55. **CAREER** Prof exegesis & Old Testament, Mission House Sem, 54-58; from asst prof to assoc prof, 58-66, Prof Old Testament, Divinity Sch, Yale Univ, 66-, Guggenheim fel, Hebrew Univ, 63-64; Am Coun Learned Soc res fel, Cambridge Univ, 70-71; Nat Endowment Hum res grant, 77-78; Fulbright fel, 81. **HONORS AND AWARDS** DD, Univ Aberdeen, 81. **MEMBERSHIPS** Soc Bibl Lit; Soc Old Testament Studies; Am Acad ARts & Sci, 95. **RESEARCH** Old Testament theol; comp relig; New Testament theol. **SELECTED PUBLICATIONS** Auth, Myth and Reality in the Old Testament, 60, Memory and Tradition in Israel, 62 & Isaiah and the Assyrian Crisis, 67, SCM Press, London; Biblical Theology in Crisis, 70, The Book of Exodus, 74, & Old Testament Books for Pastor and Teacher, 77, Westminster; Introduction to the Old Testament as Scripture, Fortress, 79; Biblical Theology of the Old and New Testaments, Fortress, 92. **CONTACT ADDRESS** Divinity Sch, Yale Univ, 409 Prospect St, New Haven, CT, 06511.

CHILDS, JAMES M., JR.
DISCIPLINE CHURCH AND SOCIETY **EDUCATION** Concordia Sr Col, BA, 61; Concordia Sem, MDiv, 65; Union Theol Sem, STM, 66; Lutheran Sch Theol, PhD, 74. **CAREER** Assoc prof, ch, Div Theol, Concordia Sr Col, 68-76; lectr, Purdue Univ, 70, 71, 76; assoc prof, Valparaiso Univ, 76-78; assoc prof, 78-87; prof, 87-; dean Acad Aff, 81-; interim pres, 89-90; adj prof, Grad Sch Bus Admin, Capital Univ, 93-; Joseph A. Sittler prof, 97-. **MEMBERSHIPS** Amer Acad Rel; Soc Christian Ethics; Inst Theol Encounter with Sci and Tech; assoc mem, Inst Soc Ethics and the Life Sci. **SELECTED PUBLICATIONS** Auth, Ethics and the Promise of God: Moral Authority and the Church's Witness, The Promise of Lutheran Ethics, Fortress, 98; Anna, Ambiguity, and the Promise: A Lutheran Theologian Reflects on Assisted Death, Must We Suffer Our Way To Death?, SMU, 96; Ethics in Business: Faith at Work, Fortress, 95; Faith, Formation and Decision: Ethics in the Community of Promise, Fortress, 92. **CONTACT ADDRESS** Hist, Theol, Soc Dept, Trinity Lutheran Sem, 2199 E Main St, Columbus, OH, 43209-2334. **EMAIL** jchilds@trinity.capital.edu

CHILDS, WINSTON
PERSONAL Born 02/14/1931, Savannah, GA, s **DISCIPLINE** LAW **EDUCATION** Amer Univ, AB 1957, JD 1959. **CAREER** Booker T Washington Found, special counsel; Minority Consult & Urbanologists, natl assn; GEOC, CIO Labor Union, pres; stock broker; private law pratice; DC Republican Central Committee, gen counsel; Natl Business League, gen counsel; Graham Building Associates Real Estate Development Company, pres; Amer Univ Law School, adjunct prof; MSI Services Inc, a systems engineering and mgmt consulting firm, Washington DC, founder, chairman, CEO, 1976-. **MEMBERSHIPS** DC Bar Assn; Amer Management Assn; Armed Forces Communication and Electronics Assn; Republican Senatorial Inner Circle; DC Metropolitan Boys/Girls Club; bd mem, Georgetown Symphony Orchestra; John Sherman Myers Society. **CONTACT ADDRESS** MSI Services, Inc, One Farragut Sq S, Ste 610, Washington, DC, 20006.

CHILES, ROBERT EUGENE
PERSONAL Born 03/01/1923, Convoy, OH, m, 1945, 1 child **DISCIPLINE** THEOLOGY **EDUCATION** Kent State Univ, AB, 44; Northwestern Univ, MA, 47; Garrett Theol Sem, BD, 47; Columbia Univ, PhD, 64. **CAREER** Clergyman, Concord Methodist Church, Dayton, 50-60; coordr adult educ prog, Hunter Col, 60-64, asst dean gen studies, 64-67; exec asst to pres, 67-68, assoc prof philos & dean students, 68-72, Prof Relig Studies, 72-88, PROF EMER, 88- , COL STATEN ISLAND, 64- . **RESEARCH** Wesleyan and American Methodist theology. **SELECTED PUBLICATIONS** Coauth, A Compend of Wesley's Theology, Abingdon, 54; auth, Methodist apostasy: From free grace to free will, Relig in Life, 58; A glossary of Tillich terms, Theol Today, 60; Theological Transition in American Methodism, 1790-1930, Abingdon, 65; The rights of patients, New England J Med, 67; Grace & Freewill, In: World Dict Methodism, Abingdon, 74; Scriptural Christianity, Francis Asbury Press, 84; The Philosophy they Bring to Class, Tchg Philos, 97. **CONTACT ADDRESS** Dept of Philos, Col of Staten Island, CUNY, Staten Island, NY, 10314.

CHILTON, BRUCE
PERSONAL Born 09/27/1949, Roslyn, NY, m, 1982, 2 children **DISCIPLINE** RELIGION **EDUCATION** Bard Col, BA, 71; General Theol Seminary, MDiv, 74; Cambridge Univ, PhD, 76. **CAREER** Tutor, General Theol Seminary, 74; Supvr

Studies, St. John's Col, Univ Cambridge, 74-76; Lectr, Sheffield Univ, 76-85; Burghley Preacher, St. John's Col, 77-78; Franz Delitzsch Lectr, Inst Judaicum Delitzschianum, 81; Vis Prof, Union Theol Seminary, 83; Assoc Prof, 85-87, Lillian Claus Assoc Prof New Testament, Yale Univ, 86-87; Prof Relig & Chaplain, 87-, Bernard Iddings Bell Prof Relig & Philos, Bard Col, 89-; Fel Pew charitable Trusts, 87-98. **HONORS AND AWARDS** Fel, Episcopal Church Found, 74-76; Res & Travel Grants, Sheffield Univ; Heinrich Hertz Stiftung, Bundesrepublik Deutschland, 81; A. Whitney Griswold Res Fund, Yale Univ, 86; Theol Development Grant, Episcopal Church, 87; Asher Edelman Fel, Bard Col, 92; Bishop Henry Martin Memorial Lectr, Univ Col Emmanuel & St. Chad, 96; Igor Kaplan Lectr Jewish Studies, Sch Theol, Univ Toronto, 97; Fel, Pew Charitable Trusts' Evangelical Schol Prog, 97-98. **MEMBERSHIPS** Akademie der Wissenschaften; British Asn Jewish Studies; British New Testament Conf; Europ Asn Jewish Studies; Inst Bibl Res; Nat Conf Christians & Jews; Oriental Club; Soc Bibl Lit; Studiorum Novi Testamenti Soc; The Tyndale House Gospels Res Project; Jesus Seminar; Inst Advanced Theol (founder). **SELECTED PUBLICATIONS** Auth, The Five Gospels. The Search for the Authentic Words of Jesus, HarperSanFranciso, 93; A Feast of Meanings. Eucharistic Theologies from Jesus through Johannine Circles: Supplements to Novum Testamentum 72, Brill, 94; coauth, The Body of Faith. Israel and the Church: Chritianity and Judaism -- The Formative Categories 2, Trinity Press Int, 96; Forging a Common Future. Catholic, Judaic, and Protestant Relations for a New Millenium, Pilgrim, 97; The Acts of Jesus. The Search for the Authentic Deeds of Jesus, HarperSanFrancisco, 98; author of numerous other publications and articles. **CONTACT ADDRESS** Bard Col, Annandale-on-Hudson, NY, 12504.

CHINCHAR, GERALD T.
DISCIPLINE RELIGIOUS STUDIES **EDUCATION** St John's Univ, MA, 73; Univ Notre Dame du Lac, MA, 77; United Theolog Sem, DMin, 92. **CAREER** Dir, Christian Initiation Processes; prof, Univ Dayton. **MEMBERSHIPS** North Amer Acad Liturgy. **RESEARCH** Liturgy and Initiation in the Catholic Tradition. **SELECTED PUBLICATIONS** Auth, Journal Keeping in the Inquiry Period, Catechumenate Mag, 92; Sunday Word, Catechumenate Magazine 15:1, 93; Liturgy of the Hours: Pastoral Perspective, Liturgical Ministry 2, 93; rev, A Promise of Presence, Liturgical Ministry 3, 94; Liturgy With Style and Grace, 97. **CONTACT ADDRESS** Dept of Religious Studies, Univ of Dayton, 300 College Park, 211 Liberty Hall, Dayton, OH, 45469-1679. **EMAIL** gerald.chinchar@udayton.edu

CHING, JULIA
PERSONAL Shanghai, China **DISCIPLINE** RELIGION/CHINESE CULTURE **EDUCATION** Col New Rochelle, NY, BA, 58; Catholic Univ America, MA, 61; Australian Nat Univ, PhD, 72; St. Andrews Col, NC, LHD, 93. **CAREER** Lectr, Australian Nat Univ, 71-74; assoc prof, Columbia Univ, 74-75; assoc prof, Yale Univ, 75-78; assoc prof, 78-81, PROF, VICTORIA COL, UNIV TORONTO 94-. **MEMBERSHIPS** Chinese Cult Ctr Greater Toronto; Royal Soc Can; Can Pugwash Gp. **SELECTED PUBLICATIONS** Auth, Probing China's Soul, 90; auth, Chinese Religions, 93. **CONTACT ADDRESS** Victoria Col, Univ Toronto, Toronto, ON, M5S 1K9. **EMAIL** jching@chass.utoronto.ca

CHINNICI, JOSEPH PATRICK
PERSONAL Born 03/16/1945, Altadena, CA **DISCIPLINE** HISTORY THEOLOGY **EDUCATION** San Luis Rey Col, BA, 68; Grad Theol Union, MA, 71; Franciscan Sch Theol, MDiv, 72; Oxford Univ, DPhil(hist, theol), 76. **CAREER** ASST PROF CHURCH HIST, FRANCISCAN SCH THEOL, 75- & ASST PROF, GRAD THEOL UNION, 75-; Univ Notre Dame travel grant, 78. **MEMBERSHIPS** AHA; Am Cath Hist Asn; US Cath Hist Soc. **RESEARCH** Church and the Enlightenment; American Catholicism; American religious history. **SELECTED PUBLICATIONS** Auth, The French Disease--The Catholic-Church and Radicalism in Ireland, 1790-1800, Amer Hist Rev, Vol 0101, 96. **CONTACT ADDRESS** Franciscan Sch of Theol, 1712 Euclid Ave, Berkeley, CA, 94709-1294.

CHISMAR, DOUGLAS
PERSONAL Born 06/27/1952, Pittsburgh, PA, m, 1973, 1 child **DISCIPLINE** PHILOSOPHY, ETHICS **EDUCATION** Am Univ, BA; Ashland Theol Sem, MDiv, 76; Ohio State Univ, PhD, 83. **CAREER** Asst prof to assoc prof to chair philos, Ashland Univ, 80-97; DIR, CHOWAN COL CTR FOR ETHICS, ASSOC PROF, PHILOS, CHOWAN COL, 98-. **HONORS AND AWARDS** Mentor Award, Ashland Univ, 93, 89; Outstanding Fac Member, Ashland Univ, 87; Sears-Roebuck Fnd Award for Teach Excel, Campus Ldrshp, Ashland Univ, 90. **MEMBERSHIPS** Am Philos Asn; NC Philos Asn; Soc Christian Philos; Asn Practical & Prof Ethics; Asn Moral Educ. **RESEARCH** Empathy and moral decision-making; mystery in science, religion and aesthetics; technology and human nature. **SELECTED PUBLICATIONS** Auth, "Lipps and Scheler on Aesthetic Empathy," Jour of Comp Lit and Aesthetics, 17, 94; rev of Stan Van Hooft, The Ethics of Caring, Ethics107, 96; rev of Ellen Singer More, Maureen Milligan, The Empathic Practitioner, Ethics 106, 96. **CONTACT ADDRESS** Center for Ethics, Chowan Col, Box 1848, Murfreesboro, NC, 27855. **EMAIL** Chismd@chowan.edu

CHIU, HUNGDAH
PERSONAL Born 03/23/1936, Shanghai, China, m, 1966, 1 child **DISCIPLINE** INTERNATIONAL LAW & RELATIONS **EDUCATION** National Taiwan Univ, LLB, 58; Long Island Univ, MA, 62; Harvard Univ, LLM, 62, SJD(int law), 65. **CAREER** Assoc res, Chinese law, EAsian Res Ctr, Harvard Univ, 64-65, res assoc, Law Sch, 66-70 & 72-74; assoc prof int law, Col Law, Nat Taiwan Univ, 65-66; prof, Nat Chengchi Univ & Nat Taiwan Univ, 70-72; assoc prof, 74-77, prof Int Law, Univ Md Law Sch, 77-, Reviewer, Nat Endowments for Humanities, 79-; fel, Inst Sino-Soviet Studies, George Washington Univ, 77-79; reviewer, NSF, 81-; vis prof, Dept Govt & Foreign Affairs, Univ Va, 80-81. **HONORS AND AWARDS** Cert Merit, Am Soc Int Law, 76; Inst Chinese Cult ann award, 80; Toulmin Medal, Soc Am Military Engrs, 82. **MEMBERSHIPS** Am Soc Int Law; Asn Asian Studies; Am Asn Chinese Studies. **RESEARCH** Chinese law and politics; Sino-American relations. **SELECTED PUBLICATIONS** Auth, The Capacity of International Organizations to Conclude Treaties, Martinus Nijhoff, The Hague, 66; The People's Republic of China and the Law of Treaties, Harvard Univ Press, 72; co-ed & contrib, Law in Chinese Foreign Policy, Oceana, 72; ed & contrib, China and the Taiwan Question: Documents and Analysis, Praeger, 73; coauth, People's China and International Law: A Documentary Study (2 vols), Princeton Univ Press, 74; ed & contrib, China and the Taiwan Issue, 79 & auth, Agreements of the People's Republic of China, 1966-1980, A Calandar, 81, Praeger; co-ed & auth, Multisystem Nations and International Law, Occas Papers & Reprint Ser Contemp Asian Studies, No 8, 81; coauth, International Law of the Sea: Cases, Documents and Readings, Elsevier, 81; co-ed & contrib, The Future of Hong Kong: Toward 1997 and Beyond, Greenwood, 87; coauth, Criminal Justice in Post-Mao China: Analysis and Documents, State Univ Press of NY, 85. **CONTACT ADDRESS** Law School, Univ Md, 500 W Baltimore St, Baltimore, MD, 21201-1786.

CHO, KAH-KYUNG
PERSONAL Born 06/07/1927, Seoul, Korea, 1 child **DISCIPLINE** PHILOSOPHY **EDUCATION** Seoul Nat Univ, BA, 52; Univ Heidelberg, PhD(philos), 57. **CAREER** Prof philos, Seoul Nat Univ, 57-70; prof philos, State Univ NY, Buffalo, 70-, Vis Fulbright prof, Yale Univ, 61-62; vis Asian prof, Fulbright Prof in conjunction with Univs Buffalo, RI, Western Mich & Cent Mich, 62-63; vis res prof, Husserl Arch, Univ Cologne, 63; Humboldt vis prof, Frankfurt, 76; vis prof, Univ Tex, Austin, 77; vis prof Univ Bochum, 83; vis prof, Osaka, 90; vis prof, Soon Sil Univ, 91. **HONORS AND AWARDS** SUNY Chancellor's Award for Excellence, 90; Fel of Japan Soc for Promotion of Science, 91; SUNY Dist Teaching Prof, 94; SOWU Book prize , 96. **MEMBERSHIPS** Ed Board, Philosophy and Phenomenological Research, 75-90; Husserl Studies, 83-; General Ed, Orbis Phenomenologicus, 93; Ed Board, Phaenomenologie-Texte und Kontexte, 98-. **RESEARCH** Contemporary European philosophy; phenomenology. **SELECTED PUBLICATIONS** Auth, Philosophy of Existence, Pak Yong-Sa, 61, 2nd ed, 69, 3rd ed, 72; Anschauung und Abstraktion, In: Kongressbericht IX Dusseldorf, Anton Hain, 71; Uber das Bekannte, In: Phanomenologie Heute, Martinus Nijhoff, 72; Mediation and immediacy for Husserl, In: Phenomenology and Natural Existence, State Univ NY, 73; Naturbild und Lebenswelt, In: Zu Werk, Univ Wirkung von W Heisenberg, Munich, 77; Anonymes Subjekt und phanomenologische Beschreibung, & Leben und Wirken M Fathers fur die Phanomenologie in US, In: Phanomenologische Forschugen, Alber, Freiburg, 82; Philosophy of Existence, Pak Yong Sa, 12th ed, 95. **CONTACT ADDRESS** Dept of Philosophy, SUNY, Buffalo, PO Box 601010, Buffalo, NY, 14260-1010. **EMAIL** KCho@ACSU.buffalo.edu

CHOPER, JESSE H.
PERSONAL Born 08/19/1935, Wilkes-Barre, PA, m, 1961, 1 child **DISCIPLINE** LAW **EDUCATION** Wilkes Col, BS, 57, LHD, 67; Univ Pa, LLB, 60. **CAREER** Instr accounting, Univ Pa, 57-60; law clerk, 60-61; from asst prof to assoc prof law, Univ Minn, 61-65; PROF, 65-82, DEAN LAW SCH, UNIV CALIF, BERKELEY, 82-, Vis prof law, Harvard Univ, 70-71; vis scholar, Syracuse Univ Col Law, 79. **HONORS AND AWARDS** DHL, Wilkes Col, 67. **RESEARCH** Constitutional law; corporation law; separation of church-state. **SELECTED PUBLICATIONS** Auth, Benchmarks, Aba Jour, Vol 0079, 93; Thoughts on the Federalist Vision of Representative Democracy as Viewed at the End of the 20th-Century--How Have We Used the Legacy of the Federalist, Harvard Jour Law and Pub Policy, Vol 0016, 93; Religion and Race Under the Constitution--Similarities and Differences, Cornell Law Rev, Vol 0079, 94; In-Memoriam--Lockhart, William,B. and Witkin, Bernard, E, Hastings Law Jour, Vol 0047, 96. **CONTACT ADDRESS** Law Sch, Univ of Calif, 220 Boalt Hall, Berkeley, CA, 94720-7201.

CHOPP, REBECA S.
PERSONAL Born 04/24/1952, KS, m, 1995, 1 child **DISCIPLINE** THEOLOGY **EDUCATION** Kans Wesleyan Univ, BA, 74; St. Paul Sch of Theol, M Div, 77; Univ Chicago Divinity Sch, PhD, 83 **CAREER** Provost and exec vpres, Emory Univ; dean of fac and acad affairs, Emory Univ, Candler Sch of Theol, 93-97; PROF OF SYST THEOL, 82- . **HONORS**

AND AWARDS Alumna of the Year, Univ Chicago, 97; Luce fel, Emory Univ, 90; Charles Howard Candler Chair of Theol, 96 **MEMBERSHIPS** Am Acad of Relig. **RESEARCH** Feminist and liberation theologies **SELECTED PUBLICATIONS** auth, Christian Moral Imagination, A Feminist Practical Theology and the Future of Theological Education, Int Jour of Practical Theol, 97; auth, Bearing Witness: Traditional Faith in Contemporary Expression, Quart Rev, 97; auth, American Feminist Theology, The Modern Theologians, 97; auth, Theorizing Feminist Theology, Horizons in Feminist Theology, 97; ed with Sheila Davaney, Differing Horizons: Feminist Theory and Theology, 97. **CONTACT ADDRESS** Emory Univ, 404 Administration Building, Atlanta, GA, 30322. **EMAIL** rchopp@emory.edu

CHORNENKI, GENEVIEVE A.
DISCIPLINE LAW **EDUCATION** Osgoode Hall Law Sch, LLB, 78. **CAREER** Instr; Founded, Mediated Solutions Incorporated **MEMBERSHIPS** Can Bar Asn. **SELECTED PUBLICATIONS** Auth, pubs on monographs about ADR. **CONTACT ADDRESS** Fac of Law, Univ Toronto, 78 Queen's Park, Toronto, ON.

CHRISTENSEN, MICHAEL
DISCIPLINE THEOLOGY; RELIGIOUS STUDIES; HISTORICAL THEOLOGY **EDUCATION** Point Loma Col, BA, 77; Yale Univ Divinity School, MA, 81; M.Phil, 95, PhD, 97, Drew Univ. **CAREER** Asst Prof, 97-, Dir of Doctor of Ministry Program, 95-, Drew Univ. **HONORS AND AWARDS** John Wesley Fel, 93-97; Will Herberg Merit Scholarship, Drew Univ, 93-96; Crossroads Scholar Program (research stipend for writing public policy monograph on nuclear issues in former Soviet Union), 94-96; Research Fel, Newark Project, 94-95; Recipient of the Helen Le Page and William Hale Chamberlain Prize awarded for the PhD Dissertation that is singularly distinguished by creative thought and excellent prose style, 97; Recipient of the Martin Luther King Jr. and Abraham Joshua Heschel Humanitarian Award for Spirituality and Social Justice, 98; Research Fel, Senior Research Scholar for Russia, The Princeton Project on Youth, Globalization and the Church, 98-01. **MEMBERSHIPS** Amer Acad of Religion; Phi Delta Lamba Honor Soc; The Patristic Soc; Soc for the Study of Eastern Orthodoxy and Evangelicalism; Charles Williams Soc. **RESEARCH** Theology and Culture; Russian Eschatology; Spirituality **SELECTED PUBLICATIONS** Auth, C.S. Lewis on Scripture, 79 (reprinted 96); Coauth, Children of Chernobyl: Raising Hope from the Ashes, 93; Auth, AIDS Ministry and the Article of Death: A Wesleyan Pastoral Theological Perspective, Catalyst, 95; Theosis and Sanctification: John Wesley's Reformulation of a Pastoric Doctrine, Wesleyan Theological Journal, 96; Evangelical-Orthodox Dialogue in Russia, The Journal of Ecumenical Studies, 96; Evangelism, Ecumenism and Mission, Religion in Eastern Europe, 96; The World after Chernobyl: Social Impact and Christian Response, Crossroads Monograph Series on Faith and Public Policy, 97. **CONTACT ADDRESS** Drew Univ, 12 Campus Dr., Madison, NJ, 07940. **EMAIL** mchriste@drew.edu

CHRISTIE, DREW
DISCIPLINE PHILOSOPHY **EDUCATION** MIT Univ, PhD, 83. **CAREER** Assoc prof. **RESEARCH** Environmental philosophy; political philosophy; pragmatism; philosophy of law; logic. **SELECTED PUBLICATIONS** Auth, Judging in Good Faith (rev); The Human Prospect (rev). **CONTACT ADDRESS** Philosophy Dept, Univ of New Hampshire, Hamilton Smith Hall, Durham, NH, 03824. **EMAIL** drewc@christa.unh.edu

CHRISTOL, CARL QUIMBY
PERSONAL Born 06/28/1914, Gallup, SD, m, 1949, 2 children **DISCIPLINE** INTERNATIONAL LAW, POLITICAL SCIENCE **EDUCATION** Univ SDak, AB, 34; Fletcher Sch Law & Diplomacy, AM, 36; Inst Univ Hautes Etudes Int, Geneva, cert int law, 38; Univ Chicago, PhD(polit sci), 41; Yale Univ, LLB, 47. **CAREER** Atty, Guthrie, Darling & Shattuck, 48-49; assoc prof, 49-56, PROF INT LAW & POLIT SCI, UNIV SOUTHERN CALIF, 56-, Atty, Fizzolio, Fizzolio & McLeod, 49-; Rockefeller fel int law & jurisp, 58-59; Stockton chair int law, US Naval War Col, 62-63; mem, Comn Study Organ Peace, 68-78; adv panel int law, US Dept State, 70-74. **HONORS AND AWARDS** Assoc Award for Excellence in Teaching, Univ Southern Calif, 77; Outstanding Prof & Raubenheimer Fac Award, Univ Southern Calif, 82-; LLD, Univ SDak, 77. **MEMBERSHIPS** Am Br Int Inst Space Law (vpres, 71-72, pres, 73-74); Am Soc Int Law; Am Bar Asn; Am Inst Aeronaut & Astronaut; Am Polit Sci Asn. **RESEARCH** The international law of outer space; international environmental law; international and national civil and political rights and liberties. **SELECTED PUBLICATIONS** Auth, The Never-Ending Dispute--Delimitations of Air Space and Outer-Space, Amer Jour Intl Law, Vol 0091, 97; International Aviation and Outer-Space Law and Relations, Amer Jour Intl Law, Vol 0091, 97; Contemporary International-Law--The Utilization of Ultraterrestrial Space--Spanish, Amer Jour Intl Law, Vol 0087, 93. **CONTACT ADDRESS** Dept of Polit Sci, Univ of Southern Calif, Los Angeles, CA, 90007.

CHRISTOPHER, RUSSELL L.
PERSONAL Born 08/07/1961, Goshen, NY, s **DISCIPLINE** PHILOSOPHY **EDUCATION** Hamilton Col, AB, 83; Univ Mich, Sch of Law, JD, 88. **CAREER** Res assoc, Columbia Univ Sch of Law, 4/94-8/96; judicial clerkship and atty, Judge John T. Noonan, Jr., US Ct of Appeals, Ninth Circuit, 8/96-8/97; res scholar, fac of law, Columbia Univ Sch of Law, 9/97-. **HONORS AND AWARDS** Robert Leet Patterson prize, philos, 81-83. **MEMBERSHIPS** NY State Bar; Ctr for Law and Philos; Columbia Univ Sch of Law. **RESEARCH** Substantive and theoretical criminal law. **SELECTED PUBLICATIONS** Auth, Self-Defense and Defense of Others, 27, Philos & Pub Affairs, 123, no 2, Spring, 98; auth, Self-Defense and Objectivity: A Reply to Judith Jarvis Thomson, 1, Buffalo Criminal Law Rev, 537, 98; auth, Unknowing Justification and the Logical Necessity of the Dadson Principle in Private Defense, 15, Oxford Jour of Legal Studies, 229, 95; auth, Mistake of Fact in the Objective Theory of Justification: Do Two Rights Make Two Wrongs Make Two Rights...?, 85, Jour of Criminal Law & Criminol, 295, 94; auth, Control and Desert: A Comment on Moore's View of Attempts, 5, Jour of Contemp Legal Issues, 111, 94. **CONTACT ADDRESS** Law Sch, Columbia Univ, 435 W. 116th St., New York, NY, 10027. **EMAIL** rchris@law.columbia.edu

CHRISTOPHER, THOMAS WELDON
PERSONAL Born 10/08/1917, Duncan, SC, m, 1950, 1 child **DISCIPLINE** LAW **EDUCATION** Washington & Lee Univ, BA, 39; Univ Ala, LLB, 48; NY Univ, LLM, 50, JSD, 57. **CAREER** Prin, Cross Keys Sch, Union, SC, 39-41 & Lorton Sch, Va, 41-42; mem fac, Law Sch, Emory Univ, 50-61, assoc dean, 54-61; prof law, Law Sch, Univ NC, 61-65; prof & dean sch law, Univ NMex, 65-71; prof law & dean sch law, 71-81, Sims PROF, LAW SCH, UNIV ALA, 81-, Mem exec comt, Asn Am Law Schs, 58; atty legal dept, Corn Prod Co, New York, 60-61. **MEMBERSHIPS** Am Bar Asn. **RESEARCH** Food and drug law; constitutional and property laws. **SELECTED PUBLICATIONS** Auth, Untitled--Comment, Natural Resources Jour, Vol 0036, 96. **CONTACT ADDRESS** Sch Law, Univ New Mexico, Albuquerque, NM, 87131.

CHRYSSAVGIS, JOHN
PERSONAL Born 04/01/1958, Sydney, Australia, m, 1984, 2 children **DISCIPLINE** THEOLOGY **EDUCATION** Greek Conserv Music, Dipl Byz Mus, 79; Univ Oxford, DPhil, 83; Univ Athens, Lic Th, 80. **CAREER** Lectr, 86-95, Univ Sydney; sub-dean, 85-95, St Andrew's Theol Col, Sydney; acting dean, 97-98, Hellenic Col, Holy Cross; prof, 95-, Holy Cross Sch Theol. **MEMBERSHIPS** N Amer Patristics Soc; Int Relig & Sci Comm. **RESEARCH** Spirituality; environ; ascetic theol. **SELECTED PUBLICATIONS** Auth, Fire and Light, 87; auth, Ascent to Heaven, 89; auth, Repentance and Confession, 90; auth, The Desert is Alive, 91; auth, Love, Sexuality, Marriage, 95; auth, The Way of the Fathers, 98; auth, Beyond the Shattered Image, 99. **CONTACT ADDRESS** 50 Goddard Ave, Brookline, MA, 02445. **EMAIL** JChryss@omaccess.com

CHUANG, RUEYLING
DISCIPLINE WORLD RELIGIONS **EDUCATION** Tamkang Univ, BA, 87; CA State Univ , MA, 92; OH Univ, PhD, 92. **CAREER** Tchg Asst, CA State Univ; Grad Tchg Assoc, OH Univ; Asst prof, St John's Univ,95-. **HONORS AND AWARDS** MacPherson Grant, Service Learning Grant; Fac Develop Grant; Barry Spiker Award; John Houk Res Grant; Ohio Univ Sch Interpersonal Comm Int Res Grant; John Houk Memorial Grant; Tish & Ray Wagner Int Stud Sch; Int Lion's Club Fel; I-Lan County Government Outstanding Student Award. **MEMBERSHIPS** Asn for Chinese Comm Studies; Chinese Comm Asn; Central States Comm Asn; Eastern Comm Asn; Int Comm Asn; Interpersonal Network Personal Relationships; Speech Comm Asn; Western States Comm Asn. **SELECTED PUBLICATIONS** Coauth, Die Partei und Wahl, Central Books, 87; Das Theater, Central Books, 87; Gender and ethnicity influences on student attitudes toward speech restrictions, political correctness, and educational models, Southern Ill Univ Press, 96; Auth, Economic prosperity or environmental protection comes first?: An examination of Taiwanese (anti)environmental rhetoric, World Col Journalism & Comm Jour Hum; Coauth, Global versus local advertising in Taiwan, Gazette, 97. **CONTACT ADDRESS** Saint John's Univ, Collegeville, MN, 56321-7155. **EMAIL** rchuang@csbsju.edu

CHUNG, BONGKIL
PERSONAL Born 05/20/1936, Korea, m, 1975, 2 children **DISCIPLINE** PHILOSOPHY **EDUCATION** Mich State Univ, PhD, 79. **CAREER** Visiting asst prof, Fla Intl Univ, 79-80; lectr, Towson State Univ, 80-81; asst prof, Fla Intl Univ, 81-86; assoc prof, Fla Intl Univ, 86-. **MEMBERSHIPS** Amer Philos Asn; Intl Soc for Chinese Philos; Intl Soc for Asian and Comparative Philos. **RESEARCH** Buddhist philosophy; Metaphysics. **SELECTED PUBLICATIONS** Auth, The Ethics of Triple Identity for Universal Harmony, Jour of Chinese Philos, vol 25, no 3; auth, Benefiance as the Moral Found in Won Buddhism, Jour of Chinese Philos, vol 23, no 2. **CONTACT ADDRESS** Philosophy Dept., Florida Intl Univ, Miami, FL, 33199. **EMAIL** chungb@fiu.edu

CHUNG, CHAI-SIK
PERSONAL Born 07/14/1930, Wonju, Korea, m, 1962, 2 children **DISCIPLINE** SOCIAL ETHICS **EDUCATION** Yonsei Univ, M Th, 57; Harvard Univ, BD, 59; Boston Univ, PhD, 64. **CAREER** Waler G Muelder prof Social Ethics, Boston Univ, 90-; Koret vis prof, Univ Calif Berkeley, 76-78; vis scholar, Univ Calif Berkeley, 74; prof Sociol, Yonsei Univ, 83-87; prof & chair Sociol, Heidelberg Col, 72-80; assoc prof Sociol, Heidelberg Col, 69-72; asst prof, Boston Univ, 66-69; asst prof, Bethany Col, 64-66; instr, Emory Univ, 62-63. **MEMBERSHIPS** Amer Acad Relig; Assoc Asian Studies; Soc Christian Ethics. **RESEARCH** Ethics and Modernization in East Asia and Korea. **SELECTED PUBLICATIONS** Korea's Initial Search for Civil Society: Problems of Perception and Adaptation, Etat, Societe Civile et Sphere Publique en Asie de L'Est, Univ Montreal, 98; Between Korean Religious Tradition and Western Impact, Jrnl Korean Thought, Stony Brook, 98; foreward, Nu ingraend wa han'guk saieso, Methodist Theol Seminary, 97. **CONTACT ADDRESS** Dept. of Theology, Boston Univ, 19 Brook St, Sherborn, MA, 01770. **EMAIL** Sikchung@aol.com

CHURCHILL, JOHN HUGH
PERSONAL Born 04/01/1949, Hector, AR, m, 1972, 3 children **DISCIPLINE** PHILOSOPHY OF RELIGION **EDUCATION** Southwestern at Memphis, BA, 71; Oxford Univ, BA, 73, MA, 80; Yale Univ, MA, 75, MPhil, 76, PhD(relig studies), 78. **CAREER** Asst Am secy, Rhodes Scholar Trust, 74-77; asst prof, 77-82, Assoc Prof Philos & Chmn, Dept of Philos, Hendrix Col, 82-84; VPRES, ACADEMIC AFFAIRS, DEAN, PROF PHILOS, HENDRIX COL, 84-. **HONORS AND AWARDS** Rhodes Scholarship **MEMBERSHIPS** Soc Philos, Relig; Am Asn Rhodes Scholars. **RESEARCH** Wittgenstein and philosophy of religion; the logic of ethical argument. **SELECTED PUBLICATIONS** Auth, many articles on Wittgenstein, philosophy of religion, and liberal arts. **CONTACT ADDRESS** Office of the Dean, Hendrix Col, 1600 Washington Ave, Conway, AR, 72032-3080. **EMAIL** churchill@hendrix.edu

CHURCHILL, MARY
DISCIPLINE RELIGIOUS STUDIES **EDUCATION** Univ Calif Santa Barbara, PhD. **CAREER** Asst prof. **RESEARCH** Native American religious traditions; women and religion; cultural studies. **SELECTED PUBLICATIONS** Auth, Balance and Synthesis: Toward a Dialogical Interpretation of Cherokee Women's Literature. **CONTACT ADDRESS** Religious Studies Dept, Univ of Colorado, Boulder, Boulder, CO, 80309. **EMAIL** Mary.Churchill@Colorado.edu

CHURCHLAND, PAUL M.
DISCIPLINE PHILOSOPHY **EDUCATION** Univ Pittsburgh, PhD, 69. **CAREER** Instr, Univ Toronto; Univ Manitoba; Inst Adv Stud, Princeton; PROF, PHILOS, UNIV CALIF, SAN DIEGO. **RESEARCH** Artificial intelligence and cognitive neurobiology, epistemology, and perception. **SELECTED PUBLICATIONS** Auth, "A Feedforward Network for Fast Stereo Vision with Movable Fusion Plane," Android Epistemology: Human and Machine Cognition, AAAI Press/MIT Press, 94; The Engine of Reason, The Seat of the Soul: A Philosophical Journey into the Brain, MIT Press, 95; "The Neural Representation of Social Reality," Mind and Morals, The MIT Press, 95. **CONTACT ADDRESS** Dept of Philos, Univ Calif, San Diego, 9500 Gilman Dr, La Jolla, CA, 92093.

CIORRA, ANTHONY J.
PERSONAL Born 10/11/1946, Elizabeth, NJ, s **DISCIPLINE** RELIGIOUS STUDIES **EDUCATION** Seton Hall, MA, 78, Mdiv, 95; St Bonanenture, MA, 84; Fordham, PhD, 91. **CAREER** Assoc prof of theology, dir, Ctr for Theology and Spiritual Development. **HONORS AND AWARDS** Pro Ecclesia et Pontifice, 98. **MEMBERSHIPS** Catholic Theological Society of Amer; Amer Acad of Relig. **RESEARCH** History of theology; relationships of theology and psychology. **SELECTED PUBLICATIONS** Auth, Everyday Mysticism, Crossroad, 95; auth, Moral Formation in the parish, 98. **CONTACT ADDRESS** Col of Saint Elizabeth, 2 Convent Rd, Morristown, NJ, 07960. **EMAIL** azambar@aol.com

CIULLA, JOANNE B.
PERSONAL Born 06/16/1952, Rochester, NY, m, 1990 **DISCIPLINE** PHILOSOPHY **EDUCATION** Univ Maryland, BA, 73; Univ Delaware, MA, 75; Temple Univ, PhD, 85. **CAREER** Harvard Post-Doctoral fel Bus & Ethics, Harvard Univ Grad School Bus Admin, 84-86; vis scholar, Oxford Univ, 89; sr fel, Wharton School Univ Penn, 86-91; Assoc prof, Coston Family Chr Leadership & Ethics, Jepson School Leadership Studies, Univ Richmond, 91- . **MEMBERSHIPS** Acad Mgt; Am Asn Univ Prof; Am Philos Asn; Asn Practical & Prof Ethics; Int Soc Bus, Econ & Ethics; Europ Bus Ethics Network; Soc Bus Ethics. **RESEARCH** Leadership studies; business ethics; philosophy of work. **SELECTED PUBLICATIONS** Auth, Casuistry and the Case for Business Ethics, Bus Ethics and Hum, Oxford Univ Press, 94; Leadership Ethics: Mapping the Territory, & Leadership Ethics: A Starter Kit and Annotated Bibliography, The Bus Ethics Quart, 95; Ethics nd Critical Thinking in Leadership Education, The Jour of Leadership Studies, 96; Business Leadership and Moral Imagination in the Twenty-First Century, Moral Values: The Challenge of the Twenty-First Century, Univ Texas Press, 96; Ethics, Chaos and the Demand for Good Leaders, Teaching Leadership: Essays in Theory and Practice, Peter Lang Publ, 96; Meaningful Work, Blackwell Encyclo Bus Ethics, Oxford, 97; Fantasy, Wishful Thinking and Truth, The Bus Ethics Quart, 98; Information, Trust, and the Ethics of Business Leaders, Int Bus Ethics: Challenges and Approaches, Univ Notre Dame & Hong Kong Univ Press, 98; ed, Ethics, The Heart of Leadership, Quorum Books, 98. **CONTACT ADDRESS** Jepson School of Leadership Studies, Univ Richmond, Richmond, VA, 23173. **EMAIL** jciulla@richmond.edu

CLADIS, MARK S.
DISCIPLINE PHILOSOPHY, RELIGION **EDUCATION** Univ Calif Santa Barbara, BA, 80; Princeton Univ, MA, 85; PhD, 88. **CAREER** Vis prof, Univ NC, 86-88; vis asst prof, Stanford Univ, 88-90; asst prof, Vassar Coll, 90-95; assoc prof and chair of Rel Dept, Vassar Coll, 95-. **HONORS AND AWARDS** Franco-Am Commission for Educ Exchange Grant, 93; Nat Endowment for the Humanities Stipend, 92; Fulbright Res Award, 92-93; Rockefeller Foundation, 98. **MEMBERSHIPS** Environmental Studies Colloquium; Asn for the Sociol of Rel; Soc fort he Scientific Study of Rel; Am Acad of Rel. **RESEARCH** Philosophy of Religion, Western Religious Thought, and Religious Ethics; Social Theory and Political Philosophy. **SELECTED PUBLICATIONS** Auth, Politics of the Heart: Rousseau, Religion, and the Relation between the Public and Private Life, forthcoming; ed, Durkheim and Foucault: Punishment and Education, 98; The Elementary Forms of the Religious Life, forthcoming. **CONTACT ADDRESS** Dept of Religion, Vassar Col, Box 228, PO Box 228, Poughkeepsie, NY, 12604-0028. **EMAIL** macladis@vassar.edu

CLAPPER, GREGORY
PERSONAL Born 10/03/1951, Chicago, IL, m, 1973, 2 children **DISCIPLINE** RELIGION; SYSTEMATIC THEOLOGY **EDUCATION** Emory, PhD. **CAREER** Huntingdow, 94-98; Westmar Col, 85-91; Senior pastor, UMC, 91-94; Assoc prof, Univ Indianapolis, 98- . **HONORS AND AWARDS** Soc of John Westley Fels. **MEMBERSHIPS** AAR; Wesleyan Theological Soc. **RESEARCH** Wesley Studies; Christian Spirituality. **SELECTED PUBLICATIONS** Auth, John Wesley on Religious Affections, 89; auth, As if the Heart Mattered: A Wesleyan Spirituality, 97; auth, When the World Breaks Your Heart-Spirtual Ways of Coping with Tragedy, 99. **CONTACT ADDRESS** 243 Hawthorne Ln, Greenwood, IN, 46147. **EMAIL** gclapper@vindy.edu

CLARK, AUSTEN
DISCIPLINE PHILOSOPHY **EDUCATION** Wesleyan Univ, BA, 75; Oxford Univ, PhD, 77. **CAREER** Res asst prof, Dartmouth Med Sch, 78-82; asst prof, Univ Tulsa, 83-86; assoc prof, Univ Tulsa, 87-94; prof, 94-. **HONORS AND AWARDS** Postdoc fel, Univ NC, 82-83. **MEMBERSHIPS** Mem, Amer Philos Assn; Philos of Sci Assn; Soc Philos Psychol. **RESEARCH** Philosophy of psychology; philosophy of mind. **SELECTED PUBLICATIONS** Auth, Beliefs and Desires Incorporated, Jour of Philos, 94; Contemporary Problems in the Philosophy of Perception, Amer Jour of Psychol, 94; Three varieties of visual field, Philos Psychol, 96; True Theories, False Colors, Philos of Sci, PSA Supplemental Issue, 96; rev, Review of Martha Farah's Visual Agnosia, Philos Psychol, 94; Review of Robert Schwartz, Vision: Variations on Some Berkeleian Themes, Philos Psychol, 96. **CONTACT ADDRESS** Dept of Philos, Univ Conn, 1266 Storrs Rd, Storrs, CT, 06269. **EMAIL** aclark@uconnvm.uconn.edu

CLARK, DAVID
DISCIPLINE NEW TESTAMENT **EDUCATION** Univ Notre Dame, PhD. **CAREER** Prof; dir, Grad Stud Prog; leads workshops on the life & writings of C S Lewis. **SELECTED PUBLICATIONS** Auth, 2 articles; presented a paper at, Soc Bibl Lit. **CONTACT ADDRESS** Dept of Relig, Southern California Col, 55 Fair Dr., Costa Mesa, CA, 92626.

CLARK, DON
DISCIPLINE LAW **EDUCATION** Univ London, LLB, 62, Cambride Univ, LLM, 65. **CAREER** Prof, 62- **RESEARCH** Ontractual remedies; judicial review **SELECTED PUBLICATIONS** Auth, Contingency Agreements, 94, Rethinking the Role of Specific Relief in the Contractual Setting, 91, Recent Developments in the Law of Contracts, 93, co-ed, Self-Determination: International Perspectives, Macmillan, 96. **CONTACT ADDRESS** Col of Law, Univ Saskatchewan, 15 Campus Dr, Saskatoon, SK, S7N 5A6. **EMAIL** Clark@law.usask.ca

CLARK, GERARD J.
DISCIPLINE LAW **EDUCATION** Seton Hall Univ, BA, 66; Columbia Univ, JD; 69. **CAREER** Prof. **RESEARCH** Constitutional law; federal courts; professional responsibility. **SELECTED PUBLICATIONS** Auth, Kronman's the Lost Lawyer: A Celebration of the Oligopoly of the Elite Lawyer, 96; The Product of the General Court in 1993: Summary and Critique, 95. **CONTACT ADDRESS** Law School, Suffolk Univ, Beacon Hill, Boston, MA, 02114. **EMAIL** gclark@acad.suffolk.edu

CLARK, J. MICHAEL
PERSONAL Born 09/02/1953, Morristown, TN, m, 1989 **DISCIPLINE** RELIGIOUS STUDIES **EDUCATION** Emory & Henry Col, Emory, VA, BA, 75; Candler School of Theol, Emory Univ, Atlanta, M Div, 78; Graduate Inst of Liberal Arts, Emory Univ, Atlanta, PhD, 83. **CAREER** Instr, Science Talent Enrichment Prog, Emory Univ, summers 91, 92, 93; adjunct asst prof, Human and Natural Ecology Prog, Emory univ, 93-96, vis asst prof, 96; asst prof, Dept of Relig Studies, Agnes Scott Col, Decatur, GA, 97; vis scholar, Iliff School of Theol, Univ of Denver, CO, 97; instr, Dept of English, GA State Univ, Atlanta, 84-, instr, Program in Relig Studies, 98-. **HONORS AND AWARDS** Am Academy of Relig res assistance grant, 87-88; Keynote speaker, Am Men's Studies Asn Annual Meeting, 97; Vis Scholar Appointment, Iliff School of Theology, 97. **MEMBERSHIPS** Am Academy of Relig, (87-; prog unit book series co-ed, 89-96; prog unit co-chair, 87-93); Soc of Christian Ethics (97-); Sheffield Academic Press (ed bd, 96-); Journal of Men's Studies (assoc ed, 92-, special issue co-ed, 95-96). **RESEARCH** Ecology; sexual ethics; gender studies. **SELECTED PUBLICATIONS** Auth, A Place to Start: Toward an Unapologetic Gay Liberation Theology, Monument Press, 89; A Defient Celebration: Theological Ethics and Gay Sexuality, Tangelwuld Press, 90; Masculine Socialization and Gay Liberation: A Conservation on the Work of James Nelson and Other Wise Friends, with Bob McNeir, The Liberal Press, 92; Beyond Our Ghettos: Gay Theology in Ecological Perspective, Pilgrim Press, 93; An Unbroken Circle: Ecotheology, Theodicy, and Ethics, Monument Press, 96; Defying the Darkness: Gay Theology in the Shadows, Pilgrim Press, 97; Doing the Work of Love: I Men's Studies at the Margins, J of Men's Studies 5 4, May 97; Doing the Work of Love: II An Extended Case Study, with Bob McNeir, J of Men's Studies 5 4, May 97; A Gay Man's Wish-List for the Future of Men's Studies in Religion, J of Men's Studies 7 2, winter 99; Teaching the Apocalypse in Ecotheology, in Teaching Apocalypse, ed T Pippin, Scholar's Press, in press; numerous other articles in refereed journals and series. **CONTACT ADDRESS** 585 Glenwood Pl SE, Atlanta, GA, 30316. **EMAIL** bmcrr@ibm.net

CLARK, JACK LOWELL
PERSONAL Born 01/15/1929, Albert Lea, MN, m, 1954 **DISCIPLINE** RELIGION **EDUCATION** Gustavus Adolphus Col, AB, 52; Northwestern Lutheran Theol Sem, BD, 55; Univ Minn, MA, 57; Yale Univ, AM, 59; PhD(New Testament), 62. **CAREER** Asst Bible, Northwestern Lutheran Theol Sem, 55-57; from asst prof to assoc prof relig, 62-70, Prof Relig & Classics, Gustavus Adolphus Col, 70-, Assoc ed, Dialogue, 68-69. **MEMBERSHIPS** Am Acad Relig; Soc Bibl Lit; Soc Sci Studies Relig. **RESEARCH** Historical methodology in the study of primary religious documents; the concept of religious authority; the correlation between personality and religious stance. **CONTACT ADDRESS** Dept of Religion, Gustavus Adolphus Col, 800 W College Ave, St. Peter, MN, 56082-1498.

CLARK, KELLY J.
PERSONAL Born 03/03/1956, Muncie, IN, m, 1978, 3 children **DISCIPLINE** PHILOSOPHY **EDUCATION** Univ Notre Dame, PhD 85, MA SC 82; Western Kentucky Univ, MA Phil 80; Michigan State Univ, BA 78. **CAREER** Calvin Col, assoc prof 89-; Univ St Andrews Scotland, vis prof 95-96; Gordon Col, asst prof 85-89. **MEMBERSHIPS** APA; SCP. **RESEARCH** Philosophy of religion and ethics. **SELECTED PUBLICATIONS** Auth, Reader in Philosophy of Religion, Broadview Press, forthcoming; Ethics Through History, under consideration; When Faith is not Enough, Eerdmans Pub Co, 97; Philosophers Who Believe, ed, InterVarsity Press, 93; Perils of Pluralism, Faith and Philo, 97; Knowing the Unknowable God, Books and Culture, 97; Trinity or Tritheism?, Religious Studies; Reformed Epistemology, Modern Reformation Mag, 98; I Believe in God the father Almighty, Intl Philo Quart; The Literature of Confession, in: Philosophers Who Believe, InterVarsity Press, 93; Return to Reason, Eerdmans Pub Co, 90. **CONTACT ADDRESS** Dept of Philosophy, Calvin Col, Grand Rapids, MI, 49546. **EMAIL** kclark@calvin.edu

CLARK, MARY T.
PERSONAL Philadelphia, PA **DISCIPLINE** PHILOSOPHY **EDUCATION** Manhattanville Col, BA; Fordham Univ, PhD, 55. **CAREER** Prof, chr, Philos Dept, Manhattanville Col, 51-84; prof emer Manhattanville, 86-. **MEMBERSHIPS** Am Philos Asn; Am Cath Philos Asn; Metaphysical Soc; Soc Medieval Renaissance Philos. **RESEARCH** Augustine of Hippo; freedom; person. **SELECTED PUBLICATIONS** Auth, Augustine, 94; auth, An Aquinas Reader, 88; auth, Augustine, Philosopher of Freedom, 59. **CONTACT ADDRESS** Philosophy Dept, Manhattanville Col, Purchase, NY, 10577. **EMAIL** mclark@mville.edu

CLARK, W. ROYCE
DISCIPLINE CONTEMPORARY RELIGIOUS THOUGHT **EDUCATION** Abilene Christian Univ, BA, 60, MA, 61; Univ Iowa, PhD, 73; Pepperdine Univ, JD, 85. **CAREER** Instr, Columbia Christian Col, 61-67; prof, 70-; vis prof, Pepperdine's London prog, 89-90; assoc, Seaver Col, 90-92; vis prof, Pepperdine's Japan prog, 92. **HONORS AND AWARDS** Res grant, 86; spec serv award, Comm of Credentials, Calif, 93; Irvine fel, 93; awarded, 95-96; Tyler outstanding tchr yr, Seaver Col, 95-96. **MEMBERSHIPS** Mem, Am Acad Rel; N Am Paul Tillich Soc; Soc Bibl Lit; Soc Buddhist-Christian Studies. **SELECTED PUBLICATIONS** Auth, The Supreme Court and the Legal Status of Religious Studies in Public Higher Education, Beyond the Classics: Essays in Religious Studies and Liberal Education, Scholars Press, 90; The Fourth Gospel and Christology in Modern Dogmatic and Systematic Theology, Johannine Studies: Essays in honor of Frank Pack, Pepperdine UP, 89. **CONTACT ADDRESS** Dept of Relig, Pepperdine Univ, 24255 Pacific Coast Hwy, Malibu, CA, 90263. **EMAIL** rclark@pepperdine.edu

CLARK KROEGER, CATHERINE
DISCIPLINE CLASSICAL AND MINISTRY STUDIES **EDUCATION** Bryn Mawr Col, AB; Univ Minn, MA, PhD. **CAREER** Instr Hamilton Col; Univ Minn; adj assoc prof, Gordon-Conwell Theol Sem, 90-. **HONORS AND AWARDS** Chaplain, Hamilton Col; founding organizer, Christians for Biblical Equality. **MEMBERSHIPS** Mem, Amer Acad Rel; Soc Biblical Lit; Evangel Theol Soc. **RESEARCH** Women in ancient religion and human sexuality and biblical mandate. **SELECTED PUBLICATIONS** Co-ed, The Goddess Revival. **CONTACT ADDRESS** Gordon-Conwell Theol Sem, 130 Essex St, South Hamilton, MA, 01982.

CLARKE, ANNE-MARIE
PERSONAL St. Louis, MO, m, 1979 **DISCIPLINE** LAW **EDUCATION** Forest Park Comm Coll, 1967-68; Northwest MO State Univ, BA, 1970; St Louis Univ School of Law, JD, 1973. **CAREER** Arthur D Little Inc, researcher, 1974-94; Northeast Utilities, asst corp sec, 1974-77; Bi-State Develop Agency, staff counsel, 1977-79; Self Employed, private practice of law, 1980-92; City of St Louis, hearing officer, family court, 1986-. **HONORS AND AWARDS** Natl Council of Negro Women Bertha Black Rhoda Section, Achievement Award, 1990; Natl Organization of Blacks in Law Enforcement (NOBLE), Achievement Award, 1993; MO Legislative Black Caucus, Jordan-McNeal Award, 1994. **MEMBERSHIPS** The MO Bar, bd of governors, 1986-90, 1991-95; Mound City Bar Assn, pris, 1981-83; Confluence St Louis, chair, prevention of juvenile crime task force, 1993; Delta Sigma Theta Sorority, Inc; The Bar Plan Mutual Insurance Co., director, 1986-. **SELECTED PUBLICATIONS** The History of the Black Bar, St Louis bar Journal, Spring 1984. **CONTACT ADDRESS** Bd of Police Commissioners, St Louis Police Dept, 1200 Clark, St. Louis, MO, 63103.

CLARKE, BOWMAN LAFAYETTE
PERSONAL Born 09/19/1927, Meridian, MS **DISCIPLINE** PHILOSOPHY **EDUCATION** Millsaps Col, AB, 48; Emory Univ, BD, 51, MA, 52, PhD, 61; Univ Miss, MA, 57. **CAREER** Instr philos, Univ the South, 59-60; res assoc applied logic, Emory Univ, 60-61; from asst prof to assoc prof, 61-67, head dept philos & relig, 72-79, PROF PHILOS, UNIV GA, 67-, Danforth Found grant, 57-58; E L Cabot Trust Fund grant, 60-61; ed, Int J Philos Relig. **MEMBERSHIPS** Southern Soc Philos & Psychol; Soc Philos Relig (pres, 73-74); Am Philos Asn; Am Acad Relig; Metaphys Soc Am. **RESEARCH** Logic and metaphysics. **SELECTED PUBLICATIONS** Auth, 2 Process Views of God, Intl Jour Philos Rel, Vol 0038, 95. **CONTACT ADDRESS** Dept of Philos, Univ of Ga, Athens, GA, 30605.

CLARKE, GRAEME
DISCIPLINE EDUCATION **EDUCATION** Auckland Univ, Oxford Univ, Univ Melbourne. **CAREER** From dep dir to dir, Hum Res Ctr, Australian Natl Univ, 82-95; chrmn, Classical Studies, Univ Melbourne, 69-81; vis fels Nuffield Foundation, Inst Classical Studies, Univ London, Inst Advanced Study, Princeton Univ, Churchill Col, Cambridge Univ, Natl Hum Ctr, NC. **HONORS AND AWARDS** FAHA, FSA. **SELECTED PUBLICATIONS** Auth, The Octavius of Marcus Minucius Felix, 74; Letters of St Cyprian of Carthage, vols 1-2, 84, vol 3, 86, vol 4, 89; ed, Rediscovering Hellenism: the Hellenic Inheritance and the English Imagination, 89; ed, Reading the Past in Late Antiquity, 90; auth, Dionysius of Alexandria: the Letters and Fragments, pending, Cyprian, pending, de Lapsis, pending, and Jebel Khalid on the Euphrates, pending. **CONTACT ADDRESS** Dept of Education, Australian National Univ.

CLARKE, MURRAY
DISCIPLINE COGNITIVE SCIENCE AND PHILOSOPHY OF SCIENCE **EDUCATION** W Ontario Univ, PhD. **CAREER** Prof; ch. **RESEARCH** Implications of evolutionary psychology, empirical psychology. **SELECTED PUBLICATIONS** Auth, Doxastic Voluntarism and Forced Belief, Philos Stud Volume 50, 86; Epistemic Norms and Evolutionary Success, Synthese, Volume 85, 86; Natural Selection and Indexical Representation, Logic and Philosophy of Science in Quebec, Volume II, Boston Stud in the Philos of Sci, 96; "Darwinian Algorithms and Indexical Representation," Philos of Sci, Volume 63, Number 1, 96. **CONTACT ADDRESS** Dept of Philos, Concordia Univ, Montreal, 1455 de Maisonneuve W, Montreal, PQ, H3G 1M8. **EMAIL** eud@vax2.concordia.ca

CLARKE, W. NORRIS
PERSONAL Born 06/01/1915, New York, NY **DISCIPLINE** PHILOSOPHY **EDUCATION** Catholic Univ of Louvain, Belgium, PhD, 50. **CAREER** Asst prof Philos, Woodstock Col, MD, 49-52; prof Philos, 55-85, Emeritus prof Philos, Fordham Univ, 85- . **HONORS AND AWARDS** Aquinas Medal, Amer Cath Philos Asn, 80; H. Morary Dr of Laws, Villanova Univ, 82; Dr Hum, Wheeling Jesuit Col, 93. **MEMBERSHIPS** Amer Cath Philos asn; Amer Philos asn; Metaphysical Soc Amer; Intl St Thomas soc. **RESEARCH** Metaphysics; St.Thomas; Philosophy of Person. **SELECTED PUBLICATIONS** Auth, Interpersonal Dialogue as Key to Realism, in Person and Community, NY, Fordham UP, 75, 141-154; Analogy and the Meaningfulness of Language about God: A Reply to Kai Nielson, The Thomist, 40, 76, 61-95; Action as the Self-Revelation of Being: A Central Theme in the Thought of St.Thomas, in History of Philosophy in the Making, Washington, UP of America, 82, 63-80; The Metaphysics of Religious Art, in Graceful Reason: Essays in Honor of Joseph Owens, Toronto, Pontifical Inst of Medieval Stud (s), 83, 303-314; Charles Hartshorne's Philosophy of God: A Thomistic Critique, in Charles Hartshorne's Concept of God: Philosophical and Theological Responses, Hingham, MS, Kluwer, 89, 103-123; Thomism and Contemporary Philosophical Pluralism, Modern Schoolman, 67, 90, 123-139; The We Are of Interpersonal Dialogue as the Starting Point of Metaphysics, 69, 92, 357-368; To Be Is To Be Substance-in-Relation, in Metaphysics as Foundation: Essays in Honor of Ivor Leclerc, Albany, SUNY Press, 92; Is a Natural Theology Still Viable Today? In Prospects for Natural Theology, Washington, Catholic Univ Amer Press, 92, 151-183; Person and Being, Aquinas Lecture, 1993, Milwaukee, Marquette UP, 93; Explorations in Metaphysics: Being-God-Person, U of Notre Dame P, 94; Living on the Edge: The Human Person as Frontier Being and Microcosm, Int Phil Quart, 36, 96, 183-200. **CONTACT ADDRESS** Fordham Univ, Loyola Hall, Bronx, NY, 10458.

CLARKE, WILLIAM NORRIS
PERSONAL Born 06/01/1915, New York, NY **DISCIPLINE** PHILOSOPHY **EDUCATION** Col St Louis, England, PhL, 39; Fordham Univ, MA, 40; Woodstock Col, STL, 46; Cath Univ Louvain, Belg, PhD(philos), 49. **CAREER** From instr to asst prof philos, Woodstock Col, 49-52; asst prof, Bellarmine Col, 52-55; from asst prof to assoc prof, 55-67, PROF PHILOS, FORDHAM UNIV, 67-, Ed, Int Philos Quart, 61- **HONORS AND AWARDS** LHD, Villanova Univ, 82. **MEMBERSHIPS** Am Philos Asn; Metaphys Soc Am (pres, 67-68); Am Cath Philos Asn (pres, 68-69). **RESEARCH** Metaphysics, especially mediaeval; St Thomas Aquinas; Plotinus. **SELECTED PUBLICATIONS** Auth, The Perfection of the Universe According to Aquinas--A Theological Cosmology, Theol Stud, Vol 0054, 93. **CONTACT ADDRESS** Dept of Philos, Fordham Univ, Bronx, NY, 10458.

CLAUDE, RICHARD P.
PERSONAL Born 05/20/1934, St. Paul, MN, 3 children **DISCIPLINE** POLITICAL SCIENCE,CONSTITUTIONAL LAW **EDUCATION** Univ of St. Thomas, BA, 56; Fla State Univ, BS,Govt, 60; Univ of Va, PhD, Polit Sci, 65. **CAREER** Instr, Vassar Col, Polit Sci, 62-64; vis asst prof, govt, William and Mary Col 64-65; asst prof, Univ of Md, 65-68; assoc prof, Univ of Md, 68-78; prof, Univ of Md, 78-93; PROF EMER, UNIV OF MD, 93-. **HONORS AND AWARDS** Pulitzer Prize Nomination, 71; Best Acad Book, 90. **RESEARCH** Human rights education **SELECTED PUBLICATIONS** auth, The Supreme Court and the Electoral Process, Johns Hopkins Univ Pr, 70; prin auth & ed, "Comparative Human Rights," Johns Hopkins Univ Pr, 78; coauth, Health Professionals and Human Rights in the philippines, Am Asn for the Advan of Sci, 87; co-ed, Human Rights in the World Community: Issues and Action, Univ Of Penn Pr, 89; co-ed, Human Rights and Statistics, Getting the Record Straight, Univ of Penn Pr, 91; auth, Human Rights Education in the Philippines, Kalikasan Pr, 92; coauth, "Medicine Under Siege: Violations of Medical Neutrality in the Former Yugoslavia, 1991-1995," Physicians for Human Rights, 96; auth, Educating for Human Rights: The Philippines and Beyond, Univ of Philippines Pr, 96; co-ed, Human Rights for the 21st Century, Univ of Pa Pr, 97; auth, The Bells of Freedom, with Resource Materials for Facilitators of Non-Formal Education and 24 Human Rights Echo Sessions, Action Prof Asn, 95. **CONTACT ADDRESS** Dept of Govt and Polit, Univ of Md, College Park, MD, 20742. **EMAIL** profclaude@aol.com

CLAYTON, MARCUS
PERSONAL Born 06/14/1931, Atlanta, GA, m, 1956, 4 children **DISCIPLINE** PHILOSOPHY **EDUCATION** Emory Univ, AB, 55, LLB, 56, PhD(philos), 67. **CAREER** From asst prof to assoc prof philos, 59-71, Prof Philos, Paine Col, 71- **MEMBERSHIPS** Metaphys Soc Am; Soc Ancient Greek Philos; Hegel Soc Am; Am Philos Asn. **RESEARCH** Contemporary epistemology and metaphysics; ancient philosophy; early modern philosophy. **SELECTED PUBLICATIONS** Contribr, A defense of individuals, Paine Col J, 71; auth, "Blanchard's Theory of Universals," contribr, Philosophy of Brand Blanchard; Library of Living Philosophers Series. **CONTACT ADDRESS** Dept of Philosophy, Paine Col, 1235 15th St, Augusta, GA, 30901-3182.

CLAYTON, PHILIP
PERSONAL Born 04/03/1956, Berkeley, CA, m, 1981, 2 children **DISCIPLINE** PHILOSOPHICAL THEOLOGY; RELIGION & SCIENCE; MODERN RELIGIOUS THOUGHT **EDUCATION** Westmont Col, BA, 78; Fuller Theolog Sem, MA, 80; Ludwig-Maximilians-Universitat, Munich, MA, 81-83; Yale Univ, MA, 84; Yale Univ, M.Phil, 85; Yale Univ, PhD, 86. **CAREER** Sonoma St Univ, 91-; Williams Col, 86-91; vis asst prof, Haverford Col, 86 **HONORS AND AWARDS** CSU Grant, 97; Templeton Grant, 97; Univ Merit Award, 96; Univ Best Prof, 95; Alexander von Humboldt Prof, Ludwig-Maximilians-Universitat, 94-95; Fulbright Senior Res Fel, Univ Munich, 90-91. **MEMBERSHIPS** Amer Acad Relig; Amer Philos Assoc; Center for Theolog & Natural Sci; Pacific Coast Theolog Soc; Leibniz Soc N Amer; Metaphysical Soc Amer; Soc Study of Process Philos. **SELECTED PUBLICATIONS** Beyond Apologetics: Integrating Scientific Results and Religious Explanations, Fortress Pr, forthcoming; Infinite and Perfect? The Problem of God in Modern Philosophy, forthcoming; Das Gottesproblem. Moderne Losungsversuche, forthcoming; God and Contemporary Science, Edinburg Univ Pr, forthcoming. **CONTACT ADDRESS** Dept. of Philosophy, Sonoma State Univ, Rohnert Park, CA, 94928. **EMAIL** clayton@sonoma.edu

CLEARY, JOHN J.
PERSONAL Born 06/18/1949, County Mayo, Ireland, m, 1973 **DISCIPLINE** PHILOSOPHY **EDUCATION** Univ Col Dublin, BA, 72, MA, 75; Boston Col, PhD, 82. **CAREER** Boston Col, Asst prof, assoc prof, prof, 81-. **HONORS AND AWARDS** Elected Member Royal Irish Acad, NEH fel, Alexander von Humbolt fel. **MEMBERSHIPS** APA, BACAP, IHV. **RESEARCH** Ancient philosophy; Plato, Aristotle, Proclus; history and philosophy of science; ancient and modern political theory. **SELECTED PUBLICATIONS** Auth, Aristotle on the many Senses of Priority, Carbondale: S IL Univ Press, 88; Aristotle and Mathematics: aporetic method in Cosmology and Metaphysics, Brill: Leiden, 95; art, Some Aspects of the Problem of Evil, Studies, 77; auth, The Mathematical Cosmology of Plato's Timaeus, Synthesis Philosophica, 90; auth, Working Through Puzzles with Aristotle, Jour Neoplatonic Stud, 93; auth, The rationality of the Real: Proclus and Hegel, At the Heart of the Real, ed F. O'Rourke, Irish Acad Press: Dublin, 91; auth, Text Matters: Interview with H. G. Gadamer, States of Mind: Dialogues with Contemporary Thinkers, ed. R. Kearney, Manchester Univ Pr, 95; auth, Plato's Teleological Atomism, Interpreting the Timaeus-Critias, ed., T Calvo & L Brisson, Academia Verlag: Sankt Augustin, 97; ed, The Perennial Tradition of Neoplatonism, 97. **CONTACT ADDRESS** Dept of Philosophy, Boston Col, Chestnut Hill, MA, 02467. **EMAIL** john.cleary@bc.edu

CLEGG, JERRY STEPHEN
PERSONAL Born 09/29/1933, Heber City, UT, m, 1960, 3 children **DISCIPLINE** PHILOSOPHY **EDUCATION** Univ Wash, PhD, 62. **CAREER** From instr to assoc prof, 62-76, prof Philos, Mills Col, 76-. **RESEARCH** Aesthetics; epistemology; history of philosophy. **SELECTED PUBLICATIONS** Auth, The Structure of Plato's Philosophy, Bucknell Univ, 77; On Genius: Affirmation and Denial from Schopenhauaz to Wittgenstein, Peter Lang, 94. **CONTACT ADDRESS** Dept of Philosophy, Mills Col, 5000 MacArthur Blvd, Oakland, CA, 94613-1000. **EMAIL** sleggj@mills.edu

CLEGG, LEGRAND H., II
PERSONAL Born 06/29/1944, Los Angeles, CA **DISCIPLINE** LAW **EDUCATION** UCLA, BA 1966; Howard Univ Sch Law, JD 1969. **CAREER** City of Compton CA, deputy city atty; Compton Community Coll, instructor; Robert Edelen Law Offices, atty 1975-; LA, legal aid found 1972-74; Compton CA, admin asst 1970-72; Dept Justice Washington, legal intern 1968-69. **HONORS AND AWARDS** Guest lecturer Vassar Coll/NY U/UCLA/U of So CA 1978-79. **MEMBERSHIPS** Mem LA Bar Assn; CA Lawyers Criminal Justice; Langston Law Club; Nat Conf Black Lawyers; Compton Cultural Commn; Assn Black Psychol; Pilgrim Missionary Bapt Ch. **SELECTED PUBLICATIONS** Pub in LA Times 1974; current bibliography on African Affairs 1969, 1972. **CONTACT ADDRESS** Compton City Hall, Compton, CA, 90224.

CLEMENT, GRACE
DISCIPLINE MORAL THEORY **EDUCATION** PhD. **CAREER** Salisbury State Univ **SELECTED PUBLICATIONS** Auth, Care, Autonomy, and Justice: Feminism; Ethic Care. **CONTACT ADDRESS** Salisbury State Univ, Salisbury, MD, 21801-6862. **EMAIL** GACLEMENT@SSU.EDU

CLEMENTS, TAD S
PERSONAL Born 08/13/1922, Buffalo, NY, m, 7 children **DISCIPLINE** PHILOSOPHY **EDUCATION** Univ Buffalo, BS, 48; PhD, 62; Univ N Mex, MS, 54. **CAREER** Cur, live exhibs, 50-54, Buffalo Mus Sci; jr sci, 60, Rosewell Prk Mem Just; inst 60-61, Univ N Dakota; asst prof, 61-64, Univ Akron; asst prof, 64-65, Univ Idaho; prof, 65-85, SUNY Col Brockport. **RESEARCH** Phil of sci; phil of relig. **SELECTED PUBLICATIONS** Auth, Ethics and Human Nature, Building a World Community, Prometheus Bks, 89; co-ed, Religion and Human Purpose, Stud in Phil & Relig Ser, Martinus Nijhoff, 87; auth, art, Religion Versus Science, Encycl of Unbelief, Prometheus Bks, 85; auth, Science vs Religion, Prometheus Bks, 91. **CONTACT ADDRESS** Dept of Philosophy, SUNY, Col, Brockport, NY, 14420.

CLERMONT, KEVIN MICHAEL
PERSONAL Born 10/25/1945, New York, NY **DISCIPLINE** LAW, CIVIL PROCEDURE **EDUCATION** Princeton Univ, AB, 67; Harvard Univ, JD, 71. **CAREER** Law clerk to Judge Murray Gurfein, 71-72; assoc, Cleary, Gottlieb, Steen & Hamilton, 72-74; from asst prof to prof, 74-89, Flanagan Prof Law, Law Sch, Cornell Univ, 89-; Fulbright scholar, Univ Nancy, France, 67-68. **HONORS AND AWARDS** Phi Beta Kappa; Sigma Xi; Order of the Coif. **RESEARCH** Federal courts. **SELECTED PUBLICATIONS** Coauth, Materials for a Basic Course in Civil Procedure, Found Press, 7th ed, 97; Law: Its Nature, Functions, and Limits, West Publ Co, 3rd ed, 86; auth, Civil Procedure, West Publ Co, 4th ed, 95. **CONTACT ADDRESS** Law Sch, Cornell Univ, Myron Taylor Hall, Ithaca, NY, 14853-4901. **EMAIL** kmc12@cornell.edu

CLIFFORD, RICHARD J.
PERSONAL Born 05/27/1934, Lewiston, ME, s **DISCIPLINE** BIBLICAL STUDIES **EDUCATION** Boston Col, Ab, 59; Weston Jesuit Sch Theology, STL, 67; Harvard Univ, PhD, 70. **CAREER** Weston Jesuit Sch Theo, Dean, 83-87; Asst prof to prof, 70-98. **HONORS AND AWARDS** Gen ed, Cath Bib Quart; Pres, Cath Bib Asn; Sabbatical Res Gnts. **MEMBERSHIPS** CBA; Soc Bib Lit; Am Sch Oriental Res. **RESEARCH** Wisdom lit; biblical poetry; psalms. **SELECTED PUBLICATIONS** Proverbs: A commentary, Old Test Lib, Louisville, Westminster John Knox, 99; The Origin and Early Development Themes of Apocalyptic, in: the Encyclopedia of Apocalypticism, ed, J J Collins, NY, Continuum, 98; The Rocky Road to the New Lectionary, America, 97; The Wisdom Literature, Interpreting the Biblical Text, Nashville, Abingdon, 98; numerous book reviews. **CONTACT ADDRESS** Weston Jesuit Sch of Theol, 3 Phillips Place, Cambridge, MA, 02138. **EMAIL** rclifford@wjst.edu

CLINTON, ROBERT N.
PERSONAL Born 08/01/1946, Detroit, MI, m, 1970, 3 children **DISCIPLINE** LAW **EDUCATION** Univ Mich, BA, 68; Univ Chicago, JD, 71. **CAREER** Assoc atty, Devoe, Sadur, Krupp, Miller, Adelman & Hamilton, 71-72; asst prof, 73-76, assoc prof, 76-79, PROF LAW, UNIV IOWA COL OF LAW, 79-, Vis prof law, Univ San Diego Sch Law, 78 & Cornell Univ Law Sch, 80-81. **MEMBERSHIPS** Am Bar Asn; Am Asn Law Schs. **RESEARCH** Native American, constitutional and federal jurisdiction law. **SELECTED PUBLICATIONS** Auth, Lone-Wolf V Hitchcock--Treaty-Rights and Indian-Law at the End of the 19th-Century, Jour Amer Ethnic Hist, Vol 0016, 97. **CONTACT ADDRESS** Col of Law, Univ of Iowa, Iowa City, IA, 52240.

CLOSIUS, PHILLIP J.
DISCIPLINE LAW **EDUCATION** Univ Notre Dame, BA; Columbia University, JD. **CAREER** Prof. **SELECTED PUBLICATIONS** Auth, Rejecting the Fruits of Action, Univ Notre Dame, 95; Social Justice and the Myth of Fairness, Univ Nebraska, 95. **CONTACT ADDRESS** Col Law, Univ of Toledo, Toledo, OH, 43606. **EMAIL** pclosiu@utnet.utoledo.edu

CLOTHEY, FREDERICK WILSON
PERSONAL Born 02/29/1936, Madras, India, m, 1962, 4 children **DISCIPLINE** HISTORY OF RELIGIONS **EDUCATION** Aurora Col, BA & BTh, 57; Evangel Theol Sem, BD, 59; Univ Chicago, MA, 65, PhD(hist relig), 68. **CAREER** Dir youth work, Advent Christian Gen Conf, 59-62; from instr to asst prof relig Boston Univ, 67-77; Assoc Prof Hist Relig, Univ Pittsburgh, 77-, Chmn Dept Relig Studies, 78-88; 95-98, Resident coordr, Great Lakes Cols Asn Year in India Prog, 71-72; producer & dir films, Yakam: A Fire Ritual in South India, spring 73, Skanda-Sasti: A Festival of Conquest, fall 73 & Pankuni Uttiram: A Festival of Marriage, spring 74. **HONORS AND AWARDS** Fulbright fel, 78, 82, 91, 98; AIIS Fellow 66-67, 81, 85, 91, 94. **MEMBERSHIPS** Am Acad Relig; Soc Indian Studies; Conf Indian Relig; Soc Sci Study Relig; Asn Asian Studies. **RESEARCH** Religion in South India; nature of myth, symbol, ritual; ethnic religion in America. **SELECTED PUBLICATIONS** Auth, The many faces of Murukan: The history and meaning of a South Indian God, Mouton, The Hague, 78; contribr, Chronometry, cosmology and the festival calendar of the Murukan Cultus, In: Interludes: Festivals of South India and Sri Lanka, Manohar Bks, 82; "Sasta-Aiyanar-Aiyappan: The God as prism of social History," Images of Man: Relgion and Historical Process in South Asia, 82; The construction of a temple in an American city & The acculturation process, In: Rythm & Intent: Ritual Studies from South India, Blackie & Son, 82; auth, Quiscence and passion: The vision of Arunakiri, Tamil Mystic Austin and Winfield, 1996; Rhythm & intent: Ritual studies from South India, Blackie & Son, 82; ed, Experiencing Siva: Encounters with a Hindu Deity, Manohar Bks, 82; Images of man: Religion and historical process, New Era Publ, 82. **CONTACT ADDRESS** Dept of Relig Studies, Univ of Pittsburgh, 2604 Cathedral/Learn, Pittsburgh, PA, 15260-0001. **EMAIL** clothey+@pitt.edu

CLOUD, W. ERIC
PERSONAL Born 02/26/1946, Cleveland, OH, m **DISCIPLINE** LAW **EDUCATION** Morris Brown Coll, BA (cum laude) 1973; Dag Hammarskjold Coll, fellowship (highest honors) 1974; Antioch Sch of Law, JD 1977; George Washington Law Sch, LLM Intl & Comparative Law 1980. **CAREER** Pvt Practice Intl Law, atty; US Dept of Treasury, consult 1979-80; US Dept of Labor, spl asst to intl tax counsel 1976-78; Cloud, Henderson & Cloud, Attorney, 1982-; Washington Afro-American Newspaper, correspondent, 1988-; Morris Brown College, lecturer, 1990-. **HONORS AND AWARDS** Good Samaritan of the Year Mayor Carl Stokes 1968; fellowship Dag Hammarskjold Coll Dag Hammarskjold Found 1973; Four Walls/Eight Window, 1990; Award for Best Article of 1990. **MEMBERSHIPS** Mem, Am Bar Assn 1977; mem, Nat Bar Assn; mem, Morris Brown College Alumni Assn, 1988-. **SELECTED PUBLICATIONS** Article in George Washington Law Review "Tax Treaties: The Need for the US to Extend its Treaty Network to Developing Countries in Light of the New International Economic and Political Realities" **CONTACT ADDRESS** Cloud and Henderson, 10605 Woodlawn Blvd, Largo, MD, 20772.

CLOUSER, KARL DANNER
PERSONAL Born 04/26/1930, Marion, OH, m, 1952, 2 children **DISCIPLINE** PHILOSOPHY **EDUCATION** Gettysburg Col, AB, 52; Lutheran Theol Sem, BD, 55; Harvard Univ, MA, 58, PhD, 61. **CAREER** Instr philos, Dartmouth Col, 61-64; asst prof, Carleton Col, 64-68; assoc prof, 68-76, prof humanities 76-90, univ prof humanities, 91-96; univ prof emer, 97-, Col Med PA State Univ, 76-; bd dirs, Lutheran Theol Sem, 70-81; assoc ed, Encycl Bioethics, 73-78; dir, Hastings Ctr Workshops Med Ethics, 74-81; **HONORS AND AWARDS** Humane Lett Thomas Jefferson Univ, 81; Dr Humane Lett, Gettysburg Col, 83; Henry Beecher Award, 96; Inst Med, 97. **MEMBERSHIPS** Fel Hastings Ctr. **RESEARCH** Medical ethics; philosophy of medicine. **SELECTED PUBLICATIONS** Auth, The sancitity of life: An analysis of a concept, Ann Internal Med, 1/73; What is medical ethics?, Ann Internal Med, 5/74; Medical ethics: Uses, abuses and limitations, New England J Med, 8/75; Biomedical ethics: Some reflections and exhortations, Monist, 1/77; Allowing or causing: Another look, Ann Internal Med, 11/77; Bioethics, In: Encycl Bioethic, Macmillan & Free Press, 78; Teaching Bioethics: Strategies, Problems, and Resources, Hastings Ctr, 80; coauth, A Critique of Principlism. Jour Med and Philos, 90; coauth, Morality vs Principlism, Prin Am Hea Care Ethics, Wiley & Sons, 94; coauth, Morality and The New Genetics, Jones & Bartlett, 96; Biomedical Ethics, Encycl Philos Suppl, Simon & Schuster, 96; coauth, Bioethics: A Return to Fundamentals. Oxford Univ Press, 97; coauth, Malady What is Disease, Humana Press, 97. **CONTACT ADDRESS** Hershey, PA, 17033-0850.

CLOUSER, ROY A.
PERSONAL Born 12/20/1937, Philadelphia, PA, m, 5 children **DISCIPLINE** PHILOSOPHY **EDUCATION** Gordon Coll, BA; Reformed Episcopal Sem, BD; Univ of Penn, MA, PhD. **CAREER** Instr, La Salle Univ; Instr, Rutgers Univ; Prof, Coll of New Jersey. **HONORS AND AWARDS** Templeton Course Awd. **MEMBERSHIPS** APSA, SCP, CPJ, ASA. **RESEARCH** Philosophy of Religion, metaphysics. **SELECTED PUBLICATIONS** Auth, The Myth of Religious Neutrality, An Essay on the Hidden Pole of Religious Beliefs in Theories, Univ Notre Dame Press, 91; Knowing with the Heart, Religious Experience and Belief in God, InterVarsity Press, 98; auth, Is God Eternal? in: The Rationality of Theism, ed A G Sienra, Rodopi Pub Amsterdam, forthcoming; A Critique of Historicism, in: Critica, 97; On the General Relation of Religion, Metaphysics and Science, in: Facets of Faith and Science, ed J Van der Meer, Univ press of Amer, 96; The Uniqueness of Dooyeweerd's Program for Philosophy and Science, Whence the Difference?, in: Christian Philo at the Close of the 20th Century, ed Griffeon & Balk, Kampen Kok Netherlands, 95. **CONTACT ADDRESS** 204 Bradley Ave, Haddonfield, NJ, 08033-2904. **EMAIL** royclouser@aol.com

CLUCHEY, DAVID P.
DISCIPLINE LAW **EDUCATION** Yale Univ, AB; SUNY at Albany, MA; Harvard Univ, JD. **CAREER** Prof; Fulbright lectr to Russ, 94; past consult to, US AID Rule of Law prog to Russ; past co-spe coun, Maine Atty Gen; past consult, several comt(s), Maine Supreme Judicial Ct; fac, Louisiana Tech Univ, 79-; past prac atty, Maine, 6 yrs; assoc dean law sch, Louisiana Tech Univ, 87-91; **MEMBERSHIPS** Treas, Maine Bar Found; past-ch, Sect on NAmer Coop, Asn Amer Law Sch. **RESEARCH** International trade and business relations. **SELECTED PUBLICATIONS** Coauth, 3-vol bk, Maine Criminal Practice; publ on, int trade regulation; antitrust and health care law. **CONTACT ADDRESS** School of Law, Univ of Southern Maine, 96 Falmouth St, PO Box 9300, Portland, ME, 04104-9300.

COAN, RICHARD W.
PERSONAL Born 01/24/1928, Martinez, CA, d, 4 children **DISCIPLINE** CLINICAL PSYCHOLOGY **EDUCATION** Univ of Southern Calif, PhD, 55. **CAREER** Res Assoc in Psychol, Univ Ill, 55-57; Asst Prof to Prof of Psychol, Univ of Ariz, 57-89; Prof Emeritus, Univ Ariz, 89-. **MEMBERSHIPS** Am

Psychol Asn. **RESEARCH** Psychology of myths & tales; human personality; symbolism. **SELECTED PUBLICATIONS** Auth, The optimal personality, an empirical and theoretical analysis, Routledge & Kegan Paul, 74; auth, Hero, artist, sage, or saint? A survey of views on what is variously called mental health, normality, maturity, self-actualization and human fulfillment, Univ Colombia Press, 77; auth, Psychologists: Personal and theoretical pathways, Irvington, 79; auth, Psychology of adjustment: Personal experience development, Wiley, 83; auth, Human consciousness and its evolution: A multidimensional view, Greenwood, 87. **CONTACT ADDRESS** 4185 E Waverly St, Tucson, AZ, 85712.

COATES, ROBERT CRAWFORD
PERSONAL Born 01/31/1937, Torrance, CA, d, 2 children **DISCIPLINE** LAW **EDUCATION** San Diego St Univ, BS, 59; Natl Univ, MB, 59; Calif Western Sch Law, JD, 70. **CAREER** Jr civil engg, 59-61, Engg dept, admin analyst, 61-63, city mngrs staff, 61-63, City of San Diego; atty, 71-82, Partner, Coates & Miller; Law Forum dir, 84-87, adj prof, 81-95, Univ San Diego Law Sch; judge, Municipal Ct, 82-, San Diego Judicial Dist. **HONORS AND AWARDS** One of Ten San Diego Citizens of the Yr, City Club, 91; Dist Svc Rotary, 91; Warren Williams Award of Am & Calif Psychiatric Asns, 91; Paul Harris Fel, Rotary Intl, 95; Award of Excel, Consumer Atty of San Diego, 97; God and Country Award, BSA, 98. **MEMBERSHIPS** Am Asn of Mining Engg; Am Geol Inst; Anza-Borrego Hist Soc; The Baja Group, Calif Mining Asn; San Diego Asn of Geol, San Diego Nat Hist Mus; Sierra Club, St Stephens Church of God in Christ; Theodore Roosevelt Asn, Torrey Pines Asn; Yosemite Asn; E Clampus Vitus, Mission Valley East Rotary Club. **RESEARCH** Mental health law, natural resources law, judicial ethics. **SELECTED PUBLICATIONS** Auth, A Street is Not a Home: Solving America's Homeless Dilemma, 90; auth, The Guys Who Can't Cook's Cookbook, 84; auth, Asserting Mineral Rights Against the US Government in Federal Court, 20 Cal WL Rev 377, 84. **CONTACT ADDRESS** 220 W Broadway, San Diego, CA, 92101.

COBB, JOHN BOSWELL
PERSONAL Japan, m, 4 children **DISCIPLINE** CONSTRUCTIVE THEOLOGY **EDUCATION** Canadian Academy, Kobe, Japan, 39; Newnan High School, Ga, 39-41; Emory-at-Oxford, Ga, 41-43, Univ Mich, 44; Univ Chicago, MA, 49, PhD, 52. **CAREER** Instr, Young Harris Col, 50-53; instr, 53-58, Ingraham Prof, Candeler School of Theology, Emory Univ, 58-90; Avery prof, CGS, 60-90; Fulbright prof, Univ of Mainz, 65-66; vis prof, Rikkyo Univ, Tokyo, 78; vis prof, Chicago Divinity School, 80; vis prof, Harvard Divinity School, 87; vis prof, Iliff School of Theology, 91; vis prof, Vanderbilt Divinity School, 93; CO-DIR, CENTER FOR PROCESS STUDIES, VICE-CHAIR, STEERING COMT MOBILIZATION FOR THE HUMAN FAMILY, PROF EMERITUS, CLAREMONT SCHOOL OF THEOLOGY & CLAREMONT GRAD SCHOOL, 98-. **HONORS AND AWARDS** Honorary degrees from the Univ Mainz, Emory Univ, Linfield Col, DePauw Univ, and Univ Victoria; Fulbright Prof, Univ Mainz; Fel, Woodrow Wilson Int Center for Scholars; Alumus of the Year, Chicago Divinity School; Distinguished Alumnus Award, Univ Chicago. **MEMBERSHIPS** Am Acad of Religion; Metaphysical Soc; Center for Process Studies. **RESEARCH** Inter-religious dialogue; process philosophy; theology & economics. **SELECTED PUBLICATIONS** Auth, Becoming a Thinking Christian, 93; Lay Theology, 94; Sustaining the Common Good, 94; Grace and Responsibility, 95; Reclaiming the Church, 97; coauth, The Green National Product: A Proposed Index of Sustainable Economic Welfare, 94. **CONTACT ADDRESS** School of Theology at Claremont, 1401 N College Ave., Claremont, CA, 91711.

COBB, JOHN HUNTER, JR.
PERSONAL Born 05/05/1953, Rocky Mount, NC, m **DISCIPLINE** LAW **EDUCATION** Hampton Univ, BA 1975; Howard Univ, JD 1979. **CAREER** Michie Company, senior editor 1979-85; Robinson Buchanan & Johnson, associate 1985-88; VIRGINIA UNION UNIVERSITY, BUSINESS LAW PROF 1985-86; SOLO PRACTICIONER 1988-. **HONORS AND AWARDS** Litigation Section VA State Bar 1985-. **MEMBERSHIPS** Mem Old Dominion Bar Assoc 1979-; Young Lawyers Conf VA State Bar 1979-; legal advisor Time Investment Corp 1985-; mem VA Trial Lawyers Assoc 1985-; comm mem Guardian Ad Litem Seminar 1987. **CONTACT ADDRESS** 2025 E Main St, Richmond, VA, 23223.

COBB, KELTON
PERSONAL Born 10/08/1958, CA, m, 1990 **DISCIPLINE** RELIGION **EDUCATION** George Fox Col, BA, 81; Princeton Sem, MDiv, 85; Univ Iowa, PhD, 94. **CAREER** Hartford Sem, prof, 95-. **MEMBERSHIPS** AAR, SCE, NAPTS **RESEARCH** Theol and Cult theory; theol ethics; comp relig ethics. **SELECTED PUBLICATIONS** Auth, Ernst Troeltech and Vaclav Havel on the Ethical Promise of Historical Failures, Jour Relig Ethics, 94; Reconsidering the Status of Popular Culture in Tillich's Theology of Culture, Jour Amer Acad Relig, 95. **CONTACT ADDRESS** Dept of Theology, Hartford Sem, 77 Sherman St, Hartford, CT, 06105. **EMAIL** kcobb@hartsem.edu

COBURN, ROBERT C.
DISCIPLINE PHILOSOPHY **EDUCATION** Yale Univ BA, 51; Univ of Chicago, Div School, BD, 54; Harvard Univ, MA, 58, PhD, 58. **CAREER** Ohio State Univ, inst, 58-59; Dartmouth Col, inst, 59-60; Univ of Chicago, asst prof, assoc prof, prof, 60-71; Univ Of Washington, prof, 71-. **HONORS AND AWARDS** Univ Pittsburgh, Andrew Mellon, 61-62; Univ Washington, Grad School Release-Time Award, 85 **MEMBERSHIPS** APA, AAUP **RESEARCH** Metaphysics; Ethics; Social philo. **SELECTED PUBLICATIONS** Auth, The Strangeness of the Ordinary: Issues and Problems in Contemporary Metaphysics, Rowman & Littlefield Pub, 90; Identity and Spatio-temporal Continuity, in: Identity and Individuation, NY Univ Press, 71; Personal Identity Revisited, in: Personal Identity, Dartmouth Pub Co, 95. **CONTACT ADDRESS** Dept of Philosophy, Washington Univ, PO Box 353350, Seattle, WA, 98195-3350. **EMAIL** coburn@u.washington.edu

COBURN, THOMAS BOWEN
PERSONAL Born 02/08/1944, New York, NY, d, 2 children **DISCIPLINE** HISTORY OF RELIGION **EDUCATION** Princeton Univ, AB, 65; Harvard Univ, MTS, 69, PhD(comp relig), 77. **CAREER** Teaching fel relig, Phillips Acad, 65-66; instr math & physics, Am Community Sch, Lebanon, 66-67; from Instr to Prof, 74-90, Charles A. Dana Prof Rel Studies, St Lawrence Univ, 90-, Vice Pres St Lawrence Univ and Dean of Acad Affairs, 96-. **HONORS AND AWARDS** Sr res fel, Am Inst Indian Studies, 81-82; Nat Endowment for Humanities fel, 82. **MEMBERSHIPS** Am Orient Soc; Am Acad Relig; Asn Asian Studies; Asia Network. **RESEARCH** South Asian religion, especially the literature and mythology of popular religion in India; goddesses; methods in comparative study. **SELECTED PUBLICATIONS** Auth, Religion departments in liberal arts colleges: An inquiry, Ctr Study World Relig, Harvard Univ Bull, summer 77; Consort of none, Sakti of all: The vision of the Devi-Mahatmya, In: The Divine Consort: Radha and the Goddesses of India, Berkeley Res Publ, 1982, rev ed, 95; The Crystallization of the Goddess Tradition: The Sources and Context of the Devi-Mahatmya, Motilal Banarsidass, New Delhi, 84; The Conceptualization of Religious Change and the Worship of the Great Goddess, St Lawrence Univ, 80; Rethinking Scripture, SUNY Press, repr 89; Encountering the Goddess: A Trans. of the Devi-Mahatmya and a Study of Its Interpretation, State Univ of NY Press, 91; guest ed, Education About Asia, 2/97; author of numerous other journal articles. **CONTACT ADDRESS** Vice Pres and Dean of Acad Affairs, St Lawrence Univ, Canton, NY, 13617-1499. **EMAIL** tcob@ccmaillink.stlawu.edu

COCCHIARELLA, NINO BARNABAS
DISCIPLINE PHILOSOPHY, MATHEMATICAL LOGIC **EDUCATION** Columbia Univ, BS, 58; Univ Calif, Los Angeles, MA & PhD, 66. **CAREER** Instr, Exten, UCLA, 63-64; asst prof philos, San Francisco State Col, 64-68; vis assoc prof, Wayne State Univ, 68; Prof Philos, Ind Univ, Bloomington, 68. **HONORS AND AWARDS** Nat Sci Found grants, 71-74; Nat Endowment for Hum grant, 77-78, 88-89. **MEMBERSHIPS** Central Div Am Philos Asn; Asn Symbolic Logic; Asn Philos Sci; Royal Inst Philos. **RESEARCH** Formal philos; philosophical linguistics; general metaphysics. **SELECTED PUBLICATIONS** Auth, Conceptual Realism versus Quine on Classes and Higher-Order Logic, Synthese, 92; Knowledge Representation in Conceptual Realism, Int J Human-Computer Studies, 95; Conceptual Realism as a Formal Ontology, In: Formal Ontology, Kluwer, 96; Reference in Conceptual Realism, Synthese, vol 114, 98; Logic and Ontology, In: Logic, Philosophy and Ideology: Essays in Memory of Joseph Bochenski, 98; auth of numerous other articles and publ. **CONTACT ADDRESS** Dept of Philos, Indiana Univ, Bloomington, 1 Indiana University, Bloomington, IN, 47405. **EMAIL** cocchiar@indiana.edu

COCHRAN JR., ROBERT F.
DISCIPLINE FAMILY LAW **EDUCATION** Carson-Newman Col, BA, 73; Univ VA, JD, 76. **CAREER** Law clk, US Court Appeals Fourth Circuit, 76-77; assoc, Boyle and Bain, 78-83; vis prof, Univ Richmond, 87-88; vis prof, Wake Forest Univ, 94; prof, 94-. **HONORS AND AWARDS** Rick J Caruso res fel, 94-95. **SELECTED PUBLICATIONS** Co auth, Lawyers, Clients, and Moral Responsibility, W Publ Co, 94; Cases and Materials on the Rules of the Legal Profession, W Publ Co, 96. **CONTACT ADDRESS** Sch of Law, Pepperdine Univ, 24255 Pacific Coast Hwy, Malibu, CA, 90263.

CODE, MICHAEL
DISCIPLINE LAW **EDUCATION** Univ Toronto, BA, 72, LLB, 76, LLM, 91. **CAREER** Lawyer, Ruby and Edwardh, 81-91; Lawyer, Sack Goldblatt Mitchell, 96- **HONORS AND AWARDS** Ed, Can Rights Reporter. **SELECTED PUBLICATIONS** Auth, pubs on criminal and constitutional litigation. **CONTACT ADDRESS** Fac of Law, Univ Toronto, 78 Queen's Park, Toronto, ON.

CODY, AELRED
PERSONAL Born 02/03/1932, Oklahoma City, OK **DISCIPLINE** THEOLOGY **EDUCATION** St Meinrad Col, BA, 56; Univ Ottawa, STL, 58, STD, 60; Pontifical Bibl Inst, SSL, 62; Pontifical Bibl Comn, Rome, SSD, 68; Royal Col of Music, ARCM, 74; Royal Col of Organists, ARCO, 75. **CAREER** Prof, Old Testament and ancient Near East hist, Pontifical Atheneum of Sant'Anselmo and Pontifical Bibl Inst, 68-78; organist, Abbazia Primaziale, 68-76; master of novices & jrs, St Meinrad Archabbey, 78-92; assoc ed and ed, Cath Bibl Q, 92- ; mem, Official Oriental Orthodox-Roman Cath Consultation in the USA, 81- ; trustee, 84-87 and mem, 92- , exec bd, Cath Bibl Asn of Am. **HONORS AND AWARDS** Christian Res Found Prize, Harvard Univ, 60. **MEMBERSHIPS** Int Asn for Coptic Stud; Am Oriental Soc; Cath Bibl Asn of Am; Soc of Bibl Lit. **RESEARCH** Hebrew language and literature; history of the ancient and Christian Near East; eastern Christian liturgy. **SELECTED PUBLICATIONS** Auth, Heavenly Sanctuary and Liturgy in the Epistle to the Hebrews, Grail, 60; auth, A History of Old Testament Priesthood, Pontifical Biblical Institute, 68; auth, Ezekiel, Michael Glazier, 84; contribur, The New Jerome Biblical Commentary, Prentice Hall, 90; contribur, The Coptic Encyclopedia, Macmillan, 91; contribur, The Oxford Companion to the Bible, Oxford University, 93; auth, High Priest, in McBrien, ed, The Harper-Collins Encyclopedia of Catholicism, Harper San Francisco, 95; contribur, Oriental Orthodox-Roman Catholic Interchurch Marriages and Other Pastoral Relationships, National Conference of Catholic Bishops, 95. **CONTACT ADDRESS** St Meinrad Archabbey, St Meinrad, IN, 47557-1010.

CODY, MARTIN LEONARD
PERSONAL Born 08/07/1941, Peterborough, England, m, 1980, 4 children **DISCIPLINE** ZOOLOGY, MATH **EDUCATION** Univ Edinburgh, MA, 63; Univ Pa,PhD, 66. **CAREER** Asst prof, Zool, Univ Calif, LA, 66-72; PROF, BIOL, UNIV CALIF, LA, 72- **MEMBERSHIPS** Am Soc Natur; Ecol Soc Am; Cooper Ornith Soc **RESEARCH** Community ecology; Birds & plants. **SELECTED PUBLICATIONS** Monitoring Breeding Bird Populations in Grand Teton National Park," Univ Wy Nat Park Ser Res Center, 94; "Short-Term Evolution of Reduced Dispersal in Island Plant Populations," J Ecol, 96; "Long-Term Studies of Vertebrate Communities," Acad Press, 96; "An Introduction to Neotropical Species Diversity," Diversity & Conser in Neotropics, 97; Birds of North America: California Thrasher Toxostoma Redivivum, 97; Birds of North America: Crissal Thrasher Toxostoma Redivivum, 98; "Assembly Rules in Plant and Bird Communities," Assembly Rules in communities, 98. **CONTACT ADDRESS** Dept Biol, Univ Calif, Los Angles, CA, 90024. **EMAIL** mlcody@ucla.edu

COE, WILLIAM JEROME
PERSONAL Born 11/15/1935, Malone, NY, m, 1977, 3 children **DISCIPLINE** PHILOSOPHY **EDUCATION** Dartmouth Col, AB, 57; Vanderbilt Univ, MA, 59; PA State Univ, PhD, 67. **CAREER** Vis lectr philos, Baldwin-Wallace Col, 61-62; from instr to asst prof, Southeast MO State Col, 62-67; asst prof, Northern IL Univ, 67-71; assoc prof Philos, 71-81, PROF PHILOS, FR LEWIS COL, 82-. **MEMBERSHIPS** Western Div Am Philos Asn; Soc Phenomenol & Existential Philos. **RESEARCH** Metaphilosophy; metaphysics; conceptual analysis. **SELECTED PUBLICATIONS** Conceptsof Leisure in Western Thought, with B. Dare and G. Welton, Kendall Hunt Pub Co, 87, 2nd ed, 98. **CONTACT ADDRESS** Dept of Philos, Fort Lewis Col, 1000 Rim Dr, Durango, CO, 81301-3999. **EMAIL** coe_w@fortlewis.edu

COGGINS, GEORGE CAMERON
PERSONAL Born 01/27/1941, Pontiac, MI, m, 1968, 1 child **DISCIPLINE** LAW **EDUCATION** Cent Mich Univ, AB, 63; Univ Mich, JD, 66. **CAREER** Assoc atty, McCutchen, Doyle, Brown & Enersen, San Francisco, 66-70; assoc prof law, 70-73, PROF LAW, UNIV KANS, 73-, Vis prof law, Law Sch, Univ NC, Chapel Hill, 81 & Northwestern Law Sch, Lewis & Clark Col, 83. **RESEARCH** Environmental law; civil procedure. **SELECTED PUBLICATIONS** Auth, Concessions Law and Policy in the National-Park System, Denver Univ Law Rev, Vol 0074, 97. **CONTACT ADDRESS** Law Sch, Univ of Kans, Green Hall, Lawrence, KS, 66045-0001.

COHEN, ANDREW I.
DISCIPLINE PHILOSOPHY **EDUCATION** SUNY at Binghamton, BA, 88; Univ NC, Chapel Hill, MA, 90, PhD, 94. **CAREER** Asst prof; Univ Wis-SP, 97-. **RESEARCH** Hobbesian political theory and contemporary social philosophy. **SELECTED PUBLICATIONS** Auth, Virtues, Opportunities, and the Right to do Wrong, J Soc Philos, Vol 28, 97. **CONTACT ADDRESS** Dept of Philosophy, Univ Wis-SP, Stevens Point, WI, 54481. **EMAIL** acohen@uwsp.edu

COHEN, ARNOLD B.
DISCIPLINE BUSINESS ACQUISITIONS **EDUCATION** Brown Univ, AB; Univ Pa Sch law, LLB. **CAREER** Prof, Villanova Univ; past clerk, US Dist Ct Judge; past assoc-in-Law, Univ Calif Sch Law Berkeley. **MEMBERSHIPS** Order of the Coif; Amer and Philadelphia Bar Ass; Amer Bankruptcy Inst; Eastern Dist Pa Bankruptcy Conf; bd dir, Consumer Bankruptcy Asst Proj. **RESEARCH** Bankruptcy and secured transactions. **SELECTED PUBLICATIONS** Auth, Bankruptcy and Secured Transactions, 3d ed, Lexis-Nexis, 97; Guide to Secured Lending Transactions, Warren, Gorham & Lamont, 88; Bankruptcy, Secured Transactions and Other Debtor-Creditor Mat-

ters, Bobbs-Merrill, 81; coauth, Bankruptcy, Article 9 and Creditors' Remedies, 2d ed, Michie Co, 89; Debtors' and Creditors' Rights, Michie Co, 84 & Debtor-Creditor Relations Under the Bankruptcy Act of 1978, Bobbs-Merrill; Consumer Bankruptcy Manual, 2d ed, Warren, Gorham & Lamont, 91, suppl through 97. **CONTACT ADDRESS** Law School, Villanova Univ, 800 Lancaster Ave, Villanova, PA, 19085-1692. **EMAIL** cohen@law.vill.edu

COHEN, BURTON I.
DISCIPLINE RELIGION **EDUCATION** Univ Chicago, MA, PhD; Roosevelt Univ, BA. **CAREER** Dir, Camp Ramah, 59-89; assoc prof. **HONORS AND AWARDS** Nat Comn Service Awd. **MEMBERSHIPS** United Synagogue Comn Jewish Educ; Nat Exec Comt Jewish Educr Assembly. **SELECTED PUBLICATIONS** Auth, Case Studies in Jewish School Management, Behrman House, 92; ed, Women and Ritual: An Anthology, Nat Ramah, 86; co-ed, Studies in Jewish Education and Judaica in Honor of Louis Newman, Ktav, 84. **CONTACT ADDRESS** Dept of Jewish Educ, Jewish Theol Sem of America, 3080 Broadway, PO Box 3080, New York, NY, 10027. **EMAIL** bucohen@jtsa.edu

COHEN, DAVID
DISCIPLINE LAW **EDUCATION** McGill Univ, BS, 71; Univ Toronto, LLB, 75; Yale Univ, LLM, 79. **CAREER** Vis prof, Osgoode Hall Law Sch; prof, 80-. **HONORS AND AWARDS** Pres, Consumers' Asn Can. **MEMBERSHIPS** Legal Services Soc British Columbia; Can Standards Asn; W Coast Environ Law Asn. **RESEARCH** Law and regulatory policy; commercial law and planning; contract law; law and economics. **SELECTED PUBLICATIONS** Auth, pubs on contract theory, governmental liability, product safety regulation, dispute resolution, and environmental policy and regulation. **CONTACT ADDRESS** Fac of Law, Univ Victoria, PO Box 2400, Victoria, BC, V8W 3H7. **EMAIL** lawdean@uvic.ca

COHEN, DEBRA R.
DISCIPLINE ADVANCED BUSINESS ORGANIZATIONS, CIVIL PROCEDURE **EDUCATION** Brown Univ, AB, 85; Emory Univ Sch Law, JD, 88. **CAREER** Assoc, Sullivan & Cromwell; assoc couns, Scholastic Inc, 92; vis asst prof, Emory Univ, 93; assoc prof, 95-. **HONORS AND AWARDS** JD with hon(s), 88. **MEMBERSHIPS** Order of the Coif. **SELECTED PUBLICATIONS** Ed, Emory Law Jour. **CONTACT ADDRESS** Law Sch, W Va Univ, PO Box 6009, Morgantown, WV, 26506-6009.

COHEN, ELLIOT
DISCIPLINE PHILOSOPHY **EDUCATION** Brown Univ, PhD, Philo, 77; AM Philo, 76; Farleigh Dickinson Univ, BA, Philo, 74. **CAREER** Ed In Chief and Founder, The International Journal of Applied Philosophy, 82-; Asst Prof, Assoc Prof to Prof, Philo, 80-, Indian River Comm Coll; Adjunct Prof of Philo, 86-92, Barry Univ; Instr, Dept of Behavioral Stud, 78-79, Univ of Florida; Lect, Philo of Law, 74-77, Providence Coll; Tech Asst, 76-77, Brown Univ. **HONORS AND AWARDS** Pres Amer Assoc for Philo, Counsellor and Psychotherapy; Co-Founder and Executive Board Member, Amer Assoc Philo, Couns and Psychotherapy; Pews Florida Philo Assoc; Lilly Post-Doctoral Award Hum; Scholarship Brown Univ; Phi Beta Kappa. **RESEARCH** Applied and Professional Ethics, law and medicine, journalism, Critical Thinking, Philosophy of Psychotherapy. **SELECTED PUBLICATIONS** Co-auth, Journalistic Ethics, ABC-CLIO Publishing Co, 97; AIDS, Crisis in Professional Ethics, Temple University Press, 94; auth, Caution, Faulty Thinking Can Be Harmful to Your Happiness, Self-Help, ed, Trace Wilco, 92; Philosophical Issues in Journalism, Oxford University Press, 92; ed, Philosophers at Work, An Introduction to the Issues and Practical Uses of Philosophy, Holt, Rinehart and Winston, 89; Making Value Judgments: Principles of Sound Reasoning, Robert E Krieger, Inc, 85; Belief-Scan 3.1, Artificial Intelligence for Detecting and Diagnosing Faulty Thinking, US Patent No 5,503,561, w/Operating Manual. **CONTACT ADDRESS** Dept Philosophy, Indian River Comm Col, 3209 Virginia Ave, Fort Pierce, FL, 34981-5599. **EMAIL** cohene@mail.firn.edu

COHEN, GEORGE M.
PERSONAL Born 11/22/1960, Brooklyn, NY, m, 1987, 3 children **DISCIPLINE** LAW **EDUCATION** Yale Univ, BA, 82; Univ of Pennsylvania, JD, 86, PhD, 92. **CAREER** Law clerk, U.S. court of appeals for the third circuit, 87-88; asst prof, Univ of Pittsburg Sch of Law, 88-93; visiting asst prof, Univ of Virginia Sch of Law, 92-93, assoc prof of law, 93-95, prof of law, 95-present, research prof, july 97-july 2000. **MEMBERSHIPS** Assn of Amer Law Sch (AALS); Amer Law & Economics Assn (ALEA); Amer Bar Assn (ABA); NY Bar; NJ Bar. **RESEARCH** Law and Economics, contract law, legal ethics, agency law **SELECTED PUBLICATIONS** Auth, The Negligence-Opportunism Tradeoff in Contract Law, 20 Hofstra Law Review 941, 92; The Fault Lines in Contract Damages, 80 Virginia Law Review 1225, 94; Under Cloak of Settlement, 82 Virginia Law Review 1051, 96; Legal Malpractice Insurance and Loss Prevention: A comparative Analysis of Economic Institutions, 4 Connecticut Insurance Law Journal 305, 97; Interpretation and Implied Terms in Contract Law, Encyclopedia of Law and Economics, forthcoming fall 98; When Law and Economics Met Professional Responsibility, forthcoming Fordham Law Review, fall 98. **CONTACT ADDRESS** School of Law, Univ of Virginia, 580 Massie Rd, Charlottesville, VA, 22903. **EMAIL** gmc3y@virginia.edu

COHEN, JONATHAN ALLAN
PERSONAL Born 12/04/1939, Troy, NY, m, 1995, 3 children **DISCIPLINE** PSYCHIATRY **EDUCATION** Univ Cal LA, BS 63, Sch Med, MD 67. **CAREER** Private Practice, psychiatry and psychoanalysis, 74-. **MEMBERSHIPS** APA; FAS; PNHP. **RESEARCH** Psychoanalytic theory and practice. **SELECTED PUBLICATIONS** Auth, Apart for Freud: Notes for a Rational Psychoanalysis, in: Freud's Subversion of Meaning, SF, City Lights Press, in press, 99; Freudianism and the human moral system. In: Against Normalization, eds, C. Ware A. Molino, SF, City Lights Press, 98; A View of the Moral Landscape of Psychoanalysis, Jour of Amer Acad Psychoanalysis, 94. **CONTACT ADDRESS** 2005 Franklin St., Suite 500, Denver, CO, 80205-5401. **EMAIL** jon.cohen@interfold.com

COHEN, MARTIN AARON
PERSONAL Born 02/10/1928, Philadelphia, PA, m, 1953 **DISCIPLINE** JEWISH HISTORY AND THEOLOGY **EDUCATION** Univ Pa, BA, 46, MA, 49; Hebrew Union Col, Ohio, BHL, 55, MAHL, 57, PhD(Jewish hist), 60. **CAREER** Asst instr Roman lang, Univ Pa, 46-48, instr, 48-50; instr, Rutgers Univ, New Brunswick, 50-51; instr Jewish hist, Jewish Inst Relig, Hebrew Union Col, Ohio, 60-62; from asst prof to assoc prof, 62-69, PROF JEWISH HIST, JEWISH INST RELIG, HEBREW UNION COL, NY, 69-, Nat chaplain, Am Vets World War II & Korea, 61-62; vis lectr, Antioch Col, 61-62; vis prof, Temple Univ, 63-65 & Hunter Col, 73-74; chmn, Nat Comt Jewish-Cath Rels Anti-Defamation League, B'rith, 76- **HONORS AND AWARDS** Chadabee Award for Outstanding Achievement, Nat Fedn Temple Brotherhoods, 76. **MEMBERSHIPS** Am Jewish Hist Soc; Cent Conf Am Rabbis; Soc Bibl Lit; Am Acad Relig; Am Soc Sephardic Studies (pres, 76-66). **RESEARCH** General Jewish history; Sephardic history; Jewish theology. **SELECTED PUBLICATIONS** Auth, The Sephardic Phenomenon--The Story of Sephardic Jews in the America and Their Subsequent Universalization Through Diaspora-A Reappraisal, Amer Jewish Archv, Vol 0044, 92. **CONTACT ADDRESS** Jewish Inst of Relig, Hebrew Union Col, 40 W 68th St, New York, NY, 10023.

COHEN, SHELDON M.
DISCIPLINE PHILOSOPHY **EDUCATION** Northwestern Univ, PhD, 70. **CAREER** Prof. **RESEARCH** Ancient philosophy; medieval philosophy; war and morality. **SELECTED PUBLICATIONS** Auth, Arms and Judgment: Law, Morality, and the Conduct of War in the Twentieth Century, Westview, 89; Aristotle on Nature and Incomplete Substance, Cambridge, 96; Aristotle on Elemental Motion, Phronesis, 94; Moral Philosophy, International Law, and the deaths of Innocents, Longwood, 91; Luck and Happiness in the Nicomachean Ethics, Soundings, 90; New Evidence for the Dating of Aristotle's Meteorology 1-3, Class Philol, 90; Aristotle and a Star Hidden by Jupiter, Sky and Telescope, 92; Defining a Higher Education: the Curriculum Question, Edwin Mellen, 90. **CONTACT ADDRESS** Dept of Philosophy, Knoxville, TN, 37996.

COHEN, STEPHEN MARSHALL
PERSONAL Born 09/27/1929, New York, NY, m, 1964, 2 children **DISCIPLINE** PHILOSOPHY **EDUCATION** Dartmouth Col, BA, 51; Harvard Univ, MA, 53; Oxford Univ, MA, 77. **CAREER** Asst prof philos, Harvard Univ, 58-62; asst prof and assoc prof, Univ Chicago, 62-67; assoc prof Rockefeller Univ, 67-70; prof philos CUNY, 70-83, exec officer prog in philos Grad Ctr, 75-83; prof philos and law, 83-97, dean div hum, 83-94, interim dean Col Lett Arts & Sci, 93-94, Univ S Calif, now Prof Emer Philos & Law, and Dean Emer Col of Lett, Arts & Sci. **HONORS AND AWARDS** Vis fel All Souls Col, Oxford, 76-77; mem Inst for Advanced Study, Princeton, 81-82. **RESEARCH** Moral, legal and political philosophy; aesthetics. **SELECTED PUBLICATIONS** Ed, The Philosophy of John Stuart Mill, 61; ed, Philosophy and Public Affairs, 70- ; ed, Philosophy and Society series, 77-83; ed, Ethical, Legal and Political Philosophy series, 83- ; co-ed, Film Theory and Criticism, 74, 79, 85, 92, 98; auth, War and Moral Responsibility, 74; auth, The Rights and Wrongs of Abortion, 74; auth, Equality and Preferential Treatment, 77. **CONTACT ADDRESS** Law School, Univ of Southern California, Los Angeles, CA, 90089-0071. **EMAIL** mcohen@law.usc.edu

COHEN, TED
PERSONAL Born 12/13/1939, Danville, IL, m, 1994, 2 children **DISCIPLINE** PHILOSOPHY **EDUCATION** Univ Chicago, AB, 62; Harvard Univ, MA, 65, PhD(philos), 72. **CAREER** From asst prof to assoc prof, 67-79, Prof Philos, Univ Chicago, 79-, Chmn Dept, 74-79, mem Comt on the Visual Arts and Comt on General Studies in the Humanities; William R. Kenan Jr Distinguished Prof in the Humanities, Col William and Mary, 86-87. **HONORS AND AWARDS** ACLS travel grants, 80, 85; Ill Philos Asn Keynote Address, 80; Quantrell Award for Excellence in Undergraduate Teaching, 83; Pushcart XVI prize, 91. **MEMBERSHIPS** Am Philos Asn; Am Soc Aesthetics (pres, 97-99). **RESEARCH** Philosophy of art; 18th century aesthetics; philosophy of language. **SELECTED PUBLICATIONS** Co-ed and contribr, Essays in Kant's Aesthetics, Univ Chicago Press, 82; auth, Jokes, In: Pleasure, Preference, and Value: Studies in Philosophical Aesthetics, Cambridge Univ Press, 83; Sports and Art: Beginning Questions, In: Human Agency, Stanford univ Press, 88; Representation: Pictorial and Photographic, In: International Encyclopedia of Communications, Oxford Univ Press, 89; co-ed and contribr, Pursuits of Reason: Essays in Honor of Stanley Cavell, Texas Tech Univ Press, 93; auth, The Relation of Pleasure to Judgement in Kant's Aesthetics, In: Kant and Critique: New Essays in Honor of W.H. Werkmeister, Kluwer Acad Publ, 93; Partial Enchantments of the Quixote Story in Hume's Essay on Taste, In: Institutions of Art: Reconsiderations of George Dickie's Philosophy, Penn State Univ Press, 94; On Consistency in One's Personal Aesthetics, In: Aesthetics and Ethics: Essays at the Intersection, Cambridge Univ Press, 98; author of numerous journal articles. **CONTACT ADDRESS** Dept of Philos, Univ of Chicago, 1050 E 59th St, Chicago, IL, 60637-1512. **EMAIL** tedcohen@midway.uchicago.edu

COHN, SHERMAN LOUIS
PERSONAL Born 07/21/1932, Erie, PA, m, 1998, 5 children **DISCIPLINE** LAW **EDUCATION** Georgetown Univ, BSFS, 54, JD, 57, LLM, 60. **CAREER** Law clerk, US Circuit Court of Appeals, DC, 57-58; staff atty, Appellate sect, civil div, US Dept Justice, 58-62, asst chief, 62-65; Prof Law, Georgetown Univ, 65-, Staff dir, Found Fed Bar Asn, 58-61; nat chmn comt younger lawyers, Fed Bar Asn, 62-63, comt uniform rules fed appellate procedure, 63-70, nat coun, 63-66, 68-70 & 72-74, chmn comt fed rules & pract, 64-66 & 68-69, coun fed courts, 68-69; assoc mem, Inst World Policy, Georgetown Univ, 62-, co-dir, Inst Law, Human Rights & Social Values, 66-73; chmn, Coun Community Affairs, 64-66; mem standing comt civil legal aid, Judicial Conf, 64-68, mem conf, 65-73; secy spec comt on adv comt rules & practice, Judicial Coun DC Circuit, 66-67; Washington dir, Practicing Law Inst, 66-68; mem civil rules comt, DC Judicial Conf, 68-73, DC Superior Court, 71-73; vis prof, Am Univ Law Sch, 69-78, 92-93, 94-95. **HONORS AND AWARDS** Younger Fed Lawyer Award, 64; 1978 Presidential Citation, 1980 John Carroll Award, 1984 Univ Recognition Award for Outstanding Fac, Georgetown Univ Alumni Asn; Honorary Diplomat, Am Bd Trial Advocates, 90; Hon M Ac, Traditional Acupuncture Inst, 93; Civil Justice Award, 93. **MEMBERSHIPS** Am Law Inst; Am Bar Asn; Fed Bar Asn; Am Inns of Court Found (pres 85-96); Nat Acad of Acupuncture & Oriental Med; Nat Acupuncture Found; Tai Hsuan Found; Traditional Acupuncture Inst. **RESEARCH** Constitutional law; civil procedure; conflicts. **SELECTED PUBLICATIONS** Auth, Overview of Acupuncture in America, 1971-1993: A Historical Perspective, In: The Oriental Medicine Resources Guide, 93; monthly article on federal practice and procedure, Fed Practice Digest, Barclays Legal Publ, 93-96; Privilege or Coverup?, Nat Law J, 3/97; A Perspective on Progress, Washington Lawyer, 4/97; Professionalism & the Trial Advocate, Voir Dire, Spring 96; The Organizational Client: Attorney-Client Privilege and the No-Contact Rule, Georgetown J of Legal Ethics 10, 97; author of numerous other articles, books, and reviews. **CONTACT ADDRESS** Law Ctr, Georgetown Univ, 600 New Jersey N W, Washington, DC, 20001-2022. **EMAIL** cohn@law.georgetown.edu

COHN, STUART R.
DISCIPLINE LAW **EDUCATION** Univ Ill, BA; Oxford Univ, BA; Yale Univ, LLB. **CAREER** Prof, Univ Fla, 77-. **MEMBERSHIPS** Amer Bar Asn Fed Regulation Securities Comm, 80-; Drafting comm for revisions to Fla corporate laws securities laws; Ill Bar; Phi Beta Kappa; Phi Kappa Phi. **RESEARCH** Corporate & securities law, jurisprudence. **CONTACT ADDRESS** School of Law, Univ of Florida, PO Box 117625, Gainesville, FL, 32611-7625. **EMAIL** cohn@law.ufl.edu

COHON, RACHEL
DISCIPLINE PHILOSOPHY **EDUCATION** UCLA, PhD. **CAREER** Asst prof, Univ Albany, State Univ NY. **RESEARCH** Ethics, philosophy of action, history of ethics. **SELECTED PUBLICATIONS** Auth, The Common Point of View in Hume's Ethics, Philos and Phenomenological Res, 97; Internalism about Reasons for Action, Pacific Philos Quart, 93. **CONTACT ADDRESS** Dept of Philosophy, Univ at Albany, SUNY, Albany, NY, 12222. **EMAIL** rcohon@cnsunix.albany.edu

COLE, KENNETH
DISCIPLINE LAW **EDUCATION** Osgoode Hall Law Sch, LLB, 74. **CAREER** Partner, Epstein, Cole **MEMBERSHIPS** Law Soc Upper Can. **SELECTED PUBLICATIONS** Auth, pubs on family law, enforcement of support orders, and procedural issues. **CONTACT ADDRESS** Fac of Law, Univ Toronto, 78 Queen's Park, Toronto, ON.

COLE, RICHARD
PERSONAL Born 10/28/1929, Evanston, IL, m, 1958, 3 children **DISCIPLINE** PHILOSOPHY **EDUCATION** Univ TX, BA, 58; Univ Chicago, PhD, 62. **CAREER** Instr philos, CO

Col, 61-62; asst prof, Grinnell Col, 62-65; assoc prof, 65-69, Prof Philos, Univ KS, 69, Res Grants, Univ KS, 74, 75, 76, 77 & 78; referee, NOUS, 77- **MEMBERSHIPS** Philos Sci Asn; Am Philos Asn; Mind Asn; Southwestern Philos Soc(pres, 77-78); Metaphys Soc Am. **RESEARCH** Philos of physical sci; philos of mathematics; logic. **SELECTED PUBLICATIONS** Auth, Ptolemy and Copernicus, Philos Rev, 10/62; Falsifiability, Mind, 1/68; Appearnance, reality and falsification, Int Philos Quart, 6/68; coauth, Concept of Order, Univ Wash, 68; Hard and soft intensionalism, 70 & auth, Causality and sufficient reason, 74, Rev Metaphysics; Causes and explanations, NOUS, 77; Possibility matrices, Theoria, 78. **CONTACT ADDRESS** Dept of Philos, Univ of Kansas, Lawrence, KS, 66045-0001. **EMAIL** nobledog@aol.com

COLEMAN, ARTHUR H.
PERSONAL Born 02/18/1920, Philadelphia, PA, m, 1987 **DISCIPLINE** LAW **EDUCATION** PA State U, BS 1941; Howard U, MD 1944; Golden Gate Coll, LlB 1956; Golden Gate Coll, JD 1968. **CAREER** Medicine, pvt practice 1948-; San Francisco Med Assoc, pres. **HONORS AND AWARDS** Bay Area Howard Univ Alumni Award 1966; SF Bay Area Council Certificate 1965-67; SF bd of supres Certificate of Award 1968; SF Dept of Health Commendation 1976; Omega Psi Phi Award for Distingushed Serv 1973; numerous articles and other publications; Distinguished Alumnus, Penn State Univ 1977. **MEMBERSHIPS** Bd dir Sec Drew Inv Corp 1952; pres co-founder Amer Health Care Plan 1973; bd dir Fidelity Savings & Loan Assn 1966; co-founder pres SF Med Assn Inc; exec dir Hunters Point Baypoint Comm Health Serv 1968-72; chmn SF Econ Opportunity Council 1964-67; pres chmn of bd Trans-Bay Fed Savings & Loan Assn 1964-66; guest lectr Golden Gate Coll of Law 1958-60; lectr Univ CA 1968; mem Pathway Comm for Family Med Univ CA Med Ctr 1970; internship Homer G Phillips Hosp 1945; mem AMA 1948; mem CA Med Assn 1948; mem SF Med Soc 1948-; pres Natl Med Assn 1976-77; pres John Hale Med Soc 1970-71; fellow Amer Acad of Forensic Sci 1958; fellow bd of govs Amer Coll of Legal Med 1961; pres Northern California Med Dental Pharm Assn 1964; pres bd Dir Golden State Med Assn 1970-74; memWorld Med Assn 1971-; mem Acad of Med 1971; coord com SF Alliance for Health Care; vice pres Amer Cancer Soc 1969-71; bd of dir SF Hunters Point Boys Club; bd dir adv council SF Planning & Ren Assn 1969-75; pres Amer Coll of Legal Medicine 1983-84; vice pres bd of dir Drew Medical Univ 1987; pres Port of San Francisco 1984-87. **CONTACT ADDRESS** San Francisco Medical Assoc, 6301 Third St, San Francisco, CA, 94124.

COLEMAN, JOHN ALOYSIUS
PERSONAL Born 03/27/1937, San Francisco, CA **DISCIPLINE** SOCIOLOGY OF RELIGION **EDUCATION** St Louis Univ, BA, 60, MA, 61; Univ Santa Clara, STM, 68; Univ Calif, Berkeley, PhD(sociol), 74. **CAREER** Asst prof relig & soc, Jesuit Sch Theol & Grad Theol Union, Berkeley, 74-77; res fel, Woodstock Ctr, Georgetown Univ, 77-78; ASST PROF RELIG & SOC, JESUIT SCH THEOL & GRAD THEOL UNION, BERKELY, 78-, Fel social ethics, Univ Chicago Divinity Sch, 73-74. **MEMBERSHIPS** Cath Theol Soc Am; Am Acad Relig; Am Soc Christian Ethics. **RESEARCH** Sociology of comparative Catholicism; history of social Catholicism; human rights. **SELECTED PUBLICATIONS** Auth, On Being the Church in the United-States--Contemporary Theological Critiques of Liberalism, Theol Stud, Vol 0057, 96; Religion and Politics in Latin-America--Liberation-Theology and Christian Democracy, Jour Rel, Vol 0073, 93; Pious Passion--The Emergence of Modern Fundamentalism in the United-States And Iran--Comparative-Studies in Religion and Society, Theol Stud, Vol 0055, 94; Sociology and Social-Justice--The Case-Study of Fichter, Joseph Sj Research, Sociol Rel, Vol 0057, 96. **CONTACT ADDRESS** Graduate Theol Union, 2465 Le Compte Ave, Berkeley, CA, 94709.

COLLIER, CHARLES W.
DISCIPLINE LAW **EDUCATION** Reed Col, BA; Yale Univ, MA, MPhil, PhD; Stanford Univ, JD. **CAREER** Prof, aff prof, Univ Fla, 86-. **MEMBERSHIPS** Law and Soc Asn; Amer Philos Asn. **RESEARCH** Constitutional law, jurisprudence, legal theory. **CONTACT ADDRESS** School of Law, Univ of Florida, PO Box 117625, Gainesville, FL, 32611-7625. **EMAIL** Reid@law.ufl.edu

COLLINGE, WILLIAM JOSEPH
PERSONAL Born 07/14/1947, Erie, PA, m, 1972, 3 children **DISCIPLINE** RELIGION **EDUCATION** Georgetown Univ, AB, 69; Yale Univ, MPhil, 71, PhD(Philos), 74. **CAREER** Asst prof Philos, Loyola Marymount Univ, 74-80; assoc prof Theol & chmn dept, Mt St Marys Col (MD), 80-89; actg chmn Philos Dept, Loyola Marymount Univ, 78-79; prof of Theology and Philosophy, Mt St Mary's Col, MD, 89. **MEMBERSHIPS** Am Philos Asn; Soc Medieval & Renaissance Philos; Col Theol Soc; Cath Theol Soc Am. **RESEARCH** Philosophy of religion; ancient and medieval Christian thought. **SELECTED PUBLICATIONS** Auth, Peter Maurin and the green revolution, Metanoia, 76, Cath Agitator, 76 & Cath Worker, 77; Structures and the science of man in Claude Levi-Strauss, Spring 77 & Hospitality and required philosophy courses, Spring 78, Metanoia; De Trinitate and the understanding of religious language, Augustinian Studies (in press); Augustine and theological falsification, Augustinian Studies, 82; Saint Augustine, Four Anti-Pelagian Writings, with John A Mourant, DC: Catholic University of American Press, 92; Historical Dictionary of Catholicism; MD: Scarecrow, 97. **CONTACT ADDRESS** Dept Theol, Mount Saint Mary's Col, 16300 Old Emmitsburg Rd, Emmitsburg, MD, 21727-7700.

COLLINS, ARDIS B.
DISCIPLINE PHILOSOPHY **EDUCATION** Univ Toronto, PhD, 68; **CAREER** Assoc prof, Loyola Univ Chicago, 68-; dir, undergrad majors & graduate Philos; philos rep, Acad Coun Col Arts & Sci(s); PhD coun rep, Graduate Stud Coord Bd; 4 terms dir, 2 counr, VP, organizer 92 conf & treas, Exec Coun Hegel Soc Am; fac, St. Mary's Col, Notre Dame, Ind, 66-68; ed consult, Hist Philos Quart; ed in chief, Owl of Minerva, jour the Hegel Soc Am, 96. **RESEARCH** Medieval and renaissance philosophy; modern philosophy, especially Kant and Hegel; metaphysics. **SELECTED PUBLICATIONS** Auth, The Secular Is Sacred: Platonism and Thomism in Marsilio Ficino's Platonic Theology, Martinus Nijhoff, 74; Ed, Hegel on the Modern World, SUNY Press, 95; articles in, J Hist Philos, Method and Speculation in Hegel's Phenomenology-Humanities Press, 82, Hegel and His Critics-SUNY Press, 89, Cardozo Law Rev, Am Catholic Philos Quart. **CONTACT ADDRESS** Dept of Philosophy, Loyola Univ, Chicago, 820 N. Michigan Ave., Chicago, IL, 60611.

COLLINS, DAISY G.
PERSONAL Born 02/05/1937, Butler, AL, d **DISCIPLINE** LAW **EDUCATION** OH State Univ, Acct major, 1955-58, BS Business Admin (cum laude) 1958; Howard Univ Sch of Law, JD (cum laude) 1970. **CAREER** Mgt trainee, Commonwealth Edison Co, Chicago, 1958-60; acct, City of Detroit, 1960-64; General Foods Corp, White Plains, cost & budget anal, 1964-66; Student asst to asst legal advisor, US State Dept, African Affairs, 1969; N MS Rural Legal Serv Greenwood, staff atty, 1970-71; OH Turnpike Comm, asst gen cnsl & stflwyr, 1973-74; No Dist of OH, asst us atty, 1975-77; Capital Univ Law School, vis assc prof of law, 1981-82; Equal Opportunity Commn Cleveland Dist Office, administrative judge, 1986-90; administrative law judge, Office of Hearings & Appeals, Social Security Administration, 1990-94; part-time instructor, Business Law & Acct, Cleveland State Univ & Cuy CC. **HONORS AND AWARDS** Hon Mention, Cleveland Federal Exec Bd for Community Service, 1976; Cleveland Bar Assn Meritorious Serv Awards, 1972-73; Six Am Jurisprudence Awds for Exc Achievement; Appreciation Award Law Beta Gamma Sigma Natl Comr Hon 1956; Beta Alpha Psi; Phi Chi Theta Scholarship Key Most Outstanding Grad Woman Coll C & Admin. **MEMBERSHIPS** exec sec Cleveland Branch NAACP 1979-80; Alpha Kappa Alpha Sor, life mem, NAACP. **SELECTED PUBLICATIONS** Articles in Howard Law Journal & Crnt Bibliography of African Affairs; HLJ Notes Editor.

COLLINS, JOHN J.
PERSONAL Born 02/02/1966, Ireland, m, 1973, 3 children **DISCIPLINE** BIBLICAL STUDIES **EDUCATION** Harvard, PhD, 72. **CAREER** Assoc Prof, Munde Lein Sem, 76-78; Assoc Prof, Prof, DePaul, 78-86; Prof, Notre Dame, 86-91; Prof, Univ Chi, 91-. **HONORS AND AWARDS** NEH Fel, 87-88; Exec Com, Soc of Bibl Lit, 89-94; Pres, Cath Bibl Assn, 97. **MEMBERSHIPS** Soc of Bibl Lit; Catholic Bibl Asn **RESEARCH** Apocalypticism; wisdom; dead sea scrolls. **SELECTED PUBLICATIONS** Auth, The Scepter and the Star. The Messiahs of the Dead Sea Scrolls and Other Ancient Literature, Dbl Day, 95; auth, Isaia, Brescia:Q, 95; coauth, Qumran Cave 4.XVII. Parabliblical Tests, Part 3, 96; coauth, Families in Ancient Israel, Westmin, 97; Apolcalypticism in the Dead Sea Scrolls, Routledge, 97; auth, Seers, Sibyls and Sages in Hellenistic-Roman Judaism, Brill, 97; auth, Jewish Wisdom in the Hellenistic Age, Old Test Lib, Westmin, 97; auth, The Apolcalyptic Imagination, Eerdmans, 98; co-ed, The Encyclopedia of Apocalypticism, Cont, 98. **CONTACT ADDRESS** 1019 Brassie, Flossmoor, IL, 60422. **EMAIL** jj.collins@uchicago.edu

COLLINS, KENNETH L.
PERSONAL Born 08/23/1933, El Centro, CA, m **DISCIPLINE** LAW **EDUCATION** UCLA, BA 1959; UCLA, JD 1971. **CAREER** LA Co, probation ofcr 1957-68; San Fernando Valley Juvenile Hall, acting dir; Fed Pub Defenders Office, pub defender 1972-75. **HONORS AND AWARDS** UCLA Chancelors Award 1971. **MEMBERSHIPS** Mem Langston Law Club; CA Attys for Criminal Justice; CA State Bar; chmn bd dir Black Law Journal; past pres Kappa Alpha Psi Upsion 1957-58; cofounderBlack Law Journal; distinguished serv. **CONTACT ADDRESS** 3701 Wilshire Blvd, Ste 700, Los Angeles, CA, 90010.

COLLINS, MARY
PERSONAL Born 09/16/1935, Chicago, IL **DISCIPLINE** RELIGIOUS STUDIES **EDUCATION** Mt St Scholastica Col, AB, 57; Cath Univ Am, PhD(relig studies), 67. **CAREER** Asst prof Relig & chmn dept, Mt St Scholastica Col, 67-70, assoc prof, 70-77; vis prof, Kans Sch Relig, Univ Kans, 69-72, vis lectr, 72-73, assoc prof, 73-78; prof Relig, Cath Univ Am, 78-, chmn dept Relig Studies, Benedictine Col, 71-72; mem, Kans Comt Humanities, 72-75; mem, Am Benedictine Acad. **HONORS AND AWARDS** Berakah Award, North Am Acad of Liturgy; Michael Mathis Award, Notre Dame Center for Pastoral Liturgy. **MEMBERSHIPS** Col Theol Soc; Am Acad Relig; NAm Acad Liturgy; Catholic Theological Society of America. **RESEARCH** Worship and ritual; contemporary religious thought; ritual and society. **SELECTED PUBLICATIONS** Auth, Eucharistic proclamation of God's presence, Worship, 11/67; Local liturgical legislation: United States, Concilium, 2/72; Taking peace education seriously, Living Light, Summer 73; Liturgy in America: The Scottsdale conference, 2/74, Liturgical methodology and the cultural evolution of worship in the United States, 2/75 & Ritual symbols and the ritual process: the work of Victor Turner, 7/76, Worship; Response to Charles David's religion and the Sense of the Sacred, Pro Cath Theol Soc Am, 12/76; contribr, Climb Along the Cutting Edge: The Renewal of Religious Life, Paulist, 77. **CONTACT ADDRESS** Catholic Univ of America, 620 Michigan Ave N E, Washington, DC, 20064-0002. **EMAIL** collinsm@cua.edu

COLLINS, ROBERT H.
PERSONAL Born 07/10/1934, Chicago, IL **DISCIPLINE** THEOLOGY **EDUCATION** Wilson Jr Clg Chicago IL, AA 1954; Michael Resse Sch of Med Tech, MT 1955; Roosevelt Univ Chicago IL, BS 1957; Concordia Theology Smnry Springfield, IL,BD 1964, MDiv 1965; Concordia Smnry St Louis, Master of Sacred Theology 1974. **CAREER** Univ of IL R&E Hospital, medical tech 1955-56; Northwestern Univ, research chemist 1956; Lab of Vit Tech, chem quality control 1957-59; Concordia Seminary, Springfield IL, 1959-63; Bethlehem Lutheran Church, Col GA, pastor 1963-73; St James Lutheran Church, Bakersfield CA, pastor 1973-77; Northern IL Dist LC-MS, missionary-at-large; Corcordia Theological Seminary, Ft Wayne IN, prof of prctl theology counseling 1977-85. **HONORS AND AWARDS** Meritorious Serv City of Col GA 1971, 72-73; Cert of Aprctn Pres Nixon GA State Advsr Com on Edc 1972; Cert of Aprctn TB Assc, Legal Aid Soc, Sr Citizens; mem Bd of Dir 1972-73. **MEMBERSHIPS** Mem Scan 1982-; vacancy pstr Shepherd of the City Luth Ft Wayne 1983-; mem Resolve; vol chpln Parkview Meml Hosp Ft Wayne, IN; part-time chpln Cnty Jail; vacancy pastor Mount Calvary Luth Church; consultant cross-cultural ministry Trinity Luth Church. **CONTACT ADDRESS** Counseling/Evng, Concordia Theol Sem, 6600 N Clinton, Fort Wayne, IN, 46825.

COLOMBO, JOHN D.
DISCIPLINE LAW **EDUCATION** Univ Ill, AB; JD. **CAREER** Law clerk, Judge Phyllis Kravitch, US Court Appeals; prof, Univ Ill Urbana Champaign. **HONORS AND AWARDS** Ed, Univ Ill Law Rev. **RESEARCH** Tax issues relating to tax-exempt organizations. **SELECTED PUBLICATIONS** Co-auth, The Charitable Tax Exemption, Westview, 95. **CONTACT ADDRESS** Law Dept, Univ Ill Urbana-Champaign., 52 E Gregory Dr, Champaign, IL, 61820. **EMAIL** jcolombo@law.uiuc.edu

COLSON, DARREL D.
DISCIPLINE PHILOSOPHY **EDUCATION** Louisiana State Univ, BA, 77; Vanderbilt Univ, MA, 82, PhD, 87. **CAREER** Instr, Western Carolina Univ, 82-87; assoc prof, Louisiana Scholars Col at Northwestern State Univ, 87-96; Fletcher Jones prof of Great Books, Pepperdine Univ, 96-. **MEMBERSHIPS** APA; Southern Soc for Philos and Psych; Soc for Ancient Greek Philos; Hume Soc; Asn for Core Texts and Courses. **RESEARCH** Plato's Socratic Dialogues. **SELECTED PUBLICATIONS** Auth, Crito 51A-C: To What Does Socrates Owe Obedience? Phronesis, 89; auth, rev of Pangle, ed, The Rebirth of Political Rationalism: An Introduction to the Thought of Leo Strauss: Essays and Lectures by Leo Strauss, Ancient Philos, 91; auth, rev of Arieti, Interpreting Plato: The Dialogues as Drama, Tchg Philos, 93; co-ed, Senior Thesis Bulletin: Abstracts and Selected Excerpts from Honors Theses, 1990-1993, Northwestern State, 96. **CONTACT ADDRESS** Humanities and Teacher Education Div, Pepperdine Univ, 24255 Pacific Coast Hwy, Malibu, CA, 90263-4225. **EMAIL** dcolson@pepperdine.edu

COLVIN, CHRISTOPHER
PERSONAL Born 05/26/1954, Salzburg, Austria, m, 1995 **DISCIPLINE** PHILOSOPHY **EDUCATION** Yale Univ, BA, 76; Northwestern Univ, MA, 80, MA, 81; Univ Texas-Austin, PhD, 87. **CAREER** Vis asst prof, Bowdoin Col, 87-88; vis asst prof, Univ Dallas, 88-91; instr, Univ Texas-Austin, 91-92 & 93-94; vis asst prof, Southwestern Univ, 92-93; vis instr, Vytautes Maguus Univ (Lithuania), 94-95. **RESEARCH** Plato; Idealist metaphysics; Greek mathematics. **SELECTED PUBLICATIONS** Transl Fichte Schlegel und der Infinitismus in der Platondeutuns, Grad Jour Philos. **CONTACT ADDRESS** St Stephens Episcopal School, PO Box 1868, Austin, TX, 78767. **EMAIL** ccolvin@sss.austin.tx.us

COLWELL, CHAUNCEY
PERSONAL Born 10/28/1954, Bryn Mawr, PA, s **DISCIPLINE** PHILOSOPHY **EDUCATION** Lebanon Valley Col, BS, 78; Villanova Univ, MA, 82; Temple Univ, PhD, 92. **CAREER** Adj prof Philosophy, 88-96, vis asst prof, 96-, Villanova

Univ, 88-. **MEMBERSHIPS** Amer Philos Asn; Soc Phenomenol & Existential Philos; Int Asn Philos & Lit. **RESEARCH** 20th Century Continental Philosophy; Philosophy of the Bio-Sciences; Social/Political Philosophy. **SELECTED PUBLICATIONS** Auth, Signs of War: Myth, Media and the Selling of Desert Storm, Jour Peace & Justice Studies, 93; The Retreat of the Subject in the Late Foucault, Philos Today, 94; Typology, Racism and The Bell Curve, Jour Peace & Justice Studies, 95; Postmodernism and Medicine: Discourse and the Limits of Practice, Conttinental and Postmodern Perspectives in the Philosophy of Science, Avebury Press, 95; Discourses of Liberation and Discourses of Transformation, Liberalism, Oppression and Empowerment, Edwin Mellen Press, 95; Deleuze, Sense and the Event of AIDS, Postmodern Culture, 96; The Virtual Body of Medicine, International Studies in Philosophy, 96; Discipline and Control: Butler and Deleuze on Individuality and Dividuality, Philosophy Today, 96; Deleuze and Foucault: Series, Event, Genealogy, Theory and Event, 97; Deleuze and the Prepersonal, Philosophy Today, 97. **CONTACT ADDRESS** Philosophy Dept, Villanova Univ, Villanova, PA, 19085. **EMAIL** ccolwell@email.vill.edu

COLYER, ELMER M.
PERSONAL Born 04/07/1950, Ludington, MI, m, 1980, 3 children **DISCIPLINE** THEOLOGY **EDUCATION** Univ Wisc, Platteville, BS, 81; Univ Dubuque Theol Sem, MDiv, 85; Boston Col, Andover Newton, PhD, 92. **CAREER** Min, New Hope/Retreat UM Churches, Desoto, Wisc, 81-88; tchg asst, Boston Col, 90-91; scholar in residence, Carter UM Church, Needham, Mass, 88-92; assoc prof of Historical Theology, Stanley Chair of Wesley Stud, Univ Dubuque Theol Sem, 93- . **HONORS AND AWARDS** Loetscher traveling fel, 84; John Wesley fel, 88-92; Bradley fel, 91-92; CHARIS Award, Univ Dubuque, 96, 98. **RESEARCH** Modern theology; Wesleyan theology; theological method. **SELECTED PUBLICATIONS** Auth, Thomas F Torrance, in Musser, ed, A New Handbook of Christian Theologians, Abingdon, 96; auth, A Theology of Word and Spirit: Donald Bloesch's Theological Method, J for Chr Theol Res, 96; auth, rev of Luther's Theology of the Cross, by Alister, Relig Stud Rev, 96; auth, rev of God the Almighty, by Bloesch, Reformation & Revival J, 97; auth, rev of The Christian Doctrine of God, by Torrance, Relig Stud Rev, 97; auth, rev of The Christian Doctrine of God, by Torrance, Scottish J of Theol, 97; auth, rev of Reasoning and Rhetoric in Religion, by Murphy, Tchg Theol and Relig, forthcoming; auth, rev of Worship, Community & the Triune God, by Torrance, Relig Stud Rev, forthcoming; auth, rev of The Cambridge Companion to Christian Doctrine, ed, Gunton, Chr Today, forthcoming; auth, Evangelical Theology in Transition: Theologians in Dialog with Donal Bloesch, InterVarsity, 99. **CONTACT ADDRESS** Univ Dubuque Theological Sem, 2000 Univ Ave, Dubuque, IA, 52001. **EMAIL** ecolyer@dbq.edu

COMBES, RICHARD E.
PERSONAL Born 04/15/1954, Pittsfield, MA, m, 1992, 3 children **DISCIPLINE** PHILOSOPHY **EDUCATION** Eisenhower Col, BA, 76; Univ Iowa, PhD, 85. **CAREER** Vis asst prof, Iowa State Univ, 86-91; asst prof, 91-94, assoc prof, 94- , Univ South Carolina, Spartansburg. **HONORS AND AWARDS** Nations Bank Excellence in Tchg and Advising Award, 97. **MEMBERSHIPS** APA; South Carolina Soc for Philos. **RESEARCH** Philosophy of mind; history of modern philosophy; ethics; philosophy of technology. **CONTACT ADDRESS** 168 Timberlake Dr, Inman, SC, 29349. **EMAIL** rcombes@gw.uscs.edu

COMFORT, PHILIP W.
PERSONAL Born 10/28/1950, Pittsburgh, PA, m, 1971, 3 children **DISCIPLINE** NEW TESTAMENT **EDUCATION** Ohio State Univ, MA, 78; Fairfax, PhD, 89; Univ South Africa, DPhil, 97. **CAREER** Adj prof. NT & Greek, Wheaton College and presently, Trinity Seminary; Sr Editor, Bible ref, 15 yrs, Tyndale House Pub. **MEMBERSHIPS** SBL **RESEARCH** New Testament Manuscripts. **SELECTED PUBLICATIONS** Auth, Early Manuscripts and Modern Translations of the New Testament, Tyndale, 91, 2nd edition, Baker, 96; The Complete Texts of the Earliest New Testaments Manuscripts, Baker, 98; The Complete Guide to Bible Versions, Tyndale, 92, 2nd edition 97; I am The Way, Baker, 94; coauth, Opening the Gospel of John, Tyndale, 94; The Quest for the Original Text of the New Testament, Baker, 92. **CONTACT ADDRESS** 307 Hagley Rd, Pawleys Island, SC, 29585. **EMAIL** pc@tyndale.com

COMPIER, DON H.
DISCIPLINE THEOLOGY **EDUCATION** Univ Pacific, BA; Park Col, MA; Emory Univ, PhD. **CAREER** Assoc prof, Church Divinity Sch Pacific. **SELECTED PUBLICATIONS** Auth, Theological Themes, Lectionary Homiletics, 97; The Holocaust, Postmodernism, and Public Theology, History of European Ideas: Proc 1996 ISSEI Conf, MIT Press, 97; Hooker on the Authority of Scripture in Matters of Morality, The Interpreted Establishment: Richard Hooker and the Construction of Christian Community, Medieval and Renaissance Texts and Stud, 97; Problematizing Diakonia, Theol, Vol 3: Revisioning the Church, Graceland/Park Col Press, 95; The Incomplete Recovery of Rhetorical Theology, Dialog, 95; The Eucharist and World Hunger, Anglican Theol Rev, 91. **CONTACT ADDRESS** Church Divinity Sch of the Pacific, 2451 Ridge Rd, Berkeley, CA, 94709-1217.

COMPTON, JOHN J.
PERSONAL Born 05/17/1928, Chicago, IL, m, 1950, 3 children **DISCIPLINE** PHILOSOPHY **EDUCATION** College of Wooster, BA, 49; Yale Univ, MA, 51, PhD, 53. **CAREER** Asst prof, 52-55, assoc prof, 55-68, prof, philos, 68-98, prof emer, 98- , chemn, 67-73, 94-95, Vanderbilt Univ; vis prof philos, Colorado Col, 77; vis prof philos, Wesleyan Univ, 84. **HONORS AND AWARDS** Phi Beta Kappa; Kent fel, 51; Belgian Am Educ Fund fel, 56-57; Danforth Found award for distinguished tchg, 66; vis fel, Princeton Univ, 68; sr fel NEH, 74-75; assoc fel, Ctr for Hum, Wesleyan Univ, 74-75; Distinguished Alumni Award, Wooster Col, 79; Alumni Prof Award of Vanderbilt Alumni Asn, 82; Distinguished Alumnus Award, Asheville Sch, 84; Distinguished Tchg Award, Peabody Col, 90. **MEMBERSHIPS** APA; AAAS; AAUP; Metaphysical Soc of Am; Soc for Phenomenology and Existential Philos; Philos of Sci Asn; Soc for Values in Higher Educ; Soc of Christian Philos. **RESEARCH** Metaphysics; philosophy of science; phenomenology; philosophy of mind; philosophy of nature. **SELECTED PUBLICATIONS** Auth, Science and God's Action in Nature, in Barbour, ed, Earth Might Be Fair: Essays in Religion, Ethics, and Ecology, Prentice-Hall, 72; auth, Death and the Philosophical Tradition, Soundings, 78; auth, Science, Anti-Science, and Human Values, Key Reporter, 78-79; auth, Reinventing the Philosophy of Nature, Rev of Metaphysics, 79; auth, Sartre, Merleau-Ponty, and Human Freedom, J of Philos, 82; auth, Phenomenology and the Philosophy of Nature, Man and World, 88; auth, Some Contributions of Existential Phenomenology to the Philosophy of Natural Science, Am Philos Q, 88; auth, Merleau-Ponty's Thesis of the Primacy of Perception and the Meaning of Scientific Objectivity, in Pietersma, ed, Merleau-Ponty: Critical Essays, Univ Press of America, 90. **CONTACT ADDRESS** 3708 Whitlane Ave, Nashville, TN, 37205. **EMAIL** jjcompton@aol.com

CONARD, ALFRED FLETCHER
PERSONAL Born 11/30/1911, Grinnell, IA, m, 1939, 2 children **DISCIPLINE** LAW **EDUCATION** Grinnell Col, AB, 32; LLD, 71; Univ Pa, LLB, 36; Columbia Univ, LLM, 39, JD, 42. **CAREER** Asst prof law, Univ Kans City, 39-42, acting dean law sch, 41-42; atty, Off Price Admin, 42-43 & Off Alien Property Custodian, 45-46; from assoc prof to prof law, Univ Ill, 46-54; PROF LAW, UNIV MICH, ANN ARBOR, 54-, Vis prof, Univ Mo, 38, Univ Calif, 47, Univ Tex, 52, Univ Colo, 57, Istanbul, Turkey, 58-59, Luxembourg, 58-59 & Mex, 63; mem assembly behav & soc sci, Nat Res Coun, 73- **RESEARCH** Enterprise organization; European company law; automobile accident compensation. **SELECTED PUBLICATIONS** Auth, A Treatise on the Law of Stock and Stockholders, as Applicable to Railroad, Banking, Insurance, Manufacturing, Commercial, Business, Turnpike, Bridge, Canal, and Other Private Corporations, Mich Law Rev, Vol 0093, 95; A Lovable Law Review, Jour Legal Edu, Vol 0044, 94. **CONTACT ADDRESS** Sch of Law, Univ of Mich, Ann Arbor, MI, 48104.

CONCANNON, JAMES M.
DISCIPLINE APPELLATE PROFACTICE, CIVIL PROFOCEDURE, AND EVIDENCE **EDUCATION** Univ KS, BS, 68, JD, 71. **CAREER** Res Atty, Kans Suprofeme Court; Vis prof, WA Univ Sch Law. **HONORS AND AWARDS** Dean,Law Sch; Prof. **SELECTED PUBLICATIONS** Sr contrib ed, Evidence in Am: The Federal Rules in the States. **CONTACT ADDRESS** Washburn Univ Topeka, 1700 SW College, Topeka, KS, 66621.

CONCES, RORY J.
PERSONAL Born 08/08/1954, East Chicago, IN, m, 1977, 3 children **DISCIPLINE** PHILOSOPHY **EDUCATION** Creighton Univ, BA, 76; DePaul Univ, MA, 80; Univ Missouri, Columbia, PhD, 91. **CAREER** Adj instr, Columbia Col, 85; adj instr, Moberly Area Jr Col, 90; lectr, philos, Creighton Univ, 94- ; lectr, vis asst prof, philos, Univ of Nebraska, 92- . **MEMBERSHIPS** APA; Phi Beta Delta; Central States Philos Asn; Soc for Social and Polit Philos. **RESEARCH** Ethics; social and political philosophy. **SELECTED PUBLICATIONS** Auth, Aesthetic Alienation and the Art of Modernity, Southwest Philos Rev, 94; auth, A Participatory Approach to the Teaching of Critical Reasoning, APA Newsl on Tchg Philos, 95; auth, The Semblance of Ideaologies and Scientific Theories and the Constitution of Facts, Rev J of Philos and Soc Sci, 96; coauth, Ethics and Sovereignty, Int Third World Stud J and and Rev, 96; auth, A Participatory Approach to the Teaching of Critical Reasoning, in Kasachkoff, ed, In the Socratic Tradition: Essays on Teaching Philosophy, Rowman & Littlefield, 97; auth, Contract, Trust, and Resistance in the Second Treatise, Locke Newsl, 97; auth, Blurred Visions: Philosophy, Science, and Ideology in a Troubled World, Peter Lang, 97; auth, Consensual Foundations and Resistance in Locke's Second Treatise, Theoria, 98. **CONTACT ADDRESS** Dept of Philosophy and Religion, Univ of Nebraska, Omaha, NE, 68182-0265. **EMAIL** rconces@cwis.unomaha.edu

CONDIT, RICHARD E.
DISCIPLINE ENVIRONMENTAL LAW **EDUCATION** NJ Inst Technol, BS, 80; Antioch Sch Law, JD, 86. **CAREER** Adja prof; past staff mem, US Env Protection Agency; past staff atty, Govt Accountability Proj, GAP & co-dir, GAP's EPA Watch Prog. **SELECTED PUBLICATIONS** Coauth, Citizens' Handbook on Env Rights. **CONTACT ADDRESS** School of Law, Univ of District of Columbia, 4200 Connecticut Ave Northwest, Washington, DC, 20008.

CONE, JAMES H.
PERSONAL Born 08/05/1938, Fordyce, AK, w, 1958, 4 children **DISCIPLINE** SYSTEMATIC THEOLOGY **EDUCATION** Philander Smith Col, BA, 58; Garrett Theol Sem, BD, 61; Northwestern Univ, MA, 63, PhD, 65. **CAREER** Asst prof philos & relig, Philander Smith Col, 64-66; asst prof relig, Adrian Col, 66-69; asst prof, 69-73, assoc prof, 70-73, prof, 73-77, prof of syst theol, 77-87, Briggs disting prof 87- , Union Theol Sem, NY. **HONORS AND AWARDS** Am Black Ach, Ebony mag, 94; Theolog Scholar and res Award fr Am Acad of relig. **MEMBERSHIPS** Am Acad Relig; Soc Study Black Relig; Ecumenical Assn Third World Theology. **RESEARCH** Relig; philos; hist. **SELECTED PUBLICATIONS** Auth, Black Theology ans Black Power; A Black Theology of Liberation; The Spirituals and the Blues: An Interpretation; God of the Oppressed; Black Theology: A Documentary History, 66-79; My Soul Looks Back; For My People; Speaking the Truth; Martin & Malcolm & America; Theology: A Documentary History, 80-92. **CONTACT ADDRESS** Dept of Theol, Union Theol Sem, 3061 Broadway, New York, NY, 10027-5710.

CONGDON, HOWARD KREBS
PERSONAL Born 12/13/1941, Syracuse, NY, m, 1973, 1 child **DISCIPLINE** PHILOSOPHY **EDUCATION** Syracuse Univ, AB, 63; Wesley Theol Sem, MDiv, 66; Purdue Univ, West Lafayette, MA, 68, PhD, 70. **CAREER** Minister, St George Island United Methodist Churches, 67-68; instr philos, Purdue Univ, 69-70; asst prof, 70-73, ASSOC PROF PHILOS, LOCK HAVEN STATE COL, 73-; Commonwealth teaching fel, 79-80. **HONORS AND AWARDS** Pa Cert Excellence in Teaching, 80. **MEMBERSHIPS** Am Philos Asn; AAUP. **RESEARCH** Philosophy of mind; significance of altered states of consciousness; philosophy of religion; philosophy of death. **SELECTED PUBLICATIONS** Auth, Drugs and religion, Lock Haven Rev, 72; Salzburg as a setting for academic studies, Acad Notes Intercult Affairs & Foreign Study, 72; The Pursuit of Death, Abingdon, 77; Abortion and the law, Philos Res & Anal, spring 78. **CONTACT ADDRESS** Dept of Philos, Lock Haven Univ, Pennsylvania, 401 N Fairview St, Lock Haven, PA, 17745-2390. **EMAIL** lcongdon@eagle.lhup.edu

CONGELTON, ANN
PERSONAL Born 08/26/1936, Dayton, OH, m, 1972, 2 children **DISCIPLINE** PHILOSOPHY **EDUCATION** Wellesley Col, BA (philos), 58; Yale Univ, PhD (philos), 62. **CAREER** Member of the Mechanical Translation Group of the Research Lab of Electronics, MIT, 62-64; asst prof to PROF, DEPT OF PHILOS, WELLESLEY COL, 64-. **MEMBERSHIPS** Amer Philos Assoc; Soc for Women in Philos. **RESEARCH** Plato; feminist theory. **CONTACT ADDRESS** Dept of Philos, Wellesley Col, Wellesley, MA, 02481.

CONKLIN, WILLIAM E.
DISCIPLINE JURISPRUDENCE; PHENOMENOLOGY; SEMIOTICS; CONSTITUTIONAL THEORY; POLITICAL PHILOSOPHY; ETHICS AND CIVIL LIBERTIES **EDUCATION** Univ Toronto, BA; London, MSc; Univ Toronto, LLB; Columbia, LLM; York, PhD. **CAREER** Prof; Osgoode Hall, Barrister-at-Law. **SELECTED PUBLICATIONS** Auth, In Defense of Fundamental Rights and Images of a Constitution, U of Toronto P, 93. **CONTACT ADDRESS** Col of Business Administration, Educ and Law, Univ of Windsor, 401 Sunset Ave, Windsor, ON, N9B 3P4. **EMAIL** wconkli@uwindsor.ca

CONLEY, CHARLES S.
PERSONAL Born 12/08/1921, Montgomery, AL, m, 1987 **DISCIPLINE** LAW **EDUCATION** Ala State Univ, BS, 1942; Univ of MI, AM, educ, 1947, AM, histroy, 1948; NY Univ, JD, 1955. **CAREER** FL A&M College of Law, prof, 1956-60; AL State U, 1962-64; Dr Martin Luther King SCLC, counsel; Recorder's CT, judge 1968-73; Macon County CT Common Pleas, 1972-, Macon County Attorney, 1986; Alabama District Court, judge, 1977. **MEMBERSHIPS** Am Nat AL Bar Assns. **CONTACT ADDRESS** 315 S Bainbridge St, Montgomery, AL, 36104.

CONLEY, J.
PERSONAL Born 11/25/1951, Philadelphia, PA **DISCIPLINE** PHILOSOPHY **EDUCATION** Univ Pa, BA, 73, Fordham Univ, MA, 77, Centre Sevres, Paris, Lth, 83; Cath Univ Louvain, PhD, 98. **CAREER** Instr, Wheeling Col, 77-79; assoc prof, Fordham Univ, 88- . **HONORS AND AWARDS** Reed Prize, 73; Pax Christi Award, 91., Phi Beta Kappa; Phi Sigma Tau; Alpha Sigma Nu. **MEMBERSHIPS** Amer Philos Assoc **RESEARCH** Ethics; aesthetics; French philos. **SELECTED PUBLICATIONS** Auth, Problems of Cooperation in an Abortive Culture, Life & Learning, 97; Narrative, Act, Structure: John Paul II's Method of Moral Analysis, Choosing Life: A Dialogue on Evangelium Vitae, Georgetown, 97; At the Origins of the Person, Homiletic & Pastoral Rev, 97; Identity and Recognition: Moral Problems concerning Student Organizations,

Proceedings of the Jesuit Philosophical Association, Barbar, 98; Natural Theology in an Anthropological Key, Josephinum Journal of Theology, 98. **CONTACT ADDRESS** Fordham Univ, Spellman Hall, Bronx, NY, 10458. **EMAIL** jconley@murray.fordham.edu

CONLEY, JOHN A.
PERSONAL Born 03/10/1928, Springfield, IL, m **DISCIPLINE** LAW **EDUCATION** Univ of Pgh, BS 1952, JD 1955, MSW 1961. **CAREER** Univ of Pittsburgh, prof 1969-; housing developer. **MEMBERSHIPS** Mem Hill House Assn 1955-69; Neighborhood Ctrs Assn 1963-65; Allegheny Co, PA Bar Assns; bd dirs Pgh Public Schs; Freedom House Enterprise Inc; chmn bd Neighborhood Rehab Inc **CONTACT ADDRESS** Dept of Social Work, Univ of Pittsburgh, 2201 C1, Pittsburgh, PA, 15260.

CONLEY, PATRICK THOMAS
PERSONAL Born 06/22/1938, New Haven, CT, m, 1962, 5 children **DISCIPLINE** AMERICAN HISTORY, CONSTITUTIONAL LAW **EDUCATION** Providence Col, AB, 59; Univ Notre Dame, MA, 61, PhD(hist), 70; Suffolk Univ, JD, 73. **CAREER** PROF HIST, PROVIDENCE COL, 63-, Spec asst to Congressman Robert O Tiernan, RI, 67-74; secy, RI Constitutional Convention, 73; chmn, RI Bicentennial Comn/Found, 74-; trustee, Bicentennial Coun of the 13 Original States, 77- **MEMBERSHIPS** AHA; Orgn Am Historians. **RESEARCH** Rhode Island history; American ethnic history; constitutional history. **SELECTED PUBLICATIONS** Auth, Brotherly Love--Murder and Politics of Prejudice in 19th-Century Rhode-Island, New Eng Quart-Hist Rev New Eng Life and Letters, Vol 0068, 95. **CONTACT ADDRESS** Dept of Hist, Providence Col, Providence, RI, 02918.

CONLON, JAMES J.
PERSONAL Born 09/30/1946, NJ **DISCIPLINE** PHILOSOPHY **EDUCATION** Marquette, PhD, 75. **CAREER** Mount Mary Col, prof, 74-. **SELECTED PUBLICATIONS** Auth, Why Lovers Can't Be Friends, in: Philosophical Perspective on Love and Sex, ed R. Stewart, Oxford Univ Press, 95; Silencing the Lambs and Educating Women, in: Post Script: Essays in Film and the Humanities, 92; Kansas, Oz and the Function of Art, Jour of Aesthetic Education, 90; Making Love, Not War: The Solder Male in Top Gun and Coming Home, Jour of Pop Film & TV, 90; The Place of Passion: Reflections on Fatal Attraction, Jour of Pop Film and TV, 89; Stanley Cavell and the Predicament of Philosophy, Proceedings of the American Catholic Philosophical Association, 83. **CONTACT ADDRESS** Dept of philosophy, Mount Mary Col, 2900 N Menomonee River Pkwy, Milwaukee, WI, 53222. **EMAIL** conlon@mtmary.edu

CONN, CHRISTOPHER
PERSONAL Born 08/18/1965, Livonia, MI, m, 1989, 2 children **DISCIPLINE** PHILOSOPHY **EDUCATION** Syracuse Univ, PhD, 96 **CAREER** Asst Prof, Univ of the South, present **RESEARCH** Metaphysics; epistemology; modern philosophy **CONTACT ADDRESS** Dept of Philosophy, Univ of the South, 735 University Ave., Sewanne, TN, 37383. **EMAIL** cconn@sewanne.edu

CONN, HARVIE MAITLAND
PERSONAL Born 04/07/1933, Regina, SK, Canada, m, 1956, 5 children **DISCIPLINE** MISSIOLOGY, COMPARATIVE RELIGIONS **EDUCATION** Calvin Col, AB, 54; Westminster Theol Sem, BD, 57, ThM, 58. **CAREER** Pastor, Orthodox Presby Church, 57-60, foreign missionary in Korea, 60-72; from Assoc Prof to Prof, 72-98, Prof Missions Emeritus, Westminster Theol Sem, 98-; Ed, Studies in World Church and Missions Series, Presby & Reformed Publ Co, 72-82; mem, Theol Working Group, Lausanne Comn for World Evangelization, 76-; mem of exec comnr, Comn for Theol Educ Reformed Ecumenical Synod, 76-; lectr, Ctr Urban Theol Studies, 81. **MEMBERSHIPS** Am Soc Missiol; Asn Prof Missions; Int asn Mission Studies; Evangelical Theol Soc; Asn Evangelical Prof Missions. **RESEARCH** Applied missionary anthropology; Christian encounter with living religions; history of Christianity in Korea. **SELECTED PUBLICATIONS** Auth, Contemporary World Theology, Presby & Reformed Publ, 73; Introduction to New Testament studies, Presby Theol Sem Publ Co, Korea, 76; ed, Theological Perspectives on Church Growth, 76 & contribr, Evangelicans and Liberation, 77, Presby & Reformed Publ Co; contribr, Discipling the City, Baker Book House, 79; Tensions in Contemporary Theology, Moody Press, 79; auth, Bible Studies on World Evangelization and the Simple Lifestyle, Presby & Reformed Publ Co, 81; Evangelism; Doing Justice and Proclaiming Grace, Zondervan Publ House, 82; A Clarified Vision for Urban Mission, Zondervan Publ House, 87; contribr, The Good News of the Kingdom, Orbis Books, 93; auth, The American City and the Evangelical Church, Baker Book House, 94; ed, Planting and Growing Urban Churches, Baker Book House, 96; contribr, Constructive Christian Theology in the Worldwide Church, Eerdmans Publ Co, 97; Biographical Dictionary of Christian Minions, Macmillan, 98. **CONTACT ADDRESS** Westminster Theol Sem, PO Box 27009, Philadelphia, PA, 19118-0009. **EMAIL** hconn@mindspring.com

CONN, MARIE A.
PERSONAL Born 01/09/1944, Rockville Center, NY, s **DISCIPLINE** RELIGIOUS STUDIES **EDUCATION** Univ Notre Dame, PhD 93, MA 90; Mary Wood Univ, MS 86, BA 66; Villanova Univ, MA 75. **CAREER** Chestnut Hill Col, assoc prof, 92-; Mary Wood Col, asst prof, 86-90; Various HS, 66-86. **HONORS AND AWARDS** John Templeton Foun Prize; ASA Lect Gnt. **MEMBERSHIPS** NAAL; CTS; CTSA; SL. **RESEARCH** Women in Western Christianity; Health Care Reform; Women in Scripture. **SELECTED PUBLICATIONS** Auth, Noble Daughters: Unheralded Women In Western Christianity, 13th to 18th Centuries, Westport, Greenwood Press, forthcoming; auth, The Anderson Pontifical: An Edition and Study, London, Henry Bradshaw Soc, forthcoming; auth, The Pontifical of Dunstun: An Edition and Study, London, Bradshaw Soc, forthcoming; auth, Rites of King-Making in 10th Century England, Proceedings, Groningen Nthlnds 98; Cracking Open Symbols: An Interdisciplinary Experience In Art and Religion, coauth, Arts, 97; Wisdom Born of Pain, Sisters Today, 97; auth, Health-Care Reform: A Human Rights Issue, Proceedings, 97; contrib, RP McBrien, ed, Encycl of Catholicism, Harper Collins, San Francisco, 95. **CONTACT ADDRESS** 50 S Penn St # 405, Hatboro, PA, 19040-3238. **EMAIL** mconn@chc.edu

CONN, WALTER EUGENE
PERSONAL Born 07/11/1940, Providence, RI, m, 1972 **DISCIPLINE** RELIGIOUS STUDIES, THEOLOGICAL ETHICS **EDUCATION** Providence Col, AB, 62; Boston Col, MA, 66; Columbia Univ, PhD(relig), 73. **CAREER** Instr philos, Boston Col, 66-69; from asst prof to assoc prof Christian ethics, St Patrick's Sem, 73-78; PROF RELIG STUDIES, VILLANOVA UNIV, 78-, Bk rev ed, Horizons, 78-80, ed, 80- **HONORS AND AWARDS** Col Theol Soc, best article, 78, best bk, 82. **MEMBERSHIPS** Am Acad Relig; Cath Theol Soc Am; Col Theol Soc; Soc Christian Ethics; Am Cath Philos Soc. **RESEARCH** Foundational theological ethics; moral-religious development; conversions. **SELECTED PUBLICATIONS** Auth, Transforming Light--Intellectual Conversion in the Early Lonergan, Theol Stud, Vol 0056, 95; Persons--What Philosophers Say About You, Horizons, Vol 0023, 96; In Over Our Heads--The Mental Demands of Modern Life, Horizons, Vol 0024, 97. **CONTACT ADDRESS** Relig Studies Dept, Villanova Univ, 845 E Lancaster Ave, Villanova, PA, 19085.

CONNOLLY, JOHN M.
PERSONAL Born 09/20/1943, New York, NY, m, 1969, 2 children **DISCIPLINE** PHILOSOPHY **EDUCATION** Fordham Col, BA, 65; Oxford Univ, MA, 67; Harvard Univ, PhD, 71. **CAREER** Instr, Elms Col, 71-73; from asst prof to assoc prof to prof, Smith Col, 73-; provost, Smith Col, 98-. **HONORS AND AWARDS** Pres scholar, Fordham Univ, 61-65; Danforth Fel, 65-71; Humboldt Fel, 78-82. **MEMBERSHIPS** Am Philos Asn. **RESEARCH** Philosophy of mind; Wittgenstein; philosophical Hermeneutics; academic freedom. **SELECTED PUBLICATIONS** Auth, The Academy's Freedom, The Academy's Burden, Professorial Passions, 98. **CONTACT ADDRESS** Provost/Dean of Faculty, Smith Col, Northhampton, MA, 01063. **EMAIL** jconnolly@smith.edu

CONSER, WALTER H., JR.
PERSONAL Born 04/04/1949, Riverside, CA, m, 1986, 3 children **DISCIPLINE** AMERICAN RELIGIOUS HISTORY **EDUCATION** Univ Calif Irvine, BA, 71; Brown Univ, MA, 74, PhD, hist, 81. **CAREER** James A. Gray fel in relig, Univ NC Chapel Hill, 82-84; adjunct facul, Univ San Francisco, 85; vis asst prof to asst prof, 85-89, assoc prof, 89-94, chemn, 92-98, prof relig, 94-, Univ NC Wilmington; fel, Albert Einstein Inst for Nonviolent Alternatives, 84-87; vis prof, JF Kennedy Inst for North Amer Studies, Free Univ Berlin, 90; prof, hist, Univ NC Wilmington, 95-. **MEMBERSHIPS** Amer Acad of Relig; Amer Hist Asn. **SELECTED PUBLICATIONS** Auth, Religious Diversity and American Religious History, Univ Ga Press, 97; auth, God and the Natural World: Religion and Science in Antebellum America, Univ SC Press, 93; co-ed, Experience of the Sacred: Readings in the Phenomenology of Religion, Brown Univ Press, 92; auth, James Marsh and the Germans, New Eng Quart, 86; auth, Conservative Critique of Church and State, Jour of Church and State, 83; auth, John Ross and the Cherokee Resistance Campaign, Jour of Southern Hist, 78; auth, Cherokee Reponses to the Debate Over Indian Origins, Amer Quart, 89; co-auth, Cherokees in Transition, Jour of Amer Hist, 77. **CONTACT ADDRESS** Dept. of Philosophy and Religion, Univ of North Carolina at Wilmington, 601 S. College Rd., Wilmington, NC, 28403.

CONVER, LEIGH E.
DISCIPLINE RELIGION **EDUCATION** E Baptist Col, BA; S Baptist Theol Sem, MDiv, ThM, PhD; Med Col Va, dipl; addn stud, Wash Sch Psychiatry, Shalem Inst for Spiritual Formation. **CAREER** Lawrence and Charlotte Hoover Professor, S Baptist Theol Sem, 91. **HONORS AND AWARDS** Fel, Amer Assn Pastoral Counselors. **MEMBERSHIPS** Mem, Soc Pastoral Theol; clinical mem, Assn Clinical Pastoral Edu; Amer Assn of Marriage and Family Therapy; Amer Gp Psychotherapy Assn. **SELECTED PUBLICATIONS** Ed, Jour Family Ministry; co-auth, Self-Defeating Lifestyles. **CONTACT ADDRESS** Ministry Stud Div, Southern Baptist Theol Sem, 2825 Lexington Rd, Louisville, KY, 40280. **EMAIL** lconvern@sbts.edu

CONVERSE, HYLA STUNTZ
PERSONAL Born 10/31/1920, Lahore, Pakistan, m, 1951, 2 children **DISCIPLINE** HISTORY OF RELIGIONS, SOUTH ASIAN LITERATURE **EDUCATION** Smith Col, BA, 43; Union Theol Sem, BD, 49; Columbia Univ, PhD(hist of relig), 71. **CAREER** Relief & rehab worker, Eglise Reforme France, 45-48; dir student work, Judson Mem Church, New York, 52-55; dir lit & study, Nat Student Christian Fed, 57-63; asst prof Asian relig & humanities, 68-78, chmn humanities fac, 73-78, assoc prof, 78-80, PROF ASIAN RELIG & HUMANITIES, OKLA STATE UNIV, 80-, Fulbright res fel, India, 74-75; Am Inst Pakistan Studies fel, 78-79. **MEMBERSHIPS** Am Orient Soc; Bhandarkar Oriental Res Inst. **RESEARCH** Religions of South Asia; literature of South Asia; arts of South Asia. **SELECTED PUBLICATIONS** Auth, An Ancient Sudra Account of the Origins of Castes, Jour Amer Oriental Soc, Vol 0114, 94. **CONTACT ADDRESS** Dept Relig Studies, Oklahoma State Univ, Stillwater, OK, 74074.

CONWAY, GERTRUDE D.
DISCIPLINE CONTEMPORARY PHILOSOPHY **EDUCATION** Col New Rochelle, BA; Fordham Univ, MA, PhD. **CAREER** Taught 2 yrs, Shiraz Univ, Iran; fac, Mt Saint Mary's Col, 79-; assoc dean, Undergrad Stud at Mt Saint Mary's Col, 87-91. **HONORS AND AWARDS** Delaplaine Distinguished tchg prof Humanities, 97-2000. **RESEARCH** Issue of cross-cultural understanding from a Wittgensteinian perspective. **SELECTED PUBLICATIONS** Auth, Wittgenstein on Foundations. **CONTACT ADDRESS** Dept of Philosophy, Mount Saint Mary's Col, 16300 Old Emmitsburg Rd, Emmitsburg, MD, 21727-7799. **EMAIL** conway@msmary.edu

CONWILL, GILES
PERSONAL Born 12/17/1944, Louisville, Kentucky, s **DISCIPLINE** PHILOSOPHY **EDUCATION** University of San Diego, BA, philosophy, 1967; Emory University, PhD, cultural studies, 1986; Athenaeum of OH, MDiv, 1973. **CAREER** Barona & Santa Ysabel Missions, religious education instructor, 1965-67; Miramar Naval Air Station, chaplain's assistant, 1966-67; St Henry's School, elementary school teacher, 1967-68; Verona Fathers Seminary, choir director, assistant organist, 1968-69; St Rita's Church, associate pastor, 1973-76; San Diego Religious Vocations Office, diocesan coordinator, premarriage instructor, 1975; National Office of Black Catholics, Department of Church Vocations, director, 1976-80; St Anthony's Church, Atlanta, associate pastor, 1980-85; St Joseph's Cathedral, San Diego, associate pastor, 1985-86; Morehouse College, Department of History, asso professor, 1987-; Inst for Black Catholic Studies, Xavier Univ, New Orleans, assoc prof, 1990. **HONORS AND AWARDS** City of Selma, Alabama, Key to the City, first city-wide Black Catholic revival; Upper Room Publishing Co., interdenominational sermon contest winner; numerous other awards. **MEMBERSHIPS** Southeast San Diego Interdenominational Ministerial Alliance, vp, 1975; Black Catholic Clergy Caucus, 1975; Assn for the Study of African American Life & History, 1987-; Southern Conference of African Amer Studies, Inc, 1987-; Ass of Southern Historians, 1992-; Georgia Assn of Historians, 1992; Amer Anthropological Assn, 1994; Black Catholic Theological Symposium, 1990. **SELECTED PUBLICATIONS** Author, "The Word Becomes Black Flesh: A Program for Reaching the American Black," What Christians Can Learn from One Another, Tyndale House Publishers, 1988; workshop presenter: "Understanding Transitions: How to Relate to Candidates from Various Backgrounds," Seventh Annual Formation Workshops, Bergamo Center, July 8-10, 1988; African-American history lecture, Shrine of Immaculate Conception, Jan 1991; "Blackology vs Ecology," Leadership Council of the Laity Conference, Feb 1991; Liturgical Sensitivity to the Black Aesthetic, in The Critic, Summer, 1986; Tell It Like It Is: A Black Catholic Perspective on Christian Educ, Natl Black Sisters Conference, 1983; Black Music: The Spirit Will Not Descend Without Song, Pastoral Life, Vol XXXII, June 1983; Blackology vs Ecology, Leadership Council of the Laity. **CONTACT ADDRESS** Professor, Department of History, Morehouse Col, 830 Westview Dr SW, Brawley Hall, Ste 204, Atlanta, GA, 30314.

CONYERS, A.J.
PERSONAL Born 05/29/1944, San Bernardino, CA, m, 1964, 2 children **DISCIPLINE** SYSTEMATIC THEOLOGY **EDUCATION** Univ Ga, BA, 66; So Baptist Sem, MDiv, 71; So Baptist Theol Sem, PhD, 79. **CAREER** Prof of Bible, Central Missouri State Univ, 79-87; chemn, Dept Relig, Charleston So Univ, 87-94; prof theol, G.W. Truett Sem, Baylor Univ, 94- . **HONORS AND AWARDS** Staley Distinguished Scholar; Ed Bd, Review and Expositor. **MEMBERSHIPS** Am Acad Relig; Evangelical Theolog Soc; William Gilmore Simms Soc. **RESEARCH** Christianity and culture. **SELECTED PUBLICATIONS** Auth, God, Hope, and History: Jurgen Moltmann's Christian Concept of History, Mercer, 88; auth, The Eclipse of Heaven, InterVarsity, 92; auth, The End: What the Gospels Say About the Last Things, InterVarsity, 95; auth, A Basic Christian Theology, Broadman & Holman, 95. **CONTACT ADDRESS** 500 N Park Ave, Waco, TX, 76708. **EMAIL** Chip_Conyers@baylor.edu

COOEY, PAULA M.
PERSONAL Hays, KS, m, 1 child **DISCIPLINE** RELIGION, THEOLOGY AND COMPARATIVE LITERATURE **EDUCATION** Univ Ga, BA, philos, 68; Harvard Divinity Sch, MTS, 74; Harvard Univ, grad sch of arts & sci, PhD, 81. **CAREER** Visiting instr, Conn Col, 9/79-9/80; instr part-time, relig, Univ Mass, Harbor Campus, 9/80-1/81; asst prof, relig, Trinity Univ, 9/81-7/87; assoc prof, relig, Trinity Univ, 8/87-8/93; prof, relig, Trinity Univ, 8/93-. **HONORS AND AWARDS** Co-dir, Southwest Regional Amer Acad of Relig workshop on teaching for jr facul, 94-96; Sears-Roebuck Found award for excellence in teaching & campus leadership, 91; Trinity Univ nom for CASE award, 88. **MEMBERSHIPS** Amer Acad of Relig; Soc for Buddhist-Christian Studies; Soc for the Sci Study of Relig; Amer Asn of Univ Prof. **RESEARCH** Death and dying from a feminist perspective. **SELECTED PUBLICATIONS** Auth, Family, Freedom, and Faith: Building Community Today, Westminster John Knox Press, ix-131, 96; auth, Religious Imagination and the Body: A Feminist Analysis, Oxford Univ Press, vii-184, 94; article, Bad Women: The Limitations of Theory and Theology, Horizons in Feminist Theology, Fortress, 97; article, Kenosis, Popular Religiosity, Religious Pluralism, Dict of Feminist Theol, John Knox Westminster Press, 96; article, Re-Membering the Body: A Theological Resource for Resisting Domestic Violence, Theol & Sexuality, 3, 27-47, 95; article, Mapping the Body through Religious Symbolism: The Life and Work of Frida Kahlo as Case Study, Imagining Faith: Essays in Honor of Richard R. Niebuhr, Scholars Press, 105-125, 95; article, Backlash, Jour of Feminist Studies, 10, 1, 109-111, 94. **CONTACT ADDRESS** Dept. of Religion, Trinity Univ, 715 Stadium Dr., San Antonio, TX, 78212-7200. **EMAIL** pcooey@trinity.edu

COOK, D. NOAM
DISCIPLINE PHILOSOPHY **EDUCATION** San Fran State Univ, BA, MA; MIT, PhD. **CAREER** Assoc prof of Philos, San Jose State Univ; consult res; Xerox, Palo Alto Res Ctr. **RESEARCH** Knowledge, know-how and technological change in social contexts. **CONTACT ADDRESS** Dept of Philosophy, San Jose State Univ, San Jose, CA, 95192-0096.

COOK, DANIEL JOSEPH
PERSONAL Born 06/27/1938, Philadelphia, PA, m, 1977 **DISCIPLINE** GERMAN AND SOCIAL PHILOSOPHY **EDUCATION** Haverford Col, BA, 60; Columbia Univ, MA, 63, PhD(philos), 68; Hebrew Union Col, BHebrew Lit, 64. **CAREER** From instr to asst prof philos, Herbert H Lehman Col, 67-71; res assoc, Univ Bonn, 71-72; ASSOC PROF PHILOS, DEPT PHILOS, BROOKLYN COL, 72-. **MEMBERSHIPS** Am Philos Asn; Soc Asian Comp Philos; Hegel Soc Am. **RESEARCH** Hegel; Marx; Leibniz. **SELECTED PUBLICATIONS** Auth, Response to Saussy,Haun Review of Writings on China, Philos E and W, Vol 0047, 97. **CONTACT ADDRESS** Dept Philos, Brooklyn Col, CUNY, 2901 Bedford Ave, Brooklyn, NY, 11210-2813.

COOK, E. DAVID
DISCIPLINE CHRISTIAN ETHICS **EDUCATION** Arizona State Univ, BA; Edinburgh Univ, MA; Oxford Univ, MA; New Col, Edinburgh Univ, PhD. **CAREER** Clinical ethicist, John Radcliffe Hospital; Instr, Oxford Univ; prof, S Baptist Theol Sem. **HONORS AND AWARDS** Listed, Who's Who in the World; Oxford Univ Dictionary of Experts. **RESEARCH** Christian perspective on such issues as euthanasia, medical ethics, genetics, AIDS, homosexuality, and pornography. **SELECTED PUBLICATIONS** Auth, The Moral Maze; Blind Alley Beliefs; Medical Ethics Today: Its Practice and Philosophy; Christianity Confronts. **CONTACT ADDRESS** Dept Christian Ethics, Southern Baptist Theol Sem, 2825 Lexington Rd, Louisville, KY, 40280. **EMAIL** dcook@sbts.edu

COOK, J. THOMAS
PERSONAL Born 08/07/1951, SC, m, 1989 **DISCIPLINE** PHILOSOPHY **EDUCATION** Johns Hopkins, BA, 72; Vanderbilt, Ma, 78, PhD, 81. **CAREER** Vis lectr, Stetson Univ, 79-80; vis asst prof, Williams Col, 80-92; prof, Rollins Col, 92-; NEH Summer Sem; tchg awards. **MEMBERSHIPS** Am Philos Asn; N Am Spinoza Soc; Spinoza Gesalschaft; Soc Philos & Psychol. **RESEARCH** Spinoza; Enlightenment; Philosophy of mind. **SELECTED PUBLICATIONS** Auth Do Persons Follow from Spinoza's God, The Personalist Forum, 92; Strange Science of Paradoxical Desires: Reply to De Dijn, Ethica, 94; Did Spinoza Lie to His Lanlady?, Studia Spinozana, 95. **CONTACT ADDRESS** Dept of Philosophy, Rollins Col, 1000 Holt Ave, Box 2659, Winter Park, FL, 32789. **EMAIL** tcook@rollins.edu

COOK, JONATHAN A.
DISCIPLINE PHILOSOPHY **EDUCATION** Harvard Univ, BA; Columbia Univ, MA, 88, MPhil, 91, PhD, 93. **CAREER** IND SCHOLAR **MEMBERSHIPS** AM Antiquarian Soc **SELECTED PUBLICATIONS** Auth, Satirical Apocalypse: An Anatomy of Melville's "The Confidence Man," 96. **CONTACT ADDRESS** 4405 SE Alder St, Portland, OR, 97215.

COOK, JOYCE MITCHELL
PERSONAL Born 10/28/1933, Sharon, PA, d **DISCIPLINE** PHILOSOPHY **EDUCATION** Bryn Mawr Coll, AB 1955; Oxford U, BA 1957, MA 1961; Yale U, PhD 1965. **CAREER** White House Staff, staff asst 1977-81; Howard Univ, spec asst for communications, 1981-89, dir of honors prog, mem dept of philosophy 1966-68, 1970-76; CT Coll, dept of philosophy 1968-70; Office of Economic Opportunity, publ Head 1965-66; US Dept of State, foreign serv reserve officer 1964-65; Wellesley Coll, dept of philosophy 1961-62; Yale Univ, dept of philosophy 1959-61. **MEMBERSHIPS** Mng editor Review of Metaphysics 1959-61; consult Inst for Serv to Educ 1972-76; mem Am Philosophical Assn; Com on Blacks in Philosophy 1970-76; prog com Eastern Div 1974-76.

COOK, JULIAN ABELE, JR.
PERSONAL Born 06/22/1930, Washington, DC, m **DISCIPLINE** LAW **EDUCATION** PA State Univ, BA, 1952; Georgetown Univ, JD, 1957; Univ of Virginia, LLM, 1988. **CAREER** Judge Arthur E Moore, law clerk, 1957-58; private practice, attorney, 1958-78; State of MI, special asst, attorney general, 1968-78; Univ of Detroit-Mercy, adjunct prof of law, 1970-74; East Dist of MI, US Courthouse, Detroit, US Dist Judge, 1978-, chief judge, 1989-96, SR JUDGE, 1996-; TRIAL ADVOCACY WORKSHOP, HARVARD UNIV, INSTRUCTOR, 1988-. **HONORS AND AWARDS** Distinguished Citizen of the Year, NAACP, Oakland Co, MI, 1970; Citation of Merit, Pontiac, MI Area Urban League, 1971; chmn, Civil Rights Commn, achieved resolution, State of MI, House of Representatives, 1971; Boss of the Year, Legal Secretary Assn, 1973-74; Pathfinders Award, Oakland Univ, 1977; Serv Award, Todd-Phillips Home Inc, 1978; Focus & Impact Award Oakland Univ, 1985; Distinguished Alumnus Award, Pennsylvania State Univ, 1985; Distinguished Alumnus Award, John Carroll Award, Georgetown Univ, 1989; Augustus Straker Award, 1988; Absalom Jones Award, Union of Black Episcopalians, Detroit Chapter, 1988; Bench-Bar Award, Wolverine, Detroit Bar Assn, 1987; Presidential Award, North Oakland Co, NAACP, 1987; Honor Soc, Univ of Detroit School of Law, 1981; B'nai B'rith Barrister, 1980; Federal Bar Assn, 1978; MI Lawyers Weekly, voted 1 of 25 Most Respected Judges in MI, 1990, 1991; Detroit Monthly, voted 1 of the best Judges in the Metro Detroit area, 1991; Georgetown University, Doctor of Law, Honoris Causa, 1992; Jewish Law Veterans of the US, Brotherhood Award, 1994; MI State Bar, Champion of Justice Award, 1994; Univ of Detroit-Mercy, Doctor of Laws, Honoris Causa, 1996; Wayne State Univ, Doctor of Laws, Honoris Causa, 1997; Georgetown Univ, Paul R Dean Award, 1997; Pontiac, MI, City Wide Choir Union, Humanitarian Award. **MEMBERSHIPS** Amer & Natl Bar Assns; Am Bar Found; co-chmn, Prof, Devel Task Force, MI Bar Assn; MI Assn of Black Judges; Fed Bar Assn; Oakland Univ Proj Twenty Comm, chmn, bd of dirs, 1966-68; Pontiac Area Urban League, pres, 1967-68; MI Civil Rights Comm, chair, 1968-71; Todd Phillips Children's Home, bd of dirs, 1968-78; Amer Civil Liberties Union, bd of dirs, 1976-78; Amer Inn of Court, pres, master of the bench, chap XI, 1994-96; Cont Legal Educ Comm, Oakland County Bar Assn, 1968-69, judicial liaison, Dist Court Comm, vice chair, 1977; Cont Legal Educ Comm, 1977; Unauthorized Practice of Law, 1977; MI Supreme Court Defense Serv Comm, 1977; exec bd of dir, past pres, Child & Family Serv of MI; chmn, Sixth Circuit Comm on Standard Jury Instruction; bd of dirs, Amer Heart Assn of MI; Amer Bar Assn, fellow, 1981-; Detroit Urban League, bd of dirs, 1983-85; Brighton Health Svcs Corp, 1985-92; Georgetown Univ Alumni Assn; Judicial Conference of the US, chmn, 1990-93; Harvard Univ, trial advocacy workshop, instructor, 1988-; life mem, NAACP; PA State Univ, Alumni Assn, alumni coun, 1986-92; Hutzel Hosp, bd of dirs, 1984-95; Georgetown Univ, bd of visitors, 1991-; NY Univ Root Tilden Snow Scholarship Prog, screening panel, 1991-; Mediation Tribunal Assn; Third Judicial Circuit of MI, bd of dirs, 1992-; Amer Law Inst, 1996-; Judicial Coun of the Sixth Circuit, sr judge personnel comm, 1996-97; MI Bar Foundation, fellow, 1987-, chair, 1993-. **SELECTED PUBLICATIONS** Published: Jurisprudence of Original Intention, co-author, 1986; A Quest for Justice, 1983; Some Current Problems of Human Administration, co-author, 1971; The Changing Role of the Probation Officer in the Federal Court, article, Federal Sentencing Reporter, vol 4, no 2, p 112, 1991; An Overview of the US District Court for the Eastern District of Michigan, article, Inter Alia, vol 28, no 1, winter 1990; Rule 11: A Judicial Approach to an Effective Administration of Justice in the US Courts, 15 Ohio N U L 397, 1988; ADR in the United States District Court for Eastern District of Michigan, Michigan Pleading and Practice ADR, Section 62A-405-62A-415, 1994; Thurgood Marshall and Clarence Thomas: A Glance at Their Philosophies, Michigan Bar Journal, March 1994, Vol 73, No 3, p298; George A Googasian-58th President of the State Bar of Michigan, Michigan Bar Journal, Oct 1992, Vol 71, No 10; "Family Responsibility, Federal Sentencing Reporter," 1995; Federal Civil Procedure Before Trial: Sixth Circuit, 1996; "Dream Makers: Black Judges on Justice," Univ of MI Law Review, 1996; "Death Penalty," co-author Cooley Law Review, 1996; "Closing Their Eyes to the Constitution: The Declining Role of the Supreme Court in the Protection of Civil Rights," co-author, Detroit Coll of Law, 1996. **CONTACT ADDRESS** Eastern District of Michigan, 231 W Lafayette, Detroit, MI, 48226.

COOK, MICHAEL J.
PERSONAL Born 01/15/1942, Altoona, PA, m, 1984, 5 children **DISCIPLINE** NEW TESTAMENT **EDUCATION** Haverford Col, BA, 64; Hebrew Un Col, PhD, 74 **CAREER** Asst Prof, 73-77; Assoc Prof, 77-81; Prof, 81-91; Prof, 92-pres **HONORS AND AWARDS** Phi Beta Kappa, Haverford Col; Exc in Tch Awd **MEMBERSHIPS** Soc of Bibl Lit **RESEARCH** New Testament; Christian-Jewish Relations **SELECTED PUBLICATIONS** Auth, Rabbinic Judaism & Early Christianity, Review & Expositor, 87; Auth, Images of Jesus in the Arts, Proceedings of the Center for Jewish-Christian Learning 10, 96, 46-56 **CONTACT ADDRESS** Hebrew Union Col, 3101 Clifton Ave, Cincinnati, OH, 45220. **EMAIL** cookmj@aol.com

COOK, MICHAEL L.
DISCIPLINE THEOLOGY **EDUCATION** Gonzaga Univ, AB, 59, MA, 60; Santa Clara Univ, STM, 67; Alma Col, STL, 67; Grad Theol Union, ThD, 74. **CAREER** Adj to ASSOC PROF, Jesuit Sch Theol, Berkeley, 71-82; assoc prof, Gonzaga Univ, 82-86; vis prof, La Pontificia Univ Cat Santiago, Chile, 87-88; assoc prof, 89-95, PROF, 95-, GONZAGA UNIV. **CONTACT ADDRESS** Gonzaga Univ, Spokane, WA, 99258.

COOK, STEPHEN L.
PERSONAL Born 07/21/1962, CT, m, 1988 **DISCIPLINE** HEBREW BIBLE AND OLD TESTAMENT **EDUCATION** Yale Univ, PhD, 92. **CAREER** Asst prof, old testament, Union Theol Sem, 92-96; asst prof, old testament, Va Theol Sem, 96-. **HONORS AND AWARDS** The Two Brothers fel, Yale Univ, 87; Phi Beta Kappa, 84. **MEMBERSHIPS** Soc of Bibl Lit; Amer Acad of Relig; Amer Sch of Orient Res; Cath Bibl Asn. **RESEARCH** Apocalypticism and post exile Israelite religion; The social roots of biblical Yahwism. **SELECTED PUBLICATIONS** Rev, The Ladies and the Cities: Transformation and Apocalyptic Identity in Joseph and Aseneth, 4 Ezra, the Apocalypse and the Shepherd of Hermas, Jour of Bibl Lit, 117, 2, 375-377, 98; rev, Prophets of Old and the Day of the End: Zechariah, the Book of Watchers and Apocalyptic, Cath Bibl Quart, 59, 757-758, 97; rev, The Five Fragments of the Apocryphon of Ezekiel: A Critical Study, Jour of Bibl Lit, 115, 3, 532-534, 96; rev, Psalms and the Transformation of Stress: Poetic-Communal Interpretation and the Family, Jour of Relig and Health, 35, 3, 263-264, 96; auth, Reflections on Apocalypticism at the Approach of the Year 2000, Union Sem Quart Rev, 49, 1-2, 3-16, 95; guest ed, Countdown to 2000: Essays on Apocalypticism, Union Sem Quart Rev, vol 49, no 1-2, 95; rev, Second Zechariah and the Deuteronomic School, Cath Bibl Quart, 57, 4, 780-781, 95; auth, Innerbiblical Interpretation in Ezekiel 44 and the History of Israel's Priesthood, Jour of Bibl Lit, 114, 2, 193-208, 95; auth, Prophecy and Apocalypticism: The Post-exilic Social Setting, Fortress Press, 95; auth, The Text and Philology of 1 Samuel xiii 20-1, Vetus Testamentum, 44, 2, 250-254, 94; auth, The Metamorphosis of a Shepherd: The Tradition History of Zechariah 11:17 + 13:7-9, Cath Bibl Quart, 55, 3, 453-466, 93; auth, Apocalypticism and the Psalter, Zeitschrift fur die alttestamentliche Wissenschaft, 104, 1, 82-99, 92. **CONTACT ADDRESS** 3737 Seminary Rd., Alexandria, VA, 22304. **EMAIL** scook@vts.edu

COOK, WILLIAM ROBERT
PERSONAL Born 12/27/1943, Indianapolis, IN **DISCIPLINE** MEDIEVAL HISTORY, HISTORY OF CHRISTIANITY **EDUCATION** Wabash Col, AB, 66; Cornell Univ, MA, 70, PhD(medieval hist), 71. **CAREER** Asst prof hist, 70-77, ASSOC PROF HIST, STATE UNIV NY COL GENESEO, 77-, Nat Endowment for Humanities fel in residence, Harvard Univ, 76-77; adj prof lit, Attica Correctional Facil, 80 & 81; adj prof relig studies, Siena Col, NY, 81. **MEMBERSHIPS** AHA; Mediaeval Acad Am; Am Soc Church Hist; Am Friends Bodley; Dante Soc Am. **RESEARCH** Medieval Franciscanism; Monasticism; Siena, Italy. **SELECTED PUBLICATIONS** Auth, Aurora, Their Last Utopia--Oregon Christian Commune, 1856-1883, Ore Hist Quart, Vol 0095, 94. **CONTACT ADDRESS** Dept of Hist, State Univ of NY Col, 1 College Cir, Geneseo, NY, 14454-1401.

COOLEY, JAMES F.
PERSONAL Born 01/11/1926, Rowland, NC, m **DISCIPLINE** THEOLOGY **EDUCATION** Johnson C Smith Univ, AB Soc Sci 1953, BD Theol 1956; Interdenom Theol Center, DM 1973; World Univ Tucson, AZ, PhD Soc Sci 1982; Life Science Coll, DD 1972; St John Univ NE, MA Sociology 1972; Law Enforcement Official, certified; Law Enforcement Instructor of Jail Opers and Jail Admin, certified. **CAREER** Grant Chapel Presb Ch, minister 1956-57; St Andrews Presb Ch, minister 1957-69; Forrest City Spec Sch Dist #7, 1957-69; St Francis Co, juv prob ofcr 1959-68, assoc juv judge 1963-64; Shorter Coll, polit sci dir/minister of svc/dean of men/acad dean 1969-73; State Rep Art Givens Jr, chf legisl on comm affairs; 5th Div Circ Ct for Judge Jack Lessenberg, prob ofcr; Tucker Prison, first black chaplain in AR 1971; Attorney Genl's Office, agent consumer protection; Pulaski County, deputy registrar; County Contact Comm Inc, founder/exec dir. **MEMBERSHIPS** Police commr Wrightsville PD 1984; chaplain Pulaski Co Sheriff Dept 1985; AR Cncl on Human Rel; Natl Hist Soc; Urban League; Early Amer Soc; Natl Conf of Christians and Jews Inc; Postal

Commem Soc; Natl Black Veterans Organ Inc; major genl Natl Chaplains Assn; foot distrib for the poor AR Food Bank Network; Amer Legion, Natl Sheriff's Assn; sr warden, comm mem 33rd Degree Mason; Boy Scouts of Amer; bd of dirs AA AWARE Drug and Alcohol Prevention Prog; Worshipful Master, Welcome Lodge #457 masonic 1987-; life member, Disabled American Veteran; life member, Veteran of Foreign Wars. **CONTACT ADDRESS** County Contact Comm Inc, PO Box 17225, N Little Rock, AR, 72117.

COONEY, BRIAN PATRICK
PERSONAL Born 09/04/1943, Montreal, PQ, Canada, m, 1968, 2 children **DISCIPLINE** PHILOSOPHY **EDUCATION** St Louis Univ, BA, 65; McGill Univ, MA, 69, PhD, 72. **CAREER** Asst prof philos, Univ Notre Dame, 71-72; asst prof, Univ Tex, Austin, 72-80; from Asst Prof to Assoc Prof, 80-91, Prof Philos, Centre Col, 91-. **HONORS AND AWARDS** Am Coun Learned Soc fel, 76-77. **MEMBERSHIPS** Am Philos Asn. **RESEARCH** History of modern philosophy; philosophy of mind. **SELECTED PUBLICATIONS** Auth, John Sergeant's Criticism of Locke's Theory of Ideas, Mod Schoolman, 1/73; Descartes and the external darkness, New Scholasticism, summer 75; Arnold Geulincx: A Cartesian idealist, J Hist Philos, 78; The biological basis of mind, Int Philos Quart, 12/78; The neural basis of self-consciousness, Nature and System, 3/79; A Hylomorphic Theory of Mind, Peter Lang Publ, 91; Dennett's Fictional Selves, SW Philos Rev, 1/94. **CONTACT ADDRESS** Dept of Philos, Centre Col, 600 W Walnut St, Danville, KY, 40422-1394. **EMAIL** cooneyb@centre.edu

COONEY, WILLIAM
PERSONAL Born 11/18/1952, Rockford, IL, m, 1975, 3 children **DISCIPLINE** PHILOSOPHY **EDUCATION** Marquette Univ, PhD. **CAREER** Prof, Briar Cliff Col. **HONORS AND AWARDS** Burlington No Fac Excel, 92; Dist Alumni, Marquette Univ, 93. **MEMBERSHIPS** Am Philos Asn. **RESEARCH** Aesthetics; philos and psychology. **SELECTED PUBLICATIONS** Contrib ed, The Human Person and the Human Community, Ginn Press, 88; ed, Reflections on Gabriel Marcel: A Collection of Essays, Edwin Mellon Press, 89; coauth, Ten Great Thinkers: An Integrative Study in Philosophy and Psychology, Univ Press Am, 90; auth, A Fallacy in Person-Denying Arguments for Abortion, J of Applied Philos, Oct 91; coauth, From Plato to Piaget: The Greatest Educational Theorists From Across the Centuries and Around the World, Univ Press Am, 6th print, 93; auth. Affirmative Action Revisited: A Response to Professor Jordan, The Doctrine of Double Effect: Philosophers Debate a Controversial Moral Principle, Univ Notre Dame Press, 96; rev article, on Seymour Cain's Gabriel Marcel's Theory of Religious Experience, Int Stud in Philos, 97; auth, Rights Theory, Encycl of Applied Ethics, Ctr for Professional Ethics, Univ Cent Lancashire, UK, Acad Press, 97; auth, The Death Poetry of Emily Dickinson: A Philosophical Exploration, Omega, the Nat J of Death and Dying, 98; auth, The Quest for Meaning: An Exploration into the Human Journey as Revealed in Philosophy and the Arts, Rowman & Littlefield, forthcoming. **CONTACT ADDRESS** Briar Cliff Col, 3303 Rebecca, Sioux City, IA, 51104. **EMAIL** cooney@briar-cliff.edu

COOP, JACK
DISCIPLINE LAW **EDUCATION** Univ Manitoba, BA, 78; Osgoode Hall Law Sch, LLB, 83. **CAREER** Senior counsel, Ontario Ministry of the Attorney General **HONORS AND AWARDS** Seconded, Legal Services Branch, Ontario Ministry Environ Energy. **MEMBERSHIPS** Law Soc. **RESEARCH** Environmental law. **SELECTED PUBLICATIONS** Auth, pubs on environmental regulation and environmental assessment law. **CONTACT ADDRESS** Fac of Law, Univ Toronto, 78 Queen's Park, Toronto, ON.

COOPER, ALMETA E.
PERSONAL Born 12/27/1950, Durham, NC, m, 1984 **DISCIPLINE** LAW **EDUCATION** Wells Coll, BA 1972; Northwestern Univ Sch of Law, JD 1975. **CAREER** Vedder Price Kaufman & Kammholz, assoc 1975-77; Amer Med Assn, asst dir of health law div 1977-82; Tuggle Hasbrouck & Robinson, partner 1980-82; Meharry Medical Coll, corporate secretary & general counsel, 1982-88; St Thomas Hospital, Nashville, TN, general counsel, 1988-; College of St Francis, Nashville, TN, adjunct faculty, 1989-. **HONORS AND AWARDS** Chicago Urban League; Alumnae Assns of Wells & Spelman Colleges; Outstanding Alumna Spelman Coll; Outstanding Volunteer Chicago Urban League; Natl Finalist White House Fellowship 1982; publications have appeared in Journal of the Amer Med Assn and in St Louis Univ Law Journal. **MEMBERSHIPS** Lecturer Joint Comm on Accreditation of Hospitals; lecturer Amer College of Hospital Administrators; lecturer New England Hosp Assembly; mem Amer Soc of Hospital Attorneys; bd of dir Minority Legal Educ Resources; alternate mem Hines Veterans Admin Cooperative Studies Prog Human Rights Comm; pres bd of dir IL Family Planning Council; mem Renaissance Women; appointed mem Nashville Private Industry Council; fin comm League of Women Voters Nashville; mem Leadership Nashville 1986-87, Music City Chap of the Links, TN Bar Assn, Napier-Looby Bar Assn, Amer Acad of Hospital Attorneys. **CONTACT ADDRESS** Office of Legal Affairs, St Thomas Hospital, 4220 Harding Rd, Nashville, TN, 37205.

COOPER, BURTON
PERSONAL Born 06/13/1932, New York, NY, m, 1955, 4 children **DISCIPLINE** THEOLOGY, PHILOSOPHY OF RELIGION **EDUCATION** Columbia Univ, BA, 54; Union Theol Sem, PhD(syst theol), 68. **CAREER** Instr relig, Wooster Col, 65-68; asst prof, Mary Washington Col, 68-70; PROF PHILOS THEOL, LOUISVILLE PRESBY THEOL SEM, 70-. **RESEARCH** Process theology; liberation theology. **SELECTED PUBLICATIONS** Auth, A Scandalous Providence--The Jesus Story of the Compassion of God, Theol Today, Vol 0053, 96. **CONTACT ADDRESS** Louisville Presbyterian Theol Sem, 1044 Alta Vista Rd, Louisville, KY, 40205-1758.

COOPER, CLARENCE
PERSONAL Born 05/05/1942, Decatur, GA, m **DISCIPLINE** LAW **EDUCATION** Clark Coll, BA 1960-64; Emory Univ Sch Law, JD 1965-67; MIT Comm Flws Prgm, flwsp 1977; Harvard Univ John F Kennedy Sch Govt Pub Admin, 1977-78. **CAREER** Atlanta Legal Serv Prog, atty 1967-68; Fulton Co GA, asst dist atty 1968-76; Atlant Muncpl Ct, assoc judge 1976; Fulton County Superior Ct, judge; US District Court, judge. **HONORS AND AWARDS** Schlrsp Clark Coll 1960-64. **MEMBERSHIPS** Mem Natl Bar Assn, Gate City Bar Assn, Natl Conf Black Lawyers, State Bar GA, Atlanta Bar Assn; mem exec bd Atlanta Br NAACP; mem Natl Urban League; bd dir Amistrad Prod, EOA's Drug Prog; past mem Atlanta Judicial Comm. **SELECTED PUBLICATIONS** "The Judiciary & Its Budget: An Administrative Hassle". **CONTACT ADDRESS** US District Court, Northern District of GA, 75 Spring St, SW, Atlanta, GA, 30303.

COOPER, CLEMENT THEODORE
PERSONAL Born 10/26/1930, Miami, FL, m **DISCIPLINE** LAW **EDUCATION** Lincoln Univ, AB 1952; Boston Univ, attended 1954-55; Howard Univ Sch of Law, JD 1958; CO State Christian Coll, Hon PhD 1973; Hastings Coll of Law Univ of CA, first natl coll of advocacy 1971. **CAREER** Private Practice, attorney-at-law 1960-. **MEMBERSHIPS** Mem MI State Bar 1960; mem DC Bar 1960; mem US Sup Ct Bar, US Ct Appeals, DC & Tenth Cir CO, US Ct Mil Appeals, Third Cir Phila, US Ct of Claims, US Second Circuit Ct of Appeals, US Fourth Circuit Ct of Appeals, US Sixth Circuit Ct of Appeals, US Ct of Appeals for Federal Circuit; mem Natl Bar Assn; Amer Bar Assn; Amer Trial Lawyers Assn; mem Amer Judicature Soc; Amer Civil Liberties Union; Pub Welfare Adv Council 1966-68; mem Ch of the Ascension & St Agnes Wash DC; life mem Alpha Phi Alpha; arbitrator, Natl Assoc of Securities Dealers. **SELECTED PUBLICATIONS** Auth, "Sealed Verdict" 1964; auth, "Location of Unpatented Mining Claims" CA Mining Journal Jan-May 1975 Vol 44; contrib ed, Natural Resources Section Amer Bar Assn "Significant Adminis Legislative & State Court Decisions Affecting the Petrol Ind in States East of the Mississippi River" 1979-80. **CONTACT ADDRESS** Law Offices of Clement T Cooper, PO Box 76135, Washington, DC, 20013-6135.

COOPER, CORINNE
DISCIPLINE LAW **EDUCATION** Univ Ariz, BA, JD. **CAREER** Prof **RESEARCH** Banking law; contracts; commercial transactions; sales; secured transactions; negotiation; lawyering skills. **SELECTED PUBLICATIONS** Auth, Getting Graphic (TM): Visual Tools for Teaching and Learning Commercial Law; Getting Graphic 2 (TM): Visual Tools for Teaching and Learning Law; ed, The Portable UCC; co-ed, A Drafter's Guide to an Alternative Dispute Resolution. **CONTACT ADDRESS** Law Dept, Univ of Missouri, Kansas City, 5100 Rockhill Rd, Kansas City, MO, 64110-2499. **EMAIL** cooperc@umkc.edu

COOPER, JOSEPH
PERSONAL Hemingway, SC **DISCIPLINE** LAW **EDUCATION** Univ of Utah Sacramento City Coll, AA 1965; University of the Pacific, McGeorge Law School, JD (honors), 1969. **CAREER** Pres, First Capital Real Estate; atty gen pract 1969-; Joseph Cooper Court Corp, president, currently; Northwestern California University, School of Law, dean of academic affairs. **HONORS AND AWARDS** City of San Francisco, Distinguished Service Award. **MEMBERSHIPS** Former mem, board of directors, California Trial Lawyers Assn; member, American Trial Lawyers Assn; Success Institute of America Inc, pres/founder. **CONTACT ADDRESS** 1310 H St, Sacramento, CA, 95814.

COOPER, M. WAYNE
DISCIPLINE PHILOSOPHY **EDUCATION** UTMB, MA, 69; Texas Tech, MA, phil, 89. **CAREER** Assoc prof, 78-89, Texas Tech Univ; prof, 79-91, Mich St Univ; prof, 91-95, Univ Texas Health Ctr, Tyler. **HONORS AND AWARDS** OKO; AEO **MEMBERSHIPS** Amer Col Cardiology; Amer Col Physicians; APS. **RESEARCH** Medical ethics. **CONTACT ADDRESS** 115 W 5th St, Tyler, TX, 75701. **EMAIL** mwaylooy@flashnet.com

COOPER STEPHENSON, KEN
DISCIPLINE LAW **EDUCATION** Univ London, LLB, 64; Cambridge Univ, LLM, 66. **CAREER** Asst dean, 81-82, prof, 64- **SELECTED PUBLICATIONS** Auth, Personal Injury Damages in Canada, Carswell, 96, Tort Theory, Captus, 93; co-ed, Charter Damages Claims, Carswell, 90. **CONTACT ADDRESS** Col of Law, Univ Saskatchewan, 15 Campus Dr, Saskatoon, SK, S7N 5A6. **EMAIL** CooperSt@law.usask.ca

COOPER-LEWTER, NICHOLAS CHARLES
PERSONAL Born 06/25/1948, Washington, DC **DISCIPLINE** RELIGIOUS STUDIES, PSYCHOTHERAPY **EDUCATION** Ashland Coll, BA 1970; Ecumenical Ctr, African-American church studies, adv studies, DMin prog 1978; Univ of MN, MSW 1978; CA Coast Univ, PhD 1988. **CAREER** Univ of MN, Ctr for Youth Devel Rsrch, rsrch specialist, 1972-73; teaching asst, 1974-75; City of St Paul Human Rights Dept, field investigator, 1974; consultant, various Christian churches, 1976-; Cooper Lewter Hypnosis Ctr NB, dir owner 1978-83; New Garden of Gethsemane, senior pastor, 1985-90; CRAVE Christ Ministries Inc, founder, psychotherapist, author; Bethel College and Seminary, professor of social work, visiting instructor of cross cultural counseling, 1990-95; Cooper-Lewter Rites of Passage, founder, 1995-; McKnight Multi Cultural Grant, coordinator, 1991-95; Metropolitan State Univ. Psychology and Social Work Faculty, 1997-. **HONORS AND AWARDS** University of MN School of Social Work, Deans Grad Fellowship, 1974; Teamer School of Religion, Honorary LHD, 1978; Bethel College and Seminary, Distinguished Faculty Service Award, 1992; St Paul Urban League, SE Hall Community Service Award, 1992; Society of Medical Hypnoanalysts, Outstanding Contributor to the Field of Medical Hypnoanalysis, 1983; Los Angeles Olympic Committee, Judgeship, 1984. **MEMBERSHIPS** Founder, 1st basileus, Xi Theta Chap, Omega Psi Phi, 1966-70; bd dir, American Academy of Med Hypnoanalysis, 1977-; NASW; NUL; NAACP; AAMH; ACSW; board member, Adoptive Families of America Inc; TURN Leadership Foundation: Salvation Army. **SELECTED PUBLICATIONS** Author, works include: "Concerns of Working Youth," People Human Svs MN, 1974, "Working Youth: Selected Findings from Exploratory Study," Jrnl Youth & Adolescence, 1974, "Sports Hypnotherapy: Contenderosis & Self Hate," Jrnl of Med Hypnoanalysts, 1980; "The Initial Environmental Experience: A Powerful Took for Psychotherapy & Hypnotherapy," Journal of Medical Hypnoanalysts, 1981; "Keep On Rollin' Along: The Temptations and Soul Therapy," The Journal of Black Sacred Music, vol 6, num 1, Spring 1992; "My Jesus was Jim Crowed!" Colors Magazine Vol 3 Issue 3 May/June 1994. co-author: Soul Theology: The Heart of American Black Culture, Harper and Row, 1986, re-published, Abingdon Press, 1991; Black Grief and Soul Therapy, Univ of Richmond, Tubman Press, 1998; consultant: various Olympic Team members, 1980-; US Junior Olympic Team NRA, 1983-; California State Fullerton Football Program, 1983-84; UCLA Basketball Program, 1984-85; lecturer: Bishop College; LK Williams Institute, 1985; SMU Perkins School of Theology, 1986. **CONTACT ADDRESS** Cooper-Lewter Rites of Passage, 253 E 4th St, Ste 201, St Paul, MN, 55101.

COPELAND, M. SHAWN
PERSONAL Born 08/24/1947, Detroit, MI, s **DISCIPLINE** SYSTEMATIC THEOLOGY **EDUCATION** Boston Col, PhD, 91 **CAREER** Inst, 83-87, St. Norbert Col; Lect, Assoc Prof, 89-94, Yale Univ Div Sch; Assoc Prof, 94-pres, Marquette Univ **HONORS AND AWARDS** Sojourner Truth Awd, 74; Sabbatical Grant, 96; Fac Res Award, 90 **MEMBERSHIPS** Amn Acad of Relig; Cath Theol Soc of Am **RESEARCH** Political Theology; African American Religious Experience **SELECTED PUBLICATIONS** Auth, Concilium Violence Against Women, 94; Auth, Editorial Reflections, 94; "Difference as a Category in Critical Theologies for the Liberation of Women," in Concilium: Feminist Theologies in Different Context, 96 **CONTACT ADDRESS** Dept of Theol, Marquette Univ, Coughlin Hall, PO Box 1881, Milwaukee, WI, 53201-1881. **EMAIL** copelands@vms.csd.mu.edu

COPELAND, WARREN R.
PERSONAL Born 09/20/1943, Davenport, IA, m, 1965, 2 children **DISCIPLINE** ETHICS AND SOCIETY, DIVINITY SCHOOL **EDUCATION** MacMurray Coll, AB, 65; Christian Theol Sem, Mdiv, 68; Univ of Chicago, AM, 71, PhD, 73. **CAREER** Illinois Conf of Churches, 73-77; Wittenberg Univ, 77-. **HONORS AND AWARDS** Dist Alumnus, MacMurray Coll. **MEMBERSHIPS** Amer Acad Rel; Soc of Christian Ethics; Soc Ethics Seminar. **RESEARCH** Economic Policy; Poverty and Welfare Policy; Urban Government. **SELECTED PUBLICATIONS** Auth, Issues of Justice, Mercer Univ Press, 88; Economic Justice, Abingdon Press, 88; And the Poor Get Welfare, Abingdon Press, 93. **CONTACT ADDRESS** Wittenberg Univ, Box 720, Springfield, OH, 45501. **EMAIL** wcopeland@wittenberg.edu

COPENHAVER, JOHN D.
PERSONAL Born 03/04/1949, Roanoke, VA, m, 1979, 1 child **DISCIPLINE** RELIGION AND RELIGIOUS STUDIES **EDUCATION** Wash & Lee Univ, BA; Fuller Theol Sem, M div; Cath Univ of Amer, PhD. **CAREER** Assoc prof, Shenandoah Univ; chaplain, Shenandoah Univ; pastor, United Meth Church; campus minister, James Madison Univ. **HONORS AND AWARDS** Exemplary Tchr award; Templeton Award for Course in Sci & Relig. **MEMBERSHIPS** Amer Acad of Relig;

Soc for the Study of Christ Spirituality. **RESEARCH** Christian spirituality; Theological anthropology; Philosophy of the mind. **SELECTED PUBLICATIONS** Auth, Prayerful Responsibility; Prayer and Social Responsibility in the Religious Thought of Douglas Steere, Univ Press of Amer, 92. **CONTACT ADDRESS** 215 Laurel Hill Dr., Stephens City, VA, 22655. **EMAIL** jcopenha@su.edu

CORCORAN, JOHN
PERSONAL Born 03/20/1937, Baltimore, MD **DISCIPLINE** PHILOSOPHY **EDUCATION** John Hopkins Univ, BES, 59, MA, 62, PhD(philos), 63. **CAREER** Mem res staff ling, res lab, Int Bus Mach Corp, Yorktown, NY 63-64; vis lectr philos, Univ Calif, Berkeley, 64-65; asst prof ling, Univ Pa, 65-69; assoc prof philos, 69-73, dir, Grad Studies, 71-74, prof philos, State Univ NY Buffalo, 73-, vis assoc prof philos, Univ Mich, Ann Arbor, 69-70; vis prof, Univ Santiago de Compostela, Spain, 95. **MEMBERSHIPS** Am Philos Asn; Asn Symbolic Logic. **RESEARCH** Logic; linguistics; mathematics. **SELECTED PUBLICATIONS** Coauth, Variable Binding Term Operators, Zeit f Math Logik u Grundlagen, 72; auth, Conceptual Structure of Classical Logic, Philos & Phenomenol Res, 72; Completeness of an Ancient Logic, J Symbolic Logic, 72; Aristotle's Syllogistic, Arch fur Geschichte der Philos, 73; ed, Ancient Logic and Its Modern Interpretations, Reidel Holland, 74; coauth, String Theory, J Symbolic Logic, 74; Ockham's Theory of Supposition, Franciscan Studies, 78; Categoricity, Hist & Philos Logic, 80; ed, Alfred Tarski's Logic, Semantics, Metamathematics, Hackett Publ Co, 83. **CONTACT ADDRESS** Dept of Philos, State Univ of NY, PO Box 601010, Buffalo, NY, 14260-1010. **EMAIL** corcorau@acsu.buffalo.edu

CORCORAN, KEVIN J.
PERSONAL Born 05/30/1964, Annapolis, MD, m, 2 children **DISCIPLINE** PHILOSOPHY **EDUCATION** Univ Maryland, BA, 88; Yale Univ, MA, 91; Purdue Univ, PhD, 97. **CAREER** Asst prof of philos, Calvin Col, 97- . **HONORS AND AWARDS** Vis grad fel, Univ Notre Dame Center for Philos of Relig, 96-97; Paul Hutner scholar of philos theol, Yale Univ, 89-91. **MEMBERSHIPS** APA; Soc of Christian Philo. **RESEARCH** Metaphysics; philosophy of mind; philosophy of religion. **SELECTED PUBLICATIONS** Auth, Persons, Bodies and the Constitution Relation, Southern J of Philos; auth, Persons and Bodies, Faith and Philos; auth, Is Theistic Experience Phenomenologically Possible? Relig Stud. **CONTACT ADDRESS** Dept of Philosophy, Calvin Col, 3201 Burton St SE, Grand Rapids, MI, 49546-4301. **EMAIL** kcorcora@calvin.edu

CORDELL, LADORIS HAZZARD
PERSONAL Born 11/19/1949, Bryn Mawr, PA, d **DISCIPLINE** LAW **EDUCATION** Antioch Coll, BA 1971; Stanford Law School, JD 1974. **CAREER** NAACP Legal Defense & Educ Fund, staff attorney 1974-75; attorney private practice 1975-82; Stanford Law School, asst dean 1978-82; State Court of Appeal Sixth Dist, justice pro tem 1986-87; Municipal Ct Santa Clara Co, judge 1982-88; Superior Ct Santa Clara Co, judge 1988-. **HONORS AND AWARDS** Black History Award Tulip Jones Womens Club 1977; nominated for Black Enterprise Magazine Annual Achievement Award in under 30 category 1977, 1978; Comm Involvement Award East Palo Alto Chamber of Comm 1982, 1983; Public Serv Awd Delta Sigma Theta 1982; Public Serv Awards Natl Council of Negro Women 1982; Outstanding Mid-Peninsula Black Woman Award Mid-Peninsula YWCA 1983; Political Achievement Award CA Black Women's Coalition & the Black Concerns Assn 1982; Featured in Ebony Magazine 1980, 1984; Implemented a minority recruitment program at Stanford Law School as asst dean; First Black Woman Judge in Northern CA; elected presiding judge of the Municipal Court 1985-86 term; Achievement Award, Western Center on Domestic Violence 1986; Santa Clara County Woman of Achievement Award 1985; Recipient of first Juliette Gordon Lowe Award for Community Serv 1987; first black woman on Superior Court in Northern California 1988-; Distinguished Citizen Award, Exchange Club 1989; Don Peters Outstanding Volunteer Award, United Way of Santa Clara County, 1991; Baha'i Community Service Award, 1992; Special Recognition Award, Human Relations Commission of Santa Clara County, 1994; Youth Service Award, Legal Advocates for Children & Youth, 1996; Unsung Heroes Award, Minority Access Committee, Santa Clara County Bar Assoc, 1996; Social Justice award, San Fran Women's Center, 1996; Legal Impact Award, Asian Law Alliance, 1996, Advocate for Justice Award, Legal Aid Society of Santa Clara County, 1996. **MEMBERSHIPS** Mem Natl Bar Assn; mem American Bar Assn; mem NAACP; mem CA Judges Assn; mem CA Women Lawyers; chairperson bd of dirs Manhattan Playhouse East Palo Alto 1980; bd of dirs & steering comm Natl Conf on Women and the Law 1980, 1984-85; policy bd Center for Rsch on Women Stanford Univ 1980-82; chairperson bd of dirs East Palo Alto Comm Law Project 1984-87; bd of trustees, United Way of Santa Clara County 1987-; bd of dir, Police Activities League (PAL), San Jose Chapter 1987-89; Natl Conf of Christians & Jews Inc, Santa Clara County 1988-; bd of trustees, Mills College, Oakland, CA, 1996-; bd of dir, Lucik Packard Fndtn for Children, Stanford, CA, 1997-; mem Silicon Valley Forum Council, Commonwealth Club of CA 1997-; bd of dir, Asian Law Alliance, San Jose, CA, 1997, mem Advisory bd, Healthy Alternatives for African American Babies, San Jose,

CA, 1994-; mem American Law Institute, 1996-. **SELECTED PUBLICATIONS** Auth, "Before Brown v Bd of Educ--Was It All Worth It?" Howard Law Journal Vol 23 No 1 1980; co-auth, "The Appearance of Justice: Judges' Verbal and Nonverbal Behavior in Criminal Jury Trials" Stanford Law Review Vol 38, No 1, 1985; "Black Immigration, Disavowing the Stereotype of the Shiftless Negro" Judges' Journal Spring 1986; Co-author, "Musings of a Trial Court Judge," Indiana Law Journal, vol 68, No 4, 1993. **CONTACT ADDRESS** Superior Court, 191 N First St, San Jose, CA, 95113.

CORDERO, RONALD ANTHONY
PERSONAL Born 06/22/1940, Manila, Philippines, m, 1961, 1 child **DISCIPLINE** PHILOSOPHY **EDUCATION** Univ Pa, BA, 62; Univ Ill, MA, 64, PhD(philos), 69. **CAREER** From instr to prof, 67-, prof philos, Univ Wis-Oshkosh, 77-. **RESEARCH** Ethics and Social Philosophy. **SELECTED PUBLICATIONS** Auth, Law, Morality and La Reconquista, Pub Affairs Quart, 10/90; Classics, Culture, and Curricula, Core and Canon: The Great Debat, ed L Robert Stevens, Univ North Tex Press, 93; Unwitting Discrimination, J Social Philosophy, Spring, 96; Aristotle and Fair Admissions, Pub Affairs Quart, January, 97; The demise of morality, J Value Inquiry, fall 74; Having it both ways with ought, Southern J Philos, winter 75; Ethical theory and the teaching of values, Educ Forum 1/76; Ought, Midwestern J Philos, spring 77. **CONTACT ADDRESS** Dept of Philosophy, Univ Wisconsin, Oshkosh, 800 Algoma Blvd, Oshkosh, WI, 54901-8601. **EMAIL** cordero@uwosh

CORDUAN, WINFRIED
PERSONAL Born 08/17/1949, Hamburg, Germany, m, 1971, 2 children **DISCIPLINE** THEOLOGY, PHILOSOPHY **EDUCATION** Univ MD, BS, 70; Trinity Evangel Divinity Sch, MA, 73; Rice Univ, PhD, 77. **CAREER** Asst prof, 77-80, assoc prof 80-87, prof relig & philos, Taylor Univ, 87. **HONORS AND AWARDS** Distinguished Prof of Year, 85, 98 **MEMBERSHIPS** Evangel Theol Soc; Evangel Philos Soc; Am Philos Asn; Soc Christian Philos **RESEARCH** Philosophical theology, world relig(s), logic. **SELECTED PUBLICATIONS** Auth, Mandmaid to Theology: An Essay in Philosophical Prolegomena, Baker, 81; co-auth, Philosophy of Religion, 2nd ed, Baker, 88; auth, Mysticism: An Evangelical Option?, Zondervan, 91; auth, Reasonable Faith, Broadman & Holman, 93; ed, I & II Chronicles Shepherd's Notes, Broadman & Holman, 98; auth, Neighboring Faiths, InterVarsity, 98. **CONTACT ADDRESS** Taylor Univ, 236 W Reade Ave, Upland, IN, 46989-1001. **EMAIL** wncorduan@tayloru.edu

CORLETT, J. ANGELO
PERSONAL Born 08/27/1958, Pomona, CA **DISCIPLINE** PHILOSOPHY **EDUCATION** Azusa Pacific Univ, BA, 79; Univ Louisville, MA, 85; Univ Calif, Santa Barbara, MA, 88; Univ Arizona, MA, 90, PhD, 92. **CAREER** Asst prof philos, San Diego State Univ. **MEMBERSHIPS** APA; Am Soc for Polit and Legal Philos; AAUP; Calif Fac Asn; Calif Tchrs Asn; Natl Educ Asn; Soc for Ethics. **RESEARCH** Ethics; legal, moral, social and political philosophy; theory of knowledge. **SELECTED PUBLICATIONS** Auth, Racism and Affirmative Action, J of Soc Philos, 93; auth, Foundations of a Kantian Theory of Punishment, So J of Philos, 93; auth, The Problem of Collective Moral Rights, Can J of Law and Jurisp, 94; auth, Goldman and the Foundations of Social Epistemology, Argumentation, 94; auth, Marx and Rights, Dialogue: Can Philos Rev, 94; auth, Corporate Responsibility for Environmental Damage, Environ Ethics, 96; auth, Can Terrorism be Morally Justified? Public Affairs Q, 96; auth, Analyzing Social Knowledge, Rowman & Littlefield, 96; auth, Corporate Punishment and Responsibility, J of Social Philos, 97; auth, What is Civil Disobedience? Philos Papers, 97; auth, Interpreting Plato's Dialogues, Class Q, 97; auth, A Marxist Approach to Business Ethics, J of Business Ethics, 98; auth, Analyzing Racism, Public Affairs Q, 98; auth, Social Epistemology and Social Philosophy, Fenomenologia e Societa, 98; auth, The Morality and Constitutionality of Secession, J of Social Philos, 98; auth, Is There a Moral Duty to Die? Biomed Ethics Rev, forthcoming; auth, Surviving Evil: Jewish, African, and Native-Americans, J of Social Philos, forthcoming; auth, Reparations to Native Americans? in Jokic, ed, War Crimes: Moral and Legal Issues, forthcoming; auth, Political Violence and Collective Responsibility in Jokic, ed, From History to Justice, forthcoming. **CONTACT ADDRESS** Dept of Philosophy, San Diego State Univ, San Diego, CA, 92182. **EMAIL** corlett@rohan.sdsu.edu

CORLISS, RICHARD LEE
PERSONAL Born 10/17/1931, Chicago, IL, m, 1953, 2 children **DISCIPLINE** PHILOSOPHY **EDUCATION** Taylor Univ, BA, 54; Northern Baptist Theol Sem, BD, 57; Univ Ill, Urbana, MA, 59, PhD(philos), 68. **CAREER** From asst prof to assoc prof, 66-75, PROF PHILOS, ST CLOUD STATE UNIV, 75- **MEMBERSHIPS** Am Philos Asn. **RESEARCH** Philosophy of language; philosophy of religion and ethics. **SELECTED PUBLICATIONS** Auth, Schleiermacher Hermeneutic and its Critics, Rel Stud, Vol 0029, 93. **CONTACT ADDRESS** 1729 13th Ave S St, Cloud, MN, 56301.

CORMIER, MICHEAL J.
DISCIPLINE LAW **EDUCATION** Univ Waterloo, BA, 76; Windsor Univ, LLB, 81; Osgoode Hall Law Sch, 94. **CAREER** Prof, Community Legal Services and the Faculty's Clinical Legal Education Programs **RESEARCH** Civil procedure; contracts; advocacy; practice skills. **SELECTED PUBLICATIONS** Auth, pubs on legal process and the manner in which law affects the poor. **CONTACT ADDRESS** Fac of Law, Univ Western Ontario, London, ON, N6A 3K7.

CORNWALL, ROBERT D.
PERSONAL Born 03/03/1958, Los Angeles, CA, m, 1983, 1 child **DISCIPLINE** HISTORICAL THEOLOGY **EDUCATION** Northwest Christian Col, BS, 80; Fuller Theol Sem, M Div, 85, PhD, 91. **CAREER** Dir of the Lib, 92-94, William Carey Int Univ; vis asst prof of Church Hist, 94-95, Fuller Theol Sem; assoc prof Theol, 95-97, Manhattan Christian Col; pastor, First Christian Church, Santa Barbara, CA, 98-. **HONORS AND AWARDS** Winner, Land O' Lakes Essay Competition, Shaw Hist Library, 91. **MEMBERSHIPS** North Am Conf of Brit Stud; Am Acad of Relig; Am Soc of Church Hist. **RESEARCH** Anglicanism 17th & 18th century; church-state issues; Nonjurors; Jacobites; Sacramental Theol. **SELECTED PUBLICATIONS** Auth, Visible and Apostolic: The Constitution of the Church in High Church Anglican and Non-Juror Thought 1688-1745, Univ DE Press, 93; auth, The Later Non-Jurors and the Theological Basis of the Usages Controversy, Anglican Theol Rev, 75, 93; auth, The Church and Salvation: An Early Eighteenth-Century High Church Anglican Perspective, Anglican and Episcopal History, 62, 93; auth, Advocacy of the Independence of the Church from the State in Eighteenth Century England: A Comparison of a Nonjuror and a Nonconformist View, Enlightenment and Dissent, 12, 93; auth, The Crisis in Disciples of Christ Ecclesiology: The Search for Identity, Encounter 55, 94; auth, Unity, Restoration, and Ecclesiology: Why the Stone-Campbell Movement Divided, J of Relig Stud, 19, 95; auth, The Ministry of Reconciliation: Toward a Balanced Understanding of the Global Mission of the Christian Church (Disciples of Christ), Lexington Theol Sem Quart, 30, 95; auth, Education for Ministry in the Augustan Age: A Comparison of the Views of Gilbert Burnet and George Bull and Their Implications for the Modern Church, Anglican Theol Rev, 78, 96; auth, The Scandal of the Cross: Self-Sacrifice, Obedience, and Modern Culture, Encounter 58, 97; ed, Gilbert Burnet, Discourse of the Pastoral Care, Edwin Mellon Press, 97; auth, The Agricultural Revolution: An Interpretive Essay, in Events that Changed the World in the Eighteenth Century, Greenwood Press, 98. **CONTACT ADDRESS** First Christian Church, 1905 Chapala St, Santa Barbara, CA, 93101. **EMAIL** bobcornwall@juno.com

CORR, CHARLES A.
PERSONAL Born 10/11/1937, Montreal, PQ, Canada, m, 1962, 3 children **DISCIPLINE** PHILOSOPHY **EDUCATION** John Carroll Univ, BS, 59; St Louis Univ, AM, 62, PhD(philos), 66. **CAREER** From instr to assoc prof, 65-78, PROF PHILOS, SOUTHERN IL UNIV, EDWARDSVILLE, 78-. **HONORS AND AWARDS** Charles A. Corr Award for Lifetime Achievement (literature), from Children's Hospice Int; for Death Education, from Asn for Death Education and Counseling. **MEMBERSHIPS** Am Philos Asn; AAUP; Asn for Death Ed and Counseling; Int Work Group on Death, Dying, and Bereavement. **RESEARCH** Classical Modern Philosophy, Especially 17th and 18th centuries; Death and Dying. **SELECTED PUBLICATIONS** Coauth, Handbook of Childhood Death and Bereavement, Springer, NYC, 96; Handbook of Adolescent Death and Bereavement, Springer, NYC, 96; Death and Dying, Life and Living, 2nd ed, Brooks/Cole, Pacific Grove, CA, 97. **CONTACT ADDRESS** Dept of Philos Studies, Southern Illinois Univ, Box 1433, Edwardsville, IL, 62026-1433. **EMAIL** ccorr@siue.edu

CORRIGAN, JOHN
DISCIPLINE RELIGION; AMERICAN STUDIES **EDUCATION** Univ of Chicago, PhD; 82 **CAREER** Asst prof, rel stud, Univ Va; current, PROF, AM STUD, ARIZ STATE UNIV **MEMBERSHIPS** Am Antiquarian Soc **RESEARCH** 18th century religion **SELECTED PUBLICATIONS** Auth, The Hidden Balance: Religion and the Social Theories of Charles Chauncy and Jonathan Mayhew, 87; auth, The Prism of Piety: Catholic Congregational Clergy at the Beginning of the Enlightenment, 91; auth, "Habits from the Heart: The American Enlightenment and Religious Ideas about Emotion and Habit," Jour of Rel 73, 93; Jews, Christians, Muslims, 97; coauth, Religion in America, 98. **CONTACT ADDRESS** 15236 N 6th Cir, Phoenix, AZ, 85023. **EMAIL** john.corrigan@asu.edu

CORRIGAN, KEVIN
PERSONAL Born 08/04/1948, United Kingdom, m, 1976, 4 children **DISCIPLINE** PHILOSOPHY; CLASSICS **EDUCATION** Lancaster, BA, 75; MA, 77, PhD, 80, Dalhousie **CAREER** Asst Prof, Col of Notre Dame, Saskatchewan, 82-86; Asst Prof, Assoc Prof, Full Prof, 86-, Dean, 91-, St. Thomas More Col, Univ of Saskatchewan. **RESEARCH** Philosophy; Classics; Ancient/Medieval Plato; Aristotle; Plotinus **SELECTED PUBLICATIONS** Auth, Plotinus Theory of Matter-Evil and the Question of Substance:Plato, Aristotle, and Alex-

ander of Aphrodisias, 96. **CONTACT ADDRESS** 1437 College Dr., Saskatoon, SK, S7N 0W6. **EMAIL** corrigan@usask.sask.ca

CORT, JOHN E.
DISCIPLINE RELIGION **EDUCATION** Univ Wi, BA, 74, MA, 82; Harvard Univ, AM, 84, PhD, 89. **CAREER** Lectr, 89-92, Harvard Univ; vis prof, 94-95, Columbia Univ; asst prof to assoc prof, 92-, Denison Univ. **HONORS AND AWARDS** Asian Cultural Counc Grant, 95-96; Getty Sr Grant, 96-98. **MEMBERSHIPS** Amer Coun of S Asian Art; Assoc of Asian Stud; Amer Acad of Relig; Conf on Relig in S India. **RESEARCH** Jainism; relig; culture; soc in S Asia. **SELECTED PUBLICATIONS** Auth, Defining Jainism: Reform in the Jain Tradition, Univ Toronto, 95; auth, Absences and Presences: Ganesh in the Shvetambar Jain Tradition, Marg Publ, 95; art, Religion, and Material Culture: Some Reflections on Method, J Amer Acad of Relig, 96; art, Recent Fieldwork Studies of the Contemporary Jains, Relig Stud Rev, 97. **CONTACT ADDRESS** Dept of Relig, Denison Univ, Granville, OH, 43023. **EMAIL** cort@denison.edu

CORVINO, JOHN F.
DISCIPLINE PHILOSOPHY **EDUCATION** St John's Univ, BA, 90; Univ Tex, Austin, PhD, 98. **CAREER** Asst inst, Univ Tex, Austin, 95-97; LECTR, WAYNE STATE UNIV, 98-. **CONTACT ADDRESS** Dept Philosophy, Wayne State Univ, 51 W Warren Ave, Rm 3001, Detroit, MI, 48201. **EMAIL** j.corvino@wayne.edu

COSCULLSIA, VICTOR
PERSONAL Born 02/20/1966, San Juan, Puerto Rico, m, 1991 **DISCIPLINE** PHILOSOPHY **EDUCATION** Univ of Miami, PhD, 93. **CAREER** Teaching Philosophy courses in Florida, Connecticut and NY since 89. **HONORS AND AWARDS** Full tuition Acad Scholarship, Univ of Miami. **MEMBERSHIPS** APA **RESEARCH** Philosophy of Religion, Ethics. **SELECTED PUBLICATIONS** Auth, Nine articles in: The Ethics of Suicide, 95. **CONTACT ADDRESS** 400 Amaifi Ave, Coral Gabias, FL, 33146. **EMAIL** Dustyouare@hotmail.com

COSTA, MICHAEL J.
PERSONAL Born 07/21/1945, Cincinnati, OH, m, 1968, 1 child **DISCIPLINE** PHILOSOPHY **EDUCATION** Princeton Univ, AB, 67; Univ Kent, MA, 77; Ohio State Univ, PhD, 81. **CAREER** Oberlin Coll, vis asst prof, 81-83; asst prof, 83-89; Assoc Prof, Univ SC, 89-. **HONORS AND AWARDS** Nat Merit Scholar, 63067; Haggin Fel Univ Kent, 76-77; Univ Fel Ohio State Univ, 77-78; Willaim H Fink Award, Ohio State Univ, 80; NEH Summer Stipend, Ind Univ, 84; Philos Dept and Coll of Humanities Stipend Computers Programs for Tchg Logic, 87. **MEMBERSHIPS** Am Philos Asn; southern Soc for Philos and Psychol; Hume Soc; SC Soc for Philos. **RESEARCH** Philosophy of David Hume. **SELECTED PUBLICATIONS** Auth, Hume and Justified belief, David Hume: Critical Assessments, 95; Why Be Just?: Hume's Response in the Inquiry, David Hume: Critical Assessments, 95; Hume and Belief in the Existence of an External World, David Hume: Critical Assessments, 95; rev, A New Justification of the Moral Rules, 95. **CONTACT ADDRESS** Dept of Philosophy, Univ of S Carolina, Columbia, SC, 29208. **EMAIL** mjcosta@sc.edu

COSTEN, MELVA WILSON
PERSONAL Born 05/29/1933, Due West, South Carolina, m, 1953 **DISCIPLINE** THEOLOGY **EDUCATION** Harbison Jr Coll, Irmo SC, 1947-50; Johnson C Smith Univ, Charlotte NC, AB Educ 1950-52; Univ of North Carolina, Chapel Hill NC MAT Music 1961-64; Georgia State Univ, Atlanta GA, PhD Curriculm and Instruction/Music 1973-78. **CAREER** Mecklenburg County School, Charlotte NC, elementary teacher, 1952-55; Edgecombe County, Rocky Mount Nashville NC, elementary teacher, 1956-57; Nash County, Nashville NC, elementary and music teacher 1959-65; Atlanta Public Schools Atlanta GA, intinerant music teacher 1965-73; Interdenominational Theological, Atlanta GA, Helmar Emil Nielsen Professor of Worship and Music, 1973-. **HONORS AND AWARDS** Conducted 500-voice elementary chorus, Music Educators Natl Conference 1970; Teacher of the Year, Slater School, Atlanta Ga, 1973; Teacher of the Year, Interdenominational Theological Center, 1975; Golden Dove Award, Kappa Omega Chapter, Alpha Kappa Alpha Sorority 1981; conducted 800-voice adult choir, Reuniting Assembly of Presbyterian Church 1983; Two Doctor of Humane Letters, Erskine Coll, Due West SC, 1987 and Wilson College, Chambersburg PA; chairperson, Presbyterian Hymnal Committee, 1985-90. **MEMBERSHIPS** Regional director, Natl Assn of Negro Musicians 1973-75; co-chair, choral div, District V Georgia Music Educators Assoc 1981-82; mem of bd Presbyterian Assn of Musicians 1982-86; chairperson, Presbyterian Church Hymnal Committee 1984-1990; mem of bd Liturgical Conference 1985-91; mem of bd Mid-Atlanta Unit, Cancer Society of America, 1985-87; artistic dir, Atlanta Olympics, 1996-99; Atlanta University Ctr Choruses, 1996. **SELECTED PUBLICATIONS** Published book African-American Christian Worship, Nashville, Abingdon press, 1993. **CONTACT ADDRESS** Music/Worship Office, Interdenominational Theol Ctr, 700 Martin Luther King Jr Dr, SW, Atlanta, GA, 30311.

COSTIGAN, RICHARD F.
PERSONAL Born 03/22/1931, Ottawa, KS **DISCIPLINE** THEOLOGY **EDUCATION** St Louis Univ, AB, 57; Yale Univ, MA, 69; Univ Ottawa (Canada), PhD, 72. **CAREER** Asst prof of theology, 75; assoc prof, 81, Loyola Univ. **MEMBERSHIPS** Am Acad of Relig; Cath Theol Soc of Am. **RESEARCH** Hist of ecclesiology; papacy. **SELECTED PUBLICATIONS** Auth, Rohrbacher and the Ecclesiology of Ultramontanism, Gregorian Univ, 80; auth, Boussuet and the Consensus of the Church, Theological Studies, 95; auth, Behind the Walls: A Theologian Examines our Relationship with the Vatican, Loyola Magazine, 96; auth, Papal Supremacy: From Theory to Practice, The Vital Nexus, 96. **CONTACT ADDRESS** Loyola Univ, 6525 N Sheridan Rd, Chicago, IL, 60626.

COSWAY, RICHARD
PERSONAL Born 10/20/1917, Neward, OH **DISCIPLINE** LAW **EDUCATION** Denison Univ, AB, 39; Univ Cincinnati, JD, 42. **CAREER** Prof law, Univ Cincinnati; PROF LAW, UNIV WASH, 58-, Comnr, Uniform State Laws for Wash, 65-; vis prof law, Southern Methodist Univ, 66-67 & Hastings Col Law, 81-82. **SELECTED PUBLICATIONS** Auth, Professor Rombauer as Friend and Colleague, Wash Law Rev, Vol 0069, 94. **CONTACT ADDRESS** Col of Law, Univ of Washington, Seattle, WA, 98105.

COTTER, JAMES FINN
PERSONAL Born 07/05/1929, Boston, MA, m, 1960, 3 children **DISCIPLINE** ENGLISH LITERATURE, PHILOSOPHY **EDUCATION** Boston Col, AB, 54, MA, 55; Fordham Univ, MA, 58, PhD(English), 63. **CAREER** From instr to asst prof English, Fordham Univ, 60-63; assoc prof, 63-68, prof English, Mt St Mary Col, NY, 68-; Fulbright-Hays lectr, Univ Oran, 70-71. **MEMBERSHIPS** MLA; Conf Christianity & Lit; Dante Soc. **RESEARCH** Dante; Renaissance poetry; Sir Philip Sidney; Gerard Manley Hopkins. **SELECTED PUBLICATIONS** Auth, Visions of Christ in Dante's Divine Comedy, Nemla Studies, 83-84; Hopkins: The Wreck of the Deutschland, 28, The Explicator, 85; Apocalyptic Imagery in Hopkins That Nature is a Heraclitean Fire and of the Comfort of the Resurrections, Victorian Poetry, 86; Look at it loom there! The Image of the Wave in Hopkins' The Wreck of the Deutschland, The Hopkins Quart, 87; Dante and Christ: The Pilgrim as Beatus Vir, The Italian Quart, 88; The Book Within the Book in Medieval Illumination, Florilegium 12, 93; The Song of Songs in The Wreck of the Deutschland in GM Hopkins and Critical Discourse, AMS Press, 94; Augustine's Confessions and The Wreck of the Deutschland in Saving Beauty: Further Studies in Hopkins, Garland, 95; The Divine Comedy and the First Psalm in Dante: Summa Medievalis, Stony Brook: Forum Italicum, 95. **CONTACT ADDRESS** 330 Powell Ave, Newburgh, NY, 12550-3412. **EMAIL** cotter@msmc.edu

COTTER, THOMAS F.
DISCIPLINE LAW **EDUCATION** Univ Wis-Madison, BS, MS, JD. **CAREER** Asst prof, Univ Fla, 94-; former assoc, Jenner Block, Chicago, and Cravath, Swaine Moore, NY; clerk, Judge Lawrence W. Pierce, US Ct Appeals, 2nd Circuit; sr articles ed, Wis Law Rev. **HONORS AND AWARDS** Ladas mem awd, 96. **MEMBERSHIPS** Amer Law and Econ Asn; Soc for the Advancement of Socioeconomics; Ill Bar; Order of the Coif. **RESEARCH** Civil procedure, evidence, intellectual property, law and economics. **CONTACT ADDRESS** School of Law, Univ of Florida, PO Box 117625, Gainesville, FL, 32611-7625. **EMAIL** cotter@law.ufl.edu

COTTON, ROGER D.
PERSONAL Born 07/11/1952, Harvey, IL, m, 1973, 2 children **DISCIPLINE** THEOLOGY **EDUCATION** Concordia Sem St Louis, ThD, 83. **CAREER** Assemblies of God Theol Sem, prof, 87-, ordained minister, 94-. **MEMBERSHIPS** ETS, IBR, SBL, AofG. **RESEARCH** Laws of Pentateuch; Pentateuch, holiness; Old Testament theology. **SELECTED PUBLICATIONS** Auth, Commentary on Leviticus, The Complete Biblical Library: Old Testament Study Bible, eds., T. Gilbrent and G. A. Lint, Springfield MO: World Library Press, 95; auth, Wonderful- God's Name, Signs and Wonders in Ministry Today, eds., B. C. Aker and G.B. McGer, Springfield MO: Gospel Pub House, 96. **CONTACT ADDRESS** Dept of Old Testament, Assemblies of God Theol Sem, 1435 N Glenstone Ave, Springfield, MO, 65802. **EMAIL** rcotton@agseminary.edu

COTTRELL, JACK WARREN
PERSONAL Born 04/30/1938, Scott County, KY, m, 1958, 3 children **DISCIPLINE** HISTORY OF DOCTRINE **EDUCATION** Cincinnati Bible Coll, AB, 59, ThB, 60; Univ Cincinnati, AB, Philos, 62; Westminster Theol Sem, MDiv, 65; Princeton Theol Sem, PhD, 71. **CAREER** Stud instr, Cincinatti Bible Coll, 59-62; PROF, THEOL, CINCINATTI BIBLE SEM, 67-. **MEMBERSHIPS** Evan Theol Sem **SELECTED PUBLICATIONS** Auth, Feminism and the Bible: An Introduction to Feminism for Christians, Coll Press, 92; auth, Gender Roles and the Bible: Creation, the Fall, and Redemption. A Critique of Feminist Biblical Interpretation, Coll Press, 94; Faith's Fundamentals: Seven Essentials of Christian Belief, Standard Publ, 95; TheCollege Press NIV Commentary: Romans, Volume 1, Coll Press, 96; auth, The College Press NIV Commentary: Romans, Volume 2, Coll Press, 98. **CONTACT ADDRESS** Jack Cottrell, 2700 Glenway Ave, Cincinnati, OH, 45204. **EMAIL** Jack.Cottrell@cincybible.edu

COTTROL, ROBERT JAMES
PERSONAL Born 01/18/1949, New York, NY, m, 1987 **DISCIPLINE** LAW **EDUCATION** Yale Univ, BA 1971, PhD 1978; Georgetown Univ Law Ctr, JD 1984. **CAREER** CT Coll, instructor 1974-77; Emory Univ, asst prof 1977-79; Georgetown Univ, lecturer 1979-84; Boston Coll Law School, asst prof of law 1984-87, assoc prof of law, 1987-90; Rutgers School of Law, Camden, NJ, assoc prof, 1990-. **MEMBERSHIPS** Consult GA Commn on the Humanities 1978-79; mem Amer Historical Assoc 1974-, Amer Soc for Legal History 1982-, Amer Bar Assoc 1985-; mem Law and Society Assoc 1985-. **SELECTED PUBLICATIONS** Auth, The Afro Yankees, Providence's Black Community in the Antebellum Era, Greenwood Press 1982. **CONTACT ADDRESS** Rutgers School of Law, Fifth and Penn Sts, Camden, NJ, 08102.

COULSON, RICHARD
PERSONAL Panhandle, TX **DISCIPLINE** LAW **EDUCATION** Oklahoma City Univ, JD, 68. **CAREER** Law clerk, 68-69, united states court of appeals 10th circuit; prof, 69-83, Oklahoma City Univ Sch of Law, dean, 73-76; assoc and member of Rainey, Ross, Rice and Binns, 83-88; Kline and Kline, 83-85; prof of law, 85-88, prof of law, 88-present, Oklahoma City Univ. **MEMBERSHIPS** Oklahoma Bar Assn; bar of the United States Supreme Court **RESEARCH** Legal hist; jurisprudence; bankruptcy law and evidence law **SELECTED PUBLICATIONS** Auth, Fradulent Transfers: History, Overview, and Developments-StateLaw, 50 Consumer Fin, 95; 1995 Consumer Bankruptcy Developments, 96; 1996 consumer bankruptcy Developments, 97; Case developments in consumer Bankruptcy Highlight Need for Statutory Refor **CONTACT ADDRESS** Sch of Law, Oklahoma City Univ, 2501 N. Bl, Oklahoma City, OK.

COUNTEE, THOMAS HILAIRE, JR.
PERSONAL Born 08/07/1939, Washington, DC, d **DISCIPLINE** LAW **EDUCATION** Amer Univ, Washington, DC, BA, 1963; Georgetown Univ Law Center, JD, 1967; Harvard Business School, MBA, 1971. **CAREER** Countee, Countee & Assoc, Inc, chmn, CEO, 1988-; chief exec officer, 1978-88; MD, Natl Capital Park & Planning Commn, gen counsel, 1977-78; Office of Mat & Budget, legislative counsel; exec offce of pres, 1975-76; MODEDCO Inv Co, pres, 1971-75; Howard Univ, Washington, DC, prof, 1973; Fed City Coll, prof, 1973; Poloroid Corp, Cambridge MA, asst general counsel, 1971; Roxbury Small Business Devel Center, Boston, consultant, 1970; Securities & Exchange Commn, Washington, DC, Attorney, 1969. **HONORS AND AWARDS** Harvard Univ Scholarship, 1956-58; Harvard Business School Fellowship, 1969-71; Georgetown Law School, Lawyers Co-op Publishing Co Prizes; State of Maryland Disabled Person of the Year, 1980. **MEMBERSHIPS** Mem, DC Bar; Practiced before US Dist Court, DC, US Court of Appeals for DC, and US Court of Mil Appeals; mem, bd of dir, New Life, Inc 1972-; National Council for Therapeutic Riding, 1980-; alumni recruiter, Phillip's Acad, 1979, Harvard Business School, 1971; mem, Kappa Alpha Psi. **SELECTED PUBLICATIONS** Auth, History of Black-Owned & Operated Finance Institutes

COUNTRYMAN, L. WM
PERSONAL Born 10/21/1941, Oklahoma City, OK **DISCIPLINE** CLASSICS, NEW TESTAMENT **EDUCATION** Univ of Chicago, BA, 62, MA, 74, PhD, 77; Grand Theol Sem, STB, 65 **CAREER** Lect, 74-76, Univ of Chicago; Asst Prof, 76-79, SW Mission St Univ; Asst Prof, 79-83 TX Christ Univ; Prof, 83-pres, Church Div Sch of the Pac **HONORS AND AWARDS** Phi Beta Kappa **MEMBERSHIPS** Soc of Bibl Lit; Assoc of Anglican Bibl Schols; Soc for Study of Christian Spirituality **RESEARCH** Spirituality; Sexual Orientation **SELECTED PUBLICATIONS** Auth, The Rich Christian in the Church of the Early Empire, Edwin Mellen Press, 80; Auth, The Mystical Way in the Fourth Gospel, Crossing Over into God, Fortress Press, 87; Living on the Border of the Holy: The Priesthood of Humanity and the Priesthoods of the Church, Morehouse Publ, 99; Forgiven and Forgiving, Morehouse Publ, 98 **CONTACT ADDRESS** Church Divinity Sch of the Pacific, 2451 Ridge, Berkeley, CA, 94709. **EMAIL** bcountryman@cdsp.edu

COUTURE, PAMELA D.
DISCIPLINE RELIGION **EDUCATION** Univ Chicago, PhD 90; Garrett-Evangelical Theological Sem, Mdiv 82; Ashland College, BA 72. **CAREER** Colgate Rochester Divinity Sch, assoc prof 98-; Assoc of Theological Sch, dir 97-98; Chandler Sch of Theol, asst prof 89-97, dir 91-93; Samaritan Inst, past coun 83-89; N IL Conf BD of Ordained Ministry, 84-92; United Meth Ch, ordained 81; Arlington Hts and Roselle IL, past staff, assoc past 78-83. **MEMBERSHIPS** IAPT; AAPC; SPT; OIMTS; AAR **SELECTED PUBLICATIONS** Auth, Feminist Wesleyan Practical Theology and the Practice of Pastoral Care, in: Liberating Faith Practices: Feminist Practical Theologies in Context, eds, Riet Bons Storm, Denise Ackerman, Kok-Pharos, 98; When the Last are First: Poor Children as a Challenge to the

Church, Sisters Today, 97; Rethinking Private and Public Patriarchy, in: Feminism Rel and the Fam, eds, Anne Carr, Emily Stewart VanLeewen, Louisville, Westminster John Knox Press, 96; Weaving the Web: Pastoral Care in an Individualistic Society, in: Through the Eyes of Women: Insights for Pastoral Care, ed, Jean Stevenson Moessner, Minn, Fortress Press, 96; Review of David Blankenhorn's Fatherless America: Confronting Our Most Urgent Social Problem, in: The Christ Century, 95. **CONTACT ADDRESS** Dept of Theology, Colgate Rochester Divinity Sch, 24 Dyson St, Rochester, NY, 14609. **EMAIL** pcouture@crds.edu

COVELL, RALPH
PERSONAL m, 3 children **DISCIPLINE** MISSIONS **EDUCATION** E Baptist Col, BA; E Baptist Theol Sem, BD, BT; Fuller Theol Sem, ThM; Denver Sem, Ddiv, PhD. **CAREER** Sr prof, Denver Sem. **HONORS AND AWARDS** Bd ch, Chinese Childen Adoption Intl; mem, CBFMS (now CBInt), Chian, Taiwan; transl consult, Bible Soc(s) Taiwan. **SELECTED PUBLICATIONS** Transl, New Testament Into the Language of the Sediq, a Malayo-Polynesian People Living in the Mountains of Taiwan; auth, Confucius, the Buddha, and Christ; Liberating Gospel in China; Mission Impossible: The Unreached Nosu. **CONTACT ADDRESS** Denver Conservative Baptist Sem, PO Box 10000, Denver, CO, 80250. **EMAIL** ralph@densem.edu

COVER, JAN
DISCIPLINE EARLY MODERN PHILOSOPHY, METAPHYSICS **EDUCATION** Syracuse Univ, PhD. **CAREER** Assoc prof, Purdue Univ; coed, Central Themes in Early Modern Philosophy. **SELECTED PUBLICATIONS** Published articles on Leibniz, causality, and space and time. **CONTACT ADDRESS** Dept of Philos, Purdue Univ, 1080 Schleman Hall, West Lafayette, IN, 47907-1080.

COWAN, LAURIE
PERSONAL Born 04/23/1961, Burlington, NC, m, 1996, 1 child **DISCIPLINE** PHILOSOPHY **EDUCATION** Emory Univ, MA, 90, PhD, 96; Bryn Mawr Col, AB, 83 **CAREER** Course Devel, 97-pres, Digital Lrn Grp; Inst, 96-97, DeKalb Col; Inst, 92-93, Auburn Univ **HONORS AND AWARDS** Univ Fel, Emory Univ, 85-89; Richard W Weaver Fel, 85 **MEMBERSHIPS** Am Philos Assoc **RESEARCH** Hist of Philosophy **SELECTED PUBLICATIONS** Auth, Dissertation: The Interpretation of Scripture in Hobbes's Leviathan, 96 **CONTACT ADDRESS** 208 Willow Ln, Decatur, GA, 30030. **EMAIL** lcmarion@aol.com

COWAN, RICHARD O.
PERSONAL Born 01/24/1934, Los Angeles, CA, m, 1958, 6 children **DISCIPLINE** CHURCH HISTORY **EDUCATION** Occidental Col, BA, 58; Stanford Univ, MA, 59, PhD, 61. **CAREER** Asst prof religious instr, 61-65, assoc prof history religion, 65-71, prof history religion, Brigham Young Univ, 71-; Danforth Fel, 58. **HONORS AND AWARDS** Phi Beta Kappa, 57. **MEMBERSHIPS** Mormom Hist Asn. **RESEARCH** Latter-day Saint history and theology. **SELECTED PUBLICATIONS** Coauth, Mormonism in the Twentieth Century 64, auth, The Doctrine and Covenants: Our Modern Scripture, 67, Temple Building Ancient and Modern, 71 & coauth, The Living Church, 74, Brigham Young Univ; Church in the Twentieth Century, 85; Doctrine and Covenants: Our Modern Scripture, 84; Temples to Dot the Earth, 89; Joseph Smith and the Doctrine and Covenants, 92; California Saints, 96; LDS Church History Encyclopedia, (pending). **CONTACT ADDRESS** Brigham Young Univ, 270L Joseph Smith Bldg, Provo, UT, 84602. **EMAIL** richard_cowan@byu.edu

COWAN, S.B.
PERSONAL Born 04/06/1962, Hattiesburg, MS, m, 1986 **DISCIPLINE** PHILOSOPHY **EDUCATION** Southern Miss, BA, 87; Southwestern Bapt Theol Sem, M. Div, 91; Univ Ark, MA, 93; PhD, 96. **CAREER** Adjunct prof, christ ethics and New Testament, Southern Bapt Theol Sem, 97; adjunct prof, philos, Univ Ark, 97-98; adjunct prof, philos of relig, Midwestern Bapt Theol Sem, 98. **MEMBERSHIPS** Evang Theol Soc; Evang Philos Soc; Soc of Christ Philos. **RESEARCH** Philosophical theology; Free will and determinism; Reformed theology. **SELECTED PUBLICATIONS** Auth, Review of Richard Swinburne's The Christian God in Philosophia Christi, vol 19, no 2, Fall, 96; A Reductio ad Absurdum of Divine Temporality, Relig Studies, vol 32, no 4, Sep, 96; On the Epistemological Justification of Miracle Claims, Philos Christi, vol 18, no 1, Spr, 95; Why Be a Christian?, The Student, vol 73, no 5, Nov, 94; The What and Why of Theology, The Student, vol 73, no 5, Nov, 94; Aristotelian' Logic in the Old Testament: A Biblical Refutation of a Strict Dichotomy Between Greek and Hebrew Thought, Bull of the Evang Philos Soc, vol 14, no 2, 91; Common Misconceptions of Evangelicals Regarding Calvinism, Jour of the Evang Theol Soc, vol 33, no 2, Jun, 90. **CONTACT ADDRESS** 1775 Janice Av., Fayetteville, AR, 72703. **EMAIL** sbcowan@juno.com

COWARD, HAROLD G.
PERSONAL Born 12/13/1936, Calgary, AB, Canada **DISCIPLINE** RELIGION/HISTORY **EDUCATION** Univ Alta, BA, 58, BD, 67, MA, 69; McMaster Univ, PhD, 73. **CAREER** Prof, Univ Calgary, 73-92, head relig stud, 76, 79-83, assoc dean hum, 77, dir, univ press, 81-83; dir, Calgary Inst Hum, 80-92; DIR, CENTRE FOR STUDIES IN RELIGION AND SOCIETY & PROF HISTORY, UNIV VICTORIA, 92-. **HONORS AND AWARDS** Fel, Royal Soc Can **MEMBERSHIPS** Pres, Can Soc Stud Relig, 84-86; pres, Shastri Indo-Can Inst, 86-88; pres, Can Corp Stud Relig, 87-90; pres, Can Fedn Hum, 90-91. **RESEARCH** Eastern religions; Hindu thought & religion; religious pluralism. **SELECTED PUBLICATIONS** Auth, Bhartrhari, 76; auth, Sphota Theory of Language, 80; auth, Jung and Eastern Thought, 85; auth, Pluralism: Challenge to World Religions; auth, Sacred Word and Sacred Text: Scripture in the World Religions, 88; auth, Hindu Ethics: Purity, Euthanasia and Abortion, 88; Derrida and Indian Philosophy, 90; coauth, Psychological Epistemology, 78; coauth, Humanities in Alberta, 84; coauth, Philosophy of the Grammarians, 90; coauth, Mantra: Hearing the Divine in India, 91; ed, Mystics and Scholars, 77; ed, Revelation in Indian Thought, 77; ed, Religion and Ethnicity, 78; ed, Humanities in the Present Day, 79; ed, Scholarly Communication, 80; ed, Calgary's Growth: Bane or Boon? 81; ed, Ethical Issues in the Allocation of Health Care Resources, 82; ed, Studies in Indian Thought, 82; ed, Religions in Contact and Change, 83; ed, The Role of the Modern Union, 85; ed, Modern Indian Responses to Religious Pluralism, 87; ed, Silence, Sacred and the Word, 88; ed, Readings in Eastern Religions, 88; ed, Hindu-Christian Dialogue, 89; ed, Privacy, 89; ed, The Future of Fossil Fuels, 91; ed, Derrida and Negative Theology, 92; ed, Reflections on Cultural Policy, 93; ed, Aging and Dying: Legal, Scientific and Religious Challenges, 93; ed, Anger in Our City: Youth Seeking Meaning, 94; ed, Population, Consumption and the Environment, 95; ed, Life After Death in World Religions, 97. **CONTACT ADDRESS** Ctr for Stud in Relig & Society, Univ of Victoria, Victoria, BC, V8W 3P4. **EMAIL** csrs@uvic.ca

COX, ARCHIBALD
PERSONAL Born 05/17/1912, Plainfield, NJ, 3 children **DISCIPLINE** LAW **EDUCATION** Harvard Univ, AB, 34, LLB, 37. **CAREER** Atty, Ropes, Gray, Best, Coolidge & Rugg, Boston, 38-41; atty, Off Solicitor Gen, US Dept Justice, 41-43; assoc solicitor, Dept Labor, 43-45; lectr law, 45-46, prof, 46-61, mem, Bd Overseers, 62-65, Williston Prof law, 65-76, Carl M Loeb Univ Prof, Harvard Law Sch, 76-, Chmn, Wage Stabilization Bd, 52; co-chmn, Construction Indust Stabilization Comt, 51-52; Solicitor Gen, US Dept Justics, 61-65, spec prosecutor, Watergate Hearings, 73; vis Pitt Prof Am hist & insts & lectr, Cambridge Univ, Eng, 73. **HONORS AND AWARDS** LLD, Loyola Univ, Chicago, 64, Univ Cincinnati, 67, Rutgers Univ, 74, Univ Denver, 74, Amherst Col, 74, Harvard Univ, 75, Univ MI, 76, Wheaton Col, 77, Northeastern, 78, Clark Univ, 80; LHD, Hahnemann Med Col, 80, Univ MA, 81. **MEMBERSHIPS** Am Bar Asm; Am Acad Arts & Sci; Am Philos Soc. **SELECTED PUBLICATIONS** Auth, Cases in Labor Law, 48; coauth, Law and the National Labor Policy, 60; auth, Civil Rights, The Constitution and the Courts, 67; The Warren Court: Constitutional Decision as an Instrument of Reform, 68; The Role of the Supreme Court in American Government, 76; Freedom of Expression, 81. **CONTACT ADDRESS** Law Sch, Harvard Univ, 1563 Massachusetts Ave, LILC 308, Cambridge, MA, 02138.

COX, CHANA B.
PERSONAL Born 10/28/1941, Detroit, MI, m, 1967, 5 children **DISCIPLINE** PHILOSOPHY **EDUCATION** Columbia Univ, PhD, 71. **CAREER** St Lectr Humanities, Lewis & Clark Col. **CONTACT ADDRESS** Lewis & Clark Col, 0615 SW Palatine Hill, Box 83, Portland, OR, 97219. **EMAIL** cox@lclark.edu

COX, CLAUDE E.
PERSONAL Born 09/23/1947, Meaford, ON, Canada, m, 1989, 3 children **DISCIPLINE** RELIGION **EDUCATION** Abilene Christian Univ, BA, 69; Knox Col, MDiv, 72; Union Theol Sem-VA, ThM, 73; Univ Toronto, MA, 74, PhD, 79. **CAREER** Asst prof Dept Near E Stud, Univ Toronto, 79-80; asst prof Dept of Relig, 80-84, Chr, 82-84; adj assoc prof of Old Testament & Hebrew, McMaster Divinity Col, 94-; Can Coun Doctoral fel, 75-79; Can-USSR Exch fel, 77-78. **MEMBERSHIPS** Int Orgn Septuagint and Cognate Stud; Soc Bibl Lit; Can Soc Bibl Stud; Soc Armenian Stud; Asn Int des Etudes Armeniennes; Ont Chaplains Asn. **RESEARCH** Old Testament; Septuagint studies; Armenian Bible. **SELECTED PUBLICATIONS** Ed The Campbell-Stone Movement in Ontario, Studies in the Campbell-Stone Movement, Edwin Mellen, 95; The Vocabulary for Good and Evil in the Armenian Translation of the New Testament, Text and Context: Studies in the Armenian New Testament, Scholars, 95; Aquila, Symmachus and Theodotion in America, Scholars, 96; The Armenian Bible, Krikor and Clara Zohrab Information Center Occasional Papers Series, 96; The Reading of the Personal Letter as the Background for the Reading of the Scriptures in the Early Church, The Early Church in Context: Essays in Honor of Everett Ferguson, Brill, 98. **CONTACT ADDRESS** 18 Roslyn Rd, Barrie, ON, L4M 2X6. **EMAIL** c.cox@sympatico.ca

COX, HOWARD A.
PERSONAL Born 10/10/1958, Jacksonville, TX, m, 1988, 2 children **DISCIPLINE** THEOLOGY **EDUCATION** Stephen F Austin State Univ, BA, 81; Abilene Christian Univ, MA, 83; Theolg Univ of Am, DRE, 94. **CAREER** Instr, Lamar Univ, 90-92; instr 88-90, asst prof, 94-, Magnolia Bible Col. **HONORS AND AWARDS** Who's Who in Am Educ; Miss Asn of Cols Outstanding Faculty Member; Sigma Tau Delta Writer's Key Award., Phi Delta Kappa; Alpha Chi; Sigma Tau Delta; Phi Iota. **MEMBERSHIPS** MLA; MLA; CCCC; Evangelical Theological Asn. **RESEARCH** 20th Century Am Lit; Post WWI Expatriates; assesment & evolution **SELECTED PUBLICATIONS** Auth, Imitating Christ's Forgiveness, 95; auth, Magnolia Bible College Conducts Research on Student's Knowledge of Safety and Security, 95; auth, A New Reading of the Feeding of the Five Thousand, 96; auth, The Christian's Response to Suicide, 97. **CONTACT ADDRESS** PO Box 1109, Kosciusko, MS, 39090.

COX, STEVEN L.
PERSONAL Born 07/16/1956, Greenville, SC, m, 1975, 2 children **DISCIPLINE** THEOLOGY **EDUCATION** Anderson Col, AP, 79; Central Wesleyan Col, BA, 82; Erskine Theol Sem, M Div, 86; Southern Baptist Theol Sem, PhD, 91. **CAREER** Asst prof of NT & Greek, Luther Rice Sem, 92-94; ASST PROF OF NT & GREEK, MID-AMERICA BAPTIST THEOL SEM, 95-. **HONORS AND AWARDS** Am Bible Soc Award, 86 (Erskine)., Nat Deans List, 82; lectured in Germany, Switzerland, and Japan; Salutatorian (Erskine), 86; Cambridge Univ, summer 99. **MEMBERSHIPS** Evangelical Theol Soc; Soc of Biblical Lit; Tyndale Fel; Inst of Biblical Res. **RESEARCH** New Testament issues; historiography; NT Greek. **SELECTED PUBLICATIONS** Auth, A History and Critique of Scholarship Concerning the Markan Endings, Mellen, 93; Essentials of New Testament Greek: A Student's Guide, Broadman/Holman, 95; Tychicus: A Profile, The Biblical Illustrator, summer 95; An Anecdote to Violence: 1 Corinthians 13, The Rev and Expositor, fall 96; Three Millenial Views, SBC Sunday School Board, Life and Works Series, spring 96; contrib to the Eerdmans Dictionary of the Bible, submitted 7/19/96; The Parable of the Sower in Luke 10:25-37: What Does Love Look Like?, The Mid-America Theol J, June 97; The Jewish Concept of Ghosts in Light of Matthew 14:26, The Biblical Illustrator, winter 97; book reviews in various theological journals, 89-98; several publications forthcoming. **CONTACT ADDRESS** Mid-America Baptist Theol Sem, 2216 Germantown Rd., South, Germantown, TN, 38138-3815. **EMAIL** slcox@ix.netcom.com

COYLE, J. KEVIN
PERSONAL Born 04/25/1943, Iroqouis Falls, ON, Canada, s **DISCIPLINE** EARLY CHRISTIAN HISTORY **EDUCATION** Univ of Ottawa, BA, BPh, 63; Catholic Univ of Amer, BTh, LTh, 65 and 67; Univ de Fribourg en Suisse, DTh, 79. **CAREER** Lectr, 76-79, Asst Prof, 79-84, Assoc Prof, 84-87, Full Prof, 87-, Universite Saint-Paul, Ottawa. **MEMBERSHIPS** Canadian Soc of Patristic Studies; North Amer Patristic Soc; Intl Assoc for Patristic Studies; Intl Assoc of Manichaean Studies; Societe quebecoise pour l etude de las religion; Soc of Biblical Lit. **RESEARCH** History of early Christianity; Latin Palaeography; Development of Christian Thought; Manichaeism **SELECTED PUBLICATIONS** Auth, De moribus ecclesiae catholicae: Augustin chretien a Rome, De moribus ecclesiae catholicae et de moribus Manichaeorum: De quantitate animae, 91; Mary Magdalene in Manichaeism, Le Museon, 91; Augustine's Millenialism Reconsidered, Charisteria Augustiniana Iosepho Oroz Reta dicata, 93; Recent Reviews on the Origins of Clerical Celibacy, Logos, 93; Hands and the Impositions of Hands in Manichaesim, Pegrina Curiositas: Eine Reise durch den orbis antiquus. Zu Ehren von Dirk van Damme, 94; Early Monks, Prayer and the Devil, Prayer and Spirituality in the Early Church, 98. **CONTACT ADDRESS** St. Paul Univ, 223 Main St., Ottawa, ON, K1S 1C4. **EMAIL** JKCOYLE@AIX1.UOTTAWA.CA

COYNE, ANTHONY M.
PERSONAL Born 09/16/1949, Richmond, VA, m, 1975, 2 children **DISCIPLINE** PHILOSOPHY **EDUCATION** Univ NC Chapel Hill, PhD, 74; Wash and Lee Univ, BS, summa cum laude 70, BA, summa cum laude 70. **CAREER** Assoc Dean, 97-, Univ S Carolina; Prof, 78-97, Univ N Carolina; Asst Prof, 76-78, Elon College; vis Asst Prof, 75, Univ NC Chapel Hill. **HONORS AND AWARDS** Phi Beta Kappa; John Motley Morehead Fel. **MEMBERSHIPS** APA; AIL; HS; NAHE; AAPT. **RESEARCH** History of Philosophy; Logic. **SELECTED PUBLICATIONS** Auth, Introduction to Inductive Reasoning, UPA, 84; auth, Paul and the Value of Philosophy, Explorations, 87; Philosophy and the Modern Mind: A Criticism, S J of Philo, 78; revs in Zentralblatt fur Mathematik: Keith Devlin, Sets Functions and Logic: An Introduction to Abstract Mathematics; Raymond Smullyan, Godel's Incompleteness Theorems; Mary Tiles, Mathematics and the Image of Reason; Anthony Galton, Logic for Information Technology; Wesley C Salmon, Logik; Paul Teller, A Modern Formal Logic Primer, vol 1 and vol 2. **CONTACT ADDRESS** Univ South Carolina Sumter, Sumter, SC, 29150. **EMAIL** acoyne@uscsumter.edu

CRABTREE, ARTHUR BAMFORD
PERSONAL Born 05/05/1910, Stalybridge, England, m, 1938, 1 child **DISCIPLINE** THEOLOGY **EDUCATION** Univ Manchester, BA, 33, BD, 35; Univ Zurich, Dr(theol), 46. **CAREER** Prof theol, Baptist Theol Sem, Switz, 49-57 & Eastern Baptist theol Sem, Pa, 57-68; assoc prof, Villanova Univ, 68-76, PROF THEOL, 76-80; Retired. **MEMBERSHIPS** N Am Acad Ecumenists; Col Theol Soc. **RESEARCH** Ecumenical and Protestant theology. **SELECTED PUBLICATIONS** Auth, Thou in Our Midst--An Ecumenical Prayer-Book-German, Jour Ecumenical Stud, Vol 0028, 91; Why and How to Pray--The Answer to World Religions--German, Jour Ecumenical Stud, Vol 0028, 91. **CONTACT ADDRESS** Dept of Theol, Villanova Univ, Villanova, PA, 19085.

CRADDOCK, JERRY RUSSELL
PERSONAL Born 05/19/1935, Pueblo, CO, m, 1961 **DISCIPLINE** ROMANCE PHILOLOGY, MEDIEVAL HISPANIC LITERATURE **EDUCATION** Tex Western Col, BA, 58; Univ Calif, Berkeley, PhD, 67. **CAREER** Asst prof Span, Univ Calif, Davis, 65-68, from asst prof to assoc prof Span & Romance philol, 68-76, PROF SPAN, UNIV CALIF, BERKELEY, 76-. **MEMBERSHIPS** Ling Soc Am; MLA; Mediaeval Acad Am. **RESEARCH** Linguistics. **SELECTED PUBLICATIONS** Auth, The Spanish Spoken in the Southwest of the United-States--Materials for Its Study--Spanish, Hisp Rev, Vol 0061, 93; A Decade of Alfonsine Studies--Working Notes and Bibliography, Romance Philol, Vol 0049, 95; A History of the Spanish-Language, Jour Hisp Philol, Vol 0017, 92; Medieval Judeo-Hispanic Documents from Castile and Aragon-Italian, Speculum-Journal Medieval Stud, Vol 0069, 94; Documents for the Linguistic History of Spanish-America, 16th-18th Centuries--Spanish, Romance Philol, Vol 0051, 97; Etymology, Romance Philol, Vol 0049, 95; Foreword--On Romance-Philologys 50th-Year of Publication, Romance Philol, Vol 0050, 97; Linguistic Documents of New-Spain--Altiplano-Central-Spanish, Romance Philol, Vol 0051, 97; Documents for the Linguistic History of Spanish-America, 16th-18th Centuries--Spanish, Romance Philol, Vol 0051, 97; Supplement to Malkiel,Yakov a Tentative-Autobibliography--New and Updated Entries Title Index, Romance Philol, Vol 0048, 95; Philological Notes on the Hammond and Rey Translation of the Relacion de la Entrada Que Hizo en el Nuevo Mexico Francisco Sanchez Chamuscado en Junio de 1581 by Gallegos, Hernan, Notary of the Expedition, Romance Philol, Vol 0049, 96. **CONTACT ADDRESS** Dept of Span & Port, Univ of Calif, 4319 Dwinelle Hall, Berkeley, CA, 94720-2591.

CRAIG, WILLIAM LANE
PERSONAL Born 08/23/1949, Peoria, IL, m, 1972, 2 children **DISCIPLINE** PHILOSOPHY, THEOLOGY **EDUCATION** Univ Birmingham UK, PhD, 77; Univ Munchen, DTh. **CAREER** Asst Prof, 80-86, Trinity Evang Div Sch; Assoc Prof, 86-87, Westmont College; indep res 87-94, Katoiike Univ Belgium; Res Prof 94-, Talbot Sch Theol. **HONORS AND AWARDS** Humboldt Fel. **MEMBERSHIPS** APA; AAR; SBL; SCP; ASA; SRF; PTS; ETS; EPS. **RESEARCH** Theism and Cosmology; Omniscience; Philosophy of Time; Resurrection. **SELECTED PUBLICATIONS** Auth, On Hasker's Defense of Anti-Molinism, Faith and Philo, 98; Creation and Conservation Once More, Religious Stud, 98; McTaggart's Paradox and the Problem of Temporary Intrinsics, Analysis, 98; Divine Timelessness and Personhood, Intl J for Philo of Religion, 98; coauth, Will the Real Jesus Please Stand Up? ed Paul Copan, Grand Rapids MI, Baker Bookhouse, 98; auth, John Dominic on the Resurrection of Jesus, in: The Resurrection, ed S Davis, D Kendall, G O Collins, Oxford, Oxford Univ Press, 97; On the Argument for Divine Timelessness from the Incompleteness of Temporal Life, Heythrop J, 97; Adams on Actualism and Presentism, Philosophia, 97; In Defense of the Kalam Cosmology Argument, Faith and Philo, 97; A Critique of Grdem's Formulation and Defense of the Doctrine of Eternity, Philosophica Christi, 96; The New B-Theory's Tu Quoque Argument, Synthese, 96; A response to Grunbaum on Creation and Big Bang Cosmology, Philosophia Naturalis, 94; Should Peter go to the Mission Field? Faith and Philo, 93; Talbot's Universalism Once More, Religious Stud, 93; Divine Foreknowledge and Human Freedom: The Coherence of Theism: Omniscience, Studies in Intellectual History, Leiden, EJ Brill, 90. **CONTACT ADDRESS** 1805 Danforth Dr, Marietta, GA, 30062.

CRAIG-TAYLOR, PHYLISS
DISCIPLINE LAW **EDUCATION** Univ Ala, BS, JD; Columbia Univ, LLM. **CAREER** Asst prof, Univ Fla, 95-. **MEMBERSHIPS** Ala Bar; NC Bar. **RESEARCH** Law, bankruptcy, poverty law, and public benefits. **CONTACT ADDRESS** School of Law, Univ of Florida, PO Box 117625, Gainesville, FL, 32611-7625. **EMAIL** c-taylor@law.ufl.edu

CRAIGHEAD, HOUSTON ARCHER
PERSONAL Born 01/24/1941, San Antonio, TX, m, 1964, 2 children **DISCIPLINE** PHILOSOPHY **EDUCATION** Baylor Univ, BA, 62, MA, 64; Univ Tex, Austin, PhD(philos), 70. **CAREER** Asst prof philos, ECarolina Univ, 66-70; assoc prof, 70-80, PROF PHILOS, WINTHROP COL, 80- **MEMBERSHIPS** Am Philos Asn; Metaphys Soc Am; Southwestern Philos Soc; Soc Studies Process Philos; Soc Philos Relig. **RESEARCH** Metaphysics, primarily in the concept of non-being; philosophy of religion; existentialism. **SELECTED PUBLICATIONS** Auth, The Life of Irony and the Ethics of Belief, Intl Jour Philos Rel, Vol 0037, 95. **CONTACT ADDRESS** Dept of Philos, Winthrop Univ, Rock Hill, SC, 29730.

CRAMTON, ROGER C.
PERSONAL Born 05/18/1929, Pittsfield, MA, m, 1952, 4 children **DISCIPLINE** LAW **EDUCATION** Harvard Univ, BA, 50; Iniv Chicago, JD, 55; Oxford Univ, LLD, 88. **CAREER** Univ Chicago, 57-61; Univ Mich, 61-73; CORNELL UNIV, 73-. **HONORS AND AWARDS** Guggenheim Fel, 88-89. **MEMBERSHIPS** Am Acad Arts & Sci; Am Law Inst Coun **RESEARCH** Legal ethics; Legal profession. **SELECTED PUBLICATIONS** Conflict of Laws: Cases, Comments, Questions, West Publ Co, 93; The Law and Ethics of Lawyering, Found Press, 94. **CONTACT ADDRESS** Cornell Law Sch, Cornell Univ, Ithaca, NY, 14850. **EMAIL** cramton@law.mail.cornell.edu

CRANFORD, LORIN L.
DISCIPLINE RELIGIOUS STUDIES **EDUCATION** Wayland Baptist Univ, BA; Southwestern Baptist Theol Seminary, ThD. **CAREER** Tchr, Southwestern Baptist Theol Seminary 75-98; prof, 98-. **MEMBERSHIPS** Soc Bibl Lit; Inst Bibl Res. **SELECTED PUBLICATIONS** Auth, Revelation, Garland; Inspiration, Garland; Lost and Found, Decision Magazine. **CONTACT ADDRESS** Dept of Religious Studies and Philosophy, Gardner-Webb Univ, PO Box 997, Boiling Springs, NC, 28017. **EMAIL** lcranford@gardner-webb.edu

CRANOR, CARL
DISCIPLINE PHILOSOPHY **EDUCATION** UCLA, PhD. **CAREER** PROF, ASSOC DEAN, HUMAN AND SOC SCI, UNIV CALIF, RIVERSIDE. **RESEARCH** Moral, legal and political philosophy. **SELECTED PUBLICATIONS** Auth, "Some Moral Issues in Risk Assessment," Ethics Vol 101, 90; "Science Courts, Evidentiary Procedures, and Mixed Science Policy Decisions," Risk: Issues in Health and Safety, Vol 4, 93; Regulating Toxic Substances: A Philosophy of Science and the Law, Oxford Univ Press, 93; Are Genes Us?, The Social Consequences of the New Genetics, Rutgers Univ Press, 94; "Toxic Substances and Agenda 21: Ethics and Policy Issues in the Science and its Implementation," Sustainable Development: Science, Ethics, and Policy, Kluwer, 95; "The Social Benefits of Expedited Risk Assessment," Risk Analysis, 95; "Improving the Regulation of Carcinogens by Expediting Cancer Potency Estimation," Risk Analysis, 95; "Learning from the Law for Regulatory Science," Law and Philos, 95; "Judicial Boundary-Drawing and the Need for Context-Sensitive Science in Toxic Torts after Daubert v. Merrell-Dow Pharmaceutical," The Va Environ Law Jour, 96; "The Normative Nature of Risk Assessment: Features and Possibilities," Risk: Health, Safety, and Environ, 97; "A Philosophy of Risk Assessment and the Law: A Case Study of the Role of Philosophy in Public Policy," Philos Stud, 97; "Eggshell Skulls and Loss of Hair from Fright: Some Moral and Legal Principles which Protect Susceptible Subpopulations," Environ Toxicology and Pharmacology, 98. **CONTACT ADDRESS** Dept of Philos, Univ Calif, 1156 Hinderaker Hall, Riverside, CA, 92521-0209. **EMAIL** carl@chss.ucr.edu

CRANSTON, MECHTHILD
PERSONAL Berlin, Germany **DISCIPLINE** ROMANCE LANGUAGES AND LITERATURES **EDUCATION** Univ Calif, Berkeley, BA, 58, PhD(Romance lang & lit), 66. **CAREER** Assoc French, Univ Calif, Berkeley, 64-66, instr, 66; asst prof, Univ San Francisco, 66-68 & Calif State Col Hayward, 68-69; chmn dept foreign lang, Univ NC, Asheville, 71-72, assoc prof French, 72-77; ASSOC PROF FRENCH, CLEMSON UNIV, 80-, US deleg & Belg Govt grant, Apollinaire Symp, Belg, 68; vis prof, Phillipps-Univ, Marburg, Ger, 70; Am Coun Learned Soc fel, 73-74; Nat Endowment for Humanities grant, 77. **MEMBERSHIPS** Am Asn Teachers Fr; MLA; Amis Rimbaud; Amis Guillaume Apollinaire; SAtlantic Mod Lang Asn. **RESEARCH** Poetry; music; criticism. **SELECTED PUBLICATIONS** Auth, Au-Dela Des Cercles, World Lit Today, Vol 0067, 93; The Connection Between Literary-Theory and the Representation of the Body in French Literature of the 17th-To-19th-Centuries--German, Fr Rev, Vol 0067, 93; L Ombre du Double, World Lit Today, Vol 0068, 94; Poetry in France Since 1960--29 Women--French, World Lit Today, Vol 0069, 95; The Artificial Paradise in 19th-Century French Literature--German, Fr Rev, Vol 0069, 95; A la Courte Paille, World Lit Today, Vol 0069, 95; From Blick to Augenblick--Rilke Panther on the Move, Neophilologus, Vol 0078, 94; Pangeia--French, World Lit Today, Vol 0071, 97; Hivernale--French, World Lit Today, Vol 0071, 97; Le Roman Dadam et Eve--French , World Lit Today, Vol 0071, 97; Nouvelles Cantates, en Lisant en Ecrivant--French, World Lit Today, Vol 0070, 96; Contemporary French Women Poets, Vol 1, From Chedid and Dohollau to Tellermann and Bancquart, Vol 2, from Hyvrard and Baude to Etienne and Albiach, World Lit Today, Vol 0070, 96; Sonnets Dispars Suivis de Cinq Autres Sonnets, Une Fabule et Deux Ampliations, World Lit Today, Vol 0068, 94; From Blick to Augenblick--Rilke Panther on the Move, Neophilologus, Vol 0078, 94; Sous-Main, Retouches, World Lit Today, Vol 0070, 96; L Ete, Temps Poetique, World Lit Today, Vol 0069, 95. **CONTACT ADDRESS** Dept of Lang, Clemson Univ, Clemson, SC, 29631.

CRAWFORD, CLAN
PERSONAL Born 01/25/1927, Cleveland, OH, m, 1949, 3 children **DISCIPLINE** LAW **EDUCATION** Oberlin Col, AB, 48; Univ of Mich, JD, 52. **CAREER** Assoc, Roscoe O. Bonisteel, Ann Arbor, Mich, 53-57; Ann Arbor city councilman, 57-58; pvt practice, Ann Arbor, Mich, 57- ; of counsel, Schlussel, Lifton, Simon, Rands, Galvin & Jackier, 89-90, Ellis, Talcott & Ohlgren, P. C., Ann Arbor, 90- ; lectr in field. **MEMBERSHIPS** Mich Soc Planning Officials; ABA; Mich Bar Asn, Washtenaw County Bar Asn. **RESEARCH** Land use and zoning, incl. planning. **SELECTED PUBLICATIONS** Michigan Zoning and Planning, 65, 3rd ed, 88; Strategy & Tactics in Municipal Zoning, 69, 2nd ed, 79; Handbook of Zoning and Land Use Ordinances with Forms, 74. **CONTACT ADDRESS** 1215 Brooklyn Ave, Ann Arbor, MI, 48104.

CRAWFORD, DAN
DISCIPLINE EPISTEMOLOGY, COGNITIVE SCIENCE, AND PHILOSOPHY OF RELIGION **EDUCATION** Univ Pittsburgh, PhD, 72. **CAREER** Vis prof, Univ Nebr, Lincoln. **SELECTED PUBLICATIONS** Published in the areas of knowledge and perception, the cosmological argument, Augustine, and W. Sellars. **CONTACT ADDRESS** Univ Nebr, Lincoln, Lincoln, NE, 68588-0417.

CRAWFORD, DAVID R.
DISCIPLINE PHILOSOPHY **EDUCATION** Eastern Col, BA; Penn State Univ, MA; DePaul Univ, PhD. **CAREER** Assoc prof, ch, Univ Detroit Mercy, 70-. **HONORS AND AWARDS** NEH grant. **RESEARCH** 19th and 20th century Continental Philosophy. **CONTACT ADDRESS** Dept of Philosophy, Univ of Detroit Mercy, 4001 W McNichols Rd, PO Box 19900, Detroit, MI, 48219-0900. **EMAIL** CRAWFODR@udmercy.edu

CRAWFORD, TIMOTHY G.
PERSONAL Born 11/19/1957, Huntsville, AL, m, 1982, 1 child **DISCIPLINE** RELIGION **EDUCATION** Southern Sem, Louisville, KY, PhD, 90; Southwestern Sem, Ft. Worth, TX, Mdiv, 84; Sanford Univ, Birmingham, AL, BA, 80. **CAREER** Assoc Prof, Chr of Hum Div, 90-, Bluefield Coll; Instr of Old Testament Hist and Interp, 88-90, Southern Sem. **HONORS AND AWARDS** Outstanding Faculty Award. **MEMBERSHIPS** Soc Biblical Lit; Natl Assoc of Prof of Hebrew; Natl Assoc of Baptist Prof of Rel. **RESEARCH** Masorah; Intertextuality. **SELECTED PUBLICATIONS** Auth, The Masorah of Biblia Hebraica Stuttgartensia, coauth, Eerdmans, 98; co-auth, Handbook to Biblical Hebrew Grammar, Eerdmans, 94; auth, Taking the Promised Land, Leaving the Promised Land: Luke's Use of Joshua for a Christian Foundation Story, Review and Exposition, 98; Blessing and Curse in Syro-Palestinian Inscriptions of the Iron Age, Peter Lang, Pub, 92; co-auth, Mercer Dictionary of the Bible, Seven articles. **CONTACT ADDRESS** Bluefield Col, 3000 College Dr, Box 16, Bluefield, VA, 24605. **EMAIL** tcrawford@mail.bluefield.edu

CRAWFORD, WILLIAM EDWARD
PERSONAL Born 12/15/1927, Key West, FL, m, 1962, 3 children **DISCIPLINE** LAW **EDUCATION** La State Univ, BA, 51, JD, 55. **CAREER** Atty at law, Chaffe, McCall, Phillips, Burke & Hopkins, 55-65; assoc prof, 66-71, asst dean sch, 66-69, prof law, Law Sch, La State Univ, Baton Rouge, 71-; dir, La State Law Inst, 78-. **RESEARCH** Trial practice; torts; legal profession. **SELECTED PUBLICATIONS** Auth, Trial and Appellate Advocacy, La State Univ, 72; Faculty symposium, The Work of the Louisiana Appellate Courts for the 1970-1971 Term, Civil Procedure, 72, Faculty symposium, The Work of the Louisana Appellate Courts or the 1971-1972 Term, Torts, 73 & Executory Process and Collateral Mortgages--Authentic Evidence of the Hand Note?, summer 73, La Law Rev; Torts, Louisiana Cases and Materials, La State Univ, 73; coauth, New Code of Civil Procedure in France: Bk I (English transl), Oceana, 78; Louisiana Code of Civil Procedure, 1982 ed, Crawford-West's Publ Co, 81. **CONTACT ADDRESS** Law Sch, Louisiana State Univ, Baton Rouge, LA, 70803-0001.

CREAMER, DAVID G.
PERSONAL Born 08/20/1946, Saint John, NB, Canada **DISCIPLINE** MORAL EDUCATION **EDUCATION** St Mary's Univ, BS (Chem), 68; Mem Univ, BEd, 72; Regic Coll, Toronto School of Theol, 77; Med (moral edu), Univ Toronto, 78; EdD (moral edu), 82. **CAREER** Teacher, High School, St John's, 71-74; dir, St Paul's High School, 82-88; asst and assoc prof, Univ Manitoba, 89-. **MEMBERSHIPS** Asn of Moral Edu; Nat Cath Edu Asn; Relig Edu Asn. **RESEARCH** Moral and Religious education; Psychology of Religion. **SELECTED PUBLICATIONS** Auth, rev Caths at the Gathering Place: Historical Essays on the Archdiocese of Tornoto, Can J of Urban Res, 93; Guides for the Journey, John MacMurray, Bernard Lonergan, James Fowler, 96; rev The Jesuit Mystique, Can Cath Rev, 96; rev, The Politics of Spirituality: A Study of a Renewal Process in an English Diocese, Can J of Urban Res, 97; Bernard J F

Lonergan: The Possibilty of Ethics, Life Ethics in World Religs, 98; The Jesus Wars, Jesuit Centre for Cath Studies, 98. **CONTACT ADDRESS** Jesuit Ctr, St. Paul's Col, 70 Dysart Rd, Winnipeg, MB, R3T 2M6. **EMAIL** creamer@ms.umanitoba.ca

CREASE, ROBERT P.
PERSONAL Born 10/22/1953, Philadelphia, PA, m, 1994, 2 children **DISCIPLINE** PHILOSOPHY **EDUCATION** Amherst Col, BA, 76; Columbia Univ, PhD, 87. **CAREER** Vis prof, asst prof, assoc prof, dir, grad prog, SUNY Stony Brook, 87- . **HONORS AND AWARDS** Fulbright-Hayes fel, 79-80. **MEMBERSHIPS** APA; AAAS. **RESEARCH** Philosophy and history of science. **SELECTED PUBLICATIONS** Co-auth, The Second Creation: Makers of the Revolution in Twentieth Century Physics; auth, The Play of Nature: Experimentation as Performance, Indiana, 93; ed, Hermeneutics and the Natural Sciences, Kluwer, 97; auth, Making Physics: A Biography of Brookhaven National Laboratory, Chicago, 99. **CONTACT ADDRESS** Dept of Philosophy, SUNY Stony Brook, 213 Harriman Hall, Stony Brook, NY, 11794. **EMAIL** rcrease@ccmail.sunysb.edu

CREED, BRADLEY
PERSONAL Born 04/20/1957, Jacksonville, TX, m, 1980, 3 children **DISCIPLINE** RELIGION **EDUCATION** Baylor Univ, BA, 79; MDiv, 82, PhD, 86, Southwestern Baptist Theological Seminary. **CAREER** Pastor, 80-93; Assoc Dean, 93-96, Truett Seminary; Dean and Prof of Christian History, 96-, George W. Truett Theological Seminary, Baylor Univ. **HONORS AND AWARDS** President's Merit Scholar in School of Theology, SWBTS, 83-85; Recipient of the Albert Venting Award, SWBTS, 82; Recipient of the Mayor's Achievement Award for the City of Natchitoches, LA, 92. **MEMBERSHIPS** Natl Assoc of Baptist Profs of Religion; North Amer Patristics Soc; Amer Acad of Religion; Conference on Faith and History; Amer Soc of Church History; Texas Baptist Historical Soc. **RESEARCH** History of Christianity; free church studies; ministry studies **SELECTED PUBLICATIONS** Auth, Church Leadership in the Southern Baptist Convention, Has Our Theology Changed? Southern Baptist Thought since 1845, 94; The Servant People of God, Proclaiming the Baptist Vision: The Church, 96. **CONTACT ADDRESS** George W. Truett Theological Seminary, Baylor Univ, Waco, TX, 76798-7126. **EMAIL** bradley_creed@baylor.edu

CRENSHAW, JAMES L.
PERSONAL Born 12/19/1934, Sunset, SC, m, 1956, 2 children **DISCIPLINE** RELIGION **EDUCATION** Furman Univ, BA, 56; S Baptist Theol Sem, BD, 60; Vanderbilt Univ, PhD, 64. **CAREER** Prof Old Testament, Atlantic Christian Col, 64-65; Mercer Univ, 65-69; Vanderbilt Univ Divinity Sch, 70-87; Duke Univ Divinity Sch, 87- . **HONORS AND AWARDS** Phi Beta Kappa; Soc for Relig in Higher Ed fel, 72-73; AATS fel, 78-79, 90-91; Guggenheim Fel, 84-85; NEH fel, 90-91; hon doctorate, Furman univ, 93; univ wide distinguished prof, 93- ; PEW Evangelical scholar, 96-97; ed, Soc of Bibl Lit monograph series. **MEMBERSHIPS** Soc Bibl Lit; Catholic Bibl Asn; Int Org for the Study of the Old Testament; Soc for Old Testament Study; Colloquium for Bibl Res. **RESEARCH** Hebrew Bible, language and literature. **SELECTED PUBLICATIONS** Auth, Trembling at the Threshold of a Biblical Text, Eerdmans, 94; auth, Joel, Doubleday, 95; auth, Urgent Advice and Probing Questions, Mercer, 96; auth, Sirach, Abingdon, 97; auth, Education in Ancient Israel, Doubleday, 98; auth, Old Testament Wisdom, rev ed, Westminster, 98. **CONTACT ADDRESS** Duke Univ, PO Box 90967, Durham, NC, 27708. **EMAIL** jlcren@mail.duke.edu

CRENSHAW, RONALD WILLIS
PERSONAL Born 01/04/1940, St. Louis, MO, m **DISCIPLINE** LAW **EDUCATION** Fist U, BA 1962; Univ of SD Sch of Med, grad; Univ of SD Coll of Law, JD 1971. **CAREER** Ronald W Crenshaw & Asso PC, atty 1976-; State of MI, spl asst atty gen 1974-; Elliard Crenshaw & Strong, partner 1973-76; Zechman & Crenshaw, partner 1972-73; US Atty's Ofc, law clrk 1971; Fredrikson Byron & Colborn Law Ofcs, legal intern 1970; Univ of SD Sch of Med, resrch asst 1968; Dept of Aero-Space Med Mcdonnell Aircraft Corp, asso physiologist 1964-67; Dept of Biochemistry Cntrl Resrch Div Monsanto Co, resrch biochemist 1964; Dept of Radiophysics Sch of Med Wash Univ St Louis, resrch asst 1962-64. **HONORS AND AWARDS** Fellow awd Univ of SD 1967; contestant Moot Ct 1969; Am Jurisprudence Awd Univ of SD 1970; gunderson seminar awd Univ of SD 1971. **MEMBERSHIPS** Mem State Bar of MI; mem Wolverine Bar Assn; mem Fed Bar Assn; mem Am Bar Assn; mem num other Bar Assn; mem public adv com on jud cands Detroit Bar Assn; chmn of adm com Detroit Bar Assn 1978-79; vice pres bd of dirs Don Bosco Hall Juvenile Home; chmn Kappa Alpha Psi Frat; found & chmn Martin Luther King Jr Meml Scholar Found Univ of SD 1968-71; chmn Martin Luther King Jr Meml Day Activities 1968-70; mem Hon Code Rev Com Univ of SD 1969; memConstl Rules Com 1969-70; pres Vermillion Chap Phi Delta Phi Legal Frat; licensed State Cts of MI; Fed Dist Ct for the E Dist of MI; US Ct of Appeals 6th Cir. **SELECTED PUBLICATIONS** "The Vagrancy Statute: To Be or Not To Be", "The Purposeful Inclusion of Am Indians". **CONTACT ADDRESS** 405 Riverd, Ste 100, Detroit, MI, 48207.

CREPEAU, PAUL-ANDRE
PERSONAL Born 05/20/1926, Gravelbourg, SK, Canada **DISCIPLINE** LAW (COMPARATIVE) **EDUCATION** Univ Ottawa, BA, 46, LPh, 47; Univ Montreal, LLL, 50; Univ Oxford, BCL, 52; Univ Paris, Docteur en droit, 55. **CAREER** Appele au Barreau de Montreal, 50; Pres de l'Office de revision du Code civil du Quebec, 65-77; Conseil de la reine, 69; Dir du Centre de recherche en droit prive et compare du Quebec, 75-96; PROF EMER, FACULTE DE DROIT, UNIV McGILL; PRESIDENT, ACADEMIE INT DE DROIT COMPARE. **HONORS AND AWARDS** Prix du Barreau du Quebec, 62; Medaille, Fondation Edouard-Montpetit, 88; Medaille, Barreau du Quebec, 90; Prix de l'Asn que de droit compare, 93; Prix du Gouverneur general pour le droit, 93; LLD(hon), Univ Ottawa, 71; LLD(hon), York Univ, 84; LLD(hon), Dalhousie Univ, 89; LLD(hon), Strasbourg Univ, 90; LLD(hon), Univ Montreal, 94. **MEMBERSHIPS** Asn can des prof de droit (pres, 64-65); Asn que des prof de droit (pres, 65-66); Inst int de droit d'expression francaise; Asn que pour l'etude compare du droit (pres, 74-85); Asn de droit int; Academie des sciences de Pologne. **SELECTED PUBLICATIONS** Auth, Les codes civils-Edition critique, annuelle 81-93; L'intensite de l'obligation juridique, 89; L'affaire Daigle et la Cour supreme du Canada ou la meconnaissance de la tradition civiliste dans Melanges Briere, 93; Essai de lecture du message legislatif dans Melanges Beetz, 95; Les Principes d'Unidroit et le Code civil du Quebec: Valeurs Partagees?/The Unidroit Principles and the Civil Code of Quebec: Shared Values?, 97; coauth, Code civil/Civil code 1866-1980, 81; coauth, Dictionnaire de droit prive et Lexiques bilingues, 85, 2nd ed, 91; Private Law Dictionary and Bilingual Lexicons, 88, 2nd ed, 91; **CONTACT ADDRESS** 5 Place du Vesinet, Montreal, PQ, H2V 2L6.

CRESS, DONALD ALAN
PERSONAL Born 12/20/1945, Los Angeles, Calif **DISCIPLINE** MEDIEVAL PHILOSOPHY, CARTESIANISM **EDUCATION** St John's Col, BA, 67; Marquette Univ, MA, 69, PhD(philos), 72. **CAREER** Instr philos, Carroll Col, 71-73; asst prof, 73-79, Assoc Prof Philos, Northern Ill Univ, 79-94, prof, 94-98, Chmn Dept, 81-85, 86-88; assoc dean, Col of Liberal Arts and Scis, N Ill Univ, dean, Col of Arts and Scis, Univ Wisc - Parkside **HONORS AND AWARDS** Andrew Mellon Post-Doc fel, ACE fel, NEH res fel, Fulbright Inst, Woodrow Wilson Doctoral fel, Grant, Northern Ill Univ Grad Sch, 75, 77, 78 & 81 **MEMBERSHIPS** Leibniz Soc; Soc Medieval & Renaissance Philos; Soc Study Hist Philos; Int Soc Neo-Platonic Studies; Am Philos Asn. **RESEARCH** Medieval philosophy, renaissance Aristotelianism, Cartesianism **SELECTED PUBLICATIONS** Auth, Truth, Error, and the Order of Reasons: Descartes' Puzzling Synopsis of the Fourth Meditation, Reason, Will and Sensation: Studies in Cartesian Metaphysics, 94; auth, Descartes' Doctrine of Volitional Infinity, S Jou of Phil, 89; auth, A Defense of Augustine's Privation Account of Evil, Augustinian Stu, 89. **CONTACT ADDRESS** Col of Arts and Scis, Univ of Wisc - Parkside, PO Box 2000, Kenosha, WI, 53141. **EMAIL** cress@uwp.edu

CRESSON, BRUCE COLLINS
PERSONAL Born 10/27/1930, Lenoir, NC, m, 1955, 2 children **DISCIPLINE** RELIGION, ARCHEALOGY **EDUCATION** Wake Forest Col, BA, 52; Southeastern Baptist Theol Sem, BD, 55, ThM, 56; Duke Univ, PhD(relig), 64. **CAREER** Instr Hebrew, Southeastern Baptist Theol Sem, 62-63; instr relig, Duke Univ, 63-66; assoc prof, 66-77, PROF RELIG, BAYLOR UNIV, 77-, Mem, excavation staff, Aphek-Antipatris, 74-76, Wendeh, 77; dir, excavation to Tel Dhalia, 78- **MEMBERSHIPS** Am Sch Org Res; Soc Bibl Lit. **RESEARCH** Edom; history of Old Testament and intertestamental period in its world setting; Biblical archaeology. **SELECTED PUBLICATIONS** Auth, Ammon, Moab and Edom--Early States-Nations of Jordan in the Biblical Period, Biblical Archaeol, Vol 0059, 96. **CONTACT ADDRESS** Dept of Relig, Baylor Univ, Waco, TX, 76703.

CRIBBET, JOHN E.
DISCIPLINE LAW **EDUCATION** Ill Wesleyan Univ, AB, LLD; Univ Ill, JD. **CAREER** Dean emer, Univ Ill Urbana Champaign. **RESEARCH** Concentrated most of his teaching and research efforts on the law of property. **SELECTED PUBLICATIONS** Co-auth, Cases and Materials on Property; Principles of the Law of Property. **CONTACT ADDRESS** Law Dept, Univ Ill Urbana Champaign, 52 E Gregory Dr, Champaign, IL, 61820. **EMAIL** jcribbet@law.uiuc.edu

CRITES, STEPHEN DECATUR
PERSONAL Born 07/27/1931, Elida, OH, m, 1955, 4 children **DISCIPLINE** PHILOSOPHY OF RELIGION **EDUCATION** OH Wesleyan Univ, BA, 53; Yale Univ, BD, 56, MA, 59, PhD(philos theol), 61. **CAREER** Instr philos & relig, Colgate Univ, 60-61; from asst prof to assoc prof relig, Prof Relig & PROF PHILOS, WESLEYAN UNIV, 69-; Managing ed, Christian Scholar, 63-65; ed, Studies Relig, 71-. **MEMBERSHIPS** Soc Relig Higher Educ; Am Philos Asn; Am Acad Relig. **RESEARCH** Hegel; post-Hegelian developments in 19th century philosophy and theology; philosophy of religion in modern existentialism. **SELECTED PUBLICATIONS** Transl, Crisis in the Life of an Actress and Other Essays on Drama, Collins & Harper Torch, 67; auth, In the twilight of Christendom: Hegel vs Kierkegaard on faith and history, Studies Relig, 72; Pseudonymous Authorship as Art and as Act, In: Kierkegaard: A Collection of Critical Essays, Doublday Anchor, 72; Continuities, Soundings, fall 73; Angels We Have Heard, In: Religion as Story, Harper & Row, 76; Dialectic and Gospel in the Development of Hegel's Thinking, PA State Univ Press, 98. **CONTACT ADDRESS** Dept of Philos, Wesleyan Univ, Middletown, CT, 06457. **EMAIL** scrites@wesleyan.edu

CRITTENDEN, CHARLES
PERSONAL Born 11/11/1933, Durham, NC, d, 3 children **DISCIPLINE** PHILOSOPHY **EDUCATION** Univ NC-Chapel Hill, BA, 54, MA, 57; Cornell Univ, PhD, 64. **CAREER** Instr, Univ Fla, 60-65; asst prof, Fla State Univ, 65-70; prof, 76-, Cal State Univ-Northridge, 70-; Phi Eta Sigma; Phi Beta Kappa. **MEMBERSHIPS** Am Philos Asn. **RESEARCH** Philosophy of language; Philosophy of mind; Philosophy of religion; Social and political philosophy. **SELECTED PUBLICATIONS** auth Unreality: The Metaphysics of Fictional Objects, Cornell Univ Press, 92; In Support of Paganism: Polytheism as Earth-based Religion, Midwest Stud Philos, 97. **CONTACT ADDRESS** Dept of Philosophy, California State Univ, Northridge, Northridge, CA, 91330-8253. **EMAIL** charlescrittenden@csun.edu

CROCKETT, WILLIAM
PERSONAL Born 09/05/1946, Tisdale, SK, Canada, m, 1970, 2 children **DISCIPLINE** NEW TESTAMENT **EDUCATION** Univ Winnipeg, BA; Princeton Seminary, MDiv; Univ Glasgow (Scotland), PhD. **CAREER** Prof New Testament; Alliance Theol Seminary, 80-. **MEMBERSHIPS** SBL **SELECTED PUBLICATIONS** Through No Fault of Their Own?, 91; ed, Four Views on Hell, 92. **CONTACT ADDRESS** Alliance Theol Sem, 350 N. Highland Ave., Nyack, NY, 10960.

CROKE, PRUDENCE MARY
PERSONAL Woonsocket, RI **DISCIPLINE** THEOLOGY, SCRIPTURE **EDUCATION** Salve Regina Col, BA, 56; Cath Univ Am, MA, 68; Boston Univ, PhD, 75. **CAREER** Tchr gen educ, St Mary's Sch, 47-56; tchr Eng & relig, St Catherine Acad, 56-59; missionary & tchr, Inst Maria Regina, 59, tchr relig, St Xavier's Acad, 61-68; instr Theol & Scripture, Salve Regina Univ, 68-71; teacher theol & scripture, St Mary's-Bay View, 75-77; from Asst Prof to Assoc Prof, 77-83, Prof Theol & Scripture, Salve Regina Univ, 82-; Prof diocesan, Inst Lay Ministry. **MEMBERSHIPS** Cath Theol Asn; Col Theol Soc; Mercy Higher Educ Colloquium; Mercy Asn Scripture & Theol. **RESEARCH** Systematic theology; sacramental theology; New Testament. **SELECTED PUBLICATIONS** Auth, Roman Cath Concepts of the Eucharist and Spiritual Growth in Interrelation with Erikson's Theory of Development in the Life Span, Univ Micro, 75; Eucharistic Devotions Throughout History, Salve Regina Univ, 92; Worship, Sacraments, Salve Regina Univ, 93. **CONTACT ADDRESS** Salve Regina Univ, Newport Univ, 100 Ochre Point Ave, Newport, RI, 02840-4192. **EMAIL** croke@salve.edu

CRONK, GEORGE
PERSONAL Born 12/24/1938, Haledon, NJ **DISCIPLINE** LAW **EDUCATION** Paterson State College, BA, 63; Rutgers Univ, MA, 65; S IL Univ, PhD, 71; Rutgers Univ, JD, 84. **CAREER** Attorney solo practice 91-, George Cronk, JD PhD, Attorney at Law; Asst Prof, Assoc Prof, Prof, 72-, Bergen Comm College; Asst Prof 70-72, College Misericordia; teach Asst 68-69, S IL Univ; instr 66-68, Union College NJ; teach Asst 64-65, Rutgers Univ. **HONORS AND AWARDS** NJ Dept Higher Edu Fel; Princeton Grad Fel; SIU Univ Fel; Ntl Defen Grad Fel; Kappa Delta Pi Acad Schlshp. **MEMBERSHIPS** APA; CLS; SAAP; NJRPA; CCHA; NJSB; SCP; CCGEA. **RESEARCH** History of Philosophy; Philosophical Theology and Anthropology; Epistemology; Traditional and Modern Logic; Comparative Religions; Biblical Studies. **SELECTED PUBLICATIONS** Auth, The Philosophical Anthropology of George Herbert Mead, NY, Peter Lang, 87; The Message of the Bible: An Orthodox Christian Perspective, Crestwood NY, St Vladimir's Seminary Press, 82; translated, Eight Philo Classics: Intro Readings from, Plato, Aristotle, Anselm of Canterbury, Thomas Aquinas, Rene Descartes, David Hume, Immanuel Kant, Jean-Paul Sarte, Orlando FL, Harcourt Brace, 95; Six Classics of Eastern Philosophy: Selections from Confucius, Lao Tzu, Nagarjuna, Vasubandhu, Shamkara, Ramanuja, Orlando FL, Harcourt Brace, 98; The Gospel of John, Orthodox Study Bible: New Testament and Psalms, Nashville, Thomas Nelson Pub, 93. **CONTACT ADDRESS** Dept of Philosophy and Religion, Bergen Comm Col, Paramus, NJ, 07652. **EMAIL** george9252@msn.com

CROOMS, LISA A.
DISCIPLINE CONTRACTS, CRITICAL RACE THEORY, AND GENDER AND LAW **EDUCATION** Howard Univ, BA, 84; Univ Mich, JD, 91. **CAREER** Assoc prof. **MEMBERSHIPS** Adv bd, Women's Rights Proj of Human Rights Watch. **RESEARCH** US obligations under the International Convention for the Elimination of All Forms of Racial Discrimination. **SELECTED PUBLICATIONS** Auth, Indivisible Rights and Intersectional Indentities or, What Do Women's Human Rights

Have to Do with the Race Convention, 40 Howard Law J, 97; Speaking Partial Truths and Preserving Power: Deconstructing White Supremacy, Patriarchy, and the Rape Corroboration Rule in the Interest of Black Liberation, 40 Howard Law J, 97; Stepping into the Projects: Lawmaking, Storytelling, and Practicing the Politics of Identification, 1 Mich J Race & Law 1, 96; An Age of ¤ImlPossibility: Rhetoric, Welfare Reform, and Poverty, 94 Mich Law Rev 1953, 96; Don't believe the hype: black women, patriarchy and the new welfarism, 38 Howard Law J 611, 95; Single Motherhood, the Rhetoric of Poverty and Welfare Reform: A Case of Gender Discrimination in the United States, in From Basic Needs to Basic Rights: Shaping the Women's Rights Agenda for the 90s and Beyond, Inst for Women, Law & Develop, 95; Women, Work, and Family: The National Welfare Reform Debate, Black Political Agenda, 3rd Quart, 94 & Legal Medicine for Sexual Harassment of Health Care Workers, 10:7 Healthspan 12, 93. **CONTACT ADDRESS** Dept of Law, Howard Univ, 2400 Sixth St NW, Washington, DC, 20059.

CROSBY, DONALD A.
PERSONAL Born 04/07/1932, Mansfield, OH, m, 1956, 2 children **DISCIPLINE** PHILOSOPHY, RELIGION **EDUCATION** Davidson Col, BA, 53; Princeton Theol Sem, BD, 56, ThM, 59; Columbia Univ, PhD, 63. **CAREER** Asst prof, philos, relig, Centre Col of Ky, 62-65; asst, assoc, prof, philos, Colorado State Univ, 65- . **HONORS AND AWARDS** Honors prof, 81; Burlington Northern award for grad tchg and res, 89; John N. Stern distinguished fac award, 94. **MEMBERSHIPS** APA; Am Acad Relig; Highlands Inst for Am Relig and Philos Thought; Soc for Advancement of Am Philos. **RESEARCH** Philosophy of nature; pragmatism. **SELECTED PUBLICATIONS** Auth, Horace Bushnell's Theory of Language, in the Context of Other Nineteenth-Century Philosophies of Language, Mouton, 75; auth, Interpretive Theories of Religion, Mouton, 81; auth, The Specter of the Absurd: Sources and Criticisms of Modern Nihilism, SUNY, 88; co-ed, Religious Experience and Ecological Responsibility, Peter Lang, 96; co-ed, Pragmatism, Neo-Pragmatism, and Religion: Conversations with Richard Rorty, Peter Lang, 97. **CONTACT ADDRESS** 5000 Boardwalk Dr, Unit 17, Fort Collins, CO, 80526. **EMAIL** donaldcrosby@compuserve.com

CROSSLEY, JOHN
PERSONAL Born 12/27/1929, Oakland, CA, m, 1984, 2 children **DISCIPLINE** THEOLOGY **EDUCATION** San Francisco Theol Sem, ThD, 62. **CAREER** Prof, Hastings Col, 62-70; Assoc Prof, Dir, Univ of Southern CA, 70-. **HONORS AND AWARDS** Who's Who in Amer, 74; Dart Awd for Acad Innovation, USC, 75; Raubenheimer Awad for Excellence in Tchg, USC, 83. **MEMBERSHIPS** Amer Acad of Religion; Soc of Christian Ethics; Pacific Coast Theol Soc; Soc for Values in Higher Education **RESEARCH** 19th Century theol and ethics; contemp theol and ethics; relig and culture; church and state. **SELECTED PUBLICATIONS** The Relation between Schleiermachers Philosophical and Theological Ethics, The Ann of the Soc of Christian Ethics, 98. **CONTACT ADDRESS** Univ of Southern California, School of , Los Angeles, CA, 90089-0355. **EMAIL** crossley@bcf.usc.edu

CROSSON, FREDERICK J.
PERSONAL Born 04/27/1926, NJ, m, 1953, 5 children **DISCIPLINE** PHILOSOPHY **EDUCATION** Cath Univ Am, BA, 49, MA, 50; Univ Notre Dame, PhD, 56 **CAREER** Inst, Asst Prof, Assoc Prof, Prof, 53-67, Dean, 68-75, Prof of Philos, 76-84, Prof of Humanities, 84-, Univ Notre Dame **HONORS AND AWARDS** Knights of Columbus Fel, 49-50; French Govmt Fel, 51-52 **RESEARCH** Phenomenology, Philos of Relig **SELECTED PUBLICATIONS** Auth, The Narrative of Conversion: Newman and Augustine, Tradition and Renewal, Louvain, 93; Rejoinder to Bruce marshal, Thomist, 93 **CONTACT ADDRESS** Dept of Philosophy, Univ of Notre Dame, Notre Dame, IN, 46556.

CROSTHWAITE, JANE FREEMAN
PERSONAL Born 11/07/1936, Salisbury, NC, m, 1964 **DISCIPLINE** AMERICAN RELIGIOUS HISTORY **EDUCATION** Wake Forest Univ, BA, 59; Duke Univ, MA, 62, PhD(-relig), 72. **CAREER** Asst dean women & instr philos, Wake Forest Univ, 62-64; head corp rec, Harvard Bus Sch Libr, 64-65q instr English, Queens Col, NC, 69-72, registr, 72-74, assoc prof relig, 74-76; lectr philos & relig, Univ NC, Charlotte, 76-79; ASST PROF RELIG, MOUNT HOLYOKE COL, 79- **MEMBERSHIPS** Am Acad Relig; MLA; Church Hist Soc. **RESEARCH** American religious history; Emily Dickinson; women in American religion. **SELECTED PUBLICATIONS** Auth, Spiritual Spectacles--Vision and Image in Mid-19th-Century Shakerism, Jour Interdisciplinary Hist, Vol 0026, 95; The Carmelite Adventure--Dickinson, Clare,Joseph Journal of the Trip To America and Other Documents, Church Hist, Vol 0063, 94. **CONTACT ADDRESS** Dept of Relig, Mount Holyoke Col, 50 College St, South Hadley, MA, 01075-1461.

CROUCH, MARGARET
DISCIPLINE PHILOSOPHY **EDUCATION** Colo State Univ, BA, 78; Univ Minn, PhD, 85. **CAREER** Prof, Eastern Michigan Univ. **HONORS AND AWARDS** Distinguished tchg awd, 94. **RESEARCH** Feminist philosophy, philosophy of language. **SELECTED PUBLICATIONS** Auth, A 'Limited' Defense of the Genetic Fallacy; Feminist Philosophy and the Genetic Fallacy; The Social Etymology of Sexual Harassment. **CONTACT ADDRESS** Dept of History and Philosophy, Eastern Michigan Univ, 701 Pray-Harrold, Ypsilanti, MI, 48197.

CROUTER, RICHARD
PERSONAL Born 11/02/1937, Washington, DC, m, 1960, 2 children **DISCIPLINE** HISTORY OF THEOLOGY **EDUCATION** Occidental Col, AB, 60; Union Theol Sem, BD, 63, ThD, 68. **CAREER** From instr to asst prof 67-73, assoc prof, 73-79, prof relig, Carleton Col, 79-, John M. and Elizabeth Musser Prof of Religious Studies, 97-, Univ Toronto, 72-73; Am Coun Learned Soc fel, 76-77; sr Fulbright scholar, Univ Marburg, 76-77, 91-92. **MEMBERSHIPS** Am Soc Church Hist; Am Acad Relig; Hegel Soc Am. **RESEARCH** History of Christian thought; Schleiermacher, Hegel, Kierkegaard. **SELECTED PUBLICATIONS** Auth, Michael Novak and the study of religion, J Am Acad Relig, 3/72; H Richard Niebuhr and stoicism, J Relig Ethics, 2/74; Hegel and Schleiermacher at Berlin: A many-sided debate, J Am Acad Relig, 3/80; Rhetoric and substance in Schleiermacher's revision of The Christian Faith, 1821-1822, J Relig, 7/80; ed and trans, Friedrich Schleiermacher, On Religion: Speeches to its Cultured Despisers, Cambridge: Cambridge Univ Press, 88, 96. **CONTACT ADDRESS** Dept of Relig, Carleton Col, 1 N College St, Northfield, MN, 55057-4044. **EMAIL** rcrouter@carleton.edu

CROUTER, RICHARD E.
PERSONAL Born 11/02/1937, Washington, DC, m, 1960, 2 children **DISCIPLINE** THEOLOGY **EDUCATION** Occidental Col, AB, 60; BD, 63, PhD, 68, Union Theol Sem. **CAREER** From instr to asst prof to assoc prof to prof to chemn, 67-, Carleton Col. **HONORS AND AWARDS** Fel, Inst for Ecumenical and Cultural Res, 71; Postdoctoraal Cross-disciplinary Fel, 72-73, Univ Toronto; Fac Develop Grant, 87, 90, 91, 97, Carleton Col; Senior Fulbright Res Fel, 87, Univ Queensland. **MEMBERSHIPS** Am Acad Religion; Fulbright Alumni Asn; German Std Asn; Soren Kierkegaard Society. **SELECTED PUBLICATIONS** Auth, Schleiermacher and the Theology of Bourgeois Society: A Critique of the Critics, 86; coauth,Traveling with Luther and Marx: On and Off the Luther Trail in the GDR, 84; auth, Ambrose, Bishop of Milan, 87; Auth, A Historical Demurral,88; auth, Revolution and the Religious Imagination in Kierkegaard's Two Ages, 91. **CONTACT ADDRESS** Carleton Col, Northfield, MN, 55057. **EMAIL** rcrouter@carleton.edu

CROWE, FREDERICK E.
PERSONAL Born 07/05/1915, Jeffries Corner, NB, Canada **DISCIPLINE** THEOLOGY **EDUCATION** Univ NB, BS, 34; Loyola Col, Univ Montreal, BA, 43; Gregorian Univ (Rome), STD, 53; Col de l'Immaculee-Conception (Montreal), LPhil, 62; DLitt(hon), St Mary's Univ, 71; DD(hon), Trinity Col, Univ Toronto, 77; LLD(hon), St Thomas Univ, 82; DD(hon), Univ St Michael's Col, 86. **CAREER** Tchr, St Mary's Col (Halifax), 43-46; ordained priest, 49; tchr theol, 53-75, res prof, 75-80, PROF EMER, REGIS COL (Toronto), 80-, dir, Lonergan Res Inst, 85-91; vis prof, Gregorian Univ (Rome), 64, 84. **HONORS AND AWARDS** John Courtney Murray Award, 77. **MEMBERSHIPS** Can Theol Soc; Cath Theol Soc Am; Jesuit Philos Asn. **SELECTED PUBLICATIONS** Auth, A Time of Change, 68; auth, Escatologia e missione terrena in Gesu di Nazareth, 76; auth, Theology of the Christian Word: A Study in History, 78; auth, The Lonergan Enterprise, 80; auth, Old Things and New: A Strategy for Education, 85; auth, Appropriating the Lonergan Idea, 89; auth, Lonergan, 92; ed, Spirit as Inquiry, 64; ed, Collection: Papers by Bernard Lonergan, 67; ed, A Third Collection: Papers by Bernard Lonergan, 85; ed, Collected Works of Bernard Lonergan, 88; contribur, New Catholic Encyclopedia, 67, 74, 79. **CONTACT ADDRESS** Lonergan Research Inst, 500-10 St. Mary St, Toronto, ON, M4Y 1P9.

CROWELL, STEVEN G.
PERSONAL Born 06/02/1953, San Diego, CA, m, 1992 **DISCIPLINE** PHILOSOPHY **EDUCATION** Univ Calif, Santa Cruz, BA, 74; Northern Ill Univ, MA, 76; Yale Univ, PhD, 81. **CAREER** Vis asst prof, Fordham Univ, 82-83; asst prof, 83-87, assoc prof, 88-97, prof, 98-, Rice Univ. **HONORS AND AWARDS** DAAD; NEH. **MEMBERSHIPS** APA; Soc for Phenomenology and Existential Philos; Husserl Cir; N Am Kant Soc; N Am Nietzsche Soc; Heidegger Conf. **RESEARCH** Phenomenology; European philosophy since Kant; aesthetics; philosophy of history. **SELECTED PUBLICATIONS** Auth, Making Logic Philosophical Again, (1912-1916), in Kisiel, ed, Reading Heidegger from the Start, SUNY Albany, 94; auth, Solipsism, Modalities of the Strange, in Crowell, ed, The Prism of the Self, Kluwer, 95; auth, Heidegger's Phenomenological Decade, Man and World, 95; ed, The Prism of the Self: Philosophical Essays in Honor of Maurice Natanson, Kluwer, 95; auth, Being Truthful, in Drummond, ed, The Truthful and the Good: Essays in Honor of Robert Sokolowski, Kluwer, 96; auth, The Mythical and the Meaningless: Husserl and The Two Faces of Nature, in Nenon, ed, Issues in Husserl's Ideas II, Kluwer, 96; auth, The Cunning of Modernity: Ibanez-Noe, Heidegger, and Nietzsche, Int Stud in Philos, 96; auth, Husserl, Derrida, and the Phenomenology of Expression, Philos Today, 96; auth, Emil Lask: Aletheiology as Ontology, Kant-Studien 87, 96; auth, Dogmatic Anti-Foundationalism, Semiotica, 96; auth, Ontology and Transcendental Phenomenology Between Husserl and Heidegger, in Hopkins, ed, Husserl in Contemprary Context, Kluwer, 97; auth, Philosophy As A Vocation: Heidegger and University Reform in The Early Interwar Years, Hist of Philos Q, 97; auth, Neighbors in Death, Res in Phenomenology XXVII, 97; auth, Neo-Kantianism, in Critchley, ed, A Companion to Continental Philosophy, Blackwell, 98; auth, Mixed Messages: The Heterogeneity of Historical Discourse, Hist and Theory, 98. **CONTACT ADDRESS** Dept of Philosophy, Rice Univ, MS-14, Houston, TX, 77005-1892. **EMAIL** crowell@rice.edu

CROWLEY, SUE MITCHELL
PERSONAL Born 10/31/1933, Columbus, OH, m, 1954, 2 children **DISCIPLINE** RELIGION AND LITERATURE **EDUCATION** St Mary's College Notre Dame, BA, cum laude 55; Ohio State Univ, MA, 68; Univ Iowa, PhD. **CAREER** Instr, lectr, Asst Dir, 72 to 84-, Univ Missouri; Instr, 82-84, Stephens College; lectr, Instr, 68-79, Univ Iowa; teacher, 67, Ursuline Acad. **HONORS AND AWARDS** Honors Teacher of the Year. **MEMBERSHIPS** AAR; MLA; Cen MO Colloquium on the Study of Religion. **RESEARCH** John Updike; Walker Percy; Robert Lowell; Toni Morrison. **SELECTED PUBLICATIONS** Coed, Critical Essays on Walker Percy, Boston, GK Hall, 89; auth, Tenderness detached from the source of tenderness, The Thanatos Syndrome: Walter Percy's Tribute to Flannery O'Connor, Walker Percy: Novelist and Philosopher, Jackson, Univ Mississippi Press, 91; coauth, Walker Percy's Grail, King Arthur Through the Ages, eds, Valerie M Lagorio, Mildred Leake Day, NY, and London, Garland Pub, 90. **CONTACT ADDRESS** 409 South Greenwood, Columbia, MO, 65203.

CROWNFIELD, DAVID R.
PERSONAL Born 06/24/1930, Quincy, MA, 3 children **DISCIPLINE** RELIGION **EDUCATION** Harvard Univ, AB, 51, ThM, 58, ThD, 64; Yale Univ, BD, 54. **CAREER** Instr Relig, Middlebury Col, 61-62; asst prof Philos & Relig, Alma Col, Mich, 62-64; from asst prof to assoc prof, 64-71, prof Philos & Relig, Univ Northern Iowa, 71-98; prof Emeritus, 98-. **HONORS AND AWARDS** Iowa Regents Award for Excellence, 93. **MEMBERSHIPS** Soc Phenomenol & Existential Philos; Am Theol Soc; Am Acad Relig; Am Philos Asn; NAm Heideger Conf. **RESEARCH** Phenomemology of religious experience; hermeneutics; Heidegger; God. **SELECTED PUBLICATIONS** Auth, Karl Barth: 1886-1968, N Am Rev, Spring 69; Tradition, domination, and resurrection, McCormick Quart, 3/70; The curse of Abel: An essay in biblical ecology, N Am Rev, Summer 73; Religion in the cartography of the unconscious, Summer 75 & The self beyond itself: Hermeneutics and transpersonal experience, Summer 79, J Am Acad Relig; Postmodern perspectives in theology and philosophy of religion, contemporary philos, 89; God among the signifiers, Man and World, 93; The question of God: Thinking after Heidegger, Philosophy Today, 96. **CONTACT ADDRESS** Dept of Philosophy & Religion, Univ of Northern Iowa, Cedar Falls, IA, 50614-0001.

CROY, MARVIN J.
DISCIPLINE PHILOSOPHY OF SCIENCE, PHILSOPHY OF EDUCATION, PHILOSOPHY OF TECHNOLOGY **EDUCATION** FL State Univ, BA, 69, PhD, 79. **CAREER** Assoc prof, Univ NC, Charlotte. **HONORS AND AWARDS** NEH grant, summer sem, Univ MD, College Park, 83; Nat Sci Found grant, 90, 91, 97; NEH, summer inst, 94. **RESEARCH** Educ applications of computer tech, espec using computers to teach logic. **SELECTED PUBLICATIONS** Auth, Collingridge and the Control of Educational Computer Technology, Soc for Philos and Technol Electronic Quart J, 1(4), 1-15, 96; An Incrementalist View of Proposed Uses of Information Technology in Higher Education, Philosophy in the Contemporary World, 4, 1-9, 97; coauth, Assessing the Impact of a Proposed Expert System via Simulation, J of Educ Comput Res, 13, 1-15, 95. **CONTACT ADDRESS** Univ N. Carolina, Charlotte, Charlotte, NC, 28223-0001. **EMAIL** mjcroy@email.uncc.edu

CRUISE, WARREN MICHAEL
PERSONAL Born 06/03/1939, Baltimore, MD, d **DISCIPLINE** LAW **EDUCATION** Morgan St U, AB 1963; Howard Univ Law Sch, JD 1970. **CAREER** Nat Ed Assn, legal cnsl 1985; Nghbrhd Legal Srv Prg, staff atty. **HONORS AND AWARDS** MJ Naylor Meml Award; high acad achvmt in field of Philosophy. **MEMBERSHIPS** Vp, bd of dir NEA Credit Union; mem Retirement Bd, NEA Kappa Alpha Psi Frat; Phi Alpha; Delta Law Frat; NAACP; Nat Bar Assn; Conf of Black-Lwyrs; Am Bar Assn. **CONTACT ADDRESS** 1201 16th St NW, Washington, DC, 20036.

CRUMBLEY, DEIDRE H.
PERSONAL Born 12/12/1947, Philadelphia, PA, s **DISCIPLINE** ANTHROPOLOGY: RELIGION & CULTURE **EDUCATION** Temple Univ, BA, 70; North Western, MA, 84, PhD, 89; Harvard, MTS. **CAREER** Jr res fel, 82-84, African Studies Dept; Univ of Ibadan Nigeria West Africa, 82-86; jr lectr, 84-

86, Arecheology & Anthropology; Rollins Col, 88-91, Anthropology; Univ FL, Anthropology, 91-98; asst prof, 98, NC State Univ, Africana Studies, Multidisciplinary Studies Div. **HONORS AND AWARDS** Lilly Fel, 79; Fuebrigher Hays, 85; Ford Post doc fel, 91. **MEMBERSHIPS** Amer Anthropological Assn; Amer Acad Religion; **RESEARCH** Religion and change in Africa and the African disapora **SELECTED PUBLICATIONS** Auth, West African Journal of Archeology & Anthropology, vol 16, Ibadan, Nigeria, 88; Impurity and Power: Women in Aladura churches, Africa, 92; Even a Woman: Sex Roles and Mobility in an Aldura Hierarchy, Sept 14, 1998 **CONTACT ADDRESS** Africana Studies/Div of Multidisciplinary Studies, No Carolina State Univ, Raleigh, NC, 27695-7107. **EMAIL** deidre_crumbley@ncsu.edu

CRUMP, ARTHEL EUGENE
PERSONAL Born 10/19/1947, New York, NY, m, 1970 **DISCIPLINE** LAW **EDUCATION** Nebraska Wesleyan Univ, 1965-67; Univ of Nebraska at Lincoln, BA, sociology, 1973; Univ of Nebraska College of Law, JD 1976. **CAREER** Legal Service of Southeast Nebraska, Attorney, 1976-82; Nebraska Gov Robert Kerrey, legal counsel, 1983-85; Nebraska Dept of Justice, deputy atty general, 1985-91, general counsel, chief deputy tax commissioner, 1991; Nebraska Wesleyan University, Criminal Justice Department, visiting instructor, 1992, 1995, 1998; Central Interstate Low-Level Radioactive Waste Commission, general counsel, executive director, 1991-. **HONORS AND AWARDS** Nebraska Law College, scholarship; Kelso Morgan Scholarship; Council on Legal Educ Opportunity Stipend; Alumni Achievement Award, Nebraska Wesleyan University; Silver Key Award, Law Student Division, American Bar Assn; Community Leaders of America; Univ of Nebraska-Lincoln, Maurice Kremer lecturer. **MEMBERSHIPS** Nebraska State Bar Assn House of Delegates; Natl Assn of Atty Generals; Natl Gov's Assn; Educ Comm of the States; board of directors, Univ of NE Gymnastic Booster Club; board of directors, Family Serv Assn of Lincoln; board of directors, United Way of Lincoln & Lancaster Cos; board of directors, Theater Arts for Youth; board of directors, Malone Comm Ctr; board of directors, Lincoln Comm Playhouse, board of directors, Malone Headstart Program; panel mem Nebraska Arts Council; Touring Artists' Progs; Minority Arts Adv Comm; NAACP; Nebraska Civil Liberties Union; Coalition of Black Men; Univ of Nebraska Booster Club Womens' Athletics; bd of trustees, Nebraska Wesleyan Univ; advs comm, Lincoln Public Schools Gifted Children; advs committee, Lancaster Co Child Care; advs committee, NE Leg Sub-Comm Revision of Licensing Regulations for Child Care Insts; advs committee, Lincoln Public Schools Multi-Cultural Educ; reorganization of cofare advs comms, Lancaster Co Ad Hoc Comm; Malone Area Citizens Council; Lincoln Public Schools Evaluation of Student Health Educ Project; State Dept of Public Welfare Comm to Review Daycare Center Licensing Standards; board of directors, Pinewood Bowl Assn; board of directors, Leadership Lincoln; Nebraska State Bar Assn Ways, Means and Planning Comm, board of directors; Nebraska Supreme Court Judicial Nomination Commission; Lincoln Bar Assn; Midwest Bar Assn; Natl Low-Level (Radioactive) Waste Forum Commission Rep; Lincoln Interfaith Council; Cornhusker Council BSA, board of directors; Crucible Club; Troop 49 Boy Scouts of America, Arborland Dist; Nebraska Urban League; NAACP; Foundation for Educational Funding, board of directors; First Natl Bank/Lincoln, board of directors; Nebraska Wesleyan Univ, board of directors; Newman United Methodist Church; Board of Higher Educ & Campus Ministry, Nebraska United Methodist Church. **CONTACT ADDRESS** Central Interstate Low-Level Radioactive Waste Commission, 1033 "O" St, Ste 530, Lincoln, NE, 68508. **EMAIL** acrump@cillrwcc.org

CRUMP, DAVID
PERSONAL Born 02/26/1956, Los Angeles, CA, m, 1976 **DISCIPLINE** NEW TESTAMENT STUDIES **EDUCATION** Univ Aberdeen, Scotland, PhD, 88. **CAREER** Minister, Christian Reformed Church, 88-97; assoc prof, Calvin Col, 97-. **MEMBERSHIPS** Soc of Bibl Lit. **RESEARCH** New Testament Theology; First Century Judaism. **SELECTED PUBLICATIONS** Auth, "The Virgin Birth in New Testament Theology," 89; "The Preaching of George Whitefield and His Use of Matthew Henry's 'Commentary,'" 89; "Jesus, the Victorious Scribal-Intercessor in Luke's Gospel," 92; "Truth," 92; Jesus the Intercessor: Prayer and Christology in Luke-Acts, 92; "Applying the Sermon on the Mount: Once You Have Read It, What Do You Do With It?," 92; "Gone to Hog Heaven," 99. **CONTACT ADDRESS** Dept of Religion & Theology, Calvin Col, 3201 Burton St SE, Grand Rapids, MI, 49546. **EMAIL** dcrump@calvin.edu

CRUZ, DAVID B.
DISCIPLINE CONSTITUTIONAL LAW **EDUCATION** Univ Calif, Irvine, BS , BA 88; Stanford Univ, MS,91; NY Univ, JD,94. **CAREER** Assoc prof,Univ Southern Calif, clerked for, Honorable Edward R. Becker, Circuit Judge US Ct Appeals 3rd Circuit; bristow fel to, Off Solicitor Gen Wash, DC. **RESEARCH** Civil rights & constitutional law. **SELECTED PUBLICATIONS** Auth, Piety & Prejudice: Free Exercise Exemption from Laws Prohibiting Sexual Orientation Discrimination. **CONTACT ADDRESS** School of Law, Univ Southern Calif, University Park Campus, Los Angeles, CA, 90089.

CRUZ, VIRGIL
PERSONAL Born 12/21/1929, New York, NY, m **DISCIPLINE** THEOLOGY **EDUCATION** Houghton Coll, BA Greek major 1953; Pittsburgh Seminary, MDiv 1956; Vrije Universiteit Amsterdam, Neth, PhD 1973. **CAREER** Hebron United Presb Ch, 1956-60; Univ of Dubuque Seminary, prof of New Testament 1966-82; Western Theol Seminary, prof of Biblical studies 1982-86; Louisville Presbyterian Theological Seminary, professor, 1986-. **HONORS AND AWARDS** Purdy Scholarship Pittsburgh Seminary 1954; Lee Church Hist Award Pittsburgh Seminary 1956; Foreign Student Scholarship Vrije Univ 1960; Grant from German Govt for language study 1968; Higgins Fellowship (2 times); Presb Grad Fellowship 1972; Houghton College, LHD, 1991; Westminster College, DD, 1992. **MEMBERSHIPS** Moderator Albany Presbtery 1959-60; chair Natl Comm for Ordination Examin 1979-80; mem Gen Assembly Cncl of Presby Ch 1984-; mem The Soc of Biblical Literature 1968-; mem The Soc for the Study of Black Religion 1975-; dir Presbyterians United for Biblical Concerns 1985-; dir Found for Educ & Rsch 1985-. **SELECTED PUBLICATIONS** Auth, The Mark of the Beast, A Study of Charagma in the Apocalypse, Amsterdam Acad Press, 1973. **CONTACT ADDRESS** New Testament, Louisville Presbyterian Theol Sem, 1004 Alta Vista Rd, Louisville, KY, 40205.

CRYSDALE, CYNTHIA S. W.
PERSONAL Born 09/08/1953, Pittsburgh, PA, m, 1976, 2 children **DISCIPLINE** THEOLOGY AND ETHICS; MORAL DEVELOPMENT **EDUCATION** Univ St Michaels Col, Toronto, PhD, 87. **CAREER** Asst to assoc prof, Cath Univ Amer, Wash DC, 89-; **HONORS AND AWARDS** Christian Faith & Life Sabbatical grant Louisville Inst, 98. **MEMBERSHIPS** Soc Christian Ethics; Col Theol Soc; Can Theol Soc; Cath Theol Soc Am. **RESEARCH** Feminist ethics; Theology of suffering; Women in church & society; Ethics & genetics. **SELECTED PUBLICATIONS** Auth, Reason, Faith, and Authentic Rekigion, The Struggle Over the Past: Religious Fundamentalism in the Modern World, Univ Press Amer, 93; Gilligan and the Ethics of Care: An Update, Relig Studies Rev, 94; ed, Women and the Social Construction of Self-Appropriation, Lonergan & Feminism, 94; auth, Lonergans Philosophy and the Religious Phenomenon: A Commentary, Method: Jour of Longergan Studies, 94; Horizons that Differ: Women and Men and the Flight From Understanding, Cross Currents, 94; Religious Education and Adult Life Stages, Evangelical Outlook, 94; ed, Lonergan and Feminism, Univ Toronto Press, 94; auth, Revisioning Natural Law: From the Classicist Paradigm to Emergent Probability, Theol Studies, 95; auth, Christian Marriage and Homosexual Monogamy, Our Selves, Our Souls and Bodies, Cowley Press, 96; Feminist Theology: Ideology, Authenticity, and the Cross, Eglise et Theologie, 97. **CONTACT ADDRESS** Dept of Religion & Religious Education, Catholic Univ of America, Washington, DC, 20064. **EMAIL** crysdale@cua.edu

CRYSLER, NATHAN M.
DISCIPLINE CONTRACTS, PROFESSIONAL RESPONSIBILITY, AND INCOME TAX **EDUCATION** Univ PA, BS, 68; Emory Univ, JD, 71; Harvard Univ, LLM, 76. **CAREER** Roy Webster prof & dir, Ctr on the Legal Prof and Soc. **SELECTED PUBLICATIONS** Coauth, Problems on Contract Law. **CONTACT ADDRESS** School of Law, Univ of S. Carolina, Law Center, Columbia, SC, 29208. **EMAIL** Nathan@law.law.sc.edu

CSIKSZENTMIHALYI, MARK
DISCIPLINE RELIGION **EDUCATION** Harvard, AB, 87; Stanford Univ, PhD, 94. **CAREER** Fac, 94-; asst prof. **HONORS AND AWARDS** Fel Nat Hum Ctr, Res Triangle Pk NC, 97-98. **RESEARCH** China's Han Dynasty (202 BCE-220 CE). **SELECTED PUBLICATIONS** Auth, Fivefold Virtue: Reformulating Mencian Moral Psychology in Han Dynasty China, Religion. **CONTACT ADDRESS** Davidson Col, 102 N Main St, PO Box 1719, Davidson, NC, 28036.

CUA, ANTONIO S.
PERSONAL Born 07/23/1932, Manila, Philippines, m, 1956, 1 child **DISCIPLINE** PHILOSOPHY **EDUCATION** Far Eastern Univ Manila, BA, 52; Univ of Cal Berkeley, MA, 54, PhD, 58. **CAREER** Teach Asst, 55-58, Univ of Cal, Berkeley; Instr, Asst Prof, 58-62, Ohio Univ; Prof, dept Chmn Philo, 62-69, SUNY Coll at Oswego; vis Prof Philo, 68-69, Catholic Univ Amer; vis Prof Philo, 74-75, Univ Missouri; vis Prof Philo, 75, George Mason Univ; vis Prof Philo, 76-77, Univ Hawaii; external examiner, 87-89, Presby School Christ Edu; external examiner, 84-, Chin Univ Hong Kong, 87-88, Macquarie Univ, 91-, Academia Sinica; consultant, 91-97, NSC Taiwan; vis pro Lectr, 95, Nat Tsing Hua Univ Hsin Chu Taiwan; Prof Philo, 69-95, Emeritus Prof, 96-, Cath Univ Amer. **HONORS AND AWARDS** SUNY res fel; Woodrow Wilson fel; Chiang Ching-Kuo Foundation res scholar. **MEMBERSHIPS** APA, SACP, Intl Soc Chinese Philo. **RESEARCH** Chinese ethics, moral philosophy, history of ethics. **SELECTED PUBLICATIONS** Auth, Reason and Virtue, A Study in the Ethics of Richard Price, Athens Ohio Univ Press, 66; Dimensions of Moral Creativity, Paradigms Principles and Ideas, Univ Park, Penn State Univ Press, 78; The Unity of Knowledge and Action, A Study in Wang Yang-ming's Moral Psychology, Honolulu, Univ Hawaii Press, 82; Ethical Argumentation, A Study in Hsun Tzu's Moral Epistemology, Honolulu Univ Hawaii Press, 85; Moral Vision and Tradition, Essays in Chinese Ethics, Wash Cath Univ Press, 98; Between Commitment and Realization, Wang Yang-ming's Vision of the Universe as a Moral Community, in: Philo East & West, 93; A Confucian Perspective on Self-Deception, in: Self and Deception, eds, R Ames and W Dissanayake, Albany, SUNY Press, 96; Reason and Principle in Chinese Philosophy, in: A Companion to World Philosophy, eds, E Deutsch and R Bontekoe Oxford Blackwell, 97; Confucian Philosophy, Chinese, in: Routledge Encyclopedia of Philosophy, London Routledge 98. **CONTACT ADDRESS** School of Philosophy, Catholic Univ of America, Washington, DC, 20064. **EMAIL** cua@cua.edu

CUBIE, DAVID LIVINGSTON
PERSONAL Born 02/12/1928, Perth, Scotland, m, 1952, 4 children **DISCIPLINE** RELIGION **EDUCATION** Eastern Nazarene Col, AB, 51; Nazarene Theol Sem, BD, 54; Boston Univ, PhD, 65. **CAREER** Pastor, Church of the Nazarene, 54-57 & Congregational Christian Churches, 57-66; asst prof Bible & theol, 66-71, assoc prof then prof, relig, 69-71, Eastern Nazarene Col; Chmn Div Philos & Relig, Mt Vernon Nazarene Col, 71-93. **HONORS AND AWARDS** Co teach of the yr, Eastern Nazarene Coll, 69; teach of the yr, Mount Vernon Nazarene Coll, 79, 91; Distinguished Fac Lect, Mount Vernon Nazarene Coll, 82; Gould Lect, Eastern Nazarene Coll, 82. **MEMBERSHIPS** North American Academy of Ecunemilists; Relig Educ Assn; Wesleyan Theol Soc. **RESEARCH** The theology of John Wesley and its origins; contemporary church history. **SELECTED PUBLICATIONS** Art, A Wesleyan Perspective on Christian Unity, Wesleyan Theological Journal, 97-98. **CONTACT ADDRESS** Div of Philos & Relig, Mount Vernon Nazarene Col, 800 Martinsburg Rd, Mount Vernon, OH, 43050-9500. **EMAIL** dcubie@mvnc.edu

CUDD, ANN E.
DISCIPLINE PHILOSOPHY **EDUCATION** Swarthmore Col, BA, 82; MA Philosophy, 84, MA, Economics, 86, PhD, 88, Univ Pittsburgh **CAREER** Asst Prof, 91-93, Occidental Col; Asst Prof, 88-94, Assoc Prof, 94-, Univ Kansas **CONTACT ADDRESS** Dept of Philos, Univ Kansas, Lawrence, KS, 66045.

CULBERTSON, DIANA
PERSONAL Born 09/18/1930, Atlanta, GA **DISCIPLINE** COMPARATIVE LITERATURE, RELIGION **EDUCATION** Siena Heights Col, BA, 52: John Carroll Univ, MA, 58; Univ NC, Chapel Hill, PhD(comp lit), 71; Aquinas Inst Theol, Iowa, MA, 80. **CAREER** Lectr world lit, St John Col Cleveland, 63-65; instr English, Univ NC, Chapel Hill, 70-71; asst prof, 71-76, ASSOC PROF COMP LIT, KENT STATE UNIV, 76-, Danforth Found fel, 76. **MEMBERSHIPS** MLA; Am Acad Relig; Am Comp Lit Asn; Cath Theol Soc Am. **RESEARCH** Comparative literature; religion; theology. **SELECTED PUBLICATIONS** Auth, Aint-Nobody-Clean, the Liturgy of Violence in Glory--Self-Sacrificing Racial Violence in Zwick, Edward Film, Rel and Lit, Vol 0025, 93; Inscribing the Other, So Hum Rev, Vol 0028, 94; The Jews Body, So Hum Rev, Vol 0028, 94. **CONTACT ADDRESS** Dept of English, Kent State Univ, PO Box 5190, Kent, OH, 44242-0001.

CULLINAN, ALICE R.
DISCIPLINE RELIGIOUS STUDIES **EDUCATION** Carson-Newman Col, BA; Southwestern Baptist Theol Seminary, PhD. **CAREER** Prof. **SELECTED PUBLICATIONS** Auth, Time for a Checkup: Assessing Our Progress in Spiritual Growth, Christian Lit Crusade, 94; pubs on spiritual growth in various Christian periodicals. **CONTACT ADDRESS** Dept of Religious Studies and Philosophy, Gardner-Webb Univ, PO Box 997, Boiling Springs, NC, 28017. **EMAIL** drac@shelby.net

CULP, SYLVIA
DISCIPLINE PHILOSOPHY OF SCIENCE, BIOLOGY, AND ETHICS **EDUCATION** Univ Calif, PhD, Univ Va, PhD. **CAREER** Asst prof, W Mich Univ; dir, grad asst. **SELECTED PUBLICATIONS** Articles, Philos Sci; British Jour Philos Sci; Nature; Jour Immunology; **CONTACT ADDRESS** Kalamazoo, MI, 49008. **EMAIL** culp@wmich.edu

CULPEPPER, R. ALAN
PERSONAL Born 03/02/1946, Little Rock, AR, m, 1967, 2 children **DISCIPLINE** THEOLOGY **EDUCATION** Baylor Univ, BA, 67, MDiv 70, Southern Baptist Theological Seminary; attended Goethe Institute, 70; Duke Univ, PhD, 74; Sabbaticals: Cambridge Univ, 80-81; Louisville Kentucky, 87-88. **CAREER** Pastor, Macedonia Baptist Church, 68-70; part-time instr, Duke Univ, 71; research asst for W.D. Davies, 71-73; asst prof of New Testament Interpretation, 74-80, assoc prof of New Testament Interpretation, 80-85, assoc dean, sch of theology, 84-87, 88-91, James Buchanan Harrison prof of New Testament Interpretation, 85-91, Southern Baptist Theological Seminary; vis prof, 83, Vanderbilt Divinity Sch; vis prof, 91-92, prof of relig 92-95, Baylor Univ; dean, 95- , McAfee Sch of Theology, Mercer Univ. **MEMBERSHIPS** Westar Institute; Studiorum Novi Testamenti Societas; Society of Biblical Lit, Literary As-

pects of the Gospels Group, chairperson 86-91, Semeia, editorial board, 91-; Natl Assn of Baptist Professors of Religion, president elect, 98; **SELECTED PUBLICATIONS** Auth, John, the Son of Zebedee: The Life of a Legend, 94, received 1995 Choice Outstanding Academic Book Award; auth, The Gospel of Luke, The New Interpreter's Bible, 95; coed, Exploring the Gospel of John, 96; ed, Critical Readings of John 6, 97; The Gospel and Letters of John, 98. **CONTACT ADDRESS** McAfee Sch of Theol, Mercer Univ, 3001 Mercer Univ Dr, Atlanta, GA, 30341-4115. **EMAIL** culpepper_ra@mercer.edu

CUMING, RON
DISCIPLINE LAW **EDUCATION** Univ Saskatchewan, BA, 62, LLB, 63; Univ Columbia, LLM, 67. **CAREER** Prof, 66- **HONORS AND AWARDS** Tchg Excellence Awd, 93, Distinguished Res Awd, 98. **RESEARCH** National and international secured financing law; debtor-creditor law and bankruptcy. **SELECTED PUBLICATIONS** Auth, Alberta Personal Property Security Act Handbook, Carswell, 96; Alberta Personal Property Security Act Handbook, Carswell, 97; co-auth, Saskatchewan and Manitoba Personal Property Security Handbook, Carswell, 95; Commercial and Consumer Transactions; Cases, Text and Materials, 95. **CONTACT ADDRESS** Col of Law, Univ Saskatchewan, 15 Campus Dr, Saskatoon, SK, S7N 5A6. **EMAIL** Cuming@law.usask.ca

CUMMINS, W. JOSEPH
DISCIPLINE PHILOSOPHY; CLASSICS **EDUCATION** Xavier Univ, AB, 70; Emory Univ, MA, 71, PhD, 75; Univ Cincinnati, MA, 76, PhD, 89. **CAREER** Asst prof, Old Dominion Univ, 76-80; from asst prof to assoc prof, 84-, Grinnell Col. **RESEARCH** Greek and Roman philosophy; intellectual history **CONTACT ADDRESS** Dept of Philosophy, Grinnell Col, Grinnell, IA, 50112. **EMAIL** cummins@ac.grin.edu

CUNNINGHAM, JACK R.
DISCIPLINE CHRISTIAN EDUCATION **EDUCATION** Cent Baptist Col BA; Mid-Am Sem, MA; SW Baptist Theol Sem, PhD. **CAREER** Adj instr, Cent Baptist Col; instr, Inst Christian Stud Southwestern Sem; admin distance edu, Sem Extension of the S Baptist Convention; J.M. Frost assoc prof, S Baptist Theol Sem. **RESEARCH** Areas of experiential learning assessment, distance education and adult education. **SELECTED PUBLICATIONS** Auth, ed, ten teachers' and study guides on the subjects of Old Testament, New Testament and teaching; pub(s), on non-traditional education methodology. **CONTACT ADDRESS** Sch Christian Edu and Leadership, Southern Baptist Theol Sem, 2825 Lexington Rd, Louisville, KY, 40280. **EMAIL** jcunningham@sbts.edu

CUNNINGHAM, L.A.
PERSONAL Born 07/10/1962, Wilmington, DE **DISCIPLINE** LAW **EDUCATION** Univ Delaware, BA 85; Benjamin N Cardozo Sch Law, JD 88. **CAREER** Benjamin N. Cardozo Sch Law, asst prof, assoc prof, prof, 92 to 97-; Samuel and Ronnie Heyman Cen, co-dir, dir, 95-97; St. John's Univ Sch Law, vis prof, 95,96,97; Cravath Swaine Moore, assoc, 88-92, 92-94; Skadden Arps Slate Meagher Flom, assoc, 87. **HONORS AND AWARDS** Phi Alpha Theta; NY Bar Assoc Leg Ethics Prize; Samuel Belkin Awd; Who's Who Amer Law. **MEMBERSHIPS** ABA; NYSBA; ABCNY; **RESEARCH** Corporate Governance; Finance; Accounting; Contracts; Markets; Ethics. **SELECTED PUBLICATIONS** Auth, The Essays of Warren Buffet: Lessons for Corporate America, Cunningham, 98; Introductory Accounting and Finance for Lawyers, west 97; Corporate Finance and Governance: Cases, Materials and Problems, with Lawrence E. Mitchell and Lewis D. Solomon, Carolina 96; Corbin on Contracts, Annual Supplements, with Arthur J. Jacobson, West 96; Warren Buffet on the Role of the Board, The Corp Bd, 98; The Modern Sensibility of New York's New Business Corporation Law, Aspen Law Bus, 98; Preventive Corporate Lawyering: Averting Accounting Scandals, Cardozo Life, 97; Game Theory and Non-Rundable Retainers: A Response to Professors Croson and Mnookin, with Lester Brickman, Harv Neg Law Rev, 97. **CONTACT ADDRESS** Benjamin N. Cardozo Sch of Law, Yeshiva Univ, 55 Fifth Av, NYC, NY, 10003. **EMAIL** cunning@ymail.yu.edu

CUNNINGHAM, SARAH B.
PERSONAL Born 04/15/1967, Pittsfield, MA **DISCIPLINE** PHILOSOPHY **EDUCATION** Kenyon Coll, BA, 89; Vanderbilt Univ, MA, 97; PhD candidate, 98. **CAREER** Instr, Belmont Univ, 96-97; asst prof, Univ Maine, 97-98; dir of develop, Verde Valley School, 98-99. **HONORS AND AWARDS** Burke Tchg Fel, Vanderbilt Univ. **MEMBERSHIPS** Am Philos Asn; German Studies Asn. **RESEARCH** Eighteen Century Aesthetics (Kant, Rousseau); Continental Philosophy; Social and Political Thought. **CONTACT ADDRESS** Univ of Maine, 5776, Orono, ME, 04469. **EMAIL** developuus@sedena.net

CUNNINGHAM, SARAH GARDNER
DISCIPLINE HISTORY AND RELIGION **EDUCATION** Princeton Univ, BA, 79; Union Theol Sem, MDiv, 89, PhD, 84. **CAREER** Macmillan Lib Ref, Simon and Schuster Acad Ref, 94-98; Marymont Sch, upper Sch History, 98-. **MEMBERSHIPS** AAR; AHA; ASCH. **RESEARCH** US Religious History; Hist of Christianity; Gender Studies. **CONTACT ADDRESS** 1735 York Ave, #6C, New York, NY, 10128. **EMAIL** sarah_cunningham@marymont.kiz.ny.us

CUNNINGHAM, SUZANNE M.
PERSONAL Albany, NY, m, 1977 **DISCIPLINE** PHILOSOPHY **EDUCATION** Fla State Univ, PhD, 72. **CAREER** Prof emer, Loyola Univ, Chicago, 98. **HONORS AND AWARDS** Res fel, Inst for Adv Studies in the Humanities, Univ Edinburgh, Scotland, fall, 85; honors teacher of the yr, Loyola Univ, 83-84; Danforth assoc, 76-81; Marion Hay Dissertation award, Fla State Univ, 73; Woodrow Wilson Dissertation fel, 71-72; Univ fel, Fla State Univ, 68-69. **MEMBERSHIPS** Amer Philos Asn; Philos of Sci Asn; Soc for Women in Philos; Soc for Adv of Amer Philos. **RESEARCH** Mind/brain; Evolution and 20th century philosophy. **SELECTED PUBLICATIONS** Article, Two Faces of Intentionality, Philos of Sci, 64, 445-460, Sept, 97; auth, Darwinism and Ethics, Blackwell's Dict of Bus Ethics, Oxford, Blackwell, 97; auth, Ordinary Language Philosophy and Phenomenology, Encycl of Phenomenol, Dordrecht, Kluwer, 97; auth, Classical Modern Philosophy and Husserl's Phenomenology, Encycl of Phenomenol, Dordrecht, Kluwer, 97; auth, Philosophy and the Darwinian Legacy, Univ Rochester Press, 96; article, Dewey on Emotions: Recent Experimental Evidence, Transactions of the C. S. Peirce Society: A Quarterly Journal in American Philosophy, 31, 4, 865-874, Fall, 95; article, Herbert Spencer, Bertrand Russell, and the Shape of Early Analytic Philosophy, Russell, Jour of the Bertrand Russell Archiv, 14, 1, 7-29, Summer, 94. **CONTACT ADDRESS** Dept. of Philosophy, Loyola Univ, Chicago, IL, 60626. **EMAIL** scunnin@orion.it.luc.edu

CURD, MARTIN
DISCIPLINE THE PHILOSOPHY OF SCIENCE, EPISTEMOLOGY **EDUCATION** Pittsburgh, PhD. **CAREER** Assoc prof, Purdue Univ. **RESEARCH** The logic of discovery; the Copernican revolution; the direction of time; incongruent counterparts. **SELECTED PUBLICATIONS** Auth, Argument and Analysis; coauth, Principles of Reasoning. **CONTACT ADDRESS** Dept of Philos, Purdue Univ, 1080 Schleman Hall, West Lafayette, IN, 47907-1080.

CURD, MARTIN VINCENT
PERSONAL Born 04/25/1951, Luton, United Kingdom, m, 1975 **DISCIPLINE** HISTORY & PHILOSOPHY OF SCIENCE **EDUCATION** Univ Cambridge, BA, 72; Univ Pittsburgh, MA, 74, PhD, 78. **CAREER** Instr hist & philos sci, Univ Pittsburgh, 75-77; Mellon instr humanities & philos, Vanderbilt Univ, 77-78; Asst Prof, 78-84, Assoc Prof Philos, Purdue Univ, 84-. **MEMBERSHIPS** Am Philos Asn; Philos Sci Asn. **RESEARCH** Scientific revolution; direction of time; logic of scientific discovery. **SELECTED PUBLICATIONS** Auth, The Logic of Discovery: An Analysis of Three Approaches, in Scientific Discovery, Logic and Rationality: Proceedings of the First Leonard Conf, D Reidel, Dordrecht, Holland, 80; The Rationality of the Copernican Revolution, PSA, 82; coauth, Professional Responsibility For Harm, Kendall/Hunt Publ Co, 84; Principles of Reasoning, St. Martin's Press, 89; auth, Argument and Analysis: An Introduction to Philosophy, West, 92; coauth, Philosophy of Science: The Central Issues, W.W. Norton, 98. **CONTACT ADDRESS** Dept of Philos, Purdue Univ, LAEB - 1360, West Lafayette, IN, 47907-1360. **EMAIL** curd@purdue.edu

CURRAN, VIVIAN
PERSONAL Born 10/30/1955, Philadelphia, PA, m, 1990, 2 children **DISCIPLINE** LAW **EDUCATION** Univ of Penn, BA, 75; Columbia Univ, MA, 77, MPh, 79, PhD, 80, JD, 83. **CAREER** Univ of Pittsburgh School of Law, instr, 89-95, vis asst prof, 94-95, asst prof, 95- . **MEMBERSHIPS** Int Assoc of Legal Semiotics; Int Assoc of Legal Methodology; East-Central Soc for Eighteenth Century Stud; APA; European Community Stud Assoc. **RESEARCH** Law and society, law and language; legal methodology; comparative law. **SELECTED PUBLICATIONS** Auth, Developing and Teaching F Foreign-Language Course for Law Students, J of Legal Educ, 93; auth, Deconstruction, Structuralism, Antisemitism and the Law, Boston Col Law Rev, 94; auth, Cour d'Appel de Grenoble: Ytong v Lasaosa, lc 16 juin, 1993, Law and Commerce, 95; auth, Learning French Through the Law: A French/English Comparative Treatment of Terms in a Legal Context, Columbia Univ, 96; auth, Metaphor Is the Mother of All Law, in Kevelson, ed, Law and the Conflict of Ideologies, Lang, 96; auth, Interpretive Decisions Applying CISG: Translation of Claude Witz's The First Decision of France's Court of Cassation Applying the UN Convention on Contracts for the International Sale of Goods, J Law and Commerce, 97; auth, What Should One Think of Judicial Ritual in Law? in Lindgren, ed, Ritual and Semiotics, 97; auth, Vichy France: A Crisis in Legality, Legitimacy and Identity, in European Memory at the Millennium, MIT, 97, (CD ROM); auth, Cultural Immersion, Difference and Categories in US Comparative Law, J Comp Law, 98; auth, Herder and the Holocaust: A Debate about Difference and Determinism in the Context of Comparative Law, in De Coste, ed, The Holocaust: Art, Politics, Law, Education, forthcoming; auth, Dealing in Difference: Comparative Law's Potential for Broadening Legal Perspectives, Am J Comp Law, forthcoming. **CONTACT ADDRESS** Univ Pittsburgh School of Law, 3900 Forbes Ave, Pittsburgh, PA, 15260. **EMAIL** curran@law.pitt.edu

CURREN, RANDALL R.
PERSONAL Born 09/19/1955, New Orleans, LA, m, 1987, 3 children **DISCIPLINE** PHILOSOPHY **EDUCATION** Univ New Orleans, BA, philos, 77; Univ Pittsburgh, MA, 81, PhD, 85. **CAREER** Andrew Mellon instr, philos, Calif Inst of Tech, 85-87; instr, philos, Calif Inst of Tech, 87-88; asst prof, 88-95, assoc prof, 95-, Univ Rochester. **HONORS AND AWARDS** Andrew Mellon fel, 77-78; Charlotte Neucombe fel, 83-84; NEH summer stipend, 91; Spencer fel, 91-92; Spencer found grant, 93-94; NEH grant, 97-98. **MEMBERSHIPS** Asn for Philos of Educ; Philos of Educ Soc; Amer Philos Asn; Amer Educ Res Asn; AMINTAPHIL; Amer Soc for Polit and Legal Philos; Soc for Ancient Greek Philos. **RESEARCH** Political philosophy; Philosophy of education; Philosophy of law; Ethics; Ancient philosophy. **SELECTED PUBLICATIONS** Article, Coercion and the Ethics of Grading and Testing, Educ Theory, 45, no 4, 425-441, fall 95; article, Punishment and Inclusion: The Presuppositions of Corrective Justice in Aristotle and What They Imply, The Can Jour of Law and Jurisprudence, 8, no 2, 259-274, jul, 95; article, Justice and the Threshold of Educational Equality, Philos of Educ 1994, 239-248, 95; article, Justice, Instruction, and the Good: The Case For Public Education in Aristotle and Plato's Laws, Part III: Why Education Should Be Public And The Same For All, Studies in Philos and Educ, 13, no 1, 1-31, 94. **CONTACT ADDRESS** Dept. of Philosophy, Univ of Rochester, Rochester, NY, 14627. **EMAIL** rcrn@troi.cc.rochester.edu

CURRIE, DAVID P.
PERSONAL Born 05/29/1936, Macon, GA, m, 1959, 2 children **DISCIPLINE** LAW **EDUCATION** Univ Chicago, AB, 57; Harvard Univ, LLB, 60. **CAREER** From asst prof to assoc prof, 62-68, PROF LAW, UNIV CHICAGO, 68-, Chmn, Ill Pollution Control Bd, 70-72. **RESEARCH** Federal jurisdiction; conflict of laws; natural resources. **SELECTED PUBLICATIONS** Auth, The Constitution in Congress--The 3rd Congress, 1793-1795, Univ Chicago Law Rev, Vol 0063, 96; The Constitution in Congress--Substantive Issues in the 1st Congress, 1789-1791, Univ Chicago Law Rev, Vol 0061, 94; Ex-Parte Young After Seminole Tribe, NY Univ Law Rev, Vol 0072, 97; Separation of Powers in the Federal-Republic-Of-Germany, Amer Jour Comp Law, Vol 0041, 93; The Constitution in Congress--The 2nd Congress, 1791-1793, Northwestern Univ Law Rev, Vol 0090, 96. **CONTACT ADDRESS** Sch of Law, Univ of Chicago, 1111 E 60th St, Chicago, IL, 60637-2702.

CURRIE, JOHN H.
DISCIPLINE LAW **EDUCATION** Univ Toronto, BS, LLB, LLM. **CAREER** Vis prof. **RESEARCH** International law; prosecution of crimes against humanity. **SELECTED PUBLICATIONS** Co-auth, Injunctions, Carswell, 96; Supreme Court of Canada Manual: Practice and Advocacy, Can Law Bk, 96. **CONTACT ADDRESS** Fac Common Law, Univ Ottawa, 550 Cumberland St, PO Box 450, Ottawa, ON, K1N 6N5.

CURRY, ALLEN
DISCIPLINE CHRISTIAN EDUCATION **EDUCATION** Temple Univ, PhD. **CAREER** Acad dean; Hugh and Sally Reaves prof. **HONORS AND AWARDS** Dir, Edu Svc(s), cord, Production, Great Commn Publ. **SELECTED PUBLICATIONS** Auth, The God We Love and Serve. **CONTACT ADDRESS** Dept of Christian Education, Reformed Theol Sem, 5422 Clinton Blvd, Jackson, MS, 39209-3099.

CURTIS-HOWE, E. MARGARET
PERSONAL Essex, England **DISCIPLINE** RELIGION **EDUCATION** Univ Sheffield, BA, 60; Univ London, cert educ, 61; Univ Manchester, PhD(New Testament & contempt lit), 64. **CAREER** Teacher relig & hist, Withington Girls' Sch, 64-69; asst prof, 72-81, Prof Middle Eastern Stud, Western KY Univ, 81-, Lectr, Ky Humanities Coun, 81-82. **HONORS AND AWARDS** Fulbright scholar, 96-97, Yemen. **MEMBERSHIPS** Soc Bibl Lit; Inst Bibl Res; North Am Patristic Soc; Bibl Archaeol Soc; Am Schs of Oriental Res; TESOL; Midwest Asn Latin Am Stud. **RESEARCH** New Testament; Dead Sea Scrolls; patristics. **SELECTED PUBLICATIONS** A reappraisal of factors influencing the Easter faith of the early Christian community, J Evangelical Theol Soc, summer 75; The place of feeling in religious experience, Collage, fall 75; Women and church leadership, Evangelical Quart, 4-6/79; The Positive Case for the Ordination of Women, In: Perspectives on Evangelical Theology, Baker, 79; Interpretations of Paul in the Acts of Paul and Thecla, In: Pauline Studies, Paternoster, UK, 80, Eerdmans, 80; Women and Church Leadership, Zondervan, 82; Commentary on the Greek Text of I Corinthians, Word Publ (in prep). **CONTACT ADDRESS** Dept of Philos & Relig, Western Kentucky Univ, 1 Big Red Way St, Bowling Green, KY, 42101. **EMAIL** margaret.curtis@wku.edu

CURTLER, HUGH M.
PERSONAL Born 12/31/1937, Charlottesville, VA, m, 1962, 2 children **DISCIPLINE** PHILOSOPHY **EDUCATION** St John's Coll, BA, 59; Northwestern Univ, MA, 62, PhD, 64. **CAREER** Asst Prof, 64-66, Univ of Rhode Island; Assoc Prof, 66-68, Midwestern Coll; 68-. Southwest State Univ of MN. **HONORS AND AWARDS** Northwestern Univ Fellowship, 61-64; NEH Fellowship, 71. **MEMBERSHIPS** APA. **RE-**

SEARCH Value Theory; Philosophy of Criticism. **SELECTED PUBLICATIONS** Auth, Ethical Argument, Paragon, 93; Rediscovering Values, M.E. Sharpe, 97. **CONTACT ADDRESS** Box 102, Cottonwood, MN, 56229. **EMAIL** curtler@ssu.southwest.MSUS.edu

CURZER, HOWARD J.
DISCIPLINE PHILOSOPHY **EDUCATION** Wesleyan Univ, BA, 74, MA, 75; Univ TX, Austin, PhD, 85. **CAREER** Instr, Univ Houston; assoc prof, TX Tech Univ, 85-. **RESEARCH** Ancient philos; ethics. **SELECTED PUBLICATIONS** His work has appeared in The Can J of Philos, Class Quart, Apeiron, Australasian J of Philos, J of Med and Philos, and Hypatia. **CONTACT ADDRESS** Texas Tech Univ, Lubbock, TX, 79409-5015. **EMAIL** AUCUR@ttacs.ttu.edu

CUSSINS, ADRIAN
DISCIPLINE PHILOSOPHY **EDUCATION** Oxford Univ, PhD. **CAREER** Asst prof, Univ Ill Urban Champaign. **RESEARCH** Meaning; reference; representation; information; content; experience; philosophy of mind and language; metaphysics; epistemology; philosophy of science. **SELECTED PUBLICATIONS** Auth, Content, Embodiment and Objectivity; Connectionist Construction of Concepts; Limitations of Pluralism; Varieties of Psychologism. **CONTACT ADDRESS** Philosophy Dept, Univ Ill Urbana Champaign, 52 E Gregory Dr, Champaign, IL, 61820. **EMAIL** acussins@uiuc.edu

CUST, KENNETH F.T.
PERSONAL Born 01/29/1953, Edmonton, AB, Canada, m, 1992, 1 child **DISCIPLINE** PHILOSOPHY **EDUCATION** Bowling Green St Univ, PhD, 93. **CAREER** Assoc prof, phil, 95-, found dir, Ctr for Appl & Prof Ethics, Cent Mo St Univ. **HONORS AND AWARDS** Fac Achieve Award, 95. **MEMBERSHIPS** Amer Soc Phil; Counseling & Psychotherapy; Tenn Phil Assn. **RESEARCH** Phil coun & consult; phil in a prof pvt pract; soc, moral, pol phil; appl phil. **SELECTED PUBLICATIONS** Art, Assault: Just Part of the Job?, Canadian Nurse, 86; art, Hypothetical Contractarianism and the Disclosure Requirement Problem in Informed Consent, J Med Hum 12:3, 91; art, Medicine, Morality, and Concept Reduction, J Med Hum 13:1, 92; authart Contractarianism and Rational Choice, Australian J Pol Phil 27:1, 93; art, Justice and Rights to Health Care, Reason Papers 18, 93; auth, A Just Minimum of Health Care, Univ Press Amer, 97. **CONTACT ADDRESS** Ctr for Applied & Professional Ethics, Central Missouri State Univ, Warrensburg, MO, 64093. **EMAIL** kencust@sprintmail.com

CUSTER, JOHN S.
PERSONAL Born 07/17/1958, Jersey City, NJ **DISCIPLINE** SACRED SCRIPTURE, THEOLOGY, CLASSICS **EDUCATION** Seton Hall Univ, BA (Classics), 79; Pontificia Universita Gregoriana, Rome, STB (Theol), 82; Pontificio Istituto Biblico, Rome, SSL (Sacred Scripture), 85; Pontificia Universita Gregoriana, Rome, STD (Sacred Scripture), 87. **CAREER** Instr, Marymount Int School, Rome, 83-86; adjunct prof, Western CT State Univ, Danbury, 88-89; adjunct prof, St Charles Borromeo Sem, Relig Studies Div, Wynnewood, PA, 90-; asst prof, Pontifical Col Josephinum, Col of Liberal Arts, Columbus, OH, 93-96, dean, 93-94, Dir of Pastoral Formation, 93-94, coord of Pastoral Formation, 94-95, dir of recruitment, 94-96, chmn, Dept of Relig Studies, 94-96; instr of Old Testament, Permanent Diaconate Prog, Eparchy of Newton, St Gregory the Theologian Sem, Newton, MA, 95-; prof of Scripture, Byzantine Cath Sem, Pittsburgh, PA, 96-, dean, 96-. **MEMBERSHIPS** Cath Biblical Soc; Soc for Biblical Lit; North Am Patristic Soc. **RESEARCH** Biblical studies; Byzantine Christian studies; Patristics. **SELECTED PUBLICATIONS** Auth, An Ironic Scriptural Wordplay in Byzantine Hymnography, St Vladimir's Theological Quart 37, 93; Byzantine Rite Slavs in Philadelphia: 1886-1916, Record of the Am Cath Hist Soc 104, 93; Qohelet and the Canon: The Dissenting Voice in Dialogue, The Josephinum J of Theol, 1, 94; The Harp, the Psaltery and the Fathers: A Biblical Image and Its Interpreters, The Downside Review, no 394, 96; The Old Testament: A Byzantine Perspective, God With Us Pubs, 96; Why a Hymn? Form and Content in St Ephrem's Hymn 31 on Virginity, St Vladimir's Theol Quart, 40, 96; Uzhorod, Balamand and Beyond: A Uniate Looks to the Millennium, J of Ecumenical Studies, 97; several other publications. **CONTACT ADDRESS** Byzantine Catholic Sem, 3605 Perrysville Ave, Pittsburgh, PA, 15124. **EMAIL** Jackcus@aol.com

CUTLER, NATHAN S.
PERSONAL Born 11/18/1949, Hainsburg, PA, m, 1988, 3 children **DISCIPLINE** PHILOSOPHY **EDUCATION** Calif Inst Integral Stud, PhD, 96. **CAREER** Independent scholar, instr, Univ Calif Santa Cruz Extension, Arts and Humanities. **MEMBERSHIPS** Am Acad Relig; Independent Scholars of South Asia. **RESEARCH** Tibetan studies; pilgrimage studies; nature and religion. **SELECTED PUBLICATIONS** Auth, The early rulers of Tibet: Their Lineage and Burial Rites, Tibet J, 91; auth, The Tibetan Guidebook: Narrative of Tise, Gangs Rinpoche, Proc of the 11th Cong of the Int Assn of Buddhist Stud, 94; auth, Mt. Kailasa: Source for the Sacred in Early Indian and Tibetan Tradition, UMI, 97; auth, An Offering Prayer to the Mountain Deity of Kailasa, Ti-se Lha-btsan, Proc of the 8th Sem of the Int Assn for Tibetan Stud, 98; auth, A Buddhist Pilgrim in the Sahdow of Mt. Kailasa, Traveler's Tales, forthcoming. **CONTACT ADDRESS** 1617 8th St, Berkeley, CA, 94710. **EMAIL** Btiseri@aol.com

CUTROFELLO, ANDREW
DISCIPLINE PHILOSOPHY **EDUCATION** Northwestern Univ, PhD, 89. **CAREER** Assoc prof, Loyola Univ, 94-; fac, St. Mary's Col Ind, 89-94. **RESEARCH** Contemporary French philosophy; contemporary European philosophy; psychoanalysis, Hume, Kant, Hegel, Nietzsche. **SELECTED PUBLICATIONS** Auth, Imagining Otherwise: Metapsychology and the Analytic A Posteriori, Northwestern UP, 97; The Owl at Dawn: A Sequel to Hegel's Phenomenology of Spirit, State Univ NY Press, 95; Discipline and Critique: Kant, Poststructuralism, and the Problem of Resistance, State Univ NY Press, 94. **CONTACT ADDRESS** Dept of Philosophy, Loyola Univ, Chicago, 820 N. Michigan Ave., Chicago, IL, 60611.

D

D'AGOSTINO, PETER R.
PERSONAL Born 12/22/1962, New York, NY, s **DISCIPLINE** RELIGIOUS STUDIES; HISTORY **EDUCATION** Brown Univ, BA, 80-84; Univ Chicago, MA, 86-87; Univ Chicago, PhD, 87-93 **CAREER** Visiting asst prof, Univ Ill, 94-95; asst prof Relig Studies & History, Stonehill Col, 95 **HONORS AND AWARDS** PEW Grant for Relig in Amer History, 98-99; Fulbright Jr Fac Res Fel, 96; Jr Fel, Univ Chic, 91-92; Giovanni Agnelli Found Italian Amer Studies Fel, 90-91; John T. McNeil Fel, 88-89 **MEMBERSHIPS** Orgn Amer Historians; Immigration History Soc; Amer Italian Historical Assoc; Amer Cath Historical Assoc; Amer Soc Church History; Amer Acad Relig **RESEARCH** U.S. Immigration History; U.S. Religious History; U.S. Society, 1877-1945; Modern Italy **SELECTED PUBLICATIONS** "The Sacraments of Whiteness: Racial Ambiguity and Religious Discipline Among Italians in Urban America," Religion and the City, forthcoming; "Urban Restructuring and the Religious Adaptation: Cardinal Joseph Bernardin of Chicago (1982-1995)," Public Religion and Urban Transformation, NY Univ Pr, forthcoming; "The Crisis of Authority in American Catholicism: Urban Schools and Cultural Conflict," Records of the American Catholic Historical Association of Philadelphia, forthcoming **CONTACT ADDRESS** 22 Bradbury St, Allston, MA, 02134. **EMAIL** pdagostino@stonehill.edu

D'AMICO, ROBERT
PERSONAL Born 01/15/1947, Buffalo, NY, m, 2 children **DISCIPLINE** PHILOSOPHY **EDUCATION** SUNY Buffalo, BA, 69, PhD, 74. **CAREER** Asst prof, 74-79, assoc prof, fall 79, actg ch, 79-80, ch, 98-, Dept of Phil Univ Fla. **MEMBERSHIPS** APA. **RESEARCH** Philosophy of social science. **SELECTED PUBLICATIONS** Auth, Historicism and Knowledge, 88; Contemporary Continental Philosophy, 98. **CONTACT ADDRESS** Dept of Philosophy, Univ of Florida, 330 Griffin-Floyd Hall, Gainsville, FL, 32611-8545. **EMAIL** rdamico@phil.ufl.edu

DAHL, NORMAN
DISCIPLINE PHILOSOPHY **EDUCATION** Univ Calif Berkeley, PhD. **RESEARCH** Ancient Greek philosophy; ethics. **SELECTED PUBLICATIONS** Auth, Plato's Defense of Justice, Philos Phenomenol Res, 91; On the Moral Status of Weakness of the Will, Logos, 89; Morality and the Meaning of Life: Some First Thoughts, Can J Philos, 87; Obligation and Moral Worth: Reflections on Prichard and Kant, Philos Studies, 86; Practical Reason, Aristotle, and Weakness of the Will, Univ Minn, 84; Paternalism and Rational Desire, Univ Minn, 83. **CONTACT ADDRESS** Philosophy Dept, Univ of Minnesota, Twin Cities, 355 Ford Hall, 224 Church St SE, Minneapolis, MN, 55455. **EMAIL** dahlx005@maroon.tc.umn.edu

DAISE, BENJAMIN
PERSONAL Born 05/21/1942, St. Helena Island, SC **DISCIPLINE** PHILOSOPHY **EDUCATION** Morehouse Col, BS, 65; Univ TX, Austin, PhD, 73. **CAREER** Prof Philos, Hobart & William Smith Col, 70. **RESEARCH** Kierkegaard studies; Plato. **SELECTED PUBLICATIONS** Auth, Kierkegaard and the absolute paradox, J Hist Philos, 1/76; The will to truth in Kierkegaard's Philosophical Fragments, J Philos Relig, 1/92. **CONTACT ADDRESS** Dept of Philos, Hobart & William Smith Cols, 4133 Scandling Center, Geneva, NY, 14456-3382. **EMAIL** daise@hws.edu

DALE, WALTER R.
PERSONAL Born 12/23/1944, Chicago, Illinois, d **DISCIPLINE** LAW **EDUCATION** University of Illinois, BS, finance, 1966; Governors State University, MBA, 1981; IIT Chicago Kent Law School, JD, 1985; John Marshall Law School, LLM, tax, 1988. **CAREER** Small Business Administration, loan servicing officer, 1971-72; Chicago City Bank & Trust Co, commercial loan officer, 1972-75; Jackson Park Hospital, internal auditor and patient accounts manager, 1980-81; Chicago State University, professor of accounting and finance, 1987-; United States Department of the Treasury, Internal Revenue Service, revenue agent, field auditor, tax law researcher, 1981-85; Caldwell & Hubbard, tax attorney, 1985-86; Brown & Porter, entertainment, tax and corporate lawyer, currently. **MEMBERSHIPS** Alpha Phi Alpha; Chicago Black Attorneys in Sports & Entertainment, president; Black Entertainment & Sports Lawyers Association; National Academy of Recording Arts & Sciences. **SELECTED PUBLICATIONS** "A New Approach to Federal Taxation," Midwest Accounting Society, March 1993. **CONTACT ADDRESS** Brown & Porter, 1130 S Wabash, Ste 501, Chicago, IL, 60605.

DALE LEA, THOMAS
PERSONAL m, 3 children **DISCIPLINE** NEW TESTAMENT **EDUCATION** Miss State Univ, BS, 60; Southwestern Baptist Theol Sem, BD, 64, ThD, 67. **CAREER** Prof, 79-. **HONORS AND AWARDS** Pastor, Vineyard Grove Baptist Chruch, 64-66; asst pastor, Cliff Temple Baptist Church, 66-68; pastor, Liberty Baptist Church, 68-72; Hunter St Baptist Church, 72-79. **MEMBERSHIPS** Evangel Theol Soc; Inst Biblical Res; Soc Biblical Lit. **SELECTED PUBLICATIONS** Auth, The New Testament: Its Background and Message, Broadman & Holman, 96; Saved by Grace, Convention Press, 94; 1, 2 Timothy, Broadman & Holman, 92; Step by Step Through the New Testament, Baptist Sunday Sch Bd, 92. **CONTACT ADDRESS** Sch Theol, Southwestern Baptist Theol Sem, PO Box 22000, Fort Worth, TX, 76122-0418. **EMAIL** tdalel@swbts.swbts.edu

DALEY, BRIAN EDWARD
PERSONAL Born 01/18/1940, Orange, NJ **DISCIPLINE** HISTORICAL THEOLOGY, CHRUCH HISTORY **EDUCATION** Fordham Univ, BA, 61; Oxford Univ, BA, 64, MA, 67, DPhil(theol), 79; Loyola Sem, PhL, 66; Hochschule Sankt Georgen, Frankfurt, Lic theol, 72. **CAREER** Instr classics, Fordham Univ, 66-67; ASST PROF HIST THEOL, WESTON SCH THEOL, 78-, Ed, Traditio, 78-; trustee, Le Moyne Col, 79-. **MEMBERSHIPS** Asn Int Etudes Patristiques; Am Soc Church Hist; Soc Values Higher Educ; Am Asn Rhodes Scholars. **RESEARCH** Greek patristic theology; history of spirituality; Neoplatonism. **SELECTED PUBLICATIONS** Auth, Position and Patronage in the Early-Church--Distinguishing Between Personal or Moral Authority and Canonical or Structural Jurisdiction in the Early-Christian Community and Civil-Society--The Original Meaning of Primacy-Of-Honor, Jour Theol; Regnum-Caelorum--Patterns of Future Hope in Early Christianity, Jour Theol Stud, Vol 0045, 94; Apollo as a Chalcedonian--Tracing the Trajectory of a Christian Oracle and Christological Apologia--A New Fragment of a Controversial Work From Early 6th-Century Constantinople, Traditio-Stud Ancient and Medieval Hist Thought and Rel. **CONTACT ADDRESS** Dept of Hist Theol, Weston Jesuit Sch of Theol, Cambridge, MA, 02138.

DALLEN, JAMES
PERSONAL Born 04/16/1943, Concordia, KS **DISCIPLINE** THEOLOGY, RELIGIOUS STUDIES **EDUCATION** St Mary's Col, KY, BA, 65; Cath Univ Am, STB, 68, MA, 69, STD, 76. **CAREER** Instr theol, Rosemont Col, 75-76, asst prof, 76-82; asst prof, 82-84, assoc prof, 84-94, prof theol, Gonzaga Univ, 94-. **MEMBERSHIPS** N Am Acad Liturgy; Cath Theol Soc Am; Col Theol Soc; Am Acad Relig. **RESEARCH** Sacrament of Penance; Eucharistic prayer, Cultural adaptation of liturgy. **SELECTED PUBLICATIONS** Auth, Liturgical Celebration: Patterns (4 vols), NAm Liturgy Resources, 71-75; The Mass Today, NAm Liturgy Resources, 76; The Reconciling Community, Liturgical Press, 86; Removing the Barriers, Liturgy Training Pubs, 91; Dilemma of Priestless Sundays, Liturgy Training Pubs, 94. **CONTACT ADDRESS** Dept of Religious Studies, Gonzaga Univ, 502 E Boone Ave, Spokane, WA, 99258-0001. **EMAIL** dallen@gonzaga.edu

DALLEY, GEORGE ALBERT
PERSONAL Born 08/25/1941, Havana, Cuba, m, 1970 **DISCIPLINE** LAW **EDUCATION** Columbus Coll, AB 1963; Columbua Univ School of Law, JD 1966; Columbia Univ Grad School & Business, MBA 1966. **CAREER** Metropolition Appl Res Cntr, assis to the pres 1962-69; Stroock & Stroock & Lavan, assoc cousnel 1970-71; US House of Representatives Comm on the Judiciary, assist counsel 1971-72; Congressman Charles Rangel, admin asst 1973-76; US Dept of State, deputy asst sec of state 1977-79; US Civil Aero Bd, mem 1980-82; Mondale for Pres, deputy camp mgr 1983-84; Cong Charles Rangel, coun and staff dir 1985-1989; senior vice pres Neill and Company Inc, 1989-93; Neill and Shaw, partner, 1989-93; Holland & Knight, partner, 1993-; Adjunct prof Am Univ Schl of Law 1981-; **MEMBERSHIPS** Avat human rights Am Bar Assoc; Intl law comm Nat'l Bar Assoc Fed Bar Assoc 1976-; mem Transafrica, NAACP, Urban League 1974-; Crestwood Comm Assn 1986-; mem bd of dir Africare, Transafrica DC Support Group; consultant, United Nations Devel Program 1989-; American Bar Association; American Bar Foundation; DC Judicial Nominating Commission. **SELECTED PUBLICATIONS** Article, Federal Drug Abuse Enforcement; speeches Dem Corp Select Process 1976; various mag articles. **CONTACT ADDRESS** Holland & Knight, 2100 Pennsylvania Ave, NW, Ste 400, Washington, DC, 20036.

DALLMAYR, FRED REINHARD
PERSONAL Born 10/18/1928, Ulm, Germany, m, 1957, 2 children **DISCIPLINE** PHILOSOPHY **EDUCATION** Univ Munich, 49-53, JD, 55; Duke Univ, PhD Polit Sci, 60. **CAREER** Asst Prof, Milwaukee Downer Col, 61-63; from asst prof to prof, Purdue Univ, 63-71; prof, Univ Georgia, 71-73; Prof & Dept Head, 73-78; PACKEY J. DEE PROF, UNIV NOTRE DAME, 78-. **HONORS AND AWARDS** Phi Beta Kappa, 60; NEH Fel, 78-79; Fulbright Res Grant, 91. **MEMBERSHIPS** Amer Polit Sci Assn; Int Polit Sci Assn; Soc for Asian and Comparative Philos; Soc for Phenomenon & Existential Philos. **RESEARCH** Modern and contemporary social and polit philos; comparative philos; cross-cultural studies; critical theory. **SELECTED PUBLICATIONS** Auth, Between Freiburg and Frankfurt, 91; The Other Heidegger, 93, Hegel: Modernity and Politics, 93; Beyond Orientalism: Essays on Cross-Cultural Encounter, 96; Alternative Visions: Paths in the Global Village, 98. **CONTACT ADDRESS** Dept. of Govt., Univ Notre Dame, Notre Dame, IN, 46556-0368. **EMAIL** Fred.R.Dallmayr.1@nd.edu

DALMAN, RODGER
PERSONAL Born 07/14/1948, Holland, MI, m, 1976, 3 children **DISCIPLINE** BIBLICAL STUDIES **EDUCATION** Northwestern Bible Col, BA, 70; Biblical Sem, MDiv, 79; Concordia Sem, ThD, 90. **CAREER** Adjunct prof, Trinity Col and Sem, current. **MEMBERSHIPS** Evangelical Theol Soc; Soc of Bibl Lit. **RESEARCH** Old Testament; Archaeology; Ancient Near Eastern history; Literature; Mythology; Geology. **SELECTED PUBLICATIONS** Auth, Research Guide for the Study of Basic Old Testament Theology; Research Guide for Understanding the Egyptian Influence on the Old Testament and the Polemics of Israel's Sea Crossing. **CONTACT ADDRESS** 9441 Bass Creek Cir, New Hope, MN, 55428. **EMAIL** rwdalman@laxs.net

DALTON, PETER C.
DISCIPLINE PHILOSOPHY **EDUCATION** Northwestern Univ, BA, 68; Univ Rochester, MA, 71, PhD, 73. **CAREER** Tchg asst, 69-70; instr, Univ Rochester, 72; asst prof, 72-77; assoc prof, Fla State Univ, 77-. **HONORS AND AWARDS** Tchg Incentive Prog Awd, 94. **MEMBERSHIPS** Am Philos Asn; Asn of Jour Editors; Fla Philos Asn. **RESEARCH** Modern philosophy; 19th century philosophy; metaphysics. **SELECTED PUBLICATIONS** Auth, A Theological Escape from the Cartesian Circle?, Int Jour Philos Relig, 97; Extended Acts, Philos, 95; The Examined Life, Metaphilos, 92. **CONTACT ADDRESS** Dept of Philosophy, Florida State Univ, 211 Wescott Bldg, Tallahassee, FL, 32306. **EMAIL** pdalton@mailer.fsu.edu

DALTON, STUART
PERSONAL Born 04/18/1964, Provo, UT, m, 1986, 2 children **DISCIPLINE** PHILOSOPHY **EDUCATION** Villanova Univ, MA, 92; Emory Univ, PhD, 97. **CAREER** Instr, Georgia State Univ, 94-97; Dean's Teaching Fel, Emory Univ, 96-97; Asst Prof, Univ Hartford, 97-. **HONORS AND AWARDS** Robert Russell Graduate Fel, Villanova Univ, 90-92; Graduate Fel and Teaching Assistantship, Emory Univ, 92-96; Phi Betta Kappa, Emory Univ, 95; Dean's Teaching Fel, Emory Univ, 96-97; NEH Summer Stipend Nominee, Univ Hartford, 97. **MEMBERSHIPS** Amer Assoc of Univ Professors; Amer Phil Assoc. **RESEARCH** 19th and 20th century continental philosophy; 17th and 18th century modern philosophy; social, political and moral philosophy; aesthetics **SELECTED PUBLICATIONS** Auth, Lyotard's Peregrination: Three (and a half) Responses to the Call of Justice, Philosophy Today, 94; Foucalt on Freedom and the Space of Transgression, PoMo2.1, 96; The General Will and the Legislator in Rousseau's On the Social Contract, Southwest Philosophy Review, 96; Heidegger's Return to the Greeks: Three Stories about Origins, Existentia, forthcoming; Beginnings and Endings in Nietzsche's Beyond Good and Evil, The Journal of Nietzsche Studies, forthcoming. **CONTACT ADDRESS** Hillyer College, Univ of Hartford, West Hartford, CT, 06117. **EMAIL** dalton@mall.hartford.edu

DALY, MARKATE
DISCIPLINE PHILOSOPHY **EDUCATION** Univ Wisc, Madison, PhD, 84. **CAREER** Adj prof & dir Ctr for Public Philos, San Francisco State Univ. **MEMBERSHIPS** Soc for Philos and Psychol; Int Soc for Social Philos. **RESEARCH** Philosophy of mind/person; ethics; social philosophy. **SELECTED PUBLICATIONS** Auth, Communitarianism: A New Public Ethic, Wadsworth, 94. **CONTACT ADDRESS** 2730 Parker St, Berkeley, CA, 94704. **EMAIL** mdaly@sfsu.edu

DAM, KENNETH W.
PERSONAL Born 08/10/1932, Marysville, KS, m, 1962 **DISCIPLINE** LAW **EDUCATION** Univ KS, BS, 54; Univ Chicago, JD, 57. **CAREER** Law clerk, Mr Justice Whittaker, US Supreme Court, 57-58; vis asst prof, 60-61, from assoc prof to prof, 61-76, Harold J. & Marion F. Green Prof Law, 76-, Max Pam Prof Am and Foreign Law, Univ Chicago, 92-, Provost, 80-82; Asst dir, US Off Mgt & Budget, 71-73; exec dir, US Coun Econ Policy, 73; Deputy Secy of State, 82-85; vpres, IBM Corp, 85-92. **MEMBERSHIPS** Am Law Inst; Am Acad Arts & Sci; Am Acad Diplomacy. **RESEARCH** International and constitutional law; trade regulation. **SELECTED PUBLICATIONS** Auth, Law and International Economic Policy--the Gatt, 70 & Oil Resources--Who Gets What How?, 76, Univ Chicago; coauth, Economic Policy Beyond the Headlines, W.W. Norton, 78, 2nd ed, 98; auth, The Rules of the Game: Reform and Evolution in the International Monetary System, 82. **CONTACT ADDRESS** Law Sch, Univ of Chicago, 1111 E 60th St, Chicago, IL, 60637-2702. **EMAIL** Kenneth_dam@law.uchicago.edu

DANAHER, JAMES P.
PERSONAL Born 12/24/1947, Jersey City, NJ, m, 1981, 2 children **DISCIPLINE** PHILOSOPHY **EDUCATION** City Univ NY, PhD, 90. **CAREER** Prof and hd, Dept Philos, Nyack Col, 90-; chm, gen ed dept, Berkeley Col, 80-. **HONORS AND AWARDS** Philos residence, Whitehall Mus, 93. **MEMBERSHIPS** Am Philos Asn; Evangel Philos Soc; Int Berkeley Soc. **RESEARCH** History of philosophy; philosophy of love. **SELECTED PUBLICATIONS** Auth, Love in Plato and the New Testament, Europ Jour Theol, 98; auth, Why Wives Shouldn't Leave Their Husbands, Preachers Mag, 98; auth, On Faith and Knowledge, Covenant Quart, Feb, 98; auth, Toward an Understanding of Love: Human and Divine, Encounter, Fall, 97; auth, Socrates and Homosexuality, Philos Christi, Fall, 96; auth, On Loving and Liking, Philos Christi, Fall, 95; auth, Submit Therefore to God, Fel Today, Nov, 93. **CONTACT ADDRESS** Dept of Philosophy, Nyack Col, 44 Bailey Ave., Oakland, NJ, 07436. **EMAIL** Danaherj@nyack.edu

DANIEL, E. RANDOLPH
PERSONAL Born 04/15/1935, Richmond, VA, m, 1960, 3 children **DISCIPLINE** THEOLOGY **EDUCATION** Davidson Col, BA, 58; Union Theol Seminary, BD, 61; Harvard Univ, ThM, 64; Univ Virginia, PhD, 66. **CAREER** Asst Prof, 66-72, Assoc Prof, 72-83, Prof, 83-, Chr, 84-88, Univ Kentucky **HONORS AND AWARDS** NDEA Fel, 63-66. **MEMBERSHIPS** Amer Historical Assoc; Medieval Acad of Amer. **RESEARCH** Apocalypticism and religious orders in the middle ages **SELECTED PUBLICATIONS** Auth, The Franciscan Concept of Mission in the High Middle ages, reprinted, 92; auth, Joachimism and John Calvin: New Approaches, Storia e figure dell 'Apocalisse fra '500 e '600, 96; auth, Reformist Apocalypticism and the Friars Minor, That Others may Know and Love: Essays in Honor of Zachary Hayes OFM, 97. **CONTACT ADDRESS** Dept of History, Univ Kentucky, Lexington, KY, 40506. **EMAIL** erdani01@pop.uky.edu

DANIEL, WILEY YOUNG
PERSONAL Born 09/10/1946, Louisville, KY, m **DISCIPLINE** LAW **EDUCATION** Howard Univ, BA 1968; Howard Univ Sch of Law, JD 1971. **CAREER** Volunteer legal work; Dickinson Wright McKean Cudlip & Moon, Attorney 1971-77; Gorsuch Kirgis Campbell Walker & Grover, Attorney 1977-88; Popham, Haik, Schnobrich & Kaufman, partner, 1988-95; US District Court, judge, 1995-. **HONORS AND AWARDS** 1986 Disting Serv Awd Sam Cary Bar Assoc, Colorado Assoc of Black Attorneys; Fellow, American Bar Foundation; Fellow, Colorado Bar Foundation; USA Speaker Aboard, Nigeria, 1995. **MEMBERSHIPS** Mem Natl Bar Assn; pres-elect, 1991-92, pres, 1992-93, CO Bar Assn; trustee, Denver Bar Assn, 1990-93; Amer Bar Assn; Managing Ed Howard LLJ; mem Delta Theta Phi Law Frat, Alpha Phi Alpha Social Frat; Law Journal 1970-71; mem Detroit Coll of Law part-time faculty 1974-77; Univ of CO School of Law 1978-81; mem Iliff Sch of Theology; mem, Colorado State Bd of Agriculture, 1989-95. **CONTACT ADDRESS** US District Court, District of Colorado, 1929 Stout St, Denver, CO, 80294.

DANIELS, CHARLES B.
DISCIPLINE PHILOSOPHY OF MIND **EDUCATION** Univ Chicago, AB; Univ Oxon, PhD. **CAREER** Instr, Yale Univ; Ind Univ; prof, 71-. **RESEARCH** Ethics; aesthetics; logic; philosophy of religion and ontology. **SELECTED PUBLICATIONS** Auth, The Evaluation of Ethical Theories; Toward an Ontology of Number; Mind; Sign; What Really Goes On In Sophocles' Theban Plays; pub(s), articles in Philos Stud; Jour Philos Logic. **CONTACT ADDRESS** Dept of Philosophy, Victoria Univ, PO Box 3045, Victoria, BC, V8W 3P4. **EMAIL** cbd@uvic.ca

DANKER, FREDERICK W.
PERSONAL Born 07/12/1920, Frankenmuth, MI, m, 1948, 2 children **DISCIPLINE** NEW TESTAMENT THEOLOGY, LIGUISTICS **EDUCATION** Concordia Sem, BA, 42, BD, 50; Univ Chicago, PhD, 63. **CAREER** From asst prof to prof New Testament exec theol, 54-74; PROF NEW TESTAMENT EXEC THEOL, CHRIST SEM-SEMINEX, 74-. **MEMBERSHIPS** Am Philol Asn; Soc Bibl Lit; Am Soc Papyrologists; Societas Novi Testamenti Studiorum; Cath Bibl Asn. **RESEARCH** Greek tragedy; Greek and Latin Epigraphy; Greek Lexicography. **SELECTED PUBLICATIONS** Auth, Apollonios-Of-Tyana in New-Testament Exegesis--Research Report and Continuing Discussion--German, Cath Bibl Quart, Vol 0058, 96; The Preface to Luke Gospel--Literary Convention and Social-Context in Luke-I,1-4 and Acts-I,1, Cath Bibl Quart, Vol 0057, 95; Paul the Accused--His Portrait in the Acts of the Apostles, Cath Bibl Quart, Vol 0058, 96; A Translator Freedom--Modern English Bibles and Their Language, Cath Bibl Quart, Vol 0057, 95. **CONTACT ADDRESS** 6928 Plateau Ave, St Louis, MO, 63139.

DANLEY, JOHN ROBERT
PERSONAL Born 01/12/1948, Kansas City, MO, m, 1969, 1 child **DISCIPLINE** ETHICAL THEORY, SOCIAL-POLITICAL PHILOSOPHY **EDUCATION** Kalamazoo Co, BA, 70; Union Theol Sem, NY, MDiv, 73; Univ Rochester, MA, 76, PhD, 77. **CAREER** Instr, 76-77, asst prof, 77-80, assoc prof philos, Southern Ill Univ, Edwardsville, 80-93; prof, 93-. **MEMBERSHIPS** Am Philos Assn; Am Acad Mgt; Southwestern Philos Assn; Soc Bus Ethics; Intl Assoc for Bus Soc. **RESEARCH** Contractarianism; corporate responsibility. **SELECTED PUBLICATIONS** Auth, The Modern Corporation and Its Role in a Free Society, University of Notre Dame Press, 94; art, HR's View of Ethics in the Workplace: Are the Barbarians at the Gate?, The Journal of Business Ethics, 96; art, Robert Nozick, Classical and Managerial Business Ideologies, The Blackwell Encyclopedic Dictionary of Business Ethics, London: Basil Blackwell, 97. **CONTACT ADDRESS** Dept of Philos Studies, Southern Illinois Univ, 6 Hairpin Dr, Edwardsville, IL, 62026-0001. **EMAIL** jdanley@siue.edu

DANNER, DAN GORDON
PERSONAL Born 07/05/1939, Salt Lake City, UT, m, 1961, 2 children **DISCIPLINE** RELIGION, HISTORY OF CHRISTIAN THOUGHT **EDUCATION** Abilene Christian Col, 61, MA, 63; Univ Iowa, PhD(relig), 69. **CAREER** Dir, Church Christ Bible Chair Bibl Lit, Tyler Jr Col, 62-66; asst prof, 69-73, assoc prof, 73-81, Prof theol, Univ Portland 81- **MEMBERSHIPS** Am Acad Refig; Am Soc Reformation Res; Am Soc Church Hist. **RESEARCH** Reformation; Reformation in England; Puritanism and the Geneva exiles, 1555-1560. **SELECTED PUBLICATIONS** Auth, Revelation 20: 1-10 in a history of interpretation of the Restoration movement, Restoration Quart, 63; Anthony Gilby: Puritan in exile--a bibliographical approach, Church Hist, 71; Women's lib or Adam's rib--the problem of women and the church, 72 & Not peace but a sword--an essay on war and peace, fall 76, Univ Portland Rev; Christopher Goodman and the English Protestant tradition of civil disobedience, Sixteenth Century J, 77; The contributions of the Geneva Bible of 1560 to the English Protestant tradition, Sixteenth Century J, 81; Resistance and the ungodly magistrate in the sixteenth century: The Marian Exiles, J Am Acad Relig, 81; auth, Pilgrimage to Puritanism: History and Theology of the Manan Exiles at Geneva, 1555 to 1560, Peter Lang, 98. **CONTACT ADDRESS** Dept of Theol, Univ of Portland, 5000 N Willamette, Portland, OR, 97203-5798.

DARBY, DERRICK
DISCIPLINE PHILOSOPHY **EDUCATION** Pittsburgh, PhD. **CAREER** Asst prof, Northwestern Univ. **RESEARCH** Moral and political philosophy. **SELECTED PUBLICATIONS** Works in Progress: Are Worlds Without Rights Morally Impoverished; The Proliferation of Rights. **CONTACT ADDRESS** Dept of Philosophy, Northwestern Univ, 1801 Hinman, Evanston, IL, 60208.

DARDEN, CHRISTOPHER A.
PERSONAL Born 04/08/1956, Martinez, CA, s **DISCIPLINE** LAW **EDUCATION** San Jose State Univ, BA, administrative justice, 1977; Univ of California-Hastings College of Law, JD, 1980. **CAREER** National Labor Relations Board, attorney, 1980-81; Los Angeles County, assistant head deputy, Special Investigations Division, begin 1981; Los Angeles County District Attorney's Office, deputy district attorney; SOUTHWESTERN UNIV SCHOOL OF LAW, PROF, 1995-. **HONORS AND AWARDS** San Jose State Univ, Dept of Admin Justice, Alumnus of the Year Award, 1995. **MEMBERSHIPS** California Bar, Criminal Law Section, exec comm, 1994-97; National Black Prosecutors Assn, board member, 1989; Loved Ones of Homicide Victims, past pres, bd of dirs, 1987-; Los Angeles County Assn of Deputy District Attorneys, board member, 1986-87; John M Langston Bar Assn, 1995. The People vs Orenthal James Simpson, BA097211, part of prosecuting team; appeared in television movie. **SELECTED PUBLICATIONS** Co-author, In Contempt, 1996. **CONTACT ADDRESS** Sch of Law, Southwestern Univ, 625 S West Moreland Ave, Los Angeles, CA, 90005-3905.

DARDEN, GEORGE HARRY
PERSONAL Born 03/14/1934, Cadiz, KY, m **DISCIPLINE** LAW **EDUCATION** KY State Univ, BS 1955; Salmon P Chase College of Law, JD 1964. **CAREER** Hamilton Cnty, OH, asst cnty prosecutor 1964-66; Cincinnati, OH, Hopkinsville, KY, priv pract 1964-69; Legal Serv Proj Ctr OH, chief attny 1967-68; Lincoln Hts, OH, city solicitor 1967-68; EEOC, Washington, DC, staff attny 1969-71, supervisory 1973, chief legal consel div 1973-75; Equal Employment Opportunity Commission, regional Attorney, Atlanta, GA, 1975-. **HONORS AND AWARDS** Citations EEOC Houston Hearings 1972-73, Chief Judge, Cincinnati Muncpl Ct 1968, WCIN Radio Station 1968; Cincinnati Herald Paper 1968. **MEMBERSHIPS** Pres Double Dollar Co 1965-68; chrmn, legal comm Hopkinsville, KY, NAACP 1968-69; chrmn, legal redress comm Denver, CO 1984-. **CONTACT ADDRESS** Atlanta Division, US Equal Employment Opportunity Commission, 75 Piedmont Ave, NE, Ste 1100, Atlanta, GA, 30335.

DARDEN, LINDLEY
PERSONAL Born 12/17/1945, New Albany, MS **DISCIPLINE** PHILOSOPHY AND HISTORY OF SCIENCE **EDUCATION** Southwestern at Memphis, BA, 68; Univ Chicago, AM, 69, SM, 72, PhD, 74. **CAREER** Asst prof, 74-78, ASSOC PROF PHILOS AND HIST, UNIV MD, COLLEGE PARK, 78-, NSF grant, 78-80; Am Coun Learned Soc fel, 82. **MEMBERSHIPS** Philos Sci Asn; Hist Sci Soc; AAAS. **RESEARCH** Theory construction in science; emergence of new fields in biology. **SELECTED PUBLICATIONS** Auth, Discovery and Explanation in Biology and Medicine, Stud Hist and Philos Sci, Voi 0027, 96; Discovering Complexity--Decomposition and Localization as Strategies in Scientific-Research, Bioln and Philos, Vol 0012, 97. **CONTACT ADDRESS** Dept of Philos, Univ of Md, College Park, MD, 20783.

DARDEN, LINDLEY
PERSONAL Born 12/17/1945, New Albany, MS **DISCIPLINE** PHILOSOPHY **EDUCATION** Rhodes Col, BA, 68; Univ Chicago, AM, 69, SM 72, PhD, 74. **CAREER** Instr, 69-70, Moriane Valley Comm Col; asst prof, 74-79, chmn, Comt on Hist & Phil of Sci, 84-86, assoc prof, 79-92, mem, Comt on Cognitive Stud, 89-, mem, Comt on Hist & Phil of Sci, 74-, prof, 92-, Univ Maryland Col Park. **RESEARCH** Phil of sci, phil of biology, hist of genetics. **CONTACT ADDRESS** Dept of Philosophy, Univ of Maryland, College Park, MD, 20742. **EMAIL** darden@carnap.umd.edu

DARWALL, STEPHEN L.
PERSONAL Born 09/09/1946, Richmond, VA, m, 1980, 2 children **DISCIPLINE** PHILOSOPHY **EDUCATION** Yale Univ, BA, 68; Univ Pittsburgh, PhD, 72. **CAREER** Ast prof, prof, Univ North Carolina Chapel Hill, 72-84; prof, Univ Michigan Ann Arbor, 84- . **HONORS AND AWARDS** NEH Fel, 78-9, 86-87, 93-94, 98-99; Phi Beta Kappa. **MEMBERSHIPS** Amer Philos Assoc; David Hume Soc. **RESEARCH** Moral philosophy; history of ethics. **SELECTED PUBLICATIONS** Auth, The British Moralists and the Internal Ought, Cambridge, 95; Philosophical Ethics, Westview, 97. **CONTACT ADDRESS** Dept of Philosophy, Univ of Michigan, Ann Arbor, MI, 48109. **EMAIL** sdarwall@umich.edu

DAUBE, DAVID
PERSONAL Born 02/08/1909, Freiburg im Breisgau, Germany, d, 3 children **DISCIPLINE** ROMAN LAW, BIBLICAL STUDIES **EDUCATION** Univ Gottingen, DrJur, 32; Cambridge Univ, PhD, 35; Oxford Univ, MA & DCL, 55. **CAREER** Fel, Caius Col, Cambridge, 38-46, lectr law, univ, 46-51; prof jurisp, Univ Aberdeen, 51-55; Regius prof civil law, Oxford Univ & fel, All Souls Col, 55-70; PROF LAW & DIR ROBBINS COLLECTION, UNIV CALIF, BERKELEY, 70-, Rockefeller award, 61-62; sr fel, Yale Univ, 62; Gifford lectr, Edinburgh, 62 & 63; Ford rotating prof polit sci, Univ Calif, Berkeley, 64; Gray lectr, Cambridge Univ, 66; hon prof law, Uiv Knostanz, 66-; Lionel Cohen lectr, Jerusalem, 70; Messenger lectr, Cornell Univ, 71; hon fel, Oxford Univ Centre Post-grad Hebrew Studies, 73- & Caius Col, 74- **HONORS AND AWARDS** Gerard lectr, Univ Calif, Irvine, 81., LLD, Univ Edinburgh, 60, Univ Leicester, 64, Cambridge Univ, 81; Dr, Univ Paris, 63; CHL, Hebrew Union Col, 71; DrJur, Univ Munich, 72. **MEMBERSHIPS** Fel Am Acad Arts & Sci; fel Brit Acad; corresp fel Acad Sci, Gottingen & Bavarian Acad Acad Sci; hon fel Royal Irish Acad; Soc Hist Ancient Law, France (pres, 57-58). **RESEARCH** Hebrew law; Old and New Testament. **SELECTED PUBLICATIONS** Auth, Judas, Calif Law Rev, Vol 0082, 94. **CONTACT ADDRESS** Sch of Law, Univ of California, Boalt Hall, Berkeley, CA, 94720.

DAUER, FRANCIS W.
PERSONAL Born 08/17/1939, Leipzig, Germany, m, 1995, 2 children **DISCIPLINE** PHILOSOPHY **EDUCATION** Dartmouth Coll, AB, 60; Harvard Univ, MA, 64; PhD, 70. **CAREER** Lectr, Univ Calif Santa Barbara, 69; asst prof 69-75; assoc prof, 75-82; vis prof, Int Christian Univ, japan, 87-90; guest prof, Osaka Univ Ja Japan, 90; prof, Univ Calif Santa Barbara 82-. **MEMBERSHIPS** Am Philos Asn; Hume Soc; Am Asoc for Aesthetics. **RESEARCH** Philosophy: Hume, Epistemology, Emotions. **SELECTED PUBLICATIONS** Auth, Between Belief and Fantasy: A Study of the Imagination, Pursuits of Reason,93; The Nature of Fictional Characters and the Referential Fallacy, J of Aesthetics and Art Criticism, 95; Hume Skepticism with Regard to Reason: A Reconsideration, Hume Studies, 96. **CONTACT ADDRESS** Dept of Philosophy, Univ Calif Santa Barbara, Santa Barbara, CA, 93106. **EMAIL** dauer@humanitas.ucsb.edu

DAURIO, JANICE
PERSONAL Born 06/26/1946, Brooklyn, NY, m, 1985 **DISCIPLINE** PHILOSOPHY **EDUCATION** Hunter Coll City Univ NY, AB, 68; Claremont Grad School, MA Philos, 73; Mount St Mary's Coll Calif, 88; Claremont Grad School, PhD Philos, 94. **CAREER** Marymount High School, 78-89; Mount St Mary's Coll, 78-84; Loyola Marymount Univ, 84-89; St John's Coll, 90-91; W Coast Univ, 95; Ventura Coll, 93; prof, Moorpark Coll, 94-. **HONORS AND AWARDS** Phi Sigma Tau. **MEMBERSHIPS** Ventura Co Fedn of Coll Teachers; Am Philos Asn; Soc for Anal Feminism; Am Cath Philos Asn; Soc of Christian Philos. **RESEARCH** Philosophy; Ethics. **SELECTED PUBLICATIONS** Auth, The Downside Review, 88; book revs, New Oxford Rev, 90-04; Sidgwick's Method of Ethics and Common Sense Morality, History of Philos Quart, 97; book rev, Faith and Philosophy, 97. **CONTACT ADDRESS** Moorpark Col, 7075 Campus Rd, Moorpark, CA, 93021. **EMAIL** Jdaurio@aol.com

DAUSCHMIDT, KENNETH G.
PERSONAL Born 10/12/1956, Des Moines, IA, m, 1980, 3 children **DISCIPLINE** LAW **EDUCATION** Univ Wisconsin, BA, 78; Univ Michigan, MA, 81; Univ Michigan, JD, 81; Univ Mich, PhD, 84 **CAREER** Prof Law, Indiana Univ, 92-; Prof Law, Univ Wisconsin, 94-97; Prof Law, Univ Cincinnati **HONORS AND AWARDS** Teaching Excellence Recognition Award, Indiana Univ, 98; John S. Hastings Fac Fel, Indiana Univ, 93-; Leonard D. Fromm Pub Interest Fac Award, Indiana Univ, 97 **MEMBERSHIPS** AAUP; AEA; L&SA; ALEA; IRRA; Indiana Bar Assoc; Amer Bar Assoc; Wisconsin Bar Assoc **RESEARCH** Labor and Employment Law; Law and Economics **SELECTED PUBLICATIONS** "The First Century of Department of Justice Antitrust Enforcement." Rev Indust Org; "The Execution of Sir William Wallace: Toward a Richer Economic Theory of Punishment." Graven Images; "Preference Shaping by the Law." New Palgrave Dictionary Econ Law, 98 **CONTACT ADDRESS** Indiana Univ, Bloomington, 211 S Indiana Ave., Bloomington, IN, 47401. **EMAIL** kensauschmidt@law.indiana.edu

DAVENPORT, CHARLES
PERSONAL Born 01/24/1933, Laredo, MO, m, 1962, 4 children **DISCIPLINE** LAW **EDUCATION** Chico State Col, AB, 54; Harvard Univ, JD, 57. **CAREER** Atty, Brobfeck, Phleger & Harrison, 60-67; prof taxation, Univ Calif, Davis, 69-75; asst dir, Cong Budget Off, Washington, 75-79; Prof Taxation, Rutgers Univ, 79-; Atty, Tax Legis Coun, Dept Treas, 67-69; vis prof, Law Ctr, Georgetown Univ, 73-74; dir, Internal Revenue Serv Proj Conf US, 74-75; tax consult, Structure of Agr Proj, Dept Agr, 79-81; Special Reports Ed, 85-90; ed in chief, 90-96; consult ed, tax Analysts, 96-. **RESEARCH** Federal taxation; legislative process; tax policy. **SELECTED PUBLICATIONS** Auth, A bountiful tax harvest, 48 Tex Law Rev 1, 69; ed & auth, Report on Administrative Procedures of the Internal Revenue Services, Govt Printing Off, Sen Doc 94-266, 75; coauth, Collection of delinquent federal taxes, 28 USC Tax Inst 589, 76; auth, The role of taxation in the regulation of energy consumption and production, 78 & The impact of the congressional budget process on tax legislation, 79, The effects of federal tax policy on American agriculture, Govt Printing Off, 82; Taxes and the family farm, Acad Polit Sci, 82; Nat Tax J; The Farm Income Tax Manual, Lexis Law Publishing, 98. **CONTACT ADDRESS** Law School, Rutgers Univ, 15 Washington St, Newark, NJ, 07102-3192. **EMAIL** cDavenport@Kinoy.Rutgersedu

DAVENPORT, GENE LOONEY
PERSONAL Born 10/09/1935, Sylacauga, AL, d, 2 children **DISCIPLINE** PSYCHOLOGY, RELIGION, OLD TESTAMENT, BIBLICAL THEORY **EDUCATION** Birmingham-Southern Col, BA(psychol), 57; Vanderbilt Divinity School, BD, 60; Vanderbilt Univ, PhD(religion:Old Testament, Biblical theol), 68. **CAREER** Prof of Relig, Lambuth Univ, 63-. **MEMBERSHIPS** Soc of Biblical Lit. **RESEARCH** Apocrypha and pseudepigrapha; theol of culture; Sermon on the Mount; the Book of Revelation. **SELECTED PUBLICATIONS** Auth, The Eschatology of the Book of Jubilees, E J Brill, 71; The Anointed of the Lord in Psalms of Solomon 17, Ideal Figures in Ancient Israel, Scholars Press; Into the Darkness: Discipleship in the Sermon on the Mount, Abingdon Press, 88. **CONTACT ADDRESS** Dept of Relig and Philos, Lambuth Univ, Jackson, TN, 38301. **EMAIL** davenpor@lambuth.edu

DAVENPORT, HARBERT WILLIAM
PERSONAL Born 07/09/1940, Dallas, TX, m, 1998, 3 children **DISCIPLINE** PHILOSOPHY **EDUCATION** Univ Houston, BA, 63; Univ Ill, Urbana, MA, 69, PhD(philos), 77. **CAREER** Asst prof philos, Cent Mo State Col, 70-72; instr, Purdue Univ, Lafayette, 72-73; Assoc Prof Philos, Western Ill Univ, 74-, Contrib ed, Peirce Ed Proj, Ind Univ-Purdue Univ, Indianapolis, 76-. **HONORS AND AWARDS** Nat Endowment for Humanities summer sem fel, 78; Am Coun Learned Soc travel grant, 79. **MEMBERSHIPS** Am Philos Asn; Charles S Peirce Soc; Soc Advan Am Philos. **RESEARCH** American philosophy; history of philosophy; history and philosophy of science. **SELECTED PUBLICATIONS** Auth, Peirce's evolutionism and his logic: Two connections, In: Proceedings of the C S Peirce Bicentennial International Congress, Tex Tech Univ, 81; Peirce on Evolution, In: Frontiers in American Philosophy, vol 2, Texas A&M Univ, 95. **CONTACT ADDRESS** Dept of Philos & Relig Studies, Western Illinois Univ, 1 University Cir, Macomb, IL, 61455-1390. **EMAIL** Bill_Davenport@ccmail.wiu.edu

DAVENPORT, MANUEL MANSON
PERSONAL Born 06/14/1929, Colorado Springs, CO, m, 1978, 6 children **DISCIPLINE** PHILOSOPHY **EDUCATION** Bethany Nazarene Col, AB, 50; Colo Col, MA, 53; Univ Ill, PhD, 57. **CAREER** Teacher elem sch, Colo, 50-52; instr, Colo Col, 56-57; from asst prof to assoc prof, Colo State Univ, 57-67; head dept philos, 67-76, Prof Philos, Tex A&M Univ, 67-; consult, UN Comn on the Future, 72; distinguished vis prof, US Air Force Acad, 80-81, 94-95. **HONORS AND AWARDS** Distinguished Teaching Award, 59, 60, 69, 78, 82, 89; Rockefeller grant, 62. **MEMBERSHIPS** Southwestern Philos Soc; AAUP; Am Philos Asn; Am Soc Aesthet. **RESEARCH** Metaethics; existentialism; Schweitzer's moral and political philosophy. **SELECTED PUBLICATIONS** Auth, Self-determinism and the conflict between naturalism and non-naturalism, J Philos, 7/59; Kant and Maritain on the nature of art, Brit J Aesthet, 10/72; The moral paternalism of Albert Schweitzer, Ethics, 1/74. **CONTACT ADDRESS** Dept of Philosophy, Texas A&M Univ, College Station, TX, 77843-4237. **EMAIL** m-davenport@philosophy.tamu.edu

DAVEY, WILLIAM J.
DISCIPLINE LAW **EDUCATION** Univ Mich, BA; JD. **CAREER** Law clerk, Justice Potter Stewart, US Supreme Court; prof, Univ Ill Urbana Champaign. **HONORS AND AWARDS** Ed, Mich Law Rev. **RESEARCH** Teaches international trade policy **SELECTED PUBLICATIONS** Auth, pubs on international trade issues; co-auth, Handbook of GATT Dispute Settlement and Legal Problems of International Economic Relations. **CONTACT ADDRESS** Law Dept, Univ Ill Urbana Champaign, 52 E Gregory Dr, Champaign, IL, 61820. **EMAIL** wdavey@law.uiuc.edu

DAVID, GERALD
PERSONAL Born 08/05/1941, Brooklyn, NY, m, 1967, 6 children **DISCIPLINE** PHD-CLINICAL PSYCHOLOGY, DHL-MODERN PHILOSOPHY **EDUCATION** Dr. of Hebrew Literature, 75, Bernard Reval Graduated School, Yeshiva Univ, Professional License, 72, New York State Department of Educ Specialization, PhD, 71, Ferkauf Graduate School, Yeshiva Univ, Professional Diploma, 68, New York State Dept of Educ, Ordination(Semicha), 66, Rabbi Isaac Elechanan Theol Seminary, Yeshiva Univ, Master of Sci in Educ, 66, City Univ of New York, Naster of Sci in Educ, 65, Ferkauf Graduate School, Yeshiva Univ, BA, 63, Yeshiva College. **CAREER** Admin Supvr and Clin Psychol positions, 66-present, New York City Bd of Educ, Supv, Diry and Psychol positions at Ohel Family Serv, 79-present. **HONORS AND AWARDS** Hon Pres-Jewish Community Council at Rockaways, Hon Chm-JASH Senior Center, Hon Chm-Jewish Services Co-ulitius. **MEMBERSHIPS** Amer Psychological Associates. **RESEARCH** Pshchol, Philos, Rel. **SELECTED PUBLICATIONS** Man's Search for Immortality: A Positivist Approach, Yeshiva Univ Press, 78, "Preschool Intellectual Assessment with the Ammons Quick Test",in Psychology in the Schools, 75, 12, 430-431, "The Effects of Special Class Placement on Multiple Disabled Children", in Reading Improvement, 75, 14, 138-143, " The Russians: A New Community in Our Midst", in Proceedings of the Association of Orthodox Jewish Scientists, 82, " A Study of the Needs of Russian Immmigrant Youth", 80, Research Study Monograph sponsored by Ahudath Israel of Amer, funded by the New York City Youth Bd. **CONTACT ADDRESS** 861 East 27th St., Brooklyn, NY, 11216.

DAVID, KEITH R.
PERSONAL Born 08/20/1929, Arkansas City, KS, m, 1949, 4 children **DISCIPLINE** SOCIOLOGY AND PHILOSOPHY **EDUCATION** Okla Baptist Univ, BA; Wichita State Univ, MA; Southern Ill Univ, PhD. **CAREER** Detail engr, Boeing Airplane Co, 48-51; Baptist minister, 51-69; lectr, philos, 60-61, dept of eng res, eng grade 3, 54-60, Wichita State Univ; doctoral asst, 62-64, lectr, philos, 64-69, Southern Ill Univ; asst prof to assoc prof to full prof, philos, William Jewell Col, 69-98. **HONORS AND AWARDS** Outstanding Facul Mem, William Jewell Col, 84; Profile in Excellence, Okla Baptist Univ, alumni office, 91; Prof emer, William Jewell Col, 94. **MEMBERSHIPS** Amer Philos Asn; Baptist Philos Teachers Asn. **RESEARCH** American philosophy; Philosophy of religion; Medical ethics. **SELECTED PUBLICATIONS** Auth, Historical Note: The Paul Carus Collection, The Monist, 75; auth, Percept and Concept in William James, The Philos of William James, Felix Meiner Verlag, 76; eng res publ, Aerodynamics, dept of defense, 55-58, Wichita State Univ, dept of eng res. **CONTACT ADDRESS** 1029 Broadmore Ln., Liberty, MO, 64068.

DAVID, MARIAN
DISCIPLINE PHILOSOPHY **EDUCATION** Univ Ariz, MA, 89, PhD, 90. **CAREER** Assoc prof. **RESEARCH** Philosophy of language; epistemology. **SELECTED PUBLICATIONS** Auth, Correspondence and Disquotation: An Essay on the Nature of Truth, 94; Analyticity, Carnap, Quine, and Truth, Philos Perspectives, 96; Two Conceptions of the Synthetic A Priori, 97; Kim's Functionalism, 97. **CONTACT ADDRESS** Philosophy Dept, Univ of Notre Dame, 336/7 O'Shaughnessy, Notre Dame, IN, 46556. **EMAIL** david.1@nd.edu

DAVIDSON, DONALD
PERSONAL Born 03/06/1917, Springfield, MA, m, 1984, 1 child **DISCIPLINE** PHILOSOPHY **EDUCATION** Harvard, BA, 39, PhD, 49. **CAREER** Asst in Philos, 41-42, 46, Harvard; instr, 47-51, Queens Coll; asst prof, 51-56, assoc prof, 56-60,

prof, 60-67, Stanford Univ; prof, 67-70, Princeton Univ; prof, 70-76, The Rockefeller Univ; lectr with rank of prof, 70-75, Princeton; univ prof, 76-81, The Univ Chicago; prof, 81-86, The Univ CA, Berkeley; appointed Willis S. and Marion Slusser prof of philos, 86-. **HONORS AND AWARDS** Amer Council of Learned Soc Fel, 58-59; Natl Science Found Sr Research Fel 63-64; Fel, Ctr for Advanced Study in the Behavioral Sci, 69-70; Guggenheim Memorial Fel, 73-74; fel, Bellagio Study and Conf Ctr, 91; Hegel Prize, awarded by the City of Stuttgart, 91; honorary degree, doctor of letters, Univ of Oxford, 95. **MEMBERSHIPS** Amer Philos Assn; Council for Philos Studies; Amer Acad of Arts and Sciences; Institute Intl de Philosophie; Guggenheim Found Edu Adv Brd; Correspond Fel British Academy; Fel Amer Assoc Advancement Science; Comite d'honneur; Norwegian Acad of Sci and Letters, elected 87; Life Fel of the Acad of Philos at Lake Sevan, elected 91. **RESEARCH** Philos of Language, mind, epistemology **SELECTED PUBLICATIONS** Auth, Esaays on Actions and Events, 80, various reprint 82, 85, 86, 89; A Coherence Theory of Truth and Knowledge, orig 83, various reprint 85, 86, 88, 91, 92, 95, 97; Inquiries into Truth and Interpretation, 84, various reprint 90, 91, 93, 94; Knowing One's Own Mind, Proceedings and Addresses of the American Philosophical Association, 87, various reprint 92, 94, 95, 96; Readings in the Philosophy of Social Science, 94; The Philosophy of Action, 97; Readings in the Philosophy of Language, 97; Meaning, Truth, Method: Introduction to Analytical Philosophy I, 97. **CONTACT ADDRESS** Philos Dept, Univ California-Berkely, 614 Moses Hall, Berkeley, CA, 94720. **EMAIL** davidson@socrates.berkely.edu

DAVIES, ALAN T.
PERSONAL Born 06/24/1933, Westmount, PQ, Canada **DISCIPLINE** RELIGION **EDUCATION** McGill Univ, BA, 54, BD, 57; Union Theol Sem (NY), STM, 60, PhD, 66. **CAREER** Ordained min, United Church Can, 57; min, NW Interlake Pastoral Charge, Man, 57-59; min, Wesley United Church, Toronto, 64-67; J. Clarence & Corale B. Workman postdoctoral fel, Hebrew Union Col Cincinnati, 67-68; lectr to assoc prof, 69-89, PROF RELIGION, VICTORIA COL, UNIV TORONTO, 89-. **SELECTED PUBLICATIONS** Auth, Anti-Semitism and the Christian Mind, 69; auth, Infected Christianity: A Study of Modern Racism, 88; coauth, How Silent Were the Churches?: Canadian Protestantism and the Jewish Plight During the Nazi Era, 97; ed, Antisemitism and the Foundations of Christianity, 79; ed, Antisemitism in Canada: History and Interpretation, 92. **CONTACT ADDRESS** Victoria Col, Univ Toronto, Toronto, ON, M5S 1K7.

DAVIES, BRIAN
DISCIPLINE PHILOSOPHY OF RELEGION **EDUCATION** Univ London, PhD. **CAREER** Prof, Fordham Univ. **HONORS AND AWARDS** Bk rev ed, Intl Philos Quart. **SELECTED PUBLICATIONS** Auth, An Introduction to the Philosophy of Religion, Oxford UP, 82; Thinking About God, Chapman, 85; The Thought of Thomas Aquinas, Oxford UP, 92. **CONTACT ADDRESS** Dept of Philos, Fordham Univ, 113 W 60th St, New York, NY, 10023.

DAVIES, DAVID
DISCIPLINE PHILOSOPHY **EDUCATION** Oxford Univ, BA, 70; Univ Manitoba, MA, 79; Univ Western Ontario, PhD, 87. **CAREER** Prof. **RESEARCH** Metaphysics; philosophies of language, mind, psychology, art, lit; aesthetics. **SELECTED PUBLICATIONS** Auth, Fictional Truth and Fictional Authors, British J Aesthet, 96; art, Dennett's Stance on Intentional Realism, Southern Jour Philos, 95; art, Putnam's Brain-Teaser, Can Jour Philos, 95; auth, Perspectives on Intentional Realism, 92. **CONTACT ADDRESS** Philosophy Dept, McGill Univ, 845 Sherbrooke St, Montreal, PQ, H3A 2T5.

DAVIES, GORDON F.
PERSONAL Born 07/25/1954, Kenora, ON, Canada **DISCIPLINE** OLD TESTAMENT STUDIES **EDUCATION** Univ Toronto, BA, 76; Ottawa Univ, BTh, 81; Saint Paul Univ, STB, 81; Biblicum, SSL, 87; Gregorian, STD, 92. **CAREER** Dean of stud, 90-96, asst prof, 90-95, spiritual dir, 90-, assoc prof, 95-, sr acad dean, 97-, St. Augustine's Sem; lectr, Ontario Ministry of Ed, relig ed, 95-. **HONORS AND AWARDS** Gov Gen Gold Medal, 76; Summa Cum Laude, 90; jr fel, Can Bibl Assoc, 96. **MEMBERSHIPS** Soc Bibl Lit; Catholic Bibl Assoc; Catholic Bibl Assoc of Can; Can Soc of Bibl Stud; Qahal; Soc for Interpreting the Old Testament as Scripture. **RESEARCH** Narrative criticism; rhetorical criticism; Exodus; Ezra-Nehemiah. **SELECTED PUBLICATIONS** Auth, Israel in Egypt: Reading Exod 1-2, JSOT, Sheffield, 92; Auth, Creed and Criticism: The Complementarity of Faith and Exegesis, The New Jerusalem, Food for the Journey, Taking God Seriously, Can Catholic Rev, 95; auth, How to Believe, The Easter Vigil, Paschaltide, Faith and Gratitude, The Last Things, Can Catholic Rev, 96; auth, Disobedience, Covenants, Seeing Stars, Three Short Questions, Massaccio's Peter, On Asking Stupid Questions, Can Catholic Rev, 97; auth, The Parish, The Bible and Everything Else: Scripture and Our Common Quest to Make Sense, New Blackfriars, 98; auth, Ezra-Nehemiah, Liturgical, forthcoming. **CONTACT ADDRESS** St. Augustine's Sem, 2661 Kingston Rd, Scarborough, ON, M1M 1M3. **EMAIL** gj.davies@utoronto.ca

DAVIES, HORTON
PERSONAL Born 03/10/1916, Cwmavon, Wales, m, 1940, 3 children **DISCIPLINE** RELIGION **EDUCATION** Univ Edinburgh, MA, 37, BD, 40; Oxford Univ, DPhil(ecclesiastical hist), 43; Univ SAfrica, DD(church hist), 51. **CAREER** Prof divinity, Rhodes Univ, SAfrica, 46-53, dean fac of divinity, 51-53; head joint dept church hist, Mansfield & Regent's Park Cols, Oxford Univ, 53-56; prof, 56-60, PUTNAM PROF RELIG, PRINCETON UNIV, 60-, Old St Andrew's Mem lectr, Emmanuel Col, Victoria Univ; Carnegie traveling fel, 52; Guggenheim fels, 59 & 64; consult, Int Missionary Coun & World Coun Churches, 56-; ed adv, Studia Liturgica, 62-; assoc ed, Worship, 67-; lectr, Union Theol Sem, Va, spring 68 & 69 & Drew Univ, 69; Scott lectr, Christian Theol Sem, fall 77. **HONORS AND AWARDS** Gunning Divinity Prize, Univ Edinburgh, 40., LittD, La Salle Col, 66; DLitt, Oxford Univ, 70. **MEMBERSHIPS** Am Soc Church Hist; Am Theol Soc. **RESEARCH** English church history; medieval pilgrimages; doctrine of providence in the 17th century in England and New England. **SELECTED PUBLICATIONS** Auth, Christian Plain Style--The Evolution of a Spiritual Ideal, Church Hist, Vol 0065, 96; The English Bible and the 17th-Century Revolution, Amer Hist Rev, Vol 0100, 95. **CONTACT ADDRESS** Dept of Relig, Princeton Univ, Princeton, NJ, 08540.

DAVIS, CASEY W.
PERSONAL Born 06/05/1958, Springfield, OH, m, 1980, 2 children **DISCIPLINE** NEW TESTAMENT **EDUCATION** Un Theol Sem, PhD, 96; Asbury Theol Sem, MDiv, 85; Miami Univ, BS **CAREER** Chaplain, 98, Roberts Wesleyan Col; Prof of Relig, 97-98, Cent Col; Adj Facul, 97, Youngstown St Univ; Lect, 94, Hampden Sydney Col **MEMBERSHIPS** Am Acad of Relig; Inst for Bibl Res; Soc of Bibl Lit; Wesleyan Theolog Soc; Evangel Theolog Soc **RESEARCH** New Testament; Orality; Rhetoric; Pauline Studies **SELECTED PUBLICATIONS** Oral Biblical Criticism: The Influence of the Principles of Orality on the Literary Structure of Paul's Epistle to the Philippians, Sheffield Acad Pr, forthcoming **CONTACT ADDRESS** 47 W Forest Dr, Chili, NY, 24624. **EMAIL** daviscw@roberts.edu

DAVIS, DANIEL CLAIR
DISCIPLINE CHURCH HISTORY **EDUCATION** Wheaton Col, AB, 53, MA, 57; Westminster Theol Sem, BD, 56; Georg-August Univ, Guttingen, ThD, 60. **CAREER** Asst prof, Olivet Col, 60-63; vis prof, asst prof, Wheaton Col, Grad Sch Theol, 63-66; prof, Westminster Theol Sem, 66-. **SELECTED PUBLICATIONS** Contrib, John Calvin: His Influence in the Western World; Challenges to Inerrancy; Inerrancy and the Church; Pressing Toward the Mark; Theonomy: A Reformed Critique. **CONTACT ADDRESS** Westminister Theol Sem, PO Box 27009, Philadelphia, PA, 19118. **EMAIL** cdavis@wts.edu

DAVIS, DEREK H.
PERSONAL Born 07/14/1949, Laredo, TX, m, 1970, 2 children **DISCIPLINE** LAW **CAREER** Nat Coun of Churches RLC, mem 95-; Intl Acad Freedom of Relig and Belief, fel 95-; Jour of Church and State, editor 93-; Baylor Univ JM Dawson Inst, dir 95-; Dawson, Sodd, Davis, Moe, TX, partner 75-90. **HONORS AND AWARDS** Pew Ch Trsts; Lilly Foun Gnt; Baylor L Rev Ed; Harris Honor Soc; Omicron Delta Kappa. **MEMBERSHIPS** APSA; AAR; ABA; WBA; STATE OF TX Bar Assoc. **SELECTED PUBLICATIONS** Auth, Original Intent: Chief Justice Rehnquist and the Course of American Church-State Relations, 91; auth, Religion and the Continental Congress 1774-1789: Contr to Orig Intent, 99; auth, The Separation of Church and State Defended: Selected Writings of James E Wood Jr, ed, 95; auth, Welfare Reform and Faith-based Organizations, co-ed, 99; auth, Legal Deskbook for Administrators of Independent Colleges and Univ's, co-ed, 94. **CONTACT ADDRESS** JM Dawson Inst Church State Studies, Baylor Univ, Waco, TX, 76798. **EMAIL** derek.davis@baylor.edu

DAVIS, ELLEN F.
DISCIPLINE OLD TESTAMENT LANGUAGES AND LITERATURE **EDUCATION** Univ Calif, AB, 71; Oxford Univ, Cert Theol, 82; Church Divinity Sch Pacific, MDiv, 83; Yale Univ, PhD, 87. **CAREER** Asst prof, Union Theol Sem, 87-89; asst prof, Yale Divinity Sch, 89-91; assoc prof, Yale Divinity Sch, 91-96; assoc prof, Va Theol Sem, 96-. **SELECTED PUBLICATIONS** Co-auth, And Pharaoh Will Change His Mind (Ezek. 32:31): Dismantling Mythical Discourse, Theol Exegesis Essays in Conversation, Eerdmans, 97; auth, Imagination Shaped: Old Testament Preaching in the Anglican Tradition, Trinity Press Intl, 95. **CONTACT ADDRESS** Va Theol Sem, 3737 Seminary Rd, Alexandria, VA, 22304. **EMAIL** EDavis@vts.edu

DAVIS, JEFFREY
DISCIPLINE LAW **EDUCATION** Univ Calif, Los Angeles, BS; Loyola Univ, Los Angeles, JD; Univ Mich, LLM. **CAREER** Prof, Univ Fla, 81-. **MEMBERSHIPS** Exec Coun, Fla Bar Bus Law Sect, 91-; Amer Bar Asn Comt on Consumer Financial Serv, 79-; Calif Bar; Fla Bar; past ch, Fla Bar Bankrupt-cy/Uniform Commercial Code Comt. **RESEARCH** Contracts, bankruptcy. **CONTACT ADDRESS** School of Law, Univ of Florida, PO Box 117625, Gainesville, FL, 32611-7625. **EMAIL** davis@law.ufl.edu

DAVIS, JOHN JEFFERSON
PERSONAL m, 5 children **DISCIPLINE** SYSTEMATIC THEOLOGY, CHRISTIAN ETHICS **EDUCATION** Duke Univ, BS, PhD; Gordon-Conwell Theol Sem, MA. **CAREER** Prof, Gordon-Conwell Theol Sem, 75-. **HONORS AND AWARDS** Danforth Grad Fel; Phi Beta Kappa grad, Duke Univ., Ch, Bd Dir(s) Mass Citizens for Life; founding mem, Bd Dir(s) Birthright of Greater Beverly; pres, Evangel Philos Soc; bd dir(s), Value of Life Comm; adv bd, Presbyterians for Democracy and Religious Freedom; delegate to the White House Conf on Families. **SELECTED PUBLICATIONS** Ed, The Necessity of Systematic Theology; auth, Theology Primer; Foundations of Evangelical Theology; Abortion and the Christian; Your Wealth in God's World; Handbook of Basic Bible Texts; Evangelical Ethics; The Christian's Guide to Pregnancy and Childbirth; Christ's Victorious Kingdom: Postmillennialism Reconsidered. **CONTACT ADDRESS** Gordon-Conwell Theol Sem, 130 Essex St, South Hamilton, MA, 01982.

DAVIS, JOHN WESLEY
PERSONAL Born 11/01/1943, Detroit, MI, m, 1966 **DISCIPLINE** LAW **EDUCATION** Wabash Coll, AB, 1964; Univ of Denver, JD, 1971. **CAREER** Int Assn Human Rights, EEO Program, dir, 1975-76; Natl Bar Assn, EEO Program, exec dir, 1976-78; Howard Univ, Reggie Program, exec dir, 1980-84, law professor, 1978-85; Self Employed, Attorney, 1985-. **HONORS AND AWARDS** NAACP, Award of Merit, 1975, Certificate of Appreciation, 1980; Natl Bar Assn, Equal Justice Award, 1977. **MEMBERSHIPS** DC Neighborhood Legal Services, bd mem, 1992-; Natl Bar Assn, life mem, NBA journal editorial board; NAACP, life mem, 1979-, cooperating Attorney, 1977-. **SELECTED PUBLICATIONS** Employment Discrimination Litigation Manual, 1977; Law Review Article, NCCU Law Journal, The Supreme Court Rationale for Racism, 1976. **CONTACT ADDRESS** 601 Indiana Ave NW, Ste 1000, Washington, DC, 20004.

DAVIS, KENNETH G.
PERSONAL Born 09/16/1957, Louisville, KY **DISCIPLINE** PASTORAL THEOLOGY, CROSS-CULTURAL COMMUNICATION **EDUCATION** St. Louis Univ, BA, cum laude, 80; Washington Theol Union, MA, 85; Pacific Sch of Theol, DMin, 91. **CAREER** Deaconate in Honduras, 85-86; found dir, Hispanic ministry, 86-88; assoc pastor, St. Paul the Apostle Church, San Pablo, CA, 88-91; staff, intl office RENEW, 91-94; found dir, DMin, Oblate Sch Theol, 94-97; asst prof, Mundelein Sem, 97- . **MEMBERSHIPS** ACHTUS; Amer Acad Rel; Asn DMin Eduuc; CORHIM; Inst de Litugia Hispana; Nat Org Catechesis for Hispanics; Nalt Catholic Coun Hispanic Ministry. **RESEARCH** Religious faith of US Hispanics. **SELECTED PUBLICATIONS** Auth, Child Abuse in the Hispanic Community: A Christian Perspective, Apuntes, 12(3), Fall, 92, 127-136; Auth, Cuando El Tomar Ya No Es Gozar, LA, Franciscan Comm Press, 93; What's New in Hispanic Ministry, Overheard, Fall 93; auth, Primero Dios, Susquehanna UP, 94; Following the Yellow Brick Road: Rahner Reasons Through Petitionary Prayer, Living Light, 30(4), Summer, 94, 25-30; The Hispanic Shift: Continuity Rather than Conversion, in An Enduring Flame: Studies on Latino Popular Religiosity, NY, Bildner Ctr W Hemispheric Studs, 94, 205-210; The Hispanic Shift: Continuity Rather Than Conversion, Jour Hispanic/Latino Theol, 1(3), May 94, 68-79; Preaching in Spanish as a Second Language, in Perspectivas, Kansas City, Sheed and Ward, 95; Presiding in Spanish as a Second Language, AIM, Wint 95, 22-24; Encuentros, in New Catholic Encycl, vol 19, Wash DC, Catholic UP, 95; Afterward, in Discovering Latino Religion, NY, The Bildner Ctr W Hemispheric Studs, 95; Selected Pastoral Resources, in Perspectivas, Kansas City, Sheed and Ward, 95; Las Bodas de Plata de Una Lluvia de Oro, Revista Latinoamericana de Teologia, 12(37), April, 96, 79-91; coauth, The Attraction and Retention of Hispanics to Doctor of Ministry Programs, Theol Ed, 33(1), Autumn, 96, 75-82; Presiding in Spanish as a Second Language, in Misa, Mesa y Musa, Schiller Park, IL, J.S. Paluch Co, 97; Misa, Mesa y Musa, Schiller Park, IL, J. S. Paluch, 97; From Anecdote to Analysis: A Case for Applied Research in the Ministry, Pastoral Phychol, 46(2), 97, 99-106; La Catequesis ante la Experiencia Rligiosa, Catequetica, 1, 97, 3-8; Introduction, Listening: Jour of Rel and Cult 32(3), Fall, 97, 147-151; Challenges to the Pastoral Care of Central Americans in the United States, Apuntes 17(2), Summer 97, 45-56; A New Catholic Reformation? Chicago Studs, 36(3), Dec 97, 216-223; Petitionary Prayer: What the Masters Have to Say, Spiritual Life, Summer 97, 91-99; A Survey of Contemporary US Hispanic Catholic Theology, Theol Dig, 44(3), fall 97, 203-212; co-ed, Listening: Journal of Religion and Culture, vol 32, no 3, Fall, 97; co-ed, Chicago Studies, vol 36, no 3, Dec, 97; co-ed, Theol Today, vol 54, no 4, Jan, 98; Visions and Dreams, Theol Today, 54(4), Jan 98, 451-452. **CONTACT ADDRESS** Dept of Theology, Mundelein Sem, 1000 E Maple Ave, Mundelein, IL, 60060. **EMAIL** kenonel@interaccess.com

DAVIS, LAWRENCE H.
PERSONAL Born 08/21/1943, Chicago, IL, m, 1970, 3 children **DISCIPLINE** PHILOSOPHY; ETHICS **EDUCATION** Columbia Univ, AB, 64; Univ Mich, Ann Arbor, PhD(philos), 69. **CAREER** Asst prof philos, Johns Hopkins Univ, 68-75; asst prof, 76-79, Assoc Prof Philos, Univ Mo-St Louis 79-,

Chmn Dept, 88-94. **HONORS AND AWARDS** Nat Endowment for Humanities younger humanist fel, 72-73; vis fel, Cornell Univ Prog on Sci, Technol & Soc, 75-76. **MEMBERSHIPS** Am Philos Asn; Soc Philos & Psychol. **RESEARCH** Foundation of ethics; theory of action; philosophy of religion. **SELECTED PUBLICATIONS** Auth, They deserve to suffer, Analysis, 3/72; The intelligibility of rule-utilitarianism, Philos Studies, 10/73; Disembodied brains, Australasian J Philos, 8/74; Prisoners, paradox and rationality, Am Philos Quart, 10/77; Theory of Action, Prentice-Hall, 79; Functionalism and absent qualia, Philos Studies, 3/82; Cerebral Hemispheres, Philos Studies, 9/97. **CONTACT ADDRESS** Dept of Philosophy, Univ of Missouri, St. Louis, 8001 Natural Bridge, St. Louis, MO, 63121-4499. **EMAIL** slhdavi@umslvma.umsl.edu

DAVIS, MICHAEL PETER
PERSONAL Born 12/19/1947, Albany, NY, m, 1969, 2 children **DISCIPLINE** PHILOSOPHY **EDUCATION** Cornell Univ, AB, 69; Penn State Univ, MA, 73, PhD, 74. **CAREER** Vis asst prof Philos, Dickinson Col, 74-75; vis asst prof Philos, Wesleyan Univ, 75-76; asst prof Philos, Alfred Univ, 76-77; prof Philos, Sarah Lawrence Col, 77-; adj prof Philos, New Sch Soc Res, 81-88; vis prof Polit Philos, Dept Polit Sci, Fordham Univ, 95-. **MEMBERSHIPS** Am Philos Asn; APSA; Soc Greek Polit Thought. **RESEARCH** Ancient philosophy; political philosophy; philosophy and literature. **SELECTED PUBLICATIONS** Auth, Aristotle's Poetics: The Poetry of Philosophy, 92; auth, The Politics of Philosophy: A Commentary on Aristotle's Politics, 96; auth, Euripides Among the Athenians, St, John's Rev, 98; auth, The Autobiography of Philosophy: Rousseau's The Reveries of the Solitary Walker, 99. **CONTACT ADDRESS** Dept of Philosophy, Sarah Lawrence Col, Bronxville, NY, 10708. **EMAIL** mdavis@mail.slc.edu

DAVIS, MORRIS E.
PERSONAL Born 08/09/1945, Wilmington, NC **DISCIPLINE** LAW **EDUCATION** NC A&T State U, BS 1967; Univ IA Coll of Law, JD 1970; Univ CA Sch Pub Health, MPH 1973. **CAREER** Dept Housing & Urban Devel San Francisco, atty-adv 1970-72; University of California Berkeley, Inst of Industrial Relations, Labor Occupational Health Prog, executive director, 1974-80; Journal of Black Health Perspectives, managing editor 1973-74; US Merit Systems Protection Board, administrative judge, 1980-85, abritrator and mediator, 1986-. **MEMBERSHIPS** CA Bar Assn; IA Bar Assn; The Am Arbtrtn Assn; Am Pub Health Assn; fellow Univ CA (San Fran) Schl of Med 1974; fellow Univ CA (Berkeley) Schl Pub Hlth 1972-73. **CONTACT ADDRESS** American Arbitration Association, 417 Montgomery St, 5th Fl, San Francisco, CA, 94104-1113.

DAVIS, MORRIS E.
PERSONAL Born 08/09/1945, Wilmington, NC **DISCIPLINE** LAW **EDUCATION** NC A&T State U, BS 1967; Univ IA Coll of Law, JD 1970; Univ CA Sch Pub Health, MPH 1973. **CAREER** Dept Housing & Urban Devel San Francisco, atty-adv 1970-72; University of California Berkeley, Inst of Industrial Relations, Labor Occupational Health Prog, executive director, 1974-80; Journal of Black Health Perspectives, managing editor 1973-74; US Merit Systems Protection Board, administrative judge, 1980-85, abritrator and mediator, 1986-. **MEMBERSHIPS** CA Bar Assn; IA Bar Assn; The Am Arbtrtn Assn; Am Pub Health Assn; fellow Univ CA (San Fran) Schl of Med 1974; fellow Univ CA (Berkeley) Schl Pub Hlth 1972-73. **CONTACT ADDRESS** American Arbitration Association, 417 Montgomery St, 5th Fl, San Francisco, CA, 94104-1113.

DAVIS, PETER L.
DISCIPLINE LAW **EDUCATION** Harvard Univ, BA, 69; NY Univ, JD, 72. **CAREER** Clin instr, New York University School of Law; trial atty, Criminal Defense Div of the Legal Aid Soc, NYC; assoc prof Law, Touro Col. **HONORS AND AWARDS** Root-Tilden scholar, NY Univ. **MEMBERSHIPS** Chp, bd dir, Andrew Glover Youth Prog, NYC. **SELECTED PUBLICATIONS** Ed, Legal Systems and Institutions: The Criminal Justice System as Paradigm; coed, N.Y.U. Criminal Law Clinic: Materials and Forms, 80, 81. **CONTACT ADDRESS** Touro Col, Brooklyn, NY, 11230.

DAVIS, RALPH
DISCIPLINE OLD TESTAMENT **EDUCATION** S Baptist Theol Sem, PhD. **CAREER** Carl W. McMurray prof. **HONORS AND AWARDS** Pastor, Westminster Reformed Presbyterian Church; sr pastor, Aisquith Presbyterian Church. **SELECTED PUBLICATIONS** Auth, Such A Great Salvation; No Falling Words; Looking on the Heart. **CONTACT ADDRESS** Dept of Old Testament, Reformed Theol Sem, 5422 Clinton Blvd, Jackson, MS, 39209-3099.

DAVIS, RICHARD
PERSONAL Born 10/14/1951, Parkersburg, WV, m, 1978, 1 child **DISCIPLINE** RELIGIOUS STUDIES **EDUCATION** Univ Chicago, BA, 73; Univ Toronto, MA, 78; Univ Chicago, PhD, 86. **CAREER** Instr, Univ Chicago, 87; vis lectr, School of thr Art Inst Chicago, 86-87; asst, assoc prof, Yale Univ, 87-97; Assoc Prof, Bard Coll, 97-. **HONORS AND AWARDS** Univ Toronto Open Fel, 76-78; Univ Chicago Humanities Fel, 78-79; NDEA Title VI Lang Fel, 79-81; AIIS Lang Fel, 81-82; Fulrbight-Hays Lr Res Fel, 83-84; Comm on southern Asian Studies Grant, Univ Chicago, 85; Mrs Giles Whiting Found Fel, 85-86; Paul Moore Fund for Undergraduate Instruction, Yale Univ, 88; A Whitney Griswold Faculty Res Grant, Yale Univ, 89; AIIS Short-term Res Grant, 90; Morse Fel in the Humanities, Yale Univ, 90-91; Whitney Humanities Center Fel, Yale Univ, 93-94; Nat Endowment for the he Humanities Fel for Univ Tchrs, 94. **MEMBERSHIPS** Asn for Asian Studies; Am Acad of Rel; Coll Art Asn; Am Oriental Soc; Am Comm for Sputhern Asian Art. **SELECTED PUBLICATIONS** Auth, Three Styles in Looting India, Hist and Anthropol, 94; Trophies of War: The Case of the Calukya Intruder, Perceptions of South Asia's Visual Past, 94; Carr-Gregg et al (1997) Brief History of Religion in India; The Rebuilding of a Hindu Temple; The Origin of Linga Worship, Rel of India in Practice, 95; The Iconography of Ram's Chariot, Contesting the Nat: Rel, Community and the Politics of Democracy in India, 96; Lives of Indian Images, 97; The Story of the Dissapearing Jains: Retelling the Saiva-Jain Encounter in Medieval South India, Open Boundaries: Jain Communities and Cultures in Indian Hist, 98; ed, Images, Miracles, and Authority in Asian Religious Traditions, 98. **CONTACT ADDRESS** 926 Ridge Rd, Hamden, CT, 06517. **EMAIL** rdavis@bard.edu

DAVIS, ROBERT N.
PERSONAL Born 09/20/1953, Kewanee, Illinois, m, 1979 **DISCIPLINE** LAW **EDUCATION** University of Hartford, BA, 1975; Georgetown University Law School, JD, 1978. **CAREER** US Department of Education, attorney; United State Attorney, special assistant; CFTC, attorney; University of MS School of Law, professor, currently. **HONORS AND AWARDS** Teacher of the Year, 1990; Department of Defense Reserve Officers Foreign Exchange Program, 1996; Scholar in Residence, Office of General Counsel, US Olympic Committee, 1996. **MEMBERSHIPS** American Arbitration Association, mediator/arbitrator. **SELECTED PUBLICATIONS** Founder of Journal of National Security Law. **CONTACT ADDRESS** Professor, Univ of Mississippi, University, MS, 38677. **EMAIL** rdavis@olemiss.edu

DAVIS, ROBERT PAUL
PERSONAL Born 07/03/1926, Malden, MA, m, 1953, 3 children **DISCIPLINE** PHYSICIAN, EDUCATOR **EDUCATION** Harvard Univ, AB, 47, MD , 51, AM, 55; Brown Univ, AM, 67. **CAREER** Intern, 51-52, asst med, 52-55, sr asst res phys, 55-56, ch res phys, 56-57, Peter Brent Brigham Hosp; jr fel, 52-55, Soc of Fellows Harvard; asst med, 56-57, Harvard Med School; asst prof med, 57-59, Univ NC; asst prof med, 59-66, assoc prof, 67, Albert Einstein Col Med; career sci, 62-67, Health Res Coun, NY; asst vis phys, 59-65, assoc vis phys, 66-67, Bronx Munic Hosp Center; phys in ch, 67-74, dir renal and metabolic diseases, 74-79, Miriam Hosp, Providence; prof med sci, 67-84, prof emeritus, 84-, chmn sect in med div biol & med scis, 71-74, Brown Univ; vis sci, 65-66 Ins Biol Chem of Univ Copenhagen; ensign, USNR, 44-46, Lt (jg) MC, 51; past mem, Corp Butler Hosp, Jewish Family & Childrens Serv; mem sci adv coun NE Reg Kidney Prog; v chmn RI Advisory Comm Med Care & Ed Found, chmn med adv bd, RI Kidney Found; past bd dirs Assoc Alumni Brown Univ; member med adv bd N Eng sect Am Liver Found, 86-; trustee, N Eng Organ Bank, Boston, 69-, treas, 70; pres End-Stage Renal Disease Coord Coun Network 28, N Eng, 78-79; assoc ed, RI Med J, 71-80. **HONORS AND AWARDS** Traveling fel, Commonwealth fund, 65-66; Willard O. Thompson Memorial traveling scholar, ACP, 65; fel AAAS, ACP. **MEMBERSHIPS** Am Fed Clin Res; Am Soc Transplant Physicians; Harvey Soc; Biophys Soc; NY Academy Medicine; Am Heart Asn; NY Academy Science; Am Soc Cell Biology; Soc Gen Physiologists; Am Physiol Soc; Am Soc Artificial Internal Organs; Int Soc Nephrology Clin; Diabetes Soc RI (pres 70-71); Providence, RI Med Socs; Am Soc Nephrology; Am Soc Pediatric Nephrology; Soc for Health and Human Values; Am Philos Asn; Phi Beta Kappa; Sigma XI. **CONTACT ADDRESS** Brown Univ, 245 Waterman St., Ste. 105, Providence, RI, 02906-5215.

DAVIS, RONALD E.
PERSONAL Born 11/05/1963, Key West, FL, m, 1989, 3 children **DISCIPLINE** BIBLICAL STUDIES **EDUCATION** Howard Payne Univ, BA 85; Southern Baptist Theol Sem, MDiv 89, PhD 94. **CAREER** Minister of Education, 95-; Prof, Sem ext 97-. **MEMBERSHIPS** SBL **RESEARCH** Rhetorical Critical Analysis of Biblical Texts; Themes Canonical Interpretations. **CONTACT ADDRESS** 7053 McClellan Rd, Mechanicsville, VA, 23111. **EMAIL** davisfive@juno.com

DAVIS, WAYNE ALAN
PERSONAL Born 12/10/1951, Detroit, MI, 1 child **DISCIPLINE** PHILOSOPHY **EDUCATION** Univ Mich, BA, 73; Princeton Univ(philos), 77. **CAREER** Lectr philos, Univ Calif, Los Angeles, 76; vis asst prof, Philos Dept, Rice Univ, 77-78 & Washington Univ, St Louis, 78-79; asst prof philos, Georgetown Univ, 79-92, prof, 93-, chair, 90-. **MEMBERSHIPS** Am Philos Asn. **RESEARCH** Philosophy of language; philosophy of mind; logic. **SELECTED PUBLICATIONS** Auth, Indicative and Subjunctive Conditionals, Philos Rev, 79; A Theory of Happiness, Am Philos Quart, 81; A Causal Theory of Enjoyment, Mind, 82; A Casual Thoery of Intending, Am Philos Quart, 21: 43-54, 84, reprinted in Readings in the Philosophy of Action, Oxford Readings in Philosophy, ed by A. Mele, Oxford: Oxford Univ Press, 97; The Two Senses of Desire, Philos Studies, 45: 181-195, 84; expanded and reprinted in Ways of Desire, ed by Joel Marks, 63-82, Precedent Press, 86; An Introduction to Logic (600 pp), Prentice-Hall, 86; The Varieties of Fear, Philosophical Studies, 51: 287-310, 87; Fundamental Troubles with Coherence, with J.W. Bender, ed, The Current State of the Coherence Theory, Philosophical Studies Series, Kluwer Academic Pub,89, 52-68; Technical Flaws in the Coherence Theory, with J.W. Bender, Synthese, 79: 257-78, 89; Speaker Meaning, Linguistics and Philosophy, 15: 223-252, 92; Implicature: Intentions, Conventions, and Principles; or: The Failure of Gricean Theory, Cambridge: Cambridge Univ Press, 98. **CONTACT ADDRESS** Philos Dept, Georgetown Univ, 1421 37th St N W, Washington, DC, 20057-0001. **EMAIL** DavisW@Gunet.georgetown.edu

DAVIS, WILLIAM V.
PERSONAL Born 05/26/1940, Canton, OH, m, 1971, 1 child **DISCIPLINE** ENGLISH, RELIGION **EDUCATION** Ohio Univ, AB, 62, MA, 65, PhD(English), 67; Pittsburgh Theol Sem, MDiv, 65. **CAREER** Asst prof English, Ohio Univ, 67-78, Cent Conn State Col, 68-71, Tunxis Community Col, 71-72 & Univ Ill, Chicago Circle, 72-77; asst prof, 77-78, assoc prof, 78-79, PROF ENGLISH & WRITER IN RESIDENCE, BAYLOR UNIV, 79-, Sr Fulbright fel, Univ Vienna, Austria, 79-80. **HONORS AND AWARDS** Yale Series of Younger Poets Prize, 79. **MEMBERSHIPS** MLA; Poetry Soc Am; Assoc Writing Prog. **RESEARCH** Twentieth century English and American literature; creative writing; contemporary American poetry. **SELECTED PUBLICATIONS** Auth, Lowell,Robert and the Sublime, Amer Lit, Vol 0068, 96; Another Room, West Hum Rev, Vol 0046, 92; Stave Church, West Hum Rev, Vol 0046, 92; The Visit, Shenandoah, Vol 0043, 93; Summer Celestial, Shenandoah, Vol 0043, 93; To-Step-Lightly-Lightly-All-The-Way-Through-Your-Ruins, Wright,James Ohio Poems, Midwest Quart Jour Contemp Thought, Vol 0037, 96. **CONTACT ADDRESS** Dept of English, Baylor Univ, Waco, TX, 76703.

DAVIS, WILLIE J.
PERSONAL Born 09/29/1935, Fort Valley, GA, m **DISCIPLINE** LAW **EDUCATION** Morehouse Coll, BA 1956; New England School of Law, JD 1963. **CAREER** MA Commiss Against Discrimination, field rep 1963; Commonwealth of MA, asst attny gen 1964-69; Dist of MA, asst US attny 1969-71, former US magistrate; Private practice, attny, currently. **HONORS AND AWARDS** Ten Outstanding Young Men Awd Boston Jr C of C 1971; Hon Deg JD New England School of Law 1972; Hon Deg DSc Lowell Tech Inst 1973; inducted into the Southern Intercollegiate Athletic Conference Hall of Fame, 1998. **MEMBERSHIPS** Mem Amer Bar Assoc, Amer Judicature Soc, Alpha Phi Alpha; Sigma Phi Fraternity; Natl Assn of Guardsmen; pres emeritus, Morehouse College Natl Alumni Assn; vice chairman, Morehouse College Board of Trustees; bd mem, Committee for Public Counsel Services, Commonwealth of Massachusetts; board of directors, Massachusetts Bay Transportation Authority. **CONTACT ADDRESS** Northeastern Univ, 15 Court Sq, Boston, MS, 02108.

DAVIS, WINSTON
PERSONAL Born 11/05/1939, Jamestown, NY, m, 1974, 2 children **DISCIPLINE** HISTORY OF RELIGION **EDUCATION** Univ Chicago, PhD, 73. **CAREER** Wash and Lee Univ, 92-; Southwestern Univ, 83-92; Kwansei Gakuin Japan, 79-83; Stanford Univ, 73-79. **HONORS AND AWARDS** Phi Beta Kappa; NEH Fel; Dist Lectr, Univ Lectr, U of AZ. **MEMBERSHIPS** AAAR; ASSR. **RESEARCH** Max Weiber; The Ethics of Responsibility. **SELECTED PUBLICATIONS** Auth, DoJo: Magil and Exorcism in Modern Japan; Japanese Religion and Society; The Moral and Political Naturalism of Baron Kate Hiroyuki. **CONTACT ADDRESS** Dept of Religion, Washington and Lee Univ, Lexington, VA, 24450. **EMAIL** davis.w@wlu.edu

DAWE, DONALD GILBERT
PERSONAL Born 07/12/1926, Detroit, MI, m, 1957, 2 children **DISCIPLINE** RELIGION **EDUCATION** Wayne State Univ, BS, 49; Union Theol Sem, BD, 52, ThD(hist theol), 60. **CAREER** Asst dean students & asst prof theol, Union Theol Sem, 58-61; from asst prof to assoc prof relig, Macalester Col, 61-69; PROF THEOL, UNION THEOL SEM, VA, 69-, Eli Lilly Endowment fel, Univ Tubingen, 64-65; Inst Int Educ fel, Harvard Ctr Studies World Relig, 68-69; consult, Asian Med & Social Studies Group, Med Col Va, Va Commonwealth Univ, 73. **MEMBERSHIPS** Fel Soc Relig Higher Educ; Soc Sci Studies Relig; Am Teilhard Soc; AAUP. **RESEARCH** Systematic theology; modern developments of Hinduism and Buddhism; phenomonology of religion. **SELECTED PUBLICATIONS** Auth, Abraham--Sign of Hope for Jews, Christian, and Muslims, Interpretation-Jour Bible and Theol, Vol 0050, 96; Deuteronomy 4.32-40, Interpretation-Jour Bible and Theol, Vol 0047, 93; Reclaiming the Jesus of History--Christology Today, Jour Bible and Theol, Vol 0048, 94; Jesus in Global Contexts, Theol Today, Vol 0050, 93; Judaism--Between Yesterday and Tomorrow, Jour Bible and Theol, Vol 0048, 94. **CONTACT ADDRESS** Dept of Theol, Theol Sem, Richmond, VA, 23227.

DAWN, MARVA J.
PERSONAL Born 08/26/1948, Napoleon, OH, m, 1989 **DISCIPLINE** THEOLOGY **EDUCATION** Univ Notre Dame, MA 86, PhD 92; Pacific Lutheran Theol Sem, ThM 83; Western Evange Sem, MDiv 78; Univ Idaho, MA 72; Concordia Tchrs Col, BA 70. **CAREER** Regent Col BC, adj prof 98-2002; CEM, theol, auth, educ, 79-; Univ Notre Dame, grad/teach asst, 84-86; Good Shep Lutheran Church, dir spec min, 76-79; Concordia Lutheran Church Campus Minister, dir yth/edu, 72-75; Univ Idaho, teacher/stud guide/auth, 70-72. **MEMBERSHIPS** SBL; AAR; PJRS; LPF. **SELECTED PUBLICATIONS** Auth, I'm Lonely Lord- How Long?: The Psalms for Today, 83, 2nd edition, Eerdmans, 98; auth, Truly the Community: Romans 12 and How to Be the Church, Eerdmans, 92, reissued, 97; auth, Is It a Lost Cause? Having the Heart of God for the Church's Children, Eerdmans, 97; auth, To Walk and not Faint: A Month of Meditations from Isaiah 40, 2nd ed, Eerdmans, 97; auth, Reaching Out Without Dumbing Down: A Theology of Worship for the Turn-of -the -Century Cultur, Eerdmans, 95; auth, Joy in Our Weakness: A Gift of Hope from the Book of Revelations, Concordia, 94; auth, Pop Spirituality or Genuine Story? Word and World, 98; auth, How does Contemporary Culture Yearn for God?, Welcome to Christ: A Lutheran Intro to the Catechumenate, Minneapolis, Augsburg Fortress, 97; auth, Worship that Develops Strong Community, Reformed Worship, 97; auth, Beyond the Worship Wars, Christian Century, 97; auth, Practical Theology for a Post-Modern Society, Oslo Norway, Ung Teologi, 96; auth, Are Christianity and Homosexuality Incompatible?, Caught in the Crossfire, Abingdon, 94. **CONTACT ADDRESS** Dept of Theology, Christians Equipped for Ministry, 304 Fredericksburg Way, Vancouver, WA, 98664-2147.

DAWSON, GEORGE L.
DISCIPLINE LAW **EDUCATION** Princeton Univ, AB; Univ Chicago, JD. **CAREER** Prof; assoc dean, Acad Aff, Univ Fla, 81-. **MEMBERSHIPS** Colo Bar. **RESEARCH** Commercial paper, contracts, estates & trusts. **CONTACT ADDRESS** School of Law, Univ of Florida, PO Box 117625, Gainesville, FL, 32611-7625. **EMAIL** Reid@law.ufl.edu

DAY, J. NORFLEETE
PERSONAL Born 09/14/1945, Birmingham, AL, s **DISCIPLINE** BIBLICAL STUDIES **EDUCATION** Samford Univ, Ba, 67; Univ Alabama, MLS, 75; Beeson Div Sch, MDiv, 93; Baylor Univ, PhD candidate. **CAREER** Assoc dir, Birmingham Public Lib, 75-93; adj fac, 92-96, instr, 96- , Beeson Div Sch. **MEMBERSHIPS** NABPR; SBL. **RESEARCH** New Testament Gospels and Acts; inter-testamental period; Gospel in art and literature. **CONTACT ADDRESS** Beeson Divinity School, 800 Lakeshore Dr, Birmingham, AL, 35229. **EMAIL** jnday@samford.edu

DAY, KATE N.
DISCIPLINE LAW **EDUCATION** Univ Ca, JD, 80. **CAREER** Prof, 93-. **RESEARCH** Civil procedure; constitutional law and race; constitutional law; constitutional theory; gender and the law. **SELECTED PUBLICATIONS** Auth, Lost Innocence and the Moral Foundation of Law, Am Univ Jour Gender and Law, 93; The Report of Task force on Technology and Justice of the Chief Justice's Commission on the Future of The Courts, 92. **CONTACT ADDRESS** Law School, Suffolk Univ, Beacon Hill, Boston, MA, 02114. **EMAIL** kday@acad.suffolk.edu

DAY, LOUIS A.
DISCIPLINE MEDIA LAW AND ETHICS **EDUCATION** Ohio Univ, PhD, 73. **CAREER** Prof, La State Univ. **SELECTED PUBLICATIONS** Auth, Broadcaster Liability for Access Denial, in Jour Quart, 83; In Search of a Scholar's Privilege, Commun and the Law, 83; Media Access To Juvenile Courts, in Jour Quart, 84; Media Access to Military Courts, in Commun and the Law, 86; The Pro Athlete's Right of Publicity in Live Sports Telecasts, in Jour Quart, 88; Ethics in Media Communications: Cases and Controversies, Wadsworth Publ Co, 96. **CONTACT ADDRESS** The Manship Sch of Mass Commun, Louisiana State Univ, Baton Rouge, LA, 70803. **EMAIL** lday@unix1.sncc.lsu.edu

DAY, PEGGY
PERSONAL Winnipeg, MB, Canada **DISCIPLINE** RELIGIOUS STUDIES **EDUCATION** Univ BC, BA, 75, MA, 77; Harvard Divinity Sch, MTS, 79, PhD, 86. **CAREER** Tchr fel, Harvard Univ, 81-86; instr Biblical Hebrew, Harvard Divinity Sch, 83-86; asst prof, Trinity Col, Univ Toronto, 86-89; ASSOC PROF & CHAIR RELIGIOUS STUDS, UNIV WINNIPEG 89-. **MEMBERSHIPS** SBL; Hebrew Scriptures & Cognate Lit. **SELECTED PUBLICATIONS** Auth, An Adversary in Heaven: Satan in the Hebrew Bible, 88; auth, Gender and Difference in Ancient Israel, 89; auth, The Bible and the Politics of Exegesis, 91. **CONTACT ADDRESS** Dept of Religious Studies, Univ Winnipeg, Winnipeg, MB, R3B 2E9. **EMAIL** peggy.day@uwinnipeg.ca

DAY, TERENCE PATRICK
PERSONAL Born 02/02/1930, London, England, m, 1969, 3 children **DISCIPLINE** HISTORY OF RELIGIONS, BUDDHISM **EDUCATION** London Col Divinity, ALCD, 59; Univ London, BD Hons, 60; King's Col, MTh, 63, PhD(hist of relig), 66. **CAREER** Lectr philos, St John's Col, Univ Agra, India, 66-71; lectr hist of relig, Univ Nairobi, Kenya, 71-73; ASST PROF HIST OF RELIG, UNIV MANITOBA, 74- **MEMBERSHIPS** Can Soc Study Relig; Am Acad Relig; Int Asn of Buddhist Studies; Am Oriental Soc; Can Asian Studies Assoc. **RESEARCH** Iconography of religions; folk religion; modern movements in religion. **SELECTED PUBLICATIONS** Auth, The Rajneesh Papers, Stud Rel-Sciences Religieuses, Vol 0025, 96. **CONTACT ADDRESS** Dept of Relig, Univ of Manitoba, Winnipeg, MB, R3T 2N2.

DAYE, CHARLES EDWARD
PERSONAL Born 05/14/1944, Durham, NC, m **DISCIPLINE** LAW **EDUCATION** NC Central Univ, BA high honors 1966; Columbia Univ, JD honors 1969. **CAREER** UNC Chapel Hill School of Law, prof 1972-81; NCCU School of Law, visiting prof 1980-81; dean & prof 1981-85; UNC Chapel Hill School of Law, prof 1985-; Henry P Brandis Dist Professor, 1991-. **HONORS AND AWARDS** Lawyer of the Year NC Assn Black Lawyers 1980; Civic Award Durham Community Affairs Black People 1981; Honorary Order of the Coif. **MEMBERSHIPS** Law clerk Hon Harry Phillips 6th Cir 1969-70; assoc Covington & Burlington 1970-72; NC Assoc of Black Lawyers, pres 1976-78, exec sec 1979-; mem bars of, US Supreme Ct, NY, DC, NC; chmn Triangle Housing Devel Corp, 1979-91, mem, 1977-; bd dir United Way of Greater Durham 1984-88; president Law School Admission Council 1991-93; mem Amer Bar Assn, NC State Bar, NC Bar Assn. **SELECTED PUBLICATIONS** Co-auth, Casebook Housing & Comm Devel 1999 ; co-auth, NC Law of Torts. **CONTACT ADDRESS** Law Sch, Univ of No Carolina, CB#3380, Chapel Hill, NC, 27599-3380.

DAYTON, DONALD WILBER
PERSONAL Born 07/25/1942, Chicago, IL, m, 1969 **DISCIPLINE** THEOLOGY, AMERICAN RELIGIOUS HISTORY **EDUCATION** Houghton Col, AB, 63; Yale Univ, BD, 69; Univ Ky, MS in LS, 69; Univ Chicago, PhD(Christian theol), 78. **CAREER** From asst to asst prof theol, Asbury Theol Sem, 69-72, acquisitions librn, B L Fisher Libr, 69-72; asst prof theol, North Park Theol Sem, 72-77, assoc prof, 77-80, dir, Mellander Libr, 72-80; PROF THEOL, NORTHERN BAPTIST THEOL SEM, 80-, Mem bd dir, Urban Life Ctr, 72-; bk ed, Sojourners, 75-; ed assoc, The Other Side, 75-; chmn comn social action & mem bd admin, Christian Holiness Asn, 73-; Staley lectureship, Anderson Col, 77; contrib ed, The Epworth Pulpit, 77-; fac, Sem Consortium Urban Pastoral Educ, 77- **MEMBERSHIPS** Karl Barth Soc NAm; Wesleyan Theol Soc; Am Theol Libr Asn; Am Soc Church Hist; Am Acad Relig. **RESEARCH** Theology and ethics of Karl Barth; 19th century American religious thought; holiness and Pentecostal churches. **SELECTED PUBLICATIONS** Auth, Creationism in 20th-Century America--A 10-Volume Anthology of Documents, 1903-1961, Zygon, Vol 0032, 97. **CONTACT ADDRESS** Dept of Theol, No Baptist Theol Sem, Lombard, IL, 60148.

DE BOLT, DARIAN C.
PERSONAL Born 10/11/1946, Marshalltown, IA, m, 1967 **DISCIPLINE** PHILOSOPHY **EDUCATION** Univ Okla, BA, 68, MA, 85, PhD, 93. **CAREER** Adj prof, Univ Central Okla, Edmond, 93-94; vis asst prof, Univ Okla, Norman, 94-95; adj prof, Univ Central Okla, Edmond, 95-98; spec mem grad fac, Univ Okla, Norman, 94-2001. **HONORS AND AWARDS** Phi Kappa Phi; Phi ESA Sigma. **MEMBERSHIPS** APA; Southwestern Philos Soc; Central States Philos Asn; Australasian Asn of Philos. **RESEARCH** Ethics; social and political philosophy; Byzantine philosophy. **SELECTED PUBLICATIONS** Auth, Kant and Clint: Dirty Harry Meets the Categorical Imperative, Southwest Philos Rev, 97; auth, George Gemistos Plethon on God: Heterodoxy in Defense of Orthodoxy, Proc of the Twentieth World Cong of Philos, 99. **CONTACT ADDRESS** Dept of Philosophy, Univ of Oklahoma, 1518 Lindale Circle, Norman, OK, 73069. **EMAIL** dcdeboltphil@worldnet.att.net

DE GRAZIA, EDWARD
DISCIPLINE INTERNATIONAL TRANSACTIONS, COMMUNICATIONS LAW **EDUCATION** Univ Chicago, BA, 48; JD 51. **CAREER** Prof; **HONORS AND AWARDS** Dir, Georgetown Univ Prog Pretrial Diversion Accused Offenders to Community Mental Health Treatment Prog; Asso fel, Inst Policy Studies. **MEMBERSHIPS** Office Dir Gen UNESCO, 56-59; U.S. Dept State; U.S. Agency Int Devel; PEN Am Ctr. **RESEARCH** International transations; community law; first admenment legislation. **SELECTED PUBLICATIONS** Coath, Censorship Landmarks and Banned Films: Movies, Censors; First Amendment; auth, Girls Lean Back Everywhere: The Law of Obscenity and the Assault on Genius, Random House, 92. **CONTACT ADDRESS** Yeshiva Univ, 55 Fifth Ave, NY, NY, 10003-4301.

DE LAURENTIIS, ALLEGRA
PERSONAL Born 04/01/1952, Roma, Italy, m, 2 children **DISCIPLINE** PHILOSOPHY **EDUCATION** W V Goethe-Univ Frankfurt Ger, PhD, 82. **CAREER** Asst prof, Dept Philos, Villanova Univ, 87-90; Asst prof, Philos, Miami Univ Ohio, 91-94; Sr Res Assoc, Dept Philos, SUNY Stonybrook, 94- . **MEMBERSHIPS** APA; SWIP; Hepel Soc Am **RESEARCH** Hepel studies; Aristotle; 19th Century interpretations of Greek antiquity. **SELECTED PUBLICATIONS** Auth, A Prophet Turned Backwards: Materialism and Mysticism in W Benjamins Notion of History, Rethinking Marxism, 94; And Yet It Moves: Hepel on Zenos Arrow, Jour Speculative Philos, 95; Logic and History of Consciousness, Introduction to Hepels Encyclopedia; SW Philos Rev, 98. **CONTACT ADDRESS** Philosophy Dept, State Univ of NY Stony Brook, Harriman Hall, Stony Brook, NY, 11794. **EMAIL** DELAURENTIIS@CCMAIL.SUNYSB.EDU

DE S. CAMERON, NIGEL M.
DISCIPLINE MEDICAL ETHICS **EDUCATION** Univ Cambridge, BA, MA; Univ Edinburgh, BD, PhD. **CAREER** Philos, Trinity Int Univ. **HONORS AND AWARDS** Found ed, Eu Jour Theol. **SELECTED PUBLICATIONS** Auth, The New Medicine: Life and Death after Hippocrates; Ed, Universalism and the Doctrine of Hell; Dictionary of Scottish Church History and Theology. **CONTACT ADDRESS** Trinity Int Univ, 2065 Half Day Road, Deerfield, IL, 60015.

DE SOUSA, RONALD B.
PERSONAL Born 02/25/1940, Lausanne, Switzerland **DISCIPLINE** PHILOSOPHY **EDUCATION** New Col, Oxford Univ, BA, 62; Princeton Univ, PhD, 66. **CAREER** Asst to assoc prof, 66-81, PROF PHILOSOPHY, UNIV TORONTO, 81-; vis assoc prof, Univ Calif Santa Barbara, 71-72; vis prof, Univ BC, 84; vis prof, Dartmouth Col, 89; vis prof, Lanzhou (China), 89. **MEMBERSHIPS** Can Philos Asn; Am Philos Asn; Int Soc Res Emotions. **SELECTED PUBLICATIONS** Auth, The Rationality of Emotion, 87. **CONTACT ADDRESS** Dept of Philosophy, Univ Toronto, 1008-215 Huron St, Toronto, ON, M5S 1A1.

DE VRIES, PAUL
DISCIPLINE PHILOSOPHY **EDUCATION** Calvin Col, BA, 67; Univ Va, MA, 76; Univ Va, PhD, 78. **CAREER** Instr Math and Philos, Piedmont Va Community Col, 75-78; Instr Philos, Univ Va, 75-78; Asst Prof Philos, Lenore-Rhine Col, 78-79; Asst Prof Philos, Wheaton Col, 79-83; Assoc Prof Philos, Wheaton Col, 83-86; Coordr Gen Educ, Wheaton Col, 83-89; Tenured Assoc Prof Philos, Wheaton Col, 86-89; Founder, Dir, Ctr for Appl Christian Ethics, Wheaton Col, 87-89; Endowed Chair Ethics and the Marketplace, Prof Bus, Relig, Philos, The King's Col, 89-94; Ctr Dean, Prof Theology and Ethics, Seminary of the East, 94-96; Interim Dean, Northern Baptist Theological Seminary, 96; Pres, NY Evangelical Seminary Fund, Inc., 97-present. **HONORS AND AWARDS** Res grants, Mellon Found, Henry Luce Found, Pew Charitable Trusts. **MEMBERSHIPS** Am Asn Advan Slavic Studies; Am Philos Asn; Baptist Ministers Conf Greater NY and Vicinity; Hastings Ethics Ctr; Leadership Excellence, Inc; NY Christian Higher Educ Consortium; Society for Bus Ethics; Society of Christian Philosophers. **RESEARCH** Applied ethics; philosophical hermeneutics; ethics theory; social crisis and change; hermeneutics of ethics. **SELECTED PUBLICATIONS** Contrib auth, Ethics Applied, McGraw Hill, 93; Contrib auth, Religion in New York City, NY Univ Press, 98; Sr ed, New York Christian Higher Education, 94; auth, Ethics Applied, Second Edition, Simon and Schuster, 98; auth, Business Ethics Applied, Simon and Schuster, 98. **CONTACT ADDRESS** NYES Fund, 236 West 72nd St, New York, NY, 10023. **EMAIL** NYESFund@aol.com

DE VRIES, WILLEM
PERSONAL Born 09/16/1950, New York, NY, m, 1982, 2 children **DISCIPLINE** PHILOSOPHY **EDUCATION** Haverford Coll, BA, 72; Univ of Pittsburgh, MA, 75, PhD, 81. **CAREER** Asst Prof, 71-85, Amherst Coll; Vis Prof, 87-88, Tufts; Asst Prof, Assoc Prof, Prof, 88-; Chr, 95-2000, Univ Of New Hampshire. **HONORS AND AWARDS** Fulbright Doctoral Fellow; Fulbright Sr Res Fellow; NEH Fellow; Mellow Postdoc; Faculty Scholar Fellow. **MEMBERSHIPS** APA; North Amer Soc; Soc for Philos and Psychol. **RESEARCH** Philosophy of Mind; German Idealism; Metaphysical and Epistemology. **SELECTED PUBLICATIONS** Auth, Hegel's Theory of Mental Activity, Ithaca, NY, Cornell Univ Press, 88; Reality, Knowledge and the Good Life: An Historical Introduction to Philosophy, NY, St Martin's Press, 91; Hegel's Logic and Philosophy of Mind, Routledge History of Philosophy, vol VI: The Age of German Idealism, 98; Who sees with equal eye, Atoms or systems into ruin hurled: Comment on Brian McLaughlin, Philosophica Studies, vol 71, 93; Experience and the Swamp Creature, Philosophical Studies, 96. **CONTACT ADDRESS** Dept of Philosophy, Univ of New Hampshire, Durham, NH, 03824. **EMAIL** Willem.devries@aol.edu

DEAN, WILLIAM D.
PERSONAL Born 07/12/1937, South Bend, IN, m, 1960, 2 children **DISCIPLINE** THEOLOGY **EDUCATION** Carleton Col, BA, 59; Divinity Sch, Univ Chicago, MA, 64, PhD, 67. **CAREER** Asst prof Philos & Relig, Northland Col, 66-68; prof Relig, Florence & Raymond Sponberg Ch Ethics, Gustavus Aldolphus Col, 68-96; prof Constructive Theol, Iliff Sch Theol,

96-. **HONORS AND AWARDS** Lilly Fac Fel; Edgar A. Carlson Award Distinguished Tchg; John Templeton Found; Sci Relig Course Competition; AAR Award Excellence Study Relig. **MEMBERSHIPS** Am Acad Relig; Highlands Inst Am Relig & Philos Thought. **RESEARCH** American religious thought; religious historicism; religious pragmatism. **SELECTED PUBLICATIONS** Auth, The Religious Critic in American Culture, 94; auth, The Scholar's Norms and the Public's Forms, Relig Studies News, May, 95. **CONTACT ADDRESS** Dept of Theology, Iliff Sch of Theol, 2201 S University Ave., Denver, CO, 80210. **EMAIL** wdean@du.edu

DEAN MOORE, KATHLEEN
PERSONAL m, 2 children **DISCIPLINE** LEGAL REASONING **EDUCATION** Univ Colo, PhD. **CAREER** Philos, Oregon St Univ. **HONORS AND AWARDS** Burlington Northern Found Fac Achievement Award; Meehan Excellence Tchg Award., Chair, dept Philos. **RESEARCH** Philos law. **SELECTED PUBLICATIONS** Auth, Pardons: Justice, Mercy, and the Public Interest, NY: Oxford UP, 89; Reasoning and Writing, Macmillan, 93; Inductive Arguments: The Critical Thinking Skills; Riverwalking, Lyons and Burford, 95. **CONTACT ADDRESS** Dept Philos, Oregon State Univ, Corvallis, OR, 97331-4501. **EMAIL** kmoore@orst.edu

DEARMAN, JOHN ANDREW
PERSONAL Born 12/06/1951, Columbia, SC, m, 3 children **DISCIPLINE** BIBLICAL STUDIES **EDUCATION** Univ NC, Chapel Hill, BA, 74; Princeton Theol Sem, MDiv, 77; Emory Univ, PhD, 81. **CAREER** Instr Jeremiah, Candler Sch Theol, 79; instr New Testament & Old Testament, La State Univ, 81, asst prof Bible introd Western archeol relig, 81-82; Prof Old Testament Introd, Austin Theol Sem, 82-, Acad Dean, 98-; Vis Schol, Univ Erlangen-Nurnberg, 89-90, Univ Stellenbosch, SAfrica, 95. **HONORS AND AWARDS** Recipient of numerous honors and grants **MEMBERSHIPS** Soc Bibl Lit; Am Schs Orient Res; Bibl Archaeol Soc. **RESEARCH** The impact of ancient civilization on Israelite foreign relations; Moab in the Iron Age. **SELECTED PUBLICATIONS** Auth, Some observations on early Hebrew works and teachers in America 1726-1823, Hebrew Studies, No 20, 79 & No 21, 80; Religion and Culture in Ancient Israel; Studies in the Mesha Inscription and Moab; author numerous papers, reviews, and entries in Harper's Dictionary of the Bible. **CONTACT ADDRESS** Dept of Old Testament, Austin Presbyterian Theol Sem, 100 E 27th, Austin, TX, 78705-5711. **EMAIL** adearman@mail.austinseminary.edu

DEBRACY, WARREN
PERSONAL Born 03/28/1942, Chicago, IL, m **DISCIPLINE** LAW **EDUCATION** Loyola Univ Chicago, BS Soc Sci 1964; Rutgers Univ New Brunswick, NJ, MA Pol Sci 1966; Cornell Univ Ithaca, NY, JD Law 1971. **CAREER** Rutgers Univ NJ, asst inst 1966; Loyola Univ Law Sch New Orleans, asst prof 1971-72; Univ of Detroit Law Sch, asst prof 1972-73; Univ of Toledo Law Sch, assoc prof 1973-79; Loyola Univ, New Orleans, LA, visiting prof, 1986; Valparoiso Univ, Valparoiso, IN, visiting prof, 1988-89. **HONORS AND AWARDS** 1st yr moot court champion Cornell Law Sch 1969; best affimative debator Gennett Newpaper Tournament Rochester 1962. **MEMBERSHIPS** Mem MI Democratic State Central Comm 1985-89; treas 2nd Cong Dist Dem Comm MI 1983-85, vice-chair 1979-81; mem, Rules Comm, Democratic Natl Convention, 1988; delegate, 1980 Democratic Natl Convention. **SELECTED PUBLICATIONS** Legality of Affirmative Action, Journal of Urban Law, 1974-75. **CONTACT ADDRESS** Sch of Law, No Carolina Central Univ, Durham, NC, 27707.

DECEW, JUDITH W.
PERSONAL Born 10/19/1948, Oberlin, OH, m, 1969, 3 children **DISCIPLINE** PHILOSOPHY **EDUCATION** Univ of Rochester, BA, 70; Univ of Mass, MA, 76, PhD, 78. **CAREER** Asst prof, 78-87, MIT; asst prof, 87-90, assoc prof, 90-98, prof, 98- , Clark Univ. **HONORS AND AWARDS** Elected to Natl APA Committee on Philosphy and Law, 90-93; listed in Who's Who in the East, The World Who's Who of Women, 92- ; listed in Who's Who in American Education, 93- ; Oliver & Dorothy Hayden Faculty Fel, Clark University, 93-94; Research Fel, Natl Endowment for the Humanities, 93-94; Higgins School of Humanities Fels, Clark Univ, 94-98, 90-91; Secretary/ Treasurer, Amer Soc for Political and Legal Phil, 97- . **RESEARCH** Ethics, philosophy of law, social and political theory. **SELECTED PUBLICATIONS** Auth, The Combat Exclusion and the Role of Women in the Military, Hypatia, 95; auth, Privacy and Information Technology, Center for the Study of Ethics in Society, Western MI Univ, Kluwer, 97; auth, Codes of Warfare, Encyclopedia of Applied Ethics, Academic Press, 97; auth, Discretion: Its Role in Judicial Decision-Making, The Philosophy of Law: An Encyclopedia, Garland, forthcoming. **CONTACT ADDRESS** 260 Chestnut St, West Newton, MA, 02465. **EMAIL** jdecew@clarku.edu

DECHANT, DELL
PERSONAL Born 07/06/1954, St. Petersburg, FL, m, 1981 **DISCIPLINE** RELIGION **EDUCATION** Univ S Fla, MA, 84. **CAREER** From adj instr to vis prof to instr & undergrad dir, Univ S Fla, 84-. **HONORS AND AWARDS** Outstanding undergrad adv award, 98. **MEMBERSHIPS** Am Acad Relig; Col Theol Soc; Soc Study Metaphysical Relig. **RESEARCH** New religious movements; ethics; methodology; religion and popular culture. **SELECTED PUBLICATIONS** Auth, Charles and Myrtle Fillmore, Nona Brooks, Ernest Holmes, Am Nat Biog, 98; auth, Hermeneutics for Allegorical Exegesis in Postmodern Idealistic Religious Systems: Comments and Guidelines, Study of Metaphysical Relig, Spring, 98; auth, Reflections on a Peculiar Religious Culture and Its Emerging Academic Community, Jour Soc Study Metaphysical Relig, Spring, 96; auth, Response to Robert Ellwood's 'Why Are Mythologists Political Reactionaries?', Relig & Soc Order, 95; auth, The Allegorical Trajectory, Int New Thought Quart, Fall, 94; auth, Myrtle Fillmore and Her Daughters, Women's Leadership in Marginal Relig, 93. **CONTACT ADDRESS** Dept of Religious Studies, CPR 315, Tampa, FL, 33620-5550. **EMAIL** ddechant@luna.cas.usf.edu

DECHERT, CHARLES RICHARD
PERSONAL Philadelphia, PA, m, 1957 **DISCIPLINE** SOCIAL AND POLITICAL PHILOSOPHY **EDUCATION** Cath Univ Am, AB, 49, MA, 50, PhD, 52. **CAREER** Vis prof comp econ & soc policy, Int Univ Soc Studies, Rome, 57-59; assoc prof govt, Purdue Univ, West Lafayette, 59-65, prof polit sci, 65-67; Prof Polit, Cath Univ AM, 67-, Instr, Our Lady of the Lake Col, 53-54; consult, Ist L'Addestramento nell'Industria, Milan, 57-59, Ministero di Grazia e Giustizia, Rome, 57-59, Grad Sch Bus, Columbia Univ, 59, Inst Defense Anal, 60, Joint Econ Comt, US Cong, 61 & Comt House Admin, US House Rep, 70; Fulbright-Hays award, Italy, 65-66 & 82. **HONORS AND AWARDS** Harmon Prize, Am Cath Philos Asn, 64. **MEMBERSHIPS** Am Polit Sci Asn; Am Cath Philos Asn; Soc Gen Syst Res; corresp mem Ist Luigi Sturzo, Rome; Intl Studies Asn; Am Soc Cybernetics; Fellowship of Cath Scholars; Intl Maritian Soc; Natl Cap Area Pol Sci Asn, Pres, 75-76. **RESEARCH** Soc-polit syst; philos of sci; sociology of knowledge. **SELECTED PUBLICATIONS** Auth, Ente nazionale idcoauthocarburi: Profile of a state corporation, Brill, Leiden, 63; Cybernetics and the human person, Int Philos Quart, 65; ed & contribr, The Social Impact of Cybernetics, Univ Notre Dame, 66, Simon & Schuster, 67; coauth, Congress: The First Branch of Government, Am Enterprise Inst, 66, Doubleday, 67; Positive Feedback, Pergamon, 68 & Systems in Society, Soc Gen Syst Res, 73; ed, Sistemi, paradigmi e societa (Systems Paradigm), Angeli, Milano, 78; El Nuevo Mundo de la Filosofia y la Tecnologia, 90; Recovering the Sacred Cath Faith, Worship, Practice, 90; Church and State in Am, 92; Freedom and Choice in a Democracy, 93; Religion in Public Life, 94; Christian Humanism, 95; Civil Society and Social Reconstruction, 96; Civil Society-Who belongs?, 97; Democracy Culture and Values, 91-92; Freedom and Choice in a Democracy, 92-93. **CONTACT ADDRESS** Dept Polit, Catholic Univ of America, 620 Michigan Ave N E, Washington, DC, 20064-0002.

DECK, ALLAN F.
PERSONAL Born 04/19/1945, Los Angeles, CA, s **DISCIPLINE** THEOLOGY; LATIN AMERICAN STUDIES **EDUCATION** St Louis Univ, BA, 69, PhD, 74; Jesuit Sch of Theol at Berkeley, MDiv, 76; Gregorian Univ, STD, 88. **CAREER** Admin, Our Lady of Guadalupe Church, 76-79; Dir, Hispanic Ministry, Diocese of Orange, 79-85; Asst Prof of Theology, Jesuit Sch of Theol, 87-92; Assoc Prof of Theol, Loyola Marymt Univ, 92-96; Exec Dir, Loyola Inst for Spirituality, 97-. **HONORS AND AWARDS** Catholic Press Asn 1st Place Award Pro Book Category, 89. **MEMBERSHIPS** Acad of Catholic Hispanic Theol of the US, (co-founder & 1st pres); Nat Catholic Counc for Hisp Ministry, (co-founder & 1st pres). **RESEARCH** Hispanic religious expressions & spirituality. **SELECTED PUBLICATIONS** Auth, Francisco Javier Alegre: A Study in Mexican Literary Criticism, Historical Inst of the Soc of Jesus, 76; auth, The Second Wave, Paulist Press, 89; auth, Perspectivas: Hispanic Ministry, Sheed & Ward, 95; Hispanic Catholic Culture in the US, Univ Notre Dame Press, 94. **CONTACT ADDRESS** 480 S Batavia St, Orange, CA, 92868. **EMAIL** deck8@juno.com

DEETER, ALLEN C
PERSONAL Born 03/08/1931, Dayton, Ohio, m, 1952, 3 children **DISCIPLINE** RELIGION, HISTORY **EDUCATION** Manchester Col, BA, 53; Bethany Theol Sem, BD, 56; Princeton Univ, MA, 58, PhD(hist Christianity), 63. **CAREER** Instr relig, 59-60, from asst prof to assoc prof, 60-72, dir, Peace Studies Inst & Prog Conflict Resolution, 67-80, assoc acad dean, 69-80, Prof Relig & Philos, Manchester Col, 72-; Adminr, Brethren Cols Abroad, 75-, Vchmn bd gov, John F Kennedy Am Haus, Marburg, 65-66; dir Brethren Cols Abroad, Univ Marburg & Univ Strasburg, 65-66; Soc Relig Higher Educ grant, 68-69; lectr, Punjabi Univ & Dibrugarh Univ, India, spring 69; exec secy, Consortium Peace Res, Educ & Develop, 71-72; consult on world order studies, various cols, univs & consortia, 71-; ed, Bull, Peace Studies Inst, Manchester Col, 71-80; spring inaugural lectr, Christian Theol Sem, Indianapolis, 72. **HONORS AND AWARDS** Hon Doctorate, Bridgewater Col. **MEMBERSHIPS** Int Studies Asn; Am Soc Church Hist; Am Acad Relig. **RESEARCH** The origins of modern radical religious and political thought; mysticism and pietism East and West, especially as related to social ethics; Tolstoyan and Gandhian political, social and religious tactics of transformation. **SELECTED PUBLICATIONS** Coauth, In His Hand, Brethren Press, 64; auth, Pietist views of the Church, Brethren Life & Thought, winter 64; Western mysticism and social concern, J Inst Traditional Cult, spring 69; Religion as a social and political force in America, Bull Ramakrishna Inst, fall 69; Toyohiko Kagawa: Mystic and Social Activist, Punjabi Univ, 70; Heirs of a Promise, Brethern Press, 72; auth, The Paradoxical Necessity of Realism and Idealism, Bull of Peace Stu Inst, 98. **CONTACT ADDRESS** Dept of Relig, Manchester Col, 601 E College Ave, N Manchester, IN, 46962-1226.

DEHART, PAUL
PERSONAL Born 12/10/1964, Memphis, TN, s **DISCIPLINE** SYSTEMATIC THEOLOGY **EDUCATION** Univ Chicago, AB, 87; The Divinity School, MAR, 90; Univ Chicago, PhD, 97. **CAREER** ASST PROF, THEOLOGY, VANDERBILT UNIV, 97-. **HONORS AND AWARDS** Phi Beta Kappa; Century fel, Chicago, 90-94; Harper Dissertation grant, 96-97. **MEMBERSHIPS** Am Acad Relig. **RESEARCH** Nineteenth and twentieth century theology; philos and theol doctrines of God; Christian theological method and the university. **SELECTED PUBLICATIONS** Auth, Eberhard Jungel on the Structure of Theology, Theol Studies 57, 96; Divine Simplicity: Theistic Reconstruction in Eberhard Jungel's Trinitarian Glaubenslehre (dissertation), 97. **CONTACT ADDRESS** The Divinity School, Vanderbilt Univ, Nashville, TN, 37240-2701. **EMAIL** paul.j.dehart@vanderbilt.edu

DEIBLER, TIMOTHY
DISCIPLINE THEOLOGY; PHILOSOPHY **EDUCATION** Dallas Baptist Univ, BA, 73; Dallas Theological Sem, ThM, 77; MA, 87, PhD, 89, Rice Univ. **CAREER** Interim Asst Prof, Huntington Col, 89-90; Interim Asst Prof, Northwestern Col, 90-91; Asst Prof, Liberty Univ, 91-93; Dialectic and Rhetoric Faculty, New Covenant Schools, 93-. **MEMBERSHIPS** Amer Phil Assoc; Amer Scientific Affil. **RESEARCH** Philosophy of Religion and Science; Philosophical Theories of Metaphor; Hermeueutics; Theology. **CONTACT ADDRESS** 2000 Weeping Willow Dr., Apt B, Lynchburg, VA, 24501.

DEIGH, JOHN
DISCIPLINE PHILOSOPHY **EDUCATION** UCLA, PhD. **CAREER** Assoc prof, Northwestern Univ. **RESEARCH** Moral and political philosophy. **SELECTED PUBLICATIONS** Auth, The Sources of Moral Agency: Essays in Moral Psychology and Freudian Theory; ed, Ethics and Personality. **CONTACT ADDRESS** Dept of Philosophy, Northwestern Univ, 1801 Hinman, Evanston, IL, 60208.

DEIGNAN, KATHLEEN P.
PERSONAL Born 12/17/1947, London, England **DISCIPLINE** THEOLOGY; SPIRITUALITY **EDUCATION** Fordham Univ, PhD, 86. **CAREER** Assoc prof Relig Studies, Iona Col, 81-98. **HONORS AND AWARDS** McCabe Award Soc Studies, 82; Iona Women of Achievement, 96; Kate Connelly-Weinert Award AAR, 97. **MEMBERSHIPS** Amer Acad Relig; Cath Theolog Soc Amer; Soc for Study Christian Spirituality. **RESEARCH** Classical and Contemporary Spirituality. **SELECTED PUBLICATIONS** Road to Rapture: Thomas Merton's Itinerarium mentis in Deum, Franciscan Studies; Prisoners of Necessity: Thomas Merton's Rain and Rhinoceros, Merton Annual; Christ Spirit: The Eschatology of Shaker Christianity, Scarecrow Pr, 92. **CONTACT ADDRESS** Dept of Theology, Iona Col, New Rochelle, NY, 10801. **EMAIL** kpdeignan@aol.com

DEJNOZKA, JAN
PERSONAL Born 12/20/1951, Saratoga Springs, NY, m, 1992, 2 children **DISCIPLINE** PHILOSOPHY **EDUCATION** Syracuse Univ, BA, 73; Univ of Iowa, MA, PhD, 76, 79; Univ of Michigan, School of Law, JD, 96. **CAREER** Univ of Iowa, tchg asst, 74-79; US Naval Acad, asst prof, 85-88; Univ of Michigan Ann Arbor, vis scholar, 91-94, 96-98; Union Col, res assoc, 80-98; Hon J. W. Callahan, Law clerk, 98. **RESEARCH** Analytic philos; ethics; logic; philos of language; mathematics; science; religion and law. **SELECTED PUBLICATIONS** Auth, Bertrand Russell on Modality and Logical Relevance, Ashgate Pub. Ltd., forthcoming; auth, Note on Continuing and Exclusive Jurisdiction over Child Support Orders, in: Mich Family Law Jour, 98; The Ontology of the Analytic Traditions and Its Origins, Lanham MD: Littlefield Adams, 96; auth, Quine: Whither Empirical Equivalence?, S African Jour Philos, 95; auth, A Reply to Umphrey's The Meinongian-Antimeinongian Dispute Reviewed, Grazer Philosophische Studien, 88; auth, Frege on Identity, Intl Stud Philos, 81. **CONTACT ADDRESS** Dept of Philosophy, Univ of Michigan, 4814 Washtenaw A8, Ann Arbor, MI, 48108-1446.

DEKAR, PAUL R.
PERSONAL Born 02/08/1944, San Francisco, CA, m, 1967, 2 children **DISCIPLINE** POLITICAL SCIENCES, THEOLOGY **EDUCATION** Univ Calif Berkeley, Polit Sci, AB, 65; Colgate Rochester Divinity School, MDiv, 71; Univ Chicago, AM, 73; PhD, 78. **CAREER** US Dept of the State Postings Wash, DC and Cameroon, 67-70; asst to the Chaplan, Univ Rochester, 70-71; asst to ed, Church Hist, 73-75; inst, Central Mich Univ, 75-76; asst prof, McMaster Divinity Coll, 76-79; assoc prof, McMaster Divinity Coll, 79-86; prof, McMaster Divinity Coll,

86-91; acting dir, Center for Peace Studies, McMaster Univ, 91-91; fac, McMaster Univ, 88-94; centenary prof, McMaster Divinity Coll, 91-94; prof, Memphis Theol Sem, 95-. **HONORS AND AWARDS** Polit Sci Scholar Univ Calif, 61-65; Doctoral Fel Univ Chicago, 73-75; Res Leave, Israel, Palestine, 82-83; Arts Res Bd grant, McMaster Univ, 84-85; Pres Can Soc of Church His, 87; Arts Res Bd grant, McMaster Univ,88-89; Res Leave Oxford Eng, 90-91; Hamilton World Citizen of the Year, 94; Delivered Rattan Lectres, Univ Melbourne Australia, 98. **RESEARCH** Political Science; Theology. **SELECTED PUBLICATIONS** Auth, The Renewal We Seek, 82; Crossing Barriers in World Mission, 83; A Study Guide to the Position Paper on the Middle East, 90; For the Healing of the Nations, 93; co-ed, In the Great Tradition, Essays in Honor of Winthrop S Hudson, 82; Celebrating the Canadian Baptist Heritage; The McMaster Conference, 85. **CONTACT ADDRESS** Memphis Theol Sem, 168 E Pkwy S, Memphis, TN, 38104-4395. **EMAIL** pdekar@mtscampus.edu

DEKONINCK, THOMAS
PERSONAL Born 05/26/1934, Louvain, Belgium, m, 1960, 3 children **DISCIPLINE** PHILOSOPHY, THEOLOGY **EDUCATION** Laval Univ, BA & BPh, 54, LPh, 56, PhD, 70; Oxford Univ, MA, 63. **CAREER** From instr to asst prof, 60-64, auxiliary prof, 64-70, assoc prof, 70-77, dean philos, 74-78, PROF PHILOS, LAVAL UNIV, 77-, Alexander von Humboldt Stiftung scholar, 72-73. **RESEARCH** Greek philosophy; metaphysics; ethics. **SELECTED PUBLICATIONS** Auth, Science and God and the Synthetic Theory of Evolution, Laval Theol et Philos, Vol 0050, 94; Anaximander--Fragmenta and Testimonia--Greek and French, Laval Theol et Philos, Vol 0050, 94; In-Memoriam--Dumont,Fernand, Laval Theol et Philos, Vol 0053, 97; The Meaning of Culture, Laval Theol et Philos, Vol 0052, 96. **CONTACT ADDRESS** 642 Charron Ste, Ste-Foy, PQ, G1X 3L6.

DEL CARMEN, ALEX
DISCIPLINE CRIMINOLOGY AND CRIMINAL JUSTICE **EDUCATION** FL State Univ, PhD. **CAREER** Asst prof, Univ of Tampa. **RESEARCH** Theoretical criminology, penology; crime prevention; juvenile delinquency. **SELECTED PUBLICATIONS** Auth, Campus Crime: An Environmental Assessment, J Security Admin, 97; rev, The Ecology of Aggression, J Social Pathology, 96; Prisons in Crisis, J Soc Pathology, 95. **CONTACT ADDRESS** Criminology and Criminal Justice Prog, Univ of Texas at Arlington, 303 Univ Hall, PO Box 19595, Arlington, TX, 76019-0595. **EMAIL** adelcarmen@uta.edu

DEL COLLE, RALPH
PERSONAL Born 10/03/1954, New York, NY, m, 1985, 2 children **DISCIPLINE** THEOLOGY **EDUCATION** New York Univ, BA, 76; Union Theol Sem, MDiv, 81, MPhil, 86, PhD, 91. **CAREER** Adj instr, Fordham Univ, 85; adj lectr, Dutchess Community Col, 88; instr, St. Anselm Col, 88-91; from asst to assoc prof, Barry Univ, 91-95; asst prof, Marquette Univ, 95-. **HONORS AND AWARDS** Mellon Grant for Summer Inst, Israel, 97; Union Theol Sem Fel, 81-85; Roothbert Fel, 78-81. **MEMBERSHIPS** Am Acad of Relig; Soc for Pentecostal Studies; Cath Theol Soc of Am; Col Theol Soc; Karl Barth Soc of North Am; Karl Rahner Soc. **RESEARCH** Systematic theology; Trinity; Christology; Holy Spirit; Doctrine of Grace. **SELECTED PUBLICATIONS** Auth, Christ and the Spirit: Spirit-Christology in Trinitarian Perspective, 94; "Trinity and Temporality: A Pentecostal/Charismatic Perspective," 95; "The Two-Handed God: Communion, Community and Contours for Dialogue," 96; "Ecumenism and the Holy Spirit: The Pneumatological Center of Ut Unum Sint," 97; "Reflections on the Filioque," 97; "Oneness and Trinity: A Preliminary Proposal for Dialogue with Oneness Pentecostalism," 97. **CONTACT ADDRESS** Dept of Theology, Marquette Univ, Coughlin 100, Box 1881, Milwaukee, WI, 53201-1881. **EMAIL** Ralph.DelColle@marquette.edu

DELACRE, GEORGES
PERSONAL Born 11/09/1922, Buenos Aires, Argentina, m, 1953, 3 children **DISCIPLINE** PHILOSOPHY OF SCIENCE **EDUCATION** Univ Buenos Aires, MA, 50; Univ Paris Sorbonne, PhD, 61. **CAREER** Prof, eng, logic & psychol, Colegio Nacional Gral. Roca, Argentina, 50-55; instr/asst prof, span, humanities, Univ Puerto Rico Mayag & R. Piedras, 55-59; asst prof, humanities, dir, general educ prog, Univ Puerto Rico, 61-67; full prof, philos, assoc dean of studies, Rio Piedras Campus, Univ Puerto Rico, 67-81; prof, philos, chair, grad sch of humanities, Rio Piedras, Univ Puerto Rico, 81-85. **HONORS AND AWARDS** Visiting fel, Princeton Univ, fall, 75; Chevalier de l'Ordre des Palmes Academiques, 77-. **MEMBERSHIPS** Asn Argentina de Filosofia, 77; Amer Philos Asn, 82-. **RESEARCH** Philosophy of science. **SELECTED PUBLICATIONS** Auth, El Tiempo en Perspectiva, Introduccion a Una Filosofia del Tiempo, UPR ed; auth, La Teoria Causal del Tiempo: Recapitulacion, Escritos de Filosofia, Buenos Aires; auth, Los Nireles Temporales Segun J.T. Fraser y el Orden Subyacente Segun D. Bohm, Revista Latinoamericana de Filosofia. **CONTACT ADDRESS** 5573 Seminary Rd., Apt. 304, Falls Church, VA, 22041.

DELANEY, CORNELIUS F.
DISCIPLINE PHILOSOPHY **EDUCATION** St. Thomas Sem, AA, 58; St. John's Sem, BA, 61; Boston Col, MA, 62; St Louis Univ, PhD. **CAREER** Prof. **RESEARCH** Pragmatism; political philosophy; history of modern philosophy. **SELECTED PUBLICATIONS** Auth, Science, Knowledge and Mind: A Study in the Philosophy of C.S. Peirce, 93; ed, Liberty and Community Values: The Liberalism-Communitarianism Debate, 93; Peirce on the Conditions of the Possibility of Science, 93. **CONTACT ADDRESS** Philosophy Dept, Univ of Notre Dame, 336/7 O'Shaughnessy, Notre Dame, IN, 46556. **EMAIL** delaney.1@nd.edu

DELANEY, DAVID K.
PERSONAL Born 10/05/1957, York, PA, m, 1980, 2 children **DISCIPLINE** EARLY CHRISTIANITY **EDUCATION** Univ Va, PhD, 96. **CAREER** Lutheran pastor, St. John Lutheran Church, Roanoke VA. **MEMBERSHIPS** AAR; SBL; N Amer Patristics Soc; Amer Soc of Church Hist. **RESEARCH** History of Biblical interpretation. **CONTACT ADDRESS** St. John Lutheran Church, 4608 Brambleton Ave SW, Roanoke, VA, 24018. **EMAIL** dkd7s@ix.netcom.com

DELEEUW, PATRICIA ALLWIN
PERSONAL Born 04/29/1950, Frankfurt, Germany, m, 1971 **DISCIPLINE** CHURCH AND MEDIEVAL HISTORY **EDUCATION** Univ Detroit, BA, 71, PhD(medieval studies), 79; Univ Toronto, MA, 72; Pontifical Inst Medieval Studies, MSL, 75. **CAREER** ASST PROF THEOL, BOSTON COL, 79-. **MEMBERSHIPS** Mediaeval Acad Am; Am Soc Church Hist. **RESEARCH** Religious social history; early medieval Germany; history of pastoral care. **SELECTED PUBLICATIONS** Auth, Hincmar-Of-Reims as Administrator of His Diocese and Ecclesiastical Province--Gerard, Speculum-Journal of Medieval Stud, Vol 0069, 94; Medieval Handbooks of Penance--A Translation of the Principal Libri Poenitentiales and Selections from Related Documents, Church Hist, Vol 0062, 93; Background on Fulrad-De-Saint-Denis C.710-784--French, Speculum-Jour Medieval Stud, Vol 0070, 95; Faith to Creed--Ecumenical Perspectives on the Affirmation of the Apostolic Faith in the 4th-Century, Jour Ecumenical Stud, Vol 0029, 92; Luther,Martin--Faith in Christ and the Gospel--Selected Spiritual Writings, Jour Ecumenical Stud, Vol 0033, 96; Medieval Handbooks of Penance--A Translation of the Principal Libri Poenitentiales and Selections from Related Documents, Church Hist, Vol 0062, 93. **CONTACT ADDRESS** Dept of Theol, Boston Col, Chestnut Hill, MA, 02167.

DELIO, ILIA
PERSONAL Born 08/20/1955, Newark, NJ **DISCIPLINE** HISTORICAL THEOLOGY **EDUCATION** Fordham Univ, PhD 96. **CAREER** Washington Theo Union, asst prof 97-; Trinity Col CT, vis prof, 96-97. **MEMBERSHIPS** AAR; SSLB **RESEARCH** Medieval mystics; Franciscan theology **SELECTED PUBLICATIONS** Auth, The Humility of God in a Scientific World, New Theol Rev, 98. **CONTACT ADDRESS** Dept of Theology, Washington Theological Union, 6897 Laurel St, Washington, DC, 20012. **EMAIL** delio@wtu.edu

DELL'AGOSTINO, DAVID
PERSONAL Born 12/24/1968, Sacramento, CA, m, 1993 **DISCIPLINE** PHILOSOPHY **EDUCATION** SFSK, MA, 95; UCSB PhD student, 97-. **CAREER** Instr; var community coll in SF Bay area; De Anza Coll. **HONORS AND AWARDS** Outstanding Grad Student, SFSK, 95. **MEMBERSHIPS** Am Philos Asn. **RESEARCH** Epistemology; Modern Philosphy. **CONTACT ADDRESS** 779 Madrona Walk Apt E, Goleta, CA, 93117-3049. **EMAIL** dellagostino@yahoo.com

DELLAPENNA, JOSEPH W.
DISCIPLINE INTERNATIONAL TRADE LAW **EDUCATION** Univ Mich, BBA, 65; Detroit Col Law, JD, 68; Nat Law Ctr, George Washington Univ, LLM, 69; Columbia Univ Sch Law, LLM, 75. **CAREER** Prof, Villanova Univ. **MEMBERSHIPS** Past consult to, Assoc(s) for Middle East Res, Inc; People's Repub China; Repub China & Water Resources Comt Int Law Asn; ch Model Water Code Proj, Amer Soc Civil Engineers; Water Regulatory Standards Comt, Amer Soc Civil Engineers; Comt on Chinese Law; past ch Comt in Int Litigation, ABA Sect Int Law and Practice; Law of the Pac Region Interest Gp; Int Legal Educ Comt, Amer Soc Int Law; Amer Law Inst; Consultative Gp on the Uniform Commercial Code; exec coun, Amer Soc Int Law. **RESEARCH** Chinese law, water rights, transnational litigation. **SELECTED PUBLICATIONS** Auth, Water in the Middle East: The Limits and Potential of Law, 97; coauth, Natural Resources Law Manual, 95; Waters and Water Rights, 91 ed; Abortion and the Constitution, 87; Suing For Governments and Their Corporations, 88. **CONTACT ADDRESS** Law School, Villanova Univ, 800 Lancaster Ave, Villanova, PA, 19085-1692. **EMAIL** dellapen@law.vill.edu

DELLUMS, LEOLA M. ROSCOE
PERSONAL Born 12/12/1941, Berkeley, CA, m, 1962 **DISCIPLINE** LAW **EDUCATION** San Francisco State University, BA, 1966; California State Teaching Credential, adult education, 1967; Georgetown University Law Center, JD, 1982. **CAREER** Institute for Services to Education, consultant, 1976; American Civil Liberties Union, development director/publicist, 1976-1978; Zuko Interior Designs, Public Relations, advertising mgr, 1978-79; Congressman Mickey Leland, special assistant, 1983; Superior Court of District of Columbia, judicial law clerk, 1984-85; Assembly California Legislature, principal consultant, Assembly Office of Research, Washington, District of Columbia, rep, 1985-92; Washington & Christian, Attorney at law, 1993-96; US Dept of Commerce, 1996-97; Sole Practioner, Attorney at law, 1997-. **HONORS AND AWARDS** The Ella Hill Hutch Award, Black Women Organized for Political Action, 1992; Inductee Berkeley High School Hall of Fame; The Sojourner Truth Meritorious Service Award, National Association of Negro Business and Professional Women's Club Inc, 1991; AT&T Volunteer Activist Award of Washington DC, Area, 1985; Congressional recognition for efforts in attaining passage of HR 1580. **MEMBERSHIPS** National Bar Association; Pennsylvania Bar; California State Society; American Bar Association; The Rainbow Fund; Potomac Links Inc; Alpha Kappa Alpha Sorority; Committee of 21 Human Rights Caucus; Congressional Club; American Society of Composers, Authors and Publishers; San Francisco State Univ Alumni Assn; Berkeley High School Alumni Association; US Supreme Court Bar; District Of Columbia Court of Appeals Bar; US District Court for the District of Columbia Bar; Center to Prevent Handgun Violence, Sasha Bruce Youth Work; Rap Inc Drug Prevention; Minority Breast Cancer Resource Ctr. **SELECTED PUBLICATIONS** Songs published under RREPCO Publishing Company; poetry published in "The Sheet"; prescriptive diagnostic research paper, "Teaching English as a Second Language to Native Born"; hosted "Cloth-A-Thon"; co-hosted "The Place;" hosted local Emmy award-winning television show "Cloth-A-Thon," WGLA; co-hosted local Emmy award-winning television show, "The Place," WRC. **CONTACT ADDRESS** 5423 28th St NW, Washington, DC, 20015.

DELOGU, ORLANDO E.
DISCIPLINE LAW **EDUCATION** Univ Utah, BS; Univ Wis, MS, JD. **CAREER** Prof; past city councilor, Portland; law sch career, 66-; asst, Thai govt on env, 91. **MEMBERSHIPS** Past ch, Env Law Sect, Asn Amer Law Sch; Maine's Bd Env Protection, 5 yrs. **RESEARCH** Environmental issues. **SELECTED PUBLICATIONS** Auth, bk on Maine Land Use Law; coauth, 2-vol, Federal Environmental Regulation. **CONTACT ADDRESS** School of Law, Univ of Southern Maine, 96 Falmouth St, PO Box 9300, Portland, ME, 04104-9300.

DEMARCO, DON
DISCIPLINE RELIGIOUS STUDIES **EDUCATION** Stonehill Col, BS; BA; St. John's Univ, MA; PhD. **CAREER** Prof **SELECTED PUBLICATIONS** Auth, Abortion: Legal and Philosophical Considerations; Human Experimentation; In Vitro Fertilization and Implantation; Men and Woman, Their Difference and its Importance; Moral and Philosophical Implications of Sex-Preselection; Moral Anesthesia-The Decline of Private Guilt; Paradox as an Analogue for Dialectical Thinking; Technologized Parenthood and the Attenuation of Motherhood and Fatherhood; The Baby M. Case: Why Surrogate Motherhood Must Be Disallowed; The conflict between reason and will in the Legislation of Surrogate Motherhood; The Foundation of Morality and the Function of Authority; The Nature of Chastity. **CONTACT ADDRESS** Dept of Religious Studies, St. Jerome's Univ, Waterloo, ON, N2L 3G3.

DEMAREST, BRUCE
DISCIPLINE SYSTEMATIC THEOLOGY **EDUCATION** Wheaton Col, BA; Adelphi Univ, MS; Trinity Evangel Divinity Sch, MA; Univ Manchester, Eng, PhD. **CAREER** Prof, Denver Sem, 75-. **RESEARCH** Area of spiritual formation and direction. **SELECTED PUBLICATIONS** Auth, A History of Interpretation of Hebrews 7:10 From the Reformation to the Present, Who is Jesus?; General Revelation: Historical Views and Contemporary Issues; co-auth, Integrative Theology; co-ed, Challenges to Inerrancy: A Theological Response; pub(s), New Intl Dictionary of the Christian Church; New Intl Dictionary of New Testament Theol; Evangel Dictionary of Theol; New Dictionary of Theol; Baker Encycl of the Bible. **CONTACT ADDRESS** Denver Conservative Baptist Sem, PO Box 10000, Denver, CO, 80250.

DEMECS, DESIDERIO D.
PERSONAL Born 11/08/1923, s **DISCIPLINE** HUMANITIES AND PHILOSOPHY **EDUCATION** Univ degli studi de Bologna, Bologna, Italy, PhD, econ & commerce, 55; State Univ NY Buffalo, PhD, philos, 65. **CAREER** Teaching fel, State Univ NY Buffalo, 62-65; assoc prof and head, dept philos, Uinv Dubuque, 65-66; prof, humanities & philos, Univ Ark Pine Bluff, 67-94; prof emer, philos & res, Univ Ark, 94-. **HONORS AND AWARDS** NEH grant; Amer Asn of State Col and Univ delegate, 78; conference dir, Ark Endow for the Humanities, 76, 80, 85, Ark Humanities Coun, 92; outstanding svc award, Pan-Hellenic Coun, Univ Ark Pine Bluff, 84; contr-dir and princ investigator, US Army Community Support Rev, 87; dir, Hungarian Exposition, Univ Ark Pine Bluff, 88; community svc award, Leadership Pine Bluff Alumni & Greater Pine Bluff Chamber of Commerce, 88. **MEMBERSHIPS** Amer Philos Asn; Ark Philos Asn; Soc of Christ Philos. **SELECTED PUB-**

LICATIONS Auth, Fixing Environment, Human Rights, Rational Laws, Free Market Economy and Democracy Globally Especially in South-Southeast-East Asia's Conditions, UAPB Res Forum, 98; auth, The Failure of the Wicked Communist Don Quixote/Sancho Panza in Central and Eastern Europe and the Problems of the Integration of the Region Into the EU and NATO, UAPB Res Forum, 97, 96; auth, Haiti: A Struggle for Democracy, Human Rights and Law, UAPB Res Forum, 95; auth, The Communist Don Quixote in Cuba, UAPB Res Forum, 95. **CONTACT ADDRESS** Univ of Arkansas, Pine Bluff, AR, 71601.

DEMENCHONOK, EDWARD V.
PERSONAL Born 01/01/1942, Vitebsk, Belarus, m, 1993, 2 children **DISCIPLINE** PHILOSOPHY **EDUCATION** Musical Col, Minsk, BA, 61; Moscow State Univ, MA, 69; Inst of Philos of the Russ Acad Sci, PhD, 77. **CAREER** Res, then sr res, Inst of Philos of the Russ Acad Sci, 70-95; assoc prof, Moscow State Univ, 82-84; vis prof, Univ Colombia, 88-90; prof Moscow State Pedag Univ, 91-92; prof, Acad Slavic Cult, Moscow, 91-92; vis prof Univ Georgia, 92-93; assoc prof, Brewton Parker Col, 94-95; assoc prof, Fort Valley State Univ, 95- . **HONORS AND AWARDS** Listed, Who's Who in the South and Southwest, Who's Who in America; Who's Who in the World, 98. **MEMBERSHIPS** APA; MLA; Int Soc for Universalism; Latin Am Stud Asn; Soc for Iberian and Latin Am Thought; Southeastern Council on Latin Am Stud; Russian Philos Soc. **RESEARCH** Philosophy of culture; social philosophy; ethics; Latin American philosophy. **SELECTED PUBLICATIONS** Auth, Contemporary Technocratic Thought in the USA, Moscow: Nauka, 84; auth, Filosofia Latinoamericana: Problemas y Tendencias, Bogota: El Buho, 90; auth, America Latina en la Epoca de la Revolucion Cientifico-technica, Bogota: COLCIENCIAS, 90; auth, Filosofia en el Mundo Contemporaneo, Bogota: UNINCCA, 90; auth, Discovering the Other and Finding Ourself, Fur Enrique Dussel: Aus Anlas Seines 60 Geburstages, Augustinus-Buchhandlung, 95; auth, Latin American Philosophy in Russia, Concordia, 96; auth, Latin American Philosophy and Multiculturalism, Secolas, 99. **CONTACT ADDRESS** 1516 Buford Carey Rd, Hull, GA, 30646. **EMAIL** demenche@usa.net

DEMKOVICH, MICHAEL
PERSONAL Born 01/30/1954, Berwyn, IL **DISCIPLINE** THEOLOGY **EDUCATION** Catholic Univ of Louvain Belgium, PhD, STD, 91. **CAREER** Aquinas Col Grand Rapids, lectr, 81-86; Dominican Studium St Louis, asst prof, 91-96; Univ NM, adj prof, 96-, Blackfriar Oxford Univ, adj prof, 97-, Dominican Ecclesial Inst, founding dir, 96-. **MEMBERSHIPS** AAR, SBL, CTSA. **RESEARCH** Spirituality **SELECTED PUBLICATIONS** Auth, Beyond Subjectivity: Opening the Ego, Listening, 94; auth, Work as Worth: Money or Meaning, Connections Between Spirit and Work, ed., Bloch & Richmond, Danes-Black, 97. **CONTACT ADDRESS** 1815 Las Lomas NE, Albuquerque, NM, 87106. **EMAIL** lumen@sprynet.com

DEMOPOULOS, WILLIAM
PERSONAL Born 02/21/1943, m, 1964, 2 children **DISCIPLINE** PHILOSOPHY, PHILOSOPHY OF SCIENCE **EDUCATION** Univ Minn, BA, 64; Univ Western Ont, PhD(philos), 74. **CAREER** ASSOC PROF PHILOS, UNIV WESTERN ONT, 72-, Lectr philos, Univ NB, 70-73, asst prof, 73-75; consult, NSF & Soc Sci & Humanities Res Coun. **MEMBERSHIPS** Philos of Sci Asn; Soc for Philos & Psychol. **RESEARCH** Philosophy of science, especially physics and cognitive science; philosophy of logic and language. **SELECTED PUBLICATIONS** Auth, In-Memoriam--1928-1997, Synthese, Vol 0112, 97; Frege, Hilbert, and Tte Conceptual Structure of Model-Theory, Hist and Philos Logic, Vol 0015, 94; Frege, Hilbert, and the Conceptual Structure of Model-Theory, Hist and Philos Logic, Vol 0015, 94. **CONTACT ADDRESS** Dept of Philos, Univ of Western Ont, London, ON, N6A 3K7.

DEMOTT, DEBORAH A.
PERSONAL Born 07/21/1948, Collingswood, NJ **DISCIPLINE** LAW **EDUCATION** Swarthmore Col, BA, 70; NY Univ, JD, 73. **CAREER** Law clerk, Southern Dist of NY, 73; assoc, Simpson, Thacher & Bartlett, 74-75; asst prof, 75-77, assoc prof, 78-80, Eugene T Bost res prof law, 81, PROF LAW, DUKE UNIV, 81-, Vis asst prof law, Sch of Law, Univ Tex, 77-78. **MEMBERSHIPS** Am Law Inst. **RESEARCH** Corporate law. **SELECTED PUBLICATIONS** Auth, Oppressed But Not Betrayed--A Comparative-Assessment of Canadian Remedies for Minority Shareholders and Other Corporate Constituents, Law and Contemp Problems, Vol 0056, 93; Our Partners Keepers--Agency Dimensions of Partnership Relationships, Law and Contemp Problems, Vol 0058, 95; Modern Equity, Law and Contemp Problems, Vol 0056, 93; Down the Rabbit-Hole and Into the Nineties--Issues of Accountability in the Wake of Eighties-Style Transactions in Control, George Washington Law Rev, Vol 0061, 93; Progressive Corporate-Law, Cornell Law Rev, Vol 0081, 96; Equitable Doctrines and Remedies in Contemporary Regulatory Settings, Law and Contemp Problems, Vol 0056, 93. **CONTACT ADDRESS** Sch of Law, Duke Univ, Durham, NC, 27706.

DEMPSEY, CAROL J.
PERSONAL Born 04/16/1955, Ridgewood, NJ **DISCIPLINE** THEOLOGY **EDUCATION** Caldwell Col, BA, 78; St. Louis Univ, MA, 86; Catholic Univ Am, PhD, 94. **CAREER** Tchr, Sacred Ht Grade Sch, 73-75; tchr, St Thomas More Grade Sch, 75-76; Tchr, Essex Cty Corr Ctr, 76-78; tchr, Mt St Dominic Grade Sch, 78-79; tchr, Lacordaire Acad, Upper Montclair NJ, 79-86; instr, bibl stud, Albertus Magnus Col, 86-89; asst prof of bibl stud and theology, Univ Portland, 94- . **HONORS AND AWARDS** Cum laude, 78; NEH grant, 80; Natl Catholic Ed Asn Awd, 93; Soc of Bibl Lit Regional Scholar Awd, 96; Natl Regional Scholar, 97-98; Arthur Butine Awd,97. **MEMBERSHIPS** Catholic Bibl Asn; Am Acad of Relig; Soc of Bibl Lit; Col Theol Soc; MLA. **RESEARCH** Hebrew Bible/Old Testament; Pentateuch; Prophets; Wisdom; biblical narrative and poetry; biblical theology and spirituality; biblical ethics; literature of the New Testament; exegesis; hermeneutics; biblical languages. **SELECTED PUBLICATIONS** Auth, Listen, O Peoples, All of You: Justice and Economic Issues in Micah 1-3, in Bible Today, 94; auth, Will and Testament, Tribes, Plagues,Nations, Exodus, in Pastoral Dictionary of Biblical Theology, Liturgical, 96; auth, Abraham and Sarah: Called, Uprooted, and Graced, in Vocations and Prayer, 97; auth, Ask the Animals, and They Will Teach You: the Gift of Wisdom and the Natural World, in Bible Today, 97; auth, Compassion: The Embrace of Life, in Mast, 97; auth, Moses: Wonderfully Surprised, in Vocations and Prayer, 97; auth, Samuel: Called from Slumber to Prophecy, in Vocations and Prayer, 97; auth, Jeremiah: Called from the Womb, in Vocations and Prayer, 98; auth, Metaphorical Language and the Expression of Love in the Song of Songs, in Bible Today, 98; The Whore of Ezekiel 16: The Impact and Ramifications of Gender-Specific Metaphors in Light of Biblical Law and Divine Judgment, in Gender and Law in the Hebrew Bible and Ancient Near East, Sheffield Academic, 98; contrib, Eerdmans Dictionary of the Bible, Eerdmans, 99; auth, The Prophets: A Liberation Critical Reading, Fortress, 99; auth, All Creation Is Groaning, Liturgical, 99. **CONTACT ADDRESS** Dept of Theology, Univ of Portland, 5000 N Willamette Blvd, Portland, OR, 97203-5798. **EMAIL** dempsey@up.edu

DEMPSEY, JOSEPH P.
PERSONAL Born 03/08/1930, Nashville, NC, m, 1958 **DISCIPLINE** THEOLOGY **EDUCATION** Fayetteville State Univ, BS 1958; Shaw Div Sch, BD 1964; NC Cen Univ, MA 1971; Shaw Div Sch, MDiv 1972; Jacksonville Theological Seminary, Florida, DTh, 1982; Faith Evangelical Lutheran Seminary, Tacoma WA, DMin 1988. **CAREER** Pastor various locations since 1961; NC CEN UNIV, INSTRUCTOR 1971-, ASSOC DIR 1988-; Pine Grove Baptist Church, Creedmoor NC, pastor 1986-87; Elementary & High School, instructor; Worthdale United Baptist Church Raleigh, NC, pastor; NCCU Counseling Ctr, assoc dir, currently; NCCU, GRAD SCHOOL OF EDUCATION, ADJUNCT ASST PROF, 1991-. **HONORS AND AWARDS** Teacher of t e Yr 1967; Raleigh, NC Christian Family of the Yr 1972; Outstanding Serv Award NC Central Univ 1973-74. **MEMBERSHIPS** Mem Min Bd Wake Baptist Assn 1964; NC Personnel & Guid Assn; Am Personnel & Guid Assn; Exec Com, Wake Co Dem Party; bd dir NC General Baptist Con, bd dir YMCA 1967-; bd dir Comm Day Carde Center; mem Goals for Raleigh Educ Outreach; mem The Raleigh-Wake Martin Luther King Celebration Comm 1989. **CONTACT ADDRESS** Grad Sch of Education, NCCU, PO Box 19688, Durham, NC, 27707.

DEMY, TIMOTHY J.
PERSONAL Born 12/06/1954, Brownsville, TX, m, 1978 **DISCIPLINE** THEOLOGY & HISTORY **EDUCATION** Tex Christian Univ, BA, 77; Dallas Theol Sem, Th M, 81, ThD, 90; Salve Regina Univ, MA, 90; Univ Tex at Arlington, MA, 94. **CAREER** Military chaplain, 81-; adj instr, Naval War Col, 96-. **HONORS AND AWARDS** Phi Alpha Theta; Outstanding Young Men in Amer; Who's Who in the South and Southwest; numerous military awards. **MEMBERSHIPS** Evang Theol Soc; Soc of Bibl Lit; Orgn of Amer Hist; Ctr for Bioethics and Human Dignity. **RESEARCH** Bioethics; The crusades; Evangelical theology; Church history. **SELECTED PUBLICATIONS** Co-auth, Basic Questions on Suicide and Euthanasia, Basic Questions on End of Life Decisions, Basic Questions on Sexuality and Reproductive Technology, Basic Questions on Alternative Medicine, Kregel Publ, 98; co-ed, Suicide: A Christian Response, Kregel Publ, 98; co-auth, Maximizing Your Marriage, Kregel Publ, 98; co-auth, Prophecy Watch, Harvest House, 98; auth, Onward Christian Soldiers? Christian Perspectives on War, The Voice, 98; auth, Suicide and the Christian Worldview, Conservative Theol Jour, 97; auth, Chaplain Walter Colton and the California Gold Rush, Navy Chaplain, 97; co-auth, The Coming Cashless Society, Harvest House, 96; auth, A Dictionary of Premillennial Theology, Kregel Books, 96; co-ed, When the Trumpet Sounds!, Harvest House, 95; auth, Blackwell's Dictionary of Evangelical Biography, Blackwells, 95; co-auth, The Rapture and an Early Medieval Citation, Bibliotheca Sacra, 95. **CONTACT ADDRESS** 7 Ellen Rd., Middletown, RI, 02842. **EMAIL** tdemy@wsii.com

DEN OUDEN, BERNARD
DISCIPLINE PHILOSOPHY **EDUCATION** Calvin Col, BA; Hartford Col, MA, PhD. **CAREER** Prof, Univ of Hartford. **RESEARCH** 19th century philos; philos of lang; nature philos of creativity; Third World develop. **SELECTED PUBLICATIONS** Auth, The Fusion of Naturalism and Humanism Language and Creativity Reason; Will, Creativity, and Time. **CONTACT ADDRESS** Philos Dept, Univ Hartford, Bloomfield Ave, PO Box 200, W Hartford, CT, 06117.

DENBY, DAVID A.
PERSONAL Born 12/24/1963, Cheltenham, United Kingdom, m, 1994 **DISCIPLINE** PHILOSOPHY **EDUCATION** Univ Coll, London Univ, BA, 86; Univ Oxford, B Philos, 88; Univ Mass, PhD, 97. **CAREER** Instr, Univ Mass, 90-94; instr, Randolph-Macon Woman's Coll, 95; instr, Dartmouth Coll, 95; Suffolk Univ, Boston, 96-; Tufts Univ Medford, 96-. **HONORS AND AWARDS** British Acad Fel, 86-88; Univ Fel, Univ Mass, 91-92. **MEMBERSHIPS** Am Philos Asn. **RESEARCH** Metaphysics; Philosophy of language; Logic. **CONTACT ADDRESS** 8 Rocky Nook Terrace, Jamaica Plain, MA, 02130. **EMAIL** David.Denby2@gte.net

DENICOLA, ROBERT C.
PERSONAL Born 10/15/1949, Union City, NJ, m, 1987, 2 children **DISCIPLINE** LAW **EDUCATION** Princeton Univ, BSE, 71; Harvard Univ, JD, 74, LLB, 76. **CAREER** Law, Univ Nebr-Lincoln, 76- **HONORS AND AWARDS** Distinguished Prof prize, Univ Nebr Found, 80; Ladas Prize, Int Trademark Asn, 84; ALI Reporter, for: Restatement of Unfair Competition. **MEMBERSHIPS** Copyright Soc US; Am Law Inst. **RESEARCH** Copyright law; trademark law. **SELECTED PUBLICATIONS** Coauth, Restatement of Unfair Competition, ALI, 95; Cases on Copyright, Unfair Competition and Related Topics, Found Press, 98. **CONTACT ADDRESS** Col of Law, Univ of Nebr, Lincoln, NE, 68583-0902. **EMAIL** rdenicol@unlinfo.unl.edu

DENNETT, DANIEL C.
DISCIPLINE PHILOSOPHY **EDUCATION** Harvard Univ, BA, 63; Oxford, D Phil, 65. **CAREER** Lectr, Oxford Col Tech, 64-65; asst prof, 65-70, assoc prof, 70-71, Univ Calif, Irvine; vis asst prof, 68, assoc prof, 71-75, PROF, 75-, chair, dept philos, 76-82, co-dir, curricular software studio, 85-89, DIST PROF ARTS, SCIS, 85-, DIR CTR COGNITIVE STUDS, 85-, TUFTS UNIV; vis assoc prof, Harvard Univ, 73; vis prof, Univ Pittsburgh, 75; vis lectr, Oxford Univ, 79. **MEMBERSHIPS** Acad Scientiarum et Artum Europaea; Am Acad ARtr, Scis; Am Asn Artificial Intelligence; Am Asn Univ Profs; Am Philos Asn; Cognitive Sci Soc; Counc Philos Studs; Memory Disorder Soc; Soc for Philos, Psychol. **SELECTED PUBLICATIONS** Auth, Elbow Room: The Varieties of Free Will Worth Wanting, MIT Press, Oxford Univ Press, 84, German ed, 86, Span ed, 92; auth, The Intentional Stance, MIT Press/A Bradford Book, 87, Fr ed, 90, Span ed, 91; auth, Consciousness Explained, Little Brown, 91, Penguin, 92, Dutch, It, Fr, Ger, Gr eds, 93; auth, Darwin's Dangerous Idea, Simon & Schuster, 95; auth, Kinds of Minds, Basic Books, 96. **CONTACT ADDRESS** Ctr Cognitive Studies, Tufts Univ, 11 Miner Hall, Medford, MA, 02155. **EMAIL** ddennett@tufts.edu

DENNY, FRED
DISCIPLINE RELIGIOUS STUDIES **EDUCATION** Univ Chicago, PhD. **CAREER** Prof. **RESEARCH** Qur'anic studies; comparative ritual; Islamic education in Malaysia and Indonesia; Islam and Muslim communities in North America. **SELECTED PUBLICATIONS** Auth, An Introduction to Islam; Islamic Theology in the New World: Some Issues and Prospects; Islam in the Americas; Qur'anic Recitation. **CONTACT ADDRESS** Religious Studies Dept, Univ of Colorado, Boulder, Boulder, CO, 80309. **EMAIL** Frederick.Denny@Colorado.edu

DENSON, FRED L.
PERSONAL Born 07/19/1937, New Brighton, PA, m **DISCIPLINE** LAW **EDUCATION** Rehsselaer Poly Inst, BChemE 1959; Georgetown U, JD 1966. **CAREER** WOKR-TV ABC, host black dimensions 1972-; Urban League of Rochester, exec dir 1970-71; Eastman Kodak Co, atty 1967-70. **HONORS AND AWARDS** Rochester Comm Serv Awd 1974-76. **MEMBERSHIPS** Bd mem NYS Pub Employ Relat Bd; exec dir Nat Patent Law Assn; dir Armarco Mktg; pres Genessee Region Home Care Assn; chmn adv counc NYS Div of Human Rights Am Bar Assn; Nat Bar Assn; Monroe Co Bar Assn; Nat Patent Law Assn; Am Arbitraton Assn **SELECTED PUBLICATIONS** Author, Know Your Town Justice Court; Minority Involvement in the US Patent System. **CONTACT ADDRESS** 14 E Main St, Webster, NY, 14580.

DENZEY, NICOLA
DISCIPLINE RELIGION **EDUCATION** Princeton Univ, PhD, 98. **CAREER** Vis Asst prof, Bowdoin Col, 97-98; vis asst prof, Skidmore Col, 98-99; Andrew Mellon postdoctoral fel, Northwestern Univ, 99-2001. **HONORS AND AWARDS** Lilly fel, Wabash Ctr for Tchg and Lrng, 98-2001; Andrew Mellon postdoctoral fel, Northwestern Univ, 99-2001. **MEMBERSHIPS** AAR/SBL; AAUW; Can Soc for Patristic Stud; Can Soc for Bibl Stud; Can Soc for Stud in Relig. **RESEARCH** Early heterodox forms of Christianity; social history of early Christianity; religions in the Greco-Roman world. **CONTACT ADDRESS** Ladd Hall, Skidmore Col, Saratoga Springs, NY, 12966. **EMAIL** ndenzey@skidmore.edu

DEPASCUALE, JUAN E.
PERSONAL Born 08/13/1950, Rio Cuarto, Argentina, m, 1989, 4 children **DISCIPLINE** PHILOSOPHY **EDUCATION** Queens Col, BA, 73; Brown Univ, MA, 80, PhD, 87; Louvain Univ, Belgium, LPhil, 81. **CAREER** Tchg fel, Brown Univ, 78-80; instr, Notre Dame Univ, 80-84; assoc prof, Kenyon Col, 84- . **HONORS AND AWARDS** Alum awd disting tchg, Kenyon, 94; Amer Philos asn awd for excellence in tchg Philos, 95; Telluride found tchg grant, 97. **MEMBERSHIPS** Amer Philos Asn. **RESEARCH** Contemporary Continental Philosophy; Philosophy of art; Philosophy of Religion. **CONTACT ADDRESS** Dept of Philosophy, Kenyon Col, Gambier, OH, 43022. **EMAIL** depascuale@kenyon.edu

DEPAUL, MICHAEL R.
DISCIPLINE PHILOSOPHY **EDUCATION** Univ Notre Dame, BA, 76; Ohio St Univ, MA, 79; Brown Univ, PhD, 83. **CAREER** Assoc prof. **RESEARCH** Ethics; epistemology. **SELECTED PUBLICATIONS** Auth, Two Conceptions of Coherence Methods in Ethics, Mind, 87; The Problem of the Criterion and Coherence Methods in Ethics, Can J Philos, 88; Naivete and Corruption in Moral Inquiry, Philos Phenomenological Res, 88; Argument and Perception: The Role of Literature in Moral Inquiry, J Philos, 88; Moral Statuses, Australasian J Philos, 88; The Highest Moral Knowledge and the Truth Behind Moral Internalism, S J Philos, 90; Balance and Refinement: Beyond Coherentism in Moral Inquiry, 93. **CONTACT ADDRESS** Philosophy Dept, Univ of Notre Dame, 336/7 O'Shaughnessy, Notre Dame, IN, 46556. **EMAIL** depaul.1@nd.edu

DER OTTER, SANDRA
DISCIPLINE PHILOSOPHY **EDUCATION** Oxford Univ, DPhil, 90. **CAREER** Dept Philos, Queen's Univ **RESEARCH** Intellectual, cultural, gender and imperial history of late 18th and 19th century Britain. **SELECTED PUBLICATIONS** Auth, The British Idealists, Oxford, 96. **CONTACT ADDRESS** Philosophy Dept, Queen's Univ, Kingston, ON, K7L 3N6. **EMAIL** denotter@qucdn.queensu.ca

DERBY, DANIEL H.
DISCIPLINE LAW **EDUCATION** Univ IL, BA, 74; DePaul Univ, JD, 78; Columbia Univ, 80, LLM. **CAREER** Judicial Law Clk, IL Appellate Ct; lectr, DePaul Univ; asst prof, Univ Akron; prof Law, Touro Col. **MEMBERSHIPS** Int Asn Penal Law. **SELECTED PUBLICATIONS** Author of articles on international criminal law and conflicts of law. **CONTACT ADDRESS** Touro Col, Brooklyn, NY, 11230. **EMAIL** DanD@tourolaw.edu

DERDAK, THOMAS J.
DISCIPLINE PHILOSOPHY **EDUCATION** Butler Univ Indianapolis, BA; Univ Chicago, MA, PhD. **CAREER** Adj prof, Loyola Univ, 79-; exec dir, Global Alliance for Africa. **RESEARCH** Philosophy of religion; aesthetics; ethics; epistemology. **SELECTED PUBLICATIONS** Publ articles on res interest. **CONTACT ADDRESS** Dept of Philosophy, Loyola Univ, Chicago, 820 N. Michigan Ave., Chicago, IL, 60611.

DERR, THOMAS SIEGER
PERSONAL Born 06/18/1931, Boston, MA, m, 1956, 5 children **DISCIPLINE** SOCIAL ETHICS, AMERICAN RELIGIOUS HISTORY **EDUCATION** Harvard Univ, AB, 53; Union Theol Sem, NY, MDiv, 56; Columbia Univ, PhD, 72. **CAREER** Asst chaplain, Stanford Univ, 56-59; asst chaplain, 63-65, from asst prof to assoc prof relig, 66-76, dir, Jr Yr Int Studies, Geneva, Switz, 70-71 & 77-78, Prof Relig, Smith Col, 77-; Consult, Dept Church & Soc, World Coun Churches, Geneva, 66-, comn faith & order, 75-; mem fac, Rush Med Col, Chicago, 80-84; fel, Inst Adv Study Relig, Univ Chicago, 81. **MEMBERSHIPS** Soc Christian Ethics. **RESEARCH** Ecumenical studies; environmental ethics; med ethics. **SELECTED PUBLICATIONS** Auth, Ecology and Human Need, Westminster, 75; coauth, Church, State and Politics, The Roscoe Pound-American Trial Lawyer Found, 81; auth, Barriers to Ecumenism: The Holy See and the World Council of Churches on Social Questions, Orbis Books, 83; coauth, Believable Futures for American Protestantism, Eerdmans, 88; Creation at Risk, Eerdmans, 95; author, Environmental Ethics and Christian Humanism, Abingdon, 96. **CONTACT ADDRESS** Dept of Relig, Smith Col, Northampton, MA, 01063-0001. **EMAIL** tderr@smith.edu

DERSHOWITZ, ALAN MORTON
PERSONAL Born 09/01/1938, Brooklyn, NY, d, 2 children **DISCIPLINE** LAW **EDUCATION** Brooklyn Col, BA, 59; Yale Univ, LLB, 62. **CAREER** Asst prof criminal law, 64-67, PROF LAW, LAW SCH, HARVARD UNIV, 67-, Consult human rights and media, Ford Found, 77-78; mem adv panel sentencing and parole, Deputy Mayor for Criminal Justice, NY, 77-78; Guggenheim Found fel, 78-79. **RESEARCH** Criminal law; international human rights; prediction and prevention of crime. **SELECTED PUBLICATIONS** Auth, Inadmissible Lies, Aba J, Vol 81, 95; Court Tv--Its Commercialism Hides its Potential, Aba J, Vol 80, 94. **CONTACT ADDRESS** Law Sch, Harvard Univ, 1525 Massachusetts, Cambridge, MA, 02138-2903.

DESAUTELS, PEGGY
PERSONAL Born 12/01/1955, Traverse City, MI, m, 1997, 2 children **DISCIPLINE** PHILOSOPHY **EDUCATION** Principia Col, BA, 77; Wash Univ, MS, 88, MA, 93, PhD, 95. **CAREER** Asst prof, Principia Col, 81-89, 94-95; teaching fel, Wash Univ, 90-94; teaching fel, 95-96, asst prof, 96-; asst dir of Ethics Center, 97-. **HONORS AND AWARDS** Olin Fel for Women, Wash Univ, 90-94; Frances Elvidge Post-Doctoral Fel, Univ of South Fl, 95-96. **MEMBERSHIPS** Am Philos Asn; Southern Soc for Philos and Psychol **RESEARCH** Biomedical ethics; cognitive science; ethical theory. **SELECTED PUBLICATIONS** Co-auth, Praying for a Cure: When Medical and Religious Practices Conflict, 99; auth, "Christian Science, Rational Choice, and Alternative World Views," 98; "Religious Women, Medical Settings, and Moral Risk," 99; "Gestalt Shifts in Moral Perception," 96; "Two Types of Theories: The Impact on Churchland's 'Perceptual Plasticity'," 95; "Psychologies of Moral Perceivers," 98. **CONTACT ADDRESS** Ethics Center, Univ of South Florida, 100 5th Ave S, St. Petersburg, FL, 33701. **EMAIL** desautel@bayflash.stpt.usf.edu

DESCHNER, JOHN
PERSONAL Born 10/23/1923, Stillwater, MN, m, 1949, 3 children **DISCIPLINE** THEOLOGY **EDUCATION** Univ Tex, BA, 44; Yale Univ, BD, 47; Univ Basel, DTheol, 60. **CAREER** From asst prof to assoc prof, 56-62, PROF THEOL AND GRAD PROG RELIG STUDIES, PERKINS SCH THEOL, SOUTHERN METHODIST UNIV, 62-, Vchmn, World Univ Serv, 52-53; vchmn, World Student Christian Fedn, 52-56; Am Asn Theol Schs fel, Heidelberg, 62-63; deleg gen conf, United Methodist Church, 68 and 70; DELEG, IV AND V ASSEMBLIES AND MEM, COMN FAITH AND ORDER, WORLD COUN CHURCHES, 68-, chmn theol comn consult church union, 73-75; vmoderator, Comn Faith Order, 76-. **HONORS AND AWARDS** DD, Southwestern Univ, 68. **MEMBERSHIPS** Am Theol Soc; fel Soc Relig Higher Educ; Am Acad Relig. **RESEARCH** Systematic theology; history of doctrine; ecumenics. **SELECTED PUBLICATIONS** Auth, What Could Santiago Accomplish, Ecumenical Rev, Vol 45, 93. **CONTACT ADDRESS** Perkins Sch of Theol, Southern Methodist Univ, Dallas, TX, 75275.

DESLAURIERS, MARGUERITE
DISCIPLINE PHILOSOPHY **EDUCATION** McGill Univ, BA; Univ Toronto, MA, PhD. **RESEARCH** Ancient philos; feminist theory. **SELECTED PUBLICATIONS** Auth, Social and civic implications of Aristotle's Notion of Authority, Sheffield, 93; rev, Principles and Premises: Interpreting Aristotle's Posterior Analytics, Can Jour Philos, 93; auth, Plato and Aristotle on Division and Definition, 91; auth, Aristotle's Four Types of Definition, 90; auth, Character and Explanation in Aristotle's Ethics and Poetics, 90. **CONTACT ADDRESS** Philosophy Dept, McGill Univ, 845 Sherbrooke St, Montreal, PQ, H3A 2T5.

DESMANGLES, LESLIE GERALD
PERSONAL Born 09/28/1941, Port-au-Prince, Haiti, m, 1968, 2 children **DISCIPLINE** ANTHROPOLOGY OF RELIGION **EDUCATION** Eastern Col, BA, 64; Eastern Baptist Theol Sem, MDiv, 67; Temple Univ, PhD(anthop relig), 75. **CAREER** Instr, Eastern Col, 69-70; instr, Ohio Wesleyan Univ, 70-75 & asst prof, 75-76; asst prof, DePaul Univ, 76-78; assoc prof Relig, Trinity Col, 78-, instr, Ohio Univ, 75-76; consult, Miami Univ of Ohio, 73-74 & Hispanic Health Coun of Hartford, 81-; Nat Endowment for Humanities & Trinity Col res grant, 80; dir, Prog Intercult Studies, Trinity Col, 81-. **MEMBERSHIPS** Asn Sociol Relig; Am Acad Relig; Caribbean Studies Asn; Pres, Haitian Studies Asn. **RESEARCH** African traditional religions; Caribbean religions. **SELECTED PUBLICATIONS** Auth, African interpretations of the Christian cross in Haitian Vodun, Sociol Analysis, 76; Rites baptismaux: Symbiose du Vodou et du Catholicisme a Haiti, Concilium, 77; The way of Vodun death, J Relig Thought, 80; Vodun baptismal rites, J Inter-Denominational Theol Ctr, 81; The Faces of the Gods: Vodou and Roman Catholicism in Haiti, Univ of NC Press, 93. **CONTACT ADDRESS** Dept Relig & Intercult, Trinity Col, 300 Summit St, Hartford, CT, 06106-3186. **EMAIL** leslie.desmangles@mail.trincoll.edu

DESMOND, LAWRENCE ARTHUR
PERSONAL Born 12/07/1929, St. John, NB, Canada, m, 1959, 1 child **DISCIPLINE** MEDIEVAL CHURCH HISTORY **EDUCATION** St Thomas Univ, NB, BA, 52; Fordham Univ, MA, 54, PhD (hist), 67. **CAREER** From asst prof to assoc prof hist, St Paul's Col, Man, 59-69, dean, 74-80, ASSOC PROF HIST, UNIV MAN, 69-, Can Counc fel, 69-70. **MEMBERSHIPS** Medieval Acad Am; Can Cath Hist Asn (vpres, 68-69); Selden Soc; Am Comt Irish Studies. **RESEARCH** Medieval Cistercian history; English legal history; New Brunswick local history. **SELECTED PUBLICATIONS** Auth, ATLAS OF CISTERCIAN LANDS IN WALES - WILLIAMS,DH/, SPECULUM-A J MEDIEVAL STUDIES, Vol 68, 1993 ATLAS OF CISTERCIAN LANDS IN WALES - WILLIAMS,DH/, SPECULUM-A J MEDIEVAL STUDIES, Vol 68, 1993 **CONTACT ADDRESS** Off of Dean, St Paul's Col Univ of Man, Winnipeg, MB, R3T 2M6.

DESPLAND, MICHEL
PERSONAL Born 07/25/1936, Lausanne, Switzerland **DISCIPLINE** RELIGION **EDUCATION** Univ Lausanne, LTheol, 58; Harvard Univ, ThD, 66. **CAREER** PROF RELIGION, CONCORDIA UNIV, 74-. **HONORS AND AWARDS** Royal Soc Can, 97. **SELECTED PUBLICATIONS** Auth, Kant on History and Religion, 73; auth, Le Choc des Morales, 73; auth, La Religion en Occident, 79; auth, The Education of Desire: Plato and the Philosophy of Religion, 85; auth, Christianisme: dossier corps, 87; auth, Les sciences religieuses au Quebec depuis 1972, 88; auth, La tradition francaise en sciences religieuses, 91; auth, Religion in History, 92; auth, Reading an Erased Code: Romantic Religion and French Literary Aesthetics, 94. **CONTACT ADDRESS** Dept of Religion, Concordia Univ, Montreal, 1455 Boul de Maisonneuve O, Montreal, PQ, H3G 1M8.

DETERDING, PAUL E.
PERSONAL Born 02/19/1953, Jacksonville, IL, m, 1989, 3 children **DISCIPLINE** EXEGETICAL THEOLOGY **EDUCATION** Concordia Seminary, Th D, 81. **CAREER** Pastor, Our Savior Lutheran Church, Satellite Beach Fla, 81-94; pastor, Christ Lutheran Church, Jackson Miss, 94-. **MEMBERSHIPS** Soc Bibl Lit **RESEARCH** Bible; New Testament **SELECTED PUBLICATIONS** Daniel: Encouragement for Faith, God's Word for Today, Concordia Pub, 96; bk revs, Concordia Theological Quarterly, 93, 94, 95; The New Testament View of Time and History, Concordia jour, 95. **CONTACT ADDRESS** 4423 I-55 North, Jackson, MS, 39206.

DETLEFSEN, MICHAEL
PERSONAL Born 10/20/1948, Scottsbluff, NE, m, 1969, 2 children **DISCIPLINE** PHILOSOPHY **EDUCATION** Wheaton Col, AB, 71; Johns Hopkins Univ, PhD, 75. **CAREER** Prof. **RESEARCH** Logic; philosophy of mathematics. **SELECTED PUBLICATIONS** Auth, Hilbert's Program, 86; Proof, Logic, Formalization, 91; Proof and Knowledge in Mathematics, 91; Wright on the Non-mechanizability of Intuitionist Reasoning, Philos Mathematica, 95; Philosophy of Mathematics in the 20th Century, Philos Sci, 96. **CONTACT ADDRESS** Philosophy Dept, Univ of Notre Dame, 336/7 O'Shaughnessy, Notre Dame, IN, 46556. **EMAIL** detlefsen.1@nd.edu

DEUTSCH, CELIA
DISCIPLINE RELIGION **EDUCATION** Univ Toronto, MA, PhD. **CAREER** Adj assoc prof. **RESEARCH** Early Judaism; early Christianity. **SELECTED PUBLICATIONS** Auth, Hidden Wisdom and the Easy Yoke and Lady Wisdom, Jesus and the Sages. **CONTACT ADDRESS** Dept of Religion, Columbia Col, New York, 2960 Broadway, New York, NY, 10027-6902. **EMAIL** cdeutsch@barnard.colubia.edu

DEUTSCH, ELIOT
PERSONAL Born 01/08/1931 **DISCIPLINE** PHILOSOPHY **EDUCATION** Univ Wisc, BS, 52; Univ Chicago, 52; Harvard Univ, 52-53; Columbia Univ, PhD, 60. **CAREER** Prof, Rensselaer Polytechnic Inst, 60-67; vis prof, Univ Chicago, 66; vis prof, Harvard Univ, 85; Dir, 6th East-West Philosopher's Conf, 87-89; Ed, Philos East & West, 67-87; Chmn, Dept Philos, Univ Hawaii, 86-87, 94, grad chmn, Philos, 91-96; prof, philos, Univ Hawaii, 86- **HONORS AND AWARDS** Faculty Fel, Am Inst of Indian Stud, 63-64; NY St Faculty Schol, 65-67; NEH Sr Fel, 73-74; **MEMBERSHIPS** Soc for Asian and Comparative Philos; Amer Philos Assn; Amer Soc for Aesthetics; Assn for Asian Studies; Metaphysical Soc of Amer; Brit Soc for Aesthetics; Int Metaphysical Soc. **SELECTED PUBLICATIONS** Auth, Bhagavad: An English Translation from the Sanskrit with Introductory Essays and Philosophical Analyses, Gita, Holt, Rinehart & Winston, 68; auth, Advaita Vedanta: A Philosophical Reconstruction, East-West Ctr, 69; auth, Humanity and Divinity: An Essay in Comparative Metaphysics, Univ Hawaii, 70; coauth, A Sourcebook of Advaita Vedanta, Univ Hawaii, 71; auth, Studies in Comparative Aesthetics, Univ Hawaii, 75; auth, On Truth: An Ontological Theory, Univ Hawaii, 79; auth, Personhood, Creativity and Freedom, Univ Hawaii, 82; coed, Interpreting Across Boundaries: New Essays in Comparative Philosophy, Princeton Univ, 88; ed, Culture and Modernity, Univ Hawaii, 91; auth, Creative Being: The Crafting of Person and World, Univ Hawaii, 92; auth, Religion and Spirituality, St Univ NY, 95; auth, Essays on the Nature of Art, St Univ NY, 96; Introduction to World Philosophies, Prentice-Hall, 96; auth, Companion to World Philosophies, Blackwell, 97; auth, Time and History: East and West, Radhakrishna Centenary Vol, 90; auth, Community as Ritual Participation, On Community, 91; auth, Concept of the Body, Self as Body in Asian Thought & Practice, St Univ NY, 92; auth, On the Comparative Study of the Self, Selves, People and Persons, Notre Dame Univ, 92; auth, The Person as Knower and Known, J of Indian Coun of Philos Res, 93; auth, Truth and Mythology, Myths & Fictions, EJ Brill, 93; auth, Creative Friendship, The Changing Face of Friendship, Univ Notre Dame, 94; auth, Self-Deception: A Comparative Study, Self & Deception, St Univ NY, 96; auth, Foreword to Alexander Eliot, The Timeless Myths, Continuum, 96; auth, Seyyed Hossein Nasr's Philosophy of Art, Libr of Living Philosophers, 96. **CONTACT ADDRESS** 1245 Aloha Oe Dr., Kailua, HI, 96734.

DEVENISH, PHILIP EDWARD
PERSONAL Born 02/09/1946, Bridgeport, CT, m, 1968, 1 child **DISCIPLINE** CHRISTIAN THEOLOGY **EDUCATION** Hamilton Col, AB, 67; Southern Methodist Univ, PhD (relig), 77. **CAREER** ASST PROF THEOL, UNIV NOTRE DAME, 77-, Nat Endowment for the Humanities fel, 79; travel fel, Zahm Found, Notre Dame, 81. **SELECTED PUBLICATIONS** Auth, Sharing Faith--A Comprehensive Approach to Religious Education and Pastoral Ministry, J Rel, Vol 74, 94; The Sovereignty of Jesus and the Sovereignty of God, Theol Today, Vol 53, ; Evil Revisited--Responses and Reconsiderations, J Rel, Vol 73, 93; Biblical Faith and Natural Theology, J Rel, Vol 74, 94; Testimony--A Philosophical Study, J Rel, Vol 73, 93. **CONTACT ADDRESS** 1726 N Sherman, South Bend, IN, 46616.

DEVIDI, DAVE
DISCIPLINE PHILOSOPHY **EDUCATION** Univ Western Ontario, PhD, 94. **RESEARCH** Mathematical and philosophical logic; philosophy of mathematics; philosophy of language and metaphysics; history of analytic philosophy; philosophy of science. **SELECTED PUBLICATIONS** Auth, pub(s) on relationship between ontological and logical principles, and relationship between non-classical logics and anti-realism. **CONTACT ADDRESS** Dept of Philosophy, Waterloo Univ, 200 University Ave W, Waterloo, ON, N2L 3G1. **EMAIL** ddevidi@uwaterloo.ca

DEVINE, PHILIP E.
PERSONAL Born 12/18/1944, Evanston, IL, m, 1986 **DISCIPLINE** PHILOSOPHY **EDUCATION** Yale Univ, BA cum laude, 66; Univ CA, Berkeley, PhD, 71; fel, Law and Philos, Harvard Law School, 80-81. **CAREER** Prof in res, Stonehill Col, 87-89; instr, Tufts Univ, 88; instr, continuing ed, Emerson Col, 88-89; ADJUNCT ASST PROF TO PROF, PROVIDENCE COL, 90-. **HONORS AND AWARDS** Listed, Who's Who in the East, 26th ed; testified by invitation before the President's Commission on Bioethics, on the care of handicapped newborns, Jan 82. **MEMBERSHIPS** Amer Philos Assoc; Amer Cath Philos Assoc; Soc Christian Philos; RI Humanities Forum; Nat Assoc of Scholars; RI Assoc of Scholars, pres, 97-. **RESEARCH** Ethics; metaphysics; social and political philos. **SELECTED PUBLICATIONS** Auth, The Ethics of Homicide, Cornell Univ Press, 78, paperback ed with new preface, Notre Dame Univ Press, 90; Theory and Practice in Ethics, Moral Theory and Moral Judgement, Baruch Brody, ed, Kluwer Academic (Philos and Medicine Series), 88; Relativism, Nihilism, and God, Univ Notre Dame Press, 89; Articles on double effect and euthanasia, in The Cambridge Dictionary of Philosophy, Robert Audi, ed, Cambridge Univ Press, 95; A Fallacious Argument Against Moral Absolutes, Argumentation, Nov 95; Human Diversity and the Culture Wars: A Philosophical Examination of Contemporary Cultural Conflict, Praeger, 96; Creation vs Evolution, Relig Studies, 96; Academic Freedom in the Postmodern World, Public Affairs Quart, July 96; 'Conservative' Views on Abortion, in New Essays on Abortion and Bioethics, Rem Edwards, ed, Advances in Bioethics, vol 2, JAI Press, 97; Homicide, Criminal vs Excusable, and Publish-or-Perish Syndrome, in The Encyclopedia of Applied Ethics, Academic Press, vols 2 and 3, 98. **CONTACT ADDRESS** Dept Philos, Providence Col, River at Eaton Streets, Providence, RI, 02981. **EMAIL** pdevine@providence.edu

DEVITT, MICHAEL
PERSONAL Born 09/29/1938, Kuala Lumpur, Malaysia, m, 2 children **DISCIPLINE** PHILOSOPHY **EDUCATION** Univ Sydney, BA, 66; Harvard Univ, MA, 70, PhD, 72. **CAREER** Lect, assoc prof, 71-87, Univ of Sydney; prof, 88-, Univ of Maryland. **HONORS AND AWARDS** Fel of Australian Academy of Humanities **MEMBERSHIPS** APA; Australasian Asn of Phil **RESEARCH** Philosophy of language, philosophy of mind/psychology, metaphysics. **SELECTED PUBLICATIONS** Auth, Designation, NY Columbia Univ Press, 81; auth, Realism and Truth, Oxford Basil Blackwell, 84; coauth, Language and Reality An Introduction to the Philosophy of Language, Oxford Basil Blackwell, 87; auth, Coming to Our Senses A Naturalistic Program for Semantic Localism, Cambridge Univ Press, 96; art, Localism and Analyticity, Phil and Phenom Res, 93; art, A Critique of the Case for Semantic Holism, Phil Persp 7 Language and Logic, 93; art, Semantic Localism Who Needs a Principled Basis, Phil and the Cogn Sciences, 94; art, the Methodology of Naturalistic Semantics, Jour of Phil, 94; art, The Metaphysics of Nonfactualism, Phil Persp 10 Metaphysics, 96; art, Meanings and Psychology A Response to Mark Richard, Nous 31, 97; art, Precis of Coming to Our Senses A Naturalistic Program for Semantic Localism, Phil Issues 8, 97; art, A Priori Convictions about Psychology A Response to Sosa and Taylor, Phil Issues 8, 97; art, On Determining Reference, Sprache und Denken Language and Thought, 97; art, Responses to the Maribor Papers, Maribor Papers in Naturalized Semantics, 98; art, Putting Metaphysics First A Response to James Tomberlin, Phil Persp 12 Language Mind and Ontology, 98; art, Reference, Routledge Encyl of Phil, vol 8, 98; art, Naturalism and the Priori, Phil Stud 92, 98. **CONTACT ADDRESS** Dept of Philosophy, Univ of Maryland, College Park, MD, 20742. **EMAIL** devitt@umiacs.umd.edu

DEVOS, JEAN
PERSONAL Paris, France, m, 1990, 1 child **DISCIPLINE** PHILOSOPHY **EDUCATION** Univ Paris, MA, 86, PhD, 88. **CAREER** Prof, Lycee Bayen, 90-91; Lycee Delamare-Deboutteville, 91-93; French Intl School, 93-. **HONORS AND AWARDS** Vis res, Georgetown Univ, 93-99. **MEMBERSHIPS** Am Philos Asn; Can Philos Asn; Int Asn for Philos and Lit; Metaphysical Soc of Am; MLA; North-Am Sartre Soc; World Phenomenol Inst. **RESEARCH** Philosophy. **CONTACT ADDRESS** French Intl Sch, 9802 Broad St, Bethesda, MD, 20814. **EMAIL** j.devos@erols.com

DEVRIES, DAWN A .
PERSONAL Born 06/11/1961, Hammond, IN, m, 1990, 1 child **DISCIPLINE** THEOLOGY **EDUCATION** Univ Chicago, BA, 83, MA, 84, PhD (theology), 94. **CAREER** Asst prof, San Francisco Theol Sem, 88-90; asst and assoc prof, McCormick Theol Sem, 90-95; assoc prof, Union Theol Sem, Richmond, VA, 95-97; prof, Union Theol Sem, Richmond, VA, 97-. **HONORS AND AWARDS** Charlotte W Newcombe fel, 88-89; Deutscher Akademische Austauschdienst, 88-89; Henry W Aluce, III, fel, 97-98. **MEMBERSHIPS** Am Academy of Relig; Am Soc Church Hist; Schleirmachen Gesellschaft. **RESEARCH** History of Christian thought, especially Continental Reformation-modern systematic theology; reformed tradition; history of preaching; women's studies. **SELECTED PUBLICATIONS** Trans and ed, Servant of the Word: Selected Sermons of Friedrich Schleiermacher, Fortress Press, 87; auth, Jesus Christ in the Preaching of Calvin and Schleiermachen, Westminster John Knox, 96. **CONTACT ADDRESS** Union Theol Sem, 3401 Brook Rd, Richmond, VA, 23227. **EMAIL** ddevries@utsva.edu

DEVRIES, PAUL
PERSONAL Born 10/08/1945, MI, m, 1970, 2 children **DISCIPLINE** RELIGION **EDUCATION** Calvin Col, BA, 67; Univ Va, MA, 76, PhD, 78. **CAREER** Pres, NY Evangel Sem Fund, 97-; interim dean, N Baptist Theol Sem, 96; center dean & prof, Sem East, 94-96; prof & ch, King's Col, 89-94; from asst prof to assoc prof to dir and coord, Wheaton Col, 79-89; asst prof, Lenore-Rhine Col, 78-79; instr, Univ Va, 75-78; instr, Piedmont Va Comm Col, 75-78. **HONORS AND AWARDS** Mellon Found grant; Henry Lucce Found grant; Pew Charitable Trust grant. **MEMBERSHIPS** Am Asn Advan Slavic Studies; Am Philos Asn; Baptist Ministers' Conf Greater NY & Vicinity; Hastings Ethics Ctr; Leadership Excellence, Inc.; NY Christian Higher Educ Consortium; Soc Bus Ethics; Soc Christian Philos. **RESEARCH** Applied ethics; philosophical Hermeneutics; ethics theory; social crisis and change; Hermeneutics of Ethics. **SELECTED PUBLICATIONS** Auth, Business Ethics Applied, 98; auth, Ethics Applied, 98; ed, New York Christian Higher Education Directory, 94, 95, 98; contribur, Religion in New York City, 98. **CONTACT ADDRESS** 49 Somerstown Rd., Ossining, NY, 10562. **EMAIL** NYESfund@aol.com

DEVRIES, WILLEM
DISCIPLINE PHILOSOPHY **EDUCATION** Univ Pittsburgh, PhD, 81. **CAREER** Prof. **SELECTED PUBLICATIONS** Auth, Theory of Mental Activity (rev), Cornell, 88; pubs on Hegel, philosophy of history, and Plato; co-auth, Knowledge, Mind, and the Given: Reading Sellars; Empiricism and the Philosophy of Mind; ed, Reality, Knowledge, and the Good Life: A Historical Introduction to Philosophy, St Martin's Univ, 91. **CONTACT ADDRESS** Philosophy Dept, Univ of New Hampshire, Hamilton Smith Hall, Durham, NH, 03824. **EMAIL** wad@cisunix.unh.edu

DEWART, LESLIE
PERSONAL Born 12/12/1922, Madrid, Spain **DISCIPLINE** RELIGION/PHILOSOPHY **EDUCATION** Univ Toronto, BA, 51, MA, 52, PhD, 54, LLB 79. **CAREER** Prof philos of relig, St Michael's Col, Univ Toronto, 56-88; PROF EMER RELIGION, UNIV TORONTO, 88-; SR RES ASSOC, TRINITY COL, 95-. **SELECTED PUBLICATIONS** Auth, Evolution and Consciousness: The Role of Speech in the Origin and Development of Human Nature, 89. **CONTACT ADDRESS** Trinity Col, Univ Toronto, Toronto, ON, M5S 1K7.

DEWITT, FRANKLIN ROOSEVELT
PERSONAL Born 05/25/1936, Conway, SC, m **DISCIPLINE** LAW **EDUCATION** South Carolina State University, BS Bus Admin 1962, JD 1964; Georgia State Univ, Certificate Housing Mgmt 1973. **CAREER** US Justice Dept, summer law clerk 1963; US Civil Serv Comm Washington DC, trial attny 1965-67; Atlantic Beach SC, town attny; Private practice, attny; National Football League Players Association, contract advisor. **HONORS AND AWARDS** Usher of the Year Cherry Hill Baptist Church 1978; Executive of the Year, 1998. **MEMBERSHIPS** Municipal consult Glenarden MD 1965-67; mem Conway SC City Council 1969-84; delegate Natl Dem Party Conv in Miami Beach FL 1972; appt by gov of SC Spec Study Committed on Home Rule 1972; mem US Court of Appeals for Fourth Circuit, Washington DC Bar, US Supreme Court, mem SC State Bar Assoc, Amer Bar Assoc, Fed Bar Assoc; chmn, bd dir Horry-Georgetown Mental Health Clinic; life mem NAACP; contract advisor, National Football League Player Association; Natl Dem Party Conv, delegate, 1980; National Bar Association, life member; Kappa Alpha Psi, life member. **SELECTED PUBLICATIONS** Auth, Super Redskins Pay Bills in Full, 1992; Washington Just Super, Super Bowl, 1988; History of a Family from Slavery to Freedom, 1985. **CONTACT ADDRESS** 510 Highway 378, Conway, SC, 29526.

DI FILIPPO, TERRY
PERSONAL Bronx, NY, s **DISCIPLINE** PHILOSOPHY, LAW **EDUCATION** Dartmouth Col, AB, 68; SUNY Buffalo, JD, 74, PhD, 87. **CAREER** Practicing Attorney, 75- ; vis asst prof, SUNY Binghamton, 87-88. **RESEARCH** History of Modern Philosophy; Philosophy of Law **SELECTED PUBLICATIONS** Auth, Mitchell Franklin and Roman Law, Telos, 86-87; auth, Pragmatism, Interest Theory & Legal Philosophy, Transactions of CS Pierce Soc, 88. **CONTACT ADDRESS** 434 Himrod St, Brooklyn, NY, 11237. **EMAIL** terence@mindspring.com

DI NORCIA, VINCENT
DISCIPLINE PHILOSOPHY **EDUCATION** Univ Toronto, PhD. **SELECTED PUBLICATIONS** Auth, Ethics, Technology Development and Innovation, Bus Ethics Quarterly, 94; auth, Sciences economiques et nouvelles Ethiques, 93; art, Communication, Power and Time: An Innisian Perspective, Can Jour Polit Sci, 90; art, An Enterprise/Organization Ethic, Bus Prof Ethics Jour, 89; art, The Leverage of Foreigners: Multinationals in South Africa, Jour Bus Ethics, 89. **CONTACT ADDRESS** Philosophy Dept, Laurentian Univ, 935 Ramsey Lake Rd, Sudbury, ON, P3E 2C6.

DICENSO, JAMES
PERSONAL Born 09/13/1957, Montreal, PQ, Canada **DISCIPLINE** RELIGION **EDUCATION** Syracuse Univ, PhD, 87. **CAREER** Assoc Prof, Univ Toronto. **MEMBERSHIPS** Am Acad Rel. **RESEARCH** Modern religious thoughts. **SELECTED PUBLICATIONS** Auth, Symbolism and Subjectivity: A Lacanian Approach to religion, J of Rel, 94; Contemporary Approaches to Psychoanalysis and Religion: Julia Kristeva'a Black Sun, Studies in Re/Sci Rel, 95; The Displaced Origin: Masuzawa's Analysis of Freud, Method and Theory in the Study of Rel, 96; Totem and Taboo and the Constitutive Function of Symbolic Forms, J of Am Acad of Rel, 96; The Other Freud, Religion, Culture, and Psychoanalysis, 99; The Psychoanalytic Movement, The Routledge Encycl of Postmodernism, forthcoming; Sigmund Freud, The Routledge Encycl of Postmodernism, forthcoming; religion and the Psycho-Cultural Formation of Ideals, What is Rel? Origins, Explanations, and Definitions, forthcoming. **CONTACT ADDRESS** Dept of Religious Studies, Trinity Col Univ of Toronto, Toronto, ON, M5S 1H8. **EMAIL** James.Dicenso@utoronto.ca

DICICCO, MARIO
PERSONAL Born 01/15/1933, Memphis, TN, s **DISCIPLINE** THEOLOGY **EDUCATION** Quincy Univ, BA 56; Univ Chicago, MA 64; Case Western Reserve, PhD 70; Loyola Univ, MA psychol, 74; Cath Theol Union, MA theol, 82; Lutheran Sch Theol, ThD 93. **CAREER** Quincy Univ, asst prof; Hales Franciscan HS, Principal; Cath Theol Union, adj prof; Lutheran Sch Theol, adj prof; Franciscan Sch Theol, adj prof. **MEMBERSHIPS** SBL; CBA. **RESEARCH** New Testament World, exegesis, introduction; Rhetoric. **CONTACT ADDRESS** Franciscan Sch of Theol, 1712 Euclid Ave, Berkeley, CA, 94709. **EMAIL** MarioD@aol.com

DICK, MICHAEL B.
DISCIPLINE RELIGIOUS STUDIES **EDUCATION** Cath Univ Am, BA, 66, MA, 66; Gregorian Univ, Rome, STB & STL, 70; Johns Hopkins Univ, MA, 77, PhD, 77. **CAREER** Post-doctoral work, Johns Hopkins Univ, 77-78; worked, W Semitic res Inst, 97. **SELECTED PUBLICATIONS** Auth, Job XXVIII 4: A New Translation, Vetus Testamentum 29, 79; The Legal Metaphor in Job 31, Catholic Bibl Quart 41, 79; Job 31, The Oath of Innocence, and the Sage, Zeitschrift fur alttestamentliche Wissenschaft 95, 83; Prophetic Poiesis and the Verbal Icon, Catholic Bibl Quart 46, 84; Conversion in the Bible, in Conversion and the Catechumenate, Paulist Press, 84; Elisha and Holy War, Voices, 83; A Syntactic study of the Book of Obadiah, Semitics 9, 84; Conversion in the Old Testament, New Catholic World 229, 86; An Inductive Reading of the Hebrew Bible, Prentice-Hall, 88; The Ethics of the Old Greek Book of Proverbs in Studia Philonica, 91; coauth, Born in Heaven Made on Earth: The Making of the Cult Image. **CONTACT ADDRESS** Dept of Relig Studies, Siena Col, 515 Loudon Rd., Loudonville, NY, 12211-1462. **EMAIL** dick@siena.edu

DICKER, GEORGES
PERSONAL Born 11/08/1942, Geneva, Switzerland, 1 child **DISCIPLINE** PHILOSOPHY **EDUCATION** San Francisco State Col, BA, 65; Univ Wis-Madison, PhD(philos), 69. **CAREER** Instr philos & relig, Colgate Univ, 69-70; asst prof, 70-73, assoc prof, 73-80, Prof Philos, State Univ NY Brockport, 80-, Nat Endowment for Humanities fel, 75-76. **MEMBERSHIPS** Am Philos Asn; Creighton Club. **RESEARCH** Theory of knowledge; history of modern philosophy, Dewey. **SELECTED PUBLICATIONS** Auth, John Dewey: Instrumentalism in Social Action, Trans Charles S Peirce Soc, fall 71;

Knowing and Coming-to-Know in John Dewey's Theory of Knowledge, Monist, 4/73; Certainty Without Dogmatism: A Reply to Unger's An Argument for Scepticism, Philos Exchange, summer 74; Dewey's Theory of Knowing, Philos Monogr, 76; Primary and Secondary Qualities: A Proposed Modification of the Lockean Account, Southern J of Philos, winter 77; Is There a Problem About Perception and Knowledge?, Am Philos Quart, 7/78; Perceptual Knowledge: An Analytical and Historical Study, Reidel, 80; The Concept of Immediate Perception in Berkeley's Immaterialism, In: Critical and Interpretive Essays, Univ Minn Press, 82; auth, Descartes: An Analytical and Historical Introduction, Oxford, 93; auth, Hume's Epistemology and Mrtaphysics: An Introduction, Routledge, 98. **CONTACT ADDRESS** 350 New Campus Dr, Brockport, NY, 14420-2914. **EMAIL** gdicker@acs.brockport.edu

DICKER, GEORGES
PERSONAL Born 11/08/1942, Geneva, Switzerland, d, 1 child **DISCIPLINE** PHILOSOPHY **EDUCATION** Univ Wisconsin, PhD, 69. **CAREER** Instr, philos and relig, Colgate Univ, 69-70; asst prof, philos, assoc prof, prof of philos, then prof and chemn, SUNY Brockport, 70- . **HONORS AND AWARDS** NEH fel in residence for col tchrs, 75-76; council for philos stud summer inst, 72, 80; NEH summer sem, 81, 84. **MEMBERSHIPS** APA; Hume Soc; Int Berkeley Soc; Creighton Club. **RESEARCH** History of modern philosophy; epistemology. **SELECTED PUBLICATIONS** Auth, Dewey's Theory of Knowing, Philos Monographs, 76; auth, Perceptual Knowledge: An Analytical and Historical Study, Reidel, 80; auth, The Concept of Immediate Perception in Berkeley's Immaterialism, in Turbayne, ed, Berkeley: Critical and Interpretive Essays, Univ Minn, 82; auth, Leibniz on Necessary and Contingent Propositions, Studia Leibnitiana, 82; auth, An Idea Can Be Like Nothing But An Idea, Hist of Philos Q, 85; auth, A Refutation of Rowe's Critique of Anselm's Ontological Argument, Faith and Philos, 88; auth, The Limits of Cartesian Dualism, in Hare, ed, Doing Philosophy Historically, Prometheus, 88; auth, Hume's Fork Revisited, His of Philos Q, 91; auth, Berkeley on the Immediate Perception of Objects, in Cummins, ed, Minds, Ideas, and Objects: Essays in the Theory of Representation in Modern Philosophy, Ridgeview, 92; auth, Descartes: An Analytical and Historical Introduction, Oxford, 93; auth, Epistemology Reburied, Trans of the Charles S. Peirce Soc, 95; auth, Hume's Epistemology and Metaphysics: An Introduction, Routledge, 98. **CONTACT ADDRESS** Dept of Philosophy, SUNY Brockport, Brockport, NY, 14420. **EMAIL** gdicker@acs.brockport.edu

DICKERSON, DENNIS CLARK
PERSONAL Born 08/12/1949, McKeesport, Pennsylvania, m **DISCIPLINE** THEOLOGY **EDUCATION** Lincoln Univ, BA 1971; Washington Univ, MA 1974, PhD 1978; Hartford Seminary, additional study; Morris Brown Coll, LHD, 1990. **CAREER** Forest Park Comm Coll, part-time instructor 1974; PA State Univ, Ogontz Campus, part-time instructor 1975-76; Williams Coll, asst prof history 1976-83, assoc prof history 1983-85; Rhodes Coll, assoc prof history 1985-87; Carter Woodson Inst Univ of VA, visiting scholar 1987-88; Williams Coll, assoc prof history, 1987-88, prof 1988-; Stanfield professor of history, 1992-; chair, Dept of History, 1998-; African Methodist Episcopal Church, historiographer, 1988-; Secretary General Officers Council; Payne Theological Seminary, visiting professor, 1992, 1996, 1998; Yale Divinity School, visiting prof of amer religious history, Spring 1995. **HONORS AND AWARDS** Fellowship Natl Endownment for the Humanities 1982; Moody Grant Lyndon B Johnson Found 1983; Grant-in-aid Amer Council of Learned Soc 1983-84; Fellowship Rockefeller Found 1983-84; articles in New Jersey History, Church History, Pennsylvania Heritage, New York State Journal of Medicine, Methodist History, Western PA Historical Magazine, AME Church Review; Journal of Presbyterian History; contributing author: Encyclopedia of Amer Business History and Biography: Iron and Steel in the 20th Century, Bruccoli Clark Layman Boo, 1994, Historical Dictionary of Methodism, Scarecrow Press, 1996, Blackwell Dictionary of Evangelical Biography, Blackwell Publishers, 1995; Black Apostles at Home and Abroad, GK Hall 1982; Biographical Dictionary of Amer Labor Leaders, Greenwood Press 1984; Encyclopedia of Southern Culture, University of North Carolina Press, 1989; Biographical Dictionary of Amer Social Welfare, Greenwood Press 1986; Life and Labor, SUNY Press 1986. **MEMBERSHIPS** Pastor, Payne AME Church Chatham NY 1980-85; mem, IBPOEW; Alpha Phi Alpha Fraternity; mem, NAACP; pastor, St Mark AME Church Munford TN 1985-87; board of corporators, Williamstown Savings Bank, 1992-; board of trustees, 1992-95; North Adams State College; GRE History Committee Educational Testing Service, 1990-96; American Society of Church History; Organization of American Historians; American Historical Association; Southern Historical Association; World Methodist Historical Society; Wesley Historical Society; American Bible Study Society, board of trustees, 1995-. **SELECTED PUBLICATIONS** Author "Out of the Crucible, Black Steelworkers in Western Pennsylvania 1875-1980," Alb State Univ of NY Press 1986; author, Religion, Race and Region: Research Notes on AME Church History, Nashville AME Sunday School Union, 1995; Militant Mediator: Whitney M Young, Jr, Univ Press of Kentucky, 1998. **CONTACT ADDRESS** Dept of History, Williams Col, Williamstown, MA, 01267.

DICKEY, WALTER J.
PERSONAL Born 11/11/1946, Bronx, NY, m, 1970, 2 children **DISCIPLINE** LAW **EDUCATION** Univ Wis, BA, 68, JD, 71. **CAREER** Fel, Int Legal Ctr, 71-73; asst prof criminal law, 76-80, Assoc Prof Criminal Law, Univ Wis Law Sch, 80-, Dir, Legal Assistance to Instnl Persons Prof, Univ Wis Law Sch, 75-. **RESEARCH** Criminal law; corrections; criminal justice. **SELECTED PUBLICATIONS** Coauth, Legal assistance for the institutionalized, Southern Ill Law Rev, 76; auth, The lawyer and the quality of service to the poor, DePaul Law Rev, 78; The lawyer and the accuracy of the presentence report, Fed Probation, 79; Incompetency and the nondangerous mentally ill client, Criminal Law Bull, 80; coauth, Law, trial judges and the psychiatric witness, Int J Law & Psychol, 81; auth, Wisconsin Administrative Code Corrections, State of Wis, 79-82; coauth, Criminal Justice Administration, Michie Co, rev ed, 82. **CONTACT ADDRESS** Law Sch, Univ Wisconsin, Madison, 975 Bascom Mall, Madison, WI, 53706-1301. **EMAIL** 1hicks@gacstaff.wisc.edu

DICKIE, GEORGE T.
PERSONAL Born 08/12/1926, Palmetto, FL, m, 1977, 2 children **DISCIPLINE** PHILOSOPHY **EDUCATION** Florida State Univ, BA 49; Univ Cal Los Angeles, PhD 59. **CAREER** Univ Illinois, prof emer 95-, prof 67-95, assoc prof 65-67; Univ Houston, assoc prof 64-65; Washington State Univ, inst, assoc prof 56-64. **HONORS AND AWARDS** Univ Ill Hum Inst Fel; NEH; NEH Sr Fel; Guggenheim Fel. **MEMBERSHIPS** ASA; APA; IPA **RESEARCH** Aesthetics **SELECTED PUBLICATIONS** Auth, Introduction to Aesthetics: An Analytical Approach, Oxford UP, 97, revised version of Aesthetics: An Introduction, Pegasus Press 71; The Century of Taste: The Philosophical Odyssey of Taste in the Eighteenth Century, Oxford UP, 96; Evaluating Art, Temple Univ Press, 88; The Art Circle: A Theory of Art, Haven, 84. **CONTACT ADDRESS** Dept of Philosophy, Univ of Illinois, Apt 9A, Chicago, IL, 60660.

DICKSON, DAVID FRANKLIN
PERSONAL Born 01/20/1933, St. Louis, MO, m **DISCIPLINE** CONSTITUTIONAL LAW, POLITICAL SCIENCE **EDUCATION** Princeton Univ, AB, 54; Yale Univ, LLB, 59; Fla State Univ, MS, 64, PhD(govt), 66. **CAREER** Assoc, Watts, Oakes & VanderVoort, NY, 61-63; res assoc Polit Sci, inst Govt Res, 65-66, from asst prof to assoc prof Law, 66-73, asst dean, 71-72, prof Law, Col Law, Fla State Univ, 73-, VDean Col, 72-, Mem, Fla Law Revision Comn, 67-70. **RESEARCH** Public law; state constitutional revision. **SELECTED PUBLICATIONS** Auth, Proposed amendments to the Florida Constitution of 1885, 66 & Comments on the Drafting of a New Constitution for Florida, 66, Fla State Univ. **CONTACT ADDRESS** Col of Law, Florida State Univ, 425 W Jefferson St, Tallahassee, FL, 32306.

DICKSON, MICHAEL
DISCIPLINE PHILOSOPHY OF SCIENCE **EDUCATION** Univ SC, BA, 90; Univ Notre Dame, PhD, 95. **CAREER** Asst prof. **RESEARCH** General philosophy of science; general philosophy of physics; philosophy of quantum mechanics; relation between quantum mechanics and relativity theory; Hellenistic philosophy. **SELECTED PUBLICATIONS** Auth, Lorentz-Invariance in Modal Interpretations, 98; On the Plurality of Dynamics, 98; Quantum Chance and Quantum Non-Locality, Cambridge, 98; Logical Foundations for Modal Interpretations, 96; An Empirical Reply to Empiricism: Protective Measurement Opens the Door for Quantum Realism, 95; Is There Really No Projection Postulate in the Modal Interpretation?", 95; Faux-Boolean Algebras and Classical Models, 95. **CONTACT ADDRESS** Dept of History and Philosophy of Science, Indiana Univ, Bloomington, 300 N Jordan Ave, Bloomington, IN, 47405. **EMAIL** midickso@indiana.edu

DIENER, PAUL W.
DISCIPLINE RELIGION AND ETHICS **EDUCATION** Lebanon Valley Col, BA; Temple Univ, PhD.. **SELECTED PUBLICATIONS** Auth, Religion and Morality: An Introduction, Westminster John Knox. **CONTACT ADDRESS** York Col, Pennsylvania, 441 Country Club Road, York, PA, 17403.

DIENES, C. THOMAS
PERSONAL Born 01/09/1940, Chicago, IL, m, 1965 **DISCIPLINE** LAW, POLITICAL SCIENCE **EDUCATION** Loyola Univ, BS, 61; Northwestern Univ, JD, 64, PhD (polit sci), 68. **CAREER** Asst prof law and polit sci, Col Law, Univ Houston, 69-70; assoc prof law and govt, Am Univ, 70-73, prof law, 73-80; Prof Law, Nat Law Ctr, George Washington Univ, 80-, Lectr constitutional law, Bar Rev Inc, Del and Md, 71-; hearing examr, Off Educ Title I Audit Hearing Bd, 73-78; vis prof law, Cornell Univ, 78-79 and George Washington Nat Law Ctr, 79-80. **MEMBERSHIPS** Am Polit Sci Asn; Law and Soc Asn; Am Acad Polit and Soc Sci. **RESEARCH** Law and the social sciences; constitutional law. **SELECTED PUBLICATIONS** Auth, Implied Libel, Defamatory Meaning, and State of Mind--The Promise of New York Times, Iowa Law Rev, Vol 78, 93. **CONTACT ADDRESS** College of Law, American Univ, Massachusetts and Nebraska Ave NW, Washington, DC, 20016.

DIGIOVANNI, GEORGE
DISCIPLINE PHILOSOPHY **EDUCATION** Univ Toronto, BA, MA, PhD. **RESEARCH** German idealism; nineteenth century philosophy; phenomenology; conceptual realism. **SELECTED PUBLICATIONS** Auth, Immanuel Kant: Religion and Rational Theology, Cambridge, 96; auth, Friedrich Heinrich Jacobi: The Main Philosophical Writings and the Novel 'Allwill', McGill-Queen's, 94; auth, Hegel's Jena Logic and Metaphysics, McGill-Queen's, 86; auth, Between Kant and Hegel, SUNY, 85. **CONTACT ADDRESS** Philosophy Dept, McGill Univ, 845 Sherbrooke St, Montreal, PQ, H3A 2T5.

DILLER, MATTHEW
DISCIPLINE CIVIL PROCEDURE, SOCIAL WELFARE LAW **EDUCATION** Harvard Col, AB, 81; Harvard Univ, JD, 85. **CAREER** Law clk, US Court of Appeals, 85-86; staff atty, The Legal Aid Soc, 86-93; adj asst, prof, NY Univ Sch Law, 89, 93; assoc prof, 93. **SELECTED PUBLICATIONS** Rev, Poverty Lawyering in the Golden Age, Mich Law Rev 1401, 95; auth, Introductory Remarks: Is the Issue Welfare or Poverty? 22 Fordham Urban Law Jour 875, 95; Entitlement and Exclusion: The Role of Disability in the Social Welfare System, 44 UCLA Law Rev 361, 96; Dissonant Disability Policies: The Tensions Between the Americans with Disabilities Act and Federal Disability Benefit Programs, 76 Tex Law Rev 1003, 98; Working without a Job: The Shifting Social Messages of the New Workfare, 9 Stanford Law & Policy Rev 19, 98. **CONTACT ADDRESS** Law Sch, Fordham Univ, 113 W 60th St, New York, NY, 10023. **EMAIL** mdiller@mail.lawnet.fordham.edu

DILLEY, FRANK B.
PERSONAL Born 11/17/1931, Athens, OH, m, 1953, 3 children **DISCIPLINE** PHILOSOPHY **EDUCATION** Ohio Univ, AB, 52, MA, 53; Union Theol Sem, MDiv, 55; Columbia Univ, PhD (philos of relig), 61. **CAREER** Tutor, Union Theol Sem, 55-57; instr, Sarah Lawrence Col, 56-57; from instr to asst prof relig, Smith Col, 57-61; assoc prof philos and chmn dept, Millikin Univ, 61-65 and 66-67; Am Coun Educ fel acad admin, Univ Denver, 65-66; prof, 67-70, assoc provost, 70-74, Prof Philos and Chmn, Dept, Univ Del, 74-. **MEMBERSHIPS** Am Philos Asn; Am Acad Relig; Parapsychology Asn. **RESEARCH** Metaphysics; philosophy of religion. **SELECTED PUBLICATIONS** Auth, Death and Personal Survival--The Evidence for Life After Death, Intl J Philos Rel, Vol 37, 95; Beyond Death--Theological and Philosophical Reflections on Life After Death, Intl Journal Philoso Rel, Vol 42, 97; Reincarnation--A Critical Examination, Intl J Philos Rel, Vol 42, 97; The Non Reality of Free Will, Intl J Philos Rel, Vol 34, 93. **CONTACT ADDRESS** Dept of Philosophy, Univ of Delaware, Newark, DE, 19711.

DILLEY, PATRICIA E.
DISCIPLINE LAW **EDUCATION** Swarthmore Col, BA; Univ Pa, MA; Georgetown Univ, JD; Boston Univ, LLM. **CAREER** Assoc prof, 98-, Univ Fla; asst and assoc prof, Seattle Univ Sch Law, 93-98; fmr assoc, Arnold Porter, Wash, DC & Downs, Rachlin Martin, Burlington Vermont. **MEMBERSHIPS** US House Ways and Means Comt, 81-87; staff dir & ch coun, Soc Security Subcomt, 85-87; past ch, Asn Amer Law Schools Sect on Employee Benefits; Amer Bar Asn Employee Benefits Comt; Nat Acad Soc Insurance. **RESEARCH** Deferred compensation, individual income taxation, corporate taxation, international taxation, advanced employee benefit law and retirement income policy. **CONTACT ADDRESS** School of Law, Univ of Florida, PO Box 117625, Gainesville, FL, 32611-7625. **EMAIL** dilley@law.ufl.edu

DILLON, M.C.
PERSONAL Born 12/07/1938 **DISCIPLINE** PHILOSOPHY **EDUCATION** Univ Virginia, BA, 60; Univ Calif, Berkeley, MA, 64; Yale Univ, MPhil, 68, PhD, 70. **CAREER** Instr, philos, Washington and Lee Univ, 65-66; instr, 68-70, from asst prof, philos, to prof, 70-93, dir, Undergrad Stud, Philos, 78-90, distinguished tchg prof, 93- , Binghamton Univ; instr, Corporate Prof Educ, IBM, Inc., 86-93. **HONORS AND AWARDS** Woodrow Wilson fel, 63-64; Yale Univ fel, 66-67, 67-68; SUNY Chancellor's Award for Excellence in Tchg, 74; SUNY Fac Res Grant, 71, 73, 78, 80. **MEMBERSHIPS** Merleau-Ponty Circle; Int Asn for Philos and Lit; Int Husserl and Phenomenological Res Soc; APA; Soc for Phenomenology and Existential Philos; NY State Philos Asn; Soc for the Philos of Sex and Love; Human Sci Res Conf; Can Soc for Hermeneutics and Postmodern Thought. **SELECTED PUBLICATIONS** Auth, Merleau-Ponty's Ontology, Indiana, 88, 2d ed, Northwestern, 97; ed, Merleau-Ponty Vivant, SUNY Press, 91; auth, Semiological Reductionism: A Critique of the Deconstructionist Movement in Postmodern Thought, SUNY Press, 95; ed, Ecart & Differance: Merleau-Ponty and Derrida on Seeing and Writing, Humanities, 97. **CONTACT ADDRESS** Dept of Philosophy, SUNY, Binghamton, Binghamton, NY, 13902-6000. **EMAIL** mdillon355@aol.com

DILWORTH, JOHN
DISCIPLINE ETHICS **EDUCATION** Bristol Univ, PhD. **CAREER** Assoc prof, W Mich Univ. **RESEARCH** Aesthetics, cognitive science. **SELECTED PUBLICATIONS** Articles, Jour Aesthetics & Art Criticism; Philos Forum; Professional Ethics. **CONTACT ADDRESS** Kalamazoo, MI, 49008. **EMAIL** dilworth@wmich.edu

DINGILIAN, DER STEPANOS
PERSONAL Born 12/19/1954, Alexandria, Egypt, m, 1990, 2 children **DISCIPLINE** THEOLOGY **EDUCATION** Sch of Theol, Claremont, PhD, 96. **CAREER** Pastor, 91-96, relig educr, 96- , Armenian Apostolic Church. **MEMBERSHIPS** AAR; SBL. **RESEARCH** Theology and psychology of hope; spirituality in relationships. **SELECTED PUBLICATIONS** Auth, A Spiritual Journey Through the Holy Badarak; auth, The Last Frontier: Hope for the Family. **CONTACT ADDRESS** 1330 E Foothill Blvd #64, Glendora, CA, 91741. **EMAIL** drstepanos@aol.com

DINKINS, DAVID N.
PERSONAL Born 07/10/1927, Trenton, New Jersey, m **DISCIPLINE** LAW **EDUCATION** Howard Univ, BS 1950; Brooklyn Law School, JD, 1956. **CAREER** Dyett, Alexander, Dinkins, Patterson, Michael, Dinkins, Jones, attorney-partner 1956-1975; NY State Democratic Party, district leader 1967-; NY State Assembly, state assemblyman 1966; City of New York, pres bd of elections 1972-73, city clerk 1975-85, Manhattan borough pres 1986-90, mayor, 1990-93; Columbia Univ, prof, 1993-. **HONORS AND AWARDS** Pioneer of Excellence, World Inst of Black Communications, 1986; Righteous Man Award, NY Board of Rabbis, 1986; Man of the Year Award, Corrections Guardians Assn, 1986; Distinguished Service Award, Federation of Negro Civil Service Org , 1986; Man of the Year Award, Assn of Negro Bus and Prof Women's Clubs; Father of the Year Award, Metropolitan Chapter, Jack and Jill of America Inc, 1989; first black mayor of New York City. **MEMBERSHIPS** NY State Amer for Democratic Action, bd of dir; Urban League, mem; 100 Black Men, bd of dir; March of Dimes, bd of dir; Assn for a Better NY, bd of dir; Manhattan Women's Political Caucus, first male mem; NAACP, life mem; Black-Jewish Coalition, mem; Vera Institute of Justice, mem; Nova Anorca & NY State Urban Development Corp; Malcolm King Harlem Coll, bd of trustees; Marymount Manhattan Coll, pres advisory council; Assn of the Bar of the City of NY, exec committee. **CONTACT ADDRESS** Prof, Sch of Intl and Public Affairs, Columbia Univ, 420 W 118th St, 14th Fl, New York, NY, 10027.

DIPUCCI, WILLIAM
PERSONAL Born 12/26/1958, Cleveland, OH, m, 1992, 2 children **DISCIPLINE** RELIGION **EDUCATION** Marquette Univ, PhD 94. **CAREER** Mount Union Col, adj prof of relig, 94-97. **MEMBERSHIPS** AAR/SBL, ETS, ASCH, NAPS **RESEARCH** Early church; hermeneutics; science and faith; 19th cen amer relig. **SELECTED PUBLICATIONS** Auth, The Interior Sense of Scripture: The Sacred Hermeneutics of John W. Nevin, Mercer Press, 98. **CONTACT ADDRESS** 291 Berwin Place, Munroe Falls, OH, 44262. **EMAIL** bdipuccio@stratus.net

DISCHER, MARK R.
PERSONAL Born 03/10/1964, Chicago, IL, s **DISCIPLINE** RELIGION; PHILOSOPHY **EDUCATION** Wheaton Col, Ba; Fuller Theolog Sem; M.Div; Yale Univ, STM; Oxford Univ, D. Phil, 98. **CAREER** Asst prof, chemn, Ottawa Univ. **MEMBERSHIPS** AAR/SBL; SCE; APA. **RESEARCH** Foundations of Mortality. **SELECTED PUBLICATIONS** Auth, art, Jonah and the Universality of Devine Care, 96; auth, Does Finnis Get Natural Rights for Everyone, 99. **CONTACT ADDRESS** Ottawa Univ, 1001 S Cedar, Ottawa, KS, 66067. **EMAIL** discher@ott.edu

DITTES, JAMES EDWARD
PERSONAL Born 12/26/1926, Cleveland, OH, m, 1948, 4 children **DISCIPLINE** PSYCHOLOGY OF RELIGION **EDUCATION** Oberlin Col, BA, 49; Yale Univ, BD, 54, MS, 55, PhD(psychol), 58. **CAREER** Instr sci, Am Sch, Turkey, 50-52; from instr to assoc prof relig, 55-67, prof psychol relig, Yale Univ, 67-, chm dept relig studies, 75-; Gug genheim fel, 65-66; Fulbright res fel, Rome, 65-66; Nat Endowment for Humanities sr fel, 72-73; ed, J Sci Studies Relig, 66-71. **MEMBERSHIPS** Soc Sci Studies Relig (pres, 72-73); Am Psychol Asn; Am Acad Relig. **RESEARCH** Motivation and vocational dilemmas of clergymen; development and decay of self-transcending commitments; continuity between biography and theology of major religious figures. **SELECTED PUBLICATIONS** Coauth, Psychological Studies of Clergymen, Nelson, 65; auth, The Church in the Way, Scribners, 67; Psychology of Religion, In: Handbook of Social Psychology, Addison-Wesley, 69; Minister on the Spot, United Church, 70; Bias and the Pious, Augsburg, 73; Beyond William James, In: Beyond the Classics, Harper, 73; The Investigator as an Instrument of Investigation, In: Encounter With Erikson, Scholars, 77; When People Say No, Harper, 79; The Male Predicament, Harper, 85; Driven by Hope, Westminster John Knox, 96; Men At Work, Westminster John Knox, 96; Pastoral Counseling, Westminster John Knox, 99. **CONTACT ADDRESS** Dept of Religious Studies, Yale Univ, PO Box 208287, New Haven, CT, 06520-8287. **EMAIL** james.dittes@yale.edu

DMOCHOWSKI, HENRY W.
PERSONAL Born 11/16/1942, Jersey City, NJ, s **DISCIPLINE** PHILOSOPHY **EDUCATION** Seton Hall Univ, AB, 64; Villanova Univ, MA, 67; New York Univ, PhD, 74. **CAREER** Adj Tchr, Gwynedd Mercy Col, 66-68; St Josephs Univ, 68-73; Voc Coord, Therapeutic Center at Fox Chase, 75-77; Coord of Voc Rehab Svc, Eagleville Hosp, 77-83; Adj Tchr, Lincoln Univ, 79-81; Rowan Univ, 85-89; Temple Univ, 90-95; LaSalle Univ, 95-. **RESEARCH** History of Philosophy, Ethics. **CONTACT ADDRESS** 116 Buckingham Dr, Rosemont, PA, 19010.

DOBBS, DAN BYRON
PERSONAL Born 11/08/1932, Ft Smith, AR, m, 1953, 4 children **DISCIPLINE** LAW **EDUCATION** Univ Ark, Ba, 56, LLB, 56; Univ Ill, Urbana, LLM, 61. JSD, 66. **CAREER** Partner, Dobbs, Pryor & Dobbs, Ft Smith, 56-60; from Asst prof to prof law, Univ NC, Chapel Hill, 61-78; Mem Fac, Law Col, Univ Ariz,78-Law clerk, US Dist Judge John E Miller, 57-59; consult, NC Courts Comn, 63-64; vis prof law, Univ Minn, 66-67, Cornell Univ Law Sch, 68-69 & Univ Va Law Sch, 74. **RESEARCH** Remedies; torts. **SELECTED PUBLICATIONS** Auth, Beyond bootstrap, Minn Law Rev, 1/67; The validation of void judgments, Va Law Rev, part 1, 6/67, part 2, 10/67; Contempt of court, Cornell Law Rev, 1/71; Et al Remedies, West, 73; Law of Remedies, (2d ed 3 vols), 93; Torts and Compensation, (with Paul Hayden, (3d ed 97); Prosser and Keeton on Torts (5th ed with Page Keeton, Robert Keeton and David Owen, 84). **CONTACT ADDRESS** Law Col, Univ Ariz, 1 University of Az, Tucson, AZ, 85721-0001. **EMAIL** Dobbs@nt.law.arizona.edu

DOBBYN, JOHN FRANCIS
PERSONAL Born 08/31/1937, Boston, MA, m, 1969, 1 child **DISCIPLINE** LAW **EDUCATION** Harvard Univ, AB, 59, LLM, 69; Boston Col, JD, 65. **CAREER** Law clerk, Fed Dist Ct, Dist Mass, 65-57; atty, Burns & Levinson, Boston, 67-68; Prof Law, Law Sch, Villanova Univ, 69-. **RESEARCH** Corporation law; insurance law; equitable remedies. **SELECTED PUBLICATIONS** Auth, Injunctions in a Nutshell, 74 & So You Want to Go to Law School, 75, West Publ; Insurance Law in a Nutshell, West Publ, 81. **CONTACT ADDRESS** Law School, Villanova Univ, 299 N Spring Mill Rd, Villanova, PA, 19085-1597. **EMAIL** dobbym@law.vill.edu

DOBSEVAGE, ALVIN P
PERSONAL Born 11/29/1922, New York, NY, m, 1949, 3 children **DISCIPLINE** PHILOSOPHY, FOREIGN LANGUAGE **EDUCATION** City Col New York, BA, 42; Harvard Univ, MA, 48; Columbia Univ, MPhilos, 52; Cent Conn State Univ, MA, 82. **CAREER** Instr philos, Brooklyn Col, 51-53; vconsul info off, US Info Serv, Salisbury, Rhodesia, 55-58; teacher Latin, Wilton High Sch, Conn, 58-65; asst prof, 65-82, ASSOC PROF FRENCH, LATIN AND LING, WESTERN CONN STATE COL, 82-, CHMN DEPT MOD LANG, 81-, Adj asst prof Latin, Saturday Sch Lang, NY Univ, 60-68; adj asst prof philos, Danbury State Col, 60-; lectr, Univ Conn, Stamford Br, 63-64; ed, Hermes Americanus; Nat Endowment for Humanities grant, Am Acad Rome, 82. **HONORS AND AWARDS** Letter of Commendation from Off Personnel, Dept of Army for Work as Mem Haines Bd Study Group, 40, regarding civil affairs, Psychol Oper, 67. **MEMBERSHIPS** Am Philos Asn; Am Philol Asn; Mediaeval Acad Am; Class Asn New England; MLA. **RESEARCH** Gaston Bachelard's theory of imagination; aesthetics and metaphysics; teaching French and Latin. **SELECTED PUBLICATIONS** Auth, The Metamorphoses of Apuleius--On Making an Ass of Oneself, Class W, Vol 89, 96. **CONTACT ADDRESS** 45 Dodgingtown Rd, Bethel, CT, 06801.

DOCKERY, DAVID S.
PERSONAL Born 10/28/1952, Tuscaloosa, AL, m, 1975, 3 children **DISCIPLINE** HISTORY; RELIGION **EDUCATION** Texas Christian Univ, MA, 86; Univ TX, PhD, 88. **CAREER** Dean & Acad VP, S Baptist Theol Sem, 88-96; pres, Union Univ, 96-. **HONORS AND AWARDS** Who's Who Relig; Who's Who Bibl Studies **MEMBERSHIPS** Soc Bibl Lit; Inst Bibl Res; Amer Acad Relig; Evangelical Theol Soc **RESEARCH** New Testament Studies; Hermeneuties; Baptist Theology. **SELECTED PUBLICATIONS** Auth, New Dimensions in Evangelical Thought, Intervarsity; Our Blessed Hope, LifeWay; Christian Scripture, Broadman & Holman; Biblical Interpretation Then and Now, Baker; auth, Ephesians, Convention; Holman Bible Handbook, Holman. **CONTACT ADDRESS** 1050 Union Univ Dr., Jackson, TN, 38305. **EMAIL** ddockery@buster.uu.edu

DODD, VICTORIA J.
DISCIPLINE LAW **EDUCATION** Harvard Univ, BA, 70; Univ Southern Ca, JD, 78. **CAREER** Prof. **SELECTED PUBLICATIONS** Auth, Becoming Gentlemen, Mass Law Jour, 97; Contributor, Analysis of the Code of Civil Procedure Governing the Courts of Estonia for the Republic of Estonia, 95; Introduction to Symposium on Law and Education, 94. **CONTACT ADDRESS** Law School, Suffolk Univ, Beacon Hill, Boston, MA, 02114. **EMAIL** vdodd@acad.suffolk.edu

DODSON, JUALYNNE
DISCIPLINE RELIGIOUS STUDIES **EDUCATION** Univ Calif Berkeley, PhD. **CAREER** Assoc prof. **HONORS AND AWARDS** Ed, J Am Acad Relig. **RESEARCH** African religions in the America. **SELECTED PUBLICATIONS** Auth, Protestant and African Derived Religious Traditions of Cuba, Women Ministries and the AME Tradition; U.S. African American Denominations in Cuba; There's Nothing Like Church Food. **CONTACT ADDRESS** Religious Studies Dept, Univ of Colorado, Boulder, Boulder, CO, 80309. **EMAIL** Jualynne.Dodson@Colorado.edu

DOERMANN, RALPH W.
PERSONAL Born 06/25/1930, Kodaikanal, India, m, 1953, 4 children **DISCIPLINE** RELIGION, OLD TESTAMENT **EDUCATION** Capital Univ, AB, 52; Lutheran Theol Sem, BD, 58; Duke Univ, PhD(Old Testament), 62. **CAREER** Pastor, Trinity Lutheran Church, Albert Lea, Minn, 61-63; from instr to assoc prof Hebrew & Old Testament, 63-72, Prof Hebrew & Old Testament, Trinity Lutheran Sem, 72-, Land of the Bible workshop fel, NY Univ, 66; James A Montgomery fel, Am Sch Orient Res, 69-70; mem staff, Joint Archaeol Exped, Tell el-Hesi, Israel, 70-; field supvr, Idalion, Cyprus, 72-74; ann prof, Albright Inst Archaeol Res, Jerusalem, 76-77, 84-85. **MEMBERSHIPS** Soc Bibl Lit; Am Schs Orient Res; Am Inst Archaeol. **RESEARCH** Biblical archaeology; Old Testament theology; heremeneutics in the intertestamental period. **SELECTED PUBLICATIONS** Auth, Luther's principles of Biblical interpretation, In: Interpreting Luther's Legacy, Augsburg, 69; Biblical Concern for the Poor, Comn Church & Soc, Am Lutheran Church, 72; Idalion 1972: the east Acropolis, Suppl Bull Am Schs Orient Res, 73; God's Hand Stretched Out: A Study of the Bood of Isiah, Am Lutheran Church Women, 76; Salvation in the Hebrew Scriptures: A Christian Perspective, Tantur Yrbk, 76-77; Salvation: Our Common Gift, In: These Things We Hold in Common, Augsburg, 81. **CONTACT ADDRESS** Dept of Old Testament, Trinity Lutheran Sem, 2199 E Main St, Columbus, OH, 43209-2334. **EMAIL** rdoerman@trinity.capital.edu

DOHERTY, BARBARA
PERSONAL Born 12/02/1931, Chicago, IL **DISCIPLINE** THEOLOGY, HISTORY OF RELIGIONS **EDUCATION** St Mary-of-the-Woods Col, BA, 53; St Mary's Col, MA, 63; Fordham Univ, PhD (theol), 79. **CAREER** Assoc prof theol, St Mary-of-the-Woods Col, 63-75; PROV SUPER, SISTERS OF PROVIDENCE, 75-, Chairperson, Leadership Conf Women Relig, Region 8, 79-82. **RESEARCH** Eastern and western spirituality. **SELECTED PUBLICATIONS** Auth, Music for 2 or More Players at Clavichord, Harpsichord, Organ--An Annotated Bibliography, Notes, Vol 49, 93; The Modern Classical Organ--A Guide to Its Physical and Musical Structure and Performance Implications, Notes, Vol 49, 93; Organ and Harpsichord Music by Women Composers--An Annotated Catalog, Notes, Vol 49, 93; Saintsaens and the Organ, Notes, Vol 51, 94. **CONTACT ADDRESS** 215 Ridge Terrace Park, Ridge, IL, 60068.

DOLAN, JAY P.
DISCIPLINE AMERICAN RELIGIOUS HISTORY **EDUCATION** Gregorian Univ, Italy, STL, 62; Univ Chicago, PhD, 70. **CAREER** Asst prof, Univ San Francisco, 70-71; asst prof, 71-77, dir, Ctr for Stud of Am Cath, 77-93, assoc prof, 77-86, prof, Univ Notre Dame, 86-; Fulbright prof, Univ Col, Ireland, 86; vis instr, Boston Col, 91; chemn, publ ser, Notre Dame Stud in Am Cath, Univ Notre Dame Press, 77-93; publ comt, Immigration Hist Soc, 77-80; ed bd, J of Am Ethnic Hist, 80-; ed bd, Church Hist, 82-86; ed bd, Hebrew Un Co-Jewish Inst of Relig, 84-89; ed bd, Sources of Am Spirituality, publ ser, Paulist Press, 86-90; ed bd, Statue of Liberty-Ellis Island Centennial publ ser, Univ Ill Press, 86-; assoc ed, Am Nat Biogr Mid-America, 88-; assoc ed, Am Nat Biogr, 89-; ed bd, Rel and Am Cult: J of Interp, 89-; ed bd, Church Hist, 94-. **HONORS AND AWARDS** Rockefeller fel, Univ Chicago, 69-70; O'Brien Fund grant, Univ Notre Dame, 72; fac res grant, Univ Notre Dame, 73; fel, Princeton Univ, 73-74; John Gilmary Shea Award, Am Cath Hist Asn, 75; res grant, Word of God Inst, 76; Frank O'Malley Award, Univ Notre Dame, 77; fel, Am Coun of Learned Soc, 78-79; fac develop grant, Univ Notre Dame, 80; Alumnus of the Yr, Univ Chicago, 87; Emily Schossberger Award, Univ Notre Dame Press, 88; res grant Lilly Endowment, 81, 81-87, 83-84, 86-88, 90-93, 91-92. **MEMBERSHIPS** Pres, Am Soc of Church Hist, 87; pres, Am Cath Hist Asn, 95; Immigration Hist Soc; Am Acad of Relig. **SELECTED PUBLICATIONS** Auth, Patterns of Leadership in the Congregation, in James P Wind and James W Lewis, eds, American Congregations, vol 2: New Perspectives in the Study of Congregations, Univ Chicago Press, 94; Conclusion, in Jay P Dolan and Allan Figueroa Deck, SJ, eds, Hispanic Catholic Culture in the U.S., Univ Notre Dame Press, 94; The People As Well As The Prelates: A Social History of a Denomination, in R Mullin and R Richey, eds, Reimagining Denominationalism: Interpretive Essays, Oxford UP, 94; coed, Mexican Americans and the Catholic Church. 1900-1965, Univ Notre Dame Press, 94; Puerto Rican and Cuban Catholics in the U.S. 1900-1965, Univ Notre Dame Press, 94; Hispanic Catholic Culture in the U.S.: Issues and Concerns, Univ Notre Dame Press, 94. **CONTACT ADDRESS** Dept of Hist, Univ Notre Dame, Notre Dame, IN, 46556.

DOLAN, JOHN M.
DISCIPLINE PHILOSOPHY **EDUCATION** Stanford Univ, PhD. **RESEARCH** Philosophy of language; moral philosophy; medical ethics. **SELECTED PUBLICATIONS** Auth, Is Physician-Assisted Suicide Possible?, Duquesne Law Rev, 96; Inference and Imagination, Archimedean Point, 94; Brain Injury Controversies, J Head Trauma Rehabilitation, 94; Counterfactual Reasoning, Reciprocity, and the Logic of Euthanasia, UFL, 94; Death by Deliberate Dehydration and Starvation: Silent Echoes of the Hungerhauser, Issues Law Medicine, 91. **CONTACT ADDRESS** Philosophy Dept, Univ of Minnesota, Twin Cities, 355 Ford Hall, 224 Church St SE, Minneapolis, MN, 55455. **EMAIL** dolan001@maroon.tc.umn.edu

DOLL, MARY A.
PERSONAL Born 06/04/1940, New York, NY, d, 1 child **DISCIPLINE** RELIGION, LITERATURE **EDUCATION** Conn Col, BA, 62; Johns Hopkins Univ, MA, 70; Syracuse Univ, PhD, 80. **CAREER** Lectr, Comm Col Baltimore, 70-71; lectr English, SUNY-Oswego, 76-81; asst prof English, SUNY, 82-84; lecrt English, Univ Redlands, 85-88; Supervisor English ed stud, Calif State Univ, 86-88; lectr Eng, Calif State Univ, 86-88; vis asst prof Eng, Tulane Univ, 88-89; asst prof, Loyola Univ, 88-89; asst prof, Our Lady Holy Cross Col, 89-91; assoc prof Eng, Our Lady Holy Cross Col, 91-95; prof Eng, Our Lady Holy Cross Col, 95- ; ch, Eng Dept, 89- ; Chr, Hon Convocation Comm, 90- . **HONORS AND AWARDS** SUNY Summer Res Grant, 82; Directory of Amer Scholars, Amer Biographical Inst, 82; Hon Mention, Amer Poetry Assn Contest, 86; acad excellence awd tchg, Univ Redlands, 86; In the Shadow of the Giant, selected as one of Choice mag 89-90 Outstanding academic bks; Sears-Roebuck tchg excellence and campus leadership awd, Our Lady of Holy Cross Col, 91; Nominated for La Humanist of the Yr Awd, 91; Who's Who in Amer Educ, 89-94; Contemporary Authors, 90; Who's Who in Rel, 91; Who's Who in the South and Southwest, 91-94; ed comm for College writing skills, 95-97; Reader for NEH: The Correspondence of Samuel Beckett, 95; Mem, Kappa Delta Pi, Sigma Pi Chapter, Intl hon soc in educa, 97; Mem, Kappa Gamma Pi, Natl Cath Col grad hon soc, 97- . **MEMBERSHIPS** Amer Acad Rel; Modern Lang Asn; S Atlantic Modern Lang Asn; Thomas Wolfe Soc, VP, 97- ; Samuel Beckett Soc; Natl Coun Tchrs Eng. **RESEARCH** The intersection of literature; education; cultural studies; and women's studies. **SELECTED PUBLICATIONS** Auth, Beyond the Window: Dreams and Learning, Jour of Curriculum Theorizing, 4, 1, Winter 82, 35-39; Love Song to Rocks, poem, Escarpments, 4, 1, Spring 83; Hearing Images, Jour Mental Imagery, 7, 1, 83, 135-142; Lewis Turco, Dictionary of Literary Biography Yearbook, 84, 331-338; Doris Lessing, DLBY, 85, 284-292; Joan Didion, Dictionary of Literary Biography Yearbook, 86, 247-252; The Monster in Children's Dreams: Night Alchemies, Jour Mental Imagery, 10, 2, 86, 53-60; Measures of Despair: The Demeter Myth in Beckett, Jour of Beckett Stud, II, Fall 86, 109-122; The Temple Symbol in Scripture, Soundings, LXX, 1-2, Spring/Summer, 87, 145-154; Rites of Story: The Old Man at Play, in Myth and Ritual in the Plays of Samuel Beckett, Katherine H. Burkman, ed, Neew Jersey, Fairleigh Dickenson UP, 87, 73-85; In the Shadow of the Giant: Thomas Wolfe, ed, Athens, OH, Ohio UP, 88; Beckett and Myth: An Archetypal Approach, New York, Syracuse UP, 88; Walking and Rocking, Make Sense Who may: Selected Essays in Honor of Samuel Beckett's 80th Birthday, Robin J. Davis and Lance St. John Butler, eds, New York, Barnes and Nobles, 89; The Monster in Children's Dreams: Its Metaphoric Awe, The Jour Curriculum Theorizing, 8, 4, Spring 90, 89-99; The Power of Wilderness: Joseph Campbell and the Ecological Imperative, in Uses of Comparative Mythology: Essays on the Work of Joseph Campbell, Kenneth L. Golden, ed, New York, Garland Press, 92, 223-234; Tom Stoppard's Theatre of Unknowing, in British Drama Since 1960, London, Macmillan Press, 94, 117-129; Ghosts of Themselves: The Demeter Women in Beckett, in Images of Persephone, Elizabeth Hayes, ed, UP of Florida, 94, 121-135; Ashborn, poem, and To Larry, With Love, poem, in Taboo, 1, 4, spring 96, 73-74; To the Lighthouse and Back: Writings on Teaching and Living, New York: peter Lang Publ, 95; Winging It, Jour Curriculum Theorizing, 13, 1, Spring 97, 41-44; Winging It, in Reading Curriculum Identity: Shared Readings, Paula Salvio and Dennis Sumara, eds, NY, Tchrs, Col Press, 97; Queering the Gaze, in Studies in Curriculum Theory, William F. Pinar, ed, New Jersey, Lawrence Erlbaum Assoc, 98; Why I Teach, L'Image, Fall 97; The Is-ness of Teaching, English Education, Dec, 97; co-ed, How we Work, New York, Peter Lang, 99. **CONTACT ADDRESS** Dept of English, Our Lady of Holy Cross Col, 4154 State St Dr, New Orleans, LA, 70125. **EMAIL** mdoll4444@aol.com

DOLLING, LISA M.
PERSONAL Born 05/03/1962, m, 1990, 1 child **DISCIPLINE** PHILOSOPHY **EDUCATION** Manhattanville Col, BA, 84; Fordham Univ, MA, 88; City Univ NY, PhD, 95. **CAREER** Asst prof Philos, St. John's Univ. **MEMBERSHIPS** Am Philos Asn; Philos Sci Asn; ACPA. **RESEARCH** Philosophy of science; aesthetics. **CONTACT ADDRESS** Dept of Philosophy, St. John's Univ, 775 Tiffany Ave., River Vale, NJ, 07675.

DOMBROWSKI, DANIEL
PERSONAL Born 08/08/1953, Philadelphia, PA, m, 1977, 2 children **DISCIPLINE** PHILOSOPHY **EDUCATION** Univ Main, BA, 74; St Louis Univ, PhD, 78. **CAREER** Asst prof, St Joseph's Univ, 78-82; assoc prof, Creighton Univ, 82-88; prof, Seattle Univ, 88- . **MEMBERSHIPS** APA; Soc for Stud of Process Philos; Soc for Study of Ethics and Animals. **RESEARCH** Process philosophy; applied ethics; history of philosophy. **SELECTED PUBLICATIONS** Auth, The Philosophy of Vegetarianism, Massachusetts, 84; auth, Hartshorne and the Metaphysics of Animal Rights, SUNY, 88; auth, Christian Pacifism, Temple, 91; auth, St John of the Cross, SUNY, 92; auth, Analytic Theism, Hartshorne, and the Concept of God, SUNY, 96; auth, Babies and Beasts: The Argument from Marginal Cases, Illinois, 97; auth, Kazantzakis and God, SUNY, 97. **CONTACT ADDRESS** Department of Philosophy, Seattle Univ, Seattle, WA, 98122. **EMAIL** ddombrow@seattleu.edu

DOMINO, BRIAN
DISCIPLINE PHILOSOPHY **EDUCATION** Univ Ariz, BA, 88; Penn State Univ, MA, 90, PhD, 93. **CAREER** Asst prof, Eastern Michigan Univ. **HONORS AND AWARDS** Provost's new fac res awd, 96-97. **RESEARCH** Social and political philosophy, ethics, 19th century philosophy, history of medicine. **SELECTED PUBLICATIONS** Auth, Form as Substance and Its Relation to Matter in Metaphysics Z 17, Dialogue, 89; Vincenzo's Portrayal of Nietzsche's Socrates, Philos and Rhetoric, 93; Two Models of Abductive Inquiry, Philos and Rhetoric, 94; The Electronic Agora: Using a Mainframe Computer in Introductory Courses, Teaching Philos, 95; A Concordance to The Will to Power, J Nietzsche Stud, 95. **CONTACT ADDRESS** Dept of History and Philosophy, Eastern Michigan Univ, 701 Pray-Harrold, Ypsilanti, MI, 48197.

DONAGHY, JOHN A.
PERSONAL Born 11/01/1947, Philadelphia, PA, s **DISCIPLINE** PHILOSOPHY **EDUCATION** Univ of Scranton, AB, 70; New Schl for Soc Res, MA, Grad Fac, 72; Boston Col, PhD, 90. **CAREER** Campus Minister, St Thomas Aquinas Church and Cath Stud Center, 83-. **MEMBERSHIPS** APA; AAR; Amer Cath Phil Assoc **RESEARCH** Ethics and population/consumption; war/peace; liberation theology; religious ethics; El Salvador. **SELECTED PUBLICATIONS** Art, The Ideology of Arms Control, in: Philos and Soc Critic, 84; art, Pacifism and Revolution, in: The Interest of Peace :a Spectrum of Philos Views, 90; art, Justice as Participation: An Emerging Understanding, First Intl Conf on Soc Values: Proceedings, 91. **CONTACT ADDRESS** 2321 Baker St, Ames, IA, 50014. **EMAIL** jdonaghy@igc.apc.org

DONAKOWSKI, CONRAD L.
PERSONAL Born 03/13/1936, Detroit, MI, m, 1961, 2 children **DISCIPLINE** HISTORY, MUSIC, RELIGION **EDUCATION** Xavier Univ, BA, 58, MA, 59; Columbia Univ, PhD, 69. **CAREER** Instr humanities, Mich State Univ, 66-69; coordr, James Madison Col, Mich State Univ, 67-72; from asst to assoc prof humanities, 69-78, prof, 78-81, prof music hist, Mich State Univ, 81-, asst dean arts & lett, 79-, Am Coun Learned Soc grant, 73. **HONORS AND AWARDS** American Revolutionary Bicentennial Article Prize, Ohio Hist Comt, 76; Rockefeller Found grants, 76 & 77. **MEMBERSHIPS** AHA; Am Soc Eighteenth Century Studies; Am Soc Church Hist; Soc Fr Hist Studies. **RESEARCH** Romanticism; enlightenment; popular culture; nonverbal communication of values; music. **SELECTED PUBLICATIONS** Auth, A Muse for the Masses: Ritual and Music in an Age of Democratic Revolution, Univ Chicago, 77. **CONTACT ADDRESS** Dept of Humanities, Michigan State Univ, 102 Music Bldg, East Lansing, MI, 48824-1043. **EMAIL** donakows@pilot.msu.edu

DONALDSON, DANIEL J.
PERSONAL Born 09/01/1941, Connersville, IN, m, 1961, 3 children **DISCIPLINE** RELIGION **EDUCATION** Johnson Bible Col, BA, 63; Lincoln Christian Col, MA, 68; Univ Mo, EdD, 81. **CAREER** Min, 63-73, prof, 67-69, Registr, 73-80, St. Louis Christian Col; acad dean, San Jose Christian Col, 80-81; registr, 82-89, min, Fla Christian Col, 90-97; acad dean, Nebr Christian Col, 97-. **MEMBERSHIPS** Accrediting Asn Bible Cols. **RESEARCH** Higher education admin; leadership moral education **SELECTED PUBLICATIONS** Auth, art, Effecting Moral Development in Preprofesional College Students, 79; auth, art, Every Scripture Profitable, 84; auth, art, Making Disciples at Home, Pt I-III, 90; auth, Nebraska Christian College Style Sheet, 97. **CONTACT ADDRESS** Nebraska Christian Col, 1800 Syracuse Ave, Norfolk, NE, 68701. **EMAIL** ddonaldson@nechristian.edu

DONEGAN, CHARLES EDWARD
PERSONAL Born 04/10/1933, Chicago, IL, m **DISCIPLINE** LAW **EDUCATION** Wilson Jr Coll, AA 1953; Roosevelt, BSC 1954; Loyola, MSIR 1959; Howard, JD 1967; Columbia, LLM 1970. **CAREER** US Commisson on Civil Rights, legal intern 1966; Poor Peoples Campaign, legal counsel 1968; F B McKissick Enterprises, staff counsel, 1969; SUNY at Buffalo, first asst prof of law 1970-73; Howard Univ, assoc prof of law 1973-77; OH State Univ, visiting assoc prof 1977-78; First US EPA, asst reg counsel 1978-80; So Univ, prof of law 1980-84, visiting professor of law 1992; CE Donegan & Assoc, atty at law; LA State Univ Law Sch, visiting prof 1981; North Carolina Central Univ Law School, visiting prof 1988-89. **HONORS AND AWARDS** Most outstanding Prof So Univ Law Sch 1982; Ford Fellow Columbia Univ Law Sch 1972-73; NEH Fellow Afro Am Studies Yale Univ 1972-73; Speaker & Participant at National & Regional Conferences; named one of top 45, 42, 56, 61 Lawyers in Washington, DC Area; Washington African-American Newspaper, 1993-96. **MEMBERSHIPS** Labor arbitrator Steel Inds Postal AAA 1971-; consultant US Dept of Ag 1972; asst counsel NAACP Legal Defense Fund Inc 1967-69; hrng officer Various Govtl Agy 1975-; officer mem Am Natl Dist of Columbia Chicago Bar Assn 1968-; mem NAACP Urban League; Alpha Phi Alpha; Phi Alpha Delta; Phi Alpha Kappa; labor arbitrator FMCS 1985; counsultant Dist of Columbia Govt Dept of Public Works; mem, District of Columbia Consumer Claims Arbitration Bd 1987-; chmn, legal educ committee, Washington Bar Assn, 1984-91; mem, District of Columbia Attorney-Client Arbitration Board, 1990-91; mem, advisory committee, District of Columbia of Education, Ward 4, 1991; moot court judge, Georgetown, Howard, Balsa, 1987-; vp, Columbia Law Alumni Assn, Washington DC, 1994-; pres, vp, mem, Society of Labor Relations Professionals (SFLRP), 1987-; Natl Bar Assn, Arbitration Section, chair; Natl Assn of Securities Dealers, arbitrator, 1994-; Natl Futures Assn, arbitrator, 1994-; New York Stock Exchange, arbitrator, 1996-; Natl Conference of Black Lawyers, founding mem; Washington Bar Assn; Industrial Relations Research Association; Society of Professionals in Dispute Resolution. **SELECTED PUBLICATIONS** Articles in professional journals; contrib, Dictionary of Am Negro Bio, 1982; Washington Afro-American Newspaper, 1993, 1994, 1995. **CONTACT ADDRESS** 601 Pennsylvania Ave NW, Ste 900, S Bldg, Washington, DC, 20004.

DONELAN, JAMES
PERSONAL Born 09/08/1961, Springfield, MA, m, 1983, 2 children **DISCIPLINE** PHILOSOPHY **EDUCATION** SUNY Stony Brook, PhD, 95. **CAREER** Adjunct asst prof, Hofstra Univ, 96; lctr, New England Col, 96-98; lctr, Franklin Pierce Col, 97-. **MEMBERSHIPS** Amer Philos Assoc **RESEARCH** Political Theory **CONTACT ADDRESS** Dept of Philosophy, 35 Blueberry Ln, Peterborough, NH, 03458. **EMAIL** jed@monad.net

DONEY, WILLIS
PERSONAL Born 08/19/1925, Pittsburgh, PA **DISCIPLINE** PHILOSOPHY **EDUCATION** Princeton Univ, BA, 46, MA & PhD, 49; Dartmouth Col, AM, 67. **CAREER** Instr philos, Cornell Univ, 49-52; asst prof Ohio State Univ, 53-57; assoc prof, 58-66, prof philos, Dartmouth Col, 66-; vis lectr, Univ Mich, 53; vis lectr, Harvard Univ, 63; Santayana fel, 56; Ford-Dartmouth fel, 70; mem, Inst Advan Studies, 72-73; Camargo Found fel, 78-79; Edinburgh Univ fel, 80. **MEMBERSHIPS** Am Philos Asn; Aristotelian Soc; AAUP; Soc Medieval & Renaissance Philos; Comite de Patronage Studia & Analecta Cartesiana. **RESEARCH** Theory of knowledge; history of philosophy, especially 17th and 18th century. **SELECTED PUBLICATIONS** Art, Spinoza's Ontological Proof, The Philosophy of Baruch Spinoza, Catholic Univ, 80; ed transl, Nicolas Malebranche: Dialogues on Metaphysics, Abaris, 80; auth, Is Berkeley's a Cartesian Mind, Berkeley, Critical and Interpretive Essays Minnesota, 82. **CONTACT ADDRESS** Dept of Philosophy, Dartmouth Col, Hanover, NH, 03755. **EMAIL** D2980@aol.com

DONFRIED, KARL P.
PERSONAL Born 04/06/1940, New York, NY, m, 1960, 3 children **DISCIPLINE** RELIGION, BIBLICAL LITERATURE **EDUCATION** Columbia Univ, BA, 60; Harvard Div Sch, BD, 63; Union Theol Sem, STM, 65; Univ Heidelberg, DTheol, 68. **CAREER** PROF, REL, BIBL LIT, SMITH COL, 68-; vis prof, Hebrew Univ- Jerusalem, Yale Univ Div Sch, Univ Harrisburg-Hamburg, W Germany, Brown Univ, Amherst Col, Mt Holyoke Col, Assumption Col, St Hyacinth Col, Sem. **SELECTED PUBLICATIONS** Auth, Romans--A New Translation with Introduction and Commentary, Theol Stud, Vol 55, 94; The Reconciled Reconciler--The Apostle Paul as Indispensable Mediator in the Salvific Event Between God and the Christian Community According To 2 Corinthians Ii,14 Vi,4, Cath Biblical Quart, Vol 58, 96; Justification by Faith--The Origin and Development of a Central Pauline Theme, J Biblical Lit, Vol 114, 95. **CONTACT ADDRESS** Dept of Relig, Bibl Lit, Smith Col, Northampton, MA, 01063. **EMAIL** KDONFRIE@sophia.smith.edu

DONKEL, DOUGLAS L.
PERSONAL Born 01/20/1959, Portland, OR, m, 1991 **DISCIPLINE** PHILOSOPHY **EDUCATION** Univ Oregon, PhD, 90. **CAREER** Adj asst prof, phil, 92-, Univ of Portland. **MEMBERSHIPS** APA; Soc for Phenomenology and Existential Phil. **RESEARCH** Continental phil; classical Amer phil; metaphysics; phil of religion; phil of technology; applied phil; theory of difference. **SELECTED PUBLICATIONS** Auth, The Understanding of Difference in Heidegger and Derrida, Amer Univ Studies, Series V, Phil Vol 143, Peter Lang Pub, 93; art, Formal Contamination: A Reading of Derrida's Argument, Phil Today 40(2), 96. **CONTACT ADDRESS** 4423 S. E. Lexington St, Portland, OR, 97206. **EMAIL** donkel@up.edu

DONNELLY, JOHN
PERSONAL Born 03/30/1941, Worcester, MA, m, 1968, 2 children **DISCIPLINE** PHILOSOPHY **EDUCATION** Holy Cross Col, BSc, 63; Boston Col, MA, 65; Brown Univ, MA, 67, PhD(philos), 69. **CAREER** Asst prof philos, Univ Notre Dame, 69-70; asst prof, Fordham Univ, 70-75, dir grad studies, 70-72; vis prof, State Univ NY, Fredonia, 75-76; assoc prof, 76-81, prof philos & chp, Univ San Diego, 81-, Nat Endowment for Humanities grant, 80; coordr, Catholic Studies Minor, Univ San Diego, 98-. **HONORS AND AWARDS** Pres, Soren Kierkegaard Soc, 88-89. **MEMBERSHIPS** Am Philos Asn. **RESEARCH** Thamatology, metaphysics; ethics; philosophical theology. **SELECTED PUBLICATIONS** Auth, Some Remarks on Geach's Predicative and Attributive Adjectives, Notre Dame J Formal Logic, 71; contribr & ed, Logical Analysis and Contemporary Theism, Fordham Univ, 72; contribr & co-ed, Conscience, Alba House, 73; auth, Conscience and Religious Morality, Relig Studies, 73; contribr, Analysis and Metaphysics, D Reidel, 75; contribr, Infanticide and the Value of Life, Prometheus Bks, 78; contribr & ed, Language, Metaphysics and Death, Fordham Univ, 78, 2nd ed, 94; contribr, Kierkegaard's Fear and Trembling: Critical Appraisals, Univ Ala, 81; auth, Thinking Clearly about Death, Philosophia, 86; Self-Knowledge and the Mirror of the Ward, In: International Kierkegaard Commentary: The Sickness Unto Death, Mercer Univ, 87; contribr and ed, Reflective Wisdom: Richard Taylor on Issues that Matter, Prometheus, 89; contribr and ed, Suicide, Right or Wrong, Prometheus, 2nd ed, 98. **CONTACT ADDRESS** Dept of Philos, Univ of San Diego, 5998 Alcala Park, San Diego, CA, 92110-2492.

DONOHUE, JOHN WALDRON
PERSONAL Born 09/17/1917, New York, NY **DISCIPLINE** HISTORY & PHILOSOPHY OF EDUCATION **EDUCATION** Fordham Univ, AB, 39; St Louis Univ, MA, 44; Woodstock Col, STL, 51; Yale Univ, PhD, 55. **CAREER** Teacher high sch, NY, 44-47; from assoc prof to prof hist & philos of educ, Sch Educ, Fordham Univ, 55-70, adj prof, 77-80; Assoc Ed, America, 72- . **HONORS AND AWARDS** Mem, Society of Jesus, 39- ; ordained Roman Catholic priest, 50; Trustee, Fordham Univ, 69-77, 78-87, St Peter's Col, 80- ; St Louis Univ, 67-81. **MEMBERSHIPS** Philos Educ Soc; Nat Cath Ed Asn. **RESEARCH** Theory of Christian education; contemporary problems concerning religion and education. **SELECTED PUBLICATIONS** Auth, Work and Education, Loyola Univ, 59; Jesuit Education: An Essay on the Foundations of Its Idea, Fordham Univ, 63; St Thomas Aquinas and Education, Random, 68; Catholicism and Education, Harper, 73. **CONTACT ADDRESS** America 106 W 56th St, New York, NY, 10019.

DONOVAN, JOHN F.
DISCIPLINE LATE MODERN GERMAN PHILOSOPHY AND THE PHILOSOPHY OF RELIGION **EDUCATION** Fordham Univ, MA; Georgetown Univ, PhD. **CAREER** Taught, Georgetown Univ, 4 yrs; Mt Saint Mary's Col, 89-. **RESEARCH** The German Enlightenment and the Origins of Religious Studies. **SELECTED PUBLICATIONS** Auth, Doing and Don'ting: A Workbook in Moral Identity. **CONTACT ADDRESS** Dept of Philosophy, Mount Saint Mary's Col, 16300 Old Emmitsburg Rd, Emmitsburg, MD, 21727-7799. **EMAIL** donovan@msmary.edu

DONOVAN, MARY ANN
PERSONAL Cincinnati, OH **DISCIPLINE** HISTORICAL THEOLOGY **EDUCATION** St Michaels, Toronto, 77 **CAREER** Prof, 94-pres, Jesuit Sch of Theol, Assoc Prof, 81-94, Assist Prof, 77-81 **HONORS AND AWARDS** Col Theology Bk Award, 98; Elizabeth Seton Medal, Distinguished Woman Theologian **MEMBERSHIPS** Cath Theol Soc of Am; Col Theology Soc; N Amer Patristics Soc; Soc for Study of Christian Spirituality **RESEARCH** History, Spirituality; Early Christianity; Women's Issues **SELECTED PUBLICATIONS** Auth, One Right Reading? A Guide to Irenaeus, Liturgical Press, 97; Auth, Sisterhood as Power, The Past and Passion of Ecclesial Women, Crossroad, 89 **CONTACT ADDRESS** Jesuit Sch of Theol, Berkeley, 1735 LeRoy Ave, Berkeley, CA, 94709. **EMAIL** mdonovan@jstb.edu

DOODY, JOHN A.
DISCIPLINE PHILOSOPHY **EDUCATION** La Salle Col, BA, 65; Univ Notre Dame, PhD, 74. **CAREER** Prof, asst dean, Villanova Univ. **SELECTED PUBLICATIONS** Auth, Radical Hermeneutics, Critical Theory and the Political, Int Philos Quart, 91; MacIntyre and Habermas on Practical Reason, Amer Cath Philos Quart, 91 and Communitarianism, Liberalism, and Social Responsibility, Edwin Mellen Press, Lewiston, NY, 91; The Right Way to Think about the Rights of the Bill of Rights, in Studies in Social and Political Theory: Social Philosophy Today, The Edwin Mellen Press, Lewiston, NY, 93. **CONTACT ADDRESS** Dept of Philosophy, Villanova Univ, 800 Lancaster Ave, Villanova, PA, 19085-1692.

DOOHAN, HELEN
DISCIPLINE NURSING, RELIGIOUS STUDIES, EDUCATIONAL LEADERSHIP **EDUCATION** Adelphi Univ, BA, 71; Gonzaga Univ, MA, 76, PhD, 83. **CAREER** PROF REL STUD, GONZAGA UNIV, 76-. **CONTACT ADDRESS** 6126 E Willow Springs Rd, Spokane, WA, 99223. **EMAIL** hdoohan@gonzaga.edu

DOOLEY, PATRICIA
DISCIPLINE MASS COMMUNICATION, AND MEDIA ETHICS AND LAW **EDUCATION** Univ Minn, MA, PhD. **CAREER** Writer, Minn Hist Soc; asst prof, Univ Maine; dir, Kans Scholastic Press Assn District Four; asst prof. **RESEARCH** History of mass communication; media ethics and law. **SELECTED PUBLICATIONS** Auth, book on the history of journalism as an occupational group. **CONTACT ADDRESS** Dept of Commun, Wichita State Univ, 1845 Fairmont, Wichita, KS, 67260-0062. **EMAIL** dooley@elliott.es.twsu.edu

DOOLEY, PATRICK KIARAN
PERSONAL Born 06/23/1942, Fargo, ND, m, 1969 **DISCIPLINE** PHILOSOPHY **EDUCATION** St Paul Sem, Minn, BA, 64; Univ Notre Dame, MA, 67, PhD (philos), 69. **CAREER** From asst prof to assoc prof, 69-77, PROF PHILOS, ST BONAVENTURE UNIV, 77-, Researcher, Finger Lakes Col Consortium, 71-72; mem, Coun Philos Studies, Calvin Col, 73; Nat Endowment for Humanities grant, Duke University, 75 and vis scholar, 77; Nat Endowment for Humanities grant, Univ Kansas, 78; fac res grant, St Bonaventure Univ, 78; Nat Endowment for Humanities grant, Univ Ill, 81. **MEMBERSHIPS** Am Philos Asn; Am Cath Philos Asn. **RESEARCH** American philosophy; William James; philosophy and psychology. **SELECTED PUBLICATIONS** Auth, The Correspondence of James,William, Vol 2--William and Henry, 1885-1896, Nineteenth Century Prose, Vol 21, 94; Halfway to Revolution--Investigation and Crisis in the Works of Adams, Henry, James, William and Stein, Gertrude, 19th Century Prose, Vol 20, 93; The Correspondence of James, William, Vol 1--William and Henry, 1861-1884, 19th Century Prose, Vol 21, 94; The Trial of Curiosity--James, Henry, James, William and the Challenge of Modernity, 19th Century Prose, Vol 21, 94. **CONTACT ADDRESS** Dept of Philos, St Bonaventure Univ, St Bonaventure, NY, 14778.

DOOLITTLE, JAMES
PERSONAL Born 10/08/1917, Morristown, NJ, m, 1944, 6 children **DISCIPLINE** ROMANCE LANGUAGES AND LITERATURES **EDUCATION** Princeton Univ, AB, 39, MA, 42, PhD, 48. **CAREER** Teacher French and English, Thacher Sch, Calif, 39-40; instr French, Princeton Univ, 46-49; from asst prof to prof, Ohio State Univ, 49-61; prof Romance lang and head dept, Univ Cincinnati, 61-65; PROF FRENCH LIT, UNIV ROCHESTER, 65-, Ohio State Univ fel, 59-60; Guggenheim fel, 62-63 and 65; Am Coun Learned Soc grant, 69-70. **RESEARCH** History of ideas in France, 1600-1900; French literature of the 17th, 18th and 19th centuries; 17th century French memoirs. **SELECTED PUBLICATIONS** Auth, The Hungry Spirit, Selected Plays and Prose of Gowan, Elsie, Park, Theatre Rsrc Can Recherches Theatrales Can, Vol 13, 1992 The Nowlan, Alden Papers--An Inventory of the Archive at the University Of Calgary Libraries, Theatre Rsrc Int, Vol 19, 94. **CONTACT ADDRESS** Dept of Foreign Lang, Lit and Ling, Univ of Rochester, Rochester, NY, 14627.

DOORLEY, MARK J.
PERSONAL Born 08/03/1961, Lima, OH, m, 1998 **DISCIPLINE** PHILOSOPHY **EDUCATION** St Alphonsus Col, BA, 84; Washington Theol Union, M Div, 88; Boston Col, PhD, 94. **CAREER** Adj fac, 94-96, St John's Univ; adj fac, 96-97, vis asst prof, 97-, Villanova Univ. **MEMBERSHIPS** APA; Am Cath Philos Asn; The Lonergan Philos Asn; The Soc for Philos in the Contemp World. **RESEARCH** Ethical theory; the thought of Bernard Lonergan, S J. **SELECTED PUBLICATIONS** Auth, The Place of the Heart in Lonergan's Ethics: The Role of Feelings in the Ethical Intentionality of Bernard Lonergan, Univ Press Am, 96; auth, Resting in Reality: Reflections on Crowe's Complacency and Concern, Lonergan Workshop: The Structure and Rhythms of Love: In Honor of Frederick Crowe, SJ, vol 13, Boston Col, 97; auth, The Teaching of Ethics, J of Philos in Contemp World, vol 3, no 1, 96; auth, To Thine Own Self Be True: Self-Appropriation and Human Authenticity, Philos & Everyday Life: A Narrative Intro, Univ KS Press, forthcoming. **CONTACT ADDRESS** Core Ethics Prog, Villanova Univ, 800 Lancaster Ave, Villanova, PA, 19085. **EMAIL** mdoorley@email.vill.edu

DOPPELT, GERALD D.
DISCIPLINE PHILOSOPHY OF SCIENCE **EDUCATION** Johns Hopkins Univ, PhD, 69. **CAREER** Instr, Univ Pa, 66-73; vis lectr, Univ Calif-Berkeley; Univ Ill; PROF, PHILOS, UNIV CALIF, SAN DIEGO. **RESEARCH** Political theory; Philos of Science. **SELECTED PUBLICATIONS** Auth, "Dretske's Conception of Perception and Knowledge," Philos of Sci, 73; "Walzer's Theory of Morality in International Relations," Philos and Public Aff, 78; "Kuhn's Epistemological Relativism: An Interpretation and Defense," Inquiry, 78; "Incorrigibility and the Mental," Australasian Jour Philos, 78; "Rawls's System of Justice: A Critique from the Left," Nous, 81; "Rawls's Kantian Ideal and the Viability of Modern Liberalism," Inquiry, 88; "The Philosophical Requirements for an Adequate Conception of Scientific Rationality," Philos of Sci, 88; "Is Rawls's Kantian Liberalism Coherent and Defensible?," Ethics, 89. **CONTACT ADDRESS** Dept of Philos, Univ Calif, San Diego, 9500 Gilman Dr, La Jolla, CA, 92093.

DORN, LOUIS
PERSONAL Born 07/01/1928, Detroit, MI, m, 1953, 4 children **DISCIPLINE** OLD TESTAMENT THEOLOGY **EDUCATION** Lutheran Schl Theol, Chicago, PhD, 80. **CAREER** Ed, Helps for Translators, 78-, United Bible Soc. **MEMBERSHIPS** Soc of Biblical Lit **RESEARCH** Translation theory; studies in Hosea and Joel. **SELECTED PUBLICATIONS** Art, The Unexpected as a Speech Device; Shifts of Thematic Expectancy in Jeremiah, Bible Translator, 86; art, Struggling with Prophets in Translation, Bible Translator, 87; art, Philippine Poetry and Translation; a General Survey, Bible Translator 45: 301; art, Learning How to Use a Handbook, Bible Translator, 95. **CONTACT ADDRESS** 32 Larch Ave, Dumont, NJ, 07628-1223. **EMAIL** louis-dorn@compuserve.com

DORNISH, MARGARET HAMMOND
PERSONAL Born 07/25/1934, St. Marys, PA **DISCIPLINE** HISTORY OF RELIGIONS **EDUCATION** Smith Col, AB, 56; Claremont Grad Sch, MA, 67, PhD(relig), 69. **CAREER** Teacher English, Orme Sch, 60-65; asst prof relig, 69-74, assoc prof, 74-92, prof relig & chair, relig studies, Pomona Col, 93-. **MEMBERSHIPS** Am Acad Relig; Pac Coast Theol Soc; Asn Asian Studies; Int Asn Buddhist Studies. **RESEARCH** Buddhist studies. **SELECTED PUBLICATIONS** Auth, D T Suzuki's early interpretation of Buddhism and Zen, Eastern Buddhist, 70. **CONTACT ADDRESS** Dept of Religion, Pomona Col, 551 N College Way, Claremont, CA, 91711-6319. **EMAIL** mdornish@pomona.edu

DORON, PINCHAS
PERSONAL Born 07/05/1933, Poland, m, 1969, 5 children **DISCIPLINE** HEBREW LANGUAGE, BIBLE **EDUCATION** Hebrew Univ, Jerusalem, BA, 62, MA, 64; NY Univ, PhD (Hebrew studies), 75. **CAREER** Instr Hebrew and Talmud, Jewish Theol Sem, 64-65; lectr Hebrew, Hunter Col, 65-66; ASST PROF HEBREW, QUEENS COL, 66-, Instr, The Ulpan Ctr, 69-70. **MEMBERSHIPS** Asn Jewish Studies; Nat Asn Professors Hebrew. **RESEARCH** Biblical research; Hebrew language and literature; medieval Hebrew literature. **SELECTED PUBLICATIONS** Auth, Labor, Crafts and Commerce in Ancient Israel, Cath Biblical Quart, Vol 57, 95; New Evidence for the Pentateuch Text in the Aleppo Codex, Cath Biblical Quart, Vol 56, 94. **CONTACT ADDRESS** 730 E 7th St, Brooklyn, NY, 11218.

DORRIEN, GARY J.
PERSONAL Born 03/21/1952, m, 1 child **DISCIPLINE** RELIGION **EDUCATION** Alma Col, BA (summa cum laude), 74; Union Theological Seminary, MDiv, 78; Princeton Theological Seminary, MA, 79, ThM, 79; Union Grad School, PhD, 89. **CAREER** Teacher, Parsons Center School for emotionally disturbed students, 79-82; chaplian and rel dept chair, the Doane Stuart School, 82-87; assoc pastor, St Andrew's Episcopal Church, 82-87; ASST/ASSOC/FULL PROF OF RELIGION & DEAN OF STETSON CHAPEL, KALAMAZOO COL, 87-. **HONORS AND AWARDS** Harold Baker Honors Scholar, Alma Col, 70-74; Omicron Delta Kappa honor Soc, 73; Harvard Divinity School Honors Scholar, 74-76; Mrs T. Outstanding Teacher Award, Univ of Chicago Prog on Secondary School Teaching, 87; Florence J. Lucasse Award for Outstanding Scholar, Kalamazoo Col, 94. **MEMBERSHIPS** Am Acad of Religion; Amnesty Int; Asn for Religion and Intellectual Life; Col Theology Soc; Episcopal Diocese of Kalamazoo; Episcopal Peace Fel; Fel of Reconciliation; Greenpeace; NAACP; Nat Asn of Col and Univ Chaplains; Nat Org of Men Against Sexism; Soc of Christian Ethics. **SELECTED PUBLICATIONS** Auth, Soul in Society: The Making and Renewal of Social Christianity, Fortress Press, 95; auth, The Word as True Myth: Interpreting Modern Theology, Westminster John Knox Press, 97; auth, The Remaking of Evangelical Theology, Westminster John Knox Press, 98; auth, Theology Without Weapons: The Making of Barthian Dialectic, forthcoming; auth, Norman Thomas, The Am Radical, Routledge, 94; auth, Review of Sins of Omission: A Primer on Moral Indifference by S. Dennis Ford, Critical Rev of Books in Relig 1993 Vol 4, 94; auth, Beyond State and Market: Christianity and the Future of Economic Democracy, Cross Currents, 95; auth, Spirit in the World: Christianity and the Clash of Interests, Word & World, 95; auth, Neoliberal, not Neoconservative, Cross Currents, winter 95-96; auth, Beyond the Twilight of Socialism: Rethinking Economic Democracy, Harvard Divinity Bull, 96; auth, The Postmodern Barth?: The Word of God as True Myth, The Christian Century, 97; auth, Communitarianism, Christian Realism, and the Crisis of Progressive Christianity, Cross Currents, 97; auth, Inventing an American Conservatism: The Neoconservative Episode, Unraveling the Right: The New Conservatism in Am Thought and Politics, Westview Pubs, 98. **CONTACT ADDRESS** Dept of Religion, Kalamazoo Col, 1200 Academy St, Kalamazoo, MI, 49006.

DORSEN, NORMAN
PERSONAL Born 09/04/1930, New York, NY, m, 3 children **DISCIPLINE** CONSTITUTIONAL LAW, CIVIL LIBERTIES **EDUCATION** Columbia Univ, BA, 50; Harvard Univ, LLB, 53. **CAREER** Stokes Prof Law, NY Univ, 61-; dir, Arthur Garfield Hays Civil Lib Mem Prog, 61-; vis prof law, London Sch Econ, 68, Univ Calif, Berkeley, 74-75 & Harvard Univ,

80 & 83; exec dir, Spec Comt Courtroom Conduct, New York Bar Asn, 70-73; chmn, Health, Educ & Welfare Rev Panel new drug regulation in US, 75-77; consult, US Violence Comn, Random House, Nat Educ TV & Brit Broadcasting Corp; trustee, Am Friends London Sch Econ; chmn, Lawyers Comt for Human Rights, 97-. **HONORS AND AWARDS** Recipient of numerous awards and 2 honorary degrees; Fel of the Am Acad of Arts and Sci., LLD, Ripon Col, 81; founding dir and fac chair of NYU's Global Law Program; founding pres, Soc of Am Law Teachers (1973). **MEMBERSHIPS** Am Law Inst; Soc Am Law Teachers (past pres); Coun of For Relations. **RESEARCH** Antitrust law; criminal law; legal process. **SELECTED PUBLICATIONS** Coauth, Political and Civil Rights in the United States, 67 & 76; Frontiers of Civil Liberties, 68; ed, The Rights of Americans, 71; coauth, Disorder in the Court, 73; ed & coauth, None of Your Business: Government Secrecy in America, 74; auth, coauth, and/or ed of numerous other articles and books. **CONTACT ADDRESS** 40 Washington Sq S, New York, NY, 10012-1005. **EMAIL** norman.dorsen@nyu.law

DORSEY, ELBERT
PERSONAL Born 10/04/1941, St. Louis, MO, m **DISCIPLINE** LAW **EDUCATION** Harris-Stowe State Coll, BA 1966; St Louis Univ School of Law, JD 1973. **CAREER** St Louis Comm Coll Dist, asst librarian 1965-66; St Louis Bd of Educ, teacher 1966-70; St Louis Legal Aid Soc, law clerk 1971-72; Small Business Admin, loan officer/Attorney 1973-74; Collier, Dorsey, & Williams, Attorney. **HONORS AND AWARDS** Ford Fellowship World Conf of Peace 1973; Humanitarian Award St Louis Alumni Chptr Kappa Alpha Psi 1985; Dedication Award Mound City Bar Assn of St Louis 1983. **MEMBERSHIPS** Historian Mound City Bar Assc; mem Judicial Conf Advy Com for the Eighth Circuit Ct of Appeals; chmn/bd of dir Yeatman/Union-Sarah Jnt Commn on Health; Polemarch St Louis Alumni Chptr Kappa Alpha Psi Frat; chmn/advsry bd St Louis Comprehensive Hlth Cntr Home Hlth Bd. **CONTACT ADDRESS** Law Office of Collier, Dorsey & Williams, 625 N Euclid, Ste 402, St. Louis, MO, 63108.

DORTER, KENNETH
PERSONAL Born 07/30/1940, New York, NY, m, 1964, 2 children **DISCIPLINE** PHILOSOPHY **EDUCATION** Queens Col, NY, BA, 62; Pa State Univ, MA, 64, PhD (philos), 67. **CAREER** From instr to asst prof, 66-72, assoc prof, 72-82, PROF PHILOS, UNIV GUELPH, 82-. **MEMBERSHIPS** Can Philos Asn; Hegel Soc Am; Soc Ancient Philos; North Am Nietzche Soc. **RESEARCH** Philosophy of art; history of philosophy; metaphysics. **SELECTED PUBLICATIONS** Auth, Incantation and Aporia in Plato Rhetoric, Philos Rhetoric, Vol 29, 96; 3 Disappearing Ladders in Plato, Philos Rhetoric, Vol 29, 96. **CONTACT ADDRESS** Dept of Philosophy, Univ of Guelph, Guelph, ON, N1G 2W1.

DOSS, BARNEY J.
DISCIPLINE PHILOSOPHY **EDUCATION** Univ Oklahoma, PhD, 94. **CAREER** Instr, 95-, Southeast Arkansas Col **CONTACT ADDRESS** 4410 W. 28th St., Pine Bluff, AR, 71603.

DOSS, SEALE
DISCIPLINE EPISTEMOLOGY, PHILOSOPHY OF NATURAL SCIENCE, HISTORY OF PHILOSOPHY, THEORY **EDUCATION** Univ TX, BA, MA; Univ CA, Berkeley, PhD. **CAREER** Prof Philos, May Bumby Severy Distinguished Serv Prof, Ripon Col. **SELECTED PUBLICATIONS** Ed, Critical Thinking as a Philosophical Movement, Ripon Col Press. **CONTACT ADDRESS** Ripon Col, Ripon, WI. **EMAIL** DossS@mac.ripon.edu

DOSTAL, ROBERT J.
PERSONAL Born 06/12/1947, Fort Benton, MT, m, 1971, 3 children **DISCIPLINE** PHILOSOPHY **EDUCATION** Pennsylvania St Univ, PhD, 77. **CAREER** Asst Prof, 76-80, Memphis St Univ; Prof, 80-98, Provost, 94-98, Bryn Mawr Col. **HONORS AND AWARDS** Humboldt Fel, 82-82, 87, 89. **RESEARCH** Metaphysics; ethics political theory; hermenuetics; Kant & Post-Kantian German Philosophy; Phenomenology. **SELECTED PUBLICATIONS** Das Ubersetzen Kants ins Englische Ubersetzen verstehen Brucken bauen Gottinger Beitrage zur Internationalen Ubersetzungsforschung, Berlin, 93; Eros Freundschaft und Politik Heideggers Versagen Athenaeum, Budapest, 94; The Public and the People Heideggers Illiberal Politics, Rev of Metaphysics, 94; The Experience of Truth for Gadamer and Heidegger Taking Time and Sudden Lightning, Hermeneutics and Truth, Northwestern Press, 94; Gadamers Continuous Challenge Heideggers Plato Interpretation, The Philos of Hasn-Georg Gadamer the library of Living Philos, 97; The End of Metaphysics and the Possibility of non Hagelian Speculative Thought, Hegel Hist and Interp, 97; Gadamer Hans-Georg, Ency of Phenomenolgy, 97. **CONTACT ADDRESS** Bryn Mawr Col, Dept of Philos, Bryn Mawr, PA, 19010. **EMAIL** rdostal@brynmawr.edu

DOTY, RALPH
PERSONAL Born 05/22/1945, Sapulpa, OK, m, 1983 **DISCIPLINE** PHILOSOPHY **EDUCATION** Univ Okla, BA, 67; Columbia Univ, MA, 69, PhD, 73. **CAREER** Instr, E Los Angeles Col, 77-79; Instr, Rose State Col, 80-82; Asst prof, 83-91, assoc prof, 91-, Univ Oklahoma, 83-. **HONORS AND AWARDS** Baldwin Award Study Prize Super Tchg, 89; Who's Who among Amer Teachers, 94. **MEMBERSHIPS** Amer Philol Asn; Class Asn Mid W & S **RESEARCH** Xenophon **SELECTED PUBLICATIONS** Auth, How High is the Sky?, Class Bull, 91; The Criterion of Truth, Peter Lang Publ, 92; Xenophons Gynaikologia: The Training of a Greek Housewife, Class Asn New Eng, 94; Xenophone: Oeconomicus VII-XIII, Bristol Class Press, 94; Attitude Change and Right Brain Thinking, Jour of Thought, 96. **CONTACT ADDRESS** Dept of Classics, Univ of Okla, 780 Van Vleet Oval, Rm 101, Norman, OK, 73019. **EMAIL** rdoty@ou.edu

DOUBLES, MALCOLM CARROLL
PERSONAL Born 08/14/1932, Richmond, VA, m, 1956, 3 children **DISCIPLINE** RELIGION, PHILOLOGY **EDUCATION** Davidson Col, BA, 53; Union Theol Sem, Va, BD, 57; Univ St Andrews, PhD, 62. **CAREER** Pastor, Lebanon & Castlewood Presby Churches, VA, 60-65; asst prof Old Testament, St Andrews Presby Col, 65-69, mem Christianity & cult team, 65-74, chmn freshman Christianity & cult team, 67-71, assoc prof relig, 69-76, dean students, 74-76; prof Relig & Dean Col, 76-97, DISTINGUISHED PROF INTL STUDIES, COKER COL, 97-; Fulbright fel, Pakistan, 84, P R China, 88; NEH younger humanist fel, 71-72; managing ed, St Andrews Rev, 72-76; managing ed, Prog for Comput & Publ Targumic Lit, 74-. **MEMBERSHIPS** Soc Bibl Lit; Int Orgn for Study Old Testament; Asn Targumic Studies 2E **RESEARCH** Aramaic language and literature, with particular reference to Targumic studies; linguistics, with particular reference to Hebrew and Greek; New Testament background, with particular reference to Jewish history. **SELECTED PUBLICATIONS** Auth, Toward the publication of the Palestinian Targum(s), Vetus Testamentum, Vol XV, No 1; Indications of antiquity in the Fragment Targum, in In Memoriam Paul Kahle, Topelmann, 68; contribr, The History of the Jews in the Time of Christ, T&T Clark & Sons, 73. **CONTACT ADDRESS** Coker Col, 300 E College Ave, Hartsville, SC, 29550-3797. **EMAIL** mdoubles@aol.com

DOUGHERTY, JAMES E.
PERSONAL Born 05/04/1923, Philadelphia, PA, m, 1950, 4 children **DISCIPLINE** POLITICAL SCIENCE; POLITICAL PHILOSOPHY; INTERNATIONAL RELATIONS **EDUCATION** St. Joseph's Col, BS, 50; Fordham Univ, MA, 54; Univ Pa, PhD, 60. **CAREER** Inst/asst/assoc prof, St. Joseph's Univ, 51-63; prof, 63-92; prof emeritus, 92- ; visiting prof, Nat War Col, 64-65; res assoc, For Policy Res Inst, 55-76; sr res assoc, Inst For Policy Anal, 76-89. **HONORS AND AWARDS** Lindback Teaching Award, 63. **MEMBERSHIPS** Am Polit Sci Asoc (ret); Int Studies Asoc (ret); Int Inst for Stragic Studies, London (ret). **RESEARCH** Arms control; US-Soviet Cold War relations; disarmament; international relations theories; US foreign policy; Europoean Monetary Union and the single currency. **SELECTED PUBLICATIONS** Auth, The Bishops and Nuclear Weapons, 84; auth, American Foregin Policy: FDR to Reagan, 86; auth, Communism, The New Dictionary of Social Thought, 94; auth, The Politics of European Monetary Union, Current Hist, 97; auth with Robert L. Pfaltzgraff, Jr., Contending Theories of International Relations, 97. **CONTACT ADDRESS** 590 Spring Ln., Philadelphia, PA, 19128-1002.

DOUGHERTY, JUDE
PERSONAL Born 07/21/1930, Chicago, IL, m, 1957, 4 children **DISCIPLINE** METAPHYSICS, HISTORY OF AMERICAN PHILOSOPHY **EDUCATION** Catholic Univ Amer, PhD, 60. **CAREER** Instr, 57-58, Marquette Univ; Instr, Asst Prof, Assoc Prof, 58-66, Bellarmine Coll; Assoc Prof, Ordinary Prof, 66-98, Dean, Sch Philos, 67-, Catholic Univ Amer. **HONORS AND AWARDS** Cardinal Wright Award, Fellowship of Catholic Scholars; Aquinas Medal, Amer Cath Philos Assoc; Pres of, ACPA; Metaphys Soc Amer; Soc Philos Rel. **MEMBERSHIPS** Metaphysical Soc Amer; Soc Philos of Rel; Amer Philos Assoc; Amer Catholic Philos Assoc. **RESEARCH** History American Philosophy, Social and Political Philosophy. **SELECTED PUBLICATIONS** Auth, The Necessity of Punishment, The World and I, 93; Wilsonian Morality, Crisis, 94; Santayana on the Role of Religion in Society, Modern Age, 95; Thomism, Encyclopedia of Applied Ethics, 97; Professional Responsibility, The World and I, 96; The Failure of Positivism and the Enduring Legacy of Comte, forthcoming; Do Majorities Have Rights?, Modern Age, 98. **CONTACT ADDRESS** School Philosophy, Catholic Univ of America, Washington, DC, 20017. **EMAIL** DOUGHERJ@CUA.edu

DOUGHERTY, JUDE PATRICK
PERSONAL Born 07/21/1930, Chicago, Ill, m, 1957, 4 children **DISCIPLINE** PHILOSOPHY **EDUCATION** Cath Univ Am, AB, 54, MA, 55, PhD, 60. **CAREER** Instr philos, Marquette Univ, 57-58; from instr to assoc prof, Bellarmine Col, Ky, 58-66; assoc prof, 66-76, Prof Philos, Cath Univ Am, 76-, Dean, Sch Philos, 67-, Ed, Rev Metaphys, 71-; vis prof philos, Univ Louvain, 74-75. **HONORS AND AWARDS** William T Miles Award, Bellarmine Col, 64; Cardinal Wright Awd, fel of Cath Schol, 94. **MEMBERSHIPS** Am Philos Asn; Am Cath Philos Asn (treas, 66-71, pres, 74-75); Metaphys Soc Am (pres, 83-84); Soc Philos Relig (pres, 78-79); Pontifical Acad of St. Thomas Aquinas; European Acad of Scis and Arts. **RESEARCH** Philosophy of religion; ethics; metaphysics. **SELECTED PUBLICATIONS** Auth, Recent American Naturalism, Cath Univ Am, 60; John H Randall's Notion of Substance, Proc Am Cath Philos Asn, 62; coauth, Approaches to Morality, Harcourt, Brace & World, 66; auth, Nagel's concept of science, Philos Today, 66; Lessons from the history of science and technology, Studies Philos and Hist of Philos, 69; Randall's Interpretation of Religion, 74; Finding of law, Proc Am Cath Philos Asn, 75; Dewey on the value of religion, New Scholasticism, 77; ed, The Good Life and Its Pursuit, Paragon, 84; ed, Studies in Philosophy and the History of Philosophy, 74-. **CONTACT ADDRESS** Sch of Philos, Catholic Univ of America, 620 Michigan Ave N E, Washington, DC, 20064-0002. **EMAIL** dougherj@cua.edu

DOUGHERTY, RAY CORDELL
PERSONAL Born 09/18/1940, Brooklyn, NY, m, 1982, 3 children **DISCIPLINE** LINGUISTICS, PHILOSOPHY OF LANGUAGE **EDUCATION** Dartmouth Col, BA, 62, MS, 64; Mass Inst Technol, PhD, 68. **CAREER** Res assoc ling, Mass Inst Technol, 68-69; asst prof, 69-72, Assoc Pr of Ling, NY Univ, 72-; Fulbright prof ling, Univ Salzburg, Austria, 76-77. **MEMBERSHIPS** Ling Soc Am; Philos Sci Asn. **RESEARCH** Grammar; semantics; history of science. **SELECTED PUBLICATIONS** Auth, A grammar of coordination: I,II, Language, 12/70; coauth, Appositive NP constructions, 1/72 & auth, A survey of linguistic methods, 11/73, Found Lang. **CONTACT ADDRESS** Dept of Ling, New York Univ, 719 Broadway, New York, NY, 10003-6806. **EMAIL** dougher@acfz.nyu.edu

DOUGLAS, JAMES MATTHEW
PERSONAL Born 02/11/1944, Onalaska, TX, m **DISCIPLINE** LAW **EDUCATION** TX Southern Univ, BA Math 1966, JD Law 1970; Stanford Univ, JSM Law 1971. **CAREER** Singer Simulation Co, computer analyst 1966-72; TX Southern Univ Sch of Law, asst Prof 1971-72; Cleveland State Univ Sch of Law, asst Prof 1972-75; Syracuse Univ Sch of Law, assoc dean assoc prof 1975-80; Northeastern Univ Sch of Law, prof of law 1980-81; TX Southern Univ Sch of Law, dean & prof 1981-95, interim provost and vp academic affairs, 1995; pres 1995-. **MEMBERSHIPS** State Bar of TX; Houston Jr Bar Assc; Amer Bar Assc Chrmn of Educ Comm of Sci & Tech Section; bd dir Hiscock Legal Soc; fac adv to Natl Bd of Black Amer Law Students; bd of dirs Gulf Coast Legal Foundation; mem Natl Bar Assoc Comm on Legal Educ; mem editorial bd The Texas Lawyer; life mem Houston Chamber of Commerce; bd of dirs, Law School Admission Council; chmn, Minority Affairs Committee, Law Shool Admission Council. **SELECTED PUBLICATIONS** "Some Ideas on the Computer and Law" TX Southern Univ Law Review 20 1971; "Cases & Materials on Contracts". **CONTACT ADDRESS** Texas So Univ, 3100 Cleburne Ave, Houston, TX, 77004.

DOUGLAS, WALTER
PERSONAL Born 02/02/1935, Grenada, WI, m, 1963, 3 children **DISCIPLINE** THEOLOGY **CAREER** Prof, Andrews Univ Theol Sem, 70-. **HONORS AND AWARDS** Andrews Medallion Scholar. **MEMBERSHIPS** AAR; DBL; Can Soc for Relig Studies; Adventist Soc for Relig Studies. **CONTACT ADDRESS** Andrews Univ, Berrien Springs, MI, 49103.

DOURLEY, JOHN PATRICK
PERSONAL Born 02/20/1936, Ottawa, ON, Canada **DISCIPLINE** RELIGION **EDUCATION** St Patrick's Col, BA, 57; Univ Ottawa, LPh, 60, STL and MTh, 64; St Michael's Col, Univ Toronto, MA, 66; Fordham Univ, PhD (theol), 71; C G Jung Inst, Switz, dipl Jungian psychol, 80. **CAREER** Asst prof, 71-75, ASSOC PROF RELIG, CARLETON UNIV, 75-. **MEMBERSHIPS** Am Acad Relig; Am Teilhard de Chardin Asn; Can Theol Soc (treas, 72-74); Can Soc Sci Study Relig. **RESEARCH** Paul Tillich's relation to early Franciscan theology, especially Bonaventure's; Tillich; C G Jung. **SELECTED PUBLICATIONS** Auth, The Implications of Jung, Carl, Gustav Critique of the Symbol of Trinity, Stud Religion Sci Religieuses, Vol 23, 94; Boehme, Jacob and Tillich, Paul on Trinity and God--Similarities and Differences, Religious Stud, Vol 31, 95. **CONTACT ADDRESS** Dept of Relig St Patrick's Col, Carleton Univ, 1125 Colonel By Dr, Ottawa, ON, K1S 1N4.

DOWD, NANCY E.
DISCIPLINE LAW **EDUCATION** Univ Conn, BA; Univ Ill, MA; Loyola Univ Chicago, JD. **CAREER** Prof, Univ Fla, 89-; instr, Suffolk Univ, 84-89, vis prof, Univ Auckland, New Zealand; Univ Western Australia; Murdoch Univ, Australia; past assoc, Choate, Hall Stewart, Boston; clerk, Judge Robert A. Sprecher, US Ct Appeals, 7th Circuit; pract law in Boston. **HONORS AND AWARDS** Rockefeller Found grant; teacher Yr, 90-91. **MEMBERSHIPS** Law and Soc Asn; Mass Bar; Phi Beta Kappa; Phi Kappa Phi; Alpha Lambda Delta; Mortar bd. **RESEARCH** Contracts, family law, employ discrimination, women and the law **SELECTED PUBLICATIONS** Auth, Defense of Single-Parent Families. **CONTACT ADDRESS** School of Law, Univ of Florida, PO Box 117625, Gainesville, FL, 32611-7625. **EMAIL** dowd@law.ufl.edu

DOWD, SHARYN
PERSONAL Born 02/14/1947, Atlanta, GA, s **DISCIPLINE** NEW TESTAMENT **EDUCATION** Wake Forest Univ, BA, 69; Southeastern Baptist Theolog Seminary, Mdiv, 80; Emory Univ, PhD, 86 **CAREER** Instr, Wake Forest Univ, 84-87; assoc prof, Lexington Theolog Seminary, 87-92; prof, Lexington Theolog Seminary, 92- **HONORS AND AWARDS** President, NABPR, 91 **MEMBERSHIPS** Soc Bibl Lit; Ntl Assoc Baptist Professors Relig; Baptist Women in Ministry **RESEARCH** New Testament Theology; Gospel of Mark; Pauline Studies **SELECTED PUBLICATIONS** "Galatians," IVP Women's Bible Commentary, Intervarsity Pr, forthcoming; "Review Essay: The Gospel and the Sacred: Poetics of Violence in Mark by Robert G. Hammerton-Kelly," Lexington Theolog Quart; ed, "Inspiration and Authority According to 2 Timothy," Common Ground, 98 **CONTACT ADDRESS** Lexington Theol Sem, 631 S Lime, Lexington, KY, 40508. **EMAIL** sdowd@lextheo.edu

DOWNES, STEPHEN M.
PERSONAL Born 12/21/1960, United Kingdom **DISCIPLINE** PHILOSOPHY **EDUCATION** Manchester Univ, BA; Warwick Univ, MA; Virginia Polytechnic & State Univ, PhD. **CAREER** Vis asst prof, philos, Univ of Cincinnati, 90-91; post-doctoral fel, Northwestern Univ, 91-92; asst prof, 92-98, assoc prof, philos, 98- , University of Utah. **MEMBERSHIPS** APA; Philos of Sci Asn. **RESEARCH** Philosophy of biology; human nature; genome project; cloning. **SELECTED PUBLICATIONS** Auth, The Importance of Models in Theorizing: A Deflationary Semantic Approach, in Hull, ed, Proceedings of the Philosophy of Science Association, vol 1, 92; auth, Modelling Scientific Practice: Paul Thagard's Computational Approach, New Ideas in Psych, 93; auth, Socializing Naturalized Philosophy of Science, Philos of Sci, 93; auth, Science, and, Logical Positivism, and, Logical Empiricism, in Garrett, ed, The Encyclopedia of Empiricism, Greenwood, 97; auth, Constructivism, in Craig, ed, Routledge Encyclopedia of Philosophy, Routledge, 98; auth, Ontogeny, Phylogeny and Scientific Development, in Hardcastle, ed, Biology Meets Psychology: Constraints, Conjectures, Connections, MIT, forthcoming. **CONTACT ADDRESS** Dept of Philosophy, Utah Univ, Salt Lake City, UT, 84112. **EMAIL** s.downes@mcc.utah.edu

DOYLE, DENNIS M.
PERSONAL m, 4 children **DISCIPLINE** RELIGIOUS STUDIES **EDUCATION** Cath Univ Am, PhD. **CAREER** Assoc prof, Univ Dayton, 84-. **RESEARCH** Ecclesiology, Catholic thought, systematics & religious education. **SELECTED PUBLICATIONS** Auth, The Church Emerging from Vatican II. **CONTACT ADDRESS** Dept of Religious Studies, Univ of Dayton, 300 College Park, Dayton, OH, 45469-1679. **EMAIL** doyled@checkov.hm.udayton.edu

DOYLE, JAMES F.
PERSONAL Born 05/16/1927, AK, m, 1954, 4 children **DISCIPLINE** PHILOSOPHY **EDUCATION** Louisiana State Univ, BS, 49; Yale Univ, MA, 57; PhD, 64. **CAREER** Instr, philos, Carleton Col, 58-60; asst prof, philos, Claremont Men's Col, 60-66; assoc prof, prof, philos, Univ Missouri, 66-98. **HONORS AND AWARDS** NEH grant, 85-86. **MEMBERSHIPS** APA; Int Asn for Philos of Law and Social Philos; Am Soc for Polit and Legal Philos. **SELECTED PUBLICATIONS** Auth, Police Discretion, Legality, and Morality, in Police Ethics,, ed, Hefferman, John Jay, 85; auth, Democratic Autonomy: Fulfilling Revolutionary Promises, Archiv fur Rechts- und Sozialphilosophie, 90; auth, Empowering and Restraining the Police: How to Accomplish Both, Criminal Justice Ethics, 92; auth, A Radical Critique of Criminal Punishment, in Griffin, ed, Radical Critiques of the Law, Univ Press of Kansas, 97; auth, Legal Accommodation of Social Diversity, Rechtstheorie, 98. **CONTACT ADDRESS** 6334 Pershing Ave, St Louis, MO, 63130-4703. **EMAIL** sjfdoyl@umslvma.umsl.edu

DRAGE-HALE, ROSEMARY
DISCIPLINE RELIGION **EDUCATION** Univ Harvard, PhD, 92. **CAREER** Assoc prof. **HONORS AND AWARDS** Co-ch, Hist of Christianity Section, Amer Acad of Rel; ed bd, Harvard Theol Rev and Mystics Quart. **RESEARCH** History of Christianity in the European Middle Ages and early modern period. **SELECTED PUBLICATIONS** Auth, Joseph as Mother: Adaptation and Appropriation of Marian Imagery, Medieval Mothering, Feminae Medievalia 4, Univ Toronto Press, 96; Taste and See, for God is Sweet: Sensory Perception and Memory in Medieval Christian Mystical Experience, Vox Mystica: Essays in Honor of Valerie Lagorio, Boydell and Brewer, 95; "The Return of the Grateful Dead: The Case for Spiritism in Late Medieval Germany," Jour of Rel and Cult Summer, 94; The Silent Virgin: Marian Imagery in the Sermons of Meister Eckhart and Johannes Tauler, De Ore Domini: Preacher and Word in the Middle Ages, Medieval Inst Publ, 94; co-ed, Models of Holiness: Paradigms of Virtue in Medieval Sermons, Intl Fed of Inst Medieval Stud, Brepols, 95. **CONTACT ADDRESS** Dept of Rel, Concordia Univ, Montreal, 1455 de Maisonneuve W, Montreal, PQ, H3G 1M8.

DRAKE, DANA BLACKMAR
PERSONAL Born 12/18/1926, Macon, GA **DISCIPLINE** ROMANCE LANGUAGES, LAW **EDUCATION** Davidson Col, AB, 48; Univ Va, LLB, 51; NY Univ, LLM, 52; Middlebury Col, MA, 66; Univ NC, Chapel Hill, PhD (Span), 67. **CAREER** Jr Partner, Young and Hollis, Columbus, Ga, 52-55; attorney, Joint Comt Taxation, 55-59; asst mgr real estate, Trust Dept, Citizens Southern Nat Bank, 59-62; instr Span, Univ NC, Chapel Hill, 62-67; asst prof, 67-71, assoc prof, 71-82, PROF SPAN, VA POLYTECH INST AND STATE UNIV, 82-. **MEMBERSHIPS** Am Asn Teachers Span and Port; MLA; Cervantes Soc Am. **RESEARCH** Cervantes. **SELECTED PUBLICATIONS** Auth, Rossetti Goblin Market, Explicator, Vol 51, 92; Ibsen A Doll House, Explicator, Vol 53, 94. **CONTACT ADDRESS** 210 University Club, Blacksburg, VA, 24060.

DRANE, JAMES FRANCIS
PERSONAL Born 04/06/1930, Chester, PA **DISCIPLINE** PHILOSOPHY, THEOLOGY **EDUCATION** Little Rock Col, AB, 51; Pontif Gregorian Univ, Rome, BD, 53; Middlebury Col, MA, 61; Univ Madrid, PhD(philos), 64. **CAREER** Asst philos, St John's Sem, Ark, 56-67; assoc prof relig studies, Webster Col, 67-69; prof Philos, Edinboro State Col, 69-, Assoc, Danforth Found, 73-; interdisciplinary fel psychiat, Menn Sch Psychiat, 76-77; res scholar, Kennedy Inst Bioethics, Georgetown Univ, 81 & Univ Tenn, Memphis, Med Complex, 82. **HONORS AND AWARDS** Distinguished Teaching Chair Pa, Pa Dept Educ, 76. **MEMBERSHIPS** Cath Philos Asn; Am Philos Asn; Soc Phenomenol & Existential Philos; Soc Sci Studies Relig; Soc Christian Ethics. **RESEARCH** Philosophy of man; medical ethics; ethics and psychiatry. **SELECTED PUBLICATIONS** Auth, Las Bases de la Tolerancia (2 vols), Univ Madrid, 64; Pilgrimage to Utopia, 65 & Authority and Institution, 69, Bruce; La Rusia Actual, Ed Juventud, 67; A New America Reformation, Littlefield & Adams, 74; Natural Law and Politics, J Value Inquiry, 74; The Possibility of God, Littlefield & Adams, 76; Religion and Ethics, Paulist Press, 77; auth, Your Emotional Life, Thomas Moore, 84; auth, Becoming A Good Doctor, Sheed & Ward, 89; auth, Making Life and Death Decisions for Others: Applying the Quality of Life Concept, Quinnipiac Col, 91; auth, Como Ser Un Buen Medico, San Pablo, 93; auth, Clinical Bioethics: Theory and Practice in Medical-Ethical Decision Making, Sheed & Ward, 94; auth, Caring to the End, Lake Area Health Education Center, 97. **CONTACT ADDRESS** Dept of Philosophy, Edinboro Univ of Pennsylvania, Edinboro, PA, 16444.

DRANGE, THEODORE MICHAEL
PERSONAL Born 03/14/1934, New York, NY, m, 1959, 2 children **DISCIPLINE** PHILOSOPHY **EDUCATION** Brooklyn Col, BA, 55; Cornell Univ, PhD(philos), 63. **CAREER** Lectr Philos, Brooklyn Col, 60-62; from instr to asst prof, Univ Ore, 62-65; asst prof, Idaho State Univ, 65-66; from asst prof to assoc prof, 66-74, prof Philos, West Va Univ, 74-, ed assoc, J Critical Analysis, 74-. **MEMBERSHIPS** Eastern Div Am Philos Asn. **RESEARCH** Philosophy of language, theory of knowledge; philosophy of science. **SELECTED PUBLICATIONS** Auth, Type Crossings, Mouton, The Hague, 66; Reply to Martin on type crossings, Philos & Phenomenol Res, 69; Paradox regained, Philos Studies, 69; Harrison and Odegard on type crossings, Mind, 69; Truth and necessary truth, J WVa Philos Soc, 73; A critical review of E Erwin's The Concept of Meaninglessness, J Critical Analysis, 75; Some applications of epistemology, J WVa Philos Soc, 75; Evolution vs Creation, Apeiron, 81. **CONTACT ADDRESS** Dept of Philosophy, West Virginia Univ, PO Box 6312, Morgantown, WV, 26506-6312. **EMAIL** tdrange@wvi/edu

DRAPER, DAVID E.
DISCIPLINE THEOLOGY **EDUCATION** Frostburg State Univ, BS, 71; Winebrenner Sem, MDiv, 79; Bowling Green State Univ, MEd, 85, PhD, 88. **CAREER** Dir develop, 82-85; VP inst advancement, 85-88; pres, dir, Churches of God, General Conf, 92-94; pres, Wiinebrenner Theol Sem, 1988-. **HONORS AND AWARDS** Outstanding Young Man Am, 86., Assoc ministry, Churches of God, Gen Conf; ed, Church Advocate; chaplain, CGYA Workshop. **MEMBERSHIPS** Mem, Impact Admin Comm; bd mem, Great Commn Ministries; mem, Fel Evangel Sem Pres(s). **SELECTED PUBLICATIONS** Ed, Youth Advance mag; Reach 'n Rejoice; pub(s), Church Advocate; The Gem; co-auth, co-author, Bound But Free, Churches of God. **CONTACT ADDRESS** Winebrenner Theol Sem, 701 E Melrose Ave, PO Box 478, Findlay, OH, 45839.

DRAY, WILLIAM HERBERT
PERSONAL Born 06/23/1921, Montreal, PQ, Canada, m, 1943, 2 children **DISCIPLINE** PHILOSOPHY **EDUCATION** Univ Toronto, BA, 49; Oxford Univ, BA, 51, MA, 55 DPhil-(philos), 56. **CAREER** Lectr philos, Univ Toronto, 5 3-55, from asst prof to prof, 56-68; prof and chmn dept, Trent Univ, 68-73; prof, Duke Univ, 73-74 and Trent Univ, 74-76; PROF PHILOS, UNIV OTTAWA, 76-, Am Coun Learned Soc fel, 60-61; Can Coun fel, 71-72 and 78-79,78-79; Killam fel, 80-81. **MEMBERSHIPS** Am Philos Asn; Can Philos Asn; Royal Soc Can; Can Hist Asn; Societi de philosophic du Quebec. **RESEARCH** Analytic philosophy; philosophy of history; philosophy of mind. **SELECTED PUBLICATIONS** Auth, Philosophical Foundations of Historical Knowledge, Clio J Lit Hist PhilosHist, Vol 24, 95; Collingwood, R. G.--The Idea of History--Revised Edition Including Collingwood Lectures of 1926-1928, Clio J Lit Hist PhilosHist, Vol 24, 94; Explanation and Understanding in the Human Sciences, Clio J Lit Hist Philos Hist, Vol 23, 93. **CONTACT ADDRESS** Dept Philos, Univ Ottawa, Ottawa, ON, K1N 6N5.

DREFCINSKI, SHANE
PERSONAL m, 2 children **DISCIPLINE** PHILOSOPHY **EDUCATION** Univ Minn, MA, 92, PhD, 96. **CAREER** Asst prof. **RESEARCH** Ancient Greek & Roman philosophy; medieval philosophy; early modern philosophy; philosophy of education; ethics. **SELECTED PUBLICATIONS** Auth, pubs on Aristotle's ethical theory. **CONTACT ADDRESS** Dept of Philosophy, Univ of Wisconsin, Platteville, 1 University Plaza, Platteville, WI, 53818-3099. **EMAIL** drefcinski@uwplatt.edu

DREHER, JOHN PAUL
PERSONAL Born 08/28/1934, Jersey City, NJ, m, 1959, 3 children **DISCIPLINE** PHILOSOPHY **EDUCATION** St Peter's Col, AB, 55; Fordham Univ, MA, 59; Univ Chicago, PhD, 61. **CAREER** Asst prof philos, Univ NC, 61-63; asst prof, 63-68, assoc prof & chmn dept philos, 68-69, prof, 89-, Lawrence Univ. **HONORS AND AWARDS** Outstanding Teacher Award, 89 **MEMBERSHIPS** Am Philos Assn. **RESEARCH** History of philosophy; applied ethics; pragmatism. **SELECTED PUBLICATIONS** Art, Moral Objectivity, Southern J Philos, 66; art, The Driving Ration in Plato's Divided Line, Ancient Philosophy, 90. **CONTACT ADDRESS** Dept of Philosophy, Lawrence Univ, PO Box 599, Appleton, WI, 54912-0599. **EMAIL** john.p.dreher@lawrence.edu

DREIER, JAMES
PERSONAL Born 04/05/1960, New York, NY, m, 1989, 3 children **DISCIPLINE** PHILOSOPHY **EDUCATION** Harvard Univ, AB, 82; Princeton, PhD, 88. **CAREER** Sr vis lectr, Monash Univ, 93-94; ASST PROF OF PHILOS, 88-95, ASSOC PROF OF PHILOS, BROWN UNIV, 95-. **MEMBERSHIPS** Am Philos Asn. **RESEARCH** Meta-ethics; rationality; decision theory. **SELECTED PUBLICATIONS** Auth, Internalism and Speaker Relativisim, Ethics; The Supervenience Argument against Moral Realism, Southern J of Philos; Expressivist Embeddings and Minimalist Truth, Philos Studies; Rational Preference: Decision Theory as a Theory of Practical Rationality, Theory and Decision; Accepting Agent Centered Norms, Australasian J of Philso; Humean Doubts, Ethics and Practical Reason, Oxford Univ Press, 97. **CONTACT ADDRESS** Dept of Philos, Brown Univ, Box 1418, Providence, RI, 02912. **EMAIL** James_Dreier@brown.edu

DREISBACH, DONALD FRED
PERSONAL Born 06/25/1941, Allentown, PA, d **DISCIPLINE** PHILOSOPHY & HISTORY OF RELIGION **EDUCATION** MA Inst Technol, BS, 63; Northwestern Univ, MA, 69, PhD, 70. **CAREER** Assoc prof, 69- 80, Prof Philos, Northern MI Univ, 80. **MEMBERSHIPS** AAUP; Am Acad Relig; Am Philos Asn; NAm Paul Tillich Soc. **RESEARCH** Philosophical theology; Paul Tillich. **SELECTED PUBLICATIONS** Auth, Paul Tillich's Herrmeneutic, J Am Acad Relig, Vol XLIII, No 1; Paul Tillich's Doctrine of Religious Symbols, Encounter, Vol 37, No 4; On the love of God, Anglican Theol Rev, Vol LIX, No 1; Circularity and consistency in Descartes, Can J Philos, Vol VIII, No 1; Agreement and obligation in the Crito, New Scholasticism, Vol LII, No 2; The unity of Paul Tillich's existential analysis, Encounter, Vol 41, No 4; On the hermeneutic of symbols: The Buri-Hardwick debate, Theologische Zeitschrift, 9-10/79; Essence, existence and the fall: Paul Tillich's analysis of existence, Harvard Theol Rev, Vol 73, No 1-2; Symbols and Salvation, Univ Press Am, 93. **CONTACT ADDRESS** Dept of Philos, No Michigan Univ, 1401 Presque Isle Av, Marquette, MI, 49855-5301. **EMAIL** ddreisba@nmu.edu

DREYFUS, HUBERT LEDERER
PERSONAL Born 10/15/1929, Terre Haute, IN, m, 1974, 2 children **DISCIPLINE** PHILOSOPHY **EDUCATION** Harvard Univ, BA, 51, MA, 52, PhD, 64. **CAREER** Instr philos, Brandeis Univ, 57-59; from instr to assoc prof, Mass Inst Technol, 60-68; assoc prof, 68-72, PROF PHILOS, UNIV CALIF, BERKELEY, 72-96, PROF EMER, 96-; French Govt grant, 64-65; res assoc computer sci, NSF grant, Harvard Univ, 68; Am Coun Learned Soc grant, 68-69; consult NEH, Nat Bd Consult, 76- **HONORS AND AWARDS** Guggenheim, 85; ACLS grant, 1968-1989; Phi Beta Kappa lectr, 92-93. **MEMBERSHIPS** Am Philos Asn; Soc Phenomenol & Existential Philos. **RESEARCH** Phenomenology and existential philosophy; artifical intelligence and computer simulation of cognitive processes; philosophy in literature. **SELECTED PUBLICATIONS** Coauth, The landscape of Dante's Inferno, Ital Quart, spring 62; auth, Alchemy and Arificial Intelligence, Rand Corp, 65; Why Computers must have bodies in order to be intelligent, Rev Metaphy, 9/67; The perceptual noema: The suppressed originality of Aron Gurwitsch, in Life-World and Consciousness, Northwestern Univ, 71; What Computers Can't Do: A Critique of Artificial Reason, Harper, 72 & What Computers Still Can't Do, MIT Press, 92; coauth, The computer as a mistaken model of the mind, in Philosophy & Psychology, Macmillan, 74; auth, Human temporality, in The Study of Time II, Springer, Verlag, 75; The priority of The World to My World: Heidegger's an-

swer to Husserl (and Sartre), Man & World, 75; co-auth, Michel Foucault, Univ Chicago press, 82; co-auth, Mind Over machines, Free Press, 86; Being in the World, MIT Press, 91; co-auth, Disclosing New Worlds, MIT Press, 97. **CONTACT ADDRESS** Dept of Philosophy, Univ of California, 314 Moses Hall, Berkeley, CA, 94720-2391. **EMAIL** dreyfus@cogsci.berkeley.edu

DRINAN, ROBERT FREDERICK
PERSONAL Born 11/15/1920, Boston, MA **DISCIPLINE** LAW **EDUCATION** Boston Col, BA, 42, MA, 47; Georgetown Univ, LLB, 49, LLM, 50; Gregorian Univ, Rome, STD, 54. **CAREER** Dean & prof law, Law Sch, Boston Col, 59-70; US Rep, Mass, 71-81; prof law, Law Ctr, Georgetown Univ, 81-; contrib ed, Am Mag, 58-70; chmn, Adv Comt Mass, US Comn Civil Rights, 62-70; vis prof, Law Sch, Univ Tex, Austin, 66-67; vis lectr, Andover-Newton Theol Sem, 66-68; ed, Family Law Quart, 67-70; mem, Exec Comt, House Democratic Study Group, 77-78 & New England Congressional Caucus, 79-81; columnist, Nat Cath Reporter, 80-. **RESEARCH** Nuclear arms control; international human rights; civil rights and liberties. **SELECTED PUBLICATIONS** Auth, Religion, The Courts and Public Policy, McGraw Hill, 63; ed, The Right to be Educated, Corpus Books, 68; auth, Democracy, Dissent and Disorder, Seabury Press, 69; auth, Vietnam and Armageddon, Sliced & Ward, 70; auth, Honor the Promise: America's Commitment to Israel, Doubleday, 77. **CONTACT ADDRESS** Law Ctr, Georgetown Univ, 600 New Jersey NW, Washington, DC, 20001-2022. **EMAIL** drinan@law.geocites.edu

DRINKARD, JOEL F., JR.
DISCIPLINE OLD TESTAMENT **EDUCATION** Univ NC, BA; Southeastern Baptist Theol Sem, MDiv, ThM; S Baptist Theoll Sem, PhD; additional stud, Regent's Park Col, Johns Hopkins Univ, Univ Chicago. **CAREER** Prof, S Baptist Theol Sem, 83-. **HONORS AND AWARDS** Curator, Joseph A. Callaway Museum. **RESEARCH** Biblical archaeology. **SELECTED PUBLICATIONS** Assoc ed, contrib auth, Mercer Bible Dictionary; co-auth, Word Biblical Commentary on Jeremiah 1-25. **CONTACT ADDRESS** Old Testament Dept, Southern Baptist Theol Sem, 2825 Lexington Rd, Louisville, KY, 40280. **EMAIL** jdrinkard@sbts.edu

DRIVER, TOM FAW
PERSONAL Born 05/31/1925, Johnson City, TN, m, 1952, 3 children **DISCIPLINE** THEOLOGY, LITERATURE **EDUCATION** Duke Univ, AB, 50; Union Theol Sem, NY, MDiv, 53; Columbia Univ, PhD, 57. **CAREER** Instr drama, 56-58, from asst prof to assoc prof theol, 58- 67, prof theol & lit, 67-73, Paul J Tillich Prof Theol & Cult, 73-93, emeritus, 93- , Union Theol Sem; Kent fel, 53-56; Mars lectr, Northwestern Univ, 61; Guggenheim fel, 62; Earl lect, Pac Sch Relig, 62; vis assoc prof, Columbia Univ, 64-65; vis prof, Univ Otago, NZ, 76, Vassar Col, 78 & Montclair State Col, 81. **HONORS AND AWARDS** DLitt, Dennison Univ, 70. **MEMBERSHIPS** Soc Values Higher Educ; Am Acad Relig; New Haven Theol Discussion Gp; Witness for Peace. **RESEARCH** Classical and modern drama; contemporary theology; ritual studies. **SELECTED PUBLICATIONS** Auth, The Sense of History in Greek and Shakespearean Drama, Columbia Univ, 60; co-ed, Poems of Belief and Doubt, Macmillan, 64; auth, The Shakespearian Clock, Shakespeare Quart, fall 64; Jean Genet, Columbia Univ, 66; History of the Modern Theatre, Delta, 71; The Twilight of Drama: From Ego to Myth, In: Humanities, Religion and the Arts, 72; Patterns of Grace: Human Experience as Word of God, Harper & Row, 77; Christ in a Changing World, Crossroad, 81; auth, The Magic of Ritual, Harper San Francisco, 91; auth, Liberating Rites: Understanding the Transformative Power of Ritual, Westview, 97. **CONTACT ADDRESS** 501 W 123rd St, #14G, New York, NY, 10027. **EMAIL** tfd2@columbia.edu

DROST, MARK P.
DISCIPLINE PHILOSOPHY **EDUCATION** Univ Rochester, PhD, 90. **CAREER** Asst prof, Mankato State Univ, 93-94; asst prof, Bloomsburg Univ, 95; adj assoc prof, Monroe Commun Col, current. **RESEARCH** Philosophy of mind; phenomenology; aesthetics. **CONTACT ADDRESS** 5584 Canadice Lake Rd, Springwater, NY, 14560. **EMAIL** csophia@prodigy.net

DRUART, THERESE-ANNE
PERSONAL Born 12/23/1945, Brussels, Belgium **DISCIPLINE** PHILOSOPHY **EDUCATION** Universite Catholique de Louvain, BA, 67, MA, 68, MA 71, PhD, 73; Univ de Tunis, certificate of third level of Arabic, summer course, 69; Univ of Oxford, BPhil, 75. **CAREER** Research fel, 75-76, Harvard Univ; researcher exchanged between the Belgian Scientific Research and the British Acad, 76-77; researcher exchanged between the Universite Catholique de Louvain and the Universita Cattolic del Sacro cuore, 77-78; asst prof, 78-83, assoc prof, 83-87, Georgetown Univ; assoc prof, 87-97, prof, 97- , The Catholic Univ of Amer; vis prof, 93, Universidad de Navarra. **HONORS AND AWARDS** Teacher of the Month **MEMBERSHIPS** APA; Amer Catholic Philosophy Assn; Soc for Medieval and Renaissance philosophy. **RESEARCH** Medieval Arabic philosophy; Greek philosophy. **SELECTED PUBLICATIONS** Ed, Arabic Philosophy, East and West: Continuity and Interaction, 88; auth, There is no god but God..., New Catholic World, 88; auth, Al-farabi, Ethics and First Intelligibles, Documentie Studi sulla tradizione filosofica medievale, 97; auth, Medieval Islamic Philosophy and Theology Bibliographical Guide, Bulletin de Philosophie medievale, 97; auth, Le Sommaire du Livre des Lois de Platon par Abu Nasr al-Farabi, Bulletin d'Etudes Orietnales, 98. **CONTACT ADDRESS** Sch of Philosophy, Catholic Univ of America, Washington, DC, 20064-0001. **EMAIL** druart@cua.edu

DRUMMOND, JOHN J.
DISCIPLINE CONTEMPORARY EUROPEAN PHILOSOPHY **EDUCATION** Georgetown Univ, BA. PhD, 75. **CAREER** Taught at, Coe Col in Cedar Rapids, Iowa, 12 yrs; vis prof, Georgetown Univ, 1 yr; fac, Mt Saint Mary's Col, 88-; past dept ch & recently app, Distinguished prof Philos. **RESEARCH** Husserl's account of moral intentionality, the moral good, and community. **SELECTED PUBLICATIONS** Auth, a bk on Husserl's theory of intentionality & ed, 2 collections of essays on the work of Husserl and special ed jour Amer Cath Philos Quart devoted to Husserl's philos; gen ed, bk ser Contrib to Phenomenolo publ by Kluwer Acad Publ in the N. **CONTACT ADDRESS** Dept of Philosophy, Mount Saint Mary's Col, 16300 Old Emmitsburg Rd, Emmitsburg, MD, 21727-7799. **EMAIL** drummond@msmary.edu

DRURY, KEITH
PERSONAL Warren, PA **DISCIPLINE** RELIGIOUS STUDIES **EDUCATION** United Wesleyan Col, BS, 69; Princeton Theol Seminary, MRE, 71; Wesley Biblical Seminary, DD, 89; Ind Wesleyan Univ, LhD, 96. **CAREER** Prof. **SELECTED PUBLICATIONS** Auth, Holiness for Ordinary People; Spiritual Disciplines for Ordinary People, Money; Sex, & Spiritual Power; So, What Do You Think?. **CONTACT ADDRESS** Dept of Religion and Philosophy, Indiana Wesleyan Univ, 4201 S Wash St, Marion, IN, 46953.

DUBAY, THOMAS E.
PERSONAL Born 12/30/1921, Minneapolis, MN **DISCIPLINE** PHILOSOPHY **EDUCATION** Cath Univ Am, MA, 51, PhD, 57. **CAREER** Instr theol, Notre Dame Sem, 52-54 & Marist Col, DC, 54-56; instr philos, Notre Dame Sem, 56-67; prof, Marycrest Col, 67-68; researcher, Russell Col, 68-70; lectr theol, Chestnut Hill Col, 70-73; PVT LECTR, 73-, Lectr, Cath Univ Am, 56. **MEMBERSHIPS** Cath Theol Soc Am; Fel Cath Scholars. **RESEARCH** Philosophy of state; life and regimen of religious orders and their members. **SELECTED PUBLICATIONS** Auth, Ecclesial Women, Alba, 70; God Dwells Within Us, 72, Can Religious Life Survive?, 73 & Caring: Biblical Theology of Community, 73, Dimension Bks; Pilgrims Pray, Alba, 74; Authenticity, Dimension, 77; What Is Religious Life?, 79 & Happy Are You Poor, 81, Dimension Bks; Faith and Certitude, Ignatius Press, 85; Five Within, Ignatius Press, 89; Seeking Spiritual Direction, Servant Pub, 93. **CONTACT ADDRESS** 4408 8th St NE, Washington, DC, 20017.

DUBOFF, LEONARD DAVID
PERSONAL Born 10/03/1941, Brooklyn, NY, m, 1967, 2 children **DISCIPLINE** ART LAW, BUSINESS LAW **EDUCATION** Hofstra Univ, BES, 68; Brooklyn Law Sch, JD, 71. **CAREER** Teaching fel legal res and writing, Stanford Law Sch, 71-72; asst prof, 72-75, assoc prof, 75-77, PROF BUS LAW AND ART LAW, LEWIS AND CLARK LAW SCH. 77-, comnr, Ore Comn Blind, 79-; bd mem, Ore Comt Humanities, 81 **MEMBERSHIPS** Am Soc Int Law. **CONTACT ADDRESS** 12440 SW Iron Mountain Blvd, Portland, OR, 97219.

DUBOIS, JAMES M.
PERSONAL Born 09/21/1967, Springfield, MA, m, 1988, 4 children **DISCIPLINE** PHILOSOPHY **EDUCATION** Int Acad Philos, Liechtenstein, PhD, 92; Univ Vienna, DSc, 97. **CAREER** Asst prof, Feanciscan Univ, Austria, 92-94; asst prof, Int Acad Philos, Liechtenstein, 94-97; asst prof, St Louis Univ, 97- . **MEMBERSHIPS** APA; Am Cath Philos Asn; Asn for Moral Educ; Am Soc for Bioethics and Hum. **RESEARCH** Health care ethics; descriptive ethics; moral development and education. **SELECTED PUBLICATIONS** Ed, "Judgment and Sachverhalt," Kluwer, 95; ed, "Moral Issues in Psychology," UPA, 97. **CONTACT ADDRESS** Cntr for Health Care Ethics, St Louis Univ, St Louis, MO, 63104. **EMAIL** duboisjm@wpogate.slu.edu

DUBOIS, SYLVIE
DISCIPLINE SOCIOLINGUISTICS, CAJUN **EDUCATION** Univ Laval, PhD, 93. **CAREER** Asst prof, La State Univ. **SELECTED PUBLICATIONS** Auth, Le discours direct au quotidien, 96; L'analyse quantitative du discours en sociolinguistique, 96; Cajun is Dead: Long Live Cajun, J of Sociolinguistics, 96. **CONTACT ADDRESS** Dept of Fr Grad Stud, Louisiana State Univ, Baton Rouge, LA, 70803.

DUCHARME, HOWARD M.
PERSONAL Born 06/04/1950, Saginaw, MI, m, 1975, 2 children **DISCIPLINE** PHILOSOPHY **EDUCATION** Hope Col, BA, 72; Trinity Divinity Sch, MA, 80; Oxford Univ, Dphil, 84. **CAREER** Asst prof, 84-85, Univ Tenn; asst prof, 86, Univ Fla; from asst to assoc prof to chemn, 86-, Univ Akron. **HONORS AND AWARDS** Who's Who of Professionals; Who's Who in the World; Who's Who in Am; Who's Who in Am Educ; Who's Who in Am Tchrs; Who's Who in the Midwest; Strathmore's Who's Who; Men of Achievement; Int Who's Who of Contemporary Achievement; Post Doctorate Award for Stds at Inst for Advanced Std Seminar on Christianity and Religious Pluralism., Who's Who Among Am Tchrs; Publ in Professional Philos, Medical and Bioethics Jour. **MEMBERSHIPS** Am Philos Asn; Kennedy Inst Ethics; Hastings Ctr; Am Asn Bioethics; Int Asn Bioethics; Society for Health and Human Values. **RESEARCH** The nature of persons; bioethics; history of ethics. **SELECTED PUBLICATIONS** Auth, The Metaphysics of Defining Death, 90; coauth, Physician Participation in Assisted Suicide, 90; auth, The Vatican's Dilemma: On the Morality of IVF and the Incarnation, 91; auth, Can a Person Be Happily Wicked, 93; coauth, Withholding Therapy, 93. **CONTACT ADDRESS** Dept of Philosophy, Univ of Akron, 302 Olin Hall, Akron, OH, 44325-1903. **EMAIL** ducharme@uakron.edu

DUCLOW, DONALD F.
PERSONAL Born 01/11/1946, Chicago, IL, m, 1970 **DISCIPLINE** ENGLISH, PHILSOSOPHY, MEDIEVAL STUDIES **EDUCATION** DePaul Univ, BA, English, philosophy, 68, MA, philosophy, 69; Bryn Mawr Coll, MA, medieval studies, 72, PhD, philosophy, 74. **CAREER** Visiting prof, philosophy, Fordham Univ, 78; asst prof of philosophy, 74-79, assoc prof of philosophy, 79-89, prof of philosophy, 89-, Gwynedd-Mercy Coll. **HONORS AND AWARDS** Mellon Fellow in the Humanities, Univ Pa, 80-81; NEH summer seminars, 87, 93. **MEMBERSHIPS** Amer Acad Religion; Medieval Acad Am; sec, Amer Cusanus Soc; Amer Assn Univ Profs; pres, Gwynedd-Mercy Coll Chap, 96-97. **RESEARCH** Medieval philosophy and religion. **SELECTED PUBLICATIONS** Auth, "Divine Nothingness and Self-Creation in John Scotus Eriugena," The Journ of Religion, vol 57, 77; "'My Suffering Is God': Meister Eckhart's Book of Divine Consolation," Theological Studies, vol 44, 83, reprinted in Classical and Medieval Literature Criticism, 93; "Into the Whirlwind of Suffering: Resistance and Transformation," Second Opinion, Nov 88; "Nicholas of Cusa," in Medieval Philosophers, vol 15, Dictionary of Literary Biography, 92; "Isaiah Meets the Seraph: Breaking Ranks in Dionysius and Eriugena?" in Eriugena: East and West, 94. **CONTACT ADDRESS** Gwynedd-Mercy Col, Gwynedd Valley, PA, 19437-0901.

DUDE, CARL K.
PERSONAL Born 12/11/1938, Brooklyn, NY **DISCIPLINE** RELIGION **EDUCATION** Trinity Hall Col and Sem CO, Dr Div 94, Dr Hum 96; NY Academy of Science and Amer Assoc Adv Science, Post doctoral fellow; Polytech Univ NY and Univ RI, undergrad: engineering, science, admin. **CAREER** United Faith Ministry, Ordained Bishop, 98-; American Ministerial Assoc, Pastor; NY Academy of Science, active mem. **HONORS AND AWARDS** NYS Conspicuous Ser Medal; President's National Medal Patriotism; Who's Who in the World., Post Doctoral Fel; Bishop. **MEMBERSHIPS** ACS; ACA; ACC; NA; IIE; AMP; APS; NAS. **RESEARCH** Theology; psychology; sociology; engineering and science **SELECTED PUBLICATIONS** Auth, Century Walk, Engraved Brick, My Honor, Univ RI. **CONTACT ADDRESS** United Faith Ministry, 80-08 45th Av, Elmhurst, NY, 11373.

DUDZIAK, MARY L.
DISCIPLINE LAW **EDUCATION** Univ Calif, Berkeley, AB,78; Yale Univ, JD,84; MA,86, MPhil 86; PhD 92.. **CAREER** Prof, Univ Southern California **RESEARCH** Impact of foreign affairs on US civil rights policy after World War II. **SELECTED PUBLICATIONS** Auth, Desegregation as a Cold War Imperative; The Little Rock Crisis: Race, Resistance, & the Image of American Democracy; The Supreme Court and Racial Equality During World War II & Josephine Baker, Racial Protest & the Cold War. **CONTACT ADDRESS** School of Law, Univ Southern Calif, University Park Campus, Los Angeles, CA, 90089. **EMAIL** mdudziak@law.usc.edu

DUERLINGER, JAMES
PERSONAL Born 02/08/1938, Milwaukee, WI, m, 1987, 5 children **DISCIPLINE** PHILOSOPHY **EDUCATION** Univ Wisc, BA, 61, PhD; Univ Wash, MA, 63. **CAREER** Asst prof, 66-71, Univ Wisc - Madison; assoc prof, 71-88, prof, 88-, Univ Iowa. **RESEARCH** Indian phil, Buddhism, Greek phil, phil of relig, comparative phil. **CONTACT ADDRESS** Philosophy Dept, Univ of Iowa, Iowa City, IA, 52242. **EMAIL** james-duerlinger@uiowa.edu

DUFFY, STEPHEN JOSEPH
PERSONAL Born 10/14/1930, Philadelphia, PA **DISCIPLINE** RELIGION, PHILOSOPHY **EDUCATION** Marist Col, BA, 51; Pontif Gregorian Univ, STL, 58; Cath Univ Am, STD(theol), 69. **CAREER** Lectr patristics, Marist Col, 56; assoc prof and chmn relig studies, Loyola Univ, La, 70-80; LECTR THEOL, NOTRE DAME SEM, 61-, Jesuit Coun Theol Reflection res grant, 75; La Comm Humanities lectureship grant, 77-78. **MEMBERSHIPS** Am Acad Relig; Cath Theol Soc Am; Col Theoll Soc; AAUP. **RESEARCH** Systematic theology; historical theology. **SELECTED PUBLICATIONS**

Auth, The Fall to Violence-Original Sin in Relational Theology, Theological Studies, Vol 56, 95; Grace and Disgrac--A Theology of Self Esteem, Soc Hist, Theol Studs, Vol 55, 94. **CONTACT ADDRESS** Notre Dame Sem, 6363 St Charles Ave, New Orleans, LA, 70118-6195.

DUHAN KAPLAN, LAURA
DISCIPLINE FEMINIST PHILOSOPHY, PHILOSOPHY OF EDUCATION, PHILOSOPHY OF PEACE, PHENOMEN **EDUCATION** Brandeis Univ, BA, 80; Cambridge Col, MEd, 83; Claremont Grad Sch, MA, 87, PhD, 91. **CAREER** Assoc prof, coord, Women's Stud prog, Univ NC, Charlotte. **RESEARCH** Family life, from the perspective of existential phenomenology. **SELECTED PUBLICATIONS** Auth, Speaking for Myself in Philosophy, Philos and the Contemp World, 1:4, 94; My Mother the Mirror, The Trumpeter, 11:4, 94; Teaching As Applied Philosophy, Tchg Philos , 17:1, 94; Woman as Caretaker: An Archetype That Supports Patriarchal Militarism, Hypatia: A J of Feminist Philos, 9:2, 94; Persons and Mystery: Art, Conflict and Self-Knowledge, in Becoming Persons, ed, Robert N. Fisher, Oxford: App Theol Press, 94; The Parable of the Levite's Concubine, in From the Eye of the Storm: Regional Conflicts and the Philosophy of Peace, eds, Laurence F. Bove and Laura Duhan Kaplan, Rodopi, 95; Physical Education for Domination and Emancipation: A Foucauldian Analysis of Aerobics and Hatha Yoga, in Philosophical Perspectives on Power and Domination: Theories and Practices, eds, Laura Duhan Kaplan and Laurence F. Bove, Rodopi, 96; Devaluing Others to Enhance our Self-Esteem: A Moral Phenomenology of Racism, in Institutional Violence, eds, Robert Litke and Deane Curtin, Rodopi, 96; coauth, Paradigms for the Philosophy of Peace, in From the Eye of the Storm: Regional Conflicts and the Philosophy of Peace, eds, Laurence F. Bove and Laura Duhan Kaplan, Rodopi, 95; coed, From the Eye of the Storm: Regional Conflicts and the Philosophy of Peace, Rodopi, 95; Philosophical Perspectives on Power and Domination: Theories and Practices, Rodopi, 97. **CONTACT ADDRESS** Univ N. Carolina, Charlotte, Charlotte, NC, 28223-0001. **EMAIL** ldkaplan@email.uncc.edu

DUKE, STEVEN BARRY
PERSONAL Born 07/31/1934, Mesa, AZ, m, 1956, 6 children **DISCIPLINE** CRIMINAL LAW & PROCEDURE **EDUCATION** Ariz State Univ, BS, 56; Univ Ariz, JD, 59; Yale Univ, LLM, 61. **CAREER** Law clerk, US Supreme Court, 59-60; fel law, Yale Univ, 60-61, from asst prof to assoc prof, 61-65; vis prof, Univ Calif, Berkeley, 65-66; prof law, Yale Univ, 66-, Dir, New Haven Legal Assistance, Inc, 67-71; mem, Conn Comn on Medico-Legal Investigations, 77-. **MEMBERSHIPS** Nat Asn Criminal Defense Coun; ACLU. **RESEARCH** Criminal law and drug policy. **SELECTED PUBLICATIONS** Auth, The Right to Appointed Counsel, Am Criminal Law Rev, 3/75; Bail Reform for the Eighties: A Reply to Senator Kennedy, Fordham Law Rev, 6/81; America's Longest War: Rethinking Our Tragic Crusade Against Drugs, 94; Drug Prohibition: An Unnatural Disaster, 27 Conn Law Rev, 95. **CONTACT ADDRESS** Law Sch, Yale Univ, PO Box 208215, New Haven, CT, 06520-8215.

DUKEMINIER, JESSE
PERSONAL Born 08/12/1925, West Point, MS **DISCIPLINE** LAW **EDUCATION** Harvard Univ, AB, 48; Yale Univ, LLB, 51. **CAREER** Atty at law, New York, 51-53; asst prof law, Univ Minn, 54-55; from assoc prof to prof, Univ Ky, 55-63; PROF LAW UNIV CLIF, LOS ANGELES, 63-. **HONORS AND AWARDS** Distinguished Teaching Award, Univ Calif, Los Angeles, 76. **MEMBERSHIPS** Am Bar Asn; Am Inst Planners. **RESEARCH** Property; estate planning; land planning and development. **SELECTED PUBLICATIONS** Auth, The Uniform Probate Code Upends the Law of Remainders, Michigan Law Rev, Vol 94, 95. **CONTACT ADDRESS** Law School, Univ of California, Los Angeles, CA, 90024.

DUMAIN, HAROLD
PERSONAL Born 03/03/1927, Utica, NY, m, 1965, 2 children **DISCIPLINE** PHILOSOPHY **EDUCATION** SUNY at Buffalo, BA, 50, MSW, 52. **CAREER** Gowanda Psychiatric Center, Dir of Soc Serv, 71-83. **HONORS AND AWARDS** US Victory Medal, WW II, US Army, Occupation Medal. **RESEARCH** Psychiatry; schizophrenia **SELECTED PUBLICATIONS** Auth, A Synthesis of Philosophy, Philo Lib, NY, 75; Professional Problems Contingent to Theory, Jour of Psychiatric Soc Work, 54; Jour of Hospital and Community Psychiatry, coauth, 71. **CONTACT ADDRESS** 4628 Pinecrest Terrace, Eden, NY, 14057.

DUMAIS, MONIQUE
PERSONAL Born 09/08/1939, Rimouski, PQ, Canada, s **DISCIPLINE** THEOLOGY; ETHICS **EDUCATION** Universite du Quebec a Rimouski, BA, 70; Harvard Univ, ThM, 73; Union Theol Seminary, PhD, 77. **CAREER** Prof, 70-, Dept Head, 85-89, Universite du Quebec a Rimouski **HONORS AND AWARDS** Bourse de recherche libe du CRSH du Canada **MEMBERSHIPS** Societe canadienne de theologie; Soc canadienne des sciences religieuses; Soc quebecoise des sciences religieuses; Amer Acad of Religion; Assoc des theologiens pour l etude de la morale **RESEARCH** Women and religion; women and the catholic church; ethics in feminist discourses; ethics and women **SELECTED PUBLICATIONS** Auth, Os direitos da mulher, 93; Los derechos de la mujer, 93; Diversite des utilisations feministes de concept experiences des femmes en sciences religieuses, 93; L'autre Parole, lieu de convergence d'une militance et d'une recherche feministes, L'autre Parole no 69, 96; Preoccupations ecologiques et ethique feministe, Religiologiques 13, 96; Ethique feministe de relation et perspectives sur le corps, Laval theologique et philosophique 53, 97; Une ethique de relation soutenue par une dynamique feministe dans las sphere pedagogique, Ethica, 97; Christa et la reconnaissance des femmes, L'autre Parole, 98; Traversees ethiques dans les langages de femmes, Reseaux, 98; Femmes et Pauvrete, 98; avec Marie Beaulieu, Mener sa barque a bonport. Cathier de reflexion ethique sur les interventions aupres des femmes en situation de pauvrete, 98. **CONTACT ADDRESS** Dept de sciences religieuses et d'ethique, Univ du Quebec, Rimouski, PQ, G5L 3A1. **EMAIL** monique_dumais@uqar.uquebec.ca

DUNAWAY, BAXTER
DISCIPLINE REAL ESTATE FINANCE AND TRANSACTIONS **EDUCATION** Auburn Univ, BS, 50; G Wash Univ, JD, 60. **CAREER** Chem engr, 50-56; US Patent off examr, 56-60; patent atty, Petro-Tex Chemical Corporation, 60-63; Patent Attorney, Ethyl Corporation, 64; Counsel, Petro-Tex Chem Corp, 65-73; regist patent atty, US Patent Off. **HONORS AND AWARDS** JD with hon(s). **MEMBERSHIPS** Mem, State Bar TX; Am Bar Assn, Conejo Bd of Realtors. **SELECTED PUBLICATIONS** Auth, Law of Distressed Real Estate, 85-92; FIRREA: Law and Practice, 92; co-ed, Distressed Business and Real Estate Newsletter. **CONTACT ADDRESS** Sch of Law, Pepperdine Univ, 24255 Pacific Coast Hwy, Malibu, CA, 90263.

DUNCAN, CHARLES TIGNOR
PERSONAL Born 10/31/1924, Washington, DC, w **DISCIPLINE** LAW **EDUCATION** Dartmouth Coll, BA (cum laude) 1947; Harvard Law Sch, JD 1950. **CAREER** Reeves Robinson & Duncan, partner 1953-60; US Atty for DC, princ asst 1961-65; US Equal Employment Oppor Commn, general counsel 1965-66; corporation counsel DC, 1966-70; Epstein Freidman Duncan & Medalie, partner 1970-74; Howard Univ Sch of Law, dean prof law 1974-78; Peabody Lambert & Meyers Washington, partner 1978-82; Reid & Priest Washington, partner 1982-90, senior counsel, 1990-94; Iran-United States Claims Tribunal, mem, 1994-. **HONORS AND AWARDS** Hon LLD Dartmouth Coll 1986. **MEMBERSHIPS** Mem NY Bar 1951, DC Bar 1953, MD Bar 1955, US Supreme Ct Bar 1954, US Seventh Circuit Ct of Appeals Bar 1962; bd of dirs of Nat Bank of Wash 1973-79, Procter & Gamble Co 1982-88, Eastman Kodak Co 1978-95, TRW Inc 1984-95; mem DC Labor Rels Board 1973-75; chmn DC Judic Nomin Commin 1975-80; mem Dartmouth Coll Alumni Counc 1975-78; bd of dir, NAACP Legal Def & Education Fund; mem ABA Nat Bar Assn Wash Bar Assn & Dist of Colum Bar, pres 1973-74; Phi Beta Kappa, Alpha Phi Alpha; Sigma Pi Phi; Delta Theta Phi, Mason; act partic prepar & present of Sch Desegregation cases 1953-55; FAA Lic instr rated comm pilot. **CONTACT ADDRESS** Iran-U.S. Claims Tribunal, Parkweg 13, The Hague, ..

DUNCAN, ELMER H
PERSONAL Born 05/26/1933, Fullerton, KY, m, 1956 **DISCIPLINE** PHILOSOPHY **EDUCATION** Univ Cincinnati, BA, 58, MA, 60, PhD (philos), 62. **CAREER** From asst prof to assoc prof, 62-71, PROF PHILOS, BAYLOR UNIV, 71-, Am Coun Learned Soc travel grant, 8th Int Cong Aesthetics, Darmstadt, Ger, 76. **MEMBERSHIPS** Western Div Am Philos Asn; Am Soc Aesthet; Southwestern Philos Soc(pres, 74-). **SELECTED PUBLICATIONS** Auth, Presbyteries and Profits--Calvinism and the Development of Capitalism in Scotland, 1560-1707, J Church State, Vol 37, 95; Scotland in the Age of the Disruption, J Church State, Vol 37, 95; Philosophy and Architecture, J Aesthetic Educ, Vol 31, 97. **CONTACT ADDRESS** Dept of Philos Col Arts and Sci, Baylor Univ, Waco, TX, 76703.

DUNCAN, JOHN C., JR.
PERSONAL Born 06/05/1942, Philadelphia, PA, m, 1989 **DISCIPLINE** LAW **EDUCATION** DePauw Univ, BA 1964; Univ of MI, MS, MA 1965-66; Stanford Univ, PhD 1971; Yale Law Schl, JD 1976; Southeastern Univ, MBPA 1985. **CAREER** Iraklion AS, Crete, Greece, Staff Judge Advocate 1978-79; Tactical Air Command, Chief Civil Law 1979-81; Hurlburt Field, FL, Staff Judge Advocate 1981-82; AF JAG Career Mgmnt, Chief Military Manpower & Analysis (JAG) 1982-84; Legal Advisor to the Asst to the Secretary of Defense (Intelligence Oversight); Deputy Judge Advocate, United Nations Command, US Forces in Korea, Deputy Staff Judge Advocate, HQ Tactical Ser Command, Langley AFB, VA. **HONORS AND AWARDS** Rector Scholar, DePauw Univ 1960-64; Graduate w/distinction DePauw Univ, Leopold Schepp Found Schlrshp 1965-66; Schlrshp Stanford Univ 1967; Flwshp Richardson Dilworth Fellow Yale 1974-76; Outstanding New Teacher Award, Southeastern Univ 1985. **MEMBERSHIPS** Life mem Alpha Phi Alpha 1968; prof various Univer 1976-; cnslr Marriage Family & Child 1976-; ODO 1976, Amer Assoc of Marriage & Family Therapists 1976; Inter Amer Bar Assoc 1983; ABA, FBA, NBA. **CONTACT ADDRESS** Headquarters Tactical Air Command, Hampton, VA, 23665.

DUNDON, STANISLAUS
PERSONAL Born 07/18/1935, Milwaukee, WI, m, 1990, 9 children **DISCIPLINE** PHILOSOPHY **EDUCATION** PhD **CAREER** Cal Poly San Luis Obispo; Univ Calif Davis; Calif State Univ Sacramento, nat coordr, Sould of Agr Proj, 99-; Cong Sci fel; Rockafeller Found grant; NSF fel; Joyce Found. **MEMBERSHIPS** APA; Agr, Food, & Hum Values Soc. **RESEARCH** Agricultural ethics. **SELECTED PUBLICATIONS** Auth Sources of Eikst Principles for an Agricultural Ethic. **CONTACT ADDRESS** PO Box 72084, Davis, CA, 95617. **EMAIL** sjdundon@davis.com

DUNLAP, ELDEN DALE
PERSONAL Born 11/01/1921, Rose Hill, KS, m, 1944, 3 children **DISCIPLINE** THEOLOGY **EDUCATION** Southwestern Col, AB, 43; Garrett Theol Sem, BD, 45; Northwestern Univ, MA, 47; Yale Univ, PhD (contemp theol), 56 **CAREER** From instr to east prof relig, Southwestern Col, 51-55, assoc prof and dean col, 55-59; assoc prof theol, 59-64, actg pres, 72-73, PROF THEOL, SAINT PAUL SCH THEOL, 64-, DEAN, 70-, MEM, BD HIGHER EDUC AND MINISTRY, UNITED METHODIST CHURCH, 80-, chmn, Ministry Study Comt, 80-84. **HONORS AND AWARDS** DD, Southwestern Col. Kans, 71. **MEMBERSHIPS** Am Theol Soc; Am Soc Church Hist; Am Acad Relig; NAm Acad Ecumenists. **RESEARCH** Development of Methodist theology; ecumenical movement. **SELECTED PUBLICATIONS** Auth, The Limits of So Called Love Divine--Wesley, John Response to Antinomianism and Enthusiasm, Church Hist, Vol 63, 94; The Evangelist of Desire--Wesley, John and the Methodists, Church Hist, Vol 62, 93; The Presence of God in the Christian Life--Wesley, John and the Means of Grace, Church Hist, Vol 65, 96. **CONTACT ADDRESS** St Paul Sch of Theology, Truman Rd and Van Brunt Blvd, Kansas City, MO, 64127.

DUNLOP, CHARLES
DISCIPLINE PHILOSOPHY **EDUCATION** Stanford Univ, BA, 65; Wright State Univ, MS, 87; Duke Univ, MA, 69, PhD, 73. **CAREER** Prof & ch dept philos, Univ Mich Flint **RESEARCH** Cognitive science; philosophy of mind; social aspects of computing. **SELECTED PUBLICATIONS** Auth, Philosophical Essays on Dreaming, Cornell UP, 77 & Computer Ethics, Encycl of Comput Sci, 4th ed, 98; coauth, Glossary of Cognitive Science, Paragon House, 93 & Computerization and Controversy: Value Conflicts and Social Choices, Acad Press, 91; rev, William Calvin's How Brains Think, in Minds and Machines, 98. **CONTACT ADDRESS** Dept of Philosophy, Univ of Michigan-Flint, Flint, MI, 48502-2186.

DUNN, JON MICHAEL
PERSONAL Born 06/19/1941, St. Wayne, IN, m, 1964, 2 children **DISCIPLINE** PHILOSOPHY LOGIC **EDUCATION** Oberlin Col, AB, 63; Univ Pittsburg, PhD (philos), 66. **CAREER** Asst prof philos, Wayne State Univ, 66-69; assoc prof, 69-76, PROF PHILOS, IND UNIV, BLOOMINGTON, 76-, CHMN, 80-, Vis asst prof, Yale Univ, 68-69; Fulbright-Hays sr res scholar, Australian-Am Educ Found, 75-76; vis fel, Inst Advan Studies, Australian Nat Univ, 75-76; sr vis, Math Inst, Oxford Univ, 78; ed, J Symbolic Logic, 82-. **MEMBERSHIPS** Asn Symbolic Logic; Am Philos Asn; AAAS; Philos of Sci Asn; Soc Exact Philos. **RESEARCH** Algebraic logic; propositional calculi; entailment. **SELECTED PUBLICATIONS** Auth, , Southern Baptists Observed--Multiple Perspectives on a Changing Denomination, J Sci Stu Rel, Vol 33, 94. **CONTACT ADDRESS** Dept of Philosophy, Indiana Univ, Bloomington, Bloomington, IN, 47401.

DUNNAVANT, ANTHONY L.
PERSONAL Born 06/23/1954, Hagerstown, MD, m, 1975, 4 children **DISCIPLINE** RELIGION **EDUCATION** Fairmont State, BA, 74; West VA Univ, MA, 76; Vanderbilt, MDiv, 79, MA, 81, PhD, 84. **CAREER** Cent Mich Univ, asst prof, 86-87; Lexington Theo Sem, asst prof, 87-88, assoc. prof, 88-93, prof, 93-, dean 98-. **MEMBERSHIPS** AAR, AAUP, ASCH, ASR, RRA **RESEARCH** Christianity in Appalachia; congreg studies; Christ primitivism of Stone-Campbell trad. **SELECTED PUBLICATIONS** Auth, Backgrounds for Congregational Portraits: Ideas and Resources for Local Church Historians in the Stone-Campbell tradition, forward by James M. Seale, Nash, TN, Disciples of Christ Hist Soc, 94; Restructure: Four Historical Ideals in the Campbell-Stone Movement and the Development of the Policy of the Christian Church, Theol and Rel, NY, Peter Lang, 93; ed Christian Faith Seeking Historical Understanding: Essays in Honor of H. Jack Forstman Mercer Univ. Press, 97; Explorations in the Stone-Campbell Traditions: Essays in Honor of Herman A. Norton, Disciples Divinity House at Vanderbilt, 95; art, History and Ecclesiology in Recent Disciples Literature, in: Mid-Stream, 93; Evangelization and Eschatology: Lost Link in the Disciples Tradition?, Lexington Theol Quart, 93. **CONTACT ADDRESS** Lexington Theol Sem, 631 South Limestone, Lexington, KY, 40508.

DUNNE, JOHN SCRIBNER
PERSONAL Born 12/03/1929, Waco, TX **DISCIPLINE** PHILOSOPHY, THEOLOGY **EDUCATION** Univ Notre Dame, AB, 51; Gregorian Univ, Rome, STL, 54, STD, 58. **CAREER** From instr to assoc prof, 57-69, PROF THEOL, UNIV NOTRE

DAME, 69-, Rockefeller res and writing grant, 60-61; vis prof, Divinity Sch, Univ Chicago, 68; Thomas More lectr, Yale Univ, 71, lectr relig studies, 72-73; adv ed, Rev Politics; Sarum lectr, Oxford Univ, 76-77. **HONORS AND AWARDS** Harbison Distinguished Teaching Award, 69. **MEMBERSHIPS** Am Aced Relig. **RESEARCH** Mysticism; autobiography; death and myth. **SELECTED PUBLICATIONS** Auth, Myth and Culture in Theology and Literature, A Conversation With Dunne, John, S., Reli Lit, Vol 25, 93. **CONTACT ADDRESS** Univ of Notre Dame Press, 327 Oshaugnessy Hall, PO Box L, Notre Dame, IN, 46556.

DUNNING, STEPHEN NORTHROP
PERSONAL Born 06/17/1941, Philadelphia, PA, m, 1974, 3 children **DISCIPLINE** MODERN WESTERN RELIGIOUS THOUGHT **EDUCATION** Goddard Col, BA, 64; Harvard Univ, MDiv, 69, PhD(Study Relig), 77. **CAREER** Instr, 77-78, asst prof Mod Western Relig Thought, Univ Pa, 78-84; from assoc prof to prof, 84-98. **HONORS AND AWARDS** Nat Endowment for Humanities fel, 82-83. **MEMBERSHIPS** Hegel Soc Am; Sorenkierbegaard Society; Am Acad Relig. **RESEARCH** Philosophy of history; religious language; hermeneutics. **SELECTED PUBLICATIONS** Auth, The Tongues of Men: Hegel and Hamann on Religious Language and History, Am Acad Relig Dissertation Ser, No 27, Scholars Press, 79; Kierkegaard's Dialectic of Inwardness: A structural Analysis of the Theory of Stages, Princeton, 85; Dialetical Readings: Three Type of Interpretation, Penn State Press, 97. **CONTACT ADDRESS** Dept of Relig Studies, Univ of Pennsylvania, Logan Hall, 249 S 86th St, Philadelphia, PA, 19104-6304. **EMAIL** sdunning@ccat.sos.upenn.edu

DURHAM, KEN R.
PERSONAL Born 03/21/1948, m, 1973, 2 children **DISCIPLINE** RELIGION AND COMMUNICATION **EDUCATION** David Lipscomb Col, BA, 70; La State Univ, MA, 72, PhD, 74; post doc grad work Austin Presbyterian theol sem, Abilene Christian Univ. **CAREER** Instr, Inst Christian Studies, 77-78; vis fac, 88; lectr, Okla Christian Univ, 91; David Lipscomb Univ, 89; adjunct fac, Harding Univ Grad Sch Rel, 89; contrib ed, 21st Century Christian, 93-; vis fac, 97-. **SELECTED PUBLICATIONS** Auth, Speaking From the Heart: Richer Relationships Through Communication, Sweet Publ, 86; Jesus, Our Mentor and Model, Baker Bk House, 87; co-auth, Becoming Persons of Integrity, Baker Bk House, 88; Anchors For the Asking, Baker Bk House, 89. **CONTACT ADDRESS** Dept of Relig, Pepperdine Univ, 24255 Pacific Coast Hwy, Malibu, CA, 90263. **EMAIL** kdurham@pepperdine.edu

DURNBAUGH, DONALD F.
PERSONAL Born 11/16/1927, Detroit, MI, m, 1952, 3 children **DISCIPLINE** CHURCH HISTORY, MODERN EUROPEAN HISTORY **EDUCATION** Manchester Col, BA, 49; Univ Mich, MA, 53; Univ Pa, PhD (hist), 60. **CAREER** Dir, Brethren Serv Comn, Austria, 53-56; lectr Brethren hist, Bethany Theol Sem, 58; from instr to asst prof hist, Juniata Col, 58-62; assoc prof, 62-70, PROF CHURCH HIST, BETHANY THEOL SEM, 70-, Alternate serv, Brethren Serv Comn, Austria and Ger, 49-51 and 53-56; dir in Europe, Brethren Cols Abroad, 64-65; adj prof church hist, Northern Baptist Theol Sem, 68-71; assoc, Ctr Reformation and Free Church Studies, Chicago Theol Sem, 68-; Nat Endowment for Humanities res fel, 76-77. **MEMBERSHIPS** Am Soc Church Hist; Orgn Am Historians; NAm Acad Ecumenists; AHA; Am Soc Reformation Res. **RESEARCH** Modern European church history; German sectarian movements in America; Communitarian societies. **SELECTED PUBLICATIONS** Auth, Spiritual Life in Anabaptism, Church Hist, Vol 66, 97; The German Peasant War and Anabaptist Community of Goods, Church Hist, Vol 63, 94; Mennonite Entrepreneurs, Church Hist, Vol 66, 97; The German Peasant War and Anabaptist Community of Goods, Church Hist, Vol 63, 94; Spiritual Life in Anabaptism, Church Hist, Vol 66, 97; Mennonite Entrepreneurs, Church Hist, Vol 66, 97; The Writings of Philips, Dirk, J Church State, Vol 35, 93. **CONTACT ADDRESS** Bethany Theol Sem, Oak Brook, IL, 60521.

DUSEK, RUDOLPH VALENTINE
PERSONAL Born 09/20/1941, Toronto, ON, Canada, m, 1968 **DISCIPLINE** PHILOSOPHY **EDUCATION** Yale Univ, BA, 63; Univ Tex, Austin, PhD(philos),72. **CAREER** Instr, 66-70, asst prof, 70-81, Assoc prof Philos, Univ NH, 81-. **MEMBERSHIPS** Philos Sci Asn; hist sci so, Soc Lit & Sci; AAUP; Am Philos Assn; ISHPSSB, HOPOS, Radical Phil Assn. **SELECTED PUBLICATIONS** Auth, contribr, Geodesy and the earth sciences in the philosophy of C S Peirce, In: Bicentennial Conference on History of Geology, New Eng Univ, 78; co-ed, Sociobiology: The debate evolves, 82 & coauth, Sociobiology: The unnatural selection of a new paradigm, 82, Philos Forum; Philos of Math and Physics in the Sokal Affair, Social Text, 97; Brecht and Lukaes as Teachers of Feyerabend and Lakotos, Hist of Hum Scis, 98. **CONTACT ADDRESS** Univ of New Hampshire, 125 Technology Dr, Durham, NH, 03824-4724. **EMAIL** valdusek@aol.com

DUSEK, VAL
DISCIPLINE PHILOSOPHY **EDUCATION** Univ Tex, PhD, 72. **CAREER** Assoc prof. **RESEARCH** Philosophy of biology; philosophy of the history of science; social epistemology; alternate approaches to science; marxism. **SELECTED PUBLICATIONS** Auth, pubs on Peirce, sociobiology debate, and Bukharin. **CONTACT ADDRESS** Philosophy Dept, Univ of New Hampshire, Hamilton Smith Hall, Durham, NH, 03824. **EMAIL** Valdusek@aol.com

DUSKA, RONALD F.
PERSONAL Born 03/01/1937, Erie, PA, m, 2 children **DISCIPLINE** PHILOSOPHY **EDUCATION** St Mary's Col, BA, 58; St John's Univ, MA, 61; Northwestern Univ, PhD, 70. **CAREER** St. John's Univ, tchr fel, inst, 61-63; Rosemount Col, inst, asst prof, assoc prof, prof, 63-96; Villanova Univ, adj prof, 80-; St Joseph's Univ, adj prof, 85-; Penn State Univ, adj prof, 93-95; Univ Pennsylvania, adj prof, 94-96; The Am Col, Charles Lamont Post Ch of Ethics and the Professions, 96-. **MEMBERSHIPS** SBE, APA, Acad of Mgmt, IASB, ACPA, SASE, Amantifil **RESEARCH** Business ethics; ethical theory; moral development; ethics of finance and insurance. **SELECTED PUBLICATIONS** Auth, Ethics and Corporate Responsibility: Theory, Cases and Dilemmas, NY: Amer Heritage Custom Pub Group, 95; auth, Education, Leadership and Business Ethics: Essays on the Work of Clarence Walton, Dordrecht, Kluwer Acad Publ, 98; auth, To Disclose or Not to Disclose? That is the Question, Jour of the Am Society of CLU & ChFC, 97; auth, Whistleblowing, in: Encycl Dict of Bus Ethics, ed. P. Werhane & R.E. Freeman, Blackwell, 97; auth, Ethics and Compliance, Jour Am Society of CLU & ChFC, 98; auth, Employee Rights, Anthology of Bus ethics, ed. B. Frederick, Blackwell, 98. **CONTACT ADDRESS** The American Col, 270 S Bryn Mawr Ave, Bryn Mawr, PA, 19010. **EMAIL** ronaldd@amercoll.edu

DUTCHER-WALLS, PATRICIA
PERSONAL Born 03/17/1952, Glen Ridge, NJ, m, 1983, 2 children **DISCIPLINE** BIBLICAL STUDIES **EDUCATION** Col of Wooster, BA, 74; Harvard Div Sch, MDiv, 78; Graduate Theol Union, ThD, 94. **CAREER** Adj asst prof, Old Testament, United Theol Sem, 94-95; asst prof Old Testament & Hebrew Bible, Knox Col, 95- . **HONORS AND AWARDS** BA with honors; MDiv with honors; ThD with honors. **MEMBERSHIPS** AAR/SBL; Can Soc of Bibl Stud. **RESEARCH** Deuteronomistic history; feminist hermeneutics; sociological method. **SELECTED PUBLICATIONS** Auth, Political Correctness, The Reformed Tradition, and Pluralism: Implications for Theological Education, Theol Educ, 92; auth, Incarnation: Interaction as a Means of Grace in Carter, ed, Of Human Bondage and Divine Grace: A Global Testimony, Open Court, 92; auth, Narrative Art, Political Rhetoric: The Case of Athaliah and Joash, Sheffield Academic, 96; auth, The Social Location of the Deuteronomists: A Sociological Study of Factional Politics in Late Pre-Exilic Judah, in Chalcraft, ed, Social-Scientific Old Testament Criticism, Sheffield Academic, 97; auth, Sociological Directions in Feminist Biblical Studies, Social Compass, 99. **CONTACT ADDRESS** Knox Col, 59 St George St, Toronto, ON, M5S 2E6.

DWORKIN, GERALD
DISCIPLINE PHILOSOPHY **EDUCATION** Univ CA Berkeley, MA, PhD. **CAREER** Prof, Univ IL at Chicago. **RESEARCH** Ethics; polit philos; philos of law. **SELECTED PUBLICATIONS** Auth, The Serpent Beguiled Me and I did Eat: Entrapment and the Creation of Crime, Law and Philos, 85; The Theory and Practice of Autonomy, Cambridge, 88; Equal Respect and the Enforcement of Morality, Soc Philos Policy, 90. **CONTACT ADDRESS** Philos Dept, Univ Illinois Chicago, S Halsted St, PO Box 705, Chicago, IL, 60607.

DWORKIN, ROGER BARNETT
PERSONAL Born 01/19/1943, Cincinnati, OH, m, 1964, 2 children **DISCIPLINE** LAW TORTS **EDUCATION** Princeton Univ, AB, 63; Stanford Univ, JD, 66. **CAREER** Asst prof, 68-71, assoc prof, 71-74, PROF LAW, SCH OF LAW, IND UNIV, BLOOMINGTON, 74-, Vis prof, Sch of Med, Univ Washington, summers, 74-79, prof biomed hist, 80-82; vis prof law, Sch of Law, Univ Va, 78-79. **MEMBERSHIPS** Soc Health and Human Values; Inst Soc Ethics and Life Sci; AAAS. **RESEARCH** Law and biology; law and medicine. **SELECTED PUBLICATIONS** Auth, Medical Law ad Ethics in the Post Autonomy Age, Indiana Law J, Vol 68,93; Emerging Paradigms in Bioethics--Introduction, Indiana Law J, Vol 69, 94. **CONTACT ADDRESS** Sch of Law, Indiana Univ, Bloomington, 1 Indiana University, Bloomington, IN, 47405-1000.

DWYER, JAMES G.
PERSONAL Born 09/27/1961, Albany, NY, m, 1992, 2 children **DISCIPLINE** LAW **EDUCATION** Boston Col, BA, 84; Yale Law School, JD, 87; Stanford Univ, PhD, 95. **CAREER** Chicago - Kent Col Law, v asst prof, 96-98; Univ WY Col Law, asst prof, 98-. **HONORS AND AWARDS** Cornell Univ, Young Scholar Award, 98. **MEMBERSHIPS** ABA **RESEARCH** Children and the law; religion and the law. **SELECTED PUBLICATIONS** Auth, Parent's Religion and Children's Welfare: Debunking the Doctrine of Parents' Rights, Calif Law Rev, 94; The Children We Abandon: Religious Exemptions to Child Welfare and Education Laws as Denials of Equal Protection to Children of Religious Objectors, N C Law Rev, 96; Religious Schools v. Children's Rights, Cornell Press, 96. **CONTACT ADDRESS** College of Law, Univ of Wyoming, 21st/Willet, Laramie, WY, 82070. **EMAIL** jdwyer@uwyo.edu

DWYER, SUSAN
DISCIPLINE PHILOSOPHY **EDUCATION** Adelaide Univ, BA; MIT, PhD. **RESEARCH** Theoretical and applied ethics. **SELECTED PUBLICATIONS** Ed, The Problem of Pornography, Wadsworth, 95; co-ed, The Problem of Abortion, Wadsworth, 97. **CONTACT ADDRESS** Philosophy Dept, McGill Univ, 845 Sherbrooke St, Montreal, PQ, H3A 2T5.

DYCH, WILLIAM V.
PERSONAL Born 06/25/1932, Philadelphia, PA **DISCIPLINE** SYSTEMATIC THEOLOGY **EDUCATION** Univ Munster, Ger, Dr Theol, 71. **CAREER** Prof Theol, Fordham Univ, 81- . **MEMBERSHIPS** Amer Acad Rel; Catholic Theol Soc Am. **RESEARCH** Systematic Theology, Christology **SELECTED PUBLICATIONS** Auth, Karl Rahner, London, Geoffrey Chafmon, 92; The Mystery of Faith, Collegeville, NM, Michael Glazrs, 95. **CONTACT ADDRESS** Fordham Univ, Loyola Hall, Bronx, NY, 10458.

DYCK, ARTHUR JAMES
PERSONAL Born 04/27/1932, Saskatoon, SK, Canada, m, 1952, 2 children **DISCIPLINE** ETHICS, PSYCHOLOGY **EDUCATION** Tabor Col, Bs, 53; Univ Kans, MA, 58 and 59; Harvard Univ, PhD (relig ethics), 66. **CAREER** Res asst psychol, Univ Kans, 57-60; spec lectr philos, Univ Sask, 64-65; asst prof social ethics, 65-69, MARY B SALTONSTALL PROF POPULATION ETHICS, SCH PUB HEALTH, HARVARD UNIV, 69-, MEM FAC, DIVINITY SCH, 69-, Co-dir, Joseph P Kennedy, Jr Found interfac prog med ethics, Harvard, 71-. **MEMBERSHIPS** Am Soc Christian Ethics; Population Asn Am; Am Acad Relig; Am Pub Health Asn. **RESEARCH** Ethical theory; ethical analysis of population policy; topics in medical ethics. **SELECTED PUBLICATIONS** Auth, Justice and Christian Ethics, J Rel, Vol 77, 97; Rethinking Rights, Preserving Community , J Rel Ethics, Vol 25, 97. **CONTACT ADDRESS** Harvard Divinity Sch, Harvard Univ, 45 Francis Ave, Cambridge, MA, 02138-1994.

DYCK, CORNELIUS JOHN
PERSONAL Born 08/20/1921, Russia, m, 1952, 3 children **DISCIPLINE** HISTORY/HISTORICAL THEOLOGY **EDUCATION** BA, Bethel Col, N Newton KS, 53; MA Wichita State Univ, 55; BD Divinity School Univ Chicago, 59, PhD, 62. **CAREER** Prof Assoc Mennonite Seminaries, 59-89; Dir Inst of Mennonite Studies, 58-79; Exec Sec, Mennonite World Conf, 61-73. **MEMBERSHIPS** Mennonite Hist Soc, Goshen IN; Mennonitischer Geschichtsverein, Weierhof Germany; Doopsgezind Historische Kring, Amsterdam; Doc for Reformation Res; NA Soc Of Church Hist. **RESEARCH** 16th century Dutch Anabaptism. **SELECTED PUBLICATIONS** Mennonite Encyclopedia vol V ed, 90; Introduction to Mennonite History, 3rd ed, 93; Spiritual Life in Anabaptism, 95. **CONTACT ADDRESS** Associated Mennonite Biblical Sem, 3003 Benham Ave, Elkhart, IN, 46514. **EMAIL** 105152.311@compuserve.com

DYE, JAMES WAYNE
PERSONAL Born 12/22/1934, Appalachia, VA, m, 1985, 1 child **DISCIPLINE** PHILOSOPHY, HISTORY OF PHILOSOPHY **EDUCATION** Carson-Newman Col, AB, 55; New Orleans Baptist Theol Sem, BD, 58; Tulane Univ, PhD, 60. **CAREER** Teaching asst philos, Tulane Univ, 58-59; from instr to asst prof, Washington Univ, 60-66; assoc prof, 66-76, dir, Philos Inst, 67-70, prof philos, Northern Ill Univ, 76-, assoc ed, The Philos Forum, 67-70. **MEMBERSHIPS** Am Philos Asn; Soc Ancient Greek Philos; Hume Soc; S Soc Philos Psy Psychol, Pres, 94-95. **RESEARCH** Ancient Greek philosophy; philosophy of religion and culture; German idealism; Hume. **SELECTED PUBLICATIONS** Coauth, Religions of the World, Appleton, 67, Irvington, 75; auth, Denton J Snider's interpretation of Hegel, Mod Schoolman, 1/70; Unspoken philosophy: The presuppositions and applications of thought, Studium Gererale, 71; Kant as ethical naturalist, J Value Inquiry, 78; Plato's concept of causal explanation, Tulane Stud Philos, 78; Aristotle's matter as a sensible principle, Int Studies Philos, 78; Nikolai Bendyaev and his ideas on ultimate reality, J Ultimate Reality & Meaning, 79; The sensibility of intelligible matter, Int Studies Philos, 82; In Search of the Philosopher-King, Archeol News, 82; The Poetization of Science, Studies in Sci and Cult II, 86; Hume on Curing Superstition, Hume Stud, 86; Superhuman Voices and Biological Books, Hist Philos Quart, 88; A Word on Behalf of Demea, Hume Stud, 89; Demea's Departure, Hume Stud, 93. **CONTACT ADDRESS** Dept of Philosophy, No Illinois Univ, 1425 W Lincoln Hwy, De Kalb, IL, 60115-2825. **EMAIL** jdye@niu.edu

DYER, JAMES MARK
DISCIPLINE THEOLOGY **EDUCATION** St Anselm Col, BA, 59; Univ Ottawa, MTh, STL, 65; Episcopal Sem Southwest, DD, 89; Muhlenberg Col, DD, 90. **CAREER** Rector, Christ Church of Hamilton and Wenham, 78-82; prof, Va Theol

Sem, 96-; dir, Spiritual Formation. **HONORS AND AWARDS** Bishop, Diocese of Bethlehem, 82-95; ed, Lambeth Conf, 98. **SELECTED PUBLICATIONS** Auth, The Anglican, Lambeth Conf, 98; Doing Theology Together, Forward Movement Publ, 94. **CONTACT ADDRESS** Va Theol Sem, 3737 Seminary Rd, Alexandria, VA, 22304. **EMAIL** MDyer@vts.edu

DYKEMAN, KING JOHN
PERSONAL Born 06/01/1934, Seattle, WA, m, 1997, 4 children **DISCIPLINE** PHILOSOPHY **EDUCATION** Creighton Univ, AB, 57; Univ Chicago, MA, 66, PhD, 69. **CAREER** Lectr lib arts, Univ Chicago, 64-67, asst dir lib arts prog adults, 66-67; from instr to asst prof, 67-73, ASSOC PROF PHILOS, FAIRFIELD UNIV 73-; ed consult, Choice, 69-; assoc adv mem for US, Centre Superiore de Logica e Scienza Comparate, 72-; Danforth Found fel, 75-; pres bd dir, Greater Bridgeport Area Coun Alcoholism, 77-79. **MEMBERSHIPS** Am Philos Asn; Charles S Peirce Soc; Soc Advan Am Philos. **RESEARCH** Concord school of philos; Am philos; history of philos. **SELECTED PUBLICATIONS** Auth, Croce, Creativity and Contemporary Philosophy, Rivista Studi Crociani, 7-12/72; The J S Mill-W Whewell feud: Categories and Their Consequences, Proc 4th Int Cong Logic, Methodology & Philosophy of Sci, Bucharest, 72; coauth, Science, Technology and Man in the Philosophy of Spirit, 73 & auth, Charles Sanders Peirce: The Minute Logic, 73, Proc IVth World Cong Philos, Varna; History of Science and Technology, Choice, 2/74; The Unity and Diversity of Science, Ethics and Aesthetics, Akten des 4 Int Kant-Long, Ger, 74; The Discovery of Significance, Proc World Cong Humanities, GA, 12/74; The principles of induction: J S Mill and C S Pierce, 5th Int Cong Logic, Methodol & Philos of Sci, CAN, 75; American Women Philosophers, Mellon Press, 93. **CONTACT ADDRESS** Dept of Philos, Fairfield Univ, 1073 N Benson Rd, Fairfield, CT, 06430-5195. **EMAIL** Dykeman@Fair1.fairfield.edu

DYKSTRA, WAYNE A.
PERSONAL Born 06/24/1944, Lebanon, OR, m, 1966, 2 children **DISCIPLINE** RELIGION **EDUCATION** Puget Sound Christian Col, BA, 87; Pacific Christian Col, MA, 91; Emmanual Sch of Rel, Mdiv, 94; Abilene Christian Univ, Dmin; 99. **CAREER** Assoc min, First Christian Church; assoc prof, Nebraska Christian Col. **HONORS AND AWARDS** Validictorian, Puget Sound Christian Col. **MEMBERSHIPS** Fel of Professors **RESEARCH** 19th century reformation of the church. **SELECTED PUBLICATIONS** Auth, A New Venture in Christian Higher Education: A History of Puget, 94; auth, Leadership Development in Christian Churches and Churches of Christ in Northeast Nebraska, 99. **CONTACT ADDRESS** Nebraska Christian Col, 1800 Syracuse Ave, Norfolk, NE, 68701. **EMAIL** wdykstra@nechristian.edu

DYMALE, HERBERT RICHARD
PERSONAL Born 07/23/1925, Murke, Poland, m, 1951, 3 children **DISCIPLINE** RELIGION **EDUCATION** United Theol Sem, MDN, 51; Princeton Theol Sem, ThM, 53; Univ Iowa, PhD(hist theol), 66. **CAREER** Asst prof hist & relig, Cascade Col, 64-67; assoc prof, 67-73, Prof Theol, Malone Col, 73- **MEMBERSHIPS** Evangel Theol Soc; Conf Faith & Hist; Wesleyan Theol Soc. **SELECTED PUBLICATIONS** Auth, What kind of hope is adequate, Christianity Today, 6/71; Paul Tillich's dialectical humanism, Christian Scholar's Rev, 11/73; contribr, Baker's Dictionary of Christian Ethics, Baker Bk, 73. **CONTACT ADDRESS** Dept of Relig & Philos, Malone Col, 515 25th St N W, Canton, OH, 44709-3897. **EMAIL** hdymale@malone.edu

E

EAGAN, JENNIFER
PERSONAL Born 11/09/1969, Arlington, VA, m, 1995 **DISCIPLINE** PHILOSOPHY **EDUCATION** Mary Washington Col, BA, 91. **CAREER** Adjunct instr, Laroche Col, fall 96-spring 97; adjunct instr, Point Park Col, spring 95; adjunct instr, Carlow Col, fall 94- spring 97; grad instr, Duquesne Univ, fall 93-94; adjunct instr, Erie County Community Col, fall 98; adjunct instr, Buffalo State Col and Canisius Col, fall 97-. **HONORS AND AWARDS** Phi Beta Kappa; Mortar Board. **MEMBERSHIPS** Amer Philos Asn; Intl Asn for Philos and Lit; North Amer Kant Soc; Soc for Phenomenological and Existential Philos; Soc of Women in Philos. **RESEARCH** Kant; Feminism; Postmodernism; Ethics. **SELECTED PUBLICATIONS** Auth, Philosophers and the Holocaust: Mediating Public Disputes, Intl Studies in Philo, XXIX, 1, winter, 97. **CONTACT ADDRESS** 396 Highgate Av., Buffalo, NY, 14215-1108. **EMAIL** eaganjl@buffalostate.edu

EAGLESON, IAN
PERSONAL Born 06/24/1959, Philadelphia, PA, d **DISCIPLINE** PHILOSOPHY **EDUCATION** UC San Diego, Phd, expected, 99. **CAREER** Vis asst prof Univ Cincinnati. **MEMBERSHIPS** APA. **RESEARCH** Kant; Epistemology. **CONTACT ADDRESS** 3240 Biship St, #5, Cincinnati, OH, 45220. **EMAIL** eaglesi@email.uc.edu

EAKIN, FRANK EDWIN
PERSONAL Born 09/04/1936, Roanoke, VA, m, 1958 **DISCIPLINE** BIBLICAL STUDIES **EDUCATION** Univ Richmond, BA 58; Southern Baptist Theological Seminary, BD 61; Duke Univ, PhD, 64. **CAREER** Wake Forest Univ, vis asst prof 64-65; Duke Univ, instr 65-66; Univ Richmond, asst prof 66-69, assoc prof 69-75, prof 75. **HONORS AND AWARDS** Phi Beta Kappa; Omicron Delta Kappa; Gurney Harris Kearns Fell; Humanities Scholar; Amer Coun Fell; Weinstein-Rosenthal Prof. **MEMBERSHIPS** Soc Bibl Lit **RESEARCH** Jewish-Christian rel; Bibl theol. **SELECTED PUBLICATIONS** What Price Prejudice? Christian Anti-semitism in America, Paulist Press 98; We Believe in One God: Creed and Scripture, Wyndam Hall Press, 85; The Bible and Anti-semitism, in: Biblical v Secular Ethics: The Conflict, Prometheus Books, 88. **CONTACT ADDRESS** Dept of Relig, Univ of Richmond, Richmond, VA, 23173.

EAMES, ELIZABETH R.
PERSONAL Born 02/18/1921, Toronto, ON, Canada, w, 1952, 2 children **DISCIPLINE** PHILOSOPHY **EDUCATION** Univ Toronto, BA, 43, MA, 44; Bryn Mawr Col, PhD, 51. **CAREER** Instr, asst prof, 48-52, Univ Mo; lectr, Wash Univ, 52-63; from lectr to assoc prof to prof, 63-90, chair, 85-88, Southern Ill Univ, Carbondale. **HONORS AND AWARDS** Grad Fel Bryn Mawr, 44-46; Carnegie Fel, 47-48, Britain; Awards for res, SIU, Am Philos Soc, NEH. **MEMBERSHIPS** Am Philos Asn; Mo Philos Asn; Ill Philos Asn; Soc for Women in Philos. **RESEARCH** Analytic philosphy; Bertrand Russell; American philosophy and feminism. **SELECTED PUBLICATIONS** Auth, Bertrand Russell's Theory of Knowledge; ed, auth, Russell's 1913 Manuscript on Theory of Knowledge; coauth, Lectures in the Far East; coauth, Logical Methods. **CONTACT ADDRESS** 512 Orchard Dr, Carbondale, IL, 62901. **EMAIL** eames@siu.edu

EARHART, HARRY BYRON
PERSONAL Born 01/07/1935, Aledo, IL, m, 1956, 3 children **DISCIPLINE** HISTORY OF RELIGIOUS, ASIAN STUDIES **EDUCATION** Univ Chicago, BD and MA, 60, PhD, 65. **CAREER** Asst prof relig, Vanderbilt Univ, 65-66; from asst prof to assoc prof, 66-69, PROF RELIG, WESTERN MICH UNIV, 75-, Fac res fels, 68 and 73; Fulbright res grant and prof relig, Int Summer Sch Asian Studies, Ewha Womans Univ, Korea, 73; adv Far Eastern relig, Encycl Britannica; ed, Relig Studies Rev, 75-80. **MEMBERSHIPS** Am Acad Relig; Asn Asian Studies; Am Soc Study Relig. **RESEARCH** History of Japanese religion; Japanese new religions; new religious movements. **SELECTED PUBLICATIONS** Auth, Women and Millenarian Protest in Meiji Japan--Deguchi, Nao and Omotokyo, Monumenta Nipponica, Vol 48, 93. **CONTACT ADDRESS** Dept of Relig, Western Michigan Univ, Kalamazoo, MI, 49001.

EARLEY, JOSEPH E.
PERSONAL Born 04/06/1932, Providence, RI, m, 1956, 3 children **DISCIPLINE** CHEMISTRY **EDUCATION** Providence Col, BS, 54; Brown Univ, PhD, 57. **CAREER** Univ Chicago, 58; Georgetown Univ, 58- , prof of chemistry, dept chair, 84- 90. **HONORS AND AWARDS** Potter Prize of Brown Univ, 57. **MEMBERSHIPS** Amer Chemistry Soc; AAAS; APA; Amer Catholic Philos Assn; Soc for Process Philosophy. **RESEARCH** Philosophy of Chemistry; Inorganic Chemistry. **SELECTED PUBLICATIONS** Auth, Individuality and Cooperative, Gu Press, 91. **CONTACT ADDRESS** Georgetown Univ, 2348 Greenwich St, Falls Church, VA, 22046-2315. **EMAIL** earleyj@gusun.georgetown.edu

EASLEY, RAY
PERSONAL Born 07/09/1951, Altus, OK, m, 3 children **DISCIPLINE** THEOLOGY **EDUCATION** Covenant Found Col, ThB, 73; Anderson Univ, M Div, 79; Univ Arkansas, EdD, 87. **CAREER** Acad dean, 9 yrs, Covenant Found Col; vice pres, enrollment & stud affairs, 2 yrs, vice pres, acad affairs, 10 yrs, Wesley Biblical Sem. **CONTACT ADDRESS** PO Box 9938, Jackson, MS, 39286. **EMAIL** rayeasley@aol.com

EASTON, LOYD D.
PERSONAL Born 07/29/1915, Rockford, IL, m, 1963, 5 children **DISCIPLINE** PHILOSOPHY **EDUCATION** DePauw Univ, AB, 37; Boston Univ, MA, 39, PhD, 42. **CAREER** From instr to assoc prof philos, 46-55, chmn dept, 52-76, prof, 55-80, emer and part-time prof philos, Ohio Wesleyan Univ, 80-; prof, philos of relig, Methodist Theol Sch, Ohio, 60-61; Am Counc Learned Soc grant, 61-62; Am Asn State & Local Hist grant, 63; consult philos terms, Webster's New World Dictionary, 66-98; Nat Endowment for Humanities fel, 76. **HONORS AND AWARDS** Phi Beta Kappa, 37; fel, Natl Coun on Religion in Higher Educ, 40; Commendation Medal, HQ US Army European Theater of Operations, 46; hon Dr of Humane Lett, Ohio Wesleyan Univ, 90. **MEMBERSHIPS** Am Philos Asn; Hegel Soc Am; Soc Philos Studies Marxism; Soc for Advanc of Am Philos. **RESEARCH** Social philosophy; history of 19th century thought; American philosophy. **SELECTED PUBLICATIONS** Auth, Alienation and Empiricism in Marx's Thought, Social Res, fall 70; ed, Philosophical Analysis and Human Welfare: Selected Essays and Chapters from Six Decades by D S Miller, Reidel, 75; auth, Marx and Individual Freedom, Philos Forum, spring 81 & winter-spring 81-82; contribur, American National Biography, 99. **CONTACT ADDRESS** 998 Braumiller Rd, Delaware, OH, 43015-3114.

EASTON, PATRICIA ANN
DISCIPLINE PHILOSOPHY **EDUCATION** Univ Western Ontario, PhD, 92. **CAREER** Vis prof, 93-95, post-doctoral fel, 93-94, Univ Toronto; post-doctoral fel, Univ of Western Ontario, 92-93; asst prof of philos, Claremont Graduate Univ, 95-. **HONORS AND AWARDS** Soc Sci and Hum Res Council of Canada, doctoral fel, 88-92, post-doctoral fel, 92-94. **MEMBERSHIPS** APA; Canadian Philos Asn. **RESEARCH** History of early modern philosophy; Descartes. **SELECTED PUBLICATIONS** Coauth, The Cartesian Empiricism of Francois Bayle, Garland, 92; coauth, Bibliographia Malebranchiana: An Annotated Bibliography of the Malebranche Literature into 1989, So Illinois, 92; auth, Rorty's History-of- philosophy-as-story-of-progress, Etudes Maritainiennes/Maritainian Stud, 95; auth, Logic and the Workings of the Mind: The Logic of Ideas and Faculty Psychology in Early Modern Philosophy, in Easton, ed, North American Kant Society Studies in Philosophy Series, Ridgeview, 97; auth, Robert Desgabets, and, Antoine LeGrand, in Craig, ed, Routledge Encyclopedia of Philosophy, Routledge, 98; auth, Jacques Rohault, and Samuel Sorbiere, in Ayers, ed, Biographical Appendix in, The Cambridge History of Seventeenth Century Philosophy, Cambridge, 98. **CONTACT ADDRESS** Dept of Philosophy, Claremont Graduate Sch, 736 N College St, Claremont, CA, 91711. **EMAIL** Patricia.Easton@cgu.edu

EATON, KENT A.
PERSONAL Born 12/08/1957, Abilene, TX, m, 1980, 3 children **DISCIPLINE** RELIGION **EDUCATION** Dallas Theol Sem, ThM, 84; Univ Barcelona, 86; Univ Wales, PhD, 98. **CAREER** Prof Church Hist, Facultad Protestante de Teologica, 86-97; dir, lectr, Bethel Sem, 97-. **MEMBERSHIPS** Am Acad Relig; Evangel Theol Soc. **RESEARCH** Mission history; church history. **SELECTED PUBLICATIONS** Auth, Beware the Trumpet of Judgment: John N. Darby and the Nineteenth Century Brethren, The Coming Deliverer, 97; auth, Los Hermanos de Plymouth en el contexto del no-conformismo britanico, Agenda Teologica, Jan, 97; auth, The Work of the Brethren in Spain, Brethren Archs and Hists Network Rev, Autumn, 97. **CONTACT ADDRESS** Dept of Theology, Bethel Sem, San Diego, 6116 Arosa St., San Diego, CA, 92115-3902. **EMAIL** k-eaton@bethel.edu

EATON, MARCIA M.
PERSONAL Born 10/05/1938, Galesburg, IL, m, 1964, 1 child **DISCIPLINE** PHILOSOPHY **EDUCATION** Knox Col, BA, 60; Stanford Univ, PhD, 68. **CAREER** Instr philos, Stanford Univ, 62-63; instr, Iowa State Univ, 64-65; from vis asst prof to asst prof, Univ Ill, Chicago Circle, 67-71; vis asst prof, Copenhagen Univ, 71-72; asst prof, 72-75, assoc prof, 75-81, PROF PHILOS, UNIV MINN, MINNEAPOLIS, 81. **HONORS AND AWARDS** Scholar in Residence, Rockefeller Center, Bellagio, Italy, 92. **MEMBERSHIPS** Am Soc Aesthet (pres, 95-97); Am Philos Soc; Brit Soc Aesthet. **RESEARCH** Aesthetics; philosophy of language. **SELECTED PUBLICATIONS** Auth,The truth value of literary statements, Brit J Aesthet, spring 72; Aesthetic pleasure and aesthetic pain, J Aesthet & Art Criticism, summer 73; Liars, ranters and dramatic speakers, in Language and Aesthetics, Univ Kans, 73; On being a character, Brit J Aesthet, winter 76; Metaphor & The Casual Theory of Expression, Personalist, 8/77; Truth in pictures, fall 80 & Strange king of sadness, 82, J Aesthet & Art Criticism; Art & Non-Art, Fairleigh Dickinson Press, 82; Art and Nonart, Asoc Univ Presses, 83; Aesthetic and the Good Life, Assoc Univ Presses, 89; Laughing at the death of Little Nell: Sentimental art and sentimental people, Am Philos Quart, 90; Where's the spear? The nature of aesthetic relevance, Brit J Aesthetics, 92; The intrinisic, nonsupervenient nature of aesthetic properties, J Aesthetic and Art Criticism, 94; Aesthetics: The mother of ethics?, J Aesthetic and Art Criticism, 96. **CONTACT ADDRESS** Dept of Philos, Univ of Minn, 224 Church St SE, Minneapolis, MN, 55455-0493. **EMAIL** eaton001@tc.umn.edu

EBBS, GARY
DISCIPLINE PHILOSOPHY **EDUCATION** Univ Mich, PhD, 88. **CAREER** Asst prof, Univ Ill Urban Champaign. **RESEARCH** Philosophy of language and mind; skepticism; self-knowledge; history of analytic philosophy. **SELECTED PUBLICATIONS** Auth, Rule-Following and Realism, Harvard, 97; Skepticism, Objectivity and Brains in Vats; Realism and Rational Inquiry; Can We Take Our Words at Face Value?. **CONTACT ADDRESS** Philosophy Dept, Univ Ill Urbana Champaign, 52 E Gregory Dr, Champaign, IL, 61820. **EMAIL** garyebbs@uiuc.edu

EBERLE, ROLF A.
PERSONAL Born 02/07/1931, Aarau, Switzerland, m, 1958, 3 children **DISCIPLINE** PHILOSOPHY **EDUCATION** Univ Calif Los Angeles, PhD, 65. **CAREER** Asst prof, Kans State Univ, 65-67; asst prof, Univ Rochester, 67-69; assoc prof, 69-75; prof, 75-91; prof emer, 91-. **HONORS AND AWARDS**

Woodrow Wilson Nat Fel, 60-61. **MEMBERSHIPS** Amer Philos Asn. **RESEARCH** Logic; Metaphysics. **SELECTED PUBLICATIONS** Auth, Logic and Proof Techniques, 96; "Semantic Analysis Without Reference to Abstract Entities," 97; "Goodman on Likeness and Differences of Meaning," 97. **CONTACT ADDRESS** 5167 Canadice Hill Rd, Hemlock, NY, 14466-9628. **EMAIL** hie7rae@aol.com

EBERTS, MARY
DISCIPLINE LAW **EDUCATION** Univ Western Ontario, BA, 68, LLB, 71: Harvard Univ, LLM, 72. **CAREER** Assoc prof; Practicing Law, Eberts Symes Street & Corbett **HONORS AND AWARDS** Founder, Women's Legal Edu Action Fund. **SELECTED PUBLICATIONS** Auth, pubs on constitutional and human rights litigation and professions with emphasis on equality rights issues affecting women. **CONTACT ADDRESS** Fac of Law, Univ Toronto, 78 Queen's Park, Toronto, ON.

ECHELBARGER, CHARLES G.
PERSONAL Born 06/20/1942, Fostoria, OH, m, 1968, 1 child **DISCIPLINE** PHILOSOPHY **EDUCATION** Ohio State Univ, PhD, 69. **CAREER** PROF OF PHILOS, SUNY AT OSWEGO, 70-. **MEMBERSHIPS** Amer Philos Assoc; Hume Soc. **RESEARCH** Hume; philos of mind; hist of modern European philos. **CONTACT ADDRESS** Dept of Philos, SUNY Col at Oswego, Oswego, NY, 13126. **EMAIL** echel@oswego.oswego.edu

ECHOLS, MARSHA A.
DISCIPLINE INTERNATIONAL LAW AND INTERNATIONAL BUSINESS TRANSACTIONS **EDUCATION** Howard Univ, BA, 65; Georgetown Univ Law Ctr, JD, 68; Free Univ Brussels, LLM, 73; Columbia Univ Law Sch, LLM, 96. **CAREER** Prof; Howard Univ, 86-; dir, Master Compe Jurisp MCJ prog; taught at, Univ Va Sch Law & George Washington Univ Nat Law Ctr. **MEMBERSHIPS** Ch, Task Force on Reg Econ Integration of the ABA & mem, Coun For Relations. **RESEARCH** Nontariff barriers for international trade in foods and agriculture. **SELECTED PUBLICATIONS** Auth, The International Tower of Babel: The Small Business Pespective, 51 Food & Drug Law J 175, 96 & Sanitary and Phytosanitary Measures, in The World Trade Organization, 96; contrib chap, WTO agreement on Sanitary and Phyto sanitary measures to an ABA bk on the WTO int trade agreement & article on int food labeling to the Food and Drug Law J. **CONTACT ADDRESS** Dept of Law, Howard Univ, 2400 Sixth St NW, Washington, DC, 20059.

ECKARDT, ALICE LYONS
PERSONAL Born 04/27/1923, Brooklyn, NY, m, 1944, 2 children **DISCIPLINE** HISTORY OF RELIGIONS **EDUCATION** Oberlin Col, BA, 44; Lehigh Univ, MA, 66. **CAREER** Lectr, 72-75, ASST PROF RELIG STUDIES, LEHIGH UNIV, 76-, Vis prof, Judaic Studies Dept, City Univ New York, 73; assoc, Rockefeller Found Grant, 75-76; Spec adv, President's Comn on the Holocaust, 79 and US Holocaust Mem Coun, 81-; vis scholar, Oxford Ctr postgrad Hebrew Studies, 82 and Cedar Crest Col, 81 and 82. **MEMBERSHIPS** Am Acad Relig; Nat Inst Holocaust; Am Professors Peace Mid East. **RESEARCH** History and theology of Jewish-Christian relations; the Holocaust, and post-Holocaust theology; sexism and world religions. **SELECTED PUBLICATIONS** Auth, The Other in Jewish Thought and History--Constructions of Jewish Culture and Identity, J Ecumenical Stud, Vol 33, 96; A Jewish Appraisal of Dialogue--Between Talk and Theology, J Ecumenical Stud, Vol 33, 96. **CONTACT ADDRESS** Beverly Hill Rd, Box 619A, Coopersburg, PA, 18036.

ECKENWILER, LISA A.
DISCIPLINE PHILOSOPHY, BIOETHICS **EDUCATION** Univ Wis, BA, 89; Univ Tenn, MA, 91, PhD, 97. **CAREER** Tchr, St. Mary's Med Ctr, Tenn, 93; tchr, Univ Tenn Med Ctr, Tenn, 94; Dept Philos, Univ Tenn-Knoxville, 91-94; Med Human Prog, Stritch Sch Med, Loyola Univ, 96; Grad Prog Pub Hea, Eastern Va Med Sch, 98; Dept Philos, Old Dominion Univ, 97- . **MEMBERSHIPS** Am Philos Assn; Amer Soc Bioethics Human; Intl Assn Bioethics; Network Feminist Approaches to Bioethics; SE Va Bioethics Network. **RESEARCH** Specialization in moral philosophy; biomedical ethics; Competence in feminist philosophy; history of philosophy. **SELECTED PUBLICATIONS** Co-ed, Institutional Policy in Paediatric Practice: Documenting Canadian Experience, Toronto, The Hospital for Sick Children Dept Bioethics, 94; Women and Communities in Clinical Research: Questioning the Influence of Communitarian Ideals, in Soc Philos Today, vol 13, ed, Yeager Hudson, Lewiston, NY, Edwin Mellen Press, 98. **CONTACT ADDRESS** Dept of Philosophy, Old Dominion Univ, 4100 Powhatan Ave, Norfolk, VA, 23529.

ECKLEBARGER, KERMIT A.
PERSONAL Born 12/10/1935, Chicago, IL, m, 1956, 2 children **DISCIPLINE** NEW TESTAMENT AND EARLY CHRISTIAN LITERATURE **EDUCATION** Wheaton Col, BA, 58, MA, 61; Univ Chicago, PhD, 87. **CAREER** New Testament prof, London Col of Bible and Missions, 60-68; New Testament prof, Ont Bible Col, 68-72; assoc prof New Testament, 72-, Vpres & Acad Dean, 93-, Denver Sem; ATS grant curric develop, 77-78. **MEMBERSHIPS** Evangelical Theol Soc; Soc Bibl Lit; Inst Bibl Res. **RESEARCH** Hermenentics; Greek grammar and exegeice. **SELECTED PUBLICATIONS** Auth Growing Towards Spiritual Maturity, 88; Nelson's Illustrated Bible Dictionary, 86; Computer Bible Study, Word, 93; Introduction to Biblical Interpretation, Word, 93. **CONTACT ADDRESS** 8981 S Coyote St, Highlands Ranch, CO, 80126. **EMAIL** kermit@densem.edu

ECKSTEIN, JEROME
PERSONAL Born 06/25/1928, 3 children **DISCIPLINE** PHILOSOPHY **EDUCATION** Brooklyn Col, BA, 49; Columbia Univ, PhD (philos), 61. **CAREER** Lectr philos, Brooklyn Col and City Col NY, 55-60; isntr philos and contemporary civilization, Columbia Univ, 60-63; from asst prof to assoc prof philos, Dowling Col, 63-66; prof philos educ, 66-70, chmn dept, 70-74, PROF JUDAIC STUDIES, STATE UNIV NY ALBANY, 70-, State Univ NY fac res fel, classification and anal of Babylonian Talmud, 68-72; Am Coun Learned Soc fel, 72-73. **MEMBERSHIPS** Soc Advan Am Philos. **RESEARCH** Religion; Plato; epistemology. **SELECTED PUBLICATIONS** Auth, Biographical Misunderstandings, Tradition J Orthodox Jewish Thought, Vol 30, 96. **CONTACT ADDRESS** Dept of Judaic Studies, State Univ of NY, 1400 Washington Ave, Albany, NY, 12222-1000.

ECONOMOU, ELLY HELEN
PERSONAL Thessaloniki, Greece **DISCIPLINE** BIBLICAL AND MODERN LANGUAGES **EDUCATION** Pac Union Col, BA, 66; Andrews Univ, MA, 67; Univ Strasbourg, France, PhD, 75. **CAREER** Instr French, 67-70, instr French & Greek, 70-72, Prof Bibl Lang & Relig, Andrews Univ, 72-77. **MEMBERSHIPS** Soc Bibl Lit; MLA; Int Platform Asn; Am Class League. **RESEARCH** Ecumenical studies; religion, the Greek Orthodox church, patristic lit; papyrology. **SELECTED PUBLICATIONS** Auth, Beloved Enemy, Pac Press Publ Asn, 68; numerous articles in Youth's Beakon & Children's Friend, 51-72. **CONTACT ADDRESS** Dept of Relig, Andrews Univ, 100 US Hwy 31, Berrien Springs, MI, 49104-0001.

EDELBERG, WALTER
DISCIPLINE PHILOSOPHY **EDUCATION** Univ Pittsburgh, PhD. **CAREER** Assoc prof, Univ IL at Chicago. **RESEARCH** Philosophical logic; metaphysics; philos of lang; hist of early mod philos. **SELECTED PUBLICATIONS** Auth, The Fifth Meditation, Philos Rev, 90; Intentional Identity and the Attitudes, Ling Philos,92; Propositions, Circumstances, Objects, Jour Philo Logic, 94. **CONTACT ADDRESS** Philos Dept, Univ Illinois Chicago, S Halsted St, PO Box 705, Chicago, IL, 60607. **EMAIL** edelberg@uic.edu

EDELMAN, DIANA
DISCIPLINE BIBLICAL STUDIES; ANCIENT SYNO-PALESTINIAN HISTORY & ARCHAEOLOGY **EDUCATION** Smith Col, AB, 75; Univ Chicago, MA, 78, PhD, 86. **CAREER** Lectr, St Xavier Univ, 90-91; assoc prof, James Madison Univ, 93-; **HONORS AND AWARDS** Grant-in-aid Amer Coun Learned Studies, 88; vis prof Ecole biblique et archeol Jerusalem, 96. **MEMBERSHIPS** Soc Bibl Lit; Amer Schools of Orient Res; Cath Bibl Asn. **RESEARCH** Ancient Syno-Palestinian history & archaelology; Deuteronomistic history; Ancient Israelite religion; 2nd temple Judaism. **SELECTED PUBLICATIONS** Auth, King Saul in the Historiography of Judah, Journal for the Study of the Old Testament Supplement Series, 91; ed, The Fabric of History: Text, Artifact, & Israels Past, Journal for the Study of the Old Testament Supplement Series, 91; auth, You Shall Not Abhor an Edomite for He is Your Brother: Edom and Seir in History and Tradition, Archaeology and Biblical Studies, 95; The Triumph of Elohim: From Yahuisims to Judaisms, Biblical Exegesis and Theology, 95. **CONTACT ADDRESS** Dept of Philosophy & Religion, James Madison Univ, MSC 7504, Harrisonburg, VA, 22807. **EMAIL** edelmadj@jmu.edu

EDELMAN, DIANE PENNEYS
DISCIPLINE LEGAL WRITING **EDUCATION** Princeton Univ, AB, 79; Brooklyn Law Sch, JD, 83. **CAREER** Prof, Villanova Univ Sch Law, 93-. **HONORS AND AWARDS** Brooklyn J Int Law, 81-83; Ed-in-Ch, 82-83; Philip C. Jessup Int Law Moot Ct Team,82; Best Oralist, Eastern Region; First Runner-Up Team, Eastern Region; Alexander Mehr Mem prize; Oceana Publ prize; Moot Ct Honor Soc; Honorable Mention, Best Brief awd, 81. **MEMBERSHIPS** Amer Soc Int Law; co-founder and Vice Ch, Innovations in Tchg Int Law Interest Gp Ch, 96-98; bd ed, Legal Writing: The Journal of the Legal Writing Institute, 98-; Philadelphia and Amer Bar Asn; Princeton Univ, Alumni Schools Comt; bd dir, Trinity Nursery and Kindergarten, 94-; Wayne Art Ctr, 94-98; Philadelphia Volunteer Lawyers for the Arts & Philadelphia Area Repertory Theatre, 89-95. **RESEARCH** Teaching international law moot court as an alternative to traditional legal writing instruction. **SELECTED PUBLICATIONS** Auth, How They Write:Our Students' Reflections on Writing, 6:1 Perspectives 24, 97; Opening Our Doors to the World:Introducing International Law in Legal Writing and Legal Research Courses,5:1 Perspectives 1, 96; Coauth, Overcoming Language and Legal Differences in the Global Classroom:Teaching Legal Research and Legal Writing to International Law Graduates and International Law Students, 96 Proceedings Issue,3 Legal Writing: J Legal Writing Inst 127, 97; From Product to Process:Evolution of a Legal Writing Program, 58 Pittsburgh Law Rev 719, 97. **CONTACT ADDRESS** Law School, Villanova Univ, 800 Lancaster Ave, Villanova, PA, 19085-1692. **EMAIL** edelman@law.vill.edu

EDGAR, TIMOTHY W.
DISCIPLINE LAW **EDUCATION** Univ Western Ontario, BA, 82, LLB, 85; Osgoode Hall Law Sch, LLM, 88. **CAREER** Prof, 89-. **SELECTED PUBLICATIONS** Co-ed, Materials on Canadian Income Tax. **CONTACT ADDRESS** Fac of Law, Univ Western Ontario, London, ON, N6A 3K7.

EDGAR, WILLIAM
DISCIPLINE APOLOGETICS **EDUCATION** Harvard Univ, BA, 66; Westminster Theol Sem, MDiv, 69; Columbia Univ, grad stud; Univ de Geneve, Thd, 93. **CAREER** Fac, Brunswick Sch, 70-78; prof, Faculte Libre de Theologie Reformee, Aix-en-Provence, France, 79-89; prof, Westminster Theol Sem, 89-. **SELECTED PUBLICATIONS** Auth, Sur le Rock; Bibliographie D'ouvrages Apologetique; Reasons of the Heart; L'Apologetica di Cornelius Van Til, Studi di teologia VII/1, 95; No News is Good News: Modernity, the Postmodern, and Apologetics, Westminster Theol Jour 57, 95; Un' Accomppaniata Insolita: Jazz e Vangelo, Studi di Teologia 15, VIII/1, 96. **CONTACT ADDRESS** Westminister Theol Sem, PO Box 27009, Philadelphia, PA, 19118. **EMAIL** wedgar@hslc.org

EDGAR, WILLIAM JOHN
PERSONAL Born 01/20/1933, Charlottesville, VA, m, 1962, 4 children **DISCIPLINE** PHILOSOPHY **EDUCATION** Cornell Univ, BA, 59; Syracuse Univ, MA, 66, PhD(philos), 72. **CAREER** Syst analyst, Advan Elec Ctr, Gen Elec Co, 59-62 & Elec Lab, 62-65; instr Philos, Syracuse Univ, 68-69; asst prof, 69-74, assoc prof, 74-79, Distinguished Teaching Prof Philos, State Univ NY, Geneseo, 79-, chairperson Dept, 78-. **HONORS AND AWARDS** Chancellor's Award for Excellence in Teaching, State Univ NY, 74 & 76. **MEMBERSHIPS** Am Philos Asn; Mind Asn. **RESEARCH** Theory of knowledge; foundations of mathematics and science; philosophy of mind. **SELECTED PUBLICATIONS** Auth, Professor Gotesky and the law of non-contradiction, Philos & Phenomenol Res, 12/71; Is modesty a virtue?, J Value Inquiry, Winter, 72; Is intuitionism the epistemically serious foundation for mathematics?, Philosophia Mathematica, Winter 73; Continuity and the individuation of modes in Spinoza's physics, In: Spinoza's Metaphysics, Van Gorcum, 76; Locations, Can J Philos, 79; Evidence, Univ Am Press, The Elements. **CONTACT ADDRESS** Dept of Philosophy, SUNY, Geneseo, 1 College Cir, Geneseo, NY, 14454-1401. **EMAIL** edgar@uno.cc.geneseco.edu

EDGE, HOYT LITTLETON
PERSONAL Born 02/23/1944, Louisville, KY, m, 1967 **DISCIPLINE** PHILOSOPHY OF MIND, PARASYCHOLOGY **EDUCATION** Stetson Univ, BA, 66; Vanderbilt Univ, MA, 68, PhD(Philos), 70. **CAREER** Asst prof, 70-74, assoc prof, 74-81, prof Philos, Rollins Col ,81-. **HONORS AND AWARDS** McKean Prof of Philosophy, 97. **MEMBERSHIPS** Am Soc Psychical Res; Soc Psychial Res; Southern Soc Philos & Psychol; Parapsychological Asn. **RESEARCH** Creativity and altered states of consciousness; experiments in ESP, PK and paranormal healing; philosophical implications of parapsychology; cross-cultural concepts of self. **SELECTED PUBLICATIONS** Auth, Rorty on Identity, J Value Inquiry, Fall 74; co-ed, Philosophical Dimensions of Parapsychology, Charles Thomas, 76; auth, Do Spirits Matter: Survival and Disembodied Spirits, 7/76 & Rejoinder to Dr Weatley's Note-on Do Spirits Matter, 10/76, J Am Soc Psychical Res; The Place of Paradigms in Parapsychology, In: The Philosophy of parapsychology, Parapsychology Found, 77; coauth, A Possible Case of the Displacement Effect in a Token Object Test, New Eng J Parapsychology, 3/78; auth, A Philosophical Justification for the Conformation Behavior Model, J Am Soc Psychical Res, 7/78; Spirituality in the Natural and Social Worlds, Revision, 95; Possession in Two Balinese Trance Ceremonies, Anthropology of Consciousness, 96. **CONTACT ADDRESS** Dept of Philosophy, Rollins Col, 1000 Holt Ave, Winter Park, FL, 32789-4499. **EMAIL** Hoyt.Edge@Rollins.edu

EDINGER, ELIZABETH
DISCIPLINE LAW **EDUCATION** Univ British Columbia, BA, 64; LLB, 67; Oxford Univ, BCL, 77. **CAREER** Asst prof, 78-87; assoc prof, 87-88; assoc dean, 88-92; prof, 92-97; assoc dean, 97-. **RESEARCH** Constitutional Law; conflicts; creditor debtor law. **SELECTED PUBLICATIONS** Auth, pubs about conflict of laws, constitutional law, and creditors' remedies. **CONTACT ADDRESS** Fac of Law, Univ British Columbia, 1822 East Mall, Vancouver, BC, V6T 1Z1. **EMAIL** edinger@law.ubc.ca

EDLER, FRANK H. W.
PERSONAL Born 09/02/1947, Amorbach, West Germany, m, 1985, 2 children **DISCIPLINE** PHILOSOPHY **EDUCATION** Univ Rhode Island, BA, 71; New York Univ, MA, 74; Univ Toronto, PhD, 92. **HONORS AND AWARDS** Twice alternate for Fulbright. **MEMBERSHIPS** Am Philos Asn; Heidegger Conf N Am. **RESEARCH** Heidegger; Hermeneutics; Phenomenology; Technology, Classical Philology; Literature. **SELECTED PUBLICATIONS** Auth Philosophy, Language, and Politics; Heideggers Attempt to Steal the Language of the R evolution in 1933-34, Soc Res, 90; Retreat from Radicality: Poggeler on Heideggers Politics, Grad Fac Philos Jour, 91; trans Selected Letters from the Heidegger-Blochmann Correspondence, Grad Fac Philos Jour, 91; auth Heideggers Interpretation of the German Revolution, Res in Phenomenol, 93; rev Heideggers Crisis: Philosophy and Politics in Nazi Germany, Jour Hist Philos, 95; auth Heidegger and Werner Jaeger on the Eve of 1933: A Possible Rapprochement?, Res In Phenomenol, 97. **CONTACT ADDRESS** 4622 Cass St, Omaha, NE, 68132. **EMAIL** fedler @metropo.mccneb.edu OR fedler@ne.uswest.net

EDWARDS, ABIYAH, JR.
PERSONAL Born 12/23/1927, Princeton, KY, s **DISCIPLINE** RELIGION **EDUCATION** Institute of Divine Metaphysical Research Inc, DD, 1971. **CAREER** UAW Local 600-Ford, CIO, 1949-65; Ford Motor Co, Dearborn, MI, 1965-92; Kaiser Jeep; Enjoy Restaurant/Palace, creative consultant/mgr, 1988-89; Third Baptist Church, associate pastor; Institute of Divine Metaphysical Research Inc, recruiter, lecturer; UNIVERSAL SCHOOL OF SPIRITUAL AWARENESS, DEAN, currently. **HONORS AND AWARDS** Project Head Start, Volunteer Service Award, 1992. **SELECTED PUBLICATIONS** Author, The Beauty of it All, 1995. **CONTACT ADDRESS** Universal School of Spiritual Awareness, 5300 Newport Ave, Detroit, MI, 48213.

EDWARDS, CLIFFORD WALTER
PERSONAL Born 07/02/1932, Southampton, NY, m, 1956, 2 children **DISCIPLINE** RELIGION **EDUCATION** Drew Univ, BA, 54; Garrett Theol Sem, BD, 58; Northwestern Univ, PhD(Bibl study & world relig), 64. **CAREER** Prof relig, Wesleyan Col, Ga, 63-68; prof & chmn dept, Randolph-Macon Col, 68-75; ASSOC PROF RELIG, VA COMMONWEALTH UNIV, 75-; Ed, Wesleyan Quart Rev, 65-68. **MEMBERSHIPS** Am Acad Relig; Soc Bibl Lit **RESEARCH** World Religions; religion and culture; biblical studies. **SELECTED PUBLICATIONS** Auth, Christian Being and Doing: A Study-commentary of James and I Peter, Ed Missions, Methodist Church, 65; ed, Methodism in Cuba, 66 & Japanese Contributions to the Study of John Wesley, 67; auth, VanGogh and God: A Creative Spiritual Quest. **CONTACT ADDRESS** Dept of Philos & Relig Studies, Commonwealth Col, Richmond, Box 2025, Richmond, VA, 23284-2025. **EMAIL** cedwards@saturn.vcu.edu

EDWARDS, DOUGLAS R.
PERSONAL Born 01/09/1950, Superior, NE, m, 3 children **DISCIPLINE** NEW TESTAMENT AND CHRISTIAN ORIGINS **EDUCATION** Boston Univ, MDiv, 78; Boston Univ Grad School Arts & Sci, PhD, 87. **CAREER** Vis instr, Univ Vermont, 84-85; instr, Col of Holy Cross, 85-87; asst prof, 87-92, assoc prof of Relig, 92-, Univ Puget Sound; NEH fel, 91-92; sr fel Albright Inst Archaeol Res Jerusalem, 92; Deans Tchg Award, 96; Soc Bibl Res grant, 98; NWACC grant, 98; vis fel, Wolfson Col Oxford, 98. **MEMBERSHIPS** Am Acad Relig; Am Schools Oriental Res; Archael Inst Am; Cath Bibl Asn; Class Soc Am Acad Rome; Soc Bibl Lit. **RESEARCH** Old World archaeology with an emphasis on Israel, the Crimea, and Asia Minor from the Hellenistic through the Byzantine periods; the Gospel of Luke and Acts; Ancient romances religion and power in antiquity. **SELECTED PUBLICATIONS** Auth Yodefat, 1992, Israel Explor Jour, 95; The 1994 Black Sea Project Excavations at Chersonesus: A Preliminary Report, Ukrainian Acad Arts & Sci, 95; The 1995 Black Sea Project Excavations at Chersonesus: A Preliminary Report, Ukrainian Acad Arts & Sci, 96; Religion and Power: Pagans, Jews, and Christians in the Greek East, Oxford Univ Press, 96; Archaeology and the Galilee: Texts and Contexts in the Greco-Roman and Byzantine Periods, Scholars Press, 97; The 1996 Black Sea Project Excavations at Chersonesus: A Preliminary Report, Ukrainian Acad Arts and Sci, 97; Cappadocia, Jotapata, Miletus, Oxford Encycl Archael in the Near East, Oxford Univ Press, 97; The Ancient Road of Sepphoris: A Cultural and Historical Study, Archaeology and the Galilee: Texts and Contexts in the Graeco-Roman and Byzantine Periods, 97; Pleasurable Reading or Symbols of Power: Religious Themes and Social Context in Chariton, Ancient Fiction and Early Christian Narrative, Scholars Press, 98. **CONTACT ADDRESS** Relig Dept, Univ Puget Sound, 1500 N Warner, Tacoma, WA, 98416. **EMAIL** dedwards@ups.edu

EDWARDS, HARRY T.
PERSONAL Born 11/03/1940, New York, NY **DISCIPLINE** LAW **EDUCATION** Cornell Univ, BS 1962; Univ of Michigan Law School, JD, 1965. **CAREER** Seyfarth, Shaw Fairweather & Geraldson, Chicago, attorney, 1965-70; Univ of Michigan Law School, professor, 1970-75, 1977-80; Harvard Univ Law School, prof 1975-77; Amtrak, bd dir, 1977-80, chmn bd 1979-80; US Ct of Appeals, Washington, DC, judge 1980-94, chief judge, 1994-. **HONORS AND AWARDS** Honorary Doctor of Law degrees from Williams Coll, Univ of Detroit, Georgetown University, Brooklyn College, State University of New York, John Jay College of Criminal Justice, Lewis & Clark College, St Lawrence Univ; Whitney North Seymour Medal, Amer Arbitration Assn, 1988; Society of Amer Law Teachers Award for distinguished contributions to teaching and public service, 1982. **MEMBERSHIPS** Amer Law Institute; Amer Bar Assn; Amer Academy of Arts & Sciences; Amer Judicature Society; Unique Learning Center, mentor, instructor, bd of directors. **SELECTED PUBLICATIONS** Co-author, Labor Relations Law in the Pub Sector, 1985, The Lawyer as a Negotiator, 1977, Collective Bargaining & Labor Arbitration, 1979, Higher Educ & the Law, 1980; author of more than 75 scholarly articles. **CONTACT ADDRESS** US Court of Appeals - DC Circuit, 333 Constitution Ave NW, Washington, DC, 20001-2866.

EDWARDS, JAMES R.
PERSONAL Born 09/28/1945, CO, m, 1968, 2 children **DISCIPLINE** THEOLOGY **EDUCATION** Whitworth Col, BA, 67; Princeton Theol Sem, M Div, 70; Univ of Zurich, Switzerland, 70-71; Fuller Theol Sem, PhD, 78. **CAREER** Min of Stud, 71-78, First Presbyterian, CO; prof, 78-97, Jamestown Col; prof, 97-, Whitworth Col, WA. **RESEARCH** biblical stud, Holocaust **CONTACT ADDRESS** 404 W Graves Rd, Spokane, WA, 99218. **EMAIL** jedwards@whitworth.edu

EDWARDS, JAMES R.
PERSONAL Born 10/28/1945, Colorado Springs, CO, m, 1968, 2 children **DISCIPLINE** BIBLICAL STUDIES; NEW TESTAMENT **EDUCATION** Whitworth Col, BA, 67; Princeton Theol Sem, MDiv, 70; Univ Zurich, 71; Fuller Theol Sem, PhD, 78. **CAREER** Minister of students, First Presbyterian Church, Colorado Springs, CO, 71-78; prof Relig, Jamestown Col, Jamestown, ND, 78-97; PROF RELIG, WHITEWORTH COL, SPOKANE, WA, 97-. **HONORS AND AWARDS** Prof of Year, Jamestown Col, 84; Sears-Roebuck Teaching Award, 90; Deutscher Akademischer Austauschdienst, 93; Templeton grant in Science and Relig, 96; Pew-Gordon summer res grant, 98. **MEMBERSHIPS** SBL; NY C. S. Lewis Soc. **RESEARCH** Gospels; Patristics; Holocaust; OT-NT. **SELECTED PUBLICATIONS** Auth, Commentary on the Epistle to the Romans, Community Bible Study, 84; Commentary on the Gospel of Mark, Community Bible Study, 87; The Layman's Overview of the Bible, co-auth with George Knight, Nashville: Thomas Nelson Pubs, 87; Commentary on the Epistle to the Ephesians, Community Bible Study, 88; Romans, New International Biblical Commentary, vol 6, Peabody: Hendrickson's, 92; Commentary on 1 and 2 Peter, Community Bible Study, 93; A Confessional Church in a Pluralistic World, Proceedings of the Wheaton Theology Conference, vol 1, Wheaton, 92, reprinted in Touchstone 6/1, 93; Life in Three Dimensions, Touchstone 6/3, 93; Citizens of History, Small Town 24/6, 94; Old Testament or Hebrew Scriptures?, Pro Ecclesia 3/4, fall 94; The Spiritual Bodies of Angels, chapter 1 in All the Angels in the Bible, ed Herbert Lockyer, Jr, Peabody: Hendrickson's, 95; New Quest, Old Errors, The Fallacies of the New Quest for the Historical Jesus, Touchstone, 9/1, 96; Ernst Lohmeyer--ein Schlusskapitel, Evangelische Theologie 56/4, 96; The Right Choice, co-auth with Gary Watts, The Presbyterian Outlook, Jan 97; Aren't They All the Same?, The Uniqueness of Christianity Among World Religions, Student Leadership J 9/2, 96; No One Righteous, No, Not One, Christian Advancement 1/1, 97; Angels of Light, Christian Advancement 1/2, 98; The Irony of Our Calling, reNEWS, June 98. **CONTACT ADDRESS** Whitworth Col, MS 1502, Spokane, WA, 99251-1502. **EMAIL** jedwards@whitworth.edu

EDWARDS, REM B.
PERSONAL Born 10/02/1934, Washington, GA, m, 1962, 2 children **DISCIPLINE** PHILOSOPHY **EDUCATION** Emory Univ, AB, 56; Yale Univ, BD, 59; Emory Univ, PhD, 62. **CAREER** Asst prof Philos, Jacksonville Univ, 62-66; assoc prof Philos, Univ Tenn, 66-70; prof Philos, Univ Tenn, 70-97. **HONORS AND AWARDS** Phi Beta Kappa; Danforth Grad Fel; Chancellor's Res Scholar; Distinguished Emory-at Oxford Alumnus; Lindsay Young prof. **MEMBERSHIPS** Tenn Philos Assoc Pres, 73-74; Soc for Philos Relig Pres, 81-82; S Soc Philos & Psychol Pres, 84-85; RS Hartman Value Inst, 89-. **RESEARCH** Ethics; Medical Ethics; Philos Relig; Ethics and Animals; Axiology; Cosmology. **SELECTED PUBLICATIONS** Fetz's Misunderstanding of Formal Axiology, Kriterion, 98; Co-ed, Bioethics for Medical Education, JAI Pr, 98; Values, Ethics, and Alcoholism, JAI Pr, 97. **CONTACT ADDRESS** Dept of Philosophy, Tennessee Univ, 8709 Longmeade Dr, Knoxville, TN, 37923. **EMAIL** redwards@utkux.utcc.utk.edu

EDWARDS, RICHARD ALAN
PERSONAL Born 12/31/1934, West Mahanoy Twp, PA, m, 1958, 3 children **DISCIPLINE** NEW TESTAMENT **EDUCATION** Princeton Univ, BA, 56; Univ Chicago, MA, 62, PhD, 68. **CAREER** Instr relig, Bethany Col, Kans, 62-63; instr, Susquehanna Univ, 63-66; assoc prof, Thiel Col, 68-72; assoc prof, Va Polytech Inst & State Univ, 72-78; assoc prof New Testament, Marquette Univ, 78-; Lutheran Church Am res & creativity grant, 69-70. **MEMBERSHIPS** Soc Bibl Lit; Studiorum Novi Testamenti Societas; Cath Bibl Asn. **RESEARCH** Synoptic Gospels and Acts; theology of Matthew. **SELECTED PUBLICATIONS** Coauth, The Sentences of Sextus, Scholars Press, 81; auth, Matthew's Story of Jesus, Fortress, 85; auth, Matthew's Portrait of Disciples: How the Text-Connoted Reader is Informed, Trinity International, 97. **CONTACT ADDRESS** Theol Dept, Marquette Univ, Milwaukee, WI, 53233. **EMAIL** edwardsr@vms.csd.mu.edu

EDWARDS, RICHARD W.
DISCIPLINE LAW **EDUCATION** Cornell Univ, BA, JD. **CAREER** Prof. **SELECTED PUBLICATIONS** Auth, International Monetary Collaboration, Transnational, 85; International Monetary Policy: The Next 25 Years, Vanderbilt J Transnational Law, 92; Reservations to Treaties, Mich J Int Law, 89. **CONTACT ADDRESS** Col Law, Univ of Toledo, Toledo, OH, 43606.

EDWARDS, RUTH MCCALLA
PERSONAL Born 04/23/1949, Cleveland, OH, m **DISCIPLINE** LAW **EDUCATION** Hiram Coll, BA 1971; Univ of Cincinnati Coll of Law, JD 1974. **CAREER** Legal Aid Soc of Cincinnati, atty & office mgr 1974-77; Private Law Practice, atty 1977-79; Hamilton County Public Defender Comm, atty 1979; Univ of Cincinnati, atty, prog coord, paralegal prog 1979-. **HONORS AND AWARDS** Hon Degree of Tech Letters Cincinnati Tech Coll 1985; YMCA Black Achievers Awd 1985. **MEMBERSHIPS** Admitted OH State Bar 1974; admitted Fed Bar So Dist of OH 1974; mem bd trustees Cincinnati Tech Coll 1977-; mem Amer, Cincinnati Bar Assns; mem & past pres Black Lawyers Assn of Cincinnati; past bd mem Legal Aid Soc of Cincinnati; bd mem & officer Winton Hills Med & Halth Ctr; bd mem & past officer Comprehensive Comm Child Care; bd mem Cincinnati Tech Coll; mem Alpha Kappa Alpha Sor; arbitrator Better Business Bureau Arbitration Prog; mem Assn of Comm Coll Trustees; sec Central Region Minority Affairs Assembly of the Assn of Comm Coll Trustees; mem Amer Assn for Paralegal Education Inc; chairperson bd trustees Cincinnati Tech Coll 1983-84; past bd mem, officer Winton Hills Med & Health Ctr; arbitrator Amer Arbitration Assoc; chair Central Region Minority Affairs Comm of the Assoc of Conity Coll Trustees. **CONTACT ADDRESS** Paralegal Program, Univ of Cincinnati, Cincinnati, OH, 45221.

EDWARDS, SANDRA
DISCIPLINE MEDIEVAL PHILOSOPHY **EDUCATION** Univ Pa, PhD. **CAREER** Philos, Univ Ark **SELECTED PUBLICATIONS** Transl, St. Thomas Aquinas's Quaestiones Quodlibetales I & II, Pontifical Inst Medieval Studies, 83. **CONTACT ADDRESS** Univ Ark, Fayetteville, AR, 72701. **EMAIL** sandrae@comp.uark.edu

EELLS, ELLERY T.
PERSONAL Born 03/26/1953, Lynwood, CA, m, 1981, 2 children **DISCIPLINE** PHILOSOPHY **EDUCATION** Univ CA, Santa Barbara, BA, 75, Berkeley, MA, 78, PhD(philos), 80. **CAREER** Vis asst prof, NC State Univ, Raleigh, 80-81; asst prof, 81-83, assoc prof, 84-87, prof philos, Univ WI-Madison, 87-. **HONORS AND AWARDS** Guggenheim; ACLS; NSF. **MEMBERSHIPS** Am Philos Asn; Philos of Science Asn. **RESEARCH** Philosophical foundations of probability theory; theory of rational decision; philosophy of science; logic, inductive logic; probabilistic causality and the question of transitivits. **SELECTED PUBLICATIONS** Auth, Causality, Utility and Decision, Synthese, 8/81; Rational Decision and Causality, Cambridge Univ Press, 9/82; coauth (with Elliott Sober), Probalistic Causality, Cambridge, 91. **CONTACT ADDRESS** Dept Philos, Univ Wisconsin, 600 North Park St, Madison, WI, 53706-1403. **EMAIL** eteells@facstaff.wisc.edu

EGAN, HARVEY DANIEL
PERSONAL Born 11/06/1937, CT **DISCIPLINE** THEOLOGY **EDUCATION** Worcester Polytech Inst, BS, 59; Boston Col, MA, 65; Woodstock Col, MA, 69; Univ Munster, ThD, 73. **CAREER** Res engr, Boeing Airplane Co, 59-60; lectr philos, Holy Cross Col, 65-66; asst prof theol, Santa Clara Univ, 73-75; asst prof, 75-80, ASSOC PROF THEOL, BOSTON COL, 80-, Jesuit priest, R C Priesthood, Soc Jesus, New Eng, 60-. **MEMBERSHIPS** Cath Theol Soc Am; Col Theol Soc; Am Acad Relig. **RESEARCH** Christian mysticism; theology of Karl Rahner; systematic theology. **SELECTED PUBLICATIONS** Auth,The Growth of Mysticism--Gregory the Great Through the 12th Century--Mcginn, B, Theol Stud, Vol 56, 95; The Letters of Hildegard of Bingen, Vol 1, Theol Stud, Vol 57, 96; Rahner, Karl, Thought Rev Cult Idea, Vol 67, 92. **CONTACT ADDRESS** Theol Dept, Boston Col, 140 Commonwealth Ave, Chestnut Hill, MA, 02167-3800.

EGLESTON, DON
DISCIPLINE LAW **EDUCATION** Saskatchewan, BA, 66; LLB, 67. **CAREER** Law, Univ of BC **HONORS AND AWARDS** Co-ed, Can Criminal Law Practice. **RESEARCH** Criminal law; criminal procedure; clinical law; advanced criminal law; trial advocacy. **SELECTED PUBLICATIONS** Auth, pubs about criminal law. **CONTACT ADDRESS** Fac of Law, Univ British Columbia, 1822 East Mall, Vancouver, BC, V6T 1Z1. **EMAIL** egleston@law.ubc.ca

EICHELBERGER, WILLIAM L.
PERSONAL Born 02/07/1922, Salisbury, NC, m **DISCIPLINE** THEOLOGY **EDUCATION** Lincoln U, AB 1959; Princeton Theol Sem, MDiv 1962, MTheol 1963; NY Theol Sem, MST 1968. **CAREER** Christian Soc Ethics, Louisville Presby Theological Seminary, assoc prof; Rutgers Univ & Newark Coll of Engineering, Protestant chaplain 1967-72; NY Theological Seminary, visiting lecturer Theology & Ethics 1968-70; Newark Coll of Engineering, educ consultant 1968-69, instructor Contemp Literature & Expostry Writing 1968-72; Univ Coll, instructor Political Science dept 1971-72; Laconia Comm Presbytery Church, pastor 1965-67; Southern Univ Baton Rouge, campus pastor 1963-65; various positions as chaplain & instructional seminars; soc Ethics & Theology, lecturer; consultant in comm devel & soc change. **HONORS AND AWARDS** Dist alumni awd Lincoln U; elec to roll of hon Ministries to Blacks in Hghr Edn. **MEMBERSHIPS** Mem KY Commn on Hum Rights 1975; mem Soc for Study of Blk Rel; Assn for Study of Afro-Am Life & Hist; Am Civ Lib Union; NAACP; Urban Leag; PUSH;pres bd dir Louisville Oppor Indstrlztn Ctrs Inc 0a05 1943-46, 48-58. **SELECTED PUBLICATIONS** Auth, Reality in Black & White; contrib various periodicals. **CONTACT ADDRESS** Camden Metro Ministries, 3513 Merriel Ave, Camden, NJ, 08105.

EICHORN, LISA
DISCIPLINE CIVIL PROCEDURE AND LEGAL RESEARCH & WRITING **EDUCATION** Princeton Univ; BA, 87; Duke Law Sch, JD, 90. **CAREER** Litigation assoc, Bingham, Dana & Gould; prof, 92; lectr, dir, Acad Support Prog. **HONORS AND AWARDS** BA with hon(s), 87; JD with hon(s). **RESEARCH** Disability law, employment law. **SELECTED PUBLICATIONS** Style ed, Law & Contemp Problems, an interdisciplinary law jour. **CONTACT ADDRESS** Law Sch, W Va Univ, PO Box 6009, Morgantown, WV, 26506-6009.

EIESLAND, NANCY L.
DISCIPLINE THEOLOGY **EDUCATION** Central Bible Coll, BA, 86; Emory Univ, MDiv, 91, PhD, 95. **CAREER** Instr, Emory Univ, 92-94; ASST PROF, SOCIOL RELIG, CANDLER SCH THEOLOGY, GRAD DIV REL, EMORY UNIV, 95-. **MEMBERSHIPS** Am Acad Rel; Asn Sociol Relig; Am Sociol Asn; Relig Res Asn; Soc Disability Stud; Soc Scient Stud Relig. **RESEARCH** Sociol relig; gender; sociol culture; orgs; qualitative res methods; soc theory; disability stud in relig; Am relig soc hist. **SELECTED PUBLICATIONS** Co-ed, Human disability and the Service of God: Reassessing Religious PRactice, Abingdon Press, 98; co-ed, Contemporary American Religion: An Ethnographic Reader, AltaMira Press, 97; auth, The Disabled God: Toward a Liberatory Theology of Disability, Abingdon Press, 94; auth, Irreconcilable Differences: Conflict, Schism, and Religious Restructuring in a United Methodist Church, in Pentecostal Currents in American Protestantism, Univ Ill Press, forthcoming; co-auth, Ecology: Seeing the Congregation in Context, in Studying Congregations, Abingdon Press, 98; auth, Mapping Faith: Choice and Change in Local Religious Organizational Environments, in Re-Forming the Center: American Protestantism, 1960 to the Present, Eerdmans Publishers, 98; auth, Barriers and Bridges: RElating the Disability Rights Movement and REligious Organizations, in Human Disability and the Service of God: REassessing Religious Practice, Abingdon Press, 98; auth, Things Not Seen: Women with Disabilities, Oppression, and Practical Theology, in Liberating Faith Practices: Feminist Practical Theologies in Context, Peeters, 98; auth, Contending with a Giant: The Impact of a Megachurch on Exurban Religious Institutions, in Contemporary American Religion: An Ethnographic Reader, AltaMira Press, 97; auth, congregational profile in Congregation and Community: Stability and Change in American Religioun, Rutgers Univ Press, 97; auth, A Strange Road Home: Adult Women Converts to Classical Pentecostalism, in Mixed Blessings: Gender and Religious Fundamentalism Cross Culturally, Routledge, 97; co-auth, Mainline Protestantism in Atlanta, in Religions of Atlanta: Religious Diversity in the Centennial Olympic City, Scholars Press, 96; co- auth, Physical Ability as a Diffuse Status Characteristic: Implications for Small Group Interaction, in Advances in Group Processes, JAI Press, 96. **CONTACT ADDRESS** Candler Sch Theol, Emory Univ, 6 Bishops Hall, Atlanta, GA, 30322. **EMAIL** neiesla@emory.edu

EIGO, FRANCIS AUGUSTINE
PERSONAL Born 12/10/1925, Smithville, NJ **DISCIPLINE** THEOLOGY **EDUCATION** LaSalle Coll, BA, 48; Cath Univ Am, STL, 64, MA, 65, STD, 69. **CAREER** From instr to asst prof, 66-73, dir admissions, 66-68, chmn relig studies dept, 72-77, Assoc Prof Theol, Villanova Univ, 73-, Dir Theol Inst, 73-, Chmn Relig Studies Dept, 80-90. **MEMBERSHIPS** NAm Acad Ecumenists; Am Acad Relig; Cath Theol Soc Am; Col Theol Soc; Soc Sci Studies Relig. **RESEARCH** Sacramental theol; French stylistics, poetic imagery; liturgy. **SELECTED PUBLICATIONS** Auth, The Images of Unfulfillment in the Poetry of Andre Chenier, 64 & The Easter Vigil: An Historical, Theological, Pastoral Study, 69, Cath Univ Am; contribr, Liturgy: shaped by and the shaper of the ongoing Christian community, Proc Villanove Univ Theol Inst, 70; ed, The Sacraments: Gods Love and Mercy Actualized, 79, Who Do People Say I Am?, 80, Whither Creativity, Freedom, Suffering?: Humanity, Cosmos, God, 81, Dimensions of Contemporary Spirituality, 82, Villanova Univ Press; Contemporary Spirituality: Responding to the Divine Initiative, 83; Modern Biblical Scholarship: Its Impact on Theology and Proclamation, 84; Called to Love: Towards a Contemporary Christian Ethic, 85; The Professions in Ethical Context: Vocations to Justice and Love, 86; The Human Experience of Conversion: Persons and Structures in Transformation, 87; A Discipleship of Equals: Towards a Christian Feminist Spirituality, 88; The Spirit Moving the Church in the United States, 89; Suffering and Healing in Our Day, 90; Imaging Christ: Politics, Art, Spirituality, 91; The Works of Mercy: New Perspectives on Ministry, 92; Rethinking the Spiritual Works of Mercy, 93; All Generations Shall Call Me Blessed, 94; New Perspectives in Beatitudes, 95; Teach Us to Pray, 96: Prayer the Global Experience, 97; At the Threshold of the Third Millenium, 98, Villanova Univ Press. **CONTACT ADDRESS** Dept of Theol & Relig Studies, Villanova Univ, 800 E Lancaster Ave, Villanova, PA, 19085.

EISELE, THOMAS DAVID
PERSONAL Born 08/26/1948, Madison, WI, m, 1972 **DISCIPLINE** PHILOSOPHY, LAW **EDUCATION** Univ Wis, BA, 70; Harvard Univ, JD, 73. **CAREER** Atty, Isham, Lincoln and Beale, 73-76; dep dir, Lake Mich Fedn, 76-78; Bigelow teaching fel, Univ Chicago Law Sch, 78-79. **SELECTED PUBLICATIONS** Auth, The Poverty of Socratic Questioning--Asking and Answering in the Meno, Univ Cincinnati Law Rev, Vol 63, 94; Freedoms Law--The Moral Reading of the American Constitution, Mich Law Rev, Vol 95, 97; Symposium on Law, Literature, and the Humanities, Introduction--Conducting our Educations in Public, Univ Cincinnati Law Rev, Vol 63, 94. **CONTACT ADDRESS** 5898 N Globe Ave, Westland, MI, 48185.

EISENBAUM, PAMELA
PERSONAL Born 02/24/1961, Washington, DC, s **DISCIPLINE** RELIGION; BIBLICAL STUDIES **EDUCATION** Harv Univ Divinity Sch, MTS, 86; Columbia Univ, PhD, 95 **CAREER** Asst Prof, 95-pres, Sch of Theol **HONORS AND AWARDS** Pres Fel, 87; Mrs. Giles Whiting Fel 94 **MEMBERSHIPS** Am Acad of Relig; Soc of Bibl Lit **RESEARCH** Jewish Background of the New Testament **SELECTED PUBLICATIONS** Auth, "The Jewish Heroes of Christian History: Hebrews 11 in Literary Context," Scholars Press, 97; Coauth, "Heroes and History in Hebrews 11," in Early Christian Interpretation of the Scriptures of Israel, JSOT Press, 97 **CONTACT ADDRESS** Iliff Sch of Theol, 2201 S University, Denver, CO, 80210. **EMAIL** peisenba@du.edu

EISENBERG, MELVIN ARON
PERSONAL Born 12/03/1934, New York, NY, 2 children **DISCIPLINE** LAW **EDUCATION** Columbia Col, AB, 56; Harvard Univ, LLB, 59. **CAREER** Vis prof law, Harvard Law Sch, 69-70; PROF, SCH LAW, UNIV CALIF, BERKELEY, 66-, Asst coun, President's Comn on Assassination of President Kennedy, 64; asst corp coun, City NY, 66; REPORTER, AM LAW INST, 81-. **RESEARCH** Contracts; corporations; the legal process. **SELECTED PUBLICATIONS** Auth, The Divergence of Standards of Conduct and Standards of Review in Corporate Law, Fordham Law Rev, Vol 62, 93; An Overview of the Principles of Corporate Governance, Bus Lawyer, Vol 48, 93; 73rd Party Beneficiaries Columbia Law Review, Vol 1992, Pg 1376, 1992 Columbia Law Rev, Vol 92, 92; The Limits of Cognition and the Limits of Contract, Stanford Law Rev, Vol 47, 95; Expression Rules in Contract Law and Problems of Offer and Acceptance, Calif Law Rev, Vol 82, 94; The World of Contract and the World of Gift, Calif Law Rev, Vol 85, 97. **CONTACT ADDRESS** Sch of Law, Univ of Calif, 220 Boalt Hall, Berkeley, CA, 94720-7201.

EISENBERG, PAUL D.
PERSONAL Born 07/07/1939, Worcester, MA, m, 1978, 1 child **DISCIPLINE** PHILOSOPHY **EDUCATION** Clark Univ, BA, 61; Harvard Univ, MA, 65, PhD, 67. **CAREER** Harvard Univ, tchg fel, 63-66; MIT, Inst, 64; Indiana Univ, Asst Prof, 66-70; Univ of ILL (Champaign-Urbana) Vis Asst Prof, 70; Indiana Univ, Assoc Prof, 70-78, Chmn, Dept of Phil, 74-80; Indiana Univ, Prof, 78-; Univ of MA, Vis Adj Prof, 80; Indiana Univ, Adj Prof, 89, Chmn, Dept of Phil, 89-94, Pres, Bloomington Fac Coun, 93-95, Co-Sec Univ Fac Coun, 93-95. **HONORS AND AWARDS** Scholar, Clark Univ, 57-61; Harvard Fel, 61-64; Indiana Univ Course Devel Grant, 86; IU Multi-disciplinary Seminar Grant, 88; Bloomington Campus Distinguished Svc Award, 97; Pinnell Award, 98., Pres, Phi Beta Kappa, 92-93; Univ of Indiana Panel Chmn, Hobbes Tercentenary Con, 79; VPres, 68-69, 78-79, Pres, 69-70, 79-80, Indiana Phil Assoc; Ed Bd, Nigerian Phil Jour, 80-84; Exec Bd Mem, Amer Assoc Tchrs of Phil, 91-; Harvard fel, 61-64. **MEMBERSHIPS** Phi Beta Kappa; APA; Fac Prof Assoc; Indiana Phil Assoc; Soc for Ancient Greek Phil; Hegel Soc of Amer; North Amer Nietzsch Soc; Amer Assoc Tchrs of Phil **RESEARCH** History of Ethics; Spinoza; Nineteenth-Century Continental Philosophy; especially Nietzsche. **CONTACT ADDRESS** Professor, Indiana Univ, Bloomington, Philosophy Sycamore Hall 026, Bloomington, IN, 47405. **EMAIL** eisenber@indiana.edu

EISENSTAT, STEVEN M.
DISCIPLINE LAW **EDUCATION** Univ Ca, BA, 72, MEd, 74; Northeastern Univ, JD, 80. **CAREER** Prof, 93-. **RESEARCH** AIDS and the law; civil procedure; legal practice skills; torts. **SELECTED PUBLICATIONS** Auth, Capping Health Insurance Benefits for AIDS: An Analysis of Disability-Based Distinctions Under the Americans with Disabilities Act, Va Jour Law Polit, 94; The HIV Infected Health Care Worker: the New AIDS Scapegoat, Rutgers, 92; An Analysis of the Rationality of Mandatory Testing for the HIV Antibody; Balancing the Governmental Public Health Interests with the Individuals' Privacy Interest, Univ Pittsburgh Law Rev, 91. **CONTACT ADDRESS** Law School, Suffolk Univ, Beacon Hill, Boston, MA, 02114. **EMAIL** seisenst@acad.suffolk.edu

EISLER, BETH A.
DISCIPLINE LAW **EDUCATION** Univ Wash, BA, JD. **CAREER** Prof. **SELECTED PUBLICATIONS** Auth, pubs on contracts, commercial law, and wills and estates. **CONTACT ADDRESS** Col Law, Univ of Toledo, Toledo, OH, 43606. **EMAIL** beisler@utnet.utoledo.edu

EKEYA, BETTE J.
PERSONAL Kenya **DISCIPLINE** RELIGION **EDUCATION** PhD, 86. **CAREER** Univ Nairobi Kenya, lectr; Egerton, Univ dept head; OLGS Seminary Scranton, tchr. **RESEARCH** OT; Prophetic movement; sacrifice and holiness. **CONTACT ADDRESS** RR6, PO Box 6496-u, Moscow, PA, 18444.

EKLUND, EMMET ELVIN
PERSONAL Born 05/01/1917, Smolan, KS, m, 1945, 2 children **DISCIPLINE** RELIGION **EDUCATION** Bethany Col, Kans, BA, 41; Augustana Theol Sem, Bd, 45; Univ Chicago, MA, 58; Boston Univ, PhD (Am church hist), 64. **CAREER** Assoc prof relig and philos and vpres, Bethany Col, 45-47; assoc prof and chmn dept, 64-70, PROF RELIG, PAC LUTHERAN UNIV, 70-, Regency prof, Pac Lutheran Univ, 78-79. **MEMBERSHIPS** Am Acad Relig; Am Soc Church Hist. **RESEARCH** Modern church history; American church history in relation to 19th century Swedish immigration. **SELECTED PUBLICATIONS** Auth, The Oxford Group, Group Revivalism, and the Churches in Northern Europe, 1930-1940, with Special Reference to Scandinavia and Germany, Church Hist, Vol 65, 96; From Revival Movement to Denomination--The Swedish Pentecostal Mission on the Islands of the North Atlantic, Church Hist, Vol 63, 94. **CONTACT ADDRESS** Dept of Relig, Pac Lutheran Univ, Tacoma, WA, 98447.

EKMAN LADD, ROSALIND
DISCIPLINE PHILOSOPHY **EDUCATION** Wheaton Col, BA; Brown Univ. MA, PhD. **CAREER** Philos, Wheaton Col. **RESEARCH** Ethics, med ethics, philos & lit, ancient philos; children rights. **SELECTED PUBLICATIONS** Auth, Children's Rights Re-Visioned; co-auth, Ethical Dilemmas in Pediatric Medicine. **CONTACT ADDRESS** Wheaton Col, 26 East Main St, Norton, MA, 02766. **EMAIL** rladd@wheatonma.edu

ELDER, CRAWFORD L.
DISCIPLINE METAPHYSICS **EDUCATION** Yale Univ, BA, 70; PhD, 75. **CAREER** Dept Philos, Univ Conn **SELECTED PUBLICATIONS** Auth, Higher and Lower Essential Natures, Amer Philos Quart, 94; Proper Functions Defended, Analysis, 94; Laws, Natures, and Contingent Necessities, Philos and Phenomenol Res, 94; A Different Kind of Natural Kind, Australasian Jour Philos,. 95; Realism and Determinable Properties, Philos and Phenomenol Res, 96; Contrariety and Carving Up Reality, Amer Philos Quart, 96; Content and the Subtle Extensionality of ' Explains , Philos Quart, 96; On the Reality of Medium-Sized Objects, Philos Stud, 96; Essential Properties and Coinciding Objects, Philos and Phenomenol Res, 98. **CONTACT ADDRESS** Dept of Philos, Univ Conn, 1266 Storrs Rd, Storrs, CT, 06269.

ELDRIDGE, MICHAEL
DISCIPLINE PHILOSOPHY **EDUCATION** Yale Univ, BD; Columbia Univ, MA; Univ FL, PhD. **CAREER** Instr, ch, dept Philos and Relig, Queens Col; instr, Spring Hill Col, Univ Fla; prof, Univ NC, Charlotte. **RESEARCH** Critical thinking and soc reform. **SELECTED PUBLICATIONS** Auth, Transforming Experience: John Dewey's Cultural Instrumentalism, Vanderbilt UP, 98. **CONTACT ADDRESS** Univ N. Carolina, Charlotte, Charlotte, NC, 28223-0001. **EMAIL** mleldrid@email.uncc.edu

ELFSTROU, GERARD
PERSONAL Born 02/26/1945, Rockford, IL **DISCIPLINE** PHILOSOPHY **EDUCATION** Cornell Col, BA, 67; Emory Univ, MA, 69, PhD, 75. **CAREER** Prof, Auburn Univ, 97-. **MEMBERSHIPS** Am Philos Asn **RESEARCH** Ethics; Social and Political Philosophy **CONTACT ADDRESS** Auburn Univ, 6080 Haley Ctr, Auburn, AL, 36849-5210.

ELHARD, LELAND E.
DISCIPLINE PASTORAL THEOLOGY **EDUCATION** Capital Univ, BA, 53; Evangel Lutheran Theol Sem, BD, 57; Univ

Chicago, MA, 63, PhD, 65. **CAREER** Instr, ELTS, 65-68; assoc prof, ELTS, 68-78; assoc prof, 78-81; prof, Trinity Lutheran Sem, 81-. **SELECTED PUBLICATIONS** Auth, The Faithful Person Leads: Self-differentiation and Pastoral Leadership, Trinity Sem Rev, 97; A Dane With The Danes, Case Studies, Assn for CASE Tchg, 96; Law and Order, Case Studies, Assn for CASE Tchg, 95; Narcissism and the Relation Between Pastor and Congregation, Trinity Sem Rev, 92; Special Review on Current Pastoral Care Literature, Trinity Sem Rev, 91. **CONTACT ADDRESS** Hist, Theol, Soc Dept, Trinity Lutheran Sem, 2199 E Main St, Columbus, OH, 43209-2334. **EMAIL** lelhard@trinity.capital.edu

ELIADE, MIRCEA
PERSONAL Born 03/09/1907, Bucharest, Romania, m, 1950 **DISCIPLINE** HISTORY OF RELIGIONS **EDUCATION** Univ Bucharest, MA, 28, PhD, 33. **CAREER** Asst prof metaphys, Univ Bucharest, 33-39; vis prof hist relig, Ecole des Hautes Etudes, Sorbonne, 46-49; from vis prof to prof, 56-61, DISTINGUISHED SERV PROF HIST RELIG, UNIV CHICAGO, 62-. **HONORS AND AWARDS** Dr, Yale Univ, 66. **MEMBERSHIPS** Am Soc Study Relig (pres, 63-67); Societe Asiatique; AAAS. **RESEARCH** History of religions. **SELECTED PUBLICATIONS** Auth, Initiation and Literature, Sinn Form, Vol 48, 96; Mantras, Parabola Myth Tradition Search Meaning, Vol 20, 95. **CONTACT ADDRESS** Divinity Sch, Univ Chicago, Chicago, IL, 60637.

ELIAS, JAMAL J.
DISCIPLINE RELIGIOUS STUDIES **EDUCATION** Yale Univ, PhD, 91. **CAREER** Asst prof, Amherst Coll, 89-96; assoc prof, Amherst Coll, 96-. **SELECTED PUBLICATIONS** The Throne-Carrier of God, 95; Death before Dying, 98; Islam, 99. **CONTACT ADDRESS** Dept of Religion, Amherst Col, Amherst, MA, 01002. **EMAIL** jjelias@amherst.edu

ELKAYAM, MOSHE
PERSONAL Born 11/09/1941, Mogador, m, 1973, 1 child **DISCIPLINE** BIBLICAL STUDIES **EDUCATION** Univ Paris VIII, PhD, 92. **CAREER** Paris, 85-92; Dir of Jewish Studies, Coll Hillel, Ville Saint-Laurent, 93-96; Scholar in Residence, Temple Emam-Eb, Montreal, 92-. **HONORS AND AWARDS** Highest Honor for PhD Thesis; Eric and Esther Exton Educ Award. **MEMBERSHIPS** AAR; SBL; AJS; JESNA; NATE; EDA; TU. **RESEARCH** Biblical Studies; Old Testament; Dead Sea Scrolls and Ancient Near Eastern regions and cultures. **SELECTED PUBLICATIONS** Auth, poetry and prose in Hebrew; pubs in folklore and tradition; pubs on Jewish Studies. **CONTACT ADDRESS** 6525 Cote St Luc, Box 506, Montreal, PQ, H4V 1G5.

ELKINS, JAMES R.
DISCIPLINE LAW **EDUCATION** Univ Ky, BA, JD; Yale Univ, LLM. **CAREER** Trial atty, Econ Stabilization Sect; asst US atty, US Atty's Office; asst prof, DePaul Univ; vis asst prof, Univ Ky; vis fel, Health Law Inst; vis prof, Wash and Lee Univ; vis adj prof, Univ Mass; prof, 77-; Benedum distinguished scholar, 95. **HONORS AND AWARDS** Order of the Coif., Ed bd, Jour of Legal Edu. **SELECTED PUBLICATIONS** Ed, Legal Stud Forum; Legal Ethics and the Legal Profession; Law and Psychiat; Psychol for Lawyers, Practical Moral Philos for Lawyers; Environmental Justice; Author, Legal Interviewing and Counseling in a Nutshell; Lawyers and Lit. **CONTACT ADDRESS** Law Sch, W Va Univ, PO Box 6009, Morgantown, WV, 26506-6009.

ELLENS, JAY HAROLD
PERSONAL Born 07/16/1932, McBain, MI, m, 1954, 7 children **DISCIPLINE** PSYCHOLOGY; RELIGION **EDUCATION** Calvin Coll, BA, 53; Calvin Theol Sem, MDiv, 56; Princeton Theol Sem, ThM. 65; Wayne State Univ, PhD, 70; Univ Mich, PhD. **CAREER** Univ tchg, 65-85; clin psychol, 70-; Presby Theol, Pastor, Pastoral Counr, 56- ; US Army Chaplain (COL), 55-92; Princeton tchg fel; Finch lectr, Fuller; Wheaton Distinguished lectr; Stob lectr ethics and religion; distinguished lectr, Austin Theol Sem. **HONORS AND AWARDS** Meritorious Serv Medals (4), Legion Merit, numerous for serv, unit, merit citations, medals, ribbons (16), US Army. **MEMBERSHIPS** CAPS; SBL; AAR; AIA; ROA; MOWW; AL. **RESEARCH** Psychology of human development; Christians origins and their roots in ancient Judaism. **SELECTED PUBLICATIONS** auth Models of Religious Broadcasting, 74; God's Grace and Human Health, 82; Turning Points in Pastoral Care, 89; Christian Perspectives on Human Development, 90. **CONTACT ADDRESS** 26707 Farmington Road, Farmington Hills, MI, 48334-4329. **EMAIL** jharoldellens@Juno.com

ELLICKSON, ROBERT CHESTER
PERSONAL Born 08/04/1941, Washington, DC, m, 1971, 2 children **DISCIPLINE** LAW **EDUCATION** Oberlin Col, AB, 63; Yale Univ, LLB, 66. **CAREER** Asst prof law, Univ Southern Calif, 70-72, assoc prof, 72-75, prof, 75-81; Prof Law, Stanford Univ, 81-. **RESEARCH** Land-use controls; law and economics; housing. **SELECTED PUBLICATIONS** Auth, Liberty, Property, and Environmental Ethics, Ecol Law Quart, Vol 21, 94; Takings Legislation, Harvard J Law Policy, Vol 20, 96; Liberty, Property, and Environmental Ethics--Discussion, Ecol Law Quart, Vol 21, 94; Property in Land, Yale Law J, Vol 102, 93; Controlling Chronic Misconduct in City Spaces--Of Panhandlers, Skid Rows, and Public Space Zoning, Yale Law J Vol 105, 96. **CONTACT ADDRESS** Law Sch, Stanford Univ, Stanford, CA, 94305.

ELLIN, JOSEPH S.
PERSONAL Born 10/31/1936, Brooklyn, NY, m, 1962, 2 children **DISCIPLINE** PHILOSOPHY **EDUCATION** Columbia Univ, BA, 57; Yale Univ, MA, 59, PhD, 62. **CAREER** From instr to asst prof, 62-67, chmn dept, 69-75 & 77-78, assoc prof, 67-79, Prof Philos, Western Mich Univ, 79- **MEMBERSHIPS** Am Philos Asn; Soc Values Higher Educ; Am Soc Polit & Legal Philos; Soc Bus & Prof Ethics. **RESEARCH** Political philosophy; philosophy of law; medical and professional ethics. **SELECTED PUBLICATIONS** Auth, Fidelity to law, Soundings, winter 68; Sterilization, privacy and the value of reproduction, Contemp Issues Bioethics, 79; Consent in political philosophy, Archiv fur Rechts-und Sozialphilosophic, No 12, 79; Collective responsibility in the professions, Dayton Rev, winter 81; Lying and deception: The solution to a dilemma in medical ethics, Westminster Rev, 5/81; Special professional morality and the duty of veracity, Bus & Prof Ethics J, Vol 1; Again: Hume on Miracles, Hume Studies, 4/93; Morality and the Meaning of Life, Harcourd Brace, 95; Assisted Suicide in Michigan, Bioethics, 1/96; Liberalism, Radicalism, Middlism, In: Radical Critiques of Law, Kansas, 97. **CONTACT ADDRESS** Dept of Philosophy, Western Michigan Univ, 1201 Oliver St, Kalamazoo, MI, 49008-3805. **EMAIL** ellin@wmich.edu

ELLINGSEN, MARK
PERSONAL Born 06/18/1949, Brooklyn, NY, m, 1973, 3 children **DISCIPLINE** RELIGION/PHILOSOPHY **EDUCATION** Gettysburg Col, BA, 71; Yale Univ, M.Div, 74; Yale Univ, MA, 75; Yale Univ, PhD, 80 **CAREER** Assoc prof, Interdenominational Theology Center, 93-; instr, Randolf Community Col, 92-93; assoc prof, Institute Ecumenical Res, 82-88; asst prof, Luther-Northwestern Lutheran Seminaries, 79-82; pastor, Evangelical Lutheran Church in America, ordained, 76 **HONORS AND AWARDS** Phi Beta Kappa; Yale Univ Day Fel; AAL Fel; Undergraduate Departmental Honors in Relig and Philos **MEMBERSHIPS** Amer Acad Relig; Amer Soc Church Hist **RESEARCH** History of Christian Thought and Ethics; Reformation Studies; Ecumenics; Hermeneutics; Religion and Science **SELECTED PUBLICATIONS** auth, Reclaiming Our Roots: An Inclusive Introduction to Church History, Trinity; auth, A Word That Sets Free, C.S.S.; auth, Making Black Ecumenism Happen: A History of the Interdenominational Theological Center As a Paradigm for Christian Unity, ITC; auth, A Common Sense Theology: The Bible, Faith, and American Society, Mercer Univ **CONTACT ADDRESS** Interdenominational Theol Ctr, 700 Martin Luther King Jr. Dr., Atlanta, GA, 30314.

ELLINGTON, JOHN
PERSONAL Born 12/09/1963, Moultrie, GA, m, 1963, 4 children **DISCIPLINE** BIBLICAL LITERATURE **EDUCATION** Emory Univ, BA, 59; Columbia Theological Seminary, ThM, 64; Univ of Wisconsin, PhD, 77. **CAREER** Pastor, 62-63, First Presbyterian Church, Manchester, GA; Missionary, 64-83, Presbyterian Church, US,; Bible Trans Consult, United Bible Societies, Kinshesa, Zaire, Dakar, Dengal, Bouake, Cote d'Ivoire, 75-. **MEMBERSHIPS** SBL **RESEARCH** Common Language Translatuion; Bantu Languages of Rep Dem du Congo. **SELECTED PUBLICATIONS** Auth, A Handbook of Kinshasa Lingala, Kinshasa, Zaire, 74; English-Lingala Dictionary, Kinshasa, Zaire, 82; Basic Lingala, Montreat, NC, 83; co-ed, A Translator's Handbook on Leviticus, NY, United Bible Societies, 90; A Handbook on Daniel, NY, United Bible Societies, 93; A Handbook on Paul's Second Letter to the Corinthians, NY, United Bible Societies, 93. **CONTACT ADDRESS** Box 1018, Montreat, NC, 28757. **EMAIL** johne@buncombe.main.nc.us

ELLIOT, ROBIN
DISCIPLINE LAW **EDUCATION** Univ British Columbia, BS, 69; LLB, 73; London Univ, LLM, 75. **CAREER** Asst prof, 76-83; assoc prof, 83-91; prof, 91-; assoc dean, 91-93. **HONORS AND AWARDS** Off, Supreme Court Can. **RESEARCH** Constitutional law and theory; human rights legislation. **SELECTED PUBLICATIONS** Auth, pubs about charter and Canadian federalism. **CONTACT ADDRESS** Fac of Law, Univ British Columbia, 1822 East Mall, Vancouver, BC, V6T 1Z1. **EMAIL** elliot@law.ubc.ca

ELLIOTT, CARL
DISCIPLINE PHILOSOPHY **EDUCATION** Glasgow Univ, PhD. **RESEARCH** Moral philosophy; medicine and culture. **SELECTED PUBLICATIONS** Auth, The Rules of Insanity: Moral Responsibility and Mental Illness, State Univ NY, 96; A Philosophical Disease: Bioethics, Culture and Identity, Routledge, 98; Why Can't We Go on as Three?, Hastings Center Report, 98. **CONTACT ADDRESS** Philosophy Dept, Univ of Minnesota, Twin Cities, 355 Ford Hall, 224 Church St SE, Minneapolis, MN, 55455. **EMAIL** ellio023@tc.umn.edu

ELLIOTT, CAROLYN S.
PERSONAL Born 02/20/1947, Glen Ridge, NJ, m, 1970, 2 children **DISCIPLINE** RELIGION AND CULTURE; HISTORY **EDUCATION** Syracuse Univ, BA, 70, MA, 73; SUNY, MLIS, 94. **CAREER** From dir to adj fac to full-time fac, 72-, Keystone Col. **HONORS AND AWARDS** Theta Chi Beta; Beta Phi Mu. **MEMBERSHIPS** Am Libr Asn; Asn Col & Res Librs; Pa Libr Asn. **RESEARCH** Religion and culture of Asia; library computing options. **SELECTED PUBLICATIONS** Auth, art, NREN Update, 1993: Washington Policy, 94. **CONTACT ADDRESS** Miller Library, Keystone Col, One College Green, La Plume, PA, 18440-0200. **EMAIL** celliott@kstone.edu

ELLIOTT, DENI
PERSONAL Born 11/16/1953, Nanticoke, PA, m, 1988, 1 child **DISCIPLINE** PHILOSOPHY **EDUCATION** Univ Maryland, BA, 74; Wayne State Univ, MSTC, 78, MA, 82; Harvard Univ, PhD, 84. **CAREER** Harvard Univ, tchg fel, 82-84; Wayne State Univ, p-t inst, 80-84; Utah State Univ, asst prof, assoc prof, 85-88; Dartmouth Col, adj asst prof, res asst prof, adj assoc prof, res assoc prof, 88-92; Univ Montana Missoula, adj prof, prof, Mansfield Prof, 92-. **HONORS AND AWARDS** Marion and Jasper Whiting Foundation fel, Rockefeller Fel, Outstanding Young Woman in Am Award, Bronze Plaque Award, Silver Apple Award, Who's Who listings: in the East, Authors and Writers, World of Women, in the World, in the West, Am Women and Among Am Tchrs., Dartmouth Col, Ethics Inst, dir, 88-92; Univ Montana Practical Ethics Ctr, dir, 96-. **MEMBERSHIPS** APPE, APA, AEJMC, SPJ, IMH, Citizen Review Board. **SELECTED PUBLICATIONS** Coauth, Contemporary Ethical Issues: Journalism, ABC-CLIO, 98; coauth, The Ethics of Scientific Research: A Guidebook for Course Development, Hanover NH: Univ Press of New Eng, 97; coauth, The Ethics of Asking: Dilemmas in Higher Education Fund Raising, ed, John Hopkins Univ Press, 95; coauth, The Burden of Knowledge: Moral Dilemmas in Prenatal Testing, writer and co-producer, Distrib :Direct Cinema Ltd, 94; coauth, Responsible Journalism, ed, SAGE 86. **CONTACT ADDRESS** Practical Ethics Ctr, Univ of Montana, Missoula, Missoula, MT, 59812. **EMAIL** deni@selway.umt.edu

ELLIOTT, JOHN HALL
PERSONAL Born 10/23/1935, New York, NY, m, 1962, 2 children **DISCIPLINE** THEOLOGY **EDUCATION** Concordia Sem, MO, BA, 57, BD, 60; Univ Munster, Dr Theol, 63. **CAREER** Asst prof theol, Concordia Sem, MO, 63-67; from asst prof to assoc prof, 68-75, prof theol & relig studies, Univ San Francisco, 75-; vis prof, Webster Col, 65-67 & Pontif Bibl Inst, Rome, 78; guest prof, Honore F Zabala Chair of Theol, Univ San Francisco, 67-68; adj prof exegetical theol, Grad Theol Union, Berkeley, Calif, 77-; resident res scholar, Disciples' Inst zur Erforschung des Urchristentums, Tubingen, WGer, 77; vis prof, Pontif Bibl Inst, Cath Bibl Asn Am, Rome, 78 & Univ Notre Dame, 81; Am Coun Learned Soc grant, 81. **HONORS AND AWARDS** Am Coun Learned Soc Travel grant, 81; USF Distinguished Res Award, 82; NEH Summer stipend, 92; USF Distinguished Teaching Award, 92. **MEMBERSHIPS** Soc of New Testament Scholars; Franz Delitzsch Ges; Soc Bibl Lit; Cath Bibl Asn Am; AAUP; Context Group. **RESEARCH** Exegesis; historical sociology; history. **SELECTED PUBLICATIONS** Auth, The Elect and the Holy, Brill, 66; The Christ Life: Jesus Christ the Sacrament and Sacramental Living, Walther League, 68; Man and the Son of Man in the Gospel According to Mark, In: Humane Gesellschaft (H D Wendland Festschrift), Zwingli, 70; Pentecost 3, Fortress, 76; Peter: Estrangement and Community, Franciscan Herald Press, 79; A Home for the Homeless: A Sociological Exegesis of 1 Peter, Its Situation and Strategy, Fortress, 81, 2nd ed, 90; 1 and 2 Peter and Jude, Augsburg Commentary on the New Testament, Augsburg, 82; ed, Social-Scientific criticism of the New Testament and Its Social World, Semeia 35, Scholars Press, 86; auth; Temple vs Household in Luke-Acts: A Contrast in Social Institutions, in The Social World of Luke-Acts, Hendrickson, 91; Matthew 20: 1-15: A Parable of Invidious Comparison and Evil Eye Accusation, Bibl Theol Bull, 92; Peter, First Epistle of, Second Epistle of, Anchor Bible Dictionary, vol 5, Doubleday, 92; What is Social-Scientific Criticism?, Fortress, 93; The Epistle of James in Rhetorical and Social Scientific Perspective: Holiness-Wholeness and Patterns of Replication, Bibl Theol Bull, 93; Sorcery and Magic in the Revelation of John, Listening, J of Relig and Culture, 93; The Evil Eye and the Sermon on the Mount: Contours of a Pervasive Belief in Social Scientific Perspective, Biblical Interpretation, 94; Disgraced Yet Graced: The Gospel According to 1 Peter in the Key on Honor and Shame, Bibl Theol Bull, 95; The Jewish Messianic Movement: From Faction to Sect, in Modeling Early Christianity: Social-Scientific Studies of the New Testament in its Context, Routledge, 95. **CONTACT ADDRESS** Dept of Theol & Relig Studies, Univ San Francisco, 2130 Fulton St, San Francisco, CA, 94117-1080. **EMAIL** elliottj@usfca.edu

ELLIOTT, SUSAN ELLI
PERSONAL Born 10/27/1952, Evanston, IL **DISCIPLINE** NEW TESTAMENT, EARLY CHRISTIANITY **EDUCATION** Jesuit Sch of Theol-Chicago, MDiv, summa cum laude, 78; Loyola Univ, PhD, 97. **CAREER** Pastor, Douglas Park Church, Chicago, 87-90; dir, Justice and Peace Network, 90-92;

Lectr, tchg fel, 93-97, vis asst prof, Loyola Univ, 97; Pastor, Zion United Church of Christ, Sterling, Colo, 97- . **HONORS AND AWARDS** Arthur J. Schmitt diss fel, Loyola Univ, 95-96; Loyola Univ tchg fel, 94-95; student paper competition prize, Midwest soc Bibl lit, 93. **MEMBERSHIPS** Soc Bibl Lit; N Amer Patristics Soc; Chicago Soc Bibl Res; Westar Inst fel; Catholic Bibl Asn. **RESEARCH** Greco-Roman mystery cults; Slavery and family in Greco-Roman Antiquity; Pauline Letts. **SELECTED PUBLICATIONS** Auth, John 15:15-Not Slaves but Friends: Slavery and Friendship Imagery and the Clarification of the Disciples' Relationship to Jesus in the Johannine Farewell Discourse, in Proceedings of the Eastern Great Lakes and Midwest Society of Bibl Lit, Toronto, vol 13, 93, 31-46; Who is Addressed in Revelation 18:6-7, Bibl Res, vol 40, 95, 98-113; Paul's Gentile Audiences: Mystery Cults, Anatolian Popular Religiosity, and Paul's Claim of Divine Authority in Galatians, in Listening: A Jour of Rel and Cult, 31, 96, 117-136; rev, Cybele, Attis, and Related Cults: Essays in Memory of M.J. Vermaseren, Rels in the Greco-Roman World, Leiden: E.J. Brill, 96. **CONTACT ADDRESS** Zion United Church of Christ, 414 Elm St, Sterling, CO, 80751. **EMAIL** ellielliott@msn.com

ELLIS, ANTHONY JOHN
PERSONAL Born 06/15/1945, England, m, 1978, 3 children **DISCIPLINE** THEOLOGY; PHILOSOPHY **EDUCATION** King's Col, London, BA, 67; MA, 68. **CAREER** Dir, Inst for Ethics & Pub Policy, Virginia Commonwealth Univ, 94-; prof Philos, Virginia Commonwealth Univ, 90-; Univ Fel, Univ of Wollongong, 89; vis prof Philos, Virginia Commonwealth Univ, 87-88; Sr lctr, Univ St Andrews, 87-90; ch Dept Moral Philos, Univ St Andrews, 85-90; lctr Dept Moral Philos, Univ St Andrews, 71-87. **HONORS AND AWARDS** Univ London Fac of Arts Tutorial Studentship, 70; Shelford Prize, 67; McCaul Prize, 67; Univ Fel in Univ of Wollongong, 89; Vis Fel in Australian Ntl Univ in Canberra, 87; Univ Fel in Univ Wollongong, 87; Fulbright Travel Award, 87. **MEMBERSHIPS** Amer Philos Assoc; Royal Inst of Philos **RESEARCH** Philosophy of Law **SELECTED PUBLICATIONS** Criminal Attempts," in Jour of Applied Philos, forthcoming; Punishment and the Principle of Fair Play, Utilitas, 97; Morality and Scripture, Tchg Philos, 96; Censorship and the Media, in Media Ethics, Routledge, 98. **CONTACT ADDRESS** Dept of Philosophy, Virginia Commonwealth Univ, PO Box 842025, Richmond, VA, 23284-2025. **EMAIL** aellis@saturn.vcu.edu

ELLIS, EDWARD EARLE
PERSONAL Born 03/18/1926, Ft Lauderdale, FL **DISCIPLINE** THEOLOGY, HISTORY **EDUCATION** Univ Va, BS, 50; Wheaton Col, Ill, MA and BD, 53; Univ Edinburgh, PhD (Bibl studies), 55. **CAREER** Asst prof Bible and philos, Aurora Col, 56-58; asst prof New Testament interpretation, Southern Baptist Theol Sem, 58-60; from vis prof to prof Bibl Studies, 62-77, RES PROF NEW TESTAMENT, NEW BRUNSWICK THEOL SEM, 77-, Am Asn Theol Schs fel, 68-69; von Humbolt scholar, 68-69 and 75-76; lectr, Princeton Theol Sem, 74, 76, 78; Guggenheim fel, 75-76; lectr, Drew Univ, 67-68 and Univ Tubingen, 75-76; vis distinguished prof Evangel Christianity, Juniata Col, 78-79; Bye fel, Robinson Col, Cambridge Univ, 82-83; exec Comt, Soc Studies New Testament, 67-69. **HONORS AND AWARDS** DD, Wheaton Col, Ill, 82. **MEMBERSHIPS** Soc Bibl Lit (treas, 67-68); Soc Studies New Testament; Inst Biblical Res. **RESEARCH** Early Christian history and thought; Biblical studies. **SELECTED PUBLICATIONS** Auth, The Gospel of Jesus--The Pastoral Relevance of the Synoptic Problem, Interpretation J Bible Theol, Vol 50, 96; Paul and the Jewish Law--Halakha in the Letters of the Apostle to the Gentiles, Interpretation J Bible Theol, Vol 47, 93. **CONTACT ADDRESS** Dept of Bibl, Studies New Brunwick Theol Sem, New Brunswick, NJ, 08901.

ELLIS, ROBERT
PERSONAL Born 07/08/1955, Fort Worth, TX, m, 1989, 2 children **DISCIPLINE** OLD TESTAMENT AND BIBLICAL HEBREW **EDUCATION** Hardin Simmons Univ, BS, 77; Southwest Baptist Theol Sem, MD, 81; PhD, 88. **CAREER** Instr, Hardin-Simmons Univ, 84-86; asst prof, Southwest Baptist Theol Sem, 86-96; prof, Hardin-Simmons Univ, 98-. **HONORS AND AWARDS** Distinguished Alumnus of Logsdon School of Theol. **MEMBERSHIPS** Nat Asn of baptist Porf of Rel; Soc of Bibl Lit. **RESEARCH** Old Testament Prophets and Wisdom Literature; Biblical Hebrew. **SELECTED PUBLICATIONS** Auth, Divine Gift and Human Response: An Old Testament Model for Stewardship, Southwestern J of Theol, 95; Are There Any Cows of Bashan on Seminary Hill?, Southwestern J of Theol, 95; article in New Int Dictionary of Old Testament Theol and Exegesis, 97; The Theological Boundaries of Inclusion and Exclusion in the Book of Joshua, Rev and Expositor, 98. **CONTACT ADDRESS** Box 16235, Abilene, TX, 79698-6235. **EMAIL** rellis@hsutx.edu

ELLIS SMITH, MARSHA A.
DISCIPLINE RELIGION **EDUCATION** Ouachita Baptist Univ, BME; Southwestern Baptist Theol Sem, MDiv, PhD. **CAREER** Instr, Baptist Theol Sem Zambia; adj prof, assoc VP, S Baptist Theol Sem. **SELECTED PUBLICATIONS** Gen ed, The Holman Book of Biblical Charts; Maps; Reconstructions; contrib, Holman Bible Dictionary; Holman Bible Handbook; The Woman's Study Bible; Biblical Illustrator. **CONTACT ADDRESS** Southern Baptist Theol Sem, 2825 Lexington Rd, Louisville, KY, 40280. **EMAIL** mellissmith@sbts.edu

ELLSWORTH, RANDALL
DISCIPLINE LAW **EDUCATION** McGill Univ, BA, 84; Osgoode Hall Law Sch, LLB, 87. **CAREER** Law clerk, Ontario Supreme Court; assoc prof. **MEMBERSHIPS** St Health Comun Nursing Found; Metropolitan Toronto Soc Planning Coun. **SELECTED PUBLICATIONS** Auth, pubs on maintenance programs and government consultations and law reform; ed, Poverty Law in Ontario: The Year in Review, Jour Law Soc Policy. **CONTACT ADDRESS** Fac of Law, Univ Toronto, 78 Queen's Park, Toronto, ON.

ELLWOOD, GRACIA F.
PERSONAL Born 07/17/1938, Lynden, WA, m, 1965, 2 children **DISCIPLINE** PHILOSOPHY OF RELIGION **EDUCATION** Claremont Grad Univ, PhD, 98. **CAREER** Private scholar. **HONORS AND AWARDS** Univ Chicago Scholar, 61-64. **MEMBERSHIPS** Amer Soc for Psychical Res; Parapsychol Asn; Intl Asn for Near-Death Studies. **RESEARCH** Near-death studies. **SELECTED PUBLICATIONS** Auth, Distressing Near-Death Experiences as Photographic Negatives, Jour of Near-Death Studies, 96; co-auth, In a Faraway Galaxy: A Literary Analysis of Star Wars, Extequer Press, 84; auth, Psychic Visits to the Past, New Amer Libr, 71; auth, Good News from Tolbein's Middle Earth, Eerdmans, 70; auth, The Cheltenham Haunting: An Interpretations, Jour Amer Soc for Psychical Res, 69; auth, The Soal-Cooper-Davis Communal J, Intl Jour of Parapsychol, 68. **CONTACT ADDRESS** 997 Athens St., Altadena, CA, 91001. **EMAIL** graciafay@hotmail.com

ELLWOOD, ROBERT S.
DISCIPLINE RELIGION **EDUCATION** Univ Chicago, PhD, 67. **CAREER** Prof, Univ Southern Calif. **RESEARCH** Religions of East Asia; Zen Buddhism; Shintoism. **SELECTED PUBLICATIONS** Auth, The Sixties Spiritual Awakening; Islands of the Dawn: The Story of Alternative Spirituality in New Zealand; Japanese Religion: A Cultural Perspective. **CONTACT ADDRESS** East Asian Studies Center, Univ Southern Calif, University Park Campus, Los Angeles, CA, 90089.

ELROD, LINDA DIANE HENRY
PERSONAL Born 03/06/1947, Topeka, KS, m, 1971, 2 children **DISCIPLINE** LAW **EDUCATION** Washburn Univ, BA, 69, JD, 71. **CAREER** Res asst, Kans Judicial Coun, 72-74; asst prof, 74-78, assoc prof, 78-82, Prof Law, Washburn Univ, 82-, Consult, Kans Judicial Coun, 75, 76 & 79; mem, Kans Govt Ethics Comn, 78-; ed, The Circuit Rider, Washburn Law Sch Assn, 78-; vchmn, Kans Pub Disclosure Comn, 81-. **HONORS AND AWARDS** Distinguished Svc Award, Wasburn Law Sch Assoc, 86; Outstanding Svc Award, Kansas Bar Assoc, 87; Phi Beta Delta, Hon Soc for Int Scholars; one of Best Lawyers in America in Family Law, 97-98; YWCA Woman of Distinction Award, 97; NONOSO, Woman's Hon. **RESEARCH** Family law; urban planning-growth management. **SELECTED PUBLICATIONS** Art, Practicing Law in a Unified Kansas Court System, Washburn Law J, 77; art, Land Transactions: A Survey of Basic Property Principles Relating to the Sale of Real Estate, Washburn Univ Sch of Law, 79; art, Housing Alternatives for the Elderly, J of Family Law, 80; art, Vanishing Farmlands And Decaying Downtowns--The Case For Growth Management, Kans Bar Assn J, 82. **CONTACT ADDRESS** Sch of Law, Washburn Univ, 1700 SW College Ave, Topeka, KS, 66621-0001.

ELSAMAHI, MOHAMED
PERSONAL Born 04/11/1949, Egypt, m, 1993 **DISCIPLINE** PHILOSOPHY OF SCIENCE **EDUCATION** Coll Med Cairo Univ, MD, 71; Univ Calgary Philos PhD, 96. **CAREER** Asst prof, Cairo Univ, 77-90; instr, Univ Calgary, 95-96; instr, SW Mo State Univ, 96-98. **MEMBERSHIPS** Egyptian Med Asn; Can Philos Asn; Am Philos Asn; Am Philos of Sci Asn. **RESEARCH** Philosophy of Science; Epistemology. **SELECTED PUBLICATIONS** Auth, Could Theoretical Entities Save Realism?, 94. **CONTACT ADDRESS** 11314 McFarland Ln, Carbondale, IL, 62901.

ELSBERND, MARY
PERSONAL Born 07/09/1948, Decoral, IN **DISCIPLINE** MORAL THEOLOGY, WOMEN'S STUDIES **EDUCATION** Briar Cliff Col, BA, 68; St. John's Univ, MA, 77; Katholieke Univ Leuven, Belgium, Sacrae Theologiae Baccalauraum, 82, Sacrae Theologiae Licentiatam, 83, BA, 81, MA, 82, PhD, 85, Sacrae Theologiae Doctor, 86. **CAREER** Asst prof, 92-96, assoc prof Pastoral Stud in Social Ehtics, 96- , Grad Dir Master Div prof, 95, Loyola Univ; asst prof Theology, 85-89, assoc prof, 89-92, Briar Cliff Col; Instr Theol, Briar Cliff Col, 79-80; Rel tchr in Wahlert and Aquin Catholic High Schools, 68-79; French Tchr Aquin Cath High Sch, 68-73; vis guest prof, Katholieke Univ Leuven, fac Moral Theol and Women's Stud, 97; Vrij asst for the Moral Theol Dept, Katholieke Univ, 84; res asst with Ctr of Concern, Wash DC, summer 90; fac mem in the Sioux City Diocesan Church Ministries Prog, 88-92; dir, Briar Cliff Peace Stud Prog, 87-92; **HONORS AND AWARDS** Study leave, Loyola Univ, Chicago, Fall 97; Loyola Univ Scholar Recipient to Faith and the Intellectual Collegium, Summer 95; Res Support Grant, Summer 94, Loyola Univ, for Young Adult Volunteer Proj; Briar Cliff Col nominee to NEH, summer grant, 92; Briar Cliff nominee for Kellogg Natl Fel Prog for the development fo "effective and broad leadership skills and abilities: 89; Briar Cliff Col finalist for Burlington Northern Outstand Tchr, 87; Vrij Asst for the Moral Theol Dept, Katholieke Univ Leuven, 84; Acad Scholar Katholieke Univ Leuven, 81-85. **MEMBERSHIPS** Cath Theol Soc Am; AAR; Soc Christian Ethics; Cath Comm on Intell Cultural Affairs. **RESEARCH** Justice and John; Women's Leadership. **CONTACT ADDRESS** Institute of Pastoral Studies, Loyola Univ, 6525 N Sheridan Rd, Chicago, IL, 60626. **EMAIL** melsber@luc.edu

ELWELL, WALTER ALEXANDER
PERSONAL Born 04/29/1937, Miami, Fla, m, 1959, 2 children **DISCIPLINE** NEW TESTAMENT, THEOLOGY **EDUCATION** Wheaton Col, BA, 59; Wheaton Grad Sch, MA, 61; Univ Edinburgh, PhD(New Testament), 70. **CAREER** Instr Greek, Wheaton Col, 59-61; instr, North Park Col, 62-63; assoc prof Bible and Greek, Belhaven Col, 71-75; chmn dept theol studies, 76-81, Prof New Testament, Wheaton Grad Sch, 75-, Bk ed, Christianity Today.; Dean, Wheaton Col Grad Sch, 81-86. **HONORS AND AWARDS** Outstanding Prof of the Year, Belhaven Col, 64. **MEMBERSHIPS** Soc Bibl Lit; Inst Bibl Res; Marketplace Ministries; Evangelical Theol Soc. **SELECTED PUBLICATIONS** Contribr, Current Issues in Biblical & Patristic Interpretation, Eerdmans, 75; Zondervan Pictorial Encycl of the Bible, Zondervan, 76; auth, The Living Bible Study Reference Ed, 76; ed, Evangelical Dictionary of Theology, Baker, 84; ed, Baker Encyclopedia of the Bible, Baker, 88; ed, Evangelical Commentary on the Bible, Baker, 89; ed, Topical Analysis of the Bible, Baker, 91; ed, Handbook of Evangelical Theologians, Baker, 93; ed, Evangelical Dictionary of Biblical Theology, Baker, 96; coauth, Encountering the New Testament, Baker, 97. **CONTACT ADDRESS** 501 College Ave, Wheaton, IL, 60187. **EMAIL** walter.elwell@wheaton.edu

EMERY, SARAH W.
PERSONAL Born 08/08/1911, Pleasant City, OH, w, 1948, 2 children **DISCIPLINE** PHILOSOPHY, ENGLISH **EDUCATION** Emory Univ, AB, 33; Ohio State Univ, MA, 38; PhD, 42. **CAREER** Tchg asst, Ohio State Univ, 38-42; tchg asst, Univ Ill, 42-43; instr, Packer Collegiate Inst, 43-46; instr, Syracuse Univ, 46-47; asst prof, Hollins Coll, 47-48; asst prof, Duke Univ, 51-52. **MEMBERSHIPS** Am Philos Asn; Phi Beta Kappa, The Poetry Soc of Tex. **SELECTED PUBLICATIONS** Auth, A Donkey's Life, A Story for Children, 79; They Walked into the Rose Garden and Other Poems, 92; Plato's Euthyphro, Apology and Crito, Arranged for Dramatic Presentation from the Jowett Translation with Chornses, 96. **CONTACT ADDRESS** Box 683, Denton, TX, 76202-0683.

EMINHIZER, EARL EUGENE
PERSONAL Born 05/22/1926, Greenville, SC, m, 1955 **DISCIPLINE** RELIGION **EDUCATION** Furman Univ, BA, 48; Youngstown Col, BS, 51; Crozer Theol Sem, BD, 55, ThM, 56; Southern Calif Sch Theol, ThD (hist), 68. **CAREER** Instr relig, Denison Univ, 56-58; instr, 58-77, ASSOC PROF PHILOS AND RELIG, YOUNGSTOWN STATE UNIV, 77-, Minister, Brookfield Christian Church, Ohio; instruct improv grant, 82-83. **MEMBERSHIPS** AHA; Am Soc Church Hist; Am Philos Asn; Soc Bibl Lit; Am Acad Relig. **RESEARCH** American Baptist history, 1800-1865; Disciples of Christ history, 1800-1864. **SELECTED PUBLICATIONS** Auth, A Case Studyo of Mainstream Protestantism--The Disciples Relation to American Culture, 1880-1989, Church Hist, Vol 62, 93; Victorian America and the Civil War, Church Hist, Vol 63, 94; Victorian America and the Civil War, Church Hist, Vol 63, 94. **CONTACT ADDRESS** 1125 Trumbull Ave, SE Warren, OH, 44484.

EMLER, DONALD
PERSONAL Born 06/01/1939, Kansas City, MO, m, 1968, 2 children **DISCIPLINE** RELIGIOUS STUDIES **EDUCATION** Univ Kansas City, Missouri, BA 60; Garrett Evang Theol Sem, M.Div, 63; Indiana Univ, Ed.D, M.Ed, 73. **CAREER** Dean, Wimberly School of Relig, Okla City Univ, 89-; Site Coordinator, Okla Grad Theol Studies Prog, Perkins School Theol, 98-; prof Religious Educ, Centenary Col La, 76-89; lctr, Univ Missouri, 74-76; Chaplain & instr, Central Meth Col, 66-68, 73. **HONORS AND AWARDS** Omicron Delta Kappa Member; Outstanding Young Men of Amer, 72; Who's Who in South & Southwest, 84, 90; Who's Who in Relig, 85, 92; Who's Who in Educ, 91; Who Who in Amer, 98; Centenary Col Fac Study Grant, 86. **MEMBERSHIPS** Assoc of Prof & Res of Relig Educ; United Meth Assoc of Scholars of Christian Educ; Relig Educ Assoc; Christian Educ Fel; Amer Acad Relig/ Soc Bibl Lit; Okla Conference of United Meth Church. **SELECTED PUBLICATIONS** Adult Learning and Development, 4 video lectures for OCU PLUS Program, 86; The Gospel of Matthew: Using the International Lesson Series, OCU-TV, 95; History of World Religions: Teacher's Guide, Okla Pub Schools, 98; The Bible as/in Literature: Tchrs Guide, Okla Pub Schools, 98; Content and Morals: The Dialogue of Theology

and Religious Education, Okla St Univ, 97. **CONTACT ADDRESS** Wimberly School of Religion, Oklahoma City Univ, Oklahoma City, OK, 73106. **EMAIL** dgemler@frodo.okcu.edu

EMPEREUR, JAMES L.

PERSONAL Born 12/21/1933, Tigerton, WI, s **DISCIPLINE** LITURGICAL THEOLOGY **EDUCATION** St Louis Univ, BA, 58, PhL, 59; Woodstock Col, STL, 66; Grad Theol Union, Berkley, PhD, 72. **CAREER** Ed chief, Modern Liturgy Mag, 73-83; prof liturgical and systematic theology, Jesuit School Theology Berkeley, 69-93; founder Inst Spirituality and Worship, 73-93; Parochial Vicar & Liturgist, San Fernando Cathedral; Lectr, Religious studies, Our Lady of the Lake Univ. **HONORS AND AWARDS** Catholic Press Award **MEMBERSHIPS** Am Acad Relig; Cath Theol Soc; Col Soc; NA Acad Liturgy; Soc Liturgica. **RESEARCH** Inculturation of liturgy and sacraments; Liturgy and Hispanic popular religion; Relationship between art and spirituality; Spirituality and psychological growth; Spirituality of homosexuality. **SELECTED PUBLICATIONS** Auth, Prophetic Anointing: God's Call to the Sick, Elderly, and Dying, Michael Glazier, 82; Worship: Exploring the Sacred, Pastoral Press, 87; Models of Liturgical Theology, Grove Books, 87; The Liturgy That Does Justice, Michael Glazier, 90; Starvation in the Midst of Plenty, Liturgical Ministry, 94; Hispanic Celebrations: Popular Religion in Action, Christian Life Communities, 95; Is Liturgy an Art Form?, Liturgical Ministry, 96; The Enneagram and Spiritual Guidance: Nine Paths to Spiritual Guidance, Continuum, 97; Popular Religion and the Liturgy: The State of the Question, Liturgical Ministry, 98. **CONTACT ADDRESS** San Fernando Cathedral, 115 Main Plaza, San Antonio, TX, 78205. **EMAIL** pgdy19a@prodigy.com

ENC, BERENT

PERSONAL Born 05/24/1938, Istanbul, Turkey **DISCIPLINE** PHILOSOPHY **EDUCATION** Princeton Univ, MSE, 62; Oxford Univ, Dipl hist & philos of sci, 64, DPhil, 67. **CAREER** Instr elec eng, Bucknell Univ, 61-62; vis lectr philos, 67-69, Assoc Prof, 71-76, Prof Philos, Univ Wis-Madison, 76-. **MEMBERSHIPS** Philos Sci Asn; Am Philos Soc. **RESEARCH** Philosophy of science; metaphysics; philosophy of mind; action theory. **SELECTED PUBLICATIONS** Auth, Numerical identity and objecthood, Mind, 1/75; Necessary properties and Linnaean essentialism, Can J Philos, 9/75; On the theory of action, J Theory Social Behav, 75; Spiral dependence between theories and taxonomy, Inquiry, 75; Reference of theoretical terms, Nous, 76; Identity statements and microreductions, J Philos, 76; author numerous other articles. **CONTACT ADDRESS** Dept of Philos, Univ of Wis, 600 North Park St, Madison, WI, 53706-1403. **EMAIL** benc@facstaff.wisc.edu

ENGEL, J. RONALD

PERSONAL Born 03/17/1936, Baltimore, MD, m, 1957, 2 children **DISCIPLINE** RELIGIOUS & ENVIRONMENTAL STUDIES **EDUCATION** Johns Hopkins Univ, BA, 58; Meadville Theol Sch Lombard Col, BD, 64; Univ Chicago, MA, 71, Phd, 77. **CAREER** Assoc Prof Social Ethics, Meadville Theol Sch Lombard Col, 70-, Lectr, Divinity Sch, Univ Chicago, 77. **MEMBERSHIPS** Am Acad Relig; Am Soc Environ Hist; Soc Christian Ethics; Int Soc Environmental Ethics. **RESEARCH** Environmental ethics; civil relig; Am philos and theol. **SELECTED PUBLICATIONS** Auth, Sacred Sands: the Struggle for Community in the Indiana Dunes, Wesleyan Univ Press, 83; The Democratic Faith, Am Jour Theolog & Philos, 5 & 9/85; co-ed, the Ethics of Environment and Development: Global Challenge, International Response, Belhaven Press and Ariz Univ Press, 90; Liberal Democracy and the Fate of the Earth, In: Spirit and Nature: Why the Environment is a Religious Issue - An Interfaith Dialogue, Beacon Press, 92; Co-auth, Ecology, Justice, and Christian Faith: A Critical Guide to the Literature, Greenwood Press, 95; Religion and Environment and Sustainable Development, In: The Encyclopedia of Bioethics, rev ed, Macmillan Publ Co, 95; James Luther Adams: Religious and Political Liberalism, Am Jour Theolog & Philos, 1/96; The Religious Authority of Democracy: James Luther Adams's Agenda for Empirical Theology, Am Jour Theolog & Philos, 1/96. **CONTACT ADDRESS** Meadville/Lombard Theol Sch, 5701 S Woodlawn Ave, Chicago, IL, 60637-1602. **EMAIL** jengel@niia.net

ENGEL, RONALD J.

PERSONAL Born 03/17/1937, Baltimore, MD, m, 1957, 2 children **DISCIPLINE** RELIGIOUS SOCIAL ETHICS **EDUCATION** Johns Hopkins, BA, 58; Meadville Lombard, BD, 64; Univ Chicago, PhD, 77. **CAREER** Prof, Meadville Lombard Theol School, 83-; Environ Studies FAC, Univ Chicago, 96-; Lectr, Divinity School, 77-. **HONORS AND AWARDS** Chicago Geog Soc Book Award, 84; Melcher Nat Book award, 84. **MEMBERSHIPS** Am Acad of Rel; Int Soc for Environ Ethics. **RESEARCH** Environmental ethics, philosophy and history; Democratic philosophy and theology. **SELECTED PUBLICATIONS** Auth, Sacred Sands: The Struggle for Community in the Indiana Dunes, 83; numerous articles on religious social ethics; coauth, Ecology, Justice, and Christian Faith: A Critical Guide to the Literature, 95; ed, Voluntary Associations: Sociocultural Analyses and Theological Interpretation, 86; co-ed, The Ethics of Environment and Development: Global Challenge, International Response, 90. **CONTACT ADDRESS** 5701 S Woodlawn Ave, Chicago, IL, 60637. **EMAIL** jengel@niia.net

ENGELHARDT, HUGO TRISTRAM, JR.

DISCIPLINE PHILOSOPHY **EDUCATION** Univ Texas, Austin, PhD, 69; Tulane Schl Med, MD, 72. **CAREER** Asst, psychiatry, 71-72, Tulane Schl Med; asst prof, 72-75, Inst for Med Hum, Univ Texas; adj asst prof, phil, 74-75, S Methodist Univ; assoc prof, prev med & commun health, 75-77, Univ Texas Med; adj assoc prof, phil, 76-77, S Methodist Univ; Rosemary Kennedy Prof, phil of med, 77-82, sr res fel, 77-82, Kennedy Inst of Ethics, Ctr for Bioethics, prof, dept commun & family med, 77-82, fac mem, 77-78, Schl of Foreign Svc, prof, phil, 77-82, Georgetown Univ; vis prof, fac of med, 81, Javeriana Univ; adj res fel, 83-, Inst of Rel, Houston TX; prof, phil, 83-, Rice Univ; prof, med & commun med, 83-, prof, med ethics, obstetrics & gynecology, 90-, Baylor Col of Med; mem, Ctr for Med Ethics & Health Policy, Baylor Col of Med, Houston TX, affil with Inst of Rel & Rice Univ, 83-. **HONORS AND AWARDS** Natl Defense Ed Act Fel, 66-69; Fulbright Grad Fel, 69-70; Woodrow Wilson Vis Fel, Westminster Col, 88; Fel Inst for Advan Stud, Berlin W Germany, 88-89. **MEMBERSHIPS** Amer Assn for Advan of Science; Amer Assn for History of Med; APA; European Soc for Phil of Med & Health Care; Hegel Soc of Amer; History of Science Soc; Intl Soc for Advan of Hum Stud in Gynecology; Metaphysical Soc of Amer; Soc for Health & Human Values; SW Phil Soc, Sigma XI. **RESEARCH** Ethics; bioethics; phil of med. **SELECTED PUBLICATIONS** Auth, Sanctity of Life and Menschenwurde: Can these Concepts Help Direct the Use of Resources in Critical Care? Sanctity of Life & Hum Dignity, Kluwer, 96; coauth, From Pagan Greece to Post-Modern Europe, European Phil of Med & Health Care 4, 96; auth, Manners in the Ruins of Community, Gentility Recalled, Soc Affairs Unit, 96; coauth, Ethical Self-Reflections in the Humanities an Social Sciences, The Responsible Scholar, Watson, 96; auth, Germ-Line Genetic Engg & Moral Diversity: Moral Controversies in a Post-Christian World, Soc Phil & Policy 13, 96; art, Suffering, Meaning, and Bioethics, Christian Bioethics 2, 96; art, Unavoidable Pluralism: Rethinking Secular Morality and Community at the End of the 20th Century, Dialektik, 96; art, Bioethics Reconsidered: Theory and Method in a Post-Christian Post-Modern Age, Kennedy Inst of Ethics J, 96; art, Equality in Health Care: Christian Engagement with a Secular Obsession, Christian Bioethics 2, 96; auth, An Orthodox Approach to Bioethics, Living Orthodoxy in the Modern World, London, Soc for Promoting Christian Knowledge, 96; auth, Japanese and Western Bioethics: Studies in Moral Diversity, Japanese & Western Bioethics, Kluwer, 97; auth, Moral Puzzles Concerning the Human Genome: Western Taboos, Intuitions, and Beliefs at the End of the Christian Era, Japanese & Western Bioethics, Kluwer, 97; art, The Crisis of Virtue: Arming for the Cultural Wars and Pellegrino at the Limes, Theoretical Med 18, 97; auth, The Foundations of Bioethics and Secular Humanism: Why is There No Canonical Moral Content?, Reading Engelhardt, Kluwer, 97; auth, Bioetica come termine plurale: di fronte alla diversita morale della fine del secondo millenio, Bioetica: la ragioni della vita e della scienza, Prometheus Intl, 22, 97; auth, Il Camp Seccolare Della Bioetica, Bioetica, Editrice Elle Di Ci 97; art, Holiness, Virtue, and Social Justice: Contrasting Understandings of the Moral Life, Christian Bioethics 3, 97; art, Freedom and Moral Diversity: The Moral Failures of Health Care in the Welfare State, Soc Phil & Policy 14, 97; auth, Bioethics and the Philosophy of Medicine Reconsidered, Phil of Med & Bioethics, Kluwer, 97; auth, Sins, Voluntary and Involuntary: Recognizing the Limits of Double Effect, Christian Bioethics 3, 97; auth, Respect for Life and the Foundations of Bioethics, The Ethics of Life, Unesco Pub, 97; auth, The Foundations of Bioethics: Liberty and Life with Moral Diversity, Reason Papers 22, 97; auth, Human Nature Genetically Re-engineered: Moral Responsibilities to Future Generations, Germ-Line Intervention & our Responsibilities to Future Generations, Kluwer, 98; coauth, Emergency Patients: Serious Moral Choices, with Limited Time, Information, and Patient Participation, Ethics in Surgery, Oxford Univ Press, 98; auth, Solidaritat: Postmoderne Perspektiven, Solidaritat, Suhrkamp, Frankfurt, 98; coauth, Medicine, Philosophy of, Encycl of Phil, Routledge, 98; art, Physician-Assisted Death: Doctrinal Development vs Christian Tradition, Christian Bioethics 4, 98; art, Physician-Assisted Suicide Reconsidered: Dying as a Christian in a Post-Christian Age, Christian Bioethics 4, 98. **CONTACT ADDRESS** Ctr for Medical Ethics, Baylor Col of Med, One Baylor Plaza, Houston, TX, 77030.

ENGERMAN, STANLEY LEWIS

PERSONAL Born 03/14/1936, New York, NY, m, 1963, 3 children **DISCIPLINE** ECONOMICS, HISTORY **EDUCATION** NY Univ, BS, 56, MBA, 58; Johns Hopkins Univ, PhD(-econ), 62. **CAREER** Asst prof econ, Yale Univ, 62-63; from asst prof to assoc prof, 63-71, prof hist & econ, Univ Rochester, 71-, Nat Sci Found sci fac fel, 69-70; Nat Endowment for Humanities sr fel, 74-75; John Simon Guggenheim mem fel, 80-81. **MEMBERSHIPS** Am Econ Asn; Econ Hist Asn; AHA. **RESEARCH** Slavery; American social and economic history. **SELECTED PUBLICATIONS** Co-ed, The Reinterpretation of American Economic History, Harper, 71; coauth, Time on the Cross: The Economics of American Negro Slavery, Little, Brown, 74; co-ed, Race and Slavery in the Western Hemisphere: Quantitative Studies, Princeton Univ, 75. **CONTACT ADDRESS** Dept of Econ, Univ of Rochester, 500 Joseph C Wilson, Rochester, NY, 14627-9000.

ENGLE, JAMES R.

PERSONAL Born 11/12/1940, Pennsylvania, PA, m, 7 children **DISCIPLINE** RELIGION **EDUCATION** Univ Pitts, PhD. **CAREER** Freeman Jr Col, prof 79-84; Eastern Mennonite Sem, prof 84-. **HONORS AND AWARDS** Sr Fel W. F Albright Inst Israel; Teach Meserete Christos Coll Ethiopia **MEMBERSHIPS** SBL; ASOR **RESEARCH** Archaeology Iron-age Palestine; Asherah and Canaanite deities. **SELECTED PUBLICATIONS** Auth, Adult Bible Study Guide, vol 61:1, 96 and vol 62:1, 97, Intl SS Lesson, Scottsdale PA, Mennonite Pub House. **CONTACT ADDRESS** Dept of Old Testament, Eastern Mennonite Univ, Harrisonburg, VA, 22802. **EMAIL** englej@ema.edu

ENGLISH, LEONA

PERSONAL Born 11/10/1963, NF, Canada **DISCIPLINE** EDUCATION **EDUCATION** Memorial Univ Newfoundland, BA, 84, BEd, 84; Univ Toronto, MRE, 89; Columbia Univ, EdD, 94. **CAREER** Asst prof, 96-. **MEMBERSHIPS** Asn of Prof and Res in Relig Educ; Can Asn for the Study of Adult Educ; Relig Educ Asn of Canada. **RESEARCH** Adult education; Informal learning; Mentoring. **SELECTED PUBLICATIONS** Auth, Mentoring in Religious Education, 98; auth, "Mentoring for Adult Religious Educators," in Caravan, 98; "The Tradition of Teresa of Avila and its Implications for Mentoring of Religious Educators," 96. **CONTACT ADDRESS** St. Francis Xavier Univ, PO Box 5000, Antigonish, NS, B2G 2W5. **EMAIL** lenglish@stfx.ca

ENNIS, ROBERT H.

PERSONAL Born 11/01/1927, New York, NY, s, 2 children **DISCIPLINE** PHILOSOPHY AND PHILOSOPHY OF EDUCATION **EDUCATION** Univ Wisc, BA, 50; NY Univ, MA, 51; Univ Ill, PhD, 58. **CAREER** Asst to assoc to full prof, Cornell Univ, 58-70; prof, Univ Ill, 70-94. **HONORS AND AWARDS** Ctr for Advan Study in the Behavioral Sci, 83-84. **MEMBERSHIPS** Amer Philos Asn; Philos of Educ Soc; Philos of Sci Asn; Asn for Informal Logic and Critical Thinking; Amer Asn of Philos Teachers. **RESEARCH** Critical thinking; Causality; Philosophy of language. **SELECTED PUBLICATIONS** Auth, Critical thinking, Prentice-Hall, 96; auth, Is critical thinking culturally biased?, Teaching Philos, 98; auth, Incorporating critical thinking in the curriculum: An introduction to some basic issues, Inquiry, 97; co-auth, Gender bias in critical thinking: continuing the dialogue, Educ Theory, 95; auth, Critical thinking assessment, Theory in Practice, 93; auth, Critical thinking: What is it?, Philos of educ 1992, Philos of Educ Soc, 93. **CONTACT ADDRESS** 495 E. Lake Rd., Sanibel, FL, 33957. **EMAIL** rhennis@uiuc.edu

ENO, ROBERT BRYAN

PERSONAL Born 11/12/1936, Hartford, CT **DISCIPLINE** PATRISTICS, CHURCH HISTORY **EDUCATION** Cath Univ Am, BA, 58, MA, 59; Inst Cath de Paris, STD, 69. **CAREER** Asst prof, St Mary's Sem, Baltimore, 68-70; ASST PROF, 70-79, ASSOC PROF PATRISTICS, CATH UNIV AM, 79-, CHMN, DEPT CHURCH HIST, AND ASSOC CHMN, DEPT THEOL, 80-, Ed, Corpus Instrumentorum, 66-70; mem, NAT LUTHERAN-ROMAN CATH DIALOGUE, 76-; vis lectr, Princeton Theol Sem, spring, 77 and 80. **MEMBERSHIPS** NAm Patristic Soc; Asn Int des Etudes Patristiques; Am Soc Church Hist; Cath Hist Asn. **RESEARCH** Latin fathers, especially Augustine; ecclesiology; eschatology. **SELECTED PUBLICATIONS** Auth, Church, Book and Bishop--Conflict and Authority in Early Latin Christianity, Cath Hist Rev, Vol 83, 97; Historical Awareness in Augustine--Ontological, Anthropological and Historical Elements of an Augustinian Theory of History, Cath Hist Rev, Vol 80, 94; A Translation of Jerome Chronicon with Historical Commentary, Cath Hist Rev, Vol 83, 97; Desire and Delight--A New Reading of Augustine Confessions, Cath Hist Rev, Vol 79, 93; After the Apostles--Christianity in the 2nd Century, Church History, Vol 64, 95; Augustine, Arianism and Other Heresies, Cath Hist Rev, Vol 83, 97; Novitas Christiana - the Idea of Progress in the Old Church Before Eusebius, Cath Hist Rev, Vol 81, 95; Sacred and Secular--Studies on Augustine and Latin Christianity, Cath Hist Rev, Vol 83, 97; Augustine, Cath Hist Rev, Vol 83, 97; Augustine and the Catechumenate, Cath Hist Rev, Vol 83, 97; The Collection Sources Chretiennes--Editing the Fathers of the Church in the Xxth Century, Cath Hist Rev, Vol 83, 97; Chiliasm and the Myth of the Antichrist--Early Christian Controversy Regarding the Holy Land, Cath Hist Rev, Vol 80, 94; The Early Church--An Annotated Bibliography in English, Cath Hist Rev, Vol 80, 94; The Significance of the Lists of Roman Bishops in the Anti Donatist Polemic, Vigiliae Christianae, Vol 47, 93; Divine Grace and Human Agency--A Study of the Semi Pelagian Controversy, Theol Stud, Vol 57, 96; Reading the Apostolic Fathers--An Introduction, Cath Hist Rev, Vol 83, 97; After the Apostles--Christianity in the 2nd Century, Church Hist, Vol 64, 95. **CONTACT ADDRESS** Catholic Univ of America, 401 Michigan Ave NE, Washington, DC, 20017.

EPHRAIM, CHARLESWORTH W.
DISCIPLINE PHILOSOPHY **EDUCATION** USAF Tech Sch, radio operations honors 1964; USAF Instr Training Sch, 1964; State Univ of NY, BA honors purchase valedictorian 1973; Yale U, MA, MPhil, PhD 1979; Nat Fellow Ford Found, 1973-78. **CAREER** US Air Force, tech instructor, sgt, radio op US & overseas 1964-68; Bankers Trust Co NY, supr 1968-73; State Univ of NY Coll at Purchase, Yale U, instructor; SUNY Empire State Coll, faculty; Mercy Coll, Dept of Philosophy, associate professor, philosophy, currently. **HONORS AND AWARDS** Completed USAF morse-code course in half time; first person in USAF hist to receive 24 GPM while in training, Keesler AFB MS 1964; grad coll in 2 1/2 yrs; rsch being done in Philosophy of the Black Experience; Awarded, Summer Rsch Grant, NY African Amer Inst to study. **MEMBERSHIPS** Mem Com for Vets Affairs; mem NY Metropolitan Assoc for Developmental Education; mem Amer Philosophical Assn; mem NAACP; mem Urban League; founder Free Community School of Mt Vernon 1980. **SELECTED PUBLICATIONS** The Logic of Black Protest, 1988. **CONTACT ADDRESS** Mercy Col, 555 B'way, Dobbs Ferry, NY, 10522.

EPP, ELDON JAY
PERSONAL Born 11/01/1930, Mountain Lake, MN, m, 1951 **DISCIPLINE** CHRISTIAN ORIGINS, MANUSCRIPT STUDIES **EDUCATION** Wheaton Col, Ill, AB, 52; Fuller Theol Sem, BD, 55; Harvard Univ, STM, 56, PhD (hist, philos relig), 61. **CAREER** Spec res asst, Princeton Theol Sem, 61-62; from asst prof to assoc prof relig, Grad Sch Relig, Univ Southern Calif, 62-67, assoc prof classics, 66-68; from assoc prof to profrelig, 68-71, Fel Claremont Grad Sch, 66-68; AM EXEC COMT, INT GREEK NEW TESTAMENT PROJ, 68-; ASSOC ED, J BIBL LIT, 71-; Guggenheim fel, 74-75. **MEMBERSHIPS** Soc Bibl Lit; Am Acad Relig; Soc Study New Testament; Cath Bibl Asn; Soc Mithraic Studies. **RESEARCH** New Testament textual criticism; Greek and Latin manuscript studies; Greco-Roman religions. **SELECTED PUBLICATIONS** Auth, The International Greek New Testament--Project Motivation Hist, Novum Testamentum, Vol 39, 97. **CONTACT ADDRESS** Off of the Dean Case, Case Western Reserve Univ, 10900 Euclid Ave, Cleveland, OH, 44106-4901.

EPPS, VALERIE C.
DISCIPLINE LAW **EDUCATION** Univ Birmingham, BA, 65; Boston Univ, JD, 72. **CAREER** Prof. **RESEARCH** Constitutional law; international law; international law. **SELECTED PUBLICATIONS** Auth, International Law for Undergraduates: Documentary Supplement, 98; The New Dynamics of Self-Determination, 97; Treaties - U.S. - U.K. Extradition Treaties - Rule of Expanded Political Offense - type Exception: In Re Requested Extradition of Smyth, Am Jour Int Law, 96; Towards Global Government: Reality or Oxymoron?, Jour Int Comp Law, 96; Elizabeth F. Defeis International Law Video Course, 96; Enforcing Human Rights, 94. **CONTACT ADDRESS** Law School, Suffolk Univ, Beacon Hill, Boston, MA, 02114. **EMAIL** vepps@acad.suffolk.edu

EPSTEIN, EDWIN M.
DISCIPLINE POLITICAL SCIENCE, LAW **EDUCATION** Univ Pa, BA, 58; Yale Univ, LLB Law, 61; Univ Calif Berkeley, MA Polit Sci, 66. **CAREER** Instr, Univ Pa, 62-64; Lectr, 64-67; asst prof, 67-69; assoc prof, 69-73; prof, 73-91; prof Emeritus, Univ Calif Berkeley, 91-; adj prof, grad Theol Union Calif, 76-; Dean and prof St Mary's Coll Calif, 94-. **HONORS AND AWARDS** Fel, Univ Reading UKI, 71; Fellow Woodrow Wilson Int Center for Scholars Wash, 77-78; Inau gural Jayes/ Quantas Vis Lectr Univ Newcastle Aus, 81; Elected Honorary Mem, Golden Key Nat Honor Soc, 87; Outstanding Fac Mem Award, Polit Economy Students Asn, 87; Elected Honorary Mem, Phi Beta Kappa, 88; Japan Soc for the Promotion of Sci Fel, 89; Howard Chase Book Award, 89; Summer Marcus Distinguished Award, Acad of Mgt, 89; The Berkeley Citation, 91. **MEMBERSHIPS** Acad of Mgt; Acad of Legal Studies in Bus; Am Bar Asn; Am Polit Sci Asn; Bars of Calif, PA ans Supreme Ct of the US; Int Asn for Bus and Soc; Int Soc of Bus, Economics and Ethics; Soc for Bus Ethics. **RESEARCH** Political Science; Law. **SELECTED PUBLICATIONS** Auth, We've Come a Long Way ...From ABLA to ALBS - A Thirty Year Personal Reflection, The J of Legal Studies Educ, 96; Bus Ethics and Corporate Social Policy: reflections on an Intellectual Journey, 1964-1996, and beyond, Bus and Soc, 98. **CONTACT ADDRESS** School of Bus and Administration, Univ of Calif, Berkeley, CA, 94720.

EPSTEIN, RICHARD ALLEN
PERSONAL Born 04/17/1943, New York, NY, m, 1972 **DISCIPLINE** LAW **EDUCATION** Columbia Univ, AB, 64; Oxford Univ, BA, 66; Yale Univ, LLB, 68. **CAREER** From asst prof to assoc prof, Univ Southern Calif, 68-73; PROF LAW, UNIV CHICAGO, 73-, Vis assoc prof, Univ Chicago, 72-73; fel, Ctr Advan Studies Behav Sci, 77-78. **MEMBERSHIPS** Am Soc Polit and Legal Philos. **RESEARCH** Torts, taxation. **SELECTED PUBLICATIONS** Auth, Additional Modes of Feminist Religious Expression Within an Halakhic Framework, Tradition J Orthodox Jewish Thought, Vol 31, 97; History Lean--The Reconciliation of Private Property and Representative Government, Columbia Law Rev, Vol 95, 95; 2 Challenges for Feminist Thought, Harvard J Law Public Policy, Vol 18, 95; The Ubiquity of the Benefit Principle, Southern Calif Law Rev, Vol 67, 94; Bramwell at the end of the 20th Century--Introduction, Am J Legal Hist, Vol 38, 94; Regulatory Takings--Law, Economics, and Politics, Mich Law Rev, Vol 94, 96; The Tort Crime Distinction--A Generation Later, Boston Univ Law Rev, Vol 76, 96; Surrogacy--The Case for Full Contractual Enforcement, Va Law Rev, Vol 81, 95; Lucas V South Carolina Coastal Council--A Tangled Web of Expectations, Stanford Law Rev, Vol 45, 93; The Federalist Papers--From Practical Politics to High Principle, Harvard J Law Public Policy, Vol 16, 93; For A Bramwell Revival, Am J Legal Hist, Vol 38, 94; Legal Education and the Politics of Exclusion, Stanford Law Rev, Vol 45, 93; Babbitt V Sweet Home Chapters of Oregon--The Law Economics Habitat Preservation, Supreme Court Rev, Vol 5, 97; Constitutional Faith and the Commerce Clause, Notre Dame Law Rev, Vol 71, 96; A Clear View of the Cathedral--The Dominance of Property Rules, Yale Law Journal, Vol 106, 97; The Moral and Practical Dilemmas of an Underground Economy, Yale Law J, Vol 103, 94; Some Doubts on Constitutional Indeterminacy, Harvard J Law Public Policy, Vol 19, 96; Law and Economics--Its Glorious Past and Cloudy Future, Univ Chicago Law Rev, Vol 64, 97; The Legal Regulation of Genetic Discrimination--Old Responses to New Technology, Boston Univ Law Rev, Vol 74, 94; Holdouts, Externalities, and the Single Owner--One More Salute to Coase, Ronald, J Law Economics, Vol 36, 93; The Chief Justiceship of Fuller,Melville, W. 1888-1910, Am J Legal Hist, Vol 40, 96; Takings, Exclusivity and Speech--The Legacy of Pruneyard V Robins, Univ Chicago Law Rev, Vol 64, 97; The Permit Power Meets the Constitution, Iowa Law Rev, Vol 81, 95; Some Reflections on the Gender Gap in Employment, Georgetown Law J, Vol 82, 93; Judicial Control Over Expert Testimony--Of Deference and Education, Northwestern Univ Law Rev, Vol 87, 93; The Status Production Sideshow--Why the Antidiscrimination Laws are Still a Mistake, Harvard Law Rev, Vol 108, 95; The Remote Causes of Affirmative Action, or School Desegregation in Kansas City, Missouri, Calif Law Rev, Vol 84, 96; Caste and the Civil Rights Laws--From Jim Crow to Same Sex Marriages, Michigan Law Rev, Vol 92, 94. **CONTACT ADDRESS** Law Sch, Univ Chicago, 1111 E 60th St, Chicago, IL, 60637-2702.

ERDEL, TIMOTHY PAUL
PERSONAL Born 08/07/1951, Decatur, IN, m, 1977, 3 children **DISCIPLINE** PHILOSOPHY; HISTORY; THEOLOGICAL LIBRARIANSHIP **EDUCATION** Fort Wayne Bible Col, BA, 73; Trinity Evangelical Divinity School, M Div, 76; Univ Chicago, AM, 78; Trinity Evangelical Divinity School, Th M, 81; Univ Ill, MA, 86. **CAREER** Asst prof of Relig & Philos, Bethel Col, 94-; lctr Historical & Philos Theol, Jamaica Theol Seminary, 87-93; tchg asst Philos & Relig Studies, Univ Ill, 82-87. **HONORS AND AWARDS** Jamaica Theol Seminary Tchr of Year, 92-93. **MEMBERSHIPS** Amer Acad Relig; Amer Philos Assoc; Amer Soc Church History; Amer Theolog Libr Assoc; Anabaptist/Mennonite Theol Librn; Conference on Faith & History; Evangel Missiological Soc; Evangel Missiological Soc; Evangelical Theolog Soc; Ill Mennonite Historical & Genealogical Soc; Mennonite Historical Soc; Methodist Librn Fel; Soc Bibl Lit; Soc Amer Archivists; Soc Christian Philos; Soc Ind Archivists; Wesleyan Theol Soc **RESEARCH** History of Missionary Church; History of Ecuador; Faith and Reason; Theological Librarianship. **SELECTED PUBLICATIONS** From Egly Amich to Global Mission: The Missionary Church Association, 98; The Missionary Church: From Radical Outcast to the Wild Child of Anabaptism, 97; compiler, Guide to the Preparation of Theses, Carribean Grad School of Theol, 89; coauth, Religions of the World, St Martin's Pr, 88. **CONTACT ADDRESS** Bethel Col, 56111 Frances Ave, Mishawaka, IN, 46545-7507. **EMAIL** erdelt@bethel-in.edu

ERICKSON, MILLARD J.
PERSONAL Born 06/24/1932, Stauchfield, MN, m, 1955, 3 children **DISCIPLINE** THEOLOGY **EDUCATION** Univ Minn, BA, 53; Northern Baptist Theol Sem, BD, 56; MPhil, 58, Univ Chicago; PhD, 63, Northwestern Univ. **CAREER** Instr, bibl & apologetics, 64-69, Wheaton Col; asst, assoc prof, chmn, bibl & phil, 69-92, Bethel Theol Sem; assoc prof, prof, theol, dean, vp, exec vp, 92-96, Southwester Baptist Theol Sem; res prof, dist prof, theol, 96-, Truett Sem of Baylor Col. **HONORS AND AWARDS** Phi Beta Kappa. **MEMBERSHIPS** Amer Theol Soc; APA; Soc of Christian Ethics; Evangel Theol Soc; Evangel Phil Soc. **RESEARCH** Systematic theology; contemporary theology. **SELECTED PUBLICATIONS** Auth, Where Is Theology Going? Issues and Perspectives on the Future of Theology, Baker Bks, 94; auth, Does It Matter How I Live? Applying Biblical Beliefs to Your Daily Life, Baker Bks, 94; auth, God in Three Persons: A Contemporary Understanding of the Trinity, Baker Bks, 95; auth, How Shall They Be Saved? The Destiny of Those Who Do Not Hear of Jesus, Baker Bks, 96; auth, Does It Matter If God Exists? Understanding Who God Is and What He Does For Us, Baker Bks, 96; auth, Does It Matter That I'm Saved? What the Bible Teaches About Salvation, Baker Bks, 96; coauth, Old Wine in New Wine Skins: Doctrinal Preaching in A Changing World, Baker Bks, 97; auth, The Evangelical Left: Encountering Postconservative Evangelical Theology, Baker Bks, 97; auth, Christian Theology, Baker Bks, 98; auth, A Basic Guide to Eschatology: Making Sense of the Millennium, Baker Bks, 98; auth, God the Father Almighty: A Contemporary Exploration of the Divine Attributes, Baker Bks, 98; auth, Postmodernizing the Faith: Evangelical Responses to the Challenge of Postmodernism, Baker Bks, 98. **CONTACT ADDRESS** 2677 Lake Court Cir, Mounds View, MN, 55112-4101.

ERICKSON, STEPHEN ANTHONY
PERSONAL Born 09/01/1940, Fairmont, MN, m, 1961, 2 children **DISCIPLINE** PHILOSOPHY **EDUCATION** St Olaf Col, BA, 61; Yale Univ, MA, 63, PhD (philos), 64. **CAREER** From instr to assoc prof, 64-73, PROF PHILOS, POMONA COL AND CLAREMONT GRAD SCH, 78-. **MEMBERSHIPS** Am Philos Asn; Soc Phenomenol and Existential Philos. **RESEARCH** Meaning and language as approached from a phenomenological point of view; philosophical dimensions of and problems in anthropology. **SELECTED PUBLICATIONS** Auth, Mead and Merleau Ponty--Toward a Common Vision, J Am Acad Rel, Vol 63, 95. **CONTACT ADDRESS** Dept of Philos, Pomona Col, Claremont, CA, 91711.

ERICSON, NORMAN R.
PERSONAL Born 07/21/1932, Loomis, NE, m, 1954, 4 children **DISCIPLINE** NEW TESTAMENT **EDUCATION** Univ NE, BA; Trinity Ev Div School, BD; Univ Chicago, PhD. **CAREER** Assoc prof, 62-74, Trinity Intl Univ; prof, 74-77, Trinity Ev Divinity School; prof, 77-, Wheaton Col. **MEMBERSHIPS** SBL; IBR; ETS; Chicago Soc Bib Lit. **RESEARCH** General Epistles; synoptic gospels. **SELECTED PUBLICATIONS** Auth, Implications from the New Testament for Contextualization, Theology and Mission, Baker, 78; auth, Interpreting I Peter, II Peter and Jude, Lit and Meaning of Scripture, Baker, 81; coauth, John: A New Look at the Fourth Gospel, Tyndale, 81; rev, J.R. Michaels, I Peter, Themelios; rev, Perkins, First and Second Peter, James and Jude, Trinity Jour; gen rev, Letters and Revelation in The Bible: New Living Translation, Tydale, 96. **CONTACT ADDRESS** on 651 Herrick Dr, Wheaton, IL, 60187.

ERICSON, RICHARD
DISCIPLINE LAW **EDUCATION** Guelph Univ, BA, 69; Univ Toronto, MA, 71; Cambridge Univ, PhD, 74; DLitt, 91. **CAREER** Prof, 93-. **HONORS AND AWARDS** Co-ed, Can Jour Soc, 75-. **RESEARCH** Criminal justice; law and communication; law reform; policing and regulation. **SELECTED PUBLICATIONS** Auth, pubs about criminology and sociology; co-auth, Policing the Risk Society Univ Toronto, 97. **CONTACT ADDRESS** Fac of Law, Univ British Columbia, 1822 East Mall, Vancouver, BC, V6T 1Z1. **EMAIL** ericson@law.ubc.ca

ERNST, CARL W.
PERSONAL Born 09/08/1950, Los Angeles, CA, m, 1974, 2 children **DISCIPLINE** RELIGIOUS STUDIES **EDUCATION** Stanford Univ, AB, 73; Harvard Univ, PhD, 81. **CAREER** Asst prof, 81-87, assoc prof, 87-92, ch, 91-92, Pomona Col; prof, 92- , ch 95- , Univ NC at Chapel Hill. **HONORS AND AWARDS** Natl Endowment Hum, dir summer sem Col tchrs, summer res grant, 93, Transl grant, Arabic, 89-90; Fulbright res fel, Pakistan, 90, 86, India, 78-79; res grant, Amer inst Pakistan stud (s), 98; Elect to Amer soc stud Rel, 96; Amer res inst Turkey Travel grant, 90; Amer Coun of learned soc, Ger, 89; sr res fel, Amer inst Indian stud (s), 81; Lang fel, Persian, 76-78 NDFL, 79-80 FLAS; Harvard Grad Sch Arts and Sci merit awd, 79. **MEMBERSHIPS** Amer Acad Rel; Middle East stud (s) asn; soc Iranian stud (s); Amer inst Pakistan stud (s); Amer soc stud (s) Rel, Carolina-Duke-Emory inst for the stud of Islam (co-founder.) **RESEARCH** Islamic Studies; Religion in South Asia. **SELECTED PUBLICATIONS** Auth, Works of Ecstasy in Surfism, SUNY Series in Islam, SUNY Press, 85; From Hagiography to Martyrology: Conflicting Testimonies to a Sufi Martyr of the Delhi Sultanate, History of Religions, XXIV, May 85, 308-327; Controversy Over Ibn Arabi's Fusus: The Faith of Pharaoh, Islamic Culture LIX, 85, 259-266; The Symbolism of Birds and Flight in the Writings of Ruzbihan Baqli, in The Legacy of Mediaeval Persian Sufism, ed Leonard Lewisohn, London, Khaniqahi Nimatullahi, 92, 353-366, also in Sufi, 11, Autumn 91, 5-12; The Spirit of Islamic Calligraphy: Daba Shah Isfahani's Adab al-Mashq, Jour Amer Oriental Soc, 112, 92, 279-286; Mystical Language and the Teaching Context in the early Sufi Lexicons, in Mysticism and Language, ed Steven T. Katz, Oxford UP, 92, 181-201; Eternal Garden: Mysticism, History, and Politics at a South Asian Sufi Center, SUNY Series in Muslim Spirituality in South Asia, SUNY Press, 92; The Man Without Attributes: Ibn Arabi's Interpretation of Abu Yazid al-Bistami, Jour Muhyiddin Ibn Arabi Soc, XIII, 93, 1-18; assoc ed, Manifestations of Sainthood in islam, Istanbul, The Isis Press, 93, also auth, Introduction, xi-xxviii, and An Indo-Persian Guide to Sufi Shrine Pilgrimage, 43-67; The Stages of Love in Persian Sufism, from Rabi'a to Ruzbihan, in Classical Persian Sufism from its Origins to Rumi, ed Leonard Lewisohn, London, Khaniqahi Nimatullahi, 94, 435-455; Ruzbihan Baqli on Love as Essential Desire, in God is Beautiful and He Loves Beauty: Festschrift fur Annemarie Schimmel, ed Alma Giese and J. Christoph Burgel, Bern, Peter Lang, 94, 181-189; The Interpretation of the Classical Sufi Tradition in India: The Shama'il al-atqiya of Rukn al-Din Kashani, Sufi, 22, 94, 5-10; Trans for Religions of India in Practice, ed Donald S.

Lopez, jr., Princeton Readings in Religions, 1, Princeton UP, 95: Lives of Sufi Saints, 495-512, Conversations of Sufi Saints, 513-517, and India as a Sacred Islamic Land, 556-64; Sufism and Yoga According to Muhammad Ghawth, Sufi, 29, Spring, 96, 9-13; Ruzbihan Baqli: Mysticism and the Rhetoric of Sainthood in Persian Sufism, Curzon Sufi Series, 4, London, Curzon Press, 96; Local Cultural Nationalism as Anti-Fundamentalist Strategy in Pakistan, Comparative Studies of South Asia, Africa, and the Middle East, 16, 96, 68-76; The Shambhala Guide to Sufism, Boston, Shambhala Pub (s), 97; Ruzbihan Baqli, The Unveiling of Secrets: Diary of a Sufi Master, transl from Arabic, Chapel Hill, NC, Parvardigar Press, 97; Persecution and Circumspection in the Shattari Sufi Order, in Islamic Mysticism Contested: Thirteen Centuries of Debate and Conflict, ed Fred De Jong and Berndt Radtke, Islamic History and Civilization, Leiden, E.J. Brill, 98; Admiring the Works of the Ancients: The Ellora Temples as Viewed by Indo-Muslim Authors, in Beyond Turk and Hindu: Rethinking Religious Identity in Premodern South Asia, ed David Gilmartin and Bruce B. Lawrence, State U of Florida P, 99; **CONTACT ADDRESS** Dept of Religion, Univ of No Carolina, Chapel Hill, NC, 27599-3225. **EMAIL** cernst@email.unc.edu

ERWIN, JAMES OTIS
PERSONAL Born 04/28/1922, Marion, NC, m **DISCIPLINE** THEOLOGY **EDUCATION** Johnson C Smith U, BA 1943; Garrett Theol Sem, MDiv 1946; Iliff Sch Theology, MRE 1953, STM 1979; Rust Coll, LLD 1971; WV Wesleyan U, LLD 1972. **CAREER** United Methodist Church, ordained to ministry 1946; Morristown Coll TN, chaplain, instructor 1946-48; Wiley Coll TX, pres 1970-72, chmn dept religion, philosophy, chaplain 1948-53; Lincoln Univ MO, asst prof 1953-66; Wesley Found Univ of IA, founder 1966-67; Philander Smith Coll AR, dean of students, chaplain 1967-70; Wesley United Methodist Church, pastor 1968-70; St James United Methodist Church Chicago, pastor 1972-76. **MEMBERSHIPS** Mem Douglas-Cherokee Ofc Econ Opportunity 1970-72; dist supt The United Meth Ch; mem Cherokee Guidance Center Morristown 1970-72; vice-chmn Little Rock BSA 1968-70; mem Intl Platform Assn; Alpha Phi Omega; Phi Beta Sigma. **SELECTED PUBLICATIONS** Contrib articles to professional jours. **CONTACT ADDRESS** 77 W Washington St, Ste 1806, Chicago, IL, 60602.

ERWIN, PAMELA
DISCIPLINE YOUTH AND FAMILY MINISTRIES **EDUCATION** Univ NC, BS; Denver Sem, MA; Univ Colo, PhD. **CAREER** Prof, Denver Sem. **RESEARCH** Educational leadership and innovation. **SELECTED PUBLICATIONS** Co-auth, Youth and Family Ministry, New Directions for Youth Ministry; auth, Principles of Mentoring, Youth Ministry Mentoring Manual; ed, Community-Based Family Ministry. **CONTACT ADDRESS** Denver Conservative Baptist Sem, PO Box 10000, Denver, CO, 80250.

ESAU, ALVIN
DISCIPLINE LAW **EDUCATION** Univ Alberta, BA, 73, LLB, 76; Harvard Univ, LLM, 77. **CAREER** Asst prof, 77-81; assoc prof, 81-85; prof, 85-. **RESEARCH** Legal systems; criminal law; professional responsibility; jurisprudence; computer applications. **SELECTED PUBLICATIONS** Ed, Radon and the Law, 90; The Winnipeg General Strike Trials: Research Source, 90. **CONTACT ADDRESS** Fac of Law, Univ Manitoba, Robson Hall, Winnipeg, MB, R3T 2N2. **EMAIL** esau@cc.umanitoba.ca

ESCHELBACH, MICHAEL A.
PERSONAL Born 10/11/1957, Ann Arbor, MI, m, 1983, 5 children **DISCIPLINE** THEOLOGY **EDUCATION** E Mich Univ, BS, 79; Concordia Theo Sem, MDiv, 85; Westminster Theo Sem, PhD, 98. **CAREER** VP, 74-81, Ann Arbor Craftsmen Inc; Pastor, 85-88, Mount Olive Luth Church; Pastor, 88-, Peace Luth Church. **MEMBERSHIPS** ETS, SBL. **RESEARCH** New Testament studies **CONTACT ADDRESS** 78 Flynn, Sandusky, MI, 48471.

ESKRIDGE, CHRIS W.
PERSONAL Born 07/20/1952, Berkeley, CA, m, 1975, 2 children **DISCIPLINE** CRIMINOLOGY; CRIMINAL SCIENCE **EDUCATION** BYU, BS 75; Ohio State Univ, MA 77, PhD 78. **CAREER** Univ Nebraska, prof, 78-; Univ Canterbury NZ, fel, 92; Lincoln Foundation, asst to Pres, 83; US Air Force, res assoc, 81; Utah Cnt Attorney's Office, crim investigator, 75-76. **HONORS AND AWARDS** Herbert Bloch Awd; ASC various teaching Awds. **MEMBERSHIPS** ACJS; ASC; IASOC; WSC. **RESEARCH** Organized Crime; Intl Crime. **SELECTED PUBLICATIONS** Auth, Criminal Justice: Concepts and Issues, contrib ed, 3rd ed, LA, Roxbury Press, 99; Liberty v Order: The Ultimate Confrontation, Dubuque IA, Kendall/Hunt, 93; Hist and Devel of Modern Correctional Practices in NZ, co-ed, in: Richter Moore, Charles Fields, eds, Comparative Crim Justice, IL, Waveland, 96; Justice and The Amer Justice Network, in: Crim Justice: Concepts and Issues, LA, Roxbury Press, 96; The Mexican Cartels: A Challenge for the 21st Century, coauth, Crim Organizations, 98; Crime and Justice in Post Cold War Hungary, Fed Probation, 96; The Great Transition: Post War Corrections in Poland, coauth, Jour of Offender Rehab, 96; Crime and Justice in NZ, coauth, Intl, 94; Penal Innovation in NZ: He Ara Hou, coauth, Jour of Offender Rehab, 94. **CONTACT ADDRESS** Dept of Criminal Justice, Nebraska Univ, Lincoln, NE, 68588-0630. **EMAIL** ceskridg@unlinfo.unl.edu

ESKRIDGE, JOHN CLARENCE
PERSONAL Born 06/06/1943, Pittsburgh, PA, s **DISCIPLINE** PHILOSOPHY **EDUCATION** Duquesne Univ Pittsburgh, BA 1966, MA 1971; Pacific So Univ CA, PhD Philosophy 1978. **CAREER** Comm Coll, prof philosophy 1978-; Carlow Coll, dir turial instructor 1973-74; Comm Coll Allegheny County, philosophy faculty 1969-; "Le Sacre Corps" Dance Co, artistic dir 1969-79; Pittsburgh Child Guidance Clinic, program dir, creative recreational arts program 1969-70; Comm Coll Allegheny County Campus, dir black studies 1969-71, coll speakers bureau 1978-88; First Baptist Church Pittsburgh, bd of deacons 1970-73; Pittsburgh High School of Creative & Performing Arts, adv bd 1979-90; Community College Allegheny County, department chairman, 1983-; Hot Lix Concert Jazz Band, leader/producer, 1978-89; Orpheo Concert Latin Band, leader/producer, 1989-. **HONORS AND AWARDS** NDEA study fellowship Duquesne Univ 1967-70; faculty spl serv award Comm Coll Allegheny Co Student Union 1978; College Blue Ribbon Faculty Award, Community College Allegheny County, 1981-82. **MEMBERSHIPS** Mem Soc for Phenomenology & Existential Philosophy 1967-80; mem Am Philos Assn 1969-80; founding chmn Hermeneutic Circle 1977-80; bd dirs Inst For Collective Behavior & Memory 1980-87; vice pres, African American Federation of the Americas, 1983-89; member, Pittsburgh Musicians Society, 1967-. **SELECTED PUBLICATIONS** various **CONTACT ADDRESS** Dept Phil & For Lang, Comm Col of Allegheny County, Allegheny, 808 Ridge Ave, Pittsburgh, PA, 15212.

ESS, CHARLES
DISCIPLINE PHILOSOPHY **EDUCATION** PA State Univ, PhD. **CAREER** Prof, Drury Col. **HONORS AND AWARDS** Joe Wyatt Challenge Awd 91. **RESEARCH** Hist of philos; ethics; logic; feminist philos; world relig(s); computer mediated commun. **SELECTED PUBLICATIONS** Auth, Cosmopolitan Ideal or Cybercentrism, Comput and Philos, 98; Is There Hope for Democracy in Cyberspace, Center Technol Cult, 97; Prophetic Communities On-line?, Presbyterian Church, 97; Values Analysis: an Experiment in Interdisciplinary Ethics, Am Philos Asn Newsletter on Tchg, 97. **CONTACT ADDRESS** Relig and Philos Dept, Drury Col, N Benton, PO Box 900, Springfield, MO, 65802.

ESTEP, MYRNA LYNN
PERSONAL Born 01/07/1944, Whitesville, WV, m, 1971, 1 child **DISCIPLINE** PHILOSOPHY; EPISTEMOLOGY **EDUCATION** Ind Univ, PhD 75, MA 71, BA 70. **CAREER** Univ of Incarnate Word, adj fac, 96-98; Our Lady of Lake Univ, adj fac, 98; Univ Zimbabwe, grad fac, 87-89; Acad Hea Sciences, sys analyst, edu spec, 81-84; San Antonio Col, instr, 78-81; Univ Texas SA, asst prof, 75-78; Ind Univ, assoc instr, 72-75. **HONORS AND AWARDS** Who's Who in: Amer, South and SW, Media and Comm, World of Women; Directory of: Am Scholars, Women Hist Of Science; Dictionary of Int Biography; 2 Commendation Letters from Peter Rowe USMC Colonel Commander The Basic School USMCCDC and from David Osborn Captain USN Commanding Officer USNTEC; Best Paper Awd Designing and Systems Vienna Aust; Phi Kappa Phi; Int Affil OSK Univ Vienna; NY Acad of Science Mem. **MEMBERSHIPS** AAAS; MAA; OSK; ISGSR; APA; IUAA. **RESEARCH** Philosophy; mathematics; philosophy of science; logic; philosophy of mathematics; computer science; systems design and development; information theory; epistemology; cognitive science; behavioral research in education. **SELECTED PUBLICATIONS** Auth, Canned Hunts: Women Students at the Univ of Texas, The Shatter the Glass Ceiling, GCCC, Greenville SC, 98; Canned Hunts: Women at the Univ of Texas, Online Jour of Feminist Construction, San Francisco CA, 98; rev, Common Threads: Women Mathematics and Work, by Mary Harris, Initiatives, Washington DC, 98; auth, Fear and Loathing: The History of Affirmative Action in Texas, Feminista, Online Jour of Feminist Reconstruction, 98; auth, What Godel said : On the Non-algoithmic Nature of the Second Theorem, Systems Res, EMCSR, 98; auth, Teaching the Logical Paradoxes: On Mathematical Insight or Is There a Non-algorithmic Element in Godel's Second Theorem? Abstracts, Am Math Soc, 99; auth, A Theory of Immediate Awareness and Knowing How, Jour of Consciousness Stud, Imprint Acad, UK, 96, and Times Higher Educ Sup, Essex UK, 96. **CONTACT ADDRESS** Dept of Philosophy, Incarnate Word Univ, 16022 Oak Grove, San Antonio, TX, 78255. **EMAIL** Estepm@universe.uiwtx.edu

ESTLUND, DAVID
PERSONAL Born 02/20/1958, Clintonville, WI, m, 1986, 3 children **DISCIPLINE** PHILOSOPHY, POLITICS **EDUCATION** Univ of Wis, PhD, 86. **CAREER** Univ of Calif at Irvine, 86-91; BROWN UNIV, 91-. **HONORS AND AWARDS** Fel, Am Coun of Learned Soc, 89-90; fel, prog in ethics & the professions, Harvard Univ, 93-94; NEH fel, 98. **MEMBERSHIPS** Am Philos Asn. **RESEARCH** Polit & moral philos. **SELECTED PUBLICATIONS** Auth, Opinion Leaders, Independence, and Condorcet's Jury Theorem, Theory and Decision, 94; Beyond Fairness and Deliberation: The Epistemic Dimension of Democratic Authority, Deliberative Democracy, MIT Press, 97; The Visit & The Video: Publication and the Line Between Sex and Speech, Sex, Preference, and Family, Oxford Univ Press, 97; The Insularity of the Reasonable: Why political Liberalism Must Admit the Truth, ETHICS, 98; Political Quality, Soc Philos and Policy, forthcoming. **CONTACT ADDRESS** 88 Hudson St, Providence, RI, 02909. **EMAIL** David_Estlund@brown.edu

ESTRICH, SUSAN
DISCIPLINE CRIMINAL LAW **EDUCATION** Wellesley Col, BA,74; Harvard Univ, JD,77. **CAREER** Robert Kingsley prof Law and Political Sci, Univ Southern Calif; clerked for, Honor J. Skelly Wright, Judge US Ct Appeals DC Circuit & Honor John Paul Stevens, Assoc Justice US Supreme Ct; taught at, Harvard Law Sch; past spec asst to, Senator Edward M. Kennedy; staff coun and spec asst to, ch coun US Senate Judiciary Comt; national campaign manager, Dukakis-Bentsen campaign, 88; weekly columnist, USA Today; contrib ed, Los Angeles Times. **MEMBERSHIPS** National Governing board, pres, 1983-89; 90-. **RESEARCH** Law & politics; criminal law; gender discrimination. **SELECTED PUBLICATIONS** Auth, Getting Away with Murder: Politics, Crime, & the Rule of Law; Real Rape & Sex at Work; coauth, Dangerous Offenders. **CONTACT ADDRESS** School of Law, Univ Southern Calif, University Park Campus, Los Angeles, CA, 90089.

ETZKORN, GIRARD J.
PERSONAL Born 09/18/1927, Kirkwood, MO **DISCIPLINE** PHILOSOPHY, FRENCH **EDUCATION** Quincy Col, BA, 53; St Joseph Sem, Ill, STB, 57; Cath Univ Louvain, PhD (philos), 61. **CAREER** From instr to assoc prof philosophy, Quincy Col, 61-71; assoc prof, Southern Ill Univ, CArbondale, 71-72; RES PROF CRITICAL ED OF WILLIAM OCKHAM, FRANCISCAN INST, 73-, Am Philos Soc grant, 65-66. **MEMBERSHIPS** Int Soc Study Medieval Philos; Am Philos Asn; AAUP. **RESEARCH** Critical editions of medieval manuscripts; French and German phenomenology and existentialism; translating of French philosopher Michel Henry. **SELECTED PUBLICATIONS** Auth, William De La Mare, Scriptum in Secundum Librum Sententiarum, Speculum J Medieval Stud, Vol 72, 97; Bonaventure Sermons de Diversis, Speculum J Medieval Stud, Vol 70, 95. **CONTACT ADDRESS** Franciscan Inst, St Bonaventure, NY, 14778.

EULA, MICHAEL JAMES
PERSONAL Born 05/18/1957, Passaic, NJ, m, 1993, 2 children **DISCIPLINE** HISTORY, LAW **EDUCATION** Rutgers Univ, BA (cum laude), 80; Calif State Univ, MA, 83; Univ of Calif at Irvine, MA, 84, PhD, 87; Newport Univ School of Law, JD, 98. **CAREER** Teaching asst/assoc, visiting asst prof of hist, Univ of Calif at Irvine, 91; lectr in hist, Calf State Univ, 89; PROF OF HIS, EL CAMINO COL, 89-. **HONORS AND AWARDS** Nat Endowment for the Humanities Fel, 90 & 95; New Jersey Hist Comn Fel, 92; Fac Res Fel, UCLA, 93; Phi Alpha Theta Iota Kappa, Rutgers Univ, 79. **MEMBERSHIPS** Am Hist Asn; Am Italian Hist Asn. **RESEARCH** Italian Americans; social history of ideas; legal history. **SELECTED PUBLICATIONS** Auth, Cultural Identity, Foodways, and the Failure of American Food Reformers Among Ital Immigrants in New York City 1891-1897, Ital Americana, forthcoming; auth, Using Theory in the Introductory History Course: One Strategy for a Postmodern Era, The Hist Teacher, forthcoming; Langage, Time, and the Formation of Self Among Italian-American Workers in New Jersey and New York 1880-1940, Ital Americana, 97; auth, Between Peasant and Urban Villager: Italian Americans of New Jersey and New York 1880-1980. The Structures of Counter Discourse, Peter Lang, 93; auth, Cultural Continuity and Cultural Hegemony: Italian Catholics in New Jersey and New York 1880-1940, Relig, 92; auth, Thinking Historically: Using Theory in the Introductory History Classroom, The Hist Teacher, 93. **CONTACT ADDRESS** Dept of History, El Camino Col, Torrance, CA, 90506.

EVANS, C. STEPHEN
PERSONAL Born 05/26/1948, Atlanta, GA, m, 1969, 3 children **DISCIPLINE** PHILOSOPHY **EDUCATION** Yale Univ, Mphil 71, PhD 74; Wheaton Col, BA high hon 69. **CAREER** Calvin College, prof 94-, dean res and sch 97-, Wm Spoelhof Teacher-Scholar 94-96; St Olaf Col , Howard and Edna Hong Kierkegaard Lib, prof curator 86-94, assoc prof 84-86; Wheaton Col, asst prof, assoc prof, prof, 74-82; Trinity Cole, asst prof 72-74; Western Kentucky Univ, vis assoc prof 80-81; Regent Col BC, vis prof 90, 92, 95; Northern Baptist Sem, adj prof 82-84; Trinity Evangel Div Sch, vis lectr 76. **HONORS AND AWARDS** Co-Winner Best Christian Sch Bk Awd; Wm Spoelhof Teach-Sch; Pew Evangel Sr Sch; NEH Fel; George C Marshall Fel; Cen Faith Devel Fel; Danforth Fel. **MEMBERSHIPS** ISC; KRC; IACS; APA; KS; SCP; AAR. **RESEARCH** Philosophy of Kierkegaard; religion; human sciences; phenomenology and existentialism; philosophical psychology. **SELECTED PUBLICATIONS** Auth, Faith Beyond Reason, Edinburgh, Edinburgh Univ Press, 98, and Grand Rapids MI, Wm B. Eerdmans, 98; The Historical Christ and the Jesus of Faith: The In-

carnational Narrative as History, Oxford, Oxford Univ Press, 96; Why Believe: Reason and Mystery as Pointers to God, revised InterVarsity Press 86, Grand Rapids, Wm Eerdmans, 96, Christian Perspectives on Religious Knowledge, co-ed, Wm Eerdmans, 93; Do Robots Have Free Will?, in: Books and Cultures, 98; Soren Kierkegaard's Fear and Trembling, in: Invitation to the Classics, eds Louise Cowan, Os Guinness, Grand Rapids MI, Baker Books, 98; The Concept of Authority in Kierkegaard's Works of Love, in: The Kierkegaard Studies Yearbook 1997, Berlin and NY, Walter de Gruyter, 97; Who is the Other in The Sickness Unto Death?, God and Human Relations in the Constitution of the Self, in: The Kierkegaard Studies Yearbook 1996, Berlin and NY, Walter de Gruyter, 96. **CONTACT ADDRESS** Dept of Philosophy, Calvin Col, 3201 Burton St SE, Grand Rapids, MI, 49546. **EMAIL** sevans@calvin.edu

EVANS, DALE WILT
PERSONAL Born 09/27/1939, Philadelphia, PA **DISCIPLINE** PHILOSOPHY, CLASSICS **EDUCATION** Pa State Univ, BA, 65, MA, 66, PhD (Philos), 73. **CAREER** Instr philos, Univ Wyo, 69-72; programmer, Sperry Univac, 74-75; ASST PROF PHILOS, PA STATE UNIV, 75-, Fulbright fel, 70-71. **MEMBERSHIPS** Am Philos Soc. **RESEARCH** Contemporary philosophy; contemporary man. **SELECTED PUBLICATIONS** Auth, Pronunciation, Mod Lan J, Vol 80, 96. **CONTACT ADDRESS** Dept of Philos, Pennsylvania State Univ, Du Bois, PA, 15801.

EVANS, DONALD D.
PERSONAL Born 09/21/1927, Thunder Bay, ON, Canada **DISCIPLINE** RELIGION/PHILOSOPHY **EDUCATION** Univ Toronto, BA, 50; Oxford Univ, BPhil, 53, DPhil, 62; McGill Univ, BD, 55; Laurentian Univ, DD, 82. **CAREER** Ordained United Church Can, 55; Pastor, Grand Forks, BC, 55-58; asst prof divinity, McGill Univ, 60-64; assoc prof to prof, 64-93, PROF EMER PHILOSOPHY, UNIV TORONTO, 93-. **HONORS AND AWARDS** Killam sr res scholar, 75-77. **SELECTED PUBLICATIONS** Auth, The Logic of Self-Involvement, 63; auth, Communist Faith and Christian Faith, 64; auth, Struggle and Fulfillment, 80; auth, Faith, Authenticity and Morality, 80; auth, Spirituality and Human Nature, 92; coauth, Analytic Philosophy in Canada, 82; ed & coauth, Peace Power and Protest, 67; ed, Against the Psychologist's Act, 78. **CONTACT ADDRESS** Victoria Col, Univ Toronto, Toronto, ON, M5S 1K7.

EVANS, JOHN WHITNEY
PERSONAL Born 08/06/1931, Kansas City, MO **DISCIPLINE** UNITED STATES CHURCH HISTORY **EDUCATION** St Paul Sem, Minn, MA, 57; Cath Univ Am, MA, 58; Univ Minn, PhD (hist, philos educl, 70. **CAREER** Instr social probs, Cathedral High Sch, Minn, 58-62; chaplain and lectr psychol and educ, Univ Minn, Duluth, 66-69; coord res campus ministry, Ctr Applied Res in Apostolate, Washington, DC, 69-71; dir, Nat Ctr Campus Ministry, Mass, 71-73; CHAPLAIN AND ASST PROF HIST AND RELIG STUDIES, COL ST SCHOLASTICA, 73-, Mem comn campus ministry, Nat Cath Educ Asn, 69-73; Underwood fel, 72-73. **HONORS AND AWARDS** Cath Campus Ministry Asn Serv Award, 73. **MEMBERSHIPS** Nat Cath Educ Asn; Soc Sci Study Relig; AHA; Am Cath Hist Asn; Relig Educ Asn. **RESEARCH** History and religion in American higher education; philosophy of education; student movements. **SELECTED PUBLICATIONS** Auth, Adapting to America--Catholics, Jesuits, and Higher Education in the 20th Century, Am Hist Rev, Vol 98, 93; Fremont, John, Charles Character as Destiny, Ore Hist Quart, Vol 94, 93; The Journals of the Lewis and Clark Expedition, March 23 June 9, 1806, Vol 7, Ore Hist Quart, Vol 94, 93; In Memoriam Crunican, Paul, Eugene 1928-1994, Cath Hist Rev, Vol 80, 94. **CONTACT ADDRESS** Off of Chaplain, Col of St. Scholastica, 1200 Kenwood Ave, Duluth, MN, 55811-4199.

EVANS, ROD L.
DISCIPLINE ETHICS AND POLITICAL PHILOSOPHY **EDUCATION** Univ Va, PhD, 87. **CAREER** Philos, Old Dominion Univ. **RESEARCH** Bioethics, business ethics. **SELECTED PUBLICATIONS** Ed, Fundamentalism: Hazards and Heartbreaks ;Drug Legalization: For and Against ;The Right Words ;The Quotable Conservative. **CONTACT ADDRESS** Old Dominion Univ, 4100 Powhatan Ave, Norfolk, VA, 23058.

EVANS, WARREN CLEAGE
PERSONAL Born 12/30/1948, Detroit, Michigan, d **DISCIPLINE** LAW **EDUCATION** Madonna College, Livonia, MI, BA, 1975; University of Detroit, Detroit, MI, MA, 1980; Detroit College of Law, Detroit, MI, JD, 1986. **CAREER** Wayne County Sheriffs Dept, Detroit, MI, undersheriff, 1970-90; Wayne County Board of Commissioners, Detroit, MI, dir of administration, 1990-91; Office of County Executive, director of community corrections, 1991-. **HONORS AND AWARDS** Distinguished Corrections Service Award, 1988; Spirit of Detroit Award, Detroit City Council, 1987. **MEMBERSHIPS** Vice pres, Detroit Board of Water Commissioners, 1989-; parlamentarian, nati; advisory board, Criminal Justice Comm, WCCC, 1990-; advisory board, Criminal Justice Comm, U of D, 1988-; advisory board, BCN Law Center, 1986-. **CONTACT ADDRESS** Director of Community Corrections, Office of County Executive, 640 Temple St, Ste 210, Detroit, MI, 48215.

EVANS, WILLIAM
PERSONAL Born 11/18/1951, Memphis, TN, m, 1977, 2 children **DISCIPLINE** RELIGIOUS STUDIES **EDUCATION** Univ of Memphis, BS Microbiology, 79; Harding Grad School, MD Church History, 89; Hebrew Union Coll Jewish Inst Rel, MA Bible Lit, 96. **HONORS AND AWARDS** Minister, Church of Christ and Baptist Church. **MEMBERSHIPS** SBL. **RESEARCH** Christian Origins. **CONTACT ADDRESS** 10251 Pendery Dr, Cincinnati, OH, 45242-5345. **EMAIL** evansBible@aol.com

EVERETT, RALPH B.
PERSONAL Born 06/23/1951, Orangeburg, SC, m, 1974 **DISCIPLINE** LAW **EDUCATION** Morehouse Coll, BA 1973; Duke Univ Law School, JD 1976. **CAREER** NC Dept of Justice, assoc Attorney general 1976; NC Dept of Labor, admin asst for legal affairs 1976-77; Senator Fritz Hollings, spec asst 1977-78, legislative asst 1978-83; US Senate, Comm on Commerce, Sci & Transportation, attny, democratic chief counsel, staff dir 1983-86; US Senate, comm on sci & transportation chief counsel and staff dir 1987-89; Paul Hastings, Janofsky and Walker, LLP partner, 1989-. **HONORS AND AWARDS** Phi Beta Kappa; Phi Alpha Theta Intl Hon Soc in History; Earl Warren Legal Scholar. **MEMBERSHIPS** Mem NC & DC Bars; admitted to US Dist Court for DC; US Court of Appeals for DC Court; US Tax Court; US Court of Claims; US Supreme Court; mem Amer Bar Assoc, Alpha Phi Alpha; mem, Alumni Board of Visitors, Duke Univ Law School; former trustee, Natl Urban League; bd of dir, Ctr for Natl Policy; Ambassador, 1998 Intl Telecommunication Union's Plenipotentiary Conference, Head of United States Delegation to the Intl Telecommunication Union's second World Telecommunication Development Conference, 1998. **SELECTED PUBLICATIONS** various **CONTACT ADDRESS** Paul, Hastings, Janofsky and Walker, LLP, 1299 Pennsylvania Avenue, NW, Washington, DC, 20004-2400.

EVERETT, WILLIAM J.
PERSONAL Born 11/18/1940, Washington, DC, m, 1982, 3 children **DISCIPLINE** RELIGION, RELIGIOUS STUDIES **EDUCATION** Wesleyan Univ, BA, 62; Yale Div Sch, BD, 65; Harvard Univ Grad Sch, PhD, 70 **CAREER** Guest Prof, 98, Univ of Western Cape; Guest Prof, 91, Un Theol col; Guest Prof, 91-92, Ruprecht-Karls Universitat; Guest Prof, 77, Berea Col; Dir, 85-94, Candler Sch of Theol; Prof, 69-84, St Francis Sem Sch **MEMBERSHIPS** Am Acad of Relig; Soc of Christian Ethics **RESEARCH** Religion and society **SELECTED PUBLICATIONS** Auth, Religion, Federalism, and the Struggle for Public Life: Cases from Germany, India and America, Oxford Univ Press, 97; The Politics of Worship: Reforming the Language and Symbols of Liturgy, United Church Press, 99 **CONTACT ADDRESS** Andover Newton Theol Sch, Newton Centre, MA, 02459. **EMAIL** weverett@ants.edu

EVERSLEY, WALTER V.L.
DISCIPLINE THEOLOGY **EDUCATION** Moravian Col, BA, 69; Harvard Univ, MA, 74, PhD, 76; Columbia Univ, JD, 81. **CAREER** Dir, Interchurch Youth Org; British Civil Svc; admin, personnel dir, Ministry of Home Aff, 58-66; instr, Harvard Divinity Sch, 73-75; adj prof, New Brunswick Theol Sem, 75-86; adj prof, Col New Rochelle, 75-86; prof, NY Theol Sem, 75-86; assoc prof, 88-91; prof, Va Theol Sem, 91-. **HONORS AND AWARDS** Asst pastor, South Church, 69-72; assoc pastor, Church of All Nations, 72-75; pastor, John Hus Moravian Church, 75-85; org pastor, Grace Moravian Church, 77-80; org pastor, Brooklyn Moravian Fel, 85; org pastor, Faith Moravian Church of Nation's Capital, 85-88; priest assoc, St. Mary's Episcopal Church, 89-; **SELECTED PUBLICATIONS** Auth, The Willing Heart: A Theology of Evangelism for the Mainline Church; The Heart of the Priesthood, An Ordination Sermon, Va Sem Jour, 92. **CONTACT ADDRESS** Va Theol Sem, 3737 Seminary Rd, Alexandria, VA, 22304. **EMAIL** WEversley@vts.edu

EVNINE, SIMON
PERSONAL Born 12/06/1959, London, England, m, 1996 **DISCIPLINE** PHILOSOPHY **EDUCATION** Univ Calif Los Angeles, PhD, 96. **CAREER** Asst prof, Calif Poly, 96-. **MEMBERSHIPS** APA. **RESEARCH** Epistemology; Philosophy of logic; Philosophy of mind. **SELECTED PUBLICATIONS** Auth, Entry on Davidson, Companion to the Philosophers, Blackwell, 98; auth, Hume, Conjectural History, and the Uniformity of Human Nature, Jour of the Hist of Philos, 93; auth, Donald Davidson, Stanford Univ Press and Polity Press, 91; auth, Understanding Madness?, 89; auth, Freud's Ambiguous Concepts, Jour of Speculative Philos, 89; auth, Innate Principles and Radical Interpretation, The Locke Newsletter, 87. **CONTACT ADDRESS** Dept. of Philosophy, California Polytech State Univ, San Luis Obispo, CA, 93407. **EMAIL** sevnine@calpoly.edu

F

FABBRO, AMATA
PERSONAL Born 08/20/1928, Grand Rapids, MI **DISCIPLINE** RELIGIOUS STUDIES **EDUCATION** Aquinas Col, BA, 61; St Mary's Col, Ind, MA, 65, PhD(sacred scriptures & theol), 67. **CAREER** From instr to asst prof, 67-72, assoc prof scripture, Aquinas Col, 72-87, prof and dept head, 88-, head dept scriptures, Diocese of Grand Rapids Permanent Deaconate Prog, 71-80. **MEMBERSHIPS** Cath Bibl Soc Am; Cath Theol Soc Am; Col Theology Soc; Interfaith Dialogue Asn. **RESEARCH** Charismatic renewal in the Catholic Church; Old Testament typology. **SELECTED PUBLICATIONS** Co-auth with E. O'Connor a chapter in Perspectives on the Charismatic Renewal, 74; auth, paper on Women in the Ministerial Priesthood, presented for Scholar in Residence Weekend at Ahavis Israel Synagogue, Grand Rapids, Mi, 85; book review on Contemplation and the Charismatic Renewal by Paul Hennebusch, Spirituality for Today, 88; contrib to The Catholic Vision; several feature articles for The Catholic Connector. **CONTACT ADDRESS** Dept of Relig Studies, Aquinas Col, Michigan, 1607 Robinson Rd S E, Grand Rapids, MI, 49506-1799. **EMAIL** fabbrama@aquinas.edu

FACKENHEIM, EMIL
PERSONAL Born 06/22/1916, Halle, Germany **DISCIPLINE** PHILOSOPHY/RELIGION **EDUCATION** Univ Halle(Ger), 37-38; Aberdeen Univ, 39-40; Univ Toronto, PhD, 45. **CAREER** Ordained Rabbi, 39; Rabbi, Congregation Anshe Sholom, Hamilton, Ont, 43-48; lectr to prof, 48-81, PROF EMER PHILOSOPHY, UNIV TORONTO, 81-; vis prof, 81-84, fel, Inst Contemporary Jewry, Hebrew Univ, 86-; Newman Distinguished Fel, Int Inst Univ Stud Jewish Civilization, 85-86. **HONORS AND AWARDS** Guggenheim fel, 57-58; Killam fel, 77-78; LLD, Laurentian Univ, 69; LLD, Sir George Wiliams Univ, 71; DD, St Andrews Col, 72; DHuL, Hebrew Union, 74; LitD, Barry Col, 83. **MEMBERSHIPS** Central Conf Am Rabbis. **SELECTED PUBLICATIONS** Auth, Paths to Jewish belief, 60; auth, Metaphysics and Historicity, 61; auth, The Religious Dimension in Hegel's Thought, 68, 82; auth, Quest for Past and Future: Essays in Jewish Theology, 68; auth, God's Presence in History, 70, 72, 97; auth, Encounters Between Judaism and Modern Philosophy, 73, 94; auth, The Jewish Return Into History, 78; auth, To Mend the World: Foundations of Future Jewish Thought, 82, 89, 94; auth, What is Judaism, 87, 88; auth, The Jewish Bible After the Holocaust: A Re-Reading, 91; auth, The God Within: Kant, Schelling and Historicity, 96; auth, Jewish Philosophers and Jewish Philosophy, 96; co-ed, Jewish Philosophy and the Academy, 96. **CONTACT ADDRESS** 3/7 Elroi St, Jerusalem, ., 92108.

FACKRE, GABRIEL JOSEPH
PERSONAL Born 01/25/1926, Jersey City, NJ, m, 1945, 5 children **DISCIPLINE** THEOLOGY **EDUCATION** Univ Chicago, BD, 48, PhD, 62. **CAREER** Pastor, Duquesne-West Mifflin, Pa, 51-60; from asst prof to assoc prof hist theol & Christian ethics, 61-66, prof theol & cult, 66-71, Lancaster Theol Sem; prof theol, 71-80, Abbot Prof Christian Theol, 80-96, emeritus, 96-, Andover Newton Theol Sch; Am Asn Theol Schs sr res fel, Mansfield Col, Oxford Univ, 67-68; vis prof relig, Univ Hawaii, 70; vis scholar, Westminster-Cheshent Col, Cambridge Univ, 74-75; vis prof theol, Claremont Sch Theol, 76 & 80, Univ Theological Sem Va, 78; vis prof, Vancouver Sch Theol, 82, 87, 91; vis prof, Pittsburgh Theol Sem, 97. **MEMBERSHIPS** Am Theol Soc (pres, 90-91). **RESEARCH** Systematic theology; mission of the church; Christology. **SELECTED PUBLICATIONS** Auth, The Religious Right and Christian Faith, Eerdmans, 82; auth, The Christian Story, v.2, Eerdmans, 87; auth, Christian Basics, Eerdmans, 91, 94, 98; auth, The Doctrine of Revelation, Edinburgh, 97; auth, Discovering the Center, Intervarsity, 98; coauth, Affirmation and Admonition, Eerdmans, 98. **CONTACT ADDRESS** Andover Newton Theol Sch, 210 Herrick Rd, Newton Centre, MA, 02159. **EMAIL** fackre@juno.com

FACTOR, RALPH LANCE
PERSONAL Born 08/23/1944, Zanesville, OH, 2 children **DISCIPLINE** PHILOSOPHY **EDUCATION** Ohio State Univ, BA, 65; Univ Ga, MA, 67, PhD, 70. **CAREER** From Asst Prof to Assoc Prof, 69-85, Prof Philos, Knox Col, 85-; Danforth assoc, 73-79; assoc ed, Int J Philos of Relig, 73-85 & J Critical Anal, 77-80. **HONORS AND AWARDS** Phi Beta Kappa **MEMBERSHIPS** Central Div Am Philos Asn. **RESEARCH** Symbolic logic; philosophy of science; philosophy of religion. **SELECTED PUBLICATIONS** Auth, A note on the analysis of mass terms, Southern J Philos, 76; Newcomb's paradox and omniscience, Int J Philos of Relig, 77; Self deception and the functionalist theory of mental processes, Personalist, 77; Value Presuppositions in Science Textbooks, 80; Principle of Singular Difference, Southern J Philos, 82; What is the Logic in Buddhist logic?, Philos East & West, 82; Poetry and Logic of Abduction, 86; A Peircean Theory of Metaphor, 89; Points, Regions and Boundaries, 92; Mercator Decoded, 95. **CONTACT ADDRESS** Knox Col, Galesburg, IL, 61401. **EMAIL** lfactor@knox.knox.edu

FADNER, DONALD E.
PERSONAL m **DISCIPLINE** RELIGIOUS STUDIES **EDUCATION** Univ Chicago, PhD, 74. **CAREER** Assoc prof; Univ Wis-SP, 74-; letters & sci adv comt, 95-97; stud conduct hearing bd, 91-92. **SELECTED PUBLICATIONS** Auth, The Responsible God: A Study of the Christian Philosophy of H. Richard Niebuhr, Chico, Calif: Scholars Press for the Amer Acad Rel Dissertation Ser, 75. **CONTACT ADDRESS** Dept of Religious Studies, Univ Wis-SP, Stevens Point, WI, 54481. **EMAIL** dfadner@uwsp.edu

FAGAN, EILEEN M.
PERSONAL Born 04/20/1942, New York, NY, s **DISCIPLINE** SYSTEMATIC THEOLOGY **EDUCATION** Col Mount St. Vincent, BA, 70; Fordham Univ, MA, 89; PhD, 97. **CAREER** Relig and math teacher, Archbishop Stepinac High Sch, 80-88; adj asst prof, Marymount Col, 88-98; adj instr, St. John's Univ, 97; adj instr, Fairfield Univ, 98. **HONORS AND AWARDS** Outstanding Part-Time Teacher Award, Marymount Col, 92. **MEMBERSHIPS** Am Acad of Relig/Soc of Bibl Lit; Cath Bibl Asoc; Cath Theol Soc of Amer; Col Theol Soc. **RESEARCH** Liberation theology; Christology; ecclesiology. **SELECTED PUBLICATIONS** An Interpretation of Evangelization: Jon Sobrino's Christoloyg and Ecclesiology in Dialogue, 98; Foreword to Pillars of Catholic Social Teaching: In the Form of a Brief Social Catechism, 99. **CONTACT ADDRESS** 170 Truman Ave., Yonkers, NY, 10703-1022.

FAGER, JEFF
PERSONAL Born 11/04/1952, Redkey, IN, m, 1975 **DISCIPLINE** HEBREW BIBLE **EDUCATION** Univ Evansville, BA, 75; So Methodist Univ, MTh, 79; Vanderbilt Univ, PhD, 87. **CAREER** Prof relig and philos, Kentucky Wesleyan Col, 86- . **MEMBERSHIPS** Soc of Bibl Lit; Am Acad of Relig. **RESEARCH** Ethics of the Hebrew Bible. **SELECTED PUBLICATIONS** Auth, Land Tenure in the Biblical Jubilee: A Moral World View, Hebrew Annual Rev, 88; auth, Back to the Past: Two Instances of Mentoring in the Hebrew Bible, Int J of Mentoring, 88; auth, Land Tenure and the Biblical Jubilee: Discovering a Moral World View through the Sociology of Knowledge, Sheffield Academic, 93; auth, Chaos and the Deborah Tradition, Q Rev, 93; auth, Miriam and Deborah: Legends of women in Power in an Ancient Patriarchal Society, Bible Tod, 94; auth, rev of Janzen, Old Testament Ethics: A Paradigmatic Approach, Princeton Sem Bull, 95; auth, book note on Habel, The Land is Mine: Six Biblican Land Ideologies, Theol Today, 96. **CONTACT ADDRESS** Kentucky Wesleyan Col, PO Box 1039, Owensboro, KY, 42302-1039. **EMAIL** jeffreyf@kwc.edu

FAIN, HASKELL
PERSONAL Born 07/01/1926, New York, NY, m, 1949 **DISCIPLINE** PHILOSOPHY **EDUCATION** Univ Ill, BS, 48, MA, 49; Univ Calif, MA, 51, PhD (philos), 56. **CAREER** Assoc prof, 56-57, chmn dept, 68-70 and 72-73, PROF PHILOS, UNIV WIS-MADISON, 67-, Fulbright lectr, Univ Bergen, 61-62; vis assoc prof, Univ BC, 63-64; prof, Fla State Univ, 70-71; vis fel, Linacre Col, Oxford Univ, 66-67, vis lectr, 67; consult, Empire State Col, 72-73; Nat Endowment for Humanities fel, 75-. **MEMBERSHIPS** Am Philos Asn. **RESEARCH** Social and political philosophy; philosophy of the social sciences; philosophy of history. **SELECTED PUBLICATIONS** Auth, Plausible Worlds--Possibility and Understanding in History and the Social Sciences, Hist Theory, Vol 32, 93. **CONTACT ADDRESS** Dept of Philos, Univ of Wis, Madison, WI, 53706.

FAINSTEIN, LISA
DISCIPLINE LAW **EDUCATION** Univ Manitoba, BA, 76; LLB, 79. **CAREER** Asst prof, 81-. **RESEARCH** Legal methods, property law, family law. **SELECTED PUBLICATIONS** Co-ed, Manitoba Queen's Bench Act and Rules, Annotated, 89; Introduction to Motions Court, 89; Equality Issues in Family Law: Considerations for Test Case Litigation. **CONTACT ADDRESS** Fac of Law, Univ Manitoba, Robson Hall, Winnipeg, MB, R3T 2N2. **EMAIL** lfainst@cc.umanitoba.ca

FAIR, BRYAN K.
DISCIPLINE LAW **EDUCATION** Duke Univ, BA, 82; UCLA, JD,85. **CAREER** Prof, Univ Ala, 91-. **RESEARCH** Constitutional law, civil rights, and women and the law. **SELECTED PUBLICATIONS** Auth, Notes of a Racial Caste Baby: Color Blindness and the End of Affirmative Action, NYU Press, 96. **CONTACT ADDRESS** Law Dept, Univ of Alabama, Box 870000, Tuscaloosa, AL, 35487-0383. **EMAIL** bfair@law.ua.edu

FAIR, FRANK KENNETH
PERSONAL Born 06/19/1944, Tallahassee, FL, m, 1967, 2 children **DISCIPLINE** PHILOSOPHY **EDUCATION** Xavier Univ, AB, 66; Boston Col, MA, 68; Univ Ga, PhD(philos), 71. **CAREER** From Asst Prof to Assoc Prof, 71-87, Prof Philos, Sam Houston State Univ, 87-. **MEMBERSHIPS** Am Philos Asn; Philos Sci Asn; Southern Soc Philos &, Psychol; Southwestern Philos Soc; AAAS. **RESEARCH** Philosophy of science; contemporary moral problems. **SELECTED PUBLICATIONS** Auth, The fallacy of many questions: Or, How to stop beating your wife, Southwestern J Philos, spring 74; J J Katz' logic of questions: New departure or dead end?, Philos Studies, 4/75; Two problems with Chisholm's Perceiving, Philos & Phenomenol Res, 6/76; On interpreting a philosophy of science: A response to Gareth Nelson, Syst Zool, 3/77; coauth, Morality on the Line: The Role of Ethics in Police Decision Making, Am J of Police, Vol X, No 2, 91. **CONTACT ADDRESS** Dept of Psychol & Philos, Sam Houston State Univ, P O Box 2447, Huntsville, TX, 77341-2447. **EMAIL** psy.fkf@shsu.edu

FAIRCHILD, MARK R.
PERSONAL Born 07/23/1954, Corry, PA, m, 1978, 4 children **DISCIPLINE** BIBLICAL STUDIES; NEW TESTAMENT; GREEK **EDUCATION** Pa State Univ, BS, bio, 76; Toccoa Falls Col, BA, bible & theol, 80; Asbury Theol Sem, M Div, spec curricul, 82; Drew Univ, M Phil, bibl studies, 85; Drew Univ, PhD, new testament studies, 89. **CAREER** Assoc prof, bible & relig, Huntington Col, 86-. **HONORS AND AWARDS** Huntington Col, teacher of the yr, 96-97. **MEMBERSHIPS** Soc of Bibl Lit; Cath Bibl Asn; Evangel Theol Soc. **RESEARCH** Gospels; Q research; Intertestamental literature. **SELECTED PUBLICATIONS** Rev, Jesus Under Fire: Modern Scholarship Reinvents the Historical Jesus, Christ Scholar's Rev, vol 25, 525-528, 96; rev, Mercer Dictionary of the Bible, Jour of the Evangel Theol Soc, vol 38, 250-251, 95; rev, The Lost Gospel: The Book of Q and Christian Origins, Christ Scholars Rev, vol 24, 93-95, 94; rev, Luke 1-9:20, vol 35A, Word Biblical Commentary, Jour of the Evangel Theol Soc, vol 37, 431-432, 94; rev, Sociology and the Jesus Movement, Jour of the Evangel Theol Soc, vol 37, 427-429, 94; rev, The Nag Hammadi Library in English, Jour of the Evangel Theol Soc, vol 37, 438-439, 94; rev, The NIV Compact Dictionary of the Bible, Jour of the Evangel Theol Soc, vol 37, 134-135, 94; rev, The Formation of Q: Trajectories in Ancient Wisdom Collections, Jour of the Evangel Theol Soc, vol 34, 123-24, 91; rev, The Evidence for Jesus, Jour of the Evangel Theol Soc, vol 31, 473-74, 88; auth, History and the Historical Jesus in the Nag Hammadi Literature, The Asbury Seminarian, vol 37, 4-17, 82. **CONTACT ADDRESS** 1531 Avon Pl., Huntington, IN, 46750. **EMAIL** mfairchi@huntington.edu

FAKHRID-DEEN, NASHID ABDULLAH
PERSONAL Born 02/24/1949, Monticello, Arkansas, m **DISCIPLINE** THEOLOGY **EDUCATION** Grand Valley State Univ, BA 1978; Western MI Univ, grad work 1978-79; Univ of Baltimore, School of Law, JD 1984-88. **CAREER** Nation of Islam, minister 1975-79; Grand Valley State Univ, asst dir of talent search 1980-83, asst dir of admissions 1979-83; Bowie State Univ, coordinator of recruitment, assoc dir of admissions 1988-90; Kentucky State University, Frankfort, KY, exec asst to the pres 1990-91; Kentucky State Univ, exec asst to the pres, 1990-91; Ohio Univ, coordinator minority student affairs, 1992-94; Univ of Kentucky Commun Coll System, coordinator minority affairs community college system, 1994-. **HONORS AND AWARDS** Outstanding Community Service World Community of Islam 1981, 1982; Grand Valley St Univ, Outstanding Service Talent Search Prgm 1983; Office of Admissions, Outstanding Service Award 1983; Outstanding Community Service, 1980-82; Charles Hamilton Houston Award, Univ of Baltimore Black Law Students Assn 1988; Freedom Fighter Award, NAACP, Bowie State University Chapter, 1991. Ohio Univ, Asante Award, 1993, Romeo Award, 1993; Hopeville Community Coll, Significant Contribution Award to Project PARADE, 1995. **MEMBERSHIPS** General business mgr Nation of Islam 1972-76; mem bd dirs Climbing Tree School 1977-78; mem bd dirs Family Services Outreach 1982-83; mem Mid-America Assn of Educ Oppor Program Personnel; Exec Council Black Law Students, Univ of Baltimore; Admissions/Retention Committee; Moot Court Board, 1986-88; Developer/presentator of CARE (motivational workshop), Baltimore/Washington Metro Area; pres, Black Law Students Assn, Univ of Baltimore School of Law 1987-88. **CONTACT ADDRESS** Executive to the President, Kentucky State Univ, Hume Hall, Lexington, KY, 40514.

FALES, EVAN MICHAEL
PERSONAL Born 12/10/1943, Bryn Mawr, PA, 2 children **DISCIPLINE** PHILOSOPHY **EDUCATION** Haverford Col, BA, 64; Temple Univ, MA, 71, PhD, 74. **CAREER** Asst prof, 74-79, Assoc Prof Philos, Univ Iowa, 79- **MEMBERSHIPS** Am Philos Asn; Philos Sci Asn. **RESEARCH** Philosophy of science; metaphysics; epistemology; philosophy of religion. **SELECTED PUBLICATIONS** Auth, Truth, tradition and rationality, 6/76 & The ontology of social roles, 6/77, Philos Social Sci; Essentialism and the Elementary Constituents of Matter, MidWest Studies in Philos XI, 86; Causation and Universals, 90; Divine Freedom and the Choice of a World, Int J Philos of Relig 35, 94; A Defense of the Given, 96; Plantinga's Case Against Naturalistic Epistemology, Philos Sci 63, 96; Scientific Explanations of Mystical Experience, Parts I & II, Relig Studies 32, 96. **CONTACT ADDRESS** Dept of Philos, Univ of Iowa, 269 English Phil Bld, Iowa City, IA, 52242-1408.

FALK, ARTHUR
PERSONAL Born 05/28/1938, New York, NY, m, 1967, 2 children **DISCIPLINE** PHILOSOPHY **EDUCATION** Fordham Univ, BA, 60; Yale Univ. **CAREER** Western Mich Univ, prof 64- , dept chemn 87-93. **HONORS AND AWARDS** Fulbright vis lectr to India, 84 **MEMBERSHIPS** APA **RESEARCH** Evolutionary semiotics **SELECTED PUBLICATIONS** Auth, Ifs and Newcombs, in: the Philo's Annual, 87; Wisdom Updates, Philo of Science, 95, Essays on Natures Semeiosis, Jour Philo Research, 95; Gaia = Maya, Hist and Philo of Life Sciences, 95; William's Domains and Reductionism, in: Quart Rev of Bio, 97; The Judger in Russell's Theories of Judgement, Russell: the Jour of the Bertrand Russell Archives, 97-98. **CONTACT ADDRESS** Dept of Philosophy, Western Michigan Univ, 1201 Oliver St, Kalamazoo, MI, 49008-5022. **EMAIL** falk@wmich.edu

FALK, ARTHUR EUGENE
PERSONAL Born 05/28/1938, New York, NY, 2 children **DISCIPLINE** PHILOSOPHY OF SCIENCE, EPISTEMOLOGY **EDUCATION** Fordham Univ, AB, 60; Yale Univ, MA, 62, PhD, 65. **CAREER** From instr to assoc prof, 64-77, Prof Philos, Western Mich Univ, 77- **RESEARCH** Philosophy of social sciences; theory of knowledge. **SELECTED PUBLICATIONS** Coauth, Computerized help in finding logic proofs, Proc 1972 Conf Comput in Undergrad Curricula, 72; A language acquisition program for the retarded, In: Language Intervention With the Retarded, 72; auth, QUINC, On Line, 72; Learning to report one's introspections, Philos Sci, 75; The state of the question about fate, Philos Res Arch, Vol 6, No 4; Some modal confusions in compatibilism, Am Philos Quart, 4/81; Purpose, feedback and evolution, Philos of Sci, 6/81. **CONTACT ADDRESS** Dept of Philos, Western Michigan Univ, 1201 Oliver St, Kalamazoo, MI, 49008-3805. **EMAIL** falk@wmich.edu

FALK, NANCY ELLEN
PERSONAL Born 09/03/1938, Bethlehem, PA, m, 1967, 2 children **DISCIPLINE** HISTORY OF RELIGIONS **EDUCATION** Cedar Crest Col, AB, 60; Univ Chicago, AM, 63, PhD(hist of relig), 72. **CAREER** Asst prof, 66-71, assoc prof, 71-79, chmn dept, 72-75, PROF RELIG, WESTERN MICH UNIV, 79-. **HONORS AND AWARDS** Fulbright, India, 84-85; AIIS sr fel, 91-92. **MEMBERSHIPS** Am Acad Relig; Asia Soc **RESEARCH** South Asian religion; women in religion. **SELECTED PUBLICATIONS** Co-ed (with Rita M Gross), Unspoken worlds: Women's religious lives in non-Western cultures, 80; auth, Women in Religion: An Annotated Bibliography of Sources in English, 1975-1992, 94. **CONTACT ADDRESS** Dept of Comp Relig, Western Michigan Univ, 1201 Oliver St, Kalamazoo, MI, 49008-3805. **EMAIL** nancy.falk@wmich.edu

FALKENSTEIN, LORNE
DISCIPLINE PHILOSOPHY **EDUCATION** Univ Toronto, PhD. **RESEARCH** History of 18th century philosophy. **SELECTED PUBLICATIONS** Auth, Kant's Intuitionism, Toronto, 95; Intuition and Construction in Berkeley's Account of Visual Space, Jour Hist Philos, 94; Was Kant a Nativist?, Jour Hist Philos, 90; Hume on Manners of Disposition and the Ideas of Space and Time, 77; Naturalism, Normativity, and Scepticism in Hume's Account of Belief, Hume Stud, 77. **CONTACT ADDRESS** Dept of Philosophy, Western Ontario Univ, London, ON, N6A 5B8. **EMAIL** lfalkens@julian.uwo.ca

FALLDING, HAROLD J.
PERSONAL Born 05/03/1923, Cessnock, Australia **DISCIPLINE** SOCIOLOGY/RELIGION **EDUCATION** Univ Sydney, BS, 50, BA, 51, Dip Ed, 52, MA, 55; Australian Nat Univ, PhD, 57. **CAREER** High sch tchr, Australia, 52-53; sr res fel, Univ Sydney, 56-58; sr lectr, Univ NSW, 59-62; vis assoc prof, grad sch Rutgers, State Univ NJ, 63-65; prof sociol, 65-88, DISTINGUISHED PROF EMER, UNIV WATERLOO, 89-. **MEMBERSHIPS** Clare Hall, Cambridge Univ; Stratford Shakespearean Found Can; Am Sociol Asn; Can Soc Sociol Anthrop; Asn Sociol Relig; Int Sociol Asn; Int Conf Sociol Relig; Can Inst Int Affairs. **SELECTED PUBLICATIONS** Auth, The Sociological Task, 68; auth, The Sociology of Religion: An Explanation of the Unity and Diversity in Religion, 74; auth, Drinking, Community and Civilization: The Account of a New Jersey Interview Study, 74; auth, The Social Process Revisited: Achieving Human Interests through Alliance and Opposition, 90; auth, Collected Poetry, 97. **CONTACT ADDRESS** 40 Arbordale Walk, Guelph, ON, N1G 4X7.

FALLER, THOMPSON MASON
PERSONAL Born 04/26/1938, Louisville, KY, m, 1969, 1 child **DISCIPLINE** PHILOSOPHY **EDUCATION** St Mary's Col, Ky, BA, 62; Xavier Univ, Ohio, MA, 64; Univ Salzburg, PhD, 69. **CAREER** From instr to asst prof, 64-73, assoc prof, 73-80, prof philos, Univ Portland, 80-, Danforth assoc, 76; Fulbright fel. **HONORS AND AWARDS** Outstanding Educr Am; Clifford Campbell Award; Culligan Award; Knight Holy Sepulchre; Pilgrim Shell. **MEMBERSHIPS** Am Philos Asn (pres, 75-76); Am Cath Philos Asn; AAUP. **RESEARCH** Justice; love; phenomenology of Franz Brentano. **SELECTED PUBLICATIONS** Auth, Augustin: Ein Philosoph, Salzburg Jahrbuch fuer Philos, 69; Challenges for today's philosophers, Univ Portland Rev, fall 77; Educating the Magnanimous Person, Univ Portland Rev; The Proper Limits of Reason as a Natural Law, Vera Lex; Ownership of our Schools, NEA Notes; Goals

200 and the School Board, Vera Lex. **CONTACT ADDRESS** Dept of Philos, Univ Portland, 5000 N Willamette, Portland, OR, 97203-5798. **EMAIL** faller@up.edu

FANT, GENE C., JR.
PERSONAL Born 06/30/1963, Laurel, MS, m, 1989, 2 children **DISCIPLINE** THEOLOGY/EDUCATION **EDUCATION** James Madison Univ, BS, 84-; Old Dominion Univ, MA, 87; New Orleans Baptist Theolog Sem, Mdiv, 91; Univ Southern Miss, MED, 95, PhD, 95. **CAREER** Asst dir, Univ Southern Miss, 94-95; asst prof, dir, Miss Col, 95-. **HONORS AND AWARDS** Dave-Maher Prize, 94; Linwood Orange Award & Fel, 94; Who's Who in the World, 99., Doctoral Fel, USM. **MEMBERSHIPS** MLA; SCMLA; Conf on Christianity and Lit; Miss Philol Asn; Int Arthurian Society. **RESEARCH** Medieval/Renaissance English literature; Bible as literature; popular culture. **SELECTED PUBLICATIONS** Auth, Petrarchan Hagiography, Gender, and Subjectivity in Mary Wroth's Pamphilia to Amphilanthus, 95; auth, art, Pun's on the Name of the Beloved in Wroth's Pamphilia to Amphilanthus, 96; auth, art, Peachwood Remembered: The Photography of Marian Stark Gaines, 97; auth, art, John Stewart Bryan, Eugene S. Pulliam, Theodore Lothrop Stoddard, 98; coauth, Expectant Moments, 99. **CONTACT ADDRESS** Mississippi Col, PO Box 4022, Clinton, MS, 39058. **EMAIL** fant@mc.edu

FARAH, CAESAR E.
PERSONAL Born 03/13/1929, Portland, OR, m, 1987, 7 children **DISCIPLINE** HISTORY, RELIGION **EDUCATION** Stanford Univ, BA, 52; Princeton Univ, MA, 55, PhD, 57. **CAREER** Pub aff asst & educ exchange attache, US Info Serv, Delhi & Karachi, 57-59; asst prof hist & Near E lang, Portland State Col, 59-63; consult US Army 62-63; asst prof hist, Los Angeles State Col, 63-64; vis prof Harvard Univ 64-65; assoc prof Near Eastern lang & lit, Ind Univ, Bloomington, 64-69; prof Middle Eastern Studies, Univ Minn, Minneapolis, 69-, Consult, spec oper res off, Am Univ, 60; cult attache's comt, Arab Embassies in Washington, DC, 61; consult, col bks div, Am Libr Asn, 64-; Ford Found grant, 66-67; guest lectr Arabic Ottoman rels, Lebanese Univ, 66 & Univ Baghdad, 67; Fulbright award, Turkey, 67-68; Am Philos Soc res grant, 70-71; guest lectr For Min Spain, Iraq, Lebanon, Iran; Min Higher Educ Saudi Arabia, Yemen, Kuwait, Qatar, Tunisia, Morocco; Syrian Acad Sci, Acad Scis Beijing; vis scholar Cambridge Univ 74; rsrc person on Middle East svc gp MN, 77; bd dir chemn Upper Midwest Consortium for Middle East Outreach, 80-; vis prof Sanaa Univ, Yemen, 84, Karl-Franzens Univ, Austria, 90, Ludwig_Maximilian Univ, Munich, 92-93; exec secy ed Am Inst Yemeni Stud 82-86; secy-gen exec bd dir Int Comt for Pre-Ottoman & Ottoman Studies, 88-; fel Res Ctr Islamic Hist, Istanbul, 93; Ctr Lebanese Stydues & St Anthony Col, Oxford, Eng, 94; vis Fulbright-Hays scholar Univ Damascus, 94. **HONORS AND AWARDS** Cert of Merit Syrian Min Higher Educ, 66-67; Stanford Univ Alumni Asn Ldr Recognition Award. **MEMBERSHIPS** Am Orient Soc; Am Asn Arabic Studies; AHA; Royal Asiatic Soc; MidE Studies Asn NAm; Asn Tchr Arabic; Turkish Studies Asn; Pi Sigma Alpha; Phi Alpha Theta. **RESEARCH** Modern Arab world, sociopolitical changes; Islamic religion and mysticism; the West and the Arab world in the 19th century. **SELECTED PUBLICATIONS** The Lebanese uprising of 1840 and the powers, J Asian Hist, 68; The Addendum in Medieval Arabic Historiography, 68; Eternal Message of Muhammad, 3rd edition, 64; Ibn-al-Najjar, Encycl of Islam, 68; Necib Pasa and the British in Syria, Archivum Ottomanicum, Budapest & Leiden, 72; Islam and revitalization, Quartet, London, 80; The quadruple alliance and proposed Ottoman reforms in Syria, 1839-41, Int J Turkish Studies II, 81; Tarikh Baghdad Ii-Ibn-al-Najjar, 80-83, 3 vols 2 edit 86; Al-Ghazali on Abstinence in Islam, 92; Decision Making in the Ottoman Empire, 92; The Road to Intervention: Fiscal Policies in Ottoman Mount Lebanon, 92; The Politics of Interventionism in Ottoman Lebanon, 2 vols, 97. **CONTACT ADDRESS** Afro-American Studies, Univ of Minnesota, Twin Cities, 267 19th Ave S, Minneapolis, MN, 55455-0499. **EMAIL** farah001@maroon.tc.umn.edu

FARBER, DANIEL ALAN
PERSONAL Born 07/16/1950, Chicago, IL, m, 1971, 1 child **DISCIPLINE** LAW **EDUCATION** Univ Ill, BA, 71, MA, 72, JD, 75. **CAREER** Asst prof, Univ Ill, 78-81; assoc prof to prof Law, Univ Minn, 81-95; prof, Univ Minn, 96-. **RESEARCH** Law and economics; constitutional law; environmental law. **SELECTED PUBLICATIONS** Auth, The First Amendment, Found Press, 98; Eco-Pragmatism: Making Sensible Environmental Decision in an Uncertain World, 99. **CONTACT ADDRESS** Law Sch, Univ Minn, 229 19th Ave S, Minneapolis, MN, 55455-0401. **EMAIL** farbe001@tc.umn.edu

FARLEY, BENJAMIN WIRT
PERSONAL Born 08/06/1935, Manila, Philippines, m, 1962, 2 children **DISCIPLINE** HISTORICAL THEOLOGY, PHILOSOPHY **EDUCATION** Davidson Col, AB, 58; Union Theol Sem, Va, BD, 63, ThM, 64, ThD, 76. **CAREER** Pastor, Franklin Presby Church, 64-68 & Cove & Rockfish Presby Churches, 68-71; instr relig, Lees-McRae Col, 73-74; assoc prof to Younts Prof Bible, Religion, and Philos, Erskine Col, 74-. **HONORS AND AWARDS** Excellence in Teaching Award, Erskine Col, 77. **MEMBERSHIPS** Am Acad Refig; pres 97-99, Calvin Studies Soc. **RESEARCH** Reformation studies; philosophy of religion; literature and religion. **SELECTED PUBLICATIONS** Auth, Erskine Caldwell: Preacher's son and Southern prophet, fall 78 & George W Cable: Presbyterian Romancer, Reformer Bible Teacher, summer 80, J Presby Hist; John Calvin's Sermons on the Ten Commandments, 81 & Calvin's Treatises Against the Anabaptists and the Libertines, 82, Baker Book House; The Hero of St Lo and Other Stories, Attic Press, 82; The Providence of God, Baker Book House, 88; Calvin's Ecclesiastical Advice, Westminster/John Knox Press, 91; In Praise of Virtue, Eerdmans, 95; Mercy Road, Cherokee Publishing Co, 86; Corbin's Rubi-Yacht, Sandlapper Press, 92. **CONTACT ADDRESS** Erskine Col, Hc 60, PO Box 595, Due West, SC, 29639-9801. **EMAIL** farley@erskine.edu

FARLEY, MARGARET ANN
PERSONAL Born 04/15/1935, St. Cloud, MN **DISCIPLINE** ETHICS **EDUCATION** Univ Detroit, AB, 57, MA, 60; Yale Univ, MPhil, 70, PhD (relig studies), 73. **CAREER** Asst prof philos, Mercy Col Detroit, 62-67; ASSOC PROF ETHICS, YALE UNIV, 71-, Danforth teacher grant, 67-69; Kent fel, 69-71; pres, bd dir, Network, 77-79. **MEMBERSHIPS** Am Acad Relig; Soc Christian Ethics; Cath Theol Soc Am. **RESEARCH** Medical ethics; history of theological ethics; women's studies. **SELECTED PUBLICATIONS** Auth, A Feminist Version of Respect for Persons, J Feminist Stud Rel, Vol 9, 93. **CONTACT ADDRESS** Divinity Sch, Yale Univ, 409 Prospect St, New Haven, CT, 06510.

FARMER, CRAIG S.
PERSONAL Born 10/02/1961, Urbana, IL, m, 1982, 2 children **DISCIPLINE** HISTORY OF CHRISTIANITY **EDUCATION** Haverford Col, BA, 83; Univ Chicago, MA, 84; Duke Univ, PhD, 92. **CAREER** Asst prof of history and humanities, 93-98; assoc prof of hist and humanities, 98-present, Milligan Col. **MEMBERSHIPS** Amer Soc of Church Hist; Amer Acad of Relig; Medieval Acad of Amer; Sixteenth Century Studies Conf. **RESEARCH** Reformation theology; hist of biblical interpretation. **SELECTED PUBLICATIONS** Auth, Changing Images of the Samaritan Woman in Early Reformed Commentaries on John, Church History, 96; Eucharistic Exhibition and Sacramental Presence in the New Testament Commentaries of Wolfgang Musculus, Wolfgang Musculus, 97; The Gospel of John in the Sixteenth Century: The Johannine Exegesis of Wolfgang Musculus, The Oxford Studies in Historical Theology, Oxford University Press, 97. **CONTACT ADDRESS** Milligan Col, Milligan College, TN, 37682. **EMAIL** csfarmer@milligan.edu

FARMER, EDWARD L.
DISCIPLINE HISTORY; PHILOSOPHY **EDUCATION** Stanford Univ, BA, 57; Harvard Univ, MA, 62, PhD, 68. **CAREER** Fulbright fel, Taiwan, 65-67; prof, Univ Minn Twin Cities, 68-. **HONORS AND AWARDS** Ed, Ming Studies, 75-85. **RESEARCH** Comparative early modern history; Ming institutions; social legislation. **SELECTED PUBLICATIONS** Auth, Early Ming Government: The Evolution of Dual Capitals, Harvard, 76; co-auth, Comparative History of Civilizations in Asia, 77; A World History: Links Across Time and Space, 87; ed, Encyclopedia of Asian History, 88. **CONTACT ADDRESS** History Dept, Univ of Minnesota, Twin Cities, 614 Social Sciences Tower, 267 19th Ave. S, Minneapolis, MN, 55455. **EMAIL** farme001@tc.umn.edu

FARNSWORTH, EDWARD ALLAN
PERSONAL Born 06/30/1928, Providence, RI, m, 1952, 4 children **DISCIPLINE** LAW **EDUCATION** Univ Mich, BS, 48; Yale Univ, MA, 49; Columbia Univ, LLB, 52. **CAREER** From asst prof to prof, 54-70, ALFRED MCCORMACK PROF LAW, LAW SCH, COLUMBIA UNIV, 70-, Vis prof, Univ Istanbul, 60; Ford fel, France, 61; vis prof, Univ Chicago, 63; consult, Ford Found, Dakar, Senegal, 63-64; dir orientation prog Am law, Asn Am Law Schs, 65-67; US rep, Comt Int Inst Unificatio Pvt Law, Rome, 67; chmn comt foreign and comp law, Asn Bar City New York, 67-70; vis prof Law Sch, Harvard Univ, 70-71; US deleg, UN Comn Int Trade Law, 70-80; reporter, Restatement (Second) of Contracts, 71 80; vis prof, Univ Paris, 74-75; US deleg dipt conf on Int Agency, Bucharest, 79; PVT LAW, ROME, 79-. **MEMBERSHIPS** Am Bar Asn; Am Law Inst. **RESEARCH** Commercial law; contracts. **SELECTED PUBLICATIONS** Auth, A Common Lawyers View of his Civilian Colleagues, Louisiana Law Rev, Vol 57, 96; Promises to Make Gifts, Am J Comparative Law, Vol 43, 95; Contract Law in a Changing World, Am J Comparative Law, Vol 40, 92. **CONTACT ADDRESS** Law Sch Bldg, Columbia Univ, 435 W 116th St, New York, NY, 10027-7201.

FARQUHAR, KEITH
DISCIPLINE LAW **EDUCATION** Wellington Univ, LLB, 64; LLM, 67; Univ Mich, LLM, 68. **CAREER** Assoc prof, 76-90; prof, 90-. **HONORS AND AWARDS** Ed, Can Jour Family Law. **RESEARCH** Family law; matrimonial property; trusts and estates; private international law. **SELECTED PUBLICATIONS** Auth, pubs about family law and trusts. **CONTACT ADDRESS** Fac of Law, Univ British Columbia, 1822 East Mall, Vancouver, BC, V6T 1Z1. **EMAIL** farquhar@law.ubc.ca

FARRELL, FRANK
DISCIPLINE CHURCH HISTORY **EDUCATION** Edinburgh Univ, PhD. **CAREER** Instr, Alliance Theol Sem; prof. **HONORS AND AWARDS** Founding ed, Christianity Today. **RESEARCH** Puritans. **SELECTED PUBLICATIONS** Ed-in-Chief, World Vision mag. **CONTACT ADDRESS** Dept of Church History, Reformed Theol Sem, 1015 Maitland Ctr Commons, Maitland, FL, 32751.

FARRELL, HOBERT K.
PERSONAL Born 02/15/1939, Charleston, WV, m, 1962, 2 children **DISCIPLINE** BIBLICAL STUDIES **EDUCATION** Wheaton Col, BA, 61, MA, 64; Gordon-Conwell Theol Sem, BD, 64; Union Theol Sem, ThM, 66; Boston Univ, PhD, 72. **CAREER** Instr Greek, Boston Univ, 67-71; prof Bibl Studies, John Wesley Col, 71-78; prof Bibl Studies, Le Tourneau Univ, 78-. **MEMBERSHIPS** Soc Bibl Lit; Inst Bibl Res; Evangel Theol Soc. **RESEARCH** Luke; Acts. **SELECTED PUBLICATIONS** Auth, The Structure and Theology of Lake's Central Section, Trin Jour, 86. **CONTACT ADDRESS** Dept of Biblical Studies, Le Tourneau Univ, PO Box 7001, Longview, TX, 75607. **EMAIL** farrellh@letu.edu

FARTHING, JOHN L.
DISCIPLINE RELIGION AND CLASSICAL LANGUAGES **EDUCATION** Univ Tulsa, BA, 69; Duke Univ, MDiv, 74, PhD, 78. **CAREER** Prof Relig and Clas Lang, 78, ch, dept Relig, Hendrix Col. **RESEARCH** Medieval, Reformation, and Renaissance theology. **SELECTED PUBLICATIONS** Auth, Thomas Aquinas and Gabriel Biel; transl, Jean-Claude Margolin, auth, Humanism in Europe at the Time of the Renaissance. **CONTACT ADDRESS** Hendrix Col, Conway, AR, 72032.

FASANARO, CHARLES N.
PERSONAL Born 10/25/1943, New York, NY **DISCIPLINE** PHILOSOPHY **EDUCATION** Manhattan Col, BS, 65; Iliff Sch of Theol, MAR, 80; Univ Denver, PhD, 83. **CAREER** Philos dept, 80-85, writing prog and asst to dir, 85-91, Univ of Colo, Boulder; prof, Center for Study of Philos and Relig, 83; prof, St. John's Col, 91-. **HONORS AND AWARDS** Univ Colo tchg award; Alumni of the Year, Iliff Sch of Theol; R. L. Stearns Award for outstanding fac achievement. **MEMBERSHIPS** APA; AAR. **RESEARCH** Philosophy of religion; comparative philosophy; ethics; theology and science. **SELECTED PUBLICATIONS** Auth, Velocities of Rage, Cadmus, 83; auth, Fellowship of Reconciliation, Music and the Vietnam War, Buddhists, in Tucker, ed, The Vietnam War: An Encyclopedia, Garland, 95; auth, Hunting with the Moon, Pinon Hill, 97. **CONTACT ADDRESS** PO Box 8242, Santa Fe, NM, 87504-8242. **EMAIL** cnfasanaro@aol.com

FATE NORTON, DAVID
DISCIPLINE PHILOSOPHY **EDUCATION** Claremont Grad Sch, MA; Univ Calif San Diego, PhD. **RESEARCH** Early modern philosophy; Hume. **SELECTED PUBLICATIONS** Auth, How a Sceptic May Live Scepticism, Faith, Scepticism and Personal Identity, Univ Alberta, 94; auth, David Hume: Common-Sense Moralist, Sceptical Metaphysician, Princeton Univ, 82; co-auth, The David Hume Library, 95; ed, The Cambridge Companion to Hume, Cambridge, 93. **CONTACT ADDRESS** Philosophy Dept, McGill Univ, 845 Sherbrooke St, Montreal, PQ, H3A 2T5.

FAULCONER, JAMES E.
PERSONAL Born 09/27/1947, Warrensburg, MO, m, 1970, 4 children **DISCIPLINE** CONTINENTAL PHILOSOPHY **EDUCATION** Brigham Young Univ, BA, 71; PA State Univ, MA, 75, PhD, 77. **CAREER** From Instr to Assoc Prof, 75-93, prof philos, Brigham Young Univ, 93, Karl G. Maeser Gen Educ Prof, 91-94, Assoc Dean, 94-97, Actg Dean, 97-98, Dean, Gen Educ & Honors, 98; Vis Prof, Inst Philos, Cath Univ Leuven Belgium, 95-96; Ed, Epoch: A Journal for the Hist Philos. **HONORS AND AWARDS** Designated "University Scholar" at graduation, Brigham Young Univ, 72; graduated "High Honors with Distinction", BYU, 72; Prof of the Month, Assoc Students BYU and Blue Key Honor Soc, 10/80; Outstanding Tchr Award, Philos Dept, Student Alumni Asn, BYU, 85, 94, 97; Honors Prof of the Year, BYU, 88; Alcuin Gen Educ Fel, BYU, 88-91; P.A. Christenson Lectr, Col Humanities, BYU, 91; Thursday Lectr, Cath Univ Leuven, Belgium, 2/96. **MEMBERSHIPS** Soc Phenomenol & Existential Philos; Heidegger Conf NAm; Am Philos Asn; Collegium Phenomenologicum; Int Phenomenol Symposium. **RESEARCH** The nature of community: philosophical anthrop as it relates to the phenomenon of community; the philos of psychol. **SELECTED PUBLICATIONS** Coauth, Introduction to Logic, D. Van Nostrand, 80; Reconsidering Psychology: Perspectives from Contemporary Continental Philosophy, Duquesne Univ Press, 90; auth, Newton, Science, and Causation, J Mind & Behavior, Winter 95; The Uncanny Interruption of Ethics: Gift, Interruption, or..., The Grad Fac Philos J, 97; Tools for Scripture Study, FARMS, 98; Levinas and the Unconscious, Levinas and the Philosophy of Psychology ; Scripture as Incarnation, Brigham Young Univ ; auth of numerous other articles and bk chapters. **CONTACT ADDRESS** Dept of Philos, Brigham Young Univ, 3196 Jkhb, Provo, UT, 84602-6279. **EMAIL** james_falconer@byu.edu

FAUPEL, WILLIAM
PERSONAL Born 05/28/1944, Cass City, MI, m, 1992, 2 children **DISCIPLINE** THEOLOGY **EDUCATION** Univ of Birmingham England, PhD, 89. **CAREER** Exec Dir library ser, 78-, Dir Wes/Holiness Stud Cent, 92-, Asbury Theo Sem; Exec Sec, 96-, Soc for Pent Stud. **MEMBERSHIPS** AAR, WTS, ATSPS, KLA, LAWMHS, EPTA. **RESEARCH** Pentecostalism, Anglican theology of history, Methodist theology and history. **SELECTED PUBLICATIONS** Auth, The Everlasting Gospel, The Significance of Eschatology in the Development of Pentecostal Thought, Sheffield ENG, Sheffield Academic Press, 96; advisory ed, The Higher Christian Life, Sources for the Study of the Holiness Movement, A Biographical Essay Pentecostal and Keswick Movements, NY Garland Publishing Co, 85; auth, Resources for Research, A Guide to Selected Bibliographic and Reference Tools, Wilmore KY, Asbury Sem Press, 71; Glossolalia as Foreign Language, Investigation of the Early Twentieth-Century Pentecostal Claim, in: Wesleyan Theo J, 96. **CONTACT ADDRESS** 3291 Nantucket Dr, Lexington, KY, 40390. **EMAIL** bill_faupel@ats.wilmore.ky.us

FAVAZZA, JOSEPH A.
PERSONAL Born 05/25/1954, Memphis, TN, m, 1991, 3 children **DISCIPLINE** RELIGIOUS STUDIES **EDUCATION** Cath Univ Louvain, Belgium MA/STB, 79; Cath Univ Louvain, Belgium, PhD, 87. **CAREER** Asst prof Religious Studies, Rhodes Col. **MEMBERSHIPS** Cath Theolog Soc Amer, 87-; Amer Acad Relig, 93-; N Amer Patristics Soc, 93-; N Amer Acad Liturgy, 98-. **RESEARCH** Institutional Life in early Christian Literature; Roman Catholic Theology; Social Reconciliation Rituals & Symbols; Roman Catholic Studies. **SELECTED PUBLICATIONS** The Efficacy of Ritual Resistance: The Case of Catholic Sacramental Reconciliation, Worship, 98; A Reconciliation Sourcebook, Liturgy Training Publ, 97; Can Reconciliation Be Postmodern? New Theolog Rev, 97. **CONTACT ADDRESS** Dept of Religious Studies, Rhodes Col, Memphis, TN, 38112-1690. **EMAIL** favagga@rhodes.edu

FAWKES, DON
PERSONAL Born 02/20/1946, Kansas City, MO, m, 1976, 1 child **DISCIPLINE** PHILOSOPHY **EDUCATION** Univ Ariz, BS, 71; MA, 76; PhD, 93. **CAREER** Assoc Prof, James Madison Univ, 97-; asst prof, Fayetteville St Univ, 94-97; adjunct asst prof, Fayetteville St Univ, 91-94; adjunct prof, Fayetteville St Univ, 89-91; asst prof, US Air Force Acad, 79-81; instr, US Air Force Acad, 76-78. **HONORS AND AWARDS** Scholarship of Josephson Inst of Ethics, 98; Marquis Who's Who in World; NEH Member; Marquis Who's Who in Sci & Engineering; Excellence in Teaching Award, Fayetteville St Univ, 94; US Air Force Scholarship in Philos, 74-76; Beta Gamma Sigma; Phi Kappa Phi; NEH Fel, Univ Ariz, 92-93. **MEMBERSHIPS** Philos Sci Assoc; Amer Philos Assoc; Intl Soc for Performance Improvement; Amer Assoc Advancement of Sci; Southwestern Philos Soc; Smithsonian Inst; Libr of Congress Assoc; Phi Kappa Phi. **RESEARCH** Philosophy of Science; Epistemology; Metaphysics; Critical Thinking & Logic; Tchg Methodologies & Philosophy of Education; Analytical Philosophy; Ethics; Philosophy of Law; Asian Studies; Philosophy and Humanities; American Philosophers; Theology & Comparative Religions. **SELECTED PUBLICATIONS** Of Tolerance, Analytic Teaching, 98; The Values of Science and the Value of Science, James Madison Univ Annl Arts & Sci Symposium, 98; Critical Thinking and Its Courses, Inquiry, 96; "On Teaching Premise/Conclusion Distinctions, Inquiry, 96. **CONTACT ADDRESS** Dept of Philosophy, James Madison Univ, 492 C Longview Dr, Harrisburg, VA, 22802.

FEAGIN, SUSAN LOUISE
PERSONAL Born 07/11/1948, New York, NY, m, 1977 **DISCIPLINE** PHILOSOPHY **EDUCATION** Fla State Univ, BA, 69; Univ Wis-Madison, MA, 73, PhD (philos), 75. **CAREER** Vis asst prof philos, Bowling Green State Univ, 76-77; ASST PROF PHILOS, UNIV MO, KANSAS CITY, 77-. **MEMBERSHIPS** Am Philos Asn; Am Soc Aesthet. **RESEARCH** Aesthetics; epistemology. **SELECTED PUBLICATIONS** Auth, Showing Pictures--Aesthetics and the Art Gallery, J Aestet Educ, Vol 27, 93; Philosophy and Art Education, J Aesthet Educ, Vol 29, 95. **CONTACT ADDRESS** Dept of Phillos, Univ of Mo, 5100 Rockhill Rd, Kansas City, MO, 64110-2499.

FEASTER, BRUCE SULLIVAN
PERSONAL Born 07/13/1961, Flint, MI, m, 1993 **DISCIPLINE** LAW **EDUCATION** MI State Univ, BA, 1983; Univ of TX Law School, JD, 1986. **CAREER** WCNLS Children's Ctr for Justice and Peace, dir, currently. **HONORS AND AWARDS** National Mens Scholar. **MEMBERSHIPS** Alpha Phi Alpha; Metro Detroit Optimist. **CONTACT ADDRESS** WCNLS Children's Ctr for Justice & Peace, 3400 Cadillac Towers, Detroit, MI, 48226.

FEE, ELIZABETH
PERSONAL Born 12/11/1946, Belfast, Northern Ireland **DISCIPLINE** HISTORY AND PHILOSOPHY OF SCIENCE **EDUCATION** Cambridge Univ, BA, 68, MA, 75; Princeton Univ, MA, 71, PhD (hist and philos sci), 78. **CAREER** Teaching asst hist med, Princeton Univ, 71-72; instr hist sci, State Univ NY Binghamton, 72-74; archivist, 74-78, asst prof, Sch Health Serv, 74-78, ASST PROF HIST PUBL HEALTH, SCH HYG PUBL HEALTH, JOHNS HOPKINS UNIV, 78-, Ed consult, Int J Health Serv, 79-; consult, Col Allied Health Sci, Thomas Jefferson Univ, 79-80. **MEMBERSHIPS** Am Asn Hist Med; Hist Sci Soc; AHA; Berkshire Conf Women's Hist; Am Publ Health Asn. **RESEARCH** History of public health research and practice; history of Johns Hopkins School of Hygiene and Public Health; women and science and women and health. **SELECTED PUBLICATIONS** Auth, Sexual Knowledge, Sexual Science--The History of Attitudes to Sexuality, Am Hist Rev, Vol 101, 96; The Emerging Histories of Aids--3 Successive Paradigms, Hist Philos Life Scis, Vol 15, 93; Dirt and Disease, Am Hist Rev, Vol 99, 94; The Emerging Histories of Aids--3 Successive Paradigms, Hist Philos Life Sci, Vol 15, 93. **CONTACT ADDRESS** Sch of Hygiene and Publ Health, Johns Hopkins Univ, 3400 N Charles St, Baltimore, MD, 21205.

FEERICK, JOHN DAVID
PERSONAL Born 07/12/1936, New York, NY, m, 1962, 6 children **DISCIPLINE** LAW **EDUCATION** Fordham Col, BS, 58; Fordham Univ, LLB, 61. **CAREER** Assoc adj prof labor law, 76-82, dean, Sch Law, Fordham Univ, 82-; assoc, Skadden, Arps, Slate, Meagher & Flom, 61, partner, 68-82. **SELECTED PUBLICATIONS** Auth, From Failing Hands: The Story of Presidential Succession, Fordham Univ Press, 65; coauth, The Vice Presidents of the United States, Franklin Watts, Inc, 74; coauth, NLRB Representation Elections-Law, Practice and Procedure, Harcourt Brace Jovanovich, 80; auth, The Twenty-Fifth Amendment, Fordham Univ Press, 92. **CONTACT ADDRESS** Sch of Law Lincoln Ctr, Fordham Univ, 140 W 62nd St, New York, NY, 10023-7407.

FEINBERG, WALTER
PERSONAL Born 08/22/1937, Boston, MA, m, 1964, 2 children **DISCIPLINE** PHILOSOPHY, PHILOSOPHY OF EDUCATION **EDUCATION** Boston Univ, AB, 60, AM, 62, PhD, 66. **CAREER** Asst prof philos educ, Oakland Univ, 65-67; from asst prof to assoc prof, 67-75, Prof Philos Educ, Univ IL, Urbana, 75-, Assoc ed, Educ Theory, 67-; mem, Bur Educ Res, Univ IL, 77. **HONORS AND AWARDS** Spencer Grant, 94-95, 96-97; Univ Chicago Baton Scholar, 95-96; Assoc, Univ IL Center for Advan Study, 88, 98. **MEMBERSHIPS** Philos Educ Soc (pres, 88-89); Am Philos Asn; Philos Sci Asn; Am Educ Studies Asn (pres, 77-); Soc Advan Am Philos. **RESEARCH** Am educ philos; racial and ethnic considerations in Am educ; principles regarding the distribution of knowledge. **SELECTED PUBLICATIONS** Auth, Reason and Rhetoric, John Wiley, 75; co-ed, Work, Technology and Education, Univ Ill, 75; Understanding Education, Cambridge, 83; Japan & The Pursuit of a New American Identity, Routledge, 93; On Higher Ground: Education & The Case for Affirmative Action, Teachers Col Press, 97; Common Schools, Uncommon Identities: Cultural Differences/National Unity, Yale, 98. **CONTACT ADDRESS** 1310 S 6th St, Champaign, IL, 61820-6925. **EMAIL** wfeinber@uiuc.edu

FEINGOLD, HENRY L.
PERSONAL Born 02/06/1931, Germany, m, 1954, 2 children **DISCIPLINE** UNITED STATES DIPLOMACY & AMERICAN JEWISH HISTORY **EDUCATION** Brooklyn Col, BA, 53, MA, 54; NY Univ, PhD, 66. **CAREER** Tchr hist, Sec Schs, NY, 53-65; lectr, City Univ NY, 67-68; from instr to assoc prof hist, 68-76, grad ctr, 75, prof hist, Baruch Col, City Univ NY, 76-, Prof Emeritus, 98-, Dir, Jewish Resource Center, Baruch Col, CUNY; Lectr exten prog in Ger, Univ MD, 55-56; adj prof, Stern Col, Yeshiva Univ, 71-73; adj lectr, Inst Advan Study Hum Jewish Theol Inst Am, 73-76. **HONORS AND AWARDS** Leon Jolson Award for best bk on Holocaust, 77; Presidential Award for Excellence in Scholarship, Baruch Col, May 86; Lee Friedman Award in Am Jewish Hist, 94; Morim Award, Jewish Tchr(s) Asn, 95. **MEMBERSHIPS** Labor Zionist Alliance (pres, 89-92); Jewish Community Relations Coun (board of dir); World Zionist Org (gen coun); Jewish Agency for Israel (gen assembly); Am Zionist Movement (cabinet). **RESEARCH** Holocaust. **SELECTED PUBLICATIONS** Auth, The Politics of Rescue: The Roosevelt Administration and the Holocaust, 1938-1945, Rutgers Univ Press, 70; Zion in America: The Jewish Experience from Colonial Times to the Present, Twayne, 74; A Midrash on the History of American Jewry, NY State Univ Press, 82; A Time for Searching: Entering the Mainstream, 1920-1945, Johns Hopkins Univ Press, 92; Bearing Witness: How American and its Jews Responded to the Holocaust, Univ Syracuse Press, 95; Lest Memory Cease, Finding Meaning in the American Jewish Past, Univ Syracuse Press, 96. **CONTACT ADDRESS** Baruch Col, CUNY, 17 Lexington Ave, New York, NY, 10010-5518. **EMAIL** jrc@baruch.cuny.edu

FEINMAN, JAY M.
PERSONAL Born 01/22/1951, Easton, PA, m, 2 children **DISCIPLINE** LAW **EDUCATION** American Univ, BA, 72; Univ Chicago, JD, 75. **CAREER** Instr, Univ Miami School of Law, 75-76; assoc, Dechert Price and Rhoads, Philadelphia, PA, 76-77; vis prof of law, Northwestern Univ School of Law, Chicago, IL, fall 90; vis prof of law, Karl Franzens Univ, Graz, Austria, spring 95; asst and assoc prof of law, 77-88, prof of law, 88-96, distinguished prof of Law, Rutgers State Univ of NJ, School of Law, 96-, assoc dean, Curriculum Development and Lawering progs, 92-95, acting dean, 97-98. **HONORS AND AWARDS** Grants: Rutgers Committee for the Improvement of Teaching, 82-83, 87-88; NJ State Bar Found, proj dir, Rutgers Elderlaw Clinic, 93-95; US Dept of Ed, proj dir, Rutgers Elderlaw Clinic, 94-95; various res grant s from Rutgers Res Coun and law school. **MEMBERSHIPS** Am bar Asn; NJ State Bar Asn; Camden County Bar Asn; Conference on Critical Legal Studies. **SELECTED PUBLICATIONS** Auth, Economic Negligence: Liability of Professionals and Businesses to Third Parties for Economic Loss, Little, Brown & Co, 95; Economic Negligence in Construction Litigation, 15, The Construction Lawyer 34, 95; Simulations: An Introduction, 45, J of Legal Ed 469, 95; Attorney Liability to Nonclients, 31 Tort and Insurance Law J 735, 96; Economic Negligence Actions: A Remedy for Third Parties, Trial, June 96; Doctrinal Classification and Economic Negligence, 33 San Diego Law Rev 137, 96; Economic Negligence in Residential Real Estate Transactions, 25 Real Estate Law J 110, 96; Implied Warranty, Products Liability, and the Boundaries Between Contract and Tort, 75 Washington Univ Law Quart 469, 97; Law School Grading, 65 UMKC Law Rev 647, 97; The Future History of Legal Education, 29 Rutgers Law J 475, 98; numerous other publications. **CONTACT ADDRESS** School of Law, Rutgers Univ, 217 N Fifth St, Camden, NJ, 08102-1203. **EMAIL** feinman@camden.rutgers.edu

FEISS, HUGH
PERSONAL Born 05/08/1939, Lakeview, OR **DISCIPLINE** THEOLOGY **EDUCATION** Mount Angel Seminary, BA, 62, MA, 66, Mdiv, 66; The Gothic Univ, PhL, 73, STL, 67; Ansohmiaium, Rome, STD, 80; Univ of Iowa, MLS, 87. **CAREER** Prof of Philo, 67-72, Prof of Theo and Hum, 74-96, Mt Angel Seminary. **HONORS AND AWARDS** NEH Summer Seminar. **MEMBERSHIPS** CTS, SBL, AAR, CPA, SSSR, ABA. **RESEARCH** 12th Century Theology. **SELECTED PUBLICATIONS** Auth, Hildegard of Bingen, Explanation of the Rule of St Benedict, ed, H Feiss, Toronto, Peregrina, 90; The Many Lives and Languages of Birgitta of Sweden and her Order, Studia Monastica, 93; co-auth, Birds in Beinecke MS189, Yale Univ Library Gazette, 94; A Poet Abbess from Notre Dame de Saintes, Magistra, 95; Environment, eds, D Christiansen & W Grazer, Washington, DC, US Catholic Conference, 96; The Christology of Greet Groote's Getijdenboek, Amer Benedictine Review, 97. **CONTACT ADDRESS** Ascension Priory, 541 E 100 S, Jerome, ID, 83338-5655. **EMAIL** hughf@magicl.K.com

FEIT, NEIL
PERSONAL Born 06/17/1966, New York, NY **DISCIPLINE** PHILOSOPHY **EDUCATION** Columbia Coll, BA, 88; Univ Mass, PhD, 96. **CAREER** Asst prof, Western Wash Univ, 97-. **MEMBERSHIPS** Am Philos Asn. **RESEARCH** Philosophy of Mind and Language; Metaphysics. **SELECTED PUBLICATIONS** Auth, On a Famous Counterexample to Leibniz's Law, Proceedings of the Aristotelian Soc, 96; More on Brute Facts, Australasian J of Philos, forthcoming; Self-Ascription and Belief De Re, Philos Studies, forthcoming. **CONTACT ADDRESS** Dept of Philosophy, Western Washington Univ, Bellingham, WA, 98225-9054. **EMAIL** nfeit@cc.wwu.edu

FELD, ALAN L.
PERSONAL Born 02/05/1940, New York, NY, m, 1962, 3 children **DISCIPLINE** FEDERAL TAX LAW **EDUCATION** Columbia Col, AB, 60; Harvard Law Sch, LLB, 63. **CAREER** Assoc prof, 71-75, PROF LAW, BOSTON UNIV, 75-, Assoc, Paul, Weiss, Rifkind, Wharton and Garrison, 64-67 and Barrett, Knapp, Smith and Schapiro, 67-71; vis prof, Law Sch, Univ Pa, 77-78. **MEMBERSHIPS** Am Law Inst. **RESEARCH** Federal taxation, the Congress, Law and the Arts. **SELECTED PUBLICATIONS** Auth, Legal Differences Without Economic Distinctions--Points, Penalties, and the Market for Mortgages, Boston Univ Law Rev, Vol 77, 97. **CONTACT ADDRESS** Law Sch, Boston Univ, 765 Commonwealth Ave, Boston, MA, 02215-1401.

FELDER, CAIN HOPE
PERSONAL Born 06/09/1943, Aiken, South Carolina, d, 1973 **DISCIPLINE** THEOLOGY **EDUCATION** Howard University, Washington, DC, BA, 1966; Oxford University, Oxford, England, dip theol, 1968; Union Theological Seminary, New York, NY, MDiv, 1969; Columbia University, New York, NY, MPhil, 1978, PhD, 1982. **CAREER** Black Methodists for Church Renewal, Atlanta, GA, national executive director, 1969-72; Morgan State University, Baltimore, MD, director of federal relations/associate professor of philosophy, 1972-74; Grace United Methodist Church, New York, NY, pastor, 1975-78; Princeton Theological Seminary, Princeton, NJ, instructor, 1978-81; Howard University School of Divinity, professor, 1981-. **HONORS AND AWARDS** Fellowships awarded by the National Fellowship Fund, The Crusade Fellowship, Union Theological Seminary Graduate Fellowship and Minority Fund, The Rockefeller Brothers Fund-Protestant and Doctoral Fellowships, Columbia University Faculty Fellowship; has received numerous scholarships; Outstanding Leadership Citation, Black Methodists for Church Renewal, The Black Caucus of the Methodist Church, 1973; Martin Luther King, Jr., Scholar-Service Award, Providence and Vicinity Council of Churches;

Progressive Natl Baptist Convention, Martin Luther King Jr Freedom Award; AME, 2nd Episcopal Dist, Excellence in Scholarship Award, 1995; public speaker at institutions of higher learning. **MEMBERSHIPS** Mem, Society of Biblical Literature; mem, Society for the Study of Black Religion; mem, Amer Academy of Religion; mem, Middle East Studies Assn; mem, bd of dirs, 1978-, exec committee, 1984-86, chair, 1985, 1986, Natl Convocation Planning Committee, Black Theology Project; bd mem, Interreligious Foundation for Comm Organization, 1970-72; founder, Enterprises Now, Inc; founder, Narco House (drug rehabilitation center), Atlanta, GA; mem, 1985-98, Coun of Univ Senate, Howard Univ; chair, Theology Search Comm, Howard Univ School of Divinity, 1987; founder, chair, the Biblical Inst for Social Change, Washington, DC. **SELECTED PUBLICATIONS** editor and author, Stony the Road We Trod: African American Biblical Interpretation, Fortress Press, 1990; author, Troubling Biblical Waters: Race, Class, and Family, Orbis Books, 1989; author, "Cost of Freedom in Urban Black Churches," Vision of Hope, 1989; author, "The Bible and Re-contextualization," African-AmericanReligious Studies: Anthology, 1989; author, "The Holy Spirit in Jesus' Formative Years," Pacific Theological Review, 1988; author, The Season of Lent,, 1993; general editor, The Original African Heritage Study Bible, Winston Derek Publishing Co, 1993; editor, Journal of Religious Thought; author of numerous other articles and book reviews. **CONTACT ADDRESS** Professor of Biblical Studies, Howard Univ, 1400 Shepherd St, NE, Washington, VT, 20017.

FELDER, DAVID W.
PERSONAL Born 04/25/1945, Providence, RI, m, 1977 **DISCIPLINE** PHILOSOPHY **EDUCATION** Boston Univ, BA, 67; Wayne State Univ, MA, 69; Florida State Univ, PhD, 78. **CAREER** Prof, Florida A & M Univ, 76-. **HONORS AND AWARDS** NEH Fel, African Thought Systems at NYU, 77, Enlightenment at Boston Univ, 91, German Social Thought Univ Chicago, 96. **MEMBERSHIPS** Amer Phil Assoc; Florida Phil Assoc. **RESEARCH** Social theory **SELECTED PUBLICATIONS** Auth, Kids Conflicts, Teenage Conflicts, Family Conflicts, Relationships and Ethics, Marital Conflicts, Divorce Conflicts, Institutional Conflicts, and Courtroom Conflicts, 95; auth, Key to High Scores on Standardized Tests: Based on the Logic Used in Test Development, 98; coauth, Freedom and Culture in German Social Theory, 99. **CONTACT ADDRESS** 9601-30 Miccosukee Rd., Tallahassee, FL, 32308. **EMAIL** felderdave@aol.com

FELDMAN, RICHARD HAROLD
PERSONAL Born 06/20/1948, Maplewood, NJ, m, 1974, 1 child **DISCIPLINE** PHILOSOPHY **EDUCATION** Cornell Univ, BA, 70; Univ Mass, MA & PhD, 75. **CAREER** Instr philos, Franklin & Marshall Col, 74-75, asst prof, 75-81, Assoc Prof Philos, Univ Rochester, 81-97, prof, Univ Rochester, 91. **MEMBERSHIPS** Am Philos Asn. **RESEARCH** Epistemology; philos of mind; metaphysics. **SELECTED PUBLICATIONS** Auth, An Alleged Defect in Getter Counterexamples, Australasian J Philos, 5/75; Co auth, Evidentialism, Philosophical Studies, 85; Reliability and Justification, 85, Proper Functionalsim, 93. **CONTACT ADDRESS** Dept of Philos, Univ of Rochester, 500 Joseph C Wilson, Rochester, NY, 14627-9000. **EMAIL** feldman@philosophy.rochester.edu

FELDTHUSEN, BRUCE P.
DISCIPLINE LAW **EDUCATION** Queen's Univ, BA, 72; Univ Western Ontario, LLB, 76; Univ Mich, LLM, 77, SJD, 79. **CAREER** Prof. **RESEARCH** Administrative law; human rights; debtor-creditor rights; remedies; regulated industries; legal theory. **SELECTED PUBLICATIONS** Auth, Economic Negligence; co-auth, Cases and Materials on the Law of Torts. **CONTACT ADDRESS** Fac of Law, Univ Western Ontario, London, ON, N6A 3K7.

FELIX, ROBERT E.
DISCIPLINE CONFLICT OF LAWS, LAW AND LITERATURE, PRODUCTS LIABILITY, AND TORTS **EDUCATION** Univ Cincinnati, AB, 56, LLB, 59, AB, 59; Univ Brit Columbia, MA, 62; Harvard Univ, LLM, 67. **CAREER** James P Mozingo III prof, Legal Res. **SELECTED PUBLICATIONS** Coauth, treatise & casebk on, conflict of laws & a treatise on the SC Law of Torts. **CONTACT ADDRESS** School of Law, Univ of S. Carolina, Columbia, SC, 29208. **EMAIL** Felix@law.law.sc.edu

FELL, ALBERT PRIOR
PERSONAL Born 10/01/1929, Toronto, ON, Canada, m, 1965, 2 children **DISCIPLINE** PHILOSOPHY **EDUCATION** Univ Toronto, BA, 52; St Andrews Univ, BPhil, 56; Columbia Univ, AM, 54, PhD (philos), 63. **CAREER** Teaching fel, 56-58, from lectr to assoc prof, 58-71, assoc dean students, 69-72, PROF PHILOS, QUEEN'S UNIV, ONT, 71-. **MEMBERSHIPS** Can Philos Asn; Am Soc Aesthe; NAm Nietzsche Soc. **RESEARCH** Philosophy of history and art. **SELECTED PUBLICATIONS** Auth, Balancing Act--Editing Queens Quart in the Mid 1960s, Queens Quart, Vol 100, 93. **CONTACT ADDRESS** Dept of Philos, Queen's Univ, Kingston, ON, K7L 3N6.

FELL, JOSEPH PHINEAS
PERSONAL Born 05/22/1931, Troy, NY, w, 1958, 2 children **DISCIPLINE** PHILOSOPHY **EDUCATION** Williams Col, BA, 53; Columbia Univ, MA, 60, PhD(philos), 63. **CAREER** Instr philos, PA State Univ, 62-63; from asst prof to assoc prof, 63-71, Prof Philos, Bucknell Univ, 71-83, John Howard Harris Prof, 83-93, Presidential Prof, 87-93, Head Dept, 77-83, 85-90, Bucknell Univ fac fel, 65, 67 & 73; Nat Endowment for Hum fel, 69-70, Emer pro, 93. **HONORS AND AWARDS** Clarke F Ansley Award, Columbia Univ, 63; Lindback Award, 69. **MEMBERSHIPS** Soc Phenomenol & Existential Philos; Am Philos Asn. **RESEARCH** Existentialism and phenomenology; philo psych; philo of hist. **SELECTED PUBLICATIONS** Auth, Emotion in the Thought of Sartre, Columbia Univ, 65; Sartre's words: an existential self-analysis, Psychoanalytic Rev, Vol LV, No 3; Sartre's theory of motivation, J Brit Soc Phenomenol, 5/70; Heidegger's notion of two beginnings, Rev Metaphys, 12/71; Was Freud a follower of Kant?, In: Der Idealismus und seine Gegenwart, Felix Meiner, 76; coauth, Emotion, Brooks/Cole, 77; Heidegger and Sartre, Columbia Univ, 79; Battle of the giants over being, In: The Philosophy of Jean-Paul Sartre, Open Court, 81; ed, The Philosophy of John William Miller, Bucknell Univ, 90; The Familiar and the Strange, in reading Heidegger Blackwell, 92; Seeing a Thig in a Hidden Whole, Heidegger Studies, Vol X, 94. **CONTACT ADDRESS** Dept of Philosophy, Bucknell Univ, Lewisburg, PA, 17837.

FELLER, DAVID EDWARD
PERSONAL Born 11/19/1916, New York, NY, m, 1947, 4 children **DISCIPLINE** LABOR LAW **EDUCATION** Harvard Univ, AB, 38, LLB, 41. **CAREER** Lectr law and econ, Law Sch, Univ Chicago, 41-42; law clerk, US Supreme Ct, 48-49; assoc gen counsel, United Steelworkers Am and Cong Indust Orgns, 49-61; gen counsel, United Steelworkers Am, 61-65 and Ind Union Dept, AFL-CIO, 61-66; PROF LAW, UNIV CALIF, BERKEY, 67-, DIR, NAT ASN ADVAN COLORED PEOPLE DEFENSE AND EDUC FUND, INC, 60-. **MEMBERSHIPS** Nat Acat Arbitrators; Indust Rel Res Assoc. **SELECTED PUBLICATIONS** Auth, End of the Trilogy--The Declining State of Labor Arbitration, Arbitration J, Vol 48, 93. **CONTACT ADDRESS** Sch of Law, Univ of Calif, Berkeley, CA, 94720.

FELSENFELD, CARL
DISCIPLINE BANKING LAW **EDUCATION** Dartmouth, AB, 48; Columbia, MS, 50, JD, 54. **CAREER** Prof, 83, Fordham Univ. **HONORS AND AWARDS** Rep, UN Comm Intl Trade Law; adv, Nat Conf of Commnr on Uniform State Laws. **SELECTED PUBLICATIONS** Auth, Holder in Due Course, Under Proposed Article 3, 3 NY State Banking Jour 18, 95; Banking Regulation in the United States; 96; Bankruptcy Law, 96; A Comment About Separate Bankruptcy System, 64 Fordham Law Rev 2521, 96. **CONTACT ADDRESS** Law Sch, Fordham Univ, 113 W 60th St, New York, NY, 10023.

FELT, JAMES WRIGHT
PERSONAL Born 01/04/1926, Dallas, TX **DISCIPLINE** PHILOSOPHY **EDUCATION** Gonzaga Univ, BA, 49, MA, 50; Alma Col, Calif, STL, 57; St Louis Univ, MS, 61, PhD, 65. **CAREER** Instr math, Loyola Univ, Calif, 50-52; instr, St Ignatius High Sch, San Francisco, 52-53; asst prof, 65-70, chmn dept, 74-80; assoc prof, Santa Clara Univ, 70-. **MEMBERSHIPS** Metaphys Soc Am; Am Philos Assn; Am Cath Philos Assn. **RESEARCH** Process philosophy; metaphysics. **SELECTED PUBLICATIONS** Art, Fatalism and Truth about the Future, The Thomist, 2/92; auth, Making Sense of Your Freedom, Ccornell U Pr, 94; art, Why Possible Worlds Aren't, Rev Met 96. **CONTACT ADDRESS** Dept of Philosophy, Santa Clara Univ, 500 El Camino Real, Santa Clara, CA, 95053-0001. **EMAIL** jfelt@mailer.scu.edu

FENNER, G. MICHAEL
DISCIPLINE CONSTITUTIONAL LAW **EDUCATION** Kansas Univ, BA, 65; Univ Missouri-Kans City, JD, 69. **CAREER** Prof; Creighton Univ, 72-; trial atty, Honors Law Grad Prog US Dept Justice, 69-72; reporter, Nebr Supreme Ct Comt on Practice and Procedure. **HONORS AND AWARDS** US Dept Justice Spec Achievement awd, 70; Nebr State Bar Found-(s) Shining Light awd, 92. **MEMBERSHIPS** Nebr Supreme Ct Comt on Practice and Procedure; House Deleg, Nebr Bar Asn; past chp Evidence sec, Asn Amer Law Sch. **SELECTED PUBLICATIONS** Publ in, Creighton Law Rev; Harvard Civil Rights-Civil Liberties Law Rev; Notre Dame Law Rev; Nebr Law Rev; Wash Univ Law Quart; Univ Mo- Kans City Law Rev and Trial. **CONTACT ADDRESS** School of Law, Creighton Univ, 2500 California Plaza, Omaha, NE, 68178. **EMAIL** fenner@culaw.creighton.edu

FEREJOHN, JOHN
DISCIPLINE LAW **EDUCATION** Stanford Univ, PhD. **CAREER** Vis prof. **RESEARCH** American governmental institutions and practices; British electoral politics; federalism; interrelations of law and politics. **SELECTED PUBLICATIONS** Auth, pubs on social choice theory and the application of game theory to political and legal institutions. **CONTACT ADDRESS** Fac of Law, Univ Toronto, 78 Queen's Park, Toronto, ON.

FEREJOHN, MICHAEL T.
DISCIPLINE PHILOSOPHY **EDUCATION** Univ CA Irvine, PhD, 76. **CAREER** Prof, Duke Univ. **RESEARCH** Ancient philos; metaphysics; epistemology; philosophical logic. **SELECTED PUBLICATIONS** Auth, The Origins of Aristotelian Science, Yale Univ, 91. **CONTACT ADDRESS** Philos Dept, Duke Univ, West Duke Bldg, Durham, NC, 27706. **EMAIL** mtf@acpub.duke.edu

FERGUSON, EVERETT
PERSONAL Born 02/18/1933, Montgomery, TX, m, 1956, 3 children **DISCIPLINE** HISTORY, PHILOSOPHY OF RELIGION **EDUCATION** Abilene Christ Univ, BA, 53, MA, 54; Harvard Univ, STB, 56, PhD, 60. **CAREER** Dean, Northeast Christ Jr Coll, 59-62; PROF, ABILENE CHRIST UNIV, 62-. **MEMBERSHIPS** North Am Patristics Soc; Am Soc Church Hist; Soc Biblical Lit; Ecclesiastical Hist Soc; Asn Int d'Etudes Patristiques; Inst Biblical Res **RESEARCH** Backgrounds Early Christianity; Early church history **CONTACT ADDRESS** Abilene Christian Univ, 609 E N 16th St, Abilene, TX, 79601. **EMAIL** Ferguson@bible.acu.edu

FERGUSON, GERRY
DISCIPLINE LAW **EDUCATION** St. Patrick's Univ, BA, 68; Ottawa Univ, LLB, 71; Univ NY, LLM, 72. **CAREER** Asst prof, 73-76; assoc prof, 76-81; prof, 81-; assoc dean, 80-82. **MEMBERSHIPS** Nat Advis Coun Law Comn Can; Int Centre Criminal Law Reform and Criminal Justice policy; Int Soc Reform Criminal Law; Can Bar Asn; Continuing Legal Edu Soc. **RESEARCH** Criminal law; criminal procedure; sentencing; and mental health law. **SELECTED PUBLICATIONS** Coauth, Canadian Criminal Jury Instructions. **CONTACT ADDRESS** Fac of Law, Univ Victoria, PO Box 2400, Victoria, BC, V8W 3H7. **EMAIL** gferguso@uvic.ca

FERGUSON, KENNETH D.
DISCIPLINE LAW **EDUCATION** Drake Univ, BA; Coburn Sch Law, JD. **CAREER** Law clerk, US Bankruptcy Court; asst prof **RESEARCH** Bankruptcy; corporate law. **SELECTED PUBLICATIONS** Auth, Repose or Not? Informal Objections To Claims of Exemptions After Taylor v. Freeland, Okla Law Rev, 97; Does Payment by Check Constitute a Transfer upon Delivery of Payment?, Am Bank Law J, 90; Discourse and Discharge: Linguistic Analysis and Abuse of the 'Exemption Declaration' Process in Bankruptcy, Am Bank Law J, 96. **CONTACT ADDRESS** Law Dept, Univ of Missouri, Kansas City, 5100 Rockhill Rd, Kansas City, MO, 64110-2499. **EMAIL** fergusonk@umkc.edu

FERGUSON, KENNETH G.
PERSONAL Born 10/05/1948, Beckley, WV, s **DISCIPLINE** PHILOSOPHY **EDUCATION** Univ Rochester, PhD, philos, 85. **CAREER** Visiting asst prof, Ariz State Univ, 86-87; visiting lectr, Appalachian State Univ, 87-88; visiting asst prof, East Carolina Univ, 88-93, 95-98. **HONORS AND AWARDS** Dissertation Essay Award, 85. **MEMBERSHIPS** Amer Philos Asn; Southern Soc for Philos and Psychol. **RESEARCH** Philosophical logic; Evolutionary ethics. **SELECTED PUBLICATIONS** Abstracts, Proceedings and Addresses of the American Philosophical Association, 85, 87, 89, 92; rev, History and Philosophy of Logic; article, An Intervention into the Flew/Fogelin Debate, Hume Studies, 18, 105-12, 92; article, Existing by Convention, Relig Studies, 28, 185-194, 92; article, Equivocation in the Surprise Exam Paradox, The Southern Jour of Philos, 29, 291-302, 91; article, Truth Conditions for Might Counterfactuals, The Review of Metaphysics, 40, 483-94, 87. **CONTACT ADDRESS** Philosophy Dept., East Carolina Univ, Greenville, NC, 27858. **EMAIL** fergusonk@mail.ecu.edu

FERGUSON, MARIANNE
PERSONAL Born 12/25/1932, Rochester, NY **DISCIPLINE** RELIGIOUS STUDIES, THEOLOGY **EDUCATION** State Univ NY Col Buffalo, BSEd, 53; St Bonaventure Univ, MA, 68; State Univ NY Buffalo, MS, 74; McMaster Univ, PhD(relig), 80. **CAREER** Teacher elem schs, Dioceses Buffalo & Brooklyn, 55-61; teacher relig & hist, De Sales Cath High Sch, 61-64; instr relig, Damon Col, 68-74; asst prof to assoc prof Relig Studies, State Univ NY Col Buffalo, 75-, lectr adult educ, Diocese Buffalo, 68-; coordr relig educ, Newman Ctr, State Univ NY Col Buffalo, 68-; adj prof psychol educ, Christ King Sem, 68-79; lectr, Head Start teacher training workshops, 75-76. **MEMBERSHIPS** Col Theol Soc (secy, 69-70); Soc Sci Study Relig; Relig Educ Asn; Cath Campus Ministries. **RESEARCH** Attitude of college students toward religion; staying power of religious denominations; women in religion. **SELECTED PUBLICATIONS** Auth, Must Religious Flee the World, Cord Mag, 3/66; Influence of Religious Education on Religious Commitment, Catechist Mag, 11-12/81; Influence of Private Schools on Religious Committment, Private Sch Quart, spring 82; auth, Women and Religion, Prentice Hall, 95; Encyclopedia references, Sage Publ. **CONTACT ADDRESS** Dept of Philos & Relig Studies, State Univ NY Col, 1300 Elmwood Ave, Buffalo, NY, 14222-1095. **EMAIL** fergusmc@buffalostate.edu

FERGUSON, PAUL
PERSONAL Born 06/20/1938, Elgin, IL, m, 1958, 8 children **DISCIPLINE** THEOLOGY **EDUCATION** Univ Tulsa, BS, 62; Wheaton Col, MA, 65, Mdiv, 70; Chicago Theolog Sem, PhD, 88; Hebrew Univ, Post doc, 95-99. **CAREER** Prof, Christian Life Col, 84-; prof, SIM Cols, 96-98; prof, ICI Univ, 96-. **MEMBERSHIPS** Nat Educ Asn; Chicago Society Biblical Res; Society Int Missionaries. **RESEARCH** Minor prophets; Elijah-Elisha; comparitive semitics; Jonah; Pentateuch; Daniel. **SELECTED PUBLICATIONS** Auth, Baker's Encyclopedia of Biblical Theology, 95; auth, Biblical Hebrew with Jonah-Stroke by Stroke, 95; auth, Biblical Languages for Fun and Profit, 97; auth, The OT: What's in it For Me, 98; auth, art, Nebuchadnezzar, Gilgamesh and the Babylonian Job, 98. **CONTACT ADDRESS** 577 Glenwood Ave, Elgin, IL, 60120.

FERGUSON, WILLIAM DEAN
PERSONAL Born 07/31/1928, Shinglehouse, PA, m, 1955, 3 children **DISCIPLINE** LAW **EDUCATION** Lebanon Valley Col, AB, 49; Cornell Univ, LLB, 55; Univ Va, SJD(law), 75. **CAREER** Assoc, Bliss & Bouch, Albany, NY, 57-62; asst prof law, Univ SDak, 62-63; from asst prof to prof, 63-68, Prof Law, 68-98, PROF EMER, EMORY UNIV, 98-. **MEMBERSHIPS** Nat Acad Arbitrators **RESEARCH** Procedure **SELECTED PUBLICATIONS** Auth, Pendent personal jurisdiction in federal courts, Villanova Law Rev, 65; The Statutes of Limitation Savings Statutes, Michie Co, 78. **CONTACT ADDRESS** Sch Law, Emory Univ, 1364 Clifton Rd N E, Atlanta, GA, 30322-0001.

FERM, DEANE WILLIAM
PERSONAL Born 05/22/1927, Lebanon, PA, m, 1949, 4 children **DISCIPLINE** RELIGION **EDUCATION** Col Wooster, BA, 49; Yale Univ, BD, 52, MA, 53, MDiv, 53, PhD, 54. **CAREER** Dir sch relig, Mont State Univ, 54-59; Dean, Col Chapel, Mt Holyoke Col, 59-, Asst dir, Danforth Found, spring, 58; guest preacher & lectr, cols & univs; vis lectr, Smtih Col, 60-61, 62-63; Danforth Found campus ministry grant, 65-66; Poulson fel, Am Scand Found, 65-66. **MEMBERSHIPS** Nat Asn Col & Univ Chaplains. **RESEARCH** Religion in higher education; contemporary theology. **SELECTED PUBLICATIONS** Auth, Responsible Sexuality Now, Seabury, 71; William James: Moralism, the will to believe and theism, Relig in Life, autumn 72; Honest to Jesus, 3/72 & Taking God seriously, 5/73, Christian Century; Reflections of a college chaplain, Theol Today, 4/76; Protestant liberalism reaffirmed, Christian Century, 5/76; The women's movement and the teaching of religion, Theol Today, 1/78. **CONTACT ADDRESS** Dean of Col Chapel, Mount Holyoke Col, South Hadley, MA, 01075.

FERM, ROBERT L.
PERSONAL Wooster, OH, m, 1952, 2 children **DISCIPLINE** RELIGION **EDUCATION** Col Wooster, BA, 52; Uale Univ, BD, 55, MA, 56, PhD 58. **CAREER** From instr to asst prof relig, Pomona Col, 58-63, from John Knox McLean assoc prof to John Knox McLean prof, 63-69, chmn dept, 60-69; prof relig & chmn dept, 69-, Tillinghast Prof of Rel, 88, Middlebury Col; Haynes Found fel, 61; assoc prof, 63-67, prof, 67-69, Claremont Grad Sch; vis assoc prof, Midddlebury Col, 64-65; Am Coun Learned Soc grant-in-aid, 77-78. **HONORS AND AWARDS** ACLS/Ford Fel, 83; Dew Endowment Fel, 98-99. **MEMBERSHIPS** Am Soc Church Hist; Am Studies Assn; Am Acad Relig. **RESEARCH** American and historical theology. **SELECTED PUBLICATIONS** Auth, Piety Purity Plenty: Images of Protestantism in American, Fortress, 91; auth, Evangelicals and Conservations in the Early South, 1940-1861, 87; auth, The Loyalist Perception and Other Essays, 89; Dumnion and L. Laty, 94. **CONTACT ADDRESS** Dept of Relig, Middlebury Col, Middlebury, VT, 05753-6001.

FERNANDEZ, EDUARDO
PERSONAL Born 04/28/1958, El Paso, TX, s **DISCIPLINE** RELIGION **EDUCATION** Loyola Univ of the South, BA, 80; Jesuit Sch Theol Berk, MDiv, 91; Univ Tex Austin, MA, 86; Gregorian Pontifical Univ, Rome, STD. **CAREER** RC Jesuit Priest, 92; Jesuit School of Theo, vis asst prof, 98-. **HONORS AND AWARDS** ASN, 80; PKP, 85; Hispanic Theol Inst, Postdoc res Grant, 97 **MEMBERSHIPS** AHO, ILH, AAR, JHMC **RESEARCH** Hist art and cult Mex/Southwest; missiology; ecumenism; dialogue between culture and religion **SELECTED PUBLICATIONS** Auth, La Cosecha: Harvesting Contemporary US Hispanic Theology, 00; Celebrating Sacraments in a Hispanic Context, coauth; Reading the Bible in Spanish, 94; US Hispanic Catholics: Trends and Works, in: Rev Relig, 94; Reflexiones Sobre la Realidid de los Hispanos en los Estados Unidos: Sombras y Luces, in : Reflex Catequ: Encuentro de San Antonio TX, 95; Seven Tips on the Pastorial CARE of Catholics of Mexican Decent in the United States, in: Chicago Stud, 97; Educating for Inculturation: Why the Arts Cannot Be Ignored, in: Future Arts Wor and Relig Edu, ed Doug Adams and Michael E, Moynahan. **CONTACT ADDRESS** Jesuit Sch of Theol, Berkeley, 1735 LeRoy Ave, Berkley, CA, 94709. **EMAIL** efernand@jstb.edu

FERRAIOLO, WILLIAM D.
PERSONAL Born 02/12/1969, Lyndhurst, NJ, s **DISCIPLINE** PHILOSOPHY **EDUCATION** Univ Okla, PhD, 97. **CAREER** Instr, philos, San Joaquin Delta Community Col, 96-. **HONORS AND AWARDS** Kenneth R. Merrill Teaching award, Univ Okla, 96-97. **MEMBERSHIPS** Amer Philos Asn; Central States Philos Asn. **RESEARCH** Realism & relativism; Abortion; Problem of evil. **SELECTED PUBLICATIONS** Auth, Black's Twin-Globe Counterexample, Southwestern Philos Rev, 97; auth, Individualism and Descartes, Teorema, 96. **CONTACT ADDRESS** 1559 Mosaic Way, Apt. #3, Stockton, CA, 95207. **EMAIL** bferraiolo@sjdccd.cc.ca.us

FERRARA, LOUIS F.
PERSONAL Born 01/27/1933, Brooklyn, NY, s **DISCIPLINE** THEOLOGY **EDUCATION** Wagner College, BA 54; Yale Divinity School Berkeley, STM 57. **CAREER** George Mercer Jr Memorial Sch of Theology, Diocese of Long Island, Episcopal Priest and Teacher, 40 Years. **HONORS AND AWARDS** Res Fell Yale Div Sch. **MEMBERSHIPS** AAR; SBL. **RESEARCH** Biblical Studies; Hebrew Bible. **SELECTED PUBLICATIONS** Auth, Various Diocesan and Parish Publications. **CONTACT ADDRESS** Apt# 11C, Brooklyn, NY, 11226-1252.

FERRARIN, ALFREDO
PERSONAL Born 10/07/1960, Thiene, Italy, m, 1996 **DISCIPLINE** PHILOSOPHY **EDUCATION** Scuola Noritale Superiore, Pisa Italy, PhD, 90 **CAREER** Asst Prof, 95-pres, Boston Univ **RESEARCH** Aristotle; Kant; Hegel **SELECTED PUBLICATIONS** Auth, Hegel interprete di Aristotele, Pisa, ETS, 90 **CONTACT ADDRESS** Dept of Philos, Boston Univ, 745 Commonwealth Ave, Boston, MA, 02215. **EMAIL** ferrarin@bu.edu

FERST, BARRY JOEL
PERSONAL Born 01/13/1946, Chicago, IL, m, 1979 **DISCIPLINE** PHILOSOPHY OF SCIENCE & RELIGION **EDUCATION** Univ IL, BA, 68; Univ KS, MA, 69; Tulane Univ, PhD(philos), 76. **CAREER** Asst prof Philos, 80-94, PROF, CARROLL COL, 95-. **MEMBERSHIPS** Am Philos Asn. **RESEARCH** Roman science and religion. **CONTACT ADDRESS** Philos Dept, Carroll Col, Montana, 1601 N Benton Ave, Helena, MT, 59625-0002.

FESMIRE, STEVEN A.
PERSONAL Born 11/06/1967, Memphis, TN **DISCIPLINE** PHILOSOPHY **EDUCATION** So Ill Univ, Carbondale, PhD, 94. **CAREER** Adj prof, 93-94; asst prof, E Tenn St Univ, 95-. **HONORS AND AWARDS** Ford Found Fel, Millsapps Col, 89-90; Summa cum laude, Millsapps Col, 90; Phi Beta Kappa; Hon mention for Douglas Greenlee Prize, Soc for Advancement of Am Philos, 92; Doctoral fel, 92-93, Diss res fel, So Ill Univ, Carbondale, 93-94. **MEMBERSHIPS** APA; Soc for the Advancement of Am Philos. **RESEARCH** Am philos, especially pragmatism; ethics; theory of metaphor. **SELECTED PUBLICATIONS** Auth, Embodied Reason, Kinesis, vol 20, no 1, 93; auth, Aerating the Mind: The Metaphor of Mental Functioning as Bodily Functioning, Metaphor and Symbolic Activity, vol 9, no 1, 94; auth, What is Cognitive About Cognitive Linguistics?, Metaphor and Symbolic Activity, vol 9, no 2, 94; auth, Educating the Moral Artist: Dramatic Rehearsal in Moral Education, Stud in Philos & Ed, vol 13, no 3-4, 94 Ed & the New Scholarship on Dewey, Kluwer Press, 94/95; auth, Dramatic Rehearsal and the Moral Artist: A Deweyan Theory of Moral Understanding, Transactions of the Charles S. Pierce Soc, vol 31, no 3, 95; auth, The Social Basis of Character: An Ecological Humanist Approach, in Practical Ethics, Blackwell Press, 96; auth, The Art of Moral Deliberation, in Democracy and the Aesthetics of Intelligence: Stud in Deweyan Reconstruction, SUNY Press, 97; auth, The Moral Artist: A Deweyan Theory of Moral Imagination, Vanderbilt Univ Press. **CONTACT ADDRESS** Dept of Philosophy, East Tennessee State Univ, Box 70656, Johnson City, TN, 37614-0656. **EMAIL** fesmires@etsu.edu DAS 063 1-90 proofed, Anne Marie Nickert DAS 063 90-100 entered, Anne Marie Nickert

FETZER, JAMES HENRY
PERSONAL Born 12/06/1940, Pasadena, CA, m, 1977, 4 children **DISCIPLINE** HISTORY AND PHILOSOPHY OF SCIENCE **EDUCATION** Princeton Univ, AB, 62; Ind Univ, MA, 68; Ind Univ, PhD, 70. **CAREER** Asst prof, Univ Ky, 70-77; vis assoc prof, Univ Va, 77-78; vis assoc prof, Univ Cincinnati, 78-79; vis NSF res prof, Univ Cincinnati, 79-80; vis lectr, Univ NC at Chapel Hill, 80-81; vis assoc prof, New Col, Univ South Fla, 81-83; MacArthur vis distinguished prof, New Col, Univ South Fla, 83-84; adjunct prof, Univ South Fla, Fall, 84-85; vis prof, Univ Va, Spring, 84-85; res scholar, New Col, Univ South Fla, 85-86; prof, Univ Minn, Duluth, 87-96; dept chair, Univ Minn, Duluth, 88-92; dir, Master of Liberal Studies Program, Univ Minn, Duluth, 96-present; distinguished McKnight univ prof, Univ Minn, 96-present. **HONORS AND AWARDS** McKnight Endowment Fel, Univ Minn; Summer Faculty Res Fel, Univ Minn; Outstanding Res Award, Univ Minn; Lansdowne Lectr, Univ Victoria; Pres, Minn Philosophical Society; Vice-pres, Minn Philosophical Society; Medal of the Univ of Helsinki; Summer Fac Res Fel, Univ Minn; Postdoctoral Fel in Computer Sci, Wright State Univ; Postdoctoral Res Fel, Nat Sci Found; Distinguished Teaching Award, Univ Ky; Summer Fac Res Fellow, 72; Graduate Res Asst, Ind Univ; Fel of the Fac, Colombia Univ; NDEA Title IV Fel, Ind Univ; The Dickinson Prize, Princeton Univ; Magna Cum Laude, Princeton. **MEMBERSHIPS** Philos of Sci Asn; Am Philosophical Asn; Asn for Computing Machinery; Human Behavior and Evolution Society; Int Society for Human Ethnology; Am Asn of Univ Profs; Society for Machines and Mentality; Am Asn for the Advanc of Sci. **RESEARCH** Philosophy of science; computer science; artificial intelligence; cognitive science. **SELECTED PUBLICATIONS** Auth, Philosophy of Science, Paragon House Publ, 93; coauth, Glossary of Epistemology/Philosophy of Science, Paragon House Publ, 93; coauth, Glossary of Cognitive Science, Paragon House Publ, 93; ed, Foundations of Philosophy of Science, Paragon House Publ, 93; co-ed, Program Verification Fundamental Issues in Computer Science, Kluwer Academic Publ, 93; auth, Philosophy and Cognitive Science, Paragon House Publ, 96; coauth, Assassination Science: Experts Speak Out on the Death of JFK, Catfeet Press, 98, co-ed, The New Theory of Reference: Kripke, Marcusk, and Its Origins, Kluwer Academic Publ, 98. **CONTACT ADDRESS** Dept of Philosophy, Univ of Minnesota, Duluth, MN, 55812. **EMAIL** jfetzer@d.umn.edu

FEUERHAHN, RONALD R.
PERSONAL Born 12/01/1937, Cape Girardeau, MO, m, 1963, 3 children **DISCIPLINE** HISTORICAL THEOLOGY **EDUCATION** Concordia Sr Col, BA, 59; Concordia Sem, MDiv, 63; Univ Cambridge, England, MPhil, 80, PhD, 92. **CAREER** Pastor, St. David's, Cardiff, Wales, 64-70; pastor, Resurrection, Cambridge, Eng, 70-77; preceptor, Westfield House, Cambridge, England, 77-86; asst prof, 86-95, assoc prof hist theol, 95- , asst chaplain and coord musical and cultural activities, 90-92, acting dean of chapel, 98, Concordia Sem. **MEMBERSHIPS** Cambridge Theol Soc; Soc for Liturgial Stud (Gr Britain); Societas Liturgica; Luther Acad; Lutheran Missiology Soc; Am Soc of Church Hist; Luthern Hist Conf. **RESEARCH** Liturgy and worship; ecumenical movement; law and Gospel; Hermann Sasse; movements of thought (Pietism, Rationalism. **SELECTED PUBLICATIONS** Co-ed, Scripture and the Church: Selected Essays of Hermann Sasse, Concordia Seminary, 95; auth, A Bibliography of Dr. Hermann Sasse, Scarecrow, 95; auth, Hermann Sasse: Confessional Ecumenist, Lutherische Theologie und Kirche, 95; auth, Hermann Sasse-Gesetz und Evangelium in der Geshcichte, in Diestelemann, ed, Eintrachtig Lehren: Festrschrift fuer Bischof Dr. Jobst Schone, Heinrich Harms, 97. **CONTACT ADDRESS** Concordia Sem, 801 DeMun Ave, St. Louis, MO, 63105. **EMAIL** feuerhahnr@csl.edu

FIDELER, PAUL ARTHUR
PERSONAL Born 05/16/1936, Passaic, NJ, m, 1963, 2 children **DISCIPLINE** BRITISH AND EUROPEAN HISTORY, WESTERN POLITICAL THOUGHT, WORLD PHILOSOPHIES **EDUCATION** St Lawrence Univ, BA, 58; Brandeis Univ, MA, 62, PhD(hist), 71. **CAREER** Instr, Framingham State Col, 64-68; asst prof to prof hist, 69-91, prof hist and humanities, Lesley Col, 73-; adv ed, Brit Studies Monitor. **HONORS AND AWARDS** Fel in NEH Summer Seminars and Inst, 74, 76, 77, 84, 89; Res Fel, The Folger Shakespeare Library, spring 90; Am Coun of Learned Soc Fel in Humanities Curriculum Development and Vis Schol, Harvard Univ, 92-93. **MEMBERSHIPS** AAUP; AHA; New Eng Hist Asn (pres 87-88); Am Philos Asn; Conf for the Study of Political Thought; N Am Conf on Brit Studies; NE Conf on Brit Studies (pres 91-93). **RESEARCH** Poor relief policy and political theory in early modern England; historiography and humanities methodologies; character, values, ethics, and justice in the curriculum, K-16. **SELECTED PUBLICATIONS** Auth, Christian Humanism and Poor Law Reform in Early Tudor England, Societas, fall 74; Have Historians Lost Their Perspective on the Past?, Change, Jan/Feb 84; Toward a Ccurricula of Hope: The Essential Role of Humanities Scholarship in Public School Teaching, Am Coun of Learned Soc, Occasional Paper, No. 23, 94; Rescuing Youth Culture: Cultivating Children's Natural Abilities as Philosophers, Lesley Mag, winter 94; coauth, Autobiography in the Classroom: A Triptych, Teaching the Humanities, spring 95; auth, Societas, Civitas and Early Elizabethan Poverty Relief, In: State, Sovereigns and Society: Essays in Early Modern English History, St. Martins, 98. **CONTACT ADDRESS** Humanities Faculty, Lesley Col, 29 Everett St, Cambridge, MA, 02138-2790. **EMAIL** pfideler@lesley.edu

FIELD, HARTRY
PERSONAL Born 11/30/1946, Boston, MA, 1 child **DISCIPLINE** PHILOSOPHY **EDUCATION** Univ Wis, BA, 67; Harvard Univ, PhD, 72. **CAREER** Asst prof, Princeton Univ, 70-76; assoc prof, Univ Southern Calif, 76-81; full prof, 81-91; prof, City Univ NY, 91-97; prof, 97-. **HONORS AND AWARDS** Guggenheim Fel. **MEMBERSHIPS** Am Philos Asn; Philos of Sci Asn. **RESEARCH** Epistemology; Metaphysics; Philosophy of mathematics. **SELECTED PUBLICATIONS** Auth, Realism: Mathematics and Modality, 89; Sciences Without Numbers, 80. **CONTACT ADDRESS** Philosophy Dept, New York Univ, New York, NY, 10003. **EMAIL** hf18@is4.nyu.edu

FIELD, THOMAS TILDEN
PERSONAL Born 09/09/1949, Hardwick, VT, m, 1977, 1 child **DISCIPLINE** ROMANCE AND THEORETICAL LINGUISTICS **EDUCATION** Wheaton Col, BA, 71; Cornell Univ, MA, 75, PhD (ling), 78. **CAREER** Instr French, State Univ NY Col Oswego, 78-79; ASST PROF LING AND FRENCH, UNIV MD BALTIMORE COUNTY, 79-, BIBLIOGR, COMP ROMANCE LING NEWSLETTER, 81-; consult, Charlotte-Mecklenburg Sch, NC, 82. **HONORS AND AWARDS** Gilbert Chinard Prize in Pedagogy, 82. **MEMBERSHIPS** Ling Soc Am; MLA; Am Asn Teachers French; Asn Int d'Etudes Occitanes. **RESEARCH** Occitan and French linguistics; textual analysis; phonology. **SELECTED PUBLICATIONS** Auth, Renaissance or Substitution--Sociolinguistic Research on the Occitan Language in the Cantal Region, Romance Philol, Vol 47, 94; Renaissance or Substitution--Sociolinguistic Research on the Occitan Language in the Cantal Region, Romance Philol, Vol 47, 94. **CONTACT ADDRESS** Dept of Mod Lang and Ling, Univ of Md, Baltimore County, Catonsville, MD, 21228.

FIELDER, JOHN H.
DISCIPLINE PHILOSOPHY **EDUCATION** Tulane Univ, BS; Univ Tex-Austin, PhD, 70. **CAREER** Prof, Villanova Univ. **HONORS AND AWARDS** Consultant grant from the Nat Endowment for the Humanities, through grants from, Asn Amer Col, Exxon Educ Found; Villanova Fac Summer Res grants, 91; shared grant, Asn for Continuing Higher Educ Res grant; Sears-Roebuck Found Tchg Excellence and Campus Leadership awd, 90; adj sr fel, Leonard Davis Inst Health Econ, Univ Pa., Develop and taught courses in, prof ethics for engineers, health care prof, and bus managers; develop, ethical decision making component of the grad course, Admin Decision Making. **MEMBERSHIPS** Amer Philos Assoc; Soc for Philos and Technol, Newsl Ed, 89-93; bd dir, Airline Safety Adv Panel, Airline Passengers Assoc N Am, 90-92; assoc ed, Consulting Medtronic, Inc. **RESEARCH** Professional ethics, case studies in technology and society, and ethical decision making. **SELECTED PUBLICATIONS** Auth, Abusive Peer Review and Health Care Reform, Health Care Crisis: The Search for Answers, Frederick, MD: Univ Publ Gp, 95; The Shiley Heart Valve - Continued, Engineering in Med and Biology, Vol 13, 94; Discarding Doctors, Engineering in Med and Biology, Vol 14, 95; How well do Medical Devices Work, Engineering in Med and Biology, Vol 13, 94 & Ethical Experts and Dr. Ethics, Engineering in Medicine and Biology, Vol 12, 94; coauth, The Ford Pinto Case: A Study in Applied Ethics, Technology, and Society, Albany, NY: SUNY Press, 94; Analyzing Ethical Problems in Medical Products: The Role of Conflicting Ethical Theories, Clinical Res and Regulatory Aff, Vol 11, 94; But Doctor, It's My Hip!: The Fate of Failed Medical Devices, Kennedy Inst Ethics J Vol 5, 95; The Ethics and Politics of Auto Regulation, in The Ford Pinto Case: A Study in Applied Ethics, Technology, and Society, Albany, NY: SUNY Press, 94. **CONTACT ADDRESS** Dept of Philosophy, Villanova Univ, 800 Lancaster Ave, Villanova, PA, 19085-1692.

FIELDS, MILTON
PERSONAL Born 04/26/1941, Millport, AL, m, 1965, 1 child **DISCIPLINE** ELEMENTARY EDUCATION, SUPERVISION, SCHOOL ADMINISTRATION, READING **EDUCATION** Free Will Baptist Bible Coll, BA, 67; Univ Ala Birmingham, BS, 76; Univ S Ala, MD, 80; Univ S Miss, PhD, 83. **CAREER** Asst Prin, EscatAwardpa Elem School, Moss Point, Miss, 76-83; Chairman of Bd Post Sec Prog for Ment Retared Adults, Columbus, Miss, 83-86; Prin, Carrollton Elem School, Carrollton, Ala, 86-88; P rin, Caledonia and W Lowndes Mid School, Columbus, Miss, 88-92; Prin, Fairview Elem School, Columbus, Miss, 92-92; Prof, Free Will Baptist Bibl Coll, Nashville, Tenn, 94-; Acad dean, Free Will Baptist Bibl Coll, Nashville, Tenn, 94-. **MEMBERSHIPS** Coll Rep Metrop Coun of Teacher Educrs; Tenn Asn of Independent Lib Arts Colls; Tenn Asn of Tecacher Educrs; Exec Bd of TATE. **RESEARCH** Christian Education; Communication Anxiety. **SELECTED PUBLICATIONS** Auth, Anxiety Among Elementary Teachers According to Various Formats and Levels of Written Memoranda, 83; Decision-making, Mgt, Educ articles, Contact, 82; Educ artciles, Free Will Baptist Bibl Coll Bull, 94. **CONTACT ADDRESS** Free Will Baptist Bible Col, 3606 West End Ave, Nashville, TN, 37025. **EMAIL** mfields@fwbbc.edu

FIELDS, STEPHEN MICHAEL
PERSONAL Born 06/19/1952, Baltimore, MD, s **DISCIPLINE** PHILOSOPHICAL; SYSTEMATIC THEOLOGY **EDUCATION** Yale Univ, PhD 93, MPhil 90, MA 88; Weston Sch Theol, STL 87, MDiv 86; Oxford Univ PC, MA 83, BA 77. **CAREER** Georgetown Univ, asst prof 93-; St Joseph's Univ, vis instr 81-83; Santa Clara Univ, Bannon Fel 96-97. **HONORS AND AWARDS** Bannan Res Lectr Fel; 4 Georgetown Res Gnts; Yale Diss Fel, decl Fulbright; Yale Univ Fel. **MEMBERSHIPS** AAR; CTSA; MS; JPS; Catholic Comm Intell and Cultural Affs. **RESEARCH** Thomism; Idealism; Newman; Rahner. **SELECTED PUBLICATIONS** Auth, Balthasar Christianity and Metaphysics, The Presidential Address, The Proceedings of the Jesuit Philosophical Association 1997, ed, Michael J. Barber, 98; auth, Doctrine as Symbol: Johann Adam Mohler in Dialogue with Kant and Hegel, The Legacy of the Tubingen School: The Relevance of Nineteenth Century Theology for the twenty-first Century, eds, Donald J Dietrich, Michael J. Himes, NY, Crossroad, 97; auth, The Metaphysics of Symbol in Thomism: Aeterni Patris to Rahner, Intl Philos Quart, 97; auth, Balthasar and Rahner on the Spiritual Senses, Theol Studies, 96; auth, Chartres Platonism and Christian Love, Modern Age: Quart Rev, 94. **CONTACT ADDRESS** Dept of Theology, Georgetown Univ, 3700 O St NW, Washington, DC, 20057. **EMAIL** fieldss@gunet.georgetown.edu

FIENSY, DAVID A.
PERSONAL McCleansboro, IL, m, 1971, 2 children **DISCIPLINE** RELIGION; NEW TESTAMENT **EDUCATION** Duke Univ, PhD, 80. **CAREER** Assoc prof, Ky Christ Col, 80-87; Inst Scholar, Inst zur Erforschung des Urchristentums, Ger, 87-89; Pastor, Church of Christ, Jamestown, OH, 89-95; prof, Ky Christian Col, 95- . **HONORS AND AWARDS** Appalachian Col Asn summer fel, 98. **MEMBERSHIPS** Soc Biblical Lit; Context; Evangelical Theol Soc. **RESEARCH** Historical Jesus; Social Scientific Criticism of New Testament; Second Temple; Judaism. **SELECTED PUBLICATIONS** Auth, Prayers Alleged to be Jewish: An Examination of the Constitutiones Apostolorum, Scholars Press, Chico, CA, 85; The Social History of Palestine in the Herodian Period: The Land is Mind, Edwin Mellen Press, Lampeter, Lewiston, Queenston, 91; The Hellenistic Synagogal Prayers, in Anchor Bible Dictionary, Doubleday, 93; Craftsmen as Brokers, Proceedings of the Eastern Great Lakes Biblical Soc, 94; New Testament Introduction, College Press, Jopin, MO, 94; Faith in Practice: Studies in the Book of Acts, co-ed, EES, Atlanta, GA, 95; The Composition of the Jerusalem Church, in Acts in Its Palestinian Setting, Eerdmans, 95; Poverty and Wealth in the Gospels and Acts, in Faith in Practice: Studies in the Book of Acts, EES, D.A. Fiensy and W. Howden, eds, 95; The Message and Ministry of Jesus: An Introduction Textbook, UP of America, Lanham, MD, 96; Jesus' Socio-Economic Background in Hillel and Jesus, eds, J.H. Charlesworth and L. Johns, Fortress, 97. **CONTACT ADDRESS** Dept of Religion, Kentucky Christian Col, 100 Academic Pkwy, Grayson, KY, 41143. **EMAIL** dfiensy@email.kcc.edu

FILLINGIM, DAVID
DISCIPLINE PHILOSOPHY **EDUCATION** Mercer Univ, Macon, BA, 82; Southeastern Baptist Theol Sem, Mdiv, 85; clin Pastoral educ, 9 units: Baptist Med Ctr, Columbia, 86-87; Ga Reg Hosp at Augusta, 85-86; John Umstead Hosp, Butner, 84; Southern Baptist Theol Sem, PhD, 96. **CAREER** Asst prof; past dir, Independent Stud: Feminist Theol and Ethics; VP, Fac Forum, 97-98; ch, Comt on Stud Internet Access; Alpha Chi Hon Soc Comt; Fac Develop Comt; Admissions Comt; SACS Comt on Tchr Improvement Prog; Ad Hoc Comt to Draft Ethics Prog Proposal; Registration Comt for Presidential Inauguration; acad adv, Relig and Undecided majors; min trng ldr, Christian Stud Un; reg church leadership trng fac, NC Baptist Conv; adj prof, Shaw Univ Ctr for Alternative Prog in Educ, CAPE, 97; vis instr, Theol Dept, Bellarmine Col, Louisville, 96; instr, Southern Baptist Theol Sem, Louisville, 94-96; instr, Philos Dept, Jefferson Commun Col, Downtown Campus, Louisville, 94 & 95; instr, Philos Dept, Georgetown Col, 94-95; instr, Jefferson Commun Col, LaGrange, 94-95; Pastor, Pleasant Plain Baptist Church, Kershaw, 88-91; gp therapist, Baptist Med Ctr, Columbia, 87-88; Struct Gp Ldr, Lexington-Richland Alcohol and Drug Abuse Coun, Columbia, 87-88; Chaplain Resident, Baptist Med Ctr, Columbia, 86-87; Clin Cha. **MEMBERSHIPS** Exec coun, Popular Cult Asn in the S & Am Cult Asn in the South, 95-97; Am Acad Rel; Soc Christian Ethics; Nat Asn Baptist Prof Rel; Southern Humanities Coun; Baptist Asn Philos Tchr(s); Asn for Practical and Prof Ethics. **CONTACT ADDRESS** Dept of Relig and Philos, Chowan Col, Murfreesboro, NC, 27855.

FILONOWICZ, JOSEPH
DISCIPLINE HISTORY OF ETHICS, SOCIAL AND POLITICAL PHILOSOPHY **EDUCATION** Hope Col, BA; Columbia Univ, MA, MPhil, PhD. **CAREER** Assoc prof, Long Island Univ. **MEMBERSHIPS** Ch, Long Island Philos Soc. **RESEARCH** History of the ideas of the British sentimental moralists, moral philosophy, psychology of ethics, American philosophy. **SELECTED PUBLICATIONS** Wrote on ethical sentimentalism for the History of Philos Quart. **CONTACT ADDRESS** Long Island Univ, Brooklyn, NY, 11201-8423. **EMAIL** JFilonow@eagle.liunet.edu

FINDLAY JR, JAMES F.
DISCIPLINE RECENT US HISTORY, AMERICAN RELIGION, AND THE CIVIL RIGHTS MOVEMENT **EDUCATION** Northwestern Univ, PhD, 61. **CAREER** Dept Hist, Univ RI **HONORS AND AWARDS** URI Res Excellence awd. **RESEARCH** Protestant churches in the Civil Rights movement. **SELECTED PUBLICATIONS** Auth, biography of Dwight L. Moody. **CONTACT ADDRESS** Dept of Hist, Univ of RI, 8 Ranger Rd, Ste. 1, Kingston, RI, 02881-0807.

FINE, ARTHUR
DISCIPLINE PHILOSOPHY **EDUCATION** Chichago Univ, PhD. **CAREER** John Evans prof, Northwestern Univ. **RESEARCH** Philosophy of physics, philosophy of natural and social science. **SELECTED PUBLICATIONS** Auth, The Shaky Game: Einstein, Realism and Quantum Theory; Science Made Up: Constructivist Sociology of Scientific Knowledge, The Disunity of Science: Boundaries, Contexts and Power, 95; Indeterminism and the Freedom of the Will, Philosophical Problems of the Internal and External Worlds, 93; Causes of Variation: Disentangling Nature and Nurture, Midwest Studies in Philosophy, 90; co-ed, Bohmian Mechanics and Quantum Theory: An Appraisal. **CONTACT ADDRESS** Dept of Philosophy, Northwestern Univ, 1801 Hinman, Evanston, IL, 60208.

FINE, KIT
PERSONAL Born 03/26/1946, United Kingdom, s, 2 children **DISCIPLINE** PHILOSOPHY **CAREER** Prof, NYU. **RESEARCH** Logic, philosophy. **CONTACT ADDRESS** 100 Washington Square E, Philo Main, New York, NY, 10003-6688. **EMAIL** kf14@.s4.nyu.edu

FINEGAN, EDWARD J.
DISCIPLINE LINGUISTICS LAW **EDUCATION** Iona Col, BS; Ohio Univ, MA; Univ Mich, MA; Ohio Univ, PhD. **CAREER** Prof; post-doc, Univ Southern Calif; Ohio State Univ, Ling Inst & Harvard Law Sch; Liberal Arts fel, Harvard Law Sch. **MEMBERSHIPS** Past dir, Amer Lang Inst/Nat Iranian Radio and Tv. **RESEARCH** Legal writing. **SELECTED PUBLICATIONS** Auth, Language: Its Structure and Use; coauth, Looking at Languages. **CONTACT ADDRESS** School of Law, Univ Southern Calif, University Park Campus, Los Angeles, CA, 90089.

FINGER, THOMAS
PERSONAL Born 05/12/1942, Chicago, IL, m, 1969, 2 children **DISCIPLINE** PHILOSOPHY **EDUCATION** Wheaton Col, AB, 65; Gordon Divinity School, MA & BD, 68; Claremont Grad School, PhD, 75. **CAREER** Asst to assoc prof of Philosophy, E Mennonite Col, 73-76; instr Sem Consortium Urban Pastoral Educ, 76-78; asst to assoc to full prof Systematic Theol, N Baptist Sem, 76-86; prof, systematic & spiritual theol, E Mennonite Sem, 89-; int pastor, Circle Evangelical Free Church, 78; fel, Inst Advanced Study Relig, Univ Chicago Divinity School, 80; pastor, N Bronx Mennonite Church, 87-89. **MEMBERSHIPS** Christian Environ Coun Evangelical Environ Network, 94; Soc Study E Orthodoxy and Evangelicalism. **RESEARCH** Systematic, Contemporary, and Historical Theology; Spiritual Theology; Environmental Theology. **SELECTED PUBLICATIONS** Auth, Modern Alienation and Trinitarian Creation, Evangelical Rev Theol, 93; Konrad Raisers View of a New Ecumenical Paradigm, Ecumenical Trends, 93; Modernity, Postmodernity--what in the world are they?, Transformation, 93; Anabaptism and Eastern Orthodoxy: some unexpected similarites?, Jour Ecumenical Studies, 94; In Praise of Sophia, Christianity Today, 94; auth, Trinity, Ecology, and Panentheism, Christians Scholars Rev, 97; Self, Earth and Society, InterVarsity, 97; A Mennonite Theology for Interfaith Relations, Grounds for Understanding, 98. **CONTACT ADDRESS** Eastern Mennonite Univ, Harrisonburg, VA, 22802. **EMAIL** fingert@cmu.edu

FINKELSTEIN, RONA
PERSONAL Born 11/07/1927, Rochester, NY, w, 1950, 2 children **DISCIPLINE** ART; PHIOSOPHY **EDUCATION** Connecticut Col, BA, 49; MA, 61, PhD, 64, Univ Rochester. **CAREER** Delaware State Col, 64-70, chairperson, 66-70; Univ Delaware, Col Parallel Program, 70-72; Exec Dir, Delaware Humanities Forum, 72-81. **MEMBERSHIPS** APA **RESEARCH** Mind-Body **CONTACT ADDRESS** 115 Sorrel Dr., Surrey Pk., Wilmington, DE, 19803. **EMAIL** rfinkel850@aol.com

FINKEN, BRYAN W.
PERSONAL Born 03/23/1961, Denver, CO, s **DISCIPLINE** PHILOSOPHY **EDUCATION** Metropolitan State Col, Denver, BA; Univ Illinois, Urbana Champaign, PhD, 93. **CAREER** Vis asst prof, Univ Arkansas, 92-93; vis lectr, Univ Witwatersrand, Johannesburg, 93-95; temp asst prof, Auburn Univ, 96-97; instr, Metropolitan State Col, 97-98. **HONORS AND AWARDS** Named six times to The Incomplete List of Teachers Ranked as Excellent by their Students, at Univ Ill. **MEMBERSHIPS** APA; N Am Nietzsche Soc; S Af Philos Asn. **RESEARCH** Theory of illusion; sciolism in the twentieth century; postmodernism as a hate movement; moral psychology; political theory; degradation of standards in the humanities; Nietzsche's metaphysics. **CONTACT ADDRESS** 2168 S Everett St, Lakewood, CO, 80227. **EMAIL** finkenb@mscd.edu

FINKIN, MATTHEW W.
DISCIPLINE LAW **EDUCATION** Ohio Wesleyan Univ, AB; Univ NY, LL.B; Yale Univ, LL.M. **CAREER** Prof, Univ Ill Urbana Champaign. **HONORS AND AWARDS** Humboldt Foundation's Res Awd. **MEMBERSHIPS** Am Asn Univ Prof, 76-78. **RESEARCH** Labor law; labor law II; higher education law; individual employee relations. **SELECTED PUBLICATIONS** Auth, pubs on labor and employment law, higher education law, and comparative law; ed, Privacy in Employment Law, BNA, 95; The Case for Tenure, Cornell, 96; co-ed, Labor Law, Foundation, 96; Introduction to German Law, Kluwer, 96. **CONTACT ADDRESS** Law Dept, Univ Ill Urbana Champaign, 52 E Gregory Dr, Champaign, IL, 61820. **EMAIL** mfinkin@law.uiuc.edu

FINLAYSON, ARNOLD ROBERT
PERSONAL Born 06/30/1963, Washington, DC, s **DISCIPLINE** LAW **EDUCATION** Bowie State Coll, BS, 1985; Howard University School of Law, JD, 1989. **CAREER** US Dept of State, procurement analyst, 1987-90; Hon George W Mitchell, assoc judge, DC Superior Court; judicial law clerk; 1990-92; Shaw, Pittman, Potts & Trowbridge, govt contracts associate, 1992-. **HONORS AND AWARDS** Howard University School of Law, Wiley A Branton Leadership Award, 1989, American Jurisprudence Award, Professional Responsibility, 1989, American Jurisprudence Award, Natl Moot Court, 1989. **MEMBERSHIPS** District of Columbia Bar, 1992; Bar of the Commonwealth of Pennsylvania, 1989; US Court of Appeals for the Federal Circuit, 1993; Amer Bar Assn, 1989; Kappa Alpha Psi Fraternity, Inc, 1983. **SELECTED PUBLICATIONS** Co-Author, Financing Govt Contracts, 1993. **CONTACT ADDRESS** Shaw, Pittman, Potts & Trowbridge, 2300 N St NW, 6th Floor, Washington, DC, 20037.

FINLEY, THOMAS JOHN
PERSONAL Born 10/29/1945, Jacksonville, FL, m, 1969, 2 children **DISCIPLINE** OLD TESTAMENT, ANCIENT SEMITIC LANGUAGES **EDUCATION** Biola Col, BA, 67, MDiv, 71; Univ Calif, Los Angeles, MA, 74, PhD, 79. **CAREER** Prof Old Testament & Semitics, Talbot Theol Sem, Biola Col, 77-. **MEMBERSHIPS** Soc Bibl Lit; Evangel Theol Soc. **RESEARCH** Old Testament biblical Hebrew, Aramaic & Akkadian languages; Studies on Joel, Amos and Obadiah. **SELECTED PUBLICATIONS** Auth, Joel, Obadiah, and Micah, Everymen Bible Commentary; Moody, 95; auth, A Bilingual Concordance to the Targum of the Prophets: Ezekiel, Brill, 98. **CONTACT ADDRESS** Talbot Theol Sem, Biola Univ, 13800 Biola Ave, La Mirada, CA, 90639-0002. **EMAIL** tom_finley@peter.biola.edu

FINN, DANIEL R.
PERSONAL Born 04/30/1947, Rochester, NY, m, 1978, 2 children **DISCIPLINE** RELIGIOUS SOCIAL ETHICS; ECONOMICS **EDUCATION** St John Fisher Col, BS, 68; Univ Chicago, MA, 75, PhD, 77. **CAREER** Asst prof, 77-84, assoc prof, 84-91, prof, 91- , chair, dept of economics and theology, 82-84, dean, sch of theology, 84-89, St John's Univ. **HONORS AND AWARDS** Clemens Chair in Economics and the Liberal Arts, St John's Univ, 89- . **MEMBERSHIPS** Soc of Christian Ethics; MN Consortium of Theological Schs; Assn for Social Economics; Midwest Assn of Theological Schs; Amer Economics Assn; Assn for Evolutionary Economics; Catholic Theological Soc of Amer; History of Economics Soc; Midwest Economics Soc; MN Economics Assn. **SELECTED PUBLICATIONS** Coauth,Toward a Christian Economic Ethic: Stewardship and Social Power, Winston, 85; auth, Self-Interest, Markets and the Four Problems of Economics Life, Annual of the Society of Chritian Ethics, 89; auth, Employment in the US: Public Discourse and Longterm Trends, Forum for Social Economics, 94; auth, Three Cheers for the Gas Tax, The Christian Century, 96; auth, Just Trading: On the Ethics and Economics of International Trade, Abingdon, 96. **CONTACT ADDRESS** Dept. of Economics, St Johns Univ, Collegeville, MN, 56321. **EMAIL** dfinn@csbsju.edu

FINN, THOMAS M.
PERSONAL Born 03/18/1927, New York, NY, m, 1968, 1 child **DISCIPLINE** PATRISTICS **EDUCATION** St. Paul's Col, AB, 56, MA, 58; Cath Univ Am, STL, 61, STD, 65. **CAREER** Chancellor Prof Relig. Col William and Mary, 73-. **HONORS AND AWARDS** Melone Fel, Coun on U.S. Arab Relations, 90; Res Fel, Inst Ecumenical and Cultural Res, 95. **MEMBERSHIPS** Am Acad Relig; Cath Bibl Asn; NAm Patristic Soc; Int Patristic Soc. **RESEARCH** Ritual in Greco-Roman antiquity, paganism, Judaism, and Christianity. **SELECTED PUBLICATIONS** Auth, Early Christian Baptism and the Catechumenate: Italy, North Africa and Egypt, Litturgical Press, 92; Early Christian Baptism and the Catechumenate: West and East Syria, Litturgical Press, 92; From Death to Rebirth: Conversion in Antiquity, Paulist Press, 97; Quodvultdeus; The Preacher and the Audience: The Homilies on the Creed, Studia Patristica 31, 97; Ritual and Conversion: The Case of Augustine, Nova & Vetera: Patristic Studies in Honor of Thomas Patrick Halton, Cath Univ Am Press, 98. **CONTACT ADDRESS** Religion Dept, Col of William and Mary, 310 Wren Building, Williamsburg, VA, 23187-8795. **EMAIL** tmfinn@facstaff.wm.edu

FINNEY, PAUL CORBY
DISCIPLINE HISTORY, ART & ARCHAEOLOGY, RELIGION **EDUCATION** Yale Univ, AB, 62; Maximilians Univ, Germany, 62-63; Harvard Univ, MA, PhD, 73. **CAREER** ASST PROF, ASSOC PROF, PROF, UNIV MO, ST LOUIS, 73-; area supervisor, Am Schs Oriental Res excavation Cathage, Tunisia, 75- 77; sen lectr, Hebrew Univ, Jerusalem, 79; vis lectr, Princeton Theol Sem, 83; sen assoc, Am Sch Class Stud, Athens, 87; assoc archaeologist, Gr Ministry Antiquities, 87; vis fel, Princeton Univ, 92, 95, 98, 99. **CONTACT ADDRESS** Dept of History, Univ of Missouri, 8001 Natural Bridge Rd, St. Louis, MO, 63121. **EMAIL** spcfinn@umslvma.umsl.edu

FINOCCHIARO, MAURICE A.
PERSONAL Born 06/13/1942, Florida, Italy, m, 1966 **DISCIPLINE** PHILOSOPHY **EDUCATION** MIT, BS, 64; Univ Calif, Berkeley, PhD, 69. **CAREER** From asst to assoc prof, 70-77, prof 77- , Distinguished Prof 91- , philos, Univ Nev, Las Vegas; vis scholar, hist sci, Harvard Univ, 98-99. **HONORS AND AWARDS** NSF res grant 76-77; NEH fel 83-84; ACLS fel 91-92; NEH res grant 92-95; Nevada State Bd of Regents Res 93; Guggenheim fel 98-99; NSF res grant, 98-01. **MEMBERSHIPS** APA; Philos Sci Asn; Hist Sci Soc; Asn Informal Logic and Critical Thinking; Am Asn It Stud. **RESEARCH** Philosophy of science; informal logic; Galileo; Antonio Gramsci; Benedetto Croce; Gaetano Mosca. **SELECTED PUBLICATIONS** Auth, History of Science as Explanation, Wayne State Univ, 73; auth, Galileo and the Art of Reasoning, Kluwer-Reidel, 80; auth, Gramsci and The History of Dialectical Thought, Cambridge, 88; auth, Gramsci Critico e la Critica, Armando, 88; transl and ed, The Galileo Affair, Univ Calif, 89; auth, Beyond Right and Left: Democratic Elitism in Mosca and Gramsci, Yale, 99. **CONTACT ADDRESS** Dept of Philosophy, Univ of Nevada, Las Vegas, Las Vegas, NV, 89154-5028. **EMAIL** mauricef@nevada.edu

FIORE, ROBIN N.
DISCIPLINE PHILOSOPHY **EDUCATION** Georgetown Univ, PhD, 97. **CAREER** Frances Elridge Post doct res fel, ethics, 97-98, Ethics Ctr, St Petersburg, FL; asst prof, ethics, 98-, Fla Atlantic Univ **HONORS AND AWARDS** Andrew Mellon Dist Fel, 96. **MEMBERSHIPS** APA; Fla Bioethics Network; Soc for Women in Phil. **RESEARCH** Bioethics; managed care; aging. **SELECTED PUBLICATIONS** Auth, Realizing Liberalism: Toward a Feminist Theory of Equality, 97; auth, Caring for Ourselves: Peer Care in Autonomous Aging, Mother Time: Women, Aging, and Ethics, Rowman & Littlefield, 99. **CONTACT ADDRESS** Florida Atlantic Univ, PO Box 3091, Boca Raton, FL, 33431. **EMAIL** rfione@fau.edu

FIORENZA, ELIZABETH SCHUSSLER
PERSONAL Germany **DISCIPLINE** NEW TESTAMENT STUDIES **EDUCATION** Univ Munster, Dr theol, 70; Univ Wurzburg, Lic theol, 63, MDiv, 62. **CAREER** Instr theol, Univ Munster, 65-66; asst prof, 70-75, assoc prof, 75-80, PROF THEOL, UNIV NOTRE DAME, 80-, Vis prof theol, Union Theol Sem, NY, 74-75; scripture coordr clergy educ, Notre Dame Inst Clergy Educ, 76-77; distinguished vis scholar, Col Wooster, 82. **MEMBERSHIPS** Cath Bibl Asn; Soc Bibl Lit; Studiorum Novi Testamenti Soc; Am Acad Relig; Col Theol Soc. **RESEARCH** New Testament studies and early Christianity; women's studies in religion; pastoral theology. **SELECTED PUBLICATIONS** Auth, Speaking Out, J Fem Stud Rel, Vol 12, 96; Feminist Issues Regarding Family Values and the Famil, J Feminist Stud Rel, Vol 12, 96. **CONTACT ADDRESS** Dept of Theol, Univ of Notre Dame, Notre Dame, IN, 46556.

FIRMAGE, EDWIN BROWN
PERSONAL Born 10/01/1935, Provo, UT, m, 1955, 7 children **DISCIPLINE** LAW **EDUCATION** Brigham Young Unv, BS, 60, MS, 62; Univ Chicago, JD, 63, LLM & SJD, 64. **CAREER** Asst prof law, Univ Mo, 64-65; White House fel, Vpres Humphrey's Staff, DC, 65-66; from Asst Prof to Prof Law, 66-90, Samuel D. Thurman Prof Law, Univ Utah, 90-; UN vis scholar, 70-71; Int rel fel at arms control negotiations, Geneva, Switz, Coun Foreign Relat, 70-71; fel law & humanities, Harvard Law Sch, 74-75, Univ Tex Law Sch, summer, 79; vis prof, Univ London, 92; Kellogg Lectr, Episcopal Divinity Sch, Cambridge, MA, 93. **HONORS AND AWARDS** Univ Distinguished Tchg Award, Univ UT, 77; Reynolds Lectr, Univ UT, 87; Charles Rodd Prize in Humanities, 88; First Place Prize, Alpha Sigma Nu, for "Zion in the Courts...", 89; McDougall Lectr, 89; Governor's Award in the Humanities, 89; Turner-Fairbanks Award for contributions to Peace & Justice, 91; Rosenblatt Prize for Excellence, 91. **MEMBERSHIPS** Am Bar Asn; Am Soc Int Law; Am Judicature Soc; Order of the Coif; Coun For Rel. **RESEARCH** International Law; torts; comp law. **SELECTED PUBLICATIONS** Auth, Removal of the President: Resignation and the procedural law of impeachment, Duke Law J, 75; The Utah Supreme Court and the rule of law: Phillips and the Bill of Rights in Utah 1975, Utah Law Rev, 76; Law and the Indo-China War: a retrospective view, In: The Vietnam War and International Law, Princeton Univ, 76; Vladivostok and beyond: An analysis of Salt II, Columbia J Trans Law, 76; The war powers and the political question doctrine, Univ Colo Law Rev, 78; MX: National Security and the Destruction of Society's Values, That Awesome Space, 81; Allegiance & Stewardship, Christianity and Cirsis, 3/82; Zion in the Courts, Ill Press, 88; coauth, The War Powers in History & Law, Ill Press, 89; auth, Religion and Law: Islamic, Jewish, and Christian Perspectives, Eisenbraun's, 90; The International Legal Systems, Foundation Press, 95. **CONTACT ADDRESS** Col of Law, Univ UT, Salt Lake City, UT, 84112-1107.

FISCELLA, JOAN B.
PERSONAL Born 12/24/1939, Chicago, IL **DISCIPLINE** PHILOSOPHY; LIBRARY SCIENCE **EDUCATION** St. Mary's Col, S Bend, Ind, BA, 63; Univ Notre Dame, PhD, 77; Univ Mich, AMLS, 83. **CAREER** Asst prof, Mary Manse Col, Toledo, Oh, 73-75; vis asst prof, Univ Il, 80-81; asst prof, Wayne St Univ, Detroit, Mich, 75-82; head, Auraria Library, 84-86; head, Univ Houston Libr, 88-90; bibliographer, asst prof to assoc prof, Univ Il Chicago, 90- . **HONORS AND AWARDS** Beta Phi Mu, Libr Sci Honor Soc, 83 **MEMBERSHIPS** Amer Libr Assoc; Amer Soc Infor Sci **RESEARCH** Characteristics of interdisciplinary lit & its implications for scholarly commun **SELECTED PUBLICATIONS** Coauth, Independent Office Collections and the Evolving Role of Academic Librarians, Libr Resources & Tech Svc, 94; An Approach to Assessing Faculty Use of Locally Loaded Databases, Col & Res Libr, 95; Collection Development, in Managing Business Collections in Libraries, Greenwood Press, 96; auth, Bibliography as an Interdisciplinary Service, Libr Trends, 96; Interdisciplinary Education: A Guide to Resources, New York, The Col Bd, 99. **CONTACT ADDRESS** Collections Develop Dept, Univ Il Chicago Libr, PO Box 8198 M/C 234, Chicago, IL, 60680. **EMAIL** jbf@uic.edu

FISCHEL, DANIEL R.
PERSONAL Born 12/10/1950, New York, NY, 1 child **DISCIPLINE** CORPORATION LAW **EDUCATION** Cornell Univ, BA, 72; Brown Univ, MA, 74; Sch of Law, Univ Chicago, JD, 77. **CAREER** Law clerk, Judge Thomas E Fairchild, Chief Judge, Seventh Circuit Court of Appeals, 77-78 and Assoc Justice Potter Stewart, US Supreme Court, 78-79; atty, Levy and Erens, 79-80; PROF LAW, NORTHWESTERN UNIV, 80-, Consult, Lexecon, Inc, 81-; vis prof law, Sch of Law, Univ Chicago, 82-83. **SELECTED PUBLICATIONS** Auth, Corporate Crime, J Legal Stud, Vol 25, 96; Clustering and Competition in Asset Markets, J Law Economics, Vol 40, 97; Contract and Fiduciary Duty, J Law Economics, Vol 36, 93. **CONTACT ADDRESS** Sch of Law, Northwestern Univ, Chicago, IL, 60611.

FISCHER, DAVID ARNOLD
PERSONAL Born 05/10/1943, St. Louis, MO, m, 1969, 1 child **DISCIPLINE** LAW **EDUCATION** Lincoln Col, AA, 63; Univ Mo-Columbia, AB, 65, JD, 68. **CAREER** From asst prof to assoc prof, 72-78, PROF LAW, UNIV MO-COLUMBIA, 78-. **MEMBERSHIPS** Am Bar Asn, **RESEARCH** Products liability. **SELECTED PUBLICATIONS** Auth, Proportional Liability--Statistical Evidence and the Probability Paradox, Vanderbilt Law Rev, Vol 46, 93. **CONTACT ADDRESS** Sch of Law, Univ of Mo, 310 Watson Pl, Columbia, MO, 65211-0001.

FISCHER, JOHN MARTIN
DISCIPLINE PHILOSOPHY **EDUCATION** Cornell Univ, PhD. **CAREER** DIR, HONORS PROG, PROF, UNIV CALIF, RIVERSIDE. **RESEARCH** Metaphysics; Moral philosophy; Philosophy of mind; Philosophy of religion. **SELECTED PUBLICATIONS** Ed, Moral Responsibility, Cornell Univ Press, 86; God, Foreknowledge and Freedom, Stanford Univ Press, 89; The Metaphysics of Death, Stanford Univ Press, 93; co-ed, Ethics: Problems and Principles, Harcourt Brace Jovanovich, 91; Perspectives on Moral Responsibility, Cornell Univ Press, 93; coauth, Responsibility and Control: A Theory of Moral Responsibility, Cambridge Univ Press, 97; auth, The Metaphysics of Free Will: An Essay on Control, Blackwell, 94. **CONTACT ADDRESS** Dept of Philos, Univ Calif, 1156 Hinderaker Hall, Riverside, CA, 92521-0209. **EMAIL** fischer@ucrac1.ucr.edu

FISCHER, MARILYN R.
DISCIPLINE SOCIAL PHILOSOPHY, ETHICS **EDUCATION** Boston Univ, Phd, 78. **CAREER** Dept Philos, Univ Dayton **RESEARCH** Philosophy of music. **SELECTED PUBLICATIONS** Auth, The Orchestral Workplace, Jour Soc Philos, 94; Philanthropy and Injustice in Mill and Addams, Nonprofit and Voluntary Sector Quart, 95; Rawls, Assns and the Political Conception of Justice, Jour Soc Philos, 97. **CONTACT ADDRESS** Dept of Philos, Univ Dayton, 300 Col Park, Dayton, OH, 75062. **EMAIL** fischer@checkov.hm.udayton.edu

FISCHER, NORMAN ARTHUF
PERSONAL Born 02/12/1943, Norway, MI, m, 3 children **DISCIPLINE** PHILOSOPHY **EDUCATION** Univ Wis-Madison, BA, 65; Univ Wash, MA, 68, Phd(philos), 75. **CAREER** Instr, 74-75, asst prof philos, Kent State Univ, 75-. **MEMBERSHIPS** Am Philos Asn; Hegel Soc Am. **RESEARCH** Marxism;Frankfort School, Social philosophy; Philosophy of Art, Film, Law, Environment. **SELECTED PUBLICATIONS** Auth; Economy and Self, Greenwood, 79; Marx's Early Concept of Democrat and the Ethical Bases of Socialism, Cambridge, 81; Hegelian Marxism and Ethics, Canadian Journal of Political and Social Theory, 84; Lucien Goldmann and Tragic Marxist Ethics, Philosophy and Social Criticism, 87; From Aesthetic Education to Environmental Aesthetics, CLIO, 96; Jurgen Habermas' Recent Philosophy of Law and the Optimum Point Between Universalism and Communitarianism, Kansas, 97; Frankfort School Marxism and Ethical Analysis of Art, Communication Theory, 97. **CONTACT ADDRESS** Dept of Philos, Kent State Univ, PO Box 5190, Kent, OH, 44242-0001. **EMAIL** parsquix@aol.com

FISCHER, ROBERT HARLEY
PERSONAL Born 04/26/1918, Williamsport, PA, m, 1942, 1 child **DISCIPLINE** PHILOSOPHY **EDUCATION** Gettysburg Col, AB, 39; Lutheran Theol Sem, Gettysburg, BD, 42; Yale Univ, PhD, 47. **CAREER** Minister, Hartland Community Parish, BT, 44-45; asst pastor, Zion Lutheran Church, Sunbury, Pa, 47-49; PROF HIST THEOL, LUTHERAN SCH THEOL, CHICAGO, 49-, Guest prof, McCormick Theol Sem, 51, 53, Garrett Theol Sem, 55, 66, Augustana Theol Sem, 61, Evangel Theol Sem, 63, Marquette Univ, 66, Kirchliche Hochschule, Berlin, 73 and Lutheran Sem, Tokyo, 80; tutor, Mansfield Col, Oxford Univ, 57-58; Am Asn Theol Schs fel, Tubingen, 64-65; assoc ed, Lutheran Quart, 65-72. **MEMBERSHIPS** Am Theol Soc Midwest Div; Am Soc Reformation Res (pres, 54); NAm Acad Ecumenists; Am Soc Church Hist; Lutheran Hist Conf (vpres, 72-76). **RESEARCH** Reformation history, especially theology of Luther; 19th century American Lutheranism; ecumenics. **SELECTED PUBLICATIONS** Auth, Roly--Chronicle of a Stubborn Nonconformist, Church Hist, Vol 63, 94. **CONTACT ADDRESS** Lutheran Sch of Theol, 1100 E 55th St, Chicago, IL, 60615.

FISH, ARTHUR
DISCIPLINE LAW **EDUCATION** Univ Toronto, BA, 80; Osgoode Hall Law Sch, LLB, 82; Oxford Univ, BCL, 86; Univ Toronto, SJD, 94. **CAREER** Chair, Ontario Mental Health Foundation **RESEARCH** Health law; estates and trusts. **SELECTED PUBLICATIONS** Auth, pubs on mental competency assessment, health-care and bioethics; co-auth, When the Mind Fails, Univ Toronto, 94. **CONTACT ADDRESS** Fac of Law, Univ Toronto, 78 Queen's Park, Toronto, ON.

FISHBURN, JANET FORSYTHE
PERSONAL Born 01/18/1937, Wilkensburg, PA, m, 1958, 3 children **DISCIPLINE** AMERICAN CHURCH AND CULTURAL HISTORY **EDUCATION** Monmouth Col, BA, 58; Pa State Univ, PhD (Am relig studies), 78. **CAREER** Dir Christian educ, 1st United Presby Church, Cleveland Heights, Ohio, 58-60; Instr humanities and Am studies, Pa State Univ, 77-78; ASST PROF CHRISTIAN EDUC AND CHURCH HIST, THEOL SCH, DREW UNIV, 78-. **MEMBERSHIPS** Am Acad Relig; Asn Prof and Researchers Relig Educ; Asn Theol Sch; Asn Field Educ; Asn Prof Educ Ministry. **RESEARCH** American church history and contemporary Christian ministry; family studies and intergenerational education; theological education and contemporary Christian ministry. **SELECTED PUBLICATIONS** Auth, Cultural Diversity and Seminary Teaching, Rel Educ, Vol 90, 95; Tennent, Gilbert, Established Dissenter, Church Hist, Vol 63.95; Preacher, Sunday, Billy and Big Time American Evangelism, Am Presbyterians J Presbyterian Hist, Vol 74, 96. **CONTACT ADDRESS** Theol Sch, Drew Univ, Madison, NJ, 07940.

FISHER, DAVID HICKMAN
PERSONAL Born 08/28/1943, San Bernardino, CA, m, 1966, 3 children **DISCIPLINE** RELIGION, PHILOSOPHY **EDUCATION** Carleton Col, BA, 65; Columbia Univ and Union Theol Sem, MA, 67; Vanderbilt Univ, MA, 73, PhD (relig), 76. **CAREER** Instr theol, Sch Theol, Univ of the South, 74-76; resident clin pastoral educ, Iowa Methodist Med Ctr, Des Moines, 76-77; asst prof relig, Kalamazoo Col, 77-78; asst prof relig and philos, Blackburn Col, 78-80; ASST PROF RELIG AND PHILOS, GEORGE WILLIAMS COL, 80-, Priest-in-charge, St John's Episcopal Church, Ionia, Mich, 77-78 and Holy Cross Episcopal Church, Fairview Heights, Ill, 79-80; LECTR, C G JUNG CTR, EVANSTON, 80-. **MEMBERSHIPS** Am Acad Relig; Col Theol Soc; Conf Anglican Theologians; Int Asn Philos and Lit. **RESEARCH** Religion and culture (psychology and religion, relation between myth story and belief); post structuralism and theology; process philosophy and theology. **SELECTED PUBLICATIONS** Auth, Public Art and Public Space, Soundings, Vol 79, 96; Nietzsche Dionysian Masks, Hist Reflections Reflexions Historiques, Vol 21, 95. **CONTACT ADDRESS** Humanities Div, George Williams Col, Downers Grove, IL, 60515.

FISHER, ELI D.
PERSONAL Born 11/11/1953, Warren, OH, m, 1990, 3 children **DISCIPLINE** RELIGION (OLD TESTAMENT) **EDUCATION** Vanderbilt Univ, PhD, 98. **CAREER** Author **MEMBERSHIPS** Soc of Bibl Lit **CONTACT ADDRESS** 9265 S Douglas Ave, Nashville, TN, 37204. **EMAIL** efisher@gbod.org

FISHER, EUGENE J.
PERSONAL Born 09/10/1943, m, 1 child **DISCIPLINE** RELIGION **EDUCATION** Sacred Heart Seminary, BA, 65; Univ Detroit, MA, 68; NY Univ, PhD, 76. **CAREER** Adj Prof, Univ Detroit. 69-77; Adj Prof, St. John's Seminary, 73-75; Lectr, St. Francis Sch Christian Educ, 69-71; Dir Catechist Formation, Office Relig Educ, Archdiocese Detroit, 71-77; Exec Dir, Secretariat for Cath-Jewish Relations, Nat Conf Cath Bishops, 77-90; Assoc Dir, Secretariat for Ecumenical & Interreligious Affairs, Nat Conf Cath Bishops, 90-. **HONORS AND AWARDS** Valedictorian, Austin Cath Preparatory Sch, 61; Kittay Fel, NY Univ, 70-71; Morris L. Kirsch Award for Excellence in Hebrew Studies, 70; Sh. Y. Agnon Award for Excellence in Hebrew Studies, 71; Walter A. Romig Distinguished Alumnus Award, Sacred Heart Col, 81; Edith Stein Guild Award for Extraordinary Contributions to Catholic-Jewish Relations, 83; Nat Workshop - Christian-Jewish Relations Special Award, 87; Raoul Wallenberg Tribute Award for Contributions to Christian-Jewish Relations, 95; Lamp of Understanding Award, Shalom Ctr for Understanding Between Christians, 95; 1995 Nat Jewish Bk Coun Award for best book in the Jewish-Christian Category, for: John Paul II, Spiritual Pilgrimage: Texts on Jews and Judaism 1970-1995. **MEMBERSHIPS** Soc Bibl Lit; Cath Bibl Asn; Nat Asn Prof Hebrew; Bibl Archaeol Soc; Service Int de Documentation Judeo-Chretienne; Am Acad Relig; Fel Reconciliation; Christian Study Group Judaism & Jewish People; Nat Inst Holocaust; Ctr Holocaust Studies; Churches' Ctr Theol & Public Policy; Vatican Comn Relig Relations Jewish People; Nat Asn Ecumenical Officers. **SELECTED PUBLICATIONS** Auth, The New Catechism, Catholics and Jews: Cardinal Ratzinger in Jerusalem, Nat Cath Register, 10/94; Jesus and His Fellow Jews, Cath Standard, 1/95; coauth, John Paul II, Spiritual Pilgrimage: Texts on Jews and Judaism 1970-1995, Crossroad Publ, 95; auth, Catholic-Jewish Relations, 1996 Catholic Almanac, Our Sunday Visitor, 96; The Church and Anti-Semitism: Rome is Due to Pronounce, Nat Cath Register, 7/96; The Rochester Agreement in Its Historical Context, The Rochester Agreement, Anti-Defamation League, 97; The Start of the Healing Process, Brotherhood 12, 98; author of numerous other articles and publications. **CONTACT ADDRESS** 3211 Fourth St. NE, Washington, DC, 20017-1194.

FISHER, ROBERT THADDEUS
PERSONAL Born 03/08/1926, Detroit, MI, m, 1947, 2 children **DISCIPLINE** PHILOSOPHY **EDUCATION** Wayne State Univ, BS, 48, MEd, 50, JD, 66; Mich State Univ, EdD, 59. **CAREER** Prof philos, Calif State Col, Pa, 61-66; a8st prof, 66-80, ASSOC PROF BUS LAW AND FINANCE, SAN DIEGO STATE UNIV, 80-. **MEMBERSHIPS** Am Psychol Asn. **RESEARCH** Existential analysis; philosophy of law and education. **SELECTED PUBLICATIONS** Auth, Swimming with the Current, Russ Hist Histoire Russe, Vol 21, 94; Hazard, John, N. 1909-1995--In Memoriam, Slavic Rev, Vol 54, 95; War, Revolution, and Peace in Russia--The Passages of Golder, Frank, 1914-1927 - Emmons, T, Patenaude, B, Russ Rev, Vol 52, 93; The Russian Syndrome--1000 Years of Political Murder, Russ Revi Vol 53, 94. **CONTACT ADDRESS** Dept of Bus Law and Finance, San Diego State Univ, San Diego, CA, 92115.

FISHER, ROGER
PERSONAL Born 05/28/1922, IL, m, 1948, 2 children **DISCIPLINE** LAW **EDUCATION** Harvard, LLB, 48. **CAREER** Lecturer, 58-60, Prof, Harvard Law School, 60-76, Samuel Williston Prof Law, 76-92; Iran Hostage Crisis, works with White House and Iranian leadership re: Algerian Mediation, 79; Dir Harv Neg Proj, 80-; Fndr Sr Consul, Conflict Mgmt Grp, 84-; Sr Princ, Conflict Mgmt, 84-; South Africa, works with NPA, ANC, Inkatha Freedom Party, 91; Samuel Williston Prof Law Emer, Harvard Law Sch, 92-; Ecuador Peru, leads joint session to gen options re: boundary war, 95; Georgia-Ossetia Conflict, help resolve conflict with invit by Pres Shevardnadze, 95-. **HONORS AND AWARDS** Guggenheim Fel, Vis Prof, Dept Intl Rela, London Sch Econo, 65-66; Szilard Peace Prize, 81; Cen for Pub Resources Pract Ach Award, 93; LHD, CT Col, 94., Orig and Exec Ed,The Advocates, pub TV, 69-70; Co-orig and Exec Ed, TV series Arabs and Israelis, 74-75. **MEMBERSHIPS** Board Memberships, Council for a Viable World, Conflict Management, Conflict Management Group Inc, Hudson Inst Trustee Emer, Program On Neg, Council on Foreign Relations. **SELECTED PUBLICATIONS** Getting It Done: How to Lead When You Are not in Charge, Roger Fisher and Alan Sharp with John Richardson, Harper Business, 98; Coping With International Conflict: A Systematic Approach to Influence in International Negotiation, with Andrea Kupfer Schneider, Eliz Borgwardt, Brian Ganson, Prentice Hall, 97; Getting Ready to Negotiate: The Getting to Yes Workbook, with Danny Ertle, Penguin Books, 95; Beyond Machiavelli: Tools for Coping With Conflict, with Eliz Kopelman, Andrea Kupfer Schneider, Harvard Univ Press, 94; Getting to Yes: Negotiating Agreement Without Giving In, second ed, Roger Fisher, William Ury, Bruce Patton, Penguin Books, 91. **CONTACT ADDRESS** Law Sch, Harvard Univ, Pound Hall 500, Cambridge, MA, 02138.

FISHER, SAUL
DISCIPLINE PHILOSOPHY **EDUCATION** Grad Sch and Univ Ctr, City Univ of NY, PhD, 97. **CAREER** Prog assoc, Andrew W. Mellon Found, 98-. **HONORS AND AWARDS** Fulbright for study in Fr, 94-95. **MEMBERSHIPS** Amer Philos Asn; Philos of Sci Asn; Hist of Sci Soc; Hist of Philos of Sci Working Grp. **RESEARCH** History and philosophy of science; Aesthetics of architecture. **SELECTED PUBLICATIONS** Rev, Gassendi's Ethics, Brit Jour for the Hist of Sci, 98. **CONTACT ADDRESS** 3636 Fieldston Rd., Bronx, NY, 10463. **EMAIL** sf@mellon.org

FISS, OWEN M.
PERSONAL Born 02/24/1938, m, 1959, 3 children **DISCIPLINE** LAW **EDUCATION** Dartmouth Col, BA, 59; Oxford Univ, BPhil, 61; Harvard Univ, LLB, 64. **CAREER** Law Clerk to Judge Thurgood Marshall, Court of Appeals, 64-65 & to Justice William J Brennan, US Supreme Court, 65-66; spec asst to John Doar, Asst Atty Gen, Civil Rights Div, Dept Justice, 66-68; from assoc prof to prof law, Univ Chicago, 68-74; Vis prof, Law Sch, Stanford Univ, 73-74; Prof Law, 74-82, Alexander M. Bickel Prof Public Law, 82-92, Sterling Prof Law, Yale Univ, 92-. **HONORS AND AWARDS** Summa Cum Laude, Valedictory Standing, Phi Beta Kappa, Rufus Choate Schol & Reynolds Fel, Dartmouth Col; Fulbright Schol, Oxford Univ; Magna Cum Laude, Prize Schol, and Law Rev, Harvard Law Sch. **RESEARCH** History of the Supreme Court-Holmes devise. **SELECTED PUBLICATIONS** Auth, Affirmative Action as a Strategy of Justice, Philos & Pub Policy 37, 97; op ed, Beyond Diversity, Washington Post, 5/7/97; Speech and Power Symposium, Is First Amendment Absolutism Obsolete?, The Nation, 7/21/97; Libertad de Expresion y Estructura Social, Fontamera, 97; Discipline and Passion, In: Rechstheorie, Zeitschrift fur Logik, Methodenlehre, Kybernetik und Sozologie des Rechts, Duncker & Humblot, 98; Money and Politics, Columbia Law Rev 2470, 98; Hong Kong Democracy, Columbia J Transnational Law 493; 98; Globalization and Its Consequences for Democracy: The Case of the World Bank (in press); Political Violence and Freedom of Speech (in press); Abortion Protest and the Limits of Free Speech (in press); author of numerous other articles and publications. **CONTACT ADDRESS** Law Sch, Yale Univ, PO Box 208215, New Haven, CT, 06520-8215. **EMAIL** owen.fiss@yale.edu

FITTIPALDI, SILVIO EDWARD
PERSONAL Born 11/09/1937, Philadelphia, PA **DISCIPLINE** RELIGION, PSYCHOLOGY **EDUCATION** Villanova Univ, AB, 60; Augustinian Col, MA, 64; Temple Univ, PhD (relig), 76. **CAREER** Instr relig, Villanova Univ, 72-76, asst prof, 76-82, chmn dept, 77-80. **MEMBERSHIPS** Col Theol Soc; Cath Theol Soc Am; Friends Conf Relig and Psychol; Asn Humanistic Psychol. **RESEARCH** The encounter of world religions; religion and psychology; mysticism. **SELECTED PUBLICATIONS** Auth, Invisible Harmony--Essays on Contemplation and Responsibility, J Ecumenical Stud, Vol 33, 96; In the Path of the Masters--Understanding the Spirituality of Buddha, Confucius, Jesus, and Muhammad, J Ecumenical Stud, Vol 32, 95. **CONTACT ADDRESS** 1325 S Broad St, Philadelphia, PA, 19147.

FITTS, LEROY
PERSONAL Born 07/06/1944, Norlina, NC, m, 1963 **DISCIPLINE** THEOLOGY **EDUCATION** Shaw Univ, BA 1967; Southeastern Bapt Theo Sem, M Div 1970; VA Sem, D Div 1975, DHL, 1990; Princeton Univ, (NEH Inst) 1984; Baltimore Hebrew University, MA 1985. **CAREER** First Bapt Ch of Jacksonville, NC, pastor 1968-72; First Bapt Church, Baltimore, MD, pastor 1972-; Comm Coll of Baltimore, adjunct prof 1978-80; VA Sem & Coll, pres 1981; ad; prof, Black Church History, St Mary's Seminary & University, Baltimore, MD. **MEMBERSHIPS** Editor Loft Carey Baptist Convention 1975-90; brd of mgrs VA Sem & Coll 1980; mem NAACP, Assoc for the Study of Negro Hist 1978-; bd of mgrs, St. Marys Seminary & University. **SELECTED PUBLICATIONS** Author, Lott Carey First Black Msnry to Africa 1978, A History of Black Baptists 1985; article "The Church in the South & Social Issues", Faith & Mission vol II, No I, Fall 1984. **CONTACT ADDRESS** First Baptist Church, 525 N Caroline St, Baltimore, MD, 21205.

FITZ, HOPE K.
DISCIPLINE PHILOSOPHY **EDUCATION** Claremom Grad School **CAREER** CT St Univ, prof, phil, 10 yrs. **HONORS AND AWARDS** NEH grant, 86; fac grant, Mount St. Mary's Col, 86; fac sum develop funds, Eastern CT St Univ, 90; Ct St Univ travel grant, 93. **MEMBERSHIPS** APA; Soc for Asian & Comparative Phil, **RESEARCH** South Asian Phil; esp Hinduism; Gandhi's ethical, religious, political thought. **SELECTED PUBLICATIONS** Art, The Mystical Experience From a Heideggerian Perspective, Jour of Relig Stud, 90; auth, The Importance of Overcoming the False Self in the Process of Self-Development, Miami Univ OH, 90; art, The Role of Self-Discipline in the Process of Self-Realization, Jour of Rel Stud, Vol XIX, 91; art, The Nature and Significance of Intuition in Patanjali's Yoga Sutra and in the Philosophical Writings of Radhakrishnan, AAS, 93; art, The Nature and Significance of Intuition in Patanjali's Yoga Sutra and in the Philosophical Writings of Radhakrishnan, Jour of Relig Stud, Vol XXVI, 95; auth, Intuition and Revelation as They Relate to Transcendence, 95; art, Gandhi's Ethical/Religious Tradition, Jour of Relig Stud, Vol XXVII, 96. **CONTACT ADDRESS** Eastern Connecticut State Univ, Classroom Bldg 356, Willimantic, CT, 06226. **EMAIL** fitzh@ecsu.ctstateu.edu

FITZGERALD, DESMOND J.
DISCIPLINE PHILOSOPHY **EDUCATION** BA, 46, MA, 47, Univ Toronto; Univ California-Berkeley, PhD, 54 **CAREER** Prof, 48-, Chr 70-96, Emeritus, 98, Univ San Francisco **CONTACT ADDRESS** Univ San Francisco, San Francisco, CA, 94117.

FITZGERALD, DESMOND J.

PERSONAL Born 01/18/1924, Toronto, ON, Canada, m, 1947, 2 children **DISCIPLINE** PHILOSOPHY, HUMANITIES **EDUCATION** Univ Toronto, BA, 46, MA, 47; Univ CA, Berkeley, MA, 50, PhD, 54. **CAREER** Instr philos, St Louis Univ, 47; from instr to assoc prof, 48-63, PROF TO PROF EMERITUS, PHILOS, UNIV SAN FRANCISCO, 63-; vis prof polit sci, Dominican Col, 57; res fel, Inst Philos Res, 58-61; Fulbright res fel, Italy, 66-67; commentator Can Affairs, World Press educ TV prog, KQED, San Francisco, 69-. **HONORS AND AWARDS** Mercier Gold Medal, 46. **MEMBERSHIPS** Am Philos Asn; Am Cath Philos Asn (pres, 75-76); Renaissance Soc Am; Hist Sci Soc. **RESEARCH** Hist of philos; philos and science; metaphysics and epistemology. **SELECTED PUBLICATIONS** Auth, Descartes--Defender of the Faith, Thought, autumn 58; Problem of the Projectile Again, 64, Is There an Unchanging Human Nature?, 69 & Liberty Versus Equality, 76, Proc Am Cath Philos Asn. **CONTACT ADDRESS** Dept of Philos, Univ of San Francisco, 2130 Fulton St, San Francisco, CA, 94117-1050. **EMAIL** fitzgeraldd@usfca.edu

FITZGERALD, JOHN JOSEPH

PERSONAL Born 10/17/1928, North Adams, MA, m, 1954, 6 children **DISCIPLINE** PHILOSOPHY **EDUCATION** Univ Notre Dame, BA, 49; St Louis Univ, MA, 53; Tulane Univ, PhD(philos), 62. **CAREER** From instr to asst prof philos, Univ Notre Dame, 58-66; assoc prof, 66-71, Prof Philos, 71-94, prof emeritus, Univ Mass, Dartmouth. **MEMBERSHIPS** Am Cath Philos Asn; Am Philos Asn; Am Fedn Teachers (1st vpres, 71-72, pres, 73-76). **RESEARCH** Classical realism; American philosophy. **SELECTED PUBLICATIONS** Auth, Peirce's How to Make our Ideas Clear, New Scholasticism, 65; Peirce's Theory of Signs as Foundation for Pragmatism, Mouton, The Hague, 66; Peirce's theory of inquiry, Trans C S Peirce Soc, 68; Peirce's argument for thirdness, New Scholasticism, summer 71; Ambiguity in Peirce's Theory of Signs, Trans C S Peirce Soc, 76; auth, Peirce's Doctrine of Symbol, in Colapietro, ed, Peirce's Doctrine of Signs, de Gruyter, 96. **CONTACT ADDRESS** 14 Sugarmill Dr, Okatie, SC, 29910.

FITZGERALD, JOHN THOMAS, JR.

PERSONAL Born 10/02/1948, Birmingham, AL, m, 1970, 2 children **DISCIPLINE** RELIGIOUS STUDIES; NEW TESTAMENT **EDUCATION** Yale Univ, PhD, 84. **CAREER** Instr, Univ Miami, 81-84; asst prof, Univ Miami, 84-88; assoc prof, Univ Miami, 88-; visiting assoc prof, Brown Univ, spring, 92; visiting assoc prof, Yale Divinity Sch, 98-99. **HONORS AND AWARDS** Soc of Bibl Lit res grant, 97-00; Max Orovitz summer res award, 85, 87, 94-95, 98. **MEMBERSHIPS** Asn of Ancient Hist; Soc of Bibl Lit; Studiorum Novi Testamenti Soc. **RESEARCH** New Testament/Early Christianity; Hellenistic philosophy & literature. **SELECTED PUBLICATIONS** Article, Eusebius and The Little Labyrinth, The Early Church in its Context: Essays in Honor of Everett Ferguson, E. J. Brill, 120-46, 98; article, The Catalogue in Ancient Greek Literature, The Rhetorical Analysis of Scripture: Essays from the 1995 London Conference, Sheffield Acad Press, 275-93, 97; article, Friendship, Encycl of Early Christianity, Garland Publ, 1, 439-42, 97; article, Introduction, Greco-Roman Perspectives on Friendship, Scholars Press, 1-11, 97; article, Friendship in the Greek World Prior to Aristotle, Greco-Roman Perspectives on Friendship, Scholars Press, 13-34, 97; article, Introduction, Friendship, Flattery and Frankness of Speech, E. J. Brill, 1-4, 96; article, Philippians in the Light of Some Ancient Discussions of Friendship, Friendship, Flattery and Frankness of Speech, E. J. Brill, 141-60, 96; article, The Problem of Perjury in Greek Context: Prolegomena to an Exegesis of Matthew 5:33, 1 Timothy 1:10, and Didache 2.3, The Social World of the First Christians: Essays in Honor of Wayne A. Meeks, Fortress Press, 156-77, 95; article, The Ancient Lives of Aristotle and the Modern Debate about the Genre of the Gospels, Restoration Quart, 36, 209-21, 94. **CONTACT ADDRESS** Dept. of Religious Studies, Univ of Miami, PO Box 248264, Coral Gables, FL, 33124-4672. **EMAIL** jtfitz@umiami.ir.miami.edu

FITZGERALD, PATRICK

PERSONAL Born 05/26/1966, Marysville, OH, s **DISCIPLINE** PHILOSOPHY/ETHICS **EDUCATION** Miami Univ, BA, 88; Univ Arizona, MA, 91, PhD, 96; Oxford Univ, M.Phil, Politics, 93. **CAREER** Grad tchng asst, 88-91 & 93-94, Univ of Ariz; asst prof of Phil, 95-, Louisana St Univ. **HONORS AND AWARDS** NEH Sum Sem Fel, Brown Univ, 96; John M. Olin Fel, 91-93; Claude Lambe Fel, 89-91; Humane Studies Residential Fel, 91; Reisen Prize, 90; Hall Prize, 87 & 88. **MEMBERSHIPS** APA **RESEARCH** Ethical theory, political phil, bioethics. **SELECTED PUBLICATIONS** Coauth, Secrecy, Human Radiation Experiments and Intentional Releases, The Human Radiation Experiments: Final Report of the Pres Adv Comm, Oxford Univ Press, 96; coauth, Atomic Veterans: Human Experimentation in Connection with Atomic Tests, The Human Radiation Experiments: Final Report of the Pres Adv Comm, Oxford Univ Press, 96; art, Service-Learning and the Socially Responsible Ethics Class, Tchng Phil 20:3, 97. **CONTACT ADDRESS** Dept of Philosophy, Louisiana State Univ, Baton Rouge, LA, 70803.

FITZMYER, JOSEPH AUGUSTINE

PERSONAL Born 11/04/1920, Philadelphia, PA **DISCIPLINE** BIBLICAL LITERATURE AND LANGUAGES **EDUCATION** Loyola Univ, Ill, AB, 43, AM, 45; St Albert Louvain, Belgium, STL, 52; Johns Hopkins Univ, PhD (Semitic lang), 56; Pontif Bibl Inst, Italy, SSL, 57. **CAREER** Instr Latin and Greek, Gonzaga High Sch, Washington, DC, 45-48; asst prof New Testament, Woodstock Col, 58-59, from assoc prof to prof Bibl lit and lang, 59-69; prof Near East lang and civilizations, Univ Chicago, 69-71; prof New Testament, and Bibl lang, Fordham Univ, 71-74 and Weston Sch Theol, 74-76; PROF BIBL LANG AND NEW TESTAMENT, CATH UNIV AM, 76-, Fel, Am Sch Orient Res, Jerusalem, Jordan, 57-58; vis lectr Semitic lang, Johns Hopkins Univ, 58-61; Am Coun Learned Soc fel, 63; vis lectr Semitic lang, Univ Pa, 65-66; vis prof New Testament, Yale Univ Divinity Sch, 67-68; mem int study comn, Lutheran World Fedn and Vatican Secretariate for Promoting Christian Unity, 67-71; ed, J Bibl Lit, 71-76; speaker's lectr Bibl studies, Oxford Univ, 74-75; ED, CATH BIBL QUART, 80-. **HONORS AND AWARDS** LittD, Col Holy Cross, 79; LHD, Univ Scranton, 79, Fairfield Univ, 81; Teol H Dr, Lunds Univ, Lund, Sweden, 81. **MEMBERSHIPS** Cath Bibl Asn Am (pres, 69-70); Soc Bibl Lit (pres, 79); Soc Studies New Testament; Cath Comm Intellectual and Cult Affairs; AAUP. **RESEARCH** Aramaic language, Dead Sea Scrolls and their relation to the New Testament; New Testament literature. **SELECTED PUBLICATIONS** Auth A Critical and Exegetical Commentary on the Acts of the Apostles, Vol 1-- Preliminary Introduction and Commentary on Acts I Xiv, Theological Studies, Vol 57, 96; Christian Palestinian Aramaic Grammar, Vol 1 - Phonology, Morphology, And Orthography, Cath Biblical Quart, Vol 55, 93; The Qumran Community-- Essene or Sadducean, Heythrop J Quart Rev Philos Theol, Vol 36, 95; Preliminary Publication of Pap qtob A Ar, Fragment 2, Biblica, Vol 75, 94; The Damascus Document Reconsidered, J Am Orient Soc, Vol 113, 93; Revelation and Mystery in Ancient Judaism and Pauline Christianity, J Am Orient Soc, Vol 113, 93; A Greek English Lexicon of the Septuagint--12 Prophets, Cath Biblical Quart, Vol 56, 94; Another Query about the Lucan Infancy Narrative and its Parallels, J Biblical Lit, Vol 114, 95; 4q246 The So Called Son of God Document from Qumran, Biblica, Vol 74, 93; Textbook of Aramaic Documents From Ancient Egypt, Vol 3, Lit, Accounts, J Am Orient Soc, Vol 115, 95; Paul--Apostle to the Gentiles, Theol Today, Vol 51, 94; New Testament Apocrypha, Vol 2--Writings Relating to the Apostles, Apocalypses, and Related Subjects, Theol Stud, Vol 54, 93; Noncanonical Writings and New-Testament Interpretation, Biblica, Vol 76, 95; The Aramaic and Hebrew Fragments of Tobit from Qumran Cave 4 , Cath Biblical Quart, Vol 57, 95; The Dictionary of Classical Hebrew, Vol 1, Aleph, J Am Orient Soc, Vol 116, 96; The First New Testament Witnesses-- Papyrus Copies of New Testament Books, Biblica, Vol 77, 96; New Testament Theology, Theol Stud, Vol 56, 95; Kephale Leader Ruler in 1 Corinthians Xi, 3 , Interpretation J Bible Theol, Vol 47, 93; The Consecutive Meaning of Eph O in Romans V, 12 , New Testament Stud, Vol 39, 93; The Dead Sea Scrolls Today, Biblica, Vol 77, 96; The Scepter and the Star-- The Messiahs of the Dead Sea Scrolls and other Ancient Literature, Theol Stud, Vol 57, 96; Graphic Concordance to the Dead Sea Scrolls, Cath Biblical Quart, Vol 55, 93; Scripture as Norm for our Common Faith, J Ecumen Stud, Vol 30, 93. **CONTACT ADDRESS** Dept of Bibl Studies, Catholic Univ of America, Washington, DC, 20064.

FITZPATRICK, WILLIAM J.

PERSONAL Born 07/03/1964, Syracuse, NY, m, 1989 **DISCIPLINE** PHILOSOPHY **EDUCATION** Princeton Univ, BA, 86; Univ Calif, Los Angeles, MA, 88, PhD, 95. **CAREER** Lectr, Yale Univ, 96- . **MEMBERSHIPS** APA. **RESEARCH** Metaethics; normative ethics; philosophy of biology. **CONTACT ADDRESS** Dept of Philosophy, Yale Univ, PO Box 208306, New Haven, CT, 06520-8306. **EMAIL** Billjfitz@aol.com

FLANAGAN, JAMES F.

DISCIPLINE CIVIL PROCEDURE, EVIDENCE, FEDERAL PRACTICE AND ALTERNATE DISPUTE RESOLUTIO **EDUCATION** Univ Notre Dame, AB, 64; Univ PA, LLB, 67. **CAREER** Prof, Univ of SC **RESEARCH** Procedural aspects of litigation. **SELECTED PUBLICATIONS** Coauth, treatise on SC civil procedure; publ on, civil procedure. **CONTACT ADDRESS** School of Law, Univ of S. Carolina, Law Center, Columbia, SC, 29208. **EMAIL** Jimf@law.law.sc.edu

FLANAGAN, KATHLEEN

DISCIPLINE RELIGIOUS STUDIES **EDUCATION** Col St Elizabeth, BA; St John's Univ, MA; Union Theol Sem, MPhil, PhD. **CAREER** Relig, Col St. Elizabeth **RESEARCH** Church hist; Sacraments; Christology; Elizabeth Seton. **SELECTED PUBLICATIONS** Auth, Some Aspects of Elizabeth Seton's Spiritual-Theological World in Vincention Heritage XIV, 93. **CONTACT ADDRESS** Dept of Relig Studies, Col of Saint Elizabeth, 2 Convent Rd., Morristown, NJ, 07960. **EMAIL** flanagan@liza.st-elizabeth.edu

FLANAGAN, OWEN

DISCIPLINE PHILOSOPHY **EDUCATION** Boston Univ, PhD, 77. **CAREER** Prof philos, Wellesley Col, 85-86; adj prof, chair dept, Duke Univ, 93-. **HONORS AND AWARDS** Pres, Soc Philos Psychol, 94-95. **MEMBERSHIPS** Soc Philos Psychol. **RESEARCH** Philos of mind; philos of psych; philos of soc sci; ethics; contemp ethical theory; moral psych. **SELECTED PUBLICATIONS** Auth, Varieties of Moral Personality: Ethics and Psychological Realism, Harvard Univ, 91; Consciousness Reconsidered, MIT, 92; Self Expressions: Mind, Morals, and the Meaning of Life, Oxford Univ, 96; ed, The Science of the Mind, MIT, 91; Identity, Character, and Morality: Essays in Moral Psychology, MIT, 90. **CONTACT ADDRESS** Philos Dept, Duke Univ, West Duke Bldg, Durham, NC, 27706. **EMAIL** ojf@acpub.duke.edu

FLANNERY, MICHAEL T.

DISCIPLINE LEGAL WRITING AND APPELLATE ADVOCACY **EDUCATION** Univ Del, BA, 87; Cath Univ Am Columbus Sch Law, JD, 91. **CAREER** Prof, Villanova Univ Sch Law, 96-; worked in, Wolf, Block, Schorr and Solis-Cohen; assoc, Gold-Bikin, Clifford and Young, 94; asst city solicitor, Philadelphia, 91-94. **CONTACT ADDRESS** Law School, Villanova Univ, 800 Lancaster Ave, Villanova, PA, 19085-1692. **EMAIL** flannery@law.vill.edu

FLANNIGAN, ROB

DISCIPLINE LAW **EDUCATION** Univ Alberta, BS, 76, LLB, 80; Univ Toronto, LLM, 82, SJD, 88. **CAREER** Prof, 85-. **RESEARCH** Contract law; business organizations; trust law. **SELECTED PUBLICATIONS** Auth, The Economic Structure of the Firm, 95; The Legal Construction of Rights of First Refusal, Can Bar Rev, 97. **CONTACT ADDRESS** Col of Law, Univ Saskatchewan, 15 Campus Dr, Saskatoon, SK, S7N 5A6.

FLEISCHACKER, SAM

PERSONAL Born 04/22/1961, London, England, m, 1998, 2 children **DISCIPLINE** MORAL, POLITICAL PHILOSOPHY **EDUCATION** Yale Col, BA, summa cum laude, 81; Yale Univ, MA, 84, MPhil, 84; PhD, 89. **CAREER** Vis asst prof, Haverford and Bryn Mawr Col (s), 88-90; fel, Univ Ctr Human Values, Princeton Fellow, Inst Adv Stud Human, Edinburgh, 94-95; assoc prof Philos, Williams Col, 91-99; assoc prof Philos, Univ Ill Chicago, 99-. **HONORS AND AWARDS** Gaudino Memorial Scholar at Williams, 97- ; Amer Philos assn fel, IASH, Edinburgh, 95; Laurance S. Rockefeller fel, UCHV, Princeton, 94-95; John M. Olin fel in Hist and Political Theory, 94-95; ACLS Recent Recipient of the PhD fel, 90-91; Charlotte W. Newcombe fel, 87-88; prize tchg fel, 86-87; various Yale fel, 82-85; Mary Cady Tew prize, 83; Phi Beta Kappa, 81; Gulf Scholar, 78-81. **RESEARCH** Scottish Enlightenment Philosophy; Nineteenth Century Philosophy, esp Hegel and Kierkegaard; Aesthetics; Philosophy of Religion; Wittgenstein. **SELECTED PUBLICATIONS** Auth, Religious Questions: Kafka and Wittgenstein on Giving grounds, Sophia, Ap 82; A Fifth Antinomy, Philosophia, May 89; On the Enforcement of Morality: Aquinas and Narcotics Prohibition, Pub Affairs Quart, Spring 90; Philosophy in Moral Practice: Kant and Adam smith, Kant-Studien, 82, 3, 91; Kant's Theory of Punishment, Kant-studien, 79,4,88, reprinted in Howard Williams, ed, Essays on Kant's Political Philosophy, U of Chicago P, 92; Integrity and Moral Relativism, Leiden, E.J. Brill, 92; The Ethics of Culture, Ithaca: Cornell Univ Press, 94; Frustrated Contracts, Poetry, and Truth, Raritan, Spring, 94, reprinted in Richard Eldridge, ed, Beyond Representation: Philosophy and Poetic Imagination, Cambridge Univ Press, 96; Multiculturalism as a Western Tradition, Academe, Spring 96; Values Behind the Market: Kant's Response to the Wealth of Nations, History of Political Thought, Fall 96; Free Speech and the Education of Governments, The Responsive Community, Winter 97; bk rev, Ethics and the Arts, Ethics, Jan 98; Insignificant Communities, in Amy Gutmann, ed, Freedom of Association, Princeton Univ Press, 98; A Third Concept of Liberty: Judgment and Freedom in Kant and Adam Smith, Princeton Univ Press, 99; **CONTACT ADDRESS** Dept of Philosophy, Williams Col, 42 South St, Williamstown, MA, 01267. **EMAIL** sfleisch@williams.edu

FLEMING, JOHN G.

PERSONAL Born 07/06/1919, m, 1946, 4 children **DISCIPLINE** LAW **EDUCATION** Oxford Univ, MA, 39, DPhil, 48, DCL, 59. **CAREER** Lectr law, King's Col, Univ London, Eng, 46-48; sr lectr, Australian Nat Univ, 49-55, Robert Garran prof and dean, 55-60; vis prof, 57-58, prof, 60-74, SHANNON CECIL TURNER PROF LAW, UNIV CALIF, BERKELEY, 74-, Mem, Eng Bar, 47; Carnegie Corp traveling grant, 54-55; ed-in-chief, Am J Comp Law, 71-. **MEMBERSHIPS** Am Law Inst; Int Acad Comp Law; Int Asn Legal Soc. **SELECTED PUBLICATIONS** Auth, Mass Torts, Am J Compar Law, Vol 42, 94. **CONTACT ADDRESS** Law Sch, Univ of Calif, Berkeley, CA, 94720.

FLETCHER, DAVID B.

PERSONAL Born 05/10/1951, Chicago, IL, m, 1976, 1 child **DISCIPLINE** PHILOSOPHY **EDUCATION** Trinity Coll, BA, 73; Loyola Univ of Chicago, MA, 77; Univ of IL, PhD, 84. **CAREER** Asst Prof to Assoc Prof Philo, 81- Wheaton Coll.

HONORS AND AWARDS Visiting Scholar, Oxford Univ, 91; Fellow, Center for Bioethics and Human **MEMBERSHIPS** Vice Pres, IL Philo Assoc, 97-99; Amer Philo Assoc, Soc of Christian Philos. **RESEARCH** Ethics; Social Philos. **SELECTED PUBLICATIONS** Auth, Particular Divine Commands, in: Christian Theism and Moral Philosophy, eds, M Nelson, M Beatty, C Fisher, Mercer Univ Press 98; Social and Political Perspectives in the Thought of Soren Kierkegaard, Univ Press of Amer, 81; co-auth, How a Christian Thinks about Medical Ethical Issues, in: New Issues in Medical Ethics, ed, J Hollman, Russian ed, 97; contributing auth, Professional Ethics, Population Policy, Dehumanization, Professional Ethics, Karl Marx, Alienation, Preproductive Technology, Sterilization, Birth Control, Medical Malpractice, Martin Luther King Jr, and Surrogate Mothers, in: New Dictionary of Christian Ethics and Pastoral Theology, eds, DJ Atkinson, DF Dield, A Holmes & O O'Donovan, Intervarsity Press, 95; Can Christian Ethics be Philosophical?, in: Festschrift for Harold O.J. Brown, eds, JS Feinberg and P Feinberg, Crossway Books, forthcoming; Response to Nigel de S. Cameron's Bioethics and the Challenge of a Post Consensus Society, Ethics and Medicine, 95. **CONTACT ADDRESS** Dept of Philosophy, Wheaton Col, Wheaton, IL, 60187. **EMAIL** david.b.fletcher@wheaton.edu

FLETCHER, GEORGE PHILIP

PERSONAL Born 03/05/1939, Chicago, IL, m, 1962, 2 children **DISCIPLINE** LAW, PHILOSOPHY **EDUCATION** Univ Calif, BA, 60; Univ Chicago, JD, 63, MCompL, 65. **CAREER** Asst prof Law, Univ Fla, 65-66; asst prof, Univ Wash, 66-69; acting assoc prof, 69-72, PROF LAW, UNIV CALIF, LOS ANGELES 72-, Vis assoc prof, Boston Col, 68-69. **RESEARCH** Comparative law; criminal and tort theory; legal philosophy. **SELECTED PUBLICATIONS** Auth, On the Moral Irrelevance of Bodily Movements, Univ Pennsylvania Law Rev, Vol 142, 94; The Brothel Boy and other Parables of the Law, Mich Law Rev, Vol 91, 93; Domination in Wrongdoing, Boston Univ Law Rev, Vol 76, 96; The Philosophers Brief, NY Rev Bks, Vol 44, 97; Risks and Wrongs, Harvard Law Rev, Vol 106, 93; Domination in the Theory of Justification and Excuse, Univ Pittsburgh Law Rev, Vol 57, 96; Blackmail--The Paradigmatic Crime, Univ Pennsylvania Law Rev, Vol 141, 93. **CONTACT ADDRESS** Sch of Law, Univ of Calif, Los Angeles, CA, 90024.

FLETCHER, ROBERT E.

PERSONAL Born 12/12/1938, Detroit, MI, m **DISCIPLINE** LAW, FILM **EDUCATION** Fisk Univ, attended 1956-59; Wayne State Univ, BA 1961; Natl Educ TV Film Training Sch, attended 1970; Comm Film Workshop Council TV News Cinematography Prog 1971; Natl Acad of TV Arts & Sci/Third World Cinema Prod Inc 1976-77; New York University School of Law, JD, 1990. **CAREER** No Student Movement Harlem, field organizer 1963-64; SNCC Jackson MS, Selma AL Atlanta GA, photographer field coord editorial & air dir 1964-68; freelance photographer journalist & film maker 1968-; Brooklyn Coll, adj prof dept of film studies 1975-76; "Vote for Your Life", prod/dir 1977; "Weatherization, What's It all About?"; Video & TV Prod, summer 1977; WPIX-TV, bi-weekly talk show; "A Nation in View", co-producer; Cravath, Swaine & Moore, attorney, 1991-. **HONORS AND AWARDS** Cinematographer dir "A Luta Continva" 1971; documentary film on liberation struggle in Mozambique "O Povo Organizado" 1975; panelist "Voices of the Civil Rights Movement" Smithsonian Inst 1980. **MEMBERSHIPS** Mem Intl Photographers of the Motion Picture Indus; chmn bd dir Rod Rodgers Dance Co 1973-; photographs pub in Ebony, Essence, Black Enterprises, Tuesday, Life, Redbook, NY Mag; author of publ in MS. **CONTACT ADDRESS** Cravath, Swaine & Moore, 825 Eighth Ave, New York, NY, 10019-7415.

FLINT, THOMAS P.

PERSONAL Born 12/14/1954, Cleveland, OH, m, 1983, 1 child **DISCIPLINE** PHILOSOPHY **EDUCATION** St Ambrose Col, BA, 75; Univ Notre Dame, PhD, 80. **CAREER** Harper instr, Univ Chicago, 80-82; asst prof, 82-88, ASSOC PROF, UNIV NOTRE DAME, 88-. **MEMBERSHIPS** Soc of Christian Philos; Amer Philos Assoc; Amer Cath Philos Assoc. **RESEARCH** Philos theology; metaphysics. **SELECTED PUBLICATIONS** Co-ed and co-auth of intro with Eleonore Stump, Hermes and Athena: Biblical Exegesis and Philosophical Theology, Univ Notre Dame Press, 93; auth, Providence and Predestination, in Philip L. Quinn and Charles Taliaferro, eds, A Companion to the Philosophy of Religion, Oxford: Blackwell Pubs, 97; Praying for Things to Have Happened, Midwest Studies in Philosophy 21, 97; Divine Providence: The Molinist Account, Ithaca, NY: Cornell Univ Press, 98. **CONTACT ADDRESS** Philos Dept, Univ Notre Dame, 336 O'Shaughnessy Hall, Notre Dame, IN, 46556-5639. **EMAIL** thomas.p.flint.1@nd.edu

FLORIDA, ROBERT E.

PERSONAL Born 09/16/1939, St. Louis, MO, m, 1963, 2 children **DISCIPLINE** RELIGION **EDUCATION** Univ Cincinnati, 62; Tufts Univ, BD, 65; McMaster Univ, MA, 69, PhD, 73. **CAREER** PROF, DEPT REL, 69-, rel dept chair, 74-75, 78-82, 84-86, 91, DEAN FAC ARTS, 93-, BRANDON UNIV. **MEMBERSHIPS** Am Acad Rel; Can Soc Stud of Rel; Int Asn Buddhist Hist. **RESEARCH** Buddhist ethics, health care ethics. **SELECTED PUBLICATIONS** Auth, "Buddhist Ethics" in Religious Humanism, 94; "Buddhism and the Four Principles," in Principles of Health Care Ethics, 94; "Introduction" and "Bioethics in the Lotus Sutra" J Buddhist Ethics, 98. **CONTACT ADDRESS** Faculty of Arts, Brandon Univ, Brandon, MB, R7A 6A9. **EMAIL** Florida@BrandonU.ca

FLOURNOY, ALYSON CRAIG

DISCIPLINE LAW **EDUCATION** Princeton Univ, BA; Harvard Univ, JD. **CAREER** Prof, Univ Fla, 88-. **MEMBERSHIPS** DC Bar. **RESEARCH** Administrative law, environmental law, property. **CONTACT ADDRESS** School of Law, Univ of Florida, PO Box 117625, Gainesville, FL, 32611-7625. **EMAIL** flournoy@law.ufl.edu

FLOWERS, RONALD BRUCE

PERSONAL Born 01/11/1935, Tulsa, OK, m, 1959, 3 children **DISCIPLINE** RELIGION, AMERICAN CHURCH HISTORY **EDUCATION** Tex Christian Univ, BA, 57; Vanderbilt Univ, BD, 60, STM, 61; Univ Iowa, PhD(relig, Am church hist), 67. **CAREER** Asst prof, 66-72, assoc prof relig, Tex Christian Univ, 72-83, prof 84-. **HONORS AND AWARDS** Danforth assoc, 71-; Weatherly Prof of Religion, 98. **MEMBERSHIPS** Disciples of Christ Hist Soc; Am Acad of Relig. **RESEARCH** The history of religion in America; church and state relationships in America. **SELECTED PUBLICATIONS** Auth, An Introduction to Church-State Relationships, Encounter, summer 71; Piety in Public Places, Christianity & Crisis, 11/71; A Selected Bibliography on Religion and Public Education, J Church & State, autumn 72; The Supreme Court's Three Tests of the Establishment Clause, Religion in Life, spring 76; coauth, Toward Benevolent Neutrality: Church, State, and the Supreme Court, Baylor Univ, 77, rev ed, 82, 5th rev ed, 84; Freedom of Religion Versus Civil Authority in Matters of Health, Ann Am Acad Pol Soc Sci, 11/79; The Supreme Courts Interpretation of the Free Exercise Clause, Relig Life, fall 80; The 1960's: A Decisive Decade in American Church-State Relationships, Encounter, summer 82;auth, Religion in Strange Times: The 1960's and 1970's, 84; co-auth, The Naturalization of Rosika Schwimmer, Journal of Church and State, spring 90; auth, In Praise of Conscience: Marie Averil Bland, Angelican and Episcopal History, March 93; Government Accomodation of Religious-Based Conscientious Objection, Seton Hall Law Rev, 93; That Godless Court?: Supreme Court Decisions on Church-State relationships, 94. **CONTACT ADDRESS** Dept of Relig, Tex Christian Univ, Box 298100, Fort Worth, TX, 76129-0002. **EMAIL** r.flowers@tcu.edu

FLOWERS, WILLIAM HAROLD, JR.

PERSONAL Born 03/22/1946, Chicago, IL, m **DISCIPLINE** LAW **EDUCATION** Univ of CO, BA 1967, Law School JD 1971. **CAREER** Adams County, deputy district Attorney; Private Practice, 1979-; Holland & Hart, Denver CO, partner, 1989-97; Hurth Yeager & Sisk LLP, 1997-. **HONORS AND AWARDS** Outstanding Alumnus, Univ of CO Black Students Alliance, 1990; Award in Business-Community Action, Boulder County, CO, 1990; Presidential Award, Natl Bar Assn, 1987. **MEMBERSHIPS** Bd of dirs KGNU Radio Station 1981-84; bd of dirs CO Criminal Defense Bar 1982-83; regional dir Natl Bar Assoc 1984-85, vice pres, 1990-91, bd of governors 1985-95; exec bd Boy Scouts of Amer 1983-; pres elect 1986, pres 1987 Sam Cary Bar Assoc; mem Comm Corrections Bd 1984-90; bd of governors, Colo Trial Lawyers Assn, beg 1988, pres-elect, 1998-99; mem, Judicial Nominating Comm 1988-94; bd of dir, CO ACLU, 1990. **CONTACT ADDRESS** Hurth Yeager & Sisk, LLP, 4860 Riverbend Rd, Boulder, CO, 80308.

FLOYD, JULIET

PERSONAL Born 03/12/1960, Boston, MA, m, 1995 **DISCIPLINE** PHILOSOPHY **EDUCATION** Wellesley Col, BA, 82; Harvard Univ, MA, PhD, 90. **CAREER** Asst prof, City Col NY, 90-95; dir grad studies, Boston Univ, 95-. **HONORS AND AWARDS** ACLS Senior fel, 98-99; Dibnet Inst MIT fel, 98-99. **MEMBERSHIPS** Am Philos Asn; Am Asn of Univ Women. **RESEARCH** Philosphy. **SELECTED PUBLICATIONS** Auth, "The Uncaptive Eye: Solipsism in Tractatus," 98; auth, "Frege, Semantics and the Double-Definition Stroke," 97; auth, "Heautonomy and the Critique of Sound Judgment: Kant on Reflective Judgment and Systematicity," 98; auth, "On Saying What You Really Want to Say: Wittgenstein, Godel and the Trisection of the Angle," 95. **CONTACT ADDRESS** Dept of Philosphy, Boston Univ, 745 Commonwealth Ave, Boston, MA, 02215.

FLOYD, MICHAEL H.

PERSONAL Born 08/05/1946, Kingstree, SC, m, 1975, 3 children **DISCIPLINE** OLD TESTAMENT STUDIES **EDUCATION** Trinity Col, BA, 69; Episcopal Theol Sch, BD, 71; Claremont Grad Sch, MA, 76, PhD, 80. **CAREER** Asst prof rel, Tex Wesleyan Col, 79-82; assoc prof Old Testament, 82-85, full prof, Episcopal Theol Sem SW, 85- . **MEMBERSHIPS** Soc Bibl Lit; Anglican Asn Bibl Scholars. **RESEARCH** Prophecy and Psalms; form criticism. **SELECTED PUBLICATIONS** Auth, How Can We Sing the Lord's Song?, Reformed Liturgy and Mus 20, 86, 95-101; Obadiah, in Harper's Bible Commentary, Harper, 88, 726-727; Falling Flat on Our Ars Poetica, Or Some Problems in Recent Studies of Hebrew Poetry, in the Psalms and Other Studies on the Old Testament, Festschrift, Cincinnati, Forward Movement Publ, 90, 118-131; Sex and the Bible, Anglican Theol Rev, 72, 90, 95-103; Prophetic Complaints about the Fulfillment of Oracles in Habakkuk 1:2-17 and Jeremiah 15:10-18, Jour Bibl Lit 110, 91, 397-418; Psalm LXXXIX: A Prophetic Complaint about the Fulfillment of the Oracle, Vetus Testamentum 42, 92, 442-257; Prophecy and Writing in Habakkuk 2:1-5, Zeitschrift fur die Alttestamentliche Wissenschaft 105, 93, 462-481; Are the Scriptures Still Sufficient? The Concept of Biblical Authority in the Thirty-Nine Articles, In Our Heritage and Common Life, UP of America, 94, 47-64; The Chimerical Acrostic in Nahum 1:2-10, Jour Bibl Lit, 113, 94, 421-437; The Nature of the Narrative and the Evidence of Redaction in Haggai, Vetus Testamentum 45, 95, 470-490; The Evil in the Ephah: Reading Zechariah 5:1-5 in Its Literary Context, Catholic Bibl Quart 58, 96, 51-68; Cosmos and History in Zechariah's View of the Restoration (Zech 1:7-6:15), in Problems in Biblical Theology, Grand Rapids, Eerdmans, 97, 125-144. **CONTACT ADDRESS** Dept of Old Testament, Episcopal Theol Sem of the Southwest, PO Box 2247, Austin, TX, 78768-2247. **EMAIL** mfloyd@etss.edu

FLYNN, THOMAS R.

PERSONAL Born 06/02/1936, Spokane, WA **DISCIPLINE** PHILOSOPHY **EDUCATION** Columbia Univ, PhD, 70. **CAREER** Asst prof, Cath Univ, 71-75; asst, assoc, prof and Samuel Candler Dobbs Prof, Emory Univ, 78- . **HONORS AND AWARDS** Fel, Nat Hum Ctr, N Carolina, 91-92; mem, Inst for Advanced Study, Princeton Univ, 98-99. **MEMBERSHIPS** APA; ACPA; SPEP. **RESEARCH** Contemporary continental, especially French, philosophy. **SELECTED PUBLICATIONS** Auth, Sartre and Marxist Existentialism: The Test Case of Collective Responsibility, Univ Chicago, 84; co-ed and contribur, Dialectic and Narrative, SUNY, 93; auth, Sartre, Foucault, and Historical Reason, v.1: Toward an Existentialist Theory of History, Univ Chicago, 97; auth, Phenomenology of Ethics, Sartrean, in Embree, ed, The Encyclopedia of Phenomenology, Kluwer, 97; auth, Sartre (1905-1980) in Critchley, ed, A Companion to Continental Philosophy, Blackwell, 98; **CONTACT ADDRESS** Dept of Philosophy, Emory Univ, Atlanta, GA, 30322. **EMAIL** tflynn@emory.edu

FOARD, JAMES HARLAN

PERSONAL Born 07/09/1948, Washington, DC, m, 1970, 1 child **DISCIPLINE** RELIGIOUS STUDIES **EDUCATION** Col of Wooster, BA, 70; MA, 72, PhD, 77, Stanford Univ. **CAREER** Asst Prof, 77-83, Assoc Prof, 83-97, Prof, 97-, Arizona State Univ. **MEMBERSHIPS** Amer Acad of Religion; Assoc of Asian Studies **RESEARCH** Japanese Religion **SELECTED PUBLICATIONS** Auth, Prefiguration and Narrative in Medieval Hagiography: the Ippen Hijiri E, Flowing Traces: Buddhism in the Literary and Visual Arts of Japan, 92; The Universal and the Particular in the Rites of Hiroshima, Communities in Question: Religion and Authority in Southeast and East Asia, 94; Text, Place and Memory in Hiroshima, Senri Ethnological Studies 95; Ritual in the Buddhist Temples of Japan, Object as Insight: Japanese Buddhist Art and ritual, 95; Ippen and Pure Land Buddhist Wayfarers in Medieval Japan, The Pure Land Tradition: History and Development, 96; Imagining Nuclear Weapons: Hiroshima, Armageddon, and the Annihilation of the Students of Ichijo School, Journal of the American Academy of Religion, 97; What One Kamakura Story Does: Practice, Place and Text in the Account of Ippen at Kumano, Revisioning Kamakura Buddhism, 98; Pure Land Belief and Popular practice: The Odori Nembutus of Ippen Shonin, Engaged Pure Land Buddhism: Studies in Honor of Professor Alfred Bloom, 98. **CONTACT ADDRESS** Religious Studies Dept, Arizona State Univ, Tempe, Tempe, AZ, 85287-3104. **EMAIL** james.foard@asu.edu

FOERST, ANNE

PERSONAL Born 03/24/1966, Germany, m **DISCIPLINE** THEOLOGY; COMPUTERSCIENCE; RELIGION & SCIENCE **EDUCATION** Univ Bonn, BA, 90; Church in Rhineland, M.Div, 92; Univ Bochum, PhD, 96. **CAREER** Res Fel, Harvard Divinity School, 95; Post-Doctoral Fel, MIT, 95; dir, God & Computers Project, 97-. **HONORS AND AWARDS** Templeton Course Award, 97. **MEMBERSHIPS** AAR; IRAS **RESEARCH** Religion & Science; Technology; Myths & Christian Theology **CONTACT ADDRESS** 545 Technology Sq NE 43-934, Cambridge, MA, 02139. **EMAIL** annef@ai.mit.edu

FOGELMAN, MARTIN

PERSONAL Born 03/16/1928, New York, NY, m, 1952, 2 children **DISCIPLINE** LAW **EDUCATION** Syracuse Univ, BA, 48, JD, 50. **CAREER** Confidential law clerk, chief judge, NY Court of Appeals, 50-54; from asst prof to assoc prof, 56-64, prof law, Sch Law, Fordham Univ, 64-86, McGivney Prof of Law, 86-; Assoc, Saxe, Bacon, O'Shea & Bryan, 54-59; consult, NY State Law Revision Comn, 66-, proj dir, 75-; hearing off, Assoc Hosp Serv, 70-. **MEMBERSHIPS** Am Bar Asn. **RESEARCH** Business corporations; not for profit corporations; mortgages. **SELECTED PUBLICATIONS** Coauth, Cases on Mortgages, Corydon M Johnston, 63; auth, Wests McKinneys Forms and Text-Business Corporation Law, West,

65 & ann suppl; The Deed Absolute as a Mortgage, Fordham Law Rev, 64; Insurance, Syracuse Law Rev, 65 & 66; Wests McKinneys Forms--Not for Profit Corporation Law, West, 72 & ann suppl. **CONTACT ADDRESS** Sch of Law, Fordham Univ, 140 W 62nd St, New York, NY, 10023-7407. **EMAIL** McGivney@aol.com

FOLEY, W. TRENT
DISCIPLINE RELIGION **EDUCATION** Kalamazoo Col, BA; McCormick Theol Sem, MDiv; Univ Chicago, AM and PhD. **CAREER** Fac, 84-; Prof, Davidson Col. **HONORS AND AWARDS** Vice-Pres, Am Acad Relig SW region. **MEMBERSHIPS** Am Soc Church Hist; N Am Patristics Soc'; Am Acad Relig. **RESEARCH** Christianity in early Anglo-Saxon England. **SELECTED PUBLICATIONS** Auth, Images of Sanctity in Eddius Stephanus' Life of Bishop Wilfrid, Edwin Mellen, 92. **CONTACT ADDRESS** Davidson Col, 102 N Main St, PO Box 1719, Davidson, NC, 28036.

FOLLIS, ELAINE R.
PERSONAL Born 01/28/1944, Quincy, MA, s **DISCIPLINE** BIBLICAL STUDIES **EDUCATION** Tufts Univ, AB, 65; BD, 68; Boston Univ, PhD, 76 **CAREER** Prof, 74-pres, Principia Col; Assoc Dean of Fac, 97-, Principia **HONORS AND AWARDS** Phi Beta Kappa, 64 **MEMBERSHIPS** Soc of Bibl Lit **RESEARCH** Holocaust Studies; Cultural History of Israel **SELECTED PUBLICATIONS** Auth, Directions in Biblical Hebrew Poetry, 87 **CONTACT ADDRESS** Principia Col, Elsah, IL, 62028. **EMAIL** erf@prin.edu

FOLSE, HENRY J., JR.
PERSONAL Born 05/02/1945, New Orleans, LA, m, 1972, 2 children **DISCIPLINE** PHILOSOPHY **EDUCATION** Harvard Col, BA, 67; Tulane Univ, MA, 70, PhD, 72. **CAREER** Assoc prof, 75-80, Col of Clarkston; assoc prof, 80-85, prof, 85-, Loyola Univ New Orleans. **HONORS AND AWARDS** NEH Fel. **MEMBERSHIPS** APA; Phil of Sci Assn; So Soc for Phil & Psychol; Metaphysical Soc of Amer. **RESEARCH** Quantum revolution; phil of physics; scientific rationality. **SELECTED PUBLICATIONS** Auth, The Philosophy of Niels Bohr: The Framework of Complementarity, N Holland Physics Pub, 85; art, The Environment and the Epistemological Lesson of Complementarity, Environ Ethics 15, 93; art, Bohr's Framework of Complementarity and the Realism Debate, Niels Bohr & Contemporary Phil: Boston Stud in Phil of Sci 153, Kluwer Acad Pub, 94; coauth, "Introduction" to Niels Bohr and Contemporary Philosophy: Boston Studies in the Philosophy of Science 153, 94; coauth, Bearers of Properties in the Quantum Mechanical Description of Nature, Intl Stud in Phil of Sci 8, 94; co-ed, Niels Bohr and Contemporary Philosophy: Boston Studies in the Philosophy of Science 153, Kluwer Acad Pub, 94; auth, The Bohr-Einstein Debate and the Philosophers' Debate over Realism versus Anti-Realism, Realism & Anti Realism in Phil of Sci; Beijing Intl Conf, 1992, Kluwer, 96. **CONTACT ADDRESS** Dept of Philosophy, Loyola Univ, New Orleans, LA, 70118. **EMAIL** folse@loyno.edu

FOLTZ, BRUCE
DISCIPLINE PHILOSOPHY **EDUCATION** Pa State Univ, PhD. **CAREER** Assoc prof. **RESEARCH** History of philosophy; recent European methodologies; philosophy of religion. **SELECTED PUBLICATIONS** Auth, Inhabiting the Earth: Heidegger; Environmental Ethics; Metaphysics of Nature; pubs on Heidegger and the the philosophy of the natural environment. **CONTACT ADDRESS** Dept of Philosophy, Eckerd Col, 54th Ave S, PO Box 4200, St Petersburg, FL, 33711.

FOLTZ, HOWARD L.
DISCIPLINE DIVINITY; GLOBAL EVANGELIZATION **EDUCATION** Southwestern Assemblies of God Col, BS; Assemblies of God Grad Sch; Denver Theol Sem, DMin. **CAREER** Prof, 85. **SELECTED PUBLICATIONS** Auth, Triumph: Missions Renewal in the Local Church, 94; How to Put Your Church on the Cutting Edge of World Missions, Ministries Today, 94; Building the Home-Base for Global Outreach, Intl Jour of Frontier Missions, 94; Sharpening Your Church's Mission Commitment, Mission Today, 95; Do Miracles Still Happen?, Decision Mag, Messenger Press, 96; How To Have A Healthy Church In A Sick World, Messenger Press, 97. **CONTACT ADDRESS** Dept of Divinity, Regent Univ, 1000 Regent Univ Dr, Virginia Beach, VA, 23464-9831.

FONTAINE, CAROLE R.
PERSONAL Born 04/11/1950, Lima, OH, m, 1972 **DISCIPLINE** OLD TESTAMENT **EDUCATION** FL State Univ, BA, 72; Yale Univ, MAR, 76; Duke Univ, PhD, 79. **CAREER** Tchg asst, Duke Univ, 76-79; Prof Hebrew Scriptures, Andover Newton Theol Sch, 79-, Instr wisdom lit, Duke Univ, 79; instr Old Testament, Univ NC, Greensboro, 79; bk rev ed, Andover Newton Quart, 79-81; joint grad fac, Boston Col & Andover Newton Theol Sch, 82-85. **HONORS AND AWARDS** Zion Found Scholarship; Gurney Harris Kearns fel; Artist-in-Residence, ANTS. **MEMBERSHIPS** Cath Bibl Asn; Soc Bibl Lit. **RESEARCH** Hebrew Bible wisdom; structural anthrop; women's studies. **SELECTED PUBLICATIONS** Auth, A modern look at ancient wisdom: The instruction of Ptahhotep, revisited, Bibl Archaeol, 44: 155-60; Traditional sayings in the Old Testament: A contextual study, Bible & Lit, Almond Press, Sheffield, England, 85; Proverbs, Ecclesiastes, In: Womens Bible Commentary (Carol Newsom & Sharon Ringe, ed), Westminster/John Knox, 92; A Feminist Companion to Reading the Bible: Approaches, Methods, Strategies (Athalya Brennere and Carole Fontaine, ed), Sheffield Acad Press, U K, 97. **CONTACT ADDRESS** Andover Newton Theol Sch, 210 Herrick Rd, Newton, MA, 02459-2236. **EMAIL** cfontaine@ants.edu

FONTINELL, EUGENE
PERSONAL Born 05/22/1924, Scranton, PA **DISCIPLINE** PHILOSOPHY **EDUCATION** Univ Scranton, BA, 48; Fordham Univ, MA, 50, PhD (philos), 57. **CAREER** Instr philos, Iona Col, 51-54; asst prof, Col New Rochelle, 54-58, assoc prof and chmn dept, 58-61; from asst prof to assoc prof, 61-70, chmn dept, 66-72, Prof Philos, Queens Col, NY, 70-. **MEMBERSHIPS** Am Philos Asn; Am Cath Philos Asn. **RESEARCH** American philosophy; philosophy of religion; philosophy of history. **SELECTED PUBLICATIONS** Auth, Submitting to Freedom--The Religious Vision of James, William, 19th Century Prose, Vol 21, 94. **CONTACT ADDRESS** Dept of Philos, Queens Col, CUNY, Flushing, NY, 11367.

FORBES, A. DEAN
PERSONAL Born 03/02/1941, Pomona, CA, m, 1971 **DISCIPLINE** PHYSICS, OLD TESTAMENT **EDUCATION** Harvard Col, AB, 62; Pacific School of Rel, MDiv, 69. **CAREER** Mem of Technical Staff, Hewlett-Packard Co, 70-90; Proj mgr, Medical Dept, 90-93; Principle Medical Dept Scientist, 93- ; Editorial bd, 84-93, Algorithms ed, 93-97, Jour of Clinical Monitoring; Algorithms editor, Jour of Clinical Monitoring & Computing, 98- ; vis scholar, Stanford Univ, 86-89. **HONORS AND AWARDS** Who's Who in America, 53rd ed. **RESEARCH** Noninvasive measurements; pattern recognition; statistics/stochastic processes; statistical-linguistic analyses of the orthography and syntax of Biblical Hebrew. **SELECTED PUBLICATIONS** Auth, A Synoptic Concordance to Hosea, Amos, Micah, Volume VI of the Computer Bible, Wooster, Bibl Res Assoc, 74; Eight Minor Prophets: A Linguistic Concordance, Volume X of the Computer Bible, Wooster: Bibl Res Assoc, 76; A Linguistic Concordance of Ruth and Jonah: Hebrew Vocabulary and Idion, Volume XI of the Computer Bible, Wooster, Bibl Res Assoc, 76; A Linguistic Concordance of Jeremiah: Hebrew Vocabulary and Idiom, Volume XIV of the Computer Bible, Wooster, Bibl Res Assoc, 78; Prose Particle Counts of the Hebrew Bible, in The Word of the Lord Shall Go Forth: Essays in Honor of David Noel Freedman in Celebration of His Sixtieth Birthday, Winona Lake, Eisenbrauns and American Schools for Oriental Res, 83, 165-183; Orthography and Text Transmission, TEXT 2, 85, 25-53; Problems in Taxonomy and Lemmatization, in Proceedings of the First International Colloquium: Bible and the Computer-the Text, Paris-Geneva, Champion-Slatkine, 86, 37-50; Further Studies in Hebrew Spelling, Conference on the History of Hebrew Spelling, Univ Calif San Diego, April 86; Spelling in the Hebrew Bible, Rome, The Pontifical Biblical Inst Press, 86; Syntactic Sequences in the Hebrew Bible, in E.G. Newing and E. W. Conrad, eds, Perspectives on Language and Text: Essays and Poems in Honor of Francis Ian Andersen on His Sixtieth Birthday, Winona Lake, Eisenbrauns, 87, 59-70; Methods and Tools for the Study of Old Testament Syntax, in Proceedings of the Second International Colloquium: Bible and the Computer-Methods, Tools, Results, Paris-Geneva, Champion-Slatkine, 89, 61-72; The Vocabulary of the Old Testament, Rome, The Pontifical Bibl Inst Press, 89, 2nd printing 92; A Key-Word-in-Context Concordance to Psalms, Job, and Proverbs, Volume XXXIV of the Computer Bible, Wooster, Bibl Res Assoc, 92; Statistical Research on the Bible, in David Noel Freedman, ed, The Anchor Dictionary of the Bible, Garden City, NY, Doubleday, 92, VI, 185-206; On Marking Clause Boundaries, in Proceedings of the Third International Colloquium: Bible and the Computer-Methods, Tools, Results, Paris-Geneva, Champion-Slatkine, 92, 181-202; A Critique of Statistical Approaches to the Isaiah Authorship Problem, in Proceedings of the Third Intl Colloquium: bible and the Computer-Methods, Tools, Results, Paris-Geneva, Champion-Slatkine, 92, 531-545; Studies in Hebrew and Aramaic Orthography, vol 2 of Biblical and Judaic Studies from the Univ Calif, San Diego, ed William Henry Propp, Winona Lake, Eisenbrauns, 92; A Key-Word-in-Context Concordance to the Pentateuch, Volume XXXVa/b of the Computer Bible, Lewiston, NY, Mellen Bibl Press, 95; Opportune Parsing: Clause Analysis of Deuteronomy 8, in Proceedings of the Fourth International Colloquium: Bible and the Computer-Desk & Discipline, Paris, Editions Honore Champion, 95, 49-75; Syntactic Ambiguity in the Hebrew Bible, in Proceedings of the Fourth International Colloquium: Bible and the Computer-Desk & discipline, Paris, Editions Honore Champion, 95, 356-367; Shards, Strophes, and Stats, in A. Beck, ed, Fortunate the Eyes that See: Essays in Honor of David Noel Freedman in Celebration of His Seventieth Birthday, Grand Rapids, Academie Publ Co, 95, 310-321; Towards a Clause-Type Concordance of TNK, in Proceedings of the Fifth International Colloquium: Bible and the Computer-Translation, Paris, Editions Honore Champion, 98; Approximate Graph-Matching as an Enabler of Example-Based Translation, in Proceedings of the Fifth International Colloquium: Bible and the Computer-Translation, Paris, Editions Honore Champion, 98. **CONTACT ADDRESS** 820 Loma Verde Ave, Palo Alto, CA, 94303. **EMAIL** adforbes@ix.netcom.com

FORBES, GRAEME
DISCIPLINE PHILOSOPHY **EDUCATION** Oxford Univ, DPhil, 80. **CAREER** Prof, Tulane Univ; Celia Scott Weatherhead distinguished ch. **SELECTED PUBLICATIONS** Auth, The Metaphysics of Modality, Oxford; Modern Logic, Oxford; pub(s) in, Philos Rev; Nous; J Philos; Ling and Philos. **CONTACT ADDRESS** Dept of Philosophy, Tulane Univ, 6823 St Charles Ave, New Orleans, LA, 70118. **EMAIL** forbes@mailhost.tcs.tulane.edu

FORD, JAMES L.
PERSONAL Born 03/21/1957, Richmond, VA, m **DISCIPLINE** EAST ASIAN RELIGION **EDUCATION** Priceton Univ, PhD, 98. **CAREER** Ast prof, Wake Forest Univ, 98- **MEMBERSHIPS** AAR; AAS. **RESEARCH** Medieval Japanese Buddhism. **CONTACT ADDRESS** Dept of Religion, Wake Forest Univ, 107 Wingate Hall, Winston-Salem, NC, 27109. **EMAIL** fordj@wfu.edu

FORD, JOHN THOMAS
PERSONAL Born 11/21/1932, Dallas, TX **DISCIPLINE** SYSTEMATIC & HISTORICAL THEOLOGY **EDUCATION** Univ Notre Dame, AB, 55; Holy Cross Col, DC, MA, 59; Gregorian Univ, Italy, STL, 60, STD, 62. **CAREER** Instr theol, Univ of Notre Dame, 62; prof, Holy Cross Col, DC, 62-68; asst prof, 68-71, from assoc prof to prof theol, Cath Univ Am, 71-, Chm Dept, 77-83, Assoc Dean, 91-96. **MEMBERSHIPS** NAm Acad Ecumenists(pres, 76-78); Cath Theol Soc Am; Am Acad Relig; Cath Hist Asn; AAUP. **RESEARCH** Nineteenth century Roman Catholic theology. **SELECTED PUBLICATIONS** Auth, A Centre of Light and Truth, Cath Hist Rev, 89; Differences about Infallibility, Church and Theol, 95; Newman's View of Education, Lit and Educ Effects, 95; co-ed, Twelve Tales Untold, Eerdmans, 93; ed, Religious Liberty: Paul VI and Dignitatis Humanae, Studium, 95. **CONTACT ADDRESS** Catholic Univ of America, 125 Caldwell Hall, Washington, DC, 20064-0002. **EMAIL** ford@cua.edu

FORD, JUDITH DONNA
PERSONAL Born 08/30/1935, Eureka, CA **DISCIPLINE** LAW **EDUCATION** Univ of CA at Berkeley, BS 1957; University of California-Berkeley, JD 1974. **CAREER** Petty Andrews Tufts & Jackson, assoc atty 1974-79; Consumer Fraud Crime Div SF Dist Atty's Office, dir 1977-79; Fed Trade Comm, dir 1980-82; Oakland-Piedmont-Emeryville Jud Dist, judge 1983-. **MEMBERSHIPS** CA Judges Assn; Alameda Co Trauma Review Comm; US Magistrate Merit Selection Comm; San Francisco Bar Assn Lawyer Referral Serv Comm 1976; NSF SoftwareAuditing Wkshp 1976; Comm for Admin of Justice 1976-79; delegate from San Fran Bar Assn Lawyer Refrl Serv Comm 1976; chair E Oakland Planned Prnthd Adv Comm 1977-80; spkr Bank Admin Inst 1977; spkr EDP Audit Cntrls Wkshp 1977; spkr CPA Soc 1977; various TV & Radio appearances; spoke to comm groupson consult fraud 1977-79; spkr Joint meeting of IIA and EDPA 1978; dir Planned Prnthd 1978-80; chair Blk Women Lawyers, N CA Finance Comm 1979-80; San Fran Lawyers Comm Urban Affairs 1979-80; chair SF Bar Assn Comm Legal Ed Comm 1979-80; bd mem Consumer Union 1979-82; ref St Bar Ct 1979-82; cnclr Law CntrBd of Cnclrs 1979-83; radio & TV spkr on FTrade Comm 1980-82; SF Bar Assoc Judiciary Comm 1981-82; Chas Houston Bar Assoc 1974-; CA Assoc of Black Lawyers 1978-; bd mem Peralta Serv Corp 1983-, judicial council, 1991-94; chair, CTC Privacy & Access Subcommittee, 1995-96; Judicial Council Court Technology, advisory comm, 1995-98; trustee, Alameda County Law Library; board member, California Judges Association, 1996-98. **SELECTED PUBLICATIONS** California Criminal Law Procedure & Practice, (CEB 1994, 2nd Ed), co-author, chapters 4 & 6. **CONTACT ADDRESS** Oakland-Piedmont Emeryville, 661 Washington St, Oakland, CA, 94607.

FORD, LEWIS S.
PERSONAL Born 11/18/1933, Leonia, NJ, m, 1957, 2 children **DISCIPLINE** PHILOSOPHY **EDUCATION** Yale Univ, AB, 55, AM, 59, PhD, 63. **CAREER** Asst prof philos and relig, MacMurray Col, 60-62; from asst prof to assoc prof, Raymond Col, Univ of the Pac, 63-70; assoc prof philos, Pa State Univ, University Park, 70-73; Nat Endowment Humanities sr fel, 73-74; PROF PHILOS, OLD DOMINION UNIV, 74-, Soc Relig Higher Educ cross-disciplinary studies fel, 68-69; ed, Process Studies, 71-. **MEMBERSHIPS** Am Philos Asn; Am Acad Relig; Soc Relig Higher Educ; Metaphys Soc Am. **RESEARCH** Process philosophy; philosophical theology; Biblical studies. **SELECTED PUBLICATIONS** Auth The Openness of God--A Biblical Challenge to the Traditional Understanding df God, Int J Philos Rel, Vol 41, 97; Behind the Masks of God--An Essay Toward Comparative Theology, Int J Philos Rel, Vol 34, 93; The God who Acts--Philosophical and Theological Explorations, Int J Philos Rel, Vol 39, 96; The Unchanging God of Love--A Study of the Teaching of Thomas Aquinas on Divine Immutability in View of Certain Contemporary Criticism of this Doctrine, Int J Philos Religion, Vol 33, 93; Theology and the University--Essays in Honor of Cobb, John, B., J Religion, Vol 73, 93; Hartshorne, Charles Concept of God, Int J Philos Religion, Vol 33, 93. **CONTACT ADDRESS** Dept of Philos, Old Dominion Univ, Norfolk, VA, 23508.

FORDE, GERHARD OLAF
PERSONAL Born 09/10/1927, Starbuck, MN, 3 children **DISCIPLINE** CHURCH HISTORY, SYSTEMATIC THEOLOGY **EDUCATION** Luther Col, BA, 50; Luther Theol Sem, BTh, 55; Harvard Divinity Sch, ThD, 67; Oxford Univ, MA, 68. **CAREER** Instr relig, St Olaf Col, 55-56; lectr church hist, Luther Theol Sem, 59-61; asst prof relig, Luther Col, 61-63; assoc prof church hist, 64-71, Prof Syst Theol, Luther Theol Sem, 71-, Lutheran World Fed lectr, Mansfield Col, Oxford Univ, 68-70; Frederick A Schiotz fel, 72-73. **MEMBERSHIPS** Am Acad Relig. **RESEARCH** Theology of Martin Luther; 19th century theology. **SELECTED PUBLICATIONS** Auth, The Law-Gospel Debate, 69, Where God Meets Man, 72 & coauth, Free To Be, 75, Augsburg; Justification By Faith: A Matter of Death & Life, 82; Theology is for Proclamation, 90; On Being a Theologian of the Cross, 97. **CONTACT ADDRESS** Luther Sem, 2481 Como Ave, St. Paul, MN, 55108-1445. **EMAIL** gfonde@luthersem.edu

FORELL, CAROLINE
PERSONAL Born 11/04/1950 **DISCIPLINE** LAW **EDUCATION** Univ Iowa, BA, 73, JD, 78. **CAREER** Instr, Asst dean, Asst Prof, Assoc Prof, Prof, 78 to 94-, Univ Oregon. **HONORS AND AWARDS** Phi Beta Kappa, Order of the Coif. **MEMBERSHIPS** OSBA **RESEARCH** Women and the Law; Civil Liability. **SELECTED PUBLICATIONS** Auth, What's Wrong With Faculty-Student Sex? The Law School Context, J Legal Edu, 97; Essentialism Empathy and the Reasonable Women, 1994 IL L Rev, 94; Attorney-Client Sex: Ethical and Liability Issues in Oregon, Willamette L Rev, 93; The Reasonable Women standard of Care, Univ Tasmania L, 92; Lawyers Clients and Sex: Breaking the Silence on the Ethical and Liability Issues, Golden Gate L Rev, 92. **CONTACT ADDRESS** School of Law, Univ of Oregon, Eugene, OR, 97403. **EMAIL** cforell@law.uoregon.edu

FORELL, GEORGE WOLFGANG
PERSONAL Born 09/19/1919, Breslau, Germany **DISCIPLINE** THEOLOGY **EDUCATION** Lutheran Theol Sem, Philadelphia, BD, 42; Princeton Theol Sem, ThM, 43; Union Theol Sem, NY, ThD, 49. **CAREER** From asst prof to assoc prof philos, Gustavus Adolphus Col, 47-54; from asst prof to assoc prof relig, State Univ Iowa, 54-58; prof theol, Chicago Lutheran Sem, 58-61; dir sch: 66-71, prof theol, 61-73, CARVER DISTINGUISHED PROF, SCH RELIG, UNIV IOWA, 73-, Vis prof, Univ Hamburg, 57-58, Japan Lutheran Theol Col, 68, Gurukul Theol Res Inst, Madras, India, 78. **HONORS AND AWARDS** DD, Wartburg Theol Sem; LHD, Gustavus Adolphus Col, 74. **MEMBERSHIPS** Fel Soc Relig Higher Educ; Am Soc Reformation Res (pres, 59); Am Soc Church Hist; Am Philos Asn; Int Cong Luther Res. **RESEARCH** Reformation history; Zinzendorf and the Moravian Missions among the American Indians; history of Christian ethics. **SELECTED PUBLICATIONS** Auth, Luther Theology in its Historical Development and its Context, 16th Century J, Vol 28, 97; Spalding, James, Colwell, 1921-1996, 16th Century J, Vol 27, 96; Luther, Martin, his Life and Thought, 16th Century J, Vol 28, 97; Christian Ethics--A Historical Introduction, Church Hist, Vol 65, 96; Christian Ethics--A Historical Introduction, Church Hist, Vol 65, 96. **CONTACT ADDRESS** Sch of Relig, Univ of Iowa, Iowa City, IA, 52242.

FOREMAN, JONATHAN BARRY
DISCIPLINE LAW **EDUCATION** Northwestern Univ, BA 73; Univ Iowa, MA 75; Univ Michigan Law, JD magna cum laude, 78; George Washington Univ, MA 83. **CAREER** Univ Oklahoma Law, prof 97-; OK City Univ Law, adj prof, 95, 96; Brigham Young Univ Law, vis prof 91; Univ Colorado Law, vis prof 87; Univ San Diego Law, vis prof 85; Tax Notes, ed staff 85; Sen D. P. Moynihan NY, tax coun 83,84; US Dept Justice, trial att, tax div 79-83; Antioch Sch Law, adj prof 81-85; Hon R.J. Yock, US Court Clms, jud clk 78-79. **HONORS AND AWARDS** Nat Summit Del; ATPI Trustee; Halliburton Fac Awd; NALJF Fel; US Supreme Court Judicial Fel finalist. **MEMBERSHIPS** Dist Columbia Bar Assoc; ABA; NTA; ACTC, ATPI; AEA; EBRI; World bank. **SELECTED PUBLICATIONS** Auth, The Once and Future Social Security Tax Expenditure, Benefits Quart, 97; auth, What Can Be Done About Marriage Penalties?, Fam Law Quart, 96; auth, Poverty Levels and Federal Tax Thresholds: 1996, Tax Notes, 96; Simplification for Low Income taxpayers: Some Options, OH State Law Jour, 96; auth, How to Reduce the Compliance Burden of the Earned Income Tax Credit on Low Income Workers and on the Internal Rev Service, OK Law Rev, 95; auth, Reconsidering the Income Tax Treatment of the Elderly: It's Time for the Elderly to Pay Their Fair Share, Univ Pitt Law Rev, 95; auth, Improving the Delivery of Benefits to the Working Poor: Proposals to Reform the Earned Income Credit Program, coauth, Amer Jour of Tax Policy. **CONTACT ADDRESS** College of Law, Univ of Oklahoma, 300 Timberdell Rd, Norman, OK, 73019. **EMAIL** jforeman@ou.edu

FOREMAN, PEGGY E.
PERSONAL Born 02/18/1958, Houston, TX, s **DISCIPLINE** LAW **EDUCATION** Univ of Pennsylvania, 1976-78; Univ of Houston, BBA, 1981; TSU, Thurgood Marshall School of Law, JD, 1985. **CAREER** Peggy Foreman, Attorney, 1985-89; Burney and Foreman, partner, 1990-. **HONORS AND AWARDS** Houston Business and Professional Men's Club, Special Recognition; Iota Phi Lambda Sorority Inc, Beta Delta Chapter, Woman of the Year. **MEMBERSHIPS** American Bar Assn; National Bar Assn; State Bar of Texas; Texas Young Lawyers Assn; Harris County Young Assn; Houston Lawyers Assn, Houston Bar Assn, Young Lawyers Assn; National Assn of Bond Lawyers; Texas Trial Lawyers Assn; Gulf Coast Black Women Lawyers Assn; Phi Delta Phi Legal Fraternity Alumni Chap; Thurgood Marshall School of Law Alumni Assn. **SELECTED PUBLICATIONS** Author/Speaker, "Effective Rainmaking", Women in the Law Section Institute, State Bar of Texas, April 1993; Author/Speaker, Wills and Trusts in Texas, Harris County Young Lawyers Assn and Texas Lawyers Assn, May 1989; Author/Speaker, Client Satisfaction, How to Thrive, Not Just Survive in a Solo/Small Firm Practice, State Bar of Texas, December 1993; numerous others. **CONTACT ADDRESS** Burney & Foreman, 5445 Almeda, Ste 400, Houston, TX, 77004.

FOREMAN, TERRY HANCOCK
PERSONAL Born 03/12/1943, Long Beach, CA, d, 2 children **DISCIPLINE** RELIGIOUS STUDIES, PHILOSOPHY **EDUCATION** Stanford Univ, AB, 64; Pa State Univ, MA, 68; Yale Univ, PhD(relig studies), 75. **CAREER** Asst prof philos, Earlham Col, 72-73; acting asst prof, Univ CA, San Diego, 74-75; asst prof & coordr relig studies, 75-78, asst prof, 78-81, ASSOC PROF PHILOS & RELIG STUDIES, MURRAY STATE UNIV, 81-, Chmn Dept, 78-96. **MEMBERSHIPS** Am Acad Relig. **RESEARCH** Role of scientific ideas in shaping concepts of religion in 18th and 19th centuries; varieties of the Bildung view of personal development in post-Enlightenment Germany. **SELECTED PUBLICATIONS** Auth, Schleiermacher's Natural History of Religion: Science and the Interpretation of Culture in the Speeches, J Relig, 4/78; Difference and Reconciliation: G. E. Lessing as Partner in Ecumenical Conversation, in Christian Faith Seeking Understanding: Essays in Honor of H. Jack Forstman, ed James O. Duke and Tony A. Dunnavant, Mercer Univ Press, 97; Henry E. Allison, Kant's Doctrine of Freedom, the Lessing Yearbook, XXVII, 96; Herder's Copernican Revolution in Philosophy and the Study of Religion, Max Muller, Founder Mytheme for Comparative Religion, forthcoming; The Sublime Conception of Religion in 18th-Century Critical poetics, forthcoming. **CONTACT ADDRESS** Dept of Philos & Relig Studies, Murray State Univ, PO Box 9, Murray, KY, 42071-0009. **EMAIL** terry.foreman@murraystate.edu

FORGUSON, LYND W.
PERSONAL Born 01/15/1938, Paducah, KY **DISCIPLINE** PHILOSOPHY **EDUCATION** Baldwin-Wallace Col, BA, 60; Northwestern Univ, MA, 61, PhD, 64. **CAREER** Fulbright-Hayes fel, Oxford Univ, 63-64; asst prof, State Univ NY, 64-67; NEH fel, Oxford Univ, 67-68; PROF PHILOSOPHY, UNIV TORONTO, 68-, prin, Univ Col, 89-97. **MEMBERSHIPS** Can Asn Univ Tchrs; Can Philos Asn; Soc Philos Psychol. **SELECTED PUBLICATIONS** Auth, Common Sense, 89. **CONTACT ADDRESS** Dept of Philosophy, Univ of Toronto, 15 King's College Cir, Toronto, ON, M5S 1A1.

FORMAN, ROBERT
DISCIPLINE RELIGION - SPIRITUAL AND MYSTICAL EXPERIENCE **EDUCATION** Columbia Univ, PhD, 88. **CAREER** Vassar Col, 88-90; Hunter Col, CUNY, 90- ; ed, J Consciousness Studies. **HONORS AND AWARDS** Numerous grants; Fetzer; New World Found; CUNY. **MEMBERSHIPS** AAR; Forge Inst. **RESEARCH** Spiritual experience; spirituality in America; mysticism. **SELECTED PUBLICATIONS** Auth, Problem of Pure Consciousness; auth, Mysticism; auth, Mind Consciousness; auth, Innate Capacity. **CONTACT ADDRESS** 383 Broadway, Hastings on Hudson, NY, 10706. **EMAIL** rforman383@aol.com

FORRESTER, WILLIAM RAY
PERSONAL Born 01/14/1911, Little Rock, AR, m, 1942, 4 children **DISCIPLINE** LAW **EDUCATION** Univ AR, AB, 33; Univ Chicago, JD, 35. **CAREER** Atty, Defrees, Buckingham, Jones & Hoffman, Chicago, IL, 35-41; prof law, Tulane Univ, 41-49; prof & dean, law sch, Vanderbilt Univ, 49-52; lby prof & dean, Tulane Univ, 52-63; Stevens prof, law sch, Cornell Univ, 63-78, dean sch, 63-73; PROF LAW, UNIV CA, HASTINGS COL LAW, 78-; vis prof, Univ London, Queen Mary Col, 74; Labor arbitrator; Board of Gov, Nat Academy of Arbitrators; L.A. member, Comm on Uniform State Laws; public member, admin conferences of the U. S., 75-78. **HONORS AND AWARDS** LLD, Univ AR, 63; LLD, Tulane Univ, 95. **RESEARCH** Federal jurisdiction and procedure; constitutional law. **SELECTED PUBLICATIONS** Auth, Constitutional Law, 59, cases & materials suppl 61 & 63, coauth, Federal Jurisdiction and Procedure, 70 & suppl to Federal Jurisdiction and Procedure, 73, 3rd ed, 77, West Publ, suppl, 81. **CONTACT ADDRESS** Dept of Law, Univ Calif, 200 McAllister St, San Francisco, CA, 94102-4907.

FORSBERG, RALPH P.
PERSONAL Born 08/28/1948, Chicago, IL, m, 1970, 1 child **DISCIPLINE** PHILOSOPHY **EDUCATION** Bradley Univ, BS, 70; Roosevelt Univ, MA, 73; Loyola Univ, PhD, 87. **CAREER** Lectr, adj prof, Loyola Univ, 74-87; lectr, adj prof, Harper Coll, 74-87; cis asst prof, Ripon Coll, 88-89; Assoc Prof, Delta Coll, 89-. **HONORS AND AWARDS** Mem Sigma Alpha Nu Honor Soc; Loyola Univ Grant-In-Aid; Roosevelt Univ Grad Scholar. **MEMBERSHIPS** Am Philos Asn; Am Asn of Philos Tchrs; Am Asn of Univ Profs; Comt on Employee Responsibilities and Rights; Int Soc of Bus, Economics, and Ethics; Med Ethics Resources Network Of Mich; Marketing Mgt Asn: Ethics Section; Midwest Acad of Legal Studies in Bus; Soc for Bus Ethics. **RESEARCH** Environmental Ethics and Ecology; Applied Ethics, Medical and Business; Native Am Philos. **SELECTED PUBLICATIONS** Auth, Ethics on the Job: Cases and Strategies, 93; random Selection and the Allocation of Scarce Medical Resources, J of Philos and Med, 94; R L Ewin, Thomas Hobbes's Theory of Morality, Int J of Philos, 94; Richard Flathman, Thomas Hobbes: Skepticism, Individuality and Chastened Politics, Int J of Philos, 95; Seth Allcorn, Anger in the Workplace: A Review, Employee Responsibilities and Rights J. **CONTACT ADDRESS** Dept of Philosophy, Delta Col, University Ctr, MI, 48710. **EMAIL** rpforsbe@alpha.delta.edu

FORSHEY, HAROLD ODES
PERSONAL Born 07/27/1934, Cambridge, OH, m, 1966, 2 children **DISCIPLINE** RELIGION **EDUCATION** Abilene Christian Col, BA, 56, MA, 61; Harvard Univ, STB, 62, ThD, 73. **CAREER** From instr to asst prof, 66-77, assoc prof, 77-82, prof Relig, Miami Univ, 82-, chmn dept, 79-84, 95-; Staff, Lahav Res Proj, 77; act dean, Coll of Arts and Science, 90-91; assoc dean, Col of Arts and Science, 91-94. **MEMBERSHIPS** Cath Bibl Asn; Soc Bibl Lit; Am Sch Orient Res; Archaeol Inst Am; Am Oriental Soc. **RESEARCH** Religion of ancient Israel; ancient Near Eastern languages and literature; archaeology of Near East. **SELECTED PUBLICATIONS** Auth, Circumcision: an initiatory rite in ancient Israel?, Restoration Quart, 73-74; Segullah and Nachalah as designations of the covenant community, Hebrew Abstr, 74; The construct chain nahalat YHWHV/'elohim, Bull Am Schs Orient Res, 75-76; The Bronze Age Settlements at Tell Halif: Phase II Excavations, 83-87, with Joe D Seger, Paul Jacobs, and others, Bulletin of the American Schools of Oriental Research, Supplement 26, 90. **CONTACT ADDRESS** Dept of Relig, Miami Univ, 500 E High St, Oxford, OH, 45056-1602. **EMAIL** forsheho@muohio.edu

FORTNA, ROBERT TOMSON
PERSONAL Born 05/05/1930, Lincoln, NE, m, 1960, 3 children **DISCIPLINE** RELIGION, NEW TESTAMENT **EDUCATION** Yale Univ, BA, 52; Cambridge Univ, BA, 54, MA, 59; Church Divinity Sch Pac, BD, 55; Union Theol Sem, NY, ThD(New Testament), 65. **CAREER** Tutor theol and instr Greek, Church Divinity Sch Pac, 55-56; lectr New Testament, 56-58; dir exten, 58-60; tutor New Testament, Union Theol Sem, NY, 60-62, lectr, 62-63; from instr to assoc prof relig, 63-74, fac fel, 67-68, dean freshman, 69, chmn dept, 69-71, 74-77 and 80-81, PROF RELIG, VASSAR COL, 74-, William F Albright fel, Am Sch Orient Res, Jerusalem, 67-68; Am Coun Learned Soc fel, 67-68; resident scholar, Ecumenical Inst Advan Theol Studies, Jerusalem, 72 and 78; prof, Albright Inst, Jerusalem, 79. **MEMBERSHIPS** Am Schs Orient Res; Soc New Testament Studies; Cath Bibl Asn Am; Soc Bibl Lit. **RESEARCH** Fourth Gospel. **SELECTED PUBLICATIONS** Auth, The Gospel of John and the Sociology of Light Language and Characterization in the 4th Gospel, J Biblical Lit, Vol 116, 97; The Signs Source in the 4th Gospel Historical Survey and Critical Evaluation of the Semeia Hypothesis, J Biblical Lit, Vol 115, 96. **CONTACT ADDRESS** Dept of Relig, Vassar Col, Poughkeepsie, NY, 12601.

FORTNER, JOHN D.
PERSONAL Born 01/13/1949, Greencastle, IN, m, 1971, 1 child **DISCIPLINE** HEBREW BIBLE AND LANGUAGE LITERATURE, CULTURE **EDUCATION** Hebrew Union Col-Jewish Inst Relig, PhD, 97. **CAREER** Asst prof Bible, Lubbock Christian Col, 78-82; Pulpit ministries in Ohio & Tenn, Church of Christ, 82-90; assoc prof Hebrew Bible & The Ane, Harding Univ Asn, 90-. **MEMBERSHIPS** Soc Bibl Lit; Am Orient Soc; Am Schools Orient Res. **RESEARCH** Old Babylonian Law; Biblical exegesis. **SELECTED PUBLICATIONS** Contrib to New Eerdmans Dictionary of Bible, 98; in progress, NIV Bible Commentary on Exodus, College Press. **CONTACT ADDRESS** Harding Univ, 900 E Center St, Box 12280, Searcy, AR, 72149-0001. **EMAIL** jdfortner@harding.edu

FOSL, PETER S.
DISCIPLINE EARLY MODERN PHILOSOPHY, SKEPTICISM, SOCIAL-POLITICAL PHILOSOPHY, FEMINISM **EDUCATION** Bucknell Univ, BA, summa cum laude; Emory Univ, PhD. **CAREER** Asst prof, Hollins Col. **HONORS AND AWARDS** Fulbright Scholar, Univ Edinburgh; Prize for Excellence in Grad Res, Emory Univ. **RESEARCH** Skepticism. **SELECTED PUBLICATIONS** His publ(s) have addressed David Hume, Stanley Cavell, Cicero, Sextus Empiricus, Gilles Deleuze, animal rights, and early Am deism. **CONTACT ADDRESS** Hollins Col, Roanoke, VA, 24020. **EMAIL** pfosl@hollins.edu

FOSS, JEFFREY E.
DISCIPLINE PHILOSOPHY **EDUCATION** Univ Alberta, BA; Univ W Ontario, MA, PhD. **CAREER** Instr, Univ Saskatchewan; Univ Alberta; Univ Regina; Univ Winnipeg; Univ Manitoba; assoc prof, 84. **RESEARCH** Philosophy of mind; philosophy of science; and philosophical psychology. **SELECTED PUBLICATIONS** Pub(s), Can Jour Philos; Philos Sci; Transactions of the Charles Peirce Soc; Amer Philos Quart. **CONTACT ADDRESS** Dept of Philosophy, Victoria Univ, PO Box 3045, Victoria, BC, V8W 3P4. **EMAIL** june19@uvvm.uvic.ca

FOSTER, DOUGLAS A.
PERSONAL Born 08/30/1952, Sheffield, AL, m, 1979, 2 children **DISCIPLINE** RELIGIOUS HISTORY **EDUCATION** David Lipscomb Univ, BA, 74; Harding Grad Sch of Religion, 76; Scarritt Col, MA, 80; Vanderbilt Univ, PhD, 86. **CAREER** Assoc Min, Jackson Park Church of Christ, 74-83; Arch, Gospel Adv Co, 88-91; Retention, Inst, Asst Prof, David Lipscomb Univ, 85-91; Asst Prof, Assoc Prof, Abilene Christian Univ, 91-94. **HONORS AND AWARDS** Outstanding Tchr Awd, College of Bibl Stud, ACU 94; Outstanding Tchr Awd, DLU, 89; Mayhew Fel Vanderbilt Univ, 83-83. **MEMBERSHIPS** Amer Soc of Church History, Amer Acad of Religion, Conf on Faith and History, disciples of Christ Hist Soc, Rel Res Assn, Soc for the Scientific Stud of Rel, Southern Baptist Hist Soc, Southwest Archivists, TN Archivists. **SELECTED PUBLICATIONS** Holding Back the Tide: T.B. Larimore and the Disciples of Christ and Churches of Christ, Discipliana, 93; Will the Cycle Be Unbroken: Churches of Christ Face the Twenty-First Century, ACU, 94; The Many Faces of Christian Unity: Disciples Ecumenism and Schism, 1875-1900, Nashville Disciples for Christ Hist Soc, 95; Millennial Harbinger, Pop Rel Mag of the USA, 95; Rethinking the History of Churches of Christ: Responses to Richard Hughes, Rest Quart, 96; Reflections on the Writing of Will the Cycle Be Unbroken: Churches of Christ Face the Twenty-First Century, Discipliana, 97. **CONTACT ADDRESS** Abilene Christian Univ, ACU 29429, Abilene, TX, 79699-9429. **EMAIL** foster@bible.acu.edu

FOSTER, HAMAR
DISCIPLINE LAW **EDUCATION** Queen's Univ, BA, 70; Sussex Univ, MA, 71; Univ British Columbia, LLB, 74; Auckland Univ, MJ, 89. **CAREER** Law clerk, Chief Justice British Columbia, 74-75; asst prof, 78-93; prof, 93-. **MEMBERSHIPS** Can Law Soc Asn; British Columbia Civil Liberties Asn. **RESEARCH** Legal process; criminal law; the law of evidence; legal history; aboriginal law. **SELECTED PUBLICATIONS** Auth, pubs on comparative criminal law, fur trade and colonial legal history, and aboriginal history and law; co-ed, Law for the Elephant, Law for the Beaver: Essays in the Legal History of the North American West and Essays in the History of Canadian Law. **CONTACT ADDRESS** Fac of Law, Univ Victoria, PO Box 2400, Victoria, BC, V8W 3H7. **EMAIL** hamarf@uvic.ca

FOSTER, JAMES HADLEI
PERSONAL Born 04/29/1938, Valdosta, GA, m, 1982 **DISCIPLINE** RELIGION **EDUCATION** Morris Brown Coll, Atlanta GA, BA, 1960; Pittsburgh (PA) Theological Sem, 1969-70; United Theological Sem, Dayton OH, MDIV, 1973; Vanderbilt Univ, NashvilleTN, DMIN, 1981. **CAREER** Massachusetts Council of Churches, Boston MA, dept pastoral serv, 1962-63; Albany State College, Albany GA, dean of the chapel/instr, 1962-66; Alcorn State Univ, Lorman MS, chaplain/asst prof, 1966-68; Christian Assoc of Metro Erie, Erie PA, assoc dir, 1970-73; Wilberforce Univ, Wilberforce OH, chaplain/assoc prof, 1973-80; Dartmouth Coll, Hanover NH, assoc chaplain/lecturer, 1980-84; A Better Chance, Boston MA, Northern New England regional dir, 1980-82; Mercy Coll, Dobbs Ferry NY, prof of religion, 1984-; St Marks AME Church, East Orange, NJ, associate pastor, 1985-. **HONORS AND AWARDS** Union Coll, LHD, 1971. **MEMBERSHIPS** Mem, Optimist Club, 1975-; assoc pastor, St Mark's AME Church, East Orange NJ, 1985-; mem, Community Relations Commission, NJ Council of Churches, 1985-88; mem, Special Task Force, E Orange Bd of Education, 1985-86; pres, Jersey Chapter, Morris Brown Coll Alumni Assn, 1988-. **CONTACT ADDRESS** Dept of Religion, Mercy Col, 555 Broadway, Dobbs Ferry, NY, 10522.

FOSTER, JOHN
DISCIPLINE LAW **EDUCATION** Univ Saskatchewan, BA, 62; Univ Toronto, MA, 63, PhD, 77. **CAREER** Prof. **SELECTED PUBLICATIONS** Auth, Strengthening Civil Society in Mexico: From Clientalism to Citizenship, Can For Policy, 97; co-auth, U.N. Futures, U.N. Reforms and the Social Agenda, 97. **CONTACT ADDRESS** Col of Law, Univ Saskatchewan, 15 Campus Dr, Saskatoon, SK, S7N 5A6.

FOSTER, LAWRENCE
PERSONAL Born 07/08/1939, Jersey City, NJ, m, 1964 **DISCIPLINE** PHILOSOPHY **EDUCATION** Univ Pa, BA, 61, PhD (philos), 66. **CAREER** From instr to assoc prof, Univ Mass, Amherst, 65-75, assoc dir law and justice prog, 75-76, ASSOC PROF PHILOS, UNIV MASS, BOSTON, 75-, DIR LAW AND JUSTICE PROG, 76-, CONSULT, NAT ENDOWMENT FOR HUMANITIES, 77-. **RESEARCH** Ethics; induction; legal and political philosophy. **SELECTED PUBLICATIONS** Auth, Brunson, Ruth, Huskey, Law Lib J, Vol 87, 95; Access to Academic Law Library Services, Law Lib J, Vol 84, 92; Aall Task Force on Citation Formats Report March 1, 1995, Law Lib J, Vol 87, 95; Religion and Sexuality in Am Lit, Am Lit, Vol 65, 93; American Cath Arts and Fictions--Culture, Ideology, Aesthetics, Am Lit, Vol 65, 93; Alcatraz is not an Island, Am Indian Cult Res J, Vol 18, 94; The Shaker Experience in America--A History of the United Society of Believers, Am Hist Rev, Vol 98,93. **CONTACT ADDRESS** Prof of Law and Justice Harbor Campus, Univ of Massachusetts, Amherst, 100 Morrissey Blvd, Boston, MA, 02125-3300.

FOSTER, MATTHEW
DISCIPLINE RELIGION, PSYCHOLOGY, ETHICS AND SOCIETY **EDUCATION** Earlham Col, BA, 74; Univ Chicago Divinity Sch, MA, 77, PhD, 87. **CAREER** Lectr, Univ Chicago, continuing educ prog, 83, 84; adjunct instr, DePaul Univ, 84; visiting instr, John Carroll Univ, 85; part-time instr, Lakeland Community Col, 87; lectr, John Carroll Univ, 87-88; asst prof, Molloy Col, 92-. **MEMBERSHIPS** Amer Acad of Relig; Soc of Buddhist-Christian Studies. **RESEARCH** Theology/philosophy of religions; Inter-religious dialogue; Contemporary theology; Theology and science; Pluralism as theological, philosophical, social issue; Environmental ethics; World religions. **SELECTED PUBLICATIONS** Auth, Gadamer and Practical Philosophy: The Hermeneutics of Moral Confidence, Scholar Press, 91. **CONTACT ADDRESS** Molloy Col, 1000 Hempstead Ave, Rockville Centre, NY, 11571-5002. **EMAIL** mfoster@molloy.edu

FOTI, VERONIQUE MARION
PERSONAL Born 09/05/1938, Miscolc, Hungary, 4 children **DISCIPLINE** PHILOSOPHY **EDUCATION** Oglethorpe Univ, BA, 62; Simmons Col, MLS, 74; Boston Col, PhD (philos), 78. **CAREER** Asst prof philos, Univ KY, 78-80; asst prof, Col of the Holy Cross, 80-81; Asst Prof Philos, Grad Faculties, New Sch Of Social Res, 81-. **MEMBERSHIPS** Am Philos Asn; Int Soc Neoplatonic Studies; Merleau-Ponty Circle; Soc Phenomenol and Existential Philos. **RESEARCH** Continental rationalism; ancient philosophy; phenomenology. **SELECTED PUBLICATIONS** Auth, Representation Represented--Foucault, Velazquez, Descartes, Postmodern Cult, Vol 7, 96; Holocaust Visions--Surrealism and Existentialism in the Poetry of Celan, Paul, Philos Lit, Vol 19, 95. **CONTACT ADDRESS** New Sch for Social Research, 65 Fifth Ave, New York, NY, 10003.

FOTION, NICHOLAS
DISCIPLINE MORAL PHILOSOPHY **EDUCATION** Univ NC, PhD, 57. **CAREER** Philos, Emory Univ. **HONORS AND AWARDS** Fulbright Prof, Yonsei Univ. **SELECTED PUBLICATIONS** Auth, Moral Situations and Military Ethics: Looking Toward the Future; Coauth, Military Ethics and Toleration; Coed, Hare and Critics: Essays on Moral Thinking. **CONTACT ADDRESS** Emory Univ, Atlanta, GA, 30322-1950.

FOUKE, DANIEL C.
DISCIPLINE MODERN PHLIOSOPHY, PHILOSOPHY OF RELIGION **EDUCATION** Univ Chicago, PhD, 86. **CAREER** Dept Philos, Univ Dayton **RESEARCH** History of science and technology. **SELECTED PUBLICATIONS** Auth, Mechanical and Organical Models in Seventeenth-Century Explanations of Biological Reproduction, Sci in Context, 89; Emanation and the Perfections of Being: Divine Causation and the Autonomy of Nature, Leibniz, Archiv fur Geschichte der Philos, 94; The Enthusiastical Concerns of Dr. Henry More: Religious Meaning and the Pyschology of Delusion, Brill, 97. **CONTACT ADDRESS** Dept of Philos, Univ Dayton, 300 Col Park, Dayton, OH, 75062. **EMAIL** fouke@checkov.hm.udayton.edu

FOULK, GARY J.
DISCIPLINE PHILOSOPHY **EDUCATION** Portland State Univ, BS, 57; Univ of Oregon, MA, 62, PhD, 66. **CAREER** Instr, philos, Univ Oregon, 63-64; instr, philos, Portland State Univ, 64-66; asst prof, assoc prof, prof, chemn, philos, Indiana State Univ, 66-95. **HONORS AND AWARDS** Outstanding undergraduate tchg, Portland State Univ, 66. **MEMBERSHIPS** APA. **RESEARCH** Ethics; ethics and animals; medical ethics. **SELECTED PUBLICATIONS** Coauth, The Moral Foundation of Nursing: Yarling and McElmurry and Their Critics, Anthology on Caring, National League for Nursing, 91; auth, Ethics and Technology Education: Fact, Possibility, and Value, in Proceedings, Technology Education Symposium XIII, Indiana, 91; coauth, Rationality and Principles: A Criticism of the Ethic of Care, Int J of Applied Philos, 92; auth, Three Reviews of Illiberal Education, Public Affairs Q, 92; coauth, The Perception of Ethical Dilemmas in Clinical Practice: Empirical Diagnosis and Philosophical Therapy, Int J of Applied Philos, 98. **CONTACT ADDRESS** 1511 SW Park Ave, Apt 419, Portland, OR, 97201.

FOWLER, VIVIA
PERSONAL Born 08/20/1954, Allendale, SC, m, 1976, 2 children **DISCIPLINE** RELIGIOUS STUDIES **EDUCATION** Columbia Col, BA, 76; Lutheran Theol S Sem, MA, 80; Univ SC, PhD, 94. **CAREER** Assoc prof of Religion & assoc dean undergraduate studies & asst dir honors, Columbia Col, 86-. **HONORS AND AWARDS** Outstanding Fac Mem, 96; ODK Fac Mem Yr, 95. **MEMBERSHIPS** AAR; SC Acad Relig; REA **RESEARCH** Women in religion; Women in Bible; Religious altitudes; Instruction. **CONTACT ADDRESS** Columbia Col, So Carolina, 1301 Columbia Col Dr, Columbia, SC, 29203. **EMAIL** vfowler@colacoll.edu

FOX, CHARLES W.
PERSONAL Born 12/30/1936, Steubenville, OH, d, 4 children **DISCIPLINE** RELIGION **EDUCATION** Baylor Univ, BA, 58; Harvard Univ, PhD, 78. **CAREER** Asst prof religion, Williams Col, 65-70; lectr philos, State Univ NY, 70-74; mentor hum, State Univ NY/Empire State Col, 74-. **HONORS AND AWARDS** S Regional Fel, 59-62; Woodrow Wilson Fel, 58-59; Rockefeller Doctoral Fel, 62-63. **MEMBERSHIPS** Am Acad Relig. **RESEARCH** Christian Thought; Origins of Christianity; Meso-American Indian Religions. **CONTACT ADDRESS** Dept of Humanities, Suny/Empire State Col, 37 Belden St., Williamstown, MA, 01267. **EMAIL** cfox@sescva.esc.edu

FOX, CHRISTOPHER B.
DISCIPLINE PHILOSOPHY OF SCIENCE **EDUCATION** Cleveland State Univ, BA, 71; State Univ NY Binghamton, MA, 74, PhD, 78. **CAREER** Assoc dean, arts and letters, dir, inst for Schol in lub arts, prof, Univ Notre Dame. **RESEARCH** Interactions between literature and medicine; psychology and science during the 18th century. **SELECTED PUBLICATIONS** Auth, How to Prepare a Noble Savage: the Spectacle of Human Science, 95; Swift and the Spectacle of Human Science, 95; ed, Gulliver's Travels: A Case Study in Contemporary Criticism, 94; Gulliver's Travels: Complete Authoritative Text, 95; Walking Naboth's Vineyand: New Studies of Swift; co-ed, Inventing Human Science: Eighteenth Century Domains, 95. **CONTACT ADDRESS** History and Philosophy of Science Dept, Univ of Notre Dame, Notre Dame, IN, 46556. **EMAIL** Christopher.B.Fox.1@nd.edu

FOX, DOUGLAS A.
PERSONAL Born 03/20/1927, Mullumbimby, Australia, m, 1958, 2 children **DISCIPLINE** THEOLOGY, HISTORY OF RELIGIONS **EDUCATION** Univ Sydney, BA, 54; Univ Chicago, MA, 57; Pac Sch Relig, STM, 58, ThD, 63. **CAREER** From asst prof to assoc prof, 63-74, Prof Relig, Colo Col, 74-. **MEMBERSHIPS** Am Acad Relig. **RESEARCH** Mahayana Buddhism; philosophy of religion; philosophical theology. **SELECTED PUBLICATIONS** Auth, Rheumatoid Arthritis--Heresies and Speculations, Perspectives Biol Med, Vol 40, 97. **CONTACT ADDRESS** Dept of Relig, Colorado Col, Colorado Springs, CO, 80903.

FOX, ELEANOR M.
PERSONAL Born 01/18/1936, Trenton, NJ, m, 3 children **DISCIPLINE** LAW **EDUCATION** Vassar Col, AB, 56; NY Univ Law Sch, LLB, 61. **CAREER** Assoc prof, 76-78, Prof Law, NY Univ Sch Law, 78-, Assoc, Simpson Thacher & Bartlett, 62-70, partner, 70-76; comnr, Nat Comn Rev Antitrust Laws & Procedure, 78-79. **HONORS AND AWARDS** Great Tchr Awd, NYU Alum Asn. **MEMBERSHIPS** Am Law Inst; Am Bar Found; Int Compet Policy Advis Comt; TriNat NAFTA Task Force; Cnl on For Rels. **RESEARCH** Competition and trade, United States and the world; industry organization; political economy. **SELECTED PUBLICATIONS** Coauth, Corporate Acquisitions and Mergers, Vol I, 68, Vol II, 70 & Vol III, 71, Matthew Bender & Co; auth, W L Esquire (novel), Marando Press, 77; co-ed & contribr, Industrial Concentration and the Market System: Legal, Economic, Social & Political Perspectives, Am Bar Asn, 79; auth, Reign of Reason (poem), Corporate Coun Ann, 79; The modernization of antitrust: A new equilibrium, Cornell Law Rev, 66: 1140; co-ed, A Visit with Whitney North Seymour, 84; co-ed, Industrial Concentration and the Market System, 79; co-ed, Antitrust Policy in Transition: The Convergence of Law and Economics, ABA, 84; co-ed, Collaborations Among Competitors: Antitrust Policy and Economics, ABA, 92; co-auth, Corporate Acquisitions and Mergers, Matthew Bender, 98; coauth, Antitrust: Cases and Materials, West, 89; co-ed, Revitalizing Antitrust in its Second Century, Quorum, 91; coauth, The Competition Dimension of NAFTA, ABA, 94; coauth, Competition Policy and the Transformation of Central Europe, Ctr for Econ Policy Res, 96; coauth, European Community Law: Cases and Materials, West, 93. **CONTACT ADDRESS** 40 Washington Sq S, New York, NY, 10012-1005. **EMAIL** foxe@turing.law.nyu.edu

FOX, ELEANOR M.
PERSONAL Born 01/18/1936, Trenton, NJ, 3 children **DISCIPLINE** LAW **EDUCATION** Vassar Col, AB, 56; NY Univ Law Sch, LLB, 61. **CAREER** Assoc prof, 76-78, dir, Root-Tilden Prog, NYU Law Sch, 78-81, WALTER J DERENBERG PROF TRADE REGULATION, NY UNIV SCH LAW, 78-, assoc dean, J D Div, NY Univ Sch Law, 87-90; vis scholar, Competition Dir Comm European Communities, winter 83; Counsel & partner, Simpson Thacher & Bartlett; lectr, new fed judges, Fed Jucial Center; comnr, Nat Comn Rev Antitrust Laws & Procedure, 78-79; Mem, Intl Competition Policy Adv Comt to Attorney General & Asst Attorney General for Antitrust; Mem, bd dir & exec comt, Lawyer's Comt Civil Rights

Under Law; US chair, Tri-Nat NAFTA Task Force; fel, Am Bar Asn & NY Bar Found; trustee, NY Univ Law Center Found, 74-92; vpres & trustee, Fed Bar Coun, 74-77; vpres, Am Foreign Law Asn, 79-82; chair, Sect Antitrust & Econ Reg, Asn Am Law Sch 80-82; vpres, Asn Bar City of NY, 89-90, mem exec comt, 76-80, 89-90; vchair, ABA Antitrust Sect, 92-94; mem, advis bd or ed bd, Antitrust Bull, Antitrust Law & Econ Rev, Rev Industrial Org, Bureau Nat Affairs Antitrust & Trade Reg Report, EEC Merger Control Reporter, NY Law J, La Gaceta Juridica de la C E, Int jour NY Univ, Columbia, Fordham & George Mason law schs. **HONORS AND AWARDS** NYU Law Review, Note & Comment ed, 60; Great Teacher Award, NYU Alumni Asn, 91. **MEMBERSHIPS** Am Asn Law Schs; Am Law Inst; Am Bar Found. **RESEARCH** Antitrust; European Union law; International & comparative competition and trade policy; torts. **SELECTED PUBLICATIONS** Coauth, Corporate Acquisitions and Mergers, Vol I, 68, Vol II, 70 & Vol III, 71, rev, 98, Matthew Bender & Co; auth, W L Esquire (novel), Marando Press, 77; co-ed & contribr, Industrial Concentration and the Market System: Legal, Economic, Social & Political Perspectives, Am Bar Asn, 79; auth, Reign of Reason (poem), Corporate Coun Ann, 79; The Modernization of Antitrust: A New Equilibrium, Cornell Law Rev, 81; co-ed, Antitrust Policy in Transition: The Convergence of Law and Economics, ABA, 84; co-ed, A Visit with Whitney North Seymour, 84; Consumer Beware Chicago, Mich Law Rev, 86; Monopilization and Dominance in the United States and the European Community - Efficiency, Opportunity, and Fairness, Notre Dame Law Rev, 86; Antitrust in Its Second Century: the Phoenix Rises from Its Ashes, Antitrust Bull, 86; The Politics of Law and Economics in Judicial Decision Making: Antitrust as a Window, NYUL Rev, 86; The Battle for the Soul of Antitrust, Calif Law Rev, 87; Extraterritoriality, Antitrust, and the New Restatement: Is Reasonableness the Answer?, NYU J Int Law & Pol, 87; Chairman Miller, the Federal Trade Commission, Econimics and Rashomon, Law & Contem Prob, 87; co-auth, Antitrust - Retrospective and Prospective: Where Are We Coming from? Where Are We Going?, NYU Law Rev, 87; Being a Woman, Being a Lawyer, and Being a Human Being - Women and Change, Ford Law Rev, 89; Harnessing the Multinational Corporation to Enhance Third World Development - The Rise and Fall and Future of Antitrust as Regulator, Cardozo law Rev, 89; co-auth, Antitrust: Cases and Materials, West, 89, supl, 95, update, 97; co-ed, Revitalizing Antitrust in its Second Century, Quorum, 91; The End of Antitrust Isolationism: The Vision of One World, Univ Chicago Legal Forum, 92; co-ed, Collaborations among Competitors: Antitrust Policy and Economics, ABA, 92; European Community Law: Cases and Materials, West, 93; supl, 98, doc supl, 98; Antitrust, Trade and the Twenty-First Century -- Rounding the Circle, The Handler Lecture, Record Asn Bar City of NY, 12/93; co-auth, The Competition Dimension of NAFTA, ABA, 94; Competition Law and the Next Agenda for WTO: Forging the Links of Competition and Trade, Pacific Rim Law & Pol J, 95; co-auth, The Harmonization of Competition and Trade Law: The Case for Modest Linkages of Law and Limits to Parochial State Action, World Competition Law & Econ Rev, 12/95; co-auth, Competition Policy and the Transformation of Central Europe, Centre for Econ Policy Res, 96; Antitrust, Competitiveness, and the World Arena: Efficiencies and Failing Firms in Perspective, Antitrust Law J, 96; Trade Competition, and Intellectual Property -- TRIPS and its Antitrust Counterparts, Vand J Transnat Law, 96; The Central European nations and the EU Waiting Room - Why Must the Central European Nations Adopt the Competition Law of the European Union?, Brook J Intl Law, 97; Toward World Antitrust and Market Access, Am J Intl Law, 97; Lessons from Boeing: a Modest Proposal to Keep Politics Out of Antitrust, Antitrust Report, 11/97; Antitrust Regulation across National Borders: The United States of Boeing versus the European Union of Airbus, Brookings Rev, winter 98; International Antitrust: Against Minimum Rules: For Cosmopolitan Principles, Antitrust Bull, spring 98; Globalization and Its Challenges for Law and Society, Loyola Univ Chicago Law J, summer 98. **CONTACT ADDRESS** 40 Washington Sq S, New York, NY, 10012-1005. **EMAIL** fox@turning.law.nyu.edu

FOX, JAMES WALKER
PERSONAL Born 10/14/1929, Kearney, NE, m, 1962, 2 children **DISCIPLINE** CRIMINAL JUSTICE, CRIMINOLOGY **EDUCATION** Ind Univ, Bloomington, BA, 57, MS, 59, EdD, 61; Univ Va, PhD (sociol), 74. **CAREER** Instr interdisciplinary soc sci, Univ Akron, 61-64; prof higher educ, Kent State Univ, 64-67; prof educ and dean student serv and educ develop, Madison Col, Va, 67-73; dir, Ctr Criminal Justice, 73-76, PROF CORRECTIONAL SERV, EASTERN KY UNIV, 73-, Part-time prof sociol and criminol, Southern Sem, 72-73; dir criminal victimization study, Univ Va, 72-74; dir, Ky Parole Recidivism Study, 78-79; consult, Tenn Bd Paroles, 80-82 and various state parole/probation agencies, 78-; PRES, J WALKER FOX CRIMINAL JUSTICT CONSULTS, INC, 81-. **MEMBERSHIPS** Am Asn Higher Educ; Am Polit Sci Asn; Am Soc Criminol; Am Correctional Asn; Acad Criminal Justice Sci. **RESEARCH** Criminal justice system; Political sociology; victimization. **SELECTED PUBLICATIONS** Auth, The Structure, Stability, and Social Antecedents of Reported Paranormal Experiences, Sociological Analysis, Vol 53, 92. **CONTACT ADDRESS** Dept of Correctional Serv, Univ of Kentucky, Stratton Bldg Room 101 Eastern, Richmond, KY, 40475.

FOX, LAWRENCE J.
PERSONAL Born 07/17/1943, Philadelphia, PA, m, 1998, 2 children **DISCIPLINE** LAW **EDUCATION** Univ Penn, BA, 65, LLB, 68. **CAREER** Clerk, Justice Samuel Roberts, Penn Supreme Court, 68-69; Reginald Hever Smith Commun Lawyer Fel, Commun Action for Legal Serv, NY, 69-72; assoc, 72-76, partner, 76- , mng partner, 89-91, 93-97, Drinker Biddle & Reath LLP. **MEMBERSHIPS** ABA; Am Law Inst; Am Col of Trial Lawyers; Penn Bar Asn; Philadelphia Bar Asn; Authors Guild. **RESEARCH** Legal ethics and professional responsibility; death penalty jurisprudence. **SELECTED PUBLICATIONS** Auth, Cowboy Ethics on the Main Line, Litigation, 93; auth, Can This Marriage be Saved? Natl Law J, 93; auth, Marketing or Mayhem? The Firm is Mythical; the Nightmare is Real, Business Law Today, 94; auth, Lawyers Can't Serve Two Masters Honestly, Natl Law J, 94; auth, Reap As You Sow, Business Law Today, 95; auth, Firing the Client, Litigation, 95; auth, Leave Your Clients at the Door, Litigation, 95; auth, Politics is Threatening the Federal Judiciary, Natl Law J, 96; auth, Advocates for the System; Advocates for Ourselves, Litigation Docket, 96; auth, Money Didn't Buy Happiness, Dickinson Law Rev, 96; auth, Why Does Gift Limit Single out Bond Lawyers? Natl Law J, 97; auth, It's OK To Discuss Billing, Solo, 97; auth, Litigating Conflicts: Is it Time to Revive the Appearance of Impropriety? Professional Lawyer, 98. **CONTACT ADDRESS** Philadelphia National Bank Bldg, 1345 Chestnut St, Philadelphia, PA, 19107-3496. **EMAIL** foxlj@dbr.com

FOX, MICHAEL
PERSONAL Born 12/12/1940, Detroit, MI, m, 1961, 2 children **DISCIPLINE** BIBLE STUDIES; ANCIENT NEAR EASTERN STUDIES **EDUCATION** Univ Mich, BA, 62; MA, 63; Hebrew Union Col, Rabbinical ordination, 68; Hebrew Univ Jerusalem, PhD, 72. **CAREER** Lectr, Haifa Univ, 71-74; lectr, Hebrew Univ Jerusalem, 75-77; asst prof to prof, Univ Wis-Madison, 77- . **MEMBERSHIPS** Soc for Bibl Lit; Nat Asoc of Profs of Hebrew. **RESEARCH** Biblical literature; ancient Egyptian literature. **SELECTED PUBLICATIONS** Auth, Ideas of Wisdom in Proverbs 1-9, JBL, 97; auth, Words for Folly, ZAH, 97; auth, What the Book of Proverbs is About, VTSup, 97; auth, Qohelet's Catalogue of Times, JNSL, 98; auth, Tearing Down and Building Up: A Rereading of Ecclesiastes, forthcoming. **CONTACT ADDRESS** Univ of Wisconsin-Madison, 1220 Linden Dr., Rm. 1346, Madison, WI, 53706. **EMAIL** mfox@lss.wisc.edu

FOX, MICHAEL ALLEN
DISCIPLINE PHILOSOPHY **EDUCATION** Univ Toronto, PhD. **CAREER** Dept Philos, Queen's Univ **RESEARCH** Environmental ethics; ethics and animals; nineteenth-century continental philosophy; existentialism; philosophy of peace. **SELECTED PUBLICATIONS** Auth, Taking the Animal's Viewpoint Seriously, 90; Peace, 91; Environmental Ethics and the Ideology of Meat Eating, 93; Planet for the Apes, 96; On the 'Necessary Suffering', 97. **CONTACT ADDRESS** Philosophy Dept, Queen's Univ, Kingston, ON, K7L 3N6.

FOX, RICHARD MILAN
PERSONAL Born 06/15/1931, Cleveland, OH, m, 1955, 3 children **DISCIPLINE** PHILOSOPHY **EDUCATION** Ohio Univ, BA, 55; Georgetown Univ, MA, 63; Univ Waterloo, PhD, 67. **CAREER** Asst prof Am civilization, Am lang ctr, Am Univ, 57-61; asst prof, Am lang inst, Georgetown Univ, 61-62; instr philos, Notre Dame Col, Ohio, 62-65; lectr, St Jerome's Col, Univ Waterloo, 65-67; asst prof, Cleveland State Univ, 67-71, actg chmn dept, 76-78 assoc prof to prof, Philos, Cleveland State Univ, 71-87; dept chair, 76-78, 83-90; ed, Philos in Context, 78-79. **HONORS AND AWARDS** Woodrow Wilson Fel, 55 **RESEARCH** Ethics; metaethics; metaphysics. **SELECTED PUBLICATIONS** Art, The Immorality of Promising, Journal of Value Inquiry, 93; art, The Immorality of Promising, Journal of Value Inquiry, 93; art, On Making and Keeping Promises, Journal of Applied Philosophy, 96; **CONTACT ADDRESS** Dept of Philosophy, Cleveland State Univ, 1983 E 24th St, Cleveland, OH, 44115-2440.

FOX, SAMUEL
PERSONAL Born 02/25/1919, Cleveland, OH, m, 1942, 1 child **DISCIPLINE** PHILOSOPHY, RELIGION **EDUCATION** Yeshiva Univ, BA, 40; Butler Univ, MA, 44; Harvard Univ, PhD (semitics), 59. **CAREER** Asst prof, 68-80, ASSOC PROF RELIG STUDIES, MERRIMACK COL, 80-, Chaplain, Brigham Women's Hosp, 76. **MEMBERSHIPS** Asn Jewish Studies; AAUP; Am Acad Relig; Col Theol Soc; Rabbinical Coun Am. **RESEARCH** Jewish customs and ceremonies; Jewish philosophy; ancient religion. **SELECTED PUBLICATIONS** Auth, By the Sweat of the Brow, Literature and Labor in Antebellum America, Am Lit, Vol 66, 94; Evans, Chris Could Always be Relied on to Pull a Fast One, Smithsonian, Vol 26, 95; Raising General Awareness of Language Learning Strategies--A Little Bit Goes a Long Way, Hisp J Devoted Teaching Span Port, Vol 78, 95; An Illustrated Glossary of Early Southern Architecture and Landscape, J Southern Hist, Vol 61, 95; Raising General Awareness of Language Learning Strategies--A Little Bit Goes A Long Way, Hisp J Devoted Teaching Span Port, Vol 78, 95; Dugout to Deco--Building in West Texas, 1880-1930, J Southern Hist, Vol 61, 95; Inside Texas--Culture, Identity, and Houses, 1878-1920, J Southern Hist, Vol 59, 93; The Life and Death of Stubbe, Peter, Lit Rev, Vol 40, 97; Sacred Pedestrians, J Southwest, Vol 36, 94; The Making of Virginia Architecture, J Southern Hist, Vol 60, 94. **CONTACT ADDRESS** 145 Lynn Shore Dr, Lynn, MA, 01902.

FOX, SANFORD J.
PERSONAL Born 09/28/1929, New York, NY, m, 1954, 3 children **DISCIPLINE** LAW, JUVENILE DELINQUENCY **EDUCATION** Univ Ill, AB, 50; Harvard Univ, LLB, 53. **CAREER** Teaching fel law, Harvard Univ, 57-58; asst dir, Proj Effective Justice, Columbia Univ, 58-59; Prof Law, Law Sch, Boston Col, 59- Nat Inst Mental Health fel psychiat aspects of delinquency, 60-61; Ford Found law fac fels, law and sci, 61-62, 63-64; Off Juvenile Delinquency and Youth Develop, Dept Health Educ and Welfare grant to direct Boston Col juvenile Delinquency training prog, 66-68; sr fel, Nat Endowment for Humanities, 71-72; chief counsel, Maine Criminal Law Rev Comn, 72-75 and Vt Criminal Code Rev Comn, 73-75; reporter for sentencing and corrections, Am Law Inst Proj to Revise Model Penal Code Comments, 76-78; CONSULT CHILD ABUSE AND NEGLECT, US DEPT HEALTH, EDUC AND WELFARE, 76-. **RESEARCH** Juvenile delinquency; law and science; criminal law. **SELECTED PUBLICATIONS** Auth, Beyond the American Legal System for the Protection of Childrens Rights, Family Law Quart, Vol 31, 97. **CONTACT ADDRESS** 44 Summer Rd, Brookline, MA, 02146.

FRANCES, BRYAN R.S.
PERSONAL Born 09/18/1963, IL, m, 1993, 1 child **DISCIPLINE** PHILOSOPHY **EDUCATION** Univ Ill, BS 87; Univ Souther Calif, MA, 89; Univ Minn, MA, 93, PhD, 98. **CAREER** Vis asst prof, Carleton Col, 99-. **MEMBERSHIPS** Am Philos Asn. **RESEARCH** Philosophy of the mind; Philosophy of language. **SELECTED PUBLICATIONS** Auth, "Plato's Response to the Third Man Argument in the Paradoxical Exercise of the 'Parmenides'", in Ancient Philos, 96; "On the Explanatory Deficiencies of Linguistic Content," in Philos Studies, 98; "Defending Millian Theories," in Mind, 98; "Arguing for Frege's Fundamental Principle," in Mind and Language, 98; "Contradictory Belief and Epistemic Closure Principles," in Mind and Language, 99. **CONTACT ADDRESS** 3739 21st Ave S, Minneapolis, MN, 55407. **EMAIL** stew0020@msn.com

FRANCK, THOMAS M.
PERSONAL Born 07/14/1931, Berlin, Germany **DISCIPLINE** LAW **EDUCATION** Univ BC, BA, 52, LLB, 53; Harvard Univ, LLM, 54, SJD, 59; Univ BC, Hon LLD, 95. **CAREER** Asst prof, Univ Nebr Law Sch, 54-56; assoc prof, 60-62, dir ctr Int Studies, 65-, prof law, Law Sch, NY Univ, 62-, vis lects, US Naval War Col, 60; Can deleg, Conf Rule of Law in Africa, 61; vis prof, Stanford Univ Sch Law, 62; Can deleg, Conf African Customary Law, 64; mem, Comn Legal Educ, Sierra Leone, 64; vis lectr, Col Law, Univ EAfrica, 63-66; consult, US Agency Int Develop, 70-72; consult to Fla Int Univ on starting a Ctr Int Studies, Miami, 72; vis prof law, Osgoode Hall Law Sch, York Univ, 72-76, prof, 74-76; Guggenheim Found res grant, 73-74 & 82-83; dir Int Law prog, Carnegie Endowment Peace, 73-79; vis prof. Woodrow Wilson School, Princeton Univ, 79; mem adv coun procedural aspects, Int Law Inst; mem adv coun, US Inst Human Rights; dir res, UN Inst Training & Res, 80-82; lectr, Hague Acad of Int Law, 93; vis Fellow, Trinity Col, Cambridge, England, 96-97. **HONORS AND AWARDS** Guggenheim Fellowship, 73-74, 82-83; Christopher Medal, for Resignation in Protest, 76; Cert of Merit, awarded by the Am Soc of Int Law, in recognition of United States Foreign Relations Law: Documents and Sources, 81; Cert of Merit, Am Soc Int Law, in recognition of Nation Against Nation: What Happened to the U.N. Dream and What the U.S. Can Do About It, 86; Elected member, Institut de Droit Int, 93-; Cert of Merit, Am Soc Int Law, in recognition of Political Questions/Judicial Answers: Does the Rule of Law Apply to Foreign Affairs?, 94; John E. Read Medal, awarded by the Can Council on Int Law, 94; Cert of Merit, Am Soc Int Law, in recognition of Fairness in International Law and Institutions, 96. **MEMBERSHIPS** Am Soc Int Law(member, exec council, 79-94, pres, April, 94-); Int League Rights of Man; Am Bar Asn; African Law Asn Am (dir, 70-73); Int Law Asn (secy-treas Am branch, 68-69, vpres, 73-94, hon vpres, 94-); Council on Foreign Relations, 78-; The Century Asn of New York, 79-; Advisory Bd, Int Human Rights Law Group; board of dir, Friends of the Hague Academy of Int Law, Inc, 80-; NYU Soc of Fellows, 84-; Admin Council, The Jacob Blaustein Inst for the Advancement of Human Rights, 88-; bd mem, Africa Watch, 89-; board of dir, Int Peace Acad, 91-; Ger Soc Int Law; Societe francaise de doit international; Can Council on Int Law; U.S. Member, Comm on Int Human Rights Law and Practice, Int Law Asn, 95. **RESEARCH** Resources of the seabed; control of terrorism; international and constitutional law. **SELECTED PUBLICATIONS** Auth, The Structure of Impartiality, Macmillan, 68; Comparative Constitutional Process, Sweet & Maxwell, London, 68, Praeger, 68; coauth, Word Politics: Verbal Strategy Among the Superpowers, 71 & Secrecy and Foreign Policy, Oxford Univ, 73; Resignation in Protest, Viking, 75; Foreign Policy by Congress, Oxford, 79; Foreign Relations Law, Oceana, 80; auth, The Tethered Presidency, NY Univ Press, 81; coauth, Human Rights in the Third World Perspective, vols I-

III, Oeana pubs, 84; coauth, United States Foreign Relations Law: Documents and Sources, vols IV-V, Oceana pubs, 84; auth, Nation Against Nation: What Happened to the U.N. Dream and What the U.S. Can Do About It, Oxford Univ Press, 85; Judging the World Court, NY: The Twentieth Century Fund, 86; coauth, Foreign Relations and National Security Law, St. Paul: West Pub Co, 87, 2nd ed, 93; auth, The Power of Legitamacy Among Nations, Oxford Univ Press, 90; Political Questions/Judicial Answers: Does the Rule of Law Apply to Foreign Affairs?, Princeton Univ Press, 92; Fairness in the International Legal and Institutional System, The Hague: Acad of Int Law, Recueil des cours, vol 240, 93-III; co-ed, International Law Decisions in National Courts, Transnational Pubs, 96. **CONTACT ADDRESS** Ctr for Int Studies, New York Univ, 40 Washington Sq S, New York, NY, 10012-1005.

FRANCO, ABEL B.
PERSONAL Born 05/26/1969, Salamanca, Spain, s **DISCIPLINE** PHILOSOPHY **EDUCATION** Universidad de Salamanca Spain, LD, 92, LD, 97, PhD, 99; CUNY, MA, 98. **CAREER** Adjunct Lectr at: CUNY, 96; Manhattan Comm Col, 97; Lehman Col, 97-98; John Jay Col, 98; Univ Pitt, tchg asst, 98. **HONORS AND AWARDS** Erasmus fel, CAJA de Madrid Found res fel; Univ Pitt full tuition scholar. **MEMBERSHIPS** RSA, APA, HSSA. **RESEARCH** Mediaeval history of science in Iberian peninsula. **SELECTED PUBLICATIONS** Auth, The Mathematization of Space Before Galileo: The Double Birth of Modern Pictorial Perspective and the Scientific Revolution, ALDEEU, eds., R. Corbalan, G. Pina, N. Toscan, forthcoming; auth, The Definition and Defense of God in and from Newton's Physical Writings, UCLA Hist Jour, 99. **CONTACT ADDRESS** Dept of History, Univ of Pittsburgh, 4041 Bigelow Blvd Apt 311, Pittsburgh, PA, 15213-1229. **EMAIL** abfst6@pitt.edu

FRANK, DANIEL H.
PERSONAL Born 08/16/1950, San Francisco, CA, m, 4 children **DISCIPLINE** PHILOSOPHY **EDUCATION** Univ of Cal at Berk, BA 73; Cambridge Univ, BA, 75, MA, 82; Univ Pittsburgh, PhD, 82. **CAREER** UCLA, vis assoc prof of philo, 88-89; Univ of Kentucky, asst prof, 81-86, assoc prof, 86-97, prof of philo, 97-, Dir of JSP, 96-. **HONORS AND AWARDS** Brit Acad, Res Fel, 94; Univ of Judaism, Finkelstein Res Fel, 87-89, UCLA Medieval and Renais Stud, Res Fel, 86 **MEMBERSHIPS** APA, AJP, AJS, SAGP, SMRP **RESEARCH** Greek philo; medi Islamic and Jewish philo **SELECTED PUBLICATIONS** Auth, The Cambridge Companion to Medieval Jewish Thought, Cambridge Univ Press, forthcoming; The Jewish Philosophy Reader, Routledge Press, forthcoming; Pride, Humility and Anger: Aristotle and Maimonides on Virtue and the Self, SUNY Press, forthcoming; History of Jewish Philosophy, Routledge Press, 97; Maimonides: Guide of the Perplexed, rev ed, Hackett, 95; Commandment and Community : New Essays in Jewish Legal and Political Philosophy, SUNY Press, 95; art, Ibn Gabirol, Joseph Albo, and Political Philosophy in Islam, in: The Routledge Encyclopedia of Philosophy, Routledge, 98; What is Jewish Philosophy? in: History of Jewish Philosophy, Routledge, 97; Teaching for a Fee: Pedagogy and Friendship in Socrates and Maimonides, in: Friendship East and West, Curzon, 96; Ethics, in: History of Islamic Philosophy, Routledge, 96. **CONTACT ADDRESS** Dept of Philosophy, Univ of Kentucky, Lexington, KY, 40506-0027. **EMAIL** dfrank@ukcc.uky.edu

FRANK, WILLIAM A.
DISCIPLINE PHILOSOPHY OF EDUCATION, ETHICS **EDUCATION** Hampton Inst, BA; Cath Univ Am, MA, PhD. **CAREER** Dept Philos, Univ Dallas **SELECTED PUBLICATIONS** Co-auth, Duns Scotus, Metaphysician, Series in the Hist Philos, Purdue Univ Press, 95; Duns Scotus on Autonomous Freedom and Divine Cocausality, Medieval Philosophy and Theology, Univ Notre Dame Press, 92. **CONTACT ADDRESS** Dept of Philos, Univ Dallas, 1845 E Northgate Dr, Irving, TX, 75062.

FRANKFORTER, ALBERTUS DANIEL
PERSONAL Born 05/17/1939, Waynesboro, PA, m, 1972 **DISCIPLINE** MEDIEVAL ECCLESIASTICAL HISTORY **EDUCATION** Franklin and Marshall Col, Artium Baccalaureie, 61; Drew Univ, MDiv, 65; Pa State Univ, MA, 69, PhD (medieval hist), 71. **CAREER** Actg chaplain, Williams Col, 63-64; asst prof, 70-80, ASSOC PROF ANCIENT and MEDIEVAL HIST, BEHREND COL, PA STATE UNIV, 80-. **MEMBERSHIPS** Mediaeval Acad Am; Am Soc Church Hist; AHA. **RESEARCH** Medieval English Episcopal registers; medieval female authors. **SELECTED PUBLICATIONS** Auth, A Rural Society After the Black Death--Essex 1350-1525, Church Hist, Vol 64, 95; Between Church and State--The Lives of 4 French Prelates in the Late Middle Ages, Church History, Vol 64, 95; England, Rome and the Papacy, 1417-1464--The Study of a Relationship, Church Hist, Vol 64, 95; Women, Sainthood and Power--The So Called Biographies of Latin Female Saints from the 4th Century to the 7th Century, Church Hist, Vol 64, 95; Between Church And State--The Lives of 4 French Prelates in the Late Middle Ages, Church Hist, Vol 64, 95; Gilbert of Sempringham and the Gilbertine Order, C. 1130-1300, Church History, Vol 66, 97; Unity and Variety--A History of the Church in Devon and Cornwall, Church Hist, Vol 63, 94; Unity and Variety--A History of the Church in Devon and Cornwall, Church Hist, Vol 63, 94; England, Rome and the Papacy, 1417-1464--The Study of a Relationship, Church Hist, Vol 64, 95; The Collegiate Church of Wimborne Minster, Church Hist, Vol 66, 97; Knowledge, Power, and the Struggle for Representation, Coll Eng, Vol 57, 95; The Collegiate Church of Wimborne Minster, Church Hist, Vol 66, 97; Crossfire , Ling Fr, Vol 5, 95; Women, Sainthood and Power--The So Called Biographies of Latin Female Saints from the 4th Century to the 7th Century, Church Hist, Vol 64, 95; Gilbert of Sempringham and the Gilbertine Order, C. 1130-1300, Church Hist, Vol 66, 97. **CONTACT ADDRESS** Dept of Hist, Pennsylvania State Univ, Erie, Station Rd, Erie, PA, 16510.

FRANKFURTER, DAVID
PERSONAL Born 02/24/1961, New York, NY, m, 1988, 2 children **DISCIPLINE** RELIGION **EDUCATION** Princeton Univ, PhD 90, MA 88; Harvard Univ, MTS 86; Wesleyan Univ, BA 83. **CAREER** Univ New Hampshire, asst to assoc prof, 95 to 98-; Col of Charleston, asst prof, 90-95. **HONORS AND AWARDS** Fairchild fel; NEH **MEMBERSHIPS** AARSBL; EES; IACS **RESEARCH** Apocalyptic lit; magic and ritual; roman Egypt; Christianization; popular religion. **SELECTED PUBLICATIONS** Auth, Religion in Roman Egypt: Assimilation and Resistance, Prin, Prin Univ Press, 98; Elijah in Upper Egypt: The Coptic Apocalypse of Elijah and Early Egyptian Christianity, studies in antiquity and Christianity, Minneapolis, Fortress Press, 93; Pilgrimage and Holy Space in Late Antique Egypt, ed, Leiden, E. J. Brill, 98; Early Christian Apocalypticism: literature and Social world, in: Encycl Apocaly, Jewish and Christian Origins of Apocalypticism, ed John J. Collins, NY, Continuum, 98; Apocalypses Real and Alleged in the Mani Codex, Numen 44, 97; The Legacy of the Jewish Apocalypse in Early Christian Communities: Two Regional Trajectories, in: The Jewish Apocal Hert in Early Christ, ed James C. VanderKam and William Adler, Minneapolis, Fortress Press, 96; Narrating Powert: The Theory and Practice of the Magical Historiola in Ritual Spells, in: Ancient Magic and Ritual Power, ed Marvin Meyer and Paul Mirecki, Leiden, Brill, 95; The Magic of Writing and the Magic of Writing: The Power of the Word in Egyptian and Greek Traditions, Helios, 94. **CONTACT ADDRESS** Dept of History, Univ of New Hampshire, Durham, NH, 03824-3586. **EMAIL** davidtf@hopper.unh.edu

FRANKLIN, ALLAN DAVID
PERSONAL Born 08/01/1938, Brooklyn, NY, m, 1974 **DISCIPLINE** HISTORY & PHILOSOPHY OF SCIENCE **EDUCATION** Columbia Col, AB, 59; Cornell Univ, PhD(physics), 65. **CAREER** Res assoc physics, Princeton Univ, 65-66, instr, 66-67; asst prof, 67-73, asoc prof physics, Univ Co, 73-82, prof, 82-. **HONORS AND AWARDS** Ch elect, Forum on History of Physics, Am Phys Soc; Exec Bd, Phil of Sci Asn.; Centennial speaker, Am Physical Soc. **MEMBERSHIPS** Fellow of Am Physical Soc; Hist Sci Soc; Phil of Sci Asn. **RESEARCH** The role of experiment in physics. **SELECTED PUBLICATIONS** Auth, The Principle of Inertia in the Middle Ages, CO Assoc Univ, 76; The Discovery and Nondiscovery of Partly Nonconservation, Studies in Hist & Philos of Sci, 10/79; The Neglect of Experiment, Cambridge Univ Press, 1986; Experiment, Right or Wrong, Cambridge Univ Press, 1990; The Rise and Fall of the Fifth Force, Am Institute of Physics, 1993; The Appearance and Disappearance of the 17-keV Neutrino, Rev. Modern Physics, 1995. **CONTACT ADDRESS** Dept of Physics & Astrophysics, Univ Colo, Box 390, Boulder, CO, 80309-0390. **EMAIL** Allan.Franklin@Colorado.edu

FRANKLIN, CARL M.
DISCIPLINE LAW **EDUCATION** Univ Wash, AB,31; Stanford Univ, MA,39; Columbia Univ, MA,40; Harvard Univ, MBA,48; Univ Va, JD,56; Yale Univ, JSD,56. **CAREER** Prof & VP Emer, Univ Southern Calif; past VP, Financial Aff; past VP, Legal Aff, USC; hon ch, Int Law; past lect & consult, Naval War Col. **SELECTED PUBLICATIONS** Auth, Law of the Sea. **CONTACT ADDRESS** School of Law, Univ Southern Calif, University Park Campus, Los Angeles, CA, 90089.

FRANKLIN, FLOYD
PERSONAL Born 12/26/1929, Hot Springs, m **DISCIPLINE** LAW **EDUCATION** KY State Coll, BA 1953; CA State Coll, MA 1957; San Fernando Vly Coll, JD 1969. **CAREER** CA Community Coll, instructor in law. **HONORS AND AWARDS** Man yr Omega Psi Phi 1966; supporter yr Urban League & YMCA. **MEMBERSHIPS** ABA; CA State Bar Assoc; Langston Law Club; CA Parole Assoc NAACP; bd of dir Legal Aid Found; mem Omega Psi Phi Frat; cosmo Golf Club; pres KY State Club LA Chap 1965-71. **CONTACT ADDRESS** 5140 Crenshaw Blvd, Los Angeles, CA, 90043.

FRANKLIN, NAOMI P.
PERSONAL Born 11/22/1946, New York, NY, d **DISCIPLINE** RELIGIOUS STUDIES **EDUCATION** Community Col NY, BA, 70; Brandeis Univ, MA, 71; Union Theol Sem, MDiv, 81; Duke Univ, PhD, 90. **CAREER** Adjunct asst prof, Nassau Community Col; assoc prof, Touro Col. **MEMBERSHIPS** Soc of Bibl Lit. **RESEARCH** Women in Biblical times; Jews of the Caribbean; Native American history and culture. **SELECTED PUBLICATIONS** Auth, Women and Development in Third World Countries; How To Do Historical Research. **CONTACT ADDRESS** 3626 Marolla Pl, Bronx, NY, 10466.

FRANKLIN, ROBERT MICHAEL
PERSONAL Born 02/22/1954, Chicago, IL, m **DISCIPLINE** THEOLOGY, AFRICAN-AMERICAN STUDIES **EDUCATION** Morehouse College, attended; University of Durham, England, BA 1975; Harvard University Divinity School, MDiv 1978; University of Chicago, PhD 1985. **CAREER** St Paul Church of God In Christ, asst pastor 1978-84; St Bernard's Hosp, prot chaplain 1979-81; Prairie St College, instr in psych 1981; University of Chicago, instr in rel & psych, field ed dir 1981-83; Harvard Univ, Divinity Sch, assoc dir of ministerial studies, 1984-85, visiting lecturer in ministry and Afro-American religion, 1986-88; Colgate Rochester Divinty School, dean/prof of Black Church Studies, 1985-89; Emory Univ, CANDLER SCH OF THEOLOGY, asst prof, 1989-91, DIR OF BLACK CHURCH STUDIES, 1989-, ASSOC PROF OF ETHICS AND SOCIETY, 1991-; FORD FOUNDATION, RIGHTS AND SOCIAL JUSTICE, PROG DIR, 1995-; INTERDENOMINATIONAL THEOLOGICAL CENTER, PRESIDENT, currently. **HONORS AND AWARDS** American Acad of Religion; Soc for the Scientific Study of Rel; Assn for the Sociology of Rel; Soc for the Study of Black Rel; Black Doctoral Fellowship FTE 1978-80; BE Mays Fellowship FTE 1975-78; Phi Beta Kappa, Morehouse Coll 1975; Publications, Union Seminary Qtrly Review 1986, The Iliff Review 1985, Criterion 1984; Liberating Visions: Human Fulfillment and Social Justice in African-American Thought, Augsburg Fortress Press, 1990. **CONTACT ADDRESS** Interdenominational Theol Ctr, 700 Martin Luther King Jr. Dr., Atlanta, GA, 30314.

FRANSON, ROBERT T.
DISCIPLINE LAW **EDUCATION** Cornell Univ, BEP, 62; Univ Calif, JD. **CAREER** Asst prof, 69-73; assoc prof, 73-90; assoc prof emer 90-. **HONORS AND AWARDS** Dir, IBM-UBC Cooperative Project Law Comput. **MEMBERSHIPS** Dir, IBM-UBC Cooperative Project in Law and Computers, 86-89; Consultant, Law Reform Commission of Canada, 76-77 **SELECTED PUBLICATIONS** Auth, pubs about administrative law; environmental law; computers and law. **CONTACT ADDRESS** Fac of Law, Univ British Columbia, 1822 East Mall, Vancouver, BC, V6T 1Z1. **EMAIL** franson@law.ubc.ca

FRAZEE, CHARLES AARON
PERSONAL Born 07/04/1929, Rushville, IN **DISCIPLINE** BYZANTINE AND CHURCH HISTORY **EDUCATION** St Meinrad Col, AB, 51; Cath Univ Am, MA, 54; Ind Univ, PhD (hist), 65, cert, Russ and Europ Inst, 65. **CAREER** Assoc prof hist, Marian Col, Ind, 56-70; assoc prof, 70-80, PROF HIST, CALIF STATE UNIV, FULLERTON, 80-. **MEMBERSHIPS** Cath Hist Soc; Am Asn Slavic Studies; Mod Greek Studies Asn; Am Soc Church Hist. **RESEARCH** Christian communities in Eastern Europe and the Middle East. **SELECTED PUBLICATIONS** Auth, Russian Society and the Greek Revolution, Russ Rev, Vol 55, 96; Rodezianko--An Orthodox Journey from Revolution to Millennium, 1917-1988, Church Hist, Vol 64, 95; Religion and Society in Russia--The 16th Century and the 17th Century, Church Hist, Vol 63, 94; Bulgaria Between East and West, Slavic Rev, Vol 54, 95; The Road that Led to Istanbul, 1526-1528, Slavonic East Europ Rev, Vol 74, 96; Notables and Clergy in Mount Lebanon--The Khazin Sheiks And the Maronite Church 1736-1840, Cath Hist Rev, Vol 83, 97; The Greeks of Asia Minor--Confession, Community, and Ethnicity in the 19th Century Am Hist Rev, Vol 98, 93; Christianity and the Eastern Slavs, Vol 1--Slavic Cultures in the Middle Ages, Church Hist, Vol 64, 95; Christianity and the Arts in Russia, Church Hist, Vol 64, 95; Religion and Society in Russia--The 16th Century and the 17th Century, Church Hist, Vol 63, 94; The Spring of Nations--Churches in the Rebirth of Central and Eastern Europe, Church Hist, Vol 63, 94; Rodezianko--An Orthodox Journey from Revolution to Millennium, 1917-1988, Church Hist, Vol 64, 95; Christianity and the Eastern Slavs, Vol 1--Slavic Cultures in the Middle Ages, Church Hist, Vol 64, 95. **CONTACT ADDRESS** Dept of Hist, California State Univ, Fullerton, Fullerton, CA, 92634.

FREDDOSO, ALFRED J.
DISCIPLINE PHILOSOPHY **EDUCATION** St John Vianney Sem, BA, 68; Univ Notre Dame, PhD, 76. **CAREER** Prof. **RESEARCH** Metaphysics; medieval philosophy; philosophy of religion. **SELECTED PUBLICATIONS** Auth, Francisco Suarez, On Efficient Causality: Metaphysical Disputations 17-19, 94; God's General Concurrence with Secondary Causes: Pitfalls and Prospects, 94; The Openness of God: A Reply to Hasker, 98; Ockham on Faith and Reason, 98; ed, The Existence and Nature of God, 83. **CONTACT ADDRESS** Philosophy Dept, Univ of Notre Dame, 336/7 O'Shaughnessy, Notre Dame, IN, 46556. **EMAIL** freddoso.1@nd.edu

FREDERICK, G. MARCILLE
PERSONAL Born 09/30/1960, Freeport, IL, m, 1998 **DISCIPLINE** THEOLOGY **EDUCATION** Beloit Col, BA, 82; Univ Wisc - Madison, MLS, 91, MA, 93; Inst Christian Stud, M Phil F, 92. **CAREER** Dir, libr & info svc, 93-98, Inst for Christian

Stud; dir, libr svc, 98-, King's Univ Col, Edmonton, AB. **RESEARCH** Historiography, Philosophical bibliography **CONTACT ADDRESS** 9125 - 50 Street, Edmonton, AB, T6B 2H3. **EMAIL** mfrederick@kingsu.ab.ca

FREDRICKSON, DAVID
DISCIPLINE NEW TESTAMENT **EDUCATION** Carleton Col, BA, 75; Luther Sem, MDiv, 80; Yale Univ, MA, 85, MPhil, 87, PhD, 90. **CAREER** Instr, 87; assoc prof, 92-. **HONORS AND AWARDS** Assoc pastor, St John Lutheran Church, Janesville, Wis. **MEMBERSHIPS** Mem, Soc of Bibl Lit. **SELECTED PUBLICATIONS** Auth, Human Sexuality and the Christian Faith, Resource, Augsburg Fortress, 93; Three Objections to Hamerton-Kelly's Interpretation of the Pauline Epistles, 93; Free Speech in Pauline Political Theology, Word and World, 92; Reading the New Testament, Augsburg Home Bible Study Series, 92; Pentecost: Paul the Pastor in 2 Corinthians, Word & World, 91. **CONTACT ADDRESS** Dept of New Testament, Luther Sem, 2481 Como Ave, St. Paul, MN, 55108. **EMAIL** dfredric@luthersem.edu

FREDRIKSEN, P.
PERSONAL Born 01/06/1951, RI, d, 3 children **DISCIPLINE** RELIGION & HISTORY **EDUCATION** Wellesley, BA, 73; Oxford, Dipl Theol, 74; Princeton, PhD, 79. **CAREER** Asst prof, History Dept, Univ Calif Berkeley, 81-86; assoc prof, Religious Studies, Univ Pitts, 86-89; aurelio prof, scripture, Boston Univ, 90-. **HONORS AND AWARDS** Lady Davis vis prof Jerusalem, 94; NEH Univ res grant, 92-93. **MEMBERSHIPS** Amer Acad Relig; Soc Bibl Lit; Nat Asn Patristic Studies **RESEARCH** Historical Jews; Jews & Gentiles in antiquity; Augustine. **SELECTED PUBLICATIONS** Auth, Augustine on History, the Chruch, and the Flesh, St Augustine the Bishop, Garland Publ, 94; From Jesus to Christ The Contribution of the Apostle Paul,Jews and Christians Speak to Jesus, 94; Torah Observance and Christianity: The Perspective of Roman Antiquity, Mod Theol, 95; What You See is What You Get: Context and Content in Current Research on the Historical Jesus, Theol Today, 95; Did Jesus Oppose the Purity Laws?, Bibl Rev, 95; Excaecati Occulta Iustitia Dei: Augustine on Jews and Judaism, Jour Early Christian Studies, 95; Jerusalem in Christian Thought, The City of the Great King: Jerusalem from David to the Present, Harvard Univ Press, 96; coauth, The Two Souls and the Divided Will, Self, Soul and Body in Religious Experience, E J Brill, 98. **CONTACT ADDRESS** Dept of Relig, Boston Univ, Boston, MA, 02215. **EMAIL** augfred@bu.edu

FREED, BRUCE
DISCIPLINE PHILOSOPHY **EDUCATION** Kenyon Col, BA, 59; Oxford Univ, MA, 61; Univ Calif Berkeley, PhD, 65. **CAREER** Prof **RESEARCH** Philosophies of language and mind; epistemology; American pragmatism. **SELECTED PUBLICATIONS** Auth, Reliability, Reasons, and Belief Contexts, Can Jour Philos, 88; Critical Notice: Alvin I. Goldman, Epistemology and Cognition, Can Jour Philos, 88; Modest Scepticism, Dialogue, 86; Education and the Limits of Authority, Monograph, 76; co-ed, Contemporary Research in Philosophical Logic and Linguistic Semantics, Reidel, 75. **CONTACT ADDRESS** Dept of Philosophy, Western Ontario Univ, London, ON, N6A 5B8. **EMAIL** bfreed@julian.uwo.ca

FREEMAN, DONALD DALE
PERSONAL Born 02/24/1937, De Smet, SD, m, 1956, 3 children **DISCIPLINE** PHILOSOPHY, RELIGION **EDUCATION** Huron Col, BS, 57; Oberlin Col, AM, 59, BD, 61; Drew Univ, PhD, 69. **CAREER** Asst prof philos, Union Col, 65-68; asst prof to assoc prof, 68-72, chmn dept, 69-72, Point Park Col; pastor, Christ United Church of Christ, Latrobe, Pa, 72-77; assoc prof, 77-80, prof Theol & Ministry, prof Congregational Life, 97, Lancaster Theol Sem, 80-97; pres, Alternative Learning Lab, Inc, Pittsburgh, 72-77; coordr, Partners Educ Ministries, 74-. **MEMBERSHIPS** Am Philos Asn; Assn for D Min Edu **RESEARCH** Kant, especially his philosophy of religion; ecclesiology, especially ministry congregational studies of laity and clergy; faith development. **SELECTED PUBLICATIONS** Coauth, Logic and the Forms of Thought, Experimental Ed, Point Park Col, 71. **CONTACT ADDRESS** 555 W James St, Lancaster, PA, 17603-2830. **EMAIL** dfreeman@lts.org

FREEMAN, EDWARD C.
PERSONAL Beta, NC, w **DISCIPLINE** LAW **EDUCATION** Knoxville Coll, AB; TX So Univ Sch of Law, LLB JD; Howard Univ Sch of Law, attnd legal sem; Univ of MI Sch of Law; Univ of TN Law Sch; Harvard Univ Sch of Law. **CAREER** Pvt Prac, atty couns 1951-; social worker 18 yrs; TN Valley Auth, mail clerk. **MEMBERSHIPS** Dir Nat Yth & Adm; dir Social Welfare for Mil Manhattan Dist; mem Nat Bar Assn; mem TN & TX Bar; licensed to prac before all State Cts Fed Ct & Supreme Ct of US; v chmn Knox Co Tax Equal Bd; Knox Co Dem Primary Bd; deL Dem Nat Conv 1976; mem steering com election of Jimmy Carter; mem TN Voters Coun; charter mem Soc Workers of Am; charter mem Magnolia Fed Savings & Loan Assn; former scout master; mem Sect of Am Bar Assn on Continuing Legal Edn; mem Am Bar Assn; Knoxville Bar & TN Bar Assn; exec bd NAACP; Omega Psi Phi Frat; Elks & Mason; exec com Dem Party; Mount Zion BaptCh; hon trst Juvenile Ct for Knox Co TN. **CONTACT ADDRESS** 2528 McCalla Ave, Knoxville, TN, 37914.

FREEMAN, EUGENE
PERSONAL Born 02/16/1906, New York, NY, m, 1930, 2 children **DISCIPLINE** PHILOSOPHY **EDUCATION** Univ Calif, Los Angeles, AB, 26; Northern Ill Col Optometry, OD, 34; Univ Chicago, PhD, 37. **CAREER** Asst prof physiologic optics and prof ethics, Northern Ill Col Optometry, 33-36, from assoc prof to prof, 36-43; asst prof philos, Ill Inst Technol, 47-53; vpres and dean, Chicago Col Optometry, 49-56; ed-in-chief, Open Court Publ Co, Ill, 59-64; assoc prof, 64-65, prof, 65-73, EMER PROF PHILOS, SAN JOSE STATE UNIV, 73-, ED, MONIST, 59-; DIR PHILOS DIV, OPEN CT PUBL CO, 73-. **MEMBERSHIPS** Am Philos Asn; Metaphys Soc Am; Charles S Peirce Soc. **RESEARCH** Visual perception and rehabilitation; philosophy of Charles Peirce; Bioethics. **SELECTED PUBLICATIONS** Auth, Talbot, Charles, Holwell, 1906-93, Med Hist, Vol 38, 94; Nuns in the Public Sphere--Aelred of Rievaulx De Sanctimoniali de Wattun and the Gendering of Authority, Comitatus J Medieval Renaissance Stud, Vol 27, 96; All of Fame Questions, Down Beat, Vol 64, 97; The Public and Private Functions of Heloise Letters, J Medieval Hist, Vol 23, 97; Gaimar, Geffrei, Vernacular Historiography, and the Assertion of Authority, Stud Philol, Vol 93, 96; Gaimar, Geffrei, Vernacular Historiography, and the Assertion of Authority, Stud Philol, Vol 93, 96; Representations of Belief--Essays in Memory of Banks, Fr Stud, Vol 47, 93. **CONTACT ADDRESS** Ed Off Philos Div, Hegeler Inst, PO Box 1908, Los Gatos, CA, 95031.

FREEMAN, JAMES B.
PERSONAL Born 03/27/1947, Patterson, NJ, s **DISCIPLINE** PHILOSOPHY **EDUCATION** Drew Univ, BA, 68; Indiana Univ, AM, 71, PhD, 73. **CAREER** Lectr, 73 & 74, Indiana Univ; adj lectr, Butler Univ, 74, Bloomfield Col, 74-75; res assoc, Univ Victoria, 75-78; adj asst prof, 78-80, asst prof, 80-84, assc prof, 85-92, prof, 93-, Hunter Col CUNY, 78-. **HONORS AND AWARDS** Summa cum laude Drew Univ. **MEMBERSHIPS** Amer Philos Asn; Asn Informal Logic Critical Thinking; Soc Christian Philos **RESEARCH** Informal logic; Arguementation theory; Epistemology; Philosophy of religion. **SELECTED PUBLICATIONS** Auth, Thinking Logically: Basic Concepts for Reasoning, Prentice Hall, 88 & 93; The Place of Informal Logic in Logic, New Essays in Informal Logic, Informal Logic, 94; The Appeal to Popularity and Presumption by Common Knowledge, Fallacies: Classical and Contemporary Readings, PA State Univ Press, 95 Premise Acceptability, Deontology, Internalism, Justification, Informal Logic, 95; Epistemic Justification and Premise Acceptability, Argumentation 10, 96; Consider the Source One Step in Assessing Premise Acceptability, Argumentation 10, 96. **CONTACT ADDRESS** Dept of Philosophy, Hunter Col, CUNY, 695 Park Ave, New York, NY, 10021. **EMAIL** james.freeman@hunter.cuny.edu

FREEMAN, THOMAS F.
PERSONAL Born 06/27/1920, Richmond, VA, m **DISCIPLINE** THEOLOGY **EDUCATION** Univ of Ghana, Ghana E Africa; VA Union U, BA 1939; Andover Newton Theol Sch, BD 1942; Univ of Chicago, PhD 1948; Howard U, further study; Boston U, further study; Univ of Vienna, Austria, further study; African U. **CAREER** Weekend Coll, dean; TX Southern Univ, dir continuing educ; Model Cities Training Ctr TSU, dir 1970-74; Coll of Arts & Sci TSU, asst dean 1968-70, dept head Philosophy 1950-67; Carmel Baptist Church, minister 1944-50; VA Union Univ, prof Practical Theology 1944-49; Monumental Baptist Church Chicago, assoc minister 1942-44; Pleasant St Baptist Church, Westerly RI, minister 1940-44; Concord Baptist Church, Boston MA, asst minister 1939-40; Mt Horem Baptist Church; Rice Univ, visiting prof. **HONORS AND AWARDS** Recip Clarke Scholarship VA Union Univ 1939; turner fellowship Andover Newton 1939-42; fellowship Univ of C 1942-46; Univ Divinty Univ Faculty Mem of Yr 1950-51; TSU-PI CC Award TSU 1974. **MEMBERSHIPS** Pres Alpha Kappa Mu Nat Honor Soc 1962-66; alumni dir Alpha Kappa Mu Nat Honor Soc 1966; bd dir Andover Newton Alumni Assn; bd dir Assn of Churches; mem NAACP; mem Boy Scouts; Urban League. **SELECTED PUBLICATIONS** Choices of The Pew 1963; Am Press co-author "From Separation to Special Designation" 1975.

FREIDAY, DEAN
PERSONAL Born 06/20/1915, Irvington, NJ, m, 1946, 2 children **DISCIPLINE** THEOLOGY, ECUMENISM **EDUCATION** Univ Rochester, BA, 36. **CAREER** CO-ED, QUAKER RELIG THOUGHT, THEOL J, 80-, MEM, CHRISTIAN AND INTERFAITH RELATIONS COMT, FRIENDS GEN CONF, 58-, chmn, 66-72, Co-Opted, 72-; delegate, 4th World Conf Faith and Order of the World Coun of Churches, 63; observer and consult, 3rd World Cong of the Lay Apostolate Vatican City, 67; mem exec comt, US Conf for the World Coun of Churches, 67-72; SPONSOR, CATH AND QUAKER STUDIES, 71-; delegate, 6th Gen Assembly World Coun of Churches, 83. **MEMBERSHIPS** Quaker Theol Discussion Group. **RESEARCH** The theology of 17th century England, especially Quakers; scriptural exegesis and hermeneutics; Roman Cath theology. **SELECTED PUBLICATIONS** Auth, Quakers, Ecumenism and the World Council of Churches Wcc, Ecumenical Rev, Vol 46, 94. **CONTACT ADDRESS** 1110 Wildwood Ave, Manasquan, NJ, 08736.

FREIN, BRIGID C.
PERSONAL Born 01/19/1957, St. Paul, MN, m, 1979, 4 children **DISCIPLINE** THEOLOGY **EDUCATION** Gonzaga Univ, BA, 79; St. Louis Univ, PhD, 89. **CAREER** From asst prof to assoc prof to chemn, 88-, Univ Scranton. **MEMBERSHIPS** Catholic Biblical Assoc; Society Biblical Literature. **RESEARCH** New Testament; Gospel of Luke. **SELECTED PUBLICATIONS** Auth, art, Fundamentalism and Narrative Criticism of the Gospels, 92; auth, art, The Literary and Theological Significance of Misunderstanding in the Gospel of Luke, 93; auth, art, Old Testament Prophecies, Narrative Predictions, and Luke's Sense of Fulfillment, 94; auth, art, Scripture in the Life of the Church, 97. **CONTACT ADDRESS** Dept of Theology/Religious Studies, Univ of Scranton, Scranton, PA, 18510. **EMAIL** freinb1@uofs.edu

FRENCH, LOUISE
PERSONAL Born 06/23/1918, Indianapolis, IN **DISCIPLINE** PHILOSOPHY **EDUCATION** Mundelein Col, AB, 40; Marquette Univ, AM, 48; St Louis Univ, PhD (philos), 61. **CAREER** Assoc prof philos and chmn dept, Clarke Col, 56-68; PROF PHILOS AND CHMN DEPT, MUNDELEIN COL, 68-. **MEMBERSHIPS** Metaphys Soc Am; Cath Philos Asn; Am Philos Asn. **RESEARCH** Metaphysics; existentialism; ancient philosophy, medieval philosophy. **SELECTED PUBLICATIONS** Auth, Approaches to Teaching Mann Death in Venice and Other Short Fiction, Ger Quart, Vol 68, 95; Mereaubrentano, Sophie. Freedom, Love, Femininity--Tricolor of Social and Individual Self Determination Ca.1800, Ger Quart, Vol 69, 96; The Experience of Other Countries--Papers Presented at Wiepersdorf Colloquium on Arnim, Achim, Von and Arnim, Bettina, Von, Ger Quart, Vol 69, 96; Merrill, Helen-In Memoriam, Tci, Vol 31, 97. **CONTACT ADDRESS** Dept of Philos, Mundelein Col, 6363 Sheridan Rd, Chicago, IL, 60660.

FRENCH, PETER A.
PERSONAL Born 03/19/1942, Newburgh, NY, m, 1964, 2 children **DISCIPLINE** PHILOSOPHY **EDUCATION** Gettysburg Col, BA, 63; Univ Southern Calif, MA, 64; Univ of Miami, PhD, 71. **CAREER** Instr, 65-66; asst prof, Ariz State Col/Northern Ariz Univ, 66-68; asst prof, Miami-Dade Col, 68-71; vis prof, Dalhousie Univ, 76; from asst prof to prof, Univ Minn, 71-81; coord of philos, Univ Minn, 72-73 & 77-78; Exxon Distinguished Res Prof, Center for the Study of Values, Univ Delaware, 80-81; Lennox Distinguished Prof Hum and Prof Philos, Trinity Univ, 81-94; chmn dept philos, Trinity Univ, 82-88; Dir, Ctr for Undergraduate Philos Res, Trinity Univ, 86-91; prof philos,Univ S Fla, 94-; ch ethics, 94-; Dir, ethics ctr, 95-; ch, dept philos, 97- . **MEMBERSHIPS** APA, Soc for Philos and Pub Aff; Soc for Bus Ethics; Soc of Philos J Eds;N Am Soc for Soc Philos; Inst for Criminal Justice Ethics. **RESEARCH** Ethics; ethical theory. **SELECTED PUBLICATIONS** Auth, The Spectrum of Responsibility, St Martin's Pr, 91; coauth, Corporations in the Moral Community, Harcourt Brace, 92; auth, Responsibility Matters, Univ Pr Kansas, 92; auth, Corporate Ethics, Harcourt Brace, 95; auth,Cowboy Metaphysics: Ethics and Death in Westerns, Rowman and Littlefield, 97; auth, Why did Wittgenstein Read Tagore to the Vienna Circle?, in Proto Soziologie, 93; auth, Responsibility and the Moral Role of Corporate Entities, in Business as a Humanity, 94; auth, The Practical and Ethical Costs of Corp Reengineering, in Business and Prof Ethics J, winter, 94; auth, Action Theory, Ration-Choice Theory, and Ethics, in Business Ethics Qtly, Summer, 95; auth, Corp Moral Agency, in the Blackwell Encyclopedic Dict of Bus Ethics, 96; auth Normativity and Private Persons: 1. Responsibility, 2. Status: Individual and Group Membership, in the Philos of Law: an Encyclopedia, 96; auth, the Compensatory Opportunities of Re-engineering, in Perspectives on the Professions, Spring, 96; auth, Rationality and Ethics, in Proto Soziologie, 96; auth, Integrity, Intentions, and Corporations, in American Business Law J, 96; auth, Spatial and Temporal Ethics, in Frontiers in Amer Philos, 96; auth, Moral Principles, Rules, and Policies, in Ethical Policy Making in Local Schools, 97; auth, Forward to Collective Responsibility, in Collective Responsibility, 98; auth, Unchosen Evil and War Crimes, in War Crimes Revisited, forthcoming. **CONTACT ADDRESS** Dept of Philosophy, Univ of South Florida, CPR 107, Tampa, FL, 33620. **EMAIL** French@boyflash.stpt.usf.edu

FRENCH, RICHARD FREDERIC
PERSONAL Born 06/23/1915, Randolph, MA **DISCIPLINE** MUSIC, RELIGION **EDUCATION** Harvard Univ, BS, 37, MA, 39. **CAREER** Mem Soc Fellows, Harvard Univ, 41-42, 46-47, asst prof music, 47-51; vpres, Assoc Music Publ, NY, 51-59; pres, NY Pro Musica, 58-70; prof sacred music, Union theol Sem, 66-73; PROF MUSIC, INST MUSIC and WORSHIP, YALE UNIV, 73-, Trustee, Brooklyn Music Sch, 60-70 and Schola Musicae Liturgicae, NY, 73-; adj prof sacred music, Union theol Sem, 73-77. **MEMBERSHIPS** Am Musicol Soc. **RESEARCH** Music and liturgy; Russian; graduate educational curricula. **SELECTED PUBLICATIONS** Auth, Libraries, History, Diplomacy, and the Performing Arts--Essays in Honor of Smith, Carleton, Sprague, Notes, Vol 49, 93. **CONTACT ADDRESS** Sch of Music, Yale Univ, New Haven, CT, 06520.

FRENCH, STANLEY G.
PERSONAL Born 12/24/1933, Hamilton, ON, Canada **DISCIPLINE** PHILOSOPHY **EDUCATION** Carleton Univ, BA, 55; Univ Rochester, MA, 57; Univ Va, PhD, 58. **CAREER** Asst to assoc prof, Univ Western Ont, 59-68; prof, Sir George Williams Univ, 68-74, ch philos, 69-71; PROF PHILOSOPHY, CONCORDIA UNIV, 74-, dir, Hum Interdisciplinary doctoral prog, 92-95. **HONORS AND AWARDS** Philip Francis du Pont fel, 58-59; Can Coun grant, 68; Brit Coun visitorship, 72, 84, 92. **MEMBERSHIPS** Can Philos Asn; Can Bioethics Soc; Am Philos Asn; Mind Asn. **SELECTED PUBLICATIONS** Auth, The Northwest Staging Route, 57; auth, Philosophers Look at Canadian Confederation, 79; auth, Interpersonal Violence, Health and Gender Politics, 93; auth, Violence Against Women: Philosophical Perspectives, 98. **CONTACT ADDRESS** Dept of Philos, Concordia Univ, Montreal, 1455 de Maisonneuve Blvd W, Montreal, PQ, H3G 1M8.

FRENCH, WILLIAM
PERSONAL Born 03/24/1951, Washington, DC, m **DISCIPLINE** THEOLOGY **EDUCATION** Dickinson Coll, BA, 73; Harvard Univ, MDiv, 77; Univ of Chicago, PhD, 85. **CAREER** Special edu teach, 73-74, National Children's Center Wash DC; teach, dept head, 78-79, Willibrord Catholic High School; summer Instr, 80, 81, Prairie State Coll Chicago; Asst Prof, Assoc Prof, 85-, Loyola Univ Chicago, Dir 94-, Peace Stud Prog. **MEMBERSHIPS** AAR, SCE, Peace Studies Assoc. **RESEARCH** Religious & environmental ethics, war & peace issues. **SELECTED PUBLICATIONS** Auth, Character and Cruelty in Huckleberry Finn, Why the Ending Works, in: Soundings 81, 98; Knowing Where You Are, in: Peace Review, A Transnational Qtly, 96; Against Biosherical Egalitarianism, in: J of Environmental Ethics, 95; Chaos and Creation, in: The Bible Today, 95; God and Biospheres as Superpowers, in: Peace Review, A Transnational Qtly, 94; Soil And Salvation, Theological Anthropology Ecologically Informed, in: The Whole and Divided Self, ed J McCarthy, New York Crossroad, 97; The World as God's Body, Theological Ethics and Pantheism, in: Broken and Whole, Essays on Religion and the Body, eds, M A Tilly & S A Ross, Lanham Univ Press of Amer, 95. **CONTACT ADDRESS** Dept of Theology, Loyola Univ, Chicago, 6525 N Sheridan, Chicago, IL, 60626. **EMAIL** wfrench@luc.edu

FRERICHS, ERNEST S.
PERSONAL Born 04/30/1925, Staten Island, NY, m, 1949, 3 children **DISCIPLINE** RELIGIOUS STUDIES, BIBLICAL STUDIES **EDUCATION** Brown Univ, AB, 48; Harvard Univ, AM, 49; Boston Univ, STB, 52, PhD, 57. **CAREER** Chmn, Dept of Religious Studies, 64-70, prof, Religious Studies and Judaic Studies, 66-95, Dean, graduate school, Brown Univ, 76-82, dir, Prog in Judaic Studies, 82-95, prof Emeritus, 96-; Pres, Albright Inst of Archaeological Research, Jerusalem, 76-82; Vice-pres, Am Schools of Oriental research, 95-97; exec dir, Dorot Found, 95-. **HONORS AND AWARDS** Lilly Postdoctoral fel; Distinguished Alumnus Award, Boston Univ, 94. **MEMBERSHIPS** Soc of Biblical Lit; Am Academy of Relig; Am Schools of Oriental Res. **RESEARCH** History of Biblical interpretation; history of Biblical translation. **SELECTED PUBLICATIONS** Ed, Bible and Bibles in America, Scholars Press, 88; Joint ed, with Leonard Lesko, Exodus, The Egyptological Evidence, Eisenbraun's, 97. **CONTACT ADDRESS** Dorot Found, 439 Benefit St, Providence, RI, 02903. **EMAIL** ErnieF@Dorot.org

FRETHEIM, TERENCE E.
DISCIPLINE OLD TESTAMENT **EDUCATION** Luther Col,BA, 56; Luther Sem, MDiv, 60; Princeton Sem, ThD, 67. **CAREER** Instr, Augsburg Col and Sem, 61-63; asst prof, Augsburg Col, 67-68; vis prof, lectr, Univ Chicago Divinity Sch; asst prof, 68; dean of acad aff, 78-88; act ch, Old Testament dept, 77-78; ch, curriculum comm, 76-77; prof, 78-. **HONORS AND AWARDS** Phi Beta Kappa, 95; Fulbright scholar; grad scholar, Lutheran Brotherhood Sem; Martin Luther scholar; Fredrik A. Schiotz fel award; ATS scholar., Co-ch, Theol Consult for the Evangel Lutheran Church in Am; pres, Minn Consortium of Theol Sch(s); bk ed, Jour Bibl Lit; pastor, Dennison Lutheran Church, 68-71. **MEMBERSHIPS** Mem, Cath Bibl Assn; Soc of Bibl Lit. **SELECTED PUBLICATIONS** Auth, Genesis, New Interpreter's Bible, 94; Exodus, Interpretation Series, John Knox, 91; Deuteronomy-II Kings, Search Units 9 and 10, 85; The Suffering of God: An Old Testament Perspective, 84; Deuteronomic History, 83; The Message of Jonah: A Theological Commentary, 77; Our Old Testament Heritage, 70-71; Creation, Fall and Flood, Stud (s) in Genesis 1-11, 69. **CONTACT ADDRESS** Dept of Old Testament, Luther Sem, 2481 Como Ave, St. Paul, MN, 55108. **EMAIL** tfrethei@luthersem.edu

FREUND, NORM
PERSONAL Born 07/21/1953, Davenport, IA, m, 1975, 2 children **DISCIPLINE** PHILOSOPHY **EDUCATION** St. Ambrose Col, BA, philos, BS, bio, 75; Southern Ill Univ, MA, philos, 77, PhD, philos, 80. **CAREER** Asst prof, philos, Luther Col, 80-81; asst prof, 81-85, assoc prof, 86-88, full prof, 89-, philos, Clarke Col. **HONORS AND AWARDS** Title III grants for Computer Hypertext Res, 95, 96; Meneve Dunham award for excellence in teaching, 88. **MEMBERSHIPS** Amer Philos Asn; Amer Asn of Philos Teachers; Concerned Philos for Peace. **RESEARCH** History of philosophy and applied ethics; Philosophy of peace and war. **SELECTED PUBLICATIONS** Rev, A Strategy of Nonviolent Defense, A Gandhian Approach, Civilian-Based Defense, Mar, 96; auth, If It's Tuesday This Must Be Bentham, Teaching Philos, Dec, 93; rev, What is Justice?, Contemporary and Classical Readings, Teaching Philos, Sept, 92; rev, The Ethics of War and Peace, Warism to Pacifism: A Moral Continuum, Teaching Philos, Dec, 91; auth, The Just War Theory: Historical Development and Contemporary Analysis, Gandhi Marg, 12, Jul-Sept, 90; rev, Toynbee's Philosophy of World History and Politics, Jour of Social Philos, 19, Fall, 88; auth, Peace: A Myriad of Meanings, The Personalist Forum 4, Spring, 88; auth, A Humanistic Sexual Ethic, Contemporary Philos, 12, Apr, 88; auth, Nonviolent National Defense: A Philosophical Inquiry into Applied Nonviolence, Univ Press of Amer, 87. **CONTACT ADDRESS** 1550 Clarke Dr., Dubuque, IA, 52001. **EMAIL** nfreund@keller.clarke.edu

FREUND, RICHARD A.
PERSONAL m, 2 children **DISCIPLINE** PHILOSOPHY AND RELIGION **EDUCATION** Jewish Theol Sem of Am, MA, PhD. **CAREER** Isaacson Prof Relig, ch, dept Philos & Relig, dir, Bethsaida Excavations Proj, Univ Nebr, Omaha; ch ed, Spotlight on Tchg, Am Acad of Relig. **HONORS AND AWARDS** Lilly Endowment tchg fel, 91, Univ-wide res award, 92, tchg award, 95, Univ Nebr, Omaha., Founder, Bethsaida Excavations Proj, Univ Nebr, Omaha. **MEMBERSHIPS** Nat secy, Soc of Bibl Lit. **SELECTED PUBLICATIONS** Auth, 1st two Vols of Bethsaida: A City by the North Shore of the Sea of Galilee. **CONTACT ADDRESS** Univ Nebr, Omaha, Omaha, NE, 68182.

FREYER, TONY ALLAN
DISCIPLINE LAW **EDUCATION** San Diego State Univ, AB, 70; Ind Univ, MA, 72, PhD, 75. **CAREER** Prof, Univ Ala, 81-. **HONORS AND AWARDS** University of Alabama's Burnum Distinguished fac awd, 92; sr Fulbright awd, Australia, 93; Abe Fellowship, Soc Sci Res Coun to Japan, 95-06. **RESEARCH** Legal history **SELECTED PUBLICATIONS** Auth, Forums of Order, 79; Harmony and Dissonance: The Swift and Erie Cases in American Federalism, 81; The Little Rock Crisis, 84; Justice Hugo L. Black and the Dilemma of American Liberalism, 90; Hugo L. Black and Modern America, 90; Regulating Big Business: Antitrust in Great Britain and America, 1880-1990, 92; Producers versus Capitalists: Constitutional Conflict in Antebellum America, 94; Democracy and Judicial Independence: A History of Alabama's Federal Courts, 95; **CONTACT ADDRESS** Law Dept, Univ of Alabama, Box 870000, Tuscaloosa, AL, 35487-0383. **EMAIL** tfreyer@law.ua.edu

FREYFOGLE, ERIC T.
DISCIPLINE LAW **EDUCATION** Lehigh Univ, BA; Univ Mich, JD. **CAREER** Prof, Univ Ill Urbana Champaign. **HONORS AND AWARDS** Ed, Mich Law Rev; dir, Ill Environ Council. **RESEARCH** Property; environmental law & policy; natural resources; land use planning; modern environmental theory; and wildlife law. **SELECTED PUBLICATIONS** Auth, Justice and the Earth and Bounded People, Boundless Lands. **CONTACT ADDRESS** Law Dept, Univ Ill Urbana Champaign, 52 E Gregory Dr, Champaign, IL, 61820. **EMAIL** efreyfog@law.uiuc.edu

FRICK, FRANK SMITH
PERSONAL Born 04/02/1938, Ponca City, OK, m, 1961, 2 children **DISCIPLINE** RELIGION **EDUCATION** Phillips Univ, AB, 60, BD, 63; Princeton Univ, PhD (relig), 70. **CAREER** Campus minister, United Ministries Higher Educ, Okla State Univ, 64-66; asst prof, 69-77, ASSOC PROF RELIG STUDIES, ALBION COL, 77-, EDUC CONSULT, WMICH CONF, UNITED METHODIST CHURCH, 69-; resident dir, Gt Lakes Cols Asn Mid East prog, Israel, 73-74; vis prof relig, Hebrew Univ Jerusalem, 73-74; mem staff, Archaeol Excavations at Tel Dan, Israel, 77-78; Nat Endowment for Humanities grant, 82. **MEMBERSHIPS** Am Schs Orient Res; Soc Bibl Lit; Cath Bibl Soc. **RESEARCH** Sociology of biblical religion; comparative study of religion; Palestinian archaeology. **SELECTED PUBLICATIONS** Auth, Where are you Staying John I, 38 - The House from the Biblical World--In Honor of Professor Couturier, Guy on the Occasion of his 65th Birthday, Cath Biblical Quart, Vol 58, 96; The Armies of the Hasmoneans and Herod--From Hellenistic to Roman Frameworks, J Biblical Lit, Vol 112, 93; Social World of Ancient Israel, 1250-587,, Biblical Archaeol, Vol 58, 95; Lectures on the Religion of the Semites, Cath Biblical Quart, Vol 59, 97; The Forging of Israel--Iron Technology, Symbolism, and Tradition in Ancient Society, Cath Biblical Quart, Vol 55, 93; Srael and the Book of the Covenant--An Anthropological Approach to Biblical Law, Interpretation J Bible Theology, Vol 49, 95. **CONTACT ADDRESS** Dept of Relig Studies, Albion Col, 611 E Porter St, Albion, MI, 49224-1831.

FRIED, CHARLES
PERSONAL Born 04/15/1935, Czechoslovakia, m, 1959, 2 children **DISCIPLINE** LAW, LEGAL PHILOSOPHY **EDUCATION** Princeton Univ, AB, 56; Oxford Univ, BA, 58; Columbia Univ, LLB, 60. **CAREER** Law clerk, Justice Harlan, US Supreme Court, 60-61; asst prof, 61-65, prof law, Law Sch, Harvard Univ, 65-, consult, US Treas & Internal Revenue Serv, 61-62; assoc reporter, Model Code Pre-Arraignment Procedure, Am Law Inst, 64; vis prof, Mass Inst Technol, 68-69; dir, Nat Court Crime & Delinquency; consult, Dept Transp, White House, 81-; Solicitor General of the U.S., 85-89; Assoc Justice, Supreme Judicial Court of Mass, 95-. **MEMBERSHIPS** AAAS; IOM. **SELECTED PUBLICATIONS** Auth, The Value of Life, Harvard Law Rev, 69; An Anatomy of Values, Harvard Univ, 70; contribr, Ethical Issues in Human Genetics, Plenum 73; Ethics of AID and Embryo Transfer, Ciba, 73; Markets and Morals, Hemisphere Publ, 77; auth, The University as Church and as Part, Bull Am Acad Arts St Sci, 12/77; Right and Wrong, Harvard Univ, 78; Contract as Promise, A Theory of Contractual Obligation, Harvard Univ, 81; Law and Order, Simon and Schuster, 91. **CONTACT ADDRESS** 1525 Massachusetts, Cambridge, MA, 02138-2903. **EMAIL** fried@law.harvard.edu

FRIEDLAND, B.
PERSONAL Born 08/30/1956, Cape Town, South Africa, m **DISCIPLINE** MEDICINE **EDUCATION** BChD, MSc, JD. **CAREER** Harvard Sch Dental Med, inst 85-88, lect 89-93; Robert W Joyce, P C, Newton Ma, law clk, legal intern, paralegal, 91-93, attorney, 91-93; Harvard Sch Dent Med, inst 93-97, asst prof, 97-. **HONORS AND AWARDS** Dist facul Awd; Dean's List Suffolk Sch Law; OKU; HOS **MEMBERSHIPS** ASL; OKU; ABA; AAOMR; HOS; IADR **RESEARCH** Medicolegal and ethical issues facing the medical and allied health professions and society. **SELECTED PUBLICATIONS** Auth, Oral Radiology in: Sonis ST, Dental secrets, Haley and Balus, Phil Pa, in press; Managed Care and the Expanding Scope of Primary Care Physician's Duties, Jour Law Med Ethics, 98; HIV Infection and the Duty to Treat: The Americans with Disabilities Act, Summons 98; Clinical Radiologic Issues in Orthodontic Practice, Semin Orthod, 98; Responding to Attorney requests for patient Information, with J. M. Haggerty, Jour MA Dent Soc, 97; Advanced Imaging Techniques asst in Implant Planning, with R. W. Valachovic, Jour MA Dent Soc, 97. **CONTACT ADDRESS** Harvard Sch Dental Medicine, Harvard Univ, 188 Longwood Ave, Boston, MA, 02115. **EMAIL** friedlan@warren.med.harvard.edu

FRIEDMAN, HARVEY MARTIN
PERSONAL Born 09/23/1948, m, 1973 **DISCIPLINE** LOGIC, FOUNDATIONS OF MATHEMATICS **EDUCATION** Mass Inst Technol, PhD (math), 67. **CAREER** Asst prof philos, Stnaford Univ, 67-69, assoc prof, 69-73; vis prof math, State Univ NY, Buffalo, 72-73, prof, 73-77; PROF MATH, OHIO STATE UNIV, 77-, Vis assoc prof math, Univ Wis, Madison, 70-71. **MEMBERSHIPS** Asn Symbolic Logic. **RESEARCH** Philosophy of mathematics; intuitionism. **SELECTED PUBLICATIONS** Auth, Races Undesirable from a Military Point of-View, J Pac Hist, Vol 32, 97; The Beast in Paradise--The United-States Navy in Micronesia, 1943-1947, Pac Hist Rev, Vol 62, 93; Guam Trial of the Century--News, Hegemony, and Rumor in the American Colony, Pac Hist Rev, Vol 63, 94; Arguing Over Empire--American Interservice and Interdepartmental Rivalry over Micronesia, 1943-1947, J Pac Hist, Vol 29, 94. **CONTACT ADDRESS** Dept of Math, Ohio State Univ, 231 W 18th Ave, Columbus, OH, 43210-1174.

FRIEDMAN, HOWARD M.
DISCIPLINE LAW **EDUCATION** Ohio State Univ, BA; Harvard Univ, JD; Georgetown Univ, LLM. **CAREER** Prof. **SELECTED PUBLICATIONS** Auth, Securities Regulation In Cyberspace, Bowne, 97; Ohio Securities Law & Practice, Anderson, 96; Securities and Commodities Enforcement, Lexington Bk, 81. **CONTACT ADDRESS** Col Law, Univ of Toledo, Toledo, OH, 43606.

FRIEDMAN, LAWRENCE M.
PERSONAL Born 04/02/1930, Chicago, IL, m, 1955, 2 children **DISCIPLINE** LAW **EDUCATION** Univ Chicago, AB, 48, JD, 51, LLM, 53. **CAREER** From asst prof to assoc prof law, St Louis Univ, 57-61; from assoc prof to prof, Univ Wis, 61-68; Prof Law, Stanford Univ, 68-. **HONORS AND AWARDS** Triennial Coif Award, Asn Am Law Schs, 76., LLD, Univ Puget Sound, 77. **MEMBERSHIPS** Law and Soc Asn (past pres); Am Soc Legal Hist; Am Acad Arts and Sci. **RESEARCH** American legal history; sociology of law and social welfare legislation; property and succession. **SELECTED PUBLICATIONS** Auth, Constitutionalism and Democracy--Transitions in the Contemporary World, J Interdisciplinary Hist, Vol 26, 95; Borders--On the Emerging Sociology of Transnational Law, Stanford J Int Law, Vol 32, 96; Guardians--A Research Note, Am J Legal Hist, Vol 40, 96. **CONTACT ADDRESS** Sch of Law, Stanford Univ, Stanford, CA, 94305-1926.

FRIEDMAN, LESLEY
PERSONAL Born 06/13/1965, New York, NY, m, 1994 **DISCIPLINE** PHILOSOPHY **EDUCATION** Union Col, BA; Univ Albany, MA; Univ Buffalo, PhD, SUNY. **CAREER** Asst Prof, Lynchburg Col, 5 yrs. **HONORS AND AWARDS** Wil-

liam T Parry Prize for Outstanding Scholarship in Philos, 92; Res Grant, Lynchburg Col, 95, 97. **MEMBERSHIPS** APA; Soc for the Advancement of Amer Philos; Hume Soc; Intl Berkeley Soc; Charles S. Peirce Soc **RESEARCH** Amer Philos; Charles S. Pierce; Modern European Philos. **SELECTED PUBLICATIONS** Remembrance of of Darkness Past A Rejoinder to Flage, Hume Stud, 93; Another Look at Flages Hume, Hume Stud, 93; C.S. Pierces Reality & Berkeleys Blunders, Jour of the Hist of Philos, 97; Contrib, Pragmatism An Annotated Bibliography 1898-1940 Value Inquiry Book Ser, 98. **CONTACT ADDRESS** Philosophy Dept, Lynchburg Col, 1501 Lakes, Lynchburg, VA, 24501-3199. **EMAIL** friedman@acavax.lynchburg.edu

FRIEDMAN, MARILYN A.
DISCIPLINE PHILOSOPHY **EDUCATION** Univ Western Ontario, PhD, 74. **CAREER** Assoc Prof, Wash Univ 91-. **HONORS AND AWARDS** Nat Endowment for the Humanities Fel, 88-89. **MEMBERSHIPS** Am Philos Asn; soc for Women in Philos. **RESEARCH** Ethics; Feminist Theory; Social and Political Philosophy. **SELECTED PUBLICATIONS** Auth, What are Friends For?: Feminist Perspective on Personal Relationship and Moral Theory, 93; coauth; Political Correctness: For and Against, 95; co-ed, Feminism and Community, 95; Mind and Morals: Essays on Ethics and Cognitive Science, 95. **CONTACT ADDRESS** Dept Of Philosophy, Wash Univ, Box 1073, St. Louis, MO, 63130. **EMAIL** friedman@artsci.wustl.edu

FRIEDMAN, MAURICE STANLEY
PERSONAL Born 12/29/1921, Tulsa, OK, 2 children **DISCIPLINE** PHILOSOPHY **EDUCATION** Educ. Harvard Univ, BS, 42; Ohio State Univ, AM, 47; Univ Chicago, PhD, 50; Int Col Am, PhD, 83. **CAREER** Res asst & statistician, Harvard Univ, 42; asst English, Ohio State Univ, 46-47; teaching asst humanities, Univ Chicago, 48-49; instr basic col prog, Washington Univ, 49-50; instr philos, Ohio State Univ, 50-51; mem fac philos & lit, Sarah Lawrence Col, 51-55, prof philos, 55-64; prof, Manhattanville Col, 66-67; prof relig, Temple Univ, 67-73, grant, 71-72; prof, 73-91, PROF EMERITUS REL STUDIES, PHILOS, COMP LIT, 91-, SAN DIEGO STATE UNIV; Lectr, New Sch Soc Res, 54-66; vis prof, Hebrew Union Col, 56-57; mem fac, Wash Sch Psychiat, 57-59; guest lectr, William Alanson White Inst Psychol, Psychoanal & Psychiat, 58-60; Lucius N Littaeur Found res grant, Israel & Europe, 59-60; treas & mem exec comt, Conf Jewish Philos, 63-69; mem fac, Pendle Hill-Quaker Ctr for Studies & Dialogue, 64-65, 67-73 & I Meier Segals Ctr for Advan Judaism, Can, 65-72; Gustav N Wurzweiler Found grants work on Buber biog, Israel & America, 65-67; vis prof, Union Theol Sem, 65 & 67; vis lectr, Vassar Col, 67; Am Philos Asn fel, 69; vis distinguished prof, Calif State Univ, San Diego, 72; vis fel, Ctr Studies Person, La Jolla, Calif, 72; mem fac, Calif Sch Prof Psychol, San Diego, 73-75; field fac, Union Grad Sch West, 75-; guild tutors, Int Col, 76-86; res adv, Fielding Inst, 77-80; vis prof rel, Univ Hawaii, 75; vis prof, Gandhi Nat Ctr Arts, New Delhi, 92; prof Sch Psychol Stud, Sand Diego, 86; DHL, Hebrew Union Col Jewish Inst of Rel, 98. **HONORS AND AWARDS** Nat Jewish Book Award for Biography, 85, LLD, Univ Vt, 61. **MEMBERSHIPS** Am Philos Asn; Metaphys Soc Am; Relig Educ Asn; Am Asn Existential Psychol & Psychiat; Asn Humanistic Psychol. **RESEARCH** Religious and dialogical existentialism; the image of man in the great religions and in modern literature; the inter-relations of philosophical anthropology, ethics, and psychology. **SELECTED PUBLICATIONS** Auth, The Modern Promethean: A Dialogue with Today's Youth, Pendle Hill, 70; Touchstones of Reality: Existential Trust and the Community of Peace, Dutton, 72, 74; coauth, Searching in the Syntax of Things: Experiments in Religion, Fortress, 72; auth, The Worlds of Existentialism: A Critical Reader, Univ Chicago & Phoenix Bks, 73; The Hidden Human Image, Delacorte & Delta Bks, 74; Martin Buber's Life and Work: The Early Years-1878-1923, Dutton & Search, 82; The human way: A dialogical approach to religion and human experience, Anima, 82; Martin Buber's Life and Work: The Middle Years-1923-1945, Dutton 83, and The Later Years-1945-1965, Dutton, 84; auth, Martin Buber and the Eternal, Human Science, 86; auth, Abraham Joshua Heschel and Elie Wiesel: You Are My Witnesses, Farrar, Straus, Giroux, 87; auth, A Dialogue with Hasidic Tales: Hallowing the Everyday, Human Science, 88; auth, Encounter on the Narrow Ridge: A Life of Martin Buber, Paragon House, 91, paperback, Span ed, 93, Jap trans, 99, Ger trans, 99; auth, Dialogue and the Human Image: Beyond Humanistic Psychology, Sage, 92; auth, Religion and Psychology: A Dialogical Approach, Paragon House, 92; auth, A Heart of Wisdom: Religion and Human Wholeness, State Univ NY Press, 92; auth, Intercultural Dialogue and the Human Image: Maurice Friedman at the Indira Gandhi Centre for the Arts, New Delhi, India, 95; ed-in-chief, Martin Buber and the Human Sciences, State Univ NY Press, 96; auth, The Affirming Flame: A Poetics of Meaning, Prometheus Books, 99. **CONTACT ADDRESS** 421 Hilmen Pl, Solana Beach, CA, 92075. **EMAIL** friedma3@mail.sdsu.edu

FRIEDMAN, MICHAEL
DISCIPLINE PHILOSOPHY **EDUCATION** Queens Col, BA, 69; Priceton Univ, PhD, 73. **CAREER** Prof. **HONORS AND AWARDS** Franklin J. Matchette Prize, 85; Lakatos Award, 87. **MEMBERSHIPS** Am Philos Asn; Am Acad Sci. **RESEARCH** Relationship between the history of science and the history of philosophy in the period from Kant to Carnap; history and philosophy of the exact sciences. **SELECTED PUBLICATIONS** Auth, Foundations of Space-Time Theories: Relativistic Physics and Philosophy of Science, 85; Geometry, Convention, and the Relativized A Priori, Univ Pittsburgh, 94; Poincare's Conventionalism and the Logical Positivists, 95; Overcoming Metaphysics: Carnap and Heidegger, Univ Minn, 96. **CONTACT ADDRESS** Dept of History and Philosophy of Science, Indiana Univ, Bloomington, 300 N Jordan Ave, Bloomington, IN, 47405. **EMAIL** mlfriedm@indiana.edu

FRIEDMAN, PHILIP ALLAN
PERSONAL Born 07/19/1927, Brooklyn, NY **DISCIPLINE** ENGLISH LITERATURE, AMERICAN PHILOSOPHY **EDUCATION** NY Univ, BA, 48; Columbia Univ, MA, 49; Univ Heidelberg, cert ling and philol, 55. **CAREER** Reporter and bk reviewer, Jewish Examiner, 48-49; prof asst, Toby Press, New York, 50-51; asst ed, Random House, Inc, New York, 51-52; instr English compos and contemp lit, Wayne State Univ, 53-54, 55-58; from asst prof to assoc prof Am Lit and studies, Calif State Univ, Los Angeles, 59-77, prof, 77-80., Consult, State Dept Comt For Visitors, Mich, 53-54, 55-58; consult and mem bd, Jewish Community Libr, Jewish Fed Coun Greater Los Angeles, 72; consult drama, Henry Street Settlement Children's Theater, 77-; referee and consult history, Hist, 78-. **MEMBERSHIPS** AAUP. **RESEARCH** Am Lit and culture; philosophy of science. **SELECTED PUBLICATIONS** Auth, Slapping Back, Aba J, Vol 82, 96. **CONTACT ADDRESS** 100 N Detroit Los, Los Angeles, CA, 90036.

FRIEDMAN, RICHARD ELLIOTT
DISCIPLINE BIBLE, NEAR EASTERN LANGUAGES AND LITERATURES **EDUCATION** Harvard Univ, ThD, 78. **CAREER** Assoc Prof Bible, Univ Calif, San Diego, 76-. **RESEARCH** Literary and historical research in bible. **SELECTED PUBLICATIONS** Auth, The Refiners Fire--The Making of Mormon Cosmology, 1644-1844, J Interdisciplinary Hist, Vol 27, 96; Religion in a Revolutionary Age, Pennsylvania Mag Hist Biog, Vol 121, 97; Law and Ideology in Monarchic Israel, J Am Orient Soc, Vol 114, 94. **CONTACT ADDRESS** Dept of Lit C-005, Univ of Calif, 9500 Gilman Dr, La Jolla, CA, 92093-5003.

FRIEDMAN, WILLIAM HILLEL
PERSONAL Born 03/21/1937, Philadelphia, PA, m, 1968, 2 children **DISCIPLINE** PHILOSOPHY **EDUCATION** Gratz Col, Bhl, 58; Univ Pa, 60, MA, 62; Univ Va, PhD (philos), 70. **CAREER** Instr math, Philadelphia Pub Schs, 61-66; instr philos, Pa State Univ, 63-66; asst prof, Mary Washington Col, 66-67; asst instr, Univ Va, 67-69; asst prof, Va Commonwealth Univ, 69-75; ASST PROF PHILOS, VA STATE COL, 77-, Evaluator, Project Opportunity, 68. **MEMBERSHIPS** Am Philos Asn: Southern Soc Philos and Psychol. **RESEARCH** Logic; philosophy of science; contemporary philosophy. **SELECTED PUBLICATIONS** Auth, The Nlrb Suffers Institutional Amnesia--The Paramax Decision, Labor Law J, Vol 44, 93. **CONTACT ADDRESS** 5613 Indigo Rd, Richmond, VA, 23230.

FRIEL, JAMES P.
PERSONAL Bronx, NY, m, 1976 **DISCIPLINE** PHILOSOPHY, LITERATURE **EDUCATION** Marist Col, BA, 56; Fordham Univ, MA, 65. **CAREER** Teacher English, Marist Bro Schs, 56-63 & Cent Sch Dist, Syosset, 63-68; prof philos, Marist Col & Col of Mt St Vincent, 68-69; Prof English & Philos, State Univ NY Farmingdale, 70-, Ed, Aitia Mag, 72-; State Univ NY grant, 73; Matchette Found grant & dir study group, 76-80; chmn two-yr teaching comt, Am Philos Asn, 77-82. **MEMBERSHIPS** Am Philos Asn; Nat Workshop Conf; Nat Info & Resource Ctr Teaching Philos. **RESEARCH** Metaphysics; humor; citizenship. **SELECTED PUBLICATIONS** Ed, Philosophy of Religion, State Univ NY, 73; auth, Citizen apprenticeship, Aitia Mag, 74-75; ed, Philosophy, Law, Modern Citizen, State Univ NY Farmingdale, 75; auth, Report on National Workship Conference, Aitia Mag, 76; Paying through the nose to lift those Sunday blues, Newday, 10/76; The mall the merrier, or is it?, NY Times, 11/76; ed, Nineteenth Century American Literature, State Univ NY, (in press). **CONTACT ADDRESS** SUNY, Farmingdale, 1250 Melville Rd, Farmingdale, NY, 11735-1389. **EMAIL** frieljp@suny.farmingdale.edu

FRIEL, MICHAEL K.
DISCIPLINE LAW **EDUCATION** Harvard Univ, BA, JD; NY Univ, LLM. **CAREER** Assoc dean, prof; Univ Fla, 86-, assoc dean, 90 and dir, Grad Tax Prog, 88-; instr, Willamette Univ, 83-87; NY Univ, 82-83; pvt pract, Salem, Oregon 76-81; Oregon Govt Ethics Comt; past dir, Marion-Polk Legal Aid Serv, Salem; VISTA Volunteer Lawyer, Oregon 69-71. **MEMBERSHIPS** Oregon Bar. **RESEARCH** Taxation. **SELECTED PUBLICATIONS** Coauth, Taxation of Individual Income. **CONTACT ADDRESS** School of Law, Univ of Florida, PO Box 117625, Gainesville, FL, 32611-7625. **EMAIL** friel@law.ufl.edu

FRIESEN, DUANE K.
PERSONAL Born 04/27/1940, Newton, KS, m, 1962, 2 children **DISCIPLINE** SOCIAL ETHICS **EDUCATION** Bethel Col, BA, 62; Mennonite Bibl Sem, BD, 65; Harvard Divinity Sch, Harvard Univ, ThD, 72. **CAREER** Prof, bibl & relig, Bethel Col, 70-. **HONORS AND AWARDS** Ralph B. Schrag, Distinguished Teaching Award, 89; David H. Richert Award for Distinguished Scholar, 86; summer stipend for younger humanists, Nat Endow for the Humanities, 73. **MEMBERSHIPS** Soc of Christ Ethics; Amer Acad of Relig; Intl Peace Rcs Asn. **RESEARCH** Theology and culture; Peace and nonviolence. **SELECTED PUBLICATIONS** Co-auth, Just Peacemaking: Ten Practices for Abolishing War, Cleveland, Oh, Pilgrim Press, 98; co-auth, A New Paradigm: Just Peacemaking Theory, Fuller Theol Sem, Overcoming Violence: Local and Global Strategies for Christian Peacemaking, Herald Press, 98; article, Religion and Nonviolent Action, Encycl of Nonviolent Action, Albert Einstein Inst, Cambridge, MA, Garland Publ Inc, 97; auth, Toward a Theology of Culture: A Dialogue with Gordon Kaufman, Mennonite Theology in Face of Modernity Essays in Honor of Gordon D. Kaufman, Bethel Col, 96; auth, Living on the Boundary: Singing God's Song as Citizens and Aliens, A Drink From the Stream II, Bethel Col, 96; auth, A Personal Response to J. L. Burkholder's Autobiographical Reflections, The Limits of Perfections: A Conversation with J. Lawrence Burkholder, Inst of Anabaptist-Mennonite Studies, Conrad Grebel Col, Waterloo, Ontario, Can, 93; auth, Means and Ends: Reflections on Opposing Theologies of History, Nonviolent America: History Through the Eyes of Peace, N. Newton, Kans, Bethel Col, 93; article, Toward a Theology of Culture: A Dialogue with John Howard Yoder and Gordon Kaufman, The Conrad Grebel Rev, 39-64, spring, 98; article, What I Learned from John Howard Yoder, Mennonite Life, mar, 98; article, Towards an Anabaptist Political Philosophy, Transformation: An International Evangelical Dialogue on Mission and Ethics, oct-dec, 97; ed, Mennonite Life, Theology of Gordon Kaufman, mar, 97; article, Singing God's Song as Citizens and Aliens: A Christian Theology of Culture, The Mennonite Quart Rev, apr, 97; article, A People's Movement as a Condition for the Development of a Just Peacemaking Theory, The Merton Annual, 9, 96; article, An Anabaptist Theology of Culture for a New Century, Conrad Grebel Rev, 33-53, winter, 95. **CONTACT ADDRESS** Box 31, North Newton, KS, 67117. **EMAIL** dfriesen@bethelks.edu

FRIGGE, S. MARIELLE
DISCIPLINE RELIGIOUS STUDIES **EDUCATION** Mt Marty Col, BA, 67; Wash Theol Union, MA, 79; Boston Col, PhD, 92. **CAREER** Prof. **MEMBERSHIPS** Benedictine Sisters of Sacred Heart Monastery; Theta Alpha Kappa; Cath Bibl Asn & Amer Benedictine Acad. **SELECTED PUBLICATIONS** Auth, Mundane Mysteries: Daily Life as Sacrament, Amer Benedictine Acad, Atchison, KS, 94 & Modern Feminism and Monastic Women: A Dialogue, triennial chap of the Benedictine Fed St Gertrude the Great, Yankton, SD, 90; assoc ed, Amer Benedictine Rev, 95-97. **CONTACT ADDRESS** Dept of Religious Studies, Mount Marty Col, 1105 W 8th St, Yankton, SD, 57078-3724. **EMAIL** mfrigge@rs6.mtmc.edu

FRISCH, MATHIAS F.
PERSONAL Born 04/07/1964, Munich, Germany, m, 1990 **DISCIPLINE** PHILOSOPHY **EDUCATION** Univ Calif Berkeley, PhD, 98. **CAREER** Asst Prof, Northwest Univ, 98-. **MEMBERSHIPS** Am Philos Asn; Phil of Sci Asn; Gesellrchaft fur Analytische Philosophie. **RESEARCH** Philosophy of Science. **CONTACT ADDRESS** Northwestern Univ, 1818 Hunman Hall, Evanston, IL, 60208. **EMAIL** m-frisch@nwu.edu

FRITSCHE, JOHANNES
DISCIPLINE PHILOSOPHY **EDUCATION** Free Univ Berlin, PhD, 82. **CAREER** Assoc prof, Eugene Lang Col. **RESEARCH** Ancient philos; medieval philos; early Frankfurt School. **SELECTED PUBLICATIONS** Auth, Method and Aim in The First Book of Aristotle's Physics, 86. **CONTACT ADDRESS** Eugene Lang Col, New Sch for Social Research, 66 West 12th St, New York, NY, 10011.

FRITZ, RON
DISCIPLINE LAW **EDUCATION** Windsor Univ, LLB, 71; London Univ, LLM, 72. **CAREER** Assoc prof, 74- **SELECTED PUBLICATIONS** Auth, The Saskatchewan Electoral Boundaries Case and Its Implications, 92; Effective Representation Denied: MacKinnon v. Prince Edward Island, 94; Drawing Electoral Boundaries in Compliance with the Charter: The Alberta Experience, 96. **CONTACT ADDRESS** Col of Law, Univ Saskatchewan, 15 Campus Dr, Saskatoon, SK, S7N 5A6. **EMAIL** Fritz@law.usask.ca

FRIZZELL, LAWRENCE E.
PERSONAL Born 05/28/1938, Calgary, AB, Canada **DISCIPLINE** BIBLICAL STUDIES **EDUCATION** Univ Oxford, PhD, 74; Pontifical Bibl Inst, SSL, 67; Univ Ottawa, STL, 62. **CAREER** Instr, St. Joseph's Sem, 62-64, 67-70; assoc prof, Seton Hall Univ, 75-; dir, Inst Judaeo-Christian Studies, 93-. **HONORS AND AWARDS** Can Coun grant for doctorate studies, 70-73. **MEMBERSHIPS** Soc Bibl Lit; Cath Bibl Asn;

Bibl Theol. **RESEARCH** Christian origins; Christian-Jewish relations. **SELECTED PUBLICATIONS** Auth, Temple and Community: Foundations for Johannine Spirituality, Mystics of the Book, 93; auth, Twenty-five Years Since Vatican II on the Jewish People: An Assessment, New Visions: Historical and Theological Perspectives on the Jewish-Christian Dialogue, 93; auth, Paul the Pharisee, Jewish-Christian Relations Throughout History, 94; auth, Spoils from Egypt Between Jews and Gnostics, Hellenization Revisited: Shaping the Christian Response within the Greco-Roman World, 94; auth, Mary and the Biblical Heritage, Marian Studies, 95; auth, Law at the Service of Humankind, Seeds of Reconciliation, 96; auth, The Bible and the Holy Land: Pastoral Letter from Jerusalem, New Blackfriars, 94; Jewish-Christian Relations and the Dialogue with World Religions, SIDIC, 95; auth, Rabbi, Theologische Realenzyklopadie, 96. **CONTACT ADDRESS** Dept of Judaeo Christian Studies, Seton Hall Univ, South Orange, NJ, 07079. **EMAIL** frizzela@shu.edu

FROEHLICH, CHARLES DONALD
PERSONAL Born 05/07/1927, Goose Creek, TX **DISCIPLINE** THEOLOGY, CLASSICS **EDUCATION** Concordia Sem, BA, 52, BD, 55, STM, 58; Univ Tex, Austin, MA, 52. **CAREER** Instr hist, Greek & Latin, St John's Col, Kans, 50-52; instr, New Testament & Greek, Concordia Sem, 55-57; instr, theol & Latin, Lutheran High Schs, St Louis, 57-62; assoc prof, 62-80, Prof Theol & Class Lang, Concordia Teachers Col, Ill, 80- **MEMBERSHIPS** Class Asn Midwest & S. **RESEARCH** New Testament; medieval Christianity; patristics. **SELECTED PUBLICATIONS** Auth, Logophiles of the world, unite!, Lutheran Educ, 11-12/73. **CONTACT ADDRESS** Dept of Theol, Concordia Univ, Illinois, 7400 Augusta St, River Forest, IL, 60305-1402.

FROHLICH, MARY
PERSONAL Born 06/15/1950, Athens, OH **DISCIPLINE** SPIRITUALITY **EDUCATION** Antioch Coll, BA, 73; Cath Univ , MA, 82; PhD, 90. **CAREER** Lectr, Trinity Coll, 90-02; lectr, Wheeling Jesuit Coll, 91-92; lectr, Cath Univ Am, 86-88 and 91-92; lectr, Georgetown Univ, 91-92; lectr, St Michael's Coll, 94; asst prof, Cath Theol Univ, 93-. **HONORS AND AWARDS** AAUW Dissertation Fel, 88. **MEMBERSHIPS** Soc for the Study of Christian Spirituality; Am Acad of Rel; Cath Theol Soc of Am; Coll Theol Soc. **RESEARCH** Spiritual Classics; Spirituality and Psychology; Ecospirituality. **SELECTED PUBLICATIONS** Auth, Praying with Scripture, 93; The Intersubjectivity of the Mystic: A Study of Teresa of Avila's Interior Castle, 93; articles on spirituality, 81-97. **CONTACT ADDRESS** Catholic Theol Union at Chicago, 5401 S Cornell Ave, Chicago, IL, 60615. **EMAIL** frohlich@ctu.edu

FROST, JERRY WILLIAM
PERSONAL Born 03/17/1940, Muncie, IN, m, 1963, 1 child **DISCIPLINE** AMERICAN & CHURCH HISTORY **EDUCATION** DePauw Univ, BA, 62; Univ WI, MA, 65, PhD, 68. **CAREER** Asst prof Am hist, Vassar Col, 67-73; assoc prof & dir relig, Friends Hist Libr, 73-79, prof, 79, Jenkins prof Quaker hist & res, Swarthmore Col, 80-, Fel, John Carter Brown Libr, 70; USIP Fel, 85, Philadelphia Inst for Early Am Studies Fel, 80, Lang Fel, 81, 97; ed, Pa Mag Hist & Biog, 81-86. **HONORS AND AWARDS** Brit Friends Hist Asn, pres, 98. **MEMBERSHIPS** Friends Hist Soc; Am Soc Church Hist. **RESEARCH** Quakers; Am family; peace research. **SELECTED PUBLICATIONS** Auth, Quaker Family in Colonial America, St Martins, 73; Connecticut Education in the Revolutionary Era, Pequot, 74; Origins of the Quaker crusade against slavery: A review of recent literature, spring 78, Quaker Hist; ed, The Keithian Controversy in Early Pennsylvania, 80 & Quaker Origins of Antislavery, 81, Norwood; Years of crisis and separation: Philadelphia yearly meeting, 1790-1860, In: Friends in the Delaware Valley, 81; Seeking the Light, Essays in Quaker History, Pendle Hill, 87; co-auth, The Quakers, Greenwood, 88; auth, A Perfect Freedom: Religious Liberty in Pennsylvania, Cambridge, 90; Our deeds carry our message: The early history of the American Friends Service Committee, Quaker Hist, 92; co-auth, Christianity: a Social and Cultural History, Prentice Hall, 98. **CONTACT ADDRESS** Friends Hist Libr, Swarthmore Col, 500 College Ave, Swarthmore, PA, 19081-1306.

FRUG, GERALD ELLISON
PERSONAL Born 07/31/1939, Berkeley, CA, m, 1968, 2 children **DISCIPLINE** LAW **EDUCATION** Univ Calif, Berkeley, BA, 60; Harvard Univ, LLB, 63. **CAREER** Law clerk to Chief Justice Roger Traynor, Supreme Ct Calif, 64-65; atty, Heller, Elhrman, White & McAuliffe, 65-66; special asst to chmn, Equal Employment Opportunity Comm, 66-69; atty, Cravath, Swaine & Moore, 69-70; gen coun & adminr, Health Serv Admin, New York, 70-74; prof law, Univ Pa, 74-81; Prof Law Harvard Univ, 81-, Vis prof, Law Sch, Harvard Univ, 78-79. **MEMBERSHIPS** Law as ideology; legal states of decentralized institutions (cities and property owners); jurisprudence. **SELECTED PUBLICATIONS** Auth, City Services, 4/98, NYU Law Rev; Geography of Community 5/96, Stanford Law Review; The city as a legal concept, Harvard Law Rev,4/80. **CONTACT ADDRESS** Law School, Harvard Univ, 1525 Massachusetts Ave, Cambridge, MA, 02138-2903. **EMAIL** frug@law.harvard.edu

FRY, MICHAEL G.
PERSONAL Born 11/05/1932, Brierley, England, m, 1957, 3 children **DISCIPLINE** ECONOMICS, HISTORY **EDUCATION** London Sch of Econ, B Sc, 56, PhD, 63. **CAREER** Prof Hist, 66-77, Carleton Univ, Ottawa, Can; dean & prof, 77-80, Grad Sch of Int Stud, Univ Denver; dir & prof, 80-98, Univ So Calif, School of Int Affairs. **HONORS AND AWARDS** NATO fel; vpres Int Stud Asn; fel of the Royal Hist Soc, UK. **MEMBERSHIPS** Int Stud Asn; Royal Hist Asn; SHAFR. **RESEARCH** North Atlantic relations; north Pacific relations; British foreign policy; Middle East. **SELECTED PUBLICATIONS** Auth, Eisenhower, Dulles and the Suez Crisis of 1956, Reexamining the Eisenhower Presidency, Greenwood Press, 93; auth, The Forgotten Crisis of 1957: Gaza and Sharm-el-Sheikh, Int Hist Rev 15, 1, 93, Revue d'Histoire Diplomatique, 93; auth, Epistemic Communities: Intelligence Studies & International Relations, Intel & Nat Security, 8, 3, 93; auth, Epistemic Communities: Intelligence Studies and International Relations, Espionage: Past, Present and Future, Cass, 94; auth, The Pacific Dominion and the Washington Conference, 1921-22, The Wash Conf, 1921-22 and The Road to Pearl Harbor, Cass, 94; auth, The United States, the United Nations and the Lebanon Crisis, 1958: Intelligence and Statecraft, in Intelligence and National Security 10,1, 95; auth, British Revisionism, Ctr for Ger & European Stud, Univ Calif, 95; auth, British Revisionism, in The 1919 Peace Settlement and Germany, Cambridge Univ Press, 96; auth, The North Pacific Triangle at Century's End: Canada, Japan and the United States, 98; ed, The Guide to Modern Politics and Diplomacy, Oxford Univ Press. **CONTACT ADDRESS** School of Int Relations, Univ of Southern California, VKC 330, Univ Park, Los Angeles, CA, 90089-0043.

FRYMER-KENSKY, TIKVA SIMONE
PERSONAL Chicago, IL, m, 2 children **DISCIPLINE** BIBLICAL STUDIES **EDUCATION** CUNY, AB 65; Jewish Theol Sem, BHL, 65; Yale Univ, MA, 67, PhD, 77. **CAREER** Vis assoc prof, 88, JTS grad schl; vis assoc prof, 91-93, Jewish Theol Sem; dir, bibl stud, 88-96, Reconstructionist Rabbinical Col; prof, Hebrew Bible, 95-, Univ Chicago Div Schl. **HONORS AND AWARDS** Dropsie Fel, 97-98; Annenberg Res Fel, 9091; NEH, 80-81; Wayne St Univ Fac Res Grant, 78; Danforth Found Grad Fel, 65; Woodrow Wilson Grad Fel, 65. **MEMBERSHIPS** AAR/SBL; AOS; Bibl Colloquim. **RESEARCH** Biblical law; women in Bible; mythology & Bible; theol. **SELECTED PUBLICATIONS** Auth, In the Wake of the Goddesses: Women, Culture and the Biblical Transformation of Pagan Myth, Macmillan, 92; auth, Motherprayer: The Pregnant Women's Spiritual Companion, Putnam-Riverhead, 95; auth, From Jerusalem to the Edge of Heaven: Meditations on the Soul of Israel, Jew Pub Soc, 96. **CONTACT ADDRESS** Divinity Sch, Univ of Chicago, 1025 E 58th St, Chicago, IL, 60637. **EMAIL** tfrymerk@midway.uchicago.edu

FUERST, WESLEY J.
DISCIPLINE OLD TESTAMENT **EDUCATION** Central Lutheran Theol Sem; Princeton Theol Sem, PhD. **CAREER** Dean of fac; dir of grad stud; prof-. **SELECTED PUBLICATIONS** Auth, Key Bible Words; Cambridge Bible Commentary on The Books of Ruth Esther; Ecclesiastes; The Songs of Songs, Lamentations: The Five Scrolls. **CONTACT ADDRESS** Dept of Old Testament, Lutheran Sch of Theol, 1100 E 55th St, Chicago, IL, 60615. **EMAIL** wfuerst@lstc.edu

FUERST, WESLEY J.
PERSONAL Born 10/23/1930, Hildreth, NE, 3 children **DISCIPLINE** THEOLOGY **EDUCATION** Midland Col, BA, 51; Cent Lutheran Theol Sem, BD, 54; Princeton Theol Sem, ThD, 58. **CAREER** Prof Old Testament, Cent Lutheran Theol Sem, 57-61; Facultad Luterana de Teol, Arg, 62-64 & Cent Lutheran Theol Sem, 65-66; Prof Old Testament Lutheran Sch Theol at Chicago, 66-, Dean Fac, 69-79. **HONORS AND AWARDS** Franklin Clark Fry fel, 69-70, D D Midland Luth Col, 85. **MEMBERSHIPS** Soc Bibl Lit. **RESEARCH** Jeremiah; Megilloth. **SELECTED PUBLICATIONS** Auth, Key Bible Words, Fortress, 64; The Five Scrolls, in Cambridge Bible Commentary, 75. **CONTACT ADDRESS** Lutheran Sch of Theol, 1100 E 55th St, Chicago, IL, 60615-5199.

FULLER, ALFREDIA Y.
PERSONAL Born 06/19/1958, Miami, FL, d **DISCIPLINE** LAW **EDUCATION** University of Maryland, BSBA, 1982; Antioch School of Law, JD, 1986. **CAREER** Skadden, Arps, law clerk, 1986-88; Fidelity Mortgage Company, president, 1990-91; George Washington University, Washington Saturday College, lecturer, 1992-93; Law Offices of Alfredia Y Fuller, Attorney, 1988-. **MEMBERSHIPS** National Bar Association, chairman, Bankruptcy Law Section, 1993-95; National Association of Black Women Attorneys, 1995; District of Columbia Superior Court, certified mediator, 1985-; District of Columbia Bar Association, 1989-; Isle of Patmos Baptist Church WDC, trustee, 1989-91; National Bar Association, board of governors, 1993-; Washington Saturday College, board of trustees, 1992-. **SELECTED PUBLICATIONS** Contributing Writer, National Bar Association Magazine, 1994-95. **CONTACT ADDRESS** Law Offices of Alfredia Y. Fuller, 601 Pennsylvania Ave NW, Ste 700, Washington, DC, 20004.

FULLER, GEORGE CAIN
DISCIPLINE PRACTICAL THEOLOGY **EDUCATION** Haverford Col, BS, 53; Princeton Theol Sem, MDiv, 56; Westminster Theol Sem, ThM, 62, ThD, 64; Babson Col, MBA, 76. **CAREER** Prof, Northwestern Col, 63-66; assoc prof, Reformed Theol Sem, 71-72; exec dir, Nat Presbyterian and Reformed Fel, 76-83; prof, Westminster Theol Sem, 78-. **HONORS AND AWARDS** Pastor, Covenant Presbyterian Church, 92-. **SELECTED PUBLICATIONS** Auth, Save Time and Invest People, Eternity, 82; Game of Life, Eternity, 84; The Life of Jesus, After The Ascension, Westminster Theol Jour, 94. **CONTACT ADDRESS** Westminister Theol Sem, PO Box 27009, Philadelphia, PA, 19118.

FULLER, REGINALD H.
DISCIPLINE NEW TESTAMENT **EDUCATION** Univ Cambridge, BA, 37, MA, 41; Gen Theol Sem, STD; Philadelphia Divinity Sch, STD; Seabury-Western Theol Sem, DD; Nashota House, DHL; Univ South, DD. **CAREER** Lectr, Queen's Col, 46-50; Birmingham Univ, 46-50; prof, St David's Univ Col, 50-55; Seabury-Western Theol Sem, 55-66; Baldwin prof, Union Theol Sem, 66-72; Molly Laird Downs prof, 72-85; prof emeri, Va Theol Sem, 85-. **SELECTED PUBLICATIONS** Auth, The Quest of the Historical Mary, Hopes and Visions: Papers of the Ecumenical Society of the Blessed Virgin Mary in the United States of America, 96; Biblical studies 1955-1990, Anglican Theol Rev, 94; Christ and Christianity: Studies in the Formation of Christology, Trinity Press Intl, 94; Jesus as Prophet, Va Sem Jour, 94. **CONTACT ADDRESS** Va Theol Sem, 3737 Seminary Rd, Alexandria, VA, 22304.

FULLER, ROBERT CHARLES
PERSONAL Born 05/06/1952, Grand Rapids, MI, m, 1975, 2 children **DISCIPLINE** RELIGION **EDUCATION** Denison Univ, BA, 74; Univ Chicago, PhD, 78. **CAREER** PROF RELIGIOUS STUDIES, BRADLEY UNIV, 78- . **RESEARCH** Contemporary American Religion **SELECTED PUBLICATIONS** "Religion and Ritual in American Wine Culture," Jour of Am Culture, 93; Alternative Therapies, The Encycl of Bioethics, Macmillan, 94; "Wine, Symbolic Boundary Setting, and American Religious Communities," Jour Am Acad Relig, 95; Holistic Health Practices, Spirituality and the Secular Quest, Crossroad, 96; Erikson, Psychology, and Religion, Pastoral Psychol, 96; "The Will to Believe: A Centennial Reflection," Jour Am Acad Religion, 96; Religion and Wine, Univ Tenn Press, 96; Naming the Antichrist, Oxford Univ Press, 95. **CONTACT ADDRESS** Dept of Religious Studies, Bradley Univ, Peoria, IL, 61625. **EMAIL** rcf@bradley.bradley.edu

FULLER, RUSSELL T.
DISCIPLINE OLD TESTAMENT **EDUCATION** Bob Jones Univ, BS, MA; Dropsie Col, dr stud; Hebrew Union Col, MPhil, PhD. **CAREER** Asst prof, Mid-Continent Col; asst prof, S Baptist Theol Sem, 98-. **RESEARCH** Ancient Near Eastern languages, literature and history. **SELECTED PUBLICATIONS** Contrib auth, Zondervan's The New International Dictionary of Old Testament Theology. **CONTACT ADDRESS** Old Testament Dept, Southern Baptist Theol Sem, 2825 Lexington Rd, Louisville, KY, 40280. **EMAIL** rfuller@sbts.edu

FULOP, TIMOTHY E.
PERSONAL Born 09/02/1960, Yokohama, Japan, m, 1982, 4 children **DISCIPLINE** RELIGION **EDUCATION** Wheaton Col, BA; Princeton Theol Sem, M Div, 87; Princeton Univ, MA, 90, PhD, 92. **CAREER** Instr, Drew Univ, 91-92; lectr, Princeton Univ, 92-93; visiting asst prof, Harvard Univ, 93-95; asst dean of fac, Columbia Theol Sem, 95-98; acad dean and vpres, King Col, 98-. **MEMBERSHIPS** Amer Soc of Church Hist; Conf on Faith & Hist; Amer Acad of Relig. **RESEARCH** African-American religion; New religious movements; American Evangelism. **SELECTED PUBLICATIONS** Ed, African-American Religion: Interpretive Essays in History & Culture, Routledge, 97. **CONTACT ADDRESS** King Col, 1350 King College Rd., Bristol, TN, 37620. **EMAIL** tefulop@king.edu

FUMERTON, RICHARD A.
PERSONAL Born 10/07/1949, Toronto, ON, Canada, m, 2 children **DISCIPLINE** PHILOSOPHY **EDUCATION** Univ Toronto, BA, 71; AM, 73, PhD, 74, Brown Univ. **CAREER** Asst Prof, 74-79, Assoc Prof, 79-85, Full Prof, 85-, Univ Iowa. **HONORS AND AWARDS** Woodrow Wilson Fellowship, 71-72; Canada Council Fellowship, 73-74. **MEMBERSHIPS** Amer Phil Assoc. **RESEARCH** Epistemology; metaphysics; value theory **SELECTED PUBLICATIONS** Auth, Reason and Morality: A Defense of the Egocentric Perspective, 90; auth, Metaepistemology and Skepticism, 96. **CONTACT ADDRESS** Dept of Philosophy, Univ of Iowa, 262 EPB, Iowa City, IA, 52242-1408. **EMAIL** richard-fumerton@uiowa.edu

FUNK, DAVID A.
PERSONAL Born 04/22/1927, Wooster, OH, 4 children **DISCIPLINE** LAW **EDUCATION** Col Wooster, BA, 49; Western Reserve Univ, JD, 51; Ohio State Univ, MA, 68; Case Western Reserve Univ, LLM, 72; Columbia Univ, LLM, 73. **CAREER** Partner, Funk, Funk & Eberhart, 51-72; assoc prof to prof, 73-

97, Prof Emeritus Law, Ind Univ Sch of Law, Indianapolis, 97-; Vis lectr, Col Wooster, 62-63; chairperson, Law & Religion Sect, Asn Am Law Sch, 77-81. **MEMBERSHIPS** Am Soc for Legal Hist. **RESEARCH** Philosophy of law. **SELECTED PUBLICATIONS** Auth, Historische Rechstatsachenforschung in Theorie und Praxis, In: Rechtsgeschichte und Rechtssoziologie, West Berlin, Duncker & Humblot, 85; Juridicial Science Paradigms as Newer Rhetorics in 21st Century Jurisprudence, N Ky Law Rev 12, 85; Applications of Political Science to the Analysis and Practice of Law, Ind Law Rev 21, 88; Varieties of Juridicial Science Paradigms For 21st Century Legal Philosophy, In: Nuovi moti per la Formazione del Diritto, CEDAM, Padova, Italy, 88; Traditional Orthodox Hindu Jurisprudence: Justifying Dharma and Danda, S.U. Law Rev 15, 88; Traditional Chinese Jurisprudence: Justifying Li and Fa, S.U. Law Rev 17, 90; Traditional Japanese Jurisprudence: Justifying Loyalty and Law, S.U. Law Rev 17, 90; Traditional Islamic Jurisprudence: Justifying Islamic Law and Government, S.U. Law Rev 20, 93; Cotterrell's Politics of Jurisprudence, Ratio Juris 6, 93; author of numerous other journal articles. **CONTACT ADDRESS** Law Sch, Indiana Univ-Purdue Univ, Indianapolis, 6208 N Delaware St, Indianapolis, IN, 46220-1824.

FURNISH, VICTOR PAUL
PERSONAL Born 11/17/1931, Chicago, IL, m, 1963, 2 children **DISCIPLINE** THEOLOGY **EDUCATION** Cornell Col (Iowa), BA, 52; Garrett-Evangelical Theological Seminary, BD, 55; Yale Univ, PhD, 60. **CAREER** Instr, 59-60, Asst Prof, 60-65, Assoc Prof, 65-71, Prof, 71-83, Univ Distinguished Prof, 83-, Perkins School of Theology, Southern Methodist Univ. **HONORS AND AWARDS** Phi Beta Kappa; United Methodist Church Scholar/Teacher Award, 93-94; SMU Alumni Award for Faculty Excellence, 94; D.H.L. Cornell Col, 95; Festschrift (ed by E. Lovering and J. Sumney), 96. **MEMBERSHIPS** Soc of Biblical Lit; Studioru Novi Testamenti Societas **RESEARCH** Pauline studies; Hellenistic ethics; New Testament theology **SELECTED PUBLICATIONS** Auth, Jesus According to Paul. Understanding Jesus Today, 93; On Putting Paul in His Place, Journal of Biblical Literature, 94; The Bible and Homosexuality: Reading the Texts in Context, Homosexuality in the Church: Both Sides of the Debate, 94; Where is the Truth in Paul's Gospel, Pauline Theology: Looking Back Pressing On, 97; The Theology of the First Letter to the Corinthians, 99. **CONTACT ADDRESS** 6806 Robin Rd., Dallas, TX, 75209. **EMAIL** vfurnish@mail.smu.edu

FURROW, DWIGHT
PERSONAL Born 02/09/1950, Bangor, ME, m, 1982, 1 child **DISCIPLINE** PHILOSOPHY **EDUCATION** Univ CA, Riverside, PhD, 93. **CAREER** VIS ASST PROF, COL OF WILLIAM AND MARY, 96-. **MEMBERSHIPS** Amer Philos Assoc. **RESEARCH** Contemporary European philos; ethics. **SELECTED PUBLICATIONS** Auth, The Discomforts of Home: Nature and Technology in Hand's End, in Research in Philosophy and Technology, fall 95; Review of Richard A. Cohen, Elevations: the Height of the Good in Rosenzweig and Levinas, in Can Philos Rev, June 95; Against Theory: Continental and Analytic Challenges in Moral Philosophy, Routledge, 95; Review of Ronald Bontekoe, Dimensions of the Hermeneutic Circle, in Can Philos Rev, fall 97; Schindler's Compulsion: A Essay on Practical Necessity, in Amer Philos Quart, vol 35, no 3, July, 98; Postmodern Ethics, forthcoming in The Encyclopedia of Ethics, 2nd ed, ed Lawrence C. Becker, Garland Pub. **CONTACT ADDRESS** Dept of Philos, Col of William and Mary, Williamsburg, VA, 23187. **EMAIL** BQNR32A@Prodigy.com

FUSS, PETER L.
PERSONAL Born 02/11/1932, Berlin, Germany, m, 1961, 2 children **DISCIPLINE** PHILOSOPHY **EDUCATION** Fordham Univ, BS, 54; Harvard Univ, MA, 56, PhD, 62. **CAREER** Lectr philos, Univ Mich, 60-61; lectr, Univ Calif, Riverside, 61-62; from asst prof to assoc prof, 62-69; assoc prof, 69-75, PROF PHILOS, UNIV MO, ST LOUIS, 75-; Vis assoc prof philos, Univ Washington, 66 67. **MEMBERSHIPS** Conf Study Polit Thought; Hegel Soc Am; AAUP. **RESEARCH** Kant, Hegel and history of 19th century philosophy; political and moral philosophy. **SELECTED PUBLICATIONS** Coauth, Five Philosophers, Odyssey, 63; auth, The Moral Philosophy of Josiah Royce, 65 & co-ed & translr, Nietzsche: A Self-Portrait from His Letters, 71, Harvard Univ; auth, Some perplexities in Nietzsche, Dialogues Phenomenol, 75; Theory and practice in Hegel and Marx, Polit Theory & Praxis, 77; Royce's concept of the self, Am Philos, 77; Hannah Arendt's Conception of Political Community, Hannah Arendt, 79; coauth, Spirit as Recollection: Hegel's Theory of the Internalizing of Experience, 81; The Silhouette of Dante in Hegel's Phenomenology, Clio, 82; Hegel: 3 Essays, Notre Dame, 84; Rousseau's engagement with amour-propre, Canadian J Pol and Soc Theory, 86; The Two-in-One, Idealistic Studies, 88; James Madison and the classical Republican tradition, Philos Res Archives, 89; Kant's teleology of nature, European Studies Conf, 91; Passion and the genesis of self-consciousness, Mo Philol Asn, 93. **CONTACT ADDRESS** Dept of Philos, Univ Mo, 8001 Natural Bridge, Saint Louis, MO, 63121-4499.

FYKES, LEROY MATTHEWS, JR.
PERSONAL Born 10/23/1945, Indianapolis, IN **DISCIPLINE** LAW **EDUCATION** Univ of So CA, BS 1967; Harvard U, MBA 1974; UCLA, JD 1972; NYU, LlM 1976. **CAREER** Seton Hall Univ Law Ctr, asst prof; Pfizer Inc, atty 1972-75; Nat Black MBA Assn, dir, bd chmn, bd sec 1974-; NYCTI Assn Inc, dir 1975-; Am Arbtrn Assn, arbtrn panel. **MEMBERSHIPS** Mem NY Bar Trustee, bd sec Studio Mus in Harlem 1973; mem 100 Black Men Inc of NYC. **CONTACT ADDRESS** 1111 Raymond Blvd, Newark, NJ, 07102.

G

GABRIELE, EDWARD
PERSONAL Born 04/15/1952, Philadelphia, PA, s **DISCIPLINE** INTERDISCIPLINARY THEOLOGY **EDUCATION** Villanova Univ, BA/BS, 75; Catholic Theological Union, Mdiv, 80; Catholic Univ, DMin, 85. **CAREER** Dir, Office of Res Admin, Naval Medical Res Center, Bethesda, MD; Ecumenical Resident Theologian, Christ the Servant Community, Gaithersburg, MD. **MEMBERSHIPS** Am Acad of Religion; Soc of Res Admins; Nat Coun of Univ Res Admins. **RESEARCH** Ritual analysis; contemporary theological critique; theological literacy. **SELECTED PUBLICATIONS** Auth, Acting Justly, Loving Tenderly, Walking Humbly: Prayers for Peace and Justice, St. Mary's Press, 95; auth, From Many, One. Praying Our Rich and Diverse Cultural Heritage, Ave Maria Press, 95; auth, My Soul Magnifies the Lord: Celebrating Mary in Prayer, Ave Maria Press, 96; auth, Cloud Days and Fire Nights: Canticles for a Pilgrimage Out of Exile, St. Mary's Press, 97; auth, Prayer with Searchers and Saints, St. Mary's Press, 98; auth, Choosing Life and Death: Looking in the Lenten Mirror, Communication, 95; auth, Rending the Veil: The God of Theology Made Manifest, Emmanuel, 95; auth, Partaking at the Table of Justice: The Witness of Christians in Contemporary American Political Life, Emmanuel, 96; auth, Hungering for Peace, Thirsting for Justice: Praying as Jesus Taught Us, Emmanuel, 96. **CONTACT ADDRESS** 20460 Afternoon Ln, Germantown, MD, 20874. **EMAIL** efg52@erols.com

GAETKE, EUGENE ROGER
PERSONAL Born 09/12/1948, St. Paul, MN, m, 1971, 2 children **DISCIPLINE** LAW **EDUCATION** Univ Minn, Minneapolis, BA, 71, JD, 74. **CAREER** Atty, Swanson and Gaetke, Grand Marias, Minn, 74-75; special asst to atty gen, Off Atty Gen, State Minn, 75-77; hearing examiner, Off Hearing Examiners, State Minn, 77-78; asst prof, 78-82, Assoc Prof Law, Col Law, Univ Ky, Lexington, 82-, VIS PROF LAW, LAW SCH, IND UNIV, BLOOMINGTON, 82-. **RESEARCH** Public lands; occupational safety and health; legal ethics. **SELECTED PUBLICATIONS** Auth, Government Lawyers and Their Private Clients under the Fair Housing Act, George Washington Law Rev, Vol 0065, 97. **CONTACT ADDRESS** Law Sch, Indiana Univ, Bloomington, Bloomington, IN, 47402.

GAFFIN, RICHARD BIRCH, JR.
DISCIPLINE PRACTICAL THEOLOGY **EDUCATION** Calvin Col, BA, 58; Westminster Theol Sem, BD, 61, ThM, 62, ThD, 69; Georg-August Univ, Guttingen, grad stud, 65. **CAREER** Prof, Westminster Theol Sem, 65. **SELECTED PUBLICATIONS** Auth, The Centrality of the Resurrection, (Resurrection and Redemption); Perspectives on Pentecost; The Holy Spirit and Eschatology, Kerux, 89. **CONTACT ADDRESS** Westminister Theol Sem, PO Box 27009, Philadelphia, PA, 19118. **EMAIL** rgaffin@hslc.org

GAFFNEY, JOHN PATRICK
PERSONAL Born 04/04/1928, New York, NY **DISCIPLINE** THEOLOGY, PHILOSOPHY **EDUCATION** St Louis de Montfort Sem, STB, 54; Pontif Univ St Thomas, Rome, STL, 56, STD, 57. **CAREER** Prof dogmatic theol, St Louis de Montfort Sem, 57-61, rector and prof Mariol, 62-66; lectr theol, Cath Univ PR and Inter-Am Univ PR, 66-67; assoc profand mem bd dirs divinity sch, 69-74, chmn dept, 69-75, PROF THEOL, ST LOUIS UNIV, 74-,Prof theol, Seat of Wisdom Col, 59-61; supvr, Montfort House Studies, St Louis, Mo, 68-75; examr, NCent Asn Cols and Univs, 69-; vchmn theol comn, St Louis Archdiocese, 70-; assoc ed, Horizons, Col Theol Soc, 80; vis lectr, Mt St Mary's Col, Los Angeles, 82. **HONORS AND AWARDS** Nancy McNeir Ring for Best Teacher of Year, St Louis Univ, 72. **MEMBERSHIPS** Col Theol Soc; Am Acad Relig; Mariological Soc Am. **RESEARCH** Christology; Mariology. **SELECTED PUBLICATIONS** Auth, Mary for All Christians, J Ecumenical Stud, Vol 0029, 92; The Virgin Goddess--Studies in the Pagan and Christian Roots of Mariology, J Ecumenical Stud, Vol 0031, 94; The Church in the Movement of the Spirit, J Ecumenical Stud, Vol 0033, 96. **CONTACT ADDRESS** Dept of Theol Studies, St Louis Univ, St Louis, MO, 63103.

GAFNI, ABRAHAM J.
DISCIPLINE TRIAL PRACTICE **EDUCATION** Yeshiva Univ, BA, BHL, 60; Harvard Law Sch, JD, 63. **CAREER** Prof & dir,Villanova Univ, 94. **HONORS AND AWARDS** Distinguished serv awd, Pa Conf State Trial Judges; Outstanding serv awd, Pa Dist Attorneys Asn; Distinguished serv awd, Philadelphia Bar Asn. **MEMBERSHIPS** Past Justice, Supreme Ct of the World Zionist Orgn; chem resolutions comt, Jewish Agency Assembly; Steering Comt, Pa Futures Comn on Justice in the 21st Century; Medical Ethics Comt, Philadelphia Geriatric Ctr. **RESEARCH** Trial advocacy; dispute resolution. **SELECTED PUBLICATIONS** Publ in, Temple Law Quart & Pa Law Quart. **CONTACT ADDRESS** Law School, Villanova Univ, 800 Lancaster Ave, Villanova, PA, 19085-1692. **EMAIL** gafni@law.vill.edu

GAGNON, CAROLLE
DISCIPLINE PHILOSOPHY **EDUCATION** Laval Univ, PhD. **RESEARCH** Logic; linguistics; semiotics; aesthetics. **SELECTED PUBLICATIONS** Auth, Metaphor as a particular case of influence, Semiotica, 98; auth, Analyse logique de la declaration des droits de la femme et de la citoyenne, Olympe de Gouges, 95; auth, Nouvelles societes, nouveaux mythes?, Philosophiques, 94; auth, Le feminisme est-il une ideologie?, Les Cahiers du Grad, 93. **CONTACT ADDRESS** Philosophy Dept, Laurentian Univ, 935 Ramsey Lake Rd, Sudbury, ON, P3E 2C6.

GAINES, ROBERT N.
DISCIPLINE PHILOSOPHY OF COMMUNICATIONS **EDUCATION** Univ IA, PhD, 82. **CAREER** Assoc prof; grad dir, Univ MD. **RESEARCH** Rhetorical theory in ancient times. **SELECTED PUBLICATIONS** Auth, Cicero's Response to the Philosophers in De oratore, Book 1, Rhetoric and Pedagogy: Its History, Philosophy, and Practice. Essays in Honor of James J. Murphy, Lawrence Erlbaum Assoc, Inc, 95; Knowledge and Discourse in Gorgias' On the Non-Existent or On Nature, Philos & Rhet 30, 97. **CONTACT ADDRESS** Dept of Commun, Univ MD, 4229 Art-Sociology Building, College Park, MD, 20742-1335. **EMAIL** rg1@umail.umd.edu

GAISER, FREDERICK J.
DISCIPLINE OLD TESTAMENT **EDUCATION** Kalamazoo Col, BA, 59; Evangel Lutheran Theol Sem, MDiv, 63; Univ Heidelberg, Ger, ThD, 85. **CAREER** Instr, CENCOAD, Augustana Col, Sioux Falls; act dean of students, 86-88; lectr, 73; registrar, 75-77; dir, Grad Stud (s); prof, 81-. **HONORS AND AWARDS** Res chemist, Upjohn Pharm, 59-60; interim pastor, Emmanuel Lutheran Church, Warren, Ohio, 63; pastor, St. Paul Lutheran Church, 69-74. **MEMBERSHIPS** Mem, Soc Bibl Lit. **SELECTED PUBLICATIONS** Auth, Psalms, Search Bible Stud, Unit 13; contrib, A Handbook on Conversion; A Primer on Christian Prayer; ed, Word & World, 88. **CONTACT ADDRESS** Dept of Old Testament, Luther Sem, 2481 Como Ave, St. Paul, MN, 55108. **EMAIL** fgaiser@luthersem.edu

GALANTER, MARC
PERSONAL Born 02/18/1931, Philadelphia, PA, m, 1967, 3 children **DISCIPLINE** LAW, SOCIOLOGY OF LAW **EDUCATION** Univ Chicago BA, 50, MA, 54, JD, 56. **CAREER** Instr law, Univ Chicago, 56-57; asst prof, Stanford Univ, 58-59; from vis asst prof to assoc prof soc sci, Univ Chicago, 59-71; prof law, State Univ NY Buffalo, 71-76; vis prof, 76-77, Prof Law & S Asian Studies, Law Sch, Univ Wis, 77-, Sr fel, Law & Modernization Prog, Yale Univ, 70-71; ed, Law & Soc Rev, 72-76; mem comt on law & soc sci, Soc Sci Res Coun, 75-84; mem adv panel for law & soc sci prog, NSF, 76-78; fel, Nat Endowment for Humanities, 79-80; fel, Van Leer Jerusalem Found, 80; consult, Ford Found, New Delhi, 81-84; Guggenheim Found fel, 85-86; chmn, Int Union Anthrop Ethnol Sci Comn on Folk Law & Legal Pluralism, 81-83; pres, Law & Soc Asn, 83-85; Dir, disputes processing res prog, 84-; Dir, Inst Legal Studies, 90-98; fel, Center Advan Studies Behavioral Sci, 97-98. **HONORS AND AWARDS** Kalven Prize, Las & Soc Asn; Hon prof, Nat Law Sch India. **MEMBERSHIPS** Law & Soc Asn; Am Law Inst; Am Acad Arts & Sci. **RESEARCH** Law and soc change; lawyers, litigation; law and relig. **SELECTED PUBLICATIONS** Auth, Religious freedoms in the United States: A turning point, Wis Law Rev, 66; The abolition of disabilities: Untouchability and the law, In: The Untouchables in Contemporary India, Univ Ariz, 72; auth, Why the haves come out ahead: Speculations on the limits of legal change, 74; Justice in many rooms: Courts, private ordering and indigenous law, J Legal Pluralism, 81; Reading the Landscape of Disputes, UCLA Law Rev, 83; Competing Equalities and the Backward Classes: Law in India, Univ of Calif Press, 1984; Law and Society in Modern India, Oxford Univ Press, 89; Tournament of lawyers, Univ Chicago Press, 91; News from Nowhere, Denver Law Rev, 92; Real World Torts, Md Law Rev, 96. **CONTACT ADDRESS** Law Sch, Univ of Wisconsin, 975 Bascom Mall, Madison, WI, 53706-1301. **EMAIL** msgalant@facstaff.wisc.edu

GALGAN, GERALD J.
PERSONAL Born 06/12/1942, New York, NY **DISCIPLINE** PHILOSOPHY **EDUCATION** Fordham Univ, PhD, 71. **CAREER** St Francis Col, Brooklyn, prof, ch dept philos, 66-. **MEMBERSHIPS** APA, ACPA, HSA. **RESEARCH** Modern and medieval philosophy. **SELECTED PUBLICATIONS** Auth, The Logic of Modernity, NY univ Press, 82; God and Subjectivity, Lang, 90; auth, Interpreting the Present, Univ Press Amer, 93. **CONTACT ADDRESS** Dept of Philosophy, St Francis Col, 180 Remsen St., Brooklyn, NY, 11201.

GALIS, LEON
PERSONAL Born 05/16/1939, Athens, GA, m, 1968 **DISCIPLINE** PHILOSOPHY **EDUCATION** Univ GA, AB, 61; Univ NC, PhD, 66. **CAREER** From Asst Prof to Assoc Prof, 65-92, Prof Philos, Franklin & Marshall Col, 92. **MEMBERSHIPS** Am Philos Asn. **RESEARCH** Soc philos; ethics. **SELECTED PUBLICATIONS** Auth, Merely Academic Diversity, J Higher Educ, 64; Of Words and Tools Again, Inquiry, 68; co-ed, Knowing: Essays in the Analysis of Knowledge, Random, 70; auth, The Democratic Case Against the Democratic College, J of Higher Educ, 73; The State-Soul Analogy in Plato's Argument that Justice Pays, J Hist of Philos, 74; The Real and Unrefuted Rights Thesis, Philos Rev, 92; Medea's Metamorphosis, Eranos, 92. **CONTACT ADDRESS** Franklin and Marshall Col, PO Box 3003, Lancaster, PA, 17604-3003. **EMAIL** LeonGalis@aol.com

GALL, ROBERT S.
PERSONAL Born 01/13/1958, Los Angeles, CA, s **DISCIPLINE** RELIGIOUS STUDIES; PHILOSOPHY OF RELIGION **EDUCATION** Univ. Penn, BA, 78; Temple Univ, MA, 80, PhD, 84. **CAREER** Univ N Iowa, asst prof, 84-85; Univ Wiscon, lectr, 85-86; Blackburn Col, asst prof, 86-87; Sinclair Com Col, asst prof, 88-95; Park Col, asst prof, 95-. **HONORS AND AWARDS** NEH Grant, 90; NEH SS Grant, 91,94; Who's Who Relig, 92-94; Who's Who Amer Tchr, 98 **MEMBERSHIPS** APA, SPEP, IAPL, CSPA, AAR **RESEARCH** Philo Relig; Contemp Euro Philo. **SELECTED PUBLICATIONS** Auth, Beyond Theism and Atheism: Heidegger's Significance for Religious Thinking, 87; art, Living on (Happily) Ever After: Derrida, Philosophy and the Comic, Philo Today, 94; Toward a Tragic Theology: The Piety of Thought in Heidegger and Tragedy, Jour Lit and Theol, 93; Review of Religion, Ontotheology and Deconstruction, Crit Rev of Bks in Relig, 91. **CONTACT ADDRESS** Dept of Philosophy and Religion, Park Col, Box 29, Parkville, MO, 64152. **EMAIL** rsgall@tfs.net

GALLAGHER, DAVID M.
PERSONAL Born 12/19/1956, Binghamton, NY, s **DISCIPLINE** PHILOSOPHY **EDUCATION** Univ Navarra, Spain, BA, 80; Catholic Univ of Am, MA, 84, PhD, 89. **CAREER** Asst prof, 88-94, assoc prof, 94- , Catholic Univ of Am. **MEMBERSHIPS** APA; Am Catholic Philos Asn; Societe Int pour la Etude de la Philos Medievale. **RESEARCH** Ethics; Thomas Aquinas. **SELECTED PUBLICATIONS** Ed, Thomas Aquinas and His Legacy, Catholic University of America, 94; auth, Thomas Aquinas, in Roth, ed, Ready Reference: Ethics, Salem, 94; auth, Free Choice and Free Judgement in Thomas Aquinas, Archiv fur Geschichte der Philosophie, 94; auth, Person and Ethics in Thomas Aquinas, Acta Philos, 95; auth, Aquinas, Abelard and the Ethics of Intention, in Lockey, ed, Studies in Thomistic Theology, Univ of Notre Dame, 96; auth, Desire for Beatitude and Love of Friendship in Thomas Aquinas, Mediaeval Stud, 96; auth, Moral Virtue and Contemplation: A Note on the Unity of the Moral Life, Sapientia, 96. **CONTACT ADDRESS** School of Philosophy, Catholic Univ of America, Washington, DC, 20008. **EMAIL** gallagher@cua.edu

GALLAGHER, SHAUN
DISCIPLINE PHILOSOPHY **EDUCATION** Villanova Univ, MA, 76; SUNY, MA, 87; Bryn Mawr Col, PhD, 80. **CAREER** Adj instr, Villanova Univ, 77-81; asst prof, Gwynedd-Mercy Col, 80-81; asst prof, 81-86, assoc prof, 86-93, dir, cognitive science, 96-, prof, philosophy, 93-, Canisius Col, 81-; invited vis sci, Med Res Coun: Cognitive Brain Sci Unit Cambridge Univ, 94. **HONORS AND AWARDS** Whiting Found Fel, 79-80; Lowery Fac Res Fel, 84; Fac Res Fel Canisius Col, 89, 92, 97; Chercheur libre: Inst Sup de Philos KU Louvain, 79-80. **MEMBERSHIPS** Amer Philos Asn; Merleau-Ponty Circle; Soc Phenomenol & Existential Philo; Int Forum on Persons. **RESEARCH** Philosophy of mind; Cognitive science esp personal identity, embodiment; Phenomenology, Hermeneutics; Critical Theory, Philosophy of Time. **SELECTED PUBLICATIONS** Auth, Hermeneutics and Education, SUNY Press, 92; ed, Merleau-Ponty, Hermeneutics, and Postmodernism, SUNY Press, 92; auth, The Place of Phronesis in Postmodern Hermeneutics, Philos Today, 93; The Historikerstreit and the Critique of Nationalism, History of European Ideas, 93; Body Schema and Intentionality,Teh Body and the Self, MIT/Bradford Press, 95; coauth, Body Schema and Body Image in a Deafferented Subject, Jour Mind & Behavior, 95; auth, Some Particular Limitations on Postconventional Universality: Hegel and Habermas, Phenomenology, Interpretation, and Community, SUNY Press, 96; Critique and Extension: A Response to Robert Young, Studies in Philosophy and Education, 96; coauth, The Earliest Sense of Self and Others: Merleau-Ponty and Recent Developmental Studies, Philosophical Psychology, 96; auth, The Moral Significance of Primitive Self-Consciousness, Ethics: an international journal of social, political and legal philosophy, 96; Hermeneutical Approaches to Educational Research, Hermeneutics in Educational Discourse, 97; Hegel, Foucault, and Critical Hermeneutics, Hegel, History, and Interpretation, SUNY Press, 97; Mutual Englightenment: Recent Phenomenology in Cognitive Science, Jour Consciousness Stud, 97; ed, Models of the Self, Jour Consciousness Stud, 97; Hegel, History, and Interpretation, SUNY, 97; The Inordinance of Time, NW Univ Press, 98. **CONTACT ADDRESS** Dept of Philosophy, Canisius Col, 2001 Main St, Buffalo, NY, 14208. **EMAIL** gallaghr@canisius.edu

GALLOWAY, J. DONALD C.
DISCIPLINE LAW **EDUCATION** Edinburgh Univ, LLB, 74; Harvard Univ, LLM, 75. **CAREER** Prof, 90-. **RESEARCH** Administrative law; jurisprudence. **SELECTED PUBLICATIONS** Auth, pubs on criminal law, tort law, and legal theory. **CONTACT ADDRESS** Fac of Law, Univ Victoria, PO Box 2400, Victoria, BC, V8W 3H7. **EMAIL** galloway@uvic.ca

GALSTON, M.
DISCIPLINE JURISPRUDENCE, BANKRUPTCY, CORPORATIONS **EDUCATION** Univ Chicago, PhD, 73; Yale Law School, JD, 82. **CAREER** Vis asst prof, Univ TX, Austin, 76; asst prof, Brandeis Univ, 77-79; lawyer, private practice (tax), 82-90; Law prof, George Washington Univ Law School, 90-. **CONTACT ADDRESS** Law School, George Washington Univ, 2000 H Street NW, Washington, DC, 20052. **EMAIL** MGalston@main.nlc.gwu.edu

GAMBLE, CHARLES W.
DISCIPLINE LAW **EDUCATION** Jacksonville State Univ, BS, 65; Univ Ala, JD, 68; Harvard Univ, LLM, 71. **CAREER** Prof, Univ Ala, 82-. **MEMBERSHIPS** Order of the Coif. **RESEARCH** Evidence and torts. **SELECTED PUBLICATIONS** Auth, McElroy's Alabama Evidence, 5th ed, 95; Gamble's Alabama Rules of Evidence: A Trial Manual for Making and Responding to Objections, 94; Alabama Law of Damages, 95; Character Evidence: A Comprehensive Approach, A Lawyer's Guide, 87. **CONTACT ADDRESS** Law Dept, Univ of Alabama, Box 870000, Tuscaloosa, AL, 35487-0383. **EMAIL** cgamble@law.ua.edu

GAMBLE, RICHARD C.
DISCIPLINE SYSTEMATIC THEOLOGY **EDUCATION** Univ Basel, Switzerland, PhD. **CAREER** Instr, Freie-Evangel Theol Akad, Basel; dir, H. Henry Meeter Ctr for Calvin Stud; prof, Calvin Theol Sem; prof-. **HONORS AND AWARDS** Fel of Natl Lib, Fed Rep Ger, The Herzog-August Bibliothek, 93. **RESEARCH** Calvinism. **SELECTED PUBLICATIONS** Auth, Augustinus contra Maximinum: An Analysis of Augustine's anti-Arian Writings; ed, encycl Calvin and Calvinism; co-ed, Pressing Toward the Mark. **CONTACT ADDRESS** Dept of Systematic Theology, Reformed Theol Sem, 1015 Maitland Ctr Commons, Maitland, FL, 32751.

GANGADEAN, ASHOK KUMAR
PERSONAL Born 09/26/1941, Trinidad, West Indies, m, 1960, 2 children **DISCIPLINE** PHILOSOPHY **EDUCATION** City Col New York, BA, 63; Brandeis Univ, PhD(philos), 71. **CAREER** Asst prof, 68-74, assoc prof, 74-80, PROF PHILOS, HAVERFORD COL, 80-, Fel, Am Inst Indian Studies, 71-72; vis lectr, Univ Poona, 71-72. **MEMBERSHIPS** Am Philos Asn; Soc Asian & Comp Philos; Asn Asian Studies; Am Acad Relig; NAm Buddhist Soc. **RESEARCH** Logical theory; metaphysics; Indian philosophy. **SELECTED PUBLICATIONS** Auth, The Quest for the Primal Word, and What is the Origin of Language, Parabola-Myth Tradition and the Search for Meaning, Vol 0020, 95; The Awakening of Primal Knowledge, and How the Traditions Point Beyond the Ego, Parabola-Myth Tradition and the Search for Meaning, Vol 0022, 97. **CONTACT ADDRESS** Dept of Philos, Haverford Col, 370 Lancaster Ave, Haverford, PA, 19041-1392.

GANNAGE, MARK
DISCIPLINE LAW **EDUCATION** Queen's Univ, BA; Osgoode Hall Law Sch, LLB, LLM. **CAREER** Lctr **MEMBERSHIPS** Ontario British Columbia Bars. **SELECTED PUBLICATIONS** Auth, pubs on copyright and designs law, criminal law and procedure, and company law. **CONTACT ADDRESS** Fac of Law, Univ Toronto, 78 Queen's Park, Toronto, ON.

GANZ, DAVID L.
PERSONAL Born 07/28/1951, New York, NY, m, 1996, 3 children **DISCIPLINE** LAW **EDUCATION** Georgetown Univ, BSFS (Int Affairs), 73; St John's Univ Law School, JD, 76; Int Law Prog, Temple Univ Law School, Rome, Italy, 75; NY Univ Law School, LLM Prog, 77-79. **CAREER** Attorney at Law; NY, NJ, DC, before the Supreme Court of the United States, the US Tax Court, federal and state appellate and trial courts; member of Ganz, Hollinger, & Towe, Esqs, and Ganz & Sivin, PA; consultant to the Subcommittee on Historic Preservation & Coinage on the House Committee on Banking, Housing & Urban Affairs, 94th and 95th Congresses. **HONORS AND AWARDS** Phi Sigma Alpha; Numismatic Literary Guild Clement F Bailey Memorial Award, 91; Order of St Agatha (Commander) by the Republic of San Marino, July 94; Glenn Smedley Memorial Award, Am Numismatic Asn, 95; Medal of Merit, Token & Medal Soc, 97; listed in several Who's Who honorary directories. **MEMBERSHIPS** Token & Medal Soc; Am Numismatic Asn (Vice-pres, 91-93, Pres, 93-95); Bd of Dirs, Georgetown Univ Lib Assoc, 82-; Founding member, Bd of dirs, Industry Council for Tangible Assets. **SELECTED PUBLICATIONS** Auth, Landlord/Tenant, in MacGraw Hill Real Estate Handbook, 93; Government Regulation of the Coin Industry, 106 The Numismatic 64 et seq, Jan & Feb, 93; Partition ch 111 in NY Real Estate Guide, 5 vols, Matthew Bender, 93; The World of Coins & Coin Collecting, Scribners, 80, 2nd ed, 85, 3rd ed, Bonus Books, 98; The 90 Second Lawyer, with Robert Irwin, John Wiley & Sons, 96; The 90 Second Lawyer's Guide to Buying Real Estate, with Robert Irwin, John Wiley & Sons, 97; How to Obtain an Instant Mortgage, with Robert Irwin, John Wiley & Sons, 97; Planning Your Rare Coin Retirement, Bonus Books, 98; numerous other publications. **CONTACT ADDRESS** 1394 3rd Ave, New York, NY, 10021. **EMAIL** DavidLGanz@aol.com

GARBER, DANIEL ELLIOT
PERSONAL Born 09/26/1949, Schenectady, NY, 2 children **DISCIPLINE** PHILOSOPHY, HISTORY OF SCIENCE **EDUCATION** Harvard Univ, AB, 71, AM, 74, PhD, 75. **CAREER** Teaching fel philos, Harvard Univ, 73-75; asst prof, 75-82, assoc prof philos, prof philos, 86-, Lawrence Kimpton Distinguished Serv prof, 96, Univ Chicago, 82-, vis asst prof philos, Univ Minn, spring 79 & Johns Hopkins Univ, 80-81; vis assoc prof philos, Princeton Univ, 82-83. **MEMBERSHIPS** Am Philos Asn; Int Berkeley Soc; Philos Sci Asn; Hist Sci Soc; Leibniz Soc. **RESEARCH** Philosophy of science; 17th century philosophy and science. **SELECTED PUBLICATIONS** Auth, Mind, body and the laws of nature in Descartes and Leibniz, Midwest Studies Philos, Vol 8; Old evidence and logical omniscience in Bayesian conformation theory, Minn Studies Philos Sci, Vol 10; Descartes Metaphysical Physics, Univ Chicago, 92; ed, The Cambridge History of Seventeenth-Century Philosophy, Cambridge Univ, 98. **CONTACT ADDRESS** Dept of Philos, Univ Chicago, 1010 E 59th St, Chicago, IL, 60637-1512. **EMAIL** garb@midway.uchicago.edu

GARBER, MARILYN
PERSONAL Brooklyn, NY, 2 children **DISCIPLINE** HISTORY, LAW **EDUCATION** Univ Calif, Los Angeles, BA, 57, MA, 60, PhD(hist), 67; Southwestern Univ, JD, 77. **CAREER** Prof hist, Calif State Univ, Dominguez Hills, 80-. **MEMBERSHIPS** Calif State Bar. **RESEARCH** Utopia; legal history; labor law; negotiation; conflict resolution **SELECTED PUBLICATIONS** Natural Law Liberalism, 67. **CONTACT ADDRESS** Dept Hist, California State Univ, Dominguez Hills, 1000 E Victoria, Carson, CA, 90747-0005. **EMAIL** mgarber@dhlx20.csudh.edu

GARCIA, ALBERT L.
PERSONAL Born 05/02/1947, Havana, Cuba, m, 1968, 2 children **DISCIPLINE** THEOLOGY **EDUCATION** FL Atlantic Univ, BA, 68; Concordia Theol Sem, M Div, 74; Lutheran School of Theol, Th M, 78, PhD, 87. **CAREER** Asst prof, 79-87, Concordia Theol Sem; vis prof, 87-89, Fla Intl Univ-; assoc prof, 92-., Concordia Univ, Wis **HONORS AND AWARDS** Elected to Phi Sigma Tau, 68; Lutheran Brotherhood Fel, 86. **MEMBERSHIPS** AAR; Assn Ed Teologica Hispana. **RESEARCH** Christology; faith and culture, ethics in particular in relationship to US Hispanic theologies and Latin Am. **SELECTED PUBLICATIONS** Co-ed, contrib, Christ and Culture in Dialogue, Concortia Publ House, 98; contrib essay, Christological Reflections on Faith and Culture, Diccionario de Teologos/Terologas, Nueva Creatcion, forthcoming; auth, Hispanic/Latino Theology in the U.S.A., Concordia J, Jan 98; auth, Luther's Theology of Suffering: An Evangelical Catholic Perspective Toward Latinola Anthropology and Spitituality, Apuntes, 98. **CONTACT ADDRESS** Concordia Univ, Wisconsin, 1200 N Lake Shore Dr, Megrion, WI, 53097. **EMAIL** Albert_Garcia@cuw.edu

GARCIA, AURELIO A.
PERSONAL Born 06/06/1958, Arecibo, Puerto Rico, m, 1995, 1 child **DISCIPLINE** HISTORY OF CHRISTIAN DOCTRINE, REFORMATION STUDIES **EDUCATION** Temple Univ, BA, 79; Princeton Theol Sem, MDiv, 83, PhD, 89. **CAREER** Instr Church Hist, 88-92, adj facC, 92-, Evangelical Sem of PR; Ordained Min Presby Church USA; Pastor, Huto Rey Presby Church. **MEMBERSHIPS** AAR; Calvin Stud Soc. **RESEARCH** Historiography; Reformation studies; Heinrich Bollinger. **SELECTED PUBLICATIONS** Auth Eusebius Theophany: A Christian Neoplatonist Response, The Patristic and Bizantine Rev, 87; The Theology of History and Apologetic Historiography in Heinrich Bullinger, Mellen Res Univ Press, 92. **CONTACT ADDRESS** Entre Rios 137 Plaza Serena, Trujillo Alto, PR, 00976.

GARCIA, LAURA
PERSONAL Born 06/04/1955, Portland, OR, m, 1983, 4 children **DISCIPLINE** PHILOSOPHY **EDUCATION** Westmont Col, BA, 77; Univ Notre Dame, PhD, 83. **CAREER** Instr, Calvin Col, 79-80; instr, Univ St Thomas, 82-84; adjunct prof, Univ Notre Dame, 84-86; vis lctr, Cath Univ Amer, 86-87; vis asst prof, Georgetown Univ, 88-92; lctr, Rutgers Univ, 93-98. **MEMBERSHIPS** Amer Philos Assoc; Amer Cath Philos Assoc; Soc Christian Philos. **RESEARCH** Philosophy of Religion; Metaphysics **SELECTED PUBLICATIONS** Modal Versions of the Ontological Argument, Philosophy of Religion, Broadview Pr, forthcoming; Religious Values and Politics, Proceedings of the Theology Institute, Villanova Univ, forthcoming; Pluralism and Natural Theology, Recovering Nature: Essays in Natural Philosophy, Ethics, and Metaphysics in Honor of Ralph McInerny, Cath Univ Pr, forthcoming; rev, Is There a God?, First Things, 98 . **CONTACT ADDRESS** Dept of Philosophy, New Jersey State Univ, 26 Nichol Ave, New Brunswick, NJ, 08901. **EMAIL** llgarcia@aol.com

GARCIA-GOMEZ, JORGE
PERSONAL Born 01/14/1937, Havana, Cuba, m, 1961, 3 children **DISCIPLINE** PHILOSOPHY, LITERATURE **EDUCATION** Univ Santo Tomas Villanueva, BA, 58; New Sch Social Res, MA, 65, PhD(Philos), 71. **CAREER** Asst prof Philos, Sacred Heart Univ, 66-69; assoc prof, 69-80, prof Philos, Southampton Col, Long Island Univ, 81-. **MEMBERSHIPS** Am Philos Asn; Am Cath Philos Asn; Am Asn Teachers Span & Port; AAUP. **RESEARCH** Metaphysics; phenomenology; aesthetics. **SELECTED PUBLICATIONS** Auth, A meditation of liberty, Abraxas, New York, fall 70; Ciudades, Ed Plenitud, Madrid, 74; ed & transl Aron Gurwitsch, El Campo de la Conciencia, Madrid, 78; Jose Ortega oy Gasset, Encyclopedia et Phenomenolozy, 97; A Bridge to Temporality, St Augustine's Confessions, Analecta Husser-liana, LII, 98 **CONTACT ADDRESS** Humanities Div Southampton Col, Long Island Univ, 239 Montauk Hwy, Southampton, NY, 11968-4198.

GARDINER, DAVID
PERSONAL Born 08/07/1957, Washington, DC, m, 1984, 2 children **DISCIPLINE** RELIGION **EDUCATION** Amherst Col, BA, 80; Univ Virginia, MA, 86; Stanford Univ, PhD, 95. **CAREER** Asst prof, 94-95, Simpson Col; asst prof, 95-97, Hawaii Pacific Univ; asst prof, 97-98, Univ San Diego; asst prof, 98-, Colorado Col. **RESEARCH** Japanese Religion (premodern), Buddhism. **CONTACT ADDRESS** Dept of Religion, Colorado Col, 14 E. Cache La Poudre, Colorado Springs, CO, 80903. **EMAIL** dgardiner@coloradocollege.edu

GARDNER, CATHERINE
PERSONAL Born 03/17/1962, Chesterfield, England, m, 1996 **DISCIPLINE** PHILOSOPHY **EDUCATION** Univ Leicester, BA, 85; Univ Col of Swansea, Wales, MA, 89; Univ Va, PhD, 96. **CAREER** Asst prof, philos, Univ Mich Flint, 96-. **MEMBERSHIPS** Amer Philos Asn; Soc for the Study of the Study of Women Philos. **RESEARCH** Feminist ethics; Women moral philosophers from the history of philosophy. **SELECTED PUBLICATIONS** Auth, Catharine Macaulay's Letters on Education: Odd But Equal, Hypatia, vol 13, no 1, 118-137, Winter, 98. **CONTACT ADDRESS** Univ of Michigan, 544 Crob, Flint, MI, 48502-2186. **EMAIL** cagard@umich.edu

GARDNER, RICHARD NEWTON
PERSONAL Born 07/09/1927, New York, NY, m, 1956, 1 child **DISCIPLINE** INTERNATIONAL LAW, ECONOMICS **EDUCATION** Harvard Univ, AB, 48; Yale Univ, LLB, 51; Oxford Univ, PhD(int econ), 54. **CAREER** Atty, Coudert Bros, NY, 54-57; from assoc prof to prof, 57-66, Henry L Moses Prof Law & Int Orgn, Columbia Univ, 66-; Dep asst to Secy State Int Orgn Affairs, 61-65; US Ambassador to Italy, 77-81; US Ambassador to Spain, 93-97; mem, Coun Foreign Rels. **MEMBERSHIPS** Am Econ Asn; Royal Econ Soc; Am Soc Int Law (vpres); Am Acad Arts & Sci. **RESEARCH** International law and organization, especially economic and political organization. **SELECTED PUBLICATIONS** Auth, New Directions in US Foreign Economic Policy, Sterling-Dollar Diplomacy, In Pursuit of World Order, Praeger, 64; Blueprint for Peace, McGraw, 66; coauth, The Global Partnership, Praeger, 68. **CONTACT ADDRESS** School of Law, Columbia Univ, 435 W 116th St, New York, NY, 10027-7201.

GARET, RONALD R.
DISCIPLINE CONSTITUTIONAL LAW **EDUCATION** Harvard Univ, BA; Yale Univ, religious stud, MA, MPhil, PhD; Univ Southern Calif, JD. **CAREER** Carolyn Craig Franklin prof Law and Rel, Univ Southern Calif; taught at, Yale Univ. **MEMBERSHIPS** Pats fac adv, Public Interest Law Found. **RESEARCH** Role of interpretation in law, theology, and literature and in the legal and moral rights of social groups. **SELECTED PUBLICATIONS** Auth, Creation and Commitment: Lincoln, Thomas, & the Declaration of Independence; Dancing to Music: an Interpretation of Mutuality; Gnostic Due Process. **CONTACT ADDRESS** School of Law, Univ Southern Calif, University Park Campus, Los Angeles, CA, 90089.

GARFINKEL, STEPHEN PAUL
PERSONAL m, 2 children **DISCIPLINE** RELIGIOUS STUDIES **EDUCATION** Univ Pa, BA; Columbia Univ, MA 73; Mphil, PhD, 83. **CAREER** Vis fac, Yale Univ; adj fac, Hunter Col; asst prof, grad schl, Jewish Theol Sem. **HONORS AND AWARDS** JTS Stroock fac fel, Jewish Theol Sem; Dancinger Fellowship; grants, Nat Found Jewish Cult., Bd gov and educ comm, Solomon Schechter Day Schl Essex-Union. **MEMBERSHIPS** Asn Jewish Studies; Columbia Univ Hebrew Biblical Sem; Soc Biblical Lit. **RESEARCH** Early popular perceptions about Moses. **SELECTED PUBLICATIONS** Auth and/or ed over fifteen books for informal Jewish education use; scholarly pubs, Vetus Testamentum, Conser Judaism, Jour Ancient Near Eastern Soc. **CONTACT ADDRESS** Jewish Theol Sem of America, 3080 Broadway, New York, NY, 10027. **EMAIL** stgarfinkle@jtsa.edu

GARLAND, JOHN WILLIAM
PERSONAL Born 10/24/1944, Harlem, NY, m, 1975 **DISCIPLINE** LAW **EDUCATION** Central State University, BA, 1971; Ohio State University College of Law, JD, 1974. **CAREER** Hayes & White, PC, sr attorney, 1983-84; Law Office of John W Garland, attorney, 1984-88; University of the District of Columbia, general counsel, 1988-91; University of Virginia, assoc gen counsel, 1991-93, exec asst to the pres, 1993-96, assoc vp for intellectual property, 1996-97; CENTRAL STATE UNIVERSITY, PRES, 1997-. **HONORS AND AWARDS** District of Columbia, Federation of Civic Association, Father of the Year, 1978; TransAfrica Award, 1987. SPA Legal Svcs of the Coastal Plains, founding dir. **MEMBERSHIPS** National Association of College & University Attorneys; National Conference of Black Lawyers, bd of dirs; Association of University Technology Managers; Washington Lawyers Committee for Civil Rights Under Law, bd of dirs; National Veterans Legal Svcs Proj, bd of dirs; Journal of College & University Law, editorial bd; US Supreme Ct; Supreme Ct of NC: Supreme Ct of Virginia; Court of Appeals, District of Columbia; US Ct of Military Appeals; LeDroit Park Civic Association, pres, 1974-76. **CONTACT ADDRESS** Central State Univ, Ohio, 1400 Brush Row Rd, Wilberforce, OH, 45384. **EMAIL** jgarland@cesvxa.ces.edu

GARLAND, MICHAEL JOHN
PERSONAL Born 12/11/1936, Denver, CO, m, 1972, 2 children **DISCIPLINE** BIOETHICS, RELIGIOUS STUDIES **EDUCATION** St Louis Univ, BA, 61; Univ Notre Dame, MA, 68; Univ Strasbourg, Dr Sci Relig, 71. **CAREER** Asst prof relig studies, Regis Col, 70-72; lectr bioethics, Sch Med, Univ Calif, San Francisco, 73-77; asst prof med ethics, sch med, Ore Health Sci Univ, 78-; vis asst prof ethics, Pac Sch Relig, Berkeley, 76-77; vis asst prof bioethics, Portland State Univ, 77-78. **HONORS AND AWARDS** Teacher of the Year, Regis Col Student Senate, 71. **MEMBERSHIPS** Am Soc Bioethics and Hum; Am Pub Health Assn; Pub Health Assn. **RESEARCH** Social ethics of American health care system; social responsibility and the medical practice; interpersonal medical ethics. **SELECTED PUBLICATIONS** Auth, Oregon's contribution to definish adequate health care, Health Care Reform: A Human Rights Approach, 94; coauth, Health Insurance, Encyclopedia of Bioethics, 95; auth, Community Responsibility for Health Policy: Tools, Structure, and Financing, 95; coauth, Consumers want choice and voice, Grading Health Care, 98; coauth, Translating the human genome project into social policy: a model for participatory democracy, Genes and Morality: New Essays, 98. **CONTACT ADDRESS** Dept of Pub Health, Oregon Health Sciences Univ, 3181 SW Sam Jackson, Portland, OR, 97201. **EMAIL** garlandm@ohsu.edu

GARRETT, DON JAMES
PERSONAL Born 06/05/1953, Salt Lake City, UT, m, 1975, 2 children **DISCIPLINE** PHILOSOPHY **EDUCATION** Univ Utah, BA, 74; Yale Univ, PhD, 79. **CAREER** Asst prof philos, Harvard Univ, 79-82; asst prof to assoc prof, philos, Univ Utah, 82-99; KENAN DISTINGUISHED PROF, UNIV NC, CHAPEL HILL, 99-. **MEMBERSHIPS** Am Philos Asn; Hume Soc. **RESEARCH** History of modern philosophy; philosophy of mind; metaphysics. **SELECTED PUBLICATIONS** Auth, Cognition and Commitment in Hume's Philosophy, Oxford, 97; ed, The Cambridge Companion to Spinoza, Cambridge, 96. **CONTACT ADDRESS** Dept of Philos, Univ Utah, 260 Central Campus Dr, Salt Lake City, UT, 84112-8916. **EMAIL** don.garrett@m.cc.utah.edu

GARRETT, GERALD R.
PERSONAL Washington, DC **DISCIPLINE** SOCIOLOGY, CRIMINOLOGY. **EDUCATION** Whitman Col, AB, 62, MA, 66; Washington State Univ, PhD, 71. **CAREER** Vis prof, Univ of Alaska, 79-86; vis prof, Wash State Univ, 77-78, 94, & 96; Asst prof to prof , Univ Mass, Dir, grad prof in Applied Sociology, 81-84, Dir, Alcohol & Substance Abuse Studies, 86-, Dir, Center for Criminal Justice, Univ Mass, 92-. **MEMBERSHIPS** Northeastern Asn of Criminal Justice Sci; Int Coalition of Addictions Studies Ed; Eastern Sociological Soc. **RESEARCH** Alcohol and other drugs; homelessness; alcohol/drug-related crime; deviance. **SELECTED PUBLICATIONS** Coauth, Substance Use and Abuse Among UMASS Boston Studies, 98; Crime, Justice, and Society, General-Hall Inc, 96; Responding to the Homeless, Plenum Pub, 92; Manny: A Criminal-Addict's Story, Houghton-Mifflin, 77; Women Alone, Lexington Books, 76; auth, Working with the Homeless, Center for Commun Media, 90. **CONTACT ADDRESS** Dept. of Sociology, Univ of Mass-Boston, Harbor Campus, 100 Morrissey Blvd., Boston, MA, 02125-3393. **EMAIL** GARRETT@UMBSKY.cc.umb.edu

GARRETT, JAMES LEO
PERSONAL Born 11/25/1925, Waco, TX, m, 1948, 3 children **DISCIPLINE** SYSTEMATIC AND HISTORICAL THEOLOGY **EDUCATION** Baylor Univ, BA, 45; Southwest Baptist Theol Sem, BD, 48, ThD, 54; Princeton Theol Sem, ThM, 49; Harvard Univ, PhD, 66. **CAREER** Instr/asst prof/assoc prof, prof, Theol, Southwest Baptist Theol Sem, 49-59; prof, Christian Theol, South Baptist Theol Sem, 59-73; dir, JM Dawson Stud in Church & State, Baylor Univ, 73-79; prof, REL, Baylor Univ, 73-79; PROF/PROF EMER, SOUTHWEST BAPTIST THEOL SEM, 79-. **MEMBERSHIPS** Am Soc Church Hist; AmAcad Rel; Conf Faith & Hist; South Baptitst Hist Soc **RESEARCH** Baptist theology; Systematic theology; Theology of Augustine Hippo; Theology of Luther & Calvin; church; Church-state religion; Religious liberty; Theolology of American cults. **SELECTED PUBLICATIONS** edr, TheConcept of the Believer's Church, 70; edr, Baptist Relations with Other Christians, 74; coauth, Are Southern Baptists "Evangelicals?", 83; Living Stones: The Centennial History of Broadway Baptist Church, Fort Worth, Texas, 1882-1982, 85; Systematic Theology: Biblical, Historical, and Evangelical, 95. **CONTACT ADDRESS** Southwest Baptist Theol Sem, PO Box 22117, Fort Worth, TX, 76122. **EMAIL** jlg@swbts.edu

GARRETT, ROBERT I., JR.
PERSONAL Born 09/24/1950, Orange, TX, m, 1970, 3 children **DISCIPLINE** NEW TESTAMENT **EDUCATION** Baylor, BA, 72; S Baptist Theol Sem, Mdiv, 75, PhD, 81 **CAREER** Prof, 80-95, NT Sem **MEMBERSHIPS** Am Soc of Missiology **RESEARCH** Biblical foundations of missions **CONTACT ADDRESS** Southwest Baptist Sem, PO Box 22000, Fort Worth, TX, 76122-0418. **EMAIL** rgarrett@swbts.swbts.edu

GARRISON, ROMAN
PERSONAL Born 05/09/1953, Cincinnati, OH, m, 1976, 2 children **DISCIPLINE** EARLY CHRISTIANITY **EDUCATION** Westminster Col, BA, 75; Pittsburgh Theological Seminary, MA, 77; Oxford Univ, MliH, 79; Univ of Toronto, PhD, 89. **CAREER** Instr, asst prof, minister. **MEMBERSHIPS** SBL. **RESEARCH** Early Christianity. **SELECTED PUBLICATIONS** Auth, Redemptive Almsgiving in Early Christianity, Sheffield Acad Press; auth, The Graeco-Roman Context of Early Christian Literature, Sheffield Acad Press. **CONTACT ADDRESS** 225 Beechwood Rd., New Wilmington, PA, 16142.

GARRO, A.M.
PERSONAL Born 04/08/1950, LaPlata, Argentina, m, 1977, 1 child **DISCIPLINE** LAW **EDUCATION** Ntl Univ Of LaPlata, JD, 75; LA State Univ, LLM, 79; Columbia Univ, JSD, 90. **CAREER** Lectr, law, 81-94, Columbia Univ; Asst Prof 80-81, LSU; collab sci, 83-85, Swiss Inst Comp Law. **MEMBERSHIPS** ABA; Colegio de Abogados de la Provincia de Buenos Aires, Colegio de Abogados de Madrid. **RESEARCH** Comparative Law; Latin Amer Law; Intl Comm Arbitration. **SELECTED PUBLICATIONS** Auth, Compraventa Intl de Mercaderias, Buenos Aires, 90. **CONTACT ADDRESS** Law School, Columbia Univ, 435 West 116th St, New York, NY, 10027. **EMAIL** garro@law.columbia.edu

GARRY, ANN
PERSONAL Born 09/12/1943, Bristol, VA, m, 3 children **DISCIPLINE** PHILOSOPHY **EDUCATION** Monmouth Col, BA, 65; Univ Chicago, MA, 66; Univ MD, College Park, PhD(philos), 70. **CAREER** Asst prof, 69-77, assoc prof, 77-82, prof philos, CA State Univ, Los Angeles, 82-. **HONORS AND AWARDS** ACLS sr fellowship. **MEMBERSHIPS** Am Philos Asn; Soc Women Philos. **RESEARCH** Feminist philosophy; epistemology; philosophical method; applied ethics. **SELECTED PUBLICATIONS** Auth, Mental images, Personalist, 77; Pornography and Respect for Women, Soc Theory & Pract, 78; Why are Love and Sex Philosophically Interesting, Metaphilosophy, 80; Narcissism & Vanity, Soc Theory & Pract, 82; Abortion: Modeling Responsibility, Law and Philosophy, 83; A Minimally Decent Philosophical Method? Analytic Philosophy and Feminism, Hypatio, 95; Women, Knowledge, and Reality: Explorations in Feminist Philosophy, 2nd ed, Routledge, 96; Sex from Somewhere Liberally Different, Philos Studies, 98. **CONTACT ADDRESS** Dept Philos, California State Univ, Los Angeles, 5151 Rancho Castillo, Los Angeles, CA, 90032-8114. **EMAIL** agarry@calstatela.edu

GARVER, NEWTON
PERSONAL Born 04/24/1928, Buffalo, NY, m, 1957, 4 children **DISCIPLINE** PHILOSOPHY **EDUCATION** Swarthmore Col, AB, 51; Oxford Univ, BPhil, 54; Cornell Univ, PhD, 65. **CAREER** Prof, 71-91, Distinbuished Serv Prof, SUNY-Buffalo, 91- ; vis prof, Mich, Friends World Col, Rochester, NW, & San Diego State Univ; NEH Summer Sem SUNY, 92. **MEMBERSHIPS** Am Philos Asn; Law & Soc Asn; AMINTAPHIL; Austrian Wittgenstein Soc. **RESEARCH** Wittgenstein; Kant; violence; non-violence. **SELECTED PUBLICATIONS** Auth, Jesus, Jefferson and the Task of Friends, Pendle Hill Pamphlet #250, 83; Naturalism and Rationality, Prometheus Books, 86; Justice, Law, and Violence, Temple Univ Press, 91; Derrida and Wittgenstein, Temple Univ Press, 94; This Complicated Form of Life, Open Court, 94; Violence in America, John Lectures, San Diego State Univ, 94; Nonviolence and Community, Pendle Hill Pamphet, 95; **CONTACT ADDRESS** State Univ of NY, 662 Baldy Hall, Box 601010, Buffalo, NY, 14260-0104. **EMAIL** garver@acsu.buffalo.edu

GARVEY, JOHN LEO
PERSONAL Born 03/22/1927, Covington, KY, m, 1952, 2 children **DISCIPLINE** LAW **EDUCATION** Xavier Univ, AB, 45; Cath Univ Am, LLB, 48; Univ MI, SJD, 67. **CAREER** Atty, 48-51; instr, 51-57, asst prof, 57-61, assoc prof, 61-65, assoc dean, Sch Law, 63-69, dean, 77-79, prof law, Cath Univ Am, 65. **HONORS AND AWARDS** LLD, Xavier Univ, 78. **MEMBERSHIPS** Am Bar Asn; Am Col Probate Coun; Am

Law Inst. **RESEARCH** Probate reform; will substitutes. **SELECTED PUBLICATIONS** Auth, Probate Court Practice in the District of Columbia Supplements, West Publ Co, 60; Some aspects of the merger of law and equity, Cath Univ Law Rev, 61; Revocable gifts of legal interests in land, KY Law J, 65; Revocable gifts of personal property, Cath Univ Law Rev, 68; contribr, Comparative Probate Law Studies, Am Law Inst, 76. **CONTACT ADDRESS** Columbus Sch of Law Cath, Univ of Am, 620 Michigan Ave N E, Washington, DC, 20064-0002.

GASS, WILLIAM HOWARD
PERSONAL Born 07/30/1924, Fargo, ND, m, 1952, 5 children **DISCIPLINE** PHILOSOPHY **EDUCATION** Kenyon Col, AB, 47; Cornell Univ, PhD, 54. **CAREER** Instr philos, Col Wooster, 51-55; from asst prof to prof, Purdue Univ, 55-69; prof philos, 69-78, Dist Prof Humanities, Washington Univ, 79-, Vis lectr English & philos, Univ Ill, 58-59; Rockefeller Found grant fiction, 66-67; Guggenheim award fiction, 69-70; judge fiction, Nat Bk Awards, 73 & 75; lectr, Salzburg Sem in Am Studies, 73; judge Pen-Faulkner Prize, 81. **HONORS AND AWARDS** DHL, Kenyon Col, 74 & George Washington Univ, 82. **MEMBERSHIPS** Am Philos Asn; PEN; Am Acad Arts & Sci; Am Acad Arts & Lts; Int Parliament Writers. **RESEARCH** Aesthetics; Greek philosophy; fiction. **SELECTED PUBLICATIONS** Auth, Omensetter's Luck (novel), New Am Libr, 66; In the Heart of the Heart of the Country, Harper, 68; Willie Masters' Lonesome Wife, 68 & Fiction and the Figures of Life 71; introd, The Geographical History of America, Random House, 73; On Being Blue, Godine, 76; The World Within The Word, Knopf, 78; auth, Habitations of the Word, 83; auth, The tunnel, Knopf, 95; auth, Finding a Form, Knopf, 96; auth, Cartesian Sonata, Knopf, 98. **CONTACT ADDRESS** Dept of Philosophy, Washington Univ, St. Louis, MO, 63130. **EMAIL** iwc@artsci.wvstl.edu

GASTON, LLOYD
PERSONAL Born 12/02/1929, Morgantown, WV, m, 1951, 3 children **DISCIPLINE** NEW TESTAMENT **EDUCATION** Dartmouth Col, BA, 52; Univ Basel, ThD(New Testament), 67. **CAREER** Res asst Old Testament, Princeton Theol Sem, 60-61; pastor, First Presby Church, Hamburg, NJ, 61-63; from instr to assoc prof relig, Macalester Col, 63-73; assoc prof, 73-78, PROF NEW TESTAMENT, VANCOUVER SCH THEOL, 78-. **MEMBERSHIPS** Soc Bibl Lit; Studiorum Novi Testamenti Societas; Can Soc Bibl Studies. **RESEARCH** Synoptic gospels; Paul. **SELECTED PUBLICATIONS** Auth, Divorce in the New-Testament, Stud in Relig-Sciences Religieuses, Vol 0023, 94. **CONTACT ADDRESS** Vancouver Sch of Theol, 6000 Iona Dr, Vancouver, BC, V6T 1J6.

GATES, GARY
PERSONAL Born 05/11/1951, Lebanon, PA, m, 1981, 2 children **DISCIPLINE** WORLD RELIGIONS, RELIGIOUS STUDIES, INTERDISCIPLINARY HUMANITIES, WRITING **EDUCATION** Messiah Col, Temple Univ, BA; Penn State Univ, MA. **CAREER** Adjunct prof, Harrisburg Area Community Col. **MEMBERSHIPS** Am Acad of Rel; Central Pa Writer's Org; Soc of Biblical Lit; Capital Area Writing-Project Board. **RESEARCH** The historical Jesus; history of Christianity; comparative religion/spirituality; science & religion. **SELECTED PUBLICATIONS** Several local books on the Pa Dutch. **CONTACT ADDRESS** 419 W. Pine St., Palmyra, PA, 17078.

GAUKER, CHRISTOPHER P.
PERSONAL Minneapolis, MN, m **DISCIPLINE** PHILOSOPHY **EDUCATION** Univ Chicago, BA, 79; Univ Pittsburgh, PhD, 84. **CAREER** Tchg asst, fel, 79-84, instr, 85, Univ Pittsburgh; vis asst prof, Wesleyan Univ, 85-86; postdoctoral fel, Univ Cincinnati, 86-87; vis asst prof, Univ Wyoming, 87-88; asst prof, 88-93, assoc prof, 93-, Univ Cincinnati; vis assoc prof, Johns Hopkins Univ, 99. **HONORS AND AWARDS** Phi Beta Kappa, 79; Taft Postdoctoral Fel, 86-87; Taft Grants in Aid, 89, 94, 97; Taft Fac Fel, 92; Taft Sabbatical Grant, 95-96. **RESEARCH** Philosophy of language; philosophy of psychology; history of modern philosophy; philosophical logic. **SELECTED PUBLICATIONS** Auth, An Extraterrestrial Perspective on Conceptual Development, Mind and Lang, 93; auth, Thinking Out Loud: An Essay on the Relation between Thought and Language, Princeton, 94; auth, A New Skeptical Solution, Acta Analytica, 95; auth, Domain of Discourse, Mind, 97; auth, Universal Instantiation: A Study of the Role of Context in Logic, Erkenntnis, 97; auth, What is a Context of Utterance? Philos Stud, 98; auth, Social Externalism and Linguistic Communication, in Acero, ed, The European Review of Philosophy, suppl vol, Cambridge, forthcoming. **CONTACT ADDRESS** Dept of Philosophy, Univ of Cincinnati, Cincinnati, OH, 45221-0374. **EMAIL** gaukercp@email.uc.edu

GAUSS, CHARLES E.
DISCIPLINE PHILOSOPHY AND MUSIC **EDUCATION** Georgetown Univ, AB, 32, MA, 33; Johns Hopkins Univ, PhD, 41. **CAREER** Owner, music studio, 32-40; instr, hist, Western Md Col, 40-43; asst prof, 45-47, assoc prof, 47-49, prof philos and dept chemn, 49-64, George Wash Univ. **HONORS AND AWARDS** Phi Beta Kappa; ACLS scholar, 42. **MEMBERSHIPS** Amer Soc for Aesthetics; Amer Philos Asn. **RESEARCH** Aesthetics; American philosophy. **SELECTED PUBLICATIONS** Auth, Aesthetic theories of French Artists - Realism to Surrealism, Johns Hopkins Press; articles and rev, Jour of Aesthetics. **CONTACT ADDRESS** 508 S. Riverside Dr., Pompano Beach, FL, 33062.

GAUSTAD, EDWIN SCOTT
PERSONAL Born 11/14/1923, m, 1946, 3 children **DISCIPLINE** AMERICAN RELIGIOUS HISTORY **EDUCATION** Baylor Univ, AB, 47; Brown Univ, AM, 48, PhD, 51. **CAREER** Instr relig, Brown Univ, 51-52; Am Coun Learned Soc scholar, 52-53; dean and prof relig and philos, Shorter Col, Ga, 53-57; assoc prof humanities, Univ Redlands, 57-65; assoc prof hist, 65-67, PROF HIST, UNIV CALIF, RIVERSIDE, 67-, Am Coun Learned Soc grant-in-aid, 63-64 and 72-73. **MEMBERSHIPS** Am Soc Church Hist (pres, 78); Am Studies Asn; Am Acad Relig; AHA; Orgn Am Historians. **SELECTED PUBLICATIONS** Auth, Williams, Roger and Puritan Radicalism in the English Separatist Tradition, Church Hist, Vol 0061, 92; A History of Christianity in the United-States and Canada, Cath Hist Rev, Vol 0079, 93; The Churching of America, 1776-1990--Winners and Losers in Our Religious Economy, J Relig, Vol 0073, 93; Quakers and Baptists in Colonial Massachusetts, J Interdisciplinary Hist, Vol 0024, 93; Jeffersonian Legacies, J Southern Hist, Vol 0060, 94; American Congregations, Vol 1--Portraits of 12 Religious Communities, Church His, Vol 0064, 95; American Congregations, Vol 2--New Perspectives in the Study of Congregations, Church Hist, Vol 0064, 95; Barbarians and Memory, J Church and State, Vol 0037, 95; When in the Course, William and Mary Quart, Vol 0052, 95; The Shaker Experience in America--A History of the United-Society-of-Believers, J Ecclesiastical Hist, Vol 0047, 96; The Separation of Church and State Defended--Selected-Writings of Wood, James, E, J Church and State, Vol 0038, 96; Modern American Religion, Vol 3--Under God, Indivisible, 1941-1960, Cath Hist Rev, Vol 0083, 97; A Time for Planting--the First Migration, 1654-1820, J Am Ethnic Hist, Vol 0016, 97; Reviving the Ancient Faith--the Story of Churches-of-Christ in America, Cath Hist Rev, Vol 0083, 97. **CONTACT ADDRESS** Dept of Hist, Univ of Calif, Riverside, CA, 92521.

GAUTHIER, CANDACE
DISCIPLINE PHILOSOPHY AND RELIGION **EDUCATION** SUNY, Oswego, BA; SUNY, Potsdam, MS; Univ NC, Chapel Hill, MA, PhD. **CAREER** Assoc prof, Philos and Relig, clin asst prof, Schl Med, Univ NC, Wilmington. **MEMBERSHIPS** Amer Philos Asn; Soc Health & Hum Values **RESEARCH** Ethical theory; ethics, law, and public policy. **SELECTED PUBLICATIONS** Auth, Philosophical Foundations of Respect for Autonomy, Kennedy Inst of Ethics J, 3:1, 93; The Value of Emotionally Expressive Visual Art in Medical Education, J of Med Hum, 17:2, 96; Teaching the Virtues: Justifications and Recommendations, Cambridge Quart of Healthcare Ethics, 6:3, 97. **CONTACT ADDRESS** Dept of Philosophy & Religion, Univ N. Carolina, Wilmington, Bear Hall, Wilmington, NC, 28403-3297. **EMAIL** gauthierc@uncwil.edu

GAUTHIER, JEFF
PERSONAL Born 12/24/1957, Plattsburgh, NY, s **DISCIPLINE** PHILOSOPHY **EDUCATION** Wadhams Hall Col, BA, 80; Bowling Green State Univ, MA, 85; Univ Mich, PhD, 92. **CAREER** Adj prof, Univ Mich, 91-92; asst prof, 92-98, assoc prof, 98-, Univ Portland. **MEMBERSHIPS** Amer Philos Asn; Hegel Soc of Amer; Soc for Phenomenol and Existential Philos; Ore Acad of Sci. **RESEARCH** Ethics; Feminism; Hegel; Kant; Political philosophy. **SELECTED PUBLICATIONS** Rev, Signs of Paradox: Irony, Resentment and Other Mimetic Structures, Philos in Rev , 98; auth, The Real Lives of Women and Children, Portland: The Univ of Portland Mag, 98; auth, Schiller's Critique of Kant's Moral Psychology: Reconciling Practical Reason and an Ethics of Virtue, Can Jour of Philos 27, dec, 97; auth, Hegel and Feminist Social Criticism: Justice, Recognition, and the Feminine, State Univ of NY Press, 97; rev, Listening to the Thunder: Advocates Talk About the Battered Women's Movement, Activist Epizine, 96; rev, Merleau-Ponty's Hermeneutics and Postmodernism, Can Philos Rev, 94. **CONTACT ADDRESS** Dept. of Philosophy, Univ of Portland, Portland, OR, 97203. **EMAIL** gauthier@up.edu

GAUTHIER, YVON
PERSONAL Born 02/01/1941, Drummondville, PQ, Canada, m, 1964, 2 children **DISCIPLINE** PHILOSOPHY **EDUCATION** Univ Montreal, MA, 62; Univ Heidelberg, Dr Phil (philos), 66. **CAREER** Lectr philos, Sem St Hyacinthe, Que, 62-63; from asst prof to assoc prof, Univ Sudbury, 66-72; assoc prof, Laurentian Univ, 72; vis assoc prof philos, Univ Toronto, 72-73; assoc prof, 73-77, PROF PHILOS, UNIV MONTREAL, 77-, Res fel math, Univ Calif, Berkeley, 72; bd experts, Dialogue, 76- **MEMBERSHIPS** Can Philos Asn; Asn Symbolic Logic. **RESEARCH** Logic; foundations of mathematics; philosophy of science. **SELECTED PUBLICATIONS** Auth, Hilbert and the Internal Logic of Mathematics, Synthese, Vol 0101, 94. **CONTACT ADDRESS** Dept of Philos, Univ of Montreal, Montreal, PQ, H3C 3J7.

GAVIL, ANDREW I.
DISCIPLINE CIVIL PROCEDURE **EDUCATION** Queens Col, CUNY, BA, 78; Northwestern Univ Sch Law, JD, 81. **CAREER** Prof; counsel, Chicago law firm of Bell, Boyd & Lloyd, and past consult, Fed Trade Comn; consult, Int Law Inst & IRIS at, Univ Md; ch, Law School's Student Aff & Libr Prog Plan Comt, 97-98; mem, Committees on Admissions, Warren Rosmarin Awd & Understanding. **SELECTED PUBLICATIONS** Auth, An Antitrust Anthology, Anderson, 96. **CONTACT ADDRESS** Dept of Law, Howard Univ, 2400 Sixth St NW, Washington, DC, 20059.

GAVIN, WILLIAM
DISCIPLINE PHILOSOPHY **EDUCATION** Fordham Univ, PhD. **CAREER** Prof; taught philos at, USM, for 28 yrs; 3rd recipient, Walter E. Russell Ch in Philos and Educ; teaches the USM Honors Course entitled, Progress, Process, or Permanence: All That is Solid Melts Into Air; ed-in-ch, The Maine Scholar. **RESEARCH** American philosophy; Ancient philosophy; philosophy of science; death and dying. **SELECTED PUBLICATIONS** Auth, William James and the Reinstatement of the Vague, Temple UP, 92; Cuttin' the Body Loose: Historical, Biological and Personal Approaches to Death and Dying, Temple UP, 95. **CONTACT ADDRESS** Dept of Philosophy, Univ of Southern Maine, 96 Falmouth St, PO Box 9300, Portland, ME, 04104-9300. **EMAIL** gavin@usm.maine.edu

GAY, WILLIAM CARROLL
PERSONAL Born 04/25/1949, Clearwater, FL, m, 1971, 1 child **DISCIPLINE** PHILOSOPHY **EDUCATION** Carson-Newman Col, BA, 71; Boston Col, PhD(philos), 76. **CAREER** Lectr philos, Brandeis Univ, 76-78; vis asst prof philos, Amherst Col, 78-79, Ind-Purdue Univ, 79-80; asst prof philos, Univ NC, 80-86, assoc prof philos, 86-96, prof philos, Charlotte, 96-, asst ed, Cult Hermeneutics, 75-77 & Philos & Social Criticism, 78-86, ed Concerned Philos for Peace newsletter, 87-. **MEMBERSHIPS** Am Philos Asn; Concerned Philosophers for Peace; IPPNO; North Carolina Philos Soc; Radical Philos Asn. **RESEARCH** War and Peace Studies; Social and political Philosophy; Philosophy of Language; 19th- and 20th-Century Continental Philosophy. **SELECTED PUBLICATIONS** Auth, Ricoeur on metaphor and ideology, Darshana Int, 92; From Wittgenstein to applied philosophy, Int J Applied Philos, 94; Bourdieu and the social conditions of Wittgensteinian language games, Int J Applied Philos, 96; Nonsexist public discourse and negative peace, The Acorn: J Gandhi-King Soc, 97; Exposing and overcoming linguistic alienation and linguistic violenc, Philos and Soc Criticism, 98. **CONTACT ADDRESS** Dept Philosophy, Univ of No Carolina, 9201 University City, Charlotte, NC, 28223-0002. **EMAIL** wcgay@email.uncc.edu

GEAREY, AMELIA J.
DISCIPLINE CHRISTIAN EDUCATION **EDUCATION** State Univ NY, BS; Fla State Univ, MS, PhD. **CAREER** Asst prof, 90; asst dir, Ctr Ministry of Tchg; assoc ed, Episcopal Children's Curriculum; assoc prof, 92; dir, Ctr Ministry of Tchg; ed, Episcopal Curriculum for Youth. **SELECTED PUBLICATIONS** Auth, Episcopal Children's Curriculum Director's Guide, Morehouse, 98; The Theological Challenge of Writing Curriculum, Engaging the Curriculum, 97; Young Children and the Expression of Faith, NAES, Worship in Episcopal Schools; Teaching Teenagers: The Joy and the Challenge, Youth and Young Adults. **CONTACT ADDRESS** Va Theol Sem, 3737 Seminary Rd, Alexandria, VA, 22304. **EMAIL** AGearey@vts.edu

GEIGER, MARY VIRGINIA
PERSONAL Born 02/02/1915, Irvington, NJ **DISCIPLINE** PHILOSOPHY, HISTORY **EDUCATION** Col Notre Dame, Md, AB, 37; Cath Univ Am, MA, 41, PhD(hist, philos), 43. **CAREER** Instr hist, 38-56, PROF PHILOS, Col Notre Dame, MD, 56-. **HONORS AND AWARDS** DHL, Col Notre Dame, Md, 76. **MEMBERSHIPS** Am Cath Philos Asn; Am Hist Asn. **SELECTED PUBLICATIONS** Auth, Daniel Carroll II, One Man and His Descendants, 1730-1978, 78; Daniel Carroll, Signer of the Constitution, Cath Univ Am, 43; Genealogy of Charles Carroll of Carrollton, 98; articles in: Catholic Encyclopedia, McGraw, 67; Encyclopedia of American Catholic History, Glazier Shelley Book, Liturgical Press, 97. **CONTACT ADDRESS** Dept of Philosophy, Col of Notre Dame of Maryland, 4701 N Charles St, Baltimore, MD, 21210-2404. **EMAIL** VGEIGER@NDM.EDU

GEIMAN, KEVIN
DISCIPLINE PHILOSOPHY **EDUCATION** Xavier Univ, AB, 83; WA, AM, 87; PhD, 88. **CAREER** Philos, Valparaiso Univ. **HONORS AND AWARDS** Univ res prof, Valparaiso Univ, 96-97; NEH Younger Scholars Awd, 95; fac rsch grant, Valparaiso Univ, 91; NEH texts transl grant, 91; NEH Summer Sem, 89. **MEMBERSHIPS** Am Philos Asn; N Am Kant Soc; N Am Soc Pol Legal Philos; Soc Phenom and Exist Philos. **RESEARCH** Soc and polit philos; mod philos; ethics; contemp europ philos; asian philos; environmental philos. **SELECTED PUBLICATIONS** Auth, Enlightened Cosmopolitanism: The Political Perspective of the Kantian 'Sublime', in What is Enlightenment?: Eighteenth Century Answers and Twentieth Century Questions, Univ Calif P, 96; Lyotard's 'Kantian Social-

ism', Philos and Soc Crit, 90; Habermas' Early Lifeworld Appropriation: A Critical Assessment, Man and World, 90; trans, Karl Leonhard Reinhold, Thoughts on Enlightenment in What is Enlightenment?; Jean-Francois Lyotard, Political Writings, Univ Minn P, 93; Michel Foucault, What is Critique? in What is Enlightenment?; co-trans, Christoph Martin Wieland, A Couple of Gold Nuggets, from the...Wastepaper, or Six Answers to Six Questions in What is Enlightenment?. **CONTACT ADDRESS** Valparaiso Univ, 1500 E Lincoln Way, Valparaiso, IN, 46383-6493.

GEISLER, NORMAN LEO

PERSONAL Born 07/21/1932, Warren, MI, m, 1955, 6 children **DISCIPLINE** PHILOSOPHY **EDUCATION** William Tyndale Coll, 55, ThB, 64; Univ Detroit, 56-57, grad school, philosophy, 65-66; Wheaton Coll, BA, philos, 58; Wheaton Graduate School, MA, theology, 60; Wayne State Univ Grad School, philosophy, 64; Northwestern Univ, philosophy, 68; Loyola Univ, Chicago, PhD, philosophy, 70. **CAREER** Dir, Northwest Suburban Youth for Christ, Detroit, 52-54; pastor, Dayton Center Church, Silverwood, MI, 55-57, ordained, 56; asst pastor, River Grove Bible Church, IL, 58-59; Grad asst, Bible-Philosophy Dept, Wheaton Coll, 59; part-time instr in Bible, 59-62; full-time asst prof of Bible and apologetics, 63-66, Detroit Bible Coll; pastor, Memorial Baptist Church, Warren, MI, pastor, 60-63; speaker at churches, retreats, pastor's confs, universities, radio, and television, 60-; pres, Alumni of Detroit Bible Coll, 61-62; several interim pastorates in Michigan, Illinois, and Texas, 65-; full-time assoc prof of philos, Trinity Coll, 70-71; visiting prof philos of religion, 69-70, chm, philos of religion, 70-79, Trinity Evangelical Divinity School; prof systematic theology, Dallas Theologoical Seminary, 79-88; dean liberty, Center Research Evangelical Seminary, Veritas Graduate School. **HONORS AND AWARDS** Elected to Wheaton Scholastic Honor Soc, 77; listed in Who's Who in Religion, Writer's Who Who, Men of Achievement; Alumnus of the Year, William Tyndale Coll, 81; When Skeptics Ask (book) nominated for Medallion Award of the year, missions/evangelism category, 91. **MEMBERSHIPS** Evangelical Theological Soc, 64-; Amer Philos Soc, 68-; Evangelical Philso Soc, 76-; Amer Scientific Assn, 80-; Amer Theological Soc, 80; Amer Acad Religion, 82-. **RESEARCH** Apologetics, theology, epistemology. **SELECTED PUBLICATIONS** Auth, Love Is Always Right, 96; auth, Creating God in the Image of Man?, 97; auth, When Cultists Ask, 97; auth, The Counterfeit Gospel of Mormonism, 98; auth, Legislating Morality, 98. **CONTACT ADDRESS** Southern Evangelical Sem, 4298 McKee Rd., Charlotte, NC, 28270.

GEISSLER, SUZANNE BURR

PERSONAL Born 11/12/1950, Somerville, NJ **DISCIPLINE** AMERICAN AND CHURCH HISTORY **EDUCATION** Syracuse Univ, BA, 71, PhD(hist), 76; Rutgers Univ, MA, 72; Drew Univ, MTS, 79. **CAREER** Instr, State Univ NY Col Cortland, 75-77; lectr, Drew Univ, 77-79; LECTR HIST, UPSALA COL, 79-, Vis lectr, Theol Sch, Drew Univ, 81. **MEMBERSHIPS** Am Soc Church Hist; Am Studies Asn; AHA; Orgn Am Historians. **RESEARCH** Early American religious history. **SELECTED PUBLICATIONS** Auth, A Sense of Deity--The Republican Spirituality of Rush, Benjamin, J Am Hist, Vol 0079, 93. **CONTACT ADDRESS** 4 Midwood Dr, Florham Park, NJ, 07932.

GELLER, DAVID A.

DISCIPLINE LAW **EDUCATION** Boston Univ, BS; New Eng Sch Law, JD. **CAREER** Adj prof Law, Thomas Col, 95-. **SELECTED PUBLICATIONS** Putting the 'Parens' Back into Parens Patriae: Parental Custody of Juveniles as an Alternative to Pretrial Juvenile Detention, 21:2 New Eng J on Criminal and Civil Confinement. **CONTACT ADDRESS** Thomas Col, Admin Bldg, Waterville, ME, 04901-5097. **EMAIL** gellerd@thomas.edu

GELLHORN, GAY

DISCIPLINE CONTRACTS I AND II, ADVANCED CONTRACTS, AND ALTERNATIVE DISPUTE RESOLUTION **EDUCATION** Radcliffe Col, BA, 60; Harvard Univ, MA, 61; Seattle Univ Sch Law, 82. **CAREER** Prof; co-dir, HIV-AIDS/Publ Entitlements Clin; past law clk, Judge James L Oakes, US Ct of Appeals, 2nd Circuit & Justice Thurgood Marshall, US Supreme Ct; assoc, Wilmer, Cutler & Pickering, DC, 84-89. **MEMBERSHIPS** DC Bar. **SELECTED PUBLICATIONS** Publ on, disability and welfare reform, public interest attorney's fees, client interviewing, equal protection. **CONTACT ADDRESS** School of Law, Univ of District of Columbia, 4200 Connecticut Ave Northwest, Washington, DC, 20008.

GELWICK, RICHARD

PERSONAL Born 03/09/1931, Briston, OK, m, 1955, 2 children **DISCIPLINE** THEOLOGY, ETHICS **EDUCATION** Southern Methodist Univ, BA, 52; Yale Univ, MDV, 56; Pacific Sch of Religion, PhD, 65 **CAREER** Intern, 54-55, Campus Ministry, Temple Univer; chaplin, asst prof, Washington at Lee Univ, 56-58; dir of religious activities, Oberlin Coll, 58-60; Danforth Campus Ministry Research Fel, 60-63; United Church of Christ Campus Ministry, Univ of CA, Berkeley, 63-66; Asst prof, 66-67, Chapman Coll; prof and chair, 67-88, Stephens Coll; research assoc, 88-89, Bowdoin Coll; prof and chair, 88-98, research fel, 98-present, Univ of New England. **HONORS AND AWARDS** Rockefeller Doctoral Fel, 61-62; Soc for Relig in Higher Education post- doctoral fel, 73-74; Distinguished Alumnus Award, Pacific Sch of Relig, 97. **MEMBERSHIPS** Amer Acad of Relig; Amer Assn for Bioethics and Humanities; Maine Bioethics Network; The Polangi Soc **RESEARCH** Michael Polangi Philosophy; Medical Ethics; Theology in Belief and in Action **SELECTED PUBLICATIONS** Auth, The Planyi-Tillich Dialogue of 1963: Polanyi's Search for a Post-Critical Logic In Science and in Theology, Tradition & Discovery, 95-96; The Calling of Being Human, Polanyiana, 96; Patient, Not Physician Assisted Dying, The Dissident, 97; Rationing Maine Medicaid, A Bioethics Case Study, Bulletin of the General Theological Library of Bangor Theological Seminary, 97; Rationing Maine Medicaid, A Bioethics Case Study, Bulletin of the General Theological Library of Bangor Theological Seminary, 97; Faith as the First Principle of Charles McCoy's Theology and Ethics, Tradition & Discovery, 97-98. **CONTACT ADDRESS** RR#5 Box 2440, Brunswick, ME, 04011. **EMAIL** rprogel@juno.com

GENDIN, SIDNEY

PERSONAL Born 01/03/1934, New York, NY, m, 1958, 2 children **DISCIPLINE** PHILOSOPHY **EDUCATION** Brooklyn Col, BA, 55; NY Univ, MA, 60, PhD, 65. **CAREER** Instr philos, NY Univ, 63-65; asst prof, State Univ NY Stony Brook, 65-70; assoc prof, 70-80, PROF PHILOS, EASTERN MICH UNIV, 80-. **MEMBERSHIPS** Am Philos Asn. **RESEARCH** Ethics; philosophy of law; epistemology. **SELECTED PUBLICATIONS** Co-ed, A plausible theory of retribution, J Value Inquiry, winter 70; Insanity and criminal responsibility, Am Philos Quart, 4/73; Philosophy; A Contemporary Perspective, Wadsworth, 74; auth, A critique of the theory of criminal rehabilitation, in Punishment & Human Rights, Schenkman, 74. **CONTACT ADDRESS** Dept of Philos, Eastern Michigan Univ, 701 Pray Harrold, Ypsilanti, MI, 48197-2201. **EMAIL** phi_gendin@online.emich.edu

GENNARO, ROCCO J.

PERSONAL Born 10/13/1963, Brooklyn, NY, m, 1990, 1 child **DISCIPLINE** PHILOSOPHY **EDUCATION** Syracuse Univ, PhD, 91. **CAREER** Adjunct asst prof, LeMoyne Col, 91-95; asst prof, 95-. **MEMBERSHIPS** Am Philos Asn; Soc for Philos and Psych. **RESEARCH** Philosophy of psychology; History of early modern philosophy; Applied ethics. **SELECTED PUBLICATIONS** Co-ed, New Essays on the Rationalists, 99; auth, Consciousness and Self-Consciousness: A Defense of the Higher-Order Thought Theory of Consciousness, 96; Mind and Brain: A Dialogue on the Mind-Body Problem, 96; "Leibniz on Consciousness and Self-Consciousness," 99; "The Relevance of Intentions in Morality and Euthanasia" in Int Philos Quart, 96. **CONTACT ADDRESS** Dept of Philosophy, Indiana State Univ, Terre Haute, IN, 47809. **EMAIL** rocco@cube.indstate.edu

GENOVA, ANTHONY CHARLES

PERSONAL Born 08/02/1929, Chicago, IL, m, 1953, 1 child **DISCIPLINE** PHILOSOPHY **EDUCATION** Univ Chicago, PhB, 57, BA, 58, MA, 58, PhD, 65. **CAREER** Instr philos, Roosevelt Univ, 59-61; lectr liberal arts, Basic Prog Liberal Educ Adults, Univ Chicago, 59-62; instr philos, Ill Inst Technol, 62; prof & chmn dept, Wichita State Univ, 62-72; Prof Philos, Univ Kans, 72-, Chmn Dept, 78-, Mem regional selection comt, Woodrow Wilson Fel Found, 66-72; Coun Philos Study Grant, Southampton Col, 68; dept grant, Wichita State Univ, 70; Wichita State Univ res grants, 68-69, 69-70, 70-71, 71-72; Am Philos Soc grants, 69-70, 71-72; Univ Kans res grant, 73-74, 74-75, 75-76, 76-77, 77-78. **MEMBERSHIPS** AAUP; Am Philos Asn; Metaphys Soc Am; Soc Phenomenol & Existential Philos; Soc Phenomenol Res. **RESEARCH** Metaphysics; philosophy of Kant; contemporary analytic philosophy. **SELECTED PUBLICATIONS** Auth, Institutional facts and Brute values, Ethics, 70; Searle's use of 'ought', Philos Studies, 73; Kant and alternative frameworks and possible worlds, Kongressakten, Int Kant Cong, Mainze, 4/74; On Anscombe's exposition of Hume, Analysis, 74; Kant's epigenesis of pure reason, Kant-Studien, 74; Speech acts and illocutionary opacity, Found Lang, 75; Speech acts and non-extensionality, Rev Metaphysics, 76; Linsky on Quine's way out, Philos & Phenomenol Res, 76; Good Transcendental Arguments, Kant-Studien, 84; Ambiguities About Realism and Utterly Distinct Objects, Erkenntris, 88; Fantastic Realisms and Global Skepticism, Philos Quart, 88; Craig on Davidson, a Thumbnail Refutation, Analysis, 91; Objectivity Without Causality, SW Philos Rev, 97; On the Very Idea of Massive Truth, Libr Living Philos (forthcoming). **CONTACT ADDRESS** Dept of Philos, Univ of Kans, Lawrence, KS, 66045-0001. **EMAIL** acg@falcon.cc.ukans.edu

GENOVESI, VINCENT JOSEPH

PERSONAL Born 10/09/1938, Philadelphia, PA **DISCIPLINE** CHRISTIAN ETHICS, THEOLOGY **EDUCATION** Fordham Univ, AB, 62, MA, 66; Woodstock Col, Md, PhL, 63, MDiv, 69; Emory Univ, PhD, 73. **CAREER** Instr philos, Loyola Col, Md, 63-66; asst prof, 73-78, from assoc prof to prof Theol, 78-87, St Joseph's Univ, Pa. **HONORS AND AWARDS** The Christian R and Mary F Lindback Award for Disting Teaching, 85; The Catholic Press Assoc Third Place, for In Pursuit of Love: Catholic Morality and Human Sexuality,97. **MEMBERSHIPS** Soc Christian Ethics; Hastings Inst Soc, Ethics & Life Sci; Cath Theol Soc Am. **RESEARCH** Contemporary Christian ethics; ethical implications of the theology of hope and political theology; medical ethics. **SELECTED PUBLICATIONS** Auth, In Pursuit of Love: Catholic Morality and Human Sexuality, 2nd ed, The Liturgical Press, 96; auth, To Suffer and Die in Christ: Spirituality and Catholic Morality, America, 96; auth, The Touch of God: Marriage as Sacrament, America, 97; auth, Is Jesuit Education Fulfilling Its Mission?, America, 98. **CONTACT ADDRESS** Dept of Theol, St. Joseph's Univ, 5600 City Ave, Philadelphia, PA, 19131-1376. **EMAIL** vgenoves@sju.edu

GENSLER, HARRY J.

PERSONAL Born 05/05/1945, Detroit, MI, s **DISCIPLINE** PHILOSOPHY **EDUCATION** Sacred Heart Sem, BA, 67; Wayne State Univ, MA, 69; Loyola Univ Chic, MDiv, 74; Univ Mich, MA, 76, PhD, 77. **CAREER** Univ Detroit, 69-70; John Carroll Univ, 70-72 & 98-; Gonzaga Univ, 77-81; Loyola Univ Chicago, 81-96; Univ Scranton, 96-98. **MEMBERSHIPS** Amer Philos Asn; Jesuit Philos Asn **RESEARCH** Logic and ethics. **SELECTED PUBLICATIONS** Auth, Godels Theorem Simplified, Univ Press Am, 84; Logic: Analyzing and Appraising Arguments, Prentic Hall, 89; Symbolic Logic: Classical and Advanced Systems, Prentice Hall, 90; Formal Ethics, Routledge, 96; Ethics: A Contemporary Introduction, Routledge, 98. **CONTACT ADDRESS** Philosophy Dept, John Carroll Univ, 20700 N Park Blvd, Cleveland, OH, 44118. **EMAIL** gensler@jcu.edu

GENTRY, PETER J.

PERSONAL Born 04/15/1954, Dallas, TX, m, 1979, 2 children **DISCIPLINE** OLD TESTAMENT/SEPTUAGINT **EDUCATION** Univ of Toronto, BA, 75, BA 78, MA, 79, PhD, 94. **CAREER** Tchg asst, Near Eastern Stud, Univ Toronto, 82-84; lectr, Ontario Theol Sem, 88-92; prof of bibl lang, Toronto Baptist Sem, 84-97; guest lectr, Univ Acadia, 96; fac, Heritage Theol Sem, 96-97; fac, Toronto Baptist Sem, 98-99; res assoc, Near & Middle Eastern Stud., Univ Toronto, 97-99. **HONORS AND AWARDS** Helen E Rogers Admission, 72-73, 74-75; Ontario grad scholar, 78-79; William E Staples Gold Medal in Near Eastern Studies, 78; William E Staples Scholar, 78; Ruby M Jolliffe Scholar, 78-79; open doctoral fel, 82-83, 83-84; TJ Meek Prize in Hebrew Syntax, 83. **MEMBERSHIPS** Soc Bibl Lit; Int Orgn for Septuagint and Cognate Stud. **RESEARCH** Hebrew linguistics; Septuagint; the Gottingen Septuaginta edition. **SELECTED PUBLICATIONS** Auth, Word Processing in Ancient Greek and Hebrew, in Revue Informatique et Statistique dans les Sciences Humaines, 92; auth, The Asterisked Materials in the Greek Job, Scholars Pr, 95; auth, The Place of Theodotion-Job in the Textual History of the Septuagint, in Origen's Hexapla and Fragments, 98; auth, The System of the Finite Verb in Classical Biblical Hebrew, in Hebrew Stud, 98; coauth Towards a New Collection of Hexaplaric Material for the Book of Genesis, in X Vongress of the International Organization for Septuagint and Cognate Studies,98. **CONTACT ADDRESS** 55 Ambercroft Blvd, Scarborough, ON, M1W 2Z6. **EMAIL** pjg@interlog.com

GEORGE, KATHRYN PAXTON

PERSONAL Born 06/12/1943, Northville, MI, m, 1985, 2 children **DISCIPLINE** GENETICS AND PHILOSOPHY **EDUCATION** Wash State Univ, BA, 80, MA, 82, PhD, 85. **CAREER** Asst Prof, Assoc Prof, Dept ch, 89 to 94-, Univ Idaho; Asst Prof, philo, Asst Prof vet, 87-89, Wash State Univ; vis Asst Prof, 85-87, Univ Idaho. **HONORS AND AWARDS** NSF Fel; AAAUW Fel., Editor of Internet/Online pub, EnvironWest. **MEMBERSHIPS** ATHENA; NOW. **RESEARCH** Bioethics; Feminism and science. **SELECTED PUBLICATIONS** Coed, Agricultural Ethics: Issues for the 21st Century, Madison WI, Tri-Soc Pub 94; Feminist Critiques of Science, in: John Norbury, ed, Proceedings of Pions and Beyond 1998, in press; Reply to Adams Donovan Gruen and Gaard, Signs: J Women in Cult and Soc, 95; Discrimination and Bias in the Vegan Ideal, J Agri and Enviro Ethics, 94; Use and Abuse Revisited: Response to Pluhar and Varner, J Agri and Enviro Ethics, 94; Values of Residents of Rural America, in: Encyc of Rural America, ed, Gary A Goreham, Santa Barbara CA, ABC-CLIO, 97; coauth, Internet/Online pub: EnvironWest, research and service entity of Univ Idaho Philo Dept, hosting Martin Inst and Geographic Analysis Prog of US Dept of Interior, originally funded by NSF. **CONTACT ADDRESS** Dept of Philosophy, Univ Idaho, 407 Morrill Hall, Moscow, ID, 83844-3016. **EMAIL** kpgeorge@uidaho.edu

GEORGE, ROLF A.

DISCIPLINE PHILOSOPHY **EDUCATION** Mich State Univ, PhD. **RESEARCH** Theory of knowledge; logic; hist of philos; Kant; Brentano; Bolzano. **SELECTED PUBLICATIONS** Auth, pub(s) on philos of Kant, logic, and philosophical problems in pub policy. **CONTACT ADDRESS** Dept of Philosophy, Waterloo Univ, 200 University Ave W, Waterloo, ON, N2L 3G1. **EMAIL** rgeorge@uwaterloo.ca

GERAETS, THEODORE F.
PERSONAL Born 03/12/1926, The Hague, Netherlands **DISCIPLINE** PHILOSOPHY **EDUCATION** Heythrop Col, Berchmanianum LPh, 51, Canisianum LTh, 57; Gregorianum, Sorbonne, Paris, PhD, 69. **CAREER** Lectr, Berchmanianum Nijmegen, 57-59; lectr to prof, 66-94, dean & ch philos, 76-80, PROF EMER PHILOSOPHY, UNIV OTTAWA, 94-. **MEMBERSHIPS** Can Philos Asn; Hegel Soc Am; Int Hegel Ver; Int Hegel Ges; Int Ges Dialektische Philos; Soc Phenomenol & Exist Philos; Merleau-Ponty Cir. **SELECTED PUBLICATIONS** Auth, Vers une nouvelle philosophie transcendantale, 71; auth, Lo Spirito Assoluto Come Apertura del Sistema Hegeliano, 85; auth, La Logica di Hegel tra Religione e Storia, 96; co-transl, Hegel: The Encyclopaedia Logic, 91. **CONTACT ADDRESS** Dept of Philosophy, Univ of Ottawa, 70 Laurier E, Ottawa, ON, K1N 6N5.

GERARD, JULES BERNARD
PERSONAL Born 05/20/1929, St. Louis, MO, m, 1953, 3 children **DISCIPLINE** CONSTITUTIONAL LAW **EDUCATION** Washington Univ, St Louis, AB, 57, JD, 58. **CAREER** Asst prof law, Sch Law, Univ Mo, 60-62; from asst prof to assoc prof, 62-80, PROF LAW AND CONSTITUTIONAL LAW, WASHINGTON UNIV, ST LOUIS, 80-, Ford Found fel, Univ Wis, 63. **RESEARCH** Judicial power and authority; amending the constitution; changing standards of civil commitment and of the insanity defense. **SELECTED PUBLICATIONS** Auth, The 1st-Amendment in a Hostile Environment--A Primer on Free Speech and Sexual Harassment, Notre Dame Law Rev, Vol 0068, 93. **CONTACT ADDRESS** Sch Law, Washington Univ, 1 Brookings Dr, Box 1120, Saint Louis, MO, 63130-4899.

GERATY, LAWRENCE THOMAS
PERSONAL Born 04/21/1940, St. Helena, CA, m, 1962, 2 children **DISCIPLINE** NEAR EASTERN ARCHEOLOGY, OLD TESTAMENT **EDUCATION** Pac Union Col, AB, 62; Andrews Univ, AM, 63, BD, 65; Harvard Univ, PhD(Near Eastern lang & lit), 72. **CAREER** Asst prof, 72-76, assoc prof, 76-80, PROF ARCHAEOL and HIST ANTIQ, ANDREWS UNIV, 80-, Ed, Andrews Univ Monographs, 72-; res grants, Ctr for Field Res, 76 and Nat Endowment for Humanities, 77; trustee, Am Ctr Orient Res, Amman, Jordon, 76-; cur, Andrews Univ Archaeol Mus, 76-; assoc ed, Andrews Univ Sem Studies, 77-. **MEMBERSHIPS** Am Schs Orient Res; Soc Bibl Lit; Am Inst Archaeol; Nat Asn Prof Hebrew; Asn Adventist Forums (pres, 72-73). **RESEARCH** Palestinian archaeology; semitic inscriptions; Old Testament exegesis. **SELECTED PUBLICATIONS** Auth, A Tribute to Horn, Siegfried, H.--March-17, 1908 November-28, 1993--In-Memoriam, Biblical Archaeol, Vol 0057, 94. **CONTACT ADDRESS** Theol Sem, Andrews Univ, Berrien Springs, MI, 49104.

GERBER, WILLIAM
PERSONAL Born 07/12/1908, Philadelphia, PA, w, 1933, 1 child **DISCIPLINE** PHILOSOPHY **EDUCATION** Univ PA, BA, 29; George Wash Univ, MA, 32; Columbia Univ, PhD, 45. **CAREER** Res positions, 30-70, US Dept of State & US Dept of Labor; instr, 63-73, Univ Md. **HONORS AND AWARDS** Phi Beta Kappa; Meritorious Serv Award, US Dept of State. **MEMBERSHIPS** APA. **RESEARCH** Ethics and metaphysics. **CONTACT ADDRESS** 3077 Chestnut St NW, Washington, DC, 20015.

GERHART, MARY
PERSONAL Born 03/04/1935, Stacyville, IA **DISCIPLINE** THEOLOGY, LITERATURE **EDUCATION** Col St Teresa, Minn, BA, 62; Univ Mo, MA, 68; Univ Chicago, MA, 70, PhD(relig, lit), 73. **CAREER** Asst prof, 72-80, Assoc Prof Relig Studies, Hobart & William Smith Cols, 80-, Ed Chair, Relig Studies Rev, 78-, Nat Endowment for Humanities grant, 76 & Fulbright grant, 82-83. **HONORS AND AWARDS** D J Bowden lectr, Ind Univ, 72; Ida Mae Wilson lectr, Vanderbilt Univ, 80. **MEMBERSHIPS** AAUP; Am Acad Relig; Cath Theol Soc Am. **RESEARCH** Hermeneutical theory; the contemporary novel; metaphor and genre in science and religion. **SELECTED PUBLICATIONS** Auth, Paul Ricoeur's Hermeneutical theory as resource for theological reflection, Thomist, 7/75; Paul Ricoeur, la metaphore vive, Relig Studies Rev, 1/76; Paul Ricoeur's notion of diagnostics: Toward a philosophy of the human, J Relig, 4/76; Generic studies: Their renewed importance in religious and literary interpretation, J Am Acad Relig, 9/77; The ironic mode of religious imagination in Heinrich Boll, CTSA Proc, 77; The question of belief in literary criticism: An intorduction to the hermeneutical theory of Paul Ricoeur, Verlag Hans-Dieter Heniz, 79; The new literature and contemprorary religious conciousness, Angelican Theol Rev, 1/80; Resentfulness transformed: The religious vision of James Joyce, Cross Currents, 3/81. **CONTACT ADDRESS** Dept of Relig Studies, Hobart & William Smith Cols, Scandling Center, Box 4040, Geneva, NY, 14456-3382. **EMAIL** gerhart@hws.edu

GERIG, WESLEY LEE
PERSONAL Born 09/17/1930, Ft Wayne, IN, m, 1952, 4 children **DISCIPLINE** RELIGION, HEBREW, THEOLOGY **EDUCATION** Ft Wayne Bible Col, AB, 51; Fuller Theol Sem, M div, 54, ThM, 56; Univ Iowa, PhD(relig), 65. **CAREER** From instr to assoc prof Bible & theol, 57-69, acad dean, 71-73, Prof Bible & Theol, Ft Wayne Bible Col, 69-91, Chmn Dept Bibl Studies, 62-91; Taylor Univ, 92-;Instr Bibl lang & dir admis, prof Bibl & theol; Winona Lake Sch Theol, 64-. **MEMBERSHIPS** Evangel Theol Soc; Am Acad Relig. **RESEARCH** The Hebrew-Gentile relations in the Old Testament; the social ethics of the Apostolic Fathers; Koine Greek. **CONTACT ADDRESS** Div Bibl Studies, Taylor Univ, Ft. Wayne, 1025 W Rudisill Blvd, Fort Wayne, IN, 46807-2197. **EMAIL** wsgerig@tayloru.edu

GERKIN, CHARLES VINCENT
PERSONAL Born 07/30/1922, Garrison, KS, m, 1945, 6 children **DISCIPLINE** RELIGION AND PERSONALITY **EDUCATION** Washburn Municipal Univ, BA, 45; Garrett Theol Sem, BD, 47. **CAREER** Assoc pastor, First Methodist Church, 47-49, chaplain, Vet Admin Hosp, 49- 51 and Boys Indust Sch, Topeka, 51-56; dir chaplaincy serv, Grady Mem Hosp, Atlanta, 57-62; exec dir, Ga Asn Pastoral Care, 62-70; PROF PASTORAL PSYCHOL, EMORY UNIV, 70-, Guest prof pastoral care, Columbia Theol Sem, 59-70; sr group therapist, Ga Clinic Alcoholism, 60-71; asst prof preventive med and community health, Sch Med, Emory Univ, 63-70. **HONORS AND AWARDS** DD, Baker Univ, 73. **MEMBERSHIPS** Asn Clin Pastoral Educ (pres, 70-71); Am Asn Pastoral Counr; Am Asn Marriage & Family Ther. **RESEARCH** Contemporary forms of crisis experience; pastoral theology and personality theory; pastoral theology and changing social values. **SELECTED PUBLICATIONS** Auth, Care of Persons, Care of Worlds--A Psychosystems Approach to Pastoral Care and Counseling, Theol Today, Vol 0050, 94. **CONTACT ADDRESS** Candler Sch of Theol, Emory Univ, Atlanta, GA, 30322.

GERRISH, BRIAN ALBERT
PERSONAL Born 08/14/1931, London, England, m, 1955, 2 children **DISCIPLINE** RELIGION, HISTORY **EDUCATION** Cambridge Univ, BA, 52, MA, 56; Westminster Col, Eng, cert, 55; Union Theol Sem, STM, 56; Columbia Univ, PhD(philos relig), 58. **CAREER** From instr to assoc prof church hist, McCormick Theol Sem, 58-65; assoc prof hist theol, 65-68, prof hist theol and Reformation hist, 68-72, PROF HIST THEOL, DIVINITY SCH, UNIV CHICAGO, 72-, Am Asn Theol Schs fac fel, 6i-62; John Simon Guggenheim Mem Found fel, 70-72; CO-ED, J RELIG, 72-; Nat Endowment for Humanities fel, 80-81. **MEMBERSHIPS** Am Acad Relig; Am Soc Reformation Res; Am Soc Church Hist (pres, 79). **RESEARCH** Continental Protestant thought in the 16th and 19th centuries. **SELECTED PUBLICATIONS** Auth, Natural Religion and the Nature of Religion--The Legacy of Deism, J Relig, Vol 0073, 93; Religion and the Religions in the English Enlightenment, J Relig, Vol 0073, 93; Atheism from the Reformation to the Enlightenment, J Relig, Vol 0074, 94. **CONTACT ADDRESS** Univ Chicago, 18541 Klimm Ave, Homewood, IL, 60430.

GERT, BERNARD
PERSONAL Born 10/16/1934, Cincinnati, OH, m, 1958, 2 children **DISCIPLINE** PHILOSOPHY **EDUCATION** Univ Cincinnati, BA, 56; Cornell Univ, PhD, 62. **CAREER** From instr to assoc prof philos, 59-70, chemn dept, 71-74, 79-81, & 98-, Prof Philos, Dartmouth Col, 70-, Stone Prof Intellectual & Moral Philos, 81-92, 98-, Eunice and Julian Cohen Prof for the study of Ethics and Human nature, 92-98; vis assoc prof philos, Johns Hopkins Univ, 67- 68; adj prof psychiat, Dartmouth Med Sch, 76-. **HONORS AND AWARDS** Nat Endowment for Humanities-Nsf sustained develop award, 80-84; Nat Endowment for Humanities fel, 69-70; Fulbright Award, Israel, 85-86, Argentina, 95; Grant from Nat Inst of Health, 90-93; Susan Linn Sage Fel in Philos, 58-59., Delegate, USA-USSR Exch Prog in Applied Ethics, 88; consult Comm Med Educ, Group for Adv Psych, 90; Panel on Sci Respon and Conduct Res, (COSEP-UP)NAS/NAEIM 90-92; found Inst Study Applied and Prof Ethics, Dartmouth Col; co-chr, 82-85; exec bd, 89-92; consult ed, Encyclopedia Philos, 93-96; consult, Comm Rev Am Anthrop Asn, 95; Ethics Adv Comm, Mary Hitchcock Mem Hosp, 83-; fel, Hastings Ctr; 86-. **MEMBERSHIPS** Am Philos Asn; Am Soc Polit & Legal Philos; Soc Bus Ethics; Soc Prof Ethics. **RESEARCH** Ethics; philosophy of psychology; philosophy of medicine. **SELECTED PUBLICATIONS** Coauth, The Moral Rules; A New Rational Foundation for Morality, Harper, 70, 73 & 75; ed, Hobbes' Man and Citizen, Doubleday-Anchor, 72; Philosophy in Medicine: Conceptual and Ethical Issues in Medicine and Psychiatry, Oxford, 82; auth, Morality: It's Nature and Justification, Oxford Univ Press, 98; Bioethics: A Return to Fundamentals, Oxford Univ Press, 97; Morality and the New Genetics: A Guide for Students and Health Care Providers, Jones and Bartlett Pubs, 96. **CONTACT ADDRESS** Dept of Philosophy, Dartmouth Col, 6035 Thornton Hall, Hanover, NH, 03755-3592. **EMAIL** bernard.gert@dartmouth.edu

GERT, HEATHER
DISCIPLINE PHILOSOPHY **EDUCATION** Brown Univ, PhD, 91. **CAREER** Asst prof, 91-97, assoc prof, 97- , Texas A&M Univ. **MEMBERSHIPS** APA. **RESEARCH** Wittgenstein; philosophy of mind/language; ethics. **SELECTED PUBLICATIONS** Auth, "Alternative Analyses," Southern J of Philos, 95; "Viability," International J of Philos Stud, 95; "Family Resemblances and Criteria," Synthese, 95; "Wittgenstein on Description," Philos Stud, 97; "Anger and Chess," Midwest Stud in Philos, forthcoming. **CONTACT ADDRESS** Dept of Philosophy, Texas A&M Univ, College Station, TX, 77843-4237. **EMAIL** heather@snaefell.tamu.edu

GETCHES, DAVID H.
PERSONAL Born 08/17/1942, Abington, PA, m, 1964, 3 children **DISCIPLINE** LAW **EDUCATION** Occidental Col, AB, 64; Univ Southern Calif, JD, 67. **CAREER** Instr polit sci, Univ Calif, San Diego, 69-70; dir, Native Am Rights Fund, 70-76; ASSOC PROF LAW, SCH LAW, UNIV COLO, 79-, Vis lectr, Col Law, Univ Denver, 75; adj prof, Ctr Northern Educ Res, Univ Alaska, 75. **MEMBERSHIPS** Asn Am Law Sch; Rocky Mountain Mineral Law Found. **RESEARCH** Indian law; water law; natural resources. **SELECTED PUBLICATIONS** Auth, American-Indian Law Deskbook--Conference of Western Attorneys-General, Western Hist Quart, Vol 0025, 94; Conquering the Cultural Frontier--the New Subjectivism of the Supreme-Court in Indian Law, Calif Law Rev, Vol 0084, 96; Dedication to Professor Johnson, Ralph, W, Wash Law Rev, Vol 0072, 97. **CONTACT ADDRESS** Sch Law, Univ Colo, P O Box 401, Boulder, CO, 80309-0401.

GEYER, ALAN
PERSONAL Born 08/03/1931, Dover, NJ, m, 1985, 6 children **DISCIPLINE** POLITICAL SCIENCE, CHRISTIAN ETHICS **EDUCATION** Ohio Wesleyan Univ, BA, 52; Boston Univ, STB, 55, PhD, 61. **CAREER** Pastor, Trinity Methodist Church, NJ, 58-60; asst to assoc prof, polit sci, Mary Baldwin Col, 60-65; Dir Int Rel, United Church of Christ, 65-68; ed, Christian Century, 68-72; Dag Hammarskjold Prof of Peace Stud and Pol Sci, Colgate Univ, 72-77; exec dir, Churches' Ctr for Theol & Public Policy, 77-87; prof polit ethics & ecumenics, Wesley Sem, 87-96; Canon Ecumenist, Wahington Nat Cathedral, 97-. **HONORS AND AWARDS** Phi Beta Kappa; Omicron Delta Kappa; Delta Sigma Rho; Alpha Kappa Delta; Robinson Fel; Kent Fel; Dempster Fel; LittD, hon, Ohio Wesleyan Univ; distinguished alumnus awards; James K Mathews Distinguished Service Award; Satterwhite Award in Christian Social Ethics. **MEMBERSHIPS** Am Polit Sci Asn; Soc of Christian Ethics; Arms Control Asn. **RESEARCH** Ethics and foreign policy; religion and politics. **SELECTED PUBLICATIONS** Auth, Piety and Politics, 63; auth, The Idea of Disarmament! Rethinking the Unthinkable, 82; auth, Redeeming the City, 82; auth, Christianity and the Superpowers: Religion, Politics, and History in US-USSR Relations, 90; auth, Lines in the Sand: Justice and the Gulf War, 92; auth, Ideology in America: Challenges to Faith, 97. **CONTACT ADDRESS** 5014 Smallwood Dr, Bethesda, MD, 20816. **EMAIL** 75254.2405@compuserv.com

GHOSH, SHUBA
PERSONAL Born 12/08/1964, India, m, 1994 **DISCIPLINE** LAW **EDUCATION** Amherst Col, BA, 84; Univ of Mich, PhD, 88; Stanford Law Sch, JD, 94. **CAREER** Asst prof, Univ of Tex, 88-91; asst prof, Okla City Univ, 96-98; assoc prof, Georgia State Univ, 98-. **MEMBERSHIPS** Am Law & Econ Asn; Law & Soc; Am Econ Asn; Soc for Evolutionary Anal of Law. **RESEARCH** Social Science in Law; Game Theory and Law; Law and Economic Development, especially in India and South Asia; Law and Literature, especially its critics. **SELECTED PUBLICATIONS** Auth, An Economic Analysis of the Common Control Exception to Gray Market Exclusion, in 15 Univ of Penn J of Int Bus Law 373, 94; Understanding Immigrant Entrepreneurs, in Reframing the Immigration Debate, 96; Property Rules, Liability Rules, and Termination Rights: A Fresh Look at the Employment at will Debate with Applications to Franchising and Divorce, in 75 Ore. L.Rev. 101, 96; Takings, the Exit Option, and Just Compensation, in 17 Int Rev of Law and Econ 157, 97; An Intellectual Property Optimist Looks at Article 9 and Bankruptcy, in 7 Fordham Intellectual Property, Media & Entertainment L.J., 97; The Legal, Policy, and Economic Implications of Immigrant Entrepreneurs for the Immigration Reform Debate, in 5 UCLA Asian Pacific Law Rev, 98; Methods, Conclusions, and the Search For Scientific Validity in Economics and Other Social Sciences, in Legal Forum, 98. **CONTACT ADDRESS** Col of Law, Georgia State Univ, 140 Decatur St, Rm 442, Atlanta, GA, 30303. **EMAIL** sgosh@gsu.edu

GIANNELLI, PAUL CLARK
PERSONAL Born 05/21/1945, New York, NY, m, 1970, 2 children **DISCIPLINE** LAW **EDUCATION** Providence Col, BA, 67; Univ VA, JD, 70; George Washington Univ, MS, 73; Univ Va, LLM, 75. **CAREER** Atty criminal law, US Army, 70-75; PROF EVIDENCE AND CRIMINAL LAW, CASE WESTERN RESERVE UNIV, 75-. **RESEARCH** Evidence; criminal procedure; criminal law. **SELECTED PUBLICATIONS** Auth, Junk Science--The Criminal-Cases, J Criminal Law and Criminology, Vol 0084, 93. **CONTACT ADDRESS** 3129 Chadbourne Rd, Shaker Heights, OH, 44120.

GIBBARD, ALLAN FLETCHER
PERSONAL Born 04/07/1942, Providence, RI, m, 1972, 1 child **DISCIPLINE** PHILOSOPHY **EDUCATION** Swarthmore Col, BA, 63; Harvard Univ, PhD(Philos), 71. **CAREER** From asst prof to assoc prof Philos, Univ Chicago, 69-74; assoc prof, Univ Pittsburg; prof Philos, Univ Mich, Ann Arbor, 77-.

HONORS AND AWARDS Phi Beta Kappa; Sigma Xi assoc mem; Blanshard philos essay prize. **RESEARCH** Ethics; social choice theory; foundations of modal logic. **SELECTED PUBLICATIONS** Auth, Utilitarianism--merely an illusory alternative?, Australasian J Philos, 65; Doing no more harm than good, Philos Studies, 73; Manipulation of voting schemes: A general result, Econometrica, 74; Wise Chice, Apt Feelings, Harvard Univ Press, 90. **CONTACT ADDRESS** Dept of Philosophy, Univ of Michigan, 435 S State St, Ann Arbor, MI, 48109-1003. **EMAIL** gibbard@umich.edu

GIBBS, JACK GILBERT, JR.
PERSONAL Born 08/11/1953, Columbus, OH, m, 1992 **DISCIPLINE** LAW **EDUCATION** MI State Univ, BA, 1975; Capital Univ Law School, JD, 1981. **CAREER** Columbus Public Schools, teacher, 1976-78; Ohio Attorney General, legal intern, 1980-81; Ben Espy, law clerk, 1982; Self Employed, Attorney, 1982-. **HONORS AND AWARDS** Ohio House of Representatives, resolution, 1983; Columbus Dispatch, Community Service Award, 1988; Capital Law School, Service Award, 1990; Ohio State Univ, Business School, Comm Service Award, 1989; Hilltop Civic Council Inc, Service Award, 1994. **MEMBERSHIPS** Hilltop Civic Council Inc, bd mem, pres, 1987-93; Centenary United Methodist Church, Chairman admin bd, 1987-95; Columbus Bar Assn, 1982-; Ohio State Bar Assn, 1982-; American Bar Assn, 1982-; American Inns of Court, 1994-; Capital Law School Black Alumni, pres, 1990-; UNCF Star Panelist, star panelist, 1993-. **SELECTED PUBLICATIONS** Lecture to community groups; Teach one seminar to Attorneys a year; testified as an expert witness on Probate Law; Written serveral articles on Probate Law & Estate Planning. **CONTACT ADDRESS** 233 S High St, Ste 208, Columbus, OH, 43215.

GIBBS, JEFFREY A.
PERSONAL Born 03/04/1952, Trenton, NJ, m, 1973, 4 children **DISCIPLINE** THEOLOGY **EDUCATION** Rice Univ, BA, 74; Concordia Theol Sem, MDiv, 79, STM, 88; Union Theol Sem, PhD, 95. **CAREER** Pastor, Calvary, St. Helens, Ore, 79-86; pastor, Grace, Scappoose, Ore, 79-89; asst prof, 92-97, assoc prof, exegetical theol, 97- , asst acad adv, 96- , Concordia Sem. **MEMBERSHIPS** Soc of Bibl Lit; Cath Bibl Asn. **RESEARCH** Gospel of Matthew; New Testament eschatology. **SELECTED PUBLICATIONS** Auth, The Grace of God as the Foundation for Ethics, Concordia Theol Q, 84; auth, Parables of Atonement and Assurance: Matthew 13-44-46, Concordia Theol Q, 87; auth, The Search for the Idiosyncratic Jesus, Concordia J, 94; auth, An Exegetical Case for Closed Communion, Concordia J, 95. **CONTACT ADDRESS** Concordia Sem, 801 DeMun Ave, St. Louis, MO, 63105. **EMAIL** gibbsj@csl.edu

GIBBS, LEE WAYLAND
PERSONAL Born 03/07/1937, Natchitoches, LA, m, 1960, 3 children **DISCIPLINE** RELIGION **EDUCATION** Macalester Col, AB, 59; Harvard Univ, STB, 62, ThD, 68. **CAREER** Asst prof hist Christian thought, Case Western Reserve Univ, 67-71; asst prof, 71-73, assoc prof, 73-82, prof church hist & psychol of Relig, Cleveland State Univ, 82-. **HONORS AND AWARDS** NEH grant, 77-78 **MEMBERSHIPS** Am Acad Relig; Am Soc Church Hist; AAUP. **RESEARCH** History of Christian thought; myth, ritual and symbol; psychology of religion. **SELECTED PUBLICATIONS** Art, Richard Hooker's Via Media Doctrine of Justification, Harvard Theol Rev, 11/81; art, Religion and Science in a High Technology World, Bulletin of Science, Technology & Society, 97. **CONTACT ADDRESS** Dept of Relig Studies, Cleveland State Univ, 1983 E 24th St, Cleveland, OH, 44115-2440. **EMAIL** ligibbs@popmail.csuohio.edu

GIBBS, PAUL J.
PERSONAL Born 11/20/1966, Boston, MA, m, 1990, 2 children **DISCIPLINE** PHILOSOPHY **EDUCATION** Univ Cincinnati, PhD, 94. **CAREER** Vis asst prof, 96-. **HONORS AND AWARDS** NEH grant, 98. **MEMBERSHIPS** Am Philos Asn; Asn for the Advan of Philos and Psych. **RESEARCH** Philosophy; Psychology. **SELECTED PUBLICATIONS** Auth, "Schizophrenia as Solipsism: A Grounding for Philosophical Counseling" in Contemp Philos, 98; "Ethical Connectionism" in Contemp Philos, 97. **CONTACT ADDRESS** Dept of Philosophy, John Carroll Univ, 20700 N Park Blvd, Cleveland, OH, 44118. **EMAIL** PGIBBS@jcuaxa.jdcu.edu

GIBLIN, CHARLES HOMER
PERSONAL Born 01/22/1928, Chicago, IL **DISCIPLINE** SACRED SCRIPTURE **EDUCATION** Loyola Univ, Ill, AB, 50, MA, 52; WBaden Univ, STL, 59; Pontif Bibl Inst, Rome, SSD, 67. **CAREER** Instr New Testament, Hebrew and Bibl Greek, Bellarmine Sch Theol, 59, asst prof New Testament, 64-65; from asst prof to assoc prof theol, New Testament, 67-76, PROF THEOL, NEW TESTAMENT, FORDHAM UNIV, 77-. **MEMBERSHIPS** Cath Bibl Asn Am; Soc Bibl Lit; Soc New Testament Studies. **RESEARCH** Pauline theology; Lucan theology. **SELECTED PUBLICATIONS** Auth, Mary Anointing for Jesus Burial-Resurrection (John-XII,1-8): A Note on the Tripartite Narrative and the Bipartitie Sign-Thematic Literary Structures of the Johannine Gospel, Biblica, Vol 0073, 92; Recapitulation and the Literary Coherence of John Apocalypse, Cath Biblical Quart, Vol 0056, 94; Evangelization and Conflict--Investigations on the Literary and Thematic Coherence of the Account of the Conversion of Cornelius (Acts-X,1-XI,18), J Biblical Lit, Vol 0114, 95. **CONTACT ADDRESS** Dept of Theol, Fordham Univ, 501 E Fordham Rd, Bronx, NY, 10458-5191.

GIBLIN, MARIE J.
PERSONAL Born 05/23/1944, Newark, NJ **DISCIPLINE** CHRISTIAN ETHICS **EDUCATION** Union Theol Sem, PhD, 86. **CAREER** Maryknoll Sch of Theol, 86-94; Xavier Univ, 94-. **MEMBERSHIPS** Am Acad of Relig; Col Theol Soc; Soc of Christian Ethics; Catholic Theol Soc of Am. **RESEARCH** Health care ethics. **SELECTED PUBLICATIONS** Auth, World Health Care Financing and the World Bank : An Ethical Reflection, Jour of Theol and Pub Policy, 93; auth, Corporatism, and, Quadragesimo Anno, in Dwyer, ed, The New Dictionary of Catholic Social Thought, Liturgical, 94; auth, Dualism, Empowerment, Hierarchy, in Russell, ed, Dictionary of Feminist Theologies, John Knox, 96; auth, The Prophetic Role of Feminist Bioethics, Horizons, 97. **CONTACT ADDRESS** Dept of Theology, Xavier Univ, 3800 Victory Pky, Cincinnati, OH, 45207-4442. **EMAIL** giblin@xavier.xu.edu

GIBSON, SCOTT M.
DISCIPLINE MINISTRY, PREACHING **EDUCATION** Penn State Univ, BS; Gordon-Conwell Theol Sem, MDiv; Princeton Theol Sem, ThM; Knox Col, Univ Toronto, MTh; Univ Oxford, DPhil. **CAREER** Sem archivist; dir, Mentored Ministry; asst dean; asst prof, Gordon-Conwell Theol Sem, 92-. **HONORS AND AWARDS** Fel, Case Stud inst., Minister, Amer Baptist Churches, USA; pres, Amer Baptist Evangel. **MEMBERSHIPS** Mem, Acad Homiletics. **RESEARCH** Contemporary issues in preaching, pastoral ministry concerns, the history of preaching, history of evangelicalism. **SELECTED PUBLICATIONS** Ed, ABE Jour; co-ed, Integrity, Proj Timothy. **CONTACT ADDRESS** Gordon-Conwell Theol Sem, 130 Essex St, South Hamilton, MA, 01982.

GIBSON, WILLIAM M.
PERSONAL Born 09/11/1934, Hackensack, NJ, m, 1989 **DISCIPLINE** CRIMINAL LAW **EDUCATION** Rutgers, BA 1956; Law Review Boston Univ Law, JD 1959; Boston Coll, MSW 1966; Harvard Business School, AMP Certificate 1973; Valordictorian MDiv Virginia Magna Cum Laude 1989. **CAREER** US Dept of Justice, asst US Atty 1961-64; Boston Univ Law, dir law & poverty project 1966-70; Boston Univ School Afro Amer Studies, Assoc Prof 1968-71; Office Economic Opportunity, regional counsel 1970-72; FTC, regional dir 1972-78; Fuller Mental Health Center, supt area dir; Boston, Metro Dist, deputy district manager; St Paul's Baptist Church, minister of educ and singles; Medical College of VA Hospital, Richmond, staff chaplain, 1990-91; SAINT STEPHEN'S BAPTIST CHURCH, PASTOR, currently; VA UNION UNIV, CRIMINOLOGY & CRIMINAL JUSTICE DEPT, INSTRUCTOR, 1993-; Policy Academy, recruit class chaplain, 1998. **HONORS AND AWARDS** 10 Outstanding Young Men Award Boston Jr CC 1968; Boston Univ Law School, Young Lawyers Chair, 1969; Community Serv Award Roxbury YMCA 1969; Outstanding Performance Award FTC 1972; Outstanding Govt Serv Award NAACP Boston 1975; Outstanding Serv Award Salvation Army 1980; Samuel H James, Sr Theological Award, VA Union School of Theology, 1989; St Stephens Bapt Church, Man of the Year, 1996. **MEMBERSHIPS** Mem Natl Assoc Social Work 1966; mem Academy Certified Social Worker 1968; mem MA Bar Assoc 1984; Sports Anglers Club, VA; Henrico County Criminal Justice Commission; Richmond Police Citizens Academy Board. **CONTACT ADDRESS** Saint Stephen's Baptist Church of Central Point, 1202 West Graham Rd, Richmond, VA, 23220.

GIER, NICHOLAS F.
DISCIPLINE PHILOSOPHY **EDUCATION** OR State Univ, BA, 66, MA, 69; PhD, 73. **CAREER** Prof, Univ ID. **HONORS AND AWARDS** Alumni Awd, 91. **SELECTED PUBLICATIONS** Auth, God, Reason and the Evangelicals: The Case Against Evangelical Rationalism, Univ Am, 87; Wittgenstein and Phenomenology: A Comparative Study of the Later Wittgenstein, NYU, 81; Process Philosophy and Theology in Religious Studies (rev), 92; Charles Hartshorne's Concept of God in Religious Studies (rev), 92; The Rehabilitation of Whitehead in Journal of the American Academy of Religion (rev), 91; Evil Revisited in Religious Studies (rev), 93; Criss-Crossing a Philosophical Landscape in Canadian Philosophical Reviews (rev), 93; Purana Perennis, Asian Folklore Studies (rev), 94; Stubborn Fact and Creative Advance: An Introduction to the Metaphysics of Alfred North Whitehead in Religious Studies Review, 95. **CONTACT ADDRESS** Philos Dept, Univ ID, W 6th St, PO Box 415, Moscow, ID, 83844. **EMAIL** ngier@uidaho.edu

GIERE, RONALD N.
DISCIPLINE PHILOSOPHY **EDUCATION** Cornell Univ, PhD. **RESEARCH** Nonlinguistic modes of representation for theoretical models and experimental data; study of science and technology as human and cultural activities. **SELECTED PUBLICATIONS** Auth, Visual Models and Scientific Judgment, Univ Toronto, 95; Science Without Laws of Nature, Laws Nature, 95; The Cognitive Structure of Scientific Theories, Philos Sci, 94; Science and Technology Studies: Prospects for an Enlightened Post-Modern Synthesis, Sci Tech Human Values, 93; The Cognitive Construction of Scientific Knowledge, Social Studies Sci, 92; ed, Cognitive Models of Science, Univ Minn, 92. **CONTACT ADDRESS** Philosophy Dept, Univ of Minnesota, Twin Cities, 355 Ford Hall, 224 Church St SE, Minneapolis, MN, 55455. **EMAIL** giere@tc.umn.edu

GIFFORD, DANIEL JOSEPH
PERSONAL Born 01/07/1932, Utica, NY, m, 1960, 3 children **DISCIPLINE** LAW **EDUCATION** Holy Cross Col, AB, 53; Harvard Univ, LLB, 58 **CAREER** Assoc, Cleary, Gottlieb, Steen and Hamilton, 58-62; from asst prof to assoc prof law, Vanderbilt Univ, 62-65; Ford fel, Columbia Univ, 65-66; prof law, State Univ NY, Buffalo, 66-77; PROF LAW, UNIV MINN, 77-, Reporter admin law, Tenn Law Revision Comn, 63-64; consult, Ark Govt Studies Comn, 68 and Admin Conf US, 68-69; vis fel, Univ Warkwick, UK, 73. **MEMBERSHIPS** AAUP. **RESEARCH** Administrative law; antitrust law. **SELECTED PUBLICATIONS** Auth, Agenda For Reform--The Future of Employment Relationships and the Law, Iowa Law Rev, Vol 0080, 94; Strike--The Daily-News War and the Future of American Labor, Notre Dame Law Rev, Vol 0072, 96; Federal Administrative-Law Judges--The Relevance of Past Choices To Future-Directions, Admin Law Rev, Vol 0049, 97. **CONTACT ADDRESS** Law Sch, Univ Minn, 229 19th Ave S, Minneapolis, MN, 55455-0401.

GIGGER, HELEN C.
PERSONAL Born 12/24/1944, Houston, TX, m **DISCIPLINE** LAW **EDUCATION** TX South U, BA Pol Sci 1965; TX So U, JD 1968. **CAREER** State of OK, OK crime comm, legal coun, planner; Dean of Law Sch, res asst; Houston Leg Found, legal intern; Okla City & Co Comm Act Prog Inc, prog analyst. **HONORS AND AWARDS** Grad with Hons in 1961, 1965 & at top of Law Class in 1968; re chrprsn of Reg VI NAACP Conf 1974; Parli; Nat Delta Conv 1973; Delta Cen Reg Parli 1974; mem of Greater Cleves CME Ch; Ch Prog Chrprsn. **MEMBERSHIPS** Mem Am Nat & OK Bar Assns; sec JJ & Bruce Law Soc; mem Amer Judiccature Soc; EEOC off Okla Crime Comm; mem Nat Spa Courts Plan Org; lect Crim Just OK City U; mem YWCA; Urban League; League of Women Voters Georgia Brown's Demo Women's Club; OK Black Pol Cau; past pres Delta Sigma Theta Sor Inc; sec Local & State NAACP; elected Nat Scholarship & Standards Com 4 yr term; policy making com Delta Sigma Theta Inc 1975. **CONTACT ADDRESS** 3033 N Walnut, Oklahoma City, OK, 73105.

GIGNAC, FRANCIS THOMAS
PERSONAL Born 02/24/1933, Detroit, MI **DISCIPLINE** PHILOLOGY, THEOLOGY **EDUCATION** Loyola Univ, Ill, AB, 55, MA, 57, MA, 68; Oxford Univ, DPhil(Greek), 64. **CAREER** Instr Greek, Loyola Univ, Ill, 65-67; from asst prof to assoc prof Theol, Fordham Univ, 68-74; assoc prof Bibl Studies & chmn dept, Cath Univ Am, 74-, NSF travel grant, 67. **MEMBERSHIPS** Cath Bibl Asn; Am Philol Asn; Am Soc Papyrologists. **RESEARCH** The language of the non-literary Greek papyri; the language of the Greek New Testament; textual criticism. **SELECTED PUBLICATIONS** Auth, The language of the non-literary Greek papyri, Am Studies Papyrology, 70; The text of Acts in Chrysostom's homilies, Traditio, 70; The pronunciation of Greek stops in the papyri, Trans & Proc Am Philol Asn, 70; An Introductory New Testament Greek Course, Loyola Univ, 73; A Grammar of the Greek Papyri of the Roman and Byzantine Periods (2 vols), Cisalpino-La Goliardica, Milan, 76 & 81. **CONTACT ADDRESS** Dept of Biblical Studies, Catholic Univ of America, 620 Michigan Ave NE, Washington, DC, 20064-0002. **EMAIL** gignac@cua.edu

GILBERT, JOSEPH
PERSONAL Born 12/01/1934, New York, NY, m, 1960, 2 children **DISCIPLINE** ETHICS, CONTEMPORARY PHILOSOPHY **EDUCATION** Brooklyn Col, BA, 62; NY Univ, MA, 63, PhD(philos), 69. **CAREER** Assoc prof, 66-74, prof Philos, State Univ NY Col Brockport, 74-, chairperson, 77-, dir & ed, Proc Ctr Philos Exchange, 75-, dir ctr philos exchange, 78-. **MEMBERSHIPS** Am Philos Asn; Philos Soc Studies Sport. **RESEARCH** Moral philosophy; philosophy of religion. **SELECTED PUBLICATIONS** Auth, Foot-notes, Philos Exchange, Summer 71; Neutrality and universalizability, Personalist, Autumn 72; Moral notions, Folio Humanistica, 74. **CONTACT ADDRESS** Dept of Humanities & Philos, SUNY, Brockport, 350 New Campus Dr, Brockport, NY, 14420-2914.

GILBERT, MARGARET
DISCIPLINE PHILOSOPHY **EDUCATION** Cambridge Univ, BA, 65; Oxford Univ, MA, 67; PhD, 78. **CAREER** Prof Philos, Univ Conn, 89-; assoc prof Philos, Univ Conn, 83-89; vis prof, King's Col London, 96-98. **HONORS AND AWARDS** ACLS fel, 89-90; mem/fel, Inst Advan Study, 78-79. **MEMBERSHIPS** Am Philos Asn. **RESEARCH** Philosophical Social Theory; Political Philosophy. **SELECTED PUBLICATIONS** Auth, On Social Facts, 89; auth, Living Together: Rationality, Sociality, and Obligation. **CONTACT ADDRESS** Dept of Philosophy U-54, Univ of Connecticut, Storrs, CT, 06269. **EMAIL** gilbert@u_connvm.uconn.edu

GILDRIC, RICHARD P.
PERSONAL Born 04/18/1945, Norfolk, VA, m, 1966, 2 children **DISCIPLINE** HISTORY & PHILOSOPHY **EDUCATION** Eckerd Col, BA, 66; Univ Va, MA, 68, PhD, 71. **CAREER** Prof, Austin Peay State Univ, 70-. **HONORS AND AWARDS** Kenneth S. Lafaurette Prize. **MEMBERSHIPS** OIEAHC; OAH; AHA; AAUP **RESEARCH** Colonial America; early modern Britian. **SELECTED PUBLICATIONS** Auth, The Profane, The Civil & the Godly: The Reformation of Manners in Orthodox New England 1679-1749, 94. **CONTACT ADDRESS** Dept of History & Philosophy, Austin Peay State Univ, Clarksville, TN, 37044. **EMAIL** gildrier@apsu01.apsu.edu

GILES, THOMAS RANSOM
PERSONAL Born 04/10/1937 **DISCIPLINE** PHILOSOPHY **CAREER** Research, 94-. **MEMBERSHIPS** APA. **SELECTED PUBLICATIONS** Auth Dictionary of Philosophers and Terms, Univ Press Univ Sao Paulo, 93. **CONTACT ADDRESS** PO Box 16678, Jersey City, NJ, 07306.

GILKES, CHERYL TOWNSEND
PERSONAL Born 11/02/1947, Boston, Massachusetts, s **DISCIPLINE** THEOLOGY **EDUCATION** Northeastern Univ, BA 1970, MA 1973, PhD 1979. **CAREER** Harvard Univ the Divinity Sch, research assoc, visiting lecturer 1981-82; faculty fellow Bunting Inst, & Radcliffe Coll; Union Baptist Church, assoc minister 1982-; Boston Univ, asst prof of sociology 1978-. **HONORS AND AWARDS** Eastern Sociological Society, I Peter Gellmon awrd 1986. **MEMBERSHIPS** Sec Cambridge Civic Unity Comm 1978-; asst dean Congress of Christian Education United Baptist Convention of MA, RI, NH 1986-; mem Amer Sociological Assoc, Assoc of Black Sociologist, Delta Sigma Theta 1983-. **CONTACT ADDRESS** Boston Univ, 96-100 Cummington St, Boston, MA, 02215.

GILL, DAVID W.
PERSONAL Born 02/02/1946, Omaha, NE, m, 1967, 2 children **DISCIPLINE** ETHICS **EDUCATION** Univ Calif, Berkeley, BA, 68; San Francisco State, MA, 71; Univ So Calif, PhD, 79. **CAREER** Asst prof, 79-82, assoc prof, 82-86, prof, 86-90, ethics, New College, Berkeley; prof, applied ethics, North Park Univ, 92- . **MEMBERSHIPS** APA; Asn for Practical and Prof Ethics; Conf on Faith and Hist; Natl Asn for Sci, Technol and Soc; Soc of Christian Ethics; Soc of Christian Philos. **RESEARCH** Technology and ethics; virtue ethics. **SELECTED PUBLICATIONS** Auth, The Unique Role of the Church in a Troubled Society, in Hawkinson, ed, Leadership Is Serving, v 2, Covenant, 93; auth, My Journey with Ellul, Ellul Forum, 94; auth, articles in Atkinson, ed, New Dictionary of Christian Ethics, InterVarsity, 95; auth, Two Calls to Christian Action, Covenant Companion, 95; auth, The Moral Character of Means and Ends, The Real Issue, 95; guest ed, The Ellul Forum for the Critique of Technological Civilization, Univ So Fla, 96; ed, Should God Get Tenure? Essays on Religion and Higher Education, Eerdmans, 97; auth, articles in Banks, ed, The Complete Book of Everyday Christianity, InterVarsity, 97; auth, Educating for Meaning and Morality: The Contribution of Technology, Bull of Sci, Technol and Soc, 97; coauth, Trends and Connections: Business, Technology and Values at the Dawn of a New Century, forthcoming; auth, Doing Right: Principles and Practices for Biblical People, forthcoming; auth, Becoming Good: Character and Community for Biblical People, forthcoming. **CONTACT ADDRESS** Dept of Philosophy, No Park Col, 3225 W Foster Ave, Chicago, IL, 60625. **EMAIL** dgill@northpark.edu

GILL, MICHAEL
DISCIPLINE 20TH CENTURY ETHICS, THE HISTORY OF MODERN PHILOSOPHY **EDUCATION** NC Univ, Chapel Hill, PhD. **CAREER** Asst prof, Purdue Univ. **RESEARCH** 17th and 18th Century British ethics. **SELECTED PUBLICATIONS** Published articles on moral justification, and on Hutcheson and Hume. **CONTACT ADDRESS** Dept of Philos, Purdue Univ, 1080 Schleman Hall, West Lafayette, IN, 47907-1080.

GILL, SAM
DISCIPLINE RELIGIOUS STUDIES **EDUCATION** Univ Chicago, PhD. **CAREER** Prof. **SELECTED PUBLICATIONS** Auth, Storytracking: Texts, Stories; Histories in Centrak Australia; Mother Earth: An American Story and the Dictionary of Native American Mythology; ed, The Arts of Living. **CONTACT ADDRESS** Religious Studies Dept, Univ of Colorado, Boulder, Boulder, CO, 80309. **EMAIL** Sam.Gill@Colorado.edu

GILLAN, GARTH J.
PERSONAL Born 02/14/1939, Washington, DC, m, 1964, 1 child **DISCIPLINE** PHILOSOPHY **EDUCATION** St John's Univ, Minn, AB, 62; Duquesne Univ, MA, 64, PhD(philos), 66. **CAREER** Asst prof philos, Seton Hill Col, 65-66; asst prof, Canisius Col, 66-69; assoc prof, 69-80, Prof Philos, Southern Ill Univ, Carbondale, 80-. **MEMBERSHIPS** Soc Phenomenol & Existential Philos; Am Philos Asn. **RESEARCH** Phenomenology; structuralism; critical theory. **SELECTED PUBLICATIONS** Auth, Language meaning and symbolic presence, Int Philos Quart, 69; The temporality of language and the symbolic, Philos & Rhetoric, 70; The noematics of reason, Philos & Phenomenol Res, 72; ed, Horizons aof the Flesh: Critical Perspectives on the Thought of Merleau-Ponty, Southern Ill Univ, 73; auth, Toward a critical conception of semiotics, 76 & coauth, The new alternative in critical sociology; Foucault's discursive analysis, 77, Cult Hermeneutics; auth, From Sign to Symbol, Harvester Press, 81; coauth, Michel Foucault: Social Theory and Transgression, Columbia Univ Press, 82; Rising from the Ruins: Reason, Being & The Good after Anschwitz, SUNY Press, 98. **CONTACT ADDRESS** Dept of Philosophy, Southern Illinois Univ, Carbondale, IL, 62901-4300. **EMAIL** gjgillan@siu.edu

GILLEN, MARK R.
DISCIPLINE LAW **EDUCATION** Univ Toronto, BC, 81, LLM, 87; York Univ, MBA, 93, LLB, 85. **CAREER** Asst prof, 87-92; assoc prof, 92-. **MEMBERSHIPS** Can Asn Law Tchr. **RESEARCH** Corporate and securities law. **SELECTED PUBLICATIONS** Auth, Securities Regulation in Canada, Carswell; pubs on Malaysian constitutional law; co-auth, Corporations Principles and Policies, Emond Montgomery; Corporations and Partnerships: Canada, Kluwer. **CONTACT ADDRESS** Fac of Law, Univ Victoria, PO Box 2400, Victoria, BC, V8W 3H7. **EMAIL** mgillen@uvic.ca

GILLETT, CARL
PERSONAL Born 03/13/1967, Oxford, England, s **DISCIPLINE** PHILOSOPHY **EDUCATION** Cambridge Univ, BA, 89; Rutgers, PhD, 97. **CAREER** Asst prof, Illinois Wesleyan Univ, 96-. **RESEARCH** Cosmology; philosophy of science; metaphysics. **CONTACT ADDRESS** Dept of Philosophy, Illinois Wesleyan Univ, PO Box 2900, Bloomington, IL, 61702-2900. **EMAIL** cgillett@titan.iwu.edu

GILLETTE STURM, FRED
DISCIPLINE PHILOSOPHY OF ART AND AESTHETICS, LATIN AMERICAN AND IBERIAN PHILOSOPHY, CH **EDUCATION** Allegheny Col, AB, 46; Union Theological Seminary, MDiv, 48; Rochester, AM, 50; Columbia Univ, PhD, 61; Vanderbilt, cert, 49; Tunghai, cert, 63. **CAREER** Prof, Univ NMex. **MEMBERSHIPS** Int Ctr for Asian Stud; Royal Asiatic Soc; Int Sinological Comt; co-dir; REs Gp for Chinese & Comp Aesthet; Int Soc for Chinese Philos; Ctr de Estudos Luso-Brasileiros; Acad Brasileira de Filosofia; pres, Soc for Iberian and Lat Am Thought. **SELECTED PUBLICATIONS** Auth, American Indians: Time in Outlook and Language, in Encycl of Time, Garland, 95; Radhakrishnan's Philosophy of Art, in New Essays in the Philosophy of Sarvepalli Radhakrishnan,Indian Bk Ctr, 95; Philosophy and the Intellectual Tradition, in Latin America: Its Problems and Its Promise, 3rd ed, Boulder & London, 97; Brazil, Philosophy, in Encycl of Philos, Routledge, 98. **CONTACT ADDRESS** Univ NMex, Albuquerque, NM, 87131.

GILLIS, CHESTER
PERSONAL Born 07/20/1951, Providence, RI, m, 1986, 1 child **DISCIPLINE** THEOLOGY **EDUCATION** Catholic Univ Louvain, MA, 77, PhL 74, PhB 73; Univ Chicago, PhD, 86. **CAREER** Asst prof, 87-88, Drew Univ; asst prof, 88-94, assoc prof, 94-present, Georgetown Univ **MEMBERSHIPS** Amer Acad Relig **RESEARCH** Interreligious dialogue; catholicism; philosophical theology **SELECTED PUBLICATIONS** Auth, A Question of Final Belief: John Hick's Pluralistic Theory of Salvation, Macmillan, London, St. Martin, NY, 89; Pluralism A New Paradigm for Theology, Lueven Peeters, Grand Rapids, 93; Roman Catholicism in America, Columbia Univ Press, NY, 99. **CONTACT ADDRESS** Dept of Theology, Georgetown Univ, PO Box 571135, Washington, DC, 20057-1135. **EMAIL** Gillisc@gunet.georgetown.edu

GILLMAN, FLORENCE MORGAN
DISCIPLINE BIBLICAL STUDIES **EDUCATION** Cath Univ Louvain, Belgium, PhD, STD. **CAREER** Dept Theo, Univ San Diego **SELECTED PUBLICATIONS** Publ, 2 bks and numerous articles on, churches and theol of Paul and women in the NT era. **CONTACT ADDRESS** Dept of Theological and Relig Studies, Univ of San Diego, 5998 Alcal Park, Maher 292, San Diego, CA, 92110-2492. **EMAIL** gillman@acusd.edu

GILLMAN, NEIL
PERSONAL Quebec, PQ, Canada **DISCIPLINE** JEWISH PHILOSOPHY **EDUCATION** McGill Univ, BA, 54; Columbia Univ, PhD, 75. **CAREER** Aaron Rabinowitz and Simon H. Rifkind prof and chm dept Jewish phil, Jewish Theol Sem. **SELECTED PUBLICATIONS** Auth, Gabriel Marcel on Religious Knowledge, Univ Press Am, 80. **CONTACT ADDRESS** Jewish Theol Sem of America, 3080 Broadway, New York, NY, 10027. **EMAIL** negillman@jtsa.edu

GILMORE, GEORGE BARNES
PERSONAL Born 02/19/1939, New York, NY, m, 1995, 3 children **DISCIPLINE** THEOLOGY, PHILOSOPHY **EDUCATION** Fordham Univ, BA, 62, MA, 64, PhD, 75; Woodstock Col, PhL, 63, BD, 69. **CAREER** Instr classics & chmn dept, Gonzaga Col High Sch, 63-66; adj instr philos, Fordham Univ, 70-72; asst prof, 74-79, assoc prof, 79-83, PROF HUMANITIES, SPRING HILL COL, 84-, Chmn Dept Theol, 77-80. **HONORS AND AWARDS** Teacher of the Year, Spring Hill Col, 76, 87 & 93. **MEMBERSHIPS** Am Acad Relig; Col Theol Soc. **RESEARCH** Religious language; Zen; Buddhist/Christian dialogue. **SELECTED PUBLICATIONS** Auth, J A Mohler on Doctrinal Development, Heythrop J, 10/78. **CONTACT ADDRESS** Spring Hill Col, 4000 Dauphin St, Mobile, AL, 36608-1791. **EMAIL** ggilmore@shc.edu

GILMORE, ROBERT MCKINLEY, SR.
PERSONAL Born 05/14/1952, Houston, Texas **DISCIPLINE** THEOLOGY **EDUCATION** TX Southern Univ, BA 1980, MA 1981, MA 1984; Univ of Houston, EdD 1985; Houston Graduate School of Theology M.D.V. 1989. **CAREER** City of Houston, asst dir 1982-84; Texas Southern Univ, instructor 1981-83; Univ of Houston, grad asst 1982-85; Prairie View A&M Univ, asst prof 1985-89; Houston Graduate School of Theology urban ministry program director; Real Urban Ministry, pres. **HONORS AND AWARDS** PV Choice Award Prairie View A&M Univ 1989. **MEMBERSHIPS** Asst to pastor Barbers Memorial Bapt Church 1979-89; radio producer and host KTSU and KPVU 1980-85; pres Real Productions 1980-; consultant Baptist Ministers Assoc 1985-95; mem Phi Delta Kappa Univ of Houston 1985-89; Prairie View A&M Univ 1986-89; dir of Drug Training Programs Independent Missionary Baptist Assn; pres Real Educ Alternatives for Leadership & Learning 1989-91; pres One Church/One Child 1988-90; drug educ consultant City of Houston. **SELECTED PUBLICATIONS** Publication "Effective Communication a Drug Education Solution," 1986. **CONTACT ADDRESS** Executive Director, Real Urban Ministry, 3253 Winbern, Houston, TX, 77004.

GILMORE, VANESSA D.
PERSONAL Born 10/26/1956, St Albans, NY, s **DISCIPLINE** LAW **EDUCATION** Hampton Univ, BS, 1977; Univ of Houston College of Law, JD, 1981. **CAREER** Foley's Dept Store, fashion buyer, 1977-79; Sue Schecter & Assoc, attorney, 1985-86; Vickery, Kilbride, Gilmore & Vickery, attorney, 1986-94; US Courts, US district Judge, 1994-. **HONORS AND AWARDS** Houston Defender Newspaper, Citizen of the Month, 1990; National Black MBA Assn, Distinguished Service Award, 1994; Holman Street Baptist Church, Community Service Award, 1994; Human Enrichment of Life, Houston's Young Black Achiever, 1989. **MEMBERSHIPS** Houston Bar Assn; NAACP, chairperson for church committee, 1989-93; YWCA, pres, bd of dirs, 1990-92; Links Inc, chairperson for LEAD, 1990-91; Univ of Houston Alumni Bd, 1993-; Texas Dept of Commerce, chairperson, 1992-94; Texans for NAFTA, chairperson. **CONTACT ADDRESS** Judge, US Courts, 515 Rusk Avenue, Room 9513, Houston, TX, 77002.

GILMOUR, JOHN C.
PERSONAL Born 01/23/1939, Pittsburgh, PA, m, 1976, 2 children **DISCIPLINE** PHILOSOPHY **EDUCATION** Emory Univ, PhD, 66. **CAREER** Inst, Asst Prof, Hofstra Univ, 63-68; Asst Prof, Norwich Univ, 68-70; Prof, Alfred Univ, 70-. **HONORS AND AWARDS** Woodrow Wilson Fel; Alfred Univ Order of Merit. **MEMBERSHIPS** Amer Soc for Aesthetics; Intl Assoc for Phil & Lit; APA **RESEARCH** Philosophy of Art, philosophy of Nietzsche, Post Modern theory. **SELECTED PUBLICATIONS** Educating Imaginative Thinkers, the Tchr's Col Record, 94; Genealogy, Interpretation, and Historical Masks, Hist Reflections/Reflexions Historiques, 95; Ed Nietzsch: Voices, Masks, and Histories, Hist Reflections/ Reflexions Historiques, 95; Fire on the Earth: Anselm Kiefer and the Postmodern World, Temple Univ Press, 90. **CONTACT ADDRESS** 10476 Cross St, Hammondsport, NY, 14840-9616. **EMAIL** Fgilmour@bigvax.alfred.edu

GILMOUR, PETER
PERSONAL Born 11/25/1942, Chicago, IL **DISCIPLINE** MINISTRY **EDUCATION** Univ of St. Mary of the Lake, PhD. **CAREER** Assoc Prof, Loyola Univ Chicago **MEMBERSHIPS** Religous Education Assoc; Assoc of Prof and Researchers in Religous Education **RESEARCH** Literatue and Religion **SELECTED PUBLICATIONS** coauth, A Companion to Pastoral Care of the Sick, 90; auth, The Wisdom of Memoir: Reading and Writing Life's Sacred Texts, 97; Growing in Courage, 98. **CONTACT ADDRESS** Inst of Pastoral Studies, Loyola Univ, Chicago, 6525 N. Sheridan Rd., Chicago, IL, 60626. **EMAIL** pgilmou@wpo.it.luc.edu

GILPIN, W. CLARK
DISCIPLINE RELIGION **EDUCATION** Univ Okla, BA, 67; Lexington Theol Sem, MDiv, 70; Univ Chicago, MA, 70, PhD,74. **CAREER** Assoc prof, Grad Sem, Phillips; current, DEAN, DIV SCH, UNIV CHICAGO. **MEMBERSHIPS** Am Antiquarian Soc **SELECTED PUBLICATIONS** Auth, The Millenarian Piety of Roger Williams, 79; auth, "The Seminary Ideal in American Protestant Ministerial Education, 1700-1808," Theol Educ 20, 84; auth, A Preface to Theology, Univ Chicago Press, 96; **CONTACT ADDRESS** Div Sch, Univ of Chicago, 1025 E 58th St, Chicago, IL, 60637. **EMAIL** wgilpin@midway.uchicago.edu

GILSON, GREG
PERSONAL Born 09/16/1966, Green Bay, WI, s **DISCIPLINE** PHILOSOPHY **EDUCATION** Univ Wisc-Madison, BS, MA, PhD. **CAREER** Lecturer, Univ Wisc-River Falls. **MEMBERSHIPS** APA **RESEARCH** Metaphysics and epistemology **CONTACT ADDRESS** 1495 Riverside Dr, #210, River Falls, WI, 54022. **EMAIL** gregory.gilson@vwrf.edu

GINGERICH, RAY C.
DISCIPLINE THEOLOGY AND ETHICS **EDUCATION** Eastern Mennonite Univ, BA; Goshen Biblical Sem, Mdiv; Vanderbilt Univ, PhD. **CAREER** Theol Dept, Eastern Mennonite Univ **SELECTED PUBLICATIONS** Articles: Festival Quart; Mennonite Weekly Rev; Conrad Grebel Rev. **CONTACT ADDRESS** Eastern Mennonite Univ, 1200 Park Road, Harrisonburg, VA, 22802-2462.

GINI, ALFRED
DISCIPLINE PHILOSOPHY **EDUCATION** Northern Ill Univ, BA; Aquinas Inst Philos, MA, PhD. **CAREER** Assoc prof; managing ed, Bus Ethics Quart. **RESEARCH** Business ethics; contemporary moral issues. **SELECTED PUBLICATIONS** Auth, Philosophical Issues in Human Rights, Random House; coauth, Heigh-Ho! Heigh-Ho! Funny, Insightful, Encouraging and Sometimes Painful Quotes About Work, ACTA Publ; It Comes With the Territory: An Inquiry Into the Nature of Work, Random House; co-ed Case Stud in Business Ethics, Prentice-Hall. **CONTACT ADDRESS** Dept of Philosophy, Loyola Univ, Chicago, 820 N. Michigan Ave., Chicago, IL, 60611.

GIRARDOT, NORMAN J.
PERSONAL Born 04/19/1943, 2 children **DISCIPLINE** HISTORY OF RELIGIONS **EDUCATION** Col Holy Cross, BS, 65; Univ Chicago, MA, 72, PhD, 74. **CAREER** Ed asst, Hist Relig J, 68-70; asst prof Theol, Notre Dame Univ, 72-79; vis asst prof, Oberlin Col, 79-80; assoc prof & chmn, Relig Studies Dept, Lehigh Univ, 80-; prof, 89; Nat Endowment for Humanities fel, 83, 93-95; Chiang Ching-kuo fel, 93-95; Pacific Cult Found fel, 93-95; exec comt, Soc Study Chinese Relig, 75-78; reader Univ Chicago Press, Univ Notre Dame Press, Scholars Press & Greenwood Press. **HONORS AND AWARDS** Phi Beta Kappa . **MEMBERSHIPS** Am Soc for the Study of Religion; Am Acad Relig; Asn Asian Scholars; Soc Study Chinese Relig. **RESEARCH** Taoism; Chinese religion and myth; Western study of Asian religion; Visionary folkart; polular religion. **SELECTED PUBLICATIONS** Auth, The problem of creation mythology in the study of Chinese religion, Vol 15, 76 & co-ed, Current perspectives in the study of Chinese religions, Vol 17, 78, Hist Relig; auth, Returning to the Beginning and the arts of Mr Huntun in the Chuang Tzu, J Chinese Philos, Vol 5, 78; Chaotic order and benevolent disorder in the Chuang Tau, Philos East & West, Vol 28, 78; Taoism, In: Encycl of Bioethics, 78; co-ed, China and Christianity, Notre Dame Univ Press, 79; Imagination and Meaning: The Scholarly and Literary Worlds of Mircea Eliade, Seabury Press, 82; auth, Myth and Meaning in Early Taoism, Univ Calif Press, 82, rb, 89; trans, I Robinet's Tavist Meditation, SUNY, 93. **CONTACT ADDRESS** Relig Studies Dept, Lehigh Univ, 9 W Packer Ave, #5, Bethlehem, PA, 18015-3082. **EMAIL** nvgo@lehigh.edu

GIROUX, MICHEL
DISCIPLINE LAW **EDUCATION** Univ Ottawa, BA, LLB. **CAREER** Assoc prof. **RESEARCH** Constitutional law; criminal law. **CONTACT ADDRESS** Law and Justice Dept, Laurentian Univ, 935 Ramsey Lake Rd, Sudbury, ON, P3E 2C6.

GITELMAN, MORTON
PERSONAL Born 02/07/1933, Chicago, IL, m, 1956, 3 children **DISCIPLINE** LAW **EDUCATION** Roosevelt Univ, cert personnel admin, 53; DePaul Univ, LLB, 59; Univ Ill, LLM, 65. **CAREER** Teaching fel law, Univ Ill, 59-60; res assoc, Duke Univ, 60-61; from asst prof to assoc prof, Univ Denver, 61-65; assoc prof, 65-69, PROF LAW, UNIV ARK, FAYETTEVILLE, 69-, PROF ARCHIT, 78-, Chmn, Ark Adv Comt US Comn Civil Rights and mem planning comn, City Fayetteville, 67-; vis prof, Univ Ill, 70-71. **MEMBERSHIPS** Am Civil Liberties Union. **RESEARCH** Constitutional law; jurisprudence; land use controls. **SELECTED PUBLICATIONS** Auth, The First Chancery Court in Arkansas: An 1855 Creation of The Arkansas General-Assembly, Ark Hist Quart, Vol 0055, 96. **CONTACT ADDRESS** Sch of Law, Univ of Ark, Fayetteville, AR, 72701-1202.

GITHIGA, JOHN GATUNGU
PERSONAL Born 07/27/1942, Muranga, Kenya, m, 1968 **DISCIPLINE** RELIGION **EDUCATION** Makerere University, theology diploma, 1974; University of the South, MDiv, 1979; International Bible Institute and Seminary, DREd, 1980; University of the South, DMin, 1981. **CAREER** Diocese of Nakuru, director of St Nicholars Children Center, five years; St Paul's United Theological College, department head, pastoral theology, 1980-86; African Association for Pastoral Studies and Counseling, founder, president, 1985-88; St Cyprian Church, vicar, 1986-91; Ecumencial Christian Fellowship, founder, president, 1992-; Lakeview Center, telephone crisis counselor, Kairos spiritual director, voluntary, 1992-; Extended Arms Outreach Center, field counselor to juvenile offenders & their parents, 1992-96; WEST TEXAS A & M UNIV, CHAPLAIN, 1996-; GRAMBLING STATE UNIV, VICAR, CHAPLAIN, currently. **HONORS AND AWARDS** Pensacola Junior College, certificate of appreciation for presentation, 1987; Kiwanis Club of Greater Pensacola, certificate of appreciation for presentation, 1988; Martin Luther King Commemorative Comm, cert of appreciation for planning, 1989; Kiwanis Cert of Appreciation for Spiritual leadership and Service to community, 1989; Initiation & Pastoral Psychology. **MEMBERSHIPS** University of West Florida Select Committee on Minority Affairs, 1987-92; Martin Luther King Jr Celebration Committee, 1989; Ecumenical and Interfaith Committee, 1987-91; Greater Kiwanis of Pensacola, 1988-92; Association of Theological Institutions in Eastern Africa, 1980-85; National Christian Council of Kenya Youth Department, Nakuru, secretary, 1966-68; Diocese of Nakuru Youth Department, secretary, 1968-71; The First Nakuru Company of the Boys Brigade, captain, 1967-68. **SELECTED PUBLICATIONS** Author, Christ & Roots, 1988; The Spirit in the Black Soul, 1984; "The Use of Psychology in Pastoral Counseling in Africa," Theological Journal, 1982; "Family in Transition," Beyond, July 1987; co-author, Ewe Ki Jana (Oh Young Man), 1971. **CONTACT ADDRESS** St. George's Church West, Texas A & M Univ, 2216 4th Ave, Canyon, TX, 79015.

GIURLANDA, PAUL
PERSONAL Born 01/14/1946, Detroit, MI, s **DISCIPLINE** THEOLOGY **EDUCATION** Cath Univ, BA, 69; Syracuse Univ, MS, 74; Grad Theol Un, MA, 78, PhD, 85 **CAREER** Fac, 78-pres, St Marys Col of CA **MEMBERSHIPS** Cath Theol Soc of Am; Am Acad of Relig; AAUP; Col Theology Soc **RESEARCH** Foundational Theology; Gender and Religion **SELECTED PUBLICATIONS** Auth, Faith and Knowledge A Critical Inquiry, University Press of America, Lanham Maryland, 87 **CONTACT ADDRESS** 250 Whitmore St, Oakland, CA, 94611. **EMAIL** paulg63223@aol.com

GIURLANDA, PAUL
PERSONAL Born 01/14/1946, Detroit, MI, s **DISCIPLINE** THEOLOGY **EDUCATION** Cath Univ, BA, 69; Syracuse Univ, MS, 74; Grad Theol Un, MA, 78, PhD, 85 **CAREER** Fac, 78-pres, St Marys Col of CA **MEMBERSHIPS** Cath Theol Soc of Am; Am Acad of Relig; AAUP; Col Theology Soc **RESEARCH** Foundational Theology; Gender and Religion **SELECTED PUBLICATIONS** Auth, Faith and Knowledge A Critical Inquiry, University Press of America, Lanham Maryland, 87 **CONTACT ADDRESS** 250 Whitmore St, Apt. 401, Oakland, CA, 94611. **EMAIL** paulg63223@aol.com

GIVELBER, DANIEL JAMES
PERSONAL Cleveland, OH, m, 1963, 2 children **DISCIPLINE** COMMON LAW SUBJECTS, LAW AND SOCIETY **EDUCATION** Harvard Col, BA, 61, JD, 64. **CAREER** Pvt pract law, Cahill, Gordon, Reindel and Ohl, New York, NY, 64-67; asst US atty, Off US Atty, Dist of Columbia, 67-69; PROF LAW, SCH OF LAW, NORTHEASTERN UNIV, 69-. **RESEARCH** Developments in law protecting emotional well being; developments in law protecting emotional well being; developments in defamation law. **SELECTED PUBLICATIONS** Auth, Learning Through Work--An Empirical-Study of Legal Internship, J Legal Educ, Vol 0045, 95. **CONTACT ADDRESS** Sch of Law, Northeastern Univ, 400 Huntington Ave, Boston, MA, 02115-5005.

GLADSON, JERRY A.
PERSONAL Born 04/21/1943, Dalton, GA, m, 1965, 2 children **DISCIPLINE** OLD TESTAMENT **EDUCATION** Southern Adventist Univ, BA, 65; Vanderbilt Univ, MA,73, PhD, 78. **CAREER** Prof, Southern Adventist Univ, 72-87; dean, Psychol Stud Inst, 87-92; sr minister, First Christian Church, Garden Grove, Calif, 93-97; sr minister, First Christian Church, Marietta, GA 97-. **HONORS AND AWARDS** Tchr of the Year, Southern Adventist Univ, 81. **MEMBERSHIPS** Soc of Biblical Lit, Catholic Biblical Asn, Christian Asn for Psychol Stud, Acad of Parish Clergy **RESEARCH** Hebrew Wisdom; Old Testament Theology and Exegesis. **CONTACT ADDRESS** 4128 Lake Mist Dr., NW, Kennesaw, GA, 30144-5112. **EMAIL** jgladson1@juno.com

GLADWIN, LEE ALLAN
PERSONAL Washington, DC **DISCIPLINE** METHODOLOGY, PHILOSOPHY **EDUCATION** Fairmont State Col, BA, 66; Cath Univ, MA, 68; Carnegie-Mellon Univ, DA, 80. **CAREER** Asst prof hist, Shenandoah Col, 68-76; ASST PROF HUMAN SERV, NAT GRAD UNIV, 82-, Consult, Oakton Res Corp, 81-82. **MEMBERSHIPS** Am Soc Training & Develop; Nat Soc Performance & Instr. **RESEARCH** Artificial intelligence; problem solving. **SELECTED PUBLICATIONS** Auth, Hollywood Propaganda, Isolationism, and Protectors of the Public Mind, 1917-1941, Prologue-Quart of the Nat Arch, Vol 0026, 94; Turing, Alan, Enigma, and the Breaking of German Machine-Ciphers in World-War-II, Prologue-Quart of the Nat Arch, Vol 0029, 97. **CONTACT ADDRESS** Rt 3, Box 225, Winehester, VA, 22601.

GLANNON, JOSEPH WILLIAM
PERSONAL Born 03/22/1946, New York, NY **DISCIPLINE** LAW **EDUCATION** Harvard Univ, BA, 68, MAT, 71, JD, 77. **CAREER** Asst dean, Bates Col, 71-74; law clerk, Massachusetts Appeals Ct, 77-78; asst corp coun, City of Boston, 78-79; from Instr to Assoc Prof, 79-86, Prof Law, Suffolk Univ, 86-, Dir, Legal Practice Skills Prog, 80-87, Chair, Fac Admin Comt, 90-96, Chair, Grading Policy Comt, 96-98, Chair, Fac Appointments Comt, 91-92; Legal consult, City of Boston, 78-80 & 82; exec comt mem, AALS Civil Procedure Section, 95-97. **HONORS AND AWARDS** Phi Beta Kappa; Cornelius J. Moynihan Award for Excellence in Tchg, 91. **RESEARCH** Civil procedure; local government law. **SELECTED PUBLICATIONS** Auth, Liability for Public Duties under the Tort Claims Act: The Legislature Reconsiders the Public Duty Role, Mass Law Rev, 94; The Law of Torts: Examples and Explanations, Little, Brown & Co, 95; Fireside Civil Procedure (9-hour audiotape series), Little, Brown & Co, 96; Civil Procedure: Examples and Explanations, 3rd ed, 97; coauth, Coordinating Civil Procedure and the Legal Research and Writing Course: A Field Experiment, J Legal Educ, 97; Politics and Personal Jurisdiction: Suing State Sponsors of Terrorism under the 1996 Amendments to the Foreign Sovereign Immunities Act (in prep); auth numerous other articles and publ. **CONTACT ADDRESS** Suffolk Law Sch, 41 Temple St, Boston, MA, 02114-4241.

GLAZEBROOK, PATRICIA
DISCIPLINE PHILOSOPHY **EDUCATION** Univ Toronto, PhD, 93. **CAREER** Asst prof, Colgate Univ. **HONORS AND AWARDS** Res grant, DAAD, Freiburg, Ger, 92. **SELECTED PUBLICATIONS** Auth, Heidegger on the Experiment, Philos Todav, 98. **CONTACT ADDRESS** Dept of Philos and Relig, Colgate Univ, 13 Oak Drive, Hamilton, NY, 13346. **EMAIL** pglazebrook@mail.colgate.edu

GLAZIER, STEPHEN D.
PERSONAL Born 06/10/1949, New London, CT, m, 1975, 1 child **DISCIPLINE** ANTHROPOLOGY, SOCIOLOGY, THEOLOGY **EDUCATION** Eastern Col, AB, 71; Princeton Univ Sem, MDiv, 74; Univ Conn, PhD, 81. **CAREER** Lectr, Univ Conn, Storrs, 79-81; vis asst prof, Trinity Col, 81-82; vis asst prof, Conn Col, 82-83; asst prof, Wayland Baptist Univ, 83-86; assoc prof, Westmont Col, 86-88; assoc prof, ch, Univ Nebr, Kearney, 88-91; assoc prof, grad fac fel, Univ Nebr, 91-94; prof, grad fac fel, Univ Nebr, 94- . **HONORS AND AWARDS** Sec, Soc Sci Stud Rel, 98- ; VP, Anthrop Rel Sec, Amer Anthrop Assn, 98-99; Prog ed, AnthropRel Sec, 97th Ann Mtg, Am Anthrop Asn, Philadelphia; Delegate, Consciousness stud sum Inst, Univ Ariz and Fetzer Inst, Flagstaff, AZ, 97; tchg fellow, Amer Acad Rel/Lilly Found Wksps, 97-98; Prof Development Leave, vis res fel, Yale Univ Div Sch/Inst Sacred Mus, fall 96; vis scholar, Rackham Grad Sch, Inst Human, Univ Mich, 96; fel, NEH Summer Inst Col Tchrs, 96; fellow, NEH Summer Sem Col Tchrs, 95; Recipient, Pratt-Heins Awd, Univ Nebr at Kearney, 93; fel, NEH Summer Inst, 93; fel, NEH Summer Sem Col Tchrs, 92; fel, NEH Summer Inst Col Tchrs, 91; mem, Exec Coun, Soc Sci stud Rel, 91-93; Participant, UNESCO Conf, Port of Spain, Trinidad, 90; fel, NEH Summer Sem Col Tchrs, Yale Univ, 89; summer fel, Transatlantic Encounters prog, Herman Dunlop Smith Ctr Hist Cartography, Newberry Lib, Chicago, 87; fel, NEH Summer Inst Afro-Amer Rel Hist, Princeton Univ, 86; Mellon Wksp Rel Revivalism, Rice Univ, 86-87; fel, NEH Summer Sem Col Tchrs, Univ Colo, 85. **MEMBERSHIPS** Amers Anthrop Asn; Royal Anthrop Inst; Amer Acad Rel; Soc Anthrop Rel; Soc Sci Stud Rel; Assn Sociol Rel; Intl Assn Caribbean Archaelolgist; Soc des Am de Paris; Amer Folklore Soc; Caribbean Stud Assn; Soc Anthrop Consciousness. **RESEARCH** Anthropology; Religion; Race and Ethnicity; Ethnohistory; Caribbean and Latin America. **SELECTED PUBLICATIONS** Ed, Perspectives on Pentecostalism: Case Studies from the Caribbean and Latin America, Washington, DC, Univ Press Amer, 80; Marchin' the Pilgrims Home: Leadership and Decision-Making in an Afro-Caribbean Faith, Westport, CT, Greenwood, 83; ed, Caribbean Ethnicity Revisited, NY and London, Gordon and Breach, 85; Syncretism and Separation: Ritual Change in an Afro-Caribbean Faith, Jour Am Folklore, 98, 387, 49-62, 85; Mourning in the Afro-Baptist Tradition: A Comparative Study of Religion in the American South and Trinidad, Southern Quart, 23, 3, 85, 141-156; Religion and Social Justice: Caribbean Perspectives, Phylon, 46, 2, 85, 283-299; Caribbean Religions: Pre-Columbian, The Encyclopedia of Religion, 3, M. Eliade, gen ed, NY, Free Press, Macmillan, 87, 81-90; Marchin' the Pilgrims Home: A Study of the Spiritual Baptists of Trinidad, Salem, WI, Sheffield Publ, 91; A Comparative Study of Caribbean Pilgimages: Haiti and Trinidad, Sacred Journeys: The Anthropology of Pilgrimage, A. Morinis, Ed, Westport, CT, Greenwood, 92, 135-147; Slavery and Social Death by O. Patterson; and The Content of Our Character, by S. Steele, in Masterpieces in African-American Literature, F.N. Magill, ed, NY, HarperCollins, 92; Responding to the Anthropologist: When the Spiritual Baptists of Trinidad Read What I Write About Them, in When They Read What We Write: The Politics of Ethnography, C.B. Brettell, ed, NY, Bergin and Garvey, 93, 37-48; Guest editor's introduction: Special issue: Spiritual Baptists, Shango, and other African-Derived Religions in the Caribbean Quart, 39, S.D. Glazier, ed, v-viii, 1-11, 93; New Religions Among Afro-Americans (Caribbean and South America), and New Religions: Afro-Suriname, HarperCollins

Dictionary of Religion, J.Z. Smith, gen ed, San Francisco, HarperCollins, 95; New Religious Movements in the Caribbean: Identity and Resistancc, Born Out of Resistance: Caribbean Cultural Creativity as a Response to European Expansion, Wim Hoogbergen, ed, Utrecht: Univ Utrecht/ISOR Pres, 95, 253-262; Latin American Perspectives on Religion and Politics, Latin Am Res Rev, 30, 1, 247-255; Changes in the Spiritual Baptist Religion, 1976-1990, Ay BoBo:Afro-Caribbean Cults: Identity and Resistance, Teil 1, Kulte, M. Kremser, Ed, Wien, Institut fur Volkerkunde der Universitat Wien, 96, 107-114; Five entries, American Folklore: An Encyclopedia, J. Brunvand, gen ed, NY, Garland, 96; Authenticity in Afro-Caribbean Religions: Contested Constructs, Contested Rites, Religion and the Social Order, L.F. Carter and D. Bromley, ed, Greenwich, CT, JAI Press, 96, 207-225; New World African Ritual: Genuine and Spurious, Jour Sci Stud Rel, 35, 4, 421-432; ed, Anthropology of Religion: A Handbook, Westport, CT, Greenwood, 97; assoc ed, Forward, Migrants, Regional Cultures, and Latin American Cities, Soc for Latin Amer Anthrop Publ Series 13, Wash DE, Amer Anthrop Assn, 97; Embedded Truths: Creativity and Context in Spiritual Baptist Music, Latin Am Mus Rev, 18, 1, 44-56; ed, Anthropology and Contemporary Religions, Westport CT, Greenwood, 98; Anthropology and Theology: The Legacies of a Link, in Explorations in Anthropology and Theology, Lanham, MD, Univ Press Am, 98; The Noise of Astonishment: Spiritual Baptist Music in Context, Religion, Diaspora and Cultural Identity: A Reader in the Anglophone Caribbean, ed, J.W. Pulis, NY and London, Gordon and Breach, 98, 277-294; Contested Rites of the Aftican Diaspora, in New Trends and Developments in African Religions, P.B. Clarke, ed, London, Greenwood; Anthropology of Religion, and nineteen shorter entries, in The Encyclopedia of Religion and Society, W.H. Swatos, Jr, ed, Walnut Creek, CA, AltaMira Press, Sage, 98; William Wallace Fenn, John Mifflin Brown, and Benjamin W. Arnett, in American National Biography, J.A. Garraty, Ed, NY, Oxford UP, 99. **CONTACT ADDRESS** Dept of Sociology and Anthropology, Nebraska Univ, Kearney, NE, 68849. **EMAIL** glaziers@platte.unk.edu

GLAZIER-MCDONALD, BETH
DISCIPLINE RELIGION **EDUCATION** Gorge Washington University; Univ Chicago, M.Div, Ph.D.-residence and guest speaker at Temple Adath Israel in Lexington, as scholar-in-residence at Keneseth Israel Congregation in Allentown, Penn. **CAREER** Asst prof, Penn State Univ; fac, Centre Col, 80-; NEH Assoc Prof Relig, current. **SELECTED PUBLICATIONS** Contrib auth, Eerdman's Dic of Bible; conribu, Atiqot, Jour Roman Archaeol. **CONTACT ADDRESS** Centre Col, 600 W Walnut St, Danville, KY, 40422. **EMAIL** glzrmcd@centre.edu

GLENN, JOHN DEAVENPORT, JR.
PERSONAL Born 03/08/1942, Wellington, TX, m, 1967, 1 child **DISCIPLINE** PHILOSOPHY **EDUCATION** Univ Texas, Austin, BA, 64; Yale Univ, MA, 66, PhD, 68. **CAREER** Asst prof, 68-74, assoc prof philos, 74- , chemn Dept of Philos, 96-99, Tulane Univ. **HONORS AND AWARDS** Phi Beta Kappa, 64; Woodrow Wilson fel, 64-65; Woodrow Wilson dissertation fel, 67-68. **MEMBERSHIPS** Soc for Philos of Relig. **RESEARCH** Modern philosophy; Kant; Kierkegaard; philosophy of religion. **SELECTED PUBLICATIONS** Auth, A Highest Good, An Eternal Happiness: The Human Telos in Kierkegaard's Concluding Unscientific Postscript, in, International Kierkegaard Commentary, v.12: Concluding Unscientific Postscript to Philosophical Fragments; auth, Kierkegaard and Anselm, in, International Kierkegaard Commentary, v.7: Philosophical Fragments and Johannes Climacus; auth, The Definition of the Self and the Structure of Kierkegaard's Work, in, International Kierkegaard commentary, v. 19: Sickness unto Death; auth, The Behaviorism of a Phenomenologist--the Structure of Behavior and The Concept of Mind, Philos Topics. **CONTACT ADDRESS** Dept of Philosophy, Tulane Univ, 105 Newcomb Hall, New Orleans, LA, 70118. **EMAIL** glenn@mailhost.tcs.tulane.edu

GLIDDEN, DAVID
DISCIPLINE PHILOSOPHY **EDUCATION** Princeton Univ, PhD. **CAREER** PROF, UNIV CALIF, RIVERSIDE. **MEMBERSHIPS** Mem, Calif Coun Hum. **RESEARCH** Ancient applied ethics and social philosophy. **SELECTED PUBLICATIONS** Auth, Death Angels & Physician Assisted Suicide, Jour of Forensic Psychiatry, 95; Moral Vision, Orthos Logos, and the Role of the Phronimos, APEIRON Spec Issue, 96; Josiah Royce's Reading of Plato's Theaetetus, Hist of Philos Quart, 96; Requiem for Philosophy, Rel, 97; Augustine's Hermeneutics and the Principle of Charity, Ancient Philos, 97. **CONTACT ADDRESS** Dept of Philos, Univ Calif, 1156 Hinderaker Hall, Riverside, CA, 92521-0209. **EMAIL** glidden@ucracl.ucr.edu

GLIDDEN, JOCK
DISCIPLINE PHILOSOPHY **EDUCATION** Middlebury Col, AB, 58; Univ Edinburgh, MA, 63; Univ Colo, PhD, 69. **CAREER** Assoc prof, Waynesburg Col. **RESEARCH** British empiricism, wittgenstein, environmental philosophy, medical ethics, philosophy of science and aesthetics. **SELECTED PUBLICATIONS** Auth, Can We Treat Nature Morally, Univ Edinburgh, 73; coauth, Teaching by the Group Method in Philosophy 101, Col Tchg, 90. **CONTACT ADDRESS** Dept of Political Science, Waynesburg Col, 51 W College St, Waynesburg, PA, 15370. **EMAIL** jglidden@weber.edu

GLOVER, RAYMOND F.
DISCIPLINE MUSIC IN LITURGY **EDUCATION** Univ Toronto, BM, 52; Union Theol Sem, MSM, 54; Va Theol Sem, LHD, 86; Berkeley Divinity Sch at Yale, MusD, 87. **CAREER** Instr, Hartford Sem Found, 63-65; Berkeley Divinity Sch, 64-70; hd mus dept, St Catherine's Sch, 76-80; prof, Va Theol Sem, 91-. **HONORS AND AWARDS** Gen ed, Church Hymnal Corp, 80-91. **SELECTED PUBLICATIONS** Auth, A Commentary on New Hymns, The Church Hymnal Corp, 87. **CONTACT ADDRESS** Va Theol Sem, 3737 Seminary Rd, Alexandria, VA, 22304. **EMAIL** RGlover@vts.edu

GLOWIENKA, EMERINE FRANCES
PERSONAL Born 03/09/1920, Milwaukee, WI **DISCIPLINE** PHILOSOPHY, SOCIOLOGY **EDUCATION** Marquette Univ, BA, 42, MA, 51, PhD(Philos), 73; St Louis Univ, PhD-(Sociol), 56. **CAREER** Elem & sec teacher, Acad Sacred Heart, Ill, 45-53; instr Philos & Sociol, Barat Col, 55-58; assoc prof Sociol & chmn dept, Duchesne Col, 61-62; prof Sociol & Social Welfare, San Francisco Col Women, 62-70, chmn dept, 61-70; asst prof Philos, Univ San Diego, 71-74; prof Philos & Sociol & chairperson Dept, Gallup Br Col, Univ NMEX, 74-, prof Philos, Gallup Diocesan Sem, 74-. **MEMBERSHIPS** Am Philos Asn; Am Cath Philos Asn; Soc Women Philos. **RESEARCH** Ethics; metaphysics; personalization. **SELECTED PUBLICATIONS** Auth, Social philosophy as a synthesis of the social sciences, Am Cath Sociol Rev, Fall 63; Notes on consciousness in matter, New Scholasticism, Fall 69; Why do we teach?, Mod Soc, 1/70; A brighter side of the new genetics, Bioscience, 2/75; The counsel of poverty: Gospels versus acts, Rev Relig, 3/75; On demythologizing philosophy, Southwest Philos Studies, 4/81; Aquinas With the Realists and the Conceptualists, Southwest Philosophical Studies, 18, 96. **CONTACT ADDRESS** Dept of Philos Gallup Br Col, Univ New Mexico, 200 College Rd, Gallup, NM, 87301-5603.

GLUCK, ANDREW L.
PERSONAL Born 03/21/1944, New York, NY, m, 3 children **DISCIPLINE** PHILOSOPHY **EDUCATION** Univ of Fl, BA, 65; Columbia Univ, MA, 73; NY Univ, MS, 90; Columbia Univ, EdD, 97. **CAREER** Adjunct fac, Bramson ORT Tech Inst, 94-; adjunct fac, Berkeley Col, 97-; adjunct fac, Empire State Col, 98-. **MEMBERSHIPS** Am Philos Asn; Nat Asn of Forensic Econ; Am Law and Econ Asn; Am Soc for Philos, Coun and Psychotherpay. **RESEARCH** Consciousness studies; Medieval philosopy; Forensic economics. **SELECTED PUBLICATIONS** Auth, "Maimonides' Arguments for Creation Ex Nihilo in the 'Guide of the Perplexed'" in Medieval Philos and Theol, 99; "Philosophical Counseling, Rationality and Healing" in Socrates Mag, 98; "The Consciousness Problem and the Human Sciences" in J of Consciousness Studies, 98; "Philosophical Practice in Career and Management Consulting" in Perspectives in Philosophical Practice, 96; "Chaos Theory and Its Application to Vocational Counseling: A Critical Reappraisal" in The J: Counseling and Values, 96; "Regarding the New Worklife Tables" in The J of Forensic Econ, 96; "Karl Popper's Three Worlds and its Implications for the Study of Consciousness" in The J of Consciousness Studies, 96. **CONTACT ADDRESS** 392 Central Park W, Apt 8C, New York, NY, 10025. **EMAIL** Andy_Gluck@msn.com

GLYMOUR, CLARK
DISCIPLINE PHILOSOPHY **EDUCATION** Ind Univ, PhD, 69. **CAREER** Instr, Princeton; Chicago Univ; Okla Univ; Univ Ill; Univ Pittsburgh; Carnegie Mellon; PROF, PHILOS, UNIV CALIF, SAN DIEGO. **RESEARCH** History of late nineteenth and early 20th century science. **SELECTED PUBLICATIONS** Auth, Thinking Things Through, MIT Press, 93; coauth, "Causation, Prediction and Search", Springer Lecture Notes in Statistics, 93. **CONTACT ADDRESS** Dept of Philos, Univ Calif, San Diego, 9500 Gilman Dr, La Jolla, CA, 92093.

GLYNN, SIMON
PERSONAL Born 06/11/1940, England, d, 2 children **DISCIPLINE** PHILOSOPHY **EDUCATION** Keele Univ, BA, 71; McMaster Univ, MA, 76; Manchester Univ, PhD, 86. **CAREER** Lectr, 83-85, Manchester Univ; Lectr, 85-87, Liverpool Univ; Asst Prof, 87-88, Central Michigan Univ; Visiting Asst Prof, 88-89, Univ Georgia; Asst Prof, 89-91, Assoc Prof, 91-98, Prof, 98-, Florida Atlantic Univ. **MEMBERSHIPS** Amer Phil Assoc; Soc for Phenomenology and Existential Phil; British Soc for Phenomenology **RESEARCH** Contemporary continental philosophy; philosophy of natural Science; philosophy of technology; philosophy of psychology; political philosophy **SELECTED PUBLICATIONS** Auth, Continental and Postmodern Perspectives in the Philosophy of Science, 95; A Reply to Wil Coleman's Simon Glynn on a Unified Epitemology of the Natural and Human Sciences, Journal of the British Society for Phenomenology, 95; World Starvation and our Moral Bankruptcy, The Emergence of the 21st Century Woman, 95; On the Idea of Continental and Postmodern Perspectives in the Philosophy of Science, Ibid, 95; The Deconstruction of Some Paradoxes in Relativity Quantum Theory and Particle Physics, Continental and Postmodern Perspectives in the Philosophy of Science, 95; From Transcendental Logic to a Phenemenology of the Life-World, Analecta Husserliana, 96; Ethical Issues in Environmental Decision Making and the Limitations of Cost Benefit Analysis, Lectures in Environmental Ethics, 96; Understanding Others: The Structure and Dynamics of Interpersonal and Cross Cultural Communication, Proceedings of the 5th Japanese/American Phenomenology Conference, 96; Identity, Perception, Ation and Choice in Contemporary and Traditional No Self Theories, Ibid; Identity, Intersubjectivity and Communicative Communion, Proceedings of the 20th World Congrss of Philosophy, 98. **CONTACT ADDRESS** Dept of Philosophy, Florida Atlantic Univ, Boca Raton, FL, 33431. **EMAIL** glynn@au.jau.edu

GNUSE, ROBERT
PERSONAL Born 12/04/1947, Quincy, IL **DISCIPLINE** OLD TESTAMENT, HISTORY OF CHRISTIAN THOUGHT **EDUCATION** Concordia Sem Exile, MDiv, 74, STM, 75; Univ Chicago, STM, 75; Vanderbilt, MA, 78, PhD(Old Testament), 80. **CAREER** Asst prof Old Testament, Univ Va, 78-79; asst prof relig, NC Wesleyan Col, 79-80; ASST PROF OLD TESTAMENT, LOYOLA UNIV, 80-, Vacancy parish pastor, St Paul's Lutheran Church, Nashville, Tenn, 76-78 and Trinity Lutheran Church, Rocky Mount, NC, 79-80. **MEMBERSHIPS** Soc Bibl Lit; Cath Bibl Asn; Col Theol Soc; Am Schs Orient Res. **RESEARCH** World religions. **SELECTED PUBLICATIONS** Auth, The Origins of Biblical Law--The Decalogues and the Book of the Covenant, Cath Biblical Quart, Vol 0055, 93; The Temple Experience of Jaddus in the 'Antiquities' of Josephus--A Report of Jewish Dream-Incubation, Jewish Quart Rev, Vol 0083, 93; Apocalypse--On the Psychology of Fundamentalism in America, Relig, Vol 0024, 94; Psalm and Story--Inset Hymns in Hebrew Narrative, J Biblical Lit, Vol 0113, 94; The 1st Book of Moses, Genesis-XXV,12-XXXVII,1--Isaac and Jacob, Cath Biblical Quart, Vol 0056, 94; The 'Book of the Covenant'--A Literary Approach, Cath Biblical Quart, Vol 0057, 95; In the Wilderness--The Doctrine of Defilement in the Book of Numbers, Cath Biblical Quart, Vol 0057, 95; Dreams in the Night--Scholarly Mirage or Theophanic Formula--The Dream-Report as a Motif of the So-Called Elohist Tradition, Biblische Zeitschrift, Vol 0039, 95; Poets and Petitioners--Late Old-Testament Theologians, Cath Biblical Quart, Vol 0057, 95; A Literary-Theological Evaluation of the Covenant Formulas, Cath Biblical Quart, Vol 0058, 96; The Israelite Judicial Process of Deuteronomistic Law, Cath Biblical Quart, Vol 0058, 96; Josephus, Flavius, the Zealots and Yavne--Towards a Rereading of the 'War of the Jews,' J Church and State, Vol 0039, 97; Corporate-Responsibility in the Hebrew Bible, Interpretation-J Bible and Theol, Vol 0051, 97; Investigations on Deuteronomistic Literature and Deuteronomic Name Theology, Cath Biblical Quart, Vol 0059, 97. **CONTACT ADDRESS** Loyola Univ, 6363 St Charles Ave, New Orleans, LA, 70118.

GODSEY, JOHN DREW
PERSONAL Born 10/10/1922, Bristol, TN, m, 1943, 4 children **DISCIPLINE** THEOLOGY **EDUCATION** Va Polytech Inst, BS, 47; Drew Univ, BD, 53; Univ Basel, DTheol, 60. **CAREER** From instr to asst prof syst theol and asst to dean, Drew Univ, 56-62, from asst prof to assoc prof hist and syst theol, 62-66, prof syst theol, 66-68; assoc dean, 68-71, PROF SYST THEOL, WESLEY THEOL SEM, 68-, Fulbright res grant, Univ Goettingen, 64-65. **MEMBERSHIPS** Am Theol Soc; Am Acad Relig; Bibl Theologians; Int Bonhoeffer Soc; Karl Barth Soc NAm. **RESEARCH** History of Christian thought; contemporary theology; philosophy. **SELECTED PUBLICATIONS** Auth, Reclaiming Bonhoeffer, Dietrich--The Promise of His Theology, Theol Stud, Vol 0056, 95. **CONTACT ADDRESS** 8306 Bryand Dr, Bethesda, MD, 20034.

GOERGEN, DONALD J.
PERSONAL Born 08/16/1943, Iowa **DISCIPLINE** THEOLOGY **EDUCATION** Aquinas Inst Of Theol, Dubuque, Iowa, PhD, Systematic Theol, 72. **CAREER** Asst Prof, Prof, Theo, 71-, Aquinas Inst; Church admin, Dubuque, Iowa, 85-94. **MEMBERSHIPS** Amer Acad of Rel; Catholic Theol Soc of Amer. **RESEARCH** Religious Pluralism; Theology and Culture. **SELECTED PUBLICATIONS** Auth, The Sexual Celibate, NY, Seabury Press, 75; The Power of Love, Chicago, Thomas More Press, 79; A Theology of Jesus, Vol 1, The Mission and Ministry of Jesus, Wilmington, Michael Glazier, Inc, 86; Vol 2, The Death and Resurrection of Jesus, Wilmington, Michael Glazier Inc, 87; Vol 3, The Jesus of Christian History, Clooegeville, MN, The Liturgical Press, 92; Vol 4, Jesus: Son of God, Son of Mary, Immanuel, Collegeville, MN, The Liturgical Press, 94, ed, Process Thought and Ecumenical Theology, Listening, 79. **CONTACT ADDRESS** 97 Waterman Pl, St. Louis, MO, 63112-1820. **EMAIL** goergend@mac.domcentral.org

GOETSCH, JAMES R.
DISCIPLINE PHILOSOPHY **EDUCATION** Emory Univ, PhD. **CAREER** Asst prof. **RESEARCH** Ancient philosophy; eighteenth century philosophy; Buddhist thought. **SELECTED PUBLICATIONS** Auth, Vico's Axioms: The Geometry of the Human World. **CONTACT ADDRESS** Dept of Philosophy, Eckerd Col, 54th Ave S, PO Box 4200, St Petersburg, FL, 33711. **EMAIL** goetscjr@eckerd.edu

GOFF, EDWIN L.
DISCIPLINE PHILOSOPHY **EDUCATION** Vanderbilt Univ, BA, 67; Boston Col, MA, 68, PhD, 74. **CAREER** Assoc prof & dir, Univ Honors Prog, Villanova Univ,70-. **HONORS AND AWARDS** NEH Summer Sem, Tufts Univ, 75; NEH Summer Sem, Univ Pa, 78. **MEMBERSHIPS** AAUP & pres, Villanova Chap, 85-88; Amer Soc for Political and Legal Philos; Int Asn for Philos of Law and Soc Philos; Soci for the Study of Black Philos; NAm Soc for Soc Philos. **RESEARCH** Social justice and the grounding of a liberal democratic theory of social change. **SELECTED PUBLICATIONS** Auth, Injustice in American Liberal Democracy: Foundations for a Rawlsian Critique, J Value Inquiry, Vol 18, 84; Justice as Fairness: The Practice of Social Science in a Rawlsian Model, Soc Res Vol 50, 83; John Rawls' A Theory of Justice: A Review in Retrospect, Soc and Thought Vol 1, 83 & Affirmative Action, John Rawls, and a Partial Compliance Theory of Justice, Cultural Hermeneutics, Vol 4, 76. **CONTACT ADDRESS** Dept of Philosophy, Villanova Univ, 800 Lancaster Ave, Villanova, PA, 19085-1692.

GOFORTH, CAROL R.
PERSONAL Born 10/12/1960, Fayetteville, AR, m, 1992, 3 children **DISCIPLINE** PSYCHOLOGY/LAW **EDUCATION** Univ AR, BA, 81; JD, 84. **CAREER** Assoc attorney, Derner, Stuart, Saunders, Daniel & Anderson, OK, 84-89; adjunct prof, Col Law, Univ Tulsa, 87-88; instr, Seton Hall Parma prog, Parma, Italy, summer 90; asst prof law, 89-92, assoc prof law, School of Law, Seton Hall Univ, Newark, NJ, 92-93; vis assoc prof law, 93-94, assoc prof law, 94-97, prof law, 97-98, Arkansas Bar found prof of Law, Univ AR School of Law, Fayetteville, 98-. **HONORS AND AWARDS** Selected AR Bar Found Prof, June 98. **MEMBERSHIPS** Am Bar Asn; AR Bar Asn. **RESEARCH** Corporate law; securities law; limited liability companied; limited liability partnerships. **SELECTED PUBLICATIONS** Co-auth, with L Beard, The Arkansas Limited Liability Company, M & M Press, 94; auth, Limited Liability Partnerships: Does Arkansas Need Another Form of Business Enterprize?, 1995 AR L Notes 57; The Rise of the Limited Liability Company: Evidence of a Race Between the States, but Heading Where?, 45 Syracuse L Rev, 1193, 95; What is She? How Race Matters, and Why It Shouldn't, 46 DePaul Univ L Rev 1, 96; Limiting the Liability of General Partners in LLPs: An Analysis of Statutory Alternatives, 75 OR L Rev 1139, 97; Continuing Obstacles to Freedom of Choice for Management Structure in LLC's, 1 Lewis & Clark J of Small and Emerging Bus L, 165, 97; Limited Liability Partnerships: The Newest Game in Town, AR L Notes 25, 97; An Update on Arkansas Limited Liability Companies: New Tax Regulations and New State Laws, 1997 AR L Notes 11; Reflections on What Lawyers Should Reflect On, 30 So TX L Rev, 585, 98; co-auth, with Michael L Closen and Gary S Rosin, Agency & Partnership, Problems and Statutes, supp 96 & supp 97; with Michael L Closen and Gary S Rosin, Agency and Partnership, Cases and Materials, supp 96 & supp 97; with L Beard, Arkansas LLCs. LLPs, LLLPs, M & M Press, forthcoming; with Michael L Closen and Gary S Rosin, Agency & Partnership, Cases and Materials, 2nd ed, forthcoming; auth, Treatment of LLC Membership Interests Under the Arkansas Securities Act, 1998 AR L Notes, forthcoming; Not In My Back Yard! Restrictive Covenants as a Basis for Opposing the Construction of Cellular Towers, 46 Buffalo L Rev, forthcoming 98. **CONTACT ADDRESS** School of Law, Univ of Arkansas, Fayetteville, AR, 72701. **EMAIL** goforth@comp.uark.edu

GOH, DAVID T.
PERSONAL Born 01/27/1959, Calcutta, India, m, 1984, 2 children **DISCIPLINE** NEW TESTAMENT **EDUCATION** Univ of Durham, United Kingdom, PhD, 94. **CAREER** Sr Pastor, Bakersfield Community Church; Adjunct Prof, Fuller Theological Seminary; VP, Harvest Intl School **CONTACT ADDRESS** 2010 O St., Bakersfield, CA, 93301. **EMAIL** docgoh@aol.com

GOLD, JEFF
DISCIPLINE PHILOSOPHY **EDUCATION** Ohio State Univ, PhD. **CAREER** Prof, E Tenn State Univ. **RESEARCH** Ancient philosophy; philosophy of religion; mysticism. **SELECTED PUBLICATIONS** Auth, Plato in the Light of Yoga, Philos E W, 96; Utilitarianism and Deontological Approaches to Criminal Justice Ethics, Justice Ethics, Anderson, 96; The Heroic Transformation of Bilbo Baggins, ETSU, 92; The Soul's Relation to the Forms: Plato's Account of Knowledge. Caravan Bk, 92; Criminal Justice Ethics: A Survey of Philosophical Theories, Anderson, 92; Is Fukuyama a Liberal?, E T S U, 91; Spiritual Zionism, Dialogue Alliance, 91; co-auth, Peacemaking, Justice, and Ethics, Anderson, 96. **CONTACT ADDRESS** Philosophy Dept, East Tennesee State Univ, Box 70717, Johnson City, TN, 37614- 0717. **EMAIL** goldj@etsu.edu

GOLD, JONATHAN
PERSONAL Born 04/19/1941, New Rochelle, NY, m, 1975 **DISCIPLINE** PHILOSOPHY **EDUCATION** Queens Col, BA, 70; SUNY Stony Brook, PhD, 81; Philadelphia Theol Sem, MDiv, 82. **CAREER** Prof Philos and Rel, W Liberty State Col; adj prof Philos, Wheeling Jesuit Univ; adj prof, Col of NJ; adj prof, Thomas Jefferson Univ. **HONORS AND AWARDS** Woodrow Wilson fel, 70-71; Who's Who Among tchrs, 95, 98. **MEMBERSHIPS** Amer Philos Asn. **RESEARCH** Logic; Metaphysics; Philosophy of Religion; Theology; Biblical Studies. **SELECTED PUBLICATIONS** Auth, Logic, Ordinality, and Pomplexity, 81; Modal Metaphysics, 92; Truth, Translations, and Trees, 92. **CONTACT ADDRESS** Dept of Humanities, West Liberty State Col, West Liberty, WV, 26074.

GOLD, RICHARD E.
DISCIPLINE LAW **EDUCATION** McGill Univ, BS, 84; Univ Toronto, LLB, 88; Univ Michigan, LLM, 92, SJD, 95. **CAREER** Law clerk, Justice Cory, Supreme Court Can; prof. **SELECTED PUBLICATIONS** Auth, Body Parts: Property Rights and the Ownership of Human Biological Materials, Georgetown. **CONTACT ADDRESS** Fac of Law, Univ Western Ontario, London, ON, N6A 3K7.

GOLD, VICTOR ROLAND
PERSONAL Born 09/18/1924, Garden City, KS, m, 1947, 3 children **DISCIPLINE** OLD TESTAMENT STUDIES **EDUCATION** Wartburg Theol Sem, BD, 46; Johns Hopkins Univ, PhD(ancient Near Eastern studies), 51. **CAREER** Guest lectr Contemp Am Denominations, Lutheran Deaconess Motherhouse, Baltimore, Md, 51; asst prof Old Testament, Hamma Divinity Sch, 52-53; pastor, Trinity Evangel Lutheran Church, Kalamazoo, Mich, 53-56; guest prof, 56, assoc prof, 56-61, prof Old Testament Studies & dean, Grad Studies, Pac Lutheran Theol Sem, 61-, Lutheran World Fed guest prof, Kirchliche Hochsch, Berlin, Ger, 59 & 68; mem fac & bd dirs, Laymen's Sch Relig, Berkeley, Calif, 59-69; mem fac, Grad Theol Union, Berkeley, 59, chmn, Area I, 65-68; hon assoc, Am Schs Orient Res, 62-64; mem, Comn Comprehensive Studies Ministry, Lutheran Church Am, 66-70; dir, Educ Div, Inst Mediter Studies, Berkeley, 67-73, exec dir inst, 69-74; vis prof, Dept Near Eastern Lang, Univ Calif, Berkeley, 68-; mem, Inter-Lutheran Comn Worship, 69-; mem, Am Lutheran Church-Lutheran Church Am Joint Comn Communion Practices, 74-76; mem, Nat Coun Churches US, 81-; trustee, 81-84; annual prof, Albright inst Arch Res, 86-. **MEMBERSHIPS** Am Schs Orient Res; Soc Bibl Lit; Am Orient Soc; Archaeol Inst Am. **RESEARCH** Near Eastern archaeology, languages and history; Old Testament exegesis and theology; international studies. **SELECTED PUBLICATIONS** Auth, Mosaic map of Medeba, 59 & Gnostic manuscripts of Chenoboskion, Bibl Archaeol; ed, Episkope, Fortress, 68; auth, Notes on Isaiah, Jeremiah, Ezekiel, In: Annotated Bible, Oxford Univ, 73, 91; ed New Testament & Psalmn. An Inclusive version, Oxford Univ, 95. **CONTACT ADDRESS** 2770 Marin Ave, Berkeley, CA, 94708-1530. **EMAIL** the_Mcgolds@ecunet.org

GOLDBERG, HILLEL
PERSONAL Born 01/10/1946, Denver, CO, m, 1969, 4 children **DISCIPLINE** JEWISH ETHICS **EDUCATION** Yeshiva Univ, BA, 69; Brandeis Univ, MA, 72, PhD(near Eastern & Judaic studies), 79. **CAREER** Lectr Talmud, Machseke Torah Inst, 71-72; lectr Jewish ethical thought, Jerusalem Col Women, 73-77; vis asst prof Judaic studies, Emory Univ, 78; LECTR JEWISH ETHICS AND INTELLECTUAL HIST, HEBREW UNIV, JERUSALEM, 79-. **MEMBERSHIPS** Am Acad Relig; Asn Jewish Studies; Am Hist Asn; Ctr Study Psychol & Judaism; World Union Jewish Studies. **RESEARCH** Rabbinic, medieval and modern Jewish ethics; Jewish intellectual history; Holocaust. **SELECTED PUBLICATIONS** Auth, Homosexuality, A Religious and Political-Analysis, Tradition-J Orthodox Jewish Thought, Vol 0027, 93; Religious Zionism Revisited: Responses to Questions on Fundamental Issues Concerning Religious and Secular Nationalism, and Non-Zionist Orthodoxy in the State of Israel Today--A Symposium, Tradition-J Orthodox Jewish Thought, Vol 0028, 94; Homosexuality, a Religious and Political-Analysis--A Rejoinder to Goldwasser, Hershel, Tradition-J Orthodox Jewish Thought, Vol 0029, 95; Philosophy of Halakha--The Many Worlds of Mikve, Tradition-J Orthodox Jewish Thought, Vol 0030, 96; Responding to 'Rupture and Reconstruction': Soloveitchik, R. Haym Transformation of Contemporary Jewish Orthodoxy, Tradition-J Orthodox Jewish Thought, Vol 0031, 97. **CONTACT ADDRESS** 915 Monaco, Denver, CO, 80220.

GOLDBERG, SANFORD C.
PERSONAL Born 11/22/1967, Brooklyn, NY, m, 1994, 3 children **DISCIPLINE** PHILOSOPHY **EDUCATION** Rutgers Univ, BA, 89; Columbia Univ, PhD, 95. **CAREER** Asst prof, Grinnell Col, 95-. **MEMBERSHIPS** Amer Philos Asn; Soc Philos Psych; S Soc Philos Psych. **RESEARCH** Philosophy of mind and language; epistemology; metaphysics **SELECTED PUBLICATIONS** Coed, The Twin Earth Chronicles, 96; coauth, Gray Matters: An Introduction to the Philosophy of Mind, 97; auth, art, Self-Ascription, Self-Knowledge, and the Memory Argument, 97; auth, art, The Very Idea of Computer Self-Knowledge and Self-Deception, 97. **CONTACT ADDRESS** Dept of Philosophy, Grinnell Col, Box 805, Grinnell, IA, 50112. **EMAIL** goldberg@ac.grin.edu

GOLDEN, DONALD LEON
PERSONAL Born 01/03/1940, Walnut Cove, NC, m **DISCIPLINE** LAW **EDUCATION** Howard Univ, BA 1972; Howard Univ Law School, JD 1972. **CAREER** US Attorney's Office, law clerk 1971; Judicial Panel on Multi-Dist Litigation, temp rsrch asst 1971; Howard Law School Library, 1971-72; US Dist Court, law clerk 1972-73; Covington & Burling, assoc 1973-77; Howard Univ Law School, adjunct prof 1974-81; Asst US Attorney's Office, atty 1977-81; Howard Univ Law School, prof 1981-. **CONTACT ADDRESS** Sch of Law, Howard Univ, 2935 Uptown St, NW, Washington, DC, 20008-1194.

GOLDEN, EVELYN DAVIS
PERSONAL Born 06/01/1951, Moultrie, GA, m **DISCIPLINE** LAW **EDUCATION** York Coll of the City Univ of NY, BA1972; Univ of FL, JD 1976. **CAREER** Dept of Legal Affairs, asst atty gen 1980-; Valencia Community Coll Orlando FL, instr prog dir 1977-79; Central FL Legal Serv, legal intern 1976-77; Pub Defender's Office Gainesville FL, legal intern 1974-75; Legal Aid Soc Brooklyn NY, legal asst 1973. **HONORS AND AWARDS** Outstd young women of Am Bd of Dir for Outstd Young Woman of Am 1977. **MEMBERSHIPS** Mem FL Bar 1978-; mem FL Chap of the Nat Bar Assn 1978-; mem FL Assn of Women Lawyers 1979-; v chmn Ch 24 Seminole Co Prog Adv Com 1976-79; parli Delta Sigma Theta Sorority Inc 1979-80; bd of dir Citrus Council of Girl Scouts 1979-. **CONTACT ADDRESS** Dept of Legal Affairs, 125 N Ridgewood Ave, Daytona Beach, FL, 32114.

GOLDFARB, RONALD L.
PERSONAL Born 10/16/1933, NJ, m, 1957, 3 children **DISCIPLINE** LAW **EDUCATION** Syracuse Univ, AB, 54, LLB, 56; Yale Law School, LLM, 60, JSD, 62. **CAREER** U.S. Air Force, JAG, 57-60; Dept of Justice, 61-64; speech writer, 64; pres task force to establish the Office of Economic Opportunity; special counsel, U.S. House of Representatives Select Committee, 67; chemn, Special Review Committee, 75-76; LAWYER, RONALD GOLDFARB & ASSOCS, 96-. **MEMBERSHIPS** DC, NY, and Calif Bars; Bar of the U.S. Supreme Court; chemn of the board/dir, Law Sci Coun; pres & general counsel, Main-Street, 84-; bod of dir, Va Center for the Creative Arts, 92-; bd of dis, Alliance for Justice, 97-. **SELECTED PUBLICATIONS** Auth, Perfect Villains, Imperfect Heroes: Robert F. Kennedy's War Against Organized Crime, Random House, 95; auth, TV or NOT TV: Courts, Television and Justice, The Twentieth Century Fund, NY Univ Press, 98; auth, The Encyclopedia of Publishing and the Book Arts, Henry Holt, 95; contribur, The Encyclopedia of Criminology, Macmillan, 94; contrib, The Encyclopedia of the United States Congress, Simon & Schuster, 94; contrib, The Macmillan Encyclopedia, 97. **CONTACT ADDRESS** 918 16th St, NW, Washington, DC, 20006.

GOLDIN, OWEN MICHAEL
PERSONAL Born 06/07/1957, Philadelphia, PA, 2 children **DISCIPLINE** PHILOSOPHY **EDUCATION** St. John's Col, Santa Fe, BA, 79; Univ Chicago, MA, 82; Univ Texas Austin, PhD, 87. **CAREER** Asst prof, 87-94, asoc prof, 94-, Marquette Univ. **MEMBERSHIPS** APA; Metaphysical Soc Am; Soc Ancient Greek Philos; Int Plato Soc. **RESEARCH** Ancient philosophy; metaphysics; ethics. **SELECTED PUBLICATIONS** Auth, "Self, Sameness and Soul in Alcibiades I and the Timaeus," Freiburger Zeitschrift fur Philos und Theol, 93; "Parmenides on Possibility and Thought," Apeiron, 93; "Aristotle on Good and Bad Actualities," J of Neoplatonic Stud, 93; Explaining an Eclipse, Univ Mich, 96; Human Life and the Natural World, Broadview, 97; "The Ecology of the Critias and Platonic Metaphysics," The Greeks and the Environment, Rowman and Littlefield, 97; "Plato and the Arrow of Time," Ancient Philos, 98. **CONTACT ADDRESS** Dept of Philosophy, Marquette Univ, PO Box 1881, Milwaukee, WI, 53201-1881. **EMAIL** 6145goldino@vms.csd.mu.edu

GOLDING, MARTIN P.
DISCIPLINE PHILOSOPHY **EDUCATION** Columbia Univ, PhD, 59. **CAREER** Prof, 76-, Duke Univ. **MEMBERSHIPS** Am Soc Polit Legal Philos. **RESEARCH** Philos of law; ethical problems in bio medl tech. **SELECTED PUBLICATIONS** Auth, Philosophy of Law, Prentice Hall, 75; Legal Reasoning, Knopf, 84; ed, The Nature of Law, Random House, 66; Jewish Law and Legal Theory, NYU, 94. **CONTACT ADDRESS** Philos Dept, Duke Univ, West Duke Bldg, Durham, NC, 27706. **EMAIL** mgolding@acpub.duke.edu

GOLDINGAY, JOHN
PERSONAL Born 06/20/1942, Birmingham, England, m, 1967, 2 children **DISCIPLINE** THEOLOGY **EDUCATION** Oxford Univ, BA, 64; Notingham Univ, PhD, 83; Lambeth Univ, DD, 97. **CAREER** Lectr, theol, St John's Theol Col, Nottingham UK, 70-97; Dana Allan Hubbard prof of Old Testament, Fuller Theol Sem, 97- . **MEMBERSHIPS** SOTS; SBL. **CONTACT ADDRESS** 111 S Orange Grove, #108, Pasadena, CA, 91105. **EMAIL** johngold@fuller.edu

GOLDMAN, ALAN H.
PERSONAL Born 08/07/1945, New York, NY, m, 1968, 2 children **DISCIPLINE** PHILOSOPHY **EDUCATION** Yale Univ, BA, 67; Columbia Univ, PhD, 72. **CAREER** Asst prof, Ohio Univ, 72-74; asst prof, Univ Idaho, 74-76; from assoc prof to prof 77-, chemn, 88-98, Univ Miami; vis assoc prof, Univ Mich, 80; vis prof, Univ Auckland, 96. **HONORS AND AWARDS** Excellence in Tchg Award, 97, Univ Miami. **MEMBERSHIPS** Am Philos Asn; Am Soc Aesthetics. **RESEARCH**

Ethics, Aesthetics; Epistemology; Philosophy of law. **SELECTED PUBLICATIONS** Auth, Justice and Reverse Discrimination, 79; auth, The Moral Foundations of Professional Ethics, 80; auth, Empirical Knowledge, 88; auth, Moral Knowledge, 88; auth, Aesthetic Value, 95. **CONTACT ADDRESS** Dept of Philosophy, Univ of Miami, Coral Gables, FL, 33124. **EMAIL** agoldman@umiami.ir.miami.edu

GOLDMAN, ALVIN I.
PERSONAL Born 10/01/1938, New York, NY, m, 1969, 2 children **DISCIPLINE** PHILOSOPHY **EDUCATION** Columbia Univ, BA, 60; Princeton Univ, MA, 62, PhD, 65. **CAREER** Asst prof to prof, Univ Mich, 63-80; prof, Univ Illinois at Chicago, 80-83; regents prof, Univ Arizona, 83-. **MEMBERSHIPS** Pres, Pacific Div, 92, member, Amer Philos Assn; pres, 88, member, Soc Philos and Psychol; Philos Sci Assn. **RESEARCH** Epistemology; cognitive science; philosophy of mind, political and legal philosophy. **SELECTED PUBLICATIONS** Auth, "Consciousness, Folk Psychology, and Cognitive Science," Consciousness and Cognition, vol 2, 93; coauth, "Speech, Truth and the Free Market for Ideas," Legal Theory, vol 2, 96; auth, "Science, Publicity, and Consciousness," Philosophy of Science, vol 64, 97; coauth, "Games Lawyers Play: Legal Discovery and Social Epistemology," Legal Theory, vol 4, 98; auth, "Why Citizens Should Vote: A Casual Responsibility Approach," Social Philosophy & Policy, 99. **CONTACT ADDRESS** Dept of Philosophy, Univ of Arizona, Tucson, AZ, 85721-0027. **EMAIL** goldman@u.arizona.edu

GOLDMAN, EDWARD A.
PERSONAL Born 03/25/1941, Toledo, OH, m, 1966, 2 children **DISCIPLINE** RABBINIC LITERATURE **EDUCATION** Harvard Col, BA, 63; Hebrew Union Col, MAHL, 69, PhD, 74. **CAREER** Prof of Rabbinics, Hebrew Union Col, 72- . **MEMBERSHIPS** Cent Conf of Am Rabbis; AAUP; Soc for Bibl Lit; Nat Asn of Prof of Hebrew; Jewish Law Asn; Asn for Jewish Stud. **RESEARCH** Midrash. **SELECTED PUBLICATIONS** Rev, Parables in Midrash: Narrative and Exegesis in Rabbinic Literatyre, by Stern, J of the Am Oriental Soc, 93; rev, Techniques and Assumptions in Jewish Exegesis before 70 CE by Brewer, J of the Am Oriental Soc, 94; rev, Introduction to the Talmud and Midrash by Strack, J of the Am Oriental Soc, 96; rev, The Bavli: An Introduction, and, The Bavli's Massive Miscellanies: The Problem of Agglutinative Discourse in the Talmud of Babylonia, by Neusner, in, Critical Rev of Books in Relig, 1994, 96; ed, Jewish Law Association Studies VIII: The Jerusalem 1994 Conference Volume, 96; auth, The Midrash and Healing, The Living Pulpit, 97; rev, Sukkah, Horayot, Shebuot, Temurah, Meilah and Tamic, South Florida Academic Commentary, by Neusner, in, Critical Rev of Books in Relig, 1996, 97; ed, Jewish Law Association Studies IV: The London 1996 Conference Volume, 97. **CONTACT ADDRESS** Hebrew Union Col, 3101 Clifton Ave, Cincinnati, OH, 45220. **EMAIL** Edwgold@aol.com

GOLDSTEIN, ABRAHAM SAMUEL
PERSONAL Born 07/27/1925, New York, NY, m, 1947, 2 children **DISCIPLINE** LAW **EDUCATION** City Col New York, BBA, 46; Yale Univ, LLB, 49, MA, 61. **CAREER** Law clerk, Circuit Judge David L Bazelon, US Court of Appeals, 49-51; partner, Donohue & Kaufmann, 51-56; assoc prof law, 56-61, dean law sch, 70-75, prof law, 61-75, STERLING PROF, LAW SCH, YALE UNIV, 75-, Provost Univ, 78-79; Mem bar, US Dist Court, Washington, DC, 49- & US Supreme Court, 54; mem adv bd community serv, CT Dept Mental Health, 62-66; vis fel, Inst Criminology & fel, Christ's Col, Cambridge Univ, 64-65; Guggenheim fel, 64-65 & 75-76; consult, President's Comn Law Enforcement, 66-67; mem, Comn to Revise Conn Criminal Code, 66-69, CT Bd Parole, 67-69 & CT Planning Comt Criminal Admin, 67-71; vis prof, Hebrew Univ, Jerusalem, 76, Tel Aviv, 86; vpres, CT Bar Found, 76-78. **HONORS AND AWARDS** MA, Cambridge Univ, 64; LLD, New York Law Sch, 79; De Paul, 87. **MEMBERSHIPS** Am Acad Arts & Sci; Am Bar Asn; Am Jewish Cong (sr vpres, 77-84). **RESEARCH** Criminal law; criminal procedure; evidence. **SELECTED PUBLICATIONS** Auth, Conspiracy to Defraud the United States, 59 & The State and the Accused: Balance of Advantage in Criminal Procedure, Yale Law J, 60; The Insanity Defense, Yale Univ, 67; co-ed, Crime, Law and Society, Free, 71; coauth, Criminal Procedure, Little, 74; The Passive Judiciary: Prosecutorial Discretion and the Guilty Plea, LA State Univ Press, 81. **CONTACT ADDRESS** Law Sch, Yale Univ, PO Box 208215, New Haven, CT, 06520-8215.

GOLDSTEIN, IRWIN
PERSONAL Born 07/12/1947, Windsor, ON, Canada, d, 2 children **DISCIPLINE** PHILOSOPHY **EDUCATION** Univ Edinburgh, PhD, 79; Univ Bristol, M. Lit, 74; Carleton Univ, BA, 70. **CAREER** Prof, Davidson Col, 98-; asst prof, Davidson Col, 83-87 **HONORS AND AWARDS** Davidson Col Res Grants; Postdoctorate Fel, Univ Edinburgh; Vans Dunlop Scholar, Univ Edinburgh; Carleton Univ Grant. **MEMBERSHIPS** Amer Philos Assoc; Intl Soc Value Inquiry; S Soc Philos Psychol; NC Philos Assoc **SELECTED PUBLICATIONS** Ontology, Epistemology, and Private Ostensive Definition, Philos and Phenomenological Res, 96; Identifying Experiences: A Celebrated Working Hypothesis Refuted, Australasian Jour Philos, 94; "Pleasure and Pain: Unconditional Intrinsic Values," Philos and Phenomenological Res, 89 **CONTACT ADDRESS** Dept of Philosophy, Davidson Col, Davidson, NC, 28036. **EMAIL** irgoldstein@davidson.edu

GOLDSTEIN, LEON JAY
PERSONAL Born 02/06/1927, Brooklyn, NY, m, 1964, 2 children **DISCIPLINE** PHILOSOPHY **EDUCATION** Brooklyn Col, AB, 49; Yale Univ, MA, 50, PhD(philos), 54. **CAREER** Instr philos, Brandeis Univ, 55-57; lectr, Univ Md Overseas Prog, 58; researcher, Am Jewish Comt, 58-63; assoc prof soc sci and philos, 63-64, assoc prof philos, 64-66, chmn dept, 65-68, PROF PHILOS, STATE UNIV NY BINGHAMTON, 66-, Lectr, City Col New York, 59-63. **MEMBERSHIPS** Am Philos Asn; Am Anthrop Asn; Hegel Soc Am. **RESEARCH** Philosophy of history and social science; epistemology; hermeneutics. **SELECTED PUBLICATIONS** Auth, What Is the Use of Jewish History, Mod Judaism, Vol 0014, 94. **CONTACT ADDRESS** Dept of Philos, State Univ of NY, Binghamton, NY, 13901.

GOLDSTEIN, PAUL
PERSONAL Born 01/14/1943 **DISCIPLINE** LAW **EDUCATION** Brandeis Univ, BA, 64; Columbia Univ, LLB, 67. **CAREER** Asst prof law, State Univ NY Buffalo, 67-69, assoc prof, 69-71; Prof Law, Stanford Univ, 75-, Via assoc prof law, Stanford Univ, 72-73. **SELECTED PUBLICATIONS** Auth, Comments on a Manifesto Concerning the Legal Protection of Computer-Programs, Columbia Law Rev, Vol 0094, 94. **CONTACT ADDRESS** Sch of Law, Stanford Univ, Stanford, CA, 94305-1926.

GOLDTHWAIT, JOHN T.
PERSONAL Born 03/31/1921, Duluth, MN, m, 1948, 1 child **DISCIPLINE** PHILOSOPHY **EDUCATION** USN Res Midship Sch, Ensign, 43, Columbia Univ; Oglethorpe Univ, Atlanta, GA, BA, MA, 44; Northwestern Univ, D Phil, 57. **CAREER** Instr, 41-43, Oglethorpe Univ; naval serv, 43-46; instr, 46-50, Oglethorpe Univ; grad tchng asst, 50-52, Northwestern Univ; instr, 52-55, Sacramento St Col; instr, 56-57, asst prof, 58-64, Univ Calif; fac, 62, Pacific Philos Inst; prof, chmn, div of Hum, dean, fac of Hum, 64-85, SUNY. **HONORS AND AWARDS** Fac summer res fel, Univ CA, 58; Plattsburgh Col Found grant, 71 **MEMBERSHIPS** APA; Am Soc for Aesthetics; Nat Coun of Tchrs of Eng; Col Conf on Composition and Commun; Speech Asn of Am; Am Transl Asn; Speech Arts Asn of Northern Calif; Calif div, Am Soc for Aesthetics; Cent Calif Philos Asn; Berkeley Aesthetics Seminar; Asn for Philos of Ed; Philos of Ed Soc; Asn for Process Philos of Ed; FL Philos Asn. **RESEARCH** Aesthetics; theory of value; ethics; process philos. **SELECTED PUBLICATIONS** Transl & ed, Immanuel Kant, Observations on the Feeling of the Beautiful and Sublime, Univ Calif Press, 60, 81; auth, Value, Language, and Life, Prometheus Bks, 85; auth, Ought Never Is: A Response to Oliver A. Johnson, J of Value Inquiry, 92; auth, A General Education Program Seen Fifty Years Later, J of Gen Ed, vol 43, no 1, 94; Values: What They Are and How We Know Them, Prometheus Bks, 96; auth, Values and Education: Helping History Along, The J of Value Inquiry, 96; auth, The Forward Look of Value Judgements, The J of Value Inquiry, 96. **CONTACT ADDRESS** 49 Sandpiper Dr, St. Augustine Beach, FL, 32084-6987.

GOLDWORTH, AMNON
PERSONAL Born 07/11/1927, Breast-Litovsk, Poland, m, 1949, 2 children **DISCIPLINE** PHILOSOPHY **EDUCATION** Queens Col, NY, BA, 50; Stanford Univ, PhD, 60. **CAREER** Univ Washington, ta, 50-51; Stanford Univ, ta, 52, 54; San Jose State Univ, inst, asst prof, assoc prof, prof, 56-95, Queens Col, lectr, 64; Stanford Univ, School of Med, clin prof pedi, 95-. **HONORS AND AWARDS** Univ Wash, Univ Tchg Fel, 50-51; Stanford Univ, Abraham Rosenberg Fel, 53; Stanford Univ, vis prof, 72; Stanford Univ, Center for Biomedical Ethics, vis scholar, 90-93; Amer Assoc of Tissue Banks, Ethics Comm / Consultant, 94- **MEMBERSHIPS** APA, AATB, AAP, SCCMS, NCTB **RESEARCH** Biomedical ethics in med practice; informal consent in htt; moral and ethical education for med student. **SELECTED PUBLICATIONS** Ed, The collected Works of Jeremy Bentham: Deontology Together with A Table of the Spring of Action and Articles on Utilitarianism, Oxford Univ Press, 83; co-ed, Ethics and Perinatology: Issues and Perspectives, Oxford Univ Press, 95; co-auth, Considerations of the Appropriateness of Intensive CAR e Applications, in: Fetal and Neonatal Brain Injury: Mechanisms, Management and the Risk of Malpractice, B.L. Decker Inc, 89; Standards of Disclosure in Informed Consent, in: Ethics and Perinatology: Issues and Perspectives, Oxford Univ Press, 95; Medical Technology and the Child, in: Birth to death: Biology, Science and Bioethics, Cambridge Univ Press, 96. **CONTACT ADDRESS** School of Medicine, Stanford Univ, 750 Welch Rd, Palo Alto, CA, 94304. **EMAIL** amnon@leland.stanford.edu

GOLLUBER, MICHAEL
PERSONAL Born 02/22/1966, Philadelphia, PA, m, 1998 **DISCIPLINE** PHILOSOPHY **EDUCATION** Sarah Lawrence Col, BA, 88; SUNY Stony Brook, MA, 91; Tulane Univ, PhD, 98. **CAREER** Vis instr, Southwestern Univ, 96-98, vis instr, Loyola Univ, 98; adj instr, Xavier Univ, 98; vis instr, Tulane Univ, 98- . **RESEARCH** Ancient philosophy; history of philosophy. **SELECTED PUBLICATIONS** Auth, Aristotle on Philosophy and the Sense of Touch, J of Philos Res, forthcoming. **CONTACT ADDRESS** 2033 Fern St, New Orleans, LA, 70118.

GOLPHIN, VINCENT F.A.
PERSONAL Born 08/07/1952, Youngstown, Ohio, s **DISCIPLINE** THEOLOGY **EDUCATION** Sacred Heart Seminary, Detroit, MI, BA, history, 1974; University of Dayton, Dayton, OH, MA, theology, 1979; Union Graduate School, PhD, religion/psychology, 1981. **CAREER** New York State Assembly, Albany, NY, senior executive asst, 1980-82; National Catholic Reporter, Washington, DC, writer, 1982-87; Charles County Community College, Waldorf, MD, adjunct professor, 1986-87; Herald-Journal, Syracuse, NY, editor/columnist, 1987-95; Onondaga Community College, Syracuse, NY, adjunct professor, 1990-95; Syracuse University, SI School of Public Communications, adjunct professor, 1995-; The Writing Co. Inc, president, currently. **HONORS AND AWARDS** NISOD, Teacher Excellence Award, 1994. **MEMBERSHIPS** President, Syracuse Press Club, 1989-91; member, Theta Chi Beta (religion honorary), 1990-; member, Phi Delta Kappa (education honorary), 1984-; member, Phi Alpha Theta (history honorary), 1972-. **CONTACT ADDRESS** President, The Writing Co., Inc, 10198 Carousel Center, Syracuse, NY, 13290.

GOMBERG, PAUL
PERSONAL Born 02/11/1943, San Francisco, CA, m, 1965, 1 child **DISCIPLINE** PHILOSOPHY **EDUCATION** Univ of CA, Berkley, BA, 64; Harvard Univ, PhD, 72. **CAREER** Inst, to Asst Prof, Univ of Missouri-St Louis, 71-72, 72-78; Vis Asst Prof , Univ of Illinois, 86-87; Asst Prof, 87-90, Assoc Prof, 90-94, Prof, 94-, Chicago St Univ. **HONORS AND AWARDS** NEH, 92; Fulbright Fel UK, 67-68, Woodrow Wilson Dissertation Fel, 67-68; Harvard Schl, 65-66, 66-67; Woodrow Wilson Fel, 65-66, Dept Citation in Phil, Univ CA, Berkley, 64. **MEMBERSHIPS** APA **RESEARCH** Social and political philosophy; social philosophy of morality; marxism; racism. **SELECTED PUBLICATIONS** Art, Friendship in the Context of a Consequentialist Life, Ethics 102, 92; art, Against Racism, Against Patriotism, APA News, 93; art, Universalism and Optimism, Ethics 104, 94; art, Autonomy and Free Expression, Jour Soc Phil, 94; art, Against Competitive Equal Opportunity, Jour of Soc Phil, 95; art, How Morality Works and Why it Fails: On Political Philosoph and Moral Consensus, Jour of Soc Phil, 97. **CONTACT ADDRESS** Chicago State Univ, 9501 S King Dr, History, P, Chicago, IL, 60628-1598. **EMAIL** P-Gomberg@csu.edu

GOMEZ LOBO, ALFONSO
DISCIPLINE PHILOSOPHY **EDUCATION** Univ Munich, PhD, 66. **CAREER** Prof. **RESEARCH** Greek philosophy; Greek historiography; early Christian thought; history of ethics; contemporary natural law theory. **SELECTED PUBLICATIONS** Auth, The Foundations of Socratic Ethics; pubs on Herodotus, Thucydides, Plato and Aristotle. **CONTACT ADDRESS** Dept of Philosophy, Georgetown Univ, 37th and O St, Washington, DC, 20057.

GONZALEZ, CATHERINE GUNSALUS
PERSONAL Born 05/20/1934, Albany, NY, m, 1973 **DISCIPLINE** HISTORICAL AND SYSTEMATIC THEOLOGY **EDUCATION** Beaver Col, BA, 56; Boston Univ, STB, 60, PhD(syst theol, hist doctrine), 65. **CAREER** From asst prof to assoc prof Bible and relig, WVa Wesleyan Col, 65-70, dir student relig life, 65-70; assoc prof hist theol, Louisville Presby Thcol Sem, 70-73; assoc prof church hist, 74-78, PROF CHURCH HIST, COLUMBIA THEOL SEM, 78-, Mem comt on status of women, Gen Assembly, United Presby Church, 67-70, comt on baptism, 70-72; mem, Faith and Order Comn, Nat Coun Churches, 73-. **MEMBERSHIPS** Presby Hist Soc. **RESEARCH** Liturgical theology; women and theology; comparative systematic theology. **SELECTED PUBLICATIONS** Auth, Between Text and Sermon--Isaiah 43, 8-15, Interpretation-J Bible and Theol, Vol 0048, 94. **CONTACT ADDRESS** Dept of Church Hist, Columbia Theol Sem, PO Box 520, Decatur, GA, 30031-0520.

GONZALEZ, JUSTO LUIS
PERSONAL Born 08/09/1937, Havana, Cuba, m, 1973, 1 child **DISCIPLINE** HISTORICAL THEOLOGY **EDUCATION** Union Theol Sem, Cuba, STB, 57; Yale Univ, STM, 58, MA, 60, PhD, 61. **CAREER** Prof, 61-68, dean, 68-69, Evangel Sem PR; assoc prof world Christianity, 69-77, Candler Sch Theol, Emory Univ; res & writing, 77-78; Ed, Apuntes; Journal Hispanic Theol, 79-; res fels hist theol, Yale Univ, 68 & 69; consult theol educ, Protestant Episcopal Church, 71-72 & 73-74; mem, Comn Faith & Order, Nat Coun Churches, 73-81; dir, 87-, Hispanic Sum Prog; exec dir, 96-, Hispanic Theol Initiative. **HONORS AND AWARDS** Hon degree, Divinas Letras, Seminario Evangelico de Puerto Rico, 94; Virgilio Elizondo Award; Acad of Cath Hispanic Theologians in US, 91; Gold Medallion Bk Award, Evangelical Christian Publ Assn, 93; Orlando Costas Award, Latino Pastoral Action Ctr, 98. **RESEARCH** Patristics; liberation theology; contemporary Latin American theology.

SELECTED PUBLICATIONS Auth, Mana: Christian Theology from a Hispanic Perspective, 90; auth, Faith and Wealth, Harper, 90; auth, Out of Every Tribe and Nation: Christian Theology at the Ethnic Roundtable, Abingdon, 92; auth, Santa Biblia: The Bible Through Hispanic Eyes, Abingdon, 96. **CONTACT ADDRESS** PO Box 520, Decatur, GA, 30031. **EMAIL** jgonz02@emory.edu

GONZALEZ, LUIS G.
PERSONAL Born 04/28/1969, Ponce, PR, m, 1989 **DISCIPLINE** PHILOSOPHY **EDUCATION** Andrews Univ, BA, 92; Western Mich Univ, MA, 94; Valparaiso Univ, JD, 94. **CAREER** Vis asst prof, Grand Valley State Univ, 96-. **MEMBERSHIPS** Am Philos Asn; Am Bar Asn. **RESEARCH** Philosophy of law; Professional ethics; Latin American philosophy. **SELECTED PUBLICATIONS** Auth, Sereno en Flor, 94. **CONTACT ADDRESS** 460 Ferndale Ave NW, Walker, MI, 49544. **EMAIL** gonzluis@river.it.gvsu.edu

GOOCH, PAUL W.
PERSONAL Born 06/24/1941, Toronto, ON, Canada **DISCIPLINE** PHILOSOPHY/RELIGION **EDUCATION** Bishop's Univ, BA, 63; Univ Toronto, MA, 65, PhD, 70. **CAREER** Asst prof, 70, assoc prof, 73, ch div hum, 77-82, prof, 88, dir grad ctr relig stud, 86-88, assoc dean hum, sch grad stud, 88-90, asst dean to dean, sch grad stud, 90-94, VICE-PROVOST, UNIV TORONTO, 94-; Commonwealth fel, St John's Col, Cambridge, 82-83. **MEMBERSHIPS** Can Philos Asn; Class Asn Can; Can Soc Stud Relig; Can Soc Bibl Stud; Soc Christian Philos. **RESEARCH** Greek philosophy; Biblical studies; philosophy of religion. **SELECTED PUBLICATIONS** Auth, Partial Knowledge: Philosophical Studies in Paul, 87; auth, Reflections on Jesus and Socrates: Word and Silence, 96. **CONTACT ADDRESS** Simcoe Hall, Univ of Toronto, 27 King's Col Cir, Toronto, ON, M5S 1A1.

GOOD, ROBERT C.
DISCIPLINE ETHICS AND RELIGION IN AMERICA **EDUCATION** Princeton Univ, AB; Univ Wis, MA, PhD. **CAREER** Instr, Rider Univ, 82; prof. **HONORS AND AWARDS** AB with honors; three NEH fel(s); Lindback Award, 91. **RESEARCH** Philosophy of religion, Imperative logic, tele-evangelism **SELECTED PUBLICATIONS** Nat and intl publ(s), philos rel, imperative logic and tele-evangelism. **CONTACT ADDRESS** Dept of Art and Sci, Westfield State Col, 577 Western Ave, Westfield, MA, 01085.

GOODE, JAMES EDWARD
PERSONAL Born 11/18/1943, Roanoke, VI **DISCIPLINE** THEOLOGY **EDUCATION** Immaculate Conceptn Coll, BA 1969; Coll of St Rose, MA 1971; St Anthony Theol Sem, MDiv 1972, MTh 1974; PhD; Univ of Louvain Belgium, post-doctoral studies 1980. **CAREER** OUR LADY OF CHARITY, PASTOR 1974-; CITY UNIV NY, ADJ PROF 1975-, CHAPLAIN 1975-; CENTER FOR POSITIVE DIRECTN, DIR 1976-; Black Religious Expernc Inst, co-dir; Directions A Jour of Black Ch/Comm Studies, editor; Black Cath Day, founder; Survival & Faith Inst of NY, cons; Juvenile Justice Task Force of Cntrl Brooklyn, cons; Offc for Black Ministry Diocese of Brooklyn, bd dirs; Bldg a Better Brooklyn, bd dirs; lectr, psychlgy & theology. **HONORS AND AWARDS** Dr of Humane Letters VA Theol Sem; Preacher of First Black Cath Revival in US Chicago 1974; Martin Luther King Schlrshp NY Univ 1975-76; Black Cath Leadrshp Awrd; proclmtn declaring Nov 18 1978 Father James E Goode Day New York City 1978; proclmtn declaring Nov 16 1979 Father James E Goode Day Mayor of Brooklyn 1979; Nat Black Cath Clergy Tribute Award 1979; proclmtn NY State Assembly; lead Nat Protest Prayer Serv Against Budget Cuts in Human Servs. **MEMBERSHIPS** Mem New York City Comm Sch Bd; mem Central Brooklyn Yth & Fmly Svcs; mem Juvenile Prevntv Pgms Brooklyn; mem New York City Comm Plnng Bd; mem Culture & Worship Adv Bd Nat Offc for Black Cath; mem Coalition of Concerned Black Eductrs of NY; mem Black Ministers Cncl; mem Nat Black Cath Clergy; Nat Assn of Black Social Wrkrs; Educ Task Force for Positive Direction of NY Urban Commn. **CONTACT ADDRESS** 1669 Dean St, Brooklyn, NY, 11213.

GOODEN, WINSTON EARL
DISCIPLINE THEOLOGY **EDUCATION** Muskingum College, BA; Yale Univ, MDiv, MS, PhD. **CAREER** Two Churches in CT, pastored; Unoja Juvenile Program, co-founder & director; Univ of IL at Chicago, asst prof; Fuller Theological Seminary, asst prof. **HONORS AND AWARDS** Presented papers across the nation. **SELECTED PUBLICATIONS** Published many articles. **CONTACT ADDRESS** Fuller Theol Sem, 135 N Oakland, Pasadena, CA, 91101.

GOODING-WILLIAMS, ROBERT
DISCIPLINE PHILOSOPHY **EDUCATION** Yale Univ, PhD. **CAREER** Prof, Northwestern Univ. **RESEARCH** Nietzsche, Du Bois, Nineteenth-Century European philosophy, literary theory and African-American literature, social theory, race and racism. **SELECTED PUBLICATIONS** Auth, The Massachuettes Review, Special Issue on Du Bois, 94; co-ed, The Souls of Black Folk, 97. **CONTACT ADDRESS** Dept of Philosophy, Northwestern Univ, 1801 Hinman, Evanston, IL, 60208.

GOODMAN, LENN EVAN
PERSONAL Born 03/21/1944, Detroit, MI, m, 1965, 2 children **DISCIPLINE** PHILOSOPHY **EDUCATION** Harvard Univ, BA, 65; Oxford Univ, DPhil(Arabic philos), 68. **CAREER** Asst prof philos and Near Eastern lang, Univ Calif, Los Angeles, 68-69; asst prof, 69-74, assoc prof, 74-81, PROF PHILOS, UNIV HAWAII, MONOA, 81-, Consult, Sch Jewish Studies, Univ Tel Aviv, 74-77 and Hawaiian Humane Soc, 78-79. **HONORS AND AWARDS** Baumgardt Prize, Am Philos Asn, 78; Littman lectr, Oxford Ctr for Postgrad Hebrew Studies, 79. **MEMBERSHIPS** Am Philos Asn; Am Orient Soc; Mid East Studies Asn NAm; Acad Jewish Philos. **RESEARCH** Jewish and Islamic philosophy; metaphysics; ethics. **SELECTED PUBLICATIONS** Auth, Anselm, Saint--A Portrait in a Landscape, Biogr-Interdisciplinary Quart, Vol 0016, 93. **CONTACT ADDRESS** Dept of Philos, Univ of Hawaii, Manoa Honolulu, HI, 96822.

GOODMAN, MICHAEL F.
PERSONAL Born 03/23/1950, CA, m, 1975, 4 children **DISCIPLINE** PHILOSOPHY **EDUCATION** Mich State Univ, PhD, 86. **CAREER** Humboldt State Univ, prof. **MEMBERSHIPS** APA, MA **RESEARCH** Logic; epistemology **SELECTED PUBLICATIONS** Auth, First Logic, UPA, 97; Contemporary Readings in Epistemology, co-auth w/ R. A. Snyder, Prentice-Hall, 93; What is a Person? Humana Press, 88; Decision and Practice, coauth, Humboldt Jour of Soc Rel, 87; Concept of Person in: Philo of Edu: An Encycl, 96; A Sufficient Condition for Personhood, Personalist Form, 92; What is a Program?, Contemp Philo, 88. **CONTACT ADDRESS** Dept Philosophy, Humboldt State Univ, Arcata, CA, 95521. **EMAIL** mfgl@axe.humboldt.edu

GOODMAN, RUSSELL B.
PERSONAL Born 05/28/1945, Pyoto, TX, m, 1971, 2 children **DISCIPLINE** PHILOSOPHY **EDUCATION** Univ Penn, BA, 66; Oxford, MA, 70; Johns Hop Univ, PhD, 71. **CAREER** Univ New Mex, asst prof, 71-79; Cambridge Univ, v sch, 77-78; Univ New Mex, assoc prof, 79-90; Cent & Auton Univ Barcelona, Full sr lect, 93; Univ New Mex, chmn Philo dept, 90-96, prof 91-. **HONORS AND AWARDS** Univ Penn, E. B. Williams Schlshp, 62-66; Oxford Univ, Thouron Brit-Amer Exch Fel 66-68; Jesus Col Oxford W Montgomerie Prize, 67; John Hop Univ, NDEA Fel, 68-71; NEH, 89-90; Fulbright SL/R Award, 93 **MEMBERSHIPS** APA, SAAP **RESEARCH** Amer philo; philo and lit. **SELECTED PUBLICATIONS** Auth, American Philosophy and the Romantic Tradition, CUP, 90; Pragmatism: A Contemporary Reader, Routledge, 95; Moral Perfectionism and Democracy in Emerson and Nietzsche, ESQ.: Jour of Amer RNA, 97; Wittgenstein and Pragmatism, Parallax 98; American Philosophy in the 18th and 19th Centuries, w/ William C. Doweling, Rout Encycl Philo, 98; Ralph Walled Emerson, Rout Encycl Philo, 98; Emerson's Mystical Empiricism, in: The Perennial Tradition of Neoplatonism, ed John J. Cleary, Leuven UP, 97; Emerson the European and Heidegger the American, in: American and European National Identities: Faces in the Mirror, ed Stephen Fender, Keele UP, 96; What Wittgenstein Learned from William James, Hist Philo Quart, 94. **CONTACT ADDRESS** Dept of Philosophy, Univ of New Mexico, Albuquerque, NM, 87131. **EMAIL** rgoodman@unm.edu

GOODMAN, SUSANNE R.
DISCIPLINE LAW **EDUCATION** Univ Toronto, BA, 77; Windsor Univ, LLB, 80. **CAREER** Lectr, 89-. **SELECTED PUBLICATIONS** Auth, pubs on family law. **CONTACT ADDRESS** Fac of Law, Univ Toronto, 78 Queen's Park, Toronto, ON.

GOODMAN-DELAHUNTY, JANE
PERSONAL Born 02/17/1952, Johannesburg, South Africa, 1 child **DISCIPLINE** PSYCHOLOGY/LAW **EDUCATION** Univ Witwatersrand, Johannesburg, S Africa, BA, 72, MA, 73; Univ Seattle Sch of Law, JD, 83; Univ Wa Seattle, PhD, 86. **CAREER** Assoc, 83-84, Bricklin & Gendler, Seattle; trial atty, 84-88, US Equal Employ Opportunity Comm, Seattle; litigation atty, 89-92, Frank & Rosen, Seattle; mediator, arbitrator, 94-, Judicial Arbitration & Mediation Svc, Endispute, Calif; admin judge, 92-, US Equal Employ Opportunity Comm. **HONORS AND AWARDS** Conrad Linder Mem Award, 73; Amer Jurisprudence Award, 82, 83; PhD Scholar, 83; Grad Res Fel, 85; Dissertation Prize, 87; Special Commendation, 88; Pres, Amer Psychol-Law Soc, 94; Chairman's Innov Award, 95; Amer Psychol-Law Soc Fel, 96. **MEMBERSHIPS** Amer Bar Assoc; Amer Judicature Soc; Amer Psychol Assoc; Amer Psychol-Law Soc; Amer Psychol Soc; Int Assoc Applied Psychol; Int Cong Law & Mental Health; Law & Soc Assoc; San Diego Psych-Law Soc; Seattle-King Co Bar Assoc; Soc for Psychol Study of Soc Issue; Wa St Bar Assoc. **RESEARCH** Psychol & law; scientific & expert evidence; employ discrimination; sexual harassment; cultural diversity; collective & political violence; dispute resolution; procedural & distributive justice; causal reasoning; decisionmaking; stereotyping; eyewitness reliability; jury behavior. **SELECTED PUBLICATIONS** Art, Employment Discrimination and Stereotyping, Encyclopedia of psychology, Oxford Univ Press, Amer Psychol Assoc, 99; art, Civil law: Employment and Discrimination, Perspectives on Psychology and Law: The State of the Discipline, Plenum Press, 99; art, Pragmatic Considerations Supporting the Reasonable Victim Standard in Hostile Workplace Sexual Harassment Cases, Psychology, Public Polit & Law, 99, coauth, Juror Decisions About Damages in Employment Discrimination Cases, Behavioral Sci & the Law, 99; art, Same-Sex Harassment: Implications of The Oncale Decision for Forensic Evaluations of Plaintiffs, Behavioral Sci & the Law, 99. **CONTACT ADDRESS** 2407 Calle Madiera, San Clemente, CA, 92672. **EMAIL** JANEGDEL@AOL.COM

GOODWIN, JAMES OSBY
PERSONAL Born 11/04/1939, Tulsa, OK, m **DISCIPLINE** LAW **EDUCATION** Univ of Notre Dame, BA 1961; Univ of Tulsa, JD 1965. **CAREER** Atty; OK Eagle Newsppr, publisher. **HONORS AND AWARDS** Award for Serv as mem bd chmn Tulsa Comprehensive Hlth Ctr 1973. **MEMBERSHIPS** Chmn Tulsa Human Srvc Agncy 1978-80; bd chmn Tulsa Comprhnsv Hlth Ctr 1973; mem Tulsa City Co Bd of Hlth; mem OK Bar Assn; Am Trial Lawyers; sec, vice pres OK Trial Lawyers; mem Tulsa Co Bar Assn; Tulsa Co Legal Aid; ACLU Award for Serv as Chmn Tulsa City Co Bd of Hlth 1975. **CONTACT ADDRESS** 122 N Greenwood, Tulsa, OK, 74120.

GORANSON, STEPHEN
PERSONAL Born 11/05/1950, Surrey, England **DISCIPLINE** RELIGION AND HISTORY **EDUCATION** Brandeis Univ, BA, 72; Duke Univ, PhD, 90. **CAREER** Wake Forest Univ; Univ NC Wilmington; NC State Univ; vis asst prof, Duke Univ, 98-. **SELECTED PUBLICATIONS** Auth, Essene Polemic in the Apocalypse of John, Legal Texts, Legal Issues, Proceedings of the Second Meeting of International Organization for Qumran Studies, Cambridge 1995: Published in Honour of Joseph M. Baumgarten, Cambridge, England, STJD, 23, Leiden, E. J. Brill, 97; auth, The Text of Revelation 22:14, New Testament Studies, 97; auth, 7 vs. 8--The Battle Over the Holy Day at Dura-Europos, Bible Rev, 96; auth, Inkwell, Ostracon with Maria Graffito, Sepphoris in Galilee: Crosscurrents of Culture, NC Mus of Art, 96; auth, The Exclusion of Ephraim in Rev. 7:4-8 and Essene Polemic Against Pharisees, Dead Sea Discoveries, 95; auth, Posidonius, Strabo, and Marcus Vipsanius Agrippa as Sources on Essenes, Jour of Jewish Studies, 94; auth, Sectarianism, Geography, and the Copper Scroll, Jour of Jewish Studies, 92; auth, Nazarenes and Ebionites, Anchor Bible Dict, 92; auth, Essenes: Etymology from 'asah, Revue de Qumran, 84. **CONTACT ADDRESS** 706 Louise Cir., #30-J, Durham, NC, 27705. **EMAIL** goranson@duke.edu

GORDON, DANE R.
PERSONAL Born 06/15/1925, London, England, m, 1952 **DISCIPLINE** PHILOSOPHY, THEOLOGY **EDUCATION** Cambridge Univ, BA, 51, MA, 56; Univ London, BD, 56; Univ Rochester, MA, 60. **CAREER** Minister, Cent Presby Church, Rochester, 57-61; from asst prof to assoc prof sci & humanities, 62-74, chemn dept, 74-76, actg dean, Col Gen Studies, 76-77, asst dean, 77-79, prof philos & relig, Rochester Inst Technol, 74-, assoc dean Col Gen Studies, 79-88; vis lectr, philos and relig, New Bulgarian Univ, 99-2000. **HONORS AND AWARDS** Eisenhart Outstanding Teacher Award, 97; NEH Int Research and Exchange Grant, 95. **MEMBERSHIPS** Am Philos Asn; AAUP; Soc for Ancient Greek Philos; Christian Asn of Relig in Eastern Europe. **RESEARCH** Hellenistic Philos; Political and Soc Philo; Ethics in the Old Testament. **SELECTED PUBLICATIONS** Ed & contrib, Criticism and Defense of Rationality in Contemporary Philosophy, Rodopi Press, 98; auth, Thinking and Reading in Philosophy of Religion, Haven Publs Inc, 94; The Old Testament: A Beginning Survey, Prentice Hall, 85; The History of the Rochester Institute of Technology, Edwin Mellen Press, 82; Who is My Neighbor?-New Ecological Answers to an Old Theological Question, Religiologique, Mar 95; Semiotics Before Semiotics, The Journal of Visual Sociology, Winter 87. **CONTACT ADDRESS** Col of Gen Studies, Rochester Inst of Tech, 1 Lomb Memorial Dr, Rochester, NY, 14623-5603. **EMAIL** drggla@rit.edu

GORDON, MICHAEL W.
DISCIPLINE LAW **EDUCATION** Univ Conn, BS, LLB; Trinity Col, MA; Univ Iberoamericana, Mexico, Maestria en Derecho. **CAREER** Chesterfield Smith prof, Univ Fla, 68-. **MEMBERSHIPS** Bd dir, US-Mexico Law Inst; Amer Soc Comp Law; bd ed, UCLA Pacific Basin Law J; adv bd, Syracuse J Int Law Commerce; NAFTA Rev; Amer For Law Asn; Amer Soc Int Law; Brit Inst Int Comp Law; Conn Bar. **RESEARCH** Corporate law, international business transactions, comparative law, international litigation. **SELECTED PUBLICATIONS** Coauth, Intl Trade and Investment in a Nutshell; Intl Business Transactions in a Nutshell. **CONTACT ADDRESS** School of Law, Univ of Florida, PO Box 117625, Gainesville, FL, 32611-7625. **EMAIL** Reid@law.ufl.edu

GORDON, ROBERT M.
DISCIPLINE PHILOSOPHY OF MIND, PHILOSOPHY AND COGNITIVE SCIENCE, ETHICAL THEORY **EDUCATION** Columbia Univ, PhD, 65. **CAREER** Instr, Univ Fla; instr, Univ Wis, Madison; vis prof, Univ Helsinki; prof, Univ Mo, St Louis; bd of ed consult, Am Philos Quart. **HONORS AND AWARDS** Am Coun of Learned Soc fel; NEH fel. **RE-**

SEARCH Folk psychology and mental simulation. **SELECTED PUBLICATIONS** Auth, Folk Psychology as Simulation, The Simulation Theory: Objections and Misconceptions, Reply to Stich & Nichols, and Reply to Perner and Howes, in Folk Psychology: The Theory of Mind Debate, eds, Martin Davies and Tony Stone, Blackwell, 95; Simulation Without Introspection or Inference From Me to You, in Mental Simulation: Evaluations and Applications, eds, Martin Davies and Tony Stone, Blackwell, 95; Sympathy, Simulation, and the Impartial Spectator, Ethics, 95; Articles on "Emotion " and "James-Lange Theory, Cambridge Dictionary of Philosophy, Cambridge UP, 95; 'Radical' Simulationism, n Theories of Theories of Mind, eds, Peter Carruthers and Peter Smith, Cambridge UP, 96; coauth, Autism and the 'Theory of Mind' Debate, in George Graham & Lynn Stephens, eds, Philosophical Psychopathology: A Book of Readings, MIT Press, 94. **CONTACT ADDRESS** Univ Mo, St Louis, St Louis, MO, 63121.

GORDON, ROBERT MORRIS
PERSONAL Born 07/01/1932, New York, NY, 1 child **DISCIPLINE** PHILOSOPHY **EDUCATION** Carleton Col, BA, 54; Columbia Univ, MA, 58, PhD, 65. **CAREER** Instr philos, Univ Fla, 62-64; lectr, 64-65, asst prof, 65-70, Univ Wis Madison; assoc prof philos, Univ Mo St Louis, 70-. **HONORS AND AWARDS** Am Coun Learned Soc fel, 74-75; Fel Nat Endow for the Hum Soc. **MEMBERSHIPS** Am Philos Assn; Soc Philos & Psychol. **RESEARCH** Ethics; philosophy of psychology; action and emotion. **SELECTED PUBLICATIONS** Art, The Simulation Theory: Objections and Misconceptions, Folk Psychology: The Theory of Mind Debate, Blackwell, 95; art, Stimulation Without Introspection or Inference From Me to You, Mental Simulation: Evaluations and Applications, Blackwell, 95; art, Radical Simulationism, Theories of Theories of Mind, Cambridge University Press, 96; art, Sympathy, Simulation, and the Impartial Spectator, Ethics, Summer, 95; coauth, Autism and the Theory of Mind Debate, Philosophical Psychopathology: A Book of Readings, MIT Press, 94; art, Empathy and Simulation Theory, Cambridge Dictionary of Philosophy, 99; art, Stimulation Theory, MIT Encyclopedia of Cognitive Science, 99. **CONTACT ADDRESS** Dept of Philosophy, Univ of Missouri, 8001 Natural Bridge, St. Louis, MO, 63121-4499. **EMAIL** gordon@umsl.edu

GORDON, RUTH E.
DISCIPLINE INTERNATIONAL ENVIRONMENTAL LAW **EDUCATION** NY Univ, BA, 77; NY Univ Sch Law, JD, 80; London Sch Econ and Political Sci, LLM, 87. **CAREER** Prof, Villanova Univ; Riesenfeld Fel in Public Int Law, Univ Calif at Berkeley; Revson Fel Scholar, City Col City Univ NY Ctr for Legal Educ & Urban Policy; repr, island nation of Vanuatu in the UN & served as, legal adv to the island's Permanent Mission to the UN. **MEMBERSHIPS** Bd dir, Amer Soc Int Law & Amer Bar Asn Int Law and Practice Section; Amer Bar Asn Standing Comt on World Order Under Law. **RESEARCH** International law and development. **SELECTED PUBLICATIONS** Coauth, United Nations Council for Namibia's Study Addressing Namibia's Violations of UN Decrees and Resolutions; publ on, Roles the UN Plays in Develop Countries, in Cornell Int Law J & Michigan J Int Law. **CONTACT ADDRESS** Law School, Villanova Univ, 800 Lancaster Ave, Villanova, PA, 19085-1692. **EMAIL** gordon@law.vill.edu

GORDON, WALTER LEAR, III
PERSONAL Born 03/06/1942, Los Angeles, CA, m **DISCIPLINE** LAW **EDUCATION** Ohio State Univ, BA 1963; UCLA, MPA 1965, JD 1973, PhD 1981. **CAREER** UCLA Law School, lecturer 1978-82; private practice, attorney, currently. **MEMBERSHIPS** Bd mem SCLC-West 1980-85; mem Langston Bar Assoc 1986. **SELECTED PUBLICATIONS** Published "The Law and Private Police," Rand 1971, "Crime and Criminal Law," Associated Faculty Press 1981; has also published several articles. **CONTACT ADDRESS** 2822 S Western Ave, Los Angeles, CA, 90018.

GORDON, WALTER MARTIN
PERSONAL Born 03/05/1928, San Francisco, CA **DISCIPLINE** ENGLISH, THEOLOGY **EDUCATION** Gonzaga Univ, MA, 53; Col St Albert de Louvain, STL, 60; Univ London, PhD(English), 66. **CAREER** Instr English, Univ Santa Clara, 55-56; asst prof, Loyola Univ, Calif, 67-71; asst prof, 72-79, ASSOC PROF ENGLISH, UNIV GA, 79-. **MEMBERSHIPS** Amici Thomae More; Renaissance Soc Am; SAtlantic Mod Lang Asn; MLA. **RESEARCH** Dramatic form in Thomas More's writings; More's writings on the Eucharist; seriocomic art of More and Erasmus. **SELECTED PUBLICATIONS** Auth, The Complete Works of More, Thomas, Vol 7--The 'Letter to Bugenhagen', the 'Supplication of Souls', the 'Letter Against Frith,' Moreana, Vol 0029, 92; Maiestas in More, Thomas Political-Thought, Moreana, Vol 0034, 97. **CONTACT ADDRESS** Dept of English, Univ of Ga, 0 Georgia University, Athens, GA, 30602-0001.

GORDON, WENDY J.
DISCIPLINE LAW **EDUCATION** Cornell Univ, BA, 71; Penn Univ, JD, 75. **CAREER** Law clerk, Judge Theodore Newman Jr., Superior Court District Columbia, 75-76; vis prof. **SELECTED PUBLICATIONS** Auth, What's Yours is Ours: Ethics, Economics and Intellectual Property; pubs on intellectual property theory. **CONTACT ADDRESS** Fac of Law, Univ Toronto, 78 Queen's Park, Toronto, ON.

GORE, BLINZY L.
PERSONAL Born 06/13/1921, Hinton, WV, m **DISCIPLINE** LAW **EDUCATION** West Virginia State College, Institute, WV, BS, education, 1946; IA Univ, JD 1950; NY Univ, MA 1958, PhD 1967. **CAREER** South Carolina State College, Orangeburg, SC, law professor, 1950-66; private practice of law, 1956-; South Carolina State College, Orangeburg, SC, associate professor of social science, 1966; Claflin College, Orangeburg, SC, vice president for academic affairs, 1967-85. **HONORS AND AWARDS** Founders Day Award NY Univ 1967; Kappa Man of 1975 Orangeburg Alumni Chap Kappa Alpha Psi 1975; Orangeburg Kappa Achievement Award, 1994; Claflin Coll Presidential Citation, 1994. **MEMBERSHIPS** Mem IA Bar & SC Bar; Pi Gamma Mu 1974; life mem NAACP; past pres Assn of Coll Deans, Registrars and Admissions Officers; United Methodist Church. **SELECTED PUBLICATIONS** Auth, On A Hilltop High, The Origin & History of Claflin College to 1994. **CONTACT ADDRESS** 1700 Belleville Rd, Orangeburg, SC, 29115.

GORMAN, MICHAEL J.
PERSONAL Born 11/03/1955, MD, m, 1976, 3 children **DISCIPLINE** NEW TESTAMENT, EARLY CHURCH HISTORY AND THEOLOGICAL ETHICS **EDUCATION** BA, Gordon Col, 77; M Div, Princeton Theol Sem, 82; PhD, 89. **CAREER** Tchg fel, 81-85, instr, 86, Princeton Theol Sem; adjunct facul, 91-93, assoc dean, 93, assoc prof, 93-98, acting dean, 94-95, dean, 95-, prof, 98-, Ecumenical Inst of Theol, St Mary's Sem & Univ Baltimore. **MEMBERSHIPS** Soc of Bibl Lit. **RESEARCH** NT/early Christian ethics; Paul; Abortion; Non-violence. **SELECTED PUBLICATIONS** Auth, Texts and Contexts, 89, 97; Abortion and the Early Church, 82. **CONTACT ADDRESS** Ecumenical Institute of Theology, St. Mary's Sem & Univ, 5400 Roland Av., Baltimore, MD, 21210. **EMAIL** migorman@aol.com

GORMAN, ROSEMARIE E.
PERSONAL Born 08/30/1946, Danbury, CT **DISCIPLINE** THEOLOGY **EDUCATION** Yale Divinity Sch, MAR, 86; Cath Univ of Am, PhD, 96. **CAREER** Lectr, Loyola Col; lectr, Sacred Heart Univ; lectr, Fairfield Univ, 93-. **MEMBERSHIPS** Cath Theol Soc of Am; Soc of Christian Ethics; Am Acad of Relig. **RESEARCH** Moral theology. **CONTACT ADDRESS** 17 Grassy Plain Terr, Bethel, CT, 06801.

GOROFF, DAVID B.
DISCIPLINE LAW **EDUCATION** Univ Ill, BA; Columbia Univ, JD. **CAREER** Law clerk, Judge Richard Cudahy, US Court Appeals; adj prof,Univ Ill Urbana Champaign. **HONORS AND AWARDS** Robert C. Watson Awd., Ed, Columbia Law Rev. **SELECTED PUBLICATIONS** Auth, pubs on First Amendment and copyright law. **CONTACT ADDRESS** Law Dept, Univ Ill Urbana Champaign, 52 E Gregory Dr, Champaign, IL, 61820.

GORRELL, DONALD KENNETH
PERSONAL Born 01/24/1928, Cleveland, OH, m, 1951, 3 children **DISCIPLINE** CHURCH HISTORY **EDUCATION** Miami Univ, BA, 49; Western Reserve Univ, MA, 51, PhD, 60; Yale Univ, BD, 55. **CAREER** Minister to students, Ohio State Univ, 55-60; asst prof, 60-68, PROF CHURCH HIST, UNITED THEOL SEM, OHIO, 68-, Am Asn Theol Sch fac fel, 65-66; secy, Gen Comn Arch and Hist, United Methodist Church, 68-72, 76-80 and 80-84 fel, Case-Study Inst, Mass, 72. **MEMBERSHIPS** AHA; Am Soc Church Hist; Orgn Am Historians; World Methodist Hist Soc. **RESEARCH** Social Gospel in the Progressive Era, 1900-1920; American church history in the twentieth century; United Methodist Church history. **SELECTED PUBLICATIONS** Auth, Ambivalent Churchmen and Evangelical Churchwomen--The Religion of the Episcopal Elite in North-Carolina, 1800-1860, J Am Hist, Vol 0081, 94. **CONTACT ADDRESS** United Theol Seminary, 1810 Harvard Blvd, Dayton, OH, 45406.

GOSS, JAMES
PERSONAL Born 08/21/1939, San Pedro, CA, m, 1961, 3 children **DISCIPLINE** RELIGION & LITERATURE **EDUCATION** Univ Southern Calif, BA, 60; Southern Calif Sch Theol, MTh, 63; Claremont Grad Sch, PhD, 70. **CAREER** Assoc prof & campus minister, Cornell Col, 65-67; asst prof, 69-80, from prof to chemn, Relig Studies, Calif State Univ, Northridge, 80-98; exec assoc to the pres, 98. **MEMBERSHIPS** Soc Bibl Lit; Am Acad Relig. **RESEARCH** Religion in literature; New Testament. **SELECTED PUBLICATIONS** Auth, Camus, God and process thought, Process Studies, summer 74; art, O'Connor's redeemed man: Christus et/vel Porcus?, Drew Gateway, winter-spring 74; art, The double action of mercy in The Artificial Nigger, Christianity & Lit, spring 74; art, Eschatology, autonomy, and individuation: The evocative power of the kingdom, Jour Am Acad of Relig, 81. **CONTACT ADDRESS** President's Office, 18111 Nordhoff St, Northridge, CA, 91330-8200. **EMAIL** james.goss@exec.csun.edu

GOSSAI, HEMCHAND
PERSONAL Born 04/11/1954, Guyana, m, 3 children **DISCIPLINE** RELIGION **EDUCATION** Concordia Col Moorhead, BA, 79; Luther Sem, MDiv, 83; Univ St. Andrews Scotland, PhD, 86. **CAREER** Luther Sem, lect, 87; Concordia Col, asst prof, 90-91; Culver-Stockton Coll, assoc prof, 92-. **HONORS AND AWARDS** Helsabeck Award, Faculty Mentorship Award, Governor's Award. **MEMBERSHIPS** SBL, CBA. **RESEARCH** Marginality issue in Genesis; social critique in the prophets. **SELECTED PUBLICATIONS** Auth, Justice, Righteousness and the Social Critique of the Eighth Century Prophets, Peter Lang Pub, 93; auth, Power and Marginality in the Abraham Narrative, Univ Press of Am, 95; auth, Genesis, Augsburg/Fortress Pub House, 93; auth, Power and Marginality in the Hagar Narrative, Ex Scientia, 95; auth, Divine Vulnerability and Human Marginality in the Akedah: Exploring a Tension, in: Horizons in Biblical Theology: An International Dialogue, 97. **CONTACT ADDRESS** Dept of Religion and Philosophy, Culver-Stockton Col, Canton, MO, 63435. **EMAIL** hgossai@culver.edu

GOSSE, RICHARD
DISCIPLINE LAW **EDUCATION** McGill Univ, BA, 47; Univ British Columbia, LLB, 50; Oxford Univ, DPhill, 60. **CAREER** Prof, 60- **SELECTED PUBLICATIONS** Auth, Continuing Poundmaker and Riel's Quest. **CONTACT ADDRESS** Col of Law, Univ Saskatchewan, 15 Campus Dr, Saskatoon, SK, S7N 5A6. **EMAIL** der@law.usask.ca

GOSTIN, LO
PERSONAL Born 10/19/1949, New York, NY, m, 1977, 2 children **DISCIPLINE** LAW **EDUCATION** Duke Univ, JD 73. **CAREER** Georgetown Univ Law, Prof of Law, 5 years; ASL Med;ethics, Exec Dir, 6 years; NCCL UK, Gen Sec, 3 years; MIND Ntl assoc Mental Hlth UK, Legal Dir, 5 years. **HONORS AND AWARDS** Rosemary Delbridge Memorial Awd. **RESEARCH** Public Health and the Law. **SELECTED PUBLICATIONS** Auth, Public Health and Human Rights in the HIV Pandemic, coauth, WHO, Oxford U Press, 97; Law Science and Medicine, coauth, U Case Bk Series, Foundation Press, 96; Rights of Persons Who are HIV Positive: The Authoritative Guide to the Rights of People Living with HIV Disease and Aids, coauth, Carbondale IL, S IL U Press, 96; The Americans with Disabilities Act: What it Means for All Americans, co-ed, Brookes Pub Co, 93; Health Legislation and Communicable Diseases: The Role of Law in an Era of Microbial Threats, Intl Digest of Health Legisl, 98; Piercing the Veil of Secrecy in HIV/AIDS and Other Sexually Transmitted Diseases: Theories of Privacy and Disclosure in Partner Notification, coauth, Duke J of Gender L and Policy, 98; The Names Debate: The Case for Ntl HIV Reporting in the United States, coauth, Albany L Rev, 98; HIV Infection and AIDS in the Public Health and Health Care Systems: The Role of Law and Litigation, coauth, J. A. M. A., 98; The AIDS Litigation Project: HIV/AIDS in the Courts in the 1990s, Part one, AIDS and Pub Policy Jour, 97, Part two, in press; Ntl HIV case Reporting for the United States: A defining Moment in the History of the Epidemic, New Eng Jour Med, 97; Deciding Life and Death in the Court Room: From Quinlan to Cruzan Glucksberg and Vacco-A Brief History and Analysis of Constitutional Protection of the Right to Die, J. A. M. A. , 97. **CONTACT ADDRESS** Law Center, Georgetown Univ, 600 New Jersey Ave NW, Washington, DC, 20001. **EMAIL** gostin@law.georgetown.edu

GOTANDA, JOHN YUKIO
DISCIPLINE INTERNATIONAL COMMERCIAL ARBITRATION **EDUCATION** Univ Hawaii, BA, 84; William S. Richardson Sch Law, Univ Hawaii, JD, 87. **CAREER** Asst prof, 94-96, assoc prof, 96-98, prof, 98-, Villanova Univ Sch Law. **MEMBERSHIPS** Dist Columbia Bar; Mass Bar; Hawaii State Bar; US Ct Appeals for the Dist of Columbia Circuit Bar; US Dist Ct for the Dist of Columbia Bar; Amer Soc Int Law; London Ct Int Arbitration; Int Law Asn; Amer Bar Asn. **RESEARCH** Damages in private international law, international commercial arbitration. **SELECTED PUBLICATIONS** Auth, Supplement Damages in Private International Law, Kluwer Law Int, 98; awding Punitive Damages in International Commercial Arbitrations in the Wake of Mastrobuono v. Shearson Lehman Hutton, Inc, 38 Harvard Int Law J 59, 97; awding Interest in International Arbitration, 90 American Journal of International Law 40, Amer Soc Int Law, 96; Glomar Denials Under FOIA: A Problematic Privilege and a Proposal for Alternative Procedures of Review, 56 Univ Pittsburgh Law Rev 165, 94; The Emerging Standards for Issuing Appellate Stays, 45 Baylor Law Rev 810, 93; coauth, The Responsible Corporate Officer: Designated Felon or Legal Fiction, 25 Loyola Univ Chicago Law J 169, 94. **CONTACT ADDRESS** Law School, Villanova Univ, 800 Lancaster Ave, Villanova, PA, 19085-1692. **EMAIL** Gotanda@law.vill.edu

GOTTLIEB, ROGER SAMUEL
PERSONAL Born 10/20/1946, White Plains, NY **DISCIPLINE** PHILOSOPHY, SOCIAL THEORY **EDUCATION** Brandeis Univ, BA, 68, PhD, 75. **CAREER** Vis asst prof philos, Univ CT, Storr, 74-77; asst prof, Tufts Univ, 78-80; Asst Prof Philos, Dept Hum, Worcester Polytech Inst, 80-, Nat Endowment for Hum fel, 80-81. **MEMBERSHIPS** Am Philos

Asn; Marxist Activist Philosophers. **RESEARCH** Marxism; soc theory; existentialism; environment; spirituality. **SELECTED PUBLICATIONS** Auth, A Marxian concept of ideology, 75 & A critique of Kierkegaard's doctrine of subjectivity, 78, Philos Forum; Habermas and critical relfective emancipation, Univ Ottawa, 78; The dialectics of National Identity Zionism and the Arab-Israeli conflict, Socialist Rev, 79; Marxism and the three forms of social primacy, J Philos, 78; Kierkegaard's ethical individualism, Monist, 79; The contemporary theory of Jurgen Habermans, Ethics, 79; Some implications of the Holocaust for ethics and social philosophy, Philos & Social Criticism, 82; History and subjectivity, Temple Univ Press, 87; An anthology of western Marxism, Oxford, 89; Thinking the unthinkable, Paulist Press, 90; Marxism 1844-1990, Routledge, 92; Radical Philosophy, Temple Univ Press, 93; This sacred earth, Routledge, 96; The ecological community, Routledge, 97. **CONTACT ADDRESS** Dept of Hum, Worcester Polytech Inst, 100 Institute Rd, Worcester, MA, 01609-2247. **EMAIL** gottlieb@wpi.edu

GOTTLIEB, STEPHEN ELLIOT
PERSONAL Born 06/02/1941, New York, NY, m, 1967, 2 children **DISCIPLINE** CONSTITUTIONAL LAW **EDUCATION** Princeton Univ, BA, 62; Yale Univ, LLB, 65. **CAREER** Assoc, 67-69, Golenback and Barrell; mem staff & managing atty, 69-72, Legal Aid Soc, St Louis; asst gen coun, 73-76, Commun Action for Legal Serv, New York; assoc prof clin tchng & constitutional law, 76-79 Col Law, WVa Univ; assoc prof, 79-82, prof constitutional law & jurisprudence, 82, Albany Law Sch, Union Univ; consult, 74-76, Legal Serv Training Prog. **HONORS AND AWARDS** Marquette Univ Law Schl, Robert F Boden Dist Vis Chmn, 97; Cleveland-Marshall Col of Law, Joseph C Hostetler-Baker and Hostetler vis chmn in las, 95-96; res grant division of res prog, NEH, 86-88. **MEMBERSHIPS** Bd dir, New York Civil Liberties Union **RESEARCH** Mass communications law; election and political campaign law; constitutional history, theory and the US Supreme Court. **SELECTED PUBLICATIONS** Ed & contrib, Public Values in Constitutional Law, Univ Mich Press, 93; art, The Paradox of Balancing Significant Interests, 45 Hastings Law J 825, 94; art, Three Justices in Search of A Character: The Moral Agendas of Justices O'Connor, Scalia and Kennedy, 49 Rutgers Law Rev, 96; art, The Philosophical Gulf on the Rehnquist Court, 29 Rutgers Law J, 97. **CONTACT ADDRESS** Albany Law Sch, Union Univ, 80 New Scotland Ave, Albany, NY, 12208-3494. **EMAIL** sgott@mail.als.edu

GOTTSCHALK, ALFRED
PERSONAL Born 03/07/1930, Oberwesel, Germany, m, 1977, 2 children **DISCIPLINE** JEWISH RELIGIOUS THOUGHT **EDUCATION** Brooklyn Col, BA, 52; Hebrew Union Col, MA, 55; Univ Southern Calif, PhD(philos), 65. **CAREER** Asst prof, 59-62, assoc prof, 62-65, Prof Bible & Jewish Relig Thought, Jewish Inst Relig, Hebrew Union Col, 65-, Via prof Near Eastern studies, Univ Calif, Los Angeles, 60- 62, 65, 68 & 70; pres Hebrew Union Col, 70-95; Chancellor, 95-; Smithsonian Inst res grant, 67; Bertha Guggenheimer fel, 67 & 69; mem, Pres Johnson Comt, Equal Employ, Pres Carter's Comt, Holocaust, 80-81 & US Holocaust Memorial Coun, 81-; chemn, Academic Com US Holocaust Memorial Coun. **HONORS AND AWARDS** Am Jewish Comt Human Rel Award, 71; Tower of David Award for Cult Contrib, Israel & Am Israel Govt, 72; Gold Medallion Award, Jewish Nat Fund, 72; fel Hebrew Univ, Jerusalem, 75; Myrtle Wreath Award, Southern Pac Coast Region of Hadassah, 77; Louis Dembitz Brandeis Award, Zionist Orgn Am, 77; Nat Brotherhood Award, Nat Conf Christians & Jews, 79., DLit, Dropsie Univ, 74; LLD, Univ Southern Calif, 76, Univ Cincinnati, 76 & Xavier Univ, Ohio, 81; DRelEd, Loyola Univ, 77. **MEMBERSHIPS** Albright Inst Archeol Res; Am Schs Oriental Res; Am Acad Relig; Israel Exploration Soc; World Union of Jewish Studies. **RESEARCH** Jewish intellectual history; modern Hebrew literature; history and archeology of the Ancient Near East. **SELECTED PUBLICATIONS** Auth, Hesed in the Bible, Hebrew Union Col Press, 6/67; The light of reason and the light of spirit: Spinoza and Ahad Ha-Am, In: Festschrift for President Zalman Shazar, Brit Ivrit Olamit, Jerusalem, fall 70; Ahad Ha-Am as Biblical Critic--A Profile, Studies in Jewish Bibliog Hist & Lit, KTAV Publ House, 71; The use of reason in Maimonides--An evaluation by Ahad Ha-Am, Proc 5th World Cong Jewish Studies, Vol III, Jerusalem, 72; United States of America: Perspectives, In: The Yom Kippur War: Israel and the Jewish People, Arno Press, 74; The image of man in Genesis and in the Ancient Near East, In: Social Psychiatry Vol II, The Range of Normal in Human Behavior, Grune & Stratton Publ, 76; From tradition to modernity: Ahad Ha-Am's quest for a spiritual Zionism, In: Shiv'im: Essays and Studies in Honor of Ira Eisenstein, Ktav Publ House, 76; Ahad Ha-Am and Leopold Zunz: Two perspectives on the Wissenschaft Des Judentums, Judaism, Vol 29, No 3; The German-Jewish Legacy: A Question of Fate, American Jewish Archives, November, 88; Ahad Ha'Am and the Jewish National Spirit, Hebrew, Hassifriya, Haziyonit, 92; At the Crossroads, World Jewry Faces Its Future, Gesher, Janmuary, 96. **CONTACT ADDRESS** 3101 Clifton Ave, Cincinnati, OH, 45220-2404.

GOTTSCHALK, PETER
DISCIPLINE HISTORY OF RELIGION **EDUCATION** Col of the Holy Cross, BA, 85; Univ Wis, MA, 89; Univ Chicago, PhD, 97. **CAREER** Asst prof, Southwestern Univ, 97- . **MEMBERSHIPS** AAR; AAS **RESEARCH** Narrative, identity, Hinuism, and Islam in South Asia; Time and space in religion. **CONTACT ADDRESS** Dept of Religions, Southwestern Univ, Box 6318, Georgetown, TX, 78756. **EMAIL** gottschp@southwestern.edu

GOTTWALD, NORMAN KAROL
PERSONAL Born 10/27/1926, Chicago, IL **DISCIPLINE** OLD TESTAMENT **EDUCATION** Eastern Baptist Theol Sem, AB & ThB, 49; Union Theol Sem, MDiv, 51; Columbia Univ, PhD(Bibl lit), 53. **CAREER** Assoc relig, Columbia Univ, 53-54, asst prof, 54-55; from assoc prof to prof Old Testament, Andover Newton Theol Sch, 55-62, Lowry prof, 62-65; prof Old Testament and Bibl theol and ethics, Grad Theol Union, 65-80; W W WHITE PROF BIBL STUDIES, NEW YORK THEOL SEM, 80-, Vis asst prof, Princeton Univ, 55; Fulbright res scholar, Jerusalem, 60-61; vis lectr, Brown Univ, 62-63 and Brandeis Univ, 63-65; prof Old Testament, Am Baptist Sem West, 65-73; vis prof, Univ Calif, Santa Cruz, 67; res fel, Hebrew Union Col Bibl and Archaeol Sch, Jerusalem, 68-69; lectr, Ecumenical Inst Advan Theol Studies, Jerusalem, 73-74; vis prof environ ethics, Univ Calif, Berkeley, 74-75, vis prof relig, Univ of the Pac, 75-76, vis prof hist of relig, Bryn Mawr Col, 77-78, vis prof Old Testament, Union Theol Sem, 82-83. **MEMBERSHIPS** Cath Bibl Asn; Am Acad Relig; Soc Bibl Lit. **RESEARCH** Sociology, history and religion of ancient Israel; Biblical theology and the sociology of religion; sociology of the Bible and political theology. **SELECTED PUBLICATIONS** Auth, Lamentations, Cath Biblical Quart, Vol 0055, 93; Social-Class as an Analytic and Hermeneutical Category in Biblical Studies, J Biblical Lit, Vol 0112, 93. **CONTACT ADDRESS** New York Theol Sem, New York, NY, 10011.

GOUGH, RUSSELL W.
DISCIPLINE ETHICAL THEORY, MORAL EDUCATION **EDUCATION** David Lipscomb Univ, BA, 84; Vanderbilt Univ, MA, 88, PhD, 90. **CAREER** Asst prof Univ Vanderbilt Univ Med Ctr, 87-88; vis lectr, 87-89; instr, David Lipscomb Univ, 88-89; assoc prof, 90-. **HONORS AND AWARDS** Freshman Sem Excellence tchg award, Pepperdine Univ, 95; Sports Ethics fel, Univ RI, 94, 95;Irvine Found grant, 93; Graves Found Res award, 92; Sears-Roebuck Asian studies fellow, 90-91. **MEMBERSHIPS** Mem, Am Philos Assn; Philos Soc Study Sport; Soc Christian Philosophers. **SELECTED PUBLICATIONS** Auth, Character Is Destiny: The Value of Personal Ethics in Everyday Life, Prima Pub, 98; Facilitating Self-reflection Concerning Personal Character Development in Physical Education and Sport, Jour Phys Edu, 98; Moral Development Researchers' Quest for Objectivity: On Whether the Judgment-Passing Hurdle Can Be Cleared, in McNamee, M.J. & Parry S.J., Chapman and Hall, 97; Character Is Everything: Promoting Ethical Excellence In Sports, Harcourt Brace Col Publ, 97; On Reaching First Base with a 'Science' of Moral Development in Sport: Problems with Scientific Objectivity and Reductivism, Jour Philos Sport, Vol XXII, 95; NCAA Policy's Strangling Effect on Ethics, Record, Vol 5, 94; Testing, Scoring, and Ranking Athletes' Moral Development: The Hubris of Social Science as Moral Inquiry, Nat Rev Athletics, 94. **CONTACT ADDRESS** Dept of Philos, Pepperdine Univ, 24255 Pacific Coast Hwy, Malibu, CA, 90263. **EMAIL** rgough@pepperdine.edu

GOUINLOCK, JAMES
DISCIPLINE PHILOSOPHICAL ANTHROPOLOGY **EDUCATION** Columbia Univ, PhD, 69. **CAREER** Philos, Emory Univ. **SELECTED PUBLICATIONS** Auth, John Dewey's Philosophy of Value; Excellence in Public Discourse; and Rediscovering the Moral Life: Philosophy and Human Practice; Ed, The Moral Writings of John Dewey; Coed, Ethics in the History of Western Philosophy. **CONTACT ADDRESS** Emory Univ, Atlanta, GA, 30322-1950.

GOULD, JOSIAH B.
PERSONAL Cleveland, OH, m, 1980, 3 children **DISCIPLINE** PHILOSOPHY **EDUCATION** Johns Hopkins Univ, PhD, 1962. **CAREER** Dist tchg prof Philos, Univ Albany, SUNY, 69- . **MEMBERSHIPS** Amer Philos Asn, E Div. **RESEARCH** Greek philosophy; history and Philosophy of Logic. **CONTACT ADDRESS** Dept of Philosophy, SUNY, 1400 Washington Ave, PO Box 22630, Albany, NY, 12222. **EMAIL** jbg@csc.albany.edu

GOULD, WILLIAM BENJAMIN
PERSONAL Born 07/16/1936, Boston, MA, m, 1963, 3 children **DISCIPLINE** LAW **EDUCATION** Univ RI, AB, 58; Cornell Law Sch, LLB, 61. **CAREER** Asst gen coun labor law, United Automobile Workers, 61-62; atty, Nat Labor Rel Bd, Washington, DC, 63-65; assoc, Battle, Fowler, Stokes anf Kheel, 65-68; prof law, Wayne State Univ Law Sch, 68-71; PROF LAW, STANFORD UNIV LAW SCH, 72-, Via prof law, Harvard Law Sch, 71-72; vis scholar, Univ Tokyo Law Fac, 75; fel anf vis scholar, Churchill Col, Cambridge, England, 75; Guggenheim fel anf vis scholar, Univ Tokyo Law Fac, 78; Fulbright-Hays distinguished lectr, Kyoto-Am Studies Summer Sem, 78. **MEMBERSHIPS** Am Bar Asn; Am Arbitration Asn; Nat Acad Arbitrators. **RESEARCH** Labor law with special interest in labor arbitration; comparative labor law and industrial relations with special interest in Japan; employment discrimination law. **SELECTED PUBLICATIONS** Auth, Assessing the Work of the United-Nations War-Crimes Tribunals--Introductory-Remarks, Stanford J Int Law, Vol 0033, 97. **CONTACT ADDRESS** Stanford Law Sch, Stanford Univ, Stanford, CA, 94305-1926.

GOULDING, JAMES ALLAN
PERSONAL Born 09/09/1937, Berea, OH, m, 1969, 2 children **DISCIPLINE** RELIGION **EDUCATION** DePauw Univ, BA, 59; Yale Univ, BD, 63, STM, 64; Claremont Grad Sch, PhD, 71. **CAREER** Instr relig, Hamline Univ, 69-70; pastor, Orwell-United Methodist Church, 72-74; asst prof, 74-80, assoc prof philos & relig & chaplain, Macmurray Col, 80-. **MEMBERSHIPS** Am Soc Church Hist; Am Acad Relig; Nat Assn Col & Univ Chaplains. **RESEARCH** Puritanism; American religion; biomedical ethics. **CONTACT ADDRESS** MacMurray Col, 447 E College Ave, Jacksonville, IL, 62650-2510. **EMAIL** goulding@mac.edu

GOUREVITCH, VICTOR
PERSONAL Born 07/13/1925, Berlin, Germany, m, 1954, 2 children **DISCIPLINE** PHILOSOPHY **EDUCATION** Univ Wisconsin, BA, 46; Univ Chicago, PhD, 55. **CAREER** Vis prof, Yale Univ; Hebrew Univ, Jerusalem; Fordham Univ; grad fac of The New Sch for Soc Res; dir, Wesleyan Ctr for Hum, 70-73; William Griffin Prof of Philos, emer, Wesleyan Univ. **HONORS AND AWARDS** Fel, Institut fur Interdisziplinare Forschung, 78-79; fel, Wesleyan Ctr for the Hum, 86-87; fel, Wissenschaftskolleg zu Berlin, 87-88. **MEMBERSHIPS** APA. **RESEARCH** Practical philosophy; Rousseau. **SELECTED PUBLICATIONS** Auth, Philosophy and Politics I-II, Rev of Metaphysics, 68; auth, Rousseau on the Arts and Sciences, Jour of Philos, 72; auth, Jean-Jacques Rousseau: The First and Second Discourses Together with the Replies to Critics and Essay on the Origin of Languages, Harper & Row, 86; auth, The First Times' in Rousseau's Essay on the Origin of Languages, Essays in Honor of Richard Kennington, Grad Philos Jour, 86; auth, Rousseau's Pure State of Nature, Interpretation, 88; trans, Leo Strauss, On Tyranny, rev ed, Macmillan, 91; auth, The Political Argument of Rousseau's Essay on the Origin of Languages, in Pursuits of Reason: Essays in Honor of Stanley Cavell, Texas Tech, 93; auth, Jean-Jacques Rousseau: The Discourses and Other Early Political Writings, Cambridge, 97; auth, Jean Jacques Rousseau: The Social Contract and Other Later Political Writings, Cambridge, 97; auth, Rousseau on Providence, in The Wisdom of Humility: Essays in Ancient and Literary Imagination in Honor of David Grene, Chicago, 99. **CONTACT ADDRESS** 120 Duane St, New York, NY, 10007. **EMAIL** vgourevitch@mail.wesleyan.edu

GOURQUES, MICHEL
PERSONAL Born 08/22/1942, St. Michel, PQ, Canada **DISCIPLINE** BIBLICAL STUDIES **EDUCATION** Col Dominicain, MA, 71; Inst Cath, ThD, 76. **CAREER** Prof, Col Dominicain de Philos et de Theol, 76-98; dean, 78-87; vis prof, Ecole Bibl et Archaeol, 96-97. **MEMBERSHIPS** Cath Bibl Asn; Asn Cath des Etudes Bibl au Can; Studiorum Novi Testamenti Soc; Soc of Bibl Lit. **RESEARCH** New Testament Christology; Gospel of John; Parables of the Gospel. **SELECTED PUBLICATIONS** Auth, Le Parabole di Luca. Dalla Sorgente Alla Foce, 98; Les Deux Livres de Luc. Cles de Lecture du Troisieme Evangile et des Actes, 98; Fede, Felicita et Sensor Della Vita. Rileggere Oggi le Beatitudini, 97; Les Paraboles de Luc. D'Amont en Aval, 97; Os Hinos do Novo Testamento, 95; auth, "The Priest, the Levite and the Samaritan Revisited: A Critical Notes on Luke 10:31-35," in J of Bibl Studies, 98; "Sur l'Articulation des Beatitudes Mattheennes (Mt 5.3-12: Une Proposition," in New Testament Studies, 98. **CONTACT ADDRESS** Faculte de Theologie, Col Dominicain de Philosophie et de Theologie, 96, ave Empress, Ottawa, ON, K1R 7G3. **EMAIL** ec522@freenet.carleton.ca

GOUWENS, DAVID J.
PERSONAL Born 05/06/1948, South Holland, IL, m, 1990 **DISCIPLINE** THEOLOGY **EDUCATION** Hope Col, BA, 70; Mdiv, 73, StM, 74, Yale Divinity School; PhD, 82, Yale Univ. **CAREER** Visiting Lectr, Hope Col, 76; Asst Prof, 83-89, Acting Dir of Doctor of Ministry Studies, 89-90, Interim Asst Dean for Academic Affairs 90-91, Assoc Prof, 89-, Brite Divinity School, Texas Christian Univ. **HONORS AND AWARDS** Univ Fel, Yale Univ, 74-77 and 79-80; Douglas Clyde MacIntosh Fel, Yale Univ, 77-78; Brite Divinity School nominee for Burlington Northern Teaching Award 89, 90; The Louise Clark Brittan Endowed Memorial Faculty Exellence Award, Brite Divinity School, 98; Brite Divinity School nominee for TCU Chancellor's Award for Distinguished Teaching, 98. **MEMBERSHIPS** Minister of Word and Sacrament, Presbyterian Church; The Soren Kierkegaard Soc; The Karl Barth Soc of North Amer; Amer Acad of Religion **RESEARCH** Kierkegaard; Theology and Aesthetics; Modern Christian Theology; Systematic Theology **SELECTED PUBLICATIONS** Auth, Heresy, New Handbook of Christian Theology, 92; Understanding, Imagination, and Irony in Kierkegaard's Repetition, Inter-

national Kierkegaard Commentary: Fear and Trembling and Repetition, 93; Kierkegaard's Either/Or Part 1: Patterns of Interpretation, International Kierkegaard Commentary: Either/Or, Part 1, 95; Kierkegaard as Religious Thinker, 96; Imagination and Introspection, Dictionary of Existentialism, forthcoming. **CONTACT ADDRESS** Brite Divinity School, Texas Christian Univ, Fort Worth, TX, 76129. **EMAIL** d.gouwens@tcu.edu

GOVAN, REGINALD C.
PERSONAL Born 12/02/1953, New York, NY **DISCIPLINE** LAW **EDUCATION** Carnegie-Mellon University, BA, 1975; University of Pennsylvania Law School, JD, 1978. **CAREER** Squire, Sanders & Dempsey, associate, 1978-79; US Court of Appeals, 6th Circuit, Judge Nathaniel R Jones, sr law clerk, 1979-81; Manhattan District Attorney, assistant district Attorney, 1981-83; sole practitioner, federal civil rights and general litigation, 1983-85, 1987-89; US Senate, Committee on the Judiciary, counsel, 1985-87; US House of Representatives, Education & Labor Committee, counsel, 1989-94; Organization Resource Counselors, Inc, sr consultant, 1995-. **MEMBERSHIPS** District of Columbia Bar, Attorney-Client Arbitration Board, chairman, 1991-94, Disciplinary Review Committee, 1991-93, Task Force on Continuing Legal Education, 1992-94; National Bar Assn, 1984-; Washington Bar Association, 1990-. **SELECTED PUBLICATIONS** "Employment Law is a Fishbowl: Coping with Less Privilege and Confidentiality," Employee Relations L.J., Vol. 23, No.3 (Winter 1997); "Honorable Compromises and the Moral High Ground: The Conflict Between the Rhetoric and the Content of the Civil Rights Act of 1991," 46 The Rutgers Law Review 7, 1993; "Framing Issues and Acquiring Codes: An Overview of the Legislative Sojourn of the Civil Rights Act of 1991," 41 The DePaul Law Review 1057, 1992; One Nation, Indivisible: The Civil Rights Challenge for the 1990's, Washington, DC, Citizens' Commission on Civil Rights, 1989. **CONTACT ADDRESS** Organization Resource Counselors, 1211 Avenue of Americas, 15th Fl, New York, NY, 10036.

GOVIG, STEWART D.
PERSONAL Born 03/30/1927, Walnut Grove, MN, m, 1954, 3 children **DISCIPLINE** RELIGION **EDUCATION** St Olaf Col, BA, 48; Luther Theol Sem, BTh, 52; Princeton Theol Sem, MTh, 54; NY Univ, PhD(relig educ, philos), 66. **CAREER** Pastor, Am Lutheran Church, Grand Marais, Minn, 54-57; assoc prof relig, 58-76, PROF RELIG, PAC LUTHER UNIV, 76-, Clergyman, Am Lutheran Church, 52-; Martin Luther fel, Nat Lutheran Educ Conf; prof dir grant relig and pub schs, Washington Comn for Humanities, 76. **RESEARCH** Religion and literature; modern church history. **SELECTED PUBLICATIONS** Auth, Religious-Education and Mental-Illness--A Higher-Education Model, Relig Educ, Vol 0091, 96. **CONTACT ADDRESS** Dept of Relig Pac, Pacific Lutheran Univ, 12180 Park Ave S, Tacoma, WA, 98447-0014.

GOWAN, DONALD E.
PERSONAL Born 01/31/1929, Cleghorn, IA, m, 1958, 2 children **DISCIPLINE** OLD TESTAMENT **EDUCATION** Univ SDak, BA, 51; Dubuque Theol Sem, BD, 57; Univ Chicago, PhD(Bible), 64. **CAREER** Pastor, Presby Church, Princeton, Iowa, 55-59; asst pastor, Presby Church Roseland, Chicago, Ill, 59-60; head dept Bible, NTex State Univ, 62-65; asst prof Old Testament, 65-69, assoc prof, 69-78, prof Old Testament, Pittsburgh Theol Sem, 78-. **HONORS AND AWARDS** Phi Beta Kappa. **MEMBERSHIPS** Soc Bibl Lit. **RESEARCH** Old Testament prophets; post-exilic period; intertestamental Judaism; biblical theology. **SELECTED PUBLICATIONS** Auth, When Man Becomes God: Humanism and Hybris in the Old Testament, 75 & Bridge Between the Testaments: A Reappraisal of Judaism from the Exile to the Birth of Christianity, 76, Pickwick; The Triumph of Faith in Habakkuk, John Knox, 76; Reclaiming the Old Testament for the Christian Pulpit, John Knox, 80; Ezekiel, John Knox, 85; Eschatology in the Old Testament, Fortress, 86; From Eden to Babel: Genesis 1-11; Eerdmans, 88; Theology in Exodus, Westminster John Knox, 94; Theology of the Prophetic Books, Westminster John Knox, 98. **CONTACT ADDRESS** Pittsburgh Theol Sem, 616 N Highland Ave, Pittsburgh, PA, 15206-2525. **EMAIL** gowandon@msn.com

GOWANS, CHRISTORHER W.
DISCIPLINE CONTEMPORARY MORAL AND POLITICAL PHILOSOPHY **EDUCATION** Univ Notre Dame, PhD. **CAREER** Dir, grad stud; prof, Fordham Univ. **RESEARCH** French moral philos from the Reformation to the Revolution. **SELECTED PUBLICATIONS** Auth, Moral Dilemmas, Oxford UP, 87; Innocence Lost: An Examination of Inescapable Moral Wrongdoing, Oxford UP, 94; Moral Theory, Moral Dilemmas and Moral Responsibilities, Moral Dilemmas and Moral Theory, Oxford UP, 96; Intimacy, Freedom and Unique Value: A Kantian' Account of the Irreplaceable and Incomparable Value of Persons, Amer Philos Quart, 96. **CONTACT ADDRESS** Dept of Philos, Fordham Univ, 113 W 60th St, New York, NY, 10023.

GOWLER, DAVID B.
DISCIPLINE PHILOSOPHY **EDUCATION** Univ IL, Champaign, BA, 81; Southern Sem, Louisville, Mdiv, 85; Cambridge Univ, Engl, 87; Southern Sem, Louisville, PhD, 89. Yale Univ NEH Summer Sem, 95. **CAREER** Assoc prof ; asst dean Acad Aff, Chowan Col, 96-; assoc prof, Chowan Col, 90-; asst prof, 90-94; dir, Global Educ Prog, Chowan Col, 97-; dir, Thinking and Writing Across the Curric prog, Chowan Col, 95-; asst prof, Berry Col, Rome, Ga, 89-90; assoc ed, Emory Stud in Early Christianity, Schol Press, 92-; assoc ed, Emory Stud in Early Christianity, Peter Lang Press, 91-93; instr, Southern Sem, Louisville, 88-89; res asst, Dr R Alan Culpepper, Southern Sem, 87; Garrett tchg fel, Southern Sem, 84-87. **SELECTED PUBLICATIONS** Auth, Host, Guest, Enemy and Friend: Portraits of the Pharisees in Luke and Acts, Emory Stud in Early Christianity, vol. 1, NY, Bern, Frankfurt am Main, Paris: Peter Lang Publ, 91; ed, New Boundaries in Old Territory: Form and Social Rhetoric in Mark, Emory Studies in Early Christianity, vol 3, NY, Bern, Frankfurt am Main: Peter Lang Press, 94; co-ed, Recruitment, Conquest and Conflict: Strategies in Judaism, Early Christianity and the Greco-Roman World, Emory Stud in Early Christianity, vol 6, Atlanta: Scholars Press, 98; H. Wayne Merritt, In Word and Deed: Moral Integrity in Paul, Emory Stud in Early Christianity, vol 2, NY, Bern, Frankfurt am Main: Peter Lang Press, 93; Jan Botha, Subject to Whose Authority Multiple Readings of Romans 13, Emory Stud in Early Christianity, vol 4, Atlanta: Scholars Press, 94; Kjell Arne Morland, The Rhetoric of Curse in Galatians: Paul Confronts a Different Gospel, Emory Stud in Early Christianity, vol 5, Atlanta: Scholars Press, 95. **CONTACT ADDRESS** Dept of Relig and Philos, Chowan Col, 200 Jones Dr, PO Box 1848, Murfreesboro, NC, 27855.

GRABER-MILLER, KEITH A.
PERSONAL Born 05/08/1959, Kokomo, IN, m, 2 children **DISCIPLINE** RELIGION **EDUCATION** Franklin Col, BA 81; Goshen Bibl Sem, Mdiv, 88; Emory Univ, PhD, 94. **CAREER** Ed & Mgr, (Bureau Ch , Kokomo Tribune) Howard County News, IN, 81-83; Int Min, Asst Prof of Comm, Goshen Col, 87-89; Tchg Asst, Emory Univ, 89-93; Assoc Prof, Goshen Col, 93-; Vis Fac, Assoc Mennonite Bibl Sem, IN, 97-. **HONORS AND AWARDS** Summa cum laude, Franklin Col, 81; Grad Fel & Tuition Scholar, Emory Univ, 89-93; Schowalter Fnd Grant, 92-93; Res Grant, IN Univ Center on Philanthropy, 92-93; Dissertation fel, Louisville Inst, 93-94; Goshen Col Multicultural Affairs Grant, 94-95, 98-99; Faculty Res Grant, Goshen Col, 97-98, 98-99. **MEMBERSHIPS** Soc for the Scientific Stud of Religion; Amer Acad of Religion; Soc of Christian Ethics; Anabaptist Soc and Anthropology Assoc. **RESEARCH** Religion and Politics; Church-Related Higher Education; Christian Ethics; Human Sexuality; Dynamics of Religious Collectivities; Mennonite History and Theology; Peacemaking. PUB Auth, Mennonite Lobbyist in Washington, The Annual of the Soc of Christian Ethics, 95; Bumping into the State: Developing a Washington Presence, Mennonite Quart Rev, 96; Wise as Serpents, Innocent as doves: American Mennonites Engage Washington, Univ of TN Press, 96; Teaching the Bible in the Classroom: Vision and Goals, The Word Among Us, PPP, 97; Worshiping with the Early Anabaptists, Gospel Herald 90:34, 97; Mennonite Mutual Aid: A Margin of Difference?, Building Com of Compassion Mennonite Mutual Aid in Theory and Practice, Harold/Pandora Press, 98; CoAuth, Worshipping with the Early Anabaptist, What Mennonites Are Thinking, 98. **CONTACT ADDRESS** Goshen Col, Goshen, IN, 46526. **EMAIL** keithgm@goshen.edu

GRACIA, JORGE JESUS EMILIANO
PERSONAL Born 07/18/1942, Camaguey, Cuba, m, 1966, 2 children **DISCIPLINE** PHILOSOPHY **EDUCATION** Wheaton Col, BA, 65; Univ Chicago, MA, 66; Pontif Inst Mediaeval Studies, Toronto, MSL, 70; Univ Toronto, PhD, 71. **CAREER** Asst prof, 71-76, assoc chairperson dept, 74-76, assoc prof, 76-80, prof philos & chmn dept, State Univ NY Buffalo, 80-85; Can Coun grant, 71; vis prof philos, Univ PR, 72-73; Nat Endowment for Humanities grant, 82. **HONORS AND AWARDS** NY Coun for Hum grant, 87; John N Findlay prize Metaphysical Soc Am, 92. **MEMBERSHIPS** Am Cath Philos Asn; Am Philos Asn; Can Philos Asn; Medieval Acad Am; Metaphysical Soc Am; Soc for Iberian and Latin Am Thought; Soc for Medieval and Renaissance Philos; Soc de Philos Iberoamericana; Int Federation of Latin Am and Caribbean Stud; Federation Int de Soc de Philos. **RESEARCH** Medieval philosophy; ontology; Hispanic philosophy. **SELECTED PUBLICATIONS** Auth, Philosophy and its History: Issues in Philosophical Historiography, 91; ed, Individuation in Scholasticism, 94; co-ed, Individuation and Identity in Early Modern Philosophy, 94; auth, A Theory of Textuality: The Logic and Epistemology, 95; **CONTACT ADDRESS** Dept of Philosophy, SUNY, Buffalo, PO Box 601010, Buffalo, NY, 14260. **EMAIL** gracia@acsu.buffalo.edu

GRAD, FRANK P.
PERSONAL Born 05/02/1924, Vienna, Austria, m, 1946, 2 children **DISCIPLINE** LAW **EDUCATION** Brooklyn Col, AB, 47; Columbia Univ, LLb, 49. **CAREER** Assoc law, 49-50, from asst dir to assoc dir, legis drafting res fund, 53-69, lectr law, 54-65, adj prof legis, 64-69, prof law & dir legis drafting res fund, 69-95, Joseph P Chamberlain Prof Legis, 82-95, emeritus, 95-, Columbia Univ; consult, Depts of Health & State Constitutional Convs, 60-; coun, Nat Munic League, 67-89; mem legal adv comt, US Coun Environ Quality, 70-72; assoc ed, Health & Soc, 72-76. **HONORS AND AWARDS** Magna cum laude, 47; 10th Horace E. Read Mem lectr, Dalhouse Law Sch, 84; **MEMBERSHIPS** Am Bar Asn; fel Am Pub Health Asn; AAUP; Am Law Inst; NY Bar Asn; Am Soc Law and Medicine; World Conservation Union; Human Genome Orgn; Int Coun Environ Law; NY Soc Medical Jurisprudence. **RESEARCH** Legislation; environmental law; public health law. **SELECTED PUBLICATIONS** Coauth, The Automobile and the Regulation of Its Impact on the Environment, Okla Univ, 75; Physicians License and Discipline, 79; auth, Public Health Law Manual, APHA, 90. **CONTACT ADDRESS** Law Sch, Columbia Univ, 435 W 116th St, New York, NY, 10027-7201.

GRAGLIA, L.A.
PERSONAL Born 01/22/1930, Brooklyn, NY, m, 1954, 3 children **DISCIPLINE** LAW **EDUCATION** City Col NY, BA, 52; Columbia Univ Law Sch, LLB, 54. **CAREER** Atty, Dept Justice, 54-57; private prac, 57-66; teaching, Univ Tex Sch Law, 66- . **RESEARCH** Judicial review, race discrimination. **SELECTED PUBLICATIONS** Auth, Disaster by Decree: The Supreme Court Decisions on Race and the Schools, Cornell Univ, 76. **CONTACT ADDRESS** Sch of Law, Univ of Tex, 727 E 26th St, Austin, TX, 78705. **EMAIL** LGRAGLIA@mail.law.utexas.edu

GRAHAM, GEORGE
PERSONAL Born 09/03/1945, Brooklyn, NY, m, 1972, 1 child **DISCIPLINE** PHILOSOPHY **EDUCATION** Brandeis, PhD, 75. **CAREER** Chmn, prof, phil, prof, psychol, 75-, Univ Ala, Birmingham **HONORS AND AWARDS** 3 tchng awards; 4 scholar awards. **MEMBERSHIPS** APA; Soc Phil & Psychol. **RESEARCH** Philosophical psychopathology; phil of mind & cognitive sci. **SELECTED PUBLICATIONS** Coauth, Philosophical Psychopathology, MIT, 94; auth, Philosophy of Mind, Blackwells, 98; coauth, A Companion to Cognitive Science, Blackwells, 98. **CONTACT ADDRESS** Dept of Philosophy, Univ of Alabama, Birmingham, AL, 35294. **EMAIL** ggraham@uab.edu

GRAHAM, GEORGE JACKSON
PERSONAL Born 11/12/1938, Dayton, OH, d, 1 child **DISCIPLINE** POLITICAL SCIENCE, POLITICAL PHILOSOPHY **EDUCATION** Wabash Coll, Hist, AB, 60; Ind Univ. PhD, Govt, 65. **CAREER** Instr, Vanderbilt Univ, 63-64; asst prof, Vanderbilt Univ, 65-72; assoc prof, Vanderbilt Univ, 72-77; PROF, VANDERBILT UNIV, 77-. **MEMBERSHIPS** Am Polit Sci Asn **RESEARCH** Political philosophy; Ethics & public policy **SELECTED PUBLICATIONS** "Contextualizing Regime Change: Transformation Windows and Systemic Reforms in Eastern Europe," Agenda Formation, Univ Mich Press, 93; "Pluralism, Parliaments, and the Public," Budapest Papers on Democratic Transition, 97. **CONTACT ADDRESS** Dept Polit Sci, Vanderbilt Univ, Nashville, TN, 37235. **EMAIL** grahamgj@ctrvax.vanderbilt.edu

GRAHAM, J. MICHELE
PERSONAL Born 06/08/1952, Long Beach, CA, s **DISCIPLINE** THEOLOGY **EDUCATION** Fuller Theol Sem, Pasadena CA, MDiv, 80; Univ Aberdeen, Scotland, PhD, 93. **CAREER** Asst prof, 94-97, Sterling Col, KS; asst prof, 97-, Whitworth Col. **RESEARCH** Trinity, atonement, women in ministry issues. **CONTACT ADDRESS** Whitworth Col, 300 W Hawthorne Rd., Spokane, WA, 99251. **EMAIL** mgraham@whitworth.edu

GRAHAM, STEPHEN R.
PERSONAL Born 12/29/1957, m, 1977, 2 children **DISCIPLINE** RELIGIOUS STUDIES **EDUCATION** Wheaton Col, BA, 82; Wheaton Grad School, MA, 84; Univ Chicago, PhD, 89. **CAREER** Instr, United Pentecostal Bibl Col, 79-80; vis instr, Governors State Univ, 86; adjunct prof, North Park Theol Sem, 86-87; asst prof, 88-93; assoc prof, 94-97; full prof, 97-. **MEMBERSHIPS** Am Acad of Relig; Am Soc of Church Hist. **RESEARCH** Religious studies. **SELECTED PUBLICATIONS** Auth, Cosmos in the Chaos: Philip Schaff's Interpretation of Nineteenth-Century American Religion, 95; "Looking Forward and Looking Backward: Schaff and Nevin at Mercersburg" in John Williamson Nevin: A Collection of Essays, 96; "Philip Schaff: Organic Development in Christianity" in Broadman Handbook of Church Historians, 95; "Thus Saith the Lord: Biblical Hermeneutics in the Early Pentecostal Movement" in Ex Auditu, 96. **CONTACT ADDRESS** No Park Theol Sem, 3225 W Foster Ave, Chicago, IL, 60625. **EMAIL** srg@northpark.edu

GRAHAM, W. FRED
PERSONAL Born 10/31/1930, Columbus, OH, m, 1953, 4 children **DISCIPLINE** RELIGION, HISTORY **EDUCATION** Tarkio Col, BA, 52; Pittsburgh Theol Sem, BD, 55; Louisville Presby Sem, ThM, 58; Univ Iowa, PhD(relig), 65. **CAREER** From instr to asst prof relig, 63-65, from asst prof to assoc prof dept relig studies, 66-73, PROF RELIG, MICH STATE UNIV, 73-. **MEMBERSHIPS** Am Soc Church Hist; Calvin Studies Soc; Am Acad Relig; Soc 16th Century Studies. **RESEARCH** Reformation, particularly 16th century Geneva and Calvin; relationship between religion and social, economic and political life and thought; science and religion. **SELECTED PUBLICATIONS**

CATIONS Auth, An Uncounseled King--Charles-I and the Scottish Troubles, 1637-1641, Church Hist, Vol 0062, 93; Calvin, John Preaching, Church Hist, Vol 0063, 94; Where Shall Wisdom Be Found--Calvin Exegesis of Job from Medieval and Modern Perspectives, 16th Century J, Vol 0026, 95; Calvinism in Europe, 1540-1610--A Collection of Documents, Church Hist, Vol 0064, 95; Ecclesia-Reformata--Studies on the Reformation, Vol 2, 16th Century J, Vol 0026, 95; Humanism and Reform--The Church in Europe, England and Scotland, 1400-1643, Church Hist, Vol 0064, 95; Calvin, John Concept of the Law, Church Hist, Vol 0064, 95; Sin and the Calvinists--Morals Control and the Consistory in the Reformed Tradition, Cath Hist Rev, Vol 0082, 96; Politics, Religion, and Diplomacy in Early-Modern Europe--Essays in Honor of Jensen, de, Lamar, Church Hist, Vol 0065, 96; The Uses of Reform--Godly Discipline and Popular Behavior in Scotland and Beyond, 1560-1610, 16th Century J, Vol 0028, 97. **CONTACT ADDRESS** Dept of Relig Studies, Michigan State Univ, East Lansing, MI, 48823.

GRAHAM, WILLIAM A.
PERSONAL Born 08/16/1943, Raleigh, NC, m, 1983, 1 child **DISCIPLINE** ISLAMIC STUDIES, HISTORY OF RELIGIONS **EDUCATION** Univ NC, Chapel Hill, Comp Lit, AB, 66; Harvard Univ; AM, 70, PhD, 73, Comp Rel and Islamics. **CAREER** Lectr, Asst Prof, 73-, Harvard Univ; Assoc Prof, Sr Lectr, Prof, Hist of Rel and Islamic Stud, M of Currier House, 91-; Chr, 87-90, Dir, Center for Middle Eastern Stud, 90-96, Chr, Dept of Near Eastern Lang and Civilization, 97-, Harvard Admin Posts. **HONORS AND AWARDS** Danforth; Woodrow Wilson Grad Fellowship; ACLS, Hist Rel Books Award; J.S. Guggenheim Fellowship. **MEMBERSHIPS** Amer Soc for the Stud of Rel; Middle East Stud Assoc; Amer Oriental Soc; Amer Acad of Rel. **RESEARCH** History of Religion; Scripture, Pilgrimage; Islamic Studies, Qur'an, Rituals, Traditionalism **SELECTED PUBLICATIONS** Auth, Divine Word and Prophetic Word in Early Islam, Mouton, 78; Beyond the Written Word, Cambridge Univ, 87; coauth, The Heritage of World Civilizations, Practice Hall, 4th ed, 97. **CONTACT ADDRESS** Currier House, Harvard Univ, 64 Linnaean St, Cambridge, MA, 02138. **EMAIL** wgraham@fas.harvard.edu

GRAHAM, WILLIAM C.
PERSONAL Born 04/16/1950, Duluth, MN **DISCIPLINE** HISTORICAL THEOLOGY **EDUCATION** Fordham Univ, PhD, 93. **CAREER** Assoc prof, Caldwell Col, NJ; dir, Caldwell Pastoral Ministry Inst. **HONORS AND AWARDS** Asst ed, Listening; columnist for Natl Cath Reporter. **MEMBERSHIPS** Am Acad Relig; Asn of Grad Prog in Ministry; New Jersey Consortium for Grad Prog in Theol; N Am Acad of Relig. **SELECTED PUBLICATIONS** Co-ed, Common Good, Uncommon Questions: A Primer in Moral Theology, Liturgical, 95; auth, Half Finished Heaven: The Social Gospel in American Literature, Univ Pr Am, 95; ed, More Urgent Than Usual: The Final Homilies of Mark Hollenhorst, Liturgical, 95; auth, Is There A Case Against St. Therese As Doctor of the Church? Sisters Today, 95; auth, Sadness of the City, in Legalized Gambling, Greenhaven, 98; auth, Up In Smoke: Preparation for Ash Wednesday, Mod Liturgy, 97/98; auth, Television, Resistance and Orthodoxy, Natl Cath Reporter, 98; auth, The Preacher and the Abortion Opponent, Celebration, 98. **CONTACT ADDRESS** 326 W 14th St, New York, NY, 10014. **EMAIL** wcgnycpl@aol.com

GRAMMER, MICHAEL B.
PERSONAL Born 10/26/1961, Wheeling, WV, m, 1994, 3 children **DISCIPLINE** LITURGY **EDUCATION** Wheeling Jesuit Col, BA, 84; Univ Notre Dame, MS, 92-, MA, 94. **CAREER** Instr, relig stud, 81-82, Mont de Chantal Vis Acad; dir, relig ed, 86-90, St Ladislaus & St Mary Churches; assoc pastor, 91-93, Church of St Boniface; tchng asst, 93-94, Cath Univ of Am; bus mngr, 93-94, N Am Forum on the Catechumenate; asst prof, spec fac, 94-96, Notre Dame Ctr for Pastoral Lit, Notre Dame; dir, Off Initiation & Spiritual Formation, 96-, Diocese of Greensburg, PA. **MEMBERSHIPS** Asn for Relig & Intel Life; Natl Cath Ed Asn; Relig Ed Asn; Liturgy Network, NA Forum, NCCL; NCEA; NALM; REACH; CACE; NACARE. **RESEARCH** Liturgical Catechesis; RCIA. **SELECTED PUBLICATIONS** Auth, Ideas and Illustrations, Homily Svc 27, 94; auth, Liturgically Minded People: A History of the Notre Dame Center for Pastoral Liturgy, Assembly 21:2, 95; auth, The Heart of Catechesis, Cath Accent 36:13, 96; auth, Is There Gravity In Heaven?, Cath Accent, 97; auth, Focus on Prayer, Cath Accent, 98; auth, Baptism, Cath Accent, 98. **CONTACT ADDRESS** Office of Spiritual Formation, Diocese of Greensburg, 723 E Pittsburgh St, Greensburg, PA, 15601-2697. **EMAIL** mgrammer@westol.com

GRANDY, RICHARD E.
PERSONAL Born 12/06/1942, Pittsburgh, PA, 2 children **DISCIPLINE** PHILOSOPHY **EDUCATION** Univ Pittsburgh, BS, 63; Princeton Univ, PhD, 67. **CAREER** Asst prof philos, Princeton Univ, 67-74; assoc prof philos, 74-79, prof, 79-80, Univ NC, Chapel Hill; prof philos, 80-, Rice Univ; NSF fel, 70-71; Am Coun Learned Soc study fel, 76. **MEMBERSHIPS** Asn Symbolic Logic; Philos Sci Asn; Am Philos Asn. **RESEARCH** Philosophy of science; philosophy of mathematics; logic. **SELECTED PUBLICATIONS** Art, A Definition of Truth for Theories With Intensional Definite Description Operators, J Philos Logic, 72; art, Reference, Meaning and Belief, J Philos, 9/73; ed, Theories and Observation in Science, Prentice-Hall, 73; Advanced Logic for Applications, D Reidel, 77. **CONTACT ADDRESS** Dept of Philosophy, Rice Univ, Houston, TX, 77251. **EMAIL** rgrandy@rice.edu

GRANGE, JOSEPH
DISCIPLINE PHILOSOPHY **EDUCATION** Fordham Univ, PhD, 70. **CAREER** Prof; taught at, USM, for over 25 yrs; taught in, Hawaii, Ireland, China, and, Belgium; dir, Soc for the Study of Process Philos. **MEMBERSHIPS** Metaphysical Soc Am. **RESEARCH** Philosophy of the environment; metaphysics; Asian philosophy; American philosophy; philosophy of religion. **SELECTED PUBLICATIONS** Auth, Nature: An Environmental Cosmology, SUNY Press; The City: An Urban Cosmology, SUNY Press. **CONTACT ADDRESS** Dept of Philosophy, Univ of Southern Maine, 96 Falmouth St, PO Box 9300, Portland, ME, 04104-9300. **EMAIL** grange@usm.maine.edu

GRANGER, CHRISTOPHER
DISCIPLINE LAW **EDUCATION** Southern Univ, LLB; Univ Mich, LLM. **CAREER** Prof. **SELECTED PUBLICATIONS** Auth, pubs on contracts, conflicts and criminal procedure, Canadian Coroner Law and Canadian Criminal Jury Trials. **CONTACT ADDRESS** Fac Common Law, Univ Ottawa, 550 Cumberland St, PO Box 450, Ottawa, ON, K1N 6N5.

GRANGER, HERBERT
PERSONAL Born 10/25/1944, Beaumont, TX, m **DISCIPLINE** PHILOSOPHY **EDUCATION** Trinity Univ, BA, 67; Univ Tex, PhD, 77. **CAREER** Asst prof, Univ SDak, 77-81; asst prof, Univ Tex, 82-83; asst prof, Univ Ariz, 84; asst prof, Ariz State Univ, 85; asst prof, Univ Colo, 86; from lectr to prof, Wayne State Univ, 87-. **HONORS AND AWARDS** NEH Summer Stipend, 89; Wayne State Univ Career Develop Ch, 92. **MEMBERSHIPS** Am Asn Univ Prof; Am Philos Asn; Soc Ancient Greek Philos. **RESEARCH** Ancient Greek philosophy; Aristotle; Plato; Presocratic philosophers. **SELECTED PUBLICATIONS** Auth, Aristotle's Idea of the Soul, 96; auth, Aristotle on the Subject Head of Form, Oxford Studies Ancient Philos, 95; auth, Aristotle on the Analogy Between Action and Nature, Class Quart, 93; auth, Aristotle and the Functionalist Debate, Apeiron, 90; auth, The Scala Naturae and the Continuity of Kinds, Phronesis, 85; auth, Aristotle an Genus and Differentia, Jour Hist Philos, 84. **CONTACT ADDRESS** Dept of Philosophy, Wayne State Univ, Detroit, MI, 48202.

GRANQUIST, MARK
PERSONAL Born 01/29/1957, Waukegan, IL, m, 1982, 2 children **DISCIPLINE** RELIGION **EDUCATION** St. Olaf Col, BA, 79; Yale Divinity Sch, MDiv 84; Univ Chicago, PhD, 92. **CAREER** Asst prof relig, St. Olaf Col, 92-. **MEMBERSHIPS** Am Soc Church Hist; Am Acad Relig; Soc Bibl Lit. **RESEARCH** Immigration and religion in America; Lutheranism; history of biblical interpretation. **SELECTED PUBLICATIONS** Auth, Smaller Religious Groups in the Swedish-American Community, Swedish-Am Hist Quart, Oct, 93; auth, A Comparison of Swedish- and Norwegian-American Religious Traditions, 1860-1920, Lutheran Quart, Autumn, 94; auth, Lithuanian-Americans, Estonian-Americans, and Swedish Americans, Gale Encycl Multicultural Am, 95; auth, Conrad Bergendoff and the LCA Merger of 1962, Swedish-Am His Quart, July, 95; auth, The Lutheran Witness, Popular Relig Mag of the US, 95; auth, The Religious Vision and Academic Quest at St. Olaf, Models for Christian Higher Educ: Strategies for Success in the Twenty-First Century, 97; auth, Lutherans in the United States, 9130-1960: Searching for the Center, Reforming the Ctr: Am Protestantism, 1900 to the Present, 98; auth, Five American Lutheran Histories, Lutheran Quart, Summer, 98. **CONTACT ADDRESS** Dept of Religion, St. Olaf Col, Northfield, MN, 55057. **EMAIL** granquis@stolaf.edu

GRANT, ISABEL
DISCIPLINE LAW **CAREER** Law Clerk, Justice Willard Estey, Supreme Court Can, 86-87; asst prof, 87-92, assoc prof, 92-. **RESEARCH** Criminal law; constitutional law; mental health law. **SELECTED PUBLICATIONS** Auth, The Law of Homicide in Canada; pubs about criminal law and charter and mental health law. **CONTACT ADDRESS** Fac of Law, Univ British Columbia, 1822 East Mall, Vancouver, BC, V6T 1Z1. **EMAIL** grant@law.ubc.ca

GRANT, JACQUELYN
PERSONAL Born 12/19/1948, Georgetown, South Carolina, s **DISCIPLINE** THEOLOGY **EDUCATION** Bennett Coll, BA 1970; Interdenominational Theol Ctr, MDiv 1973; Union Theol Seminary, MPhil 1980, PhD 1985. **CAREER** Union Theol Seminary, tutor & relief teacher 1975-77; Harvard Divinity School, assoc in rsch 1977-79; Candler School of Emory/ Theol Univ, visiting lecturer 1981; Princeton Theol Seminary, visit lectr 1985; Interdenominational Theol Center, prof 1980-. **HONORS AND AWARDS** DuBois Fellowship Harvard Univ 1979-80; Dissertation Fellowship Fund for Theological Educ 1979-80; Amer Black Achievement Awd nominee Johnson Publishing Co 1982; Woman of the Year in Religion nominee Iota Phi Lambda Sorority 1984; Martin Luther King, Jr Ministry Award, 1986; Colgate/Rochester Theological Seminary, Outstanding Alumni: Turner Theological Seminary at ITC. **MEMBERSHIPS** Assoc minister Allen AME Church 1973-80; itinerant elder African Methodist Episcopal Church 1976; assoc minister Flipper Temple AME Church 1980-93; Victory AME Church, 1993; founder/dir Black Women in Church & Soc 1981; bd of dirs Black Theology Project in the Americas. **CONTACT ADDRESS** Systematic Theology, Interdenominational Theol Ctr, 700 Martin Luther King Jr Dr, Atlanta, GA, 30314.

GRANT, JOHN W.
PERSONAL Born 06/27/1919, Truro, NS, Canada **DISCIPLINE** RELIGION **EDUCATION** Dalhousie Univ, BA, 38, MA, 41; Princeton Univ, grad stud politics, 38-39; Pine Hill Divinity Hall (NS), Cert Theol, 43; Oxford Univ, DPhil, 48. **CAREER** Ordained, 43; min, West Bay, NS, 43; dir relig infor, Wartime Infor Bd, 43-45; lectr, Pine Hill Divinity Hall, 45-46; Woodward Found Prof Church Hist, Union Col, BC, 49-59; ed-in-chief, The Ryerson Press, 60-63; prof church hist, Emmanuel Col, Univ Toronto, 63-84. **SELECTED PUBLICATIONS** Auth, Free Churchmanship in England 1870-1940, 55; auth, God's People in India, 59; auth, George Pidgeon: A Biography, 62; auth, God Speaks... We Answer, 65; auth, The Canadian Experience of Church Union, 67; auth, The Church in the Canadian Era, 72; auth, Moon of Wintertime, 84; auth, A Profusion of Spires, 88; ed, Salvation! O the Joyful Sound: the Selected Writings of John Carroll, 67; ed, Die unierten Kirchen, 73; co-ed, The Contribution of Methodism to Atlantic Canada, 92. **CONTACT ADDRESS** 86 Gloucester St, #1002, Toronto, ON, M4Y 2S2.

GRANT LUCKHARDT, C.
DISCIPLINE WITTGENSTEIN, ETHICS, GREEK PHILOSOPHY, INFORMAL LOGIC, PHILOSOPHY OF LAW, **EDUCATION** Emory Univ, PhD, 72. **CAREER** Prof, Ga State Univ. **SELECTED PUBLICATIONS** Auth, How To Do Things with Logic and Wittgenstein: Sources and Perspectives; transl, Wittgenstein's Last Writings on the Philosophy of Psychology, vols I and II, & Remarks on the Philosophy of Psychology, vol II. **CONTACT ADDRESS** Georgia State Univ, Atlanta, GA, 30303. **EMAIL** dascgl@panther.gsu.edu

GRASSIE, WILLIAM
PERSONAL Born 05/03/1957, Wilmington, DE, m, 1984, 2 children **DISCIPLINE** RELIGION **EDUCATION** Temple Univ, PhD, 94. **CAREER** Asst prof, Intellectual Heritage Prog, Temple Univ, 94-99. **HONORS AND AWARDS** Templeton Science and Religion Course Program, Roothbert fel, AFSC fel. **MEMBERSHIPS** AAR; IRAS. **RESEARCH** Philos of Science and Relig. **SELECTED PUBLICATIONS** Auth, Reinventing Nature: Science Narratives as Myths for an Endangered Planet, doctoral dissertation, Temple Univ, defended May 94; Cyborgs, Tricksters, and Hermes: Donna Haraway's Metatheory of Science and Religion, Zygon: J of Relig and Science, June 96; Powerful Pedagogy in the Science and Religion Classroom, Zygon: J of Relig and Science, Sept 97; Postmodernism: What One Needs to Know, Zygon: J of Relig and Science, March 97; Wired for the Future: Kevin Kelly's Techno-Utopia, Terra Nova: Nature & Culture, 2:4, fall 97. **CONTACT ADDRESS** PO Box 586, Unionville, PA, 19375. **EMAIL** grassie@voicenet.com

GRATZ, DELBERT L.
PERSONAL Born 03/05/1920, Allen Co, OH, m, 1943, 4 children **DISCIPLINE** CHURCH HISTORY **EDUCATION** Bluffton Col, AB, 42; Ohio State Univ, MA, 45; Univ Bern, DPhil-(hist), 50; Univ Mich, Ann Arbor, AMLS, 52. **CAREER** LIBRN, MENNONITE HIST LIBR AND COL LIBR AND PROF HIST, BLUFFTON COL 50-, Scholar, Nordrhein-Westfalen Ministry of Educ, Bonn, Ger, 64; fel, Pro Helvetia, Zurich, Switz, 64-65; Ger Acad Exchange Serv fel, Bad Godesberg, 64-65; res scholar, Baptist Theol Sem, Zurich, 64-65 and 71-72; Fulbright travel grant, 71-72. **MEMBERSHIPS** Church Hist Soc; Am Soc Reformation Res; Swiss Am Hist Soc; Mennonite Hist Soc. **RESEARCH** Anabaptist and Mennonite research; genealogical research. **SELECTED PUBLICATIONS** Auth, Helvetia-Sacra--Section 8, Vol 1, The History and Life of the Congregations in Switzerland, 16th-18th-Century, Church Hist, Vol 0065, 96. **CONTACT ADDRESS** Mennonite Hist Libr, Bluffton Col, Bluffton, OH, 45817.

GRAVEL, PIERRE
PERSONAL Born 03/13/1942, Montreal, PQ, Canada **DISCIPLINE** PHILOSOPHY, LITERATURE **EDUCATION** Univ Montreal, BPaed, 63; Univ Aix-Marseille, MA, 69, DPhil, 71. **CAREER** Asst lectr, Inst Am Univs and Univ Aix-Marseille, 68-71; prof, Col Maisonneuve, 71-73; asst prof, 73-78, ASSOC PROF PHILOS, UNIV MONTREAL, 78-, Consult philos, Rev Philos, 75-; mem, Comite de Lear, Rev Etudes Francaises, 78-; dir, Determinations, 82. **MEMBERSHIPS** Can Philos Asn. **RESEARCH** History of philosophy; aesthetics. **SELECTED PUBLICATIONS** Auth, 'Macbeth'--Shakespeare Depiction of the Workings of Power, Laval Theol et Philos, Vol 0051, 95. **CONTACT ADDRESS** 2910 Ed Montpetit, Montreal, PQ, H3C 3J7.

GRAVLEE, G. SCOTT
DISCIPLINE PHILOSOPHY **EDUCATION** Univ Wash, BA, 88; Stanford Univ, PhD, 96. **CAREER** Fel, Stanford Univ, 94-95; instru, 95-96; lectr, Christopher Newport Univ, 97-98; vis asst prof, Col of William and Mary, 96-98; asst prof, 98-. **HONORS AND AWARDS** Mellon fel, 89-91. **MEMBERSHIPS** Am Philos Asn; Soc for Ancient Greek Philos; Southern Soc for Philos and Psychol; Soc of Christian Philos. **RESEARCH** Aristotelian philosophy; Ancient Greek philosophy; Ethics. **SELECTED PUBLICATIONS** Auth, "The Pluralist University: Christian Graduate Students," 92. **CONTACT ADDRESS** Dept of Religion and Philosophy, Mount Union Col, Alliance, OH, 44601. **EMAIL** GravleGS@muc.edu

GRAY, BONNIE JEAN
PERSONAL Born 08/19/1947, Alexandria Bay, NY **DISCIPLINE** PHILOSOPHY, ETHICS & VALUE THEORY **EDUCATION** Hope Col, BA, 69; Syracuse Univ, MA, 71, PhD(philos), 73. **CAREER** Asst prof, 74-78, assoc prof philos, Eastern KY Univ, 78-83, full prof, 83-, dir, honors program, 88-. **MEMBERSHIPS** Am Philos Asn; AAUP; Hastings Ctr Inst. **RESEARCH** Hume scholarship; business ethics. **SELECTED PUBLICATIONS** Ed & contribr, Seminar in Post-Watergate Morality, Eastern Ky Univ, 77; coauth, What to Bid? & Promoters, Entertainers and Audience: A Question of Ethics (intercol cases), Clearing House, 77; Criteria for Resolving Ethical Dilemmas in Organizations, Credo; coauth, Are You Ready for Tomorrow's Management Style?, 11-12/79 & What Price Allegiance?, A Case of Managerial Ethics, 1-2/81, Business. **CONTACT ADDRESS** Eastern Kentucky Univ, 521 Lancaster Ave, Richmond, KY, 40475-3102. **EMAIL** HONGRAY@acs.eku.edu

GRAY, CHRISTOPHER
DISCIPLINE PHILOSOPHY OF LAW **EDUCATION** Cath Univ Am, PhD; McGill Univ, BCL, LLB. **CAREER** Dept Philos, Concordia Univ **SELECTED PUBLICATIONS** Pub(s), in prof and philos jour(s) on philos of law and associated topics; ed, Philosophy of Law: An Encyclopedia, 96. **CONTACT ADDRESS** Dept of Philos, Concordia Univ, Montreal, 1455 de Maisonneuve W, Montreal, PQ, H3G 1M8. **EMAIL** graycb@vax2.concordia.ca

GRAY, DONALD P.
PERSONAL Born 03/29/1937, Rochester, NY, m, 1961, 4 children **DISCIPLINE** RELIGIOUS STUDIES **EDUCATION** Univ Toronto, BA, 61; Univ Notre Dame, MA, 63; Fordham Univ, PhD(theol), 68. **CAREER** From instr to assoc prof, 62-78, prof theol, Manhattan Col, 78-. **MEMBERSHIPS** Theol Soc Am; Col Theol Soc; Am Acad Relig; Am Teilhard de Chardin Asn. **RESEARCH** Christology; death and dying; Christian systematics. **SELECTED PUBLICATIONS** Auth, The One and the Many, Herder & Herder, 69; Sacramental consciousness-raising, Worship, 3/72; Was Jesus a convert?, Relig Life, winter 74; The phenomenon of Teilhard, Theol Studies, 3/75; Patience: Human and divine, Cross Currents, winter 75; The Divine and the human in Jesus Christ, Proc Cath Theol Soc Am, 76; Finding God Among Us, St Mary's Col, 77; Jesus, the Way to Freedom, St Mary's Press, 79. **CONTACT ADDRESS** Dept of Relig Studies, Manhattan Col, 4513 Manhattan Coll, Bronx, NY, 10471-4004.

GRAY, PATRICK T.R.
PERSONAL Born 10/16/1940, Toronto, ON, Canada **DISCIPLINE** THEOLOGY/HUMANITIES **EDUCATION** Univ Toronto, BA, 62, Trinity Col, STB, 65, ThD, 73; Yale Univ, STM, 66. **CAREER** Divinity tutor, Trinity Col, 67-69; assoc rector, Ch St Simon the Apostle, 69-71; instr & vis asst prof, 72-75, sr tutor, Stong Col, York Univ, 73-76; res assoc, Pontif Inst Medieval Stud, 76-78; asst to assoc prof hist & philos theol, McMaster Divinity Col, 78-84; PROF HUMANITIES, ATKINSON COL, YORK UNIV, 84-. **HONORS AND AWARDS** Killam res scholar, 76-78. **MEMBERSHIPS** Can Fedn Hum (dir 84-87); Can Soc Patristic Stud (pres 77-79); Asn Int Etudes Byzantines. **SELECTED PUBLICATIONS** Auth, The Defense of Chalcedon in the East (451-553), 79. **CONTACT ADDRESS** Atkinson Col, York Univ, 4700 Keele St N, North York, ON, M3J 1P3.

GRAY, RONALD A.
PERSONAL Born 12/15/1952, Blackstone, VI, m, 1985 **DISCIPLINE** LAW **EDUCATION** Ohio University, BA, economics, 1975; Case Western Reserve University, College of Law, JD, 1978. **CAREER** Federal Trade Commission, Attorney, 1978-81; American Express, Attorney, 1981-85, associate counsel, 1985-87, counsel, 1987-91, senior counsel, 1991-95, managing counsel, 1995-. **HONORS AND AWARDS** Harlem Black Achieves in Industry Award, 1998; Ohio University, Gene Chapin Memorial Award, 1975. **MEMBERSHIPS** American Bar Association, 1978-; City of New York Bar Association, vice chair, Committee on Minorities, 1994-; City Bar Arbitration Committee; South African Legal Services and Legal Assistance Project, board member, 1993-; Childrens Hope Foundation, board member, 1991-94; MFY Legal Services, board member, 1996-; New York State Bar Assoc, Corporate Counsel Executive Committee, 1997-; Committee on Multi-Discipline Practice, 1998-. **SELECTED PUBLICATIONS** Companies Aim for Diversity, New York Law Journal, 1993; Employees at Risk, New York Law Journal, 1994; Chairman, Succeeding in the Business Card Market, Cred Card Institute, Executive Enterprises, 1997. **CONTACT ADDRESS** American Express Co, 200 Vesey St, New York, NY, 10285-4911.

GRAY, SHERMAN W., JR.
PERSONAL Born 07/04/1943, Montague, MA, s **DISCIPLINE** NEW TESTAMENT **EDUCATION** Catholic Univ, STL, 70; Pontifical Bib Inst, Rome Italy, SSL, 76; Catholic Univ, PhD, 87. **CAREER** Asst prof, scripture, 76-81, St Joseph Sem Yonkers NY; asst prof, scripture, Mt St Mary's Sem, Emmitsburg MD, 82-85; assoc prof, 87-, St Basil Col, Stamford CT. **MEMBERSHIPS** CBA; SBL. **RESEARCH** Gospel of Matthew, Matt 25:31-46, last judgement pericope. **SELECTED PUBLICATIONS** Auth, The Least of My Brothers, SBLDS 114, Soc of Bibl Lit, 89. **CONTACT ADDRESS** 4 Pulaski St, Stamford, CT, 06902. **EMAIL** HNCSWG@aol.com

GRAY, WALLACE
DISCIPLINE PHILOSOPHY AND RELIGION **EDUCATION** Cent Methodist Col, BA; Southern Methodist Univ, BD; Vanderbilt Univ, PhD. **CAREER** Kirk prof; Southwestern Col, 56-96; chem, Div Soc Sci, 60-66; vis prof, Friends Univ & Wichita State Univ; asst prof, Southern Methodist Univ; lectr, Univ Tenn & Vanderbilt Univ; vis scholar, Hiroshima Inst Technol, 71-72 & Univ Hawaii, 71 & 69, acad yr in E-W Philos, 63-64; lectr on China, Huron Univ, SDak; Univ Northern Iowa; Emporia State Univ, Kans; N Georgia Col; Shorter Cole, Ga; Campbell Univ, SC; Converse Col, SC; Bradley Univ, Ill; Univ Wis, Stevens Point Delegate to Population Confe, Wash, & on population at Okla State Univ. **HONORS AND AWARDS** Citizen Ambassador to China, 93. **MEMBERSHIPS** Mem, E-W Philos Conf, 64, 69 & 84, Unive Hawaii & E-W Ctr; Med Ethics Comt, Newton Mem Hosp, Winfield & Rotary Int; chem, Task Force on Upgrading Human Life, Wesley Med Ctr, Wichita, Kan. **RESEARCH** Global history of philosophy. **SELECTED PUBLICATIONS** Cheng and Tucker: A Comparative Appraisal of Two Important Recent Confucian and Neo-Confucian Studies, J Chinese Philos, Vol. 20, 93; Slavery and Oppression in Japanese History: A Case Study in Scholarly Works on Japan, Proce 14th Int sym on Asian Stud, 92, Hong Kong: Asian Res Serv, 94; Women in Ancient Japanese History, Asian Profile, Vol 22, 94 & Return of the Scarlet Letter: A Literary and Biblical Convergence with Medical Technology," Metanoia, Vol 4, 94. **CONTACT ADDRESS** Dept of Philosophy and Religion, Southwestern Col, 100 College St, Winfield, KS, 67156. **EMAIL** bumsteds@jinx.sckans.ed

GRCIC, JOSEPH M.
PERSONAL Olib, Croatia **DISCIPLINE** PHILOSOPHY **EDUCATION** CUNY, BA; Univ Notre Dame, PhD. **CAREER** Prof Philos, Ind State Univ. **HONORS AND AWARDS** Phi Beta Kappa. **MEMBERSHIPS** Amer Philos Asn. **RESEARCH** Political Philosophy; ethics; applied ethics. **SELECTED PUBLICATIONS** Auth, Moral Choices, Perspectives on the Family. **CONTACT ADDRESS** Dept of Philosophy, Indiana State Univ, Terre Haute, IN, 47809. **EMAIL** pigrcic@root.indstate.edu

GRECO, JOHN
DISCIPLINE PHILOSOPHY **EDUCATION** Brown Univ, PhD. **CAREER** Assoc prof; interim dir grad stud, Fordham Univ.. **RESEARCH** Moral responsibility. **SELECTED PUBLICATIONS** Auth, Modern Ontology and the Problems of Epistemology, Amer Philos Quart, 95; Reid's Critique of Berkeley and Hume: What's the Big Idea?, Philos and Phenomenol Res, 95; A Second Paradox Concerning Responsibility and Luck, Metaphilos, 95; Catholics vs. Calvinists on Religious Knowledge, Amer Cath Philos Quart, 95. **CONTACT ADDRESS** Dept of Philos, Fordham Univ, 113 W 60th St, New York, NY, 10023.

GREELEY, ANDREW MORAN
PERSONAL Born 02/05/1928, Chicago, IL **DISCIPLINE** SOCIOLOGY, ENGLISH LITERATURE, RELIGION **EDUCATION** St Mary Lake Sem, STL, 54; Univ Chicago, MA, Soc, 61, PhD, 62. **CAREER** Sr stud dir, Nat Opinion Res Center, Univ Chicago, 62-68; prog dir, High Educ, univ Chicago, 68-70; lectr, Soc dept, Univ Chicago, 63-72; PROF, SOC, UNIV ARIZ, 78-; PROF, SOC SCI, UNIV CHICAGO, 91-. **SELECTED PUBLICATIONS** Religion as Poetry, Trans Publ, 95; Sociology and Religion: A Collection of Readings, Harper Collins Coll Publ, 95; coauth, Common Ground, Pilgrim Press, 96; coauth, Forging a Common Future, Pilgrim Press, 1997; I Hope You're listening God, Crossroads Publ, 97. **CONTACT ADDRESS** Nat Opinion Res Center (NORC), Univ Chicago, 1155 E 60th St, Chicago, IL, 60637. **EMAIL** agreel@aol.com

GREEN, BARBARA S.
DISCIPLINE LAW **EDUCATION** Smith Col, BA, 66; Boston Univ, JD, 71, LLM, 80. **CAREER** Asst to ed, Amer Trial Lawyers' Asn, 71-72; pvt prac, Peabody, Mass, 74-80; prof, Creighton Univ. **SELECTED PUBLICATIONS** Pub(s) on taxation, Creighton Law Rev. **CONTACT ADDRESS** School of Law, Creighton Univ, 2500 California Plaza, Omaha, NE, 68178. **EMAIL** bgreen@culaw.creighton.edu

GREEN, CLIFFORD JAMES
PERSONAL Born 04/29/1934, Sydney, Australia, m, 1955, 3 children **DISCIPLINE** THEOLOGY, ETHICS **EDUCATION** Univ Sydney, BA, 55; Melbourne Col Divinity, BD, 59; Union Theol Sem, NY, STM, 64, PhD(theol), 72. **CAREER** From instr to asst prof relig, Wellesley Col, 66-72; asst prof, Goucher Col, 72-75, assoc prof, 75-79; Prof Theol & Dir, Pub Policy Ctr, Hartford Sem, 81-, Vis lectr, Univ Md, College Park, 73-75; Am Coun Learned Soc res grant, 75; lectr relig, Bates Col, 75-76; adj prof, Ecumenical Inst, St Mary's Sem, Baltimore, 77-81; vis assoc prof, Hollins Col, 80. **MEMBERSHIPS** Soc of Christian Ethics; Am Acad Relig; NAm Karl Barth Soc; Soc Values Higher Educ; Int Bonhoeffer Soc. **RESEARCH** Contemporary theology; Bonhoeffer studies. **SELECTED PUBLICATIONS** Coauth, Critical Issues in Modern Religion, Prentice-Hall, 73, 2nd ed, 90; auth, Liberation theology?, Karl Barth on women and men, Union Sem Quart Rev, spring-summer 74; Bonhoeffer: The Sociality of Christ and Humanity, Scholars, 75, 2nd ed, 99; contribr, Psychohistory and religion: The case of young man Luther, Fortress, 77; ed, Bonhoeffer, Fiction from prison, Fortress, 81; contribr, A Bonhoeffer Legacy, Eerdmans, 81; coauth, Bonhoeffer Bibliography, Primary Sources and Secondary Literature in English, Am Theol Lib Asn, 92; co-ed, Jugend und Studium, 1918-1927, Kaiser, 86; ed, contrib auth, Karl Barth: Theologian of Freedom, Collins & Harper, 89; ed, contrib auth, Churches, Cities, and Human Community, Urban Ministry in the United States, 1945-1985, Eerdmans, 96; coed, Ethik, 92, 2nd ed, 98; ed, Sanctorum Communio, Fortress, 98. **CONTACT ADDRESS** Hartford Sem, 77 Sherman St, Hartford, CT, 06105-2279. **EMAIL** green@hartsem.edu

GREEN, GARRETT
PERSONAL Born 06/01/1941, Oakland, CA, m, 1970, 2 children **DISCIPLINE** PHILOSOPHY **EDUCATION** Stanford Univ, AB, 63; Union Theol Sem, MDiv, 67; Yale Univ, MPhil, 70; PhD, 71 **CAREER** Grad tchng prof, 68-70, vis prof, 89, Yale Univ; asst prof, 70-76, assoc prof, 76-82, chmn, 77-79, prof, 82-, Conn Col. **HONORS AND AWARDS** Alexander von Humboldt res fel, Univ Tubingen, Ger, 76-77, 79-80; Sr Fulbright Scholar, Fed Rep Ger, 76-77; Student Fulbright Scholar, Univ Munster, Ger, 63-64. **MEMBERSHIPS** AAR; APA; 19th Century Theol Group; Duodecim Theol Soc; Karl Barth Soc of N Am. **RESEARCH** Hermeneutical issues in relig & theol; the concept of imagination in modern & post modern relig thought; Christian theol & post modern phil; Karl Barth's theory of relig. **SELECTED PUBLICATIONS** Auth, Imagining God: Theology and the Religious Imagination, Harper & Row, 89; auth, Kant as Christian Apologist: The Failure of Accommodationist Theology, Pro Ecclesia 4, 95; auth, The Hermeneutic Imperative: Reading the Bible as Scripture, Nederlands Theol Tijdshrift 50, 96; auth, The Sociology of Dogmatics: Niklas Luhmann's Challenge to Theology, Theol & Sociology: A Reader, Cassell, 96; auth, Who's Afraid of Ludwig Feuerbach? Suspicion and the Religious Imagination, Christian Faith Seeking Hist Understanding: Essays in Hon of H Jack Forstman, Mercer Univ Press, 97. **CONTACT ADDRESS** Connecticut Col, 270 Mohegan Ave, Box 5525, New London, CT, 06320-4196. **EMAIL** ggre@conncoll.edu

GREEN, J. PATRICK
DISCIPLINE LAW AND MEDICINE **EDUCATION** Creighton Univ, BA, 63, JD, 65. **CAREER** Prof, Creighton Univ, 71-; pvt prac, Omaha, 65-66, 69-71; in Chicago, 68; Fed Power Comn, Wash, DC, 66-68; judge, Nebr Ct Indust Rel, 75-79, **SELECTED PUBLICATIONS** Pub(s) in, Creighton Law Rev. **CONTACT ADDRESS** School of Law, Creighton Univ, 2500 California Plaza, Omaha, NE, 68178.

GREEN, JOEL B.
PERSONAL Born 05/07/1956, Lubbock, TX, m, 1979, 2 children **DISCIPLINE** NEW TESTAMENT STUDIES **EDUCATION** Tex Tech Univ, BS, 78; Perkins Sch of Theol Southern Meth Univ, M Th, 82; Univ Aberdeen, Scotland, PhD, 85. **CAREER** Asst and assoc prof, new testament, New Col Berkeley, 85-92; assoc prof, new testament, Amer Bapt Sem of the West and Grad Theol Union, Berkeley, 82-97; prof, new testament interpretation, Asbury Theol Sem, 97-. **HONORS AND AWARDS** Soc of New Testament Studies. **MEMBERSHIPS** Soc of Bibl Lit; Cath Bibl Asn; Inst for Bibl Res; Tyndale Fel. **RESEARCH** Hermeneutics; New Testament theology and ethics; Luke-Acts. **SELECTED PUBLICATIONS** Auth, Witnesses of his Resurrection: Resurrection, Salvation, Discipleship, and Mission in the Acts of the Apostles in Life in the Face of Death: The Resurrection Message of the New Testament ed. Richard N. Longenecker, McMaster New Testament Studies 3, Grand Rapids, Mich, W. B. Eerdmans, 98; auth, Bodies-That Is, Human Lives: A Re-examination of Human nature in the Bible, in Whatever Happened to the Soul? Scientific and Theological Portraits of Human Nature, ed. Warren S. Brown, Nancey C. Murphy, H. Newton Malony, Theology and the Sciences, Minneapolis, Fortress 98; auth, The Death of Jesus and the Ways of God: Jesus and the Gospels on Messianic Status and Shameful Suffering, Interpretation 52, 98; auth, Salvation to the End of the Earth (Acts 13:47): God as Saviour in the Acts of the Apostles, in The Theolofy of Acts, ed. I. Howard Marshall and David Perterson, Grand Rapids, Mich, W. B. Eerdmans, 98; auth, The Gospel of Luke, New Intl Commentary on the New Testament, Grand Rapids, Mich, W. B. Eerdmans, 97; co-auth,

The Death of Jesus in Early Christianity, Peabody, Mass, Hendrickson, 95; auth, Hearing the New Testament: Strategies for Interpretation, Grand Rapids, Mich, W. B. Eerdmans, 95; auth, The Theology of the Gospel of Luke, New Testament Theol 3, Cambridge, Cambridge Univ, 95; co-ed, Jesus of Nazareth: Lord and Christ. **CONTACT ADDRESS** Asbury Theol Sem, 204 N Lexington Ave, Wilmore, KY, 40390-1199. **EMAIL** joel_green@ats.wilmore.ky.us

GREEN, JUDITH
DISCIPLINE AMERICAN PHILOSOPHY **EDUCATION** Univ MN, PhD. **CAREER** Asst prof, Fordham Univ. **SELECTED PUBLICATIONS** Co-auth, Notorious Philosopher: the Transformative Life and Work of Angela Davis, Hypatia's Daughters: Fifteen Hundred Years of Women Philosophers, Ind UP, 96. **CONTACT ADDRESS** Dept of Philos, Fordham Univ, 113 W 60th St, New York, NY, 10023.

GREEN, MICHAEL
DISCIPLINE PHILOSOPHY **EDUCATION** Univ KS, BA, 73; Univ Chicago, PhD, 79. **CAREER** Lctr, IN Univ NE, 76-79; asst prof, Marquette Univ, 79-81; asst prof, SUNY Col Oneonta, 81-88; to assoc prof, 88-95; to prof, 95-. **MEMBERSHIPS** Am Philos Asn; Am Soc 18th Century Studies; Interdisciplinary 19th Century Studies; N Am Kant Soc; Am Pop Cult Asn; N Am Soc Study of Jean-Jacques Rousseau; Creighten Club, NY State Philos Asn; Dante Soc Interdisciplinary Values Indigenous Cults Net; Southern Mktg Asn. **RESEARCH** Ethics; Philos of Action; Applied Ethics; Issues in: War, Abortion, World Hunger and Racism and Sexism; Polit and Soc Philos; Hist of Philos (Ethics, Plato, Aristotle, Medieval, Rationalists, Hume, Kant, 19th Century Philos); African Philos; Business Ethics; Native Am Philos. **SELECTED PUBLICATIONS** Auth, Images of Justice, Int Jour Semiotics Law, 94; Cultural Identity and the Twenty-first Century Issues in Native American Culture Identity in Center for the Semiotic Study of Law, Politics and Government, Peter Lang, 94; Cultural Themes in European Philosophy, Law, and Economics, Hist Europ Ideas, 94; Images of Native Americans in Advertising, Some Moral Issues, Jour Business Ethics, 93; ed, Center for the Semiotic Study of Law, Politics, and Government, Peter Lang, 94 and 95. **CONTACT ADDRESS** SUNY Col at Oneonta, Oneonta, NY, 13820. **EMAIL** Greenmk@Oneonta.edu

GREEN, MICHAEL J.
PERSONAL Born 12/20/1966, St. Louis, MO, s **DISCIPLINE** PHILOSOPHY **EDUCATION** Univ Michigan, Ann Arbor, BA, 89; Univ Calif, Berkeley, PhD, 97. **CAREER** Lectr, philos, McGill Univ, 96-97; lectr, philos, Stanford Univ, 97-99. **HONORS AND AWARDS** Phi Beta Kappa, 88; Ralph W. Church Scholarship, 89-90; outstanding grad student instr award. 94; chancellor's fel, 95-96. **RESEARCH** Ethics; political philosophy; history of political philosophy. **SELECTED PUBLICATIONS** Auth, National Identity and Liberal Political Philosophy, Ethics & Int Affairs, 96; auth, Review of Brian Barry: Justice as Impartiality, Ethics & Int Affairs, 97; auth, the Idea of a Momentary Self and Hume's Theory of Personal Identity, British J for the Hist of Philos, forthcoming. **CONTACT ADDRESS** Dept of Philosophy, Stanford Univ, Stanford, CA, 94305. **EMAIL** michael.green@stanford.edu

GREEN, O. HARVEY
DISCIPLINE PHILOSOPHY **EDUCATION** Vanderbilt Univ, PhD, 66; Oxford Univ, DPhil, 70. **CAREER** Assoc prof, Tulane Univ. **SELECTED PUBLICATIONS** Auth, The Emotions, Kluwer; pub(s) in, Philos; Amer Philos Quart; Analysis; Mind. **CONTACT ADDRESS** Dept of Philosophy, Tulane Univ, 6823 St Charles Ave, New Orleans, LA, 70118.

GREEN, RONALD MICHAEL
DISCIPLINE RELIGION, ETHICS **EDUCATION** Brown Univ, AB, 64; Harvard, PhD, 73. **CAREER** Asst prof, 73-79, assoc, 79-84, PROF ETHICS, 84-, COHON PROF FOR STUD ETHICS & HUMAN, DARTMOUTH COL. **CONTACT ADDRESS** Ethics Inst, 6031 Parker House, Hanover, NH, 03755. **EMAIL** ronald.m.green@dartmouth.edu

GREENAWALT, ROBERT KENT
PERSONAL Born 06/25/1936, New York, NY, m, 1995, 5 children **DISCIPLINE** CONSTITUTIONAL LAW, JURISPRUDENCE **EDUCATION** Swarthmore Col, AB, 58; Oxford Univ, BPhil, 60; Columbia Univ, LLB, 63. **CAREER** Law clerk, US Supreme Court, 63-64; spec asst, AID, 64-65; from asst prof to assoc prof, 65-69, Prof Law, 69-75, cARDOZO pROF OF jURISPRUDENCE, 75-90, uNIV pROF, 90- , Columbia Univ; Chief ed, Columbia Law Rev, 62-63; Am Coun Learned Soc fel & vis fel, Cambridge Univ, 72-73; dep solicitor gen, US Dept Justice; vis fel, All Souls Col, Oxford Univ, 79. **HONORS AND AWARDS** Mem, Am Philos Soc; fel, Am Acad of Arts and Sci. **MEMBERSHIPS** Am Soc Legal & Polit Philos (pres 92-93); ed bd, J of Philos, Ethics, Law and Philos; ed bd, J of Church and State; ed bd, Ratio Juris; ed bd, Criminal Justice Ethics; ed bd, Legal Theory; ed bd, J of Criminal Law and Criminol. **RESEARCH** Free speech; religion and political participation; legal theory; legal obligation; religious liberty. **SELECTED PUBLICATIONS** Auth, Discrimination and Reverse Discrimination, Knopf, 83; auth, Religious Convictions and Political Choice, Oxford, 88; auth, Speech, Crime, and the Uses of Language, Oxford, 89; auth, Law and Objectivity, Oxford, 92; auth, Fighting Words, princeton, 95; auth, Private Consciences and Public Reasons, Oxford, 95. **CONTACT ADDRESS** 435 Riverside Dr, New York, NY, 10025.

GREENBERG, GERSHON
PERSONAL Born 09/05/1940, New York, NY **DISCIPLINE** RELIGION, PHILOSOPHY **EDUCATION** Columbia Univ, PhD(philos relig), 69. **CAREER** Asst prof relig, Dartmouth Col, 68-77; ASSOC PROF PHILOS AND RELIG, AM UNIV, 77-. **RESEARCH** Nineteenth century German-Jewish religious philosophy. **SELECTED PUBLICATIONS** Auth, Ben Hurban Leyeshua, Teguvot Shel Hagut Haredit Leshoa Bezemana, Mod Judaism, Vol 0017, 97. **CONTACT ADDRESS** Dept Philos and Relig, American Univ, 4400 Mass Ave NW, Washington, DC, 20016-8200.

GREENFIELD, MICHAEL M.
DISCIPLINE COMMERCIAL & CONSUMER LAW **EDUCATION** Grinnell Col, AB, 66; Univ Tex, Austin, JD, 69. **CAREER** Prof Law, Washington Univ, 69-, Vis prof, Univ Calif, Davis, 74-75. **RESEARCH** Consumer protection. **SELECTED PUBLICATIONS** Art, Coercive Collection Tactics: An Analysis Of The Interests And The Remedies, Washington Univ Law Quart, 72; art, Consumer protection in service transactions: Implied warranties and strict liability in tort, Utah Law Rev, 74; art, A Constitutional limitation on the enforcement of judgments: Due process and exemptions, Washington Univ Law Quart, 75; art, Debtor proceedings, Becker, Savin & Becker, Legal Checklists, Callaghan & Co, 78. **CONTACT ADDRESS** Sch of Law, Washington Univ, 1 Brookings Dr, St. Louis, MO, 63130-4899.

GREENHAWARD, DAVID M.
PERSONAL Kansas City, MO **DISCIPLINE** THEOLOGY, PREACHING AND WORSHIP **EDUCATION** Univ Kans, BGS, 76; Eden Theol Sem, MD, 79; Drew Univ, PhD, 87. **CAREER** Asst prof Vanderbilt Univ Divinity School, 86-90; Assoc prof and dean of the Sem Lancaster Theol Sem, 90-97; Pres and prof of preaching and Worship, Eden Theol Sem, 97-. **MEMBERSHIPS** AAL/SBL. **RESEARCH** Hermeneutics; Liturgical Theology. **SELECTED PUBLICATIONS** Auth, Proclamation IV: Pentecost 2: aids for Interpreting the Lessons of the Church Year, 91; As One With Authority: The Status of Concepts, Preaching, Intersections: Preaching and Biblical Interpretation, 94; Theology of Preaching, Encyclopedia of Preaching, 95; Passion Sunday, Seasons of Preaching, 96; David Buttrick and the Formation of Consciousness, World, Gospel, Scripture: Preaching as a Theological Task, 96. **CONTACT ADDRESS** Eden Theol Sem, 475 E Lockwood Ave, St Louis, MO, 63119. **EMAIL** dgreenhAward@eden.edu

GREENSPAHN, FREDERICK E.
PERSONAL Born 10/07/1946, Los Angeles, CA, m, 1997, 2 children **DISCIPLINE** BIBLICAL STUDIES **EDUCATION** Univ Calif, Santa Cruz, BA, 68; Hebrew Union Col, Jewish Inst of Relig, MA, 73; Brandeis Univ, PhD, 77. **CAREER** Lectr, relig stud, Assumption Col, Worcester MA, 77-79; asst prof, 79-85, assoc prof, 85-93, prof, 93-, Relig and Judaic Stud, Univ Denver. **HONORS AND AWARDS** Phi Beta Kappa, 91; ed, Hebrew Stud, 94-98; Univ Denver United Methodist Church Scholar- Tchr Award, 95. **MEMBERSHIPS** Soc of Bibl Lit; Assoc for Jewish Stud; Natl Assoc of Prof of Hebrew; Central Conf of Am Rabbis. **RESEARCH** Hebrew Bible; history of Jewish Biblical interpretation; Hebrew language. **SELECTED PUBLICATIONS** Auth, Hapax Legomena in Biblical Hebrew, Scholars, 84; auth, Why Prophecy Ceased, Jour of Bibl Lit, 89; auth, How Modern are Modern Biblical Studies, in Brettler, ed, Minhah le-Nahum, Biblical and Other Studies Presented to Nahum M Sarna in Honour of His 70th Birthday, JSOT, 93; auth, A Mesopotamian Proverb and its Biblical Reverberations, Jour of the Am Oriental Soc, 94; auth, When Brothers Dwell Together: The Preeminence of Younger Siblings in the Hebrew Bible, Oxford, 94; auth, An Introduction to Aramaic, Scholars, forthcoming. **CONTACT ADDRESS** Dept of Religion, Univ of Denver, Denver, CO, 80208. **EMAIL** fgreensp@du.edu

GREENSPAN, EDWARD L.
DISCIPLINE LAW **EDUCATION** Univ Toronto, BA, 65; Osgoode Hall Law Sch, LLB, 68. **CAREER** Lectr, 72-. **HONORS AND AWARDS** Ed, Martin's Ann Criminal Code; ed, Martin's Related Criminal Statutes; ed, Martin's Ontario Criminal Practice. **SELECTED PUBLICATIONS** Auth, pubs on criminal law. **CONTACT ADDRESS** Fac of Law, Univ Toronto, 78 Queen's Park, Toronto, ON.

GREENSPOON, LEONARD JAY
PERSONAL Born 12/05/1945, Richmond, VA, m, 1968, 2 children **DISCIPLINE** BIBLICAL STUDIES **EDUCATION** Univ Richmond, BA, 67, MA, 70; Harvard Univ, PhD(Near Eastern lang and civilizations), 77. **CAREER** Instr, 75-77, ASST PROF HIST, RELIG AND LATIN, CLEMSON UNIV, 77-. **MEMBERSHIPS** Int Orgn Septuagint & Cognate Studies (secy, 81-); Asn Jewish Studies; Soc Bibl Lit; Soc Values Higher Educ. **RESEARCH** Greek translations of the Old Testament; Judaism in the Hellenistic period; history of Biblical scholarship. **SELECTED PUBLICATIONS** Auth, The LXX-Version--A Guide to the Translation Technique of the Septuagint, Cath Biblical Quart, Vol 0055, 93. **CONTACT ADDRESS** Dept Hist, Clemson Univ, Clemson, SC, 29631.

GREENSTEIN, HAROLD
PERSONAL Born 11/07/1936, New York, NY, m, 1962 **DISCIPLINE** PHILOSOPHY **EDUCATION** City of New York, BA, 60; NY Univ, MA, 64, PhD(philos), 68. **CAREER** Asst prof philos, State Univ NY Col Geneseo, 65-68; from asst prof to assoc prof, 68-76, prof philos, State Univ NY Col Brockport, 76-, State Univ NY Res Found rea fel, 69; pres, Senate Fac State Univ NY Col Brockport, 77-78. **MEMBERSHIPS** Am Philos Asn; Mind Asn; Am Acad Polit & Soc Sci. **RESEARCH** Philosophy of history and the behaviorial sciences; philosophical psychology; philosophy of social sciences; philosophy of law; social and political philosophy. **SELECTED PUBLICATIONS** Coauth, Biologists as philosophers, Biosci, 11/66; Intrinsic values and the explanation of behavior, J Value Inquiry, 76; The logic of functional explanations, Philosophia, 73. **CONTACT ADDRESS** Dept of Philos, State Univ of NY, 350 New Campus Dr, Brockport, NY, 14420-2914. **EMAIL** hgreenst@acspr1.acs.brockport.edu

GREGORY, DAVID D.
DISCIPLINE LAW **EDUCATION** Duke Univ, BA; Univ Maine Sch Law, LLB; Harvard Univ, LLM. **CAREER** Prof; past dir appellate unit, Civil Rights Div, Dept Justice; past coun, York Co Dist Att; past exec sec, Comt on Judicial Responsibility and Disability; past spec master, US Dist ct overseeing implementation of the Pineland Ctr consent decree; spec coun, Maine House of Rep in its first impeachment proceedings; chem, Maine Comn on Mental Health. **SELECTED PUBLICATIONS** Coauth, treatise on Maine Tort Law. **CONTACT ADDRESS** School of Law, Univ of Southern Maine, 96 Falmouth St, PO Box 9300, Portland, ME, 04104-9300.

GREGORY, DAVID L.
DISCIPLINE LAW **EDUCATION** Catholic Univ Am, BA, 73; Wayne State Univ, Grad Sch of Business, MBA, 77; Univ Detroit Mercy Sch Law, JD, 80; Yale Univ Law Sch, LLM, 82, JSD, 87. **CAREER** Asst prof, 82-84, assoc prof, 84-86, prof, 86- , St. John's Univ School of Law. **HONORS AND AWARDS** Magna cum laude, 80; Kenneth Wang Res Prof, 87-88; Vincentian Ctr for Church and Soc Award, 98; **MEMBERSHIPS** Who's Who in Am Law; New York State Bar Asn; Michigan Bar Asn; Am Law Inst; Asn of the Bar of the City of NY; ABA; Am Arbitration Asn; Asn of Am Law Sch; Fel of Cath Scholars; Industrial Rel Res Asn; Soc of Policy Scientists; Federal Mediation and Conciliation Service; NY State Public Employment Rel Bd; NY City Office of Collective Bargaining. **SELECTED PUBLICATIONS** Auth, Labor Law, NYU and Dartmouth, 93; bd contrib ed, Handling Employment Disputes in New York, Lawyers Cooperative, 95; auth, Legal Arguments Against The Death Penalty, in Kelly, ed, St John's Univ Vincentian Chair of Social Justice and Center for Church and Society, 95; auth, Labor Law and Religion, in Finkelman, ed, The Encyclopedia of Religion and the Law, Garland, 98; coauth Labor-Management Relations and the law, Foundation, 99; ed, Labor and the Constitution, Garland, 99; auth, Catholic Social Teaching, in Carmlla, ed, Christian Perspective on Law, 99; auth, From Negligence Theory to Negligence in Employment, in Feliu, ed, Negligence in Employment, Bureau of Natl Affairs, 99. **CONTACT ADDRESS** School of Law, St. John's Univ, 8000 Utopia Pky, Jamaica, NY, 11439. **EMAIL** dgregory@sjulawfac.stjohns.edu

GREGORY, WANDA TORRES
PERSONAL Born 09/04/1958, San Juan, PR **DISCIPLINE** PHILOSOPHY **EDUCATION** Universidad de Puerto Rico, BA, 83, 84, MA, 87, PhD, 95. **CAREER** Tchg fel, 87, lectr, 88, Universidad de Puerto Rico; tchg fel, 88-90, lectr, 95, Boston Univ; vis jr fel, Institut fur die Wissenschaften vom Menschen, Vienna, 90, 92; lectr Metropolitan Col, Boston, 91, 93; lectr Univ Mass, Boston, 95-96; lectr Simmons Col, 95-97; master lectr, Suffolk Univ, 92-98; vis asst prof Simmons Col, 97-99. **HONORS AND AWARDS** Highest honors, 83, 87; Hum Scholar Award, 94; Philos Soc Fac Award, 96; nom Tchr of the Year, 96. **MEMBERSHIPS** APA. **RESEARCH** Ethics, Heidegger, philosophy of language; Quine. **SELECTED PUBLICATIONS** Auth, Indeterminacy of Translation/ Subdeterminacy of Theory: A Critique, Dialogos, 89; auth, Heidegger y Quine: La Posibilidad de un Dialogo, Dialogos, 94; auth, Traditional Language and Technological Language, Jour of Philos Res, 98; auth, Quine and Heidegger on Meaning, Dialogos, 98; auth, Heidegger on Traditional Language and Technological Language, Proceedings, Twentieth World Congress of Philosophy, 99. **CONTACT ADDRESS** Dept of Philosophy, Simmons Col, Boston, MA, 02115. **EMAIL** wgregory@simmons.edu

GREIG, ALEXANDER JOSEF
PERSONAL Born 11/18/1938, Lander, WY, m, 1961 **DISCIPLINE** THEOLOGY **EDUCATION** Union Col, BA, 61; Andrews Univ, MA, 62; Seventh-day Adventist Theol Sem, BD,

63; Edinburgh Univ, PhD(Old Testament), 74. **CAREER** Pastor, Seventh-day Adventist Church, 64-71; Asst Prof Relig, Andrews Univ, 71-. **MEMBERSHIPS** Soc Bibl Lit. **RESEARCH** Old Testament theology; Biblical studies. **CONTACT ADDRESS** Andrews Univ, 100 US Hwy 31, Berrien Springs, MI, 49104-0001. **EMAIL** greigj@andrews.edu

GREIG, GARY S.
DISCIPLINE OLD TESTAMENT **EDUCATION** Hebrew Univ, BA; Univ Chicago, MA, PhD. **CAREER** Assoc prof, 95. **RESEARCH** Near eastern languages and civilizations. **SELECTED PUBLICATIONS** Auth, The World with Power, Ventura: Regal, 93; Signs and Wonders: Bibl Overview, Third Wave Movement, A Practical Encycl of Evangel and Church Growth, Ventura, Regal, 95; Repenting of the Sins of Our Fathers, Ministries Today, 97. **CONTACT ADDRESS** Dept of Old Testament, Regent Univ, 1000 Regent Univ Dr, Virginia Beach, VA, 23464 9831.

GRELLE, BRUCE
PERSONAL Born 04/20/1956, Indianapolis, IN, m, 1974, 1 child **DISCIPLINE** RELIGION **EDUCATION** Univ Chicago, PhD, 93. **CAREER** Instr, Univ Tenn, 86-89; asst prof, 89-95, assoc prof and dir, Relig and Public Educ Resource Ctr, Calif State Univ, Chico, 95- . **MEMBERSHIPS** Am Acad Relig; Soc of Christian Ethics. **RESEARCH** Comparative religion; ethics; religion and society; religion and public education. **SELECTED PUBLICATIONS** Auth, Comparative Religious Ethics as a Form of Critical Inquiry, Annual of the Soc of Christian Ethics, 93; auth, Hegemony and the Universalization of Moral Ideas: Gramsci's Significance for Comparative Religious Ethics, Soundings, 95; coauth, Comparative Religious Ethics and Human Rights: A New Venue, Annual of the Soc of Christian Ethics, 95; coauth, Beyond Socialization and Multiculturalism: Rethinking the Task of Citizenship Education in a Pluralistic Society, Social Educ, 96; auth, Scholarship and Citizenship: Comparative Religious Ethicists as Public Intellectuals, in Twiss, ed, Explorations in Global Ethics: Comparative Religious Ethics and Interreligious Dialogue, Westview, 98; co-ed, Explorations in Global Ethics: Comparative Religious Ethics and Interreligious Dialogue, Westview, 98. **CONTACT ADDRESS** Dept of Religious Studies, California State Univ, Chico, Chico, CA, 95929-0740. **EMAIL** bgrelle@csuchico.edu

GRENZ, STANLEY J.
PERSONAL Born 01/07/1950, Alpena, MI, m, 1971, 2 children **DISCIPLINE** THEOLOGY **EDUCATION** Univ Colorado, BA, 73; Denver Conservative Baptist Sem, MDiv, 76; Univ Munich, DTheol, 80. **CAREER** Adj prof, Univ Winnipeg and Providence Sem, 80-81; prof theol, North Am Baptist Sem, 81-90; prof, Carey/Regent Col, 90- ; affil prof, Northern Baptist Theolog Sem, 96- . **HONORS AND AWARDS** Phi Beta Kappa, 73; Robert G. Kay Scholastic Awd, 76; Magna Cum Laude, 80; Outstanding Young Men of Am,82; Fulbright Scholar, 87-88; listed, Who's Who in Religion, 92-93, Men of Achievement, 93; Theol Scholar and Res Awd, 93; Intl Man of the Year, 93. **MEMBERSHIPS** Can Evangel Theolog Asn; Am Acad of Relig; Natl Asn of Baptist Prof of Relig. **SELECTED PUBLICATIONS** Auth, Revisioning Evangelical Theology, InterVarsity, 93; auth, Theology for the Community of God, Broadman & Holman, 94; co-auth, Betrayal of Trust: Sexual Misconduct in the Pastorate, InterVarsity, 95; auth, Women and the Church: A Biblical Theology of Women in Ministry, InterVarsity, 95; auth, A Primer on Postmodernism, Eerdmans, 96; auth, Created for Community: Connecting Christian Belief with Christian Living, Baker/BridgePoint, 96; coauth, Who Needs Theology? An Invitation to the Study of God, InterVarsity, 96; auth, Sexual Ethics: An Evangelical Perspective, John Knox, 97; auth, The Moral Quest: Foundations for Christian Ethics, InterVarsity, 97; auth, What Christians Really Believe...and Why, John Knox, 98; coauth, The Fortress Introduction to Contemporary Theology, Fortress, 98; auth, Welcoming But Not Affirming: An Evangelical Response to Homosexuality, John Knox, 98; auth of numerous articles. **CONTACT ADDRESS** 5920 Iona Dr, Vancouver, BC, V6T 1J6. **EMAIL** sgrenz@unixg.ubc.ca

GRESCHNER, DONNA
DISCIPLINE LAW **EDUCATION** Univ Saskatchewan, BC, 79, LLB, 80; Oxford Univ, BCL, 82. **CAREER** Prof, 82- **SELECTED PUBLICATIONS** Auth, pubs on women and the constitution, Aboriginal peoples, and human rights legislation. **CONTACT ADDRESS** Col of Law, Univ Saskatchewan, 15 Campus Dr, Saskatoon, SK, S7N 5A6. **EMAIL** Greschne@law.usask.ca

GREY, THOMAS C.
PERSONAL Born 09/01/1941, San Francisco, CA, 1 child **DISCIPLINE** LAW **EDUCATION** Stanford Univ, BA, 63; Oxford Univ, BA, 65; Yale Univ, L1B, 68. **CAREER** Asst prof, 71-74, assoc prof, 74-78, PROF LAW, STANFORD UNIV, 78-. **RESEARCH** Constitutional law; legal philosophy; history of legal thought. **SELECTED PUBLICATIONS** Auth, Thayer Doctrine--Notes on Its Origin, Scope, and Present Implications, Northwestern Univ Law Rev, Vol 0088, 93; Justice Holmes, Oliver, Wendell--Law and the Inner Self, NY Rev of Bks, Vol 0042, 95; The Collected Works of Justice Holmes--Complete Public Writings and Selected Judicial Opinions of Holmes, Oliver, Wendell, NY Rev of Bks, Vol 0042, 95; The Complete Holmes--A Reply, NY Rev of Bks, Vol 0042, 95; The Essential Holmes--Selections from the Letters, Speeches, Judicial Opinions, and Other Writings of Holmes, Oliver, Wendell, NY Rev of Bks, Vol 0042, 95; Objectivity and Hagiography in Judicial Biography--Commentary--Unrepeatable Lessons, NY Univ Law Rev, Vol 0070, 95; Patterns of American Jurisprudence, Yale Law J, Vol 0106, 96. **CONTACT ADDRESS** Law Sch, Stanford Univ, Stanford, CA, 99305.

GRIENER, GEORGE E.
PERSONAL Born 02/04/1942, Atlanta, GA, s **DISCIPLINE** THEOLOGY **EDUCATION** Spring Hill Col, BS, 67' Regis Col, MDiv, 73; St Michael's Col U of T, MA, 75; Univ Tubingen, ThD, 88. **CAREER** Jesuit School Theol Berkeley, asst prof, assoc prof, acad dean, 89-. **MEMBERSHIPS** AAR, CTSA, USCHS. **RESEARCH** 18th and 19th century theological history. **CONTACT ADDRESS** Jesuit Sch of Theol, Berkeley, 1735 LeRoy Ave, Berkeley, CA, 94709. **EMAIL** ggriener@jstb.edu

GRIFFIN, NICHOLAS
PERSONAL Born 10/22/1947, Loughborough, England, m, 1971, 1 child **DISCIPLINE** PHILOSOPHY **EDUCATION** Univ Leicester, BA, 70; Australian Nat Univ, PhD(philos), 75. **CAREER** Asst lectr gen studies, Grimsby Col Technol, 70-71; fel philos, Victoria Univ, Wellington, 75-76; asst prof, 76-82, ASSOC PROF PHILOS, MCMASTER UNIV, 82-. **MEMBERSHIPS** Can Philos Asn. **RESEARCH** Philosophical logic; Bertrand Russell; philosophy of science. **SELECTED PUBLICATIONS** Auth, Russell,Bertrand as a Critic of Religion: Natural Theology, Christian Tradition, and Freethinkers in the Reactionary Obstructionism and Theological Emancipation of 19th-Century Britain, Stud in Relig-Sci Religieuses, Vol 0024, 95. **CONTACT ADDRESS** Dept Philos, McMaster Univ, 1280 Main St W, Hamilton, ON, L8S 4K1.

GRIFFIN, PAUL R.
PERSONAL Born 02/27/1944, Bridgeport, OH, m, 1970, 2 children **DISCIPLINE** RELIGIOUS HISTORY **EDUCATION** Emory Univ, PhD, 83. **CAREER** Asst prof, assoc prof, acad dean, prof, Payne Theol Sem, 79-88; asst prof, assoc prof, chemn, dept of relig, dir African and African American Stud, Wright State Univ, 88- . **HONORS AND AWARDS** Founder, dir, of Black Relig Conf, Wright State Univ, 95; Parity 2000 Award in recognition of acad achievement and commun serv, 97. **MEMBERSHIPS** Am Acad Relig; Am Soc of Church Hist; Am Hist Assoc; Soc for Stud of Black Relig. **RESEARCH** American racism; African American religious history. **SELECTED PUBLICATIONS** Auth, The Struggles for A Black Theology of Education: The Pioneering Efforts of Post Civil War Clergy, Interdenominational Theol Center, 93; auth, Absalom Jones: A Dissenting Voice, Va Sem Jour, 95; auth, Theological Ideas Gone Awry: The Shaping of American Racism, in Turner, ed, Dissent and Empowerment: Essays in Honor of Gayraud S. Wilmore, Westminster, 99; auth, Seeds of Racism in the Soul of America, Pilgrim, 99. **CONTACT ADDRESS** Dept of Religion, Wright State Univ, Dayton, OH, 45435. **EMAIL** PGriffin@desire.wright.edu

GRIFFIN, RONALD CHARLES
PERSONAL Born 08/17/1943, Washington, m **DISCIPLINE** LAW **EDUCATION** Hampton Inst, BS 1965; Harvard Univ, attended 1965; Howard Univ, JD 1968; Univ VA, LLM 1974. **CAREER** Office Corp Counsel Dist of Columbia Govt, legal intern 1968-69, legal clerk 1969-70, asst corp counsel 1970; the JAG School AUS, instructor 1970-74; Univ of OR, asst prof; Notre Dame Univ, visiting prof 1981-82; Washburn Univ, prof of law. **HONORS AND AWARDS** Rockefeller Found Grant; Outstanding Young Men of Amer Awd 1971; Outstanding Educators of Amer Awd 1973; Intl Men of Achievement 1976; Outstanding Young Man of Amer Awd 1979; William O Douglas Awd Outstanding Prof 1985-86. **MEMBERSHIPS** Mem Legal Educ Com Young Lawyers Sect Amer Bar Assn; Young Lawyers Liaison Legal Educ & Admission to Bar Sect Amer Bar Assn; mem Bankruptcy Com Fed Bar Assn; mem OR Consumer League 1974-75; grievance examiner Mid-West Region EEOC 1984-85; mediator NE Kansas Region Consumer Protection Complaints Better Business Bureau 1984-87, pres Central States Law School Assn 1987-88; vice chairperson, Kansas Continuing Legal Education Commission, 1989-90; board member, The Brown Foundation. **CONTACT ADDRESS** Sch of Law, Washburn Univ, 17th and MacVicar, Topeka, KS, 66621.

GRIFFITH, ELWIN JABEZ
PERSONAL Born 03/02/1938, m **DISCIPLINE** LAW **EDUCATION** Long Island Univ, BA 1960; Brooklyn Law Sch, JD 1963; NYU, LLM 1964. **CAREER** Modern HS, teacher 1955-56; Chase Manhattan Bank, asst couns 1964-71; Cleveland Marshall Law Sch, asst prof 1968; Tchrs Ins & Annuity Assn, asst consl 1971-72; Drake Univ, asst dean & asst prof 1972-73; Univ of Cincinnati Coll of Law, assoc dean & prof 1973-78; DePaul Law School, dean & prof 1978-85; FLorida State Univ Coll of Law, prof 1986-. **MEMBERSHIPS** Barbados Indp Com 1966; Bedford-Stuyvesant Jr C of C 1970-72; mem Black Exec Exchg Prof 1971; mem NY State Bar Assn; Amer Bar Assn. **SELECTED PUBLICATIONS** Publ "Final Payment & Warranties Under the Uniform Commercial Code" 1973; "Truth-in-Lending & Real Estate Transactions" 1974; "Some Rights & Disabilities of Aliens" 1975; "Deportation of Aliens - Some Aspects" 1975; "The Creditor, Debtor & the Fourteenth Amendment Some Aspects" 1977. **CONTACT ADDRESS** Law Sch, Florida State Univ, Tallahassee, FL, 32306.

GRIFFITH, GWENDOLYN
DISCIPLINE ALTERNATIVE DISPUTE RESOLUTION; FAMILY LAW; FEDERAL TAXATION **EDUCATION** Rollins Col, BA, 78; Stanford Univ, JD, 81. **CAREER** Attache de Recherche, Europ Univ Inst, Florence, 81-82; assoc, Akin, Gump, Strauss, Hauer & Feld, Dallas, 82-86; asst prof, Fla State Univ, 86-87; assoc prof, 87-93; prof, 93-. **MEMBERSHIPS** Mem, Stanford Law Rev. **SELECTED PUBLICATIONS** Coauth, Corporate Taxation, 92; editor-in-ch, Stanford Jour Intl Law. **CONTACT ADDRESS** Sch of Law, Willamette Univ, 900 State St, Salem, OR, 97301. **EMAIL** ggriffit@willamette.edu

GRIFFITH, STEPHEN R.
PERSONAL Born 07/01/1943, Williamsport, PA, m, 1965, 4 children **DISCIPLINE** PHILOSOPHY **EDUCATION** Cornell Univ, AB, 66; Univ Pittsburgh, MA, 68, PhD, 73. **CAREER** Prof, philos, Lycoming Col, 70-. **HONORS AND AWARDS** Phi Beta Kappa, Cornell; Phi Sigma Tau; Phi Kappa Phi; NDEA Title IV Fel; Andrew Mellon Fel; Woodrow Wilson Dissertation Fel; NEH Summer Seminars. **MEMBERSHIPS** Amer Philos Asn; Soc of Christ Philos. **RESEARCH** Philosophy of religion; Philosophy of science; Ethics; Political philosophy; Philosophy of mind. **SELECTED PUBLICATIONS** Auth, Miracles and the Shroud of Turin, Faith and Philos; vol 13, no 1, jan, 96; auth, Could It Have Been Reasonable For the Disciples to Have Believed That Jesus Had Risen From the Dead?, Jour of Philos Res, vol XXI, 96; auth, Fetal Death, Fetal Pain, and the Morality of Abortion, Pub Affairs Quart, vol 9, no 2, apr, 95; auth, Prayer in Public School, Pub Affairs Quart, vol 1, no 2, 97-109, apr, 87; auth, How Not to Argue About Abortion, Philos Res Archives, vol XI, 347-354, mar, 86; rev, The Actor and the Spectator, Philos Rev, vol 86, 418-421, jul, 77. **CONTACT ADDRESS** 136 Huffman Av., Williamsport, PA, 17701. **EMAIL** griffith@uplink.net

GRIFFITH, THOMAS D.
DISCIPLINE TAXATION **EDUCATION** Brown Univ, AB,71; Harvard Univ, MAT,72, JD,82. **CAREER** John B. Milliken prof, Univ Southern Calif; private practice, Boston. **RESEARCH** Contracts, corporate taxation, criminal law &federal income tax. **SELECTED PUBLICATIONS** Auth, Do Three Strikes Make Sense? Habitual Offender Statutes as a Method of Crime Control & Theories of Personal Deductions in the Income Tax; coauth, Fed Income Tax: Examples & Explanation; Social Welfare & the Rate Structure: A New Look at Progressive Taxation. **CONTACT ADDRESS** School of Law, Univ Southern Calif, University Park Campus, Los Angeles, CA, 90089.

GRIGSBY, MARSHALL C.
PERSONAL Born 08/18/1946, Charlotte, NC, m **DISCIPLINE** THEOLOGY **EDUCATION** Morehouse Coll, BA 1968; Univ of Chicago Div Sch, MTh 1970, DMn 1972. **CAREER** Black Legislative Clearing House, exec dir 1970-72; First Unitarian Church of Chicago, assoc minister 1970-75; S Shore Comm Planning Assn, project dir 1972; Assn of Theology Schools, assoc dir 1973-75; Howard Univ School of Religion, asst dean/assoc professor, 1976-85; BENEDICT COLLEGE, COLUMBIA, SC, PRESIDENT, 1985-. **HONORS AND AWARDS** Fellowship recipient So Fellowships Fund Inc 1968-71; Fellowship recipient Fund for Theol Educ Inc 1969-71; Regional Finalist White House Fellows Program 1978. **MEMBERSHIPS** Ordained minister Unitarian Universalist Ch 1970-; mem Soc for the Study of Black Religion 1973-; consult Assn of Theol Schs 1975-; natl selection panel Fund for Theol Educ Inc 1976; consult Religion Div of the Lilly Endowment 1977-; mem Natl Counc of Negro Women 1979-; member, Columbia City Board of South Carolina National; member, Junior Achievement of Greater Columbia; board of trustees, ETV Endowment of South Carolina. **CONTACT ADDRESS** Benedict Col, Harden & Blanding St, Columbia, SC, 29204.

GRILL, T.R.
PERSONAL Born 10/02/1946, Rochester, NY **DISCIPLINE** PHILOSOPHY OF SCIENCE **EDUCATION** Univ Ky, BS, 68; Univ Calif, Berkeley, MA, 70, PhD, 73. **CAREER** Asst prof, Lawrence Univ, Wisc, 74-76; instr, Univ Calif, Santa Cruz exten, 86-92; sr tech writer, ed, Univ Calif, Lawrence Livermore Nat Lab, 78- . **HONORS AND AWARDS** Phi Beta Kappa; assoc fel, Soc for Tech Commun, 92; assoc, Faxon Inst, 91-92; ed in chief, Jour of Computer Documentation, 95-; assoc ed, Tech Commun, 83-90. **MEMBERSHIPS** Philos of Sci Asn; British Soc Philos of Sci; Hist of Sci Soc; APA; ASIS; Soc Tech Commun. **RESEARCH** Scientific explanation; online text structure; information access; text usability. **SELECTED PUBLICATIONS** Auth, Among the Professions, Soc for Tech Commun, 91; auth, Extended Subject Access to Hypertext On-

line Documentation, JASIS, 91; auth, Information Chunking as an Interface Design Issue for Full- text Databases, in Dillon, ed, Interfaces for Information Retrieval, Greenwood, 91; auth, Hierarchical Search Support for Hypertext Online Documentation, Int Jour of Man-Machine Stud, 92; auth, Contributions of the Open-Commentary Journal, Proceeddings of the 1997 IEEE International Professional Communication Conference, IEEE, 97. **CONTACT ADDRESS** Lawrence Livermore National Laboratory, Univ of California, Santa Cruz, L-72, PO Box 808, Livermore, CA, 94550. **EMAIL** trg@llnl.gov

GRILLO, LAURA
PERSONAL Born 08/22/1956, New York, NY, m, 1998 **DISCIPLINE** HISTORY OF RELIGIONS **EDUCATION** Brown Univ, Ab, 78; Union Theol Sem NY, MDiv, 86; Univ Chicago, PhD, 95. **CAREER** Asst prof, Millsaps Coll, 95-97; Sr Fel, Inst for Advanced Study of Rel, Univ Chicago, 97-98; Vis Asst Prof, Coll Wooster, 98-99. **HONORS AND AWARDS** Charles M Ross Trust grants 80-84, 89-90; Joseph M Kitagawa Scholar, Award in Hist of Rel, 87-88; Jr Fel, Inst for Advanced Study of Rel, 92-93; am Acad of Rel grant, 96; west African Res Asn grant, 97; Nat Endowment for Humanities grant, 97; Inst for Advanced Study of Rel, Univ Chicago Sr Fel, 97-98. **MEMBERSHIPS** Am Acad of Rel; African Studies Asn; West African Res Asn; Int Asn of Hist of Rel; am Asn Univ Prof. **RESEARCH** Method and theory of the Study of Religions; African Religions; Anthropology; Comparative Ethics; Philosophy of religion. **SELECTED PUBLICATIONS** Auth, African Traditional Religions, Encarta Encycl, 97; Divination in Contemporary Urban West Africa, Rel Study News, 98; The Body in African Religions, Purification, The Circle and African Religions, Encycl of Women and World Rel, forthcoming; Dogon: religionsgeschichtlich, Rel in Geschichte und Gegenwart, forthcoming. **CONTACT ADDRESS** 1046 Mindy Ln, #3, Wooster, OH, 44691. **EMAIL** lgrillo@acs.wooster.edu

GRIM, JOHN A.
PERSONAL Born 10/07/1946, ND, m, 1978 **DISCIPLINE** HISTORY OF RELIGION **EDUCATION** St. John's Univ, BA, 68; Fordham Univ, MA, 75, PhD, 79. **CAREER** Adj lectr, Col of Mt St Vincent, 76-79; adj lectr, St Francis Col, 79; adj lectr, Col of New Rochelle, 79-80; vis prof, Fordham Univ, 79-80; vis prof, Maryknoll Grad Sch of Theol, 80-81; assoc prof, Elizabeth Seton Col, 77-87; Hum Div, Sarah Lawrence Col, 86-89; assoc prof, 89-98, PROF, CHAIR RELIG DEPT, BUCKNELL UNIV, 98-; COORD, FORUM ON RELIG AND ECOLOGY, 89-. **HONORS AND AWARDS** V.Kann-Rasmussen Awd, 98; Aga Khan Trust for Culture Grant, 98; Sacharuna Found Grant, 97; Laurance Rockefeller Found Grant, 97; Sr Fel, Center for the Study of World Religions, Harvard Univ, Spring 97. **SELECTED PUBLICATIONS** Auth, The Shaman: Patterns of Siberian and Ojibway Healing, Civilization of the Am Indian Series, Univ of Okla Press, 83, 87; Native North and South American Mystical Traditions, An Anthology of Mysticism, Univ of Calif Press, forthcoming; An Awful Feeling of Loneliness: Native North American Mystical Traditions, Doors of Understanding: Conversations on Global Spirituality in Honor of Ewert Cousins, Franciscan Press, 97; A Comparative Study in Native American Philanthropy, Philanthropy and Culture: A Comparative Perspective, Indiana Univ Press, 97; Rituals Among Native Americans, Handbook in Anthrop of Relig, Greenwood Press, 97; co-ed, Worldviews and Ecology: Religion, Philosophy, and the Environment, Bucknell Univ Press, 93, Orbis Press, 94. **CONTACT ADDRESS** Dept of Relig, Bucknell Univ, Lewisburg, PA, 17837. **EMAIL** grim@bucknell.edu

GRIM, PATRICK
PERSONAL Born 10/29/1950, Pasadena, CA, m, 1977 **DISCIPLINE** PHILOSOPHY **EDUCATION** Univ Calif, Santa Cruz, AB(philos), 71, AB(anthrop), 71; Univ St Andrews BPhil, 75; Boston Univ, MA and PhD(philos), 76. **CAREER** Vis asst prof philos, State Univ NY, Stony Brook, 76-77; Mellon fac fel, Wash Univ, 77-78; ASST PROF PHILOS, STATE UNIV NY, STONY BROOK, 78-, Fulbright fel, 71-72; Mellon fac fel, 77-78. **MEMBERSHIPS** Am Philos Asn; Soc Philos Study of Paranormal; Ctr Sci Anomalies Res. **RESEARCH** Philosophy of science; contemporary philosophy of religion; ethics, medical ethics and philosophy of law. **SELECTED PUBLICATIONS** Auth, Operators in the Paradox of the Knower, Synthese, Vol 0094, 93. **CONTACT ADDRESS** Dept Philos, State Univ NY, 100 Nicolls Rd, Stony Brook, NY, 11794-0002.

GRIMES, DOUGLAS M.
PERSONAL Born 08/11/1942, Marshall, TX, m **DISCIPLINE** LAW **EDUCATION** CA St Coll BA 1965; Howard Univ Sch of Law, JD 1968. **CAREER** Pvt Practice, Grimes, Barnes & Gill, atty 1971-; Univ of IL Coll of Law, asst prof of Law & dir Comm Involvement 1970-71; Cont IL Nat Bank & Co Chicago, adm asst 1968-70. **MEMBERSHIPS** Has taught real estate IN U; asst city atty City of Gary; Police Civil Serv Commn; Gary Fire Commn; pres Legal Aid Soc of Gary; pres Thurgood Marshall Law Assn; legal adv Minority Businessmens Steering Com; legal adv Lake Co Corner; mem Gary Jaycees; Urban League of NW IN Inc adv bd NW IN UrbanLeague; mem Gary Frontiers Serv Club; sec treas bd mem Gary Leased Housing Corp; mem IN St Black Assembly; mem Gary chap IN St Black Assembly; del Nat Black Assembly Conv 1972-74; bd dir Gary Gus Resource Ctr; past mem Chicago Jaycees, Southend Jaycees; former public dfndr, Gary City Ct; former legal & counsel IN Jaycees. **CONTACT ADDRESS** 562 Washington St, Gary, IN.

GRIMES, JOHN ALLEN
PERSONAL Born 01/24/1948, Berkeley, CA, m, 1979, 1 child **DISCIPLINE** PHILOSOPHY AND RELIGION **EDUCATION** Univ Madras, PhD, 85. **CAREER** Asst prof, Univ Lethbridge, 89-93; asst prof, Singapore Univ, 95-96; asst prof, Mich State Univ, 97-. **MEMBERSHIPS** AAR; APA. **RESEARCH** Adraita vedanta; Ganesha; Ancient India education; Heidegger. **SELECTED PUBLICATIONS** Auth, A Concise Dictionary of Indian Philosophy, State Univ NY SUNY Press, 96; auth, Ganapati: Song of the Self, State Univ NY SUNY Press, 95; auth, Problems and Perspectives in Religious Discourse, Advaita Vedanta Implications, State Univ NY SUNY Press, 94; auth, Crest Jewel of Discrimination (Vivekacudamani), text, trans, and commentary, State Univ NY SUNY Press, in press. **CONTACT ADDRESS** Dept. of Religious Studies, Michigan State Univ, 116 Morrill Hall, East Lansing, MI, 48824. **EMAIL** grimesj@pilot.msu.edu

GRIMES, RONALD L.
PERSONAL Born 05/19/1943, San Diego, CA, m, 1984, 2 children **DISCIPLINE** RELIGION **EDUCATION** Ky Wesleyan Col, BA, 61; Emory Univ, MDiv, 64; Columbia Univ & Union Theol Sem, PhD, 70. **CAREER** Asst prof, Lawrence Univ, 70-74; PROF RELIGION & CULTURE, WILFRID LAURIER UNIV, 74-; vis prof, Univ Pittsburgh, 85-86; vis prof, Univ Notre Dame, 87; vis prof, Univ Colo, 92-94. **HONORS AND AWARDS** Westview Press award of excellence, 96. **MEMBERSHIPS** Am Acad Rel; Am Anthro Asn; Can Soc Study Rel; Soc Cult Anthro; Soc for Study Native Am Rel Traditions. **RESEARCH** Ritual studies; rel and contemporary North Am cult; rel and the soc scis. **SELECTED PUBLICATIONS** Auth, The Divine Imagination, 72; auth, Symbol and Conquest, 76, 2nd ed, 92; auth, Beginnings in Ritual Studies, 82, 2nd ed, 94; auth, Research in Ritual Studies, 85; auth, Ritual Criticism, 90; auth, Reading, Writing and Ritualizing, 93; auth, Marrying & Burying, 95; auth, Readings in Ritual Studies, 96. **CONTACT ADDRESS** Dept of Religion, Wilfrid Laurier Univ, Waterloo, ON, N2L 3C5. **EMAIL** rgrimes@mach1.wlu.ca

GRIMSRUD, THEODORE G.
DISCIPLINE THEOLOGY & PHILOSOPHY **EDUCATION** Univ OR, BS, 76; Assoc Mennonite Biblical Sem, MA, 83; Grad Theol Union, PhD, 88. **CAREER** Theol Dept, Eastern Mennonite Univ **SELECTED PUBLICATIONS** Auth, Triumph of the Lamb, Herald Press, 87; Peace Theology and the Justice of God in the Book of Revelation, Inst Mennonite Studies, 88; Mennonite Theology and Historical Consciousness: A Pastoral Perspective, Mennonite Theol Face Modernity, 96. **CONTACT ADDRESS** Eastern Mennonite Univ, 1200 Park Road, Harrisonburg, VA, 22802-2462.

GRITSCH, ERIC W.
PERSONAL Born 04/19/1931, Neuhaus, Austria, m, 1955 **DISCIPLINE** RELIGION, HISTORY **EDUCATION** Yale Univ, STM, 55, MA, 58, PhD(relig), 60; Univ Vienna, BD, 56. **CAREER** Instr Bible, Wellesley Col, 59-61; PROF CHURCH HIST, LUTHERAN THEOL SEM, GETTYSBURG, 61-, DIR INST LUTHER STUDIES, 70-, Asn Am Theol Schs fel, Univ Heidelberg, 67-68; rep scholar, Lutheran-Roman Cath Dialog in USA, 72-. **MEMBERSHIPS** Am Soc Church Hist; Am Soc Reformation Res; AAUP. **RESEARCH** German Reformation to 1900; European history of theology; Thomas Muenzer and Martin Luther. **SELECTED PUBLICATIONS** Auth, The Radical Reformation, 3rd ed, Cath Hist Rev, Vol 0080, 94; Revelation and Revolution--Basic Writings of Muntzer, Thomas, Cath Hist Rev, Vol 0080, 94; The Term Argernis in the Reformation--Concept-Historical Approach to the Biblically Legitimized Political-System of Ethics, Cath Hist Rev, Vol 0083, 97. **CONTACT ADDRESS** Dept of Church History, Gettysburg Col, Gettysburg, PA, 17325.

GROARKE, LEO A.
PERSONAL Born 07/18/1953, London, England **DISCIPLINE** PHILOSOPHY **EDUCATION** Univ Calgary, BA, 75, MA, 77; Univ Western Ont, PhD, 82. **CAREER** Fac mem, 83-94, PROF PHILOSOPHY, WILFRID LAURIER UNIV, 94-. **MEMBERSHIPS** Can Philos Asn; Int Soc Stud Argumentation; Concerned Philos Peace. **RESEARCH** History of philosophy, logic, & ethics. **SELECTED PUBLICATIONS** Auth, Greek Skepticism: Anti-Realist Trends in Ancient Thought, 90; coauth, Good Reasoning Matters!, 89, rev ed, 96; co-ed, Nuclear War: Philosophical Perspectives, 85. **CONTACT ADDRESS** Dept of Philosophy, Wilfrid Laurier Univ, Waterloo, ON, N2L 3C5. **EMAIL** lgroarke@mach1.wlu.ca

GROMADA, CONRAD T.
PERSONAL Born 01/18/1939, Youngstown, OH, m, 1987 **DISCIPLINE** ROMAN CATHOLIC THEOLOGY; SYSTEMATIC THEOLOGY **EDUCATION** Duquesne Univ, Pittsburgh, PhD, 88. **CAREER** Dean Arts & Sciences, Ursuline Col. **MEMBERSHIPS** Am Acad Relig; Col Theol Soc; Cath Theol Soc Am **RESEARCH** Sacraments; Ecclesiology; Christology. **SELECTED PUBLICATIONS** Auth, Theology of Ministry in the Lima Document: A Roman Catholic Critique, Int Scholars Press, 95. **CONTACT ADDRESS** Ursuline Col, 2550 Lander Rd., Pepper Pike, OH, 44124-4398. **EMAIL** cgromada@ursuline.edu

GRONBACHER, GREGORY
PERSONAL Born 05/27/1965, New York, NY, s **DISCIPLINE** PHILOSOPHY **EDUCATION** Milltown Institute of Theology and Philosophy, PhD, 95. **CAREER** Asst prof of theology and philosophy, Mt Aloysius Col, 94-95; Dir of Academic Research, Acton Institute, 95- . **RESEARCH** Philosophy of economics; social theory; Catholic social thought. **CONTACT ADDRESS** 161 Ottawa NW, #301, Grand Rapids, MI, 49503. **EMAIL** ggbacher@acton.org

GROOME, THOMAS H.
PERSONAL Born 09/30/1945, Dublin, Ireland, m, 1985 **DISCIPLINE** RELIGIOUS EDUCATION **EDUCATION** St Patrick's Sem IR, MDiv, 68; Fordham Univ, MS, Rel/Edu, 71; Union Theol SEM, Doc Rel/Edu, 75. **CAREER** Prof Theol, presently, Boston College. **MEMBERSHIPS** AAR; CTSA; APRRE. **RESEARCH** Interface of Ideology and Contemporary Culture. **SELECTED PUBLICATIONS** Auth, Educating for Life: A Spiritual Vision for Every Teacher and Parent, Allen TX, Thomas Moore Press, 98; Sharing Faith: A Comprehensive Approach to Religious Education and Pastoral Ministry, San Francisco, Harper and Row, 91; Language for a Catholic Church, KA City, Sheed and Ward, 91; primary auth of new revised, Coming to Faith, series, WH Sadlier, 95. **CONTACT ADDRESS** Inst of Religious Education, Boston Col, Chestnut Hill, MA, 02167. **EMAIL** groomet@bc.edu

GROOTHUIS, DOUGLAS
PERSONAL m **DISCIPLINE** PHILOSOPHY OF RELIGION AND ETHICS **EDUCATION** Univ Wis-Madison, MA; Univ Ore, PhD. **CAREER** Prof, Denver Sem, 93-. **SELECTED PUBLICATIONS** Auth, Unmasking the New Age; Confronting the New Age; Christianity That Counts; Deceived by the Light; Jesus in an Age of Controversy and The Soul in Cyberspace; pub(s), scholarly jour(s), Rel Stud, Sophia, Jour of the Evangel Theol Soc, Trinity Jour; Christianity Today; Moody Magazine; Christian Res Jour; ed, auth, Women Caught in the Conflict and Good News for Women. **CONTACT ADDRESS** Denver Conservative Baptist Sem, PO Box 10000, Denver, CO, 80250. **EMAIL** doug@densem.edu

GROS, JEFFREY
PERSONAL Born 01/07/1938, Memphis, TN **DISCIPLINE** THEOLOGY **EDUCATION** Marquette Univ, MA, 65; Forham Univ, PhD, 73. **CAREER** Seminary/Univ teaching, Christian Brothers Univ/Memphis Theol Sem, 72-81; ecumenical administration, Faith and Order, Nat Coun of Churches, 81-91; Ecumenical Affairs, Nat Conf of Cath Bishops, 91-. **HONORS AND AWARDS** Chicago Heart Asn, fel, 60, 61; Cath Diocesean Ecumenical Officers Award, 84. **MEMBERSHIPS** Cath Theol Soc; Col Theol Soc; Am Academy Relig; Nat Asn of Evangelicals; North Am Academy of Ecumenists. **RESEARCH** Ecclesiology: Catholicism, the Reformation Churches, Am Evangelicalism; Sacramental Theol: Eucharist, Ministry, Baptism; Church History: Reformation, US churches, ecumenism. **SELECTED PUBLICATIONS** Ed, The Search for Visible Unity, Pilgrim Press, 84; Building Unity, co-ed with Joseph Burgess, Paulist Press, 89; Growing Consensus, co-ed with Joseph Burgess, Paulist Press, 94; Common Witness to the Gospel, Documents on Anglican-Roman Catholic Relations 1983-1995, co-ed with Rozanne Elder and Elen Wondra, US Catholic Conf, 97; Deepening Communion, co-ed with William G Rusch, US Cath Conf, 98; co-auth, with Ann Riggs, Eamon McManus, Introduction to Ecumenism, Paulist Press, 98; auth, Challenges to Lasallian Leadership in Christian Reconciliation, Lasalliana, 44, May-August 98; A Pilgrimage Together: Ecumenical Decisions before US Churches, Catechetical Leadership, Dec 98; Grace: A Challenge Together for Lutherans and Catholics, Catechetical Leadership, April/May 98; Toward a More Perfect Communion: Ecumenical Agreement and Sacramental Preparation, Catechetical Leadership, summer 98; author of numerous other articles. **CONTACT ADDRESS** Secretariat for Ecumen & Interre, National Conf of Catholic Bishops, 3211 4th St NE, Washington, DC, 20017. **EMAIL** seiamail@nccbuscc.org

GROSS, RITA M.
PERSONAL Born 07/06/1943, Rhinelander, WI **DISCIPLINE** HISTORY OF RELIGIONS **EDUCATION** Univ Wis-Milwaukee, BA, 65; Univ Chicago, MA, 68, PhD(hist relig), 75. **CAREER** Instr theol, Loyola Univ, Chicago, 70-71; instr Indian rel, New Col, Fla, 71-73; instr, 73-75, asst prof, 75-80, ASSOC PROF EASTERN RELIG, UNIV WIS-EAU CLAIRE, 80-, Mem, rev bd relig, Anima; An Experiental J, 73- and Nat Endowment Humanities, 77-. **MEMBERSHIPS** Soc Values Higher Educ; Am Acad Relig; Women's Caucus Am Acad Relig. **RESEARCH** Hindu Theism, especially the Hindu God-

desses; Hindu inconography and mythology. **SELECTED PUBLICATIONS** Auth, Why Me--Methodological-Autobiographical Reflections of a Wisconsin Farm Girl Who Became a Buddhist Theologian when She Grew Up, J Feminist Stud in Relig, Vol 0013, 97; Toward a Buddhist Environmental Ethic: Religious Responses to Problems of Population, Consumption, and Degradation of the Global Environment, J Am Acad of Relig, Vol 0065, 97. **CONTACT ADDRESS** Dept of Philos and Relig Studies, Univ of Wis, Eau Claire, WI, 54701.

GROSSMAN, NEAL
DISCIPLINE PHILOSOPHY **EDUCATION** Univ IN, PhD. **CAREER** Assoc prof, Univ IL at Chicago. **HONORS AND AWARDS** Silver Circle Tchg Awd. **RESEARCH** Philos of sci; Spinoza; psychotherapy; mysticism. **SELECTED PUBLICATIONS** Auth, pubs in Journal of Philosophy; Metaphilosophy; Philosophy of Science; and Synthese. **CONTACT ADDRESS** Philos Dept, Univ Illinois Chicago, S Halsted St, PO Box 705, Chicago, IL, 60607.

GROTH, MILES
PERSONAL Born 12/04/1946, Greensburg, PA **DISCIPLINE** PHILOSOPHY; PSYCHOLOGY **EDUCATION** Franklin and Marshall Col, AB; Fordham Univ, PhD. **CAREER** Asst prof, dept of psychology, Wagner Col; existential psychotherapy & psychoanalysis, private practice. **HONORS AND AWARDS** Outstanding Educators in Amer, 76. **MEMBERSHIPS** Amer Philos Asn; Soc Existential Anal; Amer Heidegger Conf; Asn Study Philos Unconscious; Int Soc Phenomenol & Human Sci. **RESEARCH** Heidegger; Existential analysis **SELECTED PUBLICATIONS** Auth, Preparatory Thinking in Heideggers Teaching, Philos Libr, 87; Newsletter of the Society for Existential Analysis, 96; Existential Therapy on Heideggerian Principles, Jour Soc Existential Anal, 97; Some Precursors of Poppers Evolutionary Theory of Knowledge, Philos Sci, 97; Acknowledgement on the Conferment of the National Hebel Memorial Prize, Delos, 97; The Voice That Thinks: Heidegger Studies, Eadmer Press, 97. **CONTACT ADDRESS** Dept of Psychology, Wagner Col, 111 Parker Hall, Staten Island, NY, 10301. **EMAIL** mgroth@wagner.edu

GROUNDS, VERNON
PERSONAL m, 1939 **DISCIPLINE** ETHICS AND COUNSELING **EDUCATION** Rutgers Univ, BA; Faith Theol Sem, BD; Gordon Col, LHD; Wheaton Col, DD; Drew Univ, PhD. **CAREER** Sr prof, Denver Sem, 79. **HONORS AND AWARDS** Contrib ed, Christianity Today; intl ed, Themelios. **SELECTED PUBLICATIONS** Auth, The Reason for Our Hope; Evangelicalism and Social Responsibility; Revolution and the Christian Faith; Emotional Problems and the Gospel, Radical Commitment; co-auth, Is God Dead? **CONTACT ADDRESS** Denver Conservative Baptist Sem, PO Box 10000, Denver, CO, 80250.

GROVER, DOROTHY
DISCIPLINE PHILOSOPHY **EDUCATION** Univ Pittsburgh, PhD. **CAREER** Prof, Univ IL at Chicago . **RESEARCH** Philosophical logic; philos of lang; metaphysics; epistemology. **SELECTED PUBLICATIONS** Auth, A Prosentential Theory of Truth, Princeton, 92; Truth and Language-World Connections, Journal Philo, 90; Death and Life, Can Jour Philos, 87. **CONTACT ADDRESS** Philos Dept, Univ Illinois Chicago, S Halsted St, PO Box 705, Chicago, IL, 60607.

GROVER, ROBINSON ALLEN
PERSONAL Born 02/15/1936, New York, NY **DISCIPLINE** PHILOSOPHY **EDUCATION** Yale Univ, BA, 58; Brown Univ, MA, 62, PhD(philos), 69; Yale Univ Law Sch, MA, 76. **CAREER** Instr philos, Univ CT, Storrs, 64-68; Lectr, Chapman Col, World Campus Afloat Prog, 68-69; asst prof, 69-80, Assoc Prof Philos, Univ CT, Torrington, 80-. **MEMBERSHIPS** AAUP; Am Philos Asn; Soc Legal & Polit Philos. **RESEARCH** Thomas Hobbes; Ethics; Philo of Law; Polit Theory. **SELECTED PUBLICATIONS** Auth, The Ranking Assumption, J Theory & Decision, fall 74; The Legal Origins of Thomas Hobbes's Doctrine of Contract," Spring 80; Thomas Hobbes and International Law, 89; Individualism, Absolutism, and Contract in Thomas Hobbes's Political Theory. **CONTACT ADDRESS** Dept of Philosophy, Univ of CT, 855 Univ Dr, Torrington, CT, 06790-2635. **EMAIL** grover@uconnvm.uconn.edu

GROVES, HARRY EDWARD
PERSONAL Born 09/04/1921, Manitou Springs, CO, m **DISCIPLINE** LAW **EDUCATION** Univ of CO, BA 1943; Univ of Chicago, JD 1949; Harvard Univ, LLM 1959. **CAREER** TX So Univ, dean/sch of law 1956-60; Univ of Singapore, dean/faculty of law 1960-64; Central State Univ, pres 1965-68; Sch of Law of Cincinnati, prof 1968-70; NC Central Univ Durham, dean/sch of law 1976-81; Univ of NC, prof sch of law 1981-86; Memphis State Univ, Herbert Heff visiting prof of law, 1989-90; University of Minnesota, visiting professor of law, 1992. US Olympic Committee Ethics Committee Chair, 1993. **HONORS AND AWARDS** Phi Beta Kappa; Phi Delta Kappa; Kappa Delta Pi; president, Wake County North Carolina Phi Beta Kappa 1989-90; sire archon, Alpha Tau Chapter of Sigma Pi Phi 1986-88; The Constitution of Malaysia, 4th ed. (with Sheridan) 1979; Malayan Law Journal (PTE.) LTD; Tun Abdul Razak Memorial Lecturer, Kuala Lumpur Malaysia 1983; Judge John J Parker Award, North Carolina Bar Association, 1986; American Bar Association, Robert L Kutak Award, 1997. **MEMBERSHIPS** Elected mem City Council Fayetteville NC 1951-52; chmn Gov's Task Force on Sec & Privacy 1979-; bd of dir Mutual Svgs & Loan Assn 1979-80; pres NC Prisoner Legal Serv Inc 1979-81; pres Legal Serv of NC 1983-85; mem Sigma Pi Phi, Alpha Phi Alpha Frat; mem NC, TX, OH Bar Assns; vice pres bd of gov NC Bar Assn 1986-87; board of directors, American Bar Foundation, 1986-; member, American Bar Association Council of the Section on Legal Education and Admission to the Bar, 1989-95, sec, 1998-99; board of directors, Law School Admissions Council, 1980-82. **SELECTED PUBLICATIONS** "Comparative Constitutional Law Cases & Materials" Oceana Publs Inc 1963; "The Constitution of Malaysia" Malaysia Publs Ltd 1964; pub more than 30 other books & articles. **CONTACT ADDRESS** Sch of Law, Univ of No Carolina, Chapel Hill, NC, 27599-3380.

GRUENDER, CARL DAVID
PERSONAL Born 05/24/1927, Cleveland, OH, m, 1955, 3 children **DISCIPLINE** PHILOSOPHY **EDUCATION** Antioch Col, AB, 51; Univ Chicago, AM, 53; Univ Wis, PhD, 57. **CAREER** From instr to asst prof philos, Kans State Univ, 57-63; asst prof, Case Inst Technol, 63-67; assoc prof, 67-71, chmn dept, 72-78, Prof Philos, Fla State Univ, 71-. **MEMBERSHIPS** AAAS; Western Div Am Philos Asn; Philos Sci Asn; Hist Sci Soc. **RESEARCH** Theory of knowledge; philosophy and history of science; metaphysics. **SELECTED PUBLICATIONS** Auth, Wittgenstein on Explanation and Description, J Philos, 62; auth, On Distinguishing Science from Magic, Proc 10th Int Cong Hist Sci, 64; auth, The Achilles Paradox and Transfinite Numbers, Brit J Philos Sci, 66. **CONTACT ADDRESS** Dept of Philosophy, Florida State Univ, Tallahassee, FL, 32306-1500. **EMAIL** gruender@phil.fsu.edu

GRUENLER, ROYCE GORDON
PERSONAL m, 4 children **DISCIPLINE** NEW TESTAMENT **EDUCATION** Williams Col, BA; Philadelphia Theol Sem, BD; Kings Col, Univ Aberdeen, Scotland, PhD. **CAREER** Prof, Gordon-Conwell Theol Sem, 79-. **HONORS AND AWARDS** Fulbright Scholar, Kings Col, Univ Aberdeen; post-grad Fulbright res grant, Univ Heidelberg, Ger., Sr pastor, Second Congregational Church. **MEMBERSHIPS** Mem, Phi Beta Kappa; Soc Biblical Lit; Evangel Theol Soc. **RESEARCH** Jesus and the Gospels, Romans, Pauline thought and process theology. **SELECTED PUBLICATIONS** Auth, Jesus, Persons, and the Kingdom of God, 67; New Approaches to Jesus and the Gospels, 82; The Inexhaustible God: Biblical Faith and the Challenge of Process Theism, 83; The Trinity in the Gospel of John: A Thematic Commentary on The Fourth Gospel, 86; contrib auth, Process Theology, Baker Bk House, 87; Baker's Evangelical Commentary on the Bible, Mark and Romans, 89; Meaning and Understanding: The Philosophical Framework for Biblical Interpretation, Zondervan, 91. **CONTACT ADDRESS** Gordon-Conwell Theol Sem, 130 Essex St, South Hamilton, MA, 01982.

GRUNBAUM, ADOLF
PERSONAL Born 05/15/1923, Cologne, Germany, m, 1949 **DISCIPLINE** PHILOSOPHY **EDUCATION** Wesleyan Univ, BA 43; Yale Univ, MS, 48, PhD(philos), 51. **CAREER** Physicist, Div War Res, Columbia Univ, 44, 46, consult physicist, Div Govt-Aided Res, 46-48; from instr to prof philos, Lehigh Univ, 50-56, Selfridge prof, 56-60; dir, Ctr Philos Sci, 60-78, MELLON PROF PHILOS, UNIV PITTSBURGH, 60-, Chmn Res Prof Psychiat, 79-, Ford Found fac fel, 54-55; res prof, Ctr Philos Sci, Univ Minn, 55-56; Matchette Lectr, Wesleyan Univ, 66; Louis Clark Vanuxem Lectr, Princeton Univ, 67; Monday lectr, Univ Chicago, 68; Thalheimer lectr, Johns Hopkins Univ, 69; lectr hist sci, Univ London, 76; Einstein Centennial lectr, Inst Advan Study, Princeton, 79-80. **HONORS AND AWARDS** Robinson Award, Lehigh Univ, 53; J Walker Tomb Prize, Princeton Univ, 58. **MEMBERSHIPS** AAAS; Am Acad Arts & Sci; Philos Sci Asn (pres, 65-70); Eastern Div Am Philos Asn (pres, 82). **RESEARCH** Philosophy of physics; philosophy and methodology of the natural sciences; philosophy of psychiatry. **SELECTED PUBLICATIONS** Auth, Narlikar Creation of the Big-Bang Universe Was a Mere Origination--Discussion, Philos of Sci, Vol 0060, 93; 'Freuds Permanent Revolution': A Response to Nagel, Thomas--An Exchange, NY Rev of Bks, Vol 0041, 94; Empirical Evaluations of Theoretical Explanations of Psychotherapeutic Efficacy--A Reply to Greenwood, John, D, Philos of Sci, Vol 0063, 96. **CONTACT ADDRESS** Ctr for Philos of Sci, Univ of Pittsburgh, 1001 Cathedral/Learn, Pittsburgh, PA, 15260-0001.

GRUNFELD, JOSEPH
PERSONAL Born 08/13/1924, Berlin, Germany, m, 1955, 2 children **DISCIPLINE** PHILOSOPHY **EDUCATION** Hebrew Univ, BA, 52; Hebrew Univ, MA, 55; Hebrew Univ, PhD, 59. **CAREER** Part time lectr, Hebrew Univ, 57-63; asst prof, 63-66, assoc prof, 66-70, Haile Sellassie I Univ, Addis Ababa, Ethiopia; assoc prof, 70-90, prof, 90-, Drexel Univ, Philadelphia, Penn. **MEMBERSHIPS** Amer Philos Asn; Intl Metaphysical Soc; Inst of Human Values. **RESEARCH** Philosophy of logic; Aesthetics. **SELECTED PUBLICATIONS** Auth, Incomplete Coherence, Sci et Espirit, 98; auth, Fuzzy Logic, Sci et Esprit, 95; auth, Conceptual Relevance, B. R. Gruner, Amsterdam, 89; auth, Changing Rational Standards, A Survey of Modern Philosophy of Science, Univ Press of Amer, 85; auth, Method and Lang, B. R. Gruner, Amsterdam, 82; auth, Science and Values, B. R. Gruner, Amsterdam, 73. **CONTACT ADDRESS** Nesbitt College, Drexel Univ, Philadelphia, PA, 19104.

GUDORF, CHRISTINE E.
PERSONAL Born 06/13/1949, Louisville, KY, m, 1968, 3 children **DISCIPLINE** RELIGION **EDUCATION** IN Univ BS 71; Columbia Univ, MA 76, Mphil 78, PhD 79. **CAREER** Xavier Univ, asst prof, assoc prof, prof 78-93; FL Intl Univ, assoc prof, 93-95, prof dept rel stud 95-. **HONORS AND AWARDS** Visiting Professorships, Temple Univ, Pacific Sch of Rel, Seminario San Jose in Peru, Cath Press Awds, Gutavos Meyer Awd. **MEMBERSHIPS** AAR; SCE; CTSA. **RESEARCH** Ethics in world relig soc theory; Women in world relig(s), sexuality, economic develop. **SELECTED PUBLICATIONS** Ethics and World Religions: Crosscultural Case Studies, with Regina Wolfe, Orbis 99; Body, Sex and Pleasure: Reconstructing Christian Sexual Ethics, Pilgrim, 94; Christian Ethics: A Case Method Approach, 2d ed, with R Stivers, R Evans, A Evans, Orbis, 94; Who Says the Church Can't Change? Us Catholic, 98; On the McCagheys and Children as God's Gifts, Pk Ridge Cen Bull, 98; Sacrifice and Mutuality In Catholic Spirituality, US Catholic, 97; Could I Be a Racist Too?, US Catholic, 94; Sexual Violence: It's Too Sinful to Remain Silent, SALT, Catholic Journal of Soc Just, 93. **CONTACT ADDRESS** Dept of Relig Studies, Florida Intl Univ, Miami, FL, 33199.

GUILD, SONNY
DISCIPLINE GENESIS-ESTHER, JOB-MALACHI **EDUCATION** Harding Univ, BA, 66; ACU, MDiv, 69, Dmin, 96. **CAREER** Missionary-in-Residence, 93-. **HONORS AND AWARDS** African Mission fel. **SELECTED PUBLICATIONS** Auth, Biblia Inasemaje, 82; Prepping the Mission Team, Gospel Advocate 139, 97. **CONTACT ADDRESS** Dept of Missions, Abilene Christian Univ, Abilene, TX, 79699-9000. **EMAIL** guild@bible.acu.edu

GUINAN, MICHAEL DAMON
PERSONAL Born 02/16/1939, Cincinnati, OH **DISCIPLINE** SEMITICS, SYRIAC PATRISTICS **EDUCATION** San Luis Rey Col, BA, 61; Old Mission Theol Sem, STB, 65; Cath Univ Am, STL, 67, MA, 70, PhD(Semitics), 72. **CAREER** Prof Bibl Theol & Semitic Lang, Franciscan Sch Theol, Grad Theol Union, 72-. **MEMBERSHIPS** Cath Theol Soc Am; Cath Bibl Asn; Soc Bibl Lit; Soc for Study of Christian Spirituality. **RESEARCH** Old Testament; Syriac patristic theology. **SELECTED PUBLICATIONS** Auth, The Making of Many Images: Scripture Film and Religious Education, Multimedia Int, 73; Convenant in the Old Testament, Franciscan Herald, 75; Where are the dead?, Purgatory and immedicate retribution in James of Sarug, Proc Syriac Symp of 1972; Jacob of Sarug, In: New Cath Encycl, Vol XVI; The Creation Story of Genesis: Does It Really Establish Evolution?; Angels: Their Meaning for Today; The Menila and the Millenium; Christian Spirituality: Many Styles, One Spirit-Catholic Update, 94, 95, 97, 98. **CONTACT ADDRESS** Franciscan Sch of Theol, 1712 Euclid Ave, Berkeley, CA, 94709-1294. **EMAIL** mdguinan@aol.com

GUINIER, CAROL LANI
PERSONAL m **DISCIPLINE** LAW **EDUCATION** Radcliffe College, BA, 1971; Yale Law School, JD, 1974. **CAREER** US District Judge, Damon Keith, clerk, 1974-76; Wayne County Juvenile Court, referee, 1976-77; US Dept of Justice, Civil Rights Division, 1977-81; NAACP Legal Defense Fund, 1981-88; Univ of Pennsylvania, law prof, 1992-. **HONORS AND AWARDS** Univ Penn Law School, Harvey Levin Teaching Award, 1994. **MEMBERSHIPS** Open Society Institute, trustee, 1996-; Commonplace, Inc, founder/president, 1994; Juvenile Law Ctr, Philadelphia, PA, bd of dirs, 1992-. **SELECTED PUBLICATIONS** Christian Science Monitor, essay, 1991; Lift Every Voice, author, 1998; became the first African American woman member of the Harvard law faculty, 1998. **CONTACT ADDRESS** Professor of Law, Univ of Pennsylvania, 3400 Chestnut St, Philadelphia, PA, 19104.

GULLEY, ANTHONY D.
PERSONAL Born 04/27/1930, Watervliet, NY **DISCIPLINE** PHILOSOPHY **EDUCATION** St Joseph's Sem, NY, BA, 52; St Bernardine of Siena Col, MS, 58; Cath Univ Am, PhD, 61. **CAREER** From instr to assoc prof philos, 61-73, Prof Educ, Col St Rose, 73- **MEMBERSHIPS** Am Cath Philos Asn; Nat Cath Educ Asn; NEA. **CONTACT ADDRESS** Col of Saint Rose, Albany, NY, 12203-1490.

GUMMS, EMMANUEL GEORGE, SR.
PERSONAL Born 01/16/1928, Opelusas, LA, w **DISCIPLINE** THEOLOGY **EDUCATION** Leland College, AB cum laude 1954; Union Seminary, BD 1955; Inter Baptist Theologi-

cal, ThD 1974, LLD 1976; Universal Bible Institute, PhD 1978; Straigth Business Coll, exec sec 1960. **CAREER** West NO Baptist Assn, president 1972-76; LA Cristian Training Institute, president 1973-75; CHRISTIAN BIBLE COLLEGE OF LA, ACADEMIC DEAN 1976-; FIRST NEW TESTAMENT B C, PASTOR 1958-. **HONORS AND AWARDS** Outstanding leadership 2nd Congress LBA 1978; communicator West Bank American Muslem 1980; dedicated service ML King Comunity Center 1981. **MEMBERSHIPS** Supervisor LSU Dental School 1971-77; secretary Jefferson Parish Ministers Union 1973-81; bd chairman Jefferson Parish Voters League 1975-84; general secretary LA Progressive Baptist Assn 1978-; chaplain Veterans of Foreign Wars #2403 1981-. **CONTACT ADDRESS** First New Testament BC, 6112 W Bank Expy, Marrero, LA, 70072.

GUNDERSON, KEITH
DISCIPLINE PHILOSOPHY **EDUCATION** Princeton Univ, PhD. **RESEARCH** Philosophy of artifical intelligence; aesthetics. **SELECTED PUBLICATIONS** Auth, Leibniz's Walk-In Machine, Perception, and the Perils of Physicalism, Univ Am, 88; Mentality and Machines, Univ Minn, 85; Purposes and Poetry, Body Mind and Method, 79; A Continual Interest in the Sun and Sea; Inland Missing the Sea, Nodin, 76; ed, Language, Mind and Knowledge, Univ Minn, 75. **CONTACT ADDRESS** Philosophy Dept, Univ of Minnesota, Twin Cities, 355 Ford Hall, 224 Church St SE, Minneapolis, MN, 55455. **EMAIL** gunde002@tc.umn.edu

GUNDRY, ROBERT H.
PERSONAL Born 10/15/1932, Los Angeles, CA, m, 1954, 3 children **DISCIPLINE** RELIGION **EDUCATION** Los Angeles Baptist Col & Sem, BA, 54, BD, 57; Univ Manchester, England, PhD, 61. **CAREER** From asst prof to assoc prof Bibl studies, 62-70, chmn dept relig studies, 66-75, 90-96, prof, 70-97, KATHLEEN SMITH PROF RELIG STUDIES, WESTMONT COL, 97-. **HONORS AND AWARDS** Teacher of Year, 69, 79 & 96. **MEMBERSHIPS** Soc New Testament Studies; Soc Bibl Lit; Inst Bibl Res. **RESEARCH** Biblical studies, higher and textual criticism; theology. **SELECTED PUBLICATIONS** Auth, The Use of the Old Testament in St Matthew's Gospel, Brill, Leiden, 67; A Survey of the New Testament, 70 & The Church and the Tribulation, 73, Zondervan; Soma in Biblical Theology, Cambridge Univ, 76; Matthew: A Commentary on His Literary & Theological Art, Eerdmans, 82; Mark: A Commentary on His Apology for the Cross, Eerdmans, 93. **CONTACT ADDRESS** Dept of Relig Studies & Philos, Westmont Col, 955 La Paz Rd, Santa Barbara, CA, 93108-1099. **EMAIL** gundry@westmont.edu

GUNTER, PETE A.Y.
PERSONAL Born 10/20/1936, Hammond, IN, m, 1969, 1 child **DISCIPLINE** PHILOSOPHY **EDUCATION** Univ Tex Austin, BA, 58; Columbia Univ, BA, 60; Yale Univ, PhD, 63. **CAREER** Asst prof, Auburn Univ, 62-65; assoc prof, Univ Tenn, 65-69; full prof, Univ North Tex, 69-; regents' prof, Univ North Tex, 98-. **HONORS AND AWARDS** Marshall scholar, 58-60; Dallas Phi Beta Kappa facul excellence award, 84; Lone Star Sierra Club special svc award, 97. **MEMBERSHIPS** Amer Philos Soc; Southwestern Philos Soc; Found for Philos of Creativity, 81-; Soc for Process Philos of Educ, 93-. **RESEARCH** Philosphy of science; Process-relational philosophy especially Henri Bergson, Alfred North Whitehead; Philosophy and ecology. **SELECTED PUBLICATIONS** Co-auth, Texas Land Ethics, 98; auth, The Big Thicket: An Ecological Reconsideration, 93; co-auth, Founders of Constructive Postmodernism, 93; auth, Creativity in George Herbert Mead, 90; co-ed, Bergson and Modern Thought: Towards a Unified Science, 87; auth, Henri Bergson: A Bibliography, 87; auth, What is Living and What is Dead in the Philosophy of Hegel, 85; ed and contrib, Present, Tense, Future, Perfect, 85; auth, River in Dry Grass, Shearer, 85; co-auth, W. R. Strong: His Memoirs, Denton County Hist Comn, 81; co-auth, Process Philosophy: Basic Writings, Univ Press of Amer, 78; auth, Henri Bergson: A Bibliography, Philos Doc Ctr, 74; auth, The Big Thicket, Jenkins, 72; auth, Bergson and the Evolution of Physics, Univ Tenn, 69. **CONTACT ADDRESS** 225 Jagoe, Denton, TX, 76201. **EMAIL** gunter@po6.cas.unt.edu

GUNTHER, GERALD
PERSONAL Born 05/26/1927, Germany, m, 1949, 2 children **DISCIPLINE** AMERICAN CONSTITUTIONAL LAW AND HISTORY **EDUCATION** Brooklyn Col, AB, 49; Columbia Univ, MA, 50; Harvard Univ, LLB, 53. **CAREER** Law clerk, Judge Learned Hand, 53-54 and Chief Justice Earl Warren, 54-55; from assoc prof to prof law, Sch Law, Columbia Univ, 56-62; prof, 62-72, WILLIAM NELSON CROMWELL PROF LAW, SCH LAW, STANFORD UNIV, 72-; Res dir, Inter-Law Sch Comn Const Simplification, 57-58; Guggenheim fel, 62-63; Fulbright lectr, Ghana, 69; fel, Ctr Advan Studies Behav Sci, 69-70, vis prof const law, Harvard Law Sch, 72-73; Nat Endowment for Humanities fel, 80-81. **HONORS AND AWARDS** Distinguished Alumnus Award, Brooklyn Col, 61. **MEMBERSHIPS** Fel Am Acad Arts & Sci; Am Philos Soc; AHA; Am Law Inst; Orgn Am Historians. **RESEARCH** Judicial biography. **SELECTED PUBLICATIONS** Auth, Learned Hand--Outstanding Copyright Judge--The 24th Annual Donald-C-

Brace-Lecture, J Copyright Soc of USA, Vol 0041, 94; Objectivity and Hagiography in Judicial Biography--Transcript, NY Univ Law Rev, Vol 0070, 95; Contracted Biographies and Other Obstacles to Truth, NY Univ Law Rev, Vol 0070, 95; Members of the Warren-Court in Judicial Biography--Transcript, NY Univ Law Rev, Vol 0070, 95; Judge Hand, Learned: Examining the Life of an American Jurist--The Choices and Satisfactions of a Biographer, Proc of Am Philos Soc, Vol 0140, 96. **CONTACT ADDRESS** Sch of Law, Stanford Univ, Stanford, CA, 94305.

GUPTA, ANIL K.
PERSONAL Born 02/05/1949, Ambala, India, m, 1995, 1 child **DISCIPLINE** PHILOSOPHY **EDUCATION** Univ of London, BS with honors, 69; Univ of Pittsburgh, MA, 73, PhD, 77. **CAREER** Asst prof, 75-79, assoc prof, 80-82, McGill Univ; visiting asst prof, Univ of Pittsburgh, 79-80; assoc prof, Univ of Ill at Chicago, 82-89; visiting prof, Univ of Padua, Italy, 85; PROF, 89-95, RUDY PROF OF PHILOS, 95-, IND UNIV, 95. **HONORS AND AWARDS** Andrew Mellon Fel, 70-71 & 73-74; Humanities Res Grants, 77-78, 78-79, & 81-82; Ed-Developmental Grant, 81; fel, Inst for the Humanities, Univ of Ill at Chicago, 85-86; NEH Fel, 88-89 & 95-96; Summer fac fel, Ind Univ, 94; Teaching Excellence Recognition Award, 98; fel, Center for Advanced Study in the Behavioral Sci, Stanford, 98-99. **MEMBERSHIPS** Am Philos Asn; Asn for Symbolic Logic. **RESEARCH** Logic; philosophy of language; metaphysics. **SELECTED PUBLICATIONS** Auth, The Logic of Common Nouns, Yale Univ Press, 80; auth, Truth and Paradox, J of Philos Logic, 82; auth, Remarks on Definitions and the Concept of Truth, Proceedings of the Aristotelian Soc, 88-89; auth, Two Theorems Concerning Stability, Truth or Consequences, Kluwer Acad Press, 90; auth, A Critique of Deflationism, Philos Topics, 93; auth, Definition and Revision: A Response to McGee and Martin, Philos Issues, 97; auth, Meaning and Misconceptions, Language, Logic, and Concepts: Essays in Honor of John Macnamara, The MIT Press, forthcoming; coauth, The Revision Theory of Truth, The MIT Press, 93. **CONTACT ADDRESS** Dept of Philos, Indiana Univ, Bloomington, Sycamore Hall 026, Bloomington, IN, 47405. **EMAIL** agupta@indiana.edu

GUPTA, NEENA
DISCIPLINE LAW **EDUCATION** Queen's Univ, BA, 84, LLB, 87; Univ Toronto, LLM, 94. **CAREER** General civil litigator, Goodman and Carr **MEMBERSHIPS** Can Bar Asn; Law Soc Upper Can; Law Soc Saskatchewan. **RESEARCH** Employment and human rights law. **SELECTED PUBLICATIONS** Auth, pubs on Ontario human rights, pay equity act and the employment standards act. **CONTACT ADDRESS** Fac of Law, Univ Toronto, 78 Queen's Park, Toronto, ON.

GURINDER, SINGH MANN
PERSONAL Born 12/10/1949, Batala, India, m, 1978, 2 children **DISCIPLINE** RELIGION **EDUCATION** MTS, Harvard Divinity Sch, 87; PhD, Relig, Columbia Univ, 93. **CAREER** Assoc prof, relig, Columbia Univ, 97-99; Kapany prof, sikh studies, Univ Calif Santa Barbara, 99-. **MEMBERSHIPS** Amer Acad of Relig. **RESEARCH** Early Sikh manuscripts; Religion and society in the Punjab; Punjabi literature; Sikhs in the USA. **SELECTED PUBLICATIONS** Auth, The Goindual Potnis, Cambridge, Harvard Oriental Series, 51, 96; co-ed, with J. S. Hawley, Studying the Sikhs issues for North America, Albany, SUNY Press, 93. **CONTACT ADDRESS** Dept. of Religion, Columbia Univ, New York, NY, 10027. **EMAIL** gm7@columbia.edu

GURTLER, GARY M.
PERSONAL Born 02/27/1947, Rochester, NY **DISCIPLINE** PHILOSOPHY **EDUCATION** Fordham Univ, PhD, 78. **CAREER** Asst Prof, 80-91, Assoc Prof, 91-92, Loyola Univ of Chicago; Assoc Prof, 92-97, Boston Coll; Miller Prof of Classics, 98-, John Carrol Univ. **HONORS AND AWARDS** Pres, Jesuit Philo Assoc. **MEMBERSHIPS** APA, APAED, ACPA, ISNS, JPA. **RESEARCH** Plotinus, Plato, Aristotle, ancient and medieval philosophy, Spanish philosophy. **SELECTED PUBLICATIONS** Auth, Plotinus, the Experience of Unity, Bern, Peter Lang Pub Co, 88; art, Meeting on Philosophy's Own Ground, Zubiri's Critic of Plato's Dualism, in: Intl Philo Qtly, 98; La Noetica de Zubiri y Noetica Aristotles, in: Analogia Revista de Filosofia, forthcoming; Plotinus and the Alienation of the Soul, in: The Perennial Tradition of Noeplatonism, Leuven Univ Press, 97; Plotinus and the Platonic Parmenides, in: Intl Philo Qtly, 92; Plotinus and Byzantine Aesthetics, in: The Mod Schoolman, 89. **CONTACT ADDRESS** Dept of Philosophy, Boston Col, Chestnut Hill, MA, 02467. **EMAIL** gurtlerg@bc.edu

GUSHEE, DAVID P.
PERSONAL Born 06/17/1962, VA, m, 1984, 3 children **DISCIPLINE** CHRISTIAN ETHICS **EDUCATION** Union Theol Sem, PhD, 93. **CAREER** Assoc Prof, Dir Cen Christ Ldshp, 3 yrs, Union Univ TN. **HONORS AND AWARDS** Phi Beta Kappa; 2 Evang Press Assoc Awds., Hosts Radio Program; Writer of column in Jackson Sun. **MEMBERSHIPS** SBC **SELECTED PUBLICATIONS** Auth, The Righteous Gentiles of the Holocaust, Fortress Press. **CONTACT ADDRESS** 156 Claiborne Dr, Jackson, TN, 38305. **EMAIL** dpgushee@usip.net

GUSTAFSON, DAVID
PERSONAL Born 01/25/1942, Cokate, MN, m, 1964, 2 children **DISCIPLINE** CHURCH HISTORY **EDUCATION** Hamline Univ, BA, 64; M. Div Lutheran School of Theol, 68; Luther Seminary, Th Y, 73; Union Inst, PhD, 90. **CAREER** Lutheran Pastor, 68-98, Univ of St Thomas, St Paul, MN, 98-. **HONORS AND AWARDS** Concordia Hist Inst Book Award, 94. **MEMBERSHIPS** ASCH, LHC, AAR, Sixteenth Century Soc. **RESEARCH** American Religious History. **SELECTED PUBLICATIONS** Auth, The Church: Community of the Crucified or Community that Crucifies?, Lutheran Forum, 97; The ELCA and Ecumenism: Past, Present, and Future, Pieper Lectures in St Louis MO, 97; The ELCA: Its Past, Present, and Future, Epis, Eastertide, 96; A Quiet Week in the ELCA, Forum Letter, 95; Reflections on Bishop Chilstrom's Visit, Lutheran Forum, 95; Suggestions for a New Bishop, Lutheran Forum., 95; Review, A Speaking Life: The Legacy of John Keble, ed, Charles R. Henry, Church Hist, 97. **CONTACT ADDRESS** 5220 Oakley St., Duluth, MN, 55804. **EMAIL** DAGusto@aol.com

GUSTASON, WILLIAM
DISCIPLINE LOGICAL THEORY, INDUCTIVE LOGIC, EARLY 20TH-CENTURY ANALYSIS **EDUCATION** Univ Mich, PhD. **CAREER** Assoc prof, Purdue Univ. **RESEARCH** Frege and Wittgenstein. **SELECTED PUBLICATIONS** Auth, Reasoning From Evidence: Inductive Logic; coauth, Elementary Symbolic Logic. **CONTACT ADDRESS** Dept of Philos, Purdue Univ, 1080 Schleman Hall, West Lafayette, IN, 47907-1080.

GUTTING, GARY MICHAEL
PERSONAL Born 04/11/1942, St. Louis, MO, m, 1965, 3 children **DISCIPLINE** PHILOSOPHY OF SCIENCE **EDUCATION** St Louis Univ, BA, 64, PhD(philos), 68. **CAREER** Instr philos, St Louis Univ, 67-68; Fulbright fel, Cath Univ Louvain, 68-69; asst prof, 69-75, assoc prof, 75-82, prof philos, Univ Notre Dame, 82-; visiting prof, Free Univ of Amsterdam, 87; chemn, dept philos, Univ Notre Dame, 90-96. **MEMBERSHIPS** Philos Sci Asn; Am Philos Asn. **RESEARCH** Philosophy of science; continental philsophy; of religion. **SELECTED PUBLICATIONS** Auth, Religious Belief and Religious Skepticism, Univ Notre Dame Press, 82; Michel Foucault's Archaelogy of Scientific Reason, Cambridge Univ Press, 89; Pragmatic Liberalism and the Critique of Modernity, Cambridge Univ Press, 98; Einstein's Discovery of Special Relativity, Philos Sci, 72; contrib, Scientific Realism, In: The Philosophy of Wilfrid Sellars, Reidl, 78; Continental Philosophy of Science, In: Current Research in Philosophy of Science, Philos Sci Asn, 78; auth, Husserl and Scientific Realism, Philos & Phenomenol Res, 78; Science as Discovery, Rev Int de Philos, 80; ed, Paradigms and Revolutions: Applications and Appraisals of Thomas Kuhn's Philosophy of Science, Univ Notre Dame, 80; auth, Religious Belief and Religious Skepticism, Univ Notre Dame, 82; Can Philosophical Beliefs Be Rationally Justified?, Am Philos Quart, 82. **CONTACT ADDRESS** Dept of Philosophy, Univ of Notre Dame, Notre Dame, IN, 46556. **EMAIL** Gary.M.Gutting.1@nd.edu

GUTTMAN, EGON
PERSONAL Born 01/27/1927, Neuruppin, Germany, m, 1966, 2 children **DISCIPLINE** SECURITIES & COMMERCIAL LAW **EDUCATION** London Univ, LLB, 50, LLM, 52. **CAREER** Mem law fac, Northwestern Univ, 58-59; mem law fac, Rutgers Univ, 59-60; mem law fac, Univ Atlanta, 60-62; prof law, Sch Law, Howard Univ, 62-68; Prof Law, Com Law & Securities Regulations, WA Col, Am Univ, 68-, Barrister, Mid Temple, 52-; lectr law, Univ Khartoum, Sudan & Fac Law, Univ London, 53-58; lectr, Practicing Law Inst, 66-; adj prof law, Sch Law, Howard Univ, 68-96; spec adv to gen coun, Securities & Exchange Comn, 76-77; spec adv to dir, Enforcement, 78-80; Louis P Levitt Mem Scholar, WA Col Law, 82. **HONORS AND AWARDS** John Sherman Myers Phi Delta Phi Award, 72. **MEMBERSHIPS** Am Law Inst; Am Bar Asn; Brit Inst Int & Comp Law; Soc Pub Teachers Law; Hardwick Soc Inns of Ct England. **RESEARCH** Securities regulations, transfer of securities; international finance; economic crimes. **SELECTED PUBLICATIONS** Crime, Cause & Treatment, Sudan Judiciary, Khartoum, Sudan, 57; Article 8 of the Uniform Commercial Code, Rutgers Law Rev, Vol 136, 62; Broker-dealers bankruptcies, NY Univ Law, Vol 887, 73; The development & exercise of appellate powers in adverse action appeals, Am Univ Law Rev, Vol 323, 70; Modern Securities Transfers Supplements Annually, Warren, Gorham & Lamont, 72, 3rd ed, 87; The Futures Trading Act of 1978: Reaffirmation of coordinated CFTC-SEC jurisdiction, Am Univ Law Rev, Vol I, 79; Toward an uncertificated security, Washington & Lee Law Rev, Vol 717, 80; The transfer of securities in organized markets, USA, Britain, Canada, Osgood Hall Law Rev, Vol 400, 81. **CONTACT ADDRESS** WA Col of Law, American Univ, 481 Mass Ave N W, Washington, DC, 20016. **EMAIL** guttman@wcl.american.edu

GUY, DANIEL SOWERS
PERSONAL Born 07/12/1928, Columbus, OH, m, 1962, 2 children **DISCIPLINE** LAW **EDUCATION** Ohio Wesleyan Univ, BA, 49, JD, 52; Univ Mich, Ann Arbor, LLM, 56, SJD,

70. **CAREER** Asst atty gen, Ohio, 57-58; from asst prof to prof Law, Ohio Northern Univ, 59-73, asst dean, 64-73; prof, Univ NDak, 73-77; prof Law, Ohio Northern Univ, 77-98, dean, 78-84, atty, Ohio, 52-73; fel, Inst Soc Sci Methods in Legal Educ, Univ Denver, 67. **HONORS AND AWARDS** Phi Beta Kappa. **MEMBERSHIPS** Am Bar Asn; Am Judicature Soc. **RESEARCH** Eminant domain law; condemnation law. **SELECTED PUBLICATIONS** Contribr, State Taxation of Interstate Commerce, Judiciary Comt, US House of Rep, 64; auth, State Highway Condemnation Procedures, Int Continuing Legal Educ, 71; Empirical study of fact-finders, Ohio Northern Univ Law Rev, 73; Comparison of condemnation procedures, 74 & Open meetings and open records in North Dakota, 76, Univ NDak Law Rev. **CONTACT ADDRESS** Col of Law, Ohio Northern Univ, 525 S Main St, Ada, OH, 45810-1555.

GUZELDERE, GUVEN
PERSONAL Born 01/23/1963, Ankara, Turkey **DISCIPLINE** PHILOSOPHY **EDUCATION** Bogazici Univ, BS, 86; Indiana Univ, MS, 89, MA, 89; Stanford Univ, PhD, 97. **CAREER** Asst Prof, 97-, Duke Univ. **MEMBERSHIPS** APA, CSS, AAAI, APS, Soc for Neuroscience. **RESEARCH** Philosophy of mind, consciousness, foundations of artificial intelligence. **SELECTED PUBLICATIONS** Ed, The Nature of Consciousness, MIT Press, 97. **CONTACT ADDRESS** Dept of Philosophy, Duke Univ, 201 W Duke Bldg, Box 90743, Durham, NC, 27708. **EMAIL** guven@acpub.duke.edu

GYATSO, J.
DISCIPLINE BUDDHIST STUDIES **EDUCATION** Univ CA, Berkeley, PhD, 87. **CAREER** Assoc prof, Relig Dept, Amherst Col. **RESEARCH** Tibet; Buddhism; religion; philos; cultural studies. **SELECTED PUBLICATIONS** Ed, In the Mirror of Memory: Reflections on Mindfulness and Remembrance in India and Tibetan Buddhism, Albany: SUNY Press, 89; auth, Apparitions of the Self: The Secret Autobiographies of a Tibetan Visionary, Princeton, 98. **CONTACT ADDRESS** Amherst Col, Amherst, MA, 01002. **EMAIL** jbgyatso@amherst.edu

GYUG, RICHARD F.
DISCIPLINE MEDIEVAL LITURGY, RELIGION AND SOCIETY **EDUCATION** Univ Toronto, PhD. **CAREER** Dir, grad stud; assoc prof, Fordham Univ. **RESEARCH** Studying the liturgical manuscripts of the Beneventan region. **SELECTED PUBLICATIONS** Auth, Missale ragusinum: The Missal of Dubrovnik, 90; The Diocese of Barcelona during the Black Death: The Register 'Notule communium' 15, 94; The Pontificals of Monte Cassino, L'Eta dell'abate Desiderio, 92. **CONTACT ADDRESS** Dept of Hist, Fordham Univ, 113 W 60th St, New York, NY, 10023.

H

HAACK, SUSAN
PERSONAL Born 07/23/1945, England **DISCIPLINE** PHILOSOPHY **EDUCATION** Oxford, BA, 66, B Phil, 68; Cambridge, PhD, 72. **CAREER** Lectr, 69-71, New Hall, Cambridge UK; Lectr, 71-76, Univ of Warnick UK; Reader, 76-82, Prof, 82-90; Prof of Philos, 90-, Cooper Sr Scholar in Arts and Sci, 98-, Univ of Miami. **HONORS AND AWARDS** Harfness Fellow; Romaness Phi Beta Kappa Prof. **MEMBERSHIPS** APA, Charles S.Pein Soc; CSICOP. **RESEARCH** Philosophy of logic and language, Epistemology and Philosophy of Science, Metaphysics, Prymarism. **SELECTED PUBLICATIONS** Auth, Dry Truth and Real Knowledge, Epistemologies of Metaphor and Metaphors of Epistemology, in: Aspects of Metaphor, ed, J. Hintikka, Kluwer Academic Pub, 94; Puzzling Out Science, in: Academic Questions, 95; As For that phrase 'studying in a literary spirit...' Proceedings of the American Philosophical Perspectives, 96; Reflections on Relativism, From Momentous Tautology to Seductive Contradiction, in: Philo Perspectives, Metaphysics, ed, JE Tomberlin, Blackwell, Oxford, 96; The Ethics of Belief' Reconsidered in The Philosophy of R.M. Chisholm, ed, L Hahn, Open Court, La Salle, IL, 97; We pragmatists: Pierce and Rorty in Conversation, Partisan Review, 97; Between the Scylla of Scientism and the Charybdis of Apriorism in The Philosophy of Sir Peter Strawson, ed, L Hahn, Open Court, La Salle, IL, 98. **CONTACT ADDRESS** Dept of Philosophy, Univ of Miami, Coral Gables, FL, 33124.

HAAKONSSEN, KNUD
PERSONAL Born 07/09/1947, Tingsted, Denmark, m, 1987, 1 child **DISCIPLINE** PHILOSOPHY **EDUCATION** Univ Copenhagen, cand art, 68, mag art, 72; Univ Edinburgh, PhD, 78; Univ Copenhagen, Dr Phil, 96. **CAREER** Tutor in Philos, Krogerup Folk High School, Copenhagen, 68-69; tutor, dept of philos, Univ Copenhagen, 69-70; part-time lect in philos, Folkeuniversitetet, Copenhagen, 70-73; sr tutor, Dept of Philos, Monash Univ, Melbourne, 76-79; lect, School of Political Science, Victoria Univ of Wellington, 79-82; res fel, sr res fel, fel, sr fel, Res School of Social Studies, Inst for Advanced Studies, Australian Nat Univ, 82-94; prof, Dept of Philos, and assoc fac, Dept of Political Science, Boston Univ, 95-; vis fel at the following: Australian Nat Univ, 80-81, 95, 96, 98, Univ Aarhus, 85, Univ Ediburgh, 86, 89, Max-Planck-Institut fur Geschichte, Gottingen, 89, McGill Univ, Montreal, 92-93; fel, Woodrow Wilson Int Center for Scholars, Washington, DC, 88; co-dir, prog on the Bicentenary of the Bill of Rights, Woodrow Wilson Int Center for Scholars, Washington, DC, 89-91; lect, Int Hume Soc, Nat Endowment for the Humanities, Dartmouth Col, 90; Distinguished Vis, Univ Manitoba, Winnipeg, 92; co-ed, Newsletter of the IVR, 87-91; ed bd, Edinburgh Studies in Intellectual History, Edinburgh Univ Press, 92-97; ed adv, British J for the Hist of Philos, 92-; ed bd, Hist of European Ideas, 97-; consul ed, J of the Hist of Ideas, 92-98; ed bd, Reid Studies, 97-; bd of ed, J of the Hist of Ideas, 98-. **HONORS AND AWARDS** Gold Medal of the Univ of Aarhus, Denmark, 70; fel, Academy of Social Sciences in Australia, 92; foreign member, Royal Danish Academy of Sciences and Letters, 95. **MEMBERSHIPS** Am Philos Asn; Australian Soc of Legal Philos; Int Asn for Philos of Law and Social Philos; British Sioc for the History of Philos; Am Soc for Eighteenth-Century Studies; Australasian & Pacific Soc for Eighteenth-Century Studies; Deutsche Gesellschaft fur die Erforschung des achtzehnten Jahrhunderts; Int Soc for Eighteenth-Century Studies; Int Hume Soc; Eighteenth-Century Scottish Studies Soc; The Conference for the Study of Political Thought, Lessing Akademie, Wolfenbuttel; Int Soc for Intellectual Hist; North Am Kant Soc. **RESEARCH** History of early modern philos; legal and political philos. **SELECTED PUBLICATIONS** Auth, The Science of a Legislator, The Natural Jurisprudence of David Hume and Adam Smith, Cambridge Univ Press, 81, paperback, 89, French trans, Presses Universitaires de France, 98, Japanese trans, Tokyo: Minerva Shobo, forthcoming; ed, Traditions of Liberalism, Essays on John Locke, Adam Smith and John Stuart Mill, CIS, 88; ed, Thomas Reid, Practical Ethics: being Lectures and Papers on Natural Religion, Self-Government, Natural Jurisprudence and the Law of Nations, ed with intro and commentary, Princeton Univ Press, 90; ed, A Culture of Rights: The Bill of Rights in Philosophy Politics and Law-1791 and 1991, ed with M J Lacey, Cambridge Univ Press, 91, paperback ed, 92; ed, David Hume, Political Essays, ed with intro, Cambridge Texts in the History of Political Thought, Cambridge Univ Press, 94; ed, Enlightenment and Religion: Rational Dissent in Eighteenth-Century Britain, Ideas in Context, Cambridge Univ Press, 96; auth, Natural Law and Moral Philosophy, from Grotius to the Scottish Enlightenment, Cambridge Univ Press, 96; ed, Adam Smith, International Library of Critical Essays in the History of Philosophy, Dartmouth Pub Co, 98; gen ed, The Edinburgh Edition of Thomas Reid, Edinburgh Univ Press, 94-; forty scholarly articles; twenty opuscula; three dozen book-reviews; translations into Danish of Kuhn, Magee, Popper, and Russell. **CONTACT ADDRESS** Dept of Philosophy, Boston Univ, 745 Commonwealth Ave, Boston, MA, 02215. **EMAIL** haakon@bu.edu

HAAR, CHARLES MONROE
PERSONAL Born 12/03/1920, Antwerp, Belgium, m, 1946, 3 children **DISCIPLINE** LAW **EDUCATION** NY Univ, AB, 40; Univ Wis, MA, 41; Harvard Univ, LLB, 48. **CAREER** Pvt practice law, New York city, 49-52; from asst prof to prof, Law Sch, Harvard Univ, 52-66; asst secy, Dept Housing and Urban Develop, Washington, DC, 66-69; prof, 69-72, LOUIS D BRANDEIS PROF LAW, HARVARD UNIV, 72-, Chief reporter, Proj Model Code Lang Develop, Am Land Inst, 64-66; chmn, Joint Ctr Urban Studies, Mass Inst Technol-Harvard Univ, 69-; dir, Charles River Assocs, Cambridge, Mass; consult, Agency Int Develop, Housing and Home Finance Agency and US Senate Subcomt Govt Opers; mem, Cambridge Redevelop Authority Metrop Area Planning Coun; chmn, President's Task Forces Suburban Probs, Model Cities and Reservation Natural Beauty; chmn, Mass Home Finance Agency; mem, Mass Gov Management Task Force. **HONORS AND AWARDS** LLD, Lake Erie Univ, 68. **MEMBERSHIPS** Fel AAAS; Am Inst Planners; Brit Town Planning Inst; Am Law Inst. **RESEARCH** Law education. **SELECTED PUBLICATIONS** Auth, Preface, Harvard Environ Law Rev, Vol 0020, 96. **CONTACT ADDRESS** Law Sch, Harvard Univ, FOB 300, Cambridge, MA, 02138.

HAAS, PETER J.
PERSONAL Born 11/29/1947, Detroit, MI, m, 1971, 3 children **DISCIPLINE** HISTORY OF RELIGIONS AND JUDAISM **EDUCATION** Univ Mich, BA, 70; Hebrew Union Col, MAHL, 74; Brown Univ, PhD, 80. **CAREER** Asst prof, Vanderbilt Univ, 80-88; assoc prof, Vanderbilt Univ, 88-. **HONORS AND AWARDS** Fel, sci and soc, Robert Penn Warren Ctr, Vanderbilt Univ, 94; Lilly endow teaching fel, 95; Templeton Sci Relig course award, 97. **MEMBERSHIPS** AAR; SBL; Asn of Jewish Studies; Western Jewish Studies Asn; Central Conf of Amer Rabbis Jewish Law Asn. **RESEARCH** Jewish ethics; Rhetoric of Jewish ethics; Science and religion. **SELECTED PUBLICATIONS** Auth, Responsa: Literary History of a Rabbinic Genre, Atlanta, Scholar Press, Semeia Studies, 96; ed, Recovering the Role of Women: Power and Authority in Rabbinic Jewish Society, Atlanta, Scholar Press, 92; article, The sacred and the Mundane: The Message of Leviticus, The Christ Century, 114, 27, 877-882, 8 oct, 97; rev essay, A Time to Kill and a Time to Heal, Jews, Medicine and Medical Society, Menorah Rev, 38, 3-4, fall, 96; rev essay, Who Do You Say I Am?, A Rabbi Talks with Jesus, Menorah Rev, 37, 1-2, spring/summer, 96; article, The Emergence of Rabbinic Legal Rhetoric: The Sheelot Uteshuvot Genre, Jewish Law Asn Studies, VIII, Atlanta, Scholar Press, 55-63, 96; article, What We Know Today that We Didn't Know Fifty Years Ago: Fifty Years of Holocaust Scholarship, CCAR Jour, 1-15, fall, 95; article, Nineteenth Century Science and the Formation of Nazi Policy, The United Theol Sem Jour of Theol, XCIX, 6-30, 95; article, How to Develop the Moral Personality: Immanuel Etke's Rabbi Israel Salanter and the Musar Movement: Seeking the Torah of Truth, Menorah Rev, 35, 6-7, fall, 95; article, The Quest for Hebrew Bible Ethics: A Jewish Response, Ethics and Politics in the Hebrew Bible, Semeia, 66, 151-159, 95. **CONTACT ADDRESS** Religious Studies Dept., Vanderbilt Univ, Box 1556, Nashville, TN, 37235. **EMAIL** peter.j.haas@vanderbilt.edu

HABERMAN, DAVID L.
DISCIPLINE RELIGIOUS STUDIES **EDUCATION** Univ Chicago, PhD, 84. **CAREER** Assoc prof. **RESEARCH** History of South Asian religions; Indian arts and aesthetics; ritual studies; theories of religion; native American religions. **SELECTED PUBLICATIONS** Auth, Acting as a Way of Salvation: A Study of Raganuga Bhakti Sadhana, Oxford, 88; Journey through the Twelve Forests, Oxford, 94. **CONTACT ADDRESS** Dept of Religious Studies, Indiana Univ, Bloomington, 300 N Jordan Ave, Bloomington, IN, 47405.

HABERMEHL, LAWRENCE L.
PERSONAL Born 06/13/1937, Joplin, MO, d, 3 children **DISCIPLINE** PHILOSOPHY; PHILOSOPHY OF RELIGION **EDUCATION** Phillips Univ, AB, 59; Union Theol Sem, NYC, BD, 61; Boston Univ, PhD, 67. **CAREER** Teaching fel, Dept of Philos, Boston Univ, 65-66; instr, asst prof, ASSOC PROF, AM INT COL, SPRINGFIELD, MA, 66-. **MEMBERSHIPS** Amer Philos Assoc; Amer Assoc Univ Profs; Metaphysical Soc Amer. **RESEARCH** Contemporary moral issues; contemporary relig issues; superstitious and pseudoscience in popular culture. **SELECTED PUBLICATIONS** Auth/ed, Morality in the Modern World: Ethical Dimensions of Contemporary Human Problems, 76; auth, The Counterfeit Wisdom of Shallow Minds: A Critique of Some Leading Offenders of the 1980's, 94. **CONTACT ADDRESS** Dept of Philos, American Intl Col, 1000 State St., Springfield, MA, 01109. **EMAIL** LawLH@aol.com

HABIBI, DON A.
DISCIPLINE SOCIAL AND POLITICAL PHILOSOPHY, ETHICS, LEGAL THEORY **EDUCATION** Cornell Univ, MA, PhD. **CAREER** Assoc prof Psihol and Relig, Univ NC, Wilmington. **RESEARCH** 19th century British philosophy (Liberalism, Utilitarianism); political culture of the contemporary Middle East. **SELECTED PUBLICATIONS** Auth, The Positive/Negative Liberty Distinction and J.S. Mill's Theory of Liberty, Arch fur Rechts- und Soc Philos, 81:3, 95; J.S. Mill's Grand, Leading Principle, Iyyun: The Jerusalem Philos Quart 45, 96; coauth, Law, Ethics, and the Dilemma of Modern Liberalism, Midwest Law Rev 13, Spg, 95. **CONTACT ADDRESS** Univ N. Carolina, Wilmington, Bear Hall, Wilmington, NC, 28403-3297. **EMAIL** Habibid@uncwil.edu

HACKETT, DAVID H.
DISCIPLINE AMERICAN RELIGIOUS HISTORY, SOCIOLOGY OF RELIGION **EDUCATION** Emory Univ, PhD, 86. **CAREER** Assoc prof. **RESEARCH** Gender and American culture, American catholicism. **SELECTED PUBLICATIONS** Auth, Religion and American Culture: A Reader, Routledge, 95; Gender and Religion in American Culture, 1870-1930, Rel and Amer Cult, 95; The Silent Dialogue: Zen Letters to a Trappist Monk, Continuum, 96. **CONTACT ADDRESS** Dept of Rel, Univ Fla, 226 Tigert Hall, Gainesville, FL, 32611. **EMAIL** dhackett@religion.ufl.edu

HACKETT, ELIZABETH
PERSONAL Born 12/19/1961, Detroit, MI **DISCIPLINE** PHILOSOPHY **EDUCATION** Univ Notre Dame, BA, 83; Univ Pa, PhD, 96. **CAREER** Vis asst prof, 97-. **MEMBERSHIPS** Soc for Women in Philos; Am Philos Asn. **RESEARCH** Intersections of race and gender. **CONTACT ADDRESS** Univ of Michigan, 234 West Hall, Ann Arbor, MI, 48109. **EMAIL** bhackett@umich.edu

HACKETT, JEREMIAH M.
PERSONAL Born 02/27/1968, m, 1998, 2 children **DISCIPLINE** PHILOSOPHY **EDUCATION** Univ Toronto, PhD, 83. **CAREER** Asst prof, 82-84, Notre Dame Col, Oh; asst prof, 84-91, assoc prof, 91-99, grad dir, 96-98, Univ S Carolina. **RESEARCH** Medieval/Renaissance phil, Roger Bacon. **CONTACT ADDRESS** Dept of Philosophy, Univ of So Carolina, Columbia, SC, 29205. **EMAIL** hackettj@garnet.cla.sc.edu

HACKING, IAN
PERSONAL Born 02/18/1936, Vancouver, BC, Canada, m, 1984, 3 children **DISCIPLINE** PHILOSOPHY **EDUCATION** Univ British Columbia, BA, 56; Cantab, BA, 58, MA, PhD, 62. **CAREER** Prof, Univ Toronto, 83-; Stewart prof, Stanford, 74-82; Cambridge Univ, lectr, 69-74; Univ Brit Col, asst, assoc,

prof, 64-69. **HONORS AND AWARDS** Fel, Royal Soc Canada; fel, Am Hd of Arts. **MEMBERSHIPS** Fel British Academy **RESEARCH** Philos **SELECTED PUBLICATIONS** The Social Construction of What?, forthcoming, Harvard Press, 99; Mad Travelers: Reflections on the Reality of Transient Mental Illnesses, VA Univ Press, 98; Rewriting the Soul: Multiple Personality and the Sciences of Memory, Princ, Princ Univ Press, 95; Le Plus pur nominalisme, L'enigme de Goodman: Vleu' et usages de Vleu', Combas, Ed de l'Eclat, 93; The Taming of Chance, Cambridge Univ Press, 90; Several other titles. **CONTACT ADDRESS** Univ Toronto, Dept Philos, 215 Huron St, Toronto, ON, M5S 1A1.

HAFFNER, MARLENE ELISABETH
PERSONAL Born 03/22/1941, m, 1963 **DISCIPLINE** MEDICINE, HEALTH **EDUCATION** Western Reserve Univ, BA Chem, 58-61; George Washington Univ, Dr of Medicine, 61-65; Johns Hopkins Univ, Master of Public Health, 89-91; harvard Univ, Program for Sr Mgrs in Govt, 95. **CAREER** Chief, Adult Outpatient Dept, Gallup Indian Mex Center, 71-74; chief, Dept of Internal Med, Gallup Indian Mex Center, 71-74; preceptor, Univ of Calif San Diego, 75, 81; dir, NAIHS Arizona, 74-81; Assoc dir for Health Affairs, Bureau of Med Devices FDA, 81-82; dir for Health Affairs, Center ofr Devices and Radiological Health, FDA, 82-87; instr, F Edward Hebert School of Med, 85, 87; mentor for FDA-sponsored students, 90; clinical asst prof, adj assoc prof, F Edward Hebert School of Med, 95-; FDA rep to the Off of the Surgeon General, 87-; dir, Off of Orphan Products Develop FDA, 87-. **HONORS AND AWARDS** Award of Recognition, NORD, 88; Nat Hemophilia Found, 92; Outstanding Service to the Public Health Award NORD 96; Robert Brutsche Award COA, 96; numerous professional awards by PHS and academic awards. **MEMBERSHIPS** Am Public Health Asn; Am Med Asn; Commissioned Offrs Asn, Anchor and Caduceus Soc; Asn of Mil Surgeons of USA; Nat Nil families Asn; numerous health professional organizations. **RESEARCH** Public Health. **SELECTED PUBLICATIONS** Auth, Orphan Products - Origins, Progress and Prospects, Annual Rev of Pharmacology and Toxicology, 91; numerous articles, presentations and interviews on public health; coauth, Home Health Care Devices, Encycl of Med Devices and Instrumentations, 88; The Incentives of the Orphan Drug Act and Immunosuppressive Drug Development, Principles of Drug Develop in Transplantation and Autoimmunity, 96. **CONTACT ADDRESS** Office of Orphan Products Development, US FDA, 5600 Fisher Ln, Rockville, MD, 20857. **EMAIL** mhaffner@bangate.fda.gov

HAGEDORN, RICHARD B.
DISCIPLINE AGENCY AND PARTNERSHIP; COMMERCIAL LAW; COMMERCIAL PAPER; CONTRACTS; CORPOR **EDUCATION** Ore State Univ, BS, 70; Willamette Univ, JD, 83. **CAREER** Partner, Weatherford, Thompson, Horton, Brickey & Powers, Albany, 73-77; asst prof, Univ Mo, 77-79; asst prof, Gonzaga Univ, 79-81; assoc prof, Gonzaga Univ, 81-85; vis assoc prof, Univ Ore, 82; prof, 84-. **HONORS AND AWARDS** Comm, Uniform Commercial Code of the Amer Bar Assn, 89-. **MEMBERSHIPS** Mem, Phi Kappa Phi; Amer Law Inst; Wash State Bar Assn, 79-82. **SELECTED PUBLICATIONS** Co-auth, Secured Transactions in a Nutshell, 88; The Law of Debtors and Creditors, 91; auth, Brady on Bank Checks, 92; The Law of Promissory Notes, 92. **CONTACT ADDRESS** Sch of Law, Willamette Univ, 900 State St, Salem, OR, 97301. **EMAIL** rhagedor@willamette.edu

HAGGARD, THOMAS R.
DISCIPLINE EMPLOYMENT DISCRIMINATION, LABOR LAW, CONTRACTS AND LEGAL DRAFTING **EDUCATION** Univ TX, BA, 64, LLB, 67. **CAREER** David W. Robinson ch prof, Univ of SC. **SELECTED PUBLICATIONS** Publ on, employment law issues & regular columnist on legal writing. **CONTACT ADDRESS** School of Law, Univ of S. Carolina, Law Center, Columbia, SC, 29208. **EMAIL** Tom@law.law.sc.edu

HAGNER, DONALD A.
PERSONAL Born 07/08/1936, Chicago, IL, m, 1962 **DISCIPLINE** BIBLICAL STUDIES; NEW TESTAMENT **EDUCATION** NW Univ, BA, 58; Fuller Theol Sem, BD, ThM, 66; Univ Manchester, PhD, 69. **CAREER** Asst, assoc prof, Wheaton Col, 69-76; prof New Testament, 76-93, george eldon ladd prof new testament, 93-, Fuller Theol Sem, 76-. **HONORS AND AWARDS** C Davis Weyerhaeuser Award Excellence. **MEMBERSHIPS** Studiorum Novi Testamenti Soc; Soc Bibl Lit; Tyndale Fel; Inst Bibl Res; Uppsala Exeg Soc. **RESEARCH** Matthew; Paul; Apostolic Fathers; Second Temple Judaism. **SELECTED PUBLICATIONS** Auth, The Use of the Old and New Testaments in Clement of Rome, Supplements to Novum Testamentum, E. J. Brill, 73; The Epistle to the Hebrews, Good News Bible Commentaries, Harper & Row, 83; The Jewish Reclamation of Jesus: An Analysis and Critique of Modern Jewish Study of Jesus, Zondervan, 84; Matthew 1-13, Word Biblical Commentary, 93; coed, Anti-Semitism and Early Christianity: Issues of Polemic and Faith, Fortress, 93; ed, George Eldon Ladd, A Theology of the New Testament, Eerdmans, 93; coedm, New International Greek Testament Commentary, Eerdmans, 94; auth, Matthew 14-28, Word Biblical Commentary, Word, 95; New Testament Exegesis and Research: A Guide for Seminarians, FTS, 98. **CONTACT ADDRESS** Fuller Theol Sem, Pasadena, CA, 91182. **EMAIL** dhagner@fuller.edu

HAILE, GETATCHEW
PERSONAL Born 04/19/1931, m, 1964, 4 children **DISCIPLINE** LINGUISTICS, RELIGION **EDUCATION** Am Univ Cairo, BA, 57; Coptic Theol Col Cairo, BD, 57; Univ Tubingen, PhD(semitic philol), 62. **CAREER** Lectr, Amharic, Ge'ez and Arabic, HSI Univ, Ethiopia, 62-64, asst prof Amharic, Ge'ez and Arabic and chmn dept Ethiopian lang, 64-69; exchange scholar ling, Univ Calif, Los Angeles, 69-70; vis prof African studies, Okla State Univ, 70-71; assoc prof Amharic, Ge'ez and Arabic, HSI Univ, Ethiopia, 71-75; CATALOGUER, HILL MONASTIC MANUSCRIPT LIBR, ST JOHN'S UNIV, MINN, 76-, Contrib ed, Northeast African Studies, Mich State Univ. **RESEARCH** Ge'ez literature; Amharic grammar. **SELECTED PUBLICATIONS** Auth, From Emperor Selassie, Haile to Polotsky, H. J.--An Ethiopian and Semitic Miscellany, J Royal Asiatic Soc, Vol 0006, 96. **CONTACT ADDRESS** Hill Monastic Ms Libr, St John's Univ, Collegeville, MN, 56321.

HAINES, DIANA
PERSONAL Born 03/04/1955, Brooklyn, NY, s **DISCIPLINE** LAW **EDUCATION** Oberlin College, BA, 1977; George Washington University Law Center, JD, 1980; Antioch University, MA, legal education, 1985. **CAREER** Antioch Law School, clinical law professor, 1982-86; Department of Consumer & Regulatory Affiars, chief office of compliance, 1986-92; American University Law School, adjunct instructor, 1986-; DC Government, Civilian Complaint Review Board, executive director, 1992-. **MEMBERSHIPS** My Sister's Place, Shelter for Battered Women, staff attorney, 1990-; DC Bar, Consumer Affairs Section, steering committee, 1992-; Coalition of 100 Black Women, 1986-; Christian Social Action Committee, United Church of Christ, chairperson, 1991-. **CONTACT ADDRESS** Executive Director, Civilian Complaint Review Board, 1010 Massachusetts Ave NW, 4th Fl, Washington, DC, 20001.

HAJDIN, MANE
PERSONAL Born 09/30/1959, Belgrade, Yugoslavia, s **DISCIPLINE** PHILOSOPHY **EDUCATION** Univ Belgrade, BA, 82; McGill Univ, PhD, 88. **CAREER** Teaching asst, 83-86, reader, 85, 86, facul lectr, 86, lectr, 87, McGill Univ; lectr, Univ Papua New Guinea, 87-90; vis lectr, 90, lectr, 90-96, sr lectr, 96-97, Univ Waikato New Zealand; res assoc, Ctr for the Study of Law and Soc, Univ Calif Berkeley, 94-95, 96-97; lectr, Sonoma State Univ, 97-98; adj lectr, Santa Clara Univ, 97-98; lectr, Dominican Col of San Rafael, 98; lectr, Calif State Univ, 98. **MEMBERSHIPS** Amer Philos Asn; Can Philos Asn; Intl Asn for Philos of Law and Soc Philos; North Amer Soc for Soc Philos; Soc for the Philos of Sex and Love; Soc for the Study of Ethics & Animals. **RESEARCH** Ethics; Philosophy of law; Social & political philosophy. **SELECTED PUBLICATIONS** Co-auth, Sexual Harassment: A Debate, Littlefield Publ, 97; auth, Sexual Harassment and Negligence, Jour of Soc Philos, 97; rev, Utilitarianism, Philos in Rev, 97; book note, Social Ethics: A Student's Guide, Australasian Jour of Philos, 97; auth, The Boundaries of Moral Discourse, Loyola Univ Press, 94; article, Sexual Harassment in the law: The Demarcation Problem, Jour of Social Philos, 94; auth, Sanctions and the Notion of Morality, Dialogue, 93; auth, External Reasons and the Foundations of Morality: mother Teresa vs. Thrasymachus, Jour of Value Inquiry, 92; auth, Is There More to Speech Acts Than Illocutionary Force and Propositional Content?, Nous, 91; auth, External and Now-For-Then Preferences in Hare's Theory, Dialogue, 90; auth, A Defence of Rights-Duties Correlativism, Contemporary Yugoslav Philosophy: The Analytic Approach, Kluwer Acad Publ, 88; auth, Criminals as Gamblers: A Modified Theory of Pure Restitution, Dialogue, 87. **CONTACT ADDRESS** 839 Post St., #309, San Francisco, CA, 94109.

HALBERSTAM, MALVINA
DISCIPLINE LAW **EDUCATION** Brooklyn Col, BA, 57; Columbia Univ, JD, MIA, 61. **CAREER** Law clerk, to Judge Edmund L. Palmieri, 61-62; res assoc, Columbia Proj on Int Procedure, 62-63; asst district atty, NY county, 63-67; pvt pract, Rifkind and Sterling, Los Angeles, 67-68; sen atty, Nat Legal Prog on Health Problems of the Poor, 69-70; prof, Loyola Univ Sch of Law, 70-76; vis prof, Univ of Southern Calif Gould Law Ctr, 72-73; vis prof, Univ of Tex, 74; vis prof, Univ of Va, 75-76, reporter, Am Law Inst, Mode Penal Code Proj, 77-79; vis prof, Hebrew Univ of Jerusalem, 84-85; counr on Int Law, U.S. Dept of State, Off of the Legal Adviser, 85-86; consult, U.S. Dept of State, Off of the Legal Adviser, 86-92; prof, Yeshiva Univ, 92-. **HONORS AND AWARDS** Biographical listings include Who's Who in Am, Who's Who in Am Law, World's Who's Who of Women, Who's Who of Am Women, Who's Who in Am Educ, Int Dictionary of Biographies, Community Leaders and Noteworthy Americans, Who's Who in World Jewry. **MEMBERSHIPS** AALS; Am Bar Asn; Am Law Inst; Am Soc of Int Law; Asn of the Bar of the City of NY; Columbia Law Sch Alumni Asn; Int Asn of Jewish Lawyers and Jurists; Int Law Asn; Phi Beta Kappa Asn. **SELECTED PUBLICATIONS** Questions of Sovereignty and Self-Determination in the Arab-Israeli Conflict, in 6 Int Litigation Quart 131, 90; Interest Analysis and Dina de-Malkhuta Dina, A Comment on Aaron Kirschenbaum, The Sovereign Power of the State: A Proposed Theory of Accommodation in Jewish Law, in 12 Cardozo Law Rev 951, 91; The Use of Legislative History in Treaty Interpretation: The Dual Treaty Approach, in 12 Cardozo Law Rev 1645, 91; In Defense of the Supreme Court Decision, Alvarez-Machain, in 86 Am J Int Law 736, 92; The Copenhagen Document: Intervention in Support of Democracy, in 34 Harvard J Int Law 163, 93; A Treaty is a Treaty is A Treaty, in 33 Va J Int Law 51, 93; The Myth that Israel's Presence in Judea and Samaria is Comparable to Iraq's Presence in Kuwait, in 19 Syracuse J Int Law and Com. 1, 93; Nationalism and the Right to Self-Determination: The Arab-Israeli Conflict, in 26 N.Y.U. J of Int Law and Politics 1001, 94; The Legality of Humanitarian Intervention, in 3 Cardozo J of Int and Comp Law 1, 95; How Serious Are We About Prohibiting International Terrorism and Punishing Terrorists?, in The Jewish Lawyer 1, 96; The Jerusalem Embassy Act, in 19 Fordham Int Law J 1379, 96; The Right to Self-Defense once the Security Council Takes Action, in 17 Mich J of Int Law 229, 96; What Price Peace: From Nuremberg to Bosnia to the Noble Peace Prize, in 3 ILSA J of Int & Comp Law 229, 97; Ruth Bader Ginsburg: The First Jewish Woman on the United States Supreme Court, in 19 Cardozo Law Rev 1441, 98; United States Ratification of the Convention on the Elimination of all Forms of Discrimination Against Women, in 31 George Washington J Int Law and Economics 49, 98; Crimes Against International Maritime Navigation and Installations in the High Seas, in Int Criminal Law, ed. C. Bassiouni, 98. **CONTACT ADDRESS** Benjamin N. Cardozo Sch of Law, Yeshiva Univ, 55 Fifth Ave, New York, NY, 10003.

HALBERSTAM, MICHAEL
DISCIPLINE PHILOSOPHY **EDUCATION** Yale Univ, PhD, 96 **CAREER** Asst prof, 95-, Univ SC. **MEMBERSHIPS** APA **RESEARCH** German philosophy, political philosophy **SELECTED PUBLICATIONS** Auth, Totalitarianism as a Problem for the Modern Conception of Politics, Pol Theory vol 26, 98; auth, The Meaning of Totalitarianism for the Modern Conception of Politics, Yale Univ Press, 99. **CONTACT ADDRESS** Dept of Philosophy, Univ of South Carolina, Columbia, SC, 29208. **EMAIL** Halberstamm@garnet.cla.sc.edu

HALBERSTAM (GUGGENHEIM), MALVINA
DISCIPLINE LAW **EDUCATION** Brooklyn Coll, BA, 57; Columbia Univ, MIA, 64; JD 61. **CAREER** Prof- **HONORS AND AWARDS** Kint Scholar (2); Harlan Fiske Stone scholar; Jane Marks Murphy Prize., Counsel, Int Law, U.S. Dept State. **MEMBERSHIPS** Am Law Inst; Am Soc Int Law; Int Law Asn; Jacob Blaustein Inst Advancement Human Rights; Advisory Comt A.B.A. Standing Comt Law & Nat Security; Phi Beta Kappa. **RESEARCH** International law; human rights, US foreign relations law. **SELECTED PUBLICATIONS** Couth, Women's Legal Rights: International Agreements an Alternative to the E.R.A.? **CONTACT ADDRESS** Yeshiva Univ, 55 Fifth Ave, NY, NY, 10003-4301.

HALES, STEVEN
PERSONAL Born 01/07/1966, Chicago, IL, m, 1993 **DISCIPLINE** PHILOSOPHY **EDUCATION** Brown Univ, PhD, 92 **CAREER** Assoc Prof, 94-pres, Bloomsburg Univ **HONORS AND AWARDS** Richard M Griffith Mem Award, 95 **MEMBERSHIPS** Am Philos Assoc; N Amer Nietzsche Soc; Southern Soc for Philos & Psychol **RESEARCH** Epistemology, Metaphysics, Nietzsche **SELECTED PUBLICATIONS** Coauth, Nietzsche's Perspectivism, U of I Press, forthcom; Auth, Metaphysics: Contemporary Readings, Wadsworth Publishing Co, 99 **CONTACT ADDRESS** Dept Philos, Bloomsburg Univ of Pennsylvania, Bloomsburg, PA, 17815. **EMAIL** hales@bloomu.edu

HALIVNI, DAVID
DISCIPLINE RELIGION **EDUCATION** Columbia Univ, PhD. **CAREER** Prof. **RESEARCH** Talmud and Rabbinics. **SELECTED PUBLICATIONS** Auth, Peshat and Derash: Plain and Applied Meaning in Rabbinic Exegesis, 91; Revelation Restored: Divine Writ and Critical Responses, 97; The Book and the Sword: A Life of Learning in the Shadow of Destruction. **CONTACT ADDRESS** Dept of Religion, Columbia Col, New York, 2960 Broadway, New York, NY, 10027-6902. **EMAIL** dw13@columbia.edu

HALL, BENJAMIN LEWIS, III
PERSONAL Born 03/13/1956, Laurens, SC, m, 1981 **DISCIPLINE** LAW **EDUCATION** University of South Carolina, BA (cum laude), 1977; Duke Divinity School, MDiv, 1979; Rheinische Friedrich-Wilheims Universitat, BONN Fed'l Fulbright Rep of Germany Scholar-DAAD, 1980-82; Duke University Graduate School, PhD, 1985; Harvard Law School, JD, 1986. **CAREER** South Texas College of Law, adjunct professor of law, 1991; Vinson & Elkins LLP, trial lawyer, special counsel, 1986-92; University of Houston Law Center, adjunct professor of law, 1987-; City of Houston, city attorney, 1992-95; O'Quinn and Laminack, attorney, currently. **HONORS AND AWARDS** Rockefellar Scholar, 1977-78; Benjamin E Mays Scholar, 1978-79; Duke Black Grad Fellow, 1979-80; German Research Fellow, Bonn Universitat, 1980; James B

Duke Grad Fellow, 1980-81; DADD Scholar to Germany, 1981-82; Black Doctoral Dissertation Fellow, 1982-83; Shell Fellow to Lambarene, Gabon, Africa, 1982-83; Duke Merit Scholar, 1977-79; Merrill Griswold Scholar, 1986. **CONTACT ADDRESS** O'Quinn and Laminack, 2300 Lyric Centre Building, 440 Louisiana, Houston, TX, 77002.

HALL, DAVID
DISCIPLINE PHILOSOPHY **EDUCATION** Texas Western Col, BA; Chicago Theol Sem, BD; Yale Univ, PhD. **CAREER** Fac, Univ Tex at El Paso, 69-. **RESEARCH** Contemporary China; American intellectual history; fictionalized travel essays. **SELECTED PUBLICATIONS** Auth, The Civilization of Experience, 73; The Uncertain Phoenix, 82; Eros and Irony, 82; Richard Rorty - Prophet and Poet of the New Pragmatism, 94; The Arimaspian Eye, 92; coauth, Thinking Through Confucius, 87; Anticipating China, 95; Thinking From the Han, 97. **CONTACT ADDRESS** Dept of Philosophy, Univ of Texas, El Paso, 500 W University Ave, El Paso, TX, 79968. **EMAIL** dhall@utep.edu

HALL, DAVID
PERSONAL Born 05/26/1950, Savannah, GA, m, 1990 **DISCIPLINE** LAW **EDUCATION** Kansas State Univ, BA political sci 1972; Univ of Oklahoma, MA human relations 1975, JD 1978; Harvard Law School, LLM, 1985, SJD, 1988. **CAREER** Federal Trade Commission, staff attorney 1978-80; Univ of Mississippi Law School, asst prof of law 1980-83; Univ of Oklahoma Law School, assoc prof of law 1983-85; NORTHEASTERN UNIV SCHOOL OF LAW, assoc professor of law, 1985-88, associate dean & professor, 1988-98, PROVOST/SR VICE PRES, 1998-; Sabbatical research, South Africa, beginning 1992. **HONORS AND AWARDS** Outstanding Senior Award, Oklahoma Bar Assn 1978; Professor of the Year, Oxford Miss Branch of NAACP; Floyd Calvert Law Faculty Award, Univ of Oklahoma Law School 1984; Order of the Coif, Univ of Oklahoma Law School Chapter 1984; Robert D Klein, Northeastern Univ; Floyd Calvert Law Faculty, Univ of OK; professor of the year, NAACP, Oxford, MS; Outstanding KS State Student. **MEMBERSHIPS** Natl Conference of Black Lawyers 1978-80; Oklahoma Bar Assn 1978-; attorney, Fed Trade Commn, Chicago, IL, 1978-80; Amer Bar Assn. **CONTACT ADDRESS** Northeastern Univ, 400 Huntington Ave, Boston, MA, 02115.

HALL, DAVID LYNN
PERSONAL Shreveport, LA, 2 children **DISCIPLINE** PHILOSOPHY OF CULTURE AND RELIGION **EDUCATION** Tex Western Col, BA, 61; Chicago Theol Sem, BD, 64; Yale Univ, PhD(philos theol), 67. **CAREER** Asst prof philos, Univ Tulsa, 67-69; assoc prof, 69-75, PROF PHILOS, UNIV TEX, EL PASO, 75-, Nat Endowment for Humanities res grant, 78-. **HONORS AND AWARDS** Phi Kappa Phi; Distginguished Res Awd. **MEMBERSHIPS** Southwestern Philos Soc; Soc Studies Process Philos; Soc Asian & Comp Philos; Soc Philos of Creativity. **RESEARCH** Contemporary philosophy of culture; Asian and comparative philosophy; American Philosophy. **SELECTED PUBLICATIONS** Auth, Eros and Irony, SUNY, 82; auth, Thinking Through Confucius, SUNY, 82; auth, The Arimaspian Eye, SUNY, 92; auth, Anticipating China, SUNY, 96; auth, Richard Rorty- Poet and Prophet of New Pragmatism, SUNY, 94; auth, Thinking from the Han, SUNY, 98; auth, The Democracy of the Dead, Open Court, 98. **CONTACT ADDRESS** Dept of Philos, Univ of Tex, 500 W University Ave, El Paso, TX, 79968-0001. **EMAIL** dhall@utep.edu

HALL, JAMES
PERSONAL Born 10/20/1933, Houston, TX, m, 1957, 3 children **DISCIPLINE** PHILOSOPHY **EDUCATION** John Hopkins Univ, AB, 55; BD, 58, ThM, 60, Southeastern Seminary; UNC-Chapel Hill, PhD, 64. **CAREER** Instr, 60-62, UNC-Chapel Hill; Asst Prof, 63-65, Furman Univ; Assoc Prof, 65-74, Prof, 74-, Univ Richmond. **HONORS AND AWARDS** Thomas Chr in Phil, 82-. **MEMBERSHIPS** Amer Phil Assoc; AAUP **RESEARCH** Philosophy of religion **SELECTED PUBLICATIONS** Coauth, Biblical & Secular Ethics, 88; Auth, Logic Problems, 91; **CONTACT ADDRESS** Philosophy/North Ct., Univ of Richmond, Richmond, VA, 23173. **EMAIL** jhall@richmond.edu

HALL, JOHN
PERSONAL Washington, DC **DISCIPLINE** PHILOSOPHY **EDUCATION** Vanderbilt Univ, PhD, 70. **CAREER** Asst prof, assoc prof, Randolph-Macon Col, 68-78; assoc prof, prof, Virginia Commonwealth Univ, 79-87; prof, Davidson Col, 87-. **MEMBERSHIPS** Am Phil Asn; Phil of Sci Asn; Soc for Phil and Psych, Southern Soc for Phil and Psych; N Carolina Phil Soc. **RESEARCH** Philosophy of mind; metaphysics; epistemology. **SELECTED PUBLICATIONS** North Am ed, Phil Quart; auth, Logic and Language, Univ Pr of Am, 78; Perception and Cognition, Univ of Calif, 83; Nature of True Minds, Cambridge Univ, 92; First-Order Logic, Jones and Bartlett, 94; Philosophy of Mind, Routledge, 98. **CONTACT ADDRESS** Dept of Philosophy, Davidson Col, Davidson, NC, 28036. **EMAIL** joheil@davidson.edu

HALL, PAMELA M.
DISCIPLINE ETHICS AND MORAL PSYCHOLOGY **EDUCATION** Vanderbilt Univ, PhD, 87. **CAREER** Philos, Emory Univ. **SELECTED PUBLICATIONS** Auth, Narrative and the Natural Law: An Interpretation of Thomistic Ethics. **CONTACT ADDRESS** Emory Univ, Atlanta, GA, 30322-1950.

HALL, RICHARD JOHN
PERSONAL Born 07/11/1937, Vancouver, BC, Canada, m, 1959, 1 child **DISCIPLINE** PHILOSOPHY **EDUCATION** Oberlin Col, BA, 59; Princeton Univ, PhD(philos of math), 63. **CAREER** From instr to assoc prof philos, Franklin and Marshall Col, 62-69; assoc prof, 69-80, PROF PHILOS, MICH STATE UNIV, 80-. **MEMBERSHIPS** Am Philos Asn. **RESEARCH** Epistemology. **SELECTED PUBLICATIONS** Auth, The Evolution of Color-Vision without Colors, Philos of Sci, Vol 0063, 96. **CONTACT ADDRESS** Dept of Philos, Michigan State Univ, 503 S Kedzie Hall, E Lansing, MI, 48824.

HALL, ROBERT WILLIAM
PERSONAL Born 04/06/1928, Arlington, MA, m, 1958, 6 children **DISCIPLINE** PHILOSOPHY **EDUCATION** Harvard Univ, AB, 49, MA, 51, PhD, 53. **CAREER** Vis asst prof philos, Vanderbilt Univ, 55-57; vis asst prof, 57-63, assoc prof, 63-67, chmn dept, 64-72, Prof Philos & Relig, Univ Vt, 67, Church Soc Col Work fel, 63-64; ed, Apeiron, 67; Shedd fel, relig in higher educ, 68-69. **MEMBERSHIPS** Soc Ancient Greek Philos (secy-treas, 63-73); Brit Studies Group in Greek Polit Thought; Am Soc Polit & Legal Philos. **RESEARCH** Plato and Greek philos; philos of relig; aesthetics. **SELECTED PUBLICATIONS** Auth, Plato and the Individual, Martinus Nijhoff, 63; Gorgias, In: Essays in Ancient and Greek Philosophy, State Univ NY, 71; Plato's just and happy man: Fact or fallacy?, J Hist Philos, 71; Egalitarianism and justice in the Republic, Apeiron, 72; Plato's theory of art: A reassessment, J Aesthet & Art Criticism, 74; Plato's political analogy: Fallacy or analogy, J Hist Philos, 74; Plato, Allen and Unwin, 81; Plato and Totalitarianism, Polis, 88; Art and Morality in Plato, A Reappraisal, Jour Aesthetic Educ, 90; Natural law Revisited, Studies in Political Thought, 92; Hanslick and Musical Expressiveness, Jour Aesthetic Educ, 95; Hanslick with Feeling, Canadian Aesthetics Jour, 98. **CONTACT ADDRESS** Dept of Philos, Univ of VT, 70 S Williams St, Burlington, VT, 05401-3404.

HALL, RONALD L.
PERSONAL Born 01/02/1945, Moultrie, GA, m, 1965, 2 children **DISCIPLINE** PHILOSOPHY, RELIGION **EDUCATION** Stetson Univ, BA, 67; Duke Univ, MDiv, 70; Univ NC, Chapel Hill, PhD(Philo), 73. **CAREER** Asst prof, 73-80, Assoc Prof, 80-85, Prof, Philos & Relig, Francis Marion Univ, 85-. **HONORS AND AWARDS** NEH Summer Seminar, Purdue Univ, 78; NEH Summer Seminar, Harvard Univ, 84. **MEMBERSHIPS** Am Philos Asn; Am Acad Relig; kierkegaard Soc; Polany Soc; Soc Philos Relig. **RESEARCH** Metaphysics and epistemology. **SELECTED PUBLICATIONS** Auth, Responsibility and intention: Reflections on the problem of God's will and human suffering, Perspectives Relig Studies, summer 79; Wittgenstein and Polanyi: The problem of privileged self-knowledge, Philos Today, fall 79; Freedom: Merleau-Ponty's critique of Sartre, Philos Res Arch, winter 80; The ontological context of God's omniscience and man's freedom, Perspectives Relig Studies, spring 81; The origin of alienation: Some Kierkegaardian reflections on Merleau-Ponty's phenomenology of the body, Int J Philos Relig, summer 81; Word and Spirit: A Kierkegaardian Critique of the Modern Age, Indiana Univ Press, 93; The Human Embrace: The Love of Philosophy and the Philosophy of Love, Kierkegaard, Cavell, Nussbaum, Penn State Press (forthcoming). **CONTACT ADDRESS** Dept of Philosophy, Francis Marion Univ, Florence, SC, 29501-0547. **EMAIL** Rhall@FMarion.edu

HALL, THOR
PERSONAL Born 03/15/1927, Larvik, Norway, m, 1950, 1 child **DISCIPLINE** THEOLOGY **EDUCATION** Scand Methodist Sem, Sweden, BD, 50; Duke Univ, MRE, 59, PhD, 62. **CAREER** Asst minister, Hamar Methodist Church, Norway, 46-47; minister, Odalen Methodist Church, Kongsvinger, 51-53; nat dir Christian educ, Methodist Bd Educ, Norway, 53-57; minister, Ansonville Methodist Church, NC, 58-59; asst to minister, First Presby Church, Durham, DC, 60-62; asst preaching, Divinity Sch, Duke Univ, 61-62, from asst prof to assoc prof preaching and theol, 62-72; DISTINGUISHED PROF RELIG STUDIES, UNIV TENN, CHATTANOOGA, 72-, Ed, Var Ungdom, 53-57; Am Asn Theol Schs fac fel, Sweden, 68-69; mem, Gen Bd Evangelism, United Methodist Church, 68-72; chmn, Workgroup Scand Theol, Am Acad Relig, 74-81; vis prof, Oslo Univ, spring sem, 77, Sbarnga Sch Theol, Siberia, 80. **HONORS AND AWARDS** James Sprunt lectr, Union Theol Sem Va, 70. **MEMBERSHIPS** Am Acad Relig; Soc Philos Relig; Soc Sci Studies Relig; AAUP. **RESEARCH** Philosophy of religion; theological methodology; systematic theology. **SELECTED PUBLICATIONS** Auth, Academia-et-Ecclesia--Studies in Honor of Cleve, Fredric, Scand Stud, Vol 0065, 93; The Hedstroms and the Bethel-Ship Saga--Methodist Influence on Swedish Religious Life, Scand Stud, Vol 0066, 94. **CONTACT ADDRESS** Dept of Philos and Relig, Univ of Tenn, Chattanooga, TN, 37401.

HALLBERG, FRED WILLIAM
PERSONAL Born 08/13/1935, Minneapolis, MN, m, 1985, 5 children **DISCIPLINE** PHILOSOPHY **EDUCATION** Iowa St Univ, MS, 74; Univ Minn, MA, 63, PhD, 69. **CAREER** Instr, Univ Minn, 64-67; assoc prof, Univ N Iowa, 67-98. **MEMBERSHIPS** APA; Am Acad Relig. **RESEARCH** Theory of knowledge; philosophy of religion; philosophy of science. **SELECTED PUBLICATIONS** Auth, "Is Lady Philosophy Being Straight with Boethius," Carmina Philos, 93; "Neo-Kantian Constraints on Legitimate Religious Belief," Am Jrnl of Theol and Phil, 95; rev of Paul Jerome Croce, Science and Religion in the Era of William James, Am Jrnl of Theol and Phil, 96; Demythologization of Eschatological Environmentalism," Proc of 2nd Int Conf on Philos and Theol, 98; "Satisfaction and Power Components of the Pragmatic Definition of Truth," Pragmatism in Am Relig Thought, 98. **CONTACT ADDRESS** 630 Main St., PO Box 323, Janesville, IA, 50647. **EMAIL** hallberg@uni.edu

HALLBORG, ROBERT B., JR.
PERSONAL Born 05/24/1947, Newport, RI, m, 1971, 2 children **DISCIPLINE** PHILOSOPHY **EDUCATION** SUNY Buffalo, JD, 80, PhD, 84. **CAREER** Criminal appeals atty, Legal Aid Bureau of Buffalo, 87- . **HONORS AND AWARDS** Boldy Found Fel. **MEMBERSHIPS** Am Philos Asn; NY St Public Defenders Asn; Natl Asn Criminal Def Lawyers. **RESEARCH** Philosophy of Criminal Law justifications; Necessity Defense. **SELECTED PUBLICATIONS** Auth, Comparing Harms: The Lesser Evil Defense and the Trolley Problem, in Legal Theory 3, 97, 291-316. **CONTACT ADDRESS** Dept of Criminal Appeals, Legal Aid Bureau, 237 Main St, Ste 1602, Buffalo, NY, 14203-2723.

HALLEN, BARRY
PERSONAL Born 04/05/1941, Chicago, IL **DISCIPLINE** PHILOSOPHY **EDUCATION** Carleton Col, BA, 63; Boston Univ, MA, 68, PhD, 70. **CAREER** Lectr, 70-75, Univ of Lagos, Nigera; reader in philosophy, 75-88, Univ of Ife, Nigera; visiting prof, 97-99, Morehouse Col, **HONORS AND AWARDS** Dir, UNESCO Intercultural Project, 88-98; research fel, W.E.B. DuBois Institute for Afro-Amer Research, Harvard Univ, 95-99. **MEMBERSHIPS** ACASA; ASA; APA **RESEARCH** Africana Philosphy; interdisciplinary and intercultural studies. **SELECTED PUBLICATIONS** Auth, What's It Mean?: 'Analytic' African Philosophy, in Quest Philosophical Discussions, 96; auth, African Meanings, Western Words, African Studies Review, The African Studies Association, 97; coauth, Knowledge, Belief, and Witchcraft: Analytic Experiments in African Philosophy, 97; auth, Moral Epistemology: When Propositions Come Out of Mouths, 98; auth, entries on Aesthetics, African and on Yoruba Epistemology for the Encyclopedia of Philosophy, 98; auth, entry on African Aesthetics for the Encyclopedia of Aesthetics, 98. **CONTACT ADDRESS** Philosophy & Relig, Morehouse Col, Sale Hall, Atlanta, GA, 30314-3773. **EMAIL** ablesus@aol.com

HALLETT, MICHAEL
DISCIPLINE PHILOSOPHY **EDUCATION** Univ London, BS, PhD. **RESEARCH** Philos and hist of mathematics; philos of sci; hist of logic; logic and set theory; development of set theory; development of analytic philos. **SELECTED PUBLICATIONS** Auth, Cantorian Set Theory and Limitation of Size, Clarendon, 88; Physicalism, reductionism and Hilbert, Reidel, 90; auth, Hilbert's Axiomatic Method and The Laws of Thought, Oxford, 94; auth, Putnam and the Skolem paradox, 94; auth, Logic and Mathematical Existence, 95; auth, Hilbert and logic, Kluwer, 95. **CONTACT ADDRESS** Philosophy Dept, McGill Univ, 845 Sherbrooke St, Montreal, PQ, H3A 2T5.

HALLMAN, JOSEPH MARTIN
PERSONAL Born 10/08/1939, Chicago, IL, m, 1966, 3 children **DISCIPLINE** CONTEMPORARY & PATRISTIC THEOLOGY **EDUCATION** St Francis Sem, BA, 62; Marquette Univ, MA, 65; Fordham Univ, PhD(theol), 70. **CAREER** Instr theol, Webster Col, 64-67; asst prof, Wheeling Col, 70-76, assoc prof, 77-81; Assoc Prof Theol, Col Of St Thomas, 81-. **MEMBERSHIPS** Am Acad Relig; Cath Theol Soc Am; Soc for the Philos of Relig. **RESEARCH** Process theology; patristic theology, especially the understanding of the nature of God. **SELECTED PUBLICATIONS** Auth, The Seed of Fire - Divine Suffering in the Christology of Cyril-Of-Alexandria And Nestorius-Of-Constantinople, J Early Christian Studies, Vol 0005, 97; The Seed of Fire - Divine Suffering in the Christology of Cyril-Of-Alexandria and Nestorius-Of-Constantinople, J Early Christian Studies, Vol 0005, 97. **CONTACT ADDRESS** Dept of Theol, Col of St. Thomas, 2115 Summit Ave, Saint Paul, MN, 55105-1096.

HALLMAN, MAX
PERSONAL Born 02/21/1952, Lexington County, SC, 3 children **DISCIPLINE** PHILOSOPHY **EDUCATION** Univ SC, BA, 74, MA, 76; Tulane Univ, PhD, 86. **CAREER** Instr, Loyala Univ, 83-85; prof, coordr, Merced Col, 86-. **HONORS AND AWARDS** Phi Theta Kappa Giles Distinguished Advisor, 94; Phi Theta Kappa Advisor Continued Excellence Award, 97; Phi Theta Kappa Moselle Scholar, 95; NISOD Tchg Excel-

lence Award, 93. **MEMBERSHIPS** Am Philos Asn **RESEARCH** Nietzsche; environmental philosophy; native American Philosophy, comparative cultures. **SELECTED PUBLICATIONS** Auth, The Shattered Self: Self-Overcoming and the Transfiguration of Nature in the Philosophy of Nietzsche, 88; auth, art, Nietzsche's Environmental Ethics, 91; auth, art, Becoming Multiculturally Literate, 93; auth, Expanding Philosophical Horizons: A Non-Traditional Philosophy Reader, 95; auth, Traversing Philosophical Boundaries, 98. **CONTACT ADDRESS** Dept of Philosophy, Merced Col, 3600 M St, Merced, CA, 95340. **EMAIL** hallmanm@merced.cc.ca.us

HALPER, EDWARD CHARLES
PERSONAL Born 09/28/1951, Barberton, OH, m, 1979, 3 children **DISCIPLINE** PHILOSOPHY **EDUCATION** Univ Chicago, BA, 73; Columbia Univ, MA, 75; Univ Toronto, PhD, 80. **CAREER** Tchng fel, 80, Canisius Col; asst prof, 80-84, Gustavus Adolphus Col; asst prof, 84-87, assoc prof, 87-92, prof, 92-, Univ GA. **HONORS AND AWARDS** Grad fel, 73-74, Columbia Univ; Grad Fel, 76-77. 77-78, 78-79, Univ Toronto; George Paxton Young Mem Fel, 79; NEH Grants, 80-81, 83, 86; Aristotle's Metaphysics and Epistemology, FL ST Univ; Univ GA Res Found Grant, 88, 90, 97; Univ GA Humanities Center Fel, 95-96. **MEMBERSHIPS** APA, Can Phil Asn, Hegel Soc of Amer, Intl Asn for Greek Phil, Intl Plato Soc, Metaphysical Soc of Amer, Soc for Ancient Greek Phil, Soc for Medieval & Renaissance Phil. **RESEARCH** Ancient phil; medieval phil; 19th century German phil; metaphysics. **SELECTED PUBLICATIONS** Auth, One and Many in Aristotle's Metaphysics: The Central Books, Oh St Univ Press, 89; auth, Form and Reason: Essays in Metaphysics, SUNY Press, 93, art, The Substances of Aristotle's Ethics, Crossroads of Norm & Nature: Essays on Aristotle's Ethics and Metaphysics, 94; art, Virtue and the State, Aristotelian Pol Phil, Vol 2, 95; auth, "Aitia,"" Autarkia,"" Dianoia," "Elenchus," "Nous," " One-Many Problem," "Ousia," "Telos", Cambridge Dict of Phil, Cambridge Univ Press, 95; auth, The Logic of Hegel's Philosophy of Nature: Nature, Space, and Time, Essays on Hegel's Phil of Nature, SUNY Press, 98. **CONTACT ADDRESS** Dept of Philosophy, Univ Ga, Athens, GA, 30602-1627. **EMAIL** ehalper@uga.cc.uga.edu

HALPERIN, STEPHEN H.
DISCIPLINE LAW **EDUCATION** Concordia Univ, BA, 72; McGill Univ, BCL, 75, LLB, 78. **CAREER** Lectr; Partner, Goodman Phillips & Vineberg **MEMBERSHIPS** Editorial Board, Corporate Financing Quarterly; Advisory Board, CCH Ontario Corporations Law Guide **SELECTED PUBLICATIONS** Auth, pubs on corporate and securities law matters. **CONTACT ADDRESS** Fac of Law, Univ Toronto, 78 Queen's Park, Toronto, ON.

HALPERN, BETH
PERSONAL Born 07/28/1962, New York, NY, m, 1994 **DISCIPLINE** PHILOSOPHY **EDUCATION** Binghamton Univ, PhD, 95. **CAREER** Landmark Col, asst prof, 95-. **MEMBERSHIPS** APA **RESEARCH** Ideas of Selfhood and value inquiry; literature and the ethical imagination; eastern representations; Development of overseas program of studies in Tibetan culture and thought in Dharansaya, India. **SELECTED PUBLICATIONS** Auth, Conflicting Values, Fractured Selves, Intl Philo Quart, Fordham Univ Press, 98; books rev, The Self in Social Theory, by CF Alford, 97; The Authentic Self, by R. Ehman, Intl Stud Philos, 97; auth, The Site of Our Lives: The Self and the Subject from Emerson to Foucault, by J. S. Hans, Intl Stud Philos, forthcoming; auth, For Love of Country: Debating the Limits of Patriotism, by MC Nussbaum, Intl Stud Philos, forthcoming. **CONTACT ADDRESS** Landmark Col, RR 1, PO Box 1000, Putney, VT, 05346. **EMAIL** Batya222@aol.com

HALSTEAD, THOMAS
PERSONAL CA, m, 1977, 3 children **DISCIPLINE** RELIGION **EDUCATION** CAL St Univ, MS; Talbot Theol Sem, Mdiv; Nova SE Univ, EdD **CAREER** Chair, 14 yrs, The Masters Col **HONORS AND AWARDS** Tchr of yr, 94 **MEMBERSHIPS** Evang Theol Soc **CONTACT ADDRESS** Newhall, CA, 91321. **EMAIL** thalstead@masters.edu

HALWANI, RAJA
PERSONAL Born 04/22/1967, Beirut, Lebanon, s **DISCIPLINE** PHILOSOPHY **EDUCATION** Am Univ of Beirut, BA, 88; Syracuse Univ, MA, 95, PhD, 96 **CAREER** Visit Asst Prof, 96-97, Rollins Col; Asst Prof, 97-pres, Sch of the Art Inst of Chicago **MEMBERSHIPS** Am Philos Assoc **RESEARCH** Ethics, Sexuality **SELECTED PUBLICATIONS** In Journals of Aesthetic Edu; Social Philos; Homosexuality **CONTACT ADDRESS** Liberal Arts, School of the Art Institute of Chicago, 37 S Wabas, Chicago, IL, 60613. **EMAIL** rhalwa@artic.edu

HAMBRICK, A. FRED
PERSONAL Born 03/14/1935, Dallas, TX, m, 1963, 4 children **DISCIPLINE** RELIGION **EDUCATION** Okla Baptist Univ, BA, 57; City Univ, MAT, 68; Southwestern Seminary, BD (MDiv), 60; Luther Rice Seminary, DMin, 84. **CAREER** Teacher, Putnam City High School, 65-70; asst principal, Put-

nam City West High School, 70-72; Pastor, First Baptist Church, 72-73 & 75-83; Pastor, First United Methodist Church, 80-91; Superintendent Headmaster, Moody Christian Acad, 72-75; Principle, Okmulgee High School, 75-80; prof, Redlands Community Col, 90-97; AM BIBLE COL AND SEMINARY, 98-; PASTOR, FRANKLIN ROAD BAPTIST CHURCH, 92-. **MEMBERSHIPS** Nat Asn of Sec Sch Prin; Okla Sec Sch Prin Asn. **CONTACT ADDRESS** 200 23rd Ave, NE, Norman, OK, 73071. **EMAIL** RNALOL@aol.com

HAMBRICK, CHARLES HILTON
PERSONAL Born 05/14/1931, Atlanta, GA, m, 1955, 3 children **DISCIPLINE** HISTORY OF RELIGIONS, JAPANESE STUDIES **EDUCATION** Vanderbilt Univ, BA, 52; Drew Univ, BD, 59; Univ Chicago, MA, 67, PhD(hist of relig), 71. **CAREER** From instr to asst prof, 69-75, Assoc Prof Hist Of Relig, Vanderbilt Univ, 75- **MEMBERSHIPS** Am Acad Relig; Asn Asian Studies. **RESEARCH** Japanese religion; religion and Eastern cultures; methods in the study of religion. **SELECTED PUBLICATIONS** Auth, Religion and Society in Modern Japan--Selected-Readings, Monumenta Nipponica, Vol 0049, 94. **CONTACT ADDRESS** Dept of Relig Studies, Vanderbilt Univ, Sta B, Box 64, Nashville, TN, 37235.

HAMELIN, LEONCE
PERSONAL Born 12/04/1920, St. Narcisse, PQ, Canada **DISCIPLINE** THEOLOGY **EDUCATION** Laval Univ, BA, 45; Franciscan Int Univ, Rome, DTh, 54. **CAREER** Prof theol, Franciscan Sem Theol, 51-52 & 54-67, dean, 57-61; Prof Theol, Univ Montreal, 55-, Mem ed comt, Concilium, 65-; asst Prof, Univ Louvain, 72. **MEMBERSHIPS** Can Soc Theol: Int Soc Medieval Studies; Mediaeval Acad Am. **SELECTED PUBLICATIONS** Auth, In the Belly of the Narrative--Reading Bessette, Voix & Images, Vol 0020, 95. **CONTACT ADDRESS** 5750 Rosemont Blvd, Montreal, PQ, H1T 2H2.

HAMILTON, CHARLES VERNON
PERSONAL Born 10/19/1929, Muskogee, Oklahoma, m, 1956 **DISCIPLINE** LAW **EDUCATION** Roosevelt University, Chicago, IL, BA, 1951; Loyola University, School of Law, Chicago, IL, JD, 1954; University of Chicago, Chicago, IL, MA, 1957, PhD, 1964. **CAREER** Tuskegee University, Tuskegee, AL, assistant professor, 1958-60; Rutgers University, Newark, NJ, assistant professor, 1963-64; Lincoln University, Oxford, PA, professor, 1964-67; Roosevelt University, Chicago, IL, professor, 1967-69; Columbia, University, New York, professor, 1969-. **HONORS AND AWARDS** University of Chicago, Alumni Award, 1970; Roosevelt University Alumni Award, 1970; Lindback Teaching Award, Lincoln University, 1965; Van Doren Teaching Ward, Columbia University, 1982; Great Teacher Award, Columbia University, 1985. **MEMBERSHIPS** Board of trustees, Twentieth Century Foundation, 1973-; board member, NAACP, 1975-; board of editors, Political Science Quarterly, 1975-. **SELECTED PUBLICATIONS** Adam Clayton Powell Jr, 1991. **CONTACT ADDRESS** Professor, Columbia Univ, 420 W 118th St, Room 727, New York, NY, 10027.

HAMILTON, EUGENE NOLAN
PERSONAL Born 08/24/1933, Memphis, TN, m, 1956 **DISCIPLINE** LAW **EDUCATION** Univ of Illinois, BA, 1955, JD, 1959. **CAREER** US Army, judge advocate officer, 1959-61; US Dept of Justice, trial attorney, 1961-70; SUPERIOR COURT OF DC, JUDGE, 1970-; HARVARD LAW SCHOOL, lecturer, 1995, TEACHER, 1985-. **HONORS AND AWARDS** Washington Bar Assn, Ollie Mae Cooper Award, 1993; National Bar Assn, Wiley A Branton Issues Symposium Award; Oldender Foundation Generous Heart Award; Charles Hamilton Houston, Medallion of Merit. **MEMBERSHIPS** American Bar Assn, executive committee, 1970-; Washington Bar Assn, 1970-; Bar Assn of DC, 1990-; DC Bar Assn, 1970-. **CONTACT ADDRESS** Superior Court of District of Columbia, 500 Indiana Ave, NW, Washington, DC, 20001.

HAMILTON, ROBERT W.
PERSONAL Born 03/04/1931, Syracuse, NY, m, 1953, 3 children **DISCIPLINE** LAW **EDUCATION** Swarthmore Col, BA, 52; Univ Chicago, JD, 55. **CAREER** From assoc prof law to prof, 64-72, Vinson & Elkins prof, 72-81, Benno C Schmidt Prof Bus Law, Univ Tex, Austin, 81-, vis prof, Univ Minn, 66-67; consult, Admin Conf US, 70-; vis prof, Univ Ariz, 71-72; vis prof, Univ Pa, 78; vis prof, Washington Univ, St Louis, 82; Minerva House Drysdale Regents Chair in Law, 87-98; Godfrey Vis Prof, Univ of Maine, 87, 92. **SELECTED PUBLICATIONS** Auth, Procedures for the Adoption of Rules of General Applicability: The Need for Procedural Innovation in Administrative Rulemaking, Calif Law Rev, 72; Rulemaking on a Record by the Food and Drug Administration, Univ Tex Law Rev, 72; Texas Law and Practice: Business Organizations, (2 vols), 73 & Cases & Materials on Corporations, 76, 2nd ed, 81, West Publ, 3rd ed, 86, 4th ed, 90, 5th ed, 94, 6th ed, 98; Fundamentals of Modern Business, Little Brown, 89; Money Management for Lawyers and Clients, Little Brown, 93; Registered Limited Liability Partnerships, Colo L Review, 95; Business Organizations, Aspen, 96; Black Leather on Corporations, West, 97; Corporate General Partners of Limited Partnerships, Int Small Bus Law, 97; Limited Liability and the Real World (with Ribstein), Wash

and Lee L. Rev, 97. **CONTACT ADDRESS** Sch of Law, Univ Of Tex, 727 E 26th St, Austin, TX, 78705-3224. **EMAIL** rhamilton@mail.law.utexas.edu

HAMILTON, VICTOR PAUL
PERSONAL Born 09/26/1941, Toronto, ON, Canada, m, 1965, 4 children **DISCIPLINE** OLD TESTAMENT STUDIES, ANCIENT NEAR EASTERN HISTORY **EDUCATION** Houghton Col, BA, 63; Asbury Theol Sem, BD, 66, ThM, 67; Brandeis Univ, MA, 69, PhD, 71. **CAREER** From asst prof to assoc prof, 71-85, prof Old Testament, Asbury Col, 85-. **MEMBERSHIPS** Soc Bibl Lit; Evangelical Theol Soc. **RESEARCH** Old Testament languages. **SELECTED PUBLICATIONS** Auth, The Shepherd Psalm: Psalm 23, Asbury Seminarian, 72; Handbook on the Pentateuch, Baker, 82; Genesis Chapters 1-17, Eerdmans, 92; Genesis, Chapters 18-50, Eerdmans, 95. **CONTACT ADDRESS** 1 Macklem Dr, Wilmore, KY, 40390-1198. **EMAIL** victor.hamilton@asbury.edu

HAMLIN, ERNEST LEE
PERSONAL Born 12/09/1943, Sussex County, VA, m, 1978 **DISCIPLINE** RELIGION **EDUCATION** Virginia Union University, BA, 1970, School of Theology, MDiv, 1974; Presbyterian School of Christian Education, 1976; Virginia Commonwealth University, pastoral education, 1976-77. **CAREER** Bethesda Baptist Church, pastor, 1981-83; Richmond Virginia Seminary, theology and christian education, professor, 1982-89; Ebenezer Baptist Church, supply pastor, 1984; Union Hill United Church of Christ, pastor, 1986-89; Christian Education Ministries, president, 1990-; Emmanuel-St Mark's United Church of Christ, pastor, 1990-92; Tubman-King Community Church, senior pastor, 1992-. **HONORS AND AWARDS** Emmanuel-St Mark's UCC, Outstanding Leadership Award, 1992; Richmond Virginia Seminary, Outstanding Service Award, 1986; United Negro College Fund, Honorary Chairperson, 1983. **MEMBERSHIPS** Habitat for Humanity, board of directors, 1992-; Northeast Ministerial Alliance, executive vice pres, 1991-92; East Side Ecumenical Fellowship, executive secretary, 1990-91, executive vice pres, 1991-92; OIC Metro Saginaw, board of directors, 1990-92; One Church One Child of Michigan, board of directors, 1991-92; SCLC, Virginia State Unit, board of directors, 1982-90, Richmond Chapter, board of directors, 1981-85. **SELECTED PUBLICATIONS** "A True Mother and Christ," published poem, 1990 **CONTACT ADDRESS** Senior Pastor, Tubman-King Community Church, 425 N Seneca St, Daytona Beach, FL, 32114.

HAMM, MICHAEL DENNIS
PERSONAL Born 01/18/1936, Cincinnati, OH **DISCIPLINE** NEW TESTAMENT, BIBLE **EDUCATION** Marquette Univ, BA, 58; St Louis Univ, MA, 64, PhD(Theol), 75. **CAREER** Instr English, Creighton Preparatory Sch, 64-65; instr, 65-67, asst prof, 75-81, from assoc prof to prof Theol, Creighton Univ, 81-91, Managing ed, Theol Digest, 70. **MEMBERSHIPS** Soc Bibl Lit; Cath Bibl Asn; Col Theol Soc, 85. **RESEARCH** Gospel of Luke; Acts of the Apostles. **SELECTED PUBLICATIONS** Auth, Preaching Biblical Justice, Church, Spring, 96; Ascension, The Pastoral Dictionary of Biblical Theology, Collegeville, MN: Liturgical Press, 96; Pentecost, The Pastoral Dictionary of Biblical Theology, Collegeville, MN: Liturgical Press, 96; Spirit of God/Holy Spirit--New Testament, The Pastoral Dictionary of Biblical Theology, Collegeville, MN: Liturgical Press, 96. **CONTACT ADDRESS** Dept of Theology, Creighton Univ, 2500 California Plz, Omaha, NE, 68178-0001. **EMAIL** dhamm@creighton

HAMMER, JANE R.
PERSONAL Born 04/09/1916, Charlotte, NC, m, 1937, 3 children **DISCIPLINE** PHILOSOPHY **EDUCATION** Central High Schl, 33; UNC-Chapel Hill, AB, 36, MA, 37; Radcliffe/Harvard, 38-39. **CAREER** Tchr, 48-60, Spelman Col; Adult Citizen Ed tchr, League of Women Voters Ed Fund (Overseas Ed Fund). **HONORS AND AWARDS** Kenan Fel, 36-37, 38-39, UNC-CH; 500 Environ Achiever, Friends of UN Environ Prog, 87; Woman of The Year, ABI & IB Congress 92, 98; Millennium Hall of Fame, 98; ABI Raleigh. **MEMBERSHIPS** Soc List of Wash; Cromwell Assn; US Woman's Natl Dem Club; Fri Morning Music Club. **RESEARCH** Phil & eEthics; governance - dem, constitutions & prac of citizen resp; biography. **SELECTED PUBLICATIONS** Auth, Logic for Living, Lectures of Horace Williams, Phil Lib NY, 52; auth, Origin of Belief by H Williams, UNC-CH Dept Phil, & HWP Soc, 72; auth, Protector: A Life History of Richard Cromwell, Vantage Press, 97. **CONTACT ADDRESS** 521 Holly Rd, Edgewater, MD, 21037-3846.

HAMMOND, GUY BOWERS
PERSONAL Born 11/07/1930, Birmingham, AL, m, 1959, 2 children **DISCIPLINE** PHILOSOPHY, RELIGION **EDUCATION** Washington & Lee Univ, BA, 51; Yale Univ, BD, 55; Vanderbilt Univ, PhD, 62. **CAREER** Assoc prof, 62-67, Prof Philos & Relig, VA Polytech Inst & State Univ, 67- **MEMBERSHIPS** AAUP; Am Acad Relig; Paul Tillich Soc NAm. **RESEARCH** Contemporary theology and philosophy of religion; religion and culture. **SELECTED PUBLICATIONS** Auth, A Theology of Power--Being Beyond Domination, J Church State, Vol 0036, 94. **CONTACT ADDRESS** Dept of Philos & Relig, Va Polytech Inst & State Univ, Blacksburg, VA, 24060.

HAMRE, JAMES S.
PERSONAL Born 10/28/1931, Montevideo, MN, m, 1957, 2 children **DISCIPLINE** RELIGION IN AMERICAN HISTORY **EDUCATION** Augsburg Col, BA, 53; Luther Theol Sem, Minn, BTh, 57; Univ Chicago, MA, 59; Univ Iowa, PhD(Relig), 67. **CAREER** Prof Religion & Philosophy, Waldorf Col, Iowa, 78-94; Emeritus prof, 94-; visiting lec, Luther Theo Sem, MN, Spring 76, Augsburg Col, MN, Spring 81, District College, Volda, Norway, Spring 95. **HONORS AND AWARDS** Endowment for Humanities, 74, 87; Regents Outstanding Fac Award, Waldorf Col, 84; Holmen Fac Achievement Award, Waldorf Col, 92. **MEMBERSHIPS** Norwegian-American Historical Association. **RESEARCH** Life and thought of Georg Sverdrup; Norwegian immigrant experience; American religious history. **SELECTED PUBLICATIONS** Auth, Georg Sverdrup concerning Luther's principles in America, Concordia Hist Inst Quart, 70; Georg Sverdrup's concept of theological education in the context of a free church, Lutheran Quart, 70; A Thanksgiving Day Address by Georg Sverdrup, Norweg-Am Studies, 70; The Augsburg Triumvirate and the Kvartal-Skrift, Luther Theol Sem Rev, 72; Georg Sverdrup and the Augsburg Plan of Education, Norweg-Am Studies, 74; John O Evjen: Teacher, theologian, biographer, 74 & Georg Sverdrup's Errand into the Wilderness: Building the Free and Living Congregation, 80, Concordia Hist Inst Quart; Norwegian immigrants respond to the common school: A case study of American values and the Lutheran Tradition, Church Hist, 81; The Creationist-Evolutionist Debate and the Public Schools, Journal of Church and State, 91. **CONTACT ADDRESS** Dept of Religion & Philosophy, Waldorf Col, 106 S 6th St, Forest City, IA, 50436-1713. **EMAIL** hamrej@Waldorf.edu

HAN, JIN HEE
PERSONAL Born 07/18/1956, Seoul, Korea, m **DISCIPLINE** OLD TESTAMENT STUDY **EDUCATION** Princeton Theological Seminary, PhD 88, M Div 83; Sogang Univ, Korea, BA 79. **CAREER** NY Theological Seminary, prof, 91-; Drew Univ, adj prof, 92-; Alliance Theol Seminary, 90-91. **MEMBERSHIPS** SBS **RESEARCH** Eregesis; Biblical Interpretations; History of Eregesis. **SELECTED PUBLICATIONS** Auth, The Sacrifice of Abraham, Pulpit Digest, 98; The Word that Gives Life, in: The Upper Room Disciplines 88, Nashville Upper Room Books, 97; How Does the Holy Spirit Enter into Preaching:, Living Pulpit, 96; Biblical Understanding of the Year of Jubilee, Korea Daily News, 95; Consultant for the Korean translation of Rule of the Community, in its Intl ed of the Dead Sea Scrolls Project, Princeton Theol Sem. **CONTACT ADDRESS** Dept of Old Testament, New York Theol Sem, 5 W 29th St, New York, NY, 10001.

HANCHEY, HOWARD
DISCIPLINE PASTORAL THEOLOGY **EDUCATION** Univ NC, BA, 63; Va Theol Sem, MDiv, 67; Union Theol Col, DMin, 75; St George's Col, Jerusalem, 90. **CAREER** Rector, Piedmont Parish, 67-69; asst to rector, missioner to the deaf, St Paul's Episcopal Church, 69-72; assoc rector, E Shore Chapel, 72-76; fac mem, Union Theol Sem; rector, chaplain, St Andrew's Episcopal Church, 76-78; Arthur Lee Kinsolving prof, 78-. **HONORS AND AWARDS** Fel, Col of Chaplains; 1984 Tenure Granted, 84., Chaplain supvr, Assn for Clinical Pastoral Edu; chaplain supvr, Med Col Va of Va Commonwealth Univ, 69-72; organizer, first Episcopal parish based , ACPE certified prog of Clin Pastoral Edu, 74-76; presiding priest, founding pastor, St Peter's in the Woods Episcopal Church, 89-90; chaplain supvr, theologian in residence, St Luke's Episcopal Hospital, 93, 96. **MEMBERSHIPS** Assembly of Episcopal Hospital Chaplains. **SELECTED PUBLICATIONS** Auth, From Survival to Celebration, Leadership For the Confident Church, Cowley Publ, 94; Church Growth and the Power of Evangelism, Ideas that Work, Cowley Publ, 90; Christian Edu Made Easy, Morehouse Publ, 89; Creative Christian Edu, Morehouse Publ, 86. **CONTACT ADDRESS** Va Theol Sem, 3737 Seminary Rd, Alexandria, VA, 22304. **EMAIL** HHanchey@vts.edu

HAND, MICHAEL
DISCIPLINE PHILOSOPHY **EDUCATION** Univ SC, BS, 75, MA, 83; Fla State Univ, PhD, 85. **CAREER** Prof, Tex A&M Univ, 97-; assoc prof, Tex A&M Univ, 92-97; asst prof, Tex A&M Univ, 89-92. **HONORS AND AWARDS** Associates' Distinguished Lectr, Univ Okla, 87-88; Univ fel, Fla State Univ, 81-85; Phi Kappa Phi, Fla State Univ, 84; Phi Beta Kappa, Univ SC, 75. **SELECTED PUBLICATIONS** Auth, Informational Variability, Synthese 99, 94; What the Null Set Could Not Be, Australasian J Philos 73, 95; coauth, Logic Primer, Cambridge, MA: MIT Press, 92. **CONTACT ADDRESS** Dept of Philosophy, Texas A&M Univ, College Station, TX, 77843. **EMAIL** mhand@tamu.edu

HANDWERK-NORAGON, PATRICIA
PERSONAL Born 12/02/1941, Philadelphia, PA, m, 1969, 2 children **DISCIPLINE** PHILOSOPHY **EDUCATION** Swarthmore Coll, 63; Ohio State Univ, PhD, 68. **CAREER** Lectr, Waterloo Lutheran Univ, 67-68; asst prof,68-89; asst prof, Baldwin Wallace Coll, 69-75; adj asst prof, Cleveland State Univ, 75-76; adj asst prof, Kenyon Coll, 88; lectr, 79-97; sr lectr, Ohio State Univ Marion, 98-. **MEMBERSHIPS** Am Philos Asn. **RESEARCH** Teaching Philosophy to Undergraduates. **CONTACT ADDRESS** 1015 Beechview Dr S, Worthington, OH, 43085. **EMAIL** noragon.i@osu.edu

HANDY, WILLIAM TALBOT, JR.
PERSONAL Born 03/26/1924, New Orleans, LA, m, 1948 **DISCIPLINE** THEOLOGY **EDUCATION** Attended Tuskegee Institute, 1940-43; Dillard University, New Orleans, BA, 1948; Gammon Theological Seminary, Atlanta, GA, M Div, 1951; Boston Univ School of Theology, Boston, MA, STM, 1982. **CAREER** Newman Methodist Church, Alexandria, LA, pastor, 1952-59; St Mark Methodist Church, Baton Rouge, LA, pastor, 1959-68; The Methodist Publishing House, Nashville, TN, publishing representative, 1968-70; The United Methodist Publishing House, Nashville, TN, vice-president, personnel and public relations, 1970-78; Baton Rouge-Lafayette, LA, district superintendent, 1978-80; resident bishop, 1980-92; Missouri Area, United Methodist Church, bishop; United Methodist Publishing House, chaplain, 1996-; DREW UNIVERSITY THEOLOGICAL SCHOOL, ADJUNCT DIR, DOCTOR OF MINISTRY PROGRAM, 1996-. **HONORS AND AWARDS** Honorary DD, Huston-Tillotson College, Austin, TX, 1973; Honorary DD, Wiley College, Marshall, TX, 1973; Honorary DD, Centenary College, Shreveport, LA, 1979; Honorary LLD, Dillard University, New Orleans, LA, 1981; Honorary LHD, Philander Smith College, Little Rock, AR, 1982; Honorary DD, Central Methodist Coll, 1991; Tuskegee University & Dillard University, NAFEO Distinguished Alumnus. **MEMBERSHIPS** General bd of publication, 1988-92, past chmn, bd of trustees, St Paul School of Theology; past chmn, bd of trustees, Interdenominational Theological Center; past chmn, bd of trustees, Gammon Theological Sem; past sec, Southern Methodist Univ, bd of trustees; life and Golden Heritage member, NAACP; Hymnal Revision Committee, United Methodist Church, 1984-88; Bishop's Special Committee on SMU, 1986-87. **CONTACT ADDRESS** The United Methodist Church, 201 8th Ave S, Nashville, TN, 37202.

HANEY, MARY-ANN
DISCIPLINE LAW **EDUCATION** Trent Univ, BA, 79; Queens Univ, LLB, 83. **CAREER** Partner, McMillan Binch **SELECTED PUBLICATIONS** Auth, pubs on public and private, domestic and cross-border financing transactions, and international tax planning. **CONTACT ADDRESS** Fac of Law, Univ Toronto, 78 Queen's Park, Toronto, ON.

HANFORD, JACK
PERSONAL Born 08/30/1932, Jackson, KY, m, 1967, 5 children **DISCIPLINE** RELIGION **EDUCATION** Albion Col, AB, 52; Garrett Theol Sem, MDiv, 59; Northwestern Univ, MA, 61; Iliff Sch Theol Denver Univ, ThD, 74. **CAREER** Pastor & tchr, DePauw Univ, 59-60; pastor & instr, Univ N Iowa, 62-68; prof philos & relig, Ferris State Univ, 70-. **HONORS AND AWARDS** Soc Sci Study Relig Fel, 94; Nat Recognized Fac, Ferris State Univ, 95. **MEMBERSHIPS** Am Philos Asn; Am Acad Relig; Soc Sci Study Relig; Asn Moral Educ; Soc Creative Philos; Hastings Ctr; Kennedy Inst Ethics; Mich Med Ethics Rsrc Network; Soc Bus Ethics; Asn Relig Intellectual Life; Inst Relig Age Sci; Park Ridge Ctr Study Health, Faith, Ethics; Soc Values Higher Educ; Mich Acad Arts Sci; Soc Christian Philos; Soc Health Human Values. **RESEARCH** Biomedical ethics; psychology of religion; moral and faith development. **SELECTED PUBLICATIONS** Auth, Religion, Medical Ethics and Transplants, Jour Med Hum, 93; auth, Is the Faith of Faith Development Christian Faith?, Jour Pastoral Psychol, 93; auth, Advancing Moral Reasoning within a Biomedical Ethics Course, Insider: Ferris Fac and Staff Jour, April, 96. **CONTACT ADDRESS** 17220 Valley Dr., Big Rapids, MI, 49307.

HANIGAN, JAMES P.
PERSONAL Born 04/16/1938, New York, NY, m, 1976 **DISCIPLINE** THEOLOGY; ETHICS **EDUCATION** Fordham Univ, MA, 65; Woodstock Col, MDiv, 68; Duke Univ, PhD, 73. **CAREER** Asst Prof, Marquette Univ, 73-75; Asst Prof, Villa Maria Col, 75-79; Asst Prof to Assoc Prof, 79-86, Prof, Duquesne Univ, 86-, Dir Grad Studies, 86-94, Dept Chair, 94-97. **HONORS AND AWARDS** President's Univ Award for Excellence in Scholarship, 88. **MEMBERSHIPS** Am Acad Relig; Soc Christian Ethics; Cath Theol Soc Am; Col Theol Soc. **RESEARCH** Sexual ethics; social ethics. **SELECTED PUBLICATIONS** Auth, What Are They Saying About Sexual Morality?, Paulist Press, 82; Martin Luther King, Jr and the Foundations of Nonviolence, Univ Press Am, 84; As I Have Loved You: The Challenge of Christian Ethics, Paulist Press, 86; Homosexuality: The Test-Case for Christian Se Sexual Ethics, Paulist Press, 88; author of numerous articles and book chapters. **CONTACT ADDRESS** Theology Dept, Duquesne Univ, Pittsburgh, PA, 15282. **EMAIL** hanigan@duq.z.cc.duq.edu

HANKS, DONALD
DISCIPLINE PHILOSOPHY OF RELIGION, PHILOSOPHICAL PSYCHOLOGY, SOCIAL AND POLITICAL PHIL **EDUCATION** Univ Denver, BA, 56, MA, 65; Duke Univ, BD, 60; Univ New Orleans, ThD, 67; Tulane Univ, PhD, 70. **CAREER** Assoc prof, Univ New Orleans. **HONORS AND AWARDS** Amoco Found Award, LSU Syst, 81. **SELECTED PUBLICATIONS** Auth, Statistical Victims and Their Rights, Contemp Philos, Vol XVI, No 5, 94; Pluralism: Truth and World Community, Contemp Philos, Vol XVII, No 5, 95; The Judicial Surcharge: A Violation of Prisoner Rights, Contemp Philos, Vol XVII, No 6, 95; Christ as Criminal: Antinomian Trends for a New Millennium, Edwin Mellen Press, 97. **CONTACT ADDRESS** Univ New Orleans, New Orleans, LA, 70148. **EMAIL** dkhpl@uno.edu

HANNAN, BARBARA
DISCIPLINE PHILOSOPHY OF MIND, PHILOSOPHY OF SCIENCE, EARLY ANALYTIC PHILOSOPHY, WITTG **EDUCATION** Randolph-Macon Woman's Col, BA, 79; Univ Ariz, JD, 82, PhD, 89. **CAREER** Assoc prof, Univ NMex. **SELECTED PUBLICATIONS** Auth, Subjectivity and Reduction, Westview, 94; contribur, Love Analyzed, Westview, 96. **CONTACT ADDRESS** Univ NMex, Albuquerque, NM, 87131.

HANS, JAMES STUART
PERSONAL Born 05/06/1950, Elgin, IL, m, 1974, 1 child **DISCIPLINE** ENGLISH LITERATURE, PHILOSOPHY **EDUCATION** Southern IL Univ, Edwardsville, BA, 72, MA, 74; Washington Univ, St Louis, PhD(English), 78. **CAREER** Teaching asst English, Southern IL Univ, 72-74; asst prof, Kenyon Col, 78-82; asst to prof English, Wake Forest Univ, 82-; ed consult, Kenyon Rev, 79-82; dir, Kenyon & Exeter Prog, Exeter Univ, England, 80-81. **RESEARCH** Twentieth century literature; literary theory; contemporary philosophy. **SELECTED PUBLICATIONS** Auth, Gaston Bachelard and the Phenomenology of the Reading Consciousness, J Aesthetics & Art Criticism, spring 77; Hans-Georg Gadamer and Hermeneutic Phenomenology, Philos Today, spring 78; Derrida and Freeplay, Mod Lang Notes, 5/79; Presence and Absence in Modern Poetry, Criticism, fall 80; Hermeneutics, Play, Deconstruction, Philos Today, winter 80; The Play of the World, Univ MA Press, 81; Form and Measure in the Postmodern World, Kenyon Rev; Imitation and the Image of Man, John Benjaminis, 87; The Question of Value: Thinking Through Nietzsche, Heidegger and Freud, SIU Press, 89; The Value(s) of Literature, SUNY Press, 90; The Fate of Desire, SUNY Press, 90; The Origins of the Gods, SUNY Press, 91; Contextual Authority and Aesthetic Truth, SUNY Press, 92; The Mysteries of Attention, SUNY Press, 93; The Golden Mean, SUNY Press, 94; The Site of Our Lives: The Self and the Subject from Emerson to Foucault, SUNY Press, 95. **CONTACT ADDRESS** Dept English, Wake Forest Univ, PO Box 7387, Winston Salem, NC, 27109-7387. **EMAIL** hans@wfu.edu

HANSEN, CARL L.
PERSONAL Born 03/15/1938, Denver, CO, m, 1960, 4 children **DISCIPLINE** PHILOSOPHY, THEOLOGY **EDUCATION** Bethany Col, KS, BA, 60; Augustana Theol Sem, BD, 63; Princeton Theol Sem, ThM, 64; Univ CO Boulder, PhD, 76. **CAREER** Pastor, Holy Trinity Lutheran Church, Camden, NJ, 64-66; from instr to assoc prof, Bethany Col, Kans, 66-76, dir continuing educ, 69-76, prof philos & relig, 76-78, Johann Seleen distinguished prof, 78-81; Pres, Midland Lutheran Col, Nebr, 81-, Consult, US 7th Army Chaplains, Heidelberg, Ger, 76-77. **HONORS AND AWARDS** Johann Seleen Distinguished Professorship, Bethany Col, 78. **RESEARCH** Philos of relig; interpersonal growth; death and dying. **SELECTED PUBLICATIONS** Auth, Ethical issues in death and dying, Lutheran Women, 75; The learning society, Bethany Col Mag, 75; Dear Sara, Lutheran Mag, 76; Roots and wings, Bethany Col Mag, 78. **CONTACT ADDRESS** Midland Lutheran Col, 900 N Clarkson, Fremont, NE, 68025-4254. **EMAIL** hansen@admin.mlc.edu

HANSON, BRADLEY
PERSONAL Born 08/02/1935, Mankato, MN, m, 1962, 3 children **DISCIPLINE** SYSTEMATIC THEOLOGY **EDUCATION** St. Olaf Col, BA, 57; Luther Theol Sem, BD, 61; Yale Univ, MA, 63; Princeton Theol Sem, PhD, 70. **CAREER** Prof relig, Luther Col, 68- ; Dennis M. Jones distinguished tchg prof, 98- . **HONORS AND AWARDS** Phi Beta Kappa; Malone Fel. **MEMBERSHIPS** Am Acad Relig; Soc for the Stud of Christian Spirituality. **RESEARCH** Lutheran spirituality. **SELECTED PUBLICATIONS** Auth, Isms and Issues, Augsburg Fortress, 77; auth, The Call of Silence, Augsburg, 80; auth, Teach Us to Pray, Augsburg, 90; ed, Modern Christian Spirituality, Scholars, 90; auth, Introduction to Christian Theology, Fortress, 97. **CONTACT ADDRESS** 810 Ridge Rd, Decorah, IA, 52101. **EMAIL** hansonbr@luther.edu

HANSON, BRUCE
PERSONAL Born 03/31/1952, Park Rapids, MN, m, 1982, 1 child **DISCIPLINE** RELIGION; PHILOSOPHY **EDUCATION** Claremont Grad Univ, MA, PhD, 91. **CAREER** Assoc prof, Philosophy & Religious studies. **MEMBERSHIPS** AAR; APA **CONTACT ADDRESS** Fullerton Col, 321 E Chapman Ave, Fullerton, CA, 92632. **EMAIL** hanson1ful@aol.com

HANSON, PAUL DAVID
PERSONAL Born 11/17/1939, Ashland, WI, m, 1966, 3 children **DISCIPLINE** OLD TESTAMENT **EDUCATION** Gustavus Adolphus Col, BA, 61; Yale Univ, BD, 65; Harvard Univ, PhD, 70. **CAREER** Asst prof Old Testament, 70-74, prof, 75-81, Bussey Prof Divinity, Divinity Sch, Harvard Univ, 81-89,

Lamont prof, 89-; Fulbright, 61-62; Woodrow Wilson, 65-66; Danforth, 66-70; Thayer fel archaeol, Am Sch Orient Res, 69-70; Von Humboldt, 81-82. **MEMBERSHIPS** Soc Bibl Lit; Am Sch Orient Res; Cath Bibl Asn. **RESEARCH** Late Bibl prophecy, Jewish apocalyptic lit; Bibl theology; ancient Near Eastern lang and civilizations. **SELECTED PUBLICATIONS** Auth, Jewish apocalyptic against its Near Eastern environment, Rev Biblique, 1/71; The Dawn of Apocalyptic, Fortress, 75, 2nd ed, 79; Masculine metaphors for God and sex-discrimination in the Old Testament, Ecumenical Rev, 75; Apocalypticism, In: Interpreters Dict of the Bible, suppl vol, Abingdon, 76; Rebellion in Heaven, Azazel and Euhemeristic heroes in I Enoch 6-11, J Bibl Lit, 77; The theological significance of contradiction within the Book of the Covenant, In: Canon and Authority, 77, Dynamic Transcendence, Fortress, 78; The Diversity of Scripture, 82, Fortress; The People Called, 86, Fortress; Isaiah 40-66, 95. **CONTACT ADDRESS** Divinity Sch, Harvard Univ, 45 Francis Ave, Cambridge, MA, 02138-1994. **EMAIL** pdhanson@fas.harvard.edu

HANSON, WILLIAM H.
DISCIPLINE PHILOSOPHY **EDUCATION** Yale Univ, PhD. **RESEARCH** Logic and philosophy of logic. **SELECTED PUBLICATIONS** Auth, Algorithmic Translation in Propositional Logic, Comput Philos, 92; Indicative Conditionals Are Truth-Functional, Mind, 91; Second-Order Logic and Logicism, Mind, 90; Two Kinds of Deviance, Hist Philos Logic, 89; First Degree Entailments and Information, Notre Dame J Formal Logic, 80; co-auth, Validity in Intensional Languages: A New Approach, Notre Dame J Formal Logic, 85. **CONTACT ADDRESS** Philosophy Dept, Univ of Minnesota, Twin Cities, 355 Ford Hall, 224 Church St SE, Minneapolis, MN, 55455. **EMAIL** whanson@maroon.tc.umn.edu

HAPPEL, STEPHEN P.
PERSONAL Born 08/18/1944, Indianapolis, IN, s **DISCIPLINE** RELIGION & THE ARTS; HERMENEUTICS; SACRAMENTS; FOUNDATIONAL THEOLOGY. **EDUCATION** St. Meinrad Col, BA, 66; Ind Univ, MA, 69; Hoger Inst voor Wijsbegeerte, PhB, 74; Katholieke Univ te Leuven, PhD, 77, STD, 79. **CAREER** Instr to Asst Prof, Cath Univ Am, 73-78; Assoc Prof, St. Meinrad Sch Theol, 78-83; Assoc Prof, Cath Univ Am, 83-; Vis Assoc Prof, Univ Notre Dame, 84, 85; Vis Assoc Prof, Boston Col, 84; Flannery Vis Prof Theol, Gonzaga Univ, 92-93. **HONORS AND AWARDS** All degrees granted "summa cum laude". **MEMBERSHIPS** Mod Lang Asn; Cath Theol Soc Am; Am Acad Relig; Am Cath Philos Asn; Am Soc Aesth; Soc Liturgica; Soc Arts, Relig, & Contemp Cult; Christianity & Lit; Soc Values Higher Educ. **RESEARCH** Religion and the arts; religion and science; hermeneutics; philosophical theology. **SELECTED PUBLICATIONS** Auth, Divine Providence and Instrumentality: Metaphors for Time in Self-Organizing Systems and Divine Action, Chaos, Complexity and Self-Organization: Perspectives on Divine Action, Vatican Observatory Publ, 95; coauth, Geography of the Soul: An Intellectual Map, In: Nourishing the Soul: Discovering the Sacred in Everyday Life, HarperSanFrancisco, 95; auth, Double Marginality and the Name of Love: Literary AIDS and the Power of Religion, Marginality and Dissent, Macmillan, 97; Communion with Fast Food: The Spirituality of Work and Sacrament, The Way, 97; God's Journey in Time: Metaphors for Time in Science and Religion, Macmillan, 99; ed, Artwork as Revelation: Religious Meanings in Works of Imagination, Univ St. Thomas (forthcoming). **CONTACT ADDRESS** Religion Dept, Catholic Univ of America, Washington, DC, 20064. **EMAIL** Happel@cua.edu

HARBIN, MICHAEL A.
PERSONAL Born 05/24/1947, Vincennes, France, m, 1971, 3 children **DISCIPLINE** BIBLICAL STUDIES, OLD TESTAMENT AND SEMITIC STUDIES, ENGLISH LITERATURE **EDUCATION** US Naval acad, BS, 69; Calif State Univ, MA, 93; Dallas Theol Sem, ThM, 80, ThD, 88. **CAREER** Adj prof of Bible, Le Tourneau Univ, 90-93; adj prof English, El Centro Col, 90-93; assoc prof Biblical Stud (s), Taylor Univ, 93- . **HONORS AND AWARDS** Who's Who in Amer, 98; Who's Who in Rel, 92-93; Who's Who in the Midwest, 95, 96; Phi Kappa Phi, 93. **MEMBERSHIPS** Soc Bibl Lit; Near East Archaeol soc; Inst Bibl res; Evangel Theol Soc. **RESEARCH** Old Testament History. **CONTACT ADDRESS** Dept of Biblical Studies, Taylor Univ, 269 W Reade Ave, Upland, IN, 46989. **EMAIL** mcharbin@tayloru.edu

HARDIMON, MICHAEL O.
DISCIPLINE EUROPEAN PHILOSOPHY **EDUCATION** Univ Chicago, PhD, 85. **CAREER** PROF, PHILOS, UNIV CALIF, SAN DIEGO. **RESEARCH** Kant philos through the nineteenth century; Ethics; Social and polit philos. **SELECTED PUBLICATIONS** Auth, "The Project of Reconciliation," Philos and Public Aff, 92; Hegel's Social Philosophy, Cambridge Univ Press, 94; "Role Obligations," Jour of Philos 91, 94. **CONTACT ADDRESS** Dept of Philos, Univ Calif, San Diego, 9500 Gilman Dr, La Jolla, CA, 92093.

HARDIN, CLYDE LAURENCE
PERSONAL Born 08/27/1932, Des Moines, IA, m, 1967, 3 children **DISCIPLINE** PHILOSOPHY **EDUCATION** Johns Hopkins Univ, AB, 53; Univ Ill, AM, 54; Princeton Univ, PhD, 58. **CAREER** Instr philos, Univ Tex, 57-59; from instr to asst prof philos, 59-64, Assoc Prof Philos, Syracuse Univ, 64-, Dir Honors Prog, 68-, NSF sci fac fel, 63-64. **MEMBERSHIPS** Am Philos Asn. **RESEARCH** History and philosophy of science; logic; epistemology. **SELECTED PUBLICATIONS** Auth, Vanbrakel and the Not-So-Naked Emperor, British J Philos Sci, Vol 0044, 93; Color-Vision--A Study In Cognitive Science and the Philosophy of Perception, British J Philos Sci, Vol 0047, 96. **CONTACT ADDRESS** Dept of Philosophy, Syracuse Univ, Syracuse, NY, 13210.

HARDING, ROBERT E., JR.
PERSONAL Born 05/31/1930, Danville, KY, m **DISCIPLINE** LAW **EDUCATION** KY State Univ, BA 1954; Univ KY, JD 1957. **CAREER** USPHS, corr officer 1952-58; Natl Labor Relations Bd, atty 1958-74; EEO consultant 1980-86; labor arbitrator 1981-; Univ New Mexico, tchr Afro-Amer studies 1974-87. **HONORS AND AWARDS** New Mexico Reg Medical Prog, Certificate of Recognition, 1976; Better Bus Bur of New Mexico, Arbitrator of the Year, 1987; Governor of New Mexico Toney Anaya, Certificate of Appreciation, 1984; Sickle Cell Council of New Mexico, Certificate of Appreciation, 1990; Women United for Youth, Certificate of Recognition, 1993. **MEMBERSHIPS** Mem KY, NM, Natl, Fed, Albuquerque Bar Assns; New Mexico Black Lawyers Assn; mem US Dist Ct NM; mem US Court of Appeals 10th Circuit; US Ct Appeals DC & Supreme Ct; mem Phi Alpha Delta Legal Frat; pres, Albuquerque Branch NAACP, 1971; pres, bd dir Albuquerque Child Care Centers 1980-81; mem NM Adv Comm to the US Commiss on Civil Rights 1981-97; Better Business Bureau, Albuquerque, volunteer arbitrator, 1983-. **CONTACT ADDRESS** PO Box 14277, Albuquerque, NM, 87191.

HARDWIG, JOHN R.
PERSONAL Born 09/10/1940, Waverly, IA, m, 1997 **DISCIPLINE** PHILOSOPHY **EDUCATION** Univ of TX, PhD, 75. **CAREER** Lect, Wellesley Col, 67-69; Inst, Univ of TN, 69-74 & 78-79; Lect, Humbolt St Univ, 75-78; Inst, Maryville Col, 79-82; Lect, E TN State Univ, 82-. **HONORS AND AWARDS** NEH Fel **MEMBERSHIPS** APA **RESEARCH** Bioethics **SELECTED PUBLICATIONS** The Problem of Proxies With Interests of Their Own, UT Law Rev, 92; Toward and Ethics of Expertise, Prof Ethics and Soc Resp, 94; Support and the Invisible Family, Hastings Center Rep, 95; Privacy Self-Knowledge and the Commune Toward an Epistemology of the Family, Fem Refl On Family, 96; Elder Abuse Context and Ethics, JAI Press, 96; Dying at the Right Time-Reflections on Assisted and Unassisted Suicide, Ethics in Prac, 96; Autobiography Biography and Narrative Ethics, Stories and Their Limits Nar Appr to Bioethics, 97; Is There a Duty to Die?, Hastings Center Rep, 97. **CONTACT ADDRESS** Dept of Philosophy, East Tennessee State Univ, Johnson City, TN, 37614-0656. **EMAIL** hardwigj@etsu.edu

HARDY, MICHAEL A.
PERSONAL Born 07/02/1955, New York, NY, s **DISCIPLINE** LAW **EDUCATION** Carleton College, BA, 1977; New York Law School, JD, 1988. **CAREER** NYC Health and Hospital Corp, analyst, 1977-81; NYC Tax Commission, special asst, 1981-83; Natl Alliance Newspaper, exec ed, 1983-88; Intl Law Institute, Attorney, 1988-92; Torres, Martinez, & Hardy, Attorney/partner, 1992-. **HONORS AND AWARDS** Somerset Comm Action Program, Distinguish Legal Service, 1989; Natl Action Network, Martin Luther King Service Award, 1993. **MEMBERSHIPS** Natl Bar Assn, 1988-; Assn Bar City of New York, 1988-; Natl Assn Criminal Defense Lawyers, 1990-; Natl Action Network, board member, 1989-. **SELECTED PUBLICATIONS** Author, Minister Louis Farrakhan, Practice Press, 1986; Narrator, A More Perfect Democracy, Film Documentary, 1988. **CONTACT ADDRESS** Torres, Martinez & Hardy, 11 Park Pl, Rm 916, New York, NY, 10007-2801.

HARE, DOUGLAS ROBERT ADAMS
PERSONAL Born 03/22/1929, Simcoe, ON, Canada, m, 1951, 2 children **DISCIPLINE** NEW TESTAMENT **EDUCATION** Univ Toronto, BA, 51, BD, 54; Union Theol Sem, STM, 59, ThD(New Testament), 65. **CAREER** Teaching fel New Testament, 62-63, dir continuing educ, 63-64, from instr to assoc prof, 64-74, Prof New Testament, Pittsburgh Theol Sem, 74-, Am Asn Theol Schs fac fel, Ger, 71; chmn, sem Jewish Christianity, Studiorum Novi Testamenti Soc, 76-80. **MEMBERSHIPS** Studiorum Nori Testamenti Socs; Soc Bibl Lit; Cath Bibl Asn. **RESEARCH** Jewish-Christian relations in first century; Gospel of Matthew; gnosticism. **SELECTED PUBLICATIONS** Auth, The Son-Of-Man in the Gospel Of John, J Biblical Lit, Vol 0112, 93. **CONTACT ADDRESS** Pittsburgh Theol Sem, 616 N Highland Ave, Pittsburgh, PA, 15206.

HARGIS, JEFFREY W.
PERSONAL Born 10/04/1961, Wichita Falls, TX, m, 1993 **DISCIPLINE** RELIGION **EDUCATION** Temple Univ, PhD, 98. **CAREER** Instr, Western Sem, 98- . **MEMBERSHIPS** Am Acad Relig; Soc of Bibl Lit; Evangelical Theol Soc; N Am Patristic Soc. **RESEARCH** Early church history. **SELECTED PUBLICATIONS** auth, Against the Christians: The Rise of Early Anti-Christian Polemic, Peter Lang, 99. **CONTACT ADDRESS** 8741 Church St, Gilroy, CA, 95020. **EMAIL** hindsight2020@compuserv.com

HARLEY, GAIL M.
PERSONAL Born 07/26/1943, Parris Island, SC, d, 2 children **DISCIPLINE** RELIGION IN NEW MOVEMENTS AND ASIAN RELIGIONS **EDUCATION** Fla State Univ, PhD, relig in interdisciplinary humanities, 91. **CAREER** Adjunct assoc prof, relig and humanities, Univ South Fla, 92-; acting pres, Emma Curtis Hopkins Col, 97. **HONORS AND AWARDS** Deans list, Univ South Fla, 82. **MEMBERSHIPS** Amer Acad of Relig; Soc for the Study of Metaphysical Relig. **RESEARCH** New thought movement; New religious movements; Asian cultural and religious thought; Asian humanities. **SELECTED PUBLICATIONS** Auth, Emma Curtis Hopkins, The Historical Encyclopedia of Chicago Women, vol 2, Univ Ill Press, 98; auth, Why Ramtha is worthy of scholarly study, News Tribune, Tacoma, 97; auth, New Thought and the Harmonial Family, Amer Alternative Relig, State Univ NY Press, 95; auth, Public Library & Priority, St. Petersburg Times, 4 nov, 94; auth, A Reflection of Social Conscience, St. Petersburg Times, 1 oct, 93; auth, Developers Must Be Environmentally Sensitive, St. Petersburg Times, 93. **CONTACT ADDRESS** Aripeka, FL, 34679. **EMAIL** gharley@fiber-net.com

HARLEY, PHILIP A.
PERSONAL Philadelphia, PA, m **DISCIPLINE** THEOLOGY **EDUCATION** Morgan State Coll, BA 1945; Temple U; Univ Cincinnati; Capital Univ Sch Theol; Garrett Theol Sem, MDiv 1956. **CAREER** IL, IN, OH, SD, WI, pastor; Garrett Theol Seminary, assoc prof. **MEMBERSHIPS** Chmn Regional Consultative Com Race; Mayors Com Human Relations; dist dir Research & Devel; ministries educ IN, SD; prog leadership devel Prog Council Northern IL Conf; v chmn Leadership Devel Com N Central Jurisdictron; regional vice pres Nat Com Black Churchmen; chmn Chicago Coordinating Com Black Churchmen; v chmn Serv Review Panel Comm Fund; Ch Federation Met Chicago; Chicago Conf Religion & Race; mem bd dir Welfare Council Met Chicago. **CONTACT ADDRESS** Field Education Office, Garrett-Evangelical Theol Sem, 2121 Sheridan Road, Evanston, IL, 60201.

HARLOW, DANIEL C.
PERSONAL Born 09/25/1962, Hialeah, FL, m, 1995, 1 child **DISCIPLINE** BIBLICAL STUDIES **EDUCATION** Oral Roberts Univ, BA, 84; Princeton Theol Sem, MDiv, 87; Univ of Notre Dame, MA, 91, PhD, 94. **CAREER** Instr theol, Univ Notre Dame, 92-93; asst prof bibl stud, Calvin Col, 94-96; ed bibl stud, William Eerdmans Publ, 96- . **HONORS AND AWARDS** Fulbright fel Israel, 91-92. **MEMBERSHIPS** Soc Bibl Lit. **RESEARCH** History and literature of early Judaism and Christianity. **SELECTED PUBLICATIONS** Auth, The Greek Apocalypse of Baruch (3 Baruch) in Hellenistic Judaism and Early Christianity, Brill, 96. **CONTACT ADDRESS** William Eerdmans Publ Co, 255 Jefferson Ave SE, Grand Rapids, MI, 49503. **EMAIL** dharlow@eerdmans.com

HARMS, WILLIAM F.
PERSONAL Born 11/19/1959, Baton Rouge, LA, m, 1995 **DISCIPLINE** PHILOSOPHY **EDUCATION** Univ Calif Irvine, PhD 96; Univ Calif SC, BA 90. **CAREER** Bowling Green State Univ, vis prof, 96 to 98; Univ British Columbia, post doc res, 98-99. **MEMBERSHIPS** APA; PSA. **RESEARCH** Epistemology; Philos of Biology; Cultural Evolution; Computer Modeling. **SELECTED PUBLICATIONS** Auth, Evolution and Ultimatum Bargaining, Theory and Decision, 97; auth, Discrete Replicator Dynamics for the Ultimatum Game, U of Calif Irvine, Inst Math Behav Sciences, Tech Repot Serv, 95; auth, Cultural Revolution and the Phenotype, Biology and Philos, 96; auth, Reliability and Novelty: Information Gain in Multilevel Selection Systems, Erkenntnis; The Epistemology Use of Information Theory, Philos of Science; rev, Dan Sperber's, Explaining Culture, Economics and Philos, forthcoming. **CONTACT ADDRESS** Dept of Philosophy, Bowling Green State Univ, Bowling Green, OH, 43403. **EMAIL** wfharms@bgnet.bgsu.edu

HARNED, DAVID B.
DISCIPLINE CHRISTIAN THOUGHT AND ETHICS **EDUCATION** Yale Univ, PhD, 63. **CAREER** Prof Emer, La State Univ. **SELECTED PUBLICATIONS** Auth, Faith and Virtue, United Church Press, 76; Creed and Personal Identity, Fortress, 81. **CONTACT ADDRESS** Dept of Philos and Relig Stud, Louisiana State Univ, 106 Coates Hall, Baton Rouge, LA, 70803.

HARNSBERGER, R. SCOTT
PERSONAL Born 04/16/1952, Lincoln, NE, d, 1 child **DISCIPLINE** PHILOSOPHY **EDUCATION** Univ Wisc-Madison, PhD, 81. **CAREER** Assoc prof, Newton Gresham Libr, Sam Houston State Univ, 87-. **MEMBERSHIPS** Am Libr Asn; Am Philos Asn; Texas Libr Asn. **RESEARCH** 20th Century American art. **SELECTED PUBLICATIONS** Auth Ten Precisionist Artists: Annotated Bibliographies, Greenwood Press, 92; coed Popular Culture in Libraries, Haworth Press, 96. **CONTACT ADDRESS** Sam Houston State Univ, PO Box 2179, Huntsville, TX, 77341-2179. **EMAIL** lib_rsh@shsu.edu

HARPER, BILL
DISCIPLINE PHILOSOPHY **EDUCATION** Rensselaer Polytech Inst, BS, 64; Univ Rochester, MA, 70; PhD, 74. **CAREER** Prof **RESEARCH** Newton; testing of general relativity; Kant; decision theory; game theory. **SELECTED PUBLICATIONS** Auth, Reasoning from Phenomena: Newton's Argument for Universal Gravitation and the Practice of Science, Action and Reaction: Proceedings of a Symposium to Commemorate the Tercentenary of Newton's Principia, 93; Kant on Incongruent Counterparts, Kluwer, 91; co-auth, Newton's New Way of Inquiry, Kluwer; Unification and Support: Harmonic Law Ratios Measure the Mass at the Sun, Kluwer, 94; co-ed, Causation, Chance and Credence, Kluwer, 88; Causation in Decision, Belief Change, and Statistics, Kluwer, 88; Kant on Causality, Freedom, and Objectivity, Univ Minn, 84; Ifs, Reidel, 80. **CONTACT ADDRESS** Dept of Philosophy, Western Ontario Univ, London, ON, N6A 5B8. **EMAIL** blharp@julian.uwo.ca

HARRE, ROM
PERSONAL Born 12/18/1927, New Zealand, m, 1948, 1 child **DISCIPLINE** PHILOSOPHY **EDUCATION** Auckland Univ, BSc, 48, MA, 53; Oxford Univ, BPh, 56, MA, 59. **CAREER** King's Col, Auckland, 48-53; Punjab Univ, Pakistan, 54; Leicester Univ, 58-60; Oxford Univ, 60-96; Georgetown Univ, 88-98. **HONORS AND AWARDS** Honorary doctorates from Brussels, Helsinki, and Lima. **MEMBERSHIPS** Am Psych Soc; Br Soc for Philos of Sci. **RESEARCH** Theoretical psychology; linguistic psychology. **SELECTED PUBLICATIONS** Coauth, The Emotions, Sage, 96; auth, The Singular Self, Sage, 98; coauth, Greenspeak: A Study of Environmental Discourse, Sage, 98; ed, Positionins: Moral Foundations of Social Action, Blackwell, 98. **CONTACT ADDRESS** Dept of Psychology, Georgetown Univ, Washington, DC, 20057. **EMAIL** harre@gunet.georgetown.edu

HARRELL, DAVID E., JR.
DISCIPLINE RELIGION **EDUCATION** David Lipscomb Col, MA, 54; Vanderbilt Univ, MA, 58, PhD, 62. **CAREER** Hist tchr, E Tenn State Univ, Univ Okla, Univ Georgia, Univ Ark, Univ Ala-Birmingham; Daniel F Breeden Eminent Scholar Hum, Auburn Univ-. **HONORS AND AWARDS** Fulbright lectr Allahabad, India; res fel Inst for Ecumenical & Cult Res St Johns Abbey; Dir Am Stud Res Ctr Hyderabad, India; Fulbright Award, 93. Citation from Ambassador Frank G Wisner for outstanding contrib to scholarly understanding of US in India. **SELECTED PUBLICATIONS** Auth, Oral Roberts: An American Life, Ind Univ Press, 85; Pat Robertson: A Personal, Religious, and Political Portrait, Harper & Row, 87; coed Minorities in Modern America, Ind Univ Press; Religion and American Culture, Univ Ala Press; auth of over forty articles in scholarly publications. **CONTACT ADDRESS** History Dept, Auburn Univ, 310 Thach Hall, Auburn, AL, 36849-5207.

HARRELSON, WALTER
PERSONAL Born 11/28/1919, Winnabow, NC, m, 1942, 3 children **DISCIPLINE** THEOLOGY **EDUCATION** Univ NC, AB, 47; Union Theol Sem, BD, 49, ThD, 53. **CAREER** Instr philos, Univ NC, 47; prof Old Testament, Andover Newton Theol Sch, 51-55; assoc prof Old Testament & dean divinity sch, Univ Chicago, 55-60; prof, 60-75, dean, 67-75, distinguished prof, 75-77, Harvie Branscomb distinguished prof, 77-78, Distinguished Prof Old Testament, Vanderbilt Univ, 78-, Mem comt hist relig, Am Coun Learned Soc, 56-62, chmn, 61-62; Fulbright res scholar & Am Asn Theol Schs fac fel, Rome, Italy, 62-63; chmn, Ethiopia Manuscript Microfilm Libr, 71-; rector, Ecumenical Inst Advan Theol Studies, Jerusalem, 77-78 & spring, 79. **HONORS AND AWARDS** DD, Univ of the South, 74; DLitt, Mars Hill Col, 77. **MEMBERSHIPS** Soc Bibl Lit (pres, 71-72); Soc Values Higher Educ; Am Schs Orient Res; Am Soc Study Relig. **RESEARCH** Old Testament; Semitic languages and literatures; Biblical theology. **SELECTED PUBLICATIONS** Auth, The Anchor Bible Dictionary, J Biblical Lit, Vol 0113, 94; The Inferior Religion--A Study of the Attitudes Toward Judaism Within German Old-Testament Scholarship, J Biblical Lit, Vol 0113, 94; The Land Called Holy--Palestine In Christian History and Thought, J Am Acad Relig, Vol 0063, 95. **CONTACT ADDRESS** Divinity Sch, Vanderbilt Univ, Nashville, TN, 37240.

HARRIES, KARSTEN
PERSONAL Born 01/25/1937, Jena, Germany, m, 1959, 3 children **DISCIPLINE** PHILOSOPHY **EDUCATION** Yale Univ, BA, 58, PhD, 62. **CAREER** Instr philos, Yale Univ, 61-63; asst prof, Univ Tex, 63-65; from asst prof to assoc prof, 65-70, chmn dept, 73- 78, Prof Philos, Yale Univ, 70-, Guest prof, Univ Bonn, 65-66 & 68-69; Guggenheim fel, 71-72. **MEMBERSHIPS** Am Philos Asn; Soc Phenomenol & Existential Philos; AAUP; Am Soc Aesthet. **RESEARCH** Aesthetics; German philosophy. **SELECTED PUBLICATIONS** Auth, Nietzsche And Metaphor, Philos Lit, Vol 0019, 95; Death and Forgetting-Death Notices as Expressions of Catholic Thought Regarding Death, Am Hist Rev, Vol 0099, 94; Architecture and the After-Life, Am Hist Rev, Vol 0098, 93; Architectural Principles in the Age of Historicism, Am Hist Rev, Vol 0097, 92. **CONTACT ADDRESS** Dept of Philos, Yale Univ, P O Box 208306, New Haven, CT, 06520-8306.

HARRILL, J. ALBERT
PERSONAL Born 07/02/1963, Winston-Salem, NC **DISCIPLINE** RELIGION **EDUCATION** Univ N Carolina, Chapel Hill, BA, 86; Univ Chicago, MA, 89, PhD, 93. **CAREER** Asst prof theol, Creighton Univ, 94-96; asst prof relig stud, DePaul Univ, 96- . **HONORS AND AWARDS** Phi Beta Kappa, 85; Bernard Boyd Mem Fel, 86. **MEMBERSHIPS** Sos of Bibl Lit; North Am Patristic Soc; Soc for the Promotion of Roman Stud; Catholic Bibl Asn. **RESEARCH** Greco-Roman environment of Early Christianity; ancient slavery. **SELECTED PUBLICATIONS** Auth, Ignatius, Ad Polycarp, 4.3 and the Corporate Manumission of Christian Slaves, J of Early Christian Stud, 93; auth, Paul and Slavery: The Problem of 1 Corinthians 7:21, Bibl Res, 94; auth, The Manumission of Slaves in Early Christianity, Mohr, 95; auth, The Indentured Labor of the Prodigal Son (Luke 15:15), J of Bibl Lit, 96; auth, Slavery and Society at Corinth: The Issues Facing Paul, The Bible Today, 97; auth, The Vice of Slave Dealers in Greco-Roman Society: The Use of a Topos in 1 Timothy 1:10, J of Bibl Lit, 99. **CONTACT ADDRESS** Dept of Religious Studies, DePaul Univ, 2320 N Kenmore Ave, Chicago, IL, 60614-3298. **EMAIL** jharrill@condor.depaul.edu

HARRINGTON, DANIEL JOSEPH
PERSONAL Born 07/19/1940, Arlington, MA **DISCIPLINE** BIBLICAL STUDIES, JEWISH HISTORY **EDUCATION** Boston Col, BA, 64, MA, 65; Harvard Univ, PhD(Oriental lang), 70; Weston Sch Theol, BD, 71. **CAREER** PROF NEW TESTAMENT, WESTON JESUIT SCH THEOL, 72-; Vis lectr Old Testament, Harvard Divinity Sch, 72-; ed, New Testament Abstracts, 72-; pastoral assoc, St Agnes Church, Mass, 72-; coordr, New Testament Colloquium, Boston, 77-; trustee, Holy Cross Col, Mass, 78- **MEMBERSHIPS** Cath Bibl Asn of Am, pres 85-86; Soc Bibl Lit; Soc New Testament Studies. **SELECTED PUBLICATIONS** Auth, The Gospel According to Matthew, Collegeville: Liturgical, 83; The Gospel According to Mark, NY: Sadlier, 83; The Gospel According to Luke, NY: Sadlier, 83; Pentecost 2, Series B, Philadelphia: Fortress, 85; The New Testament: A Bibliography, Wilmington: Glazier, 85; Targum Jonathan of the Former Prophets, Wilmington: Glazier, 87; The Maccabean Revolt: Anatomy of a Biblical Revolution, Wilmington: Glazier, 88; John's Thought and Theology: An Introduction, Wilmington: Glazier, 90; The Gospel of Matthew, Collegeville: Liturgical, 91; Paul on the Mystery of Israel, Collegeville: Liturgical, 92; How to Read the Gospels, Hyde Park, NY: New City Press, 96; Wisdom Texts from Oumran, London: Routledge, 96; Paul's Prison Letters, Hyde Park, NY: New City Press, 97; Romans. The Good News According to Paul, Hyde Park, NY: New City Press, 98; and author of many other articles in directories, encyclopedias, scholarly journals, and other publications. **CONTACT ADDRESS** Bibl Studies Dept, Weston Jesuit Sch of Theol, 3 Phillips Place, Cambridge, MA, 02138-3495.

HARRINGTON, HENRY R.
PERSONAL Born 12/23/1943, Evanston, IL, m, 1968, 1 child **DISCIPLINE** ENGLISH LITERATURE & THEOLOGY **EDUCATION** Williams Col, AB, 66; Stanford Univ, MA, 68, PhD, 71. **CAREER** Asst prof, 71-80, ASSOC PROF ENGLISH, UNIV MONT, 80- **MEMBERSHIPS** MLA; AAUP; Am Acad Relig. **RESEARCH** Victorian literature; comtemporary theology and literature; novel. **SELECTED PUBLICATIONS** Auth, English Travelers and the Oriental Crowd, Kinglake, Curzon, and the 'Miracle Of The Holy Fire', Harvard Library Bul, Vol 0005, 94; A Community of One, Masculine Autobiography and Autonomy in 19th-Century Britain, 19th C Prose, Vol 0022, 95. **CONTACT ADDRESS** Dept of English, Univ of Mont, Missoula, MT, 59801.

HARRINGTON, MICHAEL L.
DISCIPLINE METAPHYSICS, PHILOSOPHY OF NATURE **EDUCATION** Davidson Col, BA; Emory Univ, MA, 69, PhD, 72. **CAREER** Assoc prof, 70-, ch, dept Philos and Relig, Univ MS, 89-. **RESEARCH** Changes in mod philos and theology. **SELECTED PUBLICATIONS** Auth, Traditions and Changes: The University in Principle and in Practice, McGraw-Hill, 95. **CONTACT ADDRESS** Univ MS, Oxford, MS, 38677. **EMAIL** prmlh@olemiss.edu

HARRINGTON, MICHAEL LOUIS
PERSONAL Born 07/08/1944, Portland, OR, m, 1976, 2 children **DISCIPLINE** PHILOSOPHY **EDUCATION** Davidson Col, AB, 66; Emory Univ, Ma, 69, PhD(philos), 72. **CAREER** Asst prof, 70-75, Assoc Prof Philos, Univ Miss, 75-98; RPOF PHILOS, UNIV MISS, 98-; Consult philos, Nat Endowment Humanities, 76-78; Miss Hum Council, 94-. **MEMBERSHIPS** Am Philos Asn; Metaphys Soc Am. **RESEARCH** Metaphysics; epistemology; philosophical theol. **SELECTED PUBLICATIONS** Auth, Evangelicism and racism in the development of Southern religion, Miss Quart, spring 74; co-auth, Traditions & Changes, 95, 96, 97, 98. **CONTACT ADDRESS** Univ of Miss, Room 302, McDonnell-Barksdale, University, MS, 38677. **EMAIL** prmlk@olemiss.edu

HARRIS, BOND
PERSONAL Born 08/23/1932, Richmond, VA, m, 1956, 2 children **DISCIPLINE** PHILOSOPHY, RELIGION **EDUCATION** Univ Richmond, BA, 55; Southeastern Sem, BD, 58, ThM, 61; Drew Univ, PhD(philos relig), 70. **CAREER** Asst prof philos & relig, Ky Wesleyan Col, 68-73; asst prof, 73-75, assoc prof philos, 75-98, prof philos, Eastern Ky Univ, 98-. **MEMBERSHIPS** AAUP; Am Philos Asn; Metaphys Soc Am; Soc Phenomenol & Existential Res; Mind Soc; Hegel Soc of Am. **RESEARCH** Metaphysics, German idealism; epistemology; philosophy of religion. **CONTACT ADDRESS** Dept Philosophy, Eastern Kentucky Univ, 521 Lancaster Ave, Richmond, KY, 40475-3102. **EMAIL** phiharris@acs.eku.edu

HARRIS, CHARLES EDWIN
PERSONAL Born 06/21/1938, Nashville, TN, m, 2 children **DISCIPLINE** ETHICAL THEORY **EDUCATION** Vanderbilt Univ, AB, 60, PhD, 64. **CAREER** Assoc prof, Texas A&M Univ75-. **HONORS AND AWARDS** Danforth assoc, 70. **MEMBERSHIPS** APA; Southwestern Philos Soc. **SELECTED PUBLICATIONS** Auth, Applying Moral Theories, Wadsworth, 86 & Aborting Fetuses: The Parental Perspective, J Applied Philos, 91; couth, Engineering Ethics: Concepts and Cases, Belmont, CA: Wadsworth Publ Co, 94. **CONTACT ADDRESS** Dept of Philosophy, Texas A&M Univ, College Station, TX, 77843-4237.

HARRIS, DAVID A.
DISCIPLINE LAW **EDUCATION** Northwestern Univ, BA; Yale Univ, JD; Georgetown Univ, LLM. **CAREER** Prof. **SELECTED PUBLICATIONS** Auth, 'Driving While Black' and All Other Traffic Offenses: The Supreme Court and Pretextual Traffic Stops, J Criminal Law Criminology, 97; Superman's X-Ray Vision and the Fourth Amendment: The New Gun Detection Technology, Temple Law Rev, 96; Frisking Every Suspect: The Withering of Terry, Davis Law Rev, 95; Factors For Reasonable Suspicion: When Black and Poor Means Stopped and Frisked, Bloomington, 94. **CONTACT ADDRESS** Col Law, Univ of Toledo, Toledo, OH, 43606. **EMAIL** dharris@uoft02.utoledo.edu

HARRIS, ERROL E.
PERSONAL Born 02/19/1908, Kimberley, South Africa, w, 1946, 4 children **DISCIPLINE** PHILOSOPHY **EDUCATION** Rhodes Univ, BA, 27, MA, 29; Oxford Univ, B. Litt, 34; Witwatersrand Univ, D. Litt, 51. **CAREER** Lectr, 30-31, Fort Hare Col; Private Sec, Minister for Mines Southern Rhodesia, 34-35; asst master, 36, Uppingham Schl England; asst master, 37, Charterhouse Schl England; ed officer, Basutoland, 37-40, Zanzibar, 41-42, British Colonial Svc; military svc: S African Army Info Svc, 42-44, chief instr, 44-46, British Army Ed Corps, Middle East Command Ed Col; lectr, phil, 46-49, sr lectr, phil, 50-52, prof, dept head, phil, 53-56, Witwatersrand Univ; vis lectr, 56-57, Yale Univ; prof, 56-62, CT Col; acting head dept, logic and metaphysics, 59-60, Univ Edinburgh (Scotland); Roy Robert Dist Prof, 63-66, Univ KS; prof, 66-76, John Evans Prof, intel and moral phil, 72-80, Northwestern Univ; vis dist prof, 77-78, Marquette Univ; Cowling Prof, 78-, Carlton Col; vis dist prof of Christian phil, 82, Villanova Univ; vis prof phil, 83-84, Emory Univ; hon res fel, 85-, Center for Phil and History of Science, Boston Univ. **HONORS AND AWARDS** Alfred Beit Scholar, Rhodes Univ, 28-29; Queen Victoria Scholar, Oxford Univ, 31-33; Hugh le May Res Fel, Rhodes Univ, 49; Bollingen Fel, 64; Ford Found Fel, 67; Res Fel, Inst for Advanced Stud in Humanities, Univ Edinburgh, 78; Terry Lectr, Yale Univ, 57; Machette Lectr, Old Dominion Univ, 65, Tulane Univ, 75; Werner Lectr, Clark Univ, 74; Aquinas Lectr, Marquette Univ, 77; Suarez Lectr, Fordham Univ, 82; Gilbert Ryle Lectr, Trent Univ, 84; Pres, Metaphysical Soc of Amer, 68; Pres, Hegel Soc of Amer, 77-78; Paul Weiss Medalist, Outstanding contr to Metaphysics, 89. **MEMBERSHIPS** APA; Hegel Soc of Amer; Hegel Soc of Great Britain; Metaphysical Soc of Amer. **RESEARCH** Hegel, Spinoza, Philos of nature & science, Metaphysics, Political Philos, Intl Politics. **SELECTED PUBLICATIONS** Auth, The Spirit of Hegel, Humanities Press, 93; auth, One World or None: Prescription for Survival, Humanities Press, 93; auth, Leibniz and Modern Science, Metaphysics as Foundation, SUNY Press, 93; art, The Obstacle to Global Solutions, Med and Global Survival, 93; art, Science, Mysticism, Belief and Conscience, Conf on Science, Mystique, Poesy and Conscience, Lisbon, 94; art, Being-for-Self in the Greater Logic, Owl of Minerva, 94; art, Dialectica and Lo(?) transcendentale e tempo, Criterio 3, 95; auth, Scepticism and Dialectic, Phenomenology and Skepticism, Northwestern Univ Press, 95/6; art, Reminiscences of Hegelians I have met, Owl of Minerva, Vol 27, 95; auth, The Restitution of Metaphysics, Humanities Press, Atlantic Highlands, 98. **CONTACT ADDRESS** 9 Marie Ave, Cambridge, MA, 02139.

HARRIS, FRED O.
DISCIPLINE LAW **EDUCATION** Univ Ark, BA; JD. **CAREER** Prof, Univ Ill Urbana Champaign. **RESEARCH** Products liability; toxic torts; environmental law; and insurance law **SELECTED PUBLICATIONS** Auth, Arkansas Wrongful Death Actions; co-auth, Warranty Law in Tort and Contract Action. **CONTACT ADDRESS** Law Dept, Univ Ill Urbana Champaign, 52 E Gregory Dr, Champaign, IL, 61820. **EMAIL** fharris@law.uiuc.edu

HARRIS, HENRY SILTON

PERSONAL Born 04/11/1926, Brighton, England, m, 1952, 4 children **DISCIPLINE** PHILOSOPHY **EDUCATION** Oxford Univ, BA, 49, MA, 52; Univ Ill, PhD(philos), 54. **CAREER** Instr philos, Univ Ill, 53-54; instr, Ohio State Univ, 54-57; from asst prof to assoc prof, Univ Ill, 57-62; assoc prof univ, 62-65, Prof Philos, Glendon Col, York Univ, Ont, 65-, Am Philos Asn res fel, 57-58; Can Coun leave fel, 64-65, 71-72 & 78-79. **MEMBERSHIPS** Am Philos Asn; Can Philos Asn; G Gentile Found Studies Philos; Hegel Soc Am (vpres, 72-74, pres, 78-80); Charles S Peirce Soc. **RESEARCH** Italian philosophy; German idealism; social theory. **SELECTED PUBLICATIONS** Auth, How Philosophy Instructs the World--The Preface of Hegel 'Philosophy Of Right' in its Relation to the Work Itself, Laval Philos, Vol 0051, 95; Philosophy and Poetry--Verene, Donald, Phillip Studies of Giambattista Vico--The War Renewed, Clio, Vol 0023, 94. **CONTACT ADDRESS** Dept of Philos Glendon Col, York Univ, Toronto, ON, M4N 3M6.

HARRIS, ISHWAR C.

PERSONAL Born 07/13/1943, India, m, 1977, 2 children **DISCIPLINE** RELIGION, ASIAN STUDIES **EDUCATION** Claremont Grad School, PhD, 74. **CAREER** Asst prof Rel, Rutgers Univ, 74-81; asst to assoc prof to PROF, COLEGE OF WOOSTER, 81-. **HONORS AND AWARDS** Luce Grant Prof Res; GLCA Japan Travel Grant, 99. **MEMBERSHIPS** Am Acad Rel **RESEARCH** Modern India; Hinduism, Gandhian studies. **SELECTED PUBLICATIONS** Auth, Radhakrishnar: Profile of a Universalist, 82; Gandhians in Contemporary India, 98. **CONTACT ADDRESS** Dept of Religious Stud, Col of Wooster, Wooster, OH, 44691. **EMAIL** IHarris@acs.wooster.edu

HARRIS, JIMMIE

PERSONAL Born 07/27/1945, Winona, MS **DISCIPLINE** LAW **EDUCATION** Univ of CA Berkeley, JD 1972; Univ of IL Champaign-Urbana, IL, BS Elec Engrng 1967. **CAREER** Vidal Sassoon Inc, counsel; Daylin Inc Asso Irell & Manella, gen counsel. **MEMBERSHIPS** Mem Beverly Hills Bar Assn; LA Co Bar Assn; Langston Law Club. **SELECTED PUBLICATIONS** Pub articles, ed CA Law Review. **CONTACT ADDRESS** 2049 Century Park E, Ste 3900, Los Angeles, CA, 90067.

HARRIS, JOHN L.

PERSONAL Born 07/13/1962, Pensacola, FL, m, 1983, 2 children **DISCIPLINE** HEBREW BIBLE **EDUCATION** Univ Arkansas, 80; Cent Bap Coll, BA, 84; Southwestern Bap Theo Sem, MDiv, 88, PhD, 94. **CAREER** Asst Prof, 95-, E Texas Bap Univ. **HONORS AND AWARDS** Who's Who Among Students Amer Univ & Coll, 83-84, 91-93; Outstanding Scholarship Awd. **MEMBERSHIPS** SBL **RESEARCH** Hebrew Bible, Pentateuch & Psalms. **CONTACT ADDRESS** 10683 CR. 214, Tyler, TX, 75707. **EMAIL** jharis@etbu.edu

HARRIS, MAX R.

PERSONAL Born 03/26/1949, Rotherham, England, m, 1974, 2 children **DISCIPLINE** RELIGIOUS STUDIES **EDUCATION** Cambridge Univ, BA, 70; Univ Calif - Santa Barbara, MA, 72; Covenant Theol Seminary, MDiv, 78; Univ Va, PhD, 89. **CAREER** Pastor, Presbyterian churches in England and the US, 78-; Asst Prof, Dept Relig Studies and Psychiat Med, Univ Va, 91-93, Assoc Dir, Ctr on the Study of Mind and Human Interaction, 91-93; Exec Dir, Wis Humanities Coun, 93-. **HONORS AND AWARDS** Numerous research and travel awards from various organizations. **MEMBERSHIPS** Am Acad Relig; Medieval/Renaissance Drama Soc; Soc Int L'Etude du Theatre Medieval. **RESEARCH** Medieval theater; folk theater; the religious and theatrical aspects of fiestas in Spain and the Americas. **SELECTED PUBLICATIONS** Auth, Theatre and Incarnation, St. Martin's Press, 90; The Dialogical Theatre: Dramatizations of the Conquest of Mexico and the Question of the Other, St. Martin's Press, 93; A Catalan Corpus Christi Play: The Martyrdom of St. Sebastian with the Hobby Horses and the Turks, Comp Drama 31, 97; The Impotence of Dragons: Playing Devil in the Trinidad Carnival, The Drama Rev 42, 98; Fireworks, Turks, and Long-Necked Mules: Pyrotechnic Theater in Germany and Catalonia, Comp Drama 32, 98; author of numerous other articles and chapters. **CONTACT ADDRESS** Exec Dir, Wisconsin Humanities Coun, 802 Regent St., Madison, WI, 53715-2610. **EMAIL** mrharri1@facstaff.wisc.edu

HARRIS, NORMAN

DISCIPLINE PHILOSOPHY **EDUCATION** Univ Ind, BA, MA, PhD. **CAREER** Prof. **RESEARCH** African American Studies; creative and technical writing; African philosophy; Egyptian philosophy. **SELECTED PUBLICATIONS** Auth, The Sixties A Black Chronology, 90; African American Social Change; A Philosophical Base, 91; Education or Initiation: Reading the Interior of the Black World Experience, 94; Can the Big Dog Run?, Black Cult J, 93; A Philosophical Basis for Afrocentricity, W J Black Studies, 92; The Sixties: An Analytical Chronology, W J Black Studies, 92; Multicultural Education in A Changing World, 90. **CONTACT ADDRESS** Philosophy Dept, Union Inst, 440 E McMillan St, Cincinnati, OH, 45206-1925.

HARRIS, STEPHEN LEROY

PERSONAL Born 02/05/1937, Aberdeen, WA, m, 1965, 2 children **DISCIPLINE** HUMANITIES, RELIGIOUS STUDIES **EDUCATION** Univ Puget Sound, BA, 59; Cornell Univ, MA, 61, PhD, 64. **CAREER** Actg cur-libr, WA State Hist Soc, 63; asst prof Eng, WA State Univ, 64-65; from asst prof to assoc prof, 65-72, chmn hum dept, 72-76, 92-98; prof hum, CA State Univ, Sacramento, 74. **HONORS AND AWARDS** Woodrow Wilson Fellow, 60-61; Faculty Research Award, CSUS, 81-82. **RESEARCH** The Eng novel; rel between the Hellenic and the Judaeo-Christian traditions in hist of Western thought; Bible studies. **SELECTED PUBLICATIONS** Auth, The Humanist Tradition in World Literature, Merrill, 70; Fire and Ice: The Cascade Volcanoes, Pac Search & the Mountaineers, 76, rev ed, 80, 2nd ed, 83; Understanding the Bible, A reader's Guide and Reference, Mayfield Publ, 97; Five Mountains of the West, Mountain Press, 88, The New Testament: A Students Introduction, Mayfield Publ, 98; Classical mythology: Images and Insights, Mayfield Publ, 97; Touchstones: Classic Readings in the Humanities, Holt Reinhart Winston, 90; Agents if Chaos, Mountain Press, 90; Restless Earth, National Geographic Books, 97; Wonders of the World, contrib, National Geographics Books, 98. **CONTACT ADDRESS** Dept of Hum and Relig Study, California State Univ, Sacramento, 6000 J St, Sacramento, CA, 95819-6083. **EMAIL** sharris@csus.edu

HARRISON, FRANK RUSSELL

PERSONAL Born 11/13/1935, Jacksonville, FL, d, 1 child **DISCIPLINE** PHILOSOPHY **EDUCATION** Undergraduate, Duke Univ, 54; Loyola Univ of the S, 55; Univ of the S. Sewanee, BA, Philos, 57; Graduate, MA, Philos, 59; PhD, Philos, 61, Univ of VA. **CAREER** Graduate Asst, Univ of VA, Charlottesville, 58-61; Inst Philos, Roanoke Coll, 61-62; Asst Prof Philos, 62-66; Assoc Prof Philos, 66-72; Prof of Philos 72-; Graduate Faculty, 66-79, 92-; Vis Prof, Univ NC, Chapel Hill, 63; Vis Prof, Emory Univ, Atlanta GA, 65; GA Inst Tech School of Info and Cmpt Sci, Atlanta GA 65-66. **HONORS AND AWARDS** Hon Program Faculty, 68; Vis Prof, Keele Univ England, 84; Phi Kappa Phi; Phi Beta Delta; Phi Sigma Tau; Outstanding Educ of Amer; Gridiron Secret Soc; The Panhellenic Council Oustanding Faculty Member of the year, 91; Tchg Improvement Program Mentor, 88-90. **MEMBERSHIPS** Phi Kappa Lit Soc; Faculty advisor 90-; Athens Torch Club; Intl Assoc of Torch Clubs, 82-; Rotary Intl 81-; Intercollegiate Studies Inst Faculty Assoc 78-; Exec Comm United Way Campaign. **SELECTED PUBLICATIONS** Truth Trees and Natural Deductions-Tools of the Trade, Intl Government Mgt Info Sci, Ashville NC, 94; Perfect Decisions in an Imperfect World, Allegany Health Group, Tampa FL, 95; Patients Rights and Bottom Line Costs, Allegany Health Group, Tampa FL, 95; Virtue and Vice, Hoffberger Center for Business Ethics, Univ Baltimore MD, 96; Deductive Well, West Publ 94. **CONTACT ADDRESS** Dept Philos, Univ of Georgia, Athens, GA, 30602.

HARRISON, JEFFREY L.

DISCIPLINE LAW **EDUCATION** Univ Fla, BS, MBA, PhD; Univ NC, JD. **CAREER** Chesterfield Smith prof, Univ Florida, 83-; ch, Asn Amer Law Schools Sect Socioeconomics; prof, Univ Houston 78-84; Univ NC Greensboro 70-78; vis prof, Leiden Univ, Neth; Univ NC, Tufts Univ; staff; Univ NC Law Rev. **HONORS AND AWARDS** Fellow, National Endowment for the Humanities, Tufts University., Univ Tex; fel, NEH. **MEMBERSHIPS** Texas Bar; Order of the Coif; Phi Kappa Phi; Omicron Delta Epsilon. **RESEARCH** Antitrust, contracts. **SELECTED PUBLICATIONS** Auth, Understanding Antitrust and Its Economic Implications and Monopoly: Economic Theory and Antitrust Policy. **CONTACT ADDRESS** School of Law, Univ of Florida, PO Box 117625, Gainesville, FL, 32611-7625. **EMAIL** harrison.jef@law.ufl.edu

HARRISVILLE, ROY A., III

PERSONAL Born 11/26/1954, Mason City, IA, m, 1978, 2 children **DISCIPLINE** BIBLICAL INTERPRETATION **EDUCATION** Concordia Col, BA, 77; Luther-Northwestern Sem, M.Div, 81; Union Theol Sem, PhD, 90. **CAREER** Prof, 94-98, acad dean, 98-, Lutheran Bible Inst. **HONORS AND AWARDS** Am Lutheran Church Grad Scholar, 85-88; James A Jones Grad Fel, 85-86; Herbert Worth Jackson Jr. Fel, 87-88; Am Grad Scholar, 88-89, Evangelical Lutheran Church; Adele Mellen Award, 92; Who's Who Biblical Studies and Archaeol, 93; Who's Who Midwest, 94; Who's Who West, 96-97. **MEMBERSHIPS** Soc Biblical Lit. **RESEARCH** New Testament studies; ancient rhetoric; hermeneutics. **SELECTED PUBLICATIONS** Auth, The Figure of Abraham in the Epistles of Saint Paul: In the Footsteps of Abraham, Mellen Res Univ Press, 92; "Between Text and Sermon: Mark 1:4-11, Interpretation, 93; Augsburg Home Bible Studies, Augsburg Publishing House, 94; "Pistis Christou: Witness of the Fathers, Novum Testamentum, 94; Four Exegetical Essays (John 16:12-15; Galatians 2:15-21; Galatians 3:23-29; Luke 9:51-62), in Lectionary Homiletics, 98. **CONTACT ADDRESS** Lutheran Bible Inst of Seattle, 4221 228th Ave SE, Issaquah, WA, 98029-9299.

HARROD, HOWARD L.

PERSONAL Born 06/09/1932, Holdenville, OK, m, 1971, 2 children **DISCIPLINE** SOCIOLOGY OF RELIGION **EDUCATION** Oklahoma Univ, BA, 60; Duke Univ, BD, 60; Yale Univ, STM, 61, MA, 63, PhD, 65. **CAREER** Asst prof, Howard Univ, 64-66; assoc prof, Drake Univ, 66-68; prof, social ethics and sociol, relig, Vanderbilt Univ, 68- . **HONORS AND AWARDS** Rockefeller Doctoral Fel, 62-63; NEH, 67; Am Coun Learned Soc Fel, 81-82; Vanderbilt Univ Fel, 87-88; Rockefeller Fel, 88. **MEMBERSHIPS** Soc for the Sci Study of Relig; Soc for Values in Higher Ed; Am Acad of Relig; Soc for the Sci Study of Relig; Soc of Christian Ethics; Plains Anthrop Soc. **RESEARCH** Religion and culture; Northern Plains religions. **SELECTED PUBLICATIONS** Auth, Mission among the Blackfeet, Univ Okl, 71; auth, The Human Center: Moral Agony in the Social World, Fortress, 81; auth, Renewing the World: Plains Indians Religion and Morality, Univ Ariz Pr, 92; auth, Becoming and Remaining a People: Native American Religions on the North Plains, Univ Ariz Pr, 95; auth, numerous articles and book ch. **CONTACT ADDRESS** Divinity School, Vanderbilt Univ, Nashville, TN, 37240. **EMAIL** howard.harrod@vanderbilt.edu

HARROLD, JEFFERY DELAND

PERSONAL Born 10/16/1956, Detroit, MI, m **DISCIPLINE** THEOLOGY **EDUCATION** University of MI, BA Economics 1978; Trinity Evangelical Divinity School, MDiv. **CAREER** ADP Network Services Inc, tech analyst 1983-84; BETHEL AME CHURCH, ASST PASTOR 1984-; TRINITY AME CHURCH, ASSOC PASTOR 1984-; TRINITY COLL, DIR OF MINORITY STUDENT DEVELOP 1985-. **HONORS AND AWARDS** Kearney Black Achievement Awd Trinity Evangelical Divinity School 1985. **MEMBERSHIPS** Mem Assoc of Christians in Student Develop 1986-87; student council pres Trinity Evangelical Div Sch 1986-87; mem Omega Psi Phi Frat. **CONTACT ADDRESS** Minority Student Dev, Trinity Col, 2077 Half Day Rd, Deerfield, IL, 60015.

HARROP, CLAYTON KEITH

PERSONAL Born 02/18/1924, Berryton, KS, m, 1944, 3 children **DISCIPLINE** RELIGION **EDUCATION** William Jewell Col, AB, 49; Southern Baptist Theol Sem, BD, 52, PhD, 56. **CAREER** From instr to assoc prof, 55-68, prof New Testament, VP Acad Aff, 92-94, Sr prof New Testament, 94-, Golden Gate Baptist Theol Sem, 68-. **MEMBERSHIPS** Soc Bibl Lit; Asn Baptist Professors of Relig. **RESEARCH** Background of New Testament times; development of early Christianity; Greek. **SELECTED PUBLICATIONS** Auth, The Letter of James, Convention Press, 69; History of the New Testament in Plain Language, Word, 84. **CONTACT ADDRESS** Golden Gate Baptist Theol Sem, 201 Seminary Dr, Mill Valley, CA, 94941-3197. **EMAIL** ckharrop@aol.com

HART, BILL

DISCIPLINE PHILOSOPHY **EDUCATION** Harvard Univ, PhD, 69. **CAREER** Prof, Univ IL at Chicago . **RESEARCH** Logic; philos of mathematics; metaphysics; epistemology. **SELECTED PUBLICATIONS** Auth, The Engines of the Soul, Cambridge, 88; On Non-Well-Founded Sets, Critica, 92; Motions of the Mind, Blackwell, 92; Hat-tricks and Heaps, Philos Studies, 92. **CONTACT ADDRESS** Philos Dept, Univ Illinois Chicago, S Halsted St, PO Box 705, Chicago, IL, 60607.

HART, CHRISTOPHER ALVIN

PERSONAL Born 06/18/1947, Denver, CO, d **DISCIPLINE** LAW **EDUCATION** Princeton University, BSE, 1969, MSE 1971; Harvard Law School, JD, 1973. **CAREER** Peabody Rivlin & Lambert, assoc 1973-76; Air Transport Assoc, Attorney 1976-77; US Dept of Transportation, deputy asst genl counsel 1977-79; Hart & Chavers, managing partner 1979-90; National Transportation Safety Board, member, 1990-93; Natl Hwy Traffic Safety Admin, deputy admin, 1993-95; Federal Aviation Administration, asst admin for system safety, 1995-. **MEMBERSHIPS** Natl, Amer, Federal, Washington Bar Assns, 1973-; Princeton Engineering Adv & Resource Council, 1975-; dir/pres, Beckman Place Condo Assn, 1979-83; Federal Communications Bar Assn, 1981-; dir, WPFW-FM, 1983-; Lawyer Pilots Bar Assn, 1975-; Aircraft Owners & Pilots Assn, 1973-. **SELECTED PUBLICATIONS** "Antitrust Aspects of Deepwater Ports," Transportation Law Journal 1979; "State Action Antitrust Immunity for Airport Operators," Transportation Law Journal 1981. **CONTACT ADDRESS** Federal Aviation Administration, 800 Independence Ave SW, Rm 1016D, Washington, DC, 20591.

HART, DARRYL GLENN

DISCIPLINE CHURCH HISTORY, THEOLOGICAL BIBLIOGRAPHY **EDUCATION** Temple Univ, BA, 79; Westminster Theol Sem, MAR, 81; Harvard Univ, MTS, 83; Johns Hopkins Univ, MA, 85, PhD, 88. **CAREER** Tchg asst, Johns Hopkins Univ, 85-88; post-dr fel, lectr, Divinity Sch, Duke Univ, 88-89; dir, Inst Stud of Amer Evangelicals, Wheaton Cole, 89-93; assoc prof, Westminster Theol Sem, 93-. **HONORS AND AWARDS** Co-ed, Dictionary of the Presbyterian and Reformed Tradition in America, 91-; bk rev ed, Fides et Historia 92-96; ed, Westminster Theol Jour, 96-; **SELECTED PUBLICATIONS** Auth, J. Gresham Machen and the Crisis of Conservative Protestantism in Modern America; The Troubled Soul of the Academy: American Learning and the Problem of Religious Studies, Rel and Amer Cult, 92; The Legacy of J.

Gresham Machen and the Identity of the Orthodox Presbyterian Church, Westminster Theol Jour 53, 92. **CONTACT ADDRESS** Westminister Theol Sem, PO Box 27009, Philadelphia, PA, 19118.

HART, JAMES G.
DISCIPLINE RELIGIOUS STUDIES **EDUCATION** Univ Chicago, PhD, 72. **CAREER** Prof. **RESEARCH** Philosophy of religion; philosophical theology; peace and conflict studies. **SELECTED PUBLICATIONS** Auth, A Precise of an Husserlian Philosophical Theology, SUNY, 86; The Person and the Common Life: Studies in a Husserlian Social Ethics, Kluwer, 92. **CONTACT ADDRESS** Dept of Religious Studies, Indiana Univ, Bloomington, 300 N Jordan Ave, Bloomington, IN, 47405.

HART, JOHN
PERSONAL Born 10/05/1943, New York, NY, m, 1975, 2 children **DISCIPLINE** THEOLOGY **EDUCATION** Marist Col, NY, BA, 66; Union Theol Sem, NY, STM, 72, MPhil, 76; PhD, 78. **CAREER** Instr, asst Cath Campus Min, Pan Amer Univ, 70-73; lectr, Christian ethics, 75-76, Union Theol Sem; instr, relig, 76-77, Trinity Col; dir, Planning & Comm Devel, San Juan, 77-78; vis asst prof, 78-79, Howard Univ; adj instr, 80-81, Augustana Col SD; dir, 79-81, Heartland Proj, SD; asst prof, 81-82, Mount Marty Col, SD; dir, devel & planning, 81-82, Mount Marty Col; admin, 82-83, Live Oak Fund for Change; adj instr, 82-83, St Edward's Univ; assoc prof, 83-85, Col Great Falls, MT; dir, environ stud, 97-, Carroll Col; prof, 85-, tenured, 89, chmn, 93-, Carroll Col. **HONORS AND AWARDS** AAR/Lilly, Tchng Fel, 97-98; NEH, sum sem, 86, 85; Templeton Sci - Rel Course Award, 95; outstanding tchr, Carroll Col, 95; Delegate, UN Intl Hum Rights Comm, 87-90. **MEMBERSHIPS** AAR; Soc of Christian Ethics. **RESEARCH** Relig & environ; Native Amer spirituality; economic justice; liberation theology. **SELECTED PUBLICATIONS** Art, Indigenous Voices for Earth Summit, New World Outlook, 93; art, Indigenous Rights, Land and Nature, Christianity & Crisis, 93; art, Orchids, Eagles and Natural Rights, Horizons, Sigurd Olson Environ Inst, 94; art, Caring for Creation: Church Teachings on Environmental Responsibility, The Critic, J Amer Cath Cult, vol 50, 95; auth, The Spirit of the Earth - A Theology of the Land, Paulist Press, 84; auth, Ethics and Technology: Innovation and Transformation in Community Contexts, Pilgrim Press, 97. **CONTACT ADDRESS** 2007 University St, Helena, MT, 59601. **EMAIL** jhart@carroll.edu

HART, RICHARD E.
PERSONAL Born 07/12/1949, Columbus, OH, m, 1972, 2 children **DISCIPLINE** PHILOSOPHY **EDUCATION** Ohio Univ, BGS, 71; SUNY Stony Brook, PhD, 84. **CAREER** Dir cont Ed, Long Island Univ, CW Post campus, 80-86; prof philos, Bloomfield Col, 86- . **HONORS AND AWARDS** Phi Kappa Phi; Alpha Sigma Lamda, hon memb. **MEMBERSHIPS** APA; Soc for Advan of Am Philos; Am Assoc of Philos. **RESEARCH** Philosophy and literature; American philosophy. **SELECTED PUBLICATIONS** Ed, Ethics and the Environment, Univ Press of Am, 92; co-ed Philosophy in Experience: American Philosophy in Transition, Fordham, 97; co-ed, Plato's Dialogues: The Dialogical Approach, Edwin Mellen, 97. **CONTACT ADDRESS** Philosophy/Humanities Dept, Bloomfield Col, Bloomfield, NJ, 01003.

HART, W.D.
PERSONAL Born 02/18/1943, Ithaca, NY, m, 1974, 1 child **DISCIPLINE** PHILOSOPHY **EDUCATION** Harvard Col, BA summa cum laude, 64; Harvard Univ, PhD 68. **CAREER** Univ of Michigan, asst prof, 69-74; Univ Col London, lectr, sr lectr, reader, 74-91; Univ New Mexico, assoc prof, prof, 92-93; Univ IL, prof, ch, 93 to 94-. **HONORS AND AWARDS** Detur Awd; John Harvard Scholar; Harvard Col Scholar; Phi Beta Kappa; Woodrow Wilson Fel; Harvard Grad Ntl Fel; Arthur Lehman Scholar. **RESEARCH** History of Analytic Philosophy; Recursion Theory; Social Choice Theory and Politics. **SELECTED PUBLICATIONS** Auth, Philosophy of Mathematics, co-ed, intro, Oxford Univ Press, 96; The Engines of the Soul, Cambridge Univ Press, 88; The Syntax of the World, Critica, 96; Meaning and Verification, Routledge Encycl of Philos, ed, E Craig, Graham Forbes, forthcoming; auth, Lowenheim-Skolem Theorems and Non-Standard Models, Routledge Encycl of Philos, ed, E. Craig, M Detlefsen, forthcoming; Dualism Companion to Philo of Mind, ed, S. Guttenplan, Blackwell, forthcoming; Godel and the Soul, Companion to Metaphysics, ed J. Kim, E. Sosa, Blackwell, 94; rev, George Boolos, ed, Meaning and Method, Philos Quart, forthcoming; DH Mellor, Matters of Metaphysics, Philos Books, 93; Long Decimals, forthcoming, in a Festschrift for Burton S. Dreben. **CONTACT ADDRESS** Dept of Philosophy, Univ of Illinois, M/C 267, Chicago, IL, 60607-7114. **EMAIL** hart@uic.edu

HARTIN, PATRICK JOHN CHRISTOPHER
PERSONAL Born 12/07/1944, Johannesburg, South Africa, s **DISCIPLINE** RELIGIOUS STUDIES **EDUCATION** UNISA, BA, 66, DTh, 81, DTh, 88; Gregorian, STB, 69, STL, 71. **CAREER** Tchr, 72-81, Headmaster, 81-83, St Benedicts Col; lctr New Testament Studies, 84-87, Sr lectr, 88-89, Univ Witwatersrand, assoc prof Dept of New Testament, 90-95, dept head, 93-95, Univ S Africa; adj fac Roman Cath Chaplain, Claremont Univ Ctr, 94-95; assoc prof, Gonzaga Univ, 95-. **MEMBERSHIPS** Cath Bibl Asn Amer; Cath Theol Soc S Africa; New Testament Soc S Africa; Studiorum Novi Testamenti Soc; Soc Bibl Lit; S African Soc Gen Lit Studies **RESEARCH** Epistle of James; Traditions behind Gospels. **SELECTED PUBLICATIONS** Auth, First century Galilee as a setting for early Christianity, Jour Semitic Studies, 94; The wisdom and apocalyptic layers of the sayings Gospel Q: What is their significance?, Hervormde Teol Studies, 94; Ethics and the New Testament: How do we get from there to here, The relevance of Theology for the 1990s, Pretoria, 84; rev, Restoring the Diaspora: Discursive Structure and Purpose in the Epistle of James, Toronto Jour Theol, 93; Auth, Who is wise and understanding among you? SBL Sem Papers, 96; Call to be perfect through suffering, Biblica, 96; Documenta Q: Reconstructions of Q through two centuries of Gospel research: Excerpted, Sorted and Evaluated: Q4:1-13, 16: The Temptations of Jesus; Nazara, 96; Christian ethics in a pluralistic society: Towards a theology of compromise, Relig & Theol, 97; The poor in the epistle of James and the Gospel of Thomas, Hervormde Teol Studies, 97. **CONTACT ADDRESS** Religious Studies Dept, Gonzaga Univ, AD Box 57, Spokane, WA, 99258-0001. **EMAIL** hartin@gonzaga.edu

HARTLE, ANN
DISCIPLINE THE NATURE OF PHILOSOPHY **EDUCATION** CUNY, PhD, 76. **CAREER** Philos, Emory Univ. **HONORS AND AWARDS** Nat Endowment Hum fel, 82-83. **SELECTED PUBLICATIONS** Auth, The Modern Self in Rousseau's Confessions: A Reply to St. Augustine and Death; Disinterested Spectator: An Inquiry into the Nature of Philosophy. **CONTACT ADDRESS** Emory Univ, Atlanta, GA, 30322-1950.

HARTLE, ANTHONY E.
PERSONAL Born 12/28/1942, Wichita, KS, m, 1964, 3 children **DISCIPLINE** PHILOSOPHY, LITERATURE **EDUCATION** US Mil Acad, BS, 64; Duke Univ, MA, 71; Univ of Texas, PhD, 82. **CAREER** PROF, DEP HEAD, ENGLISH, USMA. **MEMBERSHIPS** Am Philos Asn, Joint Serv Conf on Prof Ethics. **RESEARCH** Moral philosophy; applied ethics **SELECTED PUBLICATIONS** Auth, Moral Issues in Military Decision Making; Dimensions of Ethical Thought. **CONTACT ADDRESS** Dept of English, US Mil Acad, West Point, NY, 10996-1791. **EMAIL** ca5868@usma.edu

HARTLEY, LOYDE HOBART
PERSONAL Born 07/21/1940, Parkersburg, WV, m, 1962, 3 children **DISCIPLINE** SOCIOLOGY OF RELIGION **EDUCATION** Otterbein Col, AB, 62; United Theol Sem, BD, 65; Emory Univ, PhD, 68. **CAREER** Lectr, Emory Univ, 67-68; assoc prof sociology, 71-, dir, doctoral studies, 73-75, dean, doctoral studies, 75-82, Lancaster Theol Sem. **MEMBERSHIPS** Am Sociol Assn; Soc Sci Studies Relig; Relig Res Assn. **RESEARCH** Religious beliefs and attitudes; organization of religious groups; professional characteristics of clergy. **SELECTED PUBLICATIONS** Auth, The Placement And Deployment Of Ministers in the United Church of Christ, Res Ctr Relig & Soc, Pa, 73; auth, Understanding Church Finances, Pilgrim Press, 84; auth, Cities and Churches, Scarecrow Press; 92. **CONTACT ADDRESS** Lancaster Theol Sem, 555 W James St, Lancaster, PA, 17603-2830. **EMAIL** lhartley@lts.org

HARTMAN, LAURA PINCUS
PERSONAL Born 10/06/1963, Chicago, IL, m, 1997, 2 children **DISCIPLINE** LAW **EDUCATION** Tufts Univ, BS, 85; Univ Chicago, JD, 88. **CAREER** Vis prof of bus law, Northwestern Univ, 92; assoc prof, Dept of Mgt, dir, Inst for Bus and Prof Ethics, DePaul Univ, 90- ; sr fel, Ethics Resource Ctr, Washington DC, 98; vis prof, Univ Wisc, 98- . **HONORS AND AWARDS** Magna cum laude, 85; Phi Kappa Phi; Univ Excellence in Teachg Awd, 91; Beta Gamma Sigma; Who's Who in Am Law, 92; DePaul Coll of Com Outstanding Serv Awd, 93; Best Teaching Awd, 92, 93; Who's Who in Am, 94; 2000 Notable Am Women, 94; Internatl Who's Who, 95. **MEMBERSHIPS** Midwest Acad of Legal Stud in Bus; Soc for Bus Ethics; Am Bar Asn; Chicago Bar Asn. **RESEARCH** Business ethics. **SELECTED PUBLICATIONS** Co-auth, Instructor's Manual for Irwin's Business Law, Irwin, 94; co-auth, Law, Business and Society, 4th, 5th ed, Irwin, 95; auth, legal and ethical briefs for Hornsby, Human Resource Management: A Practical Approach, West, 95; co-auth, Employment Law for Business, Irwin, 97; auth, Property Law, draft, in Taylor, et al, Contemporary Legal Studies in Business, Irwin, 97; co-auth, Legal Environment of Business: Ethical and Public Policy Concerns, Irwin, 97; auth, Perspectives in Business Ethics, Irwin, 98; auth, Ethics and Economics of Workplace Privacy, in 1999 Handbook of Business Strategy, J of Bus Strategy, 99; auth of numerous articles. **CONTACT ADDRESS** DePaul Univ, Chicago, IL, 60604. **EMAIL** lhartman@bus.wisc.edu

HARTT, JULIAN NORRIS
PERSONAL Born 06/13/1911, Selby, SD **DISCIPLINE** RELIGION **EDUCATION** Dakota Wesleyan Univ, AB, 32, DLitt, 61; Garrett Bibl Inst, BD, 37; Northwestern Univ, AM, 38; Yale Univ, PhD, 40; Bucknell Univ, DD, 73. **CAREER** Instr philos & relig, Berea Col, 40-43; assoc prof theol, Divinity Sch, Yale Univ, 43-53, Porter prof philos theol, 53-72, chmn dept relig studies, 67-72; William Kenan prof, 72-81, Emer Prof Relig Studies, Univ Va, 81-, Fulbright fel, Italy & Guggenheim fel, 63-64. **MEMBERSHIPS** Am Philos Asn; Am Asn for Advan Sci; Am Polit Sci Asn. **RESEARCH** Philosophical theology; the ontological argument for the existence of God. **SELECTED PUBLICATIONS** Auth, Moral Unintelligibility, A Commentary on the Asbury-Hauerwas Debate, Soundings, Vol 0076, 93; Metaphysical Personalism--An Analysis of Austin Farrer Metaphysics of Theism, Relig Studies, Vol 0032, 96. **CONTACT ADDRESS** Dept of Relig Studies, Univ of Va, Charlottesville, VA, 22903.

HARVEY, CAMERON
DISCIPLINE LAW **EDUCATION** Univ Toronto, BA, 61; Osgoode Univ, LLB, 64, LLM, 66. **CAREER** Prof, 66-; assoc dean, 87-. **RESEARCH** Agency; conflict of laws; wills; property. **SELECTED PUBLICATIONS** Auth, The Law of Habeas Corpus in Canada, 74; Samuel Freedman: A Great Canadian Judge, 83; Legal Wit and Whimsy, 1988, Agency Law Primer, 93. **CONTACT ADDRESS** Fac of Law, Univ Manitoba, Robson Hall, Winnipeg, MB, R3T 2N2. **EMAIL** cam_harvey@umanitoba.ca

HARVEY, CHARLES W.
DISCIPLINE PHILOSOPHY **EDUCATION** Fla State Univ, BA, 78, PhD, 83. **CAREER** Lectr, Fla State Univ, 84-85; Asst prof to prof, Central Ark Univ, 83-. **HONORS AND AWARDS** Deutscher Akademischer Austausch Dienst grant; NEH grant; UCA grants. **SELECTED PUBLICATIONS** Auth, Husserl's Phenomenology and The Foundations of Natural Science, Ohio Univ Press, 89; auth, Conundrums: A Book of Philosophical Questions, Univ Press Am, 95. **CONTACT ADDRESS** Univ Central Ark, 201 Donaghey Ave, Conway, AR, 72035-0001. **EMAIL** charlesh@mail.uca.edu

HARVEY, JAMES CARDWELL
PERSONAL Born 07/15/1925, Italy, TX, m, 1974, 2 children **DISCIPLINE** PUBLIC POLICY AND ADMINISTRATION; HUMAN RESOURCES **EDUCATION** SMU, BA, 49; Univ Texas at Austin, MA, 52, PhD, 55; Univ Ariz, MA, 69. **CAREER** Asst prof, Pan Am Col, 54-57; asst prof, Univ Texas El Paso, 57-64; assoc prof Ft Lewis Col, 64-65; assoc prof & chr Social Sciences, W New Mex Univ, 65-68; prof, 70-92, RET & ADJ PROF, JACKSON STATE UNIV, 70-; Fulbright schol, 52-53; NASVAA PA fel, 74-75; Pi Alpha Alpha; Phi Alpha Theta, Pi Sigma Alpha, Pi Gamma Mu, Pi Delta Phi. **MEMBERSHIPS** ASPA **RESEARCH** Human Resources **CONTACT ADDRESS** Jackson State Univ, 3825 Ridgewood Rd, Box 18, Jackson, MS, 39211.

HARVEY, JOHN D.
PERSONAL Born 03/11/1951, Johnstown, PA, m, 1974, 4 children **DISCIPLINE** NEW TESTAMENT **EDUCATION** Wycliffe Col, Univ Toronto, ThD, 97. **CAREER** Assoc prof, New Testament & Greek, Columbia Bibl Sem, 91- . **MEMBERSHIPS** ETS; IBR; SBL; So Carolina Acad of Relig. **RESEARCH** Paul; Gospels; New Testament theology; New Testament Greek. **SELECTED PUBLICATIONS** Auth, Toward a Degree of Order in Ben Sira's Book, ZAW, 93; auth, Citizenship, & Nature, Natural, in Elwell, ed, Evangelical Dictionary of Biblical Theology, Baker, 96; auth, Mission in Jesus' Teaching, & Mission in Matthew, in Larkin, ed, Mission in the New Testament: An Evangelical Approach, Orbis, 98; auth, Listening to the Text: Oral Patterning in Paul's Letters, Baker, 98; auth, Biblical Criticism and Mission, in Moreau, ed, Evangelical Dictionary of World Missions, Baker, forthcoming; auth, Redemption, in Freedman, ed, Eerdmans Dictionary of the Bible, Eerdmans, forthcoming. **CONTACT ADDRESS** Columbia Bible Col, PO Box 3122, Columbia, SC, 29230-3122. **EMAIL** jharvey@ciu.edu

HARVEY, LOUIS-CHARLES
PERSONAL Born 05/05/1945, Memphis, Tennessee, s **DISCIPLINE** THEOLOGY **EDUCATION** LeMoyne-Owen Coll, BS 1967; Colgate Rochester Divinity School, MDiv 1971; Union Theological Seminary, MPhil 1977, PhD 1978. **CAREER** Colgate Rochester-Divinity School, prof, 1974-78; Payne Theological Seminary, dean, 1978-79, pres, 1989-; United Theological Seminary, prof 1979-; Metropolitan AME Church, senior minister, 1996-. **HONORS AND AWARDS** Rsch grant Assn of Theological Schools 1984-85; pioneered study of Black Religion in Great Britain, 1985-86. **MEMBERSHIPS** Speaker, preacher, writer, workshop leader African Methodist Episcopal Church 1979-. **SELECTED PUBLICATIONS** Articles published Journal of Religious Thought 1983, 1987; biographer of William Crogman in Something More Than Human Cole, 1987. **CONTACT ADDRESS** Senior Minister, Metropolitan AME Church, 1518 M St NW, Washington, VT, 20005.

HARVEY, MARK S.
PERSONAL Born 07/04/1946, Binghamton, NY, m, 1983 **DISCIPLINE** RELIGIOUS STUDIES **EDUCATION** Syracuse Univ, BA, 68; Boston Univ, ThM, 71; PhD, 83. **CAREER**

Lectr, 17 yrs, MIT. **HONORS AND AWARDS** NEH Fel; Readers Digest comm Awd; Whiting Foun Fel. **MEMBERSHIPS** AAR; SSAM; ASA; DES; SARCC; ASCAP. **RESEARCH** Music Religion Culture, American Music, Jazz. **SELECTED PUBLICATIONS** Auth, Jazz Time and Our Time, in: This is How We Flow: Rhythm in Black Cultures, ed Angela S Nelson, Columbia SC, U of SC press, 99 forthcoming; Rhythm Ritual and Religion: Postmodern Musical Agonistes, in: Theomusicology: A Special Issue of Black Sacred Music : A J of Theomusicology, 94; New World a' Comin': Religious Perspectives on the Legacy of Duke Ellington, in: Scared Music of the Secular City: From Blues to Rap, J of Theomusicology, 92. **CONTACT ADDRESS** JFK Station, Box 8721, Boston, MA, 02114. **EMAIL** mharvey@mit.edu

HARVEY, WILLIAM BURNETT
PERSONAL Born 09/04/1922, Greenville, SC, m, 2 children **DISCIPLINE** LAW **EDUCATION** Wake Forest Col, 43; Univ MI, JD, 48. **CAREER** Lectr law, Univ MI, 48-49; assoc, Hogan & Hartson, Wash, DC, 49-52; prof lectr law, George Wash Univ, 50; from asst prof to prof, Univ MI, 51-66; prof law & polit sci, Ind Univ, Bloomington, 66-73, dean sch law, 66-71; Prof Law & Polit Sci, Boston Univ, 73-, Gen Coun, 82-, Rockefeller fel, Univ Heidelberg, 55-56; prof & dean fac law, Univ Ghana & dir legal educ, Ghana Govt, 62-64; mem exec comt, Asn Am Law Schs, 67-69; vis Fulbright prof law, Univ Nairobi, 71-72; vis prof, Duke Univ, 72-73, Fletcher Sch Law & Diplomacy, 75-76 & Harvard Law Sch, 77-78. **RESEARCH** Impact of law on internal Univgovernance; legal philos; law and develop, espec Africa. **SELECTED PUBLICATIONS** Coauth, Cases and Materials on Contracts and Contract Remedies; auth, Law and Social Change in Ghana, Princeton Univ, 66; Introd to Legal Systems of East Africa, E Africa Lit Bur, 74; Freedom, Univand Law: The Legal Status of Academic Freedom in the Universities of Black Africa, Lagos Univ, 78; coauth, The independence of Transkei: A largely constitutional inquiry, J Mod Africa Studies, 6/78. **CONTACT ADDRESS** 201 Newbury St, Boston, MA, 02116. **EMAIL** whervey@bu.edu

HARWOOD, ROBIN
DISCIPLINE PHILOSOPHY OF MIND, PHILOSOPHY OF RELIGION, ANCIENT AND MEDIEVAL PHILOSOPHY **EDUCATION** Reading, Eng, PhD, 95. **CAREER** Lectr, Ga State Univ. **SELECTED PUBLICATIONS** Auth, The Survival of the Self. **CONTACT ADDRESS** Georgia State Univ, Atlanta, GA, 30303. **EMAIL** phlrrh@panther.gsu.edu

HASKER, R. WILLIAM
PERSONAL Born 03/06/1935, Washington, DC, m, 1960, 2 children **DISCIPLINE** PHILOSOPHY **EDUCATION** Univ Edinburgh, PhD. **CAREER** Distinguished prof & ch Div Humanities and Bible. **HONORS AND AWARDS** Ctr for Philos Relig, Univ Notre Dame, fel. **SELECTED PUBLICATIONS** Auth, Reason and Religious Belief: An Introduction to the Philosophy of Religion, Oxford UP & God, Time, and Knowledge, Cornell UP. **CONTACT ADDRESS** Dept of Philosophy, Hunter Col, CUNY, 695 Park Ave, New York, NY, 10021. **EMAIL** whasker@huntington.edu

HASKIN, DAYTON
PERSONAL Born 09/14/1946, Ann Arbor, MI **DISCIPLINE** ENGLISH LITERATURE, REFORMATION & PURITAN THEOLOGY **EDUCATION** Univ Detroit, BA, 68; Northwestern Univ, MA, 70; Univ London, BD, 75; Yale Univ, PhD(English), 78. **CAREER** Instr English, John Carroll Univ, 70-72; ASST PROF ENGLISH, BOSTON COL, 78- **MEMBERSHIPS** MLA; Milton Soc Am. **RESEARCH** Seventeenth century English literature; English puritanism; the English Bible. **SELECTED PUBLICATIONS** Auth, The Reinvention of Love--Poetry, Politics and Culture From Sidney to Milton, J English Germanic Philol, Vol 0095, 96; Politics, Poetics and Hermeneutics in Milton Prose - Lowenstein,D, Turner,Jg/, Heythrop Journal-A Quarterly Review Of Philosophy and Theology, Vol 0034, 93; Torah and Law in 'Paradise Lost', Theol Studies, Vol 0056, 95; Anxiety In Eden, A Kierkegaardian Reading of 'Paradise Lost', Comp Lit Studies, Vol 0032, 95; The Reinvention of Love--Poetry, Politics and Culture From Sidney to Milton, J English Germanic Philol, Vol 0095, 96; A History of Donne 'Canonization' From Izaak Walton to Cleanth Brooks, J English Germanic Philol, Vol 0092, 93. **CONTACT ADDRESS** Dept of English, Boston Col, Chestnut Hill, MA, 20167.

HASSING, ARNE
PERSONAL Born 04/02/1943, Umtali, Rhodesia, m, 1966, 2 children **DISCIPLINE** RELIGION, HISTORY **EDUCATION** Boston Univ, BA, 64; Garrett-Evangel Theol Sem, MDiv, 68; Northwestern Univ, PhD(relig), 74. **CAREER** Asst Prof Humanities, Northern Ariz Univ, 73 **HONORS AND AWARDS** Jesse Lee Prize, Gen Comn Arch & Hist, United Methodist Church, 77. **MEMBERSHIPS** Am Soc Church Hist; Am Acad Relig; Soc Advan Scand Study; World Methodist Hist Soc. **RESEARCH** History of religion in Scandinavia; religion and modern culture; history of Christianity in the American Southwest. **SELECTED PUBLICATIONS** Auth, The Hedstroms and the Bethel Ship Saga--Methodist Influence on Swedish Religious Life, Am Hist Rev, Vol 0099, 94; Rome and the Counterreformation in Scandinavia, Vol 3, Jesuit Educational Strategy, 1553-1622, Vol 4, The Age Of Gustavus Aldolphus, and Queen Christina of Sweden, 1622-1656, Am Hist Rev, Vol 0098, 93. **CONTACT ADDRESS** Dept of Humanities, No Arizona Univ, Box 6031, Flagstaff, AZ, 86011-0001.

HASSING, RICHARD F.
DISCIPLINE HISTORY AND PHILOSOPHY OF SCIENCE **EDUCATION** Cornell Univ, PhD. **CAREER** Philos, Catholic Univ Am. **RESEARCH** Atistotle; hist of physics & philos of nature. **SELECTED PUBLICATIONS** Auth, The Use and Non-Use of Physics in Spinoza's Ethics; The Southwestern Jour Philos 11, 80; Wholes, Parts, and Laws of Motion; Nature and System 6, 84; Thomas Aquinas on Physics VII;1 and the Aristotelian Science of the Physical Continuum, Catholic Univ Press, 91; Animals versus the Laws of Inertia; Rev Metaphysics 46, 92, Introduction, and Modern Natural Science and the Intelligibility of Human Experience, Catholic Univ Press, 97; The Exemplary Career of Newton's Mathematics, The St John's Rev 44, 97. **CONTACT ADDRESS** Catholic Univ of America, 620 Michigan Ave Northeast, Washington, DC, 20064. **EMAIL** hassing@cua.edu

HATAB, LAWRENCE J.
DISCIPLINE 19TH- AND 20TH-CENTURY CONTINENTAL PHILOSOPHY **EDUCATION** Fordham Univ, PhD, 76. **CAREER** Chair, Philos dept. **RESEARCH** Ancient philos, and social and political philos. **SELECTED PUBLICATIONS** Auth, Nietzsche and Eternal Recurrence ;Myth and Philos ;A Nietzschean Defense of Democracy: An Experiment in Postmodern Politics **CONTACT ADDRESS** Old Dominion Univ, 4100 Powhatan Ave, Norfolk, VA, 23058. **EMAIL** LHatab@odu.edu

HATCHER, DONALD L.
PERSONAL Born 11/01/1947, Monett, MO, m, 1993, 5 children **DISCIPLINE** PHILOSOPHY **EDUCATION** Univ Kansas, PhD, 83. **CAREER** Prof, philos, Baker Univ, 78- . **HONORS AND AWARDS** Duboc Univ Prof, 92-98. **MEMBERSHIPS** APA; Asn for Informal Logic and Critical Thinking; Simon de Beauvoir Soc; Philos of Educ Soc. **RESEARCH** Critical thinking; feminism. **SELECTED PUBLICATIONS** Auth, Understanding the Second Sex, Peter Lang, 84; auth, Science, Ethics and Technological Assessment, 2d ed, American, 95; auth, Reasoning and Writing, 2d ed, Vale, 98. **CONTACT ADDRESS** Baker Univ, PO Box 65, Baldwin City, KS, 66006. **EMAIL** dhatcher@idin.net

HATCHER, RICHARD GORDON
PERSONAL Born 07/10/1933, Michigan City, IN, m **DISCIPLINE** LAW **EDUCATION** IN Univ, BS 1956; Valparaiso Univ, JD 1959. **CAREER** Lake Co IN, deputy prosecuting atty 1961-63; City of Gary, city councilman 1963-67, mayor 1967-88; Hatcher and Associates, pres, 1988-; Valparaiso Univ, law prof, 1992-; Roosevelt University, Harold Washington Professor, political science, currently. **HONORS AND AWARDS** Outstanding Achievement Civil Rights 10 Annual Ovington Awd; life mem & Leadership Awd NAACP; Man of Yr Harlem Lawyers Assn; Disting Serv Awd Capital Press Club; Disting Serv Awd Jaycees; Employment Benefactors Awd Intl Assn Personnel Employment Security; Serv Loyalty & Dedication Awd Black Students Union Prairie State Coll; Outstanding Cit Yr Awd United Viscounts IN; Inspired Leadership IN State Black Caucus; among 100 Most Influential Black Americans Ebony Magazine 1971; among 200 most outstanding young leaders of US, Time Magazine, 1974; Urban Leadership award, IN Assn of Cities and Towns, 1986; Natl League of Cities President's Award, 1987; Natl Black Caucus of Local Elected Officials Liberty Award, 1987; Honorary Doctorates, Coppin St College, DuquesneU, Fisk U, Valparaiso U, Clevnd St U. **MEMBERSHIPS** Dem Conf of Mayors 1977; instr IN Univ NW; many publs; chmn Human & Resources Devel 1974; mem Natl League of Cities; past pres, US Conf of Mayors; Natl Conf of Black Mayors; Natl Black Polit Conv; former vice chair, Natl Dem Comm; Mikulski Commn report dem party policy; Natl Urban Coalition; natl chmn bd dir Operation PUSH; mem IN Exec Bd NAACP; mem Natl Dem Comm on Delegate Selection (co-author Com Report); founder Natl Black Caucus of Locally Elected Officials; Natl Black Caucus; IN State Dem Central Com; Assn Councils Arts; chair TransAfrica Inc; Jesse Jackson for Pres Campaign; pres Natl Civil Rights Museum and Hall of Fame; mem bd of dirs Marshall Univ Socof Yeager Scholars; fellow, Kennedy School of Govt, Harvard U; chair, African American Summit, 1989. **CONTACT ADDRESS** Law Sch, Valparaiso Univ, Valparaiso, IN, 46383.

HATCHETT, JOSEPH WOODROW
PERSONAL Born 09/17/1932, Clearwater, FL, s **DISCIPLINE** LAW **EDUCATION** FL A&M Univ, AB 1954; Howard Univ, JD 1959; Naval Justice Sch, Certificate 1973; NY Univ, Appellate Judge Course 1977; Amer Acad of Jud Educ, Appellate Judge Course 1978; Harvard Law Sch, Prog Instruction for Lawyers 1980, 1990. **CAREER** Private Law Practice, Daytona Beach FL 1959-66; City of Daytona Beach, contract consul 1963-66; US Attorney, asst Jacksonville FL 1966; US Atty for the Middle Dist of FL, first asst 1967-71; Middle Dist of FL, US magistrate 1971-75; Supreme Court of FL, justice 1975-79; US Court of Appeals for the 5th Circuit, US circuit judge 1979-81; US COURT OF APPEALS FOR THE 11TH CIRCUIT, US CIRCUIT JUDGE 1981-. **HONORS AND AWARDS** Stetson Law Sch Dr Laws 1980; FL Memorial Coll Honoris Causa Dr Laws 1976; Howard Univ Post Grad Achievement Awd 1977; High Risk Awd State Action Cncl1977; President's Citation Cook Co Bar Assn 1977; Most Outstanding Citizen Broward Co Natl Bar Assn 1976; Bicentennial Awd FL A&M Univ 1976; Comm SvcsAwd Edward Waters Coll 1976; An Accolate for Juristic Distinction Tampa Urban League 1975; Medallion for Human Relations Bethune Cookman 1975; Man of the YrAwd FL Jax Club 1974; first black person apptd to the highest court of a state since reconstruction; first black personelected to public office in a statewide election in the south; first black person to serve on a federal appellate court in the south; **MEMBERSHIPS** Mem FL Bar, Amer Bar Assn, Natl Bar Assn; bd dir Amer Judicature Soc; mem Jacksonville Bar Assn; mem DW Perkins Bar Assn; mem FL Chap of Natl Bar Assn; mem Phi Delta Phi Legal Frat, Phi Alpha Delta Legal Frat, Omega Psi Phi Frat. **SELECTED PUBLICATIONS** Publs including "Criminal Law Survey-1978" Univ of Miami Law Review; "1978 Devements in FL Law" 1979; "Pre-Trial Discovery in Criminal Cases" Fedl Judicial Ctr Library 1974. **CONTACT ADDRESS** 11th Circuit Ct of Appeals, PO Box 10429, Tallahassee, FL, 32302.

HATFIELD, GARY C.
PERSONAL Born 11/25/1951, Wichita, KS **DISCIPLINE** PHILOSOPHY **EDUCATION** Wichita State Univ, BA, BFA, 74; Univ Wisc, Madison, PhD, 79. **CAREER** Asst prof, Harvard Univ, 79-81; asst prof, Johns Hopkins, 81-87; assoc prof, 87-91; prof, 91-, Univ of Penn. **MEMBERSHIPS** APA; Philos of Sci Asn; Hist of Sci Soc. **RESEARCH** History of modern philosophy; philosophy of psychology. **SELECTED PUBLICATIONS** Auth, "Reason, Nature and God in Descartes," in Essays on the Philosophy and Science of Rene Descartes, Oxford, 93; "Remaking the Science of Mind," in Inventing Human Science, Univ of Calif Press, 95; "Was the Scientific Revolution Really A Revolution in Science," in Tradition, Transmission, Transformation, Brill, 96; "The Workings of the Intellect," in Logic and the Workings of the Mind, Ridgeview, 97; ed and trans, Immanuel Kant, Prolegeoma to Any Future Metaphysics, Cambridge, 97; "The Cognitive Faculties," in Cambridge History of Seventeenth Century Philosophy, Cambridge, 98; "Wundt and Psychology as Science," Perspectives on Sci, 97. **CONTACT ADDRESS** Dept of Philosophy, Univ of Pennsylvania, 433 Logan Hall, Philadelphia, PA, 19104-6304. **EMAIL** hatfield@phil.upenn.edu

HATTAB, HELEN
PERSONAL Born 03/17/1969, Seoul, Korea, m, 1990 **DISCIPLINE** PHILOSOPHY **EDUCATION** Trenton State Coll, BA, 90; Univ Penn, MA, 94, PhD, 98. **CAREER** Vis Asst Prof, 98-, Virginia Poly Inst & State Univ. **MEMBERSHIPS** APA, HSS **RESEARCH** Renaissance philosophy & intellectual history, 17th century philosophy & history of science, Descartes views on causation in their historical context. **SELECTED PUBLICATIONS** Auth, One Cause or Many? Jesuit Influences on Descartes' Division of Causes, Proceedings of the Societe Intl d'Etudes Medievales, forthcoming; Laws of Nature, in: The Sci Revolution An Encyclopedia, ed, W Applebaum, NY, Garland Pub Inc, forthcoming. **CONTACT ADDRESS** Dept of Philosophy, Virginia Polytechnic Univ, Major Williams Hall 229, Blacksburg, VA, 24061-6367. **EMAIL** hhattab@vt.edu

HAUCK, ALLAN
PERSONAL Born 05/19/1925, Springfield, OH, m, 1942, 2 children **DISCIPLINE** PHILOSOPHY, RELIGION **EDUCATION** Kenyon Col, BA, 45; Wittenburg Univ, BD, 47; Hartford Sem Found, ThD, 50. **CAREER** Asst prof philos St Christianity, Roanoke Col, 50-51; prof, Midland Lutheran Col, 58-68; Prof, Carthage Col, 68- **MEMBERSHIPS** Am Soc Church Hist. **SELECTED PUBLICATIONS** Auth, Spanish Protestants and Reformers in the 16th Century--Supplement 1, Church Hist, Vol 0066, 97. **CONTACT ADDRESS** Dept of Relig, Carthage Col, Kenosha, WI, 53140.

HAUGELAND, JOHN CHRISTIAN
PERSONAL Born 03/13/1945, Harrisburg, IL, 1 child **DISCIPLINE** PHILOSOPHY **EDUCATION** Harvey Mudd Col, BS, 66; Univ Calif, Berkeley, PhD, 76. **CAREER** Asst prof 74-81, assoc prof, 81-86, prof philos, Univ Pittsburgh, 86. **MEMBERSHIPS** Am Philos Asn **RESEARCH** Philos of mind; metaphysics; Heidegger. **SELECTED PUBLICATIONS** Auth, Mind Design, MIT Press, 81; Artificial Intelligence: The Very Idea, MIT Press, 85; Mind Design II, MIT Press, 97; Having Thought, Harvard Univ Press, 98. **CONTACT ADDRESS** Dept of Philos, Univ of Pittsburgh, 1001 Cathedral/Learn, Pittsburgh, PA, 15260-0001. **EMAIL** haugelan@pitt.edu

HAUSER, ALAN J.
PERSONAL Born 10/15/1945, Chicago, IL, m, 1989, 4 children **DISCIPLINE** BIBLICAL STUDIES **EDUCATION** Concordia Univ, BA, 67; Concordia Sem, MAR, 68; Univ Iowa, PhD, 72. **CAREER** From asst prof to assoc prof to prof, Appalachian State Univ, 72-. **MEMBERSHIPS** Soc Bibl Lit.

RESEARCH Biblical interpretation; rhetorical criticism; the Book of Judges; early Judaism; Old Testament literature. **SELECTED PUBLICATIONS** Coauth, From Carmel to Horeb: Elijah in Crisis, 90; coauth, Rhetorical Criticism of the Bible: A Comprehensive Bibliography with Notes on History and Method, 94; auth, The Minor Judges: A Re-evaluation, Jour Bibl Lit, June, 75; auth, Israel's Conquest of Palestine: A Peasant's Rebellion?, Jour Study Old Testament, May, 78; auth, Judges 5: Parataxis in Hebrew Poetry, Jour Bibl Lit, March, 80; auth, Genesis 2-3: The Theme of Alienation, Art & Meaning: Rhetoric in Bibl Lit, 82; auth, Jonah: In Pursuit of the Dove, Jour Bibl Lit, March, 85; auth, Two Songs of Victory: A Comparison of Exodus 15 and Judges 5, Directions Bibl Hebrew Poetry, 87. **CONTACT ADDRESS** Dept of Philosophy & Religion, Appalachian State Univ, 114 Greer Hall, Boone, NC, 28608. **EMAIL** hauseraj@appstate.edu

HAUSER, RICHARD JOSEPH
PERSONAL Born 06/22/1937, Milwaukee, WI **DISCIPLINE** CHRISTIAN SPIRITUALITY **EDUCATION** St Louis Univ, BA, 61, MA & PHL, 64, STL, 69, MA, 69; Cath Univ Am, Ph-D(relig & relig educ), 73. **CAREER** Prof & Chmn Theol, Creighton Univ, 72-; dir grad prog Theol. **MEMBERSHIPS** Cath Theol Soc Am; Am Acad Relig. **RESEARCH** Role of Holy Spirit in contemporary spirituality, especially personal prayer and discernment of spirits; spirituality of Thomas Merton; history of Christian spirituality. **SELECTED PUBLICATIONS** Auth, In His Spirit: A Guide to Today's Spirituality, Paulist Press, 82; Moving in The Sp;irit: Becoming A Contemplative in Action, Paulist, 86; Finding God in Troubled Times: The Holy Spirit and Suffering, Paulist, 94. **CONTACT ADDRESS** Theol Dept, Creighton Univ, 2500 California Plz, Omaha, NE, 68178-0001. **EMAIL** hausersj@breighton.edu

HAUSER, THOMAS
PERSONAL Born 02/27/1946, New York, NY **DISCIPLINE** LAW **EDUCATION** Columbia Col, BA, 67; Columbia Law Sch, JD, 70. **CAREER** Author **HONORS AND AWARDS** Prix Lafayette; Haviva Reik Award. **SELECTED PUBLICATIONS** Missing; The Trial of Thomas Shea; For Our Children with Frank Macchiarola; The Family Legal Companion; The Black Lights: Inside the World of Professional Boxing; Final Warning: The Legacy of Chernobyl, with Dr Robert Gale; Muhammad Ali: His Life and Times; Arnold Palmer: A Personal Journey; Muhammad Ali: In Perspective; Healing: A Journey of Tolerance and Understanding; Muhammad Ali and Company; Ashworth and Palmer; Agatha's Friends; The Beethoven Conspiracy; Hanneman's War; The Fantasy; The Hawthorne Group; Harder Than it Looks; Finding the Princess; Martin Bear and Friends; The Four Chords. **CONTACT ADDRESS** 11 Riverside Dr, NY, NY, 10023.

HAUSMAN, CARL R.
DISCIPLINE PHILOSOPHY **EDUCATION** Northwestern Univ, PhD. **CAREER** Adj prof, Univ Louisville. **RESEARCH** Philosophical approaches to creativity and metaphor theory as applied to the arts. **SELECTED PUBLICATIONS** Auth, Metaphor and Art, Cambridge, 89; The Evolutionary Philosophy of Charles S Peirce, Cambridge, 93; A Discourse on Novelty and Creation, State Univ NY Press, 84; co-ed, bk(s) on the relation between pragmatism and phenomenology and an anthology, The Creativity Question. **CONTACT ADDRESS** Dept of Philos, Univ Louisville, 2301 S 3rd St, Louisville, KY, 40292.

HAUSMAN, DANIEL M.
PERSONAL Born 03/27/1947, Chicago, IL, m, 1980, 2 children **DISCIPLINE** PHILOSOPHY **EDUCATION** Harvard Col, BA, 69; NY Univ, MAT, 71; Cambridge Univ, BA, 73; MA, 77; Columbia Univ, M Phil, 75; PhD, 78. **CAREER** Teacher, NYC Public Schs, 70-71; preceptor, Columbia Univ, 75-77; asst prof, Univ MD, 78-84; assoc prof, Carnegie-Mellon Univ, 84-88; assoc prof, Univ Wis-Madison, 88-91; prof, 91-; vis prof, London Sch Econ, 94; vis res assoc, Centre du Recherche en Epistemologie Appliquee, 94; vis res assoc, THEMA, Univ Cergy-Pontoise, 94; res fel, London Sch Econ, 96-98. **HONORS AND AWARDS** Bancroft Award, Columbia Univ, 78. **MEMBERSHIPS** Am Econ Asoc; Am Philos Asoc; Hist of Econ Soc; Int Network for Econ Methodology; Philos of Sci Asoc. **RESEARCH** Philosophy of economics; social and political philosophy; metaphysics (causality). **SELECTED PUBLICATIONS** Co-auth with Michael S. McPherson, Economic Analysis and Moral Philosophy, 96; auth, Problems with Supply-Side Egalitarianism, Polit and Soc, 96; ed with Roger Backhouse, Uskali Maki, and Andrea Salanti, Economic Methodology: Crossing Disciplinary Boundaries, 98; auth, Causal Asymmetries, 98; auth, Philosophy of Economics, Routledge Encyclopedia of Philosophy, 98. **CONTACT ADDRESS** Philosophy Dept, Univ of Wisconsin, Madison, WI, 53706. **EMAIL** dhausman@macc.wisc.edu

HAVAS, RANDALL E.
DISCIPLINE PHILOSOPHY **EDUCATION** Univ Calif, Berkeley, Ba, 79; Harvard Univ, PhD, 86. **CAREER** Asst prof, assoc prof, Yale Univ, 87-97; asst prof, Willamette Univ, 97-. **MEMBERSHIPS** APA; N Am Nietzsche Soc. **RESEARCH** Nineteenth and twentieth century continental philosophy; psychoanalysis; Buddhism. **SELECTED PUBLICATIONS** Auth, Nietzsche's Genealogy: Nihilism and the Will to Knowledge, Cornell, 95. **CONTACT ADDRESS** 3005 NE 59th Ave, Portland, OR, 97213. **EMAIL** rhavas@teleport.com

HAVENS DUFOUR, JOHN H.
PERSONAL m, 3 children **DISCIPLINE** PHILOSOPHY **EDUCATION** Rutgers Univ, BA, 89; Yale Univ, MA, 93, M.Phil, 93. **CAREER** Instr, 95-, Col of Santa Fe, Albuquerque. **MEMBERSHIPS** APA; Amer Indian Phil Assn. **RESEARCH** Epistemology; ethics; phil of religion; Native Amer phil. **CONTACT ADDRESS** 2612 19th St NW, Albuquerque, NM, 87104. **EMAIL** john.havens-dufour@yale.edu

HAVIGHURST, CLARK C.
PERSONAL Born 05/25/1933, Evanston, IL, m, 1965, 2 children **DISCIPLINE** LAW **EDUCATION** Princeton Univ, AB, 55; Northwestern Univ, JD, 58. **CAREER** Assoc prof, 64-68, Prof Law, Duke Univ, 68-, Ed, Law & Contemporary Problems, 65-70; scholar in residence, Inst Med, Nat Acad Sci, 72-73; adj scholar, Am Enterprise Inst Public Policy Res. **MEMBERSHIPS** Inst Med- Nat Acad Sci. **RESEARCH** Antitrust; regulated industries; health care. **SELECTED PUBLICATIONS** Auth, The Place of Private Accrediting Among the Instruments of Government, Law Contemp Problems, Vol 0057, 94; Accrediting and the Sherman Act, Law Contemp Problems, Vol 0057, 95. **CONTACT ADDRESS** Law Sch, Duke Univ, Durham, NC, 27706.

HAWK, CHARLES NATHANIEL, III
PERSONAL Born 10/25/1957, Atlanta, GA **DISCIPLINE** LAW **EDUCATION** Morehouse Coll, BA cum laude 1979; Georgetown Univ Law Center JD 1982. **CAREER** Cooper & Weintraub PC, assoc 1982-83; Morehouse Coll, dir office of alumni affairs; Hawk Law Firm, Attorney, currently. **HONORS AND AWARDS** Serv Awd United Negro Coll Fund 1985. **MEMBERSHIPS** Sec Deacon Bd Friendship Baptist Church 1978-; mem Council for Advancement and Support of Educ 1983-; chmn United Way Campaign Morehouse Coll 1983-; mem GA Bar Assn 1983-; of counsel Law Firm Cooper & Assoc 1983-; legal counsel Natl Black Alumni Hall of Fame 1983-; legal counsel Hank Aaron Found Inc 1984-; legal counsel Council of Natl Alumni Assoc Inc 1984-. **SELECTED PUBLICATIONS** Writer and dir of "Balls, Balloons, and Butterflies" presented 1981 Washington DC; artistic achievement Georgetown Univ Church Ensemble 1982; writer & dir "Black Gold" 1982 Washington DC. **CONTACT ADDRESS** The Hawk Law Firm, 34 Peachtree St, Ste 1100, Atlanta, GA, 30303.

HAWKINS, BENJAMIN SANFORD, JR.
PERSONAL Born 09/26/1936, Miami, FL **DISCIPLINE** PHILOSOPHY **EDUCATION** Univ Miami Coral Gables, BA, 62, MA, 64, PhD, 71; advan work, Univ Birmingham, England, 64-66. **CAREER** Instr, Central Michigan Univ, 68-69; Sr tutor, Univ Western Australia, 72-73; asst prof, Calif St Col, Sonoma, 73-77; lectr, Centre for Continuing Ed, Australian Natl Univ, 79-80; lectr, Univ Ilf, Nigeria, 85-86; asst prof, Columbus Col, Georgia, 87. **HONORS AND AWARDS** Grad tchg asst, Univ Miami, 62-64, 66-68. **MEMBERSHIPS** APA; Charles Sanders Peirce Soc. **RESEARCH** History and philosophy of logic; philosophy of language/semiotics; formal ontology; work of C.S. Peirce, Frege, Wittgenstein; philosophy and logic. **SELECTED PUBLICATIONS** Auth, "Peirce and Frege, a Question Unanswered," Mod Logic, 93; "De Morgan, Victorian Syllogistic and Relational Logic," Mod Logic, 95; "Peirce and Russell," Charles S. Peirce Sesquicentennial Cong, Harvard Univ, 89, pub as On a Falsigrafis in Bertrand Russell's Principles of Mathematics, Stud in the Logic of Charles S. Peirce, Indiana Univ, 97. **CONTACT ADDRESS** 935 NE 88 St, Miani, FL, 33138-3326.

HAWKINS, MERRILL M.
PERSONAL Born 12/04/1963, Vicksburg, MS, m, 1988, 1 child **DISCIPLINE** HISTORY; THEOLOGY **EDUCATION** BA, History; PhD **CAREER** Grad Asst, Baylor Univ, 90-95; Asst Prof, Carson-Newman Col, 95-. **HONORS AND AWARDS** Outstanding Graduate Student, Baylor Univ, 93; Faculty Research Award, Carson-Newman Col, 98. **MEMBERSHIPS** Amer Soc of Church History; Amer Acad of Religion; Southern Historical Assoc. **RESEARCH** American religious history; religion in the American South; religion and social activism **SELECTED PUBLICATIONS** Coauth, Texas Baptist Educational Institutions, Texas Baptist History, 90; Auth, Private Schools, Public Funds, Report from the Capital, 90; Roger Williams on Separation, Report from the Capital, 92; The Ecumenical and Social Leadership of G. Bromley Oxnam, Methodist History, 95; Attitudes toward the White House, Baptist History and Heritage 32, 97; Will Campbell: Radical Prophet of the South, 97; J.B.Tidwell, The Handbook of Texas, forthcoming. **CONTACT ADDRESS** Carson-Newman Col, CNC Box 71919, Jefferson City, TN, 37760. **EMAIL** hawkins@cncacc.cn.edu

HAWKINS, RALPH K.
PERSONAL Born 06/24/1969, Yuma, AZ, m, 1990, 1 child **DISCIPLINE** BIBLICAL LANGUAGES **EDUCATION** David Lipscomb Univ, BA, 90, MA, 95; Univ of the South, DMin, 98. **HONORS AND AWARDS** Endow for Bibl Res, 97. **MEMBERSHIPS** Am Schools of Orient Res; Cath Bib Asn; Soc of Bibl Lit. **RESEARCH** Archaeology; Historiography of ancient Israel. **SELECTED PUBLICATIONS** Auth, A Heritage in Crisis. **CONTACT ADDRESS** 275 North Carolina Ave, Sewanee, TN, 37355. **EMAIL** Hawkirk9@sewanee.edu

HAWLEY, JOHN STRATTON
DISCIPLINE COMPARATIVE RELIGION **EDUCATION** Amherst Col, AB, 63; Union Theol Sem, MDiv, 66; Harvard Univ, PhD, 77; Univ Delhi, 72; Univ Wis, 71; Hebrew Univ, 66-67. **CAREER** Inst, St. George's Sch, Jerusalem, 67-68; asst prof, Bowdoin Col, 77-78; vis assoc prof, Grad Theol Union, 82; from asst to assoc to prof, Asian Langs & Lit, Univ Wash, 78-85; dir, Southern Asian Inst, Columbia Univ, 89-95; dir, Nat Resource Ctr S Asia, Columbia Univ, 89-97; PROF REL, BARNARD COL, COLUMBIA UNIV, PRESENTLY. **CONTACT ADDRESS** Barnard Col, New York, NY, 10027. **EMAIL** jsh3@columbia.edu

HAWORTH, LAWRENCE L.
PERSONAL Born 12/14/1926, Chicago, IL **DISCIPLINE** PHILOSOPHY **EDUCATION** Rollins Col (Fla), BA, 49; Univ Ill, MA, 50, PhD, 52. **CAREER** Prof, 65-96, assoc dean grad stud, 75-81, 84-86, ch philos, 67-70, 88-89, DISTINGUISHED PROF EMER, UNIV WATERLOO, 96-. **MEMBERSHIPS** Can Philos Asn. **RESEARCH** Fel, Royal Soc Can. **SELECTED PUBLICATIONS** Auth, The Good City, 63; auth, Decadence and Objectivity, 77; auth, Autonomy, 91; coauth, Value Assumptions in Risk Assessment, 91. **CONTACT ADDRESS** Dept of Philosophy, Univ of Waterloo, Waterloo, ON, N2L 3G1.

HAWTHORNE, GERALD F.
PERSONAL Born 08/16/1925, Los Angeles, CA, m, 1955, 3 children **DISCIPLINE** CLASSICAL GREEK, NEW TESTAMENT **EDUCATION** Wheaton Col, Ill, BA, 51, MA, 54; Univ Chicago, PhD, 69. **CAREER** From instr to assoc prof, 53-73, Prof Class Greek & New Testament Exegesis, Wheaton Col, Ill, 73- **MEMBERSHIPS** Am Acad Relig; Soc Bibl Lit; Evangel Theol Soc; Studiorum Novi Testamenti Soc; Inst Bibl Res (treas, 73-). **RESEARCH** Early Christian literature and church history; New Testament studies. **SELECTED PUBLICATIONS** Auth, Chained in Christ--The Experience and Rhetoric of Paul Imprisonments, J Biblical Lit, Vol 0116, 97. **CONTACT ADDRESS** Wheaton Col, Wheaton, IL, 60187.

HAYDEN, JOHN CARLETON
PERSONAL Born 12/30/1933, Bowling Green, KY, m **DISCIPLINE** THEOLOGY **EDUCATION** Wayne State, BA 1955; Univ of Detroit, MA 1962; Coll of Emmanuel & St Chad, LTh honors 1963; Howard U, PhD 1972; College of Emmanuel & St Chad, MDiv, 1991. **CAREER** St Mary's School for Indian Girls, teacher, 1955; Detroit Public Schools, teacher, 1956-59; St Chad's Secondary School, instructor, 1962-64; Univ of Regina, Anglican chaplain, 1963-67, instructor in history, 1965-68; St George's Church, associate rector, 1968-71, 1973-82, 1986-87, 1994-; Church of The Atonement, assistant, 1971-72; St Monica's Church, priest-in-charge, 1972-73; Howard Univ, asst professor of history, 1972-78, scholar in church history, 1978-79; Morgan State Univ, Department of History and Geography, chmn, 1979-86; Holy Comforter Church, St Andrew's Parish, rector, 1982-86; Frostburg State University, prof of history, 1986-87; Univ of the South School of Theology, associate dean, 1987-92; Episcopal Office for Black Ministries, consultant, 1992-94; St Michael and All Angels Church, Adelphi Parish, priest-in-charge, 1992-94; Montgomery College, adjunct lecturer of history, 1992-94; Episcopal/Anglican chaplain, lecturer in church history, Howard University, 1994-. **HONORS AND AWARDS** Angus Dunn Fellowship, 1973, 1974, 1978, 1989, 1995, 1998; Faculty Research in the Social Sciences Award, 1973, 1974; Spencer Foundation Award, 1975; Am Philosophical Soc Award, 1976; Commn for Black Minsters, Grant, 1976-78; Bd For Theol Education, Fellowship, 1978-79; Robert R Moton Fellowship, 1978-79; Absalom Jones Award, 1987; Grambling University Award, Grambling State University, 1990; Kanuga Conference Center Award, 1991. **MEMBERSHIPS** Ch Historical Soc; asso editor, "Episcopal Anglican History;" board of directors, 1975-85, Assn for Study of Afro-American Life & History; Am Historical Assn; Southern Historical Assn; Union of Black Episcopalians, Parliamentarian; pres, Saskatchewan Assn for Retarded Children, 1966-68; chmn youth conf, Saskatchewan Centennial Corp, 1964-67; Tuxis and Older Boys' Parlaiment Bd, 1963-68; lieutenant-gen of Saskatchewan, 1967; Royal Canadian Mountain Police, Regina, chaplain's assoc; Saskatchewan Correctional Institution, Anglican chaplain, 1963-68; Wascana Student Housing Corp, founding dir, 1965-68; Ranch Ehrlo, founding dir, 1967-68; Saskatchewan Boys' Schl, protestant chaplain, 1963-68; Com for Community Improvement; pres, Black Episcopal Clergy, Washington Diocese, 1974-76; board of directors, Washington Urban League, 1980-87; board of directors, St Patrick's Episcopal Day School, 1981-87; secretary, board of trustees, St Mary's Episcopal Center, 1988-92; board of advisors, St Andrew's/Sewanee School, 1989-; Society for the Promotion of Christian Knowledge/USA Board, 1987-92; KANUGA Conference Cen-

ter, program committee, 1989-93, diversity comm, board of advisors, 1996-; Evangelical Education Society, board of directors, 1992-; Washington Episcopal School, board of trustees, 1992-. **CONTACT ADDRESS** Howard Univ, PO Box 6, Washington, DC, 20059.

HAYES, ALAN L.
PERSONAL Born 09/29/1946, Oakland, CA **DISCIPLINE** RELIGION/CHURCH HISTORY **EDUCATION** Pomona Col, BA, 67; Brown Univ; McGill Univ, BD, 71, PhD, 75. **CAREER** Asst to assoc prof, 75-89, registr, 79-94, PROF CHURCH HIST, UNIV TORONTO, 89-, acad dean, 92-94, vice prin, 96-; priest, Anglican Church Can. **HONORS AND AWARDS** Can Coun doctoral fel, 72-75. **SELECTED PUBLICATIONS** Ed & contribur, By Grace Co-workers, 89; ed & contribur, A New Introduction to John Wycliffe, 94; ed & contribur, Church and Society in Documents 100-600 AD, 95; contribur, Dictionary of Canadian Biography. **CONTACT ADDRESS** Univ of Toronto, Toronto, ON, M5S 1H7.

HAYES, DIANA L.
PERSONAL Born 05/30/1947, Buffalo, NY **DISCIPLINE** THEOLOGY **EDUCATION** State Univ NY, BA, 69; George Wash Nat Law Ctr, JD, 73; Cath Univ Am, STB, 83, STL, 85; Cath Univ Louvain, STD, 88, PhD, 88. **CAREER** Attorney, 73-85; from asst prof to assoc prof, Georgetown Univ, 88-; adj fac, Xavier Univ Inst Black Cath Studies, 91-. **HONORS AND AWARDS** Joint Travel Grant, 97; Consortium Univ Wash Coop Grants Fac, 95-96; 11th Madeleva Lectr, St. Mary's Col, 95; Keck Fel Am Studies, 94-95; Bunn Award Fac Excellence, Georgetown Univ, 94; Off Student Affairs Outstanding Contrib Georgetown Community Award, 93; Landegger Semester Res Grant, 92; Jr Fac Summer Res Grant, 92, 93; Dr Fel 87-88; Jean Fairfax-Muskiwinni Fel Black Women Relig, 85-88. **MEMBERSHIPS** Cath Theol Soc Am; Nat Ctr Pastoral Leadership; Georgetown Univ Women's Ctr Bd Advocates & Women's Studies Bd Adv; Woodstock Theol Ctr; Am Acad Relig; Col Theol Soc; Soc Study Black Relig; Black Cath Theol Symposium. **RESEARCH** Liberation & contextual theologies in the U.S.; public religion. **SELECTED PUBLICATIONS** Auth, And Still We Rise: An Introduction to Black Liberation Theology, 96; auth, Trouble Don't Last Always: Soul Prayers, 95; auth, Hagar's Daughter's: Womanist Ways of Being in the World, 95; auth, Through the Eyes of Faith: The Nguzo Saba and the Beatitudes of St. Matthew, Jour Relig Thought, 98; auth, Different Voices: Black, Womanist and Catholic, The Tablet, 93; auth, To Be Black, Catholic and Female, New Theol Rev, May, 93; auth, My Hope is in the Lord: Transformation and Salvation in the African American Community, Embracing the Spirit: Womanist Perspectives on Hope, Salvation, and Transformation, 97; auth, The Human Face of the Other, Multicultural Experience in U.S. Church & Theol, 95; auth, Feminist Theology/Womanist Theology: A Black Catholic Perspective, Black Theol: A Documentary Hist, 93; auth, Trusting the Voices: Educating Women for the 21st Century, One Vision, One Voice: Lectures Delivered at the Mother Caroline Friess Centenary Celebrations, 93. **CONTACT ADDRESS** Dept of Theology, Georgetown Univ, Box 571135, Washington, DC, 20057-1135.

HAYES, EDWARD L.
PERSONAL m, 3 children **DISCIPLINE** CHRISTIAN EDUCATION **EDUCATION** Westmont Col, BA; Dallas Theol Sem, ThM; Univ Denver, PhD. **CAREER** Prof, pres Denver Sem, 93. **HONORS AND AWARDS** Baptist minister, First Baptist Church of Montebello, Calif; exec dir, Mount Hermon Assn, 79-92. **RESEARCH** Teaching, preaching, administering and fundraising. **SELECTED PUBLICATIONS** Auth, The Focused Life and Other Devotion; Words to Live By and The Focused Life. **CONTACT ADDRESS** Denver Conservative Baptist Sem, PO Box 10000, Denver, CO, 80250.

HAYES, ZACHARY JEROME
PERSONAL Born 09/21/1932, Chicago, IL **DISCIPLINE** HISTORY OF CHRISTIAN THEOLOGY **EDUCATION** Quincy Col, BA, 56; Univ Bonn, Ger, ThD, 64. **CAREER** Lectr syst theol, St Joseph Sem, Ill, 64-68; assoc prof, 68-74, Prof Hist Of Theol, Cath Theol Union, Chicago, 74. **HONORS AND AWARDS** Res grant, Asn of Theol Schs, 77; res scholar, 78; Scholar-in-Residence, 84, 91; J.C. Murray Award, CTSA, 85; LittD, Quincy Univ, 85., LittD, St Bonaventure Univ, 74. **MEMBERSHIPS** Cath Theol Soc Am; Soc for Sci Study Relig. **RESEARCH** Mediaeval philos and theol; contemp theological developments, particularly in Christology. **SELECTED PUBLICATIONS** Auth, The General Doctrine of Creation in the Thirteenth Century, Schoningh, 64; transl, The Theology of History in St Bonaventure, Franciscan Herald, 71; What Manner of Man? Sermons on Christ by St Bonaventure, Franciscan Herald, 64; The meaning of Convenientia in the metaphysics of St Bonaventure, Franciscan Studies, 74; Incarnation and creation in the theology of St Bonaventure, In: Studies Honoring Ignatius Brady, Franciscan Inst, 76; Christology and metaphysics, J of Relig, 78; Disputed Questions on the Trinity, Franciscan Inst, 79; The Hidden Center, Paulist, 81; Visions of a Future, Glazier, 89; Disputed Questions on the Knowledge of Christ, Franciscan Inst, 92; Reduction of the Arts to Theology, Franciscan Inst, 96; A Window to the Divine, Franciscan Press,

96. CONTACT ADDRESS Catholic Theol Union at Chicago, 5401 S Cornell Ave, Chicago, IL, 60615-6200. **EMAIL** zach@ctu.edu

HAYNES, WILLIAM J., JR.
PERSONAL Born 09/05/1949, Memphis, TN, m **DISCIPLINE** LAW **EDUCATION** Coll of St Thomas, BA 1970; Vanderbilt School of Law, JD 1973. **CAREER** TN State Atty Gen Office, asst atty general 1973-77; TN State Antitrust & Consumer Protection, dep atty general 1978-84, spec dep atty general for special litigation 1984; US DISTRICT COURT MIDDLE DISTRICT OF TN, MAGISTRATE JUDGE, 1984-. **HONORS AND AWARDS** Bennett Douglas Bell Awd Vanderbilt School of Law 1973; Federal Exec Assn; Black History Month Award, 1990. **MEMBERSHIPS** Mem Amer Bar Assn 1978, 1985, 1988-91; vice chair, State Enforcement Comm, Antitrust Section; mem 1st vice pres Nashville Bar Assn, 1980-84; dist atty gen pro tem Shelby Cty Criminal Court 1980; mem Rotary Intl, 1980-90; mem bd of dir Cumberland Museum & Sci Ctr 1981-87; mem bd of professional responsibility TN Supreme Court 1982-84; mem bd of dir Napier Lobby Bar Assn 1983-84; chmn antitrust planning comm Natl Assn of Atty General 1984; mem, bd of advisors, Corporate Practice Series, Bureau of Natl Affairs, 1989,90; Lecturer-in-law Vanderbilt School of Law, 1987-94. **SELECTED PUBLICATIONS** Author, "State Antitrust Laws" published by the Bureau of National Affairs, 1988; Contributing Author, "The Legal Aspects of Selling & Buying," Shepard's McGraw Hill, 1991. **CONTACT ADDRESS** US District Court, 649 US Courthouse, Nashville, TN, 37203.

HAYS, DANNY
PERSONAL Born 05/20/1953, San Francisco, CA, m, 1979, 2 children **DISCIPLINE** OLD TESTAMENT **EDUCATION** New Mexico State Univ, BS, 76; Dallas Theol Sem, ThM, 80; Southwestern Baptist Theol Sem, PhD, 92. **CAREER** Assoc Prof Rel, 92-, Ouachita Baptist Univ. **MEMBERSHIPS** ETS, SBL. **RESEARCH** Hermeneutics, Cushites. **SELECTED PUBLICATIONS** Auth, Verb Forms in the Expository Discourse Sections of Ecclesiastes, Journal of Translation and Textlinguistics, 95; The Sushite: A Black Nation in the Bible, Bibliotheca Sacra, 96; Ebedmelech, in: Eerdmans Dictionary of the Bible, Grand Rapids, Eerdmans, forthcoming; From the Land of the Bow: Black Soldiers in the Ancient Near East, Bible Review, 98; co-auth, Grasping the Word of God: A Hands On Approach to Reading, Interpreting and Applying the Bible, Zondervan, forthcoming. **CONTACT ADDRESS** Ouachita Baptist Univ, Box 3677, Arkadelphia, AR, 71998-0001. **EMAIL** haysd@alpha.obu.edu

HAYWOODE, M. DOUGLAS
PERSONAL Born 02/24/1938, Brooklyn, NY, d **DISCIPLINE** LAW **EDUCATION** Brooklyn Coll, BA 1959; Brooklyn Law Schl, JD 1962; LLM 1967; New Sch Social Resrch, MA 1970; PhD. **CAREER** Private Practice Law, 1962; City of NY, prof Political Science 1969; New York City Branch NAACP, counsel 1962-64; Human Resources Admin NYC, assoc gen counsel 1972-74. **HONORS AND AWARDS** Governor personal Appointee, New York Housing Corp. **MEMBERSHIPS** Mem New York City Bar Assn; Nat Conf Black Lawyers; Am Soc Intl Law; Intl African Centre; Enterprise 9 Investigation Agency, director. **CONTACT ADDRESS** 128 East 31st St, New York, NY, 10016.

HAZEN, THOMAS LEE
PERSONAL Born 09/06/1947, New York, NY, m, 1969, 1 child **DISCIPLINE** BUSINESS & TORT LAW **EDUCATION** Columbia Col, Columbia Univ, BA, 69, Law Sch, JD, 72. **CAREER** Asst prof, Col Law, Univ Nebr, 74-77, assoc prof, 77-79, prof, 79-80; Prof Law, Sch Law, Univ NC, 80- **RESEARCH** Securities law; corporate law. **SELECTED PUBLICATIONS** Auth, Defining Illegal Insider Trading--Lessons From the European Community Directive on Insider Trading, Law Contemp Problems, Vol 0055, 92. **CONTACT ADDRESS** Sch of Law, Univ of NC, Chapel Hill, NC, 27514.

HEAD, IVAN
DISCIPLINE LAW **EDUCATION** Univ Alberta, BA, 51; LLB, 52; Harvard Univ, LLM, 60; Univ Notre Dame, LLD. **CAREER** UBC Chair in South-North Studies; Prof, 63- **RESEARCH** International law; south-north relations. **SELECTED PUBLICATIONS** Auth, pubs about legal scholarship and foreign and developmental policy; co-auth, The Canadian Way. **CONTACT ADDRESS** Fac of Law, Univ British Columbia, 1822 East Mall, Vancouver, BC, V6T 1Z1. **EMAIL** head@law.ubc.ca

HEAD, JOHN W.
PERSONAL Born 03/08/1953, Hannibal, MO, m, 1979, 3 children **DISCIPLINE** LAW **EDUCATION** Univ Mo, BA, 75; Oxford Univ, MA, 77; Univ Va, JD, 79. **CAREER** Judicial clerk, DC Court of Appeals, 79-80; assoc atty, Cleary, Gottlieb, Steen and Hamilton, 80-83; counsel, Asian Development Bank, 83-88; legal counselor, Int Monetary Fund, 88-90; prof, Univ Kans, 90- . **MEMBERSHIPS** ABA; Am Soc of Int Lawyers. **RESEARCH** International law, finance and business; comparative law. **CONTACT ADDRESS** Law School - Green Hall, Univ of Kansas, Lawrence, KS, 66045.

HEADRICK, THOMAS E.
PERSONAL Born 06/28/1933, East Orange, NJ, m, 1957, 2 children **DISCIPLINE** LAW **EDUCATION** Franklin & Marshall Col, BA, 55; Oxford Univ, BLitt, 58; Yale Univ, LLB, 60; Stanford Univ, PhD(polit sci), 75. **CAREER** Law clerk, Hon Harry Foster, State Supreme Ct, Olympia, Wash, 60-61; atty, Pillsbury, Madison & Sutro, San Francisco, 61-64; mgt consult, Emerson Consult, London, 64-66 & Baxter, McDonald & Co, Berkeley, Calif, 66-67; asst dean, Stanford Law Sch, 67-70; vpres acad affairs, Lawrence Univ, 70-76; Prof Law & Dean Sch Law, State Univ NY Buffalo, 76-, Asst dir, Ansonia Redevelop Agency, Ansonia, Conn, 59-60; mgt consult, Emerson Consult, London, 64-66 & Baxter, McDonald & Co, Berkeley, Calif, 66-67. **MEMBERSHIPS** Am Polit Sci Asn; Law & Soc Asn. **RESEARCH** Medieval property law; political economy of declining regions. **SELECTED PUBLICATIONS** Auth, Crossing Bridges, Buffalo Law Rev, Vol 0044, 96. **CONTACT ADDRESS** Fac of Law & Jurisp, State Univ NY, J L O Hall, Buffalo, NY, 14260-0001.

HEALEY, ROBERT MATHIEU
PERSONAL Born 06/01/1921, New York, NY, m, 1953, 1 child **DISCIPLINE** CHURCH, HISTORY **EDUCATION** Princeton Univ, BA, 42; Yale Univ, MFA, 47, BD, 55, MA, 56, PhD(relig), 59. **CAREER** Instr English, Mercersburg Acad, 42-44 & Rensselaer Polytech Inst, 48-52; assoc prof commun, 56-63, from assoc prof to prof Am church hist, 63-74, chnin div hist & theol, 68-70, interim acad dean, 70-71, Prof Church Hist, Theol Sem, Univ Dubuque, 74-, Mem comt relig & pub educ, Nat Coun Churches, 58-62; consult, Nat Studies Conf Church & State, Ohio, 64; theologian in residence, Am Church in Paris, 65-66; mem bd dirs, Asn Theol Fac Iowa, 67-71 & 76-80; consult Gen Coun, United Presby Church USA, 71-72; resident scholar, Ecumenical Inst Advan Theol Studies, Israel, 73-74; pres, Asn Fac & Theol Educ Prof Theol Sem, Univ Dubuque, 73-77; vis prof, Univ Edinburgh, 80-81; Asn Theol Schs in US & Can basic res grant, 80-81. **MEMBERSHIPS** Am Soc Church Hist; Am Acad Relig; Presby Hist Soc. **RESEARCH** Relationships of church, state and education in the United States and in France; Andrew Melville (1545-1622), and Scottish reformation; Judaism in American religious history. **SELECTED PUBLICATIONS** Auth, The Mainstream Protestant Decline-- The Presbyterian Pattern, Church Hist, Vol 0064, 95; The Organizational Revolution--Presbyterian and American Denominationalism, Church Hist, Vol 0064, 95; The Language of Liberty 1660-1832--Political Discourse and Social Dynamics in the Anglo-American World, Church Hist, Vol 0066, 97; John Duns-Scotus, Doctor of the Church, J Ecumenical Studies, Vol 0030, 93; Waiting For Deborah-- John Knox, And 4 Ruling Queens, Sixteenth Century J, Vol 0025, 94. **CONTACT ADDRESS** Dept of Hist & Theol Theol Sem, Univ of Dubuque, Dubuque, IA, 52001.

HEATH, EUGENE
PERSONAL Born 04/03/1958, Lakeland, FL **DISCIPLINE** PHILOSOPHY **EDUCATION** Davidson Coll, BA, 80; Yale Univ, MA, 82, PhD, 88. **CAREER** Vis Asst Prof, 88-90, Coll of Wooster; vis Asst Prof, 90-91, Coll of Charleston; vis Asst Prof, 91-92, Kenyon Coll; vis Asst Prof, 92-93, Lyon Coll; Asst Prof, 93-, SUNY New Paltz. **HONORS AND AWARDS** Phi Beta Kappa. **MEMBERSHIPS** APA, Hume Soc, Adam Smith Soc. **RESEARCH** Social & political philosophy, 18th century British moral philosophy. **SELECTED PUBLICATIONS** Auth, On the Normative Implications of a Theory of Spontaneous Order, in: Time Order Chaos, The Study of Time IX, ed by JT Fraser, MP Soulsby, A Argyros, Madison Conn Intl Univ Press, 98; Mandeville's Bewitching Engine of Praise, in: Hist of Philo Qtly, 98; Two Cheers and a Pint of Worry, An On-Line Course in Political and Social Philosophy, in: Teaching Philo, 97; The Commerce of Sympathy, Adam Smith on the Emergence of Morals, in: J of Hist of Philo, 95; auth, Rules, Function and the Invisible Hand, An In Interpretation of Hayek's Social Theory, in: Philo of Social Sci, 92; How to Understand Liberalism as Gardening, Galeotti on Hayek, in: Political Theory, 89. **CONTACT ADDRESS** Dept of Philosophy, State Univ of NY, 75 S Manhelm, New Paltz, NY, 12561-2440. **EMAIL** heathe@npvm.newpaltz.edu

HECHT, NEIL S.
PERSONAL Born 07/29/1934, New York, NY, m, 1960, 3 children **DISCIPLINE** LAW **EDUCATION** Yeshiva Univ, BA, 54; Yale Univ, JD, 59; Columbia Univ, LLM, 64, JSD, 72. **CAREER** Pvt pract law, 59-62; vpres & gen counsel, John Small & Co, 62-63; assoc prof, 64-66, Prof Law, Boston Univ, 66-, Consult, Orgn Social & Tech Innovations, 67-68; bd dirs, Nat Jewish Comn Law & Pub Affairs, 70-; Am rep, Acad Comt, Bar-Ilan Univ, Israel, 71- **MEMBERSHIPS** Am Judicature Soc; Am Bar Asn. **RESEARCH** Long term leases; Jewish law; evidence. **SELECTED PUBLICATIONS** Auth, Tribute to Austin Stickells, Boston Univ Law Rev, Vol 0073, 93. **CONTACT ADDRESS** Sch of Law, Boston Univ, 765 Commonwealth Ave, Boston, MA, 02215-1401.

HECK, RICHARD
PERSONAL Born 03/21/1964, Troy, NY, m, 1998, 1 child **DISCIPLINE** PHILOSOPHY **EDUCATION** Duke Univ, BA, 85; Oxford Univ, BPhilo, 87; MIT, PhD, 91. **CAREER** Asst

Prof to Assoc Prof, 91-, Harvard, Dept of Philos. **HONORS AND AWARDS** Marshall Scholarship, 85. **MEMBERSHIPS** Amer Philos Assoc; ASL. **RESEARCH** Philos of Lang; Philos of Math; Philos of Logic; Frege. **SELECTED PUBLICATIONS** Auth, That There Might Be Vague Objects(So Far as Concerns Logic), The Monist 81, pp 277-99, 98; Grundgesetze der Arithmetik 1, 29-32, Notre Dame Journal of Formal Logic 38, pp 437-74, 98; Finitude and Hume's Principle, Journal of Philosophical Logic 26, pp 589-617, 97; Language, Thought and Logic: Essays in Honour of Michael Dummett, Oxford, Oxford Univ Press, 97; The Julius Caesar Objection, Language, Thought and Logic, pp 273-308; The Finite and the Infinite in Frege's Grundgesetze der Arithmetik, in M. Schirn, ed, Philosophy of Mathematics Today, Oxford, Oxford Univ Press, 97. Several more. **CONTACT ADDRESS** Philosophy Dept, Harvard Univ, 208 Emerson Hall, Cambridge, MA, 02138. **EMAIL** HECK@FAS.HARVARD.EDU

HECKMAN, HUGH W.
PERSONAL Born 06/25/1941, Lynchburg, VA, d, 3 children **DISCIPLINE** PHILOSOPHY **EDUCATION** Univ of Tenn, BS, 66; Ashbury Sem, BS, 70; Catholic Univ of Amer, PhD. **CAREER** Andrew Col, adj prof, 82. **HONORS AND AWARDS** USAF Commendation Medal, Morino Assoc Inc, MVE, **MEMBERSHIPS** APA, PADI, NAVI **RESEARCH** Comparative religion; Judaism; Christianity; Islam; Buddhism; Taoism; Hinduism. **CONTACT ADDRESS** RR1, PO Box 115A, Coleman, GA, 31736.

HECKMAN, PETER
PERSONAL Born 01/17/1956, NJ, m **DISCIPLINE** PHILOSOPHY **EDUCATION** Grinnell Col, BA, 78; Northwestern Univ, MA, 80; Northwestern Univ, PhD, 88. **CAREER** Neb Wesleyan Univ, asst prof, 93-. **HONORS AND AWARDS** Felshp NTI, 77; Grinnell Col, Hon in Philo, 78; Felshp School of Crit and Theory **RESEARCH** Hist of philo; aesth, bus ethics; 19th and 20th cent continental philo. **SELECTED PUBLICATIONS** Auth, The Role of Music in Nietzsche's Birth of Tragedy, Brit Jour of Aesthetics, 90; Nietzsche's Clever Animal: Metaphor in Truth and Falsity, Philo and Rhet, 91; Business and Games, Jour of Bus Ethics, 92; The Role of Science in Nietzsche's Human-all-too-Human, Man and World, 93; The Indictment of Morality in Daybreak, Intl Stud in Philo, 96. **CONTACT ADDRESS** Dept of Philosophy, Nebraska Wesleyan Univ, Lincoln, NE, 68504-2796. **EMAIL** pheckman@NebrWesleyan.edu

HEDRICK, CHARLES WEBSTER
PERSONAL Born 04/11/1934, Bogalusa, LA, m, 1955, 3 children **DISCIPLINE** RELIGIOUS STUDIES **EDUCATION** Miss Col, BA, 58; Golden Gate Southern Baptist, BD, 62; Univ Southern Calif, MA, 68; Claremont Grad Sch & Univ Ctr, PhD, 77. **CAREER** Res asst, Inst Antiquity & Christianity, 69-70, res assoc, 70-76; lectr New Testament, Claremont Grad Sch & Univ Ctr, 77-78; asst prof relig studies, Wagner Col, 78-80; asst prof New Testament, Southwest Mo State Univ, 80-, Chaplain Col ret, US Army Reserve, 67-; prof Southwest Missouri State Univ, 91. **HONORS AND AWARDS** Pres Natl Assoc Baptist Profs of Relig, 87-88; Southwest Missouri State Univ Found Excellence in Research Award, 85; John G. Gummie Distinguished Scholar Award, 98-99. **MEMBERSHIPS** Soc Bibl Lit; Soc d'Archeologie Copte; lntn Assn Coptic Studies. **RESEARCH** The Gospel of Mark; the Nag Hammamdi library; the parables of Jesus. **SELECTED PUBLICATIONS** Auth, The Apocalyspe of Adam: A Literary and Source Analysis, Scholars Press, 80; art, Paul's Conversion-Call: A Comparative Analysis Of The Three Reports in Acts, J Bibl Lit, 81; art, Christian Motifs in the Gospel of the Egyptians: Method and motive, Novum Testamentum, 81; auth, Parables as Poetic Fictions, The Creative Voice of Jesus, Hendrickson, 94. **CONTACT ADDRESS** Dept of Religous Studies, Coll of Hums & Pub Affairs, Southwest Missouri State Univ, 901 S National, Springfield, MO, 65800-0088.

HEELAN, PATRICK AIDAN
DISCIPLINE PHILOSOPHY **EDUCATION** Univ Coll, Nat Univ Ireland, BA, MA, 48; St Stanislaus Col, LicPhil, 54; Milltown Inst Theol, Philos, Dublin, STL, 59; St. Louis Univ, PhD(geophsyics), 52; Cath Univ Louvain, Belgium, PhD(philos), 64. **CAREER** Res assoc, Dublin Inst Adv Stud, 53-54, 64-65; vis fel, Fordham Univ, NY & Palmer Lab, Princeton Univ, 60-62; summer fel, Stanford Univ, Univ Colo; lectr Univ Col, Dublin 64-65; asst, assoc prof, Fordham Univ, 65-70; co-dir honors prog, Thomas More Col, Fordham Univ, 69-70; vis prof, physics, Boston Univ, 68-69; PROF PHILOS, 70-92, CHAIR DEPT, 70-74, PROF EMER, 92-, SUNY, STONY BROOK; prof hum, soc scis, Health Scis Ctr, SUNY, Stony Brook, 72-75; vpres lib stud, dean arts scis, 75-79, dean hum & fine arts, 90-92, SUNY, Stony Brook; mem, Ctr Relig Stud, 80-92, act chair, dept relig stud, 85-86, SUNY, Stony Brook; NSF sen fel, sen vis fel, Ctr Philos Sci, Univ Pittsburg, 83; exec VPres, prof philos, 92-95; WILLIAM A GASTON PROF PHILOS, 95-, GEORGETOWN UNIV. **CONTACT ADDRESS** Dept Philosophy, Georgetown Univ, Washington, DC, 20057.

HEER, LARRY G.
PERSONAL Born 09/03/1946, Decatur, IL, m, 1977, 1 child **DISCIPLINE** RELIGION **EDUCATION** Harvard Univ, PhD, 77 **CAREER** Seventh-day Adventist Sem, asst prof, assoc prof, 78-84, Can Univ Col, prof, 84-. **HONORS AND AWARDS** Albright Institute, A.P. **MEMBERSHIPS** SBL, PEF, ASOR. **RESEARCH** History, near east arch, Hebrew Bible, NW Semitic Epigraphy. **CONTACT ADDRESS** Dept of Religious Studies, Canadian Univ Col, 235 College Ave, College Heights, AB, T4L 2E5. **EMAIL** iherr@canu.ab.ca

HEFFERNAN, JAMES
DISCIPLINE PHILOSOPHY **EDUCATION** Fordham Univ, BA, 64, MA, 67; Univ Notre Dame, PhD, 76. **CAREER** Asst prof, 72-77; assoc prof, 77-82; prof, 82-, Univ Pacific. **SELECTED PUBLICATIONS** Auth, The Land Ethic: A Critical Appraisal, 93; Why Wilderness?, 93. **CONTACT ADDRESS** Philos Dept, Univ Pacific, Pacific Ave, PO Box 3601, Stockton, CA, 95211.

HEFFERNAN, JAMES DANIEL
PERSONAL Born 08/06/1940, Syracuse, NY, m, 1967, 1 child **DISCIPLINE** PHILOSOPHY **EDUCATION** Fordham Univ, BA, 64, MA, 67; Univ Notre Dame, PhD(philos), 76. **CAREER** Asst prof, 72-77, Assoc Prof Philos, Univ Of The Pac, 77-. **MEMBERSHIPS** Am Philos Asn. **RESEARCH** Philosophy of science; philosophy of mind; environmental ethics. **SELECTED PUBLICATIONS** Auth, Some doubts about tuning machine arguments, Philos Sci, 45: 638-647; coauth (with K M Sayre), The cybernetic approach to the philosophy of mind: A dialogue, Cognition and Brain Theory, 3: 101-108; auth, The land ethic: A critical appraisal, Environ Ethics, 4: 39-51. **CONTACT ADDRESS** Dept of Philosophy, Univ of the Pacific, 3601 Pacific Ave, Stockton, CA, 95211-0197. **EMAIL** jheffernan@uop.edu

HEFFNER, JOHN HOWARD
PERSONAL Born 01/13/1947, Lebanon, PA **DISCIPLINE** PHILOSOPHY **EDUCATION** Lebanon Valley Col, BS, 68, BA, 87; Univ Edinburgh, Cert philos, 70; Boston Univ, AM, 71, PhD, 76. **CAREER** Asst prof, 72-80, Assoc Prof, 80-84, PROF PHILOS, LEBANON VALLEY COL, 84-; Nat Sci Found fel psychol, Northwestern Univ, 77-78. **HONORS AND AWARDS** John Templeton Found, 97. **MEMBERSHIPS** Soc Advan Am Philos; Metaphys Soc Am; Hegel Soc Am. **RESEARCH** Philosophy of religion; philosophy of science; philosophy of perception. **SELECTED PUBLICATIONS** Auth, Husserl's critique of traditional Empiricism, J Brit Soc Phenomenol, 5/74; Some epistemological aspects of recent work in visual perception, Proc Philos Sci Asn, Vol I, 76; Perception and animal consciousness: The philosophical context, Behav & Brain Sci, 12/78; The causal theory of visual perception: Its scientific basis and philosophical implications, Int Philos Quart, 9/81; Causal relations in visual perception, in Naturalistic Epistemology: A Twenty Year Symposium, Reidel, 87; Contemporary Issues in Philosophy, in The Reader's Adviser, 14th ed, R R Bowker, 1994. **CONTACT ADDRESS** Lebanon Valley Col, 101 N College Ave, Annville, PA, 17003-1400. **EMAIL** heffner@lvc.edu

HEFT, JAMES L.
DISCIPLINE RELIGIOUS STUDIES **EDUCATION** Univ Toronto, PhD. **CAREER** Prof; chancellor, Univ Dayton. **MEMBERSHIPS** Ch, bd Dir, Asn Cath Colleges and Universities. **RESEARCH** Doctrinal and moral theology. **SELECTED PUBLICATIONS** Auth, John XXII and Papal Teaching Authority, 86; ed, Faith and the Intellectual Life, Notre Dame, 96. **CONTACT ADDRESS** Dept of Religious Studies, Univ of Dayton, 300 College Park, 466B Humanities, Dayton, OH, 45469-1679. **EMAIL** heft@checkov.hm.udayton.edu

HEGGEN, BRUCE A.
PERSONAL Born 06/18/1950, Pelican Rapids, MN **DISCIPLINE** THEOLOGY **EDUCATION** Concordia Coll, BA, 72; Lutheran Sem, MDiv, 82; McGill Univ, PhD, 96. **CAREER** Pastor, Lutheran Campus Ministry, 96-, adj Asst Prof English, 97-, Univ of Delaware. **HONORS AND AWARDS** Del Div of the Arts, Individual Artist Fel. **MEMBERSHIPS** AAR **RESEARCH** Christian theology, American religious life, Religion & Literature. **SELECTED PUBLICATIONS** Auth, Outside Yom Ha'Shoah, in: Plumbline, J of Min in Higher Edu, 98; The Spirit of God in the Life of the Institute, in: Plumbline, J Of Min IN Higher Edu; That Afternoon in Harvest, in: Vermont Woodlands, 97; Dappled Things, Poetry Ecology and the Means of Grace in Joseph Sittler's Theology for Earth, in: Union Sem Qtly Rev, 97; Beggars to God, Masculine Identity in Light of Martin Luther's Spirituality, in: Gender in World Religions, 91; Hammer-Handle Piety and the Care of the Earth, Joseph Sittler on Ecology and Christian Faith, in: ARC, J of Fac of Relig Stud, McGill Univ, 90. **CONTACT ADDRESS** Lutheran Campus Ministry, Univ of Delaware, 247 Haines St, Newark, DE, 19711. **EMAIL** heggen@udel.edu

HEIDER, GEORGE C.
PERSONAL Born 06/13/1953, Washington, DC, m, 1979, 2 children **DISCIPLINE** OLD TESTAMENT **EDUCATION** Concordia Sr Col, BA, 75; Concordia Sem, M Div, 79; Yale Univ, PhD, 84. **CAREER** Asst to assoc to full prof, theol, Concordia Col, 84-95; exec vpres, acad svc, Concordia Col, 87-95; pres, Concordia Univ, 95-. **HONORS AND AWARDS** Amer Coun on Educ Fel, 94-95. **MEMBERSHIPS** Soc of Bibl Lit; Cath Bibl Asn; Amer Asn of Higher Educ; Amer Asn of Pres of Independent Col and Univ. **RESEARCH** History of divided monarchy in Israel. **SELECTED PUBLICATIONS** Auth, Lahmu, Molech, Tannin, Dict of Deities and Demons in the Bible, Leiden, Brill, 95; auth, Molech, Anchor Bible Dict, 4, 895-898, NY, Doubleday, 92; auth, The Cult of Molek: A Reassessment, Sheffield, England, JSOT Press, 85. **CONTACT ADDRESS** Concordia Univ, Illinois, 7400 Augusta St., River Forest, IL, 60305-1499. **EMAIL** heider@curf.edu

HEIDT, SARAH L.
PERSONAL Born 11/15/1968, Roanoke, VA, m, 1 child **DISCIPLINE** PHILOSOPHY **EDUCATION** Yale Univ, BA, 91, PhD, 97. **CAREER** Lectr, Yale Univ, 97-99. **HONORS AND AWARDS** Yale Prize fel, 96-95. **MEMBERSHIPS** Am Philos Asn; North Am Kant Soc. **RESEARCH** Kant; Heidegger. **SELECTED PUBLICATIONS** Auth, "From Bestimmung to Verstimmung: Community in Hegel's Philosophy of Religion," in New Perspectives on Hegel's Philos of Relig, 92. **CONTACT ADDRESS** 306 E 96th St, Apt 16J, New York, NY, 10128. **EMAIL** sarah.heidt@yale.com

HEIL, JOHN P.
PERSONAL Born 10/13/1947, St. Louis, MO **DISCIPLINE** THEOLOGY **EDUCATION** Pontifical Bibl Inst Rome, Italy, SSD, 79. **CAREER** Kenrick Sch of Theol, prof, 79-. **MEMBERSHIPS** SNTS, CBH, SBL. **RESEARCH** Narrative and rhetorical criticism of the New Testament. **CONTACT ADDRESS** Kenrick-Glennon Sem, 5200 Glennon Dr, St. Louis, MO, 63119.

HEIM, MICHAEL R.
PERSONAL Born 11/08/1944, Milwaukee, WI, m, 1969, 1 child **DISCIPLINE** PHILOSOPHY **EDUCATION** NIU, MA, 68; Penn State Univ, Phd, 79. **CAREER** Freelance tchr/writer in S Cal. **HONORS AND AWARDS** Great Tchr Award Digital Media, Art Ctr Col Design, 95. **MEMBERSHIPS** Am Philos Soc. **RESEARCH** Impact of computerization; Designing knowledge interface. **SELECTED PUBLICATIONS** Auth Electric Language, Yale Univ Press, 87; Metaphysics of Virtual Reality, Oxford Univ Press, 93; Virtual Realism, Oxford Univ Press, 98. **CONTACT ADDRESS** 2305 Ruhland Ave, Redondo Beach, CA, 90278. **EMAIL** mike@mheim.com

HEIN, DAVID
PERSONAL Born 10/02/1954, Baltimore, MD **DISCIPLINE** RELIGION; PHILOSOPHY **EDUCATION** Univ Va, BA, 76, PhD, 82; Univ Chicago, MA, 77. **CAREER** From asst prof to assoc prof to prof, 83-, Hood Col. **HONORS AND AWARDS** Raven Society; Omicron Delta Kappa; Laughlin Award for Tchg; Service Schol; Milo Jewett Prize. **MEMBERSHIPS** AASCH; HSEC; AAR **RESEARCH** History of christianity; anglican and episcopal history. **SELECTED PUBLICATIONS** Auth, The Expository Times; auth, Historical Majeziu; auth, Anglican and Episcopal History; auth, Cross Currents; auth, Modern Age; auth, The Maryland; auth, the Journal of Eclesicstical History; coauth, Essays on Lincoln Faith and Politics. **CONTACT ADDRESS** Dept of Religion and Philosophy, Hood Col, Frederick, MD, 21701. **EMAIL** hein@hood.edu

HEIN, NORVIN
PERSONAL Born 08/19/1914, East Canton, OH, m, 1951, 3 children **DISCIPLINE** COMPARATIVE RELIGION **EDUCATION** Col Wooster, BA, 37; Yale Univ, BD, 46, PhD(relig), 51. **CAREER** Instr Eng, Ewing Christian Col, Univ Allahabad, 39-43; from instr to assoc prof, 50-76, Prof Comp Relig, Yale Univ, 76-, Dir Grad Studies, 78-, Fulbright res grant, India, 64-65; consult & panelist, Nat Endowment for Hum, 77-Emer Prof, Yale Univ. **MEMBERSHIPS** Am Orient Soc; Asn Asian Studies; Royal Asiatic Soc; Am Soc Study Relig (vpres, 72-75, pres, 75-78); Am Acad Relig. **RESEARCH** Hinduism, hist of relig; Indian hist. **SELECTED PUBLICATIONS** Auth, The Miracle Plays of Mathura, Yale Univ & Oxford Univ, 72; Hinduism, In: Reader's Guide to the Great Religions, Free Press, 65, 2nd rev & enlarged ed, 77; Caitanya's ecstasies and the theology of the name, In: Hinduism: New Essays in the History of Religion, E J Brill, 76; contribr, Die Religion in Geschichte und Gegenwart, Hinduism in Religions of the World, St. Martin's Press, 83, 3rd ed, 93. **CONTACT ADDRESS** 6 Tuttle Rd Bethany, New Haven, CT, 06525. **EMAIL** morvin.hein@yale.edu

HEIN, ROLLAND NEAL
PERSONAL Born 09/12/1932, Cedar Rapids, IA, m, 1954, 2 children **DISCIPLINE** ENGLISH, THEOLOGY **EDUCATION** Wheaton Col, BA, 54; Grace Theol Sem, BD, 57; Purdue Univ, PhD, 71. **CAREER** Assoc prof English, Bethel Col, Minn, 62-70; from Assoc Prof to Prof English, 70-97, Fac Emeritus, Wheaton Col, Ill, 97-. **MEMBERSHIPS** MLA. **RESEARCH** Life and writings of George MacDonald, 1824-1905. **SELECTED PUBLICATIONS** Auth, A biblical view of the

novel, Christianity Today, 1/73; Lilith: theology through mythopoeia, Christian Scholar's Rev, 74; ed, Life Essential: The Hope of the Gospel, 74, Creation in Christ: The Unspoken sermons of George MacDonald, 76 & George MacDonald's World: An Anthology from the Novels, 78, H Shaw; The Harmony Within 1982; Sunrise, 89; George MacDonald: Victorian Mythmaker, 93; G.K. Chesterton: Myth, Paradox, and the Commonplace, Seven: An Anglo-Am J, 96; Lilith: A Variorum Edition, Johannesen, 97; Christian Mythmakers, Cornerstone, 98. **CONTACT ADDRESS** Dept of English, Wheaton Col, 501 College Ave, Wheaton, IL, 60187. **EMAIL** Rolland N Hein@ Wheaton.edu

HEINE, STEVEN
PERSONAL Born 01/15/1950, Philadelphia, PA, m, 1981, 2 children **DISCIPLINE** EAST ASIAN RELIGIONS **EDUCATION** Univ PA, BA, 71; Temple Univ, MA, 76, PhD, 80. **CAREER** Asst prof, LaSalle Univ, 87-90; assoc prof, PA State, 91-96; prof, FL Int Univ, 97-. **HONORS AND AWARDS** Fulbright, 81-82; NEH, 96-97. **MEMBERSHIPS** Am Academy of Relig; Asn for Asian Studies; Southern Japan Seminar. **RESEARCH** Medieval Japanese Buddhism. **SELECTED PUBLICATIONS** Auth, Dogen and the Koan Tradition: A Tale of Two Shobogenzo Texts, series in philos and psychotherapy, State Univ New York Press, 94; co-ed, with Charles Wei-hsun Fu, Japan in Traditional and Postmodern Perspectives, State Univ NY Press, 95; ed, Buddhism and Interfaith Dialogue, Zen and Western Thought, Univ HI Press, 95; auth, Putting the 'Fox' Back Into the 'Wild Fox Koan": On the Intersection of Philosophical and Popular Religious Elements in the Ch'an/Zen Koan Tradition, Harvard J of Asiatic Studies 56/2, 96; Philosophical and Rhetorical Modes of Zen Discourse: Contrasting Nishida's Logic and Koan poetry, Buddhist-Christian Studies 11, 97; The Dogen Canon: Dogen's Pre-Shobogenzo Writings and the Question of Change in His Later Works, Japanese J of Religious Studies 24/1-2, 97; Sayonara Can Mean 'Hello': Rethinking the Butterfly Syndrome in Postwar American Films, Post Script 16/3, 97; ed, Zen and Comparative Studies, pt 2 of a two-vol sequel to Zen and Western Thought, Univ HI Press, 97; auth, Motion and Emotion in Medieval Japanese Buddhism, J of Chinese Philos, forthcoming; Verses From the Mountain of Eternal Peace: The Zen Poetry of Dogen, Charles E Tuttle, forthcoming; Shifting Shape, Shaping Text: Putting the 'Fox' Back in the 'Wild Fox Koan', Univ HI Press, forthcoming; numerous other articles, monographs, and reviews. **CONTACT ADDRESS** Dept of Relig Studies, Florida Intl Univ, University Park, Miami, FL, 33199. **EMAIL** heines@fiu.edu

HEINZ, JOHN P.
PERSONAL Born 08/06/1936, Carlinville, IL, m, 1967, 2 children **DISCIPLINE** LAW & POLITICAL SCIENCE **EDUCATION** Wash Univ, AB, 58; Yale Univ, LLB, 62. **CAREER** Teaching fel, Wash Univ, 58-59; atty, Off Secy Air Force, 62-65; from asst prof to prof, 65-88, Owen L. Coon Prof Law, Northwestern Univ, 88-, Prof Soc, 87-; Consult, USDA, 66; dir Russell Sage prog law & soc sci, Northwestern Univ, 68-70, dir res, Sch Law, 73-74; consult, Ill Judicial Conf, 71-73; pres, John Howard Asn, 74-75; mem res adv comt, Am Judicature Soc, 75-77; affiliated scholar, Am Bar Found, 75-; mem, bd trustees, Law & Soc Asn, 78-81; exec dir, Am Bar Found 82-86. **HONORS AND AWARDS** Harry Kalven Prize of the Law and Soc Asn, for distinguished research on law and society, 87; Award for Best Teacher in a First Year Course, Northwestern Law Sch, 96-97; Distinguished Alumni Achievement Award, Washington Univ, 98; recipient of numerous research grants. **MEMBERSHIPS** Am Polit Sci Asn; Law & Soc Asn; Am Bar Asn. **RESEARCH** Law and the behavioral sciences; the legal profession; criminal law. **SELECTED PUBLICATIONS** Coauth, A theory of Policy Analysis and some Preliminary Applications, In: Policy Analysis of Political Science, Markham, 70; Public Access to Information, Transaction Bks, 79; Chicago Lawyers: The Social Structure of the Bar, Russell Sage Found & Am Bar Found, Basic Book, 82, rev ed, Northwestern Univ Press and Am Bar Found, 94; The Hollow Core: Private Interests in National Policy Making, Harvard Univ Press, 93; The Constituencies of Elite Urban Lawyers, Law & Soc Rev, vol 31, 97; auth or coauth of numerous other journal articles. **CONTACT ADDRESS** Sch of Law, Northwestern Univ, 357 E Chicago Ave, Chicago, IL, 60611-3069. **EMAIL** j-heinz@nwu.edu

HEINZE, RUTH-INGE
PERSONAL Born 11/04/1919, Berlin, West Germany **DISCIPLINE** RELIGION, ASIAN FOLKLORE **EDUCATION** Univ Calif, Berkeley, BA, 69, MA, 71, PhD(Asian studies), 74. **CAREER** Ed text bks, Follett Publ Co, Chicago, 55-56; lectr anthrop, Exten Course, Berlin, 63-73; producer, Radio Broadcast Berlin, 63-68; lectr English, Univ Chiang Mai, Thailand, 72; Res Assoc, Ctr South & Southeast Asia Studies, Univ Calif, Berkeley, 73-, Am Inst Indian Studies travel grant, 75; lectr Southeast Asia, Univ San Francisco, 75-76; Fulbright res fel, Inst Southeast Asian Studies, Singapore, 78-79; dir & ed newslett, Asian Folklore Studies Group; nat dir, Independent Scholars Asia, 81- **MEMBERSHIPS** Asn for Asian Studies; Asian Folklore Studies Group; Independent Scholars Asia; Int Asn Study Asian Med. **RESEARCH** Historical and functional analysis of religious practices in South and Southeast Asia; psychological anthropology; translation of foreign texts. **SELECTED PUBLICATIONS** Auth, The Rock Art of Utah, Am Indian Culture Res J, Vol 0019, 95. **CONTACT ADDRESS** Ctr for South & Southeast Asia Studies, Univ of Calif, 260 Stephens Hall, Berkeley, CA, 94720.

HEISE, MICHAEL
PERSONAL Born 03/30/1960, Chicago, IL, m, 1988, 2 children **DISCIPLINE** LAW **EDUCATION** Stanford Univ, AB, 83; Univ Chicago, JD, 87; Northwestern Univ, PhD, 90. **CAREER** Asst prof law, Ind Univ School of Law, 94-. **CONTACT ADDRESS** School of Law, Indiana Univ-Purdue Univ, Indianapolis, 735 West New York St., Indianapolis, IN, 46202-5194.

HELLER, AGNES
DISCIPLINE PHILOSOPHY **EDUCATION** Lorand Eotvos Univ, PhD, 55. **CAREER** Hannah Arendt Prof Philos and Pol Sci. **RESEARCH** Ethics; polit philos; Hegel; Marx; Lukacs; existentialism; postmodernity as a philos attitude within modernity. **SELECTED PUBLICATIONS** Auth, General Ethics, 88; Beyond Justice, 87; The Power of Shame, 86; Radical Philosophy, 84; Everyday Life, 84; A Theory of History, 82; A Theory of Feelings, 79; Renaissance Man, 78; The Theory of Need in Marx, 76; ed, Lukacs Revalued, 83. **CONTACT ADDRESS** Eugene Lang Col, New Sch for Social Research, 66 West 12th St, New York, NY, 10011.

HELLERSTEIN, WALTER
PERSONAL Born 06/21/1946, New York, NY, m, 2 children **DISCIPLINE** LAW **EDUCATION** Harvard Col, AB, 67; Univ Chicago Law, JD, 70. **CAREER** May 96-, partner, Sutherland Asbill Brennan, GA ; 86-96, of counsel, Morrison Foerster, CA; 78 to 98-, prof & assoc prof, Univ GA Law; 76 to 78, assist prof, Univ Chicago Law; 73 to 75, assoc, Covington Burling, WA DC. **HONORS AND AWARDS** Phi Beta Kappa; Order of the Coif; Multistate Tax Comm 25th Ann Award, Admitted to the Bar, DC 70; IL 76; NY 89 **MEMBERSHIPS** ALI, NTA, ABA, NY Bar Assoc; State and Local Tax Advisory Bd. **SELECTED PUBLICATIONS** Coauth, State and Local Taxation, Cases and materials, 6th ed, West Pub 97; State Taxation, 97-98; auth, State Tax Notes, US Supreme Court Review and Preview 98, State Taxation of Telecommunication and Electronic Commerce 97, Supreme Court Preview 96, On the Proposed Single-Factor Formula in Michigan 95; Commerce Clause Restraints on State Tax Incentives, 97; reviews of, Federalism in Taxation: The Case for Greater Uniformity, D. Shaviro 94, Constitutional Uniformity and Equality in State Taxation 86. **CONTACT ADDRESS** School of Law, Univ of Georgia, Athens, GA, 30602-6012.

HELLMAN, GEOFFREY
DISCIPLINE PHILOSOPHY **EDUCATION** Harvard Univ, PhD. **RESEARCH** Philosophy of mathematics and logic; philosophy of physics; philosophy of language; aesthetics. **SELECTED PUBLICATIONS** Auth, Gleason's Theorem Is Not Constructively Provable, J Philos Logic, 93; Bell-Type Inequalities in the Non-ideal Case: Proof of a Conjecture of Bell, Foundations Physics, 92; Mathematics without Numbers: Towards a Modal-Structural Interpretation, Oxford, 89; Logical Truth by Linguistic Convention, 86; Review of recent work in truth theory, J Symbolic Logic, 85; Realist Principles, Philos Sci, 83; Symbol Systems and Artistic Styles, J Aesthet Art Criticism, 77; co-auth, Physicalism: Ontology, Determination, and Reduction, J Philos, 75. **CONTACT ADDRESS** Philosophy Dept, Univ of Minnesota, Twin Cities, 355 Ford Hall, 224 Church St SE, Minneapolis, MN, 55455. **EMAIL** hellm001@tc.umn.edu

HELM, THOMAS EUGENE
PERSONAL Born 01/20/1943, Hammond, IN, m, 1966, 1 child **DISCIPLINE** RELIGION & LITERATURE **EDUCATION** Earlham Col, AB, 65; Havard Univ, STB, 68; Univ Chicago, AM, 72, PhD, 77. **CAREER** Asst prof, 74-80, assoc prof, 80-86, PROF RELIG STUDIES, WESTERN ILL UNIV, 86-, dir Univ Honors, 98-, Res Coun grant, Western Ill Univ, 78; jr fel, Inst Med & Renaissance Studies, 79. **MEMBERSHIPS** Am Acad Relig; Midwest Am Acad Relig; Renaissance Soc; Soc Values Higher Educ. **RESEARCH** Renaissance and reformation studies; rhetoric. **SELECTED PUBLICATIONS** Auth, The warp of piety, the woof of politics: American civil religion, Perkins J, spring 78; Enchantment and the banality of evil, Relig Life, spring 80; The Christian Religion, Prentice Hall, 91. **CONTACT ADDRESS** Dept of Philos & Relig Studies, Western Illinois Univ, 1 University Cir, Macomb, IL, 61455-1390. **EMAIL** te-helm@wiu.edu

HELMHOLZ, R.H.
PERSONAL Born 07/01/1940, Pasadena, CA **DISCIPLINE** HISTORY, LAW **EDUCATION** Princeton Univ, AB, 61; Harvard Univ, LLB, 65; Univ Calif, Berkeley, MA, 66, PhD(hist), 70; Trinity Col, Dublin, LLD(h.c.), 92. **CAREER** Asst Prof Hist to Prof Law and Hist, Washington Univ, St. Louis, 70-81; Prof Law, 81-84, Ruth Wyatt Rosenson Prof Law, Univ Chicago, 84-; co-ed, Comparative Studies in Continental and Anglo-Am Legal Hist, 97-; assoc ed, New Dictionary of Nat Biography, 98-. **HONORS AND AWARDS** Fulbright Schol, Univ Kent, 68-69; Royal Hist Soc, Fel, 78-; Guggenheim Fel, 86-87; Cambridge Univ, Maitland Lectr and Vis Fel Commoner, Trinity Col, 86-87; Am Acad of Arts and Sci, Fel, 91-; Alexander von Humboldt Found, Res Prize, 92-93; Medieval Acad of Am, Fel, 97-; All Souls Col, Oxford, vis fel, Michaelmas term, 98. **MEMBERSHIPS** Selden Soc; Am Soc Legal Hist; Royal Hist Soc. **RESEARCH** Legal history. **SELECTED PUBLICATIONS** Auth, Canonical Defamation, Vol 15, Am J Legal Hist, 72; Marriage Litigation in Medieval England, Cambridge Univ, 74; Assumpsit and fidei laesio, Law Quart Rev, Vol 91, 75; Writs of prohibition and ecclesiastical sanctions, Minn Law Rev, 76; Support Orders, Church Courts and the Rule of Filius Nullius, Va Law Rev, Vol 63, 77; Early Enforcement of Uses, Columbia Law Rev, Vol 79, 79; Canon Law and English Common Law, London, 83; Select Cases on Defamation to 1600, Seldon Soc, Vol 101, 85; Canon Law and the Law of England, London, 87; Roman Canon Law in Reformation England, Cambridge, 90; coauth, Notaries Public in England since the Reformation, London, 91; ed and contribur, Canon Law in Protestant Lands, Berlin, 92; auth, The Spirit of Classical Canon Law, Athens, Ga, 96; coauth, The Privilege against Self-Incrimination: its Origins and Development, Chicago, 97. **CONTACT ADDRESS** Law Sch, Univ of Chicago, 1111 E 60th St., Chicago, IL, 60637-2702. **EMAIL** dick_helmholz@ law.uchicago.edu

HELMINIAK, DANIEL A.
PERSONAL Pittsburgh, PA **DISCIPLINE** SYSTEMATIC THEOLOGY, EDUCATIONAL PSYCHOLOGY **EDUCATION** Boston Coll Andover Newton Theol Sch, PhD, 79; Univ Tex, Austin, PhD, 84. **CAREER** Asst prof, Oblate Sch Theol, 81-85; pastoral couns, 89-95; asst prof, State Univ W Ga, 95-97; psychotherapist, Pittsburgh Pastoral Inst, 97-98; coord educ, Consumer Credit & Counseling Svcs, 98-. **HONORS AND AWARDS** Catholic Journalist Book Awards hon mention, 87 **MEMBERSHIPS** Am Acad Rels; Am Asn Pastoral Counrs; Am Psychol Asn'Cath Theol Soc Am; Soc Sci Stud Rel; Soc Sci Stud Sexuality. **RESEARCH** Midlife transition; relationship of psychol and theol; spirituality; sexual integration. **SELECTED PUBLICATIONS** Auth, The Same Jesus: A Contemporary Christology, Loyola Univ Press, 96; auth, Spiritual Development: An Interdisciplinary Study, Loyola Univ Press, 87; auth, What the Bible Really Says About Homosexuality, Alamo Square Press, 94; auth, The Human Cove of Spirituality: Mind as Psyche and Spirit, State Univ NY Press, 96; auth, Religion and the Human Sciences: An Approach via Spirituality, State Univ NY. **CONTACT ADDRESS** 48 MLK Dr., SW, Atlanta, GA, 30303. **EMAIL** DHelminiak@aol.com

HELYER, LARRY R.
PERSONAL Born 11/06/1942, Seattle, WA, m, 1965, 2 children **DISCIPLINE** BIBLICAL STUDIES **EDUCATION** Biola Col, BA, 65; W Conserv Baptist Sem, M.Div, 68; Fuller Theol Sem, PhD, 79. **CAREER** Asst prof, 79-84, assoc prof, 84-89, prof, 89-, Taylor Univ. **HONORS AND AWARDS** Clyde Cook Award, scholar/athlete, 65, Biola Col; Delta Epsilon Chi Natl Honor Soc, 65, Biola Col; St Dept Fel, 68-69, Amer Inst of Holy Land Stud; Dist Prof of Year, 88, Taylor Univ. **MEMBERSHIPS** Soc of Biblical Lit; Inst for Biblical Res; Evangelical Theol Soc; Near East Archaeological Soc. **RESEARCH** Old Testament, Jewish lit of the 2nd temple; New Testament, Biblical archaeology. **SELECTED PUBLICATIONS** Art, Recent Research on Col 1:15020 (1980-1990), Grace Jour, 92; art, Luke and the restoration of Israel, Jour of the Evangel Theol Soc, 93; art, Cosmic Christology and Col 1: 15-20, JETS, 94; auth, Yesterday, Today and Forever: the Continuing Relevance of the Old Testament, Sheffield Pub, 96; art, Old Testament Hero and Heroine Narratives, S Baptist Jour of Theol, 98. **CONTACT ADDRESS** Taylor Univ, 236 W Reade Ave., Upland, IN, 46989-1001. **EMAIL** lrhelyer@tayloru.edu

HEMMER, JOSEPH
DISCIPLINE COMMUNICATION LAW **EDUCATION** Bradley Univ, MA; Univ Wisc, PhD, 78. **CAREER** Law, Carroll Col. **HONORS AND AWARDS** Marquette Univ DSR-TKA Outstanding Alumni Award, 68; Wisc Comm Asn Andrew T. Weaver Award, 82., Chair, Comm dept. **SELECTED PUBLICATIONS** Auth, Communication Law: Judicial Interpretation of the First Amendment. **CONTACT ADDRESS** Carroll Col, Wisconsin, 100 N East Ave, Waukesha, WI, 53186.

HENDERSON, EDWARD H.
PERSONAL Born 04/21/1939, Atlanta, GA, m, 1973, 4 children **DISCIPLINE** PHILOSOPHY **EDUCATION** Rhodes Col, BA, 61; Tulane Univ, MA, 64, PhD, 67. **CAREER** Asst prof, Westminster Col, 64-66; from asst to full prof, 66- , chemn dept, 79- , Louisiana State Univ. **HONORS AND AWARDS** Phi Beta Kappa; Omicron Delta Kappa; Woodrow Wilson fel, 61-64; Natl Defense Educ Act Fel, 61-64; Distinguished Faculty Award, 81. **MEMBERSHIPS** Soc for Philos of Relig; Soc of Christian Philos; Scholarly Engagement with Anglican Doctrine. **RESEARCH** Philosophy of religion; philosophical theology; Austin Farrer. **SELECTED PUBLICATIONS** Co-ed, Divine Action: Studies Inspired by the Philosophical Theology of Austin Farrer, T & T Clark, 90; auth, The Divine Playwright, The Personalist Forum, 96; auth, How to be a Christian Philosopher in the Postmodern World, in, Spirituality and Theology,

John Knox, 98; auth, The Supremely Free Agent, in McLain, ed, Free-Will and Theology, University Press of America, forthcoming. **CONTACT ADDRESS** Dept of Philosophy and Religious Studies, Louisiana State Univ, Baton Rouge, LA, 70803. **EMAIL** ehender@lsu.edu

HENDERSON, HERBERT H.
PERSONAL m **DISCIPLINE** LAW **EDUCATION** WV State Coll, BS 1953; George Wash Univ Coll of Law, JD 1958. **CAREER** Attorney, civil rights & general practice; Marshall Univ, part-time instructor in black history, 1967-80; Henderson & Henderson General Practice, Huntington, WV, sr partner, currently. **HONORS AND AWARDS** W Robert Ming Award, NAACP Bd of Dirs; Justitia Officium Award, West Virginia Univ Coll of Law, 1989. **MEMBERSHIPS** Mem Cabell Co Bar Assn; bd dir WV Trial Lawyers Assn; WV State Bar; Nat Bar Assn; Am Trial Lawyers Assn; Mountaineer Bar Assn; mem bd dir Region III Assn of Mental Hlth; chmn bd trustees Huntington Dist united Methodist Ch; state United Meth Ch Conf; pres Meth Men's Club; Ebenezer Meth Ch; mem Kappa Alpha Psi Frat; mem, bd of trustees, Morristown Coll; mgr & supvr, WV NAACP Jobs Program, 1978-; state pres WV NAACP, 1966-; mem, natl bd of dirs, NAACP, 1980-. **CONTACT ADDRESS** 317 Ninth St, Huntington, WV, 25711.

HENDERSON, JOHN B.
DISCIPLINE RELIGIONS OF CHINA AND JAPAN **EDUCATION** Univ Calif, Berkeley, PhD, 77. **CAREER** Prof Hist and Relig Stud, La State Univ. **SELECTED PUBLICATIONS** Auth, Scripture, Canon, and Commentary: A Comparison of Confucian and Western Exegesis, Princeton, 91. **CONTACT ADDRESS** Dept of Philos and Relig Stud, Louisiana State Univ, 106 Coates Hall, Baton Rouge, LA, 70803.

HENDLEY, BRIAN
DISCIPLINE PHILOSOPHY **EDUCATION** Yale Univ, PhD, 66. **RESEARCH** Philos of educ; Amer philos. **SELECTED PUBLICATIONS** Auth, Dewey, Russell, Whitehead: Philosophers as Educators, Southern Ill Univ, 86; ed, Plato, Time, and Education: Essays in Honor of Robert S. Brumbaugh, SUNY, 87. **CONTACT ADDRESS** Dept of Philosophy, Waterloo Univ, 200 University Ave W, Waterloo, ON, N2L 3G1. **EMAIL** bhendley@uwaterloo.ca

HENDLEY, STEVE
PERSONAL Born 12/03/1955, Nashville, TN, m, 1986, 2 children **DISCIPLINE** PHILOSOPHY **EDUCATION** Rhodes Col, 78, BA; Vanderbilt Univ, 80, MA Philosophy; Duquesne Univ, 81, MA, Psychology, PhD Philosophy. **CAREER** Teaching asst, 82, Duquesne Univ; visiting faculty, 88, West Virginia Univ; assoc prof, 88- , Birmingham-Southern Col. **MEMBERSHIPS** Alabama Philosophical Soc, Secretary-Treasurer, 90-91; APA; The Sartre Soc of North Amer, Co-Chair, 97- ; Soc for Phenomenology and Existential Philosophy. **RESEARCH** Contemporary continental philosophy; moral and political philosophy. **SELECTED PUBLICATIONS** Auth, From Communicatve Action to the Face of the Other: Habermas and Levinas on the Foundations of Moral Theory, Philosophy Today, 96; auth, Autonomy and Alterity: Sartre and Levinas on the Grounds of Moral Obligation, Journal of the British Society for Phenomenology, Winter 96; auth, Lyotard and the Question of Community, in Phenomenology, Interpretation, and Community: Selected Studies in Phenomenology and Existential Philosophy, 96; auth, Reconsidering the Limits of Democracy with Castoriadis and Lefort, in Reinterpreting the Political: Selected Studies in Phenomenology and Existential Philosophy, 98. **CONTACT ADDRESS** Birmingham-So Col, 900 Arkadelphia Rd, Birmingham, AL, 35254. **EMAIL** shendley@bsc.edu

HENKIN, LOUIS
PERSONAL Born 11/11/1917, Russia, m, 1960, 3 children **DISCIPLINE** LAW; DIPLOMACY **EDUCATION** Yeshiva Univ, AB, 37; Harvard Univ, LLB, 40; Columbia Univ, LLD, 95. **CAREER** Law clerk, Judge Learned Hand, US Court of Appeals, 40-41; foreign affairs officer, Us Dept State, 45-46; law clerk, Justice Frankfurter, US Supreme Court, 46-47; foreign affairs officer, US Dept State, 48-57; prof law, Univ Pa Law Sch, 57-62; prof law & int law & diplomacy, 62-63, Hamilton Fish Prof Int Law & Diplomacy & Prof Law, Columbia Univ, 63-98; Harlan Fiske Stone prof const law, 78-79;Univ Prof, 79-, Mem bar, NY, 41- & US Supreme Court, 47-; consult, UN Legal Dept, 47-48, US Dept State, 58 & 61, US Arms Control & Disarmament Agency, 61-66 & Nat Coun Marine Resources & Engineering Develop, 68-70; assoc dir legis drafting res fund, Columbia Univ, 56-57; US mem, Permanent Court of Arbit, 63-69; pres, US Inst Human Rights, 70-; mem, US Adv Comt Law of Sea, 72-; Am Acad Arts & Sci fel, 74; mem human rights comt, Nat Comn for UNESCO, 77-; dir, Columbia Ctr Human Rights, 78-; co-ed-in-chief, Am J Int Law, 78-; chief reporter, Am Law Inst, 79- **HONORS AND AWARDS** DHL, Yeshiva Univ, 63; Bklyn Law School, JD (hon), 97. **MEMBERSHIPS** Am Soc Int Law; Int Law Asn; Coun Foreign Relat; Am Polit Sci Asn; Am Soc Polit & Legal Philos. **RESEARCH** United States Constitutional law; international law; human rights. **SELECTED PUBLICATIONS** Ed, Arms Control: Issues for the Public, 61; Auth, How Nations Behave: Law and Foreign Policy, Praeger, 68 & Columbia Univ, 2nd ed, 79; Law for the Sea's Mineral Resources, Inst Study Sci in Human Affairs, Columbia Univ, 68; Foreign Affairs and the Constitution, Foundation, 72; ed, World Politics and the Jewish Condition, Quadrangle, 72; co-ed, Transnational Law in a Changing Society, Columbia Univ, 72; auth, The Rights of Man Today, Westview, 78; ed, The International Bill of Rights: The Covenant on Civi and Political Rights, Columbia Univ, 81; co-ed, International Law, Cases and Materials, West, 2nd ed, 80; co auth Human Rights in Comtemporary Chine, 86; Right v Might: International Law and the Use of Force, 89; Constitutionalism and Rights: The Influence of the United States Constitution Abroad, 89; Foreign Affairs and the US Constitution, 90; The Age of Rights, 90; Constitutionalism, Democracy and Foreign Affairs, 90; International Law: Cases and Materials, 93; International Law: Politics and Values, 95; **CONTACT ADDRESS** Sch of Law, Columbia Univ, 435 West 116th St, New York, NY, 10027.

HENNESSY, ANNE
PERSONAL Born 03/30/1938, San Francisco, CA **DISCIPLINE** RELIGION **EDUCATION** Grad Theol Union, MA, 83, PhD, 88; Calif State Univ, MA, 69; St. Joseph Col, BA, 62. **CAREER** Prof, Pontifical Gregorian Univ, Rome, Italy, 93-; asst dir, Inst Living Water, Tabgha, Israel, 89-97; acad dean, Loyola Marymount Univ, 75-80; coordr, Sisters St. Joseph, 69-74. **RESEARCH** New Testament; 1st Century Galilee; historical expressions of Christian discipleship. **SELECTED PUBLICATIONS** Auth, The Formation of Adult Disciplines: A Reading of John 20-21, Emmanuel, April, 96; auth, Contemplative Pilgrimage to the Holy Land, Prayer & Serv, Jan-March, 96; auth, The Galilee of Jesus, 94; auth, Holy Land Pilgrims and Ministry to Them, Rev Relig, July-Aug, 94; coauth, The Family of Jesus, The Family: A Cath Perspective, Dec, 95; auth, Galilean Perspectives on Religious Life, Rev Relig, March-April, 93; coauth, Joseph and Mary: Their Vocations and Mission, 92; auth, The Multiplication of Loaves and Fishes: A Formative Experience, Emmanuel, Sept, 92. **CONTACT ADDRESS** 480 S Batavia St., Orange, CA, 92868.

HENRICH, DIETER
PERSONAL Born 01/05/1927, Marburg, Germany, m, 1975 **DISCIPLINE** PHILOSOPHY **EDUCATION** Heidelberg Univ, DPhil, 50, DPhil habil, 56. **CAREER** Asst prof philos, Heidelberg Univ, 56-60; prof, Free Univ Berlin, 60-65 & Heidelberg Univ, 65-81; Prof Philos, Univ Munich, 81-; Vis Prof Philos, Harvard Univ, 73-, Vis prof philos, Columbia Univ, 68-73. **MEMBERSHIPS** Int Hegel Asn (pres, 70-). **SELECTED PUBLICATIONS** Auth, Philosophy of Naturalism, Merkur-Deutsche Zeitschrift Fur Europaisches Denken, Vol 0050, 96. **CONTACT ADDRESS** Dept of Philos, Harvard Univ, Cambridge, MA, 02138.

HENRICH, SARAH
DISCIPLINE NEW TESTAMENT **EDUCATION** Muhlenberg Col, BA, 69; Bryn Mawr Univ, MA, 71; Lutheran Theol Sem, MDiv, 79; Yale Univ, PhD, 94. **CAREER** Asst prof, Lutheran Sch Theol, 89; dir, Christian edu, St. Michael's Lutheran Church, New Canaan, 83-88; ch, Bible Div; assoc prof, 92-. **HONORS AND AWARDS** Assoc ed, Word and World; asst pastor, St. Michael's Lutheran Church. **MEMBERSHIPS** Mem, Soc Biblical Lit. **SELECTED PUBLICATIONS** Pub(s) in Augsburg Fortress; auth, Great Personalities of the New Testament; See God's Grace in Action. **CONTACT ADDRESS** Dept of New Testament, Luther Sem, 2481 Como Ave, St. Paul, MN, 55108. **EMAIL** shenrich@luthersem.edu

HENRY, BRENT LEE
PERSONAL Born 10/09/1947, Philadelphia, PA, m **DISCIPLINE** LAW **EDUCATION** Princeton Univ, BA 1969; Yale Law Sch, JD 1973; Yale Univ, Master of Urban Studies 1973. **CAREER** New Haven Housing Information Ctr, counsel 1973-74; Yale Univ, lecturer in Afro-Amer studies 1973-74; Jones Day Reavis & Pogue, atty 1974-78; NYCHuman Resources Adminstrn, dept admin 1978-79; Jones Day Reavis & Pogue, atty 1979-82; Greater Southeast Comm Hospital Found, dir of business and govt affairs 1982-84; Howard Univ School of Business Admin, adjunct prof, 1982-94; Helix/Medlantic Healthcare Group, sr vice pres/gen counsel 1985-. **HONORS AND AWARDS** Frederick Abramson Award, DC Bar Association, 1996. **MEMBERSHIPS** Bd of trustees, Princeton Univ 1969-72; adv council Woodrow Wilson School of Pub & Intl Affairs Princeton Univ 1969-72; ABA; NBA; Ohio Bar Assns; DC Bar Assn; board of directors, Natl Health Lawyers Assn, 1988-96, president, 1994-95; board of directors, Mental Health Law Project 1987-98; bd of dirs, Combined Health Appeal of the Natl Capital Area, 1989-93; Princeton University Alumni Council, executive committee, 1994-, vice chair, 1995-97, chair, 1997-99; Public Welfare Foundation, bod, 1995. **SELECTED PUBLICATIONS** Auth, "The Provision of Indigent Defense Servs in Greater Cleveland" Cleveland Found. **CONTACT ADDRESS** Helix/Medlantic Health Care Group, 100 Irving St NW, Washington, DC, 20010.

HENRY, CARL F.H.
PERSONAL Born 01/22/1913, New York, NY, m, 1940 **DISCIPLINE** RELIGION **EDUCATION** Wheaton Col, BA, 38, MA, 40; North Bap Theol Sem, BD, 41, Thd, 42, Boston Univ, PhD, 49. **CAREER** North Bap Theol Sem, asst prof, prof, 40-47; Fuller Theol Sem, prof, act dean, 47-56; Eastern Bap Sem, prof, 69-74; World Vision Intl, lectr at large, 74-86; Trinity Evan Div School, vis prof, 74-97. **HONORS AND AWARDS** Boston Univ, Distinguished Alumnus, 98; South Bap Conven, 50-years Gold Service Award, 93; Hillsdale Col, Hon LLD, 89; Gordon-Conwell Theol Sem, Hon DD, 84; Northwestern Col, Hon DD, 79; Relig Herit of Amer, Faith and Freedom Award, 75 **MEMBERSHIPS** WVI, WCE, PF, RHA **SELECTED PUBLICATIONS** Auth, God, Revelation and Authority; A Plea for Evangelical Demonstration, 71; Aspects of Christian Social Ethics, 64; Remaking the Modern Mind, 48; founding editor of Christianity Today; ed, Contemporary Evangelical Thought, 57; The Bible Expositor, 60; Jesus of Nazareth: Savior and Lord, 73. **CONTACT ADDRESS** 1141 Hus Dr, #20 B, Watertown, WI, 53098.

HENRY, DANIEL JOSEPH
PERSONAL Born 01/03/1945, New York, NY, m **DISCIPLINE** LAW **EDUCATION** Columbia Univ School of Law, JD 1967-70. **CAREER** Rubin Wachtel Baum & Levin, assoc 1969-71; Bernard M Baruch Coll, adj lecturer 1971-72; NY State Spec Comm on Attica, asst counsel 1971; NY State Supreme Ct, law sec 1971-73; Carver Dem Club, counsel 1972-76; Montgomery Ward & Co, sr attny 1973-74; Caterpillar Tractor Co, attny 1976-84; Univ of MN, assoc attny. **MEMBERSHIPS** Mem Amer Bar Assoc, Natl Bar Assoc, Intl Law Sec Council, IL State Bar Assoc 1979-80; vchmn Natl Urban Coaltion Salute to Cities Dinner 1980. **CONTACT ADDRESS** Univ of Minnesota, 100 Church St SE, Minneapolis, MN, 55455.

HENRY ELROD, LINDA
DISCIPLINE FAMILY LAW, COMPARATIVE LAW AND REAL PROPERTY **EDUCATION** Washburn Univ, BA, 69, JD, 71. **CAREER** Vis prof, WA Univ; Vis prof, Univ San Diego Inst; Ed, Family Law Quart. **MEMBERSHIPS** Secy-Treas, KS Bar Asn; Chair,Family Law Section; Profes Topeka Bar Asn. **SELECTED PUBLICATIONS** Areas: family law issues. **CONTACT ADDRESS** Washburn Univ Topeka, 1700 SW College, Topeka, KS, 66621. **EMAIL** zzelro@acc.wuacc.edus

HENSLEE, WILLIAM D.
DISCIPLINE COPYRIGHT LAW, ENTERTAINMENT LAW **EDUCATION** Univ HI, BA, 77; J.D., Pepperdine Univ, JD, 84; Univ CA, MFA, 96. **CAREER** Recruitment cood, 94; admin dir, staff instr, Multistate Legal Studies, Inc, 85-88; dir, Planned Giving, 88-89; nat dir, HBJ Multistate Advantage, 89-90; asst prof; ed, ABA Career Series bk(s), 84-. **MEMBERSHIPS** Mem, AR, CA, Nmex, PA Bar Assn(s). **SELECTED PUBLICATIONS** Auth, Careers in Entertainment Law, Am Bar Assn, 90; How to Survive the First Year of Law School, ABA Law Student Div, 86; co-auth, Non-Legal Careers for Lawyers, Am Bar Assn, 94; nt **CONTACT ADDRESS** Sch of Law, Pepperdine Univ, 24255 Pacific Coast Hwy, Malibu, CA, 90263.

HERBENICK, RAYMOND M.
DISCIPLINE CLASSICAL PHILOSOPHY, LOGIC **EDUCATION** Georgetown Univ, Phd, 68. **CAREER** Dept Philos, Univ Dayton **RESEARCH** Applied ethics, history of Slavic philosophy. **SELECTED PUBLICATIONS** Auth, Remarks on Abortion, Abandonment, and Adoption Opportunities, Philosophy and Public Affairs, Princeton Univ Press, 75; Basic Logic: A Systems Approach to the Structures and Principles of Logical Reasoning, Ginn, 85; Carpatho-Rusyn American Index: A Computerized Bibliography Vols1-11 (78-88), Carpatho-Rusyn Res Ctr, 91; Augustine's Moral Thermometer of Human Goodness, Univ Dayton Rev, 94. **CONTACT ADDRESS** Dept of Philos, Univ Dayton, 300 Col Park, Dayton, OH, 75062. **EMAIL** herbenic@checkov.hm.udayton.edu

HERBERT, GARY
PERSONAL Born 12/24/1941, Loves Park, IL, m, 1967, 2 children **DISCIPLINE** PHILOSOPHY **EDUCATION** Ill Wesleyan Univ, BA, 65; The Am Univ, MA, 67; Penn State Univ, PhD, 72. **CAREER** Prof of Philos, Loyola Univ-New Orleans, 72-. **MEMBERSHIPS** Am Philos Asn. **RESEARCH** Political philosophy: Modern philosophy. **SELECTED PUBLICATIONS** Fear of Death and the Foundations of Natural Right in the Philosophy of Thomas Hobbes, Hobbes Studies, 94; Immanuel Kant: Punishment and the Moral Preconditions of Political Existence, Interpretation, 95; Transcendental Consent: The APrior; Preconditions of Political Existence, SW Philos, 96; John Locke: Natural Rights and Natural Duties, Jahrbuch fur Recht und Ethik, 96; Fichtes Deduction of Rights from Self-consciousness, Interpretation, 98. **CONTACT ADDRESS** Dept of Philosophy, Loyola Univ, New Orleans, LA, 70118. **EMAIL** gherbert@loyno.edu

HERDT, JENNIFER A.
PERSONAL Born 12/10/1967, New Delhi, India, m, 1995 **DISCIPLINE** RELIGION; ETHICS; POLITICS; PHILOSOPHY **EDUCATION** Oberlin Col, BA, 89; Princeton Univ, MA, 92, PhD, 94. **CAREER** Asst prof Rel, New Col of the Univ S

Fla, 94- ; Postdoc fel, Ctr Philos Rel, Univ Notre Dame, 98-99. **HONORS AND AWARDS** Whiting fel, 92; Mellon Grad Prize fel, 92; Mellon fel Hum, 89; Phi Beta Kappa, 88. **MEMBERSHIPS** Amer Acad Rel; Amer Philos Asn; Amer Soc 18th c stud (s); Soc Christian Ethics; Hume Soc. **RESEARCH** History of Modern Moral Philosophy; Cambridge Platonists. **SELECTED PUBLICATIONS** Auth, Cruelty, Liberalism, and the Quarantine of Irony: Rorty on the Disjunction Between Public and Private, Soundings 75, 92; Opposite Sentiments: Hume's Fear of Faction and the Philosophy of Religion, Amer Jour Theol and Philos, Sept 95; auth, Religion and Faction in Hume's Moral Philosophy, Cambridge UP, 97. **CONTACT ADDRESS** Division of Humanities, New Col of the Univ of So Florida, 5700 North Tamiami Trail, Sarasota, FL, 34243. **EMAIL** herdt@virtu.sar.usf.edu

HERMAN, ARTHUR L.
PERSONAL Born 11/16/1930, Minneapolis, MN, m, 1956, 2 children **DISCIPLINE** PHILOSOPHY **EDUCATION** Univ Minn, PhD, 70. **CAREER** Prof; Univ Wis-SP, 65-; fac adv, Philos Club, 84-; ch, Search and Screen Comt for Assoc Dean; fac adv, Col Letters and Sci; Univ Honors Soc, 86-88; dir, Univ Honors Prog, 86-88. **HONORS AND AWARDS** Univ Scholar awd, 93; Acad Letters & Sci awd for Scholarship, 90; Excellence in Tchg awd, 73 and 68. **SELECTED PUBLICATIONS** Auth, The Problem of Evil and Indian Thought, New Delhi, Oxford: 94; The Way of the Lotus:Critical Reflections on the Ethics of the Saddharmapundarika Sutra, Asian Philos, 97. **CONTACT ADDRESS** Dept Religious Studies, Univ Wis-SP, Stevens Point, WI, 54481.

HERMAN, JONATHAN
DISCIPLINE TAOISM, CONFUCIANISM, BUDDHISM, MYSTICISM **EDUCATION** Harvard Univ, PhD, 92. **CAREER** Asst prof, Ga State Univ. **HONORS AND AWARDS** Cert of Distinction in Tchg, Harvard Univ. **SELECTED PUBLICATIONS** Auth, I and Tao: Martin Buber's Encounter With Chuang Tzu. **CONTACT ADDRESS** Georgia State Univ, Atlanta, GA, 30303. **EMAIL** phljrh@panther.gsu.edu

HERMAN, ROBERT M.
PERSONAL Born 07/29/1921, Philadelphia, PA, m, 1992 **DISCIPLINE** PHILOSOPHY **EDUCATION** Univ Pittsburgh, PhD, 62. **CAREER** Indiana Univ Panna, prof, dept ch, 59-87. **MEMBERSHIPS** APA **CONTACT ADDRESS** RR # 2, PO Box 164, Marion Center, PA, 15759.

HERMAN, STEWART W.
PERSONAL Born 09/25/1948 **DISCIPLINE** SOCIAL ETHICS **EDUCATION** Univ Chicago, Divinity Sch, 88. **CAREER** Asst Prof, Concordia Coll, Moorehead, MN. **MEMBERSHIPS** SDE, AAR, SBE, Assoc of Lore Texts and Courses; Acad Mgt. **RESEARCH** Business Ethics. **SELECTED PUBLICATIONS** Auth, Durable Goods: A Covenant Ethic for Management's and Employees, Univ of Notre Dame, forthcoming; Luther, Law and Social Covenants: Cooperative Self-Obligation in the Reconstruction of Lutheran Social Ethics, Journal of Religious Ethics, 97; co-ed, Business Ethics Quarterly 7:2, Introduction, Enlarging the Conversation, Returning the Corporation to Its Roots, On Moral Business Classic, 97; The Modern Corporation and an Ethics of Trust, Journal of Religious Ethics, 92. **CONTACT ADDRESS** Dept Religion, Concordia Col, Minnesota, Moorehead, MN, 56562. **EMAIL** herman@cord.edu

HERRERA, ROBERT ANTHONY
PERSONAL Born 10/31/1933, Spring Lake, NJ, m **DISCIPLINE** MEDIEVAL PHILOSOPHY, PHILOSOPHY OF RELIGION **EDUCATION** Col St Thomas, BA, 53; New Sch Soc Res, MA, 65, PhD, 75. **CAREER** Vis asst prof philos, Rutgers Univ, 70-71; assoc prof, 73-79, Prof Philos, Seton Hall Univ, 79-97, Prof Emeritus, 98-; Adj fac, New Sch Soc Res, 68-73, Baruch Col, 70-72 & Immaculate Conception Sem, 70-71; consult, Judeao-Christian Inst, Seton, 76- & Christendom Col, 77. **HONORS AND AWARDS** Seton Hall Univ res grant, 77, 78, 79, 82, 84; Canagie summer grant, 70; NS Hum grant, 82; Wilbur Found grant, 95; Earhart Found grant, 98. **MEMBERSHIPS** Am Philos Asn; Am Cath Philos Asn. **RESEARCH** Early medieval thought (emphasis on Anselm); the Augustinian tradition; 19th-20th century Span polit thought (emphasis on Donoso Cortes). **SELECTED PUBLICATIONS** Auth, John of the Cross: Introductory studies, Rev Espiritualidad, Madrid, 68; contribr, God in Contemporary Thought Nauwelaerts, Louvain, 77; auth, Anselm's Proslogion, Univ Press, 78; contribr, J Hist Philos, Mod Schoolman, Angus Triniana, Philos Today & Analecta Anselmiana; Lamps of Fire, St Bedes Pub, 79; Donoso Contes: Cassandrs of the Age; Eerdmans, 95; ed, Mystics of the Book, Peter Lang, 93; Saints Scholars and Sovereigns, Peter Lang, 94. **CONTACT ADDRESS** Dept of Philos, Seton Hall Univ, 400 S Orange Ave, South Orange, NJ, 07079-2697.

HERRUP, CYNTHIA
PERSONAL Born 03/10/1950, Miami, FL **DISCIPLINE** BRITISH STUDIES, LAW **EDUCATION** Northwestern Univ, PhD, 82. **CAREER** Asst prof, Univ of Mich, 81-84; ASST PROF, 84-88, ASSOC PROF, 88-91, PROF OF LAW, DUKE UNIV, 91-. **HONORS AND AWARDS** Distinguished vis, Centre for British Studies, Univ of Adelaide, 98; fel, Royal Hist Soc, 86-; Walter D. Love Prize, North Am Confr on British Studies, 86; NEH/Folger Shakespeare Libr Fel, 96-97; John Simon Guggenheim Fel, 89-90; NEH Fel for Univ Teachers, 88-89; ACLS Recent Recipients of the PhD Awd, 84. **MEMBERSHIPS** Am Hist Asn; Am Soc for Legal Hist; North Am Confr on British Studies. **RESEARCH** Early modern Britain; legal hist; social hist. **SELECTED PUBLICATIONS** Auth, Crimes Most Dishonorable: Sex, Law, and the 2nd Earl of Castlehaven, Oxford Univ Press, 99; The Common Peace: Participation and the Criminal Law in Seventeenth-Century England, Cambridge Univ Press, 87; The Pluck Bright Honour from the Pale-Fac'd Moon: Gender and Honor in the Castlehaven Story, Transactions of the Royal Hist Soc, 96; The Patriarch at Home. The Trial of the Earl of Castlehaven for Rape and Sodomy, Hist Workshop J, 96; Law and Morality in Seventeenth-Century England, Past & Present, 85. **CONTACT ADDRESS** Dept of Hist, Duke Univ, Box 90719, Durham, NC, 27708. **EMAIL** cherrup@acpub.duke.edu

HERTIG, PAUL
PERSONAL Born 09/06/1955, Minneapolis, MN, m, 1983, 1 child **DISCIPLINE** BIBLICAL THEOLOGY **EDUCATION** Fuller Theol Sem, PhD, 95. **CAREER** Asoc dean, prof missiology, World Mission Univ, 95-98; lectr, New Testament, Azusa Pacific Univ, 95-98; asst prof, world Christianity, United Theol Sem, 98-. **HONORS AND AWARDS** Theol award, diss, 95; Azuse Pacific Univ grant, 97, 98. **MEMBERSHIPS** Soc of Bibl Lit; Am Soc of Missiology. **RESEARCH** Matthew and mission; Luke-Acts and mission; mission and marginalization. **SELECTED PUBLICATIONS** Auth, The Role of Mission in Church Renewal: Matthean Foundations, Am Baptist Quart, 96; auth, The Galilee Theme in Matthew: Transforming Mission through Marginality, Missiology, 97; auth, Galilean Christianity, in Dictionary of the Later New Testament and Its Developments, InterVarsity, 97; auth, The Multi-Ethnic Journeys of Jesus in Matthew: Margin-Center Dynamics, Missiology, 98; auth, The Jubilee Mission of Jesus in the Gospel of Luke: Reversals of Fortunes, Missiology, 98; auth, Matthew's Narrative Use of Galilee in the Multicultural and Missiological Journeys of Jesus, Mellen Bibl, 98. **CONTACT ADDRESS** 1443 N Euclid Ave, Dayton, OH, 45406. **EMAIL** phertig@united.edu

HERTIG, YOUNG LEE
PERSONAL Born 03/02/1954, Seoul, Korea, m, 1983, 1 child **DISCIPLINE** THEOLOGY **EDUCATION** Yonsei Grad Univ, MA, 79; Bethel Theol Sem, MA, 83; Fuller Theol Sem, MA, 87, PhD, 91. **CAREER** Asst prof, 92-95, adj prof, 96-98, cross cultural ministry, Fuller Theol Sem; asst prof, Vera B Blinn Chair, World Christianity, United Theol Sem, 98- . **HONORS AND AWARDS** Assoc for Theol Sch grant, 93; Global Res Inst grant, 96. **MEMBERSHIPS** Asn of Prof of Mission; Am Acad Relig. **RESEARCH** Reconciliation and peacemaking inside out, from interdisciplinary perspectives. **SELECTED PUBLICATIONS** Auth, Coping as a Minority Female Leader, Theol News and Notes, 93; auth, On Liberating Theology from Sexual, Racial Bias, Los Angeles Times, 94; auth, Expanding and Balancing Our Horizons, Korean Christian J, 96; auth, Asian- American Women in the Workplace and the Church, in Ng, ed, People On the Way: Asian North Americans Discovering Christ, Culture, and Community, Valley Forge, 96; auth, Sugar/Sugary, in Banks, ed, The Complete Book of Everyday Christianity: An A-to-Z Guide to Following Christ in Every Aspect of Life, InterVarsity, 97; auth, The Asian-American Alternative to Feminism: A Yinist Paradigm, Missiology: An Int Rev, 98. **CONTACT ADDRESS** 1443 N Euclid Ave, Dayton, OH, 45406. **EMAIL** yhertig@united.edu

HERTZ, RICHARD C.
DISCIPLINE JUDAISM **EDUCATION** Univ Cincinnati, BA; Northwestern Univ, PhD. **CAREER** Ch, Jewish Stud; ordained, Hebrew Union Col in Cincinnati; honorary doct, Hebrew Union College-Jewish Inst Rel and Univ of Detroit Mercy; prof, Univ of Detroit Mercy, 70-. **HONORS AND AWARDS** Temple Beth El as their spirtual leader for the past forty-three years. **RESEARCH** Introduction to Judaism, Bibical courses, history of Judaism and the Jewish people, modern Jewish life and thought, and the Holocaust **CONTACT ADDRESS** Dept of Religious Studies, Univ of Detroit Mercy, 4001 W McNichols Rd, PO Box 19900, Detroit, MI, 48219-0900. **EMAIL** HERTZRC@udmercy.edu

HERWITZ, DAVID RICHARD
PERSONAL Born 12/08/1925, Lynn, MA, m, 1960, 2 children **DISCIPLINE** LAW **EDUCATION** Mass Inst Technol, BS, 46; Harvard Univ, LLB, 49. **CAREER** Assoc prof, 54-57, PROF LAW, HARVARD UNIV, 57-, Consult, US Treasury Dept, 60-63. **SELECTED PUBLICATIONS** Auth, Stock redemptions and the accumulated earnings tax, 61, Allocation of stock between services and capital, 62 & Installment repurchase of stock: Surplus limitations, 65, Harvard Law Rev; Business Planning, 66, Corporations Game Plan, 75, Accounting for Lawyers, 2nd ed, 97, with Barrett, Foundation Press. **CONTACT ADDRESS** Law Sch, Harvard Univ, 1525 Massachusetts, Cambridge, MA, 02138-2903. **EMAIL** dherwitz@law.harvard.edu

HERZOG, PETER EMILIUS
PERSONAL Born 12/25/1925, Vienna, Austria, m, 1970, 2 children **DISCIPLINE** LAW **EDUCATION** Hobart Col, BA, 52; Syracuse Univ, JD, 55; Columbia Univ, LLM, 56. **CAREER** From dep asst attorney gen to asst attorney gen, NY State Dept Law, 56-58; from asst prof to assoc prof, 58-66, law librn, 60-67, Prof Law, Col Law, Syracuse Unix, 66-, Legal asst metropolitan areas studies, NY State Joint Legis Comt, 58-60; staff mem, Prof Int Procedure, Columbia Univ Law Sch, 60-64, assoc dir, Proj European Legal Inst, 68; consult, NY State Comt Eminent Domain, 71-72; assoc prof, Univ Paris, 76-77. **MEMBERSHIPS** Am Soc Int Law; Soc Comp Legis, France. **RESEARCH** Conflict of law; comparative law; law of European communities. **SELECTED PUBLICATIONS** Auth, Brussels and Lugano, Should you Race to the Courthouse or Race for a Judgment, Am J Comp Law, Vol 0043, 95. **CONTACT ADDRESS** Col of Law, Syracuse Univ, Syracuse, NY, 13210.

HESLEP, ROBERT DURHAM
PERSONAL Born 12/18/1930, Houston, TX, m, 1964, 2 children **DISCIPLINE** PHILOSOPHY OF EDUCATION **EDUCATION** Tex Christian Univ, AB, 55; Univ Chicago, AM, 57, PhD(philos educ), 63. **CAREER** Teacher, Harvard Sch Boys, Chicago, 58-63; instr philos educ, Pestalozzi-Froebel Teachers Col, Chicago, 59-61; assoc prof educ found & philos, Edinboro State Col, 63-65; assoc prof, 65-72, prof philos of educ, Univ GA, 72-, consult, Res for Better Sch, 76-77; adv, Nat Soc for Study Educ, 76-77; mem, Philos of Educ Soc Comn to Analy Am Educ, 74-75. **MEMBERSHIPS** Philos Educ Soc (pres, 76-77); Southeast Philos Educ Soc (pres, 71-72). **RESEARCH** The concept of action; philosophy of mind; political philosophy; moral education. **SELECTED PUBLICATIONS** Auth, Thomas Jefferson & Education, Random, 69; ed, Philosophy of Education, 1971, Philos Educ Soc, 71; co-ed, Social Justice and Preferential Treatment, Univ Ga, 77; auth, The Mental in Education: A Philosophical Study, Univ Ala Press, 81; auth, Education in Democracy, Iowa State Univ Press, 89; auth, Moral Education for Americans, Praeger, 95; auth, Philosophical Thinking in Educational Practice, Praeger, 97. **CONTACT ADDRESS** Col of Educ, Univ of Ga, Athens, GA, 30602-0001. **EMAIL** rheslep@arches.uga.edu

HESS, RICHARD S.
PERSONAL Born 12/17/1954, Lancaster, PA, m, 1996, 3 children **DISCIPLINE** RELIGION **EDUCATION** Wheaton Col, BA, 76; Trinity Evangel Divinity Sch, MDiv, 79, ThM, 80; Hebrew Union Col, PhD, 84. **CAREER** Prof, Denver Sem, 97-; rd, Reohampton Inst London, 95-97; lectr, Glasgow Bibl Col, 89-95; instr, Univ Sheffield, 88-89; guest lectr, St. George's Col, 86; lectr, Loyola Univ, 84-85; lectr, Xavier Univ, 83-84; tutor, Hebrew Union Col, 81-84. **HONORS AND AWARDS** Nat Endowment Hum Fel for Col Tchrs & Independent Scholars, 96-97; Nat Endowment Hum Summer Travel Grant, 90; Tyndale House Res Fel, 86-89, 90; Fulbright Post-Dr Res Fel, 86; Nat Endowment Hum/Am Sch Oriental Res Fel, 85; David Lefkowicz Interfaith Fel, Hebrew Union Col, 79-82; Isaac & Rachel Berg Found Fel, Hebrew Union Col, 81-82; Erna & Julius Krouch Fund Fel, Hebrew Union Col, 82-84. **MEMBERSHIPS** Am Oriental Soc; Am Sch Oriental Res; British Asn Near Eastern Archaeol; Cath Bibl Asn Am; Inst Bibl Res; Int Orgn Study Old Testament; Israel Exploration Soc; Soc Study Old Testament; Soc Bibl Lit. **RESEARCH** Hebrew Bible; Genesis 1-11; Deuteronomigtic history; comparative philology; ancient Near East; West Semitic archives; personal names. **SELECTED PUBLICATIONS** Auth, Joshua: An Introduction and Commentary, 96; auth, Studies in the Personal Names of Genesis 1-11, 93; auth, Amarna Personal Names, 93; co-ed, Making the Old Testament Live, 98; co-ed, Translating the Bible, 98; co-ed, The Lord's Anointed: Interpretation of Old Testament Messianic Texts, 95; co-ed, I Studied Inscriptions from Before the Flood: Ancient Near Eastern Linguistic and Literary Approaches to Genesis 1-11, 94; co-ed, He Swore an Oath: Biblical Themes from Genesis 12-50, 94; auth, The Late Bronze Age Alalakh Texts at the Australian Institute of Archaeology, Buried Hist, March, 98; auth, The Form and Structure of the Solomonic District List in 1 Kings 4:7-19, Crossing Boundaries and Linking Horizons: Studies in Honor of Michael C. Astour, 97; auth, The Dead Sea Scrolls and Higher Criticism of the Hebrew Bible, The Scrolls and the Scriptures: Qumran Fifty Years After, 97; auth, West Semitic Texts and the Book of Joshua, Bull Bibl Res, 97; auth, Getting Personal: What Names in the Bible Teach Us, Bibl Rev, Dec, 97; auth, Hurrians and Other Inhabitants of Late Bronze Age Palestine, Levant, 97; auth, The Image of the Messiah in the Old Testament, Images of Christ: Ancient and Modern, 97; auth, Non-Israelite Personal Names in the Book of Joshua, Cath Bibl Quart, 96; auth, Asherah or Asherata?, Orientalia, 96; auth, A Typology of West Semitic Place Name Lists with Special Reference to Joshua 13-21, Bibl Archaeol, Sept, 96; auth, A Comparison of the Ugarit, Emar and Alalakh Archives, Ugarit, Religion and Culture: Proc of the Int Colloquium on Ugarit, Religion and Culture, 96; auth, Joshua 1-12 as a Centrist Document, Dort ziehen Schiffe dahin... Collected Commun to XIVth Congress of Int Org Study Old Testament, 96; auth, Genesis 1-2 and Recent Studies of Ancient Texts, Sci & Christian Belief, 95; coauth, Alalakh Text 457, Ugarit Forschungen, 94; auth, Achan and Anchor: Names and Wordplay in Joshua 7, Hebrew Annual Rev, 94; auth, Alalakh and the Bible: Obstacle or Contribution?, Scripture & Other Ar-

tifacts: Essays Archael & Bibl in Honor of Philip J. King, 94; auth, Fallacies in the Study of Early Israel: An Onomastic Perspective, Tyndale Bull, 94; auth, One Hundred Fifty Years of Comparative Studies on Genesis 1-11: An Overview, I Studies Inscriptions Before the Flood: Ancient Near Eastern Literary & Linguistic Approaches to Genesis 1-11, 94; auth, Asking Historical Questions of Joshua 13-19: Recent Discussion Concerning the Date of the Boundary Lists, Faith, Tradition, Hist: Old Testament Hist in Its Near Eastern Context, 94. **CONTACT ADDRESS** Dept of Old Testament, Denver Conservative Baptist Sem, PO Box 10000, Denver, CO, 80250-0100. **EMAIL** rick@densem.edu

HESTER, D. MICAH
PERSONAL Born 07/16/1966, Pomona, CA, m, 1993 **DISCIPLINE** PHILOSOPHY **EDUCATION** Pomona Col, BA, 88; Vanderbilt Univ, MA, 95; Phd, 98. **CAREER** Adj Asst Prof, TN State Univ, 93-98. **MEMBERSHIPS** Soc for the Adv of Amer Philo; Assoc of Pract & Prof Ethics; Amer Soc of Bioethics & Humanities; APA **RESEARCH** Bioethics; amer philo; computer ethics. **SELECTED PUBLICATIONS** The Place of Community in Medical Encounters, Jour of Med and Phil, 98; Competition or Community: Ethical Concerns in the Residency Matching Process, JAMA, 98. **CONTACT ADDRESS** 221 37th Ave N, Nashville, TN, 37209-4802. **EMAIL** d.hester@columbia.net

HESTER, JAMES D.
DISCIPLINE RELIGION **EDUCATION** Eastern Baptist Col, BA, 60; Univ Basel, PhD, 66. **CAREER** Asst prof, Univ Redlands, 67-. **HONORS AND AWARDS** Fac Service Awd, 93. **MEMBERSHIPS** Asn Gen Lib Studies; Int Soc Hist Rhet; Soc Biblical Lit; Studiorum Novi Testamentum Soc. **SELECTED PUBLICATIONS** Auth, The Rhetorical Structure of Galatians 1:11-2:14, 84; The Use and Influence of Rhetoric in Galatians 2:1-14, 86; Placing the Blame: The Presence of Epideictic in Galatians 1 and 2, Sheffield Acad, 91. **CONTACT ADDRESS** Dept of Religion, Univ Redlands, 1200 E Colton Ave, PO Box 3090, Redlands, CA, 92373-0999. **EMAIL** hester@uor.edu

HESTER, MARCUS B.
PERSONAL Born 06/20/1937, Raleigh, NC, m, 1998 **DISCIPLINE** PHILOSOPHY **EDUCATION** Wake Forest Col, BA, 60; Vanderbilt Univ, PhD, 64. **CAREER** From instr to assoc prof, 63-76, prof philos, 76-, Wake Forest Univ; fel, coop prog humanities, Univ NC, Chapel Hill, 66-67. **MEMBERSHIPS** Southern Soc Philos & Psychol; Am Soc Aesthet. **RESEARCH** Aesthetics; philosophy of mind; contemporary analytical philosophy. **SELECTED PUBLICATIONS** Auth, The Meaning of Poetic Metaphor, Mouton, 67; art, Purpose In Painting And Action, Am Philos Quart, 1/70; art, Are Paintings And Photographs Inherently Interpretative, J Aesthet & Art Criticism, winter 72; art, Sensibility And Visual Acts, Am Philos Quart, 10/75; art, Aristotle on Function of Man in Relation to Eudaimonia, Hist of Phil Quarterly, 91. **CONTACT ADDRESS** Dept of Philosophy, Wake Forest Univ, PO Box 7332, Winston Salem, NC, 27109-7332. **EMAIL** hpster@wfu.edu

HESTEVOID, H. SCOTT
PERSONAL Born 03/26/1952, Nashville, TN, m, 1979, 2 children **DISCIPLINE** PHILOSOPHY **EDUCATION** Vanderbilt Univ, BA, 74; Brown Univ, AM, 78, PhD, 78. **CAREER** Prof, Univ Ala, 78- . **HONORS AND AWARDS** Richard M. Griffith mem awd, 79, Southern Soc Philos and Psych. **MEMBERSHIPS** SSPP; APA. **RESEARCH** Analytic metaphysics; metaphysics. **SELECTED PUBLICATIONS** Auth, Conjoining, Philos and Phenomen Res, XLI, 81, 371-385; Disjunctive Desert, Amer Philos Quart, 20, 83, 357-363; Justice to Mercy, Philos and Phenomen Res, XLVI, 85, 281-291; Passage and the Presence of Experience, Philos and Phenomen Res, L, 90, 537-552, reprinted in The New Theory of Time, ed, Oaklander and Smith, Yale UP, 94; Berkeley's Theory of Time, Hist of Philos Quart, 7, 90, 179-192; The Concept of Religion, Public Affairs Quart, 5, 91, 149-162; The Anselmian Single-Divine-Attribute Doctrine, Relig Stud (s), 29, 93, 63-77; coauth, On Passage and Persistence, Amer Philos Quart, 31, 94, 269-283. **CONTACT ADDRESS** Dept of Philosophy, Univ of Alabama, PO Box 870218, Tuscaloosa, AL, 35487. **EMAIL** hhestevo@philos.as.ua.edu

HETZEL, OTTO J.
PERSONAL Born 06/02/1933, New York, NY, m, 1957, 3 children **DISCIPLINE** LAW **EDUCATION** Pa State Univ, BA, 55; Yale Univ, JD, 60; Harvard Univ, LLM, 70. **CAREER** Dept atty gen, State of Calif, 60-64 & 65-67; assoc, Hardy, Carley & Love, Palo Alto, Calif, 64-65; asst gen counsel equal opportunity & labor relat, US Dept Housing & Urban Develop, 67-68, assoc gen counsel model cities & govt relat, 68-69; prof law, Wayne State Univ, 70-75, assoc dir, Ctr Urban Studies, 70-72; vis prof, Univ Man, Inst Sci & Technol, 75-76; Prof Law, Wayne State Univ, 76-, Lectr, George Washington Univ, 69-70; consult, US Dept Housing & Urban Develop, 69-72, city of Kansas City, Mo, 72-73 & Urban Inst, Wash, DC, 75-78; ed, Urban Law & Policy, 77-; vis prof, State Univ Utrecht, Holland, 80. **MEMBERSHIPS** Am Bar Asn; Soc Am Law Teachers. **RESEARCH** Urban housing and community development programs; legislative law and process; communications law-cable television. **SELECTED PUBLICATIONS** Auth, Some Historical Lessons for Implementing the Clinton Administrations Empowerment Zones and Enterprise Communities Program--Experiences From the Model-Cities Program, Urban Lawyer, Vol 0026, 94. **CONTACT ADDRESS** Law Sch, Wayne State Univ, Detroit, MI, 48202.

HEXHAM, IRVING
PERSONAL Born 04/14/1943, Whitehaven, England **DISCIPLINE** RELIGION **EDUCATION** Univ Lancaster, BA, 70; Univ Bristol, MA, 72, PhD, 75. **CAREER** Asst prof, Bishop Lonsdale Col, 74-77; asst prof, Regent Col, 77-80; asst prof, Univ Man, 80-84; asst to assoc prof, 84-92, PROF RELIGIOUS STUDIES, UNIV CALGARY, 92-. **MEMBERSHIPS** S African Inst Race Relations; Can Soc Stud Relig; Am Acad Relig; Soc Sci Stud Relig; Berlin Missiological Soc; S African Missiological Soc; Royal Anthrop Inst. **SELECTED PUBLICATIONS** Auth, The Irony of Apartheid, 81; coauth, New Religions as Global Cultures: The Sacralization of the Human, 77; coauth, Understanding Cults and New Religions, 86; auth/comp, A Concise Dictionary of Religion, 93; ed, Texts on Zulu Religion, 86; ed, The Scripture of the Amanazaretha of Ekuphakameni, 94; co-ed, Afro-Christian Religion at the Grassroots in Southern Africa, 91; co-ed, Empirical Studies of African Independent-Indigenous Churches, 92; co-ed, The Oral History and Sacred Traditions of the Nazareth Baptist Church: Volume One-The Story of Isaiah Mdliwamafa Shembe, 96. **CONTACT ADDRESS** Dept of Religious Studies, Univ of Calgary, Calgary, AB, T2N 1N4. **EMAIL** hexham@acs.ucalgary.ca

HEYD, THOMAS
DISCIPLINE PHILOSOPHY **EDUCATION** Univ Calgary, BA, MA; Univ W Ontario, PhD. **CAREER** Instr, Univ Calgary; Univ W Ontario; Univ Alberta; sessional lectr. **RESEARCH** Philosophy of science; aesthetics, environmental philosophy; ethics and history of philosophy. **SELECTED PUBLICATIONS** Pub(s), Intl Philos Quart; Brit Jour Aesthet; Environ Ethics; Jour of the Hist of the Behavioral Sci. **CONTACT ADDRESS** Dept of Philosophy, Victoria Univ, PO Box 3045, Victoria, BC, V8W 3P4.

HICKS, H. BEECHER, JR.
PERSONAL Born 06/17/1944, Baton Rouge, LA, m **DISCIPLINE** THEOLOGY **EDUCATION** Univ of AR Pine Bluff, BA 1964; Colgate Rochester, MDiv 1967, Dr of Ministry 1975; Richmond Virginia Seminary LLD honorary. **CAREER** Second Baptist Church, intern pastorate 1965-68; Irondequoit United Church of Christ, minister to youth 1967-68; Mt Ararat Baptist Church, sr minister 1968-73; Antioch Baptist Church, minister 1973-77; METRO BAPTIST CHURCH, SENIOR MINISTER 1977-; COLGATE ROCHESTER DIVINITY SCHOOL AND UNITED THEOLOGICAL SEMINARY, ADJ PROF. **MEMBERSHIPS** Chmn Bd of Funeral Dirs 1985; vp, Eastern Reg Natl Black Pastors Conf; admin Natl Black Pastors Conf; bd Council for Court Excellence; asst sec Progressive Natl Baptist Convention, Co-chair American Baptist Ministers Council of D.C., pres Kerygma Assoc, A Religious Consulting Service; pres Martin Luther King Fellows, Inc; co-chair Ministers in Partnership (Pregnancy Prevention); board of trustees, United Theological Seminary, Dayton, OH. **SELECTED PUBLICATIONS** "Give Me This Mountain" Houston TX 1976; "Images of the Black Preacher, The Man Nobody Knows" Valley Forge PA 1977; "The Black Church as a Support System for Black Men on the Simon Syndrome" Howard Univ; Comm Leaders & Noteworthy Amers 1977; Gubernatorial Citation for Serv 1977; Martin Luther King Fellowship in Black Church Studies 1972-75; Preaching Through A Storm Zondervan Press 1987; author, Correspondence with a Cripple from Tarsus, Zondervan Press, 1990. **CONTACT ADDRESS** Metropolitan Baptist Church, 1225 R St NW, Washington, DC, 20009.

HICKS, STEPHEN R.C.
PERSONAL Toronto, ON, Canada **DISCIPLINE** PHILOSOPHY **EDUCATION** Univ Guelph, BA, MA, 85; Ind Univ, PhD, 92. **CAREER** Assoc prof & chemn, Rockford Col, 92-. **MEMBERSHIPS** Amer Philos Asn; Soc for Bus Ethics; Ayn Rand Soc. **RESEARCH** Objectivism; Intellectual history; Business ethics. **SELECTED PUBLICATIONS** Auth, Readings for Logical Analysis, WW Norton & Co, 98. **CONTACT ADDRESS** Dept. of Philosophy, Rockford Col, Rockford, IL, 61108. **EMAIL** shicks@rockford.edu

HIERS, RICHARD H.
DISCIPLINE LAW **EDUCATION** Yale Univ, BA, BD, MA, PhD; Univ Fla, JD. **CAREER** Prof Rel and aff prof Law; Univ Fla, 61-; articles; law clerk, US 5th, Circuit Judge Jerre S. Williams. **MEMBERSHIPS** Fla Bar Public Interest Law Sect, Comt on Individual Rights and Responsibilities; Bar Asn 5th Fed Circuit; US Dist Ct, Western Div Tex; adv commt, J Law and Rel; Order of the Coif; Phi Kappa Phi. **RESEARCH** Law, Ethics & Social Policy, Employment Discrimination. **SELECTED PUBLICATIONS** Ed, Fla Law Rev **CONTACT ADDRESS** School of Law, Univ of Florida, PO Box 117625, Gainesville, FL, 32611-7625. **EMAIL** hiers@law.ufl.edu

HIGGINS, KATHLEEN MARIE
PERSONAL Born 10/15/1954, Jacksonville, FL, m, 1990 **DISCIPLINE** PHILOSOPHY **EDUCATION** Univ Missouri-Kansas City, music, 77; Yale Univ, MA, 78, MPhil, 79, PhD, philos, 82. **CAREER** Instr, 82-83, asst prof, 83-89, assoc prof, 89-95, prof, 95-, Univ Texas at Austin; visiting asst prof, Univ Calif Riverside, 86-87; visiting sr lecturer, May - June 89, June - July 90, June 91, June 92, visiting prof, June 93, June 94, June 95, May 96, May 98, Univ Auckland, New Zealand. **HONORS AND AWARDS** Univ Res Inst Summer Res Award, Univ Texas at Austin, 85; resident scholar, Rockefeller Found Bellagio Study and Conf Center, 93; Outstanding Academic Books of 1988-89 (Nietzsche's Zarathustra), Choice; Univ Research Inst Faculty Award, fall 94; visiting fellow, Australian Natl Univ Philos Dept and Canberra School Music, June-Aug 97. **MEMBERSHIPS** Amer Philos Assn, Comm Status Women, 95-98; Amer Soc Aesthetics; Humanities Tech Assn; North Amer Nietzsche Soc, Exec Comm, 97-; Intl Assn Aesthetics. **RESEARCH** Nineteenth and twentieth century continental philosophy; aesthetics; philosophy of psychology; philosophy of music; ethics; feminism. **SELECTED PUBLICATIONS** Coauth, A Passion for Wisdom, 97; auth, "Death and the Skeleton," in Death and Philosophy, 98; auth, "Nietzsche's Aesthetics: Nietzsche's Literary Style," in Encyclopedia of Aesthetics, 98; coauth, "Emotions: Historical Overview," in The Encyclopedia of Aesthetics, 98; auth, Comic Relief: Nietzche's Frohliche Wissenschaft, 99. **CONTACT ADDRESS** Dept of Philosophy, Univ of Texas at Austin, Austin, TX, 78712. **EMAIL** plac645@utxvms.cc.utexas.edu

HIGH, DALLAS MILTON
PERSONAL Born 11/14/1931, Van Wert, OH, m, 1957, 3 children **DISCIPLINE** PHILOSOPHY **EDUCATION** Ohio Wesleyan Univ, BA, 56; Yale Univ, BD, 59; Duke Univ, PhD(philos relig), 65. **CAREER** From asst prof to assoc prof philos & relig, Hiram Col, 64-69; assoc prof, 69-72, chmn dept, 69-77, Prof Philos, Univ KY, 72-, Danforth assoc 71-; Rockefeller Found res fel, 75-76. **MEMBERSHIPS** Am Philos Asn; Am Acad Relig; Southern Soc Philos & Psychol; Soc Health & Human Values; Soc for Values in Higher Educ. **RESEARCH** Philosophy of religion; health and values; Ludwig Wittgenstein. **SELECTED PUBLICATIONS** Auth, Wittgenstein and Kierkegaard--Religion, Individuality, and Philosophical Method, Int J Philos Relig, Vol 0034, 93; Ethical and Legal Issues in Conducting Research Involving Elderly Subjects, Behavioral Sci Law, Vol 0013, 95. **CONTACT ADDRESS** Dept of Philos, Univ of Ky, 500 S Limestone St, Lexington, KY, 40506-0003.

HIGHFIELD, RONALD CURTIS
PERSONAL Born 06/01/1951, m, 2 children **DISCIPLINE** RELIGION **EDUCATION** Harding Univ, BA, 75; Harding Grad Sch Rel, MTh, 79; Rice Univ, MA, PhD, 88. **CAREER** Campus min, Col Church of Christ, 79-80; yputh min, Bering Drive Church of Christ, 81-84; campus min, Univ Houston, 86-88; adjunct instr, Univ St Thomas, 89; assoc prof, 89-. **HONORS AND AWARDS** Post doc fel, Rice Univ, 88; first prize, Ted Ward wrtg award contest, 84., Co-coord, Restoration Theol Res Fel. **MEMBERSHIPS** Mem, Am Acad Rel; Christian Theol Res Fel. **SELECTED PUBLICATIONS** Auth, Barth and Rahner: Toward an Ecumenical Understanding of Sin and Evil. Peter Lang, 89; The Superstitions of the Modern Mind Examined, Jour Ctr Christianity and Cult, 96; Children's Education and the Kingdom of God in America, Leaven Jour, 95; The Freedom to Say "NO"?, Karl Rahner's Doctrine of Sin, Theol Studies, 95; An Essay on the Christian Mission in Higher Education, Fac Dialogue, 95; Galileo, Scientific Creationism and Biblical Hermeneutics, Studies in Honor of Thomas H. Olbricht on the Occasion of His Sixty-Fifth Birthday , Restoration Quart, 94; rev, A Review of The Second Incarnation: A Theology for the 21st Century Church, by Rubel Shelly and Randall J Harris, Howard Pub Co, 92, Restoration Quart, 94. **CONTACT ADDRESS** Dept of Relig, Pepperdine Univ, 24255 Pacific Coast Hwy, Malibu, CA, 90263.

HIGHTOWER, ANTHONY
PERSONAL Atlanta, GA, s **DISCIPLINE** LAW **EDUCATION** Clark Coll, Atlanta GA, BA, 1983; Univ of Iowa, Iowa City IA, JD, 1986. **CAREER** Self-employed, College Park GA, Attorney, 1986-; Clark Coll, Atlanta GA, teacher, 1988-; City of College Park, College Park, GA, city councilman, 1986-90, mayor pro-tem, 1990; Clark Atlanta Univ, Atlanta, GA, adjunct prof, 1988-; State of GA, Atlanta, GA, state rep, 1991-. **HONORS AND AWARDS** Selected for Membership, Alpha Kappa Mu Honor Soc, 1981, Pi Gamma Mu Intl Honor Soc, 1981; Participated and Completed Inaugural Class of South Fulton Leadership, 1987; Golden Rule Awards Panel, United Way/J C Penny, 1988; Appreciation Award, Metro Atlanta Private Indus Council, 1988; Political Service Award, Delta Sigma Theta Sorority Inc, 1988; Leadership Institute for Municipal Elected Officials, Univ of GA, 1989. **MEMBERSHIPS** Mem, NAACP, 1979-, Alpha Phi Alpha Frat, 1980-; bd mem, Clark Coll, 1982-83; natl bd mem, Alpha Phi Alpha Frat Inc, 1982-83; mem, State Bar of Georgia, 1986-, Natl Bar Assn, 1986-, Amer Bar Assn, 1986-, Natl League of Cities, 1986-, Natl Black Caucus of Local Elected Officials, 1986-, Georgia Municipal Assn, 1986-; bd mem, Fulton County Public Safety Training Center, 1989-. **CONTACT ADDRESS** 1568 Willingham Dr, Suite 212A, College Park, GA, 30337.

HILBERT, DAVID
DISCIPLINE PHILOSOPHY **EDUCATION** Stanford Univ, PhD. **CAREER** Assoc prof, Univ IL at Chicago. **RESEARCH** Include philos of mind; philos of perception; color; philos of biology. **SELECTED PUBLICATIONS** Auth, Color and Color Perception, CSLI, 87; What is Color Vision?, Philos Studies, 92. **CONTACT ADDRESS** Philos Dept, Univ Illinois Chicago, S Halsted St, PO Box 705, Chicago, IL, 60607. **EMAIL** hilbert@uic.edu

HILDEBRAND, DAVID
PERSONAL Born 11/21/1964, New York, NY, m, 1997 **DISCIPLINE** PHILOSOPHY **EDUCATION** Univ Penn, BA, 87; Univ Tex, PhD, 97. **CAREER** Instr, Univ Tex Austin, 95-96; adjunct prof, Univ Tex, 97-99; adjunct prof, Austin Community Col, 97-99. **HONORS AND AWARDS** Travel grant, JFK Inst, Berlin. **MEMBERSHIPS** Amer Philos Asn; Soc for the Adv of Amer Philos. **RESEARCH** Figures in American philosophy, metaphysics & epistemology; Pedagogy in college teaching; Pragmatism; Process philosophy; Literary criticism; Philosophy of science. **SELECTED PUBLICATIONS** Auth, Genuine Doubt and the Community in Peirce's Theory of Inquiry, Southwest Philos Res, vol 12, no 1, 33-43, 96; auth, Was Kenneth Burke a Pragmatist?, Trans of the Charles S. Peirce Soc, vol 31, no 3, 632-658, 95; auth, Kimball on Whitehead on Perception. Process Studies, vol 22, no 1, 13-20, 93. **CONTACT ADDRESS** 2300 Enfield Rd., Apt. D, Austin, TX, 78703. **EMAIL** hilde@uts.cc.utexas.edu

HILDRETH, RICHARD GEORGE
PERSONAL Born 10/11/1943, Hollywood Beach, FL **DISCIPLINE** ENVIRONMENTAL & PROPERTY LAW **EDUCATION** Univ Mich, BSE, 65, JD, 68; Oxford Univ, dipl, 69. **CAREER** Atty, Steinhart Law Firm, 69-72; prof, Univ San Diego, 73-78; Prof Law, Univ Ore, 78-, Vis scholar, Harvard Law Sch, 75-76. **MEMBERSHIPS** Coastal Soc. **RESEARCH** Ocean and coastal law. **SELECTED PUBLICATIONS** Auth, Coastal and Maritime Zone Planning and Management--Transnational and Legal Considerations, Ocean Develop Int Law, Vol 0027, 96; Oceans Management Policy--The Strategic Dimension, Ocean Develop Int Law, Vol 0027, 96. **CONTACT ADDRESS** Sch of Law, Univ of Ore, Eugene, OR, 97403.

HILL, CHARLES
DISCIPLINE NEW TESTAMENT **EDUCATION** Cambridge Univ, PhD. **CAREER** Instr, Northwestern Col; assoc prof-. **SELECTED PUBLICATIONS** Auth, Regnum Caelorem: Patterns of Future Hope in Early Christianity, Oxford Early Christian Stud, Oxford UP, 92; The Marriage of Montanism and Millennialism, Studia Patristica XXXI, 92; Study Notes to I and II Thessalonians, The New Geneva Study Bible, Thomas Nelson Publ, 95; rev, Review of Gregory C. Jenks, The Origins and Development of the Antichrist Myth, Jour Theol Stud 43, 92. **CONTACT ADDRESS** Dept of New Testament, Reformed Theol Sem, 1015 Maitland Ctr Commons, Maitland, FL, 32751.

HILL, CHRISTOPHER
DISCIPLINE PHILOSOPHY OF LANGUAGE **EDUCATION** Harvard Univ, PhD. **CAREER** Philos, Univ Ark **HONORS AND AWARDS** Nat Hum Ctr fel. **SELECTED PUBLICATIONS** Auth, Sensations, Cambridge Univ Press, 91. **CONTACT ADDRESS** Univ Ark, Fayetteville, AR, 72701. **EMAIL** sandrae@comp.uark.edu

HILL, HARVEY
PERSONAL Born 09/07/1965, Atlanta, GA, m, 1992, 1 child **DISCIPLINE** RELIGION **EDUCATION** Yale Univ, BA, 87; Candler Sch of Theol, MTS, 91; Emory Univ, PhD, 96 **CAREER** Asst Inst, Emory Univ/Candler School of Theol, 95-96; Asst Prof Relig and Philos, Berry Coll, 96-present. **HONORS AND AWARDS** Graduate Fel, 91-94; Dissertation Travel Grant, 95; Bernadotte E. Schmitt Grant, Amer Hist Assoc, 95; Thomas Aquinas Fel, 95-96; Dean's Teaching Fel, 95-96. **RESEARCH** Nineteeth-century European and Amer Relig; Roman Catholic Modernism; The Oxford Movement; Anglican and Catholic Studies; Biblical Hermeneutics **SELECTED PUBLICATIONS** Auth, Anglican and Episcopal History 62, Worship in Ecclesiology of William White, 93; Coauth, Anglican Theol Review 76, Literary Art in the Moral Theology of Jeremy Taylor, 94; Auth, For All the Saints, Sarah Dickey, Leo the Great, Order of St. Luke Publications, 95; Auth, Jour for the History of Modern Theol, La science catholique: Alfred Loisy's Program of Historical Theology, 96; Auth, Church History, French Politics and Alfred Loisy's Modernism, forthcoming 1998; Auth, American National Biography, Ferdinand Cartwright Ewer, Thomas Gallaudet, Charles Chapman Grafton, John Stark Ravenscroft, Oxford Univ Press, forthcoming, 99. **CONTACT ADDRESS** Religion and Philosophy Dept, Berry Col, PO Box 550, Mt. Berry, GA, 30149. **EMAIL** hhill@berry.edu

HILL, JACQUELINE R.
PERSONAL Born 05/23/1940, Topeka, KS, d **DISCIPLINE** LAW **EDUCATION** Univ of CA Berkeley, BA 1957-62; Univ of Southern CA, Teachers Credential 1965-66; Southwestern Univ School of Law, JD (cum laude) 1968-72; California State Univ, Long Beach, Certitificate in Calligraphy 1987-89. **CAREER** Univ of CA Lawrence Radiation Lab, admin exec 1963-66; LA Unified School Dist, math teacher 1966-1973; LA Comm Coll Dist, evening instr 1972-75; Los Angeles County, deputy dist atty, 1973-; California State University-Long Beach, instructor, 1990-91. **HONORS AND AWARDS** Legal Book Awards Southwestern Univ School of Law 1969-72. **MEMBERSHIPS** CA State Bar; Amer Bar Association; CA State Adv Grp Juvenile Justice and Delinquency Prevention 1983-. **CONTACT ADDRESS** Los Angeles County, 210 W Temple St, Los Angeles, CA, 90012.

HILL, JASON D.
DISCIPLINE THEOLOGY **EDUCATION** Georgia State Univ, BA, 91; Purdue Univ, MA, 95, PhD, 98. **CAREER** ASST PROF PHILOS, SOUTHERN ILL UNIV. **CONTACT ADDRESS** Dept of Philos Studies, So Illinois Univ, Peck Hall, Edwardsville, IL, 62026. **EMAIL** jahill@siue.edu

HILL, R. KEVIN
DISCIPLINE PHILOSOPHY **EDUCATION** Ill Univ, PhD. **CAREER** Asst prof, Northwestern Univ. **SELECTED PUBLICATIONS** Auth, Foucault's Critique of Heidegger, Philos Today, 90; MacIntyre's Nietzsche, Int Studies in Philos, 92; Ultimate Skepsis, Int Studies in Philos, 97; Genealogy, Routledge Encyclopedia of Philos, 98. **CONTACT ADDRESS** Dept of Philosophy, Northwestern Univ, 1801 Hinman, Evanston, IL, 60208.

HILL, RENEE AFANAN
DISCIPLINE PHILOSOPHY **EDUCATION** Univ MI, Ann Arbor, BA, 74; Eastern MI Univ, Ypsilanti, MA, 78; Univ VA, Charlottesville, MA, 90, PhD, 95. **CAREER** Asst prof, VA State Univ, 94-& WV State Col Inst, 92-94; tchg asst, Univ VA, Charlottesville, 91; exec dir, Richmond Black Stud Found, 88-89; dir std activ, VA Union Univ, 85-87 & VP, Stud Aff, 86-87; instr, VA Union Univ, 81-85: instr, adj, VA Commonwealth Univ, Richmond, 83- 83; asst dir, Nataki Talibah Sch house, Detroit, 78-81. **HONORS AND AWARDS** Nat Achievement Scholar, 70; Inducted into Phi Beta Kappa, 74; SHEV fel, 87-88, 88-89, 89-90, 90-91 & 91-92 . **MEMBERSHIPS** APA; Southern Soc Philos Psychol; VA Philos Asn; WV Philos Asn. **RESEARCH** Polit philos; philos of mind; non-western philos; philos for children. **SELECTED PUBLICATIONS** Auth, Sins of the Fathers: Compensation Through the Generations, W Va Philos Asn, W Va State Col, 94; Compensation and Serendipitous Events, W Va Philos Asn, W Va Univ, Morgantown, 93; Compensatory Justice Versus Existence: A Comment on Morris, Va Philos Asn, William & Mary Col, 93. **CONTACT ADDRESS** Dept of Hist and Philos, Virginia State Univ, 1 Hayden Dr, Petersburg, VA, 23806. **EMAIL** renhill@aol.com

HILL, ROSCOE EARL
PERSONAL Born 07/04/1936, Lincoln, NE, m, 1959, 2 children **DISCIPLINE** PHILOSOPHY **EDUCATION** Carleton Col, BA, 58; Univ Chicago, MA, 63, PhD, 68. **CAREER** Instr Philos, Carleton Col, 61-62; asst prof, Yale Univ, 67-73; asst prof, 73-80, assoc prof Philos, Univ Denver, 80-; dean of Arts, Humanities, Social Sciences, 90-98. **MEMBERSHIPS** Am Philos Asn; Am Soc Legal & Polit Philos; Soc Relig Higher Educ. **RESEARCH** Philosophy of law; ethics; philosophy of mind. **SELECTED PUBLICATIONS** Coauth, Affirmative School Integration, Sage Publ, 69; Legal validity and legal obligation, Yale Law, J, 71; Virtue for its own sake, Personalist, 72. **CONTACT ADDRESS** Dept of Philosophy, Univ of Denver, 2199 S University, Denver, CO, 80210-4711. **EMAIL** rhill@du.edu

HILL, THOMAS E.
PERSONAL Born 03/25/1937, Atlanta, GA, m, 1981, 2 children **DISCIPLINE** PHILOSOPHY **EDUCATION** Harvard, BA, 59; Oxford, BPhil, 61; Harvard, MA, 64, PhD, 66. **CAREER** Johns Hopkins Univ, 65-66; Asst Prof, Pomona Col, 66-68; Asst, Assoc, Prof, Univ Calif LA, 68-84; Kenan Prof, Univ NC at Chapel Hill, 84-. **HONORS AND AWARDS** Rhodes Schol, 59-62; Danforth Fellow, 59-65; Tanner Lecturer, Stanford, 94; Dist Tchng Award for Post-BA Instr, 78. **MEMBERSHIPS** Am Philos Asn; N Am Kant Soc. **RESEARCH** Ethics; political philosophy; Kant. **SELECTED PUBLICATIONS** Autonomy and Self-Respect, Cambridge Univ Press, 91; Dignity and Practical Reason in Kant's Moral Theory, Cornell Univ Press, 92. **CONTACT ADDRESS** Dept of Philos, Univ N. Carolina at Chapel Hill, Chapel Hill, NC, 27599-3125. **EMAIL** thill@email.unc.edu

HILLAR, MARIAN
PERSONAL Born 03/22/1938, Poland, m, 1970, 2 children **DISCIPLINE** PHILOSOPHY **EDUCATION** Univ Medical School of Danzig, MD Summa cum laude, 56-72, PhD, 66. **CAREER** Univ Med School of Danzig, Biochemistry, instr to asst prof 58-69; Baylor Col of Med, sr research assoc, adj asst prof, 69-75; Texas Southern Univ, asst prof, assoc prof, prof 71-85, dir lab of molecular biology and biochemistry, 71-85; Universita degli Studi di Camerino, Italy, vis prof, 80; Ponce School of Medicine, PR, prof, dept chemn of biochem, 85-86, prof & dir of center for Philo & Socinian Studies, 86-, Corresponding Ed, Bez Dogmatu, Warsaw, 93-. **HONORS AND AWARDS** Pol Acad of Science, Research Award, 65; Univ Med School of Danzig, biomed award, listed in: Amer Men & Wom of Science, 75; Who is Who, in: Frontiers of Science, 82, Southwest, 82, Theology and Science, 92 & American Education, 93. **MEMBERSHIPS** BS, The Biochem Society, AAAS, AHA, PIASA, AF, IRAS, SAAP, APA. **RESEARCH** Hist of W and E Philo; hist of relig and relig doctrines; orig of Christianity and doctrine; socinianism **SELECTED PUBLICATIONS** Auth, Biochemical Energetics, NIH & TSU, 77; Energetics and Kinetic Mechanisms of Enzyme Function, TSU, 92; co-edit, Ethics and Humanism: Anthology of Essays, Amer Human Assoc, Houston, 92; Humanism and Social Issues, co-edit, AHA, Houston, 93; Contributors to the Philosophy of Humanism: Anthology of Essays, AHA, Houston, 94; The Philosophy of Humanism and the Issues of Today: Anthology of Essays, AHA, Houston, 95; The Case of Michael Servetus (1511-1553)- The Turning Point in the Struggle for Freedom of Conscience, Edwin Mellen Press, 97, articles, The Logos and Its Function in the Writings of Philo of Alexandria: Greek Interpretation of the Hebrew Thought and Foundations of Christianity, Parts I & II, in: A Jour from the Rad Reform, A Testimony to Biblical Unitarianism, vol 7, no 4, 98. **CONTACT ADDRESS** Dept of Philosophy, 9330 Bankside, Houston, TX, 77031-1713. **EMAIL** noam@swbell.net

HILLERS, DELBERT ROY
PERSONAL Born 11/07/1932, Chester, SD, m, 1958, 2 children **DISCIPLINE** OLD TESTAMENT, SEMITIC LANGUAGES **CAREER** Instr Hebrew, Concordia Sr Col, 58-60; from asst prof to assoc prof Hebrew & Old Testament, 63-70, Prof Semitic Lang, Johns Hopkins Univ, 70-, Ann prof, Am Sch Orient Res, Jerusalem, 68-69; Am Philos Soc grant, 68-69. **MEMBERSHIPS** Soc Bibl Lit; Am Orient Soc. **RESEARCH** Northwest Semitic languages; Old Testament. **SELECTED PUBLICATIONS** Auth, Textbook Of Aramaic Documents From Ancient-Egypt, Cath Biblical Quarterly, Vol 0057, 95. **CONTACT ADDRESS** Dept of Near Eastern Studies, Johns Hopkins Univ, 3400 N Charles St, Baltimore, MD, 21218.

HILLIARD, DAVID C.
PERSONAL Born 06/22/1937, Framingham, MA, m, 1974 **DISCIPLINE** LAW **EDUCATION** Tufts Univ, BS, 59; Univ Chicago, JD, 62. **CAREER** Adjunct prof, Northwestern Univ School of Law, 71-, chmn, Symposium on Intellectual & Law, 87-. **MEMBERSHIPS** Am Bar Asn; Am Col of Trial Lawyers. **RESEARCH** Intellectual law. **SELECTED PUBLICATIONS** Auth, Trademarks and Unfair Competition, Matthew Bender, 3rd ed, 98; Trademarks and Unfair Competiton Deskbook, 2nd ed, 98. **CONTACT ADDRESS** 1320 N State Parkway, Chicago, IL, 60610.

HILLMER, MARK
DISCIPLINE OLD TESTAMENT **EDUCATION** Northwestern Col, BA; 57; Concordia Sem, BD, 62; Univ Wis, MA, 63; Hebrew Union Col, PhD. **CAREER** Vis prof, St. John's Univ, 70-71; vis asst prof, Concordia Tchr(s) Col; asst prof, Thiel Col, 66-67; assoc prof, 67; Louise Grunow prof, 82. **HONORS AND AWARDS** Fulbright scholar, Univ Heidelberg., Asst pastor, Grace Lutheran Church, Cincinnati, 63-77 **MEMBERSHIPS** Mem, Soc Bibl Lit; Cath Bible Soc; Lutheran Coun, USA Consult on the Holy Spirit, 76-77. **SELECTED PUBLICATIONS** Contrib, Ezekiel notes, New Intl Version Study Bible, 85; Ezekiel, Minor Prophets, Lamentations, and Ecclesiastes, New Intl Version Reference Edition, 83; transl, Ruth, Malachi, and Ecclesiastes, New Intl Version, 78. **CONTACT ADDRESS** Dept of Old Testament, Luther Sem, 2481 Como Ave, St. Paul, MN, 55108. **EMAIL** mhillmer@luthersem.edu

HIMES, MICHAEL J.
PERSONAL Born 05/12/1947, New York, NY, s **DISCIPLINE** CHRISTIAN THEOLOGY **EDUCATION** Cathedral Col, Brooklyn, NY, BA, 68; Sem of the Immaculate Conception, Huntington, NY, Master of Divinity, 72; Univ of Chicago, PhD, 81. **CAREER** Prof, Sem of the Immaculate Conception, 77-87; from asst acad dean to acad dean, Sem of the Immaculate Conception, 77-87, assoc prof, Univ of Notre Dame, 87-93; collegiate dir, Univ of Notre Dame, 91-93; from assoc prof to prof, Boston Col, 93-. **HONORS AND AWARDS** Divinity Sch of the Univ of Chicago Fel, 75, 76, 77; Dr of Letters, honoris causa, conferred by St Joseph's Col, NY, 92; Catholic Press Asn Book Award in Theol, 94; Notre Dame Social Concerns Award, Ctr for Soc Concerns of the Univ of Notre Dame, 95; Cath Press Asn Book Award in Theol, 98; Sophia Award for Contribs to Cath Theol, Wash Theol Union, 99. **MEMBERSHIPS** Am Acad of Relig; AHA; Am Soc of Church Hist; Cath Hist Soc of Am; Cath Theol Soc of Am. **RESEARCH** History of theology from the seventeenth century to the present; contemporary Catholic theology. **SELECTED PUBLICATIONS** Auth, Holiness and Finitude: Creaturely Spirituality, in PACE 19, 90; Tragedy and the Goodness of Creatureliness, in PACE 19, 90; Incarnational Spirituality and the Terror of Time, in PACE 19, 90; The Trinity and Creaturely Spirituality, in PACE 19, 90; The Intrinsic Sacramentality of Marriage: The Theological Ground for the Inseparability of Validity and Sacramentality in Marriage, in The Jurist 50, 1, 90; Our Amazing Dignity: An

Address to the National Federation of Catholic Physicians' Guilds, in The Linacre Quart 58, #3, 91; Catholicism as Integral Humanism: Christian Participation in Pluralistic Moral Education, in The Challenge of Pluralism: Education, Politics, and Values, ed. F. Clark Power and D.K. Lapsley, 92; Historical Theology as Wissenschaft: Johann Sebastian Drey and the Structure of Theology, in Revisioning the Past: Prospects in Hist Theol, ed. M. Potter Engel and W.E. Wyman, 92; The Ecclesiological Significance of Reception of Doctrine, in The Heytrop Journal 33, #2, 92; Doing theTruth in Love: Conversations about God, Relationships and Service, 95; Living Conversation: Higher Education in a Catholic Context, in Conversations 8, 95; 'A Great Theologian of Our Time': Moehler on Schleiermacher, in The Heythrop Journal 37, #1, 96; Talking with Contemporary American Culture: A Catholic Starting Point, in Evangelization, Culture and Catholic Identity, ed. D.M. McCarron and H.B. Bumpus, 96; Divinizing the Church: Strauss and Barth on Moehler's Ecclesiology, in The Legacy of the Tuebingen Sch, ed. D.J. Dietrich and M.J. Himes, 97; Why Do We Need a Church?, in The Furrow 48, 97; Ongoing Incarnation: Johann Adam Moehler and the Beginnings of Modern Ecclesiology, 97. **CONTACT ADDRESS** Dept of Theology, Boston Col, Chestnut Hill, MA, 02167-3806.

HINDERER, WALTER
PERSONAL Born 09/03/1934, Ulm, Germany, m, 1966 **DISCIPLINE** GERMAN LITERATURE/PHILOSOPHY **EDUCATION** Abitur, Kepler Gymnasium, Ulm, 54; Univ Tubingen, German & Eng Lit, European History & Phil, 54-55; Univ Munich, 55-60, PhD, 60. **CAREER** Dir, Acad Div, 61-66, R. Piper & Co (publ), Munich, 61-66; asst prof, German, 66-69, Penn St Univ; assoc prof, German, 69-71, Univ CO; vis prof, 70-71, Stanford Univ; prof, German, 71-78, Univ MD; prof, German, 78-, Princeton Univ. **HONORS AND AWARDS** Fel, Inst for Res in Humanities, Univ WI, 76-77; DAAD Res Grant, 84; Fel, Inst for Advanced Study Berlin, 85-86; Fel, Franz Rosenzweig Res Center, 95, Hebrew Univ; Order of Merit of the Fed Rep of Germany, 95; Alexander von Humboldt Award, 98. **MEMBERSHIPS** Intl Vereinigung fur Germanische Sprach und Lit; Modern Language Asn; AATG; Schiller-Gesellschaft; Buchner-Gesellschaft; Heine-Gesellschaft; Gesellschaft fur Interkulturelle Germanistik. **RESEARCH** German & European lit of the 18th, 19th, and 20th centuries; concepts and ideas of German drama; political poetry; politics and lit; German soc and cult history; rhetoric and oratory; lit theory; poetics and aesthetics; history of criticism. **SELECTED PUBLICATIONS** Auth, Arbeit an der Gegenwart. Zur deutschen Literatur nach 1945, Wurzburg: Verlag Konigshausen und Neumann, 94; ed, Brechts Dramen, Intrepretationen, Verlag Philipp Reclam jun, 95; ed, Kleists Dramen Literaturstudium, Interpretationen, Verlag Philipp Reclam jun, 97; ed, Codierungen von Liebe in der Kinstperiode, Verlag Konigshausen & Neumann, 97; auth, Von der Idee des Menschen, Uber Friedrich Schiller, Verlag Konigshausen & Neumann, 98; ed, Kleists Erzahlungen, Literaturstudium, Interpretationen, Reclam Verlag, 98; auth, Die Rhetorik der Parabel. Zu ihrem asthetischen Funktionszuusammenhang und Funktionswechsel bei Friedrich Schiller, Fabel und Parabel Kulturgeschichtliche Prozesse im 18, Jahrhundert. 94; auth, Die Depotenzierung der Vernunft: Kompensationsmuster im praromantischen und romantischen Diskurs, Romantiches Erzahlen, Verlag Konigshausen & Neumann, 95; auth, Den Dichtern geht es wie dem Araukaner, Anmerkungen zu Gunter Kunerts Poetik, Kunert Werkstatt, Materialien und Studien zu Gunter Kunerts literarischem Werk, Aisthesis Verlag, 95; auth, Das Rocheln der Mona Lisa. Aspeckt von Ernst Jandels Lyrik im Kontext der sechziger Jahre, Text & Kriktik. Zeitschrift fur Literatur, 96; auth, Die Entmundigung der Mundigkeit. Zum Paradigmawechsel eines anthropologischen Konzepts im philosophischen und literarischen Diskurs der Kinstperiode, Lit und Erfahrungswandel 1789-1930, Intl Corvey-Symposiums 9 & 12, 93; auth, Im babylonischen Turm, oder: Steine aus dem Glashaus, Amerikas Kampf um den Kanon und um kulturelle Einheit, Neue Rundschau. Der postkoloniale Blick. Eine neue Weltliteratur?, Jahrgang 96; auth, Das Reich der Schatten In Interpretationen. Gedichte von Friedrich Schiller, Stuttgart Philipp Reclam Verlag, 96; auth, Torquato Tasso, Goethe-Handbuch Vol II, JB Metzler Verlag, 96; auth, Literatur als Anweisung zum Fremdverstehen, Deutsch und fur Asien, IDV-Regionaltagung Asien - Beijing, 94, Intl Cul Pub, 96; ed, Zur Liebesauffassung der Kinstperiode, Codierungen von Liebe in der Kinstperiode, Verlag Konigshausen & Neumann, 97; ed, Liebessemantik als Provokation, Codierunger von Liebe in der Kunstperiode, Verlag Konigshausen & Neumann, 97; ed, Prinz Friedrich von Homburg. Zweideutige Vorfalle, Kleists Dramen, Literaturstudium, Interpretationen, Verlag Philipp Reclam jun, 97; auth, Literarisch-Asthetische Auftakte zur Romantischen Musik, Jahrbuch der deutschen Schillergesellschaft, 1997, Alfred Kroner Verlag, 97; auth, Das Killektivindividuum Nation im deutschen Kiontext. Zu seinem Bedeutungswandel im vor-und nachrevolutionaren Diskurs, Volk-Nation-Europa. Zur Romantisierung und Entromantisierung politischer Begriffe, Verlag Konigshausen & Neumann, 98; ed, Die heilige Cacilie oder die Gewalt der Musik, Kleists Erzahlungen. Literaturstudium, Interpretationen, Reclam Verlag, 98. **CONTACT ADDRESS** Dept of Germanic Lang and Lit, Princeton Univ, 230 E Pyne, Princeton, NJ, 08544-5264. **EMAIL** Hinderer@Princeton.edu

HINDS, LENNOX S.
PERSONAL Port of Spain, Trinidad and Tobago, m **DISCIPLINE** LAW **EDUCATION** City Coll, BS; Rutgers School of Law, JD 1972. **CAREER** Natl Conf Of Black Lawyers, natl dir; Prisoner's Rights Organization Defense, dir 1971-72; Heritage Fnd, dir 1969-72; Citgo Corp, rsch sect chief 1964-69; Rutgers State Univ, prof of criminal law, chmn Administration of Justice Program, currently. **HONORS AND AWARDS** J Skelly Wright Civil Rights Award; Assn of Black Law Students Community Service Award 1973; Distguished Alumnus Award Black Amer Law Students 1974. **MEMBERSHIPS** Permanent del UN Non-Govt Organization; Intl Assn of Democratic Lawyers; Intl Bd, Organization of Non-Govt Organizations; NJ Bar Assn; Committee on Courts & Criminal Procedure; Natl Minority Adv Commn for Criminal Justice; Natl Adv Council for Child Abuse; bd mem Society Mobilization Legal Project; past natl secretary Black-American Law Students Assn; past bd mem Law Students Civil Rights Research Council; State Bar of New York, New Jersey. **SELECTED PUBLICATIONS** numerous publications. **CONTACT ADDRESS** Administration of Justice Program, Rutgers Univ, New Brunswick, NJ, 08903.

HINES, MARY E.
DISCIPLINE RELIGIOUS STUDIES **EDUCATION** Emmanuel Col, BA; Univ St. Michael's Col, MA, PhD. **CAREER** Relig, Emmanuel Col. **MEMBERSHIPS** Cath Theol Soc Am; Am Acad Relig; Col Theol Soc; Boston Theol Soc; N Am Acad Ecumenists; Anglican Roman Cath Consultation US. **SELECTED PUBLICATIONS** Auth, The Transformation of Dogma: An Introduction to Karl Rahner on Doctrine. New York: Paulist Press, 89; Rahnerian Spirituality: Implications for Ministry, In Handbook of Spirituality for Ministers, Paulist Press, 95; Community for Liberation: Church. In Freeing Theology: Contemporary Catholic Theology in Feminist Perspective, Harper, 93; Introduction to Ecclesiology, In The Church in the Nineties: Its Legacy, Its Future, Liturgical Press, 93; Mary, In The New Dictionary of Catholic Spirituality, Liturgical Press, 93; What Ever Happened to Mary?, New Theol Rev, 92; Mary and the Prophetic Mission of the Church, Jour Ecumenical Studies, 91; Ministry: The Praxis of the Kingdom of God, The Praxis of Christian Experience: An Introduction to the Thought of Edward Schillebeeckx, Harper & Row, 89; Women Religious in Transition, New Thepol Rev, 88. **CONTACT ADDRESS** Emmanuel Col, Massachusetts, 400 The Fenway, Boston, MA, 02115. **EMAIL** hines@emmanuel.edu

HINGLE, NORWOOD N., III
PERSONAL Born 05/18/1963, New Orleans, LA, m, 1989, 3 children **DISCIPLINE** NEW TESTAMENT **EDUCATION** Univ New Orleans, BS, 85; Gordon-Conwell Theol Sem, M Div, 89; Univ Aberdeen, Scotland, PhD, 95. **CAREER** Assoc minister, St. Paul's United Methodist Church, 95-; adj lectr, relig, Northeast La Univ, 96-97; ordained elder in full connection, La Conf of United Methodist Church, 97-. **MEMBERSHIPS** Amer Acad of Relig; Soc of Bibl Lit; Inst for Bibl Res. **RESEARCH** Gospels of Matthew and John; Christology; Second Temple Judaism. **SELECTED PUBLICATIONS** Rev, Evang Quart, 98; rev, Scottish Bull of Evang Theol, 96. **CONTACT ADDRESS** 1626 Milton St., Monroe, LA, 71201.

HINSDALE, MARY ANN
PERSONAL Born 04/10/1947, Chicago, IL **DISCIPLINE** RELIGIOUS STUDIES **EDUCATION** Marygrove Col, BA, 70; Cath Univ Am, MA, 71; Regis Col, STL, 83; Univ St Michael's Col, PhD, 84. **CAREER** Asst prof. **HONORS AND AWARDS** Annual Bk Awd, 87. **MEMBERSHIPS** Col Theol Soc; Am Acad Relig; Cath Theol Soc Am; Cath Press Asn; Cath Theol Soc Am; Asn Jesuit Col and Univ. **SELECTED PUBLICATIONS** Auth, Women and Theology, Orbis Bk, 95; Faith That Transforms, Paulist, 87. **CONTACT ADDRESS** Col of the Holy Cross, Worcester, MA, 01610-2395.

HINSON, E. GLENN
PERSONAL Born 07/27/1931, St. Louis, MO, m, 1956, 2 children **DISCIPLINE** CHURCH HISTORY **EDUCATION** Washington Univ; BA 54; Southern Baptist Theological Seminary; BD, ThD, 57,62; Oxford Univ; D Phil 74. **CAREER** Southern Baptist Theological Sem; prof, 62-92, prof of spirituality, John Loftis Prof of church hist, 92-99; Wake Forest Univ; prof 82-84. **HONORS AND AWARDS** Johannes Quasten Medal; Cuthbert Allen Awd; 2 ATS Fell; Prof of the Year SBTS. **MEMBERSHIPS** ASCH; AAR; IPS; EIS; NAPS; NABPR; ITMS. **RESEARCH** Early Christianity and Spirituality. **SELECTED PUBLICATIONS** Auth, Love At the Heart of Things: A Biography of Douglas V. Steer, Pendle Hill Pub, 98; The Early Church, Abingdon, 96; The Church Triumphant: A History of Christianity up to 1300, Mercer Univ, 95; A Serious Call to a Contemplative Lifestyles, rev, ed, Smith & Helwys 93. **CONTACT ADDRESS** Dept of Church History, S Baptist Theological Sem, 3400 Brook Rd, Richmond, VA, 23227.

HINTIKKA, JAAKKO
PERSONAL Born 01/12/1929, Vantaa, Finland **DISCIPLINE** PHILOSOPHY **CAREER** Jr fel of the soc of fels, 56-59, Harvard Univ; prof, 59-70, Univ Helsinki; prof, part-time, 65-82, Standford Univ; research prof, 70-81, Acad of Finland; prof, 90-present, Boston Univ. **HONORS AND AWARDS** FL State Univ Found prof, 86-90, (renamed McKenzie prof, 89); Commander of the order of the Lion of Finland, first class, 87; E.J Nystrom prize of the societas scientiarum fennica, 88; Erik Ahlman lecture, Univ of Jyvaskyla, 88; The grand prize of Suomen Kulttuurirahasto, FIN, 89; Honorary doctorate, Jagiellonian Univ of Krakow, 95. **MEMBERSHIPS** Scientific advisor and foreign member of the Internationales Forschungszentrum Salzburg, 66- ; Acad of Science and Letters of FIN, 61- ; Fel of Societas Scientiarum Fennica, 66- ; Council for Philosophical Studies, 82-86; Norwegian Acad of science and letters, 91- . **SELECTED PUBLICATIONS** Auth, Lingua Universalis vs. Calculus Ratiocinator, Kluwer, 96; auth, Language, Truth and Logic in Mathematics, Kluwer, 97; auth, Paradigms for Language Theory and Other Essays in the Foundations of Language, Kluwer, 97; auth, Language, Truth and Logic in Mathematics, Kluwer, 98; Paradigms for Language Theory and Other Essays, Kluwer, 98. **CONTACT ADDRESS** Dept of Philosophy, Boston Univ, Boston, MA, 02215.

HINTON, GREGORY TYRONE
PERSONAL Born 11/22/1949, Barrackville, WV, d **DISCIPLINE** LAW **EDUCATION** Fairmont State College, AB, 1978; West Virginia University, College of Law, JD, 1981; Kellogg Leadership Development Certification, 1995. **CAREER** Thorofare Markets Inc, stock clerk/carry-out 1968-69; Hope Natl Gas Co, casual rouster 1970-71; Montana Power Co, elec clerk 1972-73; Gibbs & Hill, elec clerk 1973-75; N Central Opportunity Indus Ctr, exec dir 1975-78; Fairmont City Council, council member 1977-86, mayor 1983-85; WV Univ Coll of Law, consultant; attorney private practice; Fairmont St Coll, prof, 1989-. **HONORS AND AWARDS** 1st black elected Mayor to a major city in WV 1983; Hon Mem Magnificent Souls 1983; Outstanding Young Man of Amer Jaycees 1979, 1984; WV Outstanding Black Atty Black Amer Law Student Assn Morgantown WV 1984; WV Outstanding Black Atty; Spec Award as Mayor from WV State Assn and PER-PDR Tri-State Conf ofCouncils IBPOEW PA-OH-WV 1984; Spec Award as Mayor from Dunbar HS class of 1947 1984; Honorary Mem Amer Soc for Nondestructive Testing Fairmont State Coll Sect 1984; Black Amer Law Student Assn Morgantown WV 1985; Outstanding WV Black attorney; Wiliam A Boram Award, Teaching Excellence, 1996, 1997; Carnegie Foundation for the Advancement of Teaching, West VA Professor of the Year, 1997. **MEMBERSHIPS** Mem Montana Valley Assn of Health Ctrs Inc 1974-; deacon Good Hope Baptists Church 1974-; corp banking & business law & minority affairs comm WV State Bar 1984-86; vstg comm WV Univ Coll of Law 1984-87; adv bd WNPB-TV 1984-86; bd mem Fairmont Gen Hosp 1985-86; consul WV Univ Coll of Law 1985-; WV Adv Comm to US Commn on Civil Rights 1985-89; pres MT State Bar Assn 1986-88; ethics comm WV State Bar 1986-87; NAACP Legal Redress Comm.

HINTZEN, PERCY CLAUDE
PERSONAL Born 01/26/1947, Georgetown, Guyana, m **DISCIPLINE** PHILOSOPHY **EDUCATION** University of Guyana, Georgetown, Guyana, BS, 1975; Clark University, Worcester, MA, MA, 1976; Yale University, New Haven, CT, MA, 1977; MPhil, 1977, PhD, 1981. **CAREER** Yale University, New Haven, CT, acting instructor, 1978-79; University of Guyana, Guyana, lecturer, 1977-78; University of California, Berkeley, CA, associate professor, 1979-; African Amer Studies, chairperson, 1994-; Peace & Conflict Studies, dir, 1994-. **MEMBERSHIPS** Member, American Sociological Society, 1979-; member, Caribbean Studies Association, 1979; member, American Political Science Association, 1979-81. **SELECTED PUBLICATIONS** The Costs of Regime Survival, Cambridge University Press, 1989. **CONTACT ADDRESS** Univ of California at Berkeley, 660 Barrows, Berkeley, CA, 94720.

HIRSTEIN, WILLIAM
DISCIPLINE PHILOSOPHY **EDUCATION** Univ Calif at Davis, PhD, 94. **CAREER** Prof, William Paterson Univ, 97; 2 yrs postdoctoral fel, Univ Calif, San Diego; asst dir, VS Ramachandran's Brain and Perception Lab, 96. **RESEARCH** Bringing current findings in neuroscience to bear on classical philosophical issues; Questions about self, and self-representation; The problem of consciousness; Questions about self-deception and confabulation. **SELECTED PUBLICATIONS** coauth, Capgras Syndrome: A Novel Probe for Understanding the Neural Representation of the Identity and Familiarity of Persons, Proceedings of the Royal Soc of London, 264, 97; Three Laws of Qualia: Clues From Neurology About the Biological Functions of Consciousness and Qualia, J of Consciousness Stud, 4, 97, part of a special issue on, Models of the Self, be publ as bk by the MIT Press. **CONTACT ADDRESS** Dept of Philosophy, William Paterson Col, 300 Pompton Rd., Atrium 267, Wayne, NJ, 07470.

HISKES, ANNE L.
DISCIPLINE PHILOSOPHY OF SCIENCE **EDUCATION** Hope Col, BA; Ind Univ, MA, PhD. **CAREER** Dept Philos, Univ Conn **RESEARCH** Philosophy and spacetime theories, theories of scientific explanation. **SELECTED PUBLICATIONS** Co-auth, Science, Technology, and Policy Decisions, Westview Press, 86; auth, Theoretical Explanation and Unifica-

tion, Logic and Philosophy of Science in Uppsala, Kluwer Acad Publ, 94. **CONTACT ADDRESS** Dept of Philos, Univ Conn, 344 Mnsfield Rd, Storrs, CT, 06269.

HITCHCOCK, DAVID
DISCIPLINE PHILOSOPHY **EDUCATION** Univ Claremont, PhD. **CAREER** Assoc prof. **RESEARCH** Philos of logic; metaphysics; philos of language. **SELECTED PUBLICATIONS** Auth, Critical Thinking. **CONTACT ADDRESS** Philosophy Dept, McMaster Univ, 1280 Main St W, Hamilton, ON, L8S 4L9.

HIZ, HENRY
PERSONAL Born 10/08/1917, Leningrad, Russia, m, 1943 **DISCIPLINE** LINGUISTICS, PHILOSOPHY **EDUCATION** Free Univ Brussels, lic en philos, 46; Harvard Univ, PhD(-philos), 48. **CAREER** Asst philos, Underground Univ Warsaw, 40-44; adj math, Univ Warsaw, 49-50; asst prof, Univ Utah, 52-54 & Pa State Univ, 55-60, assoc prof, 60-64, Prof Ling, Univ Pa, 64-, Vis lectr, Univ Pa, 51, 53, 54 & 58-59; investr, NSF Tranformation & Discourse Analysis Proj, 58-; vis prof philos, NY Univ, 69- 71 & Jagiellonian Univ, 77; vis fel philos, Clare Hall, Cambridge, Eng, 76-77; Guggenheim fel ling, 76-77. **MEMBERSHIPS** Ling Soc Am; Semiotic Sco Am (pres, 75-76); Am Philos Asn. **RESEARCH** Formal grammars; mathematical logic; philosophy of art. **SELECTED PUBLICATIONS** Auth, Zellig Harris, 23-October-1909 May-22-1992, In-Memoriam, Proceedings Am Philos Soc, Vol 0138, 94. **CONTACT ADDRESS** Dept of Ling, Univ of Pa, Philadelphia, PA, 19174.

HOAGLUND, JOHN ARTHUR
PERSONAL Born 06/15/1936, Houston, TX, m, 1966, 2 children **DISCIPLINE** PHILOSOPHY **EDUCATION** Free Univ Berlin, PhD, 67. **CAREER** Lectr Am studies, Free Univ Berlin, 67-72; asst prof philos, 72-75, assoc prof, 75-80, chmn dept, 76-79, prof philos, Christopher Newport Univ, 79-, sr Fulbright res fel, Univ Bergen, Norway, 80-81. **HONORS AND AWARDS** Am Coun Learned Soc Travel Award, 75. **MEMBERSHIPS** AAUP; Am Philos Asn; Am Soc Aesthet; Asn Informal Logic and Critical Thinking, Pres 85-87; Int Soc Study Argumentation. **RESEARCH** Aesthetics; ethics; critical thinking; informal logic. **SELECTED PUBLICATIONS** Auth, The thing in itself in English interpretations of Kant, Am Philos Quart, 73; Originality and aesthetic value, Brit J Aesthet, 76; Music as expressive, Brit J Aesthet, 80; On artistic creativity, Proe 19th Int Cong Aesthet, 80; Some Moral Problems of the Damaged Neonate, Philos in Context, 84; Reasons and Premises in Informal Logic, CT News, 88; Fiction and Belief, Primum Philosophia, 93; Critical Thinking: A Socratic Model, Argumentation, 93; ed Studies in Critical Thinking and Informal Logic, Vale Press; auth, Textbook Critical Thinking, 2nd ed, 95. **CONTACT ADDRESS** Dept Philos, Christopher Newport Univ, 1 University Pl, Newport News, VA, 23606-2949. **EMAIL** hoaglund@cnu.edu

HOBBS, TREVOR RAYMOND
PERSONAL Born 01/31/1942, Pontypridd, Wales, m, 1966, 2 children **DISCIPLINE** OLD TESTAMENT **EDUCATION** Univ London, BD, 66, PhD(theol), 73; Baptist Sem, Ruschlikon, MTh, 68. **CAREER** Lectr, 69-70, asst prof Bible studies, 70-74, assoc prof, 74-78, Prof Hebrew & Old Testament Interpretation, McMaster Divinity Col, McMaster Univ, 78- **MEMBERSHIPS** Soc Old Testament Studies, UK; Soc Bibl Lit; Can Soc Bibl Studies. **RESEARCH** Old Testament prophetic literature, theology and hermeneutics; Old Testament historical geography; Historigraphy. **SELECTED PUBLICATIONS** Auth, The End of the Bronze-Age--Changes in Warfare and the Catastrophe C.1200bc, Cath Biblical Quarterly, Vol 0057, 95; The History of Ancient Palestine from the Paleolithic Period to Alexander Conquest, Cath Biblical Quarterly, Vol 0056, 94. **CONTACT ADDRESS** McMaster Divinity Col, McMaster Univ, 1280 Main St W, Hamilton, ON, L8S 4K1.

HOBGOOD-OSTER, LAURA
PERSONAL Born 09/18/1964, Indiana, m, 1995 **DISCIPLINE** HISTORICAL THEOLOGY **EDUCATION** St Louis Univ, PhD, 97; Vanderbilt Univ, Mdiv, 89; James Madison Univ, BA, 85. **CAREER** Asst Prof of Rel, 98-, Southwestern Univ; Lectr/Instr of Rel Studies, 97-98, Cal State Univ. **HONORS AND AWARDS** Pres Fellow, 94-97, St Louis Univ; Faculty Merit Scholar, 88-89, Vanderbilt Univ. **MEMBERSHIPS** AAR **RESEARCH** Christianity in America, Theology of Nature, Gnostic Christianity, Women and Religion. **SELECTED PUBLICATIONS** Auth, As Heaven and Earth Combine: Perceptions of Nature in American Shakerism, Esoteric Studies, 98; She Glanceth From Earth to Heaven: The Phenomenon of Love Mysticism Among Women in Antebellum Virginia and Maryland, Univ Press of the South, 98; Mary Magdalene, Gnostic Revealer, Koinonia Journal, Princeton Seminary Graduate Forum 96; Sexuality-One of God's Gifts, A Year in the Life, St Louis, Chalice Books, 93; Building Self Esteem, Christian Children's Fellowship Manual, Chalice Books, 92; ed, The Sabbath Journal of Judith Lomax, Scholar Press, Texts and Translations Series, forthcoming; **CONTACT ADDRESS** Southwestern Univ, 1001 E University, Georgetown, TX, 78626. **EMAIL** hoboster@southwestern.edu

HOCHBERG, STEPHEN
DISCIPLINE LAW **EDUCATION** NY Univ, BA, 67; Yale Univ, JD, 70. **CAREER** Asst instr, Yale Univ; US Ct of Appeals for the Third Circuit; gen coun, Lefrak Orgn, NY; asst prof, NY Law Schl; pvt pract, NYC; founding assoc prof Law, Touro Col. **SELECTED PUBLICATIONS** Ed, Cooperative Conversions: A Tenants Survival Guide, 80. **CONTACT ADDRESS** Touro Col, Brooklyn, NY, 11230.

HOCKENBERY, JENNIFER D.
PERSONAL Born 07/16/1971, London, OH, m, 1996 **DISCIPLINE** PHILOSOPHY **EDUCATION** Bowdan Col, BA, 93; Boston Univ, MA, 96, PhD, 98. **CAREER** Univ of Mass, lectr, 96-97; Mt Mary Col, lecrt, asst prof, 97-. **HONORS AND AWARDS** Boston Univ, Pres Fel, Outstanding TA Award. **MEMBERSHIPS** APS, Phi Beta Kappa **RESEARCH** Augustine; Ancient philo; Christ philo; philo of relig. **CONTACT ADDRESS** Dept of Philosophy, Mount Mary Col, 5224 West Luebbe Lane, Milwaukee, WI, 53223. **EMAIL** hockenberyj@mtmary.edu

HODDER, ALAN
DISCIPLINE COMPARATIVE RELIGION **EDUCATION** Harvard Col, BA; Harvard Divinity Sch, MTS; Harvard Univ, MA, PhD. **CAREER** Assoc prof, dir, undergrad educ in Comp Stud of Relig, Harvard Univ; vis assoc prof, Hampshire Col. **SELECTED PUBLICATIONS** Publ include studies of Puritan pulpit rhetoric, orientalism, American transcendentalism, and the Bengal renaissance. **CONTACT ADDRESS** Hampshire Col, Amherst, MA, 01002.

HODES, HAROLD T.
DISCIPLINE PHILOSOPHY **EDUCATION** Columbia Col, BA, 70; Harvard Univ, PhD, 77. **CAREER** Assoc prof, Cornell Univ. **RESEARCH** Philosophy. **CONTACT ADDRESS** Dept of Philosophy, Cornell Univ, 218 Goldwin Smith Hall, Ithaca, NY, 14853.

HODGES, DONALD CLARK
PERSONAL Born 10/22/1923, Fort Worth, TX, m, 1949, 5 children **DISCIPLINE** PHILOSOPHY **EDUCATION** NY Univ, BA, 47; Columbia Univ, MA, 48, PhD(philos), 54. **CAREER** Instr humanities, Hobart & William Smith Cols, 49-50, instr philos, 50-52; from instr to assoc prof, Univ Mo, 52-63, chmn humanities, 56-61; prof philos, Univ Nebr, 63; prof, Univ SFla, 63-64; chmn dept, 64-69, Prof Philos, Fla State Univ, 64-, Univ Mo res grants, 58, 61, 62; vis prof philos, Univ Hawaii, 65-66; consult ed, Indian Sociol Bull, 65-69; Fla State Univ res grant, 67-68; dir, Fla Ctr Studies Soc Philos, 67-71; assoc ed, Soc Theory & Practice, 69-72, co-ed, 72-; assoc ed, Philos Currents, 72-; assoc mem, Inst Social Philos, Pa State Univ, 72-; mem adv bd, Centro Superiore di Logica e Scienze Comparate, Univ Bologna, 72- **MEMBERSHIPS** Am Philos Asn; Soc Philos Studies Dialectical Materialism (secy-treas, 63-73). **RESEARCH** Social and political philosophy; philosophy of the social sciences; philosophy of economics, history, and political science. **SELECTED PUBLICATIONS** Auth, Mariategui and Latin-American Marxist Theory, Hisp Am Hist Rev, Vol 0074, 94; Divine Violence, Spectacle, Psychosexuality, and Radical Christianity in the Argentine Dirty-War, Hisp Am Hist Rev, Vol 0073, 93; Radical Thought in Central-America, Am Hist Rev, Vol 0098, 93; Dossier-Secreto--Argentina Desaparecidos and the Myth of the Dirty-War, Am Hist Rev, Vol 0099, 94; Marxism in Latin-America From 1909 to the Present--An Anthology, Americas, Vol 0051, 94. **CONTACT ADDRESS** Dept of Philos, Florida State Univ, 600 W College Ave, Tallahassee, FL, 32306-1096.

HODGES, LOUIS WENDELL
PERSONAL Born 01/24/1933, Eupora, MS, m, 1954, 2 children **DISCIPLINE** RELIGION & JOURNALISM **EDUCATION** Millsaps Col, BA, 54; Duke Univ, BD, 57, PhD, 60. **CAREER** From asst prof to assoc prof, 60-68, prof relig, 68-97, dir ethics, 74-97, Knight Prof Journalism, 97-, Univ Prog Soc & Professions, Washington & Lee Univ. **MEMBERSHIPS** Am Soc Christian Ethics. **RESEARCH** Theology of race relations; theology and ethics, ethics and the press. **SELECTED PUBLICATIONS** Art, Christian Ethics and Non-Violence, Relig in Life, 62; art, The Roots of Prejudice, Christian Advocate, 62; coauth, The Christian and His Decisions, Abingdon, 69. **CONTACT ADDRESS** Dept of Journalism, Washington & Lee Univ, Lexington, VA, 24450. **EMAIL** hodgesl@wlu.edu

HODGES, MICHAEL P.
PERSONAL Born 11/23/1941, Youngstown, OH, m, 1991, 2 children **DISCIPLINE** PHILOSOPHY **EDUCATION** William & Mary, AB, 63; Univ Va, MA, 66, PhD, 67. **CAREER** Asst Prof, Univ Tenn, 67-70; Asst Prof, Vanderbilt Univ, 70-76; Assoc Prof, Vanderbilt Univ, 76-91; Prof, Vanderbilt Univ, 91-. **HONORS AND AWARDS** NEH Fellow, 94. **MEMBERSHIPS** APA; S Soc for Philos & Psychol. **RESEARCH** Wittgenstein; Philosophy of Religion; American Philosophy. **SELECTED PUBLICATIONS** Auth, Transcendence and Wittgenstein's Tractatus, Temple Univ Press, 90; auth, The Ontological Project Considered: The Displacement of Theoretical by Practical Unity, The S J of Philos, Spring 92; auth, The States of Ethical Judgements in the Philosophical Investigations, Philos Investigations; 18:2, 4/95; co-auth, Thinking in the Ruins: Two Overlooked Responses to Contingency, Overheard in Seville, no 13, 108, 95; auth, Sensibility, Pragmatism, and Modernity, Bulletin of the Santayana Soc; no 15, 97; auth, Faith: Transcendence and Genealogy, Claremont Stud in the Philos of Relig, forthcoming. **CONTACT ADDRESS** Dept of Philos, Vanderbilt Univ, 111 Furman Hall, Nashville, TN, 37240. **EMAIL** hodgesmp@ctrvax.vanderbilt.edu

HODGSON, PETER C.
PERSONAL Born 02/26/1934, Oak Park, IL, m, 1960, 2 children **DISCIPLINE** THEOLOGY **EDUCATION** Princeton Univ, AB, 56; Yale Univ, BD, 59, MA, 60, PhD, 63. **CAREER** Asst prof, Trinity Univ, 63-65; Vanderbilt Univ Divinity Sch, from asst prof to assoc prof, 65-73; prof 73-; ch, grad dept of relig, 75-80 & 90-97; grad fac coun, 75-80 & 90-97; univ res coun, 78-80; grad dean search comt, 83-84; ch, divinity fac, 85-86; fac sen, 85-86; univ comt on promotion and tenure, 87-88; divinity dean search comt, 88-89; ch, divinity acad prog comt, 88-89; grad dept of relig long range planning comt, 90-94; ch, New Testament, Homiletics, and Church Hist Search Comts, 93-96. **HONORS AND AWARDS** Phi Beta Kappa, 56; cum laude, 59; Woodrow Wilson Fel, 56-57; Danforth Fel, 56-62; Guggenheim Fel, 74-75; Fulbright Scholar, 81; NEH, 81-87; Vanderbilit Univ Fel, 80-81, 86-87, & 92-93; Lilly Endowment, 98. **MEMBERSHIPS** Soc for Values in Higher Ed; Am Acad Relig; Hegel Soc Am; 19th C. Theology Group; Workgroup on Constructive Christian Theology. **RESEARCH** Modern theology. **SELECTED PUBLICATIONS** Auth, The Formation of Historical Theology: A Study of Ferdinand Christian Baur, Harper & Row, 66; auth, Jesus--Word and Presence: An Essay in Christology, Fortress, 71; auth, Children of Freedom: Black Liberation in Christian Perspective, Fortress, 74; auth, New Birth of Freedom: A Theology of Bondage and Liberation, Fortress, 76; auth, Revisioning the Church: Ecclesial Freedom in the New Paradigm, Fortress, 88; auth, God in History: Shapes of Freedom, Abingdon, 89; auth, Winds of the Spirit: A Constructive Christian Theology, John Knox, 94; auth of numerous articles and essays. **CONTACT ADDRESS** Vanderbilt Divinity School, Vanderbilt Univ, Nashville, TN, 37240. **EMAIL** peter.c.hodgson@vanderbilt.edu

HOEFER, CARL
DISCIPLINE PHILOSOPHY **EDUCATION** Stanford Univ, PhD. **CAREER** Assoc Prof, Univ Calif, Riverside; VIS PROF, LONDON SCH ECON, ENG, 98-99. **RESEARCH** Philosophy of physics, metaphysics, philosophy of science. **SELECTED PUBLICATIONS** Coauth, "Substantivalism and the Hole Argument," Philosophical Problems of the Internal and External Worlds, Univ Pittsburgh Press, 94; "The Metaphysics of Space-time Substantivalism," The Jour Philos, 96; "On Lewis' Objective Chance: Human Supervenience Debugged," MIND vol 106, 97. **CONTACT ADDRESS** Dept of Philos, Univ Calif, 1156 Hinderaker Hall, Riverside, CA, 92521-0209. **EMAIL** carl@einstein.ucr.edu

HOEFFNER, KENT
PERSONAL Born 08/02/1958, Dallas, TX, m, 1986, 1 child **DISCIPLINE** THEOLOGY **EDUCATION** S Baptist Theol Sem, PhD. **CAREER** Asst prof, Truett-McConnell Col, 96-. **MEMBERSHIPS** AAR/SBL, Baptist Asn Philos Tchr. **RESEARCH** Post-modernism and Christianity; pedagogy and theology. **CONTACT ADDRESS** Dept of Theology, Truett-McConnell Col, 1201 Bishop Farms Pkwy, Watkinsville, GA, 30677. **EMAIL** kent@truett.cc.ga.uc

HOEFLIN, RONALD K.
PERSONAL Born 02/23/1944, Richmond Heights, MO, s **DISCIPLINE** PHILOSOPHY **EDUCATION** New Sch for Soc Res, PhD, 87 **CAREER** Self Employed, Test Designer & Editor of various journals **HONORS AND AWARDS** Rockefeller Prize, 88; Who's Who in Amer; Who's Who in World **MEMBERSHIPS** Amer Philos Assoc **RESEARCH** Metaphysics; Categories; Metaphilosophy **CONTACT ADDRESS** PO Box 539, New York, NY, 10101.

HOEKEMA, DAVID A.
PERSONAL Born 06/10/1950, Peterson, NJ, m, 1972, 2 children **DISCIPLINE** PHILOSOPHY **EDUCATION** Calvin Col, BA, 72; Princeton Univ, PhD, 81. **CAREER** Asst prof, 77-84, St Olaf Col; exec dir, Amer Phil Asn, & assoc prof, phil, 84-92, Univ Del; dean, Nat Sci & Math, & Contextual Disc, prof, phil, 92-98, dir grad stud, 93-94, actng v pres, Student Life, 98-99, Calvin Col **HONORS AND AWARDS** Calvin Ctr for Christian Scholar grant; Am Coun of Learned Soc grant, 87-88; Danforth Fel, 72; Nat Merit Scholar, 68; Alvin M Bentley Scholar, 68; Who's Who in Am; Who's Who in the World; Dict of Intl Biog. **MEMBERSHIPS** Soc of Christian Phil; Bd of Trustees, Grand Rapids Art Mus; APA; Soc for Values in Higher Ed; Am Asn of Advancement of Sci; Am Coun of Learned Soc; Int Asn for Phil of Law, Soc Phil. **RESEARCH** Political phil; phil of art; hist of phil; phil of relig. **SELECTED PUBLICATIONS** Auth, Rights and Wrongs: Coercion, Punishment, and the State, Susquehanna Univ Press, 86; auth, Handbook for Administrators of Learned Societies, ACLS, NY 90; auth, Campus Life and Moral Community: In Place of In Loco Parentis, Rowman

& Littlefield, 94; auth, Liberalism Revisited: Religion, Reason, Diversity, Christian Century 111:29, 94; auth, Conversations for Christian Higher Education: Introduction, Calvin Col, 96; auth, College Life in America: Historical Context and Legal Issues, Contemp Issues in Judicial Affairs, Jossey-Bass, 96; auth, Politics, Religion, and Other Crimes Against Civility, Academe 82:6, 96; co-ed, Christianity and Culture in the Crossfire, Eerdmans, 97. **CONTACT ADDRESS** Calvin Col, Grand Rapids, MI, 49546. **EMAIL** dhoekema@calvin.edu

HOFBECK, JOSEF
PERSONAL Born 05/30/1938, Germany, m, 1964, 4 children **DISCIPLINE** THEOLOGICAL STUDIES, ETHICS **EDUCATION** Sorbonne Univ, CES, 63 & 65; Inst Cath Paris, STL, 64, STD, 67. **CAREER** Asst prof, 67-72, chmn dept theol studies, 72-75, Assoc Prof Theol, Concordia Univ, Loyola Campus, 72- **MEMBERSHIPS** Soc Can Theol; Cath Theol Soc Am; Am Soc Christian Ethics; Prov Asn Teachers Ethics & Relig. **RESEARCH** Fundamental theology; Christian ethics. **SELECTED PUBLICATIONS** Auth, The Irony of Theology and the Nature of Religious Thought, Studies Relig, Vol 0021, 92. **CONTACT ADDRESS** Concordia Univ, Montreal, 7141 Sherbrooke St W, Montreal, PQ, H4B 1R6.

HOFF, TIMOTHY
DISCIPLINE LAW **EDUCATION** Tulane Univ, AB, 63; Tulane Univ, JD, 66; Harvard Law Sch, LLM, 70. **CAREER** Prof, Univ Ala, 70-. **HONORS AND AWARDS** Student Bar Association's Outstanding fac mem awd, 86. **MEMBERSHIPS** Phi Beta Kappa; Fla Bar; Al Bar. **RESEARCH** Admiralty, civil procedure, conflict of laws, law in literature, federal jurisdiction, and law and religion. **SELECTED PUBLICATIONS** Auth, Alabama Limitations of Actions and Notice Provisions, 2d, 92. **CONTACT ADDRESS** Law Dept, Univ of Alabama, Box 870000, Tuscaloosa, AL, 35487-0383. **EMAIL** thoff@law.ua.edu

HOFFECKER, W. ANDREW
DISCIPLINE CHURCH HISTORY **EDUCATION** Dickinson Col, BA; Gordon-Conwell, MDiv; Brown Univ, PhD. **CAREER** Prof, Grove City Col; prof. **HONORS AND AWARDS** Captain, US Army. **SELECTED PUBLICATIONS** Auth, Piety and the Princeton Theologians; ed, Building a Christian World View. **CONTACT ADDRESS** Dept of Church History, Reformed Theol Sem, 5422 Clinton Blvd, Jackson, MS, 39209-3099.

HOFFMAN, JOHN C.
PERSONAL Born 12/07/1931, Toronto, ON, Canada **DISCIPLINE** THEOLOGY **EDUCATION** Univ Toronto, BA, 54; McGill Univ, PhD, 57, BD, 59, STM, 60; Union Theol Sem (NY), ThD, 64. **CAREER** Prof relig stud, Univ Windsor, 64-90, prin Iona Col, 64-85, dean students, 87-90; prin, Emmanuel Col, 90-96, PROF THEOLOGY, EMMANUEL COL, UNIV TORONTO, 90-. **SELECTED PUBLICATIONS** Auth, Ethical Confrontation in Counselling, 79; auth, Law, Freedom and Story, 86; auth, Faithfull Stories, 94. **CONTACT ADDRESS** Emmanuel Col, Univ of Toronto, 75 Queen's Park Cr, Toronto, ON, M5S 1K7.

HOFFMAN, MARK G.
DISCIPLINE RELIGION **EDUCATION** Univ Ill, BA, 78; Luther Northwestern Theol Sem, MDiv, 83; Yale Univ, MA, 85, MPhil, 87, PhD, 96. **CAREER** Instr Greek and New Testament, Luther Northwestern Theol Sem, 87-88; pastor, Faith Lutheran Church, Spicer, MN, 88-92; pastor, Hope Lutheran Church, Fargo, ND, 92-. **MEMBERSHIPS** Soc Bibl Lit; Cath Bibl Asn. **RESEARCH** New Testament. **CONTACT ADDRESS** Dept of Ministry, Hope Lutheran Church, 3246 Elm St., Fargo, ND, 58102-1126. **EMAIL** mgvh@minister.com

HOFFMAN, PAUL
DISCIPLINE HISTORY OF EARLY MODERN PHILOSOPHY **EDUCATION** UCLA, PhD. **CAREER** ASSOC PROF, UNIV CALIF, RIVERSIDE. **RESEARCH** Moral psychology; Philosophy of mind. **SELECTED PUBLICATIONS** Coauth, "Alternative Possibilities: A Reply to Lamb," Jour Philos 91, 94; "Responses to Chappell and Watson," Philos Stud 77, 95; "Strength and Freedom of Will: Descartes and Albritton," Philos Stud 77, 95; "The Being of Leibnizian Phenomena," Studia Leibnitiana 28, 96; "Descartes on Misrepresentation," Jour Hist of Philos 34, 96. **CONTACT ADDRESS** Dept of Philos, Univ Calif, 1156 Hinderaker Hall, Riverside, CA, 92521-0209. **EMAIL** phoffman@ucracl.ucr.edu

HOFFMAN, PETER TOLL
PERSONAL Born 05/05/1946, Schenectady, NY, m, 1973, 1 child **DISCIPLINE** LAW **EDUCATION** Mich State Univ, BA, 68; Univ Mich, JD, 71. **CAREER** Instr & dir clinical law prog, Univ Mich Sch Law, 72-73; asst prof to assoc prof, 74-82, Earl Dunlap Prof of Law, Univ Nebr Col Law, 82-; Vis assoc prof, Univ Hawaii Sch Law, 77-78; Vis Sr Fel, City Univ of Hong Kong, 92; Assoc Justice, Supreme Court of Palau, 94-96; Vis Prof, Univ of San Diego, 99. **RESEARCH** Lawyering skills. **SELECTED PUBLICATIONS** Auth, Trial court responses to claims for relief under the Nebraska Post Conviction Act: A taxonomy, Nebr Law Rev, 57: 355; Clinical course design and the supervisory process, Ariz State Law Rev, 82; Valuation of Cases for Settlement: Theory and Practice, J Dispute Resolution, 91; coauth, The Effective Deposition, 2nd ed, 96. **CONTACT ADDRESS** Col of Law, Univ of Nebr, East Campus, Lincoln, NE, 68583.

HOFFMAN, PIOTR
DISCIPLINE HISTORY OF PHILOSOPHY AND CONTINENTAL PHILOSOPHY **EDUCATION** Univ Paris, Sorbonne, PhD, 70. **CAREER** Prof, Univ Nev, Reno. **RESEARCH** Ontological implications of the political philosophies of Hobbes, Locke, and Rousseau. **SELECTED PUBLICATIONS** Auth, The Anatomy of Idealism, Kluwer/Martinus Nijhoff, 82; The Human Self and the Life and Death Struggle, Univ Fla, 83; Doubt, Time, and Violence, Univ Chicago, 86; Violence in Modern Philosophy, Univ Chicago, 89; The Quest for Power: Hobbes, Descartes and the Emergence of Modernity, Hum Press, 96. **CONTACT ADDRESS** Univ Nev, Reno, Reno, NV, 89557. **EMAIL** unrug@unr.edu

HOFFMAN, VALERIE J.
PERSONAL Born 04/27/1954, New York, NY, M, 1998, 3 children **DISCIPLINE** RELIGION **EDUCATION** Univ Chicago **CAREER** Univ IL, vis lectr, asst prof, assoc prof, 83-. **HONORS AND AWARDS** Full Re Grant, 87-88; NEH Fel, 91-92; Univ Ill, Univ Schol, 96 **MEMBERSHIPS** MESANA, AAR, AMEWS, AIMS, AAS **RESEARCH** Islamic thought and pop relig; late med & mod n and e Africa; Islamic gender ideology; woman's relig lives. **CONTACT ADDRESS** Program for the Study of Religion, Univ of Illinois, 707 S Mathews Ave, Urbana, IL, 61801. **EMAIL** vhoffman@staff.uiuc.edu

HOFFMASTER, BARRY
DISCIPLINE PHILOSOPHY **EDUCATION** Dartmouth Col, BA, 69; Univ Minn, MA, 78; PhD, 75. **CAREER** Prof **RESEARCH** Methodological approaches to bioethics. **SELECTED PUBLICATIONS** Auth, Hanging Out a Shingle: The Public and Private Services of Professionals, Can Jour Law Jurisprudence, 96; Dragons in the Sunset: The Allure of Assisted Death, 94; The Forms and Limits of Medical Ethics, Social Sci Medicine, 94; Morality and Culture: Putting Ethical Issues in Context, 94; coauth, Bioethics for Clinicians: 7. Truth Telling, Can Medical Asn Jour, 97; A Decision-making Aid for Long-term Care Waiting List Policies: Modelling First-come, First-served vs Needs-based Criteria, 96; co-ed, Deadlines and Diversity: Journalism Ethics in a Changing World, Fernwood, 96; Health Care Ethics in Canada, Harcourt Can, 95. **CONTACT ADDRESS** Dept of Philosophy, Western Ontario Univ, London, ON, N6A 5B8. **EMAIL** choffmas@julian.uwo.ca

HOFSTADTER, DOUGLAS RICHARD
PERSONAL Born 02/15/1945, New York, NY, w, 1985, 2 children **DISCIPLINE** PHILOSOPHY, PSYCHOLOGY, HISTORY, PHILOSOPHY OF SCIENCE, COMPARATIVE LIT **EDUCATION** Stanford Univ, BS, 65; Univ of Ore, MS, 72; PhD, 75. **CAREER** Visiting Scholar, inst for Math Studies in the Social Sci, Stanford Univ, 75-77; asst prof of computer sci, 77-80, assoc prof of computer sci, 80-83, Ind Univ; visiting scholar, computer sci dept, Stanford Univ, 80-81; columnist, Sci Am, 81-83; visiting sci, Artificial Intelligence Lab, MIT, 83-84; Walgreen Prof for the Study of Human Understanding and prof of psychology and cognitive sci, Univ of Mich, 84-88; visiting scholar, Center for Computer-Assisted Res in the Humanities, Stanford Univ, 97; DIR, CENTER FOR RES ON CONCEPTS AND COGNITION, 88-, ADJUNCT PROF OF PSYCHOLOGY, PHILOS, HIST, PHILOS OF SCI, & COMPARATIVE LIT, 88-, COL PROF OF COGNITIVE SCI AND COMPUTER SCI, 88-, IND UNIV. **HONORS AND AWARDS** Pulitzer Priz, 80; Am Book Award, 80; Guggenheim Fel, 80-81; Polya Prize, 83; Senior Fel, Mich Soc of Fels, 85; Arts and Sci Alumni Fels Award, Univ of Ore, 97; Tracy M. Sonneborn Award, Ind Univ, 98. **RESEARCH** Cognitive science; philosophy of the mind; creativity in translation; the mechanisms underlying discovery and creation in mathematics. **SELECTED PUBLICATIONS** Coauth, Fluid Concepts and Creative Analogies: Computer Models of the Fundamental Mechanisms of Thought, Basic Books, 95; auth, Rhapsody on a Theme by Clement Marot, Grace A. Tanner Center for Human Values, 95; auth, Le Ton beau de Marot: In Praise of the Music of Language, Basic Books, 97; auth, Breaking Out of Egocentrisms and Chauvinisms: The Many-layered Process of Building a Modern Mind, Evolution: Entwicklung und Organisation in der Natur, Rowohlt, 93; auth, Speechstuff and Thoughtstuff: Musings on the Resonances Created by Words and Phrases via the Subliminal Perception of their Buried Parts, Of Thoughts and Words: The Relation between Language and Mind, 95; On Seeing A's and Seeing As, Stanford Humanities Rev, 95; auth, Popular Culture and the Threat to Rational Inquiry, Sci, 98. **CONTACT ADDRESS** Center for Research on Concepts and Cognition, Indiana Univ, Bloomington, 510 N Fess St., Bloomington, IN, 47408-3822. **EMAIL** dughof@cogsci.indiana.edu

HOGAN, MELINDA
DISCIPLINE PHILOSOPHY **EDUCATION** Univ Calif, Berkeley, AB, 79; Univ Wis, MA, 85, PhD, 89. **CAREER** Asst prof. **RESEARCH** Philosophy of mind, philosophy. of language, metaphysics. **SELECTED PUBLICATIONS** Auth, What is wrong with an Atomistic Account of Mental Representation?, Synthese, 94; "Natural Kinds and Ecological Niches," Biol and Philos, 92. **CONTACT ADDRESS** Dept of Philos, Dalhousie Univ, Halifax, NS, B3H 3J5. **EMAIL** melinda.hogan@dal.ca

HOGAN, WILBUR C.
PERSONAL Born 12/27/1903, Kansas City, MO, m, 1992, 3 children **DISCIPLINE** PHILOSOPHY, LOGIC, MATH **EDUCATION** US Coast Guard Acad; BS, 28; Purdue Univ, MS, 59. **CAREER** Coast Guard officer, 28-58; commander, Coast Guard Inst, 50-52; Calif Polytech Inst, 59-73. **HONORS AND AWARDS** Number One Student at USCG Acad, 28; Number One Student at Purdue Univ Grad Prog, 59; Emeritus Prof, Calif Polytech Inst, 73. **MEMBERSHIPS** Naval Inst; Am Philos Soc. **RESEARCH** World religions of the ancient world - Sumeria and Mexico. **SELECTED PUBLICATIONS** Auth, articles in The Naval Inst Preceedings, 54-56. **CONTACT ADDRESS** 162 Serrano Heights, San Louis Obispo, CA, 93401.

HOGENSON, GEORGE B.
PERSONAL Born 02/23/1948, Rochester, MN, m, 1987, 1 child **DISCIPLINE** PHILOSOPHY **EDUCATION** St. Olaf Col, BA, 70; Yale Univ, PhD, 79. **CAREER** Asst prof, Yale Univ, 79-86; prog officer, MacArthur Found, 86-89; private practice, Jungian analyst, 89-. **RESEARCH** History and philosophy of psychoanalysis; Evolutionary theories of cognitive development. **SELECTED PUBLICATIONS** Auth, Jung's Struggle with Freud. **CONTACT ADDRESS** 711 S. Dearborn, Apt. 801, Chicago, IL, 60605. **EMAIL** hogenson@msn.com

HOITENGA, DEWEY J.
PERSONAL Born 02/05/1931, Hancock, MN, m, 1953, 4 children **DISCIPLINE** PHILOSOPHY OF RELIGION **EDUCATION** Calvin Col, AB, 52; Calvin Theological Seminary, BD, 55; MA, 57, PhD, 59, Harvard Univ. **CAREER** Instr, Worcester Jr Col, 59; Asst Prof, 59-61, Assoc Prof, Chr, 61-65, Chr, Humanities Dept, 62-62, Chr, Committee for guest Lectrs and Performing Artists, 63-65, Juniata Col; Assoc Prof, 65-69, Prof, 69-, Grand Valley State Univ. **HONORS AND AWARDS** Adjunct Fel, Univ Notre Dame, 87-88; Michigan Assoc of Governing Boards of State Univ Distinguished Fac Award, 92; Henry Stob Lectureship, Calvin Col, 93; Meeter Center Colloqium Series (invited lectureship), 95. **MEMBERSHIPS** Amer Phil Assoc; Soc of Christian Philosphers **RESEARCH** Epitemology; philosophy of mind; philosophy of religion; specialty and reformed epistemology **SELECTED PUBLICATIONS** Auth, Faith and Reason from Plato to Plantinga: An Introduction to Reformed Epitemology, 91; Faith Seeks Understanding: Augustine's Alternative to Nature Theology, Collectanea Augustiniana, 93; Happiness: Goal or Gift? Two Lectures on the Relationships Between Knowledge, Goodness, and Happiness in Plato and Calvin, The Stob Lectures, 94; John Calvin on the Will: Critique and Corrective, 97. **CONTACT ADDRESS** Grand Valley State Univ, 221 Lake Superior Hall, Allendale, MI, 49401. **EMAIL** hoitengd@gvsu

HOLDER, ARTHUR G.
DISCIPLINE CHRISTIAN SPIRITUALITY **EDUCATION** Duke Univ, AB, PhD; Gen Theol Sem, MDiv. **CAREER** Prof; dean, Acad Aff, Church Divinity Sch Pacific **SELECTED PUBLICATIONS** Co-auth, Bede: A Biblical Miscellany, Liverpool UP, 98; auth, (Un)Dating Bede's De Arte Metrica, Northumbria's Golden Age, Sutton, 98; Styles of Clerical Address in the Letters of Augustine, Studia Patristica, 97; Bede: On the Tabernacle, Liverpool UP, 94; The Mosaic Tabernacle in Early Christian Exegesis, Studia Patristica, 93; Saint Basil the Great on Secular Education and Christian Virtue, Rel Edu, 92. **CONTACT ADDRESS** Church Divinity Sch of the Pacific, 2451 Ridge Rd, Berkeley, CA, 94709-1217.

HOLIFIELD, E. BROOKS
PERSONAL Born 01/05/1942, Little Rock, AR, m, 1963, 2 children **DISCIPLINE** AMERICAN RELIGIOUS HISTORY **EDUCATION** Hendrix Col, BA, 63; Yale Div Sch, BD, 66; Yale Univ, PhD, 70. **CAREER** Asst prof, 70-75, assoc prof, 75-80, prof, 80-84, C H Candler prof, 84-, Emory Univ. **HONORS AND AWARDS** Woodrow Wilson fel, 63; Danforth fel, 63; Yale Sterling fel, 69; NEH fel, 76, 83, 91; Lilly and PEW fel, 98. **MEMBERSHIPS** Am Soc of Church Hist; Am Acad of Relig; Am Hist Asn; Orgn of Am Hist. **RESEARCH** Religious thought in America. **SELECTED PUBLICATIONS** Auth, The Covenant Sealed, 74; auth, The Gentlemen Theologians, 78; auth, History of Pastoral Care in America, 83; auth, Health and Medicine in the Methodist Tradition, 86; auth, Era of Persuasion: American Thought and Culture, 1521-1680, 89. **CONTACT ADDRESS** Bishops Hall, Emory Univ, Atlanta, GA, 30322. **EMAIL** eholifi@emory.edu

HOLLADAY, CARL R.
PERSONAL Born 10/18/1943, Huntingdon, TN, m, 1964, 3 children **DISCIPLINE** THEOLOGY **EDUCATION** Abilene Christian Univ, BA, 65, MDiv, 69; Princeton Theo Sem, MTh, 70; Cambridge Univ, PhD, 75. **CAREER** Asst Prof, 75-78, Assoc Prof, 78-80, Yale Univ Div School; Assoc Prof, 80-90, Prof NT, 90-, Assoc Dean, 83-85, act Dean, 85, Assoc Dean, 86-91, Dean fac & acad affairs, 92-94, Emory Univ Candler School Theo. **MEMBERSHIPS** SBL, SSNT, AAUP. **RESEARCH** New Testament literature & history, Greek speaking Judaism in the Hellenistic-Roman world. **SELECTED PUBLICATIONS** Auth, Fragments from Hellenistic Jewish Scholars, SBL, Scholars Press, 83-95; Theios Aner in Hellenistic Judaism, SBL, Scholars Press, 77; co-auth, Biblical Exegesis, A Beginners Handbook, Atlanta John Knox Press, 87. **CONTACT ADDRESS** 668 Clifton Rd NE, Atlanta, GA, 30307-1789. **EMAIL** theocrh@emory.edu

HOLLADAY, WILLIAM LEE
PERSONAL Born 06/23/1926, Dallas, TX, m, 1948, 4 children **DISCIPLINE** RELIGION **EDUCATION** Univ Calif, BA, 48; Pac Sch Relig, BD, 51; State Univ Leiden, THD, 58. **CAREER** Asst prof relig, Elmhurst Col, 60-63; prof Old Testament, Near East Sch Theol, 63-70; prof, 70-71, Lowry Prof Old Testament, Andover Newton Theol Sch, 71- **MEMBERSHIPS** Soc Bibl Lit. **RESEARCH** Jeremiah studies; patterns of pre-exilic Hebrew poetry. **SELECTED PUBLICATIONS** Auth, The Laments of Jeremiah and Their Contexts--A Literary and Redactional Study of Jeremiah-XI-XX, Cath Biblical Quarterly, Vol 0054, 92; The Waters Have Risen Up to My Neck--Form, History and Theology of Psalm-LXIX, Cath Biblical Quarterly, Vol 0057, 95; Jeremiah, J Biblical Lit, Vol 0113, 94; Anonymi-Glosa-Psalmorum-Ex-Traditione-Seniorum, Pt 1 - Praefatio and Psalms-I-C, Cath Biblical Quarterly, Vol 0058, 96; Isaiah and His Audience--The Structure and Meaning of Isaiah-I-XII, Biblica, Vol 0074, 93; A Hermeneutic of Curiosity and Readings of Psalm-LXI, Cath Biblical Quarterly, Vol 0058, 96. **CONTACT ADDRESS** Andover Newton Theol Sch, Newton, MA, 02159.

HOLLAND, MARGARET G.
DISCIPLINE PHILOSOPHY **EDUCATION** State Univ NY Buaaflo, PhD, 91. **CAREER** Assoc prof, current. **MEMBERSHIPS** Am Philos Asn. **RESEARCH** Ethics; Moral psychology. **SELECTED PUBLICATIONS** Auth, "Touching the Weights: Moral Perception and Attention," in Int Philos Quart, 98; "What's Wrong With Telling the Truth: An Analysis of Gossip," in Am Philos Quart, 96. **CONTACT ADDRESS** Dept of Philosophy and Religion, Univ of Northern Iowa, Cedar Falls, IA, 50614. **EMAIL** margaret.holland@uni.edu

HOLLAND, ROBERT A.
PERSONAL Born 11/24/1953, St. Louis, MO, m, 1990 **DISCIPLINE** PHILOSOPHY **EDUCATION** Univ Ill-Chicago, PhD, 89. **CAREER** Assoc Prof, Hofstra Univ, 89-. **MEMBERSHIPS** Am Philos Asn; Philos Sci Asn; Asn Symbolic Logic. **RESEARCH** Philosophy of mathematics & science; Metaphysics; Non-western philosophy. **SELECTED PUBLICATIONS** Auth Kant, Reichenbach, and Aprioricity, Philos Stud, 92; Apriority and Applied Mathematics, Synthese, 92; A Modern Formulation of Anselm's Response to Gaunilo, Tchg Philos, 93; Towards a Resolution of Sankara's Atmavidya and the Buddhist Doctrine of Anatman, Int Philos Quart, 95. **CONTACT ADDRESS** Dept of Philosophy, Hofstra Univ, 104 Heger Hall, Hempstead, NY, 11049. **EMAIL** phirah@hofstra.edu

HOLLANDER, RACHELLE D.
PERSONAL Born 07/04/1944, Balto, MD, m, 1969, 2 children **DISCIPLINE** PHILOSOPHY **EDUCATION** Goucher Col, BA, 65; UMCP, PhD, 79. **CAREER** Prog dir, US Natl Science Found, 76-. **MEMBERSHIPS** AAAS; Coun of Soc for Social Stud of Science; APA, Soc for Phil and Tech; Asn for Practical and Prof Ethics. **SELECTED PUBLICATIONS** Coed, Acceptable Evidence: Science and Values in Risk Management, Oxford Univ Press, 91. **CONTACT ADDRESS** SDEST, NSF, Rm 995, Arlington, VA, 22230. **EMAIL** rholland@nsf.gov

HOLLENBACH, PAUL WILLIAM
PERSONAL Born 05/09/1926, Lawrence, MA, m, 1952, 3 children **DISCIPLINE** RELIGION, BIBLE **EDUCATION** Wheaton Col, AB, 49; Univ Rochester, MA, 52; Union Theol Sem, NY, BD, 54; Drew Univ, PhD(Bible), 65. **CAREER** Asst prof relig, Emory & Henry Col, 59-63; asst prof philos, Cent Col Iowa, 64-67; asst prof, 67-69, Assoc Prof Philos, Iowa State Univ, 69-, Coordr Relig, 73-, Chmn Prog In Relig, 74- **MEMBERSHIPS** Am Acad Relig; Soc Bibl Lit. **RESEARCH** New Testament; life of Jesus. **SELECTED PUBLICATIONS** The Social World of Luke-Acts--Models For Interpretation, Cath Biblical Quarterly, Vol 0055, 93. **CONTACT ADDRESS** Dept of Philos, Iowa State Univ of Science and Tech, Ames, IA, 50011.

HOLLER, CLYDE
PERSONAL Born 07/05/1948, Washington, PA **DISCIPLINE** PHILOSOPHY OF RELIGION **EDUCATION** Univ Chicago, BA, 70; Episcopal Theol School, MDiv, 73; Boston Univ, PhD, 81. **CAREER** Indiana Purdue Fort Wayne; owner-manager, Buckhead Editorial Service Atlanta, 85-. **HONORS AND AWARDS** Assoc Fac in Philos Dept, 81-85. **MEMBERSHIPS** Am Acad of Rel. **RESEARCH** Black Elk; Kierkegaard; Lakota Religion; Philosophy of Religion. **SELECTED PUBLICATIONS** Auth, Tragedy in the Context of Kierkegaard's Either/Or, in Int Kierkegaard Commentary: Either/Or, 95; Black Elk's Religion: The Sun Dance and Lakota Catholicism, 95; The Black Elk Reader, forthcoming. **CONTACT ADDRESS** Buckhead Editorial Service, 3091 Maple Dr NE, Ste 204, Atlanta, GA, 30305. **EMAIL** buckword@mindspring.com

HOLLERAN, JOHN WARREN
PERSONAL Born 04/23/1928, San Francisco, CA **DISCIPLINE** SCRIPTURE, THEOLOGY **EDUCATION** St Patrick's Col, Calif, HA, 49; Univ Calif, Berkeley, MA, 60; Gregorian Univ, Rome, Italy, STL, 53, STD, 73; Univ San Francisco, MA, 77. **CAREER** Asst prof ethics, Holy Names Col, Calif, 55-57; lectr theol, Lone Mt Col, San Francisco, Calif, 57-62; spiritual dir, N Am Col, Rome, 62-68; prof scripture, St Patrick's Sem, Menlo Park, Calif, 68-. **MEMBERSHIPS** Cath Theol Soc Am; Cath Bibl Asn; AAUP. **RESEARCH** Scripture; theology; spirituality. **SELECTED PUBLICATIONS** Auth, The Synoptic Gethsemane, Gregorian Univ, 73; Christ's prayer & Christian prayer, Worship, 3/74. **CONTACT ADDRESS** Vallombrosa Ctr, 320 Middlefield Rd, Menlo Park, CA, 94025-3563.

HOLLEY, DAVID M.
DISCIPLINE PHILOSOPHY **EDUCATION** Southern Baptist Theol Sem, Louisville, Mdiv; Univ TX at Austin, PhD. **CAREER** Dept Phil, Univ S Miss **RESEARCH** Transformation of the self and strategies for avoiding wrongdoing. **SELECTED PUBLICATIONS** Publ on, studies in philosophy of religion, philosophy and rhetoric, ethics & philosophical psychology. **CONTACT ADDRESS** Dept of Philos and Relig, Univ of Southern MS, 2701 Hardy St, Hattiesburg, MS, 39406. **EMAIL** dmholley@ocean.st.usm.edu

HOLLEY, JIM
PERSONAL Born 12/05/1943, Philadelphia, PA, d **DISCIPLINE** THEOLOGY **EDUCATION** Wayne State University, Detroit MI, PhD, Higher Education; University of Chicago, Chicago, IL, Master of Divinity. **CAREER** LITTLE ROCK BAPTIST CHURCH, DETROIT, MI, PASTOR, 1972-; COGNOS ADVERTING, DETROIT, PRESIDENT, CEO, 1988-; ASHLAND THEOLOGICAL SEMINARY, DEAN. **CONTACT ADDRESS** Little Rock Baptist Church, 9000 Woodward Ave, Detroit, MI, 48202.

HOLLIS, SUSAN T.
PERSONAL Born 03/17/1939, Boston, MA, d, 2 children **DISCIPLINE** RELIGION; ANCIENT NEAR EASTERN LANGUAGES & CIVILIZATIONS **EDUCATION** Harvard, PhD, 82 **CAREER** Prof, Union Inst Los Angeles, 91-93; dean & prof, Sierra Nevada Col, 93-95; center dir & assoc dean, Central NY Center, State Univ of NY, Empire State Col, 96- **HONORS AND AWARDS** Teaching Excellence, Harvard Col; Who's Who in the West, East, America, World, Women **MEMBERSHIPS** Amer Res Egypt; Amer Acad Relig; Soc Bibl Lit; Int Assoc Egyptologist; Amer Folklore Soc **RESEARCH** Ancient Egypt; Ancient Israel; Egyptian Relations; Folklore **SELECTED PUBLICATIONS** Ed, Ancient Egyptian Hymns, Prayers, and Songs. An Anthology of Ancient Egyptian Lyric Poetry, Scholar's Press, 95; co-ed & contributor, Feminist Theory and the Study of Folklore, Univ Ill, 93; auth, "Otiose Deities and the Ancient Egyptian Pantheon," Jrnl Amer Res Center in Egypt, 98 **CONTACT ADDRESS** SUNY Empire State Col, 219 Walton St, Syracuse, NY, 13202-1226. **EMAIL** susan_hollis@sln.esc.edu

HOLLOWAY, ALVIN J.
PERSONAL Born 07/02/1926, Shreveport, LA, s **DISCIPLINE** PHILOSOPHY **EDUCATION** Spring Hill Col, BS, 49; St Louis Univ, STL, 57; Fordham Univ, PhD, 65. **CAREER** Chemn, philos dept, Loyola Univ, 67-98. **MEMBERSHIPS** APA; Am Catholic Philos Asn. **RESEARCH** Medieval philosophy; Augustine; biomedical ethics. **CONTACT ADDRESS** 6363 St Charles Ave, New Orleans, LA, 70118. **EMAIL** holloway@loyno.edu

HOLM, TAWNY
PERSONAL Born 08/29/1966, WY, s **DISCIPLINE** HEBREW BIBLE **EDUCATION** John Hopkins Univ, PhD, 97. **CAREER** Vis Lect, 95-96, Central Col; Adj Prof, 97-98, Loyola Col; Adj Prof, 97-98, St Marys Ecumenical Inst; Vis Asst Prof, 98-, DePauw Univ. **MEMBERSHIPS** Soc of Bibl Lit; Catholic Bibl Assoc **RESEARCH** The book of Daniel; Syriac philology; Demotic Egyptian story cycles. **CONTACT ADDRESS** DePauw Univ, 103e Harrison Hall, Dept of Re, Greencastle, IN, 46135. **EMAIL** tholm@depauw.edu

HOLMAN, CHARLES L.
DISCIPLINE NEW TESTAMENT **EDUCATION** Westmont Col, BA; Fuller Theol Sem, BD, ThM; Univ Nottingham, Eng, PhD. **CAREER** Instr, Jamaica Theol Sem, 64-69; dean, instr, Trinity Christian Training Inst, 72-78; asst prof, 82-86; assoc prof, 87-93; prof, 93-. **SELECTED PUBLICATIONS** Auth, A Response to Roger Stronstad's The Biblical Precedent for Historical Precedent, 93; Paul's Preaching Cognitive and Charismatic, Spirit and Renewal: Essays in Honor of J. Rodman Williams, Jour Pentecostal Theol, Supplement Series 5, Sheffield Acad Press, 94; Titus 3:5-6: A Window on World-Wide Pentecost, Jour Pentecostal Theol 8, 96; Till Jesus Comes: Origins of Christian Apocalyptic Expectation, Hendrickson, 96. **CONTACT ADDRESS** Dept of New Testament, Regent Univ, 1000 Regent Univ Dr, Virginia Beach, VA, 23464-9831.

HOLMES, RICHARD H.
DISCIPLINE PHILOSOPHY **EDUCATION** Wash Univ, PhD, 72. **RESEARCH** Contemporary European philos; philos of/in lit. **SELECTED PUBLICATIONS** Auth, The Transcendence of the World, Wilfrid Laurier, 94; ed, Moritz Geiger's The Significance of Art; Husserl Memorial Issue of Eidos. **CONTACT ADDRESS** Dept of Philosophy, Waterloo Univ, 200 University Ave W, Waterloo, ON, N2L 3G1. **EMAIL** rholmes@uwaterloo.ca

HOLMES, ROBERT ERNEST
PERSONAL Born 07/24/1943, New York, NY, s **DISCIPLINE** LAW **EDUCATION** NY U, BA 1966; NY Univ Sch of Law, JD 1969; Manhattan Sch Of Music & Univ of So CA, addl study. **CAREER** Paul Weiss Rifkind Wharton & Garrison, summer assoc 1968, part time atty 1968-69, assoc atty 1969-71; WA Sq Coll of Arts & Sci, guest lectr 1969-70, adj instr Amer Lit 1970-71; NY School of Continuing Educ, adj instr Black Amer 1969-70; Motown Record Corp, sr counsel 1971, legal counsel 1971; Columbia Pictures Music Group, sr vp, gen mgr, pres Columbia Pictures Music Publ Div. **HONORS AND AWARDS** Dean's List Temple Univ & NY Univ Sch of Law; Univ Schlrshp NY U, NY State Schlrshp NY U; Leopold Schepp Fnd Schlrshp NY U; various debate & pub spkng awrds; Am Jurisprudence Prize in Copyright; Military History Award Temple Univ 1963; recipient Fulbright-Dougherty Travel Grant 1967; Samuel Rubin SchlrshpCarnegie Fnd Schlrshp **MEMBERSHIPS** Bd dir Pacific Psychotherapy Asso CA; bd dir NAACP; bd dir Constl Rights Found CA; bd dir Black Music Assoc; past pres Black Entertainment & Sports Lawyers' Assoc. **SELECTED PUBLICATIONS** numerous publs. **CONTACT ADDRESS** Columbia Pictures Music Publ, Columbia Plaza E, Rm 231, Burbank, CA, 91505.

HOLMES, ROBERT LAWRENCE
PERSONAL Born 12/28/1935, Watertown, NY, m, 1958, 2 children **DISCIPLINE** PHILOSOPHY **EDUCATION** Harvard Univ, AB, 57; Univ MI, MA, 59, PhD, 61. **CAREER** Instr philos, Univ TX, 61-62; from asst prof to assoc prof, 62-71, Prof Philos, Univ Rochester, 71-, Am Coun Learned Soc grant-in-aid, 64; fel, Ctr Advan Studies, Univ IL, 70-71; fel, Nat Hum Inst, Yale Univ, 76-77; Sr fulb lec, moscow univ, 83; Ed, Public Affairs Quarterly, 95-99. **MEMBERSHIPS** Am Philos Asn. **RESEARCH** Ethics; philos of war; soc and polit philos. **SELECTED PUBLICATIONS** Auth, Descriptivism, supervenience and universalizability, J Philos, 3/66; John Dewey's moral philosophy in contemporary perspective, Rev Metaphysics, 9/66; co-auth, Philosophic Inquiry: An Introduction to Philosophy, 2nd ed, Prentice-Hall, 68; auth, Violence and nonviolence, In: Violence, McKay, 71; University neutrality and ROTC, Ethics, 4/73; On pacifism, Monist, 10/73; Is morality a system of hypothetical imperative?, Analysis, 1/74; Nozick on anarchism, Polit Theory, 5/77; On War and Morality, 89; Ed, Nonviolence in Theory and Practice, 90; Basic Moral Philosophy, 93, 2nd edition, 98. **CONTACT ADDRESS** Dept of Philos, Univ of Rochester Dewey, 500 Joseph C Wilson, Rochester, NY, 14627-9000. **EMAIL** HLMS@db1.cc.rochester.edu

HOLTMAN, SARAH WILLIAMS
DISCIPLINE PHILOSOPHY **EDUCATION** Col of William and Mary, BA, 82; Univ Virginia, JD, 86; UNC-Chapel Hill, PhD, 95. **CAREER** Law Clerk, Massachusetts Supreme Ct, 86-87; Law Clerk, New Hampshire Supreme Ct, 87-89; Asst Prof, 95-, Univ Minnesota-Twin Cities. **HONORS AND AWARDS** Phi Betta Kappa; Charlotte W. Newcombe Fel, Woodrow Wilson Fdn, 94-95. **MEMBERSHIPS** Amer Phil Assoc. **RESEARCH** Ethics; political philosophy; philosophy of law; Kant's practical philosophy **SELECTED PUBLICATIONS** Auth, Kant's Formula of Humanity and the Pursuit of Subjective Ends, Proceedings of the 8th International Kant Congress, 95; A Kantian Approach to Prison Reform, Jahrbuch fur Rechtund Ethik, 97; Toward Social Reform: Kant's Penal Theory Reinterpreted, Utilitas, 97. **CONTACT ADDRESS** Dept of Philosophy, Univ of Minnesota-Twin Cities, 224 Church St. S.E., 355 Ford H, Minneapolis, MN, 55455. **EMAIL** holtm001@maroon.tc.umn.edu

HOMANS, PETER
PERSONAL Born 06/24/1930, New York, NY, m, 1958, 3 children **DISCIPLINE** RELIGIOUS STUDIES, RELIGION & PSYCHOLOGY **EDUCATION** Princeton Univ, AB, 52; Va

Theol Sem, BD, 57; Univ Chicago, PhD(relig & psychol), 64. **CAREER** Lectr relig, Trinity Col, Univ Toronto, 62-64; asst prof, Hartford Sem Found, 64-65; asst prof relig & psychol, 65-68, assoc prof, 68-79, prof Psychol and Relig Studies, Univ Chicago, 80-, Soc Values Higher Educ res grant popular cult, 73-74; Asn Theol Sch res grant relig & psychol, 77. **MEMBERSHIPS** Am Psychol Asn; Am Acad Relig; Soc Values Higher Educ. **RESEARCH** The psychology of religion; psychology and culture. **SELECTED PUBLICATIONS** Ed & contribr, The Dialogue Between Theology and Psychology, Univ Chicago, 68; auth, Theology After Freud: An Interpretive Inquiry, Bobbs Merrill & Co, 70; ed & contribr, Childhood and Selfhood: Essays on Tradition, Religion and Modernity in the Psychology of Erik H Erikson, Bucknell Univ, 78; The Ability to Mourn: Disillusionment and the Social Origins of Psychoanalysis, Univ Chicago Press, 89. **CONTACT ADDRESS** Univ of Chicago, 1025-35 E 58th St, Chicago, IL, 60637-1577. **EMAIL** phomans@midway.uchicago.edu

HOMERIN, T. EMIL
PERSONAL Born 05/19/1955, Pekin, IL, m, 1977, 2 children **DISCIPLINE** RELIGION **EDUCATION** Univ Illinois, BA, 77, MA, 78; Univ Chicago, PhD, 87. **CAREER** Lect Rel Stud, DePaul Univ, 82-83; lect Islamic Civ, George Williams Col, 83; asst prof Islamic Stud, Temple Univ, 86-88; asst prof Rel to ASSOC PROF, DEPT CHAIR, UNIV ROCHESTER, 94-. **HONORS AND AWARDS** Nom, Goergen Award Dist Ach, Artistry in Teach, 97; Hon men, Golden Key Nat Hon Soc Exemplary Commitment to Higher Educ, 95; G. Granyon & Jane W. Curtis Award Exc, 93; finalist, Teach Year, 92; Abraham J. Karp Award Exc, Univ Roch, 91; Am Asn Teachers of Arabic Translation Contest; Michael A. Scherer Award, Univ Ill, 77; James Scholar, Univ Ill, 75-76., Whitehall Fnd Scholar, 73-77; Ill State Scholar, 73-77; NDFL/NDEA Fel, 77-78; Ctr Arabic Stud Abroad Fel, 79-80; Nat Defense For Lang Fel, 80-82; Fulbright-Hays Fel Res Abroad, 83-84; Mrs. Giles Whiting Fel Hum, 85-86; NEH Fel, Cairo, (declined), 88- 89; Fulbright Islamic Civ Res Fel, 88-89. **MEMBERSHIPS** Am Acad Rel; Am Oriental Soc; Am Res Ctr Egypt; Middle East Stud Asn. **RESEARCH** Arabic poetry; Islam; mysticism. **SELECTED PUBLICATIONS** Auth, From Arab Poet to Muslim Saint: Ibn al-Farid, His Verse, and His Shrine, Univ SC Press, 94; auth, "Reflections on Arabic Poetry in the Mamluk Age," Mamluk Stud Rev 1, 97; auth, "Ibn al-Farid," and Munawi's Literary Hagiography of Ibn al-Farid," in Windows on the House of Islam, Univ Calif Press, 98; auth, "Saving Muslim Souls: the Khanqah and the Sufi Duty in Mamluk Lands," Mamluk Stud Rev, 3, 99; **CONTACT ADDRESS** Dept Religion and Classics, Univ of Rochester, Rochester, NY, 14627. **EMAIL** THEH@db6.cc.rochester.edu

HONEYCUTT, DWIGHT A.
PERSONAL m, 3 children **DISCIPLINE** CHURCH HISTORY **EDUCATION** Mercer Univ, BA; Midwestern Baptist Sem, BD; Intl Baptist Theol Sem, Switzerland, ThM; New Orleans Baptist Theol Sem, ThD. **CAREER** Instr, ch, Acad Comm, Intl Baptist Theol Sem, Cali, Colombia, 77; vis prof, New Orleans Baptist Theol Sem; Midwestern Baptist Theol Sem, 87-88; prof, 88; William A. Carleton prof, Golden Gate Baptist Theol Sem, 92-. **HONORS AND AWARDS** Assoc secy, missionary personnel, S Baptist For Mission Bd, 72. **SELECTED PUBLICATIONS** Pub(s), Theol Educator; Bolotin Teologico de ABITHA; El Heraldo; Dialogo Teologica; Jour Church and State; SBC Quart Rev. **CONTACT ADDRESS** Golden Gate Baptist Theol Sem, 201 Sem Dr, Mill Valley, CA, 94941-3197. **EMAIL** DwightHoneycutt@ggbts.edu

HONG, CHANG-SEONG
PERSONAL Born 09/03/1964, Incheon, Korea, m, 1993 **DISCIPLINE** PHILOSOPHY **EDUCATION** Brown Univ, MA, 95, PhD, 99. **CAREER** Adj prof, RI Col, 97-98; asst prof, St. Cloud State Univ, 98-. **MEMBERSHIPS** Am Philos Asn; Soc Philos Psychol. **RESEARCH** Philosophy of mind; metaphysics. **SELECTED PUBLICATIONS** Auth, Natural Kinds and the Identity of Property, Teorema, 98; auth, Kripke's Reference Theory, Philos Forum, 91; auth, Falsifiability and the Growth of Knowledge, Philos Forum, 88. **CONTACT ADDRESS** Dept of Philosophy, St. Cloud State Univ, Brown Hall 123, St. Cloud, MN, 56301. **EMAIL** cshong@stcloudstate.edu

HONG, HOWARD V.
PERSONAL Born 10/19/1912, Wolford, ND, m, 1938, 8 children **DISCIPLINE** PHILOSOPHY **EDUCATION** St. Olaf Col, BA, 34; Univ Minn, PhD. **CAREER** Prof, philos, St. Olaf Col, 38-78; general ed, Kierkegaard's Writings, Princeton Univ Press, 72-. **HONORS AND AWARDS** Knight of Dannebrog; D. Hum., Carleton Col; Ll. D., McGill Univ; Th. D., Univ Copenhagen. **MEMBERSHIPS** Amer Philos Asn. **RESEARCH** Kierkegaard; Philosophical anthropology. **SELECTED PUBLICATIONS** Auth, Kierkegaard's Writings, 98. **CONTACT ADDRESS** 5174 E. 90 Olad Dutch Rd., Northfield, MN, 55057.

HONORE, STEPHAN LEROY
PERSONAL Born 05/14/1938, Urbana, OH, m **DISCIPLINE** LAW **EDUCATION** Capital Univ, BS 1960; Univ of Toledo, JD 1974. **CAREER** Peace Corps Columbia, Dominican Rep, 1961-66; US State Dept AID, 1966-68; Trans Century Corp, 1968-69; Model Cities Prog Toledo, 1970-71; Peace Corps Dominican Rep, 1978-81; Thurgood Marshall School of Law, law prof 1974-84; self-employed Houston, TX, Attorney at law, import/export business, real estate, 1984-; Telecommunications, 1994-. **MEMBERSHIPS** Student body pres Capital Univ 1960-69; presiding justice, student honor ct Univ of Toledo Coll of Law 1973-74; law reveiw, casenote editor Univ of Toledo Law 1973-74; bd of dir Immigration Counselling Ctr 1976-78; mem State Bar of TX, Natl Bar Assn, Houston Bar Assn, Amer Immigration Lawyers Assn; pres 1984-86, mem Parochial Sch Bd 1983-88; mem, bd of educ, Galueston-Houston Catholic Diocese, 1988-94, pres of bd, 1992-94. **SELECTED PUBLICATIONS** Articles on criminal & labor law, Univ of Toledo Law Review.

HOOD, EDWIN T.
DISCIPLINE LAW **EDUCATION** Univ Iowa, JD; Univ NY, LLM. **CAREER** Prof **HONORS AND AWARDS** Pearson Awd, 93. **RESEARCH** Taxation. **SELECTED PUBLICATIONS** Auth, Closely Held Businesses in Estate Planning, Aspen Law Bus, 98; co-auth, Federal Taxation of Close Corporations, Callaghan. **CONTACT ADDRESS** Law Dept, Univ of Missouri, Kansas City, 5100 Rockhill Rd, Kansas City, MO, 64110-2499. **EMAIL** hoode@umkc.edu

HOOKER, PAUL K.
PERSONAL Born 12/17/1953, Wartrace, TN, m, 1990, 2 children **DISCIPLINE** OLD TESTAMENT **EDUCATION** Univ TN, BA, 75; Union Theological Sem, VA, DMin, 79; Emory Univ, PhD, 93. **CAREER** Presbyterian minister, 20 years; PASTOR, ROCK SPRING PRESBYTERIAN CHURCH, 93-. **MEMBERSHIPS** Soc of Biblical Lit **RESEARCH** 1-2 Kings; 1-2 Chronicles; church's use of scripture. **SELECTED PUBLICATIONS** Auth, A New Chronology for the Kings of Israel and Judah, with John H. Hayes. **CONTACT ADDRESS** 1824 Piedmont Ave. NE, Atlanta, GA, 30324. **EMAIL** pkhooker@mindspring.com

HOOKS, BENJAMIN LAWSON
PERSONAL Born 01/31/1925, Memphis, TN, m, 1951 **DISCIPLINE** LAW **EDUCATION** LeMoyne College, attended, 1941-43; Howard University, attended, 1943-44; DePaul University, JD, 1948. **CAREER** Attorney, 1949-65, 1968-72; Mutual Federal Savings & Loan Assn, co-founder, vice pres, director, chairman, 1955-69; Middle Baptist Church, pastor, 1956-72; asst public defender, 1961-64; Greater New Mt Moriah Baptist Church, pastor, 1964-; Shelby County Criminal Court, judge, 1965-68; Federal Communications Commission, 1972-78; NAACP, executive director, 1977-93; Chapman Co, senior vice pres, 1993; Fisk Univ, prof of social justice, 1993-. **HONORS AND AWARDS** Howard University, honorary LLD, 1975; Wilberforce University, honorary LLD, 1976; Central State University, honorary DHL, 1974, honorary LLD, 1976; Masons, Man of the Year Award, 1964, Gold Medal Achievement Award, 1972; Optimist Club of America Award, 1966; Lincoln League Award, 1965; Tennessee Regional Baptist Convention Award; Spingarn Award, NAACP, 1986; producer/host, Conversations in Black & White; co-producer, Forty Percent Speaks; panelist, What Is Your Faith?. **MEMBERSHIPS** Natl Bar Assn, judicial council; American Bar Assn; Tenessee Bar Assn; bd trustee, LeMoyne-Owen College; bd dir, Southern Christian Leadership Conference, 1968-72; grand chancellor, Knights Pythias; bd trustee, Hampton Institute; Natl Civil Rights Museum, bd member. **CONTACT ADDRESS** Fisk Univ, 1000 17th Ave N, Nashville, TN, 37208-3051.

HOOPS, MERLIN HENRY
PERSONAL Born 10/02/1926, Byron, NE, m, 1955, 2 children **DISCIPLINE** THEOLOGY, NEW TESTAMENT **EDUCATION** Capital Univ, AB, 51; Evangel Lutheran Theol Sem, BD, 55; Univ Hamburg, ThD(New Testament), 58. **CAREER** Assoc prof, 60-71, prof, 71-81, Ernest W & Edith S Ogram Prof, 81-94, Ernest W & Edith S Ogram prof emer New Testament studies, Trinity Lutheran Sem, OH, 94-; mem, Lutheran-Orthodox Comn, 66-68 & dept of theol studies, Lutheran Coun. **MEMBERSHIPS** Soc Bibl Lit; Lutheran Acad Scholar (treas, 71-). **RESEARCH** New Testament backgrounds; Gospel of Matthew and John; liberation theology. **SELECTED PUBLICATIONS** Auth, The concept of Liberation, Lutheran Quart, 8/76; Translating the Bible: The Challenge of an Ongoing Process, Trinity Sem Rev, fall 81. **CONTACT ADDRESS** Trinity Lutheran Sem, 2199 E Main St, Columbus, OH, 43209-2334.

HOOVER, STEWART
DISCIPLINE RELIGIOUS STUDIES **EDUCATION** Univ Pa, PhD. **CAREER** Prof. **RESEARCH** Media and religion; cultural studies; contemporary American religious movements. **SELECTED PUBLICATIONS** Auth, Media and Moral Order in Post-Positivist Media Studie; Religion in the Media; co-ed, Media, Religion and Culture. **CONTACT ADDRESS** Religious Studies Dept, Univ of Colorado, Boulder, Boulder, CO, 80309. **EMAIL** Stewart.Hoover@Colorado.edu

HOPKINS, DONALD RAY
PERSONAL Born 11/14/1936, Tulsa, OK, d **DISCIPLINE** LAW **EDUCATION** University of Kansas, BA 1958; Yale University, MA 1959; University of California Berkeley, JD 1965; Harvard Law School, LLM (cum laude) 1969. **CAREER** Univ of California Berkeley, teaching asst 1960-63, asst dean of students 1965-67, asst exec v chancellor 1967-68; NAACP Legal Defense Fund Inc, staff Attorney 1969-70; Pacific Cons, exec vice pres 1970-71; Eighth California Cong Dist, dist admins 1971-; Attorney in Private Practice 1981-. **HONORS AND AWARDS** Various achievement awds; Woodrow Wilson Fellow; Phi Beta Kappa; Pi Sigma Alpha. **MEMBERSHIPS** Estate tax examiner US Treasury Dept 1965; coll teacher Univ of California Laney Coll 1966-68; Acad of Polit Sci; Arbitration Assn Bd of Arbitrators; bd dir ACLU, No California 1969-71; bd dir Univ of California Alumni Assn 1976-79; bd dir African Film Soc; bd dir Travelers Aid Soc; Kansas/Yale/Harvard/Univ of California Alumni Assn; California State, Natl, American, Federal, Alameda Cty Bar Assns; bd dir Chas Houston Bar Assn; Amer Trial Lawyers Assn; Natl Conference of Black Lawyers; Natl Lawyers Guild; California Assn of Black Lawyers; bd dir Volunteer on Parole. **SELECTED PUBLICATIONS** Co-auth "Politics & Change in Berkeley" Nathan & Scott; various articles. **CONTACT ADDRESS** District Administrator, 8th CA Cong Dist, 201-13th St, Ste 105, Oakland, CA, 94612.

HOPKINS, DWIGHT N.
PERSONAL Born 02/22/1953, Richmond, VA, m **DISCIPLINE** THEOLOGY **EDUCATION** Harvard Univ, BA, 76; Union Theol Seminary, Mdiv, 84, Mphil, 87, PhD, 88. **CAREER** Assoc Prof, 88-95, Santa Clara Univ; Assoc of Theol, 96-, Univ Chicago Divinity School. **MEMBERSHIPS** Amer Acad of Rel; Soc for the study of Black Rel; Ecumenical Assoc of Third World Theol. **RESEARCH** Rel; Polit; culture; Econ. **SELECTED PUBLICATIONS** Auth, Black Theology USA and South Africa, Maryknoll, NY, Orbis Books, 89; We Are One Voice: Essays on Black Theology in South Africa and the USA, Johannesburg, South Africa, Slotaville Press, 89; Cut Loose Your Stammering Tongue: Black Theology in the Slave Narratives, Maryknoll, NY, Orbis Books, 91' Shoes That Fit Our Feet: Sources for a Constructive Black Theology, Maryknoll, NY, Orbis Books, 93; Changing Conversations: Religious Reflection and Cultural Analysis, NY, Routledge, 96; Liberation Theologies, Postmodernity and the Americas, NY, Routledge, 97; Introducing Black Theology of Liberation, Maryknoll, NY, Orbis Books, 99. **CONTACT ADDRESS** Univ of Chicago Divinity School, 1025 E 58th St, Chicago, IL, 60637. **EMAIL** Dhopkins@MiDWAY.uchicago.EDU

HOPKINS, JASPER
DISCIPLINE PHILOSOPHY **EDUCATION** Harvard Univ, PhD. **RESEARCH** Ancient philosophy; history of medieval and Renaissance philosophy. **SELECTED PUBLICATIONS** Auth, Nicholas of Cusa on Wisdom and Knowledge, 96; A Miscellany on Nicholas of Cusa, 94; Philosophical Criticism: Essays and Reviews, 94. **CONTACT ADDRESS** Philosophy Dept, Univ of Minnesota, Twin Cities, 355 Ford Hall, 224 Church St SE, Minneapolis, MN, 55455. **EMAIL** hopki001@maroon.tc.umn.edu

HOPKINS, THOMAS J.
PERSONAL Born 07/28/1930, Champaign, IL, m, 1956, 4 children **DISCIPLINE** HISTORY OF RELIGIONS **EDUCATION** Col William & Mary & Mass Inst Technol, BS, 53; Yale Univ, BS, 58, MA, 59, PhD, 62. **CAREER** From instr to assoc prof, 61-72, Prof Relig, 72-96, EMER PROF RELIG SCI, 96-, FRANKLIN & MARSHALL COL, 61- ; Dir India Studies prog, Cent Pa Consortium, 71-75; chmn group Indian philos & relig, Coun Intercult Studies & Prog, 72-77; chr AAR Asian Relig/Hist Relig Sect, 75-80; co-chr AAR Comp Stud Relig Section, 80-87. **MEMBERSHIPS** Asn Asian Studies; Am Orient Soc; Am Acad Relig; Am Soc Study Relig. **RESEARCH** Indian history; phenomenology of religion. **SELECTED PUBLICATIONS** Auth, The social teaching of the Bhagavata Purana, In: Krishna: Myths, Rites and Attitudes, East-West, 66; The Hindu Religious Tradition, Dickenson, 71; Contribr, Six Pillars: Introduction to the Major Works of Sri Avrobindo, Conchocheague Assoc, 74; contrib Hare Krishna, Hare Krishna, Grove Press, 83; Krishna Consciousness in the West, Bucknell Univ Press, 89; Death and Afterlife: Perspectives of World Religions, Greenwood Press, 92. **CONTACT ADDRESS** 323 N West End Ave, Lancaster, PA, 17603.

HOPPE, E.A.
PERSONAL Born 10/14/1963, Seattle, WA, s **DISCIPLINE** PHILOSOPHY **EDUCATION** DePaul Univ, PhD, 99. **CAREER** Part-time instr, DePaul Univ, 95-99. **HONORS AND AWARDS** DePaul Fel. **MEMBERSHIPS** APA; SPEP; Nietzsche Soc. **RESEARCH** Plato; metaphysics. **CONTACT ADDRESS** 4539 N Whipple St, #3W, Chicago, IL, 60625. **EMAIL** eahoppe@worldnet.att.net

HOPPE, LESLIE JOHN
PERSONAL Born 09/22/1944, Chicago, IL **DISCIPLINE** HEBREW SCRIPTURES, ANCIENT NEAR EAST RELIGIONS **EDUCATION** St Francis Col, BA, 67; Aquinas Inst

Theol, MA, 71; Northwestern Univ, PhD(relig), 78. **CAREER** Asst prof Old Testament, Aquinas Inst Theol, 76-79; assoc prof, St Mary of the Lake Sem, 79-81; PROF OLD TESTAMENT, CATH THEOL UNION, 81-; Vis lectr, North Park Theol Sem, 76; vis prof, Garrett-Evangelical Theol Sem, 80-81; Studium Biblicum Franciscanum, 94, 98. **MEMBERSHIPS** Soc Bibl Lit; Cath Bibl Asn; Am Schs Orient Res **RESEARCH** Deuteronomic literature; post-exilic literature; wisdom literature. **SELECTED PUBLICATIONS** Auth, Joshua-Judges, 82; What Are They Saying About Biblical Archaeology, 84; Being Poor: A Biblical Study, 87; Deuteronomy, 86; A New Heart: The Book of Ezekiel, 91; Churches and Synagogues of Ancient Palestine, 94. **CONTACT ADDRESS** 5401 S Cornell Ave, Chicago, IL, 60615-6200. **EMAIL** 76753.3230@compuserve.edu

HOPPER, DAVID HENRY
PERSONAL Born 07/31/1927, Cranford, NJ, m, 1967, 3 children **DISCIPLINE** RELIGION **EDUCATION** Yale Univ, BA, 50; Princeton Theol Sem, BD, 53, ThD, 59. **CAREER** From Asst prof to assoc prof, 59-73, Prof Relig, Macalester Col, 73- **MEMBERSHIPS** Am Acad Relig; Int Bonhoeffer Soc, AAUP. **RESEARCH** Systematic theology; Biblical studies; existentialism. **SELECTED PUBLICATIONS** Auth, Technology and Religion, Zygon, Vol 0028, 93; auth, Technology, Theology, and the Idea of Progress, Westminster, 91. **CONTACT ADDRESS** Dept of Relig Studies, Macalester Col, 1600 Grand Ave, Saint Paul, MN, 55105-1899. **EMAIL** hopper@macalester.edu

HOPPERTON, ROBERT J.
DISCIPLINE LAW **EDUCATION** Baldwin Wallace Col, BA; Univ Toledo, MA; Ohio State Univ, JD. **CAREER** Prof. **SELECTED PUBLICATIONS** Auth, Majoritarian and Counter-Majoritarian Difficulties: Democracy, Distrust, and Disclosure in American Land-Use Jurisprudence-A Response to Professors Mandelker and Tarlock, Boston Col Environ Affairs Law Rev, 97; Standards of Judicial Review in Supreme Court Land Use Opinions: A Taxonomy, an Analytical Framework, and a Synthesis, Univ Wash J Urban Contemporary Law, 97; The Presumption of Validity in American Land Use Law: A Substitute for Analysis, A Source of Significant Confusion, Boston Col Environ Affairs Law Rev, 96; Teaching Present and Future Interests: A Methodology for Students That Unifies Estates in Land Concepts, Structures, and Principles, Univ Toledo, 95. **CONTACT ADDRESS** Col Law, Univ of Toledo, Toledo, OH, 43606. **EMAIL** rhopper@uoft02.utoledo.edu

HOPPMAN, R.A.
PERSONAL Born 08/20/1950, Charleston, SC, m, 1975, 3 children **DISCIPLINE** INTERNAL MEDICINE; RHEUMATOLOGY **EDUCATION** Univ South Carolina, BS 72, MD 82. **CAREER** East Carolina Univ, asst prof, 87-90; SC Sch of Medicine, prof, V Ch, 90-; Performing Arts Clinic, dir, 97-. **HONORS AND AWARDS** Outstanding Tchr 93-98; Ciba-Geigy Outstanding Med Resi Awd; Alpha Omega Alpha; VA Commendation; Who's Who in the South and SW. **MEMBERSHIPS** AMA; ACP; ACR; SCRA; IAMA; Nat Assoc of VA Physicians and Dentists; Performing Arts Med Assoc. **RESEARCH** Medical problems of performing artists; medical education. **SELECTED PUBLICATIONS** Auth, Musculoskeletal problems in instrumental musicians, Performing Arts Medicine, eds, Brandfonbrener, Lederman, Sataloff, Singular Pub Gp Inc, 98; Ulna nerve entrapment in a French horn player, J Clinical Rheumatology, 97; The medical history of great composers: an educational aid, Med Problems Performing Artists, 97; Pharmocologic Management of Pain in Performing Artists, Med Problems Performing Artists, 96; Musculoskeletal problems of musicians: a niche for the rheumatologist, Jour Clinical Rheumatology, 95; Nonsteroidal anti-inflammatory drugs in performing arts medicine, Med Problems Performing Artists, 93; Performing Arts Medicine: getting regional involvement, Sixteenth Annual Symposium on Medical Problems of Musicians and Dancers, Aspen CO, 98. **CONTACT ADDRESS** Dept of Medicine, South Carolina Univ, Two Richland Medical Park, #502, Columbia, SC, 29203. **EMAIL** Hoppman@richmed.medpark.sc.edu

HORNE, GERALD CHARLES
PERSONAL Born 01/03/1949, St. Louis, MO, m, 1994 **DISCIPLINE** LAW, AFRICAN-AMERICAN STUDIES **EDUCATION** Princeton Univ, BA, 1970; Univ California-Berkeley, JD, 1973; Columbia Univ , PhD, 1982. **CAREER** Affirmative Action Coord Center, dir counsel 1979-82; Sarah Lawrence Coll, prof, 1982-88; Natl Conf of Black Lawyers, exec dir, 1985-86; Local 1199 Health and Hospital Workers Union AFL-CIO, special counsel, 1986-88; Univ of California, Santa Barbara, prof; UNIV OF NORTH CAROLINA, PROF, currently. **HONORS AND AWARDS** Natl Conf of Black Lawyers, Hope Stevens Award, 1983; Univ of California, Santa Barbara, Getman Service to Students Award, 1990; Council on Intl Exchange of Scholars, Fullbright Scholar/Univ of Zimbabwe, 1995; Univ of Virginia, Carter G Woodson Fellow, 1991-92; City Univ of NY, Belle Zeller Visiting Prof, 1993-94. **MEMBERSHIPS** Natl Lawyers Guild, Intl Committee, chair, 1988-92; Natl Conf of Black Lawyers, Intl Committee, chair, 1982-85; Pears and Freedom Party, chair, 1991-92; American Federation of Teachers, Local 2274, sec/treas, 1976-78. **CONTACT ADDRESS** Univ of No Carolina, CB5250, Chapel Hill, NC, 27599-5250.

HORNE, JAMES R.
DISCIPLINE PHILOSOPHY **EDUCATION** Univ Columbia, PhD, 64. **RESEARCH** Philos of religion; ethics. **SELECTED PUBLICATIONS** Auth, Beyond Mysticism, WLU, 78; The Moral Mystic, WLU, 83; Mysticism and Vocation, WLU, 96. **CONTACT ADDRESS** Dept of Philosophy, Waterloo Univ, 200 University Ave W, Waterloo, ON, N2L 3G1. **EMAIL** jrhorne@uwaterloo.ca

HORNE, MARTHA J.
DISCIPLINE NEW TESTAMENT **EDUCATION** Duke Univ, AB, 70; Va Theol Sem, MDiv, 83; Episcopal Divinity Sch, DD, 98. **CAREER** Adj instr, field edu mentor, 83-85; asst to Vicar, St. Andrew's Episcopal Church, 83-85; asst rector, Christ Church, 85-86; asst to the dean, 86-88; assoc dean for admin, 88-94; dean, pres, Va Theol Sem, 94-. **SELECTED PUBLICATIONS** Auth, A Vision for Theological Education in North America, Anglicanism: A Global Communion, Mowbray, 98; Sabbath and Compasssion, The Living Pulpit, 98; rev, Review of Saving Work: Feminist Practices of Theological Education by Rebecca Chapp, In Trust mag, 96. **CONTACT ADDRESS** Va Theol Sem, 3737 Seminary Rd, Alexandria, VA, 22304. **EMAIL** MHorne@vts.edu

HORNE, MILTON P.
PERSONAL Born 03/19/1956, Antlers, OK, m, 1975, 2 children **DISCIPLINE** RELIGION **EDUCATION** Missouri Univ, Columbia, BA, 79; Northwestern Baptist Seminary, KC, MDiv, 83; Oxford Univ., Oxford, Eng, Dphilo, 90. **CAREER** Inst, Asst, Assoc, and Prof, William Jewell Coll, 86-present. **HONORS AND AWARDS** Wand Keavtely Award in Archaeology, NEH Summer Seminar, Tenure at William Jewell Coll. **MEMBERSHIPS** SBL; Natl Assoc of Baptist Prof of Rel. **RESEARCH** Hebrew-Wisdom Literature; sociology of religion; Academic Teaching of Bible and Religion. **SELECTED PUBLICATIONS** Auth, Rereading the Bible, Prentice-Hall, forthcoming; Proverbs and Ecclesiastes, Smith-Helwys, forthcoming. **CONTACT ADDRESS** Dept of Religion, William Jewell Col, 500 College Hill, Liberty, MO, 64068. **EMAIL** hornem@william.jewell.edu

HORNE, RALPH ALBERT
PERSONAL Born 03/10/1929, Haverhill, MA **DISCIPLINE** CHEMISTRY, PHILOSOPHY, LAW **EDUCATION** MIT, SB, 50; Univ Vermont, MS, 52; Boston Univ, MA, 53; Columbia Univ, PhD, 55; Suffolk Univ Law Sch, JD, 79. **CAREER** Tchg asst, Univ Vermont, 50-52; tchg asst, Columbia Univ, 53; res asst, Brookhaven Nat Lab, 53-55; post doc fel, MIT, 55-57; sr sci, Radio Corp Am, 57-58; sr sci, Jos Kave & Co, 58-60; sci staff, Arthur D Little Inc, 60-69, 72-78; assoc sci, Hole Ocean Inst, 70-71; faculty, MIT, 70-71; prin sci, JBP Sci Corp, 71-72; SR SCI, ENERGY 7 ENVIR ENGG INC, 80-; pres & found, Free Speech Found, 80-. **SELECTED PUBLICATIONS** Marine Chemistry, Wiley & Sons, 69; edr, Water and Aqueous Solutions, Wiley & Sons, 72; The Chemistry of Our Environment, Wiley & Sons, 78. **CONTACT ADDRESS** 9 Wellington St, Boston, MA, 02118.

HORNECKER, RONALD L.
PERSONAL m, 2 children **DISCIPLINE** MINISTRY **EDUCATION** Northwest Mo State Univ, BA; Midwestern Baptist Theol Sem, MDiv, DMin. **CAREER** Assoc, supervised ministry, 85; assoc prof, 87; prof, Golden Gate Baptist Theol Sem, 97. **HONORS AND AWARDS** PACT Church of the Yr award, Noland Road Baptist Church in Independence, Pastor, Noland Road Baptist Church in Independence; founding co-pastor, Novato Christian Fel; supvr, Midwestern Baptist Theol Sem's Field Edu prog. **MEMBERSHIPS** Mem, Assn for Theol Field Edu; S Baptist In-Service Guidance org. **SELECTED PUBLICATIONS** Contrib, Experiencing Ministry Supervision. **CONTACT ADDRESS** Golden Gate Baptist Theol Sem, 201 Sem Dr, Mill Valley, CA, 94941-3197. **EMAIL** RonHornecker@ggbts.edu

HOROVITZ, AMIR
PERSONAL Born 02/23/1959, Israel, m, 1995 **DISCIPLINE** PHILOSOPHY **EDUCATION** Tel-Aviv Univ, PhD, 93. **CAREER** Instr, 91-93, Instr Dr, 93-95, Tel-Aviv Univ; sr lectr, Suffolk Univ, 97-. **RESEARCH** Philosophy of mind and cognitive science; Philosophy of languages; Philosophy of science; Epistemalogy; Philosophy of law. **SELECTED PUBLICATIONS** Auth, Searle's Mind: Physical, irreducible, subjective and noncomputational, Pragmatics & Cognition, 94; A Note on The Intentionality of Fear, Philosophica 53, 94; Content and Sensitivity, Iyyun 44, 95; Mind and Body in the Thought of Yeshayahu Leibowitz, Yeshayahu Leibowitz, His World and Philosophy, Keter, 95; Philosophy of Mind, The Hebrew Encyclo, 95; Putnam, Searle, and Externalism, Philos Studies 81, 96; auth, A Critical Study of Mental Causation, Philosophia, 98. **CONTACT ADDRESS** 6 Ashton Pl., Cambridge, MA, 02138.

HOROWITZ, DONALD L.
PERSONAL Born 06/27/1939, New York, NY, m, 1960, 3 children **DISCIPLINE** LAW, POLITICAL SCIENCE **EDUCATION** Syracuse Univ, AB, 59, LLB, 61; Harvard Univ, LLM, 62, MA, 65, PhD(polit sci), 67. **CAREER** Law clerk to Joseph S Lord, US Dist Ct, Philadelphia, 65-66; res assoc, Ctr Int Affairs, Harvard Univ, 67-69; atty, Civil Div, US Dept Justice, 69-71; fel, Am Foreign Relations & Woodrow Wilson Ctr, 71-72; res assoc, Brookings Inst, 72-75; sr fel, Res Inst Immigration & Ethnic Studies, 75-81; Prof Law, Sch Law, Duke Univ, 80-, Consult, Ford Found, 77-82; mem, Coun on the Role Courts, 79-; Guggenheim fel, Guggenheim Found, 80-81. **HONORS AND AWARDS** Louis Brownlow Prize, Nat Acad Pub Admin, 77; McDonald-Currie lectr, McGill Univ, 80. **RESEARCH** Ethnic group relations; labor law and labor relations; legal philosophy. **SELECTED PUBLICATIONS** Auth, The Quran and the Common-Law--Islamic Law Reform and the Theory of Legal Change, Am J Comp Law, Vol 0042, 94. **CONTACT ADDRESS** Sch of Law, Duke Univ, Durham, NC, 27706.

HORSNELL, MALCOLM J.A.
PERSONAL Born 01/31/1939, London, England, m, 1965, 1 child **DISCIPLINE** BIBLICAL STUDIES **EDUCATION** Toronto Baptist Sem, BD, 67; Wilfred Laurier Univ, BA, 67; Princeton Theol Sem, ThM, 68; Univ Toronto, PhD, 74. **CAREER** Min, St John's Road Baptist Church, 75-78; asst prof, Univ Toronto, New Testament, Univ Toronto, 77-78; asst prof, assoc prof, prof, 78-, assoc dean, 93- , dir, Basic Degree Prog, 98-, McMaster Div Col. **HONORS AND AWARDS** Arts Res Bd, 81-89, McMaster Univ; Social Sci and Hum Res Coun, 86-89. **MEMBERSHIPS** Sos of Bibl Lit; Am Oriental Soc; Can Soc of Bibl Stud; Can Soc for Mesopotamian Stud. **RESEARCH** Hebrew Biblical language; Sumeria. **SELECTED PUBLICATIONS** Auth, Biblical Concepts of Aging, McMaster Jour of Theol, 93; auth, Magic, Mantic, Jewelry/Ornaments, Incision/Cutting, in, The New International Dictionary of Old Testament Theology and Exegesis, Zondervan, 97; auth, A Review and Reference Grammar for Biblical Hebrew, McMaster, 98. **CONTACT ADDRESS** McMaster Divinity Col, McMaster Univ, Hamilton, ON, L8S 4K1. **EMAIL** horsnell@mcmail.cis.mcmaster.ca

HORST, IRVIN BUCKWALTER
PERSONAL Born 05/31/1915, Lancaster, PA, m, 1944, 4 children **DISCIPLINE** HISTORY, RELIGION **EDUCATION** Goshen Col, BA, 49; Univ Pa, MA, 51; Univ Amsterdam, PhD(theol), 66. **CAREER** Dir relief in Neth, Mennonite Cent Comt, 46-48; assoc prof hist, Eastern Mennonite Col, 55-66, prof church hist, 66-67; PROF MENNONITE HIST, UNIV AMSTERDAM, 67-, Secy, Teylers Godgeleerd Genootschap & consult ed, Mennonite Quart Rev, 68-; secy commissie tot uitgave van Documenta Anabaptistica, Neerlandica, 68-; ed, Doopsgezinde Bijdragen, 77- **MEMBERSHIPS** Am Soc Church Hist; Bibliog Soc, England; Renaissance Soc Am. **RESEARCH** Dutch and English Reformation history; Anabaptists; bibliography. **SELECTED PUBLICATIONS** Auth, Between Known Men and Visible Saints--A Study in 16th-Century English Dissent, Church Hist, Vol 0065, 96. **CONTACT ADDRESS** Univ van Amsterdam Herengracht, 514-516 1017 CC, Amsterdam, ..

HORST, STEVEN
DISCIPLINE PHILOSOPHY OF MIND **EDUCATION** Boston Univ, BA; Univ Notre Dame, PhD. **CAREER** Asst prof, 90-97; Assoc prof, 97-; Chair, 98-; Wesleyan Univ. **HONORS AND AWARDS** NEH Fel; NEH Summer Inst; Prize Interdisciplinary Studies; Trustee Sch. **MEMBERSHIPS** Am Philos Asn; Soc Philos & Psychol; Phi Beta Kappa. **SELECTED PUBLICATIONS** Auth, Symbols and Computation; Divine Eternity and Special Relativity; Phenomenology and Psychophysics; Evolutionary Explanation and the 'Hard Problem' of Consciousness; Broad Content, Narrow Content, Phenomenological Content; Formalist and Conventionalist Views of Language. **CONTACT ADDRESS** Wesleyan Univ, Middletown, CT, 06459. **EMAIL** shorst@mail.wesleyan.edu

HORSTMAN, ALLEN
PERSONAL Born 08/01/1943, Seymour, IN, 2 children **DISCIPLINE** HISTORY, LAW **EDUCATION** Purdue Univ, BS, 65; Harvard Law Sch, LLB, 68; Univ Calif, Berkeley, PhD, 77. **CAREER** Prof hist, Albion Col, 77-. **MEMBERSHIPS** AHA; Am Bar Asn; Conf Brit Studies. **RESEARCH** English legal history; American legal history. **CONTACT ADDRESS** Dept of History, Albion Col, 611 E Porter St, Albion, MI, 49224-1831. **EMAIL** ahorstman@albion.edu

HOSOI, Y. TIM
DISCIPLINE HISTORY OF NON-WESTERN RELIGIOUS IDEAS **EDUCATION** Univ Chicago, PhD. **CAREER** Philos, Oregon St Univ. **HONORS AND AWARDS** Dir, Prog Ethics, Sci, Environment. **MEMBERSHIPS** Cascade-W Japan Am Soc. **RESEARCH** Japanese Religions. **SELECTED PUBLICATIONS** Contribur The Oxford Companion to World Religions. **CONTACT ADDRESS** Dept Philos, Oregon State Univ, Corvallis, OR, 97331-4501. **EMAIL** thosoi@orst.edu

HOSPITAL, CLIFFORD G.
PERSONAL Born 03/09/1937, Rockhampton, Australia **DISCIPLINE** RELIGION **EDUCATION** Univ Queensland, BA, 61, BD, 64; Harvard Univ, PhD, 73. **CAREER** Lectr to assoc

prof, 71-83, head dept, 83-90, PROF COMPARATIVE RELIGION, QUEEN'S UNIV & QUEEN'S THEOL COL, 83-. **MEMBERSHIPS** Can Soc Stud Relig; Am Acad Relig; Soc Hindu-Christian Stud. **SELECTED PUBLICATIONS** Auth, The Righteous Demon: A Study of Bali, 84; auth, Breakthrough: Insights of the great Religious Discoverers, 85; ed bd, Stud Relig, 83-86. **CONTACT ADDRESS** Dept of Religion, Queen's Univ, Kingston, ON, K7L 3N6.

HOSSEIN, ZIAI
PERSONAL Born 07/06/1944, Mashhad, Iran, m, 1970, 1 child **DISCIPLINE** PHILOSOPHY **EDUCATION** Yale BS, 67, Harvard PhD, 76. **CAREER** UCLA, dir Iranian stud, prof Islamic Iranian stud. **MEMBERSHIPS** CIS, SIP&S **RESEARCH** Post Avicennan Illuminationist; Platonist philo. **SELECTED PUBLICATIONS** Auth, Suhrawardi's The Book of Radiance, text, trans, intro & notes, Costa Mesa: Mazda Pub, 98; Entries on Islamic Philosophy, in: Oxford Comp to Philo, ed Ted Honderich, Oxford and London: Oxford UP 95; Shihab al-Din Yahya Suhrawardi, The Illuminationist Tradition, and Sadr al-Din al-Shirazi: 17th c Syncretism in Islamic Philosophy, in: Routledge Hist of Islamic Philo, ed S H Nasr and Oliver Leaman, London Routledge, 95; Shams al-Din Muhammad Shahrazuuri's Sharh Hikmat al-Ishraq, Commentary on the Philosophy of Illumination, crit ed intros notes and indexes, Cult Stud & Research Inst Tehran, 93. **CONTACT ADDRESS** Dept of Near Eastern Languages and Cultures, UCLouisiana, 405 Hilgard Ave, Los Angeles, CA, 90095-1511. **EMAIL** ziai@ucla.edu

HOULGATE, LAURENCE DAVIS
PERSONAL Born 02/19/1938, Pasadena, CA, m, 1970, 1 child **DISCIPLINE** PHILOSOPHY **EDUCATION** Los Angeles State Col, BA, 60; Univ Calif, Los Angeles, MA, 65, PhD (philos), 67. **CAREER** Instr philos, Calif State Col Fullerton, 64-66; lectr, Univ Calif, Santa Barbara, 66-67, asst prof, 67-72; vis assoc prof, Reed Col, 72-73; assoc prof, George Mason Univ, 73-79; Assoc Prof Philos, Calif Polytech State Univ, San Luis Obispo, 79- **MEMBERSHIPS** Am Philos Asn; Am Soc Polit & Legal Philos. **RESEARCH** Philosophy of law; ethics. **SELECTED PUBLICATIONS** Auth, Children--Rights and Childhood, Law Philos, Vol 0015, 96. **CONTACT ADDRESS** Dept of Philos, California Polytech State Univ, 1 Grand Ave, San Luis Obispo, CA, 93407-0001.

HOUSE, PAUL R.
DISCIPLINE OLD TESTAMENT **EDUCATION** Southwest Baptist Univ, BA; Univ Missouri-Columbia, MA; S Baptist Theol Sem, MDiv, PhD; additional stud, Ecumenical Inst Theol Res, Jerusalem; Whitefield Inst, Eng; Oxford Univ. **CAREER** Instr, Taylor Univ, 86-96; dept ch, Biblical Stud, Taylor Univ, 91-96; Martha & Talmage prof, S Baptist Theol Sem, 96-. **SELECTED PUBLICATIONS** Ed, S Baptist Jour Theol. **CONTACT ADDRESS** Old Testament Dept, Southern Baptist Theol Sem, 2825 Lexington Rd, Louisville, KY, 40280. **EMAIL** phouse@sbts.edu

HOUSER, NATHAN
PERSONAL Born 05/10/1944, IN, m, 1975, 2 children **DISCIPLINE** PHILOSOPHY **EDUCATION** Univ of Waterloo, PhD, 85 **CAREER** Pierce Edition Proj, 80-83, res asst, asst ed, assoc ed, dir, general ed, 80-93, Indiana Univ Purdue Univ Indianapolis, asst prof, assoc prof, prof, 86-. **HONORS AND AWARDS** SSHRC fel, Fulbright-Hayes Award, NEH Grant. **MEMBERSHIPS** CSPS, APA, SAAP, ADE. **RESEARCH** Charles S. Pierce; Am Philos; philos of mind; textual theory. **SELECTED PUBLICATIONS** Auth, Toward A Piercean Semiotic Theory of Learning, in: Am Jour of Semiotics, 87; Pierce and the Law of Distribution, Perspectives on the History of Mathematical Logic, ed T. L. Drucker, Boston: Birkhauser, 91; auth, Charles Sanders Pierce, in: The Encyclopedia of Philosophy Supplement, Simon & Schuster Macmillan, 96; auth,Writings of Charles S. Pierce: A Chronological Edition, vol 3, 4, & 5, asst/assoc editor, Bloomington: Indiana Univ Press, 86, 89, 93; auth, Essential Pierce: Selected Philosophical Writings, gen ed (Pierce Edition Project), Bloomington: Indiana Univ Press, 98. **CONTACT ADDRESS** Dept of Philosophy, Indiana Univ-Purdue Univ, Indianapolis, 425 University Blvd., Indianapolis, IN, 46202-5140. **EMAIL** nhouser@iupui.edu

HOWARD, ARTHUR ELLSWORTH DICK
PERSONAL Born 07/05/1933, Richmond, VA, m, 1961, 1 child **DISCIPLINE** LAW **EDUCATION** Univ Richmond, BA, 54; Univ Va, LLB, 61; Oxford Univ, BA, 60, MA, 65. **CAREER** Assoc law, Covington & Burling, Wash, DC, 61-62; law clerk, Mr Justice Black, Supreme Court US, 62-64; from assoc prof to prof, 64-76, dir grad prog, 72-74, assoc dean sch law, 67-69, White Burkett Miller Prof Law and Public Affairs, Univ Va, 76-, Vchmn Magna Carta Comn VA, 64-65; mem, Va Independence Bicentennial Comn, 67-; exec dir, Va Comn Const Revision, 68-69; counsel to Va Gen Assembly, spec session 69, regular session, 70; consult, US Senate Judiciary Comt, subcomt on const rights, 74-; Woodrow Wilson Int Ctr for Scholars fel, Wash, DC, 74-75 & 76-77; bd of ed, Am Oxonian, 68; pres, Va Acad Laureater, 81-; Coun to Gov Va, 82- **HONORS AND AWARDS** Distinguished prof Award, Univ Va, 81. **RESEARCH** Constitutional law and history; jurisprudence. **SELECTED PUBLICATIONS** Auth, Chief Enigma, Aba J, Vol 0081, 95. **CONTACT ADDRESS** Sch of Law, Univ of Va, Charlottesville, VA, 22901.

HOWARD, DAVID M., JR.
PERSONAL Born 07/21/1952, Billings, MT, m, 1979, 2 children **DISCIPLINE** RELIGION **EDUCATION** Geneva Col, BS, 74; Wheaton Col, MA, 77; Univ Mich, AM, 80, PhD, 86. **CAREER** From instr to asst prof to assoc prof, Bethel Theol Sem, 82-90; from asst to assoc prof, Trinity Evangel Divinity Sch, 90-97; from assoc prof to prof, New Orleans Baptist Theol Sem, 97-. **MEMBERSHIPS** Soc Bibl Lit; Evangel Theol Sem. **RESEARCH** Hebrew language; Hebrew poetry; Psalms; Old Testament historical narrative. **SELECTED PUBLICATIONS** Auth, An Introduction to the Old Testament Historical Books, 93; auth, The Structure of Psalms 93-100, 97; auth, Rhetorical Criticism in Old Testament Studies, Bull Bibl Res, 94; auth, Editorial Activity in the Psalter: A State-of-the-Field Survey, The Shape & Shaping Psalter, 93; auth, A Contextual Reading of Psalms 90-94, The Shape & Shaping Psalter, 93; auth, Philistines, Peoples of Old Testament World, 94; auth, All Israel's Response to Joshua: A Note on the Narrative Framework of Joshua 1, Fortunate the Eyes that See, 95. **CONTACT ADDRESS** Dept of Hebrew and Old Testament, New Orleans Baptist Theol Sem, 3939 Gentilly Blvd., New Orleans, LA, 70126. **EMAIL** dhoward@nobts.edu

HOWARD, DON A.
DISCIPLINE PHILOSOPHY OF SCIENCE **EDUCATION** Mich State Univ, BSc, 71, AM, 73; Boston Univ, PhD, 79. **CAREER** Prof. **RESEARCH** Philosophy of science; foundations of physics; history of philosophy of science. **SELECTED PUBLICATIONS** Auth, Was Einstein Really a Realist?, 93; Einstein, Kant, and the Origins of Logical Empiricism, 94; Relativity, Eindeutigkeit, and Monomorphism: Rudolf Carnap and the Development of the Categoricity Concept in Formal Semantics, 96; A Peek Behind the Veil of Maya: Einstein, Schopenhauer, and the Historical Background of the Conception of Space as a Ground for the Individuation of Physical Systems, 97; co-ed, Einstein and the History of General Relativity, 89; co-ed, The Collected Papers of Albert Einstein, 89. **CONTACT ADDRESS** History and Philosophy of Science Dept, Univ of Notre Dame, Notre Dame, IN, 46556. **EMAIL** Don.A.Howard.43@nd.edu

HOWARD, MICHAEL W.
PERSONAL Born 12/28/1952, El Dorado, KS, m, 1995, 1 child **DISCIPLINE** PHILOSOPHY **EDUCATION** Univ Chicago, BA, 74; Boston Univ, PhD, 81. **CAREER** Chemn, 93-98, assoc prof, Univ Maine, 81-. **MEMBERSHIPS** APA; RPA; Intl Inst for Self Mgt. **RESEARCH** Economic democracy; Theories of justice; Marxism. **SELECTED PUBLICATIONS** Auth, Where Do We Go From Here": Another View, Grassroots Econ Organizing Newsletter, 97; auth, Mondragon at 40, Grassroots Econ Organizing Newsletter, 96; auth, Does Generalizing the Mondragon Model Require Revising It?, Social Econ and Social Participation: The Ways of the Basques, Marcial Pons and Gezki, 96; auth, Market Socialism and the International Mobility of Capital, Radical Philos Rev of Books, 95; auth, Self-Management, Ownership, and the Media, Jour of Mass Media Ethics, 94; auth, Ethics Education in the University: Origins and Pitfalls, Focus on Public Policy, 94; auth, Reflections on Cuba, Radical Philos Newsletter, 94. **CONTACT ADDRESS** Philosophy Dept., Univ of Maine, Orono, ME, 04469. **EMAIL** mhoward@maine.edu

HOWE, LAWRENCE W.
PERSONAL Born 09/08/1953, Pensacola, FL, m, 1988 **DISCIPLINE** PHILOSOPHY **EDUCATION** Univ Mo, PhD, 83. **CAREER** Assoc prof, ch, Dept Philos, Univ W Fla. **HONORS AND AWARDS** Tchg Incentive Prog Award, Univ W Fla, 94. **MEMBERSHIPS** Am Philos Asn, Fla Philos Asn. **RESEARCH** Bergson; environmental ethics; process philosophy. **CONTACT ADDRESS** Dept of Philosophy, Pensacola, FL, 32514. **EMAIL** lhowe@uwf.edu

HOWE, LEROY T.
PERSONAL Born 08/22/1936, Coral Gables, FL, m, 1962, 2 children **DISCIPLINE** PHILOSOPHY, RELIGION **EDUCATION** Univ Miami, AB, 58, MA, 60; Yale Univ, BD, 62, MA, 63, PhD(relig studies), 65. **CAREER** Instr philos, Southern Conn State Col, 64-65; asst prof, Fla Southern Col, 65-67; asst prof, Cent Mich Univ, 67-69; assoc dean, 72-78, Prof, Perkins Sch Theol, Southern Methodist Univ, 69-, Ed, Perkins J, 71- **MEMBERSHIPS** Am Acad Relig; Am Cath Philos Asn; Soc Values Higher Educ. **SELECTED PUBLICATIONS** Auth, Theology and Pastoral Counseling--A New Interdisciplinary Approach, J Relig, Vol 0077, 97. **CONTACT ADDRESS** Perkins Sch of Theol, Southern Methodist Univ, Dallas, TX, 75275.

HOWE, RUTH-ARLENE W.
PERSONAL Born 11/21/1933, Scotch Plains, NJ, m, 1957 **DISCIPLINE** LAW **EDUCATION** Wellesley Coll, BA 1955; Simmons Coll Sch of Social Work, SM 1957; Boston Coll Law School JD 1974. **CAREER** Cleveland OH Catholic Youth Serv Bureau, casewkr 1957-61; Tufts Delta Health Ctr Mound Bayou MS, housing devel consultant 1969-70; Simmons Coll Sch of Social Work, instr soc pol 1970-78; Law & Child Dev Project DHEW/ACYF Funded B C Law Sch, asst dir 1977-79; Boston Coll Law Sch, asst prof of law 1977-81, assoc prof of law with tenure, 1981-97, prof, 1998-. **HONORS AND AWARDS** Wellesley scholar Wellesley Coll 1955; Nat'l Inst of Mental Health Fellowship 1956-57; Honored by MA Black Legislative Caucus 1988; Honored by Museum of Afro-American History as one of Sojourner's Daughters; Boston African American Women Who Make A Difference, an exhibition of portraits by photographer Lou Jones, 1991; Mary Ingraham Bunting Inst Radcliffe Coll, Hermon Dunlap Smith Fellow in Law & Social/Public Policy, 1994-95; Honored by Boston College Law School Alumni Association, 1996. **MEMBERSHIPS** Bd mem Boston League of Women Voters 1963-68; clerk Grimes-King Found for the Elderly Inc 1972-; guardian ad litem MA Family and Probate Court 1979-; ABA Tech to NCCUSL Uniform Adoption and Marital Property Acts 1980-83; reviewer CWLA Journal-Child Welfare 1984-91; mem MA Gov St Com on Child Support Enforcement 1985; mem MA Adv Comm on Child Support Guidelines 1986-; mem MA Gov/MBA Commn on the Legal Needs of Children 1986-87; NCCUSL Uniform Putative and Unknown Fathers Act Reporter 1986-88; member, editorial board, Family Advocate, ABA section of Family Law, 1989-95; mem, Massachusetts Supreme Judicial Court Commission to Study Racial & Ethnic Bias in the Courts, 1990-94; US State Department, Study Group on Intercountry Adoption, 1991-. **SELECTED PUBLICATIONS** Co-auth, Katz McGrath Child Neglect Laws in Am ABA Press 1976. **CONTACT ADDRESS** Law Sch, Boston Col, 885 Centre St, Newton Center, MA, 02459.

HOWELL, JOHN C.
PERSONAL Born 02/24/1924, Miami, FL, m, 1947, 2 children **DISCIPLINE** CHRISTIAN ETHICS **EDUCATION** Stetson Univ, BA, 49; Southwestern Baptist Theol Sem, BD, 52, ThD, 60, PhD(ethics), 75; Univ MO, Kansas City, MA, 72. **CAREER** Pastor, First Baptist Church, Crowley, Tex, 50-56; pastor, West Bradenton Baptist Church, Fla, 56-60; acad dean, 75-82, Prof Christian Ethics, Midwestern Baptist Theol Sem, 60-, Am Asn Theol Schs fel, Univ London, 67-68; coun, Midwest Christian Counseling Ctr, 69-75. **HONORS AND AWARDS** DD, Stetson Univ, 79. **MEMBERSHIPS** Am Soc Christian Ethics; Nat Coun Family Rel. **RESEARCH** Family life; sexual educ. **SELECTED PUBLICATIONS** Auth, Teaching About Sex: A Christian Approach, Broadman; Gambling and the family, In: The Gambling Menace, Broadman, 66; contribr, The Cutting Edge, Word, Vol I, 69; Extremism Right and Left, Eerdmans, 72; Growing in Oneness, Convention, 72; Teaching Your Children About Sex, Broadman, 73; auth, Senior Adult Family Life, 79 & Equality and Submission in Marriage, 79, Broadman. **CONTACT ADDRESS** Midwestern Baptist Theol Sem, 5001 N Oak, Kansas City, MO, 64118-4620.

HOWELL, ROBERT
DISCIPLINE PHILOSOPHY **EDUCATION** Univ Mich, PhD. **CAREER** Prof, Univ Albany, State Univ NY. **RESEARCH** History of modern philosophy, analytical metaphysics, aesthetics. **SELECTED PUBLICATIONS** Auth, Kant's Transcendental Deduction, Kluwer, 92. **CONTACT ADDRESS** Dept of Philosophy, Univ at Albany, SUNY, Albany, NY, 12222. **EMAIL** bobh@cnsunix.albany.edu

HOWIE, JOHN
PERSONAL Born 12/03/1929, Jackson, MS, m, 1954, 3 children **DISCIPLINE** PHILOSOPHY **EDUCATION** Vanderbilt Univ, BA, 51; Emory Univ, BD, 54, MA, 55; Boston Univ, PhD, 65. **CAREER** From assoc prof to prof, 71-94, prof, 97-, Southern Ill Univ. **HONORS AND AWARDS** Post doctoral Stud, Cambridge Univ, 72. **RESEARCH** Presently editing a volume of the Leys Memorial Lectures for publication by the SIU press. **CONTACT ADDRESS** 615 S Glenview Dr, Carbondale, IL, 62901-2245.

HOWZE, KAREN AILEEN
PERSONAL Born 12/08/1950, Detroit, MI, s **DISCIPLINE** LAW **EDUCATION** Univ of S California, BA 1972 (cum laude); Hastings Coll of Law, JD 1977. **CAREER** Detroit Free Press, reporter 1971; San Francisco Chronicle, reporter 1972-78; Newsday, Long Island, asst editor 1978-79; Gannett Newspapers, Rochester NY, asst managing editor/Sunday features editor 1979-80; USA Today, founding editor 1981, managing editor/systems 1982-86, managing editor/international edition 1986-88; Gannett Co Inc, Corporate News Systems, editor 1988-90; management consultant, 1990-; HOWZE AND ASSOCIATES, KAREN AILEEN HOWZE, PC, ATTORNEY 1990-; Howard Univ School of Communications, lecturer, 1990-92; ADOPTION SUPPORT INSTITUTE, PRESIDENT/FOUNDER 1990-; American University School of Communication, professor 1991-94. **HONORS AND AWARDS** Business Woman of the Year, Spellman Alumni, Washington DC 1986. **MEMBERSHIPS** Mem Nat Assn of Black Journal; past mem Sigma Delta Chi; past mem Women in Commun; mem Alameda Co Comm Hlth Adv Bd; guest lectu local comm coll; mem, Amer Society of Newspaper Editors; vice-chair, Minority Opportunities Comm, Amer Newspaper Publisher's Assn;

board of directors, North American CNL on Adoptable Children; board of directors MAAT Institute; board of directors Chelsea School; chairperson Mayor's Committee on Placement of Children in Family Homes; District of Columbia Bar Association & State of Maryland Bar Association, licensed to practice law in District of Columbia and Maryland. **SELECTED PUBLICATIONS** Publications: And Still We Rise, Interviews with 50 Black Americans by Barbara Reynolds, sr editor, 1987; Making Differences Work: Cultural Context in Abuse and Neglect Practice for Judges and Attorneys, 1996. **CONTACT ADDRESS** PO Box 1127, Silver Spring, MD, 20910.

HOYT, CHRISTOPHER R.
DISCIPLINE LAW **EDUCATION** Northwestern Univ, BA; Univ Wis, MS, JD. **CAREER** Prof **MEMBERSHIPS** Am Bar Asn. **RESEARCH** Federal taxation; business organizations; retirement plans; tax-exempt organizations. **SELECTED PUBLICATIONS** Auth, The Legal Compendium for Community Foundations. **CONTACT ADDRESS** Law Dept, Univ of Missouri, Kansas City, 5100 Rockhill Rd, Kansas City, MO, 64110-2499. **EMAIL** hoytc@umkc.edu

HOYT, THOMAS L., JR.
PERSONAL Born 03/14/1941, Fayette, Alabama, m **DISCIPLINE** THEOLOGY **EDUCATION** Evansville Coll and Lane Coll, BA 1962; Interdenominational Theological Center, MDiv 1965; Union Theological Seminary, STM 1967; Duke Univ, PhD 1975. **CAREER** Jefferson Park Methodist, assoc pastor 1965-67; St Joseph CME, pastor 1967-70; Fawcett Memorial, pastor 1970-72; Interdenominational Theological Center, professor 1972-78; Howard Univ, professor 1978-80; Hartford Seminary, professor 1980-. **HONORS AND AWARDS** Rockefeller Doctoral Fellowship; Assn of Theological Schools Fellowship; worked on Joint Committee, which published an Inclusive Lectionary (year A,B,C,)1983-85; Natl Assn for Equal Opportunity in Higher Education, award; Bilateral Dialogue between Methodist/Roman Catholic Churches, participant; African Methodist Episcopal Zion/Christian Methodist Episcopal Unity Committee. **MEMBERSHIPS** Society of Biblical Literature; American Academy of Religion; Society for the study of Black Religion; Theology Commission of Consultation onChurch Union; CT Bible Society, board of directors; Christian Methodist Church; Alpha Phi Alpha; NAACP; Faith and Order Commission of Natl Council and World Council of Churches; Institute for Ecumenical and Cultural Research, board of directors. **CONTACT ADDRESS** Professor, Hartford Sem, 77 Sherman St, Hartford, CT, 06105.

HOYT-O'CONNOR, PAUL E.
PERSONAL Born 04/01/1960, Brooklyn, NY, m, 1987, 1 child **DISCIPLINE** PHILOSOPHY; HISTORY **EDUCATION** Fordham Univ, BA, 92; Boston Col, PhD, 92. **CAREER** Asst prof, 94- , Spalding Univ. **MEMBERSHIPS** APA; Amer Catholic Philos Assn; Kentucky Philos Assn **RESEARCH** Social and political philos; Ethical theory. **SELECTED PUBLICATIONS** Auth, Lonegan and Bellah: Social Science in Public Philosophy, American Catholic Philosophy Quarterly, 95; auth, Progress Without End, International Philosophical Quarterly, 98. **CONTACT ADDRESS** Spalding Univ, 851 S 4th St, Louisville, KY, 40203. **EMAIL** spalding@humanities.net

HSIEH, DINGHWA EVELYN
PERSONAL Born 05/06/1961, Taipei, Taiwan, m, 1993 **DISCIPLINE** BUDDHIST STUDIES **EDUCATION** UCLA, PhD, 93 **CAREER** Asst Prof, 98-pres, Tsuman St Univ; Vis Asst Prof, 96-98, Reed Col; Vis Lect, 96-96, Harvard Div Sch; Res Fel, 93-95, UC Berkeley **HONORS AND AWARDS** Chanc Post Doc Fel **MEMBERSHIPS** AAR, Assoc of Asian Studies **RESEARCH** Zen; Literati Cult **SELECTED PUBLICATIONS** Auth, Images of Women in Ch'an Buddhist Literatire of the Sung Period, Sung Buddhism, 99 **CONTACT ADDRESS** Truman St Univ Div of Soc Sci, Kirksville, MO, 63501. **EMAIL** dhsieh@truman.edu

HUANG, SIU CHI
PERSONAL Born 07/07/1913, Fujian, China **DISCIPLINE** PHILOSOPHY **EDUCATION** Fujian Christian Univ, BA, 36; Univ Penn, MA, 39, PhD, 44. **CAREER** Prof Philos and dept ch, 50-85, Emer prof philos, Beaver Col, 96- ; vis prof, Univ Hawaii, 72; vis prof, Xiamen Univ, 80, 84; vis prof, Fudan Univ, 88. **HONORS AND AWARDS** Lindback awd for disting tchg, Beaver Col, 61; Hon dr letts, 95. **MEMBERSHIPS** Amer Philos Asn; Amer Oriental Soc; Soc Philos E and W. **RESEARCH** Neo-Confucianism and Comparative Philosophy. **SELECTED PUBLICATIONS** Auth, Lu Hsiang-Ohan A 12th Century Chinese Idealist Philosophy; Zhang Zai and Josiah Royce, in Chinese; Trans Chinese, George Berkeley's Three Dialogues Between Hylas and Philonous, and Sources of Religious Insight. **CONTACT ADDRESS** Dept of Philosophy, Beaver Col, Apt 458, Fairway, Rydal, PA, 19046.

HUBBARD, F. PATRICK
DISCIPLINE TORTS, JURISPRUDENCE, EVIDENCE, AND CRIMINAL LAW **EDUCATION** Davidson Col, BA, 66; NY Univ, JD, 69; Yale Univ, LLM, 73. **CAREER** Ronald L. Motley Tort prof Law, Univ of SC. **SELECTED PUBLICATIONS** Publ, on torts & criminal law. **CONTACT ADDRESS** School of Law, Univ of S. Carolina, Law Center, Columbia, SC, 29208. **EMAIL** Path@law.law.sc.edu

HUBER, DONALD L.
DISCIPLINE CHURCH HISTORY **EDUCATION** Capital Univ, BA, 62; Evangel Lutheran Theol Sem, BD, 66; Duke Univ, PhD, 71; Univ Mich, MALS, 73. **CAREER** Instr, ELTS, 69-72; librarian, ELTS, 73-78; librarian, 78-91; sec fac, 78-80; act dean Acad Aff, 84-85; guest lectr, Luther Sem, Adelaide, Australia, 86-87; prof, Trinity Lutheran Sem, 88-; archiv, Trinity Lutheran Sem, 91-. **SELECTED PUBLICATIONS** Auth, Luther A. Gottwald, John H. Tietjen, Dictionary of Heresy Trials in Amer Christianity, Greenwood, 97; Teddy, Rah! Theodore Roosevelt and German-Americanism, Timeline, Ohio Hist Soc, 96; Red, White, and Black: The Wyandot Mission at Upper Sandusky, Timeline XIII, 96; The Rise and Fall of Lane Seminary: An Antislavery Episode, 95. **CONTACT ADDRESS** Hist, Theol, Soc Dept, Trinity Lutheran Sem, 2199 E Main St, Columbus, OH, 43209-2334. **EMAIL** dhuber@trinity.capital.edu

HUDDLESTON, MARK
PERSONAL Born 06/12/1947, Indianapolis, IN, m, 1968, 4 children **DISCIPLINE** RELIGION **EDUCATION** Milligan Col, BA, 69; Emmanuel Sch Religion, MDiv, 75, DMin, 99; Emory Univ, 76-78; Univ Tex, MA, 84. **CAREER** Min, Beaver Creek Christian Church, 71-76; min, Christs Church, 76-78; transl, 80-88, vp, 88-92, trning, 92-97, Pioneer Bible Translators; assoc prof, Nebr Christian Col, 97-. **MEMBERSHIPS** Theta Phi; Eta Beta Rho **RESEARCH** Linguistics; Missiology **SELECTED PUBLICATIONS** Auth, Which Language for Literacy, 80; auth, Language Learning and Cross-Cultural Communication, 87; auth, Equivalent Dynamics: For Whom Do I Translate, 88; auth, Financial Planning and Accountability, 92; ed, Buku Ye Membe Mba K'Akulugu, 83. **CONTACT ADDRESS** 1007 Madison Ave, Norfolk, NE, 68701. **EMAIL** mhuddleston@nechristian.edu

HUDDLESTON, TOBIANNA W.
DISCIPLINE PHILOSOPHY **EDUCATION** Simmons Col, BA, 70; NY Univ Washington Square, NYC, MA, PhD, 77. **CAREER** Vineyard Fine Arts Crown, Edgartown, Aesthetics Programs Development. **HONORS AND AWARDS** Most Promising Genius, NYU, 77; William Barret Prize. **MEMBERSHIPS** ABP, APA, CPPS **RESEARCH** Logic **SELECTED PUBLICATIONS** Auth, Pure Philosophy Jour. **CONTACT ADDRESS** Eden Place Farm Corp Retreat, PO Box 331, Burgin, KY, 40310.

HUDEC, ROBERT EMIL
PERSONAL Born 12/23/1934, Cleveland, OH, m, 1956, 2 children **DISCIPLINE** LAW **EDUCATION** Kenyon Col, BA, 56; Cambridge Univ, BA, 58; Yale Univ, LLB, 61. **CAREER** Law clerk, US Supreme Court, 61-63; asst gen counsel, Off Spec Rep Trade Negotiations, Exec Off pres, 63-65; from asst prof to assoc prof law, Yale Univ, 66-72; prof law, Law Sch, Univ Minn, Minneapolis, 72- **HONORS AND AWARDS** LLD, Kenyon Col, 79. **RESEARCH** International trade; commercial law. **SELECTED PUBLICATIONS** Auth, The Gatt Legal System and World Trade Diplomacy, Praeger, 75, 2nd ed, Butterworths, 90; Developing Countries in the Gatt Legal System, Thames Essay No 50, Gower, Trade Policy Res Ctr, 88; Enforcing International Trade Law: The Evolution of the Modern Gatt Legal System, Butterworths, 93; co-ed, Harmonization and Fair Trade: Prerequisites for Free Trade?, MIT Press, 96. **CONTACT ADDRESS** Law Sch, Univ of Minn, 229 19th Ave S, Minneapolis, MN, 55455-0401. **EMAIL** hudec001@tc.umn.edu

HUDELSON, RICHARD HENRY
PERSONAL m, 2 children **DISCIPLINE** PHILOSOPHY **EDUCATION** De Pauw Univ, BA, 68; Univ Mich, MA, 75, PhD(philos), 77. **CAREER** Teaching asst philos, Univ Mich, 72-75; res asst hist philos, Inst Advan Studies, 76-77; Asst Prof Philos, Univ Minn, Duluth, 77-, Nat Endowment for Humanities summer res grant, 82. **MEMBERSHIPS** Am Philos Asn. **RESEARCH** History of social philosophy; history of German philosophy. **SELECTED PUBLICATIONS** Auth, Marxism and Philosophy in the Twentieth Century, Praeger, 90; auth, The Rise and Fall of Communism, Westview, 93. **CONTACT ADDRESS** Dept of Philos, Univ of Minn, 10 University Dr, Duluth, MN, 55812-2496. **EMAIL** rhudelso@ub.d.umn.edu

HUDNUT-BEUMLER, JAMES
PERSONAL Born 02/21/1958, Detroit, MI, m, 1987, 2 children **DISCIPLINE** RELIGION **EDUCATION** Princeton Univ, PhD, 89. **CAREER** Prof, Dean of Fac, 93-, Columbia Theol Sem; Prod Assoc, 91-93, Lilly Endow Inc; Lectr, 88-91, Princeton Univ. **HONORS AND AWARDS** Phi Beta Kappa; Leopold Scheap Schl. **MEMBERSHIPS** AAR; ASCH; SSSR. **RESEARCH** American Religion History. **SELECTED PUBLICATIONS** Auth, Looking for God in the Suburbs: The Religion of the American Dream and Its Critics, 1945-1965, New Brunswick, Rutgers U Press, 94; auth, Myth's and Realities in the Financing of Amer Religion, in: The Financing of America, Mark Chaves, ed, Walnut Creek CA, Alta Mira Press, 98; Religion and Suburbs, The Encyc of Cities and Their Suburbs, Westport CT, ABC-Clio, forthcoming; auth, Ecclesial Accountability in the Missional Church, The Gospel and Our Culture, 98; auth, Creating a Commonwealth: The History Ethics and Theol of Church Endowments, Congregations, 97; auth, A New Dean Meets a New Day in Theol Education, Theol Edu, 96; auth, The Tithes that Bind? Protestants and Giving, The Cultures of Giving, Dwight Forthcoming; Burlingame, ed, San Fran, Jossey Bass, 95; rev, Money Matters: Personal Giving in American Churches, by Dean Hoge, Charles Zech, Patrick McNamara, Michael J Donahue, Religious Stud Rev, forthcoming; The Fifties Spiritual Marketplace: American Religion in a Decade of Conflict, by RS Ellwood, in: American Presbyterians: The J Presby History, forthcoming; ed, Behind the Stained Glass Window: Money Dynamics in the Church, by John and Sylvia Ronsvalle, in: Theol Today, 98. **CONTACT ADDRESS** Columbia Theol Sem, Box 520, Decatur, GA, 30031. **EMAIL** hudnut-beumlerj@ctsnet.edu

HUDSON, DAVIS M.
DISCIPLINE LAW **EDUCATION** Wake Forest Univ, BS; Fla State Univ, JD; Univ Fla, LLM; Univ London, LLM. **CAREER** Prof, Univ Fla, 76-. **MEMBERSHIPS** Fla Bar. **RESEARCH** Taxation, state and local taxation, international tax, immigration law. **SELECTED PUBLICATIONS** Coauth, Black Letter on Federal Income Taxation. **CONTACT ADDRESS** School of Law, Univ of Florida, PO Box 117625, Gainesville, FL, 32611-7625. **EMAIL** hudson@law.ufl.edu

HUDSON, ROBERT
DISCIPLINE HISTORY AND PHILOSOPHY OF SCIENCE AND EPISTEMOLOGY **EDUCATION** W Ontario Univ, PhD. **CAREER** Dept Philos, Concordia Univ **RESEARCH** Contemporary experimental microbiology. **SELECTED PUBLICATIONS** Pub(s), in Synthese; Stud in Hist and Philos of Sci. **CONTACT ADDRESS** Dept of Philos, Concordia Univ, Montreal, 1455 de Maisonneuve W, Montreal, PQ, H3G 1M8. **EMAIL** hudsonr@alcor.concordia.ca

HUDSON, YEAGER
PERSONAL Born 08/14/1931, Meridian, MS, m, 1953, 2 children **DISCIPLINE** PHILOSOPHY **EDUCATION** Educ: Millsaps Col, BA, 54; Boston Univ, STB, 58, PhD, 65. **CAREER** From Instr to Prof, 59-94, Charles A. Dana Prof Philos, Colby Col, 94, Chmn Dept, 80-88; Fulbright lectr, Poona Univ & Ahmednagar Col, India, 67-68; dir self-study Ahmednagar Col under stipulation of Univ Grants Comn Indian Govt, 67-68. **MEMBERSHIPS** Am Philos Asn; Metaphys Soc Am; Soc Advan Am Philos; Philos Relig. **RESEARCH** Metaphysics; philos of educ; Indian philos. **SELECTED PUBLICATIONS** Auth, Emerson & Tagore: The Poet as Philosopher, Cross Roads Bks, 88; Philosophy of Religion, Mayfield Publ, 91; ed, Philosophy of Religion: Selected Readings, Mayfield Publ, 91; Rending and Renewing the Social Order, Edwin Mellen Press, 96; Technology, Morality, and Social Policy, Edwin Mellen Press, 97; co-ed, The Bill of Rights: Bicentennial Perspectives, Edwin Mellen Press, 93; Freedom, Dharma, and Rights, Edwin Mellen Press, 93; Liberalism, Oppression, and Empowerment, Edwin Mellen Press, 94; The Social Power of Ideas, Edwin Mellen Press, 95. **CONTACT ADDRESS** Dept of Philos, Colby Col, 4555 Mayflower Hill, Waterville, ME, 04901-8845. **EMAIL** y_hudson@colby.edu

HUENEMANN, CHARLES
DISCIPLINE PHILOSOPHY **EDUCATION** Univ Ill, Chicago, PhD, 94. **CAREER** Asst prof philos, Utah State Univ, 94- . **CONTACT ADDRESS** Dept of Languages and Philosophy, Utah State Univ, Logan, UT, 84322-0720. **EMAIL** hueneman@cc.usu.edu

HUFF, PETER A.
PERSONAL Born 11/01/1958, Atlanta, GA, m, 1994, 1 child **DISCIPLINE** HISTORICAL THEOLOGY **EDUCATION** Mercer Univ, BA, 80; Southern Baptist Theol Seminary, MDiv, 84; St Louis Univ, PhD, 94. **CAREER** Asst Prof, Univ Puget Sound, 94-95; Asst Prof Theol, St. Anselm Col, 95-. **HONORS AND AWARDS** Phi Beta Kappa. **MEMBERSHIPS** Am Acad Relig; Am Soc Church Hist; Col Theol Soc. **RESEARCH** Religion in American culture; religion and literature; catholic studies. **SELECTED PUBLICATIONS** Coauth, Knowledge and Belief in America: Enlightenment Traditions and Modern Religious Thought, Cambridge Univ Press, 95; auth, With the Body of This World: Allen Tate's Quarrel with Modern Gnosticism, Fides et Hist, 95; New Apologists in America's Conservative Catholic Subculture, Horizons, 96; Allen Tate and the Catholic Revival: Trace of the Fugitive Gods, Isaac Hecker Studies in Religion and American Culture, Paulist Press, 96; John Locke and the Prophecy of Quaker Women, Quaker Hist, 97. **CONTACT ADDRESS** Theology Dept, St. Anselm Col, 100 Saint Anselm Dr., Manchester, NH, 03102. **EMAIL** pehuff@anselm.edu

HUFFMAN, DOUGLAS S.
PERSONAL Born 01/01/1961, Minneapolis, MN, m, 1985 **DISCIPLINE** THEOLOGY **EDUCATION** Northwest Coll, BA, 83; Weaton Coll Grad School, MA, 85; Trinity Evangel Divinity School, MA, 89; PhD, 94. **CAREER** Asst Prof, Northwest Coll, St Paul MN, 94-. **HONORS AND AWARDS** Outstanding Young man of Am, 86; Trinity Fac Scholar, 89; Who's who among Am Teachers, 96. **MEMBERSHIPS** Evanegel

Theol Soc; Soc of Bibl Lit; Inst for Bibl Res. **RESEARCH** Luke-Acts; NT Greek; Christian Aplologetics. **SELECTED PUBLICATIONS** Auth, The Historical Jesus of Ancient Unbelief, JETS, 97; rev The Preface to Luke's Gospel: Literary Convention and Social Context in Luke 1:1-4 and Acts 1:1 JETS, forthcoming; rev Luke's Portrait of Paul, JETS, forthcoming; rev The Modern Search for the Real Jesus: An Introductory Survey of the Historical Roots of Gospels Criticism, JETS, forthcoming; Assassins, Bernice, Drusilla, Gentile, Yokefellow, Eerdmans Dictionary of the Bible, forthcoming; Acts, forthcoming. **CONTACT ADDRESS** Northwestern Col, 3003 Snelling Ave N, St. Paul, MN, 55113. **EMAIL** dsh@nwc.edu

HUFFMAN, JR., GORDON
DISCIPLINE CHRISTIAN MISSION **EDUCATION** Capital Univ, BA, 64; Evangel Lutheran Theol Sem, BD, 68; Chinese Univ, Hong Kong, grad stud, 76-77; Univ St Andrews, PhD, 77. **CAREER** Prof, Lutheran Theol Sem, Hong Kong, 77-79; fac, Southeast Asia Grad Sch Theol, 78-79; assoc dean, Lutheran Theol Sem, Hong Kong, 79; vis prof, 79-80; asst prof, 81-83; assoc prof, 83-91; John H. F. Kuder prof, 84-; prof, Trinity Lutheran Sem, 91-. **SELECTED PUBLICATIONS** Auth, Mission is the Heart of the Church, World Encounter, 85; The Shape of Mission, Trinity Sem Rev, 85. **CONTACT ADDRESS** Hist, Theol, Soc Dept, Trinity Lutheran Sem, 2199 E Main St, Columbus, OH, 43209-2334. **EMAIL** thuffman@trinity.capital.edu

HUGGETT, NICK
DISCIPLINE PHILOSOPHY **EDUCATION** Rutgers Univ, PhD. **CAREER** Asst prof, Univ IL at Chicago . **RESEARCH** Philos of physics. **SELECTED PUBLICATIONS** Co-auth, Interpretations of Quantum Field Theory, Philos Sci. **CONTACT ADDRESS** Philos Dept, Univ Illinois Chicago, S Halsted St, PO Box 705, Chicago, IL, 60607. **EMAIL** huggett@uic.edu

HUGHES, JOYCE A.
PERSONAL Born 02/07/1940, Gadsden, AL, s **DISCIPLINE** LAW **EDUCATION** Carleton Coll Northfield MN (magna cum laude), BA 1961; Univ Madrid Spain 1961-62; Univ MN Law Sch (cum laude), JD 1965. **CAREER** Northwestern Univ School of Law, prof, 1979-, assoc prof, 1975-79; Chicago Transit Authority, general counsel, 1984-88; Continental Illinois Bank, attorney, 1982-84; Univ MN Law Sch, assoc prof 1971-75; Peterson & Holtze Minneapolis, consult 1971-74; Auerbach Corp Philadelphia, consult 1970-71; LeFevere Lefler Hamilton & Peterson Minneapolis, atty 1967-71; Judge Earl R Larson Minneapolis, law clk 1965-67. **HONORS AND AWARDS** Phi Beta Kappa, 1961; Fulbright Scholarship 1961-62; John Hay Whitney Fellowship 1962-63; Achievement Award Carleton College Alumni 1969; 100 Top Business & Professional Women, Dollars & Sense Magazine, 1986; Superior Public Service Award, Cook County Bar Assn, 1987. **MEMBERSHIPS** Mem, Amer Bar Assn, Natl Bar Assn, Illinois Bar Assn, Cook County Bar Assn; dir, Chicago Bd of Educ, 1980-82; dir, Federal Home Loan Bank of Chicago, 1980-84; dir, First Plymouth Bank, 1971-82; trustee, Natl Urban League, 1972-78; trustee, Carleton Coll, 1969-94. **CONTACT ADDRESS** School of Law, Northwestern Univ, 357 E Chicago Ave, Chicago, IL, 60611.

HUGHES, KEVIN L.
PERSONAL Born 11/12/1969, Baltimore, MD, m, 1995, 1 child **DISCIPLINE** HISTORY OF CHRISTIANITY **EDUCATION** Univ Chicago, PhD, 97. **CAREER** Arthur J Ennis postdoc fel hum, 97-, Villanova Univ. **HONORS AND AWARDS** Phi Beta Kappa, 90; Pres Scholar, Villanova Univ, 87-91; Dist Stud Award (Relig Studies), Villanova Univ, 91; summa cum laude, Villanova Univ, 91; Valedictorian, Villanova Univ, 91; Century Fel, Univ Chicago, 91-95; jr fel, Inst for Advanced Stud of Relig, 95-96. **MEMBERSHIPS** Am Soc of Church Hist; AAR; Soc of Bibl Lit. **RESEARCH** Theology, religion, and culture of the Middle Ages; history of biblical exegesis; apocalypticism. **SELECTED PUBLICATIONS** Auth, A Theology of Antichrist? Peter Lombard's Commentary on 2 Thessalonians in its Medieval Exegetical Context, Proceed of Am Soc of Church Hist, Theol Res Exchange Network, 97; rev, Carthusian Spirituality: The Writings of Hugh of Balma and Guigo de Ponte, Church Hist, forthcoming; auth, Adso and His Sources: Notes on Antichrist and the Exegetical Tradition at the Millenium, The Apocalyptic Year 1000: Religious Expectation and Social Change in Western Europe, 968-1033, Oxford Univ Press, forthcoming; auth, Augustine and Antichrist: Strategies of Synthesis in Early Medieval Exegesis, in History, Apocalypse, and the Secular Imagination, An Interdisciplinary Symposium on Augustine's City of God, forthcoming; coauth, Second Thessalonians: Two Early Medieval Apocalyptic Commentaries, TEAMS Medieval Comm Series, forthcoming. **CONTACT ADDRESS** Core Humanities, Villanova Univ, 800 Lancaster Ave, Villanova, PA, 19085. **EMAIL** khughes@email.villanova.edu

HUGHES, PAMELA S.
DISCIPLINE LAW **EDUCATION** McGill Univ, BA, 74, LLB, 77; Univ Toronto, LLM, 78. **CAREER** Securities law, Blake, Cassels & Graydon **HONORS AND AWARDS** Dir, Capital Markets Int Markets Branch. **SELECTED PUBLICATIONS** Auth, pubs on international securities markets. **CONTACT ADDRESS** Fac of Law, Univ Toronto, 78 Queen's Park, Toronto, ON.

HUGHES, PAUL
PERSONAL Born 03/25/1954, Boston, MA, m, 1991 **DISCIPLINE** PHILOSOPHY **EDUCATION** Univ of IL Chicago, PhD, 87. **CAREER** Col of Will and Mary, vis asst prof, 86-87; Univ of Mich, Dearborn, asst prof, 87-93, assoc prof, 93-98, ch, dept of human, 98-. **MEMBERSHIPS** APA, SSPP, CSPA **RESEARCH** Ethics; philo of law and lib; polit philo; philo of relig; Marxism. **SELECTED PUBLICATIONS** Auth, Taking Ethics Seriously: Virtue, Validity and the Art of Moral Reasoning, in: Teaching Philo, 96; What is Involved in Forgiving? in: Philosophia, 97; Exploitation, Autonomy and the Case for Organ Sales, in: Intl Jour of Applied Philo, 98; Paternalism, Battered Women, and the Law, in: Jour of Soc Philo, fc, 99. **CONTACT ADDRESS** Dept of Humanities, Univ of Michigan, Dearborn, MI, 48128. **EMAIL** pmhuhges@umich.edu

HUGHES, RICHARD ALLAN
PERSONAL Born 07/30/1941, Batavia, NY, m, 1973, 2 children **DISCIPLINE** RELIGIOUS STUDIES **EDUCATION** Univ of Indianapolis, BA, 63; Boston Univ, STB, 66, PhD(-theol), 70. **CAREER** Asst prof to prof Relig, Lycoming Col, 70-. **HONORS AND AWARDS** The Szondi Prize, 93. **MEMBERSHIPS** Int Szondi Asn. **RESEARCH** Psychoanalysis; thanatology; ethics. **SELECTED PUBLICATIONS** Auth, Szondi's Theory of the Cain Complex, fall 79 & On Aggression: The Szondian View, fall 81, Am Imago; Theology and the Cain Complex, Univ Press Am, 82; The Cain Complex and the Apostle Paul, Soundings, spring 82; Bereavement and Pareschatology, Encounter, fall 82; Aggression and Expiation, Univ Press of Am, 87; The Judge and the Faith Healer, Univ Press of Am, 89; Return of the Ancestor, Peter Lang, 92; The Radiant Shock of Death, Peter Lang, 95. **CONTACT ADDRESS** 700 College Pl, Williamsport, PA, 17701-5192. **EMAIL** hughes@lycoming.edu

HUGHES, RICHARD T.
PERSONAL Born 02/21/1943, Lubbock, TX, m, 1963, 1 child **DISCIPLINE** CHRISTIAN HISTORY **EDUCATION** Harding Univ, BA (Bible), 65; Abilene Christian Univ, MA (Christian history), 67; Univ IA, PhD (Christian history), 72. **CAREER** Asst prof, relig div, Pepperdine Univ, 71-76; assoc prof and prof, Dept of Religious Studies, Southwest MO State Univ, 77-82; prof, history dept, Abilene Christian Univ, 83-88; prof, relig div, 88-94, DISTINGUISHED PROF, RELIGION DIVISION, PEPPERDINE UNIV, 94-. **HONORS AND AWARDS** Outstanding Alumnus, Col of Arts and Sciences, Harding Univ, 86; Faculty Person of the Year, Seaver Col, Pepperdine Univ, 92-93; Distinguished Alumnus, Col of Biblical and Family Studies, Abilene Christian Univ, 96. **MEMBERSHIPS** Am Soc Church Hist; Am Academy Relig. **RESEARCH** 19th century Am relig, especially restorationist movements; religion and higher ed in the US. **SELECTED PUBLICATIONS** Ed, The Primitive Church in the Modern World, Univ IL Press, 95; auth, Reviving the Ancient Faith: The Story of Churches of Christ in America, Eerdmans, 96; co-ed with Wm. B. Adrian, Models for Christian Higher Education, Eerdmans, 97. **CONTACT ADDRESS** Religion Division, Pepperdine Univ, 24255 Pacific Coast Hwy, Malibu, CA, 90263. **EMAIL** rhughes@pepperdine.edu

HUGHES, ROBERT DON
DISCIPLINE RELIGION **EDUCATION** Calif Baptist Col, BA; Golden Gate Baptist Theol Sem, MDiv; S Baptist Theol Sem, PhD. **CAREER** Assoc VP, Acad Prog, dir, Cont Edu and Extension Stud, act dir, Prof Dr Stud, S Baptist Theol Sem. **HONORS AND AWARDS** Mass media consult, Intl Mission Bd. **RESEARCH** Cross cultural missions. **SELECTED PUBLICATIONS** Auth, Satan's Whispers. **CONTACT ADDRESS** Sch Theol, Southern Baptist Theol Sem, 2825 Lexington Rd, Louisville, KY, 40280. **EMAIL** rhughes@sbts.edu

HUGLY, PHILIP
DISCIPLINE LOGIC, THE PHILOSOPHY OF MATHEMATICS **EDUCATION** Univ Calif, Berkeley, PhD, 65. **CAREER** Prof, Univ Nebr, Lincoln. **RESEARCH** Wittgenstein. **SELECTED PUBLICATIONS** Coauth, Theories of Truth and Truth-Value Gaps, Ling and Philos 16, 93; The Disquotational Theory of Truth is False, Philos 22, 93; Quantifying over the Reals, Synthese 101, 94; Intentionality and Truth: An Essay on the Philosophy of Arthur Prior. **CONTACT ADDRESS** Univ Nebr, Lincoln, Lincoln, NE, 68588-0417.

HULL, DAVID L.
PERSONAL Born 06/15/1935, Burnside, IL **DISCIPLINE** PHILOSOPHY **EDUCATION** Indiana Univ, PhD, 64. **CAREER** Univ Wisc, Milwaukee, 64-84; Northwestern Univ, 85-. **HONORS AND AWARDS** Guggenheim Fel. **MEMBERSHIPS** Am Acad of Arts and Sci; Philos of Sci Asn; Soc of Syst Biol. **RESEARCH** History and philosophy of biology. **SELECTED PUBLICATIONS** Auth, Die Rezeption von Darwin's Evolutionstheorie bei Britischen Wissenschaftsphilosophen des 19. Jahrhunderts, in Engels, ed, Die Rezeption von Evolutionstheorien im 19. Jahrhundert, Suhrkamp, 95; auth, Rainbows in Retrospect: L.A. Johnson's Contributions to Taxonomic Philosophy, Telopea, 96; auth, A Revolutionary Philosopher of Science, Nature, 96; auth, What's Wrong with Invisible-Hand Explanations? PSA, 97; auth, That Just Don't Sound Right: A Plea for Real Examples, in Earman, ed, The Cosmos of Science, Pittsburgh, 97; auth, Species, Subspecies and Races, Social Research, 98; co-ed, Philosophy of Biology, Oxford, 98. **CONTACT ADDRESS** Dept of Philosophy, Northwestern Univ, Evanston, IL, 60208. **EMAIL** d-hull@nwu.edu

HULL, MICHAEL F.
PERSONAL Born 04/01/1963, Bronx, NY **DISCIPLINE** BIBLICAL STUDIES **EDUCATION** St Joseph's Sem, MA, 93; Pontifical Gregorian Univ, STL, 96, STD (cand), 96-. **CAREER** Ordained Roman Cath Priest of the Archdiocese of New York, 93; graduate studies, Pontifical Gregorian Univ, Rome, 94-98; prof of Sacred Scripture, St Joseph's Seminary, NY, 98-. **MEMBERSHIPS** Cath Biblical Asn; Soc of Biblical Lit; Am Academy of Relig. **RESEARCH** Biblical studies; ancient Near East; theology. **SELECTED PUBLICATIONS** Auth, Prophesy and Revelation 10, 1-11; 11, 1-13: The Creative Use of the Old Testament by a New Testament Prophet, Dunwoodie Rev 16, 93; Jezebel and John: Authority in Thyatira, Dunwoodie Rev 17, 94. **CONTACT ADDRESS** St. Joseph's Sem, 201 Seminary Ave, Apt 25A, Yonkers, NY, 10704-1896. **EMAIL** mfhull@compuserve.com

HULL, N.E.H.
PERSONAL Born 08/27/1949, New York, NY, m, 1970, 2 children **DISCIPLINE** LAW, HISTORY **EDUCATION** Ohio State, Univ, BA, 74; Columbia Univ, PhD, 81; Univ of Georgia, JD, 85. **CAREER** Assoc prof, 87-93, prof, 93-97, distinguish prof of law and hist, 97-present, Rutgers Univ. **HONORS AND AWARDS** Scribes Book Award for 1998; Erwin Surrency Prize of Amer Soc for Legal Hist, 99. **MEMBERSHIPS** ABA, New Jersey Bar Assn; AHA; ASLA; OAH **RESEARCH** Amer Legal and Jurisprudential Hist **SELECTED PUBLICATIONS** Auth, Vital Schools of Jurisprudence: Roscoe Pound, Wesley Newcomb Hohfeld, and the Promotion of an Academic Jurisprudential Agenda, 1910-1919, Journal of Legal Education, 95; The Romantic Realist: Art, Literature and the Enduring Legacy of Karl Llewellyn's Jurisprudence, 40 American Journal of Legal History, 96; Roscoe Pound & Karl Llewellyn: Searching for an American Jurisprudence, 97; Back to the Future of the Institute: William Draper Lewis's Vision of the ALI's Mission During Its First Twenty-Five Years and The Implications for the Institute's Seventy-Fifth Anniversary, 98. **CONTACT ADDRESS** Sch Law-Camden, Rutger Univ, 217 N. Fifth St., Camden, NJ, 08102-1203. **EMAIL** nehhul@crab.rutgers.edu

HULL, RICHARD T.
PERSONAL Born 12/29/1939, Oklahoma City, OK, m, 1962, 1 child **DISCIPLINE** PHILOSOPHY **EDUCATION** Austin Col, MA, 63; Ind Univ, PhD, 71. **CAREER** Headmaster, Calasanctius Prep School Buffalo, NY, 83-86; scholar in res, Buffalo Gen Hosp, 95; prof Philos, SUNY-Buffalo, 67-97; Exec Dir Texas Coun Hum, 97-. **MEMBERSHIPS** Am Philos Asn; Nat Soc Fund Raising Exec. **RESEARCH** Humanities; biomedical ethics; philosophy of mind. **SELECTED PUBLICATIONS** Auth, Ethical Issues in the New Reproductive Technologies, Wadsworth, 90; A Quarter Century of Value Inquiry: Presidential Addresses of the American Society of Value Inquiry, Editions Rodopi, 94; Symposium: Russian Value Theory, The Jour of Value Inquiry, 96; William H. Werkmeister, Martin Heidegger on the Way, Editions Rodopi, 96; Presidential Addresses of the American Philosophical Association, 1901-1910 and Presidential Addresses of the American Philosophical Association, 1911-1920, Kluwer Acad Publ, 98. **CONTACT ADDRESS** Texas Council Humanities, Banister Pl 3809-A S 2nd St., Austin, TX, 78704-7058. **EMAIL** rthull@pub lic-humanities.org

HULL, WILLIAM E.
PERSONAL Born 05/28/1930, Birmingham, AL, m, 1952, 2 children **DISCIPLINE** RELIGION **EDUCATION** Samford Univ, BA, 51; S Baptist Theoll Sem, MDiv, 54, PhD, 60. **CAREER** Ordained Baptist Minister, 50; S Baptist Theol Sem, fel, inst, asst prof, assoc prof, prof, 54-75; Vis prof. at: Baptist Theol Sem, Switzerland, 63; Louisiana State Univ Sch of Med, 75-78; S Baptist Theol Sem, 79, 90-92; Nigerian Baptist Theol Sem, 82; Samford Univ, prof, 87-. **MEMBERSHIPS** AAPS, AAR, AAHE, AAUP, ASOR, NABPR, SBL **SELECTED PUBLICATIONS** Auth, The Gospel of John, Alpha-Omega Series, Broadman, 64; auth, John, Broadman Bible Commentary, Broadman, 70; auth, The Bible, Covenant, 74; auth, Love in Four Dimensions, Broadman, 82; auth, The Christian Experience of Salvation, Layman's Library of Christian Doctrine, Broadman, 87; auth, Handbook of Contemporary Preaching, Broadman, 93; auth, Proclaiming the Baptist Vision: The Bible, Smith & Helwys, 94; auth, The University Though the Eyes of Faith, Light & Life, 98. **CONTACT ADDRESS** Dept of Theology, Samford Univ, 435 Ver Club Way, Birmingham, AL, 35216-1357. **EMAIL** wehull@samford.edu

HULLETT, JAMES N.
PERSONAL Born 03/02/1939, Toledo, OH, m, 1981, 1 child **DISCIPLINE** PHILOSOPHY **EDUCATION** Brandeis Univ, PhD, 67. **CAREER** Asst prof, Dartmouth Col, 66-68; asst prof, Boston Univ, 68-75; vis prof, Burlington Col, 83-85; publ, Hackett Pub Co., 76- . **MEMBERSHIPS** APA. **CONTACT ADDRESS** Hackett Pub Co, PO Box 7, Cambridge, MA, 02139.

HULLOT-KENTOR, ROBERT
PERSONAL Born 10/09/1948, Pittsburgh, PA, m, 1977 **DISCIPLINE** AESTHETICS **EDUCATION** Univ MA, PhD, 85. **CAREER** Boston Univ, 85-86; Hobart and Willian Smith Colleges, 86-88; Harvard Univ, 88-89; Stanford Univ, 89-94; ASSOC PROF, SOUTHAMPTON COL, 97-. **HONORS AND AWARDS** Mellon fel, Harvard Univ, 89-90; J. Paul Getty fel, 90-91; J. Paul Getty Vis Scholar, 93; Orion Vis Artist, Univ Victoria, 97. **RESEARCH** Aesthetics. **SELECTED PUBLICATIONS** Ed, translator, and intro, Kierkegaard: Construction of the Aesthetic, by T. W. Adorno, Minnesota, 92; ed, translator, and intro, Aesthetic Theory, by T. W. Adorno, Minnesota, 98; auth, Terra Infirma: Sculptures of Mowry Baden, Victoria, 98. **CONTACT ADDRESS** Southampton Col, Montau E. Hwy, Southampton, NY, 11968. **EMAIL** Kentor@southampton.libnet.edu

HULTGREN, ARLAND
DISCIPLINE NEW TESTAMENT **EDUCATION** Univ Mich, MA, 63; Lutheran Sch Theol, MDiv, 65; Union Theol Sem, ThD, 71; sabbatical terms, Univ Cambridge, 84-85; Uppsala, Sweden, 90-91. **CAREER** Instr, Wagner Col, 69-77; assoc prof, 77; dept ch, 86-93; prof, 86-. **HONORS AND AWARDS** Asst pastor, Trinity Lutheran Church, 66-68; pastor, St Andrew's Lutheran Church, Minneapolis, 79-80; ed, Word & World, 81-88. **MEMBERSHIPS** Mem, Soc Bibl Lit; Studiorum Novi Testamenti Societas; Bd of Trustees, Gustavus Adolphus Col. **SELECTED PUBLICATIONS** Co-ed, All Things New: Essays in Honor of Roy A. Harrisville, 92; Christ and His Communities: Essays in Honor of Reginald H. Fulle, 90; auth, Advent-Christmas: Proclamation 4, 89; New Testament Christology: A Critical Assessment and Annotated Bibliography, 88; Christ and His Benefits: Christology and Redemption in the New Testament, 87; Paul's Gospel and Mission: the Outlook from His Letter to the Romans, 85; I-II Timothy, Titus, Augsburg Commentary on the New Testament, 84. **CONTACT ADDRESS** Dept of New Testament, Luther Sem, 2481 Como Ave, St. Paul, MN, 55108. **EMAIL** ahultgre@luthersem.edu

HULTGREN, ARTHUR J.
PERSONAL Born 07/17/1939, Muskegon, MI, m, 1965, 3 children **DISCIPLINE** NEW TESTAMENT STUDIES **EDUCATION** Augustana Col, BA, 61; Univ Mich, MA, 63; Lutheran Sch Theol Chicago, MDiv, 65; Union Theol Sem, ThD, 71. **CAREER** Instr to assoc prof, rel stud, Wagner Col, 69-77; assoc prof to PROF NEW TESTAMENT, LUTHER SEM, 77-. **HONORS AND AWARDS** Phi Beta Kappa, 61; Outstanding Alumni Achievement Award, Augustana Col, 96. **MEMBERSHIPS** Soc Bibl Lit; Studiorum Novi Testamenti Societas. **RESEARCH** Gospel of Matthew; Parables of Jesus; Epistle to the Romans. **SELECTED PUBLICATIONS** Auth, The Rise of Normative Christianity, 94; co-ed, The Earliest Christian Heretics: Readings from Their Opponents, 96. **CONTACT ADDRESS** Luther Sem, 2481 Como Ave, St. Paul, MN, 55108. **EMAIL** ahultgre@luthersem.edu

HUMBER, JAMES MICHAEL
PERSONAL Born 11/10/1942, Erie, PA, m, 1967, 2 children **DISCIPLINE** PHILOSOPHY **EDUCATION** Colgate Univ, AB, 64; State Univ NY Buffalo, MA, 67, PhD, 70. **CAREER** From Asst Prof to Assoc Prof, 69-83, Prof Philos, GA State Univ, 83. **MEMBERSHIPS** Am Philos Asn; Southern Soc Philos & Psychol; Hum Soc. **RESEARCH** Early mod hist of philos; applied ethics. **SELECTED PUBLICATIONS** Co-ed, Biomedical ethics and the Law, Plenum Press, 76, 2nd ed, 79; Biomedical Ethics Reviews: 1983, Humana Press, 83, 84, and to the present; Business Ethics, Promethus Books, 92; auth, Justifying the Foreign Corrupt Practices Act, Business Ethics, rev ed, Promethus Books, 92; Hume's Invisible Self, Am Cath Philos Quart, Summer 95; Maternity, Paternity, and Equality, Biomedical Ethics Reviews: 1995, Humana Press, 95; Hume, The Blackwell Companion to the Philosophers, Blackwell; author of numerous other articles and book reviews. **CONTACT ADDRESS** Dept of Philos, Georgia State Univ, Box 4089, Atlanta, GA, 30302-4089. **EMAIL** phljmh@panther.gsu.edu

HUMMEL, BRADFORD SCOTT
PERSONAL Born 02/06/1966, Santa Paula, CA, m, 1990, 2 children **DISCIPLINE** THEOLOGY **EDUCATION** William Corey Col, BA, 87; Hebrew Univ, 88-89; Southwestern Baptist Theol Sem, M.Div, 91, PhD, 96. **CAREER** Adj prof, Southwestern Baptist Theol Sem, 93-94, 98; asst prof, LeTourneau Univ, 98-. **HONORS AND AWARDS** Greek Award; Hebrew Award; Jenkins-Chastain Citizenship Award; President's Scholar; Rotary Int Fel. **MEMBERSHIPS** Soc Biblical Lit; Am Soc Oriental Res; Am Acad Relig; Nat Asn Baptist Profs of Relig. **RESEARCH** Hebrew Bible; Second Temple Period. **CONTACT ADDRESS** 505 Wain Dr, Longview, TX, 75604. **EMAIL** hummels@letu.edu

HUMPHREYS, FISHER
PERSONAL Born 02/05/1939, Columbus, MS, m, 1963, 2 children **DISCIPLINE** THEOLOGY **EDUCATION** MS Col, BA, 61; Loyola Univ, MA, 84; Oxford Univ, MLit, 67; New Orleans Baptist Theological Sem, BD, 64, ThD, 72. **CAREER** Prof Theol, New Orleans Baptist Theological Sem, 70-89; PROF DIVINITY, SAMFORD UNIV, 90-. **HONORS AND AWARDS** George Macon Award for Excellence in Teaching, 98. **MEMBERSHIPS** AAR; NABPR; CTS; BAPT; Christian Theol Res fel (CTRF). **RESEARCH** Doctrine of the Trinity. **SELECTED PUBLICATIONS** Auth, The Way We Were, McCracken Press, 94; Thinking About God, 94. **CONTACT ADDRESS** Beeson Divinity School, Samford Univ, Birmingham, AL, 35229. **EMAIL** fhhumphr@samford.edu

HUNT, MARY ELIZABETH
PERSONAL Born 06/01/1951, Syracuse, NY **DISCIPLINE** THEOLOGY **EDUCATION** Marquette Univ, BA (magna cum laude), theology, philos, 72; Harvard Divinity School, master theol studies, 74; Jesuit School of Theology, master divinity, 79; Graduate Theol Union, PhD, philos and systematic theol, 80. **CAREER** Visiting prof theol, frontier internship in mission, ISEDET, 80-82; co-dir, co-founder, Women's Alliance for Theol Ethics and Ritual, 83-; visiting asst prof religion, Colgate Univ, 86-87; adjunct asst prof of Women's Studies, Georgetown Univ, 95-. **HONORS AND AWARDS** Isaac Hecker Award, Paulist Center; Prophetic Figure Award, Women's Ordination Conf; Crossroads Women's Studies Prize, 90; Mary Rhodes Award, Loretto Community, 93. **MEMBERSHIPS** Amer Acad Religion, Women and Religion, chair, 92-94; Soc Christian Ethics; Inst Study Christianity and Sexuality, bd dirs; Phi Sigma Tau; Alpha Sigma Nu. **SELECTED PUBLICATIONS** Auth, Fierce Tenderness: A Feminist Theology of Friendship, 91; ed, From Woman-Pain to Woman-Vision: Writings in Feminist Theology, 89; auth, "Variety Is the Spice of Life: Doing It Our Ways," in Our Families, Our Values: Snapshots of Queer Kinship, 97; auth, "Re-Imagining Backlash," in Concilium: Feminist Theology in Different Contexts, 96. **CONTACT ADDRESS** Women's Alliance for Theol, Ethics and Ritual, 8035 13th St, Stes. 1, 3, 5, Silver Spring, MD, 20910. **EMAIL** mhunt@hers.com

HUNTER, FREDERICK DOUGLAS
PERSONAL Born 01/30/1940, Pittsburgh, PA, m **DISCIPLINE** LAW **EDUCATION** Univ of Pittsburgh, BS 1961, PhD 1967; Univ of Maryland, JD 1974. **CAREER** The Lubrizol Corp, chief patent counsel, associate general counsel; EI Dupont De Nemours & Co, corporate counsel 1972-89; W R Grace & Co, sr rsch chem 1967-72. **MEMBERSHIPS** Amer Bar Assn; Delaware Bar Assn; District of Columbia Bar Assn; AOA Fraternity; AIPLA. **SELECTED PUBLICATIONS** Publ 5 papers various sci jour. **CONTACT ADDRESS** The Lubrizol Corp, 29400 Lakeland Blvd, Wickliffe, OH, 44092-2298.

HUNTER, JERRY L.
PERSONAL Born 09/01/1942, Mt. Holly, NC **DISCIPLINE** LAW **EDUCATION** NC, BS; A&T State U, 1964; Howard Univ Schl of Law, JD 1967. **CAREER** Roundtree Knox Hunter & Parker, Partner Law firm. **HONORS AND AWARDS** Am Jurisprudence Award for Academic Achievement in Legal Methods & History. **MEMBERSHIPS** Mem US Supreme Court Bar; US Dist Court (MD & DC); US Court of Appeals & DC Court of Appeals; mem Natl Bar Assn; Am Bar Assn; DC Bar Assn; Assn of Plaintiffs Trail Atty; Sigma Delta Tau Legal Frat Alpha Kappa Mu Honor Soc; Kappa Pi Intl Honorary Art Soc **SELECTED PUBLICATIONS** Co-auth, "Current Racial Legal Developments" 12 How-L J 299, Spring 66 No 2. **CONTACT ADDRESS** Roundtree, Knox, Hunter & Parker, 1822 11th St NW, Washington, DC, 20001.

HUNTER, JOEL
DISCIPLINE PRACTICAL THEOLOGY **EDUCATION** Ohio Univ, BA; Christian Theol Sem, MDiv, DMin. **CAREER** Vis lectr **SELECTED PUBLICATIONS** Auth, The Journey To Spiritual Maturity; The Challenging Road and Prayer; Politics & Power. **CONTACT ADDRESS** Dept of Practical Theology, Reformed Theol Sem, 2101 Carmel Rd, Charlotte, NC, 28226.

HUNTER, RODNEY J.
PERSONAL Born 10/08/1940, Detroit, MI, m, 1970, 1 child **DISCIPLINE** PASTORAL THEOLOGY **EDUCATION** Yale Col, BA, 62; Princeton Theol Sem, BD, 62, PhD, 74. **CAREER** From instr to asst prof and assoc prof to prof of pastoral theol, Candler School of Theol, Emory Univ, 71- . **MEMBERSHIPS** Soc for Pastoral Theol; AAR; Asn for Practical Theol; Asn for Clinical Pastoral Educ. **RESEARCH** Theology of pastoral care and counseling; theology and personality studies; Freud, Jung and religion; psychology and religion; personal commitment. **SELECTED PUBLICATIONS** Auth, Law and Gospel in Pastoral Care, J of Pastoral Care, 76; auth, The Future of Pastoral Theology, Pastoral Psychol, 80; auth, A Perspectival Pastoral Theology, in Aden, ed, Turning Points in Pastoral Care: The Legacy of Anton Boisen and Seward Hiltner, Baker Book House, 90; ed, Dictionary of Pastoral Care and Counseling, Abingdon, 90; auth, Participation in the Life of God: Revisioning Lapsley's Salvation-Health Model, in Childs, ed, The Treasure of Earthen Vessels: Explorations in Theological Anthropology, John Knox, 94; co-ed and contribur, Pastoral Care and Social Conflict: Essays in Honor of Charles V. Gerkin, Abingdon, 95; auth, Religious Caregiving and Pedagogy in a Postmodern Context: Recovering Ecclesia, J of Pastoral Theol, 98; auth, The Power of God for Salvation: Transformative Ecclesia and the Theological Renewal of Pastoral Care and Counseling, J of the Interdenominational Theol Ctr, 98. **CONTACT ADDRESS** Candler School of Theology, Emory Univ, Atlanta, GA, 30322. **EMAIL** rhunt02@emory.edu

HURD, HEIDI M.
PERSONAL Born 10/19/1960, Laramie, WY, m, 1987, 2 children **DISCIPLINE** PHILOSOPHY; LAW **EDUCATION** Queens Univ, BA, 82; Dalhousie Univ, MA, 84; Univ Southern Calif, JD, 88, PhD, 92. **CAREER** Asst prof, law, Univ Penn, 89-94; prof, law & philos, Univ Penn, 94-; visiting asst prof, philos, Univ Iowa, 91-92; assoc dean, acad affairs, Univ Penn Law Sch, 94-96; visiting prof, law, Univ Va, 97-98. **MEMBERSHIPS** Bd of ed, Legal Theory, Cambridge Press, 93-; comt mem, AALS jurisprudence sect, 92-93, 98-99; Order of the Cole, 88-. **RESEARCH** Philosophy of law; Ethics. **SELECTED PUBLICATIONS** Article, Duties Beyond the Call of Duty, 5 Annual Rev of Law and Ethics, 97; article, The Moral Magic of Consent, 2 Legal Theory, 121-146, 95; article, The Deontology of Negligence, 76 B.U. L. Rev, 249-72, 95; article, The Levitation of Liberalism, 105 Yale Law Jour, 795-824, 95; article, Interpreting Authority, Legal Interpretation, Oxford Univ Press, 94; article, What in the World is Wrong?, 5 Jour of Comtemp Legal Issues, 157-216, 94. **CONTACT ADDRESS** Univ of Pennsylvania Law School, 3400 Chestnut St., Philadelphia, PA, 19104-6204.

HURST, THOMAS R.
DISCIPLINE LAW **EDUCATION** Univ Wis, AB; Harvard Univ, JD. **CAREER** Prof, Univ Florida. **MEMBERSHIPS** Wis Bar. **RESEARCH** Corporate law, contracts, corporate finance. **CONTACT ADDRESS** School of Law, Univ of Florida, PO Box 117625, Gainesville, FL, 32611-7625. **EMAIL** hurst@law.ufl.edu

HUSAK, DOUGLAS NEIL
PERSONAL Born 06/11/1948, Cleveland, OH **DISCIPLINE** PHILOSOPHY, LAW **EDUCATION** Denison Univ, BA, 70; Ohio State Univ, MA, PhD(Philos) & JD, 76. **CAREER** Vis asst prof Philos, Ind Univ, 76-77; asst prof Philos, Rutgers Univ, New Brunswick, 77-, vis asst prof, Univ Pittsburgh, Summer 80. **HONORS AND AWARDS** Rutgers Parents Asn Outstanding Teacher Award, 80. **MEMBERSHIPS** Am Philos Asn; Soc Am Social & Legal Philosophers; Soc Business Ethics. **SELECTED PUBLICATIONS** Auth, University practices of preferential hiring and reverse discrimination in favor of Blacks--a moral analysis, Am J Jurisp, 78; Political violence, Nous, 78; Sovereigns and third party beneficiaries, J Value Inquiry, 78 Ronald Dworkin and the right to Paternalism and autonomy, Philosophy and Public Affairs, 80 Obscenity and speech, J Value Inquiry (in prep); The presumption of freedom, Nous (in prep); Philosophy of Crimal Law, Rowman & Littlefield, 87; Drugs and Rights, Cambridge Univ Press, 92. **CONTACT ADDRESS** Dept of Philosophy, Rutgers Univ, PO Box 270, New Brunswick, NJ, 08903-0270. **EMAIL** husak@rci.rutgers.edu

HUSTWIT, RONALD E.
PERSONAL Born 04/02/1942, Pittsburgh, PA, m, 1966, 3 children **DISCIPLINE** PHILOSOPHY **EDUCATION** Westminster Coll, BA, 64; Nebraska, MA, 65; Texas, PhD, 70. **CAREER** Prof, Coll Of Wooster. **MEMBERSHIPS** Am Philos Asn. **RESEARCH** Ludwig Wittgenstein; Philosophy of Mind, Religion, Language. **SELECTED PUBLICATIONS** Auth, Something about OK Bouwsma; Wittgenstein Interest in Kiekegaand, Wittgenstein Studies,97. **CONTACT ADDRESS** 806 E Wayne Ave, Wooster, OH, 44691. **EMAIL** rhustwit@wooster.edu

HUTCHESON, RICHARD E.
PERSONAL Born 01/20/1928, Washington, DC, m, 1953, 2 children **DISCIPLINE** PHILOSOPHY **EDUCATION** Coll of William & Mary, BA, 52; Harvard Univ, MA, 54, PhD, 62. **CAREER** Asst prof, Wofford Col, 57-59; Asst prof, Allegheny Coll, 59-67; assoc prof, Kansas State, 67-69; chemn, St. Mary's Notre Dame, 69-71; prof, dean, SUNT Potsdam, 72-90. **HONORS AND AWARDS** Phi Beta Kappa; Omicron Delta Kappa. **MEMBERSHIPS** APA; Metaphysical Soc Am. **RESEARCH** Nineteenth century British metaphysics. **CONTACT ADDRESS** 387 Savage Farm Dr, Ithaca, NY, 14850.

HUTCHINSON, DOUGLAS S.
PERSONAL Born 10/13/1955, Dorval, PQ, Canada **DISCIPLINE** PHILOSOPHY **EDUCATION** Queen's Univ, BA, 76; Oxford Univ, BPhil, 78, DPhil, 83. **CAREER** Lectr philos, Balliol Col, 79-80, Corpus Christi Col, Oxford Univ, 80-83; asst prof, 83-87, ASSOC PROF PHILOSOPHY, UNIV TORONTO, 87-. **HONORS AND AWARDS** Rhodes scholar, 76; res fel, Humboldt Fedn(Ger), 93-94. **SELECTED PUBLICATIONS** Auth, The Virtues of Aristotle, 86; assoc ed, Plato: Complete Works, 97. **CONTACT ADDRESS** Dept of Philosophy, Univ of Toronto, 6 Hoskin Ave, Toronto, ON, M5S 1H8.

HUTCHINSON, ROGER CHARLES
PERSONAL Born 11/13/1935, Camrose, AB, Canada, m, 1965, 2 children **DISCIPLINE** RELIGIOUS STUDIES, SOCIAL ETHICS **EDUCATION** Univ Alta, BSc, 58; Queen's Univ, BD, 66; Univ Chicago, MA, 68; Victoria Univ, ThD, 75. **CAREER** Lectr, 69-75, asst prof, 75-78, Assoc Prof Relig Studies, Univ Toronto, 78- **MEMBERSHIPS** Can Soc Study Relig; Soc Christian Ethics. **RESEARCH** Religion and public policy in Canada; Christian socialism in Canada; inter-church coalitions. **SELECTED PUBLICATIONS** Auth, A Place in Creation, Studies Relig Sci, Vol 0023, 94. **CONTACT ADDRESS** Dept of Relig Studies Victoria Col, Univ of Toronto, Toronto, ON, M5S 1K7.

HUTCHISON, HARRY GREENE, IV
PERSONAL Born 04/12/1948, Detroit, MI, s **DISCIPLINE** LAW **EDUCATION** Wayne State University, Detroit, MI, BA, 1969, MA, 1975; University of Michigan, Ann Arbor, MI, MBA, 1977; Wayne State University, Detroit, MI, JD, 1986. **CAREER** Detroit Edison, Detroit, MI, business analyst, 1970-74; Ford Motor Co, Troy, MI, financial analyst, 1977-80; Lawrence Technological University, Southfield, MI, professor, 1981-89; UNIVERSTIY OF DETROIT, DETROIT, MI, LAW PROFESSOR, 1989-. **MEMBERSHIPS** Senior policy analyst, Mackinac Center, 1987-; board of advisors, Heartland Institute, 1990-. **CONTACT ADDRESS** Sch of Law, Univ of Detroit, 651 E Jefferson, Detroit, MI, 48226.

HUTCHISON, JOHN A.
PERSONAL Born 03/02/1912, m, 1938, 5 children **DISCIPLINE** PHILOSOPHY **EDUCATION** LaFayette Col, MA; Columbia Univ, PhD. **CAREER** Williams Col, 47-55; Columbia Univ, 55-60; Claremont Grad Sch, 60-77. **HONORS AND AWARDS** Ford fel, 53; Danforth fel, 60, 61. **MEMBERSHIPS** APA; Soc for Relig Stud. **RESEARCH** World religions; philosophy and religion. **SELECTED PUBLICATIONS** Auth, Paths of Faith, 4th ed, 95; auth, Living Options in World Faiths, 77. **CONTACT ADDRESS** 720 Mayflower Rd, Claremont, CA, 91711.

HUTSON, CHRISTOPHER R.
PERSONAL Born 01/08/1961, Chattanooga, TN **DISCIPLINE** NEW TESTAMENT STUDIES **EDUCATION** David Lipscomb Col, BA, 83; Univ Cincinnati, MA, 87; Yale Univ, MDiv, 89, PhD, 98. **CAREER** Adj instr, St Xavier Univ, 97-98; asst prof, New Testament, Hood Theol Sem, 98- . **MEMBERSHIPS** Soc of Bibl Lit; Chicago Soc of Bibl Res; Disciples of Christ Hist Soc. **RESEARCH** New Testament and Early Christianity; social history. **CONTACT ADDRESS** Hood Theol Sem, 800 W Thomas St, Salisbury, NC, 28144. **EMAIL** crhutson@salisbury.net

HUTTER, REINHARD
DISCIPLINE CHRISTIAN ETHICS; THEOLOGY **EDUCATION** Duke Divinity Sch; Univ Erlangen, ThD; post dr res, Inst for advan stud of Rel, Univ Chicago Divinity Sch. **CAREER** Assoc prof **HONORS AND AWARDS** Ed bd, Currents in Theol and Mission. **MEMBERSHIPS** Mem, Community Life Comm; Library Adv Comm; Admissions Comm. **RESEARCH** Christian beliefs and practices. **SELECTED PUBLICATIONS** Coauth, George Lindbeck's The Nature of Doctrine: Religion and Theology in a Post-Liberal Age; The Peaceable Kingdom: A Primer in Christian Ethics; co-ed, Ecumenical Ventures in Ethics: Protestants Engage Pope John Paul II's Moral Encyclicals, Eerdmans, 98; auth, Theologie als kirchliche Praktik, Gutersloher Verlagshaus, 98. **CONTACT ADDRESS** Dept of Ethics and Theology, Lutheran Sch of Theol, 1100 E 55th St, Chicago, IL, 60615. **EMAIL** rhutter@lstc.edu

HUTTON, LEWIS J.
PERSONAL Born 07/26/1921, New York, NY, m, 1948, 4 children **DISCIPLINE** ROMANCE LANGUAGES, RELIGION **EDUCATION** Columbia Univ, AB, 42, MA, 46; Princeton Theol Sem, BD, 44; Princeton Univ, MA, 48, PhD(Romance lang, Span), 50; Union Theol Sem, STM, 50. **CAREER** Instr Span, Princeton Univ, 45-48; instr, NY Univ, 48-49; minister, First Presby Church, Gowanda, NY, 51-55; sr minister, Capitol Hill Presby Church, Wash, DC, 55-62; sr minister, First Presby Church, Kirksville, Mo, 62-64; from asst prof to assoc prof Span, Drake Univ, 64-66; assoc prof, 66-72, Prof Span, Univ RI, 72-, Assoc Span, George Washington Univ, 57-62. **MEMBERSHIPS** MLA; Am Asn Teachers Span & Port; Am Soc Church Hist; Soc Bibl Lit. **RESEARCH** Sixteenth and seventeenth century Spanish literature; contemporary intellectual thought; sixteenth century ecclesiastical history. **SELECTED PUBLICATIONS** Auth, Cervantes and the Burlesque Sonnet, Sixteenth Century J, Vol 0024, 93. **CONTACT ADDRESS** Dept of Span, Univ of RI, Kingston, RI, 02881.

HUTTON, RODNEY R.
DISCIPLINE OLD TESTAMENT **EDUCATION** Dana Col, BA, 70; Evangel Lutheran Theol Sem, MDiv, 74; Univ Heidelberg, grad stud, 74-75; Claremont Grad Sch, PhD, 83. **CAREER** Instr, ELTS, 73-74; assoc, Inst Antiquity and Christianity, 76-77; asst prof, 82-87; assoc prof, 87-93; guest prof, Univ Tubingen, 89-90; prof, Trinity Lutheran Sem, 93-. **MEMBERSHIPS** Soc Biblical Lit; Cath Biblical Soc; E Great Lakes Bible Soc. **SELECTED PUBLICATIONS** Co-auth, Covenants and Care, Augsburg/Fortress, 98; auth, Innocent or Holy? Justification and Sanctification in Old Testament Theology, Word and World 17, 97; Narrative in Leviticus: The Case of the Blaspheming Son , Altorientalische und Biblische Rechtsgeschichte, Harrasowitz, 97; Magic or Street-Theater? The Power of the Prophetic Word, Zeitschrift fur die alttestamentliche Wissenschaft 107, 96; Charisma and Authority in Israelite Society, Augsburg/Fortress, 94; Moses on the Mount of Transfiguration, Hebrew Annual Rev 14, 94. **CONTACT ADDRESS** Bible Dept, Trinity Lutheran Sem, 2199 E Main St, Columbus, OH, 43209-2334. **EMAIL** rhutton@trinity.capital.edu

HWANG, TZU-YANG
PERSONAL Born 09/21/1953, Taiwan, m, 1980 **DISCIPLINE** RELIGION **EDUCATION** Tainan Theol Col, MDiv; Princeton Univ Theol Sem, MTh, 86; Chinese for Christ Theol Sem, PhD, 90. **CAREER** Tchg asst, Tainan Theol Sem; pastor, Good Shepherd Formosa Presbyterian Church; Chemn Chinese for Christian Theol Sem; adj prof Holy Light Theol Sem; pres, prof, Am Chi-Chou Neo-Philos Inst, 95- ; pres, Light Christ Church, 96- ; res assoc, Am Biographical Inst, 96- . **HONORS AND AWARDS** Mil prize, Natl Dfense Dept, Taiwan, 73; Int cultural diploma of honour; Millennium Hall of Fame Medal of Honour; fel, Am Biog Inst; listed, Five Thousand Personalities of the World, Who's Who in Religion, Who's Who in Am; Key of Success-Achievemet of Res; **MEMBERSHIPS** Int Governors Clubs; Int Order of Ambassadors; Am Acad Relig; Am Acad Relig; Soc Bibl Lit; Sci Stud Relig. **RESEARCH** Fundamental and systematic theology and culture; sixteenth to twentieth century religious thoughts and their relation to religion, philosophy and culture; methods to develop religious cultural philosophy and theology in the east and west. **SELECTED PUBLICATIONS** Auth, Theologies of Christianity and Thoughts of Chinese Culture, diss; auth, Cultural Theologies in Asia; auth, Theology and Piety; auth, Theology and Life; auth, An Impact of Hearts and Spriits Shaking; auth, A Philosophy of Religion and Theology of Christianity; auth, Cultural Theologies in Asia; auth, Theologies of Christianity and Thoughts of Chinese Culture; auth, An Approach to History of Ministry Thinking of Dr. Campbell Moody in Taiwan. **CONTACT ADDRESS** 11768 Roseglen St., El Monte, CA, 91732.

HYDE, ALAN STUART
PERSONAL Born 05/24/1951, Los Angeles, CA, m, 1976, 2 children **DISCIPLINE** LAW **EDUCATION** Stanford Univ, AB, 72; Yale Univ, JD, 75. **CAREER** Instr, New York Univ, 76-78; asst prof, 78-81, assoc prof, 87-89, Sch Law, prof, 89-, Rutgers Univ, Newark, Sidney Roitman Scholar, 91-, vis prof Michigan, 83-84, Yale, 93-94, YeShiva, 94-95, Columbia, 95-96. **RESEARCH** Labor law; sociology of law; philosophy of law. **SELECTED PUBLICATIONS** Coauth, Cases and Materials on Labor Law, Found Press, 82; auth, Bodies of Law, Princeton Univ Press, 97. **CONTACT ADDRESS** Sch Law, Rutgers Univ, 15 Washington St, Newark, NJ, 07102-3192. **EMAIL** hyde@andromeda.rutgers.edu

HYLAND, DREW ALAN
PERSONAL Born 02/09/1939, Wilkes-Barre, PA, m, 1964, 2 children **DISCIPLINE** PHILOSOPHY **EDUCATION** Princeton Univ, BA, 61; Pa State Univ, MA, 63, PhD(philos), 65. **CAREER** From lectr to asst prof philos, Univ Toronto, 64-67; asst prof, 67-74, prof philos, Trinity Col, Conn, 74-; Charles A. Dana Prof of Philos. **HONORS AND AWARDS** Brownell Prize for Excellence in Teaching, 90; Dir, Trinity Center for Collaborative Teaching and Research, 97. **MEMBERSHIPS** Mem Soc Phenomenol & Existential Philos; Heidegger Circle; Hegel Soc Am; Philos Soc for Study of Sport; IAPL; APA. **RESEARCH** Greek philosophy; Continental philosophy; philosophy of sport. **SELECTED PUBLICATIONS** Auth, Why Plato wrote Dialogues, Philos & Rhetoric, 1/68; Eros, Epithumia and Philia in Piston, Phronesis, 68; Self-reflection and knowing in Aristotle, Giornali di Metarisica, 68; Art and the happening of truth: Relections on the end of philosophy, J Aesthet & Art Criticism, 2/71; contribr, Sport and the Body: A Philosophical Symposium, Lea & Febiger, 72; auth, The Origins of Philosophy, Putnam, 73; And that is the best part of us: Human being and play, J Philos of Sport, 77; The Virtue of Philosophy: An Interpretation of Pluto's Charmidis, Ohio Univ Press, 81; The Question of Play, Univ Press of America, 84; The Philosophy of Sport, Paragon, 90; Finitude and Transcendence in the Platonic Dialogues, SUNY Press, 95. **CONTACT ADDRESS** Dept of Philos, Trinity Col, 300 Summit St, Hartford, CT, 06106-3186. **EMAIL** Drew.Hyland@Trincoll.edu

HYLTON, PETER
DISCIPLINE PHILOSOPHY **EDUCATION** Harvard Univ, PhD. **CAREER** Prof, Univ IL at Chicago. **RESEARCH** Philos of lang; logic; hist of analytic philos. **SELECTED PUBLICATIONS** Auth, Russell; Idealism; Emergence of Analytic Philosophy, Oxford, 90. **CONTACT ADDRESS** Philos Dept, Univ Illinois Chicago, S Halsted St, PO Box 705, Chicago, IL, 60607.

HYMAN, JONATHAN MORRIS
PERSONAL Born 01/09/1943, Washington, DC **DISCIPLINE** LAW **EDUCATION** Harvard Univ, AB, 65; Yale Univ, LLB, 68. **CAREER** Co-dir clinical law, Law Sch, Northwestern, 73-75; asst prof, 75-78, ASSOC PROF CRIMINAL & CLINICAL LAW & FEDERAL COURTS, LAW SCH, RUTGERS UNIV, 78- **MEMBERSHIPS** Conf Critical Legal Studies. **RESEARCH** Negotiation theory; remedies in law. **SELECTED PUBLICATIONS** Auth, Minitrials and Matchmakers--Styles of Conducting Settlement Conferences, Judicature, Vol 0080, 96. **CONTACT ADDRESS** Law Sch, Rutgers Univ, 15 Washington St, Newark, NJ, 07102-3192.

HYMERS, MICHAEL
DISCIPLINE PHILOSOPHY **EDUCATION** Univ Dalhousie, BS, 85, MA, 88; Univ Alberta, PhD, 93. **CAREER** Asst prof. **RESEARCH** Epistemology, philosophy of language, metaphysics, history of modern philosophy. **SELECTED PUBLICATIONS** Auth, "Bad Faith," Philos, 89; "Wittgenstein on Names and Family Resemblances," Eidos, 90; "Something Less Than Paradise: The Magic of Modal Realism," Australasian Jour of Philos, 91; "The Role of Kant's Refutation of Idealism," S Jour Philos, 91; "Internal Relations and Analyticity: Wittgenstein and Quine," Can Jour Philos, 96; "Truth and Metaphor in Rorty's Liberalism," Intl Stud in Philos, 96; Kant's Private-Clock Argument, Kant-Stud, 97; "Realism and Self-Knowledge," Philos Stud, 97. **CONTACT ADDRESS** Dept of Philos, Dalhousie Univ, Halifax, NS, B3H 3J5. **EMAIL** mhymers@gpu.srv.ualberta.ca

HYSON, JOHN M.
DISCIPLINE CIVIL PROCEDURE, ENVIRONMENTAL LAW **EDUCATION** Boston Col, BA, 63; Univ NC, MA, 64; Harvard Law Sch, LLB, 67. **CAREER** Prof, Villanova Univ. **MEMBERSHIPS** Rules Comt, Pa Env Hearing Bd, 84-88. **RESEARCH** Environment law and land use. **SELECTED PUBLICATIONS** Auth, Pennsylvania Exclusionary Zoning Law: A Workable Alternative to Mount Laurel, 36 Land Use Law & Zoning Digest, 84; The Impact of Act 249 of 1978 Upon the Casey Pending Ordinance Doctrine in Pennsylvania Exclusionary Zoning Litigation, 26 Vill. L. Rev 322, 81; The Problem of Relief in Developer-Initiated Exclusionary Zoning Litigation, 12 Urb L. Ann 21, 76; coauth, A Comparative Analysis of the Fed and Pennsylvania Superfund Acts," 1 Vill Env. L.J. 1, 90; co-ed, Environment Litigation, 91. **CONTACT ADDRESS** Law School, Villanova Univ, 800 Lancaster Ave, Villanova, PA, 19085-1692. **EMAIL** hyson@law.vill.edu

HYUN, INSOO
PERSONAL Born 06/28/1970, Seoul, Korea, m, 1997 **DISCIPLINE** PHILOSOPHY **EDUCATION** Stanford Univ, BA, 92, MA, 93; Brown Univ, PhD, 98. **CAREER** Asst Prof, 98-, W Mich Univ. **MEMBERSHIPS** APA, APPE **RESEARCH** Ethics, biomedical ethics. **CONTACT ADDRESS** Dept of Philosophy, Western Michigan Univ, 320 Moore Hall, Kalamazoo, MI, 49008-5022. **EMAIL** insoo.hyum@wmich.edu

I

IANNONE, A. PABLO
PERSONAL Born 09/18/1940, Buenos Aires, Argentina, m, 1985, 2 children **DISCIPLINE** PHILOSOPHY **EDUCATION** Univ Wisconsin-Madison, PhD, 75; Univ Wisconsic-Madison, MA, 72; UCLA, BA, 69. **CAREER** Prof Philos, Central Conn St Univ, 93-; assoc prof Philos, Central Conn St Univ, 87-93; vis prof Philos, Dalhousie Univ, 87; asst prof Philos, Central Conn St Univ, 83-87; Postdoctoral Tchg Fel, Univ Fla, 82-83; temporary asst prof, Iowa St Univ, 82. **HONORS AND AWARDS** Conn St Univ Res Grant, 85, 87, 89, 91, 94, 95, 96, 97, 98; Central Conn St Univ Res Grant, 83; Central Conn St Univ Minority & Staff Develop Grant, 89; Amoco Found Outstanding Tchg Award, Univ Tex at Dallas, 76; Kemper K Knapp Grad Teaching Award, Univ Wisc at Mad, 74; Ford Fel, 73; Phi Beta Kappa, 70. **MEMBERSHIPS** Amer Philos Assoc; Amer Assoc Advancement of Sci; Argentine-N Amer Assoc for Advancement of Sci, Tech, and Culture-New York; Assoc for Practical & Prof Ethics; Intl Soc for Environ Ethics; Intl Soc for Environ Ethics; Latin Amer Studies Assoc; Soc for Philos in Contemporary World; Soc for Human Econ. **RESEARCH** Ethics and Socio-Political Philosophy; Business Ethics; Ethics of Technology; Environmental Ethics; History and Philosophy of Science and Technology; Philosophy of Culture. **SELECTED PUBLICATIONS** Dictionary of World Philosophy, Routledge Ltd, forthcoming; Dealing with Diversity: Cultural Fragmentation, Intercultural Conflicts, and Philosophy, in Crossing Cultural Boundaries: Philosophy and Cultural Diversity, Humanities Pr, forthcoming; Cross-Cultural Ecologies: The Expatriate Experience, the Multiculturalism Issue, and Philosophy, In the Company of Others: Perspectives on Community, Family, and Culture, Rowman & Littlefield Pub, 96; Philosophy as Diplomacy: Essays in Ethics and Policy Making, Humanities Pr, 94. **CONTACT ADDRESS** Dept of Philosophy, Central Connecticut State Univ, 1615 Stanley St, New Britain, CT, 06050. **EMAIL** iannone@ccsua.ctstateu.edu

IANNUZZI, JOHN N.
PERSONAL Born 05/31/1935, New York, NY, m, 1979, 6 children **DISCIPLINE** LAW **EDUCATION** Fordham Col, BS-SS, 56; NY Law Sch, JD, 1962. **CAREER** Law, Iannuzzi and Iannuzzi, 63-; Adjunct Prof, Fordham Univ, Sch of Law, 88-. **HONORS AND AWARDS** Who's Who in the World, 9th and 11th eds; Who's Who in Am Law, ed 1-8. **SELECTED PUBLICATIONS** What's Happening?, Thomas Yoseloff, 63; Part 35, Richard W. Baron, 70; Sicilian Defense, Richard W Baron, 73; auth, Courthouse, Doubleday, 80; auth, J.T., Berkeley Books, 84; auth, Cross Examination: The Mosaic Art, Prentice Hall, 2nd ed, 84; auth, Trial Strategy and Psychology, Prentice Hall, 92; Disposition by Guilty Plea, Appellate Div of Supreme Court, 1st - 6th ed. **CONTACT ADDRESS** 233 Broadway, New York, NY, 10279.

IHDE, DON
PERSONAL Born 01/14/1934, Hope, KS, m, 1957, 3 children **DISCIPLINE** PHILOSOPHY **EDUCATION** Univ Kans, BA, 56; Andover Newton Theol Sch, BD, 59; Boston Univ, PhD(philos), 64. **CAREER** Lectr philos, Boston Univ, 62-64; asst prof, Southern Ill Univ, 64-67; Fulbright res fel, Univ Paris, 67-68; assoc prof, Southern Ill Univ, Carbondale, 68-69; PROF PHILOS, STATE UNIV NY STONY BROOK, 69-, Nat Endowment Humanities sr fel, 72. **MEMBERSHIPS** Southern Soc Philos & Psychol; Eastern Div Am Philos Asn; Soc Phenomenol & Existential Philos. **RESEARCH** Recent European philosophy, particulary phenomenology and existentialism; phenomenology of man-machine relations. **SELECTED PUBLICATIONS** Auth, Gadamer and Hermeneutics, Semiotica, Vol 0102, 94; From Text to Action--Essays in Hermeneutics, Semiotica, Vol 0102, 94. **CONTACT ADDRESS** Dept of Philos, State Univ of NY, Stony Brook, NY, 11794.

IHLAN, AMY
DISCIPLINE PHILOSOPHY **EDUCATION** Harvard Law School, JD, 84; Univ Minn, PhD, 95. **CAREER** Asst prof philos, Cornell Col, 94- . **HONORS AND AWARDS** Phi Beta Kappa; grad fel, Univ Minn. **MEMBERSHIPS** APA; Soc for Women in Philos; Minnesota Bar Asn. **RESEARCH** Moral particularism; ethical theory; legal reasoning; feminist ethics and jurisprudence. **SELECTED PUBLICATIONS** Auth, Wang Yang-Ming: A Philosopher of Practical Action, J of Chinese Philos, 93; auth, The Dilemma of Difference and Feminist Standpoint Theory, APA Newsl on Feminism and Philos of Law, 95; auth, Burning Crosses, Political Expression, and the First Amendment: The Case of R.A.V. v City of St. Paul, in Kaplan, ed, Philosophical Perspectives on Power and Domination, Rodopi, 97; auth, Feminism and Firearms, in Curtin, ed, Institutional Violence, Rodopi, forthcoming. **CONTACT ADDRESS** Dept of Philosophy, Cornell Col, 600 First St W, Mount Vernon, IA, 52314. **EMAIL** aihlan@cornell-iowa.edu

IKE, ALICE DENISE
PERSONAL Born 03/25/1955, Washington, DC, s **DISCIPLINE** LAW **EDUCATION** University of Maryland, Baltimore County, BA, 1977, School of Law, JD, 1981. **CAREER** Morgan State Univ, part-time instructor, 1984, 1985; Legal Services Institute, legal intern, 1980-81; Legal Aid of Maryland Inc, staff attorney, 1981-82; City of Baltimore, Office of the State's Attorney, assistant states attorney, 1983-85; Univ of Maryland, Baltimore County, part-time instructor, 1990-; Department of Health and Mental Hygiene, Office of the Attorney General, assistant attorney general, 1985-. **MEMBERSHIPS** DC Bar Assn, 1982-; State of Maryland Bar Assn, 1981-; Alliance of Black Women Attorneys, 1982-; Foster Care Review Bd of Baltimore City, chairperson of the bd, 1986-. **CONTACT ADDRESS** Assistant Attorney General, Office of the Attorney General, Department of Health and Mental Hygiene, 300 W Preston St, Ste 302, Baltimore, MD, 21201.

IMMERWAHR, JOHN
DISCIPLINE PHILOSOPHY **EDUCATION** Princeton Univ, AB, 67; Univ Mich, MA, 68, PhD, 72. **CAREER** Prof & dept ch, Villanova Univ,73-. **HONORS AND AWARDS** Lindback awd Distinguished Tchg, Villanova Univ, 92; Philadelphia Inquirer Mag Story, Ten Top Profs, 86; Silver Medalist in CASE prof Yr awd, 86; Philadelphia Mag, 84 People to Watch in 84; creation of the John Immerwahr prize in Philos, endowed by a former student, Oakland Univ, 74 & Princeton, 67, Phi Beta Kappa, Summa Cum Laude, McCosh prize. **SELECTED PUBLICATIONS** Auth, Preserving the Higher Education Legacy: A Conversation with California Leaders, San Jose: Calif Higher Educ Policy Ctr, 95; The Broken Contract: Connecticut Citizens Look at Public Education, New Haven: Graustein Memorial Fund, 94; The Socratic Classroom: Classroom Communication Strategies, J Mgt Syst 6:1, 94; Hume's Revised Racism, J Hist Ideas 53:3, 92; Hume on Tranquilizing the Passions, Hume Stud 18:2, 92; Asking Questions, Metaphilosophy 22:4, 91 & earlier version publ as, A Taxonomy of Questions, in The Newsl of the Amer Asn Philos Teachers 14:1, 91; Coauth, Race and the Modern Philosophy Course, Tchg Philos 16:1, 93; Assignment Incomplete: The Unfinished Business of Education Reform, NY: Public Agenda Found, 95; Goodwill and Growing Worry: Public Perceptions of American Higher Education, Wash, DC: Amer Coun Educ, 95; The Fragile Coalition: Public Support for Higher Education in the 1990s, Wash, DC: Amer Coun Educ, 95; Teaching Values: What does the Public Really Want, Soc for the Advan Educ, 95; What the Public Thinks of Colleges, in The Chronicle of Higher Educ, 95; First Things First: What Americans Expect from the Public Schools, NY: Public Agenda Found, 94; The Rules of Public Engagement, in Beyond the Beltway:Engaging the Public In For Policy, NY: W.W. Norton, 94 & Second Opinions: Americans' Changing Views on Healthcare Reform, NY: Public Agenda Found, 94. **CONTACT ADDRESS** Dept of Philosophy, Villanova Univ, 800 Lancaster Ave, Villanova, PA, 19085-1692.

IMWINKELRIED, EDWARD
PERSONAL Born 09/19/1946, San Francisco, CA, m, 1978, 2 children **DISCIPLINE** LAW **EDUCATION** Univ San Francisco, BA, 67, JD, 69. **CAREER** Captain, US Army Judge Advocate General's Corps, 70-74; prof, law, Univ San Diego, 74-79; prof, law, Wash Univ St. Louis, 79-85; prof, law, Univ Calif Davis, 85-. **HONORS AND AWARDS** Distinguished teacher, Univ Calif Davis Law Sch; Outstanding teacher, Wash Univ; Distinguished facul, Nat Col of District Atty. **MEMBERSHIPS** Amer Acad of Forensic Sci; Amer Bar Asn. **RESEARCH** Scientific evidence; Uncharged misconduct; Evidentiary priviledges. **SELECTED PUBLICATIONS** Auth, Where There's Smoke, There's Fire: Should the Judge or the Jury Decide the Question of Whether the Accused Committed an Alleged Uncharged Crime Proffered Under Federal Rule of Evidence 404?, 42, St. Louis Univ Law Jour, 813, 98; co-auth, Cyberspace: The Newest Challenge for Traditional Legal Doctrine, 24, Rutgers Computer and Tech Law Jour, 305, 98; auth, Evidentiary Foundations, LEXIS Law Publ, 4th ed, 98; co-auth, North Carolina Evidentiary Foundations, LEXIS Law Publ, 98; auth, Article V Priviledges, Emerging Problems Under the Federal Rules of Evidence, 3rd ed, 98; auth, Foreword, Symposium: International Perspectives on Scientific Evidence, 30, Univ Calif Davis Law Rev, 941, 97; co-auth, The Supreme Court's Decision to Recognize a Psychotherapist Priviledge in Jaffee v. Redmond, 116 S. Ct. 1923, 96; co-auth, The Meaning of Experience and the Role of Reason Under Federal Rule of Evidence 501, 65, Univ Cincinnati Law Rev, 1019, 97; co-auth, Issues Once Moot: The Other Evidentiary Objections to the Admissibility of Exculpatory Polygraph Examinations, 32, Wake Forest Law Rev, 1045, 97; ed bd, Jefferson's California Evidence Benchbook, chap 35-38, 40, 3rd ed, 97; co-auth, Criminal Evidentiary Foundations, LEXIS Law Publ, 97; auth, The Methods of Attacking Scientific Evidence, Michie Publ Co, 3rd ed, 97; auth, Evidentiary Heresy: Disregarding the Rules of Evidence at Trial!, 41, Trial Lawyer's Guide, 40, 97; auth, The Next Step in Conceptualizing the Presentation of Expert Evidence as Education: The Case for Didactic Trial Procedures, 1, Intl Jour of Evidence and Proof, 128, 97; co-auth, Federal Evidence Tactics, 97; auht, A New Threat to Plaintiff's Discovery Rights?, 33, Trial, 36, 97. **CONTACT ADDRESS** School of Law, Univ of California Davis, 400 Mrak Hall Dr., Davis, CA, 95616-5201. **EMAIL** ejimwinkelried@ucdavis.edu

INADA, KENNETH K.
PERSONAL Born 05/07/1923, Honolulu, HI, m, 1954, 1 child **DISCIPLINE** PHILOSOPHY **EDUCATION** Univ Hawaii, BA, 49; Univ Chicago, MA, 51; Univ Tokyo, Japan, PhD (Buddhist philos), 60. **CAREER** From instr to assoc prof philos, Univ Hawaii, 60-69; assoc prof, 69-71, Prof Philos, State Univ NY Buffalo, 71-, Sr fac fel, Am Inst Indian Studies, 66-67; State Univ NY Res Found grant, 70 & 74. **MEMBERSHIPS** Eastern Div, Am Philos Asn; Am Orient Soc; Asn Asian Studies; Soc Asian & Comp Philos (pres, 72-76); Int Soc Chinese Philos. **RESEARCH** Buddhist philosophy; comparative East-West philosophy. **SELECTED PUBLICATIONS** Auth, The Challenge of Buddho-Taoist Metaphysics of Experience, J Chinese Philos, Vol 0021, 94; Understanding the Chinese Mind, J Chinese Philos, Vol 0023, 96; The Chinese Doctrinal Acceptance of Buddhism, J Chinese Philos, Vol 0024, 97; A Theory of Oriental Aesthetics--A Prolegomenon, Philos East & West, Vol 0047, 97. **CONTACT ADDRESS** Dept of Philos, State Univ of NY, P O Box 601010, Buffalo, NY, 14260-1010.

INBAU, FRED EDWARD
PERSONAL Born 03/27/1909, New Orleans, LA, m, 1935, 2 children **DISCIPLINE** LAW **EDUCATION** Tulane Univ, BS, 30, LLB, 32; Northwestern Univ, LLM, 33. **CAREER** Res asst, sci crime detection lab, sch law, Northwestern Univ, 33-34, instr police sci, 34-36, asst prof law, 36-38; dir, Chicago Police Sci Crime Detection Lab, 38-41; atty-at-law, Lord, Bissel & Kadyk, 41-45; from prof to John Henry Wigmore prof, 45-77, EMER JOHN HENRY WIGMORE PROF LAW, SCH LAW, NORTHWESTERN UNIV, CHICAGO, 77-, Consult pub safety div, Off US High Comnr Ger, 51-52; consult serv admin criminal justice in US, Am Bar Found, 55-58; pres, Am for Effective Law Enforcement, Inc, 66-; ed, J Police Sci & Admin, 73-78. **MEMBERSHIPS** Am Acad Forensic Sci (pres, 55-56); Am Acad Polygraph Exam (pres, 54-56); Am Bar Asn; hon mem Nat Dist Attorneys Asn; hon mem Am Soc Questioned Doc Exam. **RESEARCH** Criminal law; scientific criminal investigation; criminal interrogation. **SELECTED PUBLICATIONS** Auth, Tributes to Haddad, J Criminal Law & Criminology, Vol 0083, 92. **CONTACT ADDRESS** Sch of Law, Northwestern Univ, Evanston, IL, 60201.

INBODY, TYRON LEE
PERSONAL Born 03/21/1940, Goshan, IN, m, 1961, 2 children **DISCIPLINE** THEOLOGY **EDUCATION** Univ Indianapolis, BA, 62; United Theol Sem, MDiv, 65; Univ Chicago, MA, 67, PhD, 73. **CAREER** Adrian Col, prof, 69-76; United Theol Sem, prof, 76-. **HONORS AND AWARDS** NEH **MEMBERSHIPS** AAR, HIART **RESEARCH** American Theology and philosophy. **SELECTED PUBLICATIONS** Auth, The Transforming God: An Interpretation of Suffering And Evil, Westminster John Knox Press, 97; auth, The Constructive Theology of Bernard Meland: Postliberal Empirical Realism, AAR Studies in Religion, Atlanta: Scholars Press, 95; ed. Changing Channels: The Church and the Television Revolution, Dayton OH: Whaleprints, 90; auth, The Power of Prayer and the Mystery of Evil, Anglican Theol Rev, 98; auth, Prayer in the Midst of Suffering, Keeping in Touch, 98; auth, Delwin Brown's Constructive Historicism as a Reconstruction of Empirical Theology, Am Jour Theol and Philos, 97. **CONTACT ADDRESS** Dept of Theology, United Theology Sem, 1810 Harvard Blvd., Dayton, OH, 45406. **EMAIL** tyinbody@aol.com

INGLES, ERNIE B.
PERSONAL Born 12/30/1948, Calgary, AB, Canada **DISCIPLINE** BIBLIOGRAPHY/HISTORY **EDUCATION** Univ Calgary, BA, 70, MA, 73; Univ BC, MLS, 75. **CAREER** Head, Rare Bks & Spec Coll, Univ Calgary, 74-84; univ librn, Univ Regina, 84-90; dir librs, 90-95, ASSOC VICE PRES LEARNING SYSTEMS, UNIV ALBERTA, 95-. **HONORS AND AWARDS** Marie Tremaine Medal Bibliog; Ruth Cameron Medal; Int Lib Sci Honour Soc. **MEMBERSHIPS** Can Libr Asn; Bibliog Soc Can; Can Asn Col Univ Librs; Can Asn Res Librs. **SELECTED PUBLICATIONS** Auth, Canada: The Printed Record, 81, 82, 83, 84; auth, Canada: World Bibliography Series, 90; auth, Bibliography of Canadian Bibliographies, 94. **CONTACT ADDRESS** Univ of Alberta, University Hall 3-16, Edmonton, AB, T6G 2J9.

INGLIS, JOHN
DISCIPLINE MEDIEVAL PHILOSOPHY **EDUCATION** Univ Ky, PhD, 93. **CAREER** Dept Philos, Univ Dayton **RESEARCH** Relation between philosophy and theology. **SELECTED PUBLICATIONS** Auth, Philosophical Anatomy and the Historiography of Medieval Philosophy, Brit Jour Hist Philos, 97. **CONTACT ADDRESS** Dept of Philos, Univ Dayton, 300 Col Park, Dayton, OH, 75062. **EMAIL** inglis@checkov.hm.udayton.edu

INGRAM, DAVID B.
PERSONAL Born 01/27/1952, Whittier, CA **DISCIPLINE** PHILOSOPHY **EDUCATION** Univ Calif San Diego, PhD, 80. **CAREER** Asst to assoc prof, Univ Northern Iowa, 80-87; assoc to full prof, Loyola Univ of Chicago, 87-. **HONORS AND AWARDS** Alpha Sigma Nu prize for best book in philos/theol, 92-95. **MEMBERSHIPS** Amer Philos Asn; Soc for Phenomenol and Existential Philos. **RESEARCH** Social and political philosophy; French; German philosophy. **SELECTED PUBLICATIONS** Auth, Reason: History and Politics, State Univ of NY Press, 95; auth, Critical Theory and Philosophy, Paragon House, 90; Habermas and the Dialectic of Reason, Yale Univ Press, 87. **CONTACT ADDRESS** Dept. of Philosophy, Loyola Univ, Chicago, IL, 60626. **EMAIL** dingram@orion.it.luc.edu

INYAMAH, NATHANIEL GINIKANWA N.
PERSONAL Born 01/21/1934, Mbaise, Nigeria, m **DISCIPLINE** THEOLOGY **EDUCATION** Univ Nigeria, Diploma Tehol 1958; STM NW Seminary MN, BD MDiv 1969; Temple, MA 1973f Temple, PhD 1976;1971. **CAREER** Nigeria, tchr 1951-53; Nigeria HS, 1954-55; Holy Trinity & Lutheran Nigeria, pastor 1959-66; LCA, asst & supply pastor; Camden NJ, teacher; positions in Nigeria Traditional Priest Earth Goddess; Trinity Lutheran Church, pastor & founder. **HONORS AND AWARDS** Crowned chief Okonko Igbo Soc US Lutheran Missionary At Large 1967-71; Aid Assn Lutheran Ins Scholarship 1967; NW Students Assn Scholarship 1968; Lutheran Wmn Missionary & League Scholarship 1969; Elmer O & Ida Preston Educ Trust Award 1969-71; Temple Univ Grad Sch Award 1972, 73. **MEMBERSHIPS** Bd dir & vice pres Lutheran Ch; pres Ezinihitte Cultural Union; vice pres Owerri Divisional Union, Owerri Provincial Union; WHO; exec mem Eastern Nigeria Soc Welfare Soc; youth prog dir; Utheran Commn Soc Equality Justice; Educ Com Minority Group; African Studies Assn. **CONTACT ADDRESS** PO Box 9786, Philadelphia, PA, 19140.

IORIO, DOMINICK ANTHONY
PERSONAL Born 09/13/1931, Trenton, NJ, m, 1957, 2 children **DISCIPLINE** PHILOSOPHY **EDUCATION** Seton Hall Univ, AB, 55; Fordham Univ, AM, 60, PhD(philos), 66. **CAREER** Instr hist, Trenton Jr Col, 57-61, asst prof philos, 61-65, coordr lib arts, 62-65; asst prof philos, 65-68, asst dean sch lib arts & sci, 71-73, ASSOC PROF PHILOS, RIDER COL, 68-, Dean Sch Lib Arts & SCI, 73-, Consult, Dept Higher Educ, NJ, 77; chmn, Educ Adv Comt, NJ, 82. **HONORS AND AWARDS** Cor ad Cor Loquitor Medal, Nat Newman Fedn, 62; Christian R & Mary Lindback Award for Distinguished Teaching, Rider Col, 71. **MEMBERSHIPS** Am Philos Asn; Am Cath Philos Asn; Renaissance Soc Am. **RESEARCH** Italian Renais-

sance philosophy; Cartesianism, with special emphasis on Nicolas Malebranche; social philosophy, with special emphasis on phenomenological and existential methods. **SELECTED PUBLICATIONS** Auth, Descartes--An Intellectual Biography, Renaissance Quart, Vol 0050, 97. **CONTACT ADDRESS** Off of Dean, Rider Col, 2083 Lawrenceville, Lawrenceville, NJ, 08648-3099.

IOZZIO, MARY JO
PERSONAL Born 11/25/1956, Paterson, NJ, m, 1994 **DISCIPLINE** THEOLOGY **EDUCATION** Penn State Univ, BA, 77; Providence Col, MA, 86; Fordham Univ, MA, 82, PhD, 94. **CAREER** Asst prof, Barry Univ, 92- . **HONORS AND AWARDS** Fulbright award, 98-99; professional development award, 95, 96, 97, 98; Barry Univ Honors Students Teaching Award, 95. **MEMBERSHIPS** Am Acad Relig; Catholic Theol Soc of Am; Soc of Christian Ethics. **RESEARCH** Fundamental moral theology; bioethics; virtue theory and application. **SELECTED PUBLICATIONS** Auth, Three Perspectives of Virtue Theory, Providence: Stud in Western Civilization, 93; auth, Self-Determination and the Moral Act: A Study of the Contributions of Odon Lottin, OSB, Peeters, 95; auth, Science, Ethics, and Cloning Technologies, Linacre Q, 97; auth, Justice is a Virtue Both in and out of Healthcare, Irish Theol Q, 98; auth, Old Wine, New Skins: A Study of the Catechetical Tradition in Transition, in Allsopp, ed, Christian Ethics and the New Catechism, Scranton, forthcoming; ed and auth, Recovering the Traditions: Religious Perspectives in Medical Ethics, Scranton, 99. **CONTACT ADDRESS** Dept of Theology and Philosophy, Barry Univ, 11300 Northeast Second Ave, Miami Shores, FL, 33161. **EMAIL** miozzio@mail.barry.edu

IRELAND, RODERICK LOUIS
PERSONAL Born 12/03/1944, Springfield, MA, d **DISCIPLINE** CRIMINAL JUSTICE, LAW **EDUCATION** Lincoln U, BA 1966; Columiba Law Sch, JD 1969; Harvard Law, LLM 1975. **CAREER** Boston Juvenile Ct, judge 1977-90; Bd of Appeal on Motor Vehicle Policies & Bonds, chmn of bd 1977; Sec of Adminstrn & Finance MA, counsel 1975-77; Harvard Law Sch, teaching fellow 1975; Roxbury Defenders Com, dir 1971-74, Massachusetts Appeals Court, judge, begin 1990; MA SUPREME COURT, JUSTICE, currently; NORTHEASTERN UNIVERSITY SCHOOL OF LAW, FACULTY, currently, COLLEGE OF CRIMINAL JUSTICE, FACULTY, currently. **HONORS AND AWARDS** Recip 10 Outstndg yng ldrs of Boston award Boston Jaycees 1979; 10 outstndg men of Am award US Jaycees 1980. First African American justice On Massachusetts Supreme Court. **MEMBERSHIPS** Bd of dirs Columbia Law Sch Alumni Assn; mem MA Bar Assn; mem Boston Bar Assn; mem ABA; mem MA Black Lawyers Assn; mem NY Bar Assn Bd Dirs Proj Aim; bd dirs First Inc; bd dirs Roxbury YMCA; bd dirs MA Minority Council on Alcoholism; mem Omega Psi Phi; mem Lincoln Alumni. **CONTACT ADDRESS** Massachusetts Supreme Court, 1500 New Courthouse, Boston, MA, 02108.

IRVINE, DALE T.
PERSONAL Born 01/26/1955, OH, m, 1978, 2 children **DISCIPLINE** RELIGION **EDUCATION** Union Theolo Sem, NY, PhD; Princeton Theol Sem, MDiv; Thomas Edison College, BA. **CAREER** New York Theol Sem, prof 89 to 98-. **SELECTED PUBLICATIONS** Auth, Christian Traditioning, Christian Histories: Rendering Accounts, Orbis 98; The Agitated Mind of God: Theology of Koyama with Akintunde Akuinde, Orbis 96. **CONTACT ADDRESS** Dept of Theology, New York Theol Sem, 5 W 29th St, NYC, NY, 10001. **EMAIL** dirvin@drew.edu

IRVINE, STUART
PERSONAL Born 05/11/1954, Los Angeles, CA, m, 1981, 4 children **DISCIPLINE** RELIGION **EDUCATION** Pomona Col, BA, 76; Yale Univ, MDiv, 80; Emory Univ, PhD, 89. **CAREER** Louisiana State Univ, assoc prof 98-. **MEMBERSHIPS** SBL/AAR **RESEARCH** Hebrew; Prophecy **SELECTED PUBLICATIONS** Auth, Isaiah, Ahaz, and the Syro-Ephraimitic Crisis, in Scholars, 90; Isaiah's She'ar-yashub and the Davidic House, in Biblische Zeitschrift NF 36, 93. **CONTACT ADDRESS** Dept of Religious Studies, Louisiana State Univ, 1848 Glendale Ave, Baton Rouge, LA, 70808.

IRWIN, JOYCE LOUISE
PERSONAL Born 11/04/1944, Joplin, MO, m, 1980 **DISCIPLINE** REFORMATION & POST-REFORMATION THOUGHT, HISTORY OF CHRISTIANITY **EDUCATION** Wash Univ, AB, 66; Yale Univ, MA, 68, MPhil, 69, PhD(relig studies), 72. **CAREER** Asst prof hist, Univ Ga, 70-77; ASST PROF PHILOS & RELIG, COLGATE UNIV, 77-82. **MEMBERSHIPS** Am Soc Reformation Res; Am Acad Relig; Am Soc Church Hist. **RESEARCH** Theology and music; women in religion. **SELECTED PUBLICATIONS** Auth, Crautwald and Erasmus--A Study in Humanism and Radical Reform in 16th-Century Silesia, Renaissance Quart, Vol 0047, 94; The Radical Reformation, Renaissance Quart, Vol 0047, 94. **CONTACT ADDRESS** Colgate Univ, 8 West Kendrick, Hamilton, NY, 13346.

IRWIN, WILLIAM HENERY
PERSONAL Born 10/25/1932, Houston, TX **DISCIPLINE** BIBLE PHILOSOPHY **EDUCATION** Univ Toronto, BA, 56, MA, 58; Pontif Univ St Thomas Aquinas, STL, 61; Pontif Bibl Inst, Rome, SSL, 63, SSD, 74; Ecole Biblique, Jerusalem, Eleve titule, 64. **CAREER** Asst prof, 65-70, asst dir, Toronto Sch Theol, 77-80, Assoc Prof sacred Scripture, St michael's Col, Univ Toronto, 73-, DEAN FAC THEOL, ST MICHAEL'S COL, 80-, Assoc ed, Cath Bibl Quart, 76-79. **MEMBERSHIPS** Cath Bibl Asn; Can Soc Bibl Studies. **RESEARCH** Hebrew poetry; Old Testament; Ugaritic literature. **SELECTED PUBLICATIONS** Auth, Reading Isaiah, Cath Bibl Quart, Vol 0055, 93; The so Called City of Chaos in Isaiah-Xxiv, 10 and the Genitive of Result + The Treatment of the Genitive in Biblical Hebrew Syntax and its Function in Translation and Interpretation, Biblica, Vol 0075, 94; Cyrus in Deutero Isaiah--A Redaction-History of the Origins and Theology of Isaiah-Xl-Lv, Cath Bibl Quart, Vol 0056, 94; The Servant of Yhwh and Cyrus--A Reinterpretation of the Exilic Messianic Program in Isaiah-Xl-Lv, Cath Bibl Quart, Vol 0056, 94; Fear of God, the Analogy of Friendship and Ben-Sira Theodicy + An Examination of the Traditional Concept of Divine Testing From the Book of Sirach, Biblica, Vol 0076, 95; Conflicting Parallelism in Job-V,13, Isaiah-Xxx,28, Isaiah-Xxxii,7 + A Note on a Stylistic Phenomenon in Hebrew Poetic Phrases, Biblica, Vol 0076, 95; Rhetorical Criticism and the Poetry of the 'Book of Job, Cath Bibl Quart, Vol 0058, 96; The Book Called 'Isaiah'--'Deutero-Isaiah's Role in Composition and Redaction, J Bibl Lit, Vol 0116, 97. **CONTACT ADDRESS** Fac of Theol St Michael's Col, Univ of Toronto, 81 St Mary St, Toronto, ON, M5S 1J4.

IRWIN, WILLIAM T.
PERSONAL Born 04/01/1970, Bronx, NY **DISCIPLINE** PHILOSOPHY **EDUCATION** State Univ of NY at Buffalo, PhD, 96; Fordham Univ, BA, 92. **CAREER** Asst Prof Philos, 98-, King's Coll Wilkes-Barre, PA; Tchg Fellow, State Univ of NY, 93-96; Res Asst to Jorge J.E. Gracia, 92. **HONORS AND AWARDS** Phi Beta Kappa, Fordham Univ; Outstanding Russian Lang Stud Award, Fordham Univ; Phi Sigma Tau, Intl Honor Soc in Philos; Hughes Award for the Outstanding Stud of Philos at Fordham Univ; Recipient of the King's Coll Summer Res Grant. **MEMBERSHIPS** Amer Philos Assoc; Soc Phenomenal and Existential Philos; North Amer Nietzsche Soc; The North Amer Sartre Soc; Amer Catholic Philos Assoc; Assoc Devel of Philos Tchg; Referee for Journal of Value Inquiry. **RESEARCH** 19th and 20th Century Continental Philosophy, Hermeneutics, Phenomenal and Existentialism, History of Philosophy. **SELECTED PUBLICATIONS** Auth, Sartre, Freedom and the Gambler, Contemporary Philosophy 16, pp 9-13, 94; Intention and Foresight in the British Law of Murder, Sorites, 98; Plato's Two Immortalities, Contemporary Philosophy, forthcoming; Philosophy and Seinfield: A Book about Nothing and Everything, La Salle, IL, Open Court Press, forthcoming; The Closed Nature of a Poem, Syracuse Univ Graduate Philosophy Conference, 93; Texts Have No Meaning, A Critique of Hirsch in Defense of Humpty Dumpty, Central Division Meeting of the American Philosophical Association Pittsburgh, PA, 97. **CONTACT ADDRESS** Dept of Philosophy, King's Col, Wilkes Barre, PA, 18711. **EMAIL** wtirwin@rs01.Kings.edu

ISAAC, GORDON L.
DISCIPLINE ADVENT CHRISTIAN STUDIES, CHURCH HISTORY **EDUCATION** Seattle Pacific Univ, BA; Western Evangel Theol Sem, MDiv; Luther Theol Sem, MTh; Marquette Univ, PhD. **CAREER** Berkshire asst prof, Gordon-Conwell Theol Sem, 97-. **HONORS AND AWARDS** Dir, Ctr Advent Christian Stud. **MEMBERSHIPS** Mem, Sixteenth Century Soc; Amer Soc Church Hist. **RESEARCH** Theology of Martin Luther, history of exegesis, Trinitarian theology, the Early Church Fathers. **SELECTED PUBLICATIONS** Assoc ed, Luther Digest. **CONTACT ADDRESS** Gordon-Conwell Theol Sem, 130 Essex St, South Hamilton, MA, 01982.

ISADORE, HAROLD W.
PERSONAL Alexandria, LA **DISCIPLINE** LAW **EDUCATION** Southern Univ, BS 1967; Southern Univ Schl of Law, JD 1970; SUNY at Buffalo Law Schl, Cert 1978. **CAREER** US Dept of Labor Office of the Solicitor, atty 1970-73; Baton Rouge Legal Aid Scty, atty 1973-74; Public Defender of Baton Rouge, atty 1974-75; Southern Univ School of Law, assoc law libririan 1975-. **HONORS AND AWARDS** Serv awrd Stdnt Bar Assoc, SU Law Schl 1970; Humanitarian Award, Louis A Martinet Legal Society; Southern Univ Law Center, Staff Award, 1980-81, 1985-87, 1990-94. **MEMBERSHIPS** Mem Am Bar Assn, Natl Bar Assn, Delta Theta Phi Law Frat, Am Assn of Law Libraries, Kappa Alpha Psi Frat, Inc. **SELECTED PUBLICATIONS** Hypotext on Security Devices Southern • Univ Pblshr 1979; Hypotext on Civil Procedure Vols 1 and 11 S Univ Pblshr 1980-81. **CONTACT ADDRESS** Law Sch, So Univ, Baton Rouge, LA, 70813.

ISASI-DIAZ, ADA MARIA
PERSONAL Born 03/22/1943, La Habana, Cuba, s **DISCIPLINE** CHRISTIAN EHTICS **EDUCATION** Union Theological Seminary, PhD, 90. **CAREER** Prof of Christian Ethics and Theology, 91- , Drew Univ. **HONORS AND AWARDS** One of 26 prominent contemporary thinkers in Questions of Faith II and Faces of Faith videos, produced by UMCom and Trinity Parish of New York, 89; Honorary Degree, Doctor of Laws, Lynchberg Col, 93. **SELECTED PUBLICATIONS** auth, En La Lucha-A Hispanic Women's Liberation Theology, 93; auth, Women of God, Women of the People, 95; co-ed and contributor, Hispanic/Latino Theology-Challenge and Promise, 96; auth, Mujerista Theology: A Theology for the 21st Century, 96. **CONTACT ADDRESS** 100 Overlook Terrace, #818, New York, NY, 10040. **EMAIL** aisasidi@drew.edu

ISEMINGER, GARY
PERSONAL Born 03/03/1937, Middleboro, MA, m, 1965, 2 children **DISCIPLINE** PHILOSOPHY **EDUCATION** Wesleyan Univ, BA, 58; Yale Univ, MA, 60, PhD, 61. **CAREER** Instr, Yale Univ, 61-62; vis prof, Univ Minn, 79; Mayo Med Sch, 86-87; Lancaster Univ, 94; prof, Carleton Col, 62-. **HONORS AND AWARDS** Phi Beta Kappa, 57; Woodrow Wilson fel, 58; NSF-Coun for Philos Studies Summer Inst Grant, 68; Bush Found Summer Grant, 83; Sloan Found Summer Grant, 84. **MEMBERSHIPS** Minn Philos Soc; Minn Humanities Comn; Am Philos Asn; Am Soc for Aesthetics; Com of the Am Soc for Aesthetics. **RESEARCH** Philosophy; Aesthetics; Logic. **SELECTED PUBLICATIONS** Auth, An Introduction to Deductive Logic, 68; Knowledge and Argument, 84; "An Intentional Demonstration?," 92; "Actual Intentionalism vs. Hypothetical Intentionalism," 96; "The Intentional Fallacy," 98; Ed, Logic and Philosophy: Selected Readings, 80; Intention and Interpretation, 92. **CONTACT ADDRESS** Dept of Philosophy, Carleton Col, Northfield, MN, 55057. **EMAIL** giseming@carleton.edu

ISENBERG, SHELDON ROBERT
PERSONAL Born 10/21/1941, Fall River, MA **DISCIPLINE** HISTORY OF JUDAISM & EARLY CHRISTIANITY **EDUCATION** Columbia Univ, AB, 62; Harvard Univ, MA, 65, PhD (relig), 69. **CAREER** Asst prof relig, Duke Univ, 68-69 & Princeton Univ, 69-73; asst prof relig, 73-76, ASSOC PROF RELIG, CTR JEWISH STUDIES, UNIV FLA, 76-, Assoc Dir Ctr, 73-, Soc Relig Higher Educ cross-disciplinary fel, 72-73. **MEMBERSHIPS** Asn Jewish Studies; Soc Values Higher Educ; Am Acad Relig; Soc Bibl Lit. **RESEARCH** Judaism in Greco-Roman Palestine; Biblical text criticism; historical method from social psychological and social anthropoligical perspectives. **SELECTED PUBLICATIONS** Auth, The Lamp of God--A Jewish Book of Light, J Amer Acad Rel, Vol 0060, 92; Education for Shalom--Religion Textbooks and the Enhancement of the Catholic and Jewish Relationship, J Ecumenical Stud, Vol 0034, 97. **CONTACT ADDRESS** Ctr for Jewish Studies, Univ of Fla, Gainesville, FL, 32611.

ISERSON, KENNETH V.
PERSONAL Born 04/08/1949, Washington, DC, m, 1973 **DISCIPLINE** BIOEMEDICAL ETHICS **EDUCATION** Univ Md, College Pk, MD, MS, bio educ, 71; Univ Md Sch of Med, Baltimore MD, 75; Univ Phoenix, Tucson, MBA, 84-86; sr fel, bioethics, Ctr for Clinical Med Ethics, Univ Chicago, Pritzker Sch of Med, 7/90-6/91. **CAREER** Clinical asst prof, dept of emergency med, Col of Osteopathic Med, Ft Worth, 79-82; chair, dept of emergency med, fac, family practice residency, Carswell AFB Regional Hospital, Ft Worth, 78-80; clinical assoc dir, emergency med residency, Darnall Army Hospital, Ft Hood, Tex, 80-81; chair and clinical assoc prof, div of emergency med, Tex A&M Univ Col of Med, Temple, Tex, 80-81; asst prof, sect of emergency med, dept of surgery, Univ Ariz Col of Med, 81-85; residency dir, 82-91, assoc prof, 85-92, prof, 92-, sect of emergency med, dept of surgery, Univ Ariz Col of Med; dir, Ariz Bioethics Prog, Univ Ariz Col of Med, 91-. **HONORS AND AWARDS** Intl Authors and Writers Who's Who, 99; Emergency Med Residents' Teacher of the yr, 97; Who's Who of Medicine and Healthcare, 96; Contemporary Authors, 95; NY Public Libr award, 95; Pew Charitable Trusts Sr fel, Ctr for Clinical Med Ethics, Univ Chicago, 90-91; Intl Who's Who of Professionals, 94; Global Business Leaders, 93; Who's Who of Emerging Leaders in America, 89; Amer Men and Women of Sci, 89; Who's Who in the West, 89; Valedictorian, Univ Phoenix, Tucson, 87; Amer Med Asn Physician Recognition award, 80, 83, 86, 89, 93, 94, 97; fel, Amer Col of Emergency Physicians, 82; diplomat, Amer Bd of Emergency Med, 80, 90. **MEMBERSHIPS** Amer Col of Emergency Physicians; Amer Med Asn; Amer Philos Asn; Amer Soc for Bioethics and Humanities; Europ Soc for Philos of Med & Health Care; Nat Asn of Advisors for Health Professionals; Soc for Acad Emergency Med; Wilderness Med Soc. **RESEARCH** Ethical issues related to emergency medical care, end-of-life issues, and medicine's future. **SELECTED PUBLICATIONS** Auth, Asking the Right Questions--Physician-Assisted Suicide and Emergency Medical Systems, Acad Emergency Med, 847-9, 98; auth, Nonstandard Advance Directives: A Pseudoethical Dilemma, Jour of Trauma, 139-42, 98; auth, Elegant Emergency Medicine, Jour of Emergency Med, 483-4, 98; co-auth, Financial Relationships with Patients, Surgical Ethics, Oxford Univ Press, 322-41, 98; auth, Bioethics, Emergency Medicine: Concepts and Clinical Practice, 4th ed, C. V. Mosby, 212-221, 98; auth, Bioethical Dilemmas in Emergency Medicine and Prehospital Care, Health Care Ethics: Critical Issues for the 21st Century, Aspen Publ, 138-145, 97; auth, Human Subjects in Trauma Research, Emergency Medicine, 2nd ed, Galen Press Ltd, 134-142, 95;

auth, Practicing Procedures on the Newly Dead, Emergency Medicine, 2nd ed, Galen Press Ltd, 123-129, 95; auth, Ethics of Wilderness Medicine, Wilderness Medicine: Management of Wilderness and Environmental Emergencies, 3rd ed, C. V. Mosby, 1436-1446, 95; auth, Bioethical Dilemmas in Emergency Medicine and Prehospital Care, Health Care Ethics: Critical Issues, Aspen Publ, 146-150, 94. **CONTACT ADDRESS** Arizona Bioethics Program, Univ of Arizona Col of Medicine, 1501 N. Campbell Av., Box 245057, Tucson, AZ, 85724. **EMAIL** kvi@u.uug.arizona.edu

ISH, DANIEL
DISCIPLINE LAW **EDUCATION** Univ Saskatchewan, BA, 70, LLB, 70; Osgoode Hall Law Sch, LLM, 74. **CAREER** Prof, 75- **SELECTED PUBLICATIONS** Auth, The Law of Canadian Co-operatives, Carswell, 81; Absenteeism Attendance Programs, 95; co-auth, Legal Responsibilities and Duties of Directors in Canadian Co-operatives, 95; Co-operatives in Principle and Practice, 92. **CONTACT ADDRESS** Col of Law, Univ Saskatchewan, 15 Campus Dr, Saskatoon, SK, S7N 5A6. **EMAIL** Ish@law.usask.ca

ISOM, DALLAS W.
DISCIPLINE ANTITRUST, CIVIL PROCEDURE, FEDERAL JURISDICTION, PLEADING **EDUCATION** Univ Utah, JD, 65. **CAREER** Grad fel, Stanford Univ, 65-66; tchg fel, Stanford Univ, 65-66; private practice, King, Miller, Anderson, Nash & Yerke, 66-68; asst prof, 68-70; assoc prof, 70-74; prof, 74. **MEMBERSHIPS** Mem, Order of the Coif. **SELECTED PUBLICATIONS** Auth, Oregon Civil Pleading and Practice Handbook, 74, 78, 80; ed, note ed, Utah Law Rev. **CONTACT ADDRESS** Sch of Law, Willamette Univ, 900 State St, Salem, OR, 97301. **EMAIL** disom@willamette.edu

ISRAEL, JEROLD H.
PERSONAL Born 06/14/1934, Cleveland, OH, m, 1959, 3 children **DISCIPLINE** LAW **EDUCATION** Western Reserve Univ, BBA; Yale Univ, LLB. **CAREER** Ed Rood Eminent scholar, Trial Advocacy and Procedure, Univ Fla, 93-; Stephen C. O'Connell vis prof, 91; Alene and Allen F. Smith prof emer, Univ Mich Law Sch, 61-96. **MEMBERSHIPS** Ohio Bar; Mich Bar; Order of the Coif. **RESEARCH** Criminal procedure, white collar crime. **SELECTED PUBLICATIONS** Coauth, White Collar Crime: Law and Pract. **CONTACT ADDRESS** School of Law, Univ of Florida, PO Box 117625, Gainesville, FL, 32611-7625. **EMAIL** israel@law.ufl.edu

IVES, CHRISTOPHER
PERSONAL Born 12/11/1954, Torrington, CT, s **DISCIPLINE** PHILOSOPHY **EDUCATION** Claremont Graduate School, PhD, 88. **CAREER** Asst Prof, 87-93, Assoc Prof, 93-, Univ Puget Sound **HONORS AND AWARDS** Phi Beta Kappa, Cum Laude, Williams Col, 76; Claremont Graduate School Univ Fel, 81-85; Phi Kappa Phi, Univ Puget Sound, 93. **MEMBERSHIPS** Amer Acad of Religion; Assoc for Asian Studies; Intl Assoc of Buddhist Studies; Intl Soc for Asian and Comparative Phil; Soc for the Study of Japanese Religion; Soc for Buddhist-Christian Studies **RESEARCH** Japanese Buddhism and ethics **SELECTED PUBLICATIONS** Auth, Zen Awakening and Society, 92; Divine Emptiness and Historical Fullness: A Buddhist-Jewish-Christian Conversation with Maseo Abe, 95; Response: Visions and Revisions in Buddhist Ethics, Journal of Buddhist Ethics 3, 95; Ethical Pitfalls in Imperial Zen and Nishida Philosophy: Ichikawa Hakugen's Critique, Rude Awakenings: Zen, the Kyoto School, & the Question of Nationalism, 95; The Return to the Relative: Sunyata and the Realm of Ethics, Divine Emptiness and Historical Fullness: A Buddhist-Jewish-Christian Conversation with Maseo Abe, 95; What Are We Anyway? Buddhists, Buddhologists, or Buddhologians, Buddhist Christian Studies, 98; Maseo Abe and his Dialogical Mission, Maseo Abe: A Zen Life of Dialogue, 98. **CONTACT ADDRESS** Dept of Religion, Univ of Puget Sound, Tacoma, WA, 98416. **EMAIL** ives@ups.edu

IYER, NITYA
DISCIPLINE LAW **EDUCATION** Univ Toronto, BA, 83, LLB, 86; Harvard Univ, LLM, 89. **CAREER** Asst prof, 90-94; assoc prof, 94-. **RESEARCH** Feminist theory; race and racism; family law; constitutional law. **SELECTED PUBLICATIONS** Auth, pubs about constitutional and human rights, family law, feminist and anti-racist analyses of law, and reproduction and the law. **CONTACT ADDRESS** Fac of Law, Univ British Columbia, 1822 East Mall, Vancouver, BC, V6T 1Z1. **EMAIL** iyer@law.ubc.ca

J

JABLONSKI, LEANNE M.
DISCIPLINE RELIGIOUS STUDIES **EDUCATION** McGill Univ, PhD. **CAREER** Post-doc scholar, Ohio State Univ; rel stud adj fac mem and Assoc Dir, Marianist Env Educ Ctr at Mt St John/Bergamo in Dayton. **RESEARCH** Plant Ecology and the impacts of Global Climate Change. **CONTACT ADDRESS** Dept of Religious Studies, Univ of Dayton, 300 College Park, 473 Humanities, Dayton, OH, 45469-1679. **EMAIL** jablonsk@checkov.hm.udayton.edu

JACKMAN, BARBARA
DISCIPLINE LAW **EDUCATION** Windsor Univ, BA, 72; Univ Toronto, LLB, 76. **CAREER** Lectr; Practicing Immigration & Refugee Law, Jackman & Associates **MEMBERSHIPS** Can Bas Asn; Law Union Ontario; Can Civil Liberties Asn. **SELECTED PUBLICATIONS** Auth, pubs on immigration and refugee law, administrative law and constitutional law. **CONTACT ADDRESS** Fac of Law, Univ Toronto, 78 Queen's Park, Toronto, ON.

JACKMAN, HENRY
PERSONAL Born 04/04/1965 **DISCIPLINE** PHILOSOPHY **EDUCATION** Columbia Univ, BA; Pittsburgh Univ, MA, PhD. **CAREER** Prof, Univ Toledo. **RESEARCH** Philos of lang; Am Pragmatism; philos of mind; hist of analytic philos; epistemology; hist of mod philos; William James; philos of sci; metaphysics; logic. **SELECTED PUBLICATIONS** Auth, Review of Declerck: Tense In English: Its structure and use in discourse, Language, 93; Radical Interpretation and the Permutation Principle, Erkenntnis; James on Prudential Arguments and the Will to Believe, 97; James' Pragmatic Account of Intentionality and Truth, 98; Individualism and Interpretation, SW Philos Rev, 98. **CONTACT ADDRESS** Dept of Philos, Univ Toledo, Toledo, OH, 43606. **EMAIL** hjackma@uoft02.utoledo.edu

JACKSON, CAROL E.
DISCIPLINE LAW **EDUCATION** Wellesley College, BA, 1973; Univ of Michigan, JD, 1976. **CAREER** Thompson & Mitchell, attorney, 1976-83; Mallinckrodt Inc, counsel, 1983-85; US District Court, Eastern District MO, magistrate, 1986-92, DISTRICT JUDGE, 1992-; WASHINGTON UNIV, ADJUNCT PROF OF LAW, 1989-92. **MEMBERSHIPS** St Louis Art Museum, trustee, 1987-91; National Assn of Women's Judges; Federal Magistrate Judges Assn; Missouri Bar; St Louis County Bar Assn; Metro St Louis; Mound City Bar Assn; Lawyers Assn of St Louis. **CONTACT ADDRESS** US District Court-Eastern Missouri, 1114 Market St, St. Louis, MO, 63101-2043.

JACKSON, GORDON EDMUND
PERSONAL Born 01/11/1918, Spokane, WA, m, 1939, 2 children **DISCIPLINE** PASTORAL THEOLOGY **EDUCATION** Monmouth Col, AB, 40; Pittsburth-Xenia Theol Sem, BD, 43; Tarkio Col, DD, 53; Univ Chicago, PhD, 54. **CAREER** Minister, Westminster United Presby Church, Olympia, Wash, 44-49; prof philos of relig, 49-70, dean, 55-77, HUGH THOMSON KERR PROF PASTORAL THEOL, PITTSBURGH THEOL SEM, 75-, Mem comn on accrediting, Asn Am Theol Schs, 62-68; adj prof relig studies, Univ Pittsburgh, 69- **MEMBERSHIPS** Soc Sci Studies Relig; Am Acad Relig. **RESEARCH** Concept of the image of God and its implications for Christian education; hostility in man; spiritual formation of the self. **SELECTED PUBLICATIONS** Auth, The Diaconate--A Full and Equal Order--A Comprehensive-Study and Critical Study of the Origin, Development, and Decline of the Diaconate in the Context of the Churchs Total Ministry and the Renewal of the Diaconate Today With Re, J Ecumenical Stud. **CONTACT ADDRESS** Pittsburgh Theol Sem, 616 N Highland Ave, Pittsburgh, PA, 15206.

JACKSON, JARED JUDD
PERSONAL Born 07/26/1930, New Haven, CT, m, 1953, 4 children **DISCIPLINE** OLD TESTAMENT SEMITIC STUDIES **EDUCATION** Harvard Univ, AB, 52; Episcopal Theol Sch, BD, 58; Union Theol Sem NY, ThD(Old Testament), 62. **CAREER** Asst prof Old Testament, Huron Col Ont & Univ Western Ont, 62-64; vis prof relig, Williams Col, 64-65; from asst prof to prof, 65-97, Prof Emeritus Old Testament, Pittsburgh Theol Sem, 97-; adj prof grad studies relig, Univ Pittsburgh, 69-. **HONORS AND AWARDS** Church Soc Col Work fel, 58-60; Rockefeller Bros Fund fel, 60-62; Am Asn Theol Schs fac fel, 68-69. **MEMBERSHIPS** Soc Bibl Studies; Soc Study Egyptian Antiq; Soc Bibl Lit; Am Schs Orient Res. **RESEARCH** Ugaritic and Egyptian studies in relation to Old Testament. **SELECTED PUBLICATIONS** Contribr to the interpreter's dictionary of the Bible, Abingdon, 62; co-ed, Rhetorical Criticism, 74. **CONTACT ADDRESS** Pittsburgh Theol Sem, 616 N Highland Ave, Pittsburgh, PA, 15206-2525. **EMAIL** jjackson@pitt.edu

JACKSON, JOSEPH HOLLISTER
PERSONAL Born 10/13/1912, Springfield, VT, m, 1941, 1 child **DISCIPLINE** PHILOSOPHY, PSYCHOLOGY **EDUCATION** Middlebury Col, AB, 35; Brown Univ, MA, 37, PhD(philos), 40. **CAREER** Personnel dir, Columbia Broadcasting Syst, Inc, 44-50; training dir, Am Electric Power Co, 50-54; publ dir, Soc Advan Mgt, 54-55; managing ed, Ronald Press Co, 55-60; consult ed sci, Encycl Americana, 60-64; writer, Sci Fortnightly & Dateline in Sci, Richard Sigerson, 64-65; ed-in-chicf, Investigating the Earth, Houghton, 65-67; instr philos, New Sch Social Res, 66-67; asst prof, Univ Conn, 68-72; Res & Writing, 72-, Nat Sci Found fel, Conn Res Found, 68-69; proj ed, Earth Sci Curriculum Proj, Nat Sci Found, 65-67; WRITER HARVARD PHYSICS PROF, 68-. **MEMBERSHIPS** Am Philos Asn; AAAS. **RESEARCH** Ethics; motivation; developmental and social psychology. **SELECTED PUBLICATIONS** Auth Pictorial guide to the Planets, 65, 3rd ed, 81 & coauth, Pictorial Guide to the Moon, 69, 3rd ed, 73, Crowell; Spaceship Earth-Earth Sciences, Houghton, 73, 2nd ed, 80; contribr, Psychology 73/74, Dushkin, 73; auth, Measurement of ethical values, Perceptual & Motor Skills, 36: 1075-1088; coauth, Investigating Behavior, Harper, 76; Infant Culture, Crowell, 78. **CONTACT ADDRESS** 57 Attawan Ave, Niantic, CT, 06357.

JACKSON, RANDOLPH
PERSONAL Born 10/10/1943, Brooklyn, NY **DISCIPLINE** LAW **EDUCATION** NY U, BA 1965; Brooklyn Law Sch, JD 1969. **CAREER** Mudge Rose Guthrie & Alexander, asso atty 1969-70; Private Practice of Law, 1971-81; New York City Family Court, hearing examiner 1981; Civil Court, Housing Part, judge 1981-87; Civil Court, judge 1987-88; Supreme Court Brooklyn NY, justice 1988-. **MEMBERSHIPS** Life mem Nat Bar Assn 1971-; mem Brooklyn Bar Assn 1971-; mem Crown Hgts Lions Club 1980-; Sigma Pi Phi. **SELECTED PUBLICATIONS** Book, "How to Get a Fair Trial By Jury" 1978. **CONTACT ADDRESS** Supreme Court, Kings County, 360 Adams St, Brooklyn, NY, 11201.

JACKSON, ROGER
DISCIPLINE RELIGIONS OF SOUTH ASIA AND ISLAM **EDUCATION** Wesleyan, BA; Wisconsin, MA, PhD. **CAREER** Religion, Carleton Univ. **SELECTED PUBLICATIONS** Coauth, The Wheel of Time: Kalachakra in Context, 85; Auth, Is Enlightenment Possible?, 93; Coed, Tibetan Literature: Studies in Genre, 96. **CONTACT ADDRESS** Carleton Col, 100 S College St., Northfield, MN, 55057-4016.

JACKSON, WILLIAM JOSEPH
PERSONAL Born 08/31/1943, Rock Island, IL, m, 1968, 1 child **DISCIPLINE** RELIGION **EDUCATION** Lyndon (VT) St Col, BA, 75; Harvard Univ, PhD, 84. **CAREER** Asst prof, 85-92, assoc prof, 92-, Indiana Univ, Purdue. **HONORS AND AWARDS** Danforth Fel to Grad Schl, 75. **MEMBERSHIPS** AAR. **RESEARCH** S Indian religious music; Hindu singer-saints; fractals in humanities. **SELECTED PUBLICATIONS** Auth, Tyagaraja: Life and Lyrics, Oxford Univ Press, 91; auth, J.L. Mehta on Heidegger, Hermeneutics and Indian Tradition, Netherlands, 92; art, Features of the Kriti: A Song Form Developed by Tyagaraja, Asian Music Jour, Cornell Univ, 93; auth, The Power of the Sacred Name: V Raghavan's Studies on Namasiddhanta and Indian Culture, India Book Center, 94; art, Purandaradasa's Songs on the Holy Name, Jour of Vaisnava Stud, 94; auth, Tyagaraja and the Renewal of Tradition: Translations and Reflections, New Delhi, 95; art, Music as Reflectaphor for Cosmic Order in the Vijayanagara Empire, Jour of Vaisnava Stud, 96; art, Annamacarya's Spiritual Thinking, Jour of Vaisnava Stud, 96; auth, The Songs of Three Great South Indian Saints, Oxford Univ Press, 98; art, Fractals of Love: Self-Similarity in the Bhakti Community, Jour of Vaisnava Stud, 98. **CONTACT ADDRESS** 5750 Broadway St, Indianapolis, IN, 46220. **EMAIL** wjackson@iupui.edu

JACOB, BRUCE ROBERT
PERSONAL Born 03/26/1935, Chicago, IL, m, 1962, 3 children **DISCIPLINE** LAW **EDUCATION** FL State Univ, BA, 57; Stetson Univ, JD, 59; Northwestern Univ, LLM, 65; Harvard Univ, SJD, 80; Univ FL, LLM(taxation), 95. **CAREER** Asst atty gen, Off of the Atty Gen of Fla, 60-62; assoc, Holland, Bevis & Smith, Attys, 62-64; from asst prof to assoc prof criminal law, Sch Law, Emory Univ, 65-69; res assoc, Ctr Criminal Justice, Harvard Law Sch, 69-70; staff atty, Community Legal Assistance Off, Cambridge, Mass, 70-71; from assoc prof to prof & dir clinical progs, Col Law, Ohio State Univ, 71-78; prof & dean, Sch Law, Mercer Univ, 78-81; Prof, Dean & Vpres, Col Law, Stetson Univ, 81-94; Prof and Dean Emer, 94-, Special officer, conscientious objector cases, US Dept Justice, 65-68; mem, Ga Governor's Comn on Crime & Justice, 67-68. **MEMBERSHIPS** Am Judicature Soc. **RESEARCH** Correctional law; criminal procedure; criminology; administrative law; taxation **SELECTED PUBLICATIONS** Coauth, Sit-in demonstrations: Are they punishable in Florida?, Univ Miami Law Rev, 60-61; auth, Reparation or restitution by the criminal offender to his victim, J Criminal Law, Criminol & Police Sci, 70; Prison discipline and inmate rights, Harvard Civil Rights- Civil Liberties Law Rev, 70; coauth, Justice after trial: Prisoners' need for legal services in the criminal-correctional process, Kans Law Rev, 70, contribr, The Concept of Restitution: An Historical Overview, In: Restitution in Criminal Justice, Lexington Books, 77. **CONTACT ADDRESS** Col of Law, Stetson Univ, 1401 61st St S, Saint Petersburg, FL, 33707-3299. **EMAIL** jacob@hermes.law.stetson.edu

JACOBS, DAVID C.
DISCIPLINE PHILOSOPHY **EDUCATION** Ca State Univ, BA; New Sch Soc Res, MA, 90; Vanderbilt Univ, PhD, 93. **CAREER** Instr, Vanderbilt Univ, 92; Adj prof, 93-96; asst prof, 96-. **RESEARCH** Contemporary European philosophy; philosophy of the body. **SELECTED PUBLICATIONS** Auth, Introduction: Heidegger, the History of Being, the Presocratics; Parmenides' Ontological Education; Martin Heidegger and the Phenomenon of Natural Science (rev), 95; The Tain of the Mirror, in Auslegung (rev), 90; co-ed, Heidegger and the Political, Graduate Fac Philos Jour, 91. **CONTACT ADDRESS** Dept of Philosophy, 615 McCallie, Chattanooga, TN, 37403. **EMAIL** david-jacobs@utc.edu

JACOBS, ENNIS LEON, JR.
PERSONAL Born 01/19/1954, Tampa, FL, m, 1976 **DISCIPLINE** LAW **EDUCATION** Florida A & M Univ, Magna Cum Laude, BS, technology, 1976; Florida State Univ Coll of Law, JD, 1986. **CAREER** Eastman Kodak Co, systems analyst, 1976-80; RCA Corp, systems representatives, 1980-82; Florida Public Service Commission, staff Attorney, 1986-89; Florida Attorney General, staff Attorney, 1989-91; Florida Senate, staff Attorney, 1991-93; Florida Legislative House, staff Attorney, 1993-. **MEMBERSHIPS** Tallahassee Habitat for Humanity, pres of board; National Bar Assn; Amer Bar Assn; Leon County Guardian Ad Litem. **SELECTED PUBLICATIONS** Author, "State Regulation of Information Services," Barrister, ABA Young Lawyers Division, Spring 1991. **CONTACT ADDRESS** Florida House of Rep-Comm on Insurance, House Office Bldg, Rm 302, The Capitol, Tallahassee, FL, 32399-1300.

JACOBS, JONATHAN
DISCIPLINE MORAL PHILOSOPHY, EPISTEMOLOGY, METAPHYSICS **EDUCATION** Univ PA, PhD, 83. **CAREER** Assoc prof, Colgate Univ. **SELECTED PUBLICATIONS** Auth, Practical Realism and Moral Psychology, 95; Plasticity and Perfection: Maimonides and Aristotle on Character, 97; Why is Virtue Naturally Pleasing, 95. **CONTACT ADDRESS** Dept of Philos and Relig, Colgate Univ, 13 Oak Drive, Hamilton, NY, 13346. **EMAIL** jjacobs@mail.colgate.edu

JACOBS, MICHELLE S.
DISCIPLINE LAW **EDUCATION** Princeton Univ, AB; Rutgers Univ, JD. **CAREER** Prof, Univ Fla, 93-; past supv atty, Rutgers Univ Urban Legal Clinic; pvt pract, McGee Jacobs, NY, 85-90; prof, Columbia Univ Fair Housing Clinic. **MEMBERSHIPS** NJ Bar; NY Bar. **CONTACT ADDRESS** School of Law, Univ of Florida, PO Box 117625, Gainesville, FL, 32611-7625. **EMAIL** jacobsm@nervm.nerdc.ufl.edu

JACOBSON, ARLAND D.
PERSONAL Born 09/25/1941, Mitchell, SD, m, 1964, 2 children **DISCIPLINE** RELIGION **EDUCATION** Augustana Col, BA, 63; Univ Chicago Div Sch, 64-65; Luther Sem, BD, 67; Claremont Grad Univ, PhD, 78. **CAREER** Pastor, Humboldt Lutheran Church, SD, and Scranton Luthern Parish, ND, 74-76; vis asst prof relig stud, Loyola Marymount Univ, 78-79; asst prof relig, 79-83, dir, CHARIS Ecumenical Ctr and Fargo-Moorhead Communiversity, 83- , Concordia College. **HONORS AND AWARDS** Scholar in residence, Inst for Ecumenical and Cultural Res, Collegeville MN, 90; Bush Summer Fel, 92; Who's Who in Relig, 92; scholar in residence, Tantur Ecumenical Inst, Jerusalem, 97; Who's Who in America, forthcoming. **MEMBERSHIPS** Soc of Bibl Lit; Catholic Bibl Asn of Am; Westar Inst; Soc for the Advan of Cont Educ for Ministry. **RESEARCH** The synoptic gospel source Q; anti-family tendencies in the Jesus movement; social context of first-century Galilee; ecumenical shared ministry. **SELECTED PUBLICATIONS** Coauth, Exploring the yearly Lectionary, Fortress, 91; auth, The First Gospel: An Introduction to Q, Polebridge, 92; auth, Apocalyptic and the Sayings Source Q, in Van Segbroeck, ed, The Four Gospels 1992: Festschrift Frans Neirynck, v 1, Leuven Univ, 92; coauth, Ecumenical Shared Ministry: Bringing Congregations Together From Different Denominations, Alban Inst, 93; auth, Which Was the First Gospel? The Fourth R, 93; auth, Q, in Miller, ed, The Complete Gospels, rev ed, Polebridge, 94; auth, The Literary Unity of Q, in Kloppenborg, ed, The Shape of Q: Signal Essays on the Sayings Gospel, Fortress, 94; auth, Divided Families and Christian Origins, in Piper, ed, The Gospel Behind the Gospels, Brill, 95; coauth, Ecumenical Shared Ministry and the United Methodist Church, General Commission on Christian Unity and Interreligious Concerns, 95; auth, Q and the Deuteronomistic Tradition Revisited, in The Quest for Q: Dankesgabe an James M Robinson, 99. **CONTACT ADDRESS** CHARIS Ecumenical Center, Concordia Col, Minnesota, Moorhead, MN, 56562. **EMAIL** jacobson@cord.edu

JACOBSON, DIANE L.
DISCIPLINE OLD TESTAMENT **EDUCATION** Connecticut Col, BA, 70; Columbia Univ/Union Theol Sem, MA, 75, MPhil, 82, PhD, 90. **CAREER** Instr, NY Theol Sem, 80-82; tutor, instr, Union Theol Sem, 76-78, 79; asst prof, 82; assoc prof, 90-; ch, Bibl Div, 93. **MEMBERSHIPS** Mem, Soc Bibl Lit. **SELECTED PUBLICATIONS** Coauth, Beginner's Guide to the Bible, 91; auth, Psalms: A Prayer Tutor, 86. **CONTACT ADDRESS** Dept of Old Testament, Luther Sem, 2481 Como Ave, St. Paul, MN, 55108. **EMAIL** djacobso@luthersem.edu

JACOBSON, PAUL KENNETH
PERSONAL Born 06/21/1946, Bayonne, NJ, m, 1968, 2 children **DISCIPLINE** PHILOSOPHY, INTELLECTUAL HISTORY **EDUCATION** Seton Hall Univ, AB, 67; Duquesne Univ, MA, 70, PhD(philos), 75. **CAREER** Instr philos, St Peter's Col, 70-71; asst prof, Marywood Col, 72-77; assoc prof philos, 77-85, prof philos, 85-, dean, col of arts and sci, 87-98, assoc vp acad affairs, 82-87, dir honors prog, 78-89, registrar, St Ambrose Univ, 79-87. **HONORS AND AWARDS** NDEA Fel, 68-70. **MEMBERSHIPS** Am Philos Asn; Soc Phenomenol & Existential Philos; Merleau-Ponty Circle US; Consult/evaluator, 91-, team chemn, 95-, accrditation rev coun, 96-, North Central Asn of Col and Schools. **RESEARCH** Phenomenology; epistemology; philosophical anthropology. **SELECTED PUBLICATIONS** Auth, Plato's theory of Anamnesis, 66 & Longinus's conception of the sublime, 67, Bayley Rev; One more new botched beginning: Review of Merleau-Ponty's La Prose du Monde, 72 & Dirty work: Gurwitsch on the phenomenological theory of science and constitutive phenomenology, 76, Res Phenomen; The return of Alcibiades: An approach to the meaning of sexuality through the works of Freud and Merlear-Ponty, Philos Today, 78. **CONTACT ADDRESS** Dept Philosophy, St. Ambrose Univ, 518 W Locust St, Davenport, IA, 52803-2898. **EMAIL** pjacobsn@savnix.sau.edu

JACOBSON, STEPHEN
DISCIPLINE EPISTEMOLOGY, PHILOSOPHY OF MIND, PHILOSOPHY OF SCIENCE, METAPHYSICS, PHILO **EDUCATION** Univ Mich, PhD, 89. **CAREER** Lectr, Ga State Univ. **SELECTED PUBLICATIONS** Publications in Synthese, Pacific Philos Quart and Australasian J of Philos. **CONTACT ADDRESS** Georgia State Univ, Atlanta, GA, 30303. **EMAIL** phlsrj@panther.gsu.edu

JACOBUS, LEE ANDRE
PERSONAL Born 08/20/1935, Orange, NJ, m, 1958, 2 children **DISCIPLINE** ENGLISH, PHILOSOPHY **EDUCATION** Brown Univ, AB, 57, AM, 59; Claremont Grad Sch, PhD(English), 68. **CAREER** Instr, Western Conn State Col, 60-68; PROF ENGLISH, UNIV CONN, 68-. **MEMBERSHIPS** MLA; James Joyce Soc; Milton Soc Am; Am Comt Irish Studies. **RESEARCH** Milton; 17th century English authors; modern Irish literature. **SELECTED PUBLICATIONS** Auth, Milton, John Burden of Interpretation, Theolog Stud, Vol 0056, 95. **CONTACT ADDRESS** Dept of English, U-25 Univ of Conn, Storrs, CT, 06268.

JAINI, PADMANABH S.
PERSONAL Born 10/23/1923, Mangalore, India, m, 1956, 1 child **DISCIPLINE** LINGUISTICS, SOUTH & SOUTHEAST ASIAN RELIGIONS **EDUCATION** HPT Col, India, BA, 47; BJ Inst Res, Ahmedabad, MA, 49; Vidyodaya Pirivena, Ceylon, Tripitakacarya, 51; Univ London, PhD (Sanskrit Lit) 59. **CAREER** Lectr Sanskrit & Pali, Benaras Hindu Univ, 52-56; Pali & Buddhist Sanskrit, Univ London, 56-64, reader, 65-67; vis lectr Buddhism, Univ Mich, Ann Arbor, 64-65, prof Indic Lang, 67-72; prof Buddhism, Univ Calif, Berkeley, 72-94; prof Emeritus, grad school, 94. **RESEARCH** Pali and Buddhist Sanskrit language and literature; Abhidharma studies; comparative study of Indian religions. **SELECTED PUBLICATIONS** Ed, Abhidharmadipa, K P Jayawal Inst, 52; auth, On the theory of two Vasubandhus, 58 & The Vaibhasika theory of words, 59, Bull Sch Orient & African Studies, Univ London, ed, Milinda-Tika, Pali Text Soc London, 61; auth, The story of Sudhana and Manohara, 66, Aloka of Haribhadra and the Saratama of Ratnakarasanti: A comparative study of the two commentaries of the Astasahasrika, 72 & Jina Rsabha as an avatara of Visnu, 77, Bull Sch Orient & African Studies, Univ London; The Jaina Path of Purification, Univ Calif, 78; Gender and Salvation: Jaina Debates on the Spiritual Liberation of Women, foreword by R Goldman, xxiv, Preface 4, Univ of Berkeley Press, Berkeley, 91. **CONTACT ADDRESS** Dept of South and Southeast Asian Lang & Lit, Univ of California, Berkeley, 7303 Dwinelle Hall, Berkeley, CA, 94720-0001.

JAMES, ALLIX BLEDSOE
PERSONAL Born 12/17/1922, Marshall, TX, m **DISCIPLINE** THEOLOGY **EDUCATION** VA Union Univ, AB 1944, MDiv 1946; Union Theol Seminary, ThM 1949, ThD 1957. **CAREER** Third Union Baptist Church, former minister; Mount Zion Baptist Church, former minister; Union Zion Baptist Church, former minister; VIRGINIA UNION UNIV, instr Biblical studies 1947-50, dean of students 1950-56, dean of sch of theology 1956-70, vice pres 1960-70, pres 1970-79, pres emeritus, 1979-85, CHANCELLOR, 1985-. **HONORS AND AWARDS** Alpha Phi Alpha, Beta Gamma Lambda Chapter, Outstanding Achievement Award, 1981; Richmond First Club, Good Government Award, 1985; Metropolitan Business League, MF Manuel Community Service Award, 1991; Fullwood Foods Inc, Exemplary Vision Award, 1992; International Ministers' Wives Association, The Shirley A Hart Award for Global Humanitarian Service, 1992; Honorary Degrees: University of Richmond, LLD, 1971; St Paul's College, DD, 1981. The University Chapel was named in his honor, The Alex B. James Chapel, 1992. **MEMBERSHIPS** National Conference of Christians and Jews Inc, board of directors, national executive board; Richmond Gold Bowl Sponsors, co-founder, president, board of directors; National Council for America's First Freedom, board of directors; Black History Museum and Cultural Center of Virginia Inc, president, board of trustees; Richmond Tommorrow, education task force, chairman; Leadership Roundtable, founder, chairman, board of directors; Virginia Electric and Power Co., board of directors; Consolidated Bank and Trust Co., board of directors; American Council of Life Insurance, university advisory council; Beekne Investment Co. Inc, board of directors; Alpha Phi Alpha Fraternity Inc; Sigma Pi Phi Fraternity Inc, Alpha Beta Boule; Moore Street Baptist Church, board of trustees. First African-American to serve as president of Virginia State Board of Education; Association of Theological Schools in the US; National Conference of Christians and Jews, Virginia Region; first African-American chairman, Richmond Planning Commission; Board of trustees, Virginia Union University named the restored University Chapel in Coburn Hall, The Allix B James Chapel, 1992; guest of the Government of Republic of Taiwan to explore possiblities for educational cooperation, 1976; conferences with European theological educators from Germany, Switzerland, Italy, France, and England, 1969; study of higher education in USSR, 1973. **SELECTED PUBLICATIONS** Contributing editor, The Continuing Quest; author: Calling a Pastor in a Baptist CHurch; numerous articles, local and national publications and professional journals. **CONTACT ADDRESS** Virginia Union Univ, 1500 N Lombardy St, Richmond, VA, 23220.

JAMES, BERNARD
DISCIPLINE CONSTITUTIONAL LAW **EDUCATION** Univ MI, BGS, 77, JD, 83. **CAREER** Law clk, Mich Court Appeals, 83-84; lectr, Nat Criminal Justice Inst; prof. **HONORS AND AWARDS** Am jurisp awards. **MEMBERSHIPS** Mem, Am Bar Assn; Nat Org Legal Problems Edu; The Am Sch Bd(s) Assn. **SELECTED PUBLICATIONS** Contrib ed, ABA Preview US Supreme Court Jour; contrib columnist, Nat Law Jour; contrib writer, Sch Safety J. **CONTACT ADDRESS** Sch of Law, Pepperdine Univ, 24255 Pacific Coast Hwy, Malibu, CA, 90263.

JAMES, FRANK
DISCIPLINE CHURCH HISTORY **EDUCATION** Oxford Univ, PhD. **CAREER** Instr, Ctr for Medieval and Renaissance Stud, affil Keble Col, Oxford Univ; assoc prof-. **HONORS AND AWARDS** Transl, ch, Ed Comm of the Peter Martyr Lib. **SELECTED PUBLICATIONS** Auth, Peter Martyr Vermigli: Praedestinatio Dei in the Thought of an Italian Reformer; ed/transl, Selected Works of Peter Martyr Vermigli: Theological Treatises; co-ed, Via Augustini: Augustine in the Later Middle Ages, Renaissance and Reformation; gen ed, Peter Martyr Lib; sr ed, Library of Classical Protestant Theology Texts on CD-ROM; consult ed, The Blackwell Encycl of Medieval, Renaissance and Reformation Christian Thought. **CONTACT ADDRESS** Dept of Church History, Reformed Theol Sem, 1015 Maitland Ctr Commons, Maitland, FL, 32751.

JAMES, FRANK SAMUEL, III
PERSONAL Born 08/10/1945, Mobile, AL, m **DISCIPLINE** LAW **EDUCATION** Campbell Coll, BS 1973; Univ of AL, JD 1978; US Army War College, graduate, 1990. **CAREER** Fed Judge Virgil Pittman, law clerk 1978-80; US Dept of Justice, asst us atty 1980-86; Univ of AL School of Law, prof, asst dean 1986-90; Berkowitz, Lefkovits, Isom and Kushner, partner, 1990-. **HONORS AND AWARDS** Bench and bar Legal Hon Soc 1978; Distinguished Alumnus, Campbell University, 1987. **MEMBERSHIPS** Mem Amer Bar Assoc 1978-, AL State Bar 1978-, Birmingham Bar Assoc 1980-; bd of mgmt YMCA of Metro Birmingham 1996-; mem of council Synod of the Mid South 1985-86; moderator, mem of council Birmingham Presbytery 1986; pres of bd 1988-90, chmn of bd, 1991-, Alabama Capital Representation Resource Center 1991-; director, Columbia Theological Seminary, 1991-; trustee, Farrah Law Society, 1990-; trustee, The Presbytery of Sheppards and Lapsley, 1990-98. **SELECTED PUBLICATIONS** Auth, Contingent Fees in Domestic Relations Actions 3 Jrnl of the Legal Prof 209 1978; co-auth, Perspectives on the Evidence Law of Alabama: A Decade of Evolution 1977-87, 40 Alabama Law Review 95, 1988; auth, Protecting Final Judgments: A Critical Overview of Provisional Injunctive Relief in Alabama, 20 Cumberland Law Review 227, 1990. **CONTACT ADDRESS** Berkowitz, Lefkovits, Isom & Kushner, 1600 Southtrust Tower, Birmingham, AL, 35203.

JAMES, H. RHETT
PERSONAL Born 12/01/1928, Baltimore, MD, m **DISCIPLINE** EDUCATION, THEOLOGY **EDUCATION** VA Union U, AB 1950; Our Lady of the Lake Coll, MEd 1951; VA Union U, MDiv 1957; TX Christian U, MTh 1961; Harvard Univ Inst of Mgt, 1974; Univ ofIN, Memphis Univ Insts on on Mgt-Commun Servs 1974-75; Univ of TX at Arlington, PhD 1974. **CAREER** Urban Affairs & Community Devel Center, asst prof of soc sci, assoc dir of devel, dir; New Careers for the Handicapped Program Bishop Coll TX, dir 1962-; New Hope Baptist Church TX, pastor 1958-; VA Union Univ, instructor 1955-58; San Antonio School System St Phillips Jr Coll, instructor 1950-55. **HONORS AND AWARDS** Goals for Dallas Commun Serv Aw; OIC Commun Serv Aw; Urban Leag Disting Serv Aw; NKOK Radio Sta Commun Serv Aw; Big Bros Commun Serv Aw; Disting Serv Aw Urban Leag; Trail Blazers Aw; Dllas City Counc Serv Aw. **MEMBERSHIPS** Educ com chmn Dallas NAACP 1961; pres Dallas NAACP 1962; bd of dir TX Counc of Chs; del Pres Com on Equal Employ Opportun; fdr, 1st pres Dallas Frontiers Internat; pres Dallas Dem Men; bd mem Family Guid Ctr; bd mem Am Civ Lib Union; ret bd mem Dallas Urban Leag; bd mem TX Assn of Devlpng Colls 1970-74; bd mem City of Dallas; mem Am Mensa Soc; bd mem N Dallas Am Cancer Soc; mem So Histl Assn; mem Am Assn of Univ Profs; bd mem Am Bapt Conv Chs of the S; mem Sigma Pi Phi & Kappa Alpha Psi Frat. **CONTACT ADDRESS** New Hope Baptist Church, 5002 S Central Expressway, Dallas, TX, 75215.

JAMES, MARQUITA L.
PERSONAL Born 11/09/1932, Philadelphia, PA **DISCIPLINE** LAW **EDUCATION** Wilberforce Univ Wilberforce OH, BA 1955; Seton Ahll Univ S Orange NJ, MA 1966; Candidacy NY U, PhD 1974. **CAREER** Nassau Comm Coll Garden City, Long Island NY, assoc prof History 1969-; Wyandanch Schools, Wydandanch NY, chmn 1964-68; Freeport NY, Afro-Amer History curr coor 1968-69. **HONORS AND AWARDS** Listed among black edrs in Black Hist Museum Hempstead LI NY; natl def educ award Tchrs Coll Columbia Univ NY UL,; inst intl educ award Univ of Ghana Legon W Africa 1969; m l kingr jr grad fellow award NY Univ 1968-71. **MEMBERSHIPS** Hist & ldr crea of estab of Afro-Am Hist Soc in Freeport & Long Island NY; activist leader in successful fight to deseg sch buses & discrim prac in Freeport Schls 1968-69; mem Assn Univ Prof Assn Afro-Am Edn; Am Hist Assn; Afro-Am Black Heritage Assn; Cong of Racial Equal; Coun on Interracl Books for Child; Alpha Kappa Alpha Sor; Nat Black Feminist Org; pres Nassau-Suffolk Br Assn for Study of Afro-Am Life & Hist. Univ of TN, asst prof & asst librarian 1973-77; Univ of KY, asst prof of law/law librarian; assoc prof of law/law librarian Univ of KY 1977-82; prof of law/law lib 1982-88; Villanova Univ, prof of law/dir of law library, 1988-95, associate dean for information svcs & professor of law, 1995-. **CONTACT ADDRESS** Villanova Univ, Villanova, PA, 19085.

JAMES, ROBERT N.
PERSONAL Born 03/25/1931, Denver, CO, m, 1971, 2 children **DISCIPLINE** RELIGIOUS STUDIES **EDUCATION** Empire State Col, SUNY, BA, 75; Greenwich Univ, MA, 96, Doctoral Candidate. **CAREER** Retired **RESEARCH** Monistic Theology **CONTACT ADDRESS** 28350 Winthrop Cir, Bonita Springs, FL, 34134. **EMAIL** numa@mci2000.com

JAMES, WILLIAM
DISCIPLINE LEGAL RESEARCH **EDUCATION** Morehouse Col, BA, 67; Howard Univ Sch Law, JD, 72; Atlanta Univ Sch Libr Sci, MSLS, 73. **CAREER** Prof, Villanova Univ; dir, Law Libr, 88-; assoc dean, Inf serv, 95-. **MEMBERSHIPS** Asn Amer Law Schools Comt on Libr; bd adv, Legal Reference serv Quart; Amer Asn Law Libraries, served on comt for Placement, Educ, Minorities, Scholarship and grants; chem, Minorities Comt, 85-87; past chep, Scholarship and Nomination Comt, Southeastern Asn Law Librarians **RESEARCH** Legal research. **SELECTED PUBLICATIONS** Auth, Law Libraries Which Offer serv to Prisoners, Am Ass'n of Law Libraries Comt on Law Libr serv to Prisoners, 75; Recommended Collections for Prison Law Libraries, 75;"Legal Reference Materials and Law Library servs, Am Ass'n of Law Libraries Comt on Law Libraries serv to Prisoners, 76; Legal Reference Materials and Law Library servs, U Ken Continuing Legal Educ, 76; contrib, Fundaments of Legal Research, 77; co-contrib, Law and Psychiatry, 79 & Natural Resources and Development, 87. **CONTACT ADDRESS** Law School, Villanova Univ, 800 Lancaster Ave, Villanova, PA, 19085-1692. **EMAIL** wjames@law.vill.edu

JAMES, WILLIAM CLOSSON
PERSONAL Born 05/20/1943, Sudbury, ON, Canada, m, 1964, 3 children **DISCIPLINE** RELIGION, ENGLISH LITERATURE **EDUCATION** Queen's Univ, Ont, BA, 65, BD, 68; Univ Chicago, MA, 70, PhD(relig & lit), 74. **CAREER** Lectr, 73-75, asst prof, 75-80, chmn undergrad studies relig, 78-81, ASSOC PROF RELIG & LIT, QUEEN'S UNIV, ONT, 80-, Exec bd mem relig, Can Soc for Study Relig, 75-78; mem bd dirs relig, Can Corp for Studies Relig, 78-; book rev ed, Studies in Relig, 79-. **MEMBERSHIPS** Can Soc for Study Relig; Am Acad Relig. **RESEARCH** Religion and literature; modern Canadian fiction; heroism and the quest in literature. **SELECTED PUBLICATIONS** Auth, Nature and the Sacred in Canada + Role of Geography and Climate in Shaping a Canadian Identity, Stud in Religion Sciences Religieuses, Vol 0021, 92. **CONTACT ADDRESS** Dept of Relig, Queen's Univ, Kingston, ON, K7L 3N6.

JAMROS, DANIEL
PERSONAL Born 03/11/1942, Adams, MA **DISCIPLINE** THEOLOGY **EDUCATION** Vanderbilt, PhD, 86. **CAREER** Assoc Prof, 85-, Canisius College. **MEMBERSHIPS** AAR, HSA, CTS of A, **RESEARCH** Hegel, Catholic theology, philosophy of religion. **SELECTED PUBLICATIONS** Auth, The Human Shape of God, Religion in Hegel's Phenomenology of Spirit, NY Paragon House, 94; art, Hegel on the Incarnation, Unique or Universal, in: Theological Studies, 95; The Appearing God' in Hegel's Phenomenology of Spirit, CLIO, 90; Satisfaction for Sin, Aquinas on the Passion of Christ, in: Irish Theo Qtly, 90; review, Thomas Steinherr, Der Begriff Absoluter Geist in der Philosophie G W Hegels, Erzabtei St Ottilien, EOS Verlag, in: Hegel-Studien, 95. **CONTACT ADDRESS** Canisius Col, 2001 Main St, Buffalo, NY, 14208-1098. **EMAIL** jamros@canisius.edu

JANZEN, JOHN GERALD
PERSONAL Born 08/09/1932, Meadow Lake, SK, Canada, m, 1959, 2 children **DISCIPLINE** OLD TESTAMENT **EDUCATION** Univ Sask, BA, 58, LTh, 59; Harvard Univ, PhD, 66. **CAREER** Prof Old Testament, Col Emmanuel & St Chad, 65-68; MacAllister-Pettigrew prof Old Testament, Christian Theol Sem, Emmanuel Col, 68-. **MEMBERSHIPS** Am Acad Relig; Soc Bibl Lit. **RESEARCH** Biblical interpretation. **SELECTED PUBLICATIONS** Auth, Studies in the Text of Jeremiah (Harvard Semitic Monographs, Vol 6), Harvard Univ, 73; Commentaries on Job. 85; Genesis 12-50, 93; Exodus, 97; articles in Catholic Biblical Quart, Harvard Theological Review, Journal of Biblical Literature, Journal of Religion, Journal for the Study of the New Testament, Journal for the Study of the Old Testament, Letington Theological Quart, Religion and Literature, Semela, Vetus Testamentum. **CONTACT ADDRESS** PO Box 88267, Indianapolis, IN, 46208-0267. **EMAIL** jgjanzeu@cts.edu

JAROW, E.H.
DISCIPLINE RELIGIONS OF INDIA, COMPARATIVE LITERATURE **EDUCATION** Columbia Univ, PhD, 91 **CAREER** ASST PROF, REL STUD, VASSAR COL, 94-. **CONTACT ADDRESS** Dept of Relig, Vassar Col, Poughkeepsie, NY, 12604. **EMAIL** ehjarow@vassar.edu

JARRETT, JAMES L.
PERSONAL Born 10/07/1917, Little Rock, AR, m, 1956, 7 children **DISCIPLINE** PHILOSOPHY **EDUCATION** Univ Utah, BS, 39, MS, 40; Univ Mich, PhD, 48. **CAREER** Instr English & speech, Murray High Sch, Utah, 39-40; instr sec educ, Univ Utah, 40-41, 42-43, from instr to prof philos, 43-44, 46-55; regional dir, Great Bks Found, 55-57, pres, 58-59; lectr philos, Univ Mich, 57-58; prof philos & pres, Western Wash State Col, 59-64; PROF EDUC, UNIV CALIF, BERKELEY, 64-, Vis assoc prof philos, Columbia Univ, 51-52; mem, Res Adv Coun, 61-64, chmn, 63-64; assoc dir, Univ Calif Studies Ctr UK & Ireland, 72-74. **MEMBERSHIPS** Am Philos Asn. **RESEARCH** Aesthetics; philosophy of literature and education; logic of language. **SELECTED PUBLICATIONS** Auth, Jung,Carl,Gustav 'Psychology of Religion and Synchronicity', J Amer Acad Rel, Vol 0061, 93. **CONTACT ADDRESS** Sch of Educ, Univ of Calif, 1501 Tolman Hall, Berkeley, CA, 94720-1671.

JARRETT, JON
DISCIPLINE PHILOSOPHY **EDUCATION** IA State Univ, BS, 75; Cornell Univ, MS, 77; Univ Chicago, PhD, 83. **CAREER** Assoc prof, Univ IL at Chicago. **RESEARCH** Philos of sci; logic; metaphysics; epistemology. **SELECTED PUBLICATIONS** Auth, Bell's Theorem: A Guide to the Implications, Philos Consequences Quantum, 89. **CONTACT ADDRESS** Philos Dept, Univ Illinois Chicago, S Halsted St, PO Box 705, Chicago, IL, 60607.

JARVIE, IAN CHARLES
PERSONAL Born 07/08/1937, South Shields, England, m, 1962, 2 children **DISCIPLINE** PHILOSOPHY, ANTHROPOLOGY **EDUCATION** Univ London, BS, 58, PhD(philos), 61. **CAREER** Lectr philos, Univ Hong Kong, 62-66; chmn dept, 76-79, PROF PHILOS, YORK UNIV, 67-. **MEMBERSHIPS** Royal Anthrop Inst; Brit Soc Philos Sci; Soc Cinema Studies. **RESEARCH** Philosophy of the social sciences; anthropological theory; movies. **SELECTED PUBLICATIONS** Auth, Shared Pleasures--A History of Movie Presentation in the United States, Hist J Film Radio and Television, Vol 0014, 94. **CONTACT ADDRESS** Dept of Philos, York Univ, Downsview, ON, M3P 1P3.

JASANOFF, SHEILA S.
PERSONAL Born 02/15/1944, Calcutta, India, m, 1968, 2 children **DISCIPLINE** LAW; SCIENCE & TECHNOLOGY POLICY **EDUCATION** Harvard Univ, AB, 64, PhD, 73, JD, 76; Univ Bonn, MA, 66. **CAREER** Assoc, Bracken Selig & Baram, 76-78; res asst to sr res asst, 78-84, assoc prof, 84-89, prof, 90-98, Cornell Univ, 78-98; prof, Harvard Univ, 98-; res scholar, Italy, Rockefeller Found, 96. **HONORS AND AWARDS** Distinguished Achievement Award, Soc Risk Anal, 92; Don K Price Book Award, 98. **MEMBERSHIPS** Mass Bar; Amer Asn Advan Sci; Soc Stud Sci, Sigma XI **RESEARCH** Law, science, and technology; Science and public policy; Comparative politics of science and technology. **SELECTED PUBLICATIONS** Auth, Bridging the Two Cultures of Risk Analysis, Risk Analysis, 93; ed, Learning From Disaster: Risk Management After Bhopal, Univ Penn Press, 94; coed, Handbook of Science and Technology Studies, Sage Publ, 95; auth, Science at the Bar: Law, Science, and Technology in America, Harvard Univ Press, 95; Is Science Socially Constructed--And Can It Still Inform Public Policy, Science and Engineering Ethics, 96; Research Subpoenas and the Sociology of Knowledge, Law and Contemporary Problems, 96; NGOs and the Environment: From Knowledge to Action, Third World Quart, 97; ed, Comparative Science and Technology Policy, Cheltenham Gos UK, 97; auth, Civilization and Madness: The Great BSE Scare of 1996, Public Understanding of Science, 97; coauth, Conversations with the Community: AAAS at the Millennium, Science, 97. **CONTACT ADDRESS** John F Kennedy School of Govt, Harvard Univ, 79 John F. Kennedy St, Cambridge, MA, 02138. **EMAIL** sheila_jasanoff@harvard.edu

JAY, STEWART
PERSONAL Born 06/27/1950, Havre, MT **DISCIPLINE** LAW, PHILOSOPHY **EDUCATION** Georgetown Univ, AB, 73; Harvard Univ, JD, 76. **CAREER** Law clerk to Judge George L Hart Jr, US Dist Ct, Washington, DC, 76-77 & Chief Justice Warren Burger, US Supreme Ct, 77-78; asst prof law, Univ NC, 78-80; ASSOC PROF LAW, UNIV WASH, 81-, Vis Prof, Sch Law, Univ Tex, 80. **RESEARCH** Philosophy of law; Federal jurisdiction; civil procedure. **SELECTED PUBLICATIONS** Auth, Tourism in Southeast-Asia, Bull of the Sch of Oriental and African Stud-Univ London, Vol 0056, 93; No Money, no Honey--A Study of Street Traders and Prostitutes in Jakarta, Bull of the Sch of Oriental and African Stud-Univ London, Vol 0056, 93; The Original Misunderstanding--The English, the Americans and the Dialectic of Federalist Jurisprudence, Buffalo Law Rev, Vol 0041, 93; Society and Exchange in Nias, Bull Sch Oriental and African Stud-Univ London, Vol 0056, 93; Classical Dance and Theater in South-East Asia, Bull Sch of Oriental and African Stud-Univ London, Vol 0057, 94; Servants of Monarchs and Lords--The Advisory Role of Early English Judges, Amer J Legal Hist, Vol 0038, 94; Anthropology, Art and Aesthetics, Bull Sch of Oriental and African Stud-Univ London, Vol 0057, 94; Women and Culture--Between Malay Adat and Islam, Bull Sch of Oriental and African Stud-Univ London, Vol 0057, 94; Hanging Without a Rope--Narrative Experience in Colonial and Postcolonial Karoland, Bull Sch Oriental and African Stud-Univ London, Vol 0058, 95; Zapin--Folk-Dance of the Malay World, Bull of the Sch of Oriental and African Stud-Univ London, Vol 0058, 95; in the Realm of the Diamond-Queen--Marginality in an Out-Of-The-Way Place, Bull Sch Oriental and African Stud-Univ London, Vol 0058, 95. **CONTACT ADDRESS** Sch of Law, Univ of Wash, 1100 N E Campus Pky, Seattle, WA, 98195-6605.

JEAL, ROY R.
PERSONAL Born 06/28/1952, Vancouver, BC, Canada, m, 1972, 3 children **DISCIPLINE** BIBLICAL STUDIES **EDUCATION** Univ Sheffield, PhD, 90. **CAREER** Assoc prof, William & Catherine Booth Coll, 95-. **MEMBERSHIPS** Can Soc of Bibl Studies; Soc of Bibl Lit. **RESEARCH** New Testament; Paul the Apostle; Critical Method. **SELECTED PUBLICATIONS** Auth, A Strange Style of Expression, Ephesians 1:23, Filologia Neotestamentaria, 97. **CONTACT ADDRESS** William & Catherine Booth Col, 447 Webb Pl, Winnipeg, MB, R3B 2P2. **EMAIL** jeal@mb.sympatico.ca

JEFFERIES, CHARLOTTE S.
PERSONAL Born 03/08/1944, McKeesport, PA, s **DISCIPLINE** LAW **EDUCATION** Howard U, BS 1966; Rollins Coll, postgrad 1967; Duquesne Univ Sch of Law, JD 1980. **CAREER** Seminole Co FL, teacher 1966-67; OIC of Erie, dir of couns 1967-70; Urban Coalition of RI, health planner 1970-71; Student Serv OIC of RI, dir 1971-72; Career Develop Brown Univ, assoc dir 1973-77; Neighborhood Legal Serv McKeesport, legal intern 1978-79; Office of US Attorney Dept of Justice, law clerk 1979-80; Honorable Donald E Ziegler Judge US Dist Ct Western Dist of PA, law clerk 1980-81; Horty Springer & Mattern PC, partner, 1981-. **HONORS AND AWARDS** Aptmt law clerk Office of US Attorney 1979; appellate moot court bd Duquesne Univ 1979-80; Outstanding Student of the Year Black Amer Law Student Assoc Duquesne Univ Chap 1980; Richard Allen Awd Outstanding Civic contributions 1980; chmn Merit Selection Panel US Magistrates Western Dist of PA 1987, 1988. **MEMBERSHIPS** Mem Delta Sigma Theta Inc; mem Amer Natl PA and Allegheny Bar Assocs; mem Homer S Brown Law Assoc, Soc of Hospital Attorneys; city councilperson Cityof Duquesne; mem YWCA of McKeesport; mem NAACP, Howard Univ Alumni Club; Allegheny County Air Pollution, advisory com, municipal advisory comm, mon valley commission; Natl Health Lawyers Assn. **CONTACT ADDRESS** Horty Springer & Mattern PC, 4614 Fifth Ave, Pittsburgh, PA, 15213.

JEFFERS, CLIFTON R.
PERSONAL Born 02/08/1934, Roxboro, NC, m **DISCIPLINE** LAW **EDUCATION** TN State Univ, AB (magna cum laude) 1956; Hastings Coll Law Univ CA, JD 1964. **CAREER** State of CA, state deputy atty, 1964-69; US Dept HUD, reg admin, 1969-76; State of CA, chief asst state pub defender, 1976-84; JAMES & JEFFERS, SR PARTNER, currently. **HONORS AND AWARDS** Outstanding Pres Awd NAACP 1967, 1969; Amer Jurisprudence Awd; US Dept HUD Equal Empl Oppt Awd; US Dept HUD Cert of Fair Housing Achvmt; NAACP Meritorious Serv Awds; guest lectr in Criminology Univ of CA Berkeley; Outstanding Performance Awd HUD; commendations San Francisco bd of supervisors; Certificate of Honor San Francisco bd of supervisors; guest lecturer Stanford Univ Law School; guest lecturer, Univ of Southern CA School of Law. **MEMBERSHIPS** Mem Natl, CA, San Francisco Bar Assns; Charles Houston Bar Assn; bd of dir Bar Assn of SF 1984-; bd dirs Lawyers Club of San Francisco 1981-82; mem Amer Judicature Soc; pres SF NAACP 1966-69; bd dir Amer Civil Liberties Union of No CA 1969-73; SF Coun of Chs 1967-72; SF Econ Oppt Coun 1967-68; founding president William Hastie Lawyers Assn; bd dir Frederick Douglas Haynes Gardens; gen counsel 3rd Baptist Ch; bd dir CA Rural Legal Assistance Found; founding mem San Francisco Black Leadership Forum; trustee 3rd Bapt Ch; bd dir NAACP; bd of dir First Dis-

trict Appellate Project; co-founder, State Bar Standing Comm on Legal Services to Criminal Defendants; mem, CA Assn of Black Lawyers; co-founder and dir Third Baptist Gardens, Inc.; mem Afro-Amer Agenda Council. **CONTACT ADDRESS** James & Jeffers, 870 Market St, Ste 1200, San Francisco, CA, 94102.

JEFFERSON, M. IVORY
PERSONAL Born 09/10/1924, Logan, WV, w **DISCIPLINE** LAW, THEOLOGY **EDUCATION** Attended, Univ of So CA, Univ of Manila; Emmanus Bible Sch, grad; Robert H Terrell Sch of Law, LLB LLD 1950. **CAREER** Manpower Commn & Housing Div of Newport News Ofc of Human Affrs, consult in field of pastoral counseling; Sixth Mt Zion Baptist Temple, Hampton, VA, pastor, 1966-96, pastor emeritus, 1996; Richmond Virginia Seminary, professor of systematic theology, 1990-. **HONORS AND AWARDS** Authority in fields of pastoral counseling, taxation and domestic relations. **MEMBERSHIPS** Admitted to VA Bar 1951; admitted to US Supreme Ct Bar 1956; licensed & ordained in Gospel Ministry 1961 1963; moderator Tidewater Peninsula Bapt Assn; legal adv Progressive Natl Baptist Conv; mem validating Comm for the Fund of Renewal Amer Bapt Ch Inc; consult Office of Offender Aid & Restoration Newport News; chairman, Riverside Regional Medical Center Clergy Relations, 1990-; board member, Peninsula AIDS Foundation, 1988-; member, Peninsula Crime Line, 1988-; Peninsula Aids Foundation, chairman of bd, 1994-; Peninsula Crime Line, pres, 1995-. **CONTACT ADDRESS** Sixth Mt Zion Bapt Temple, 2003 Kecoughtan Rd, Hampton, VA, 23661.

JEFFERSON, OVERTON C.
PERSONAL Port Arthur, TX, m **DISCIPLINE** LAW **EDUCATION** Xavier U, New Orleans, AB 1949; NC Cntrl U, JD; NY Univ Sch Law, LLM. **CAREER** Houston Legal Found, central office dir 1985; TX Southern Univ School of Law, asst prof 1953-58. **CONTACT ADDRESS** 609 Fannin Ave, Ste 1909, Houston, TX.

JEFFREY, RICHARD C.
PERSONAL Born 08/05/1926, Boston, MA, m, 1955, 2 children **DISCIPLINE** PHILOSOPHY **EDUCATION** Univ Chicago, MA, 52; Princeton Univ, PhD(philos), 58. **CAREER** Asst prof elec engr, Mass Inst Technol, 59-60; asst prof philos, Stanford Univ, 60-64; Vis mem math, Inst Advan Studies, 63; vis assoc prof philos, Princeton Univ, 64; assoc prof, City Col New York, 64-67; prof, Univ Pa, 67-74; PROF PHILOS, PRINCETON UNIV, 74-. **MEMBERSHIPS** Am Philos Asn; Asn Symbolic Logic; Philos Sci Asn; Am Acad Arts & Scis. **RESEARCH** Decision theory; probability theory; logic. **SELECTED PUBLICATIONS** Auth, The Logic of Decision, 65 & 82 & Formal Logic: Its Scope and Limits, 67, 81, 91, McGraw; co-ed (with Rudolf Carnap), Studies in Inductive Logic and Probability, Vol 1, 71, Vol 2, 80; coauth, Computability and Logic, Cambridge Univ, 74, 80, 89; Probability and the Art of Judgment, 92. **CONTACT ADDRESS** Dept of Philosophy, Princeton Univ, Princeton, NJ, 08544. **EMAIL** dickjeff@princeton.edu

JEGSTRUP, ELSEBET
PERSONAL Born 05/17/1937, Copenhagen, Denmark **DISCIPLINE** POLITICAL PHILOSOPHY **EDUCATION** Loyola Univ Chicago, PhD, 92. **CAREER** Asst prof of Philos, Augusta State Univ, 93-. **MEMBERSHIPS** Am Philos Asn; Soc Phenomenol & Existential Philos; Int Asn Philos & Lit; Kierkegaard Soc. **RESEARCH** Kierkegaard; Political philosophy; Contemporary continental philosophy; Plato. **SELECTED PUBLICATIONS** Auth A Questioning of Justice: Kieregaard, the Postmodern Critique and Political Theory, Political Theory, 95; Kieregaard on Tragedy: the Aporias of Interpretation, Philos Today, 96; rev Kieregaard in Post/Modernity, Tchg Philos, 98; rev Becoming a Self: A Reading of Kierkegaard's Concluding Unscientific Postscript, Tchg Philos, 98. **CONTACT ADDRESS** Dept of Polit Sci & Philos, Augusta State Univ, Augusta, GA, 30904. **EMAIL** jegstrup@aug.edu

JENEMANN, ALBERT HARRY
PERSONAL Born 08/16/1927, Philadelphia, PA **DISCIPLINE** PHILOSOPHY, THEOLOGY **EDUCATION** Spring Hill Col, AB, 54; Boston Col, STL, 61; Gregorian Univ Rome, PhL, 67, PhD(philos), 69. **CAREER** Instr math, Loyola High Sch, Baltimore, Md, 54-57, instr philos, Loyola Col, Baltimore, Md, 62-63; from instr to asst prof, Wheeling Col, 63-66, from asst prof to assoc prof, 69-74, super, Jesuit Commun, 70-74, chmn dept, 73-74; assoc prof philos, St Joseph's Univ, PA, 74-, chm dept philos, 74-80; ordained Jesuit priest, 60; mem bd trustees, Loyola Col, Md, 72-78 & Wheeling Col, 74-82; Ethics Comm, St Agnes Hosp, Philadelphia, 76-; ed, Jesuit Philos Asn Ann Proc, 77-80; dir Faith-Justice Inst, 80-83; VP Student Life, 85-89. **HONORS AND AWARDS** Alpha Sigma Nu (Honorary), 82; Barbelin Award, SJU, 86; Greek Advisor of the Year, SJU, 97. **MEMBERSHIPS** Am Cath Philos Asn (pres, Philadelphia Chap, 80-81); Am Philos Asn; Jesuit Philos Asn (secytreas, 77-80, pres, 93-94). **RESEARCH** Medical ethics; French existentialism; contemporary scholasticism. **SELECTED PUBLICATIONS** Auth, The Political Freedom of John Stuart Mill, Gregorian Univ, 69; ed, An Institutional Profile of Wheeling College (2 vols), Wheeling Col, 71; co-ed, Hunger and the American Conscience, St Joseph's Col, 76; auth, Philosophy and the Right to Food, Int Symp Hunger, 8/76; auth, Medical Decisions: Ethical and Economic Dimensions, Quality Assurance and Utilization Rev, Feb 87; Multiple Pregnancy, Confidentiality, Discontinuing Treatment, etc, Proc JPA, Feb 95; coauth, Application of Medical and Surgical Interventions Near the End of Life, J of Am Col of Cardiology, April 98. **CONTACT ADDRESS** St Joseph's Univ, 5600 City Ave, Philadelphia, PA, 19131-1395. **EMAIL** ajeneman@sju.edu

JENKINS, JOHN
DISCIPLINE PHILOSOPHY **EDUCATION** Univ Notre Dame, BA, 76, MA, 78; Jesuit Sch of Theol at Berkley, Mdiv, 88; Oxford Univ, Bphil, 87, STL, 88, Dphil, 89. **CAREER** Assoc prof. **RESEARCH** Medieval philosophy; philosophical theology; Aristotle. **SELECTED PUBLICATIONS** Auth, Aquinas on the Veracity of the Intellect, J Philos, 91; Yearly, Aquinas, and Comparative Method, J Relig Ethics, 93; Good and the Object of Natural Inclinations in St. Thomas Aquinas, Medieval Philos Theol, 93; Expositions of the Text: Aquinas's Aristotelian Commentaries, Medieval Philos Theol, 96; Knowledge and Faith in Thomas Aquinas, 97. **CONTACT ADDRESS** Philosophy Dept, Univ of Notre Dame, 336/7 O'Shaughnessy, Notre Dame, IN, 46556. **EMAIL** jenkins.1@nd.edu

JENSEN, DEBRA J.
PERSONAL Born 07/29/1953, Wetaskiwin, AB, Canada, 2 children **DISCIPLINE** PHILOSOPHY OF RELIGION **EDUCATION** Univ Calgary, BA, 86, MA, 89; Univ Toronto, PhD, 95. **CAREER** Sessional instr, Relig Stud, Univ Calgary, 93-96; Tenurable Instr, Relig Stud, Mount Royal Col, 96-. **HONORS AND AWARDS** Judith Sloman Mem Award Womens Stud & Eng, Univ Calgary, 84 & 85; Lizzie Arthur Russell Theosophical Scholar, 87-88; Grad Asst Res Univ Calgary, 88-89; Special Entrance fel, 90; Soc Sci & Hum Res Coun Can Doctoral fel, 90-93; Soc Sci & Hum Res Can Post-doctoral fel, 95-96. **MEMBERSHIPS** Am Acad Relig; Can Soc Stud Relig; Gender Inst-Univ Calgary; Mount Royal Col Fac Asn; Asn Transpersonal Psychol; Soc Phenomenol & Existentialist Philos. **RESEARCH** Nature of religion, especially philosophy and psychology of religion; religious experience, especially mysticism; women and religion. **SELECTED PUBLICATIONS** Auth, Soteriology From a Christian and Hindu Perspective, Jour of Dharma, 89; Presentation on Death, Dying and the Regeneration of Life, The Multi-Faith Gathering: Where Traditions Meet, Calgary, 96; Self, Identity and Gender in the Life and Work of Simone Weil, Grail: An Ecumenical Jour, 96; Florence Nightingales Mystical Vision and Social Action, Scottish Jour Relig Stud, 98. **CONTACT ADDRESS** Humanities Dept, Mount Royal Col, 4825 Richard Rd SW, Calgary, AB, T3E 6K6. **EMAIL** djensen@mtroyal.ab.ca

JENSEN, GORDON A.
PERSONAL Born 02/09/1956, Camrose, AB, Canada, m, 1979, 2 children **DISCIPLINE** THEOLOGY **EDUCATION** Univ Alberta, BA, 80; Lutheran Theol Sem SK, MDiv, 84; St Michael's Coll Toronto, PhD, 92. **CAREER** Pastor, St Olaf Lutheran Church, Swift Current Can, 84-88; PASTOR, Armene Lutheran Parish, Armena, Can, 92-. **HONORS AND AWARDS** Governor Gold Medal at Univ of St Michael's Coll, 92. **MEMBERSHIPS** AAR; Can Soc for the Study of Rel; Can Theol Soc. **RESEARCH** Luther; Contextual Theologies. **SELECTED PUBLICATIONS** Auth, The Christology of Luther's Theology of the Cross, Consesus: A Can Lutheran J of Theol, 97; A Reluctant Denomination, Practice of Ministry in Can, 98; At a Fork in the Road: Potential Paths for the Church in the 21st Century, Consesus: A Can Lutheran J of Theol, forthcoming; coauth, The Story of Jesus, 93. **CONTACT ADDRESS** Box 7, Armena, AB, T0B 0G0. **EMAIL** alparish@telusplanet.net

JENSEN, TIM
PERSONAL Edmore, MI, m, 2 children **DISCIPLINE** RELIGIONS OF ASIA **EDUCATION** Dana Col, BA, 66;Univ Chicago, MA, 70, PhD, 76. **CAREER** Instr, Mary Washington Col, 72-78; instr, Sturt Col of Advan Educ, Adelaide, S Australia, 78-82; instr, Univ Nebr, Omaha. **HONORS AND AWARDS** Off of Educ grant, 73. **RESEARCH** Christianity. **SELECTED PUBLICATIONS** Published in the areas of Hinduism and Guddhism; published an article on Danish immigration to the U.S. and Canada. **CONTACT ADDRESS** Univ Nebr, Omaha, Omaha, NE, 68182.

JERIN, ROBERT A.
DISCIPLINE LAW AND JUSTICE **EDUCATION** Univ New Haven, BS; FL State Univ, MS; Sam Houston State Univ, PhD, 87 **CAREER** Fac, N Ga Col, Salem State Col, and Appalachian State Univ; chr Law and Justice Dept, Endicott Col. **RESEARCH** Restorative justice and crime prevention. **SELECTED PUBLICATIONS** Auth, articles in the American Journal of Police and Criminal Justice Policy Review; chapters published in edited volumes on Media and Crime, Crime in the 21st Century, Crime Victims Services and the Juvenile Justice System. **CONTACT ADDRESS** Endicott Col, 376 Hale St, Beverly, MA, 01915.

JESSE, JENNIFER G.
PERSONAL Born 01/19/1959, Akron, OH, m, 1991 **DISCIPLINE** RELIGIOUS STUDIES **EDUCATION** Kent State Univ, BA, 79; Butler Univ, MA, 87; Christian Theol Sem, MDiv, 87; Univ Chicago, PhD, 97. **CAREER** Adjunct prof, St. Xavier Univ, 97-. **MEMBERSHIPS** Am Acad of Relig; Highlands Inst for Am Relig and Philos Thought. **RESEARCH** Postliberal theology; William Blake. **SELECTED PUBLICATIONS** Auth, "Radical Empiricism and the Holographic Model of Reality," 97; "Postliberal Theology in the Valley of Dry Bones," in Encounter, 97; "Mythic Logic: Theological Implications of a Melandean Epistemology," 93; "A Process Perspective of Revelation: A Nonfoundational Epistemology," in Encounter, 87. **CONTACT ADDRESS** 12207 Maple Ave, Blue Island, IL, 60406-1027. **EMAIL** jdjj@enteract.com

JOBES, KAREN H.
PERSONAL Born 07/02/1952, Trenton, NJ, m, 1980 **DISCIPLINE** BIBLICAL STUDIES **EDUCATION** Westminster Theol Sem, Philadelphia, PhD, 95. **CAREER** ASST PROF OF NEW TESTAMENT STUDIES, WESTMONT COL, 96-. **HONORS AND AWARDS** IOSCS Award for Outstanding Paper in Septuagint Res, 95. **MEMBERSHIPS** Inst for Biblical Res; Soc of Biblical Lit; Int Org for Septuagint and Cognate Studies; Evangelical Theol Soc. **RESEARCH** Septuagint; New Testament; biblical Greek. **SELECTED PUBLICATIONS** Auth, Distinguishing the Meaning of Greek Verbs in the Semantic Domain for 'Worship' in Biblical Words and their Meaning: An Introduction to Lexical Semantics, by Moises Silva, 2nd ed, Zondervan, 94; A Comparative Syntactic Analysis of the Greek Versions of Daniel: A Test Case for New Methodology, BIOSCS 28, fall 95 (recipient of the 1995 IOSCS Int award); review, The Morphology of Biblical Greek, William D. Mounce, Zondervan, 94, in JETS 39, 4, 96; For Such a Time As This: A Defining Moment in Christian Ministry, Faith and Mission 14, fall 96; The Alpha-Text of Esther: Its Character & Relationship to the Masorectic Text, SBLS 153: Atlanta: Scholars Press, 96; review, Reclaiming the Bible for the Church, ed C. E. Braaten and R. W. Jenson, Eerdmans, 95, in Ashland Theol J XXIX, 97; review of Whoredom: God's Unfaithful Wife in Biblical Theology, Raymond Ortlund, Eerdmans, 96, in Themelios 23, 2, Feb 98; How an Assassination Changed the Greek Texts of Esther, ZAW, 98; review of The Bible for Everyday Life, ed George Carey, Eerdmans, 96, in Ashland Theol J, forthcoming; NIV Application Commentary: Esther, Zondervan, in press. **CONTACT ADDRESS** Dept of Relig Studies, Westmont Col, 955 La Paz Road, Santa Barbara, CA, 93108. **EMAIL** jobes@westmont.edu

JOBLING, DAVID
DISCIPLINE JEWISH BIBLE, OLD TESTAMENT **EDUCATION** Union Theolog Sem, PhD, 72. **CAREER** Asst prof, assoc prof, Old Testament, Louisville Presby Theol Sem, 70-77; prof Old Testament St Andrews Col, 78- . **HONORS AND AWARDS** Pres, Can Soc of Bibl Stud, 92-93. **MEMBERSHIPS** SBL; AAR; Soc for Old Testament Stud. **RESEARCH** Idealogical readings of the Bible. **SELECTED PUBLICATIONS** Auth, The Sense of Biblical Narrative: Structural Analysis of Biblical Texts, 2 v, Shefffield Academic, 78; ed, Semeia: An Experimental Journal of Biblical Criticism, v. 54, 59; ed, The Bible and the Politics of Exegesis, Pilgrim, 91; ed. On Story-Telling, Polebridge, 91; coauth, The Postmodern Bible, Yale, 95; auth, I Samuel, Liturgical, 98. **CONTACT ADDRESS** St Andrews Col, 1121 College Dr, Saskatoon, SK, S7N 0W3. **EMAIL** jobling@sask.usrste.ca

JOHANSON, HERBERT A.
DISCIPLINE CONST LAW, AND LEGAL HISTORY **EDUCATION** Columbia Univ, AB, 55, MA, 61, PhD, 65; NY Law Sch, LLB, 60. **CAREER** Ernest F. Hollings prof Const Law, Univ of SC. **SELECTED PUBLICATIONS** Auth, casebk on Amer legal and const hist & textbk on the hist of criminal justice. **CONTACT ADDRESS** School of Law, Univ of S. Carolina, Law Center, Columbia, SC, 29208. **EMAIL** Hjohnson@law.law.sc.edu

JOHN, EILEEN
DISCIPLINE PHILOSOPHY **EDUCATION** Univ MI, PhD. **CAREER** Dept Philos, Univ Louisville **RESEARCH** The role of fiction in prompting moral and conceptual knowledge. **SELECTED PUBLICATIONS** Auth, Subtlety and Moral Vision in Fiction, Philos and Lit. **CONTACT ADDRESS** Dept of Philos, Univ Louisville, 2301 S 3rd St, Louisville, KY, 40292. **EMAIL** e0john01@ulkyvm.louisville.edu

JOHN, P.M.
PERSONAL Born 06/17/1929, Kerala, India, w, 1965, 2 children **DISCIPLINE** RELIGIOUS STUDIES **EDUCATION** Seramapore Col, BD, 59; SMU, STM, 61; Drew Univ, MA, 72, PhD, 73. **CAREER** Instr, 65-70, Lafayett Col; Asst prof and instr, 70-73, Northeastern Univ; Assoc and asst prof, 77-80, Pahlavi Univ; Adjunct, 81-90, Univ of Lowell, Simmons Col; Assoc and asst prof, 90-98, Framingham St Col. **HONORS AND AWARDS** Steering Cmm, NGO Forum Working Group at Habitat II, UN Conf at Istanbul, 96; Institute:Infusing Asian Studies into the Undergrad Curriculum, Univ Hawaii & E/West Ctr, 95; Amer Assoc of State Col and Univ, 91; Lyceum Lec-

ture: I Ching for Timely Decisions: Ancient Chin Phil Revisited, Framingham, 91. **MEMBERSHIPS** Amer Acad of Relig; Hegel Soc of Amer; Amer Philosophy Assn; Third World Scholars Consortium **RESEARCH** Global Thresholds in Philosophy, Education, Business and Goverance Issues in Third World Cultures. **SELECTED PUBLICATIONS** Auth, Teacher as...Hermeneut of Faith, Religion & Soc, Indian Journal of Theology, 70; auth, Issues of Religion in Early Marx, 70; auth, The World of the I Ching, A chapter in Echoes of the Wordless Word, 73; auth, On Interpreting Myths, 75; auth, Marx on Alienation: Elements of a Critique of Capitalism and Communism, 76; auth, Hindu Dharma, 79; auth, Five editorials in TWIST: A Third World Forum, 85-89; auth, Human Rights, 87; auth, Between Two Cultures, 95. **CONTACT ADDRESS** 27 Hickory Cliff Rd, Newton, MA, 02464. **EMAIL** pmjohn@twist.org

JOHNNSON, THOMAS F.
PERSONAL Born 06/01/1943, Detroit, MI, m, 1965, 3 children **DISCIPLINE** RELIGION **EDUCATION** Wayne St Univ, BPh, 65; Fuller Theo Sem, Mdiv, 68; Princeton Sem, ThM, 69; Duke Univ, PhD, 79. **CAREER** VP Acad Affairs, Sioux Falls Col, 81-83; Prof, N Amer Baptist Sem, 83-88; Pres, Univ of Sioux Falls, 89-97; Int Pres, George Fox Univ, 97-98; VP/Dean Western Evangelical Sem, 98-. **MEMBERSHIPS** AAR; Soc of Bibl Lit **RESEARCH** Johannine Studies; Biblical Theology; Christian Mysticism **SELECTED PUBLICATIONS** Auth, 1, 2 and 3 John, New Intl Bibl Comm, Hendrickson Pub, 93. **CONTACT ADDRESS** Western Ev Sem, George Fox Univ, 12753 SW 68th St, Portland, OR, 97223. **EMAIL** tjohnson@georgefox.edu

JOHNS, LOREN L.
PERSONAL Born 03/08/1955, Goshen, IN, m, 1978, 2 children **DISCIPLINE** THEOLOGY **EDUCATION** Princeton Theol Sem, PhD, 98. **CAREER** Theol book editor, Herald Press, 85-89; ASSOC PROF, RELIGION, BLUFFTON COL, 93-; chair, 98-99. **HONORS AND AWARDS** Outstanding grad bibl studies, Associated Mennonite Bibl Sem, 84. **MEMBERSHIPS** Soc of Bibl Lit; Mennonite Hist Soc. **RESEARCH** Apocalypse of John, Dead Sea Scrolls. **CONTACT ADDRESS** Bluffton Col, 280 W College Ave, Bluffton, OH, 45817. **EMAIL** johnsl@bluffton.edu

JOHNSON, BEN
PERSONAL Born 06/29/1937, m, 1960, 4 children **DISCIPLINE** THEOLOGY **EDUCATION** Gustavus Adolphus College, BA 59; Lutheran Sch Theol, Mdiv 61; Harvard Univ, ThD 66; Oxford Univ, 71-72. **CAREER** Wittenberg Univ Hamma Sch Theo, prof, dean, 65-78; Trinity Lutheran Sem, prof 78-80; Salem Lutheran Church MN, Sr pastor, 80-92; St Cloud State Univ, adj fac, 87-92; Concordia Univ Irvine, adj fac, 94-; Lutheran Bible Inst, VP, prof, 92-96; Concordia Univ, pres since 96, appointed as first Dir of the LBI House of Stud, 98-. **HONORS AND AWARDS** Danforth Fel; Soc Val Higher Edu Fel; ATS Fel; Concordia Bk Awd. **MEMBERSHIPS** SBL **RESEARCH** Unusual Religious Experiences **SELECTED PUBLICATIONS** Auth, The Didache and Christian Ethics, Let Christ Be Christ: Theology Ethics and World Religions in the Two Kingdoms, essays in honor of Charles Manske on the occasion of his sixty-fifth birthday, forth coming; How We Got the Bible, Church and Life, 98; Theology and the Bible, F O C L Point, 94; Built on a Rock, pub and preface, St Cloud MN, 82. **CONTACT ADDRESS** LBI House of Studies, Concordia Univ, California, 5321 University Dr., Suite H, Irvine, CA, 92612. **EMAIL** LBIC@aol.com

JOHNSON, CALIPH
PERSONAL Born 10/03/1938, St. Joseph, LA, m **DISCIPLINE** LAW **EDUCATION** Univ of Maryland, BA 1964; San Jose State U, MA 1968; Univ of San Francisco Sch of Law, JD 1972; Georgetown Univ Law Ctr, LlM 1973. **CAREER** Thurgood Marshall School of Law, Southwest Inst for Equal Employment, Thurgood Marshall School of Law TX Southern Univ, dir 1975-78; Office of Gen Counsel Equal Employment Opportunity Commn, appellate atty 1973-75; Inst for Public Interest Represent, atty 1972-73; Oakland Citizens Com for Urban Renewal, exec dir 1970-72; City of Oakland CA, admin analyst 1970-72; Univ of Miaduguri Nigeria, consultant 1978-80; Office of Lawyer Training Legal Serv Corp , advocacy trainer 1978-80; EEOC, hearing examiner 1979-80; Title VII Project Natl Bar Assn Bd of Dir Gulf Coast Legal Found, faculty. **MEMBERSHIPS** Mem commn on law office exon Am Bar Assn; labor law sect Nat Bar Assn; civil litigation com Fed Bar Assn; civil procedure & clin sec assn of Am Law Sch; Grad Fellowship Inst for Pub Int Rep Georgetown Univ Law Ctr 1972-73; a response to crises of enforcing fair employment Houston Lawyer 1975; **SELECTED PUBLICATIONS** Book review Let Them Be Judges Howard Univ Law Jour 1980; course material on fair empl lit TX So Univ 1976; integrated clinical curr module TX So Univ & HEW 1978-80; teamsters v US Impact on Seniority Relief TX SoNBA Law Rev 1979. **CONTACT ADDRESS** 3201 Wheeler, Houston, TX, 77004.

JOHNSON, CHAS FLOYD
PERSONAL Camden, NJ, m, 1983 **DISCIPLINE** LAW **EDUCATION** Univ of Delaware 1960-61; Howard Univ, BA 1962; Howard Univ Sch of Law, JD 1965. **CAREER** Howard Berg Law Offices, Attorney 1965; US Copyright Office, Attorney 1967-70; Swedish Ministry of Justice Stockholm, Sweden, Attorney 1970; Universal Television, prod coordinator, 1971-74, associate prod, 1974-76, producer, 1976-82, suprvsng prod 1982-, executive producer 1985-. **HONORS AND AWARDS** Emmy Award, Rockford Files, Best TV Drama; Alumni Achvmnt Award Stony Brook Coll Prep, 1979; Outstanding Alumnus Howard Univ Alumni Club of So CA, 1982; Outstanding Alumnus Howard Univ, 1985; LA Area Emmy Award Winner for producing and performing in a KCET/PBS Special "Voices of Our People, A Celebration of Black Poetry" 1981; 3 Emmy Nominations for: Rockford Files, 1978-79, 1979-80, Magnum PI 1982-83, 1983-84; City of LA, Commendations, 1982, 1993; CA State Legislature, Commendation, 1982; CA State Senate, Commendation, 1982; Hawaii State Senate, Commendation, 1988; Hawaii House of Representatives, Commendation, 1988; City of Honolulu, Commendation, 1988. **MEMBERSHIPS** Screen Actors Guild of America; Producers Guild of America, board of directors; Writers Guild of America; National Academy of Television Arts & Sciences; American Film Institute; Omega Psi Phi; Caucus for Producers, Directors and Writers, 1990-; Crossroads Theatre Arts Academy, 1990; board of directors, Kwanza Foundation, 1985; board of directors, American Independent Video Filmmakers, 1985-90; vice chairman, The Media Forum, 1978-82; Assn of Black Motion Picture and Television Producers, 1980-82. **SELECTED PUBLICATIONS** Production credits include: "Rockford Files," producer, 1974-80; "Bret Maverick," producer, 1981-82; "Magnum PI," co-executive producer, 1982-88; "BL Stryker," co-executive producer, 1988-90; "Revealing Evidence," NBC Movie of the Week, executive producer, 1990; "Quantum Leap," co-executive producer, 1992; "Baa Baa Black Sheep," pilot, producer, 1975; "Hellinger's Law," pilot, producer, 1980-81; "Simon and Simon," pilot, producer, 1980; "Silver Fox," pilot, co-creator, executive producer, 1991; "Rockford Files" Movies for TV, 1994-; author: "The Origins of the Stockholm Protocol," US Copyright Society, 1970; co-author: Black Women in Television, 1990. **CONTACT ADDRESS** Universal TV, 846 North Cahuenga Blvd, Los Angeles, CA, 90038.

JOHNSON, DALE ARTHUR
PERSONAL Born 03/13/1936, Duluth, MN, m, 1958, 3 children **DISCIPLINE** RELIGION **EDUCATION** Colgate Univ, BA, 57; Oxford Univ, BA, 59, MA, 63; Lutheran Sch Theol, BD, 62; Union Theol Sem, NY, ThD, 67. **CAREER** Asst prof relig, Luther Col, 65-69; exchange prof theol, St. John's Univ, Minn, 68-69; asst prof to prof of Church History, Divinity School, Vanderbilt Univ, 69-; dir continuing educ, 73-77; assoc dean, 85-89. **HONORS AND AWARDS** Phi Beta Kappa, Rhodes Scholarship, Albert C. Outler Prize in Ecumenical Church History, 96. **MEMBERSHIPS** Am Soc Church Hist; Am Acad Relig; Conf Brit Studies; Eccles Hist Soc. **RESEARCH** Reformation and modern European church history; 19th-century English religion; religion in America. **SELECTED PUBLICATIONS** Co-ed, Moral Issues and Christian Response, Holt, 71, rev 2nd ed, 76; auth, Between Evangelicalism and a Social Gospel: The Case of Joseph Rayner Stephens, Church Hist, 73; Church and Society in Modern History: Beyond Church and State, J Church & State, 77; Did the Nineteenth Century English Church Fail to Heed the Signs of the Times?, 77 & Pedagogy and Polemic in Modern English Hymns, 79, Hist Mag of Protestant Episcopal Church; The End of the Evidences: A Study in Nonconformist Theological Transition, J United Reformed Church Hist Soc, 79; Popular Apologetics in Late Victorian England: The Work of the Christian Evidence Soc, J Relig Hist, 81; The Methodist Quest for an Educated Ministry, Church Hist, 82; Women in English Religion, 1700-1925, Mellon, 83; Women and Religion in Britain and Ireland: An Annotated Bibliography from the Reformation to 1993, Scarecrow, 95; The Changing Shape of English Nonconformity, 1825-1925, Oxford, 98; co-ed, Moral Issues and Christian Response, Harcourt Brace, rev 6th ed, 98; articles. **CONTACT ADDRESS** Divinity Sch, Vanderbilt Univ, Nashville, TN, 37240. **EMAIL** Dale.A.Johnson@Vanderbilt.edu

JOHNSON, DAVID LAWRENCE
PERSONAL Born 01/25/1941, Minneapolis, MN, m, 1963, 1 child **DISCIPLINE** RELIGION AND PHILOSOPHY OF INDIA, ETHICS AND TECHNOLOGY **EDUCATION** Augsburg Col, AB, 66; Univ Iowa, PhD, 72. **CAREER** Asst prof, 70-76, chmn dept, 78-82, assoc prof humanities, Ind State Univ, Terre Haute, 76-, prof Relig, 82-, adj prof humanities, Rose Hulman Inst Technol, 76 & 78. **MEMBERSHIPS** Am Acad Relig; Asn Asian Studies. **RESEARCH** Modern religious thought, India; religion and politics; technology and human condition. **SELECTED PUBLICATIONS** Auth, The task of relevance: Aurobindo's synthesis of religion and politics, Philos East & West, 10/73; Religious Roots of Nationalism: Aurobindo's Early Political Thought, Mukhopadhyay, Calcutta, 74; Technology, Society and Human Development, Davis Publ, 78 & 82; Indian Thought Between Tradition and the Culture of Technology, D.K. Printworld, 95; Reason and Religion in the Traditions of China and India, The Davies Group Publ, 97. **CONTACT ADDRESS** Dept of Humanities, Indiana State Univ, 210 N 7th St, Terre Haute, IN, 47809-0002. **EMAIL** hujohnso@root.indstate.edu

JOHNSON, EDWARD
PERSONAL Born 12/26/1950, Lincoln, NE **DISCIPLINE** PHILOSOPHY **EDUCATION** Univ Nebr-Lincoln, BA, 72; Princeton Univ, PhD(philos), 76. **CAREER** Asst prof Philos, Univ New Orleans, 76-83, assoc prof Philos, Univ New Orleans, 83-90, prof Philos, 90-, chmn dept, 82-. **HONORS AND AWARDS** Alumni Award for Excellence in Teaching, 84, Outstanding Honors Faculty Member, 90. **MEMBERSHIPS** Am Philos Asn. **RESEARCH** Moral theory, environmental ethics, medical ethics, philos of technology, philos of education. **SELECTED PUBLICATIONS** Contribr, Videotheraphy in Mental Health, Charles C Thomas, 81; Ethics and Animals, Humana Press, 83; Earthbound, Random, 84; Animal Rights and Human Obligations, Prentice-Hall, 89; Encyclopedia of Ethics, Garland, 92; Cambridge Dictionary of Philosophy, Cambridge Univ Press, 95; Nagging Questions: Feminist Ethics in Everyday Life, Rowman and Littlefield, 95; Sex, Love, and Friendship, Rodopi, 97; Human Sexuality, Ashgate, 97; Encyclopedia of Applied Ethics, Academic Press, 97; auth, Animal Liberation versus the Land Ethic, Environ Ethics, 81; Ingoring Persons, Tulane Studies in Philos, 82; (E)Quality Education, Forum for Honors, 88; Contratto e Status Morale, Etica & Animali, 89; Inscrutable Desires, Philosophy of the Social Sciences, 90; Singer's Cookbook, 91; & Carruthers on Consciousness and Moral Status, 91; Between the Species: A Journal of Ethics. **CONTACT ADDRESS** Philos Dept, Univ New Orleans, 2000 Lakeshore Dr, New Orleans, LA, 70148-0001. **EMAIL** rejpl@uno.edu

JOHNSON, ELIZABETH A.
PERSONAL New York, NY, s **DISCIPLINE** THEOLOGY **EDUCATION** Catholic Univer of Amer, PhD, 81. **CAREER** Asst prof, assoc prof, 81-91, Catholic Univ of Amer; prof, distinguished prof of theology, 91- ; Fordham Univer. **HONORS AND AWARDS** Four honorary doctorates; Grawemeyer award; teacher of the year, 98, Fordham; US Catholic Award for promoting the cause of women in the church. **MEMBERSHIPS** AAR; Catholic Theological Soc of Amer; Col Theology Soc; Amer Theological Soc. **RESEARCH** Feminist theology; systematic theology. **SELECTED PUBLICATIONS** Auth, Wisdom Was Made Flesh and Pitched Her Tent Among Us, Reconstructing the Christ Symbol: Essays in Feminist Christology, 93; Does God Play Dice? Divine Providence and Chance, Theological Studies, 96; Turn to the Heavens and the Earth: Retrieval of the Cosmos in Theology, presidential address, CTSA proceedings, 96. **CONTACT ADDRESS** Dept of Theology, Fordham Univ, Bronx, NY, 10458.

JOHNSON, ERNEST L.
PERSONAL Born 08/24/1950, Ferriday, LA, m, 1992 **DISCIPLINE** LAW **EDUCATION** Grambling State University, BS, 1973; Southern University School of Law, JD, 1976. **CAREER** Johnson, Taylor & Thomas, sr partner, 1980-89; Southern University Law Center, professor; Life Savings Bank, chairman of the board, president, currently. **HONORS AND AWARDS** NAACP, National President Leadership Award, 1992; Louis A Martinet Legal Society, Leadership Award, 1991; JK Haynes Education Foundation, The Prestigious Seervice Award, 1990; Southern University Law Center, Earl Warren Fellowship, 1973-76; Scotlandville Jaycees, Scotlandville Man of the Year Award, 1990. **MEMBERSHIPS** Louisiana NAACP, exec vp, 1991-; Louisiana State Bar Association, 1976-; Louis A Martinet Legal Society, 1986-; Project Invest in Black, board of directors; Church Point Ministries Feed a Family, board of directors. **CONTACT ADDRESS** President, Life Savings Bank, 7990 Scenic Hwy, 1st Fl, Baton Rouge, LA, 70807.

JOHNSON, FREDERICK A.
DISCIPLINE PHILOSOPHY **EDUCATION** Ohio State Univ, PhD, 71. **CAREER** Prof. **SELECTED PUBLICATIONS** Auth, pubs on formal logic and philosophy of mathematics. **CONTACT ADDRESS** Philosophy Dept, Colorado State Univ, Fort Collins, CO, 80523.

JOHNSON, GERALDINE ROSS
PERSONAL Born 05/13/1946, Moline, IL, m **DISCIPLINE** LAW **EDUCATION** Augustana Coll, BA 1968, Univ of PA Sch of Social Work, MSW 1974; Univ of IA Coll of Law, JD 1982. **CAREER** Linn Co IA Dept of Soc Svcs, caseworker 1968-69; Children's Serv City of St Louis, intake case worker 1969-70; Get Set Day Care, preschool tchr 1970-72;Franciscan Mental Health Ctr, social worker 1974-78; Davenport Civil Rights Commn, Attorney 1984-86; City of Davenport Legal Dept, atty 1986-. **MEMBERSHIPS** Mem Iowa State Bar Assoc, Scott Co Bar Assoc; mem Sounds of Peace Choral Group 1981-86; mem Davenport Civil Rights Commn 1982-84; bd of dirs Family Resources Inc 1982-; mem Delta Sigma Theta Public Serv Sor Inc 1984-; volunteer United Way 1986; guest speaker Upward Bound, Marycrest Sociology Dept, MeritEmployment Council, Blackhawk Coll Alpha Ctr; mem Tabernacle Baptist Church Moline IL; mem Pulpit Comm 1986. **SELECTED PUBLICATIONS** Survey of sex educ literature on file in the British Library by request 1984. **CONTACT ADDRESS** City of Davenport, City Hall 226 W Fourth St, Davenport, IA, 52801.

JOHNSON, GOLDEN ELIZABETH
PERSONAL Born 03/21/1944, Newark, NJ **DISCIPLINE** LAW **EDUCATION** Douglass Coll, AB 1961-65; Rutgers Newark Sch of Law, JD 1968-71. **CAREER** Hoffman La Roche Inc, gen atty 1977-; Rutgers Law Sch, prof 1976-; Newark Muncpl Ct, judge 1974-77; Hoffmann-La Roche Inc, atty 1974; Comm Leagl Action Wrkshp, proj dir 1972-74; State of NJ, dep atty & gen 1971-72; US Atty Ofc, intern 1970; W Kinney Jr HS, tchr 1969; Newark Legal Serv, intern 1969; Spec Rsrch Lab, microblgst 1965-68. **HONORS AND AWARDS** Comm serv awd Rutgers Law Sch 1972; comm serv awd Donald Tucker Civic Assn 1974; achvmt awd Essex Co Civic Assn 1975; black woman achvmt awd COM-BIN-NATION 1975; life mem Guild Legal Serv; awd Nat Cncl of Negro Women 1975; achvmt awd No Reg of Fedn of Colored Women's Club 1975; oust achvmt NJFedn of Colored Women's Club 1975; achvmt awd Delta Sigma Theta Inc 1975; comm serv awd Newark Title 1 Ctrl Parents Cncl 1975; achvmt awd Neward Sect Nat Cncl of Negro Women 1975; awd of excell Oper PUSH 1975; comm serv awd Roosevelt Homes Housing Proj 1975; achvmt awd Nat Assn of Negro Bus & Professional Women's Clubs 1975; comm serv awd Essex Co Legal Serv 1975; serv awd Newark Housing Cncl Comm 1976; disgshd serv awd Seton Hall Univ 1976; certof apprctnCtrl Ward Girls Club 1976; Oper PUSH Tidewa Women Achvmt Awd 1976; achvmt awd Dr Martin Luther King Jr Comm Ctr 1976; achiev awd Guyton-Callahan Post 152 1976; outsdng Woman of Yr NJ Jaycee-ETTES 1977; hon life mem Zeta Alpha Iota 1977; Alumni Roster of Superior Merit E Side HS 1977;Outstdg Young Woman of Am 1975, 77; gen Couns to Young Dems of NJ. **MEMBERSHIPS** Mem NJ State Bar Assn; Essex Co Bar Assn; Garden State Bar Assn; present mem bd of Gov & exec comm Nat Bar Assn; past pres bd mem Women's Div Nat Bar Assn; bd of tst NJ State Opera; bd of tst & past chmn Newark-Essex Co Legal Serv & Joint Law Reform; bd of dir Ctrl Ward Girls Club; mem NJ Adv Bd US Commn on Civil Rights 1973-77; bd of dir Leaguers Inc; mem NJ Coll of Med & Denistry's Bd of Concerned Citzs 1972-75; NAACP; life mem Nat Cncl of Negro Women; chtr mem Assn of Black Women Lwyrs; mem liaison City of Newark for Essex Co Fed of Dem Women 1977; 100 Women for Integ in Govt; mem Rutgers Newark Sch of Law Alumni Assn. **CONTACT ADDRESS** 555 Mount Prospect Ave, Newark, NJ, 07104.

JOHNSON, GOLDEN ELIZABETH
PERSONAL Born 03/21/1944, Newark, NJ **DISCIPLINE** LAW **EDUCATION** Douglass Coll, AB 1961-65; Rutgers Newark Sch of Law, JD 1968-71. **CAREER** Hoffman La Roche Inc, gen atty 1977-; Rutgers Law Sch, prof 1976-; Newark Muncpl Ct, judge 1974-77; Hoffmann-La Roche Inc, atty 1974; Comm Leagl Action Wrkshp, proj dir 1972-74; State of NJ, dep atty & gen 1971-72; US Atty Ofc, intern 1970; W Kinney Jr HS, tchr 1969; Newark Legal Serv, intern 1969; Spec Rsrch Lab, microblgst 1965-68. **HONORS AND AWARDS** Comm serv awd Rutgers Law Sch 1972; comm serv awd Donald Tucker Civic Assn 1974; achvmt awd Essex Co Civic Assn 1975; black woman achvmt awd COM-BIN-NATION 1975; life mem Guild Legal Serv; awd Nat Cncl of Negro Women 1975; achvmt awd No Reg of Fedn of Colored Women's Club 1975; oust achvmt NJFedn of Colored Women's Club 1975; achvmt awd Delta Sigma Theta Inc 1975; comm serv awd Newark Title 1 Ctrl Parents Cncl 1975; achvmt awd Neward Sect Nat Cncl of Negro Women 1975; awd of excell Oper PUSH 1975; comm serv awd Roosevelt Homes Housing Proj 1975; achvmt awd Nat Assn of Negro Bus & Professional Women's Clubs 1975; comm serv awd Essex Co Legal Serv 1975; serv awd Newark Housing Cncl Comm 1976; disgshd serv awd Seton Hall Univ 1976; certof apprctnCtrl Ward Girls Club 1976; Oper PUSH Tidewa Women Achvmt Awd 1976; achvmt awd Dr Martin Luther King Jr Comm Ctr 1976; achiev awd Guyton-Callahan Post 152 1976; outsdng Woman of Yr NJ Jaycee-ETTES 1977; hon life mem Zeta Alpha Iota 1977; Alumni Roster of Superior Merit E Side HS 1977;Outstdg Young Woman of Am 1975, 77; gen Couns to Young Dems of NJ. **MEMBERSHIPS** Mem NJ State Bar Assn; Essex Co Bar Assn; Garden State Bar Assn; present mem bd of Gov & exec comm Nat Bar Assn; past pres bd mem Women's Div Nat Bar Assn; bd of tst NJ State Opera; bd of tst & past chmn Newark-Essex Co Legal Serv & Joint Law Reform; bd of dir Ctrl Ward Girls Club; mem NJ Adv Bd US Commn on Civil Rights 1973-77; bd of dir Leaguers Inc; mem NJ Coll of Med & Denistry's Bd of Concerned Citzs 1972-75; NAACP; life mem Nat Cncl of Negro Women; chtr mem Assn of Black Women Lwyrs; mem liaison City of Newark for Essex Co Fed of Dem Women 1977; 100 Women for Integ in Govt; mem Rutgers Newark Sch of Law Alumni Assn. **CONTACT ADDRESS** 555 Mount Prospect Ave, Newark, NJ, 07104.

JOHNSON, J. PRESCOTT
PERSONAL Tumalo, OR, m, 1943, 3 children **DISCIPLINE** PHILOSOPHY **EDUCATION** Northwestern Univ, PhD, 59. **CAREER** Inst, Kansas City Col & Bible Sch, 43-45; Asc prof, Bethany Nazarene Col, 49-57; ast prof, Univ Okla, 57-62; prof, 62-86 & prof emer, 86-, Monmouth Col. **MEMBERSHIPS** APA. **RESEARCH** Theory of value; philosophy of religion. **SELECTED PUBLICATIONS** "Spirituality and Community," Jrnl of Speculative Philos, 97; "Beauty of Holiness," Asbury Theol Jrnl, 97. **CONTACT ADDRESS** 1040 E. 3rd Ave., Monmouth, IL, 61462.

JOHNSON, JAMES TURNER
PERSONAL Born 11/02/1938, Crockett Mills, TN, m, 1968, 2 children **DISCIPLINE** RELIGION, RELIGIOUS ETHICS **EDUCATION** Brown Univ, AB, 60; Vanderbilt Univ, BD, 63; Princeton Univ, MA, 67, PhD(Relig), 68. **CAREER** Instr Philos & Relig, Newberry Col, 63-65; lectr Relig, Vassar Col, 68-69; asst prof, 69-77, Univ Res Coun fac fel, 72-73, assoc prof & chairperson dept, 77-82, prof Relig, Rutgers Univ, New Brunswick, 82-, Rockefeller Found Humanities fel, 76-77; Nat Endowment for Humanities grant, 76. **HONORS AND AWARDS** US Inst of Peace grants, 88-89, 90-91; Nat Endowment for Humanities fel, 92-93; Earhart Found grant, 97. **MEMBERSHIPS** Am Acad Relig; Am Soc Christian Ethics; Inst Soc, Ethics & Life Sci; Coun Relig & Int Affairs; AAUP; Am Acad Pol & Soc Science. **RESEARCH** Limitation of war; history of just war thought; religion and international law; comparative religious ethics. **SELECTED PUBLICATIONS** Auth, A Society Ordained by God: English Puritan Marriage Doctrine, Abingdon, 70; The covenant idea and the Puritan view of marriage, J Hist Ideas, 1-2/71; The meaning of noncombatant immunity in the just war/limited war tradition, J Am Acad Relig, 6/71; Toward reconstructing the Jus ad Bellum, Monist, 10/73; ed, Love and Society: Essays in the Ethics of Paul Ramsey, Scholars Press, 74; auth, Natural law as a language for the ethics of war, J Relig Ethics, Fall 75; Ideology, Reason and the Limitation of War: Secular and Religious Concepts, 1200-1740, 75 & Just War Tradition and the Restraint of War, 81, Princeton Univ; Ethics and Public Policy Center; co-ed, Beyond Confrontation, Univ of Michigan, 95; The Holy War Idea in Western and Islamic Tradition, Penn State, 97. **CONTACT ADDRESS** Dept of Religion, Rutgers Univ, 70 Lipman Drive, New Brunswick, NJ, 08901-8525. **EMAIL** jtj@rci.rutgers.edu

JOHNSON, JOHN W.
PERSONAL Born 11/06/1934, Summerfield, LA **DISCIPLINE** LAW **EDUCATION** Georgetown Univ Law Center, LlM 1964; Howard Univ Sch of Law, JD 1962; So Univ Baton Rouge, BA 1957. **CAREER** AT & T, atty 1972; NY Law Sch, law prof 1978-; US Dept of Just Wash, trial lawy 1964-68; OH Bell Tel & Co Cleveland Corp ABA, lawy 1968-72. **MEMBERSHIPS** Nat Bar Assn; NY Bar Assn; OH Bar Assn; DC Bar Assn; LA Bar Assn; World Peace thru Law; Adm to Prac before Supreme Ct of US Sigma Delta Tau Legal Frat Part in LA first "sit in" demonstrn 1960 case reviewed by US Sup Ct Garner V LA. **CONTACT ADDRESS** AT&T, 195 Broadway, New York, NY, 10007.

JOHNSON, JOHNNIE L., JR.
PERSONAL Born 11/01/1946, Nesbitt, MS, m, 1970 **DISCIPLINE** LAW **EDUCATION** Morris Brown Coll, BA 1967; OH Northern Univ, JD 1970. **CAREER** Dept of Justice, asst us atty 1970-73; Equal Employment Oppty Commission, asst reg atty 1973-75, spec asst to comm 1975-78, dir trial team II 1978-81; EEOC, assistant Gen Counsel, 1981-83; director, Legal & Special Pol Div, 1983-84; Director Special Projects, 1984-85; sr trial Attorney, 1985-. **HONORS AND AWARDS** Donnie Delaney Comm Defense Awd 1974; Outstanding Young Man of Amer 1979; participant in "Old Dominion 100 Mile Endurance Run" 1979, Empire State Run Up 1979, 1980, JFK 50 Miler 1980; Marine Corp Marathin 1979, 1980, 1981; Ohio Northern University, College of Law, 16th annual Law Review Symposium, lecturer. **MEMBERSHIPS** Pres, Natl Council of EEOC Locals 216, August 1998-; pres,AFGE Local 2667, August 1998-; pres, Morris Brown Coll Alumni Assoc 1985-92, mediator, DC Mediation Service 1989-; bd of directors, Ohio Northern Univ Law Alumni Assoc 1988-; pres, Mediterranean Villa Cluster Assn l986-; Mediator, Multi-Door Disput Resolutim Center, 1990-; president, BF Jones Bar Association, 1970-73; president, Board of Directors, Memphis & Shelby City, Legal Services Assn 1972-74; first vice president, Memphis Chapter, Federal Bar Assn, 1972-74; lecturer, Ohio Northern University College of Law 16th Annual Law Review Symposium. **CONTACT ADDRESS** Equal Employment Opportunity Comm, 1801 L St, NW, Washington, DC, 20507.

JOHNSON, JUSTIN MORRIS
PERSONAL Born 08/19/1933, Wilkinsburg, PA, m, 1960 **DISCIPLINE** LAW **EDUCATION** Univ Chicago, AB, 1954, Law School, JD, 1962; attended Univ of VA, 1982-83. **CAREER** Partner/sole proprietor, Johnson & Johnson, 1962-77; Board of Education, School District of Pittsburgh and Pittsburgh-Mt Oliver Intermediate Unit, assistant solicitor, 1964-70, solicitor and assistant secretary, 1970-78; Berkman Ruslander Pohl Lieber & Engel, partner, 1978-80; SUPERIOR COURT OF PA, JUDGE, 1980-; ADJUNCT PROFESSOR, DUQUESNE UNIV SCHOOL OF LAW. **HONORS AND AWARDS** Bond Medal, Univ Chicago, 1954; Dr Martin Luther King Jr Citizen's Medal, 1973; Top Hat Award, 1981, for distinguished judicial service; Homer S Brown Service Award, 1982; Man of the Year, Bethesda Presbyterian Church, 1983; President's Award, Pennsylvania Trial Lawyers Association, 1983; Award of Merit, Pittsburgh Young Adult Club, 1983; St Thomas More Award, 1985; Public Service Award, Pittsburgh chapter, ASPA, 1986. **MEMBERSHIPS** Active elder Bethesda Presbyterian Church; mem Natl Cong Bar Examiners 1969-83; mem, PA Bd Law Examiners 1969-89, vice chairman 1975-83, chairman 1983-89; bd of trustees Mercy Hospital 1976-93, Southside Hosp 1978-88, United Way of Allegheny Co 1979-90; Carnegie Mellon University, 1988-93, 1995-; Pittsburgh Theological Seminary, 1985-93; Princeton Theological Seminary, 1992-; Urban League of Pittsburgh; hearing comm PA Supreme Court Disciplinary Bd. **CONTACT ADDRESS** Superior Ct of Pennsylvania, 330 Grant St, Pittsburgh, PA, 15219.

JOHNSON, KEVIN R.
PERSONAL Born 06/29/1958, m, 1987, 3 children **DISCIPLINE** LAW **EDUCATION** Univ Calif Berkeley, AB, 80; Harvard Univ, JD, 83. **CAREER** Atty, Heller Ehrman Whit & McAuffe, 84-89; actg prof, Univ Calif Davis Sch Law, 89-92; prof, 92- ; assoc dean for acad affairs, 98- . **HONORS AND AWARDS** Phi Beta Kappa; Harvard Law Review. **RESEARCH** Civil procedure; immigration and refugee law. **CONTACT ADDRESS** School of Law, Univ of Calif.-Davis, Davis, CA, 95616. **EMAIL** krjohnson@ucdavis.edu

JOHNSON, LUKE TIMOTHY
PERSONAL Born 11/20/1943, Park Falls, WI, m, 1974, 1 child **DISCIPLINE** NEW TESTAMENT STUDIES, THEOLOGY **EDUCATION** Notre Dame Sem, BA, 66; St Meinrad Sch Theol, MDiv, 70; Ind Univ, MA, 70; Yale Univ, PhD(New Testament), 76. **CAREER** Asst prof relig, St Joseph Sem Col, 70-71; asst prof New Testament, Yale Divinity Sch, 76-79, assoc prof, 79-82; ASSOC PROF NEW TESTAMENT, IND UNIV, 82-. **MEMBERSHIPS** Soc Bibl Lit; Cath Bibl Asn; Soc Values Higher Educ; Soc New Testament Studies. **RESEARCH** Christian origins. **SELECTED PUBLICATIONS** Auth, The Literary Function of Possessions in Luke-Acts, Scholars, 76; Invitation to the New Testament, Epistles III, Doubleday, 80; Sharing Possessions: Mandate and Symbol of Faith, Fortress, 81; Hard Blessings, Argus, 81. **CONTACT ADDRESS** New Testament Dept, Indiana Univ, Bloomington, Bloomington, IN, 47401.

JOHNSON, PATRICIA ALTENBERND
PERSONAL Born 03/05/1945, Seattle, WA, m, 1968, 1 child **DISCIPLINE** CONTINENTAL PHILOSOPHY **EDUCATION** Eckerd Col, BA, 67; Columbia Univ, MA, 69; Univ Toronto, MA, 74, PhD, 79. **CAREER** Prof philos, Univ Dayton, 79-. **MEMBERSHIPS** Am Philos Asn; Hegel Soc Am; Soc Christian Philosophers; Soc Philos Relig. **RESEARCH** Hermeneutics; Hegel; philosophy of religion. **SELECTED PUBLICATIONS** Co-ed, With Both Eyes Open, Pilgrim Press, 88; auth, Feminist Christian Philosophy?, Faith and Philosophy, 92; Gadamer: Incarnation, Finitude, and the Experience of Divine Infinitude, Faith and Philos, 93. **CONTACT ADDRESS** Dept of Philos, Univ of Dayton, 300 College Park, Dayton, OH, 45469-1546. **EMAIL** johnsonp@checkov.hm.udayton.edu

JOHNSON, PATRICIA L.
PERSONAL Born 01/29/1956, New York, New York, s **DISCIPLINE** LAW **EDUCATION** John Jay Coll of Criminal Justice, BA 1977, MA 1979; Cornell Univ Sch of Law, pre-law prog 1978; Rutgers Sch of Law Newark, JD 1985; Office of Court Admin NY Frontline Leadership Certificate l988. **CAREER** Bureau of Alcohol Tobacco & Firearms, student aide 1977; US Rsch Svcs, branch mgr 1979-82; Bronx Family Court, notifications supervisor 1982-83; Bronx Dist Attorney's Office, legal asst 1983-85; Judicial Friends, law intern 1985; Bronx District Attorney's Office, asst dist atty 1985-86; Bronx Public Admin Office, assoc counsel l986-88; Walter Kaitz Foundation Fellowship finalist l989; John Jay Coll of Criminal Justice, New York, NY, adjunct prof, 1986; Bronx Surrogate's Court, Bronx, NY, deputy chief clerk, 1988-. **HONORS AND AWARDS** Outstanding Achievement w/Distinction Rutgers Women's Rights Reporter 1985; Assoc of Black Law Students Serv to Black Comm 1985; moderator Entertainment & Sports Law Forum Black Bar Assoc of Bronx Cty 1987; battling the motion picture assoc of Amer movie rating of "The White Girl" published in NY Law Journal 1988; Walter Kaitz Foundation Fellowship Finalist, 1989. **MEMBERSHIPS** Mem Black Women Attorneys 1981-; mem Natl Bar Assoc 1983-; mem Phi Alpha Delta Law Frat Intl 1983-; mem Professional and Business Women 1985-, NAACP 1985-, Natl Women's Political Caucus 1985-, Black Entertainment and Sports Lawyers Assoc 1986-; recording sec Black Bar Assoc of Bronx County 1986-; corresponding sec/chair program bd Black Bar of Bronx l987-89; exec dir & founder Black Entertainment & Sports Tribune l989-; Big Sister, The Big Sisters, Inc, l989; chairperson, Entertainment & Sports Law Comm for Metropolitan Black Bar Assn, 1989-; exec dir, Black Entertainment & Sports Tribune, 1989-. **CONTACT ADDRESS** Professor, Law & Police Science, John Jay Col of Criminal Justice, 899 Tenth Ave, Room 422T, New York, NY, 10019.

JOHNSON, RICK L.
PERSONAL Born 03/18/1952, Houston, TX, m, 1998, 2 children **DISCIPLINE** OLD TESTAMENT **EDUCATION** La Col, BA, 74; Southwestern Bapt Theol Sem, M Div, 77; Southwestern Bapt Theol Sem, PhD, 83. **CAREER** Instr, relig, Wayland Bapt Univ, 82-84; asst prof, relig, Wayland Bapt Univ, 84-87; assoc prof, relig, Wayland Bapt Univ, 87-90; prof, relig, Wayland Bapt Univ, 90-92; assoc prof, old testament, Southwestern Bapt Theol Sem, 92-. **HONORS AND AWARDS** Who's Who Among America's Teachers, 94; Outstanding

Facul Award, Wayland Bapt Univ, 87-88, 92; Broadman Seminarian Award, Southwestern Bapt Theol Sem, 77. **MEMBERSHIPS** Soc of Bibl Lit; Nat Asn of Bapt Prof of Relig. **RESEARCH** Old Testament theology; Literary criticism of the Bible. **SELECTED PUBLICATIONS** Auth, Introducing 1 Corinthians, Bibl Illus, 23, 13-17, summer, 97; auth, Modern Old Testament Interpretation, Biblical Hermeneutics: A Comprehensive Introduction to Interpreting Scripture, 99-115, Nashville, Broadman & Holman Publ, 96; auth, Prepare to Meet the Lion: The Message of Amos, Southwestern Jour of Theol, 38, 20-28, fall, 95; auth, A Leper's Status in Ancient Israel, Bibl Illus, 21, 76-78, spring, 95; auth, God's Jealousy, Bibl Illus, 20, 40-43, fall, 93; auth, Hosea 4-10: Pictures at an Exhibition, Southwestern Jour of Theol, 36, 20-26, fall, 93; auth, Bar-Kochba, Kidron Valley, Midian, Midianites, and Rechabites, Holman Bibl Dict, Nashville, Holman Bibl Publ, 91; auth, The Old Testament Demand for Faith and Obedience, Southwestern Jour of Theol, 32, 27-35, summer, 90; auth, Heavenly Strength for an Earthly Journey. The System of Hebrews, Religious Writings and Religious Systems. Systemic Analysis of Holy Books in Christianity, Islam, Buddhism, Greco-Roman Religions, Ancient Israel and Judaism, vol 2, 75-87, Brown Studies in Relig, Atlanta, Scholar Press for Brown Judaic Studies, 89. **CONTACT ADDRESS** Southwestern Baptist Theological Sem, PO Box 22246, Fort Worth, TX, 76122. **EMAIL** rlj@swbts.swbts.edu

JOHNSON, ROGER A.
DISCIPLINE HISTORY; THEOLOGY **EDUCATION** Northwestern Univ, BA, 52; Yale Divinity Sch, BD, 55; Harvard Divinity Sch, ThD, 66. **CAREER** Elisabeth Luce Moore Prof of Christian Studies, Wellesley Col, 59-. **CONTACT ADDRESS** 7 Appleby Rd., Wellesley, MA, 02181. **EMAIL** rjohnson@mediaone.net

JOHNSON, ROGER ALAN
PERSONAL Born 09/07/1930, Duluth, MN, m, 1953, 3 children **DISCIPLINE** RELIGION, PHILOSOPHY **EDUCATION** Northwestern Univ, BA, 52; Yale Univ, BD, 55; Harvard Univ, ThD(theol), 66. **CAREER** From instr to assoc prof, 60-74, PROF RELIG, WELLESLEY COL, 74-, Lectr, Lutheran Theol Sem Philadelphia, 66; consult, Bd Theol Educ, Lutheran Church Am, 67-69; vis prof, Chung Chi Col, Univ Hong Kong, 68-69; mem, Group Applied Psychoanal, Harvard Univ, 70-; consult, Off Res & Planning, Lutheran Church Am, 73- **MEMBERSHIPS** Am Acad Relig; Soc Relig Higher Educ; Soc Sci Studies Relig. **RESEARCH** Philosophical origins of demythologizing; existentialist theology and philosophy; psychoanalysis and theology. **SELECTED PUBLICATIONS** Auth, Is Bultmann an heir of Luther?, Dialogue, fall 67; The Origins of Demythologizing, Brill, 73; coauth, Critical Issues in Modern Religion, Prentice-Hall, 73; Psychohistory and Religion, Fortress, 77; Congregations as Nurturing Communities, 79. **CONTACT ADDRESS** Dept of Relig, Wellesley Col, Wellesley, MA, 02181.

JOHNSON, RONALD W.
PERSONAL Born 10/06/1949, Newnan, GA, m, 1970, 3 children **DISCIPLINE** THEOLOGY **EDUCATION** West GA Col, BA, 71; So Baptist Theol Sem, M Div, 74, D Min, 85; Univ SAfrica, ThD, 99. **CAREER** Ed, SBC Sunday Sch Bd, 74-79; ed, 79-91, SBC Home Mission Bd; prof, 91-93, So Baptist Sem; dir of Evangel, 93-96, GA Baptist Convention; prof, missions & evangel, 96-., Mcafee Sch Of Theol. **HONORS AND AWARDS** Outstanding Dir of GA Baptist Leaders, 95. **MEMBERSHIPS** Acad for Evangel in Theological Education. **RESEARCH** Missiology and evangelism in postmodernism. **SELECTED PUBLICATIONS** Auth, Doctrine of Salvation, Convention Press; auth, Oikos: A Practical Approach to Family Evangelism, Brodman Press; auth, Evangelism for All God's People, Brodman Press; auth, How Will They Hear If We Don't Listen, Brodman Press. **CONTACT ADDRESS** 3001 Mercer Univ Dr, Atlanta, GA, 30341. **EMAIL** Johnson_RW@Mercer.edu

JOHNSON, STEPHEN M.
PERSONAL Born 06/28/1941, St. Louis, MO, m, 1991, 2 children **DISCIPLINE** RELIGION **EDUCATION** Spring Hill Col, AB, 65; Marquette, MA, 68; Yale, MPhil, 71, PhD, 73. **CAREER** Prof, Montclair St Univ, 71-. **MEMBERSHIPS** Amer Acad of Religion; Soc for Values in Higher Ed; Amer Culture Assn; Popular Culture Asn **RESEARCH** American civil religion; civic affairs and philosophy; american religious history and american studies; religion and psychology. **SELECTED PUBLICATIONS** Popular Culture as Religion: Faiths by Which We Naturally Live, Pop Cul Rev, 94; In Uno Plures: From Civil Religion to Civic Responsibility, Pop Cul Rev, 95; Re-constructing American In(ter)dependence: Feminist Method and American Civic Tradition, Pub Affairs Quart, 96; A Southern Sense of America: From Jackson Square, Gettysburg, and the Vietnam Wall toward Tomorrow, Stud in Pop Cul, 96; Pedagogical and Civic Response-Abilities, Chron of Higher Ed, 97; Pedagogical Responsibility and Professional Self Disclosure: Liberating Classrooms from False Dilemmas, Thinking, 98. **CONTACT ADDRESS** 94 Elmwood Rd, Verona, NJ, 07044-2508. **EMAIL** johnson@saturn.montclair.edu

JOHNSON, STEVEN D.
PERSONAL Born 10/12/1958, McDowell, KY, m, 1988 **DISCIPLINE** THEOLOGY, RELIGIOUS STUDIES **EDUCATION** Case Western Univ, BA, 81; Eden Theol Sem, MDiv, 89; Drew Univ, PhD, 95. **CAREER** Minister, United Church Christ Col, Acad, Theological Sem, 98- ; adj prof Philos and Ethics, Broome Commun Col, 95-97. **HONORS AND AWARDS** Will Herberg Scholar; Niebuhn Scholar; Grad stud fel; Press Prize; Natl merit scholar. **MEMBERSHIPS** AAR **RESEARCH** Jurgen Moltmann, Hermeneutics, Theological Ethics, Theology. **CONTACT ADDRESS** Dept of Theology, United Church of Christ, 700 Prospect Ave, Cleveland, OH, 44115-1100. **EMAIL** johnsons@ucc.org

JOHNSON, WALTER THANIEL, JR.
PERSONAL Born 05/18/1940, Greensboro, NC, m, 1985 **DISCIPLINE** LAW **EDUCATION** A&T State U, BS 1961; Duke Univ Sch of Law, JD 1964; Univ of North Carolina Chapel Hill Govt Executives Inst l981; Univ of North Carolina Chapel Hill Justice Exec Program l984. **CAREER** Frye & Johnson, atty; Guilford Co Superior Ct, asst dist atty 1968-69; USAF, judge adv 1965-68; Law Office of Elreta Alexander, asso 1964-65; Redevel Com Greensboro, relocation adv 1962-63; Public Storage & Warehousing Inc, sec, exec com 1971-76; Barjo Inc, sec, exec com 1973-; Duke Univ Law Sch, adjunct prof of law 1975-; Barbee & Johnson partner l987-88; Barbee Johnson & Glenn partner 1988-. **HONORS AND AWARDS** Outstdng young men of NC NC Jaycees 1970; Freedom Guard Award NC Jaycees 1970-71; disting serv award Greensboro Jaycees 1970; Peacemaker Award Carolina Peacemaker Newspaper; vice pres Assn of Paroling Authorities l982-85; Citizens Comm on Alternatives to Inceration l981-83. **MEMBERSHIPS** Mem Greensboro Bd Dirs of NC Nat Bank 1976-; vice pres planning for United Way of Greensboro 1969-71; mem, chmn, Greensboro Cty Bd of Educ 1970-; mem Bdof Govs NC Bar Assn 1975-; chmn NC Inmate Grievance Co Com 1975-; chmn bd trustee Univ NC 1974-; bd mem Eastern Music Festival 1972-76; chmn North Carolina Parole Comm l981-85; Adjunct prof North Carolina Central School of Law l985-87; vice chmn Greensboro Vision l985-; bd mem Greensboro Economic Devel Council l988-. **CONTACT ADDRESS** Barbee Johnson & Glenn, 102 N Elm Street, Greensboro, NC, 27401.

JOHNSON, WILLARD
PERSONAL Born 05/30/1939, IA, m, 1980 **DISCIPLINE** RELIGION **EDUCATION** Oberlin Col, BA; Univ of WI, MA, PhD **CAREER** Dir, 71-76, Cal St Univ; Prof, 77-pres, San Diego St Univ **HONORS AND AWARDS** Phi Beta Cappa; Woodrow Wilson Fel **MEMBERSHIPS** Am Acad of Relig **RESEARCH** Shamanism; South & East Asian Religions **SELECTED PUBLICATIONS** Auth, Poetry and Speculation of the Rg Veda, Univ of Cal, 80; Auth, Riding the Ox Home, Beacon, 86 **CONTACT ADDRESS** Dept Relig Studies, 5500 Campanile, San Diego, CA, 92182-8143.

JOHNSTON, CAROL F.
PERSONAL Born 05/01/1951, Panama Canal, s **DISCIPLINE** PHILOSOPHY OF RELIGION AND THEOLOGY **EDUCATION** Union Theol Sem, MDiv, 78; Claremont, PhD, 94. **CAREER** Asst prof, Christian Theol Sem, 95- . **HONORS AND AWARDS** Phi Beta Kappa; Claremont Diss Fel; Presbyterian Scholar for Doctoral Stud. **MEMBERSHIPS** AAR. **RESEARCH** Theology and culture; faith and wealth, ecojustice, economics. **SELECTED PUBLICATIONS** Auth, Wealth or Health of Nations, Pilgrim, 98. **CONTACT ADDRESS** Christian Theol Sem, 1000 W 42nd St, Indianapolis, IN, 46208. **EMAIL** johnston@cts.edu

JOHNSTONE, HENRY, JR.
PERSONAL Born 02/22/1920, Montclair, NJ, m, 1948, 2 children **DISCIPLINE** PHILOSOPHY **EDUCATION** Harvard Univ, PhD, 50. **CAREER** Instr, Williams Col, 48-52; prof, Pa State Univ, 52-84. **MEMBERSHIPS** Am Philos Soc; SCA. **RESEARCH** Philosophical argumentation; Rhetoric; Epistemology; Logic; Thanatology. **SELECTED PUBLICATIONS** Auth," Philosophy and Argumentum ad Hominem," in J of Philos, 52; "'The Relevance of Philosophy to Rhetoric and of Rhetoric to Philosophy," in the Quart J of Speech, 66; "An Inductive Decision-Procedure for the Monadic Predicate Calculus," in Logique et Analyse, 66-67; "Sleep and Death," in The Monist, 75; auth, The Problem of the Self, 70. **CONTACT ADDRESS** 240 Sparks Bldg, University Park, PA, 16802. **EMAIL** hwj1@psu.edu

JOKIC, ALEKSANDER
PERSONAL Born 06/19/1960, Belgrade, Yugoslavia, m, 1990, 1 child **DISCIPLINE** PHILOSOPHY **EDUCATION** Belgrade Univ, BA, 84; UC Santa Barbara, PhD, 91. **CAREER** Exec dir Ctr for Philos Educ, Santa Barbara City Col, 97-; asst prof of Philos, W Virg Univ, 98-; October Prize City of Belgrade, 84. **MEMBERSHIPS** Am Philos Asn; Serbian Philos Soc. **RESEARCH** Moral philosophy; Metaphysics; Philosophy of science. **SELECTED PUBLICATIONS** Auth Why Potentiality Cannot Matter, Jour Soc Philos, 93; Consequentialism, Deontological Ethics, and Terrorism, Theoria, 95; Potentiality and Identity, Human Rights, 96; Aspects of Scientific Discovery, Serbian Philos Soc, 97; Kant, Supereerogation, and Praiseworthiness of Actions, Philos Stud, 97. **CONTACT ADDRESS** Dept of Philosophy, W Va Univ, 252 Stansbury Hall, PO Box 6312, Morgantown, WV, 26505-6312. **EMAIL** ajokic@sbcc.sbceo.kiz.ca.us

JOLLEY, NICHOLAS
DISCIPLINE SEVENTEENTH AND EIGHTEENTH CENTURY PHILOSOPHY **EDUCATION** Cambridge Univ, PhD, 74. **CAREER** PROF, PHILOS, UNIV CALIF, SAN DIEGO. **RESEARCH** Polit philos. **SELECTED PUBLICATIONS** Auth, The Reception of Descartes' Philosophy,The Cambridge Companion to Descartes, Cambridge Univ Press, 95; "Leibniz: Truth, Knowledge, and Metaphysics," The Renaissance and 17th Century Rationalism, Routledge Hist of Philos Vol 4, Routledge, 93; "Intellect and Illumination in Malebranche," Jour Hist of Philos 32, 94; ed, The Cambridge Companion to Leibniz, Cambridge Univ Press, 95. **CONTACT ADDRESS** Dept of Philos, Univ Calif, San Diego, 9500 Gilman Dr, La Jolla, CA, 92093.

JOLLIMORE, TROY
PERSONAL Born 01/03/1971, Liverpool, NS, Canada, m, 1997 **DISCIPLINE** PHILOSOPHY **EDUCATION** Univ of King's Col, BA, 93; Princeton Univ, MA, 96, PhD, 99. **CAREER** Georgetown Univ, vis lectr; asst prof, 98-. **MEMBERSHIPS** APA, CPA **RESEARCH** Ethics; polit; philo. **CONTACT ADDRESS** Dept of Philosophy, Georgetown Univ, 37th & 20th St, Washington, DC, 20057. **EMAIL** jolimore@princeton.edu

JOLLS, C.
DISCIPLINE LAW **EDUCATION** Stanford Univ BA 89; Harvard Law Sch, JD 93; MIT, PhD 95. **CAREER** US CT of App Judge S. Williams, law clerk, 95-96; US Sup CT Judge A. Scalia, law clerk, 96-97; Harvard Law Sch, asst prof, 94-95 and 97-. **HONORS AND AWARDS** PHI Beta Kappa. **MEMBERSHIPS** MA Bar. **RESEARCH** Employment law; Corp law; Intersection of psychology with law and economics. **SELECTED PUBLICATIONS** Auth, A Behavioral Approach to Law and Economics, coauth, Stanford L Rev, 98; auth, Theories and Tropes: A Reply to Posner and Kelman, coauth, Stanford L Rev, 98; auth, Behavioral Economic Analysis of Redistributive Legal Rules, in: Symposium: Behavioral Law and Econ, Vanderbilt L. Rev, 98; auth, Contracts as Bilateral Commitments: A New Perspective on Contract Modification, Jour of Legal Stud, 97; auth, Hands-Tying and the Age Discrimination in Employment Act, in: Symposium: The Changing Workplace, Texas L Rev, 96. **CONTACT ADDRESS** School of Law, Harvard Univ, Cambridge, MA, 02138. **EMAIL** jolls@law.harvard.edu

JONAS, HANS
PERSONAL Born 05/10/1903, Germany, m, 1943, 3 children **DISCIPLINE** PHILOSOPHY **EDUCATION** Univ Marburg, PhD, 28. **CAREER** Lectr ancient hist, 46-48, Brit Coun Sch Higher Studies, Jerusalem; tchng fel, 49-50, McGill Univ; vis prof, 50-51, Carleton Univ; assoc prof, 51-54, prof, 55-66, Alvin Johnson prof, 66-77, Emer Prof Philos, 77-, New Sch Social Res; guest lectr, 38-39 & 46-48, Hebrew Univ, Israel; Lady Davis fel, 49-50; Rockefeller fel, 59-60 & 74-75; vis lectr, 58, 61-62, Princeton Univ; Ingersoll lectr, 61, Harvard Univ; vis prof, 61, 66-67, Columbia Univ; adj prof, 63-64, Hunter Col; fel, Ctr Advan Studies, 64-65, Wesleyan Univ; vis prof, 66-67, Union Theol Sem; comt social thought, Univ Chicago, 68, 69 & 70; NEH grant, 73-74; fel, Am Acad Arts & Sci, 76. **HONORS AND AWARDS** DHL, Hebrew Union Col-Jewish Inst Relig, 62; DLL, New Sch Social Res, 76; DTheol, Philipps Univ, Marburg, 76. **MEMBERSHIPS** Am Philos Assn; Am Soc Studies Relig. **RESEARCH** History of philosophy and religion in late antiquity and early Christianity, especially gnosticism; technology and ethics; philosophy of organism. **SELECTED PUBLICATIONS** Auth, Macht oder Ohnmacht der Subjektivitat, Das Leib-Seele-Problem im Vorfeld des Prinzips Verantwortung, Ibid, Frankfurt, 81; auth, On Faith, Reason, and Responsibility, 81. **CONTACT ADDRESS** 9 Meadow Ln, New Rochelle, NY, 10805.

JONAS, W. GLENN, JR.
PERSONAL Born 06/16/1959, Gastonia, NC, m, 1989, 1 child **DISCIPLINE** RELIGION **EDUCATION** Mars Hill Col, BA, 81; SW Baptist Theol Sem, MDiv, 84; Baylor Univ, PhD, 90. **CAREER** Instr, Temple Jr Col, 89-93; oral historian, Inst Oral Hist, Baylor Univ, 93-94; asst prof relig, Campbell Univ, 94-. **HONORS AND AWARDS** Prof of the Year, Campbell Univ, 97; Grad Student Asn Fel, 89. **MEMBERSHIPS** Am Acad Relig; S Baptist Hist Soc; NC Baptist Hist Soc; Am Soc Church Hist; Tex Baptist Hist Soc; Nat Asn Baptist Prof Relig. **RESEARCH** Baptists; church history; social Christianity. **SELECTED PUBLICATIONS** Auth, A Critical Evaluation of Albert Henry Newman, Church Historian, 92; auth, Through the Dark Valley: Albert Henry Newman's Experience at the Rochester Theological Seminary, Tex Baptist Hist, 93; auth, He Lives Yet in Baylor University: The Life and Influence of John Stephenson Tanner, Tex Baptist Hist, 95; co-auth, The Baylor List of Effective Preachers, The Christian Ministry, July/Aug, 96; auth, Historical Vignettes, Bibl Recorder, Aug/Sept, 96; auth, Is Unity Really Possible, Bibl Recorder, Dec, 97; auth,

The Political Side of B.H. Carroll, Baptist Hist & Heritage, Fall, 98. **CONTACT ADDRESS** Dept of Religion, Campbell Univ, PO Box 143, Buies Creek, NC, 27506. **EMAIL** jonas@mailcenter.campbell.edu

JONES, BARNEY LEE
PERSONAL Born 06/11/1920, Raleigh, NC, m, 1944, 5 children **DISCIPLINE** AMERICAN CHURCH HISTORY, BIBLICAL LITERATURE **EDUCATION** Duke Univ, BA, 41, PhD(Am Christiani y), 58; Yale Univ, BD, 44. **CAREER** Instr Bible, Duke Univ, 48-50, chaplain, 53-56, asst dean, Trinity Col, 56-64, assoc prof relig, 64-72, PROF RELIG, 72-80. **MEMBERSHIPS** Soc Relig Higher Educ; Am Soc Church Hist. **RESEARCH** Colonial American church history, particularly New England area; Charles Chauncy, 1707-1782. **SELECTED PUBLICATIONS** Auth, John Caldwell, critic of the Great Awakening in New England, in: A Miscellany of American Christianity, Duke Univ, 63. **CONTACT ADDRESS** 2622 Pickett Rd, Durham, NC, 27705.

JONES, BARRY ALAN
DISCIPLINE RELIGION **EDUCATION** Duke Univ, PhD, 94. **CAREER** Pastor, Park View Baptist Church, Durham NC, 94-97; asst prof, Mars Hill Col, 97- . **MEMBERSHIPS** Soc of Bibl Lit. **RESEARCH** Prophetic literature. **SELECTED PUBLICATIONS** Auth, Formation of the Book of the Twelve, Scholars, 95. **CONTACT ADDRESS** Dept of Religion, Mars Hill Col, Mars Hill, NC, 28754. **EMAIL** dbjones@mhc.edu

JONES, BONNIE LOUISE
PERSONAL Born 02/03/1952, Philadelphia, PA, s **DISCIPLINE** LAW **EDUCATION** Lincoln Univ, BA 1970; NC Central Univ School of Law, JD 1982. **CAREER** VA Legal Aid Soc, law clerk 1982-83; Newport News Police Dept, permits examiner 1983-85; Hampton Roads Regional Acad of Criminal Justice, training/evaluation specialist 1985-86; Blayton Allen & Assocs, assoc Attorney 1986-88; self-employed atty Hampton VA, 1988-; McDermott, Roe & Sons, 1992-96; College of William and Mary, School of Law, adj prof, 1994-97; Hampton Gen Dist Court, judge, 1996-. **HONORS AND AWARDS** Commendation for 5 city talent show from Committee for Educ of Gifted Students Hampton School System 1979; on-air Attorney for WAVY Channel 10 Midday TV program 1990-96; series of lectures to Chinese lawyers, journalists, and economists at Hampton Univ on practicing law as a minority in Amer; on-air atty for WVEC Channel 13, midday, 1987-92. **MEMBERSHIPS** Mem Phi Alpha Delta Law Fraternity 1982-; mem Big Brother/Big Sisters of Peninsula 1985; mem Amer & VA Bar Assocs 1986; mem Assoc of Trial Attorneys of Amer; mem PA Bar Assn 1987-; Hampton Bar Assn 1988-92; council vice pres Intl Training in communication council II 1988-89; Commission in Chancery for the Hampton Circuit Courts; Girls, Inc of The Greater Peninsula, former president board of directors. **CONTACT ADDRESS** Hampton Gen District Court, P.O. Box 70, Hampton, VA, 23669.

JONES, BRUCE WILLIAM
PERSONAL Born 08/28/1935, Palo Alto, CA, d, 3 children **DISCIPLINE** HEBREW BIBLE **EDUCATION** Amherst Col, BA, 56; Grad Theol Union, PhD(Old Testament), 72; Azusa Pac Univ, MA, 80. **CAREER** Prog secy, Student Christian Movement India, 60-62; minister, United Church of Christ, Petersburg, Ill, 62-64; lectr Old Testament, Pac Sch Relig, 68-69; asst prof relig studies, Holy Names Col, 70-73; asst prof, 73-75, ASSOC PROF RELIG STUDIES, CALIF STATE COL, BAKERSFIELD, 76-, Lectr Bible, Mills Col, 69-73; therapist, Bakersfield Family Therapy Group, 81-. **MEMBERSHIPS** Soc Bibl Lit; Am Acad Relig; Am Asn Marriage & Family Therapy. **RESEARCH** Apocalyptic literature; the Book of Esther; computer assisted instruction in Bible and religion. **SELECTED PUBLICATIONS** Auth, The prayer in Daniel 9, Vetus Testamentum, 18: 488; More about the apocalypse as apocalyptic, J Bibl Lit, 87: 325; Religious studies as a test case for computer assisted instruction in the humanities, Proc 4th Conf Comput in Undergrad Curricula, Claremont Col, 73; Computer assisted instruction in religious studies, Bull Coun Study Relig, 74; Two misconceptions about the Book of Esther, Cath Bibl Quart, 39: 171; The so-called appendix to the Book of Esther, Semitics, 6: 36; Antiochus Epiphanes and the persecution of the Jews, in: Scripture in Context: Essays on the Comparative Method, Pickwick Press, 80; Using the computer to teach methods and interpretative skills in the humanities: Implementing a project, Resourses Educ, 82. **CONTACT ADDRESS** Dept of Relig Studies, California State Univ, Bakersfield, Bakersfield, CA, 93309.

JONES, CAROLYN
PERSONAL Born 12/18/1958, Burlington, NC, m, 1997 **DISCIPLINE** RELIGIOUS STUDIES **EDUCATION** Univ of VA, PhD, 91 **CAREER** Visit Lect, 86-88, Univ of NC; Adj Prof, 87, Elon Col; Asst Prof 91-98, Assoc Prof, 98-pres, LA St Univ **HONORS AND AWARDS** Fourd Found Post Doctor Fel, 93-94 **MEMBERSHIPS** Am Acad of Relig; Southeastern Comm for the Study of Relig; Toni Morrison Soc **RESEARCH** Religion & Literature; African-American Literature & Religion **SELECTED PUBLICATIONS** Auth, The Fiction and Criticism of Toni Morrison, MacMillan Press, 98 **CONTACT ADDRESS** Dept of Philos and Relig Studies, Louisiana State Univ, 106 Coastes Hall, Baton Rouge, LA, 70803.

JONES, CAROLYN M.
PERSONAL Born 12/18/1958, Burlington, NC, m, 1997 **DISCIPLINE** PHILOSOPHY **EDUCATION** Univ N Carolina, Chapel Hill, BA, 80, MA, 83; Univ Virginia, PhD, 91. **CAREER** Adj fac, 87, Elon Col; vis lectr, 86, 87, 88, UNC Chapel Hill; acting asst prof, 88-91, asst prof, 91-98, assoc prof, 98-, Louisiana St Univ. **RESEARCH** Religion & lit, African-Amer lit, classical & modern lit. **CONTACT ADDRESS** Dept of Phil & Relig, Louisiana State Univ, 106 Coates Hall, Baton Rouge, LA, 70803-3901. **EMAIL** dr_cmjones@hotmail.com

JONES, CHARLES B.
PERSONAL Born 03/24/1957, Durham, NC, m, 1980, 2 children **DISCIPLINE** RELIGIOUS STUDIES **EDUCATION** Univ of Va, PhD, 96. **CAREER** Visiting asst prof, Carleton Col, 95-96; ASST PROF, CATHOLIC UNIV OF AM, 96-. **MEMBERSHIPS** Am Acad of Religion; Asn for Asian Studies; Soc for Buddhist-Christian Studies. **RESEARCH** Chinese pure land Buddhism; interreligious dialogue. **SELECTED PUBLICATIONS** Auth, Buddhism in Taiwan: Religion and the State 1660-1990, Univ of Hawaii Press, 99. **CONTACT ADDRESS** Dept of Religion and Religious Ed, Catholic Univ of America, Washington, DC, 20064. **EMAIL** CBJones57@aol.com

JONES, DAVID CLYDE
PERSONAL Born 07/26/1937, Greenville, SC, m, 1962, 2 children **DISCIPLINE** SYSTEMATIC THEOLOGY **EDUCATION** Bryan Col, BA, 59; Westminster Theol Sem, BD, 62, ThM, 64; Concordia Sem, St Louis, ThD(syst theol), 70. **CAREER** Assoc Prof Syst Theol, Covenant Theol Sem, 68-, DEAN FAC, 78-. **MEMBERSHIPS** Soc Christian Ethics; Evangel Theol Soc. **SELECTED PUBLICATIONS** Auth, Who are the Poor?, Presbyterion, 77. **CONTACT ADDRESS** 12330 Conway Rd St, Louis, MO, 63131.

JONES, DONALD D.
DISCIPLINE THEOLOGY; ETHICS **EDUCATION** Augustana Col, BA, 57; Drew Univ Theological School, Mdiv, 61; Drew Univ, PhD, 69. **CAREER** Instr, 66, Asst Prof, 69, Assoc Prof, 74, Prof, 81-, Drew Univ. **CONTACT ADDRESS** Drew Univ, 36 Madison Ave, Madison, NJ, 07940.

JONES, DONALD L.
PERSONAL Born 08/07/1938, Xenia, OH, m, 1961, 3 children **DISCIPLINE** RELIGIOUS STUDIES **EDUCATION** Ohio Wesleyan Univ, BA, 60; Methodist Theol Sch, MDiv, 63; Duke Univ, PhD, 66. **CAREER** Asst prof relig, Earlham Col & Sch Relig, 66-67; from asst prof to assoc prof to prof Relig Studies, grad dir, Univ SC, 67-. **MEMBERSHIPS** Am Acad Relig; Soc Bibl Lit; SC Acad Relig. **RESEARCH** Luke-Acts; Roman Imperial Cult; New Testament; Christian origins. **SELECTED PUBLICATIONS** Auth, The Title 'Author of Life (Leader)' in the Acts of the Apostles, Soc Bibl Lit Seminar Papers 94, 94; auth, Religion in the 1940s, Am Decades: 1940-1949, 95; auth Emperor, Emperor Cult, HarperCollins Bibl Dict, 96. **CONTACT ADDRESS** Dept of Religious Studies, Univ of South Carolina, Columbia, SC, 29208. **EMAIL** jones-donald@sc.edu

JONES, EMMA PETTWAY
PERSONAL Born 07/29/1945, Boykin, Alabama, d **DISCIPLINE** LAW **EDUCATION** Albertus Magnus Coll, 1978-80; NH Coll, Manchester, BS 1981, MBA 1985; CUNY Law School Queens, JD 1988. **CAREER** New Haven Fed Credit Union, organizer/mgr 1979-81; EMA Assoc, pres 1980-86; Jones Turner & Wright, legal asst 1986-87; Williams & Wise, legal intern 1987; independent consultant. **HONORS AND AWARDS** Received numerous Certificates of Excellence & Outstanding Service Awards. **MEMBERSHIPS** Exec dir People Acting for Change New Haven CT; researcher Yale Univ Provost Dept; consultant, trainer Legal Assistance New Haven CT, Public Housing Prog Tenant Representative Council, NH Coll, Organizational Development Inst Cheyney State Coll, Fair Haven Mediation Prog; exec dir CT Afro-American Historical Society; chairperson Natl Econ Devel & Law Ctr; vice pres New Haven YWCA.

JONES, JAMES EDWARD, JR.
PERSONAL Born 06/04/1924, Little Rock, AR, m **DISCIPLINE** LAW **EDUCATION** Lincoln Univ, BA 1950; Univ IL Inst Labor and Indus Relations, MA 1951; University of Wisconsin School of Law, JD 1956. **CAREER** US Wage Stabilization Board, industrial relations analyst, 1951-53; US Department of Labor, legislative attorney, 1956-63, counsel for labor relations, 1963-66; Office of Labor Management Policy Development, director, 1966-67; associate solicitor, Division of Labor Relations and Civil Rights, 1967-69; Univ WI-Madison, vistg prof law and indus relations 1969-70; Inst for Rsch on Poverty, assoc 1970-71; Inst Relations, Rsch Inst, dir 1971-73; Ctr for Equal Employment and Affirmative Action, Indus Relations Rsch Inst, dir 1974-; Univ WI, prof of law 1970-, Bascom prof law 1982-91; Nathan P Feinsinger Professor of Labor Law, 1991-93; Prof Emeritus, 1993-. **HONORS AND AWARDS** Sec Labor Career Service Awd Dept Labor 1963; John Hay Whitney Fellow; contributor articles, chapters to professional publs; Smongeski Award, 1988; Alumni Achievement Award, Lincoln University, 1967; Order of the Coif, 1970; Phi Kappa Phi, 1987; Prof of the Year, UW Leo Students, 1986; Hilldale Award, Social Sci Div, 1991; Martin Luther King Humanitarian Award, City of Madison, WI, 1991; C Clyde Ferguson, Jr Memorial Award, American Assn of Law Schools Minority Group Section, 1993; Distinguished Service Awd, Wisconsin Law Alumni Association, 1995; Distinguished Alumni Awd, University of Illinois, 1996; Society of American Law, Teachers Achievement Award, 1998. **MEMBERSHIPS** National Bar Assn; member, State Bar of Wisconsin; American Bar Assn, 1985-; public review board member, UAW, 1970; advisory committee, National Research Council National Academy of Sciences, 1971-73; Wisconsin Governor's Task Force on Comparable Worth, 1984-86; Madison School District Affirmative Action Advisory Committee, 1988-91; National Academy of Arbitrators, 1982-. **CONTACT ADDRESS** Law Sch, Univ of Wisconsin, Madison, WI, 53706.

JONES, JOE FRANK
PERSONAL Born 08/02/1949, Warner Robbins, GA, m, 1983, 1 child **DISCIPLINE** PHILOSOPHY **EDUCATION** Armstrong Col, BA, 75; Univ of Ga, MA, 79; Fla State Univ, MA, 81; Fla State Univ, PhD, 83. **CAREER** Asst prof to assoc prof, relig and philos, Barton Col, 91-. **HONORS AND AWARDS** Univ fel, Univ Ga and Fla State Univ; AAAS fel, Univ Ga, Editor, The International Journal for Philosophy in the Contemporary World, 97 **MEMBERSHIPS** Amer Philos Asn; Soc for Philos in the Contemporary World; The NC Relig Studies Asn; Amer Soc for Philos; Counseling and Psychotherapy; Soc for Philos of Relig. **RESEARCH** The realism/constructionism debate; Philosophy of religion; Interpretations of the history of philosophy; Philosophical counseling. **SELECTED PUBLICATIONS** Auth, Moral Growth in Children's Literature: A Primer with Examples, Philosophy in the Contemporary World, vol 1, no 4, 10-19, winter, 94; auth, Religion and Ethics and Altruism, Magill's Ready Ref: Ethics, Pasadena, Calif, Salem Press, 95; auth, Theological Perspectives on Substance Abuse, Faith and Mission, vol IX, no 2, 3-24, spring, 92; auth, Striking Commensurate from the Oxford Translation of An Post A24, Philos Res Archives, vol X, 197-202, 84; auth, Intelligible Matter and Geometry in Aristotle, Apeiron: A Jour for Ancient Philos and Sci, vol XVII, no 2, 94-102, 83; auth, A Blackstone Bibliography, Soc Theory and Practice, vol 5, no 2, 239-242, 79. **CONTACT ADDRESS** Dept of Religion and Philosophy, Barton Col, 1701 Chamberlain Dr. NW, Wilson, NC, 27896-1561. **EMAIL** jjones@barton.edu

JONES, JUDITH A.
DISCIPLINE PHILOSOPHY **EDUCATION** Emory Univ, PhD. **CAREER** Asst prof, Fordham Univ. **RESEARCH** Questions of individualism, contemp naturalism. **SELECTED PUBLICATIONS** Auth, The Rhythm of Experience in Whitehead and Dewey, Listening: A Jour Rel and Cult, 94; Teach Us to See It: A Retrieval of Metaphysics in Ethics, Jour of Speculative Philos, 96; Introduction to reprint of Whitehead's Religion in the Making, Fordham UP, 96. **CONTACT ADDRESS** Dept of Philos, Fordham Univ, 113 W 60th St, New York, NY, 10023.

JONES, L. GREGORY
PERSONAL m, 3 children **DISCIPLINE** CHRISTIAN THEOLOGY AND ETHICS **EDUCATION** Univ Denver, BA, 80, MPA, 82; Duke Univ, MDiv, 85, PhD, 88. **CAREER** Res & tchg asst, 84-87, lectr Theol, 87-88, Duke Univ; asst prof Theol, 88-94, dir Ctr for Hum, 92-96, chr Dept of Theol, 96-97, assoc prof Ttheol 94- , Loyola Coll co-ed, Modern Theol, 91-. **HONORS AND AWARDS** Acad Pol Comt, 95- , Mem Exed Bd, 95- ,Ecumentical I nst St Mary's Sen & Univ. N Am Min fel, 83-85; John Wesley fel, 85-88; Andrew Mellon fel, 87-88; Loyola Col Summer Res grants, 89, 91, & 92. **MEMBERSHIPS** Am Acad Relig; Karl Barth Soc N Am; Soc John Wesley Fellows; Soc Christian Ethics. **SELECTED PUBLICATIONS** Co-ed, Rethinking Metaphysics, Blackwells, 95; auth Embodying Forgiveness: A Theological Analysis, Wm B. Eerdmans, 95; coed Spirituality and Social Embodiment, Blackwells, 97; coed Blackwell Readings in Modern Theology, 96-99; Forgiveness, Practicing Our Faith: A Way of Life for a Searching People, Jossey-Bass, 97; Spirituality Life: Thomas Moore' Misguided Care of the Soul, The Christian Century, 96; A Thirst for God or Consumer Spirituality? Cultivating Disciplined Practices of Being Engaged by God, Mod Theol, 97; God and The Craft of Forgiveness, The Circuit Rider, 97; Finding the Will to Embrace the Enemy, Christianity Today, 97. **CONTACT ADDRESS** New Divinity, Duke Univ, Box 90968, Durham, NC, 27708-0968. **EMAIL** lgjones@mail.Duke.edu

JONES, LAWRENCE N.
PERSONAL Born 04/24/1921, Moundsville, WV, m **DISCIPLINE** THEOLOGY **EDUCATION** WV State Coll, BS in Educ 1942; Univ of Chicago, MA in Hist 1948; Oberlin Grad Schl of Theology, BD 1956; Yale Univ Grad Schl, PhD in Religion 1957, 1961. **CAREER** Fisk Univ, dean of chapel 1960-64; Union Theological Seminary NY, dean prof 1965-75; HOWARD UNIV DIVINTIY SCHL, dean prof 1975-91, DEAN EMERITUS, 1991-. **HONORS AND AWARDS** Lucy Monroe Flwshp Oberlin Grad Schl 1956; Rosenwald Schlrshp Rosenwald Fund 1942; Rockefeller Doctoral Flwshp Rockefeller Brothers 1959-61; LLD, West Virginia State College 1965;

DHL, Jewish Theological Seminary 1971; DD, Chicago Theological Seminary 1975; DD, Shaw University, 1986; DD, Episcopal Theological Seminary in Virginia, 1992. **MEMBERSHIPS** Mem United Church Pod for World Ministries 1975-81; consult Lilly Endowment Inc, Congress of Natl Black Churches, Grad Theological Union 1983; chrmn Civil Rights Coord Comm Nashville 1962-64; pres Soc for Study of Black Religion 1974-77; secr Assc Theological Schls 1981-82; bd mem WHMM TV Public Advisory Board 1984-.

JONES, PAUL HENRY
PERSONAL Born 06/28/1949, Richmond, VA, m, 1976, 2 children **DISCIPLINE** HISTORICAL THEOLOGY **EDUCATION** Yale Univ, BA, 72; Brite Div Sch, Tex Christian Univ, MDiv, 78; Vanderbilt Univ, MA, 84, PhD, 88. **CAREER** Dean of the Chapel, assoc prof, prog dir Rel, Transylvania Univ, 85-; tchg asst, Vanderbilt Univ, 81-83. **HONORS AND AWARDS** Alpha Omicron Pi Awd for tchg excellence, 98, Transylvania Univ; Bingham Awd excellence tchg, 97, Transylvania Univ; T.A. Abbott Awd fac excellence, Div higher educ, Christian Church, 97; John H. Smith fel, Vanderbilt Univ; Theta Phi Hon Soc, Fac Bk Awd (s) in New Testament, Hebrew Bible, Rel ed, and Christian Board of Publ Awd (s) for scholastic excellence at Brite Div Sch. **SELECTED PUBLICATIONS** Auth, An Eidetics of the Eucharist, Mid-stream: An Ecumenical Jour, Jan 91; Worship as Identity Formation, Lexington Theol Quart, April 91; Tarry at the Cross: A Christian Response to the Holocaust, Perspectives, March 92; The Meaning of the Eucharist: Its Origins in the New Testament Texts, Encounter, Spring 93; Christ's Eucharistic Presence: A History of the Doctrine, NY, Peter Lang Publ, 94; Making a Differnce is Imperative, The Disciple, Aug 94; We Are How We Worship: Corporate Worship as a Matrix for Christian Identity Formation, Worship, July 95; Worship and Christian Identity, The Disciple, Dec 96; Disciples at Worship: From Ancient Order to Thankful Praise, in Christian Faith Seeking Historical Understanding, Macon, GA, Mercer UP, 97; coauth, 500 Illustrations: Stories from Life for Preaching and Teaching, Nashville, Abingdon Press, 98. **CONTACT ADDRESS** Dept of Religion, Transylvania Univ, 352 Melbourne Way, Lexington, KY, 40502. **EMAIL** pjones@mail.transy.edu

JONES, RICHARD J.
DISCIPLINE MISSION AND WORLD RELIGIONS **EDUCATION** Oberlin Col, BA, 64; Johns Hopkins Univ, MA, 66; Va Theol Sem, MDiv, 72; Univ Toronto, PhD, 88. **CAREER** Tchg Eng as for lanf, Phan-chau-Trinh sec sch, DaNang, Univ Hue, Viet-Nam, 66-69; tchg asst, Wycliffe Col, 84-88; prof, Va Theol Sem, 88-. **HONORS AND AWARDS** First coord, Episcopal Church of Ecuador, Diocesan Extension Sem, 72-75. **SELECTED PUBLICATIONS** Auth, How to talk to your Muslim Neighbor, Forward Movement Publ, 96; Wilfred Cantwell and Kenneth Cragg on Islam as a Way of Salvation, Bulletin of Missionary Res XVI, 92; rev, Review of: The Quest for Human Unity: A Religious History by Joseph Mitsuo Kitagawa, Anglican Theol Rev, 92. **CONTACT ADDRESS** Va Theol Sem, 3737 Seminary Rd, Alexandria, VA, 22304.

JONES, ROBERT ALUN
DISCIPLINE RELIGIOUS STUDIES **EDUCATION** Univ Redlands, BA, 65; Univ Pa, MA, 66; PhD, 69. **CAREER** Prof, Univ Ill Urbana Champaign,72-. **RESEARCH** American civilization. **SELECTED PUBLICATIONS** Auth, The Ethics of Research in Cyberspace, 94; The Other Durkheim: History and Theory in the Treatment of Classical Sociological Thought, Blackwell, 96; Durkheim, Rousseau, and Realism, J Hist Behavioral Sci, 96; Religion and Science in Les Formes Alimentaires de la vie religieuse; Sociology and Irony, Swiss J Sociology, 97; Metaphysicians and Ironists: Some Reflections on Sociology and Its History, Blackwell, 98; Emile Durkheim, Blackwell, 98; co-auth, Contextualization, Cognitive Flexibility, and Hypertext: The Convergence of Interpretive Theory, Cognitive Psychology, and Advanced Information Technologies, Blackwell, 95; co-ed, Durkheim's Elementary Forms of the Religious Life, Routledge, 97. **CONTACT ADDRESS** Religious Studies Dept, Univ Ill Urbana Champaign, 52 E Gregory Dr, Champaign, IL, 61820. **EMAIL** rajones@uiuc.edu

JONES, SHAWN
PERSONAL Boise, ID, m, 3 children **DISCIPLINE** MINISTRY **EDUCATION** Columbia Christian Col, BA, 81, BS, 85; Pepperdine Univ, MS, 90; Northwest Grad Sch Ministry, D. Min. **HONORS AND AWARDS** Fac Member of the Year, 98, Student Award. **MEMBERSHIPS** SBL **CONTACT ADDRESS** 9101 E Burnside, Portland, OR, 97216-1515.

JONES, THOMAS CANBY
PERSONAL Born 09/25/1921, Karuizawa, Japan, m, 1945, 1 child **DISCIPLINE** RELIGION, PHILOSOPHY **EDUCATION** Haverford Col, BA, 42; Yale Univ, BD, 52, PhD, 56. **CAREER** From asst prof to assoc prof, 55-65, chmn dept relig & philos, 59-79, chmn div humanities, 72-75, Prof, 65-95, Prof Emeritus Relig & Philos, Wilmington Col, Ohio, 95-; Dir, Thomas R Kelly Relig Ctr, 62- & Actg Dir Peace Studies, 78-, Ed, J Quaker Relig Thought, 63-69; chmn, Quaker Theol Discussion Group, 69-77; asst clerk Am sect, Friends World Comt, 68-; Woodbrooke Col fel, spring, 72; Wistar Brown fel, Haverford Col, 78-79; Founder, Friend's Asn for Higher Educ, 80; co-chair, FAHE, 80-85. **MEMBERSHIPS** Am Soc Church Hist. **RESEARCH** Seventeenth century Puritanism; historical theology. **SELECTED PUBLICATIONS** Auth,The concept of Christ as servant as motivation for Quaker service, Quaker Relig Thought, fall 63; A believing people: Contemporary relevance, In: Conference on Concept of the Believer's Church, Scottsdale, Pa Herald, 70; The message of Quakers, In: The Three M's of Quakerism, Friends United, 71; George Fox's attitude toward war, Acad Fel Annapolis, 72; ed, Quaker Understanding of Christ & Authority, Friends World Comt, 74; auth, Worship as experienced, In: Quaker Religious Thought, Quaker Theol Disc Group, Alburtis, Pa, winter 75; Biblical basis of Peacemaking, In: New Call to Peacemaking, Friends World Comt, 77; Christ the center of holism, In: Essays in Holism: A Quaker Approach, Friends United, 78; ed, The Power of the Lord is Over All: The Pastoral Letters of George Fox, Friends United Press, 89; auth, Subject of Festschrift: Essays in Honor of T. Canby Jones: Practiced in the Presence, Friends United Press, 94. **CONTACT ADDRESS** Wilmington Col, Ohio, 251 Ludovic St, Box 1323, Wilmington, OH, 45177-2499.

JONES, WILLIAM A., JR.
PERSONAL Born 02/24/1934, Louisville, KY, m **DISCIPLINE** THEOLOGY **EDUCATION** Univ of KY, BA 1958; Crozer Theol Sem, BD 1961; Benedict Coll, SC, Hon DD 1969; Colgate Rochester-Bexley Hall-Crozer Theol Sem, PhD 1975. **CAREER** 1st Baptist Church Phila, pastor 1959-62; BETHANY BAPTIST CHURCH BROOKLYN, PASTOR 1962-. **HONORS AND AWARDS** Editor Missions Outlook 1961-62; cited "Man in the News" NY Times; Man of the Yr Brooklyn Jaycees 1967; Outstanding Brooklynite NY Recorder Poll 1970; Ophelia Devore Achievement Awd 1970; Black Heritage Assn Awd 1971; Capital Formation Comm Leader Awd 1971; Comm Serv Awd Brooklyn Chap Phi Beta Sigma 1972; Frederick Douglass Awd NY Urban League 1972; Natl Assn of Health Serv Exec Awd 1975; Disting Serv Awd Colony Club First AME Zion Ch Brooklyn 1977; Freedom Awd Comm Mus of Brooklyn Inc 1978; listed in 100 Most Influential Black Amers Ebony Magazine 1979; 1 of America's 15 Outstanding Black Preachers Ebony Mag 1984. **MEMBERSHIPS** Preacher at churches, conventions, conferences univs & colls in Amer, England, Israel, India, Australia, W Africa; pres Prog Nat Bapt Conv 1968-70; prof Black Ch Studies Colgate Rochester Bexley Hall Crozer 1972-76; preacher for NBC's "Art of Living" 1977; frequently featured Conf Echoes Family Radio Network; mem Martin Luther King Jr Fellow Inc; mem Genl Council Bapt World Alliance; trustee, vis prof, Colgate Rochester Div Sch; vis prof Princeton Theol Sem; coord Min's Com on Job Oppors for Brooklyn 1963-64; bd chmn Bedford Stuyvesant Youth in Action 1965-67; founder/chmn Greater NY SCLC Operation Breadbasket 1967-72; chmn Natl SCLC Operation Breadbasket 1972-73; vis prof Practical Tehol Union Theol Sem 1975-76; chmncombd Kings Co Hosp Ctr 1970-77; adj prof romiletics Wesley Tehol Semsh DC 1976-77. **SELECTED PUBLICATIONS** Co-author "The Black Ch Looks at the Bicentennial" PNB Pub House Elgin IL 1976; author "Freedom of Conscience, The Black Experience in Amer" Religious Liberty in the Crossfire of Creeds-Ecumenical Press Philadelphia 1978; author "God in th Ghetto" PNB Pub House Elgin IL 1979. **CONTACT ADDRESS** Bethany Baptist Church, 460 Sumner Ave, Brooklyn, NY, 11216.

JONES, WILLIAM B.
DISCIPLINE PHILOSOPHY **EDUCATION** Univ Va, PhD(physics), 70; Vaderbilt Univ, PhD(philos), 75. **CAREER** Chair, dept, 85-91. **SELECTED PUBLICATIONS** Areas: philosophy of science and technology. **CONTACT ADDRESS** Old Dominion Univ, 4100 Powhatan Ave, Norfolk, VA, 23058. **EMAIL** WBJones@odu.edu

JONES, WILLIAM BOWDOIN
PERSONAL Born 05/02/1928, Los Angeles, CA, m, 1953 **DISCIPLINE** LAW **EDUCATION** Univ of CA-Los Angeles, AB 1949; Univ Southern CA, JD 1952. **CAREER** Private Practice, attorney-at-law 1952-62; US Foreign Service Officer, diplomat 1962-84; US Dept of State, Washington, deputy assistant secretary of state, 1969-73; US Dept of State, Paris France, chief, US mission to UNESCO, 1973-77; US Dept State chairman US-Japan cultural conference, Hawaii, 1973; US Dept of State, ambassador to Haiti 1977-80; Hampton University, diplomat-in-residence, 1980-81; Univ of VA, ambassador in residence 1984-85; Woodrow Wilson Foundation, Princeton, NJ, fellow, 1986-87; US House of Rep Subcommittee on Western Affairs, staff dir, 1987; The International Business Law Firm, partner, 1988-91; HAMPDEN SYDNEY COLLEGE, SYDNEY, VA, BD OF TRUSTEES, 1992-, adjunct professor, 1991; Pepperdine University, distinguished visiting professor, 1993. **HONORS AND AWARDS** Outstanding Public Serv CA Legislature 1972; Professional Achievement UCLA Alumni 1980; Merit Awd Alumni Univ So CA 1981; Key to City Los Angeles 1981. **MEMBERSHIPS** Sigma Pi Phi-Boule; Kappa Alpha Psi; Washington Intl Club; CA Bar; District of Columbia, US Supreme Court; Bar of the US Court of Intl Trade 1988; bd of dirs, American Association for the United Nations, National Capital Region, 1996-; US Council, United Nations University, 1997-; James Madison Society, Hampden-Sydney College, 1996-. First African American to be named chief of the US Mission to UNESCO, Paris

JONES, WILLIAM K.
PERSONAL Born 09/01/1930, New York, NY, m, 1952, 3 children **DISCIPLINE** LAW **EDUCATION** Columbia Univ, AB, 52; LLB, 54. **CAREER** From assoc prof to prof law, 59-71, JAMES L DOHR PROF LAW, COLUMBIA UNIV, 71-, Res asst, Am Law Inst, 59-60; res dir comt on licenses & authorizations, Admin Conf US, 61-62; consult, President's Task Force on Commun Policy, 67-68, mem, Task Force on Antitrust Policy, 67-68; consult, Ford Found, 67-68. **MEMBERSHIPS** Am Bar Asn. **RESEARCH** Antitrust policy; communications policy; regulated industries. **SELECTED PUBLICATIONS** Auth, Strict Liability for Hazardous Enterprise, Columbia Law Rev, Vol 92, Pg 1744, 92, Columbia Law Rev, Vol 0092, 92. **CONTACT ADDRESS** Sch of Law, Columbia Univ, 435 W 116th St, New York, NY, 10027-7201.

JONES, WILLIAM PAUL
PERSONAL Born 02/13/1930, Johnstown, PA, m, 1954, 5 children **DISCIPLINE** RELIGION **EDUCATION** Mt Union Col, BA, 51; Yale Univ, BD, 54; MA, 55, PhD, 60. **CAREER** Part-time instr, Divinity Sch, Yale Univ, 55-56, col, 56-57; from instr to asst prof relig, Princeton Univ, 58-65; assoc prof, 65-72, PROF PHILOS THEOL, ST PAUL SCH THEOL, MO, 72-, Soc Relig Higher Educ Kent fel, 56; Procter-Gamble & Lilly fels, France, 63-64; theol consult, Joint Strategy for Action Comt, 68- **MEMBERSHIPS** Soc Relig Higher Educ; Am Theol Soc. **RESEARCH** Philosophy of religion; religion and the arts; contemporary theology. **SELECTED PUBLICATIONS** Auth, Caring for Creation--An Ecumenical Approach to the Environmental Crisis, Theology Today, Vol 0051, 95. **CONTACT ADDRESS** St Paul Sch of Theol, Kansas City, MO, 63127.

JONTEPACE, D.
PERSONAL Born 07/07/1951, Berkeley, CA, m, 1976, 2 children **DISCIPLINE** PSYCHOLOGY OF RELIGION **EDUCATION** Univ Chicago, PhD 84. **CAREER** Santa Clara Univ, assoc prof. **HONORS AND AWARDS** Irvine Foun Gnt; Pres Res Gnt. **MEMBERSHIPS** AAR; SSSR. **RESEARCH** Psychology of Religion; Psychoanalysis and Feminism. **SELECTED PUBLICATIONS** Auth, In Defense of an Unfriendly Freud: Psychoanalysis Feminism and Theology in: Pastoral Psychology, forthcoming; Legitimation of Hatred or Inversion into Love: Religion in Kristeva's Re-Reading of Freud in: Res in the Soc Sci Stud of Religion, forthcoming; Feminists Transformations in the Psychology of Religion: New Developments in Method and Theory, Method and Theory in the Stud of Religion, forthcoming; auth, The Swami and the Rorschach: Spiritual Practice Religious Experience and Perceptions, The Innate Capacity: Mysticism Psychology and Philosophy, Robert Formen, ed, Oxford Univ Press, 98; auth, New Directions In Feminist Psychology of Religion: An Introduction, Jour of Fem Studies in Rel, 97; auth, At Home in the Uncanny: Freudian Representations of Death Mothers and the Afterlife, Jour of the Amer Acad Rel, 96; Psychoanalysis After Feminism, Rel Stud Rev, 93. **CONTACT ADDRESS** Dept of religious Studies, Santa Clara Univ, Santa Clara, CA, 95053. **EMAIL** djontepace@scu.edu

JOOHARIGIAN, ROBERT B.
DISCIPLINE PHILOSOPHY **EDUCATION** Univ of Wisconsin, PhD, 77. **CAREER** Schoolcraft Col, Livonia MI, adj prof, 81-, Macomb Comm Col, Warren MI, adj inst, 88-, Central Mich Univ, Troy, adj inst, 88-. **MEMBERSHIPS** APA **RESEARCH** Philosophy of religion. **SELECTED PUBLICATIONS** Auth, God and Natural Evil, Wyndham Hall Press, Bristol IN. **CONTACT ADDRESS** PO Box 1485, Royal Oak, MI, 48068-1485.

JOOS, ERNEST
PERSONAL Born 01/06/1923, Uraiujfalu, Hungary, m, 1949, 6 children **DISCIPLINE** PHILOSOPHY, LITERATURE **EDUCATION** McGill Univ, MA, 59; Inst d'Etudes Medievales, Montreal, Lic en Phil, 66; Univ Montreal, PhD(medieval philos), 70. **CAREER** Asst prof philos, Loyola Col, Montreal, 67-75; PROF PHILOS, CONCORDIA UNIV, 75-, Vis prof philos, Univ Laval, Quebec, 77-78 & Univ de Montreal, 79-81. **MEMBERSHIPS** Can Philos Asn; Am Cath Philos Asn. **RESEARCH** Intentionality; metaphysics-ontology. **SELECTED PUBLICATIONS** Auth, The Words for Preaching--Homiletics Lectures Given in Findenwalde, Laval Theologique Et Philosophique, Vol 0049, 93; Might the End of History Be the Beginning of Wisdom--The Alienation of the Mind in Hegel 'Phenomenology of the Spirit', Laval Theologique Et Philosophique, Vol 0051, 95; Notes on Nietzsche, Laval Theologique et Philosophique, Vol 0051, 95. **CONTACT ADDRESS** Concordia Univ, Montreal, 130 Kenaston Ave, Montreal, PQ, H3R 1M2.

JORDAN, EDDIE J., JR.
PERSONAL Born 10/06/1952, Fort Campbell, KY, m, 1974 **DISCIPLINE** LAW **EDUCATION** Wesleyan Univ, Middletown, CT, BA, 1970-74; Rutgers Law School, Newark, NJ, JD, 1974-77. **CAREER** Pepper, Hamilton & Scheetz, assoc; Southern Univ Law School, professor, 1981; US Attorney's Office, assist US attorney, 1984-87; Sessions & Fishman, assoc, 1987-90, partner, 1990-92; Bryan, Jupiter & Lewis, of counsel, 1992-

94; US DEPT OF JUSTICE, US ATTORNEY, 1994-. **HONORS AND AWARDS** Louis A Martinet Legal Society, A P Tureaud Award, 1992; Victims & Citizens Against Crime, Outstanding Prosecutor Awd, 1995; NAACP, New Orleans Chap, David Ellis Byrd Awd, 1997; Crimefighters Assn of New Orleans, Distinguished Public Svc Awd, 1998. **MEMBERSHIPS** Human Relations Commission, City of N Orleans, advisory comm human relations, 1993; LA State Bar Assn, bd of governors, 1984; Metropolitan Area Comm, bd of dirs, 1990-94; Planned Parenthood of LA, bd of dirs, 1989-94, vice pres, bd of dirs, 1991-93; St Thomas/Irish Channel Consortium, bd of dirs, 1990-94; NAACP, 1993-95; Reducing Alcohol Accessibility to Youth, adv bd; New Orleans chapter of Federal Bar Assn, bd of dirs; Pediatric AIDS Prog, adv bd; New Orleans Community, Teach for America, adv bd; Atty General's Adv Comm, Subcommittee for Controlled Substances/Drug Abuse Prevention, vice chair; Reducing Alcohol Accessibility to Youth, bd of dirs for the New Orleans Chapter of the Federal Bar Assoc, advisory bd for the Pediatric AIDS Program, New Orleans comm advisory bd for Teach for America; vice chair of the Attorney General's advisory comms, subcomm for Controlled Substances/Drug Abuse Prevention; mem, subcommittees for Justice Programs and Organized Crime/Violent Crime; 1998, two-year term on the Attorney General's, advisory comm. **SELECTED PUBLICATIONS** In Search of the Meaning of RICO, LA State Bar Assn; Changing Carnival's old ways is a progressive step, The Times Picayune; Recent Dev in the Law Manual, LA State Bar Assn, 1985-96; Louisiana Appellate Practice Handbook, Lawyers Cooperative Publishing, contributing author. **CONTACT ADDRESS** US Attorney's Office, Eastern District of Louisiana, 501 Magazine St, New Orleans, LA, 70130.

JORDAN, EMMA COLEMAN

PERSONAL Born 11/29/1946, Berkeley, CA **DISCIPLINE** LAW **EDUCATION** CA State U, BA 1969; Howard U, JD 1973. **CAREER** Stanford Law School, tching fellow 1973-74; Univ of Santa Clara, asst prof 1974-75; Georgetown Univ Law Center, prof, 1987- present. **HONORS AND AWARDS** White House Fellow, 1980-81, Outstdng Acad Achvmt Award Phi Alpha Delta 1973; grad 1st in class Howard Law Sch 1973; **MEMBERSHIPS** Exec comm, 1988-91, pres-elect, 1991-92, pres, 1992-93; Assoc of Amer Law Schools; mem Nat Conf of Black Lawyers; Nat Bar Assn; Am Soc of Intl Law; pub mem CA State Bd of Dental & Exmnrs; Am Assn of Law Schs Sects on Commercial Law & Contracts, Minority Grps; mem Charles Houston Bar Assn; bd of dir CA Assn of Black Lawyers; pres Soc of Amer Law Teachers 1986-88; chr CA St Bar Financial Inst Comm; chr AALS Financial Inst & Consumer Fin Serv Sect; bd mem Consumer Action; adv comm Natl Consumer Union Northern CA; mem Amer Law Inst; special asst, Attorney General of the US, 1981. **SELECTED PUBLICATIONS** Co-ed, Race, Gender and Power in America, Oxford Univ Press, 95; Lynching: The Dark Metaphor of American Law, Basic Books, spring 99; Litigation without representation; The Need for Intervention to Affirm Affirmative Action, Harvard Civil Liberties Civil Rights Law Rev 1979; "After the Merger of Contribution & Indemnity, What are the Limits of Comparative Loss Allocation" AR St Law Rev 1980; "Problems & Prospects of Participation in Affirmative Action Litigation" UC Davis Law Rev 1980; Limitations of the Intl Lega Mech Namibia 1972; "Ending the Floating Check Game," Hastings Law Review, 1986; "Taking Voting Rights Seriously," Nebraska Law Review, 1986. **CONTACT ADDRESS** Sch of Law, Georgetown Univ, 600 New Jersey Ave, Washington, DC, 20001-2075.

JORDAN, EMMA COLEMAN

PERSONAL Born 11/29/1946, Berkeley, CA **DISCIPLINE** EDUCATION, LAW **EDUCATION** CA State U, BA 1969; Howard U, JD 1973. **CAREER** Stanford Law School, tching fellow 1973-74; Univ of Santa Clara, asst prof 1974-75; Georgetown Univ Law Center, prof, 1987- present. **HONORS AND AWARDS** White House Fellow, 1980-81, Limitations of the Intl Lega Mech Namibia 1972; Outstdng Acad Achvmt Award Phi Alpha Delta 1973; grad 1st in class Howard Law Sch 1973; **MEMBERSHIPS** Exec comm, 1988-91, pres-elect, 1991-92, pres, 1992-93; Assoc of Amer Law Schools; mem Nat Conf of Black Lawyers; Nat Bar Assn; Am Soc of Intl Law; pub mem CA State Bd of Dental & Exmnrs; Am Assn of Law Schs Sects on Commercial Law & Contracts, Minority Grps; mem Charles Houston Bar Assn; bd of dir CA Assn of Black Lawyers; pres Soc of Amer Law Teachers 1986-88; chr CA St Bar Financial Inst Comm; chr AALS Financial Inst & Consumer Fin Serv Sect; bd mem Consumer Action; adv comm Natl Consumer Union Northern CA; mem Amer Law Inst; special asst, Attorney General of the US, 1981. **SELECTED PUBLICATIONS** co-ed, Race, Gender and Power in America, Oxford University Press, 1995; Lynching: The Dark Metaphor of American Law, Basic Books, spring 1999; Without representation; The Need for Intervention to Affirm Affirmative Action, Harvard Civil Liberties Civil Rights Law Rev 1979, After the Merger of Contribution & Indemnity, What are the Limits of Comparative Loss Allocation" AR St Law Rev 1980; "Problems & Prospects of Participation in Affirmative Action Litigation" UC Davis Law Rev 1980; Ending the Floating Check Game, Hastings Law Review, 1986; Taking Voting Rights Seriously, Nebraska Law Review, 1986. **CONTACT ADDRESS** Sch Law, Georgetown Univ, 600 New Jersey Ave, Washington, DC, 20001-2075.

JORDAN, MARK D.

DISCIPLINE PHILOSOPHY OF SCIENCE **EDUCATION** St. John's Col, Ba 73; Univ Tex, MA, 75, PhD, 77. **CAREER** Prof. **RESEARCH** Medieval natural philosophy and medicine through the 13th century. **SELECTED PUBLICATIONS** Auth, Ordering Wisdom: The Hierarchy of Philosophical Discourses in Aquinas, 86; The Invention of Sodomy in Christian Theology, 97; The Construction of a Philosophical Medicine: Exegesis and Argument in Salernitan Teaching on the Soul, 90; The Critique of Galen in Thirteenth Century Philosophy and Theology, 92; The Fortune of Constantine's Pantegni, 94. **CONTACT ADDRESS** History and Philosophy of Science Dept, Univ of Notre Dame, Notre Dame, IN, 46556. **EMAIL** Mark.D.Jordan.2@nd.edu

JORDAN, ROBERT WELSH

PERSONAL Born 12/20/1936, Miami Beach, FL, m, 1962, 1 child **DISCIPLINE** PHILOSOPHY, PHILOSOPHY OF HISTORY **EDUCATION** Univ Houston, BS, 57; New Sch Social Res, MA, 70. **CAREER** Asst prof, 70-82, ASSOC PROF PHILOS, CO STATE UNIV, 82-. **MEMBERSHIPS** Husserl Circle; Soc Phenomenol & Existential Philos; Am Soc Value Inquiry. **RESEARCH** Twentieth century Continental philosophy; German philosophy since Kant; philosophy of history and social science. **SELECTED PUBLICATIONS** Auth, Vico and Husserl: History and Historical Science, In: Giambattista Vico's Science of Humanity, John's Hopkins Univ Press, 76; Vico and the Phenomenology of the Moral Sphere, Social Res, Vol 43, 76; Das transzendentale Ich als Seiendes in der Welt, Perspecktiven Philos, Vol 5, 79; Das Gesetz, die Anklage und Klc Prozess: Franz Kafka und Franz Brentano, Jahrbuch deutschen Schillerges, Vol 24, 80; auth, intro to & transl of Husserl's Inaugeral Lecture at Freiburg im Breisgau (1917): Pure Phenomenology, its Method and its Field of Investigation, In: Husserl: The Shorter Works, Univ Notre Dame Press, 80; Extended Critical Review of Edmind Husserl's Vorlesungen uper Ethik and Wertlehre, 1908-1914, ed by Ullrich Melle (Husserliana, vol 28), Dordrecht, Boston, London: Kluwer Academic Pubs, 88, in Husserl Studies 8, 92; Phenomenalism, Idealism, and Gurwisch's Account of the Sensory Noema, in To Work at the Foundations, J. C. Evans and R. W. Stufflebeam, eds, Kluwer Academic Pubs, 97; The Part Played by Value in the Modification of Open into Attractive possibilities, Ch 5 oh Phenomenology of Values and Valuing, J. G. Hart and Lester Embree, eds, Kluwer Academic Pubs, 97; Hartmann, Nicolai, in Encyclopedia of Phenomenology, Lester Embree, gen ed, Kluwer Academic Pubs, 97; Value Theory in Encyclopedia of Phenomenology, Lester Embree, gen ed, Kluwer Academic Pubs, 97. **CONTACT ADDRESS** Dept of Philos, Colorado State Univ, Fort Collins, CO, 80523-0001. **EMAIL** rjordan@vines.colostate.edu

JORDAN, SANDRA D.

PERSONAL Born 12/03/1951, Philadelphia, Pennsylvania, m, 1973 **DISCIPLINE** LAW **EDUCATION** Wilberforce University, BS Ed, magna cum laude, 1973; University of Pittsburgh Law School, JD, 1979. **CAREER** US Dept of Justice, asst US attorney, 1979-88; US Dept of Independent Counsel, Iran Contra, assoc counsel, 1988-91; University of Pittsburgh Law School, prof, 1989-. **HONORS AND AWARDS** US Attorney General Special Commendation, 1984; Allegheny County Bar Association, Exceptionally Qualified for Judiciary, 1992. **MEMBERSHIPS** Homer S Brown Law Association, 1979-; National Bar Association, 1979-; Disciplinary Bd, Supreme Court of PA, 1990-94; Pennsylvania Judicial Conduct Bd, vice chair, 1994-. **SELECTED PUBLICATIONS** Published "Classified Information & Conflicts," Columbia Law Review vol 91, No 7, 1991. **CONTACT ADDRESS** Professor, Univ of Pittsburgh, School of Law, 3900 Forbes Ave, Rm 529, Pittsburgh, PA, 15260. **EMAIL** jordan@law.pitt.edu

JORGENSEN, DANNY L.

PERSONAL Born 01/23/1951, Sidney, MT **DISCIPLINE** RELIGION **EDUCATION** N Ariz Univ, BS, 72; W Ky Univ, MA, 74; Ohio State Univ, PhD, 79. **CAREER** Prof relig studies, 92- courtesy prof sociol, 97-, undergrad honors prg fac, 96-, Univ S Fla. **HONORS AND AWARDS** Best Article Award, John Whitmer Hist Asn, 94, 96; Outstanding Undergrad Tchg Award, Univ S Fla, 91-92. **MEMBERSHIPS** John Whitmer Hist Asn; Mormon Hist Asn. **SELECTED PUBLICATIONS** Auth, Less-Known and Historically Unimportant? Studying the Lives of Reorganized Latter Day Saint Women, Restoration Studies, 98; auth, Religion and Modernization: Secularization or Sacralization?, Relig & Political Order: Politics in Class & Contemporary Christianity, Islam & Judaism, 96; auth, Neo-Paganism in America: How Witchcraft Matters Today, The Relig Factor: Intro to How Relig Matters, 96; auth, The Old Fox: Alpheus Cutler, Differing Visions: Dissenters in Mormon Hist, 94; auth, Cutler's Camp at the Big Grove on Silver Creek: A Mormon Settlement in Iowa, 1847-1853, Nauvoo Jour, Fall, 97; auth, Sisters' Lives, Sisters' Voices: Neglected RLDS Herstories, John Whitmer Hist Asn Jour, 97; auth, Dissent and Schism in the Early Church: Explaining Mormon Fissiparousness, Dialogue: Jour Mormon Thought, Fall, 95; auth, Conflict in the Camps of Israel: The Emergence of the 1853 Cutlerite Schism, Jour Mormon Hist, Spring, 95; auth, The Scattered Saints of Southwestern Iowa: Cutlerite-Josephite Conflict and Rivalry, 1855-1865, John Whitmer Hist Asn Jour, 93. **CONTACT ADDRESS** Dept Religious Studies, South Fla Univ, 4202 E Fowler Ave. CPR 107, Tampa, FL, 33620-5550.

JOSEPH, NORMA BAUMEL

PERSONAL Born 10/12/1944, NY, m, 1965, 4 children **DISCIPLINE** RELIGION **EDUCATION** Concordia Univ, PhD, 95. **CAREER** Assoc prof. **RESEARCH** Judaism; gender, Jewish law, women & relig. **CONTACT ADDRESS** 1455 de Maisonneuve West, Montreal, PQ, H3W I5I. **EMAIL** nojo@vax2.concordia.ca

JOSEPH, STEPHEN

PERSONAL Born 11/27/1940, Worcester, MA **DISCIPLINE** PHILOSOPHY **EDUCATION** Brown Univ, BA, 62; Univ Penn, MA, 65, PhD, 79. **CAREER** Philo Dept Ch, 91-, Prof, 82-98, Framingham State College; math Teach, 82, Univ MA; philo Teach, 68-82, Boston State College. **MEMBERSHIPS** APA; MSCA. **RESEARCH** Ethics; Philosophy of Religion. **CONTACT ADDRESS** Crocker Hall, Framingham State Col, 100 State St, Framingham, MA, 01701. **EMAIL** sjoseph@fsc.edu

JOSEPHSON, GOODMAN

PERSONAL Born 07/30/1945, Tubigen, Germany, m, 1967, 2 children **DISCIPLINE** PHILOSOPHY **EDUCATION** Ohio State Univ, BA, 68; MA, 72; PhD, 81. **CAREER** Assoc prof, Columbus Coll of Art and Design, 72-; res assoc, Ohio State Univ, 87-. **MEMBERSHIPS** Am Philos Asn. **RESEARCH** Artificial Intelligence; Philosophy of Art and Design; Philosophy of Media; Illustrator. **SELECTED PUBLICATIONS** Auth, Controversies in Artificial Intelligence, The World & I, 95; Remedial Readings on Advertising, AIGA J of Graphic Design, 97; From Idolatry to Advertising: Visual Art and Contemporary Culture, 96; coauth, Architecture of Intelligence: The Problems and Current Approaches to Solutions, Artificial Intelligence and Neural Networks, 94; co-ed, What Kind of Science is Artificial Intelligence, Abductive Inference, Computations, Philosophy, Technology, 94. **CONTACT ADDRESS** 93 East Riverglen Dr, Worthington, OH, 43085. **EMAIL** sj@cis.ohio-state.edu

JOST, TIMOTHY STOLZFUS

PERSONAL Born 11/25/1948, Reedley, CA, m, 1982, 3 children **DISCIPLINE** LAW **EDUCATION** Univ CA, Santa Cruz, BA, 70; Univ Chicago, JD, 75. **CAREER** Asst Prof Law to NEWTON D. BAKER, BAKER & HOSTETLER CHAIR OF LAW AND PROF OF COL OF MEDICINE AND PUBLIC HEALTH, DIVISION OF HEALTH SERVICES AND MANAGEMENT AND POLICY, OH STATE UNIV, 81-. **HONORS AND AWARDS** OH State Univ Distinguished Scholar Award, 96; Fulbright Awards, 89, 96. **MEMBERSHIPS** Am Soc of Law, Medicine and Ethics; Am Health Lawyers Asn; Gesellschaft fur Recht und Politik im Gesundheitswesen. **RESEARCH** Law and medicine; property law. **SELECTED PUBLICATIONS** Auth, Health LawTreatise, with Barry Furrow, Thomas Greaney, Sandra Johnson, and Robert Schwartz, West, 95; Health Law Hornbook, with Barry Furrow, Thomas Greaney, Sandra Johnson, and Robert Schwartz, West, 95; Cases, Problems & Materials in Health Law, 3rd ed, with Barry Furrow, Thomas Greaney, Sandra Johnson, and Robert Schwartz, West, 97; Regulation of the health Care Professions, ed, Health Admin Press, 97; The Law of Medicare and Medicaid Fraud and Abuse, with Sharon Davies, West, 98. **CONTACT ADDRESS** Law Sch, Ohio State Univ, 55 W 12th Ave, Columbus, OH, 43210-1306. **EMAIL** jost.1@osu.edu

JOY, LYNN S.

DISCIPLINE PHILOSOPHY **EDUCATION** Harvard Univ, PhD, 82. **CAREER** Fel Bunting Inst, Radcliffe Col, 88-89; adv ed, 89-. **RESEARCH** Philos strategies of philosophers from Descartes to Kant; mod philos; continental philos; hist and philos of sci. **SELECTED PUBLICATIONS** Auth, Gassendi the Atomist: Advocate of History in an Age of Science, Cambridge Univ, 87. **CONTACT ADDRESS** Philos Dept, Duke Univ, West Duke Bldg, Durham, NC, 27706. **EMAIL** ljoy@acpub.duke.edu

JOY, PETER

PERSONAL Born 12/02/1951, Youngstown, OH, s **DISCIPLINE** LAW **EDUCATION** Case Western Reserve Univ Law School, JD, 77. **CAREER** Asst prof and dir, Milton A. Kramer Law Clinic, Case Western Univ School of Law, 84-98; prof and dir, Milton A. Kramer Law Clinic, Case Western Univ School of Law, 98; prof, Washington Univ School of Law, 98-. **MEMBERSHIPS** AALS; CLEA. **RESEARCH** Legal profession; clinical legal educ; trial practice and procedure; criminal law. **SELECTED PUBLICATIONS** Auth, "Report of the Committee on the Future of the In-House Clinic", in 42 J. Legal Ed 508, 94; auth, "The MacCrate Report: Moving Toward Integrated Learning Experiences", in 1 Clinical L Rev 401, 94; auth, "What We Talk About When We Talk About Professionalism", in 1 Geo J Legal Ethics 987, 94; auth, "A Time to Disrobe to

Save Your Honor", in National J, 95; auth, "Losing Titles", in Ohio Law, 96; auth, "Unpublished Opinions Stunt Common Law", in National J, 96; auth, "Clients Are Consumers, Too", in 82 ABAJ 120, 96; auth, "Clinical Scholarship: Improving the Practice of Law", in 2 Clinical L Rev 385. 96; auth, "Amendments to Disciplinary Rules Create New Expectations for Ohio Lawyers", in Law & Fact, 97; auth, "Ethics Perspectives: What Are the Ethical Ramifications of an 'Of Counsel' Affiliation?", in 68 Cleveland B J 20, 97; auth, "Clinical Experience Translates to Client Experience", in 11 NALP Bull, 98; auth, "Submission of the Association of American Law Schools to the Supreme Court's Student Practice Rule", in 4 Clinical L Rev 539, 98; coauth, "Access to Justice, Academic Freedom, and Political Inference: A Clinical Program Under Siege", in 4 Clinical L Rev 531, 98. **CONTACT ADDRESS** Washington Univ School of Law, One Brookings Dr., Campus Box 1120, St. Louis, MO, 63130. **EMAIL** joy@wulaw.wustl.edu

JOYNER, IRVING L.
PERSONAL Born 12/11/1944, Brooklyn, New York, d **DISCIPLINE** LAW **EDUCATION** Long Island Univ, Brooklyn NY, BS, 1970; Rutgers Univ School of Law, Newark NJ, JD. **CAREER** United Church of Christ Comm for Racial Justice, New York NY, dir of criminal justice, 1968-78; Currie & Joyner, Raleigh NC, attorney at law, 1978-80; Natl Prison Project of ACLU, Washington DC, staff attorney, 1980-81; Currie, Pugh & Joyner, Raleigh NC, attorney at law, 1981-85; NC Central Univ School of Law, Durham NC, assoc dean and prof of law, 1985-. **HONORS AND AWARDS** Outstanding Contribution to Racial Justice, Assn of Black Law Students, 1977; Paul Robeson Award, Black Amer Law Student Assn, 1977; Professor of the Year, NCCU Student Bar Assn, 1985; Living Legacy Award OA Dupree Scholarship Foundation, 1987; Outstanding Contribution to Civil Rights, Wake Forest Black Law Student Assn 1987; author of The Black Lawyer in NC, article, 1988; Conflicts of Interest, article, 1988; President's Award by LaGrange, Frink Alumni and Friends Assn, 1991; Lawyers of the Year Award by North Carolina Assn of Black Lawyers, 1995; Outstanding Teacher's Awd, North Carolina Central University Law School Student Bar Association. **MEMBERSHIPS** Mem/former pres, NC Assn of Black Lawyers, 1977-; mem, NC State Bar, 1977-; mem, Natl Bar Assn, 1977-; mem, NC Academy of Trial Lawyers, 1977-; Federal Bar Advisory Council, 1985-. **SELECTED PUBLICATIONS** Police Misconduct Litigation CLE manuscript and Law Review article, 1991; Preparation and Use of Requests for Jury Instructions, CLE manuscript, 1988; Criminal Procedure in NC, book, 1989; Supplements to Criminal Procedure in North Carolina, 1991-94; The Status of African-American Lawyers in North Carolina, article, 1992. **CONTACT ADDRESS** Professor of Law, North Carolina Central Univ School of Law, 1512 S Alston Ave, Durham, NC, 27707.

JUENGER, FRIEDRICH K.
PERSONAL Born 02/18/1930, Frankfurt, Germany, m, 1967, 2 children **DISCIPLINE** LAW **EDUCATION** Univ Mich, MCL, 57; Columbia Univ, JD, 60. **CAREER** Assoc prof, Wayne State Univ, 66-68, prof, 68-75; vis prof, 75-76, Prof Law, Univ Calif, Davis, 76-, Edward L Barrett, Jr, prof Law, 93-;Vis prof, Univ Freiburg, West Germany, 72-73, 74; vis prof Max-Planck Inst Foreign & Comparative Law 81-82; Univ Jean Moulin, Lyon, France, 84; Eaason-Weinmann vis prof Tulane Univ, 89; vis prof J W Goethe Univ, Frankfurt/Main, 92; Allen Allen & Hemsley fel, Univ Sydney, 93; vis prof Univ Francaise du Pacifique, Tahiti, 93; vis prof Univ Michigan, 94; vis prof Victoria Univ of Wellington, 98. ed, Am J Comp Law, 76-. **HONORS AND AWARDS** Volkswagen Found grant, 72-73; Fulbright-Hays prof res fel, 81-82. **MEMBERSHIPS** Am Law Inst; Am Soc Int Law; Gesellschaft fur Rechtsvergleichung; Soc Pub Teachers Law; Int Acad Comp Law. **RESEARCH** Conflict of laws; comparative law; international transactions. **SELECTED PUBLICATIONS** Coauth (with Lajos Schmidt), The German Stock Corporation Act, Commerce Clearing House, 67; Business Regulation in the Common Market Nations--West Germany, McGraw-Hill, 69; auth, Choice of law in interstate torts, 118 Univ Pa Law Rev 202, 69; Recognition of foreign divorces--British and American perspectives, 20 Am J Comp Law 1, 72; Moglichkeiten eirner Neuorientierung des Internationalen Privatrechts, 26 Neue Juristische wochenschrift 1521, 73; Trends in European conflicts law, 60 Cornell Law Rev 969, 75; Marital property and the conflict of laws: A tale of two countries, In: Symposium in Honor of Willis L M Reese, 81 Columbia Law Rev 933, 81; Parteiautonomie und objecktive Ankn-u06pfung im EG-Ubereinkommen zum Internationalen Vertragsrecht--Eine Kritik aus amerikanischer Sicht, 46 Rabels Zeitschrift 57, 82. **CONTACT ADDRESS** Law School, Univ of California, Davis, King Hall, Davis, CA, 95616-5200. **EMAIL** fkjuenger@ucdavis.edu

JUERGENSMEYER, JULIAN C.
DISCIPLINE LAW **EDUCATION** Duke Univ, AB, JD. **CAREER** Gerald A. Sohn Res scholar; prof, dir, LLM in Comp Law Prog and aff prof Urban and Regional Planning, Univ Fla, 69-. **MEMBERSHIPS** Ohio Bar; Order of the Coif; Phi Beta Kappa; Omicron Delta Kappa. **RESEARCH** Land use planning law, property, intl environmental law, agricultural law. **SELECTED PUBLICATIONS** Coauth, A Practitioner's Guide to Impact Fees; Florida Land Use and Growth Management Law; Urban Planning and Land Development Control Law. **CONTACT ADDRESS** School of Law, Univ of Florida, PO Box 117625, Gainesville, FL, 32611-7625. **EMAIL** juergens@law.ufl.edu

JULIANO, ANN CAREY
DISCIPLINE CIVIL PROCEDURE AND EMPLOYMENT DISCRIMINATION **EDUCATION** Univ Pa, BA, 89; Cornell Law Sch, JD, 92. **CAREER** Asst prof, Villanova Univ; law clerk, Honorable Stephanie K. Seymour, US Ct Appeals 10th Circuit and later to, Honorable Raymond J. Pettine, US Dist Ct Dist RI; from trial atty in the Indian Resources Sect to spec asst to asst atty gen Lois J. Schiffer, US Dept Justice; Env and Natural Resources Div; past prof lectr, George Washington Univ Nat Law Ctr. **HONORS AND AWARDS** Special Commendation for Outstanding serv, Dept Justice, 97. **RESEARCH** Employment discrimination. **SELECTED PUBLICATIONS** Auth, Did She Ask For It: The Unwelcome Requirement in Sexual Harassment Cases, 77 Cornell L. Rev 1558, 92. **CONTACT ADDRESS** Law School, Villanova Univ, 800 Lancaster Ave, Villanova, PA, 19085-1692. **EMAIL** juliano@law.vill.edu

JUNG, DARRYL
DISCIPLINE PHILOSOPHY **EDUCATION** McGill Univ, BA, 85, MA, 90; MIT, PhD, 94. **CAREER** Asst prof. **RESEARCH** Philosophy of mathematics; philosophy of logic; philosophy of language; early analytic philosophy; mathematical logic; set theory. **SELECTED PUBLICATIONS** Auth, A Formalisation of the Logical Theory of Principia Mathematica, Bull Symbolic Logic, 97; Russell's Early Mathematical Philosophy (rev), 97; On Russell's Conception of Logic: The Notion of Formal System in Principia Mathematica, Bull Symbolic Logic, 96; The Vicious-Circle Principle, Bull Symbolic Logic, 95. **CONTACT ADDRESS** Dept of Philosophy, Florida State Univ, 211 Wescott Bldg, Tallahassee, FL, 32306. **EMAIL** djung@mailer.fsu.edu

JUNG, L. SHANNON
PERSONAL Born 07/23/1943, Baton Rouge, LA, M, 1974, 3 children **DISCIPLINE** ETHICS **EDUCATION** Washington & Lee Univ, BA, 65; Union Theological Seminary, BD, 68; Yale, STM 69; Vanderbilt, PhD, 74. **CAREER** Assoc prof, 79-87, Concordin Col; prof of rural ministry and dir, 1987- , Wartburg and the Univ of Dubuque **HONORS AND AWARDS** Outstanding faculty award; NEH grants; Northwestern area, Lilly, Louisville, Pew, other grants. **MEMBERSHIPS** AAR; SCE; Amer Sociological Assn. **RESEARCH** Ecology; the implications of physical constitution of human beings for ethics; Theology of land; Rural congregations. **SELECTED PUBLICATIONS** Auth, We Are Home: A Spirtuality of the Environment, Paulist, 93; coauth, Rural Congregational Studies: A Guide for Good Shepherds, Abingon, 97; coauth, Moral Issues and Christian Response, 98; auth, Rural Ministry: The Shape of the Renewal to Come, Abingdon, 98. **CONTACT ADDRESS** 3099 St. Anne Dr., Dubuque, IA, 52001. **EMAIL** lsjung@aol.com

JUNG, PATRICIA BEATTIE
PERSONAL Born 09/21/1949, Great Falls, MN, m, 1974, 3 children **DISCIPLINE** CHRISTIAN ETHICS **EDUCATION** Unv of Santa Clara, BA, 71; Vanderbilt Univ, MA, 74, PhD, 79. **CAREER** Assoc prof, Loyola Univ Chicago, 95-; Asst prof, Concordia Col, 79-87; adj fac, Lutheran Theol Sem, 93; assoc prof, Wartburt Theol Sem, 88-95. **HONORS AND AWARDS** John and Theresa Mulcahy Res Support Grant on Cath Issues, 98; Exxon Vis Fel in Ethics and Med, Baylor Col of Med, 85. **MEMBERSHIPS** Soc of Christian Ethics; SCE; Cath Theol Soc of Amer; Amer Acad of Religion **RESEARCH** Sexual and medical ethics; Feminist ethics. **SELECTED PUBLICATIONS** Ed, Homosexuality and the Biblical Renewal of Catholic Moral Theology; coed, Good Sex; coed, Moral Issues and Christian Response, 98; coauth, Heterosexism: An Ethical Challenge, 93. **CONTACT ADDRESS** Loyola Univ, Chicago, 6525 N Sheridan Rd, Chicago, IL, 60626-5385. **EMAIL** pjung@wpo.it.luc.edu

JUNKER, KIRK W.
PERSONAL Born 05/02/1959, Pittsburgh, PA, s **DISCIPLINE** LAW; RHETORIC **EDUCATION** Penn State Univ, BA, 81; Duquesne Univ, JD, 84, Univ of Pittsburg, PhD, 96 **CAREER** Asst counsel, Pennsylvania Dept of Environmental Protection, 88-96; Adjunct Prof, Duquesne Univ, 95-present; lectr, The Open Univ, London, 96-98; lectr, Dublin City Univ, 98-present. **MEMBERSHIPS** British Assoc for the Advancement of Sci; Amer Assoc for the Advancement of Sci; Natl Communication Assoc; Internatl Soc for the Hist of Rhetoric; Society for the Social Study of Science; German-American Lawyers Assoc. **RESEARCH** Rhetoric; rhetoric and communication of sci; law; environmental policy. **SELECTED PUBLICATIONS** auth, Future Works '95: Fakten, Wege, Visionen, Citizen Participation in Environmental Protection, Amerika Haus, Munich, 96; auth, Juris, Environmental Regulation and Risk Mgt for Expansion and Direct Investment in Business in the U.S., 96; coauth, Science and the Public, More than Just Doing What's Right: Ethics in Science, The Science Wars, auth, Science, Regulation, and Standards, Informing Publics about Ozone Pollution, Open University Press, 98; Ed, Law and Science Special Issue of Social Epistemology, 99; auth, Science Communication, Scientists Communicating With Other Professionals, Open Univ Press, 99; auth, Rescuing All Our Futures: The Future of Future Studies, Cloning the Future, Adamantine Press, London, 98; coed, Science Communication: Professional Contexts, Routledge, London, 98. **CONTACT ADDRESS** 39 Palewell Pk, London, ., SW14 8JQ. **EMAIL** k.w.junker@open.ac.uk

JURISSON, CYNTHIA
PERSONAL Born 09/09/1958, Chicago, IL, m, 1990, 3 children **DISCIPLINE** RELIGIOUS STUDIES **EDUCATION** Augustova Col, BA, 80; Luther Northwestern Theol Sem, MDiv, 84; Princeton Theol Sem, PhD, 94. **CAREER** Assoc prof, 88- **MEMBERSHIPS** Am Soc of Church Hist; Am Acad of Relig; Lutheran Hist Conf. **RESEARCH** Women in the history of Christiantiy; Revivalism; History of Christian thought. **SELECTED PUBLICATIONS** Auth, Understanding One Another: A Congregational Resource for the African Methodist Episcopal Church and the Evangelical Lutheran Church in America. **CONTACT ADDRESS** Lutheran Sch of Theol, 1100 E 55th St, Chicago, IL, 60615. **EMAIL** cjurisson@lstc.edu

JUST, FELIX
PERSONAL Born 11/02/1959, Berlin, Germany, s **DISCIPLINE** RELIGIOUS STUDIES, NEW TESTAMENT **EDUCATION** Yale Univ, PhD, 98. **CAREER** Asst prof Theol Stud, Loyola Marymount Univ, 96-. **HONORS AND AWARDS** Phi Beta Kappa **MEMBERSHIPS** Catholic Bibl Asn; Soc Bibl Lit; Cath Theol Soc Am; Col Theol Soc. **RESEARCH** Gospel of John, medicine and miracles in the Greco-Roman world, Book of Revelation. **CONTACT ADDRESS** Dept of Theol Stud, Loyola Marymount Univ, 7900 Loyola Blvd, Los Angeles, CA, 90045-8400. **EMAIL** fjust@lmumail.lmu.edu

K

KAC, MICHAEL
DISCIPLINE PHILOSOPHY **EDUCATION** Univ Calif Los Angeles, PhD. **RESEARCH** Syntax and semantics of natural language; philosophical foundation of linguistics. **SELECTED PUBLICATIONS** Auth, What Is Categorial Grammar Really Good For?, John Benjamins, 93; Grammars and Grammaticality, John Benjamins, 92; A Simplified Theory of Boolean Semantic Types, J Semantics, 92; Corepresentation of Grammatical Structure, Univ Minn, 78; co-auth, Theoretical Implications of Disordered Syntactic Processing, Lang Sci, 92. **CONTACT ADDRESS** Philosophy Dept, Univ of Minnesota, Twin Cities, 355 Ford Hall, 224 Church St SE, Minneapolis, MN, 55455. **EMAIL** kac@cs.umn.edu

KADENS, MICHAEL G.
DISCIPLINE LAW **EDUCATION** Univ Mich, BA; Stanford Univ, JD. **CAREER** Prof. **SELECTED PUBLICATIONS** Auth, Practitioner's Guide to Treatment of Seller's Products Liability in Asset Acquisitions, Univ Toledo, 78; Proposed Subchapter S Amendments, Taxes, 80. **CONTACT ADDRESS** Col Law, Univ of Toledo, Toledo, OH, 43606. **EMAIL** mkadens@utnet.utoledo.edu

KADISH, MORTIMER R.
PERSONAL Born 12/02/1916, New York, NY, m, 1973, 1 child **DISCIPLINE** PHILOSOPHY **EDUCATION** Columbia Univ, PhD, 50. **CAREER** Asst, assoc, full prof, Western Reserve Univ, Case Western Reserve Univ, 50-84; chairman Dept Philos, Case Western Reserve Univ, 65-67, 72-76; dir ,Western Reserve Univ-case Program of Philos Studies, 64-66; Emeritus Prof, 85-. **HONORS AND AWARDS** Special Rockefeller Fel, 51; Ford Fel, 54-55; John Simon Guggnheim Fel, 54-55; Yadoo App as Resident, 65; Fel Am Coucil of Learned Soc, 67-68. **MEMBERSHIPS** AAUP; Easter Div Am Philos Asn. **RESEARCH** Philosophy of Art and Literature; Ethics; Political and Legal Philosophy. **SELECTED PUBLICATIONS** Auth, articles on philosophical topics; Toward a Theory of Higher Education, 91; The Ophelia Paradox, 94. **CONTACT ADDRESS** 13906 Larchmere Blvd, Cleveland, OH, 44120.

KADISH, SANFORD H.
PERSONAL Born 09/07/1921, New York, NY, m, 1942, 2 children **DISCIPLINE** LAW **EDUCATION** City Col New York, BSS, 42; Columbia Univ, LLB, 48. **CAREER** From asst prof to prof law, Col Law, Univ Utah, 51-61; prof, Univ Mich, 61-64; prof, 64-76, A F & MAY T MORRISON PROF LAW & DEAN SCH OF LAW, UNIV CALIF, BERKELEY, 76-, Fulbright lear, Univ Melbourne, 56; vis prof, Sch Law, Univ Tex, 58; E R Thayer fel, Law Sch, Harvard Univ, 60, vis prof, 61; reporter, Joint Calif Legis Comt Revise Penal Code, 64-67; consult, President's Crime Comn, DC, 66-67; fel, Ctr Advan Studies Behav Sci, Stanford, 67-68; mem, Calif Coun Criminal Justice, 67-69; vis fel, Inst Criminol, Cambridge, Eng, 68 & Addison Roach lectr, Ind Univ, 69. **MEMBERSHIPS** Nat Acad Arbitrators; Am Soc Philos & Legal Philos; AAUP (pres, 70-72). **RESEARCH** Criminal law; jurisprudence. **SELECTED PUBLICATIONS** Auth, The Criminal Law and the Luck of the Draw--Foreword, J Criminal Law & Criminology, Vol 0084, 94; The Folly of Overfederalization, Hastings Law J, Vol 0046, 95; Reckless Complicity, J Criminal Law & Criminology, Vol 0087, 97. **CONTACT ADDRESS** Sch of Law, Univ of Calif, 225 Boalt Hall, Berkeley, CA, 94720.

KAEBNICK, GREGORY E.
PERSONAL Born 11/29/1963, Gallup, NM, m, 1987, 1 child **DISCIPLINE** PHILOSOPHY **EDUCATION** Univ Minn, PhD, 98. **CAREER** Assoc ed, Hastings Ctr Reports, The Hastings Ctr. **MEMBERSHIPS** Am Soc Bioethics & Hum; Am Philos Asn. **RESEARCH** Moral realism; Particularism. **CONTACT ADDRESS** 10 Edinburgh Dr, Peekskill, NY, 10568. **EMAIL** kaebnick@thehastingscenter.org

KAELIN, EUGENE FRANCIS
PERSONAL Born 10/14/1926, St. Louis, MO, m, 1952, 3 children **DISCIPLINE** PHILOSOPHY **EDUCATION** Univ Mo, AB, 49, MA, 50; Univ Bordeaux, DES, 51; Univ Ill, PhD(philos), 54. **CAREER** Instr philos, Univ Mo, 52-53; from instr to assoc prof, Univ Wis, Madison, 55-65; assoc prof, 65-67, chmn dept, 69-72, PROF PHILOS, FLA STATE UNIV, 67-, Fel from Univ Ill, Univ Bordeaux, 54-55; assoc ed, Arts in Soc, 58-64; Am Coun Learned Soc fel, Inst Studies Humanities, Univ Wis, 60-61; res scholar, Freiburg, 64-65; mem nat adv bd, Aesthetic Educ Prog, Cent Midwestern Regional Educ Lab, Inc, 68-73; chmn ed comt, Social Theory & Pract, 72-73. **MEMBERSHIPS** Am Philos Asn; Am Soc Aesthet; Soc Phenomenol & Existential Philos; Int Soc Phenomenol & Lit. **RESEARCH** Aesthetics; contemporary phenomenology; philosophy of aesthetic education. **SELECTED PUBLICATIONS** Auth, Analecta Husserliana--The Yearbook of Phenomenological Research, Vol 33, J Aesth Educ, Vol 0027, 93; The Logic of Imaginative Education--Reaching Understanding, J Aesth Educ, Vol 0029, 95. **CONTACT ADDRESS** Dept of Philos, Florida State Univ, Tallahassee, FL, 32306.

KAHANE, HOWARD
PERSONAL Born 04/19/1928, Cleveland, OH, d, 1 child **DISCIPLINE** PHILOSOPHY **EDUCATION** Univ Calif, Los Angeles, BA, 54, MA, 58; Univ Pa, PhD, 62. **CAREER** Asst prof philos, Whitman Col, 62-64; from asst prof to assoc prof, Univ Kans, 64-70; from asst prof to assoc prof, Baruch Col, 70-76; PROF PHILOS, UNIV MD, BALTIMORE COUNTY, 76-, Nat Sci Found res grant, 67-68. **MEMBERSHIPS** Western Div Am Philos Asn; Eastern Div Am Philos Asn. **RESEARCH** Theory of knowledge; logic and philosophy of science; ethics. **SELECTED PUBLICATIONS** Auth, A difficulty on conflict and confirmation, Philos Sci, 65; Logic and Philosophy: A Modern Introduction, Wadsworth, 69, 2nd ed, 73, 3rd ed, 78 & 4th ed, 82; coauth, Hard and soft intensionalsim, Rev Metaphys, 70; auth, Logic and Contemporary Rhetoric, Wadsworth, 71, 2nd ed, 76 & 3rd ed, 80; Pathological predicates and projection, Am Philos Quart, 71; Making the World Safe for Reciprocity, in: Reason and Responsibility, Wadsworth, 5th ed, 81. **CONTACT ADDRESS** Dept of Philos, Univ of Md, Baltimore, MD, 21228.

KAHN, CHARLES H.
PERSONAL Born 05/29/1928, New Iberia, LA, m, 1951, 2 children **DISCIPLINE** HISTORY OF PHILOSOPHY **EDUCATION** Univ Chicago, BA, 46, MA, 49; Columbia Univ, PhD, 58. **CAREER** From instr to assoc prof Greek & Latin, Columbia Univ, 57-65; assoc prof, 65-68, chmn dept, 75-78, PROF PHILOS, UNIV PA, 68-, Univ Chicago exchange fel to Univ Paris, 49-50; Cutting traveling fel, Columbia Univ, 55-56; Am Coun Learned Soc res fel, 63-64; co-ed, Arch Geschichte Philos, 65-; mem managing comt, Am Sch Class Studies in Athens, 70-, vis prof, 74-75; Nat Endowment for Humanities fel, 74-75. **MEMBERSHIPS** Am Philos Asn; Soc Ancient Greek Philosophers (pres, 76-78). **RESEARCH** Greek philosophy, especially Presocratics, Plato and Aristotle; political philosophy. **SELECTED PUBLICATIONS** Auth, The Chronology of Plato Dialogs, Classical J, Vol 0088, 92; Proleptic Composition in the 'Republic', or Why Book-1 Was Never a Separate Dialogue + Plato, Classical Quart, Vol 0043, 93. **CONTACT ADDRESS** Dept of Philos/CN, Univ of Pa, 34th and Spruce St, Philadelphia, PA, 19104.

KAHN, DOUGLAS A.
PERSONAL Born 11/07/1934, Spartanburg, SC, m, 1970, 2 children **DISCIPLINE** LAW **EDUCATION** Univ NC, Chapel Hill, BA, 55; George Washington Univ, JD, 58. **CAREER** Trial atty, Civil Div, Appellate Sect, Dept Justice, 58-60 & Tax Div, Appelate Sect, 60-62; atty-at-law, Sachs & Jacobs, 62-64; from Asst Prof to Prof, 64-84, Paul G, Kauper Prof Law, Sch Law, Univ Mich, Ann Arbor, 84-; Vis prof, Law Sch, Stanford Univ, 73-74; vis prof, Duke Univ, Univ NC, 77; vis prof & George Bacon-Victor Kilkenny chair, Fordham Univ, 80-81; vis prof, Cambridge Univ, 96. **HONORS AND AWARDS** Emil Brown Found Prize, 70. **MEMBERSHIPS** Am Bar Asn. **RESEARCH** Taxation; estate planning. **SELECTED PUBLICATIONS** Auth, Mandatory buy-out agreements for stock of closely held corporations, 69, A definition of liabilities in Internal Revenue code sections 357 & 358 (d), 75 & Accelerated depreciation--tax expenditure or proper allowance for measuring net income?, 79, Mich Law Rev; coauth, Corporate Taxation, West Publ Co, 89; Corporate Income Taxation, West Publ Co, 4th ed, 94; Federal Taxation of Gifts, Trusts and Estates, West Publ Co, 3rd ed, 97; auth, Federal Income Tax, Found Press, 3rd ed, 94. **CONTACT ADDRESS** Law Sch, Univ of Mich, 625 S State St, Ann Arbor, MI, 48109-1215.

KAHN, JEFFREY C.
PERSONAL Born 10/12/1960, Santa Monica, CA, m, 2 children **DISCIPLINE** BIOETHICS **EDUCATION** Univ Calif, Los Angeles, BA, 83; Johns Hopkins Univ Sch of Hygiene and Public Health, MPH, 88; Georgetown Univ, PhD, 89. **CAREER** Dir, grad prog, asst prof, Ctr for the Stud of Bioethics, Med Col Wisc, 92-96; dir, Ctr for Bioethics, assoc prof, Univ of Minn, 96- . **MEMBERSHIPS** APA, Am Pub Hea Asn; Am Soc for Bioethics and Hum. **RESEARCH** Applied ethics; ethics and genetics; ethics and public health; research ethics; ethical theory. **SELECTED PUBLICATIONS** Ed, Kennedy Inst of Ethics J, 96; ed, Accountability in Res, 98; ed, J of Andrology, 98; Policies for Human Subjects Research, University Pub Grp, 98; Beyond Consent, Oxford, 98. **CONTACT ADDRESS** Center for Bioethics, Univ of Minnesota, 410 Church St SE, Ste N504, Boynton, MN, 55455. **EMAIL** kahnx009@tc.umn.edu

KAISER, CHRISTOPHER BARINA
PERSONAL Born 10/16/1941, Greenwich, CT, 1970, 3 children **DISCIPLINE** DIVINITY; PHYSICS **EDUCATION** Harvard Univ, AB, 63; Univ Edinburgh, PhD, 74. **CAREER** Lectr, Univ Edinburgh, 73-75; from asst to assoc to PROF OF HISTORICAL-SYSTEMATIC THEOLOGY, W THEOL SEM, 76-. **MEMBERSHIPS** Am Soc Church Hist; Soc Hist Technol **RESEARCH** New Testament Christology; Comparative historical sociology of science. **SELECTED PUBLICATIONS** auth From Biblical Secularity to Modern Secularism: Historical Aspects and Stages, Secularism versus Biblical Secularity, ITEST Faith/Science Press, 94 & 96; "The Integrity of Creations and the Social Nature of God," Scottish Jour Theol, 96; The Laws of Nature and the Nature of God, Facets of Faith and Science, Univ Press Am, 96; Scientific Work and Its Theological Dimensions: Toward a Theology of Natural Science, Facets of Faith and Science, Univ Press Am, 96; Quantum Complementarity and Christological Dialectic, Religion and Science: History, Method, Dialogue, Routledge, 96; Creational Theology and the History of Physical Science: The Creationist Tradition from Basil to Bohr, E J Brill, 97; Extraterrestrial Life and Extraterrestrial Intelligence, Reformed Review, 98; John Calvin Climbing Jacob's Ladder, Perspectives: A Journal of Reformed Thought, 98; The Nature of the Chruch from a Reformed Perspective, Reformed World, 98. **CONTACT ADDRESS** W Theol Sem, 101 E 13, Holland, MI, 49423. **EMAIL** chrisk@westernsem.org

KAISER, KEVIN
PERSONAL Born 03/17/1964, Oakland, CA, s **DISCIPLINE** BIBLICAL STUDIES **EDUCATION** San Jose State Univ, BA, 87; Grad Theol Union, Berkeley, MA, 90; Univ Calif, Berkeley, PhD, 97. **CAREER** Mus dir, Bodie Inst Bibl Arch, Berkeley CA, 90-98. **HONORS AND AWARDS** Phi Kappa Phi; ASOR summer travel grant; Univ Calif, Berkeley summer fel. **MEMBERSHIPS** ASOR. **RESEARCH** Archaeology; history; Near Eastern languages. **CONTACT ADDRESS** 14328 Cuesta Ct., Sonora, CA, 95370. **EMAIL** krkaiser@aol.com

KAISER, WALTER C., JR.
PERSONAL Born 04/11/1933, Folcroft, PA, m, 1957, 4 children **DISCIPLINE** BIBLICAL ARCHAEOLOGY **EDUCATION** Wheaton Col, AB, 55, BD, 58; Brandeis Univ, MA, 62, PhD, 73. **CAREER** Instr, 58-60, asst prof of Bible, 60-64, actg dir of archaeol & Near Eastern stud, 65-55, Wheaton Col; asst prof, 66-70, assoc prof, 70-75, chmn dept of OT, 75-79, sr vice pres, acad dean, 80-92, sr vice pres of Distance Learning, 92-93, Trinity Evangel Divin Schl; Coleman M Mockler Dist Prof of OT, 93-96; pres, 97-, Gordon Conwell Theol Sem. **HONORS AND AWARDS** Danforth Tchr Stud grant. **MEMBERSHIPS** Evangel Theol Soc; Inst of Bibl Res; Near Eastern Archaeol Soc; Soc of Bibl Lit. **RESEARCH** Old Testament Theol; Israel, history and archaeology; ethics. **SELECTED PUBLICATIONS** Auth, The Journey Isn't Over: The Pilgrim Psalms (120-134) for Life's Challenges and Joys, Baker 93; coauth, An Introduction to Biblical Hermeneutics: The Search for Meaning, Zondervan, 94; auth, The Book of Leviticus: Introduction, Commentary and Reflections, New Interpreter's Bible, Abingdon, 94; auth, Proverbs: Wisdom for Everyday Life, Zondervan, 95; auth, Psalms: Heart to Heart with God, Zondervan, 95; auth, The Messiah in the Old Testament, Zondervan, 95; auth, Hard Sayings of the Bible, InterVarsity, 96; auth, A History of Israel, Broadman & Holman, 98; auth, The Christian and the "Old" Testament, US Ctr for World Mission, 98; auth, An Urgent Call For Revival and Renewal in Our Times: Sixteen Revivals in the Old and New Testament with a Study Guide, Broadman & Holman, 99; auth, Are the Old testament Documents Reliable?, InterVarsity, 99. **CONTACT ADDRESS** Gordon-Conwell Theol Sem, 130 Essex St, South Hamilton, MA, 01982. **EMAIL** wckaiser@gcts.edu

KAJEVICH, STEVEN N.
PERSONAL Born 07/29/1937, Yugoslavia, d **DISCIPLINE** THEOLOGY **EDUCATION** Prizren, Yugoslavia, BD, 56; Belgrade, MTh, 62; DePaul Univ, MA, 71, PhD, 74. **CAREER** Priest, Scebien Orthodox Church, Paris, 66-78; asst prof philos, ethics, Lewis Univ & DePaul Univ, 85- . **HONORS AND AWARDS** World Council of Churches scholarship. **MEMBERSHIPS** APA; CPA; Writers Club. **RESEARCH** Political and social philosophy; international relations, crime and punishment. **SELECTED PUBLICATIONS** Auth, Un-Created Freedom: Origin of Being and Its Negation, Univ Press of Am, 77. **CONTACT ADDRESS** 5701 N Sheridan Rd, #4-P, Chicago, IL, 80660.

KALANTZIS, GEORGE
PERSONAL Born 04/18/1967, Athens, Greece, m, 1987, 3 children **DISCIPLINE** RELIGION **EDUCATION** Northwestern Univ, PhD, 97. **CAREER** Dir Acad Comput, 97- , fac, 98- , Northwestern Univ. **HONORS AND AWARDS** Hartman Fel; Ernest W. Saunders Endowed Fel; Ester Y Armstrong Scholar. **MEMBERSHIPS** ASA; NAPS; SBL; ASOR; ETS; ASCH. **RESEARCH** Christology; Byzantine theology; information technology in education. **SELECTED PUBLICATIONS** Auth, Ephesus, Jian Dao, 97. **CONTACT ADDRESS** Garrett-Evangelical Theol Sem, 2121 Sheridan Rd, Evanston, IL, 60621. **EMAIL** George.Kalantzis@nwu.edu

KALIN, EVERETT ROY
DISCIPLINE NEW TESTAMENT **EDUCATION** Concordia Sem, BA, MDiv; Harvard Univ Divinity Sch, ThD. **CAREER** Instr, Concordia Col; assoc prof, Concordia Sem; Christ Sem Seminex prof, 83-. **SELECTED PUBLICATIONS** Transl, Suffering by Dorothee Soelle, Fortress Press; Jesus of Nazareth by Herbert Braun, Fortress Press; Christ and Power by Martin Hengel, Fortress Press; Reconciliation, Law, and Righteousness by Peter Stuhlmacher, Fortress Press. **CONTACT ADDRESS** Dept of New Testament, Pacific Lutheran Theol Sem, 2770 Marin Ave, Berkeley, CA, 94708-1597. **EMAIL** ekalin@sirius.com

KALLENBERG, BRAD J.
PERSONAL Born 04/14/1958, Minneapolis, MN, m, 1980, 3 children **DISCIPLINE** PHILOSOPHICAL THEOLOGY **EDUCATION** Fuller Theo Sem, PhD, 98. **CAREER** Instr, 96-99, Intl School of Theol; adj Asst Prof, 94-99, Fuller Theo Sem; Instr, 98-, Azusa Pacific Univ. **HONORS AND AWARDS** Full Doc Fel, Fuller Theo Sem. **MEMBERSHIPS** APA, AAR. **RESEARCH** Wittgenstein & theology, Anglo-American postmodernism, Christian ethics. **SELECTED PUBLICATIONS** Co-ed, Virtues and Practices in the Christian Tradition, Christian Ethics after MacIntyre, Harrisburg PA Trinity Press Intl, 97; auth, Conversion Converted, A Postmodern Formulation of the Doctrine of Conversion, in: The Evangelical Qtly, 95; On Cultivating Moral Taste, in: Virtues and Practices in the Christian Tradition, Christian Ethics after MacIntyre, eds, N Murphy, M T Nation, Harrisburg PA, Trinity Press Intl, 97; Unstuck from Yale, Theological Method After Lindbeck, in: Scottish J of Theo, 97; The Gospel Truth of Relativism, in: Scottish J of Theo, forthcoming; co-auth, Ludwig Wittgenstein, A Christian in Philosophy, in: Scottish J of Theo, 98. **CONTACT ADDRESS** 3471 N Arrowhead Ave, San Bernardino, CA, 92405. **EMAIL** kallenberg@sprintmail.com

KAMBEITZ, TERESITA
PERSONAL Richmond, SK, Canada **DISCIPLINE** RELIGIOUS EDUCATION **EDUCATION** St.Angela's Acad, ARTC, 57; tchrs col, 58-59; Univ Sask, BA, 69, BEd, 69; St Paul Univ, Ottawa, Theol, 69-70; St. Michael's Col, MRE, 76; Ont Inst Stud Educ, Univ Toronto, MEd, 86, PhD, 88. **CAREER** Tchr, various schs Sask, 59-64; princ/tchr, St. Patrick, Swift Current, Sask, 64-68; tchr, Holy Cross Sch, Saskatoon, 70-85; DIR RELIGIOUS EDUC, NEWMAN THEOL COL, EDMONTON, 88-. **HONORS AND AWARDS** Peter Craigie Award, Alta Tchrs Asn. **MEMBERSHIPS** Newman Theol Col; Alta Tchrs Asn; Asn Profs Res Relig Educ; Relig Educ Asn US & Can; Ursuline Congregation Prelate. **SELECTED PUBLICATIONS** Auth, Death and Dying, 79; auth, Health Hazards of So-Called Low-Radiation, 80; auth, Ursulines Remember, vol 1, 94, vol 2, 95. **CONTACT ADDRESS** Religious Education Program, Newman Theol Col, Edmonton, AB, T5L 4H8.

KAMBER, RICHARD
DISCIPLINE AESTHETICS **EDUCATION** Claremont Grad Sch, PhD, 75. **CAREER** Philos, Col NJ. **HONORS AND AWARDS** Dean, Arts & Scis. **SELECTED PUBLICATIONS** Auth, On the Nonexistence of Literary Ideas, Philos & Lit, 79; A Modest Proposal for Defining a Work of Art, British Journal Aesthetics, 93. **CONTACT ADDRESS** Col of New Jersey, PO Box 7718, Ewing, NJ, 08628-0718.

KAMINSKY, JACK
PERSONAL Born 03/19/1922, New York, NY, m, 1947 **DISCIPLINE** PHILOSOPHY **EDUCATION** Yale, 43-44; US Army, 43-46; City Univ of NY, BSS, 44; NYU, MA, 47, PhD, 50. **CAREER** Asst Inst, 49-50, NYU; Inst, Univ of Akron, 50-51; Inst, 52-53, City Univ of NY; Chmn, Dept of Philos, 53-65, Asst Prof, 53-57, Assoc Prof, 57-61, Prof, 61-92, Prof Emeritus, 92-, Binghamton Univ. **HONORS AND AWARDS** Assistantship, NYU, 49-50; Fel, ACLU, 51-52, Fel, Binghamton Univ, 63, 66; Distinguished Res Fel, 67; Pres Creighton Philos Club, 61-62., Awarded Bronze Star in WWII, 45. **MEMBERSHIPS** APA **RESEARCH** Language; logic; epistemology; metaphysics. **SELECTED PUBLICATIONS** Logic and Language,

Knopf, 56; Language and Onotology, Univ S Illin Press, 69; Logic a Philosophical Introduction, Wesley, 74; Essays in Linguistic Ontology, Univ of S Illin Press, 82; Articles in Jour: Jour of Phil, Phil & Phenomenocological Res, Jour of the Hist of Ideas, Philos of Science, Jour of Gen Ed, Revue Intl DC Philos, Kant Studies, Indian Jour of Philos, Encyl of Philos; Art and Philos, 96. **CONTACT ADDRESS** PO Box 542, Cortland, NY, 13045. **EMAIL** akaminsky@snycurva.cortland.edu

KAMIONKOWSKI, SUSAN T.
PERSONAL Born 07/22/1963, Cleveland, OH **DISCIPLINE** BIBLICAL STUDIES **EDUCATION** Oberlin Col, BA, 85; Harvard Div Sch, MTS, 87; Brandeis Univ, PhD cand, 99. **CAREER** Lectr, Hebrew Col of Brookline MA, 92-97; Dir of Bibl Civilization, Reconstructionist Rabbinical Col, 96-98. **MEMBERSHIPS** Am Orient Soc; Soc of Bibl Lit; Asn for Judaic Stud. **RESEARCH** Biblical literature; Pentateuch and prophecy; ancient Near Eastern literature; gender studies. **CONTACT ADDRESS** Reconstructionist Rabbinical Col, 1299 Church Rd, Wyncote, PA, 19047. **EMAIL** tamarkam@aol.com

KAMISAR, YALE
PERSONAL Born 08/29/1929, New York, NY, w, 3 children **DISCIPLINE** LAW **EDUCATION** NY Univ, AB, 50; Columbia Univ, LLB, 54. **CAREER** Assoc Prof to Prof Law, Univ Minn, 57-65; Prof, 65-79, Henry K. Ransom Prof Law, 79-92, Clarence Darrow Distinguished Univ Prof, Univ Mich, 92-. **HONORS AND AWARDS** Research Award for outstanding contributions to the law and the legal profession, Am Bar Found Fels, 96. **MEMBERSHIPS** Am Law Inst; Am Acad Arts & Sci. **RESEARCH** Criminal procedure; criminal law. **SELECTED PUBLICATIONS** Coauth, Constitutional Law: Cases, Comments & Questions, 1st ed, 64, 8th ed, 65; Modern Criminal Procedure: Cases, Comments & Questions, 1st ed, 65, 8th ed, 96; auth, On the "Fruits" of Miranda Violations, Coerced Confessions, and Compelled Testimony, Mich Law Rev 93, 95; On the Meaning and Impact of Physician-Assisted Suicide Cases, Minn Law Rev 82, 98; Physician-Assisted Suicide: The Problems Presented by the Compelling Heartwrenching Case, J Criminal Law & Criminol 88, 98. **CONTACT ADDRESS** Univ Mich Law Sch, 625 S State St., 914 LR, Ann Arbor, MI, 48109. **EMAIL** ykamisar@umich.edu

KAMM, FRANCES MYRNA
PERSONAL New York, NY **DISCIPLINE** PHILOSOPHY **EDUCATION** Barnard Col, BA, 69; Mass Inst Technol, PhD(philos), 80. **CAREER** Instr, Univ Mass, Boston, 73; instr, NY Univ, 79-80, Prof Philos, NY Univ, 80-, Affiliated fac, NY Univ Law Sch, vis prof philos, UCLA, 97-98. **HONORS AND AWARDS** Amer Coun Learned Soc grant 82-83, fel Ethics, Harvard Univ, 89-90. **MEMBERSHIPS** Am Philos Asn; Soc Philos & Pub Affairs. **RESEARCH** Ethics; social and political philosophy; bioethics. **SELECTED PUBLICATIONS** Auth, Creation and Abortion, OUP, 92, Morality, Mortality, vols 1 & 2, OUP, 93, 96. **CONTACT ADDRESS** Dept of Philosophy, New York Univ, 100 Washington Sq E, New York, NY, 10003-6688. **EMAIL** fmk1@IS4.nyu.edu

KAMTEKAR, RACHANA
DISCIPLINE PHILOSOPHY **EDUCATION** Stanford Univ, BA, 87; Univ Chicago, PhD, 95. **CAREER** Asst prof, Williams Col, 95- . **HONORS AND AWARDS** Mellon Fel, 93-94; Ill Inst Tech teaching fel, 94-95; Friedrich Solmsen fel, Univ Wis-Madison, 98-99. **MEMBERSHIPS** Am Philos Asoc; Am Philol Asoc. **RESEARCH** Ancient moral and political philosophy. **CONTACT ADDRESS** 1401 Observatory Dr., Madison, WI, 53706. **EMAIL** rkamteka@williams.edu

KANE, FRANCIS
DISCIPLINE POLITICAL PHILOSOPHY **EDUCATION** PhD. **CAREER** Salisbury State Univ **SELECTED PUBLICATIONS** Areas: assisted suicide, the death and dying movement. **CONTACT ADDRESS** Salisbury State Univ, Salisbury, MD, 21801-6862. **EMAIL** FIKANE@SSU.EDU

KANE, JOHN
DISCIPLINE RELIGIOUS STUDIES, WOMEN'S ISSUES **EDUCATION** Univ Dayton, BA, 64; Univ Fribourg, Switz, STB, 68; Saint Louis Univ, MA, 70; McMaster Univ, Canada, PhD, 78. **CAREER** Prof Relig Stud, Regis Col, 80-. **MEMBERSHIPS** Am Acad of Relig; Col Theol Soc; Pax Christi, USA. **RESEARCH** Contemporary catholicism; religion and society/politics; Christianity and contemporary culture. **SELECTED PUBLICATIONS** Auth, Of Christ & Culture - Building Faith's Body, in American Catholic Teaching: Resources for Renewal, Sandra Yocum Mize and William Portier, eds, Orbis Bks, 97. **CONTACT ADDRESS** Dept of Relig Stud, Regis Col, 3333 Regis Blvd, Denver, CO, 80221.

KANE, ROBERT
PERSONAL Born 12/25/1938, Boston, MA, m, 1965, 2 children **DISCIPLINE** PHILOSOPHY **EDUCATION** Holy Cross Coll, AB, 60; Yale Univ, MA, 62; PhD, 64. **CAREER** Asst prof, Fordham Univ, 64-67; asst prof, Haverford Coll, 67-70; asst prof, Univ Tex Austin, 70-74; assoc prof, 74-85, prof 85-95. **HONORS AND AWARDS** Philosopher's Annual Selection, the Best Articles in Philosophy, 84; Acad of Distinguished Teachers inaugural member, 95; Rubert W Hamilton faculty Award, 96. **MEMBERSHIPS** Am Philos Soc; Mind Asn; Behavioral and Brain Sci Asn. **RESEARCH** Philosophy of Mind and Action; Free Will; Ethics; Theory of Values; Philosophy of Religion. **SELECTED PUBLICATIONS** Auth, The Ends of Metaphysics, Int Philos Quart, 93; Free Will: The Elusive Ideal, Philos Srudies, 94; Through the Moral Maze, 94; The Significance of Free Will, 96; Dimensions of Value and the Aims of Social Inquiry, Am Behavioral Sci, 98. **CONTACT ADDRESS** Dept of Philosophy, Univ of Tex, Austin, TX, 78712. **EMAIL** rkane@uts.cc.utexas.edu

KANE, STANLEY
DISCIPLINE PHILOSOPHY OF RELIGION, HISTORY OF PHILOSOPHY, ENVIRONMENTAL PHILOSOPHY **EDUCATION** Barrington Col, BA; Brown Univ, AM; Harvard Univ, PhD. **CAREER** Prof, Miami Univ **RESEARCH** Philosophy of religion. **SELECTED PUBLICATIONS** Publ on, problems of God and evil; nature of God; nature of religious lang; Anselm's theory of free will; Aquinas' doctrine of the soul and personal identity; 17th century mechanism philos & histl roots of the env crisis. **CONTACT ADDRESS** Dept of Philosophy, Miami Univ, Oxford, OH, 45056. **EMAIL** kanegs@muohio.edu

KANE, THOMAS ANTHONY
PERSONAL Born 06/27/1945, Philadelphia, PA **DISCIPLINE** RITUAL STUDIES, LITURGICS **EDUCATION** Univ Notre Dame, MA, 70; Cath Univ Am, STL, 73; Ohio State Univ, PhD, 82. **CAREER** Lectr relig & the arts, Cath Univ, 75-82; asst prof Pastoral Theol, Weston Jesuit Sch Theol, 83-; Lectr, Cath Mission Coun Cult & Liturgy, 79-81; vis prof, Josephinum Pontif Inst, 77-78, DeSales Sch Theol, 81-82 & Washington Theol Union, 82. **MEMBERSHIPS** Societas Liturgica; NAm Acad Liturgy. **RESEARCH** Celebration, art and ritual. **SELECTED PUBLICATIONS** Coauth, Textures of the Spirit, 1-2/79 & Psalm Dance 36, 9-10/79, Liturgy Mag; ed, Celebrating 1979, 79 & Celebrating 1980, 80, Winston Press; 1980: The Year of the Spirit, Paulist Press, 80; auth, Environmental Artists, Life Gifts, 81; The Dancing Church of Africa; The Dancing Church of South Pacific. **CONTACT ADDRESS** 3 Phillips Place, Cambridge, MA, 02138-3495. **EMAIL** TKANECSP@aol.com

KANG, WI JO
DISCIPLINE RELIGION **CAREER** Rel, Wartburg Theol. **SELECTED PUBLICATIONS** Auth, Christ and Caeser in Modern Korea, NYSU Press, 97 **CONTACT ADDRESS** Wartburg Theol Sem, 333 Wartburg Pl, Dubuque, IA, 52001. **EMAIL** kangwi.jo@mcleod.usa

KANG, WI JO
PERSONAL Born 03/10/1930, Chinju, Korea, m, 1961, 4 children **DISCIPLINE** HISTORY OF RELIGIONS, MISSIONS **EDUCATION** Concordia Sem, BA, 57, 1313, 60; Univ Chicago, MA, 62, PhD, 67. **CAREER** Instr hist of relig, Columbia Univ, 64-66; asst prof, Valparaiso Univ, 66-68; assoc prof, Concordia Sem, 68-74 & Christ Sem-Seminex, 74-78; vis prof, Yonsei Univ, Korea, 78-79; Prof of Mission, Wartburg Sem, 80-; Christ and Caesar in Modern Korea: A History of Christianity and Politics, State Univ NY Press, 97. **MEMBERSHIPS** Am Acad Relig; Am Hist Soc; Int Soc Buddhist Studies; Am Soc Missiology; Am Soc Church Hist. **RESEARCH** History of religions in Asia; history of Christian missions in East Asia; world religions and politics. **SELECTED PUBLICATIONS** Auth, Korean Religions Under the Japanese Government (in Japanese), Seibunsha, Tokyo, 76; In Search of Light (in Korean), 76 & Religion and Politics of Korea Under Japanese Rule (in Korean), 77, Christian Lit Soc Korea, Seoul; The secularization of Korean Buddhism, Actes du XXIXe Cong Int des Orient Paris L'Asiatheque, 77; Religious response to Japanese rule, Ctr for Korean Studies, Kalamazoo, Mich, 77; co-ed, Christian Presence in Japan, Seibunsha, Tokyo, 81; auth, Christianity under the government of Chung Hee Park, Missiology: Int Rev, 81; Christianity in China, Currents in Theol & Mission, 82. **CONTACT ADDRESS** Wartburg Theol Sem, 333 Wartburg Place, Dubuque, IA, 52003-5050. **EMAIL** KANGWI JO@MACLEODUSA

KAPLAN, ABRAHAM
PERSONAL Born 06/11/1918, Odessa, Russia, m, 1939, 2 children **DISCIPLINE** PHILOSOPHY **EDUCATION** Col St Thomas, BA, 37; Univ Calif, Los Angeles, PhD(philos), 42. **CAREER** Instr philos, NY Univ, 44-45; from asst prof to assoc prof, Univ Calif, Los Angeles, 46-52, prof & chmn dept, 52-63; prof, Univ Mich, Ann Arbor, 63-73; PROF PHILOS & METHODOLOGY, HAIFA UNIV, 73-, Dean Soc Sci, 74-, Guggenheim fel, 45-46; consult, Rand Corp, 47-; vis assoc prof, Univ Mich, 51-52; res assoc, Rockefeller Prof Lang & Symbolism, 51-52; vis prof, Harvard Univ, 53 & Columbia Univ, 55; Rockefeller fel, 57-58; fel, Ctr Advan Studies Behav Sci, 60-61; fel, Ctr Advan Studies, Wesleyan Univ, 62-63; dir, East-West Philosophers Conf, Univ Hawaii, 68-69; vis prof philos, Hebrew Univ Jerusalem, 63-64 & 70. **HONORS AND AWARDS** LHD, Univ Judaism, 62. **MEMBERSHIPS** Am Philos Asn; Am Soc Polit & Legal Philos; Am Acad Psychoanal; Asn Jewish Philos. **RESEARCH** Aesthetics; social philosophy; methodology of the human sciences. **SELECTED PUBLICATIONS** Coauth, Power and Society, Yale Univ, 50; auth, The New World of Philosophy, Random, 61; The Conduct of Inquiry, Chandler Publ, 64. **CONTACT ADDRESS** Div Soc Sci, Haifa Univ, Mt Carmel, Haifa, ., 31999.

KAPLAN, DAVID M.
DISCIPLINE PHILOSOPHY **EDUCATION** Fordham univ, PhD, 98. **CAREER** Adj instr, Fordham Univ, 96-98; adj instr, Hofstra Univ, 97- ; adj instr, Polytechnic Univ, 96- . **HONORS AND AWARDS** Pres scholar, Fordham Univ, 90-94. **MEMBERSHIPS** APA; Soc for Phenomenology and Existential Philos. **RESEARCH** Twentieth century continental philosophy; social/political philosophy. **CONTACT ADDRESS** 617 Manhattan Ave, Brooklyn, NY, 11222. **EMAIL** kaplan@murray.fordham.edu

KAPLAN, RICHARD L.
DISCIPLINE LAW **EDUCATION** Univ Ind, BS; Yale Univ, JD. **CAREER** Prof,Univ Ill Urbana Champaign. **HONORS AND AWARDS** Urbana-Champaign Campus Awd, 94. **RESEARCH** Income taxation; taxation of international transactions; elder law; and federal tax policy. **SELECTED PUBLICATIONS** Auth, pubs on income taxation, taxation of international transactions, and elder law. **CONTACT ADDRESS** Law Dept, Univ Ill Urbana Champaign, 52 E Gregory Dr, Champaign, IL, 61820. **EMAIL** rkaplan@law.uiuc.edu

KAPLAN, WILLIAM
DISCIPLINE LAW **EDUCATION** Univ Toronto, BA, MA; Osgoode Hall Law Sch, LLB; Stanford Univ, JSD. **CAREER** Assoc prof. **SELECTED PUBLICATIONS** Auth, Labour Arbitration Yearbook; pubs on labour law and arbitration. **CONTACT ADDRESS** Fac Common Law, Univ Ottawa, 550 Cumberland St, PO Box 450, Ottawa, ON, K1N 6N5.

KAPLOW, LOUIS
PERSONAL Born 06/17/1956, Chicago, IL, m, 2 children **DISCIPLINE** LAW **EDUCATION** Northwestern Univ, BA, 77; Harvard Law School, JD (magna cum laude), 81; Harvard Univ, MA, 81, PhD, 87. **CAREER** Law Clerk to Hon. Henry J. Friendly, United States Court of Appeals for the Second Circuit, 81-82; PROF, HARVARD LAW SCHOOL, 87-. **MEMBERSHIPS** Am Economic Asn; Nat Tax Asn; Am Law and Economics Asn. **RESEARCH** Taxation; antitrust; law & economics. **SELECTED PUBLICATIONS** Auth, Accuracy, Complexity, and the Income Tax, J of Law, Economics and Organization, 98; auth, A note on the Optimal Supply of Public Goods and the Distortionary Cost of Taxation, Nat Tax Journal, 98; auth, Tax Policy and Gifts, Am Economic Asn Papers and Proceedings, 98; auth, Tax and Non-Tax Distortions, J of Public Economics, 98; auth, Accuracy in Adjudication, The New Palgrave Dictionary of Economics and the Law, 98; auth, General Characteristics of Rules, Encycl of Law and Economics, 98; auth, Tax Treatment of Families, Encycl of Taxation and Tax Policy, 98; auth, Comment on Antitrust Issues in the Licensing of Intellectual Property, Brookings Papers on Economic Activity: Microeconomics, 97; auth, Regional Cost-of-Living Adjustments in Tax-Transfer Schemes, Tax Law Review, 96; auth, The Optimal Supply of Public Goods and the Distortionary Cost of Taxation, Nat Tax J, 96; auth, On the Divergence Between Ideal and Conventional Income Tax Treatment of Human Capital, Am Economic Asn Papers and Proceedings, 96; auth, Fiscal Federalism and the Deductibility of State and Local Taxes in a Federal Income Tax, Va Law Review, 96; coauth, Accuracy in the Assessment of Damages, J of Law and Economics, 96; auth, Antitrust Analysis, Aspen Pub, 97. **CONTACT ADDRESS** School of Law, Harvard Univ, 1575 Massachusetts Ave., Cambridge, MA, 02138.

KARABAN, ROSLYN A.
DISCIPLINE RELIGION & PERSONALITY SCIENCES **EDUCATION** Stonehill Col, BA, 75; Harvard Div Sch, MDiv, 78; Grad Theol Union, PhD, 84. **CAREER** Inst, cont educ, Stonehill Col, 74; teach asst, Harvard Div Sch, 77-78; grad asst, Pacific Sch Relig, 80-81; Inst, Pacific Sch Relig, 81; Inst, United Theol Col, Bangalore, India, 85-87; Inst, 87-88, asst prof, 88-91, ASSOC PROF, 91-, ST BERNARD'S INST, Tel Dan Archaeol Dig, assoc couns, Samaritan Pastoral Couns Ctr, 90-; act dir, DMin prog, Div Sch, Rochester NY, 94; TEACH FAC, SUPERVISOR, GENESEE REGION HOME CARE AND SAMARITAN PASTORAL COUNSELING CTR, 96-. **CONTACT ADDRESS** St. Bernard's Inst, 1100 S Goodman St, Rochester, NY, 14620.

KARAMUSTAFA, AHMET T.
PERSONAL Born 11/15/1956, Turkey, m, 1986, 3 children **DISCIPLINE** RELIGIOUS STUDIES, ISLAMIC STUDIES **EDUCATION** Hamilton Coll NY, BA, 78; McGill Univ Can, MA, 81; PhD, 87. **CAREER** Asst prof, Wash Univ, 87-94; acting chair, Wash Univ, 94; dir, Center for the Study of Islamic Socs and civilizations, Wash Univ, 94-97; Assoc Prof, Wash Univ, 94-. **HONORS AND AWARDS** Phi Beta Kappa, 78; Grad magna cum laude, Hamilton Coll, 78; Dean's List, McGill

Univ, 87. **MEMBERSHIPS** Am Acad of Rel; Am Asn of Teachers of Turkish Lang; Am Res Inst in Turkey; Middle E Studies Asn; Soc for Iranian Studies; Turkish Studies Asn. **RESEARCH** Premodern Islamic intellectual traditions. **SELECTED PUBLICATIONS** Auth, God's Unruly Friends: Dervish Groups in the Islamic Later Middle Period, 1200-1550, 94; Vahidid's Menakib-I Hvoca-I Cihan ve Nefice-I can: critical Edition and Analysis, 93; asst ed, The History of Cartography, cartography in the Traditional Islamic and South Asian Societies, 92. **CONTACT ADDRESS** Dept of Asian and Near Eastern Languages and Literature., Wash Univ, One Brookings Dr, PO Box 1111, St. Louis, MO, 63130. **EMAIL** akaramus@artsci.wustl.edu

KARDONG, TERRENCE G.
PERSONAL Born 10/22/1936, Minneapolis, MN **DISCIPLINE** MONASTIC STUDIES **EDUCATION** Catholic Univ, MA, 68; Licentiate, Theology, Sant Ansolmo, 77. **CAREER** ED, THE AMERICAN BENEDICTINE REV **HONORS AND AWARDS** Honorary doctorate, Belmont Col. **MEMBERSHIPS** Norht Am Patristic Soc. **RESEARCH** Rule of St. Benedict; pre-Benedictine sources. **SELECTED PUBLICATIONS** Auth, Benedicts Rule: Tranlation and Commentary, Liturgical Press, 96. **CONTACT ADDRESS** Assumption Abbey, Richardton, ND, 58652. **EMAIL** abredit@popctctel.com

KARMEL, ROBERTA S.
PERSONAL Born 05/04/1937, Chicago, IL, m, 1995, 4 children **DISCIPLINE** LAW **EDUCATION** Radcliff Col, BA, 59; New York Univ Schl of Law, LLB, 62. **CAREER** Comm, Securities & Exchange Com, 77-80; Prof, Brooklyn Law Schl, 86-; Partner, 87-94, Counsel, 95-, Kelly Drye & Warren LLP. **HONORS AND AWARDS** Hon doctorate of humanities, Kings Col, Wilkes Barre PA, 98. **MEMBERSHIPS** ABA; Amer Bar Found Fel; Amer Law Inst; Assoc of ME Bar of ME City of NY; Intl Bar Assoc **RESEARCH** Securities regulation; international financial law. **SELECTED PUBLICATIONS** Auth, National Treatment Harmonization and Mutual Recognition, Capital Mkts Forum Intl Bar Assoc, 93; Securities Law in the European Community Harmony or Cacophony?, Toulane Jour Intl & Comp, 93; Implications of the Stakeholder Model, Geo Wash Law Rev, 93; Barriers to Foreign Issuer Entry Into US Markets, Law & Policy in Intl Bus, 93; The Relationship Between Mandatory Disclosure and Prohibitions Against Insider Trading: Why a Property Rights Theory of Inside Information is Untenable, Brooklyn L Rev, 93; Living with US Regulations Complying with the Rules and Avoiding Litigation, Fordham Intl L Jour, 94; Is the Shingle Theory Dead? Wash & Lee Law Rev, 95; A Report on the Attitudes of Foreign Companies Regarding a US Listing, Stan JL & Bus, 97. **CONTACT ADDRESS** 250 Joralemon St, Brooklyn, NY, 11201. **EMAIL** rkarmel@brooklaw.edu

KARST, KENNETH L.
PERSONAL Born 06/26/1929, Los Angeles, CA, m, 1950, 4 children **DISCIPLINE** CONSTITUTIONAL LAW **EDUCATION** UCLA, AB, 50; Harvard Univ, LLB, 53. **CAREER** Sch of Law, UCLA **CONTACT ADDRESS** UCLouisiana School of Law, PO Box 951476, Los Angeles, CA, 90095-1476. **EMAIL** karst@law.ucla.edu

KASELY, TERRY S.
PERSONAL Born 10/06/1958, Rochester, PA, m, 1986, 3 children **DISCIPLINE** PHILOSOPHY **EDUCATION** Duquesne Univ, PhD, 92. **CAREER** Part-time inst, Indiana Univ of PA, Univ of PGH, Duquesne Univ, Penn State Univ, & Butler Comm Coll, 87-. **MEMBERSHIPS** APA **RESEARCH** History of philosophy **SELECTED PUBLICATIONS** The Method of the Geometer: A New Angle on Husserl's Cortesianism, Husserl Studies 13:141-154, 97. **CONTACT ADDRESS** 306 S Pike Road, Sarver, PA, 16055.

KASFIR, SIDNEY L.
DISCIPLINE IDOMA MASQUERADE AND SACRED KINGSHIP **EDUCATION** Univ London, PhD, 79. **CAREER** Hist, Emory Univ. **SELECTED PUBLICATIONS** Ed, West African Masks and Cultural Systems. **CONTACT ADDRESS** Emory Univ, Atlanta, GA, 30322-1950. **EMAIL** hartsk@emory.edu

KASSAM, ZAYN
DISCIPLINE THEOLOGY **EDUCATION** McGill Univ, PhD, 95. **CAREER** Asst Prof, Pomona Col, 95-. **CONTACT ADDRESS** Religious Studies, Pomona Col, 551 N College Ave, Claremont, CA, 91711. **EMAIL** zkassam@pomona.edu

KATER, JOHN L., JR.
DISCIPLINE MINISTRY DEVELOPMENT **EDUCATION** Columbia Col, AB; Gen Theol Sem, MDiv; McGill Univ, PhD. **CAREER** Prof; dir, Ctr for Anglican Lrng and Life, Church Divinity Sch Pacific. **SELECTED PUBLICATIONS** Ed, The Challenges of the Past, of the Future: Essays on Mission in the Light of Five Hundred Years of Evangelization in the Americas, CDSP, 94; auth, Campus Ministry and the Reign of God, Plumbline, 95; A Life of Practical Devotion: The Company of Mission Priests in the Church of England 1940-1993, Anglican and Episcopal Hist, 94; Whose Church Is It Anyway? Anglican Catholicity Reconsidered, Anglican Theol Rev, 94; Finding Our Way: American Christians in Search of the City of God, Cowley, 91. **CONTACT ADDRESS** Church Divinity Sch of the Pacific, 2451 Ridge Rd, Berkeley, CA, 94709-1217.

KATES, CAROL A.
PERSONAL Born 11/05/1943, Coral Gables, FL **DISCIPLINE** PHILOSOPHY **EDUCATION** Univ Calif, Berkeley, BA, 65; Tulane Univ, MA, 67, PhD(Philos), 68; Cornell Univ, MILR, 86. **CAREER** Asst prof, 68-71, from assoc prof to prof Philosophy, Ithaca Col, 71-, res assoc ling, Cornell Univ, 73; Am Coun Learned Socs res grant, 76-77; Nat Endowment for Humanities res grant, 73. **MEMBERSHIPS** Am Philos Asn; Southern Soc Philos & Psychol; Ling Asn Can & US; Soc Women Philos. **RESEARCH** Philosophy of Public Policy; phenomenology; existentialism; philosophy in literature. **SELECTED PUBLICATIONS** Auth, Psychical distance and temporality, Tulane Studies in Philos, 71; A critique of Chomsky's Theory of Grammatical Competence, 76 & Linguistic relativity and generative Semantic grammar, 77, Forum Ling; The Problem of Universals: An empiricist account of ideal objects, Man and World, Vol XII, 79; An intentional analysis of the law of contradiction, Res in Phenomenology, Vol IX, 79; A pragmatic theory of metaphor, Forum Ling, 12/79; Pragmatics and Semantics, Cornell Univ Press, 80; Art and myth: The authentic image, In: Philos & Archaic Experience, Duquesne Univ Press (in press). **CONTACT ADDRESS** Dept of Philosophy, Ithaca Col, 953 Danby Rd, Ithaca, NY, 14850-7002. **EMAIL** kates@ithaca.edu

KATSORIS, CONSTANTINE N.
DISCIPLINE TAX LAW **EDUCATION** Fordham, BS, 53, JD, 57; NY Univ, LLM, 63. **CAREER** Pvt practice, Cahill, Gordon, Reindel & Ohl, NYC, 58-64; pres, Fordham Law Rev Assn, 63-64; consult, NY Comm on Estates, 64-67; arbitrator, Nat Assn Securities Dealers, 68-; arbitrator, NY Stock Exch, 71-; dir, Fordham Law Alumni Assn, 72-; public mem, Securities Ind Conf on Arbit, 77-; pvt judge, Duke Law Sch Pvt Adjudication Ctr, 89-; arbitrator trainer, Nat Assn Securities Dealers, 94-; arbitrator trainer, NY Stock Exch, 94-; prof, 64-. **SELECTED PUBLICATIONS** Auth, Mastrobuono: Not the Last Word on Punitives, 13 Alternatives 29, 95; Ruder Report is a Delicate Compromise, 14 Alternatives 29, 96; SICA: The First Twenty Years, 23 Fordham Urban Law Jour 483, 96; The Betrayal of McMahon, 24 Fordham Urban Law Jour 221, 97. **CONTACT ADDRESS** Law Sch, Fordham Univ, 113 W 60th St, New York, NY, 10023.

KATZ, LEWIS ROBERT
PERSONAL Born 11/15/1938, New York, NY, m, 1964, 1 child **DISCIPLINE** CRIMINAL LAW **EDUCATION** Queens Col, NY, BA, 59; Ind Univ, Bloomington, JD, 63. **CAREER** Assoc, Snyder, Bunger, Cotner & Harrell, 63-65; instr law, Univ Mich, 65-66; from asst prof to prof, 66-72, John C Huthins Prof Law, Sch Of Law, Case Western Reserve Univ, 72-; Dir Ctr Criminal Justice, 73-; Lectr, US Int Commun Agency, Africa, 81-82. **RESEARCH** Criminal procedure; criminal justice administration. **SELECTED PUBLICATIONS** Auth, Ohio Criminal Law, Banks Baldwin Publ, 74, criminal procedure sections added 86, statutory commentary added 87, updated annually until 95; coauth, New York Suppression Manual: Arrest, Search and Seizure, Interrogation and Identification, West Annual Publ, 91-97; auth, Know Your Rights, West, 94; coauth, Ohio Felony Sentencing Law, West Annual Publ, 96, 97; Baldwin's Ohio Practice Criminal Law, Banks Baldwin Law Publ, 96; Ohio Criminal Justice, West Annual Publ, 97. **CONTACT ADDRESS** Sch of Law, Case Western Reserve Univ, 11075 East Blvd, Cleveland, OH, 44106-1769. **EMAIL** lrk@po.cwru.edu

KATZ, MILTON
PERSONAL Born 11/29/1907, New York, NY, m, 1933, 3 children **DISCIPLINE** LAW **EDUCATION** Harvard Univ, AB, 27, JD, 31. **CAREER** Solicitor, War Pro Bd, 41-43; Byrne prof admin law, Law Sch, Harvard Univ, 46-48; US spec rep, Europe, 50-51; Stimson prof law & dir int legal studies, Law Sch, Harvard Univ, 54-78, dir int prog taxation, 61-65, res assoc, Prog Technol & Soc, 67-69. Trustee & mem exec comn, Carnegie Endowment Int Peace, 53-78, chmn bd trustees, 71-78; lect, Nat War Col, 53-55 & US Army War Ccl, 54-56; consult, Ford Found, 54-67; lectr, Haverford Col, 55; trustee, Longy Sch Music, 55-67; trustee & mem exec comt, World Peace Found, 55-; trustee & mem exec comt, Citizens Res Found, 59-78, pres, 72-78; mem, Comt Foreign Affairs Personnel, 61-63; chmn comt manpower, White House Conf Int Coop, 65; trustee, Brandeis Univ, 66-; consult, Secy Educ, Dept Health, Educ & Welfare, 67; trustee, Case Western Reserve Univ, 67-79; trustee, Int Legal Ctr, 67-78, chmn bd trustees, 74-78; chmn comt life sci & social policy, Nat Acad Sci-Nat Res Coun, 68-76; mem technol assessment panel, Nat Acad Sci, 68-70; Sherman Fairchild vis scholar, Calif Inst Technol, 74; CHMN ENERGY ADV COMT, OFF TECHNOL ASSESSMENT, US CONG, 75-80. **HONORS AND AWARDS** LLD, Brandeis Univ, 72. **MEMBERSHIPS** Am Bar Asn; Am Asn Comp Studies Law; Am Soc Int Law; Am Law Inst; fel Am Acad Arts & Sci (pres, 79-82). **RESEARCH** International legal studies; foreign policy; science, technology and law. **SELECTED PUBLICATIONS** Coauth, Law of International Transactions and Reactions, Foundation Press, 60; auth, The Things that are Caesar's, Knopf, 66; The Relevance of International adjudication, Harvard, 68; contribr, Man's Impact on the Global Environment, Mass Inst Technol, 70; Decision making in the production of power, Sci Am, 70; auth, International Aspects of Education in Law, Cyclopedia Educ, Macmillan & Free Press, 71; contribr, Assessing Biomedical Technologies, Nat Acad Sci, 73; Technology, Trade and the US Economy, Nat Res Coun, 78. **CONTACT ADDRESS** Law Sch, Harvard Univ, Cambridge, MA, 02138.

KATZ, NATHAN
PERSONAL Born 08/11/1948, Philadelphia, PA, m, 1982 **DISCIPLINE** BUDDHIST STUDIES, COMPARATIVE RELIGIONS **EDUCATION** Temple Univ, AB, 70, MA, 75, PhD(relig), 78. **CAREER** Instr relig, Rutgers Univ, 75-78; vis prof Buddhism, Naropa Inst, 78-79; ASST PROF EASTERN RELIGS, WILLIAMS COL, 79-, Am Coun Learned Soc Travel Grant, Austria, 81, Fulbright-Hays res fel, Sri Lanka, 76-78. **MEMBERSHIPS** Fel, Royal Asiatic Soc; Int Asn Buddhist Studies; Am Acad Relig; Asn Asian Studies; Am Philos Asn. **RESEARCH** Buddhist social philosophy; biography of Indrabhuti (8th century Tantric philosopher); Hermeneutics: Buddhist and contemporary western. **SELECTED PUBLICATIONS** The Synagogues of South-india, Arts of Asia, Vol 23, 93; Between Jerusalem and Benares--Studies in Judaism and Hinduism, Int Rev Hist Religions, Vol 43, 96; The Judaisms of Kaifeng and Cochin in The Influence of Confucian and Hindu Theologies on Jewish Folk Traditions and Minhagim Local Observances--Parallel and Divergent Styles of Religious Acculturation, Int Rev Hist Religions Vol 43, 96; Contacts Between Jewish and Indo-Tibetan Civilizations Through the Ages in Rediscovering A Cross-Fertilization Between Biblical and Buddhist Thought, Judaism, Vol 43, 94. **CONTACT ADDRESS** Dept of Relig, Florida Intl Univ, Miami, FL, 33199.

KATZ, SANFORD NOAH
PERSONAL Born 12/23/1933, Holyoke, MA, m, 1958, 2 children **DISCIPLINE** LAW, BEHAVIORAL SCIENCES **EDUCATION** Boston Univ, AB, 55; Univ Chicago, JD, 58. **CAREER** Assoc prof law, Cath Univ Am, 59-64; prof, Univ Fla, 64-68; prof law, Boston Col, 68; lectr law & social work, Smith Col, 65-68; ed-in-chief, Family Law Quart, 71-; assoc law, Clare Hall, Cambridge Univ, 73; visiting fel All Souls Col, Oxford, 97. **HONORS AND AWARDS** Ford Found law fac fel, 64-65; Sterling Fel, Yale Law Sch, 63-64; dept Health, Educ & Welfare res grant, 66-78; Field Found res grant, 68-70; **MEMBERSHIPS** Am Bar Assn; Int Soc Family Law. **RESEARCH** Law and social work; family law. **SELECTED PUBLICATIONS** Auth, Judicial and Statutory Trends In The Law Of Adoption, Georgetown Law J, 62; auth, When Parents Fail: The Law's Response to Family Breakdown, Beacon, 71; ed, The Youngest Minority (2 vols), Am Bar Assn, 74; auth, Creativity in Social Work, Temple Univ, 75; coauth, Adoptions Without Agencies, Child Welfare League Am, 78; co-ed, Family Violence, 78; coauthm, Marriage and Cohabitation in Contemporary Society, Butterworths, 81; auth, Child Snatching-The Legal Response to the Abduction of Children, Am Bar Assn, 81. **CONTACT ADDRESS** Law Sch, Boston Col, 885 Centre St, Newton, MA, 02159-1100. **EMAIL** sanfnd.katz@be.edu

KAUCHECK, KEN
PERSONAL Born 10/14/1946, Highland Park, MI **DISCIPLINE** CANON LAW **EDUCATION** St. Mary's Univ, DDiv, 92; Gregorian Univ, Rome, PhD Canon Law, JCD, 94. **CAREER** Roman Catholic Priest, 78-, Archdiocese of Detroit, Sacred Heart Sem, adj prof, Metropolitan Tribunal - Judge: Defender of the Bond, 91-. **HONORS AND AWARDS** Summa Cum Laude **MEMBERSHIPS** CLSA, ATA **RESEARCH** Teaching magisterium of the church. **SELECTED PUBLICATIONS** Auth, Must the Act of Divine and Catholic Faith Be Given to Ordinatio sacerdotalis?: A Study of the Ordinary Universal Magisterium, in Studia canonica Saint Paul Univ Press, 97. **CONTACT ADDRESS** St. Anastasia Catholic Church, 4571 John R. Rd, Troy, MI, 48098. **EMAIL** kkaucheck@aol.com

KAUFMAN, GORDON DESTER
PERSONAL Born 06/22/1925, Newton, KS, m, 1947, 4 children **DISCIPLINE** THEOLOGY **EDUCATION** Bethel Col, Kans, AB, 47; Northwestern Univ, MA, 48; Yale Univ, BD, 51, PhD(philos theol), 55. **CAREER** Asst instr philos, Yale Univ, 50-52; from instr to asst prof relig, Pomona Col, 53-58; assoc prof theol, Div Sch, Vanderbilt Univ, 58-63; prof, 63-69, Edward Mallinckrodt Jr Prof Divinity, 69-95, MALLINCKRODT PROF DIV EMERITUS, HARVARD UNIV DIV SCH, 95-; Fulbright res fel, Univ Tubingen, 61-62; Guggenheim fel, Oxford Univ, 69-70; vis prof, United Theol Col, Bangalore, India, 76-77; vis prof, Dashisha Univ, Kyoto, 83; vis prof, Univ S Africa, Pretoria, 84; vis lectr, Oxford Univ, 86; vis prof, Chung Chi Col, Chinese Univ Hong Kong, 91. **HONORS AND AWARDS** LHD, Bethel Col, Kans, 73. **MEMBERSHIPS** Am Theol Soc (pres, 79-80); Am Acad Relig (pres, 81-82). **RESEARCH** Philosophical and systematic theology; philos of rel.

SELECTED PUBLICATIONS Auth, Relativism, Knowledge and Faith, Univ Chicago, 60; The Context of Decision, Abingdon, 61; Systematic Theology: A Historicist Perspective, Scribners, 68; God the Problem, Harvard Univ, 72, Fr trans, 75; An Essay on Theological Method, Scholar's Press, 75, rev ed, 79, 3d ed, 95, Jap trans, 89; Nonresistance and Responsibility, Faith & Life Press, 79; The Theological Imagination: Constructing the Concept of God, Westminster, 81; auth, Theology for a Nuclear Age, Manchester Univ Press and Westminster Press, 85, It, Jap, Ger trans; auth, In Face of Mystery: A Constructive Theology, Harvard Univ Press, 93; auth, God-Mystery-Diversity: Christian Theology in a Pluralistic World, Fortress Press, 96. **CONTACT ADDRESS** Divinity Sch, Harvard Univ, 45 Francis Ave, Cambridge, MA, 02138.

KAUFMAN, STEPHEN ALLAN
PERSONAL Born 09/11/1945, Minneapolis, MN, m, 1972, 2 children **DISCIPLINE** ANCIENT NEAR EASTERN LANGUAGES, OLD TESTAMENT **EDUCATION** Univ Minn, BA, 62; Yale Univ, PhD(Near Eastern lang and lit), 70. **CAREER** Asst prof North-West semitics, Univ Chicago, 71-76; assoc prof, 76-81, PROF BIBLE and COGNATE LIT, HEBREW UNION COL, 81-, Vis sr lectr, Haifa Univ, Israel, 74-76; ED, SOC BIBL LIT, ARAMAIC SERIES, 79- **MEMBERSHIPS** Am Oriental Soc; Soc Bibl Lit. **RESEARCH** Aramaic studies; humanities micro computing. **SELECTED PUBLICATIONS** The Causative Stem in Ugartic and the Causative Form in Semitic--A Morphologic-Semantic Analysis of the S-Stem and Disputed Non-Sibilant Causative Stems in Ugartic, J Am Oriental Soc, Vol 113, 93; Old Aramaic Grammar of Texts from 7th-8th Century BC, J Am Oriental Soc, Vol 115, 95; A Scholars; Dictionary of Jewish Palestinian Aramaic--An Article Rev of Sokoloff, Michael Dictionary, J Am Oriental Soc, Vol 114, 94; The Dead Sea Scrolls on Microfiche--A Comprehensive Facsimile Edition of the Texts from the Judean Desert, Vol 3, Inventory List of Photographs, J Am Oriental Soc, Vol 116, 96; The Function of the Niphal in Biblical Hebrew in Relationship to Other Passive-Reflexive Verbal-Systems and to the Pual and Hophal in Particular--Siebesma,Pa, Cath Bibl Quart, Vol 56, 94; Living Waters--Scandinavian orientalistic Studies Presented to Lokkegaard,Frede on His 75th Birthday, January 27th, 1990, J Am Oriental Soc, Vol 113, 93; The Dead-Sea-Scrolls on Microfiche--A Comprehensive Facsimile Edition of the Texts from the Judean Desert, Vol 2, Companion Volume, J Am Oriental Soc, Vol 116, 96; The Dead-Sea-Scrolls Catalog--Documents, Photographs, and Museum Inventory Numbers, J Am Oriental Soc, Vol 116, 96. **CONTACT ADDRESS** Dept Bible and Cognate Lit, Hebrew Union Col, Cincinnati, OH, 45220.

KAUFMAN, WILLIAM E.
PERSONAL Born 06/20/1938, Philadelphia, PA, m, 1965, 2 children **DISCIPLINE** PHILOSOPHY **EDUCATION** Univ of PA, BA, 59; Jewish Theol Sem of Amer, Rabbi, M of Hebrew Letters, 64; Boston Univ, PhD, 71. **CAREER** Congregational Rabbi for 34 yrs; Rabbi of Temple Bethel, Fall River, MA; Adjunct Prof, Philos, Rhode Island Coll. **HONORS AND AWARDS** Phi Beta Kappa. **MEMBERSHIPS** Amer Philos Assoc; Amer Acad Rel; Assoc for Jewish Stud. **RESEARCH** Modern and Contemporary Jewish Philos; Process Theol. **SELECTED PUBLICATIONS** Auth, Contemporary Jewish Philosophies, Wayne State Univ Press, 92; Journeys, An Introductory Guide to Jewish Mysticism, NY Block Pub Co, 80; The Case for God, St Louis, MO, The Chalice Press, 91; A Question of Faith, Jason A., Northvale, NJ, 94; John Wild: From Realism to Phenomenology, NY, Peter Lang, 96; The Evolving God in Jewish Process Theology, Mellen Press, Lewiston, NY, 97. **CONTACT ADDRESS** 404 Langley St, Fall River, MA, 02720.

KAUFMANN, FRANK
PERSONAL Born 12/23/1952, New York, NY, m, 1982, 3 children **DISCIPLINE** CHURCH HISTORY **EDUCATION** Vanderbuilt Univ, PhD 85. **CAREER** Pace Univ, adj prof, Univ Theol Sem, adj prof. **HONORS AND AWARDS** Vanderbilt Univ Schshp; F U Berlin Schshp. **MEMBERSHIPS** AAr **RESEARCH** Religion and society; New religions; Inter religious dialogue. **SELECTED PUBLICATIONS** Auth, Religion and the Future of South African Societies, ed, forthcoming; Christianity in the Americas, ed, NY, Paragon Pub, 98; Dialogue and Alliance, assoc ed, Quart Jour; Newsletter of the Inter-religious Federation for World Peace, assoc ed, quart; Today's World, sr ed consul, monthly; The Foundations of Modern Church History, NY, Lang Pub, 89; Religion and Peace in the Middle East, NY, New Era Books, 87. **CONTACT ADDRESS** Inter Religious Federation, Pace Univ, 4 West 43rd St, New York, NY, 10036. **EMAIL** fortl@pipeline.com

KAVANAGH, AIDAN
PERSONAL Born 04/20/1929, Mexia, TX **DISCIPLINE** RELIGION **EDUCATION** St Meinrad Sem, BA, 56; Univ Ottawa, Ont, STL, 58; Fakultat Trier, Ger, STD, 63. **CAREER** Asst prof theol, St Meinrad Sem, 62-66; from assoc prof to prof theol, Univ Notre Dame, 66-74, dir grad prog liturgical studies, 66-74; actg dir, Yale Inst Sacred Music, 75-77; PROF LITURGICS, YALE DIVINITY SCH, 74-, Dir and vpres, World Ctr Liturgical Studies, 67-68; consult, Nat Cath Off Radio and TV, 67-69 and Int Comt English in Liturgy, 67-69; mem Am Roman Cath Bishop's Subcomt Liturgy, 67-69; assoc ed, Worship, 67-; VIS PROF, DIVINITY SCH, YALE UNIV, 72-73; ASSOC ED, STUDIA LITURGICA, 72- **HONORS AND AWARDS** Berakah Award, NAm Acad Liturgy, 76; Hale Lectr, Seabury-Western Theol Sch, 82., MA, Yale Univ, 74. **MEMBERSHIPS** Nat Liturgical Conf; Am Acad Relig; Nat Asn Pastoral Musicians; Roman Cath-Oriental Orthodox Ecumenical Consultation; NAm Acad Liturgy. **RESEARCH** Hist and theory of ritual; social anthropology of symbolic forms; sacramental theology. **SELECTED PUBLICATIONS** Early Christian Baptism and the Catechumenate--Italy, North-Africa, and Egypt, Cath Hist Rev, Vol 79, 93. **CONTACT ADDRESS** Liturgics Dept, Yale Univ, New Haven, CT, 06510.

KAY, GERSIL NEWMARK
PERSONAL Philadelphia, PA, m, 1980 **DISCIPLINE** PHYSICS; BUSINESS ADMINISTRATION **EDUCATION** Univ Pa; Wharton Sch. **CAREER** Adj Prof, Drexel Univ; Pres, Conservation Lighting Int'l; Founder/Chmn, Building Conservation Int'l. **HONORS AND AWARDS** Victorian Society; Pa Hist and Mus Comn; BOMA; Asoc of Gen Contractors; 1st Pres of the United States Hist Preserv Award. **MEMBERSHIPS** AIA; CSI; IAEI; AIC; SAH; SIA; AASHH; AAM. **RESEARCH** Conservation lighting; older building construction techniques. **SELECTED PUBLICATIONS** Mechanical/Electrical Systems for Historic Buildings, 92; Fiber Opitcs in Architectural Lighting, 98. **CONTACT ADDRESS** 1901 Walnut St., Ste. 902, Philadelphia, PA, 19103.

KAY, HERMA HILL
PERSONAL Born 08/18/1934, Orangeburg, SC, 1 child **DISCIPLINE** LAW **EDUCATION** Southern Methodist Univ, BA, 56; Univ Chicago, JD, 59. **CAREER** Law clerk, Calif, Supreme Court Justice Traynor, 59-60; from asst prof to assoc prof, 60-63, prof law, Univ Calif, Berkeley, 63-, fel, Ctr Advan Studies Behav, Sci, 63-64; dir family law proj, Children's Bureau, 64-67; co-reporter, Uniform Marriage & Divorce Act, Nat Conf Comnrs on Uniform State Laws, 68-70. **RESEARCH** Family law; sex-based discrimination; conflict of laws. **SELECTED PUBLICATIONS** Coauth, Text, Cases and Materials on Sex Based Discrimination, West Publ, 74, 4th ed, 96; auth, The family and kinship system of illegitimate children in California law, Am Anthrop, 67:57; Conflict of laws: Foreign law as datum, 53:47 & A family court: The California proposal, 57:1205, Calif Law Rev. **CONTACT ADDRESS** Sch of Law, Univ of Calif, 220 Boalt Hall, Berkeley, CA, 94720-7201. **EMAIL** kayh@mail.law.berkeley.edu

KAY, JAMES F.
PERSONAL Born 05/18/1948, Kansas City, MO **DISCIPLINE** HOMILETICS; SYSTEMATIC THEOLOGY **EDUCATION** Pasadena Col, BA 69; Harvard Univ M Div 72; Union Theol Sem, M Phil 84, PhD 91. **CAREER** Northern Lakes Presby Parish MN, 74-78; Bemidji State Univ MN, campus pastor 77-79; Presby Hlth Edu Wel Assoc NY, consultant 80-82; Princeton Theological Sem, inst homiletics, asst prof, assoc prof, 88-97, Joe R Engle assoc prof, 97-. **HONORS AND AWARDS** Phi Delta Lambda; BA magna cum laude; Warrack Lectr. **MEMBERSHIPS** AH; AAR; DTS; Karl Barth Soc of N Amer. **RESEARCH** Apocalypticism; Greco-Roman rhetoric; Pauline theology. **SELECTED PUBLICATIONS** Auth, Women Gender and Christian Community, co-ed, Louisville, Westminster John Knox Press, 97; Seasons of Grace: reflections from the Christian Year, Grand Rapids, William B. Eerdmans Pub Co, 94; Christus Praesens: A Reconsideration of Rudolf Bultmann's Christology, Grand Rapids, William B. Eerdmans Pub Co, 94; Preaching at the Turn of the Ages, St Mary's Col Bull, 98; In Whose Name: Feminism and Trinitarian Baptismal Formula, Theology Today, 93. **CONTACT ADDRESS** Dept of Theology, Princeton Theol Sem, PO Box 821, Princeton, NJ, 08542. **EMAIL** james.kay@ptsem.edu

KAY, JUDITH WEBB
PERSONAL Born 12/19/1951, m, 1972, 1 child **DISCIPLINE** ETHICS **EDUCATION** Oberlin Col, BA, 73; Pac School of Relig, MA, 78; Grad Theol Union, PhD, 88. **CAREER** Prof of Prof & Med Ethics, Am Col Traditional Chinese Med, 81-88; asst prof Dept Relig, Wake Forest Univ, 88-92; asst prof Dept Relig, 92-93, actg dean Stud, 93-94, DEAN OF STUDENTS, DIV STUDENT AFFAIRS, UNIV PUGET SOUND, 94-; Woodrow Wilson Newcombe fel finalist, 87; Woodrow Wilson Womens Stud Prog finalist, 87; Roothbert Fund grad fel excellence in scholar, 75-78. **MEMBERSHIPS** Nat Asn Stud Pers Adminr; Am Acad Relig; Soc Christian Ethics. **RESEARCH** Moral psychology; Virtue ethics from a liberation perspective; Professional ethics; Bio- medical ethics. **SELECTED PUBLICATIONS** Auth Politics without Human Nature? Reconstructing a Common Humanity, Hypatia: A Jour of Feminist Philos, 94; Natural Law, Dictionary of Feminist Theol, Westminster John Knox Press, 96; Getting Egypt Out of the People: Aquinas Contributions to Liberation, Aquinas and Empowerment: Classical Ethics for Ordinary Lives, Georgetown Univ Press, 96; rev Gloria Albrecht: The Character of our Communities: Toward an Ethic of Liberation for the Church, Relig Stud Rev, 97; rev Birnab Care: Living With Ones Past: Personal Fates and Moral Pain, Jour of Relig, 98. **CONTACT ADDRESS** Univ Puget Sound, 1500 N Warner, Tacoma, WA, 98416. **EMAIL** dos@ups.edu

KAYE, LAWRENCE J.
PERSONAL Born 02/25/1960, Milwaukee, WI **DISCIPLINE** PHILOSOPHY **EDUCATION** MIT, PhD, 90. **CAREER** Univ Massachusetts, Lectr, 90-. **MEMBERSHIPS** APA **RESEARCH** Philosophy of Mind; Cognitive Science; Philos of Language; Epistemology; Metaphysics. **SELECTED PUBLICATIONS** Auth, Semantic Compositionality: Still The Only Game in Town, Analysis, 93; Are Most of Our Concepts Innate?, Synthese, 95; The Computational Account of Belief, Erkenntnis, 94; The Languages of Thought, Philo of Science, 95; A Scientific Psychologistic Foundation for Theories of Meaning, Minds and Machines, 95; rev, Another Linguistic Turn?, Language Thought and Consciousness: An Essay in Philo Psychol by Peter Carruthers, Psyche, 98. **CONTACT ADDRESS** Philosophy Dept, Univ Mass, 100 Morrissey Blvd, Boston, MA, 02125-3393. **EMAIL** kaye@umbsky.cc.umb.edu

KAYLOR, ROBERT DAVID
DISCIPLINE RELIGION **EDUCATION** Rhodes Col, AB; Louisville Presbyterian Sem, BD; Duke Univ, PhD. **CAREER** Fac, 64-; James Sprunt Prof Relig, present. **HONORS AND AWARDS** Thomas Jefferson Award, Davidson Col, 87. **MEMBERSHIPS** Omicron Delta Kappa, Soc Bibl Lit, Am Acad Relig and Presbytery of Charlotte. **RESEARCH** New Testament studies; Asian religions. **SELECTED PUBLICATIONS** Auth, Paul's Covenant Community: Jew and Gentile in Romans, Westminster John Knox, 88; Jesus the Prophet: His Vision of the Kingdom on Earth, Westminster John Knox, 94. **CONTACT ADDRESS** Dept of Relig, Davidson Col, 102 N Main St, PO Box 1719, Davidson, NC, 28036.

KEALY, SEAN P.
PERSONAL Born 03/29/1937, Thurles, Ireland, s **DISCIPLINE** BIBLICAL STUDIES **EDUCATION** Gregorian Univ, Rome, STL, 66; Univ Col Dublin, MA, 67; Bibl Inst Rome, LSS, 68. **CAREER** Dean Theol, St. Thomas Aquinas Seminary, Nairobi; Sr. Lectr, Kenyatta Univ, Nairobi; Rector, Holy Ghost Missionary Col, Dublin; Holy Ghost Provincial Coun, Dublin; Pres and Prof, Blackrock Col, Dublin; Prof Theol, Duquesne Univ, mem bd dir, chair theol. **MEMBERSHIPS** Irish Bibl Asn; Cath Bibl Asn; Cath Theol Asn. **RESEARCH** History of Exegesis; gospels; biblical studies; spirituality. **SELECTED PUBLICATIONS** Auth, The Apocalypse of John, Liturgical Press, 87; Science and the Bible, Columbia Press, 87; Jesus and Politics, Collegeville, 90; Sprituality for Today, Mercier Press, 94; Matthew's Gospel and the History of Biblical Interpretation, 2 vols, Mellen Bibl Press, 97. **CONTACT ADDRESS** Trinity Hall, Duquesne Univ, Pittsburgh, PA, 15282. **EMAIL** kealy@duq3.cc.duq.edu

KEARNS, JOHN THOMAS
PERSONAL Born 10/28/1936, Elgin, IL, m, 1963, 3 children **DISCIPLINE** PHILOSOPHY **EDUCATION** Univ Notre Dame, AB, 58; Yale Univ, MA, 60, PhD(philos), 62. **CAREER** Asst prof, 64-69, assoc prof, 69-79, prof Philos, State Univ NY Buffalo, 78-; chmn, 94-. **MEMBERSHIPS** Am Philos Assn; Assoc Symbolic Logic, Linguistics Soc of America. **RESEARCH** Logic; philosophy of language; cognitive science. **SELECTED PUBLICATIONS** Contribr, The logical concept of existence, Notre Dame J Formal Logic, 60; Combinatory logic with discriminators, J Symbolic Logic, 69; auth, Deductive Logic: A Programed Introduction, Appleton, 69; contribr, Substance and time, J Philos, 70; Vagueness and failing sentences, Logique et Analyse, 74; auth, Sentences and propositions, In: The Logical Enterprise, Yale Univ, 75; contribr, Denoting and referring, Philos & Phenomenological Res, 76; The logic calculation, Z Math Logik und Grundlagen Math, 77; Reconceiving Experience, a Solution to a Problem Inherited from Descartes, SUNY, 96; contribur, Thinking Machines, Some Fundamental Confusions, Minds and Machines, 97; contribur, Propositional Logic of Supposition and Assertion, Notre Dame J Formal Logic, 97; contribur, Representing, In: Truth in Perspective, Ashgate, 98. **CONTACT ADDRESS** Dept of Philosophy, SUNY, Buffalo, PO Box 601010, Buffalo, NY, 14260-1010. **EMAIL** kearns@acsu.buffalo.edu

KEATING, GREGORY C.
PERSONAL Born 10/15/1956, New York, NY, m, 1983, 2 children **DISCIPLINE** LAW **EDUCATION** Amherst Col, BA 79; Harvard Univ JD, 85; Princeton Univ, MA 81, PhD 93. **CAREER** USC Law School, prof 96-, assoc prof 93-96, asst prof 91-93; Palmer and Dodge, MA 87-90; Foley, Hoag and Eliot, assoc 85-87. **HONORS AND AWARDS** Phi Beta Kappa **MEMBERSHIPS** AALS **RESEARCH** Torts Prod Liability; Jurisprudence; Legal Profession. **SELECTED PUBLICATIONS** Auth, Reasonableness and Rationality in Negligence Theory, 96; The Idea of Fairness in Enterprise Liability, 97; Keeton, Sargentich & Keatings, Tort and Accident Law, 98. **CONTACT ADDRESS** School of Law, Univ Southern Calif, University Park, Los Angeles, CA, 90089-0071. **EMAIL** gkeating@law.usc.edu

KEATING, JAMES
PERSONAL Born 08/01/1961, New York, NY, m, 1991 **DISCIPLINE** THEOLOGY **EDUCATION** Cath Univ Am, PhD, 98. **CAREER** Asst prof, 96- . **MEMBERSHIPS** AAR. **RESEARCH** Biblical theology; Systems theology. **CONTACT ADDRESS** Dept of Theology, Providence Col, Providence, RI, 02918. **EMAIL** keatingjs@aol.com

KEAY, ROBERT
PERSONAL Born 08/16/1959, Brockton, MA **DISCIPLINE** BIBLE **EDUCATION** Bob Jones Univ, BA, 84, MA, 86, PhD, 91; Gordon-Conwell Theol Sem, ThM, 98. **CAREER** Dir of res, New England Inst of Relig Res, Lakeville, MA, 91-94; adjunct instr, 92-94, academic dean & prof of Bible, New England Bible Col, S Portland, ME, 94-. **HONORS AND AWARDS** Phi Alpha Chi. **MEMBERSHIPS** Soc of Biblical Lit; Evangelical Theol Soc; Evangelical Philos Soc. **RESEARCH** Pauline theol; eschatology; new religions. **SELECTED PUBLICATIONS** Auth, A Biblical-Theological Evaluation of Theonomic Ethics, PhD thesis, Bob Jones Univ, Greenville, SC, 91; A Proposal Concerning Paul's Use of Hosea in Romans 9: Canonical-Traditional-Contextual, ThM thesis, Gordon-Conwell Theol Sem, 98; The OT Background of the Firtsborn: A Preliminary Study for Understanding the Firstborn of All Creation in Colossians 1:15, J of Christian Apologetics 1, 98 (online journal- http: //www/sesdigiweb.com/journal). **CONTACT ADDRESS** 57 Woodridge Dr, Steep Falls, ME, 04085. **EMAIL** dean@nebc.edu

KECK, LEANDER E.
PERSONAL Born 03/03/1928, Washburn, ND, m, 1956, 2 children **DISCIPLINE** RELIGION **EDUCATION** Linfield Col, BA, 49; Andover Newton Theol Sch, BD, 53; Yale Univ, PhD, 57. **CAREER** Instr Bibl hist, Wellesley Col, 57-59; from asst prof to prof New Testament, Divinity Sch, Vanderbilt Univ, 59-72; PROF NEW TESTAMENT, CANDLER SCH THEOL AND CHMN DIV RELIG, GRAD SCH, EMORY UNIV, 72-, Am Asn Theol Schs fel, Tubengen, 64-65; researcher, Cambridge Univ, Eng, 71; ED MONOGR SER, SOC BIBL LIT, 73-; res award, Cambridge Univ, Eng, Asn Theol Schs, 76. **HONORS AND AWARDS** STD, Bethany Col, 75. **MEMBERSHIPS** Am Acad Relig; Soc Bibl Lit. **RESEARCH** Gospels and early traditions about Jesus; New Testament Christology; ethos and ethics en early Christianity. **SELECTED PUBLICATIONS** The Premodern Bible in the Postmodern World, Interpretation-A J Bible Theol, Vol 50, 96; The Gospel According to Mark, J Theol Studies, Vol 45, 94; Rethinking So-Called New-Testament Ethics in A Rhetorical Analysis and Historical Justification of Emergent Christian Ethics from Its Greco-Roman Environment, J Bibl Lit, Vol 115, 96; From Jewish Prophet to Gentile God--The Origins and Development of New-Testament Christology, Interpretation-A J Bible Theol, Vol 47, 93; Paul as Thinker in the Resurrection of the Crucified Jesus as an Eschatological Event in the Theology of the Apostle, INTERPRETATION-A J Bible Theol, Vol 47, 93; Studies on the Epistle to the Romans, J Theol Studies, Vol 44, 93; The Rhetoric of Righteousness in Romans-III, 21-26, J Bibl Lit, Vol 112, 93. **CONTACT ADDRESS** Sch Divin, Yale Univ, New Haven, CT, 06520.

KEE, HOWARD CLARK
PERSONAL Born 07/28/1920, Beverly, NJ, m, 1951, 3 children **DISCIPLINE** RELIGION, HISTORY **EDUCATION** Bryan Col, BA, 40; Dallas Theol Sem, ThM, 44; Yale Univ, PhD(relig), 51. **CAREER** Instr relig thought, Univ Pa, 51-53; from asst prof to prof New Testament, Drew Univ, 53-67; Rufus Jones prof hist relig, Bryn Mawr Col, 68-77; prof New Testament, 77-82, WILLIAM GOODWIN AURELIO PROF BIBLICAL STUDIES and DIR GRAD DIV RELIG STUDIES, SCH THEOL, BOSTON UNIV, 82-, Vis prof relig, Princeton Univ, 55-56; mem bd managers and chmn transl comt, Am Bible Soc, 58-; Am Asn Theol Schs fel, Marburg, Ger, 59-60; Guggenheim Found fel archaeol, Jerusalem, 66-67; ed, Soc Bibl Lit Dissertation Ser; BD ADV, YALE UNIV INST SACRED MUSIC, 79- **MEMBERSHIPS** Soc Relig Higher Educ; Soc Bibl Lit; Am Acad Relig; Aaup; Soc New Testament Studies. **RESEARCH** Hist and literature of early Christianity; archaeology of the Hellenistic and early Roman periods; social setting of early Christianity in the Graeco-Roman world. **SELECTED PUBLICATIONS** Theios-Aner and the Markan Miracle Traditions--A Critique of the Theios-Aner Concept As An Interpretative Background of the Miracle-Tradition Used by Mark, Cath Bibl Quart, Vol 54, 92; The Changing Meaning of Synagogue--A Response to Oster, Richard, New Test Studies, Vol 40, 94; Encyclopedia of Early Christianity, J Church State, Vol 35, 93; Jesus in Current Approaches to an Analysis of A Puzzling Designation in the Q-Tradition Q-VII, 18-35--A Glutton and a Drunkard, New Test Studies, Vol 42, 96; The Land Called Holy--Palestine in Christian History and Thought, Am Hist Rev, Vol 99, 94; A Century of Quests for the Culturally Compatible Jesus in an Examination of Recent Scholarship from the So-Called Jesus-Seminar and AN Overview of 20th-Century Research into the Christ Figure, Theology Today, Vol 52, 95; Defining the 1st-Century-Ce Synagogue--Problems and Progress, New Test Studies, Vol 41, 95; Foundational Writings of the Testament of the 12 Patriarchs--An Investigation on the Size, Contents and Characteristics of the Original Writings, Cath Bibl Quart, Vol 55, 93. **CONTACT ADDRESS** Sch of Theol, Boston Univ, Boston, MA, 02215.

KEEFE, ALICE ANN
PERSONAL m, 3 children **DISCIPLINE** RELIGIOUS STUDIES **EDUCATION** Syracuse Univ, PhD, 95. **CAREER** Asst prof; Univ Wis-SP, 64-; fac senate, 95-; Women's Stud Comt; adv, Stevens Point Pagan Alliance. **SELECTED PUBLICATIONS** Auth, Rapes of Women/Wars of Men, in Women, War and Metaphor, Lang and Soc in the Study of the Hebrew Bible, Semeia 61, 93; The Female Body, the Social Body and the Land: A Socio-Political Reading of Hosea 1-2, in The Feminist Biblical Commentary: The Prophets, Sheffield Acad Press; Religious Pluralism, Interreligious Dialogue, and the Academic Study of Religion:Christian Perspectives, for Soc for Buddhist-Christian Stud, 96; Men Are Not Our Enemies: 'Us' And 'Them' in Thich Nhat Hanh's Engaged Buddhism and Feminist Spirituality, for Conf on Rel, War and Peace, 96; Interconnectedness in Engaged Buddhism and Feminist Theology, for Soc for Buddhist-Christian Stud Int Conf, 96. **CONTACT ADDRESS** Dept of Religious Studies, Univ Wis-SP, Stevens Point, WI, 54481. **EMAIL** akeefe@uwsp.edu

KEEFER, DONALD R.
PERSONAL Born 06/05/1955, Baltimore, MD, m, 1993 **DISCIPLINE** PHILOSOPHY **EDUCATION** Univ MD, Baltimore Co, BA, 78; Temple Univ, PhD, 88 **CAREER** ASSOC PROF PHILOS, RHODE ISLAND SCHOOL OF DESIGN, 88-, CHAIR, DEPT OF HIST, PHILOS, SOCIAL SCIENCE, 97-2000. **HONORS AND AWARDS** NEH Summer fel, 92. **MEMBERSHIPS** Am Soc Aesthetics; Am Philos Asn; RI Philos Soc. **RESEARCH** Pragmatism; theories of culture; cognition and creativity. **SELECTED PUBLICATIONS** Auth, Review of J-J. Nattiez's Music and Discourse, J of Aesthetics and Art Criticism, spring 93; Reports on the Death of the Author, Philos and Lit, vol 19, no 1, April 95; The Rage of Innocents: On Casting the First Stone in a Sea of Cultural Pain, in States of Rage: Emotional Eruption, Violence, and Social Change, Renee Curry and Terry Allison, eds, NY Univ Press, 96; review of Michael O'Toole's The Language of Displayed Art, J of Aesthetics and Art Criticism, vol 54, no 3, summer 96; Message of the Bottle: Design Products on the Shores of Semiotics, in Zed, vol 4; Review of Shusterman, Practicing Philosophy, forthcoming in the J of Metaphilos. **CONTACT ADDRESS** 5 Burr's Lane, Providence, RI, 02904. **EMAIL** dkeefer@risd.edu

KEEGAN, JOHN E.
PERSONAL Born 04/29/1943, Spokane, WA, 2 children **DISCIPLINE** LAW **EDUCATION** Gonzaga Univ, BA (English, Psychol), 65; Harvard Law School, JD (Law), 68. **CAREER** Partner, Davis Wright Tremaine, Seattle, 86-; previously Deputy Prosecuting Attourney, King County and Office of General Counsel, Dept of Housing and Urban Development, Washington, DC. **MEMBERSHIPS** WA State Bar Asn; Am Bar Asn; Seattle-King Co Bar Asn; Author's Guild. **SELECTED PUBLICATIONS** Auth, Clearwater Summer, Carroll & Graf, 94. **CONTACT ADDRESS** Davis Wright Tremaine, 2600 Century Sq, Seattle, WA, 98101. **EMAIL** johnkeegan@dwt.com

KEEL, VERNON
DISCIPLINE MEDIA LAW, INTERNATIONAL COMMUNICATION, AND RESEARCH METHODOLOGY **EDUCATION** Univ Minn, PhD. **CAREER** Vis res, Univ Montreal; pres, Assn Sch Journalism and Mass Commun; exec comm; Assn Commun Admin; Nat Accrediting Coun Edu in Journalism and Mass Commun; steering comm, William Randolph Hearst found; founder, dir, prof, Elliott Sch Commun, 89-96. **HONORS AND AWARDS** Vis res, Univ Montreal. **SELECTED PUBLICATIONS** Ed, Communication and Community. **CONTACT ADDRESS** Wichita State Univ, 1845 Fairmont, Wichita, KS, 67260-0062. **EMAIL** keel@elliott.es.twsu.edu

KEELING, LYTLE BRYANT
PERSONAL Born 04/01/1934, Jasper, AR, m, 1970, 1 child **DISCIPLINE** ANALYTIC PHILOSOPHY, PHILOSOPHY OF RELIGION **EDUCATION** Okla Northeastern State Col, BA, 56; Southern Methodist Univ, BD, 59; Univ Chicago, MA(theol), 63, MA(philos), 64, PhD(philos theol), 71. **CAREER** From asst prof to assoc prof, 65-77, Prof Philos, Western Ill Univ, 77-. **MEMBERSHIPS** Am Philos Asn; Am Acad Relig. **RESEARCH** Interpretation of God-language; Wittgenstein's philosophy. **SELECTED PUBLICATIONS** Auth, The pantheism of Charles Hartshorne, In: Philosophy of Religion: Contemporary Perspectives, Macmillan, 74; Feeling as a metaphysical category: Hartshorne from an analytical view, Process Studies, spring 76; coauth, Beyond Wittgensteinian Fideism? A critique of Hick's concept of faith, Int J Philos Relig, winter 77. **CONTACT ADDRESS** Dept of Philosophy, Western Illinois Univ, 1 University Cir, Macomb, IL, 61455-1390. **EMAIL** Bryant_Keeling@ccmail.wiu.edu

KEENAN, J.F.
PERSONAL Born 02/15/1953, Brooklyn, NY **DISCIPLINE** RELIGION **EDUCATION** Gregorian Univ Rome, STD 88. **CAREER** Fordham Univ, asst prof 87-91; Weston Jesuit Sch Theol, asst prof, assoc prof 91 to 93-. **HONORS AND AWARDS** ATS Gnt; Inst Adv Stud Humanities Edinburgh fel; Cen Theo Inq Princeton fel. **MEMBERSHIPS** CTS; SCE **RESEARCH** Casuistry; Aquinas; Virtues; Bioethics; Puritan; Practical Divinity. **SELECTED PUBLICATIONS** Auth, Virtues for Ordinary Christians, Kansas City, Sheed Ward, 96; The Context of Casuistry, coauth, Wash DC, Georgetown Univ Press, 95; Josef Fuchs and the Question of Moral Objectivity in Roman Catholic Ethical Reasoning, Rel Stud Rev, 98; Are You Growing Up in the Virtues?, Priests and People, 98; Moral Theology Out of Western Europe, Theo Stud, 98; What's New in the Ethical and Religious Directives?, Linacre Quart, 98; Virtue Ethics, Basic Christian Ethics: An Introduction, Bernard Hoose, ed, London, Chapman, 97; Institutional Cooperation and the Ethical and Religious Directives, Linacre Quart, 97. **CONTACT ADDRESS** Dept of Theology, Weston Jesuit Sch of Theol, 3 Phillips Place, Cambridge, MA, 02138. **EMAIL** jfkweston@aol.com

KEENAN, JOHN
DISCIPLINE ASIAN RELIGIONS **EDUCATION** Charles Borromeo Sem, AB; Univ Pa, MA; Univ Wis, PhD. **CAREER** Prof; Middlebury Col, 86-. **HONORS AND AWARDS** Frederick Streng awd. **SELECTED PUBLICATIONS** Auth, The Gospel of Mark: A Mahayana Reading; How Master Mou Removes our Doubts: A Reader Response Study of the Mou-Tzu-Li-hou-lunm & The Meaning of Christ: A Mahayana Theology. **CONTACT ADDRESS** Dept of Religion, Middlebury Col, Middlebury, VT, 05753.

KEENER, CRAIG S.
PERSONAL Born 07/04/1960, s **DISCIPLINE** NEW TESTAMENT **EDUCATION** Duke Univ, PhD, 91. **CAREER** Hood Theol Seminary, 92-96; Vis Prof Bibl Studies, Eastern Seminary, 96-99. **MEMBERSHIPS** Soc Bibl Lit; Inst Bibl Res. **RESEARCH** Greco-Roman & Jewish contexts of early Christianity. **SELECTED PUBLICATIONS** Auth, ...And Marries Another: Divorce & Remarriage in the Teaching of the New Testament, Hendrickson Publ, 91; Paul, Women & Wives: Marriage & Women's Ministry in the Letters of Paul, Hendrickson Publ, 92; The IVP Bible Background Commentary: New Testament, InterVarsity Press, 93; The Spirit in the Gospels and Acts: Rebirth and Prophetic Empowerment, Hendrickson, 97; an academic commentary on Matthew (currently untitled), Eerdmans (forthcoming 99). **CONTACT ADDRESS** Eastern Baptist Theol Sem, 6 Lancaster Ave, Wynnewood, PA, 19096-3494. **EMAIL** CSKeener@compuserve.com

KEENEY, DONALD E.
PERSONAL m **DISCIPLINE** THEOLOGY **EDUCATION** Wheaton Coll, BA, 76, MA, 79; S Baptist Theo Sem, MDiv, 82, PhD, 87; Columbia Univ, MSLS, 92. **CAREER** Assoc Prof, librarian, 97-, Central Baptist Sem. **MEMBERSHIPS** SBL, NABPR, ATLA. **RESEARCH** Theology and bibliography, theology & librarianship. **CONTACT ADDRESS** Central Baptist Theol Sem, 741 N 31st St, Kansas City, KS, 66102-3964.

KEETON, MORRIS TEUTON
PERSONAL Born 02/01/1917, Clarksville, TX, m, 1944, 3 children **DISCIPLINE** PHILOSOPHY **EDUCATION** Southern Methodist Univ, AB, 35, AM, 36; Harvard Univ, AM, 37, PhD, 38. **CAREER** Instr philos, Southern Methodist Univ, 38-41; educ secy, Civilian Pub Serv Camp, 41-45, educ secy, Brethren Civilian Pub Serv, 42-45; Guggenheim fel, 46; col pastor, Antioch Col, 47-59, dir educ policy studies, 56-60, from asst prof to prof philos, 47-77, assoc dean fac, 60-63, dean, 63-67, acad vpres, 67-72, provost & vpres, 72-77; CEO, Coun Advan Experiential Learning, 77-89, Head mission in Ger, Am Friends Serv Comt, 53-55; exam, NCent Asn Cols & Sec Schs, 61-77, mem exec bd, Comn Higher Educ, 73-77; chmn, Carus lectr comt, Am Philos Asn, 64-69. **MEMBERSHIPS** Western Div Am Philos Asn (secy-treas, 59-61); Asn Higher Educ (pres, 72-73); fel Soc Relig Higher Educ; Southwestern Philos Soc (secy-treas, 40-41). **RESEARCH** Epistemology; ethical theory; adult learning. **SELECTED PUBLICATIONS** Auth, The Philosophy of Edmund Montgomery, Southern Methodist Univ, 50; Values Men Live by, Abingdon, 60; coauth, Range of Ethics, Am Bk Co, 66; Struggle and Promise ..., McGraw, 69; auth, Shared Authority on Campus, Am Asn Higher Educ, 70; coauth, Ethics for Today, Van Nostrand, 5th ed, 73; Experiential Learning, Jossey-Bass, 77. **CONTACT ADDRESS** 10989 Swansfield Rd, Columbia, MD, 21044. **EMAIL** mkeeton@polaris.umuc.edu

KEETON, ROBERT ERNEST
PERSONAL Born 12/16/1919, Clarksville, TX, m, 1941, 2 children **DISCIPLINE** LAW **EDUCATION** Univ Tex, BBA, 40, LLB, 41; Harvard Univ, SJD, 56. **CAREER** Assoc prof law, Southern, Methodist Univ, 51-53; Thayer teaching fel, 53-54, from asst prof to prof, 54-73, Langdell Prof Law, Harvard Univ, 73-, Assoc Dean Law Sch, 75-, Mem law fac, Salzburg Sem Am Studies, 61; trustee, Col Retirement Equities Fund, 65-69; MASS COMNR UNIFORM STATE LAWS, 71-; MEM FAC, NAT INST TRIAL ADVOCACY, 72-, DIR, 73-76, ED CONSULT, 76-; TRUSTEE, FLASCHNER JUDICIAL INST, 78- **HONORS AND AWARDS** Clarence Arthur Kulp Mem Award, Am Risk and Insurance Asn, 66. **MEMBERSHIPS** Am Law Inst; Am Bar Asn; Am Risk and Insurance Asn; Am Acad Arts and Sci. **RESEARCH** Torts; insurance; trial practice. **SELECTED PUBLICATIONS** Restating Strict Liability and Nuisance, Vanderbilt Law Rev, Vol 48, 95. **CONTACT ADDRESS** Law Sch, Harvard Univ, Cambridge, MA, 02138.

KEIFERT, PATRICK
DISCIPLINE SYSTEMATIC THEOLOGY **EDUCATION** Valparaiso Univ, BA, 73; Christ Sem, MDiv, 77; Divinity Sch, Univ Chicago, PhD, 82; additional stud, Univ Heidelberg; Univ

Tubingen, Ger. **CAREER** Tchg asst, Christ Sem-Seminex, 76-77; instr, 80; adj prof, Sch of Law, Hamline Univ, 84; assoc prof, 86-; dir, Lutheran Leadership Inst. **HONORS AND AWARDS** Travel grant, Fulbright-Hays lang grant, Deutscher Akademischer Austauschdienst; post dr fel, Franklin Clark Frye., Asst pastor, Pilgrim Evangel Lutheran Church, Chicago, 78-80; interim pastor, Lord of Life Lutheran church, 82; Trinity and Hope Lutheran Churches, 83; Galilee Lutheran Church, 85. **SELECTED PUBLICATIONS** Auth, Welcoming the Stranger: A Public Theology of Worship and Evangelism, 92; Worship and Evangelism: A Pastoral Handbook, 90; People Together, 94. **CONTACT ADDRESS** Luther Sem, 2481 Como Ave, St. Paul, MN, 55108. **EMAIL** pkeifert@luthersem.edu

KEIM, ALBERT N.
DISCIPLINE THEOLOGY **EDUCATION** Eastern Mennonite Univ, BA; Univ VA, MA; OH State Univ, PhDs. **CAREER** Theol Dept, Eastern Mennonite Univ **SELECTED PUBLICATIONS** Articles: Conrad Grebel Rev. **CONTACT ADDRESS** Eastern Mennonite Univ, 1200 Park Road, Harrisonburg, VA, 22802-2462.

KEIM-CAMPBELL, JOSEPH
DISCIPLINE PHILOSOPHY **EDUCATION** Rutgers Univ, BA, 83; Univ Ariz, PhD, 92. **CAREER** Asst prof, Kent State Univ, 91-94; vis asst prof, Boise State Univ, 94-97; ASST PROF, WASH STATE UNIV, 97-. **CONTACT ADDRESS** PO Box 645130, Pullman, WA, 99164-5130. **EMAIL** josephc@wsu.edu

KEITER, ROBERT B.
PERSONAL Born 07/05/1946, Bethesda, MD, m, 1976, 2 children **DISCIPLINE** LAW; HISTORY **EDUCATION** Northwestern Univ, JD 72; Washington Univ, BA 68. **CAREER** Univ Utah Col Law, Wallace Stegner prof, dir, 93-; Wallace Stegner Cen Land Resource Environ, prof, James I. Farr prof, 93-98, Univ Wyoming College of Law, assoc prof, interim dean, prof, Winston S. Howard dist prof, 78-93; Univ Utah, vis prof, 85; Southwestern Univ, assoc prof, 76-78; Idaho Legal Aid, managing att, 75-76; Appalachian Res Def Fund, Reginald Heber Smith Fel, 72-74. **HONORS AND AWARDS** Omicron delta Kappa; Phi Kappa Phi; Sr Fulbright Sch **MEMBERSHIPS** ABA; State Bars of Wyoming, Idaho, West Virginia; RMMLF Trustee. **RESEARCH** Nat Resources Law and Policy; Constitutional Law. **SELECTED PUBLICATIONS** Auth, Reclaiming the Native Home of Hope: Community Ecology and the West, ed, Univ Utah Press, 98; Visions of the Grand Staircase-Escalante: Examining Utah's Newest National Monument, co-ed, Wallace Stegner Cen Utah Museum Natural Hist, 98; The Greater Yellowstone Ecosystem: Redefining America's Wilderness Heritage, coed, Yale Univ Press, 91; Ecosystems and the Law: Toward an Integrated Approach, Ecolo Apps, Preserving Nature in the Provincial Parks: Law Policy and Science in a Dynamic Environment, rev, Denver U L, 97; Ecological Policy and the Courts: Of rights Processes and the Judicial Role, Human Ecolo Rev, 97; Greater Yellowstone's Bison: The Unraveling of an Early American Wildlife Conservation Achievement, Jour of Wildlife Mgmt, 97; Law and Large Carnivore Conservation in the Rocky Mountains of the Us and Canada, coauth, Conservation Biology, 96. **CONTACT ADDRESS** College of Law, Utah Univ, 332 S. 1400 E. Front, Salt Lake City, UT, 84112. **EMAIL** keiterb@law.utah.edu

KEITH, HEATHER
DISCIPLINE PHILOSOPHY **EDUCATION** Southern Ill Univ, PhD. **CAREER** Adj prof, E Tenn State Univ. **SELECTED PUBLICATIONS** Auth, An Interview with Martha Nussbaum, Kinesis, 97. **CONTACT ADDRESS** Philosophy Dept, East Tennesee State Univ, Box 70717, Johnson City, TN, 37614- 0717. **EMAIL** keith@etsu.edu

KEKES, JOHN
PERSONAL Born 11/22/1936, Budapest, Hungary, m, 1967 **DISCIPLINE** PHILOSOPHY **EDUCATION** Queen's Univ, Ont, Can, BA, 61, MA, 62; Australian Nat Univ, PhD(philos), 67. **CAREER** Asst prof to assoc prof Calif State Univ, Northridge, 65-71; prof, Univ Sask, Regina, Can, 71-74; prof philos & chm dept, State Univ NY Albany, 74-, Rev ed, Metaphilos, 77-80; consult ed, Am Philos Quart, 78-; consult ed, Hist Philos Quart, 84-87; gen ed, Studies in Moral Philos, 87-91; consult ed to ed, Public Affairs Quart, 87-. **HONORS AND AWARDS** W. Wilson Fel, 61; Can Coun Fel, 61; Res Scholar, Australian Nat Univ, 62-65; NEH Summer Fel, 71; Can Coun Grant, 73; Rockefeller Found, Humanities Fel, 80-81; Rockefeller Found Bellagio Study Str, 82, 89; Earhart Found Fel, 83, 88, 89, 98; Sen Res Fel, Ctr for Philos Sci Univ, Pittsburgh, 84-85; Visiting Prof, United States Mil Acad West Point, 85-86; Estonian Acad of Sci, 89; Nat Univ of Singapore, 89; Hungarian Acad of Sci, 98. **MEMBERSHIPS** Am Philos Asn; Royal Inst of Philos. **RESEARCH** Moral and political philos; public policy. **SELECTED PUBLICATIONS** Auth, A Justification of Rationality, State Univ NY Albany, 76; The Nature of Philosophy, Oxford, 80; The Examined Life, Assoc Univ Presses, 88; Moral Tradition and Individuality, Princeton Univ Press, 89; Facing Evil, Princeton Univ Press, 93; The Morality of Pluralism, Princeton Univ Press, 93; Moral Wisdom and Good Lives, Cornell Univ Press, 95; Against Liberalism, Cornell Univ Press, 97; Against Liberalism, Cornell Univ Press, 97; A Case for Conservatism, Cornell Univ Press, 98. **CONTACT ADDRESS** Dept of Philos, State Univ NY, 1400 Washington Ave, Albany, NY, 12222-1000. **EMAIL** jkekes@csc.albany.edu

KELBLEY, CHARLES A.
DISCIPLINE PHILOSOPHY **EDUCATION** Sorbonne, PhD; Fordham Univ, PhD. **CAREER** Assoc prof, Fordham Univ. **RESEARCH** Philos issues in the theory of law and justice. **SELECTED PUBLICATIONS** Auth, Legal Ethics: Discretion and Utility in Modern Rule 1.6, Fordham Urban Law Jour, 85; Hart's Legacy, Newsletter on Philosophy and Law, APA Newsletters, 96; Rawls: From Moral to Political Theory, Intl Philos Quart, 96. **CONTACT ADDRESS** Dept of Philos, Fordham Univ, 113 W 60th St, New York, NY, 10023.

KELLENBERGER, BERTRAM JAMES
PERSONAL Born 05/04/1938, San Francisco, CA, m, 1981, 2 children **DISCIPLINE** PHILOSOPHY **EDUCATION** San Jose Univ, BA, 60; Univ Calif Berkeley, MA, 63; Univ Ore, PhD, 67. **CAREER** Lectr, Cameroon Coll of Arts and Sci, 62-64; asst prof, Calif State Univ Northridge, 67-71; vis prof, Albion Coll, 71-72; assoc prof, Calif State Univ Northridge, 71-75; adj prof, Claremont Grad School, 91; prof Calif State Univ Northridge, 75-. **MEMBERSHIPS** Am Philos Asn; Soc of Christian Philos. **RESEARCH** Philosophy of Religion; Ethics. **SELECTED PUBLICATIONS** Auth, Religious Discovery: Faith and Knowledge, 72; the Cognitivity of religion: Three Perspectives, 85; God-Relationships With and Without God, 89; Relationship Morality, 95; Kierkegaard and Nietzsche: Faith and Eternal Acceptance, 97; ed, Inter-Religious Models and Criteria, 93. **CONTACT ADDRESS** Dept of Philosophy, California State Univ, Northridge, Northridge, CA, 91330-8253. **EMAIL** james.kellenberger@csun.edu

KELLER, DAVID R.
PERSONAL Born 12/17/1962, m **DISCIPLINE** PHILOSOPHY **CAREER** Instr philos, Univ Georgia, 93-94; instr philos, Univ Hawaii, 95; asst prof philos, Dept Hum and Philos, 96- , program coordinator, Center for the Study of Ethics, 98- , asst prof philos, Dept of Integrated Stud, 98- , Utah Valley State Col. **RESEARCH** Ethics; environmental philosophy; history of the Western intellectual tradition; literature; aesthetics; philosophy of science; existentialism. **CONTACT ADDRESS** Utah Valley State Col, 800 W 1200 South, Orem, UT, 84058-5999. **EMAIL** kellerda@uvsc.edu

KELLER, EVELYN FOX
PERSONAL Born 03/20/1936, New York, NY, d, 2 children **DISCIPLINE** PHYSICS **EDUCATION** Brandeis Univ, BA, 57; Radcliffe Coll, MA, 59; Harvard Univ, PhD, 63. **CAREER** Instr, Physics, New York Univ, 62-63; asst res sci, Courant Inst Math Sci, New York Univ, 63-66; asst prof, Grad Sch Med Sci, Cornell Univ Med Coll, 63-69; assoc prof, New York Univ, 70-72; lectr, math Biol, assoc prof, SUNY-Purchase, 72-82; Univ Md, 74; vis fel, MIT, Sci/Tech/Soc, 79-80; vis scholar, MIT, 80-84; vis prof, Math & Human, Northeast Univ, 81-82; vis prof, MIT, 85-86; prof, Math & Human, Northeast Univ, 82-88; prof, Univ Calif-Berkeley, Rhet & Women's Stud, 88-92; PROF, MIT, HIST & PHILOS SCI, 92-. **RESEARCH** Language, gender & science; History of explanation in developmental biology **SELECTED PUBLICATIONS** Refiguring Life: Metaphors of Twentieth Century Biology, Columbia Univ Press, 95; Feminism and Science, Oxford Univ Press, 96; Open the Social Sciences: Report of the Gulbenkian Commission on the Restructuring of the Social Sciences, Stanford Univ Press, 96. **CONTACT ADDRESS** Massachusetts Inst of Tech, 77 Massachusetts Ave, Cambridge, MA, 02139-4307. **EMAIL** efkeller@mit.edu

KELLER, JAMES ALBERT
PERSONAL Born 10/20/1939, Pittsburgh, PA, m, 1961, 3 children **DISCIPLINE** PHILOSOPHY **EDUCATION** Mass Inst Technol, BS, 61; Pittsburgh Theol Sem, MDiv, 64; Yale Univ, MPhil, 67, PhD(relig studies), 69. **CAREER** Asst prof philos, MacMurray Col, 67-72; asst prof, 72-74, ASSOC PROF PHILOS, WOFFORD COL, 74-, CHMN DEPT, 72- **MEMBERSHIPS** Am Philos Asn; Am Acad Relig; Soc Christian Philos; Ctr Process Studies. **RESEARCH** Philosophy of religion; metaphysics; thought of Alfred North Whitehead. **SELECTED PUBLICATIONS** The Hiddenness of God and the Problem of Evil, Int J Philos Relig, Vol 37, 95; The Power of God and Miracles In-Process Theism, J Am Acad Relig, Vol 63, 95; The Philosophy Of Hartshorne, C, J Relig, Vol 73, 93. **CONTACT ADDRESS** Dept of Philos, Wofford Col, Spartanburg, SC, 29301.

KELLER, PIERRE
DISCIPLINE NINETEENTH-CENTURY PHILOSOPHY **EDUCATION** Columbia Univ, PhD. **CAREER** ASSOC PROF, UNIV CALIF, RIVERSIDE. **RESEARCH** Kant; Phenomenology; 19th century philos. **SELECTED PUBLICATIONS** Auth, "Personal Identity and Kant's Third Person Perspective," Idealistic Stud, 94; "Heidegger's Destruction of Pragmatism in the History of Philosophy," Jour Hist of Ideas, 95; "Heidegger's Critique of the Vulgar Notion of Time," Intl Jour of Philos Stud, 96; "Hegel on the Nature of the Perceptual Object," Jahrbuch fuer Hegelforschung, 97; coauth, "Heidegger and the Source(s) of Intelligibility," Continental Philos Rev, 98. **CONTACT ADDRESS** Dept of Philos, Univ Calif, 1156 Hinderaker Hall, Riverside, CA, 92521-0209. **EMAIL** pierrek@ucrac1.ucr.edu

KELLOGG, FREDERIC R.
PERSONAL Born 01/27/1942, Boston, MA, m, 1993 **DISCIPLINE** PHILOSOPHY OF LAW **EDUCATION** Harvard Univ, BA, 64, LLB, 68; George Wash Univ, LLM, 78, SJD, 83. **CAREER** Attorney, 68-94; vis Prof, Fulbright fel, 96, Univ Warsaw; vis Prof, Moscow State Univ. **HONORS AND AWARDS** Dewey Essay Proj Prize; Fulbright Fel. **MEMBERSHIPS** APA; SAAP; CSPS. **RESEARCH** History and theory of law, responsibility. **SELECTED PUBLICATIONS** Auth, The Formative Essays of Justice Holmes: The Making of an American Legal Philosophy, Westport CT, Greenwood Press, 84. **CONTACT ADDRESS** 2027 Que St NW, Washington, DC, 20009. **EMAIL** 103336.1312@compuserve.com

KELLY, BALMER HANCOCK
PERSONAL Born 06/12/1914, Wytheville, VA, m, 1944, 3 children **DISCIPLINE** THEOLOGY, BIBLICAL INTERPRETATION **EDUCATION** King Col, AB, 34; Union Theol Sem, Va, Bd, 39, ThM, 40; Princeton Univ, ThD, 46. **CAREER** Prof Bible, King Col, 40-41; asst prof, 43-48, prof Bibl theol, 48-62, Aubrey Lee Brooks prof, 62-77, dean fac, 65-73, Emer prof Bibl Theol, Union Theol Sem, VA, 77-, Co-ed, Interpretation, 47-66; ed, Layman's Bible Commentary, 56- **HONORS AND AWARDS** LLD, King Col, 50. **MEMBERSHIPS** Soc Bibl Lit. **RESEARCH** New Testament Greek; Biblical theology. **SELECTED PUBLICATIONS** Auth, Ezra, Nehemia, Esther, Job, Vol, VIII, In: Layman's Bible Commentary, John Knox, 62. **CONTACT ADDRESS** PO Box 272, Reedville, VA, 22539.

KELLY, DAVID F.
PERSONAL Born 12/05/1940, Somerville, MA **DISCIPLINE** THEOLOGY **EDUCATION** Univ St Michael's Col, Toronto, Can, PhD, 78. **CAREER** Prof of Theology and Health Care Ethics and Dir, Health Care Ethics Center, Duquesne Univ, Pittsburgh, PA. **HONORS AND AWARDS** Duquesne Univ President's Award for Excellence in Scholarship, 93; NEH grant, 83; Presidential Scholarship grant, 98. **MEMBERSHIPS** CTS; CTSA; SCE; Hastings Center; SCCM; AAR. **RESEARCH** Health care ethics. **SELECTED PUBLICATIONS** Auth, The Emergence of Roman Catholic Medical Ethics in North America: An Historical, Methodological, Bibliographical Study, Edwin Mellon Press, 79, reprinted 92; Clinical Care Ethics: Treatment Decisions in American Hospitals, special pubs of the Nat Asn of Cath Chaplains, 1, no 3, Nov 85; Experimentation, Medical, Fetal Research, Organ Transplantation, and Right to Die, The HarperCollins Encyclopedia of Catholicism, ed Richard P McBrien, HarperSanFrancisco, 95; Ethics Consultation, with John W Hoyt, MD, FCCM, Critical Care Clinics, 12, no 1, Jan 96; Ethical Arguments about Physician-Assisted Suicide, St Francis J of Medicine, 96; Karl Rahner and Genetic Engineering: The Use of Theological Principles in Moral Analysis, Philosophy and Theology, 95; Medical Futility and the Ethics of Foregoing Treatment, St Francis J of Medicine, 97; Catholic Medical Ethics in America, The Encyclopedia of American Catholic History, ed Michael Glazier and Thomas Shelley, Liturgical Press, 97; Organic Transplantation, Chapter 21 of Christian Ethics, ed Bernard Hoose, Cassell, 98; The Ethics of Foregoing Treatment: The American Concensus, St Francis J of Medicine, 98; numerous other publications. **CONTACT ADDRESS** Theology Dept, Duquesne Univ, Pittsburgh, PA, 15282-0504.

KELLY, DOUGLAS
DISCIPLINE SYSTEMATIC THEOLOGY **EDUCATION** Univ of North Carolina, BA; Univ Lyon, Dipl; Union Theol Sem, BD; Univ Edinburgh, PhD. **CAREER** J. Richard Jordan prof. **HONORS AND AWARDS** Gen ed, Calvin's Old Testament Commentaries. **MEMBERSHIPS** Mem, Calvin Stud Soc; La Societe Internationale pour L'Etude de la Philosophie Medievale. **SELECTED PUBLICATIONS** Auth, Carolina Scots: An Historical and Genealogical Study of Over 100 Years of Emigration; ed, The Evangel; The Scottish Bulletin of Evangel Theol. **CONTACT ADDRESS** Dept of Systematic Theology, Reformed Theol Sem, 2101 Carmel Rd, Charlotte, NC, 28226.

KELLY, JIM KELLY
DISCIPLINE METAPHYSICS, MORAL THEORY, PHILOSOPHY OF THE HUMANITIES **EDUCATION** SUNY at Oswego, BA; Ohio State Univ, MA, PhD. **CAREER** Assoc prof, Miami Univ **RESEARCH** Intersection of metaphysics, morality, and moral theory. **SELECTED PUBLICATIONS** Auth, Wide and Narrow Interdisciplinarity, in J Gen Educ, 45 2, 96. **CONTACT ADDRESS** Dept of Philosophy, Miami Univ, Oxford, OH, 45056. **EMAIL** kellyjs@muohio.edu

KEMENY, PAUL CHARLES
PERSONAL Born 12/13/1960, Morristown, NJ, m, 1983, 1 child **DISCIPLINE** AMERICAN RELIGIOUS HISTORY **EDUCATION** Wake Forest, BA, 83; Westminster Sem, MAR, 86, MDiv, 87; Duke Univ, ThM, 88; Princeton Sem, PhD, 95. **CAREER** Vis fel, ctr stud (s) Amer Rel, Princeton Univ, 95-96; asst prof, Rel, Calvin Col, 96- . **HONORS AND AWARDS** Woodrow Wilson awd, 97 **MEMBERSHIPS** AAR; HEQ; AHA; ASOH; Conf Earth Hist. **CONTACT ADDRESS** Dept of Religion and Theology, Calvin Col, 3201 Burton St SE, Grand Rapids, MI, 49546.

KEMPF, STEPHEN W.
PERSONAL Born 10/23/1948, Chicago, IL, m, 1979, 5 children **DISCIPLINE** THEOLOGY **EDUCATION** Univ Laval, PhD, 96. **CAREER** Bible research; Wycliffe Bible Translators. **MEMBERSHIPS** SBL. **RESEARCH** Pentateuch; Old Testament studies. **SELECTED PUBLICATIONS** Auth, Genesis 3:14-19: Climax of the Discourse? Jour of Transl and Textlinguistics, 93; auth, Introducing the Garden of Eden: The Structure and Function of Genesis, Jour of Transl and Textlinguistics, 96; auth, Translator's Notes on Genesis 11:27-25: 11, Translator's Notes on Genesis, SIL, 98. **CONTACT ADDRESS** 1253 du Bellay, Sainte-Foy, PQ, G2E 4T8. **EMAIL** stevekempf@compuserve.com

KENDRICK, JOY A.
PERSONAL Born 0911, Burlington, NC, s **DISCIPLINE** LAW **EDUCATION** Univ of North Carolina at Chapel Hill, BA, 1977; State Univ of New York at Buffalo, JD, 1981; Indiana Univ, MBA, 1985. **CAREER** Alamance Technical College, orientation librarian, 1977-78; Cora P Maloney College, academic coordinator, 1980-81; Neighborhood Legal Services Inc, staff attorney, 1981-83; law clerk, 1979-81; NCR Corporation, business intern, 1984; JA Kendrick Business Enterprises Inc, president, 1985-; Law Office of Joy Kendrick, managing counsel, 1985-. **MEMBERSHIPS** Erie County Bar Association; New York State Bar Association; American Bar Association; Leadership Buffalo, 1988; Chamber of Commerce, board of directors, 1987-90; Buffalo Private Industry Council, board of directors, 1990-; Buffalo Business, contributing writer; Minority Business Council, bd of directors; Housing Assistant Center, bd of directors. **CONTACT ADDRESS** Lawyer/ Business Consultant, Law Office of Joy A Kendrick/JA Kendrick Business Enterprise, 107 Delaware Ave, Ste 327, Buffalo, NY, 14202.

KENNEDY, BRUCE
DISCIPLINE LAW **EDUCATION** Univ Mich, BA, AMLS; Univ Minn, JD. **CAREER** Assoc prof. **SELECTED PUBLICATIONS** Auth, Confidentiality of Library Records & Problems, Policies and Laws, Law Lib J, 89; A Draft User Guide to the AALL Universal Case Citation, Law Lib J, 97. **CONTACT ADDRESS** Col Law, Univ of Toledo, Toledo, OH, 43606. **EMAIL** bkenned@uoft02.utoledo.edu

KENNEDY, D. ROBERT
PERSONAL Born 08/24/1946, Jamaica, WI, m, 1970, 3 children **DISCIPLINE** THEOLOGY **EDUCATION** West Indies Col, BTh; Andrews Univ, MA; McGill Univ, STM; Columbia Univ, EdD; Greenwich Univ, PhD cand. **CAREER** Religious educator; seven years as prof of theol, relig. **HONORS AND AWARDS** AAR/Lilly tchg fel, 93-94. **MEMBERSHIPS** Soc Relig Stud; Am Acad of Relig; Soc of Bibl Lit. **RESEARCH** Silence in Heaven: a study of Revelation 8:1 with special focus on its socio-cultural understanding, and an understanding of science and spirituality. **SELECTED PUBLICATIONS** Auth, The politics of the Basin: A Study of Lost Washing, Univ Press of Am, 95; auth, The Politics of the Spirit: Understanding the Spirit in the Church, Univ Press of Am, 96. **CONTACT ADDRESS** Atlantic Union Col, PO Box 554, South Lancaster, MA, 01561. **EMAIL** drkennedy@atlantic.edu

KENNEDY, DAVID
DISCIPLINE LAW **EDUCATION** Brown Univ, BA, 76; Harvard Univ, JD, 80. **CAREER** Vis prof. **SELECTED PUBLICATIONS** Auth, pubs on European community law, evidence, international law, and international trade and legal theory. **CONTACT ADDRESS** Fac of Law, Univ Toronto, 78 Queen's Park, Toronto, ON.

KENNEDY, ROBERT E.
PERSONAL Born 06/20/1933, Brooklyn, NY **DISCIPLINE** SYSTEMATIC THEOLOGY **EDUCATION** Univ of Ottawa, Canada, PhD, 70. **CAREER** Prof, St Peter's Coll, Jersey City, NJ. **HONORS AND AWARDS** Excellent Tchg Award; Durant Prof. **MEMBERSHIPS** AAR. **RESEARCH** Buddhism, Zen; Buddhist Christian Interfaith Work. **SELECTED PUBLICATIONS** Auth, Zen Spirit, Christian Spirit, Continuum, NY, 95. **CONTACT ADDRESS** 50 Glenwood Ave, #908, Jersey City, NJ, 07306.

KENNEDY, ROBIN M.
DISCIPLINE LAW **EDUCATION** Univ Notre Dame, BA; Case Western Reserve Univ, JD. **CAREER** Assoc prof. **SELECTED PUBLICATIONS** Auth, Clinical Law in the Area of Mental Health, Univ Wis, 79; co-auth, Alternative Dispute Resolution, Ohio Jurisprudence, 97; Mediating Status Offender Cases: A Successful Approach, Mediation Quarterly, 96. **CONTACT ADDRESS** Col Law, Univ of Toledo, Toledo, OH, 43606. **EMAIL** rkenned@utnet.utoledo.edu

KENNEDY, THOMAS
PERSONAL Born 04/23/1955, Anderson, SC, m, 1976, 2 children **DISCIPLINE** PHILOSOPHY **EDUCATION** Calvin Col, BA, 75; Univ of Virginia, PhD, 86. **CAREER** Austin P State Univ, asst prof, 87-89; Valparalso Univ, asst prof, assoc prof, 89-. **HONORS AND AWARDS** Valparaiso Univ Alumni, Distinguished Tchg Award, Res Award., Ed bd, Ethics and Medicine, 95-; NEH Younger Scholars Proj Adv, 91 and 93; dir Soc Christ Philos Summer Conference, Valparaiso Univ, 91. **MEMBERSHIPS** Am Philos Asn; Soc Christ Philos; Am Soc Aesthetics; 18th-Century Scottish Studies Soc. **RESEARCH** Philos of art; ethics, philos of religion; Eighteenth century Scottish thought. **SELECTED PUBLICATIONS** Coauth, From Christ to the World, Wm. B. Eerdmans, Grand Rapids, 94. **CONTACT ADDRESS** Dept of Philosophy, Valparalso Univ, Valparalso, IN, 46383. **EMAIL** Tom.Kennedy@valpo.edu

KENNEDY, WILLIAM THOMAS, JR.
PERSONAL Born 03/18/1928, Washington, DC **DISCIPLINE** THEOLOGY **EDUCATION** Dist Columbia Tchrs, BS 1953; Wesley Theol/Drew Theol, STB/BD 1955-60; Wesley Theol, STM 1968. **CAREER** Yale Divty Schl, assoc prof 1969-78; Wesley AME Zion Chrh Phila, pastor homeo/pratl theol 1971-83; Eastern Bpt Semy adj prof preaching 1978-85; Tioga United Methd Chrh, pastor 1983-85; Drew Theol Seminary, adj prof preaching 1985-; Grace UM Church, pastor retired 1995; Consortium for Theological Education, pro preaching 1989-; Arch St UM Church, associate minister, currently. **HONORS AND AWARDS** Dr divty Livinstone Coll 1980; professional cassette Lyman Beecher Series Yale 1969; Hester Lectures, Golden Gate Theological Seminary, 1996. **MEMBERSHIPS** Prsdg elder Barbados Dist/AME Zion 1980-; prof socio/rel Eastern Coll 1977-79; prof soc Mattatuck Coll 1964-68; prest Waterbury Conn NAACP 1964-68; chrmn Waterbury Hmn Rel Comm 1964-68; town Comm Waterbury Conn 1964-70. **CONTACT ADDRESS** Arch St United Methodist Church, 55 N Broad St, Philadelphia, PA, 19107.

KENNEDY-DAY, KIKI
PERSONAL Chicago, IL, m, 1988 **DISCIPLINE** NEAR EASTERN LANGUAGES AND LITERATURE-ARABIC (ISLAMIC PHILOSOPHY) **EDUCATION** NY Univ, PhD, 96. **CAREER** St John's Univ Jamaica; Adj Asst Prof, Hofstra Univ NY, 98-. **MEMBERSHIPS** APA. **RESEARCH** Islamic Philosophy; Ibn Sina. **SELECTED PUBLICATIONS** Auth, articles about Al-Kindi, Aristotelianism in Islamic Philos, Routledge Encycl of Islamic Philos, 98. **CONTACT ADDRESS** Fort Washington Ave, 4A, New York, NY, 10033.

KENNESON, PHILIP D.
DISCIPLINE THEOLOGY AND PHILOSOPHY **EDUCATION** Butler Univ, BA, 81; Emmanuel Sch Relig, Johnson City, Mdiv, 86; Duke Univ, Durham, PhD, 91. **CAREER** Asst prof. **SELECTED PUBLICATIONS** Auth, Beyond Sectarianism: A Postliberal Re-Appraisal of Church and World. Christian Mission and Modern Culture Series, Trinity Press Int, 99; Pluralism, Political Liberalism, and the Need for a New Moral Language, Discernment 3 1, 94; There's No Such Thing as Objective Truth, and It's a Good Thing, Too, In Christian Apologetics In The Postmodern World, Downers Grove, IL: Inter Varsity Press, 95; The Alleged Incorrigibility of Postliberal Theology: Or, What Babe Ruth and George Lindbeck Have in Common, In The Nature of Confession: Evangelicals and Postliberals in Conversation, Downers Grove, IL: Inter Varsity Press, 96; Worship Wars and Rumors of Worship Wars, Rev in Relig and Theol, 96; repr in Baptists Today, 96; Spirituality American Style, Rev in Relig and Theol, 97; coauth, Selling Out the Church: The Dangers of Church Marketing, Abingdon Press, 97; rev, The Sense of a People: Toward a Church for the Human Future, In Mod Theol 10 2, 94; The One, the Three and the Many: God, Creation and the Culture of Modernity, In Mod Theol 11 2, 95; Modernity and Religion, In Relig Stud Rev 21 2, 95; Selling God: American Religion in the Marketplace of Culture, in Relig and Theolm, 96 & Essays in Critical Theology, Mod Theol 13 2, 97. **CONTACT ADDRESS** Dept of Theology and Philosophy, Milligan Col, PO Box 9, Milligan Col, TN, 37682. **EMAIL** pkenneson@milligan.edu

KENNEY, GARRETT C.
PERSONAL Born 12/31/1950, Spokane, WA, m, 1971, 4 children **DISCIPLINE** RELIGIOUS STUDIES **EDUCATION** Gonzaga Univ, educ leadership, PhD, 94. **CAREER** Adjunct instr, Gonzaga Univ, 89-94; visiting asst prof, Eastern Wash Univ, 94-. **MEMBERSHIPS** Amer Acad of Relig; Soc of Bibl Lit. **RESEARCH** New Testament; Johannine studies. **SELECTED PUBLICATIONS** Auth, Lessons in Religion, Kendall/Hunt, 96; auth, Introduction to Religion, Kendall/Hunt, 88. **CONTACT ADDRESS** Humanities Program, Eastern Washington Univ, Patterson 250, MS 25, Cheney, WA, 99004. **EMAIL** gkenney@ewv.edu

KENNEY, JOHN PETER
PERSONAL Born 05/01/1952, Lawrence, MA, m, 1974, 2 children **DISCIPLINE** PHILOSOPHY, RELIGIOUS STUDIES **EDUCATION** Bowdoin Coll, AB, 74; Brown Univ, PhD, 82. **CAREER** Asst prof, 80-85; assoc prof, 86-92; prof, Read Coll, 92-95; dean, prof, Saint Michael's Coll, 95-. **HONORS AND AWARDS** Phi Beta Kappa, 73; Nat Endowment for the Himanities Res Fel, 84-85, 91-92; Burlington Northern Faculty Achievement Award, 90. **MEMBERSHIPS** Am Acad of Rel; N Am Patristic Soc. **RESEARCH** Philosophical Theology. **SELECTED PUBLICATIONS** Auth, Mystical Monotheism A Study in Ancient Platonic Theology, 91; La presencia de la verdad in las Confesiones, San Augustin en Oxford, 95; Mysticism and Contemplation in the Enneads, Am ctah Philos Quart, 97; St Augustine and the Invention of Mysticism, Studia Patristica, 97; San Agustin y la invencion del misticismo, San Augustin en Oxord, forthcoming; Marius Victorinus, Routledge Encycl of Philos, 98; Tertulian, Routledge Encycl of Philos, 98. Ed, The School of Moses: Studies in Philo and Hellenistic Religion, 95. **CONTACT ADDRESS** Office of the Dean of the College, Saint Michael's Col, Colchester, VT, 05439. **EMAIL** Jkenney@smcut.edu

KENNICK, WILLIAM ELMER
PERSONAL Born 05/28/1923, Lebanon, IL, m, 1949, 3 children **DISCIPLINE** PHILOSOPHY **EDUCATION** Oberlin Col, BA, 45; Cornell Univ, PhD(philos), 52. **CAREER** Instr philos, Boston Univ, 50-51; instr, Oberlin Col, 47-48, 51-54, asst prof & chemn dept, 54-56; from assoc prof to prof, 56-76, William F Kenan Jr prof, 78-80, G Henry Whitcomb Prof Philos, Amherst Col, 76-, Lectr, Smith Col, 63-64; mem Comn Inst Higher Educ, New England Asn Schs & Cols, 72-75, vchmn, 75, chemn, 76; actg dean fac, Amherst Col, 80. **HONORS AND AWARDS** MA, Amherst Col, 62. **MEMBERSHIPS** Am Philos Asn; Am Soc Aesthet; Medieval Acad Am. **RESEARCH** Aesthetics; metaphysics. **SELECTED PUBLICATIONS** Auth, Does Traditional Aesthetics Rest on a Mistake?, Mind, 58; Art and Philosophy: Readings in Aesthetics, St Martins, 64; coauth, Metaphysics: Readings and Reappraisals, Prentice-Hall, 66; auth, Moore on Existence and Prediction, In: G E Moore: Essays in Retrospect, Allen & Unwin, 70; On Solipsism, In: Psychoanalysis and Philosophy, Int Univ Press, 70; Philosophy as Grammar and the Reality of Universals, In: Ludwig Wittgenstein: Philosophy and Language, Allen & Unwin, 72. **CONTACT ADDRESS** Dept of Philos, Amherst Col, Amherst, MA, 01002-5003.

KENNY, ALFREIDA B.
PERSONAL Born 03/12/1950, Richmond, VI **DISCIPLINE** LAW **EDUCATION** Syracuse U, AB 1968-72; Columbia Univ Sch of Law, JD 1972-75. **CAREER** Federal Reserve Bank of NY, staff atty 1975-76; Harper & Row Publ Inc, asst gen counsel 1976-80; Weil Gotshal & Manges, assoc 1980-84; Cooper & Kenny, partner 1984-. **HONORS AND AWARDS** Charles Evans Hughes Fellowship Columbia Law Sch 1976; Outstanding Young Women of Am US Jaycees 1978; Professional Awd for Outstanding Serv Natl Assn of Negro Business & Professional Women's Club; Columbia Univ Chap Outstanding Alumnus Awd Black Law Students Assn. **MEMBERSHIPS** Mem Phi Delta Phi Legal Frat 1973-; mem Nat Assn of Black Women Atty 1977-; mem Am Bar Assn 1977-; mem Assn of the Bar of the City of NY 1977-; pres Assn of Black Women Atty NY 1978-80; mem Com on Labor & Employ of the assn of the Bar of the City of NY; bd of dir Nat Bar Assn Women's Div 1980-82; treas 1975-80, mem bd of dirs 1975-, vice pres Alumni Assn Columbia Law Sch Class of 1975, 1980-85; vice pres Friends of Syracuse (Black Alumni Assn) 1979-80; admitted to the bar of Dist Ct for Southern Dist of NY, Dist Ct Eastern Dist for the Dist of NY, US Supreme Court 1981, Ct of Appeals for the 6th Circuit; mem Zeta Phi Beta Sor Inc 1980-; mem Paul Robeson Scholarship Comm Columbia Univ Sch of Law 1980-; Civil Court Comm of Assoc of Bar of the City of NY 1986-. **SELECTED PUBLICATIONS** "The Voting Rights Act of 1965 & Minority Access to th Polit Process" Columbia Human Rights Law Review Vol 6 No 1 1974. **CONTACT ADDRESS** Cooper & Kenny, 71 Broadway, New York, NY, 10006.

KENT, DAN GENTRY
PERSONAL Born 10/13/1935, Palestine, TX, m, 1957, 3 children **DISCIPLINE** OLD TESTAMENT PROPHECY AND CRITICISM **EDUCATION** Baylor Univ, BA, 57; Southwestern Bapt Theol Sem, BD, 59; Southwestern Bapt Theol Sem, ThD, 65. **CAREER** Assoc prof, relig, Wayland Bapt Univ, 75-80; prof, old testament, Southwestern Bapt Theol Sem, 80-. **HONORS AND AWARDS** Pastor, Brandon Baptist Church, 60-62; First Baptist Church, De Leon, 62-66; Hampton Rd Baptist Church, 66-71; Calvary Baptist Church of Oak Cliff, 71-75. **MEMBERSHIPS** Soc Biblical Lit; Nat Assn of Baptist Prof Rel. **RESEARCH** Women in the Old Testament; Social justice in the Old Testament. **SELECTED PUBLICATIONS** Auth, Joshua, Judges, Ruth (Layman's Bible Book Commentary), Broadman Press, 80; auth, Lamentations (Bible Study Commentary), Zondervan, 83; Hosea: Man, Times, and Material, Southwestern Jour of Theol, fall, 93. **CONTACT ADDRESS** Southwestern Baptist Theological Sem, PO Box 22338, Ft. Worth, TX, 76122-0338. **EMAIL** dgk@swbts.swbts.edu

KERCKHOVE, LEE
PERSONAL Born 04/15/1963, Chicago, IL **DISCIPLINE** PHILOSOPHY **EDUCATION** Univ Calif San Diego, BA, 88; Logola Univ Chicago, MA, 91; PhD, 96. **CAREER** Assoc Prof, Palomar Coll, 97-. **HONORS AND AWARDS** Fulbright Scholar, Technische Universitat, Berlin, Germany, 93-94. **MEMBERSHIPS** Am Philos Asn; North Am Nietzsche Soc. **RESEARCH** Social and Political Philosophy; Ethics; Neitzsche. **SELECTED PUBLICATIONS** Auth, Moral Fanaticism and the Holocaust: A Defense of Kant Against Silber, Philos in Contemp World, 94; Re-Thinking Ethical Naturalism: Nietzsche's 'Open Question" Argument, Man and World, 94; Emancipation Social Science and Genealogy: Habermas on Nietzsche, Philos in Contemp World, 95; coauth, Fetal Personhood and the Sorites Paradox, 98. **CONTACT ADDRESS** Dept of Philosophy, Palomar Col, 1140 W Mission Rd, San Marcos, CA, 92069. **EMAIL** lkerckhove@palomar.edu

KERLIN, MICHAEL J.
PERSONAL Born 01/13/1936, Philadelphia, PA, m, 1971, 2 children **DISCIPLINE** PHILOSOPHY **EDUCATION** LaSalle Univ, BA, 57, MA, 58, MBA, 89; Gregorian Univ, PhD, 66. **CAREER** Asst prof, 66-71, asoc prof, 71-76, prof philos, 76-, LaSalle Univ. **HONORS AND AWARDS** Lendback Award for Distinguished Tchg, 87. **MEMBERSHIPS** AAR; APA; Am Cath Philos Asn; Soc of Christian Philos. **RESEARCH** Social philosophy; business and society; philosophy of religion; Roman Catholic modernism. **SELECTED PUBLICATIONS** Auth, St. Philip Veri and 16th Century Church Renewal, America, 95; auth, Peter French, Corporate Ethics and the Wizard of Oz, 97; auth, From Kerlin's Pizzeria to MJK Reynolds : A Socratic and Cartesian Approach to Business Ethics, 97. **CONTACT ADDRESS** Dept of Philosophy, La Salle Univ, 1900 W Olney Ave, Philadelphia, PA, 19141. **EMAIL** kerlin@lasalle.edu

KERN, GILBERT RICHARD
PERSONAL Born 12/05/1932, Detroit, MI, 6 children **DISCIPLINE** CHURCH & AMERICAN HISTORY **EDUCATION** Findlay Col, AB, 54; Winebrenner Theol Sem, BD, 58; Univ Chicago, MA, 60, PhD, 68. **CAREER** From lectr to prof church hist, Winebrenner Theol Sem, 60-70, pres, 63-70; Prof Relig, 70-75, Prof Hist, 75-98, Professor Emeritus, The Univ of Findlay, 98-; Lectr Hist, Winebrenner Theol Sem, 72-84. **MEMBERSHIPS** Am Soc Church Hist; Am Hist Asn. **RESEARCH** Nineteenth century Am church. **SELECTED PUBLICATIONS** Auth, John Winebrenner: 19th Century Reformer, Cent Publ House 74; Findlay College: The first one hundred years, 82. **CONTACT ADDRESS** Dept Hist, The Univ of Findlay, 1000 N Main St, Findlay, OH, 45840-3695. **EMAIL** kern@lucy.findlay.edu

KERR LAWSON, ANGUS
DISCIPLINE PHILOSOPHY **EDUCATION** McMaster Univ, PhD, 63. **RESEARCH** Philos of George Santayana; foundations of math. **SELECTED PUBLICATIONS** Auth, pub(s) on George Santayana. **CONTACT ADDRESS** Dept of Philosophy, Waterloo Univ, 200 University Ave W, Waterloo, ON, N2L 3G1. **EMAIL** kerrlaws@uwaterloo.ca

KERSTEN, FREDERICK IRVING
PERSONAL Born 09/26/1931, Niagara Falls, NY, m, 1994, 2 children **DISCIPLINE** PHILOSOPHY **EDUCATION** Lawrence Univ, BA, 54; New School for Soc Res, MA, 59, PhD, 64. **CAREER** Insr, asst prof, assoc prof, Univ Montana, Missoula, 64-69; assoc prof, prof, Univ Wisconsin, Green Bay, 69-94. **HONORS AND AWARDS** Halle Fel, 60-61; Frankenthal prof, Univ of Wisconsin, Green Bay, 84-94. **MEMBERSHIPS** Ed bd, Human Stud; ed bd, Husserl Stud. **RESEARCH** Husserl's and Husserlian phenomenology; phenomenological philosophy in metaphysics and epistemology; philosophy and art in the Renaissance and Baroque; nineteenth century philosophy. **SELECTED PUBLICATIONS** ed, trans, Alfred Schutz, Collected Papers, Kluwer, 95; auth, "Notes from the Underground," The Prism of the Self, ed by Crowell, Kluwer, 95; Constitutive Phenomenology, Intentionality, Alfred Schutz, Encyclopedia of Phenomenology, ed Embree, Kluwer, 97; "Some Reflections on the Ground for Comparison of Multiple Realities," Alfred Schutz' Sociological Aspect of Literature, ed by Embree, Kluwer, 97; Galileo and the Invention of Opera, Kluwer, 97; Stuffed Cabbage in the Old New School Cafeteria, Hum Stud, 97; "The Purely Possible Political Philosophy of Alfred Schutz," Schutzian Social Science, ed Embree, Kluwer, 98; "Angela Thirkell," UK J of the Angela Thirkell Soc, 98; ed, Reconstruction of Alfred Schutz, Hum Stud, forthcoming. **CONTACT ADDRESS** 2355 Old Plank Rd, De Pere, WI, 54115.

KESAN, JAY P.
DISCIPLINE LAW **EDUCATION** Univ Tex Austin, MS; PhD; Georgetown Univ, JD. **CAREER** Law clerk, Judge Patrick E. Higginbotham, US Court Appeals; asst prof,Univ Ill Urbana Champaign. **HONORS AND AWARDS** Assoc ed, Georgetown Law J. **RESEARCH** Intellectual property; law and regulation of cyberspace; and science; technology and the law; Patent law; Law and Regulation of Cyberspace and Theoretical Foundations of Intellectual Property. **SELECTED PUBLICATIONS** Auth, pubs on intellectual property, law and regulation of cyberspace, and science, technology and law. **CONTACT ADDRESS** Law Dept, Univ Ill Urbana Champaign, 52 E Gregory Dr, Champaign, IL, 61820. **EMAIL** kesan@law.uiuc.edu

KESSLER, ANN VERONA
PERSONAL Born 01/28/1928, Aberdeen, SD **DISCIPLINE** MODERN & CHURCH HISTORY **EDUCATION** Mt Marty Col, BA, 53; Creighton Univ, MA, 57; Univ Notre Dame, PhD, 63. **CAREER** Teacher elem schs, 47-49, 57-59 & Mt Marty High Sch, 52-56; from instr to assoc prof, 62-73, acad dean, 63-65, head dept hist, 68-77, Prof Hist, Mt Marty Col, 73-98, Professor Emeritus, 98-; mem, Am Benedictine Acad, 67-98; mem, Fulbright Scholar Selection Comt, 77, 79. **HONORS AND AWARDS** Teaching Excellence and Campus Leadership Award, Sears-Roebuck Found, 91. **MEMBERSHIPS** Am Acad Polit & Soc Sci; AHA; Am Polit Sci Asn. **RESEARCH** Fate of religious orders in France since the revolution; modern church-state controversies; monastic history and biography of Benedictines. **SELECTED PUBLICATIONS** Auth, French Benedictines under stress, fall 66 & Political legacy to the religions in France: Laic laws of the Third Republic, 12/69, Am Benedictine Rev; Post-Revolution Restoration of French Monasticism, SDak Soc Sci Asn J, fall 77; Founded on Courage, Inspired with Vision: Mt Marty Col, In: From Idea to Institution, 89; First Catholic Bishop of Dakota: Martin Marty, In: South Dakota Leaders, 89; Benedictine Men and Women of Courage, 96. **CONTACT ADDRESS** Mount Marty Col, 1105 W 8th St, Yankton, SD, 57078-3724. **EMAIL** akessler@rs6.mtmc.edu

KESSLER, S. ANN
DISCIPLINE CHURCH HISTORY, PASTORAL MINISTRY **EDUCATION** Mt Marty Col, BA, 53;Creighton Univ, Omaha, MA, 57; Univ Notre Dame, PhD, 63. **CAREER** Prof emer, Mt Marty Col; part-time prof, Hist, Geog & Polit Sci; part-time, plan giving coordr, Develop Dept & prof. **MEMBERSHIPS** Benedictine Sisters of Sacred Heart Monastery; Phi Alpha Theta; SDak Hist Soc; Yankton Hist Soc; Hist Women Relig Organ & Amer Benedictine Acad. **SELECTED PUBLICATIONS** Auth, Benedictine Men and Women of Courage: Roots and History. **CONTACT ADDRESS** Dept of Religious Studies, Mount Marty Col, 1105 W 8th St, Yankton, SD, 57078-3724. **EMAIL** akessler@rs6.mtmc.edu

KETCHEN, JIM
DISCIPLINE LAW **EDUCATION** Univ Windsor, BA, MA, LLB. **CAREER** Lectr. **MEMBERSHIPS** Ontario Asn Family Mediation. **RESEARCH** Politics; law. **CONTACT ADDRESS** Law and Justice Dept, Laurentian Univ, 935 Ramsey Lake Rd, Sudbury, ON, P3E 2C6.

KETNER, KENNETH LAINE
PERSONAL Born 03/24/1939, Mountain Home, OK, m, 1963, 1 child **DISCIPLINE** PHILOSOPHY, FOLKLORISTICS **EDUCATION** OK State Univ, BA, 61, MA, 67; Univ CA, Los Angeles, MA, 68; Univ CA, Santa Barbara, PhD(philos), 72. **CAREER** Instr philos, OK State Univ, 64-67; res asst folklore, Univ CA, Los Angeles, 67-68; teaching asst philos, Univ CA, Santa Barbara, 69-70; asst prof, 71-75, assoc prof, 75-77, Prof, 77-81, Peirce Prof Philos, TX Tech Univ, 81-, Dir Iinst Studies In Pragmaticism, 72-. **HONORS AND AWARDS** Research Merit Award, TX Tech Univ, 80. **MEMBERSHIPS** Am Philos Asn; Charles S Pierce Soc (pres, 78). **RESEARCH** Am philos, philosophical anthropology; folkloristic method and theory. **SELECTED PUBLICATIONS** Auth, The role of Hypotheses in Folkloristics, J Am Folklore, 86: 114-130; An Emendation of R G Collingwood's doctrine of asolute presuppositions, Grad Studies TX Tech Univ, 7/73; A Comprehensive Bibliography of the Published Works of Charles S Peirce, KTO Microform, 77; Charles S Peirce: Contributions to the Nation, TX Tech Univ, 78; Proceedings, Peirce Bicentennial Int Congress, TX Tech Univ, 81. **CONTACT ADDRESS** Institute for Studies in Pragmaticism, Texas Tech Univ, Room 304A Library, Lubbock, TX, 79409-0002. **EMAIL** B90Ky@ttacs.ttu.edu

KEVELSON, ROBERTA
PERSONAL Born 11/04/1931, Brooklyn, NY, d, 2 children **DISCIPLINE** SEMIOTICS AND PHILOSOPHY **EDUCATION** Brown Univ, PhD, 78; Yale Univ, post doctoral, 79. **CAREER** Asst prof, Pa State Univ, 81; full prof, Pa State Univ, 86; distinguished prof, philos, Pa State Univ, 87; exec dir, Ctr Semiotic Res, 84-98. **HONORS AND AWARDS** Amoco award, outstanding teaching; distinguished prof of philos. **MEMBERSHIPS** APA; Intl Asn Semiotics of Law; IUR; Amintaphic Semiotic Soc of Amer. **RESEARCH** Works of Charles S. Peirce; Philosophy of law; Aesthetics; Semiotics; General theory. **SELECTED PUBLICATIONS** Auth, Peirce's Pragmatism, NY, 98; ed, Hi-Fives: A Trip to Semiotics, NY, 98; auth, Peirce, Science, Signs, NY, 96; auth, Peirce's Esthetics of Freedom, NY, 93; series ed-in-chief, Critic of Institutions, NY; series ed-in-chief, Semiotics & the Human Sciences, NY; series co-ed; Semaphores & Signs, St. Martin's Press, NY. **CONTACT ADDRESS** 104 Woodbine Ct., Williamsburg, VA, 23185. **EMAIL** bobbieke@earthlink.net

KEVERN, JOHN
DISCIPLINE CHURCH HISTORY **EDUCATION** Univ Paris-Sorbonne, Dipl Sup, 74; Univ Ill, BA, 75; Gen Theol Sem, MDiv, 80; Univ Chicago Divinity Sch, PhD, 97. **CAREER** Asst prof, Cooke Ch of Hist Theol, Bexley Hall Sem, 92-; dean, Bexley Hall Sem, 96. **SELECTED PUBLICATIONS** Auth, The Future of Anglican Theology, Anglican Theol Rev 75th Anniversary Ed, 94; Form in Tragedy: A Study in the Methodology of Hans Urs von Balthasar, In Communio, 94; The Fullness of Catholic Identity, In The Anglican Cath, 96; The Trinity and the Search for Justice, Anglican Theol Rev, 97. **CONTACT ADDRESS** Hist, Theol, Soc Dept, Trinity Lutheran Sem, 2199 E Main St, Columbus, OH, 43209-2334. **EMAIL** jkevern@trinity.capital.edu

KEYT, DAVID
PERSONAL Born 02/22/1930, Indianapolis, IN, m, 1975, 2 children **DISCIPLINE** PHILOSOPHY **EDUCATION** Kenyon Col, AB, 51; Cornell Univ, MA, 53, PhD, 55. **CAREER** Instr to PROF, Philos Chr, 71-78, actg philos chr, 67-68, 70, 86, 94, UNIV WASH, 57- ; vis asst prof, UCLA, 62-63; vis assoc prof, Cornell Univ, 68-69; vis prof, Univ Hong Kong, 87; Princeton Univ, 88-89; Univ Calif-Irvine, 90. **MEMBERSHIPS** Soc Ancient Greek Philos; Am Philos Asn **RESEARCH** Plato and Aristotle **SELECTED PUBLICATIONS** Co-ed, A Companion to Aristotles Politics, Oxford, 91; Analyzing Plato's Arguments: Plato and Platonism, Methods of Interpreting Plato and His Dialogues, Oxford, 92; auth, Supplementary Essay, Aristotle's Politics, Books III and IV, Oxford, 95; Aristotle and the Ancient Roots of Anarchism, Topoi, 96; Aristotles Politics Books V and VI, Oxford Univ Press, 98. **CONTACT ADDRESS** 12032 36th Ave. NE, Seattle, WA, 98125. **EMAIL** keyt@u.washington.edu

KHAN, ABRAHIM H.
PERSONAL Born 04/13/1943, Guyana, m, 1969, 3 children **DISCIPLINE** RELIGION **EDUCATION** Howard Univ, BS, 65; Yale Univ, BD, 68; McGill Univ, MA, 71, PhD, 73; **CAREER** Lectr, Mcgill Univ, 73-75; res assoc, McGill, 74-75; lectr, Concordia Univ & Champlain Col, 74-75; asst prof, Univ Manitoba, 75-76; asst prof Univ Toronto, 76-79; asst prof, McGill, 79-81; relig stud, Univ Toronto, 81-82; lectr, Trent Univ, 82-83; asst prof, Trent Univ, 83-84; lectr, Univ Toronto, 83-84; res assoc, Trinity Col, assoc prof, McMaster Univ, 84-85; lectr, hon fel, Univ Toronto, 85-86; lectr, Trinity Col & Univ Toronto, 86-; assoc prof, Concordia Univ, 91-92; lectr, Trinity Coll, Scarborough Coll, 92-; lectr Knox Coll, 95-; sr fel, Harvard univ, 96-97; lectr, Univ Toronto, fel Trinity Coll, 98-. **HONORS AND AWARDS** Intl Conference Travel Grant, Univ Toronto, 90-91; SSHRCC Res Grant, 85-91, Sr Fel, Harvard, 97. **MEMBERSHIPS** AAR; CPA; CSSR; CTS; SKS; AASSC; NAASR **RESEARCH** Kierkegaard studies; cross-cultural philosophy of religion; Islam; Hinduism; Caribbean studies. **SELECTED PUBLICATIONS** Salighed as Happiness, Wilfrid Laurier, 85; "Kierkegaard and the Glory of our Common Humanity," Joyful Wisdom v 3, Thought House, 94; "Melancholy: An Elusive Dimension of Depression," Jrnl Med Hum, 94; "The Center Out There for Early Pre-Islamic Pilgrims: Is the Kab'ah the Original Sacra of Meca," Year Book of Christian Archology Supplement, 95; "Challenge of Information Technol for Literary Studies," Jrnl of Relig & Technol Infor, 96; "Kierkegaard as Firechief in Denmark," Relig Stud, 96; "Identity, Personhood and Religion in Caribbean Context," Harvard Working Papers on Latin Am, 97. **CONTACT ADDRESS** Trinity College, Univ of Toronto, Toronto, ON, M5S 1H8. **EMAIL** khanah@chass.utoronto.ca

KHUSHF, GEORGE
PERSONAL Born 07/13/1961, New York, NY, m, 1986, 3 children **DISCIPLINE** BIOETHICS **EDUCATION** Rice Univ, PhD, 93, MA. 90; Texas A&M Univ, BS, 83. **CAREER** Humanities Dir, 95-, Center for Bioethics; Asst Prof, Dept of Philos, 95-, Univ of South Carolina; Mng Ed, Journal of Med and Philos, 93-95. **MEMBERSHIPS** ASBH, APA. **RESEARCH** Concepts of Health, administrative and organizational ethics, medical epistemology. **SELECTED PUBLICATIONS** Review, Hegel and the Spirit: Philosophy as Pneumatology, by A Olson, in: The Owl of Minerva, 94; auth, Ethics, Politics and Health Care Reform, in: J of Medicine and Philosophy, 94; Grammacentrism and the Transformation of Rhetoric, in: Philosophy and Rhetoric, 95; Nursing Ethics at the Juncture of Two Kinds of Care, in: South Carolina Nurse, 97; Embryo Research: On the Ethical Geography of the Debate, Journal of Medicine and Philosophy, 97; coauth, Understanding, Assessing and Managing Conflicts of Interest, Surgical Ethics, Oxford Univ Press, 98. **CONTACT ADDRESS** 1719 Oriole, Columbia, SC, 29204. **EMAIL** khushf@iopa.sc.edu

KIECKHEFER, RICHARD
PERSONAL Born 06/01/1946, Minneapolis, MN, m, 1986, 2 children **DISCIPLINE** PHILOSOPHY, HISTORY **EDUCATION** Saint Louis Univ, BA, 68; Univ Tex Austin, MA Philos, 70; PhD Hist, 72. **CAREER** Instr, Univ Tex Austin, 73-74; lectr, 74; asst prof, Philips Univ, 75; asst prof, 75-79; assoc prof, 79-84, Prof, Northwest Univ, 84-. **HONORS AND AWARDS** Tchg citation from Council for Advancement and Support of Education, 82, 83; Nat Endowment for the Humanities Fel, 87-

88; Guggenheim Found Fel, 92-93; Fel of Medieval Acad Of Am, 98. **MEMBERSHIPS** Medieval Acad Of Am; Am Soc of Church Hist; An Acad of Rel; Societas Magica. **RESEARCH** Late medieval religious culture-including mystical theology, magic and witchcraft, and church architecture to parish religion. **SELECTED PUBLICATIONS** Auth, The holy and the unholy: sainthood, witchcraft, and magic in late medieval Europe, J of Medieval And Renaissance Studies, 94; The specific rationality of medieval magi, Am Hist Rev, 94; Forbidden Rites: A Necromancer's manual of the fifteenth Century, 98; The office of inquisition and medieval heresy: the transition from personal to institutional jurisdiction, J of Ecclesiastical Hist, 95; Avenging the blood of children: anxiety over child victims and the origins of the European witch trials, the Devil, Heresy and Witchcraft in the Middle Ages: Essays in Honor of Jeffrey B Russel, 98; The Devils' contemplative: the Liber iuratus, the Liber visionum, and Christian appropriation of Jewish occultism, Conjuring Spirits: Texts and Traditions of Medieval Ritual magic, 98. **CONTACT ADDRESS** Dept of Religion, Northwestern Univ, 1940 Sheridan Rd, Evanston, IL, 60208-4050.

KIELKOPF, CHARLES F.
PERSONAL Born 04/16/1935, St. Paul, MN, m, 1957, 5 children **DISCIPLINE** PHILOSOPHY **EDUCATION** Univ Minn, BA, 58, MA, 60, PhD(philos), 62. **CAREER** Instr philos, Univ Minn, 62-63; asst prof, 63-77, Prof Philos, Ohio State Univ, 77-. **MEMBERSHIPS** Am Philos Asn. **RESEARCH** Philosophy of logic; modal logic; metaphysics, Kant, Heidegger. **SELECTED PUBLICATIONS** Auth, Strict Finitism, Mouton, The Hague, 69; Formal Sentential Entailment, Washinton D.C., 77; A Kantian Condemnation of Atheistic Despair, Peter Lang, Bern, 97. **CONTACT ADDRESS** Dept of Philos, Ohio State Univ, 230 N Oval Mall, Columbus, OH, 43210-1335. **EMAIL** kielkopf.1@osu.edu

KIERSKY, JAMES H.
PERSONAL Born 04/22/1946, Memphis, TN, m, 1988, 2 children **DISCIPLINE** PHILOSOPHY **EDUCATION** Washington & Lee Univ, BA, 68; Emory Univ, MA, 75, PhD, 83. **CAREER** Instr, Atlanta Jr Col, 75-78; instr, Spelman Col, 77-78; instr, lectr, Georgia Inst of Technol, 78-79; vis adj fac Atlanta Metropolitan Col, 95, Kennesay State Col, 95, DeKalb Col, 97; adj prof, Emory Univ, 83, 95-98; asst prof, Georgia State Univ, 78- . **HONORS AND AWARDS** DAAD, 76; Outstanding Teaching Award, 78. **MEMBERSHIPS** APA; Georgia Philos Soc. **RESEARCH** Ethics; free will and determinism; social/political philosophy; logic and critical thinking; multiculturalism. **SELECTED PUBLICATIONS** Auth, Bhopal: A Case Study & Ethical Complexities Involving Multinational Corporations, in, Snoeyenbos, ed, Business Ethics, Prometheus, 93; coauth, Thinking Critically: Techniques for Logical Reasoning, West, 95; auth, Instructors Manual with Test Bank and Solutions to Accompany Thinking Critically, West, 97; auth, A Multicultural Introduction to Philosophy, West, forthcoming. **CONTACT ADDRESS** Dept of Philosophy, Emory Univ, 214 Bowden Hall, Atlanta, GA, 30322. **EMAIL** phljhk@panther.gsu.edu

KIERSTEAD, MELANIE STARKS
PERSONAL Born 03/20/1960, Potsdam, NY, m, 1984, 2 children **DISCIPLINE** RELIGION **EDUCATION** Houghton Col, BA, 82; Bethany Bible Col, Ba, 83; Wesley Biblical Sem, M. Div, 86; Reformed Theolog Sem, Th.M, 87; Drew Univ, M. Phil, 93, PhD, 96 **CAREER** Tchr, Capital City Christian Acad, 87-88; prof, Phillips Junior Col, 88-89; campus pastor 96-97, prof, 89-90, 92-97, Bartlesville Wesleyan Col; asst prof, IN Wesleyan Univ, 97-. **HONORS AND AWARDS** Extraordinary People, 97, Houghton Col. **MEMBERSHIPS** Soc Biblical Lit; Am Acad Rel; Wesleyan Theolog Soc. **RESEARCH** 2nd Century Montanism; Luke-Acts; Pastorals. **SELECTED PUBLICATIONS** Auth, art, God of Comfort, 91; auth, art, The Word Inspires Confession, 95; auth, Calling God's people back to Hope, 95; auth, art, The Letter, 96; auth, art, Remembering the One True God's Faithful Love, 97. **CONTACT ADDRESS** 1723 Beechwood Blvd, Marion, IN, 46952. **EMAIL** mkierstead@indwes.edu

KILCOYNE, JOHN R.
DISCIPLINE LAW **EDUCATION** Univ Victoria, LLB, 78, LLM, 84. **CAREER** Asst prof, 84-90; assoc prof, 90-. **RESEARCH** Employment law; legislation and policy; computer technology. **SELECTED PUBLICATIONS** Auth, pubs on labour relations and collective bargaining. **CONTACT ADDRESS** Fac of Law, Univ Victoria, PO Box 2400, Victoria, BC, V8W 3H7. **EMAIL** jrk@uvic.ca

KIM, AI RA
PERSONAL Born 09/01/1938, Korea, s, 2 children **DISCIPLINE** RELIGION **EDUCATION** Drew Univ, PhD, 91. **CAREER** United Meth Church, ordained clergy; United Theological Sem, asst prof, 98-. **MEMBERSHIPS** AAR, RRA **RESEARCH** Women's issues in religion and culture. **SELECTED PUBLICATIONS** Auth, Women Struggling for a New Life: The Role of Religion in the Cultural Passage from Korea to America, SUNY Press, 96; Christianity and the Korean Immigrant Women in the US, in: Korean American Women Living in Two Cultures, ed Young In Song and Aileen Moon, Los Angeles: Baylor Univ Press, 97; br, Bridge Makers and Cross Bearers, (by Juug Ha Kim), in Academia Koreana, Los Angeles: Baylor Univ Press, 98. **CONTACT ADDRESS** Dept of Theology, United Theological Sem, 1624 Burbank Dr, Dayton, OH, 45406.

KIM, CHAN-HIE
PERSONAL Born 06/07/1935, Hoeryung, Korea, m, 1962, 1 child **DISCIPLINE** BIBLICAL STUDIES; NEW TESTAMENT **EDUCATION** Yonsei Univ, BA, 58; Vanderbilt, BD, 64, PhD, 70. **CAREER** Asst prof, Yonsei Univ, 72-73; prof of new testament & christian ministries, Claremont of Theol, 77-. **MEMBERSHIPS** Soc Bibl Lit; Cal-Pac Annual Conf United Meth Church **RESEARCH** New Testament; Ancient Greek epistolography **SELECTED PUBLICATIONS** Auth, Form and Function of the Greek Letter of Recommendation **CONTACT ADDRESS** 1325 N. College Ave., Claremont, CA, 91711. **EMAIL** chkim@cst.edu

KIM, WONIL
PERSONAL Born 03/15/1949, Seoul, Korea, m, 1977 **DISCIPLINE** RELIGION **EDUCATION** Claremont Grad Sch, PhD. **CAREER** Asst prof, Old Testament Studies, Sch Relig, La Sierra Univ, 94-. **MEMBERSHIPS** AAR; SBL. **RESEARCH** Theology; literary theory; ideology criticism. **CONTACT ADDRESS** Dept of Religion, La Sierra Univ, 4700 Pierce St, Riverside, CA, 92515-8247. **EMAIL** wkim@lasierra.edu

KIM, YOUNGLAE
PERSONAL Born 07/25/1961, Korea, m, 1986, 1 child **DISCIPLINE** THEOLOGY; CHRISTIAN EDUCATION **EDUCATION** Yonsei Univ, BA, 95; Drew Univ, MDiv, 90; Yale Univ, STM, 92; Columbia Univ, PhD, 96. **CAREER** Adj Prof, Drew Univ Theol School, 97- . **MEMBERSHIPS** Relig Educ Asn. **RESEARCH** Higher education; theological education; holistic education. **SELECTED PUBLICATIONS** Auth, Broken Knowledge: The Sway of the Scientific and Scholarly Ideal at Union Theological Seminary in New York, 1887-1926, Univ Press Am, 97. **CONTACT ADDRESS** 46 Minton Ave., Chatham, NJ, 07928. **EMAIL** Ylaekim@aol.com

KIMBALL, ROBERT
DISCIPLINE PHILOSOPHY **EDUCATION** Yale Univ, PhD. **CAREER** Dept Philos, Univ Louisville **RESEARCH** Intersection of epistemology. **SELECTED PUBLICATIONS** Auth, articles on the connection between thought and lang, on Wittgenstein, and on Whitehead. **CONTACT ADDRESS** Dept of Philos, Univ Louisville, 2301 S 3rd St, Louisville, KY, 40292. **EMAIL** rhkimb01@ulkyvm.louisville.edu

KIMBLE, MELVIN
DISCIPLINE PASTORAL CARE **EDUCATION** Wittenberg Univ, BA, 47; Hamma Sch Theol, MDiv, 50; S Baptist Theol Sem, ThM, 60; Univ Vienna, 60-61; US Intl Univ, PhD, 74. **CAREER** Guest prof, summer grad prog, 68, 74; vis prof, Leonard Davis Sch, Univ S Calif, 91-92; assoc prof, 65; prof, 67-; dir of intership, 65-74. **HONORS AND AWARDS** Lutheran World Federation scholar; res award, Amer Col of Health Care Administrators, 86; Edu Found of Am award, 82; post-doctoral fel, Gerontology, Andrus Gerontology Ctr, 81-82., Pastor, Grace Lutheran Church, 50-55; Calvary Lutheran Church, 55-58; head chaplain, Miss State Hospital, 59-60; pastor, Amer Protestant Church, Bonn, 61-65. **MEMBERSHIPS** Mem, Amer Soc on Aging; Assn for Hum Psychol; Gerontol Soc Am; Soc for Pastoral Theol; Viktor E. Franklin Inst of Logotherapy. **SELECTED PUBLICATIONS** Auth, Education for Ministry with the Aging, Ministry with the Aging: Designs, Challenges, Foundations, , 81; Aging and Ministry, Primary Pastoral Care, 90; Age and the Search for Meaning, Spiritual Maturity in the Later Years, 90; sr ed, Handbook on Aging, Spirituality and Religion, 95. **CONTACT ADDRESS** Dept of Pastoral Care, Luther Sem, 2481 Como Ave, St. Paul, MN, 55108. **EMAIL** mkilble@luthersem.edu

KINBALL, GAYLE
PERSONAL Born 06/12/1943, Los Angeles, CA, 1 child **DISCIPLINE** RELIGIOUS STUDIES **EDUCATION** UCSB, PhD, 76. **CAREER** Prof, CA State Univ, Chico, 72-. **RESEARCH** Gender, family. **SELECTED PUBLICATIONS** Auth, The Teen Trip; 50/50 Parenting; How to Survive Your Parents' Divorce: Kids' Advice to Kids; Everything You Need to Know to Succeed After College; 21st Century Families. **CONTACT ADDRESS** Dept of Ethinic and Women's Studies, California State Univ, Chico, Chico, CA, 95929. **EMAIL** gkimball@csuchico.edu

KIND, AMY
DISCIPLINE PHILOSOPHY **EDUCATION** Amherst Col, BA, 90; UCLA, PhD, 97. **CAREER** Asst prof, philos, 97- , Claremont McKenna Col. **HONORS AND AWARDS** Mellon Fel, 90-92; Mellon dissertation fel, 95; Phi Beta Kappa. **MEMBERSHIPS** APA. **RESEARCH** Philosophy of mind; epistemology; metaphysics. **CONTACT ADDRESS** Dept of Philosophy, Claremont McKenna Col, 850 Columbia Ave, Claremont, CA, 91711. **EMAIL** akind@benson.mckenna.edu

KING, PATRICIA ANN
PERSONAL Born 06/12/1942, Norfolk, VA, m, 1981 **DISCIPLINE** ETHICS, LAW **EDUCATION** Wheaton Coll, BA 1963; Harvard Law School, JD 1969. **CAREER** Dept of State, budget analyst 1964-66; Equal Employment Opportunity Commn, special asst to chmn 1969-71; Dept of Health Educ & Welfare, dept dir office of civil rights 1971-73; Civil Div Dept of Justice, dep asst atty general 1980-81; Georgetown Univ, assoc prof of law 1974-88; Georgetown Univ, Law Center, prof of law, 1988-. **HONORS AND AWARDS** Honorary LLD, Wheaton College 1992; Distinguished Serv Award HEW 1973; Secretary's Special Citation HEW 1973; John Hay Whitney Fellowship John Hay Whitney Found 1968. **MEMBERSHIPS** Natl Commn for Protection of Human Subjects 1974-78; sr rsch scholar Kennedy Inst of Ethics 1977-; fellow Hastings Inst NY 1977-; Recombinant DNA Adv Com 1979-82; pres Commn for the Study of Ethical Problems in Med & Rsch 1980-81; chmn Redevelopment Land Agency DC 1976-79; US Circuit Judge Nominating Com 1977-79; board, Russell Sage Foundation 1981-91; Amer Law Institute 1988-; National Academy of Sciences, Institute of Medicine; bd, Women's Legal Defense Fund, 1987-; bd of trustees, Wheaton Coll, 1989-. **SELECTED PUBLICATIONS** "The Juridicial Status of the Fetus" MI Law Review 1647, 1979; co-author "Law Science and Medicine" 1984. **CONTACT ADDRESS** Law Sch, Georgetown Univ, 600 New Jersey Ave NW, Washington, DC, 20001.

KING, SALLIE B.
PERSONAL Born 03/22/1952, Washington, DC, m, 1977, 2 children **DISCIPLINE** PHILOSOPHY AND RELIGION **EDUCATION** Smith Col, BA, 73; Univ of BC, MA, 75; Temple Univ, PhD, 81. **CAREER** Lectr, State Univ of NY at Buffalo, 79-80; asst prof, Colby Col, 81-82; asst prof, Bates Col, 82-83; from asst prof to assoc prof, Southern Ill Univ at Carbondale, 83-89; dir of undergrad studies, Southern Ill Univ at Carbondale, 85-89; from assoc prof to prof, James Madison Univ, 92-; dept head, 92-97. **HONORS AND AWARDS** Japan Found Professional Fel, 83-84; Nat Endowment for the Hums, 85; Outstanding Teacher in the Col of Liberal Arts, Southern Ill Univ, 89; Edna T. Schaeffer Humanist Award, James Madison Univ, 97. **MEMBERSHIPS** Am Acad of Relig; Am Philos Asn; Int Asn of Buddhist Studies; Asn for Asian Studies; Phi Beta Kappa; Soc for Buddhist-Christian Studies; Soc for Comp and Asian Philos. **SELECTED PUBLICATIONS** Auth, Two Epistemological Models for the Interpretation of Mysticism, in J of the Am Acad of Relig 56 (2), 88; Toward a Buddhist Model of Inter-Religious Dialogue, in Buddhist-Christian Studies 10, 90; Buddha Nature, 91; Religion as Practice, in Buddhist-Christian Studies 14, 94; On Pleasure, Choice and Authority, in Buddhist-Christian Studies 14, 94; It's a Long Way to a Global Ethic: A Response to Leonard Swidler, in Buddhist-Christian Studies 15, 95; A Buddhist Perspective on a Global Ethic and Human Rights, in J of Dharma 20 (2), 95; Charles Hartshorne: Pioneer Buddhist-Christian Dialogian, in Creative Transformation 6 (2), 97; Transformative Nonviolence: The Social Ethics of George Fox and Thich Nhat Hanh, in Buddhist-Christian Studies 18, 98; Journey in Search of the Way: The Spiritual Autobiography of Satomi Myodo, 98; coauth, Process Metaphysics and Minimalism: Implications for Public Policy, in Environmental Ethics 13, 91; A Buddhist-Christian Contribution to the Earth Charter, in Buddhist-Christian Studies 17, 97; coed, Engaged Buddhism: Buddhist Liberation Movements in Asia, 96; The Sound of Liberating Truth: Buddhist-Christian Dialogues in Honor of Frederic J. Streng, 98; rev, Kenosis and Action: A Review Article, in Buddhist-Christian Studies 12, 92. **CONTACT ADDRESS** Dept of Philosophy and Religion, James Madison Univ, Harrisonburg, VA, 22807.

KING, WILLIAM J.
PERSONAL Born 07/21/1921, Selma, AL, m, 1952 **DISCIPLINE** THEOLOGY **EDUCATION** Talladega Coll, AB 1943; Howard Univ School of Religion, MDiv 1946; Eden Theological Seminary, exchange student from Howard Univ 1946; Chapman College, Family Therapy Institute of Marin. **CAREER** Shiloh Baptist Church, pastor; private practice, licensed counselor; Third Baptist Church, pastor 1946-51; Antioch Progressive Church, interim pastor; Trinity Missionary Baptist Church, interim pastor; Solano Community College, faculty, currently. **MEMBERSHIPS** Progressive National Baptist Convention; Amer Assn of Marriage & Family Counselors; CA State Assn of Marriage Counselors; mem Natl Alliance for Family Life Inc; Alpha Phi Alpha Fraterity; NAACP.

KINGHORN, KENNETH CAIN
PERSONAL Born 06/23/1930, Albany, OK, m, 1955, 4 children **DISCIPLINE** CHURCH HISTORY **EDUCATION** Ball State Univ, BS, 52; Asbury Theol Sem, BD, 62; Emory Univ, PhD, 65. **CAREER** From prof church hist to Dean Sch Theol, Asbury Theol Sem, 65-. **MEMBERSHIPS** Am Soc Church Hist. **RESEARCH** Wesley studies; Protestant Reformation; spiritual formation. **SELECTED PUBLICATIONS** Auth, Dynamic Discipleship, Fleming H Revell, 73; Fresh Wind of the Spirit, 75, Gifts of the Spirit, 76 & Christ Can Make You Fully Human, 79, Abingdon; Discovering Your Spiritual Gifts, 81 & A Celebration of Ministry, 82, Francis Asbury Publ Co; The Gospel of Grace, Abingdon, 92. **CONTACT ADDRESS** Dept of Church Hist, Asbury Theol Sem, 204 N Lexington Ave, Wilmore, KY, 40390-1199. **EMAIL** ken_kinghorn@ats.wilmore.ky.us

KINGSBURY, JOHN MERRIAM
PERSONAL Born 07/04/1928, Boston, MA, m **DISCIPLINE** BIOLOGY **EDUCATION** Harvard Univ, AM, 52, PhD, 54. **CAREER** Asst prof, 54-59, assoc prof, 60-69, prof, 70-82, prof Emeritus, Cornell Univ, 83-. **HONORS AND AWARDS** Sc D Dickinson Col, 85; Fulbright Sr Scholar, 80; Profile of Service Award, Univ NH, 98. **MEMBERSHIPS** New England Hist Geneological Soc; Nat Geneological Soc; MA Chapter Soc of the Cincinnati; Bullard Memorial Farm Asn; Fairbanks Family of Am. **RESEARCH** The Farmers of Bogastow, MA Bay Colony, 1629-1750. **SELECTED PUBLICATIONS** Auth, Knowledge of Poisonous Plants in the United States--History and Conclusions, Econ Bot, 15, 61; Introduction, in Celia Thaxter, An Island Garden, Heritage Books, Bowie MD, rev in subsequent eds, 78; Oil and Water-The New Hampshire Story, Shoals Marine Laboratory, Ithaca, NY, 75; Botanical Vignettes from the University's Past, I, Charles Frederick Millspaugh '75, Cornell Plan Quart 37, 81; Christopher Columbus as a Botanist, Cornell Plan Quart 45, 92, also (modified) in: Arnoldia, 52 (2), 92; Interconnecting Bloodlines and Genetic Inbreeding in a Colonial Puritan Community: Eastern Massachusetts, 1630-1885, Nat Geneal Soc Quart, 84 (2), 96; Benjamin Bullard's First Wife, Martha ¤Fairbanksl Pidge, The ¤Fairbanksl Homestead Courier, winter 96; Summary Geneologies, in D Stevens, Bullard Family Papers, Bullbrier Press, Jersey Shore, PA, 96. **CONTACT ADDRESS** Cornell Univ, 135A Guterman, Ithaca, NY, 14853. **EMAIL** JMK11@Cornell.edu

KINNEY, E.D.
PERSONAL Born 01/17/1947, Boston, MA, m, 1983, 1 child **DISCIPLINE** LAW **EDUCATION** Duke Univ, AB, 69; Univ Chicago, MA, 70; Univ N Carolina, MPH, 79; Duke Univ, JD, 73. **CAREER** Prof of Law, 85- , dir, Ctr for Law and Health, 87- , Indiana Univ Sch of Law, Indianapolis. **MEMBERSHIPS** ABA; NC State Bar Asn; Am Asn of Law Schools; Nat Health Lawyers Asn; Am Soc of Law, Medicine and Ethics; Am Pub Health Asn; Indiana Pub Health Asn. **RESEARCH** Health policy; medical malpractice; quality assurance. **SELECTED PUBLICATIONS** Coauth, The Potential Role of Diabetes Guidelines in the Reduction of Medical Malpractice Claims Involving Diabetes, in Diabetes Care, 94; coauth, Bringing the Patient Back in : the Rhetoric of Victimization and Medical Malpractice, in Perspectives on Social Problems, 94; auth, Private Accreditation as a Substitute for Direct Government Regulation in Public Health Insurance Programs: When is it Appropriate?, in Law and Contemporary Problems, 94; coauth, Quality Improvement in Community-Based, Long-Term Care: Theory and Reality, in Am J of Law and Med, 94; auth, Protecting Consumers and Providers under Health Reform :An Overview of the Major Administrative Law Issues, in Health Matrix, 95; auth, Malpractice Reform in the 1990s: Past Disappointments, Future Success?, in J of Health Politics, Policy and Law, 95; coauth, Collaborative Quality Improvement in Community-Based, Long-Term Care: Translating Theory into Practice, in the Joint Commission J on Quality Improvement, 95; auth, Rule and Policy Making under Health Reform, in Admin Law Rev, 95; coauth, The Merits of State Action Antitrust Immunity to Promote Hospital Collaboration: A Good Idea for Indiana?, in Ind Law Rev, 95; auth, Resolving Consumer Grievances in a Managed Care Environment, in Health Matrix, 96; auth, Medicare Managed Care from the Beneficiary's Perspective, in Seton Hall Law Rev, 96; auth, Procedural Protections for Patients in Capitated Health Plans, in Am J of Law and Med, 96; coauth, History and Jurisprudence of the Patient-Physician Relation in Indiana, in Indiana Law Rev, 96; auth, Health Insurance Coverage in Indiana: is there a Problem, in IN-ROADS, 96; auth, Administrative Law Issues in Professional Regulation, in Regulation of the Healthcare Professions, Health Admin Pr, 97; coauth, Automating Assessment for Community-Based, Long-Term Care: Indiana's Experience, in Generations, 97; coauth, Serious Illness and Private Health Coverage: A Unique Problem Calling for Unique Solutions, in J of Law, Med & Ethics, 97; auth, Indiana's Medical Malpractice Reform Revisited: A Limited Constitutional Challenge, in Ind Law Rev, 98; auth, Consumer Grievance and Appeal Procedures in Managed Care Plans, in the Health Lawyer, 98. **CONTACT ADDRESS** 735 W New York St, Indianapolis, IN, 46202. **EMAIL** ekinney@iupui.edu

KIRCHHEVEL, GORDON D.
PERSONAL Born 07/06/1935, Mitchell, SD, s **DISCIPLINE** RELIGION **EDUCATION** Concordia Sem, St Louis, MO, BA, 57, BD, 60. **CAREER** Concordia Sen Col, Ft Wayne, IN, instr, 61-65. **MEMBERSHIPS** SBL **RESEARCH** Interpret of OT by NT authors. **SELECTED PUBLICATIONS** Auth, He That Cometh in Mark 1:7 and Mathew 24:30, Bull for Bib Research, 94; The Children of God and the Glory That John 1:14 Saw, Bull Bib Research, 96. **CONTACT ADDRESS** 531 W Deming Pl, Chicago, IL.

KIRGIS, FREDERIC LEE
PERSONAL Born 12/29/1934, Washington, DC, m, 1997, 2 children **DISCIPLINE** LAW **EDUCATION** Univ of Calif, Berkeley, JD, 60; Yale Univ, BA, 57. **CAREER** Asst prof to prof of law, Univ of Colo, 67-73; prof of law, UCLA, 73-78; PROF OF LAW, WASHINGTON AND LEE UNIV, 78-, dean, school of law, 83-88, law alumni asn prof, 90-. **HONORS AND AWARDS** Order of the Coif, 60; Deak Prize for int law scholar by a young scholar, 74. **MEMBERSHIPS** Amer Soc for Int Law, 94-; Amer Law Inst; Amer Bar Asn. **RESEARCH** International Law. **SELECTED PUBLICATIONS** Auth, International Organizations in Their Legal Setting, 2nd edition, West Pub Co., 93; auth, Prior Consultation in International Law: A Study of State Practice, Univ Press of Va, 83; auth, The Formative Years of the American Society of International Law, Am J. Int, 96; auth, A Mythical State's Attitude Toward the Role of the United Nations in Maintaining and Restoring Peace, Ga J. Int &Comp., 96; auth, The Security Council's First Fifty Years, Am J. Int, 95; auth, Claims Settlement and the United Nations Legal Structure, in The United Nations Compensation Commission 103, 95; chapters on specialized law-making processes, shipping, & aviation, United Nations Legal Order 109, 95; auth, The Degrees of Self-Determination in the United Nations Era, Am J. Int, 94. **CONTACT ADDRESS** School of Law, Washington and Lee Univ, Lexington, VA, 24450.

KIRK-DUGGAN, CHERYL ANN
PERSONAL Born 07/24/1951, Lake Charles, LA, m, 1983 **DISCIPLINE** THEOLOGY, MUSICOLOGY **EDUCATION** University of Southwestern Louisiana, BA 1973; University of Texas at Austin, MM 1977; Austin Presbyterian Theological Seminary, MDiv 1987; Baylor University, PhD, 1992. **CAREER** Univ of Texas at Austin, music of Black Amers coach accomp 1974-77; Austin Community College, music of Black Amers 1976-77; Prairie View A&M Univ, teacher 1977-78; The Actor's Inst, teacher 1982-83; Williams Inst CME Church, organist, choir dir 1979-83; Self-employed, professional singer, voice teacher, vocal coach 1980-85; Christian Methodist Church, ordained minister, deacons orders 1984, elders orders 1986; Baylor University, Institute of Oral History, graduate asst, 1987-89, Dept of Religion, teaching asst, 1989-90; Meredith College, assistant professor, 1993-96; CENTER FOR WOMEN & RELIGION, DIR, GRADUATE THEOLOGICAL UNION, ASST PROF, 1997-; EDITORIAL BD, CONTAGION: JOURNAL OF VIOLENCE, MIMESIS & CULTURE, 1994-; ASSN FOR BLACK AWARENESS, MEREDITH COLLEGE, ADVISOR, 1994-. **HONORS AND AWARDS** University of Southwestern Louisiana, Magna Cum Laude; University of Texas at Austin, University Fellowship, 1975-77; Fund for Theological Education, Fellowship for Doctoral Studies, 1987-88, 1988-89. **MEMBERSHIPS** Pi Kappa Lambda, 1976-; Omicron Delta Kappa, 1977-; associate pastor, Trinity CME Church, 1985-86; president, Racial Ethnic Faith Comm, Austin Seminary, 1986-87; Golden Key Honor Society, 1990; Colloquim On Violence & Religion; Society of Biblical Literature; American Academy of Religion; Center for Black Music Research; Society of Chritian Ethics; American Society for Aesthetics; Sigma Alpha Iota. **SELECTED PUBLICATIONS** Carnegie Hall debut, 1981; featured: "Life, Black Tress, Das Goldene Blatte, Bunte," 1981, 1982; recording: "Third Duke Ellington Sacred Concert," Virgil Thompson's Four Saints in Three Acts, EMI Records, 1981-82; author: Lily Teaching Fellow, 1995, 1996; Collidge Scholar with Assoc for Religion & Intellectual Life, 1996; "African-American Spirituals: Exorcising Evil Through Song," A Troubling in My Soul: Womanist Perspectives on Evil and Suffering, Orbis Press, 1991; "Gender, Violence and Transformation," Curing Violence: The Thought of Rene Girard, Polebridge Press, 1991; African-American Special Days: 15 Complete Worship Services, Abingdon Press, 1996; It's In the Blood: A Trildgy of Poetry Harvested from a Family Tree, River Vision, 1996; Exorcizing Evil: A Womanist Perspective on the Spirituals, Orbis, 1997. **CONTACT ADDRESS** Ctr for Women, Religion, 2400 Ridge Rd, Berkeley, CA, 94709-5298.

KIRKLAND GRANT, J.
DISCIPLINE LAW **EDUCATION** Univ MI, BBA, 65, JD (Cum Laude), 67. **CAREER** Vis scholar, Harvard Univ, Columbia Univ; acad dean, Touro Univ; dean, prof Law, Del Law Sch; prof Law, Univ SC; asst prof Law, Ga State Univ; asst prof, Univ Toledo; vis prof, Univ Ky; arbitrator, Am Arbit Asn; prof Law, Touro Col. **MEMBERSHIPS** Am Bar Asn; NY State Bar Asn; Am Law Inst; Scribes. **SELECTED PUBLICATIONS** Auth, New York Corporation Law Handbook, Gould Publ; Securities Arbitration, Quorum Bks, 94. **CONTACT ADDRESS** Touro Col, Brooklyn, NY, 11230. **EMAIL** KirkG@tourolaw.edu

KIRKPATRICK, FRANK GLOYD
PERSONAL Born 08/04/1942, Washington, DC, m, 1966, 2 children **DISCIPLINE** PHILOSOPHY OF RELIGION, HISTORICAL THEOLOGY, ETHICS **EDUCATION** Trinity Col, Conn, BA, 64; Columbia Univ, MA, 66; Brown Univ, PhD(relig studies), 70. **CAREER** Teaching asst relig, Brown Univ, 67-68; asst prof, 69-78, dir individualized degree prog, 73-75, assoc prof relig, Trinity Col, Conn, 78-; prof of relig, 86-. **HONORS AND AWARDS** Charles A. Dana Research Professor, 93-95. **MEMBERSHIPS** Am Acad Relig. **RESEARCH** John Macmurray; process thought; social ethics: economics. **SELECTED PUBLICATIONS** Auth, Process of agent: Models for self and God, Thought, spring 73; Subjective becoming: an unwarranted abstraction?, Process Studies, summer 73; coauth, Bellah's beliefless religion: The objectivity of God and moral value, Philos Relig, fall 73; (with R Nolan), Living Issues in Ethics, Wadsworth, 82; Community, Georgetown Univ Press, 86; Together Bound, Oxford Univ Press, 94. **CONTACT ADDRESS** Dept of Relig, Trinity Col, 300 Summit St, Hartford, CT, 06106-3186. **EMAIL** frank.kirkpatrick@mail.trincoll.edu

KIRKPATRICK, W. DAVID
PERSONAL m, 2 children **DISCIPLINE** THEOLOGY **EDUCATION** Baylor Univ, MA, 64; Southwestern Baptist Theol Sem, MDiv, 69, ThD, 74; addn stud, Univ Cambridge, 86. **CAREER** Grad tchg asst, Baylor Univ, 63-64; instr, Dallas Baptist Col, 65-69; Dallas Community Col, 70; assoc prof, Wayland Baptist Col, 71-75; prof, Southwestern Baptist Theol Sem, 80-. **HONORS AND AWARDS** Albert Venting Award, 68; Kenneth Moore Scholar Grad Stud, 69-74. **MEMBERSHIPS** Soc Biblical Lit; Amer Acad Rel, Southwestern Assoc Baptist Prof Rel; Nat Assn Baptist Prof Rel. **SELECTED PUBLICATIONS** Auth, Creation, Southwestern Jour Theol, 81; Theol Sects and Cults, Word and Way, 78. **CONTACT ADDRESS** Sch Theol, Southwestern Baptist Theol Sem, PO Box 22000, Fort Worth, TX, 76122-0418.

KIRSHBAUM, HAL
DISCIPLINE PHILOSOPHY **EDUCATION** Antioch Col, BA; Univ Calif Berkeley, MA, PhD. **CAREER** Prof. **RESEARCH** Philosophy of science; infant mental health; language and anthropology; ericksonian hypnosis; social philosophy; psychology of physical disability; family therapy. **SELECTED PUBLICATIONS** Auth, Disability and Humiliation, J Primary Prevention, 91; The Americans With Disabilities Act: An Opinion, Network, 91; Theories of Infant Development, 89. **CONTACT ADDRESS** Philosophy Dept, Union Inst, 440 E McMillan St, Cincinnati, OH, 45206-1925.

KIRTLAND, ROBERT
DISCIPLINE LAW **EDUCATION** St Peter's Col, BA; Univ Mich, MA, PhD. **CAREER** Adj prof. **SELECTED PUBLICATIONS** Auth, George Wythe, Lawyer, Revolutionary, Judge, 85. **CONTACT ADDRESS** Col Law, Univ of Toledo, Toledo, OH, 43606.

KIS, MIROSLAV M.
DISCIPLINE ETHICS **EDUCATION** SAS FRance, BA, 74; Andrews Univ, MDiv, 76; Mcgill Univ, PhD, 83. **CAREER** Asst Prof, 83-86, Assoc Prof, 86-90, Prof, Christian Ethics, 90-, Andrews Univ. **CONTACT ADDRESS** SDA Theol Sem, Andrews Univ, Berrien Springs, MI, 49103.

KISIEL, THEODORE JOSEPH
PERSONAL Born 10/30/1930, Brackenridge, PA, m, 1963, 2 children **DISCIPLINE** PHILOSOPHY **EDUCATION** Univ Pittsburgh, BS, 52; Duquesne Univ, MA, 61; PhD(philos), 62. **CAREER** Res metallurgist, Armour Res Found, 52-53; nuclear engr, Westinghouse Atomic Power Div, 53-58; asst prof philos, Canisius Col, 63-69; PROF PHILOS, NORTHERN ILL UNIV, 69-, Alexander von Humboldt Found sr fel philos, 70-71, 74, 81, 82; ed adv, Z fur Allgemeine Wissenschaftstheorie, 71-; vis prof philos, Northwestern Univ, 73-74; vis prof philos, Duquesne Univ, 75; Am Coun Learned Soc res fel philos, 77-78; Ger Acad Exchange Service sr fel philos, 83, 93; Fulbright res fel philos, 84-85, Germany; Fulbright prof, Bochum, Germany, 89; Presidential res prof, NIU, 98-02. **HONORS AND AWARDS** NEH transl grant, 81-83; NEH travel to collections grant, 84, 87; Inter Nationes transl award, 85. **MEMBERSHIPS** AAUP **RESEARCH** Phenomenology; philosophy of science; history of 19th & 20th century continental philosophy. **SELECTED PUBLICATIONS** Coauth, Phenomenology and the Natural Sciences, 70 & cotranslr, Werner Marx, Heidegger and the Tradition, 71, Northwestern Univ; auth, Scientific discovery: Logical, psychological, or hermeneutical?, In: Explorations in Phenomenology, Nijhoff, The Hague, 73; On the dimensions of a phenomenology of science in Husserl and the younger Dr Heidegger, J Brit Soc Phenomenol, 73; Aphasiology, phenomenology of perception, and the shades of structuralism, In: Language & Language Disturbances, Duquesne Univ, 74; New philosophies of science in the USA: A selective survey, Z fur Allgemeine Wissenschaftstheorie, 74; Heidegger and the new images of science, Res Phenomenol, 77; Habermas' purge of pure theory: Critical theory without ontology?, Human Studies, 4/78; translr, Martin Heidegger, History of the Concept of Time, Ind Univ, 85; auth, The Genesis of Heidegger's Being and Time, Univ Calif, 93; co-ed, Reading Heidegger from the Start, State Univ NY, 94; Why Students of Heidegger Will Have to Read Emil Lask, Man and World, 95; Heidegger's Gesamtausgabe: An International Scandal of Scholarship, Phil Today, 95; A Hermeneutics of the Natural Sciences? The Debate Updated, Mand and World, 97; Die formale Anzeige: Die methodische Geheimwaffe des fruehen Heidegger, In: Heidegger - neu gelesen, Koenigshausen & Neumann, Wuerzburg, 97 **CONTACT ADDRESS** Dept of Philos, No Illinois Univ, 1425 W Lincoln Hwy, De Kalb, IL, 60115-2825. **EMAIL** tkisiel@niu.edu

KISSLING, PAUL J.
PERSONAL Born 08/03/1957, Toledo, OH, m, 1979, 2 children **DISCIPLINE** BIBLICAL LANGUAGES **EDUCATION** Univ of Sheffield, PhD, 91. **CAREER** Great Lakes Christian Col MI, prof, 91-; Co-editor, Col Press, NIV Old Testament

Commentary. **MEMBERSHIPS** SBL, IBR **RESEARCH** Hebrew narrative research **SELECTED PUBLICATIONS** Auth, Reliable Characters in the Primary History, in: JSOTSup, 96. **CONTACT ADDRESS** Dept of Old Testament, Great Lakes Christian Col, 4808 Omar Dr, Lansing, MI, 48917. **EMAIL** pjk@voyager.net

KISTEMAKER, SIMON
DISCIPLINE NEW TESTAMENT **EDUCATION** Free Univ Amsterdam, PhD. **CAREER** John and Frances Gwin prof, dept ch, RTS/Jackson; prof-. **HONORS AND AWARDS** Gold Medallion, Evangel Bk of the Yr Award, New Testament Commentary., Past pres, Evangel Theol Soc. **SELECTED PUBLICATIONS** Auth, New Testament Commentary; The Parables of Jesus; The Gospels in Current Study. **CONTACT ADDRESS** Dept of New Testament, Reformed Theol Sem, 1015 Maitland Ctr Commons, Maitland, FL, 32751.

KITCHEL, MARY JEAN
PERSONAL New York, NY **DISCIPLINE** PHILOSOPHY, MEDIEVAL STUDIES **EDUCATION** Rice Univ, BA, 64; Pontif Inst Mediaeval Studies, MSL, 68; Univ Toronto, PhD, 74. **CAREER** Asst prof philos, Univ St Thomas, TX, 68-69; asst prof, Emmanuel Col, MA, 69-74; loan asst, Student Financial Aid, Houston Community Col Syst, 76-77; asst prof, 77-79, assoc dean extended educ, 80-82, Assoc Prof Philos, Univ St Thomas, TX, 79-88, Prof Phil, 88-, Dean Acad Serv, 90-93, Dept Ch Phil, 96-, Asst prof church hist, St Mary's Sem, TX, 68-69; res assoc philos & text ed, Pontif Inst Mediaeval Studies, Toronto, 73-75; Nat Endowment for Hum grant, 79. **HONORS AND AWARDS** Piper Professorship, 90; Sears-Roebuck Found Award, 90 **MEMBERSHIPS** Am Cath Philos Asn. **RESEARCH** Ed and analysis of texts of Walter Burley; philos psychol, philos of hum person; medl ethics. **SELECTED PUBLICATIONS** Auth, The De potentis animae of Walter Burley, 71, Walter Burley's Doctrine of the Soul: Another view, 77 Mediaeval Studies; Walter Burley and radical Aristotelanism, Proc World Cong on Aristotle (in press). **CONTACT ADDRESS** Dept of Philos, Univ of St Thomas, 3800 Montrose, Houston, TX, 77006-4696. **EMAIL** kitchel@stthom.edu

KITCHENER, RICHARD F.
DISCIPLINE PHILOSOPHY **EDUCATION** Univ Minn, PhD, 70. **CAREER** Prof. **RESEARCH** Philosophy of science. **SELECTED PUBLICATIONS** Ed, New Ideas in Psychology and author of Piaget's Theory of Knowledge, 86; The World View of Contemporary Physics: Does it Need a New Metaphysics?, 88; Psychology and Philosophy, 94. **CONTACT ADDRESS** Philosophy Dept, Colorado State Univ, Fort Collins, CO, 80523.

KITCHER, PATRICIA
DISCIPLINE PHILOSOPHY **EDUCATION** Princeton Univ, PhD, 74. **CAREER** Instr, Univ Vermont; CH, PHILOS, UNIV CALIF, SAN DIEGO. **RESEARCH** Philosophy of Kant and the philosophy of psychology. **SELECTED PUBLICATIONS** Auth, "Revisiting Kant's Epistemology," Nous, 95; "From Neurophilosophy to Neurocomputation:Searching for the Cognitive Forest," The Churchlands and their Critics. Blackwell's, 95. **CONTACT ADDRESS** Dept of Philos, Univ Calif, San Diego, 9500 Gilman Dr, La Jolla, CA, 92093.

KITCHER, PHILIP
PERSONAL Born 02/20/1947, London, England, m, 1971, 2 children **DISCIPLINE** PHILOSOPHY OF SCIENCE **EDUCATION** Cambridge, BA, 69; PhD, Princeton, 74. **CAREER** Asst prof, Vassar Coll, 73-74; asst prof, Univ Vt, 74-78; vis asst prof, Univ Mich, 79; assoc prof, Univ Vt, 70-83; prof, Univ Minn, 83-86; dir, Minn Center Philos Sci, 84-86; prof, Univ Calif San Diego, 86-93; presidential prof, 93-. **HONORS AND AWARDS** Henry Schuman Prize, 71; ACLS Study Fel, 81-82; Univ Vt Distinguished Scholar in Humanities and Soc Sci. **MEMBERSHIPS** US Comt, Int Union of Logic, Methodology and Philos of Sci; ICSU Working Group for Oxford Univ Press; NIH/DOE Working Group on the Ethical, Legal, and Soc Implications of the Human Genome Proj. **RESEARCH** Ethical Issues in Contemporary Biology; History and Philosophy of Biology; Growth of Scientific Knowledge; Scientific Explanation; Realism; Naturalistic Epistemology; Philosophy of Social Sciences; History and Philosophy of Mathematics. **SELECTED PUBLICATIONS** Auth, Abusing Science: The Case Against Creationism, 82; The Nature of Mathematical Knowledge, 83; Vaulting Ambition: Sociobiology and the Quest for Human Nature, 85; The Advancement of Science, 93; The Lives to Come: The Genetic Revolution and Human Possibilities, 96. **CONTACT ADDRESS** Univ Calif San Diego, 9500 Gilman Dr, La Jolla, CA, 92093-0119. **EMAIL** pkitcher@ucsd.edu

KITCHING, BENITA
PERSONAL Born 02/10/1944, Springfield, IL **DISCIPLINE** PHILOSOPHY **EDUCATION** Univ Ill, Chicago, PhD, 88. **CAREER** Vis lectr, Southern Ill Univ, Edwardsville, 81; vis lectr, Univ Ill, Springfield, 90. **HONORS AND AWARDS** Phi Beta Kappa; Richter Scholar; Magna Cum Laude. **MEMBERSHIPS** APA. **RESEARCH** Aesthetics; philosophical treatment of the spiritual. **CONTACT ADDRESS** 820 S English Ave, Springfield, IL, 62704.

KITTAY, EVA FEDER
PERSONAL Born 08/13/1946, Malmo, Sweden, m, 1967, 2 children **DISCIPLINE** PHILOSOPHY **EDUCATION** Sarah Lawrence Col, BA, 67; CUNY, PhD, 78. **CAREER** Adj lectr, John Jay College of Criminal Justice, CUNY, 85; adj lectr, Lehman Col, CUNY, 74, 75; vis asst prof, philos, Univ Md, College Park, 78-79; asst prof, 79-86, assoc prof, 86-93, prof, philos, 93-, SUNY at Stony Brook; vis prof, philos, Sarah Lawrence Col, 93. **HONORS AND AWARDS** SUNY summer fel, 82; res asst award, 81-82; subvention, Soc for Philos and Public Affairs, 84; Exxon Educ Found, 84-86; tchg commend, 86; AUUP travel grant, 87; NSF grant, 89; ACLS travel grant; Founders Fel AAUW, 89-90; CUNY Alumni Assoc Annual Achievement Award, 92. **MEMBERSHIPS** Soc for Women in Philos, NY chap & Eastern Div; APA; Philos of Sci Asn; Soc for Philos and Psychol; Soc for Philos and Public Affairs; Soc for Women in Philos; NY Acad of Sci; Soc for Philos for Social Responsibility. **RESEARCH** Feminist theory; philosophy and public policy; philosophy of language. **SELECTED PUBLICATIONS** Auth, Metaphor: Its Linguistic Structure and Its Cognitive Force, Oxford, 87; co-ed, Women and Moral Theory, Rowman and Littlefield, 87; co-ed, Frames, Fields and Contrasts: New Essays in Semantics and Lexical Organization, Lawrence Erlbaum, 92; auth, Mastering Envy: Narcissistic Wound, Symbolic Wounds, and a Vision of Healing, Psychoanalytic Rev, 94; coauth, Metaphor, in The Encyclopedia of Language and Linguistics, Pergamon, 95; auth, Taking Dependency Seriously: Social Cooperation, The Family Medical Leave Act, and Gender Equality Considered in Light of the Social Organization of Dependency Work, Hypatia, 95; auth, Human Dependency and Rawlsian Equality, in Meyers, ed, Rethinking the Self, Westview, 96; auth, Social Policy and Feminist Theory, in Jaggar, ed, Blackwell's Companion to Feminist Philosophy, Blackwell, 98; auth, Welfare, Dependency and a Public Ethic of Care, Social Justice, 98; auth, On Dependency and Welfare Justice: The Case for Scholarship and Activism, Feminist Stud, 98; auth, Love's Labor: Essays on Equality and Dependency, Routledge, 98; coauth, Concerning Expressivity and the Ethics of Selective Abortion for Disability: Conversations with My Son, in Haber, ed, Norms and Values: Essays in Honor of Virginia Held, forthcoming; auth, Not My Way, Sesha, Your Way, Slowly: Maternal Thinking in the Raising of a Child with Profound Intellectual Disabilities, in Hanisberg, ed, On Behalf of Mothers: Legal Theorists, Philosophers and Theologians Reflect on Dilemmas of Parenting, Beacon, forthcoming. **CONTACT ADDRESS** Dept of Philosophy, SUNY at Stonybrook, Stony Brook, NY, 11794-3750. **EMAIL** ekittay@cc.mail.sunysb.edu

KITTELSON, JAMES
DISCIPLINE CHURCH HISTORY **EDUCATION** St. Olaf Col, Phi Beta Kappa grad, 63; Stanford Univ, MA, 64, PhD, 69. **CAREER** Instr, Ohio State Univ, 71; vice-ch, Ohio State Univ, 74-77; ch, grad stud, Ohio State Univ, 89-91; vis grad prof, Luther Northwestern Theol Sem, 92; Concordia Univ. 97; prof, 97-; dir, Lutheran Brotherhood Res Prog. **HONORS AND AWARDS** Pres, bd of the Sixteenth Century Stud (s) Conf; exec comm, Coun Amer Soc for Reformation Res; Soc for Reformation Res; bd of dir(s), Ctr for Reformation Res. **SELECTED PUBLICATIONS** Auth, Luther the Reformer: The Story of the Man and His Career, 86; sr ed, Oxford Encycl of the Reformation, 96. **CONTACT ADDRESS** Dept of Church History, Luther Sem, 2481 Como Ave, St. Paul, MN, 55108. **EMAIL** jkittels@luthersem.edu

KITTS, MARGO
PERSONAL Born 04/01/1952, Colusa, CA, d, 1 child **DISCIPLINE** RELIGION **EDUCATION** Univ Calif, PhD, 94. **CAREER** Asst prof, Merrimack Col, 96-; adj prof, Univ San Francisco, 95-96; lectr & joint-lectr, Univ Calif Davis, 93, 94; lectr, Calif State Univ, 92. **HONORS AND AWARDS** Best Grad Student Paper, West Coast AAR, 91, 93. **MEMBERSHIPS** AAR; CTS. **RESEARCH** Homer, sacrifice; religious war and violence; Islam and the Middle East; women in world religions; Hittite language and religion. **SELECTED PUBLICATIONS** Auth, Two Expressions for Human Mortality in the Epics of Homer, Hist Relig, Nov, 94; auth, The Sacrifice of Lykaon in Iliad 21:1-125, Metis, 92. **CONTACT ADDRESS** Dept of Religious Studies, Merrimack Col, North Andover, MA, 01845. **EMAIL** mkitts@merrimack.edu

KIVY, PETER NATHAN
PERSONAL Born 10/22/1934, New York, NY **DISCIPLINE** PHILOSOPHY **EDUCATION** Univ Mich, AB, 56, MA, 58; Yale Univ, MA, 60; Columbia Univ, PhD(philos), 66. **CAREER** From asst prof to assoc prof, 67-76, Prof Philos, Rutgers Univ, 76- **HONORS AND AWARDS** Deems Taylor Award, Am Soc Composers. **MEMBERSHIPS** Am Soc Aesthet; Am Musicol Soc; Am Philos Asn. **RESEARCH** Aesthetics; 18th century philosophy; music aesthetics. **SELECTED PUBLICATIONS** Auth, Hume's standard of taste: Breaking the circle, Brit J Aesthet, 67; Child Mozart as an aesthetic symbol, J Hist Ideas, 67; Aesthetic aspects and aesthetic qualities, J Philos, 68; Speaking of Art, 73 & ed, Francis Hutcheson: Inquiry Concerning Beauty, Order, Harmony, Design, 73, Martinus Nijhoff; The Seventh Sense, B Franklin, 76; The Corded Shell: Reflections on Musical Expression, Princeton Univ Press, 80. **CONTACT ADDRESS** Dept of Philos, Rutgers Univ, P O Box 270, New Brunswick, NJ, 08903-0270.

KLAASSEN, WALTER
PERSONAL Born 05/27/1926, Laird, SK, Canada, m, 1952, 3 children **DISCIPLINE** HISTORY, THEOLOGY **EDUCATION** McMaster Univ, BA, 54; McMaster Divinity Sch, BD, 57; Oxford Univ, DPhil(hist theol), 60. **CAREER** Assoc prof Bible, Bethel Col, Kans, 60-62, chmn dept Bible and relig, 62-64; assoc prof Bible and relig, 64-70, assoc prof hist, 71-73, PROF HIST, CONRAD GREBEL COL, UNIV WATERLOO, 73-; Can Coun grants, 70-73 and 78-79. **MEMBERSHIPS** Am Soc Church Hist; Can Soc Church Hist; Mennonitischer Geschichtsverein; NAm Comt for Doc Free Church Origins (secy, 71). **RESEARCH** Just war theory; dissent in the 16th century; unilateral peace initiatives in history. **SELECTED PUBLICATIONS** Jesus, A Crucified Pharisee, J Ecumenical Studies, Vol 0029, 92; Homosexuality in the Church in Both Sides of the Debate, J Ecumenical Studies, Vol 0033, 96. **CONTACT ADDRESS** Conrad Grebel Col, Waterloo, ON, N2L 3G6.

KLARE, KARL E.
PERSONAL Born 01/08/1947, New York, NY **DISCIPLINE** LAW **EDUCATION** Columbia Col, BA, 67; Yale Univ, MA, 68; Harvard Univ, JD, 75. **CAREER** Instr polit sci, Adelphi Univ, 69-72; staff atty, Nat Labor Relations Bd, 75-76; assoc, Segal, Roitman & Coleman, 76-77; assoc prof, 77-80, Prof Law, Northeastern Univ, Mass, 80-. **MEMBERSHIPS** Conf Critical Legal Studies. **RESEARCH** Labor law; law and social theory; legal history. **SELECTED PUBLICATIONS** co-ed, The Unknown Dimension: European Marxism Since Lenin, Basic Bks, 72; auth, Judicial Deradicalization of the Wagner Act, Minn Law Rev, Vol 62, 78; Labor Law as Ideology, Indust Relations Law J, Vol 4, 81. **CONTACT ADDRESS** Sch of Law, Northeastern Univ, 400 Huntington Ave, Boston, MA, 02115-5098.

KLASS, DENNIS
DISCIPLINE RELIGION **EDUCATION** Elmhurst Col, BA, 63; Andover Newton Theol Schl, BD, 67; Univ Chicago MA, 70, Phd, 74. **CAREER** Res fel, 68-69, crse asst and clin supvr, Univ Chicago, 69; fac, 71-, adj fac, 75-92, prof, Webster Univ; ed bd, Omega:J of Death & Dying, Death Stud; mng ed, Relig & Educ. **HONORS AND AWARDS** Appreciation Award, Nat Bd of The Compassionate Friends, 92; Kemper Award for Outstanding Tchg, 95. **SELECTED PUBLICATIONS** Auth, Solace and Immortality: Bereaved Parents' Continuing Bond with Their Children, in George E. Dickinson, Michael R. Leming, and Alan C. Mermann, eds, Dying, Death, and Bereavement, 2nd ed, Dushkin Publ Gp, 94; Death and Spirituality, in Hannelore Wass and Robert A. Neimeyer, eds, Dying: Facing the Facts, 3rd ed, Taylor and Francis, 95; The Deceased Child in the Psychic and Social Worlds of Bereaved Parents during the Resolution of Grief, In Dennis Klass, Phyllis Silverman, and Steven Nickman, eds, Continuing Bonds: New Understandings of Grief, Taylor & Francis, 95; Continuing Bonds in Japanese Ancestor Worship, in Dennis Klass, Phyllis Silverman, and Steven Nickman, eds, Continuing Bonds: New Understandings of Grief, Taylor & Francis, 95 ; Managing Bonds with the Dead: Japanese Ancestor Worship, The Forum, Nov/Dec, 95; coauth, Grief and the Role of the Inner Representation of the Deceased, Omega 30:4, 94-95; Continuing Bonds: New Understandings of Griefed, Taylor & Francis, 96. **CONTACT ADDRESS** Webster Univ, St. Louis, MO, 63119. **EMAIL** klassde@websteruniv.edu

KLASSEN, WILLIAM
PERSONAL Born 05/18/1930, Halbstadt, MB, Canada, m, 1977, 3 children **DISCIPLINE** RELIGION **EDUCATION** Goshen Col, BA, 52, BD, 54; Princeton Theol Sem, PhD(New Testament), 60. **CAREER** Instr Greek, Goshen Col, 57-58; Instr New Testament, Mennonite Bibl Sem, 58-62, from assoc prof to prof, 62-69; Prof relig, Univ Man, 69-82, Head dept, 71-82; DIR DEVELOP, SIMON FRASER UNIV, BURNABY, BC, 82-; Menninger Found fel, 61-62; Vis prof, NY Theol Sem, 64-65; Exec dir, Mennonite Ment Health Serv, Inc, 65-66; Asst prof, Univ Notre Dame, 68-69; Instr, Ind Univ, South Bend, 68-69; Can Coun leave fel, 73-74; Fel, Ecumenical Inst Advan Theol Studies, Jerusalem, 73-74. **HONORS AND AWARDS** John F Funk lectr, 63; Menno Simons lectr, 64; Weyerhaueser lectr, McCormick Theol Sem, 67. **MEMBERSHIPS** Am Acad Relig; Soc Studies New Testament; Soc Bibl Lit; Can Soc Studies Relig; Int Asn Hist Relig. **RESEARCH** Stoic ethics; reformation history, especially hermeneutics; women in the early Christian movement. **SELECTED PUBLICATIONS** Auth, Theology, Cath Hist Rev, vol 0080, 94; The Sacred Kiss in the New Testament in An Example of Social Boundary Lines, New Testament Studies, vol 0039, 93; Galilean Upstarts, Jesus 1st Followers According to Q, Rev Bibl, vol 0102, 95. **CONTACT ADDRESS** Dept of Relig, Univ of Man, Winnipeg, MB, R3T 2N2.

KLEBBA, JAMES MARSHALL
PERSONAL Born 09/08/1942, Jefferson City, MO, m, 1968, 1 child **DISCIPLINE** LAW **EDUCATION** St John's Univ, BA, 64; Harvard Univ, JD, 67. **CAREER** Prof Law, Sch Law, 73- , assoc dean, 83-89, 97-99, interim dean, 89-90, Loyola Univ; Vis prof, Kansas Univ, 76, Sch Law, Univ Minn, 81-82 & Sch Law, Univ Mo, 81; consult, Comt Civil Rules, Minn Supreme Ct, 81-82; mem adv comt on code of civil procedure, La

Law Inst, 82- **MEMBERSHIPS** Am Bar Asn; Asn Am Law Schs (chemn, Civil Procedure Sect, 78-79). **RESEARCH** Civil procedure; evidence; environmental law; water rights and water resources; comparative judicial systems. **SELECTED PUBLICATIONS** Auth, The fifth circuit and environment: The quest for effective review of agency action, 74 & Fifth circuit symposium: Federal jurisdiction and civil procedure, 77, Loyola Law Rev; Insuring solar access on retrofits: The problem and some solutions, Solar Eng Mag, 1/80; auth, Water REsources for Louisiana, 82; auth, Legal and Institutional Analysis of Louisiana's Water Laws, 83; coauth, Evidence Cases and Problems, 1995; auth, Conflict and Cooperation in the American Judicial System, Univ Budapest Law Rev, 97. **CONTACT ADDRESS** Dept of Law, Sch Law Loyola Univ, 7214 St Charles Ave, New Orleans, LA, 70118-6195. **EMAIL** klebba@loyno.edu

KLECK, GARY
PERSONAL Born 03/02/1951, Elmhurst, IL, m, 1982, 2 children **DISCIPLINE** CRIMINOLOGY **EDUCATION** Univ of Ill, AB, 73, AM, 75, PhD, 79. **CAREER** Instr, 78-79, asst prof, 79-84, assoc prof, 84-91; prof, School of Criminology and Criminal Justice, Fla State Univ, 91-. **HONORS AND AWARDS** Univ of Ill Found Fel; Michael J. Hindelang Award of the Am Soc of Criminology. **MEMBERSHIPS** Am Soc of Criminology. **RESEARCH** Firearms and violence; crime control. **SELECTED PUBLICATIONS** Auth, Point Blank, 91; Targeting Guns, 97; The Great American Gun Debate, 97. **CONTACT ADDRESS** School of Criminology and Criminal Justice, Florida State Univ, 306 Hecht House, Tallahassee, FL, 32306-1127. **EMAIL** gkleck@mailer.fsu.edu

KLEIN, ANNE
DISCIPLINE RELIGIOUS STUDIES, TIBETAN BUDDHISM, CLASSICAL TIBETAN LANGUAGE **EDUCATION** Univ VA, PhD, 81. **CAREER** Prof, ch, dept Relig Stud, Rice Univ. **HONORS AND AWARDS** Fulbright dissertation res fel, India and Nepal, 80; NEH summer grant, 94; NEH transl grant, 94. **SELECTED PUBLICATIONS** Auth, Knowing, Naming, and Negation: A Sourcebook on Tibetan Sautrantika; Knowledge and Liberation; Path to the Middle: Oral Madhyamika Philosophy in Tibet: The Spoken Scholarship of Kensur Yeshey Tupden; Meeting the Great Bliss Queen:Buddhists, Feminists, and the Art of the Self, Beacon Press, 94. **CONTACT ADDRESS** Rice Univ, PO Box 1892, Houston, TX, 77251-1892. **EMAIL** klein-A@rice.edu

KLEIN, ELLEN R.
PERSONAL Born 04/15/1958, Westchester, PA **DISCIPLINE** PHILOSOPHY **EDUCATION** New Col, Univ So Fla, BA, 81; Univ So Fla, MA, 83; Univ Miami, PhD, 89. **CAREER** Instr, 88-89, Rollins Col; asst prof, 89-90, Wash Col; asst prof, 91-96, Univ N Fla; vis assoc prof, Johnston Chmn, 97, Whitman Col; asst prof, 98, Cent Wash Univ; asst prof, 99-, Flagler Col. **MEMBERSHIPS** Fla Philos Asn; APA. **RESEARCH** Epistemology; arguments against feminism; business ethics; pedagogy. **SELECTED PUBLICATIONS** Coauth, Hunting, Encycl of Bioethics, 94; auth, Nomad Come Home: A Critique of Rosi Braidotti's Feminism and Modernity, Free Inquiry, 95; auth, Philosophy for Physicians: An Introduction to Medical Ethics, Jacksonville Med, 95; auth, Philosophers as Experts: A Response to Pfeifer, Inquiry, vol XV, no 1, 95; coauth, Philosophy and the Politics of Feminism, Free Inquiry, vol 16, no 1, 95/96; auth, Feminism Under Fire, Prometheus Bks, 96; auth, Kings or Rogues: Philosophers on Biomedical Ethics Committees, APA Newsl on Med, vol 96:1, 96; auth, Professional Philosophers vs. Professionals as Philosophers, Ethically Speaking: The Newsl of the Asn for Pract & Profes Ethics, vol 6, no 1, 97; auth, Can Feminism Be Rational?, J of Interdisciplinary Stud, vol x, no 1/2, 98; auth, The Only Necessary Condition for a Successful Business Ethics Course: That it is Taught by a Philosopher, Bus Ethics Quart, 98. **CONTACT ADDRESS** 110 Ocean Hollow Ln #315, St. Augustine, FL, 32095. **EMAIL** eruthklein@aol.com

KLEIN, KENNETH
DISCIPLINE PHILOSOPHY **EDUCATION** WA Univ, AB, 52; Univ Chicago, BD, 55; Harvard Univ, PhD, 63. **CAREER** Philos, Valparaiso Univ. **HONORS AND AWARDS** Caterpillar Awd for Excel Tchg, Valparaiso Univ, 95, Rockefeller Fel Relig, Harvard Univ, 60-62; Frank Knox Mem Fel, Harvard Univ, 59-60; fel Mansfield Col, Oxford Univ. **RESEARCH** Philos of reigion; hist and philos of relig. **SELECTED PUBLICATIONS** Auth, Positivism and Christianity, Martinus Nijhoff, 74; co-ed, In the Interest of Peace: A Spectrum of Philosophical Views, Longwood Acad, 90; Issues in War and Peace: Philosophical Inquiries, Longwood Pub, 89. **CONTACT ADDRESS** Valparaiso Univ, 1500 E Lincoln Way, Valparaiso, IN, 46383-6493.

KLEIN, MICHAEL LEON
PERSONAL Born 08/05/1940, Brooklyn, NY, m, 1970, 4 children **DISCIPLINE** BIBLE AND TARGUMIC LITERATURE **EDUCATION** Brooklyn Col, BA, 54; Univ Pa, MA, 75; Hebrew Univ, Jerusalem, PhD, 79. **CAREER** Asst dean, 74-76, asst prof, 74-79, from assoc dean to dean, 79-81, ASSOC PROF ARAMAIC AND RABBINICS, HEBREW UNION COL, JEWISH INST RELIG, JERUSALEM 79-. **MEMBERSHIPS** Soc Bibl Lit; Asn Targumic Studies; Asn Jewish Studies. **RESEARCH** Targumic literature; translational theory; early medieval manuscripts. **SELECTED PUBLICATIONS** Auth, Notes on the Library of the Annenberg Research Institute and Additional Targum Manuscripts, Jewish Quart Rev, Vol 0083, 92; The Interpretation of Speech in the Pentateuch Targums in A Study of Method and Presentation in Targumic Exegesis, J Semitic Studies, Vol 0039, 94. **CONTACT ADDRESS** Jewish Inst of Relig, Hebrew Union Col, Jerusalem, ..

KLEIN, PETER DAVID
PERSONAL Born 09/17/1940, Cincinnati, OH, d, 1 child **DISCIPLINE** PHILOSOHY **EDUCATION** Earlham Col, BA, 62; Yale Univ, MA, 64, PhD, 66. **CAREER** Asst prof philos, Colgate Univ, 66-70; from asst prof to assoc prof, 70-81, Prof, Rutgers Univ, 81-, Chmn, 82-87 and 93-96, vice provost, Undergrad Educ and assoc provost for Hum and Fine Arts, 87-92; Lectr, NEH Summer Inst on Epistemology, 93; Subj ed (with R Foley), epistemology, Encyclopedia of Philosophy, Routledge. **HONORS AND AWARDS** Danforth Grad Fel, 62-66; Ford Found grant, Oxford Univ, 69-70; NJ Comn for Hum, 73-74 & 79-80, Control Data Corp, computer asst instr in elementary logic, 79-80; NEH publ prog grant, Certainty, 81; various Rutgers Res Counc grants. **MEMBERSHIPS** Am Philos Asn. **RESEARCH** Epistemology. **SELECTED PUBLICATIONS** Auth, The Private Language Argument and The Sense-Datum Theory, Australasian Jour Phil, 69; Are Strawson's Persons Immortal? -- A Reply, Philos Studies, 69; A Proposed Definition of Propositional Knowledge, Jour Philos, 71, reprinted, Knowing, Univ Press Am, 84, Knowledge and Justification, Ashgate Publ Co, 94, and On Knowing and the Known, Prometheus Books, 96; Knowledge, Causality and Defeasibility, Jour Philos, 76; Misleading Misleading, Defeators, Jour Philos, 76, reprinted, On Knowing and the Known, Prometheus Books 96; Misleading Evidence and the Restoration of Justification, Philos Studies, 80; Certainty: A Refutation of Skepticism, Univ Minn Press, 81, 2nd printing, 84; Reply to Professor Odegard, Philos Books, 82; Real Knowledge, Synthese, 83; Virtues of Inconsistency, Monist, 85; Radical Interpretation and Global Scepticism, In: Truth and Interpretation (Ernest LePore, ed), Basil Blackwell, 86; Immune Belief Systems, Philos Topics, 86; On Behalf of the Skeptic, The Possibility of Knowledge: Nozick and His Critics (S Luper-Foy, ed), Rowman & Littlefield, 87; Epistemic Compatibilism and Canonical Beliefs, In: Doubting: Contemporary Perspectives on Scepticism (M Roth & G Ross, ed), Kluwer Acad Publ, 90; Certainty, In: A Companion to Epistemology (J Dancy & E Sosa, ed), Basil Blackwell, 92; Contemporary Scepticism, In: A Companion to Epistemolgy (J Dancy & E Sosa, ed), Basil Blackwell, 92; Scepticism, In: A Companion to Epistemology (J Dancy & E Sosa, ed), Basil Blackwell, 92; Co-auth (with Ted Warfield), What Price Coherence?, Analysis, 7/94; Skepticism and Closure: Why the Evil Genius Argument Fails, Philos Topics, spring 95; Closure, In: The Cambridge Dictionary of Philosophy (R Audi, ed), Cambridge Univ Press, 95; Certainty, In: The Cambridge Dictionary of Philosophy (R Audi, ed), Cambridge Univ Press, 95; Co-auth (with Ted Warfield), No Help for the Coherentist, Analysis, 4/96; Warrant, Proper Function, Reliabilism and Defeasibility, In: Warrant and Contemporary Epistemology (Jonathan Kvanvig, ed), Rowman & Littlefield, 96; Certainty, In: Encyclopedia of Philosophy (E Craig, ed), Routledge, 98; The Concept of Knowledge, In: Encyclopedia of Philosophy (E Craig, ed), Routledge, 98; Epistemology, In: Encyclopedia of Philosophy (E Craig, ed), Routledge, 98. **CONTACT ADDRESS** Dept of Philos, Rutgers Univ, PO Box 270, New Brunswick, NJ, 08903-0270. **EMAIL** pdklein@crci.rutgers.edu

KLEIN, RALPH W.
PERSONAL m, 2 children **DISCIPLINE** OLD TESTAMENT **EDUCATION** Concordia Sem; Harvard Univ Divinity Sch, PhD. **CAREER** Dean; Christ Sem-Seminex prof. **HONORS AND AWARDS** Humboldt fel, Univ Gottingen; Humboldt Univ, Berlin., Ed, Currents in Theol and Mission, 74-. **SELECTED PUBLICATIONS** Auth, Textual Criticism of the Old Testament, Israel in Exile, 1 Samuel, Word Biblical Commentary 10; Ezekiel: The Prophet and His Message; commentary on Ezra and Nehemiah for the New Interpreter's Bible. **CONTACT ADDRESS** Dept of OldTestament, Lutheran Sch of Theol, 1100 E 55th St, Chicago, IL, 60615. **EMAIL** rklein@lstc.edu

KLEIN, RICHARD
PERSONAL Born 06/21/1943, New York, NY, m, 1961, 2 children **DISCIPLINE** LAW **EDUCATION** Univ WI, BA, 64; Columbia Univ, MA, 68, MIA, 69, doctorate, 70, Harvard Univ, JD, 72. **CAREER** Touro Law Sch, prof, 83-; Hofstra prof 82-83; Legal Aid Society, Sr Trial att, 72-82. **HONORS AND AWARDS** Fac Mem of the Yr. **MEMBERSHIPS** ABA; AATL. **RESEARCH** Intl Human Rights; Criminal Law. **SELECTED PUBLICATIONS** Auth, Human Rights in Hong Kong, The Humanist, 97; Law and Racism in an Asian Setting, Hastins Intl Law Rev, The Empire Strikes Back: Britain's Use of Law to Suppress Political Dissent, Boston U Intl L Jour, 97. **CONTACT ADDRESS** Touro Law School, Touro Col, 300 Nassau Rd, Huntington, NY, 11743.

KLEIN, WILLIAM
PERSONAL Born 02/11/1946, Weehawken, NJ, m, 1968, 2 children **DISCIPLINE** NEW TESTAMENT EXEGESIS **EDUCATION** Univ of Aberdeen, Scotland, PhD, 78 **CAREER** Inst, 77-78, Columbia Internatl Univ; Prof, 78-pres, Denver Sem **HONORS AND AWARDS** Whos Who Among Students; Whos Who in Relig; Outstanding Young Men of Amer; Who's Who in World; Men of Achievement; Who's Who in Bibl Studies & Archaeology **MEMBERSHIPS** Soc of Bibl Lit; Inst for Bibl Res, Evangelical Theolog Soc; Tyndale Fel for Bibl Res **RESEARCH** Hermeneutics; Pauline theology; Sermon on the Mount; Theology of Election **SELECTED PUBLICATIONS** Auth, "Evangelical Hermeneutics," in Initiation into Theology, JL Van Schaik, 98; "Election," in Dictionary of the Later New Testament and Its Developments, Inter Varsity Pr, 97 **CONTACT ADDRESS** Denver Conservative Baptist Sem, PO Box 10000, Denver, CO, 80250-0100. **EMAIL** billk@densem.edu

KLEIN, WILLIAM A.
PERSONAL Born 03/03/1931, Chicago, IL **DISCIPLINE** LAW **EDUCATION** Harvard Univ, AB, 52, JD, 57. **CAREER** Prof law, Univ Wis, 61-71; PROF LAW, UNIV CALIF, LOS ANGELES, 71-. **RESEARCH** Federal income taxation; legal organization of business. **SELECTED PUBLICATIONS** Auth, Tailor to the Emperor With No Clothes in The Supreme-Courts Tax Rules for Deposits and Advance Payments, UCLA Law Rev, Vol 0041, 94. **CONTACT ADDRESS** Law Sch, Univ of Calif, Los Angeles, CA, 90024.

KLEINBAUER, W. EUGENE
DISCIPLINE EARLY CHRISTIAN, BYZANTINE ART **EDUCATION** Princeton Univ, PhD. **CAREER** Prof. **SELECTED PUBLICATIONS** Auth, Modern Perspectives in Western Art History, 71; Research Guide to the History of Western Art, 83; Early Christian and Byzantine Architecture, 92. **CONTACT ADDRESS** Dept of History and Art, Indiana Univ, Bloomington, 300 N Jordan Ave, Bloomington, IN, 47405. **EMAIL** kleinbau@indiana.edu

KLEINER, SCOTT ALTER
PERSONAL Born 12/22/1938, Cincinnati, OH, m, 1960, 2 children **DISCIPLINE** PHILOSOPHY, PHILOSOPHY OF SCIENCE **EDUCATION** Williams Col, AB, 60; Univ Chicago, AM, 61, PhD(Philos), 68. **CAREER** From instr to asst prof, 65-69; asst prof, 69-77, from assoc prof to prof Philos, Univ GA, 77-97, Sarah B Moss fel, 73-74. **MEMBERSHIPS** AAAS; Philos Sci Asn; Asn Symbolic Logic. **RESEARCH** History and philosophy of natural science; foundations of physics; philosophy of biology. **SELECTED PUBLICATIONS** Auth, Erotetic logic and the structure of scientific revolution, Brit J Philos Sci, 70; Criteria for Meaning Change in Physics, In: Studies in the Foundations, Methodology and Philosophy of Science, 71; Ontological Commitment and the Methodological Commensurability of Theories, In: Boston Studies in Philosophy of Science, 71; Recent theories of theoretical meaning, Philosophica, 76; The philosophy of biology, Southern J Philos, 76; Referential Divergence in Scientific Theories, 77 & Feyerabend, Galileo and Darwin, 79, In: Studies in History & Philosophy of Science; Problem Solving and Discovery in the Growth of Darwin's Theories of Evolution, Synthese, 81; Logic of Discovery, Kluwer, 93. **CONTACT ADDRESS** Dept of Philosophy & Religion, Univ of Georgia, Athens, GA, 30602-0001. **EMAIL** skleiner@arches.uga.edu

KLEINGELD, PAULINE
PERSONAL Rotterdam, m, 1 child **DISCIPLINE** PHILOSOPHY **EDUCATION** Leiden Univ, MA, BA, PhD, 94. **CAREER** Asst prof, 93-, Washington Univ of St Louis. **HONORS AND AWARDS** Washington Univ Fac Res Grant; Lilly Endowment Tchng Fel; DAAD Fel. **MEMBERSHIPS** APA; ASECS; NAKS; NASSP; Kant-Gesellschaft. **RESEARCH** History of modern phil, esp Kant. **SELECTED PUBLICATIONS** Auth, Kant on the Nature of Reason (In Dutch), Louvain Univ Press, 93; art, The Problematic Status of Gender-Neutral Language in the History of Philosophy: The Case of Kant, Phil Forum, 93; auth, Progress and Reason: Kant's Philosophy of History, Wurzburg Konigshausen und Neumann, 95; art, What Do the Virtuous Hope For?: Re-reading Kant's Doctrine of the Highest Good, Proc of the 8th Intl Kant Congress, Memphis 95, Marquette Univ Press, 95; art, Between Copernican Turn and Grand Narrative: The Relevance of Kant's Philosophy of History, Fischer Verlag, 96; art, Kants Politischer Kosmopolitismus, Jahrbuch fur Recht und Ethik 5, 97; art, The Conative Character of Reason in Kant's Philosophy, Jour of the History of Phil 36, 98; art, Just Love? Marriage and the Question of Justice, Soc Theory and Practice 24, 98. **CONTACT ADDRESS** Dept of Philosophy, Washington Univ, One Brookings Drive, Campus Box 1073, St. Louis, MO, 63130-4899. **EMAIL** pkleinge@artsci.wastl.edu

KLEMKE, ELMER DANIEL
PERSONAL Born 07/29/1926, St. Paul, MN **DISCIPLINE** PHILOSOPHY **EDUCATION** Hamline Univ, BA, 50; Northwestern Univ, MA, 58, PhD(philos), 60. **CAREER** Asst prof philos, DePauw Univ, 59-64; prof, Roosevelt Univ, 64-74, chmn dept, 65-74; assoc dean and prof, 74-76, Prof Philos, Iowa

State Univ, 76-. **MEMBERSHIPS** Am Philos Asn; Western Div Am Philos Asn (secy-treas, 69-72); AAUP. **RESEARCH** Contemporary Brit and Am philos; philos of logic; metaphysics. **SELECTED PUBLICATIONS** Auth, Reflections and Perspectives: Essays in Philosophy, The Hague, Mouton, 74; (with A Jacobson & F Zabeeh), Readings in Semantics, Univ Ill Press, 74; auth, Studies in the Philosophy of Kierkegaard, Nijhoff, The Hague, 76; Bibliography of G E Moore scholarship, 1903-present, Southwestern J Philos, Vol VII, No 3; coauth, (with Robert Hollinger & A David Kline), Introductory Readings in the Philosophy of Science, Prometheus Bks, 80; auth, The Meaning of Life, Oxford Univ Press, 81; coauth, (with Robert Hollinger & A David Kline), Philosophy: The Basic Issues, St Martin's Press, 81; auth, A Defense of Philosophical Realism, Humanities Press, Fall 98. **CONTACT ADDRESS** Dept of Philosophy, Iowa State Univ of Science and Tech, 402 Catt Hall, Ames, IA, 50011-0002.

KLERMAN, DANIEL M.
DISCIPLINE LAW **EDUCATION** Yale Univ, BA,88; Univ Chicago, JD,91; PhD,98. **CAREER** Assoc prof, Univ Southern Calif; clerked for, Honorable Richard A. Posner, Judge US Ct Appeals 7th Circuit & Honorable John Paul Stevens, Assoc Justice US Supreme Ct. **RESEARCH** Legal history; class action lawsuits; issues in intellectual property, trademark, & unfair competition. **SELECTED PUBLICATIONS** Auth, Settling Multidefendant Lawsuits: The Advantage of Conditional Setoff Rules; An Economic Analysis of Mary Carter Settlement Agreements & Earth First? CERCLA Reimbursement Clains & Bankruptcy. **CONTACT ADDRESS** School of Law, Univ Southern Calif, University Park Campus, Los Angeles, CA, 90089. **EMAIL** dklerman@law.usc.edu

KLIBANSKY, RAYMOND
PERSONAL Born 10/15/1905, Paris, France **DISCIPLINE** PHILOSOPHY **EDUCATION** Univ Heildelberg, PhD, 28; Oxford Univ, MA, 36. **CAREER** Asst philos, Heidelberg Acad, 27-33; Hon lectr, Kings Col, Univ London, 34-36; Lectr, Oriel Col, Oxford, 36-48; Frothinghem prof, 46-75, EMER PROF LOGIC AND METAPHYSICS, MCGILL UNIV, 75-; HON FEL, UNIV LONDON, 50-; Guest prof, Inst Mediaeval Studies, Univ Montreal, 47-68; Mahlon Powell prof philos, Ind Univ, 50; Gretler Found lectr, Univ Zurich, 50; Guggenheim fel, 53 and 65; Cardinal Mercier prof philos, Cath Univ Louvain, 56; Found lectr, Univ Rome, 57; Vis prof philos, 61; Prof ordinarius (aD), Ministry Educ Baden-Wurttemberg, 59-75, Emer prof, 75-; Vis prof, Univ Genoa, 64; MEM COUN, CTR HUMANISTIC STUDIES, ROME, 49-; FEL, INT INST PHILOS, PARIS, 53-; PRES, COMN CHRONIQUES ET TRAVAUX BIBLIOG, 53-; PRES COMN PHILOS ET COMMUNAUTE MONDIALE, 58-; Pres, Inst, 66-69 and Can rep exec comt, Int Fed Philos Socs, 53-; Actg chmn nat comt hist and philos sci, Nat Res Coun Can, 69-69 and MEM NAT COMT INT COUN SCI UNIONS, 63-; FEL, ACAD ATHENS, 70-; PRES INT COMT, ANSELM STUDIES, 70-; Vis fel, Wolfson Col, Oxford, 76-78; Dir, Can Acad Ctr, Italy, 80; FEL, WOLFSON COL, OXFORD, 81-. **HONORS AND AWARDS** DPhil, Univ Ottawa, 71. **MEMBERSHIPS** Fel Royal Soc Can; Int Soc Studies Medieval Philos(vpres, 64-69, pres, 69-72, hon pres, 72-); Int Inst Philos (hon pres, 69-), fel Int Acad Hist Sci; Can Soc Hist and Philos Sci (pres, 59-72, emer pres, 72-); Royal Hist Soc. **RESEARCH** Philosophy of history and metaphysics; history of Platonism; Nicholas of Cusa. **SELECTED PUBLICATIONS** Auth, Beyond the Limits of Academic Life in An Interview with Klibansky, Raymond, a Canadian Philosopher, About Cassirer, Ernst and the Wartburg Library, Merkur-Deutsche Zeitschrift fur Europaisches Denken, Vol 0050, 96. **CONTACT ADDRESS** Dept of Philos, McGill Univ, Montreal, PQ, H3A 1B1.

KLIMA, GYULA
PERSONAL Born 10/20/1956 **DISCIPLINE** PHILOSOPHY **EDUCATION** Univ Budapest, MA, 82; PhD, 86. **CAREER** Asst prof, Yale Univ, 92-95; sr res fel, Hungarian Acad, 93-97; assoc prof Univ Notre Dame, 95-. **RESEARCH** Philosophical semantics; ontology; comparative analysis of medieval and modern theories. **SELECTED PUBLICATIONS** Auth, Saint Thomas Aquinas on Being and Essence, 90; Ars Artium, Essays in Philosophical Semantics, Medieval and Modern, 88; The Semantic Principles Underlying Saint Thomas Aquinas's Metaphysics of Being, Medieval Philos Theol, 96; Man=Body+Soul: Aquinas's Arithmetic of Human Nature, Philso Studies Relig, 97; Contemporary 'Essentialism' vs. Aristotelian 'Essentialism', 98; Saint Anselm's Proof: A Problem of Reference, Intentional Identity and Mutual Understanding, Medieval Philos Modern Times, 98. **CONTACT ADDRESS** Philosophy Dept, Univ of Notre Dame, 336/7 O'Shaughnessy, Notre Dame, IN, 46556. **EMAIL** klima.1@nd.edu

KLINE, GEORGE LOUIS
PERSONAL Born 03/03/1921, Galesburg, IL, m, 1943, 3 children **DISCIPLINE** PHILOSOPHY **EDUCATION** Columbia Univ, AB, 47, AM, 48, PhD, 50. **CAREER** Instr philos, Columbia Univ, 50-52 and 53-54, asst prof, 54-60; assoc prof philos and Russ, 60-66, chmn dept, 77-82, prof, 66-81, MILTON C NAHM PROF PHILOS, BRYN MAWR COL, 81-; Vis asst prof, Univ Chicago, 52-53; consult, USSR res prog, 52-55; Ford fel, Paris, 54-55; Inter-Univ Comt travel grant, USSR and Czech, 56 and 57; ed philos sect, Am Bibliog Slavic Studies, 57-67; consult, Foreign Area Fel Prog, 59-64; ed, J Philos, 59-64, consult ed, 64-78; Rockefeller fel, USSR, Poland, Czech, Hungary and Western Europe, 60; consult ed philos, Current Digest of the Soviet Press, 61-64; CONSULT ED, STUDIES IN SOVIET THOUGHT, 62-; J VALUE INQUIRY, 67-; PROCESS STUDIES, 70-; J HIST OF IDEAS, 76-; Slavic Rev, 77-79; vis prof philos, Johns Hopkins Univ, 68-69, Univ Pa, 80-81 and Swarthmore Col, 81-82; Nat Endowment for Humanities sr fel, 70-71, consult, 72-76; Guggenheim fel, 78-79; Fulbright res fel, Paris, 79. **MEMBERSHIPS** Am Philos, Asn; Am Asn Advan Slavic Studies; Metaphys Soc Am; Hegel Soc Am (vpres, 71-73); Int Hegel-Vereinigung. **RESEARCH** Ethics; metaphysics; Russian philosophy, especially ethical and social theory. **SELECTED PUBLICATIONS** Auth, The Scientific Mythology of Communism, Russ Rev, Vol 0056, 97. **CONTACT ADDRESS** 632 Valley View Rd, Ardmore, PA, 19003.

KLINE, MARLEE
DISCIPLINE LAW **EDUCATION** Simon Fraser Univ, BA, 82; Oxford Univ, BA, 84; Dalhousie Univ, LLB, 85; Osgoode Univ, LLM, 91. **CAREER** Asst prof, 89-94; assoc prof, 94-. **RESEARCH** Child welfare law; social welfare law; feminist legal theory; racism and law; property law. **SELECTED PUBLICATIONS** Auth, pubs about child welfare law, feminist analysis of law and structures of racism within the law. **CONTACT ADDRESS** Fac of Law, Univ British Columbia, 1822 East Mall, Vancouver, BC, V6T 1Z1. **EMAIL** kline@law.ubc.ca

KLINE, MEREDITH GEORGE
PERSONAL Born 12/15/1922, Coplay, PA, m, 1944, 3 children **DISCIPLINE** RELIGION **EDUCATION** Gordon Col, AB, 44; Westminster Theol Sem, ThB and ThM, 47; Dropsie Col, PhD (Assyriol and Egyptol), 56. **CAREER** Prof Old Testament, Westminster Theol Sem, 48-65; PROF OLD TESTAMENT, GORDON-CONWELL THEOL SEM, 65-; VIS PROF OLD TESTAMENT, Sch Theol, Claremont, 74-75 and REFORMED THEOL SEM, 80-; PROF OLD TESTAMENT, WESTMINISTER THEOL SEM, CALIF, 82-. **RESEARCH** Old Testament. **SELECTED PUBLICATIONS** Auth, Heaven On Earth in The Social And Political Agendas of Dominion Theology; J Church State, Vol 0036, 94. **CONTACT ADDRESS** Gordon-Conwell Theol Sem, South Hamilton, MA, 01982.

KLING, DAVID
PERSONAL Born 04/21/1950, Mora, MN, m, 1985, 4 children **DISCIPLINE** HISTORY OF CHRISTIANITY, RELIGION IN AMERICAN LIFE **EDUCATION** Trinity Col, IL, BA, 72; Northern IL Univ, 76; Univ Chicago, PhD, 85. **CAREER** Asst prof hist, Palm Beach Atlantic Col, 82-86; Univ administration, Univ Miami, 86-93; asst prof of relig studies, 93-95, assoc prof, Univ Miami, 95-. **HONORS AND AWARDS** Kenneth Scott Latourette Prize in Religion and Modern Hist (Best Book Manuscript), 92. **MEMBERSHIPS** Am Academy of Relig; Am Soc of Church Hist. **RESEARCH** Revivalism in Am; biblical texts in hist of Christianity. **SELECTED PUBLICATIONS** Auth, A Field of Divine Wonders: The New Divinity and Village Revivals in Northwestern Connecticut, 1792-1822, PA State Univ Press, 93; For Males Only: The Image of the Infidel and the Construction of Gender in the Second Great Awakening in New England, J of Men's Studies 3, May 95; twenty-five entries in The Blackwell Dictionary of Evangelical Biography, 1730-1860, ed Donald M Lewis, 2 vols, Blackwell Pubs, 95; The New Divinity and Williams College, 1793-1836, Religion and American Culture: A Journal of Interpretation 6, summer 96; By the Light of His Example: New Divinity Schools of the Prophets and Theological Education in New England, 1750-1825, in American Theological Education in the Evangelical Tradition, eds D G Hart and R Albert Mohler, Jr, Baker Books, 96; Smyth, Newman, in Dictionary of Heresy Trials in American Christianity, ed George H Shriver, Greenwood Press, 97; New Divinity Schools of the Prophets, 1750-1825: A Case Study in Ministerial Education, History of Ed Quart 37, summer 97. **CONTACT ADDRESS** Dept of Relig Studies, Univ of Miami, PO Box 248264, Miami, FL, 33124. **EMAIL** dkling@miami.edu

KLONOSKI, R.J.
PERSONAL Born 06/10/1952, Scranton, PA, m, 1974, 3 children **DISCIPLINE** PHILOSOPHY **EDUCATION** Univ of Scranton, BA, 74; Kent State Univ, MA, 76; Duquesne Univ, PhD, 83. **CAREER** Prof philos, Univ of Scranton, 81- . **HONORS AND AWARDS** Alpha Sigma Nu Awd, 87; res grants, 85, 89, 93, 98; vis scholar, N Carolina Ctr for Independent Higher Ed, 90; tchr of the year, 98. **MEMBERSHIPS** Soc for Ancient Greek Philos; Int Hobbes Asn; Alpha Sigma Mu; Phi Sigma Tau. **RESEARCH** Ethics; political philosophy, philosophy of education, Greek philosophy. **SELECTED PUBLICATIONS** Auth, The Preservation of Homeric Tradition: Heroic Re-Performance in the Republic and the Odyssey, CLIO, 93; auth, On Friendship as Our Ownmost Salvation, McNeese Rev, 95-96; auth, Homonoia in Aristotle's Ethics and Politics, Hist of Polit Thought, 96. **CONTACT ADDRESS** Dept of Philosophy, Univ of Scranton, Scranton, PA, 18510.

KLOSTERMAIER, KLAUS KONRAD
PERSONAL Born 06/14/1933, Munich, Germany, m, 1971, 3 children **DISCIPLINE** COMPARATIVE RELIGION **EDUCATION** Pontif Gregorian Univ Rome, B Phil, 54, Lic Phil, 55, Dr Phil, 61; Univ Bombay, PhD(ancient Indian hist and cult), 69. **CAREER** Res guide philos, Inst Orient Philos, Agra Univ, 62-64; vis prof Indian Anthrop, Tata Inst Soc Sci, Bombay-Chembur, 64-65; dir, Inst Indian Cult, Bombay Bandra, 65-70; from asst prof to assoc prof World relig, 70-73, PROF WORLD RELIG, UNIV MAN, 73-; S L Swamikannu Pillai lectr, Univ Madras, 68-69; mem bd dirs, Shastri Indo-Can Inst, Montreal-New Delhi, 72-75. **MEMBERSHIPS** Asn Asian Studies; Am Orient Soc; Can Soc Studies Relig; Int Soc Psychol Relig; Ger Soc Missions Sci. **RESEARCH** Interreligious dialogue; Indian philosophies and religions; Judian art. **SELECTED PUBLICATIONS** Transl, The Infancy of Krsna in Critical Edition of the Harivamsa Couture, J Am Orient Soc, Vol 0113, 93; Buddhism Reevaluated by Prominent 20th-Century Hindus, J Dharma, Vol 0020, 95; Studying the Sikhs in Issues for North America, Studies Relig-Scis Religieuses, Vol 0024, 95; The Hermeneutic Center in An Investigation of Interpretive Methodologies in The Study of Theology Through Dialogue and a Transcultural Understanding of Religion, J Ecumenical Studies, Vol 0034, 97; Religious Studies as World Theology J Ecumenical Studies, Vol 0034, 97; Interreligious Dialogue Between Tradition and Modernity, J Ecumenical Studies, Vol 0034, 97. **CONTACT ADDRESS** Dept of Relig, Univ of Man, Ft Garry Campus, Winnipeg, MB, R3T 2N2.

KLUGE, EIKE-HENNER W.
DISCIPLINE BIOMEDICAL ETHICS **EDUCATION** Univ Calgary, BA; Univ Mich, AM, PhD. **CAREER** Instr, Univ Calif; prof, 71; dept ch. **RESEARCH** History of philosophy and theory of perception. **SELECTED PUBLICATIONS** Auth, bk(s) and articles in medical ethics, hist philos. **CONTACT ADDRESS** Dept of Philosophy, Victoria Univ, PO Box 3045, Victoria, BC, V8W 3P4. **EMAIL** ekluge@uvvm.uvic.ca

KMIEC, DOUGLAS WILLIAM
PERSONAL Born 09/24/1951, Chicago, IL, m, 1973, 2 children **DISCIPLINE** PROPERTY AND LAND USE LAW **EDUCATION** Northwestern Univ, BA, 73; Univ Southern Calif, JD, 76. **CAREER** Atty, Vedder, Price, Kaufman and Kammholz, 76-78; asst prof property and land use, Valparaiso Univ, 78-80; adj prof environ law, Ind Univ, 80; ASSOC PROF PROPERTY, LAND USE, STATE AND LOCAL GOVT, NOTRE DAME UNIV, 80-; Fel, Inst for Humane Studies, 81 and Law and Econ Inst, 82; special asst to the President of the US and White House fel, 82-83. **HONORS AND AWARDS** Legal Writing Prize, Univ Southern Calif, 76. **MEMBERSHIPS** Am Asn Law Sch; Am Bar Asn; Intercollegiate Studies Inst. **RESEARCH** The philosophy of property; federalism and the limits of government; natural law and jurisprudence. **SELECTED PUBLICATIONS** Auth, The 91 Civil-Rights Act in A Constitutional, Statutory, and Philosophical Enigma, Notre Dame Law Rev, Vol 0068, 93; Clarifying the Supreme Courts Taking Cases in An Irreverent But Otherwise Unassumable Draft Opinion in Dolan V City of Tigard, Denver Univ Law Rev, Vol 0071, 94; Mere Creatures of The State in Education, Religion, and The Courts, a View From The Courtroomm, Notre Dame Law Rev, Vol 0070, 95; At Last, the Supreme-Court Solves the Takings Puzzle, Harvard J Law Pub Policy, Vol 0019, 95; Prof Murphy,Edward, Notre Dame Law Rev, Vol 0071, 95. **CONTACT ADDRESS** Law Sch, Univ of Notre Dame, Notre Dame, IN, 46556.

KNELLER, JANE E.
DISCIPLINE PHILOSOPHY **EDUCATION** Univ Rochester, PhD, 84. **CAREER** Assoc prof. **HONORS AND AWARDS** VP, NAm Kant Soc; ed, J Kantian Rev. **MEMBERSHIPS** Soc Women Philos; Soc Analytic Feminism; Am Soc Aesthet. **SELECTED PUBLICATIONS** Auth, pubs on history of modern philosophy, aesthetics, and feminist social and ethical theory; Autonomy and Community: Readings in Contemporary Kantian Social Philosophy, SUNY, 98; Klaus Reich's The Completeness of Kant's Table of Judgments, Stanford. **CONTACT ADDRESS** Philosophy Dept, Colorado State Univ, Fort Collins, CO, 80523.

KNIGHT, CAROLY ANN
PERSONAL Born 0807, Denver, CO, s **DISCIPLINE** THEOLOGY **EDUCATION** Bishop Coll, Dallas, TX, BA, 1977; Union Theological Seminary, New York City, MDiv, 1980; United Theoligical Seminary, Dayton, OH, DMin, 1995. **CAREER** Canaan Bapt Ch, NYC, asst pastor, 1978-87; Philadelphia Bapt Ch, NYC, pastor, 1988-93; Union Theological Seminary, NYC, asst prof, 1989-93; ITC, ATLANTA, ASST PROF, 1995-. **HONORS AND AWARDS** Ebony Magazine, 15 Greatest Black Women Preachers, 1997; Morehouse Coll, Coll of Preachers, 1996; United Negro Coll Fund, Alumni Award, 1993; Natl Coun of Negro Women, Bethune Award, 1991; Negro Professional Women Comm Svc, Laurelton Chap, 1987. **MEMBERSHIPS** Delta Sigma Theta, golden life mem, 1982-; NAACP, 1980-. **SELECTED PUBLICATIONS** "If The Worst Should Come!," sermon, 1997; "When You Talk to Yourself!," sermon, 1997; "How To Deal With Failure," Sister to Sister, devotional, 1993. **CONTACT ADDRESS** Interdenominational Theol Ctr, 700 Martin Luther King Jr Dr, SW Rm 207, Atlanta, GA, 30314-4143.

KNIGHT, DEBORAH
DISCIPLINE PHILOSOPHY **EDUCATION** Univ Carleton, BA; MA; Univ Toronto, PhD. **CAREER** Adj prof. **HONORS AND AWARDS** Assoc ed, Film Philos. **RESEARCH** Philosophy of mind; philosophy of language; philosophy of art. **SELECTED PUBLICATIONS** Auth, Aristotelians on Speed: Paradoxes of Genre in the Context of Cinema, Oxford, 97; Naturalism, Narration, and Critical Perspective: Ken Loach and the Experimental Method, Praeger. 97; Back to Basics: Film/Theory/Aesthetics, J Aesthet, 97; A Poetics of Psychological Explanation, Metaphilos, 97; Making Sense of Genre, 96; co-auth, The Case of the Disappearing Enigma, Philos Lit, 97. **CONTACT ADDRESS** Philosophy Dept, Queen's Univ, Kingston, ON, K7L 3N6. **EMAIL** knightd@post.queensu.ca

KNIGHT, GARY
PERSONAL Born 12/08/1939, St. Joseph, MO, m, 1962, 3 children **DISCIPLINE** LAW **EDUCATION** Stanford Univ, AB, 61; Southern Methodist Univ, JD, 64. **CAREER** Assoc, Nossaman, Waters, Scott, Krueger and Riordan, Los Angeles, Calif, 64-68; from asst prof to assoc prof law, 68-75, PROF LAW, LAW CTR, LA STATE UNIV, BATON ROUGE, 75-; CAMPANILE PROF MARINE RECOURCES LAW, 71-; MEM ADV COMT LAW OF SEA, US GOVT INTER-AGENCY LAW OF SEA TASK FORCE, 72-; ASSOC ED, OCEAN DEVELOP and INT LAW J, 72-; mem exec bd, Law of Sea Inst, 75-80; consult, US Dept State, 74-75; consult, Cent Intel Agency, 77-; chmn Sci and Statist Comt, Gulf of Mex Fishery Mgt Coun, 77-78; PRES, JONATHAN PUBL CO, 81-. **MEMBERSHIPS** Am Bar Asn; Am Soc Int Law. **RESEARCH** Law of the sea; ocean resources. **SELECTED PUBLICATIONS** Auth, An Inventory of the Supreme Court of the Holy-Roman-Empire from the Hauptstaatsarchiv-Stuttgart A-D, J Soc Archivists, Vol 0015, 94; Swedish Archive Bibliographies 1980-1989 J Soc Archivists, Vol 0015, 94. **CONTACT ADDRESS** Law Ctr, Louisiana State Univ, Baton Rouge, LA, 70803.

KNIGHT, HENRY H.
PERSONAL Born 01/14/1948, Atlanta, GA, m, 1979, 1 child **DISCIPLINE** THEOLOGICAL STUDIES **EDUCATION** Emory Univ, PhD, 87, BA, 70; Candler School of Theology, BA, 70. **CAREER** Asst Prof of Evangelism, Saint Paul School of Theol, 93-98; Adjunct Lectr, Candler School of Theol, 86-93. **MEMBERSHIPS** AAR; AETE; WTS; SPS. **RESEARCH** Evangelism, Wesleyan Theology, contemporary and evangelical Theology. **SELECTED PUBLICATIONS** Auth, A Future for Truth: Evangelical Theology in a Postmodern World, Abingdon Press, 97; The Presence of God in the Christian Life: John Wesley and the Means of Grace, in: Pietist and Wesleyan Studies monograph series, Scarecrow Press, 92; co-auth, On Being a Witness: Worship and Holiness in the Wesleyan and Pentecostal Traditions, in: Liturgy and the Moral Self: Humanity at Full Stretch Before God, eds, EB Anderson & BT Morrill, Liturgical Press, 98; True Affection: Biblical Narrative and Evangelical Spirituality, in: The Nature of Confession: Evangelicals and Postliberals in Conversation, eds, TR Phillips & DL Okholm, InterVarsity Press, 96; Worship and Sanctification, Wesleyan Theo J, 97; John Wesley: Mentor for an Evangelical Revival, Wesleyan Theo J, 97. **CONTACT ADDRESS** 4810 Pawnee Dr., Roeland Park, KS, 66205.

KNIKER, CHARLES R.
PERSONAL Born 08/20 1936, Austin, TX, m, 1962, 2 children **DISCIPLINE** RELIGION AND EDUCATION **EDUCATION** Elmhurst College, BA; Eden Sem, BD 62; San Francisco Sem, MA 66; Columbia U Teach College, EdD 69. **CAREER** Assoc Dir acad affs, 98-, Iowa Bd of Regents; vis Prof, 97-, Texas A&M College of Ed; pres and Prof rel and edu, 93-96, Prof, 69-93, Iowa State Univ. **HONORS AND AWARDS** ISU Outstanding Teacher; CI Cert Merit; ISU Fac Citation; 3 Lilly Endows; US Dept Edu Gnt; Global Perspectives Inc Gnt. **MEMBERSHIPS** AERA; AESA; NCR; ASCD; HES. **RESEARCH** Religion and Education. **SELECTED PUBLICATIONS** Auth, Seminary Inertia, Christian Century, 98; ch 1 & 2, Religion and Schooling in Contemporary America: Confronting our Culturalism Pluralism, NY, Garland Pub, 97; Should the Bible be Taught in Public Schools: Yes!, Bible Rev, 95, reprinted, New Conversations, 95; Religion in the Secondary Schools: A Necessary Fact of Life for Today's Adolescents, Fam Perspective, 92; Accommodating the Religious Diversity of Public School Students: Putting the CARTS Before the Horse, Rel and Pub Edu, 88; Reflections on the Continuing Crusade for Common Schools: in: Religious Schooling in America: Hist Insights and Contemporary Concerns, ed, James C Carper, Thomas Hunt, Birmingham AL, Religious Educ Press, 84; Coed, Myth and Reality, 2nd edition, Boston, Allyn and Bacon, 75; Teaching About Religion in the Pub Schools, Bloomington IN, Phi Delta Kappa Educ Foun, 85; The Values of Athletics in Schools: A Continuing Debate, Phi Delta Kappa, 74. **CONTACT ADDRESS** Old Historical Bldg, Texas A&M Univ, E 12th & Grand Ave, Des Moines, IA, 50319. **EMAIL** ckniker@iastate.edu

KNIPE, DAVID MACLAY
PERSONAL Born 11/25/1932, Johnstown, PA, m, 3 children **DISCIPLINE** HISTORY OF RELIGION, SOUTH ASIAN STUDIES **EDUCATION** Cornell Univ, AB, 55; Union Theol Sem, MA, 58; Univ Chicago, MA, 65, PhD(hist relig), 71. **CAREER** Lectr, 67-69, from instr to asst prof, 69-73, assoc prof, 73-79, PROF SOUTH ASIAN STUDIES, UNIV WISMADISON, 79-; Sr res fel, Am Inst Indian Studies, 71-72, and 80. **MEMBERSHIPS** Am Acad Relig; Asn Asian Studies; Am Soc Study Relig. **RESEARCH** Vedic religion; Hinduism Jainism; methodology and religion. **SELECTED PUBLICATIONS** Auth, Asceticism and Healing in Ancient-India in Medicine In The Buddhist Monastery Isis, Vol 0084, 93; Hindu Spirituality in Vedas Through Vedanta, J Am Orient Soc, Vol 0117, 97. **CONTACT ADDRESS** Dept of S Asian Studies, Univ of Wis, 1220 Linden Drive, Madison, WI, 53706-1557.

KNITTER, PAUL FRANCIS
PERSONAL Born 02/25/1939, Chicago, IL **DISCIPLINE** SYSTEMATIC THEOLOGY, COMPARATIVE RELIGIONS **EDUCATION** Divine Word Sem, Ill, BA, 62; Pontif Gregorian Univ, BA, 64, Licentiate, 66; Philipps Univ, WGer, PhD (theol), 72. **CAREER** Asst prof theol, Cath Theol Union, Chicago, 72-75; assoc prof, 75-78, PROF THEOL, XAVIER UNIV, OHIO, 78-. **MEMBERSHIPS** Am Acad Relig; Cath Theol Soc Am; Col Theol Soc; Am Soc Missiology. **RESEARCH** Dialogue among World religions; eastern religions; Christology. **SELECTED PUBLICATIONS** Auth, Pitfalls and Promises for a Global Ethics, J Dharma, Vol 0019, 94; In Face of Mystery in A Constructive Theology, Horizons, Vol 0022, 95. **CONTACT ADDRESS** Dept of Relig, Xavier Univ, 3800 Victory Pky, Cincinnati, OH, 45207-1092.

KNOLL, MICHAEL S.
DISCIPLINE LAW **EDUCATION** Univ Chicago, AB,77; AM,80; PhD,83; JD,84. **CAREER** Prof, Univ Southern Calif; clerked for, Honorable Alex Kozinski, Judge US Ct Appeals 9th Circuit; private practice, New York, Wash, DC; past legal adv to the vice ch, US Int Trade Comn. **RESEARCH** Corporate finance; international trade law; taxation; law & economics. **SELECTED PUBLICATIONS** Auth, An Accretion Corporate Income Tax; Legal & Economic Framework for the Analysis of Injury by the US International Trade Commission & Uncertainty, Efficiency, & the Brokerage Industry. **CONTACT ADDRESS** School of Law, Univ Southern Calif, University Park Campus, Los Angeles, CA, 90089.

KNOPOFF, L.
PERSONAL Los Angeles, CA, m, 1961, 3 children **DISCIPLINE** PHYSICS **EDUCATION** Calif Inst of Technol, PhD, 49. **CAREER** Univ Calif, 50-; Prof, Univ Calif. **HONORS AND AWARDS** Gold Medal of Royal Astron Soc; Medal of Seismological Soc Am; Wiechert Medal of Ger Geophysical Soc; Guggenheim Fel. **MEMBERSHIPS** Nat Acad Sci; Am Acad Arts and Sci; Am Philos Soc; **RESEARCH** Earthquake Physics; Earthquake Prediction Fracture Mechanics; Elasticity Theory. **CONTACT ADDRESS** Physics Dept, Univ of Calif, Los Angleles, CA, 90095. **EMAIL** knopoff@physics.ucla.edu

KNOX, GEORGE F.
PERSONAL Born 10/17/1943, Cleveland, TN, m, 1985 **DISCIPLINE** LAW **EDUCATION** MI State Univ, BS Zoology 1966; Univ of Miami School of Law, JD 1973. **CAREER** Univ of Miami School of Business Admin, lecturer 1973-74; City of Miami, FL, asst city Attorney 1974-75; Univ of AR Fayetteville, asst prof of law 1975-76; Univ of Miami School of Law, lecturer 1978-80; Nova Univ Center for the Study of Law, lecturer 1980-82; City of Miami, FL, city Attorney and dir of law dept 1976-82; Paul, Landy Beiley & Harper PA, partner 1982-84; Long & Knox, partner 1984-; Kubicki Draper Gallagher, Miami, FL, Attorney 1990-. **HONORS AND AWARDS** Jaycees Outstanding Young Men of Amer 1976; Miami-Dade Chamber of Commerce Awd of Outstanding Contribution to Social and Economic Development 1977; Black Lawyers' Assn Virgil Hawkins Achievement Award 1977; Alpha Phi Alpha Fraternity Achievement Award 1977; participant "Law and Justice in Today's Society" seminar sponsored by Natl Endowment for the Humanities Harvard Univ 1978; FL Jr Coll at Jackson ville Community Awareness Award; Beta Beta Lambda Chap Alpha Phi Alpha Fraternity Community Service Award 1981; NAACP Appreciation Award 1981; Northwest Council of Jacksonville Chamber of Commerce Jacksonville Achiever Award 1986. **MEMBERSHIPS** Mem FL, Natl, Amer, DC Bar Assns; mem, Natl Inst of Municipal Law Officers; mem Assn of Amer Law Schools, Black Lawyers Assn, FL League of Cities, Assn of Amer Trial Lawyers, Acad of FL Trial Lawyers; mem US Dist Court Southern Dist of FL, US Court of Appeals for Fifth Circuit, United States Supreme Court; mem NAACP; bd dirs Miami-Dade Community College Foundation Inc; mem Greater Miami Chamber of Commerce; mem FL Memorial College Ctr of Excellence; bd dirs YMCA of Greater Miami; Member Dade County Blue Ribbon Committee; member of board of trustees, Florida Memorial College; board of directors, United Way; member, The Miami Coalition for a Drug-Free Community. **SELECTED PUBLICATIONS** Numerous publications. **CONTACT ADDRESS** Kubicki, Draper, Gallagher & McGrane, 25 W Flagler St, Miami, FL, 33130.

KOBACH, KRIS W.
DISCIPLINE LAW **EDUCATION** Harvard Univ, BA; Oxford Univ, MPhil, PhD; Yale Sch Law, JD. **CAREER** Law clerk, Judge Deanell Reece Tacha, US Court Appeals; assoc prof **HONORS AND AWARDS** Ed, Yale Law J. **RESEARCH** Constitutional law and theory; American legal history. **SELECTED PUBLICATIONS** Auth, The Referendum: Direct Democracy in Switzerland, Dartmouth, 94; Political Capital: The Motives, Tactics, and Goals of Politicized Businesses in South Africa, Univ Am, 90; pubs on political science, constitutional law, and legal history. **CONTACT ADDRESS** Law Dept, Univ of Missouri, Kansas City, 5100 Rockhill Rd, Kansas City, MO, 64110-2499. **EMAIL** kobachk@umkc.edu

KOCH, GLENN A.
DISCIPLINE NEW TESTAMENT STUDIES **EDUCATION** Marshall Univ, BA; E Baptist Theol Sem, BD, ThM; Univ Pa, MA, PhD. **CAREER** Prof, E Baptist Theol Sem. **MEMBERSHIPS** Mem, Soc of Biblical Lit; Philadelphia Sem on Christian Origins; Nat Assn of Baptist Prof(s) of Rel. **SELECTED PUBLICATIONS** Co-auth, Learning to Read New Testament Greek. **CONTACT ADDRESS** Eastern Baptist Theol Sem, 6 Lancaster Ave, Wynnewood, PA, 19096.

KOCH, MICHAEL
DISCIPLINE PHILOSOPHY **EDUCATION** Bard Col, BA; SUNY Albany, DA; Univ IL, PhD. **CAREER** Adj lctr, Univ Albany, 94; adj lctr, SUNY Oneonta, 93-. **RESEARCH** Hist of philos: pragmatism, citical theory; continental philos: hermeneutics, phenomenology; 20th century soc and polit philos; philos of soc sci(s), tech; aesthetics. **SELECTED PUBLICATIONS** Auth, Marco's Letters: The EZLN and the Rhetoric of Nationalism in the age of Global Capitalism; The Manikin and Its Masks: The Negative Hermeneutics of Henry Adams; Aristotle's Posterior Analytics: Reconstructive Rationality for Social Scientific Inquiry. **CONTACT ADDRESS** SUNY Col at Oneonta, Oneonta, NY, 13820. **EMAIL** Shradedw@Oneonta.edu

KODDERMANN, ACHIM
DISCIPLINE PHILOSOPHY **EDUCATION** Johannes-Gutenberg-Univ; BA; MA, 88; PhD, 91. **CAREER** Vis prof, Univ Denver, 89-90; counsellor/corp planner/pers asst to CEO, Nat Ger Pub Broadcasting, 90-93; asst instr, Univ ME, 90-93; asst prof, SUNY Oneonta, 93-96; vis prof, Sripatum Univ, 96; assoc prof, SUNY Oneonta, 96-. **HONORS AND AWARDS** Richard Siegfried Fac Prize Acad Excellence, SUNY Oneonta, 95; fellow, NEH summer inst PA State Univ, 94; rep hum, Ctr Environ Studies, 89-93. **MEMBERSHIPS** APA; Deutsche Kant Gesellschaft ev.; Int Kant Soc; Dante Soc, Ger Sec;, DAIMON, Int Soc Neoplatonic Studies; Int Soc Study Europ Ideas; Soc Ancient Gr Philos; Typographe. **RESEARCH** Ethics: applied ethics, environmental ethics, professional and business ethics, media ethics; continental philos: hermeneutics, Ger idealism, romanticism, phenomenology, mod French philos; philos of law ; sci, tech and soc studies. **SELECTED PUBLICATIONS** Auth, Why the Medieval Idea of a Community-Oriented University is Still Modern, Educ Change, 95; World Debt and the Human Condition Structural Adjustment and the Right to Development (rev) in Studies in Human Rights, Greenwood, 94, and Denver Jour Int Law & Policy, 95; Television as a Moral Medium and as a Factor in an Information Society in The Image of Technology, Soc Interdisciplinary Study Soc Imagery, 94;Jere P Surber--Language and German Idealism, Fichte's Linguististic Philosophy Daimon, Revista de Filosofea, 94. **CONTACT ADDRESS** SUNY Col at Oneonta, Oneonta, NY, 13820. **EMAIL** Koeddea@Oneonta.edu

KOEGLER, HANS-HERBERT
PERSONAL Born 01/13/1960, Darmstadt, Germany **DISCIPLINE** PHILOSOPHY **EDUCATION** Goethe Univ Ger, PhD. **CAREER** Asst prof, Univ Ill, 91-97; vis scholar, Boston Univ, 97; asst prof, Univ N Fla, 97. **HONORS AND AWARDS** Honorary Fac Mem, Univ Catamarca Arg; Fel of the Ger Nat Fel Orgn. **MEMBERSHIPS** APA; Critical Theory Roundtable. **RESEARCH** Philosophy of language; Interpretive Theory; Social Philosophy. **SELECTED PUBLICATIONS** Auth, Die macht des Dialogs: Kritische Hermeneutik nach Gadamer, Foucault, und Rorty, 92; Michel Foucault: Ein anti-humanistischer Aufklarer, 94; The Power of Dialogue: Critical Hermeneutics after Gadamer and Foucault, 96; co-ed, Empathy and Agency: The Problem of Understanding in the Human Sciences,99. **CONTACT ADDRESS** History, Philosophy and Religious Studies, Univ N Fla, 4587 St John's Bluff, Jacksonville, FL, 32224. **EMAIL** hkoegler@gw.unf.edu

KOENIG, THOMAS ROY
PERSONAL Born 04/07/1934, Detroit, Mich, m, 1971, 4 children **DISCIPLINE** PHILOSOPHY, THEOLOGY **EDUCATION** Villanova Univ, BA, 57; Colegium Int Augustinianum, Rome, 61; DePaul Univ, MA, 65; Cath Univ Louvain, PhD(philos), 67. **CAREER** Teacher math & Latin, Mendel Cath High Sch, Chicago, 61-64; asst prof philos, Tolentine Col, 65-70; asst prof, 70-74, Assoc Prof Philos, Purdue Univ, Calumet Campus, 74-, Nat Found for Humanities fel philos, 70; Purdue Res Found fel, 71; participant, Ind Comt for Humanities & humanists, Midwest Ctr, 73-74; Nat Found for Humanities grant,

77-79; Fulbright fel, Belgium, 65-67. **MEMBERSHIPS** AAUP; Am Philos Asn; Am Catholic Philols Asn; Southern Soc Philos and Psychol. **RESEARCH** Problem of maturity in existential philosophy and psychology; Paul Ricoeur's interpretation of Freud; problems of leisure in a contemporary world. **SELECTED PUBLICATIONS** Auth, The Philosophy of Georges Bastide, Martinus Nijhoff, The Hague, 71; An Introduction to Ethics, MSS, 74. **CONTACT ADDRESS** Dept of Philos, Purdue Univ, 2233 171st St, Hammond, IN, 46323-2094.

KOERTGE, NORETTA
PERSONAL Born 10/07/1935, Olney, IL **DISCIPLINE** PHILOSOPHY OF SCIENCE, HISTORY OF SCIENCE **EDUCATION** Univ Ill, BS, 55, MS, 56; London Univ, PhD(philos of sci), 69. **CAREER** Instr chem, Elmhurst Col, 60-63; head chem sect, Am Col for Girls, Instanbul, Turkey, 63-64; lectr philos of sci, Ont Inst for Studies Educ, 68-69; asst prof, 70-73, assoc prof, 74-81, PROF HIST and PHILOS OF SCI, IND UNIX, BLOOMINGTON, 81-; AM REP, BRIT SOC FOR PHILOS OF SCI, 76-. **MEMBERSHIPS** Philos Sci Asn. **RESEARCH** Theories of scientific method; historical development of philosophy of science; Poppers philosophy of science. **SELECTED PUBLICATIONS** Auth. The Myth of the Framework, In Defense of Science and Philosophy of Science, Vol 0064, 97. **CONTACT ADDRESS** Indiana Univ, Bloomington, 130 Goodbody Hall, Bloomington, IN, 47401.

KOESTENBAUM, PETER
PERSONAL Born 04/06/1928, Berlin, Germany, m, 4 children **DISCIPLINE** PHILOSOPHY **EDUCATION** Stanford Univ, BA, 49; Harvard Univ, MA, 51; Boston Univ, PhD, 58. **CAREER** Prof, phil, 54-88, San Jose St Univ, CA **HONORS AND AWARDS** Outstanding Prof CA St Col & Univ System, 69 **MEMBERSHIPS** APA **RESEARCH** Philos; business **SELECTED PUBLICATIONS** Auth, Leadership: The Inner Side of Greatness, Jossey Bass. **CONTACT ADDRESS** 3927 Fairbreeze Circle, Westlake Village, CA, 91361. **EMAIL** pkipeter@ix.netcom.com

KOESTER, CRAIG R.
PERSONAL Born 08/25/1953, Northfield, MN, m, 1979, 2 children **DISCIPLINE** THEOLOGY **EDUCATION** Union Theolog Sem, PhD, 86; Luther Theolog Sem, M.Div, 80; St Olaf Col, BA, 76. **CAREER** Assoc prof New Testament, Luther Theolog Sem, 91-; asst prof New Testament, Luther Theolog Sem, 86-91; interim Pastor, Trinity Luth Church, NY City, 85-86; asst Pastor, Immanuel Luth Church, Princeton, MN, 80-83. **HONORS AND AWARDS** Who's Who in Relig; Associated Church Pr Award for Bibl Exposition, 91; Who's Who in Bibl Studies & Archaeology; Bruce Prize for New Testament Study, Luther Theolog Sem, 80 **MEMBERSHIPS** Center of Theolog Inquiry Member. **SELECTED PUBLICATIONS** Millennial Hope and the Book of Revelation, Dialog 37, forthcoming; Jesus' Resurrection as Presupposition for the New Testament, in The Quest for Jesus and the Christian Faith, Luther Sem, 97; Symbolism in the Fourth Gospel: Meaning, Mystery, Community, Fortress Pr, 95; The Unshakable Kingdom: A Study of Hebrews, Augsburg, 93. **CONTACT ADDRESS** Dept of Theology, Luther Sem, 2481 Como Ave, St Paul, MN, 55108.

KOESTER, HELMUT
PERSONAL Born 12/18/1926, Hamburg, Germany, m, 1953, 4 children **DISCIPLINE** NEW TESTAMENT STUDIES **EDUCATION** Univ Marlburg, Ger, D Theol, 54. **CAREER** Instr, Univ Heidelberg, Ger, 54-56, asst prof, 56-58; prof of New Testament Studies and Ecclesiastical Hist, Harvard Univ, 58-98. **HONORS AND AWARDS** Dr Theol, hon, Univ Geneva, Switzerland, 84. **MEMBERSHIPS** Soc of Biblical Lit; Societas Novi Testamenti Studiorum; Am Academy of Arts and Sciences. **RESEARCH** Early-Christian lit; archaeology. **SELECTED PUBLICATIONS** Auth, Athens A and Isthmia in Helmut Koester and Ann Graham Brock, eds, Archaeological Resources for New Testament Studies, vol 1 and 2, Trinity Press Int, 94; Archaologie und Paulus in Thessalonike, in Lukas Bormann, et al, eds, Religious Propaganda and Missionary Competition in the New Testament World: Essays Honoring Dieter Georgi, Brill, 94; History, Culture, and Religion of the Hellenistic Age, Introduction to the New Testament, vol 1, 2nd ed, De Gruyter, 95; Jesus' Presence in the Early Church, Cristianesimo nella Storia 15, 94; The Red Hall in Pergamon, in Michael White and O Larry Yarbrough, The Social World of the Early Christians: Essays in Honor of Wayne A Meeks, Fortress, 95; Ephesos in Early Christian Literature, in Ephesos: Metropolis of Asia, Harvard Theol Studies 41, Trinity Press Int, 95; The Sayings of Q and Their Image of Jesus, in William L Peterson et al, eds, Sayings of Jesus: Canonical and Non-Canonical: Essays in Honor of Tjitze Baarda, Brill, 97; Philippi at the Time of Paul and After His Death, with Charalambos Bakitzis, Trinity Press Int, 98; several other publications. **CONTACT ADDRESS** 45 Francis Ave, Cambridge, MA, 02138.

KOHL, MARVIN
PERSONAL Born 05/19/1932, New York, NY, m, 1955, 4 children **DISCIPLINE** PHILOSOPHY **EDUCATION** City Col New York, BA, 54; NY Univ, MA, 58, PhD(philos), 66. **CAREER** Instr philos, Long Island Univ, 61-65; from asst profto assoc prof, 65-73, PROF PHILOS, STATE UNIV NY COL FREDONIA, 73-; NIH FEL, MASS INST TECH, 70-71; CONTRIB ED, FREE INQUIRY, 80-. **RESEARCH** Ethical theory and medical ethics. **SELECTED PUBLICATIONS** Auth, Enforcing a Vision of Community in the Role of the Test Oath in Missouri Reconstruction, Civil War History, Vol 0040, 94. **CONTACT ADDRESS** Dept of Philos State, Univ of New York, Col Fredonia, NY, 14063.

KOHN, RICHARD
PERSONAL Born 07/20/1948, New York, NY, m, 1 child **DISCIPLINE** BUDDHIST STUDIES **EDUCATION** Univ Wisc, BA, MA, PhD, 98. **CAREER** Lectr, 90, Univ Calif; adj assoc cur, 90-91, Asian Art Museum of SF; vis asst prof, 92, Indiana Univ; res assoc, 93-, Ctr for South Asian Stud, lectr, 99-Univ Calif, Berkeley. **HONORS AND AWARDS** Phi Beta Kappa; Soc Sci Res Coun; Diss, abroad fel; Fulbright-Hays Fel; Red Ribbon, Amer Film Fest. **MEMBERSHIPS** AAR. **RESEARCH** Himalayan art; Tibetan relig & cult; Buddhist ritual. **SELECTED PUBLICATIONS** Art, Trance Dancers and Aeroplanes: Montage and Metaphor in Ethnographic Film, 1942-1992, 50 Years after Balinese Character. Yearbk Visual Anthropology, IUAES, vol 1, Firenze: Angelo Pontecorboli Editore, 93; coauth, Paramsukha-Chakrasamvara and Vajravarahi, Seated Vairocana with Attendants, Asian Art Mus: Selected Works, Univ Wash Press, 94; art, The Ritual Preparation of a Tibetan Mandala, Mandala & Landscape, Printworld, 97; art, A Rite of Empowerment, An Offering of Torma, A Prayer to the God of the Plain, Relig of Tibet in Pract, Princeton Univ Press, 97; art, Himalayan Buddhism, Encycl of Women & World Relig, Macmillan, 98. **CONTACT ADDRESS** 454 Beloit Ave, Kensington, CA, 94708-1114. **EMAIL** rjkohn1@socrates.berkeley.edu

KOLAK, DANIEL
PERSONAL Born 06/30/1955, Zagreb, Croatia, m, 1 child **DISCIPLINE** PHILOSOPHY **EDUCATION** Univ Md, BA; MA, 81; PhD, 86. **CAREER** Asst prof, Touson State Univ, 86-87; asst prof, Univ of Wisconsin, 87-89; dir, Cognitive Sci Lab, William Poterson Univ, 95-; CHAIRMAN PHILOS DEPT, PROF, WILLAIM POTERSON UNIV, 95-. **MEMBERSHIPS** APA. **RESEARCH** Philosophy of Mind; Philosophy of Science; Cognitive Science; Mathematics and Logic, Philosophy of Language; Philosophy of Art. **SELECTED PUBLICATIONS** Auth, The Thousand and One Question, 94; In Search of God: The Language and Logic of Belief, 94; Lovers of Wisdom, 97; In Search of Myself: Life, Death, and Personal Identity, 98; From the Presocratics to the Present: a Personal Odyssey, 98; Wittgenstein Tractatus, 98; coauth, Wisdom Without Answers, 98; ed, From Palto to Wittgenstein, 94; The Mayfield Anthology of Western Philosophy, 98; Philosophical Bridges, 99; co-ed, The Experience of Philosophy. **CONTACT ADDRESS** 38 White Birch Dr, Pomona, NY, 10970. **EMAIL** kolardan@msn.com

KOLASNY, JUDETTE M.
PERSONAL Born 10/15/1938, Tiffini, OH, s **DISCIPLINE** THEOLOGY **EDUCATION** Marquette Univ, PhD, 85. **MEMBERSHIPS** CBS, CTSA, SBL. **RESEARCH** Gospel of John **CONTACT ADDRESS** 1007 N Marshall St #314, Milwaukee, WI, 53202-3225.

KOLB, DAVID ALAN
PERSONAL Born 04/15/1939, Brooklyn, NY **DISCIPLINE** PHILOSOPHY **EDUCATION** Fordham Univ, AB, 63, MA, 65; Woodstock Col, PhL, 64; Yale Univ, MPhil, 70, PhD, 72. **CAREER** Instr philos, Fordham Univ, 64-67, asst prof, Univ Chicago, 72-77; assoc prof Philos & chmn dept, 77-88, CHARLES A. DANA PROFESSOR OF PHILOSOPHY, BATES COL, 89-. **MEMBERSHIPS** Am Philos Asn; Hegel Soc Am; Heidegger Circle. **RESEARCH** Hist of philos; philos of art, hypertext; German philos. **SELECTED PUBLICATIONS** Critique of Pure Modernity, Univ of Chicago Press; Postmodern Sophistications, Univ of Chicago Press; Socrates in the Labyrinth, Eastgate Systems. **CONTACT ADDRESS** Dept of Philos, Bates Col, 75 Campus Ave, Lewiston, ME, 04240-6018. **EMAIL** dkolb@bates.edu

KOLB, ROBERT
PERSONAL Born 06/17/1941, Fort Dodge, IA, m, 1965 **DISCIPLINE** REFORMATION HISTORY, HISTORY OF THEOLOGY **EDUCATION** Concordia Sr Col, BA, 63; Concordia Sem, BD, 67, STM, 68, MDiv, 72; Univ Wis-Madison, MA, 69, PhD(hist), 73. **CAREER** Exec dir, Found Reformation Res and res fel, 72-77; ASST PROF RELIG and HIST, CONCORDIA COL, 77-; Part-time instr church hist, Concordia Sem, 72-77; ASSOC ED, SIXTEENTH CENTURY J, 73-. **MEMBERSHIPS** Am Soc Reformation Res; Am Soc Church Hist; Sixteenth Century Studies Conf; Am Acad Relig Res. **RESEARCH** Lutheran church history 1550-1600; history of piety or popular Christianity; 16th century martyrology. **SELECTED PUBLICATIONS** Auth, Bodying the Word in Textual Resurrections in the Martyrological Narratives of Foxe, Crespin, Beze And Aubigne Sixteenth Century J, Vol 0024, 93; The Influence of Luther, Martin Galatians Commentary of 1535 on Later 16th Century Lutheran Commentaries on Galatians, Archiv Fur Reformationsgeschichte-Archive For Reformation History, Vol 0084, 93; Problems of Authority in the Reformation Debates Church Hist, Vol 0063, 94; Sermon and Society in Lutheran Orthodoxy in Ulm, 1640-1740, Am Hist Rev, Vol 0099, 94; Andreae,Johann,Valentin Collected Works, Vol 7 in Veri Christianismi Solidaeque Philosophiae Libertas, Sixteenth Century J, Vol 0026, 95; God Gift of Martyrdom in the Early Reformation Understanding of Dying for the Faith, Church Hist, Vol 0064, 95; Whether Secular Government Has the Right to Wield the Sword in Matters of Faith, A Controversy in Nurnberg, 1530, Church History, Vol 0066, 97; Obituaries, Autobiographical Writings and Cosmonexus of Andreae,Johann,Valentin, Sixteenth Century J, Vol 0028, 97. **CONTACT ADDRESS** Concordia Col, Minnesota, Hamline and Marshall Ave St, St Paul, MN, 55104.

KOLDEN, MARC
DISCIPLINE SYSTEMATIC THEOLOGY **EDUCATION** Univ Harvard, BA, 62; Luther Theol Sem, 66; Univ Chicago, MA, PhD, 69, 76. **CAREER** Instr, Hamma Sch Theol, 71-73; asst prof, 73-78; , assoc prof, 81; prof, 89-; acad dean, 96. **HONORS AND AWARDS** Assoc pastor, Our Redeemer Lutheran Church; dir, Northern Rockies Inst of Theol, 78-81. **SELECTED PUBLICATIONS** Auth, Christ Our Sure Foundation: Sermons for Pentecost, 95; Living the Faith, 92; coauth, co-ed, Called and Ordained: Lutheran Perspectives on the Office of Ministry, 90. **CONTACT ADDRESS** Dept of Systematic Theology, Luther Sem, 2481 Como Ave, St. Paul, MN, 55108.

KOLLAR, NATHAN RUDOLPH
PERSONAL Born 07/20/1938, Braddock, PA, m, 1972, 3 children **DISCIPLINE** RELIGIOUS STUDIES, HISTORY **EDUCATION** St Bonaventure Univ, BA, 60; Cath Univ Am, STL, 64, STD, 67; Univ Notre Dame, MA, 68. **CAREER** Instr theol, Whitefriars Hall, 64-67; asst prof, Washington Theol Coalition, 68-71; asst prof relig studies, St Thomas Univ, 71-74; assoc prof, 74-82, PROF RELIG STUDIES, ST JOHN FISHER COL, 82-; CHMN DEPT, 79-; Consult relig educ, Div Adult Educ, US Cath Conf, 71-73; dir relig, Ctr Study Relig N Am, 73-77; dir relig and educ, Resource Ctr Death Educ, 77. **MEMBERSHIPS** Am Acad Relig; Col Theol Soc; Soc Sci Study Relig; Can Soc Study Relig; Forum for Death Educ and Coun. **RESEARCH** North American culture and religion; dying, death and religion; eschatology. **SELECTED PUBLICATIONS** Auth, Death in the Midst of Life in Perspectives on Death From Christianity and Depth-Psychology, Horizons, Vol 0020, 93. **CONTACT ADDRESS** St John Fisher Col, Rochester, NY, 14618.

KOMONCHAK, JOSEPH ANDREW
PERSONAL Born 03/13/1939, Nyack, NY **DISCIPLINE** THEOLOGY **EDUCATION** St Josephs Sem, NY, AB, 60, Pontif Gregorian Univ, Rome, STL, 64; Union Theol Sem, NY, PhD(theol), 76. **CAREER** Assoc prof theol, St Josephs Sem, NY, 67-77; assoc prof theol, Cath Univ Am, 77-80. Mem, bd dirs, Cath Theol Soc Am, 73-75. **MEMBERSHIPS** Cath Theol Soc Am; Am Acad Relig. **RESEARCH** Thought of John Henry Newman; ecclesiology and ministry; theology of social mission of the Church. **SELECTED PUBLICATIONS** Auth, The Vatican Council Theme of Reception in French, Theol Studies, Vol 0055, 94; The Synod of Bishops in Papers and Documents in Italian, Cath Hist Rev, Vol 0080, 94; Paul-Vi and Ecclesiological Problems at the Council, Papers From the September-1986 Brescia Colloquium Italian, Catho Histl Rev, Vol 0080, 94; Paul-Vi and the Relationship Between the Church and the World at Vatican-Ii, Papers From the September-1989 Rome Symposium Italian, Cath Hist Rev, Vol 0080, 94; Papers Presented at the Central Preparatory Commission for the Vatican-Ii Ecumenical Council January-June, 1962 in Italian, Cath Hist Rev, Vol 0080, 94; Ecclesiologia in Questions on Methodology and a Proposition in Italian, Theol Studies, Vol 0056, 95; The Origin and Development of Sources Chretiennes in Edition of the Fathers of the Church in the 20th-Century in French, Theol Studies, Vol 0057, 96; Guests in Their Own House, The Women of Vatican-Ii, Horizons, Vol 0024, 97; Paul-Vi and Episcopal Collegiality in Colloquio-Internazionale-Di-Studio, Brescia, September 25-26-27, 92 Italian, Cath Hist Rev, Vol 0083, 97. **CONTACT ADDRESS** 3711 Kennedy St, Hyattsville, MD, 20783.

KONVITZ, MILTON R.
PERSONAL Born 03/12/1908, Israel, m, 1942, 1 child **DISCIPLINE** CONSTITUTIONAL LAW **EDUCATION** NYU, JD, 1930; Cornell, PhD, 1933. **CAREER** Private practice, Newark, NJ, 33-46; Newark Housing Authority, gen counsel, 38-43; NJ State Housing Authority, gen counsel, 43-45; NYU Law Sch, lectr, 38-46; NAACP Legal Def Fund, asst gen counsel, 43-46. **HONORS AND AWARDS** Honorary degrees from Syracuse Univ, Rutgers Univ, Yeshiva Univ, Jewish Thelo Sem, Hebrew Union Col; awards from NYU, Hebrew Univ. **MEMBERSHIPS** Amer Academy of Arts and Sciences, Fel. **RESEARCH** Constitutional law **SELECTED PUBLICATIONS** Auth, Constitution and Civil Rights, Expanding Liberties, Immigration and Civil Rights, Alien and Asiatic in American Law, Judaism and the American Idea, Torah and Constitution. **CONTACT ADDRESS** 150 Norwood Ave, Oakhurst, NJ, 07755-1604.

KOONTZ, GAYLE GERBER
PERSONAL Born 11/19/1946, Bluffton, OH, m, 1969, 3 children **DISCIPLINE** THEOLOGICAL ETHICS; SOCIAL ETHICS **EDUCATION** Boston Univ, PhD. **CAREER** Instr, Goshen Col, 81-82; to PROF THEOLOGY AND ETHICS, ASSOCIATED MENNONITE BIBLICAL SEM, ELKHART, IN, 82-, dean, 90-94, president, 94-95. **MEMBERSHIPS** Am Academy of Relig; Soc of Christian Ethics. **CONTACT ADDRESS** Associated Mennonite Biblical Sem, 3003 Benham Ave., Elkhart, IN.

KOPACZYNSKI, GERMAIN
PERSONAL Born 04/24/1946, Chelsea, MA **DISCIPLINE** PHILOSOPHY, THEOLOGY **EDUCATION** St Hyacinth Col, BA, 69; Seraphicum, Rome, STL, 75; Boston Col, PhD, 77; Alphonsianum, Rome, STD , 92. **CAREER** Asst Prof Philos, St Hyacinth Col Sem, 76-, Asst Acad Dean, 82. **HONORS AND AWARDS** Fr Adam Zajdel fel, St Hyacinth Clg and Sem. **MEMBERSHIPS** Am Philos Asn; Am Cath Philos Asn. **RESEARCH** Philos of God; Medieval philos; linguistic philos; feminism; biomedical ethics. **SELECTED PUBLICATIONS** Auth, Van Buren e le frontiers del linguaggio, Citta di Vita, 75; Some Franciscans on St Thomas' Essence-Existence Doctrin, Franciscan Studies 38, Ann XVI, 78; Linguistic Ramifications of the Essence-Existence Debate, Univ Press Am, 79; The essence-existence question in a linguistic key, Miscellanea Francescana 80, 80; ed, St Bonaventure: Sermon I on the Annunciation, 3/81 & St Bonaventure: Sermon II on the Assumption, 7-8/81, The Cord; auth, Review of Joseph Donceel's The Searching Mind: An Introduction to a Philosophy of God, Miscellanea Francescana 81, 81; Abstract of Linguistic Ramifications of the Essence-Existence Debate,The Monist 65, 82; Abortion's Mother: Early Works of Simone de Beauvoir, Faith and Reason, winter 94; No Higher Court: Contemporary Feminism and the Right to Abortion, Univ Scranton Press, 95; A Fight for the Work of God, Homiletic and Pastoral Rev, 7/95; auth, Review of Brad Stetson, The Silent Subject: Reflections on the Unborn in American Culture, Ethics, 4/97. **CONTACT ADDRESS** 159 Washington St, Boston, MA, 02135-4325. **EMAIL** frgermai@nchcenter.org

KOPAS, JANE
PERSONAL Garfield, NJ **DISCIPLINE** PHILOSOPHY OF RELIGION **EDUCATION** St Bonaventure Univ, BS, 66, MA, 71; Grad Theol Union, PhD(theol), 76. **CAREER** Asst prof relig, Col Wooster, 75-78; ASST PROF THEOL and RELIG STUDIES, UNIV SCRANTON, 78-. **MEMBERSHIPS** Am Acad Relig; Cath Theol Soc Am. **SELECTED PUBLICATIONS** Auth, The Voice of the Turtledove in New Catholic Women in Europe, Horizons, Vol 0021, 94; An Introduction to New-Testament Christology, Horizons, Vol 0022, 95; The Struggle for Theology Soul in Contesting Scripture in Christology, Horizons, Vol 0023, 96. **CONTACT ADDRESS** Dept of Theol and Relig Studies, Univ of Scranton, 800 Linden St, Scranton, PA, 18510-4501.

KOPELMAN, LORETTA M.
PERSONAL Born 09/05/1938, New York, NY, m, 2 children **DISCIPLINE** PHILOSOPHY, MEDICINE **EDUCATION** Syracuse Univ, BA, 60, MA, 62; Univ Rochester, NY, PhD, 66. **CAREER** Asst lect, 65-66, Univ Rochester; lect, 67-68, Univ Tenn; lect, 68-69, New Haven Col; lect, 71, Univ MD; assoc lect, 71-73 instr, 74-76, asst prof, 76-78,, Sch of Med, Jr Humanist Award, 73-74, fel, Nat Endowment for the Hum, 74-76, Univ Rochester; dir, 78-84, Hum Prog, Sch of Med; assoc prof, 78-85, chmn, 84-, prof, 85- Dept of Med Hum, E Carolina Univ, **HONORS AND AWARDS** Founder, Dept of Med Hum, E Carolina Univ Sch of Med, 78; Pres, Soc for Health and Human Values, 97-98; founding Pres, Am Soc for Bioethics & Humanities, 97-98; ed bds: J of Med & Philos, The Encycl of Bioethics (2nd ed), mem, exec coun, Am Asn for the Advancement of Philos & Psychiatry, & founding bd mem, Am Soc for Bioethics and Humanities. **MEMBERSHIPS** Phi Beta Kappa; Am Soc for Bioethics and Humanities; Asn for the Advancement of Philos and Psychiatry; APA; Soc for Health and Human Values; Aristotelian Soc; Am Asn of Univ Profs; Phi Kappa Phi; Theta Beta Phi; Asn for Fac in the Med Hum; Hastings Ctr; Kennedy Inst of Ethics; The European Soc for Philos of Med & Health Care; Soc for Law & Med; Am Asn of Bioethics; the Int Asn of Bioethics; Soc for Bioethics Consultation. **RESEARCH** Publications reflect interests in the rights and welfare of patients in research subjects including children and vulnerable populations, death and dying, moral problems in psychiatry, research ethics and other issues in philosophy of medicine and bioethics, as well as cross-cultural issues such as female genital cutting and duties to be truthful. **SELECTED PUBLICATIONS** Auth, Medical Futility, Encyclopedia of Applied Ethics, 3, 97; auth, Female Circumcism and Genital Mutilation, Encycl of Applied Ethics, 3, 97; auth, Medicine's Challenge to Relativism: The Case of Female Genital Mutilation, Philos of Med & Bioethics: A Twenty-Year Retrospective and Critical Appraisal, Kluwer Acad Pubs, vol 50, 97; coauth, Preventing and Managing Unwarranted Biases Against Patients, Surgical Ethics, Oxford Univ Press, 98; coauth, The US Health Delivery System: Inefficient and Unfair to Children, Am J of Law & Med, XXIII: 2-3, 97; coauth, Moral and Social Issues Regarding Pregnant Women Who Use and Abuse Drugs, Obstetrics and Gynecology Clinics of North Am, 98; auth, The Best-Interests Standard as Threshold, Ideal, and Standard of Reasonableness, The J of Med & Philos, 22:3, 97; auth, Children and Bioethics: Uses and Abuses of the Best-Interest Standard, Intro, The J of Med & Philos, 22:3, 97; auth, AIDS Activists and Their Legacy for Research Policy, in Health Care Ethics: Critical Issues for the 21st Century, Aspen Pubs, Inc., 98; coauth, William Carlos Williams and the Company Doctor, Acad Med, 73:10, 98; Bioethics and Humanities: What Makes Us One Field?, J of Med & Phiolos, 23:4, 98. **CONTACT ADDRESS** Dept of Medical Humanities, East Carolina Univ, Brody 2S-17, Greenville, NC, 27858. **EMAIL** kopelman@brody.med.ecu.edu

KOPERSKI, VERONICA
PERSONAL Born 08/07/1940, Detroit, MI, s **DISCIPLINE** THEOLOGY **EDUCATION** Cath Univ Louvain Belgium, PhD 91, STD 92. **CAREER** SS Cyril Methodius Sem, asst prof, 92-93; Barry Univ, asst prof, assoc prof, 93 to 96-. **HONORS AND AWARDS** Who's Who Among Amer Tchrs; CU Doctoral Fel. **MEMBERSHIPS** SBL; CBA; IBR; FCCS. **RESEARCH** New Testament and Letters of Paul. **SELECTED PUBLICATIONS** Auth, Scriptural Reflections, Jour of Liturgical Conf, 98; The Scriptures: Eastertime, Liturgy: From Ashes to Fire, Jour of Liturgical Conf; Serving the Word, in Homily service, Liturgical Conf, 95; rev, Gordon D. Fee's, Paul's Letter to the Philippians, NICNT, 95, Louvain Studies, 96; Knowledge of Christ and Knowledge of God in the Corinthian Correspondence, The Corinthian Correspondence, ed, Reimund Bieringer, Leuven, Peeters, 96; The Knowledge of Christ Jesus My Lord, The High Christology of Philippians 3:7-11, Biblical Theol and Exegesis, Kampen, Kok Pharos, 96. **CONTACT ADDRESS** Dept of Theology and Philosophy, Barry Univ, 11300 N E Second Ave, Miami, FL, 33027. **EMAIL** koperski@jeanne.barry.edu

KORN, HAROLD LEON
PERSONAL Born 06/25/1929, Bronx, NY **DISCIPLINE** LAW **EDUCATION** Cornell Univ, AB, 51; Columbia Univ, LLB, 54. **CAREER** Law clerk to Judge Stanley H Fuld, Court Appeals State NY, 54-56; dir res, NY State Adv Comt Practice & Procedure, 56-60; assoc dir legis drafting res fund, Columbia Univ, 61-63, lectr law, Law Sch, 62-63, adj assoc prof, 63-65; prof, State Univ NY Buffalo, 65-68; prof, Sch Law, NY Univ, 68-71; Prof Law, Columbia Univ, 71-, Spec consult criminal conspiracy, Am Law Inst Model Penal Code, 60; civil practice revision, NY State Senate, 60-62. **RESEARCH** Civil procedure; evidence; jurisdiction of federal courts. **SELECTED PUBLICATIONS** Coauth, Comments on procedural reform-preliminary motions in New York: A critique, 4/57; The treatment of inchoate crimes in the model penal code of the American Law Institute: Attempt, Solicitation and conspiracy, part 1, 4/61, part 2, 6/61; Catastrophic accidents in government Programs, Nat Security Indust Asn, 63 & New York civil practice (8 vols), Matthew Bender, 63-64; Chief draftsman, Model city charter, Nat Munic League, 6th ed, 64; auth, Law, fact and science, Columbia Law Rev, 6/66. **CONTACT ADDRESS** Sch of Law, Columbia Univ, 435 W 116th St, New York, NY, 10027-7201.

KORNBLITH, HILARY
PERSONAL Born 11/03/1954, New York, NY, m, 1980, 2 children **DISCIPLINE** PHILOSOPHY **EDUCATION** Cornell Univ, PhD, 80. **CAREER** Prof of Philos, Univ Vt, 91-. **HONORS AND AWARDS** NEH Fellowship for Col Teachers, 84-85. **MEMBERSHIPS** Am Philos Asn; Soc for Philos and Psychol; Philos of Sci Asn. **RESEARCH** Epistomology; philosophy of psychology. **SELECTED PUBLICATIONS** Auth, Inductive Inference and Its Natural Ground, MIT Press, 93; ed, Naturalizing Epistomology, MIT Press, 85, 2nd ed, 94; auth, Naturalistic Epistomology and Its Critics, Philos Topics, 23, 237-255, 95; auth, The Role of Intuition in Philosophical Inquiry, Rethinking Intuition, Rowman & Littlefield, 98; auth, Distrusting Reason, Midwest Stud in Philos, XXII, 98. **CONTACT ADDRESS** Dept Philos, Univ Vt, 70 S Williams St, Burlington, VT, 05401. **EMAIL** hkornbli@zoo.uvm.edu

KORP, MAUREEN
PERSONAL Born 05/18/1945, NJ, d, 1 child **DISCIPLINE** RELIGIOUS STUDIES **EDUCATION** Rutgers Univ, AB Philos, 66; MA Art Hist, 76; Univ Ottawa, MA Rel Studies, 87; PhD, 91. **CAREER** Atlantic Community Coll, 73-74; Mercer County Community Coll, 73-74; Rutgers Univ, 75-76; Thomas Edison State Coll, 76-80; Ottawa Public School Bd, 81; Univ Ottawa, 86-95, 96-98; Pacifica Grad Inst Calif, 94-98; Univ Bucharest Romania, 95-96; McGill Univ, 97-98. **HONORS AND AWARDS** Breadloaf Writers Conference Scholar, Middlebury Coll, 65, 68; Rutgers Univ, tchg assistantship, 74-76; Consulting Scholar in Humanities, the State Library of New Jersey, 78-79; Univ Ottawa res assistantship, 86-91; Univ Ottawa Merit Grad Res Scholar, 86-88; Univ Ottawa Res Excellence Scholar, 88-91; Doctoral Fel, 88-89; Margaret Denton Wagner Aluma Fel, Rutgers Univ, 89; Post-doctoral Fel, Soc Sci and Humanities Res Council Can, 91-92; can Museum of Civilization Res Assoc, 91-96; AAR/Lilly Tchg Fel, 93-94; Fulbright, 94-95; Civic Educ Project, Univ Bucharest, 95-96; Invited speaker UNESCO Conference Paris, 98. **MEMBERSHIPS** Am Acad Rel. **RESEARCH** Sacred Sites; Indigenous beliefs; Interrelationship of artistic and religious experiences and society. **SELECTED PUBLICATIONS** Auth, Problems of Prejudice in the Thwaites edition of the Jesuit Relations, Hist Reflections, 95; Teaching from the Headlines: Myth and the Media Coverage of Diana's Death, Rel Studies News, 97; Sacred Art of the earth: Ancient and Contemporary Earthworks, 97; Images of Bucharest, Do uglass, 98; Craft: Microhistorical Traditions: Encycl of Women and World Rel, 98; The Eye of the Artist, 98; Queuing, Douglass, forthcoming. **CONTACT ADDRESS** 703 B King Edward Ave, Ottawa, ON, K1N 7N9. **EMAIL** mkorp@aix1.uottawa.ca

KORSGAARD, CHRISTINE M.
PERSONAL Born 04/09/1952, Chicago, IL, d **DISCIPLINE** PHILOSOPHY **EDUCATION** Univ IL at Urbana, BA, 74; Harvard Univ, PhD, 81. **CAREER** Asst prof of philos, 80-83, Univ CA at Santa Barbara; prof of philos and general studies in the humanities, 83-91, Univ Chicago; prof of philos, 91- Havard Univ. **HONORS AND AWARDS** Fel of the Ctr for Human Values, 95-96; Phi Beta Kappa **MEMBERSHIPS** APA; int Kaut Soc; Hume Soc; Soc for Political and Legal Philosophy. **RESEARCH** Ethics; hist of ethic. **SELECTED PUBLICATIONS** Auth, From Duty and for the Sake of the Noble: Kant and Aristotle on Morally Good Action, Aristotle, Kant, and the Stoics: Rethinking Happiness and Duty, 96; auth, Creating the Kingdom of Ends, 96; coauth, The Sources of Normativity, 96; auth, Taking the Law into Our Own Hands: Kant on the Right to Revolution, Reclaiming the History of Ethics: Essays for John Rawls, 97; auth, The Normativity of Instrumental Reason, Ethics and Practical Reason, 97, auth, Self-Constituion in the Ethics of Plato and Kant, The Journal of Ethics, forthcoming; **CONTACT ADDRESS** Philosophy Dept, Harvard Univ, 208 Emerson Hall, Cambridge, MA, 02138. **EMAIL** korsgaar@fas.harvard.edu

KORSMEYER, CAROLYN
DISCIPLINE PHILOSOPHY **EDUCATION** Brown Univ, PhD, 72. **CAREER** Prof Philos, SUNY-Buffalo, 96-. **MEMBERSHIPS** APA; ASA; SWIP. **RESEARCH** Aesthetics; Philosophy of mind; Feminism. **SELECTED PUBLICATIONS** Auth Taste as Sense and as Sensibility, Philos Topics, 97; Aesthetics in Feminist Perspective, Ind Univ Press, 93; coauth Feminism and Tradition in Aesthetics, Penn State Press, 95; Aesthetics: The Big Questions, Basil Blackwell, 98. **CONTACT ADDRESS** Philosophy Dept, Univ at Buffalo, Baldy Hall, Buffalo, NY, 14260. **EMAIL** ckors@acsu.buffalo.edu

KORT, WESLEY A.
PERSONAL Born 06/08/1935, Hoboken, NJ, m, 1960, 3 children **DISCIPLINE** RELIGION **EDUCATION** Calvin Col, BA, 56; Calvin Tehol Sem, BD, 59; Univ Chicago, MA, 61, PhD, 65. **CAREER** Instr, relig, Princeton Univ, 63-65; asst prof, relig, 65-70, assoc prof, 70-77, prof, 77- , Duke Univ. **HONORS AND AWARDS** Fel, Soc for the Arts, Relig and Contemp Culture; fel, Ctr Theol Inquiry, Princeton Univ; outstanding prof award, Duke Univ. **MEMBERSHIPS** Am Acad Relig; Conf on Christianity and Lit. **RESEARCH** Religion in modern and postmodern culture; narrative and belief. **SELECTED PUBLICATIONS** Auth, Modern Fiction and Human Time: A Study in Narrative and Belief, Univ S Fla, 85; auth, Story, Text, and Scripture: Literary Interests in Biblical Narrative, Penn State, 88; auth, Bound to Differ: The Dynamics of Theological Discourses, Penn State, 92; auth, Take, Read: Scripture, Textuality and Cultural Practice, Penn State, 96. **CONTACT ADDRESS** Dept of Religion, Duke Univ, PO Box 90964, Durham, NC, 27708-0964. **EMAIL** wkort@acpub.duke.edu

KORWAR, ARATI
DISCIPLINE MEDIA LAW, FREEDOM OF EXPRESSION, MASS COMMUNICATION AND SOCIETY, VISUAL CO **EDUCATION** Univ NC, Chapel Hill, PhD, 97. **CAREER** Asst prof, La State Univ, 97-. **HONORS AND AWARDS** Freedom Forum J Scholar, 95-96; Shirley and Whitney Award, AEJMC Law Div, 97; Outstanding Graduating Ph.D. Student, UNC Sch of J and Mass Commun, 97. **SELECTED PUBLICATIONS** Auth, Daily Life, in Amherst Through the Years, Munchkin Press, 79; War of Words: Speech Codes at Colleges and Universities in the United States, 1995, Freedom Forum First Amendment Ctr, 95; coauth, Choice of Law in Multistate Media Law Cases: Have the 'Quaking Quagmires' Been Quelled?, in Jour and Mass Commun Monogr 153, 95. **CONTACT ADDRESS** The Manship Sch of Mass Commun, Louisiana State Univ, 206 Journalism Building, Baton Rouge, LA, 70803. **EMAIL** akorwar@unix1.sncc.lsu.edu

KOSROVANI, EMILIO M.
DISCIPLINE PHILOSOPHY **EDUCATION** Univ Washington, PhD, 89. **CAREER** Lectr, Humboldt State Univ, 88-90. **MEMBERSHIPS** APA. **RESEARCH** Philosophy of action. **CONTACT ADDRESS** PO Box 45165, Seattle, WA, 98145.

KOSS, DAVID HENRY
PERSONAL Born 11/24/1935, Elgin, IL **DISCIPLINE** CHURCH HISTORY **EDUCATION** NCentral Col, BA, 56; Evangelical Theol Sem, BD, 59; Princeton Theol Sem, ThM, 61; Northwestern Univ, PhD, 72. **CAREER** Clergyman, Meth-

odist Church, Earlville, Ill, 66-71; faculty relig, IL coll, 72-; Scarborough prof of relig, 90. **MEMBERSHIPS** Am Soc Church Hist; AAR. **RESEARCH** Am and Mod Europ church hist. **CONTACT ADDRESS** Dept of Relig, Illinois Col, 1101 W College Ave, Jacksonville, IL, 62650-2299. **EMAIL** koss@hilltop.ic.edu

KOSTENBERGER, ANDREAS J.
PERSONAL Born 11/02/1957, Vienna, Austria, m, 1989, 3 children **DISCIPLINE** NEW TESTAMENT AND BIBLICAL STUDIES **EDUCATION** Columbia Univ, MDiv, 88; Trinity Evan Div Sch, PhD, 93. **CAREER** Assoc Prof, Southern Baptist Theol Sem. **HONORS AND AWARDS** Scholarly Productivity Awd, Trinity Evang, 96. **MEMBERSHIPS** SBL; ETS; EMS; IBR **RESEARCH** Biblical Studies **SELECTED PUBLICATIONS** Ed, Women in the Church, Baker, 95; auth, The Mission of Jesus and the Disciples According to the Fourth Gospel, Eerdmans, 98. **CONTACT ADDRESS** Southeastern Baptist Theol Sem, 222 N Wingate St, Wake Forest, NC, 27588. **EMAIL** Akostenber@aol.com

KOTERSKI, JOSEPH W.
PERSONAL Born 11/28/1953, Cleveland, OH, s **DISCIPLINE** PHILOSOPHY **EDUCATION** Xavier Univ, HAB, class lang, 76; St. Louis Univ, PhD, philos, 82; Weston Sch of Theol, M Div, theol, 91; Weston Sch of Theol, STL, scripture, 93. **CAREER** Assoc prof, philos, Fordham Univ, Bronx, NY, 92-. **HONORS AND AWARDS** Danforth Scholar, 76. **MEMBERSHIPS** Amer Philos Asn; Amer Cath Philos Asn. **RESEARCH** Natural law ethics; Medieval philosophy. **SELECTED PUBLICATIONS** Auth, Jaspers on Realism and Idealism, Jahrbuck der Osterreichischen Karl Jaspers Gesellschaft, 11, 58-69, 98; auth, History of the Philosophy of Religion: from the thirteenth century to the twentieth century, Philos of Relig: A Guide to the Subject, London, Cassell, 12-21, 98; auth, Homilies, Homiletic and Pastoral Rev, 97, 9, 33-44, 97; auth, First, Do No Harm, Celebrate Life, 19, 2, 46, mar-apr, 97; auth, Unexpected Philosophical Progress: The Origins of the Concept of the Person, Proceedings of the 58th Annual Meeting of the Jesuit Philosophical Association, Boston Col, JPA, 24-40, mar 21, 97; auth, Unreliable Tools, Postmodernism and Christ Philos, Wash, DC, Amer Maritain Asn and The Cath Univ of Amer Press, 141-48, 97; auth, Homilies, Homiletic and Pastoral Rev, 97, 1, 33-43, 96; auth, The Doctrine of Immortality in the Old Testament, Cath Dossier, 2, 2, 44-48, 96; auth, Recognizing One of Aquina's Debts to Neoplatonism, Aquinas on Mind and Intellect: New Essays, Dowling Studies in the Humanities and the Soc Scie, Dowling Col Press, 1-14, 96; auth, C. S. Lewis and the Natural Law, CSL-The Bulletin of the NY C.S. Lewis Soc, 26, 6, 306, 1-7, apr, 95; auth, Religions as the Root of Culture, Christianity and Western Civilization: Christopher Dawson's Insights, San Francisco, Ignatius Press, 15-35, 95; auth, The Book of Wisdom as a Biblical Approach to Natural Law, Freedom, Virtue and the Common Good, Amer Maritain Asn and Univ Notre Dame Press, 253-263, 95; auth, Homilies, Homiletic and Pastoral Rev, 95, 8, 33-41, may, 95. **CONTACT ADDRESS** Dept. of Philosophy, Fordham Univ, Bronx, NY, 10458. **EMAIL** koterski@fordham.edu

KOTZ, SAMUEL
PERSONAL Born 08/28/1930, Harbin, China, m, 1963, 3 children **DISCIPLINE** MATHEMATICAL STATISTICS **EDUCATION** Cornell Univ, PhD, 60. **CAREER** Assoc prof, Univ Toronto, 63-67; prof, Temple Univ, 67-79; Univ Md, 79-97; VISITING SCHOLAR, GEORGE WASH UNIV, 97- . **HONORS AND AWARDS** Honorary Doctorate, Harbin Inst Technol. **MEMBERSHIPS** Royal Statist Soc; Inst Math Statist; Int Stat Inst. **RESEARCH** Statisitcal sciences; probability theory; quality control. **SELECTED PUBLICATIONS** ed, Encyclopedia of Statistical Sources **CONTACT ADDRESS** Dept of Op Res, George Washington Univ, Washington, DC, 20052. **EMAIL** kotz@seas.gwu.edu

KOTZIN, RHODA HADASSAH
PERSONAL Born 05/05/1933, Chicago, Ill **DISCIPLINE** PHILOSOPHY **EDUCATION** Brandeis Univ, BA, 54; Yale Univ, MA, 56, PhD(philos), 60. **CAREER** Instr Philos, La State Univ, 61 & Western Mich Univ, 61-62; from asst prof to assoc prof, 62-70, Prof Philos, Mich State Univ, 70- **HONORS AND AWARDS** Distinguished Fac Award, Mich State Univ, 81. **MEMBERSHIPS** Am Philos Asn; N Am Kant Soc; Kantgesellschaft Leibniz Soc; Soc Women Philos. **RESEARCH** History of philosophy; feminist philosophy; phenomenology; metaphysics/epistemology. **CONTACT ADDRESS** Dept of Philos, Mich State Univ, 503 S Kedzie Hall, East Lansing, MI, 48824-1032. **EMAIL** kotzin@pilot.msu.edu

KOZAR, JOSEPH F.
DISCIPLINE RELIGIOUS STUDIES **EDUCATION** Univ St Michael's Col, Toronto, MDiv, PhD. **CAREER** Prof, Univ Dayton. **SELECTED PUBLICATIONS** Pub(s), Catechist; Toronto J Theol; Proceedings Eastern Great Lakes Midwest Bible Soc. **CONTACT ADDRESS** Dept of Religious Studies, Univ of Dayton, 300 College Park, 345 Humanities, Dayton, OH, 45469-1679. **EMAIL** kozar@checkov.hm.udayton.edu

KOZYRIS, PHAEDON JOHN
PERSONAL Born 01/02/1932, Thessaloniki, Greece, m, 1956, 2 children **DISCIPLINE** LAW **EDUCATION** Univ Thessaloniki, Dipl law, 54; Univ Chicago, MCL, 55; Int Univ Comp Law, Luxembourg, Dipl droit compare, 58; Cornell Univ, JD, 60. **CAREER** Assoc atty, Cahill, Gordon, Sonnett, Reindel and Ohl, New York and Paris, 60-69; PROF LAW, OHIO STATE UNIV, 69-; Vis prof, Duke Univ, 71-72, Univ Tex, 78 and Univ Thessaloniki, Greece, 80. **MEMBERSHIPS** Am Soc Int Law; AAUP; Am Asn Law Schs. **RESEARCH** Corporate law; law of international transactions; conflict of laws. **SELECTED PUBLICATIONS** Auth, Reflections on the Impact of Membership in the European Communities on Greek Legal Culture, J Mod Greek Studies, Vol 0011, 93; Denying Human Rights and Ethnic Identity in The Greeks of Turkey, J Mod Greek Studies, Vol 0012, 94; The Conflicts Provisions of the Alis Complex Litigation Project in A Glass Half Full, La Law Rev, Vol 0054, 94; The Conflict of Laws Aspects of the New American Business Entity in The Limited Liability Company, Am J Comp Law, Vol 0043, 95; The Limited Liability Company, Does It Exist Out of State in What Law Governs It, Univ Cincinnati Law Rev, Vol 0064, 96; The Macedonians of Greece in Denying Ethnic Identity, J Mod Greek Studies, Vol 0014, 96. **CONTACT ADDRESS** Sch of Law, Ohio State Univ, Columbus, OH, 43210.

KRAABEL, ALF THOMAS
PERSONAL Born 11/04/1934, Portland, OR, m, 1956, 3 children **DISCIPLINE** RELIGIOUS STUDIES, CLASSICS **EDUCATION** Luther Col, BA, 56; Univ Iowa, MA, 58; Luther Theol Sem, BD, 61; Harvard Univ, ThD, 68. **CAREER** Asst prof classics and relig studies, 67-70, assoc prof classics and chmn rclig studies, 70-76, PROF CLASSICS and RELIG STUDIES, UNIV MINN, MINNEAPOLIS, 76-; CHMN DEPT and DIR GRAD STUDY, 80-; Assoc dir, Joint expedition to Khirbet Shema, Israel, 69-73; Sabbatical fel, Am Coun Learned Soc, 77-78. **MEMBERSHIPS** Soc Bibl Lit; Am Acad Relig; Am Soc Study Relig; Soc Values Higher Educ. **RESEARCH** Greco-Roman religions; archaeology. **SELECTED PUBLICATIONS** Auth, Jewish Communities in Asia-Minor, Cath Bibl Quart, Vol 0055, 93; Ancient Jewish Epitaphs in An Introductory Survey of a Millennium of Jewish Funerary Epigraphy Cath Bibl Quart, Vol 0055, 93; From Synagogue to Church in Public Services and offices in the Earliest Christian Communities Interpretation-A, J Bible Theol, Vol 0048, 94; Mission and Conversion in Proselytizing in the Religious History of the Roman Empire, J Early Christian Studies, Vol 0004, 96; Early Christian Epitaphs from Anatolia, Cath Bibl Quart, Vol 0058, 96. **CONTACT ADDRESS** Dept of Classics, Univ of Minn, 310A Folwell Hall, Minneapolis, MN, 55455.

KRAEMER, DAVID
PERSONAL Born 10/23/1955, Newark, NJ, m, 1977, 2 children **DISCIPLINE** THEOLOGY **EDUCATION** Brandeis Univ, BA 77; Jewish Theol Sem, MA, PhD, 84. **CAREER** Prof, Jewish Theol Sem. **HONORS AND AWARDS** Consultant, Jewish Museum. **MEMBERSHIPS** CLAL, Nat Jewish CCtr Lrng and Ldrshp. **RESEARCH** Literary analysis of rabbinic literature, particularly the Talmud, and the social and religious history of Jews in late antiquity. **SELECTED PUBLICATIONS** Auth, Jewish Death: A History of Practices and Beliefs in Late Antiquity, submitted; Reading the Rabbis: Literature and Religion in Talmudic Babylonia, Oxford U Press, 96; Responses to Suffering in Classical Rabbinic Literature, Oxford U Press, 95; Evil and Suffering, Judaic Doctrines of, in: The Millennial Encycl of Judaism, The Religion, WS Green et al eds, forthcoming; Rabbinic Sources for Historical Study, in: Judaism in Late Antiquity, Issues and Debates, J. Neusner, Alan J. Avery-Peck, eds, Leiden, EJ Brill, 98; The Spirit of the Rabbinic Sabbath, Conservative Judaism, 97; Child and Family Life in Judaism, in: Religious Dimensions of Child and Family life, Harold Coward, Phillip Cook eds, Victoria, Univ of Vict, 96; When God is Wrong, Sh'ma: A Jour of Jewish Responsibility, 95. **CONTACT ADDRESS** Jewish Theol Sem of America, 3080 Broadway, New York, NY, 10027. **EMAIL** dakraemer@jtsa.edu

KRAFT, ROBERT ALAN
PERSONAL Born 03/18/1934, Waterbury, CT, m, 1955, 4 children **DISCIPLINE** HISTORY OF WESTERN RELIGION **EDUCATION** Wheaton Col, IL, BA, 55, MA, 57; Harvard Univ, PhD, 61. **CAREER** Asst lectr New Testament studies, Univ Manchester, 61-63; from asst prof to assoc prof relig thought, 63-76, acting chmn dept, 72-73, 92, Prof Relig Studies, Univ PA, 76-, Chmn Grad Studies, 73-84, 96-, Chmn Dept, 77-84; Vis lectr, Lutheran Theol Sem, Philadelphia, 65-66; ed, Monogr ser, Soc Bibl Lit, 67-72 & Pseudepigrapha ser, 73-78; task force on scholarly publ, Coun Studies Relig, 71-72. **HONORS AND AWARDS** Fels, Guggenheim, 69-70 & Am Coun Learned Soc, 75-76. **MEMBERSHIPS** Soc Bibl Lit; Int Orgn Septuagint & Cognate Studies; NAm Patristic Soc; Studiorum Nov Testamenti Societas; Am Soc Papyrologists. **RESEARCH** Judaism in the Hellenistic era, especially Greek-speaking Judaism; Christianity to the time of Constantine, espec the second century; computers and Ancient lit. **SELECTED PUBLICATIONS** Auth, Was There a Messiah-Joshua Tradition at the Turn of the Era?, RKMESSIA ARTICLE on the IOUDAIOS Electronic Discussion Group, 6/10/92; Philo's Text of Genesis 2.18 (I will make a helper), on the IOUDAIOS Electronic Discussion Group, 6/10/93; The Pseudepigrapha in Christianity, In: Tracing the Threads: Studies in the Vitality of Jewish Pseudepigrapha, SBL Early Judaism and Its Literature 6, Scholars, 94; coauth, Jerome's Translation of Origen's Homily on Jeremiah 2.21-22 (Greek Homily 2; Latin 13), Revue Be/ne/dictine 104, 94; auth, The Use of Computers in New Testament Textual Criticism, In: The Text of the NT in Contemporary Research, Studies and Documents 46, 95; Scripture and Canon in Jewish Apocrypha and Pseudepigrapha, In: Hebrew Bible/Old Testament: The History of its Interpretation, I: From Beginnings to the Middle Ages (Until 1300), 1: Antiquity, Vandenhoeck & Ruprecht, 96; author of numerous other articles. **CONTACT ADDRESS** Relig Studies, Univ of PA, Logan Hall, Philadelphia, PA, 19104-6304. **EMAIL** kraft@ccat.sas.upenn.edu

KRAHMER, SHAWN MADISON
DISCIPLINE THEOLOGY **EDUCATION** Univ Illinois, BS, summa, cum laude, 81; Garrett-Evangelical Theol Sem, MDiv, summa, cum laude, 84; Univ Chicago, MA, 87, PhD, honors, 95. **CAREER** Asst Prof, 95-, St Joseph's Univ; Research Asst 92-94, 89-91, Data Base mgr 88-95, Univ Chicago **HONORS AND AWARDS** Phi Kappa Phi. **MEMBERSHIPS** AAR; SSCS; Del Valley Medieval Assoc. **RESEARCH** Christian Monastic Theol; Spirituality, Christian Mysticism, Ancient and Medieval Historical Theol, Feminist Theol. **SELECTED PUBLICATIONS** Auth, A Constructive Dialogue on Friendship and Eros: Towards a Theol of Right Relation, Soundings: A J Interdisciplinary Studies, 97; auth, Loving in God: An Examination of the Hierarchical Aspects of the Ordo Caritatis in Bernard of Clairvaux and Aelred of Rievaulx, Amer Benedictine Rev, forthcoming; auth, The Bride as Friend in Bernard of Clairvaux's, Sermones Super Cantica, Amer Benedictine Rev, 97; The Friend as Second Self and the Theme of Substitution, in the Letters of Bernard Clairvaux, Cistercian Studies Qtly, 96; Friend and Lover as Metaphors of Right Relation in Bernard of Clairfaux, Cistercian Stud Qtly, 95; rev, Teresa M Shaw, The Burden of the Flesh: Fasting and Sexuality in Early Christianity, Anglican Theol Rev, forthcoming; auth, Elizabeth A Johnson, Friends of God and Prophets: A Feminist Theol reading of the Communion of Saints, Anglican Theol Rev, forthcoming; Rosemary Radford Ruether, Women and Redemption: A Theol History, Anglican Theol Rev, forthcoming; Andrew D Brown, Popular Piety in Late Medieval England: The Diocese of Salisbury 1250-1550, RN Swanson, Religion and Devotion in Europe, Anglican Theol Rev, 98; Patricia Ranft, Women and the Religious Life in Premodern Europe, Anglican Theol Rev, 97. **CONTACT ADDRESS** Dept of Theology, St Joseph's Univ, 5600 City Ave, Philadelphia, PA, 19131. **EMAIL** skrahm@sju.edu

KRAKAUER, ERIC
PERSONAL Cincinnati, OH **DISCIPLINE** PHILOSOPHY MEDICAL ETHICS AND INTERNAL MEDICINE **EDUCATION** Yale Univ, Grad Schl, PhD, 91; Yale Univ, Med Schl, 92. **CAREER** Inst, Harvard Medical Schl, 97-. **HONORS AND AWARDS** Fulbright Fel. **MEMBERSHIPS** APA; Modern Language Assoc; Amer Soc for Bioethics and Humanities; AMA **RESEARCH** Ethical and cultural issues in end-of-life care. **CONTACT ADDRESS** Palliative Care Service, Massachusetts General Hospital, 55 Fruit S, Boston, MA, 02114.

KRAMER, ROBERT
PERSONAL Born 08/17/1913, Davenport, IA **DISCIPLINE** LAW **EDUCATION** Harvard Univ, AB, 35, LLB, 38. **CAREER** From assoc prof to prof law, Duke Univ, 47-59; asst atty gen of US Dept Justice, 59-61; prof, 61-79, EMER PROF LAW and DEAN, LAW SCH, GEORGE WASHINGTON UNIV 80-; Ed, Law and Contemporary Probs, 47-56 and J Legal Educ, 48-56. **MEMBERSHIPS** Am Law Inst. **SELECTED PUBLICATIONS** Auth, Against Recycling and Schubert, Heine, Song Cycles, Nineteenth Century Mus, Vol 0020, 96; Spirit at Work in Discovering the Spirituality in Leadership, J Relig Health, Vol 0036, 97. **CONTACT ADDRESS** Sch of Law, George Washington Univ, Washington, DC, 20006.

KRAMER-MILLS, HARTMUT
PERSONAL Born 12/14/1962, Jena, Germany, m, 1988, 2 children **DISCIPLINE** PROTESTANT THEOLOGY **EDUCATION** McCormick Theol Sem Chicago, MD, 88; Marburg Univ Germany, Ecclesiastical Exam, 90; Greifswald Univ Germany, PhD, 97. **CAREER** Vicar, Ev Kirche der Kirchenprovinz Sachsen Germany, 91; tchg asst, Kirchliche Hochschule Naumburg Germany, 92-93; lectr, Pedagogische Hochschule Erfurt Germany, 93-98. **HONORS AND AWARDS** World Alliance of Reformed Churches/McCormick Theol Sem: full scholar, 86-87. **MEMBERSHIPS** Am Soc of Church Hist. **RESEARCH** Christianity in Europe during the 19th century until 1945; History of the English Reformation. **SELECTED PUBLICATIONS** Auth, Von Arnoldshain und Sagorsk nach bad Urach. Anmerkungen zum gegenwartigen Dialog Zwischen der Evangelischen Kirche in Deutschland und der Russischen Orthodoxen Kirche, Die Zeichen der Zeit, 96; Wilhelminische Moderne und das fremde Christentum. Untersuchumngen zu Friedrich Naumanns "Briefe uner Religion", 97; Die Gemeinde der Heiligen. Erinnerungen an die Zukunft der Kirche. Hartmut Kramer-Mills uber Manfred Josuttis, Die Zeichen der Zeit, 98. **CONTACT ADDRESS** 123 Buckelew Ave, Jamesburg, NJ, 08831.

KRANTZ, ARTHUR A.
PERSONAL Born 09/14/1938, Edmonton, AB, Canada, m, 1965, 2 children **DISCIPLINE** PHILOSOPHY **EDUCATION** Concordia Sr Col, BA, 62; Concordia Sem, MDiv, 65; Univ Tor, MA, 67; Univ Waterloo, PhD, 72. **CAREER** Wilfred Lauier Univ, sess lecrt, lectr, 67-71; Univ Regina, Luther Col, asst prof, prof, acad dean, 71-. **MEMBERSHIPS** CPA, CSHPT, AAR, SKS, CSCP, AI, CCLA **RESEARCH** Plato; Kierkegaard; Heidegger; Nietzsche; Sartre; Gadamer. **CONTACT ADDRESS** Dept of Philosophy, Luther Col, 700 College Dr, Regina, SK, S4S 0A2. **EMAIL** Arthur.Krentz@uregina.ca

KRASSEN, MILES
DISCIPLINE JUDAIC STUDIES **EDUCATION** St. John Col, BA, 67; Ind Univ, MA, 83; Univ Pa, MA, 85, PhD, 90. **CAREER** Asst prof. **RESEARCH** Jewish mysticism, hasidism, Kabbalah texts. **SELECTED PUBLICATIONS** Au, Isaiah Horowitz: Generations of Adam. **CONTACT ADDRESS** Dept of Relig, Oberlin Col, Oberlin, OH, 44074.

KRATTENMAKER, THOMAS GEORGE
PERSONAL Born 01/15/1943, Camden, NJ, m, 1965, 2 children **DISCIPLINE** LAW **EDUCATION** Swarthmore Col, BA, 65; Columbia Univ, JD, 68. **CAREER** Asst prof, Sch Law, Univ Conn, 68-72; PROF LAW, GEORGETOWN UNIV LAW CTR, 72-; Law clerk, US Supreme Ct, 70-71; asst dir, Bur Consumer Protection, Fed Trade Comn, 71-72; secy, DC Law Revision Comm, 76-78; co-dir, Network Inquiry Staff, Fed Common Comn, 78-80. **RESEARCH** Constitutional law; antitrust law; communications law. **SELECTED PUBLICATIONS** Auth, Converging 1st Amendment Principles for Converging Communications Media, Yale Law J, Vol 0104, 95. **CONTACT ADDRESS** Law Ctr, Georgetown Univ, Washington, DC, 20001.

KRAUSZ, MICHAEL
PERSONAL Born 09/13/1942, Geneva, Switzerland, m, 1976 **DISCIPLINE** PHILOSOPHY **EDUCATION** Rutgers Univ, BA, 65; Indiana Univ, MA, 67; Univ Toronto, PhD, 69. **CAREER** Instr, York Univ, 66-67; instr, 67-68; resear assoc, Ont Instit for Studies in Edu; 68, Univ of Toronto; asst prof, Univ Toronto, Victoria Coll, 69-70; instr, Trent Univ, 69-70; asst prof, 70-76, from assoc prof to prof, 76-91; Milton C Nahm prof Philos, 91, Bryn Mawr Coll. **HONORS AND AWARDS** Bryn Mawr Col Fac Res Grant, 98; George Washington Univ Elton Lect, 98; Univ Ulm, Germany, Hans-Kupczyk Gastprofessur Lect and Award, 97; David Norton Memorial Lect, Univ Del, 97; Tata Enery Res Inst Honorary Fel, New Delhi, India; Alice Hardenberg Clark Res Grant, 89; NEH Summer Inst participant; Oxford Univ Senior Mem; Res Grant Oxford Univ; Alfred Sloan Found Grant, 86; Res Grant to Kenya, 85; Ossabaw Found Res Fel, 78, 80; Andrew W Mellon Fel, 77-78; Madge Miller Res Grant, 76, 85; Bryn Mawr Col Fac Res Grant. **MEMBERSHIPS** Amer Philos Assoc; Amer Soc Aesthetics; Intl Development Ethics Assoc; Collingwood Soc; Royal Soc of Arts; Soc of Intercultural Philos; Acad of Ethical Sci. **RESEARCH** Epistemology; Philosophy of History; Culture and Interpretation. **SELECTED PUBLICATIONS** Interpretation, Relativism and Culture: Four Questions for Margolis, Interpretation, Relativism and the Metaphysics of Culture, Humanities Pr, 98; Rightness and Reasons: A Reply to Stecker, Jour of Aesthetics and Art Crit, 97; coauth, Varieties of Relativism, Basil Blackwell Pub, 95. **CONTACT ADDRESS** Dept of Philosophy, Bryn Mawr Col, Bryn Mawr, PA, 19010.

KRAUT, BENNY
PERSONAL Born 12/24/1947, Munich, Germany, m, 1972, 3 children **DISCIPLINE** MODERN JEWISH HISTORY, MODERN JUDAISM **EDUCATION** Yeshiva Univ, BA, 68; Brandeis Univ, MA, 70, PhD(Jewish hist), 75. **CAREER** Vis asst prof Judaica, Vassar Col, 75-76; ASSOC PROF JUDAICA, UNIV CINCINNATI, 76-. **MEMBERSHIPS** Orgn Am Historians; Asn Jewish Studies; World Union Jewish Studies. **RESEARCH** Development of American Judaism; religious and theological responses to the Holocaust; Jewish-Christian relations in American history. **SELECTED PUBLICATIONS** Auth, Wise, Isaac, Mayer in Shaping American Judaism, Am Hist Rev, Vol 0099, 94; Alternatives to Assimilation in The Response of Reform Judaism to American Culture, Am Hist Rev, Vol 0101, 96. **CONTACT ADDRESS** Judaic Studies, Univ of Cincinnati, P O Box 210169, Cincinnati, OH, 45221-0169.

KRAUT, RICHARD
PERSONAL Born 10/27/1944, Brooklyn, NY **DISCIPLINE** PHILOSOPHY **EDUCATION** Univ Mich, BA, 65; Princeton Univ, PhD, 69. **CAREER** Asst prof, Philosophy, 69-76, assoc prof, Philosophy, 76-83, prof, Philosophy, 83-95, chr, Dept Philos, 88-91, res prof, Humanities, 89-95, Univ Ill Chicago, 69-95; vis prof, Univ Chicago, 97; prof philosophy, 95-, prof, classics, 97-, chr, dept philos, 97-, Northwestern Univ, 95-. **HONORS AND AWARDS** Pres, APA, 93-94. **MEMBERSHIPS** Amer Philos Asn **SELECTED PUBLICATIONS** Auth, Socrates and the State, Princeton Univ Press, 84; Aristotle on the Human Good, Princeton Univ Press, 89; ed, The Cambridge Companion to Plato, Cambridge Univ Press, 92; ed, Critical Essays on Plato's Republic, Rowman & Littlefield, 97; auth, Aristotle Politics Books VII and VIII, Clarendon Press, 97. **CONTACT ADDRESS** Dept of Philosophy, Northwestern Univ, 1818 Hinman Ave, Evanston, IL, 60208-1315.

KRAWCHUK, ANDRII
DISCIPLINE THEOLOGY **EDUCATION** McGill Univ, BA, 76, BTh, 79; Accademia Alfonsiana, Rome, LThM, 81; Univ Ottawa, PhD, 90; St Paul Univ, DTh, 90. **CAREER** Acad Prog Coordr, Harvard Ukrainian Res Inst, 90; res fel, 90-91, proj dir, 92-93, Central State Hist Archiv L'viv; ed, publ div, Greek Cath Archeparchy of L'viv, 91-92; postdoct fel, 93-94 & ed, Logos, A J of Eastern Christian Stud, lectr, St Paul Univ, 94-95; res assoc, Can Inst of Ukrainian Stud, 95-97; prof, Christian ethics, L'viv Theol Acad, 97-98. **HONORS AND AWARDS** Postdoctoral fel, Univ Alberta, 89; postdoctoral fel, Harvard Univ, 90; Can-USSR exchange fel, 90-91; Cenko Prize in Bibliog, 91; tchg and res fel, Can Inst Ukrainian Stud, 93-94; Reform through Knowledge Program, Asn of Univ and Col of Can, 96-97; Can Ethnic Studies Award, 97. **MEMBERSHIPS** Shevchenko Sci Soc Can; Can Asn of E Christian Stud; Christians Assoc for Relations with E Europe; AAR; Can Asn of Slavists; Soc of Christian Ethics. **RESEARCH** History of Christian ethics, East and West. **SELECTED PUBLICATIONS** Ed, Moral'ne Bohoslovia, by Jean-Marie Aubert, Catholic Archeparchy of L'viv, 93; comp, The Bohdan Bociurkiw Collection on Religion and Church-State Relations in the Soviet and Post-Soviet Republics: A Preliminary Inventory of Its Principal Sections, Ottawa: CIUS Reports, 94; ed, Zaklyk do pokaiannia, by Andrei Sheptytsky, Rare Books Library Series, L'viv: Svichado, 94; transl, Paps'ka Rada v Spravakh Sim'yi, L'viv: Svichado, 97; ed, Moral'ne Bohoslovia, 2d ed, L'viv: Strim, 97; auth, Christian Social Ethics in Ukraine: The Legacy of Andrei Sheptytsky, Can Inst of Ukrainian Stud, 97; ed, Andrei Sheptytsky: His Life and Works, v.2: Christian Social and Political Ethics, L'viv: Central State Historical Archives, 98; auth, A Systematic Bibliography of Ukrainian-Language Religious and Theological Periodical Literature, 1871-1939, L'viv Theolog Acad, 99. **CONTACT ADDRESS** Sheptytsky Inst, St Paul Univ, 223 Main St, Ottawa, ON, K1S 1C4. **EMAIL** akrawchuk@ustpaul.uottawa.ca

KREBS, VICTOR J.
PERSONAL Born 01/26/1957, Lima, Peru **DISCIPLINE** PHILOSOPHY **EDUCATION** Vanderbilt Univ, BA, 81; Univ Notre Dame, MA, 84, PhD, 92. **CAREER** Asst prof, 93-94, assoc prof, philos, 94- , dir grad stud in philos, 96- , Univ Simon Bolivar, Venezuela. **HONORS AND AWARDS** Phi Beta Kappa; Konrad Adenauer res fel; Inst of Int Educ scholar; Pew Teaching Leadership Award; Outstanding Young Men of Am Award. **MEMBERSHIPS** APA; North Am Kant Soc; Sociedad Venezuelana Filosofia. **RESEARCH** Wittgenstein; philosophy of psychology; aesthetics; philosophy of language and mind; Kant; archetypal psychology and psychoanalysis. **SELECTED PUBLICATIONS** Auth, El Silencio de Wittgenstein, Criterion 8, 94; auth, La Transfiguracion de la Filosofia: Wittgenstein y la Recuperacion del Sentido, Proceedings IV Congreso Nacional de Filosofia, 94; auth, El Naturalismo Trascendental de Wittgenstein, Ideas y Valores, 96; auth, Locura y Memoria del Arte, in Arte y Locura serie Conversaciones en el Museo, 98; auth, Espiritus Sobre las Ruinas: Wittgenstein y el Pensamiento Estetico, Arete X, 98; auth, La Labor Olvidada del Pensar, Argos, 98; auth, Lenguaje Mente, y Alma en Wittgenstein, Proceedings, Primer Congreso Iberamericano de Filosofia, 98; auth, Pensando con el alma y el Tonto Prejuicio Cientifico de Nuestro Tiempo, Filosofia, Merida-Venezuela, 98; auth, Lo Bueno, lo Malo, y lo Bello, La Belleza en Todas partes, Museo de Bellas Artes de Caracas, forthcoming. **CONTACT ADDRESS** CCS 90170, PO Box 025323, Miami, FL, 33102-5323. **EMAIL** vkrebs@usb.ve

KREMER, MICHAEL
PERSONAL Born 12/24/1957, New Haven, CT, m, 1989, 3 children **DISCIPLINE** PHILOSOPHY **EDUCATION** Univ Toronto, BA, 80; Univ Pittsburgh, MA, 83, PhD, 86. **CAREER** Instr, 86-87, asst prof, 87-93, assoc prof, 93-, Univ Notre Dame. **HONORS AND AWARDS** Nat Endow Hum, Fel Univ tchrs, ALTERNATE, 98-99. **MEMBERSHIPS** Amer Philos Asn; Asn Symbolic Logic. **RESEARCH** History of Analytic Philosophy; Philosophy of Language; Logic; Philosophy of Mathematics. **SELECTED PUBLICATIONS** Auth, Logic and Meaning: The Philosophical Significance of the Sequent Calculus, Mind 97, 88, 50-72; Kripke and the Logic of Truth, Jour Philos Logic 17, 88, 225-278; Set-Theoretic Realism and Arithmetic, Philos Stud (s) 64, 91, 253-271; The Multiplicity of General Propositions, Nous 26, 92, 409-426; The Argument of On Denoting, Philos rev 103, 94, 249-297. **CONTACT ADDRESS** Dept of Philosophy, Notre Dame Sem, 336 O'Shaughnessy Hall, Notre Dame, IN, 46556-5639. **EMAIL** Michael.J.Kremer.2@nd.edu

KRENTZ, EDGAR
DISCIPLINE NEW TESTAMENT **EDUCATION** Concordia Sem, MDiv; Wash Univ, MA, PhD; additional stud, Univ Chicago; Amer Sch of Class Stud at Athens, Greece. **CAREER** Christ Sem-Seminex prof. **HONORS AND AWARDS** Assoc dir, Joint Expedition to Caesarea Maritima in Israel. **RESEARCH** Pauline studies in relation to the Greco-Roman world. **SELECTED PUBLICATIONS** Auth, The Historical-Critical Method; Augsburg New Testament Commentary on Galatians; Hymnody as Epideictic Literature. **CONTACT ADDRESS** Dept of New Testament, Lutheran Sch of Theol, 1100 E 55th St, Chicago, IL, 60615. **EMAIL** ekrentz@lstc.edu

KRESS, ROBERT LEE
PERSONAL Born 09/22/1932, Jasper, IN **DISCIPLINE** THEOLOGY, PHILOSOPHY **EDUCATION** St Meinrad Col, BA, 54; Univ Innsbruck, STB, 56, STL, 58; Univ Notre Dame, MA, 64; Univ St Thomas Aquinas, Rome, STD, 68. **CAREER** Supt, Washington Cath High Sch, 59-64; lectr philos and relig, Univ Evansville, 68-70; asst prof theol, St Louis Univ, 71-73; assoc prof philos and relig, Univ Evansville, 73-74, prof, 78-79; ASSOC PROF, DEPT THEOL, CATH UNIV AM, 79-; Vis fel theol, Princeton Theol Sem, 70-71; vis prof, Lutheran Theol Sem, 80, Princeton Theol Sem, 81 and Toronto Sch Theol, 82; fel, Ctr Libertarian Studies, 82. **HONORS AND AWARDS** Outstanding Bk of Year, Col Theol Soc, 76. **MEMBERSHIPS** Col Theol Soc; Int Soc Metaphysics; Cath Theol Soc Am; Am Acad Relig. **RESEARCH** Religion and culture; gnosticism; Christian philosophy. **SELECTED PUBLICATIONS** Auth, Femininity, Castration and the Phallus, Lit Psychol, Vol 0042, 96. **CONTACT ADDRESS** Dept of Theol, Catholic Univ of America, Washington, DC, 20064.

KREY, PHILIP D.W.
DISCIPLINE EARLY; MEDIEVAL CHURCH HISTORY **EDUCATION** Univ Mass/Boston, BA, 72; Lutheran Theol Sem at Gettysburg, MDiv, 76; Cath Univ Am, MA, 85;; Univ Chicago, PhD, 90. **CAREER** Dean; prof-. **HONORS AND AWARDS** Fulbright fel, Univ Munich, 89., Co-founder, Soc Stud of the Bible in the Middle Ages. **SELECTED PUBLICATIONS** Auth, transl, medieval Franciscan's Revelation Commentary - Nicholas of Lyra; co-ed, Sources of Medieval Christian Thought, Cath UP. **CONTACT ADDRESS** Dept of History and Systematic Theology, Lutheran Theol Sem, 7301 Germantown Ave, Philadelphia, PA, 19119 1794. **EMAIL** Pkrey@ltsp.edu

KRIEG, ROBERT A.
PERSONAL Born 02/08/1946, Hackensack, NJ, s **DISCIPLINE** THEOLOGY **EDUCATION** Stonehill Col, BA, 69; Univ of Notre Dame, PhD, 76. **CAREER** Asst prof, King's Col, 75-77; Prof, Univ Notre Dame, 77-. **MEMBERSHIPS** Catholic Theological Soc of Am; Col Theology Soc. **RESEARCH** Christology; 19th and 20th Century Theology in Germany. **SELECTED PUBLICATIONS** Auth, Romano Guardini: Precursor of Vatican II, Univ of Notre Dame Press, 97; ed & contrib. Romano Guardini: Proclaiming Sacred in a Modern World, Liturgy Training Pub, 95; assoc ed & coauth, Encyclopedia of Catholicism, Harper Collins, 95; Die Rezeption Roman Guardinis in Nordamerika, Theologie und Glaube, 98; Introduction in the 1997 Edition, The Spirit of Catholicism, Crossroad, 97; Peyton, Patrick J., New Catholic Encyclopedia, Writers' Guild Inc with McGraw-Hill Book Co, 96. **CONTACT ADDRESS** Dept of Theology, Univ of Notre Dame, 327 O'Shaughnessy Hall, Notre Dame, IN, 46556-5639. **EMAIL** krieg.1@ND.EDU

KRIER, JAMES EDWARD
PERSONAL Born 10/19/1939, Milwaukee, WI, m, 1974, 2 children **DISCIPLINE** LAW **EDUCATION** Univ Wis- Madison, BS, 61, JD, 66. **CAREER** Law clerk, Supreme Court Calif, 66-67; assoc, Arnold and Porter, DC, 67-69; from actg prof to prof law, Univ Calif, Los Angeles, 69-78; prof law, Stanford Law Sch, 78-80; PROF LAW, LAW SCH, UNIV CALIF, LOS ANGELES, 80-; CONSULT, ENVIRON QUALITY LAB, CALIF INST TECHNOL, 71-; vis fel, Wolfson Col, Oxford Univ, 76. **MEMBERSHIPS** AAAS **RESEARCH** Environmental law; law and economics; property law. **SELECTED PUBLICATIONS** Auth, Science, Environment, and the Law in Round-Table Discussion, Ecol Law Quart, Vol 0021, 94; Property Rules and Liability Rules in The Cathedral in Another Light, NY Univ Law Rev, Vol 0070, 95; Regulatory Takings in Law, Economics, and Politics, Georgetown Law J, Vol 0084, 96; Internationale-Handelsgesellschaft-Mbh V Einfuhr-und-Vorratsstelle-fur-Getreide-und-Futtermittel, Texas Law Rev, Vol 0074, 96; The Cathedral At 25 in Citations and Impressions, Yale Law J, Vol 0106, 97. **CONTACT ADDRESS** Law School, Univ of Calif, Los Angeles, CA, 90024.

KRIMERMAN, LEONARD I.
DISCIPLINE PHILOSOPHY OF WORK **EDUCATION** Cornell Univ, BA, 55; PhD, 64. **CAREER** Dept Philos, Univ Conn **RESEARCH** Theory and prospects of democracy, recent political philosophy. **SELECTED PUBLICATIONS** Co-auth, When Workers Decide, New Soc Publ, 91; From the Ground Up, S End Press, 92; Education for Democratic Community and Work, Critical Education for Work: Multidisciplinary Approaches, 94; From the Kitchen to the World: Three Decades of Cooperative Development in Japan, GEO, 94; auth, Contours of Collaboration--A New State of Organizing?, GEO, 94. **CONTACT ADDRESS** Dept of Philos, Univ Conn, 344 Mansfield Rd, Storrs, CT, 06269.

KRIMM, HANS HEINZ
PERSONAL Born 01/08/1933, Tallinn, Estonia, m, 1955, 2 children **DISCIPLINE** PHILOSOPHY **EDUCATION** Johns Hopkins Univ, AB, 55, PhD(philos), 60. **CAREER** Asst, John Hopkins Univ, 57-60; from instr to asst prof philos, Utica Col, Syracuse Univ, 60-63; from asst prof to assoc prof, 63-78, prof philos, 78-98, prof emeritus, CO Col, 98-; steering comt, prog

sci, technol & humanism, Aspen Inst Humanistic Studies, 74-77; open space adv comt, Colo Springs, 76. **RESEARCH** Common sense conceptions of causality; philosophy of science and logic; the value-structure of science and technology; environmental ethics. **CONTACT ADDRESS** Dept Philos, Colorado Col, 14 E Cache La Poudre, Colo Springs, CO, 80903-3294.

KRIMSKY, SHELDON
PERSONAL Born 06/26/1941, New York, NY, m, 1970, 2 children **DISCIPLINE** PHILOSOPHY; HISTORY OF SCIENCE **EDUCATION** Brooklyn Col, BS, 63; Purdue Univ, MS, 65; Boston Univ, PhD(philos), 70. **CAREER** Assoc dir urban & environ studies, 75-78, actg dir, 78-80, from Asst Prof to Assoc Prof, 80-90, Prof Dept Urban & Environ Policy, 90-; Res assoc philos & hist sci, Boston Univ, 73-. **HONORS AND AWARDS** NDEA Fel; Distinguished Alumnus, Boston Univ **MEMBERSHIPS** AAAS **RESEARCH** Biotechnology; science and society; bioethics; chemicals and health. **SELECTED PUBLICATIONS** Auth, The Muliple-World Thought Experiment and Absolute Space, Nous, 72; The Use and Misuse of Critical Gedankenexperimente, zeitschrift fur allgemeine Wissenschafts theories Vol IV, No 2; Regulating Recombinant DNA Research in Controversy: Politics of Technical Decisions, Sage, 78; The role of the citizen court in the recombinant DNA debate, Bull Atomic Scientists, 10/78; coauth, Recombinant DNA research: The scope and limits of regulation, The Am J Pub Health, 12/79; auth, Genetic Alchemy: The Social History of the Recombinant DNA Debate, MIT Press, 82; Patents for life forms sui generis: Some new questions for science law and society, Recombinant DNA Tech Bull, 4/81; coauth, Environmental Hazards, Auburn House Publ Co, 88; Social Theories of Risk, Praeger, 92; auth, Biotechnics and Society, Praeger, 92; coauth, Agricultural Biotechnology and the Environment, Univ Ill Press, 96. **CONTACT ADDRESS** Dept of Urban Environ Policy, Tufts Univ, 97 Talbot Ave, Medford, MA, 02155-5555. **EMAIL** skrimsky@emerald.tufts.edu

KRISHNA, VERN
DISCIPLINE LAW **EDUCATION** Alta Univ, LLB; Harvard Univ, LLM. **CAREER** Prof, 81-. **HONORS AND AWARDS** Pres, Certified General Accountants Asn. **MEMBERSHIPS** Law Soc Upper Can. **SELECTED PUBLICATIONS** Auth, The Fundamentals of Canadian Income Tax; The Essentials of Income Tax Law. **CONTACT ADDRESS** Fac Common Law, Univ Ottawa, 550 Cumberland St, PO Box 450, Ottawa, ON, K1N 6N5.

KRISPIN, GERALD
DISCIPLINE SYSTEMATIC THEOLOGY **EDUCATION** Univ Alberta, BA, 81; Lutheran Theol Sem, Saskatoon, Mdiv, 83; Concordia Sem, St Louis, STM, ThD, 91. **CAREER** Assoc prof, Concordia Univ, 87-. **SELECTED PUBLICATIONS** Auth, True Lutheran Confessions, Can Lutheran, XI:1, 96; auth, Paul Gerhardt: Confessional Subscription and the Lord's Supper, Logia: A J Lutheran Theol IV:3, 95; auth, Spirituality and Spiritual Formation in the Hymnody of Paul Gerhardt, Lutheran Theol Rev VI:1, 93, Christ, the Way, Can Lutheran, 92; auth, Odo Cassel and the Kultmysterium: A Study in Liturgical Synergism, Confessional Lutheran Res Soc Newsl, 91; coauth, The Christian Faith: A Biblical Introduction, Edmonton: Pioneer Press, 96, 2nd Rev and Expanded Ed, 98. **CONTACT ADDRESS** Dept of Religious Studies, Concordia Col, Alberta, 7128 Ada Blvd, Edmonton, AB, T5B 4E4. **EMAIL** gkrispin@concordia.ab.ca

KRISTELLER, PAUL OSKAR
PERSONAL Born 05/22/1905, Berlin, Germany, m, 1940 **DISCIPLINE** PHILOSOPHY **EDUCATION** Univ Heidelberg, PhD, 28; Univ Pisa, PhD, 37. **CAREER** Lectr Ger, Inst Super Magistero, Florence, Italy, 34-35; Univ Pisa, 35-38; lectr Philos, Yale Univ, 39; assoc, 39-48, from assoc prof to prof, 48-68, F J E Woodbridge prof, 68-73, EMER F J E WOODBRIDGE PROF PHILOS, COLUMBIA UNIV, 73-; Fulbright vis prof, Univ Pisa, 52; mem, Inst Advan Studies, Princeton, 54-55, 61 and 68-69; Guggenheim fel, 58 and 68-69. **HONORS AND AWARDS** Serena Medal, Brit Acad, 58; Premio, Int Forte dei marmi, 68., PhD, Univ Padua, 62, Middlebury Col, 72, Columbia Univ, 74, Cath Univ Am, 76, Univ Rochester, 77, Duke Univ, 79, Washington Univ, 82, State Univ NY, Binghamton, 82. **MEMBERSHIPS** Am Philos Asn; fel Mediaeval Acad Am; Am Soc Church Hist; Asn Teachers Ital; Renaissance Soc Am. **RESEARCH** Renaissance philosophy; ancient and medieval philosophy; intellectual history. **SELECTED PUBLICATIONS** Auth, Musica Scientia in Musical Scholarship in the Italian Renaissance, Am Hist Rev, Vol 0098, 93; Gordan, Phyllis, Goodhart In-Memoriam, Renaissance Quart, Vol 0047, 94; Iter Kristellerianum and Honoring the Career of Kristeller, Paul, Oskar, Renaissance Scholar in The European Journey 1905-1939, Renaissance Quart, Vol 0047, 94; Humanist Jurisprudence in Studies in the Field of Jurisprudence Under the Influence of Humanism, Renaissance Quart, Vol 0048, 95; Comment on Black Athena, J Hist Ideas, Vol 0056, 95; Ferrariis, Antonio, De, Called Il-Galateo, De Educatione 1505, Renaissance Quart, Vol 0049, 96. **CONTACT ADDRESS** 1161 Amsterdam Ave, New York, NY, 10027.

KRODEL, GOTTFRIED G.
PERSONAL Born 07/14/1931, Redwitz, Germany, m, 1956, 1 child **DISCIPLINE** CHURCH HISTORY **EDUCATION** Univ Erlangen, ThD, 55. **CAREER** Instr church hist, Univ Chicago, 56-59; from asst prof to assoc prof relig, Concordia Col, Moorhead, Minn, 59-65; assoc prof hist and church hist, 65-71, PROF HIST and CHURCH HIST, VALPARAISO UNIV, 71-. **MEMBERSHIPS** Am Soc Church Hist; Am Soc Reformation Res; AHA; Renaissance Soc Am; Lutber Ges. **RESEARCH** History of Christian thought; Renaissance and humanism; constitutional history of 16th century Germany. **SELECTED PUBLICATIONS** Auth, A Mystics Passion in The Spirituality of Staupitz, Johannes, Von in His 1520 Lenten Sermons, Church Hist, Vol 0062, 93; Erasmus, Church Hist, Vol 0063, 94; Erasmus, Lee and the Correction of the Vulgate in The Shaking of the Foundations, Church Hist, Vol 0064, 95; The Kings Bedpost in Reformation and Iconography in a Tudor Group-Portrait, Church Hist, Vol 0066, 97. **CONTACT ADDRESS** Dept of Hist, Valparaiso Univ, Valparaiso, IN, 46383.

KROIS, JOHN MICHAEL
PERSONAL Born 11/24/1943, Cincinnati, OH **DISCIPLINE** PHILOSOPHY, GERMAN **EDUCATION** Ohio Univ, BA, 68, MA, 70; Pa State Univ, PhD(philos), 75. **CAREER** Asst prof philos, Tech Univ of Braunschweig, 75-77; res fel, Inst Study Philos and Humanism, Munich, 77-79; ASST PROF PHILOS, UNIV TRIER, 80-. **MEMBERSHIPS** Charles S Peirce Soc; Hegel Soc Am; Ger Soc Semiotic Studies; Am Philos Asn; Semiotic Soc Am. **RESEARCH** Natural law theory; history of philosophy; philosophy of history. **SELECTED PUBLICATIONS** Auth, Verene and Cassirer in On New Beginnings, Clio-A, J Lit Hist Philos Hist, Vol 0023, 94; A Note About Philosophy and History in the Place of Cassirer Erkenntnisproblem, Sci Context, Vol 0009, 96. **CONTACT ADDRESS** Dept of Philos, Univ of Trier, Trier, ., 5500.

KRONDORFER, BJOERN
PERSONAL Born 03/29/1959, Frankfurt, Germany, m, 1991, 2 children **DISCIPLINE** RELIGIOUS STUDIES **EDUCATION** Goethe Univ, BA (equivalent), 81; Temple Univ, MA, 84, PhD, 90. **CAREER** Adj Asst Prof, Lehigh Univ, 90; Instr, Temple Univ, 90-91; Vis Asst Prof, 92-96, Asst Prof Religious Studies, St. Mary's Col Md, 96-. **HONORS AND AWARDS** DAAD Stipend, Ger Acad Exchange Service, 83; Luther Stipend, 84; Fel Coolidge Res Colloquium, 86; Dissertation Fel, Temple Univ, 89; Post-Doctoral Fel, Temple Univ, 90-91; Selected Schol for Speakers Bureau Md Humanities Coun, 96-99. **MEMBERSHIPS** Am Acad Relig; Soc Values Higher Educ; Am Men's Studies Asn; Bibliodrama Gesellschaft/Germany. **RESEARCH** Religion and culture; religion and gender; holocaust studies; religion, bible, arts. **SELECTED PUBLICATIONS** Ed, Body and Bible: Interpreting and Experiencing Biblical Narratives, Trinity Press Int, 92; auth, Remembrance and Reconciliation: Encounters Between Young Jews and Germans, Yale Univ Press, 95; ed, Men's Bodies, Men's Gods: Male Identities in a (Post-) Christian Culture, NY Univ Press, 96; auth, The Non-Absent Body: Confessions of an African Bishop and a Jewish Ghetto Policeman, In: Revealing Male Bodies (in progress). **CONTACT ADDRESS** Dept of Religious Studies, St. Mary's Col of Md, St. Mary's City, MD, 20686. **EMAIL** bhkrondorfer@osprey.smcm.edu

KRUPP, E.C.
PERSONAL Born 11/18/1944, Chicago, IL, m, 1968, 1 child **DISCIPLINE** PHYSICS ASTRONOMY **EDUCATION** Pomona Col, BA 66; UCLA, MA 68, PhD 72. **CAREER** Griffith Observatory, Curator 72-74, Director 74. **HONORS AND AWARDS** Am Inst Physics, best writer; Bruce Medal, W Am Astron; Astro Soc of Pacific, Klumpke Roberts Awd. **MEMBERSHIPS** Astron Soc og the Pacific; AAS; Intl Astron Union. **RESEARCH** Ancient and pre-historic Astron; celestial component of belief systems. **SELECTED PUBLICATIONS** Skywatchers, Shamans & Kings: Astronomy and the Archaeology of Power, 97; Beyond the Blue Horizon: Myths and Legends of the Sun, Moon , Stars and Planets, 91; Archaeolastronomy and the Roots of Science, 84; numerous bks, papers and articles. **CONTACT ADDRESS** Griffith Observatory, 2800 East Observatory Rd, Los Angeles, CA, 90027.

KRYCH, MARGARET A.
PERSONAL m, 2 children **DISCIPLINE** SYSTEMATIC THEOLOGY AND CHRISTIAN EDUCATION **EDUCATION** Univ Western Australia, BA, 63, MA, 70, grad diploma, 68; Melbourne Col Divinity, BD, 66, Theol M, 70; Princeton, PhD, 85. **CAREER** Teacher, theol, Methodist Deaconess Community, 65; parish minister, Methodist Conf of Western Australia, 66-67; assoc dir, dept of christ educ, Western Australia Methodist Conf, 68-70; master-in-residence, Princeton Theol Sem, 70-71; ed, div for parish svc, LCA, 73-77; asst prof, christ educ, Lutheran Theol Sem, 77-82; assoc prof, christ educ, Lutheran Theol Sem, 82-88; vis lectr, Princeton Theol Sem, 88-89; prof, christ educ, Lutheran Theol Sem, 88-91; prof, christ educ and theol, Lutheran Theol Sem, 91-93; Charles F. Norton prof, christ educ and theol, Lutheran Theol Sem, 93-; assoc dean of grad educ, Lutheran Theol Sem, 97-. **HONORS AND AWARDS** Commonwealth scholar, 60-62; Hackett scholar, 63, 64; Fulbright grant, 70; J.R. Saunders prize in philos, 60; Outstanding Young Women of Amer, 76, 77. **MEMBERSHIPS** Australian-New Zealand Soc for Theol Studies, 65-70; Australian Psychol Soc, 69-70; Nat Asn for Gifted Children, 87-92; Relig Educ Asn of US and Can, 73-; Asn of Prof and Res in Relig Educ, 77-; Soc for Res in Child Develop, 77-; AAR/SBL, 91-; Asn of Dr of Ministry Educ, 97-. **SELECTED PUBLICATIONS** Auth, The Gospel Calls Us (Theology of Lifelong Learning), Lifelong Learning, Augsburg Fortress, 97; auth, The Bible and Those Difficult Topics, Parish Teacher, 95; auth, Women in Churchwide & Seminary Ministry, Lutheran Women in Ordained Ministry, 1970-1995, Augsburg, 95; auth, Seminary Commemorates 25th Anniversary of Ordination of Women, P.S., 95; auth, The Future of the Catechisms in Teaching, Currents in Theol and Mission, 94; auth, The Pastor as Christian Educator, Parish Practice Notebook, 94; contr, A Collection of Responses from ELCA Academicians and Synodical Bishops to The Church and Human Sexuality: A Lutheran Perspective, 94. **CONTACT ADDRESS** 210 Wells Ln., Springfield, PA, 19064. **EMAIL** mkrych@ltsp.edu

KUBICKI, JUDITH M.
PERSONAL Born 08/21/1946, Buffalo, NY **DISCIPLINE** RELIGION **EDUCATION** Catholic Univ of Amer, PhD, 97. **CAREER** Dir of Music, 86-93, acad dean, 97-, Christ the King Sem. **RESEARCH** Liturgy, liturgical music, symbol, semiotics ritual. **CONTACT ADDRESS** 711 Knox Rd, East Aurora, NY, 14502. **EMAIL** jkubicki@pcom.net

KUCHEMAN, CLARK ARTHUR
PERSONAL Born 02/07/1931, Akron, OH, m, 1961 **DISCIPLINE** PHILOSOPHY, RELIGION **EDUCATION** Univ Akron, BA, 52; Meadville Theol Sch of Lombard Col, BD, 55; Univ Chicgo, MA, (Economics) 59, PhD(Relig & Ethics), 65. **CAREER** From instr to asst prof Social Ethics, Univ Chicago, 61-67; prof Relig & Philos, 67-80, Arthur V Stoughton Prof Christian Ethics, Claremont McKenna Col & Claremont Grad Univ, 80-, Nat Endowment for Humanities, fel, 70. **MEMBERSHIPS** Am Acad Relig; North Amer Soc for Social Philosophy; Hegel Society of America. **RESEARCH** Ethics, especially philosophical and religious; philosophy of economic science. **SELECTED PUBLICATIONS** Auth, Professor Tillich: Justice and the economic order, J Relig; Toward a theory of normative economics, In: Social Ethics: Issues in Ethics and Society, Harper, 68; Religion, culture and religious socialism, J Relig, 7/72; Morality versus economic science in religious socialism, In: Belief and Ethics, Ctr Sci Study Relig, 78; Rationality and moral obligation, In: The Life of Choice, Beacon Press. **CONTACT ADDRESS** 850 Columbia Ave, Claremont, CA, 91711-6420. **EMAIL** clark_kucheman@mckenna.edu

KUEHN, MANFRED
DISCIPLINE THE HISTORY OF EARLY MODERN PHILOSOPHY **EDUCATION** McGill Univ, PhD. **CAREER** Prof, Purdue Univ. **RESEARCH** 18th century philosophy; Immanuel Kant, Hume, Reid. **SELECTED PUBLICATIONS** Auth, Scottish Common Sense in Germany, 1768-1800. **CONTACT ADDRESS** Dept of Philos, Purdue Univ, 1080 Schleman Hall, West Lafayette, IN, 47907-1080.

KUHN, STEVE
DISCIPLINE PHILOSOPHY **EDUCATION** Johns Hopkins Univ, BA; Stanford Univ, PhD. **CAREER** Dept Philos, Georgetown Univ **RESEARCH** Logic; philosophy of logic; ethics; metaphysics; philosophy of language. **SELECTED PUBLICATIONS** Auth, pubs on modal and tense logic, and reasoning in ordinary language. **CONTACT ADDRESS** Dept of Philosophy, Georgetown Univ, 37th and O St, Washington, DC, 20057.

KUHN, STEVEN THOMAS
PERSONAL Born 03/01/1949, Baltimore, Md, m, 1970, 1 child **DISCIPLINE** PHILOSOPHY **EDUCATION** Johns Hopkins Univ, BA, 70; Stanford Univ, PhD(philos), 76. **CAREER** Fel comput sci, Univ Pa, 77-78; Assoc Prof Philos, Georgetown Univ, 78- **MEMBERSHIPS** Am Philos Soc; Asn Symbolic Logic; Soc Exact Philos; Asn Comput Mach. **RESEARCH** Logic; philosophy of science; philosophy of language. **SELECTED PUBLICATIONS** Auth, Many Sorted Modal Logics, Uppsala Studies Philos, 77; The Pragmatics of Tense, Vol 40, Synthese; Quantifiers as modal operators, Vol 39, Studia Logica; coauth (with A K Joshi), Centered logic, Proc 1979 Int Joint Conf Artificial Intel, 79; auth, Logical expressions, constants and operation logic, Vol 78, J Philos; auth, The Domino Relation, J Phil Logic 181 coauth, Numbers without Ones, The Fibbonacci Qrt vol 30; auth, Minimal Non-Contingency Logic, Notre Dame J of Formal Logic, vol 36. **CONTACT ADDRESS** Dept of Philos, Georgetown Univ, 1421 37th St N W, Washington, DC, 20057-0001.

KUHN, THOMAS SAMUEL
PERSONAL Born 07/18/1922, Cincinnati, OH, m, 1948, 3 children **DISCIPLINE** HISTORY AND PHILOSOPHY OF SCIENCE **EDUCATION** Harvard Univ, BS, 43, MA, 46, PhD(physics), 49. **CAREER** Civilian employee, off Sci Res and Develop, Harvard Univ, 43-45, instr gen educ, 51-52, asst prof gen educ and hist of sci, 52-56; from asst prof to prof hist of

sci, Univ Calif, Berkeley, 56-74; prof, Princeton Univ, 64-68, M Taylor Pyne Prof, 69-79; PROF PHILOS and HIST SCI, MASS INST TECHNOL, 79-; Lowell lectr, 51; Guggenheim fel, 54-55; fel, Ctr Advan Studies Behav Sci, 58-59; dir, Sources Hist of Quantum Physics Proj, 61-64; bd dirs, Soc Sci Res Coun, 64-67; assoc ed physics, Dict Sci Biog, 64-; dir prog hist and philos of sci, Princeton Univ, 67-72; mem, Inst Advan Study, 72-79; MEM, ASSEMBLY BEHAV and SOC SCI, 80-. **HONORS AND AWARDS** Howard T Behrman Award, Princeton Univ, 77., LLD, Univ Notre Dame, 73; DHL, Rider Col, 78; Doctorate, Linkoping Univ, Sweden, 80. **MEMBERSHIPS** Nat Acad Sci; Am Philos Soc; Am Acad Arts and Sci; Hist Sci Soc (pres, 68-70); Am Philos Asn. **RESEARCH** Reconstruction of out-of-date scientific ideas; description and abstract analysis of the way languag an ideas change in scientific development. **SELECTED PUBLICATIONS** Auth, The Road Since Structure, Arbor Ciencia Pensamiento Cult, Vol 0148, 94. **CONTACT ADDRESS** Dept of Ling and Philos Mass, Massachusetts Inst of Tech, Cambridge, MA, 02139.

KUHNS, RICHARD
PERSONAL Born 05/03/1924, Chicago, IL, m **DISCIPLINE** PHILOSOPHY **EDUCATION** Dartmouth, BA, 47; Columbia Univ, PhD, 55 **CAREER** Prof, 50-95 Columbia Univ **CONTACT ADDRESS** 420 Riverside Dr, New York, NY, 10025.

KUJAWA, SHERYL A.
PERSONAL Born 05/30/1956, Milwaukee, WI **DISCIPLINE** RELIGIOUS STUDIES **EDUCATION** Marquette Univ, BA, 77; Sarah Lawrence Col, MA, 79; Harvard Divinity Sch, MTS, 81; Episcopal Divinity Sch, Mdiv, 83; Boston Col, PhD, 93. **CAREER** Adjunct fac, Episcopal Divinity Sch, 86-88; adjunct fac, Union Theol Sem, 92-95; assoc prof of Pastoral Theol, Episcopal Divinity Sch, 98-. **HONORS AND AWARDS** Ford Found fel, 78-79; Hist fel, Boston Col, 81-84. **MEMBERSHIPS** Asn of Prof and Res in Relig Educ; Asn of Theol Field Educ. **RESEARCH** Religious studies. **SELECTED PUBLICATIONS** Auth, "Youth Ministry: Evangelization, Conscientization, and Liberation," 98; auth, Disorganized Religion: The Evangelization of Youth and Young Adults, 98; co-auth, GodWorks: Youth and Young Adult Ministry Models...Evangelism at Work With Young People. **CONTACT ADDRESS** 99 Brattle St, Cambridge, MA, 02138. **EMAIL** Skujawa@episdivschool.org

KUKLA, REBECCA
DISCIPLINE HISTORY OF MODERN PHILOSOPHY, SOCIAL PHILOSOPHY, GENDER THEORY AND CULTURAL **EDUCATION** Univ Toronto, BA, 90; Univ Pittsburgh, PhD, 95. **CAREER** Asst prof, Univ NMex. **RESEARCH** The writing of Jean-Jacques Rousseau. **SELECTED PUBLICATIONS** Published in The Brit J for Psihol of Sci, Metaphilosophy, J of Speculative Philos, J of Brit Soc for Phenomenol, Poznan Stud, Eidos, and Anal, as well as contributing chapters to volumes on Rousseau, Feminist Theory, and Popular Cult. **CONTACT ADDRESS** Univ NMex, Albuquerque, NM, 87131.

KULSTAD, MARK ALAN
PERSONAL Born 01/08/1947, Minneapolis, MN **DISCIPLINE** PHILOSOPHY **EDUCATION** Macalester Col, BA, 69; Univ Mich, PhD(philos), 75. **CAREER** Asst prof, 75-81, ASSOC PROF PHILOS, RICE UNIV, 81-; Alexander von Humboldt Found res fel, Hanover, WGer, 79-80. **MEMBERSHIPS** Am Philos Asn; Am Leibniz Soc (pres, 81 -). **CONTACT ADDRESS** Dept of Philos, Rice Univ, Houston, TX, 77251.

KULTGEN, JOHN
PERSONAL Born 10/16/1925, Dallas, TX, m, 1980, 5 children **DISCIPLINE** PHILOSOPHY **EDUCATION** Univ Texas, Austin, BA, 46; Univ Chicago, MA, 48, PhD, 52. **CAREER** Asst prof philos, Oregon State Univ, 52-56; assoc prof and prof, philos, Southern Methodist Univ, 56-67; prof philos, Univ Missouri, Columbia, 67-. **HONORS AND AWARDS** Peace Stud Prof of the Year, 96; Byler Dist Prof, 98. **MEMBERSHIPS** APA; Southwest Philos Soc; Concerned Philos for Peace. **RESEARCH** Epistemology; ethics; war and peace; professional ethics. **SELECTED PUBLICATIONS** Auth, Purging Our Nuclear Intentions, Peace and Justice Stud, 93; auth, Ron Kovic, in DeLeon, ed, Leaders from the 1960s, Greenwood, 94; auth, Intervention and Autonomy: Parentalism and the Caring Life, Oxford, 95; auth, Military as A Profession, in Wells, ed, An Encyclopedia of War and Ethics, Greenwood, 96; auth, William James' Moral Equivalent of War at One Hundred, Jour of Peace and Justice Stud, 97; auth, The Professionalization of the Military and the Management of Violence, in Litke, ed, Institutional Violence, Rodopi, 98; auth, Slote's Free Standing Virtue Ethics and Its Props, Southwest Jour of Philos, forthcoming; co-ed, Problems for Democracy: Obstacles to Peace and Justice, in Philosophy of Peace series, Rodopi, in preparation. **CONTACT ADDRESS** Dept of Philosophy, Univ of Missouri, Columbia, MO, 65211. **EMAIL** philjohn@showme.missouri.edu

KUMAR, RAHUL
PERSONAL Born 11/08/1967, Canada, s **DISCIPLINE** PHILOSOPHY **EDUCATION** Queens Univ, Canada, BA; Univ of Oxford, MA, 92; PhD, 95. **CAREER** Post-Dr Fel, Harvard Univ, 95-97. **HONORS AND AWARDS** SSHRC Post-Dr Fel, 95-97. **MEMBERSHIPS** APA **RESEARCH** Ethical Theory and Psychology. **CONTACT ADDRESS** Dr, Univ Pennsylvania, Logan Hall # 466, Philadelphia, PA, 19104-6304. **EMAIL** rakumar@phil.penn.edu

KUMFER, EARL T.
DISCIPLINE THEOLOGY **EDUCATION** Cath Univ Am, AB, 62, MA, 63; Southern Ill Univ, Carbondale, 82. **CAREER** CHAIR, PROF PHILOS & THEOL, UNIV ST FRANCIS, 65-. **CONTACT ADDRESS** 4801 Arlington Ave, Fort Wayne, IN, 46807. **EMAIL** ekumfer@sfc.edu

KUNKEL, JOSEPH C.
DISCIPLINE ETHICS **EDUCATION** St Bonaventure Univ, PhD, 64. **CAREER** Dept Philos, Univ Dayton **RESEARCH** Philosophy of peace. **SELECTED PUBLICATIONS** Co-ed, In the Interest of Peace: A Spectrum of Philosophical Views, Longwood Acad, 90; auth, Power Politics, Human Nature, and Morality, On the Eve of the 21st Century: Perspectives of Russian and American Philosophers, Rowman and Littlefield, 94; The Rich Get Richer and the Poor Starve: Is There an Ethical Alternative?, Philosophical Perspectives on Power and Domination: Theories and Practices, Editions Rodopi, 97. **CONTACT ADDRESS** Dept of Philos, Univ Dayton, 300 Col Park, Dayton, OH, 75062. **EMAIL** kunkel@checkov.hm.udayton.edu

KUNTZ, J. KENNETH
PERSONAL Born 01/20/1934, St. Louis, MO, m, 1962, 2 children **DISCIPLINE** BIBLICAL STUDIES **EDUCATION** Grinnell Col, BA, 56; Yale Univ Div Sch, BD, 59; Union Theol Sem, PhD, 63. **CAREER** Instr, 63-65, asst prof, 65-67, relig, Wellesley Col; asst prof, 67-70, assoc prof, 70-76, prof, 76- , Sch of Relig, Univ Iowa. **HONORS AND AWARDS** NEH summer stipend, 71, 84; Alexander von Humbolt Stiftung, 71-72. **MEMBERSHIPS** Catholic Bibl Asn; Soc of Bibl Lit; Chicago Soc of Bibl Res; Soc for Old Testament Study. **RESEARCH** Biblical Hebrew poetry; Psalms studies; rhetorical criticism of Biblical texts. **SELECTED PUBLICATIONS** Auth, The Self-Revelation of God, Westminster, 67; auth, The People of Ancient Israel: An Introduction to Old Testament Literature, History, and Thought, Harper & Row, 74; auth, King Triumphant: A Rhetorical Study of Psalms 20 and 21, Hebrew Annual Rev, 86; auth, Recent Perspectives on Biblical Poetry, Relig Stud Rev, 93; auth, Engaging the Psalms: Gains and Trends in Recent Research, Currents in Research: Biblical Studies, 94; auth, The Form, Location, and Function of Rhetorical Questions in Deutero-Isaiah, in Broyles, ed, Writing and Reading the Scroll of Isaiah: Studies in an Interpretive Tradition, Brill, 97. **CONTACT ADDRESS** School of Religion, Univ of Iowa, Iowa City, IA, 52242-1376. **EMAIL** ken-kuntz@uiowa.edu

KUNTZ, PAUL G.
PERSONAL Born 11/22/1915, Philadelphia, PA, m, 1970, 4 children **DISCIPLINE** PHILOSOPHY **EDUCATION** Haverford Col, BA, 37; Harvard Univ Div, STB-STM, 40, 41, PhD, 46; Yale Univ, post doct, 54-55. **CAREER** Asst to dean, 38-41, Harvard Univ; instr, rel, 46-48, Smith Col; asst prof, phil & rel, assoc prof, 52-57, prof, 57-56, Noble Prof, 61-66, Grinnell Col; chmn, dept phil, 66-69, prof, 66-85, prof emer, 85-, Emory Univ. **HONORS AND AWARDS** Kent Fel, Natl Soc Values in Higher Ed, 45; Ford Found Fel phil, Yale Univ, 55-56; Lilly Found Res Grant, 59-60; Carnegie Corp NY: Dir Grinnell Sem on Order, 63-64; Danforth Cross Discip Fel, 66; APS, Phil Res Grants, 68-69, 70-71, 72-73; Amer Coun of Learned Soc, trvl grants, 69, 73; 8 Res Grants, Emory Univ, 66-73, 82-83; Woodrow Wilson Intl Ctr for Schlrs, Smithsonian Inst, Fel, 70-71. **MEMBERSHIPS** Metaphysical Soc Amer; Soc for Aesthetics; So Soc for Phil & Psychol; Santayana Soc; Gandhi-King Soc; Intl Soc of Metaphysics; AAR; Soc of Christian Phil; Maritain Soc; Amer Phil Catholic Soc. **RESEARCH** Metaphysics, theory of order. **SELECTED PUBLICATIONS** Auth, Doing Something for the Categories: the Cable of Categoreal Methods and the Resulting Tree of Categories, Time & Change to Consciousness: Stud in the Metaphysics of Charles Peirce, Berg Pub, 94; auth, Cosmos and Chaos: Weiss's Systematic Categorization of the Universe, Phil Paul Weiss, Lib of Living Phil, vol XXIII, Open Court, 95; art, Of Rights and Duties: A Jeffersonian Dialogue, Modern Age, vol 38, 96; art, John O'Neill, The Canadian Burkean, and His Dialectic of Covenant and Contract, Phil of Soc Sci, vol 27, 97; auth, Der Sittenkodex eines Radikalen Reformators: Paracelsus und die Zehn Gebote, Europa in der Fruhen Neuzeit: Festchrift fur Gunter Muhlpfords, Bohlau Verlag, 97; art, The Ten Commandments on Schoolroom Walls? Why did the Supreme Court Reject the 1978 Kentucky Statute (Stone v Graham)? Could such a Law Succeed? Univ Florida J of Law & Pub Pol, vol 9, 97; art, John Ruskin on Bishop Moses and the Ten Commandments, Ruskin Gazette, J of Ruskin Soc of London, 98; auth, The Moral Code of A Radical Reformer: Paracelsus and the Ten Commandments, Contentious Triangle: Church, State & Univ; A Festschrif in Honor of Prof George H. Williams, Forest Clingerman, 98; art, Jefferson as a Man of Moderation, Conor Cruise O'Brien, The Long Affair: Thomas Jefferson and the French Revolution, 1785-1800, Modern Age, vol 40, 98. **CONTACT ADDRESS** 1655 Ponce de Leon Ave NE, Atlanta, GA, 30307-1619.

KUO, LENORE
PERSONAL New York, NY **DISCIPLINE** METAPHYSICS, ETHICS AND THE HISTORY OF PHILOSOPHY **EDUCATION** Univ Wis, Madison, BA, MA, PhD. **CAREER** Assoc prof Philos and Women's Stud, Univ Nebr, Omaha, 85-. **RESEARCH** Social policy analysis. **SELECTED PUBLICATIONS** Published on topics as diverse as surrogate mothering, corruption in bureaucracy and recent U.S. attempts to require women to use Norplant (a form of birth control) as a condition of probation. **CONTACT ADDRESS** Univ Nebr, Omaha, Omaha, NE, 68182.

KUPPERMAN, JOEL J.
PERSONAL Born 05/18/1936, Chicago, IL, m, 1964, 2 children **DISCIPLINE** PHILOSOPHY **EDUCATION** Univ Chicago, AB, 54, SB, 55, Am, 56; Cambridge Univ, PhD, 63. **CAREER** From instr to assoc prof, 60-72, PROF PHILOS, UNIV CT, 72-; Nat Endowment for Humanities fel, 81; vis fel, Corpus Christi Col, Oxford, 85, Rockefeller villa at Bellagio, 88, Clare Hall, 88; Earhart Found fel, 95-96. **HONORS AND AWARDS** Excellence in Teaching Prize, Univ CT, 73. **MEMBERSHIPS** Am Philos Asn; Soc Asian & Comp Philos. **RESEARCH** Ethics; metaphysics. **SELECTED PUBLICATIONS** Auth, Ethical Knowledge, Allen & Unwin, London, 70; Precision in History, Mind, 75; Vulgar Consequentialism, Mind, 80; Foundations of Morality, Allen & Unwin, London, 83; Character, Oxford Univ Press, 91; Value...And What Follows, Oxford Univ Press, 99; Learning from Asian Philosophy, Oxford Univ Press, 99. **CONTACT ADDRESS** Dept of Philos, Univ of CT, U-54, Storrs, CT, 06269-2054. **EMAIL** JKupper@uconnvm.uconn.edu

KURLAND, ADAM H.
DISCIPLINE LAW **EDUCATION** Univ Calif, Los Angeles, BA, 78, JD, 81. **CAREER** Prof. **MEMBERSHIPS** Amer Bar Asn; participated, Cent Eastern and Europ Law Initiative Workshop in Alma-Ata Kazakhstan; active mem, ABA White Collar Crime Subcomt & Criminal Justice Sect Bk Publ Comt. **RESEARCH** Negotiating immunity and plea agreements in the state and federal criminal justice systems. **SELECTED PUBLICATIONS** Auth, Providing a Federal Criminal Defendant with a Unilateral Right to a Bench Trial: A Renewed Call to Amend Federal Rule of Criminal Procedure 23 (a), 26 UC Davis L Rev 309, 93 & First Principles of American Federalism and the Nature of Federal Criminal Jurisdiction, Emory Law J 1, 96. **CONTACT ADDRESS** Dept of Law, Howard Univ, 2400 Sixth St NW, Washington, DC, 20059.

KURLAND, PHILIP B.
PERSONAL Born 10/22/1921, New York, NY, m, 1954 **DISCIPLINE** LAW **EDUCATION** Univ Pa, AB, 42; Harvard Univ, LLB, 44, JD, 69. **CAREER** Assoc prof law, Northwestern Univ, 50-53; WILLIAM R KENAN DISTINGUISHED SERV PROF, UNIV CHICAGO, 53-; ED, SUPREME COURT REV, 60-; Chief consult, US Senate Subcomt Separation of Powers, 67-76; COUNSEL, ROTHSCHILD, BARRY and MYERS, 72-. **HONORS AND AWARDS** LLD, Univ Notre Dame, 77 and Univ Detroit, 82. **RESEARCH** Legal history and procedure; constitutional law, judicial biography. **SELECTED PUBLICATIONS** Auth, Judicial Biography in History, Myth, Literature, Fiction, Potpourri, New York Univ Law Rev, Vol 0070, 95. **CONTACT ADDRESS** Univ of Chicago, 1116 E 59th St, Chicago, IL, 60637.

KURTZ, PAUL
PERSONAL Born 12/21/1925, Newark, NJ, m, 1960, 4 children **DISCIPLINE** PHILOSOPHY **EDUCATION** NY Univ, BA, 48; Columbia Univ, MA, 49, PhD, 52. **CAREER** Instr, Queens Col, 50-52; instr to assoc prof, Trinity Col, 52-59; vis lectr New Sch of Soc Res, 60-65; assoc prof, Vassar Col, 60; prof Philos Union Col, 61-65; prof emer philos SUNY Buffalo, 65- ; pres, Prometheus Books, 70- ; chemn, com for the Sci Investigation of Claims of the Paranormal, 76- ; ed-in-chief, Free Inquiry Mag, 80- . **HONORS AND AWARDS** Fel, AAAS; John Dewey fel; Bertrand Russell Soc Award; John Dewey Fel. **MEMBERSHIPS** AAAS; Am Philos Asn; Int Acad of Humanism; Int Humanist and Ethical Union. **RESEARCH** Value theory; social philosophy; science and the paranormal. **SELECTED PUBLICATIONS** Auth, The New Skepticism: Inquiry and Reliable Knowledge, Prometheus, 92; auth, Living without Religion: Eupraxophy, Prometheus, 94; auth, Toward a New Enlightenment: The Philosophy of Paul Kurtz, Transaction, 94; coed, Challenges to the Enlightenment: In Defense of Reason and Science, Prometheus, 94; auth, The Courage to Become: The Virtues of Humanism, Praeger, 97. **CONTACT ADDRESS** PO Box 664, Amherst, NY, 14226. **EMAIL** PaulKurtz@aol.com

KURZ, WILLIAM STEPHEN
PERSONAL Born 11/09/1939, Detroit, MI **DISCIPLINE** NEW TESTAMENT, CHRISTIAN ORIGINS **EDUCATION** St Louis Univ, BA, 63, MA, 64, PhL, 64, MA, 70, STL, 71; Yale Univ, PhD(New Testament), 76. **CAREER** Instr philos, Creighton Univ, 64-65; teacher Greek and Latin, Creighton Prep Sch, 65-67; ASST PROF NEW TESTAMENT, MARQUETTE UNIV, 75-. **MEMBERSHIPS** Soc Bibl Lit; Cath Bibl Asn. **RESEARCH** Gospel of Luke-Book of Acts; the Greek Bible and Hellenistic Judaism; intertestamental and New Testament reinterpretation of earlier scriptures. **SELECTED PUBLICATIONS** Auth, The Farewell of the Word in the Johannine Call to Abide, Theol Studies, Vol 0054, 93; Host, Guest, Enemy, and Friend in Portraits of the Pharisees in Luke and Acts, Cath Biblical Quart, Vol 0055, 93; Images of Judaism in Luke Acts, J Amn Acad Rel, Vol 0061, 93; Moses or Jesus in an Essay in Johannine Christology, Theol Studies, Vol 0055, 94; Stewardship and the Kingdom of God in an Historical, Exegetical, and Contextual Study of the Parable of the Unjust Steward in Luke-Xvi,1-13, Cath Bibl Quart, Vol 0056, 94; The Apostolic Origins of the Gospels in German, Cath Biblical Quart, Vol 0057, 95; Becoming Children of God in John Gospel and Radical Discipleship, Theol Studies, Vol 0056, 95; The Legacy of Jesus and the Farewell Address of the Fathers in an Historical Investigation on the Genre of Farewell Speeches From the Gospel Perspective of John-Xiii-Xvii in German, J Bibl Lit, Vol 0115, 96; Effects of Variant Narrators in Acts-X-Xi in Functional Redundancy and Falsely Attributed Narrators Within Luke Acts of the Apostles, New Testament Studies, Vol 0043, 97. **CONTACT ADDRESS** Dept of Theol, Marquette Univ, Milwaukee, WI, 53233.

KUSHNER, JAMES ALAN
PERSONAL Born 04/14/1945, Philadelphia, PA, m, 1970, 3 children **DISCIPLINE** LAW, CONSTITUIONAL HISTORY **EDUCATION** Univ Miami, BBA, 67; Univ Md, LLB & JD, 68. **CAREER** Adj prof housing law, Univ Mo-Kansas City, 73; vis lectr, Univ Calif, Berkeley, 74-75; assoc prof, 75-78, PROF LAW, SOUTHWESTERN UNIV, CALIF, 78-; Consult, Am Bar Asn, 74-76; vis lectr, Univ Va, 81; vis prof, UCLA, 83 & 93. **MEMBERSHIPS** Am Asn Law Schs. **RESEARCH** Race and Law; urban housing and planning. **SELECTED PUBLICATIONS** Auth, Apartheid in America, Carrollton Press, 80; Urban Transportation Planning, Urban Law & Policy, Vol 4, 81; Housing & Community Development (with Mandelker et al), Michie/Bobbs-Merrill, 81, 2nd ed, 89; The Reagan Urban Policy: Centrifugal Force in the Empire, UCLA J Environ Law & Policy, 82; Non-Owner Rights in Real Property and the Impact on Property Taxes, Urban Law & Policy, 85; Government Discrimination, West, 88; DMS: The Development Monitoring System is the Latest Technique for Subdivision Review and Growth Management, Zoning and Planning Law Report, 88; Unfinished Agenda: The Federal Fair Housing Enforcement Effort, Yale Law & Pol Review, 88; Substantive Equal Protection: The Rehnquist Court and the Fourth Tier of Judicial Review, Mo Law Rev, 88; The Fair Housing Amendments Act of 1988: The Second Generation of Fair Housing, Vanderbilt Law Rev, 89; Subdivision Law and Growth Management, West, 91; Property and Mysticism: The Legality of Exactions as a Condition for Public Development Approval in the Time of the Rehnquist Court, J Land Use & Environ Law, 92; Vested Development Rights, in 1992 Zoning and Planning Law Handbook, 92; A Tale of Three Cities: Land Development and Planning for Growth in Stockholm, Berlin, and Los Angeles, Urban Lawyer, 93; Growth Management and the City, Yale Law & Pol Rev, 94; Fair Housing: Discrimination in Real Estate, Community Development and Revitalization, 2nd ed, West, 95; Growth for the Twenty-First Century: Tales from Bavaria and the Vienna Woods -- Comparative Images of Urban Planning in Munich, Salzburg, Vienna, and the United States, Southern Calif Interdisciplinary Law J, 97; co-auth, Land Use Regulation: Cases and Materials, Aspen Law and Business, forthcoming; co-auth, Housing and Community Development: Cases and Materials, 3rd ed, Carolina Acad Press, forthcoming. **CONTACT ADDRESS** School of Law, Southwestern Univ, 675 S Westmoreland Ave, Los Angeles, CA, 90005-3905. **EMAIL** jkushner@swlaw.edu

KUYKENDALL, CRYSTAL ARLENE
PERSONAL Born 12/11/1949, Chicago, IL, w, 1969 **DISCIPLINE** EDUCATION, LAW **EDUCATION** So IL Univ, BA 1970; Montclair State Univ, MA 1972; Atlanta Univ, EdD 1975; Georgetown Univ Law Ctr, JD 1982. **CAREER** Seton Hall US Orange NJ, Montclair State Univ, instr 1971-73; DC Publ School, admin intern plnng rsch & eval 1974-75; Natl Comm for Citizens in Ed, dir 1975-77; Natl School Bds Assoc Wash DC, dir urban & minority rel dept 1978-79; PSI Assoc Inc Wash DC, dir ed devel 1979-80; Natl Alliance of Black School Ed, exec dir 1980-81; Roy Littlejohn Assoc Inc, sr assoc 1982-; KIRK Inc (Kreative and Innovative Resources for Kids), president and general counsel. **HONORS AND AWARDS** Awd for Outstanding Comm Serv to Women & Minorities, Natl Coalition of Esea Title I Parents 1979; "50 Leaders of the Future" Ebony Mag 1978; Hon Citizen New Orleans State of LA, Outstanding Serv Natl Caucus of Black School Bd Mems 1979; Presidential Appointment to The Natl Advisory Council on Continuing Educ, US Pres, Jimmy Carter 1978-81, chairperson 1979-81; Black Excellence Award, Black Alumni Association of Southern IL Univ 1981; Urban League of Greater Muskegon, Service Award; Natl Assn of Blacks in Criminal Justice, Service Award. **MEMBERSHIPS** Chpsn Natl Adv Council Continuing Ed 1978-81; consult Natl Teachers Corp Proj 1978-79; cons, mem Natl Transition Team for the Office of Elem Secondary Ed 1980; mem Amer Assn of School Admin 1974-; mem ed task force Martin Luther King Jr Ctr for Soc Change 1977-; mem Black Amer Law Students Assn 1978-; mem, Amer Bar Assn, Natl Bar Assn, DC Bar Assn, 1988, assoc supvr and curriculum developer, 1992-. **SELECTED PUBLICATIONS** Author, "Comm Serv & School Bd," Publ Cross Reference Journal of Multicultural Ed 1979; You/Yours: Making the Most of this School Year, motivational calender, 1987; booklet published: "Improving Black Student Achievement Through Enhancing Self-Image," , Amer Univ Mid-Atlantic Equity Center, 1989; "From Rage to Hope: Strategies for Reclaiming Black and Hispanic Students," National Education Service Inc, 1992.

KUZMINSKI, ADRIAN
PERSONAL Born 02/21/1944, Washington, PA, m, 1966, 2 children **DISCIPLINE** HISTORY, PHILOSOPHY **EDUCATION** Amherst Coll, BA, 66; Univ of Rochester, PhD, 73. **CAREER** Prof of Hist, 71-80, Univ of Hawaii; Res Scholar in Philos, 96-, Hartwick Coll. **HONORS AND AWARDS** Fulbright and Wilson Fellow. **MEMBERSHIPS** APA **RESEARCH** Consciousness, political economy. **SELECTED PUBLICATIONS** The Soul, Peter Lang Pub, NY, 94. **CONTACT ADDRESS** RD #1, Box 68, Fly Creek, NY, 13337. **EMAIL** adrian@clarityconnect.com

KUZNIEWSKI, ANTHONY JOSEPH
PERSONAL Born 01/28/1945, Carthage, MO **DISCIPLINE** AMERICAN HISTORY, CHURCH HISTORY **EDUCATION** Marquette Univ, AB, 66; Harvard Univ, AM, 67, PhD(hist), 73; Loyola Univ Chicago, MDiv, 80. **CAREER** Teaching fel hist, Harvard Univ, 68-72; asst prof, Col Holy Cross, 74-76 and Loyola Univ Chicago, 80-81; ASST PROF HIST, COL HOLY CROSS, 81-; Res tutor hist, Kirkland, House Harvard Col, 70-72; Vis lectr, Loyola Univ Chicago, 76-77. **HONORS AND AWARDS** Oscar Halecki Award, Polish Am Hist Asn and Am Hist Asn, 81. **MEMBERSHIPS** Polish Am Hist Asn (pres, 82-83); Am Cath Hist Asn; Orgn Am Historians. **RESEARCH** Polish immigrants in the United States; the religious life of Polish Americans; the interaction of various Catholic immigrant groups in the United States. **SELECTED PUBLICATIONS** Auth, This Confident Church in Catholic Leadership and Life in Chicago, 1940-1965, Am Hist Rev, Vol 0099, 94; Contending with Modernity in Catholic Higher Education in the 20th Century, Am Hist Rev, Vol 0102, 97. **CONTACT ADDRESS** Dept of Hist, Col of the Holy Cross, Worcester, MA, 01610.

KWON, KYEONG-SEOG
PERSONAL Born 03/18/1962, Seoul, Korea, m, 1987, 1 child **DISCIPLINE** RELIGION **EDUCATION** Yale Univ, STM, 91; Claremont Grad Univ, PhD, 98. **CAREER** Adj prof, KPCA Presbyterian Theol Sem, Whittier, Calif, 95-; vis scholar, Harvard Univ, 98. **HONORS AND AWARDS** Grad student paper competition award, Am Acad of Relig, western div, 95. **MEMBERSHIPS** Am Acad Relig; APA. **RESEARCH** World religions; systematic theology; Christian thought; philosophy of religion; Asian religion and thought. **CONTACT ADDRESS** 913 La Salle Cir, Corona, CA, 91719. **EMAIL** kskwon@earthlink.net

KYMLICKA, WILL
DISCIPLINE PHILOSOPHY **EDUCATION** Queen's Univ, BA, 84; Univ Oxford, BPhil, 86, PhD, 87. **CAREER** Lectr, Queen's Univ, 86-87; Princeton Univ, 87-88; Univ Toronto, 88-89; asst prof, Univ Toronto, 89-90; sr policy analyst, Royal Commission on New Reproductive Tech, 90-91; visiting prof, Univ Ottawa, 91-93; visiting prof, 94-98; res dir, Univ Ottawa, 94-98; visiting fel, Europ Forum, Europ Univ Inst, 96-; vis prof, Inst for Adv Stud, Vienna, 97-; Queen's Nat scholar, Queen's Univ, 98-; visiting prof, Univ Pompeau Fabra, Barcelona, 98-; Nationalism Stud Prog, Cent Europ Univ, Budapest, 98-. **HONORS AND AWARDS** Commonwealth scholar, 84-86; doc fel, SSHRC, 86-87; postdoc fel, SSHRC, 87-89; Can res fel, SSHRC, 89-92; Strategic Grants award, SSHRC, 94-97; Ralph J Bunche award, Amer Polit Sci Assn, 96; Macpherson prize, Can Polit Sci Assn, 96; Strategic Grants award, SSHRC, 98. **SELECTED PUBLICATIONS** Auth, Liberalism, Community, and Culture, Oxford UP, 89; Contemp Polit Philos, Oxford UP, 90; Multicultural Citizenship, Oxford UP, 95; Finding Our Way: Rethinking Ethnocultural Relations in Canada, Oxford UP, 98; ed, Justice in Political Philosophy, Elgar, 92; The Rights of Minority Cultures, Oxford, 95; Ethnicity and Group Rights, NYU, 97. **CONTACT ADDRESS** Dept of Philos, Carleton Univ, 1125 Colonel By Dr, Ottawa, ON, K1S 5B6. **EMAIL** kymlicka@uottawa.ca

L

LACHS, JOHN
PERSONAL Born 07/17/1934, Budapest, Hungary, m, 1967, 2 children **DISCIPLINE** PHILOSOPHY **EDUCATION** McGill Univ, BA, 56, MA, 57; Yale Univ, PhD, 61. **CAREER** Asst prof to prof, William & Mary Col, 59-67; prof, 67-93, centennial prof, 93- , Vanderbilt Univ. **HONORS AND AWARDS** E. Harris Harbison Award for Distinguished Tchg; Chancellor's Cup; Madison Sanatt Prize for Excellence in Undergrad Tchg; Herbert Schneider Award for Lifetime Contrib to Am Philos. **MEMBERSHIPS** APA; Soc for the Advancement of Am Philos; Metaphysical Soc of Am. **RESEARCH** American philosophy; ethics; medical ethics; metaphysics. **SELECTED PUBLICATIONS** Auth, Intermediate Man, 81; auth, Mind and Philosophers, 87; auth, George Santayana, 88; auth, The Relevance of Philosophy to Life, 95; auth, In Love with Life, 98; auth, The Cost of Comfort, 99; coauth, Thinking in the Ruins, 99. **CONTACT ADDRESS** Dept of Philosophy, Vanderbilt Univ, Nashville, TN, 37240. **EMAIL** lachsj@ctrvax.vanderbilt.edu

LACKEY, DOUGLAS PAUL
PERSONAL Born 08/27/1945, New York, NY **DISCIPLINE** PHILOSOPHY **EDUCATION** Mich State Univ, BA, 66; Yale Univ, PhD(philos), 70. **CAREER** Ass prof philos, NY Univ, 70; asst prof, 72-76, assoc, 76-82, prof philos, Bernard Baruch Col, 82-, Nat Endowment for Humanities fel, 81. **RESEARCH** History of Bertrand Russell's philosoph; ethics. **SELECTED PUBLICATIONS** Auth, Tense and special relativity, Nous, 7 1; ed, B Russell's Essays in Analysis, Allen & Unwin, Braziller & Longanesi, 73. **CONTACT ADDRESS** Dept of Philosophy, Baruch Col, CUNY, 17 Lexington Ave, New York, NY, 10010-5518. **EMAIL** dlackey@email.gc.cuny.edu

LACY, ALLEN
PERSONAL Born 01/07/1935, Dallas, TX, m, 1958, 2 children **DISCIPLINE** PHILOSOPHY **EDUCATION** Duke Univ, AB, 56, PhD, 62. **CAREER** Ed asst, Duke Univ Press, 58-60; instr English, Clemson Col, 61-62; from asst prof to assoc prof philos, Madison Col, Va, 62-66; asst prof humanities, Mich State Univ, 66-68; assoc prof philos, Kirkland Col, 68-71; assoc prof, 71-74, actg dean soc and behav sci, 72-73, PROF PHILOS, STOCKTON STATE COL, 74-, PROF RELIG, 80-, Nat Endowment for Humanities fel, 70. **RESEARCH** Religion and culture; philosophical ideas in literature; social ethics; existentialism. **SELECTED PUBLICATIONS** Auth, The uselessness of art, Christian Scholar, spring 66; coauth, Censorship and Como se Hace una Novela, Hisp Rev, 66; auth, Miguel de Unamuno: the Rhetoric of Existence, Mouton, the Hague, 67; Marshall McLuhan, playful prophet, in: the Religious Situation, Beacon, 68; ed, Selected Works of Miguel de Unamuno in English, Vol I, Princeton Univ (in press). **CONTACT ADDRESS** 1511 Shore Rd, Linwood, NJ, 08221.

LACY, HUGH GALE
PERSONAL Born 03/23/1948, Huntsville, AL, m, 1977 **DISCIPLINE** LAW **EDUCATION** Alabama A&M University, BA, 1972, MEd, 1974; Miles Law School, JD, 1989. **CAREER** Huntsville City Board of Education, teacher corps intern, 1972-74; US Army Ballistic Missle Defense Systems Command, supply management assistant, 1974-75; US Army Ordnance Missile & Munitions Center & School, education specialist, 1975-92; Hugh G Lacy, PC, attorney, 1990-; US Army Corps of Engineers, education specialist, 1992-. **HONORS AND AWARDS** 4-H Club Leadership Award, 1974; US Army Ordnance Missile & Munition Center & School, Performance, 1985-92, Letters of Appreciation, 1982, 1988-91; US Army Missile Command, Equal Employment Opportunity Counselor Appreciation Certificate, 1992; Alpha Phi Alpha Fraternity, Inc, Brother of the Year, State of Alabama, 1990, Brother of the Year, Delta Theta Lambda, 1991. **MEMBERSHIPS** St Bartley P B Church, building & education committees, 1986-; Alpha Phi Alpha Fraternity, Inc, area director, 1982-, associated editor to Sphinx, 1990-; Alabama Lawyers Association, 1989-; Alabama Trial Lawyers Association, 1990-; American Bar Association, 1990-; National Bar Association, 1990-; NAACP, 1972-; Special Education Action Committee, counselor, 1989-; Huntsville/Madison County Bar Association, legislative committee, 1990-. **CONTACT ADDRESS** Attorney, PO Box 18341, 300 E Clinton Ave, Ste 2, Huntsville, AL, 35804.

LACY, PHILIP T.
DISCIPLINE CONTRACTS AND COMMERCIAL LAW **EDUCATION** Duke Univ, BA, 69; Univ VA, LLB, 72. **CAREER** Assoc dean & prof, Univ SC. **RESEARCH** Bankruptcy law. **SELECTED PUBLICATIONS** Coauth, a treatise on commercial law; publ on, bankruptcy and commercial law. **CONTACT ADDRESS** School of Law, Univ of S. Carolina, Law Center, Columbia, SC, 29208. **EMAIL** Phil@law.law.sc.edu

LACY, WILLIAM LARRY
DISCIPLINE PHILOSOPHY **EDUCATION** Rhodes Col, BA, 59; Univ Virginia, PhD, 63. **CAREER** Chr, Dept of Phi-

losophy, Rhodes Col. **CONTACT ADDRESS** Dept of Philos, Rhodes Col, 2000 N. Parkway, Memphis, TN, 38112. **EMAIL** lacy@rhodes.edu

LADD, ROSALIND EKMAN
PERSONAL Born 10/13/1933, Manchester, NH, m, 1963, 2 children **DISCIPLINE** PHILOSOPHY **EDUCATION** Wheaton Col, Mass, BA, 55; Brown Univ, MA, 56, PhD, 62. **CAREER** From instr to asst prof Philos, Smith Col, 59-67; assoc prof, 67-73, prof Philos, Wheaton Col, MA, 73-, vis prof, Biomed Ethics, Brown Univ, 80 & 82. **MEMBERSHIPS** Am Philos. **RESEARCH** Ethics; medical ethics; children's rights. **SELECTED PUBLICATIONS** Ed, Readings in the Problems of Ethics, Scribner, 65; auth, The paradoxes of formalism, Brit J Aesthet, 70. **CONTACT ADDRESS** Dept of Philosophy, Wheaton Col, 26 E Main St, Norton, MA, 02766-2322. **EMAIL** rladd@wheatonma.edu

LADEN, ANTHONY
DISCIPLINE PHILOSOPHY **EDUCATION** Harvard Univ, PhD, 96. **CAREER** Asst prof, Univ IL at Chicago. **RESEARCH** Moral and polit philos; liberalism; feminism; hist of moral and polit thought. **SELECTED PUBLICATIONS** Auth, Games, Fairness and Rawls's A Theory of Justice, 91. **CONTACT ADDRESS** Philos Dept, Univ Illinois Chicago, S Halsted St, PO Box 705, Chicago, IL, 60607.

LADENSON, ROBERT F.
PERSONAL Born 08/03/1943, Chicago, IL, m, 1982, 2 children **DISCIPLINE** PHILOSOPHY AND LAW **EDUCATION** Univ Wisc, BA, 65; Johns Hopkins, PhD, 70; DePaul Univ, JD, 80. **CAREER** Asst prof, 69-75, assoc prof, 75-84, prof, 84-, Ill Inst of Tech; vis assoc prof, Univ Colo Boulder, 81. **HONORS AND AWARDS** Grantee, Nat Sci Found; Nat Endow for the Humanities. **MEMBERSHIPS** Ill State Bd of Educ; Special Educ Hearing officer; Asn for Practical and Professional Ethics; Amer Philos Asn. **RESEARCH** Ethics; Political philosophy; Philosophy of law; Free speech; Disability rights; Ethics education. **SELECTED PUBLICATIONS** Auth, On the Scope of Legitimate Authority, Jour of Soc Philos, 98; auth, Is the Right of Free Speech Special?, Soc Theory and Practice, 97; auth, What is a Disability?, Intl Jour of Applied Philos, 96; auth, Ethics in the Amer Workplace, 95; auth, Values and ethics in organizational and human systems development; auth, A Philosophy of Free Expression, 82. **CONTACT ADDRESS** Dept. of Humanities, Illinois Inst of Tech, Chicago, IL, 60616. **EMAIL** ladenson@charlie.cns.iit.edu

LAFAVE, WAYNE R.
DISCIPLINE LAW **EDUCATION** Univ Wis, BS; LLB; JD. **CAREER** Prof, Univ Ill Urbana Champaign. **HONORS AND AWARDS** Ed, Wis Law Rev. **RESEARCH** Criminal procedure. **SELECTED PUBLICATIONS** Auth, pubs on criminal procedure. **CONTACT ADDRESS** Law Dept, Univ Ill Urbana Champaign, 52 E Gregory Dr, Champaign, IL, 61820. **EMAIL** wlafave@law.uiuc.edu

LAFOLLETTE, HUGH
DISCIPLINE PHILOSOPHY **EDUCATION** Vanderbilt Univ, PhD. **CAREER** Prof, E Tenn State Univ. **RESEARCH** Ethics; political philosophy; philosophy of law. **SELECTED PUBLICATIONS** Auth, Co-auth, Brute Science: The Dilemmas of Animal Experimentation, Routledge, 97; The Origin of Speciesism, Philos, 96; Util-izing Animals, J Applied Philos, 95; Two Models of Models in Biomedical Research, Philos Quarterly, 95; Animal Experimentation: The Legacy of Claude Bernard, Int Studies Philos Sci, 94; Chaos Theory: Analogical Reasoning in Biomedical Research, Idealistic Studies, 94; co-ed, Ethics in Practice: An Anthology, Blackwell, 97. **CONTACT ADDRESS** Philosophy Dept, East Tennesee State Univ, Box 70717, Johnson City, TN, 37614- 0717. **EMAIL** lafollet@etsu.edu

LAFONT, CRISTINA
DISCIPLINE PHILOSOPHY **EDUCATION** Frankfurt, PhD. **CAREER** Asst prof,Northwestern Univ. **RESEARCH** Philosophy of language, theories of rationality, phenomenology, hermeneutics, critical theory. **SELECTED PUBLICATIONS** Auth, Sprache und Welterschliessung, Zur linguistischen Wende der Hermeneutik Heideggers; La razon como lenguaje, Un analisis del giro linguistico en la filosofia del lenguaje alemana; co-ed, En torno a la filosofia de J Habermas. **CONTACT ADDRESS** Dept of Philosophy, Northwestern Univ, 1801 Hinman, Evanston, IL, 60208.

LAFRANCE, YVON
PERSONAL Born 12/01/1930, Montreal, PQ, Canada, m **DISCIPLINE** PHILOSOPHY **EDUCATION** Univ Montreal, BA, 51; Univ Sao Paulo, Brazil, LPh, 59; Univ Louvain, Beig, DPh, 67. **CAREER** Prof philos, Univ Sao Paulo, 62-64, Univ Sherbrook, 67-68 and Univ Que, 68-71; PROF PHILOS, UNIV OTTAWA, 71-, Can Coun res grant, 77-78 and 80-82. **HONORS AND AWARDS** Doctorat d'Etat en philos, Paris-Nanterre, 82. **MEMBERSHIPS** Asn Guillaume Bude; Can Asn Philos; Int Soc Neoplatonic Studies; Soc Promotion Hellenic Studies London. **RESEARCH** Greek philosophy; Plato and Aristotle. **SELECTED PUBLICATIONS** Auth, The Origin and Evolution of the Greek Concept of Phusis, Laval Theologique et Philos, Vol 0050, 94. **CONTACT ADDRESS** Dept of Philos, Univ of Ottawa, 90 Wilbrod, Ottawa, ON, K1N 6N5.

LAIDLAW, E.A.
DISCIPLINE PHILOSOPHY **EDUCATION** Univ of Rochester, PhD, 90. **CAREER** Prof, Monroe Comm Col, 93-. **HONORS AND AWARDS** Teaching **MEMBERSHIPS** APA **CONTACT ADDRESS** 191 Seneca Pkwy, Rochester, NY, 14613-1412. **EMAIL** Blaidlaw@Monroecc.edu

LAINE, JAMES W.
PERSONAL Born 05/08/1952, Midland, TX, m, 1983, 4 children **DISCIPLINE** RELIGION **EDUCATION** TX Tech, BA, 74; Harvard, MTS, 77, ThD, 84. **CAREER** Asst prof, , 83-85 CT Col; asst prof, 85-91, acad dean, 92-95, assoc prof, 95-97, prof, 98-, Macalester Col. **MEMBERSHIPS** AAR; Asn of Asian Studies. **SELECTED PUBLICATIONS** Auth, Visions of God, 89; auth, Epic of Shivaji, 99. **CONTACT ADDRESS** Relig Stud Dept, Macalester Col, 1600 Grand Ave, St. Paul, MN, 55105-1899. **EMAIL** laine@Macalester.edu

LAITOS, JAN GORDON
PERSONAL Born 05/06/1946, Colorado Springs, CO **DISCIPLINE** LAW, AMERICAN LEGAL HISTORY **EDUCATION** Yale Univ, BA, 68; Law Sch, Univ Colo, JD, 71; Law Sch, Univ Wis, SJD, 74. **CAREER** Law clerk, Colo Supreme Ct, 71-72; atty, Off Legal Coun, US Dept of Justice, 74-76; PROF LAW, LAW SCH, UNIV DENVER, 76-, Sr legal adv, Solar Energy Res Inst, 78-81; consult, Colo State Dept of Natural Resources, 79-80, US Dept of Interior, 79-80 and US Dept of Energy, 80-81. **MEMBERSHIPS** Natural resources law; energy law. **RESEARCH** Auth, Causation and the Unconstitutional Conditions Doctrine--Why the City of Tigards Exaction Was a Taking, Denver Univ Law Rev, Vol 0072, 95; National Parks and the Recreation Resource, Denver Univ Law Rev, Vol 0074, 97. **CONTACT ADDRESS** Law Sch, Univ of Denver, Denver, CO, 80208.

LAMAUTE, DENISE
PERSONAL Born 03/14/1952, St. Louis, MO, m, 1980 **DISCIPLINE** LAW **EDUCATION** Brandeis Univ, Waltham, MA, BA, (Magna cum Laude) 1973; Washington Univ, St Louis, MO, JD, 1977, LL.M. (tax) 1980. **CAREER** Teachers Insurance & Annuity Assn, sr tax Attorney, 1978-82; Ernst & Whinney, New York, NY, supvr, 1982-85; Lamaute Tax & Financial Servs, New York, NY, owner, 1985-; Lamaute Capital, Inc, pres, currently. **MEMBERSHIPS** Mem, US Tax Ct, 1981-; mem, Nzingha Soc, 1987-88; co-chmn, Natl Bar Assn, 1988-89; mem volunteer, Jr Achievement, 1989. **SELECTED PUBLICATIONS** Author "Tax Loopholes for Investors" to be published by Tab Books NY, 1989; natl speaker for "Black Enterprise" networking Forum; frequent speaker on tax & financial matters at confs around the country; frequent contributing writer to magazines, newspapers on financial issues. **CONTACT ADDRESS** Lamaute Capital, Inc, Washington, DC.

LAMB, RAMDAS
PERSONAL m, 1978, 2 children **DISCIPLINE** RELIGIOUS STUDIES **EDUCATION** Univ of California, Santa Barbara, PhD, 91. **CAREER** Assoc Prof, 91-, Dept of Rel, Univ of Hawaii. **MEMBERSHIPS** AAS; AAR; ASR. **RESEARCH** South Asian Religion; Medieval & Contemporary Hinduism; Religion & Contemporary Soc. **SELECTED PUBLICATIONS** Auth, Rapt in the Name: The Ramnam is Ramnam and the Ram Bhakti Tradition, Albany, NY, SUNY Press, forthcoming, 99; Consulting Ed, Corsini Dictionary of Psychology, Washington, DC, Taylor and Francis, 98; Religion, Atlas of Hawaii, 3rd ed, Honolulu, Univ of Hawaii Press, 98; Asceticism and Devotion: The Many Faces of Ram Bhakti in the Ramananda Sampraday, Journal of Vaisnava Studies, vol 2, #4, 94. **CONTACT ADDRESS** Dept of Religion, Univ of Hawaii Manoa, 2530 Dole St., Honolulu, HI, 96822. **EMAIL** RAMDAS@HAWAII.EDU _

LAMBERT, BENJAMIN FRANKLIN
PERSONAL Born 03/06/1933, Lowell, MA, s **DISCIPLINE** LAW **EDUCATION** Boston Univ, BA 1955; Brandeis Univ, MA 1959; Seton Hall Univ Sch of Law, JD 1968. **CAREER** Ciba Phar Co Inc, rsch chem 1957-66; Ciba Ltd, rsch asst 1962-63; Merck & Co Inc, atty 1966-70; Fitzpatrick, Cella, Harper & Scinto, atty 1970-72; Johnson & Johnson, patent atty 1973-. **HONORS AND AWARDS** Delta Hon Soc; Scarlet Key Hon Soc; Student Fac Asmbl; Augustus Howe Buck Schlr; Tchng Fellow Brandeis Univ. **MEMBERSHIPS** Mem NJ Bar Assn; Reg US Patent Ofc 1968, NJ Bar, 1969; NY Bar 1972; US Ct of Customs & Patent Appeals 1977; US Dist Ct Dist of NJ 1969; Dist Ct So Dist NY 1972; Dist Ct Eastern Dist NY 1972; NJ Patent Law Assn; Amer Patent Law Assn; NAACP 1977. **SELECTED PUBLICATIONS** numerous **CONTACT ADDRESS** Johnson & Johnson, One Johnson & Johnson Plaza, New Brunswick, NJ, 08933.

LAMBERT, BYRON C.
DISCIPLINE CHRISTIAN DOCTRINE; HISTORY OF CULTURE **EDUCATION** Univ Buffalo, BA, 45, MA, 46; Butler Univ sch Rel, BD, 50; Univ Chicago, PhD, 57. **CAREER** Assoc prof English, Milligan Col, 57-60; dean, assoc prof English, Simpson Col, 60-62; dean, 62-65, campus dean, 65-71, assoc prof Hum, 71-75, assoc dean, Col ed, 71-75, Fairleigh Dickinson Univ; Prof Philos, 75-85, actg dean, Arts and Sci, 82-83, acting Provost, Madison Campus, 81.. **HONORS AND AWARDS** Fairleigh Dickinson Univ, Campus Achieve Awd, 74; Pres James A. Garfield Awd, Emmanuel Sch Rel, Tenn, 98. **MEMBERSHIPS** Amer Philos Asn; Soc Christian Philso; Disciples of Christ Hist Soc. **RESEARCH** C.S. Lewis; Paul Elmer More; Christian theology, sacraments, Holy Spirit.. **SELECTED PUBLICATIONS** Auth, The Essential Paul Elmer More, 72; The Rise of the Anti-Mission Baptist, 80; The Recovery of Reality, 80; The Restoration of the Lord's Supper and the Sacramental Principle, 92; Experience-Different Semantic Worlds, Wasleyan Theol Jour, Spring 95; Shifting Grontiers and the Invisible Hand, Discipliana, Fall 95; The Middle Way of Frederick Doyle Kershner, 98; The Regrettable Silence of Paul Elmer More, Modern Age, Fall 98; C.S. Lewis and the Moral Law, Stone-Campbell Jour, Fall 98. **CONTACT ADDRESS** 300 North Perry St, Hagerstown, IN, 47346.

LAMBERT, J. KAREL
PERSONAL Born 04/10/1928, Chicago, IL, m, 1949, 3 children **DISCIPLINE** PHILOSOPHY **EDUCATION** Willamette Univ, BA, 50; Univ Oregon, MS, 52; Mich St Univ, PhD, 56. **CAREER** Asst prof, 56-60, assoc prof, 60-63, Univ of Alberta; prof & chmn Dept of Phil, 63-67, West Virginia Univ; Prof, 67-, Above Scale, 90-, Res Prof of Logic 7 Phil, 94-, Univ of California; honor prof, 84-, Univ of Salzburg Austria. **HONORS AND AWARDS** Fulbright Hayes Scholar, 3 times; NEH Fel, 3 times; Univ of Calif Pres Fel. **MEMBERSHIPS** Amer Phil Asn; Amer Psych Asn; Asn for Symbolic Logic. **RESEARCH** Logic; philosophy of science; experimental psychology. **SELECTED PUBLICATIONS** Art, A Theory about Logical Theories of Expressions of the Form The So and So Where The is in the Singular, Erkenntnis, 91; Coauth, Logic Bivalence and Denotation, Ridgeview, 91; ed, Philosophical Applications of Free Logic, Oxford NY & London, 91; coauth, An Introduction to the Philosophy of Science, 4th ed, Ridgeview, 92; art, Russells Version of the Theory of Definite Descriptions, Phil Stud, 92; Coauth, Outline of a Theory of Scientific Understanding, Synthese, 94; coauth, Characterizing and Classifiying Explicating a Biological Distinction, Monist, 94; art, On the Reduction of Two Paradoxes and the Philosophical Significance Thereof, Physick Philosophie und die Einheit der Wiessenschaften,Spektrum, 95; coauth, Resiliency and Laws in the Web of Belief, Laws of Nature, 95; Auth, Free Logics Their Foundations Character and Some Applications Thereof, Akademia Verlag Sankt Augustin bei Bonn, 97; art, Nonextensionality, Das weite Spektrum der Analytischen Philosophie, 97; coauth, Definitions in nonstrict positive free logic, Modern Logic, 97;ed, A Theory of Definite Descriptions, Phil Applications of Free Logic, Oxford Univ Press, 91; auth, Free logic and Definite Descriptions, New Directions in Free Logic Essays in Honor of Karel Lambert, 98. **CONTACT ADDRESS** 480 Enterprise St, Hammond, OR, 97121. **EMAIL** chainsaw3@netscape.net

LAMBERT, JEAN CHRISTINE
PERSONAL Born 06/21/1940, Berwyn, IL **DISCIPLINE** CHRISTIAN THEOLOGY **EDUCATION** North Park Col, Chicago, BA, 62; Columbia Univ, MA, 67, MPhil, 74, PhD(relig), 81. **CAREER** Asst prof, 76-82, ASSOC PROF THEOL, ST PAUL SCH THEOL, KANSAS CITY, 82-, Mem task force relig, Kansas City Metrop Regional Comn Status Women, 79-; mem, Bk of Worship Revision Comt, Evangel Covenant Church, 75-82, bd publ, 76-81. **MEMBERSHIPS** Am Acad Relig. **RESEARCH** Feminist theology; Whiteheadian and Hartshornian process philosophy. **SELECTED PUBLICATIONS** Auth, Daniel Day Williams: a bibliography, Union Sem Quart Rev, 75; Response to Penelope Washbourn's paper the Dynamics of Female Experience ..., in: Feminism and Process Thought Conference Papers, Harvard Divinity Sch, 77; Becoming human: a Whiteheadian exploration of issues underlying the discussion of abortion, in: Feminism and Process Thought, Mellin Press, 81; Response to David Cassell, Narthex, 82. **CONTACT ADDRESS** Dept of Theol, St Paul Sch of Theol, Kansas City, MO, 64127.

LAMBERT, RICHARD THOMAS
PERSONAL Born 03/28/1943, Rochester, NY, m, 1978, 3 children **DISCIPLINE** HISTORY OF PHILOSOPHY, LOGIC, ETHICS **EDUCATION** St Bernard's Col, BA, 65; Univ Notre Dame, PhD, 71. **CAREER** Asst prof, 70-80, philos dept chmn, 77-82, assoc prof 80-, prof philos, Carrol Col, Mont, Dir, Summer, 81-82, Dir, Continuing Educ, 81-85, Exchange prof philos, Loras Col, 76-77. **HONORS AND AWARDS** NY State Regents Scholar, 61-65; NDEA Grad Fel, 66-70; Exec Comt, Delta Epsilon Sigma, 90-94, vpres & pres, 94-98. **MEMBERSHIPS** Int Berkeley Soc; Am Cath Philos Asn; Am Philos Asn; Delta Epsilon Sigma. **RESEARCH** Berkeley; Aquinas; Camus. **SELECTED PUBLICATIONS** Auth, Berkeley's use of the relativity argument, Idealistic Studies, 10: 107-121; Albert Camus and the paradoxes of expressing a relativism,

Thought, 56: 185-198; A textual study of Aquinas' comparison of the intellect to prime matter, New Scholasticism, Vol 56; Berkeley's commitment to relativism, Berkeley: Critical and Interpretive Essays, Univ Minn Press, 82; Habitual knowledge of the soul in St Thomas Aquinas, Mod Schoolman, 40: 1-19; The literal intent of Berkeley's Dialogues, Philos & Lit, 6: 165-171; Nonintentional experience of oneself in Thomas Aquinas, New Scholasticism, 59: 253-275; Teaching Camus's The Plague in an introductory philosophy course, Approaches to Teaching Camus's The Plague, MLA, 85; transl, Thomas Aquinas, Disputed Question on the Soul's Knowledge of Itself, Clearinghouse for Medieval Philos Transl, 87; Conferring honors in a democratic society, Delta Epsilon Sigma Jour, 33: 59-60; President's report to the membership, Delta Epsilon Sigma Jour, 43: 77-78; Ethics column, Helena Independent Record, 90. **CONTACT ADDRESS** Carroll Col, Montana, 1601 N Benton Ave, Fac Box 49, Helena, MT, 59625-0002. **EMAIL** rlambert@carroll.edu

LAMIRANDE, EMILIEN
PERSONAL Born 05/22/1926, St-Georges de Windsor, Canada **DISCIPLINE** HISTORY OF CHRISTIANITY **EDUCATION** Univ Ottawa, BA, 49, LPh, 50, MA, 51, LTh, 55; Univ Innsbruck, DTh, 60; Union Theol Sem, NY, STM, 65;. **CAREER** Assoc prof theol, Univ Ottawa, 60-65; prof, St Paul Univ, Ont, 65-70, dean fac theol, 67-69; chmn dept, 72-74, PROF RELIG STUDIES, UNIV OTTAWA, 70-. **MEMBERSHIPS** Am Acad Relig; Can Cath Hist Asn; Can Theol Soc (vpres, 67-70); Asn Can d'Estudes Patristiques (vpres, 79-). **RESEARCH** Early Christianity; North African Church; ecclesiology. **SELECTED PUBLICATIONS** Auth, Sulpician Priests in Canada--Major Figures in Their History, Stud in Rel-Sciences Religieuses, Vol 0022, 93; Body of the Church, Body of Christ--Sources for the Ecclesiology of the Communion, Stud in Rel-Sciences Religieuses, Vol 0022, 93; Writings of the Reformation Fathers, Stud in Rel-Sciences Religieuses, Vol 0025, 96; The Aggiornamento and Its Eclipse--Free Thinking in the Church and in the Faithful, Stud in Rel-Sciences Religieuses, Vol 0025, 96. **CONTACT ADDRESS** Dept of Relig Studies, Univ of Ottawa, Ottawa, ON, K1H 8M5.

LAMM, JULIA A.
PERSONAL Born 06/06/1961, Cincinnati, OH **DISCIPLINE** THEOLOGY **EDUCATION** Col St. Catherine, BA, 83; Univ Chicago, AM, 84, PhD, 91. **CAREER** Asst prof, 89-95, ASSOC PROF, GEORGETOWN UNIV, 95-. **HONORS AND AWARDS** Alexander von Humboldt Fel, 96-97. **MEMBERSHIPS** Am Acad of Religion. **RESEARCH** Historical theology; F.D.E. Schleiermacher. **SELECTED PUBLICATIONS** Auth, The Living God: Schleiermacher's Theological Appropriation of Spinoza, Pa State Univ Press, 96; The Early Philosophical Roots of Schleiermacher's Notion of Gefuhl 1788-1794, Harvard Theological Rev, 94; Schleiermacher's Post-Kantian Spinozism: The Essays on Spinoza 1793-94, J of Religion, 94; Catholic Substance Revisited: Reversals of Expectations in Tillich's Doctrine of God, Paul Tillich: A New Catholic Assessment, Liturgical Press, 94; Tensions in a Catholic Theology of the Body, Choosing Life: A Dialogue on Evangelium Vitae, Georgetown Univ Press, 97; A Hermeneutics of Revulsion, Papers of the North Am Paul Tillich Soc, 95; Schleiermacher as a Resource for Feminist Theology, Harvard Divinity Bulletin, 95. **CONTACT ADDRESS** Theology Dept, Georgetown Univ, New North 120, Box 571135, Washington, DC, 20057-1135.

LAMM, NORMAN
PERSONAL Born 12/19/1927, Brooklyn, NY, m, 1954, 4 children **DISCIPLINE** JEWISH PHILOSOPHY **EDUCATION** Yeshiva Col, BA, 49; Yeshiva Univ, PhD, 66. **CAREER** Jacob Michael prof of Jewish philos, Yeshiva Univ, 66- ; pres, Yeshiva Univ, 76- . **HONORS AND AWARDS** Abramowitz Zeitlin Award, 72; Hon Dr Hebrew Letters, 77; Corning Glass Higher Educ Leadership Award, 86. **RESEARCH** Hasidism; Talmud. **SELECTED PUBLICATIONS** Auth, The Royal Reach, 70; A Hedge of Roses, 70; Torah Lishwah, 72; Torah Umodda, 90; Halakhot Veshallkhot, 91; Shema: Spirituality and Law in Judaism 98; The Religious Thought of Hasidism, 99. **CONTACT ADDRESS** Office of the President, Yeshiva Univ, 500 West 185th St, New York, NY, 10033. **EMAIL** nlamm@ibm.net

LAMOTHE, KIMERER L.
PERSONAL Born 07/25/1963, New York, NY, m, 1992, 2 children **DISCIPLINE** RELIGION **EDUCATION** Willaims Coll, BA, 85; Harvard Divinity School, MTS, 84; Harvard Univ, PhD, 96. **CAREER** Vis asst prof, Brown Univ, 96-97; Lectr, Head Tutor, Harvard Univ, 97-. **HONORS AND AWARDS** Phi Beta Kappa; Bok Center Teaching Award; Nat Merit Scholar; Graves Prize; Mellon Dissertation Fel; Center for the Study of World Rels Fel. **MEMBERSHIPS** AAR; Phi Beta Kappa. **RESEARCH** Religion and the performing arts; Philosophy of religion; Modern dance; Feminist and postmodern theory. **SELECTED PUBLICATIONS** Passionate Madonna: the Christian Turn of American Dancer Ruth St Denis, J of am Acad Of Rel, 98. **CONTACT ADDRESS** Harvard Univ, 12 Quincy St, Cambridge, MA, 02138. **EMAIL** klamothe@fas.harvard.edu

LANCASTER, HERMAN BURTRAM
PERSONAL Born 03/06/1942, Chicago, IL, m **DISCIPLINE** LAW **EDUCATION** Chicago State Univ, BS 1965; Rosary Coll, MA 1968; DePaul Univ, JD 1972. **CAREER** Chicago Bd of Ed, teacher 1965-66; DePaul Univ Law School, asst dir law library 1966-70; Univ of Chicago, psychiatric dept dir of info 1970-72, legal counsel 1972-73; GLENDALE UNIV LAW SCHOOL, PROF, DIR OF RESEARCH 1973-; THE LEGAL INST, LAW CONSULTANT, 1976-. **HONORS AND AWARDS** Omega Psi Phi Scholarship 1963; Grad Fellowship 1966; DePaul Law School Scholarship 1968; DePaul Law Review Scholarship 1969-72; Blue Key Law Hon Soc 1968; Man of the Year Omega Psi Phi 1966. **MEMBERSHIPS** AAA, arbitrator, 1986-; The Subcontractors Inst, advisor, 1984-; Glendale Law Review 1976-; NAACP 1975-. **SELECTED PUBLICATIONS** Has published numerous articles **CONTACT ADDRESS** The Legal Inst, 3250 W Wilshire Blvd, Ste 958, Los Angeles, CA, 90010.

LANCE, MARK
DISCIPLINE PHILOSOPHY **EDUCATION** Univ Pittsburgh, PhD. **CAREER** Prof. **RESEARCH** Political philosophy; philosophy of language; epistemology; logic; metaphysics. **SELECTED PUBLICATIONS** Auth, pubs on logic, Normativity, meaning, and Bayesianism. **CONTACT ADDRESS** Dept of Philosophy, Georgetown Univ, 37th and O St, Washington, DC, 20057.

LANCTOT, CATHERINE J.
DISCIPLINE CONSTITUTIONAL LAW, LEGAL PROFESSION **EDUCATION** Brown Univ, BA, 78; Georgetown Univ Law Ctr, JD, 81. **CAREER** Prof; Villanova Univ, 88-. **RESEARCH** Legal ethics, employment law. **SELECTED PUBLICATIONS** Auth, The Defendant Lies and the Plaintiff Loses: The Fallacy of the Pretext-Plus' Rule in Employment Discrimination Cases, 43 Hastings L J 59, 91, **CONTACT ADDRESS** Law School, Villanova Univ, 800 Lancaster Ave, Villanova, PA, 19085-1692. **EMAIL** lanctot@law.vill.edu

LANDERS, RENEE M.
PERSONAL Born 07/25/1955, Springfield, Illinois, m, 1980 **DISCIPLINE** LAW **EDUCATION** Radcliffe Coll of Harvard Univ, AB, 1977; Boston Coll Law School, JD, 1985. **CAREER** Massachusetts Secretary of State, Bookstore Div, program development specialist, 1978, admin asst to secretary of state, 1979-80, deputy secretary of state, 1980-82; Supreme Judicial Court of Massachusetts, law clerk, 1985-86; Ropes & Gray, associate, 1986-88; Boston Coll Law School, asst prof, 1988-93; Office of Policy Development, US Department of Justice, deputy assistant attorney general, 1993-96; US Department of Health & Human Services, deputy general counsel, 1996-. **HONORS AND AWARDS** Radcliffe College Alumnae Assn, Distinguished Service Award, 1992; Elected Honorary Mem, Iota of Massachusetts Chap, Phi Beta Kappa, Radcliffe College, 1995. **MEMBERSHIPS** Harvard Univ, bd of overseers, 1991-95, pres bd of overseers, 1996-97; Massachusetts Eye and Ear Infirmary, dir, 1993-96; Metropolitan District Commission, assoc commissioner, 1991-93; Big Sister Assoc of Greater Boston, vp and dir, 1988-93; Massachusetts Supreme Judicial Court, gender bias study committee, sub-committee chair, 1986-1989, racial and ethnic bias study, 1990-94; Boston Bar Assoc, council member, 1988-91, chair committee on gender and justice, 1989-93. **CONTACT ADDRESS** Deputy General Counsel, US Department of Health & Human Services, 200 Independence Ave, SW, Washington, VT, 20201.

LANDES, GEORGE MILLER
PERSONAL Born 08/02/1928, Kansas City, MO, m, 1953, 1 child **DISCIPLINE** OLD TESTAMENT **EDUCATION** Univ Mo, AB, 49; McCormick Theol Sem, BD, 52; Johns Hopkins Univ, PhD(Semitic studies), 56. **CAREER** From instr to assoc prof, 56-70, Baldwin prof sacred lit, 72-80, DAVENPORT PROF HEBREW, UNION THEOL SEM, NY, 81-, Am Coun Learned Soc fel, 67-68; annual prof, Am Sch Orient Res, Jerusalem, 67-68. **MEMBERSHIPS** Soc Bibl Lit; Am Orient Soc; Am Schs Orient Res. **RESEARCH** Old Testament history and archaeology; the semitic and cognate languages; Semitic studies. **SELECTED PUBLICATIONS** Auth, Satire and the Hebrew Prophets, Interpretation-J Bible and Theol, Vol 0048, 94; A Poetics of Jonah--Art in the Service of Ideology, Interpretation-J Bible and Theol, Vol 0049, 95; Commentary on the Prophets Haggai, Zechariah, and Malach, Cath Bibl Quart, Vol 0057, 95; Readings in Biblical Hebrew--an Intermediate Textbook, J Amer Oriental Soc, Vol 0115, 95. **CONTACT ADDRESS** Union Theol Seminary, 3041 Broadway, New York, NY, 10027.

LANDESMAN, CHARLES
PERSONAL Born 12/17/1932, Brooklyn, NY, m, 1955, 3 children **DISCIPLINE** PHILOSOPHY **EDUCATION** Wesleyan Univ, AB, 54; Yale Univ, MA, 56, PhD, 59. **CAREER** Instr philos, Yale Univ, 57-59; from asst prof to assoc prof, Univ Kans, 59-65; assoc prof, 65-70, Prof Philos, Hunter Col, 70-, Chmn Dept, 67-71, 79-82, Dir, Fac Sem Interdisciplinary Studies, 77-78. **HONORS AND AWARDS** Fulbright lectr, Ben Gurion Univ, Israel, 92-93. **MEMBERSHIPS** Am Philos Asn; Am Fedn Teachers. **RESEARCH** Philosophy of language; philosophy of mind; political philosophy; epistemology. **SELECTED PUBLICATIONS** Auth, Discourse and its Perspective, Yale Univ Press, 72; Color and Consciousness, Temple Univ Press, 89; The Eye of the Mind, Kluwer Acad Publ, 93; An Introduction to Epistemology, Blackwell, 97. **CONTACT ADDRESS** Dept of Philos, Hunter Col, CUNY, 695 Park Ave, New York, NY, 10021-5085. **EMAIL** clandesm@msn.com

LANDINI, GREGORY
PERSONAL Born 12/27/1955, Miami Beach, FL, m, 1987, 2 children **DISCIPLINE** PHILOSOPHY **EDUCATION** IN Univ, BA, 78, PhD, 86. **CAREER** Asst prof, 85-89, Ball State Univ; asst prof, 89-91, assoc prof, 92-, Univ Iowa. **MEMBERSHIPS** APA; Bertrand Russell Soc; Cent St Philos Asn. **RESEARCH** Philos of logic; foundations of mathematics; philos of language; philos of mind. **SELECTED PUBLICATIONS** Auth, The Definability of the Set of Natural Numbers in the 1925 Principia Mathematica, J of Philos Logic, 25, 96; auth, Logic in Russell's Principles of Mathematics, Notre Dame J of Formal Logic, 37, 96; auth, Decomposition and Analysis in Frege's Grundgesetze, Hist & Philos of Logic, 17, 96; auth, Russell's Intentional Logic of Prepositions: A Resurrection of Logicism?, Thought, Language & Reality, Essays in Honor of Hector-Neri Castaneda, Kluwer, 98; auth, Denoting Against Denoting, Russell, 18, 98. **CONTACT ADDRESS** Dept of Philosophy, Univ of Iowa, Iowa City, IA, 52241. **EMAIL** glandini@uiowa.edu

LANE, MARC J.
PERSONAL Born 08/30/1946, Chicago, IL, m, 1971, 3 children **DISCIPLINE** LAW **EDUCATION** Univ of Ill, BA, 67; Northwestern Univ, JD, 71; Int Asn of Registered Financial Planners, 87; Int Asn of Prof Financial Consults, 94; Int Asn of Registered Financial Consults, 95. **CAREER** Pres and atty, Law Offices of Marc J. Lane, 71- ; chemn and ceo, Marc J. Lane & Co., 85- ; pres, Longmeadow Assocs, Ltd., 84- ; pres, Longmeadow Insurance Servs, 84- ; adj prof, Univ of Ill, 96- . **HONORS AND AWARDS** Lincoln Awards, Ill State Bar Asn, 73, 77; Disting. Serv Award, Grant A Wish, Inc., 90; Crystal Globe Award, Tax Execs Inst, 92; Cert of Spec Congressional Recognition, U.S. Cong, 95; Cert of Recognition for Outstanding Contribs to the White House Conf on Small Bus, Pres William J. Clinton, 95; Recognition as a Business Leader, Small Bus Survival Comt, 96; Cert in Recognition and Appreciation of Outstanding Serv, Ill State Bar Asn, 96; Award in Appreciation for Disting. Membership, Int Asn for Financial Planning, 96; Cert of Congressional Recognition, U.S. Cong, 96; Cert in Appreciation for Serv as a mem of the Bus Advice and Financial Planning Section Coun, 97; Award for contributing immeasurably to the Center's growth and development, 97; Incl as a subject of biographical record, Contemporary Auths, Who's Who in American Law, Who's Who in Finance and Industry, Who's Who in the Midwest, Bar Register of Preeminent Attys, International Who's Who, International Who's Who of Professionals, National Directory of Who's Who in Executives and Professionals, National Registry of Who's Who, American Directory of Who's Who in Executives and Businesses, Int Auths and Writers Who's Who, Cambridge Who's Who Registry of Business Leaders, Who's Who Among Top Executives; AV (highest) rating: very high legal ability, Martindale-Hubbell, Inc.; Cert of Merit for Disting. Serv to the Community, Dictionary of Internat Biography. **MEMBERSHIPS** Int Bar Asn; ABA; Ill State Bar Asn; Chicago Bar Asn; Chicago Coun of Lawyers; Int Asn of Prof Financial Consults; Nat Acad of Elder Law Attys, Inc.; Ill Chap of the Nat Acad of Elder Law Attys; AARP; Medico-Legal Inst, Inc.; NASD; Int Asn for Financial Planning; Nat Asn of Corp Dirs; Int Trade Asn of Greater Chicago; Chicagoland Chamber of Com; NORBIC; Attys Title Guarantee Fund, Inc.; U.S. Securities and Exchange Comn and Ill Secy of State; Ill Dept of Prof Regulation; Int Asn of Registered Financial Planners; Nat Asn of Securities Dealers, Inc. **RESEARCH** Corp law; Finance; Taxation. **SELECTED PUBLICATIONS** Auth, Contracting for Communications Services, Nonprofit World, Jan-Feb, 90; Exempt Status Options--Which is Best?, Nonprofit World, Jul-Aug, 90; Challenges to Nonprofits' Tax Status: Is There Cause for Alarm?, Nonprofit World, Jul-Aug, 91; Partnerships, parts 1 and 2, Optometric Economics, Oct-Nov, 91; Does it Matter Where We Incorporate?, Nonprofit World, Nov-Dec, 91; Purchase and Sale of Small Business, 91; Purchase and Sale of Small Business: Forms, 91; Why is our Property-Tax Exemption Being Challenged?, Nonprofit World, Jan-Feb, 92; Can We Exclude Certain People from Membership?, Nonprofit World, Mar-Apr, 92; Can Our Organization Issue Stock?, Nonprofit World, May-June, 92; Can Fellowship Money Be Considered Income?, Nonprofit World, Jul-Aug, 92; Can Personal Lobbying Jeopardize Your Organization?, Nonprofit World, Nov-Dec, 92; Fundraising for Foreign Charities, Nonprofit World, Jan-Feb, 93; Exec Pay Options Ease Equity Dilemma, Crain's Small Bus, Sept, 93; Your Employees and your Retirement Plan, Nonprofit World, Nov-Dec, 93; It Might Not Pay to Delay Director's Fees, Crain's Small Bus, May, 94; Property for Profit, Winning Strategies, 1:2, sum, 94; For Exporters, Routing Goods Via Israel Can Yield Big Savings, Crain's Small Bus, Sept, 94; Lease Inducements Help Attract New Tenants, The Metro-Chicago Office Guide, 4th Quarter, 94; Partnerships Can Register With LCC Option, Crain's Small Bus, Dec-Jan, 94/95; GATT Lowers Tariffs But Raises New

Taxing Questions, Crain's Small Bus, Mar, 95; Don't Buy Off-the -Shelf Power of Attorney, Crain's Small Bus, Sept, 95; This Trust Allows Charity To Begin at Home, Crain's Small Bus, Dec-Jan, 95-96; Don't Tell It to the Judge, Try a Mediator, Crain's Small Bus, Apr, 96; Clicking on Internet Stock Plays, Crain's Small Bus, Nov, 96; New Job Reference Law Is No Blank Check, Crain's Small Bus, Feb, 97; Portable Health Care Insurance Gets Rolling, Crain's Small Bus, May, 97; Look for Integrity in Board Members, Crain's Chicago Bus, Feb 9, 98; publ, A Summary of the Family and Medical Leave Act of 1993 (P.L. 1-3.3), 93, Key Features of the Revenue Reconciliation Act of 1993, 93; Incentives and Opportunities for Israeli Companies to Do Business in the United States, 94; U.S. Credit Facilities Available to Argentine Enterprises Doing Business in the United States, 94; Long-Term Care Insurance: The New Tax Benefits, The New Design Choices, 97; coauth, Business Advice & Financial Planning for Lawyers, 95; Elder Law: Meeting the New Challenges When Advising Elderly Clients, 97. **CONTACT ADDRESS** Law Offices of Marc J. Lane, 180 North LaSalle St., Ste 2100, Chicago, IL, 60601. **EMAIL** success@marcjlane.com

LANG, BEREL
PERSONAL Born 11/13/1933, Norwich, CT, m, 1972, 2 children **DISCIPLINE** PHILOSOPHY **EDUCATION** Yale Univ, BA, 54; Columbia Univ, PhD, 61. **CAREER** Prof Philos, Univ Colorado, 61-83; prof Philos and Humanistic Stud, SUNY Albany, 83-97; prof humanities, Trinity Col, 97- . **HONORS AND AWARDS** ACLS fel; APA fel; fel, Ctr for Judaic Stud, Univ Penn; fel, Wesleyan Univ; NEH, NSF grants. **MEMBERSHIPS** AOA; MLA; Asn for Jewish Stud; Am Soc for Aesthetics; PEN. **RESEARCH** Social philosophy; aesthetics; Holocaust studies. **SELECTED PUBLICATIONS** Auth, Act and Idea in the Nazi Genocide, 90; auth, The Anatomy of Philosophical Style: Literary Philosophy and the Philosophy of Literature, 91; auth, Mind's Bodies: Thought in the Act, 95; auth, Heidegger's Silence, 96; auth, The Future of the Holocaust: Between History and Memory, 99. **CONTACT ADDRESS** Trinity Col, Hartford, CT, 06106. **EMAIL** berel.lang@trincoll.edu

LANG, MARTIN ANDREW
PERSONAL Born 05/02/1930, Brooklyn, NY, 3 children **DISCIPLINE** THEOLOGY, RELIGION **EDUCATION** Marist Col, BA, 51; Cath Univ Am, MA, 60, PhD, 64. **CAREER** Asst prof theol, Marist Col, 64-68; assoc prof, St Norbert Col, 68-70; PROF THEOL, GRAD DIV RELIG EDUC, FAIRFIELD UNIV, 77-, Dir, 70-; Union Theol Sem fel, Columbia Univ, 66-67; Fairfield Univ Fac res grant, 76. **MEMBERSHIPS** Am Acad Relig; Cath Bibl Asn Am; Relig Educ Asn; Dirs Grad Progs Relig Educ (vpres, 74-75). **RESEARCH** Religious and psychological development; religion and human sexuality; psychological and religious interrelationships in the development of God images. **SELECTED PUBLICATIONS** Auth, The Inheritance: What Catholics Believe, Pflaum, 70; contribr, Continuing Christian Development, Twenty-Third Publ, 73; auth, Prayer, The Lamp, 1/73; Maturity of thought and religious alternatives, Relig Teachers J, 1/73; contribr, Faith as a learned lifestyle, in Emerging Issues in Religious Education, 76; Acquiring Our Image of God, Paulist, 83. **CONTACT ADDRESS** Relig Studies, Fairfield Univ, 1073 N Benson Rd, Fairfield, CT, 06430-5195. **EMAIL** malang@fairi.fairfield.edu

LANG, MICHAEL B.
DISCIPLINE LAW **EDUCATION** Harvard Col, AB; Univ Pa, JD. **CAREER** Prof; app Maine Law's first Libra prof, 90; fac law sch, Louisiana Tech Univ, 83- and its assoc dean, 93-96; taught, Utah, Ill Inst Technol/Chicago Kent Col Law and Univ San Diego Col Law; prac tax law, Philadelphia and Chicago; past res fel, Yale Univ. **MEMBERSHIPS** Amer Bar Asn Sect Taxation. **SELECTED PUBLICATIONS** Collab on 1st ed, Bittker's multivolume Federal Taxation of Income, Estates and Gifts; co-compiler, Index to Federal Tax Articles; coauth, treatise on tax elections. **CONTACT ADDRESS** School of Law, Univ of Southern Maine, 96 Falmouth St, PO Box 9300, Portland, ME, 04104-9300.

LANGAN, JOHN P.
PERSONAL Born 08/10/1940, Hartford, CT, s **DISCIPLINE** PHILOSOPHY **EDUCATION** Loyola Univ - Chicago, AB, 64, PhL, 64, MA, 66; Woodstock Col, BD, 70; Univ Mich, PhD, 79. **CAREER** Instr, St. Ignatius High Sch, 64-65; Instr, Univ Detroit, 65-67; Teaching Fel, Univ Mich, 71-72; Lectr Theol, 75-79, Lectr Philos, Georgetown Univ, 79-; Res Fel, 75-83, Sr Fel, Woodstock Theol Ctr, 83-, Actg Dir, 86-87; Vis Asst Prof Soc Ethics, Yale Divinity Sch, 83; Rose F. Kennedy Prof Christian Ethics, Kennedy Inst Ethics, Georgetown Univ, 87-; Vis Prof Philos, Loyola Univ Chicago, 95-. **HONORS AND AWARDS** Nat Merit Schol, 57; Rackham Prize Fel, Univ Mich, 72-73; Vis Fel, Jesuit Inst, Boston Col, 93-94. **MEMBERSHIPS** Am Acad Relig; Am Cath Philos Asn; Am Philos Asn; Asn Applied Professional Ethics; Cath Theol Soc Am; Int Studies Asn; Soc Christian Ethics; Soc Christian Philos; Coun Christian Approaches Disarmament; Soc Bus Ethics; Soc Medieval Renaissance Philos. **SELECTED PUBLICATIONS** Ed, Catholic Universities in Church and Society: A Dialogue on Ex Corde Ecclesiae, Georgetown Univ Press, 93; auth, Just War Doctrine, The Harper Collins Encyclopedia of Catholicism, Harper, 95; Capital Punishment, The Harper Collins Encyclopedia of Catholicism, Harper, 95; Religious Pacifism and Quietism: A Taxonomic Approach and a Catholic Response, Pacifism and Quietism in the Abrahamic Traditions, Georgetown Univ Press, 96; author of numerous other publications and articles. **CONTACT ADDRESS** The Joseph and Rose Kennedy Inst Ethics, Georgetown Univ, Room 424, Healy Bldg, Washington, DC, 20057. **EMAIL** langanj@gunet.georgetown.edu

LANGER, MONIKA
DISCIPLINE PHILOSOPHY **EDUCATION** Univ Toronto, BA, MA, PhD; Univ McGill, MLS. **CAREER** Instr, Univ Toronto; Yale Univ; Univ Alberta; Dalhousie Univ; assoc prof, 82. **RESEARCH** Continental European philosophy; feminist philosophy; social/political issues and philosophy in literature. **SELECTED PUBLICATIONS** Auth, Merleau-Ponty's Phenomenology of Perception: A Guide and Commentary; pub(s), articles in Philos Today, Can Jour of Polit and Soc Theory, Tchg Philos, Thesis Eleven, The Trumpeter, Library of Living Philosophers, Philos of Jean-Paul Sartre; co-ed, The New Reality: The Politics of Restraint, Brit Columbia. **CONTACT ADDRESS** Dept of Philosophy, Victoria Univ, PO Box 3045, Victoria, BC, V8W 3P4.

LANGER, RUTH
PERSONAL Born 03/30/1960, Pittsburgh, PA, m, 1986, 2 children **DISCIPLINE** RELIGION **EDUCATION** Hebrew Union Col, Jewish Inst of Religion, PhD 94. **CAREER** Boston Col, asst prof 95-. **MEMBERSHIPS** AJS; WUJS; AAR; SBL **RESEARCH** Jewish liturgy and ritual. **SELECTED PUBLICATIONS** Auth, To Worship God Properly: Tensions between Liturgical Custom and Halakhah in Judaism, in: Heb Union Col Press, forthcoming; Rev, Leon J. Weinberger, Twilight of a Golden Age: Selected Poems of Abraham Ibn Ezra, in: The Medieval Rev, forthcoming; Liturgy, History of and Liturgy reform, in: Readers Guide to Judaism, ed, Michael Terry, Fitzroy Dearborn Pub, forthcoming; From Study to Scripture to Reenactment of Sinai, Worship, 98; Approaching Divine Holiness: Issues in the Liturgical Use of the KEDU shah, in: Proceedings of the Rabbinical Assembly, 97. **CONTACT ADDRESS** Dept of Theology, Boston Col, 1215 Commonwealth Av, West Newton, MA, 02465-2908. **EMAIL** langer@bc.edu

LANGERAK, EDWARD ANTHONY
PERSONAL Born 05/01/1944, Grand Rapids, Mich, m, 1966, 2 children **DISCIPLINE** PHILOSOPHY, INTERDISCIPLINARY STUDIES **EDUCATION** Calvin Col, BA, 66; Univ Mich, MA, 72; Princeton Univ, PhD(relig), 72. **CAREER** Asst prof, 72-78, Assoc Prof, 78-86, prof, Philos, St Olaf Col, 87-, Nat Humanities Inst fel, Univ Chicago, 78-79. **MEMBERSHIPS** Am Philos Asn; Soc Values Higher Educ; Am Soc Value Inquiry; Inst Soc, Ethics & Life Sci. **RESEARCH** Medical ethics; values and technology; tolerabce. **SELECTED PUBLICATIONS** Auth, Abortion: Listening to the middle, Hastings Ctr Report, 10/79; coauth, Christian Faith, Health, and Medical Practice, Eerdmans, 89; auth, Duties and Conventanal Ethics, Duties to Others, Kluwer, 94; auth, Theism and Toleration, Companion to Philosopy of Religion, Blackwell, 96; auth, Disagreement: The Dark Side of Tolerance, Philosophy, Religion, and the Question of Intolerance, SUNY, 97. **CONTACT ADDRESS** St Olaf Col, 1520 St Olaf Ave, Northfield, MN, 55057-1099. **EMAIL** langerk@stolaf.edu

LANGFORD, MICHAEL J.
PERSONAL Born 06/29/1931, London, England **DISCIPLINE** PHILOSOPHY **EDUCATION** Oxford Univ, BA, 54, MA, 57; Univ London, England, PhD(philos), 66. **CAREER** Asst prof, 67-72, ASSOC PROF PHILOS, MEM UNIV NFLD, 72-. **MEMBERSHIPS** Can Philos Asn. **RESEARCH** Philosophy of religion; moral philosophy. **SELECTED PUBLICATIONS** Auth, Fideist Responses to Atheism and Positivism--the Rationality of Belief Revisited, Stud in Rel-Sci Religieuses, Vol 0023, 94. **CONTACT ADDRESS** Dept of Philos, Memorial Univ of Newfoundland, St John's, NF, A1C 5S7.

LANGIULLI, NINO FRANCIS
PERSONAL Born 10/09/1932, Brooklyn, NY, m, 1959, 3 children **DISCIPLINE** PHILOSOPHY, ENGLISH **EDUCATION** Maryknoll Col, AB, 55; Hunter Col, MA, 60; NY Univ, MA, 65, PhD(philos), 73. **CAREER** Instr English, St Augustine's High Sch, Brooklyn, 57-60; instr theol, 61-65, asst prof philos, 66-71, assoc prof, 72-76, Prof Philos, St Francis Col, NY, 76-, Danforth Assoc, 66-72. **HONORS AND AWARDS** Fulbright 60-61; Sears Roebuck Teaching Exc, 91; assoc ed, Measure, 89-96; book rev ed, Telos, 98. **MEMBERSHIPS** Am Philos Asn; AAUP. **RESEARCH** Contemporary philosophy; history of philosophy; metaphysics. **SELECTED PUBLICATIONS** Auth, Machiavelli, In: Shakespeare Encycl, Crowell, 66; ed & translr, Critical Existentialism, 69 & ed, The Existentialist Tradition, 71, Doubleday; translr, Existentialism, In: Encycl Britannica, Univ Chicago, 73; Possibility, Necessity, and Existence, Temple, 92; European Existentialism, Transaction, 97. **CONTACT ADDRESS** 32 Farnum St, Lynbrook, NY, 11563.

LANGLINAIS, J. WILLIS
PERSONAL Born 08/12/1922, San Antonio, TX **DISCIPLINE** THEOLOGY **EDUCATION** Univ of Dayton, OH, BS, 43; Univ of Fribourg, Switzerland, STB, 50, STL, 52, STD, 54. **CAREER** Dir, Marianist Novitiate, Galesville, WI, 59-63; Dean of Arts and Sciences, 64-75, Academic Vice-Pres, 75-81, DIR OF INSTITUTIONAL SELF STUDY FOR ACCREDITATION, ST. MARY'S UNIV, SAN ANTONIO, 70-72, 82-. **MEMBERSHIPS** College Theol Soc; Cath Theol Soc of Am; Mariological Soc Am. **RESEARCH** Ethics; ecumenics; comparative religions. **CONTACT ADDRESS** 1 Camino Santa Maria, San Antonio, TX, 78228. **EMAIL** jwillis@alvin.stmarytx.edu

LANGUM, DAVID J.
PERSONAL m, 2 children **DISCIPLINE** LAW **EDUCATION** Dartmouth Col, AB, 62; Stanford Univ, JD, 65; San Jose State Univ, MA, 76; Univ Mich Law School, LLM, 81, SJD, 85. **CAREER** Res clerk, Hon Murray Draper, Cal Court Appeals, San Fran, CA, 65-66; assoc, Dunne, Phelps & Mills, San Fran, CA, 66-68; partner, Christenson, Hedemark, Langum & O'Keefe, San Jose, CA, 68-78; fac, San Fran Law School, 66-67, Lincoln Univ School Law, 68-78, Detroit College of Law, 78-83; prof Law, 83-85, dean, 83-84, Nevada School of Law; prof of law, 85- , chemn doctoral prog law, relig & cult, 94- , co-chemn Cumberland Colloquim Am Legal Hist, 95- , Cumberland School Law, Samford Univ. chemn, Rushton Distinguised Lect Prof, 97. **HONORS AND AWARDS** Fel, Intercultural Commun Soviet Union, 62; James Willard Hurst Prize, 88; Golieb fel, NYU, 91; Ucross Found res writing fel, 98. Caroline Bancroft Hist Prize, 91; Herbert Eugene Bolton Award, 78; Lawyers Title Award, 64-65. **MEMBERSHIPS** Calif State Bar; US Supreme Court Bar; Mich State Bar; Am Soc Legal Hist; Am Hist Asn; Al Hist Asn; Ala Asn Hist; W Hist Asn; Cal Hist Soc. **SELECTED PUBLICATIONS** Auth, Crossing Over the Line: Legislating Morality and the Mann Act, Univ Chicago Press, 94; The Legal System of Spanish California: A Preliminiary Study, W Legal Hist, 94; rev, Land Grants and Lawsuits in Northern New Mexico, Am Hist Rev, 95; Rugged Justice: The Ninth Circuit Court of Appeals and the American West, 1891-1941, Am Hist Rev, 95; A Comment on The Lost Lawyers Legal Education, Cumberland Law Rev, 96; rev, Federal Criminal Law Doctrines: the Forgotten Influence of Prohibition, Am Hist Rev, 96; Saving Old Glory: the History of the American Flag Desecration Controversy, Social Science and Modern Society, 96; From Maverick to Mainstream: Cumberland School of Law, 1847-1997, Univ Georgia Press, 97; Memoir of a Book: Writing the History of Cumberland, Cumberland Law Rev, 97. **CONTACT ADDRESS** Cumberland School of Law, Samford Univ, 800 Lakeshore Dr., Birmingham, AL, 35229. **EMAIL** djlangum@samford.edu

LANIAK, TIMOTHY
PERSONAL Born 09/27/1958, MA, m, 1981, 3 children **DISCIPLINE** RELIGION **EDUCATION** Wheaton Coll, BA, 80; Gordon-Conwell Sem, MDiv, 89; Harvard Divinity Sch, ThD, 97. **CAREER** Asst prof, Gordon-Conwell Sem. **MEMBERSHIPS** AAR; SBL; IBR; BAS. **RESEARCH** Old Testament; anthropology; Judaism; archaeology. **SELECTED PUBLICATIONS** Auth, Shame and Honor in the Book of Esther, Scholars, 98. **CONTACT ADDRESS** 2324 Wedgewood Dr, Matthews, NC, 28105. **EMAIL** tlaniak@gcts.edu

LANNING, BILL L.
PERSONAL Born 10/31/1944, Kansas City, MO, m, 1966, 2 children **DISCIPLINE** RELIGION **EDUCATION** Baylor Univ, PhD, 76; Wichita State Univ, P-doc, 89-90. **CAREER** Butler Com Col, inst, 93,96-97; Bethany Col, inst, 90-91, 93-94; Hutchinson Com Col, inst, 91-97, Blinn Col, inst, 79-88. **MEMBERSHIPS** AAR, APA, INS, IANDE, CTNS, ITEST **RESEARCH** Mind and consciousness; relig, philo and science; near-death experiences; vedic indo-euro stud. **SELECTED PUBLICATIONS** Auth, Daily Book of Prayer, United Church Press, forthcoming yr 2000; articles in: Northwest Houston Leader, Mt. Hope Clarion and Haven Jour, McPherson Sentinel; bk reviews, in: Bryan Eagle and Jour of Church and State. **CONTACT ADDRESS** 4606 Mangum Rd, Houston, TX, 77092. **EMAIL** billanni@swbell.net

LAPIDUS LERNER, ANNE
PERSONAL m, 2 children **DISCIPLINE** RELIGION **EDUCATION** Harvard Univ, AB, 64, MA, 65, PhD, 77. **CAREER** Lectr, Jewish Theol Sem Am.. **RESEARCH** Study of mod Jewish lit; the reinterpretation of texts by mod writers; position of women in Judaism. **SELECTED PUBLICATIONS** Auth, Passing the Love of Women: A Study of Gide's Saul; Who Has Not Made Me a Man: The Movement for Equal Rights for Women in American Judaism. **CONTACT ADDRESS** Dept of Jewish Lit, Jewish Theol Sem of America, 3080 Broadway, PO Box 3080, New York, NY, 10027. **EMAIL** anlerner@jtsa.edu

LAPPRAND, MARC
DISCIPLINE TWENTIETH CENTURY FRENCH LITERATURE **EDUCATION** Univ Toronto, PhD. **RESEARCH** Boris Vian; Raymond Queneau and Oulipo; literary theory. **SELECTED PUBLICATIONS** Auth, Boris Vian la vie contre: biographie critique, Ottawa, Presses de l'Universite d'Ottawa,

Paris, Nizet, 93; Trois Fous du langage: Vian, Queneau, Prevert, Nancy, Presses universitaires de Nancy, 93; Poetique de l'Oulipo, Amsterdam, Rodopi, 98. **CONTACT ADDRESS** Dept of French, Victoria Univ, PO Box 3045 STN CSC, Victoria, BC, V8W 3P4. **EMAIL** lapprand@uvic.ca

LAPSLEY, JAMES N.
PERSONAL Born 03/16/1930, Clarksville, TN, m, 1990, 2 children **DISCIPLINE** RELIGION **EDUCATION** Rhodes Col, BA, 52; Union Theol Seminary, BD, 55; Univ Chic, PhD, 61 **CAREER** Fac, Princeton Theol Seminary, 61-92; Prof Pastoral Theol, 76-92; Acad Dean, 84-89; Prof Emeritus, 92-. **HONORS AND AWARDS** Phi Beta Kappa; Rockefeller Bros Fellow, 59-61; Danforth Fellow, Menninger Fnd, 60-61. **MEMBERSHIPS** Soc for Pastoral Theol; Am Soc on Aging; Am Acad of Relig. **RESEARCH** Theological anthropology; personality characteristics and aging. **SELECTED PUBLICATIONS** Auth, Reconciliation, Forgiveness, Lost Contracts, Theol Today, XXIII, 2, 44-59, 7/66; auth, Salvation and Health, Westminster, 72; auth, The Self, Its Vicissitudes and Possibilities: An Essay in Theological Anthropology, Pastoral Psychology, 35, 23-45, 86; auth, Renewal in Late Life through Pastoral Counsleing, Paulist, 92; auth, Vengeance: The Half Hidden Pillager of Our Lives, Pastoral Psychol, 46, 4, 255-266, 3/98. **CONTACT ADDRESS** 16610 Meadow Park Dr, Sun City, AZ, 85351. **EMAIL** lapsley@interacs.com

LARKIN, ERNEST ELDON
PERSONAL Born 08/19/1922, Chicago, IL **DISCIPLINE** THEOLOGY **EDUCATION** Mt Carmel Col, PhB, 43; Pontif Univ St Thomas Aquinas, STL, 49, STD, 54. **CAREER** Instr theol, Whitefriars Hall, Washington, DC, 51-60; lectr, Cath Univ Am, 60-61, from instr to assoc prof, 61-72; PROF SPIRITUAL THEOL AND PRES, KINO INST, 72-80; LECTR AND WRITER, 80-. **MEMBERSHIPS** Theol Soc Am. **RESEARCH** Spiritual theology; prayer, comtemplation, Carmelite spirituality. **SELECTED PUBLICATIONS** Auth, John of the Cross--an Appreciation, Horizons, Vol 0022, 95; John of the Cross--Conferences and Essays by Members of the Institute of Carmelite Studies and Others, Horizons, Vol 0022, 95. **CONTACT ADDRESS** Kino Inst of Theol, Phoenix, AZ, 85020-4295.

LAROSILIERE, JEAN DARLY MARTIN
PERSONAL Born 02/04/1963, Port-au-Prince, Haiti, m, 1988 **DISCIPLINE** LAW **EDUCATION** Fairfield University, AB, 1985; Tulane University School of Law, JD, 1988; Georgetown University Law Center, LLM, 1990. **CAREER** Georgetown University Law Center, graduate teaching fellow, 1988-90; Seton Hall University School of Law, adjunct professor of law, 1992-; US Department of Justice, assistant US attorney, 1990-. **HONORS AND AWARDS** Tulane University, senior trial competition finalist, 1988; Black Law Students Association, Frederick Douglass Moot Court Champion, 1988. **MEMBERSHIPS** US Department of Justice, hiring committee, 1992-; Garden State Bar Association, 1990-; American Bar Association, 1988-; Natl Bar Assn, 1985-. **CONTACT ADDRESS** Assistant US Attorney, US Department of Justice, 970 Broad St, Rm 502, Newark, NJ, 07102.

LARRABEE, MARY J.
PERSONAL Born 02/09/1943, Sacramento, CA, m, 1973, 2 children **DISCIPLINE** PHILOSOPHY **EDUCATION** Holy Names Col, BA, 65; Indiana Univ, MA, 69; Univ Toronto, PhD, 74. **CAREER** Tchg assoc, Indiana Univ, 66-69; instr, 69-72, tutor, 72-73, Univ Toronto; lectr, 74-77, York Univ, Atkinson Col, McLaughlin Col; from asst and assoc, 77-97, to prof, 98-, philos, DePaul Univ. **HONORS AND AWARDS** Kappa Gamma Pi; Ontario Govt Fel, 70-73; DePaul Univ Fac Summer Res Grant, 83, 86, 88, 90, 95, 98; DePaul Univ Competitive Fac Leav Grant, 88, 92, 97, and Competitive Res Grant, 89, 92; listed, World Who's Who of Women, 89, Who's Who of American Women, 98. **MEMBERSHIPS** APA; Soc for Phenomenology and Existential Philos; Soc for the Study of Husserl's Philos; Soc for Women in Philos; Husserl Circle; Metaphysical Soc of Am; Nat Women's Stud Asn; Nat Asn for Women in Cath Higher Educ. **RESEARCH** Phenomenology, existentialism; postmodernism; race studies; women's studies; time; gender; consciousness and subjectivity. **SELECTED PUBLICATIONS** Ed and contribur, An Ethic of Care: Feminist and Interdisciplinary Perspectives, Routledge, 92; auth, Inside Time-Consciousness: Diagramming the Flux, Husserl Stud, 94; auth, The Time of Trauma: Husserl's Phenomenology and Post-Traumatic Stress Disorder, Human Stud, 95; auth, Toward a Feminine Imaginary: Irigaray and Voices of the Crone? in DaSilva, ed, Her Voices: Hermeneutics of the Feminine, Univ Press of America, 96; auth, Searching for Voice: Towards a Phenomenology of Autonomy and Connectedness, in Embree, ed, Feminist Phenomenology, Kluwer, 98; auth, There's No Time Like the Present: How to Mind the Now, in Brough, ed, More Phenomenology of Time, Kluwer, 99; contribur, Encyclopedia of Feminist Theory, Routledge, 99. **CONTACT ADDRESS** Philosophy Dept, DePaul Univ, 1150 W Fullerton, Chicago, IL, 60614. **EMAIL** mlarrabe@wppost.depaul.edu

LARSEN, ALLAN W.
PERSONAL Born 03/15/1936, NYC, NY, m, 1962, 3 children **DISCIPLINE** PHILOSOPHY **EDUCATION** CUNY Brooklyn Col, BA, 62; Univ Delaware, MA, 64; Duquesne Univ, PhD, 71. **CAREER** Univ Penn Slippery Rock, inst, asst prof, assoc prof, prof, 63-94; Westminister Col, part-time prof. **HONORS AND AWARDS** Professor Emeritus, 3 times Outstanding Philos Prof. **MEMBERSHIPS** APA, SPEP. **RESEARCH** Phenomenology; existential and environment philosophy; philosophy of technology. **SELECTED PUBLICATIONS** Auth, Nietzsche on the Legacy of Socrates, History of European Ideas, 96; auth,The flight from the Earth to the Universe, European Legacy, 98; auth, The Phenomenology of Mircea Eliade, An Eliade Anthology, 98. **CONTACT ADDRESS** Dept of Philosophy, Slippery Rock Univ, Slipperyrock, PA, 16057-2125. **EMAIL** allan.larsen@sru.edu

LARSON, DAVID A.
DISCIPLINE LABOR LAW **EDUCATION** DePauw Univ, BA, 76; Univ Ill, JD, 79; Univ Penn, LLM, 87. **CAREER** Prof, Creighton Univ; past managing ed, Recent Decisions Sect, Ill Bar J; pvt pract Minneapolis, Minn,; instr, Loyola Univ Chicago Sch Bus and Millsaps Col; prof in residence, Equal Employ Opportunity Comn, Appellate Div in Wash DC, 90-91. **HONORS AND AWARDS** Fac awd of Excellence, Amer Bus Law Asn, 86. **RESEARCH** Employment discrimination. **SELECTED PUBLICATIONS** Pub(s) in, Yale J Int Law; Mo Law Rev; NY Univ Rev Law and Soc Change; La Law Rev; Memphis State Univ Law Rev; Labor Law J; Seton Hall Legislative J; Univ Detroit Mercy Law Rev; Amer J Trial Advocacy. **CONTACT ADDRESS** School of Law, Creighton Univ, 2500 California Plaza, Omaha, NE, 68178. **EMAIL** larson@culaw.creighton.edu

LARSON, GERALD J.
DISCIPLINE RELIGIOUS STUDIES **EDUCATION** Columbia Univ, PhD, 67. **CAREER** Prof. **RESEARCH** Indian Philosophy; cross cultural philosophy of religion; history of religions; classical and Vedic Sanskrit studies. **SELECTED PUBLICATIONS** Auth, India's Agony Over Religion, State Univ NY, 95; Classical Samkhya: An Interpretation of Its History and Meaning, Banarsidass, 79; co-auth, Samkhya: A Dualist Tradition in Indian Philosophy, Princeton, 86; Interpreting Across Boundaries: New Essays in Comparative Philosophy, Princeton, 87. **CONTACT ADDRESS** Dept of Religious Studies, Indiana Univ, Bloomington, 300 N Jordan Ave, Bloomington, IN, 47405.

LASKY, GEOFFERY
PERSONAL Born 01/21/1954, New York, NY, d **DISCIPLINE** PHILOSOPHY **EDUCATION** Univ of Illinois, Urbana, PhD, 81. **CAREER** Long Island Univ, sr adj prof; Adelph Univ, adj prof. **MEMBERSHIPS** APA **RESEARCH** Philosophy; psychology; physics; philo of education. **SELECTED PUBLICATIONS** Auth, Thinking on the Edge: Building a Theory of Intelligence. **CONTACT ADDRESS** Dept of Philosophy, Long Island Univ, PO Box 8116, Garden City, NY.

LASS, TRIS
PERSONAL Born 09/28/1972, Okinawa, Japan **DISCIPLINE** PHILOSOPHY **EDUCATION** Univ Portland, BA, 97. **CAREER** Guest lectr, Univ Portland; tchg asst, hist and res, Portland State Univ. **HONORS AND AWARDS** Cum laude, 97; Capstone presentor, Univ Portland. **MEMBERSHIPS** APA; Am Hist Soc. **RESEARCH** German and French phenomenology; existentialism; philosophy and history of science; Russian history; East Asian history; contemporary European history; Eastern philosophy; history of Christianity and Taoism. **SELECTED PUBLICATIONS** Auth, Outsider's Call to Thought, Three Days in Exile, Baobab, 96; auth, Necessary Lie, Science as Culture, 98; auth, Merleau-Ponty and Wittgenstein, A Synthesis, Univ Portland Philos J, 98; auth, Paradox: The Historical Tradition, Univ Portland Philos J, 98. **CONTACT ADDRESS** 2174 NW Davis, #505, Portland, OR, 97210. **EMAIL** tlass@earthlink.net

LASSEK, YUN JA
PERSONAL Born 06/07/1941, Korea, 2 children **DISCIPLINE** PHILOSOPHY OF EDUCATION **EDUCATION** NY Univ, PhD, 85 **CAREER** Adjunct prof, 93-94, Rosemont Col; managing dir, 93-94, 94- , program chair, The Board of Governors, The Greater Philadelphia Philosophy Consortium. **HONORS AND AWARDS** Boston Univ, Teaching Assistanship, 65-66; The first prize award in the Liberal Arts Col for the chung-Ang Univ Sch, 63-64. **MEMBERSHIPS** APA; SAAP **RESEARCH** Critical thinking; Perception and cognition; Visual arts education **SELECTED PUBLICATIONS** Auth,Ecology and the 18th century world view, Children: Thinking in Philosophy Proceedings of the 5th International Conf on Philosphy for Children, 92. **CONTACT ADDRESS** 415 Barclay Rd., Bryn Mawr, PA, 19010. **EMAIL** 102165.3562@compuserve.com

LASSON, KENNETH L.
PERSONAL m, 3 children **DISCIPLINE** LAW **EDUCATION** Johns Hopkins Univ, AB, 63; Univ of Maryland School of Law, JD, 66; Johns Hopkins Univ, MA, 67. **CAREER** Res asst, Const Conv Comn of Maryland, 66; exec secy, Maryland School Law Rev. Comn, 66-67; tchg fel and lectr, Johns Hopkins Univ, 66-68; asst to the Dean, Univ of Maryland School of Law, 67-69; ed and admin consult, R. Nader's Ctr for Study of Responxive Law, 69-72; asst to the Pres, Goucher Col, 70-71; asst prof, Loyola Col, 72-78; guest schloar, The Brookings Institution, 75-77; lectr, Univ of Maryland School of Law, 77; affirmative action off, Loyola Col, 77-79; vis scholar, Cambridge Univ, 85; on-site dir, Aberseen summer law prog, 94; prof, Univ of Baltimore School of Law, 76- . **MEMBERSHIPS** ABA; Am Zionist Movement; Cross Country Improvement Asn; Beth Abraham Congregation; Baltimore Jewish Coun; Comt on Law and Pub Affairs; Maryland Am Civil Liberties Union, Ct of Appeals of Maryland; Fourth Circuit of Appeals, Supreme Court. **RESEARCH** Civil Liberties **SELECTED PUBLICATIONS** Auth, The Workers, 72; Proudly We Hail, 75; Private Lives of Public Servants, 78;Your Rights and the Draft, 80;Your Rights As A Vet, 81; Getting the Most Out of Wahington, 82; Representing Yourself, 83; Mousetraps and Muffling Cups, 86; Patent Pending: 200 Years of Brilliant and Bizarre Inventions, Baltimore Sun Mag, 90; Scholarship Amok: Excesses in the Pursuit of Truth and Tenure, 103 Harvard Law Rev 926, 90; Racism in Higher Education: Brown's Effect on Campus Bigotry, 7 Harvard Black Letter Jour 139, 90; Reasonable Doubts, City Paper, 91 To Stimulate, Provoke, or Incite? First Amendment Purposes and Group Defamation, 3 St. Thomas Law Rev 49, 91; On Letters and Law Reviews: A Jaded Rejoinder, 24 Conn Law Rev 201, 91; Feminism Awry: Excesses in the Pursuit of Rights and Trifles, 42 Jour of Legal Educ 1, 92; Religious Liberty in the Military: The First Amendment under Friendly Fire, 9 Jour of Law and Relig 471, 93; Mad Dogs and Englishmen: A Ditty Dedicated to First-Year Law Students, Confused on the Merits, 17 NOVA Law Rev 857, 93; Learning Law, 93; The Jews of Scotland, Los Angeles Jewish Jour, 94; Lawyering Askew: Excesses in the Pursuit of Fees and Justice, 74 Boston Univ Law Rev 301, 94; Radfems and the First Amendment, The Defender, 95; Political Correctness Askew: Excesses in the Pursuit of Minds and Manners, 63 Tenn Law Rev 689, 96; The Tintinnabulation of Bell's Letters, 36 Washburn Law Jour 18, 96; Holocaust Denial and the First Amendment: The Quest for Truth in a Free Society, 6 George Mason Law Rev 35, 97. **CONTACT ADDRESS** School of Law, Univ of Baltimore, Baltimore, MD, 21201. **EMAIL** klasson@ubmail.ubalt.edu

LATCOVICH, MARK A.
PERSONAL Born 04/15/1955, Ridgeway, PA **DISCIPLINE** THEOLOGY **EDUCATION** St Mary's Sem Wickliffe, MDiv, 81, MA, 86, Case Western Reserve Univ, PhD, 96. **CAREER** Ordained Priest, 81; St Mary's Sem, assoc prof, acad dean, 96-. **MEMBERSHIPS** ASA, GSA, RRA / SSR. **RESEARCH** Issues in Roman Catholic theology and their social impact. **SELECTED PUBLICATIONS** Auth, Ecclesial Empowerment: A Study of Roman Catholic Permanent Deacons and Their Spouses, Society for the Scientific Study of Religion, Annual Confer, 95; auth, The Emerging Role of Roman Catholic Permanent Deacons: An Application of the Role Theory of R.H. Turner, Am Socio Assoc, Annual Confer, 94; Extrinsic Religiosity as a Generalized Resistance Resource of an Older Person's Sense of Coherence, coauth, Gerontological Society of Am, Annual Confer, 93; auth, The Clergyperson and the Fifth Step, Spirituality and the Fifth Step, ed. R. Kus, Hayworth Pr, 95; auth, Special Groups and Alcoholics Anonymous, coauth, in Jour of Gay and Lesbian Studies, Hayworth Pr, 93. **CONTACT ADDRESS** Dept of Theology, St. Mary Graduate Sch, 28700 Euclid Ave, Wickliffe, OH, 44092. **EMAIL** mxl@po.cwru.edu

LATHAM, WELDON HURD
PERSONAL Born 01/02/1947, Brooklyn, NY, m **DISCIPLINE** LAW **EDUCATION** Howard Univ, BA business admin 1968; Georgetown Univ Law Ctr, JD 1971; George Washington Univ Natl Law Ctr, advanced legal courses 1975-76; Brookings Inst, exec educ prog 1981. **CAREER** Checchi & Co, mgmt consultant 1968-71; Covington & Burling, atty 1971-73; Howard Univ Sch of Law, adj prof 1972-82; The White House Ofc of Mgmt & Budget, asst genl counsel 1974-76; Hogan & Hartson, atty 1976-79; Univ of VA Law Sch, guest prof 1976-91; US Dept of Housing & Urban Develop, genl deputy asst sec 1979-81; Sterling Systems Inc, vice pres genl cnsl 1981-83; Planning Research Corp, executive assistant, counsel to the chairman and CEO, 1983-86; Reed Smith Shaw & Mc Clay, managing partner, McLean VA office 1986-92; Minority Business Enterprise Magazine, columnist, 1991-; Civilian Aide to the Secretary of the Army, 1994-; Shaw, Pittman, Potts & Trowbridge, Natl Law Firm, senior partner, 1992-. **HONORS AND AWARDS** Advocate of the Year, Minority Enterprise Development Week, US Department of Commerce, 1996; Small Business Administration, Private Industry Advocate of the Year, 1992; Northern VA Min Business & Professioal Assn Award, 1990; National Association of Equal Opportunity in Higher Education Achievement Award, 1987; Outstanding Performance Award, US Department of HUD, Sr Exec Serv Washington DC, 1980. **MEMBERSHIPS** Bd dirs Washington Hosp Center Foundation, 1996; Capital Area Advisory Board of First Union National Bank, 1995-; Burger King Corp Diversity Action Council, 1996-; Small Business Administration National Advisory Council, 1994-; Maryland Econom-

ic Development Commission, 1996-; general counsel, National Coalition of Minority Businesses, 1993-; Decomcratic National Committee, 1996; Platform Drafting COmmittee, 1996; managing trustee, Democratic National COmmittee, 1995-; bd dirs District of Columbia Foundation, Inc, 1982-88; Bar Association membership, 1972-: American District of Columbia Natl Federal Virginia; Washington; Natl Contract Mgmt Assn 1982-; legal counsel MD Mondale/Ferraro Campaign Com 1984; apptee VA Gov's Business Adv Comm on Crime Prevention 1983-86; apptee VA Gov's Regulatory Adv Bd 1982-84; Washington steering comm NAACP Legal Defense & Educ Fund 1976-96; Professional Services Council, board of directors 1984-88; editorial advisory bd Washington Business Journal 1985-88; VA Commonwealth Univ, board of directors 1986-89; Democratic Natl Committee Business Council 1986-90, and vice chair, 1994-; Washington Urban League, board of directors 1986-90; numerous others. **CONTACT ADDRESS** Shaw, Pittman, Potts & Trowbridge, 2300 N St NW, Washington, DC, 20037.

LATHROP, GORDON W.
DISCIPLINE LITURGY **EDUCATION** Occidental Col, BA, 61; Luther Sem, BD, 66; Univ Nijmigen, ThD, 69. **CAREER** Charles A. Schieren prof. **HONORS AND AWARDS** Past pres, N Amer acad of Liturgy. **MEMBERSHIPS** Mem, Societas Liturgica. **RESEARCH** Links between liturgy and culture, liturgy and ethics, liturgy and mission. **SELECTED PUBLICATIONS** Auth, Holy Things: A Liturgical Theology, Fortress, 93; gen ed, series Open Questions in Worship. **CONTACT ADDRESS** Dept of Practical Theology, Lutheran Theol Sem, 7301 Germantown Ave, Philadelphia, PA, 19119 1794. **EMAIL** Glathrop@ltsp.edu

LAU, SUE
PERSONAL Born 03/25/1935, St. Joseph, MO, m, 1955, 2 children **DISCIPLINE** RELIGIOUS STUDIES **EDUCATION** Univ Pittsburgh, PhD, 81. **CAREER** Lectr, Univ Pittsburgh, 81-; Asst Prof, Ind Univ of Pa, 91; Vis Asst Prof, WVa Univ, 98. **HONORS AND AWARDS** Phi Beta Kappa; Apple for the Teacher Award, Univ Pittsburgh, 84, 87, 93. **MEMBERSHIPS** Service Int de Documentation Judeo-Chretienne; Am Acad Relig; Soc Bibl Lit; Bibl Archaeol Soc. **RESEARCH** Women in religion. **SELECTED PUBLICATIONS** Auth, Women and Religion: A Bibliography (available on the Internet). **CONTACT ADDRESS** 540 Leger Rd., North Huntington, PA, 15642. **EMAIL** flsclau@aol.com

LAUDER, ROBERT EDWARD
PERSONAL Born 07/06/1934, Brooklyn, NY **DISCIPLINE** PHILOSOPHY **EDUCATION** Cathedral Col, BA, 56; Cath Univ Am, MA, 65; Marquette Univ, PhD(philos), 68. **CAREER** Lectr theol, St Joseph's Col, 63-64; lectr relig studies, Queens Col, 71-75; assoc prof, 75-79, PROF PHILOS, CATHEDRAL COL SEM, 80-. **MEMBERSHIPS** Am Cath Theol Soc; Am Cath Philos Soc; AUP. **RESEARCH** Existentialist philosophy; personalist philosophy. **SELECTED PUBLICATIONS** Contribr, Ingmar Bergman: Essays in Criticism, Oxford Univ, 75; auth, Loneliness is for Loving, Ave Maria, 78; The Love Explosion: Human Experience and the Christian Mystery, Living Flame, 1/79. **CONTACT ADDRESS** Cathedral Col Sem, 7200 Douglaston Pkwy, Douglaston, NY, 11362.

LAUER, EUGENE F.
PERSONAL Born 10/07/1935, Pittsburgh, PA, s **DISCIPLINE** THEOLOGY AND HISTORICAL THEOLOGY SYSTEMATICS **EDUCATION** St. Fidelis Col, 53-55; St. Vincent Col, BA, 57; St. Mary Sem and Univ, STB, 59, STL, 61; Gregorian Univ, Rome, STD, 66; Cath Univ of Amer, 84-85. **CAREER** Asst prof, relig, LaRoche Col, summer, 67; lectr, relig, Carlow Col, 66-68; assoc prof, relig, LaRoche Col, 68-73; adjunct facul mem, Duquesne Univ, 68-69; adjunct facul mem, St. Vincent Sem, 69-70; part-time asst prof, Ind Univ of Penn, 71-72; prof, relig, LaRoche Col, 73-75; ed, Middle States Report, 73; pres, acad senate, 73-75; acting acad dean, LaRoche Col, 74-75; assoc prof, theol, Duquesne Univ, 75-81; mem one-year all-univ planning comn, 78; mem search comt, 80; visiting prof, relig, Seton Hill Col, 81-82; assoc prof, theol/relig, 82-86; dir MA prog in relig educ, Wheeling Jesuit Col, 82-86; adjunct facul, Cath Univ of Amer, 84-85; prof, theol/relig, dir MA prog, Wheeling Jesuit Col, 86-87; dir, Ctr for Continuing Formation in Ministry, assoc prof specialist, Univ Notre Dame, 87-98, chair, special prof facul asn, Univ Notre Dame, 96-97; dir, Hesburgh Ctr for Continuing Formation in Ministry Cath Theol Union, 98-. **HONORS AND AWARDS** Chair, Special Professional Facul, Notre Dame, 97; chair, Nat Cath Coalition on Preaching, 92-97; chair, Facul Senate and Assembly, Wheeling Jesuit Univ, 86-87; Outstanding Facul Person award, Wheeling Jesuit Univ, 86, 87; facul rep, all-univ planning comn, 78-79; chair, facul senate, LaRoche Col, 73-75; outstanding educ award, LaRoche Col, 72. **MEMBERSHIPS** Amer Acad of Relig; Amer Asn for Higher Educ; Cath Theol Soc of Amer; Col Theol Soc. **RESEARCH** Sacraments; Religion and public affairs. **SELECTED PUBLICATIONS** Article, For What Shall We Ask: A Biblical-Theological Critique of Prayer of Petition, Studies in Formative Spirituality, XI, 2, 145-156, may, 90; rev, New Experiment in Democracy, Social Thought, XIV, 4, 60-61, fall, 88; reb, Faithful Dissent, Soc Thought, XIII, 1, 64-67, winter, 87; article, Overcoming Resistance in Power-Sharing, Health Progress, 67, 3, 46-48, 71, apr, 86; article, New Approaches to Decision-Making in Moral Theology, Health Progress, 67, 1, 42-46, 56, jan-feb, 86; article, The Holiness of Marriage: Some New Perspectives from Recent Sacramental Theology, Studies in Formative Spirituality, VI, 2, 215-226, may, 85; book rev, When Health Care Employees Strike, Health Progress, 66, 4, 66, may, 85; article, Service Strikes: The New Moral Dilemma, Issues in the Labor-Mgt Dialogue, Church Perspectives, Cath Health Asn of US, 82. **CONTACT ADDRESS** Hesburgh Center, Catholic Theol Union at Chicago, 5401 S. Cornell Av., Chicago, IL, 60615.

LAUGHLIN, JOHN C.H.
PERSONAL Born 09/05/1942, Asheboro, NC, m, 1965, 1 child **DISCIPLINE** HEBREW BIBLE STUDIES, NEAR EASTERN ANTHROPOLOGY AND PHILOSOPHY **EDUCATION** Wake Forest Univ, BA, Greek, 67; Southern Bapt Theol Sem, M Div, 71; PhD, 75. **CAREER** Pastor, Col Ave Bapt Church, Bluefield, WV, 75-76; asst prof relig, Hardin-Simmons Univ, Abilene, TX, 76-77; asst prof relig, Palm Beach Atlantic Col, West Palm Beach, Fla, 77-79; prof relig and cha, dept relig, Averett Col, Danville, Va, 79-. **MEMBERSHIPS** Nat Asn Bapt Prof of Relig; Amer Sch of Oriental Res; Soc of Bibl Lit; Bibl Archaeo Soc. **RESEARCH** Archaeology and the Bible; Near Eastern Archaeology; Biblical Studies. **SELECTED PUBLICATIONS** Articles, Mercer Dict of the Bible, 90; Capernaum from Jesus' Time and After, Bibl Archaeol Rev, 54-61, 90, 93; Joshua, Mercer Commentary on the Bible, 95; Israel and the Liberation of Canaan, Joseph A. Callaway's Faces of the Old Testament, Mercer Univ Press, 95; Digging Archaeology, The Bibl Illusr, fall, 97; Samaria the Strong, The Bibl Illusr, fall, 98. **CONTACT ADDRESS** Averett Col, 420 W. Main St., Danville, VA, 24541. **EMAIL** laughlin@averett.edu

LAUMAKIS, STEPHEN J.
DISCIPLINE MEDIEVAL PHILOSOPHY: ST. THOMAS AQUINAS **EDUCATION** St. Charles Sem, BA, 82; Villanova Univ, MA, 84; Univ Notre Dame, PhD, 91. **CAREER** Phil, St. John Vianney Col Sem **MEMBERSHIPS** MN Philos Soc; Am Philos Asn; Am Catholic Philos Asn; Soc Christian Philos. **SELECTED PUBLICATIONS** Auth, Is Christian Science Possible?,Science & Theology, Univ St Thomas, 96; The Role of Chance in the Philosophy of Teilhard De Chardin, Villanova Univ, 84. **CONTACT ADDRESS** St. John Vianney Col Sem, 2115 Summit Ave, St Paul, MN, 55105-1095.

LAWERGREN, BO
PERSONAL Born 01/04/1937, Sweden, s, 2 children **DISCIPLINE** PHYSICS **EDUCATION** Australian Natl Univ, PhD, 64. **CAREER** Prof, 70-, Hunter Col, CUNY. **RESEARCH** Musical archaeology and acoustics **SELECTED PUBLICATIONS** Auth, Harfe, MGG2, Vol, 4, 96; auth, Leier,MGG2, Vol 5, 96; auth, The Spread of Harps Between the Near and Far East During the First Millennium A. D.: Evidence of Buddhist Musical Cultures on the Silk Road, Silk Road Art & Arch 4, 96; auth, Mesopotamien (archaeological), Die Musik in Geschichte und Gegenwart (=MGG2), 97; auth, To Tune a String: Dichotomies and Diffusions between the Near and Far East, Ultra Terminum Vagari, Edizioni Quasar, 97; auth, Harp (cang), Encycl Iranica, 98; auth, Parthian Empire, New Grove Dict of Music and Musicians, 98; auth, Persia, New Grove Dict of Music and Musicians, 98; auth, Harp, New Grove Dict of Music and Musicians, 98; auth, Lyre (ancient), New Grove Dict of Music and Musicians, 98; art, The Beginning and End of Angular Harps: Causal History ca 1900bc to1600ad, Cambridge Archaeol Jour, 98; art, Distinctions among Canaanite, Philistine, and Israelite Lyres, and their Global Lyrical Contexts, Bul of Amer Schls of Oriental Res, 98. **CONTACT ADDRESS** Dept of Physics and Astronomy, Hunter Col, CUNY, 695 Park Ave, New York, NY, 10021. **EMAIL** Bo.lawergren@hunter.cuny.edu

LAWHEAD, WILLIAM F.
DISCIPLINE HISTORY OF PHILOSOPHY, PHILOSOPHY OF RELIGION **EDUCATION** Wheaton Col, BA; Univ TX, Austin, PhD. **CAREER** Prof, Univ MS, 80-. **RESEARCH** God and time. **SELECTED PUBLICATIONS** Auth, The Voyage of Discovery: A History of Western Philosophy, Wadsworth Publ Co, 96. **CONTACT ADDRESS** Univ MS, Oxford, MS, 38677. **EMAIL** wlawhead@olemiss.edu

LAWLESS, CHARLES E.
DISCIPLINE EVANGELISM AND CHURCH GROWTH **EDUCATION** Cumberland Col, BS; S Baptist Theol Sem, MDiv, PhD. **CAREER** Lectr, Univ Cincinnati; asst prof, coord, Dr Ministry Prog, S Baptist Theol Sem. **SELECTED PUBLICATIONS** Contrib, articles to denominational periodicals; auth, curriculum for the Sunday Sch Bd, S Baptist Convention. **CONTACT ADDRESS** Billy Graham Sch Missions, Evangel and Church Growth, Southern Baptist Theol Sem, 2825 Lexington Rd, Louisville, KY, 40280. **EMAIL** clawless@sbts.edu

LAWLOR, JOHN I.
PERSONAL Born 12/16/1941, Winona Lake, IN, m, 1965, 3 children **DISCIPLINE** OLD TESTAMENT STUDIES **EDUCATION** Cedarville Col, BA, 63; Grace Theological Seminary, BD, 66, THM 69; Drew Univ, MPhil, 89, PhD 91. **CAREER** Asst prof, 70-80, prof 80- , Baptist Bible Col; adjunct prof, 92- ,, Penn State Univ. **RESEARCH** Archaeology: Ammonites and Moatsites; Hebrew Bible:Narrative. **SELECTED PUBLICATIONS** Auth, Violence, Evangelical Dictionary of Biblical Theology, 96; auth, Tel el-'Umeiri: Field A: The Ammonite Citadel, 1989, in Madaba Plains Project, 3: The 1989 Season at Tell el-'Umeiri and Vicinity, 97; auth, Karak Resources Project, 1997, American Journal of Archaeology, 98; auth, orthcoming: The Kerak Resources Project, 1997, Annual of the Department of Antiquities of Jordon; Tel el-'Umeiri: The Western Citadel: 1996, 1998, in Madaba Plains Project, 4: The 1994 Season at Tell el-'Umeiri and Vicinity; Tel el-'Umeiri: The Western Citadel: 1992, 1994, in in Madaba Plains Project, 4: The 1992 Season at Tell el-'Umeiri and Vicinity; A Corpus of Bone Carvings from the Excavation of the Esbus North Church, in a Festschrift for James A. Sauer. **CONTACT ADDRESS** 116 Maple Ave, Clarks Summit, PA, 18411. **EMAIL** jlawlor@bbc.edu

LAWRENCE, JOHN SHELTON
PERSONAL Born 03/30/1938, Amarillo, TX, m, 1961, 2 children **DISCIPLINE** PHILOSOPHY **EDUCATION** Stanford Univ, BA, 60; Tex Univ, PhD(philos), 64. **CAREER** From instr to asst prof philos, Univ Devner, 64-66; asst prof, 66-69, assoc prof, 69-79, PROF PHILOS, MORNINGSIDE COL, 80-, HEAD DEPT, 66-. **MEMBERSHIPS** Am Philos Asn. **RESEARCH** Ethics; value theory; aesthetics. **SELECTED PUBLICATIONS** Auth, The Persian Gulf Conflict and the Vanishing Heroes + Hostages, Journalism and Desert Storm, J Amer Culture, Vol 0017, 94; Operation Desert Storm--the Public Spectacle--Editors Introduction, J Amer Culture, Vol 0017, 94; The Emperors Virtual Clothes--the Naked Truth about Internet Culture, J Amer Culture, Vol 0019, 96. **CONTACT ADDRESS** Dept of Philos, Morningside Col, Sioux City, IA, 51106.

LAWRENCE, LARY
DISCIPLINE LAW **EDUCATION** Univ Calif, Los Angeles, BA, 70; Univ Calif, Berkeley, JD, 73. **CAREER** Prof, Loyola, 84-; prof & Harriet L. Bradley Ch Contract Law Contracts, Sales and Payments; Bigelow tchg fel; instr, Univ Chicago Sch of Law; assoc prof, Univ Mo-Columbia Sch of Law, 77-79; fac, Univ NC Sch of Law, attened rank tenured assoc prof, 79-84; vis prof, Hofstra; Univ San Diego; Univ Hawaii; Univ Bus and Econ(s), Beijing; Monash Univ, Melbourne, Australia. **SELECTED PUBLICATIONS** Published on, commercial law. **CONTACT ADDRESS** Law School, Loyola Marymount Univ, 7900 Loyola Blvd, Burns 425, Los Angeles, CA, 90045. **EMAIL** llawrenc@lmulaw.lmu.edu

LAWRY, EDWARD GEORGE
PERSONAL Born 02/25/1944, Pittsburgh, PA, d, 2 children **DISCIPLINE** EXISTENTIALISM **EDUCATION** Fordham Univ, BA, 66; Univ Pittsburgh, MA, 67; Univ Tex, Austin PhD (philos), 71. **CAREER** Asst prof to assoc prof, 71-89, Prof Philos, Okla State Univ, 89-; Chm, Mountain-Plains Philos Conf, 77-78 & 80-81; vis fel, Dept Art Hist, Yale Univ, 78-79. **MEMBERSHIPS** Am Philos Asn; Southwestern Philos Soc; Mountain-Plains Philos Conf(secy-treas, 73-74); Int Asn Philos & Lit. **RESEARCH** Aesthetics; ethics. **SELECTED PUBLICATIONS** Auth, The work-being of the work of art in Heidegger, Man & World, Vol II, No 1 & 2; Did Kant refute idealism?, Idealistic Studies, 1/80; Literature as philosophy, Moviegoer, 10/80. **CONTACT ADDRESS** Dept of Philos, Oklahoma State Univ, Stillwater, OK, 74078-5064. **EMAIL** elawry@okway.okstate.edu

LAWSON, E.T.
PERSONAL Born 11/27/1931, Capetown, South Africa, m, 1966, 2 children **DISCIPLINE** RELIGION **EDUCATION** Univ Chicago, PhD, 63. **CAREER** Western Mich Univ, 61-; prof and chair, comparative relig, 76-. **HONORS AND AWARDS** Distinguished facul sch; excellence in teaching award. **MEMBERSHIPS** Northern Amer Asn for the study of relig; Amer Soc for the study of relig; Soc for philos psychol. **RESEARCH** Cognitive science; African religions. **SELECTED PUBLICATIONS** Auth, Religions of Africa, Waveland Press, 98; auth, Rethinking Religion, Cambridge Univ Press, 90. **CONTACT ADDRESS** Dept of Comparative Religion, Western Michigan Univ, 121 Monroe St., Kalamazoo, MI, 49008. **EMAIL** lawson@umich.edu

LAWSON MACK, RANETA
DISCIPLINE CRIMINAL LAW **EDUCATION** Univ Toledo, BA, 85, JD, 88. **CAREER** Prof, Creighton Univ; assoc, Davis, Graham & Stubbs, Denver, 88-91; USWEST fel, Creighton Univ, 97. **HONORS AND AWARDS** Outstanding Advocate awd; Amer Jurisp awd, Univ Toledo; Alumni Excellence in Law awd, Univ Toledo Black Law Stud Asn, 94. **SELECTED PUBLICATIONS** Auth, A Lay Person's Guide to Criminal Law, 98; pub(s) in, Ind Int and Comp Law Rev; Creighton Law Rev; Ariz State Law J; St Thomas Law Rev; Thurgood Marshall Law Rev; Creighton Lawyer. **CONTACT ADDRESS** School of Law, Creighton Univ, 2500 California Plaza, Omaha, NE, 68178. **EMAIL** mack@culaw.creighton.edu

LAYMAN, FRED DALE
PERSONAL Born 09/27/1931, Marshfield, MO, m, 1952, 1 child **DISCIPLINE** THEOLOGY, BIBLICAL THEOLOGY **EDUCATION** Asbury Col, AB, 54; Asbury Theol Sem, BD, 56; Princeton Theol Sem, ThM, 57; Univ Iowa, PhD(relig), 72. **CAREER** Prof Bible and philos, Friends Univ, 58-63; assoc prof New Testament Greek, Asbury Col, 67-68; PROF BIBL THEOL, ASBURY THEOL SEM, 68-. **MEMBERSHIPS** Soc Bibl Lit. **RESEARCH** Old Testament theology; New Testament theology. **SELECTED PUBLICATIONS** Auth, The Figure of Abraham in the Epistles of Paul--in the Footsteps of Abraham, Interpretation-J Bible and Theol, Vol 0048, 94. **CONTACT ADDRESS** Sch Divin, Asbury Theol Sem, 204 N Lexington Ave, Wilmore, KY, 40390-1199.

LAYWINE, ALISON
DISCIPLINE PHILOSOPHY **EDUCATION** Univ Ottawa, BA; Univ Montreal, MA; Univ Chicago, PhD. **RESEARCH** Hist of pol philos; Jewish philos; ancient Greek philos. **SELECTED PUBLICATIONS** Auth, Kant's Early Metaphysics and the Origins of the Critical Philosophy, Ridgeview, 95; art, Intellectual Appearances, British Jour Hist Philos, 95. **CONTACT ADDRESS** Philosophy Dept, McGill Univ, 845 Sherbrooke St, Montreal, PQ, H3A 2T5.

LAZAROFF, DANIEL E.
DISCIPLINE LAW **EDUCATION** State Univ NY at Stony Brook, BA, 71;, NY Univ, JD, 74. **CAREER** Prof, Loyola, 83-; prof & Leonard E. Cohen ch Law & Econ(s); fac, Univ Detroit Mercy Sch of Law, attained rank tenured assoc prof, 78-83. **SELECTED PUBLICATIONS** Publ on, antitrust and sports law. **CONTACT ADDRESS** Law School, Loyola Marymount Univ, 7900 Loyola Blvd, Burns 345, Los Angeles, CA, 90045. **EMAIL** dlazarof@lmulaw.lmu.edu

LAZEROWITZ, ALICE AMBROSE
PERSONAL Born 11/25/1906, Lexington, IL, w, 1938 **DISCIPLINE** PHILOSOPHY **EDUCATION** Millikin Univ, AB, 28; Univ Wisc, MA, 29, PhD, 32; Cambridge Univ, PhD, 38. **CAREER** Instr, phil, 35-37, Univ Mich; asst prof - prof, 37-72, (Sophia & Austin Smith Prof of Phil 64), Emeritus Prof Phil, 72-, Smith Col; phil ed, 53-65, Jour of Symbolic Logic; dist vis prof phil, 75, Univ Del; vis prof, 79-, Carelton Col. **HONORS AND AWARDS** Alice Freeman Palmer Fel, Wellesley Col, 32; Marion Kennedy Studentship, Newham Col, 33-34, 34-35; LLD, Millikin Univ, 58; Vice Pres, APA, Eastern Div, 75; Head, Northampton United Way. **MEMBERSHIPS** APA; Amer Asn of Univ Prof; Hospice of Hampshire County; Amer Civil Liberty Union. **RESEARCH** Philosophy of mathematics. **SELECTED PUBLICATIONS** Coauth, Fundamentals of Symbolic Logic, Holt, Rinehart & Winston, 62; auth, Essays in Analysis, Allen & Unwin, 66; coed & contr, G.E.Moore, Essays in Retrospect, Muirhead Lib of Phil, Allen & Unwin, 70; coed & contr, Ludwig Wittgenstein, Philosophy and Language, Allen & Unwin, 72; ed, Wittgenstein's Lectures, Cambridge, 1932-1935, Blackwell, 79; coauth, Philosophical Theories, Mouton & Co. 76; coauth, Essays in the Unknown Wittgenstein, Prometheus Books, 84; coauth, Necessity and Language, Croom Helm, 85: ed, Lectures on Metaphysics 1934-1935, Peter Lang, 92. **CONTACT ADDRESS** 126 Vernon St, Northampton, MA, 01060.

LEA, THOMAS DALE
PERSONAL Born 09/20/1938, MS, m, 3 children **DISCIPLINE** THEOLOGY **EDUCATION** Southwestern Baptist Theol Sem, PhD, 67. **CAREER** Southwestern Baptist Theol Sem, pastor, assoc prof, prof, dean, 66-. **MEMBERSHIPS** SBL, ETS, IBR, NABPR. **RESEARCH** Johannine studies; hermeneutics; pastoral epistles. **SELECTED PUBLICATIONS** Auth, How to Study the Bible, Nashville TN, Convention Press, 87; auth, Step by Step Through the New Testament, Nashville TN: Baptist Sunday School Board, 92. **CONTACT ADDRESS** Southwestern Baptist Theology Sem, PO Box 22000, Fort Worth, TX, 76122-0140. **EMAIL** tdalel@swbts.swbts.edu

LEAR, ELIZABETH T.
DISCIPLINE LAW **EDUCATION** Univ NC, BA; Univ Mich, JD. **CAREER** Prof, Univ Fla, 90-; vis prof, Univ San Diego & Calif Western Sch Law; past assoc, Williams and Connolly, Wash, DC; clerk, Judge J. Edward Lumbard, US Ct Appeals, 2nd circut, NY; pvt pract. **MEMBERSHIPS** Order of the Coif; Pa Bar. **RESEARCH** Federal sentencing and the 11th amendment, criminal law, federal practice, civil procedure. **CONTACT ADDRESS** School of Law, Univ of Florida, PO Box 117625, Gainesville, FL, 32611-7625. **EMAIL** lear@law.ufl.edu

LEARY, DAVID E.
DISCIPLINE HISTORY & PHILOSOPHY OF PSYCHOLOGY **EDUCATION** San Luis Rey Col, CA, BA, 68; San Jose State, CA, MA, 71; Univ Chicago, IL, PhD, 77. **CAREER** Vis asst prof of Psychology, Graduate Theol Union, Berkeley, CA, 71-72; instr Psychol, Holy Names Col, Oakland, CA, 72-74; instr psychol, San Francisco State Univ Ext Services and Univ CA Ext Services, 73-74; instr of Psychol, Univ Chicago, 75; asst prof of the History and Philos of Psychol, Univ NH, Durham, 77-81, co-dir, grad prog in the Theory and History of Psychol, 77-89, assoc prof Psychol & Humanities, 81-87; fel, Center for Advanced Study in the Behavioral Sciences, Stanford, CA, 82-83, co-dir, summer inst on the Hist of Social Scientific Inquiry, 86; assoc prof Humanities, Cambridge Univ Summer prog, 84; Chairperson, Dept of Psychol, 86-89, prof of Psychol, Hist, and the Humanities, Univ NH, Durham, 87-89; prof of Psychology, dean of Arts and Sciences, Univ Richmond, VA, 89-. **HONORS AND AWARDS** San Luis Rey College Memorial Fund Scholarship, 63-68; Special Honors, PhD dissertation, 77; Univ NH Merit Award, 78, 82; Asn of Am Pubs Award, 85; Phi Beta Kappa, 87; numerous grants, fellowships, and stipends from the NEH, Univ NH, Nat Sci Found, Mellon Found, and others. **MEMBERSHIPS** Am Asn of Higher Ed; Am Conf of Academic Deans (member of the bd, 93-2000, chair of the bd, 98-99); Am Hist Asn; Am Psychol Asn (Pres, 83-84, Pres, Div of Theoretical and Philos Psychol, 94-95); Am Psychol Soc; Asn of Am Colleges and Universities; Cheiron: Int Soc for the History of the Behavioral and Social Sciences; Forum for the Hist of Human Science; Hist of Science Soc; Soc for the Hist of Science in Am. **RESEARCH** The intellectual, social, and cultural history of psychology, with a special focus on the relations between psychology and the humanities (eg, literature, philosophy, and religion) and the other sciences. **SELECTED PUBLICATIONS** Auth, An Introduction to the Psychology of Guilt, Lansford Co, 75; A Century of Psychology as Science, co-ed with Sigmund Koch, MacGraw-Hill, 85 (recipient of the Asn of Am Pubs Award, 85), 2nd ed reissued with a new postscript, Am Psychol An, 92; Metaphors in the History of Psychology, Cambridge Univ Press, 90, paperback, 94; William James, the Psychologist's Dilema, and the Historiography of Psychology: Cautionary Tales, Hist of Human Sciences, 8, 95; Naming and Knowing: Giving Forms to Things Unknown, Social Res 62, 95; William James and the Art of Human Understanding, in Ludy T Benjamin, Jr, ed, A History of Psychology: Original Sources and Contemporary Research, 2nd ed, McGraw-Hill, 97 (reprinted from 92); Sigmund Koch (1917-1996), co-auth with Frank Kessel and William Bevan, Am Psychologist 53, 98; numerous other publications. **CONTACT ADDRESS** Dean of Arts and Sciences, Univ of Richmond, Richmond, VA, 23173.

LECK, GLORIANNE MAE
DISCIPLINE PHILOSOPHY **EDUCATION** Univ Wis, BS, 63, MS, 66, PhD(educ philos), 68. **CAREER** Social fac residence halls, Univ Wis, 65-66, teaching asst, 65-67; instr, Wis State Univ, 67-69; asst prof, Pa State Univ, 69-73; assoc prof, 74-80, Prof Educ & Philos, Youngstown State Univ, 80-, Sect chairperson, Cultural Found of Educ, Pa State, 70-71; vis asst prof educ & philos, NY Univ, summer, 72; chairperson, Dept Educ Found, Youngstown State Univ, 75-77; chair, Comt Acad Standards & Accreditation, Am Educ Studies Asn, 78-79; The Politics of Adolescent Sexual Identity and Queer Responses, Gerald Unks, ed, The Gay Teen, Routledge, 95; A Lavender-tongued reliably queer lesbian does language on language, William Leap, ed, Beyond the Lavender Lexicon: Authenticity, Imagination, and Appropriation in Lesbian and Gay Literature, Gordon and Breach, 96; An Oasis: The LGBT Student Group on a Commuter Campus, Ronni Sanlo, ed, Working with Lesbian, Gay, Bisexual and Transgendered, College Students: A guide for Faculty, Staff and Administrators, Greenwood, 98. **HONORS AND AWARDS** O E A Holloways/Human and Civil Rights Commission Award, 94; Proclamation from Mayor and City Council for service on Human Relations Commission, 96; Distinguished Professorship for Community Service, Youngstown State, University Honors, Convocation, 97; **MEMBERSHIPS** Am Educ Studies; Am Philos Asn; Soc Women Philos; Philos Educ Soc; NEA. **SELECTED PUBLICATIONS** Coauth, Philosophical assumptions of research on gender differences of: Two by two and we'll never get through, Speech Commun Asn, summer 75; Standards for academic and professional instruction in foundations of education, educational studies & educational policy studies, Educ Studies Press, 77; auth, Hearts and minds: The common journey of Simone de Beavoir & Jean-Paul Sartre, winter 78 & Schooling, teaching and learning American education, spring 79, Educ Studies; Teacher education and social action concerns, J Ohio Asn Supv & Curric Develop, spring 79; Review of Jean-Paul Sartre by himself, Educ Studies, summer 80; A reflection on consequences, J Ohio Coun Elementary Sc Sci, 1/81; Other cultural perspectives: Field experiences and opportunities, The Forum, spring 81. **CONTACT ADDRESS** Research & Founds, Youngstown State Univ, One University Plz, Youngstown, OH, 44555-0002. **EMAIL** f0036363@cc.ysu.edu

LEDDY, T.
PERSONAL Born 09/30/1949, Oakland, CA, m, 1985 **DISCIPLINE** PHILOSOPHY **EDUCATION** Boston Univ, PhD, 83; San Francisco State, MA 74; Univ Cal Santa Cruz, BA 71; Col San Mateo, AA 69. **CAREER** San Jose State Univ, asst prof, assoc prof, prof, 83-95-; Alfred Univ, asst prof, 82-83; Napa Col, inst, 75-77; Chabot Col, inst, 74-75. **HONORS AND AWARDS** ASA Mem Bd Trustees **RESEARCH** Aesthetics; philo of art. **SELECTED PUBLICATIONS** Auth, Analytic Anti-Essentialism, The Encycl of Aesthetics, ed Michael Kelly, OUP, 98; Sparkle and Shine, Brit Jour of Aesth, 97; rev, Caroline Van Eck, Organicism in Nineteenth Century Architecture, in: The Jour of Aesth and Art, 97; rev, Jean Babbert Harrell, Profundity: A Universal Value, PUP 92, in: Jour of Aesth and Crit, 96; Everyday Surface Aesthetic Qualities: Neat Messy Clean Dirty, Jour of Aesth and Art Crit, 95; Metaphor and Metaphysics, Metaphor and Symbolic Activity, 95; Nietzsche On Unity of Style, Hist Reflections, 95; A Pragmatist Theory of Artistic Creativity, The J of Value Inq, 94; Dialogical Architecture, Philo and Arch, ed, Michael H. Mitias, Amster, Rudolpi, 94; American Society for Aesthetics: 50th Anniversary Meeting, The Jour of Value Inq, 94. **CONTACT ADDRESS** Dept of Philosophy, San Jose State Univ, San Jose, CA, 95192. **EMAIL** twleddy@email.sjsu.edu

LEDER, DREW L.
DISCIPLINE PHILOSOPHY **EDUCATION** Yale Univ, BA, MD; SUNY, PhD. **CAREER** Assoc prof; first Scholars-in-Residence on Aging, Chicago's Park Ridge Center **SELECTED PUBLICATIONS** Auth, Spiritual Passages: Embracing Life's Sacred Journey,Tarcher-Putnam, 97; The Absent Body, Univ Chicago Press, 90; ed, The Body in Medical Thought and Practice, Kluwer, 92; asst ed, The Encyclopedia of Bioethics, Macmillan, 95. **CONTACT ADDRESS** Dept of Philosophy, Loyola Col, 4501 N Charles St, Baltimore, MD, 21210.

LEDERLE, HENRY
PERSONAL Born 01/22/1946, Durban, South Africa, m, 1982, 2 children **DISCIPLINE** SYSTEMATIC THEOLOGY **EDUCATION** Univ of Orange Free St, BA, MA, 66, 68, 69; Univ of Stellenbosch, Bth, 72; Univ of S Africa, Dth 85 **CAREER** Assoc Prof, 78-90, Univ of S Africa; Prof, 90-95 Oral Roberts Univ; Assoc Pastor, 95-98 First Presby Church; Prof, 98-pres, ORU **HONORS AND AWARDS** Von Humboldt Scholar, 88-89 **MEMBERSHIPS** AAR; Soc for Pentecostal Studies **RESEARCH** Reformed Theology **SELECTED PUBLICATIONS** Auth, Treasures Old and New, Hendrickson Publ, 88 **CONTACT ADDRESS** 2312 W Indianola St, Broken Arrow, OK, 74012.

LEDFORD, KENNETH F.
PERSONAL Born 08/17/1953, Gulfport, MS, m, 1977, 2 children **DISCIPLINE** HISTORY; LAW **EDUCATION** Univ NC, BA, 75, JD, 78; Johns Hopkins Univ, BA, 84, PhD, 89. **CAREER** Adjunct asst prof history, Univ MD, 88-89; vis asst prof history, 89, lectr Paul H. Nitze School Adv Int Studies, 88-91, Johns Hopkins Univ; res fel/ed, German Hist Inst, 89-91; asst prof history & law, 91-97, ASSOC PROF HISTORY & LAW, 97-, CASE WESTERN RESERVE UNIV, 91-; German Marshall Fund US res fel, 98-99; Fulbright fel, 97-98; ed bd Law Hist Rev, 96-; DAAD fel, 85-86; Mellon Found fel, 82-84; John Motley Morehead fel Univ NC, 75-78; Phi Beta Kappa, 74; Phi Eta Sigma, 72. **HONORS AND AWARDS** John Snell Mem Essay Prize S Hist Asn, 83; Seymour W Wurfel Prize Int Law Univ NC, 78. **MEMBERSHIPS** Am Hist Asn' Am Soc Legal Hist; Conf Grp Cent Europ Hist; S Hist Asn; Ger Stud Asn; Law Soc Asn; VA State Bar. **RESEARCH** German social history; German and European legal history; history of Central European professions; history of the German Burgertum; historiography of German. **SELECTED PUBLICATIONS** Conflict within the Legal Professions: Simultaneous Admission and the German Bar 1903-1927, German Professions, 1800-1950, Oxford Univ Press, 90; Lawyers, Liberalism, and Procedure: The German Imperial Justice Laws of 1877-79, Central European History, 93; "German Lawyers and the State in the Weimar Republic," Law and History Review, 95; "Identity, Difference, and Enlightenment Heritage: Comment on The Right to Be Punished," Law and History, 98; Lawyers and the Limits of Liberalism: The German Bar in the Weimar Republic, Lawyers and the Rise of Western Political Liberalism, Clarendon Press, 98; From General Estate to Special Interest: German Lawyers 1878-1933, Cambridge Univ Press, 96. **CONTACT ADDRESS** Dept of History, Case Western Reserve Univ, Cleveland, OH, 44106-7107. **EMAIL** KXL15@po.cwru.edu

LEDOUX, ARTHUR
PERSONAL Born 09/01/1948, Melrose, MA, m, 1982, 1 child **DISCIPLINE** PHILOSOPHY **EDUCATION** Tufts Univ, Medford MA, BA, 70; Univ Notre Dame, Notre Dame IN, PhD, 77. **CAREER** ASSOC PROF PHILOS, MERRIMAC COL, N. ANDOVER, MA, 75-; DEAN OF LIBERAL ARTS, 97-98. **HONORS AND AWARDS** Fulbright fel to Sri Lanka, 86. **MEMBERSHIPS** Am Philos Asn. **RESEARCH** Asian philos; comparative philos; philos of relig. **SELECTED PUBLICATIONS** Auth, review, The Middle Works of John Dewey, vols 1-2, in The New Scholasticism (J of Am Cath Philos Asn), vol LII, no 4, 9/78; Dewey on Meditation, in Insights (J of the John Dewey Soc), vol 15, no 2, 12/78; discussion article, Meditation in the Classroom: A Reply, AAPT News (Newsletter of the Am Asn Philos Teachers), vol 17, no 1&2, March, July 94; paper anthologized, On the Complementary Core Pradoxes of Faith and Effort in Theravada Buddhism and Christianity, in East-West Encounters in Philosophy and Religion, ed by Ninian Smart and Srinivasa Murthy, Long Beach Pubs, 96. **CONTACT ADDRESS** Dept of Philos, Merrimack Col, North Andover, MA, 01845. **EMAIL** ALedoux@Merrimac.edu

LEE, DONALD S.
DISCIPLINE PHILOSOPHY **EDUCATION** Yale Univ, PhD, 61. **CAREER** Assoc prof, Tulane Univ. **SELECTED PUBLI-**

CATIONS Auth, Hartshorne and Pragmatic Metaphysics, The Philosophy of Charles Hartshorne; pub(s) in, Southern J Philos; Dialectica; Philos and Rhetoric; Metaphilos. **CONTACT ADDRESS** Dept of Philosophy, Tulane Univ, 6823 St Charles Ave, New Orleans, LA, 70118.

LEE, DONALD SOULE
PERSONAL Born 09/02/1933, New Orleans, LA, m, 1962, 3 children **DISCIPLINE** PHILOSOPHY **EDUCATION** Tulane Univ, BS, 55, MA, 58; Yale Univ, PhD(philos), 61. **CAREER** From instr to asst prof philos, Wash Univ, 60-64; asst prof, 64-69, Assoc Prof Philos, Tulane Univ, 69-. **MEMBERSHIPS** Southern Soc Philos & Psychol (secy, 78-81 & pres, 81-82); Southwestern Philos Soc; Soc Advan Am Philos. **RESEARCH** Philosophy of science; epistemology; pragmatism. **SELECTED PUBLICATIONS** Auth, The construction of empirical concepts, Philos & Phenomenol, 12/66; Ultimacy and the philosophic field of Metaphysics, Tulane Studies Philos, 66; Scientific method as a stage process, Dialectics, 1/68; Hypothetic inference in systematic philosophy, Int Philos Quart, 9/69; Pragmatic ultimates: Contexts and common sense, Southern J Philos, winter 77; The structure of substitution, Southern J Philos, summer 80. **CONTACT ADDRESS** Dept of Philos, Tulane Univ, 6823 St Charles Ave, New Orleans, LA, 70118-5698.

LEE, GRANT S.
DISCIPLINE PHILOSOPHY **EDUCATION** Temple Univ, PhD, 75. **RESEARCH** Oriental philosophy. **SELECTED PUBLICATIONS** Auth, Life and Thought of Yi Kwang-su, 84. **CONTACT ADDRESS** Philosophy Dept, Colorado State Univ, Fort Collins, CO, 80523.

LEE, JUNG YOUNG
PERSONAL Born 07/20/1935, Sunchun, Korea, m, 1965 **DISCIPLINE** SYSTEMATIC THEOLOGY, ASIAN RELIGIONS **EDUCATION** Findlay Col, BA, 57; Garrett Theol Sem, BD, 61; Western Reserve Univ, MS, 62; Boston Univ, ThD(syst theol), 68. **CAREER** Assoc minister, Alderstate United Methodist Church, Ohio, 60-61; minister, Oehloff Methodist Church, 61-63; actg librn, Howard Univ Sch Relig, 63-64; assoc minister, Ohmer Park Methodist Church, 65-66; asst prof relig and philos, Otterbein Col, 68-72; PROF RELIG STUDIES, UNIV N DAK, 72-, Fulbright-Hays sr fel, 77; DIR, FAR EASTERN CULT INST, 77-; vis lectr, Seoul Nat Univ, Ewha Woman's Univ, 77, San Francisco Theol Sem and Grad Theol Union, 79-80, Ilift Sch Theol, 80 and Garrett-Evangelical Theol Sem, 82; vis scholar, Univ Calif, Berkeley, 79-80. **MEMBERSHIPS** Am Acad Relig; Asn Asian Studies; Am Philos Asn; Korean Soc Relig Studies in NAm (pres, 77-). **RESEARCH** Comparative religion (Christian encounter with other religions); Korean religion (Shamanism); Chinese philosophy (I Ching). **SELECTED PUBLICATIONS** Auth, Eating + the Significance about the Lotus in the 'Pisan Cantos', Paideuma-J Devoted to Ezra Pound Scholarship, Vol 0022, 93; A Lotus of Another Color--an Unfolding of the South Asian Gay and Lesbian Experience, Amerasia J, Vol 0020, 94. **CONTACT ADDRESS** Univ Calif Berkeley, Berkeley, CA, 94720.

LEE, K. SAMUEL
PERSONAL Born 12/20/1957, Korea, m, 1982, 2 children **DISCIPLINE** PASTORAL COUNSELING; PASTORAL THEOLOGY **EDUCATION** Yale Univ, MDiv, 83; Ariz State Univ, PhD, 95. **CAREER** Assoc Dean, 95-98, Asst Prof, Wesley Theol Seminary, 98-. **MEMBERSHIPS** APA; AAR. **RESEARCH** Cross-cultural psychology; pastoral care. **CONTACT ADDRESS** Wesley Theol Sem, 4500 Massachusetts Ave. NW, Washington, DC, 20016. **EMAIL** RevSL@aol.com

LEE, LENA S. KING
PERSONAL AL, w **DISCIPLINE** LAW **EDUCATION** Morgan State Coll, BA 1939; NYU, MA, 1947; MD Univ of Law, LLB 1951, JD. **CAREER** Citizens Commn on Recreation 1956; Urban Renewal and Housing Com 1955-61; Redevel Com 1955; Kennedy's Civil Rights Conf, pres 1961; Pres's Com on Govt Contractors & Conf 1958; Commn on Mfg Tax 1958; Justice of the Peace 1959-61. **HONORS AND AWARDS** Numerous awards and honors; inducted into Hall of Fame Women's Commission of Maryland, 1989; Charter member of Thurgood Marshall (Legal) Society, 1992; Honored as "Living Legend" by (Thelma Cox) Heritage Society, 1995, contributed article to MD Univ, Law School Journal. **MEMBERSHIPS** House of Delegates, MD, 1982; Mem MD Gen Assembly House of Dels 1966-; mem Am Judicature Soc, Monumental, Baltimore Bar Assns, Center for Dispute Settlement, Nat Assn of Parliamentarians; coms Herbert M Frisby Hist Soc, Intl Platform Assn, Lambda Kappa, Sigma Gamma Rho, Bus & Professional Women's Club, Du Bois Circle, MD League of Women's Clubs, Cheyney Alumni Assn; alumni Univ MD Law School; univ club mem Univ of MD; gov comm on Criminal Justice 1968; gov comm on Juvenile Justice 1970; joint comm on Corrections 1973; comm Family Court & Domestic Relations 1973; comm on Chesapeake Bay Affairs 1980-83.

LEE, MI KYOUNG MITZI
DISCIPLINE PHILOSOPHY **EDUCATION** Col of Columbia Univ, BA, 89; Harvard Univ, PhD, 96 **CAREER** Asst Prof of Philos; 96-pres, Univ of IL **HONORS AND AWARDS** Whiting Dissertation Fel, 94-5 **MEMBERSHIPS** Am Philos Assoc **RESEARCH** History of Ancient Greek and Roman Philosophy **CONTACT ADDRESS** Dept of Philos, Univ of Illinois, 601 S Morgan, Chicago, IL, 60607. **EMAIL** mmlee@vic.edu

LEE, MI KYOUNG MITZI
DISCIPLINE PHILOSOPHY **EDUCATION** Col of Columbia Univ, BA, 89; Harvard Univ, PhD, 96 **CAREER** Asst Prof of Philos; 96-pres, Univ of IL **HONORS AND AWARDS** Whiting Dissertation Fel, 94-5 **MEMBERSHIPS** Am Philos Assoc **RESEARCH** History of Ancient Greek and Roman Philosophy **CONTACT ADDRESS** Dept of Philos, Univ of Illinois, 601 S Morgan, Chicago, IL, 60607. **EMAIL** mmlee@vic.edu

LEE, RICHARD
DISCIPLINE ETHICAL THEORY **EDUCATION** Stanford Univ, PhD. **CAREER** Philos, Univ Ark **SELECTED PUBLICATIONS** Articles; Analysis, Idealistic Studiess. **CONTACT ADDRESS** Univ Ark, Fayetteville, AR, 72701. **EMAIL** rlee@comp.uark.edu

LEE, SANDER H.
PERSONAL Born 01/30/1951, Dallas, TX, m, 1984, 1 child **DISCIPLINE** PHILOSOPHY, PSYCHOLOGY **EDUCATION** George Washington Univ, Undergrad in Philos and Psychol; Georgetown Univ, Doctorate Philos. **CAREER** Pres of The Conf of Philos Soc and the Soc for the Philos Stud of the Contemp Visual Arts. Tchg at Howard Univ; Consult Ed Journals. **MEMBERSHIPS** Past Pres Intl Soc for Value Inquiry; **RESEARCH** Aesthetics Soc Theory. **SELECTED PUBLICATIONS** Auth, Woody Allen's Angst, Philosophical Commentaries on his Serious Films, Auth, McFarland Publishing Co, 97; Consult ed, The Journal of Value Inquiry and Film Philosophy. **CONTACT ADDRESS** Philosophy Dept, Keene State Col, Parker Hall, Keene, NH, 03435-1402. **EMAIL** clong@lawschool.edu slee@keene.edu

LEE, SANDER H.
PERSONAL Born 01/30/1951, Dallas, TX, m, 1984, 1 child **DISCIPLINE** PHILOSOPHY **EDUCATION** George Wash Univ, BA, 73; Univ Wien-Sommer Hoshsch, Dipl, 74; Georgetown Univ, MA, 76; PhD, 78; Brit Studies Prog in Philos and Criminal Justice, Inst of Anglo-Am Studies, London, 81; **CAREER** Prof, Keenes Coll, 86-; fac adv, 86-; asst prof, Howard Univ, 80-86; pres, The Intl Soc for Value Inquiry, 88-93;pres, Soc for the Philos Study of the Contemp Vis Arts, 89-; ch, Acad Overview Subcomm on the Grad Prog, 91-92; intl coord, Intl Soc for Value Inquiry, Finland and Russia, 93; ch, Philos Search Comm, 93; assoc ed, The Jour of Value Inquiry, 90-93; ed, Jour of Value Inquiry on Philos and Film, 95; ch, Admin Comm and Adv Act, 96-98; consult ed, The Jour of Value Inquiry and the Value Inquiry Bk Series, 93-; consult ed, Philos and Film, 93-; pres and Intl Cord for the Conf of Philos Soc, 96-. **HONORS AND AWARDS** Bd of Trustee's Scholar, George Wash Univ, 69-73; spec honors in philos, George Wash Univ, 73; Phi Beta Kappa, George Wash Univ 73; Univ Fel(s), Georgetown Univ, 73-76; Fel, Univt Wien-Summer Hoshsch, 74; Tchg Asstship, Georgetown Univ, 76-77., Intl coord, Soc for the Philos Study of the Contemp Vis Arts, Conf of Philos Soc, USA, 98; Proj Hum, The Crisis in Bosnia: Political Responsibility, History and Cultural Understanding, 95. **MEMBERSHIPS** Mem, Hist/Philos DPEC Subcomm, 95; mem, Commun Maj Comm, 93-; mem, VP, Acad Aff Search Comm, 94-95; mem, Hist/Philos DPEC Subcomm, 96; mem, Commun Search Comm, 95; mem, Commun Maj Comm, 94-;. **RESEARCH** Contemporary analytic philosophy, contemporary continental philosophy, epistemology. **SELECTED PUBLICATIONS** Co-auth, Philos Self-Study for the Prog Rev, 91-92; **CONTACT ADDRESS** Dept of Philos, Keene State Col, 229 Main St, Keene, NH, 03405-1402. **EMAIL** slee@keene.edu

LEE, STEVEN PEYTON
PERSONAL Born 05/19/1948, Schenectady, NY, m, 1981, 3 children **DISCIPLINE** PHILOSOPHY **EDUCATION** Univ Del, BA, 70, MA, 73; York Univ, Toronto, PhD(philos), 78. **CAREER** Asst prof Philos, Bowling Green State Univ, 78-80; asst prof Philos, Hobart & William Smith Col, Geneva, NY, 81-, Nat Endowment for Humanities fel, Ind Univ, 80-81; asst prof, 81-85; assoc prof to prof, 85-91, Hobart and William Smith Colls. **HONORS AND AWARDS** Faculty Research Award, Hobart and William Smith Colleges, 91; Harvard Fell in Law and Lib Arts, 94-95, Harvard Law School. **MEMBERSHIPS** Am Philos Asn. **RESEARCH** Ethics; social philosophy; action theory. **SELECTED PUBLICATIONS** Auth, Poverty alnd Violence, Social Theory and Practice 22, no 1, Spring, 96; Democracy and the Problem of Persistent Minorities, in Larry May et al, eds Groups and Group Rights, Lawrence, KS, Univ of Kansas Press, 97. **CONTACT ADDRESS** Philosophy Dept, Hobart & William Smith Cols, Geneva, NY, 14456. **EMAIL** lee@hws.edu

LEE, SUKJAE
DISCIPLINE PHILOSOPHY **EDUCATION** Seoul Natl Univ, BA, 90, MA, 92; Yale Univ, PhD program, 94- . **CAREER** Author **HONORS AND AWARDS** Korean Found for Advanced Stud Prize Fel, 94; Jacob Cooper Prize, Yale Univ, 97; tchg fel, Yale Univ, 98. **SELECTED PUBLICATIONS** Auth, Scotus on the Will: The Rational Power and The Dual Affection, Vivarium, 98. **CONTACT ADDRESS** 405 Canner St, #3, New Haven, CT, 06511. **EMAIL** sukjae.lee@yale.edu

LEE, SUNGHO
PERSONAL Born 04/21/1959, South Korea, m, 1987, 2 children **DISCIPLINE** RELIGION, THEOLOGY **EDUCATION** Northwester Univ, PhD, 97. **CAREER** Pastor, United Methodist Church, Northern Ill Conf, 93- . **MEMBERSHIPS** SBL **RESEARCH** Old Testament Theol, Immigrants. **CONTACT ADDRESS** No Illinois Conf, 46W 742 Main St, Kaneville, IL, 60144. **EMAIL** sle312@megsinet.net

LEE JR., MILTON C.
DISCIPLINE CRIMINAL LAW & PROCEDURE, EVIDENCE, WILLS & ESTATES, TRIAL ADVOCACY **EDUCATION** Am Univ Sch Justice, BS, 82; Cathc Univ Sch Law, JD, 85. **CAREER** Assoc prof; supvr, Juvenile Justice Clin; staff atty, Publ Defender Serv, 85-90 & Dep Trial Ch, 90-93; vis assoc prof, Georgetown Univ Law Ctr, 90-91; adj fac, Georgetown Univ; Bd Dir, Law Stud in Court Prog. **MEMBERSHIPS** DC Bar Comt, Individual Rights & Criminal Law. **SELECTED PUBLICATIONS** Publ an article on, use of preventive detention in juvenile cases, 95. **CONTACT ADDRESS** School of Law, Univ of District of Columbia, 4200 Connecticut Ave Northwest, Washington, DC, 20008.

LEFCOE, GEORGE
DISCIPLINE LAW **EDUCATION** Dartmouth Col, BA,59; Yale Univ, LLB,62.. **CAREER** Florine & Ervin Yoder prof Real Estate Law, Univ Southern Calif; past pres, Los Angeles City Plan Comn; past ch, Los Angeles Co Regional Plan Comn and Commissioner of the Los Angeles Convention Ctr; ch, USC Law School's Property Forum; **RESEARCH** Urban redevelopment; affordable housing; real estate lending; financing major real estate transactions. **SELECTED PUBLICATIONS** Auth, Land Development in Crowded Places: Lessons from Abroad & Real Estate Transactions. **CONTACT ADDRESS** School of Law, Univ Southern Calif, University Park Campus, Los Angeles, CA, 90089.

LEFEBURE, LEO D.
PERSONAL Born 11/20/1952, Chicago, IL **DISCIPLINE** CHRISTIAN SYSTEMATIC THEOLOGY **EDUCATION** Univ Chicago PhD, 87; St Mary of the Lake Seminary STL, Mdiv, 78. **CAREER** Univ of St Mary of the Lake, Dean of the Eccle Fac of Theol, 92-98, Chair dept Syst Theo, 89-92, Prof Syst Theol, 94-, Assoc prof, 91-94. **HONORS AND AWARDS** ATS Jr Scholars Prog, 89; Louisville Inst, Christian Faith Life Sabb Grant, 98. **MEMBERSHIPS** AAR; CTSA; COVER; Soc Buddhist Christ Stud. **RESEARCH** Buddhist Christian Dialogue; revelation; interreligious dialogue; Christology **SELECTED PUBLICATIONS** The Budda and the Christ: Explor in Budd-Christ Dialo, Maryknoll NY, Orbis Books, 93; Life Transformed: Meditations on the Christian Scriptures in Light of Buddhist Perspectives, Chicago, ACTA pub, 89; Toward a Contemporary Wisdom Christology: A Study of Karl Rahmer and Norman Pittenger, Lanham MD, Univ Press Am, 88; Christianity and Other Religions in the Year 1000, forthcoming, Chicago Studies 37, 98; Beyond Scapegoating: A Conversation with Rene Girard and Ewert Cousins, The Christian Century 115/11, 98; 200 Years in Tibet: Glimpses of Fact and Film, The Christian Century, 115/8, 98; Awakening and Grace: Rel Ident in the Thought of Masao Abe and Karl Rahner, Cross Currents 47/4, 98; Report on Hindu-Catholic Dialogue, Pro Dialogo 9, 98; Approaches to Revelation and Theology, Chicago Studies, 36/2, 97. **CONTACT ADDRESS** Univ St Mary of the Lake, 1000 E Maple St, Mundelein, IL, 60060-1174. **EMAIL** canondean@aol.com

LEFTOW, BRIAN
PERSONAL Born 09/25/1956, Brooklyn, NY, m, 1980 **DISCIPLINE** PHILOSOPHY **EDUCATION** Grove City Coll, BA, 77; Yale, MA, 78; MPhilos, 81; PhD, 84. **CAREER** Vis asst prof, Reed Coll, 84-84; Fordham Univ, 85-; Assoc Prof, Fordham Univ, 92-. **HONORS AND AWARDS** Distinguished Scholar Fel, Univ Notre Dame, 92-93; Evangel Scholars' Grant, 91-92. **MEMBERSHIPS** Am Philos Asn; Soc of Christian Philos; Soc for Medieval and Renaissance in Philos; Philos of Time Soc. **RESEARCH** Philosophical Theology; Analytic Metaphysics; Medieval Philosphy. **SELECTED PUBLICATIONS** Auth, Anselm on the Necessity of the Incarnation, Rel Studies, 95; Can Philosophy Argue God's Existence?, The Rationality of Belief and the Plurality of Faith, 95; Anselm on the Beauty of the Incarnation, The Modern Schoolman, 95; Anselm on Cost of Salvation, Medieval Philos and Theol, 97; Divine Action and Embodiment, Proceedings of the ACPA, 97; Eternity, The Cambridge Companion to Philos of Rel, 97; Omnipresence; Necessary Being; Divine Simplicity; Concepts of God, The Encycl of Philos, 98; A God Beyond Space and Time, Theos, Antropos, Christos, 98; The Eternal Present, god and Time, 99;

Anti Social Trinitarianism, The Trinity, 99; Aquinas on the Infinite, Preceedings of the XX World Congress of Philos, forthcoming; Divine Ideas, forthcoming. **CONTACT ADDRESS** 66 Wood Ave, Ardsley, NY, 10502. **EMAIL** leftow@murray.fordham.edu

LEHMAN, SCOTT
DISCIPLINE PHILOSOPHY **EDUCATION** Swarthmore Col, BA, 64; Univ Chicago, PhD, 70. **CAREER** Dept Philos, Univ Conn **RESEARCH** Foundations of economics, policy analysis, environmental ethics. **SELECTED PUBLICATIONS** Auth, Strict Fregean free logic, Philos Logic, 94; Privatizing Public Lands, Oxford Univ Press, 95, Privatizing public lands: a Bad Idea, Jour of Environmental Law & Policy, 96. **CONTACT ADDRESS** Dept of Philos, Univ Conn, 1266 Storrs Rd, Storrs, CT, 06269.

LEHRBERGER, JAMES
DISCIPLINE EARLY MODERN PHILOSOPHY, PHILOSOPHY OF RELIGION **EDUCATION** Univ SF, BA; Univ Dallas, MA, PhD; further advan stud, S Methodist Univ. **CAREER** Dept Philos, Univ Dallas **SELECTED PUBLICATIONS** Co-ed, Intelligo ut Cream: St. Augustine's Confessions, The Thomist, 88; auth, Crime Without Punishment: Thomistic Natural Law and the Problem of Sanctions, Law and Philos: The Practice of Theory, Ohio State Univ Press, 92; Saints, Sovereigns, and Scholars: Studies in Honor of Frederick D. Wilhelmsen, Peter Lang, 93; Deontology, Teleology, and Aquinas' Virtue Ethic in Saints, Sovereigns, and Scholars, Peter Lang, 93; Dialectical and Demonstrative Arguments in Aristotle's Account of the Eternal Cosmos, il cannocchiale, rivista di studi filosofici, 96. **CONTACT ADDRESS** Univ of Philos, Univ Dallas, 1845 E Northgate Dr, Irving, TX, 75062.

LEIBOWITZ, CONSTANCE
PERSONAL New York, NY **DISCIPLINE** PHILOSOPHY **EDUCATION** New York Univ, BA, 60, MA, 64, PhD, 73. **CAREER** Asst prof, 67-74, Assoc Prof Philos, Univ NH, 74-85, prof philos, Plymouth State Col Univ NH, Chmn, Philos Dept, 83. **HONORS AND AWARDS** Univ Hons Scholar, New York Univ, 60 & 74. **MEMBERSHIPS** Am Philos Asn; Am Asn Philos Tchr(s), Northern New England Philos Asn. **RESEARCH** Ethics, death, law. **CONTACT ADDRESS** Dept of Philos, Plymouth State Col, Univ System of New Hampshire, 15 Holderness Rd, Plymouth, NH, 03264-1600. **EMAIL** Constancel@psc.plymouth.edu

LEIBOWITZ, FLORA L.
DISCIPLINE PHILOSOPHY OF ART/AESTHETICS **EDUCATION** SUNY-Stony Brook, BA, 73; The Johns Hopkins Univ, MA, 75, PhD, 79. **CAREER** Asst prof, 77-84, assoc prof, 84-93, prof, 93- , Dir Grad Stud, 94- , Dept of Philos, Oregon State Univ; vis asst prof, Dept Philos, Univ Texas-Austin, 83. **HONORS AND AWARDS** Phi Kappa Phi; ACLS Travel Award, L L Stewart Fac Develop Oregon State Univ, 95. **MEMBERSHIPS** Am Philo Asn; Am Soc Aesthet; Brit Soc Aesthet. **RESEARCH** Philosophy of art, especially the mass arts and electronic media. **SELECTED PUBLICATIONS** Auth, The Logic of Humes Conversion Theory, Jour Aesthet and Art Critocosm, 93; Pornography and Persuasion, Philos & Lit, 94; Apt Feelings, or Why Womens Films Aren't Trivial, Post-Theory: Reconstructing Film Studies, Univ Wisc Press, 96; Agency, Theories of Expression, and the Movies, Film Theory and Philosophy, Oxford Univ Press, 97; Pianists in the Movies, Philosophy and Literature, 97; Robert Solomons Sexual Paradigms: Twenty Years After, Sex, Love, and Friendship, Rodopi, 97; **CONTACT ADDRESS** Dept of Philososphy, Oregon State Univ, Corvallis, OR, 97331. **EMAIL** fleibowitz@orst.edu

LEIES, JOHN A.
PERSONAL Born 04/24/1926, Chicago, IL **DISCIPLINE** THEOLOGY **EDUCATION** Univ Dayon, OH, BS (Ed), 48; Univ Fribourg, Switzerland, STD, 59. **CAREER** Prof, Academic VP, Pres, St. Mary's Univ, San Antonio, TX; ed of four books; author of more than 160 aticles; TV TALK SHOW HOST, 95-. **HONORS AND AWARDS** Distinguished Faculty, St. Mary's Univ, 98. **MEMBERSHIPS** Fel of Cath Scholars; Fel of the Nat Cath Bioethics Center, Boston. **RESEARCH** Bioethics; moral theology. **SELECTED PUBLICATIONS** Auth, Religion and Sanctity According to St. Thomas Aquinas, St. Paul's Press, Fribourg, Switzerland, 63; Evil as a Way to Good?, Ethics and Medics, Nov 88; Handbook on Critical Sexual Issues & Handbook on Critical Life Issues, revised ed, co-ed with Donald G. McCarthy and Edward J. Bayer, Pope John Center Pub, 89; Human Sexuality and Personhood, revised ed, ed, Pope John Center Pub, 90; Yes, There Was a 'Sexual Revolutions', Human Sexuality and Personhood, revised ed, Pope John Center Pub, 90; Magisterial Teaching on Human Sexuality and Marriage, 1980-1990, Human Sexuality and Personhood, revised ed, Pope John Center Pub, 90; Family and Incompetent Patient, Ethics and Medics, Nov 90; Advance Directives for Health Care Decisions, with Roy Klister, JD, Ethics and Medics insert, Nov 91; Human Sexuality, Marriage, and the Family: Contemporary Readings, second provisional ed, St. Mary's Univ Pubs, 92; Death Revised, Ethics and Medics, June 96; Advance Directives for Health Care Decisions, Ethics and Medics, Aug 96; numerous articles for the San Antonio Archdiocesan newspaper, Today's Catholic, Aug 89-Jan 99. **CONTACT ADDRESS** St. Mary's Univ, San Antonio, TX, 78228. **EMAIL** theojohn@stmarytx.edu

LEIGHTON, STEPHEN
DISCIPLINE PHILOSOPHY **EDUCATION** Univ Alberta, BA; MA; Univ Tex Austin, PhD. **CAREER** Dept Philos, Queen's Univ **RESEARCH** Ancient philosophy; philosophical psychology; ethics. **SELECTED PUBLICATIONS** Auth, Aristotle and the Emotions, Garland, 95; What We Love, Australasian J Philos, 93; Relativizing Moral Excellence in Aristotle, Apeiron, 92; On Feeling Angry or Elated, J Philos, 88. **CONTACT ADDRESS** Philosophy Dept, Queen's Univ, Kingston, ON, K7L 3N6. **EMAIL** leighton@post.queensu.ca

LEIGHTON, TAIGEN DANIEL
PERSONAL Born 01/23/1950, Baltimore, MD, d **DISCIPLINE** EAST ASIAN BUDDHISM **EDUCATION** Columbia Col, BA, 77; Calif Inst Integral Studs, MA, 88; Berkeley Grad Theol U, PhD. **CAREER** Adj prof, John F. Kennedy Univ, Oriada, Calif, 93; adj prof, Univ San Francisco, 96; adj prof, Calif Inst Integral Stud, 96-98; adj prof, Inst Buddhist Stud, Berkeley Grad Theol Sem, 94-99. **HONORS AND AWARDS** Pres Scholar, Grad Theol Union. **MEMBERSHIPS** Am Acad Rel. **RESEARCH** Soto Zen; Dogen; East Asian Mahoyana praxis and its contemporary implications. **SELECTED PUBLICATIONS** Ed, transl, Cultivating the Empty Field: The Silent Illumination of Zen Master Mongzhi, N Point Press, 91; Review of The Book of Serenity, The Eastern Buddhist, 91; ed, transl, Dogen's Pure Standards for the Zen Community: A Translation of 'Eihei Shingi,' State Univ of NY Press, 96; Being Time Through Deep Time, Tricycle, 96; Now is the Past of the Future, Shambhala Sun, 96; Comparative Review of Transmission of Light and The Record of Transmitting the Light, The E Buddhist, 97; ed, transl, The Wholehearted Way: A Translation of Eihei Dogen's Bendowa and Commentary by Kisho Uchiyama Roshi, Tuttle, 97; Budhisattra Archetypes: Classic Buddhist Guides to Awakening and their Modern Expression, Penguin, 98; Masters of Spirit and Words, Dagen and Dylan, Kyoto Jour, 98. **CONTACT ADDRESS** 94 Laurel Dr, Fairfax, CA, 94930. **EMAIL** taigen@sirius.com

LEIMAN, SID ZALMAN
PERSONAL Born 11/03/1941, New York, NY **DISCIPLINE** HISTORY, RELIGION **EDUCATION** Brooklyn Col, BA, 64; Mirrer Yeshivah, BRE, 64; Univ Pa, PhD(Orient studies), 70. **CAREER** Lectr Jewish hist and lit, Yale Univ, 68-70, from asst prof to assoc prof relig studies, 70-78; prof Jewish hist and dean, Vervard Revel Grad Sch, Yeshiva Univ, 78-81; PROF AND CHMN DEPT JUDAIC STUDIES, BROOKLYN COL, 81-, Nat Found Jewish Cult res grant, 67-68; Morse fel, Yale Univ, 71-72; vis scholar Jewish law and ethics, Kennedy Inst Ethics, Georgetown Univ, 77-78; Mem Found Jewish Cult res grant, 81-82. **MEMBERSHIPS** Am Schs Orient Res; Soc Bibl Lit; Am Acad Relig; Asn Jewish Studies; Am Jewish Hist Soc. **RESEARCH** Jewish history; Jewish ethics; Biblical studies. **SELECTED PUBLICATIONS** Auth, Horowitz, Jacob on the Study of Scripture--From the Pages of 'Tradition', Tradition-J Orthodox Jewish Thought, Vol 0027, 92; From the Pages of Tradition--Friedman, David of Karlin--the Ban on Secular Study in Jerusalem, Tradition-J Orthodox Jewish Thought, Vol 0026, 92; Dwarfs on the Shoulders of Giants + the Study of Torah Despite a Theology of Generational Regression, Tradition-J Orthodox Jewish Thought, Vol 0027, 93; Carlebach, Joseph, Wuerzburg and Jerusalem--a Conversation Between Bamberger, Seligmann, Baer and Salant, Shmuel, Tradition-J Orthodox Jewish Thought, Vol 0028, 94; Ha Kohen Kook, Abraham, Isaac--Invocation at the Inauguration of the Hebrew-University--Excerpt From the Pages of Tradition April-1, 1925, Tradition-J Orthodox Jewish Thought, Vol 0029, 94; Rabbi Schwab,Shimon + Respone on the Torah and Derekh-Eretz Movement Concerning Jewish Education--a Letter Regarding the Frankfurt Approach--From the Pages of 'Tradition', Tradition-J Orthodox Jewish Thought, Vol 0031, 97. **CONTACT ADDRESS** Dept of Judaic Studies, Brooklyn Col, CUNY, Brooklyn, NY, 11367.

LEISER, BURTON M.
DISCIPLINE PHILOSOPHY **EDUCATION** Univ Chicago, BA, 51; Yeshiva Univ, MHL, 56; Brown Univ, PhD, 68; Drake Univ, JD, 81. **CAREER** Assoc prof, State Univ Coll, 65-69; vis prof, Sir George William Univ Montreal, 69-72; prof, Drake Univ, 72-83; Prof, Pace Univ, 83-. **MEMBERSHIPS** Int Soc for Philos of Law; am Soc for Value Inquiry; Am Bor Asn. **RESEARCH** Ethics; legal and Political Philosphy. **SELECTED PUBLICATIONS** Auth, Custom, Law, and Morality, 69; values in Conflict: life, Liberty, and the Rule of Law, 76; Liberty, Justice, and Morals: Contemporary Value Conflicts, 86. **CONTACT ADDRESS** Dept of Philosophy, Pace Univ, 1 Pace Plaza, Briarcliff Manor, NY, 10510-2256. **EMAIL** Bleiser@pace.edu

LEITH, JOHN HADDON
PERSONAL Born 09/10/1919, Due West, SC, m, 1943, 2 children **DISCIPLINE** THEOLOGY **EDUCATION** Erskine Col, AB, 40; Columbia Theol Sem, BD, 43; Vanderbilt Univ, MA, 46; Yale Univ, PhD, 49. **CAREER** Minister, Second Presby Church, Nashville, Tenn, 44-46 and First Presby Church, Auburn, Ala, 48-59; PROF HIST THEOL, UNION THEOL SEM, VA, 59-, Lectr relig, Auburn Univ, 49-58; vis prof, Columbia Theol Sem, 55-57 and Univ Edinburgh, 74; Folger Shakespeare Libr fel, 65. **HONORS AND AWARDS** DD, Erskine Col, 72 and Davidson Col, 78. **RESEARCH** History of theology; reformation. **SELECTED PUBLICATIONS** Auth, Luther and Calvin on Secular Authority, 16TH Century J, Vol 0024, 93; Christian Confessions--a Historical Introduction, Theol Today, Vol 0054, 97. **CONTACT ADDRESS** Union Theol Sem, 3401 Brook Rd, Richmond, VA, 23227.

LELAND, CHARLES WALLACE
PERSONAL Born 03/22/1928, Culver, IN **DISCIPLINE** ENGLISH LITERATURE, SCANDANAVIAN DRAMA **EDUCATION** Oberlin Col, AB, 50; Oxford Univ, BA, 53, MA, 56; Univ Toronto, STB, 58. **CAREER** Lectr English, 59-62, asst prof, 62-69, ASSOC PROF ENGLISH, UNIV TORONTO, 69-, Roman Cath priest, Congregation of St Basil, 59-. **MEMBERSHIPS** Asn Advan Scand Studies Can; Ibsen Soc Am; Soc Advan Scand Study. **RESEARCH** Ibsen; Strindberg; literature of the English Renaissance. **SELECTED PUBLICATIONS** Auth, Catiline and the Burial Mound, Mod Drama, Vol 0038, 95. **CONTACT ADDRESS** St Michael's Col Univ of Toronto, Toronto, ON, M5S 1J4.

LELWICA, MICHELLE M.
PERSONAL Born 03/13/1964, San Francisco, CA, s **DISCIPLINE** RELIGIOUS STUDIES; WOMEN'S STUDIES **EDUCATION** Col of St. Benedict, BA, 86; Harvard Divinity School, MTS, 89, ThD, 96. **CAREER** Asst prof of religious studies & women's studies, St Mary's Col, Calif. **MEMBERSHIPS** AAR **RESEARCH** Women and religion; Religion and culture; Religion and the body. **SELECTED PUBLICATIONS** Auth, Nudity, Encyclo of Women & World Relig, Macmillan Publ, 98; Losing Their Way to Salvation: Women, Weight-Loss, and the Salvation Myth of Culture Life, Religion and Popular Culture in America, Univ Calif Press, 98; From Superstition, to Enlightenment, to the Race for Pure Consciousness: Anti-Religious Currents in Popular and Academic Feminist Discourse, Jour Feminist Studies Relig, 98. **CONTACT ADDRESS** 2536 College Ave., #9B, Berkeley, CA, 94704. **EMAIL** mlelwica@stmarys-ca.edu

LEMIEUX, LUCIEN
PERSONAL Born 04/30/1934, St-Remi, PQ, Canada **DISCIPLINE** HISTORY, RELIGION **EDUCATION** St-Jean Col, BA, 54; Univ Montreal, LTh, 58; Gregorian Univ, DHist, 65. **CAREER** Prof hist, St-Jean Col, 65-68; asst prof church hist, Univ Montreal, 67-73, ASSOC PROF, 73-79. Mem, Centre Hist Relig Can, 67-. **HONORS AND AWARDS** Prix Litteraire Du Quebec, 68. **MEMBERSHIPS** Can Soc Theol. **RESEARCH** Religious history of citizens of Quebec, 1760-1840. **SELECTED PUBLICATIONS** Auth, Leger, Paul, Emile--Evolution of his Philosophy, 1950-1967, Revue D Histoire De L Amerique Francaise, Vol 0048, 95; The Seminaire-De-Quebec From 1800 to 1850, Revue D Histoire De L Amerique Francaise, Vol 0049, 96. **CONTACT ADDRESS** Dept of Theol, Univ of Montreal, Montreal, PQ, H3C 3J7.

LEMKE, WERNER ERICH
PERSONAL Born 01/31/1933, Berlin, Germany, m, 1959, 3 children **DISCIPLINE** OLD TESTAMENT, ANCIENT HISTORY **EDUCATION** Northwestern Univ, BA, 56; NPark Theol Sem, BD, 59; Harvard Univ, ThD(Old Testament), 64. **CAREER** Asst prof Bibl interpretation & lectr ancient hist, NPark Col & Theol Sem, 63-66; assoc prof, 66-69, actg dean, 73-74, Prof Old Testament Interpretation, Colgate Rochester Divinity Sch, 69-, Archaeol fel, Hebrew Union Col, Jerusalem, 69-70; prof, W F Albright Inst Archaeol Res Jerusalem, 72-73; vis prof in relig studies, Univ Rochester, 70, 74, 77. **MEMBERSHIPS** Colloquium Old Testament Res (secy-treas, 69-); Soc Bibl Lit; Am Schs Orient Res. **RESEARCH** Hebrew; Old Testament interpretation; ancient Near Eastern languages, literatures and history. **SELECTED PUBLICATIONS** Auth, The snyoptic problem in the chronicler's history, Harvard Theol Rev, 10/65; Nebuchadrezzar, my servant, Cath Bibl Quart, 1/66; Magnalia Dei: The Mighty Acts of God, Essays on the Bible and Archaeology presented to G Ernest Wright, Doubleday, 76; The way of obedience: I Kings 13 and the structure of the Deuteronomistic history, In: Magnalia Dei, Doubleday, 76; The near and distant God, J Bibl Lit, 12/81; Revelation through history in recent Biblical theology, Interpretation, 1/82. **CONTACT ADDRESS** Colgate Rochester Divinity Sch, 1100 S Goodman St, Rochester, NY, 14620-2530. **EMAIL** wlemke@crds.edu

LEMONCHECK, LINDA
PERSONAL Born 07/02/1954, Los Angeles, CA, m, 1984 **DISCIPLINE** PHILOSOPHY; FEMINIST THEORY **EDUCATION** Occidental Col, AB, 76; UCLA, MA, PhD, 81. **CAREER** Lctr, Occidental Col, 78-81, UCLA, 81-83, Calif State Univ, LongBeach, 81-83, 90-92, 94-96, USC 96 & 98- ; **HONORS AND AWARDS** Phi Beta Kappa; Women's Studies Award, Calif State Univ, Long Beach, 93; Editor, Oxford Univ Press, 98-.. **MEMBERSHIPS** Am Philos Asn; Soc Women

Philos; Nat Coun Res Women. **RESEARCH** Feminist applied ethics, specifically womens sexual and reproductive issues: promiscuity, sexual preference and deviance, pornography and prostitution, sexual harassment and sexual violence, new reproductive technologies. **SELECTED PUBLICATIONS** Auth, Dehumanizing Women: Treating Persons as Sex Objects, Rowman & Littlefield, 85; Loose Women. Lecherous Men: A Feminist Philosophy of Sex, Oxford Univ Press, 97; Sexual Harassment: A Debate, Rowman & Littlefield, 97. **CONTACT ADDRESS** 128 6th St., Seal Beach, CA, 90740. **EMAIL** llemon@msn.com

LEMOS, RAMON M.
PERSONAL Born 07/07/1927, Mobile, AL, m, 1994, 4 children **DISCIPLINE** PHILOSOPHY **EDUCATION** Univ Alabama, BA, 51; Duke Univ, MA, 53, PhD, 55. **CAREER** Instr, asst prof, assoc prof, prof, philos, Univ Miami, 56-99, chemn, 71-84. **HONORS AND AWARDS** Phi Beta Kappa; Fulbright Scholar, 55-56; Outstanding Teacher, 68; Distinguished Fac Scholar, 97. **MEMBERSHIPS** APA; Southern Soc for Philos and Psychol. **RESEARCH** Metaphysics; philosophy of mind, moral and political; philosophical theology; history of philosophy. **SELECTED PUBLICATIONS** Auth, Experience, Mind, and Value: Philosophical Essays, Brill, 69; auth, Rousseau's Political Philosophy: An Exposition and Interpretation, Georgia, 77; auth, Hobbes and Locke: Power and Consent, Georgia, 78; auth, Rights, Goods, and Democracy, Delaware, 86; auth, Metaphysical Investigations, Associated Univ Presses, 88; auth, The Nature of Value: Axiological Investigations, Florida, 95. **CONTACT ADDRESS** Dept of Philosophy, Univ of Miami, Coral Gables, FL, 33124.

LEMPERT, RICHARD OWEN
PERSONAL Born 06/02/1942, Hartford, CT, m, 1967, 1 child **DISCIPLINE** SOCIOLOGY OF LAW, EVIDENCE LAW **EDUCATION** Oberlin Col, AB, 64; Univ Mich, JD, 68, PhD, 71. **CAREER** Asst prof, 66-68, Assoc To Prof, Sch Law, Univ Mich, 68-, Mem panel on law & soc sci, NSF, 75-79; Mason Ladd vis distinguished prof law, Univ Iowa Law Sch, 81; vis fel, Ctr Socio-Legal Studies, Wolfson Col, Oxford, 82; mem, Comt Law Enforcement & Criminal Justice, Nat Res Coun, 80-; Fel Ctr AdvanStud in Behav, 94-95; Russell Sage Found Fel, 98-99. **HONORS AND AWARDS** Harry Kalven Prize, 97. **MEMBERSHIPS** Law & Soc Asn; Am Sociol Asn; Soc Am Law Teachers. **RESEARCH** Sociology of law; law and psychology; evidence. **SELECTED PUBLICATIONS** Auth, Strategies of research design in the legal impact study: The control of plausible rival hypotheses, 66 & Norm-making in social exchange: A contract law model, 71, Law St Soc Rev; Uncovering non-discernable differences: Empirical research and the jury-size cases, 75 & Modeling relevance, 77, Univ Mich Law Rev; coauth, A modern approach to evidence, West Publ Co, 77; auth, More tales of two counts: Exploring changes in the dispute settlement function of trial courts, Law & Soc Rev, 78; Desert and deterrence: An assessment of the moral bases for capital punishment, 81 & Civil juries and complex cases: Let's not rush to judgement, 81, Mich Law Rev; A Modern Approach to Evidence, West Publ; An Invitation to Law & Social Science: Desert, Disputes and Dirtribution, Pa Press, 90; Under the Influence, Drugs and the American Work Force; Cultural Differences and Discrimination: Samoans Before A Public Housing Eviction Board, Am Soc Rev, 94; After the DNA Wars: A Mopping Up Operation, Israel Law Rev, 97; Civil Juries and Complex Cases: Taking Stock after Twelve Years, Verdict, Brookings Inst, Wash, DC, 93. **CONTACT ADDRESS** Sch of Law, Univ Mich, 625 S State St, Ann Arbor, MI, 48109-1215.

LENNON, THOMAS M.
DISCIPLINE PHILOSOPHY **EDUCATION** Manhattan Col, BA; Ohio State Univ, PhD. **RESEARCH** Early modern philosophy. **SELECTED PUBLICATIONS** Auth, The Battle of the Gods and Giants: The Legacies of Descartes and Gasendi 1655-1715, Princeton, 93; co-auth, Bibliographia Malebranchiana: A Critical Guide to the Malebranche Literature into 1989, 92; The Cartesian Empiricism of Francois Bayle, Garland, 92. **CONTACT ADDRESS** Dept of Philosophy, Western Ontario Univ, London, ON, N6A 5B8. **EMAIL** tlennon@julian.uwo.ca

LENNOX, JAMES GORDON
PERSONAL Born 01/11/1948, Toronto, ON, Canada, m, 1969, 1 child **DISCIPLINE** ANCIENT PHILOSOPHY, PHILOSOPHY OF BIOLOGY **EDUCATION** York Univ, BA(hons), 71; Univ Toronto, MA, 73, PhD(philos and Greek), 78. **CAREER** ASST PROF HIST AND PHILOS SCI, UNIV PITTSBURGH, 77-, Mem med ethics, Prog Human Values Health Care, 77-. **MEMBERSHIPS** Am Philos Asn; Soc Ancient Greek Philos; Philos Sci Asn; His Sci Soc. **RESEARCH** Ancient Greek metaphysics and science; medical ethics; history and philosophy of biology. **SELECTED PUBLICATIONS** Auth, Darwin Was a Telegist, Biology and Philos, Vol 0008, 93; Aristotles Physicsa, Isis, Vol 0084, 93; Natural-Selection and the Struggle for Existence, Stud in Hist and Philos of Sci, Vol 0025, 94; Teleology by Another Name--a Reply, Biology and Philos, Vol 0009, 94; The Meaning of Evolution--the Morphological Construction and Ideological Reconstruction of Darwin Theory, Philos Sci, Vol 0061, 94. **CONTACT ADDRESS** Dept of Hist and Philos of Sci, Univ Pittsburgh, 1017 Cathedral/Learn, Pittsburgh, PA, 15260-0001.

LENNOX, STEPHEN J.
PERSONAL Born 12/17/1957, Philadelphia, PA, m, 1982, 2 children **DISCIPLINE** THEOLOGY **EDUCATION** Drew Univ, PhD, 92. **CAREER** Asst prof to assoc prof to abstractor and assoc ed to dir, 94-. **HONORS AND AWARDS** Who's Who in Am Educ, 95; Doctoral Dissertation Award, 92; Outstanding Young Man of Am. **MEMBERSHIPS** Soc Bibl Lit; Wesleyan Theolog Society. **RESEARCH** Biblical Interpretation **SELECTED PUBLICATIONS** Auth, art, The Eschatology of George D. Watson, 94; auth, Commentary on Proverbs, 98; auth, art, Biblical Interpretation in the American Holiness Movement, 98. **CONTACT ADDRESS** Indiana Wesleyan Univ, 4201 S Washington St, Marion, IN, 46953. **EMAIL** slennox@indwes.edu

LEONARD, ELLEN L.
PERSONAL Born 08/26/1933, Toronto, ON, Canada **DISCIPLINE** THEOLOGY **EDUCATION** Reaching Certificate, Toronto Teacher's Coll, 55; Univ Toronto, BA, 67; Manhattan Coll, MA, 71; St Micheal's Coll, PhD, 78. **CAREER** Tchr, Holy Rosary School Toronto, 55-57; tchr, St James School Colgan, 57-59; St Joseph School Merriton, 59-62; tchr, principal, Holy Spirit Toronto, 62-69; tchr, Metropolitan Separate School Bd, 70-73; tchg asst, Univ Toronto, 74-75; tchg asst, St Michael's Coll,77-78; lectr, St Michael's Coll, 77-78; asst prof, 78-82; assoc prof, 82-91; ADVANCED DEGREE FAC, TORONTO SCHOOL OF THEOL, 83-; PROF, ST MICHAEL'S COLL, 91-; FAC, Centre for the study of Rel Univ Toronto, 94-. **HONORS AND AWARDS** Vis fel, St Edmund's Coll, Cambridge, 88, 91; numerous grants from SSHRC. **MEMBERSHIPS** Am Acad of Rel; Can Theol Soc; cath Theol Soc of Am. **RESEARCH** Roman Catholic Modernism; Feminist Theory; Chritology. **SELECTED PUBLICATIONS** Auth, George Tyrrell and the Catholic Tradition, 82; Unresting Transformation: the Theology and Spirituality of Maude Petre, 91; Creative Tension: The Spiritual Legacy of Friedrich von Hugel, 97; numerous chapters in books and articles in refereed journals. **CONTACT ADDRESS** Faculty of Theology, Univ of St Michael's Col, 81 St Mary St, Toronto, ON, M5S 1J4. **EMAIL** leonard@chass.utoronto

LEONARD, WALTER J.
PERSONAL Born 10/03/1929, Alma, GA, m **DISCIPLINE** LAW **EDUCATION** Savannah State Coll, 1947; Morehouse Coll Atlanta, 1959-60; Atlanta Univ Grad Schl of Business, 1961-62; Howard Univ Sch of Law, JD 1968; Harvard Univ Inst of Educ Mgmt, 1974; Harvard Univ, AMP 1977. **CAREER** Ivan Allen Jr Atlanta, asst campaign mgr 1961; The Leonard Land Co Atlanta, owner/operator 1962-65; Sam Phillips McKenzie, campaign asst 1963; Dean Clarence Clyde Ferguson Jr Sch of Law Howard Univ, legal rsch asst 1966-67; Washington Tech Inst, admin asst to pres 1967-68; Howard Univ Sch of Law, asst dean & lectr 1968-69; Harvard Univ Law Sch, asst dean/asst dir admiss & finan aid 1969-; US Office of Econ Oppty, hearing examiner 1969-70; Univ of CA/ Univ of VA, visit prof summers 1969-72; Harvard Univ, asst to pres 1971-77; Fisk Univ, pres 1977-84; Howard Univ, disting sr fellow 1984-86; US Virgin Islands, executive assistant to governor, 1987-89; private consulting, 1989-90; Cities in Schools, Inc. (National/International), executive director, 1990-94. **HONORS AND AWARDS** Award for Disting Serv to Assn & Office of Pres 1972; Apprec Award Harvard Black Students' Assn 1971; Walter J Leonard Day and key to city of Savannah, GA 1969; 1st Annual Melnea A Cass Comm Award Boston YWCA 1977; New England Tribute Dinner to Walter J Leonard spons by Hon Thomas P O'Neill Jr, Hon Edw M Kennedy, Hon Edw W Brooke, Pres Derek Bok of Harvard Univ 1977; Paul Robeston Award Black Amer Law Students Assn 1977; Frederick Douglass Pub Serv Award Greater Boston YMCA 1977; Special Orator Celebration of 50th Birthday of Martin Luther King Jr Boston, MA 1979; Alumni Achievement Award Morehouse Alumni Club of New England 1977; Apprec Dinner and Award Urban League of Eastern MA 1977; Exemplary Achieve Award Faculty Resolution Grad Sch Educ Harvard Univ 1976; Service Award and Appreciation Citation, Governor of US Virgin Islands; Oxford Scholar, 1997; more than 250 other awards, citations, and 5 honorary degrees. **MEMBERSHIPS** Mem Assn of Amer Law Schs; Council on Legal Educ Oppty; Law Sch Admissions Council; Amer Assn of Univ Prof; Howard Univ Law Sch Alumni Assn; bd of visitors USN Acad; bd trustees Natl Urban League; bd trustees Natl Pub Radio; Intl Assn of Y's Men's Club Inc; NAACP; pres Natl Bar Assn; consult The Ford Found NY 1969-71; Committee on Policy for Racial Justice, Joint Center for Economic and Political Studies; Harvard Alumni; NAACP life member; Omega Psi Phi Fraternity; Sigma Pi Phi Fraternity; board of trustees, US Naval Academy Foundation; board of directors, Cities in Schools, Inc. **SELECTED PUBLICATIONS** "Our Struggle Continues-Our Cause is Just" The Crisis, May 1978; "Reflecting on Black Admissions in White Colleges" The Morning After A Retrospective View, 1974; articles in, The Boston Globe, USA Today, The Harvard Law School Bulletin. **CONTACT ADDRESS** Howard Univ, 2400 Sixth St NW, Washington, DC, 20059.

LEPARD, BRIAN
DISCIPLINE LAW **EDUCATION** Princeton Univ, BA; Yale Univ, JD. **CAREER** Asst prof **HONORS AND AWARDS** Ed, Yale J Int Law. **RESEARCH** Income taxation; international human relations. **SELECTED PUBLICATIONS** Co-auth, Unrelated Business Income Tax Issues in Health Care, 86. **CONTACT ADDRESS** Law Dept, Univ of Nebraska, Lincoln, 103 Ross McCollum Hall, PO Box 830902, Lincoln, NE, 68588-0420. **EMAIL** blepard@unlinfo.unl.edu

LEPLIN, JARRETT
PERSONAL Born 11/20/1944, Houston, TX **DISCIPLINE** HISTORY AND PHILOSOPHY OF SCIENCE **EDUCATION** Amherst Col, BA, 66; Univ Chicago, MA, 67, PhD(philos), 72. **CAREER** Instr philos, Ill Inst Technol, 67-70 and Univ Md Baltimore County, 70-71; asst prof, 71-76, ASSOC PROF PHILOS, UNIV NC, GREENSBORO, 76-. **MEMBERSHIPS** Am Philos Asn; Hist Sci Asn; AAAS; Brit Soc Hist Sci; Philos Sci Asn. **RESEARCH** Scientific methodology; theory comparison, philosophy of space and time. **SELECTED PUBLICATIONS** Auth, Kitcher, Philip the Advancement of Science--Science Without Legend, Objectivity Without Illusion, Philos of Sci, Vol 0061, 94. **CONTACT ADDRESS** Dept of Philos, Univ of NC, Greensboro, NC, 23412.

LEPOFSKY, DAVID M.
DISCIPLINE LAW **EDUCATION** Osgoode Hall Law Shc, LLB, 79; Harvard Univ, LLM, 82. **CAREER** Secondment, Crown Law Office - Criminal Division **MEMBERSHIPS** Canadian Association for Visually Impaired Lawyers **SELECTED PUBLICATIONS** Auth, Open Justice-the Constitutional Right to Attend and Speak about Criminal Proceedings in Canada; pubs on constitutional and human rights. **CONTACT ADDRESS** Fac of Law, Univ Toronto, 78 Queen's Park, Toronto, ON.

LEROY CONRAD, ROBERT
DISCIPLINE EDUCATIONAL MINISTRY **EDUCATION** Concordia Sem, MDiv, STM; Wash Univ, MA; Princeton Sem, PhD. **CAREER** Dir, Extension Educ; prof. **HONORS AND AWARDS** Educ Comm ch, Commn for Church and Youth Agency Relationships. **SELECTED PUBLICATIONS** Auth, What Planners and Teachers Need to Know About Today's Adults, Lifelong Learning: A Practical Guide to Adult Education in the Church, Augsburg Fortress, 97. **CONTACT ADDRESS** Dept of Educational Ministry, Lutheran Sch of Theol, 1100 E 55th St, Chicago, IL, 60615.

LESCHER, BRUCE
PERSONAL Born 06/07/1945, Corpus Christi, TX, s **DISCIPLINE** THEOLOGY **EDUCATION** Univ of Notre Dame, BA, 68; Univ of MI, MA, 73; Univ of San Fran, MAS, 82; Grad Theol Union, Berkeley, PhD **CAREER** Asst Prof, 90-95, St Edwards Univ; Assoc Prof, 95-98, Cath Theol Union; Dir, 98-, Inst for Spirit and Worship, Jesuit Sch of Theol **MEMBERSHIPS** Am Acad of Relig; Cath theol Soc of Am **RESEARCH** Spiritual formation **CONTACT ADDRESS** Jesuit Sch of Theol, Berkeley, 1735 LeRoy Ave, Berkeley, CA, 94709. **EMAIL** blescher@jstb.edu

LESCHERT, DALE
PERSONAL Born 12/31/1954, Camrose, AB, Canada **DISCIPLINE** HERMENEUTICS **EDUCATION** Providence Theo Sem, MDiv, 80; Western Sem Portland, MTh, 81, Fuller Theo Sem, PhD, 91. **CAREER** Asst Prof, 83-85, Mountainview Bib Coll; faculty, bible & theo, 87-88, Briercrest Bible Coll; adj fac, 91, Can Bap Sem, Langley; adj Prof NT, 95, Capital Bible Sem; independent research & writing, 96-. **MEMBERSHIPS** SBL, ETS. **RESEARCH** Hermeneutics, New Testament, theology, epistemology. **SELECTED PUBLICATIONS** Auth, Hermeneutical Foundations of Hebrews, in: Nat Assoc BPRDS, 94; Entries, Age, Mediator and Witness, in: Eerdmans Dictionary of the Bible, eds D N Freedman, A C Myers & A B Beck, Grand Rapids Wm b Eerdmans Pub Co, forthcoming; Hebrews, Eschatology of, in: Dictionary of Premillennial Theology, ed, M Couch, Grand Rapids Kregel Pub, 96; Why Should We Think About God and the Bible? in: First People, Thanksgiving, 93. **CONTACT ADDRESS** 2013 Seventh Ave, New Westminster, BC, V3M 2L5.

LESKE, ADRIAN M.
PERSONAL Born 04/14/1936, Gumeracha, Australia, m, 1961, 3 children **DISCIPLINE** NEW TESTAMENT **EDUCATION** Concordia Sem, STM, 67, ThD,71. **CAREER** Min, Wellington, NZ, 60-65, Walkerie, S Australia, 66-69; prof relig stud, Concordia Univ, 71-. **HONORS AND AWARDS** Exch study schol, Concordia Sem, St. Louis, 58-60, 69-71; Allan Schendel Award, 90. **MEMBERSHIPS** Soc of Bibl Lit; Can Soc of Bibl Stud; Asn for Res in Rel Stud & Theol. **RESEARCH** Gospel of Matthew; exile and post-exile prophets. **SELECTED PUBLICATIONS** Auth, "Influence of Isaiah 40-66 on Christology in Matthew and Luke: A Comparison," SBL 1994 Seminar Papers; "Influence of Isaiah on Christology in Matthew and Luke," Crisis in Christology: Essays in Quest of Resolution, Dove, 95; "Isaiah and Matthew: The Prophetic Influence in the First Gospel-A Report on Current Research," Jesus and the Suffering Servant: Isiah 53 and Christian Origins, Trinity, 1998; "Matthew," International Bible Commentary, Liturgical, 1998. **CONTACT ADDRESS** Concordia Col, Alberta, 7128 Ada Blvd, Edmonton, AB, T5B 4E4. **EMAIL** aleske@concordia.ab.ca

LESLIE, BENJAMIN C.
PERSONAL Born 05/02/1957, Anniston, AL, m, 1980, 2 children **DISCIPLINE** SYSTEMATIC THEOLOGY **EDUCATION** Samford Univ, BA, 79; Southern Baptist Theol Sem, MDiv, 83; Baptist Theol Sem, Ruschlikon, ThM, 86; Univ Zurich, D Theol, 90. **CAREER** PROF SYSTEMATIC THEOLOGY AND CHRISTIAN ETHICS, NORTH AMERICAN BAPTIST SEM, 90-98. **MEMBERSHIPS** Am Academy Relig; Soc of Christian Ethics; Nat Asn Baptist Professors of Relig. **RESEARCH** Christian theology general; Barth studies; Baptist studies. **SELECTED PUBLICATIONS** Auth, Trinitarian Hermeneutics, Peter Lung, 90; Barth, karl, A New Testament of Christian Theologians, Abingdon, 96. **CONTACT ADDRESS** No American Baptist Sem, 1525 S. Grange Ave., Sioux Falls, SD, 57105-1599. **EMAIL** BLeslie605@aol.com

LESLIE, JOHN A.
PERSONAL Born 08/02/1940, Calcutta, India **DISCIPLINE** PHILOSOPHY **EDUCATION** Oxford Univ, BA, MA, 67, MLitt, 70. **CAREER** Fac mem to prof, 68-96, PROF EMER PHILOSOPHY, UNIV GUELPH, 96-; vis prof relig stud, Univ Calgary, 86; vis fel philos, Australian Nat Univ, 87; vis fel, Univ Liege, 93. **HONORS AND AWARDS** SSHRC fel, 80-81; Fel, Royal Soc Can, 97. **MEMBERSHIPS** Can Philos Asn; Am Philos Asn; Philos Sci Asn. **SELECTED PUBLICATIONS** Auth, Value and Existence, 79; auth, Universes, 89; auth, The End of the World, 96; ed, Physical Cosmology and Philosophy, 90. **CONTACT ADDRESS** Philosophy Dept, Univ of Guelph, Guelph, ON, N1G 2W1. **EMAIL** johnlesl@uoguelph.ca

LESSARD, HESTER A.
DISCIPLINE LAW **EDUCATION** Dalhousie Univ, LLB, 85; Univ Columbia, LLM, 89. **CAREER** Asst prof, 89-94; assoc prof, 94-. **HONORS AND AWARDS** Co-ed, Can Jour Women Law. **RESEARCH** Constitutional law; feminist legal theories; family law; and legal process. **SELECTED PUBLICATIONS** Auth, pubs on feminist critiques of constitutional rights. **CONTACT ADDRESS** Fac of Law, Univ Victoria, PO Box 2400, Victoria, BC, V8W 3H7. **EMAIL** hlessard@uvic.ca

LESTER, ROBERT CARLTON
PERSONAL Born 02/01/1933, Lead, SD, m, 1954, 3 children **DISCIPLINE** COMPARATIVE RELIGION **EDUCATION** Mont State Univ, BA, 55; Yale Univ, BD, 58, MA, 59, PhD(comp relig), 63. **CAREER** From asst prof to assoc prof philos and relig, Am Univ, DC, 62-70; assoc prof, 70-72, PROF RELIG STUDIES, UNIV COLO, BOULDER, 72-, Vis lectr, Foreign Serv Inst, US Dept State, 67-; vis prof Asian studies, Cornell Univ, 68-69; Fulbright-Hays sr res fel, India, 74-75. **MEMBERSHIPS** Asn Asian Studies; Am Acad Relig; fel Soc Relig Higher Educ. **RESEARCH** Buddhism in Southeast Asia; Hinduism; South Indian Vaishnavism. **SELECTED PUBLICATIONS** Auth, The Sattada Srivaisnavas, J Amer Oriental Soc, Vol 0114, 1994 **CONTACT ADDRESS** Relig Studies, Univ of Colo, Boulder, CO, 80309. **EMAIL** Robert.Lester@Colorado.edu

LEUBSDORF, JOSHUA
PERSONAL Born 02/11/1942, New York, NY, m, 1998, 1 child **DISCIPLINE** LAW **EDUCATION** Harvard Univ, BA, 63; Stanford Univ, MA, Eng, 64; Harvard Law Sch, JD, 67. **CAREER** Assoc prof and prof, Boston Univ, 75-84; vis prof, Columbia Univ, 90-91; Univ Calif Berkeley, 93; Cornell Univ, 95; prof, Rutgers Law Sch, Newark, 84-. **HONORS AND AWARDS** Fulbright scholar, Paris, 95. **MEMBERSHIPS** Amer Law Inst. **RESEARCH** Legal Ethics and Civil Procedure. **SELECTED PUBLICATIONS** Auth, Civil Procedure, 4th ed, with F. James and G. Hazard, 92. **CONTACT ADDRESS** Rutgers Law School, 15 Washington St., Newark, NJ, 07102.

LEVESQUE, PAUL J.
PERSONAL Born 06/17/1962, Santa Monica, CA **DISCIPLINE** RELIGIOUS STUDIES **EDUCATION** Catholic Univ of Amer, Philos, BA, 84, MA, 85; Catholic Univ of Louvain, Belgium, Rel Stud, BA, 87, MA, 88, STB, 88, Masters in Morals and Rel Sic, 89, PhD, 95. **CAREER** Instr, 97-, California State Univ, Fullerton; Adjunct Prof, 93-, Mount St Mary's Coll. **HONORS AND AWARDS** Theodore T. Basselin Scholar, Cath Univ Amer, Sch of Philos. **MEMBERSHIPS** Amer Acad Rel; Amer Philos Assoc; Soc for the Sci Stud of Rel; Assoc for the Sociology of Rel; North Amer Assoc for the Stud of Rel; Assoc Rel and Intellectual Life; Cath Theol Soc Amer. **RESEARCH** Christianity and Culture, Philosophy of Religion, Catholic Studies. **SELECTED PUBLICATIONS** Auth, Symbols of Transcendence, Religious Expression in the Thought of Louis Dupre, Louvain Theological and Pastoral Monographs 22, Leuven, Peeters Press, Grand Rapids, W.B. Eerdmans, 97; A Symbolical Sacramental Methodology, Questions Liturgiques Studies in Liturgy, 95; Eucharistic Prayer Posture, From Standing to Kneeling, Questions Liturgiques/Studies in Liturgy, 93. **CONTACT ADDRESS** 24252 El Toro Rd, Laguna Hills, CA, 92653. **EMAIL** pLevesque@Fullerton.edu.

LEVI, ISAAC
PERSONAL Born 06/30/1930, New York, NY, m, 2 children **DISCIPLINE** PHILOSOPHY **EDUCATION** NY Univ, BA, 51; Columbia Univ, MA, 54, PhD, 57. **CAREER** From instr to asst prof philos, Case Western Reserve Univ, 57-62; asst prof, City Col NY, 62-64; from assoc prof to prof, Case Western Reserve Univ, 64-70, chmn dept, 68-70; Prof Philos, Columbia Univ, 70-, John Devoey Prof, 91-; Nat Sci Found awards, 63-65 & 67-69; Guggenheim fel, 66-67; Fulbright res fel, UK, 66-67; vis scholar, Corpus Christi Col, Cambridge, 73. **HONORS AND AWARDS** Vis scholar Darwin Col, Cambridge, 80, 92, Vis Fel, All Souls Col Oxford, 88; Vis fel, Wolfson Col, Cambridge, 96; Doctor honorus causa, Lund Univ, Sweden. **MEMBERSHIPS** Am Philos Asn; Philos Sci Asn; Brit Soc Philos Sci. **RESEARCH** Philos of sci; philos of soc sci. **SELECTED PUBLICATIONS** Auth, Must the Scientist Make Value Judgements?, J Philos, 60; On the Seriousness of Mistakes, Philos Sci, 62; Probability Kinematics, Brit J Philos Sci, 67; Gambling With Truth, Knopf, 67; On Indeterminate Probabilities, 74 & Direct inference, 77, J Philos; auth, The Enterprise of Knowledge, MIT, 80; auth, Decisions and Revisions, Cambridge, 84; auth, Hard Choices, Cambridge, 86; auth, The Fixation of Belief and its Undoing, Cambridge, 91; auth, For the Sake of the Argument, Cambridge, 96; auth, The Covenant of Reason, Cambridge, 97. **CONTACT ADDRESS** Dept of Philosophy, Columbia Univ, New York, NY, 10027-6900. **EMAIL** levi@columbia.edu

LEVIE, HOWARD SIDNEY
PERSONAL Born 12/19/1907, Wolverine, MI, m, 1934 **DISCIPLINE** LAW **EDUCATION** Cornell Univ, AB, 28, JD, 30; George Washington Univ, LLM, 57. **CAREER** From assoc prof to prof, 63-77, EMER PROF LAW, LAW SCH, ST LOUIS UNIV, 77-, Int law consult, Naval War Col, 65-71, Charles H Stockton chmn int law, 71-72; vpres, St Louis Coun World Affairs, 68-70. **MEMBERSHIPS** Int Soc Mil Law and Law of War; Am Bar Asn; Fed Bar Asn; Am Soc Int Law; Int Law Asn. **RESEARCH** International law. **SELECTED PUBLICATIONS** Auth, Landmines--a Deadly Legacy-Arms Project Human Rights Watch Physicians Human Rights, Amer J Int Law, Vol 0088, 94; Evaluating Present Options for an International Criminal Court, Mil Law Rev, Vol 0149, 95. **CONTACT ADDRESS** Sch Law, St Louis Univ, St Louis, MO, 63103.

LEVIN, DAVID M.
DISCIPLINE PHILOSOPHY **EDUCATION** Columbia Univ, PhD. **CAREER** Prof, Northwestern Univ. **RESEARCH** Phenomenology, esthetics, social and political philosophy, philosophy of the human sciences, postmodernism. **CONTACT ADDRESS** Dept of Philosophy, Northwestern Univ, 1801 Hinman, Evanston, IL, 60208.

LEVIN, RONALD MARK
PERSONAL Born 05/11/1950, St. Louis, MO, m, 1989 **DISCIPLINE** LAW **EDUCATION** Yale Univ, BA, 72; Univ Chicago, JD, 75. **CAREER** Law clerk, US Court of Appeals, 5th Circuit, 75-76; assoc, Sutherland, Asbill & Brennan, 76-79; from Asst Prof to Assoc Prof, 79-85, Prof Law, Washington Univ, 85-, Assoc Dean, 90-93; consult, Admin Conf U.S., 79-81, 93-95; chair, Asn Am Law Sch Sect on Admin Law, 93, Sect on Legis, 95; vice-chair, Am Bar Asn Sect Admin Law & Reg Pract, 98-99. **RESEARCH** Administrative law; legislative process. **SELECTED PUBLICATIONS** Auth, Understanding unreviewability in administrative law, Minn Law Rev, 90; Judicial review and the uncertain appeal of certainty on appeal, Duke Law J, 95; Direct finale rulemaking, George Washington Law Rev, 95; Congressional Ethics and Constituent Advocacy, Mich Law Rev, 96; coauth, State and Federal Administrative Law, West, 2nd ed, 98; Administrative Law and Process, West, 4th ed, 97. **CONTACT ADDRESS** Sch of Law, Washington Univ, Campus Box 1120, St. Louis, MO, 63130-4899. **EMAIL** levin@wulaw.wustl.edu

LEVINE, ALEXANDER
PERSONAL Born 07/21/1966, Minneapolis, MN **DISCIPLINE** EIGHTEENTH CENTURY PHILOSOPHY **EDUCATION** Reed Coll, BA, 88; Univ Calif, C Phil, 91; PhD, 94.

LEVINE, ANDREW
PERSONAL Born 11/28/1944, Philadelphia, PA, s **DISCIPLINE** PHILOSOPHY **EDUCATION** Columbia Univ, PhD, 71 **CAREER** Prof, UW, Madison **RESEARCH** Social and Political Philosophy **SELECTED PUBLICATIONS** Auth, Rethinking Liberal Equality, Cornell, 98; Auth, The General Will, Cambridge, 93 **CONTACT ADDRESS** Dept of Philos, Univ of Wisconsin, Madison, WI, 53706. **EMAIL** alevine@macc.wisc.edu

LEVINE, JULIUS B.
PERSONAL Born 02/08/1939, Waterville, ME, m, 1965, 3 children **DISCIPLINE** LAW **EDUCATION** Harvard Univ, BA, 60, JD, 64; Oxford Univ, PhD(law), 69. **CAREER** Instr law, Bd Student Adv, Harvard Law Sch, 63-64; law clerk, US Dist Ct, 64-65; assoc prof, 69-72, Prof Law, Boston Univ Sch Law, 72-, Law pract, Levine Brody & Levine, Attorneys at Law, 65-; adv uniform probate code, Law Sch Adv Coun, Am Bar Asn, 71-78; contribr ed, Am Bar Asn Sect Litigation, 76-80; legal ed, Nat Col Probate Judges Quart Newsletter, 80-81. **HONORS AND AWARDS** Omicron Chi Epsilon, 59; Phi Beta Kappa, 59; Rhodes Scholar, 60-61 & 67-69. **MEMBERSHIPS** Am Asn Law Sch. **RESEARCH** Law of procedure and litigation; wills, trusts, estates and property law. **SELECTED PUBLICATIONS** Contribr, Higher Education: Resources and Finance, McGraw-Hill, 62; coauth, Uniform probate code: Analysis and comments, Nat Col Probate Judges, 70; auth, Abuse of discovery ... are we suffering a true crisis of overdiscovery?, Am Bar Asn J, Vol 67, 81; Living probate, Nat Col Probate Judges Quart Newsletter, spring 81; Discovery: A Comparison Between English and American Civil Discovery Law with Reform Proposals, Oxford Univ Press, 82; Winning Trial Advocacy, Prentice Hall, 89. **CONTACT ADDRESS** Sch of Law, Boston Univ, 765 Commonwealth Ave, Boston, MA, 02215-1401. **EMAIL** rcoulson@lec.okcu.edu

LEVINE, MARTIN L.
DISCIPLINE CRIMINAL LAW **EDUCATION** Brandeis Univ, BA; Yale Univ, JD. **CAREER** UPS Found prof Law, Gerontology, Psychiatry, and the Behavioral Sci; Vprovost, Fac and Minority Aff; clerked for, Honorable J. Skelly Wright, Judge US Ct Appeals DC Circuit; dir, Oxford-USC Inst for Legal Theory. **MEMBERSHIPS** Pres, Int Asn Aging, Law, and Ethics. **SELECTED PUBLICATIONS** Auth, Elderlaw: Legal, Ethical, and Policy Issues of Aging Individuals and an Aging Society; Age Discrimination and the Mandatory Retirement Controversy & Law and Aging: International Variations; ed, Psychology and Law. **CONTACT ADDRESS** School of Law, Univ Southern Calif, University Park Campus, Los Angeles, CA, 90089.

LEVINSON, JERROLD
PERSONAL Born 07/11/1948, Brooklyn, NY, m, 1985, 1 child **DISCIPLINE** PHILOSOPHY **EDUCATION** MIT, BS, 69; Univ Mich, PhD, 74. **CAREER** Asst Prof, 76-81, Assoc Prof, 81-91, Prof, 91-, Univ Maryland; Vis Prof, Johns Hopkins Univ, Univ Landau, Univ Rennes. **HONORS AND AWARDS** NEH Category B Fel. **MEMBERSHIPS** APA, ASA **RESEARCH** Aesthetics; metaphysics; theory of value; philosophy of mind. **SELECTED PUBLICATIONS** Music Art and Metaphysics, Cornell, 90; Pleasures of Aesthetics, Cornell, 96; Film Music and Narrative Agency, Univ Wisconsin, 96; Evaluating Music, Revue Inter de Philo, 96; Wollheim on Pictorial Representation, J Aes & Art Crit, 98; L'art Lamusique et l'histoire, Paris, 98. **CONTACT ADDRESS** Univ of Maryland, Philosophy Dept - Skinner Bldg, College Park, MD, 20742. **EMAIL** JL32@umail.umd.edu

LEVIT, NANCY
DISCIPLINE LAW **EDUCATION** Bates Col, BA; Univ Kans, JD. **CAREER** Prof **RESEARCH** Sex segregation; feminism; constitutional law; criminal law. **SELECTED PUBLICATIONS** Auth, The Gender Line: Men, Women, and the Law, Univ NY, 98; co-auth, Jurisprudence Contemporary Readings, Problems and Narratives. **CONTACT ADDRESS** Law Dept, Univ of Missouri, Kansas City, 5100 Rockhill Rd, Kansas City, MO, 64110-2499. **EMAIL** levitn@umkc.edu

LEVMORE, SAUL
DISCIPLINE LAW **EDUCATION** Columbia Univ, BA, 73; Yale Univ, PhD, 78, JD, 80; Kent Univ, LLD, 95. **CAREER** Vis prof. **RESEARCH** Commercial Law, Comparative Law, Contracts, Corporate Tax, Corporations, Public Choice and the Law, and Torts **SELECTED PUBLICATIONS** Auth, pubs on commercial law, comparative law, contracts, and corporate tax. **CONTACT ADDRESS** Fac of Law, Univ Toronto, 78 Queen's Park, Toronto, ON.

LEVY, IAN CHRISTOPHER
PERSONAL Born 02/24/1967, New York, NY **DISCIPLINE** HISTORICAL THEOLOGY **EDUCATION** Univ of New Mexico, BA, 89; Vanderbilt, MA, 91; Marquette Univ, PhD, 97. **CAREER** Marquette Univ, tchg asst, 94-96, Nashotah House Episcopal Sem, adj prof, 97; Marquette Univ, adj prof, 97-, Carroll Col, adj prof, 98-. **HONORS AND AWARDS** Phi Beta Kappa, Marquette Univ, Schmitt fell. **MEMBERSHIPS** MAA, MAMW, SBL, ASCH **RESEARCH** Medieval Theol; esp biblical interpretations and sacraments. **SELECTED PUBLICATIONS** Auth, John Wyclif and Augustinian Realism, in: Augustiniana, 98; Biographical Dictionary of Christian Theologians, contributing auth, eds P. Carey, J. Lienhard, Greenwood Pub Co, forthcoming; auth, Was John Wyclif's Theology of the Eucharist Donatistic? in: Scottish Jour of Theol, forthcoming. **CONTACT ADDRESS** Dept of Theology, Marquette Univ, 5400 W Washington Blvd, Milwaukee, WI, 53208. **EMAIL** ian.levy@marquette.edu

LEVY, ROBERT J.
DISCIPLINE PHILOSOPHY **EDUCATION** Boston Univ, BA, MA; Duke Univ, PhD. **CAREER** Prof, 67-; **RESEARCH** Philosophy of logic, philosophy of science, contemporary philosophy, non deductive reasoning. **SELECTED PUBLICATIONS** Auth, Introductory to Logic. **CONTACT ADDRESS** Wittenberg Univ, Springfield, OH, 45501-0720.

LEWIS, CARY B., JR.
PERSONAL Born 09/13/1921, Chicago, IL, m **DISCIPLINE** LAW **EDUCATION** Univ of IL, AB 1942; Univ of Chicago, MBA 1947; Univ of IL, CPA 1950; DePaul Univ, JD 1966; Harvard Univ, AMP 1971; Teaching Certificates & Licenses, HS 1951, Jr Coll 1967, Coll 1958, Supervisory 1967. **CAREER** KY State Univ, asst prof 1947-50; So Univ, assoc prof 1950-; CPA, 1950-75; MT Washington & Co CPA's Chicago, sr auditor 1951-53; Chicago Pub Sch, 1951-57; Collier-Lewis Realty Co, auditor 1953-71; Chicago Tchrs Coll, 1957-65; AA Rayner & Sons, auditor 1960-72; Budget Coord, 1966-67; Atty at Law, 1966-; Chicago State Univ, spec asst to vice pres 1967, prof law & acctg 1957-, **HONORS AND AWARDS** Wisdon Hall of Fame, 1972; Worldwide Acad of Scholars 1975; Natl Hon Soc 1938; Sachem 1941; first black to practice as CPA LA 1951; first black atty & CPA State of IL 1966. **MEMBERSHIPS** Budgetary consult office of econ oppor 1967-69; educ consult to dept hlth educ & welfare 1968-69; auditing consult to dept of labor 1967-69; mgmt consult to Black Econ Union 1969; chmn educ adv comm Chicago NAACP; mem Amer Bar Assn, IL Bar Assn; Chicago Bar Assn; Cook Co Bar Assn; Amer Judicare Soc; Amer Bus Law Assn; Amer Inst CPA's; IL Soc CPA's; Natl Soc CPA's; Amer Acct's Assn; Amer Assn of Univ Prof's; City Club of Chicago. **CONTACT ADDRESS** 95 St at King Dr, Chicago, IL, 60628.

LEWIS, DANIEL J.
PERSONAL Born 04/07/1950, Billings, MT, m, 1970, 3 children **DISCIPLINE** WESTERN RELIGION **EDUCATION** William Tyndale Col, BRE, 84; Univ Detroit Mercy, MA, 86. **CAREER** Sr pastor, Troy Christ Chapel, 81-, guest lectr, Univ of the Nations, 91-; adjunct facul, Ecumenical Theol Sem, 98-; part-time facul, Robert H. Whitaker Sch of Theol, 87-89; adjunct facul, William Tyndale Col, 87-. **HONORS AND AWARDS** Who's Who in Amer Relig, 93; Who's Who in Amer Univ and Col, 84. **MEMBERSHIPS** Soc of Bibl Lit. **RESEARCH** Biblical theology; American railroads. **SELECTED PUBLICATIONS** Article, Building a Sellios Gas Station, N-Scale, Hundman Publ, jul/aug, 98; article, Bunker C.. .at Harlowton, N-Scale, Hundman Publ, may/jun, 98; article, Thinking Vertically, The Hobtox, NCR/NMRA, winter, 98; article, SW1200, N-Scale, Hundman Publ, nov/dec, 97; article, DPM Comes to Life, N-Scale, Hundman Publ, jul/aug, 97; article, Moving Toward the Prototype, The Hotbox, NCR/NMRA, spring, 96; article, Capturing a Mood, N-Scale, Hundman Publ, mar/apr, 96; article, Evolving Operations on a Small Railroad, Model Railroader, Kalmbach Publ, feb, 96; article, Modeling a Milwaukee Road Superdome, N-Scale, Hundman Publ, may/jun, 95; article, A Ride on the Tuscola and Saginaw Bay, The Hotbox, NCR/NMRA, fall, 95; article, Kitbashing the Bachmann Watertank, N-Scale, Hundman Publ, nov/dec, 94; article, The Three Sisters Railroad, N-Scale, Hundman Publ, mar/apr, 94; mongr; Ezra-Nehemiah, 98; mongr, The Book of Hebrews, 98; monogr, The Book of Daniel, 98; monogr; The Book of Isaiah, 97; monogr, Holy Space and Holy Time, 97; monogr, The Gospel of the Beloved Disciple, 96; monogr, Eschatology, 96; monogr, New Testament Survey, 96; monogr, Bible Characters, 96; monogr, Spiritual Life and Discipleship, 96; monogr, D-History, 96; monogr, Letters to Timothy, 95; monogr, Voices from the North, 95; monogr, The Church Catholic, 94; monogr, The Burden of Disillusionment, 94; monogr, Things That Matter Most, 94; monogr, Ezekiel: Message of Doom and Hope, 94; monogr, Christians and Culture, 94; auth, Three Crucial Questions About the Last Days, Grand Rapids: Baker, 98. **CONTACT ADDRESS** 390 E. Long Lake Rd., Troy, MI, 48098. **EMAIL** tcchapel@aol.com

LEWIS, DAVID BAKER
PERSONAL Born 06/09/1944, Detroit, MI, m **DISCIPLINE** LAW **EDUCATION** Oakland Univ, BA 1965; Univ of Chicago, MBA 1967; Univ of MI, JD 1970. **CAREER** Northern Trust Co, administrative dept, 1966; Morgan Guaranty Trust Co, corporate research analyst, 1967; Lewis & Thompson Agency Inc, 1968; Miller Canfield Paddock & Stone, summer law clerk 1969; Univ of MI, lectr Afro-Am and African Studies Dept 1970; Hon Theodore Levin US Dist Ct, law clerk 1970-71; Patmon Young & Kirk, assoc atty 1971-72; Detroit College of Law, associate professor, 1972-78; David Baker Lewis Atty at Law, sole practitioner 1972; Lewis, White & Clay, president, 1972-82, chairman of the board, founding shareholder, director, 1972-. **HONORS AND AWARDS** University of Detroit-Mercy, honorary LHD, 1991; American Jewish Comm, Learned Hand Awd, 1995. **MEMBERSHIPS** Institute of American Business, executive committee, board of directors, 1985-; Lewis & Thompson Agency Inc, board of directors, 1967-; Consolidated Rail Corp., board of directors, 1989-98, audit committee, 1989-98, chairman, 1992-98, ethics committee, 1992-95; Michigan Opera Theatre, board of trustees, 1982-; Center for Creative Studies, board of directors, 1983-96; Music Hall Center for the Performing Arts, board of directors, 1983-94; Detroit Symphony Orchestra Inc, board of directors, 1983-; Metropolitan Affairs Corp., board of directors, 1984-92; Booker T Business Association, board of directors, 1988-90; National Conference on Christians and Jews, board of directors, 1990-; SEMCOG-Regional Development Initiative Oversight Committee, 1990-92; Greater Detroit and Windsor Japan-American Society, board of directors, 1990-92; Arts Commission of the City of Detroit, board of directors, 1992-97; American Bar Association, 1970-; American Bar Foundation, 1987-; State Bar of Michigan, 1970-; Client Security Fund, 1988-; Wolverine Bar Association, 1970-; Detroit Bar Association, 1970-; National Association of Securities Professionals, 1985-; Oakland University Foundation, board of trustees, 1985-, chairman, 1998-; National Association of Bond Lawyers, 1979-; life member: Judicial Conference of the US Court of Appeals for the Sixth Circuit; University of Michigan Law School, Committee of Visitors; National Bar Association; NAACP. **CONTACT ADDRESS** Lewis & Munday, PC, 1300 First National Bldg, Detroit, MI, 48226.

LEWIS, DOUGLAS
DISCIPLINE PHILOSOPHY **EDUCATION** Univ Iowa, PhD. **RESEARCH** Early modern European philosophy. **SELECTED PUBLICATIONS** Auth, On the Aims and the Method of Spinoza's Philosophy, SW J Philos, 77; Spinoza on Extension, Studies Hist Philos, 76; The Existence of Substances and Locke's Way of Ideas, Theoria, 69; co-auth, Locke on Mixed Modes, Knowledge and Substances, J Hist Philos, 70. **CONTACT ADDRESS** Philosophy Dept, Univ of Minnesota, Twin Cities, 355 Ford Hall, 224 Church St SE, Minneapolis, MN, 55455. **EMAIL** lewis002@tc.umn.edu

LEWIS, ERIC
DISCIPLINE PHILOSOPHY **EDUCATION** Univ Cornell, BA; Univ Ill Chicago, PhD. **RESEARCH** Ancient philos; hist and philos of science; ancient natural philos. **SELECTED PUBLICATIONS** Auth, Alexander of Aphrodisias; auth, The Stoic Theory of Identity. **CONTACT ADDRESS** Philosophy Dept, McGill Univ, 845 Sherbrooke St, Montreal, PQ, H3A 2T5.

LEWIS, GORDON RUSSEL
PERSONAL Born 11/21/1926, NY, m, 1948, 3 children **DISCIPLINE** THEOLOGY PHILOSOPHY **EDUCATION** Baptist Bible Seminary, 44-46; BA, Gordon Coll, 48; M.Div Faith Seminary, 51; MA, Syracuse Univ, 53; Cornell Univ, 54; PhD, Syracuse Univ. **CAREER** Prof of Apologetic, Baptist Bible Seminary, 51-58; Prof of Theol/Philos, Denver Seminary, 58-93, Sr Prof, 93; Visiting Prof, Young Life Institute, 67; Cir Christan Training Inst, Denver Seminary, 60-70; VP and Pres of Evangelical Theol Soc, 77-78; Board Cam of Christian Res Assoc, 79-83; Founder and Board Chm Evangelical Ministries to New Rel, 82-92; Contributing Ed to Journal of Psychol and Theol. **HONORS AND AWARDS** Theta, Beta Phi Hon Philosophical Soc, Syracuse Univ; Lausanne Asso Lusanne Comm On World Evangelism; Biographical sketch in Ref book,such as Who's Who in Amer; Pres of Ecangelical Philosophical Soc, 77-87; Pres of Evangelical Theol Soc, 92; Member of Evangelical Fellowship Theol Commn, 90-96. **MEMBERSHIPS** Amer Academy of Rel; Soc of Christian Philos; Evangelical Theol Soc; World Evangelical Fellowship Commn, 90-96. **RESEARCH** Philo; Theol; Rel; Cults. **SELECTED PUBLICATIONS** Integrative Theology, 3 vol in 1, 1544pp Zondervan, 96; Testing Christianity's Truth Claims, 363pp, Univ Press of Amer, 90; What Everyone Should Know About Transcendental Meditation, 92pp, Regal, 75; Decide For Yourself: A Theological Workbook, 174pp, InterVarsity Press, 70; Confronting the Cults, 198pp, Presbyterian and Reformed Publishing Co, 66. **CONTACT ADDRESS** Denver Conservative Baptist Sem, PO Box 10000, Denver, CO, 80250. **EMAIL** Grlewis@aol.com

LEWIS, HAROLD T.
PERSONAL Born 02/21/1947, Brooklyn, New York, m, 1970 **DISCIPLINE** THEOLOGY **EDUCATION** McGill Univ, BA, 1967; Yale Divinity School, M Div, 1971; Cambridge Univ, research fellow, 1972-73; University of Birmingham (Eng), PhD, 1994. **CAREER** NYC Dept of Social Serv, social worker, 1967-68; Overseas Missionary, Honduras, 1971-72; St Monica's Church, rector, 1973-82; St Luke's Episcopal Church, assoc priest, 1983-96; Mercer School of Theology, prof of homiletics, 1988-96; Episcopal Church Cent, staff officer, 1983-94; NY Theological Seminary, prof of Homiletics, 1995-96; Calvary Episcopal Church, Pittsburgh, PA, rector, 1996-; Pittsburgh Theological Seminary, adj prof, 1996-. **HONORS AND AWARDS** Berkeley Divinity Schhol at Yale, Doctor of Divinity, 1991; Episcopal Church Foundation, Research Fellowship, 1978, Yale Univ, Research Fellowship, 1990; Operation Crossroads Office, Distinguished Alumnus Award, 1985. **MEMBERSHIPS** Sigma Pi Phi, sec, 1991-; Prophetic Justice Unit, Natl Council of Churches, exec committee, 1988-96; Racial Justice Working Group, Natl Council of Churches, 1986-96. **SELECTED PUBLICATIONS** Editor, Recruitment, Training & Devel of Black Clergy, 1980; Lift Every Voice and Sing II, 1993; Author, In Season, Out of Season, A Collection of Sermons, 1993; Yet With a Steady Beat: The Afro-Amer Struggle for Recognition in the Episcopal Church, 1996. **CONTACT ADDRESS** Calvary Episcopal Church, Pittsburgh, PA, 15206.

LEWIS, JACK PEARL
PERSONAL Born 03/13/1919, Midlothian, TX, m, 1978, 2 children **DISCIPLINE** RELIGION **EDUCATION** Abilene Christian Col, AB, 41; Sam Houston State Teacher's Col, MA, 44; Harvard Univ, STB, 47, PhD, 53; Hebrew Union Col, PhD, 62. **CAREER** From asst prof to assoc prof, 53-57, prof bible & grad sch relig, Harding Col, 57-, Thayer fel, Am Sch Orient Res, Jerusalem, 67-68; senior fel, Albright Inst for Arch Res, Jerusalem, 87-88. **HONORS AND AWARDS** Christian Education Award, 20th Century Christian, 68; Distinguished Christian Service Award, Harding Univ, 88, Pepperdine Univ, 91. **MEMBERSHIPS** Soc Bibl Lit; Nat Asn Prof Hebrew; Am Acad Relig; Evangel Theol Soc; Near East Arch Soc. **RESEARCH** The minor Prophets. **SELECTED PUBLICATIONS** Ed, The English Bible From KJV to NIV, Baker Bk, 81; auth, The Offering of Abel (Gen. 4:4): A Historical Interpretation, JETS 37, 94; The Gates of Hell Shall Not Prevail Against It (Matt. 16:18): A Study of the History of Interpretation, JETS 38, 95; Claude R. Conder, Surveyor of Palestine, NEASB, 95; Sire Charles William Wilson Discoverer of Wilson's Arch, NEASB, 96; Clermont-Ganneau and 19th Century discovery, NEASB, 96. **CONTACT ADDRESS** Grad Sch of Relig, Harding Univ, 1000 Cherry Rd, Memphis, TN, 38117-5499. **EMAIL** jackplewis@juno.com

LEWIS, JAMES F.
PERSONAL Born 06/21/1937, m, 1958, 3 children **DISCIPLINE** HISTORY OF RELIGIONS **EDUCATION** Bethel Col, BA, 60; Bethel Theol Sem, BD, 63; Univ Iowa, PhD, 76. **CAREER** Asst prof and dept chair, world relig, Union Bibl Sem, Pune, Maharashtra, India, 77-81; assoc prof and dept chair, world relig, St. Bonifacius, 81-94; assoc prof, world relig, Wheaton Col, 94-. **MEMBERSHIPS** Evang Theol Soc; Asn of Asian Studies; Amer Acad of Relig. **RESEARCH** Religion in Vietnam; Religion in Modern India. **SELECTED PUBLICATIONS** Co-auth, Religious Traditions of the World, Zondervan, 91. **CONTACT ADDRESS** 501 College Av., Wheaton, IL, 60187. **EMAIL** james.f.lewis@wheaton.edu

LEWIS, JEFFREY E.
DISCIPLINE LAW **EDUCATION** Duke Univ, BA, JD. **CAREER** Dean emer, Univ Fla, 88-96; prof, Univ Fla, 72-; dean to assoc dean, 82-96; instr, Univ Akron, 70-72; ch, ABA Accreditation Comt, 96-; ch, Planning Comt, Asn Amer Law Schools, 95 Workshop for New Teachers; past ch, Amer Bar Asn Spec Comt For Law Sch Study; past ch, ABA/AALS Comn on the Financing of Legal Educ; vis prof, Escuela Libre de Derecho, Mexico City and Fachbereich Rechtswissenschaft, Johann Wolfgang Goethe-Univ, Frankfurt, Ger. **HONORS AND AWARDS** Ful sch, Cambridge Univ. **MEMBERSHIPS** Fla Fed Judicial Nominating Comn, 93-97; Fla Supreme Ct Select Comt on Fla Bd Bar Examiners, 96-97; Law Sch Admission Coun Finance Comt, 88-90; Fla Bar Comt on Professionalism, 87-90; AALS Accreditation Comt, 84-86; ABA/AALS Accreditation Site Evaluation Teams, 82-; Ohio Bar; Omicron Delta Kappa; Phi Kappa Phi. **CONTACT ADDRESS** School of Law, Univ of Florida, PO Box 117625, Gainesville, FL, 32611-7625. **EMAIL** lewis@law.ufl.edu

LEWIS, LLOYD ALEXANDER, JR.
PERSONAL Born 11/12/1947, Washington, DC, s **DISCIPLINE** THEOLOGY **EDUCATION** Trinity College, AB, 1969; Virginia Theological Seminary, MDiv, 1972; Yale University, MA, 1975, MPhil, 1981, PhD, 1985. **CAREER** St George's Church, curate, 1972-74; General Theological Seminary, tutor, 1977, visiting professor, 1989; Virginia Theological Seminary, assistant professor of the New Testament, 1978-86, associate professor of New Testament, 1986-91; GEORGE MERCER SCHOOL OF THEOLOGY, DEAN, 1991-. **HONORS AND AWARDS** Virginia Theological Seminary, Honorary Doctorate in Divinity, 1992; Cathedral of the Incarnation, Canon Theologian, 1991; Rockefeller Doctoral Fellowship, Fellow, 1974-76. **MEMBERSHIPS** Society for the Study of Black Religion; Society of Biblical Literature; Programme for Theological Education, World Council of Churches, commissioner; Union of Black Episcopalians; Standing Liturgical Commission, The Episcopal Church, consultant. **SELECTED PUBLICATIONS** Author, "An African-American Appraisal of the Philemon Paul Onesimus Triangle," Stony the Road We Trod, 1991; author, "The Law Courts at Corinth: An Experiment in the Power of Baptism," Christ and His Communities, 1990. **CONTACT ADDRESS** George Mercer Sch of Theol, 65 4th St, Garden City, NY, 11530.

LEWIS, NEIL
DISCIPLINE PHILOSOPHY **EDUCATION** Univ Melbourne, BA; Univ Pittsburgh, PhD. **CAREER** Assoc prof. **RESEARCH** Medieval philosophy. **SELECTED PUBLICATIONS** Auth, William of Auvergne's Account of the Enuntiabile: Its Relations to Nominalism and the Doctrine of Eternal Truths, 95; Robert Grosseteste and the Church of Fathers, Brill, 97; Power and Contingency in Robert Grosseteste and Duns Scotus, Brill, 96; The First Recension of Robert Grosseteste's De libero arbitrio, Mediaeval Studies, 91. **CONTACT ADDRESS** Dept of Philosophy, Georgetown Univ, 37th and O St, Washington, DC, 20057.

LEWIS, PETER J.
PERSONAL Born 12/01/1966, Luton, England, m, 1996 **DISCIPLINE** PHILOSOPHY **EDUCATION** Oxford Univ, BA, 88; U C Irvine, MA, 92, PhD, 96. **CAREER** Texas Tech Univ, vis instr, vis asst prof, asst prof, 95-. **RESEARCH** Philo of Physics and science; epistemology. **SELECTED PUBLICATIONS** Auth, Quantum Mechanics, Orthogonality and Count-

ing, Brit Jour for Philo of Science, 97; GRW and the Tails Problem, Topoi, 95; Quantum Mechanics and Ontology, Kriterion, 93. **CONTACT ADDRESS** Dept of Philosophy, Texas Tech Univ, Box 43092, Lubbock, TX, 79409-3092. **EMAIL** plewis@ttacs.ttu.edu

LEWIS, RANDY LYNN
PERSONAL Born 07/02/1947, Brownfield, TX, m, 1975 **DISCIPLINE** PHILOSOPHY **EDUCATION** Tex Tech Univ, BA, 69; Univ Tex, Austin, PhD(philos), 75. **CAREER** Instr philos, Tex Tech Univ, 70-71 and Univ Tex, Asutin, 75-76; asst prof, Tex Tech Univ, 76-77; ASST PROF PHILOS, UNIV TEX, AUSTIN, 77-80. **MEMBERSHIPS** Western Am Philos Asn. **RESEARCH** History of modern philosophy; analytic philosophy; Marxism. **SELECTED PUBLICATIONS** Auth, Perception: a representative theory, J Interdisciplinary Study Mind, 3/78. **CONTACT ADDRESS** Univ Texas, 5812 Blythewood Dr, Austin, TX, 78745.

LEWIS, WILLIAM A., JR.
PERSONAL Born 08/16/1946, Philadelphia, PA, m **DISCIPLINE** LAW **EDUCATION** Amer Univ, 1967-68; Susquehanna Univ, BA 1968; Boston Univ Law School, JD 1972. **CAREER** City of Philadelphia PA, asst dist atty 1972-75; US Civil Rights Commission, Attorney 1975-80, dir cong lia div 1980-85, dir congressional & community relations div 1985-86, acting asst staff dir for congressional & public affairs 1987, counsel senate judiciary committee 1987-; Senate Judiciary Committee, Washington, DC, counsel, 1987-89; Equal Employment Opportunity Comm, Washington, DC, supervisory atty, 1989-92; Office of Admin and Mgt, US Dept of Energy, exec asst to dir, 1992-94; Office of Science Education Programs, director, 1994-96; Office of Employee Concerns, 1996-. **HONORS AND AWARDS** Legal Defense Fund Scholarship NAACP 1971-72. **MEMBERSHIPS** Pres, Blacks in Govt US Civil Rights Comm 1977-80; exec comm Susquehanna Univ Alumni Assoc 1980-83, 2nd vice pres 1987, pres, 1988-90; mem PA Bar Assoc 1972-, Eastern Dist Court PA 1974-; del Legal Rights & Justice Task Force White House Conf on Youth Estes Park Co 1970; pres Susquehanna Univ Alumni Assoc 1988-91; board of directors, Susquehanna Univ, 1988-. **SELECTED PUBLICATIONS** "Black Lawyer in Private Practice" Harvard Law School Bulletin 1971. **CONTACT ADDRESS** Office of Employee Concerns, US Dept of Energy, Washington, DC, 20585.

LEYERLE, BLAKE
PERSONAL Born 08/16/1960, Boston, MA, s **DISCIPLINE** HISTORY OF CHRISTIANITY **EDUCATION** Duke Univ, PhD 91. **CAREER** Univ Notre Dame, asst prof, assoc prof, 91 to 98-. **MEMBERSHIPS** NAPS; AAR. **RESEARCH** Social Hist of Early Christianity; John Chrysostom; Pilgrimage; Monasticism. **SELECTED PUBLICATIONS** Auth, Meal Customs in the Greco-Roman World, Passover and Easter: The Liturgical Structuring of a Sacred Season, eds, Paul Bradshaw, Lawrence A. Hoffman, Univ Notre dame Press, forthcoming; Appealing to Children, The Jour of Early Christian Studies, 97; auth, Landscape as Cartography in Early Christian Pilgrimage Narratives, Jour of Amer Acad Relig, 96; auth, Clement of Alexandria on the Importance of Table Etiquette, The Jour of Early Christian Studies, 95; auth, John Chrysostom on Almsgiving and the Use of Money, Harv Theol Rev, 94; auth, John Chrysostom on the Gaze, The Jour of Early Christian Studies, 93. **CONTACT ADDRESS** Dept of Theology, Univ of Notre Dame, 327 O'Shaughnessy Hall, Notre Dame, IN, 46556. **EMAIL** Leyerle@nd.edu

LI, CHENYANG
PERSONAL China, m, 2 children **DISCIPLINE** PHILOSOPHY **EDUCATION** Univ Conn, PhD. **CAREER** Assoc prof, Monmouth Col. **HONORS AND AWARDS** Best Diss Essay Award, Philo Ed Soc, 93. **MEMBERSHIPS** Asn Chinese Philosophers in Am; Amer Philos Assoc **RESEARCH** Comparative philosophy, metaphysics, ethics. **SELECTED PUBLICATIONS** Auth, "What-being," Int Philos Q, 93; "Natural Kinds," Rev of Metaphysics, 93; "Mind-Body Identity Revised," Philos: Philos Q Israel, 94; "Confucian Concept of Jen and the Feminist Ethics of Care," Hypatia, 94; "How Can One Be A Taoist-Buddhist-Confucian," Int Rev Chinese Rel & Philos, 96; "Shifting Perspectives," Philos E & W, 97; "Confucian Value and Democratic Value," J of Value Inquiry, 97; "Tao Encounters the West," SUNY, 99. **CONTACT ADDRESS** 700 E Broadway, Monmouth, IL, 61462. **EMAIL** chenyang@monm.edu

LICHTENBERT, ROBERT H.
PERSONAL Born 12/26/1945, Chicago, IL, m, 1972, 2 children **DISCIPLINE** PHILOSOPHY **EDUCATION** DePaul Univ, BA, 68; Tulane Univ, MA, 70, PhD, 75. **CAREER** Adj prof, twelve col. **HONORS AND AWARDS** Several articles in newspapers on his journal, The Meaning of Life. **MEMBERSHIPS** APA; Asn for the Develop of the Philos Teaching, pres, 91- . **RESEARCH** The meaning of life; personal philosophy in daily life; aesthetics; teaching philosophy. **SELECTED PUBLICATIONS** Auth, "Motivating Students in Philos," 93; "Developing My Philosophy Teaching," 94; "The Mystery of Getting the Point Across," 95; "Philosophical Journals," 96; J for the Develop Philos Teaching; "A Kantian Indecent Proposal," 95; "Economic Determinism in Zola's Germinal," forthcoming; Soc for the Philos Study of the Contemp Visual Arts Rev; "The Meaning of Life," 88- . **CONTACT ADDRESS** 1823 W Barry Ave, Chicago, IL, 60657.

LIDZ, JOEL W.
PERSONAL Born 03/17/1952, Wilkes-Barre, PA **DISCIPLINE** PHILOSOPHY **EDUCATION** Penn State, B Phil, 74, MA, 75; Tulane Univ, PhD, 79. **CAREER** Adj prof, 87-, Bentley Col, Waltham, MA. **MEMBERSHIPS** APA. **RESEARCH** Plato; ethics; affirmative action. **SELECTED PUBLICATIONS** Ed, Philosophy, Being and the Good, Univ Press Am, 83; auth, Reflections on and in Plato's Cave, Interpretation, vol 21, 93/94; auth, Medicine as Metaphor in Plato, J of Med & Philos, vol 19, 94; auth, 12 Angry Men, Tchng Philos, vol 18, 95. **CONTACT ADDRESS** 234 Marlborough St, Boston, MA, 02116. **EMAIL** rascalj@aol.com

LIEBERMAN, JETHRO K.
PERSONAL Born 10-23/1943, Washington, DC, m, 1990, 2 children **DISCIPLINE** LAW **EDUCATION** Yale Univ, BA, 64; Harvard Univ, JD, 67; Columbia Univ, PhD, 95. **CAREER** Lieut, Judge Advocate General's Corps, US Navy, 68-71; assoc, Arent Fox Kintner Plotkin & Kahn, 71-72; vice pres, gen counsel & dir, Stein & Day Publ, 72-73; legal affairs ed, Business Week, 73-82; vice pres and dir of publ, Center for Public Res, 82-85; vis assoc prof, Fordham Law Sch, 83-85; prof law, dir of Writing Program, NY Law Sch, 85- ;adj prof polit sci, Columbia Univ, 98- . **HONORS AND AWARDS** Silver Gavel Award, ABA, 82, 88. **MEMBERSHIPS** ABA; Ny State Bar Asn; Law and Soc Asn; Am Polit Sci Asn; Typophiles. **RESEARCH** Constitutionalism; specialization and expertise; theory of harm. **SELECTED PUBLICATIONS** Auth, The Tyranny of the Experts: How Professionals and Specialists are Closing the Open Society, Walker, 70; auth, Milestones! 200 Years of American Law, West, 76; auth, Crisis at the Bar: Lawyers' Unethical Ethics and What To Do About It, Norton, 78; auth, The Litigious Society, Basic, 81; coauth, The Lawyer's Guide to Writing Well, McGraw-Hill, 89; auth, The Evolving Constitution: How the Supreme Court Has Ruled on Issues from Abortion to Zoning, Random, 92, rev ed Univ Calif, 99. **CONTACT ADDRESS** New York Law Sch, 57 Worth St, New York, NY, 10013. **EMAIL** JLieberman@nyls.edu

LIEBERT, ELIZABETH
PERSONAL Born 07/28/1944, Seattle, WA, s **DISCIPLINE** RELIGION AND PERSONALITY **EDUCATION** Vanderbilt Univ, PhD, 86. **CAREER** Prof spiritual life and dir christ spirituality, San Francisco Theol Sem, 87-; Grad Theol Union. **MEMBERSHIPS** Amer Acad of Relig; Cath Theol Soc of Amer; Spiritual Dir Intl. **RESEARCH** Spiritual care of women; Spiritual exercises of Ignatius of Loyola; Discernment. **SELECTED PUBLICATIONS** Auth, Accompaniment in Ministry: Supervision as Spiritual Formation, Jour of Supervision in Training in Ministry, 97; auth, Linking Faith and Justice: Remarks on the Occasion of Installation, Christ Spirituality Bull, 97, Pastoral Psychol, 46, 207-212, 98; chap, Coming Home to Themselves: Women's Spiritual Care, Through the Eyes of Women: Insights for Pastoral Care, Fortress Press, 96; co-auth, The Spirituality of the Teacher, The Way Suppl, 95; auth, The Thinking Heart: Developmental Dynamics in Etty Hillesum's Diaries, Pastoral Psychol, 95; auth, The Eighteenth Annotation of the Spiritual Exercises: A Developmental Perspective and Contemporary Adaptations of the Eighteenth Annotation, A Symposium: Ignatian Spirituality: Summary of Proceedings, Loyola House, 94. **CONTACT ADDRESS** 2 Kensington Rd., San Anselmo, CA, 94960. **EMAIL** eliebert@sfts.edu

LIECHTY, DANIEL
PERSONAL Born 05/02/1954, Beatrice, NE, m, 1996, 1 child **DISCIPLINE** THEOLOGY **EDUCATION** Univ Vienna, Austria, PhD, 83; Grad Theol Found, DMin, 94. **CAREER** Group specialist, Inst Penn Hospital, 90-94; psychosocial coordr, Montgomery Hospital Hospice Prog, 95-. **MEMBERSHIPS** Asn Death Educ & Coun; Ernest Becker Found; Nat Asn Soc Workers; Acad Certified Soc Workers; Nat Coun Hospice Professionals; Am Acad Relig. **RESEARCH** Values in medicine; death and dying; effects of cultural beliefs on behavior. **SELECTED PUBLICATIONS** Auth, Abstracts of the Complete Writings of Ernest Becker, 96; Transference and Transcendence, 95; Early Anabaptist Spirituality, 94; Sabbatarianism in the Sixteenth Century, 92; Theology in Post Liberal Perspective, 90; Andreas Fischer & the Sabbatarian Anabaptists, 88. **CONTACT ADDRESS** Dept of Pastoral Counseling, Montgomery Hospital, 334 Sagamore Rd., Havertown, PA, 19083. **EMAIL** liechtyd@delconet.com

LIENHARD, JOSEPH T.
DISCIPLINE HISTORICAL THEOLOGY **EDUCATION** Fordham Univ, BA, MA,; Woodstock Univ, PhL, BD, STM; Habil, Freiburg ThD. **CAREER** Asst ch, grad stud; prof, 90, Fordham Univ. **RESEARCH** Augustine's late works. **SELECTED PUBLICATIONS** Auth, The Bible, the Church, and Authority: The Canon of the Christian Bible, Hist and Theol, Collegeville, 95; transl, Gospel according to Luke, Origen: Homilies on Luke; Fragments on Luke, Wash, 96. **CONTACT ADDRESS** Dept of Relig, Fordham Univ, 113 W 60th St, New York, NY, 10023.

LIGHTNER, ROBERT P.
PERSONAL Born 04/04/1931, Cleona, PA, m, 1952, 3 children **DISCIPLINE** THEOLOGY, MODERN HISTORY **EDUCATION** Baptist Bible Col, ThB, 55; Dallas Theol Sem, ThM, 59, ThD, 64; Southern Methodist Univ, MLA, 72. **CAREER** Instr Bible & Theol, 59-61, from Asst Prof to Assoc Prof Systematic Theol, Baptist Bible Sem, 63-68, Dept Chmn, 63-66; from Asst Prof to Prof Systematic Theol, 68-98, Adjunct Prof, Dallas Theol Sem, 98-. **HONORS AND AWARDS** Graduated with honors from Dallas Theol Sem., Started churches in NY and AR; Pastor and Interim Pastor in NY, PA, AR, OK, LA, and TX; mission trips to Paraguay, Venezuela, and Peru. **MEMBERSHIPS** Grace Evangelical Soc; Conservative Theol Soc; Pre-Trib Study Group. **RESEARCH** Pre-millennial, A-millennial, and post-millennial theology. **SELECTED PUBLICATIONS** Auth, The Toungues Tied, Speaking in Tongues and Divine Healing; The Death Christ Died: A Case for Unlimited Atonement; Prophecy in the Ring; Truth for the Good Life; James: Apostle of Practical Christianity; The God of the Bible; The Saviour and the Scriptures; Triumph though Tragedy; Neo-Liberalism; Neo-Evangelicalism Today; Church-Union: A Layman's Guide; The God of the Bible and other gods; Last Days Handbook; author of numerous other publications and articles. **CONTACT ADDRESS** 324 Clear Springs Dr, Mesquite, TX, 75150-0000.

LIGHTSTONE, JACK
DISCIPLINE RELIGION **EDUCATION** Brown Univ, PhD, 77. **CAREER** Prof. **RESEARCH** Literature of Ancient Judaism, contemporary North American Judaism. **SELECTED PUBLICATIONS** Auth, The Commerce of the Sacred: Mediation of the Divine among the Jews in the Greco-Roman Diaspora, Scholars Press, 84; Society, the Sacred and Scripture in Ancient Judaism: a Sociology of Knowledge, Wilfrid Laurier UP, 94; Ritual and Ethnic Identity: A Comparative Study of the Social Meaning of Liturgical Ritual in Canadian Synagogues, Laurier UP, 95; Form, Formularies and Meaning in the Babylonian Talmud: The Case of b. Bekorot 2a-b, New Approaches to the Study of Ancient Judaism, Vol 6, Scholars Press, 95; Ancient Jewish Perceptions of History: An Anthropological Approach, Under History's Canopy, Univ Toronto Press, 95; "The Institutionalization of the Rabbinic Academy and the Redaction of the Babylonian Talmud," Stud in Rel, 93; "The Rhetoric of the Mishnah and the Babylonian Talmud: From Rabbinic Priestly Scribes to Scholastic Rabbis," Hist Reflections, 95. **CONTACT ADDRESS** Dept of Rel, Concordia Univ, Montreal, 1455 de Maisonneuve W, Montreal, PQ, H3G 1M8.

LILLIE, BETTY JANE
PERSONAL Born 04/11/1926, Cincinnati, OH **DISCIPLINE** BIBLICAL STUDIES **EDUCATION** Col of Mt. St. Joseph, BSEd, 55, BA 61; Providence Col, MA Theology, 67, MA Biblical Studies, 75; Hebrew Union Col, PhD, 82. **CAREER** Fac, Athenaeum of OH, 82-; instr, Providence Col, 79-86; Univ of Cincinnati, 84-98; Col of Mt. St. Joseph, 80. **HONORS AND AWARDS** Lifetime Achievement Award, ABI, 97 **MEMBERSHIPS** Cathol Biblical Asn; Soc for Biblical Lit; Biblical Archaeology Soc; Eastern Great Lakes Biblical Soc; Coun on the Study of Religion; OH Humanities Coun. **RESEARCH** Biblical Studies; Biblical Archaeology; Religious Studies. **SELECTED PUBLICATIONS** Auth, A History of the Scholarship on the Wisdom of Solomon from the Nineteenth Century to Our Time. **CONTACT ADDRESS** 2704 Cypress Way, No 3, Cincinnati, OH, 45212-1773.

LIMBURG, JAMES
PERSONAL Born 03/02/1935, Redwood Falls, MN, m, 1957, 4 children **DISCIPLINE** RELIGION **EDUCATION** Luther Col, BA, 56; Luther Theol Sem, BD, 61; Union Theol Sem, Va, ThM, 62, PhD, 69. **CAREER** Teacher, High Sch, Minn, 56-57; prof relig, Augustana Col, SDak, 62-78; Prof Old Testament, Luther Sem, 78- **HONORS AND AWARDS** Distinguished Service Award, Luther Col, 78. **MEMBERSHIPS** Soc Bibl Lit; Cath Bibl Soc. **RESEARCH** Old Testament. **SELECTED PUBLICATIONS** Auth, The Prophets and the Powerless, John Knox, 77; The Old Testament for US, Augsburg, 82; Old Stories for a New Time, John Knox, 83; Psalms for Sojourners, Augsburg, 86; Hosea-Micah, in Interpretation: A Bible Commentary, John Knox, 88; Jonah: A Commentary, in The Old Testament Library, Westminster/John Knox, 93. **CONTACT ADDRESS** Dept of Bible, Luther Sem, 2481 Como Ave, Saint Paul, MN, 55108-1445. **EMAIL** jlimburg@luthersem.edu

LIMPER, PETER FREDERICK
PERSONAL Born 06/26/1939, Chicago, IL **DISCIPLINE** PHILOSOPHY **EDUCATION** Yale Univ, BA, 61, MA, 65, PhD, 75. **CAREER** Asst prof philos, Calif State Univ, Hayward, 66-71; vis instr philos, Bowdoin Col, 74-75; asst prof, 77-80, assoc prof philos, 80-91, prof philos, 91-, Dean of Arts, 93-, Christian Brothers Univ, 80-. **MEMBERSHIPS** Am Philos Asn; Soc Philos & Tech; AAAS. **RESEARCH** Process philosophy; American philosophy; science, technology and values. **SELECTED PUBLICATIONS** Auth, Process, Creativity, and Technology: Reflections on The Uncertain Phoenix, Process Stud, 86; Technology and Value: A Process Perspective, Contemp Philos, 89; Process Themes in Frederick Ferre's Philosophy of Technology, Philos and Tech, Kluwer Acad Publ, 90;

Albert Borgmann and John Dewey on Everyday Technology, Research in Philos and Tech, JAI Press, 94; Of Algorithms and Apple Pie: A Pragmatist Critique of AI, Tx A&M Stud in Philos, Tx A&M Univ, 96. **CONTACT ADDRESS** Dept Religion and Philos, Christian Brothers Univ, 650 E Parkway S, Memphis, TN, 38104-5519. **EMAIL** plimper@cbu.edu

LINCOLN, BRUCE
PERSONAL Born 03/05/1948, Philadelphia, PA, m, 1971, 2 children **DISCIPLINE** HISTORY OF RELIGIONS **EDUCATION** Haverford Col, BA, 70; Univ Chicago, MA, 73, PhD, 76. **CAREER** Asst prof Humanities, 76-79, assoc prof, 79-86, prof Comparative Studies in Discourse & Soc, 86-94, Univ Minn; PROF HISTORY OF RELIGIOUS & ASSOC MEMBER DEPT ANTHROP & CLASSICS, CTR FOR MIDDLE EASTERN STUDIES, COMM ANCIENT MEDITERRANEAN WORLD, UNIV CHICAGO, 94-; vis prof, Univ Siena, 84-85, Uppsala Univ, 85, Novosibrisk Univ, 91, Univ Copenhagen, 98; Guggenheim fel, 82-83; Scholar of the Col, Univ Minn, 90-93. **HONORS AND AWARDS** ACLS Book Award, 81. **RESEARCH** Religion & other ideological systems; Discourse and the construction of social borders and hierarchies; Politics of myth, ritual, and cosmatogy. **SELECTED PUBLICATIONS** Priest, Warriors, and Cattle: A Study in the Ecology of Religions, Univ Cal Press, 81; Emergin from the Chrylasis: Studies in Rituals of Women's Initiation, Harvard Univ Press, 81; Myth, Cosmos, and Society: Indo-European Themes of Creation and Destructions, Harvard Univ Press, 86; Discourse and the Construction of Society: Comparative Studies of Myth, Ritual, and Classification, Oxford Univ Press, 89; Death, Warm and Sacrifice: Studies in Ideology and Practice, Univ Chicago Press, 91; Authority: Construction and Corrosion, Univ Chicago Press, 94. **CONTACT ADDRESS** Swift Hall, Univ of Chicago, 1025 E 58th St, Chicago, IL, 60637. **EMAIL** blincoln@midway.uchicago.edu

LINCOLN, C. ERIC
PERSONAL Born 06/23/1924, Athens, AL, m **DISCIPLINE** RELIGIOUS STUDIES **EDUCATION** LeMoyne Coll, AB 1947; Fisk Univ, AM 1954; Univ of Chicago, BD 1956; Boston U, MEd, PhD 1960; Carleton Coll, LLD 1968; St Michael's Coll, LHD 1970. **CAREER** Duke Univ, prof of religion 1976-; Fisk Univ, prof & chmn 1973-76; Union Theol Sem, prof 1967-73; Portland State Univ, prof 1965-67; Clark Coll, prof 1954-65; Dartmouth Coll, lectr 1962-63; Vassar Coll, adj prof 1969-70; State Univ of NY, visiting prof 1970-72; Queens Coll, visiting prof 1972; Vanderbilt Univ, adj prof 1973-76; Change Magazine, consultant; Rev of Religious Research Soc, assoc editor for scientific study of religion. **HONORS AND AWARDS** Fellow Amer Acad of Arts & Sciences; Lilly Ednowment Grant; author of The Black Church Since Frazier 1974, The Black Experience in Religion 1974, A Profile of Martin Luther King Jr 1969, The Black Americans 1969, Is Anybody Listening? 1968, Sounds of the Struggle 1967, The Negro Pilgrimage in America 1967, My Face is Black 1964, The Black Muslims in America 1961; co-author of A Pictorial History of the Negro in America 1968; Lillian Smith Book Award, 1989, for first novel, The Avenue, Clayton City; author, This Road Since Freedom, poetry, 1989; author, The Black Church in the African American Experience, 1990-; William R Kenan, Jr Distinguished Professor, 1991; Teacher of the Year, Duke Univ; 11 hon degrees. **MEMBERSHIPS** Amer Sociol Assn; Authors League of Amer; founding pres, emeritus, Black Acad of Arts & Letters; NY Acad of Arts & Scis; Soc for Study of Black Religion; American Academy of Arts asnd Sciences; 32 Degree Mason; life member, NAACP; life member, Kappa Alpha Psi; Boule, Sigma Pi Phi; Fellowship of Southern Writers. **SELECTED PUBLICATIONS** Co-author, The Black Church in the African-American Experience, 1991; author, Coming through the Fire: Surviving Race and Place in America, 1996; Hymnodist; hymns appear in "United Methodist Hymnal," "Songs of Zion, (UMC)," "Lift Every Voice, (Episopalian)," etc. **CONTACT ADDRESS** Dept of Religion, Duke Univ, Durham, NC, 27706.

LINCOURT, JOHN M.
DISCIPLINE BIOMEDICAL ETHICS, AMERICAN PHILOSOPHY, MEDIEVAL PHILOSOPHY **EDUCATION** St Anselm Col, BA, 63; Niagara Univ, MA, 64; SUNY, Buffalo, PhD, 72. **CAREER** Prof Philos, Bonnie E Cone Distinguished Prof Tchg, dir, Ctr for Prof and Appl Ethics, Univ NC, Charlotte. **HONORS AND AWARDS** John Huske Anderson Award, NC Med Soc; Nations Bank Award for Excellence in Tchg; Case Prof of the Yr for NC. **RESEARCH** Anselm of Canterbury; Charles S. Peirce's epistemology and its rel to areas in the Soc Sci(s). **SELECTED PUBLICATIONS** Auth, Costs of Care: Two Vexing Cases in Health Care Ethics, Strategic Management of Health Care Organizations by Duncan, Ginter & Swayne, Blackwell Publ, 94; Case # 12: The Costs of Care, in Instr's Manual, 95; Ethics Without a Net: A Case Workbook in Bioethics, 2nd ed, Kendall/Hunt, 95. **CONTACT ADDRESS** Univ N. Carolina, Charlotte, Charlotte, NC, 28223-0001. **EMAIL** jmlincou@email.uncc.edu

LIND, MILLARD C.
PERSONAL Born 10/10/1918, Bakersfield, CA, m, 1943, 7 children **DISCIPLINE** BIBLICAL THEOLOGY, OLD TESTAMENT **EDUCATION** Goshen Col, BA, 42; Goshen Bibl Se, BD, 47; Pittsburgh-Xenia Theol Sem, ThM, 55; Pittsburgh Theol Sem, ThD(Old Testament), 63. **CAREER** Pastor, Hopewell Mennonite Church, Kouts, Ind, 43-47; writer, Mennonite Publ House, Pa, 47-60, ed mag, 55-60; actg dean Assoc Mennonite Bibl Sem, 70-71, PROF OLD TESTAMENT, GOSHEN BIBL SEM, 60-, Am Asn Theol Schs fac fel, 68-69. **MEMBERSHIPS** Am Schs Orient Res; Soc Bibl Lit. **RESEARCH** Warfare in ancient Israel; worship in the Old Testament; theology of politics in the Old Testament. **SELECTED PUBLICATIONS** Auth, Theology of the Old Testament, Vol 1--Jhwh Election and Obligation, Cath Bibl Quart, Vol 0055, 93; Theology of the Old Testament, Vol 2--Israel Path With Jhwh, Cath Bibl Quart, Vol 0056, 94; The Patriarchate in Israel in Deuteronomy, Cath Bibl Quart, Vol 0056, 94; Rudiments of Old Testament Hermeneutics, Cath Bibl Quart, Vol 0057, 95. **CONTACT ADDRESS** Associated Mennonite Biblical Sem, 1123 S 8th St, Elkhart, IN, 46517.

LINDBERG, CARTER HARRY
PERSONAL Born 11/23/1937, Berwyn, IL, m, 1960, 3 children **DISCIPLINE** THEOLOGY, HISTORY OF CHRISTIAN THOUGHT **EDUCATION** Augustana Col, AB, 59; Lutheran Sch Theol, BD, 62; Univ Iowa, PhD, 65. **CAREER** Asst prof relig, Susquehanna Univ, 65-67; asst prof theol, Col Holy Cross, 67-72; asst prof, 72-79, assoc prof, 80-84, PROF CHURCH HIST & THEOL, SCH THEOL, BOSTON UNIV, 85-. **MEMBERSHIPS** Am Soc Reformation Res; Am Soc, Church Hist; Soc 16th Century Studies (vpres, 77); Luther-Ges. **RESEARCH** Luther; ethics; historical theology in the 16th and 19th century. **SELECTED PUBLICATIONS** Auth, Martin Luther: Copernican Revolution or Ecumenical Bridge?, Una Sancta, Vol 24, No 1; Luther and Feuerbach, In:Sixteenth Century Essays and Studies, St Louis, 70; Prierias and his Significance for Luther's Development, Sixteenth Century J, 72; Luther's Theology of the Demonic, In: Disguises of the Demonic, Asn Press, 75; Theology and Politics: Luther the Radical and Muntzer the Reactionary, Encounter, 76; Luther's Views on Papal Authority, Andover Newton Quart, 77; Karlstadt, Luther and the Origins of Protestant Poor Relief, Church Hist, 77; Conflicting Models of Ministry, Concordia Theol Quart, 77; auth, The Third Reformation?, Macon: Mercer Univ Press, 83; ed and contrib, Piety, Politics, and Ethics: Reformation Studies in Honor of George W. Forell, Kirksville: Sixteenth Century J Pubs, 84; auth, Martin Luther, Nashville: United Methodist Pub House, 88; Korean Tr, Seoul: Concordia, 90; Beyond Charity: Reformation Initiatives for the Poor, Minneapolis: Fortress Press, 93; coauth, with Emily Albu Hanawalt, Through the Eye of the Needle: Judeo-Christian Contributions to Social Welfare, Kirksville: Thomas Jefferson Univ Press, 94; auth, The European Reformations, Oxford: Blackwell, 96; coauth, with Howard C. Kee, et al, Christianity: A Social and Cultural History, 2nd ed, Prentice-Hall, 98; over 60 articles and book chapters about reformation history and theology. **CONTACT ADDRESS** Sch of Theol, Boston Univ, 745 Commonwealth Ave, Boston, MA, 02215-1401. **EMAIL** clindber@bu.edu

LINDBERG, JORDAN JOHN
PERSONAL Born 04/21/1969, Traverse City, MI, m, 1993 **DISCIPLINE** PHILOSOPHY **EDUCATION** Albion Coll, BA, 91; Mich State Univ, MA, 93; Univ of Missouri, PhD, 97. **CAREER** Asst Prof, Philo Religion & Environmental Studies, 97-, Central Mich Univ. **HONORS AND AWARDS** Superior Grad Achievement Awd. **MEMBERSHIPS** APA, CSPA. **RESEARCH** Epistemology, 20th century Anglo-American philosophy, Environmental Philosophy. **CONTACT ADDRESS** Dept of Philosophy & Religion, Central Michigan Univ, 131 Anspach Hall, Mt. Pleasant, MI, 48858. **EMAIL** wildtrout@yahoo.com

LINDER, ROBERT DEAN
PERSONAL Born 10/06/1934, Salina, KS, m, 1957, 4 children **DISCIPLINE** EUROPEAN HISTORY, HISTORY OF CHRISTIANITY **EDUCATION** Emporia State Univ, BS, 56; Cent Baptist Theol Sem, MDiv, MRE, 58, Univ IA, MA, 60, PhD, 63. **CAREER** Instr western civilization, Univ IA, 58-61; asst prof hist, William Jewell Col, 63-65; from asst prof to assoc prof, 65-73, prof KS State Univ, 73-, Sr res fel, The Centre for the Study of Christianity, Macquerie Univ, Sydney, Australia, 95 , Ed, Fides et Historia, Conf Faith & Hist, 68-78, Mayor, Manhattan, KS, 71-72, 78-79; Dir, Relig Studies Prog, KS State Univ, 79-82. **HONORS AND AWARDS** KS State Univ Distinguished Tchg Award, 68; Phi Kappa Phi Outstanding Scholar, 1980; Sr Fac Award for Res Excellence, Inst for Soc & Behav Res, KS State Univ, 97. **MEMBERSHIPS** AHA; Am Soc Church Hist; Am Soc Reformation Res (secy, 71-79); Renaissance Soc Am; Rocky Mountain Soc Sci Asn; Conf Faith & Hist. **RESEARCH** Reformation and Renaissance hist; hist of Christianity; Australian relig hist. **SELECTED PUBLICATIONS** Auth, The Political Ideas of Pierre Viret, Droz, Geneva, 64; co-ed, Protest and Politics: Christianity and Contemporary Politics, Attic, 68; coauth, Calvin and Calvinism: Sources of Democracy?, Heath, 70; ed, God and Caesar: Case Studies in the Relationship between Christianity and the State, Conf Faith & Hist, 71; co-ed, The Cross and the Flag, Creation House, 72; coauth, Politics and Christianity, InterVarsity, 73; co-ed, The Eerdman's Handbook to the History of Christianity, Eerdmans, 77; coauth, Twilight of the Saints: Biblical Christianity and Civil Religion in America, InterVarsity, 78; coauth, Civil Religion and the Presidency, Zonervan, 88; co-ed, The Dictionary of Christianity in America, InterVarsity, 90; co-ed, The History of Christianity, Fortress, 90; co-ed, A Concise Dictionary of Christianity in America, InterVarsity, 95; auth, The People of God and the Great War: Australian Evangelicals in World War I, CSAC, 98. **CONTACT ADDRESS** Dept of Hist, Kansas State Univ, 208 Eisenhower Hall, Manhattan, KS, 66506-1002. **EMAIL** rdl@ksu.edu

LINDGREN, JOHN RALPH
PERSONAL Born 10/08/1933, Oak Park, IL, m, 1958, 5 children **DISCIPLINE** PHILOSOPHY **EDUCATION** Northwestern Univ, BS, 59; Marquette Univ, MA, 61, PhD(philos), 63. **CAREER** Teaching asst philos, Marquette Univ, 60-62; from instr to asst prof, Col Holy Cross, 62-65; asst prof, 65-69, assoc prof, 69-79, PROF PHILOS, LEHIGH UNIV, 79, CHMN DEPT, 73-, Vis scholar, Law Sch, Univ Pa, 77-78. **MEMBERSHIPS** Eastern Div Am Philos Asn; Philos and Pub Affairs; Conf Studies Polit Thought; Int Asn Philos Law and Social Philos. **RESEARCH** Philosophy of law; social philosophy; political economy. **SELECTED PUBLICATIONS** Auth, Peirce, Paradox, Praxis--the Image, the Conflict and the Law, Semiotica, Vol 0095, 93. **CONTACT ADDRESS** Dept of Philos, Lehigh Univ, Bethlehem, PA, 18015.

LINDQUIST, LARRY
DISCIPLINE RELIGION **EDUCATION** Trinity Intl Univ, BA; Trinity Evangel Divinity Sch, MA; Northern Ill Univ, DEd. **CAREER** Adj prof, Trinity Intl Univ; Moody Bible Inst; asst prof, Denver Sem, 98-. **RESEARCH** Youth and family ministries and educational ministry **SELECTED PUBLICATIONS** Auth, Reader's Guide; contrib auth, Reaching a Generation for Christ. **CONTACT ADDRESS** Denver Conservative Baptist Sem, PO Box 10000, Denver, CO, 80250.

LINDSEY, WILLIAM D.
PERSONAL Born 03/30/1950, Little Rock, AR **DISCIPLINE** RELIGIOUS STUDIES **EDUCATION** Loyola Univ, BA, 72; Univ St Michael's Col, Toronto School of Theol, MA, 80, PhD, 87; Tulane Univ, MA, 89. **CAREER** Asst prof and chemn, Theol Dept, Xavier Univ, 84-91; asst prof and chemn Theol Dept, Belmont Abbey Col, 91-93; independent scholar, 93- . **HONORS AND AWARDS** Fel, Loyola Univ, 68-72; Alpha Sigma Nu, 69; Phi Delta Pi, 76; C Douglas Jay award, Toronto School of Theol, 83; Charles Dana grant, 86; fel, Center for the Humanities, Oregon State Univ, 89; Bush Found Fac Develop Grant, 90; winning essay, Ctr for the Study of Relig and Am Culture Awards, 92. **MEMBERSHIPS** Am Acad Relig; Catholic Theol Soc of Am; Col Theol Soc. **RESEARCH** Social gospel movement; social ethics; development of conscience and ethical awareness. **SELECTED PUBLICATIONS** Auth, Ethics and Morality, Loyola Inst, 89; auth, Singing in A Strange Land: Praying and Acting with the Poor, Sheed & Ward, 91; auth, The Problem of Great Time: A Bakhtinian Ethics of Discourse, J of Relig, 93; auth, Richard Rorty: The Homelessness of Liberalism, The Ecumenist, 93; auth, James Joyce's The Dead, Eschatology and the Meaning of History, Toronto J of Theol, 95; auth, Shailer Mathews' Lives of Jesus: The Search for a Theological Foundation for the Social Gospel, SUNY, 96; auth, The AIDS Crisis and the Church: A Time to Heal, in Thatcher, ed, Christian Perspectives on Sexuality and Gender, Eerdmans, 96; auth, Prophetic Neopragmatism and the Double Intentionality of Religious Symbols: A Theological Response to Cornel West's Keeping Faith: Philosophy and Race in America, Toronto J of Theol, 97; auth, Crossing the Postmodern Divide: Some Implications for Academic Theology, Theol and Sexuality, 97. **CONTACT ADDRESS** 519 Ridgeway Dr, Little Rock, AR, 72205. **EMAIL** indsch19@idt.net

LINDT, GILLIAN
DISCIPLINE RELIGION **EDUCATION** London Univ, BS, 54, MA, 55, PhD, 65. **CAREER** Prof. **RESEARCH** Social theory; sociology of religion; comparative history of religion in America and Western Europe from the eighteenth century to the present. **SELECTED PUBLICATIONS** Auth, Moravians in Two Worlds: A Study of Changing Communities. **CONTACT ADDRESS** Dept of Religion, Columbia Col, New York, 2960 Broadway, New York, NY, 10027-6902. **EMAIL** gl9@columbia.edu

LINEBACK, RICHARD HAROLD
PERSONAL Born 06/05/1936, Cincinnati, OH, m, 1957, 2 children **DISCIPLINE** PHILOSOPHY **EDUCATION** Univ Cincinnati, BA, 58; Ind Univ, MA, 62, PhD, 63. **CAREER** Lectr philos, Ind Univ, 62-63; asst prof, Wichita State Univ, 63-65; from asst prof to assoc prof, 65-72, chmn dept, 68-72, prof philos, Bowling Green State Univ, 72-, Bowling Green State Univ grant computer applications in philos, 67-; ed, The Philosopher's Index, 67-; Nat Endowment for Humanities grants, 76, 77, 78 & 79. **MEMBERSHIPS** Am Philos Asn. **RESEARCH** Ethics; computers. **SELECTED PUBLICATIONS** Coauth, Encounter: An Introduction to Philosophy, Scott, 69; co-ed, International Directory of Philosophy, Philos Doc Ctr, 72, 74, 78 & 82. **CONTACT ADDRESS** Philosophers Information Ctr, 1616 E Wooster St, Bowling Green, OH, 43402.

LINEHAN, ELIZABETH ANN
PERSONAL Born 03/19/1940, Des Moines, IA **DISCIPLINE** PHILOSOPHY **EDUCATION** Mount St Agnes Col, BA, 64; Fordham Univ, MA, 70, PhD(Philos), 76. **CAREER** From instr to asst prof Philos, Spring Hill, Col, 73-76; asst prof Philos, St Joseph's Univ, 76-; chmn, Philosophy Dept, 83-92; 97. **MEMBERSHIPS** AAUP; Am Philos Asn; Hastings Ctr Soc, Ethics & Life Sci; Soc Women Philos. **RESEARCH** American philosophy; bio-medical ethics; aesthetics. **SELECTED PUBLICATIONS** Auth, Neo-cortical tests and personal death: A reply to Robert Veatch, Omega, 81-82; Ignorance, self-deception and moral accountability, J Value Inquiry; 80. **CONTACT ADDRESS** St. Joseph's Univ, 5600 City Ave, Philadelphia, PA, 19131-1376. **EMAIL** elinehan@sju.edu

LINENTHAL, EDWARD TABOR
PERSONAL Born 11/06/1947, Boston, MA, m, 1974, 1 child **DISCIPLINE** RELIGIOUS STUDIES, AMERICAN HISTORY **EDUCATION** Western Mich Univ, BA, 69; PACIFIC Sch Relig, MDiv, 73; Univ Calif, Santa Barbara, PhD(relig studies), 79. **CAREER** Lectr Am relig, Univ Calif, Santa Barbara, 78-79; ASST PROF RELIG STUDIES, UNIV WIS-OSHKOSH, 79-, asst ed bk rev sect, Relig Studies Rev, 81-. **MEMBERSHIPS** Am Soc Church Hist; Am Acad Relig. **RESEARCH** Religion and war; religion and American culture; history of religions. **SELECTED PUBLICATIONS** Auth, Iwo Jima--Monuments, Memories, and the American Hero, Rev(s) in Amer Hist, Vol 0021, 93; Committing History in Public, J Amer Hist, Vol 0081, 94; The Boundaries of Memory--the United States Holocaust Memorial Museum, Amer Quart, Vol 0046, 94; American Samurai--Myth, Imagination, and the Conduct of Battle in the 1st Marine Division, 1941-1951, J Amer Hist, Vol 0082, 95; Struggling With History and Memory, J Amer Hist, Vol 0082, 95; The A Bomb Controversy at the National Air and Space Museum, Historian, Vol 0057, 95; Remembering War the American Way, J Amer Hist, Vol 0083, 96; Responses to Glassberg,David 'Public History and the Study of Memory'--Problems and Promise in Public History, Public Historian, Vol 0019, 97. **CONTACT ADDRESS** Dept of Relig, Univ of Wis, 800 Algoma Blvd, Oshkosh, WI, 54901-8601.

LINGIS, ALPHONSO
DISCIPLINE PHILOSOPHY **EDUCATION** Loyola Univ, BA, 54; Cath Univ Louvain, Lic, 58, PhD, 61. **CAREER** From instr to assoc prof philos, Duquesne Univ, 60-66; assoc prof, 66-80, prof philos, PA State Univ, 80-. **MEMBERSHIPS** Soc Phenomenol & Existential Philos. **RESEARCH** Phenomenology and existentialist philos; hist of modern philos; ontology. **SELECTED PUBLICATIONS** Auth, Excesses: Eros and Culture, SUNY, 84; Libido: The French Existential Theories, Ind Univ, 85; Phenomenological Explanations, Martinus Nijhoff, 86; Deathbound Subjectivity, Ind Univ, 89; The Community of Those Who Have Nothing in Common, Ind Univ, 94; Abuses, Univ Calif, 94; Foreigh Bodies, Routledge, 94; Sensation: Intelligibility in Sensibility, NY Hum, 95; The Imperative, Ind Univ, 98; Dangerous Emotions, Univ Calif, 99. **CONTACT ADDRESS** Dept Philos, Pennsylvania State Univ, 240 Sparks Bldg, University Park, PA, 16802-5201.

LINGSWILER, ROBERT DAYTON
PERSONAL Born 06/05/1927, Buffalo, NY, m, 1948, 2 children **DISCIPLINE** PHILOSOPHY **EDUCATION** Heidelberg Col, AB, 49; Iliff Sch Theol, ThM, 52, ThD(philos relig), 64. **CAREER** Asst prof philos, SDak Sch Mines & Technol, 63-66; assoc prof, 66-77, Prof Philos & Chmn Dept, Baldwin-Wallace Col, 77- **MEMBERSHIPS** Am Philos Asn. **RESEARCH** Philosophy of religion and science; political philosophy; ethics. **CONTACT ADDRESS** 275 Eastland Rd, Berea, OH, 44017-2088. **EMAIL** rlingswi@bw.edu

LINKER, MAUREEN
PERSONAL Born 10/04/1963, New York, NY **DISCIPLINE** PHILOSOPHY **EDUCATION** CUNY, PhD, 96. **CAREER** Asst prof philos, Univ Mich, Dearborn, 96- . **HONORS AND AWARDS** Rackham Jr Fac fel, 97. **MEMBERSHIPS** APA; Soc for Anal Feminism. **RESEARCH** Epistemology; logic; feminist philosophy; philosophy of law. **CONTACT ADDRESS** Dept of Philosophy, Univ of Michigan, 4901 Evergreen Rd, Dearborn, MI, 48128. **EMAIL** mlinker@umich.edu

LINSENBARD, GAIL E.
PERSONAL Born 10/06/1959, Los Angeles, CA **DISCIPLINE** PHILOSOPHY **EDUCATION** Univ Colo Boulderm, PhD, 96. **CAREER** Asst prof, Mass Coll of Liberal Arts, 96-; asst adj prof, NY Univ. **HONORS AND AWARDS** Dean's Small Grant Award. **MEMBERSHIPS** Am Philos Asn; Soc for Women in Philos; Soc for Phenomenol and Existential Philos; N Am Sartre Soc; Simon de Beauvoir Circle. **RESEARCH** 19th and 20th Century Continental Philosophy; Human Rights; Ethics; Feminist Philosophy. **SELECTED PUBLICATIONS** Auth, Women's Rights as Human Rights, Women Rights as Human Rights: Activism and Social Change in Africa; An Investigation of Sartre's Notebooks for an Ethics, forthcoming. **CONTACT ADDRESS** 118 Water St #C, Williamstown, MA, 01267. **EMAIL** glinsenb@mcla.mass.edu

LINSS, WILHELM CAMILL
PERSONAL Born 03/21/1926, Erlangen, Germany, m, 1953, 3 children **DISCIPLINE** NEW TESTAMENT **EDUCATION** Univ Erlangen, BD, 50; Boston Univ, ThD(New Testament textual criticism), 55. **CAREER** Asst prof philos and Christianity, Gustavus Adolphus Col, 54-57; prof New Testament, Cent Lutheran Theol Sem, 57-67; dir admis, 68-78, registr, 68-70, PROF NEW TESTAMENT, LUTHERAN SCH THEOL CHICAGO, 67-, Res, Univ Munster, 63. **MEMBERSHIPS** Soc Bibl Lit. **RESEARCH** Textual criticism; New Testament theology; exegesis. **SELECTED PUBLICATIONS** Auth, Peter in Matthew--Discipleship, Diplomacy, and Dispraise, With an Assessment of Power and Privilege in the Petrine Office, J Bibl Lit, Vol 0113, 94. **CONTACT ADDRESS** Lutheran Sch of Theol, 1100 E 55th St, Chicago, IL, 60615.

LINTS, RICHARD
PERSONAL m, 3 children **DISCIPLINE** THEOLOGY, APOLOGETICS **EDUCATION** Westminster Col, BA; Univ Notre Dame, MA, PhD; Univ Chicago, AM. **CAREER** Instr, Trinity Col, Bristol, 84-86; Westminster Col, 82-83; sr tchg fel, Univ Notre Dame, 81; prof, Gordon-Conwell Theol Sem, 86-. **HONORS AND AWARDS** Grant, Ass Theol Sch(s) and Pew Charitable Trusts., Minister, Presbyterian Church in Am; pastor, Redeemer Presbyterian Church. **RESEARCH** Theological and cultural upheavals of the 1960's. **SELECTED PUBLICATIONS** Auth, The Fabric of Theology: A Prolegomena to Evangelical Theology, Eerdmans, 93. **CONTACT ADDRESS** Gordon-Conwell Theol Sem, 130 Essex St, South Hamilton, MA, 01982.

LIPMAN, MATTHEW
PERSONAL Born 08/24/1923, Vineland, NJ, 1 child **DISCIPLINE** PHILOSOPHY **EDUCATION** Columbia Univ, BS, 50, PhD, 54. **CAREER** From instr to prof philos, Columbia Univ, 54-72; Prof Philos, Montclair State Col, 72, Dir Inst Advan Philos Children, 74-, Instr contemp civilization, Columbia Col, 54-63; lectr philos, City Col New York, 53-66, adj assoc prof, 66-75; mem fac, Sarah Lawrence Col, 63-64; Am Coun Learned Soc grant-in-aid, 67; Nat Endowment Humanities grants, 70-73; Rockefeller grant, 78-82. **HONORS AND AWARDS** Matchette Prize, 55. **MEMBERSHIPS** Am Philos Asn; Am Soc Aesthetics; Soc Advan Am Philos. **RESEARCH** Philosophy for children; aesthetics; metaphysics. **SELECTED PUBLICATIONS** Ed & contribr, Contemporary Aesthetics, Allyn & Bacon, 73; auth, Harry Stottlemeier's Discovery, 74; co-ed, Instructional Manual to Accompany Harry Stottlemeier's Descovery, 75; auth, Lisa, 76; co-ed, Instructional Manuel to Accompany Lisa, 77; coauth, Philosophy in the Classroom, 77, & auth, Suki, 78, Inst Advan Philos Children; co-ed, Growing Up With Philosophy, Temple Univ 78. **CONTACT ADDRESS** Inst Advan Philos, Montclair State Univ, Upper Montclair, NJ, 07043. **EMAIL** lipman@saturn.montclair.edu

LIPPY, CHARLES
PERSONAL Born 12/02/1943, Binghamton, NY, s **DISCIPLINE** RELIGION **EDUCATION** Dickinson Col, BA, 65; Union Theol Sem, MDiv, 68; Princeton Univ, MA, 70, PhD, 72 **CAREER** Prof, Univ of TN, 94-pres; Asst Prof, Assoc Prof, Prof, 76-94, Clemson Univ; Visit Asst Prof, 74-75, Miami Univ; Asst Prof, 72-74, Oberlin Col; Visit Prof, 90-91, Emory Univ **HONORS AND AWARDS** Fulbright Scholar, India, 88; Summer Fel, Louisville Inst, 98; NEH Summer Stipends; NEH Summer Seminars **MEMBERSHIPS** Am Acad of Relig; Am Soc of Church Hist; Am Stud Assoc; Org of Am Historians; Soc for Scientific Study of Relig **RESEARCH** Religion in American Culture **SELECTED PUBLICATIONS** Coauth, The Evangelicals A Historical, Thematic and Biographical Guide, Greenwood Press, 99; Auth, Modern American Popular Religion A Critical Assessment and Annotated Bibliography, Greenwood Press, 96; Auth, Popular Religious Magazines of the United States, Greenwood Press, 94 **CONTACT ADDRESS** Dept of Philos and Relig, Univ of TN, 615 McCallie Ave, Chattanooga, TN, 37403. **EMAIL** charles-lippy@utc.edu

LISSKA, ANTHONY JOSEPH
PERSONAL Born 07/23/1940, Columbus, OH, m, 1968, 2 children **DISCIPLINE** PHILOSOPHY **EDUCATION** Providence Col, AB, 63; St S Stephen's Col, MA, 67; Ohio State Univ, PhD(philos), 71. **CAREER** Asst prof, 69-76, chmn dept, 73-78, assoc prof, 76-81, PROF PHILOS, DENISON UNIV, 81-, DEAN COL, 78-. **MEMBERSHIPS** Am Philos Asn; Am Cath Philos Asn; Soc Medieval and Renaissance Philos; Asn Am Cols. **RESEARCH** Medieval philosophy; history of perception; ethical naturalism. **SELECTED PUBLICATIONS** Auth, The Defense of Natural Law, Heythrop Journal-Quart Rev of Philos and Theol, Vol 0035, 94. **CONTACT ADDRESS** Dept of Philos, Denison Univ, 1 Denison University, Granville, OH, 43023-1359.

LIST, PETER C.
PERSONAL Born 10/22/1939, WI, m, 2 children **DISCIPLINE** PHILOSOPHY **EDUCATION** Mich St Univ, PhD,69. **CAREER** Instr, 67-69, ast prof, 69-75, assoc prof, 74-94, prof, 94-, Oregon St Univ. **HONORS AND AWARDS** Phi Kappa Phi, Recognition Award for Excellence in Tchg, Am Philos Asn, 95. **MEMBERSHIPS** APA; Int Soc for Environ Ethics; Soc for Philos Contemp World. **RESEARCH** Ethical issues in the natural resource sciences; public attitudes about nature; environmental ethics. **SELECTED PUBLICATIONS** Ed, Radical Environmentalism, Philosophy and Tactics, Wadworth, 93; "Some Philosophical Assessments of Environmental Disobedience," in Philosophy and the Natural Environment, Cambridge, 94; "The Land Ethic in American Forestry: Pinchot and Leopold," in The Idea of the Forest, Lang, 95; "Moving Toward an Expanded Land Management Ethic," in Nature and the Human Spirit, Venture, 96; "Leopoldian Forestry and the Ethical Acceptability of Forest Practices," in Defining Social Acceptability in Ecosystem Management: a Workshop Proceedings, USDA Forest Serv, 96 **CONTACT ADDRESS** Dept of Philosophy, Oregon State Univ, Corvallis, OR, 97332. **EMAIL** plist@orst.edu

LISZKA, JAMES
PERSONAL Born 03/18/1950, Pittsburgh, PA, m, 2 children **DISCIPLINE** PHILOSOPHY **EDUCATION** Indiana Univ of Pa, BS, 72; Univ of So Carolina, MA, 74; New Sch for Soc Res, PhD, 78. **CAREER** Hum Fel, Scarborough Col, Univ Toronto, 85-86; Univ Alaska, Anchorage, 80- . **HONORS AND AWARDS** Teaching Excellence Award, 98. **MEMBERSHIPS** APA; Semiotic Soc of Am; Charles S. Peirce Soc. **RESEARCH** Ethics; aesthetics; semiotics. **SELECTED PUBLICATIONS** Auth, The Semiotic of Myth, Indiana, 90; auth, A General Introduction to the Semeiotic of Charles S. Peirce, Indiana, 96; auth, Moral Competence, Prentice-Hall, 99. **CONTACT ADDRESS** Dept of Philosophy, Univ of Alaska, Anchorage, 3211 Providence Dr, Anchorage, AL, 99508. **EMAIL** afjjl@uaa.alaska.edu

LITCH, MARY
DISCIPLINE PHILOSOPHY **EDUCATION** Univ Mass, PhD. **CAREER** Prof, Univ Ala Birmingham, 96-. **RESEARCH** Philosophy of artificial intelligence. **SELECTED PUBLICATIONS** Auth, Computation, Connectionism and Modelling the Mind, Philos Psychol 10, 97. **CONTACT ADDRESS** Dept of Philosophy, Univ of Alabama, Birmingham, 1400 University Blvd, Birmingham, AL, 35294-1150. **EMAIL** litch@uab.edu

LITTLE, DANIEL E.
PERSONAL Born 04/07/1949, Rock Island, IL, d, 2 children **DISCIPLINE** PHILOSOPHY **EDUCATION** Univ Ill, BA, BS, 71; Harvrd Univ, PhD, 77. **CAREER** Asst prof, Univ Wisc, Parkside, 76-79; vis assoc prof, Wellesley Col, 85-87; vis scholar, 89-91, assoc, 91-95, Ctr Int Aff, Harvard Univ; asst prof, 79-85, assoc prof, 85-92, prof, 92-96, chemn, dept philos and relig, 92-93, assoc dean fac, 93-96, Colgate Univ; vpres acad aff, Bucknell Univ, 96- . **HONORS AND AWARDS** Phi Beta Kappa; Woodrow Wilson Grad fel, 71-72; res grant NSF, 87; Soc sci res postdoctoral fel, MacArthur Found, 89-91. **MEMBERSHIPS** APA; Am Soc for Polit and Legal Philos; Asn Asian Stud; Int Asn Philos of Law and Social Philos; Int Devel Ethics Asn. **SELECTED PUBLICATIONS** Auth, The Scientific Marx, 86; auth, Understanding Peasant China: Case Studies in the Philosophy of Social Science, 89; auth, Varieties of Social Explanation: An Introduction to the Philosophy of Social Science, 91; auth, On the Reliability of Economic Models, 95; auth, Microfoundations Method and Causation: On the Philosophy of the Social Sciences, 98. **CONTACT ADDRESS** VPAA Marts Hall, Bucknell Univ, Lewisburg, PA, 17837.

LITTLE, JOSEPH W.
DISCIPLINE LAW **EDUCATION** Duke Univ, BSME; Worcester Polytech Inst, MSME; Univ Mich, JD. **CAREER** Prof; alumni res scholar; Univ Fla, 67-; vis prof, Monash Univ, Australia, Univ Auckland, New Zealand, Univ Natal, Univ Stellenbosch, S Africa, Peking Univ, China; past assoc, Sutherland, Asbill Brennan, Atlanta; fmr mayor/commnr, Gainesville City Comn. **HONORS AND AWARDS** Vis fel, Wolfson Col, Oxford, England. **MEMBERSHIPS** Michigan Bar; DC Bar; Ga Bar; Fla Bar; Amer Law Inst; Phi Beta Kappa; Sigma Xi. **RESEARCH** Local government law, workers' compensation, torts, US & Fla constitutional law. **SELECTED PUBLICATIONS** Coauth, Torts: The Civil Law of Reparation for Harm Done by Wrongful Act. **CONTACT ADDRESS** School of Law, Univ of Florida, PO Box 117625, Gainesville, FL, 32611-7625. **EMAIL** little@law.ufl.edu

LITTLEFIELD, NEIL OAKMAN
PERSONAL Born 02/12/1931, North Conway, NH, m, 1958, 3 children **DISCIPLINE** LAW **EDUCATION** Univ Maine, BS, 53; Boston Univ, LLB, 57; Univ Mich, LLM, 59, SJD, 61. **CAREER** Asst prof law, Sch Law, Creighton Univ, 59-61; from assoc prof to prof, Sch Law, Univ Conn, 61-70; PROF LAW, COL LAW, UNIV DENVER, 70-, DIR BUS PLANNING PROG, 71-, Vis prof, Ind Univ, 66-67; consult, Food and Drug Admin, Consumer Access Prog, 77-78. **MEMBERSHIPS** Am Bar Asn. **RESEARCH** Commercial law; consumer law; bankruptcy law. **SELECTED PUBLICATIONS** Auth, Negotiable Instruments, Bank Deposits and Collections, and Other Payment Systems, Bus Lawyer, Vol 0048, 93; Payments--Article-3, Article-4 and Article-4a/, Bus Lawyer, Vol 0049, 94; Payments--Article-3, Article-4 and Article-4a, Bus Lawyer, Vol 0051, 96; Payments--Article-3, Article-4 and Article-4a, Bus Lawyer, Vol 0052, 97. **CONTACT ADDRESS** Col of Law, Univ of Denver, 200 W 24th Ave, Denver, CO, 80208.

LITTLEJOHN, EDWARD J.
PERSONAL Born 05/05/1935, Pittsburgh, PA, d **DISCIPLINE** LAW **EDUCATION** Wayne State Univ, BA 1965; Detroit Coll of Law, JD (cum laude) 1970; Columbia Univ Law Sch, LLM 1974, JSD 1982. **CAREER** City of Detroit, varied Gov serv 1959-70; Detroit Coll of Law, prof 1970-72; Wayne State Law Sch, assoc prof & assistant dean 1972-76, assoc dean & prof of law 1976-78, prof of law 1972-96, prof emeritus of law, 1996-; Univ of Utrecht Netherlands, visiting prof, 1974; Wayne State Center for Black Studies, faculty research assoc; The Damon J Keith Law Collection for History of African-American Lawyers and Judges of Wayne State University, founder/director. **HONORS AND AWARDS** Charles Evans Hughes Fellow Columbia Univ Law School 1973-74; WEB Dubois Scholarship Awd Phylon Soc Wayn State Univ 1986; Special Alumni Awd Wolverine Student Bar Assoc Detroit Coll of Law 1986; Trailblazer Award, Wolverine Bar Assn 1988;Black Educator of 1991 (MI & Ohio), Detroit Peace Corps; Alumni Faculty Service Award, Wayne St Alumni Assn, 1991; DH Gordon Excellence in Teaching Award, Alumni and Friends of the Law School, 1994; Champion of Justice Award, State Bar of Michigan, 1995. **MEMBERSHIPS** Apptd to Bd Police Commrs Detroit 1974-78, chmn 1977-78; mem MI Bar Assn, NBA, ABA, Wolverine Bar Assn, Alpha Phi Alpha; ed bd The Urban Educator and the Compleat Lawyer; hearing officer MI Dept of Civil Rights; consult Police Civil Liability and Citizen Complaints; reporter Amer Bar Assoc; task force on Minorities in the Legal Profession; chair, City of Detroit Board of Ethics, 1994-; trustee, Kurdish Museum and Library of NY, 1990-96; Michigan Correctional Officers, training council, 1990-93; Michigan Committee on Juvenile Justice, 1987-90. **SELECTED PUBLICATIONS** Publications in various legal journals. **CONTACT ADDRESS** Law Sch, Wayne State Univ, 468 W Ferry Mall, Detroit, MI, 48202-3620.

LIVEZEY, LOWELL W.
PERSONAL Born 02/15/1943, Erie, PA, m, 1970 **DISCIPLINE** RELIGIOUS SOCIAL ETHICS, ECONOMICS **EDUCATION** Swarthmore Col, BA, 66; Univ Chicago, DMin, 70. **CAREER** Dir, World Without War Coun, 70-81; admin dir Undergrad Prog, Woodrow Wilson School, Princeton, 83-88; exec asst to pres, Chicago State Univ, 88-92; vis prof, Res prof, Univ Ill at Chicago, 92-. **MEMBERSHIPS** Am Acad Relig; Soc Christian Ethics; Relig Res Asn; Am Sociol Asn; Asn Sociol Relig. **CONTACT ADDRESS** Rel in Urban Am Prog, Univ Ill at Chicago, 1007 W Harrison St, Chicago, IL, 60607-7136. **EMAIL** livezey@uic.edu

LIVINGSTON, DONALD W.
DISCIPLINE HISTORY OF MODERN PHILOSOPHY **EDUCATION** WA Univ, PhD, 65. **CAREER** Philos, Emory Univ. **HONORS AND AWARDS** Nat Endowment Hum fel, 78-79. **SELECTED PUBLICATIONS** Auth, Hume's Philosophy of Common Life; Coed Hume, A Re-evaluation; Liberty in Hume's "History of England"; Hume as Philosopher of Society, Politics, and History. **CONTACT ADDRESS** Emory Univ, Atlanta, GA, 30322-1950.

LIVINGSTON, JAMES CRAIG
PERSONAL Born 07/12/1930, Grand Rapids, MI, m, 1954, 2 children **DISCIPLINE** RELIGION **EDUCATION** Kenyon Col, BA, 52; Union Theol Sem, MDiv, 56; Columbia Univ, PhD(relig), 65. **CAREER** Asst prof relig, Southern Methodist Univ, 63-68; dean undergrad prog, 73-78, assoc prof Relig & chmn dept, Col William & Mary, 68-78, prof relig, 78-86, WALTER G. MASON PROF RELIG, 86-; Grad Coun Humanities Danforth fel, 65; vis fel, Clare Hall, Cambridge, 67-68; Am Coun Learned Soc fel, 72-73; Nat Endowment for Humanities fel, 79-80, 89-90; Busch fel, 79-80; Woodrow Wilson Int Center for Scholars, fel, 90. **HONORS AND AWARDS** Phi Beta Kappa; Brose Found Decemial Prize, 80; State Council of Higher Education for Virginia, Outstanding Faculty Award, 89; The Thomas Jefferson Award, Col of William and Mary, 94. **MEMBERSHIPS** Am Acad Relig. **RESEARCH** Modern religious thought; contemporary theology; Victorian religious studies. **SELECTED PUBLICATIONS** Auth, William Golding's The Spire, Seabury, 67; Paul Tillich's Christology and Historical Research, In: Paul Tillich: Retrospect and Future, Abingdon, 67; ed, M. Arnold's Literature and Dogma, Ungar, 70; auth, Modern Christian Thought, Macmillan, 71, 2nd ed, 2 vols, 97, 99; Henry Dodwell's Christianity Not Founded on Argument, 1742, revisited, J Theol Studies, 71; Matthew Arnold on the Truth of Christianity: A Reappraisal, J Am Acad Relig, 73; The Religious Creed and Criticism of Sir James Fitzjames Stephen, Victorian Studies, 3/74; The Ethics of Belief. An Essay on the Victorian Religious Conscience, Scholars, 74; Matthew Arnold and Christianity: His Religious Prose Writings, Univ NC Press, 84; Anatomy of the Sacred, Macmillan, 89, 2nd ed, 93, 3rd ed, 98; Tradition and the Critical Spirit: Catholic Modernist Writings of George Tyrrell, Fortress Press, 91. **CONTACT ADDRESS** Dept of Relig, Col of William and Mary, Williamsburg, VA, 23185.

LLEWELLYN, DON W.
DISCIPLINE LAW, INTERNATIONAL TAXATATION **EDUCATION** Dickinson Col, BA, 57; Dickinson Sch Law, JD, 61; NY Univ Sch Law, LLM, 67. **CAREER** Prof;Villanova Univ, 80-; dean grad Legal Stud, Villanova Univ, 86-88; dir gard Tax Prog, Villanova Univ, 80-86. **MEMBERSHIPS** Amer and Philadelphia Bar Ass Tax Sections; Int Fiscal Asn. **RESEARCH** Taxation,estate planning. **SELECTED PUBLICATIONS** Auth, Tax Planning for For Persons Investing in and Disposing of US Assets, Int J, 96; The Evolution of Sophisticated Tax Planning for Lifetime Gifts-What Planning Techniques Continue to be Effective, Real Prop Prob & Tr. J, 95; coauth, Planning Pitfalls and Opportunities for For Owned Corporations Under the Earnings Stripping Rules, 47 Tax Law 641, 94; Tax Planning for Lifetime and Testamentary Dispositions-Prototype Plans, ALI-ABA, 97; contrib, Tax Aspects of For Investment in US Real Estate, Real Estate Financing, 93 & Partnerships, in Advan Bus Tax Plan, 85. **CONTACT ADDRESS** Law School, Villanova Univ, 800 Lancaster Ave, Villanova, PA, 19085-1692. **EMAIL** llewelly@law.vill.edu

LLOYD, ELISABETH A.
PERSONAL Born 03/03/1956 **DISCIPLINE** HISTORY, PHILOSOPHY OF SCIENCE **EDUCATION** Queen's Univ, 74-75; Univ Colo-Boulder, BA, Sci/Polit Theory, 76-80; Princeton Univ, PhD, 80-84. **CAREER** Vis instr, Exper Stud, Univ Colo-Boulder, 80; vis scholar, Genetics, Harvard Univ, 83-84; vis lectr, Philos, Univ Calif-San Diego, 84-85; asst prof, Philos, Univ Calif-San Diego, 85-88; asst prof, Univ Calif-Berkeley, 88-90; assoc prof, Univ Calif-Berkeley, 90-97; prof, Philos, Univ Calif-Berkeley, 97-; PROF, BIOL, IND UNIV, 98-. **MEMBERSHIPS** Nat Endow Hum; Nat Sci Found; Am Philos Asn; Philos Sci Asn; Int Soc Hist, Philos, & Soc Stud of Biol **SELECTED PUBLICATIONS** The Structure and Confirmation of Evolutionary Theory, Greenwood Press, 94; co-edr, Keywords in Evolutionary Biology, Harvard Univ Press, 92; "The Anachronistic Anarchist," Philosophical Studies 81, APA West Div Sympos, 96; "Science and Anti-Science: Objectivity and its Real Enemies," Feminism, Science, and the Philosophy of Science, Kluwer, 96; "Feyerabend, Mill, and Pluralism," Philosophy of Science, Supplemental Issue: PSA 96 Symposium Papers, 97. **CONTACT ADDRESS** Hist & Philos Sci Dept, Indiana Univ, Bloomington, Goodbody Hall 130, Bloomington, IN, 47405-2401. **EMAIL** ealloyd@indiana.edu

LO, JIM
PERSONAL Born 06/26/1954, New York, NY, m, 1976, 2 children **DISCIPLINE** THEOLOGY **EDUCATION** Bartiesville Wesleyan Col, BA, 78; Ind Wesleyan Univ, MA, 82; Wheaton Grad Sch, MA, 92; Univ South Africa, PhD, 98. **CAREER** Pastor, 78-82; missionary, bible sch tchr, Wesleyan Church, Africa, 82-95; missionary, dir, bible sch tchr, Wesleyan Church, Cambodia, 95-96; asst prof, Ind Wesleyan Univ, 96-. **HONORS AND AWARDS** W. Hilbert Norton Award, 92, Wheaton Col; Tch Excellence Award, 97-98; Who's Who among Am Tchrs, 98. **MEMBERSHIPS** Evangelical Missiological Soc. **RESEARCH** Missions; intercultural issues; bible. **SELECTED PUBLICATIONS** Auth, art, Unique and United: a partnership in South Africa, 96; auth, art, When God Rocks the Boat, 97; auth, art, Staying True to God, 98; auth, art, Infanticide, 97; auth, art, Balancing Fear with Love, 97, auth, art, Christian College-An Answer to Prayer, 97. **CONTACT ADDRESS** 4201 S Washington St, Marion, IN, 46953. **EMAIL** jlo@indwes.edu

LOBEL, DIANA
DISCIPLINE RELIGIOUS STUDIES **EDUCATION** Oberlin Col, BA, 79; Harvard Divinity School, MTS, 82, Harvard Univ, PhD, 95. **CAREER** Vis fel, instr, Univ Md, 96-97; Anna Smith Fine asst prof Judaic Stud, Rice Univ, 97- . **HONORS AND AWARDS** Memorial Found for Jewish Culture grant; Danforth Award; Combined Jewish Philanthropies award; Phi Beta Kappa. **MEMBERSHIPS** APA; Asn for Jewish Stud; Am Acad Relig. **RESEARCH** Jewish and Islamic philosophy and the Classical Tradition; Judeo-Arabic thought; negative theology; comparative religious thought. **SELECTED PUBLICATIONS** Auth, Between Mysticism and Philosophy: Sufi Language of Religious Experience, SUNY, 99. **CONTACT ADDRESS** Dept of Religious Studies MS 15, Rice Univ, 6100 S Main St, Houston, TX, 77005-1892. **EMAIL** dlobel@ruf.rice.edu

LOCHTEFELD, JAMES G.
DISCIPLINE CONTEMPORARY EUROPEAN CONTINENTAL PHILOSOPHY **EDUCATION** Colgate Univ, BA; Harvard Divinity Sch, MTS; Univ Wash, MA; Columbia Univ, PhD. **CAREER** Instr, St. Olaf Col, 91-92; Asst prof, Carthahe Col,92-97; Assoc prof, Carthage Col, 97-. **HONORS AND AWARDS** Robinson Prize, 79; Hindi Language Program Fel, 85, FLAS fel, 84, 86, 87; Fulbright-IIE, 89; Charlotte W. Newcombe Doctoral Dissertation fel, 90; pres fel, 88, 89, 91; Fac summer res Grant, 96; Senior Res fel, 97-98. **MEMBERSHIPS** AOS, AAR/SBL, ASIANetwork. **SELECTED PUBLICATIONS** Auth, Reflected Splendor: The Regional Appropriation of 'All-India' Tirthas, The Vishva Hindu Parishad And The Roots Of Hindu Militancy, JAAR LXII 2, 94; New Wine, Old Skins: The Sangh Parivar and the Transformation of Hinduism, Rel, 96; The Saintly Camar: Perspectives on the Life of Ravidas, ARC: The Jour Fac Relig Studies, 98. **CONTACT ADDRESS** Carthage Col, 2001 Alford Dr., Kenosha, WI, 53140.

LODGE, JOHN G.
PERSONAL Born 08/07/1947, Chicago, IL, s **DISCIPLINE** BIBLICAL THEOLOGY, MATTHEW AND PAUL **EDUCATION** Pontifical Bibl Inst, Rome, SSL, 81; Pontifical Gregorian Univ, Rome, STD, 96. **CAREER** Parish priest and assoc pastor, 73-78; instr and assoc prof, Bible dept, Mundelein Sem, 81-; acad dean, Mundelein Sem, 84-88, 97-. **MEMBERSHIPS** Cath Theol Soc of Amer; Cath Bibl Asn; AAR/SBL. **RESEARCH** St. Paul; Romans; Gospel of Matthew. **SELECTED PUBLICATIONS** Auth, Romans 9-11: A Reader Response Analysis, Scholars Press, 96; auth, The Apostle's Appeal and Readers' Response: 2 Corinthians 8 and 9, Chicago Studies 30, 59-76, 91; auth, Matthew's Passion-Resurrection Narrative, Chicago Studies 25, 3-20, 86; auth, All Things to All: Paul's Pastoral Strategy, Chicago Studies 24, 291-306, 85; auth, The Salvation Theologies of Paul and Luke, Chicago Studies 22, 83; auth, James and Paul at Cross-Purposes? James 2,22, Biblica 62, 81. **CONTACT ADDRESS** Mundelein Sem, 1000 E Maple Ave, Mundelein, IL, 60060-1174. **EMAIL** jlodge2976@aol.com

LODGE, PAUL A.
PERSONAL Born 01/18/1968, Leeds, England, s **DISCIPLINE** PHILOSOPHY **EDUCATION** Oxford Univ, philos & psychol, BA, 90; Leeds Univ, philos of mind, MA, 91; Rutgers Univ, philos, PhD, 98. **CAREER** Visiting asst prof, Tulane Univ, Jul 98-. **HONORS AND AWARDS** Annual essay competition winner, Leibniz Soc of North Amer, 98; res grant for PhD candidates and recent PhDs, DAAD, 97; annual essay competition winner, Leibniz Soc of North Amer, 96. **MEMBERSHIPS** APA; Leibniz Soc of North Amer; Hist of Philos Sci Working Grp; Aristotelian Soc; G.W. Leibniz Gesellschaft. **RESEARCH** 17th & 18th century philosophy. **SELECTED PUBLICATIONS** Auth, Stepping Back Inside Leibniz's Mill, The Monist, 81, 554-73, 98; auth, Force and the Nature of Body, Discourse on Metaphysics, 17-18, Leibniz Soc Rev, 7, 116-24, 97; auth, Leibniz Microfilms at the University of Pennsylvania, Leibniz Soc Rev, 6, 164-69, 96; auth, Abstract of 1996 Essay Competition Winner, Leibniz Soc Rev, 6, 170-71, 96. **CONTACT ADDRESS** Dept. of Philosophy, Tulane Univ, 105 Newcomb Hall, New Orleans, LA, 70118-5698. **EMAIL** plodge@mailhost.tcs.tulane.edu

LOEB, LOUIS EDWARD
PERSONAL Born 06/25/1945, St. Louis, MO **DISCIPLINE** PHILOSOPHY **EDUCATION** Wesleyan Univ, BA, 67; Oxford Univ, BPhil, 69; Princeton Univ, PhD, 75. **CAREER** Asst prof, 74-80, assoc prof, 80-89, prof philos, Univ MI, 89, chmn, Dept Philos, 93-99; Mem bd trustees, Wesleyan Univ, CT, 74-77. **MEMBERSHIPS** Am Philos Asn; Hume Soc; Leibniz Soc. **RESEARCH** Hist of mod philos. **SELECTED PUBLICATIONS** Auth, Causal theories and causal overdetermination, J Philos, 9/74; Hume's moral sentiments and the structure of the Treatise, J Hist Philos, 10/77; From Descartes to Hume: Continental Metaphysics and the Development of Modern Philosophy, Cornell Univ Press, 81; Is there radical sisimulation in Descartes' Meditations?, In: Amelia O Rorty, ed, Essays on Descartes' Meditations, Univ Calif Press, 86; Was Descartes sincere in his appeal to the light of nature?, Jour Hist Philos, 7/88; The priority of reason in Descartes, Philos Rev, 1/90; Stability, justification, and Hume's propensity to attribute identity to related objects, Philos Topics, spring 91; The Cartesian circle, In: Cambridge Companions to Philosophy: Descartes (John G Cottingham, ed), Cambridge Univ Press, 92; Causation, extrinsic relations, and Hume's second thoughts about personal identity, Hume Studies, 11/92; Hume on stability, justification, and unphilosophical probability, Jour Hist Philos, 1/95; Instability and uneasiness in Hume's theories of belief and justification, Brit Jour Hist Philos, 9/95; Causal inference, associationism, and skepticism in Part III of Book I of Hume's Treaties, In: Logic and the Workings of the Mind (Patricia Easton, ed), North Am Kant Soc Studies in Philos, vol 5, Ridgeview, 97; Sextus, Descartes, Hume, and Peirce: On securing settled doxastic states, Nous, 3/98. **CONTACT ADDRESS** Dept of Philos, Univ of MI, 435 S State St, Ann Arbor, MI, 48109-1003. **EMAIL** lloeb@umich.edu

LOEWE, WILLIAM PATRICK
PERSONAL Born 11/28/1941, New Rochelle, NY, m, 1977 **DISCIPLINE** THEOLOGY **EDUCATION** Fordham Univ, BA, 65, MA, 66; Loyola Scm, PhL, 66; Marquette Univ, PhD(theol), 74. **CAREER** Asst prof, 73-80, ASSOC PROF THEOL, CATH UNIV AM, 80-. **MEMBERSHIPS** Am Acad Relig; Cath Theol Soc Am; Col Theol Soc. **RESEARCH** Lonergan studies; contemporary foundational and systematic theology; theology within interdisciplinary perspective. **SELECTED PUBLICATIONS** Auth, Systematic Theolog--Roman Catholic Perspectives, Vol 1-2, J Rel, Vol 0074, 94; God as Trinity--Relationality and Temporality in Divine Life, Horizons, Vol 0022, 95; Jesus Jewishness--Exploring the Place of Jesus Within Early Judaism, Horizons, Vol 0024, 97. **CONTACT ADDRESS** Dept of Relig and Relig Educ, Catholic Univ of America, 620 Michigan Ave NE, Washington, DC, 20064-0002.

LOEWY, ERICH H.
PERSONAL Born 12/31/1927, Vienna, Austria, m, 1974, 3 children **DISCIPLINE** HEALTH CARE ETHICS **EDUCATION** NY Univ, BA, 50; State Univ NY, PhD Med, 54. **CA-**

REER Demonstrator, Case Western Reserve Univ, Ohio, 60-64; clin instr, 64-70; sr clin instr, 70-77; clin asst prof, Albany Med Coll Union Univ, 77-8 -81; lectr, Adirondack Community Coll, 74-81; asst prof, Univ Connecticut School Med, 81-84; assoc grad fac, Univ Ill Grad School, 86-95; asst prof, uni Ill Coll Med, 84-87; assoc prof, 87-93; prof, 93-95; asst prof, Univ Ill Chicago, 84-89; assoc prof, 89-93; prof, 93-95; Prof, Chair Biethics Dept, Univ Calif Sacramento, 96-. **HONORS AND AWARDS** Advisor of the Year, Univ Ill, 86; Convocation Speaker, 86; Golden Apple Tchg Award, 88; Selected to hood Graduating Sr, 89, 90, 92; Marquis Who's Who in the Midwest; Marquis Who's Who in Am Law; Marquis Who's Who in Sci and Engineering; Woodrow Wilson Nat Fel. **MEMBERSHIPS** WHO Network Monitoring; Am Asn for the Advancement of Sci; NY Acad of Sci; Fel Am Coll of Physicians; Hist of Sci Soc; Paleopathology Soc; Soc of Hist of Med; Physicians for Human Rights; Int Physicians for the Prevention of Nuclear War; Physicians for Soc Responsibility; Am Philos Asn; inst Asn of Bioethics; Int Bioethics Inst; Akademie fr Ethik in der Medizin; Europ Soc fot eh Philos of Med and Health Care; Soc of Health & Human values; Hastings Center of Ethics & Life Sci. **RESEARCH** Health-care Ethics; Social Justice; Relation of individual freedom to communal needs; Allocation of service resources. **SELECTED PUBLICATIONS** Auth, numerous publications on health care ethics, 54-97; Of Cultural Practises, Ethics and Education: Thoughts about affecting changes in cultural practices, Health-Care Analysis, 98; Curiosity, Imagination, Science, compassion and Ethics: Do Curiosity and Imagination serve a central function? Theoretical Med, 98; Orchestrating the End of Life, Dignity and Physician Assisted Dying: Dangers, Opportunities and Prior Neglected Conditions, Med, Health and Philos, 98; Of Curiosity, Imagination, Justice and Health-Care Systems: What would an "ideal" health0care system look like? Health-Care Analysis, 98; Of Health-Care Professionals, Ethics and Strikes, Cambridge Quart, 98; coauth, Ethics and Managed care: Reconstructing a System and Refashioning a Society, Archive of Internal Med, 98. **CONTACT ADDRESS** Medical Ctr, Univ Calif Davis, 2221 Stockton Blvd, Sacramento, CA, 95817. **EMAIL** ehloewy@ucdavis.edu

LOEWY, ROBERTA S.
PERSONAL Born 11/22/1945, OH, m, 1974, 3 children **DISCIPLINE** ETHICS **EDUCATION** Skidmore Coll, BA, 81; Loyola Univ Chicago, MA, 92; PhD, 97. **CAREER** Instr, Ill Central Coll, 88-89; consultant, Pekin Hospital, 93-94; co-fac, Methodist Med Center, 93-97; consultant, co-chair, Ethics Team, Sacramento County Dept of Health and Human Serv, 96-98; Asst Clin Prof, Univ Calif, 97-. **HONORS AND AWARDS** State Univ NY Tchg Asst ship, 81; State Univ NY Tchg Fel, 81-82; Univ Conn, non-tchg fel; 82-83; Loyola Univ Med Center Clin Fel, 90-92; NEH Diss grant, 93; Loyola Univ Diss Fel, 94-95. **MEMBERSHIPS** Am Asn of Univ Women, Am Philos Asn; Am Soc of Bioethics and Humanities; Int Asn of Bioethics; Int Bioethics Inst; Europ Soc for Philos of Med and Health Care; Concerned Philosophers for Peace. **RESEARCH** Ethical Obligations in Medical Relationships; Hospice; Cord Blood Salvage; Palliative Care and under Managed Care. **SELECTED PUBLICATIONS** Auth, Teamwork, Cambridge Quart of Healthcare Ethics, 93; The Relationship of Medically-Assisted Nutrition and Hydration to Respect for Human Persons, Cambridge Quart of Healthcare Ethics, 93; A Critique of Tradition Relationship Models, Cambridge Quart of Healthcare Ethics, 94; Relationships in Health Care Revisited, Healthcare Ethics: Critical Issues, 94; rev, Health care Ethics Committees: The Next Generation, Doody's Health Sci Book Rev J, 94; coauth, Ethics and the Brave New World of Health Care: Repatriation of Trauma Center Patients by Managed Care Organizations; Of Cultural Practices, Ethics and Education: Thoughts About Affecting Changes in Cultural Practices, Health Care Analyses. **CONTACT ADDRESS** 11465 Ghirardelli Ct, Gold River, CA, 95670. **EMAIL** roberta.loewy@ucdms.ucdavis.edu

LOFTUS, JOHN ALLAN
PERSONAL Born 03/13/1947, Pittston, PA **DISCIPLINE** PSYCHOLOGY OF RELIGION **EDUCATION** Fordham Univ, MA, 70, AB, 72; Woodstock Col, NY, M Div, 72; Boston Univ, PhD, 83. **CAREER** Exec dir, 86-94, Southdown Emmanuel Convalescent Found; John J. Wintermeyer Chmn of Psychol, 94-98, Univ Waterloo, St. Jerome's; pres, 98-, Regis Col, Univ Toronto. **MEMBERSHIPS** APA; MA Psych Asn; Soc for the Sci Stud of Relig; AAR. **RESEARCH** Psychology and relig; sexuality; psych & spirituality issues; healing and health psychology. **SELECTED PUBLICATIONS** Auth, Clergy & Religious Exposed to AIDS, Southdown, 91; auth, A View from the Bridge: Healing in the Churches, Pastoral Press; auth, Understanding Sexual Misconduct Among the Clergy, Pastoral Press, 94; auth, Health, Healing & Social Justice, 97. **CONTACT ADDRESS** Regis Col, 15 St. Mary St, Toronto, ON, M4Y 2R5. **EMAIL** ja.loftus@utoronto.ca

LOGAN, SAMUEL TALBOT, JR.
DISCIPLINE CHURCH HISTORY **EDUCATION** Princeton Univ, BA, 65; Westminster Theol Sem, MDiv, 68; Emory Univ, PhD, 72. **CAREER** Tchg asst, Emory Univ, 69; instr, DeKalb Jr Col, 70; dir, Dept Amer Stud, Barrington Col, 70-79; asst prof, 1970-1978; prof, Barrington Col, 78-79; prof, Westminster Theol Sem, 79-. **SELECTED PUBLICATIONS** Auth, Academic Freedom at Christian Institutions, Christian Scholar's Rev; Shoulders to Stand On, Decision, 93; Theological Decline in Christian Institutions and the Value of Van Til's Epistemology, Westminster Theol Jour, 95; ed, The Preacher and Preaching: Reviving the Art in the Twentieth Century. **CONTACT ADDRESS** Westminister Theol Sem, PO Box 27009, Philadelphia, PA, 19118. **EMAIL** slogan@wts.edu

LOHR, CHARLES HENRY
PERSONAL Born 06/24/1925, New York, NY **DISCIPLINE** HISTORY OF MEDIEVAL AND RENAISSANCE PHILOSOPHY **EDUCATION** Fordham Univ, BA, 47, PhL, 56; Woodstock Col, Md, STB, 61, STL, 62; Univ Freiburg, PhD(philos), 67, Dr phil habil, 72. **CAREER** Res asst, Raimundus-Lullus-Inst, Univ Freiburg, 63-67; from asst prof to assoc prof theol, Fordham Univ, 67-72; res fel philos, Raimundus-Lullus-Inst, Univ Freiburg, 72-74; Univ dozent theol, 74-76, PROF THEOL, ALBERT LUDWIGS UNIV, FREIBURG, 76-, Guggenheim Mem found fel, 71-72; dir, Raimundus-Lullus-Inst, Univ Freiburg, 75-; Nat Endowment Humanities grant, 76-77; dean, Theol Fac, Univ Freiburg, 77-78. **HONORS AND AWARDS** Mag Phil, Maioricensis Schola Lullistica, Palma, Majorca, 72; Dr phil, Univ Fribourg, 81. **MEMBERSHIPS** Mediaeval Acad Am; Am Hist Asn. **RESEARCH** History of medieval and Renaissance philosophy. **SELECTED PUBLICATIONS** Auth, Lull, Ramon and the Epistemic Theory of Lemyesier, Thomas, Isis, Vol 0086, 95; The Intellectual Activity in the Medieval Faculty of Arts at Paris--Texts and Masters, C. 1200-1500, Vol 1--Repertory of Names Beginning With the Letters A-B, Speculum-J Medieval Stud, Vol 0071, 96. **CONTACT ADDRESS** Raimundus-Lullus-Inst, Univ of Freiburg, Werthmannplatz D-78 Freiburg im Breisgan, Wreiburg, ., 7800.

LOKKEN, LAWRENCE
DISCIPLINE LAW **EDUCATION** Augsburg Col, BA; Univ Minn, JD. **CAREER** Hugh F. Culverhouse Eminent scholar in Taxation; prof, Univ Fla, 74-82 and 94-; instr, NY Univ, 80-93; instr, Univ Ga, 68-70; vis prof, NY Univ, Duke Univ, Univ Minn, Leiden Univ, Neth; vis scholar, Harvard Univ; ed, Fla Tax Rev, 94-96; ed-in-ch, Tax Law Rev, 83-87; past res consult, Harvard Law Sch Intl Tax Prog; note and comment ed, Minn Law Rev; spec adv to UN on Intl Tax Matters, 95-. **MEMBERSHIPS** Order of the Coif. **RESEARCH** Tax issues and policy, international tax treaties. **SELECTED PUBLICATIONS** Coauth, federal taxation of income, estates and gifts; fundamentals of intl taxation. **CONTACT ADDRESS** School of Law, Univ of Florida, PO Box 117625, Gainesville, FL, 32611-7625. **EMAIL** lokken@law.ufl.edu

LOMBARD, LAWRENCE B.
PERSONAL Born 11/24/1944, New York, NY, d **DISCIPLINE** PHILOSOPHY **EDUCATION** Cornell Univ, AB, 65; Stanford Univ, PhD, 74. **CAREER** From asst prof to assoc prof to prof to chemn, 69-, Wayne State Univ. **MEMBERSHIPS** AAUP; Am Philos Asn. **RESEARCH** Metaphysics; event theory. **SELECTED PUBLICATIONS** Auth, Actions, Results, and the Time of a Killing, 78; auth, Events, 79; auth, Events and Their Subjects, 81; auth, Events and the Essentiality of Time, 82; auth, Events: A Metaphysical Study, 86. **CONTACT ADDRESS** Dept of Philosophy, Wayne State Univ, Detroit, MI, 48202. **EMAIL** l.b.lombard@wayne.edu

LOMBARDI, JOSEPH L.
PERSONAL Born 12/01/1939, Brooklyn, NY **DISCIPLINE** PHILOSOPHY **EDUCATION** Manhattan Col, BA, 61; Woodstock Col, PhL, 65, BD, 70; Fordham Univ, MA, 67; New York Univ, PhD, 75. **CAREER** Instr, Fordham Univ, 65-67; assoc prof philos, St Joseph's Univ, 74-. **HONORS AND AWARDS** NEH summer stipend, 85, 90. **MEMBERSHIPS** APA; Am Catholic Philos Asn; Jesuit Philos Asn; AAUP. **RESEARCH** Analytic philosophy; ethics; philosophy of religion. **SELECTED PUBLICATIONS** Various articles in Ethics, Relig Stud, Am Catholic Philos Quart, Jour of Relig Ethics, Am Jour of Jurisp. **CONTACT ADDRESS** Dept of Philosophy, St Joseph's Univ, 5600 City Ave, Philadelphia, PA, 19131. **EMAIL** jlombard@sju.edu

LONE, JANA M.
PERSONAL Born 04/28/1960, New York, NY, m, 3 children **DISCIPLINE** PHILOSOPHY **EDUCATION** Univ Mass, BA, 82; George Wash Law Sch, JD, 85; Univ Wash, MA, 90, PhD, 96. **CAREER** Dir, Northwest Ctr for Philos for Children, 96-. **HONORS AND AWARDS** Amer fel, Amer Asn of Univ Women Educ Found, 93-94; JD with honors; BA, magna cum laude. **MEMBERSHIPS** Bus and Prof Women's Cabinet, Jewish Fed of Greater Seattle; Northwest Women's Law Ctr; Vashon Island Connections Mentorship Prog; Vashon-Maury Island Publ Health and Safety Network; The Children's Alliance; Books for Kids; Seattle Jewish Family Svc; Shelters for Battered Women and Their Children. **RESEARCH** Ethics; Philosophy of education; Philosophy of childhood; Philosophy of law; Philosophy of feminism; Environmental ethics. **SELECTED PUBLICATIONS** Auth, Are We All Mystery Creatures? Talking Philosophy With Children Who Are At Risk, Thinking, 97; auth, Voices in the Classroom: Girls and Philosophy for Children, Thinking, 97; auth, Poetry and the Philosophical Understanding of Children, Bookbird: World of Children's Books, 96. **CONTACT ADDRESS** 22024 Monument Rd. SW, Vashon Island, WA, 98070. **EMAIL** jmohrlone@compuserve.com

LONG, BURKE O'CONNOR
PERSONAL Born 09/17/1938, Richmond, VA, m, 1964, 2 children **DISCIPLINE** RELIGION, BIBLICAL STUDIES **EDUCATION** Randoph-Macon Col, BA, 61; Yale Univ, BD, 64, MA, 66, PhD, 67. **CAREER** Instr relig, Yale Univ, 65-67 & Wellesley Col, 67-68; asst prof, 68-73, assoc prof, 73-82, Prof Relig, Bowdoin Col, 82-, Consult, Bd Educ, United Presby Church, 67-70; ed, Sources for Bibl Study, Soc Bibl Lit, 77-; Soc Bibl Lit res fel, 79-80; vis prof, Emory Univ, 82. **MEMBERSHIPS** Soc Bibl Lit; World Union Jewish Studies; Inst Antiquity & Christianity. **RESEARCH** Old Testament; ancient Near East; folklore; folkliterature. **SELECTED PUBLICATIONS** Auth, The Problem of Etiological Narrative in the Old Testament, Walter de Gruyter, Berlin, 69; Two question and answer schemata in the prophets, J Bibl Lit, 71; 2 Kings iii and genres of prophetic narrative, Vetus Testamentum, 73; contribr, Language in Religious Practice, Newbury, 76; auth, Recent field studies in oral literature and Old Testament form criticism, Vetus Testamentum, 76; co-ed & contribr, Canon and Authority: Essays in Old Testament Religion and Theology, Fortress, 77; ed & contribr, Images of Man & God: Old Testament Stories in Literary Focus, Almond, 81; auth, Social world of ancient Israel, Interpretation, 82. **CONTACT ADDRESS** Dept of Relig, Bowdoin Col, 7300 College Station, Brunswick, ME, 04011-8473.

LONG, CHARLES H.
PERSONAL Born 08/23/1926, Little Rock, AR, m **DISCIPLINE** RELIGIOUS STUDIES **EDUCATION** Dunbar Jr Coll, Diploma 1946; Univ of Chicago, BD 1953, PhD 1962; Dickinson Coll, LHD 1971. **CAREER** Univ of Chicago, instr 1956-60, asst prof 1960-64, assoc prof 1964-70, prof 1970-74; Duke Univ, prof history of religion 1974-88; Univ of NC Chapel Hill, Wm Rand Kenan jr prof 1974-88; Jeanette K Watson prof, history of religions, Syracuse Univ; Univ of CA, Santa Barbara, dir of res ctr for black studies, 1991-96. **HONORS AND AWARDS** Guggenheim Fellowship 1971; mem bd of govs Univ of NC Press Natl Humanities Faclty; consult Encyclopaedia Brittanica; Alumni of Year, Divinty School University of Chicago, 1985; Distinguished Alumni Award, University of Chicago, 1991. **MEMBERSHIPS** Past pres Amer Acad of Religion; mem Soc for Religion in Higher Edn; Intl Assn of Historians of Religion; Soc for Study of Black Religion; American Society for Study of Religion.

LONG, DOUGLAS C.
PERSONAL Born 05/25/1932, Ann Arbor, MI, m, 1961, 2 children **DISCIPLINE** PHILOSOPHY **EDUCATION** Univ Mich, BA, 54; Harvard Univ, MA, 55, PhD, 63. **CAREER** From assoc prof to prof & ch, Dept Philos, Univ NC, 67-; vis assoc prof, Brown Univ, 69; vis asst prof, Univ Wash, 65, from instr to asst prof, Univ Calif Los Angeles, 60-67. **HONORS AND AWARDS** Nat Endowment Hum Fel, 76-77; Nat Sci Found Grant, 67; Frederick Sheldon Traveling Fel to Corpus Christi Col, Oxford Univ, 58-59. **MEMBERSHIPS** Am Philos Asn; NC Philos Soc; Duke/Univ NC Med Ethics Res Group. **RESEARCH** Philosophy of mind; epistemology; action theory; metaphysics; bioethics. **SELECTED PUBLICATIONS** Auth, Why Machines Can Neither Think Nor Feel, Language, Mind & Art: Essays Appreciation & Analysis in Honor of Paul Ziff, 94; auth, One More Foiled Defense of Skepticism, Philos & Phenomenol Res, June, 94. **CONTACT ADDRESS** Dept of Philosophy, Univ of No Carolina, CB #3125, Chapel Hill, NC, 27599-3125. **EMAIL** dlong@email.unc.edu

LONG, JEROME HERBERT
PERSONAL Born 00/00/1931, Little Rock, AR, m, 1959, 2 children **DISCIPLINE** HISTORY OF RELIGIONS **EDUCATION** Knox Col, AB, 56; Univ Chicago Divinity Sch, BD, 60, MA, 62, PhD(hist of relig), 73. **CAREER** From instr to assoc prof relig, Western Mich Univ, 64-70; vis assoc prof, 70-71, ASSOC PROF RELIG, WESLEYAN UNIV, 71-, Mem, Comt on Reorgn of Curric of Relig Dept, Western Mich Univ, 65-67, mem, African Studies Comt, 65-70, secy, 66-67, mediator, Black Am Studies Prog, 68-70; mem, African Studies Comt, Wesleyan Univ, 74-75, chmn, 75-76, chmn, Search Comt for Dir for Ctr for Afro-Am Studies and interim curric coordr, Ctr for Afro-Am Studies, 75-76; VIS SCHOLAR, INST AFRICAN STUDIES, LEGON, GHANA, WEST AFRICA, UNIV GHANA, 77-. **RESEARCH** Prehistoric and primitive religions; historical approaches to religion and culture; religions of African peoples. **SELECTED PUBLICATIONS** Auth, Symbol and reality among the Trobriand Islanders, in: Essays in Divinity, Vol 1: the History of Religion, Univ Chicago, 69. **CONTACT ADDRESS** Wesleyan Univ, Middletown, CT, 06457.

LONG, JOHN EDWARD
PERSONAL Born 03/16/1941, Philadelphia, PA, m **DISCIPLINE** RELIGIOUS STUDIES **EDUCATION** Temple U, BA 1963; Theol Sem of the Reformed Episcopal Ch, BD 1966; Westminister Theol Sem, Th M 1970; Brandeis U, MA PhD 1978. **CAREER** Western KY Univ, assoc prof of religious studies present. **HONORS AND AWARDS** Dissertation Research Fellowship Fulbright-Hays Research Fellow in Algeria 1974-75; Grad Study Fellowship Ford Found Advanced Study Fellowship for Black Am 1972-73; Fellowship to Study Arabic in Tunisia N African Cntr for Arabic Studies 1972. **MEMBER-**

SHIPS Mem Am Assn of Tchrs of Arabic 1979; mem Middle East & Studies Assn 1975; mem Middle East Inst 1975; Dissertation Research Fellowship Fulbright-Hays Research Fellow in Algeria 1974-75; Grad Study Fellowship Ford Found Advanced Study Fellowship for Black Am 1972-73; Fellowship to Study Arabic in Tunisia N African Cntr for Arabic Studies 1972. **CONTACT ADDRESS** Dept Philos, Relig, Western Kentucky Univ, Bowling Green, KY, 42101.

LONG, PAUL
DISCIPLINE MISSIONS **EDUCATION** Fuller Theol Sem, PhD. **CAREER** Prof emeri. **HONORS AND AWARDS** Hubbard Awd. **SELECTED PUBLICATIONS** Auth, The Man in the Leather Hat; Citizen Soldiers of World War II. **CONTACT ADDRESS** Dept of Missions, Reformed Theol Sem, 5422 Clinton Blvd, Jackson, MS, 39209-3099.

LONG, R. JAMES
PERSONAL Born 12/15/1938, Rochester, NY, m, 1974, 3 children **DISCIPLINE** HISTORY OF MEDIEVAL PHILOSOPHY **EDUCATION** Pontif Inst Med Studies, LMS, 66; Univ Toronto, PhD(Medieval studies), 68. **CAREER** From asst prof to assoc prof, 69-78, prof philos, Fairfield Univ, 78-, Fulbright scholar medieval philos, Fulbright Comn, US Govt, 68-69; Can Coun fel philos, 68-69; Am Coun Learned Socs & Am Philos Soc grant-in-aid, 77; Nat Endowment for Humanities scholarly publ grant, 79; vis fac fel, Yale Univ, 82-83, dir hon prog, 82-91; liason faculty, program in Greek and Roman Studies, Ffld univ, 81-. **HONORS AND AWARDS** Fellow of Massey Col, Toronto, 65-68; Province of Ontario Graduate Fellowships, 66-68; Canada Council Doctoral Fellowship, 67-68; Fulbright Scholarship, Italy and U.K., 68-69; Canada Council Post-doctoral Fellowship, 69; NEH Summer Stipend, 74; Am Council of Learned Socs Grant-in-Aid, 77; Am Philos Soc Grant, 77; Assoc of Clare Hall, Cambridge Univ, 77; NEH Scholarly Publications Grant, 79; NEH Summer Seminar for College Teachers, Fordham Univ, 81; Yale Visiting Faculty Fellowship, 82-83; NEH Summer Seminar for College Teachers, Yeshiva Univ, 84; Am Philos Soc Grant, 84; Fairfield Univ Summer Stipends, 86, 89, 92; NEH Summer Seminar for College Teachers, Columbia Univ, 87; NEH Summer Stipend, 88; Warren W. Wooden Citation, PMR Conference, 89; NEH Editions/Texts Grant, ed of Richard Fishacre's Sentences-Commentary, 1-2, $130,000, 92-94; Yale Visiting Fellowship, Philosophy Dept, 96-98. **MEMBERSHIPS** Medieval Acad Am; Am Cath Philos Asn (life member); Soc Textual Scholarship; Soc Medieval & Renaissance Philos, secrt-treas, 91-; Catholic Comm on Intellectual and Cultural Affairs; Consociatio cultorum historiae Ordinis Praedicatorum; International Soc for Napoleanic Studies; Societe Internationale pour l'Etude de la Philosophie Medievale. **RESEARCH** Early thirteenth-century philosophy, particularly Oxford; 13th-century science, particularly medicine and botany; works of Richard Fishacre. **SELECTED PUBLICATIONS** Auth, Utrum iurista vel theologus plus proficiat ad regimen ecclesie . . ., 68; The Science of Theology according to Richard Fishacre: Ed of the Prologue to his Commentary on the Sentences, 72, Mediaeval Studies; In Defense of the Tournament: an ed of Pierre Dubois' De torneamentis . . ., 73; A Note on the Dating of MS Ashmole 1512, 74, Manuscripta ; Richard Fishacre and the Problem of the Soul, Mod Schoolman, 75; Richard Fishacre's Quaestio on the Ascension of Christ: An Edition, Mediaeval Studies, 78; ed, Bartholomaeus Anglicus, On the Properties of Soul and Body, Toronto Medieval Latin Texts IV, 79; auth, Botany in the High Middle Ages: An introduction, Res Publica Litterarum, 81; The Virgin as Olive-Tree: A Marian Sermon of Richard Fishacre and Science at Oxford, Archivum Fratrum Praedicatorum 52: 77-87, 82; Alfred of Sareshel's Commentary on the Pseudo-Aristotelian De plantis: A Critical Edition, Mediaeval Studies 47: 125-67, 85; The Question "'Whether the Church Could Better be Ruled by a Good Canonist than by a Theologian' and the Origins of Ecclesiology, Proceedings of the PMR Conference 10: 99-112, 85; Richard Fishacre, Dictionnaire de Spiritualite 13, cols 563-65, 87; Richard Fishacre's Way to God, A Straight Path: Studies in Medieval Philosophy and Culture, Essays in Honor of Arthur Hyman, eds Ruth Link-Salinger et al, 174-82, Washington, D.C.: The Catholic Univ of Am Press, 88: with Joseph Goering, Richard Fishacre's Treatise De fide, spe, et caritate, Bull de Philos Medievale 31: 103-11, 89; Adam of Buckfield and John Sackville: Some Notes on Philadelphia Free Library MS Lewis European 53, Traditio 45: 364-67, 89-90; The Reception and Interpretation of the Pseudo-Arostolian De Plantis at Oxford in the Thirteenth Century, Knowledge and the Sciences in Medieval Philosophy (proceedings of the Eighth Intnl Congress of Medieval Philos: S.I.E.P.M, eds Reijo Tyorinoja, Anja I. Lehtinen, & Dagfinn Follesdal: Annuals of the Finnish Soc for Missiology and Ecumenics, 55, pp 111-23, Helsinki, 90; The Moral and Spiritual Theory of Richard Fishacre: Edition of Trinity Col, MS 0.1.30, Archivum Fratrum Praedicatorum 60, 5-143, 90; The Anonymous Peterhouse Master and the Natural Philosophy of Plants, Traditio 46: 313-26, 91; Richard Fishacre, Medieval Philosophers, ed Jeremiah Hackett, Dictionary of Literary Biography, vol 115, pp 195-200, Detroit: Bruccoli Clark Layman, Inc, 92; A Thirteenth-Century Teaching Aid: An Edition of the Bodleian Abbreviatio of the Pseudo-Aristolian De Plantis, in Aspectus et Affectus: Essays and Editions in Grosseteste and Medieval Intellectual Life in Honor of Richard C. Dales, ed Gunar Freibergs with an intro by Richard Southern, AMS Studies in the Middle Ages: no 23: 87-103, New York: AMS Press, 93; Richard Fishacre's Super S. Augustini librum de haeresibus adnotationes: An Edition and Commentary, Archives d'histoire doctrinale et litteraire du moyen age 60: 207-79, 93; Botany, in Medieval Latin: An Introduction and Bibliographical Guide, ed F.A.C. Mantello and A.G. Rigg, 401-05, Washington, D.C.: The Catholic Univ of America Press, 96; Richard Fishacre's Treatise De libero arbitrio, Moral and Political Philosophies in the Middle Ages, proceedings of the 9th Itnl congress of Medieval Philos, ed B. Carlos Bazan, Eduardo Andujar, Leonard Sbrocchi, 2: 879-91, Ottawa, 17-22, Aug 92, Ottawa: Legas, 95; with Margaret Jewett, A Newly Discovered Witness of Fishacre's Sentences-Commentary: Univ of Chicago MS 156, Traditio 50: 342-45, 95; The Reception and Use of Aristotle by the Early English Dominicans, Aristotle in Britain During the Middle Ages, ed John Marenbon, pp 51-56, Turnhout (Belgium): Brepols, 96; Roger Bacon on the Nature and Place of Angels, Vivarium 35/2: 266-82, 97; Richard Fishacre, in the New Dictionary of National Biography, (in press); Adam de Buckfield, ibid; Geoffrey de Aspale, ibid; The Cosmic Christ: The Christology of Richard Fishacre, OP, Christ Among the Medieval Dominicans, UND Press (in press); Of Angels and Pinheads: The Contributions of the Early Oxford Masters to the Doctrine of Spiritual Matter, Franciscan Studies, Essays in Honor of Girard Etzkorn, ed Gordon A. Wilson and Timothy B. Noone, 56: 237-52, 98; The First Oxford Debate on the Eternity of the World, Recherches de Philosophie et Theologie Medievale 65/1: 54-98, 98; with Timothy B. Noone, Fishacre and Rufus on the Metaphysics of Light: Two Unedited Texts, Melanges Leonard Boyle (in press); The Role of Philosophy in Richard Fishacre's Theology of Creation, proceedings of the 10th Inl Congress of Medieval Philosophy, Erfurt, 25-30 August 97: 571-78, in press. **CONTACT ADDRESS** Dept of Philos, Fairfield Univ, 1073 N Benson Rd, Fairfield, CT, 06430-5195. **EMAIL** long@fair1.fairfield.edu

LONG, RODERICK T.
PERSONAL Born 02/04/1964, Los Angeles, CA **DISCIPLINE** PHILOSOPHY **EDUCATION** Harvard Col, AB, 85; Cornell Univ, MA, 88, PhD, 92. **CAREER** Instr, asst prof, 90-98, Univ NC, Chapel Hill; instr, Auburn Univ, 98-99. **RESEARCH** Ancient philosophy; moral and political philosophy. **SELECTED PUBLICATIONS** Auth, art, Mill's Higher Pleasures and The Choice of Character, 92; auth, art, Abortion, Abandonment, and Positive Rights: The Limits of Compulsory Altruism, 93; auth, art, Immanent Liberalism: The Politics of Mutual Consent, 95; auth, art, Aristotle's Conception of Freedom, 96; auth, art, Toward a Libertarian Theory of Class, 98. **CONTACT ADDRESS** Dept of Philosophy, Auburn Univ, 6080 Haley Ctr, Auburn, AL, 36849. **EMAIL** longrob@mail.auburn.edu

LONG, STEVEN A.
PERSONAL Born 07/26/1959, OH, m, 3 children **DISCIPLINE** PHILOSOPHY **EDUCATION** Trinity Int Univ, MA, 86; Marquette Univ, PhD, 95. **CAREER** Affil prof & fac and curric coordr, St Ambrose Univ, 95-98; ctr dir, Spring Arbor Col, 98-. **MEMBERSHIPS** Soc Christian Philos; Am Philos Asn. **RESEARCH** Logic of Christian doctrine; Public policy. **CONTACT ADDRESS** 231 Aberdeen Ct, Belleville, MI, 48111.

LONG III, EUGENE T.
PERSONAL Born 03/16/1935, Richmond, VA, m, 1960, 2 children **DISCIPLINE** PHILOSOPHY **EDUCATION** Randolph Macon Col, BA, 57; Duke Univ, BD, 60; Univ of Glasgow, PhD, 64 **CAREER** Asst to Assoc Prof; 64-70, Randolph-Macon Col; Assoc to Prof, 73-pres, Univ of SC; Chair Dept Philos, Univ S Carolina, 72-87 **HONORS AND AWARDS** Russell Research Award, 86; Metaphysical Soc of Amer Pres, 98; Pres Soc for Philos of Relig, 80; NEH Summer Res Fel, 68; Duke Univ of N Carolina Res Fel, 69 **MEMBERSHIPS** Am Philos Assoc; Metaphys Soc of Am; Soc for Philos of Relig **RESEARCH** Philos of Relig; 19th & 20th Century European Philos **SELECTED PUBLICATIONS** Auth, "In Search of Transcendence," Rev Metaphysics, 98; "The Gifford Lectures and the Scottish Personal Idealist, Rev Metaphysics, 95 **CONTACT ADDRESS** Dept of Philos, Univ of S. Carolina, Columbia, SC, 29208. **EMAIL** N510008@vm.sc.edu

LONGENECKER, RICHARD NORMAN
PERSONAL Born 07/21/1930, Mishawaka, IN, m, 1955, 3 children **DISCIPLINE** NEW TESTAMENT THEOLOGY **EDUCATION** Wheaton Col, Ill, BA, 53, MA, 56; Univ Edinburgh, PhD, 59. **CAREER** Instr Bible, Wheaton Col, Ill, 56-57, asst prof theol, 60-62, grad sch theol, 62-63; from assoc prof to prof New Testament, Trinity Evangel Divinity Sch, 63-73; PROF NEW TESTAMENT, WYCLIFFE COL, UNIV TORONTO, 72-, Am Asn Theol Schs fac fel, 66-67; mem sch bd, Ill Unit Dist 95, Lake Zurich, 70-72. **MEMBERSHIPS** Evangel Theol Soc (secy, 62-64, treas, 64-65, vpres, 73, pres, 74); Soc Bibl Lit; Studiorum Novi Testamenti Soc; Just Bibl Res. **RESEARCH** Pauline theology; early Jewish Christianity; inter-testamental period. **SELECTED PUBLICATIONS** Auth, Power and Politics in Palestine--the Jews and the Governing of their Land 100BC-AD70, Interpretation-J Bible and Theol, Vol 0047, 93. **CONTACT ADDRESS** Wycliffe Col, Toronto, ON, M5S 1A1.

LONGINO, HELEN
DISCIPLINE PHILOSOPHY **EDUCATION** Johns Hopkins Univ, PhD. **RESEARCH** Social nature of scientific knowledge; biological bases of human nature. **SELECTED PUBLICATIONS** Auth, Explanation v. Interpretation in the Critique of Science, Sci Context, 97; Feminist Epistemology as a Local Epistemology, 97. **CONTACT ADDRESS** Philosophy Dept, Univ of Minnesota, Twin Cities, 355 Ford Hall, 224 Church St SE, Minneapolis, MN, 55455. **EMAIL** hlongino@tc.umn.edu

LONGMAN, TREMPER, III
PERSONAL Born 09/08/1948, Princeton, NJ, m, 1973, 3 children **DISCIPLINE** THEOLOGY **EDUCATION** Ohio Wesleyan Univ, BA, 74; Westminster Theol Sem, MDiv, 77; Yale Univ, MA, 80, PhD, 83. **CAREER** Westminster Theol Sem, prof, 81-98; Westmont Col, prof, 98-. **MEMBERSHIPS** SBL, IBR. **RESEARCH** Old Testament; ancient near east. **SELECTED PUBLICATIONS** Coauth, Cry of the Soul: How Our Emotions Reveal Our Deepest Questions About God, Nav Press, 94; auth, Psalms, Geneva Study Bible, Thomas Nelson, 95; coauth, When God Declares War, Christianity Today, 96; auth, How to Read the Psalms, Discipleship Jour, 97; auth, Reading the Bible with Heart and Mind, Nav Press, 97; auth, Guilt and Compassion: Old Testament versus New Testament?, Modern Reformation, 97; coauth, Bold Purpose: Exchanging Counterfeit Happiness for the Real Meaning of Life, Tyndale House Pub, 98. **CONTACT ADDRESS** Dept of Old Testament, Westmont Col, 955 La Paz Rd, Santa Barbara, CA, 93108. **EMAIL** longman@westmont.edu

LONGSTAFF, THOMAS R.W.
PERSONAL Born 10/09/1935, Nashua, NH, m, 1969, 5 children **DISCIPLINE** RELIGIOUS STUDIES **EDUCATION** Univ Maine, BA, 64; Bangor Theol Sem, BD, 64; Columbia Univ, PhD, 73. **CAREER** Inst, Colby Col, 69-73, asst prof, 73-79, assoc prof, 79-84, full prof, 84-81, dir Amer Studies, 87-89, chmn, Soc Sci Div, 87-90, chmn, phil/relig, 89-91, dir, African-Amer Studies, 92-93, chmn, relig studies, 92-96; vis prof, Bangor Theol Sem, 75. **HONORS AND AWARDS** Woodrow Wilson Fellow, 64; Colby Col, Charles A. Dana Prof of Relig Studies, 91-94, Crawford Family Prof of Relig Studies, 94-. **MEMBERSHIPS** Am Sch Orient Res; Cath Bibl Asn of Am; Israel Exploration Soc; Maine Archaeol Asn; Maine Philos Inst; Soc of Bibl Lit; Studiorum Novi Testamenti Societas. **RESEARCH** Biblical archaeology and Christian origins; Judaism and Christianity in the Roman and Byzantine Periods. **SELECTED PUBLICATIONS** Co-auth, "Palynology and Cultural Process: An Exercise in the New Archaeology," 97; auth, Computer Recording, Analysis, and Interpretation," 97; auth, "The Gush Halav Synagogue," 96; co-auth, "Zipproi--1991," 95; co-auth, "Excavations at Sepphoris: The Location and Identification of Shikhin," pts 1-2, 94-5. **CONTACT ADDRESS** Colby Col, 4643 Mayflower Hill, Waterville, ME, 04901-8846.

LOPES, DOMINIC MCIVER
PERSONAL Born 07/03/1964, Aberdeen, Scotland, d **DISCIPLINE** PHILOSOPHY **EDUCATION** McGill Univ, BA, 86; Oxford Univ, DPhil, 92. **CAREER** Vis asst prof Philos, Perdue Univ, 91-92; asst prof Philos, 92-97, assoc prof Philos, Ind Univ-Kokomo, 97- . **MEMBERSHIPS** Amer Soc Aesthetics; Amer Philos Asn. **RESEARCH** Philosophy of art, Philosophy of mind, ethics. **SELECTED PUBLICATIONS** Auth, Understanding Pictures, Oxford UP, 96. **CONTACT ADDRESS** Dept of Humanities, Indiana Univ, Kokomo, Kokomo, IN, 46904-9003. **EMAIL** dlopes@indiana.edu

LOPEZ-MORILLAS, CONSUELO
PERSONAL Born 07/07/1944, Iowa City, IA, m, 1971, 2 children **DISCIPLINE** ROMANCE & HISPANO-ARABIC LITERATURE **EDUCATION** Bryn Mawr Col, BA, 65; Univ Calif, Berkeley, PhD, 74. **CAREER** Asst prof, Ohio State Univ, 74-77; from Asst Prof to Assoc Prof, 77-94, Prof Spanish and Near Eastern Lang, Ind Univ, 94-; Vis asst prof Arabic, Ohio State Univ, 79. **MEMBERSHIPS** MLA; Am Oriental Soc; Asociacion Internacional de Hispanistas. **RESEARCH** Hispano-Arabic language and literature; Romance linguistics; Hispanic linguistics (historical). **SELECTED PUBLICATIONS** Auth, Aljamiado akosegir and its old provencal counterparts, Romance Philol, 75; Los bereberes Zanata en la historia y la leyenda, Al-Andalus, 77; Trilingual Marginal notes in a Morisco manuscript from Toledo, J of the Am Oriental Soc, 82; La oracion como dialogo en un comentario morisco sobre la Fatiha, Nueva Revista de Filologia Hisp, 82; The Quran in 16th Century Spain: Six Morisco Versions of Sura 79, Tamesis Books, London, 82; Was the Muwashsah Really Accompanied by the Organ?, La Coronica, 85; Hispano-Semitic Calques and the Context of Translation, Bulletin of Hispanic Studies, 90; Language and Identity in Late Spanish Islam, Hispanic Rev, 95; Textos aljamiados sobre la vida de Mahoma: El profeta de los moriscos, CSIC, Madrid, 94. **CONTACT ADDRESS** Dept of Spanish & Portuguese, Indiana Univ, Bloomington, Bloomington, IN, 47405. **EMAIL** lopez@indiana.edu

LORD, TIMOTHY C.
PERSONAL Born 11/05/1960, Elizabethtown, KY, m, 1995, 1 child **DISCIPLINE** PHILOSOPHY **EDUCATION** Purdue Univ, PhD, 95. **CAREER** Prof, philos, Heartland Community

Col, 93-. **HONORS AND AWARDS** Who's Who in the Midwest, 98. **MEMBERSHIPS** Amer Philos Asn; Intl Asn for Philos and Lit; Amer Soc for Aesthetics; Soc for Phenomenol and Existential Philos. **RESEARCH** Philosophy of history; History of philosophy; Aesthetics; Epistemology. **SELECTED PUBLICATIONS** Rev, Philosophical Historicism and the Betrayal of First Philosophy, CLIO: A Jour of Lit, Hist and the Philos of Hist, 26.3, 390-97, 97; article, A Paradigm Case of Polemical History: Terry Eagleton's The Ideology of the Aesthetic, CLIO: A Jour of Lit, Hist and the Philos of Hist, 22.4, 337-56, 93; rev, Philosophy and Its History: Issues in Philosophical Historiography, CLIO: A Jour of Lit, Hist and the Philos of Hist, 22.4, 396-99, 93; article, Hegel, Marx, and Shoeless Joe: Religious Ideology in Kinsella's Baseball Fantasy, Aethlon: The Jour of Sport Lit, 10.1, 43-51, 92; rev, The Ideology of the Aesthetic, Philos and Lit, 16.2, 374-76, 92. **CONTACT ADDRESS** Heartland Comm Col, 1228 Towanda Av., Bloomington, IL, 61701. **EMAIL** tim@hcc.cc.il.us

LOREK, ROBERT
PERSONAL Born 05/02/1966, Chicago, IL, s **DISCIPLINE** PHILOSOPHY **EDUCATION** Univ Dayton, BS, bus adm, 88; Univ Nebr, MA, philos, 94. **CAREER** Adjunct prof, Elmhurst Col, Col of Dupage, Univ St. Francis. **MEMBERSHIPS** Amer Philos Asn. **RESEARCH** Ethics; Epistemology; Metaethical theory. **SELECTED PUBLICATIONS** Auth, Intuition: A Foundation for Moral Principles, Quest For Goodness, Krasemann, Simon & Schuster, 98. **CONTACT ADDRESS** 1504 W. Jackson, Chicago, IL, 60607. **EMAIL** robertl@elmhurst.edu

LOSONCY, THOMAS A.
DISCIPLINE PHILOSOPHY **EDUCATION** Sacred Heart Sem, BA, 61; Univ Detroit, MA, 63; Univ Toronto, PhD, 72. **CAREER** Assoc prof,Villanova Univ. **SELECTED PUBLICATIONS** Auth, St Augustine, in Ethics in the History of Western Philos, NY; St Martin's Press, Chap 3, 89; The Soul-Body Problem in the Thirteenth Century: Countering the Trend Toward Dualism, Stud in Medieval Cult XII, 78; St Anselm's Rejection of the 'Ontological Argument' - A Review of the Occasion and Circumstances, Amer Cath Philos Quart, LXIV, 90; Plato's Meno Argument for Recollection: Correct and Incorrect, Methexis, Etudes Neoplatoniciennes Presenteees au Professeur Evanghelos A. Moutsopoulos, Athenes: Ctr Int d'Etudes Platoniciennes et Aristoleciennes, 92 & Giles of Rome (Aegidius Romanus), Dictionary of Literary Biog Vol 115: Medieval Philos, Detroit and London: Gale Res Inc, 92. **CONTACT ADDRESS** Dept of Philosophy, Villanova Univ, 800 Lancaster Ave, Villanova, PA, 19085-1692.

LOSONSKY, MICHAEL
DISCIPLINE PHILOSOPHY **EDUCATION** Univ Rochester, PhD, 82. **CAREER** Assoc prof. **SELECTED PUBLICATIONS** Auth, pubs on philosophy of mind and history of early modern philosophy; co-auth, Readings in Language and Mind, Blackwell, 96; Beginning Metaphysics, Blackwell, 98. **CONTACT ADDRESS** Philosophy Dept, Colorado State Univ, Fort Collins, CO, 80523.

LOTT, JOHN BERTRAND
DISCIPLINE RELIGION **EDUCATION** Washington Univ, St Louis, BA, 89; Univ Pa, PhD, 95. **CAREER** Asst prof; lect, Amer Philol Asn, Chicago, 97, York Univ, Ont, 96; Amer Philol Asn, San Diego, 95; invited lect, Phi Alpha Theta lect His, Wichita State Univ, 97, Pomona Col, Wichita State Univ & Vassar Col, 97; Swarthmore Col, 95; Union Col, Schenectady, 95. **RESEARCH** The age of Augustus; Silver age Latin; ancient religion; Greek and Roman history. **SELECTED PUBLICATIONS** Auth, Philip II, Alexander and the Two Tyrannies at Eresos of IG XII 2 526, Phoenix 50 1, 96; An Augustan Sculpture of August Justice, ZPE 96; **CONTACT ADDRESS** Classics Dept, Vassar Col, Box 244, Poughkeepsie, NY, 12604. **EMAIL** jolott@vassar.edu

LOUCH, ALFRED
PERSONAL Born 02/14/1927, Fresno, CA, m, 1951, 2 children **DISCIPLINE** PHILOSOPHY **EDUCATION** Univ Calif, Berkeley, BA,49, MA, 51; Cambridge Univ, PhD, 56. **CAREER** Teaching asst, Univ Calif, Berkeley, 49-52; instr philos, Oberlin Col, 57-59; from asst prof to assoc prof, Syracuse Univ, 59-65; PROF PHILOS, CLAREMONT GRAD SCH, 65-, Vis assoc prof, Univ Calif, Los Angeles, 63-64. **RESEARCH** Philosophy of mind; philosophy of the social sciences and psychology; philosophy of law. **SELECTED PUBLICATIONS** Auth, The Myth of theory, Philos and Lit, Vol 0020, 96; The Reign of Ideology, Philos and Lit, Vol 0021, 97; Opera--Desire, Disease, Death, Philos and Lit, Vol 0021, 97; Reclaiming Truth--Contributions to a Critique of Cultural Relativism, Philos and Lit, Vol 0021, 97. **CONTACT ADDRESS** Dept of Philos, Claremont Graduate Sch, Claremont, CA, 91711.

LOUDEN, ROBERT B.
PERSONAL Born 04/08/1953, Lafayette, IN, m, 1985, 2 children **DISCIPLINE** PHILOSOPHY **EDUCATION** Univ Calif Santa Cruz, BA, 75; Univ Chi, MA, 76; PhD, 81 **CAREER** Prof Philos, Univ S Maine, 96-; vis assoc prof Philos, Emory Unif, 95; vis assoc prof Philos, Gottingen Univ Germany, 92; assoc prof Philosophy, Univ S Maine, 88-96; asst prof Philos, Univ S Maine, 82-88; vis asst prof Philos, Iowa St Univ, 80-82; adjunct lctr, Barat Col, 79-80; adjunct lctr, Ind Univ, 77-80. **HONORS AND AWARDS** Humboldt Found Res Gel, 91-92, 96-97; Ntl Endowment Humanities Fel, 96; NEH Summer Sem Fel, 83, 85, 88, 93; Amer Council Learned Soc Fel, 89-90; NEH Summer Stipend, 89. **MEMBERSHIPS** Amer Philos Assoc; Humboldt Assoc Amer **RESEARCH** Ethics; History of Moral Philosophy; Kant; Aristotle. **SELECTED PUBLICATIONS** Kant's Impure Ethics: From Rational Beings to Human Beings, Oxford Univ Pr, forthcoming; Morality and Moral Theory: A Reappraisal and Reaffirmation, Oxford Univ Pr, 92; The Education of Humanity: A Kantian Primer," Jrnl Educ, 97; What is Moral Authority? Euboulia, Sunesis, and Gnome vs. Phronesis, Ancient Philos, 97. **CONTACT ADDRESS** Dept of Philosophy, S Maine Univ, 96 Falmouth St, Portland, ME, 04104-9300. **EMAIL** louden@portland.maine.edu

LOUGHRAN, JAMES N.
PERSONAL Born 03/22/1940, Brooklyn, NY **DISCIPLINE** PHILOSOPHY **EDUCATION** Fordham Univ, BA, 64; MA, 65; PhD, 85. **CAREER** Joined SJ, 58; ordained priest, 70; instr, St. Peter's Col, 65-67; ast dean Fordham Univ, 70-73; tchr, Fordham Univ, 74-79, 82-84, dean 79-82; pres, Loyola Marymount Univ, 84-91; act pres, Brooklyn Coll, 92; Miller prof, John Carroll Univ, 92-93; interim pres, Mount St Mary's Coll, 93-94; interim acad vpres, Fordham Univ, 94-95; pres, St. Peter's College, 95- . **HONORS AND AWARDS** PhD, hon, Loyola Col, 85. **MEMBERSHIPS** APA; Am Catholic Philos Asn. **RESEARCH** Moral philosophy. **SELECTED PUBLICATIONS** "Reasons for Being Just," Value of Justice, Fordham Univ, 79; "The Moral Ideal of the Person," Int Philos Q, 86; "Francis Hutcheson," Hist of Philos Q, 86. **CONTACT ADDRESS** President's Off, St. Peter's Col, 2641 Kennedy Blvd., Jersey City, NJ, 07305. **EMAIL** loughran_j@spcvxa.spc.edu

LOUNIBOS, JOHN
PERSONAL Born 03/21/1934, Petaluma, CA, m, 1970, 2 children **DISCIPLINE** HUMANITIES, RELIGIOUS STUDIES **CAREER** Tchng, 61-, Bellarmine HS, San Jose, CA; prof, relig stud, 71-98, Dominican Col, Blauvelt **HONORS AND AWARDS** 3 NEH summer fellowships for college teachers: with John Gager, Princeton Univ, 79; with Arthur Hyman, Columbia/Yeshiva Univ, 84; with William Dever, Univ AZ, Tuscon, 95. **MEMBERSHIPS** AAR; Col Theol Soc; Int Soc for Neoplatonic Stud; Soc for Medieval Renaissance Philos. **RESEARCH** Philos and relig texts, histories, and interpretation. **SELECTED PUBLICATIONS** Co-ed, The College I Experience: Integrating Work, Leisure and Service, (ASC), 80; co-ed, Pagan and Christian Anxiety: A Response to E. R. Dodds, UAP, 84. **CONTACT ADDRESS** Dominican Col, Blauvelt, 470 Western Hwy, Orangeburg, NY, 10962. **EMAIL** JLounibos@aol.com

LOUX, MICHAEL
DISCIPLINE PHILOSOPHY **EDUCATION** Col of St. Thomas, BA, 64; Univ Chicago, MA, 65, PhD, 68. **CAREER** Prof. **RESEARCH** Ancient philosophy; metaphysics. **SELECTED PUBLICATIONS** Auth, Primary Ousia, 91; Understanding Process: Reflections on Physics, 94; Composition and Unity, 94; Kinds and Predication: Aristotle's Categories, Philos Papers, 97; Beyond Substrata and Bundles, Cont Metaphysics, 97; An Introduction to Metaphysics, 97. **CONTACT ADDRESS** Philosophy Dept, Univ of Notre Dame, 336/7 O'Shaughnessy, Notre Dame, IN, 46556. **EMAIL** loux.1@nd.edu

LOVEJOY, GRANT I.
PERSONAL m, 2 children **DISCIPLINE** THEOLOGY **EDUCATION** Baylor Univ, BA, 80; Southwestern Baptist Theol Semi, MDiv, 84, PhD, 90. **CAREER** Assoc prof, Southwwestern Baptist Theol Sem, 88-. **HONORS AND AWARDS** Col Minister, Emmanuel Baptist Church, 78-83; pastor, Kingswood ISU, 84-85; Shady Shores Baptist Church, 85-88. **MEMBERSHIPS** Acad Homiletics; Rel Speech Commun Assn; Evangel Homiletic Soc. **SELECTED PUBLICATIONS** Auth, Biblical Hermeneutics, Broadman & Holman, 96; Pastoral Preaching, Leadership Handbooks of Practical Theol, Word & Worship, Baker Bk House, 92; Pulpit Humor, Leadership handbooks of Practical Theol: Word & Worship, Baker Bk House, 92; Emotion in Preaching, Leadership Handbooks of Practical Theol: Word & Worship, Baker Bk House, 92. **CONTACT ADDRESS** Sch Theol, Southwestern Baptist Theol Sem, PO Box 22000, Fort Worth, TX, 76122-0418. **EMAIL** glovejoy@swbts.swbts.edu

LOVETT, LEONARD
PERSONAL Born 12/05/1939, Pompano Beach, FL, m **DISCIPLINE** THEOLOGY **EDUCATION** Saints Jr Coll, AA 1959; Morehouse Coll, BA 1962; Crozer Theological Seminary, MDiv 1965; Emory Univ Candler's Grad Sch of Theology, PhD 1979. **CAREER** Meml COGIC, pastor 1962-70; Health & Welfare Council Philadelphia New York City Proj, coord 1965-67; Stephen Smith Towers 202 Senior Citizens, proj mgr 1967-70; Ch Mason Theological Seminary, pioneer pres 1970-74; Fuller Theological Seminary, assoc dir Black Ministries 1977-81. **MEMBERSHIPS** Pres Soc for Pentecostal Studies 1975; mem Soc for the Study of Black Religion 1972-; reactor Vatican-Pentecostal Dialogue W Germany 1974; visit prof Grad Theological Union Berkeley 1975; prof of Ethics & Theology Ecumenical Cntr for Black Church Studies 1978-; prof of Ethics & Theology Amer Bapt Seminary of the West 1984; visiting fellow Human Behavior Amer Inst of Family Relations 1982-85; bd mem, Watts Health Foundation, United Health Plan 1985-; columnist, Black Perspective, Ministries Today Magazine 1988-. **SELECTED PUBLICATIONS** Conditional Liberation Spirit Journal 1977; What Charismatics Can Learn from Black Pentecostals Logos Journal 1980; Tribute to Martin Luther King in Outstanding Black Sermons Vol 2 Judson Press 1982; contrib Aspects of the Spiritual Legacy of the Church of God in Christ in Mid-Stream An Ecumenical Journal Vol XXIV No 4 1985, Black Witness to the Apostolic Faith Eardmans 1988; Black Holiness-Pentecostalism, Black Theology, Positive Confession Theology, Dictionary of the Pentecostal Charismatic Movement, Zondervan 1988; Doctor of Laws, Saints Jr College, 1972. **CONTACT ADDRESS** Church at the Crossroads COGIC, 9216 Parmelee Ave, Los Angeles, CA, 90002.

LOW, ROY
PERSONAL Born 11/14/1953, San Francisco, CA, m, 1985, 2 children **DISCIPLINE** BIBLICAL STDS; OLD TESTAMENT **EDUCATION** Univ Cal Berkeley, BS, 76; Dallas Theol Sem, ThM, 84; Golden Gate Baptist Theol Sem, PhD, 95. **CAREER** Civil engr, Pac Gas & Elec Co, 77-84; asst to assoc pastor, Cumberland Presby Chinese Church, 84-92; asst to assoc prof of Old Testament, W Sem, 92-99. **HONORS AND AWARDS** Who's Who Among Stud, Amer Univ & Col, 92-93. **MEMBERSHIPS** Soc Bibl Lit; Asn Prof Hebrew Evangel Theol Soc. **RESEARCH** Poetic literature (Biblical); Rhetoric **CONTACT ADDRESS** 359 Michelle Ln., Daly City, CA, 94015. **EMAIL** Roy1amylow@aol.com

LOWE, EUGENE Y., JR.
PERSONAL Born 08/18/1949, New York, NY, m, 4 children **DISCIPLINE** RELIGION; CHURCH HISTORY **EDUCATION** Princeton Univ, AB, 71; Union Theol Sem, M Div, 78; Union Theol Sem, PhD, 87. **CAREER** Res assoc and consult, Andrew W. Mellon Found, 93-97; lectr, dept of relig, Princeton Univ, 93-95; dean of students, Princeton Univ, 83-93; assoc provost, Northwestern Univ, 95-. **HONORS AND AWARDS** Phi Beta Kappa; Protestant fel; fund for Theol Educ, 76-77; Harold Willis Dodds Prize, Princeton Univ, 71; grad fel, Episcopal Church Found, 78-81. **MEMBERSHIPS** Amer Acad of Relig; Amer Soc of Church Hist; Lilly Seminar on Relig and Higher Educ. **SELECTED PUBLICATIONS** Auth, Walter Righter, Dict of Heresy Trials in American Christianity, Greenwood Press, 320-326, 97; auth, Racial Ideology, Encycl of Amer Social Hist, 335-346, Charles Scribner's Sons, 93; auth, From Social Gospel to Social Science at the University of Wisconsin, The Church's Public Role: Retrospect and Prospect, 233-251, Eerdmans, 93; auth, Mordecai Kaplan, Twentieth-Century Shapers of American Popular Religion, 210-217, Greenwood, 89. **CONTACT ADDRESS** Office of the Provost, Northwestern Univ, Crown Center 2-154, Evanston, IL, 60208.

LOWENFELD, ANDREAS F
PERSONAL Born 05/30/1930, Berlin, Germany, m, 1962, 2 children **DISCIPLINE** INTERNATIONAL LAW **EDUCATION** Harvard Univ, AB, 51, LLB, 55. **CAREER** From spec asst to dep legal adv US Dept State, 61-66, prof, 67-80, CHARLES L DENISON PROF LAW, NY UNIV, 80-. **MEMBERSHIPS** Am Soc Int Law; Am Bar Asn. **RESEARCH** Aviation law; international economic law and transactions; conflict of laws. **SELECTED PUBLICATIONS** Auth, Rules of Origin, the Canada United States Fta, and the Honda Case, Amer J Int Law, Vol 0087, 93; Thoughts about a Multinational Judgments Convention--a Reaction to the Vonmehren Report, Law and Contemp Problems, Vol 0057, 94; Remedies Along With Rights--Institutional Reform in the New Gatt, Amer J Int Law, Vol 0088, 94; Choice of Law and Multistate Justice, Amer J Int Law, Vol 0088, 94; Conflict, Balancing of Interests, and the Exercise of Jurisdiction to Prescribe--Reflections on the Insurance Antitrust Case, Amer J Int Law, Vol 0089, 95; Enforcing International Trade Law--the Evolution of the Modern Gatt Legal System, Amer J Int Law, Vol 0089, 95; The USA, the EEC, and the Gatt--the Road Not Taken, Univ Pa J Int Econ Law, Vol 0017, 96; Congress and Cuba--the Helms Burton Act, Amer J Int Law, Vol 0090, 96; Forum Shopping, Antisuit Injunctions, Negative Declarations, and Related Tools of International Litigation, Amer J Int Law, Vol 0091, 97; Nationalizing International Law--Essay in Honor of Henkin, Louis, Columbia J Transnational Law, Vol 0036, 97. **CONTACT ADDRESS** SCH LAW, New York Univ, 550 1ST AVE, NEW YORK, NY, 10012.

LOWENSTEIN, D.H.
PERSONAL Born 05/10/1943, New York, NY, m, 1970, 2 children **DISCIPLINE** LAW **EDUCATION** Yale Univ, BA 64; Harvard Univ LLB 67. **CAREER** UCLA, prof 79-; Cal Fair Pol Pract Comm, ch 75-79; Cal Deputy Sec of State, 71-75; Cal Rural Leg asst, 68-71. **MEMBERSHIPS** CSB; APSA; ALSC; MLA **RESEARCH** Election Law; Law and Lit **SELECTED**

PUBLICATIONS Auth, Election Law, Carolina Acad Press, 95; You don't have to be Liberal to hate the racial Gerrymandering cases, Stanford Law Rev, 98; The Failure of the Act: Conceptions of Law in, The Merchant of Venice, Bleak House, Les Miserables, and Richard Weisberg's Poetics, Cardozo Law Rev, 94; Are Congressional Term Limits Constitutional?, Harv Jour of La w & Pub Policy, 94. **CONTACT ADDRESS** Dept of Law, UCLouisiana, 405 Hilgard, Los Angeles, CA, 90095-1476. **EMAIL** lowenste@mail.ucla.edu

LOWERY, MARK
PERSONAL WI, m, 8 children **DISCIPLINE** THEOLOGY **EDUCATION** Marquette Univ, PhD. **CAREER** Prof, Dallas Univ. **RESEARCH** Importance and complementary nature of theological education, spiritual formation and pastoral training. **SELECTED PUBLICATIONS** Faith and Reason; Irish Theol Quart; New Oxford Rev; Catholic Faith; Homiletic and Pastoral Rev; Soc Justice Rev and Envoy. **CONTACT ADDRESS** Instit for Religious and Pastoral Studies, Univ of Dallas, 1845 E Northgate Dr, Irving, TX, 75062.

LU, MATTHIAS
PERSONAL Born 06/02/1919, China **DISCIPLINE** PHILOSOPHY, THEOLOGY **EDUCATION** Pontifical Urbanian Univ, Rome, PhD, 46. **CAREER** Prof philos, theol, Fujen Univ, Peking, 46-48; chemn Educ Comt for Parish Co-Operatives, Ontario, 51-56; instr philos Univ Notre Dame, 56-58; vis lectr St Bonaventure Univ, 58-59; asst prof St John's Univ, 59-62; res assoc Univ Calif, Berkeley, 62- ; asst prof, 62-72, res assoc philos, 72- , scholar in res, 73- , St Mary's Col of Calif; vicar for Chinese and East Asian people, Oakland CA, 69-86; dir St Thomas Aquinas Int Ctr, 74- . **HONORS AND AWARDS** Pro Ecclesia et Pontefice Medal, Pope Pius XII, 39; Gold Medal for Distinguished Service, Pope John Paul II, 85; honorary PhD, Scicluna Int Univ Found, 87; Einstein Medal, 88; honorary ThD, Albert Einstein Int Acad Found, 93. **MEMBERSHIPS** APA; Am Cath Philos Asn; Am Oriental Soc; AAAS; Am Acad Polit and Soc Sci; Cath Theol Soc Am; Chinese Hist Soc of Am; Int Soc of St Thomas Aquinas; Int Jacques Maritain Soc; Int Soc of Metaphysics; Int Asn of Symbolic Logic; Int Soc of Chinese Philos. **SELECTED PUBLICATIONS** Auth, Common People Need the Common Doctor, Moraga, 79; auth, Einstein for Peace and Harmony between Science and Religion, Int Acad of Albert Einstein, 91; auth, Human Family and Human Children for a Human World, World Forum of NGO's, U.N., 93; auth, Dialogue of Christianity with Cultures in China in Francis, ed, Christian Humanism, International Perspectives, Peter Lang, 95; Martyrdom for Truth and Liberty in the People's Republic of China: a 1949-1996 report to the Fifth World Congress of Christian Philosophy, Euntes Docete, 96; auth, Hypocrisy or Tactful Machination? Cath Int, 96; auth, A Plea for Freedom, Cath Int, 98. **CONTACT ADDRESS** St. Thomas Aquinas Center, St Mary's Col, PO Box 3014, Moraga, CA, 94575.

LUBECK, RAY
PERSONAL Born 05/29/1954, Waco, TX, m, 1981, 2 children **DISCIPLINE** OLD TESTAMENT STUDIES **EDUCATION** Multnomah Bible Col, BS, 79; Trinity Evangel Divinity Sch, MA, 86; Univ of South Africa, DTh, cand. **CAREER** Lectr, Ecola Bible Sch, 6 yrs; adj prof, Western Sem, 4 yrs; prof, Multnomah Bible Col, 8 years. **HONORS AND AWARDS** Cum laude, 86. Who's Who Among America's Tchrs, 98. **MEMBERSHIPS** Evangel Theol Soc; Soc of Bibl Lit. **RESEARCH** Old Testament; hermeneutics; Biblical theology. **SELECTED PUBLICATIONS** Auth, Studies in the Literary Structure of Johah, Trinity Evangel Divinity Sch, 86; "Prophetic Sabotage," Trinity J, 88; rev, Hermeneutics as Theological Prolegomena by Scalise, Intepretation and the Bible by McEvenue, J of the Evangel Theol Soc, 96. **CONTACT ADDRESS** Multnomah Bible Col and Biblical Sem, 8435 NE Glisan St., Portland, OR, 97220. **EMAIL** rlubeck@teleport.com

LUCAS, RAYMOND E.
PERSONAL Born 06/26/1932, Richmond, VA, m, 1962, 1 child **DISCIPLINE** PHILOSOPHY **EDUCATION** Univ Va, BA, 58, MA, 63; Tulane Univ, PhD, 67. **CAREER** Asst prof, 66-67, assoc prof, 67-70, E Tenn State Univ; assoc prof, 70-73, prof, 73-93, chr Dept Philoso, 79-90, prof Emer, 93 , Kutztown Univ. **MEMBERSHIPS** APA; S Soc Philos & Psychol. **RESEARCH** Epistemology; Social and political philosophy. **CONTACT ADDRESS** 321 Spring St, Fleetwood, PA, 19522.

LUCASH, FRANK S.
PERSONAL Born 02/06/1938, Belleville, IL, m, 1966, 2 children **DISCIPLINE** PHILOSOPHY **EDUCATION** Southern Illinois Univ, BA, 59, MA, 66, PhD, 70. **CAREER** Univ Nevada Reno, lectr, 68-70; asst prof, 70-80; assoc prof, 80-. **MEMBERSHIPS** APA, NASS **RESEARCH** Baruch Spinoza; Philo of Mind. **SELECTED PUBLICATIONS** Auth, The Philosophical Method of Spinoza's Treatise on the Emendation of the Intellect, and its Application to the Ethics, Philo and Theol, 93; Spinoza's Philosophy of Immanence -- Dogmatic or Critical? Jour of Spec Philo, 94; Does Self-Knowledge Lead to Self-Esteem?, Studia Spinozana, 92; Essence and Existence in Part # of Spinoza's Ethics, 94; Spinoza's Dialectical Method, Can Philo Rev, 95; The Co-Extensiveness of the Attributes in Spinoza, SW Philo Rev, 96. **CONTACT ADDRESS** Dept of Philosophy, Univ of Nevada, Reno, NV, 89557. **EMAIL** lucash@equinox.unr.edu

LUCE, DAVID R.
PERSONAL Born 02/22/1927, Boston, MA, m, 1962, 2 children **DISCIPLINE** PHILOSOPHY **EDUCATION** Dartmouth Col, BA, 50; Univ of Michigan, MA, 52, PhD, 57. **CAREER** Univ of Arkansas, inst, 57-59; Univ of Minnesota, inst, 59-60; Univ of Chicago, vis asst prof, 60; Univ of Wisconsin Milwaukee, asst prof, assoc prof, prof, 60-. **HONORS AND AWARDS** Phi Beta Kappa, Thayer Prize Math. **MEMBERSHIPS** APA, ASL, AAUP, PBK. **RESEARCH** Ethics; Social philosophy; philosophy of religion. **SELECTED PUBLICATIONS** Auth, Causal Relations Between Mind and Body: A New Formulation of the Mind Body Problem, Ann Arbor: Univ Microfilms, 57; auth, The Smith Act, Nixon's Smith Act and the Smith Act in the McClellan-Hruska Criminal Code Bill, in: Loyola of L. A. Law Rev, vol 9, no 2, 76; auth, A Proposal Even More Radical Than Proxmire's Bill to De-Regulate the Broadcasting Industry Entirely, Free Speech, 77; auth, Potential Personhood and the Rights of the Unconceived, in: Conscience: A Newsjournal of Prochoice Catholic Opinion, 86; auth, Civil Liberties and the Citizen, 1993 Viewpoints on War, Peace and Global Cooperation: The Annual Jour, 93; The Sociobiologist is Wearing No Clothes, Shepherd Express, 98. **CONTACT ADDRESS** 2914 N Downer Ave, Milwaukee, WI, 53211. **EMAIL** luce@csd.uwm.edu

LUCK, DONALD G.
PERSONAL Born 01/02/1933, Portchester, NY, d, 3 children **DISCIPLINE** THEOLOGY **EDUCATION** Gettysburg Col, BA, 54; Lutheran Theol Sem, BD, 57; Union Theol Sem, STM, 66, PhD, 78. **CAREER** Parish pastor, metro NY, 58-65; from asst prof to assoc prof relig, Concordia Col, 69-82; from assoc prof systematic theol to T.A. Kantonen prof systematic theol, Trinity Lutheran Sem, 82-. **MEMBERSHIPS** Am Acad Relig; Soc Buddhist/Christian Studies. **RESEARCH** Doctrinal theology; philosophical theology; Christian-Buddhist dialogue. **SELECTED PUBLICATIONS** Auth, The A-B-C's of Theology: User-Friendly Orientation for Beginners, 99; auth, Taking a Page from Paul: Facing Contemporary Temptations of Acculturated Ministry, Trinity Sem Rev, Fall/Winter, 97; auth, Anonymous Extravagance, Trinity Sem Rev, Fall, 95; auth, Reaffirming the Image of God as Father, Trinity Sem Rev, Fall, 94; auth, The New Passover, Lutheran Partners, March/April, 93. **CONTACT ADDRESS** Dept of Theology, Trinity Lutheran Sem, 2199 E Main St., Columbus, OH, 43209. **EMAIL** dluck@trinity.capital.edu

LUCK, DONALD L.
DISCIPLINE SYSTEMATIC THEOLOGY **EDUCATION** Gettysburg Col, BA, 54; Lutheran Theol Sem, BD, 57; Union Theol Sem, STM, 66, PhD, 78. **CAREER** Assoc prof, Concordia Col, 69-82; assoc prof, 82-85; vis prof, Lutheran Theol Sem, 86. T. A. Kantonen prof, 85-. **MEMBERSHIPS** Amer Acad Rel; N Amer Paul Tillich Soc; Soc Buddhist-Christian Stud. **SELECTED PUBLICATIONS** Auth, Taking a Page from Paul, Trinity Sem Rev, 97; Reaffirming the Image of God as Father, Trinity Sem Rev, 94; The New Passover, Lutheran Partners, 93; The Hamma Legacy, Trinity Sem Rev, 92. **CONTACT ADDRESS** Hist, Theol, Soc Dept, Trinity Lutheran Sem, 2199 E Main St, Columbus, OH, 43209-2334. **EMAIL** dluck@trinity.capital.edu

LUCKERT, KARL WILHELM
PERSONAL Born 11/18/1934, Winnenden-Hoefen, Germany, m, 1957, 3 children **DISCIPLINE** HISTORY OF RELIGIONS **EDUCATION** Univ Kans, BA, 63; Univ Chicago, MA, 67, PhD, 69. **CAREER** Vis lectr, rel, NCent Col, 68-69; asst prof humanities, Northern Ariz Univ, 69-79; assoc prof, 79-82, prof relig studies, Southwest Mo State Univ, 82-; gen ed, Am Tribal Relig series, Univ Nebr Press, 77-. **HONORS AND AWARDS** NEH res fel anthrop, Okla Univ, 72-73; Rockefeller Found Humanities res fel, 77-78; res assoc, Mus Northern Ariz, 77-; Burlington Northern Found Fac Achievement Award for Schol, 88; named hon prof, Univ Ningxia, China, 90; Excellence in Res Award, SMSU Found, 95. **MEMBERSHIPS** Am Acad Relig. **RESEARCH** American Indian religions; religion in evolution. **SELECTED PUBLICATIONS** Auth, The Navajo Hunter Tradition, Univ Ariz, 75; Olmec Religion: A Key to Middle America and Beyond, Okla Univ, 76; Navajo Mountain and Rainbow Bridge Religion, Mus Northern Ariz Press, 77; A Navajo Bringing-Home Ceremony, Mus Northern Ariz Univ, 78; Coyoteway, A Navajo Holyway Healing Ceremonial, Univ Ariz, 79; Egyptian Light and Hebrew Fire: Theological and Philosophical Roots of Christendom in Evolutionary Perspective, State Univ NY Press, 91; coauth, Myths and Legends of the Hui, a Muslim Chinese People, State Univ NY Press, 94; Kazakh Traditions in China, Univ Press Am, 98; Uighur Stories from Along the Silk Road, Univ Press Am, 98; author numerous journal articles. **CONTACT ADDRESS** Dept Relig Studies, Southwest Mo State Univ, 901 S National, Springfield, MO, 65804-0088. **EMAIL** luckert@dialnet.net

LUCKHARDT, C. GRANT
PERSONAL Born 10/25/1943, Palm Beach, FL, m, 1967, 1 child **DISCIPLINE** PHILOSOPHY **EDUCATION** St John's Col, AB, 65; Emory Univ, PhD(philos), 72. **CAREER** Asst prof, 71-76, assoc prof, 76-87, PROF PHILOS, GA STATE UNIV, 88-, DIR HONORS PROG, 89-; Vis tutor, St John's Col, summer, 76 & 77. **MEMBERSHIPS** Am Philos Asn. **RESEARCH** Wittgenstein; Native American thought. **SELECTED PUBLICATIONS** Wittgenstein: Investigations 50, Southern J of Philos, 77; Beyond Knowledge: Paradigms in Wittgenstein's Later Philosophy, Philos and Phenomenol Res, 78; Wittgenstein and His Impact on Contemporary Thought, 78 & Language, Logic and Philosophy, 80, Holder-Pichler-Tempsky; ed, Wittgenstein: Sources & Perspectives, Cornell Univ Press, 80; co-transl, L Wittgenstein: Remarks on the Philosophy of Psychology, Vol II, Blackwell's & Univ Chicago Press, 81; L Wittgenstein: Last Writings on the Philosophy of Psychology, vol I, Blackwell's, 82, vol II, 93; auth, Wittgenstein and Behaviorism, Synthese, 83; Lion Talk, Philos Investigations, 95. **CONTACT ADDRESS** Dept of Philos, Georgia State Univ, University Plaza, Atlanta, GA, 30303-3080. **EMAIL** dascgl@panther.gsu.edu

LUDWIG, JAN KEITH
PERSONAL Born 03/15/1942, Harrisburg, PA, m, 1965, 2 children **DISCIPLINE** PHILOSOPHY OF SCIENCE **EDUCATION** Gettysburg Col, BA, 63; Johns Hopkins Univ, PhD(-philos), 71. **CAREER** Instr, Am Univ, 67-69; from instr to asst prof, 69-75, ASSOC PROF PHILOS, UNION COL, NY, 75-, CHMN DEPT, 73-, Res fel, Harvard Univ, 76-77. **MEMBERSHIPS** Am Philos Asn; Philos Sci Asn; Hist Sci Soc. **RESEARCH** Analytic philosophy; philosophy of mind; history of science. **SELECTED PUBLICATIONS** Auth, Reading the Book of Nature--an Introduction to the Philosophy of Science, Isis, Vol 0084, 93; Philosophy of Science and its Discontents, Isis, Vol 0085, 94. **CONTACT ADDRESS** Dept of Philos Humanities Ctr, Union Col, 807 Union St, Schenectady, NY, 12308-3107.

LUDWIG, KIRK
PERSONAL Born 05/11/1959, Tulsa, OK, m **DISCIPLINE** PHILOSOPHY **EDUCATION** Univ of Calif Santa Barbara, BS, 81; Univ of Calif Berk, PhD, 90. **CAREER** Univ of Fla, asst prof, assoc prof, 90-. **HONORS AND AWARDS** R. M. Griffith Memorial Award, 2 NEH grants, IREX grant. **MEMBERSHIPS** APA, SPP, ESPP, SSPP, FPA. **RESEARCH** Philo of mind and language; epistemology. **SELECTED PUBLICATIONS** Auth, Duplicating Thoughts, Mind & Language, 96; auth, The Truth About Moods, in: Protosozioloie, Cognitive Semantics I: Concepts of Meaning, 97; auth, Truth Conditional Semantics for Tense, coauth, Tense, Time and Reference, ed. Q. Smith, Oxford: Oxford Univ Press, 98; auth, Functionalism, Causation and Causal Relevance, Psyche, 98; Semantics for Opaque Contexts, coauth, Philos Perspectives, 98; auth, Meaning, Truth and Interpretation, & Introduction to Reading Davidson, Discussions with Donald Davidson on Truth, Meaning and Knowledge, ed., U. Zeglen, Routledge, 98. **CONTACT ADDRESS** Dept of Philosophy, Univ of Florida, Gainesville, FL, 32611-8545. **EMAIL** kludwig@phil.ufl.edu

LUDWIG, THEODORE MARK
PERSONAL Born 09/28/1936, Oxford, NE, m, 1960, 4 children **DISCIPLINE** HISTORY OF RELIGIONS, ASIAN RELIGIONS **EDUCATION** Concordia Sem St Louis, BA, 58, MDiv, 61, STM, 62, ThD, 63; Univ Chicago, PhD(Hist Relig), 75. **CAREER** Asst prof, 68-73, res prof, 79-80, assoc prof Theol, Valparaiso Univ, 74-, Missionary, Nihon Ruteru Kyokai, Japan, 63-67; res assoc Hist Relig, Univ Chicago, 73-75; dir Overseas Study Ctr Reutlingen, Ger, Valparaiso Univ, 76-78; Danforth assoc, 77-; Nat Endowment for Humanities fel, 81-82. **HONORS AND AWARDS** Distinguished teaching award, Valparaiso Univ, 79-80. **MEMBERSHIPS** Soc Bibl Lit; Am Acad Relig; Asn Asian Studies; Soc for Study of Japanese Regions. **RESEARCH** Ancient Near Eastern religions; Japanese religions; Japanese tea ceremony. **SELECTED PUBLICATIONS** Auth, Jeremiah's Book of Consolation, 68, Concordia Theol Monthly; The traditions of the establishing of the earth in Deutero-Isiah, J Bibl Lit, 73; The way of tea: a religioaesthetic mode of life, Hist Relig, 74; co-ed (with Frank Reynolds), Transitions and Transformations in the History of Religions: Essays in Honor of Joseph M Kitagawa, 80 & auth, Remember not the former things: Disjunction and transformation in Ancient Israel, In: Transitions and Transformations in the History of Religions: Essays in Honor of Joseph M Kitagawa, 80, E J Brill, Leiden; Christian self-understanding and other religions, Currents in Theol & Mission, 80; Before Rikyu: Religious and aesthetic influences in the early history of the tea ceremony, Monumenta Nipponica, 81; The Sacred Paths of the West, 94; The Sacred Paths: Understanding the Religions of the World, 96. **CONTACT ADDRESS** Dept of Theology, Valparaiso Univ, Valparaiso, IN, 46383-6493. **EMAIL** Ted.Ludwig@valpo.edu.

LUDWINOWSKI, RETT R.
PERSONAL Born 11/06/1943, Skawina, Poland, m, 1995, 2 children **DISCIPLINE** COMPARATIVE AND LITERATURE LAW **EDUCATION** Jagiellonian Univ, Cracow, Po-

land, MA (law), 66, D Phil (law), 71, grad studies in law, post of legal counsellor, 73, post doctorate degree in law, habiliation, 76; **CAREER** Asst to the chair of Hist of Political Ideas, Inst of Political Science, Jagiellonian Univ, 66-67, sr lect, 67-71, adjunct prof, 71-76, asst prof, 76-81, chmn, Div of Business, 76-81, chmn, Div of Law, 80-81, assoc prof of Law, 81, supervisor, chair of Hist of Legal and Political Ideas, 81, holder of chair of the Hist of Legal and Political Ideas, 81; sr fel, Marguerite Eyer Wilbur Found, 82; vis prof of Political Science, Elizabethtown Col, PA, spring 82; vis scholar, The Hoover Inst, Stanford Univ, 83; vis prof of Politics, Alfred Univ, fall 83; vis prof of Politics, Cath Univ Am, 84; vis prof Law, Cath Univ Am, 84-85; prof of Law, 85, tenured, 86, dir, Cath Univ of Am Int Business and Trade summer prog in Poland, dir, Comparative and International Law Institute, Cath Univ Am Law School, 87-; vis scholar, Max-Planck-Inst, fall 90; Sr Fulbright Scholar, Jagiellonian Univ, 97. **HONORS AND AWARDS** Sr fel, Marguerite Eyer Wilbur Found, residential; Hoover Inst grant as vis scholar, summer 82; vis prof with grant from Earhart Found, Cath Univ of Am, 84; res grants from the following: Earhart Found, 87, 88, 91-92; Wilbur Found, 87, 89; Rosenstiel Found, 89, 90; Bartory Found, 90; Bradley Found, 92; residential fel, Max-Planck-Inst, Hamburg, Ger, 90. **SELECTED PUBLICATIONS** Auth, The Beginning of the Constitutional Era, A Comparative Study of the First American and European Constitution, co-auth with William Fox Jr, CUA Press, 93; Constitution Making in the Countries of Former Soviet Dominance: Current Develoment, GA J of Int and Comparative Law, vol 23, no 2, 93; Fundamental Constitutional Rights in the New Constitution of Eastern and Central Europe, Cardozo J of Int and Comparative Law, vol 3, no 1, spring 95; Regulations of International Trade and Business, vol I, International Trade, ABC, 96, vol II, Business Transactions, co-auth and ed, ABC, winter 96; Constitution Making in the Countries of Former Soviet Dominance, Duke Univ Press, 96; numerous other publications. **CONTACT ADDRESS** Columbus School of Law, Catholic Univ of America, Washington, DC, 20064. **EMAIL** ludwikowski@law.cus.edu

LUEBKE, NEIL ROBERT
PERSONAL Born 09/15/1936, Pierce, NE, m, 1957, 2 children **DISCIPLINE** PHILOSOPHY **EDUCATION** Midland Col, BA, 58; Johns Hopkins Univ, MA, 62, PhD(philos), 68. **CAREER** Asst prof, 61-71, assoc prof, 71-76, assoc prof & chairperson, 76-81, Prof & Head Philos, Okla State Univ, 81-84, 89-87, Regents Service Prof, 97-; Dir Exxon critical thinking proj, Exxon Educ Found, 71-74. **MEMBERSHIPS** Am Philos Asn; Am Sect Int Asn for Philos Law & Social Philos; Soc Bus Ethics; N Am Soc for Social Philos. **RESEARCH** Theories of social authority and trust; Thomas Hobbes; engineering ethics. **SELECTED PUBLICATIONS** Auth, Is Hobbes's view of property bourgeois?, Philos Topics, 81; Conflict of Interest as a Moral Category, Bus and Prof Ethics J, vol 6, no 1. **CONTACT ADDRESS** Dept of Philos, Oklahoma State Univ, 226 Hannen Hall, Stillwater, OK, 74078-5064. **EMAIL** nluebke@okway.okstate.edu

LUKE, BRIAN A.
DISCIPLINE ENVIRONMENTAL ETHICS, POLITICAL PHILOSOPHY **EDUCATION** Pittsburgh Univ, PhD, 92. **CAREER** Dept Philos, Univ Dayton **RESEARCH** Feminist theory. **SELECTED PUBLICATIONS** Auth, Solidarity Across Diversity: A Pluralistic Rapprochement of Environmentalism and Animal Liberation, Soc Theory and Pract, 95; Justice, Caring, and Animal Liberation, Beyond Animal Rights: A Feminist Caring Ethic for the Treatment of Animals, Continuum, 96; A Critical Analysis of Hunters' Ethics, Environmental Ethics , 97. **CONTACT ADDRESS** Dept of Philos, Univ Dayton, 300 Col Park, Dayton, OH, 75062. **EMAIL** luke@checkov.hm.udayton.edu

LULL, TIMOTHY F.
DISCIPLINE SYSTEMATIC THEOLOGY **EDUCATION** Williams Col, BA; Yale Divinity Sch, BD; Yale Grad Sch, MPhil, PhD. **CAREER** Tchg pastor, Harvard Divinity Sch; vis lectr, Stonehill Col; vis scholar, St Edmund's Col, Cambridge, Eng; asst prof, assoc prof, prof, Lutheran Theol Sem at Philadelphia; lectr, Churchwide Assembly, 93; Hein-Fry lectr, 96; ch, GTU Coun of Deans, 90-92; prof, 89-; pres. **HONORS AND AWARDS** GTU Core Doctoral Fac; co-ch, Lutheran/Reformed Dialogue; GTU fac trustee, 92-95; actg pres, PLTS, 94; GTU Bd Acad Comm, 1992-. **SELECTED PUBLICATIONS** Auth, Called to Confess Christ; This Church Confesses; ed, Martin Luther's Basic Theological Writings, Fortress, 89; A Common Calling, 93. **CONTACT ADDRESS** Dept of Systematic Theology, Pacific Lutheran Theol Sem, 2770 Marin Ave, Berkeley, CA, 94708-1597. **EMAIL** tlull@plts.edu

LUMPP, RANDOLPH
DISCIPLINE PERSONALITY AND SPIRITUALITY, RELIGIOUS STUDIES, CHRISTIANITY THROUGH THE C **EDUCATION** Seattle Univ, BA, 63; Marquette Univ, MA, 68; Univ Ottawa, Canada, PhD, 76. **CAREER** Prof Relig Stud, ch, dept Relig Stud, Regis Col, 72-. **HONORS AND AWARDS** Regis Col Fac Lectr of the Year, 92. **MEMBERSHIPS** Am Acad of Relig; Am Asn of Univ Prof. **RESEARCH** Psychology of religion; biblical studies. **SELECTED PUBLICATIONS** Auth, A Biographical Portrait of Walter Jackson Ong, in Oral Tradition 2, 87; Literacy, Commerce and Catholicity: Two Contexts of Change and Invention, in Oral Tradition 2, 87; Introduction to the Study of Native American Religious Traditions, in Module for RC 410 Native American Religious Traditions, RECEP II, 91; Term and Method Problems in the Study of Native American Religious Traditions, AAR/SBL Rocky Mountain - Great Plains Reg, 93; Tradition and Common Sense in the Academy: An Odyssey in Search of Dialogue, Adducere II, Regis Univ, 95. **CONTACT ADDRESS** Dept of Relig Stud, Regis Col, 3333 Regis Blvd, Denver, CO, 80221. **EMAIL** rlumpp@regis.edu

LUNCEFORD, JOSEPH E.
PERSONAL Born 01/20/1937, State Springs, MS, m, 1960, 2 children **DISCIPLINE** THEOLOGY **EDUCATION** Mississippi Col, BA, 62; New Orleans Baptist Theol Sem, BTh, 66; Baylor Univ, PhD, 79. **CAREER** Asst prof, 81-87, assoc prof, 87-94, prof relig, 94-, Georgetown Col. **RESEARCH** The revelation, Johannine stud. **CONTACT ADDRESS** Georgetown Col, PO Box 254, Georgetown, KY, 40324. **EMAIL** jluncefo@georgetowncollege.edu

LUNDBOM, JACK R.
PERSONAL Born 07/10/1939, Chicago, IL, m, 1964, 2 children **DISCIPLINE** BIBLICAL STUDIES **EDUCATION** North Park Theological Seminary, BD, 67; San Francisco Theological Seminary and Graduate Theological Union, Berkeley, PhD, 73. **CAREER** Asst Prof/Lectr, 74, 76,-77, Univ California-Berkeley; Visiting Prof, 74-75, Andover Newton Theological School; Visiting Prof, 83, Yale Divinity School; Visiting Prof, 90, 92-93, Lutheran School of Theology, Chicago; Life Member, 96-, Univ Cambridge. **HONORS AND AWARDS** Sr Fulbright Prof, Universitat Marbury, Germany, 88-89; NEH Fel, Uppsda Univ and Cambridge Univ, 91-92; NEH Fel, Albright Inst of Archaeological Research, Jerusalem and Cambridge Univ, 97-98; Mem, Princeton Ctr of Theological Inquiry, 98-99. **MEMBERSHIPS** Soc of Biblical Lit; Catholic Biblical Assoc; American Schools of Oriental Research **RESEARCH** Old Testament/Hebrew Bible; Hebrew Prophets; Jeremiah; rhetorical criticism **SELECTED PUBLICATIONS** Auth, Jeremiah 15/15-21 and the Call of Jeremiah, Scandanavian Journal of the Old Testament, 95; Mary Magdalene and Song of Songs 3: 1-4, Interpretation 49, 95; Section Markings in Bible Scrolls, Genizah Fragments 32, 96; The Inclusio and Other Framing Devices in Deuteronomy I-XXVIII, Vetus Testamentum 46, 96; Warner Sallman and His Head of Christ, Swedish-American Historical Quarterly 47, 96; Scribal Contibutions to Old Testament Theology, To Hear and Obey: Essays in Honor of Frederick Carlson Holmgren, 97; Jeremiah: A Study in Ancient Hebrew Rhetoric, 97; Coauth, Haplography in Jeremiah 1-20, Frank Moore Cross Volume, 98; Parataxsis, Rhetorical Structure, and the Dialogue over Sodom in Genesis 18, World of Genesis: Persons, Places, Perspectives, 98; Masterpainter: Warner E. Sallman, 98; Jeremiah 1-20, 99. **CONTACT ADDRESS** 5254 N. Spaulding Ave., Chicago, IL, 60625.

LUNDE, JONATHAN M.
PERSONAL Born 06/09/1960, Cameroon, m, 1984, 3 children **DISCIPLINE** BIBLICAL STUDIES **EDUCATION** Moorehead State Univ, BS (summa cum laude), 83; Lutheran Brethren Sem, MDiv (highest ranking senior), 86; Trinity Evangelical Divinity School, ThM (academic distinction), 89, PhD, 96. **CAREER** ADJUNCT FAC FOR THE GRADING OF NEW TESTAMENT EXTENSION COURSES, TRINITY EVANGELICAL DIVINITY SCHOOL, 91-; ASST PROF OF BIBLICAL STUDIES, TRINITY INT UNIV, COL OF ARTS AND SCIENCES, 96-. **MEMBERSHIPS** Soc of Biblical Lit; Evangelical Theol Soc **RESEARCH** Life of Jesus; apocalyptic lit; NT use of the OT. **SELECTED PUBLICATIONS** Auth, Heaven and Hell & Repentance, in Dictionary of Jesus and the Gospels, ed J. B. Green, S. McKnight, I. H. Marshall, InterVarsity Press, 92; Repentance, in New Dictionary of Biblical Theology, InterVarsity Press, forthcoming. **CONTACT ADDRESS** Trinity Int Univ, 2065 Half Day Rd., Deerfield, IL, 60015. **EMAIL** jlunde@trin.edu

LUPER, STEVEN
DISCIPLINE PHILOSOPHY **EDUCATION** Baylor Univ, BA, 77; Harvard Univ, PhD, 82. **CAREER** Asst prof, 82-88; assoc prof, 88-94; PROF, 94-. **RESEARCH** Epistemology; Social and Political Philosophy; Ethics. **SELECTED PUBLICATIONS** Auth, Internalism, Synthese, 88; Morality and The Self, The Monist, 91; The Possibility of Knowledge: Nozick and his Critics, 87; Problems of International Justice, 88; Invulnerability: On Securing happiness, 96; Social Ideas and Policies: Readings in Social and Political Philosophy, 98; Existing: An introduction to Existentialist Thought, 2000, coauth, Drugs, Morality and the Law, 94; The Moral Life, 97. **CONTACT ADDRESS** Philosophy Dept, Trinity Univ, 715 Stadium Dr, San Antonio, TX, 78212-7200. **EMAIL** sluper@trinity.edu

LURIE, HOWARD R.
DISCIPLINE ADMINISTRATIVE LAW **EDUCATION** W Va Univ, AB, 60; Univ Mich Law Sch, JD, 63. **CAREER** Prof; Villanova Univ, 68-.. **HONORS AND AWARDS** Army Commendation Medal, 66. **MEMBERSHIPS** Amer Bar Asn; Philadelphia Patent Law Asn; Int Asn for the Adv of Tchg and Res in Intellectual Property. **RESEARCH** Trade regulation, intellectual property and copyright law. **SELECTED PUBLICATIONS** Auth, What is Fair Use, Synthesis, Law and Policy in Higher Education, Univ Md, 89; The Ownership of Copyright in Journal Articles, 1 3 Technical serv Quart 31, 84 & Consumer Complaints: A Proposed Fed Trade Regulation Rule, 5 Mich. J. Law Reform 426, 72. **CONTACT ADDRESS** Law School, Villanova Univ, 800 Lancaster Ave, Villanova, PA, 19085-1692. **EMAIL** lurie@law.vill.edu

LUSKY, LOUIS
PERSONAL Born 05/15/1915, Columbus, OH, m, 1946, 3 children **DISCIPLINE** LAW **EDUCATION** Univ Louisville, BA, 35; Columbia Univ, LLB, 37. **CAREER** Law clerk to Supreme Court Justice Harlan F Stone, 37-38; assoc, Root, Clark, Buckner and Ballantine, NY, 38-42, 44-45; civilian mem oper analysis sect, 8th Air Force, 43-44; with legal div, US Mil Govt Ger, 45-46; partner, Wyatt and Grafton, Louisville, Ky, 47-51; private practice, 52-63; PROF LAW, COLUMBIA UNIV, 63-, Mem nat comt, Am Civil Liberties Union, 63-67, nat bd, 67-70. **MEMBERSHIPS** Am Law Inst; Am Bar Asn. **SELECTED PUBLICATIONS** Auth, Gellhorn, Walter, Columbia Law Rev, Vol 0096, 96. **CONTACT ADDRESS** Sch of Law, Columbia Univ, New York, NY, 10027.

LUYSTER, ROBERT W.
DISCIPLINE PHILOSOPHY **EDUCATION** Dartmouth Col, BA, 58; Univ Chicago, MA, 61; PhD, 64. **CAREER** Dept Philos, Univ Conn **RESEARCH** Religious myth and symbol, peace and social justice. **SELECTED PUBLICATIONS** Auth, Hamlet and Man's Being: The Phenomenology of Nausea, Univ Press Am, 94; Dionysos: The masks of madness, Parabola, 95; co-auth, Living Religions, Englewood Cliffs, Prentice Hall, 91. **CONTACT ADDRESS** Dept of Philos, Univ Conn, 1266 Storrs Rd, Storrs, CT, 06269.

LYGRE, DAVID GERALD
PERSONAL Born 08/10/1942, Minot, ND, m, 1966, 2 children **DISCIPLINE** CHEMISTRY, BIOCHEMISTRY **EDUCATION** Concordia Coll, BA, 64; Univ North Dakota, PhD, 68. **CAREER** Postdoc fel, Case Western Res Univ, 68-70; PROF, CENTRAL WASH UNIV, 70-. **MEMBERSHIPS** Am Chem Soc **RESEARCH** Enzymology of carbohydrate metabolism, aging. **SELECTED PUBLICATIONS** coauth, Chemistry: A Contemporary Approach, Wadsworth Publ, 91; General, Organic, and Biological Chemistry, Brooks-Cole Publ, 95. **CONTACT ADDRESS** Dept Chem, Central Washington Univ, Ellensburg, WA, 98926. **EMAIL** lygred@cwu.edu

LYLE, KENNETH
DISCIPLINE NEW TESTAMANT STUDIES **EDUCATION** Southern Baptist Theol Sem, PHD, 95; M DIV 91; Mississippi Col, BS, 84 **CAREER** Asst Prof of Relig, 96-pres, Bluefield Col; Adj Prof, 95-96, Southern Baptist Theol Sem **MEMBERSHIPS** Soc of Bibl Lit **RESEARCH** Apocalyptic Literature; Ethics **SELECTED PUBLICATIONS** Auth, Ethical Admonition in the Epistle of Jude, Peter Lang Press, 98 **CONTACT ADDRESS** Bluefield Col, 3000 College Dr, Box 27, Bluefield, VA, 24605. **EMAIL** klyle@mail.bluefield.edu

LYMAN, J. REBECCA
DISCIPLINE CHURCH HISTORY **EDUCATION** W Mich Univ, BA; Cath Univ Am, MA; Univ Oxford, DPhil. **CAREER** Samuel M. Garrett prof, Church Divinity Sch Pacific **SELECTED PUBLICATIONS** Auth, The Making of a Heretic: The Life of Origen in Epiphanius' Panarion 64, Studia Patristica, 97; A Topography of Heresy: Mapping the Rhetorical Creation of Arianism, Arianism after Arius, Edinburgh, 93; Lex Orandi: Heresy, Orthodoxy, and Popular Religion, The Making and Remaking of Christian Doctrine, Oxford, 93; Christology and Cosmology: Models of Divine Action in Origen, Eusebius, and Athanasius, Oxford UP, 93. **CONTACT ADDRESS** Church Divinity Sch of the Pacific, 2451 Ridge Rd, Berkeley, CA, 94709-1217.

LYNCH, JOSEPH HOWARD
PERSONAL Born 11/21/1943, Springfield, MA, m, 1965, 3 children **DISCIPLINE** MEDIEVAL & CHURCH HISTORY **EDUCATION** Boston Col, BA, 65; Harvard Univ, MA, 66, PhD, 71. **CAREER** Vis asst prof hist, Univ Ill, Urbana, 70-71; asst prof & asst dir Ctr Medieval & Renaissance Studies, 71-77, assoc prof hist, 77-85, dir ctr Medieval & Renaissance Studies, 78-83, prof hist, Ohio State Univ, 85. **HONORS AND AWARDS** Am Coun Learned Soc fel, 75, Inst Advanced Study, 88, NEH Fel, 87-88 **MEMBERSHIPS** Mediaeval Acad Am; Soc Relig Higher Educ; AHA; Am Cath Hist Assoc; Int Sermon Studies; Assoc Research History of monasticism; Medieval church hist. **RESEARCH** History of monasticism; Medieval church history. **SELECTED PUBLICATIONS** Auth, Spiritale Vinculum: the Vocabulary of Spiritual Kinship in Early Medieval Europe, 87; The Medieval Church: A Brief History, 92; auth, Christianizing Kinship: Ritual Sponsorship in Anglo-Saxon England, 98. **CONTACT ADDRESS** Dept of History, Ohio State Univ, 230 W 17th Ave, Columbus, OH, 43210-1361. **EMAIL** lynch.1@osu.edu

LYNCH, JOSEPH J.
DISCIPLINE PHILOSOPHY **EDUCATION** Claremont Grad School, PhD, 92. **CAREER** Lectr in Philos, Cal Polytechnic State Univ, 90- . **MEMBERSHIPS** Am Philos Asn; Soc Philos & Psychol; Soc for Study Ethics & Animals; Soc Study Philos & Martial Arts. **RESEARCH** Philosophy of religion; philosophy of mind. **SELECTED PUBLICATIONS** Auth, Harrison and Hick on God and Animal Pain, Sophia, 94; Is Animal Pain Conscious?, Between the Species, 95; Reply to Professor Russow, Between the Species, 97; Wittgenstein and Animal Minds, Between the Species, 97; A Reply to Professor Comstock, Between the Species, 98; Theodicy and Animal Pain, Between the Species, 98. **CONTACT ADDRESS** Philosophy Dept, California Polytech State Univ, San Luis Obispo, CA, 93405. **EMAIL** jlynch@calpoly.edu

LYNCH, MICHAEL P.
DISCIPLINE EPISTEMOLOGY, PHILOSOPHY OF MIND, EPISTEMOLOGY **EDUCATION** SUNY, Albany, BA, summa cum laude, 90; Syracuse Univ, MA, 92, PhD, 95. **CAREER** Mng tchg assoc, 92-94, sr tchg assoc, 92-94, instr, Syracuse Univ, 94-95; asst prof, Univ MS, 95-. **HONORS AND AWARDS** Phi Beta Kappa, 89; SUNYA Undergrad Award for Distinguished Work in Philos, 90; tchg fel, Syracuse Univ, 94-95; Outstanding TA Award, Syracuse Univ, 94; Syracuse Univ cert of univ tchg, 95; summer grant, Univ Miss Off of Res, 96, 97; Cora L Graham Oustanding Tchr of Freshman, Univ Miss, 98; Griffith Mem Award. Southern Soc of Philos and Psychol, 98. **RESEARCH** Pluralism and objectivity. **SELECTED PUBLICATIONS** Auth, Expanding the Graduate Student's Role in Instructional Development, Tchg Philos. 18, 95; Hume and the Limits of Reason, Hume Stud, 22, 96; Truth and Relativism: A Reply to Rappaport, Philos, 25, 97; Minimal Realism or Realistic Minimalism?, Philos Quart, 97; Three Models of Conceptual Schemes, Inquiry. 40, 97; coauth, Videotaping as a Tool for Instructional Development, in Teaching: A Guide for Graduate Students, Syracuse UP, 94; guest ed, Real Knowing: Feminist Epistemology and the Coherence Theory, Soc Epistemology, Vol 12:3, 98. **CONTACT ADDRESS** Univ MS, Oxford, MS, 38677. **EMAIL** mlynch@olemiss.edu

LYNN, RICHARDSON R.
DISCIPLINE CIVIL PROCEDURE **EDUCATION** Abilene Christian Univ, BA, 73; Vanderbilt Univ, JD, 76. **CAREER** Adjunct prof, Vanderbilt Univ Sch Law, 76-80; prof, Pepperdine Univ Sch Law, 80-86; vis prof, Campbell Univ Sch Law, 86; assoc ed, Litigation, 90-95; prof, 86-89 admin, LA West Am Inn Court, 92-93; prof, dean. **HONORS AND AWARDS** Res fel, Belmont Univ, 89-90. **MEMBERSHIPS** Mem, Am, TN, Nebr Bar Assn(s). **SELECTED PUBLICATIONS** Auth, Appellate Litigation, 93; Jury Trial Law & Practice, 86; Honest Goverunient, 92; contrib, Fed Litigation Guide; Thompson on Real Property. **CONTACT ADDRESS** Sch of Law, Pepperdine Univ, 24255 Pacific Coast Hwy, Malibu, CA, 90263.

LYON, GORDON W.
PERSONAL Born 11/09/1966, Durban, South Africa, m, 1997 **DISCIPLINE** PHILOSOPHY **EDUCATION** Univ Cambridge, PhD, 94. **CAREER** Lect, Rhodes Univ, 96-97; vis ast prof, Florida St Univ, 97-. **HONORS AND AWARDS** S African Human Sci Res Coun Doctoral Merit Award, 91-93. **MEMBERSHIPS** Am Philos Asn; Fl Philos Asn; Southern Soc Philos & Psych. **RESEARCH** Wittgenstein, philosophy of psychology, philosophy of mind. **SELECTED PUBLICATIONS** Auth, "Experience of Perceptual Familiarity," Philos, 96. **CONTACT ADDRESS** Dept of Philosophy, Florida State Univ, Tallahassee, FL, 32306-1500. **EMAIL** glyon@mailer.fsu.edu

LYON, ROBERT WILLIAM
PERSONAL Born 03/15/1929, Peoria, IL, m, 1954, 2 children **DISCIPLINE** NEW TESTAMENT **EDUCATION** Ohio Univ, BS, 51; Asbury Theol Sem, BD, 54; Princeton Theol Sem, ThM, 56; Univ St Andrews, PhD(New Testament), 59. **CAREER** Vis lectr New Testament, Princeton Theol Sem, 58-59; pastor, LePorte United Methodist Church, Elyria, Ohio, 59-66; assoc prof New Testament lang and lit, 66-72, PROF NEW TESTAMENT LANG AND LIT, ASBURY THEOL SEM, 72-, Res asst, Am Bible Soc, 58-59. **MEMBERSHIPS** Soc Bibl Lit; Studiorum Novi Testamenti Soc. **RESEARCH** Textual criticism; Greek paleography. **SELECTED PUBLICATIONS** Auth, Jesus--a Revolutionary Biog, J Church and State, Vol 0037, 95. **CONTACT ADDRESS** Asbury Theol Sem, Wilmore, KY, 40390.

LYON, STEVE
PERSONAL m, 2 children **DISCIPLINE** PASTORAL MINISTRY **EDUCATION** Univ Houston, BA, 68; Southwestern Baptist Theol Sem, MDiv, 71, PhD, 78. **CAREER** Adj prof, Midwestern Baptist Theol Sem; Baptist Theol Sem Costa Rica; prof, Baptist Theol Sem Venezuela, 88-93; prof, Southwestern Baptist Theol Sem, 93-. **SELECTED PUBLICATIONS** Auth, Should Baptist Churches Have Elders?, The Baptist Standard, 97; Deberian las Iglesias Bautistas Tener un Cuerpo de Ministros o Pastores Ancianos?, Luminar Bautista, Venezuela, 97; What About the Pastor's Family, Christian Family Mag, 97. **CONTACT ADDRESS** Sch Theol, Southwestern Baptist Theol Sem, PO Box 22000, Fort Worth, TX, 76122-0418. **EMAIL** sml@swbts.swbts.edu

LYON, THOMAS D.
DISCIPLINE LAW **EDUCATION** Dartmouth Col, BA,83; Harvard Univ, JD,87; Stanford Univ, PhD,94. **CAREER** Assoc prof,Univ Southern Calif,97-; res assoc, Harbor-UCLA Med Ctr; atty, Children's Serv Div, Los Angeles Co Coun; instructor, Stanford Univ. **MEMBERSHIPS** American Psychological Association; American Psychological Society; Society for Research in Child Development; Member, Board of Directors, &Chair of the Legal Subcommittee, American Professional Society on the Abuse of Children; Editorial Board. **RESEARCH** Law & psychology; family law; evidence. **SELECTED PUBLICATIONS** Auth, The Relevance Ratio: Evaluating the Probative Value of Expert Testimony in Child Sexual Abuse Cases; The Effects of Threats on Children's Disclosure of Sexual Abuse; False Allegations and False Denials of Child Sexual Abuse; Children's Decision-making Competency: Misunderstanding Piaget; coauth, Young Children's Understanding of Forgetting over Time. **CONTACT ADDRESS** School of Law, Univ Southern Calif, University Park Campus, Los Angeles, CA, 90089. **EMAIL** tlyon@law.usc.edu

LYONS, DANIEL D.
DISCIPLINE PHILOSOPHY **EDUCATION** Univ Chicago, PhD, 66. **CAREER** Prof. **RESEARCH** Ethical theory; social and political philosophy; logic; philosophical issues in computer science. **SELECTED PUBLICATIONS** Auth, pubs on computer logic; co-auth, Benson Strutting and Fretting. **CONTACT ADDRESS** Philosophy Dept, Colorado State Univ, Fort Collins, CO, 80523.

LYONS, DAVID
PERSONAL Born 02/06/1935, New York, NY, m, 1955, 3 children **DISCIPLINE** PHILOSOPHY **EDUCATION** Brooklyn Col, BA, 60; Harvard Univ, MA, 63, PhD, 63. **CAREER** Susan Linn Sage prof of philos emer, prof of law emer, Cornell Univ, 64-95; prof law, 95- , prof philos, 98- , Boston Univ. **HONORS AND AWARDS** Guggenheim Found fel, 70-71; Soc for Hum fel, 72-73; Clark award for dist tchg, Cornell Univ, 76; NEH fel, 77-78, 93-94; NEH Const fel, 84-85. **RESEARCH** Moral, political and legal theory. **SELECTED PUBLICATIONS** Auth, Moral Aspects of Legal theory: Essays on Law, Justice, and Political Responsibility, Cambridge, 93; auth, Normal Law, Nearly Just Societies, and other Myths of Legal Theory, in Archiv fur Rechts- und Sozialphilosophie, 93; auth, Rights, Welfare, and Mill's Moral Theory, Oxford, 94; auth, The Balance of Injustice and the War for Independence, Monthly Rev, 94; auth, Political Responsibility and Resistance to Civil Government, Philos Exchange, 95-96; auth, Mill's Utilitarianism: Critical Essays, Rowman & Littlefield, 97; auth, Moral Judgment, Historical Reality, and Civil Disobedience, Philos & Public Affairs, 98. **CONTACT ADDRESS** School of Law, Boston Univ, 765 Commonwealth Ave, Boston, MA, 02215. **EMAIL** dbl@bu.edu

LYONS, ROBIN R.
PERSONAL Born 12/09/1956, Salem, IL, m, 1992, 1 child **DISCIPLINE** RELIGIOUS STUDIES; PASTORAL THEOLOGY **EDUCATION** W Ky Univ, BA, 79; Drew Univ, M.Div, 82. **CAREER** Pastor, Murphysboro United Meth Church, 95-. **HONORS AND AWARDS** Various Seminary Awards; various Community Service Awards. **MEMBERSHIPS** AAR/SBL; Conf Board of Ordained Ministry **RESEARCH** Bonhoeffer Studies; Historical Jesus; Pastoral Theology; Church Growth Studies. **CONTACT ADDRESS** 1514 Pine St, Murphysboro, IL, 62966.

LYSAUGHT, M. THERESE
DISCIPLINE RELIGIOUS STUDIES **EDUCATION** Duke Univ, PhD. **CAREER** Asst prof, Univ Dayton. **MEMBERSHIPS** Recombinant DNA Adv Comt, Nat Inst Health. **RESEARCH** Theological ethics and medical ethics. **CONTACT ADDRESS** Dept of Religious Studies, Univ of Dayton, 300 College Park, 302 Humanities, Dayton, OH, 45469-1679. **EMAIL** lysaught@udayton.edu

LYTLE, TIMOTHY F
PERSONAL Born 05/15/1959, Williamsburg, PA, s **DISCIPLINE** PHILOSOPHY **EDUCATION** Toccoa Falls Col, BA, 80; Western Kentucky Univ, MA, 81; Univ Georgia, PhD, 89. **CAREER** Vis asst prof, 89-90, Sweet Briar Col; vis asst prof, 90-92, Mississippi St Col; vis asst prof, 92-95, Arkansas St Univ; asst prof, 95-, dept head, phil & relig, 95-98, Piedmont Col. **RESEARCH** Philosophy of relig, epistemology **CONTACT ADDRESS** PO Box 362, Demorest, GA, 30535. **EMAIL** tlytle@piedmont.edu

M

M'GONIGLE, R. MICHAEL
DISCIPLINE LAW **EDUCATION** Univ British Columbia, BA, 69; Univ London, MS, 70; Univ Toronto, LLB, 76; Yale Univ, LLM, 79, JD, 82. **CAREER** Assoc prof. **MEMBERSHIPS** Co-founder, Greenpeace Intl **SELECTED PUBLICATIONS** Auth, pubs on international law, law of the sea, and environmental issues; co-auth, Forestopia: A Practical Guide to the New Forest Economy. **CONTACT ADDRESS** Fac of Law, Univ Victoria, PO Box 2400, Victoria, BC, V8W 3H7. **EMAIL** mgonigle@uvic.ca

MABE, ALAN R.
PERSONAL Born 08/21/1942, Pilot Mountain, NC, m, 1982, 1 child **DISCIPLINE** PHILOSOPHY **EDUCATION** Guilford Col, BA, 64; Syracuse Univ, MA, 67, PhD(philos), 71. **CAREER** Asst prof philos & pub affairs, Syracuse Univ, 71-72; asst prof, 72-76, chmn ed comt, Social Theory & Pract, 73-76, Assoc Prof Philos, Fla State Univ, 76-, Chmn Dept, 77-, Dean Grad Stu, 93-, Ed, Law & Philos, Inter J Jurisp Legal Philos, 81-96. **MEMBERSHIPS** Am Philos Asn; Am Soc Polit & Legal Philos. **RESEARCH** Philosophy of law; ethics; philosophy of social science. **SELECTED PUBLICATIONS** Auth, Hart and the moral content of law, spring 72, The Relationship of Law and morality, spring 74 & Fuller and the Internal Morality of Law, 75, Southern J Philos; Coerced therapy, Social Protection, and Moral Autonomy, 75 & ed, New Techniques and Strategies of Social Contro, 75, Am Behav Sci; auth, Morality, Force and Democratic Theory, Philos Forum, 77. **CONTACT ADDRESS** Dept of Philosophy, Florida State Univ, 600 W College Ave, Tallahassee, FL, 32306-1096. **EMAIL** amabe@mailer.fsu.edu

MABERY, LUCY
PERSONAL Born 04/14/1937, Dallas, TX, m, 1997, 3 children **DISCIPLINE** THEOLOGY **EDUCATION** Dallas Theol Sem, MABS, 85, ThM, 89; Texas Womens Univ, PhD, 94. **CAREER** Prof, Dallas Theol Sem. 8 yrs. **MEMBERSHIPS** AAMFT; AACC; Am Psychotherapy Asn. **SELECTED PUBLICATIONS** Auth, Ministering to Today's Women, Word, 99. **CONTACT ADDRESS** Dallas Theol Sem, 3909 Swiss Ave, Dallas, TX, 75204. **EMAIL** lmabery@aol.com

MACARTHUR, JOHN F.
PERSONAL Born 06/19/1939, m, 4 children **DISCIPLINE** THEOLOGY **EDUCATION** Los Angeles Pacific Col, BA, 61; Talbot Theol Sem, BD, 64, MD, 70; Grace Grad School, LittD, 76; Talbot Theol Sem, 77, DD. **CAREER** Assoc pastor, Calvary Bible Church, Calif., 64-66; asst prof, Los Angeles Baptist Col, 65; fac rep, Talbot Theol Sem, 66-69; pastor of Grace Commun. Church, Sun Valley, Ca., 69- ; adj prof, Talbot Theol Sem, 70-78; pres and tchr on nat syndicated radio prog, Grace to You, 70- ; pres and tchr for Grace to You tape ministry, 70- ; adj prof, Dallas Theol Sem, 82; pres of the Master's Col, Newhall, Ca., 85- ; pres of the Master's Sem, 86- . **HONORS AND AWARDS** Grace to You, nationally syndicaticated radio program and tape ministry, is broadcast 540 times daily across America. Numerous tapes and books have been translated into more than 35 languages. Grace Community Church is the largest Protestant Congregation in LA County. **MEMBERSHIPS** Moody Bible Inst; Indep. Fundamental Churches of Am; Gifts of Grace; Coun on Biblical Manhood and Womanhood; Stewardship Services Found; Joni and Friends. **SELECTED PUBLICATIONS** Auth, The Vanishing Conscience, 94; Different by Design, 94; Reckless Faith, 94; First Love, 95; The Power of Suffering, 95; Alone With God, 95; The Love of God, 96; The Silent Sheperd, 96; The Glory of Heaven, 96; The Body Dynamic, 96; The Power of Integrity, 97; How to Get the Most from God's Word, 97; The Mac Arthur Study Bible, 97; Strength for Today, 97; The Freedom and Power of Forgiveness, 98; The Pillars of Christian Character, 98; James, 98; Our Sufficiency in Christ, 98. **CONTACT ADDRESS** Grace Comm Church, PO Box 1642, Canyon Country, CA, 91351.

MACARTHUR, STEVEN D.
PERSONAL Born 11/25/1949, Bronxville, NY, d, 2 children **DISCIPLINE** RELIGION; PHILOSOPHY **EDUCATION** Princeton Theol Sem, MDiv, 75; Univ Glasgow, PhD, 80. **CAREER** ASSOC PROF OF RELIG AND PHILOS, STERLING COL. **HONORS AND AWARDS** Phi Beta Kappa **MEMBERSHIPS** Soc of Biblical Lit; Evangelical Theol Soc. **CONTACT ADDRESS** Dept of Relig and Philos, Sterling Col, Box 149, Sterling, KS, 67579. **EMAIL** smacarthur@sterling.edu

MACAULAY, STEWART
PERSONAL Born 04/07/1931, Atlanta, GA, m, 1954, 4 children **DISCIPLINE** LAW **EDUCATION** Stanford Univ, AB, 52, LLB, 54. **CAREER** Instr law, Univ Chicago, 56-57; from asst prof to assoc prof, 57-65, PROF LAW, UNIV WIS MADISON, 65-, Mem adv comt, Am Law Inst, 60-; fel, Ctr Advan Studies Behav Sci, 66-67; dir Chile law prog, Int Legal Ctr, 70-72. **RESEARCH** Law and behavioral science; law and exchange in large-scale industry; free speech in theory and in practice. **SELECTED PUBLICATIONS** Auth, On Rattling Cages--Handler, Joel Goes to Philadelphia and Gives a Presidential-Address, Law and Soc Rev, Vol 0026, 92; The Last Word, J Law and Soc, Vol 0022, 95; Crime and Custom in Business Society, J Law and Soc, Vol 0022, 95; The More Things Change--Business Litigation and Governance in the American Automobile-Industry, Law and Soc Inquiry-J Amer Bar Found, Vol 0021, 96. **CONTACT ADDRESS** Law Sch, Univ of Wis, 975 Bascom Mall, Madison, WI, 53706-1301.

MACCORMICK, CHALMERS
PERSONAL Born 04/17/1928, Framingham, MA, m, 1953, 5 children **DISCIPLINE** RELIGION **EDUCATION** Bowdoin Coll, AB, 52; Harvard Univ, AM, 53, PhD, 59. **CAREER** From instr to asst prof relig, 58-67, chmn dept hist and philos relig, 62-71, assoc prof, 67-71, PROF HIST AND PHILOS RELIG, WELLS COL, 71-. **MEMBERSHIPS** Am Acad Relig; Soc Values Higher Educ. **RESEARCH** CHURCH HIST; religions of India; comparative study of religions. **SELECTED PUBLICATIONS** Auth, We Are People Full of Hope--Interviews With the 14th Dalai Lama, J Ecumenical Stud, Vol 0029, 92; 3rd Eye Theology--Theology in Formation in Asian Settings, J Ecumenical Stud, Vol 0029, 92; The Story of Christianity in India, Vol 4, Pt 2--the History of Christianity in Tamil Nadu From 1800 to 1975, J Ecumenical Stud, Vol 0031, 94; A New Indian Translation of the Bhagavadgita in Relation With Christian Belief, J Ecumenical Stud, Vol 0031, 94; Making All Things New--Dialogue, Pluralism, and Evangelization in Asia, J Ecumenical Stud, Vol 0032, 95; World Religions in Dialogue--Cooperating to Transform Society, J Ecumenical Stud, Vol 0032, 95; Is My God Your God--a Critical Discussion, J Ecumenical Stud, Vol 0033, 96; Great God, Hear us--Prayers of the World, J Ecumenical Stud, Vol 0033, 96. **CONTACT ADDRESS** Dept of Relig, Wells Col, Aurora, NY, 13026.

MACCRIMMON, MARILYN
DISCIPLINE LAW **EDUCATION** Univ Ca, BS, 62; Univ British Columbia, LLB, 75. **CAREER** Asst prof, 76-81; assoc prof, 81-90; prof, 90-. **SELECTED PUBLICATIONS** Auth, Trial by Ordeal, Can Criminal Law Rev, 96; pubs about process of proof, feminism and procedural rights, and the role of social science evidence in judicial decision-making. **CONTACT ADDRESS** Fac of Law, Univ British Columbia, 1822 East Mall, Vancouver, BC, V6T 1Z1. **EMAIL** maccrimmon@law.ubc.ca

MACDONALD, BURTON
PERSONAL Born 09/13/1939, Canada, m, 1980 **DISCIPLINE** BIBLE & ARCHAEOLOGY; NEAR EASTERN ARCHAEOLOGY; CHRISTIAN RELIGION **EDUCATION** Univ Ottawa, BA, 60; MA, 65; Cath Univ Am, PhD, 74. **CAREER** Sr Resident, Massey Col in Univ Tor, 95-96; prof & chair Dept Theolog & Relig Studies, St Francis Xavier Univ, Nova Scotia, 89-97; assoc prof Dept Theolog, St Francis Xavier Univ, 79-89; annual prof, Amer Center Oriental Res, Amman, Jordan, 79-80, 86-87; asst prof, St Francis Dept Theolog, St Francis Xavier Univ, 72-79; lctr Dept Theolog, St Francis Xavier Univ, 66-67; lctr Dept Theolog, Xavier Col, Sydney, Nova Scotia. **MEMBERSHIPS** Brit Inst at Amman for Archaeology & History; Can Mediter Inst; Cath Bibl Assoc Amer; Soc Bibl Lit; Amer Schools of Oriental Res. **RESEARCH** Ammonitties, Moabites, and Edomites: History & Archaeology; Biblical Site Identification East of the Jordan; Archaeological Survey of Southern Jordan. **SELECTED PUBLICATIONS** Co-ed, Ancient Ammon, EJ Brill Pub, forthcoming; Ammonite Territory and Sites, in Ancient Ammon, EJ Brill Pub, forthcoming; Ammon, Moab, and Edom: Early States/Nations of Jordan in the Biblical Period (End of the 2nd and During 1st Millennium BC), Al Kutba Pub, 94. **CONTACT ADDRESS** Dept of Religious Studies, St Francis Xavier Univ, PO Box 5000, Antigonish, NS, B2G 2W5. **EMAIL** bmacdona@stfx.ca

MACDONALD, MARY N.
PERSONAL Born 12/29/1946, Maleny, Australia, s **DISCIPLINE** HISTORY OF RELIGION **EDUCATION** Univ Chicago, PhD, 88 **CAREER** Lctr, Melanesian Inst, New Guinea, 80-83; prof Hist Relig, LeMoyne Col, 88-98 **HONORS AND AWARDS** Newcombe Dissertation Fel, 87-88 **MEMBERSHIPS** Amer Acad Relig; Assoc Social Anthropology in Oceania **RESEARCH** Religions of Oceania; Religious Movements; Ecology and Religion **SELECTED PUBLICATIONS** "Magic and the Study of Religion in Melanesia," Religiologigues, 95; "Youth and Religion in Papua New Guinea," Catalyst, 96; "Religion and Human Experience," Introduction to the Study of Religion, Orbis, 98 **CONTACT ADDRESS** Relig Studies Dept, LeMoyne Col, Syracuse, NY, 13214. **EMAIL** macdonald@maple.lemoyne.edu

MACDOUGALL, BRUCE
DISCIPLINE LAW **EDUCATION** Acadia Univ, BA, 82; Oxford Univ, BA, 84; BCL, 86; Dalhousie Univ, LLB, 85. **CAREER** Law Clerk, Justice Gerald Le Dain, Supreme Court Can, 86-87; asst prof, 87-93; prof, 93-. **RESEARCH** Law of obligations; sexual orientation and the law; secured transactions; commercial transactions. **SELECTED PUBLICATIONS** Auth, pubs about contracts, commercial transactions, secured transactions and sexual orientation. **CONTACT ADDRESS** Fac of Law, Univ British Columbia, 1822 East Mall, Vancouver, BC, V6T 1Z1. **EMAIL** bmacdougal@law.ubc.ca

MACHADO, DAISY L.
PERSONAL Born 11/08/0000, Cuba, m, 1984 **DISCIPLINE** CHRISTIAN HISTORY **EDUCATION** Brooklyn Coll, BA, 74; Hunter Coll School of Social Work, MSW, 78; Union Theo Sem, MDiv, 81; Univ Chi Div School, PhD, 96. **CAREER** Ordained minister, 79-92, Disciples of Christ; Asst Prof Hispanic stud & church hist, 92-96, Texas Christian Univ, Brite Div School; Prog Dir Hispanic Theo Initiative, 96-, Emory Univ, Atlanta. **HONORS AND AWARDS** O E Scott Scholarship, TE Fund Doc Scholarship, E S Ames Scholarship, TE Fund Diss Fel. **MEMBERSHIPS** AAR **RESEARCH** History of latin Protestant church in USA, history Protestant Missions to Mexico, Caribbean, & Central Latin America. **SELECTED PUBLICATIONS** Auth, Jesus loves me...more than you? The Bible and Racism, in: J of the Christian Church, 97; From Anglo-American Traditions to a Multicultural World, in: Discipliana Hist J Disciples of Christ Hist Soc, 97; El Cantico de Maria, in: J for Preachers, 97; Kingdom Building in the Borderlands, The Church and Manifest Destiny, in: Hispanic/Latino Theology, Challenge and Promise, eds, A M Isasi-Diaz & F Segovia, Minneapolis Fortress Press, 96; Latinos in the Protestant Establishment, Is There a Place for Us at the Feast Table?, in: Protestantes/Protestants, eds, J L Gonzalez & D Maldonado, Nashville Abingdon forthcoming. **CONTACT ADDRESS** Hispanic Theo Initiative, 1703 Clifton Rd, Ste F-2, Atlanta, GA, 30329. **EMAIL** dmachad@emory.edu

MACHAFFIE, BARBARA J.
PERSONAL Born 11/29/1949, Philadelphia, PA, m, 1972 **DISCIPLINE** RELIGIOUS STUDIES; ECCLESIASTICAL HISTORY **EDUCATION** Col of Wooster, BA, 71; Univ of Edinburgh, Scotland, BD, 74, PhD, 77. **CAREER** Ref Libr, Princeton Theol Sem, 77-80; vis asst prof, Cleveland State Univ, 81-83; instr, Marietta Col, 83-87; asst prof, Hist and Relig, Marietta Col, 92- . **HONORS AND AWARDS** Molly C. Putnam and Israel Ward Andrews Assoc prof Relig. **MEMBERSHIPS** Phi Beta Kappa; Scottish Ecclesiastical Hist Soc; Amer Acad Rel. **RESEARCH** 19th Century British Ecclesiastical History; Women and Religion. **SELECTED PUBLICATIONS** Auth, Her Story: Women in Christian Tradition, Fortress, 86; Readings in Her Story: Women in Christian Tradition, Fortress, 92. **CONTACT ADDRESS** Dept of History and Religion, Marietta Col, Marietta, OH, 45750. **EMAIL** machaffb@marietta.edu

MACHAMER, PETER KENNEDY
PERSONAL Born 10/20/1942, Cleveland, Ohio, 3 children **DISCIPLINE** PHILOSOPHY **EDUCATION** Columbia Univ, AB, 64; Cambridge Univ, BA, 66, MA, 70; Univ Chicago PhD(philos), 72. **CAREER** Instr philos, Ill Inst Technol, 67-69; from asst prof to assoc prof, Ohio State Univ, 69-76; assoc prof, 76-78, Prof Hist & Philos Sci & Chmn Dept, Univ Pittsburgh, 79-, Nat Endowment for Humanities curric develop grant & asst dir, Prog Hist Philos & Hist Sci Theories, Ohio State Univ, 72-74. **HONORS AND AWARDS** NSF Scis and Values, 98 **MEMBERSHIPS** Philos Sci Asn (governing bd, 80-84); Hist Sci Soc; Am Philos Asn; AAAS **RESEARCH** History of 17th century philosophy and science; rationality in science; philosophy of psychology. **SELECTED PUBLICATIONS** Coauth, A theory of critical reasons, In: Language and Aesthetics, Kans State Univ, 73; auth, Feyerabend and Galileo: The the interaction of theories and the reinterpretation of experience, Studies Hist & Philos Sci, 73; Causality and explanation in the philosophy of Descartes, In: Matter Space and Motion, 74 & co-ed, Matter Space and Motion, 74, Ohio State Univ; co-ed, Mindscapes, Univ Pittsburgh, 97; ed, Cambridge Companion to Galileo, Cambridge Univ, Science and Values, Critical Qrt, 98. **CONTACT ADDRESS** Dept of Hist & Philos of Sci, Univ of Pittsburgh, 1017 Cathedral/Learn, Pittsburgh, PA, 15260-0001. **EMAIL** pkmacht@pitt.edu

MACHAN, TIBOR R.
PERSONAL Born 03/18/1939, Budapest, Hungary, d, 3 children **DISCIPLINE** PHILOSOPHY **EDUCATION** Claremont McKenna Col, BA, 65; NY Univ. MA, 66; Univ Cal at Santa Barbara, PhD, 71. **CAREER** Cal State at Bakersfield, asst prof, 70-72; State Univ of NY at Fredonia, 72-82, tenured 78; Univ of Cal at Santa Barbara, vis assoc prof, 79-84; Franklin Col, Switzerland, 83,85-86 & 97; Univ of San Diego vis dist prof, 84-85; USMA West Point, v prof, 92-93; Adelphi Univ, sr J. M. Olin prof, 94; Chapman Univ, dist fel & prof, 97-, Auburn Univ, prof, 86-99. **HONORS AND AWARDS** Koch Foundation, Confer dir, 70, 72 & 80; Reason Foundation, edu pro dir, 79-84, US dept of edu, JJNGFBM, 85-90; Freedom Comm Inc, advisor, 97-. **MEMBERSHIPS** AAPS, APA, MTPS, Phila Society **RESEARCH** Political philo; meta-ethics; ethics, philo; soc; sciences. **SELECTED PUBLICATIONS** Auth, Ayn Rand, Peter Lang, 99 f/c; Classical Individualism, Routledge, 98; Generosity: Virtue in the Civil Society, Cato Institute, 98; A Primer of Ethics, Univ of Oklahoma Press, 97; Capitalism and Individualism: Reframing the Argument for the Free Society, St Martin's Pub. Co, 90; Marxism: A Bourgeois Critique, MCB Univ Press Ltd, 88. **CONTACT ADDRESS** Sch of Business and Economics, Chapman Univ, PO Box 64, Silverado, CA, 92676. **EMAIL** machan@chapman.edu

MACHINA, KENTON F.
PERSONAL Born 04/23/1942, Denver, CO **DISCIPLINE** PHILOSOPHY **EDUCATION** Valparaiso Univ, BS, math and philos, 63; Univ Calif Los Angeles, MA, philos, 66, PhD, philos, 68. **CAREER** Asst prof, philos, Ind Univ, 68-73; asst to assoc to full prof, philos, Ill State Univ, 73-. **HONORS AND AWARDS** Danforth grad fel; Outstanding sr humanities prof, Ill State Univ, 95. **MEMBERSHIPS** Amer Philos Asn; Ill Philos Asn; AAUP. **RESEARCH** Free will and determinism and moral responsibility; Vagueness and semantics. **SELECTED PUBLICATIONS** Article, Challenges for Compatibilism, Amer Philos Quart, 31, 213-333, 94; article, Induction and Deduction Revisited, Nous, 19, 571-578, 85; article, Freedom of Expression in Commerce, Law and Philos, 3, 375-406, 84; auth, Basic Applied Logic, Scott, Foresman and Co, 82; article, Belief, Truth and Vagueness, Jour Philos Logic, 5, 47-78, 76, reprinted, Vagueness: a Reader, MIT Press, 97; article, Vague Predicates, Amer Philos Quart, 9, 225-33, 72; article, Kant, Quine, and Human Experience, Philos Rev, 484-497, Oct, 72. **CONTACT ADDRESS** Illinois State Univ, Campus Box 4540, Normal, IL, 61790-4540. **EMAIL** kfmachin@ilstu.edu

MACHLE, EDWARD JOHNSTONE
PERSONAL Born 09/29/1918, Canton, China, m, 1942, 3 children **DISCIPLINE** PHILOSOPHY **EDUCATION** Whitworth Col, AB, 39; San Francisco Theol Sem, BD, 42, AM, 44; Columbia Univ, PhD, 52. **CAREER** Instr philos, Columbia Univ, 46-47; asst prof, 47-52, assoc prof, 53-63, prof, 63-81, chmn dept, 66-69, EMER PROF PHILOS, UNIV COLO, BOULDER, 81-, Pastor, churches, Concrete, Wash, San Francisco, Calif and Mineola, NY. **MEMBERSHIPS** Am Philos Asn; Am Acad Relig; Soc Asian and Comp Philos. **RESEARCH** Oriental and comparative philosophy; religious symbols; ethics. **SELECTED PUBLICATIONS** Auth, The Mind and the Shen-Ming in 'Xunzi', J Chinese Philos, Vol 0019, 92. **CONTACT ADDRESS** 515 Simmons St, Port Angeles, WA, 98362.

MACIEROWSKI, E.M.
PERSONAL Born 11/01/1948, Springfield, MA, m, 1994, 5 children **DISCIPLINE** PHILOSOPHY; MEDIEVAL STUDIES **EDUCATION** St. John's Col, BA, 70; Univ Toronto, MA, 73; Pontifical Inst of Mediaeval Studies, MSL, 76; Univ Toronto, PhD, 79. **CAREER** Tutor, Latin prog, St. Michael's Col & Univ Toronto, 78-79; lectr & asst prof, philos, Univ St. Thomas, 79-83; visiting asst prof, philos, Cath Univ of Amer, 83-86; res grant transl, Nat Endow for the Humanities, 86-87; assoc prof and chair, philos, Christendom Col, 87-93; lectr II, logic, Lord Fairfax Community Col, spring, 93; Benedictine Col, 93-. **HONORS AND AWARDS** Woodrow Wilson fel, 70-71; Can Coun Doctoral fel, 75-76; NEH Seminar in Arabic Paleography, Univ Penn, 76; Imperial Iranian Acad of Philos, Tehran, 76-77; NEH Transl grant, 86-87; guest cur, Smithsonian Inst, 87; NEH summer seminar, Columbia Univ, 93; Second Summer Thomistic Inst, Univ Notre Dame, 94; NEH Study grant, 95; pres, Kans City Area Philos Soc, mar, 97-98; speaker, Kans Humanities Coun, Aug, 97-98. **MEMBERSHIPS** Amer Cath Philos Asn; Amer Philos Asn; Fel of Cath Scholars; Kans City Area Philos Asn. **RESEARCH** History of philosophy; Logic; Greek mathematics; Philosophy of nature; Moral philosophy; Metaphysics; Mnemonics; History of cryptology; Hermeneutics. **SELECTED PUBLICATIONS** Auth, Thomas Aquina's Earliest Treatment of the Divine Essence, Ctr for Medieval and Renaissance Studies & Inst of Global Cultural Studies at Binghamton Univ; auth, On Cutting Off A Ratio, Apollonius of Perga, Critical Translation of the Treatise From the Two Extant MSS of the Arabic Version of the Lost Greek Original, The Golden Hind Press, 87; article, Latin Averroes on the Motion of the Elements, Archiv fur Geschichte der Philosophie, Band 74, Heft 2, 127-157, 92; article, John Philoponus on Aristotle's Definition of Nature: A Translation from the Greek with Notes, Ancient Philos, VIII, 73-100, Spring, 88. **CONTACT ADDRESS** Dept. of Philosophy, Benedictine Col, 1020 N 2nd St, Atchison, KS, 66002. **EMAIL** edwardm@raven.benedictine.edu

MACINTOSH, DUNCAN
DISCIPLINE PHILOSOPHY OF LANGUAGE AND SCIENCE **EDUCATION** Queen's Univ, BA, 79; Univ Waterloo, MA, 81; Univ Toronto, PhD, 86. **CAREER** Assoc prof. **RESEARCH** Epistemology, metaethics, decision and action theory, metaphysics. **SELECTED PUBLICATIONS** Auth, Preference-Revision & the Paradoxes of Instrumental Rationality, CJP, 92; "Persons and the Satisfaction of Preferences," Jour Philos, 93; "Partial Convergence & Approximate Truth," Brit Jour Philos Sci, 94; "Could God Have Made the Big Bang?," Dialogue, 94. **CONTACT ADDRESS** Dept of Philos, Dalhousie Univ, Halifax, NS, B3H 3J5. **EMAIL** duncan.macintosh@dal.ca

MACINTOSH, JOHN JAMES
PERSONAL Born 07/30/1934, North Bay, ON, Canada **DISCIPLINE** PHILOSOPHY **EDUCATION** Univ Auckland, BA, 57, MA, 58; Oxford Univ, BPhil, 61, MA, 63. **CAREER** Jr lectr philos, Univ Auckland, 59; res lectr, Merton Col, Oxford Univ, 61-63, lectr and fel, St John's Col, 63-66, CUF lectr literae humaniores, Oxford Univ, 64-66; assoc prof, 66-70, PROF PHILOS, UNIV CALGARY, 70-. **RESEARCH** Philosophy of mind; seventeenth century science; metaphysics. **SELECTED PUBLICATIONS** Auth, Belief in God Revisited + Concerning the Dual Aspect of Faith, the Nature of Performatives, and the Arousal of Belief States--a Reply to Williams, J.N., Rel Stud, Vol 0030, 94; Hypatia of Alexandria, Isis, Vol 0087, 96. **CONTACT ADDRESS** Dept of Philos, Univ of Calgary, Calgary, AB, T2N 1N4.

MACINTYRE, JAMES
DISCIPLINE LAW **EDUCATION** Univ British Columbia, BC, 56, LLB, 57; Harvard Univ, LLM, 58. **CAREER** Assoc prof, 64-68; prof, 68-. **RESEARCH** Labour law; labour arbitration law; trusts; evidence. **SELECTED PUBLICATIONS** Auth, pubs about evidence in income tax, equity, labour law and labour arbitration. **CONTACT ADDRESS** Fac of Law, Univ British Columbia, 1822 East Mall, Vancouver, BC, V6T 1Z1. **EMAIL** macintyre@law.ubc.ca

MACK, ERIC M.
DISCIPLINE PHILOSOPHY **EDUCATION** Univ Rochester, PhD, 73. **CAREER** Prof, Tulane Univ. **SELECTED PUBLICATIONS** Auth, Personal Integrity, Practical Recognition, and Rights, The Monist; pub(s) in, Philos and Public Aff; Ethics; Philos Stud; Soc Philos and Policy. **CONTACT ADDRESS** Dept of Philosophy, Tulane Univ, 6823 St Charles Ave, New Orleans, LA, 70118. **EMAIL** emack@mailhost.tcs.tulane.edu

MACKEY, LOUIS HENRY
PERSONAL Born 09/24/1926, Sidney, OH, d, 4 children **DISCIPLINE** PHILOSOPHY, COMPARATIVE LITERATURE **EDUCATION** Capital Univ, BA, 48; Yale Univ, MA, 53, PhD(philos), 54. **CAREER** From instr to asst prof philos, Yale Univ, 53-59; from assoc prof to prof, Rice Univ, 59-67; vis prof, 67-68, prof Philos, Univ Tex, Austin, 68-, Morse fel, Yale Univ, 57-58; vis prof, Haverford Col, 71-72; Nat Endowment for Humanities res fel, 76-77; vis prof, Univ of Tulsa, 83. **HONORS AND AWARDS** President's Assoc Teaching Excellence Award, 91; Award for Outstanding Grad Teaching, 94. **MEMBERSHIPS** Amer Comparative Lit Assoc, Inter Assoc for Philo and Lit. **RESEARCH** Literary theory; medieval philosophy; Kierkegaard. **SELECTED PUBLICATIONS** Auth, Soren Kierkegaard, In: Existentialism, McGraw, 64; Kierkegaard: A Kind of Poet, Univ Pa, 71; The loss of the world in Kierkegaard's ethics, In: Kierkegaard: A Collection of Critical Essays, Doubleday, 72; Entreatments of God: Reflections on Aquinas' five ways, Franciscan Studies, 77; Anatomical curiosities: Northrop Frye's theory of criticism, Tex Studies in Lang & Lit, 81; Paranoia, Pynchon and preterition, Sub-Stance, 81; Redemptive subversions: The Christian discourse of St Bonaventure, In: The Autonomy of Religious Belief, Notre Dame, 81; A ram in the afternoon: Kierkegaard's discourse of the other, Psychiat & Humanities, Vol 5, 81; Theory and Practic in the Rhetoric of I A Richards, Rheoric Soc Quarterly, 97. **CONTACT ADDRESS** Univ of Texas, Austin, TX, 78712-1026.

MACKINNON, PETER
DISCIPLINE LAW **EDUCATION** Dalhousie Univ, BA, 69; Queen's Univ, LLB, 72; Univ Saskatchewan, LLM, 76. **CAREER** Asst dean, 79-81; prof, 75- **HONORS AND AWARDS** Pres, Can Coun Law Deans, 94. **MEMBERSHIPS** Law Soc Saskatchewan; Can Asn Law Tchr. **SELECTED PUBLICATIONS** Auth, Costs and Compensation for the Innocent Accused, Can Bae Rev, 88; co-ed, After Meech Lake, Fifth House, 91; Drawing Boundaries: Legislatures, Courts and Electoral Values, Fifth House, 92. **CONTACT ADDRESS** Col of Law, Univ Saskatchewan, 15 Campus Dr, Saskatoon, SK, S7N 5A6.

MACKLER, AARON L.
PERSONAL Born 12/09/1958, Chicago, IL, m, 1986, 3 children **DISCIPLINE** PHILOSOPHY, THEOLOGY **EDUCATION** Yale Univ, BA, 80; Hebrew Univ, Grad Studies, 81-82; Jewish Theological Seminary, MA, 85; Georgetown Univ, PhD, 92. **CAREER** Staff ethicist, NY State Task Force on Life and the Law, 90-94; vis asst prof, Jewish Theological Seminary, 92-94; ASST PROF OF THEOLOGY, DUQUESNE UNIV, 94-. **MEMBERSHIPS** Am Acad of Religion; Am Philos Asn; Am Soc for Bioethics and Humanities; Asn for Jewish Studies; Catholic Theological Soc of Am; Center for Medical Ethics, Univ Pittsburgh Medical Center, Assoc; Col Theology Soc; Rabbinical Assembly; Soc of Christian Ethics. **RESEARCH** Bioethics; Jewish ethics; Jewish thought; Catholic moral theology; religious ethics. **SELECTED PUBLICATIONS** Auth, Universal Being and Ethical Particularity in the Hebrew Bible: A Jewish Response to Voegelin's Israel and Revelation, J of Religion, forthcoming; An Expanded Partnership with God? In Vitro Fertilization in Jewish Ethics, J of Religious Ethics, 97; Cases and Principles in Jewish Bioethics: Toward a Holistic Model, Contemporary Jewish Ethics and Morality, Oxford Univ Press, 95; Judaism, Justice, and Access to Health Care, Kennedy Inst of Ethics J, 91; Symbols, Reality, and God: Heschel's Rejection of a Tillichian Understanding of Religious Symbols, Judaism, 91. **CONTACT ADDRESS** 6519 Darlington Rd., Pittsburgh, PA, 15217.

MACKLIN, RUTH C.
PERSONAL Born 03/27/1938, Newark, NJ, 2 children **DISCIPLINE** PHILOSOPHY **EDUCATION** Cornell Univ, BA, 58; Case Western Reserve Univ, MA, 66, PhD, 68. **CAREER** From instr to assoc prof philos, Case Western Reserve Univ, 67-76, dir moral probs in med proj, 73-74; assoc behav studies, Hastings Ctr, 76-80; assoc prof, 80-84, Prof Bioethics, Albert Einstein Col Med, 84-, Shoshanah Trachtenberg Frackman Fac Scholor, biomedical ethics, 91, head, Div Philos and Hist Med, Dept Epidemiology and Soc Med, 93-; consult ed, Ethics & Behaviors, 90-; ed advis bd, Jour Med Ethics, 95. **MEMBERSHIPS** Eastern Div Am Philos Asn; APHA; ASBH, IAB. **RESEARCH** Bioethics, AIDS; reproductive health. **SELECTED PUBLICATIONS** Auth, Moral concerns and appeals to rights and duties, Hastings Ctr Report, 10/76; co-ed, Moral Problems in Medicine, Prentice-Hall, 76; auth, Consent, coercion, and conflicts of rights, Perspectives in Biol & Med, spring 77; Moral progress, Ethics, 8/77; Moral issues in human genetics: Counseling or control?, Dialogue, 77; co-ed, Violence and the Politics of Research, 81 & Who Speaks for the Child: The Problems of Proxy Consent, 82, Plenum Press; auth, Man, Mind, and Morality: The Ethics of Behavior Control, Prentice-Hall, 82; Predicting dangerousness and the public health response to AIDS, Hastings Center Report, 86; co-auth, AIDS research: The ethics of clinical trials, Law, Med & Health Care, 12/86; Mortal Choices: Bioethics in Today's World, Pantheon Books, 87; Mortal choices: Ethical dilemmas in moder medicine, rep, Houghton Mifflin Co, 88; Is there anything wrong with surrogate motherhood? An ethical analysis, Law, Med & Health Care, spring/summer 88, In: Surrogate Motherhood: Politics and Privacy, Ind Univ Press, 90; Ethics and human values in family planning, In: Ethics and Human Values in Family Planning, CIOMS, 89; HIV infection in children: som ethical conflicts: Tech Report on Develop Disabilities and HIV Infection, 9/89; The paradoxical case of payment as benefit to reserach subjects: IRB: A Rev of Human Subjects Res, 11-12/89; Ethics and human reproduction: International perspectives, Social Problems, 90; HIV-infected psychiatric patients: Beyond confidentiality, Ethics & Behavior, 91; Universality of the Nuremberg code, In: The Nazi Doctors and the Nuremberg Code: Human Rights in Human Experimentation, Oxford Univ Press, 92; Privacy of genetic information and control of it, In: Gene Mapping, Oxford Univ Press, 92; Antiprogestins: Ethical issues, In: Proceedings of the International Symposium on Angiprogestins, Bangladesh Asn for Prevention of Septic Abortion, 6/92; Women's health: An Ethical perspective, Jour Law, Med & Ethics, spring 93; Enemies of Patients, Oxford Univ Press, 93; Surrogates and Other Mothers, The Debates over Assisted Reproduction, Temple Univ Press, 94; Reversing the presumption: The IOM report on women in health research, Jour Am Women's Med Asn, 94; Cloning without prior approval: A response to recent disclosures of noncompliance, Kennedy Inst Ethics Jour, 95; Maternal-fetal conflict, In: Ethics and Perinatology, Oxford Univ Press, 95; Reproductive technologies in developing countries, Bioethics, 7/95; Rights in bioethics, In: Encyclopedia of Bioethics, 2nd ed, Macmillan, 95; Ethics, informed consent and assisted reproduction, Jour Assisted Reproduction and Genetics, 95; Trials and tribulations: The ethics of responsible research, In: Pediatric Ethics: From Principles to Practice, Harwood Acad Publ, 96; Disagreement, consensus and moral integrity, Kennedy Inst Ethics Jour, 96; Cultural differences and long-acting contraception, In: Controversial Contraception: Moral an dPolicy Challenges of Long-Acting Birth Control, Georgetown Univ Press, 96; Ethics and reproductive health: A principal approach, World Health Statist Quart, 96; Ethical relativism in a multicultural society, Kennedy Inst Ethics Jour, 98; Justice in international research, In: Beyond Consent: Seeking Justice in Research, Oxford Univ Press. **CONTACT ADDRESS** Dept of Epidemiology & Soc Med, Albert Einstein Col of Med, 1300 Morris Pk Ave, Bronx, NY, 10461-1926. **EMAIL** macklin@aecom.yu.edu

MACLEAN, IAIN STEWART
PERSONAL Born 01/06/1956, Bellville, South Africa, m, 1991, 1 child **DISCIPLINE** THEOLOGY, PRACTICAL THEOLOGY, RELIGION & SOCIETY **CAREER** Minister, Presbyterian Church of South Africa, 79-84; dual-standing, Presbytery of Boston (PCUSA) and United Church of Christ, 85-96; Minister at Large, Presbytery of the Peaks (PCUSA), 96-; vis asst prof, Roanoke Col, Salem, VA, 95-97; vis asst prof, Washington & Lee Univ, Lexington, VA, 97-98; asst prof of Religious Thought, James Madison Univ, Harrisonburg, VA, 98-. **HONORS AND AWARDS** Prizewinner, South African Historia, 73; Nationale Taalbond Bilingualism Award, 73; Rotary Scholarship, Cape Province Rotarians, 77-79; grad writing fels prog, Danforth Center for Teaching and Learning, Harvard Univ, 91; Distinction in Teaching Award, Bok Center for Teaching and Learning, Harvard Col, 90-91, 92-93, 94-95; Dean's Dissertation Award, Harvard Divinity School, 93-94; summer fac course dev grant, James Madison Univ, 98. **MEMBERSHIPS** Am Academy of Relig; Presbytery of the Peaks (Presbyterian Church, USA); Am Mis Soc; Karl Barth Soc. **RESEARCH** Relig and soc; relig and democracy; comparative African and Latin Am religions; relig and ethnic/nationalist conflict; hist theol; Reformed/Cath theol and ethics. **SELECTED PUBLICATIONS** Auth, Confessiom, Tradition, and Descent into Hell, in Dictionary of the Bible, ed David N Freedman, Eerdmans, forthcoming; eight entries in Encyclopedia of Minorities in American Politics, ed Jeffrey D Schultz, Oryx, forthcoming; eight entries in Reformations: Protestant and Catholic, 1500-1620: An Interdisciplinary Dictionary, ed by J Carney, Greenwood Press, forthcoming; eleven entries in Encyclopedia of Religion in American Politics, ed Jeffrey D Schultz, Oryx, forthcoming; Bahia and Zion: Religion and Races in Conflict, Afro-Brazilian Religions and African Indigenous Churches in the Process of Democratization, chapter in African Religions and the State, ed Kip S Elolia and Joseph Murphy, with foreward by Peter Paris, Eerdmans, 98; Participatory Democracy: The Brazilian Ecclesial Base as a Case of Unfulfilled Expectations, A Political Analysis of the Period 1981-1991, in Religie en Teologie, 98; assoc ed, Encyclopedia of Religion in American Politics, ed by Jeffrey D Schultz, Oryx, forthcoming; Opting for Democracy: Liberation Theologians, the Catholic Church and the Ethics of Democratization in Brazil, Studies in Religion, Politics and Public Life, II Peter Lang, 98; numerous other publications. **CONTACT ADDRESS** Dept of Philos and Relig, James Madison Univ, MSC 7504, Harrisonburg, VA, 22807. **EMAIL** macleaix@jmu.edu

MACLEOD, COLIN
DISCIPLINE PHILOSOPHY **EDUCATION** B.A. (Queens), M.A. (Dalhousie), Ph.D. (Cornell) **CAREER** Instr, Univ Brit Columbia; Simon Fraser Univ; asst prof, 98. **HONORS AND AWARDS** Vis fel, Ctr for Law and Soc, Univ Edinburgh. **RESEARCH** Contemporary political philosophy; ethics and philosophy of law. **SELECTED PUBLICATIONS** Auth, Liberalism, Justice, and Markets: A Critique of Liberal Equlaity, OUP, 98; pub(s), Polit and Soc; Can Jour for Law and Jurisprudence; Law and Philos; Dialogue. **CONTACT ADDRESS** Dept of Philosophy, Victoria Univ, PO Box 3045, Victoria, BC, V8W 3P4.

MACLEOD, GREGORY J.
PERSONAL Born 11/24/1935, Sydney Mines, NS, Canada **DISCIPLINE** PHILOSOPHY **EDUCATION** Louvain, Belgium, PhD, 69. **CAREER** PROF PHILOSOPHY, UNIV CAPE BRETON, 69-. **HONORS AND AWARDS** PhD(hon), St. Francis Xavier Univ, 94. **SELECTED PUBLICATIONS** Auth, New Age Business, 86; auth, From Mondragon to America: Experiments in Community Economic Development, 97. **CONTACT ADDRESS** Dept of Philosophy, Univ of Cape Breton, Box 5300, Sydney, NS, B1P 6L2. **EMAIL** gmacleod@sparc.uccb.ns.ca

MACNEIL, IAN RODERICK
PERSONAL Born 06/20/1929, New York, NY, m, 1952, 4 children **DISCIPLINE** LAW **EDUCATION** Univ Vt, BA, 50; Harvard Univ, JD, 55. **CAREER** Law clerk, Hon Peter Woodbury, US Court Appeals, Manchester, NH, 55-56; assoc, Sulloway Hollis Godfrey & Soden, Concord, NJ, 56-59; from asst prof to prof law, Cornell Univ, 59-72; prof, Univ Va, 72-74; prof law, Sch Law, Cornell Univ, 74-76, Ingersoll prof, 76-80; John Henry Wigmore Prof Law, Sch Law, Northwestern Univ, 80-, Fulbright vis prof law, Univ Col, Dar es Salaam, Univ EAfrica, 65-67; vis prof law, Duke Univ, 71-72; vis prof, Harvard Univ, 88-89; Guggenheim fel, 78-79. **HONORS AND AWARDS** Emil Brown Prev Law Award, 71. **MEMBERSHIPS** Am Bar Asn; Am Law Inst; Soc Pub Teachers Law; Can Asn Law Teachers; Standing Coun Scottish Chiefs. **RESEARCH** Contracts, arbitration. **SELECTED PUBLICATIONS** Auth, Bankruptcy Law in East Africa, Legal Publ & Oceana, 66; Contracts: Instruments of Social Cooperation--East Africa, Rothman, 68; coauth, Formation of Contracts: A Study of the Common Core of Legal Systems, Oceana & Stevens, 68; Students and Decision Making, Pub Affairs Press, 70; auth, The many future of contracts: Adjustment of long term economic relations, Northwestern Univ Law Rev, 78; Contracts: Exchange Transactions & Relations, Foundation, 2nd ed, 78; auth, The New Social Contract, Yale Univ, 80; American Arbitration Law, Oxford Univ, 90; coauth, Federal Arbitration Law, Little Brown, 94. **CONTACT ADDRESS** Sch of Law, Northwestern Univ, 357 E Chicago Ave, Chicago, IL, 60611-3069.

MACQUARRIE, JOHN
PERSONAL Born 06/27/1919, Renfrew, Scotland, m, 1949, 3 children **DISCIPLINE** SYSTEMATIC THEOLOGY **EDUCATION** Univ Glasgow, MA, 40, BD, 43, PhD, 54. **CAREER** Minister, St Ninian's Church, Brechin, 48-53; lectr syst theol, Univ Glasgow, 53-62; prof, Union Theol Sem, NY, 62-70; LADY MARGARET PROF DIVINITY, OXFORD UNIV, 70-, Hastie lectr, Univ Glasgow, 62; Cooper lectr, Swarthmore Col, 62; John M English lectr, Andover-Newton Divinity Sch, 63; Birks lectr, McGill Univ, 63; John XX111 lectr, St Xavier Col, Ill, 65; Page lectr, Berkeley Divinity Sch, 66; Richard lectr, Univ Va, 67; consult, Lambeth Conf, 68; Penick lectr, Univ NC, 69; dir, SCM Press, Ltd, London, 70-76; canon, Christ Church, Oxford, 70-; Prideaux lectr, Univ Exeter, 71; Firth lectr, Univ Nottingham, 72. **HONORS AND AWARDS** DLitt, Univ Glasgow, 64, DD, 69; STD, Univ of the South, 67; DD, Oxford Univ 70, Episcopal Theol Sem SW and Va Theol Sem. **MEMBERSHIPS** Soc Study Theol. **RESEARCH** Existentialism; demythologizing; contemporary religious thought. **SELECTED PUBLICATIONS** Auth, The Logic of Religious and Theological Language, J Dharma, Vol 0017, 92; God Without Being, J Rel, Vol 0073, 93; Believing 3 Ways in One God--a Reading of the Apostles Creed, Expository Times, Vol 0104, 93; Prospects for Natural Theology, J Theol Stud, Vol 0044, 93; Dictionary of Scottish Church Hist and Theology, J Theol Stud, Vol 0045, 94; Christ, Church and Society--Essays on Baillie, John and Baillie, Donald, J theol Stud, Vol 0045, 94; The Theology of Moltmann, Jugen, Expository Times, Vol 0107, 95; The Assurance of Things Hoped for--a Theology of Christian Faith, J Theol Stud, Vol 0046, 95; Bultmann, Scottish J Theol, Vol 0048, 95; Unashamed Anglicanism, Expository Times, Vol 0107, 95; God in Christian Perspective, J F Theol Stud, Vol 0046, 95; Christian Doctrine in the Light of Polanyi, Michael Theory of Personal Knowledge, Expository Times, Vol 0106,

95; Ebb and Flow of Hope, Christian Theology at the End of the 2nd Millennium, Expository Times, Vol 0107, 96; Confucianism and Christianity--a Comparative-Study of Jen and Agape, Expository Times, Vol 0107, 96; The Ecclesiology of Rahner, Karl, J Theol Stud, Vol 0047, 96; The Legacy of Bultmann, Heythrop J-Quart Rev Philos and Theol, Vol 0037, 96; Dialogue Among the World Religions/ Expository Times, Vol 0108, 97; Revelation and Reconciliation--a Window on Modernity, J Theol Stud Vol 0048, 97. **CONTACT ADDRESS** Univ Oxford, Christ Church, Oxford, ., OX1 1DP.

MACY, GARY A.
DISCIPLINE RELIGIOUS HISTORY **EDUCATION** Univ Cambridge, PhD. **CAREER** Dept Theo, Univ San Diego **SELECTED PUBLICATIONS** Publ on, medieval theol and rel, espec the theol of the Eucharist. **CONTACT ADDRESS** Dept of Theological and Relig Studies, Univ of San Diego, 5998 Alcal Park, Maher 282, San Diego, CA, 92110-2492. **EMAIL** macy@acusd.edu

MACZKA, ROMWALD
DISCIPLINE PENTATEUCH, CHRISTOLOGIES OF THE NEW TESTAMENT **EDUCATION** Wheaton Col, BA, 75; Wheaton Grad Sch, MA, 83; Leipzig Univ, PhD, 87. **CAREER** Instr, Inst Slavic Studies, 79-84;Assoc prof, Carthage Col, 89-; Res affiliate,Inst Study Christianity Marxism, 89-91; Vis asst prof, Trinity College, 88-89. **HONORS AND AWARDS** Grants: Evangelical Lutheran Church Am; Am Ctr Int Leadership; Lilly Found AmCtr Int Leadership; David C. Cook Foundation (Elgin, IL); academic sch; Stewards' Found. **MEMBERSHIPS** Mennonite Central Comt; Am Hist Asn; Conference Faith & Hist; Am Chemical Soc; American Asn Advancement Slavic Studies. **SELECTED PUBLICATIONS** Auth, Scholarly rev, Theology without Boundaries: Encounters of Eastern Orthodoxy and Western Tradition; The Rise and Decline of Thomas Muentzer, Lutheran Quart;Ed, Christianity and Marxism in U. S. Higher Education: A Handbook of Syllabi, Yesterday's Dissidents -- Tomorrow's Vanguard, 90; Glasnost and the Church; Re-theologizing Thomas Muentzer in the German Democratic Republic, Mennonite Quart Rev; Christian/Marxist Dialogue and Thomas Muentzer. **CONTACT ADDRESS** Carthage Col, 2001 Alford Dr., Kenosha, WI, 53140. **EMAIL** rom@carthage.edu

MADDEN, DANIEL PATRICK
PERSONAL Born 09/29/1931, Chicago, IL **DISCIPLINE** PHILOSOPHY, RELIGION **EDUCATION** DePaul Univ, BSC, 53; Aquinas Inst, BA, 57, MA, 63; Ment Health Inst, Iowa, cert, 61; St Paul Univ, STL, 68, STD, 72; Univ Ottawa, MTh, 68, PhD, 72. **CAREER** Prof theol, chmn dept philos & theol, counselor & chaplain, Sacred Heart Dominican Col, 61-63; instr relig, Univ Dallas, 63-64; prof theol & philos, chmn dept & dean of men, Col St Joseph on the Rio Grande, 64-66; asst prof theol, Univ Albuquerque, 66-68; dir & pastor, Aquinas Newman Ctr, Univ NMex, 68-71; asst prof theol & chaplain, St Mary's Dominican Col, 71-73; ASSOC PROF THEOL/ RELIG STUDIES & CAMPUS MINISTRY ADJ, BARRY UNIV, 73-. **HONORS AND AWARDS** Archbishop Lamy Award, Archdiocese of Santa Fe, 65. **MEMBERSHIPS** Col Theol Soc; Nat Cath Guidance Conf; Cath Theol Soc Am; Nat Liturgy Comn; Cath Campus Ministry Asn **RESEARCH** Scripture; counseling and guidance; Quakers & Catholics; spirituality of imperfection (12 steps) programs. **SELECTED PUBLICATIONS** Coauth, Teach Us to Love, Herder, 64. **CONTACT ADDRESS** Dept of Theol/Philos, Barry Univ, 11300 N E 2nd Ave, Miami, FL, 33161-6695. **EMAIL** madden@pcsa01.barry.edu

MADDEN, EDWARD
PERSONAL Born 03/18/1925, Gary, IN, m, 1946, 2 children **DISCIPLINE** PHILOSOPHY **EDUCATION** Oberlin Col, AB 46, MA 47; Univ of IA, PhD, 50 **CAREER** Asst Prof, 50-59, Univ of Connect; Assoc Prof, 59-64, San Jose St; Prof, St Univ of NY at Buffalo; Adj Prof, 92-98, Univ of KY **HONORS AND AWARDS** Herbert Schneider Awd; Phi Kappi Phi; Fulbright Prof; Vis Res Fel, Linacre Col, Oxford, England **MEMBERSHIPS** Am Philos Assoc; Soc for the Advancement of Am Philos; CS Pierce Soc; Am Council of Learned Soc **RESEARCH** American Philosophy; Philosophy of Science; Metaphysics **SELECTED PUBLICATIONS** Coauth, Theories of Scientific Method, U of WA Press, 60; Auth, Philosophical Problems of Psychology, Odyssey Press, 62; Auth, Chauncey Wright and the Foundations of Pragmatism, U of WA Press, 63 **CONTACT ADDRESS** 170 Wesley Dr, Wilmore, KY, 40390.

MADDEN, PATRICK
PERSONAL Born 07/19/1948, Long Beach, CA, s **DISCIPLINE** BIBLICAL STUDIES **EDUCATION** Cath Univ of Am, PhD, 95 **CAREER** Asst Prof, 95-98, St. Mary's Sem; Adj Prof, 98-pres, Grew Inst **MEMBERSHIPS** Cath Bibl Assoc; Notre Dame Ctr for Past Liturgy **CONTACT ADDRESS** Our Lady of Fatima Church, PO Box 4136, Monroe, LA, 71211-4136. **EMAIL** 72240.1661@compuserve.com

MADDY, PENELOPE
DISCIPLINE PHILOSOPHY **EDUCATION** Univ Calif Berkeley, BA, math, 72; Princeton Univ, PhD, 79. **CAREER** Asst prof, philos, Univ Notre Dame, 78-83; assoc prof, philos, Univ Ill Chicago, 83-87; assoc prof, philos, Univ Calif Irvine, 87-89; prof, philos, Univ Calif Irvine, 89-. **HONORS AND AWARDS** Westinghouse Sci Scholar, 68-72; Marshall fel, 72-73; NSF Scholar award, 86, 88-89, 91-92, 94-95; election, Amer Acad of Arts and Sci, 98. **MEMBERSHIPS** Amer Philos Asn; Asn for Symbolic Logis; Philos of Sci Asn. **RESEARCH** Philosophy and foundations of mathematics; Philosophy of logic. **SELECTED PUBLICATIONS** Auth, Naturalism in Mathematics, Oxford Univ Press, 97; auth, Realism in Mathematics, Oxford Univ Press, 90. **CONTACT ADDRESS** Dept. of Philosophy, Univ of California, Irvine, CA, 92697. **EMAIL** pjmaddy@uci.edu

MADISON, GARY BRENT
PERSONAL Born 09/13/1940, Kankakee, IL **DISCIPLINE** PHENOMENOLOGY, EXISTENTIALISM **EDUCATION** St Joseph's Col, Ind, BA, 62; Marquette Univ, MA, 64; Univ Paris, PhD(philos), 68. **CAREER** Lectr English, Univ Nantes, 65-67; asst philos, Univ Paris, 68-70; asst prof, 70-75, assoc prof, 75-80, PROF, MCMASTER UNIV, 80-, Can Coun fel, 76-77; affiliated prof comp lit, Univ Toronto, 79-. **MEMBERSHIPS** Can Philos Asn; Soc Phenomenol and Existential Philos. **RESEARCH** Metaphysics; philosophy of culture. **SELECTED PUBLICATIONS** Auth, The Transition From Modernity to Postmodernity, and a Postmodern Interpretation of History, Progress, Revolution, Universality, Rationality, Humanism, and Civil Society, Etudes Litteraires, Vol 0027, 94. **CONTACT ADDRESS** Dept of Philos, McMaster Univ, 1280 Main St W, Hamilton, ON, L8S 4L8.

MADSEN, CHARLES CLIFFORD
PERSONAL Born 02/13/1908, Luck, WI, m, 1934, 2 children **DISCIPLINE** THEOLOGY, PSYCHOLOGY OF RELIGION **EDUCATION** Univ Minn, AB, 31; Trinity Theol Sem, Nebr, BD, 34; Cent Baptist Theol Sem, ThD, 49. **CAREER** Pastor, Our Savior's Lutheran Church, Kansas City, Kans, 34-42; prof practical theol, Trinity Theol Sem, Nebr, 46; chmn dept Christianity, 46-56, pres, 56-71, consult, 71-73, EMER PRES, DANA COL, 73-, Knight, Royal Order Dannebrog, 68. **HONORS AND AWARDS** DD, Midland Lutheran Col, 65; LHD, Dana Col, 71. **RESEARCH** The relationship between Christian doctrine and current psychiatric practices; the doctrinal dynamics of Christian psychotherapy; psychiatry. **CONTACT ADDRESS** 2519 College Dr, Blair, NE, 68008.

MADSEN, TRUMAN GRANT
PERSONAL Born 12/13/1926, Salt Lake City, UT, m, 1953, 3 children **DISCIPLINE** PHILOSOPHY, RELIGION **EDUCATION** Univ Utah, BS, 50, MS, 51; Harvard Univ, AM, 57, PhD, 60. **HONORS AND AWARDS** Schiller Essays Prize, Univ Southern Calif, 52; Honors Prof of the Year, Brigham Young Univ, 66, Karl G Maeser Distinguished Teacher, 67, Outstanding Teacher Award, 71., Teaching asst philos, Harvard Univ, 55; from asst prof to assoc prof philos and relig, 57-71, chmn dept hist and philos relig, 60-72, dir, Inst Mormon Studies, 66-72, Richard L Evans prof Christian understanding, 71-77, PROF PHILOS AND DIR, JUDEO-CHRISTIAN STUDIES CTR, BRIGHAM YOUNG UNIV, 77-, Lectr, Northeastern Univ, 69-70 and Grad Theol Union, 73; guest ed, BYU Studies, 70-; chmn pub progs comt, Nat Endowment for Humanities, 74-. **MEMBERSHIPS** Am Philos Asn. **RESEARCH** Philosophy of language; contemporary philosophy of religion. **SELECTED PUBLICATIONS** Auth, The American Religion--the Emergence of the Post-Christian Nation, Brigham Young Univ Studies, Vol 0035, 95. **CONTACT ADDRESS** Brigham Young Univ, 165 Joseph Smith Bldg, Provo, UT, 84602.

MAFFIE, JAMES
DISCIPLINE PHILOSOPHY **EDUCATION** UCLA, BA, 73; Univ Mich, MA, 76; PhD, 88. **CAREER** Asst prof, North Carolina State Univ, 88-90; asst prof, Calif State Univ Northbridge, 90-95; asst prof, Colo State Univ, 98-. **HONORS AND AWARDS** Phi beta kappa; Postdoctorate Fel. **MEMBERSHIPS** Am Philos Asn; radical Philos; Asn of Philos of Sci Asn. **RESEARCH** Epistemology; Philosophy of Science; Mesoamerican Philosophy; Feminism. **SELECTED PUBLICATIONS** Auth, Realism, Relativism, and Naturalized Meta - Epistemology, Metaphilosophy, 93; Naturalism, Scientism, and the Independence of Epistemology, Erkenntnis, 95; Towards and Anthropology of Epistemology, The Philos Forum, 95; 'Just-So' Stories about 'Inner Cognitive Africa' : Some Doubts about Sorensen's Evolutionary Epistemology of Thought Experiments, Biol and Philos, 97; Atran's Evolutionary Psychology: 'Say It Ain't Just-So, Joe', Behavioral and Brain Sci, 98; Naturalism and Epistemological Authority: Beyond Pragmatism and Absolutism, Intellectual Hist Newsletter, 98. **CONTACT ADDRESS** Dept of Philosophy, Colorado State Univ, Ft. Collins, CO, 80523-1781. **EMAIL** maffiej@spot.colorado.edu

MAGEE, GLENN A.
PERSONAL Born 04/10/1966, Norfolk, VA, s **DISCIPLINE** PHILOSOPHY **EDUCATION** Emory Univ, PhD, 98. **CAREER** ASST PROF, GA SOUTHERN UNIV, FALL 98-. **MEMBERSHIPS** Amer Philos Assoc. **RESEARCH** German idealism; ancient philos. **SELECTED PUBLICATIONS** Auth, Hegel and the Hermetic Tradition, forthcoming. **CONTACT ADDRESS** 510 Coventry Rd, Decatur, GA, 30030. **EMAIL** gamagee@gsaix2.cc.gasou.edu

MAGGS, PETER BLOUNT
PERSONAL Born 07/24/1936, Durham, NC, m, 1960, 4 children **DISCIPLINE** SOVIET AND EAST CENTRAL EUROPEAN LAW **EDUCATION** Harvard Univ, AB, 57, JD, 61. **CAREER** From asst prof to assoc prof law, 64-69, PROF LAW, UNIV ILL, URBANA-CHAMPAIGN, 69-, Exchange student, Leningrad State Univ, 61-62; res assoc, Harvard Law Sch and assoc, Harvard Russ Res Ctr, 63-64; Fulbright res sscholar, Univ Belgrade, 67; exchange scholar, Bulgarian Acad Sci, 67; sr fel, E-W Population Inst, 72; vis cholar, Acad Sci USSR, 72; reporter, Uniform Simplification of Land Transfers Act, NCCUSL, 74-76; ed, Soviet Statues and Decisions, 76-; Fulbright lectr law, Moscow State Univ, 77. **MEMBERSHIPS** Am Asn Advan Slavic Studies. **RESEARCH** Computer-based legal education; communist legal systems. **SELECTED PUBLICATIONS** Auth, Russian Law--the End of the Soviet System and the Role of Law, Amer J Comp Law, Vol 0041, 93. **CONTACT ADDRESS** College of Law, Univ of Illinois, at Urbana, Champaign, IL, 61801.

MAGID, LAURIE
DISCIPLINE LEGAL WRITING AND APPELLATE ADVOCACY **EDUCATION** Wharton Sch Bus, Univ Pa, BS, 82; Columbia Law Sch, JD, 85. **CAREER** Instr, Villanova Univ, 97-; clerked, Honorable James Hunter III Ct Appeals Third Circuit; asst dist atty, Philadelphia Dist Attorney's Off, 86-95; past prosecutor, tried cases, wrote briefs; argued in the Pa Supreme and Superior Courts; past adj prof, Temple Law Sch; assoc prof and co-dir Legal Writing Dept, Widener Law Sch, 95. **SELECTED PUBLICATIONS** Publi in, Columbia Law Rev, Ohio State Law J, Wayne Law Rev & San Diego Law Rev, on Miranda Rights, Discriminatory Selection of Juries, Legal Writing Pedagogy and First Amendment Protections. **CONTACT ADDRESS** Law School, Villanova Univ, 800 Lancaster Ave, Villanova, PA, 19085-1692. **EMAIL** magid@law.vill.edu

MAGILL, GERARD
PERSONAL Born 10/09/1951, Scotland **DISCIPLINE** THEOLOGICAL ETHICS **EDUCATION** Gregorian Univ, Rome, PhB, STB, STL; Edinburgh Univ, PhD. **CAREER** Drygrange Col, Scotland, 76-86; Loyola Univ, 81-88; St. Louis Univ, 88- . **MEMBERSHIPS** AAUP; SCE; AAR; CTSA; CTT; ASLME; ASBH. **RESEARCH** Health care ethics. **SELECTED PUBLICATIONS** Ed, Discourse and Context: An Interdisciplinary Study, Southern Ill Univ, 93; ed, Personality and Belief: Interdisciplinary Essays; Univ of Am, 94; co-ed, Values and Public Life: An Interdisciplinary Study, Univ of Am, 95; co-ed, Abortion, Catholicism, and Public Policy: An Interdisciplinary Investigation, Univ Creighton, 96. **CONTACT ADDRESS** St Louis Univ, 1402 S Grand Blvd, St Louis, MO, 63104.

MAGNET, JOSEPH E.
DISCIPLINE LAW **EDUCATION** Univ Long Island, BA; McGill Univ, LLB, LLM, PhD. **CAREER** Prof. **SELECTED PUBLICATIONS** Auth, pubs on constitutional law and other legal subjects. **CONTACT ADDRESS** Fac Common Law, Univ Ottawa, 550 Cumberland St, PO Box 450, Ottawa, ON, K1N 6N5.

MAGNUS, BERND
DISCIPLINE NINETEENTH AND TWENTIETH-CENTURY EUROPEAN PHILOSOPHY **EDUCATION** Columbia Univ, PhD. **CAREER** PROF, UNIV CALIF, RIVERSIDE. **RESEARCH** Critical literary theory; History of modern philosophy. **SELECTED PUBLICATIONS** Auth, Nietzsche's Case: Philosophy as/and Literature, Routledge, 93; "Reading Ascetic Reading: Toward the Genealogy of Morals and the Path Back to the World," Nietzsche, Genealogy, Morality, Univ Calif Press, 94; "Postmodern Pragmatism," Pragmatism: From Progressivism to Postmodernism, Praeger, 95; Postmodern Philosophy, The Cambridge Dictionary of Philos, Cambridge Univ Press, 95; "Holocaust Child," Contemp Continental Philos in the US: A Photogrammic Presentation, 96; ed, Specters of Marx, Routledge, 94; Whither Marxism?, Routledge, 95; co-ed, The Cambridge Companion to Nietzsche, Cambridge Univ Press, 96. **CONTACT ADDRESS** Dept of Philos, Univ Calif, 1156 Hinderaker Hall, Riverside, CA, 92521-0209. **EMAIL** magnus@ucrac1.ucr.edu

MAGUIRE, DANIEL C.
PERSONAL Born 04/04/1931, Philadelphia, PA, m, 1 child **DISCIPLINE** RELIGIOUS AND PHILOSOPHICAL ETHICS **CAREER** PROF ETHICS, MARQUETTE UNIV; vis prof, Univ Notre Dame, 83-84. **HONORS AND AWARDS** Best Scholarly Book of the Year, for The Moral Choice, The

Council of WI Writers, Inc, 78; Torch Bearer Award, Cream City Business Assoc, Milwaukee; listed by MS Magazine, 82; voted one of the ten best teachers, Univ Notre Dame, 84. **MEMBERSHIPS** Soc Christian Ethics, pres, 81; The Religious Consultation on Population, Reproductive Health, and Ethics, pres, 98. **RESEARCH** Justice Theory; population; ecology; feminism. **SELECTED PUBLICATIONS** Auth, Death By Choice, 74; The Moral Choice, 75; A New American Justice: Ending the White Male Monopolies, 80; The New Subversives: Anti-Americanism of the Religious Right, 82; The Moral Revolution, 86; On Moral Grounds: The Art/Science of Ethics, 91; The Moral Core of Judaism and Christianity, 93; Ethics For a Small Planet, 98. **CONTACT ADDRESS** Marquette Univ, Milwaukee, WI, 53233. **EMAIL** 6609maguired@vms.csd.mu.edu

MAGURSHAK, DANIEL J.
DISCIPLINE CONTEMPORARY EUROPEAN CONTINENTAL PHILOSOPHY **EDUCATION** Northwestern Univ, PhD. **CAREER** English, Carthage Col. **HONORS AND AWARDS** DAAD sch, Alexander von Humboldt Fel. **SELECTED PUBLICATIONS** Areas: Heidegger and Kierkegaard. **CONTACT ADDRESS** Carthage Col, 2001 Alford Dr., Kenosha, WI, 53140. **EMAIL** magurs1@carthage.edu

MAHAN, SUSAN
PERSONAL Born 04/13/1949, San Jose, CA, m, 1997, 3 children **DISCIPLINE** HISTORIC THEOLOGY **EDUCATION** Univ South FL, BA, 71, MA, 77; Marquette Univ, PhD, 88. **CAREER** Adjunct prof: San Jose State Univ, 88-97, Santa Clara Univ, 92-97, Univ of San Francisco, 92-98; ADJUNCT PROF, LOYOLA-MARYMOUNT, 98-. **MEMBERSHIPS** AAR; CTSA; CTS. **RESEARCH** Amer spirituality; women mystics; Asceticism; spirituality and work; spirituality and marriage. **CONTACT ADDRESS** 181 Rainbow Lane, Watsonville, CA, 95076. **EMAIL** smahan@got.net

MAHER, PATRICK
DISCIPLINE PHILOSOPHY **EDUCATION** Univ Pittsburgh, PhD, 84. **CAREER** Assoc prof, Univ Ill Urbana Champaign **RESEARCH** Philosophy and history of science; probability and inductive logic; decision theory. **SELECTED PUBLICATIONS** Auth, Betting on Theories; Probabilities for New Theories; Subjective and Objective Confirmation; The Hole in the Ground of Induction; Preference Reversal in Ellsberg Problems; Depragmatized Dutch Book Arguments. **CONTACT ADDRESS** Philosophy Dept, Univ Ill Urbana Champaign, 52 E Gregory Dr, Champaign, IL, 61820. **EMAIL** garyebbs@uiuc.edu

MAHERN, CATHERINE
DISCIPLINE LAW **EDUCATION** Purdue Univ, BS, 75; Ind Univ-Indianapolis, JD, 80. **CAREER** Assoc prof & dir, Law Sch Legal Clinic, Creighton Univ; dir Elder Law Clinic Creighton Univ, Thurgood Marshall Sch Law, 85-92; legal svc(s) atty, Tex, 83-85; legal svc(s), In, 80-82. **RESEARCH** Consumer law; family law. **SELECTED PUBLICATIONS** Pub(s), legal problems of the elderly, Tex Bar J. **CONTACT ADDRESS** School of Law, Creighton Univ, 2500 California Plaza, Omaha, NE, 68178. **EMAIL** mahern@culaw.creighton.edu

MAHONEY, EDWARD P.
DISCIPLINE PHILOSOPHY **EDUCATION** Columbia Univ, PhD, 66. **CAREER** Fulbright tchg fel, Univ Rome; vis prof, Univ CA, Cath Univ Am; prof, Duke Univ. **HONORS AND AWARDS** Pres, Soc Medieval Renaissance Philos. **MEMBERSHIPS** Soc Medieval Renaissance Philos. **RESEARCH** Medieval psychology. **SELECTED PUBLICATIONS** Ed, Medieval Aspects of Renaissance Learning, Duke Univ, 74; Philosophy and Humanism, Columbia Univ, 76. **CONTACT ADDRESS** Philos Dept, Duke Univ, West Duke Bldg, Durham, NC, 27706. **EMAIL** emahoney@acpub.duke.edu

MAHONY, WILLIAM K.
PERSONAL Born 10/06/1950, Denver, CO **DISCIPLINE** RELIGION **EDUCATION** Williams Col, BA, 73; Yale Univ, MDiv, 76; Univ Chicago, PhD, 82. **CAREER** MacArthur Asst Prof Relig, 82-88, assoc prof, 88-96, prof, Davidson Col, 96-. **HONORS AND AWARDS** Nat Endowment Hum Fel Col Tchr; Hamilton-Hunter Love of Tchg Award; ODK Tchg Award. **MEMBERSHIPS** Am Acad Relig; Soc Tantric Stud. **RESEARCH** History; thought and literatures of religions originating in India. **SELECTED PUBLICATIONS** Auth, Meditation Revolution, Agama, 1997; Artful Universe, SUNY, 1998. **CONTACT ADDRESS** Department of Religion, Davidson Col, PO Box 1719, Davidson, NC, 28036-1719. **EMAIL** bimahony@davidson.edu

MAIDMAN, MAYNARD PAUL
PERSONAL Born 08/07/1944, Philadelphia, PA, m, 1971, 2 children **DISCIPLINE** ANCIENT HISTORY, BIBLICAL STUDIES **EDUCATION** Columbia Univ, AB, 66; Univ Pa, PhD(Oriental studies), 76. **CAREER** Lectr, 72-76, asst prof, 76-78, ASSOC PROF HIST AND HEBREW, YORK UNIV, 78-. **MEMBERSHIPS** Am Oriental Soc; Soc Bibl Lit. **RESEARCH** Private economic records from Late Bronze Age Iraq and their significance; the dynamics of ancient archive keeping; ancient Israelite political history. **SELECTED PUBLICATIONS** Auth, Reallexikon of Assyriology and Near Eastern Archaeology, Vol 8, Fascicles 1-2, Meek Miete, Fascicles 3-4, Miete Moab, J Amer Oriental Soc, Vol 0116, 96; Uncovering Ancient Stones--Essays in Memory of Richardson, H. Neil, J Amer Oriental Soc, Vol 0116, 96. **CONTACT ADDRESS** York Univ, N York, ON, M3J 1P3.

MAIER, HAROLD GEISTWEIT
PERSONAL Born 03/25/1937, Cincinnati, OH, m, 1963, 2 children **DISCIPLINE** LAW **EDUCATION** Univ Cincinnati, BA, 59, JD, 63; Univ Mich, LLM, 64. **CAREER** From asst prof to assoc prof law, 65-70, Prof Law, Vanderbilt Univ, 70, Dir Transnat Legal Studies, 73-, David Daniels Allen Distinguished Chair in Law, 88-; US State Dept deleg, Asn Am Law Schs Conf Yugoslavian-US Trade, Belgrade, 68; guest scholar, Brookings Inst, Washington, DC, 76-77; consult Panama Canal treaties, Off Secy of Army, 76; Counr on Int Law, Office of the Legal Advisor, U.S. Dept of State, 83-84. **HONORS AND AWARDS** Ford Inst Studies fel, Max Planck Inst Foreign & Int Patents, Univ Munich, 64-65; Paul J Hartman Outstanding Teaching Award, 76. **MEMBERSHIPS** Am Soc Int Law; Am soc Comp Law. **RESEARCH** United States foreign relations law; private international law; international civil litigation. **SELECTED PUBLICATIONS** Coauth, Private internatioanl law and its sources, Vanderbilt Law Rev, 63; auth, The bases and range of federal common law in private international matters, Vanderbilt J Transnat Law, 71; Coordination of laws in a national federal state: An analysis of the writings of Elliott Evans Cheatham, Vanderbilt Law Rev, 73; Cooperative federalism in international trade: Its constitutional parameters, Mercer Law Rev, 76; Extraterritorial jurisdiction at a cross-roads: An intersection between public and private international law, Am J Int Law, 82; Interest Balancing and Extraterritorial Jurisdiction, Am J Comp Law 31, 83; coauth, A Unifying Theory for Judicial Jurisdiction and Choice of Law, Am J Comp Law 39, 91; Finding the Trees in Spite of the Metaphorist: The Problem of State Interests in Choice of Law, Alb Law Rev 56, 93. **CONTACT ADDRESS** Law Sch, Vanderbilt Univ, 2201 W End Ave S, Nashville, TN, 37240-0001.

MAIER, WALTER A.
DISCIPLINE RELIGION **EDUCATION** Concordia Theol Sem, MDiv, 78; Harvard Univ, MA, PhD, 84. **CAREER** Concordia Univ, River Forest, IL, asst, assoc prof, 84-89; Concordia Theol Sem, Ft. Wayne, IN, 89-. **MEMBERSHIPS** SBL, ETS, IBR **RESEARCH** Cult of Anc Near East; Bib Stud. **SELECTED PUBLICATIONS** Auth, Asherah: Extrabiblical Evidence, 86; The Healing of Noaman in Missiological Perspective, Concordia Theol Quart, 97; A Henneneutics Text for the Advanced Student, Concordia Theol Quart, 98. **CONTACT ADDRESS** Dept of Theology, Concordia Theol Sem, 6600 N Clinton St, Fort Wayne, IN, 46825-4996. **EMAIL** CFWMAIER3WA@crf.cuis.edu

MAITZEN, STEPHEN
DISCIPLINE PHILOSOPHY **EDUCATION** Northwestern Univ, BA, 85; Yale Univ, Law Sch, 85-86; Cornell Univ, MA, 90, PhD, 92. **CAREER** Asst prof. **RESEARCH** Epistemology, applied ethics, philosophy of religion. **SELECTED PUBLICATIONS** Auth, "The Ethics of Statistical Discrimination," Soc Theory and Practice, 91; "Two Views of Religious Certitude," Rel Stud, 92; "Our Errant Epistemic Aim," Philos & Phenomen Res, 95; God and Other Theoretical Entities, Topoi, 95; The Knower Paradox and Epistemic Closure, Synthese, 98; "Closing the Is-Ought Gap," Can Jour of Philos, 98. **CONTACT ADDRESS** Dept of Philos, Dalhousie Univ, Halifax, NS, B3H 3J5. **EMAIL** stephen.maitzen@dal.ca

MAJOR, APRIL
DISCIPLINE COMPUTER LAW **EDUCATION** Moravian Col, BS, 93; Villanova Univ Sch Law, JD, 96. **CAREER** Vis asst prof, Villanova Univ; past dir, Technol & Operations Ctr for Inf Law and Policy; dir, Global Democracy Proj. **MEMBERSHIPS** Past mem, Nat Physics Honor Soc. **RESEARCH** Computer law and internet regulation, international law and for policy, and intellectual property. **SELECTED PUBLICATIONS** Auth, Copyright Law Tackles Yet Another Challenge: The Electronic Frontier of the World Wide Web & Internet Red Light Dists: A Domain Name Proposal For Regulatory Zoning of Obscene Content. **CONTACT ADDRESS** Law School, Villanova Univ, 800 Lancaster Ave, Villanova, PA, 19085-1692.

MAKARUSHKA, IRENA
PERSONAL Born 10/01/1946, Munich, Germany, d, 3 children **DISCIPLINE** PHILOSOPHY OF RELIGION **EDUCATION** St John's Univ, BA, 67; Boston Univ, MA, 79; Boston Univ, PhD, 86 **CAREER** Instr, Boston Col, 85-86; asst prof, Holy Cross Col, 86-90; asst prof, Bowdoin Col, 90-93; assoc prof, Bowdoin Col, 94-; chair, Religious Dept, Bowdoin Col, 95-98; assoc Dean Acad Affairs, Goucher Col, 98- **HONORS AND AWARDS** Faculty Res Grant, Bowdoin Col, 90, 91, 93, 96, 97; Faculty Development Fund, Bowdoin Col, 91, 96 **MEMBERSHIPS** Soc for Values in Higher Education; Intl Nietzsche Soc; Amer Philos Assoc; Amer Acad Relig; Member Steering Committee, Amer Acad Relig, 90-93; Member Prog Committee, Amer Acad Relig, 90-93; Program Dir, Amer Acad Relig New England, 90-92; Member Steering Committee, Film Prog Unit, Amer Acad Relig **SELECTED PUBLICATIONS** Auth, "Transgressing Goodness in Breaking the Waves," Imag-(in)ing Otherness: Filmic Visions of Living Together, Trinity St Mungo, 99; auth, "Transgressing Goodness in Breaking the Waves," Jrnl Relig & Film, 98; auth, "Dualism," Encycl Women & World Relig, Macmillan, 98 **CONTACT ADDRESS** Goucher Col, 1021 Dulan, Baltimore, MD, 21204-2794. **EMAIL** imakarus@goucher.edu

MAKAU, JOSINA M.
PERSONAL Born 04/11/1950, Oostzahn, Netherlands **DISCIPLINE** RHETORIC, PHILOSOPHY **EDUCATION** Calif State Univ, Northridge, BA, 73; Univ Calif, Los Angeles, MA, 73; Univ Calif, Berkeley, MA, 76, PhD(rhetoric), 80. **CAREER** ASST PROF COMMUN, OHIO STATE UNIV, 79-. **MEMBERSHIPS** Speech Commun Asn; Rhetoric Soc Am; Int Soc Hist Rhetoric; Cent States Speech Asn. **RESEARCH** Rhetoric and philosophy of law; modern theories of argumentation; rhetorical criticism. **SELECTED PUBLICATIONS** Auth, Argumentation, Communication, and Fallacies--a Pragma-Dialectical Perspective, Philos and Rhetoric, Vol 0028, 95. **CONTACT ADDRESS** Dept of Commun, Ohio State Univ, Columbus, OH, 43210.

MAKKREEL, RUDOLF A.
PERSONAL Born 05/29/1939, Antwerp, Belgium, m, 1967, 1 child **DISCIPLINE** PHILOSOPHY **EDUCATION** Columbia Col, BA, 60; Columbia Univ, PhD, 66. **CAREER** Instr, Rutgers Univ Col, 63-66; asst prof, Univ Calif San Diego, 66-73; asst prof, 73-76, assoc prof, 76-85, prof, 85-91, Candler Prof of philos, 91- , Emory Univ; ed, 83-98, pres, 98- , J of the Hist of Philos. **HONORS AND AWARDS** Pulitzer Prize nomination, 75; Natl Book Award nomination, 75; citation for excellence in scholar publ, Asn of Am Publ, 90; Ger Acad Exchange Scholar, 64-65; Humboldt fel, 78-79; Thyssen Found grant, 79-86; NEH grant, 81-86; Volkswagen Found grant, 82-87. **MEMBERSHIPS** Int Board of Advisors of the Ctr for Advanced Res in Phenomenology; APA; Am Soc for Aesthetics; Soc for Phenomenology and Existential Philos. **RESEARCH** History of philosophy from Kant to present; aesthetics; existentialism; philosophy of history; phenomenology; hermeneutics. **SELECTED PUBLICATIONS** Auth, Dilthey: Philosopher of the Human Studies, Princeton, 75; co-ed, Wilhelm Dilthey, Selected Works, 6 v, Princeton, 89- ; co-ed, Dilthey and Phenomenology, University Press of America, 87; auth, Imagination and Interpretation in Kant: The Hermeneutical Import of the Critique of Judgment, Chicago, 90; auth, Purposiveness in History: Its Status after Kant, Hegel, Dilthey and Habermas, Philos and Soc Criticism, 92; auth, The Confluence of Aesthetics and Hermeneutics in Baumgarten, Meier, and Kant, J of Aesthetics and Art Criticism, 96. **CONTACT ADDRESS** Department of Philosophy, Emory Univ, Atlanta, GA, 30322. **EMAIL** philrm@emory.edu

MAKUCH, STANLEY M.
DISCIPLINE LAW **EDUCATION** Univ Toronto, BA, 67; Univ Carleton, MA, 68; Osgoode Hall Law Sch, LLB, 71; Harvard Univ, LLM, 72. **CAREER** Assoc dean, 81-85; prof. **RESEARCH** Municipal planning law; environmental law. **SELECTED PUBLICATIONS** Auth, Canadian Municipal and Planning Law, Carswell; Regulation by Municipal Licensing, Univ Toronto; Spill's Bill: Duties Rights and Obligations, Butterworth's; pubs on municipal law matters. **CONTACT ADDRESS** Fac of Law, Univ Toronto, 78 Queen's Park, Toronto, ON.

MALAMENT, DAVID BARUCH
PERSONAL Born 12/21/1947, New York, NY **DISCIPLINE** PHILOSOPHY OF SCIENCE **EDUCATION** Columbia Univ, BA, 68; Rockefeller Univ, PhD(philos), 75. **CAREER** Asst prof, 75-78, assoc prof, 78-82, prof philos, 82-89, David B & Clara E Stern Prof, Univ Chicago, 89-; vis assist prof philos, Princeton Univ, spring 77; chair, Comm on the Conceptual Foundations of Science, Univ Chicago, 95-98. **HONORS AND AWARDS** N S F res Fellowship, 79-80, 86-87; Whitehead Lecturer, Harvard Univ, fall 80; fel, Center for the Philos of Science, Univ Pittsburgh, fall 83; fel, Center for Advanced Study in the Behavioral Sciences, Palo Alto, 89-90; Quantrell Award for Excellence in Undergraduate Teaching, Univ Chicago, June 91. **MEMBERSHIPS** Elected to the Am Academy of Arts and Sciences, spring 92. **RESEARCH** Mathematical and conceptual foundations of modern physics. **SELECTED PUBLICATIONS** Auth, Minimal Acceleration Requirements for Time Travel in Godel Spacetime, J Mathematical Physics, vol 26, no 4, 85; A Modest Remark on Reichenbach, Rotation, and General relativity, Philos of Science, vol 52, no 4, 85, reprinted in J Butterfield, M Hogarth, & G Belot, eds, Spacetime in the Int Res Libr of Philos, Dartmouth Pubs Co, 96; Newtonian Gravity, Limits, and the Geometry of Space, in R Colodny, ed, From Quarks to Quasars, Univ Pittsburgh Press, 86; Gravity and Spatial Geometry, in R Marcus, et al, eds, Logic, Methodology, and Philos of Science VII (proceedings of the 1983 Salzburg Congress), Elsevier Science Pubs, 86; Time Travel in the Godel Universe, PSA 1984, vol 2 (proceedings of the Philos of Science Asn meetings, Chicago, 1984), 86; A Note About Closed

Timelike Curves in Godel Spacetime, J Mathematical Physics, vol 28, no 10, 87; Critical Notice: Itamar Pitowsky, Quantum Probability--Quantum Logic, Philos of Science, vol 59, no 2, 92; Introductory essay to a previously unpublished lecture by Kurt Godel on "rotating universes" in vol III of Godel, Kurt, Collected Works, ed S Feferman et al, Oxford Univ Press, 95; Is Newtonian Cosmology Really Inconsistent?, Philos of Science, vol 62, no 4, 95; In Defense of Dogma--Why There Cannot Be a Relativistic Quantum Mechanical Theory of (Localized) particles in R Clifton, ed, Perspectives on Quantum Reality, Kluwer, 96. **CONTACT ADDRESS** Dept Philos, Univ Chicago, 1010 E 59th St, Chicago, IL, 60637-1512. **EMAIL** d-malament@uchicago.edu

MALAVET, PEDRO A.
DISCIPLINE LAW **EDUCATION** Emory Univ, BBA; Georgetown Univ, JD, LLM. **CAREER** Assoc prof, Univ Fla, 95-; adj prof, Georgetown Univ Law Ctr, 95, Pontifical Cath Univ Puerto Rico, 91-92; jr partner, Bufete Malavet Ayoroa, Ponce, Puerto Rico, 89-93; clerk, Honorable Raymond L. Acosta, US Dist Ct, San Juan, PR. **HONORS AND AWARDS** Future law prof fel, Georgetown Univ Law Ctr, 93-94. **MEMBERSHIPS** PR Bar; Order of the Coif. **RESEARCH** Comparative law, civil law, civil procedure, European union. **CONTACT ADDRESS** School of Law, Univ of Florida, PO Box 117625, Gainesville, FL, 32611-7625. **EMAIL** malavet@law.ufl.edu

MALHOTRA, ASHOK KUMAR
PERSONAL Born 04/01/1940, Ferozepur, India, w, 1966, 2 children **DISCIPLINE** PHILOSOPHY **EDUCATION** Univ Rajasthan, BA, 61, MA, 63; Univ Hawaii, PhD(philos), 69. **CAREER** Asst prof, 67-70, assoc prof, 70-80, chm dept, 76-78, Prof Philos, State Univ NY Col Oneonta, 80-, Chm Gen Studies, 75-, Campus coordr, NY State Five-Col Sem on India, 68-69; consult ed, J Humanistic & Interdisciplinary Studies, 77-; dir, India Intersession Prog, State Univ NY Col, 79-80 & 81-82; reviewer, Nat Endowment for Humanities grant proposals. **HONORS AND AWARDS** Gold Medal for obtaining the highest GPA in MA Philosophy; Suny Chancellor's Award for excellence in teaching; Certificate of Recognition for bringing cultural interchange between East and West, Univ Hawaii. **MEMBERSHIPS** Soc Asian & Comp Philos; Am Asian Studies; Am Philos Asn; Asn for Asian Studies; Soc for Comparative Study of Civilizations; Jean-Paul Sartre Soc; Int Phenomenol Soc. **RESEARCH** Comparative philosophy and religion; existentialism and phenomenology; Indian philosophy. **SELECTED PUBLICATIONS** Auth, Sartre's Existentialism in Nausea & Being and Nothingness, Writers Workshop, Calcutta, 76; Hinduism's second shot at becoming a missionary religion, Bharata Manisha, An Ing J, India, 10/76; Samkhya-yoga versus Sartre's philosophy, Asian Thought & Soc, 4/78; Tagore's Aesthetics, Asian Studies Spec Ser, 79; coauth (with Nina Malhotra), Perspectives on Meditation and Personality, New Delhi, India, 80; auth, Hesse's Novel Siddhartha: A Rare Synthesis of Hinduism, Buddhism and Existentialism, 80 & coauth (with Nina Malhotra), Guru Business: A Study of Muktananda and Rajneesh, 81, Asian Res, Hong Kong; auth, Pathways to Philosophy, 95; author of over 30 other publications. **CONTACT ADDRESS** Dept of Philos, State Univ NY Col, PO Box 4015, Oneonta, NY, 13820-4015. **EMAIL** malhotak@oneonta.edu

MALLER, MARK P.
PERSONAL Born 10/19/1947, Chicago, IL **DISCIPLINE** PHILOSOPHY **EDUCATION** Southern Ill Univ, BA, 70; Duquesne Univ, MA, 73, PhD, 96. **CAREER** Adjunct instr, Harper Col, 92-97; instr, Col of DuPage, 96-; instr, Lewis Univ, 97-. **MEMBERSHIPS** Am Philos Asn. **RESEARCH** Philosophy. **SELECTED PUBLICATIONS** Auth, "The Morality of Tipping" in Publ Affairs Quart, 93. **CONTACT ADDRESS** Col of DuPage, 22nd and Lambert Rd, Glen Ellyn, IL, 60137. **EMAIL** Marlopal@yahoo.com

MALLOY, EDWARD A.
PERSONAL Born 05/03/1941, Washington, DC **DISCIPLINE** CHRISTIAN ETHICS, THEOLOGY **EDUCATION** Univ Notre Dame, BA, 63, MA, 67, MTh, 69; Vanderbilt Univ, PhD, 75. **CAREER** From Instr to Assoc Prof, 74-81, Prof Theol, Univ Notre Dame, 81, Dir Mdiv Prog, 77, Assoc Provost, 82-87, Pres, Univ Notre Dame, 87. **MEMBERSHIPS** Am Soc Christian Ethics; Cath Theol Soc Am. **SELECTED PUBLICATIONS** Auth, Natural law theory and Catholic moral theology, 75 & Typological analysis in Christian ethics, 75, Am Ecclesiastical Rev; The ethics of responsibility--a comparison of the moral methodology of H Richard Niebuhr and Charles Curran, Iliff Rev, 77; Robert Johann--an ontological basis for an ethics of responsibility, Horizons, 77; Ethical issues in the zoning controversy, Chicago Studies, 77; The problem of methodology in contemporary Roman Catholic ethics, St Luke's J Theol, 78; Homosexuality and the Christian Way of Life, Univ Press Am, 81. **CONTACT ADDRESS** Office of the President, Univ of Notre Dame, Notre Dame, IN, 46556. **EMAIL** edward.a.malloy.5@nd.edu

MALM, HEIDI
DISCIPLINE PHILOSOPHY **EDUCATION** Univ Calif, Santa Barbara, BA; Univ Ariz, PhD. **CAREER** Assoc prof; fac, Univ Nebr-Lincoln & Univ Nebr Med Sch; 6 yrs dir undergrad Stud, Philos; 5 yrs vice-chp, Acad Coun; ed bd, Public Affairs Quart & Exec Comt, Am-Int Soc for Philos and Law. **RESEARCH** Ethical theory; applied ethics; philosophy of law. **SELECTED PUBLICATIONS** Publ in, Philos & Public Affairs, Ethics, Am Philos Quart, Philos Stud, Legal Theory and Public Affairs Quart. **CONTACT ADDRESS** Dept of Philosophy, Loyola Univ, Chicago, 820 N. Michigan Ave., Chicago, IL, 60611.

MALONEY, ELLIOTT CHARLES
PERSONAL Born 04/17/1946, Pittsburgh, PA **DISCIPLINE** NEW TESTAMENT STUDIES, BIBLICAL LANGUAGES **EDUCATION** St Vincent Col, AB, 68; Pontifical Atheneum of St Anselm, Rome, STL, 72; Fordham Univ, PhD(New Testament), 79. **CAREER** Instr, 76-81, Asst Prof New Testament Studies & Bibl Lang, 81-92; Professor New Testament Studies & Bibl Lang, 92-, St Vincent Sem, 81-. **MEMBERSHIPS** Soc Bibl Lit; Cath Bibl Asn. **RESEARCH** Greek language of the New Testament; Gospel of Mark; Epistles of Paul. **SELECTED PUBLICATIONS** Auth, Semitic interference in Marcan Syntox, Soc Bibl Lit Dissertation Series, 81; transl, Epistles of James, 1-2 Peter, Jude, In: New American Bible, rev New Testament, 86. **CONTACT ADDRESS** St Vincent Col, 300 Fraser Purchase, Latrobe, PA, 15650-2690. **EMAIL** emaloney@stvincent.edu

MALONEY, J. CHRISTOPER
PERSONAL Born 10/07/1949, Youngstown, OH **DISCIPLINE** PHILOSOPHY **EDUCATION** Cleveland State Univ, BA, 71; Ind Univ, Bloomington, MA, 75, PhD(philos), 78. **CAREER** Assoc instr philos, Ind Univ, Bloomington, 74-77, vis instr, 78; ASST PROF PHILOS, OAKLAND UNIV, 78-. **MEMBERSHIPS** Am Philos Asn. **RESEARCH** Metaphysics; epistemology. **CONTACT ADDRESS** Dept of Philos, Oakland Univ, Rochester, MI, 48063.

MALONEY, MAUREEN A.
DISCIPLINE LAW **EDUCATION** Warwick Univ, LLB, 77; Univ Toronto, LLM, 81. **CAREER** Asst prof, 81-93; prof, 93-; fac dean, 90-93. **SELECTED PUBLICATIONS** Auth, pubs on tax law, tax policy, women and the law, and aspects of the law on disadvantaged groups. **CONTACT ADDRESS** Fac of Law, Univ Victoria, PO Box 2400, Victoria, BC, V8W 3H7.

MALONEY, THOMAS
DISCIPLINE MEDIEVAL PHILOSOPHY AND THE PHILOSOPHY OF RELIGION **EDUCATION** Gregorian Univ, Rome, PhD. **CAREER** Dept Philos, Univ Louisville **RESEARCH** 13th-century logic, espec semantics. **SELECTED PUBLICATIONS** Publ(s), transl on of three treatises on universals by Roger Bacon along with an edition and annotated transl of Bacon's Compendium studii theologiae; transl, Bacon's Summulae dialectices. **CONTACT ADDRESS** Dept of Philos, Univ Louisville, 2301 S 3rd St, Louisville, KY, 40292. **EMAIL** tsmalo01@ulkyvm.louisville.edu

MAMARY, ANNE
DISCIPLINE PHILOSOPHY **EDUCATION** State Univ NY Binghamton, PhD. **CAREER** Vis Prof,State Univ NY Cortland **RESEARCH** Feminist philosophy; post colonial studies; multi cultural studies; ancient Greek philosophy. **SELECTED PUBLICATIONS** Auth, Not the Same Difference: a Review Essay of Luce Irigaray's Thinking the Difference, Int Studies Philo; Mint, Tomatoes and the Grapevine; co-ed, Cultural Activisms: Poetic Voices, Political Voices, SUNY, 98. **CONTACT ADDRESS** Philosophy Dept, State Univ NY Cortland, Box 2000, Cortland, NY, 13045-0900. **EMAIL** mamary@snycorva.cortland.edu

MAMO, NATHAN
PERSONAL Born 12/06/1952, Pasadena, CA **DISCIPLINE** NEW TESTAMENT STUDIES **EDUCATION** Jesuit Sch Theol, Berkeley, STL, 94. **CAREER** Pastor, 98-, St John the Apostle Cath Parish HI; rect, 94-98, Cathedral Our Lady Of Peace HI; Pastor, 78-91, St John V Parish HI. **MEMBERSHIPS** CBA; SBL. **RESEARCH** St Paul; Corinthian Correspondence. **CONTACT ADDRESS** 95-370 Kuahelani Ave, Mililani, HI, 96789-1103.

MANDELKER, DANIEL ROBERT
PERSONAL Born 07/18/1926, Milwaukee, WI, m, 1968, 2 children **DISCIPLINE** LAW **EDUCATION** Univ Wis, AB, 47, LLB, 49; Yale Univ, JSD, 56. **CAREER** Asst prof law, Drake Univ, 49-52; atty & adv, Housing & Home Finance Agency, Washington, DC, 52-53; from asst prof to assoc prof law, Ind Univ, 53-62; from assoc prof to prof, 62-75, Stamper Prof Law, Washington Univ, 75-; Ford Found law fac fel, London, England, 59-60; mem comn soc & behav urban res, Nat Acad Sci, 68; consult housing, bldg, planning, UN Centre, 72-73; consult, Hawaii Dept Planning & Econ Develop, 72-; mem, Am Bar Asn Adv Comn Housing & Urban Growth, 75-77. **MEMBERSHIPS** Nat Center for the Revitalization of Central Cities; APA; Development Regulations Coun, Urban Land Inst; Comm on Environmental Law, Int Union for the Conservation of Nature. **SELECTED PUBLICATIONS** Couth, State and Local Government in a Federal System, 96; Planning and Control of Land Development, 95; Corridor Preservation: Study of Legal and Institutional Barriers, Fed Highway Admin; Environmental Protection: Law and Policy, 90; auth, Land Use Law, 97; NEPA Law and Litigation, 92; Environmental Policy: The Next Generation, Dept of Land Economy, 93; Judicial Review of Land-Use Decisions in Modernizing State Planning Statutes: The Growing Smart Working Papers, Am Planning Asn, 96; Waiving the Taking Clause: Conflicting Signals from the Supreme Court, 95; Housing Issues in AIDS Law Today, 93. **CONTACT ADDRESS** School of Law, Washington Univ, 1 Brookings Dr, St. Louis, MO, 63130-4899. **EMAIL** mandelker@wwlaw.wustl.edu

MANDLE, JONATHAN
DISCIPLINE PHILOSOPHY **EDUCATION** Univ Pitt, PhD. **CAREER** Asst prof, Univ Pitt. **RESEARCH** Ethics and political theory and their history. **CONTACT ADDRESS** Dept of Philosophy, Univ at Albany, SUNY, Albany, NY, 12222. **EMAIL** mandle@cnsunix.albany.edu

MANDT, ALMER J., III
PERSONAL Born 01/29/1950, Urbana, IL **DISCIPLINE** PHILOSOPHY **EDUCATION** Trinity Coll, BA, 72; Vanderbilt Univ, MA; PhD, 78. **CAREER** Coordr of Gen Edu, Wichita State Univ, 85-88; asst and assoc prof, 76-; dir of honors program, Wichita State Univ, 95-. **HONORS AND AWARDS** Phi Beta kappa, 71; Machette Found Dissertation Fel, 75-76; Council Award for Distinguish Merit, Souther Soc for Philos nad Psychol; 81; Faculty Leadership Award, Wichita State Univ, 92. **MEMBERSHIPS** Am Philos Asn; Metaphysics Soc of Am; Soc for the Advancement of Am Philos; Am Asn of Univ Profs. **RESEARCH** Philosophy of Culture; History of Philosophy; 19th Century Philosophy; Political Philosophy. **SELECTED PUBLICATIONS** Auth, The Inconceivability of Kant's Transcendental Subject, Int Philos Quart, 83; Mill's Two View On Belief, Philos, 84; The Inevitability of Pluralism: Philosophical Practice and Philosophical Excellence, Institution of Philosophy: A Discipline in Crisis?, 89; Religious Liberty, School Prayer, and the Constitution, Soundings, 89; Fichte, Kant's Legacy, and the Meaning of Modern Philosophy, Rev of Metaphysics, 97; ed, Fichte and Contemporary Philosophy, Philos Forum, 87-88. **CONTACT ADDRESS** Dept of Philosophy, Wichita State Univ, Wichita, KS, 67260-0074. **EMAIL** mandt@twsuvm.uc.twsu.edu

MANGRUM, FRANKLIN M.
PERSONAL Born 06/01/1925, Mayfield, KY, m, 1945 **DISCIPLINE** PHILOSOPHY **EDUCATION** Washington Univ, AB, 49; Univ Chicago, PhD, 57. **CAREER** Teacher philos & humanities, Shimer Col, 56-59; distinguished fac award, ATMSU 68-69, prof, Morehead State Univ, 95, Head Dept, 66-84, prof philos emer, 95-, Fac mem bd regents, 68-71. **MEMBERSHIPS** Metaphys Soc Am; NEA; Western Div Am Philos Asn. **RESEARCH** Epistemology; metaphysics. **CONTACT ADDRESS** Dept of Philosophy, Morehead State Univ, 150 University Blvd, Morehead, KY, 40351-1684.

MANGRUM, R. COLLIN
DISCIPLINE LAW **EDUCATION** Harvard Univ, BA, 72; Univ Utah, JD, 74; Oxford Univ, Bachelor of Civil Laws, 78; Harvard Univ, Doctor of Judicial Sci, 83. **CAREER** Pvt prac, Salt Lake City, 75-77; assoc ed, Utah Law Rev; Rotary Int Found fel, 77 and 78; vis scholar, Univ Edinburgh, 86, prof Creighton Univ, 79-. **HONORS AND AWARDS** National Alpha Sigma Nu Bk awd, 89. **SELECTED PUBLICATIONS** Auth, Zion in the Courts: A Legal History of The Church of Jesus Christ of Latter-Day Saints 1830-1900, Univ Ill Press, 88; publ in, Creighton Law Rev; Duke Law J; Utah Law Rev; BYU Stud; Morman Hist J. **CONTACT ADDRESS** School of Law, Creighton Univ, 2500 California Plaza, Omaha, NE, 68178. **EMAIL** mangrum@culaw.creighton.edu

MANIATES, MARIA RIKA
PERSONAL Born 03/30/1937, Toronto, ON, Canada **DISCIPLINE** MUSICOLOGY, PHILOSOPHY **EDUCATION** Univ Toronto, BA, 60; Columbia Univ, MA, 62, PhD(musicol), 65. **CAREER** From lectr to assoc prof, 65-74, chmn dept, 73-78, PROF MUSICOL, UNIV TORONTO, 74-, Am Coun Learned Socs grant-in-aid musicol, 66-67; vis prof music, Columbia Univ, 67 and 76; appln appraiser musicol, Can Coun, 69-, res fel, 70-72; Einstein Award Comt, Am Musicol Soc, 76-79; Can Coun travel grants, 73, 75, 77, 78, 79, and 80; Univ Toronto humanities res grants, 78-79 and 79-80. **MEMBERSHIPS** Int Musicol Soc; Am Musicol Soc; Renaissance Soc Am; Can Renaissance Soc; Int Soc Hist Rhetoric. **RESEARCH** Renaissance music and culture; mannerism; philosophy and aesthetics. **SELECTED PUBLICATIONS** Auth, Musica Scientia--Musical Scholarship in the Italian Renaissance, Notes, Vol 0050, 93; The Politicized Muse--Music for Medici Festivals, 1512-1537, Renaissance and Reformation, Vol 0018, 94; Music in Renaissance Magic--Toward a Historiography of Others, J Amer Musicol Soc, Vol 0048, 95; **CONTACT ADDRESS** Fac of Music, Univ of Toronto, Toronto, ON, M5S 1A1.

MANIER, A. EDWARD
DISCIPLINE PHILOSOPHY OF SCIENCE **EDUCATION** Univ Notre Dame, BS, 53; St Louis Univ, AM, 56, PhD, 61. **CAREER** Prof. **RESEARCH** History and philosophy of biology; neuromedical sciences. **SELECTED PUBLICATIONS** Auth, The Young Darwin and His Cultural Circle, 78; Reductionist Rhetoric: Expository Strategies and the Development of the Molecular Neurobiology of Behavior, 89; Walker Percy: Language, Neuropsychology and Moral Tradition, 91. **CONTACT ADDRESS** History and Philosophy of Science Dept, Univ of Notre Dame, Notre Dame, IN, 46556. **EMAIL** A.E.Manier.1@nd.edu

MANN, GURINDER SINGH
DISCIPLINE RELIGION **EDUCATION** Columbia Univ, PhD, 93. **CAREER** Assoc prof. **SELECTED PUBLICATIONS** Auth, Studying the Sikhs: Issues for North America, SUNY, 93; The Goindval Pothis, Harvard, 96. **CONTACT ADDRESS** Dept of Religion, Columbia Col, New York, 2960 Broadway, New York, NY, 10027-6902.

MANN, WILLIAM EDWARD
PERSONAL Born 05/06/1940, Los Angeles, CA, m, 1966, 2 children **DISCIPLINE** HISTORY OF PHILOSOPHY, PHILOSOPHY OF RELIGION **EDUCATION** Stanford Univ, BA, 62, MA, 64; Univ Minn, Minneapolis, PhD(Philos), 71. **CAREER** From instr to asst prof Philos, St Olaf Col, 67-72; asst prof, Ill State Univ, 72-74; assoc prof, 74-80, prof Philos, Univ VT & chmn dept, 80-. **HONORS AND AWARDS** 1971 Dissertation Essay Competition, The Rev of Metaphys, 72. **MEMBERSHIPS** Am Philos Asn, div sec-treas, 94; Soc Ancient Greek Philos; Soc Medieval Renaissance Philos. **RESEARCH** Philosophical theology; medieval philosophy, ancient philosophy. **SELECTED PUBLICATIONS** Auth, The ontological presuppositions of the ontological argument, Rev Metaphysics, 72; The divine attributes, Am Philos Quart, 75; The perfect island, Mind, 76; The theft of the pears, Apeiron, 77; The third man--the man who never was, Am Philos Quart, 79; Anaxagoras and the homoiomere, Phronesis, 80; Divine simplicity, Relig Studies, 82; Dreams of immortality, Philos, 83; Hope in Eleonore Stump, ed, Reasoned Faith: Essays in Philosophical Theology in Honor of Norman Kretzmann, Ithaca, NY: Cornell University Press, 93; Piety: Lending a Hand to Euthyphro, Philosophy and Phenomenological Research, 98. **CONTACT ADDRESS** Dept of Philosophy, Univ of Vermont, 70 S Williams St, Burlington, VT, 05401-3404.

MANNING, BLANCHE MARIE
PERSONAL Born 12/12/1934, Chicago, IL, m **DISCIPLINE** LAW **EDUCATION** Chicago Tchrs Coll, BE 1961; John Marshall Law Sch Chicago, JD 1967; Roosevelt Univ Chicago, MA 1972; Univ of VA, Charlottesville, VA, LLM, 1992. **CAREER** Chicago Bd of Educ, teacher 1961-68; Cook Co State's Attys Office, asst states atty 1968-73; Equal Employment Oppor Commn, supervisory trial atty 1973-77; United Airlines, gen atty 1977-78; US Attys Office, asst US atty 1978-79; Circuit Ct of Cook Co, assoc judge 1979-86; 1st Municipal Dist Circuit Ct of Cook Co, supervising judge 1984-86, supervising circuit judge 1986-87; Justice of the Illinois Appellate Court, 1st District 1987-94; judge US District Court, ND IL, 1994-; Harvard Law School, Univ of Chicago Law School, Trial Advocacy Workshops, teaching team member, 1991-; De Paul University College of Law, adjunct professor, 1992-; Dept of Justice, Atty Gen Adv Inst, adj faculty mem, 1979. **HONORS AND AWARDS** Edith Sampson Meml Awd 1985; Awd of Appreciation The Intl Assoc of Pupil Personnel Workers 1985; IL Judicial Council; Kenneth E Wilson Judge of the Year Awd Cook County Bar Assn; Disting Alumna Awd Chicago State Univ 1986; Awd of Excellence in Judicial Admin Women's Bar Assn 1986; Black Rose Award, League of Black Women 1987; Thurgood Marshall Award, IIT Kent Law School BALSA 1988; Professional Achievement Award, Roosevelt Univ 1988; We Care Role Model Award, Chicago Police Department 1987-94; Distinguished Service Award, John Marshall Law School, 1989; We Care Outstanding Role Model Award, Chicago Public Schools & Chicago Police Dept, 1992-94; National Black Prosecutors Association, Distinguished Service Award, 1991; The Guardians Police Organization, Citizen's Award, 1991; Honorary Doctor of Humane Letters Degree, Chicago State Univ, 1998. **MEMBERSHIPS** Mem Natl Assn of Women Judges; Cook County Bar Association; Il Judicial Council; lecturer IL Judicial Conf New Judges Seminar, Professional Devel Prog for New Assoc Judges, IL Judicial Conf Assoc Judges Sem 1982-86; New Judges Seminar, faculty; Chicago Bar Assn Symphony Orchestra; Chicago State Univ Community Concert Band, and Jazz Band. **CONTACT ADDRESS** United States District Court, 219 S Dearborn St, Ste 2156, Chicago, IL, 60604.

MANNING, CHRISTEL
PERSONAL Born 11/11/1961, Long Beach, CA **DISCIPLINE** HISTORY OF AMERICAN RELIGION **EDUCATION** Tufts Univ, BA, economics (Magna cum laude), 84; Univ CA, Santa Barbara, MA, relig studies, 91, PhD, relig studies, 95. **CAREER** Teacher, Social Studies, Noble and Greenough School, 86-89; lect, Elderhostel, Santa Barbara, 94; instr, dept of philos and relig, Hollins Col, 94-95; ASST PROF, DEPT OF PHILOS AND RELIGIOUS STUDIES, SACRED HEART UNIV, 95-. **HONORS AND AWARDS** Omnicron Delta Epsilon (Int Honor Soc in Economics), 84; Phi Beta Kappa, 84; Distinguished Scholars fel, 89-90; CA State grad fel, 91-92, 92-93; nominated for UCSB Outstanding Teaching Asst Award, 94; Thomas O'Day Award for the Study of Religion and Soc, 94; Soc for the Scientific Study of Religion, Res Award, 94. **MEMBERSHIPS** Am Academy Relig; Asn for Soc of Relig; Soc for the Scientific Study of Relig, Nat prog chair, 97. **RESEARCH** Gender and religion; fundamentalism; new religions. **SELECTED PUBLICATIONS** Auth, Review of Margaret Lamberts Bendroth, Fundamentalism and Gender, J for the Scientific Study of Religion 33.3, 94; Cultural Conflicts and Identity: Second Generation Hispanic Catholics in the United States, with Wade Clark Roof, Social Compass, 94; Embracing Jesus and the Goddess: Towards a Reconceptualizing of Conversion to Syncretistic Religion, in Magical Religion and Modern Witchcraft, ed by James Lewis, State Univ NY Press, 95; Review of Miriam Therese Winter, Defecting in Place: Women Claiming Responsibility for Their Own Spiritual Lives, J for the Scientific Study of Relig, 96; Women in a Divided Church: Liberal and Conservative Catholic Women Negotiate Changing Gender Roles, Sociology of Relig, 97; Review of Martin Marty & Scott Appleby, Fundamentalisms Comprehended, Review of Relig Res, 97; Women in New Religious Movements, in Encyclopedia of Women and World Religions, ed by Serinity Young, Macmillan, forthcoming, 98; Return to Mother Nature: The Politics of Paganism in America and Western Europe, in The Encyclopedia of Politics and Religion, ed by Robert Wuthnow, Congressional Quart Books, forthcoming, 98; God Gave Us the Right: The Impact of Feminism on Conservative Christian and Orthodox Jewish Women, Rutgers Univ Press, forthcoming, 98; Conversations Among Women: Gender as a Bridge between Religious and Ideological Cultures, in Reflexive Ethnography: Remembering for Whom We Speak, ed by Lewis Carter, JAI Press, forthcoming, 99. **CONTACT ADDRESS** Dept Philos & Relig Studies, Sacred Heart Univ, 5151 Park Ave., Fairfield, CT, 06432. **EMAIL** manningc@sacredheart.edu

MANNS, JAMES WILLIAM
PERSONAL Born 10/16/1944, South Weymouth, MA, m, 1967 **DISCIPLINE** PHILOSOPHY **EDUCATION** Lafayette Col, BA, 66; Boston Univ, MA, 70, PhD(philos), 72. **CAREER** Instr philos, Boston Univ, 70-71; asst prof, 71-76, ASSOC PROF PHILOS, UNIV KY, 76-. **MEMBERSHIPS** Am Philos Asn; Am Soc Aesthet. **RESEARCH** Aesthetics; epistemology. **SELECTED PUBLICATIONS** Auth, Metaphor--the Logic of Poetry, Metaphor and Symbolic Activity, Vol 0009, 94. **CONTACT ADDRESS** Dept of Philos, Univ of Kentucky, 1415 Patterson Off T, Lexington, KY, 40506-0003.

MANSFIELD, MECKLIN ROBERT
PERSONAL Born 08/11/1938, Crenshaw, MS, m, 1960, 3 children **DISCIPLINE** RELIGION, NEW TESTAMENT **EDUCATION** Rhodes College, BA, 60; Duke Divinity Sch, M. Div, 63; Vanderbilt Univ, MA & PhD(Bibl Studies), 70. **CAREER** Instr Philos, Cumberland Col, 68-70; asst prof Relig & chaplain, Mt Union Col, 70-78; assoc prof, 78-80, prof New Testament, Oral Roberts Univ, 80-, minister, United Methodist Church, Tenn Conf, 65-91; OK conf, 91. **MEMBERSHIPS** Soc Bibl Lit. **RESEARCH** New Testament Gospel studies; Mark; Johannine studies. **SELECTED PUBLICATIONS** Auth, Wind and Flame: Living Faith Series, United Methodist Publ House, 78; Gospel of John: Persons who Encountered Jesus, 80 & The Person and Work of Jesus, In: Adult Bible Studies, 82, United Methodist Publ House; Spirit and Gospel in Mark, Hendrickson, 87. **CONTACT ADDRESS** Dept Relig & Philosophy, Oral Roberts Univ, 7777 S Lewis, Tulsa, OK, 74171-0001. **EMAIL** rmansfield@oru.edu

MANZIG, JOHN G.W.
DISCIPLINE CONTRACTS; MUNICIPAL LAW; LAND USE PLANNING LAW; ENVIRONMENTAL LAW; WILLS AND SUCCESSION; COMPARATIVE LAW AND CONFLICT OF LAWS **EDUCATION** Dalhousie, LLB, LLM; Cologne, Lic Jur, Dr Iur. **CAREER** Prof emer; Osgoode Hall, Barrister-at-Law & Bar NS. **MEMBERSHIPS** Dir, Can Inst of Env Law and Policy. **SELECTED PUBLICATIONS** Assoc ed, Env Law Reports. **CONTACT ADDRESS** Col of Business Administration, Education and Law, Univ of Windsor, 401 Sunset Ave, Windsor, ON, N9B 3P4. **EMAIL** jmanzig@uwindsor.ca

MARANGOS, FRANK
PERSONAL Born 04/12/1954, Lowell, MA, m, 1977, 1 child **DISCIPLINE** RELIGION **EDUCATION** Hellenic Col, BA, 76; Holy Cross Sch Theol, MDiv, 79; Southern Methodist Univ, DMin, 86; Nova Southeastern Univ, EdD. **CAREER** Asst Priest, Annunciation Cathedral, Huston, Tex, 79-83; Diocese of Denver Youth Dir, 81-83; Parish Priest, Annunciation Church, Pensacola, Fla, 83-89; Dioceseof Atlanta Clergy Syndesmo, Sec, 85-92; Rel Ed Comm, Diocese of Atlanta Recording Sec, 85-87; Editor, Praxis: National Clergy Mag, 85-95; Writer, Column: Liturgical Year, Orthodox Observer, 86-89; Rel Ed Dir, Diocese of Atlanta, 87-97; Dir, Sch Orthodox Stud, Palm Beach Comm Col, 88-97; Editor, Manna: Rel Ed Mag, 88-95; Parish Priest, St. Mark, Boca Raton, Fla, 89-97; Adj prof Orthodox Stud, Pope Vincent DePaul Theol Sch, Boynton Beach, Fla, 95-97; Dir Rel Ed for the Greek Orthodox Archdiocese of Am, present. **HONORS AND AWARDS** Pres, Stud Coun, Hellenic Col, 76; Cum Laude, Hellenic Col, 76; Who's Who in Amer Univ, 77; Boston Theol Inst Rep, 77-78; Cum Laude, Holy Cross Sch Theol, 79; Amer Bible soc awd, Holy Cross, 79; Who's Who-Clergy in Amer, 85; High Honors, Doc Diss, Perkins Theol Sch, SMU, 86; Cum Laude, Perkins Theol Sch, 86; Hon Mention, Scholars Paper Competition, NOVA, 96; Pres, grad stud coun, NOVA Southeastern Univ, 96., Built Holy Sanctuary of St Mark in Boca Raton, FL, 95-97. **RESEARCH** Distance Learning. **SELECTED PUBLICATIONS** Auth, An Examination of the Orthodox Funeral Service, Master Divinity Thesis, 79; Christ Is Risen!...Now What?, New Calif (Natl Greek Newspaper), April 10, 80; Ape or Adam , Orthodox Observer, 82; What's So New About New Week?, Orthodox Observer, April 7, 82, 10; After He Says Goodbye, Orthodox Observer, June 2, 82, 2; The Youth Rush, Orthodox Observer, Oct 20, 82, 7; Christmas: A Holiday Heresy?, Orthodox Observer, Dec 15, 82, 9; Was Jesus born Again?, Orthodox Observer, Jan 12, 83, 5; Pascha: Passion or Passage?, Orthodox Observer, Feb 24, 82, 3; Pre-Lent: Reach Out and Touch Somebody, Orthodox Observer, March 9, 83, 2; What's Become of the Light?, Theosis Mag, April 84, and Orthodox Observer; Going Home for Christmas, Orthodox Observer, Dec 84; Pentecost Revisited, Theosis Mag, June 85; Heart to Heart: A Pentecost Reflection, Orthodox Observer; Unwrapping the Indescribable Gift, Orthodox Observer; The Epitaphios: Flower or Power, Orthodox Observer; Do Your Compete with God?, Orthodox Observer; Shared Christian Praxis and Religious Education, Greek Orthodox Theol Rev, 85; Liberation Theology and Christian education Theory, Greek Orthodox Theol Rev, Winter, 85; Rev of Freedom in Mission, emilio Castro, WCC Publ, Greek Orthodox Theol Rev, 86; A Praxis of Liturgical Catechesis, Doc Diss, SMU, 86; How to Save the World Without Worshipping Nature, Greek Orthodox Theol Rev, 85; Liberation Theology and Christian Education, in ed, Jeff Astley, Theological Perspectives on Christian Education, Univ Wales, Eng, 95; **CONTACT ADDRESS** Dept of Religious Education, Greek Orthodox Archdiocese, 50 Goddard Ave, Brookline, MA, 02146-7496. **EMAIL** frfrank@omaccess.com

MARASINGHE, M. LAKSHMAN
DISCIPLINE INTERNATIONAL BUSINESS TRANSACTIONS; TORTS; LAW AND DEVELOPMENT; JURISPRUDENCE AND CONFLICTS **EDUCATION** Univ Col, London, LLB, LLM; Sch Oriental and African Stud, London, PhD. **CAREER** Prof; Osgoode Hall, Barrister-at-Law & Inner Temple, Eng; past scholar, Max-Planck-Inst. **MEMBERSHIPS** Bd directors, Third World Legal Stud. **SELECTED PUBLICATIONS** Ed, Third World Legal Stud. **CONTACT ADDRESS** Col of Business Administration, Education and Law, Univ of Windsor, 401 Sunset Ave, Windsor, ON, N9B 3P4. **EMAIL** lmarasi@uwindsor.ca

MARCH, WALLACE EUGENE
PERSONAL Born 07/08/1935, Dallas, TX, m, 1957, 2 children **DISCIPLINE** THEOLOGY; ANCIENT LANGUAGES **EDUCATION** Austin Col, BA, 57; Austin Presby Theol Sem, BD, 60; Union Theol Sem, NY, PhD(Old Testament), 66. **CAREER** From instr to assoc prof, Austin Presby Theol Sem, 64-73, prof, 73-82; Arnold B Rhodes Prof Old Testament, Louisville Presby Theol Sem, 82-, Dean, 92-. **HONORS AND AWARDS** Rockefeller Schol, 64; Advanced Rel Study Fel, 66, 74; Asn Theol Schs Theol Scholar res grant, 80. **MEMBERSHIPS** Soc Bibl Lit; Am Schs Orient Res. **RESEARCH** Prophetic literature, particularly the sixth and eighth centuries; form criticism and literary criticism; Biblical theology. **SELECTED PUBLICATIONS** Contribr, Laken: its functions and meanings, In: Rhetorical Criticism, Pickwick, 74; Prophecy, In: Old Testament Form Criticism, Trinity Univ, 74; auth, Basic Bible Study, German Press, 78; Ed, Texts and Testaments: Critical Essays on the Bible and Early Church Fathers, Trinity Univ, 80; auth, Biblical Theology, authority and the Presbyterians, J Presby Hist, 81; Israel and the Politics of Land, John Knox Press, 94; Haggai, The New Interpreter's Bible, Abingdon Press, 96. **CONTACT ADDRESS** Louisville Presbyterian Theol Sem, 1044 Alta Vista Rd, Louisville, KY, 40205-1758. **EMAIL** emarch@lpts.edu

MARCHENKOV, VLADIMIR
PERSONAL Born 06/24/1957, Leninogorsk, USSR, m, 1981, 2 children **DISCIPLINE** INTERDISCIPLINARY: PHILOSOPHY, MUSIC AND COMPARATIVE STUDIES IN THE HUMANITIES **EDUCATION** Ohio State Univ, MA, 94; PhD, 98. **CAREER** Transl, Postfactum Newsgency Moscow Russia, 89-91; grad res assoc, Ohio State Univ, 92-98. **MEMBERSHIPS** Am Philos Asn; Am Soc for Aesthetics; Am Asn of the Advancement of Slavic Studies; Am Asn of Tchrs of Slavic and Eastern Europ Lang. **RESEARCH** German Idealist Philosophy; Music Aesthetics; Russian Religious - Idealist Thought; Myth Theory; Philosophy of Art; Dialectical Logic. **SELECTED PUBLICATIONS** Auth, Conservative Ideas in Modern Russia, Slavic Almanach, 95; from The Dialectics of Myth, 96; rev of round-table Philosophy of Philology, Symposion. J of Russian Thought, 97; introd to Diasophic Odysseys: Odysses the First, Symposion. J of Russian Thought, 97; Orpheus and Vyacheslav Ivanov's Philosophy of Art, Symposion. J of Rus-

sian Thought, 97. **CONTACT ADDRESS** 1930 North Star Rd, Columbus, OH, 43212. **EMAIL** marchenkov.2@osu.edu

MARCIN, RAYMOND B.
PERSONAL Born 02/25/1938, CT, m, 1965, 4 children **DISCIPLINE** PHILOSOPHY AND THEOLOGY OF LAW **EDUCATION** St John's Sem, AB, 59; Fairfield Univ, AB, 61; Fordham Univ, JD, 64. **CAREER** Staff coun legis, Conn State Legis, 64-67; atty poverty law, Neighborhood Legal Serv Inc, 67-68, law reform dir, 69-71; staff coun civil rights, Conn Comn on Human Rights, 68-69; atty civil rights, Ctr Nat Policy Rev, 71-72; from asst to assoc prof, 72-79, PROF JURISP AND CONST LAW AND LEGIS, CATH UNIV SCH LAW, 79-, Mem, Proj Study and Appl of Humanistic Educ Law, 80-; vis prof, Delaware Law Sch, Widener Univ, 82-83. **MEMBERSHIPS** Am Law Inst. **RESEARCH** Rawlsian and other Kantian interpretations of justice; the interpretation of legislation; the nonresistancd-to-evil ethic and the litigative mind. **SELECTED PUBLICATIONS** Auth, Schopenhauer Theory of Justice, Cath Univ Law Rev, Vol 0043, 94. **CONTACT ADDRESS** Catholic Univ of America, Washington, DC, 20064.

MARCUS, DAVID
PERSONAL Dublin, Ireland **DISCIPLINE** BIBLE AND ANCIENT SEMITIC LANGUAGES **EDUCATION** Cambridge Univ, BA; Columbia Univ, PhD. **CAREER** Fac, Columbia Univ; prof, chr, Bible and Ancient Semitic Languages, Jewish Theol Sem Am. **RESEARCH** The Bible and the Ancient Near East; presently working with an international team of scholars revising the critical edition of the Hebrew Bible. **SELECTED PUBLICATIONS** Auth, From Balaam to Jonah: Anti-prophetic Satire in the Hebrew Bible, Brown Judaic Studies series; numerous scholarly articles; two language manuals, Akkadian, the ancient language of Mesopotamia, Tthe Aramaic of the Babylonian Talmud. **CONTACT ADDRESS** Jewish Theol Sem of America, 3080 Broadway, New York, NY, 10027. **EMAIL** damarcus@jtsa.edu

MARCUS, RUTH BARCAN
PERSONAL New York, NY, d, 4 children **DISCIPLINE** PHILOSOPHY **EDUCATION** New York Univ, BA, 41; Yale Univ, MA, 42, PhD, 46. **CAREER** Prof, 59-63, Roosevelt Univ; prof, dept head, 64-70, Univ Illinois; prof, 71-73, Northwestern Univ; prof, 73-92, Halleck Prof, Emeritus & Sr Scholar, Yale Univ; vis prof, 93, Univ Calif, Irvine. **HONORS AND AWARDS** Guggenheim Fel, 52-53; NSF Fel, 63-64; Intl Inst of Phil, Paris, 73; Amer Acad of Arts & Sci, 73-; Rockefeller Fel, Bellagio, 73, 90; Mellon Fel, Natl Hum Ctr, 92-93; Hon degree, Dr of Hum letters, Univ Illinois, 95; Machette Award in my honor, phil dept, 86, Yale. **MEMBERSHIPS** APA; Assn for Symbolic Logic; Phil of Science Assn; Intl Fedn of Phil Soc. **RESEARCH** Philosophy **SELECTED PUBLICATIONS** Auth, The Logical Enterprise, Yale, 75; auth, Modalities: Philosophical Essays, Oxford Univ Press, 93; auth, Logic, Methodology and Philosophy of Science VII, North Holland, 86; art, The Identity of Individuals in a Strict Functional Calculus of Second Order, J Symbolic Logic; art, "Extensionality" Mind, LXIX, repr, Reference & Modality, Oxford, 71; art, Modalities and Intensional Languages, Synthese XIII, 61; art, Interpreting Quantification, Inquiry 5, 62; auth, Does the Principle of Substitutivity Rest on a Mistake?, Logical Enterprise, Yale, 75; art, Moral Dilemmas and Consistency, J of Phil LXXVII, 80; art, Some Revisionary Proposals About Belief and Believing, Phil & Phen Res, 90; art, The Anti-Naturalism of Some Language Centered Accounts of Belief, Dialectica, 95; art, More on Moral Conflict, Moral Conflict & Moral Theory, Oxford Press, 96. **CONTACT ADDRESS** Philosophy Dept, Yale Univ, Box 208306 Yale Station, New Haven, CT, 08520-8306. **EMAIL** ruthmarcus@yale.edu

MARDER, NANCY S.
DISCIPLINE LAW **EDUCATION** Yale Univ, BA; Univ Cambridge, England, MPhil; Yale Univ, JD. **CAREER** Assoc prof,Univ Southern Calif; clerked for, Honorable John Paul Stevens, Assoc Justice US Supreme Ct; Honorable William A. Norris, Judge US Ct Appeals 9th Circuit & Honorable Leonard B. Sand, Judge US Dist Ct Southern Dist NY; private practice, NY City. **MEMBERSHIPS** American Judicature Society; National Association of Women Judges (Judicial academic Network); Society of American Law Teachers; Law and Society Association. **RESEARCH** Civil Procedure; Advanced Civil Procedure: Judges, Juries, & Trials; & a seminar on Law, Literature, & Feminism. **SELECTED PUBLICATIONS** Auth, Deliberations and Disclosures: A Study of the Post-Verdict Interviews of Jurors; Beyond Gender: Peremptory Challenges & the Roles of the Jury & Gender Dynamics & Jury Deliberations **CONTACT ADDRESS** School of Law, Univ Southern Calif, University Park Campus, Los Angeles, CA, 90089.

MARENCO, MARC
PERSONAL Born 09/15/1952, Uriah, CA, s **DISCIPLINE** PHILOSOPHY **EDUCATION** Oxford, DPhil, 92 **CAREER** ASSOC PROF, MORAL PHILOSOPHY, PACIFIC UNIV **SELECTED PUBLICATIONS** various **CONTACT ADDRESS** Dept Philosophy, Pacific Univ, 2043 College Way, Forest Grove, OR, 97116. **EMAIL** marencom@pacificu.edu

MARGOLIS, JOSEPH
PERSONAL Born 05/16/1924, Newark, NJ, m, 1968, 5 children **DISCIPLINE** PHILOSOPHY **EDUCATION** Drew Univ, BA, 47; Columbia Univ, MA, 50, PhD(philos), 53. **CAREER** From instr to asst prof philos, Long Island Univ, 47-56; asst prof, Univ SC, 56-58; assoc prof dept philos and sr res assoc dept psychiat, Univ Cincinnati, 59-64, prof philos, 64-65; prof and head dept, Univ Western Ont, 65-67; vis prof, Univ Toronto, 67-68; PROF PHILOS, TEMPLE UNIV, 68-, Lectr, Cooper Union, 53; reader, Columbia Univ, 53-54, lectr, 54; vis asst prof, Trinity Col, Conn, 55 and 56; vis assoc prof Northwestern Univ, 58, Columbia Univ, 65, Univ Minn, 64, Western Reserve Univ, 64-65, Univ Calgary, 68, Univ Utah, 68 and NY Univ, 70-71; Nimh spec fel, 62-63; Can Coun fel, 67; assoc ed, Mt Adams Rev, 70-71; mem adv bd, Social Theory and Practice, 72-; contrib ed, Bk Forum, 72-; consult, J Critical Analysis, 73-; ed, Philos Monogr, 75-; consult ed, Behaviorism, 76- and J Theory of Social Behaviour, 76-. **MEMBERSHIPS** Am Philos Asn. **RESEARCH** Theory of knowledge; philosophical psychology; value theory. **SELECTED PUBLICATIONS** Auth, Texts + Worlds Textuality Through an Analysis of Views by Kant, Wittgenstein, and Derrida, Poetics Today, Vol 0014, 93; Big Little Fest + Jazz in Rapid City, Down Beat, Vol 0062, 95; Some Remarks on Sparshott on the Dance, J Aesth Educ, Vol 0031, 97; Late Forms of Psychologism and Antipsychologism + Philosophical Theory, Philos and Rhetoric, Vol 0030, 97. **CONTACT ADDRESS** Dept of Philosophy, Temple Univ, 1114 W Berks St, Philadelphia, PA, 19122-6029.

MARIETTA, DON E.
PERSONAL Born 11/01/1926, Montgomery, AL, m **DISCIPLINE** PHILOSOPHY **EDUCATION** Vanderbilt Univ, PhD, 59. **CAREER** FL Atlan Univ, asst prof, assoc. prof, prof, dist prof, 65-98; FL Atlan Univ, prof emeritus, 98-. **HONORS AND AWARDS** FL Atlan Univ, var tchg awards **MEMBERSHIPS** APA, FPA **RESEARCH** Ethical theory and environmental ethics. **SELECTED PUBLICATIONS** Auth, For People and the Planet, 95; Philosophy of Sexuality, 97; Introduction to Ancient Philosophy, 98; Environmental Philosophy and Environmental Activism, co-ed, 98; Pluralism in Environmental Ethics, in: Topoi, 93; Reflection and Environmental Activism, in: Enviro Philo and Enviro Act, 95. **CONTACT ADDRESS** Dept of Philosophy, Florida Atlantic Univ, Apt 562, Delray Beach, FL, 33483. **EMAIL** marigord92@aol.com

MARINA, JACQUELINE
PERSONAL Born 06/28/1961, Bronx, NY, m, 1994 **DISCIPLINE** PHILOSOPHY OF RELIGION **EDUCATION** Yale Univ, PhD, 93. **CAREER** Asst prof of Philos, Perdue Univ. **HONORS AND AWARDS** Fac incentive grant, Fall 97; Purdue res found, 94 summer grant; Yale Univ Paul C. Gignilliat fel for outstanding Stud (s) Hum, 88-89; Yale Div Sch Julia A. Archibald High scholar prize. **MEMBERSHIPS** Amer Philos Asn; Amer Acad Rel; N Amer Kant Soc; Schleiermacher Group. **RESEARCH** Kant and the 19th century; esp Schleiermacher. **SELECTED PUBLICATIONS** Coauth, Faith in Philosophy, in Handbook of Faith, James Michael Lee, ed, Religious Education Press, Birmingham, 90, 47-70; The Role of Limits in Aristotle's Concept of Place, The S Jour of Philos, XXXI,2, Summer 93, 205-216; Schleiermacher's Christology Revisited: A Reply to His Critics, The Scottish Jour Theol, 49,2, 96, 177-200; Kant's Deduction of the Categorical Imperative, Kant -Studien 89, Heft 2, 98, 167-178; A Critical-interpretive Analysis of Some Early Writings by Schleiermacher on Kant's Views of Human Nature and Freedom (1789-1799), with Translated Texts, New Athanaeum/Neues Athenaeum, 5, 11-31; Kant on Grace: A Reply to his Critics, rel stud (s), 33, 379-400; The Theological and Philosophical Significance of the Markan Account of Miracles, Faith and Philos, 13, 3, July 98. **CONTACT ADDRESS** Dept of Philosophy, Purdue Univ, 1360 Liberal Arts and Education Bldg, West Lafayette, IN, 47907-1360. **EMAIL** marinaj@purdue.edu

MARKS, HERBERT J.
DISCIPLINE RELIGIOUS STUDIES **EDUCATION** Yale Univ, PhD, 85. **CAREER** Assoc prof. **RESEARCH** Hebrew Bible; history and theory of biblical interpretation; Bible in western literature. **SELECTED PUBLICATIONS** Auth, The Book of the Twelve, Lit Guide Bible; On Prophetic Stammering, The Book and the Text; co-ed, Indiana Studies in Biblical Literature. **CONTACT ADDRESS** Dept of Religious Studies, Indiana Univ, Bloomington, 300 N Jordan Ave, Bloomington, IN, 47405.

MARKS, JOEL HOWARD
PERSONAL Born 10/13/1949, New York, NY, d, 2 children **DISCIPLINE** PHILOSOPHY **EDUCATION** Cornell Univ BA, 72; Univ Conn, MA, 78, PhD, 82. **CAREER** Instr, dir lib arts, 73-75, Portland Schl Art; vis ast prof, 82-84, St John Fisher Col; asst prof, 84-88, assoc prof, 88-94, prof, phil, 94-, Univ New Haven. **HONORS AND AWARDS** Phi Bet Kappa **MEMBERSHIPS** APA; Amer Assoc of Phil Tchrs. **RESEARCH** Ethical theory, professional ethics. **SELECTED PUBLICATIONS** Ed, The Ways of Desire, 86; co-ed, Emotions in Asian Thought, 95; coed, Gerard Hoffnung Festschrift, 92; auth, Moral Moments, 96. **CONTACT ADDRESS** Dept of Philosophy, Univ New Haven, West Haven, CT, 06516.

MARLER, GRANT A.
PERSONAL Born 12/22/1957, Inglewood, CA, m, 1993, 1 child **DISCIPLINE** PHILOSOPHY **EDUCATION** Arizona State Univ, BA, 86; Old Dominion Univ, MA, 96; Claremont Grad Univ, PhD, in progress. **CAREER** Imagery anal and proj mgr, USAF, 80-94; sr anal, Int Corp, 95-96; adj instr, religion, Riverside Commun Col, 97; res asst, philos prog, Claremont Grad Univ, 98- . **MEMBERSHIPS** APA. **RESEARCH** Philosophical logic; early analytical philosophy; philosophy of mathematics. **SELECTED PUBLICATIONS** Auth, Wittgenstein on Freedom of the Will, MA thesis, 96. **CONTACT ADDRESS** 782 Stanislaus Circle, Claremont, CA, 91711. **EMAIL** grant.marler@cgu.edu

MARMURA, MICHAEL ELIAS
PERSONAL Born 11/11/1929, Jerusalem, Palestine, m, 1962, 3 children **DISCIPLINE** ISLAMIC PHILOSOPHY, ARABIC **EDUCATION** Univ Wis, BA, 53; Univ Mich, MA, 55, PhD(-Near Eastern studies), 59. **CAREER** Lectr Islamic philos and theol, 59-62, from asst prof to assoc prof, 62-69, assoc chmn dept Mid E and Islamic studies, 69-78, PROF ISLAMIC PHILOS AND THEOL, UNIV TORONTO, 69, CHMN DEPT MID E AND ISLAMIC STUDIES, 78-. **MEMBERSHIPS** Am Orient Soc; Can Philos Asn. **RESEARCH** Islamic theology. **SELECTED PUBLICATIONS** Auth, Ghazalian Causes and Intermediaries + Article Rev of Frank,Richard 'Creation and the Cosmic System', J Amer Oriental Soc, Vol 0115, 95; The Formation of Modern Arabic Scientific and Intellectual Vocabulary, Speculum-J Medieval Stud, Vol 0071, 96. **CONTACT ADDRESS** Dept of Mid E and Islamic Studies, Univ of Toronto, Toronto, ON, M5S 1A1.

MARQUIS, DONALD BAGLEY
PERSONAL Born 11/02/1935, Elkhart, IN, d, 2 children **DISCIPLINE** PHILOSOPHY **EDUCATION** Ind Univ, BA, 57, MA, 64, PhD(philos), 70; Univ Pittsburgh, MA, 62. **CAREER** Actg asst prof philos, 67-70, asst dir, Western Civilization Prof, 67-71, asst prof, 70-76, assoc prof, 76-90, PROF PHILOS, UNIV KANS, 90-. **MEMBERSHIPS** Am Philos Asn; Southwestern Philos Soc **RESEARCH** Medical ethics; ethics. **SELECTED PUBLICATIONS** Leaving Therapy to Chance: An Impasse in the Ethics of Randomized Clinical Trials, Hastings Center Report, 83; An Argument that All Prerandomized Clinical Trials Are Unethical, Jour Med and Philos, 86; Why Abortion Is Immoral, Jour Philos, 89; Four Versions of Double Effect, Jour Med and Philos, 91; Fetuses, Futures and Values: A Reply to Shirley, Southwest Philos Rev, 95; Reiman on Abortion, Jour Soc Philos, 98; Why Most Abortions are Immoral, Bioethics Med Ed, JAI Press, 98; The Weakness of the Case for Legalizing Physician-Assisted Suicide, In: Physician-Assisted Suicide: Expanding the Debate, Routledge, 98. **CONTACT ADDRESS** Dept of Philosophy, Univ of Kansas, Lawrence, KS, 66045-2145. **EMAIL** dmarquis@falcon.cc.ukans.edu

MARRAS, AUSONIO
DISCIPLINE PHILOSOPHY **EDUCATION** Colgate Univ, BA, 63; Duke Univ, PhD, 67. **CAREER** Prof **RESEARCH** Philosophy of mind; foundations of cognitive science. **SELECTED PUBLICATIONS** Auth, Metaphysical Foundations of Action-Explanation, Kluwer, 97; Action Explanation and Mental Causation, Napoli, 97; The Debate on Mental Causation: Davidson and His Critics, Dialogue, 97; The Causal Relevance of Mental Properties, Philos, 97; Nonreductive Materialism and Mental Causation, Can Jour Philos, 94; co-ed, Language Learning and Concept Acquisition, Ablex, 86. **CONTACT ADDRESS** Dept of Philosophy, Western Ontario Univ, London, ON, N6A 5B8. **EMAIL** amarras@julian.uwo.ca

MARROW, STANLEY BEHJET
PERSONAL Born 02/10/1931, Baghdad, Iraq **DISCIPLINE** NEW TESTAMENT **EDUCATION** Boston Col, BA, 54, MA, 55; Weston Col, PhL, 55, STL, 62; Pontifical Bibl Inst, Rome, SSL, 64; Gregorian Univ, Rome, STD, 66. **CAREER** Asst prof relig, Al-Hikma Univ, Baghdad, 66-68; asst prof New Testament, Pontifical Bibl Inst, 68-71; PROF NEW TESTAMENT, WESTON SCH THEOL, 71-; Assoc ed, Biblica, 68-71, New Testament Abstracts, 71- & Cath Bibl Quart, 78-87. **MEMBERSHIPS** Cath Bibl Asn; Soc Bibl Lit; Am Acad Relig; Soc New Testament Studies. **RESEARCH** Theology of the New Testament. **SELECTED PUBLICATIONS** Co-ed, AlFarabi's Commentary on Aristotle's Peri Hermeneias, Imprimerie Cath, Beyrouth, 60, 2nd ed, 71; auth, The Christ in Jesus, Paulist Press, 68; Index to Biblica 1945-1969, 70 & Basic Tools of Biblical Exegesis, 76 & 78, Biblical Inst, Rome; The Words of Jesus in Our Gospels, Paulist Press, 79; Speaking the Word Fearlessly: Boldness in the New Testament, NY: Paulist Press, 82; Paul, His Letters and His Theology, NY: Paulist Press, 86; The Gospel of John: A Reading, NY: Paulist Press, 95. **CONTACT ADDRESS** 3 Phillips Place, Cambridge, MA, 02138-3495.

MARRS, RIOCK R.
PERSONAL Born 05/28/1952, Tucson, AZ, m, 2 children **DISCIPLINE** RELIGION **CAREER** Grad tchg asst, Abilene Christian Univ, 73-79; adjunct prof, Johns Hopkins Univ, 82-83; pt time instr, St. Mary's Sem, Univ, Ecumenical Inst, 79-81; asst prof, Abilene Christian Univ, 84-86; assoc prof, Pepperdine

Univ, 87-; ch, Admission and Scholar Comm Rel, 91-92. **SELECTED PUBLICATIONS** Auth, What's Wrong with this Picture?, 21st Century Christian, 94; In the Beginning: Male and Female, Essays on Women in Earliest, Christianity, Col Press, 94; The Prophetic Faith: A Call to Ethics and Community, RQ 36, 94; rev, T. Lenchak, Choose Life!, A Rhetorical-Critical Investigation of Deuteronomy, Rel Studies Rev 20/4, 94; Gordon Mitchell, Together in the Land, A Reading of the Book of Joshua, Rel Studies Rev 20/4, 94. **CONTACT ADDRESS** Dept of Relig, Pepperdine Univ, 24255 Pacific Coast Hwy, Malibu, CA, 90263. **EMAIL** rmarrs@pepperdine.edu

MARSCHALL, JOHN PETER
PERSONAL Born 12/11/1933, Chicago, IL **DISCIPLINE** AMERICAN RELIGIOUS HISTORY **EDUCATION** Loyola Univ, Ill, AB, 56; St Louis Univ, MA, 61; Cath Univ Am, PhD(hist), 65. **CAREER** Lectr relig hist, Cath Univ Am, 65; asst prof, Viatorian Sem, Washington, DC, 61-65; asst prof Am relig hist, Loyola Univ, Ill, 66-69, mem grad fac, 68; dir, Ctr Relig and Life, 69-72, prog coordr, Ctr Relig and Life, 73-76; lectr, 69-80, ASSOC PROF AM HIST, UNIV NEV, RENO, 80-, Schmitt Found travel grant, Europe, 63-64; dir, Self-Studies Sisters of Charity, BVM, 66-68; co-dir, Self-Studies New Melleray Trappist Abbey, 68-69; mem subcomt hist, life and ministry priests, Nat Coun Bishops, 68-72; Western dir, Nat Inst for Campus Ministries, 75-79; ed consult, NICM J for Christian and Jews in Higher Educ, 75-79; asst to pres, Univ Nev, Reno, 80-. **MEMBERSHIPS** Cath Campus Ministry Asn (pres, 75-76); Am Acad Relig; Orgn Am Historians; Am Cath Hist Asn; Am Acad Polit and Soc Sci. **RESEARCH** Nineteenth century American Catholic history; history of religion in Nevada. **SELECTED PUBLICATIONS** Auth, The Premier See--a History of the Archdiocese-of-Baltimore, Church Hist, Vol 0065, 96. **CONTACT ADDRESS** Dept of Hist, Univ of Nev, Reno, NV, 89557-0001.

MARSDEN, G.M.
PERSONAL Born 02/25/1939, m, 1969, 2 children **DISCIPLINE** HISTORY OF CHRISTIANITY **EDUCATION** Haverford College, BA, honors, 59; Westminster Theol Sem, BD, 63; Yale Univ MA, 61, PhD, 65. **CAREER** Francis A McAnaney Prof of Hist, 92-, Univ Notre Dame; Prof 86-92, Duke Univ; vis Prof 86, 90, Univ Cal Berkeley; vis Prof 76-77, Trinity Evang Div Schl; Dir 80-83, Calvin College; Instr, Asst Prof, Assoc Prof, Prof, 65-86, Calvin College; Asst Instr, 64-65, Yale Univ. **HONORS AND AWARDS** Lippincott Prize; YHF for NEH; Calvin Cen Christ Schl fel; Eternity Book of the Year; Calvin Res Fel; J Howard Pew Freedom Gnt; Guggenheim Fel. **MEMBERSHIPS** ASCH. **SELECTED PUBLICATIONS** Auth, The Outrageous Idea of Christian Scholarship, NY, Oxford Univ Press, 97; The Soul of the American University: From Protestant Establishment to Established Nonbelief, NY, Oxford Univ Press, 94; coed, The Secularization of the Academy, NY, Oxford Univ Press, 92; Understanding Fundamentalism and Evangelicalism, Grand Rapids, W B Eerdmans, 91, collection of previously pub essays; Reforming Fundamentalism: Fuller Seminary and the New Evangelicalism, Grand Rapids, W b Eerdmans, 87, reissued pbk, 95. **CONTACT ADDRESS** Dept of History, Univ Notre Dame, Notre Dame, IN, 46556. **EMAIL** marsden.1@nd.edu

MARSH, JAMES L.
DISCIPLINE PHILOSOPHY **EDUCATION** Northwestern Univ, PhD. **CAREER** Prof, Fordham Univ. **RESEARCH** Aesthetics, phenomenology and hermeneutics. **SELECTED PUBLICATIONS** Auth, Post-Cartesian Meditations, Fordham UP, 88; Critique, Action, and Liberation, SUNY, 95; co-auth, Modernity and Its Discontents, Fordham UP, 92. **CONTACT ADDRESS** Dept of Philos, Fordham Univ, 113 W 60th St, New York, NY, 10023.

MARSHALL, ROBERT J.
DISCIPLINE THEOLOGY **EDUCATION** Wittenberg Univ; Chicago Lutheran Theol Sem, PhD; Univ Chicago. **CAREER** Pres, Lutheran Church in Am; pres, Lutheran World Relief; sr sch in residence-. **MEMBERSHIPS** Mem, Bd of Trustees, Muhlenberg Col. **SELECTED PUBLICATIONS** Auth, On Being a Church Member in the ELCA; The Mighty Acts of God, Augsburg Fortress Press. **CONTACT ADDRESS** Dept of Theology, Lutheran Sch of Theol, 1100 E 55th St, Chicago, IL, 60615. **EMAIL** rmarshal@lstc.edu

MARTENS, ELMER ARTHUR
PERSONAL Born 08/12/1930, Main Centre, SK, Canada, m, 1956, 4 children **DISCIPLINE** RELIGION, OLD TESTAMENT **EDUCATION** Univ Sask, BA, 54; Univ Man, BEd, 56; Mennonite Brethren Bibl Sem, CA, BD, 58; Claremont Grad Sch, PhD, 72. **CAREER** Assoc prof, 70-80, pres, Mennonite Brethren Bibl Sem, 77-86, prof Old Testament, 80-95, PROF EMERITUS,MENNONITE BRETHREN BIBL SEM, 95-; Co-translr, New Am Standard Bible, 69-70; New Living Translation, 89-96. **HONORS AND AWARDS** First Award (an expense-paid trip to Israel), Sermon writing contest sponsored by Nat Asn of Evangelicals, 62. **MEMBERSHIPS** Soc Bibl Lit; Evangelical Theological Soc; Institute of Biblical Research. **RESEARCH** Old Testament theology; Prophets. **SELECTED PUBLICATIONS** Contribr, The Church in Mission, Bd Christian Lit, 67; God's Design: A Focus on Old Testament Theology, Baker, 81, 3rd ed, Bibal Press, 98; Jeremiah, Herald Press, 86; ed, along with B. C. Ollenburger and G. Hasel, The Flowering of Old Testament Theology: A Reader in Twentieth Century Theology 1930-1990, Eisenbraun, 92; Old Testament Theology, Institute of Biblical Research Bibliographies #13, Baker, 97. **CONTACT ADDRESS** Mennonite Brethren Biblical Sem, 4824 E Butler, Fresno, CA, 93727-5014. **EMAIL** eamartens@compuserve.com

MARTHALER, BERARD LAWRENCE
PERSONAL Born 05/01/1927, Chicago Heights, IL **DISCIPLINE** RELIGIOUS EDUCATION **EDUCATION** Pontif Fac Theol, San Bonaventura, Rome, STL, 52, STD, 53; Univ Minn, MA, 56, PhD(ancient hist), 68. **CAREER** Instr church hist, Assumption Sem, 53-61; asst prof theol, Bellarmine Col, Ky, 61-63; asst prof relig educ, 63-67, assoc prof and head dept, 67-72, pres, 74-75, PROF RELIG EDUC, CATH UNIV AM, 73, CHMN DEPT, 74-. Exec ed, the Living Light, 72-. **MEMBERSHIPS** Col Theol Soc (vpres, 68-70); Am Acad Relig; Asn Prof and Researchers Relig Educ (pres, 74-75); Cath Theol Soc Am; Relig Educ Asn. **RESEARCH** Religious education as socialization. **SELECTED PUBLICATIONS** Auth, A Universal Catechism for the Catholic Church From the Council of Trent to Our Day, Theol Stud, Vol 0054, 93; The Catechisms in Quebec 1702-1963, Cath Hist Rev, Vol 0079, 93. **CONTACT ADDRESS** Dept of Relig and Relig Educ, Catholic Univ of America, Washington, DC, 20064.

MARTI, GENOVEVA
DISCIPLINE PHILOSOPHY **EDUCATION** Stanford Univ, PhD. **CAREER** Assoc prof, Univ Calif, Riverside; VIS PROF, BIRKBECK COLL, ENG, 98-99. **RESEARCH** Study of the connection between language and the world we talk about. **SELECTED PUBLICATIONS** Auth, "Aboutness and Substitutivity," Midwest Stud, 89; "The Source of Intensionality," Philos Perspectives, 93; "Do Modal Distinctions Collapse in Carnap's System?," Jour of Philos Logic, 94; "The Essence of Genuine Reference," Jour of Philos Logic, 95. **CONTACT ADDRESS** Dept of Philos, Univ Calif, 1156 Hinderaker Hall, Riverside, CA, 92521-0209. **EMAIL** gmarti@ucrac1.ucr.edu

MARTIN, CHARLES BURTON
PERSONAL Born 05/24/1924, Chelsea, MA, 4 children **DISCIPLINE** PHILOSOPHY OF MIND, METAPHYSICS **EDUCATION** Boston Univ, BA, 48; Cambridge Univ, PhD(philos), 59. **CAREER** From lectr to sr lectr & reader philos, Univ Adelaide, 54-66; prof, Univ Sydney, 66-71; PROF PHILOS, UNIV CALGARY, 71-, Vis assoc prof, Columbia Univ, summer, 61; vis asst prof, Harvard Univ, fall, 61; vis prof, Columbia Univ, 62, Univ Mich, 68 & Harvard Univ, 70, 75 & 80; vis lectr, Oxford Univ, 78. **MEMBERSHIPS** Australasian Philos Asn (pres, 68); Can Philos Asn. **RESEARCH** The role of sensory experience in concept formation; realism and anti-realism. **SELECTED PUBLICATIONS** Auth, A religious way of knowing, MIND, 52; Religious Belief, Cornell Univ Press, 59; coauth, Remembering, Philos Rev, 66; co-ed, Locke and Berkeley, Macmillan & Co, Ltd, 68; auth, People, In: Contemporary Philosophy in Australia, George Allen & Unwin, 69; Knowledge without observation, Can J Philos, 71; God, the nullset and divine simplicity, In: The Challenge of Religion Today, Sci Hist Publ, 76; Substance substantiated, Australasian J Philos, 80. **CONTACT ADDRESS** Univ Calgary, 101 5th St NW, Calgary, AB, T2N 2A8.

MARTIN, CHARLOTTE JOY
PERSONAL Born 05/26/1963, Brooklyn Park, MN, s **DISCIPLINE** THEOLOGY **EDUCATION** Col St Benedict, BA, 85; Vanderbilt Univ, MA, 90, PhD 94. **CAREER** Asst prof, 91-, assoc prof, 97-, Mount Mercy Col, Cedar Rapids IA. **HONORS AND AWARDS** Who's Who in Amer Tchrs, 96. **MEMBERSHIPS** Amer Acad of Religion **RESEARCH** Eschatology, Pedagogy, Jewish Christian Dialogue. **CONTACT ADDRESS** Religious Studies Dept, Mount Mercy Col, 1330 Elmhurst Drive NE, Cedar Rapids, IA, 52402-4907. **EMAIL** chmartin@mmc.mtmercy.edu

MARTIN, D. MICHAEL
PERSONAL m, 2 children **DISCIPLINE** NEW TESTAMENT INTERPRETATION **EDUCATION** Dallas Baptist Col, BA; Southwestern Baptist Theol Sem, MDiv, PhD; addn stud, Tyndale House; Cambridge Univ, 94. **CAREER** Tchg asst, tchg fel, Southwestern Baptist Theol Sem; vis prof, 80-81; adj prof, Golden Gate's S Calif Campus, 81-84; instr, Calif Baptist Col; ch, Div Rel, Calif Baptist Col, 82; prof, Golden Gate Baptist Theol Sem-; assoc acad dean. **SELECTED PUBLICATIONS** Pub(s), Christian Century; Biblical Illustrator; Sunday Sch Bd; contrib, Holman Bible Dictionary; auth, Vol 33, 1 & 2 Thessalonians, New American Commentary, Broadman. **CONTACT ADDRESS** Golden Gate Baptist Theol Sem, 201 Sem Dr, Mill Valley, CA, 94941-3197. **EMAIL** MichaelMartin@ggbts.edu

MARTIN, DEAN M.
PERSONAL Born 08/04/1942, Lebanon, MO, m, 1965, 2 children **DISCIPLINE** RELIGION **EDUCATION** William Jewell Col, BA, 64; Yale Univ Divinity Sch, BD, 67; Baylor Univ, PhD, 72. **CAREER** Asst prof, US Int Univ, 71-74; from asst prof to assoc prof, Campbell Univ, 74-92; vis prof Philos, Baylor Univ, 92; prof, Campbell Univ, 93-. **MEMBERSHIPS** Am Acad Relig; Soc Philos Relig; Baptist Asn Philos Tchrs; Asn Baptist Prof Relig; Soren Kierkegaard Soc. **RESEARCH** Religion and philosophy of language; Ludwig Wittgenstein; Soren Kierkegaard; religion/theology; philosophy of religion. **SELECTED PUBLICATIONS** Auth, God and Objects: Beginning with Existence, Int Jour Philos Relig, Feb, 97; auth, Learning to Become a Christian, Relig Educ, Winter, 87; auth, On Certainty and Religious Belief, Relig Studies, Dec, 84; auth, Language, Thinking, and Religious Consciousness, Int Jour Philos Relig, Fall, 79; auth, Language, Theology, and the Subject Life, Perspectives in Relig Studies, Fall, 78. **CONTACT ADDRESS** PO Box 487, Buies Creek, NC, 27506. **EMAIL** dmartin@camel.campbell.edu

MARTIN, EDWARD N.
PERSONAL MI, m, 1993, 1 child **DISCIPLINE** PHILOSOPHY **EDUCATION** Hillsdale Col, BA, 88; Trinity Evang Divinity Sch, MA, 90; Purdue Univ, PhD, 95. **CAREER** Prof, Trinity Col & Sem, 96-. **MEMBERSHIPS** Soc of Christian Phil; APA; Evangelical Theol Soc; Phil of Time Soc **RESEARCH** Contemporary Christian Philosophy of Religion; Ethics; G E Moore; Analytic Philosophy. **SELECTED PUBLICATIONS** Rev, Our Idea of God, The Crucible 2, 91; Proper Function, Natural Reason, and Evils as Extrinsic Goods, Global Jour of Classic Theol 1, 98; On Behalf of the Fool: G E Moore and Our Knowledge of the Existence of Material Objects, Sorites 2, 96; Rev, The Evidential Argument from Evil, Intl Jour for Phil of Religion, 97. **CONTACT ADDRESS** Dr, Trinity Col & Sem, 4233 Medwel Drive, Newburgh, IN, 47629-0717. **EMAIL** 75413.761@compuserve.com

MARTIN, ERNEST L.
PERSONAL Born 05/22/1932, Meeker, OK, m, 1987, 3 children **DISCIPLINE** THEOLOGY **EDUCATION** Ambassador Univ, BA, 58, MA, 60, PhD, 66. **CAREER** Sec of Bd, 60-72, Registrar, 60-65, Dean of Faculty, 65-72, Ambassador Univ, England; Chm, Dept of Theol, 73-74, Ambassador, Univ, Pasadena, CA. **HONORS AND AWARDS** Head of Coll Students for 5 yrs at the Jerusalem Excavations under Prof Benjamin Mazar, Hebrew Univ. **MEMBERSHIPS** SBL; ASOR; Planetarian Soc. **RESEARCH** Theology, chronology, history, astronomy. **SELECTED PUBLICATIONS** Auth, The Star That Astonished the World, 78; Secrets of Golgotha, 88; Restoring the Bible, 84; 101 Bible Secrets That Christians Do Not Know, 93; The People That History Forgot, 91; The Tithing Dilemma, 74; NEW: The Temples That Jerusalem Forgot, Jan 99; Angels-The Fictions and the Facts, Nov 2000. **CONTACT ADDRESS** Acad of Scriptural Knowledge, PO Box 25000, Portland, OR, 97225. **EMAIL** doctor@asklem.com

MARTIN, FRANCIS DAVID
PERSONAL Born 03/29/1920, Johnstown, PA, m, 1942, 4 children **DISCIPLINE** PHILOSOPHY **EDUCATION** Univ Chicago, AB, 42, PhD, 49. **CAREER** From asst prof to prof philos, 49-72, John Howard Harris Prof, Bucknell Univ, 72-, Fulbright res scholar, Italy, 57-59; Lilly Found fel, 66-67. **HONORS AND AWARDS** Christian Lindback Award Distinguished Tchg, 69. **MEMBERSHIPS** Am Philos Soc; Am Soc Aesthet; Nat Soc Studies Educ. **RESEARCH** Aesthetics; the philos of A N Whitehead; the philos of Martin Heidegger. **SELECTED PUBLICATIONS** Auth, Unrealized possibility in the aesthetic experience, J Philos; On the supposed incompatibility between formalism and expressionism, J Aesthet & Art Criticism; Naming paintings, Art J; Art and the Religious Experience, Bucknell Univ, 72; Sculpture and Enlivened Space: Aesthetics and History, Univ Press Ky, 81; The Humanities Throught the Arts, McGraw-Hill, 74, 5th ed, 97. **CONTACT ADDRESS** Dept of Philosophy, Bucknell Univ, Lewisburg, PA, 17837.

MARTIN, GLEN
PERSONAL Born 01/21/1944, Rochester, NY, m, 1978, 1 child **DISCIPLINE** PHILOSOPHY **EDUCATION** SUNY Buffalo, BA, 70; CUNY, MA, 76, PhD, 85. **CAREER** Prof, 85-, Radford Univ. **HONORS AND AWARDS** IPPNO Pres. **MEMBERSHIPS** APA; AAR; CPP; IPPNO; ISISR; RPA; SPPE; SACP; SPEP; Wld Co-ord Council of the Global Ratif and Elections Netwk. **RESEARCH** Global Issues; Peace Studies; Philosophy of Liberation. **SELECTED PUBLICATIONS** Auth, The Principle of Unity In diversity as the Foundation of World Peace, eds, Paul Smithka, Alison Bailey, Rodopi Press, forthcoming; Preface to: Seeking Balance: A Collection of Poetry, by Elaine Webster, Naples NY, Dawn Dancer Press, 98; auth, A Buddhist Response to Institutional Violence, in: Institutional Violence, eds, Deane Curtin, Bob Litke, Rodopi Press, forthcoming; auth, A Holistic Response to Institutional Violence: Compassion Critical Theory and Nonviolence, in: Peace in a Violent World, ed, Howard Friedman, Rodopi Press, forthcoming; Nuclear Madness, IPP Newsletter, 97, and The Human Quest, 98; Freedom in Cuba, IPP Newsletter, 97; rev, The Evidential Argument from Evil, ed Daniel Howard-Snyder, in: Teaching Philosophy, 97; rev, Joan Stambaugh, The Other Nietsche, in: Intl Studies in Philosophy, forthcoming;

Wittgenstein Language and Education for Creativity, Teaching Philo, 96; Wittgenstein and Time, Intl Encyc of Time, ed, Samuel L Macey, Garland Press, 94; Kierkegaard and Time, Intl Encyc of Time, ed, Samuel L Macey, Garland Press, 94. **CONTACT ADDRESS** 313 7th Ave, Radford, VA, 24141. **EMAIL** gmartin@runet.edu

MARTIN, JAMES AUGUST
PERSONAL Born 03/18/1938, Sarasota, FL, m, 1962, 2 children **DISCIPLINE** PHILOSOPHY **EDUCATION** Fla State Univ, BA, 61; Univ Mich, MA, PhD(philos), 69. **CAREER** Res instr philos, Dartmouth Col, 67-69, asst prof, 69-73; asst prof, 73-77, ASSOC PROF PHILOS, UNIV WYO, 77-. **MEMBERSHIPS** Am Philos Asn. **RESEARCH** Epistemology; analytic philosophy; philosophy, logic and science. **SELECTED PUBLICATIONS** Auth, How not to define truth functionality, Logique Analyse, 12/70; Arc there truth functional connectives?, Metaphilos, 7/73; coauth, What a man does he can do?, Analysis, 4/73; Outcomes and abilities, Analysis, 6/73; Objective knowledge: A review, Philos Rev, 1/75; Proving necessity, Philos Res Arch, 76. **CONTACT ADDRESS** Dept of Philosophy, Univ of Wyoming, P O Box 3392, Laramie, WY, 82071-3392.

MARTIN, JAMES LUTHER
PERSONAL Born 07/22/1917, Lone Wolf, OK **DISCIPLINE** RELIGION **EDUCATION** Oklahoma City Univ, BA, 38; Yale Univ, BD, 41, PhD(theol), 51. **CAREER** From assoc prof to prof philos & relig, Col Idaho, 46-57; PROF RELIG & CHMN DEPT, DENISON UNIV 57-, Fund Advan Educ fel, 54-55; fac training fel, Am Inst Indian Studies, 63-64. **MEMBERSHIPS** Am Acad Relig; Asn Asian Studies. **RESEARCH** History of Christian thought; Oriental religions; Hindu temple administration. **SELECTED PUBLICATIONS** Auth, The economy of the Tiru Jeer math, Studies on Asia, 66; Hindu orthodoxy in a South Indian village, J Am Acad Relig, 12/67; Variations on Tergalai orthodoxy, India Cult Quart, 12/70. **CONTACT ADDRESS** Dept of Relig, Denison Univ, Granville, OH, 43023.

MARTIN, JANE ROLAND
PERSONAL Born 07/20/1929, New York, NY, m, 1962, 2 children **DISCIPLINE** PHILOSOPHY, EDUCATION **EDUCATION** Radcliffe Col, AB, 51; Harvard Univ, M Ed, 56; Radcliffe Col, PhD, 61. **CAREER** Assoc prof of Philos, Univ MA, Boston, 72-81, prof, 81-92; PROF OF PHILOS EMERITA, 92-. **HONORS AND AWARDS** Hon doct: Univ of Umea, Sweden; Salem St Univ, MA; Guggenheim fel, 87; NSF, 84; Buntia, Inst fel, 81. **MEMBERSHIPS** APA; Philos of Ed Soc; Soc for Women in Philos; Am Ed Res Asn. **RESEARCH** Philos of ed; feminist theory and philos. **SELECTED PUBLICATIONS** Auth, Reclaiming a Conversation: The Ideal of the Educated Woman, Yale Univ Press, 85; auth, Science in a Different Style, Am Philos Quart, 25, 88; auth, Idealogical Critique and the Philosophy of Science, Philos of Science, 56, 89; auth, The Schoolhome: Rethinking Schools for Changing Families, Harvard Univ Press, 92; auth, Curriculum and the Mirror of Knowledge, Beyond Lib Ed, Routledge, 93, Defending Diversity, Univ MA Press, 94; auth, Changing the Educational Landscape: Philosophy, Women, and Curriculum, Routledge, 94; auth, Methodological Essentialism, False Difference, and Other Dangerous Traps, Signs, 19, 94; auth, Aerial Distance, Esotericism, and Other Closely Related Traps, Signs, 21, 96; auth, Bound for the Promised Land: the Gendered Character of Higher Education, Duke J of Gender Law & Pol, 4, 97. **CONTACT ADDRESS** 8 Gerry's Landing Rd, Cambridge, MA, 02138. **EMAIL** m/martin@bu.edu

MARTIN, JANICE R.
DISCIPLINE LAW **EDUCATION** University of Louisville, BS (with honors), political science; University of Louisville Law School, JD. **CAREER** Instructor, Univ of Louisville; Private practice, attorney; Jefferson County Attorney's Office, Juvenile Division, head; Jefferson County District Court, district judge, 1992-. **HONORS AND AWARDS** Distinguished Law School Alumni Award, 1992; Continuing Legal Educ Award, 1994, 1996; Kentucky Women's Leadership Class, 1994. **MEMBERSHIPS** Kentucky Task Force on Racial Bias; Women's Lawyers Assn; NAWJ. **CONTACT ADDRESS** Judge, Jefferson County District Court, Hall of Justice, 600 W Jefferson Ave, Louisville, KY, 40202.

MARTIN, JERRY LEE
PERSONAL Born 10/16/1941, Turkey, TX **DISCIPLINE** PHILOSOPHY **EDUCATION** Univ Calif, Riverside, AB, 63; Univ Chicago, MA, 66; Northwestern Univ, Evanston, PhD(philos), 70. **CAREER** Instr philos, eve div, Northwestern Univ, 65-67; asst prof, 67-73, chmn dept, 79-81, ASSOC PROF PHILOS, UNIV COLO, BOULDER, 73-, DIR, CTR STUDY VALUES & SOCIAL POLICY, 81-, Mellon Congfel, 82-83. **MEMBERSHIPS** Am Philos Asn; Soc Phenomenol & Existential Philos; Soc Historians Early Am Repub; AAUP. **RESEARCH** Epistemology; ethics and public policy; political philosophy. **SELECTED PUBLICATIONS** Auth, Has Strawson Refuted Scepticism About Other Minds?, Philos Asn; contribr, New Essays in the philosophy of mind, Can J, 75; auth, A dialogue on criteria, Philos Forum; The duality of time, Man & World; ed, the Concept of the Quality of Life: Problems of Definition and Evaluation, 82. **CONTACT ADDRESS** Dept of Philos, Univ of Colo, Boulder, CO, 80302.

MARTIN, JOAN M.
DISCIPLINE CHRISTIAN SOCIAL ETHICS **EDUCATION** Elmhurst Col, BA, 73; Princeton Theol Sem, M Div, 76; Temple Univ, MA, 89; Temple Univ, PhD, 96. **CAREER** Ordained Presbyterian minister, 76-; assoc prof, Christian ethics, Episcopal Divinity Sch, 94-. **HONORS AND AWARDS** Mary Grove Col, dr of humane letters. **MEMBERSHIPS** Amer Acad of Relig; Soc for Christ Ethics. **RESEARCH** Christian ethics--economics, humane labor, womanist/feminist theory, welfare policy. **SELECTED PUBLICATIONS** Article, Sources for Womanist Ethics: The Slave Narrative as Historical and Sacred Text, Jour of the Proceedings of the Europ Soc of Women in Theol Res, Thessaloniki, Greece, 98; auth, Sisterhood, Work, Womanist, Dict of Feminist Theol, Westminster/John Knox Press, 96; auth, The Work Ethic of Enslaved Women in The Antebellum, 1830-1865, Jour of the Interdenominational Theol Ctr, Spring, 95, Perspectives on Womanist Theol, Black Church Scholars Series, vol VII, Spring, 95; auth, Re-Imagining the Church as Spiritual Institution: Affirming Diversity and Life Sustaining Relationships, Church and Soc: Jour of the Presbyterian Church, vol 84, no 5, May/June, 94; auth, The Notion of Difference for Emerging Womanist Ethics: The Writings of Audre Lorde and Bell Hooks, Jour Feminist Studies in Relig, Spring, 93; auth, African American Women's Embodiment and Moral Agency, Probe, NARW, Spring, 93; auth, We Can't Win For Losin' or Can We?, The Acceptable Year: Sermons From Liberation Theol, Judson Press, 82; auth, Still Making The Road As We Go, Your Daughters Shall Prophesy: Feminist Alternatives in Theol Educ, The Pilgrim Press, 80. **CONTACT ADDRESS** Episcopal Divinity Sch, 99 Brattle St., Cambridge, MA, 02138. **EMAIL** jmartin@episdivschool.org

MARTIN, JOEL
DISCIPLINE RELIGION **EDUCATION** Duke Univ, PhD **CAREER** ASSOC PROF, FRANKLIN MARSHALL COL, 88-. **CONTACT ADDRESS** PO Box 3003, Lancaster, PA, 17604-3003.

MARTIN, JOSEPH RAMSEY
PERSONAL Born 10/15/1930, Paducah, KY, m, 1955, 2 children **DISCIPLINE** PHILOSOPHY **EDUCATION** Univ Va, PhD(philos), 67. **CAREER** Master English, Brooks Sch, Mass, 58-60, chmn dept, 60-62; instr, Lib Arts Sems & Dept English, Univ Va, 62-63; asst prof philos, Transylvania Col, 67-68; asst prof, 68-73, assoc prof, 73-78, PROF PHILOS, WASHINGTON & LEE UNIV, 78-. **MEMBERSHIPS** Am Philos Asn. **RESEARCH** Epistemology; philosophy of mind and language. **SELECTED PUBLICATIONS** Conceptual obsolescence and land use policy, Towards a Land Use Ethic, Piedmont Environ Coun, 79. **CONTACT ADDRESS** Dept of Philosophy, Washington & Lee Univ, Lexington, VA, 24450.

MARTIN, JUDITH G.
DISCIPLINE RELIGIOUS STUDIES **EDUCATION** McMaster Univ, MA, PhD; Union Theol Sem in NYC, MA. **CAREER** Assoc prof; past dir, Women's Stud Prog, Univ Dayton. **RESEARCH** Feminist theology, religions of the world. **SELECTED PUBLICATIONS** Auth, Why Women Need a Feminist Spirituality, Women's Stud Quart. **CONTACT ADDRESS** Dept of Religious Studies, Univ of Dayton, 300 College Park, 327 Humanities, Dayton, OH, 45469-1679. **EMAIL** martin@checkov.hm.udayton.edu

MARTIN, MARTY
PERSONAL Born 02/05/1928, West Point, NE, m, 1982, 7 children **DISCIPLINE** RELIGIOUS HISTORY **EDUCATION** Lutheran School of Theol, Chicago, STM, 54; Univ of Chicago, PhD, 56. **CAREER** Lutheran Pastor, 49-63, Washington, DC; Prof, 63-98, Univ of Chicago; Sr, Ed, Christian Century, 56-98; George B. Caldwell Sr Scholar in Residence, Park Ridge Center for Health, Faith and Ethics, 81-. **HONORS AND AWARDS** Natl Medal of Hum; Natl Book Award; Medal of the Amer Acad of Arts and Sci; 60 honorary degrees. **MEMBERSHIPS** Past Pres Amer Acad of Rel; Amer Soc of Church Hist; Amer Catholic Hist Assoc. **RESEARCH** American Religious History, 18th and 20th centuries; comparative international studies of movements such as fundamentalism and ethnonationalism. **SELECTED PUBLICATIONS** Auth, Righteous Empire: The Protestant Experience in America, Dial, 70; Pilgrims in Their Own Land: 500 Years of Religion in America, Little Brown, 84; Religion and Republic: The American Circumstance, Beacon, 87; The One and the Many: America's Struggle for the Common Good, Harvard, 97; 3 volume Modern American Religion: The Irony of It All: 1893-1919, Univ of Chicago, 86; The Noise of Conflict, 1919-1941, Univ of Chicago, 91; Under God, Indivisible, 1941-1960, Univ of Chicago, 96. **CONTACT ADDRESS** 239 Scottswood Rd, Riverside, IL, 60546.

MARTIN, MICHAEL LOU
PERSONAL Born 02/03/1932, Cincinnati, OH, m, 1962, 2 children **DISCIPLINE** PHILOSOPHY **EDUCATION** Ariz State Univ, BS, 56; Univ Ariz, MA, 58; Harvard Univ, PhD(philos), 62. **CAREER** Asst prof philos, Univ Colo, 62-65; asst prof, 65-68, assoc prof, 68-75, prof Philos, 75-97, prof emer, 97- , Boston Univ. **HONORS AND AWARDS** Fel, Inst Theoretic Psychol, Univ Alta, 69-70; lib arts fel law & philos, Harvard Law Sch, 79-80. **MEMBERSHIPS** Am Philos Asn; Philos Sci Asn. **RESEARCH** Philosophy of science; philosophy of law; philosophy of religion. **SELECTED PUBLICATIONS** Coauth, Probability, Confirmation and Simplicity, Odyssey, 66; auth, Concepts of Science Education, Scott-Foresman, 72; auth, The Legal Philosophy of H.L.A. Hart: A Critical Appraisal, Temple, 87; auth, Atheism: A Philosophical Justification, Temple, 90; auth, The Case against Christianity, Temple, 91; coauth, Readings in the Philosophy of Social Science, MIT, 94; auth, The Big Domino in the Sky and Other Atheistic Tales, Prometheus, 96; auth, Legal Realism: American and Scandinavian, Peter Lang, 97. **CONTACT ADDRESS** 8 Gerry's Landing Rd, Cambridge, MA, 02138.

MARTIN, MIKE W.
PERSONAL Born 11/06/1946, Salt Lake City, UT, m, 1968, 2 children **DISCIPLINE** PHILOSOPHY **EDUCATION** Univ Utah, BS, 69, MA, 72; Univ Calif Irvine, PhD, 77. **CAREER** Instr, grad courses, bus ethics, Fluor Corp, Calif State Polytechnic Univ, 79, 81; instr, eng ethics, 81, biomed ethics, 83, Univ Calif Irvine; co-teacher, ethics for eng deans & fac, Tex Tech Univ, Murdough Ctr, 91-93; postgrad eng & mgt prog instr, Univ Calif Los Angeles, 90-94; instr, 76-78, asst prof, 78-82, assoc prof, 82-86, prof, 86-, philos, Chapman Univ. **HONORS AND AWARDS** Distinguished lectr, Chapman Univ, 96-97; achievement award, Chapman Univ, 94; fel, Wang Distinguished Res fel, 89-91; nominee, prof of the yr award, Counc for Adv and Support of Educ, 88,89; res grant, Asn of Amer Col, 88; teaching grant, Asn of Amer Col, 87-91, 92; teaching award, Arnold L. & Lois S. Graves award, 83; fel, Nat Endow for the Humanities fel, 81-82; NEH/NSF proj & fel, 78-80; teaching award, Matchette Found, Univ Calif Irvine, 76. **RESEARCH** Applied ethics. **SELECTED PUBLICATIONS** Auth, Love's Virtues, Univ Press of Kans, 96; auth, Virtuous Giving: Philanthropy, Voluntary Service and Caring, Ind Univ Press, 94; auth, Everyday Morality: An Introduction to Applied Ethics, Wadsworth, 89, 95; auth, Self-Deception and Morality, Univ Press of Kans, 86; article, Personal Ideals and Professional Responsibilities, Applied Ethics in a Troubled World, Kluwer Acad Publ, 167-178, 98; auth, Caring About Clients, Professional Ethics, 6, 55-75, Spring, 97; auth, Advocating Values: Professionalism in Teaching Ethics, Teaching Philos, 20:1, 19-34, Mar, 97; auth, Professional Distance, Intl Jour of Applied Philos, 11:2, 39-50, Winter/Spring, 97; auth, Self-Deceiving Intentions, Behavioral and Brain Sci, 20, no 1, 122-123, 97; auth, Rape and Sexual Harassment, Philos of Sex and Love, Prentice-Hall, 344-351, 97; auth, Homosexuality and Homophobia, Soc Ethics, McGraw-Hill, 182-8, 97; auth, Moral Perspectives on Self-Deception, Dict de Philos Morale, Presses Univ de Fr, Paris, 97; auth, Self-Deception, Blackwell Encycl Dict of Bus Ethics, Blackwell, 575-6, 97; auth, Personal Ideals in Professional Ethics, Professional Ethics, 5, no 1&2, 3-27, 96; auth, Self-Deception, Bad Faith, False Consciousness, Vital Lie, Cambridge Dict of Philos, Cambridge Univ Press, 62, 262, 720-721, 842, 95; auth, Religion Ethics and Professionalism, Professional Ethics, 3, no 2, 17-35, 94; auth, Teaching Philanthropy Ethics, Teaching Philos, 17, no 3, 245-260, 94; auth, Adultery and Fidelity, Jour of Social Philos, 25, no 3, 76-91, 94. **CONTACT ADDRESS** Dept. of Philosophy, Chapman Univ, Orange, CA, 92666. **EMAIL** mwmartin@chapman.edu

MARTIN, RAYMOND ALBERT
PERSONAL Born 11/03/1925, m, 1949, 4 children **DISCIPLINE** BIBLE **EDUCATION** Wartburg Col, BA, 47; Wartburg Theol Sem, BD, 51; Princeton Theol Sem, ThM, 52, PhD(Old Testament), 57, Harvard Divinity School Post-doctoral Study (N.T.), 63-64. **CAREER** Instr Greek, Wartburg Col, 52-54; Missionary prof Old Testament & New Testament, Gurukul Luth Theol Col, India, 57-69; prof Bibl & Intertestamental Studies, Wartburg Theol Sem, 69-. **HONORS AND AWARDS** Emeritus, 98-. **MEMBERSHIPS** Soc Bibl Lit; Soc Bibl Studies, India (secy, 65-69); Int Orgn Septuagint & Cognate Studies; Chicago Society of Biblical Research. **RESEARCH** Greek language; Gospel origins; Intertestamental literature, Historical Jesus; Early Paul; Septuagint Studies. **SELECTED PUBLICATIONS** Auth Some Syntactical Criteria of Translation Greek, VT, 60; Syntactical Evidence of Aramaic Sources in Acts I-XV, NTS, 64; Some Recent Developments in the Study of Discoveries Near the Dead Sea, IJT, 65; The Earliest Messianic Interpretation of Genesis 3:15, JBL, 65; The Date of the Cleansing of the Temple in John, IJT 2:13-22, 65; Syntax of the Greek of Jeremiah 57, India List of Theological Periodicals, 67; Syntactical Evidence of Semitic Sources in Greek Documents, 74; Job in Indian Commentary on the Bible, 74; Syntax Criticism of the LXX Additions to Esther, JBL, 75; Syntactical Evidence of a Semitic Vorlage of the Testament of Joseph in Studies on the Testament of Joseph, 75; Syntax Criticism of the Testament of Abraham in Studies on the Testament of Abraham, 76; Introduction to N.T. Greek, 76,78, & 80; Syntactical and Critical Concordance to the Greek text of Baruch and the Epistle of Jeremiah, Vol XII of The Computer Bible, 77; Syntax Criticism of the Synoptic Gospels, 87; Syntactical Concordance to the Correlated Greek & Hebrew Text of Ruth, Vol XXX of The Computer Bible, 88; Syntactical Concordance to the Correlated Greek and Hebrew Texts of Ruth, Part 2, Vol XXX of The Computer Bible, 89; Syntax Criticism of Johannine Literature, The Catholic Epistles and the Gospel Passion Accounts, 90; Studies in the Life and Ministry of the Early Paul and Related

Issues, 93; Computer Generated Tools for the Study of the Greek and Hebrew Texts of Ruth, Part 3, V XXXC of The Computer Bible, 94; Computer Generated Tools for the Study of the Greek and Hebrew Texts of Obadiah in The Computer Bible, 95; Studies in the Life and Ministry of the Historical Jesus, 95; Computer Generated Tools for the Study of the Greek and Hebrew Texts of Jonah in The Computer Bible, 96; Computer Generated Tools for the Sudy of the Greek and Hebrew Texts of Nahum in The Computer Bible, 98. **CONTACT ADDRESS** Dept of Biblical Studies, Wartburg Theological Sem, 333 Wartburg Place, Dubuque, IA, 52003. **EMAIL** RAMartin7@aol.com

MARTIN, RAYMOND FREDERICK
PERSONAL Born 08/21/1941, Rochester, NY, m, 1961, 2 children **DISCIPLINE** PHILOSOPHY **EDUCATION** Ohio State Univ, BA, 62, MA, 64; Univ Rochester, PhD(philos), 68. **CAREER** Asst prof philos, Davidson Col, 67-69; asst prof, 69-72, ASSOC PROF PHILOS, UNIV MD, COLLEGE PARK, 72-, Teaching & res fel, Macalester Col, 70-71. **MEMBERSHIPS** Am Philos Asn. **RESEARCH** Causal explanation; philosophy of history; objectivity. **SELECTED PUBLICATIONS** Auth, On weighting causes, Am Philos Quart, 72; Singular causal explanations, Theory & Decision, 72; Empirically conclusive reasons and scepticism, Philos Studies, 75; History and subjectivity, Ratio, 78; Historical counter-examples and sufficient cause, Mind, 1/79; Explanatory controversy in historical studies, A case study: The classic Maya collapse, In: Time and Cause, Reidel, 80; Beyond positivism: A research program for philosophy of history, Philos Sci, 81; Causes, conditions and causal importance, Hist & Theory, 82. **CONTACT ADDRESS** Dept of Philos, Univ Md, College Park, MD, 20742-0001.

MARTIN, REX
PERSONAL Born 07/12/1935, Marion, IN, m, 1956, 2 children **DISCIPLINE** PHILOSOPHY **EDUCATION** Rice Univ, BA, 57; Columbia Univ, MA, 60, PhD, 67. **CAREER** Lectr philos, Columbia Univ, 61-62; instr polit sci, Purdue Univ, 62-65; asst prof philos, Lycoming Col, 66-68; from asst prof to assoc, prof, 68-73, chmn dept, 72-78, Prof Philos, Univ Kans, 73-, prof Polit Theory and Govt, Univ Wales, Swansea, 95-00 (joint with Univ Kans); Fulbright res scholar, Univ Helsinki, 72-73; Nat Endowment for Humanities res fel, 76; scholar in residence, Rockefeller Found, Bellagio Study Ctr, Italy, 80; vis prof philos, Univ Auckland, summer, 81; fac Law, Univ Sydney, Australia, fall 92; vis res fel, School Hist Studies, Inst Advan Studies, Princeton, 84, and Centre for Philos and Public Affairs, Univ St Andrews, Scotland, 91; pres, Am Sect, Inst Asn Philos Law & Social Philos, 91-99, vpres, 95-99; chmn Am Philos Asn Comt Philos & Law, 92-95. **MEMBERSHIPS** Am Philos Asn; Am Soc Polit & Legal Philos; Int Asn Philos Law & Social Philos; Soc Philos & Pub Affairs. **RESEARCH** Polit and legal philos; philos of hist; philos of R G Collingwood. **SELECTED PUBLICATIONS** Auth, Historical Explanation: Re-enactment and Practical Inference, Cornell Univ, 77; Rawls and Rights, Univ Press KS, 85; A System of Rights, Oxford Univ Press, 93; co-ed (with Mark Singer), G C macCallum, Legislative Intent, and Other Essays on Law, Politics and Morality, Univ Wis Press, 93; ed, R G Collingwood's Essay on Metaphysics, rev ed, Clarendon Press/Oxford Univ Press, 98. **CONTACT ADDRESS** Dept of Philos, Univ of Kansas, Lawrence, KS, 66045-2145. **EMAIL** 3950252@mcimail.com

MARTIN, ROBERT K.
PERSONAL Born 08/12/1959, Alexandria, LA, m, 1989, 2 children **DISCIPLINE** RELIGIOUS STUDIES **EDUCATION** Louisiana Col, Ba, 81; Princeton Theol Sem, MDiv, 85; Harvard Univ Divinity Sch, ThM, 88; Princeton Theol Sem, PhD, 95. **CAREER** Asst prof relig educ, Yale Divinity Sch. **HONORS AND AWARDS** Louisville Inst grant, 97-98; Wabash Ctr for Tchg and Learning in Theol and Relig grant, 98. **MEMBERSHIPS** United Methodisc Scholars in Christian Educ; Asn of Prof and Res in Relig Educ; N Am Prof of Christian Educ; Am Acad Relig. **RESEARCH** Systematic, practical, pastoral theology; organizational principles of Christian community; critical social theory; foundations of educational theory; liberation movements; postmodernism; epistemological correspondences between science and theology; theological education. **SELECTED PUBLICATIONS** Auth, Congregational Studies and Critical Pedagogy in Theological Perspective, Theol Educ, 97; auth, Theological Education in Epistemological Perspective: The Significance of Michael Polanyi's Personal Knowledge for a Theological Orientation of Theological Education, Tchg Theol and Relig, 98; auth, The Incarnate Ground of Christian Faith: Toward a Christian Theological Epistemology for the Educational Ministry of the Church, Univ Press of Am, 98; auth, Having Faith in Our Faith in God: Toward a Critical Realist Epistemology for Christian Education, Relig Educ, forthcoming; auth, Education and the Liturgical Life of the Church, Relig Educ, forthcoming; auth, Christian Ministry as Communion, J of Ecumenical Stud, forthcoming. **CONTACT ADDRESS** Divinity Sch, Yale Univ, 409 Prospect St, New Haven, CT, 06511. **EMAIL** robert.martin@yale.edu

MARTIN, ROBERT M.
DISCIPLINE PHILOSOPHY **EDUCATION** Columbia Univ, BA, 63; .Univ Mich, MA, 66, PhD, 71. **CAREER** Prof. **RESEARCH** Philosophy of language, metaphysics, practical ethics. **SELECTED PUBLICATIONS** Auth, The Meaning of Language, 87; The Philosopher's Dictionary, 91; There are Two Errors in the the Title of This Book, 92; Scientific Thinking, 97. **CONTACT ADDRESS** Dept of Philos, Dalhousie Univ, Halifax, NS, B3H 3J5. **EMAIL** r.m.martin@dal.ca

MARTIN, THOMAS
PERSONAL Born 04/12/1949, East Lansing, MI, m, 1974, 4 children **DISCIPLINE** PHILOSOPHY **EDUCATION** Univ Missouri, PhD. **CAREER** Chemn, dept of philos, Univ Nebraska, Kearney, 86- . **MEMBERSHIPS** Am Chesterton Soc. **RESEARCH** Dostoyevsky; Solzhenitsyn and Chesterton. **CONTACT ADDRESS** Dept of Philosophy, Univ of Nebraska, Kearney, NE, 68849. **EMAIL** martin@platte.unk.edu

MARTIN, TROY
PERSONAL Seminole, TX, m, 1974, 2 children **DISCIPLINE** BIBLE STUDIES **EDUCATION** Univ Chicago, PhD, 90, **CAREER** Assoc Prof, 10 yrs, ST Xavier Univ. **HONORS AND AWARDS** Excell Schlshp Awd; Sabb; DAAD Gnt. **MEMBERSHIPS** AAR; SBL. **RESEARCH** Pauline Epistles. **SELECTED PUBLICATIONS** Auth, By Philosophy and Empty Deceit, Colossians as Response to a Cynic Critique, j for Stud of the New Test Supp Ser, Sheffield, Sheffield Acad Press, 96; Metaphor and Composition in First Peter, Soc of Bib Lit, Atlanta, Scholars Press, 92; Assessing the Johannine Epithet The Mother of Jesus, Cath Bib Qtly; forthcoming; The Christian's Obligation Not to Forgive, Expository Times, forthcoming; Pagan and Judeo-Christian Time-keeping Schemes in Gal 4:10 and Col 2:16, New Test Stud, 96; Apostasy to Paganism: The Rhetorical Stasis of the Galatian Controversy of Bib Lit, 95; The Scythian Perspective in Col #:11, Novum Testamentum, 95; But Let Everyone Discern the Body of Christ, J Bib Lit, 95. **CONTACT ADDRESS** St Xavier Univ, 3700 W 103rd St, Chicago, IL, 60655. **EMAIL** martin@sxu.edu

MARTIN, WAYNE M.
DISCIPLINE HISTORY OF PHILOSOPHY **EDUCATION** Univ Calif-Berkeley, PhD, 93. **CAREER** UNDERGRAD ADV, UNIV CALIF, SAN DIEGO. **RESEARCH** Post-Kantian idealists; Phenomenology. **SELECTED PUBLICATIONS** Auth, "Without a Striving, No Object is Possible: Fichte's Striving Doctrine and the Primacy of Practice," New Perspectives on Fichte, Hum Press, 96; Fichte's Anti-Dogmatism, Ratio V:2,92. **CONTACT ADDRESS** Dept of Philos, Univ Calif, San Diego, 9500 Gilman Dr, La Jolla, CA, 92093.

MARTINEZ, FELIPE
PERSONAL New York, NY, m, 1976, 2 children **DISCIPLINE** ETHICS **EDUCATION** Drew Univ, PhD, 97. **CAREER** Dir, 92-97, Relig Life, exec dir, 97-, Ctr for Prom of Christian Faith, asst prof, phil & relig, Interamerican Univ, PR. **HONORS AND AWARDS** Dedman Scholar, 87, Drew Univ; Minority Acad Career Grant Scholar, St New Jersey, 87; Fund for Theol Ed scholar, 87. **MEMBERSHIPS** AAR; Assn of Puerto Rican Hist. **RESEARCH** Liberation movements and Christians in 60's PR; postmodern ethics in relig discourse. **SELECTED PUBLICATIONS** Auth, The Social Thought of Protestant Christians in the 1960's: Beginnings of a Puerto Rican Theology of Liberation, Drew Univ, 97. **CONTACT ADDRESS** El Senorial, 323 Gonzalo Berceo, San Juan, PR, 00926. **EMAIL** fmartin@caribe.net

MARTINEZ, H. SALVADOR
PERSONAL Born 03/31/1936, Leon, Spain **DISCIPLINE** MEDIEVAL SPANISH LITERATURE, PHILOSOPHY OF HISTORY **EDUCATION** Univ Rome, Dr Laurea, 60; Gregoriana Univ, Rome, Laurea, 68; Univ Toronto, PhD, 72. **CAREER** Prof Span lit & philos, Angelo State Univ, 72-76; Prof Medieval Span Lit, NY Univ, 76-. **MEMBERSHIPS** Soc Rencesvals; Asoc Int Hispanistas; Mediaeval Acad Am; MLA; Am Acad Res Historians Medieval Spain. **CONTACT ADDRESS** Dept of Span & Port, New York Univ, 19 University Pl, New York, NY, 10003-4556. **EMAIL** hsm1@is.nyu.edu

MARTINEZ, JACQUELINE M.
DISCIPLINE SEMIOTICS, PHENOMENOLOGY, FEMINIST THEORY, INTERCULTURAL COMMUNICATION **EDUCATION** Southern Ill Univ, PhD, 92. **CAREER** Asst prof, Purdue Univ. **SELECTED PUBLICATIONS** Auth, Radical Ambiguities and the Chicana Lesbian; Body Topographies on Contested Lands, in Spoils of War: Women of Color, Cultures, Revolutions, 97; coauth, Signifying Harassment: Communication, Ambiguity, and Power, Human Stud, 95. **CONTACT ADDRESS** Dept of Commun, Purdue Univ, 1080 Schleman Hall, West Lafayette, IN, 47907-1080. **EMAIL** martinez@purdue.edu

MARTINEZ, ROY
PERSONAL Born 01/25/1947, Dangriga, Belize, m, 1 child **DISCIPLINE** PHILOSOPHY **EDUCATION** Univ De Montreal, PhD, 86 **CAREER** Chair, 87-95, Chair, 96-pres, Spelman Col **HONORS AND AWARDS** Phi Beta Kappa, Epsilon of Georgia; Presidential Fac Award for Scholarly Achievement **MEMBERSHIPS** Am Philos Assoc; Int Assoc for Philos and Lit **RESEARCH** Kierkegaard; Hermeneutics; Ethics **SELECTED PUBLICATIONS** Ed, The Very Idea of Radical Hermeneutics, Humanities Press, 97; Auth, Speech-Acts, Kierkecaard, and Postmodern Thought, International Philosophical Quarterly, 97 **CONTACT ADDRESS** Spelman Col, PO Box 37, Atlanta, GA, 30314. **EMAIL** rmartine@spelman.edu

MARTINICH, ALOYSIUS PATRICK
PERSONAL Born 06/28/1946, Cleveland, OH, m, 1973, 3 children **DISCIPLINE** PHILOSOPHY **EDUCATION** Univ Windsor, BA, 69; Univ Calif, San Diego, MA, 71, PHD, 73. **CAREER** From Asst Prof to Assoc Prof, 73-85, Prof Philos, Univ Tex, Austin, 85-. **MEMBERSHIPS** Am Philos Asn. **RESEARCH** Philosophy of language; philosophical theology; modern philosophy. **SELECTED PUBLICATIONS** Ed, Certainty and Surface in Epistemology and Philosophical Method, The Edwin Mellen Press, 91; auth, Two Gods of Leviathan: Thomas Hobbes on Religion and Politics, Cambridge Univ Press, 92; A Hobbes Dictionary, Blackwell Publ, 95; Thomas Hobbes Perspectives on British History, MacMillan, 97, St. Martin's Press, 97; Thomas Hobbes: A Biography, Cambridge Univ Press (forthcoming 99). **CONTACT ADDRESS** Dept of Philos, Univ of Tex, Austin, TX, 78712-1026. **EMAIL** martinich@mail.utexas.edu

MARTINSON, PAUL V.
PERSONAL China **DISCIPLINE** CHRISTIAN MISSIONS; WORLD RELIGIONS **EDUCATION** St Olaf Col, BA, 57; Luther Sem, BD, 61; Univ Chicago Divinity Sch, MA, 69, PhD, 73. **CAREER** Instr, 65-67; asst prof, 72; prof, 84-. **HONORS AND AWARDS** Bd ch, Midwest China Study Resource Center; asst pastor, Truth Lutheran Church, 63-67; supervis, Lutheran Middle Sch(s), Kowloon, Yuen-long, 66-67. **MEMBERSHIPS** Mem, Assn for Asian Stud (s); Amer Acad of Rel; Amer Soc of Missiology; Intl Assn for Mission Stud (s); Assoc prof(s) of Missions; Intl Assn of Buddhist Stud (s); founding mem, Soc for Stud of Chinese Rel. **SELECTED PUBLICATIONS** Auth, A Theology of World Religions: Interpreting God, Self, and the World Semitic, Indian, and Chinese Thought, 87; Islam: An Introduction for Christians, 95. **CONTACT ADDRESS** Dept of Christian Missions and World Religions, Luther Sem, 2481 Como Ave, St. Paul, MN, 55108. **EMAIL** pmartins@luthersem.edu

MARTINSON, ROLAND
DISCIPLINE PASTORAL THEOLOGY; MINISTRY **EDUCATION** Luther Sem, BD, 68; San Francisco Theol Sem, STD, 78. **CAREER** Scholar-in-residence, Inst Rel and Wholeness, 85-86; asst prof, 77; prof, 82-. **HONORS AND AWARDS** Pastor, Salem Lutheran Church, 68-74; Hope Lutheran Church, 74. **MEMBERSHIPS** Mem, Nat Coun on Family Rel(s). **RESEARCH** Pastoral care. **SELECTED PUBLICATIONS** Auth, Gearing Up for Youth Ministry in the 21st Century, 92; Effective Youth Ministry, A Congregational Approach, 88; Bringing Up Your Child and Ministries with Families, 86; A Joyful Call to Ministry, 82. **CONTACT ADDRESS** Dept of Pastoral Care, Luther Sem, 2481 Como Ave, St. Paul, MN, 55108. **EMAIL** rmartins@luthersem.edu

MARTLAND, THOMAS RODOLPHE
PERSONAL Born 05/29/1926, Port Chester, NY, m, 1952, 2 children **DISCIPLINE** PHILOSOPHY, RELIGION **EDUCATION** Fordham Univ, BS, 51, magna cum laude; Columbia Univ, MA, 55, PhD, 59. **CAREER** Asst prof, Lafayette Col, 59-65, Jones distinguished fac, lectr, 63; assoc prof philos, Southern IL Univ, 65-66; Assoc Prof Philos, Univ at Albany, 66-84; Fac exchange scholar, State Univ NY, 76-77; mem advisory comt, Literature and the Arts, MN Conf on Comparative Lit, 76-77, mem advisory comt Conf on the Epistemological Relations between the Sci and Humanities, Miami Univ, Oxford, Ohio, 76; Assoc dir, reg resource center for the Nat Asc for Humanitities Ed, 79-82; Guest ed, Annuals of Scholar, 81; Dir Conf on Representation, Univ Albany, 81, Prof, 84-97; Prog chair, Conf on Art, Myth and Religion, James Mason Univ, Fairfax, Va, 86; Distinguished Jeannette K Watson vis prof of Relig, Syracuse Univ, 87; Dir Conf on Spaces: In Architecture & Dance, Univ Albany, 88; Dir, Relig Studies prog, 80-87, dir grad studies prog of Phil, 89-91, dir master of arts in Liberal studies, 95-97, res prof, phil, Univ at Albany 97. **HONORS AND AWARDS** Jones Fund Award for Superior Tchg, Lafayette Col, 62-63; Fac res award, Lafayette Col, 63, 64, Southern IL Univ, 65, Univ at Albany, 67, 68, 71, 87; Signum Laudis Award for Excellence in Tchg and Res, Univ at Albany, 86. **MEMBERSHIPS** Mem, Prog Comt, Am Soc for Aestheics, 79; Chair, Exec Comt Int Assoc for Phil and Relig, 80-81, mem 76-81; Mem, Advisory Comt, Conf on Deconstructionism, Univ at Stony Brook, 83; Mem, Advisory Comt Conf on Philosophy as Lit: Lit as Philos, Univ IA, IA City, 84; Ch, Eastern Div Am Soc for Aesthetics, 87-88, mem 85-88. **RESEARCH** Philos of relig; aesthetics; philos of the hum. **SELECTED PUBLI-**

CATIONS Auth, The Metaphysics of William James and John-Dewey, 69; Religion as Art: An Interpretation, 81 (4th print); Essays in books, Religion as an Aspect of the Various Disciplines, In: The Status of Religious Studies in Public Universities (Milton D. McLean, ed), 67; When is Religion Art? Answer: When It Is a Jar, In: Art, Creativity and the Sacred (Diane Apostolos-Cappadona, ed), 84; Quine's Half Entities', and Gadamer's Too, In: Philosophy as Literature: Literature as Philosophy (Donald Marshall, ed), 87; The Sublime, The Encyclopedia of Religion (Mircea Eliade, ed), 87; Other articles have appeared in Jour of Phil, Am Phil Quart, Jour Aesthetic and Art Criticism, Jour Comparative Lit and Aesthetics, Jour Am Acad of Relig, Phil and Phenomenological Res, Rev of Metaphysics, Brit Jour of Aesthetics, Relig Studies, and The Monist. **CONTACT ADDRESS** Dept of Philos, Univ at Albany, 1400 Washington Ave, Albany, NY, 12222. **EMAIL** l.martland@albany.edu

MARTOS, JOSEPH
PERSONAL Born 06/11/1943, New York, NY **DISCIPLINE** RELIGIOUS STUDIES **EDUCATION** Gregorian Univ (Rome), STB, 66; DePaul Univ, PhD, 73. **CAREER** Assoc Prof & Chmn Theol Dept, Allentown Col, PA, 85-92; Prof & Chmn, Russell Inst, Spalding Univ, LA, 92-. **MEMBERSHIPS** AAR; CTSA; CTS; NALM **RESEARCH** History; ritual; culture. **SELECTED PUBLICATIONS** Doors to the Sacred: A Historical Introduction to Sacraments in the Catholic Church, Triumph Bks, 91; Sacrament of Reconciliation, Modern Catholic Ency, 94; The Wild Man's Journey: Reflections on Male Spirituality, St Anthony Messenger Press, 96; Equal at the Creation: Sexism, Society, and Christian Thought, Univ of Toronto Press, 98. **CONTACT ADDRESS** Spalding Univ, Louisville, KY, 40203. **EMAIL** spalding8@humanities.win.net

MARTY, MARTIN EMIL
PERSONAL Born 02/05/1928, West Point, NE, m, 1952, 5 children **DISCIPLINE** MODERN RELIGIOUS HISTORY **EDUCATION** Concordia Sem, BA, 49, MDiv, 52; Lutheran Sch Theol, Chicago, STM, 54; Univ Chicago, PhD(church hist), 56. **CAREER** From assoc prof to prof relig hist, 63-78, assoc dean divinity sch, 70-75, F M CONE DISTINGUISHED SERV PROF, UNIV CHICAGO, 78-, Vis assoc prof, Lutheran Sch Theol, Chicago, 61 & Union Theol Sem, New York, 65; bd mem, Nat Humanities Ctr, 76-; assoc ed, Christian Century, ed newslet, Context & coed, Church Hist. **HONORS AND AWARDS** Nat Bk Award, 72., Nineteen from US cols & univs. **MEMBERSHIPS** Fel Am Acad Arts & Sci; Soc Am Historians; Soc Values Higher Educ. **RESEARCH** Nineteenth century religious history of United States, Great Britain and Western Europe; effects of political-industrial revolutions on religion; history of religious behavior in America. **SELECTED PUBLICATIONS** Auth, American Religious History in the 80s, Church Hist, vol 0062, 93; Dictionary of American Religious Biography, 2nd ed, Cath Hist Rev, vol 0079, 93; From the Centripetal to the Centrifugal in Culture ind Religion, Theol Today, vol 0051, 94; Religion and Radical Politics, J Relig, vol 0074, 94; Defending the Faith, J Amer Hist, vol 0082, 95; Evangelicalism, J Southern Hist, vol 0061, 95; God in the Wasteland, J Relig, vol 0076, 96; Neale, J.M. and the Quest for Sobornost, J Relig, vol 0076, 96; Religion, Public Life, and the American Polity, J Relig, vol 0077, 97. **CONTACT ADDRESS** Divinity Sch Swift Hall, Univ of Chicago, Chicago, IL, 60637.

MARTYN, JAMES LOUIS
PERSONAL Born 10/11/1925, Dallas, TX, m, 1950, 3 children **DISCIPLINE** NEW TESTAMENT **EDUCATION** Tex Agr & Mech Col, BS, 46; Andover Newton Theol Sch, BD, 52; Yale Univ, MA, 56, PhD, 57. **CAREER** Instr Bibl hist, Wellesley Coll, 58-59; from asst prof to assoc prof New Testament, 59-67, Edward Robinson Prof Bibl Theol, Union Theol Sem, NY, 67-, Fulbright fel, Univ Gottingen, 57-58; Guggenheim fel, 63-64. **MEMBERSHIPS** Soc Bibl Lit. **RESEARCH** The Fourth Gospel; Jewish Christianity. **SELECTED PUBLICATIONS** Auth, Notes and Comments on the Letter of James, United Christian Youth Movement, 62; co-ed, Studies in Luke-Acts, Abingdon, 66; auth, Epistemology at the turn of the ages, In: Christian History and Interpretation, Cambridge, 67; Attitudes ancient and modern toward tradition about Jesus, Study World, 67; History and Theology in the Fourth Gospel, Harper, 68, rev ed, Abingdon, 78; Source criticism and religionageschichte in the Fourth Gospel, Perspective, 70; The Gospel of John in Christian History, Paulist, 78. **CONTACT ADDRESS** Union Theol Sem, 3041 Broadway, New York, NY, 10027.

MARTYN, SUSAN
DISCIPLINE LAW **EDUCATION** St Olaf Col, BA, MArquette Univ, JD. **CAREER** Prof. **SELECTED PUBLICATIONS** Auth, Informed Consent in the Practice of Law, Univ Wash, 80; Peer Review and Quality Assurance for Lawyers, Univ Toledo, 88; Coming to Terms with Death: The Cruzan Case, Hastings, 91; Physician Assisted Suicide: The Lethal Flaws of the Ninth and Second Circuit Decisions, Law Rev, 97. **CONTACT ADDRESS** Col Law, Univ of Toledo, Toledo, OH, 43606. **EMAIL** smartyn@uoft02.utoledo.edu

MASCHER, SHARON
DISCIPLINE LAW **EDUCATION** McGill Univ, BA, 86; Univ Calgary, LLB, 90, LLM, 94. **CAREER** Asst prof. **SELECTED PUBLICATIONS** Auth, Australia's National Greenhouse Response: Implications for the Energy Sector, 97; Taking the Precautionary Approach: New Zealand Fisheries, Environ Planning Law Jour, 97; Environmental Protection under Common Law, 97; co-auth, Water Law in Australia: Comparative Studies and Options for Reform, 97. **CONTACT ADDRESS** Col of Law, Univ Saskatchewan, 15 Campus Dr, Saskatoon, SK, S7N 5A6.

MASCHKE, TIMOTHY
DISCIPLINE THEOLOGY **EDUCATION** Concordia Sem, MDiv, 74, STM, 81; Trinity Evang Div Sch, DMin, 84; Marquette Univ, PhD, 93. **CAREER** Asst prof, 82-87, assoc prof, 88-97, PROF, 97-, CONCORDIA UNIV. **CONTACT ADDRESS** Concordia Univ, Wisconsin, 12800 N Lake Shore Dr, Mequon, WI, 53097-2402. **EMAIL** Timothy_Maschke@cuw.edu

MASHBURN, AMY R.
DISCIPLINE LAW **EDUCATION** Eckerd Col, BA; Univ Fla, JD. **CAREER** Prof, Univ Fla, 90-; past assoc, Dean, Mead, Egerton, Bloodworth, Capouano Bozarth, Orlando, Fla; articles ed, Fla Law Rev. **MEMBERSHIPS** Fla Bar; Order of the Coif; mem, Fla Bar Prof Ethics Comt; mem. Fla Bar Standing Comt on Professionalism. **RESEARCH** Civil procedure, professional responsibility, administrative law. **CONTACT ADDRESS** School of Law, Univ of Florida, PO Box 117625, Gainesville, FL, 32611-7625. **EMAIL** mashburn@law.ufl.edu

MASK, E. JEFFEREY
DISCIPLINE THEOLOGY **EDUCATION** Univ Mississippi, BA, 77; Southeastern Baptist Theol Sem, MDiv, 81; Emory Univ, PhD, 90. **CAREER** Asst Prof, 91-95, Assoc Prof, 95-, Wesley Col. **CONTACT ADDRESS** Wesley Col, Dover, DE, 19901. **EMAIL** maskje@mail.wesley.edu

MASOLO, D.A.
DISCIPLINE PHILOSOPHY **EDUCATION** Gregorian Univ, Rome, PhD. **CAREER** Justus Bier prof of hum. **RESEARCH** The impact of cult(s) on moral and conceptual knowledge. **SELECTED PUBLICATIONS** Auth, bk chapters on ethics, social and political philos, and African philosophy; ed, co-ed, several bk(s), Philosophy and Cultures; African Philosophy In Search of Identity, Ind Univ Press, Edinburgh UP, 94. **CONTACT ADDRESS** Dept of Philos, Univ Louisville, 2301 S 3rd St, Louisville, KY, 40292. **EMAIL** damaso01@ulkyvm.louisville.edu

MASON, DAVID RAYMOND
PERSONAL Born 11/06/1936, Hagerstown, MD, m, 1963, 3 children **DISCIPLINE** PHILOSOPHICAL & CONTEMPORARY THEOLOGY **EDUCATION** WVA Univ, AB, 59; Gen Theol Sem, MDiv, 62; Univ Chicago, MA, 69, PhD, 73. **CAREER** Instr philos, Cent YMCA Community Col, 68-70 & 71-72; asst prof relig studies, 72-76, Assoc Prof Relig Studies John Carroll Univ, 77, Prof, 82, Dir Tuohy Chair, 97, Grauel fac, fel, John Carroll Univ, 79, 86. **MEMBERSHIPS** Am Acad Relig; Soc Studies Process Milos; Metaphys Soc Am. **RESEARCH** Whitehead studies; correlation of concepts of time and providence, particularly historically and present possibilities; the logic of God-lang. **SELECTED PUBLICATIONS** Auth, Three recent treatments of the ontological argument, Ohio J Relig, spring 74; An examination of Worship as a key for reexamining the God problem, J Relig, 1/75; Can we speculate on how God acts?, J of Relig, 1/77; Some abstract yet crucial thoughts about suffering, Dialog, spring 77; What sense does it make to say God knows future contingent things?, J Relig Studies, spring 79; Time and Providence, Univ Press Am, 82; Can God be both perfect and free, Relig Studies, 2/82; Selfhood, Transcendence, & the Experience of God, Modern Theology, 87; Gilkeyon God and the World, Am Jour of Theol & Philos, 95; The Self and Its Body: A Model for the God-World Relation, Jour of Relig Studies, 95. **CONTACT ADDRESS** Dept of Relig Studies, John Carroll Univ, 20700 N Park Blvd, Cleveland, OH, 44118-4581. **EMAIL** dmason@jcvaxa.jcu.edu

MASON, H.E.
DISCIPLINE PHILOSOPHY **EDUCATION** Harvard Univ, PhD. **RESEARCH** Moral and political philosophy; philosophy of the mind; Wittgenstein. **SELECTED PUBLICATIONS** Auth, Realistic Interpretations of Moral Questions, Univ Minn, 88; On the Many Faces of Morality: Reflections on Fear and Trembling, 88; AIDS: Some Ethical Considerations, Minn Medicine, 87; On the Treatment of the Notion of the Will in Wittgenstein's Later Writings, 86; On Wittgenstein's Use of the Notion of a Language Game, 78; co-auth, Some Thought Experiments about Mind and Meaning, Stanford, 90. **CONTACT ADDRESS** Philosophy Dept, Univ of Minnesota, Twin Cities, 355 Ford Hall, 224 Church St SE, Minneapolis, MN, 55455. **EMAIL** hmason@tc.umn.edu

MASON, HERBERT WARREN
PERSONAL Born 04/20/1932, Wilmington, DE, m, 1954, 3 children **DISCIPLINE** ISLAMIC HISTORY & RELIGION **EDUCATION** Harvard Univ, AB, 55, AM, 65, PhD, 69. **CAREER** Teaching fel & lectr, Harvard Univ, 62-67; UNIV PROF, BOSTON UNIV, 72-; Lectr English lit, St Joseph's Col, 60-62; vis lectr, Simmons Col, 62-63; vis lectr Islamic hist, Tufts Univ, 65-66; tranls & ed, Bollingen Found, 68-72; coed, Humaniora Islamica, 72-76; guest lectr various univ, 73-79 & Libr of Congress, 79. **MEMBERSHIPS** Am Oriental Soc; Mark Twain Soc; Medieval Acad Am; Am Acad Relig; PEN; Am Hist Asn; Am Academy of Poets. **RESEARCH** Islamic history, literature and religion, especially Sufism; Arabic: translation of sources; comparative medieval studies: Islamic, Latin European & Byzantine sources. **SELECTED PUBLICATIONS** Ed, Reflections on the Middle East Crisis, Mouton & Co, 70; auth, Gilgamesh, A Verse Narrative, Houghton Mifflin Co, 71; Two Statesmen of Medieval Islam, Mouton & Co, 72; En Parlant de Gilgamesh Avec Louis Massignon, L'Herne, Paris, 75; The Death of al-Hallaj, Notre Dame Univ Press, 79; Summer Light, Farrar, Straus and Giroux, 80; Gilpins Point, Sewanee Rev, 80; ed & transl, The Passion of al-Hallaj, Princeton Univ Press, 82; A Legend of Alexander, Notre Dame Univ Press, 86; Memoir of a Friend: Louis Massignon, Notre Dame Univ Press, 88; Testimonies and Reflections, Notre Dame Univ Press, 89; Al-Hallaj, Curzon Press, UK, 95; Haythu Taltaqi al-Anhar, novel in Arabic, Abu Dhabi Press, 98. **CONTACT ADDRESS** 745 Commonwealth Ave, Boston, MA, 02215-1401.

MASON, JEFFREY A.
PERSONAL Born 05/26/1945, Galveston, TX, m, 1977, 2 children **DISCIPLINE** PHILOSOPHY **EDUCATION** Birbeck Col, London, PhD, 75. **CAREER** Middlesex Polytech, London, 72-75, 76-82; Calif State, 75-76; Calif State, San Diego, 82-83; Middlesex Univ, 93-98. **MEMBERSHIPS** APA. **RESEARCH** Philosophy and rhetoric. **SELECTED PUBLICATIONS** Auth, Philosophical Rhetoric, Routledge, 89; auth, The Future of Thinking, Routledge, 92; auth, The Philosopher's Address, Lexington, forthcoming. **CONTACT ADDRESS** 825 12th St, Huntington Beach, CA, 92648. **EMAIL** jeff4@net999.com

MASON, SHEILA
DISCIPLINE ADVANCED ETHICS PHILOSOPHY, PHILOSOPHY OF LEISURE **EDUCATION** McGill Univ, BA, 65; Purdue Univ, MA, 67, PhD, 72. **CAREER** Assoc prof. **SELECTED PUBLICATIONS** Auth, "Enseigner l'ethique selon le paradigme du 'moi moralement lie'," Philosopher No 16, 94; Education for Leisure: Moving towards Community, Leisure and Ethics: Reflections on the Philosophy of Leisure Vol II, Amer Assoc for Leisure and Recreation, 95; L'Intelligence Morale, Actes du Colloque:'De L'Ethique aux ethiques', Ethica, 97; The Self and the Ethics of Care, The Conceptual Self in Context, Cambridge UP, 97; L'ethique Narrative et la compassion, ERES Groupe de Recherche en Ethique Sociale, 98. **CONTACT ADDRESS** Dept of Philos, Concordia Univ, Montreal, 1455 de Maisonneuve W, Montreal, PQ, H3G 1M8. **EMAIL** eud@vax2.concordia.ca

MASON, STEVE
PERSONAL Born 09/14/1957, Toronto, ON, Canada **DISCIPLINE** EARLY JUDAISM AND CHRISTIAN ORIGINS **EDUCATION** McMaster Univ, BA, 80, MA, 81; Univ St Michaels Col, PhD, 86. **CAREER** Vis asst prof, Mem Univ NF, 87-89; prof and head, Dept Classics & Ancient Mediter Stud, Penn State Univ, 96-96; asst prof, 89-92, assoc prof, 92-98, prof, 98-, York Univ-Toronto. **MEMBERSHIPS** Soc Bibl Lit; Am Philol Asn; Studiorum Novi Testamenti Soc; Can Soc Bibl Stud. **RESEARCH** Philosophy and religion in the Greco-Roman world, especially Judaism (specialization: Flavius Josephus) and early Christianity. **SELECTED PUBLICATIONS** Coed An Early Christian Reader, Can Scholars Press, 90; auth Flavius Josephus on the Pharisees, E J Brill, 91; Josephus and the New Testament, Hendrickson, 92; ed Understanding Josephus: Seven Perspectives, Sheffield Acad Press, 98. **CONTACT ADDRESS** York Univ, 219 Vanier Col, Toronto, ON, M3J 1P3. **EMAIL** smason@yorku.ca

MASSANARI, RONALD LEE
PERSONAL Born 06/04/1941, Champaign, IL, m, 1963, 2 children **DISCIPLINE** HISTORY OF CHRISTIAN THOUGHT **EDUCATION** Goshen Col, BA, 63; Univ Wis-Madison, MA, 65; Garrett Theol Sem, BD, 66; Duke Univ, PhD(relig), 69. **CAREER** Vis asst prof church hist, Divinity Sch, Duke Univ, 69-70; from asst prof to assoc prof, 70-80, PROF RELIG, ALMA COL, 80-, Adj prof, San Francisco Theol Sem, 77-. **MEMBERSHIPS** Am Soc Church Hist; Am Acad Relig **RESEARCH** Religion and imagination; myth and ritual; political theology. **SELECTED PUBLICATIONS** Auth, True or false socialism: Adolf Stoecker's critique of Marxism from a Christian socialist perspective, Church Hist, 72; Christian socialism in nineteenth century Germany: A case study of a shift in anthropological perspective, Union Sem Theol Quart, 73; Vision and praxis, 77 & The politics of imagination, 77, Cross Currents; An exploration into religious symbolism, Relig in Life, 77; Time line, circle time, beneath and beyond, 78 & In the image of the father, but ..., 80, Relig in Life; A Journey with the Great Mother, Anima, 81. **CONTACT ADDRESS** Dept of Relig, Alma Col, 614 W Superior St, Alma, MI, 48801-1511.

MASSEY, GERALD J.
PERSONAL Born 02/11/1934, Wauseon, OH, m, 1957, 4 children **DISCIPLINE** PHILOSOPHY OF SCIENCE, SYMBOLIC LOGIC **EDUCATION** Univ Notre Dame, BA, 56, MA, 60; Princeton Univ, MA, 62, PhD(philos), 64. **CAREER** From Asst prof to prof philos, Mich State Univ, 63-70; chmn dept philos, 70-76, Prof Philos, Hist & Philos Sci, Univ Pittsburgh, 76, SR RES ASSOC, CTR PHILOS SCI, 76-, Mellon fel, Univ Pittsburgh, 69-70. **MEMBERSHIPS** Philos Sci Asn (secy-treas, 65-70); Asn Symbolic Logic; Am Philos Asn; Am Cath Philos Asn; AAUP. **RESEARCH** Modal logic, philosophy of physical geometry; philosophical logic. **SELECTED PUBLICATIONS** Auth, The Laboratory of the Mind, Philos Sci, vol 0062, 95. **CONTACT ADDRESS** Dept of Philos, Univ of Pittsburgh, Pittsburgh, PA, 15260.

MASSEY, JAMES EARL
PERSONAL Born 01/04/1930, Ferndale, MI, m **DISCIPLINE** THEOLOGY **EDUCATION** Detroit Bible Coll, BRE, BTh 1961; Oberlin Grad School of Theol, AM 1964; Asbury Theol Seminary, DD 1972; Pacific School of Religion, addit study 1972; Univ of MI; Boston Coll Grad School; Ashland Theological Seminary, DD, 1991; Huntington Coll, DD, 1994; Tuskegee Univ, Hum D, 1995; Warner Pacific College, DD, 1995; Anderson University, Litt D, 1995; Washington & Jefferson College, DD, 1997. **CAREER** Church of God of Detroit, assoc minister 1949-51, 1953-54; Metro Church of God, sr pastor 1954-76; Anderson Coll, School of Theol, campus minister, prof of religious studies 1969-77; Christian Brotherhood, speaker 1977-82; Anderson University, School of Theol, prof of new testament 1981-84; Tuskegee Univ Chapel & Univ Prof of Religion, dean 1984-89; ANDERSON UNIVERSITY, SCHOOL OF THEOLOGY, dean, professor of preaching and Biblical studies, 1990-95, DEAN EMERITUS & PROF AT LARGE, currently. **HONORS AND AWARDS** Danforth Foundation, Underwood Fellow, 1972-73; Staley Foundation, Staley Distinguished Christian Scholar, 1977; Wesleyan Theological Society, Lifetime Achievement Award, 1995. **MEMBERSHIPS** Lecturer Gautschi Lectures Fuller Theol Sem 1975-1986; Freitas Lectures Asbury Theol Sem 1977, Rall Co-Lecturer Garrett-Evangelical Sem 1980, Mullins Lectures So Bapt Sem 1981, Swartley Lectures Eastern Baptist Sem 1982, Jameson Jones Lecturer Iliff School of Theol 1983, Rom Lectures Trinity Evangelical DivSchool 1984; northcutt lectures Southwestern Bapt Theol Sem 1986;l bd of dir Detroit Council of Churches; theol study commiss Detroit Council of Churches; corp mem Inter-Varsity Christian Fellowship; matl comm Black Churchmen; mem Wesleyan Theol Soc; ed bd Christian Scholars Review; bd of dir Warner Press Inc; vchmn Publ Bd of the Church of God; ed adv Tyndale House Publisher 1968-69; comm chmn Christian Unity; mem Natl Assoc of Coll & Univ Chaplains; bdof dir Natl Black Evangelical oc; life mem NAACP; Lausanne Continuation Comm 1974-; pres Anderson Civil Serv Merit Commiss 1975-81; ed bd Leadership Mag; bd of dir Natl Religious Broadcasteers; ed bd Preaching Mag 1987; Resource Scholar, Christianity Today Inst 1985; sr editor, Christanity Today, 1993-95. **CONTACT ADDRESS** Sch of Theology, Anderson Univ, Anderson, IN, 46012-3462.

MATASAR, RICHARD
PERSONAL Born 06/04/1952, m, 1975, 2 children **DISCIPLINE** LAW **EDUCATION** Univ Pa, BA, 74; Univ Pa, JD, 77. **CAREER** Law Clerk, Judge Max rosenn, U.S. Court of Appeals for the Third Circuit, 77-78; assoc atty, Arnold & Porter, 78-80; assoc prof, Univ of Iowa; DEAN, COL OF LAW, UNIV FLA. **HONORS AND AWARDS** Phi Beta Kappa; Pi gamma Mu; Order of the Coif. **MEMBERSHIPS** ABA; AALS. **RESEARCH** Civil procedure; legal ethics; federal courts; professionalism; legal educ. **SELECTED PUBLICATIONS** Auth, "Rediscovering 'One Constitutional Case': Procedural Rules and the Rejection of Gibbs Test for Supplemental Jurisdiction", in 71 Calif L Rev, 83; auth, "A Pendent and Ancillary Jurisdiction Primer: The Scope and Limits of Supplemental Jurisdiction", in 17 U.C. Davis L. Rev 103, 83; coauth, "Procedural Common Law, Federal Jurisdictional Policy, and Abandonment of the Adequate and Independent State Grounds Doctrine", in 86 Colum L Rev, 86; auth, "Personal Immunities Under Section 1983: The Limits of the Court's Historical Analysis", in 40 Ark L Rev, 87; auth, "Commercialist Manifesto: Entrepreneurs, Academics, and Purity of the Heart and Soul", in 48 Fla L Rev, 96. **CONTACT ADDRESS** Univ of Florida Col of Law, PO Box 117620, Gainesville, FL, 32611-7620. **EMAIL** Matasar@law.ufl.edu

MATEJKA, GEORGE
PERSONAL Born 11/28/1950, Cleveland, OH, s **DISCIPLINE** PHILOSOPHY **EDUCATION** Cath Univ of Am, MA, 73 Philos; Gregorian Univ of Am, 81 Theol **CAREER** Asst Prof Philos, 91, Borromes Col of OH; Assoc Prof of Philos, 92-present, Notre Dame Col of OH **MEMBERSHIPS** Am Philos Assoc **RESEARCH** Umberto Eco **CONTACT ADDRESS** Notre Dame Col, 4545 College, Cleveland, OH, 44121-4293. **EMAIL** gmatejka@ndc.edu

MATHENY, PAUL DUANE
PERSONAL Born 07/13/1953, Conroe, TX, m, 1983, 1 child **DISCIPLINE** RELIGION **EDUCATION** Clarke Univ, BA; Goddard Col, MA, Princeton Theol Sem, MDiv, Yale, STM, Univ Heidelberg, DTh. **CAREER** Bellarmine Col, vis lectr; Barton Col, asst prof; Westhampton Christian Church Roanoke, VA, sr minister; First Christian Church Conroe, TX, sr minister. **MEMBERSHIPS** KBS of NA, AAR, IBS **RESEARCH** K. Barth's theology and ethics; Dietrich Bonhoeffer's life and work; theology and science. **SELECTED PUBLICATIONS** Ed. The Young Bonhoeffer, Fortress Press, forthcoming, ed. Renaissance and Reformation, T&T Clark, 92, auth, Dogmatics and Ethics, Peter Lang, 90. **CONTACT ADDRESS** First Christian Church, 549 Stephen F. Austin Dr, Conroe, TX, 77302. **EMAIL** paul.matheny.div.83@aya.yale.edu

MATHER, HENRY S.
DISCIPLINE CONTRACTS, JURISPRUDENCE, AND SECURED TRANSACTIONS **EDUCATION** Univ Rochester, BA, 59; Columbia Univ, MA, 61; Cornell Univ, JD, 70. **CAREER** Prof, Univ of SC. **SELECTED PUBLICATIONS** Publ on, contract law. **CONTACT ADDRESS** School of Law, Univ of S. Carolina, Law Center, Columbia, SC, 29208. **EMAIL** law0149@univscvm.csd.scarolina.edu

MATHEWES, CHARLES
PERSONAL Born 07/09/1969, Montclair, NJ, s **DISCIPLINE** RELIGIOUS STUDIES **EDUCATION** Univ Chicago, PhD 97, MA 92; Georgetown Univ, BA 91. **CAREER** Univ Virginia, 97-. **MEMBERSHIPS** AAR; SCE; APSA; SCP; APA. **RESEARCH** Theology; Ethics; Politics; Mural Psychology; Nature; Evil and Sin; Tradition. **SELECTED PUBLICATIONS** Auth, Augustine's Demythologizing of Evil in De Civitate Dei, in: The Unity of Belief and Practice in Early Christianity, Blackwell, forthcoming; Theology and Cultur, in: Blackwell Companion to Theol, forthcoming; Augustinian Anthropology: A Proposal and a Partial Map, Jour of Religious Ethics, forthcoming; Pluralism Otherness and the Augustine Tradition, Modern Theol, 98; rev, The Rebirth of Tragedy, Martha Nussbaum, Jonathon Lear, Bernard Williams, Anglican Theol Rev, 97. **CONTACT ADDRESS** Dept of Religious Studies, Virginia Univ, Charlottesville, VA, 22903. **EMAIL** ctmathewes@virginia.edu

MATHEWS, EDWARD G.
PERSONAL Born 06/10/1954, Albany, NY, m, 1985 **DISCIPLINE** THEOLOGY **EDUCATION** Cath univ Am, BA, 82; MA, Semitic Lang and Lit; 82; Columbia Univ NY, MA, Armenian Hist and Lit, 91; M Philos, 94; PhD, 96. **CAREER** ADJ FAC, Our lady Lebanon Maronite Sem Wash, 85; inst, Cath Univ Am Wash, 85-87; adj prof, 93; adj, Hebrew Univ Israel, 94; Evangel Theol Sem Armenia, 98; Instrm Univ Scranton, PA, 89-. **HONORS AND AWARDS** Cardinal Gibbons Scholarship, 78-82; Phi Beta Kappa, 82; Cath Univ Scholar, 84087; Cath Univ Grad Student Assoc Scholar, 86; App Pres Fel of the Fac, Columbia Univ, 90-94; Zohrab Fel, Columbia Univ, 94-96; Vis Res Fel, Hebrew Univ Jerusalem, 94-95. **MEMBERSHIPS** Soc for Bibl Lit; Asn Int des etudes armeniennes; Soc for Armenian Studies; Nat asn for Armenian Studies and Res; cath Bibl Asn; N Am Patristic Soc. **RESEARCH** History; Literature and Theology of Early Eastern Christianity; Historical biblical Exegesis; Greek Patristics. **SELECTED PUBLICATIONS** Auth, The Armenian Literary Corpus Attributed to St Ephrem the Syrian: Prolegomena to a Project, StNersess Theol Rev, 96; The Armenian Version of Ephrem's Commentary on Genesis, The Book of Genesis in Jewish and Oriental Christian Interpretation, 97; The Armenian Commentary on the Book of Genesis attributed to Ephrem the Syrian, 98. **CONTACT ADDRESS** Dept of Theology, Univ of Scranton, Scranton, PA, 18510. **EMAIL** egm381@tiger.vofs.edu

MATHEWS, MARK WILLIAM
PERSONAL Born 06/03/1955, Allentown, PA, d, 2 children **DISCIPLINE** PHILOSOPHY **EDUCATION** Colgate Univ, BA, 77; Univ Minn, PhD, 93. **CAREER** Metropolitan State Univ, asst prof, 91-. **HONORS AND AWARDS** Outstanding Tchr of the Yr. **MEMBERSHIPS** APA, ACJS. **RESEARCH** Ethics; Professional and law enforcement ethics. **CONTACT ADDRESS** Dept of Philosophy, Metropolitan State Univ, 1770 James Ave S #2, Minneapolis, MN, 55403-2827. **EMAIL** mmathews@msvs.edu

MATHIS, ROBERT
PERSONAL m, 1 child **DISCIPLINE** CHURCH ADMINISTRATION **EDUCATION** Univ Tex, MEd, 76; Southwestern Baptist Theol Sem, MRE, 78, PhD, 84; Univ Miss, EdD, 95. **CAREER** Instr, Hale Ctr ISD, 69-70; prof, NOBTS, 86-98. **HONORS AND AWARDS** S Baptist res fel; Outstanding res award, SBRF, 95., Min edu, Mountainview Baptist Church, 74-77; Ridglea Baptist Church, 77-81; assoc pastor, 81-86. **MEMBERSHIPS** Rel Res Assn, SBREA. **SELECTED PUBLICATIONS** Auth, Teacher Preparation Material, The Adult Teacher, 94; Submission, Theol Educator, 92. **CONTACT ADDRESS** Sch Edu Ministries, Southwestern Baptist Theol Sem, PO Box 22000, Fort Worth, TX, 76122-0418. **EMAIL** rrm@swbts.swbts.edu

MATILAL, BIMAL KRISHNA
PERSONAL Born 06/01/1935, Joynagar, India, m, 1958, 1 child **DISCIPLINE** INDIAN PHILOSOPHY AND LINGUISTICS **EDUCATION** Univ Calcutta, BA, 54, MA, 56; Harvard Univ, AM, 63, PhD(Indian logic), 65. **CAREER** Lectr Sanskrit lit, Govt Sanskrit Col, Univ Calcutta, 57-62; from asst prof to assoc prof, 65-71, PROF INDIAN PHILOS, UNIV TORONTO, 71-, Guest lectr, III Int Cong Orient, 67-; Can Coun travel grant, 67; UNESCO Coun Humanities & Philos grant, 67; overseas res lei, Univ Toronto, 67; assoc prof, Univ Pa, 69-70; ed, J Indian Philos, Reidel, 70-; vis sr fel, Univ London, 71-72. **MEMBERSHIPS** Am Orient Soc; Soc Asian & Comp Philos (vpres, 73-). **RESEARCH** Indian logic and epistemology; theories of linguistics and semantics in ancient India; Sanskrit literature and literary criticism. **SELECTED PUBLICATIONS** Auth, Is Prasanga a Form of Deconstruction, J Indian Philos, vol 0020, 92; A Note on Samkara Theodicy, J Indian Philos, vol 0020, 92. **CONTACT ADDRESS** Dept of Sanskrit & Indian Studies, Univ of Toronto, Toronto, ON, M5S 1A1.

MATOVINA, TIMOTHY M.
PERSONAL Born 10/13/1955, Hammond, IN, m, 1996, 1 child **DISCIPLINE** RELIGIOUS STUDIES **EDUCATION** Cath Univ of Am, PhD, 93. **CAREER** Asst prof, 95-. **MEMBERSHIPS** Am Acad of Relig; Acad of Cath Hispanic Theol; Am Hist Asn. **RESEARCH** Religion; Cultural studies; Latino studies; Catholicism; Ethnicity. **SELECTED PUBLICATIONS** Co-auth, San Fernando Cathedral: Soul of the City, 98; Mestizo Worship: A Pastoral Approach to Liturgical Ministry, 98; auth, Tejano Religion and Ethnicity: San Antonio, 1821-1860, 95; The Alamo Remembered: Tejano Accounts and Perspectives, 95; co-ed, Defending Mexican Valor in Texas: Jose Antonio Navarro's Historical Writings, 1853-1857, 95; auth, "New Frontiers of Guadalupanismo" in J of Hispanic/Latin Theol, 97; "Sacred Place and Collective Memory: San Fernando Cathedral, San Antonio, Texas" in U.S. Cath Historian, 97; "Guadalupan Devotion in a Borderlands Community" in J of Hispanic/Latino Theol, 96; "Lay Initiatives in Worship on the Texas Frontera, 1830-1860" in U.S. Cath Historian, 94. **CONTACT ADDRESS** Dept of Theological Studies, Loyola Marymount Univ, 7900 Loyola Blvd, Los Angeles, CA, 90045-8400. **EMAIL** tmatovin@popmail.lmu.edu

MATSEN, HERBERT S.
PERSONAL Born 03/15/1926, Portland, OR, m, 1987 **DISCIPLINE** PHILOSOPHY **EDUCATION** Wash State Col, BS, 50; Columbia Univ, MA, 61, PhD, 69. **CAREER** Instr, Wash Col, 60-61; instr, 62-65, asst prof, 66-68, Converse Col; asst prof, 69-72 assoc prof, 72-82, Univ S Carolina; Phi Beta Kappa; Phi Kappa Phi; Irwin Edman Scholar philos; Fulbright grant Italy, 58-60. **MEMBERSHIPS** Medieval Acad Am; Renaissance Soc Am; SIPPM. **RESEARCH** Philosophy of medicine at Bologna from 1300-1600; Alessandro Achillini (1463-1512); History of European Universities in the Middle Ages and Renaissance. **SELECTED PUBLICATIONS** Alessandro Achillini (1463-1512) and his Doctrine of Universals and Transcendentals: A Study in Renaissance Ockhamism, Bucknell Univ Press, 74; The Influence of Duns Scotus and his Followers on the Philosophy of A Achillini, Regnum Hominis et Regnum Dei, Crome, 78; Students "Arts" Disputations at Bologna around 1500, Renaissance Quart, 94. **CONTACT ADDRESS** 605 S 34th Ave, Yakima, WA, 98902-3928.

MATTER, EDITH ANN
PERSONAL Born 12/29/1949, Ft Smith, AR **DISCIPLINE** HISTORY OF CHRISTIANITY **EDUCATION** Oberline Col, BA, 71; Yale Univ, MA, 75, PhD(relig studies), 76. **CAREER** Lectr, 76, ASST PROF RELIG STUDIES, UNIV PA, 77-, Grant-in-aid text studies, Univ Pa, 78. **MEMBERSHIPS** Am Acad Relig, Women's Caucus; Mediaeval Acad Am; Am Soc Church Hist; Southeastern Medieval Asn. **RESEARCH** Biblical study in the Early Middle Ages; women in Medieval monasticism; textual editing. **SELECTED PUBLICATIONS** Auth, Paulinus of Aquileia, Opera Omnia, vol 1--Contra Felicem Libri Tres, Speculum-J Medieval Stud, vol 0068, 93; The Letters of Catherine of Siena, vol 1, Church Hist, vol 0062, 93, Friendship and Community--The Monastic Experience, 350-1250, Speculum-J Medieval Stud, vol 0068, 93; The Cult of the Virgin Mary in Anglo Saxon England, Church Hist, vol 0062, 93; Readings on the Song of Songs, Jewish Quart Rev, vol 0083, 93; Andreas De Sancto Victore, vol 6--Expositio in Ezechielem 'Exposition on Ezekiel', Speculum-J Medieval Stud, vol 0069, 94; Meanings of Sex Difference in the Middle Ages, J Interdisciplinary Hist, vol 0026, 95; Egyptian Obelisks--Politics and Culture in Rome During the Baroque Period, 16th Century J, vol 0026, 95; Angela of Foligno, Church Hist, vol 0064, 95; Eriugena--East and West, Church Hist, vol 0064, 95; Through a Speculum that Shines, Church Hist, vol 0065, 96; Eros and Allegory--Medieval Exegesis of the 'Song of Songs', Theol Stud, vol 0057, 96; A Conflict of Traditions--Women in Religion in the Early Middle Ages Ad500-840, Church Hist, vol 0065, 96; Biblical Commentaries from the Canterbury-School of Theodore and Hadrian, Speculum-J Medieval Stud, vol 0072, 97. **CONTACT ADDRESS** Dept of Relig Studies, Univ Pa, 236 S 34th St, Philadelphia, PA, 19104-3804.

MATTHAEI, SONDRA
PERSONAL Born 08/29/1942, Clay Center, KS, 1 child **DISCIPLINE** THEOLOGY **EDUCATION** Kansas State Univ, BA, 64; Saint Paul School of Theo, MRE, 69; School of Theo at Claremont, PhD, 89. **CAREER** Instr, Assoc Prof to Asst Prof, Christian Rel Edu, 89-, Saint Paul School of Theo; Outreach Min, 86-87, Dir of Christian Edu 69-, Los Feliz United Methodist Church. **HONORS AND AWARDS** Consecrated Diaconal Minister; Member Kansas West Annual Conf; Member of the Joint Candidacy Task Force of Higher Edu and Ministry of the United Methodist Church. **MEMBERSHIPS** Amer Acad of Rel; Assoc of Prof and Res in Rel Edu; Christian Edu Fellowship; Rel Edu Assoc; United Methodist Assoc of Scholars in Christian Edu. **RESEARCH** Methodist Hist. **SELECTED PUBLICATIONS** Auth, Faith Formation Through Mentoring Ministries, proposal under consideration; Transcripts of the Trinity, Communion and Community in: Formation for Holiness of Heart and Life, Quarterly Review, vol 18, 98; co-auth, Candidacy Guidebook for Deacons, Elders and Local Pastors, Nashville, Board of Higher Education and Ministry, 97; auth, Faith Matters Faith-Mentoring in the Faith Community, Valley Forge PA, Trinity Press International, 96; A Healing Ministry: The Educational Forms of Parish Nursing, Journal of Religious Education, 95. **CONTACT ADDRESS** Saint Paul Sch of Theol, 5123 Truman Rd, Kansas City, MO, 64127. **EMAIL** matthaci@spst.edu

MATTHEWS, A. WARREN
DISCIPLINE OLD TESTAMENT, NEW TESTAMENT **EDUCATION** Univ St Andrews, PhD, 59. **CAREER** Chair, dept, 79-85, 91-94; Dean, Student Affairs, 70-74; Vice Pres Student Services, 74-77. **SELECTED PUBLICATIONS** Auth, World Religions ;Abraham Was Their Father ;The Development of St. Augustine from Neoplatonism to Christianity. **CONTACT ADDRESS** Old Dominion Univ, 4100 Powhatan Ave, Norfolk, VA, 23058. **EMAIL** WMathews@odu.edu

MATTHEWS, GARETH BLANC
PERSONAL Born 07/08/1929, Buenos Aires, Argentina, m, 1958, 3 children **DISCIPLINE** PHILOSOPHY **EDUCATION** Franklin Col, AB, 51; Harvard Univ, AM, 52, PhD, 61. **CAREER** Asst prof philos, Univ Va, 60-61; from asst prof to assoc prof, Univ Minn, Minneapolis, 61-69; Prof Philos, Univ Mass, Amherst, 69-, George Santayana fel, Harvard Univ, 67- 68; vis lectr, Cambridge Univ, 76; Mead-Swing lectr, Oberlin Col, 76; dir, Nat Endowment for Humanities summer sem, 80, 85, 88, 98; contrib ed, Thinking. **MEMBERSHIPS** Am Philos Asn; Mind Asn. **RESEARCH** Mediaeval philos; ancient philos; philos and children. **SELECTED PUBLICATIONS** Auth, Thought's Ego in Augustine and Descartes, Cornell Univ Press, 92; auth, The Philosophy of Childhood, Harvard Univ Press, 94; Philosophy and the Young Child, Harvard Univ Pres, 80. **CONTACT ADDRESS** Dept of Philosophy, Univ of Mass, Amherst, MA, 01003-0525. **EMAIL** matthews@philos.umass.edu

MATTHEWS, PATRICIA
DISCIPLINE PHILOSOPHY **EDUCATION** Knox Col, BA; Univ Iowa, PhD. **CAREER** Asst prof. **HONORS AND AWARDS** Tchg Incentive Prog Awd, 96. **RESEARCH** Kant aesthetics. **SELECTED PUBLICATIONS** Auth, The Significance of Beauty: Kant on Feeling and the System of the Mind, Kluwer Acad, 97; Feeling and Aesthetic Judgment: A Rejoinder to Tom Huhn, Jour Aesthet, 97; Kant on Cognition and Taste, Marquette Univ, 95; Kant's Theory of Imagination: Bridging Gaps in Judgment and Experience (rev), Oxford, 94. **CONTACT ADDRESS** Dept of Philosophy, Florida State Univ, 211 Wescott Bldg, Tallahassee, FL, 32306. **EMAIL** pmatthew@mailer.fsu.edu

MATTHEWS, ROBERT JOSEPH
PERSONAL Born 05/19/1943, Lubbock, TX **DISCIPLINE** PHILOSOPHY **EDUCATION** Cornell Univ, BS, 65, MS, 67, PhD(French lit & philos), 74; Georgetown Univ, MA, 70. **CAREER** Asst Prof Philos, Rutgers Univ, 74-, Andrew W Mellon fac fel humanities, Harvard Univ, 77-78; ADJ PROF, INST AESTHET, TEMPLE UNIV, 77-; assoc, Behav & Brain Sci, 77-. **MEMBERSHIPS** Am Philos Asn; Am Soc Aesthet; Soc Philos & Psychol. **RESEARCH** Aesthetics; philosophy of language; philosophy of science. **SELECTED PUBLICATIONS** Auth, 3 Concept Monte--Explanation, Implementation and Systematicity, Synthese, vol 0101, 94; Border Disputes--Response to Johnston, Penelope, Hist Today, vol 0046, 96; Can Connectionists Explain Systematicity, Mind and Lang, vol 0012, 97. **CONTACT ADDRESS** Dept of Philos, Rutgers State Univ, P O Box 270, New Brunswick, NJ, 08903-0270.

MATTIE, U.
PERSONAL Born 04/22/1961, Turin, Italy, m, 1986, 2 children **DISCIPLINE** LAW; ECONOMICS **EDUCATION** Univ Torino Italy, JD 83; Univ Cal Berk, LLD 89. **CAREER** Univ Trento IT, prof 90-97; Univ Torino IT, prof 97-; Univ Cal Hastings Law Coll, Fromm Prof of Law, 96-. **HONORS AND AWARDS** AIACL; Prof invite', Fac Droit Compare. **RESEARCH** Comparative law and law economics. **SELECTED PUBLICATIONS** Auth, Comparative Law and Economics, Ann Arbor MI, 97. **CONTACT ADDRESS** Hastings Coll of Law, Univ of California, San Francisco, San Francisco, CA, 94102. **EMAIL** matteiu@uchastings.edu

MATTINGLY, RICHARD EDWARD
PERSONAL Born 01/01/1938, Wichita, KS, m, 1963, 1 child **DISCIPLINE** PHILOSOPHY **EDUCATION** Univ Kans, BA, 61; Univ Tex, Austin, PhD, 71. **CAREER** Asst prof philos, 63-72, chmn joint dept philos, Westminster Col & William Woods Col, 73-77, Assoc Prof Philos, 72-, chemn dept, 96-, Westminster Col, 72, Dean Fac, 77-95, VP, 78-95. **MEMBERSHIPS** Central Div Am Philos Asn; Central States Philos Asn. **RESEARCH** Theory of knowledge; philosophy of science; political philosophy. **CONTACT ADDRESS** Dept of Philosophy, Westminster Col, 501 Westminster Ave, Fulton, MO, 65251-1299. **EMAIL** mattinre@jaynet.wcmo.edu

MATTINGLY, SUSAN SHOTLIFF
PERSONAL Born 10/12/1941, Kansas City, MO, m, 1963, 1 child **DISCIPLINE** PHILOSOPHY **EDUCATION** Univ KS, BA, 63; Univ TX, PhD, 68. **CAREER** Inst of Phil, 67-69, asst prof, 69-72, head phil dept, 72-77, assoc prof 72-94, prof philos Lincoln Univ, Head Dept of Eng, For Lang & Philos, 94-, Lectr, Westminster Col, MO, 66-67. **HONORS AND AWARDS** NEH Summer Seminar fel, 81, Woodrow Wilson fel, Phi Beta Kappa. **MEMBERSHIPS** Am Philos Asn; Soc Women in Philos; AAUP. **RESEARCH** Medical ethics, philos of medicine. **SELECTED PUBLICATIONS** The Right to Health Care & the Right to Die, Philos Res Arch, 79; Viewing Abortion from the Perspective of Transplanatation: The Ethics of the Gift of Life, Soundings, 84; Fetal Needs, Physicians Duties, Midwest Medical Ethics, 91; Professional Ethics & the Maternal-Fetal Dyad: Exploring the Two-Patient Obstetric Model, Hastings Center Report, 92; Co-auth, Family Involvement in Medical Decision Making, Family Medicine, 96; The Mother-Fetal Dyad & the Ethics of Care, Physical & Occupational Therapy in Pediatrics, 96. **CONTACT ADDRESS** Dept of Philos, Lincoln Univ, 820 Chestnut St, Jefferson City, MO, 65102-0029. **EMAIL** mattings@lincolnu.edu

MATUSTIK, MARTIN J. BECK
PERSONAL Czechoslovakia **DISCIPLINE** PHILOSOPHY **EDUCATION** Fordham Univ, PhD, 91. **CAREER** Assoc prof, Purdue Univ, 95- . **HONORS AND AWARDS** Fulbright, 98, 95. **MEMBERSHIPS** APA; SPEP; RPA. **RESEARCH** Critical theory; nineteenth and twentieth century continental philosophy. **SELECTED PUBLICATIONS** Auth, Postnational Identity, Guilford, 93; Specters of Liberation, SUNY, 95; co-auth, Kierkegaard in Post/Modernity, Indiana, 95 **CONTACT ADDRESS** Dept of Philosophy, Purdue Univ, 1080 Schleman Hall, W. LaFayette, IN, 47907-1360. **EMAIL** mmatustk@purdue.edu

MAULE, JAMES EDWARD
DISCIPLINE LAW **EDUCATION** Wharton Sch, Univ Pa, BS, 73; Villanova Univ Sch Law, JD, 76; Nat Law Ctr, George Washington Univ, LLM, 79. **CAREER** Prof, Villanova Univ; sr tax and technol partner, Villanova Ctr for Inf Law and Policy; past atty, Legislation and Regulations Div, Off Ch Coun to the Internal Revenue serv; past atty-adviser, Honorable Herbert L. Chabot, US Tax Ct; taught at, Dickinson Sch Law. **MEMBERSHIPS** Adv Bd, US Income of BNA Tax Mgt, Inc; ed adv bd, J Ltd Liability Co; Amer Bar Asn; past ed adv bd, S Corp: J Tax, Legal, and Bus Strategies. **RESEARCH** Taxation, computer law. **SELECTED PUBLICATIONS** Contrib, BNA Tax Management Portfolio ser; publ on, Taxation and First Amendment History. **CONTACT ADDRESS** Law School, Villanova Univ, 800 Lancaster Ave, Villanova, PA, 19085-1692. **EMAIL** maule@law.vill.edu

MAXEY, B. ANN
DISCIPLINE BUSINESS ORGANIZATIONS, SECURITIES REGULATIONS, CORPORATE POLICY ISSUES **EDUCATION** Tulane Univ, BS, 63, JD, 78. **CAREER** Prior to coming to the WVU College of Law in 1991, Porfessor Maxey was Sr partner, Tucson, Ariz firm of O'Connor, Cavanaugh, Anderson, Westover, Killingsworth & Beshears, 88-91; partner, Hecker, Phillips & Hooker, 81-88; law clk, US Court of Appeals for the Ninth Circuit, SF, 79-81; prof, 91. **HONORS AND AWARDS** Morrison law rev award, Order of the Coif., Cumulative index ed, mem, Tulane Law Rev. **MEMBERSHIPS** Mem, AALS; Amer Bar Assn; Secy Comm Couns Responsibility; Comm Legal Bus Ethics; State Bar Calif; ArizState Bar Assn; Ariz Bar Found; W Va Bar Assn. **SELECTED PUBLICATIONS** Auth, SEC Enforcement Actions Against Securities Lawyers: New Remedies vs. Old Policies, 22 Delaware J. Corp. Law, 97; Competing Duties? Securities Lawyers' Liability After Center Bank, 64 Fordham L Rev 2185, 96. **CONTACT ADDRESS** Law Sch, W Va Univ, PO Box 6009, Morgantown, WV, 26506-6009.

MAY, CHRISTOPHER N.
PERSONAL Born 03/05/1943, Evanston, IL, m **DISCIPLINE** AMERICAN LAW **EDUCATION** Harvard Univ, AB, 65; Yale Univ, LLB, 68. **CAREER** Dir res, Nat Inst Educ Law & Poverty, Sch Law, Northwestern Univ, 68-69; Staff atty, San Francisco Neighborhood Legal Assistance Found, 70-73; instr, Sch Law, Golden Gate Univ, 71-73; prof Law, Loyola Law Sch, Ca, 73-. **HONORS AND AWARDS** Alpha Sigma Nu Natl Jesuit Book Award, 89. **RESEARCH** Supreme Court & congressional exercises of the war powers; Presidential noncompliance with the law. **SELECTED PUBLICATIONS** Auth, A Manual on the Laws & Administrative Regulations of the General Assistance & ADC Programs in the State of Illinois, Am Civil Liberties Union, 67; Withdrawal of Public Welfare: The right to a prior hearing, 76 Yale Law J 1234, 67; coauth (with Daniel William Fessler), Amicus Curiae brief in Goldberg versus Kelly, 397 US 254, 70; auth, Supreme Court holds residency test unconstitutional, Vol 3, No 1, Administration unveils welfare reform package: Recipients must work, Vol 3, No 89 & Supreme Court approves maximum grants, Vol 3, No 321, Clearinghouse Rev; coauth (with Daniel William Fessler), The Municipal Services Equalization Suit: A Cause of Action in Quest of a Forum, Public Needs, Private Behavior, and the Metropolitan Political Economy, Resources Future, Cambridge Univ, 75; In The Name of War: Judicial Review and the War Powers since 1918, Harvard Univ, 89; coauth, The Law of Prime Numbers, NY Univ Law Rev, 73; auth, Presidential Defiance of Unconstitutional Laws: Reviving the Royal Prerogative, Hastings Const Law Quart, 94; What Do We Do Now?: Helping Juries Apply the Instructions, Loyola Los Angeles Law Jour, 95; coauth, The Jurisprudence of Yogi Berra, Emory Law Jour, 97; Constitutional Law: National Power and Federalism, Aspen Law and Bus, 98; Constitutional Law: Individual Rights, Aspen Law and Bus, 98; auth, Presidential Defiance ofUnconstitutional Laws: Reviving the Royal Prerogative, Greenwood, 98. **CONTACT ADDRESS** Law Sch, Loyola Marymount Univ, 919 S Albany St, Los Angeles, CA, 90015-0019. **EMAIL** cmay@lmulaw.lmu.edu

MAY, DAVID M.
PERSONAL Born 11/18/1958, Monett, MO, m, 1980 **DISCIPLINE** NEW TESTAMENT **EDUCATION** Northwest MO State Univ, BS, 80; Southern Baptist Theol Sem, MDiv, 83, PhD, 87. **CAREER** Baptist chair of Bible, Central MO State Univ, Warrensburg, MO, 87-90; vis prof of New Testament, Midwestern Baptist Theol Sem, Kansas City, MO, 91-94; ASSOC PROF OF NEW TESTAMENT, CENTRAL BAPTIST THEOL SEM, KANSAS CITY, MO, 94-. **HONORS AND AWARDS** Regional Scholar nominee, 96. **MEMBERSHIPS** Soc of Biblical Lit; Nat Assoc Baptist Profs of Relig. **RESEARCH** Social scientific criticism of the New Testament. **SELECTED PUBLICATIONS** Auth, Mark 3:20-35 from the Perspective of Shame/Honor, Biblical Theol Bull, vol 17, summer 87; The Social Scientific Study of the New Testament: A Bibliography, vol 4, Mercer Univ Press, 91; Mark 2:15: The House of Jesus or Levi?, New Testament Studies, vol 39, 93; Drawn from Nature and Everyday Life: Parables and Social Scientific Criticism, Rev and Expositor, vol 94, no 2, spring 97; The Straightened Woman,(Luke 1310-17): Paradise Lost and Regained, Perspectives in Religious Studies, vol 24, no 3, fall 97. **CONTACT ADDRESS** Central Baptist Theol Sem, 741 N 31st St., Kansas City, KS, 66102-3964. **EMAIL** davidmay@cbts.edu

MAY, JOHN R.
DISCIPLINE RELIGIOUS STUDIES, ENGLISH IN RELIGION AND LITERATURE **EDUCATION** Emory Univ, PhD, 71. **CAREER** Alumni prof Eng and Relig Stud, La State Univ; ed, Paulist. **HONORS AND AWARDS** Alpha Sigma Nu; Phi Kappa Phi. **RESEARCH** Southern literature; religion and film. **SELECTED PUBLICATIONS** Auth, The Pruning Word: The Parables of Flannery O'Connor, Notre Dame, 76; Ed, Image and Likeness: Religious Visions in American Film Classics, Paulist, 92. **CONTACT ADDRESS** Dept of Philos and Relig S tud, Louisiana State Univ, 106 Coates Hall, Baton Rouge, LA, 70803.

MAY, MELANIE A.
PERSONAL Born 01/06/1955, Washington, DC **DISCIPLINE** THEOLOGY **EDUCATION** Manchester Col, BA, 76; Harvard Divinity Sch, Mdiv, 79; Harvard Univ, AM, 82, PhD, 86. **CAREER** Assoc gen secy, ecumenical off, Church Brethren General Board, 86-92; prof, dean, Rochester Divinity Sch, 92-. **HONORS AND AWARDS** Decade Award, Harvard Divinity Sch, 94., Edward C. Hopkins Honor Scholar, 78-79. **MEMBERSHIPS** World Council Churches Standing Commission on Faith and Order; Nat council Churches, Faith and Order. **RESEARCH** Women and Church; women's theolog ecumenism; global christianity **SELECTED PUBLICATIONS** auth, Bond of Unity: Women, Theology, and the Worldwide Church, 89; auth, For All the Saints: The Practice of Ministry in the Faith Community, 90; auth, Women and Church: Ecumenical Challenge of Solidarity in the Age of Alienation, 91; auth, A Body Knows: A Theopoetics of Death and Resurrection, 95. **CONTACT ADDRESS** 1100 Goodman St, Rochester, NY, 14620. **EMAIL** mmay@crds.edu

MAY, RICHARD WARREN
PERSONAL Born 03/01/1944, Marlborough, MA, m **DISCIPLINE** HUMANITIES/PHILOSOPHY **EDUCATION** Univ Mass, BS 68, Cal State Univ, MA, 91. **CAREER** Res Assoc, adv bd mem, 85-, Point One Advisory Gp. **HONORS AND AWARDS** ISPE Diplomat; Who's Who in the World 3 x's., US Patent # 473992, 1988. **MEMBERSHIPS** NCIS; AAR; ISPE; JGS. **RESEARCH** Religious studies vis-...-vis Jewish genealogy. **SELECTED PUBLICATIONS** Auth, The Online Buddha and the Stars, Telicom, J the Intl Soc for Philo Enq, 95; Thinking About Mozart's Minuet K 355, Telicom. 95; Four Eastern

Philosophies, in: Thinking on the Edge, Burbank CA, Agamemnon Press, 93. **CONTACT ADDRESS** 279 Highland Ave, Buffalo, NY, 14222-1748. **EMAIL** CJ353@freenet.buffalo.edu

MAYER, DON
PERSONAL Born 03/27/1948, CA, m, 1987, 3 children **DISCIPLINE** INTERNATIONAL LAW **EDUCATION** Duke Univ Law School, JD, 73; Georgetown Univ Law Center, LLM, 85. **CAREER** Office of the Staff Judge Advocate, Francis E Warren Air Force Base, Cheyenne, WY, 73-75; private law practice, Asheville, NC, 75-83; Chief Clerk for Legal Res, Wilkes, Artis, Hendrick and Lane, Chartered, Washington, DC, 84-85; asst prof of Business Law, School of Business, Western Carolina Univ, Cullowhee, NC, 85-90; asst prof of Management, School of Business Administration, Oakland Univ, Rochester, MI, 90-94; asst adjunct prof of Law, History, and Commun, Univ MI School of Business Administration, 94; assoc prof of Management, Oakland Univ School of Business Administration, 95-. **HONORS AND AWARDS** Ralph Bunde Award, Academy of Legal Studies in Business, Int Law Section, 98. **MEMBERSHIPS** Academy of Legal Studies in Business. **RESEARCH** Ethics; international law; the environment. **SELECTED PUBLICATIONS** Auth, Labelling, Packaging and Alleged Failures to Warn: Federal Pre-emption May Void Claims Based on State Law, J of the Academy of Marketing Science, vol 22, no 3, summer 94; with Anita Cava, Social Contract Theory and Gender Discrimination: Some Reflections on the Donaldson-Dunfee Model, Business Ethics Quart, vol 5, no 2, April 95; Foreign Corrupt Practices Act, International Free Trade, International Arbitration, Negligence, Sex Discrimination, and International Law, in the Encyclopedia of Business, Gale Pub Co, 96; Arbitration of Employment Discrimination Claims and the Challenge of Contemporary Federalism, 47 South Carolina Law Rev, no 3, spring 96; Instructor's Manual and Test Bank to Accompany International Business Law and Its Environment, by Schaeffer, Earle, and Agusti, 3rd ed, West Pub Co, 95; Boundaries of the Moral Community, in Blackwell's Encyclopedic Dictionary of Business Ethics, Pat Werhane and Ed Freeman, eds, 98; Instructor's Manual and Test Bank to Accompany Fisher and Phillips' The Legal, Ethical, and Regulatory Environment of Business, 6th ed, West Pub Co, 97; Institutionalizing Overconsumption, in Westra and Werhane, eds, Consumption and the Environment, Rowman and Littlefield, forthcoming; Arbitral Alternatives to Injunctive Relief for International Letter of Credit Fraud, with Mark S Blodgett, Am Business Law J, vol 35, no 3; Environmental Law in Context: Integrating Ethics, Economics, and the International Dimension, J of Legal Studies ed, vol 16:1, forthcoming; Lessons in Law from A Civil Action, J of Legal Studies Ed, vol 16:1, forthcoming. **CONTACT ADDRESS** School of Business Administration, Oakland Univ, Rochester, MI, 48309. **EMAIL** mayer@oakland.edu

MAYNARD, ARTHUR HOMER
PERSONAL Born 08/28/1915, Centerville, MI, m, 1941, 2 children **DISCIPLINE** RELIGION **EDUCATION** Cornell Col, BA, 36; Boston Univ, MA, 38, STB, 39; Univ Southern Calif, PhD(Bible lit), 50. **CAREER** Minister, Methodist Churches, Wis & Calif, 39-50; vis prof relig, Willamette Univ, 50-52; from assoc prof to prof, Univ Miami, 52-58, chmn dept, 52-58; chmn dept relig studies, 62-75, PROF BIBLE, UNIV PAC, 58-. **MEMBERSHIPS** Soc Bibl Lit; Am Acad Relig. **RESEARCH** Gospel of John; Old Testament prophets. **SELECTED PUBLICATIONS** Auth, Born from Above--The Anthropology of the Gospel of John, J Relig, vol 0074, 94. **CONTACT ADDRESS** Dept of Religious Studies, Univ of the Pacific, Stockton, CA, 95211.

MAYNARD, PATRICK
DISCIPLINE PHILOSOPHY **EDUCATION** Univ Chicago, BA; Cornell Univ, PhD. **CAREER** Assoc prof **SELECTED PUBLICATIONS** Auth, The Engine of Visualization: Thinking Through Photography, Cornell, 97; ed, Perspectives on the Arts and Technology, 97. **CONTACT ADDRESS** Dept of Philosophy, Western Ontario Univ, London, ON, N6A 5B8.

MAYNARD, THERESE H.
DISCIPLINE LAW **EDUCATION** Univ Calif, Irvine, BA, 78; Univ Calif, Los Angeles, JD, 81. **CAREER** Prof & William M. Rains fel; Loyola Univ, 83-; practiced, Gibson, Dunn & Crutcher. **RESEARCH** Securities litigation. **SELECTED PUBLICATIONS** Publ on, securities law. **CONTACT ADDRESS** Law School, Loyola Marymount Univ, 7900 Loyola Blvd, Burns 404, Los Angeles, CA, 90045. **EMAIL** tmaynard@lmulaw.lmu.edu

MAYNARD-REID, PEDRITO U.
PERSONAL Kingston, Jamaica, m, 1970, 2 children **DISCIPLINE** NEW TESTAMENT **EDUCATION** Andrews Univ, ThD, 81 **CAREER** Pof bibl studies, W Indies Coll, Jamaica, 70-85; prof bibl studies, Antilkan Univ, Puerto Rico, 85-89; prof bibl studies, WA, 91-. **HONORS AND AWARDS** Zarara Awardard for Teaching, 93. **MEMBERSHIPS** Soc of Bibl Studies. **RESEARCH** Epistle of James. **SELECTED PUBLICATIONS** Auth, Caribbean Worship, The Complete Libr of Christian Worship, 95; African-American Worship, Libr of Christian Worship, 95; James, 96; Complete Evangelism: The Luke-Acts Model, 97; James, Introducing the Bible, 97; Samaria, Dictionary of the Later New Testament and Its Development, 97; Forgiveness, Dictionary of the Later New Testament and Its Development, 97. **CONTACT ADDRESS** 903 Highland Park Dr, College Place, WA, 99324. **EMAIL** maynped@wwc.edu

MAYR, FRANZ KARL
PERSONAL Born 03/12/1932, Linz, Austria, m, 1968, 2 children **DISCIPLINE** PHILOSOPHY OF RELIGION & LANGUAGE; METAPHYSICS; LEGAL PHILOSOPHY **EDUCATION** Univ Innsbruck, LPh, 56, PhD(philos), 57, MLaw, 62. **CAREER** Asst prof philos, Univ Innsbruck, 63-64 & 65-68; asst prof relig & philos, 64-65, assoc prof, 68-76, PROF PHILOS, UNIV PORTLAND, OR, 76- . **RESEARCH** Political philosophy; Philosophy of religion. **SELECTED PUBLICATIONS** Coauth, Lexikon fur Theologie und Kirche, Herder, Freiburg, 63; auth, Geschichte der Philosophie Antike, 64; Genos und Geschlecht: Zum Problem der Metaphysik, 65 & Der Gott Hermes und die Hermeneutik, 68, Tijdschrift voor Filos, Louvain; Trinitaet und Familie in Augustinus De TrinitateXII: Reone des Etudes Augustimiemes, Paris, 72; Der Aristolelische Gottesbeweis in Lichte de Religious Grschichte, Feitschrift fur Religious und Geistes Gerschichte, Cologne, 72; Philosophische Implikationen Amerikanischer Linguistik, Feitschrift fur Philosophische Forschung, Stuttgart, 73; Language, Sacramentune Mundi, An Encyclopedia of Theology III, New York-London, 69; Philosophische Hermenentik und Dentsche Sprache, Tydschrift von Filosofie, Louvain, 86; Horen: Lexikon fur Antike und Christentum, Bonn, 90; Der Ausschluss der Weiblich-Mutterlichen Analogie fur Gott bei Thomas von Aquin, S.C.G. IV, Theologie und Glanbe, Paderborn, 73; Trinitetsche unde theologische Anthropologie, Feitschrift fur Theologie und Kirche, 70; Die Einseitigkeit der Traditionellen Gottesche Zum Verhilhims von Anthropologie und Tneumatologie, Erfehrung und Theolgie des Hl. Geistes, Munich, 74; Tatriachales Gottesverstanduis, Theologische Quartaloschrift, Tubingen, 72; Sprache, Sprachphilosophie, Herders Theologisches Taschenlevikon, 81; coauth, Existential Sacramentum mundi: International Theological Lexicon, Herder & Herder, 69; Simbolos, Mitos y Archetypos, Antropologia Vasca: Gram Encyclopedia Vasca, Bilbao, 80; El Matriarcalismo Vasco, Bilbao, 80; coauth, El Inconsciente Colectivo Vasco, San Sebastian, 82; coauth, Arquetipos y Simbolos Colectivos: Circulo Eranos I, Barcelona, 94; Lenguaje: Diccionario de Hermenentica, Univ de Densto Bilbao, 77. **CONTACT ADDRESS** Dept of Philosophy, Univ of Portland, 5000 N Willamette, Portland, OR, 97203-5798.

MAZOR, LESTER JAY
PERSONAL Born 12/12/1936, Chicago, IL, m, 1992, 3 children **DISCIPLINE** PHILOSOPHY OF LAW, LEGAL HISTORY **EDUCATION** Stanford Univ, AB, 57, JD, 60. **CAREER** Instr law, Univ Va, 61-62; from asst prof to prof, Univ Utah, 62-70; Henry R Luce prof, 70-75, Prof Law, Hampshire Col, 75-, Reporter, Am Bar Asn Proj Standards Criminal Justice, 65-69; vis assoc prof law, Stanford Univ, 67-68; vis prof, State Univ NY Buffalo, 73-74; proj dir mat study, Am Bar Found Study Legal Educ, 74-. **MEMBERSHIPS** Law & Soc Asn; Int Soc Asn; Am Legal Studies Asn; Int Asn Philos Law & Soc Philos. **RESEARCH** Legal hist; legal and polit theory; future studies. **SELECTED PUBLICATIONS** Ed, Prosecution and Defense Functions, 67 & Providing Defense Services, 70, American Bar Asn; coauth, Introduction to the Study of Law, Found Press, 70; auth, Power and responsibility in the attorney-client relation, Stanford Law Rev, 68; The crisis of liberal legalism, Yale Law J, 72; Disrespect for law, In: Anarchism, NY Univ, 78. **CONTACT ADDRESS** Sch of Soc Sci, Hampshire Col, 893 West St, Amherst, MA, 01002-3359. **EMAIL** lmazor@hampshire.edu

MAZOUE, JIM
DISCIPLINE AMERICAN PHILOSOPHY, ETHICS, EPISTEMOLOGY **EDUCATION** Tulane Univ, PhD, 83. **CAREER** Vis instr, Univ Ala, 80; vis instr, 81-82, vis asst prof, Univ SC, Columbia, 82-83; vis asst prof, 84, Tulane Univ, 86; vis asst prof, Eastern Ky Univ; vis asst prof, Univ Tenn, Knoxville, 86-90; adj asst prof, Univ New Orleans, 91-; clin consult, Med Ctr, Univ Tenn, Knoxville, 86-90; Ethics comt, Lakeview Reg Med Ctr, Covington, La, 95-97. **HONORS AND AWARDS** NEH summer sem, Ind Univ, 86; La Educ Qual Sup Fund Enhancement grant, Philos Dept Acad Comput Lab, 97-98; City Nat Bank Award, La State Univ, 98. **RESEARCH** American philosophy; epistemology. **SELECTED PUBLICATIONS** Auth, Nozick on Inferential Knowledge, Philos Quart 35, 85; Some Remarks on Luper-Foy's Criticism of Nozickian Tracking, Australasian J of Philos 64, 86; Self-Synthesis and Self-Knowledge, in Polrocznik Filozoficzny Mlodych, Piotr Boltuc, ed, Warsaw UP, 87; Self-Synthesis, Self-Knowledge, and Skepticism, Logos, 11, 90; Diagnosis Without Doctors, J of Med and Philos 15, 90; Should Human Diagnosticians Be Replaced by Automated Diagnostic Systems?:Yes, in Controversial Issues in Mental Health, Stuart A Kirk and Susan D Einbinder, eds, Brown & Allyn, 94. **CONTACT ADDRESS** Univ New Orleans, New Orleans, LA, 70148.

MAZUR, DENNIS J.
PERSONAL Born 04/11/1949, Kittanning, PA, m, 1979, 2 children **DISCIPLINE** PHILOSOPHY **EDUCATION** Stanford Univ, BA, 73, MA, 74, MD, 79, PhD, 83. **CAREER** Assoc Prof Med, Ore Health Sci Univ, 91-; Chair, Inst Rev Bd, Dept Veterans Affairs Med Ctr, 91-. **HONORS AND AWARDS** Post-Doctoral Award, Soc Med Decision Making, 83. **RESEARCH** Informed consent; risk disclosure; patient-physician decision making; how patients interpret data and use information in medical decision making; patients preferences for information and role in decision making, particularly in the area of invasive medical interventions. **SELECTED PUBLICATIONS** Coauth, How older patients' treatment preferences are influenced by disclosures about therapeutic uncertainty: Surgery vs. expectant management for localized prostate cancer, J Am Geriatrics Soc, 96; The influence of physician explanations on patient preferences about future health care states, Med Decision Making, 97; Patients' preferences for risk disclosure and role in decision making for invasive medical interventions, J General Internal Med, 97; auth, How older patient preferences are influenced by consideration of future health outcomes, J Am Geriatrics Soc, 97; Medical Risk and the Right to an Informed Consent in Clinical Care and Clinical Research, Am Col Physician Execs, 98; author of numerous other articles and publications. **CONTACT ADDRESS** Med Service, Dept of Veterans Affairs Med Ctr, 3710 SW US Veterans Hospital Rd, Portland, OR, 97201.

MAZUR, DIANE H.
DISCIPLINE LAW **EDUCATION** State Univ NY- Binghamton, BA; Penn State Univ, MS; Univ Tex, JD. **CAREER** Assoc prof, Univ Fla, 94-; Bigelow tchg fel & lectr, Univ Chicago, 93-94; adj fac, Widener Univ, 92-93; fmr assoc, Modrall law firm, Albuquerque, NM; staff, Rev Litigation. **MEMBERSHIPS** NM Bar; Order of the Coif; Univ Tex Chancellors. **RESEARCH** Evidence, corporations, women in military service. **CONTACT ADDRESS** School of Law, Univ of Florida, PO Box 117625, Gainesville, FL, 32611-7625. **EMAIL** mazur@law.ufl.edu

MCAFFEE, THOMAS B.
DISCIPLINE CONSTITUTIONAL LAW **EDUCATION** Univ Utah, JD, 79. **CAREER** Articles ed, Utah Law Rev; instr, Southern Ill Univ; prof, Univ Nev, Las Vegas. **HONORS AND AWARDS** Fac Achievement Award for Scholar, Univ Nev, Las Vegas, 97. **SELECTED PUBLICATIONS** Published numerous articles in law journals including the Harvard J of Law and Pub Policy, Columbia Law Rev, Brigham Young Univ Law Rev, and Temple Law Rev. **CONTACT ADDRESS** Univ Nev, Las Vegas, Las Vegas, NV, 89154.

MCALISTER, ELIZABETH
DISCIPLINE PHILOSOPHY OF MIND **EDUCATION** Vassar Col, BA; Yale Univ, MA, Mphil, PhD. **CAREER** Asst prof, 90-97; Assoc prof, 97-; Chair, 98-; Wesleyan Univ. **HONORS AND AWARDS** Fel, Indiana Univ; Visitor, Mellon Seminar, Yale Univ Ctr Global Migration; Post-doctoral Fel, Rutgers Ctr Hisl Analysis; Dissertation Fel, Univ Ill, Yale Univ; Henry Hart Rice Adv Res fel. **SELECTED PUBLICATIONS** Auth, Haitian Vodou meets Italian Catholicism in Spanish Harlem: The Madonna of 115th Street Revisited; Congregations as Cultural Spaces: Immigration, Ethnicity and Religion in the United States, Temple Univ Press, 98, Angels in the Mirror: Vodou Music of Haiti. Roslyn, NY: Ellipsis Arts Publ, 97; New York, Lavalas, and the Emergence of Rara, Jour Haitian Studies, 96; A Sorcerer's Bottle: The Visual Art of Magic in Haiti, Sacred Arts of Haitian Vodou, UCLA Fowler Mus Cult Hist, 95, Vodou Music and Ritual Work, Rhythms of Rapture: Sacred Musics of Vodou, Smithsonian/Folkways, 95; 'Men Moun Yo; Here Are The People:" Haitian Rara Festivals and Transnational Popular Culture in Haiti and New York City, Yale Univ, 95; Sacred Stories from the Haitian Diaspora: A Collective Biography of Seven Vodou Priestesses in New York City, Jour Caribbean Studies, 93; Walking with the Mardi Gras Indians. FACES: Mag About People, 93; Rara Demonstrations: Traditional Ritual Turns Political Weapon in Haitian New York, Int Forum Yale, 92; Serving the Spirits Across Two Seas: Vodou Culture in Haiti and New York, Aperture, 92; Home Away From Home: Haitian Life in New York, FACES: Mag About People, 91; Haitians Make Some Noise in Brooklyn, Beat, 91; Ton Ton Club, Haiti since Duvalier, Mirabella, 90; Vodou in New York City: New Creolizations: The Economizing of Ritual Time and Space in Haitian Religion, Yale Univ, 90; Voodoo, NY Woman, 88. **CONTACT ADDRESS** Wesleyan Univ, Middletown, CT, 06459.

MCALISTER, LINDA L.
PERSONAL Born 10/10/1939, Long Beach, CA **DISCIPLINE** PHILOSOPHY **EDUCATION** Barnard Coll, BA, 62; Cornell Univ, PhD, 69. **CAREER** Asst/assoc prof, Brooklyn Coll, 68-77; Dean, San Diego State Univ Imperial Valley Campus, 77-82; Dean, Fort Myers Campus Univ S Fla, 82-85; Asst to Vice Chancellor, 85-87; Prof, Univ S Fla, 87-99. **HONORS AND AWARDS** Sr Fulbright Res Fel, 73-74; Distinguished Woman Philosopher, Soc for Women in Philos, 98. **MEMBERSHIPS** Soc for Women in Philos; am Philos Asn; Int Asn of Women Philosphers. **RESEARCH** Feminist Philos; History of

Women In Philosophy. **SELECTED PUBLICATIONS** Auth, On the Possibility of Feminist Philosophy, Hypatia, 94; Gerda Walther, Hist of Women Philosophers, 95; Feminist Cinematic Depictions of Violence Against Women: Three Representational Strategies, Krieg/War, 97; My Grandmother's Passing, Collage White: Feminist Philos Reflections on Race and Identity, forthcoming; coauth, Edith Stein, Hist of Women Philosophers, 95; Psychology From and Empirical Standpoint, 95; ed, Hypatia's daughters: 1500 Years of Women Philosphers, 96. **CONTACT ADDRESS** Women's Studies Program, Univ of S Fla, Tampa, FL, 33820. **EMAIL** mcallister@chuma1.cas.usf.edu

MCANINCH, WILLIAM S.
DISCIPLINE CONSTITUTION AND CRIMINAL LAW **EDUCATION** Tulane Univ, BA, 62; Univ AR, LLB, 65; Yale Univ, LLM, 69. **CAREER** Solomon Blatt prof, Univ of SC. **SELECTED PUBLICATIONS** Auth or coauth, 3 bks on criminal law. **CONTACT ADDRESS** School of Law, Univ of S. Carolina, Law Center, Columbia, SC, 29208. **EMAIL** Bill@law.law.sc.edu

MCARTHUR, ROBERT L.
PERSONAL Born 02/18/1944, San Mateo, CA, m, 1995, 2 children **DISCIPLINE** PHILOSOPHY, LAW, LOGIC & PHILOSOPHY OF SCIENCE **EDUCATION** Villanova Univ, BA, 67, MA, 68; Temple Univ, PhD(Philos), 72. **CAREER** Instr Philos, Villanova Univ, 69-72; from Assoc Prof to Prof Philos, 72-98, VPres and Dean of Fac, 88-98, Christian A. Johnson Prof of Integrated Learning, 98-. **HONORS AND AWARDS** Am Conn Educ fel acad admin, 75-76. **MEMBERSHIPS** Am Philos Asn; Philos Sci Asn. **RESEARCH** Logic; philosophy of language; philosophy of religion; philosophy of law. **SELECTED PUBLICATIONS** Coauth, Peter Damian and undoing the past, Philos Studies, 2/74 & Non-assertoric inference, Notre Dame J Formal Logic, 4/74; auth, Factuality and modality in the future tense, Nous, 9/74; Tense and temporal neutrality, Australasian J Philos, 5/75; Tense Logic, Reidel, 76; From Logic to Computing, Wadsworth, 91. **CONTACT ADDRESS** Dept of Philos, Colby Col, 150 Mayflower Hill, Waterville, ME, 04901-4799. **EMAIL** rlmcarth@colby.edu

MCAULIFFE, JANE D.
DISCIPLINE RELIGION **EDUCATION** Univ Toronto, BA, 68, MA, 79, PhD, 84. **CAREER** Asst prof, dept stud relig, Univ Toronto, 81-86; assoc prof, hist relig & Islamic stud, Candler Sch Theol, Emory Univ, Atlanta, 86-92; assoc dean, 90-92, assoc prof, 92-, CHAIR, DEPT STUD RELIG, DIR, CTR STUD RELIG, UNIV TORONTO 92-. **HONORS AND AWARDS** Thesis Award, Mid East Stud Asn; Guggenheim Fel, 96. **MEMBERSHIPS** Am Soc Stud relig; Am Acad Relig; Am Oriental Soc; Can Soc Stud Relig; Soc Values Higher Educ. **SELECTED PUBLICATIONS** Auth, Qur'anic Christians: An Analysis of Classical and Modern Exegesis, 91; auth, Abbasid Authority Affirmed: The Early Years of al-Mansur, 94. **CONTACT ADDRESS** Dept Stud of Religion, Univ Toronto, Toronto, ON, M5S 2E8. **EMAIL** jane.mcauliffe@utoronto.ca

MCAVOY, JANE
PERSONAL Born 05/23/1957, Burlington, IA, m, 1985 **DISCIPLINE** THEOLOGY **EDUCATION** Drake Univ, BME, 79; Lexington Theol Sem, MDiv, 85; Univ Chicago, PhD, 91. **CAREER** Assoc prof, Rel Stud (s), Hiram Col, 90-97; assoc prof, Theol, Lexington Theol Sem, 97- . **HONORS AND AWARDS** Hiram nominee for TA Abbot awd for Outstanding Disciples prof, 91; Martin awd for Outstand Contrib to Hiram Col, 92; Gerstecker-Gund scholar fel from Hiram Col, 91-95; Louisville Inst Summer Scholar Stipend, 98. **MEMBERSHIPS** Amer Acad Rel; Forrest-Moss Inst for Disciples Women Scholars of Rel; Asn Disciples Theol Discussion. **RESEARCH** Feminist Theology; Christian Mysticism. PUB Auth, God-Talk: Three Modern Approaches, Lexington Theol Quart, 22, Oct 87, 106-117; The Changing Image of Parish ministry, Lexington Theol Quart, 25, July 90, 65-80; Biblical Images of the Call to Ministry, in Celebrating God's Call to Ministry, 10-13, eds, William B. Drake and Terry Ewing, Lexington, Lexington Theol Sem, 91; In Search of a Blessing, in Bread Afresh, Wine Anew: Sermons by Disciples Women, 151-144-155, eds, Joan Campbell and David Polk, St. Louis, Chalice Press, 91; ed, Table Talk: Resources for the Communion Meal, St. Louis, Chalice Press, 93; God With Us: From Language to Liturgy, in Setting the Table: Women in Theological Conversation, eds, Rita Brock, Claudia Camp, and Serene Jones, St. Louis, Chalice Press, 95; Hospitality: A Feminist Theology of Education, in Teaching Theology and Religion, 1,1, Feb 98, 20-26. **CONTACT ADDRESS** Dept of Theology, Lexington Theol Sem, 631 S Limestone, Lexington, KY, 40508. **EMAIL** vmcavoy@lextheo.edu

MCBAIN, JAMES F., JR.
PERSONAL Born 07/09/1971, St. Louis, MO, s **DISCIPLINE** PHILOSOPHY **EDUCATION** Northeast Missouri State Univ, BA, 94; Univ Missouri, St Louis, BA, 95; Univ Missouri, Columbia, PhD program. **CAREER** Dept Philos, Univ Missouri **MEMBERSHIPS** APA; Southwestern Philos Soc; Central States Philos Asn. **RESEARCH** Philosophy of science; epistemology; philosophy of mind. **CONTACT ADDRESS** Dept of Philosophy, Univ of Missouri, Columbia, 435 General Classroom Bldg, Columbia, MO, 65211-4160. **EMAIL** c696666@showme.missouri.edu

MCBETH, HARRY LEON
PERSONAL m **DISCIPLINE** CHURCH HISTORY **EDUCATION** Wayland Baptist Univ, BA, 54; Southwestern Baptist Theol Sem, MDiv, 57, ThD, 61. **CAREER** Distinguished prof, Southwestern Baptist Theol sem, 60-. **HONORS AND AWARDS** Outstanding Young Men Am, 66, Pastor, First Baptist Church, 55-60. **MEMBERSHIPS** S Baptist Hist Soc; Amer Soc Church Hist. **SELECTED PUBLICATIONS** Auth, The Baptist Heritage: Four Centuries of Baptist Witness, Broadman Press, 87; A Sourcebook for Baptist Heritage, Broadman Press, 90; Texas Baptists: A Sesquicentennial History, Baptist Way Press, 98. **CONTACT ADDRESS** Sch Theol, Southwestern Baptist Theol Sem, PO Box 22000, Fort Worth, TX, 76122-0418. **EMAIL** hlm@swbts.swbts.edu

MCBRIDE, WILLIAM LEON
PERSONAL Born 01/19/1938, New York, NY, m, 1965, 2 children **DISCIPLINE** PHILOSOPHY **EDUCATION** Georgetown Univ, AB, 59; Yale Univ, MA, 62, PhD(philos), 64. **CAREER** From instr to assoc prof philos, Yale Univ, 64-73; assoc prof, 73-76, PROF PHILOS, PURDUE UNIV, WEST LAFAYETTE, 76-, Morse fel philos, Yale Univ, 68-69; fel, Ctr for Humanistic Studies, Purdue Univ, 81. **MEMBERSHIPS** Am Philos Asn; Soc Phenomenol & Existential Philos (exec cosecy, 77-80); Am Soc Polit & Legal Philos. **RESEARCH** Social, political, and legal philosophy; Marx and Marxism; existentialist thought, especially the philosophy of Sartre. **SELECTED PUBLICATIONS** Auth, Promotion Commotion + Response to the Report Concerning Promotion Criteria in the Philosophy Department at the University of Chicago, Lingua Franca, vol 0007, 97. **CONTACT ADDRESS** Purdue Univ, W Lafayette, IN, 47907.

MCBRIEN, RICHARD PETER
PERSONAL Born 08/19/1936, Hartford, CT, 1 child **DISCIPLINE** THEOLOGY **EDUCATION** St Thomas Sem, AA, 56; St John Sem, MA, 62; Pontifical Gregorian Univ, Rome, STL, 64, STD, 67. **CAREER** Prof theol & dean of studies, Pope John XXIII Nat Sem, 65-70; assoc prof, 70-72, prof, 72-80, dir, Inst Relig Educ, 75-80, Boston Col; Crowley-O'Brien-Walter Prof Theol, Univ Notre Dame, 80-; Assoc pastor, Our Lady of Victory Church, 62-63; chaplain, Southern Conn State Col, 62-63; syndicated columnist, Essays in Theol, 66-; chmn, Adv Coun, Notre Dame's Ecumenical Inst for Advan Theol Res, Tantur-Jerusalem, 82-87. **HONORS AND AWARDS** John Courtney Murray Award, Cath Theol Soc Am, 76; Christopher Award, The Christophers, 81. **SELECTED PUBLICATIONS** Auth, The Remaking of the Church: An Agenda for Reform, Harper & Row, 73; auth, Has the Church Surrendered?, Dimension Books, 74; auth, Roman Catholicism, Cathedral Publ, 75; auth, In Search of God, Dimension Books, 77; auth, Basic Questions for Christian Educators, St Mary's Press, 77; auth, Catholicism, Winston Press, 80; rev ed, Caeser's Coin: Religion and Politics in America, McMillan, 87; gen ed Harper Collin's Encyclopedic of Catholicism, 95; auth, Responses to 101 Questions on the Church, Paulist Press, 96; auth, Lives of the Popes, Harper San Francisco, 97. **CONTACT ADDRESS** Dept of Theol, Univ of Notre Dame, 327 Oshaugnessy Hall, Notre Dame, IN, 46556.

MCCABE, DAVID
DISCIPLINE MORAL PHILOSOPHY, POLITICAL PHILOSOPHY **EDUCATION** Northwestern Univ, PhD, 95. **CAREER** Vis asst prof, Colgate Univ. **SELECTED PUBLICATIONS** Auth, var articles in moral and polit theory. **CONTACT ADDRESS** Dept of Philos and Relig, Colgate Univ, 13 Oak Drive, Hamilton, NY, 13346. **EMAIL** dmccabe@mail.colgate.edu

MCCAFFERY, EDWARD J.
DISCIPLINE LAW **EDUCATION** Yale Univ, BA; Harvard Univ, JD; Univ Southern Calif, MA. **CAREER** Maurice Jones, Jr., prof; clerked for, Honorable Robert N. Wilentz, Ch Justice Supreme Ct NJ; off consult, Russian Fed; private practice, San Francisco. **SELECTED PUBLICATIONS** Auth, Taxing Women; Cognitive Theory and Tax; Slouching Towards Equality: Gender Discrimination, Market Efficiency, Social Change; coauth, Framing the Jury: Cognitive Perspectives on Pain and Suffering Awards. **CONTACT ADDRESS** School of Law, Univ Southern Calif, University Park Campus, Los Angeles, CA, 90089.

MCCAGNEY, NANCY
DISCIPLINE RELIGIOUS STUDIES **EDUCATION** Univ Wisc, Madison, BA, MA; Univ Calif Santa Barbara, MA, PhD. **CAREER** Asst prof, philos, Univ Delaware. **HONORS AND AWARDS** NEH fel; Regents fel. **MEMBERSHIPS** AAR; APA; ASAP; ISEE; IABS. **RESEARCH** Religion and environment. **SELECTED PUBLICATIONS** Auth, Nagarjuna and the Philosophy of Openness, Rowman & Littlfield, 97. **CONTACT ADDRESS** Pollution Ecology Lab, Rm 104, Univ of Delaware, 700 Pilottown Rd, Lewes, DE, 19958.

MCCALL, EMMANUEL LEMUEL, SR.
PERSONAL Born 02/04/1936, Sharon, PA, m **DISCIPLINE** THEOLOGY **EDUCATION** Univ of Louisville, BA 1958; So Bapt Theol Sem, BD 1962, MRE 1963, MDiv 1967; Emory Univ, DMinistry 1975. **CAREER** Simmons Bible Coll Louisville, prof 1958-68; 28th St Bapt Church Louisville, pastor 1960-68; Cooperative Ministries w/Natl Bapt So Bapt Conv, assoc dir, 1968-74; So Bapt Theol Sem Louisville, adj prof 1970-96; So Baptist Convention, dir dept of black church relations home missions bd 1974-88; Black Church Extension Division, Home Mission Board, SBC, director 1989-91; CHRISTIAN FELLOWSHIP BAPTIST CHURCH, COLLEGE PARK, GA, PASTOR, 1991-; MERCER UNIV SCHOOL OF THEOLOGY, ADJUNCT PROF, 1996-. **HONORS AND AWARDS** Hon DD Simmons Bible Coll 1965; Ambassador of Goodwill City of Louisville 1967; Hon DD United Theol Sem 1977; Victor T Glass Awd Home Mission Bd So Bapt Conv 1979; E Y Mullins Denominational Service Award, Southern Bapt Theological Seminary, 1990, E Y Mullins Humanitarian Award; American Baptist College, 1990. **MEMBERSHIPS** Bd of dir Morehouse Sch of Religion 1972-85; mem Amer Soc of Missiology 1975-80; bd of trustees Interdenominational Theol Ctr 1978-; president elect, National Alumni Assn SBTS 1990-91, president 1991-92; co-chairman, Interdenomenational Theological Center, 1990-93, chair, 1993-96; Atlanta University Center, trustee, 1993-96; Truett McConnell College, trustee, 1994-. **CONTACT ADDRESS** 1500 Norman Dr, College Park, GA, 30349.

MCCALL, JAMES RUSSELL
PERSONAL Born 08/20/1936, Nashville, TN, m, 1962, 3 children **DISCIPLINE** LAW **EDUCATION** Pomona Col, BA, 59; Harvard Univ, JD, 62. **CAREER** Atty, Breed, Robinson & Stewart, Oakland, 62-69; deputy atty gen, Off Atty Gen State Calif, 69-71; PROF LAW, HASTINGS COL LAW, UNIV CALIF, 71-, CONSULT CONSUMER PROTECTION LAW, CALIF STATE SENATE, 72- & Calif Atty Gen Off, 72-80; Distinguished vis prof Am Antitrust Law, Nihon Univ, Tokyo, 81. **MEMBERSHIPS** Am Asn Law Sch; Am Bar Asn; Soc Am Law Teachers; Am Soc Writers Legal Subj. **RESEARCH** Consumer protection law; antitrust law; trade regulation law. **SELECTED PUBLICATIONS** Auth, Greater Representation for California Consumers--Fluid Recovery, Consumer Trust Funds, and Representative Actions, Hastings Law J, vol 0046, 95. **CONTACT ADDRESS** Hastings Col of Law, Univ of Calif, Carmel Valley, CA.

MCCALL, STORRS
DISCIPLINE PHILOSOPHY **EDUCATION** McGill Univ, BA; Oxford Univ, BA, PhD. **RESEARCH** Philosophy of law. **SELECTED PUBLICATIONS** Auth, Aristotle's Modal Syllogisms, North-Holland, 63; auth, Polish Logic 1920-39, Clarendon, 67; auth, A Model of the Universe, Clarendon, 94. **CONTACT ADDRESS** Philosophy Dept, McGill Univ, 845 Sherbrooke St, Montreal, PQ, H3A 2T5.

MCCANN, EDWIN
DISCIPLINE PHILOSOPHY **EDUCATION** Univ Pa, PhD, 75. **CAREER** Assoc prof & dir, Sch Philos,Univ Southern Calif; Univ Southern Calif, 83-; asst prof, Harvard Univ, 75-78; asst prof, MIT, 78-83; past vis prof, UCLA, UC Irvine, and Claremont Grad Sch. **HONORS AND AWARDS** Fac of the Month, Mortar Brd Honors Soc, 93; USC Associate s' awd for Excellence in Tchg, 97. **RESEARCH** History of modern philosophy. **SELECTED PUBLICATIONS** Auth, The Conditional Analysis of 'Can': Goldman's 'Reductio' of Lehrer, Philos Stud 28, 75; Skepticism and Kant's B Deduction, Hist Philos Quart 2, 85; Lockean Mechanism, in Its History and Historiography, Dordrecht: D. Reidel, 85; Cartesian Selves and Lockean Substances, Monist 69, 86; Locke on Identity: Matter, Life, and Consciousness, Archiv fuer Geschichte der Philos 69, 87; rep in Essays on Early Modern Philos Vol 8: John Locke: Theory of Knowledge, NY: Garland, 92; Locke's Philosophy of Body, chap in The Cambridge Companion to Locke, Cambridge: Cambridge UP, 94; History: Philosophy of Mind in the Seventeenth and Eighteenth Centuries, chap in the Blackwell Companion to the Philosophy of Mind, Oxford: Blackwell, 94. **CONTACT ADDRESS** Dept of Philosophy, Univ Southern Calif, 3709 Trousdale Pkwy, Los Angeles, CA, 90089-0451. **EMAIL** mccann@bcf.usc.edu

MCCANN, HUGH JOSEPH
PERSONAL Born 12/27/1942, Philadelphia, PA, m, 1965, 4 children **DISCIPLINE** PHILOSOPHY **EDUCATION** Villanova Univ, BA, 64; Univ Chicago, MA, 65, PhD, 72. **CAREER** Instr, Northern IL Univ, 67-68; Prof Philos, TX A&M Univ, 68-, Dept Head, 81-85, Danforth fel, 64. **MEMBERSHIPS** AAUP; Am Philos Asn; Mind Asn; Southwestern Philos Soc; Soc Christian Philosophers. **RESEARCH** Philos of action; metaphysics of time and events; causation and explanation. **SELECTED PUBLICATIONS** Auth, Is raising one's arm a basic action?, J of Philos, 72; Volition and basic action, Philos Rev, 74; Trying, paralysis and volitions, Rev of Metaphysics, 75; Nominals facts, and two conceptions of events, Philos Studies, 79; On mental activity and passivity, 79 & The trouble with level-generation, 82, Mind. **CONTACT ADDRESS** Dept of Philos, Texas A&M Univ, 1 Texas A and M Univ, College Station, TX, 77843. **EMAIL** h-mccann@tamu.edu

MCCARTHY, DENNIS JOHN
PERSONAL Born 10/14/1924, Chicago, IL **DISCIPLINE** OLD TESTAMENT EXEGESIS, SEMITIC LANGUAGES **EDUCATION** St Louis Univ, MA, 51; Inst Cath, Paris, STD, 62; Pontifical Bibl Inst, Rome, SSL, 63. **CAREER** From asst prof to assoc prof Old Testament, St Louis Univ, 63-69; extraordinary prof, 69-74, PROF OLD TESTAMENT, PONTIFICAL BIBL INST, ROME, 74-, Assoc ed, Cath Bibl Quart, 68-76; ED, OLD TESTAMENT, BIBLICA, 79-. **MEMBERSHIPS** Soc Bibl Lit; Cath Bibl Asn Am. **RESEARCH** Old Testament historical books; folklore and literature. **SELECTED PUBLICATIONS** Society, personality and inspiration, Theol Studies, 63; II Samuel 7 and the structure of the Deuteronomic history, J Bibl Lit, 65; Der Gottesbund im Alten Testament, Katholisches Bibelwerk, Ger, 66; Prophetism, In: New Cath Encycl, 67; Kings and Prophets, Bruce, 68; Hosea, In: Jerome Commentary, Old Testament Covenant (in Ital), Blackwell & Marietti 72; Treaty and Covenant: A Study in Form in the Ancient Near Eastern Documents in the Old Testament, 2nd ed, Pontifical Bibl Inst, 78. **CONTACT ADDRESS** Via della Pilotta 25, Rome, ..

MCCARTHY, J. THOMAS
PERSONAL Born 07/02/1937, Detroit, MI **DISCIPLINE** LAW **EDUCATION** Univ Detroit, BS, 60; Univ Mich, Ann Arbor, JD, 63. **CAREER** Atty, San Francisco, 63-66; from asst prof to assoc prof law, 66-72, prof law, Univ San Francisco, 72-, consult, Limbach & Limbach, San Francisco, Calif, 83-. **HONORS AND AWARDS** Centennial Award, Am Intellectual PropertyLaw Asn, 97; Rossman Award, Patent Off Soc, 79. **MEMBERSHIPS** Am Patent Law Asn; Inst Elec & Electronics Engrs; Int Asn Advan Teaching & Res Intellectual Property. **RESEARCH** Trademark law; unfair competition law; antitrust law. **SELECTED PUBLICATIONS** Auth, Trademarks and Unfair Competition (6 vols), West, 4th edition, 96; Rights of Publicity & Privacy (2 vols), West, 87. **CONTACT ADDRESS** Law Sch, Univ of San Francisco, 2130 Fulton St, San Francisco, CA, 94117-1080. **EMAIL** mccarthyt@usfca.edu

MCCARTHY, THOMAS
DISCIPLINE PHILOSOPHY **EDUCATION** Nat Univ Ireland, PhD. **CAREER** Face, Univ Col Dublin and Merrimack Col; instr, Endicott Col, 95-. **RESEARCH** The nature of consciousness and perception. **SELECTED PUBLICATIONS** Auth, The Transcendental Ego and Its Legacy in Phenomenology. **CONTACT ADDRESS** Endicott Col, 376 Hale St, Beverly, MA, 01915.

MCCARTHY, THOMAS A.
PERSONAL Born 03/06/1940, Springfield, MA, m, 1963, 2 children **DISCIPLINE** MATHEMATICS AND PHILOSOPHY **EDUCATION** Holy Cross Col, BS, math, 61; Notre Dame Univ, MA, philos, 63, PhD, philos, 68. **CAREER** Instr, Univ Munich Ger, 68-72; asst to assoc prof, Boston Univ, 72-85; prof of philos, John Shaffer prof in the Humanities, Northwestern Univ, 85-. **HONORS AND AWARDS** Guggenheim fel; NEH fel; ACLS fel; Humboldt fel. **MEMBERSHIPS** Amer Philos Asn; Soc for Phenomenology & Existential Philos. **RESEARCH** Social & political philosophy; German philosophy. **SELECTED PUBLICATIONS** Auth, The Critical Theory of Jurgen Habermas, MIT Press, Hutchinson Press, 78; auth, Ideals and Illusions: On Reconstruction and Deconstruction in Contemporary Critical Theory, MIT Press, 91; co-auth, Critical Theory, Basil Blackwell, 94; co-ed, Understanding and Social Inquiry, Notre Dame Press, 77; co-ed, After Philosophy: End or Transformation?, MIT Press, 86; transl, Legitimation Crisis, by J. Habermas, Beacon, 75; general ed, Studies in Contemporary German Social Thought, MIT Press. **CONTACT ADDRESS** Dept. of Philosophy, Northwestern Univ, 1818 Hinman, Evanston, IL, 60208. **EMAIL** t-mccarthy@nwu.edu

MCCARTHY, TIMOTHY
DISCIPLINE PHILOSOPHY **EDUCATION** Johns Hopkins Univ, PhD, 79. **CAREER** Assoc prof, Univ Ill Urbana Champaign. **RESEARCH** Philosophical logic; philosophy of language; metaphysics; philosophy of mathematics; metaphysical issues in the philosophy of science. **SELECTED PUBLICATIONS** Auth, The Idea of a Logical Constant; Truth Without Satisfaction; Modality, Invariance, and Logical Truth. **CONTACT ADDRESS** Philosophy Dept, Univ Ill Urbana Champaign, 52 E Gregory Dr, Champaign, IL, 61820. **EMAIL** tgmccart@uiuc.edu

MCCARTNEY, DAN GALE
DISCIPLINE NEW TESTAMENT **EDUCATION** Carnegie-Mellon Univ, BFA, 71; Gordon-Conwell Theol Sem, MDiv, 74; Westminster Theol Sem, ThM, 77, PhD, 89. **CAREER** Instr, Manna Bible Inst, 78-81; prof, Westminster Theol Sem, 83-. **SELECTED PUBLICATIONS** Auth, Let the Reader Understand: A Guide to Interpreting and Applying the Bible, Why Does It Have To Hurt?: The Meaning of Christian Suffering; "Logikos in 1 Peter 2:2," Zeitschrift fur neutestamentiche Wissenschaft; Ecce Homo: The Coming of the Kingdom as the Restoration of Human Vicegerency, Westminster Theol Jour, 94. **CONTACT ADDRESS** Westminster Theol Sem, PO Box 27009, Philadelphia, PA, 19118. **EMAIL** dmccartney@wts.edu.

MCCARTNEY, JAMES J.
PERSONAL Born 09/01/1943 **DISCIPLINE** PHILOSOPHY **EDUCATION** Villanova Univ, BA, 66; Wash Theol Union-Augustinian Col, MA, 71; Cath Univ Am, MS, 72; Georgetown Univ, PhD, 81. **CAREER** Tenured assoc prof & dept ch, Villanova Univ; ethicist consult, Holy Redeemer Health Syst; ethicist consult, Cath Health E, Southeast Div; ethicist consult, Franciscan Health Partnership, Inc. **MEMBERSHIPS** Amer Soc for Bioethics and Humanities; Hastings Ctr; Kennedy Inst Ethics; Amer Philos Asn; Soc for Phenomenological and Existential Philos; Cath Theol Soc Am; ed bd, Catholic Studies in Bioethics & HEC Forum. **SELECTED PUBLICATIONS** Auth, Mergers and Sterilization: Ethics in the Board Room, HealthCare Ethics Committee Forum 9:3, 97; The Social Implications of Abortion, J for Peace and Justice Stud 7:1, 96; Consensus Statement on the Triage of Critically Ill Patients, J of the Amer Medl Assn 271:15, 94; Attitudes of Critical Care Medicine Professionals Concerning Distribution of Intensive Care Resources, Critical Care Med 22:2, 94 & Abortion, Social Implications of, in the New Dictionary of Catholic Social Thought, , A Michael Glazier Book, Collegeville, MN: The Liturgical Press, 94. **CONTACT ADDRESS** Dept of Philosophy, Villanova Univ, 800 Lancaster Ave, Villanova, PA, 19085-1692. **EMAIL** jmccartn@email.vill.edu

MCCARTNEY, SHARON
DISCIPLINE LAW **EDUCATION** Pomona Col, BA; Univ Iowa, MFA; Univ Victoria, LLB. **CAREER** Law, Univ Victoria. **SELECTED PUBLICATIONS** Auth, pubs on creative writing. **CONTACT ADDRESS** Fac of Law, Univ Victoria, PO Box 2400, Victoria, BC, V8W 3H7. **EMAIL** sharonmc@uvic.ca

MCCARTY, DORAN CHESTER
PERSONAL Born 02/03/1931, Bolivar, MO, m, 1952, 4 children **DISCIPLINE** PHILOSOPHY, THEOLOGY **EDUCATION** William Jewell Col, AB, 52; Southern Baptist Theol Sem, BD, 56, ThD(theol, philos), 63. **CAREER** Instr relig, William Jewell Col, 66-67; PROF PHILOS & THEOL, MIDWESTERN BAPTIST THEOL SEM, 67-. **MEMBERSHIPS** Soc Bibl Lit; Am Acad Relig; Am Philos Asn. **SELECTED PUBLICATIONS** Auth, Realism in Mathematics, Synthese, vol 0096, 93; Constructibility and Mathematical Existence, Synthese, vol 0096, 93. **CONTACT ADDRESS** Dept of Theol & Christian Philos, Midwestern Baptist Theol Sem, Kansas City, MO, 64118.

MCCAULEY, ROBERT N.
PERSONAL Born 06/01/1952, Gassaway, WV, m, 1975, 1 child **DISCIPLINE** PHILOSOPHY **EDUCATION** Western Mich Univ, BA 74; Univ Chicago, MA 75, PhD 79. **CAREER** Ind Cen Univ, asst prof, 79-83; Emory Univ, asst prof, assoc prof, prof, 83 to 97-. **HONORS AND AWARDS** ACLS Fel; Lilly Endow Postdoc Tchg Awd; Massee-Martin NEH Dist Tchg Prof inaug appt; Emory Williams Dist Tchg awd. **MEMBERSHIPS** SPP; PSA; SSPP; SSSR; APA; NAASR. **RESEARCH** Philosophy of Psychology; Philosophy of Science; Cognitive Approaches to the study of religion. **SELECTED PUBLICATIONS** Auth, The Churchlands and Their Critics, ed, Oxford, Blackwell Pub, 96; auth, Rethinking Religion: Connecting Cognition and Culture, coauth, Cambridge, Cam Univ Press, pbk 93, 2nd print 96; auth, Who Owns Culture?, coauth, Meth and Theory in Study of Religion, 96; auth, Crisis of Conscience, Riddle of Identity: Making Space for a Cognitive Approach to Religious Phenomena, coauth, Jour of the Amer Acad of Religion, 93. **CONTACT ADDRESS** Dept of Philosophy, Emory Univ, Atlanta, GA, 30322. **EMAIL** philrnm@emory.edu

MCCLAIN, T. VAN
PERSONAL Born 06/10/1952, Dallas, TX, m, 1977, 3 children **DISCIPLINE** OLD TESTAMENT AND HEBREW **EDUCATION** SW Baptist Theol Sem, MDiv, 77, PhD, 85. **CAREER** Assoc Prof, Dir library serv, 89-, Mid-Amer Baptist Theol Sem. **MEMBERSHIPS** ETS; SBL. **RESEARCH** Old Testament and New Testament; Semitic Languages; Cults; Hermeneutics. **SELECTED PUBLICATIONS** Auth, The Use of Amos in the New Testament, Mid-America Theol J, 95; Hosea's Marriage to Gomer, Mid-Amer Theol J, 93; Introduction to the Book Of Isaiah, Mid-Amer Theol J, 91. **CONTACT ADDRESS** Northeast Branch, Mid-America Baptist Theol Sem, 2810 Curry Rd, Schenectady, NY, 12303. **EMAIL** VMcClain@mabtsne.edu

MCCLAMROCK, RON
DISCIPLINE PHILOSOPHY **EDUCATION** Mass Inst Tech, PhD. **CAREER** Assoc prof, Univ Albany, State Univ NY. **RESEARCH** Philosophy of psychology, foundations of artificial intelligence and cognitive science, philosophy of the mind and philosophy of science. **SELECTED PUBLICATIONS** Auth, Existential Cognition: Computational Minds in the World, Univ Chicago Press, 95. **CONTACT ADDRESS** Dept of Philosophy, Univ at Albany, SUNY, Albany, NY, 12222. **EMAIL** ron@cnsunix.albany.edu

MCCLEAN, ALBERT
DISCIPLINE LAW **EDUCATION** Queen's Univ, LLB, 57; Cambridge Univ, PhD, 63. **CAREER** Prof, 68-. **HONORS AND AWARDS** Ed, Can Bar Rev, 84-94. **RESEARCH** Property law. **SELECTED PUBLICATIONS** Auth, pubs about advanced real property, equity and trusts, property and restitution. **CONTACT ADDRESS** Fac of Law, Univ British Columbia, 1822 East Mall, Vancouver, BC, V6T 1Z1. **EMAIL** mcclean@law.ubc.ca

MCCLELLAND, WILLIAM LESTER
PERSONAL Born 08/25/1924 **DISCIPLINE** HISTORY OF CHRISTIANITY **EDUCATION** Westminster Col, BA, 48; Pittsburgh Theol Sem, BD, 51, ThM, 56; Princeton Theol Sem, PhD(hist theol), 67. **CAREER** Pastor, Knox United Presby Church, Des Moines, 51-53; pastor, Avalon United Presby Church, Pittsburgh, 53-56; from asst prof to assoc prof, 56-71, dir honors, 67-72, trustee, Bd Trustees, 76-77, chmn dept, 68-74, PROF RELIG, MUSKINGUM COL, 71, CHMN DEPT RELIG & PHILOS, 77, Coordr, Div Arts & Humanities, 81-, Vis lectr, Westminster Col, Eng, 67; Am Col Switz, 69. **MEMBERSHIPS** Am Soc Church Hist; Am Acad Relig; Soc Liturgica; AAUP. **RESEARCH** American religious experience as compared with European religious experience; Reformation history; liturgical history. **SELECTED PUBLICATIONS** Auth, Underhill, Evelyn--Artist of the Infinite Life, Church Hist, vol 0063, 94. **CONTACT ADDRESS** Dept of Relig & Philos, Muskingum Col, New Concord, OH, 43762.

MCCLENDON, JAMES EM., JR.
PERSONAL Shreveport, LA, m, 2 children **DISCIPLINE** THEOLOGY **EDUCATION** Univ Tex, BA, 47; Southwestern Baptist Theol Sem, BD, 50, ThD, 53; Princeton Theol Sem, ThM, 52. **CAREER** Vis prof, Stanford Univ, 67; Univ Notre Dame, 76-77; lectr, Goucher Col, 70-71; vis assoc prof, Temple Univ 69; vis lectr, Univ Pa, 70; vis prof, Baylor Univ, 95; prof, Golden Gate Baptist Theol Sem, 54-66; prof, Grad Theol Union, 71-90; scholar in residence, Fuller Theol Sem, 90-. **HONORS AND AWARDS** Rockefeller Brothers Fund grant, 62-63. **MEMBERSHIPS** Am Soc of Church Hist; Am Philos Asn; Nat Coun of Churches; Pacific Coast Theol Soc; Am Acad of Relig; Nat Asn of Baptist Prof of Relig. **RESEARCH** Systematic theology; Radical reformation. **SELECTED PUBLICATIONS** Co-auth, Baptist Roots: A Reader in the Historic Theology of a Christian People, 99; auth, Doctrine, Systematic Theology Volume 11, 94; co-auth, Convictions: Defusing Religious Relativism, 94; Ethics: Systematic Theology Volume 1, 94; Biography as Theology, 90; auth, "Protestant Theology: USA," 93. **CONTACT ADDRESS** Fuller Theol Sem, Box 222, Pasadena, CA, 91182.

MCCOLLOUGH, C. THOMAS
DISCIPLINE RELIGION **EDUCATION** Univ Fla, BA; Duke Univ, MDiv; Univ Notre Dame, MA and PhD. **CAREER** Fac, 80-; prof, current. **RESEARCH** History of Christianity and Christian thought; Biblical history and archaeology; contemporary Middle East. **SELECTED PUBLICATIONS** Auth, contribu, Studi Patristica, Relig Studies Rev; co-ed, Archaeology and the Galilee: Text and Context in the Graeco-Roman and Byzantine Periods, Scholars Press, 97. **CONTACT ADDRESS** Centre Col, 600 W Walnut St, Danville, KY, 40422. **EMAIL** mccollog@centre.edu

MCCOLLOUGH, THOMAS ELMORE
PERSONAL Born 06/26/1926, Birmingham, AL, m, 1956, 2 children **DISCIPLINE** RELIGION **EDUCATION** Univ Tex, BBA, 47; Southern Baptist Theol Sem, BD, 50, ThD, 55. **CAREER** Asst prof relig, Stetson Univ, 55-58; assoc prof theol, Baptist Theol Sem, Switz, 58-61; asst prof, 61-66, ASSOC PROF RELIG, DUKE UNIV, 66-, Teaching fel theol, Southern Baptist Theol Sem, 50-52; Soc Relig Higher Educ cross disciplinary fel, London Sch Econ, 67-68. **MEMBERSHIPS** Am Soc Christian Ethics; Am Acad Relig; fel Soc Relig Higher Educ. **RESEARCH** Theology; ethics. **SELECTED PUBLICATIONS** Auth, Moral Fragments and Moral Community--A Proposal for Church in Society, J Church and State, vol 0036, 94. **CONTACT ADDRESS** Dept of Relig, Duke Univ, Durham, NC, 27706.

MCCONNAUGHAY, PHILIP J.
DISCIPLINE LAW **EDUCATION** Univ Ill, BA; JD. **CAREER** Assoc prof, Univ Ill Urbana Champaign, 95-. **MEMBERSHIPS** Phi Beta Kapp;Univ Ill Law Forum. **RESEARCH** Copyright; evidence; international business transactions; and international litigation and arbitration. **SELECTED PUBLICATIONS** Auth, pubs on international commercial dispute resolution, commercial law reform in emerging nations, and comparative legal ethics. **CONTACT ADDRESS** Law Dept, Univ Ill Urbana Champaign, 52 E Gregory Dr, Champaign, IL, 61820. **EMAIL** pmcconna@law.uiuc.edu

MCCONNELL, JEFF
PERSONAL Born 06/10/1953, Newport, RI **DISCIPLINE** PHILOSOPHY **EDUCATION** Harvard, AB, 77; MA Inst of Tech, PhD, 94 **CAREER** Lect, 88-pres, Tufts Univ **MEMBERSHIPS** Am Philos Assoc; Philos of Sci Assoc; Soc for Phi-

los & Psychol **RESEARCH** Metaphysics of Origins; Mind-Body Problem **SELECTED PUBLICATIONS** Auth, In Defense of the Knowledge Argument, Philosophical Topics 22, 94 **CONTACT ADDRESS** Dept of Philos, Tufts Univ, 7 Spaulding St, Medford, MA, 02155. **EMAIL** jmcconne@emerald.tufts.edu

MCCONNELL, TERRANCE C.
PERSONAL Born 12/19/1948, Zanesville, OH, m, 1970 **DISCIPLINE** PHILOSOPHY **EDUCATION** Wittenberg Univ, BA, 71; Univ MN, PhD, 75. **CAREER** Tchg asst philos, Univ MN, 71-74, instr, 74-75; asst prof, Carleton Col & St Olaf Col, 75-76; asst prof, 76-80, Assoc Prof Philos, 80-87, prof philos, Univ NC-Greensboro, 87-, Fac fel, Univ NC, Greensboro. **HONORS AND AWARDS** Nat Endowment for the Hum fel, 89-90; Nat Endowment for the Hum fel, 95-96. **MEMBERSHIPS** Am Philos Asn; Inst for Soc, Ethics & Life Sci. **RESEARCH** Ethics; polit philos; med ethics. **SELECTED PUBLICATIONS** Auth, Augustine on torturing and punishing an innocent person, Southern J Philos, Vol XVII, pages 481-492; The incentive argument for the unionization of medical workers, J Med Ethics, Vol 5, pages 182-184; Utilitarianism and Supererogatory Acts, Ratio, Vol XXII, pages 36-38; Donagan on act and agent evaluations, Philos Studies, Vol 38, pages 97-100; Utilitarianism and conflict resolution, Logique et Analyse, Vol 24, pages 245-257; Moral blackmail, Ethics, Vol 91, pages 544-567; Moral absolutism and the problem of hard cases, J Relig Ethic, Vol 9, pages 286-297; Gratitude, Temple Univ Press, 93; Moral Issues in Health Care, 2nd ed, Wadsworth Publ. **CONTACT ADDRESS** Dept of Philos, Univ of N. Carolina, 1000 Spring Garden, Greensboro, NC, 27402-6170. **EMAIL** mcconnea@iago.uncg.edu

MCCONNELL, WILLIAM HOWARD
PERSONAL Born 07/02/1930, Aylmer East, PQ, Canada, m, 1963, 2 children **DISCIPLINE** LAW, POLITICAL SCIENCE **EDUCATION** Carleton Univ, BA, 55; Univ NB, BCL, 58; Univ Toronto, PhD(polit sci), 68; Univ Sask, LLM, 70. **CAREER** Lectr polit sci, Bishop's Univ, 66-69; from asst prof to assoc prof law, 70-75, PROF LAW, UNIV SASK, 75-, Assoc prof law, Univ Windsor, 74-75; consult const law, Govt Northwest Territories, 75-78 & Govt Sask, 77-81. **MEMBERSHIPS** Can Bar Asn; Can Asn Law Teachers. **RESEARCH** Constitutional law; comparative federalism; international law. **SELECTED PUBLICATIONS** Auth, Disruptions, Constitutional Struggles from the Charter to Meech Lake, Can Hist Rev, vol 0073, 92. **CONTACT ADDRESS** Col of Law, Univ of Sask, Saskatoon, SK, S7N 0W0.

MCCORMICK, R.A.
PERSONAL Born 10/03/1922, Toledo, OH, s **DISCIPLINE** MORAL THEOLOGY **EDUCATION** Loyola Univ, BA, 45; MA, 50; Gregorian Univ, STD, 57. **CAREER** Prof, Jesuit Sch Theol, 57-73; prof, Kennedy Inst Ethics, Georgetown Univ, 74-86; prof, Univ Notre Dame, 86- . **HONORS AND AWARDS** 14 honorary degrees. **MEMBERSHIPS** Cath Theol Soc; Am Soc of Christian Ethics. **RESEARCH** Fundamental moral, medical ethics. **SELECTED PUBLICATIONS** Auth, Notes on Moral Theology 1981-1984, 84; auth, The Critical Calling: Moral Dilemmas Since Vatican II, 89; auth, Corrective Vision: Explorations n Moral Theology, 94; auth, Readings in Moral Theology No. IX, 96. **CONTACT ADDRESS** Theol. Dept., Univ of Notre Dame, 327 O'Shaughnessy Hall, Notre Dame, IN, 46556.

MCCOY, FRANCIS T.
DISCIPLINE LAW **EDUCATION** Univ Fla, AB, MA, JD. **CAREER** Prof emer, Univ Fla, 56-; past Vice Consul, US For Serv; vis prof, Johann Wolfgang Goethe Univ, Ger. **MEMBERSHIPS** Fla Bar; Phi Beta Kappa. **RESEARCH** Admiralty, legal history, family law. **CONTACT ADDRESS** School of Law, Univ of Florida, PO Box 117625, Gainesville, FL, 32611-7625. **EMAIL** McCoy@law.ufl.edu

MCCOY, JERRY
DISCIPLINE RELIGION AND PHILOSOPHY **EDUCATION** DePauw Univ, BA; Northwestern Univ, MA; Christian Theol Sem, MDiv; Columbia Univ/Union Theol Sem, PhD. **CAREER** Prof, Eureka Col. **HONORS AND AWARDS** Rep Christian Church, World Coun Churches, 95. **RESEARCH** Western relig traditions and Asian relig(s). **SELECTED PUBLICATIONS** Auth, book on Christianity and ecology. **CONTACT ADDRESS** Eureka Col, 300 E College Ave, PO Box 280, Eureka, IL, 61530.

MCCOY, PATRICIA A.
PERSONAL Born 06/20/1954, Cortland, NY **DISCIPLINE** LAW **EDUCATION** Univ Cal Berk, JD 83; Oberlin Col BA 76. **CAREER** Cleveland State Univ MC of Law, asst prof, 97-; Mayer Brown Platt DC, partner, 91-92, assoc 84-90, sum assoc 83; Hon Robert S. Vance, law clk, 83-84. **HONORS AND AWARDS** Prof of the Year; Howard L. Oleck Awd; 6 Clev Marsh Fac Res Gnts; Ger Marshall Fund; Named DC Pro Bono Lawyer. **MEMBERSHIPS** DCB **RESEARCH** Banking regulation; corp law; corp finance; post-socialist econ reforms. **SELECTED PUBLICATIONS** Auth, Special Factors Making Small Post-Socialist Economies Susceptible to Bank System Risk, in: Global Trends and Changes in East European Banking, ed, Ewa Miklaszewka, Jagiellonian Univ, 98; The Demise of the Common Law Doctrine in D'Oench Duhme, Matthew Bender, 98; Banking Law Manual, 2nd ed, Matthew Bender, forthcoming 99; Levers of Law Reform: Public Goods and Russian Banking, Cornell Intl Law Jour, 97; A Political Economy of the Business Judgment Rule in Banking: Implications for Corporate Law, Case W Res L Rev, 96; The Notional Business Judgment Rule in Banking, Cath U L Rev, 95. **CONTACT ADDRESS** Dept of Law, Cleveland State Univ, 1801 Euclid Ave, Cleveland, OH, 44115. **EMAIL** pmccoy@trans.csuohio.edu

MCCOY, THOMAS RAYMOND
PERSONAL Born 04/14/1943, Cincinnati, OH, m, 1968, 2 children **DISCIPLINE** CONSTITUTIONAL LAW **EDUCATION** Xavier Univ, BS, 64; Univ Cincinnati, JD, 67; Harvard Univ, LLM, 68. **CAREER** Asst prof, 68-71, assoc prof, 71-75, assoc dean, 71-75, prof law, Sch of Law, Vanderbilt Univ, 75-. **RESEARCH** The religion clauses in the First Amendment; judicial jurisdiction and conflict of laws; alternative dispute resolution; conceptual language and syllogistic reasoning. **SELECTED PUBLICATIONS** Auth, Commentary on Katzenbach v McClung, The Oxford Companion to the Supreme Court of the United States, 92; coauth, Conditional Spending, Encyclopedia of the American Constitution, 92; art, The Sophisticated Consumer's Guide to Alternative Dispute Resolution Techniques: What You Should Expect (or Demand) from ADR Services, Proc of the Surety Claims Inst, 92 & 26 U.Memphis L Rev, 96; art, The Whys and Ways of Mediation -- A Guide for the Sophisticated User, Business Law Today, 92; art, A Coherent Methodology for First Amendment Speech and Religion Clause Cases, 48 Vand L Rev 1335, 95. **CONTACT ADDRESS** Sch of Law, Vanderbilt Univ, 2201 West End Ave S, Nashville, TN, 37240-0001. **EMAIL** tmccoy@law.vanderbilt.edu

MCCRACKEN, CHARLES JAMES
PERSONAL Born 04/17/1933, Los Angeles, CA, m, 1956, 2 children **DISCIPLINE** PHILOSOPHY **EDUCATION** Univ Calif, Los Angeles, BA, 55; Fordham Univ, MA, 59; Univ Calif, Berkeley, PhD, 69. **CAREER** From instr to asst prof, 65-71, assoc prof, 71-80, prof philos, Mich State Univ, 80-. **HONORS AND AWARDS** MSU distinguished faculty award, 98. **MEMBERSHIPS** AAUP; Am Philos Asn. **RESEARCH** History of modern philosophy; epistemology; metaphysics. **SELECTED PUBLICATIONS** Auth, Malebranche and British Philosophy, Oxford Univ Press, 83. **CONTACT ADDRESS** Dept of Philosophy, Michigan State Univ, 503 S Kedzie Hall, East Lansing, MI, 48824-1032. **EMAIL** mccrack2@pilot.msu.edu

MCCULLAGH, MARK
DISCIPLINE PHILOSOPHY **EDUCATION** Philos, Math, BA; Philos, PhD. **CAREER** Asst Prof, SMU, 97-. **HONORS AND AWARDS** Soc Sci and Humanities Res Council Doctoral Fel; Alan Ross Anderson Fel. **MEMBERSHIPS** Am Philos Asn. **RESEARCH** Philosophy of language; Philos of Mind. **SELECTED PUBLICATIONS** Auth, Mediality and Rationality in Aristotle's Account of Excellence of Character, Aperion, 95. **CONTACT ADDRESS** Dept of Philosophy, SMU, Box 750142, Dallas, TX, 75175. **EMAIL** mcculle@mail.smu.edu

MCCULLOCH, ELIZABETH
DISCIPLINE LAW **EDUCATION** Univ Mich, BGS; Duke Law Sch, JD. **CAREER** Dir, soc pol ctr govt responsibility; governors comn on child support; state Fla human subjects rev coun; co health care bd; pres, sexual and physical abuse resource ctr; dir, Fla bar found public serv law fellows; atty, VISTA Jacksonville legal aid; staff atty & dir, family law unit, JALA. **HONORS AND AWARDS** Grant recipient, Dept Hea and Rehab Svcs, Dept Educ, State WAGES bd, AvMed, Fla Bar Found. **RESEARCH** Poverty law and policy, family law, legal services to the poor. **CONTACT ADDRESS** School of Law, Univ of Florida, PO Box 117625, Gainesville, FL, 32611-7625. **EMAIL** McCulloc@law.ufl.edu

MCCULLOH, GERALD WILLIAM
PERSONAL Born 05/03/1941, St. Paul, MN, m, 1967, 2 children **DISCIPLINE** THEOLOGY, PHILOSOPHY OF RELIGION **EDUCATION** Vanderbilt Univ, BA, 62; Harvard Univ, MDiv, 65; Univ Chicago, MA, 68, PhD(hist & systematic theol), 73. **CAREER** Instr humanities, Cent YMCA Community Col, 68; instr theol, 69-73, asst prof, 73-80, Assoc Prof Theol, Loyola Univ Chicago, 80-, Ed, 19th Century Theol Work Group Diss Set, 73-75; ed, Texts, 79; mem steering comt, 19th Century Theol Work Group, 76-; assoc Protestant Chaplain, Loyola Univ, 74-; res leave, Gottingen Univ, 81. **MEMBERSHIPS** Am Acad Relig; Am Acad Polit & Soc Sci; AAUP. **RESEARCH** Nineteenth century theology; American religious experience; history and structure of religious thought. **SELECTED PUBLICATIONS** Auth, Jurgen Moltmann, The Theology of Hope, J Relig, 1/69; Robert M Miller, How shall they hear without a preacher? The life of Ernest Fremont Tittle, Mid-Am, 4/72; Albrecht Ritschl three essays, J Relig, 1/74; ed St auth, A Bibliography of Dissertations in Nineteenth Century Theology: 1960-1976, privately publ, 76; Profiles in Belief: The Religious Bodies of the United States and Canada, Vol II, Protestant Denominations, Nat Cath news Serv, 12/78; Bibliography of Dissertations in Nineteenth Century Theology: 1960-1976, Loyola Univ, 76. **CONTACT ADDRESS** Dept of Theol, Univ of Chicago, 6525 N Sheridan Rd, Chicago, IL, 60626-5385. **EMAIL** gmccull@luc.edu

MCCULLOUGH, LAURENCE B.
PERSONAL Born 08/02/1947, Philadelphia, PA, m, 1977 **DISCIPLINE** MEDICAL ETHICS **EDUCATION** Williams Col, BA, 69; Univ Texas, Austin, PhD, 75. **CAREER** Asst prof, hum and med, Texas A & M Univ, 76-79; asst prof, 79-82, assoc prof, 82-87, prof of Family and Commun Med, Georgetown Univ; prof, med and med ethics, Baylor Col of Med, 88-. **HONORS AND AWARDS** Post-doctoral fel, 75-76; Am Coun of Learned Soc Fel, 95-96. **MEMBERSHIPS** Am Soc for Bioethics and Hum; Gerontological Soc of Am. **RESEARCH** Bioethics; history of medical ethics; Leibniz. **SELECTED PUBLICATIONS** Coauth, Ethics in Obstretics and Gynecology, Oxford, 94; ed, Long-Term Care Decisions: Ethical and Conceptual Dimensions, Johns Hopkins, 95; auth, Leibniz on Individuals and Individuation: The Persistence of Premodern Ideas in Modern Philosophy, Kluwer, 96; auth, John Gregory and the Invention of Professional Medical Ethics and the Profession of Medicine, Kluwer, 98; co-ed, Surgical Ethics, Oxford, 98; ed, John Gregory's Writings on Medical Ethics and Philosophy of Medicine, Kluwer, 98; coauth, Medical Ethics: Codes and Statements, BNA, 2000. **CONTACT ADDRESS** Center for Medical Ethics and Health Policy, Baylor Col of Med, One Baylor Plz, Houston, TX, 77030. **EMAIL** mccullou@bcm.tmc.edu

MCCULLOUGH, RALPH C., II
DISCIPLINE TORTS, LAW AND MEDICINE, DAMAGES, AND TRIAL ADVOCACY **EDUCATION** Erskine Col, BA, 62; Tulane Univ, JD, 65. **CAREER** Am Col Trial Lawyers prof, Univ of SC. **SELECTED PUBLICATIONS** Coauth, bk(s) on civil litigation in the fed courts and on SC torts law. **CONTACT ADDRESS** School of Law, Univ of S. Carolina, Law Center, Columbia, SC, 29208. **EMAIL** law0150@univscvm.csd.scarolina.edu

MCDANIEL, JOHN B.
DISCIPLINE RELIGION **EDUCATION** Vanderbilt Univ, BA, 72; Claremont Sch Theol, PhD, 78. **CAREER** Prof, Hendrix Col. **RESEARCH** Buddhism. **SELECTED PUBLICATIONS** Auth, Of God and Pelicans. **CONTACT ADDRESS** Hendrix Col, Conway, AR, 72032.

MCDANIEL, THOMAS F.
PERSONAL Baltimore, MD, m **DISCIPLINE** OLD TESTAMENT STUDIES AND HEBREW **EDUCATION** Univ Richmond, BA; E Baptist Theol Sem, BD; Univ Pa, MA, 56; Johns Hopkins Univ, PhD, 66. **CAREER** Prof, E Baptist Theol Sem. **SELECTED PUBLICATIONS** Auth, rev, Deborah Never Sang: A Philol Commentary on Judges 5, Makor Press, Jerusalem, 83. **CONTACT ADDRESS** Eastern Baptist Theol Sem, 6 Lancaster Ave, Wynnewood, PA, 19096.

MCDERMOTT, A. CHARLENE
PERSONAL Born 03/11/1937, Hazelton, PA, m, 1988, 3 children **DISCIPLINE** PHILOSOPHY **EDUCATION** Univ Penn, BA, 56, PhD, 64. **CAREER** Prof philos, 76-86, assoc dean, dir Asian Stud, 78-81, dean grad stud, 81-86, Univ New Mexico; prof philos 86-91, provost and vice-pres Acad Affairs, 86-89, CCNY; dean in residence, consultant, Council of Grad Sch, 85-86; dean for acad and student affairs, consultant, Albuquerque Acad, 91-93; acad consultant, grant writer, vis prof, 93- . **HONORS AND AWARDS** Phi Beta Kappa; Univ New Mexico res allocations comm grant; NEH fel, AAUW fel; listed, Who's Who in Am, Who's Who in Am Educ, Dict of Int Biog. **SELECTED PUBLICATIONS** Auth, An Eleventh Century Logic of Exists, Reidel of Dordrecht, Netherlands; auth, Beothius of Dacia's Treatis on the Modes of Signifying, John Benjamins, Netherlands, 80; auth, Comparative Philosophy: Selected Essays, University Press, 83. **CONTACT ADDRESS** PO Box 1814, Corrales, NM, 87048.

MCDERMOTT, GERALD D.
PERSONAL Born 10/26/1952, m, 1976, 3 children **DISCIPLINE** RELIGION/RELIGION IN AMERICA **EDUCATION** Univ Chicago, BA, New Testament and early Christian studies, 74; North Dakota State Univ, BS, history, edu, 82; Grand Rapids Baptist Seminary, MRE, 82; Univ Iowa, PhD, 89. **CAREER** Assoc prof religion & philos, Roanoke Coll, 88-. **HONORS AND AWARDS** Fellowship for Young Scholars in American Religion, Center for the Study of Religion and American Culture, 92-93; Woodrow Wilson Award for outstanding scholarly article: "Jonathan Edwards, the City on a Hill, and the Redeemer Nation: A Reappraisal", 93; selected by Roanoke Coll student body to give "Last Lecture," 93; member, Center Theol Inquiry, Aug 95 - July 96; Mednick Fellowship, Virginia Found Independent Colls, 95. **RESEARCH** Jonathan Edwards; relationship between Christianity and the world religions. **SELECTED PUBLICATIONS** Auth, One Holy and Happy Society: The Public Theology of Jonathan Edwards, 92; coauth, A Medical

and Spiritual Guide to Living with Cancer, 93; coauth, Dear God, It's Cancer, 97; auth, Jonathan Edwards Confronts the Gods: Christian Theology, Enlightenment Religion, and Non-Christian Religions, forthcoming; auth, Can Evangelicals Learn from the Buddha? Jesus, Revelation and the Religions, 99. **CONTACT ADDRESS** Dept of Religion, Roanoke Col, Salem, VA, 24153. **EMAIL** mcdermott@roanoke.edu

MCDERMOTT, JOHN J.
PERSONAL Born 02/18/1960, Britt, IA, s **DISCIPLINE** SCRIPTURE **EDUCATION** Harvard Univ, BA, 82; St. Meinrad Sch of Theol, 86; Pontifical Bibl Inst, 1992 **CAREER** Asst Prof, 92-pres, Loras Col **MEMBERSHIPS** Cath Bibl Assoc; Soc of Bibl Lit **RESEARCH** Early Israelite History **SELECTED PUBLICATIONS** Auth, "Multipurpose Genealogies," The Bible Today, 97; Auth, "What are they saying about the formation of Ancient Israel," Paulist Press, 98 **CONTACT ADDRESS** Loras Col, PO Box 222, Dubuque, IA, 52044-0178. **EMAIL** mcdermot@lcac1.loras.edu

MCDERMOTT, JOHN J.
DISCIPLINE PHILOSOPHY **EDUCATION** Fordham, PhD. **CAREER** Univ Distinguished prof, Texas A&M Univ. **SELECTED PUBLICATIONS** Auth, The Culture of Experience: Philosophical Essays in the American Grain, NYU, 76; Streams of Experience: Reflections on the History and Philosophy of American Culture, Mass, 86; ed, The Writings of William James, Chicago, 77 & The Philosophy of John Dewey, Chicago, 81. **CONTACT ADDRESS** Dept of Philosophy, Texas A&M Univ, College Station, TX, 77843-4237.

MCDEVITT, ANTHONY
PERSONAL Born 07/25/1925, Birmingham, AL, s **DISCIPLINE** THEOLOGY; CANON LAW **EDUCATION** St Mary's Univ, Baltimore, BA, 45, StL, 49; Lateran Univ, Rome, JCD, 53. **CAREER** Expert at II Vatican Council, 63-65; Judicial Vicar, Diocese of Mobile, 62-98. **MEMBERSHIPS** Cath Theol Soc Am; Canon Law Soc Am; Amer Acad Religion **RESEARCH** Theology; Canon Law **CONTACT ADDRESS** Drawer D, Mobile, AL, 36601. **EMAIL** Tonymcd@aol.com

MCDONALD, PATRICIA M.
PERSONAL Born 06/12/1946, Scarborough, England **DISCIPLINE** RELIGION **EDUCATION** Catholic Univ of America, PhD 89; Pontifical Biblical Inst Rome, LSS 86; Univ Cambridge, MPhil 83; Heythrope Col, Univ London, BD 72; Univ Cambridge England, BA, MA 68/71. **CAREER** Catholic Univ of America, asst prof, 89-90; Mount St. Mary's Col MD, asst prof, assoc prof, 90 to 96-. **MEMBERSHIPS** CBA; SBL; CTS **SELECTED PUBLICATIONS** Auth, Biblical Brinkmanship: Francis Gigot and the New York Review, in: William L. Portier and Sandra Yokum Mize, eds, American Catholic Traditions: Resources for Renewal, Col Theol Soc, Maryknoll NY, Orbis Press, 97; Three entries in: The Pastoral Dictionary of Biblical Theology, Liturgical Press, 96; Romans 5:1-11 as a Rhetorical Bridge, Jour for the Stud of the New Testament, 90. **CONTACT ADDRESS** Theology Dept, Mount St. Mary's Col, Emmitsburg, MD, 21727. **EMAIL** mcdonald@msmary.edu

MCDONALD, PETER J.T.
PERSONAL Born 02/04/1956, Germany, m, 1988, 2 children **DISCIPLINE** PHILOSOPHY **EDUCATION** Catholic Univ, MA, 80; Freiburg Univ, PhD, 97. **CAREER** Adj prof Philos, Dominican House Studies, 97-. **MEMBERSHIPS** Am Philos Asn; Martin Heidegger Gesellschaft. **RESEARCH** Phenomenology. **SELECTED PUBLICATIONS** Auth, Daseinsanalytik und Grundfrage. Zur Einheit und Ganzheit von Heideggers Sein und Ziet, 97. **CONTACT ADDRESS** 17104 Laburnum Court, Rockville, MD, 20855-2504. **EMAIL** PMcDonald@compuserve.com

MCDONOUGH, SHEILA
DISCIPLINE RELIGION **EDUCATION** McGill Univ, PhD, 63. **CAREER** Prof. **RESEARCH** 19th and 20th century South Asian Islam, Muslim/Christian relations. **SELECTED PUBLICATIONS** Auth, Gandhi's Responses to Islam, New Delhi, D.K. Printworld, 94; The Muslims of Montreal, Muslim Communities of North America, New York: SUNY, 95; Typology of Religion and State, Religion, Law and Society, WCC Press, 95; The Impact of Social Change on Muslim Women, Gender Genre and Religion, Wilfred Laurier UP: 95; India 1857-1947, Muslim and Other Religions, Oxford UP, 96; Poetry and Ethics, The Legacy of Fazlur Rahman, Univ Edmonton Press, 96; Visions du future des musulmansm, Religiologiques, 96. **CONTACT ADDRESS** Dept of Rel, Concordia Univ, Montreal, 1455 de Maisonneuve W, Montreal, PQ, H3G 1M8.

MCDORMAN, TED L.
DISCIPLINE LAW **EDUCATION** Univ Toronto, BA, 76; Dalhousie Univ, LLB, 79, LLM, 82. **CAREER** Assoc prof, 85-. **SELECTED PUBLICATIONS** Auth, pubs on ocean law and policy, trade law and comparative constitutional law. **CONTACT ADDRESS** Fac of Law, Univ Victoria, PO Box 2400, Victoria, BC, V8W 3H7. **EMAIL** tlmcdorm@uvic.ca

MCDOWELL, MARKUS
PERSONAL Born 07/21/1960, Chattanooga, TN, m, 1986, 1 child **DISCIPLINE** RELIGION **EDUCATION** Abilene Christian Univ, BS, 83; Pepperdine Univ, MS, 92, Mdiv, 96. **CAREER** Assoc min, Camarillo Church of Christ, 95-96; youth min, Camarillo Church of Christ, 88-; bk rev ed, Leaven, 95; tchg asst, 95; adjunct prof, 96-. **HONORS AND AWARDS** J P, Gloria Sanders scholar, Pepperdine Univ, 89-96; Howard A. White scholar, 89. **MEMBERSHIPS** Mem, Soc Bibl Lit; Cath Bibl Assn Am. **SELECTED PUBLICATIONS** Auth, George Eldon Ladd," Scribner's American Biography, Vol 1, Scribner & Sons, 98; L. Ron Hubbard, Scribner's American Biography, Vol 2, Scribner & Sons, 98; What Are Human Being That You Are Mindful Of Them?: A worship service based on Psalm 8, Leaven, 96; Preaching Biblical and Modern, Leaven, 95; Cyberspace Helps Spread the Gospel,Ventura County Star, 95; rev(s), Matson, David Lertis. Household Conversion Narratives in Acts: Patterns and Interpretations, Leaven, 97; Miller, Patrick, They Cried Unto the Lord: The Form and Theology of Biblical Prayer, Leaven, 96; Fee, Gordon, God's Empowering Presence: The Holy Spirit in the Letters of Paul, Leaven, 95; Brueggemann, Walter, Finally Comes the Poet: Daring Speech for Proclamation, Leaven, 95. **CONTACT ADDRESS** Dept of Relig, Pepperdine Univ, 24255 Pacific Coast Hwy, Malibu, CA, 90263. **EMAIL** mhmcdowe@pepperdine.edu

MCELENEY, NEIL JOSEPH
PERSONAL Born 08/08/1927, Charlestown, MA **DISCIPLINE** THEOLOGY **EDUCATION** St Paul's Col, DC, AB, 50, MA, 53; Cath Univ Am, STL, 54; Pontif Bibl Inst, Rome, SSB, 55, SSL, 56. **CAREER** Prof sacred scripture, St Paul's Col, DC, 56-73; prof New Testament & Greek, St Patrick's Sem, 75-78; ADJ ASSOC PROF, CATH UNIV AM, DC, 79-, Ed & contribr, Pamphlet Bible Ser, Paulist, 60-73; vis prof, Cath Univ Am, 61, Marist Col, 64, Univ Dayton, 65 & 66 & St Louis Univ, 69; res assoc, William Foxwell Albright Inst Archaeol Res in Jerusalem, 73-74. **HONORS AND AWARDS** CBA Prof, Pontif Bibl Inst, Rome, 82. **MEMBERSHIPS** Am Acad Relig; Soc Bibl Lit; Soc Old Testament Study Gt Brit; Cath Bibl Asn England; Cath Theol Soc Am. **RESEARCH** Scriptural studies; Bible. **SELECTED PUBLICATIONS** Auth, As Ministers of Christ--The Christological Dimension of Ministry in the New Testament, Cath Bibl Quart, vol 0055, 93; The Unity and Theme of Matthew VII,1-12 + An Analysis of Inner Relationships as Exemplifying Exegetical Diversity Within New Testament Gospel Passages, Cath Bibl Quart, vol 0056, 94. **CONTACT ADDRESS** Dept of Philos Cath, St Pauls Coll, Washington, DC, 20017.

MCELHANEY, JAMES WILLSON
PERSONAL Born 12/10/1937, New York, NY, m, 1961, 2 children **DISCIPLINE** LAW **EDUCATION** Duke Univ, AB, 60, LLB, 62. **CAREER** Atty, Wis, 62-63; from asst prof to prof law, Sch Law, Univ Md, Baltimore, 66-73; prof, Sch Law, Southern Methodist Univ, 74-76; vis Joseph C Hostetler prof trial pract & advocacy, 76-77, JOSEPH C HOSTETLER PROF TRIAL PRACT & ADVOCACY, SCH LAW, CASE WESTERN RESERVE UNIV, 77-, Atty, Wickham, Borgelt, Skogstad & Powell, Wis, 66; mem adv comt landlord-tenant laws, Nat Conf Comnrs on Uniform State Laws, 69-73; reporter, Governor's Comn Landlord-Tenant Law, Md, 70-73; consult, Md Comprehensive Health Planning Agency, 71-73; vis prof law, Southern Methodist Univ, 76. **MEMBERSHIPS** Am Bar Asn; Asn Am Law Sch. **RESEARCH** Conflict of laws; landlord-tenant law; litigation and evidence. **SELECTED PUBLICATIONS** Auth, Publishing the Exhibit, ABA J, vol 0079, 93; Authentication, ABA J, vol 0079, 93; The Real Message, ABA J, vol 0079, 93; Jury Voir Dire--Getting the Most Out of Jury Selection, ABA J, vol 0079, 93; Highlighting, ABA J, vol 0079, 93; Helping the Witness--Techniques for Keeping Witnesses Out of Trouble, ABA J, vol 0079, 93; Limited Admissibility--Keeping Evidence on Track, ABA J, vol 0079, 93; Focusing the Deposition--Using Your Goals to Guide Your Deposition Techniques, ABA J, vol 0079, 93; Rehabilitation, ABA J, vol 0079, 93; Understanding Character Evidence, ABA J, vol 0079, 93; Staying Out of Jail, ABA J, vol 0079, 93; Its Happening Now, ABA J, vol 0079, 93; Using the Exhibit, ABA J, vol 0080, 94; Good Ways to Lose, ABA J, vol 0080, 94; The Human Factor, ABA J, vol 0080, 94; Creative Objecting, ABA J, vol 0080, 94; Breaking the Rules of Cross--Fast Thinking Will Lift Inquiry Beyond Mediocrity, ABA J, vol 0080, 94; Showtime for the Jury, ABA J, vol 0080, 94; Liar, vol 80, Pg 74, Yr 1994, ABA J, vol 0080, 94; The Absent Witness, ABA J, vol 0080, 94; Working the File, ABA J, vol 0080, 94; Composting Files, ABA J, vol 0080, 94; The Varying Terrain of Impeachment, ABA J, vol 0080, 94; Liar, ABA J, vol 0080, 94; Blind Cross-Examination, ABA J, vol 0080, 94; How You Argue Will Affect Whether the Judge Sees Things Your Way, ABA J, vol 0081, 95; Litigating in Theory, ABA J, vol 0081, 95; Writing to the Ear, ABA J, vol 0081, 95; Advocacy in Other Forums, ABA J, vol 0081, 95; Putting the Case Together, ABA J, vol 0081, 95; Mongo on the Loose, ABA J, vol 0081, 95; Witness Profiles, ABA J, vol 0081, 95; Jury Instructions, ABA J, vol 0081, 95; Opening Statements--to Be Effective With the Jury, Tell a Good Story, ABA J, vol 0081, 95; Making Evidence, ABA J, vol 0081, 95; Finding the Right Script, ABA J, vol 0081, 95; When Admissibility Is the Issue, ABA J, vol 0081, 95; A Shot in the Foot, ABA J, vol 0082, 96; 12 Ways to a Bad Brief, ABA J, vol 0082, 96; The Case Wont Settle--Things Are Different When You Know Youre Going to Trial, ABA J, vol 0082, 96; The Art of Persuasive Legal Writing, ABA J, vol 0082, 96 ; Prepping the Ceo, ABA J, vol 0082, 96; Making the Most of Motions, ABA J, vol 0082, 96; A Matter of Style, ABA J, vol 0082, 96; Organizing the Witness List, ABA J, vol 0082, 96; Hung by Dangling Facts, ABA J, vol 0082, 96; Gestapo Impeachment, ABA J, vol 0082, 96; Reasonable Arguments, ABA J, vol 0082, 96; Winning Arguments, ABA J, vol 0082, 96; Evasive Witnesses, ABA J, vol 0083, 97; Winning Deposition Tactics, ABA J, vol 0083, 97; Disarming Tactics, ABA J, vol 0083, 97; Strategy for Dragonslayers, ABA J, vol 0083, 97; How I Solved My Evidence Problem, ABA J, vol 0083, 97; Gizmos in the Courtroom, ABA J, vol 0083, 97; Litigation--Ducking the Artful Dodger--Ethics Problems Within the Law Firm Require Special Care, ABA J, vol 0083, 97; Dont Take the Bait, ABA J, vol 0083, 97; Tactical Timing, ABA J, vol 0083, 97; Briefs That Sing, ABA J, vol 0083, 97; On Admissibility, ABA J, vol 0083, 97; Exposing Fatal Flaws, ABA J, vol 0083, 97; Terms of Enlightenment, ABA J, vol 0083, 97. **CONTACT ADDRESS** Sch of Law, Case Western Reserve Univ, 11075 East Blvd, Cleveland, OH, 44106-1769.

MCELWAIN, HUGH THOMAS
PERSONAL Born 10/24/1931, Weirton, WV, m, 1973, 3 children **DISCIPLINE** RELIGION, PHILOSOPHY **EDUCATION** Stonebridge Priory, BA, 53; Marianum Theol Fac, Rome, BD, 55, STD, 59. **CAREER** Instr theol, Stonebridge Priory, 59-61, asst prof theol & acad dean, 61-65; assoc prof philos & theol, St Mary of the Lake Col, 65-68; prof hist theol & acad dean, Cath Theol Union, 68-72; chmn dept, 73-76, asst dean grad studies, 77-81, Assoc Prof Relig Studies, Rosary Col, 73-, Am Asn Theol Schs fac fel, Divinity Sch, Univ Chicago, 72. **MEMBERSHIPS** AACU **RESEARCH** Peace studies; religion and science. **SELECTED PUBLICATIONS** Auth, Theology in an age of renewal, Chicago Studies, 66; Implications of evolution for theology, Barat Rev, 67; An Introduction to Teilhard de Chardin, Argus Commun, 67; contribr, The They May Live: Reflections on Ecology, Alba, 72; St Augustine's Doctrine on War, Abbey Press, 72. **CONTACT ADDRESS** Dean Col of Arts and Sciences, Rosary Col, 7900 W Division, River Forest, IL, 60305-1099. **EMAIL** mcelwnhu@email.dom.edu

MCFAGUE, SALLIE
PERSONAL Born 05/25/1933, Quincy, MA **DISCIPLINE** THEOLOGY, RELIGION AND LITERATURE **EDUCATION** Smith Col, BA, 55; Yale Divinity Sch, BD, 59; Yale Grad Sch, PhD(theol), 64. **CAREER** Asst prof, 72-75, dean, 75-79, assoc prof, 75-79, PROF THEOL, VANDERBILT DIVINITY SCH, 80-. Ed, Soundings, 67-75; Nat Endowment for Humanities fel, Oxford, 80-81. **MEMBERSHIPS** Am Acad Relig; Soc Values Higher Educ; Soc Arts, Relig & Contemp Cult; Am Theol Soc. **RESEARCH** Religious language; contemporary theology, religion and literature. **SELECTED PUBLICATIONS** Auth, Barbour, Ian--Theologians Friend, Scientists Interpreter, Zygon, vol 0031, 96; The Loving Eye Versus the Arrogant Eye--Christian Critique of the Western Gaze on Nature and the Third World, Ecumenical Rev, vol 0049, 97. **CONTACT ADDRESS** Vanderbilt Univ, 221 Kirkland Hall, Nashville, TN, 37232.

MCFARLAND, IAN A.
PERSONAL Born 07/26/1963, Hartford, CT, m, 1994 **DISCIPLINE** SYSTEMATIC THEOLOGY **EDUCATION** Trinity Col, Hartford, BA, 84; Union Theol Sem, (NY), M Div, 89; Lutheran School of Theology at Chicago, ThM, 90; Yale Univ, M Phil, 94, PhD, 95. **CAREER** LECT IN DIVINITY, UNIV ABERDEEN, 98-. **MEMBERSHIPS** Am Academy Relig **RESEARCH** Doctrine of God; Christology; Soteriology. **SELECTED PUBLICATIONS** Auth, The God Who Risks: Perspectives on the Trinity in Contemporary Theology, in Lutheran Forum, Pentecost (May), 94; Working From the Margins: An Evaluation of the Relationship between Authority and Responsibility in the Life of the Church, in Modern Theology 12, July 96; Why Engage in the Discipline of Theology, in Consensus: A Canadian Lutheran Journal of Theology 23:2, 97; The Ecstatic God: The Holy Spirit and the Constitution of the Trinity, in Theology Today 54, Oct 97; Listening to the Least: Doing Theology from the Outside In, Pilgrim Press, forthcoming 98. **CONTACT ADDRESS** Dept of Divinity with Relig Studies, Univ of Aberdeen, Aberdeen, ., AB24 3UB. **EMAIL** i.a.mcfarland@abdn.ac.uk

MCGARY, HOWARD
DISCIPLINE AFRICAN AMERICAN PHILOSOPHY, SOCIAL AND POLITICAL PHILOSOPHY **EDUCATION** Calif State Univ, Los Angeles, BA; Univ Minn, PhD. **CAREER** Instr, Rutgers, State Univ NJ, Livingston. **RESEARCH** Race and social justice. **SELECTED PUBLICATIONS** Auth, Rawls' Logic of Political Arguments: Political Justification Without Truth, in E. M. Barth and E. C. W. Krabbe, eds, Logic and Political Culture, Royal Neth Acad of Arts and Sci, 92; Alienation and the African American Experience, in Richard Schmitt and Thomas Moody, eds, Alienation and Social Criticism, Hum Press, 94; Police Discretion and Discrimination, in John Kleinig, ed, Handled with Discretion, Rowman & Little-

field, 96; Racism, Social Justice, and Interracial Coalitions, The J of Ethics, 1, 3, 97; coauth, Between Slavery and Freedom: Philosophy and American Slavery, Ind UP, 92. **CONTACT ADDRESS** Dept of Philos, Rutgers, State Univ NJ, Livingston Col, 141 Davison Hall, Piscataway, NJ, 08854-8045. **EMAIL** hmcgary@rci.rutgers.edu

MCGEE, HENRY W., JR.
PERSONAL Born 12/31/1932, Chicago, IL, m **DISCIPLINE** LAW **EDUCATION** NW Univ, BS 1954; DePaul Univ, JD 1957; Columbia Univ, LLM 1970. **CAREER** Cook Co, asst state's atty 1958-61; Great Lakes Region USOEO, regional legal servs dir 1966-67; Univ of Chicago Ctr for Studies in Crim Justice Juv Delinq Rsch Proj, legal dir 1967-68; Wolfson Coll Oxford Univ England, visiting fellow 1973; Visiting Prof, Univ of Florence Italy Inst of Comparative Law 1976, Univ of Puerto Rico 1979, Univ of Madrid (complutense) 1982; Fed Univ Rio de Janeiro Brazil, grad planning prog 1987; National Autonomous University of Mexico, 1988; UCLA, prof of law, currently. **HONORS AND AWARDS** Blue Key Natl Honor Frat 1957; num publ. **MEMBERSHIPS** Mem Natl Bar Assn; mem Natl Conf of Black Lawyers; draftsman Natl Conf of Bar Examiners 1974-; consult City Poverty Com London England 1973; consult & lectr Urban Plng USIS Italy 1976; past editor in chief DePaul Law Review. **CONTACT ADDRESS** Law Sch, Seattle Univ, 950 Broadway Plaza, Seattle, WA, 98122.

MCGILLIVRAY, ANNE
DISCIPLINE LAW **EDUCATION** Saskatchewan Univ, BA, LLB, 86; Univ Toronto, LLM. **CAREER** Lectr, 89-90; asst prof, 90-94; assoc prof, 94-. **RESEARCH** Children and the law; law and literature; criminal law. **SELECTED PUBLICATIONS** Auth, Different Voices, Different Choices: Playing at Law and Literature, Can Journal Law Soc, 92; Reconstructing Child Abuse: Western Definition and Non-Western Experience, 92; Ideologies Children's Rights; Abused Children in the Courts: Adjusting the Scales After Bill C-15, Manitoba Law Jour, 91. **CONTACT ADDRESS** Fac of Law, Univ Manitoba, Robson Hall, Winnipeg, MB, R3T 2N2. **EMAIL** anne@ms.umanitoba.ca

MCGILVRAY, JAMES
DISCIPLINE PHILOSOPHY **EDUCATION** Univ Toronto, PhD. **RESEARCH** Time and tense; color perception; semantics of natural languages. **SELECTED PUBLICATIONS** Auth, Constant Colors in the Head, Synthese, 94; auth, Tense, Reference, and Worldmaking, 91. **CONTACT ADDRESS** Philosophy Dept, McGill Univ, 845 Sherbrooke St, Montreal, PQ, H3A 2T5.

MCGINLEY, JOHN WILLAND
PERSONAL Born 05/11/1944, Philadelphia, PA, m, 1968, 5 children **DISCIPLINE** PHILOSOPHY, RELIGION **EDUCATION** Holy Cross Col, BA, 66; Boston Col, PhD(philos), 71. **CAREER** From asst prof to assoc prof, 70-78, prof philos, Univ Scranton, 78, chmn dept, 76-. **RESEARCH** Platonic philosophy; Jewish-Christian dialogue; Schelling. **SELECTED PUBLICATIONS** Auth, The essential thrust of Heidegger's thought, 71 & Nous poetikas, 76, Philos Today; Commentary on Plato's Parmenides, Univ Scranton, 76; The doctrine of the good in Plato's Philebus, Apeiron, 77; Does God exist?, Philos Today, 78; Aristotle's Notion of the Voluntary, Apeiron, 81; Catechism for Theologians, Univ Press Am, 81; MIASMA: Haecceitas in SCOTUS, The Esoteric in Plato, and Other Related Matters, Universtiy Press of America, Lanham Maryland, 96; What Does Others Have to do with Jerusalem?; Brother John Publications, Gunmone, Pa, 97. **CONTACT ADDRESS** Dept of Philosophy, Univ of Scranton, 800 Linden St, Scranton, PA, 18510-4501.

MCGINN, BERNARD JOHN
PERSONAL Born 08/19/1937, Yonkers, NY, m, 1971, 2 children **DISCIPLINE** HISTORY OF CHRISTIANITY **EDUCATION** St Joseph's Sem, BA, 59; Pontif Gregorian Univ, STL, 63; Brandeis Univ, PhD, 70. **CAREER** Instr theol, Cath Univ Am, 68-69; instr theol & hist Christiantiy, 69-70, asst prof hist Christianity, 70-75, assoc prof, 75-78, Prof Hist Theol & Christianity, Univ Chicago, 78-, Am Asn Theol Schs res fel, 71. **MEMBERSHIPS** AHA; Medieval Acad Am; Am Cath Hist Asn; Am Acad Relig; Am Soc Church Hist. **RESEARCH** Hist of theol; intellectual and cult hist of the Middle Ages. **SELECTED PUBLICATIONS** Auth, The abbot and the doctors, Church Hist, 71; The Golden Chain, Cistercian Publ, 72; The Crusades, Gen Learning Press, 73; Apocalypticism in the Middle Ages, Mediaeval Studies, 75; ed, Three Treatises on Man, Cistercian Publ, 77; auth, Visions of the End, Columbia, 79; transl, Apocalyptic Spirituality, 79 & coauth (with E Colledge), Meister Eckhart, 81, Paulist; Foundations of Mysticism, Crossroad, 91; Growth of Mysticism, Crossroad, 94; Flowering of Mysticism, Crossroad, 98. **CONTACT ADDRESS** Divinity Sch, Univ of Chicago, 1025-35 E 58th St, Chicago, IL, 60637-1577. **EMAIL** bmcginn@midway.uchicago.edu

MCGINN, SHEILA E.
PERSONAL Dubuque, IA, m, 1980, 2 children **DISCIPLINE** RELIGION **EDUCATION** Northwestern Univ, BA, 78; Univ TX, Irving, MA, 81; Northwestern Univ, PhD, 89. **CAREER** Tchng asst, 82, Garrett-Evangelical Theol Sem, Evanston; instr, 84; lect of theol, 84-88, 90-91, Loyola Univ Chicago; lect in Relig Studies, 87, , asst prof, 87-91, Mundelein Col, Chicago; asst prof of Theol, 91-92, Loyola Univ Chicago; asst prof of Relig Studies, 92-97, assoc prof, 97-., John Carroll Univ, Cleveland. **HONORS AND AWARDS** Univ Dallas Merit Scholar, 80-81; Northwestern Univ Res Fel, 82-85; Kahl Endowment for Intl the Curric, 96, 98; Reg Scholar for the Eastern Great Lakes & Midwest Biblical Societies, 96. **MEMBERSHIPS** AAR; Asn Int d'Etudes Patristiques, Lyons; Cath Bibl Asn; Eastern Great Lakes Bibl Soc; Int Soc for Neoplatonic Stud; N Am Patristic Soc; Soc for Bibl Lit. **RESEARCH** Early Christianity, new testament studies, Hebrew bible, relig studies and Catholic theology **SELECTED PUBLICATIONS** Auth, Galations 3: 26-29 and the Politics of the Spirit, Proceed: EGL & MWBS, 93; auth, The Acts of Thecla, in Searching the Scriptures, vol 2: A Feminist Ecumenical Commentary and Translation, Crossroads, 94; auth, Matthew's Gospel, in the Study Bible for Women: The New Testament, HarperCollins, 95, Baker, 96; auth, Not Counting ¤the| Women: A Feminist Reading of Matthew 26-28, SBL 1995 Sem Papers, ed Gene H. Lovering, Scholars Press, 95; auth, 1 Cor 11:10 and the Ecclesial Authority of Women, Listening/J of Relig & Cult, Lewis Univ; auth, The Montanist Oracles and Prophetic Theology, Studia Patristica 1995, in press; auth, Why Now the Women? Social-Historical Insights on Gender Roles in Matthew 26-28, Proceedings: EGLBS 17, 97; co-auth, Bibliographies for Biblical Research: Revelation, New Testament Series 21, Mellon Biblical Press, 97. **CONTACT ADDRESS** Dept of Relig Studies, John Carroll Univ, 20700 N Park Blvd, University Heights, OH, 44118. **EMAIL** smcginn@jcu.edu

MCGINNIS, JAMES W.
PERSONAL Born 07/08/1940, Fairfield, AL, m, 1988 **DISCIPLINE** LAW **EDUCATION** Wayne State Univ, BS 1963; San Francisco State Univ, MA 1965; Yeshiva Univ, PhD 1976; Wayne State Univ Law School, JD 1977. **CAREER** Coll Entrance Examination Bd, asst dir 1967-69; Univ of California Berkeley, instructor, 1970-72; Far West Lab for Educ Research, research assoc 1972-73; Oakland Univ, asst prof 1976-81; Private Practice, lawyer. **HONORS AND AWARDS** Fellowship Project Beacon, Yeshiva Univ 1965-66; Ford Found Fellowship Language Soc of Child, Univ of CA 1968. **MEMBERSHIPS** Pres Kappa Alpha Psi Frat Wayne State Univ 1961-62; mem Assn of Black Psychologist 1963-73; researcher Black Studies Inst Wayne State Univ 1975-76; office counsel Hall & Andary Law Firm 1982-84; chmn PAC 1982-85, mem 1982-, Natl Conf of Black Lawyers. National Bar Association 1989-. **CONTACT ADDRESS** Bell & Gardner P C, 561 E Jefferson Ave, Detroit, MI, 48226.

MCGINTY, MARY PETER
PERSONAL Born 03/02/1925, Chicago, IL **DISCIPLINE** SYSTEMATIC THEOLOGY **EDUCATION** St Xavier Col, Ill, AB, 45; Marquette Univ, MA, 58, PhD, 67. **CAREER** From lectr to asst prof theol, 62-68, Rosary Col; asst prof syst theol, St Mary of the Lake Sem, 68-73; asst prof, 73-82, dir grad theol, 74-81, assoc prof Theol, 82-, Loyola Univ, Chicago; consult relig, Scholastic Testing Serv, 58-68; lectr, Marquette Univ, 69. **HONORS AND AWARDS** Mellon Grant, 81; research grants, 82, 84-85, Loyola. **MEMBERSHIPS** Cath Theol Soc Am; Col Theol Soc; Am Acad Relig. **RESEARCH** Contemporary theology, ecclesiology, Christology, secularization, Yves Congar. **SELECTED PUBLICATIONS** Auth, The Sacrament of Christian Life, 92; auth, Secularization: Our Destiny or Our Demon?, Jesuit Assembly, 89. **CONTACT ADDRESS** Dept of Theol, Loyola Univ, Chicago, 6525 N.Sheridan Rd, Chicago, IL, 60626-5385. **EMAIL** mmcgint@wpo.it.luc.edu

MCGLONE, MARY M.
PERSONAL Born 08/28/1948, Denver, CO, s **DISCIPLINE** THEOLOGY **EDUCATION** Univ San Francisco, MA, 81; St Louis Univ, PhD, 91. **CAREER** Assoc prof theol, Avila Col, 91-98; leadership, The Sisters of St. Joseph of Carondulist, 98-. **HONORS AND AWARDS** Catholic Press Asn Best Hist, 98. **MEMBERSHIPS** CTSA; USCMA. **RESEARCH** Latin America **SELECTED PUBLICATIONS** Auth, Shining Faith Across The Hemisphere, Orbis Press, 97. **CONTACT ADDRESS** 2307 S Lindbergh, St. Louis, MO, 63131. **EMAIL** marymcgcsj@aol.com

MCGOVERN, ARTHUR F.
DISCIPLINE PHILOSOPHY **EDUCATION** Georgetown Univ, BA; Loyola Univ, MA; Univ Paris, PhD. **CAREER** Prof; past ch, Univ Core Curric Comt; prof, Univ of Detroit Mercy, 70-. **RESEARCH** Ethics, epistemology, Marxism and Christianity, social justice issues, and history of modern philosophy. **SELECTED PUBLICATIONS** Auth, Marxism: An American Christian Perspective; Ethical Dilemmas and the Modern Corporation Liberation Theology and its Critics. **CONTACT ADDRESS** Dept of Philosophy, Univ of Detroit Mercy, 4001 W McNichols Rd, PO Box 19900, Detroit, MI, 48219-0900. **EMAIL** MCGOVEAF@udmercy.edu

MCGOWEN TRESS, DARYL
DISCIPLINE PHILOSOPHY **EDUCATION** SUNY/Buffalo, PhD. **CAREER** Asst prof, Fordham Univ. **RESEARCH** Ancient philos, sci and med theories of generation. **SELECTED PUBLICATIONS** Auth, The Metaphysical Science of Aristotle's Generation of Animals and Its Feminist Critics, Rev of Metaphysics, 92; Relations in Plato's Timeaeus, Jour Neoplatonic Stud, 94; co-auth, Liabilities of the Feminist Use of Narrative: A Study of Sara Ruddick's Story in Maternal Thinking, Pub Aff Quart, 95. **CONTACT ADDRESS** Dept of Philos, Fordham Univ, 113 W 60th St, New York, NY, 10023.

MCGRADE, ARTHUR STEPHEN
PERSONAL Born 08/28/1934, Brooklyn, NY, m, 1954, 1 child **DISCIPLINE** PHILOSOPHY **EDUCATION** Univ Chicago, BA, 53, MA, 57; Yale Univ, PhD, 61; Cambridge Univ, PhD(hist), 72. **CAREER** From instr to assoc prof, 60-75, Prof Philos, Univ Conn, 76- . **HONORS AND AWARDS** Cross fel, Soc Relig Higher Educ, 64-65; prin researcher, Nat Humanities Found proj grant, 67-68; fel, Alexander von Humboldt Found, WGer, 72-73; Nat Hum Found grants, 80, 94-95; life member, Clare Hall, Cambridge, 95. **MEMBERSHIPS** Am Philos Asn; Mediaeval Acad Am; Soc Medieval and Renaissance Philos; Guild of Scholars of the Episcopal Church. **RESEARCH** Medieval philosophy; political philosophy. **SELECTED PUBLICATIONS** Auth, The Coherence of Hooker's Polity: The Books on Power, J Hist Ideas, 4/63; coauth, Fundamentals of Logic, Doubleday, 66; auth, The Public and the Religious in Hooker's Polity, Church Hist, 68; The Political Thought of William of Ockham, Cambridge, 74; co-ed, Richard Hooker: Of the Laws of Ecclesiastical Polity, Sidgwick & Jackson, 76; Ockham and the birth of individual rights, In: Authority and Power, Cambridge, 80; Ockham on Enjoyment, Rev of Metaphysics, 81; contrib, The Folger Library Edition of the Works of Richard Hooker, MRTS, 93; ed, Richard Hooker and the Construction of Christian Community, 97; auth, Natural Law and Moral Omnipotence, In: Cambridge Companion to Ockham. **CONTACT ADDRESS** 16, Chedworth St, Cambridge, ., L83 9JF. **EMAIL** asm10@cam.ac.uk

MCGUIRE, ANNE
DISCIPLINE RELIGION **EDUCATION** Barnard Col, BA, 73; Columbia Univ, MA, 76; Yale Univ, MA, 76, Mphil, 78, PhD, 83. **CAREER** Assoc prof; dept ch, 89 92; Haverford Col, 82-. **RESEARCH** Analysis and interpretation of early Christian and Gnostic literature, especially the writings of the Nag Hammadi library, discovered in Egypt in 1945. **SELECTED PUBLICATIONS** Co-ed, The Nag Hammadi Library After Fifty Years: Proceedings of the 1995 Society of Biblical Literature Commemoration, Nag Hammadi and Manichaean Stud 44, Leiden & NY: EJ Brill, 97. **CONTACT ADDRESS** Dept of Religion, Haverford Col, 370 Lancaster Ave, Haverford, PA, 19041.

MCGUIRE, ANNE M.
PERSONAL Born 10/05/1951, New Haven, CT, m, 1980, 2 children **DISCIPLINE** RELIGIOUS STUDIES **EDUCATION** Barnard Col, BA, 73; Columbia Univ, MA, 75; Yale Univ, MPhil, 80, PhD, 83. **CAREER** Instr, Villanova Univ, 80-82; asst prof, 82-90, assoc prof, 90- , Haverford Col. **HONORS AND AWARDS** Fac res grant, Haverford Col; Ford Grant for development of social justice courses. **MEMBERSHIPS** Soc of Bibl Lit. **RESEARCH** Ancient religions; Gnosticism; early Christianity; New Testament; comparative religions. **SELECTED PUBLICATIONS** Auth, Virginity and Subversion: Norea against the Powers in The Hypostasis of the Archons, in King, ed, Images of the Feminine in Gnosticism, Fortress, 88; auth, Equality and Subordination in Christ: Displacing the Powers of the Household Code in Colossians, in Gower, ed, Annual Publication of the College Theology Society, Univ Press of Am, 90; auth, Thunder, Perfect Mind, in Fiorenza, ed, Searching the Scriptures, v.2: A Feminist Commentary, Crossroad, 94; co-ed, The Nag Hammadi Library after Fifty Years: Proceedings of the 1995 Society of Biblical Literature Commemoration, Brill, 97; auth, Women and Gender in Gnostic Texts and Traditions, in Kraemer, ed, Women and Christian Origins: A Reader, Oxford, 98. **CONTACT ADDRESS** Dept of Religion, Haverford Col, Haverford, PA, 19041. **EMAIL** amcguire@haverford.edu

MCHATTEN, MARY TIMOTHY
PERSONAL Born 10/20/1931, Castle Hill, ME **DISCIPLINE** BIBLICAL STUDIES **EDUCATION** Univ Ottawa Can, PhD, 79. **CAREER** Dir of Bibl Studies, Kino Inst Phoenix Ariz, 73-89; chair of Bible Studies Dept, Mount Angel Sem St Benedict Ore, 89-. **MEMBERSHIPS** Cath Bibl Asn; Soc of Bibl Lit; Bibl Archaeol Soc. **RESEARCH** Biblical Women; Prophets; Wisdom Literature. **CONTACT ADDRESS** Mount Angel Sem, St. Benedict, OR, 97373. **EMAIL** MTMchatten@mtangel.edu

MCHENRY, LEEMON B.
PERSONAL Born 09/01/1956, NC, s **DISCIPLINE** PHILOSOPHY **EDUCATION** Univ Edinburgh, PhD, 84. **CAREER** Lectr, Loyola Marymount Univ, 96- . **HONORS AND AWARDS** Vans Dunlap Scholar in logic and metaphysics, Edinburgh. **MEMBERSHIPS** APA; Ctr for Process Stud. **RESEARCH** Logic; metaphysics; classical American philosophy.

SELECTED PUBLICATIONS Co-ed, auth, several articles in, Reflections on Philosophy: Introductory Essays, St Martins, 93; coauth, Whitehead's Approximation to Bradley, Idealistic Stud, 93; auth, Quine's Pragmatic Ontology, J of Speculative Philos, 95; auth,Whitehead's Panpsychism as the Subjectivity of Prehension, Process Stud, 95; auth, Descriptive and Revisionary Theories of Events, Process Stud, 96; auth, Bradley's Conception of Metaphysics, in Mander, ed, Perspectives on the Logic and Metaphysics of F.H. Bradley, UK: Theommes, 96; auth, Quine and Whitehead: Ontology and Methodology, Process Stud, 97; auth, Naturalized and Pure Metaphysics: A Reply to Hutto, Bradley Stud, 98. **CONTACT ADDRESS** 4900 Overland Ave, #121, Culver City, CA, 90230. **EMAIL** lmchenry@lmumail.lmu.edu

MCINERNEY, PETER K.
PERSONAL Born 12/12/1948, m **DISCIPLINE** PHILOSOPHY **EDUCATION** Yale Univ, BA, 71; Univ of TX, PhD, 76 **CAREER** Chm, 86-89, 91-97; Prof, 91-, Assoc Prof, 84-91, Oberlin Col; Visit Asst Prof, 81, Univ of MI; Asst Inst, 76, Univ of TX **HONORS AND AWARDS** NEH Fel, 85-86 **SELECTED PUBLICATIONS** Auth, Time and Experience, Temple Univ Press, 91; Introduction to Philosophy, HarperCollins Publishers, 92; Coauth, Ethics, HarperCollins, 94 **CONTACT ADDRESS** Dept of Philosophy, Oberlin Col, Oberlin, OH, 44074. **EMAIL** peter.mcinerney@oberlin.edu

MCINERNY, RALPH M.
PERSONAL Born 02/24/1929, Minneapolis, MN, m, 1953, 6 children **DISCIPLINE** PHILOSOPHY **EDUCATION** St Paul Sem, BA, 51; Univ MN, MA, 52; Laval Univ, PhL, 53, PhD, 54. **CAREER** Instr philos, Creighton Univ, 54-55; from asst prof to assoc prof, 55-69, PROF PHILOS, UNIV NOTRE DAME, 69-, MICHAEL P GRACE PROF MED STUDIES, 78-; Fulbright res scholar, BEL, 59-60; NEH fel, 77-78; vis prof, Univ Louvain, spring 82. **HONORS AND AWARDS** LHD, Benedictine Col, 79. **MEMBERSHIPS** Am Philos Asn; Am Cath Philos Asn (pres, 71, 80-81); Metaphys Soc Am; Author Guild; Soren Kierkegaard Soc; Am J of Jurisprudence, ed brd, 80; Am Maritain Soc, brd of dir, 80-81; Catholic Center for Renewal, brd of dir, 82; Center for Christianity & Common Good, Univ of Dallas, steering comm, 91-; Center J, ed brd, 81-85; Conseil scientifique of Maritain Institut, Int brd of dir, 82; Crisis, J of Lay Catholic Opinion, founder and pub, 81-; Dialogue at Notre Dame, advisory brd, 89-; Fellowship of Catholic Scholars, brd of dir, 83-86, pres, 91-93; IN Rev Foundation, advisory brd member, 89-; Institute on Christianity & Contemporary Thought, brd of dir, 82; Metaphysical Soc of Am, pres, 92-93; Int Maritain House of Study, brd of dir, 82; Philos section, annual Catholic Library Asn, ed, 65-70; Rivista de Filosofia, ed brd, 87-; Societas Internationalis Ethicae, board member, 89-; The Homeland Foundation Exec Dir, 91-92; The new Scholasticiam, Ed, 75-89; Truth, a J of Modern Thought, ed board, 91-; Univ of Notre Dame Press, ed brd, 63-73; Wethersfield Institute, dir, 89-92; Catholic campaign for America, Nat Comm Member, 92-; Int Asn of Crime Writers Hammet, Hammet Prize Comm, 92; The Ingersoll Prizes in Literature and Humanities, Jury panelist, 93; Legit: a Literary Magazine for Readers and Writers of the Great Lakes Area, ed brd, 93-; Medieval Institute, Pubs comm, Cardinal Newman Soc for the Preservation of Catholic Higher education, brd of advisors; Catholic Book Store, South Bend, In, brd of advisors; Pres, Catholic Educational Television; Catholic Dossier, ed. **RESEARCH** Medieval philosophy; ancient philosophy; Kierkegaard. **SELECTED PUBLICATIONS** Auth, From the Beginnings of Philosophy to Plotinus, In: A History of Western Philosophy, I, Regnery, 63; Thomism in an Age of Renewal, Doubleday, 66; Studies in Analogy, The Hague: Nijhoff, 68; ed, New Themes in Christian Philosophy, Notre Dame Press, 68; auth, Philosophy from St Augustine to Ockham, In: A History of Western Philosophy, II, Univ Notre Dame Press, 70; St Thomas Aquinas, In: Twayne World Authors Series, Hall, 77; Rhyme and Reason: St Thomas and Modes of Discourse, Marquette Univ Press, 81; Ethica Thomistica, Cath Univ Am Press, 82; History of the Ambrosiana, Univ of Notre Dame Press, 83; Being and Predication, The Catholic Univ of Am Press, 86; Art and Prudence, Univ of Notre Dame Press, 88; First Glance at Thomas Aquinas: Handbook for Peeping Thomists, 89; Boethius and Aquinas, The Catholic Univ of Am Press, 90; Aquinas on Human Action, Catholic Univ of Am Press, 92; The Question of Christian Ethics, Catholic Univ of Am Press, 93; Aquinas Against the Averroists, Purdue Univ Press, 93; ed, Thomas's Commentary on the Ethics, Dumb Ox Books, Notre Dame In, 93; ed, Thomas's Commentary on De Anima, Dumb Ox Books, Notre Dame, In, 94; auth, The God of Philosophers, Westminster-McMurrin Lectures, Salt Lake City, 94; ed, The Degrees of Knowledge, Vol VII, in The Collected Works of Jacques Maritain, Univ of Notre Dame Press, 95; Aquinas and Analogy, The Catholic Univ of Am Press, 95; Ethica Thomistica, rev ed, The Catholic Univ of Am Press, 97; Thomas Aquinas, Penguin Classics, 98. **CONTACT ADDRESS** Jacques Maritain Center, Univ of Notre Dame, 714 Hesburgh Library, Notre Dame, IN, 46556. **EMAIL** Ralph.M.McInerny.1@nd.edu

MCINTIRE, CARL THOMAS
PERSONAL Born 10/04/1939, Philadelphia, PA, 2 children **DISCIPLINE** MODERN HISTORY, PHILOSOPHY OF HISTORY **EDUCATION** Univ Pa, MA, 62, PhD(hist), 76; Faith Theol Sem, MDiv, 66. **CAREER** Instr hist, Shelton Col, 65-67; asst prof hist, Trinity Christian Col, 67-71; vis scholar, Cambridge Univ, 71-73; SR MEM HIST, INST CHRISTIAN STUDIES, TORONTO, 73-, Am Philos Soc res grant, 81; Soc Sci & Humanities Res Coun Can res grant, 81-82; lectr, Trinity Col, Univ Toronto, 82- **MEMBERSHIPS** AHA; Conf Faith & Hist; Am Cath Hist Asn; Am Soc Church Hist. **RESEARCH** Secularization of modern thought and society; comparative views of history: Christian, Hindu, Jewish, Marxist, Liberal and African Tribal; English politics in relation to the papacy, especially 19th century. **SELECTED PUBLICATIONS** Auth, The Knights Monks of Vichy France--Uriage, 1940-1945, Stud in Relig-Sciences Religieuses, vol 0024, 95. **CONTACT ADDRESS** Univ Toronto, 229 College St, Toronto, ON, M5S 1A1.

MCINTOSH, SIMEON CHARLES
PERSONAL Born 07/14/1944, Carriacou, Grenada **DISCIPLINE** LAW **EDUCATION** York U, BA 1971; Howard U, JD 1974; Columbia U, LlM 1975. **CAREER** Howard U, asst prof of law; Univ of OK, asst prof of law 1975-76. **MEMBERSHIPS** Soc of Am Law Tchrs; Am Legal Studies Assn. **CONTACT ADDRESS** 2935 Upton St, Washington, DC, 20008.

MCINTYRE, LEE C.
PERSONAL Born 01/02/1962, Portland, OR, m, 1986, 2 children **DISCIPLINE** PHILOSOPHY **EDUCATION** Wesleyan Univ, BA 84; Univ Michigan, MA 87, PhD 91. **CAREER** Colgate Univ, asst prof, 93-; Boston Univ, res assoc, 91-93; Tufts Experimental Col, vis lectr, 92. **HONORS AND AWARDS** Phi Beta Kappa **MEMBERSHIPS** APA; PSA **RESEARCH** Philo of natural and social sciences. **SELECTED PUBLICATIONS** Auth, Complexity: A Philosopher's Reflections, Complexity, 98; Gould on Laws in Biological Science, Biology and Philo, 97; The Case for the Philosophy of Chemistry, coauth, Synthese, 97; Readings in the Philosophy of Social Science, coed, Cambridge, MIT Press, 94; Laws and Explanation in the Social Sciences: Defending a Science of Human Behavior, Boulder CO, Westview Press, 96. **CONTACT ADDRESS** Dept Philosophy and Religion, Colgate Univ, Hamilton, NY, 13346. **EMAIL** LmcIntyre@center.colgate.edu

MCINTYRE, MONI
PERSONAL Born 02/12/1948, Detroit, MI **DISCIPLINE** THEOLOGY, CHRISTIAN ETHICS **EDUCATION** St Michael's Col, Toronto, PhD, 90. **CAREER** Asst prof, Duquesne Univ, 90-. **MEMBERSHIPS** CTE; AAR; CTSA; CTA. **RESEARCH** Feminist theol; ecological ethics; social ethics. **SELECTED PUBLICATIONS** Auth, Ethnicity and Religious Experience in the Social Ethics of Gibson Winter, in Ethnicity, Nationality and Religious Experience, ed Peter C Phan, Annual Pub of the Col Theol Soc, 91, Univ Press Am, 95; On Choosing the Good in the Face of Genocide, the Genocide Forum, 1, March 95; ed with Mary Heather Mackinnon, Readings in Ecology and Feminist Theology, Sheed & Ward, 95; auth, Capital Punishment in the Catholic Christian Tradition, New Theology Rev 9, Aug 96; review, An Agenda for Sustainability: Fairness in a World of Limits, by William M Bueler, Cross Cultural Pubs, 97, in Religious Studies Rev 24, July 98; ed with Mary Heather MacKinnon and Mary Ellen Sheehan, Light Burdens, Heavy Blessings: Essays from the Church in Honor of Margaret Brennan, IHM, Sheed & Ward, forthcoming 98; numerous other publications. **CONTACT ADDRESS** 507 Shady Ave, Apt A-6, Pittsburgh, PA, 15206. **EMAIL** mmcin@aol.com; mcintyre@duq3.cc.duq.edu

MCINTYRE, RONALD TREADWELL
PERSONAL Born 05/01/1942, New Orleans, LA, m, 1984, 1 child **DISCIPLINE** PHILOSOPHY **EDUCATION** Wake Forest Col, BS, 64; FL State Univ, MA, 66; Stanford Univ, PhD(philos), 70. **CAREER** Asst prof philos, Case West Reserve Univ, 70-77; assoc prof, 77-81, PROF PHILOS, CA STATE UNIV, NORTHRIDGE, 81-, DEPT CHAIR, 96-. **HONORS AND AWARDS** Nat Endowment for the Humanities Fel, 80; Woodrow Wilson Fel, 64; Phi Beta Kappa, 64. **MEMBERSHIPS** Am Philos Asn. **RESEARCH** Philosophy of language; phenomenology; contemporary metaphysics. **SELECTED PUBLICATIONS** Coauth, Intentionality via intensions, J Philos, 9/71; Husserl's Identification of Meaning and Noema, Monist, 1/75; Intending and Referring, in Hussert, Intentionality, and Cognitive Science, ed by H. Dreyfus, MIT Press, Bradford Books, 82; Husserl's Phenomenological Conception of Intentionality and its Difficulties, Philosophia, 11, 82; Searle on Intentionality, Inquiry, 27, 84; ed, Symposium on The Intentionality of Mind, Synthese, 61, 84; Husserl and the Representational Theory of Mind, Topoi, 5, 86, reprinted in: Perspectives on Mind, ed by H. Otto and J. Tuedio, D. Reidel, 88, Historical Foundations of Cognitive Science, ed by J-C Smith, Kluwer, 90, and trans by J. Jaze in Les Etudes Philosophiques, Phenomenologie et Psychologie Cognitive, Presses Univ de France, 91; Husserl and Frege, J of Philos, 84, 88; The Theory of Intentionality in Phenomenology and Analytic Philosophy, in Topics in Philosophy and Artificial Intelligence, ed by L. Albertazzi and R. Poli, Bozen, Italy: Inst Mitteleuropeo di Cultura, 91; Naturalizing Phenomenology?, Dretske on Qualia, in Naturalizing Phenomenology: Contemporary Phenomenology and Cognitive Science, ed by B. Pachoud et al, Stanford Univ Press, forthcoming; co-ed four other publications. **CONTACT ADDRESS** Dept of Philos, California State Univ, Northridge, 18111 Nordhoff St, Northridge, CA, 91330-8253. **EMAIL** ronald.mcintyre@csun.edu

MCKAGUE, CARLA A.
DISCIPLINE LAW **EDUCATION** Guelph Univ, BA, 70, MS, 72; Univ Toronto, LLB, 80. **CAREER** Legal Counsel, Office of the Public Guardian and Trustee **SELECTED PUBLICATIONS** Co-auth, Mental Health Law in Canada, Butterworth's, 87. **CONTACT ADDRESS** Fac of Law, Univ Toronto, 78 Queen's Park, Toronto, ON.

MCKALE, MICHAEL
DISCIPLINE WORLD RELIGIONS **EDUCATION** Univ Notre Dame, BA; Jesuit Sch Theol, MA; Grad Theol Union, PhD. **CAREER** St Francis Col **HONORS AND AWARDS** Ch, Philos & Relig Studies Dept; Dir, Pastoral Ministry Ctr Inst Ethics. **MEMBERSHIPS** Am Acad Relig, Soc Christian Ethics, Asn Catholic Cols & Univ. **SELECTED PUBLICATIONS** Areas: Global Catholicism, Social Ethics, Justice and Peace, and Religion and Personality **CONTACT ADDRESS** Saint Francis Col, PO Box 600, Loretto, PA, 15940.

MCKEE, PATRICK M.
DISCIPLINE PHILOSOPHY **EDUCATION** Univ Md, PhD, 71. **CAREER** Prof. **SELECTED PUBLICATIONS** Auth, Philosophical Foundations of Gerontology, 81; The Art of Aging, 87; pubs on epistemology and aesthetics. **CONTACT ADDRESS** Philosophy Dept, Colorado State Univ, Fort Collins, CO, 80523.

MCKELWAY, ALEXANDER JEFFREY
PERSONAL Born 12/08/1932, Durham, NC, m, 1960, 3 children **DISCIPLINE** THEOLOGY **EDUCATION** Davidson Col, AB, 54; Princeton Theol Sem, BD, 57; Univ Basel, ThD, 63. **CAREER** Instr, Dartmouth Col, 63-65; asst prof, 65-68, assoc prof, 68-81, PROF RELIG, DAVIDSON COL, 81-, Nat Endowment Humanities younger scholar fel, 69-70. **MEMBERSHIPS** Am Acad Relig; Karl Barth Soc NAm; Duodecim Soc. **RESEARCH** Contemporary theology; modern theology, systematic theology, historical theology. **SELECTED PUBLICATIONS** Auth, The Gottingen Dogmatics--Instruction the Christian Religion, vol 1, Interpretation-J Bible and Theol, vol 0047, 93; Humanization and the Politics of God--The Koinonia Ethics of Lehmann, Paul, Interpretation-J Bible and Theol, vol 0049, 95; How to Read Barth, Karl--The Shape of His Theology, Interpretation-J Bible and Theol, vol 0050, 96; Defending the Faith--Machen, J.,Gresham and the Crisis of Conservative Protestantism in Modern America, Theol Today, vol 0053, 96; Barth, Karl Critically Realistic Dialectical Theology, Interpretation-J Bible and Theol, vol 0051, 97. **CONTACT ADDRESS** Dept of Relig, Davidson Col, Po Box 1719, Davidson, NC, 28036-1719.

MCKENNA, BILL
DISCIPLINE PHENOMENOLOGY, EPISTEMOLOGY, HISTORY OF PHILOSOPHY **EDUCATION** Clark Univ, BA; New Sch Soc Res, PhD. **CAREER** Prof & dept ch, Miami Univ **RESEARCH** How we experience and know ourselves and the world with present specific interests in perception; idea of truth; concept of rationality. **SELECTED PUBLICATIONS** Ed, Husserl Stud. **CONTACT ADDRESS** Dept of Philosophy, Miami Univ, Oxford, OH, 45056. **EMAIL** mckennwr@muohio.edu

MCKENNA, MICHAEL S.
PERSONAL Born 05/20/1963, Franklin, PA, s **DISCIPLINE** PHILOSOPHY **EDUCATION** Univ VA, PhD, 93. **CAREER** Lecturer, CA State Univ, Long Beach, 93-94; ASST PROF, ITHACA COL, 94-. **RESEARCH** Free will; moral responsibility; ethics. **SELECTED PUBLICATIONS** Auth, R. J. Wallace, Responsibility and the Moral Sentiments, review, The Philos Rev, 105, 96; A Reply to the MacDonald: A Defense of the Presumption in Favor of Requirement Conflicts, J of Social Philos, vol 28, no 1, spring 97; Alternative Possibilities and the Failure of the Counter-Example Strategy, J of Social Philos, vol 28, no 3, winter 97, John Martin Fischer's The Metaphysics of Free Will, review article, Legal Theory 3, 97; Moral Theory and Modified Compatibilism, J of Philos Res, vol 23, 98; Does Strong Compatibilism Survive Frankfurt-Style Counter-Examples?, Philos Studies, forthcoming; The Limits of Evil and the Role of Moral Address: A Defense of Strawsonian Compatibilism, J of Ethics, forthcoming. **CONTACT ADDRESS** Dept of Philos and Relig, Ithaca Col, Ithaca, NY, 14850. **EMAIL** mmckenna@ithaca.edu

MCKEVITT, GERALD
PERSONAL Born 07/03/1939, Longview, WA **DISCIPLINE** AMERICAN HISTORY, THEOLOGY **EDUCATION** Univ San Francisco, AB, 61; Univ Southern CA, MA, 64; Univ CA, Los Angeles, PhD(hist), 72; Pontif Gregorian Univ, Rome, STB, 75. **CAREER** Res asst prof hist, 75-77, asst prof, 77-92, prof hist, Univ Santa Clara, 93-, dir Univ Arch, 75-85. **HONORS AND AWARDS** Oscar O Wither Award, 91. **MEMBERSHIPS** Soc Am Archivists. **RESEARCH** California history;

Jesuit education in California; Italian Jesuit exiles in America, 19th century. **SELECTED PUBLICATIONS** Auth, Gold Lake myth, J West, 10/64; The Jesuit Arrival in California and the Founding of Santa Clara College, Records Am Cath Hist Soc, 9-12/74; From Franciscan Mission to Jesuit College: a Troubled Transition at Mission Santa Clara, Southern CA Quart, summer 76; Progress Amid Poverty, Santa Clara College in the 1870s, Pac Hist, winter 76; The Beginning of Santa Clara University, San Jose Studies, 2/77; The University of Santa Clara, A History, 1851-1977, Stanford Univ, 79; Jump That Saved Rocky Mountain Mission, Pacific Hist Rev, 86; Jesuit Missionary Linguistics, Western Hist Quart, 90; Hispanic Californians and Catholic Higher education, CA Hist, 90-91; Jesuit Higher Education in US, Mis-America, 91; Italian Jesuits in New Mexico, NM Hist Rev, 92; Christopher Columbus as Civic Saint, CA Hist, winter 92-93; Art of Conversion: Jesuits and Flatheads, US Cath Hist, 94. **CONTACT ADDRESS** Dept Hist, Univ Santa Clara, 500 El Camino Real, Santa Clara, CA, 95053-0001. **EMAIL** gmckevitt@mailer.scu.edu

MCKIM, DONALD K.
PERSONAL Born 02/25/1950, New Castle, PA, m, 1976, 2 children **DISCIPLINE** THEOLOGY **EDUCATION** Westminster Col, 71; Pitts Theol Sem, MDiv, 74; Univ Pitts, PhD, 80. **CAREER** Vis fac, Relig Dept, Westminster Col; prof, Theology, Univ Dubuque Theol Sem, 81-88; acad dean & prof of theology, memphis theol sem, 94-. **HONORS AND AWARDS** Jamison Scholar; Marvin Scholar. **MEMBERSHIPS** Amer Acad Relig; Calvin Stud Soc; Karl Barth Soc; 16th Century Stud Soc **RESEARCH** Doctrine of scripture; John Calvin; Reformed theological tradition. **SELECTED PUBLICATIONS** Auth, Kerygma: The Bible and Theology I II III IV, 93; The bible in Theology and Preaching, Abingdon, 94; The Westminster Dictionary of Theological Terms, Westminster John Knox, 96; God Never Forgets: Faith, Hope, and Alzheimers Disease, Westminster John Knox, 97; ed, Historical Handbook of Major Biblical Interpreters, Inter-Varsity, 98. **CONTACT ADDRESS** Memphis Theol Sem, 168 E Parkway S, Memphis, TN, 38104-4395. **EMAIL** dmckim@mtscampus.edu

MCKIM, ROBERT
DISCIPLINE RELIGIOUS STUDIES **EDUCATION** Trinity College Dublin, BA,1975;. Univ Calgary, 1977;Ph.D, Yale University, 1982. **CAREER** Assoc prof, Univ Ill Urbana Champaign,82-. **HONORS AND AWARDS** Templeton Foundation Award, 1997; Arnold O. Beckman Research Award, Research Board, Univ Ill, Spring 1998. **RESEARCH** Philosophy of religion; history of early modern philosophy; ethics. **SELECTED PUBLICATIONS** Auth, The Theological Notion of Anonymous Christianity, Calgary Inst Humanities, 82; The Significance of Religious Diversity, Fort Worth, 94; Environmental Ethics: The Widening Vision, Relig Studies Rev, 97; co-ed, National Identity and Respect among Nations, Oxford, 97; The Morality of Nationalism, Oxford, 97. **CONTACT ADDRESS** Religious Studies Dept, Univ Ill Urbana Champaign, 52 E Gregory Dr, Champaign, IL, 61820. **EMAIL** r-mckim@uiuc.edu

MCKIM, VAUGHN R.
DISCIPLINE PHILOSOPHY OF SCIENCE **EDUCATION** Oberlin Col, BA, 62; Yale Univ, MA, 64, PhD, 66. **CAREER** Assoc prof. **MEMBERSHIPS** Philosophy of social science; philosophy of technology; contemporary metaphysical issues in philosophy of science. **RESEARCH** Scientific Rationality: Construction or Constraint?, 88; co-ed, Causality in Crisis? Statistical Methods and the Search for Causal Knowledge in the Social Sciences, 97 **SELECTED PUBLICATIONS** Auth, **CONTACT ADDRESS** History and Philosophy of Science Dept, Univ of Notre Dame, Notre Dame, IN, 46556. **EMAIL** Vaughn.R.McKim.1@nd.edu

MCKINNEY, GEORGE DALLAS, JR.
PERSONAL Born 08/09/1932, Jonesboro, AR, m **DISCIPLINE** THEOLOGY **EDUCATION** AR State AM& N Coll Pine Bluff, BA (magna cum laude) 1954; Coll, MA 1956; Univ of MI, Grad Studies 1957-58; CA Grad Sch of Theol, PhD 1974. **CAREER** ST STEPHEN'S CH OF GOD IN CHRIST, PASTOR 1962-; PRIVATE PRACTICE, MARRIAGE FAMILY & CHILD COUNSELOR 1971-; Comm Welfare Council, consult 1968-71; Econ Opportunity Com, asst dir 1965-71; San Diego Co Probation Dept, sr probation officer 1959-65; Family Ct Toledo, couns 1957-59; Toledo State Mental Hosp, prot chaplain 1956-57; Chargin Falls Park Comm Center, dir 1955-56. **HONORS AND AWARDS** Recipient JF Kennedy Award for servs to youth; outstanding pastor award San Diego State Univ Black Students; award for servs to youth Black Bus & Professional Women of San Diego; listed in Contemporary Authors; social worker of the yr award San Diego Co 1963; one of the ten outstanding men in San Diego Jr C of C 1966; outstanding man ot the yr award Intenat Assn of Aerospace Workers Dist 50 1969; outstanding contributions to the San Diego Comm in Field of Religious Activities NAACP 1975; achievement award for Religion Educ & Dedicated Serv to Youth So CA Ch of God in Christ; hon at Testimonial Dinner San Diego State Univ by the NewFriends of the Black Communications Center 1977; listed "Today" 1 of 20 hors Making Significant Contribution to Evangelical Christian Lit; named "Mr San Diego" by Rotary Club of San Diego. **MEMBERSHIPS** Mem CA Probation Parole & Correctional Assn; founder & chmn of bd of dirs St Stephen's Group Home; mem Sandiego Co Council of Chs; bd of trustees Interdenominational Theol Center Atlanta; bd of dirs C H Mason Theol Sem Atlanta; bd of dirs Bob Harrison Ministries; bd of elders Morris Cerillo World Evangelism; mem Sigma Rho Sigma Social Sci Frat; mem San Diego Rotary Club (1st black); mem Alpha Kappa Mu Nat Hon Society; mem Operation Push; vol chaplain at summer camp BSA; mem San Diego Mental Health Assn; mem NAACP; mem YMCA; mem San Diego Urban League; bd of advs Black Communication Center SanDiego State U; mem CA Mental Health Assn. **SELECTED PUBLICATIONS** "The Theol of the Jehovah's Witnesses" "I Will Build My Ch"; several other pubs; African American Devotional Bible, sr editor, 1997. **CONTACT ADDRESS** St Stephen's Church, 5825 Imperial Ave, San Diego, CA, 92114.

MCKINNEY, LAUREN D.
DISCIPLINE THEOLOGY **EDUCATION** Dickinson Col, BA; Temple Univ, MA, PhD. **CAREER** Theol Dept, Eastern Mennonite Univ **SELECTED PUBLICATIONS** Contrib, Mary Mitford: Essays, Garland. **CONTACT ADDRESS** Eastern Mennonite Univ, 1200 Park Road, Harrisonburg, VA, 22802-2462.

MCKINNEY, RICHARD I.
PERSONAL Born 08/20/1906, Live Oak, FL, m, 1967, 2 children **DISCIPLINE** PHILOSOPHY **EDUCATION** Morehouse Col, AB, 31; Andover Newton Theol Schl, BB, 34, STM, 37; Yale Univ, PhD, 42. **CAREER** Asst prof, phil & relig, 35-42 dean, schl of relig, 42-44, Virg Union Univ; Pres, 44-50, Storer Col; chmn, dept phil, 51-78, Morgan St Univ. **HONORS AND AWARDS** Phi Beta Kappa **MEMBERSHIPS** APA; Natl Ed Assn; Soc for Rel Values. **RESEARCH** Philosophy of Religion **SELECTED PUBLICATIONS** Auth, Religion in Higher Education Among Negroes, Yale Univ Press, Relig in Amer, Arno Press, 72; auth, A Philosophical Paragraph: We Hold These Truths..., Common Ground, Essays in Honor of Howard Thurman, Hoffman Press, 76; auth, History of the Black Baptists of Florida 1850-1985, FL Mem Col Press, 87; auth, Keeping the Faith - A History of the First Baptist Church, 1863-1980, 1st Baptist Church, 81; art, Howard Thurman: Apostle of Sensitiveness - An Examination of his Autobiography, Toward Wholeness, J of Ministries to Blacks in Higher Ed, 83; art, American Baptist and Black Education in Florida, Amer Baptist Quart, 92; auth, Mordecai - The Man and his Message, The Story of Mordecai Wyatt Johnson, Howard Univ Press, 97; auth, Mordecai Wyatt Johnson, College President, Notable Black Amer Men, Fisk Univ Press, 98. **CONTACT ADDRESS** 2408 Overland Ave, Baltimore, MD, 21214. **EMAIL** richmc0741@aol.com

MCKISSICK, FLOYD B., JR.
PERSONAL Born 11/21/1952, Durham, NC, m, 1990 **DISCIPLINE** LAW **EDUCATION** Clark Univ, AB, 1974; Univ of NC at Chapel Hill, School of City and Regional Planning, MRP, 1975; Harvard Univ, Kennedy School of Government, MPA, 1979; Duke Univ School of Law, JD, 1983. **CAREER** Floyd B McKissick Enterprises, asst planner, 1972-74; Soul City Com, director of planning, 1974-79; Peat, Marwick, & Mitchell, management consultant, 1980-81; Dickstein, Shapiro & Morin, Attorney, 1984-87; Faison and Brown, Attorney, 1987-88; Spaulding & Williams, Attorney, 1988-89; McKissick & McKissick, Attorney, 1989-. **MEMBERSHIPS** Durham City Council, 1994-; NC Center for the Study of Black History, president; Land Loss Prevention Project, past chairman, board member; Durham City-Council Planning Commission; St Joseph's Historical Society, board member; Museum of Life and Science, board member; Durham City of Adjustments; Rural Advancement Foundation International, board member. **SELECTED PUBLICATIONS** Co-author of Guidebook on Attracting Foreign Investment to the US, 1981; Author of When an Owner can Terminate a Contract Due to Delay, 1984; Author of Mighty Warrior, Floyd B McKissick, Sr, 1995. **CONTACT ADDRESS** McKissick & McKissick, 4011 University Dr, Ste 203, Durham, NC, 27707-2549.

MCKNIGHT, EDGAR VERNON
PERSONAL Born 11/21/1931, Wilson, SC, m, 1955, 2 children **DISCIPLINE** RELIGION, CLASSICAL LANGUAGES **EDUCATION** Col Charleston, BS, 53; Southern Baptist Theol Sem, BD, 56, PhD, 60; Oxford Univ, MLitt, 78. **CAREER** Chaplain, Chowan Col, 60-63; from asst prof to assoc prof, 63-74, assoc dean acad affairs, 70-73, prof relig & classics, 74-82, chemn, dept classics, 78-80, chemn, dept relig, 91-95, William R Kenan Prof Relig, Furman Univ, 82-; vis prof, Southern Baptist Theol Sem, 66-67; Fulbright sr res prof, Univ Tubingen, 81-82, Univ Muenster, 95-96; NEH study grant, Yale Univ, summer, 80; Bye-fel Robinson Col, Univ Cambridge, 88-89. **HONORS AND AWARDS** Bk of Year Award, MLA, 78. **MEMBERSHIPS** Soc Bibl Lit; Am Acad Relig; Am Schs Orient Res; Studiorum Novi Testamenti Soc. **RESEARCH** Biblical scholarship among American and Baptist scholars, espec A T Robertson; Biblical hermeneutics; structuralism and semiotics. **SELECTED PUBLICATIONS** Coauth, A History of Chowan College, Graphic Arts, 64; auth, Opening the Bible: A Guide to Understanding the Scriptures, Broadman, 67; coauth, Introd to the New Testament, Ronald 69; auth, What is Form Criticism?, In: Series on Introduction to Biblical Scholarship, Fortress, 69; coauth, Can the Griesbach Hypothesis be Falsified?, J Bibl Lit, 9/72; auth, Structure and Meaning in Biblical Narrative, Perspectives Relig Studies, spring 76; Meaning in Texts: The Historical Shaping of a Narrative Hermeneutics, Fortress, 78; The Bible and the Reader, Fortress, 85; Postmodern Use of the Bible, Abringdon, 88; ed, Reader Perspectives on the New Testament, Semeia 48, 89; NT ed, Mercer Dictionary of the Bible, 90; NT ed, Mercer Commentary on the Bible, Mercer, 94; co-ed, The New Literary Criticism and the New Testament, Sheffield and Trinity, 94. **CONTACT ADDRESS** Dept of Relig, Furman Univ, 3300 Poinsett Hwy, Greenville, SC, 29613-1218. **EMAIL** edgar.mcknight@furman.edu

MCKNIGHT, JOSEPH WEBB
PERSONAL Born 02/17/1925, San Angelo, TX, m, 2 children **DISCIPLINE** LEGAL HISTORY, FAMILY LAW **EDUCATION** Univ Tex, Austin, BA, 47; Oxford Univ, BA, 49, BCL, 50, MA, 54; Columbia Univ, LLM, 59. **CAREER** Legal pract, Cravath, Swaine & Moore, New York, 51-55; from asst prof to prof, 55-63, assoc dean, 77-80, Prof Law, Sch Law, Southern Methodist Univ, 63-, Consult, Hemisfair, 67-69; dir, Family Code Proj, State Bar Tex, 66-75. **HONORS AND AWARDS** Phi Beta Kappa; Rhodes Scholar; Kent fel, 58-59; Academia Mexicana de Derecho Int, 88; State Bar of Texas Family Law Section Hall of Legends, 97. **MEMBERSHIPS** Am Soc Legal Hist (vpres, 67-69); Am Soc Int Law; Nat Legal Aid & Defenders Asn. **SELECTED PUBLICATIONS** Auth, Family Law: Husband and Wife, Annual Survey of Texas Law, SMU L Rev, 93, 94, 95, 96, 97, 98; auth, Texas Community Property Law: Conservative Attitudes, reluctant Change, Law & Contemp Prob, 93; auth, The Mysteries of Spanish Surnames, El Campanario, 94; auth, Spanish Legitim in the United States: Its Survival and Decline, Am J Comp L, 96; auth, Survival and Decline of the Spanish Law of Descendent Succession on the Anglo-Hispanic Frontier of North America: Homenaje al Professor Alfonso Garcia-Gallo, 96; contribur, Tyler, ed, The New Handbook of Texas, 96; auth, Eugene L. Smith, 1933-1997, An Appreciation of His Achievements, Family Law Section Rept, 97; coauth, Texas Matrimonial Property Law, 2d ed, Lupus, 98. **CONTACT ADDRESS** Sch of Law, Southern Methodist Univ, Dallas, TX, 75275. **EMAIL** suzannes@mail.smu.edu

MCLAREN, JOHN P.S.
DISCIPLINE LAW **EDUCATION** St. Andrews Univ, LLB, 62; London Univ, LLM, 64; Univ Mich, LLM, 70; Calgary Univ, LLD, 97. **CAREER** Prof, 87-. **HONORS AND AWARDS** Founder, Can Law Soc Asn. **MEMBERSHIPS** Am Soc Legal Hist. **RESEARCH** Tort law, insurance law, Canadian legal history, social history of the law, legal education, and legal theory **SELECTED PUBLICATIONS** Auth, Essays on Revisions, the State and the Law, 98; pubs on tort law, insurance law, Canadian legal history, social history of the law, legal education, and legal theory; co-auth, Fraser Committee Report on Pornography and Prostitution in Canada; co-ed, Law for the Elephant, Law for the Beaver: Essays in the Legal History of the North American West and Essays in the History of Canadian Law. **CONTACT ADDRESS** Fac of Law, Univ Victoria, PO Box 2400, Victoria, BC, V8W 3H7. **EMAIL** jmclaren@uvic.ca

MCLAUGHLIN, JOSEPH M.
PERSONAL Born 03/20/1933, Brooklyn, NY, m, 1959, 3 children **DISCIPLINE** LAW **EDUCATION** Fordham Univ, AB, 54, LLB, 59; NY Univ, LLM, 64. **CAREER** Asst instr philos, Fordham Col, 54-55, from asst prof to assoc prof, 61-66, PROF LAW, SCH LAW, FORDHAM UNIV, 66-, Dean, 71-, Lectr, Practicing Law Inst, 63-; consult, NY Law Revision Comn, 63-; NY Judical Conf, 63-. **RESEARCH** Procedure; evidence, trail and appellate practice. **SELECTED PUBLICATIONS** Auth, Mulligan, William, Hughes--In Memoriam, Fordham Law Rev, vol 0065, 96. **CONTACT ADDRESS** Sch of Law, Fordham Univ, New York, NY, 10023.

MCLAY, TIM
PERSONAL Born 01/17/1963, St. Stephen, NB, Canada, m, 1983, 3 children **DISCIPLINE** OLD TESTAMENT **EDUCATION** Durham, PhD, 94 **CAREER** Asst Prof, Acadia Divinity Col, 96-. **MEMBERSHIPS** Soc of Biblical Lit; Intl Org for Septuagint and Cognate Studies **RESEARCH** Septuagint; use of Septuagint; Daniel **SELECTED PUBLICATIONS** auth, A Collation of variants from Papyrus 967 to Ziegler's Critical Edition of Susanna, Daniel, Bel et Draco, Textus 18, 95; Syntactic Profiles and the Characteristics of Revision: A Response to Karen Jobes, BIOSCS 26, 96; The OG and Th Versions of Daniel, 96; It's a Question of Influence: The Old Greek and Theodotion Texts of Daniel, Origen's Hexapla and Fragments, 98; Septuagint, Theodotion, Greek Versions, Chester Beatty Papyri, Eerdman's Dictionary of the Bible, forthcoming; Lexical Inconsistency: A Methodology for the Analysis of the Vocabulary in the Septuagint, 10th Congress of the IOCS, forthcoming. **CONTACT ADDRESS** Acadia Divinity Col, Wolfville, NS, B0P 1X0. **EMAIL** tmclay@acadiau.ca

MCLEAN, GEORGE FRANCIS
PERSONAL Born 06/29/1929, Lowell, MA **DISCIPLINE** PHILOSOPHY **EDUCATION** Gregorian Univ, PhB, 51, PhL,

52, STB, 54, STL, 56; Cath Univ Am, PhD, 58. **CAREER** From instr to assoc prof, 58-67, dir philos workshop, 61-68, Prof Philos, 67-93, prof emeritus, 93- , Cath Univ Am, & Coordr, Acad Exchanges, 81-, Lectr-prof, Oblate Col, 56-92; metaphys & theodicy area ed, New Cath Encycl, 61-64; vis res prof, Univ Madras, 69, 77, Univ Paris, 70, Inst for Oriental Studies, Cairo, 91, 92. **HONORS AND AWARDS** Adv prof, Fordham Univ, 94; hon prof Shanghai Acad of Sci, 98. **MEMBERSHIPS** Am Cath Philos Asn (secy, 63-80); Am Philos Asn; Metaphys Soc Am; Int Soc Metaphys (secy, 78-98); World Union Cath Philos Soc (secy, 72-98); Coun for Res in Values and Philos (secy, 81-). **RESEARCH** Metaphysics; hist of philos; philos of relig. **SELECTED PUBLICATIONS** Auth, Man's Knowledge of God According to Paul Tillich, 58; auth, Perspectives on Reality, 66; auth, An Annotated Bibliography of Philosophy in Catholic Thought, 66; auth,A Bibliography of Christian Philosophy and Contemporary Issues, 66; ed, Readings in Ancient Western Philosophy, 70, 2d ed, 97; auth, Ancient Western Philosophy, 71; auth, Plenitude and Participation, 78; auth, Tradition and Contemporary Life: Hermeneutics of Perennial Wisdom and Social Change, 86; auth, Tradition, Harmony and Transcendence, 94. **CONTACT ADDRESS** Sch of Philos, Catholic Univ of America, Washington, DC, 20064. **EMAIL** mclean@cua.edu

MCLELLAN, BRADLEY N.
DISCIPLINE LAW **EDUCATION** Univ Western Ontario, BA; Univ Toronto, LLB, 77. **CAREER** Lectr; Partner, Weir & Foulds **SELECTED PUBLICATIONS** Auth, pubs on real estate law, condominium law and environmental law; co-auth, McLellan, Perell Real Estate Law. **CONTACT ADDRESS** Fac of Law, Univ Toronto, 78 Queen's Park, Toronto, ON.

MCLELLAND, JOSEPH CUMMING
PERSONAL Born 09/10/1925, Scotland, m, 1947, 4 children **DISCIPLINE** PHILOSOPHY OF RELIGION **EDUCATION** McMaster Univ, BA, 46; Univ Toronto, MA, 49; Knox Col, Toronto, BD, 51; Univ Edinburgh, PhD, 53. **CAREER** Prof, Presby Col, Que, 57-64; PROF PHILOS RELIG, MCGILL UNIV, 64-, Dean Fac Relig Studies, 75-. **HONORS AND AWARDS** DD, Diocesan Col Montreal, 73 & Knox Col, Toronto, 76. **MEMBERSHIPS** Can Theol Soc (pres, 63-64); Can Soc Studies Relig. **RESEARCH** Philosophy and theology of relationship; analogy and mythology; modern atheism. **SELECTED PUBLICATIONS** Auth, Bucer, Martin--Reforming Church and Community, J Theol Stud, vol 0046, 95; Furcha, Edward, J. 1935-1997 + A Memorial Tribute to a Church Historian, 16th Century J, vol 0028, 97. **CONTACT ADDRESS** Fac of Relig Studies, McGill Univ, 3520 University St, Montreal, PQ, H3A 2T5.

MCMAHAN, JEFFERSON
PERSONAL Born 08/30/1954, GA, m, 1977, 2 children **DISCIPLINE** PHILOSOPHY **EDUCATION** Univ of the South, BA, 76; Oxford Univ, BA, MA, 79; Cambridge Univ, PhD, 86. **CAREER** Res fel, St. John's Col, Cambridge Univ, 83-86; asst prof, Univ Ill Urbana, 86-92; assoc prof, Univ Ill Urbana, 92-. **HONORS AND AWARDS** Rhodes scholar, 76. **SELECTED PUBLICATIONS** Co-auth, The Morality of Nationalism, Oxford Univ Press, 97; article, Wrongful Life; Paradoxes in the Morality of Causing People to Exist, Rational Commitment and Social Justice: Essays for Gregory Kavka, Cambridge Univ Pres, 208-247, 98; article, Brain Death, Cortical Death, and Persistent Vegetative State, A Companion to Bioethics, Blackwell, 250-260, 98; article, Preferences, Death, and the Ethics of Killing, Preferences, Walter de Gruyter & Co, 471-502, 98; article, A Challenge to Common Sense Morality, Ethics, 108, no 2, 394-418, 98; article, Intervention and Collective Self-Determination, Ethics and Intl Affairs, 10, 1-24, 96; article, Cognitive Disability, Misfortune, and Justice, Philos and Public Affairs, 25, no 1, 3-34, Winter, 96; article, Killing and Equality, Utilitas 7, no 1, 1-29, Apr 95; article, Innocence, Self-Defense, and Killing in War, Jour of Polit Philos, 2, no 3, 193-221, Sept 94; article, Self-Defense and the Problem of the Innocent Attacker, Ethics, 104, no 2, 252-290, Jan, 94; article, The Right to Choose an Abortion, Philos and Public Affairs, 22, no 4, 331-348, Fall, 93; article, Killing, Letting Die, and Withdrawing Aid, Ethics, 103, no 2, 250-279, Jan, 93. **CONTACT ADDRESS** Dept. of Philosophy, Univ of Illinois, 810 S. Wright St., 105 Gregor, Urbana, IL, 61801.

MCMAHAN, OLIVER
PERSONAL Born 11/15/1954, Honolulu, HI, m, 1975, 2 children **DISCIPLINE** HUMANITIES AND RELIGION **EDUCATION** Texas Christian Univ, DMin, 84; Ga State Univ, PhD, 97. **CAREER** Assoc prof, dean, Inst of External Studies, Church of God Theol Seminary. **MEMBERSHIPS** ACA. **CONTACT ADDRESS** Church of God Sch of Theol, 900 Wallcrest, Cleveland, TN, 37311. **EMAIL** amintranet@aol.com

MCMAHON, MARTIN J., JR.
DISCIPLINE LAW **EDUCATION** Rutgers Col, BA; Boston Col, JD; Boston Univ, LLM. **CAREER** Clarence J.TeSelle prof, Univ Fla, 97-; instr, Univ Ky, 79-97; vis Hugh F. Culverhouse Eminent scholar in taxation, Univ Fla, 91. **MEMBERSHIPS** Amer Law Inst; Amer Col Tax Coun; Amer Bar Asn Tax Sect. **RESEARCH** Individual income taxation, corporate taxation, partnership taxation, tax policy. **SELECTED PUBLICATIONS** Coauth, Federal Income Taxation of Individuals; Federal Income Taxation of Business Organizations. **CONTACT ADDRESS** School of Law, Univ of Florida, PO Box 117625, Gainesville, FL, 32611-7625. **EMAIL** Mcmahon@law.ufl.edu

MCMAHON, ROBERT
DISCIPLINE EPIC, PLATONIST LITERATURE, PHILOSOPHY AND LITERATURE **EDUCATION** Univ Calif, Santa Cruz, PhD, 86. **CAREER** Prof, La State Univ. **HONORS AND AWARDS** Robert L (Doc) Amborski Award, 87; Phi Kappa Phi Award, 90; Award for Excellence in Tchg Freshmen, 94; Alpha Lambda Delta, Nat Freshman Honor Soc; Amoco Award, 95; Tiger Athletic Found Award, Honors Col, 96. **RESEARCH** Voegelinian essays; Milton; Dante. **SELECTED PUBLICATIONS** Auth, Homer/Pound's Odysseus and Virgil/Ovid/Dante's Ulysses: Pound's First Canto and the Commedia, Paideuma, 87; Kenneth Burke's Divine Comedy: The Literary Form of The Rhetoric of Religion, PMLA, 89; Augustine's Prayerful Ascent: An Essay on the Literary Form of the Confession, 89; Satan as Infernal Narcissus: Interpretative Translation in the Commedia, in Dante and Ovid: Essays in Intertextuality, 91; 'Coloss. 3.3' as Microcosm, George Herbert J, 93; The Structural Articulation of Boethius' Consolation of Philosophy, Medievalia et Humanistica, 94; The Two Poets of Paradise Lost, 98. **CONTACT ADDRESS** Dept of Eng, Louisiana State Univ, 212K Allen Hall, Baton Rouge, LA, 70803.

MCMAHON, WILLIAM EDWARD
PERSONAL Born 09/25/1937, Chicago, IL, m, 1962, 2 children **DISCIPLINE** PHILOSOPHY **EDUCATION** Univ Notre Dame, AB, 59, PhD(Philos), 70; Brown Univ, MA, 61. **CAREER** Instr philos, St Cincent Col, Pa, 61-64; asst prof, John Carroll Univ, 67-69; asst prof, 69-77, assoc prof Philos, Univ Akron, 77-; assoc prof, 77-83; prof Philos, 83-. **RESEARCH** Philosophy of language and linguistics; contemporary and medieval ontologies; contemporary analytic philosophy. **SELECTED PUBLICATIONS** Auth, The problem of evil and the possibility of a better world, J Value Inquiry, Summer 69; Hans Reichenbach's Philosophy of Grammar, Mouton, 76; The teaching of philosophy: Subject matter versus pedagogy, Teaching Philos, Fall 76; A generative model for translating from ordinary language into symbolic notation, Synthese, 77; Dreadnought Battleships and Battle Cruisers, Univ Am, 78; The semantics of Ramon Llull, Studies in the History of Logic: Proceedings of III Symposium of the Hist of Logic, de Gruyter, 96; Biographies in Biographical Dictionary of American Sports, Baseball II, Greenwood, 98. **CONTACT ADDRESS** Dept of Philosophy, Univ of Akron, 302 Olin Hall, Akron, OH, 44325-1903. **EMAIL** McMahon@UAKRON.edu

MCMANUS, EDGAR J.
PERSONAL Born 03/04/1924, New York, NY, m, 1956 **DISCIPLINE** AMERICAN COLONIAL, LEGAL & CONSTITUTIONAL HISTORY **EDUCATION** Columbia Univ, BS, 52, MA, 53, PhD, 59. **CAREER** Lectr hist, Columbia Univ, 53-56; from lectr to assoc prof, 57-73, prof hist, Queens Col, NY, 73, Adj prof law, NY Law Sch, 62-66; Am Coun Learned Soc fel, 68-69. **HONORS AND AWARDS** JD, NY Univ, 59. **MEMBERSHIPS** AHA **RESEARCH** Am Negro slavery; legal origins of Am Negro slavery. **SELECTED PUBLICATIONS** Auth, The status of res ipsa loquitor in New York, NY Univ Intramural Law Rev, 11/47; Antislavery legislation in New York, J Negro Hist, 10/61; The enforcement of acceleration clauses in New York, NY Law Forum, 12/62; A History of Negro Slavery in New York, 66, Black Bondage in the North, 73, Syracuse Univ; Law and Libery in Early New England, Univ of MA, 93. **CONTACT ADDRESS** Dept of Hist, Queens Col, CUNY, 6530 Kissena Blvd, Flushing, NY, 11367-1597.

MCMANUS, FREDERICK RICHARD
PERSONAL Born 02/08/1923, Lynn, MA **DISCIPLINE** CANON LAW **EDUCATION** St John's Sem, AB, 47; Cath Univ Am, JCD, 54. **CAREER** Prof moral theol & canon law, St John's Sem, 54-58; dean sch, 67-74, PROF CANON LAW, CATH UNIV AM, 58-, VPROVOST & DEAN GRAD STUDIES, 74-, Ed, The Jurist, 58-; consult, Pontif Prep Comn Liturgy, 60-62; peritus, II Vatican Coun, 62-65, consult consilium execution const on liturgy, 64-69; dir secretariat of bishops' comt liturgy, Nat Conf Cath Bishops, DC, 64-75; treas, Int Comn English in Liturgy, 65-; consult, Pontif Comn Revision of Code of Canon Law, Rome, 67-; chmn bd, Asn Cath Col & Univ, 80-82. **HONORS AND AWARDS** Pay Christi, St John's Univ, 64; Honorary Archimandrite of Jerusalem, 70; Role of Law Award, Canon Law Soc, 73; Mathis award, Univ Notre Dame, 78; Berakah Award, North Am Acad Liturgy, 79; Prelate of Honor, Pope John Paul II, 80., LLD, St Anselm's Col, 64 & Stonehill Col, 65. **MEMBERSHIPS** Canon Law Soc Am; Cath Theol Soc Am; Liturgical Conf (pres, 59-62); NAm Acad Liturgy, Societas Liturgica; hon mem Guild Relig Archit. **RESEARCH** Liturgy **SELECTED PUBLICATIONS** Auth, The First Ordinary of the Royal Abbey of St Denis in France--Paris Bibliotheque Mazarine-526, Speculum-J Medieval Stud, vol 0068, 93. **CONTACT ADDRESS** Catholic Univ of America, Washington, DC, 20064.

MCMULLEN, MIKE
PERSONAL Born 10/14/1965, Fremont, NE, m, 1989, 1 child **DISCIPLINE** RELIGION; SOCIOLOGY **EDUCATION** Emory Univ, PhD, 95 **CAREER** Asst prof Sociol, Univ Houston, 95- **HONORS AND AWARDS** Univ Houston Res Award, 96, 97; SSSR Res Award, 94; RRA Res Award, 94; Emory Grad Tchg Award, 93. **MEMBERSHIPS** Amer Acad Relig; Amer Sociol Assoc; Assoc Sociol Relig; Soc Sci Study Relig **RESEARCH** Baha'I Faith; Religious Denominations; Religion and Peace Issues; Conflict Resolution and Mediation. **SELECTED PUBLICATIONS** The Religious Construction of a Global Identity: The Baha'i Faith in Atlanta, Rutgers Univ, forthcoming; bk rev, Sacred Acts, Sacred Space, Sacred Time, by John Walbridge, Jour Baha'I Studies, forthcoming; bk rev, The Origins of the Baha'i Community of Can, 1889-1948, by Will C Van den Hoonaard, Soc Relig, 97. **CONTACT ADDRESS** Dept of Sociology, Univ Houston, 2700 Bay Area Blvd., Houston, TX, 77058. **EMAIL** mcmullen@1.uh.edu

MCMULLIN, ERNAN
DISCIPLINE PHILOSOPHY OF SCIENCE **EDUCATION** Nat Univ of Ireland, BSc, 45; Maynooth Col, BD, 48; Univ Louvain, PhD, 54. **CAREER** Prof Emeritus, Univ Notre Dame, 94-. **HONORS AND AWARDS** Fel, Amer Acad of Arts & Sciences; Fel, Amer Assn for the Advn of Science; Fel, Intl Acad for the History of Science. **MEMBERSHIPS** APA; PSA; History of Science Soc; Metaphysical Soc of Amer; ACPA **RESEARCH** Issues in contemporary philosophy of science; history of scientific methodology; relationship of religion to the natural sciences. **SELECTED PUBLICATIONS** Auth, Newton on Matter and Activity, 78; The Inference that Makes Science, 92; Rationality and Paradigm Change in Science, 93; The Indifference Principle and the Anthropic Principle in Cosmology, 93; Religion and Cosmology, 93; Enlarging Imagination, 96; Galileo on Science and Scripture, 97; ed, Evolution and Creation, 85; Construction and Constraint: The Shaping of Scientific Rationality, 88; The Social Dimensions of Science, 92; co-ed, Philosophical Consequences of Quantum Theory, 89. **CONTACT ADDRESS** History and Philosophy of Science Dept, Univ of Notre Dame, Notre Dame, IN, 46556. **EMAIL** Ernan.McMullin.1@nd.edu

MCNAMARA, PAUL
DISCIPLINE PHILOSOPHY **EDUCATION** Univ Mass, PhD, 90. **CAREER** Asst prof. **HONORS AND AWARDS** Ed, Philos Studies. **RESEARCH** Ethical theory; deontic logic; Leibniz; philosophy of language; philosophy of mind. **SELECTED PUBLICATIONS** Auth, pubs on Leibniz, metaphysics of modality, philosophy of AI, and supererogation in deontic logic. **CONTACT ADDRESS** Philosophy Dept, Univ of New Hampshire, Hamilton Smith Hall, Durham, NH, 03824. **EMAIL** paulm@christa.unh.edu

MCNEILL, SUSAN PATRICIA
PERSONAL Born 10/03/1947, Washington, DC, s **DISCIPLINE** LAW **EDUCATION** Wilson College, BA, 1969; Creighton University, JD, 1978; Pepperdine University, MBA, 1980. **CAREER** US Air Force: Edwards AFB, Assistant Staff Judge Advocate, contract attorney, 1978-81; Norton AFB, Ballistic Missile Office, Asst Staff Judge Advocate, staff attorney, 1981-84; Lindsey Air Station, Germany, Staff Judge Advocate, chief legal officer, 1984-87; Dept of Justice, Defense Procurement Fraud Unit, trial attorney, 1987-89; Pentagon, Air Force Contract Law Division, trial attorney, 1989-91, Air Force General Counsel's Office, staff attorney, 1991-92; Defense Systems Management College, Acquisition Law Task Force, associate director, senior attorney, 1992-93; AF General Counsels Office, civilian staff attorney, 1993-95; Sawyer Myersburg, of counsel, currently. **HONORS AND AWARDS** Judge Advocate, Big Sisters of Omaha, Big Sister of the Year, 1978; Natl Coalition 100 Black Women, VA Commonwealth Chapter, Serwa Award, 1993. **MEMBERSHIPS** Nebraska Bar Assn, 1978-; Big Sisters of Omaha, 1977-78; National Contract Management Assn, Wiesbaden, Germany, chapter president, 1985-87; Air Force Cadet Officer Mentor Program, executive board, 1991-; American Bar Assn, Government Contracts Section, 1991-. **CONTACT ADDRESS** Sawyer & Myerberg, 21689 Great Mills Rd, Lexington Park, MD, 20653.

MCNULTY, JOHN K.
PERSONAL Born 10/13/1934, Buffalo, NY, d, 3 children **DISCIPLINE** PSYCHOLOGY AND LAW **EDUCATION** Swarthmore Col, AB, 56; Yale Law Sch, LLB, 59. **CAREER** Law clerk, Justice Hugo L. Black, US Supreme Ct, 59-60; atty, Jones, Day, Cockley & Reavis, 60-64; prof, Univ Calif Berkeley Sch of Law, 64-. **HONORS AND AWARDS** Guggenheim fel, 77; four prizes for standing first in class, Yale Law Sch, 56-59. **MEMBERSHIPS** Amer Law Inst; Intl Fiscal Asn; Amer Bar Asn. **RESEARCH** Law and policy of taxation (income, estate & gift, international). **SELECTED PUBLICATIONS** Auth, Federal Income Taxation of Individuals, West Publ Co, 95; auth, Federal Estate & Gift Taxation, West Publ Co, 94; coauth, Federal Income Taxation of Business Enterprises, 95; auth, Federal Income Taxation of S Corporations, Found Press, 92. **CONTACT ADDRESS** Univ of California Berkeley, 335 Boalt Hall, Berkeley, CA, 94720-7200. **EMAIL** mcnultyj@mail.law.berkeley.edu

MCNULTY, JOHN KENT
PERSONAL Born 10/13/1934, Buffalo, NY, m, 1955, 3 children **DISCIPLINE** LAW **EDUCATION** Swarthmore Col, AB, 56; Yale Univ, LLB, 59. **CAREER** Law clerk, Justice Hugo L Black, US Supreme Court, 59-60; atty, Jones, Day, Cockley & Reavis, Cleveland, 60-64; from actg assoc prof to actg prof, 64-67, prof Law, 67-91, ROGER J. TRAYNOR PROF OF LAW, UNIV CA, BERKELEY, 91-; Consult, CA Constitutional Revision Comn, CA Legis, 65-66, Continuing Educ of Bar, Univ CA Exten, 65- & Urban Studies Proj, Rand Corp, 72-; lectr, Korean Legal Ctr, Seoul, 72; consult & lectr, Am Law Inst & Am Bar Asn Comt on Continuing Legal Educ; consult, Baker & McKenzie, 74-75; Guggenheim fel, 77; vis scholar, Univ Tilburg, The Neth, 77, Cologne Univ, 77, Univ Tokyo, 79, London School of Economics, 85, Cambridge Univ, 94, Edinburgh Univ, 94, Leiden Univ, 96. **MEMBERSHIPS** Am Law Inst; Am Bar Asn; Nat Tax Asn & Tax Inst Am; Int Fiscal Asn Council, US branch. **RESEARCH** Law of taxation. **SELECTED PUBLICATIONS** Auth, Corporations and the Intertemporal Conflict of Laws, 1/67 & Tax Policy and Tuition Credit legislation, 1/73, CA Law Rev; US Taxation of Foreign Direct Investment in the United States, St Gallen Hochschule, Switz, 10/73; contribr, Fundamental Alternatives to Present Transfer Tax Systems, In: Death, Taxes and Family Property, West & Am Bar Asn Sect of Real Property, Probate & Trust Law, 77; auth, Verlagerung und zurechnung von einkommen nach Amerikanischem einkommensteuerrecht, Steuer-und-Wirtschaft, Ger, 78; Federal Estate and Gift Taxation in a Nutshell, West Pub, 79, 5th ed, 94; Federal Income Taxation of S Corporations, Found press, 92; Federal Income Taxation in a Nutshell, 5th ed, 95. **CONTACT ADDRESS** Sch of Law, Univ of Calif, 335 Boalt Hall, Berkeley, CA, 94720-7201. **EMAIL** mcnultyj@mail.law.berkeley.edu

MCNUTT, PAULA M.
PERSONAL Born 03/12/1955, Denver, CO, s **DISCIPLINE** HEBREW BIBLE, ANTHROPOLOGY AND ARCHAEOLOGY **EDUCATION** Univ Colorado, BA, 78; Univ Montana, MA, 83; Vanderbilt Univ, PhD, 89. **CAREER** Prof, Canisius Col, 87-. **HONORS AND AWARDS** NEH Fel for Col Tchr, 94-95. **MEMBERSHIPS** Amer Acad Relig; Soc Bibl Lit, Cath Bibl Asn, Amer Sch Oriental Res, Archaeol Inst Amer **RESEARCH** Social world of ancient Israel; social roles and statuses of artisans; religion and technology. **SELECTED PUBLICATIONS** Reconstructing the Society of Ancient Israel, Libr of Ancient Israel Series, Louisville, Westminster John Knox Press, 99; The Kenites, the Midianites, and the Rechabites as Marginal Mediators in Ancient Israelite Tradition, Semeia 67, p 109-132, 94; coauth with James W. Flanagan, David W. McCreery and Khair Yassin, Preliminary Report of the 1993 Excavations at Tell Nimrin, Jordan, Ann of the Dept of Antiquities of Jordan, XXXVIII, pp 205-244, 94; Kenites, P. 407 in The Oxford Companion to the Bible, Bruce M. Metzger and Michael D. Coogan eds, Oxford Univ Press, 93; The Development and Adoption of Iron Technology in the Ancient Near East, Proceedings: The Eastern Great Lakes Bibilical Society, 12, pp 47-66, 92; The African Ironsmith as Marginal Mediator: A Symbolic Analysis, Journ of Ritual Studies, 5/2, pp 75-98, 91; The Forging of Israel: Iron Technology, Symbolism, and Tradition in Ancient Society, The Social World of Biblical Antiquity Series, 8, Sheffield, Almond Press, 90; Sociology of the Old Testament, pp 835-839, Mercer Dict of the Bible, Macon, GA, Mercer Univ Press, 90; Egypt as an Iron Furnace: A Metaphor of Transformation, pp 293-301, Society of Biblical Literature 1988 Seminar Papers, David J. Lull ed, Atlanta, Schol Press, 88; Interpreting Ancient Israel's Fold Traditions, Journ for the Study of the Old Testament, 39, pp 44-52, 87. **CONTACT ADDRESS** Canisius Col, 2001 Main St., Buffalo, NY, 14208. **EMAIL** mcnutt@canisius.edu

MCPHERSON, JAMES ALAN
PERSONAL Born 09/16/1943, Savannah, GA, d, 1 child **DISCIPLINE** LITERATURE, HISTORY, LAW **EDUCATION** Morris Brown Col, BA, 65; Harvard Law School, LLB, 68; Writers Workshop, Univ IA, MFA, 71. **CAREER** Lect, Univ CA at Santa Cruz, 69-71; asst prof, Morgan State Univ, 75-76; assoc prof, Univ VA, 76-81; prof, Univ IA, 81-. **HONORS AND AWARDS** Pulitzer Prize, 78; MacArthur Prize Fellows Award, 81. **MEMBERSHIPS** ACLU; NAACP; Authors Guild; Am Academy of Arts and Sciences; fel, Center for Advanced Studies, Stanford Univ, 97-98. **RESEARCH** Law. **SELECTED PUBLICATIONS** Auth, Crabcakes, 98; Fatherly Daughter, 98. **CONTACT ADDRESS** Dept of English, Univ of Iowa, Iowa City, IA, 52242.

MCRAE, DONALD M.
DISCIPLINE LAW **EDUCATION** Otago Univ, LLB, LLM. **CAREER** Prof. **SELECTED PUBLICATIONS** Auth, pubs on international law. **CONTACT ADDRESS** Fac Common Law, Univ Ottawa, 550 Cumberland St, PO Box 450, Ottawa, ON, K1N 6N5.

MCRAE, JOHN R.
DISCIPLINE RELIGIOUS STUDIES **EDUCATION** Yale Univ, PhD, 83. **CAREER** Assoc prof. **RESEARCH** East Asian Buddhism; Zen Buddhism. **SELECTED PUBLICATIONS** Auth, The Northern School and the Formation of Early Ch'an Buddhism, Univ Hawaii, 86; **CONTACT ADDRESS** Dept of Religious Studies, Indiana Univ, Bloomington, 300 N Jordan Ave, Bloomington, IN, 47405.

MCRAY, JOHN ROBERT
PERSONAL Born 12/17/1931, Holdenville, OK, m, 1957, 3 children **DISCIPLINE** RELIGION **EDUCATION** David Lipscomb Col, BA, 55; Harding Col, MA, 56; Univ Chicago, PhD(New Testament & Early Christian lit), 67. **CAREER** Asst prof Bible, Greek & church hist, Harding Col, 58-66; assoc prof, David Lipscomb Col, 66-71; res prof archaeol & geog, Albright Inst Archaeol Res, Israel, 72-73; prof relig studies, Mid Tenn State Univ, 73-80; prof New Testament, Wheaton Col Grad Sch, 80-, Rockefeller grant, 62-63. **HONORS AND AWARDS** J W McGarvey Award, 60; Christian Res Found Award, 62; Outstanding Teacher of the Year, Mid Tenn State Univ, spring 77. **MEMBERSHIPS** Southeast Sect Soc Bibl Lit (vpres, 77-78, pres, 78-79); Inst Bibl Res; Am Schs Orient Res; Int Orgn Septuatint & Cognate Studies; North Am Patristic Soc. **RESEARCH** New Testament exegesis; New Testament backgrounds and archaeology; Pauline Studies. **SELECTED PUBLICATIONS** Auth, New Testament Introduction and Survey, Harding, 61; The Eternal Kingdom, Gospel Light, 61; auth, Scripture and tradition in Irenaeus, 67, The church fathers in the second century, 69 & To Teleion in I Corinthians 13:10, 71, Restoration Quart; Charismata in the second century, Studia Patristica, 75; Apocalyptic and atonement in the Epistle to the Hebrews, 80 & Stewardship and scholarship, 81, Restoration Quart; Archaeology and the New Testament, Baker, 91. **CONTACT ADDRESS** Dept of Relig, Wheaton Col, 501 E College Ave, Wheaton, IL, 60187. **EMAIL** John.R.McRay@wheaton.edu

MCREYNOLDS KIDD, REGGIE
DISCIPLINE NEW TESTAMENT **EDUCATION** Col William & Mary, BA, 73; Westminster Theol Sem, MAR, 75, MDiv, 77; Duke Univ, PhD, 89. **CAREER** Assoc prof; dean of the Chapel. **HONORS AND AWARDS** Pastor, Worship, Chapel Hill Bible Church. **MEMBERSHIPS** Mem, Disputed Paulines gp, Soc of Bibl Lit. **RESEARCH** Pauline epistles. **SELECTED PUBLICATIONS** Auth, dissertation Wealth and Beneficence in the Pastoral Epistles, Scholars Press. **CONTACT ADDRESS** Dept of New Testament, Reformed Theol Sem, 1015 Maitland Ctr Commons, Maitland, FL, 32751. **EMAIL** rkidd@rts.edu

MCROBERT, JENNIFER
DISCIPLINE PHILOSOPHY **EDUCATION** Mount Allison Univ, BA; Dalhousie University, MA; Univ Western Ontario, PhD. **CAREER** Asst prof, 94-. **MEMBERSHIPS** N Am Kant Soc, 93-; Can Philos Asn, 96-; Can Soc Hist Philos Sci, 95-. **RESEARCH** Early modern philosophy; history and philosophy of science. **SELECTED PUBLICATIONS** Auth, Stephen R. Palmquist. Kant's System of Perspectives: An architectonic interpretation of the Critical philosophy, Can Philos Rev, 94; I. Kant's afterword to Samuel Thomas Soemmerring's On the Organ of the Soul, 96. **CONTACT ADDRESS** Philosophy Dept, Acadia Univ, Wolfville, NS, B0P 1X0. **EMAIL** jennifer.mcrobert@acadiau.ca

MCVANN, MARK
PERSONAL Born 08/28/1950, Washington, DC, s **DISCIPLINE** BIBLICAL STUDIES **EDUCATION** Emory Univ, PhD, 84 **CAREER** Prof Relig Studies, Lewis Univ, 79-; vis prof Relig Studies, Manhattan Col, 94-95 **HONORS AND AWARDS** Cordilio Excellence in Scholar Award, 97. **MEMBERSHIPS** Cath Bibl Assoc; Amer Acad Relig; Context Group; Col Theolog Soc. **RESEARCH** Ritual and Literary Symbols **SELECTED PUBLICATIONS** Biblical Studies: A Brief Introduction, in Sacred Adventure: An Introduction to Theology, forthcoming; Rev of JB Gibson's The Temptation of Jesus in Early Christianity, Bibl Theology Bulletin, forthcoming; Rev of MD Hooker's The Gospel According to Saint Mark, Bibl Theology Bulletin, 97. **CONTACT ADDRESS** Dept of Religious Studies, Lewis Univ, Rt 53, Romeoville, IL, 60446. **EMAIL** mcvannma@lewisu.edu

MEAD, LISA M.
DISCIPLINE LAW **EDUCATION** Univ Tex, BSW,84; Univ Southern Calif, JD,89. **CAREER** Asst dean; past dir atty, Homeless Assistance Proj Public Coun; past state off prog coordr, Texas Coalition for Juvenile Justice; co-founder and bd mem, Law School's Public Interest Law Found. **HONORS AND AWARDS** Student Bar Association Faculty Appreciation Award, University of Southern California Law School, 1995-1996; University of Southern California Public Interest Law Foundation Outstanding Graduate, 1993. **MEMBERSHIPS** Member, National Association of Law Placement (NALP) since 1993; NALP Educational Programming Committee, Member 1997-98; NALP Public Service Committee, Chair 1996-97, Vice-Chair 1995-96; Los Angeles Count Bar Association (LACBA) Homeless Committee, Board Member 1989-93; LACBA Individual Rights Section, Treasurer, 1991-93, Member 1989-95; USC Public Interest Law Foundation, Board Member 1988-92, 1993-present; Women Lawyers Association of Los Angeles, member. **SELECTED PUBLICATIONS** Auth, Sharing the Obligation: How Legal Educators and Employers Engender Professionalism, Ethical Responsibility, & Accountability. **CONTACT ADDRESS** School of Law, Univ Southern Calif, University Park Campus, Los Angeles, CA, 90089. **EMAIL** lmead@law.usc.edu.

MEAD, WALTER BRUCE
PERSONAL Born 05/25/1934, Cedar Rapids, IA, 1 child **DISCIPLINE** POLITICAL PHILOSOPHY **EDUCATION** Carlton Col BA, 56; Yale Univ MA, 60; Duke Univ, MA PhD, 62-68. **CAREER** Asst Prof, Lake Forest Col, 63-67; Assoc Prof and Prof, Ill State Univ, 67-95, Prof Emer, 95-. **HONORS AND AWARDS** Lake Forest Col, Outstanding Prof; Ill State Univ, Numerous Fellowships, Research Grants. **MEMBERSHIPS** Am Pol Sci Asn; Midwest Pol Sci Asn; So Pol Sci Asn; ed bd, J Pol. **RESEARCH** Philos of Mind; Value Theory; Michael Polanyi. **SELECTED PUBLICATIONS** Extremism and Cognition, Kendall Hunt Pub, 71; The United States Constitution, Univ SC Press, 87. **CONTACT ADDRESS** 4 Kenyon Crt, Bloomington, IL, 61701. **EMAIL** wbmead@ilstu.edu

MEADE, DENIS
PERSONAL Born 10/16/1930, Des Moines, IA **DISCIPLINE** THEOLOGY, CHURCH HISTORY **EDUCATION** St Benedict's Col, Kans, AB, 52; Pontif Univ St Anselmo, Rome, STL, 56; Pontif Lateran Univ, JCD, 60. **CAREER** From instr to asst prof theol, 60-71, assoc prof, 71-80, prof relig Studies, Benedictine Col, 80-. **MEMBERSHIPS** Canon Law Soc Am; Federation Catholic Schs. **RESEARCH** Medieval monastic history: moral theology. **SELECTED PUBLICATIONS** Auth, From Turmoil to Solidarity: The Emergence of the Vallumbrosan Monastic Congregation, Am Benedictine Rev, 68. **CONTACT ADDRESS** Dept of Religious Studies, Benedictine Col, 1020 N 2nd St, Atchison, KS, 66002-1499. **EMAIL** dmeade@benedictine.edu

MEADE, E.M.
DISCIPLINE PHILOSOPHY **EDUCATION** Boston Col, PhD, 93. **CAREER** Asst prof, Cedar Crest Col, 93- . **MEMBERSHIPS** APA; SPEP. **RESEARCH** Moral judgment; axiology; biomedical ethics; ethics pedagogy. **SELECTED PUBLICATIONS** Auth, The Commodification of Values, in Hannah Arendt: Twenty Years Later, MIT, 96. **CONTACT ADDRESS** Cedar Crest Col, 100 College Dr, Allentown, PA, 18104. **EMAIL** emeade@cedarcrest.edu

MEADOR, DANIEL JOHN
PERSONAL Born 12/07/1926, Selma, AL, m, 1955, 3 children **DISCIPLINE** LAW **EDUCATION** Auburn Univ, BS, 49; Univ Ala, JD, 51; Harvard Univ, LLM, 54. **CAREER** Law clerk, Justice Thomas S Lawson, Ala Supreme Court, 53 & Justice Hugo L Black, US Supreme Court, 54-55; atty at law, Birmingham, Ala, 55-57; from assoc prof to prof law, Univ Va, 57-66; dean, Sch Law, Univ Ala, 66-70; JAMES MONROE PROF LAW, UNIV VA, 70-, Mem, Judicial Conf Fourth Circuit; Fulbright lectr, UK, 65-66; Asst Atty Gen, US, 77-79. **MEMBERSHIPS** Am Law Inst; Am Bar Asn; Am Soc Legal Hist. **RESEARCH** Federal judiciary; civil procedure; legal history. **SELECTED PUBLICATIONS** Auth, Inherent Judicial Authority in the Conduct of Civil Litigation, Tex Law Rev, vol 0073, 95. **CONTACT ADDRESS** Law School, Univ of Virginia, Charlottesville, VA, 22903.

MEADORS, GARY T.
PERSONAL Born 06/03/1945, Connersville, IN, m, 1967 **DISCIPLINE** GREEK, NEW TESTAMENT **EDUCATION** Grace Coll and Theol Sem. ThD, 83. **CAREER** Asst Prof, 79-83, Piedmont Baptist Coll; Prof of NT, 83-93, Grace Theol Sem; Prof of NT, 93-95, Baptist Sem of PA; Prof of NT, 95-, Grand Rapids Baptist Sem. **MEMBERSHIPS** ETS, IBR, SBL. **RESEARCH** New Testament; Ethics. **SELECTED PUBLICATIONS** Auth, Can a Believer Fall from Grace?, Spire 14:2, 86; Discipleship-Another Nuance to Consider, Exposition 4:3, 93; Evangelical Dictionary of Biblical Theology, ed by Walter Elwell, Grand Rapids, Baker Book House, 96; Love is the Law of Spiritual Formation, Presidential address to the Midwest Region Meeting of the Evangelical Theological Society, 98; Why Are They Looking At Jesus?, The Jesus Seminar, Baptist Bulletin, 97; Craig Blomberg, 1 Corinthians, The Application Series, JETS41, 98. **CONTACT ADDRESS** Grand Rapids Baptist Sem, 1001 E Beltline NE, Grand Rapids, MI, 49525. **EMAIL** gmeadors@cornerstone.edu

MEAGHER, ROBERT FRANCIS
PERSONAL Born 05/13/1927, Brooklyn, NY **DISCIPLINE** INTERNATIONAL LAW AND DEVELOPMENT **EDUCATION** City Col New York, BSS, 49; Yale Univ, LLB, 52. **CAREER** Leader specialist, Foreign Affairs Int Orgn State Dept grant, India, 53, Pakistan, 54; lawyer corp finance, Winthrop, Stimson, Putnam & Roberts, New York, 54-58; legal officer int law & contracts, UN, Beirut, 58-59; asst dir pub int develop finance foreign aid proj, Columbia Univ Law Sch, 61-65, assoc dir int legal res, 65-68; Prof Int Law, Fletcher Sch Law & Diplomacy, Tufts Univ, 67-, Int Legal Ctr grant, 71; Agency Int Develop grant, 72-74; adj prof law, Columbia Univ, 72; consult, Harvard Develop Adv Serv, 72-; ADJ PROF LAW, COLUMBIA UNIV, 72-; Rockefeller Found grant, 75-76; sr fel, Over-

seas Develop Corp, 75-76; Bellagie grant, 76; Am participant, Int Commun Agency India, Bangladesh, 79, Kuwait, Quatar, Nepal, Bangladesh, Thailand, Sri Lanka, Indonesia & Australia, 81; vis prof int law, Monash & Melbourne Univs, Australia, 81. **MEMBERSHIPS** African Law Asn Am (pres, 67-69); Am Foreign Law Asn; Int Law Asn; Am Bar Asn; Am Soc Int Law. **RESEARCH** Role of law in the development process; private investment and foreign aid; international economic and social organizations. **SELECTED PUBLICATIONS** Auth, The United Nations--Challenges of Law and Development--Introduction, Harvard Int Law J, vol 0036, 95. **CONTACT ADDRESS** Fletcher Sch of Law & Diplomacy, Tufts Univ, Medford, MA, 02111.

MEANS, JAMES
PERSONAL m **DISCIPLINE** PASTORAL MINISTRIES AND HOMILETICS **EDUCATION** Wheaton Col, BA; Denver Sem, BD; Univ Denver, MA, PhD. **CAREER** Prof, Denver Sem, 68-. **HONORS AND AWARDS** Gold Medallion Book Award winner., Sr pastor, S Gables Evangel Free Church; pastor, Evangel Free Churches in Loomis and Omaha, Nebr. **MEMBERSHIPS** Mem, Soc for Pastoral Theol; Assn of Practical Theol. **SELECTED PUBLICATIONS** Auth, Leadership in Christian Ministry; Effective Pastors for a New Century. **CONTACT ADDRESS** Denver Conservative Baptist Sem, PO Box 10000, Denver, CO, 80250. **EMAIL** jimm@densem.edu

MEANY, MARY WALSH
DISCIPLINE RELIGIOUS STUDIES **EDUCATION** Spalding Univ, BA, 65; Fordham Univ, MA, 67, PhD, 75. **CAREER** Instr, Franciscan Inst, St Bonaventure Univ, 97; co-ch, Hist Christianity Sect, Am Acad Rel, 88-94; Col serv, ch, Core Rev Comt, 92-95 & Franciscan Tradition Comt, 90-96; mem, Jewish Christian Inst Plan Bd; 1st Yr Stud Adv. **HONORS AND AWARDS** Co-organizer, sessions on, The Appropriation of the Vita Christi Tradition in Off and Popular Piety, Kalamazoo, 90-92 & 94-96. **SELECTED PUBLICATIONS** Auth, Angela of Foligno: Destructuring of Identity, Divine Representations: Postmodernism and Spirituality, Paulist Press, 94. **CONTACT ADDRESS** Dept of Relig Studies, Siena Col, 515 Loudon Rd., Loudonville, NY, 12211-1462.

MEDLIN, S. ALAN
DISCIPLINE TRUSTS AND ESTATES, FIDUCIARY ADMINISTRATION, REAL ESTATE TRANSACTIONS AND **EDUCATION** Univ SC, BA, 76, JD, 79. **CAREER** Prof, Univ of SC. **SELECTED PUBLICATIONS** Coed, Probate Practice Reporter; ed, Amer Bar Asn, Real Property, Probate and Trust J. **CONTACT ADDRESS** School of Law, Univ of S. Carolina, Law Center, Columbia, SC, 29208. **EMAIL** Alan@law.law.sc.edu

MEEHAN, M. JOHANNA
PERSONAL Born 02/01/1956, Winchester, MA, 2 children **DISCIPLINE** PHILOSOPHY **EDUCATION** Brandeis Univ, BA, 77; Boston Univ, MA, PhD, 90. **CAREER** Tchg asst, Instr, 79-83, Boston Univ; instr, 83-84, 89-90, Univ MS; inst, Bates Col, 86-87; instr, Brandeis Univ, 88; instr, Emerson Col, 89-90; asst prof, Grinnell Col, 90-99. **HONORS AND AWARDS** Machette Prize, 81; Borden Parker Bowne Scholar, 84; Col Lib Arts Award, 84; Grad Sch Dissertation Scholar, 85; DAAD, 85; Peter Bertocci Fel, 86; GTE Grant, 90; NEH Speaker Grant, 93; Harris Fel, 94; Committee Status Women, 98. **MEMBERSHIPS** Am Philos Asn; Soc Phenomenology; Existentialist Philos; Critical Theory Round Table. **RESEARCH** Social political philosophy; continental philosophy; feminism pychoanalytic theory. **SELECTED PUBLICATIONS** Auth, Feminists Read Habermas: Gendering the Subject of Discourse, 95; ed, intro, Feminists Read Habermas: Gendering the Subject of Discourses, 95; auth, art, Communicative Ethics, 97; auth, art, Interpretation and the Social Sciences, 97; auth, art, Plurality, Autonomy and the Right to Die, 98. **CONTACT ADDRESS** Dept of Philosophy, Grinnell Col, Grinnell, IA, 50112.

MEEKS, WAYNE ATHERTON
PERSONAL Born 01/08/1932, Aliceville, AL, m, 1954, 3 children **DISCIPLINE** RELIGION **EDUCATION** Univ Ala, BS, 53; Austin Presby Theol Sem, BD, 56; Yale Univ, MA, 63, PhD(New Testament studies), 65. **CAREER** Instr relig, Dartmouth Col, 64-65; from asst prof to assoc prof, Ind Univ, Bloomington, 66-69; assoc prof, 69-73, Prof Relig Studies, Yale Univ, 73-, Nat Endowment for Humanities fel, 75-76; Guggenheim fel, 79-80. **HONORS AND AWARDS** Fel, British Acad, 92-. **MEMBERSHIPS** Soc Bibl Lit; Soc Values Higher Educ; Am Acad Relig; Soc New Testament Studies. **RESEARCH** New Testament studies; religions in Greco-Roman world. **SELECTED PUBLICATIONS** Auth, Go From Your Father's House, John Knox, 64; The Prophet King, In: Religions in Antiquity, E J Brill, Leiden, 67; ed, The writings of St Paul, Norton, 72; co-ed & transl, Conflict at Colossae, Soc Bibl Lit, 73; co-ed, God's Christ and His People, Norwegian Univ Press, 77; coauth, Jews and Christians in Antioch, Soc Bibl Lit, 78; ed, Zur Soziologie des Urchristentums, Kaiser, 79; auth, The First Urban Christians, Yale Univ Press, 83; auth, The Moral World of the First Christians, Westminster, 86; auth, The Origins of Christian Morality, Yale Univ Press, 93; co-ed, Greeks, Romans, and Christians, Fortress, 90; co-ed, The Future of Christology, Fortress, 93; ed, The Library of Early Christianity (series), Westminster, 82-87; assoc ed, Harper Bible commentary, Harper Collins, 88; gen ed, Harper Collins Study Bible, Harper Collins, 93. **CONTACT ADDRESS** Dept of Relig Studies, Yale Univ, PO Box 208287, New Haven, CT, 06520-8287. **EMAIL** wayne.meeks@yale.edu

MEERBOTE, RALF
PERSONAL Born 05/08/1942, Merseburg, Germany **DISCIPLINE** HISTORY OF MODERN PHILOSOPHY **EDUCATION** Univ Chicago, BS, 64; Harvard Univ, MA, 67, PhD(philos), 70. **CAREER** Asst prof philos, Univ Ill, Chicago Circle, 69-73, assoc prof, 73-80; ASSOC PROF PHILOS, UNIV ROCHESTER, 80-, Fulbright sr res fel, 76-77. **MEMBERSHIPS** Am Philos Asn; Kantgesellschaft. **RESEARCH** Kant's theory of knowledge; theory of knowledge; aesthetics. **SELECTED PUBLICATIONS** Auth, Kant and Jobs Comforters, J Amer Acad Relig, vol 0060, 92. **CONTACT ADDRESS** Dept of Philosophy, Univ of Rochester, Rochester, NY, 14627.

MEHL, PETER J.
PERSONAL Born 06/28/1956, m, 2 children **DISCIPLINE** PHILOSOPHY **EDUCATION** Univ Chicago, MA, 83, PhD, 89. **CAREER** Assoc prof, dir Interdisciplinary Relig Stud, 94-, asst dean, Col Lib Arts, 96-98, interim dean, 98- . **MEMBERSHIPS** APA; Am Acad Relig; Soc for Philos in Contemp World; Counc of Colleges of Arts and Sci. **RESEARCH** Philosophical and religious ethica; applied ethica; philosophy of religion; religion and culture; moral psychology; Kierkegaard. **SELECTED PUBLICATIONS** Auth, "The Self Well Lost," Philos in the Contemp World, 95; "Religion, Philosophy and Public Life," Theol and Public Policy, 95; "Moral Virtue, Mental Health and Happiness," International Kierkegaard Commentary on Kierkegaard's Either/Or, Pt 2, Mercer Univ, 95; "William James' Ethics and the New Causuistry," Int J of Applied Philos, 96. **CONTACT ADDRESS** Col of Liberal Arts, Univ Central Arkansas, 201 Donaghey Ave, Conway, AR, 72035-5003. **EMAIL** peterm@mail.uca.edu

MEHLMAN, MAXWELL
PERSONAL Born 11/04/1948, Washington, DC, m, 1979, 2 children **DISCIPLINE** POLITICAL SCIENCE, POLITICS AND ECONOMICS, AND LAW **EDUCATION** Reed Col, BA, 70; Oxford Univ, BA, 72; Yale Law Sch, JD, 75. **CAREER** Atty, Arnold & Porter, Wash, DC, 75-84; assoc prof of law, 87-90, asst prof, 84-87; dir, The Law Med Ctr, Case Western Reserve Univ, 88-; Arthur E. Petersilge prof of law, Case Western Reserve Univ, 97-. **HONORS AND AWARDS** Rhodes Scholar, Ore, 70; Phi Beta Kappa, 70. **MEMBERSHIPS** Amer Soc of Law, Med and Ethics. **RESEARCH** Health care law and policy; Ethical, legal and policy issues in human genetics. **SELECTED PUBLICATIONS** Auth, Getting a Handle on Coverage Decisions: If Not Case Law, Then What?, 31, Ind Law Rev, 75, 98; co-auth, Genetic Testing for Cancer Risk: How to Reconcile the Conflicts, 279, JAMA, 179, 98; co-auth, Access to the Genome: The Challenge to Equality, Georgetown Univ Press, 98; co-auth, When Do Health Care Decisions Discriminate Against Persons With Disabilities? 22, Jour of Health Polit, Policy and Law, 1385, 97; co-auth, Enhancing Cognition in the Intellectually Intact: Possibilities and Pitfalls, 27, Hastings Ctr Report, 14, 97; auth, Access to the Genome and Federal Entitlement Programs, The Human Genome Project and the Future of Health Care, Ind Univ Press, 113-132, 96; auth, Historical Trends in Malpractice Litigation, Physician Exec and the Law: Issues and Trends in Liability, Amer Col of Physicians Exec, 21-44, 96; auth, Medical Advocates: A Call for a New Profession, 1, Widener Law Rev, 299, 96; co-auth, The Need for Anonymous Counseling and Testing, 58, Amer Jour Human Genetics, 393-397, 96; co-ed, Justice and Health Care: Comparative Perspectives, John Wiley & Sons, 95. **CONTACT ADDRESS** 11075 East Blvd., Cleveland, OH, 44106.

MEHTA, MAHESH MAGANLAL
PERSONAL Bombay, India **DISCIPLINE** PHILOSOPHIES AND RELIGIONS OF INDIA **EDUCATION** Univ Bombay, BA, 53, MA, 55, LLB, 57, PhD(Sanskrit), 64. **CAREER** Prof Sanskrit, Gujarat Univ, India, 58-61; lectr, Mithibai Col, Univ Bombay, 61-63 and Wilson Col, 63-67; fel, Univ Pa, 67-68, lectr Indian philos and relig, 68-69; asst prof, 69-73, ASSOC PROF INDIAN PHILOS AND RELIG, UNIV WINDSOR, 73-. **MEMBERSHIPS** Am Orient Soc; Asn Asian Studies; Can Soc Asian Studies; Bhandarkar Orient Res Inst; All-India Orient Cong. **RESEARCH** Advaita Vedanta; Mahayana Buddhism: Madhyamika and Yogacara. **SELECTED PUBLICATIONS** Auth Ocean of Eloquence--Tsongkhapa Commentary of the Yogacara Doctrine of Mind, Stud Rel Scns Religieuses, Vol 24, 95; On N9b 3p4 Chronological Strata in the Grammar of the Min Dialects, Bull Inst Hist Philol Acad Sinica, Vol 66, 95. **CONTACT ADDRESS** Dept of Asian Studies, Univ of Windsor, Windsor, ON, N9B 3P4.

MEHURON, KATE
DISCIPLINE PHILOSOPHY **EDUCATION** Col Santa Fe, BA; Univ Denver, MA; Vanderbilt Univ, PhD. **CAREER** Assoc prof, Eastern Michigan Univ. **HONORS AND AWARDS** Distinguished fac tchg awd, 92; Mich Governing Boards Distinguished fac awd, 95. **RESEARCH** History of philosophy; 19th and 20th century continental thought, feminist theory, HIV/AIDS issues. **SELECTED PUBLICATIONS** Ed, Free Spirits: Feminist Philosophers On Culture, Prentice-Hall, 95. **CONTACT ADDRESS** Dept of History and Philosophy, Eastern Michigan Univ, 701 Pray-Harrold, Ypsilanti, MI, 48197.

MEIDINGER, ERROL ELDON
PERSONAL Born 04/28/1952, Bismarck, ND, m, 1981, 2 children **DISCIPLINE** LAW, SOCIAL SCIENCE **EDUCATION** Univ ND, BA, 74; Northwestern Univ, MA, 77, JD, 79, PhD, 87. **CAREER** Sr fel, Lewis & Clark Col, 79-82; Assoc Prof, 82-87, Prof Law & Jurisprudence, State Univ NY Buffalo, 87-, Dir, Environment & Soc Inst, 98; Legis aid, NDak State Legis, 73; resident assoc, Argonne Nat Lab, 76-77. **MEMBERSHIPS** Am Soc Asn; Law & Soc Asn; Int Asn Study Common Property. **RESEARCH** Property syst and soc rel; environmental policy; "private" environmental standard setting. **SELECTED PUBLICATIONS** Auth, Applied Time Series Analysis, 80 & Interrupted Time Series Analysis, 80, Sage; The public uses of eminent domain: History and policy, Environ Law, 80; The Changing Legal Environment of Northern Forest Policy Making, In: Sustaining Ecosystems, Economies, and a Way of Life in the Northern Forests, The Wilderness Soc, 93; coauth, Science Advocacy is Inevitable: Deal with It, Proceedings of the Soc of Am Foresters, 96; Science and Policy in Natural Resources, Rennsalaerville Sci & Policy Seminar, USDA--Forest Service, 6/96; auth, Organizational and Legal Challenges for Ecosystem Management, In: Creating a Forestry for the 21st Century: The Science of Ecosystem Management, Island Press, 97; Look Who's Making the Rules: The Roles of the FSC and ISO in International Environmental Policy, Human Ecol Rev, 97; Laws and Institutions in Cross-Boundary Stewardship, In: Stewardship Across Boundaries, Island Press, 98. **CONTACT ADDRESS** Sch of Law, State Univ NY, J.L.O. Hall, Buffalo, NY, 14260-1100. **EMAIL** eemeid@aesu.buffalo.edu

MEIER, JOHN P.
PERSONAL Born 08/08/1942, New York, NY **DISCIPLINE** BIBLICAL STUDIES **EDUCATION** St Joseph Col, BA, 64; Gregorian Univ, STL, 68; Bibl Inst, SSD, 76. **CAREER** Prof of New Testament, St Joseph's Sem, 72-84; prof of New Testament, Catholic Univ of Am, 84-98; prof of New Testament, Univ of Notre Dame, 98- . **HONORS AND AWARDS** Summa Cum Laude with gold medal, 68, 76; Catholic Press Asn best book award 84; Bibl Archaeol Soc best book award, 93. **MEMBERSHIPS** CBA; SBL; SNTS; CTSA. **RESEARCH** Historical Jesus; New Testament Christology; Gospel of Matthew. **SELECTED PUBLICATIONS** Auth, Why Search for the Historical Jesus? Bible Rev, 93; auth, A Marginal Jew--Retrospect and Prospect, in Archbishop Gerety Lectures, 1992-1993, Seton Hall Univ, 93; auth, The Miracles of Jesus: Three Basic Questions for the Historian, in The Santa Clara Lectures, v.1, no.1, Santa Clara Univ, 94; auth, A Marginal Jew: Rethinking the Historical Jesus, v 2: Mentor, Message, and Miracles, Doubleday, 94; auth, Happy the Eyes That See: The Tradition, Message, and Authenticity of Luke 10:23-24 par, in Bartelt ed, Fortunate the Eyes That See: David Noel Freedman Festschrift, Eerdmans, 95; auth, Miracles and Modern Minds, Catholic World, 95; auth, The Eucharist at the Last Supper: Did It Happen? Theol Dig, 96; auth, Dividing Lines in Jesus Research Today: Through Dialectical Negation to a Positive Sketch, Interpretation, 96; auth, The Quest for the Historical Jesus as a Truly Historical Project, Grail: An Ecumenical J, 96; auth, The Miracles of Jesus: Three Basic Questions for the Historian, Dialogue: A J of Mormon Thought, 96; auth, four essays: John 1:1-18, John 20:19-23, The Jerusalem Council, The Conflict at Antioch, Mid-Stream, 97; auth, The Circle of the Twelve: Did It Exist During Jesus' Public Ministry, JBL, 97; auth, On Retrojecting Later Questions from Later Texts: A Reply to Richard Bauckham, CBQ, 97. **CONTACT ADDRESS** 1519 Marigold Way, #509, South Bend, IN, 46617. **EMAIL** John.P.Meier10@nd.edu

MEIER, SAMUEL
PERSONAL Born 09/10/1952, Tucson, AZ, m, 1978, 2 children **DISCIPLINE** RELIGION **EDUCATION** Univ Calif LA, BA, 74; Dallas Sem, ThD, 78; Harvard Univ, PhD, 87. **CAREER** Instr, Asian Theol Sem, 78-82; from asst prof to assoc prof, Ohio State Univ, 86-. **HONORS AND AWARDS** Alumni Distinguished Tchg Award; Jennie Solomon Award in Old Testament; W.H.G. Thomas Scholarship Award. **MEMBERSHIPS** Phi Beta Kappa. **RESEARCH** Communication in the ancient world; royal protocol; prophets; kingship; messengers. **SELECTED PUBLICATIONS** Auth, Speaking of Speaking: Marking Direct Discourse in the Hebrew Bible, 92; auth, The Messenger in the Ancient Semitic World, 88; auth, The Heading of Psalm 52, Hebrew Annual Rev, 94; auth, Orienting the Mappa Mundi in Judaism's Earliest Traditions, Shofar, 98. **CONTACT ADDRESS** Dept of Theology, Ohio State Univ, 1825 Weather Stone Ln, Worthington, OH, 43235. **EMAIL** meier.3@osu.edu

MEILAENDER, GILBERT
DISCIPLINE PHILOSOPHY **EDUCATION** Concordia Col Ft Wayne, BA, 68; Concordia Sem St Louis, Mdiv, 72; Princeton Univ, PhD, 76. **CAREER** Philos, Valparaiso Univ. **HON-**

ORS AND AWARDS NEH Fel Col Tchrs, 89-90 and 81-82., Bd dir, Soc Christ Ethics, 95-; ed adv bd, First Things; assoc ed, J Relig Ethics, 92-; ed bd, Dialog, 88-; ed bd, Ann Soc Relig Ethics, 88-90; assoc ed, Relig Studies Rev, 85-91; ed bd, J Relig Ethics, 82-; fel, The Hastings Ctr. **MEMBERSHIPS** Am Theol Soc; Soc Christ Ethics. **SELECTED PUBLICATIONS** Auth, Body, Soul, and Bioethics, Notre Dame UP, 95; Faith and Faithfulness: Basic Themes in Christian Ethics, Notre Dame UP, 91; Veritatis Slendor: Reopening Some Questions of the Reformation, J Relig Ethics, 95; Products of the Will: Robertson's Children of Choice, Washington and Lee Law Rev, 95; When Harry and Sally Read the Nicomachean Ethics: Friendship Between Men and Women in The Changing Face of Friendship, Notre Dame UP, 94; Terra es animata: On Having a Life, Hastings Ctr Rpt, 93; 'Love's Casuistry': Paul Ramsey on Caring for the Terminally Ill, J Relig Ethics, 91; A View From Somewhere: The Political Thought of Michael Walzer, Rel Studies Rev, 90. **CONTACT ADDRESS** Valparaiso Univ, 1500 E Lincoln Way, Valparaiso, IN, 46383-6493.

MEILKEJOHN, DONALD
PERSONAL Born 06/01/1909, Providence, RI, m, 1941, 4 children **DISCIPLINE** PHILOSOPHY **EDUCATION** Univ Wisconsin, AB, 30; Harvard Univ, PhD, 36. **CAREER** Instr, 36-38, Dartmouth; Assoc Prof, 38-46, WM & Mary; Assoc Prof to Prof, 46-63, Univ of Chicago Coll; Prof, 63-74, Syracuse Univ. **HONORS AND AWARDS** Bechtal Prize Essay, Harvard, 37; Excellence in Tchg, Chicago, 54. **MEMBERSHIPS** Amer Philos Assoc; AAUP. **RESEARCH** Political Theory. **SELECTED PUBLICATIONS** Auth, Freedom and the Public, 65; Articles in Philosophical and Legal Journals. **CONTACT ADDRESS** Box 194, East Calais, VT, 05650.

MEINKE, WILLIAM B.
PERSONAL Born 07/18/1948, Eaton Rapids, MI **DISCIPLINE** MEDICINE **EDUCATION** Univ MI, Col of Lit, Sciences and the Arts, BA (English Lit), 70; Univ MI Medical School, MD, 78; Univ CA, Davis-Sacramento Medical Center, Dept of Surgery, Internship and Residency, Surgery, 83. **CAREER** Emergency Medicine Practice (part time), Kaiser Permanente Medical Center, Emergency Dept, Sacramento, CA, 80-84; gen medical practice, multi-specialty group, Eaton Rapids Medical Clinic, MI, 85-89; emergency and occupational medical practice, Physicians' Marketing Services, Inc, Industrial Health Services, Inc, Lexington, KY, Georgetown, KY, 89-95; administrative physician, Toyota Motor Mfg, KY, Inc, Industrial Health Services, 95-, vice pres, Team Member Services, July 97. **HONORS AND AWARDS** Certified Independent Medical Examiner, Am Board of Independent Medical Examiners, spring 97; ed bd, J, Medical Problems of Performing Artists, fall 97. **MEMBERSHIPS** Am Col of Occupational and Environmental Medicine; Performing Arts Medicine Asn. **RESEARCH** Ergonomics; art medicine (performing arts). **SELECTED PUBLICATIONS** Auth, Musicians, Physicians and Ergonomics, A Critical Appraisal, Medical Problems of Performing Artists, Sept 94; The Work of Piano Virtuosity: An Ergonometric Analysis, Medical Problems of Performing Artists, June 95; A Proposed Standardized Medical History and Physical for Musicians, Medical Problems of Performing Artists, Dec 95; Common Medical Problems of Pianists-An Approach, Meinke and Savage, Presentations at Symposium: Medical Problems of Musicians and Dancers, Aspen, CO, June 97; Risks and Realities of Musical Performance, Medical Problems of Performing Artists, June 98; Historical and Physical Correlates to Technical Problems Encountered by Advanced Level Pianists, Meinke and Savage, scheduled for presentation at Symposium: Medical Problems of Performing Artists, Aspen, CO, June 98, with subsequent publication. **CONTACT ADDRESS** 1708 Woodlark Ln, Lexington, KY, 40505.

MEINWALD, CONSTANCE
DISCIPLINE PHILOSOPHY **EDUCATION** Princeton Univ, PhD, 87. **CAREER** Assoc prof, Univ IL at Chicago. **RESEARCH** Ancient philos. **SELECTED PUBLICATIONS** Auth, Plato's Parmenides, Oxford, 91; Good-bye to the Third Man, Cambridge, 92. **CONTACT ADDRESS** Philos Dept, Univ Illinois Chicago, S Halsted St, PO Box 705, Chicago, IL, 60607.

MEISEL, ALAN
PERSONAL Born 12/24/1946, Newark, NJ, m, 2 children **DISCIPLINE** LAW **EDUCATION** Yale Col, BA, 68; Yale Law School, JD, 72. **CAREER** Prof of Law, Univ Pittsburgh School of Law, 76-; Dickie, McCamey & Chilcote prof of Bioethics, 95-. **HONORS AND AWARDS** Am Asn of Publishers, Most Outstanding Book in Legal and Accounting Practice Category for The Right to Die, 89; Am Fed of Clinical Res, Nellie Westerman Prize in Medical Ethics for Ethical Factors in the Allocation of Experimental Medical Therapies: The Chronic Left-Ventricular Assist Device, 90, with L S Parker, R M Arnold, L A Siminoff, and L H Roth; fel, Hastings Center. **MEMBERSHIPS** Am Bar Asn; Am Health Lawyers Asn; Am Socv of Bioethics and Humanities; Am Soc of Law, Medicine and Ethics; Int Asn of Bioethics. **RESEARCH** Health law; bioethics; informed consent; end-of-life decision making. **SELECTED PUBLICATIONS** Auth, Legal Myths About Terminating Life Support, Archives of Internal Medicine, 91; The Legal Concensus About Foregoing Life-Sustaining Treatment: Its Status and Its Prospects, Kennedy Inst of Ethics J, 92; Barriers to Foregoing Nutrition and Hygdration in Nursing Homes, Am J of Law and Medicine, 95; The Right to Die, John Wiley & Sons, 95; The Right to Die: A Case Study in American Law Making, European J Health Law, 96; Legal Myths About Informed Consent, Archives of Internal Medicine, with M G Kucezewski, 96, condensed in Resident Physician, 97; Physician-Assisted Suicide: A Roadmap for State Courts, Fordham Urban L J, 97; numerous other publications. **CONTACT ADDRESS** School of Law, Univ of Pittsburgh, Pittsburgh, PA, 15260. **EMAIL** meisel@med.pitt.edu

MEITZEN, MANFRED OTTO
PERSONAL Born 12/12/1930, Houston, TX **DISCIPLINE** THEOLOGY **EDUCATION** Rice Univ, BA, 52; Wartburg Theol Sem, ThM, 56; Harvard Univ, PhD, 61. **CAREER** From asst prof to assoc prof relig, Rocky Mt Col, 61-65; assoc prof relig studies, 65-70, chmn prog humanities, 72-77, PROF RELIG STUDIES, WVA UNIV, 70, CHMN DEPT, 65-, Vis scholar, Christ Church Col, Oxford Univ, 73. **MEMBERSHIPS** Am Acad Relig; Am Guild Organists; Univ Prof Acad Order (1st pres, 77-79, pres, 79). **RESEARCH** Theology and culture; contemporary theology; New Testament studies. **SELECTED PUBLICATIONS** Auth, 2 Observations about Human Reason, J Relig Health, Vol 35, 96. **CONTACT ADDRESS** 119 Forest Dr, Morgantown, WV, 26505.

MELCHIONNE, KEVIN
DISCIPLINE PHILOSOPHY **EDUCATION** SUNY, Stony Brook, PhD, 95. **CAREER** Dir, exhibits, Tyler Schl of Art, Temple Univ. **HONORS AND AWARDS** Renwick Fel, Natl Museum of Amer Art, Smithsonian Inst. **MEMBERSHIPS** Col Art Assn; Amer Assn of Museums. **RESEARCH** Aesthetics; cult stud; contemporary art. **SELECTED PUBLICATIONS** Rev, Werner Muensterberger's Collecting: An Unruly Passion: Psychological Perspectives, Phil 7 Lit, vol 20, 96; rev, Christopher Reed's Not at Home: the Suppression of the Domestic in Modern Art and Architecture, J of Aesthetics & Art Criticism, vol 55, 97; art, Living in Glass Houses: Decoration, Neatness and the Art of Domesticity, J of Aesthetics and Art Criticism, Spec issue on Environ Aesthetics, vol 56, 98; auth, Artistic Dropouts, Aesthetics: The Big Questions, Blackwell, 98; auth, Drawing upon Drawing: the Reclamation Drawings of Michael Lucero, Amer Ceramics, 98; art, Re-Thinking Site-Specificity in Public Art: some Critical and Philosophical Problems, Art Criticism, vol 12, 98; art, The Aesthetics of Collecting, Phil & Lit, 98; art, Of Bookworms and Busybees: Cultural Theory in the Age of Do-It-Yourselfing, J of Aesthetics & Art Criticism, 99; art, Al Held and the Reconstruction of Painting, Amer Art, 99. **CONTACT ADDRESS** Tyler School of Art, Beech & Penrose Aves, Elkins Park, PA, 19027.

MELE, ALFRED R.
DISCIPLINE CLASSICS AND PHILOSOPHY **EDUCATION** Wayne State Univ, BA, 73; Univ MI, PhD, 79. **CAREER** Vail Prof Philos, 79. **RESEARCH** Cognitive philos; hist of ancient philos. **SELECTED PUBLICATIONS** Auth, Irrationality, Oxford UP, 87; Springs of Action, Oxford UP, 92; Autonomous Agents, Oxford UP, 95; co-edr, Mental Causation, Clarendon, 93. **CONTACT ADDRESS** Davidson Col, 102 N Main St, PO Box 1719, Davidson, NC, 28036. **EMAIL** almele@davidson.edu

MELLEMA, GREGORY
PERSONAL Born 06/22/1948, Chicago, IL, m, 1973, 2 children **DISCIPLINE** PHILOSOPHY **EDUCATION** Univ MI, MBA, 78; Univ MA, PhD, 74. **CAREER** Instr, 74-75, St. Olaf Col; asst prof, 75-76, assoc prof, prof, 78-, Calvin Col. **HONORS AND AWARDS** Who's Who in the World; Who's Who in Am Ed. **MEMBERSHIPS** APA; Soc of Christian Philos. **RESEARCH** Ethics. **SELECTED PUBLICATIONS** Auth, On Being Fully Responsible, Am Philos Quart, 84; auth, Quasi-Supererogation, Philos Stud, 87; auth, Individuals, Groups, and Shared Moral Responsibility, Peter Lang, Inc, 88; auth, Beyond the Call of Duty, SUNY Press, 91; auth, Offense and Virtue Ethics, Can J of Philos, 91; auth, Supererogation, Blame, and the Limits of Obligation, Philosophia, 94; auth, Collective Responsibility, Rodopi, 97; auth, Collective Guilt, Encycl of Applied Ethics, 98. **CONTACT ADDRESS** Dept of Philosophy, Calvin Col, Grand Rapids, MI, 49546. **EMAIL** mell@calvin.edu

MELLI, MARYGOLD SHIRE
PERSONAL Born 02/08/1926, Rhinelandr, WI, m, 1950, 4 children **DISCIPLINE** LAW **EDUCATION** Univ Wis, Ba, 47, LLB, 50. **CAREER** Fel, res and criminal law, Univ Wis Law Sch, 50-53; asst prof law, 61-66, assoc prof, 66-67, assoc dean admin, 70-72, PROF LAW, LAW SCH, UNIV WIS-MADISON. MEM BD MGRS, NAT CONF BAR EXAMRS, 80-; affil, Univ Wis Inst Res Poverty, 81-. **MEMBERSHIPS** Law and Soc Asn; Int Soc Family Law; Nat Coury Family Rel; Am Bar Asn Family Law Sect. **RESEARCH** Child support; divorce policy; legal problems of the elderly. **SELECTED PUBLICATIONS** Auth The United States-Child Support Enforcement for The 21st Century, Univ Louisville J Family Law, Vol 32, 94; The United States--Continuing Concern With the Economic Consequences of Divorce, Univ Louisville J Family Law, Vol 31, 93. **CONTACT ADDRESS** Law Sch, Univ of Wis, Madison, WI, 53706.

MELNICK, ATRHUR
DISCIPLINE PHILOSOPHY **EDUCATION** Univ Chicago, PhD, 71. **CAREER** Prof, Univ Ill Urbana Champaign. **RESEARCH** Metaphysics; history of modern philosophy; philosophy of science; philosophy of mathematics; logic. **SELECTED PUBLICATIONS** Auth, Kant's Analogies of Experience and Space; Time and Thought in Kant; pubs on Kant. **CONTACT ADDRESS** Philosophy Dept, Univ Ill Urbana Champaign, 52 E Gregory Dr, Champaign, IL, 61820. **EMAIL** amelnick@uiuc.edu

MENDELSON, ALAN
PERSONAL Born 07/30/1939, Washington, DC **DISCIPLINE** RELIGION **EDUCATION** Kenyon Col, AB, 61; Brandeis Univ, MA, 65; Univ Chicago, PhD(hist cult), 71. **CAREER** Vis lectr philos and relig, Hebrew Univ Jerusalem, 71-73; ASST PROF RELIG, MCMASTER UNIV, 76-. **MEMBERSHIPS** Philos Inst. **RESEARCH** Judaism and Christianity in Greco-Roman world. **SELECTED PUBLICATIONS** Auth, The Story of Creation--Its Origin and its Interpretation in Philo and the Fourth Gospel, J Jewish Stud, Vol 48, 97. **CONTACT ADDRESS** Dept of Relig, McMaster Univ, 1280 Main St W, Hamilton, ON, L8S 4K1.

MENDES, ERROL
DISCIPLINE LAW **EDUCATION** Exeter Univ, LLB; Univ Ill, LLM. **CAREER** Prof. **HONORS AND AWARDS** Ed, Nat Jour Const Law. **SELECTED PUBLICATIONS** Ed, Racial Discrimination: Law and Practice; co-ed, Canadian Charter of Rights and Freedoms. **CONTACT ADDRESS** Fac Common Law, Univ Ottawa, 550 Cumberland St, PO Box 450, Ottawa, ON, K1N 6N5.

MENDIETA, EDUARDO
PERSONAL Born 12/28/1963, Colombia, m, 1993, 2 children **DISCIPLINE** PHILOSOPHY **EDUCATION** Union Theol Sem, MA, 91; New School for Soc Res, PhD, 97. **CAREER** Vis prof, Univ Iberoamericans, 98; asst prof, Univ San Fran, 94-. **MEMBERSHIPS** Amer Acad Relig; Amer Pholos Asn; Soc Phenomenol Existential Philos. **RESEARCH** German & Latin American philosophy; Moral philosophy; Postcolonist & globalization theory; Habermas; Dussel; Apel. **CONTACT ADDRESS** Philosophy Dept, Univ San Fran, 2130 Fulton St, San Francisco, CA, 94117-1080. **EMAIL** mendietae@usfca.edu

MENDOLA, JOSEPH
DISCIPLINE METAPHYSICS, ETHICAL THEORY, AND PHILOSOPHY OF MIND **EDUCATION** Univ Mich, PhD, 83. **CAREER** Assoc prof, ch, dept Philos, Univ Nebr, Lincoln. **SELECTED PUBLICATIONS** Auth, Normative Realism, or Bernard Williams and Ethics at the Limit, Australasian J of Philos 67, 89; Objective Value and Subjective States, Philos and Phenomenol Res L, 90; An Ordinal Modification of Classical Utilitarianism, Erkenntnis 33, 90; Human Thought. **CONTACT ADDRESS** Univ Nebr, Lincoln, Lincoln, NE, 68588-0417.

MENDOSA, ANTONIO
DISCIPLINE CORPORATE FINANCE **EDUCATION** St Mary's Univ, BBA, 73, JD, 78. **CAREER** Prof, Pepperdine Col. **HONORS AND AWARDS** Rick J Caruso res fel, 94-95. **MEMBERSHIPS** Mem, Am Bar Assn; Am Soc Intl Lawyers; State Bar TX. **SELECTED PUBLICATIONS** Auth, The Creeping Breach Intl Law. **CONTACT ADDRESS** Sch of Law, Pepperdine Univ, 24255 Pacific Coast Hwy, Malibu, CA, 90263.

MENKE, CHRISTOPH
DISCIPLINE PHILOSOPHY **EDUCATION** Free Univ Berlin, PhD, 55. **CAREER** Assoc prof, Eugene Lang Col. **RESEARCH** Nietzsche; Hegel; aesthetics; ethics. **SELECTED PUBLICATIONS** Auth, Tragedy in Daily Life: Freedom and Justice in Hegel, 96. **CONTACT ADDRESS** Eugene Lang Col, New Sch for Social Research, 66 West 12th St, New York, NY, 10011.

MENN, STEPHEN
DISCIPLINE PHILOSOPHY **EDUCATION** Johns Hopkins Univ, MA, PhD; Univ Chicago, MA, PhD. **RESEARCH** Ancient philosophy; medieval philosophy; history and philosophy of mathematics. **SELECTED PUBLICATIONS** Auth, Plato on God as Nous, Southern Ill Univ, 95; art, Aristotle and Plato on God as Nos and as the Good, Rev Metaphysics, 92; art, The Problem of the Third Meditation, Am Cath Philos Quarterly, 93; auth, Metaphysics, Dialectic, and the Categories, 95. **CONTACT ADDRESS** Philosophy Dept, McGill Univ, 845 Sherbrooke St, Montreal, PQ, H3A 2T5.

MENSCH, JAMES
DISCIPLINE PHILOSOPHY **EDUCATION** Univ Md, BA, 67; Univ Toronto, PhD, 76. **CAREER** Author **MEMBERSHIPS** Am Philos Asn; Soc Phenomenol Existential Philos; Can Soc Hermeneutics Post Modern Thought. **SELECTED PUBLICATIONS** Auth, Knowing and Being: A Post-Modern Reversal, Penn State Univ, 96; After Modernity: Husserlian Reflections on a Philosophical Tradition, Univ NY, 96; The Beginning of the Gospel of St. John: Philosophical Perspectives, Peter Lang, 92; Freedom and Selfhood, Husserl Studies, 97; Presence and Postmodernity, Am Cath Philos Quarterly, 97; The Bible as Literature, Can Cath Rev, 95; Husserl and Sartre: A Question of Reason, J Philos Res, 94; The Mind Body Problem, Phenomenological Reflections on an Ancient Solution, Am Cath Philos Quarterly, 94. **CONTACT ADDRESS** St Francis Xavier Univ, Antigonish, NS, B2G 2W5.

MENZEL, CHRISTOPHER
DISCIPLINE PHILOSOPHY **EDUCATION** Pacific Lutheran Univ, BA, 79; Univ Notre Dame, PhD, 84. **CAREER** Assoc prof, 91-, ass prof, 86-91 researcher, 87-91, Texas A&M Univ; vis res scientist, Commonwealth Scientific and Industrial Res Org, 96; actg asst prof, 85-86 & postdoctoral fel, 84-86, Stanford Univ. **RESEARCH** Artificial intelligence, philosophical theology; 20th century Anglo-American philosophy. **SELECTED PUBLICATIONS** Auth, Modeling Method Ontologies: A Foundation for Enterprise Model Integration, in Ontological Engineering: Papers from the 97 AAAI Spring Symp, Menlo Park, AAAI Press, Technical Report SS-97-06; Alethic Modalities and Type Theory, Cambridge Dictionary of Philos, Cambridge UP, 95; coauth, Situations and Processes, Concurrent Engineering: Research and Applications 4 3, 96; A Situation Theoretic Approach to the Representation of Processes, in Modelling and Methodologies for Enterprise Integration, London, Chapman and Hall, 96; Toward a Method for Acquiring CIM Ontologies, Int J Comput Integrated Manufacturing 8 3, 95; An Ontology and Process Description Method for Design and Implementation of Information-Integrated Enterprises, Int J Flexible Automation and Integrated Manufacturing 1, 94; IDEF3 Process Descriptions and Their Semantics, in Intelligent Systems in Design and Manufacturing, ASME Press, 94. **CONTACT ADDRESS** Dept of Philosophy, Texas A&M Univ, 510 Blocker, College Station, TX, 77843-4237. **EMAIL** cmenzel@tamu.edu

MERCADANTE, LINDA A.
PERSONAL Newark, NJ, 1 child **DISCIPLINE** THEOLOGY AND HISTORY OF DOCTRINE **EDUCATION** Princeton Theol Sem, PhD, 86. **CAREER** Prof, theol, B. Robert Straker chair, Methodist Theol Sch in Oh, 87-. **HONORS AND AWARDS** Mem, Ctr of Theol Inquiry; scholar, Ecumenical Inst; grants, The Louisville Inst; grants, Asn of Theol Scholars. **MEMBERSHIPS** Amer Acad of Relig; Workgroup on Constructive Theol. **RESEARCH** Gender; Addiction; Doctrine of sin; Historical theology. **SELECTED PUBLICATIONS** Auth, Victims & Sinners: Spiritual roots of addiction & recovery, Westminster, 96; auth, Sin, Addiction & Freedom, Reconstructing Christ Theol; auth, Gender, Doctrine & God: The Shakers & contemporary theology, Abingdon, 90. **CONTACT ADDRESS** 3081 Columbus Pk., Delaware, OH, 43015. **EMAIL** lmercadante@mtso.edu

MERCER, MARK
PERSONAL Born 11/03/1957, London, ON, Canada, m, 1998 **DISCIPLINE** PHILOSOPHY; FILM STUDIES **EDUCATION** Carleton Univ, BA, 82, MA, 85; Univ Toronto, PhD, 91. **CAREER** Col prof, Okanagau Univ Col, 93-94; asst prof, Brandon Univ, 94-95; asst prof, Univ Calgary, 95-97; asst prof, Univ Manitoba, 98; asst prof, St Cloud State Univ, 98-99. **HONORS AND AWARDS** Soc Serv Hum fel, 91-93. **MEMBERSHIPS** Can Philos Asn; Amer Philos Asn **RESEARCH** Pholosophy of mind; Epistenology; Ethics. **SELECTED PUBLICATIONS** coauth, Meaning Holism and Interpretability, Philos Quart, 91; auth, On a Pragmatic Argument Against Pragmatism in Ethics, Am Philos Quart, 93; Psychological Egoism and Its Critics, S Jour Philos XXXVI, 98. **CONTACT ADDRESS** #76, 3725 Victoria Ave., MB, R7B 3C3. **EMAIL** mmercer@stcloudstate.edu

MERCHANT, CAROLYN
PERSONAL Born 07/12/1936, Rochester, NY, 2 children **DISCIPLINE** ENVIRONMENTAL HISTORY, PHILOSOPHY & ETHICS **EDUCATION** Vassar Col, AB, 58; Univ Wis, MA, 62, PhD, 67. **CAREER** Lectr hist of sci, Univ San Francisco, 69-74, asst prof, 74-78; asst prof environ hist, 79-80, assoc prof 80-, CHANCELLOR PROF ENVIRON HIST, PHILOS & ETHICS, UNIV CALIF, BERKELEY, former chmn, Dept Conserv & Resource Studies; Vis prof, Ecole Normale Superieure, Paris, 6/86. **HONORS AND AWARDS** NSF, 76-78; NEH grant, 77, 81-83; Am Counc Learned Soc fel, 78; Center Advan Studies, Behavioral Sci, 78; Fulbright sr scholar, Umea Univ, Sweden, 84; Agr Exp Station, Univ Calif, Berkeley, 80-86, 86-92, 92-; Nathan Cummings Found, 92; Am Cultures fel, Univ Calif, Berkeley, 6/90; Vis fel, School Soc Sci, Murdoch Univ, Perth, Australia, 91; John Simon Guggenheim fel, 95; Doctor Honoris Causa, Umea Univ, Sweden, 95. **MEMBERSHIPS** Hist Sci Soc; West Coast Hist Sci Soc; British Soc Hist Sci; Soc Hist Technol; Am Soc Environ Hist. **RESEARCH** Scientific revolution; American environmental history; women and nature. **SELECTED PUBLICATIONS** Auth, D'Alembert and the vis viva controversy, Studies in Hist and Philos of Sci, 8/70; Leibniz and the vis viva controversy, Isis, spring 71; The Leibnizian-Newtonian debates: Natural philosophy and social psychology, British J for the Hist of Sci, 12/73; Madame du Chatelet's metaphysics and mechanics, Studies in Hist and Philos of Sci, 5/77; The Death of Nature: Women, Ecology, and the Scientific Revolution, Harper and Row, San Francisco, 80, 2nd ed, 90; Earthcare: Women and the environmental movement, Environment, 6/81; Isis' consciousness raised, Isis, fall 82; Ecological Revolutions: Nature, Gender, and Science in New England, Univ NC Press, 89; Radical Ecology: The Search for a Liveable World, Routledge, 92; Major Problems in American Environmental History: Ecology, Humanities Press, 94; Earthcare: Women and the Environment, Routledge, 96; ed, Green Versus Gold: Sources in California's Environmental History, Island Press, 98; Reinventing Eden: Women, Nature, and Narrative, in progress. **CONTACT ADDRESS** Dept of Environ Sci, Policy & Mgt, Univ Calif, Berkeley, CA, 94720-3310. **EMAIL** merchant@nature.berkeley.edu

MERKLE, JOHN CHARLES
PERSONAL Born 12/26/1946, Philadelphia, PA **DISCIPLINE** RELIGIOUS STUDIES AND THEOLOGY **EDUCATION** St Vincent de Paul Sem, BA, 69; Cath Univ Louvain, MA, 74, PhD(relig studies), 82. **CAREER** INSTR THEOL, COL ST BENEDICT, 77-. **MEMBERSHIPS** Col Theol Soc; Relig Educ Asn. **RESEARCH** Modern and contemporary Jewish philosophy and theology; Jewish-Christian dialogue; faith development. **SELECTED PUBLICATIONS** Auth, Bound Together in God, Rel Edu, Vol 91, 96. **CONTACT ADDRESS** Dept of Theol, Col of Saint Benedict, 37 College Ave S, Saint Joseph, MN, 56374-2001.

MERLING, DAVID
PERSONAL Born 06/14/1948, Pittsburg, PA, m, 1969, 2 children **DISCIPLINE** OLD TESTAMENT STUDIES, ARCHAEOLOGY, HISTORY OF ANTIQUITY **EDUCATION** Andrews Univ, PhD, 96. **CAREER** Assoc prof of Archaeol and Hist of Antiquities, Andrews Univ, 86-; Curator, Siegfried H. Horn Archaeol Museum, 91- . **HONORS AND AWARDS** Andrews Univ Fac Res Grant, 91-92, 94; Who's Who in Bibl Stud and Archaeol, 93; Zion Res found travel grant, 84, Tell e-Umeyri, Jordan. **MEMBERSHIPS** Adventist Theol Soc; Amer Sch Oriental Res; Bibl Archaeol Soc; Evangelical Theol Soc; Inst Bibl Res; Israel Exploration Soc; Near Eastern Archaeol Soc; Soc Bibl Lit. **RESEARCH** Archaeology and the Book of Joshua. **CONTACT ADDRESS** Dept of Archaeology, Andrews Univ, Berrien Springs, MI, 49104-0990. **EMAIL** merling@andrews.edu

MERLINO, SCOTT A.
PERSONAL Born 08/23/1962, Erie, PA **DISCIPLINE** PHILOSOPHY **EDUCATION** Univ of Cal at Davis, PhD, 97. **CAREER** Amer River Col, instr; Cal State Univ, adj prof. **MEMBERSHIPS** APA, PSA, ISHP&SSB **CONTACT ADDRESS** Dept of Philosophy, American River Col, 101 Grande Ave, Davis, CA, 95616-0219. **EMAIL** samerlin@inreach.com

MERMIER, GUY R.
PERSONAL Born 10/20/1931, Grenoble, France, m, 1954, 2 children **DISCIPLINE** ROMANCE LANGUAGES AND LITERATURE **EDUCATION** Univ Grenoble, Lic es-let and DES, 53; Univ Pa, PhD, 61. **CAREER** Instr French, Amherst Col, 52-53; instr Romance lang, Univ Mass, 54-55; asst instr, Univ Pa, 55-56; instr foreign lang, Temple Univ, 56-61; from instr to asst prof Romance lang, 61-67, Rackham grant, 62, ASSOC PROF ROMANCE LANG, UNIV MICH, ANN ARBOR, 67-, Fulbright grant, Amherst Col, 52-53; Smith-Mundt fel, 52; NDEA consult, Temple Univ, 56; PROF, LAVAL UNIV, 57-; dir, Mich-Wis Jr Year in France, 67-68; PRES, ALLIANCE FRANCAISE, ANN ARBOR, 68- **MEMBERSHIPS** MLA; Am Asn Teachers French; Int Arthurian Soc; Mod Humanities Res Asn; Am Asn Teachers Ital. **RESEARCH** Medieval; Renaissance; 19th century literature and existentialist 20th century literature. **SELECTED PUBLICATIONS** Auth, Noces De Sable, World Lit Today, Vol 70, 96; The Medieval Occitan Novel, Fr Rev, Vol 68, 95. **CONTACT ADDRESS** Dept of Romance Lang, Univ of Michigan, Ann Arbor, MI, 48104.

MERON, THEODOR
PERSONAL Born 04/28/1930, Kalisz, Poland **DISCIPLINE** INTERNATIONAL LAW, HUMAN RIGHTS **EDUCATION** Hebrew Univ, MJ, 54; Harvard Univ, LLM, 55, SJD, 57. **CAREER** Legal adv, Ministry of Foreign Affairs, Israel, 67-71; ambassador to Can, 71-75; UN Rep, 77; PROF LAW, LAW SCH, NY UNIV, 78-, Fel, Rockefeller Found, 75 and 80; vis prof law, Law Fac, Univ Ottawa, 73-75 and Hebrew Univ, 77 and 79; consult, World Bank, spring, 79. **HONORS AND AWARDS** Israel Ministry for Foreign Affairs Prize, 58; Carnegie lectr, The Hague Acad Int Law, 80. **MEMBERSHIPS** Am Soc Int Law; Int Law Asn; French Soc Int Law. **RESEARCH** Public international law; international organization. **SELECTED PUBLICATIONS** Auth, International Criminalization of Internal Atrocities, Am J Int Law, Vol 89, 95; The Continuing Role of Custom in the Formation of International Humanitarian Law, Am J Int Law, Vol 90, 96; The Authority to Make Treaties in the Late Middle Ages, Am J Int Law, Vol 89, 95; The Helms Burton Act--Exercising the Presidential Option, Am J Int Law, Vol 91, 97; Rape as a Crime Under International Humanitarian Law, Am J Int Law, Vol 87, 93; The Time Has Come for the United States to Ratify Geneva Protocol I, Am J Int Law, Vol 88, 94; Lieber, Francis Code and Principles of Humanity, Col J Transnational Law, Vol 36, 97; War Crimes in Yugoslavia and the Development of International Law/, Am J Int Law, Vol 88, 94; Extraterritoriality of Human Rights Treaties, American Journal Of International Law, Vol 89, 95 Combating Lawlessness in Gray Zone Conflicts Through Minimum Humanitarian Standards, Am J Int Law, Vol 89, 95; From Nuremberg to the Hague, Mil Law Rev, Vol 0149, 95. **CONTACT ADDRESS** Sch of Law, New York Univ, 40 Washington Sq S, New York, NY, 10012-1005.

MERRILL, DANIEL DAVY
PERSONAL Born 06/01/1932, South Bend, IN, m, 1956, 2 children **DISCIPLINE** PHILOSOPHY **EDUCATION** Princeton Univ, BA, 54; Univ Minn, MA, 58, PhD, 62. **CAREER** Instr philos, Knox Col, 59-62; from asst prof to assoc prof, 62-75, chmn dept, 65-68, assoc dean, 70-73, PROF PHILOS, OBERLIN COL, 75-, Mem comt on status and future profession, Am Philos Asn, 69-72 and prog comt Western Div, 83. **MEMBERSHIPS** Western Div Am Philos Asn; Western Conf Teaching Philos (chmn, 70-72); Asn Symbolic Logic; Philos Sci Asn. **RESEARCH** History and philosophy of logic; philosophy of language; philosophy of science. **SELECTED PUBLICATIONS** Auth, Making Sense of Sollys Syllogistic Symbolism, Hist Philos Logic, Vol 17, 96. **CONTACT ADDRESS** Dept of Philosophy, Oberlin Col, 135 W Lorain St, Oberlin, OH, 44074-1076.

MERRILL, EUGENE H.
PERSONAL Born 09/12/1934, Anson, ME, m, 1960, 1 child **DISCIPLINE** OLD TESTAMENT **EDUCATION** Bob Jones Univ, BA, 57, MA, 60, PhD, 63; NY Univ, MA 70; Columbia Univ, MPhil, 77, PhD, 85. **CAREER** Prof Old Testament Stud, Bob Jones Univ, 63-66; prof of the Bible, Berkshire Christian Col, 68-75; sr prof Old Testament Stud, Dallas Theol Sem, 75- . **HONORS AND AWARDS** Vis scholar, Union Theol Sem, 63, 64; travel-study grant, Israel, US State Dept, 65; listed Who's Who in Religion, 76, 78, Outstanding Educators of America, 81-82, International Scholars Directory, 71, 73, 75. **MEMBERSHIPS** Evangelican Theol Soc; Am Schools of Orient Res; Am Orient Soc; Soc of Bibl Lit. **RESEARCH** History of Israel; Old Testament theology. **SELECTED PUBLICATIONS** Auth, Royal Priesthood: An Old Testament Messianic Motif, Bib Sac, 93; auth, Deuteronomy, New Testament Faith, and the Christian Life, in Dyer, ed, Integrity of Heart, Skillfulness of Hands, Baker, 94; auth, Haggai, Zechariah, Malachi : An Exegetical Commentary, Moody, 94; auth, Deuteronomy, Broadman & Holman, 94; contribur to The Complete Who's Who in the Bible, ed Gardner, Marshall Pickering, 95; auth, History in Sandy, ed Cracking Old Testament Codes, Broadman & Holman, 95; auth, The Late Bronze/Early Iron Age Transition and the Emergence of Israel, Bib Sac, 95; contribur to Evangelical Dictionary of Biblical Theology, ed Elwell, Baker Book, 96; co-trans, Deuteronomy, in New Living Translation, Tyndale, 96; auth, The Peoples of the Old Testament According to Genesis, Bib Sac, 97; ed and contribur New International Dictionary of Old Testament Theology and Exegesis, ed Van Gemeren, Zondervan, 97; auth, Suicide and the Concept of Death in the Old Testament in Demy, ed, Suicide: A Christian Response, Kregel, 98. **CONTACT ADDRESS** Dallas Theol Sem, 3909 Swiss Ave, Dallas, TX, 75204. **EMAIL** eugene_merrill@dts.edu

MERRILL, KENNETH ROGERS
PERSONAL Born 06/15/1932, Marshall, TX, m, 1954 **DISCIPLINE** PHILOSOPHY **EDUCATION** Bethany-Peniel Col, BA, 54; Northwestern Univ, MA, 56 PhD, 63. **CAREER** From instr to assoc prof, 58-77, chmn dept, 64-70, PROF PHILOS, UNIV OKLA, 77- **MEMBERSHIPS** Am Philos Asn; Hume Soc; Southwestern Philos Soc. **RESEARCH** Philosophy of Whitehead; British empiricism; American philosophy. **SELECTED PUBLICATIONS** Auth, State Trust Lands--History, Management, and Sustainable Use, W Am Quart, Vol 28, 97; Whose Home on the Range , W Am Quart, Vol 27, 96. **CONTACT ADDRESS** Dept of Philosophy, Univ of Oklahoma, 455 W Lindsey St, Norman, OK, 73019-2000.

MERRILL, RICHARD AUSTIN
PERSONAL Born 05/20/1937, Logan, UT, m, 1974, 2 children **DISCIPLINE** LAW **EDUCATION** Columbia Univ, AB, 59, LLB, 64; Oxford Univ, BA and MA, 61. **CAREER** Law clerk, Circuit Court Appeals, 64-65; attorney, Covington and Burning, 65-69; PROF LAW, UNIV VA, 69, DEAN, 80 , CONSULT, ADMIN CONF US, 72-; gen coun US Food and Drug Admin, 75-77; MEM, INST MED, 77-; MEM LID TOXICOL, NAT ACAD SCI, 79- **SELECTED PUBLICATIONS** Auth, The Architecture of Government Regulation of Medical Products, Va Law Rev, Vol 82, 96; The Delaney Paradox Reexamined--Regulating Pesticides in Processed Foods, Food Drug Law Jour, Vol 48, 93; The Standard of Evidence Required for Premarket

Approval under the Medical Device Amendments of 1976, Food Drug Law Jour, Vol 47, 92. **CONTACT ADDRESS** Law Sch, Univ of Va, Charlottesville, VA, 22901.

MERRITT, FRANK S.
DISCIPLINE LAW **EDUCATION** Hiram Col, BA; Case Western Reserve Univ, JD. **CAREER** Prof. **HONORS AND AWARDS** Ed, Criminal Law J Ohio, 90-93. **SELECTED PUBLICATIONS** Co-auth, Federal Rules of Criminal Procedure, 97. **CONTACT ADDRESS** Col Law, Univ of Toledo, Toledo, OH, 43606. **EMAIL** fmerrit@pop3.utoledo.edu

MERRYMAN, JOHN HENRY
PERSONAL Born 02/24/1920, Portland, OR, m, 1953, 3 children **DISCIPLINE** LAW **EDUCATION** Univ Portland, BS, 43; Univ Notre Dame, MS, 44, JD, 47; NY Univ, LLM, 50, JSD, 55. **CAREER** Assoc prof law, Univ Santa Clara, 48-53; prof, 53-71, SWEITZER PROF LAW, STANFORD UNIV, 71-, Vis prof comp law, Univ Rome, 63-64; vis res prof, Ctr Econ Res, Athens, Greece, 62 and 64; consult, Chile Law Prog, Ford Found and Int Legal Ctr, 66-70; vis res prof, Max Planck Inst Foreign St Int Pvt Law, Hamburg, 68-69; Fulbright res grant, Ger, 68-69. **HONORS AND AWARDS** Order of Merit, Italy, 70. **RESEARCH** Comparative law; art and the law; law and development. **SELECTED PUBLICATIONS** Auth, The Moral Right of Utrillo, Maurice, Am J Comparative Law, Vol 43, 95; The Wrath of Rauschenberg, Robert, J Copyright Soc USA, Vol 40, 92; The French Deviation, Am J Comparative Law, Vol 44, 96. **CONTACT ADDRESS** Crown Law, Stanford, CA, 94305-1926.

MERSKY, ROY MARTIN
PERSONAL Born 09/01/1925, New York, NY, m, 1951, 3 children **DISCIPLINE** LAW **EDUCATION** Univ Wis, BS, 48, JD, 52, MALS, 53. **CAREER** Cataloger, US Govt Doc, Univ Wis Educ Libr, 51-52; readers' adv and ref and catalog librn, Milwaukee Publ Libr, Munic Ref Libr, City Hall, 53-54; asst librn and chief readers' and ref serv, Yale Law Libr, 54-59; dir, Wash State Law Libr, 59-63; prof law and law librn, Univ Colo, 63-65; PROF LAW AND LAW LIBRN, UNIV TEX, AUSTIN, 65-, Atty, 52-54; exec secy judicial coun and comnr Wash court reporters, State of Wash, 59-63; consult, Nat Col State Trial Judges, var col law libr, legal serv prog, Off Econ Opportunity and ETexas Legal Serv; interim dir, Jewish Nat and Hebrew Univ Jerusalem Libr, 72-73; CONSULT, J REUBEN CLARK SCH LAW, BRIGHAM YOUNG UNIV, 72-73 AND ORAL ROBERTS UNIV, 77-; ED CONSULT, TRANSMEDIA PUBL CO, 72- **MEMBERSHIPS** Am Bar Asn; Am Libr Asn; Am Asn Law Libr; Am Civil Liberties Union; Asn Am Law Schs. **RESEARCH** Civil rights; legal history; legal research and writing. **SELECTED PUBLICATIONS** Auth, Aall and the Road to Diversity, Law Library Jour, Vol 85, 93. **CONTACT ADDRESS** 727 E 26th St, Austin, TX, 78705-3224.

MERTENS, THOMAS R.
PERSONAL Born 05/22/1930, Ft Wayne, IN, m, 1953, 2 children **DISCIPLINE** BIOLOGY/GENETICS **EDUCATION** Ball State Univ, BS, 52; Purdue Univ, MS, 54, PhD, 56. **CAREER** Res Assoc, Univ Wisc, 56-57; Ball State Univ, Asst Prof Biol, 57-62, Assoc Prof, 62-66, Prof, 66-93, Distinguished Prof, 88-93, Distinguished Prof Emeritus, 93-. **HONORS AND AWARDS** Fellow, Am Asn for the Adv of Sci, 82; Distinguished Svc to Sci Educ, 87; Hon member, Nat Asn of Biol Thcrs; McGuffey Award in Life Sci. **MEMBERSHIPS** AAAS; Nat Asn of Biol Tchrs (pres 85); Nat Sci Tchrs Asn; Genetics Soc of Am. **RESEARCH** Genetics education; plant cytology/genetics. **SELECTED PUBLICATIONS** Co-auth, Genetics Laboratory Investigations, Prentice Hall, 10th ed, 95, 11th ed, 98; co-auth, Tradescantia: A Tool for Teaching Meiosis, The Am Biol Tchr, 59:5, 300-304, 5/97. **CONTACT ADDRESS** Dept of Biology, Ball State Univ, 2506 W Johnson Rd, Muncie, IN, 47304.

MERWIN, PETER MATTHEW
PERSONAL Born 06/20/1944, Chicago, IL **DISCIPLINE** PHILOSOPHY **EDUCATION** DePaul Univ, BA, 67, MA, 69, PhD, 92. **CAREER** Instr, philos, DePaul Univ, 78-81; instr, English, Chicago Bd of Educ, 71-98. **HONORS AND AWARDS** Arthur J Schmitt Found fel, 78-79, 79-80; Who's Who in the Midwest, 98. **MEMBERSHIPS** APA; Soc for Phenomenological and Existential Philos; Newberry Lib Assoc; Westerners Int; Int Soc for Philos and Lit. **RESEARCH** Symbols of the American Indians; philosophy of symbolic forms of Ernst Cassirer. **SELECTED PUBLICATIONS** Auth, The People's Relationship to the Land, Univ of So Dakota, 79; auth, Revenge on the Reservation, Heartland J, 84; auth, The Philosophy of Symbolic Forms of Ernst Cassiver and the Lakotas, DePaul Univ, 92 (diss); auth, Brand Book, v 1, 2, Westerners Int, 97; auth, Brand Book, v 3, Westerners Int, 98. **CONTACT ADDRESS** 8821 O'Brien Dr, Orland Hills, IL, 60477.

METZGER, BRUCE MANNING
PERSONAL Born 02/09/1914, Middletown, PA, m, 1944, 2 children **DISCIPLINE** NEW TESTAMENT LANGUAGE & LITERATURE **EDUCATION** Lebanon Valley Col, AB, 35; Princeton Theol Sem, ThB, 38, ThM, 39; Princeton Univ, MA, 40, PhD, 42. **CAREER** Teaching fel New Testament, 38-40, from instr to prof, 40-64, George L Collord Prof New Testament Lang & Lit, Princeton Theol Sem, 64-, Chmn Am comt versions, Int Greek New Testament Proj, 50-; vis lectr, Presby Sem, Campinas, Brazil, 52; mem panel transl, Rev Standard Version of the Apocrypha, Nat Coun Churches, 53-57 & Standard Bible Comt, 59-; hon fel & corresp mem, Higher Inst Coptic Studies, Egypt, 55-; mem Kuratorium, Vetus-Latina-Inst, Ger, 59-; mem adv comt, Inst New Testament Text Res, Univ Munster, 62-; mem managing comt, Am Sch Class Studies, Athens; mem, Inst Advan Studies, Princeton, 64-65 & 73-74; Soc Bibl Lit deleg, Am Coun Learned Soc, 64-67; consult, Nat Endowment for Humanities, 68-, vis fel, Clare Col, Cambridge Univ, 74; mem adv comt, Collected Works of Erasmus, 77- **HONORS AND AWARDS** Christian Res Found Prizes, 55, 62 & 63; F C Burkitt Medal Bibl Stud, Br Acad, 84., DD, Lebanon Valley Col, 51; LHD, Findlay Col, 62; DD, Univ St Andrews, 64; DTheol, Univ Munster, 70; DLitt, Univ Potchefstroom, 85. **MEMBERSHIPS** Am Philol Asn; Am Acad Relig; Soc Bibl Lit; Soc Study New Testament; Am Papyrological Asn. **RESEARCH** New Testament; early versions of the Bible; early Church history. **SELECTED PUBLICATIONS** Auth, Chapters in the History of New Testament Textual Criticism, Brill, Leiden, 63; The Text of the New Testament, Its Transmission, Corruption, and Restoration, Oxford, 64, Ger ed, 66, Japanese ed, 73, Italian ed, 96, Russian ed, 96; The New Testament, Its Background, Growth, and Content, Abingdon, 65, Chinese ed, 77; co-ed, The Greek New Testament, Am Bible Soc, 66; auth, Index to Periodical Literature on Christ and the Gospels, 66 & Historical and Literary Studies: Pagan, Jewish, and Christian, 68, Brill, Leiden; A taxtual commentary on the Greek New Testament, United Bible Soc London, 71; Manucripts of the Greek Bible, Oxford, 81. **CONTACT ADDRESS** 20 Cleveland Lane, Princeton, NJ, 08540.

METZGER, DANIEL
PERSONAL Born 01/20/1954, Milwaukee, WI, m, 1976, 3 children **DISCIPLINE** RELIGION **EDUCATION** Mankato State Univ, MA, 85; Marquette, PhD, 94. **CAREER** Pastor, Our Savior's Lutheran Church, 80-82; instr, Bethany Lutheran College, 82-98. **MEMBERSHIPS** AAR; SBL. **RESEARCH** Fifteenth century justification theory; Eucharistic theology. **CONTACT ADDRESS** 336 N Redwood Dr, Mankato, MN, 56001. **EMAIL** dmetzger@blc.edu

MEYER, BEN FRANKLIN
PERSONAL Born 11/05/1927, Chicago, IL **DISCIPLINE** BIBLICAL LITERATURE **EDUCATION** Gonzaga Univ, BA, 50; Mt St Michael's Col, PhL, 51; Univ Santa Clara, MST, 58; Pontif Bibl Inst, STL, 61 Gregorian Univ, STD(Theol), 65. **CAREER** Asst prof scripture and theol, Alma Col, Calif, 63-68; asst prof scripture, Grad Theol Union, 66-68; PROF JUDAISM AND CHRISTIANITY, MCMASTER UNIV, 69-, Fulbright grant, Germany, 64-65. **MEMBERSHIPS** Cath Bibi Asn Am; Soc Bibl Lit; Studiorum novi Testamenti Soc. **RESEARCH** Historical Jesus; early Christian thought. **SELECTED PUBLICATIONS** Auth The 5 Gospels--The Search for the Authentic Words of Jesus, Interpretation J Bible Theol, Vol 48, 94; The Historical Jesus--The Life of a Mediterranean Jewish Peasant, Cath Biblical Quart, Vol 55, 93. **CONTACT ADDRESS** Dept of Religious Studies, McMaster Univ, 1280 Main St W, Hamilton, ON, L7S 4K1.

MEYER, LEROY N.
PERSONAL Born 02/04/1946, Arlington, VA, m, 1986, 3 children **DISCIPLINE** PHILOSOPHY **EDUCATION** Univ Va, PhD, 75. **CAREER** Asst prof, Philos, George Mason Univ, 76-77; vis schol, Philos, Univ Cambridge, 77-78; asst to assoc prof to DIR OF PHILOS, UNIV S DAKOTA, 88 -. **MEMBERSHIPS** Am Philos Asn; Iowa Philos Asn; Philos Science Asn; Realia. **RESEARCH** Philos Culture; Philos Science; Philos War, Peace. **SELECTED PUBLICATIONS** Auth, "The Shadows of August: Moral Reflections Fifty Years After Hiroshima and Nagasaki," Intl Quart 2, 95; co-auth, "Wakinyan Hotan: Inscrutability of Lakota/Dakota Metaphysics," in From Our Eyes: Learning From Indigenous People, 96; auth, "Pluralism, Perspectivism & the Enigma of Truth," Contemporary Philosophy, 97. **CONTACT ADDRESS** Dept of Philosophy, Univ S. Dakota, Vermillion, SD, 57069. **EMAIL** lnmeyer@usd.edu

MEYER, MILTON WACHSBERG
PERSONAL Born 09/08/1951, Pittsburgh, PA, m, 1991, 1 child **DISCIPLINE** PHILOSOPHY **EDUCATION** Duke Univ, BA, 73; Oxford Univ, BPhil, 75; Princeton Univ, PhD, 83. **CAREER** Instr, Univ Notre Dame, 79-84; asst prof, Cornell Univ, 84-91; lectr, Univ Penn, 95, 97. **HONORS AND AWARDS** Danforth fel, 73. **MEMBERSHIPS** APA. **RESEARCH** Ethics; political philosophy; feminist philosophy. **CONTACT ADDRESS** 316 Ogden Ave, Swarthmore, PA, 19081. **EMAIL** mwmeyer@phil.upenn.edu

MEYER, PAUL WILLIAM
PERSONAL Born 05/31/1924, Raipur, India, m, 1948, 2 children **DISCIPLINE** NEW TESTAMENT **EDUCATION** Elmhurst Col, BA, 45; Union Theol Sem, NY, BD, 49, ThD, 55. **CAREER** Lectr New Testament, Union Theol Sent, NY, 51-52, instr, 52-54; asst prof, Divinity Sch, Yale Univ, 54-62, assoc prof, 62-64; prof, Colgate Rochester Divinity Sch, 64-70; prof New Testament, Divinity Sch, Vanderbilt Univ, 70-78; HELEN H P MANSON PROF NEW TESTAMENT LIT AND EXEGESIS, PRINCETON THEOL SEM, 78-, Fulbright res grant, Univ Gottingen, 61-62; Morse fel, Yale Univ, 61-62. **MEMBERSHIPS** Soc Bibi Lit; Soc New Testament Studies; Am Theol Soc; AAUP. **RESEARCH** New Testament theology and exegesis; history of New Testament interpretation. **SELECTED PUBLICATIONS** Auth, Christians and the New Creation--Genesis Motifs in the New Testament, J Biblical Lit, Vol 0115, 96. **CONTACT ADDRESS** Princeton Theol Sem, Princeton, NJ, 08540.

MEYERS, CAROL L.
PERSONAL Born 11/26/1942, Wilkes-Barre, PA, m, 1964, 2 children **DISCIPLINE** NEAR EASTERN STUDIES/ BIBLICAL STUDIES & ARCHAEOLOGY **EDUCATION** Wellesley Col, AB, 64; Brandeis Univ, MA, 66; PhD, 75. **CAREER** Prof Religion, Duke Univ, 90-; dir Women's Studies Program, Duke Univ, 92; assoc dir Women's Studies Program, Duke Univ, 86-90, 92-; consultant, DreamWorks production of Prince of Egypt, forthcoming; Ntl Endowment Humanities Inst on Image & Reality of Women in Near East Soc, 95; vis fac, Univ Conn, 94-; Consultant, Lilith Publications Network, 94-; Consultant, "Mysteries of the Bible," for Cable TV, 93; Consultant, New Dominion Pictures, 92-93; Consultant, "Religion, Culture, and Family," Univ Chi Divinity School, 91-97; assoc prof, Duke Univ, 84-90; Res Fac, Duke Univ, 83-; co-dir, Duke Univ Summer Prog in Israel, 80-. **HONORS AND AWARDS** Intl Correspondence Fel, Bar Ilan Univ, 98; Frankfurt am Main Res Assoc, Johann Wolfgang Goethe Universitat, 95; Alumni Distinguished Undergraduate Tchg Award Nominee, 94; Severinghaus Award, Wellesley Col, 91; Princeton Univ Vis Fel, 90-91; Princeton Univ Res Member, 90-91; Ntl Endowment Humanities, 82-83, 90-91; Howard Found Fel, 85-86; Duke Univ Res Council, 83-84, 85-86, 87-88, 90-91, 92-93, 93-94; Oxford Univ Vis Res Fel, 82-83; Oxford Centre for Postgraduate Hebrew Studies Vis Scholar, 82-83; Duke Univ Fac Summer Fel, 82; Cooperative Program in Judaic Studies Publications Grant, 81. **MEMBERSHIPS** Amer Acad Relig; Amer Schools of Oriental Res; Archaeol Inst Amer; Archaeol Soc Jordan; Assoc Jewish Studies; British School of Archaeol in Jerusalem; Cath Bibl Assoc; Center for Cross-Cult Res on Women; Harvard Semitic Museum; Israel Exploration Soc; Palestine Exploration Soc; Soc Bibl Lit; Soc Values in Higher Ed; Wellesley Col Center for Res on Women; Women's Assoc of Ancient Near East Studies; Women's Caucus, Assoc for Jewish Studies. **RESEARCH** Syro-Palestinian Archaelogy; Hebrew Bible; Gender in the Biblical World **SELECTED PUBLICATIONS** Coauth, Families in Ancient Israel, Westminster/John Knox Pr, 97; coed, Sepphoris in Galilee: Cross-Currents of Culture, N Carolina Museum Art, 96; coauth, Zippori (Sepphoris) 1994, Excavations & Surveys in Israel, 97; "New Faces of Eve," Humanistic Judaism, 97-98. **CONTACT ADDRESS** Dept of Religion, Duke Univ, Box 90964, Durham, NC, 27708-0964. **EMAIL** carol@acpub.duke.edu

MEYERS, DIANA TIETJENS
DISCIPLINE ETHICS, FEMINIST THEORY, SOCIAL AND POLITICAL PHILOSOPHY **EDUCATION** Univ Chicago, AB, philosophical psychol, 69; City Univ New York Grad Center, MA, philosophy, 76, PhD, philosophy, 78. **CAREER** Visiting asst prof, State Univ New York Stony Brook, 78-79; asst prof, Government Dept , Cornell Univ, , 79-85; asst prof, Montclair State Coll, 85-87; assoc prof, 87-90, prof, 90-, Univ of Connecticut Storrs. **HONORS AND AWARDS** Univ Fellowship, 76-77; graduate fellow, res, 77-78; humanities faculty res grant, summer, 90; general educ development grant, 81; grant, Exxon Educ Found, 84-85; Rockefeller Residency Fellowship, Center for Philosophy and Public Policy (declined), 85-86; fellowship, ACLS/Ford Found, 86; Career Devel Grant, Montclair State Coll, 86-87; Special Achievements Awards, 90, 94, major res grants, 91, 93, Provost's Fellowship, spring 93, Univ Conn; Rockefeller Found Study Center at Bellagio, Italy, residency, summer 93; Who's Who in the East, 86-; Intl, Who's Who of Women, 86-; Who's Who of Amer Women, 98. **MEMBERSHIPS** Ex officio member, Comt Status Women 92-97, chair, Eastern Div Program Comt, 94-96, Amer Philosophical Assn; treas, New York Group, 97-, natl hq, Exec Comt, 80-84, 91-95, exec sec, 84-91, Soc Philosophy Public Affairs; co-chair, 87-, Women's Studies Exec Bd, Women's Studies Curriculum Courses Comt, 91-, chair, Grad Placement Center, 96-, sexual harassment officer, 94-, Dept of Philosophy, Women's Studies/ Psychol Search Comt for the Dir of Women's Studies, 97-, Univ Conn. **RESEARCH** Philosophy of law; applied ethics. **SELECTED PUBLICATIONS** Ed, Feminist Social Thought: A Reader, 97; auth, "Social Exclusion, Moral Reflection, and Rights," in Radical Critiques of the Law, 97; "Agency," in A Companion to Feminist Philosophy, 98; reviewer, Care, Gender, and Justice, 98; paper presented, "Authenticity for Real People," World Congress of Philosophy, 98. **CONTACT ADDRESS** Dept of Philosophy, Univ of Connecticut, Storrs, CT, 06269-2054. **EMAIL** dmeyers@uconnvm.uconn.edu

MEYERS, MICHAEL
PERSONAL Born 02/16/1950, Manhattan, NY, s **DISCIPLINE** LAW **EDUCATION** Antioch Coll, BA 1972; Rutgers

Law School, JD 1975. **CAREER** Marc Corp NYC, intern 1967,68, fellow 1968-75; Met Applied Rsch Ctr, asst to Dr Kenneth B Clark pres 1970-75; NAACP, asst exec dir 1975-84, dir res policy & planning 1977-84; RACE Inc NY, founder/dir/pres 1984-. **HONORS AND AWARDS** Staff Cit Comm Investigating Corpl Punishment in NYC's Publ School 1974; Law School Rep to Law Student Div Amer Bar Assoc 1972-75; Outstanding Young Men of Amer 1986. **MEMBERSHIPS** Mem spec comm HUD, Amer Bar Assoc 1974-75; bd dir Sponsors of Open Housing Investment Wash DC 1970-77; bd dir New Hope Housing Inc 1971-77; natl chmn comm of 25 SOHI 1972-74; exec comm SOHI 1970-77; bd dir Natl Child Labor Comm Inc 1976-82; bd dir NY Civil Liberties Union 1976-; exec comm Natl Coaltion Against the Death Penalty 1977-84, Amer Civil Liberties Union Equality Comm 1974-80, Acad Freedom Comm, Free Speech Assoc Comm; bd dir Amer Civil Liberties Union 1981-. **SELECTED PUBLICATIONS** Publs in Integrated Ed Mag, Youth & Soc Jrnl, Civil Liberties, Wall St Jrnl, Change Mag, LA Times, Crisis, NY Times, Wash Post, Christ Sci Monitor, Newsday, Daily News, NY Post, Village Voice; Esquire Register 1986. **CONTACT ADDRESS** RACE Inc, PO Box 1342, Riverdale, NY, 10471.

MEYERS, ROBERT
DISCIPLINE PHILOSOPHY **EDUCATION** State Univ NY, Buffalo, PhD. **CAREER** Prof, Univ Albany, State Univ NY. **RESEARCH** Theory of knowledge, history of modern empiricism, American pragmatism and Hume. **SELECTED PUBLICATIONS** Auth, The Likelihood of Knowledge, Dordrecht, 88; coauth, Early Influences on Peirce: A letter to Samuel Barnett, J Hist Philos, 93. **CONTACT ADDRESS** Dept of Philosophy, Univ at Albany, SUNY, Albany, NY, 12222.

MICHAEL, COLETTE VERGER
PERSONAL Marseille, France, 6 children **DISCIPLINE** FRENCH AND PHILOSOPHY **EDUCATION** Univ Wash Seattle, fr and philos, BA, 69; Univ Wash Seattle, romance lang, MA, 70; Univ Wisc Madison, hist of sci, MA, 75; Univ Wisc Madison, fr and minor philos, PhD, 73. **CAREER** Tchg asst, Fr and Ital Dept, Univ Wisc Madison, 9/73-12/73; lectr, extension dept, Univ Wisc Madison, 7/74-8/74; lectr, fr and ital dept, Univ Wisc Madison, 2/74-8/74; prof, humanities, Shimer Col, Mt Carroll, Ill, 75-77; asst prof, foreign lang and lit, Northern Ill Univ, 77-84; assoc prof, foreign lang and lit, Northern Ill Univ, 84-90; prof, foreign lang and lit, Northern Ill Univ, 90-. **HONORS AND AWARDS** Consulat General de France Svc Culturel, Subvention for Bulletin de la Soc Amer de Philos, Jan, 92; Facul Develop grant, Hist and Tech of Fr Cinema, Fall, 91; Deans fund for res in the humanities, Spring, 87; Deans' Fund for Res, Grad Sch, Northern Ill Univ, asst for res on Negritude, Fall, 85; Deans's Fund for Res, Grad Sch, Northern Ill Univ, asst for res on The Marquis de Sade: The Man, His Works and His Critics, Fall, 83; Res award from Dean of Grad Sch, Northern Ill Univ, Topic: Choderlos de Laclos, The Man, His Works, and His Critics, Jan 80-Jun 80; Grad Sch Summer grant, NIU Topic: The Marquis de Condorcet, His Work, His Ideology, His Influence, 78; Nat Endow for the Humanities Summer Fel for Col Tchrs, Univ Ill Univ, Champaign, Topic: The European Enlightenment in the Amer Revolution, Summer, 77; Ford Found Fel, Fr and Ital Dept, Univ Wisc Madison, 71, 72, 73; Nonresident scholar, The Grad Sch, Univ Wisc Madison, 71-72. **RESEARCH** Philosophy, 18th Century. **SELECTED PUBLICATIONS** Articles, Camus, Science and Metaphors, Bull de la Soc Amer de Philos de Lang Fr VIII, 2, 78-88, 96; A la recherche de l'absolu: le neant des ecrivains maudits, Actes du Congres Intl des Soc de Philos de lang Fr, Poitiers, Fr, 167-169, 96; L'audiovisuel et la litterature francophone, Rev Francophone, VIII, 2, 73-83, 95; Justine ou la vertu devant la violence, Actes de Ile Congres mondial sur la violence et la coexistence humaine, Montreal, Vol VII, 429-435, 95; Billy Budd: An Allegory on the Rights of Man, Allegory Old and New: Creativity and Continuity in Culture, Analecta Husserliana, XLII, 251-258, 94; Light and Darkness and the Phenomenon of Creation in Victor Hugo, Analecta Husserliana: The Elemental Dialectic of Light and Darkness, XXXVIII, 131-149; Les Lettres de Doleances: Un Genre de Cahiers, ou Cahiers d'un nouveau Genre? Lang de la Revolution 1770-1815, Inst Nat de la Lang Fr: Lexicometrie et textes polit, Paris, Klimcksieck, 251-264, 95. **CONTACT ADDRESS** 635 Joanne Ln., De Kalb, IL, 60115. **EMAIL** tc0cvml@corn.cso.niu.edu

MICHAEL, EMILY
PERSONAL Baltimore, MD, m, 2 children **DISCIPLINE** PHILOSOPHY **EDUCATION** Univ Pa, PhD, 73. **CAREER** Prof, Brooklyn Col, 73-. **HONORS AND AWARDS** NEH fel, 82-83. **MEMBERSHIPS** Am Philos Asn; Hume Soc; British Soc for the Hist of Philos; Soc for Medieval and Renaissance Philos. **RESEARCH** Philosophy. **SELECTED PUBLICATIONS** Auth, "Renaissance Theories of Body, Soul, and Mind" in Psyche and Soma in the History of Western Medicine and Philosophy, 98; "Daniel Sennert on Matter and Form" in Early Science and Medicine, 97; "Francis Hutcheson and the Glasgow School of Logic," 97; "Gassendi's Modified Epicureanism and British Moral Philosophy" in History of European Ideas, 95. **CONTACT ADDRESS** Dept of Philosophy, Brooklyn Col, CUNY, Brooklyn, NY, 11210. **EMAIL** emmbc@cunyum.cuny.edu

MICHAEL, RANDALL BLAKE
PERSONAL Born 08/17/1948, Lexington, NC, m, 1970, 1 child **DISCIPLINE** RELIGIOUS STUDIES **EDUCATION** Univ NC Chapel Hill, BA, 70; Harvard Divinity School, MDiv, 72; Harvard Univ, AM, 75, PhD, 79. **CAREER** Instr, 78-; assoc prof, 92-. **RESEARCH** Hindu bhakti movements. **CONTACT ADDRESS** Dept of Religion, Ohio Wesleyan Univ, 50 Henry St, Delaware, OH, 43015-2377. **EMAIL** rbmichae@cc.owu.edu

MICHAELSEN, ROBERT SLOCUMB
PERSONAL Born 05/16/1919, Clinton, IA, m, 1941, 3 children **DISCIPLINE** RELIGION **EDUCATION** Cornell Col, BA, 42; Yale Univ, BD, 45, PhD(Christian soc ethics), 51. **CAREER** Asst prof religh Univ Iowa, 47-52; asst prof Am Christianity, Divinity Sch, Yale Univ, 52-54; prof relig and dir sch, Univ Iowa, 54-65, res prof, 63-64; chmn dept, 65-72, PROF RELIG STUDIES, UNIV CALIF, SANTA BARBARA, 65-, Fulbright scholar, India, 61; proj consult, Soc Relig Higher Educ, 63-64. **HONORS AND AWARDS** DD, Cornell Col, 54. **MEMBERSHIPS** Fel Soc Relig Higher Educ; Am Soc Church Hist; Am Acad Relig (pres, 71-72). **RESEARCH** Religion in American; religion in higher education, especially in tax-supported universities. **SELECTED PUBLICATIONS** Auth, The 1st Freedom--Religion and The Bill of Rights, Church Hist, Vol 62, 93; Undermined Establishment-Church State Relations in America, Church Hist, Vol 62, 93; The Amendments to the Constitution--A Commentary, Church Hist, Vol 65, 96. **CONTACT ADDRESS** Dept of Religious Studies, Univ of California, Santa Barbara, CA, 93106.

MICHEL, WALTER L.
DISCIPLINE OLD TESTAMENT **EDUCATION** Univ Vienna, MDiv; Univ Wis, MA, PhD; post-dr stud, Yale Univ; Pontifical Bibl inst, Rome. **CAREER** Campus pastor, Univ Wis; lectr, Adult Forums; vis prof, Univ Chicago Divinity Sch; Spertus Col of Judaica; North Park Theol Sem; prof-. **SELECTED PUBLICATIONS** Auth, Job In the Light of Northwest Semitic; Prologue and First Cycle of Speeches Job; Biblica et Orientalia, Bibl Inst Press, 87. **CONTACT ADDRESS** Dept of Old Testament, Lutheran Sch of Theol, 1100 E 55th St, Chicago, IL, 60615. **EMAIL** wmichel@lstc.edu

MICKLER, MIKE
DISCIPLINE THEOLOGY **EDUCATION** Graduate Theological Union, PhD, 89 **CAREER** Asst Prof, Church History, 89-94, Assoc Prof, 95-, Academic Dean, 95-, Unification Theological Sem. **CONTACT ADDRESS** 10 Dock Rd., Barrytown, NY, 12507. **EMAIL** utsed@ulstn.net

MIDDLETON, DARREN J. N.
PERSONAL Born 10/06/1966, Nottingham, England, m, 1994 **DISCIPLINE** THEOLOGY **EDUCATION** Univ Manchester, 86-89; Oxford Univ, 89-91; Univ Glasgow, 92-96. **CAREER** Ast prof, Rhodes Col, 93-97; ast prof, Texas Chr Univ, 98-. **MEMBERSHIPS** AAR/SBL. **RESEARCH** Theology and literature; Rastafarianism; Baptist theology. **SELECTED PUBLICATIONS** Auth, "David Pailin's Theology of Divine Action," Process Stud, 93; "Nikos Kazantzakis and Process Theology," Jrnl of Mod Greek Stud, 94; "W. Norman Pittenger's The Word Incarnate," Mod Believing, 95; "Christ Recrucified," Notes in Contemp Lit, 95; "Nikos Kazantzakis and The Last Temptation of Christ," Christianity and the Arts, 96; "Vagabond or Companion: Kazantzakis and Whitehead on God," God's Struggler, Mercer Univ, 96; "Genesis: A Journey into Eden," Christianity and the Arts, 97; "Apophatic Boldness," Midwest Qrtly, 98; "Kazantzakis and Christian Doctrine," Jrnl of Mod Greek Stud, 98; "Chanting Down Babylon," This is How We Flow, Univ South Carolina, 99. **CONTACT ADDRESS** Texas Christian Univ, PO Box 298100, Fort Worth, TX, 76129. **EMAIL** d.middleton2@tcu.edu

MIKVA, A.J.
PERSONAL Born 01/21/1926, Milwaukee, WI, m, 1948, 3 children **DISCIPLINE** LAW **EDUCATION** Univ Chicago Law Sch, JD, 51. **CAREER** Congressman, 69-79; judge & chief judge, US Ct Appeals, 79-94; White House coun, 94-95; visiting prof, Univ Chicago Law Sch, 96-98; visiting prof, Univ Ill Col of Law, 98-. **HONORS AND AWARDS** Order of COIF; Phi Beta Kappa. **MEMBERSHIPS** Amer Law Inst. **RESEARCH** Legislative process. **SELECTED PUBLICATIONS** Auth, Legislative Process, Little Brown & Co; auth, Introduction to Statutory Interpretation, Aspen Books. **CONTACT ADDRESS** 5020 S. Lake Shore Dr., Apt. 3608, Chicago, IL, 60615. **EMAIL** amikva@uic.edu

MILES, DELOS
PERSONAL Born 11/20/1933, Florence Co, SC, m, 1953, 4 children **DISCIPLINE** THEOLOGY **EDUCATION** Furman Univ, BA, 55; Southeastern Baptist Theol Sem, BD, 58; San Francisco Theol Sem, STD, 73. **CAREER** Assoc pastor, West End Baptist Church, Va, 58-59; pastor, Crewe Baptist Church, Va, 59-63; assoc secy Evangel and assoc missions, Va Baptist Gen Bd, 63-66; dir evangel, Gen Bd SC Baptist Convention, 66-73, dir Evangel and Church serv div, 74-77; ASSOC PROF EVANGEL, MIDWESTERN BAPTIST THEOL SEM, MO, 78- **MEMBERSHIPS** Acad Evangel Prof. **RESEARCH** Evangelism; church growth; neo-pentecostalism. **SELECTED PUBLICATIONS** Auth, A Line of Time--Approaches to Archaeology in the Upper and Middle Thames Valley, England, World Archaeol, Vol 29, 97; Political Experience and Anti Big Government--The Making and Breaking of Themes in Ford,Gerald 1976 Presidential Campaign, Mich Hist Rev, Vol 23, 97. **CONTACT ADDRESS** Midwestern Baptist Theol Sem, 5001 N Oak St Trafficway, Kansas City, MO, 64118.

MILES, KEVIN THOMAS
PERSONAL Born 04/22/1956, Schenectady, NY, m, 1987, 2 children **DISCIPLINE** PHILOSOPHY **EDUCATION** DePaul Univ, PhD, 98. **CAREER** ASST PROF, DEPT PHILOS, VILLANOVA UNIV, 94-. **HONORS AND AWARDS** Lindback Minority Faculty Research Award, 98; Faculty summer research grant, Villanova Univ, 98. **MEMBERSHIPS** Soc for Phenomenology & Existential Philosophy; Int Soc for African & Ditspara Philos; Amer Philos Assoc, eastern div. **RESEARCH** Aristotle; law & politics; Du Boise; Race; Arendt; Malcolm X. **CONTACT ADDRESS** Villanova Univ, 800 Lancaster Ave., Villanova, PA, 19085. **EMAIL** kmiles@email.vill.edu

MILES, MURRAY LEWIS
DISCIPLINE PHILOSOPHY **EDUCATION** Univ Toronto, BA; Albert-Ludwigs-Univ, Freiburg, Ger, PhD. **CAREER** Instr, Ryerson Polytech Inst, 77-80; asst prof, Univ Toronto, 83-84; asst prof, 84-88; assoc prof, 88-; dept ch, 84-89; adj prof, McMaster Univ, 97. **HONORS AND AWARDS** Ger Acadc Exchange Assn scholar, 71-72; Can Coun doc fel, 72-73, 73-74, 74-75, 75-76; postdoc fel, Soc Sci and Hum Res Coun, 81-82., Ch, Brock Univ Fac Assn Comm on the Terms and Conditions of Employment, 86-87; Brock Univ Fac Assn Comm on Public Aff and Commun Liaison, 92-93, 93-93; Parent Adv Gp, Niagara Peninsula Children's Ctr, 94-. **MEMBERSHIPS** Mem, Exec Fac Bu, 87-88, 88-89; Sen Comm on Grad Stud and Res, 87-88, 88-89; Decanal Comm on the Image/Profile of the Hum, 88; Parent Adv Gp; Niagara Peninsula Children's Ctr; OCUFA Pol Rel(s) Comm, 92-93; Adv Comm, Neurodevelopmental Clinical Res Unit, 94-; Sen Comm on Res. **SELECTED PUBLICATIONS** Auth, Logik und Metaphysik bei Kant, Zu Kants Lehre vom zwiefachen Gebrauch des Verstandes und der Vernunft, Vittorio Klostermann Verlag, Frankfurt, Ger, 78; "Fundamental Ontology and Existential Analysis in Heidegger's Being and Time," Intl Philos Quart, 94; "Leibniz on Apperception and Animal Souls," Dialogue XXXIII, 94; "Philosophy and Liberal Learning," Queen's Quart 104/1, 97 **CONTACT ADDRESS** Dept of Philos, Brock Univ, 500 Glenridge Ave, St Catharines, ON, L2S 3A1. **EMAIL** mmiles@spartan.ac.brocku.ca

MILETIC, STEPHEN F.
PERSONAL Born 11/23/1952, Windsor, ON, Canada, m, 1975, 4 children **DISCIPLINE** NEW TESTAMENT, THEOLOGY **EDUCATION** Academy of Music & Performing Arts, Vienna, Austria, 71-72; Univ Windsor, BA, 75-76; Univ Windsor, MA, 77; Univ Windsor, BEd, 78; Marquette Univ, PhD, 85. **CAREER** Dir, Nat Office of Relig Educ, Canadian Conf of Catholic Bishops, 86; consult, res & relig educ, 87-88; provost & academic dean, Notre Dame Inst, 88-96, assoc prof, Franciscan Univ of Steubenville, 96-. **MEMBERSHIPS** Soc of Biblical Lit; Canadian Soc of Biblical Studies; Catholic Biblical Asn. **SELECTED PUBLICATIONS** Translat, R. Le Doaut's The Message of the New Testament and the Aramaic Bible, Pontifical Biblical Inst Press, 82; auth, "One Flesh: Ephesians 5.22024, 31. Marriage and the New Creation", in Analecta Biblica 115, Pontifical Biblical Inst Press, 88; auth, 204 brief New Testament articles for the Catholic Encyclopedia, Our Sunday Visitor, 91; auth, commentaries on biblical texts for Sunday, Cycle C for Discover the Bible, No. 1166, 92; auth, commentaries on biblical texts for 4th & 5th Sundays of Easter, Cycle A for Discover the Bible, 93; auth, commentaries on biblical texts for 1st and 2nd Sundays of Lent, Year B for Discover the Bible, 94; auth, commentaries on biblical texts for All Saints and 31st Sunday of Ordinary Time, Year C for Discover the Bible, 98. **CONTACT ADDRESS** Theology Department, Franciscan Univ of Steubenville, 1235 University Blvd., Steubenville, OH, 43952-6701. **EMAIL** smiletic@franuniv.edu

MILGROM, JACOB
PERSONAL Born 02/01/1923, New York, NY, m, 1948, 4 children **DISCIPLINE** RELIGION **EDUCATION** Brooklyn Col, BA, 43; Jewish Theol Sem, BHL, 43, MHL, 46, DHL, 53;. **CAREER** From instr to prof Old Testament, Grad Sch Relig, Va Union Univ, 54-65; assoc prof Hebrew and Bible, 65-73, PROF BIBL STUDIES, UNIV CALIF, BERKELEY, 73-, Mem staff, Encycl Judaica, 68-71; dir, Univ Calif Studies Ctr, Hebrew Univ Jerusalem, 69-71; Nat Found Jewish Cult fel, 69; Am Philos Soc and Am Coun Learned Soc grants-in-aid, 72; Jewish Mem Cult Found fel, 72-73; Univ Calif, Berkeley humanities res inst, 77; Guggenheim fel, 78. **HONORS AND AWARDS** DD, Jewish Theol Sem, 73. **MEMBERSHIPS** Soc Bibl Lit. **RESEARCH** Biblical and ancient Near Eastern culture; Cult and law of ancient Israel. **SELECTED PUBLICATIONS** Auth, Text and Concept in Leviticus 1.1-9+--A Case in Exegetical Method, Jour Am Orient Soc, Vol 0115, 95; Raising up a Faithful Priest--Community and Priesthood in Biblical

Theology, Interpretation Jour Bible Theol, Vol 49, 95; Law and Narrative and the Exegesis of Leviticus Xix, 19, Vetus Testamentum, Vol 46, 96; Futher on the Expiatory Sacrifices, Jour Biblical Lit, Vol 0115, 96; Leviticus--The 3rd Book of Moses, Cath Biblical Quart, Vol 56, 94; The Temple Scroll and the Bible--The Methodology of 11qt, Jour Am Orient Soc, Vol 0117, 97; Confusing the Sacred and the Impure, Vetus Testamentum, Vol 44, 94; At the Altar of Decision--A Workshop in Handmade Midrash, Parabola Myth Tradition and the Search for Meaning, Vol 18, 93; Purity and Monotheism--Clean and Unclean Animals in Biblical Law, Interpretation J Bible Theol, Vol 48, 94; Encroaching on the Sacred--Purity and Polity in Numbers 1-10, Interpretation Jour Bible Theol, Vol 51, 97. **CONTACT ADDRESS** Dept of Near Eastern Studies, Univ of Calif, Berkeley, CA, 94720.

MILLEN, R.L.
PERSONAL Born 02/26/1943, Brooklyn, NY, m, 1961, 3 children **DISCIPLINE** RELIGIOUS STUDIES **EDUCATION** Stern Col, BA, 65; McMaster Univ, MA, 75, PhD, 84. **CAREER** Instr, McMaster Univ, 72-74, 75-76; res assoc, Shalom Hartman Inst, Jerusalem, 76-77; lect, Pardes Grad Inst, Jerusalem, 77-79; ed consult, United Hebrew Sch of Detroit, 78-83; fac, Yeshiva Univ High Sch, 83-86; adj asst prof, Stern College for Women, 85-86; asst prof, Univ Nebr, Omaha, 87-89; fac, Wexner Heritage Found 87-89; assoc prof, Wittenberg Univ, 88- . **HONORS AND AWARDS** Samuel Belkin Mem Award for Prof Achievement; McMaster Univ Benefactors Scholar; McMaster Univ Dept of Philos Fel; Stern Col Fac Award for Academic Excellence and Character; B'Nai Zion Award for Excellence in Hebrew. **MEMBERSHIPS** Am Acad of Relig; Asn for Jewish Stud; Canadian Soc for Stud in Relig; Coalition for Alternatives in Jewish Educ; Eastern Great Lakes Bibl Soc; Midwest Jewish Stud Asn; Soc for Bibl Lit; World Union of Jewish Stud. **RESEARCH** Women and religion, Nineteenth and twentieth century German-Jewish thought. **SELECTED PUBLICATIONS** Auth, "Birkhat HaGomel," Judaism, 94; "B T Kiddushin 34a Revisited," Gender and Judaism, NYU, 95; "Monarchy and Don Isaac Abravanel," Religion in the Age of Exploration, ed Menachem Mor, Creighton Univ, 96; ed, New Perspectives on the Holocaust; NYU, 96; auth, "Pitfalls of Memory," New Perspectives on the Holocaust, ed Rochellke Millen, NYU, 96; "Gardens of Innocence?" Nietzsche and Depth Psychology, ed Jacob Golomb, SUNY, 97; "Seventy Faces," Hadassah Mag, 97; "Christians and Pharisees," Death of God Movement and the Holocaust, ed Stephen R. Haynes, Greenwood, 98; "The Desert as Focus for Ethical Exploration," Shofar, 98. **CONTACT ADDRESS** Dept of Religion, Wittenberg Univ, PO Box 720, Springfield, OH, 45501. **EMAIL** rmillen@wittenberg.edu

MILLENDER, MICHAEL J.
DISCIPLINE LAW **EDUCATION** Duke Univ, BA; Oxford Univ, BA; Princeton Univ, PhD. **CAREER** Asst prof, Univ Fla, 96-. **HONORS AND AWARDS** Mellon fel in Humanities, Princeton Univ, 90-92, 95; Marshall scholar, Oxford Univ, 88-90. **RESEARCH** American legal history. **CONTACT ADDRESS** School of Law, Univ of Florida, PO Box 117625, Gainesville, FL, 32611-7625. **EMAIL** Millender@law.ufl.edu

MILLER, A.R.
PERSONAL Born 01/27/1949, Wheeling, WV, m, 1971, 2 children **DISCIPLINE** PHILOSOPHY **EDUCATION** MA, 71, PhD, 75, philos, Mich State Univ. **CAREER** Asst prof, 75-80, assoc prof, 80-90, full prof, 90-, philos, Univ Tex San Antonio. **HONORS AND AWARDS** NEH year-long seminar, Ind Univ; NDEA Title IV fel; Woodrow Wilson fel. **MEMBERSHIPS** Amer Philos Asn. **RESEARCH** Philosophy of mind; Philosophy of language; Ethics. **SELECTED PUBLICATIONS** Auth, Survival & Diminished Consciousness; auth, Bentham on Justifying the Principle of Utility; auth, Describing Unwitting Behavior; auth, Wanting, Intending & Knowing What One is Doing. **CONTACT ADDRESS** Div. of English, Classics & Communication, Univ of Texas, 6900 N. Loop 1604 W, San Antonio, TX, 78249. **EMAIL** amiller@lonestar.jpl.utsa.edu

MILLER, ANTHONY
DISCIPLINE FAMILY LAW, PUBLIC SECTOR LABOR LAW, TORTS **EDUCATION** CA State Univ, BA, 67, MA, 72; Pepperdine Univ, JD, 77. **CAREER** Pepperdine law rev, 75-77; tchg fel, 77-78; fac mem, 83; vis prof, Univ Calif, 91; assoc dean, acad, 89-93; prof-. **MEMBERSHIPS** Mem, arbitration panels; Am Arbitration Assn; Fed Mediation and Conciliation Serv; Employ Rel Bd; CA State Bar; Am Bar Assn. **SELECTED PUBLICATIONS** Auth, Cases and Materials on Family Law, Matthew Bender; California Government Codes, Forms and Commentary, 2d ed, W Publ. **CONTACT ADDRESS** Sch of Law, Pepperdine Univ, 24255 Pacific Coast Hwy, Malibu, CA, 90263.

MILLER, BARBARA BUTLER
PERSONAL Born 05/17/1942, Chicago, IL, M, 1988, 1 child **DISCIPLINE** RELIGION **EDUCATION** Univ Mich, PhD, 94. **CAREER** Edgewood Col, assoc prof, chemn relig stud dept, 98-. **MEMBERSHIPS** SBL, CTS, CBA, NAWCHE, MBAS **RESEARCH** Women in the bible; feminist critique. **SELECTED PUBLICATIONS** Auth, Eve and Behind the Sex of God, in: Ready Reference: Women's Issues, Salem Press, 97; Bible: New Testament and Virgin Mary, in: Reader's Guide to Women's Studies, Chicago: Fitzroy Dearborn Press, 97; **CONTACT ADDRESS** Dept of Religious Studies, Edgewood Col, 5517 Hammersley Rd, Madison, WI, 53711. **EMAIL** bmiller@edgewood.edu

MILLER, BENJAMIN
PERSONAL Born 06/27/1914, West Haven, CT **DISCIPLINE** PHILOSOPHY, RELIGION **EDUCATION** Occidental Col, BA, 35; Pac Sch Relig, MA, 38. **CAREER** Asst relig, Pomona Col, 38-40; vicar, St Mark's Episcopal Church, Downey, Calif, 41-46; rector, Grace Espiscopal Church, Glendora, 46-48; prof philos, Stephens Col, 48-54; vis prof, Univ Vt, 54-55; leader, Soc Ethical Cult, 55-60 and Philadelphia Ethical Soc, 60-61; asst prof philos, Lake Erie Col, 62-71; dir serv to mil families, Lake Co Chap, Am Red Cross, 73-77; RES AND WRITING, 77-, MEM NAT COUN, ROBINSON JEFFERS COMT, 62- **RESEARCH** Philosophy of religion; ethics; aesthetics. **SELECTED PUBLICATIONS** Auth, Vocabulary Review Game , Hispania J Devoted Teaching Span Portug, Vol 77, 94; Wiederaneignung der Eigenen Biographie, Ger Life Letters, Vol 50, 97; Give them Back their Lives--Recognizing Client Narrative in Case Theory, Michi Law Rev, Vol 93, 94; A Thousand Buddhas, Ga Rev, Vol 47, 93; Money Laundering, Am Criminal Law Rev, Vol 34, 97 Miller, Buffy, 3 Feld Solos , Ballet Rev, Vol 21, 93. **CONTACT ADDRESS** 315 1/2 E Walnut Ave, Painesville, OH, 44077.

MILLER, C. DOUGLAS
DISCIPLINE LAW **EDUCATION** Univ Kans, BS, JD; NY Univ, LLM. **CAREER** Prof,Univ Fla, 73-; pst Off Coun, Miller Rainey, Orlando, Fla and Lowndes, Drosdick Doster, Orlando; past partner, Clark, Mize, Linville Miller, Salina, Kans; vis prof, Leiden Univ, Neth and Ariz State Univ. **HONORS AND AWARDS** Harry J. Rudick mem awd, NY Univ, 66. **MEMBERSHIPS** Exec Coun, Fla Bar Gen Practt Sect, 0-94, and Tax Sect, 84-85; Adv bd, Univ Calif, San Diego, Estate Planning Inst, 79-82; Fla Bar Elder Law Sect, Tax Sect, Real Property, Probate Trust Law Sect; Amer Bar Asn Tax Sect Sect Real Property, Probate Trust Law; Kans Bar; Fla Bar; Beta Gamma Sigma. **RESEARCH** Estates and trusts, estate planning, professional responsibility, sports law, taxation. **CONTACT ADDRESS** School of Law, Univ of Florida, PO Box 117625, Gainesville, FL, 32611-7625. **EMAIL** miller@law.ufl.edu

MILLER, CLARENCE
PERSONAL Born 08/05/1927, New York, NY, m, 1953, 2 children **DISCIPLINE** PHILOSOPHY **EDUCATION** New York Univ, PhD, 61; New School for Social Research, PhD, 68. **CAREER** Educr, New York Bd of Ed, Yeshiva Mesivta, Ladycliff Col, Ford Found Freedom Agenda Prog, 53-78; ed therapist and couns, SUNY, Downstate Med Ctr, Brooklyn, 77-78; writer, RGH Publ, New York, 62- ; playwright, FirstStage Theatre, Hollywood, 90- . **HONORS AND AWARDS** Deans list; Tchr of the year, 73, 74, 75, 76. **MEMBERSHIPS** APA; Dramatist Guild; FirstStage Theatre Asn; Ibsen Soc; The Shaw Project. **RESEARCH** Philosophical foundations of psychology; metaphysical implications of cosmology; philosophy of theatre; epistemology. **SELECTED PUBLICATIONS** Auth, Moore Dewey and the Problem of the Given, The Mod Schoolman, 62; auth, Body Washed Ashore, in The Mutilators, Windsor, 93; auth, Theoretical Perspectives for Directors and Actors, FirstStage, 94; auth, numerous parable plays staged yearly, FirstStage PlayWrights Express, 90-98. **CONTACT ADDRESS** 3057 Brighton 4th St, Brooklyn, NY, 11235. **EMAIL** cmiller3@worldnet.att.net

MILLER, DANNA R.
DISCIPLINE PHILOSOPHY **EDUCATION** Harvard Univ, PhD. **CAREER** Asst prof, Fordham Univ. **RESEARCH** Matter, natural philos, and metaphysics. **SELECTED PUBLICATIONS** Auth, Sargis of Re 'aina on what the celestial bodies knew, Proc Vithum Symp Syriacum, Orientalia Christiana Analecta, 94; George, bishop of Arab tribes on true philosophy, Festschrift in Honor of Sebastian Brock, Oxford UP, 96. **CONTACT ADDRESS** Dept of Philos, Fordham Univ, 113 W 60th St, New York, NY, 10023.

MILLER, DAVID
PERSONAL Born 12/16/1932, Chicago, IL **DISCIPLINE** COMPARATIVE RELIGION **EDUCATION** Harvard Divinity Sch, BD, 57-60; Univ Ill, BA, 51-55; Harvard Univ, PhD, 60-68. **CAREER** Assoc prof, 74-; assoc prof, Sir George Williams Univ, 72-74; asst prof, Sir George Williams Univ, 70-72; asst prof, Case W Reserve Univ, 68-70; lectr, Case W Reserve Univ, 65-68; vis lectr, Oberlin Col, 69-70. **RESEARCH** Study of contemporary Hindu monastics and gurus. **SELECTED PUBLICATIONS** co-auth, Hindu Monastic Life: The Monks and Monastics of Bhubaneswar, McGill-Queens UP, 76; Hindu Monastic Life, reprinted, Manamohar Press, New Delhi, 96; The Spiritual Descent of the Divine: The Life Story of Svami Sivananda, Hindu Spirituality, Vol II, 97; "Modernity in Hindu Monasticism," Intl Jour of Comparative Rel and Phil, 96; "The Chariot and the Phallus in the Temple Architecture of Orissa," Jour of Vaisnava Stud, 95. **CONTACT ADDRESS** Dept of Rel, Concordia Univ, Montreal, 1455 de Maisonneuve W, Montreal, PQ, H3G 1M8.

MILLER, DAVID LEROY
PERSONAL Born 02/25/1936, Cleveland, OH **DISCIPLINE** RELIGION **EDUCATION** Bridgewater Col, AB, 57; Bethany Theol Sem, BD, 60; Drew Univ, PhD, 63. **CAREER** Instr English, Drew Univ, 60-61; instr classics, Upsala Col, 62-63; asst prof relig, Drew Univ, 63-67; assoc prof, 67-74, PROF RELIG, 74- ,SYRACUSE UNIV; Vis asst prof comp lit, Rutgers Univ, 66-67; mem adv coun, Danforth Assocs, 73-76; lectr, Eranos Conf, Switz, 75, 77, 78, & 80. **HONORS AND AWARDS** Chancellor's prize best teacher, Syracuse Univ, 81. **MEMBERSHIPS** Am Acad Relig. **RESEARCH** Theology in relation to mythology, literature & depth psychology. **SELECTED PUBLICATIONS** Co-ed, Interpretation: The poetry of Meaning, Harcourt, 67; auth, Gods & Games, Harper, 70; The New Polytheism, Harper, 74; Images of happy ending, Eranos Jahrbuch, 77; Silenos and the poetics of Christ, Eranos Jahrbuch, 78; Between God and the Gods-Trinity, Eranos Jahrbuch, 80; Christs-Archetypical images in theology, Seabury, 81; Three Faces of God-Traces of the Trinity in Literature and Life, Fortress, 86; Hells and Holy Ghosts-A Theopoetics of Christian Belief, Abingdon, 89. **CONTACT ADDRESS** Dept of Religion, Syracuse Univ, Syracuse, NY, 13244-1170. **EMAIL** dlmiller@mailbox.syr.edu

MILLER, DONALD
DISCIPLINE SOCIOLOGY OF RELIGION **EDUCATION** Univ Southern Calif, BA, 68; USC, MA, 72, PhD, 75. **CAREER** Firestone prof; Univ Southern Calif, 75-. **RESEARCH** Sociology of religion; religion and social change in America; religion and community organizing/development; genocide. **SELECTED PUBLICATIONS** Auth or coauth, bk(s), Survivors: An Oral History of the Armenian Genocide, Univ Calif Press, 93; Homeless Families: The Struggle for Dignity, Univ Ill Press, 93; Writing and Research in Religious Studies, Prentice Hall, 92 & The Case for Liberal Christianity, Harper & Row, 81. **CONTACT ADDRESS** Dept of Religion, Univ Southern Calif, University Park Campus, Los Angeles, CA, 90089. **EMAIL** demiller@bcf.usc.edu

MILLER, DOUGLAS B.
PERSONAL Born 04/12/1955, Ft. Dodge, IA, 3 children **DISCIPLINE** OLD TESTAMENT **EDUCATION** Princeton Theol Sem, PhD, 96. **CAREER** Asst Prof, Dept ch, 5 yrs, Tabor College. **MEMBERSHIPS** SBL; CBA. **RESEARCH** Wisdom Literature; Bible Theology. **SELECTED PUBLICATIONS** Auth, Power in Wisdom: The Suffering Servant of Ecclesiastes Four, Millard Lind festschrift, Pandora Press, 99 forthcoming; Qoheleth's Symbolic Use of Hebel, J of Biblical Lit, 98; coauth, An Akkadian Handbook, Eisenbrauns, 96; Teaching the Bible: Paradigms for the Christian College, Direction, 95; coauth, Signs as Witnesses in the Forth Gospel: Reexamining the Evidence, Cath Bib Qtly, 94, auth, Meir Sternberg: Narrative Poetics and Bible Ideology, Koinonia, 91. **CONTACT ADDRESS** 601 Lincoln St S, Hillsboro, KS, 67063. **EMAIL** dougm@tcnet.tabor.edu

MILLER, DOUGLAS JAMES
PERSONAL Born 07/03/1941, Portland, OR, m, 1963, 2 children **DISCIPLINE** RELIGION AND SOCIETY **EDUCATION** Wheaton Col, Ill, AB, 63; Fuller Theol Sem, BD, 66; Claremont Grad Sch and Univ Ctr, PhD (relig and soc), 72. **CAREER** Ford Found teaching asst social ethics, Claremont Men's Col, 69; assoc prof, 70-80, PROF CHRISTIAN SOCIAL ETHICS, EASTERN BAPTIST THEOL SEM, 80- **MEMBERSHIPS** Am Soc Christian Ethics. **RESEARCH** Civil violence and social change; methodology in Christian ethics. **SELECTED PUBLICATIONS** Auth, The Human Science of Communicology--A Phenomenology of Discourse in Foucault and Merleauponty, Philos Rhetoric, Vol 28, 95; Pink Collar Trash--Semiotics of the Secretarial Position, Am J Semiotics, Vol 11, 94. **CONTACT ADDRESS** Dept of Christian Thought and Mission Eastern Baptis, Philadelphia, PA, 19151.

MILLER, ED L.
PERSONAL Born 04/06/1937, Los Angeles, CA, m, 1979, 4 children **DISCIPLINE** PHILOSOPHY; THEOLOGY **EDUCATION** Univ S Calif, BA, MA, PhD, Dr Theol. **CAREER** Instr, Calif Lutheran Col, 62-64; asst prof, St Olaf Col, 64-66; prof, Univ Colo, 66-. **MEMBERSHIPS** Amer Acad Relig; Soc for New Testament Studies; Soc of Christian Philos; Soren Kierkegaard Soc. **RESEARCH** Philosophical Theology; New Testament; Soren Kierkegaard. **SELECTED PUBLICATIONS** Coauth, Contemporary Theologies, Fortress Pr, 98; At the Centre of Kierkegaard: An Objective Absurdity, Religious Studies, 97; Question that Matter, McGraw Hill, 96. **CONTACT ADDRESS** Dept of Philosophy, Univ of Colorado, Campus Box 232, Boulder, CO, 80309. **EMAIL** Edlmiller@aol.com

MILLER, ERIC
PERSONAL Born 06/19/1957, Boston, MA, m, 1 child **DISCIPLINE** PHILOSOPHY **EDUCATION** Harvard Univ, AB, 79; Univ Goettingen non-degree grad student, 79-83; Princeton Univ, MA, 86, PhD, 92. **CAREER** Univ Gottingen, res asst, 80-83, Princeton Univ, res asst, 84-86, lecrt, 88-89; Univ Penn, lect, 89-90; Pomona Col, asst prof, 91-98, assoc prof, 98-, Clarmont Grad Univ, assoc prof, 98-. **HONORS AND AWARDS**

Harvard, B. Blume Prize, Fulbright-IIE Research Grant, J. Javits Fel, Pomona Col, Wig DT Award **MEMBERSHIPS** AAUP, APA, MLA, PAMLA, AAATG, FWPCA **RESEARCH** Philo of: lit, lang, mind and narrative. **SELECTED PUBLICATIONS** Art, Der Stechlinsee. Symbol und Struktur in Fontanes Altersroman, in: Jour of Eng and Ger Philolgy, 98; Romantic Irony and Virtual Reality, Pop Cult Rev, 98; Literary Ficton and As-If Fiction, in: Philo and Rhetoric 96; Masks of Negation: Greek eironeia and Schlegel's Irony, in: Euro Rom Rev, 97; trans, John L. Ackrill: Aristoteles. eine einfuhrung in sein Philosophieren, DeGruyter, 85. **CONTACT ADDRESS** Dept of German and Russian, Pomona Col, 550 N Harvard Ave, Claremont, CA, 91711. **EMAIL** emiller@pomona.edu

MILLER, FRANKLIN
PERSONAL Born 07/15/1948, Washington, DC, m, 1968, 3 children **DISCIPLINE** PHILOSOPHY **EDUCATION** Columbia Univ, PhD, 77. **CAREER** Assoc prof of Medical Education, June 90- , Univ VA. **HONORS AND AWARDS** Bioethicist; Sr research fel, Kennedy Institute of Ethics. **MEMBERSHIPS** APA; Amer Soc of Bioethics and the Humanities. **RESEARCH** Ethics of clinical research; death and aging; professional integrity; pramatism and bioethics. **SELECTED PUBLICATIONS** Auth, Comments on Second Report of the Attorney General's Research Working Group on Research with Decisionally Impaired Indivduals, Journal of Health Care Law & Policy, 98; coauth, Voluntary Death: A Comparison of Terminal Dehydration and Physician-Assisted Suicide, Annals of Internal Medicine, April 1, 1998; auth, Commentary: Professional Integrity in the Home, Ethics Rounds, Journal of Pain and Symptom Management, Feb 98; coauth, Clinical Pragmatism: Bridging Theory and Practice, Kennedy Institute of Ethics Journal, March 98; coauth, Dealing with Dolly: Inside the National Bioethics Advisory Commission, Health Affairs, May-June 98. **CONTACT ADDRESS** 3910 Underwood St, Chevy Chase, MD, 20815. **EMAIL** fgm3910@aol.com

MILLER, J. MAXWELL
PERSONAL Born 09/20/1937, Kosciusko, MS, m, 1962, 2 children **DISCIPLINE** HEBREW BIBLE **EDUCATION** Millsaps Col, AB, 59; Emory Univ, PhD, 64; post-doctoral, Biblisch-arcaologisches Institut, Tubingen Univ, W Ger, 74-75, 81-82; Millsaps Col, hon DD, 84. **CAREER** Instr, old testament, Interdenominational Theol Ctr, Atlanta, 62-63; grad asst instr, Hebrew, Emory Univ, 63-64; asst prof, old testament, Birmingham-Southern Col, 64-67; asst prof, 71-78, full prof, 78-, dir, grad div of relig, 83-92, Candler Sch of Theol, Emory Univ. **HONORS AND AWARDS** Nat Defense Educ Act grad fel, 60-64; Nat Found of the arts and Humanities, summer res stipend, 66; Emory Univ summer res grant, 67, 69, 72, 78, 79, 82; Alexander von Humbolt Stiftung stipend, 74-75, 81-82; Woodruff Res Support Grant, 80; Asn of Theol Sch res grant, 81-82; Nat Endow for the Humanities res grant, 87-88. **MEMBERSHIPS** Soc of Bibl Lit; Amer Sch of Oriental Res; Palestine Exploration Soc; Deutsche Verein fur Erforschung Palastinas. **RESEARCH** History and archaeology of biblical times. **SELECTED PUBLICATIONS** Auth, Separating the Solomon of History from the Solomon of Legend, The Age of Solomon: Scholarship at the Turn of the Millenium, Leiden, The Netherlands, Brill, 97; auth, Biblical Archaeologist, 60/4, Ancient Moab: Still Largely Unknown, 194-204, 97; auth, Central Moab and History of Moab, Encycl of Near Eastern Archaeol, Oxford Univ Press, 96; auth, The Ancient Near East an Archaeology, Old Testament Interpretation: Past, Present and Future, Abingdon Press, 245-260, 95; auth, Explorations in Ancient Moab, Qadmoniot, 28, 77-82, 95; auth, Introduction to the History of Ancient Israel, The New Interpreter's Bible, Abingdon Press, 244-271, 94; auth, Israel, History of, Judah, Oxford Companion to the Bible, Oxford Univ Press, 93; auth, Reading the Bible Historically: The Historian's Approach, chap I, 11-28, To Each Its Own Meaning: An Introduction to Biblical Criticisms and Their Application, Westminster/John Knox Press, 93; ed, Archaeological Survey of the Kerak Plateau, Amer Sch of Oriental Res Archaeol Reports, 1, Scholars Press, 91; co-auth, A History of Ancient Israel and Judah, Westminster Press/SCM Press, 86. **CONTACT ADDRESS** Candler School of Theology, Emory Univ, Atlanta, GA, 30322. **EMAIL** theojmm@emory.edu

MILLER, JAMES BLAIR
PERSONAL Born 08/02/1916, Mt Vernon, OH, m, 1943, 3 children **DISCIPLINE** CHRISTIAN EDUCATION, PRACTICAL THEOLOGY **EDUCATION** Bethany Col, WVa, AB, 38; Yale Univ, BD, 41; Ind Univ, EdD(educ), 55. **CAREER** Pastor, First Christian Church, Plymouth, Pa, 41-44; instr relig, Bethany Col, WVa, 44-51; asst prof Christian educ, 51-55, prof, 55-80, EMER PROF CHRISTIAN EDUC, CHRISTIAN THEOL SEM, 80-, Pastor, Mem Church, Bethany, WVa, 44-51; consult educ dept, United Christian Missionary Soc, 62-63; chmn prof and res sect, Div Christian Educ, Nat Coun Churches, 62; mem curric and prog coun, Christian Churches, 64-68 and Comn Christian Educ, Am Asn Theol Schs, 65-67. **MEMBERSHIPS** Asn Professors and Researchers in Relig Educ; Asn Christian Church Educators. **RESEARCH** Theological foundations for Christian education; history of education; learning theory. **SELECTED PUBLICATIONS** Auth, Technology, Theology, and the Idea of Progress, Interpretation J Bible Theology, Vol 47, 93. **CONTACT ADDRESS** Christian Theol Sem, 1000 W 42nd St, Indianapolis, IN, 46208.

MILLER, JEROME A.
PERSONAL Born 08/24/1946, Pittsburgh, PA, m, 1969, 3 children **DISCIPLINE** PHILOSOPHY **EDUCATION** Georgetown Univ, PhD, 72. **CAREER** Prof, Chr Dept Philos, 72-98, Salisbury State Univ. **HONORS AND AWARDS** Outstanding Faculty Award. **MEMBERSHIPS** Amer Philos Assoc. **RESEARCH** Philosophy of Religion; Theory of Knowledge. **SELECTED PUBLICATIONS** Auth, The Way of Suffering, Georgetown Univ Press, 89; In The Throe of Wonder, Santa Univ of NY Press, 92. **CONTACT ADDRESS** 303 New York Ave, Salisbury, MD, 21801. **EMAIL** jeromeamiller@yahoo.com

MILLER, JOHN F., III
PERSONAL Born 06/25/1938, Buffalo, NY **DISCIPLINE** PHILOSOPHY **EDUCATION** Gettysburg Coll, BA, 60; Univ of MD, MA, 63; NYU, PhD, 69. **CAREER** Instr, 65-66 Queens Coll, NY; Asst Prof, 65-66, Radford Coll, VA; Instr, 66-69, Univ of South FL, Tampa; Assoc Prof, 70-98, North Texas State Univ, Denton; Adjunct Prof in Philo, Univ of South FL. Hillsborough Comm Coll, Tampa, FL, St Leo Coll, St Leo FL, St Petersburg Jr C. **HONORS AND AWARDS** Phi Beta Kappa. **MEMBERSHIPS** APA, SPS, SSPP, New Mexico and West Texas Philo Soc, ARR. **RESEARCH** Ancient Philosophy, Philosophy of Religion, Parapsychology. **SELECTED PUBLICATIONS** Auth, On the Track of the Elephant: The Relevance of Psychical Research to Religious Experience for an Understanding of Reality, The J of Religion and Psychical Research, 95; American Culture and the Development of New Thought, The J Study of Metaphysical Religion, 96; Mind, Mind, What Therefore art Thou, Mind, The J of Religion and Metaphysical Research, 97; Birthmarks and Memory: Evidence for Mind-Body Dualism, The J of Religion and Physical Research, 98; Creation Meditation, Gateways to Higher Consciousness, Annual Conference Preceedings of the Academy of Religion and Psychical Research, 98. **CONTACT ADDRESS** 1004 Cedar Lake Dr, Tampa, FL, 33612.

MILLER, PATRICIA COX
PERSONAL Born 01/19/1947, Washington, DC, m **DISCIPLINE** RELIGION IN LATE ANTIQUITY **EDUCATION** Mary Washington Col of U Va, BA, 69; Univ Chicago, MA, 72; PhD, 79. **CAREER** Asst prof, Univ Wash, 75-76; asst prof, Syracuse Univ, 77-83; assoc prof, Syracuse Univ, 83-95; prof, Syracuse Univ, 95-; dir grad studies, dept relig, Syracuse Univ, 92-. **HONORS AND AWARDS** Pres, Namer Patristics Soc, 96-97; fel, NEH, 83; Kent fel, Univ Chicago, 72-75. **MEMBERSHIPS** Amer Acad Relig; Namer Patristics Soc. **RESEARCH** Religion and Aesthetics in Late Antiquity; Early Christian asceticism; Early Christian and Pagan hagiography. **SELECTED PUBLICATIONS** Auth, Dreams in Late Antiquity: Studies in the Imagination of a Culture, Princeton, Princeton Univ Press, 94; Biography in Late Antiquity: A Quest for the Holy Man, Berkeley, Univ Calif Press, 83; Articles, Differential Networks: Relics and Other Fragments in Late Antiquity, Jour of Early Christ Studies, 6, 113-38, 98; Strategies of Representation in Collective Biography: Constructing the Subject as Holy, Greek Biography and Panegyrics in Late Antiquity, ed Tomas Hagg and Philip Rousseau, Berkeley, Univ Calif Press, 98; Jerome's Centaur: A Hyper-Icon of the Desert, Jour of Early Christ Studies, 4, 209-33, 96; Dreaming the Body: An Aesthetics of Asceticism, Asceticism, ed Vincent Wimbush and Richard Valantasis, New York, Oxford Univ Press, 281-300, 95; Desert Asceticism and The Body from Nowhere, Jour of Early Christ Studies, 2, 137-53, 1994; The Blazing Body: Ascetic Desire in Jerome's Letter to Eustochium, Jour of Early Christian Studies, 1, 21-45, 93; The Devil's Gateway: An Eros of Difference in the Dreams of Perpetua, Dreaming, 2, 45-63, 92; Plenty Sleeps There: The Myth of Eros and Psyche in Plotinus and Gnosticism, Neoplatonism and Gnosticism, ed R. Wallis and J. Bregman, Stony Brook, State Univ of NY Press, 223-38, 92. **CONTACT ADDRESS** Dept. of Religion, Syracuse Univ, 501 Hall of Languages, Syracuse, NY, 13244-1170. **EMAIL** plmiller@syr.edu

MILLER, RICHARD B.
DISCIPLINE RELIGIOUS STUDIES **EDUCATION** Univ Chicago, PhD, 85. **CAREER** Assoc prof. **RESEARCH** Methods in religious ethics; history of Christian ethics; political and social ethics. **SELECTED PUBLICATIONS** Auth, Interpretations of Conflict: Ethics, Pacifism, and the Just-War Tradition, Univ Chicago, 91. **CONTACT ADDRESS** Dept of Religious Studies, Indiana Univ, Bloomington, 300 N Jordan Ave, Bloomington, IN, 47405.

MILLER, ROBERT DAVID
PERSONAL Born 09/04/1941, Chapel Hill, NC, d **DISCIPLINE** PSYCHIATRY **EDUCATION** Davidson Col, BS, 64; Duke Univ, PhD, 72, MD, 73. **CAREER** Clin assoc in psych, 76-78, Duke Univ Medical Ctr; clin asst prof, 78-81, clin assoc prof, 81-82; lect, law, 82-91, clin assoc prof of psych, 83-90, clin prof, 90-91, Univ Wis; clin assoc prof of psych, 84-91, Med Col of Wis; prof of psych, dir91-, Univ Co Health Sci Ctr; lect in law, 93-98, adj prof, law, 98, Univ Denver Col of Law; staff psych, 76-78, John Umstead Hosp, Butner, NC; dir, 78-80,, Eastern Admissions Unit, dir, 80, Adult Admissions Unit, dir, res trng, 80-82; co-dir, 80-82, Duke Univ/John Umstead Psychiatric Residency Prog; trng dir, 82-91, Forensic ctr, Mendota Mental Health Inst, Madison; ch psych, 91-95, Co Dept of Corrections; dir of res and ed, 93-, Inst for Forensic Psychiatry, Co Mental Health Inst At Pueblo; Consul, 95-, Co Dept of Corrections. **HONORS AND AWARDS** Phi Eta Sigma, 60; Phi Beta Kappa, 63; Sigma Xi, 71; Manfred S. Guttmacher Award, Am Psychiatric Asn, 89, 90; listed in The Best Doctors in America, 94, 98; Manfred S. Guttmacher Award, Am Psychiatric Asn Honorable Mention, 95. **MEMBERSHIPS** APA; Am Orthopsych Asn; NC Neuroscis Soc; Am Group Psycother Asn; NC Neuropsych Asn; WI Psych Asn; CO Psych Asn; Southeastern Group Psycother Asn; NC Group Behavior Soc; Am Acad of Psych & the Law; The Hastings Ctr, assoc member; Int Acad of Law & Mental Health; Am Acad of Forensic Scis, Psychiatry & Behavioral Sci Sect; Am Acad of Psych & Law, Midwest Chap; Wis St Med Soc; Am Bd of Forensic Psych. **SELECTED PUBLICATIONS** Auth, Involuntary Civil Commitment of the Mentally Ill in the Post-Reform Era, Charles C. Thomas, 87; coauth, Hypnosis and Dissimulation, Clin Asses of Malingering & Deception, Guilford Press, 88; auth, The US. Supreme Court Looks at Voluntariness and Consent, Int J of Law & Psychiatry, 94; coauth, Mental Health Screening and Evaluation Within Prisons, Bul of the Am Acad of Psych & Law, 94; coauth, Psychiatric Stigma in Correctional Facilities, Bul of the Am Acad of Psych & Law, 94; auth, Abolition of the Insanity Defense in the United States, Int Bul of Law & Mental Health, 94; auth, Involuntary Commitment to Outpatient Treatment, Principles & Practice of Forensic Psychiatry, Chapman & Hall, 94; coauth, Law & Mental Health Professionals: Wisconsin, APA, 95; auth, The Continuum of Coercion: Constitutional and Clinical Considerations in the Treatment of Mentally Disordered Persons, Univ Denver Law Rev, 97; auth, The Forced Administration of Sex-Drive Reducing Medications to Sex Offenders: Treatment or Punishment?, Psychol, Pub Pol & Law, in press; auth, Advance Directives for Psychiatric Treatment: A View from the Trenches, Psychol, Pub Pol & Law, in press; auth, Coerced Treatment in the Community, Psychiatric Clinics of North America, in Press. **CONTACT ADDRESS** Parker, CO, 80134.

MILLER, ROLAND
DISCIPLINE MISSIONS **EDUCATION** Concordia Sem, BA, MDiv; Kennedy Sch of Missions, MA, 54; Hartford Sem Found, PhD, 73. **CAREER** Instr, Concordia Sem, 66-67; vis sholar, Harvar Univ, 76-90; prof, Luther Col, Univ Regina, Can, 76-89; acad dean, Luther Col, 77-89; cord rel prog, Luther Col, 80-89; vis lectr, 91-92; vis prof, 93-. **HONORS AND AWARDS** Lutheran missionary, Malappuram, Kerala, southern India, 53-76. **MEMBERSHIPS** Mem, W Conf Univ Deans of Arts and Sci; Shastri Indo-Can Inst. **SELECTED PUBLICATIONS** Auth, The Mappila Muslims of Kerala, A Study in Islamic Trends, 91; The Sending of God: Essays on the Mission of God and His People, 80; Religious Studies in Manitoba and Saskatchewan, 91. **CONTACT ADDRESS** Dept of Missions, Luther Sem, 2481 Como Ave, St. Paul, MN, 55108. **EMAIL** rmiller@luthersem.edu

MILLER, RONALD H.
PERSONAL Born 04/17/1938, St. Louis, MO, d, 3 children **DISCIPLINE** RELIGION **EDUCATION** St. Louis Univ, BA, 61; Jesuit Sch Phil, PhL, 62; St Louis Univ, MA, 63; Northwestern Univ, PhD, 78. **CAREER** Regis High School and Col, tchr, 62-65; Northwestern Univ, TA, 70-74; Lake Forest Col, lectr, 74-89, assoc prof, 89-, Dept chemn, 94-. **HONORS AND AWARDS** St. Louis Univ, BA, magna cum laude; Deutsche Akademische Austauschdienst Fel, 69-70; Clement Stone Schshp, 72; Lake Forest Col, Great Tchr Award, 86, Bird Award, 93, Charlotte Simmons Prize, 94, William R. Bross Professorial Ch, 95 **MEMBERSHIPS** IFCJ **RESEARCH** Jewish Christian dialogue; NT. **SELECTED PUBLICATIONS** Auth, The Spirituality of Franz Rosenzweig, in: Western Spirituality, ed Mathew Fox, Fides, 79; Pilgrimage Without End, in: Five Spiritual Journeys, ed by L. Zirker, Iroquois House, 81; Fireball and the Lotus: Emerging Spirituality from Ancient Roots, co-ed, Bear and Co, 87; Dialogue and Disagreement: Franz Rosenzweig's Relevance for Contemporary Jewish - Christian Understanding, Univ Press of Amer, 89; Space for the Spirit, in: Finding a Way: Essays on Spiritual Practice, ed by Lorette Zirker, Tuttle Press, 96. **CONTACT ADDRESS** Dept of Religion, Lake Forest Col, Lake Forest, IL, 60045. **EMAIL** rmiller@lfc.edu

MILLER, STEPHEN R.
PERSONAL Born 09/25/1949, Jackson, TN, m, 1970, 2 children **DISCIPLINE** OLD TESTAMENT **EDUCATION** Union Univ, BS, 71; Mid-Amer Baptist Theol Sem, ThM, 76, PhD, 82. **CAREER** Prof, 82- OT/Hebrew Lang, Mid-Amer Baptist Theol Sem. **MEMBERSHIPS** Soc of Biblical Lit; Evangel Theol Sem. **SELECTED PUBLICATIONS** Auth, The Literary Style of the Book of Isaiah and the Unity Question, Mid-Amer Baptist Theol Sem, 82; art, Psalm 19: The Revelation of God, Mid-Amer Theol J, vol 8:2, 84; art, The Authorship of Isaiah, Mid-Amer Theol J, vol 15:1, 91; art, Introduction to the Book of Hosea, Mid-Amer Theol J, vol 17, 93; auth, Daniel, New Amer Comm, vol 18, Broadman & Holman, 94; art, Introduction and Outline for the Prophecy of Amos, Mid-Amer Theol J, vol 19, 95; art, Christians and the Ten Commandments, Life & Work Advan Bibl Stud, Lifeway Christian Rsrcs, 96; art, An Introduction to Old Testament Wisdom Literature, Life & Work Directions Tchr Ed, Lifeway Christian Rscrs, 96; art,

Tithes and Offerings, Bibl Illus, Lifeway Christian Rscrs, 97; art, The Prophecy of Jeremiah, Life & Work Advan Bibl Study, Lifeway Christian Rscrs, 98. **CONTACT ADDRESS** Mid-America Baptist Theol Sem, PO Box 381528, Germantown, TN, 38183-1528. **EMAIL** smiller@mabts.edu

MILLER, TEDD
PERSONAL Born 01/04/1946, Washington, District of Columbia, m, 1976 **DISCIPLINE** LAW **EDUCATION** Bethune Cookman College, BA, 1968; Rutgers School of Law, JD, 1972. **CAREER** Rutgers Univ, adjunct faculty, 1972-75; Essex County Legal Services, staff attorney, 1972-75; Council on Legal Education Opportunity, asst director, 1975-80; Georgetown Univ Law Center, director of admissions, 1980-92; Howard Univ School of Law, asst dean of director of admissions, currently. **MEMBERSHIPS** Law School Admissions Council, board of trustees, 1994-97; Assn of American Law Schools, chair section on pre legal education and admission to law school, 1994-96. **CONTACT ADDRESS** Sch of Law, Howard Univ, 2900 Van Ness St NW, Ste 200, Holy Cross Mall, Washington, VT, 20010.

MILLER, TELLY HUGH
PERSONAL Born 06/18/1939, Henderson, TX, m **DISCIPLINE** THEOLOGY **EDUCATION** Wiley Coll, BA 1962; Interdenom Theol Cntr, MDiv 1965; Vanderbilt U, DMin 1973; Prairie View A&M Univ, EdM 1980. **CAREER** St Paul Baptist Church St Albans WV, pastor 1965; WV State Coll, religious counselor 1967; Wiley Coll Marshall TX, coll minister 1968, financial aid dir 1970, assoc prof/chmn dept of religion 1973, vice pres for student affairs 1974, prof and chmn dept of religion and philosophy 1976-. **HONORS AND AWARDS** East TX Educ Oppors Ctr Awd 1980; Kappa Alpha Psi Achievement Awd 1980; Omega Psi Phi Man of the Year Awd 1983; elected first Black Commissioner for Harrison County 1983; apptd by Gov of TX to East TX Regional Review Comm for the State's Comm Develop Block Grant Prog. **MEMBERSHIPS** Relig consult Bapt WV St Coll Inst 1967; mem Am Assn Univ Profs; chmn Christmas Baskets for Needy St Albans 1967; bd dirs YMCA St Albans 1966-67; chmn mem drive NAACP 1967; mem exec com Kanawha Co chap 1967; v moder Mt Olivet Assn 1966-67; pres George Washington Carver Elem Sch PTA 1977; pres Gamma Upsilon Lambda Chap Alpha Phi Alpha Frat Inc 1977; mem Alpha Phi Alpha Frat Inc, Alpha Phi Omega Natl Serv Frat Kappa Pi Chapt, AAUP, Morgan Lodge No 10 St Albans WV, NAACP; fellowship of Christian Athletes; bd of dirs Harrison County United Way Fund Dr 1983, bd of dirs Harrison County Red Cross. **CONTACT ADDRESS** Dept of Relig/Philos, Wiley Col, 711 Rosborough Springs Rd, Marshall, TX, 75670.

MILLER, TIMOTHY ALAN
PERSONAL Born 08/23/1944, Wichita, KS, m, 1982, 2 children **DISCIPLINE** RELIGIOUS STUDIES **EDUCATION** Univ Kansas AB, 66, PhD, 73. **CAREER** Lectr, asst prof, assoc prof rel studies, prof rel studies, dept chair, 73-. **MEMBERSHIPS** Am acad rel; Communal stud asn; Soc for utopian stud; Mid Am Am stud asn; Intl commu stud. **RESEARCH** New rel move; alt rel; hist of intentional community **SELECTED PUBLICATIONS** Artists Colonies as Communal Soc in the Arts and Crafts Era, Communal Soc 16, 96; American Alt Rel, Albany, State Univ NY press, 95; The Evolution of Hippie Communal Spirituality: The Farm and Other Hippies Who Didn't Give Up, American Alt Rel, with Albert Bates, Albany, State Univ NY press, 95; Black Jews and Black Muslims, American Alt Rel, Albany, State Univ NY press, 95; The Quest for Utopia in 20th Century America, vol I, 1900-1960, Syracuse Univ press, 98; The Hippies and America Values, Univ Tenn press, 91; American Communes, 1860-1960: Bibliography, Garland Pub, 90; Following in His Steps: Biography of Charles M Sheldon, Univ Tenn press, 87. **CONTACT ADDRESS** Dept Religious Studies, Univ of Kansas, 103 Smith Hall, Lawrence, KS, 66045. **EMAIL** tkansas@ukans.edu

MILLER-MCLEMORE, BONNIE JEAN
PERSONAL Born 11/25/1955, Jacksonville, FL, m, 1980, 3 children **DISCIPLINE** THEOLOGY **EDUCATION** Kalamazoo Col, BA, 97; Univ Chi, MA, 80; Univ Chi, PhD, 86. **CAREER** Assoc prof Pastoral Theolog & Coun, Vanderbilt Univ, 95-; assoc prof Relig, Personality & Culture, Chi Theolog Sem, 92-95; asst prof Relig, Personality & Culture, Chi Theolog Sem, 87-92; vis asst prof Pastoral Care, Chi Theolog Sem, 86-87. **HONORS AND AWARDS** Lilly Found Grant Recipient, 98-; Lilly Found Grant Recipient, 90-96; Assoc Theolog Schools Young Scholar Award, 90-91; Ann E Dickerson Scholar, 80-84; Edward Scribner Aims Award, 80-81; Stevens Memorial Scholar, 79-80. **MEMBERSHIPS** Amer Acad Relig; Soc Christian Ethics; Soc of Pastoral Theology. **RESEARCH** Practical & Pastoral Theology; Feminist Theology; Feminist Psychology; Theology and Culture of Work **SELECTED PUBLICATIONS** Co-ed, Feminist and Womanist Pastoral Theology: Implications for Care, Faith, and Reflection, Abingdon, forthcoming; coauth, From Culture Wars to Common Ground: Religion and the American Debate, Westminster/John Knox, forthcoming; Also A Mother: Work and Family as Theological Dilemma, Abingdon, 94. **CONTACT ADDRESS** Dept of Religion, Vanderbilt Univ, Nashville, TN, 37240-2701. **EMAIL** bonnie.miller-mclemore@vanderbilt.edu

MILLGRAM, ELIJAH
DISCIPLINE PHILOSOPHY **EDUCATION** Harvard Univ, AB (philos), 84, PhD (philos), 91. **CAREER** Asst prof, Princeton Univ, 91-97; ASSOC PROF, VANDERBILT UNIV, 97-. **HONORS AND AWARDS** Nat Endowment for the Humanities fel, 96-97; Nat Humanities Center fel (declined), 96-97; Center for Advanced Studies in the Behavioral Sciences, Stanford Univ, fel for 99-00. **SELECTED PUBLICATIONS** Auth, An Apprentice Argument, Philos and Phenomenological Res, 54, Dec 94; Was Hume a Humean?, Hume Studies21, April 95; William's Argument Against External Reasons, Nous 30, June 96; Deliberative Coherence, with Paul Thagard, Synthese 108, July 96; book review, Henry Richardson, Practical Reasoning about Final Ends, July, 96; Hume on Practical Reasoning, Iyyun, July 97; Practical Induction, Cambridge, MA: Harvard Univ Press, 97; Varieties of Practical Reasoning, in G. Meggle, Analyomen 2, vol 3, Berlin: de Gruyter, 97; Incommensurability and Practical Reasoning, in R. Chang, Incommensurability, Incomparability, and Practical Reason, Cambridge, MA: Harvard Univ Press, 98; Deciding to Desire, in C, Fehige and U. Wessels, Preferences, Berlin: Walter de Gruyter, 98; book review, Iris Murdoch, Existentialists and Mystics, Boston Review, 23, Feb/March 98. **CONTACT ADDRESS** Philosophy-111 Furman Hall, Vanderbilt Univ, Nashville, TN, 37240. **EMAIL** elijah.millgram@vanderbilt.edu

MILLIKAN, RUTH G.
DISCIPLINE PHILOSOPHY **EDUCATION** Oberlin Col, AB, 55; Yale Univ, PhD, 69. **CAREER** Dept Philos, Univ Conn **RESEARCH** Philosophy of mind; Philosophy of language; philosophy of biology; ontology. **SELECTED PUBLICATIONS** Auth, Language, Thought, and Other Biological Categories, Bradford Bk(s)/MIT Press, 84; White Queen Psychology and Other Essays For Alice, Bradford Bk(s)/MIT Press, 93, 88; Explanation in Biopsychology, Mental Causation, Oxford Univ Press, 93, reprinted, Philosophy of Psychology: Debates on Psychological Explanation, Oxford Univ Press, 95; A Bet With Peacocke, Philosophy of Psychology: Debates on Psychological Explanation, Oxford Univ Press, 95; Pushmi-pullyu Representations, Philosophical Perspectives, Ridgeview Publ, 96, reprinted, Mind and Morals, MIT Press, 96; On Swampkinds, Mind & Language, 96; Varieties of Purposive Behavior, Anthropomorphism, Anecdotes, and Animals, SUNY Press, 96; Some Troubles with Wagner's Reading of Millikan, Philos Stud, 97. **CONTACT ADDRESS** Dept of Philos, Univ Conn, 1266 Storrs Rd, Storrs, CT, 06269.

MILLNER, DIANNE MAXINE
PERSONAL Born 03/21/1949, Columbus, OH, m, 1986 **DISCIPLINE** LAW **EDUCATION** Pasadena City Coll, AA 1969; Univ of CA at Berkeley, AB 1972; Stanford U, JD 1975. **CAREER** Hastings Coll of The Law, instructor 1977-78; Pillsbury Madison & Sutro Law Firm, Attorney 1975-80; Alexander, Millner & McGee, atty, 1980-91; Steefel, Levitt & Weiss, Attorney, 1991-94; CA Continuing Education of the Bar, atty, currently. **HONORS AND AWARDS** Pres Award Womens Div Nat Bar Assn 1980; Phi Beta Kappa UC Berkeley 1975. **MEMBERSHIPS** Dir Youth for Serv 1978-80; mem Commnty Redevel Agencys Assn 1983-94; Nat Bar Assn; Black Woman Lawyers Assn; Charles Houston Bar Assn; mem, American Assn of Univ Women, 1990-92; comm chair, Parents Division of the Natl Federation of the Blind, 1988-; mem, American Bar Assn; mem, CA State Bar. **CONTACT ADDRESS** California Continuing Education of the Bar, 2300 Shattuck Avenue, Berkeley, CA, 94704.

MILLS, CHARLES
DISCIPLINE PHILOSOPHY **EDUCATION** Univ Toronto, PhD. **CAREER** Assoc prof., Univ IL at Chicago **RESEARCH** Oppositional politl theory. **SELECTED PUBLICATIONS** Auth, The Moral Epistemology of Stalinism, Polit Soc, 94; Under Class Under Standings, Ethics, 94; Non Cartesian Sums: Philosophy and the African American Experience, Tchg Philos, 94. **CONTACT ADDRESS** Philos Dept, Univ Illinois Chicago, S Halsted St, PO Box 705, Chicago, IL, 60607.

MILLS, JON L.
DISCIPLINE LAW **EDUCATION** Stetson Univ, BA; Univ Fla, JD. **CAREER** Prof and dir,Univ Fla, 88-. **MEMBERSHIPS** Fla Bar; Order of the Coif; Phi Kappa Phi; Fla Constitution Rev Comn, 97-98; chem, CRC Style and Drafting Comt. **RESEARCH** Florida Constitutional Law, Environmental Law, Legislative Drafting. **CONTACT ADDRESS** School of Law, Univ of Florida, PO Box 117625, Gainesville, FL, 32611-7625. **EMAIL** mills@law.ufl.edu

MILLS, PATRICIA J.
PERSONAL Born 03/18/1944, Newark, NJ, 1 child **DISCIPLINE** POLITICAL PHILOSOPHY **EDUCATION** Rutgers Univ, BA, 73; SUNY Stony Brook, MA, 75; York Univ, Toronto, PhD, 84. **CAREER** Lectr, social sci and hum, York Univ, 76-81; lectr women's stud, Univ Toronto, 84-85; vis scholar, philos, 85-86, asst prof, 86-88, Univ Toronto; asst prof, assoc prof, philos, Univ Mass Amherst, 88- . **HONORS AND AWARDS** Post-doc fel, Soc Sci and Hum Res Council Canada, 83-85; fac tchg grant, 91-92; distinguished tchg award, 97; listed Who's Who in the East, 99-00; listed Who's Who in Am, 98, 99; listed Who's Who of Am Women, 97, 99. **MEMBERSHIPS** Am Polit Sci Asn; APA; Can Philos Asn; Hegel Soc Am; Soc for Phenomenol and Existential Philos; Am Soc for Aesthetica; Soc for Women in Philos; Simone de Beauvoir Soc; Natl Women's Stud Asn; SOFPHIA. **SELECTED PUBLICATIONS** Auth, Hegel's Antigone, The Owl of Minerva, 86; auth, Women, Nature, and Psyche, Yale Univ, 87; auth, Nature and Freedom: Thoughts for the 1980s, in Clark, ed, Renewing the Earth: The Promise of Social Ecology, Green Print, 90; auth, Feminism and Ecology: On the Domination of Nature, Hypatia: J of Feminist Philos, 91; auth, Feminist Sympathy and Other Serious Crimes: A Reply to Swindle, The Owl of Minerva: J of the Hegel Soc of Am, 92; auth, Hegel and The Woman Question: Regocnition and Intersubjectivity, in Clark, ed, The Sexism of Social and Political Theory: Woman and Reporduction from Plato to Nietzsche, Univ Toronto, 79, repr in Cerrito, ed, Nineteenth-Century Literature Criticism, Gale, 94; ed, Feminist Interpretations of G.W.F. Hegel, Pennsylvania State, 96; **CONTACT ADDRESS** Dept Political Science, Univ Massachusetts, Amherst, MA.

MILLSTEIN, IRA M.
PERSONAL Born 11/08/1927, New York, NY, m, 1949, 2 children **DISCIPLINE** LAW **EDUCATION** Columbia School of Law, LL.B, 49; Columbia Univ School of Engineering, BS, 47. **CAREER** Sr Partner, Weil, Gotshal & Manges, NY, NY, present; Eugene F William Jr Vis Prof, Yale Univ, 96; Lester Crown Vis Fel, Yale Univ, 92; Ch, Inst Investory Proj, Columbia Univ School of Law, 87-; adjunct prof, Columbia Univ, 87-89; Fel Fac of Govt, Harvard Univ, 83-87; Distinguished Fac Fel, Yale Univ, 83; Sloan Fel, Yale Univ, 82; adjuct prof Law, NY Univ, 67-78. **HONORS AND AWARDS** Honorary Doctorate Humane Letters, Yeshiva Univ, 88; Awarded by Fr Govt rank of"Chevalier (Knight) of the National Order of Merit. **MEMBERSHIPS** NY City Partnership Policy Center Ch; Yale School of Management Advisory Board Member; Org for Econ Develop Chair; Amer Acad Arts & Sci Fel; Ntl Assoc of Corporate Directors Brd Member; Japan Society; Appointed by Vice-Pres Gore and Russian Prime Minister Chernomyrdin to US-Russia Capital Markets Forum Working Group on Investory Protection, 97-; Amer Bar Assoc; NY State Bar Assoc; Assoc of Bar of City of NY. **SELECTED PUBLICATIONS** Coauth, The Active Board of Directors and Performance of the Large Publicly Traded Corporation, Columbia Law Rev, 98; The Responsible Board," Bus Lawyer, 97; The Professional Board, Bus Lawyer; The Evolution of the Certifying Board, Bus Lawyer, 93. **CONTACT ADDRESS** Dept of Management, Weil, Gotshal & Manges, 767 Fifth Ave, New York, NY, 10153. **EMAIL** Ira.Millstein@weil.com

MINAR, EDWARD
DISCIPLINE WITTGENSTEIN AND THE HISTORY OF ANALYTIC PHILOSOPHY **EDUCATION** Harvard Univ, PhD. **CAREER** Philos, Univ Ark **SELECTED PUBLICATIONS** Articles; Synthese, Philos & Phenomenological Res, Pacific Philos Quart. **CONTACT ADDRESS** Univ Ark, Fayetteville, AR, 72701. **EMAIL** eminar@comp.uark.edu

MINAS, ANNE C.
DISCIPLINE PHILOSOPHY **EDUCATION** Harvard Univ, PhD, 67. **RESEARCH** Social philos gender issues; feminism. **SELECTED PUBLICATIONS** Auth, Gender Basics: Feminist Perspectives on Women and Men, Wadsworth, 93. **CONTACT ADDRESS** Dept of Philosophy, Waterloo Univ, 200 University Ave W, Waterloo, ON, N2L 3G1. **EMAIL** aminas@uwaterloo.ca

MINNICH, ELIZABETH
DISCIPLINE PHILOSOPHY **EDUCATION** New Sch Soc Res, MA, PhD. **CAREER** Prof. **RESEARCH** Western philosophy. **SELECTED PUBLICATIONS** Auth, Can Virtue Be Taught? A Feminist Reconsiders, Boston Univ, 93; From Ivory Tower to Tower of Babel?, Duke Univ, 92; Judging in Freedom: Hannah Arendt On The Relation of Thinking and Judgment, 89. **CONTACT ADDRESS** Union Inst, 440 E McMillan St., Cincinnati, OH, 45206-1925.

MINNICH, NELSON H.
DISCIPLINE CHURCH HISTORY **EDUCATION** Boston Col, AB, 65, MA, 66; Gregorian Univ, STB, 70; Harvard Univ, PhD, 77. **CAREER** Instr, Loyola Acad, 66-68; teach fel, asst, 72, 74; asst, 77-83, assoc 83-93, PROF, HIST, CHURCH HIST, 93-, act chair, 78, 85, chair 79, 87-89, 98-, CHURCH HIST, CATH UNIV AM, assoc ed, 77-90, ADVIS ED, CATHOLIC HIST REV, 91-, ED, MELLVILLE STUD IN CHURCH HIST; ASSOC ED, ENCYCLOPEDIA RENAISSANCE, 96. **CONTACT ADDRESS** Dept Church History, Catholic Univ of America, 417 Caldwell Hall, Washington, DC, 20064.

MINOGUE, BRENDAN PATRICK
PERSONAL Born 04/19/1945, Brooklyn, NY, m, 1970, 2 children **DISCIPLINE** PHILOSOPHY **EDUCATION** Cathedral Col, BA, 67; OH State Univ, MA, 70, PhD, 74. **CAREER** From Asst Prof to Prof Philos, Youngstown Univ, 74, Chmn Dept, 78. **HONORS AND AWARDS** Nat Endowment Hum fel, 76; vis scholar award, Col Grad Studies, Univ WVA,76. **MEMBER-**

SHIPS Am Philos Asn; Philos Sci Asn. **RESEARCH** Philos of Sci, Metaphysics, and philos of lang. **SELECTED PUBLICATIONS** Auth, Quine on analyticity and transl, Southern J Philos, summer 76; Numbers, properties and frege, Philos Studies, 6/77; Cartesian optics and Semantic rationalism, Proc XV Int Cong Hist Sci, 8/77; Realism and intensional reference, Philos Sci, winter 79; Bioethics: A Committee Approach, Jones & Bartlett, 96; ed, Reading Engelhardt: Essays on the Thought of H. Tristram Engelhardt, Kluwer, 96. **CONTACT ADDRESS** Dept of Philos, Youngstown State Univ, 1 University Plz, Youngstown, OH, 44555-0002. **EMAIL** bpminogu@cc.ysu.edu

MINOR, ROBERT NEIL
PERSONAL Born 10/02/1945, Milwaukee, WI, m, 1970, 1 child **DISCIPLINE** ASIAN RELIGION **EDUCATION** Trinity Col, BA, 67, MA, 69; Univ Iowa, PhD(relig India), 75. **CAREER** Asst prof relig, Allegheny Col, 75-77; asst prof, 77-81, Assoc Prof Relig, Univ Kans, 81- **MEMBERSHIPS** Am Acad Relig; Asn Asian Studies. **RESEARCH** Religious thought in modern India; the Bhagavad Gita; history of religions; methodology; gender and religion. **SELECTED PUBLICATIONS** Auth, The relationship of Aurobindo's view of law and personal freedom to his ultimate concern, J Relig Thought, fall-winter, 74-75; Sri Aurobindo, the Good and the Perfect, SAsia Bks, 78; Sri Aurobindo's integral view of other religions, Relig Studies, 79; The Gita's way as the only way, Philos E & W, 7/80; Bhangavad Gita: An Exegetical Commentary, 81, Sri Aurobindo and experience: logic and otherwise, In: Religion in Modern India & Sarvepalli Radhakrishnam and Hinduism defined and defended, In: Religion in Modern India, 81, SAsia Bks; Sarvepalli Radharkrishnam on the nature of Hindu tolerance, J Am Acad Relig, 6/82; ed and contribr, Modern Indian Interpreters of the Bhagavadgita, 86; auth, The religious, the spiritual, and the secular: Auroville & Secular India, 98. **CONTACT ADDRESS** Univ of Kansas, Lawrence, KS, 66045-0001. **EMAIL** rminor@ukans.edu

MINOW, MARTHA
PERSONAL Born 12/06/1954, Highland Park, IL, m, 1 child **DISCIPLINE** LAW **EDUCATION** Univ of Mich, AB, 75; Harvard Grad School of Ed, EdM, 76; Yale Law School, JD, 79. **CAREER** Law clerk to Justice Thurgood Marshall, U.S. Supreme Court, 80-81; acting dir, Harvard Prog in Ethics and the Professions, 93-94; ASST PROF, 81-86, PROF, HARVARD LAW SCHOOL, 86-. **HONORS AND AWARDS** Honorary Doctor of Ed, Wheelock Col, 98. **MEMBERSHIPS** Fac Advisory Comt, Fac Hist and Ourselves; Board of Syndication, Harvard Univ Press; Board of Trustees, Revson Found; Sr Fel, The Prog of Ethics and the Professions, Harvard Univ; Chair of the Board, Radcliffe Public Policy Inst of Families, Children, Disabled Persons, Truth, and ReconsilIation Comns. **SELECTED PUBLICATIONS** Co-ed, Women and the Law, Foundation Press, 98; co-ed, Law Stories, Univ of Mich Press, 96; co-ed, Narrative, Violence and the Law: The Essays of Robert M. Cover, Univ of Mich Press, 92; auth, Between Vengeance and Forgiveness: Facing History After Genocide and Mass Violence, Beacon Press, forthcoming; auth, Not Only For Myself: Identity, Politics, and Law, The New Press, 97; auth, Making All the Difference: Inclusion, Exclusion, and American Law, Cornell Univ Press, 90; coauth, Civil Procedure: Doctrine, Practice and Context, Little Brown, forthcoming. **CONTACT ADDRESS** School of Law, Harvard Univ, 407 Griswold, Cambridge, MA, 02138. **EMAIL** minow@law.harvard.edu

MIRANDA DE ALMEIDA, ROGERIOR
PERSONAL Born 04/09/1953, Crato, Brazil **DISCIPLINE** PHILOSOPHY **EDUCATION** Univ Metz, PhD, 97. **CAREER** Instr, Univ Campinas, 94; asst prof, St. Vincent Col, 95-. **MEMBERSHIPS** Soc for Phemenol and Existential Philos; Am Philos Asn; Friedrich Nietzsche Soc of Great Britain. **RESEARCH** Philosophy of language; Philosophy and psychoanalysis; History of philosophy; Lacanian thought. **SELECTED PUBLICATIONS** Auth, "Freud, Nietzsche: L'Enigme du Pere," in Le Portique, 98; "La Finalite, la Providence et le Hasard Selon Nietzsche," in Revue des Sci Relig, 97; "Foucault, Nietzsche and Interpretation," in Foucault e a Destruicao das Evidencias, 95; "The True, the Non-True and Appearance According to Nietzsche," in Sintese, 94. **CONTACT ADDRESS** St. Vincent Col, 300 Fraser Purchase Rd, Latrobe, PA, 15650-2690. **EMAIL** rogerio@acad1.stvincent.edu

MIRECKI, PAUL A.
DISCIPLINE RELIGION **EDUCATION** Harvard Univ, ThD, 86 **CAREER** Vis asst prof, Univ Mich, 86-88; vis asst prof, Albion Col, 88-89; Assoc prof, Univ Ks, 89- . **HONORS AND AWARDS** NEH; ACLS, DAAD res & travel grants **MEMBERSHIPS** Amer Soc of Papyrologist; Amer Acad of Relig. **RESEARCH** Papyrology; coptic lang; ancient Mediterranean relig. **SELECTED PUBLICATIONS** Auth, The Coptic Wizard's Hoard, Harvard Theol Rev, 95; coauth, Manichaean Letter, Magical Spell, in Emerging from Darkness: Studies in the Recovery of Manichaean Sources, Brill, 97; Ancient Magic and Ritual Power, Brill, 95; The Gospel of the Savior: A New Ancient Gospel, Polebridge, 99; coed, Emerging from Darkness: Studies in the Recovery of Manichaean Sources, Brill, 97. **CONTACT ADDRESS** Dept of Relig Stud, Univ Ks, Smith Hall, Lawrence, KS, 66045. **EMAIL** LVAP@kuhub.cc.ukans.edu

MIROWSKI, PHILIP E.
DISCIPLINE PHILOSOPHY OF SCIENCE **EDUCATION** Mich State Univ, BA, 73; Univ Mich, MA, 76, PhD, 79. **CAREER** Prof. **RESEARCH** History and philosophy of economic theory. **SELECTED PUBLICATIONS** Auth, Mandelbrot's Economics After a Quarter-Century, 95; Three Ways of Thinking About Testing in Econometrics, 95; Harold Hotelling and the Neoclassical Dream, 97; Civilization and its Discounts, 95; The Economic Consequences of Philip Kitcher, 96; On Playing the Economics Trump Card in the Philosophy of Science: Why It Didn't Work for Michael Polanyi, 97; Do You Know the Way to Santa Fe?, 96; Machine Dreams: Economic Agent as Cyborg, 98; ed, Edgeworth's Writings on Chance, Probability and Statistics, 94; Natural Images in Economics: Markets Read in Tooth and Claw, 94. **CONTACT ADDRESS** History and Philosophy of Science Dept, Univ of Notre Dame, Notre Dame, IN, 46556. **EMAIL** Philip.E.Mirowski.1@nd.edu

MISNER, PAUL
PERSONAL Born 02/14/1936, Akron, OH, w **DISCIPLINE** THEOLOGY **EDUCATION** St Charles Borromeo Sem, BA, 54-58; Gregorian Univ, Rome, STL, 58-62; Univ of Munich, Dr Theol. 65-69. **CAREER** Asst Prof, 69-75, Theol, Boston Coll; Fulbright Res Prof, 75-76, Univ of Marburg; Asst, Assoc, Vis Prof, 79-, Theol, Marquette Univ; Fulbright Res Prof, 85-86, Inst for European Hist, Mainz; Vis Prof, 91, Univ of Cologne. **HONORS AND AWARDS** Fulbright Res Prof; Social Catholicism name d Book of the Year, 92; Award from Bradley Inst for Democracy and Public Values for Sabbatical support. **MEMBERSHIPS** Amer Acad Rel; Amer Catholic Hist Assoc; Amer Hist Assoc; Catholic Theol Soc Amer; North Amer Acad of Ecumenists. **RESEARCH** Modern European Christianity and Christian Thought; Roman Catholic Studies. **SELECTED PUBLICATIONS** Auth, Social Catholicism in Europe, From the Onset of Industrialization to the First World War, NY, Crossroad, 91; Social Catholicism in Nineteenth-Century Europe, A Review of Recent Historiography, The Catholic Historical Review, 92; Contributor to The New Dictionary of Catholic Social Thought, Collegeville, MN, Liturgical Press, 94. **CONTACT ADDRESS** Dept Theology, Marquette Univ, Milwaukee, WI, 53201-1881.

MISNER, ROBERT L.
DISCIPLINE ADMINISTRATION OF CRIMINAL JUSTICE, CONTRACTS, CORRECTIONS & PRISONS **EDUCATION** Univ San Francisco, BA, 68; Univ Chicago, JD, 71. **CAREER** Asst atty gen, Ore Dept Justice, Salem, 71-72; lectr, Univ Sydney Law Sch, 72-74; vis prof, Univ Minn, 74-75; assoc prof, Ariz State Univ, 75-78; dep atty gen, Ariz atty gen, 78; prof, Ariz State Univ, 78-87; vis prof, Univ Va, 81; dean, 87-94; prof, 87-. **MEMBERSHIPS** Mem, Amer Law Inst. **SELECTED PUBLICATIONS** Co-auth, Restructing of the Criminal Justice System in the Northern Territory, 73; auth, Speedy Trial: Federal and State Practice, 83; assoc ed, Univ Chicago Law Rev. **CONTACT ADDRESS** Sch of Law, Willamette Univ, 900 State St, Salem, OR, 97301. **EMAIL** rmisner@willamette.edu

MISSNER, MARSHALL HOWARD
PERSONAL Born 01/10/1942, Chicago, IL, m, 1969, 2 children **DISCIPLINE** PHILOSOPHY **EDUCATION** Univ Chicago, BA, 63, MA, 67, PhD, 70. **CAREER** Asst prof, 69-80, assoc prof philos, 80-, Univ Wis-Oshkosh; consult, Wis Humanities Comt, 77-. **MEMBERSHIPS** Am Philos Assn. **RESEARCH** Hobbes; social philosophy; philosophy of science. **SELECTED PUBLICATIONS** Art, Hobbes's Method in Leviathan, J Hist Ideas, 77; ed, Business and Ethics, Alfred Publ, 80; art, The Skeptical Basis Of Hobbe's Political Philosophy, J Hist Ideas, 83. **CONTACT ADDRESS** Dept of Philosophy, Univ of Wisconsin, 800 Algoma Blvd, Oshkosh, WI, 54901-8601. **EMAIL** missner@uwosh.edu

MITCHELL, ALAN C.
PERSONAL Born 11/16/1948, Brooklyn, NY, m, 1998 **DISCIPLINE** NEW TESTAMENT, CHRISTIAN ORIGINS **EDUCATION** Fordham Univ, AB, 72; Western Sch Theol, MDiv, 79; Yale Univ, MA, 81, MPhil, 83; PhD, 86. **CAREER** Instr, Wheeling Col, 73-76; teach fel, Yale Div Sch, Yale Col, 80 82; adj inst, Fairfield Univ, 83; asst prof, 86, ASSOC PROF, GEORGETOWN UNIV, 92-. **HONORS AND AWARDS** Phi Beta Kappa; Alpha Sigma Nu; Yale Univ fel; Landegger Sr. fel, 96-97. **MEMBERSHIPS** Cath Bibl Asn; Soc Bibl Lit. **RESEARCH** New Testament soc world; Hellenistic moral philos and early Christianity; Paul; Hebrews. **SELECTED PUBLICATIONS** Auth, Looking to the Interests of Others: Friendship and Justice in New Testament Communities, in Let Justice Roll Down Like Waters: Distinguished Lectures in Jesuit Education, Georgetown Univ Press, 93; auth, Rich and Poor in the Courts of Corinth: Litigiousness and Status in 1 Corinthians 6.1-11, New Testament Stud 39, 93; auth, Friendship, in A Modern Catholic Encyclopedia, Liturgical Press, 94; auth, Holding on to Confidence, in Friendship, Flattery, and Frankness of Speech: Studies on Friendship in the Ancient World, Nov Supp 82, 96; auth, Greet the Friends by Name: New Testament Evidence for the Greco-Roman Topon on Friendship, in Greco-Roman Perspectives on Friendship, Scholars Press, 97; auth, The Use of Scripture in Evangelium Vitae: A Response to James Keenan, in Choosing Life: A Dialogue on Evangelium Vitae, Georgetown Univ Press, 97; co-ed, Choosing Life: A Dialogue on Evangelium Vitae, Georgetown Univ Press, 97. **CONTACT ADDRESS** Georgetown Univ, Box 571135 - 123 New North Bldg, Washington, DC, 20057-1135. **EMAIL** mitchea2@gusun.georgetown.edu

MITCHELL, C. BEN
DISCIPLINE CHRISTIAN ETHICS **EDUCATION** Miss State Univ, BS; Southwestern Baptist Theol Sem, MDiv; Univ Tenn, PhD. **CAREER** Bioethics consult, S Baptist Ethics and Rel Liberty Commn; Fel, Ctr for Bioethics and Human Dignity; dir, Southern's Jordan Inst; **MEMBERSHIPS** Mem, bd adv(s), Univ Fac for Life at Georgetown Univ. **RESEARCH** Ethical implications of new genetics. **SELECTED PUBLICATIONS** Co-ed, Prescription Ethics: Pharmaceutical Representative Interactions with Health Care Professionals; ed, Ctr's jour, Ethics and Medicine: A Christian Perspective on Bioethics. **CONTACT ADDRESS** Christian Ethics Dept, Southern Baptist Theol Sem, 2825 Lexington Rd, Louisville, KY, 40280. **EMAIL** bmitchell@sbts.edu

MITCHELL, DONALD
DISCIPLINE ASIAN AND COMPARATIVE PHILOSOPHY OF RELIGION **EDUCATION** Univ Hawaii, PhD. **CAREER** Prof, Purdue Univ; assoc ed, Buddhist-Christian Stud. **RESEARCH** The Buddhist-Christian dialogue. **SELECTED PUBLICATIONS** Auth, Spirituality and Emptiness: The Dynamics of Spiritual Life in Buddhism and Christianity. **CONTACT ADDRESS** Dept of Philos, Purdue Univ, 1080 Schleman Hall, West Lafayette, IN, 47907-1080.

MITCHELL, JEFF
PERSONAL Born 03/03/1964, Lancaster, PA, m, 1995 **DISCIPLINE** PHILOSOPHY **EDUCATION** Whitman Col, BA, 86; Vanderbilt Univ, MA, 90, PhD, 93. **CAREER** Vis prof, philos, Miss State Univ, 93-94; asst prof, philos, Ark Tech Univ, 94-. **MEMBERSHIPS** Amer Philos Asn; Soc for the Advan of Amer Philos. **RESEARCH** Moral and philosophical psychology; Pragmatism; Value theory. **SELECTED PUBLICATIONS** Auth, Reason's Different Tastes, The Southern Jour of Philos, 96; auth, Danto, Dewey and the Historical End of Art, Transactions of the Charles S. Peirce Society, 89. **CONTACT ADDRESS** Social Sciences & Philosophy, Arkansas Tech Univ, WPN 255, Russellville, AR, 72801. **EMAIL** ssjm@atuvm.atu.edu

MITCHELL, SANDRA D.
DISCIPLINE PHILOSOPHY OF SCIENCE **EDUCATION** Univ Pittsburgh, PhD, 87. **CAREER** PROF, PHILOS, UNIV CALIF, SAN DIEGO. **RESEARCH** Epistemological and metaphysical issues in biology and the social sciences. **SELECTED PUBLICATIONS** Auth, "Competing Units of Selection?: A Case of Symbiosis," Philos of Sci, 54, 87; "The Units of Behavior in Evolutionary Explanations," Interpretation and Explanation in the Study of Animal Behavior, Westview Press, 90; "On Pluralism and Integration in Evolutionary Explanations," Amer Zoologist, 92; "Dispositions or Etiologies? A Comment on Bigelow and Pargetter," Jour Philos, 93; "Function, Fitness and Disposition," Biol and Philos, 95; co-auth, Self Organization and Adaptation in Insect Societies, PSA, 90, Volume Two, 91. **CONTACT ADDRESS** Dept of Philos, Univ Calif, San Diego, 9500 Gilman Dr, La Jolla, CA, 92093.

MITIAS, MICHAEL HANNA
PERSONAL Born 07/23/1939, Swaydieh, Syria, m, 1966, 3 children **DISCIPLINE** VALUE THEORY, METAPHYSICS **EDUCATION** Union Col, Ky, BA, 63; Univ Waterloo, PhD, 71. **CAREER** From instr to assoc prof philos, 67-73, distinguished prof, 71-72, Prof Philos, Millsaps Col, 73-. **RESEARCH** Aesthetics; social and political philosophy. **SELECTED PUBLICATIONS** Auth, Limits of the scientific method in the study of man, Proc 15th World Con Philos, fall 73; The Aesthetic Object: Critical Studies, Univ Press Am, 77; Another look at Hegel's concept of punishment, Hegel-Studies, 78; Law as the foundation of the state: Hegel, Interpretation, 82. **CONTACT ADDRESS** Dept of Philosophy, Millsaps Col, 1701 N State St, Jackson, MS, 39210-0001. **EMAIL** mitiamh@okra.millsaps.edu

MOBERLY, ROBERT B.
DISCIPLINE LAW **EDUCATION** Univ Wis, BS, JD. **CAREER** Trustee res fel, prof and dir, Inst Dispute Resolution, Univ Fla, 77-. **MEMBERSHIPS** Exec bd, Int Soc for Labor Law and Soc Sec, US Branch, 89-92; Fla Supreme Ct Comt on Mediation and Arbitratiabout 89-; Arbitration Panels for Railway Mediation bd, Amer Arbitration Asn, and Fed Mediation Conciliation Serv; Wis Bar; Tenn Bar; Fla Bar Fac Affe. **RESEARCH** Labor law, negotiation, mediation, collective bargaining & arbitration. **CONTACT ADDRESS** School of Law, Univ of Florida, PO Box 117625, Gainesville, FL, 32611-7625. **EMAIL** moberly@law.ufl.edu

MODICA, JOSEPH BENJAMIN
DISCIPLINE RELIGIOUS STUDIES **EDUCATION** Queens Col, City Univ New York, BA, 75; Alliance Theol Sem, MDiv, 86; MPhil, 91, PhD, 95, Drew Univ. **CAREER** Chaplain and Asst Prof, Biblical Studies, 93-, Eastern Col. **CONTACT ADDRESS** Eastern Col, 1300 Eagle Rd., St. Davids, PA, 19087-3696. **EMAIL** jmodica@eastern.edu

MOENSSENS, ANDRE A.
PERSONAL Born 01/13/1930, Hoboken, Belgium, m, 8 children **DISCIPLINE** LAW, CRIMINALISTICS **EDUCATION** Chicago-Kent Col Law of Ill Inst Technol, JD, 66; Northwestern Univ, LLM, 67. **CAREER** Head instr, Inst Appl Sci, 60-66; from instr to prof law, Chicago-Kent Col Law, 66-73, dir, Inst Criminal Justice, 67-71; Prof Law, Sch of Law, Univ Richmond, 73-95; chm, Law, W Va Univ, 93-95; emer prof law, Univ Richmond, 95- ; Doublas Stripp prof law and dir, Forensic Center Law, Med and Public Policy, Univ Mo, Kansas City, 96-. **HONORS AND AWARDS** Excellence in tchg awards, 73, 79, 84, 95; Harold A Feder Jurisp Award, AAFS, 98. **MEMBERSHIPS** Fel Am Acad Forensic Sci (secy-treas, 75-76); Am Trial Lawyers Asn; Int Assoc for Identification; Can Identification Soc; Am Soc Law, Med and Ethics; Va State Bar; Ill State Bar Assn; KCMO Bar Assn. **RESEARCH** Criminal justice; scientific evidence; criminalistics. **SELECTED PUBLICATIONS** Auth, Fingerprints and the Law , 69 & Fingerprint Techniques, 70, Chilton; coauth, Scientific Police Investigation, 72; coauth, Scientific Evidence in Civil and Criminal Cases, 73, 2nd ed 78, to 4th ed, 95; coauth, Cases on Criminal Law, 73, to 6th ed, 98; Cases on Criminal Procedure, Bobbs-Merrill, 2d ed, 87; Problems & Cases in Trial Advocacy, 81, to 5th ed, 95. **CONTACT ADDRESS** School of Law, Univ Mo, Kansas City, 5100 Rockhill Rd, Kansas City, MO, 64110-2499.

MOFFAT, ROBERT C.L.
DISCIPLINE LAW **EDUCATION** Southern Methodist Univ, BA, MA, LLB; Univ Sydney, Australia, LLM. **CAREER** Prof, aff prof Philos, Univ Fla, 66-. **HONORS AND AWARDS** Lon Fuller Prize in Jurisp, 87. **MEMBERSHIPS** Texas Bar; Law and Soc Asn; Amer Soc for Polit and Legal Philos. **RESEARCH** Jurisp, criminal law, law and society, law and public policy. **SELECTED PUBLICATIONS** Co-ed, Radical Critiques of the Law, Kans, 97. **CONTACT ADDRESS** School of Law, Univ of Florida, PO Box 117625, Gainesville, FL, 32611-7625. **EMAIL** moffat@law.ufl.edu

MOFFETT, SAMUEL HUGH
PERSONAL Born 04/07/1916, Pyongyang, Korea, m, 1942 **DISCIPLINE** HISTORY OF MISSIONS, ASIAN CHURCH HISTORY **EDUCATION** Wheaton Col, Ill, AB, 38; Princeton Theol Sem, ThB, 42; Yale Univ, PhD, 45. **CAREER** Lectr English & church hist, Yenching Univ, Peking, 48-49; asst prof church hist, Nanking Theol Sem, 49-50; vis lectr ecumenics, Princeton Theol Sem, 53-55; prof church hist, 60-81, dean Grad Sch, 66-70, assoc pres, 70-81, Presby Theol Sem, Seoul, Korea; pres, Asian Ctr Theol Studies & Mission, 74-81; prof missions & ecumenics, 81-87, Henry Winters Luce Prof of Ecumenics and Mission, emeritus, Princeton Theol Sem; bd dir, Yonsei Univ, Seoul, 57-81, Soongjun Univ, Seoul, 69-81 & Whitworth Col, Spokane, Wash, 73-79; mem, US Educ Comn, Korea, 66-67. **HONORS AND AWARDS** Order Civil Merit, Repub Korea, 81; DD, King Col, TN, 85; DD, Gordon Conwell Theol Sem, 95; DD, Presbyterian Col and Theol Sem, 96; hon PhD Soongsil Univ, SEoul, 97., LittD, Yonsei Univ, Seoul, Korea, 81. **MEMBERSHIPS** Am Soc Missiology; Int Asn Missiological Studies; Korean Church History Soc; Royal Asiatic Soc (pres, Korean Br, 68-69). **RESEARCH** Asian church history; history of missions; Korean studies. **SELECTED PUBLICATIONS** Coauth, First Encounters: Korea 1880-1910, Dragon's Eye Press, Seoul, 82; auth, History of Christianity in Asia, Beginnings to 1500, Harper Collins, 92. **CONTACT ADDRESS** 150 Leabrook Ln, Princeton, NJ, 08540.

MOHAN, ROBERT PAUL
PERSONAL Born 10/25/1920, Ashley, PA **DISCIPLINE** PHILOSOPHY **EDUCATION** Cath Univ, AB, 42, AM, 47, STL, 54. **CAREER** Instr English, St Mary's Sem, MD, 47-48; instr French & Latin, St Edward's Sem, Wash, 48-50; dean summer session & workshops, 60-72, univ marshal, 68, mem acad senate, prof Philos, Cath Univ Am, 50-, Assoc ed, Am Ecclesiastical Rev, 55; lectr ethics, sr sem, Dept of State, 80. **MEMBERSHIPS** Am Cath Philos Asn; Am Philos Asn. **RESEARCH** Social philosophy; a Thomistic philosophy of civilization and culture. **SELECTED PUBLICATIONS** Auth, Philosophy of History, McMillan- Crowell, 70. **CONTACT ADDRESS** Dept of Philos, Catholic Univ of America, Washington, DC, 20017. **EMAIL** mohan@cua.edu

MOHANTY, JITENDRA N.
DISCIPLINE PHENOMENOLOGY **EDUCATION** Univ Gottingen, PhD, 54; Univ Burdwan, DLitt, 88. **CAREER** Philos, Emory Univ. **HONORS AND AWARDS** Life Mem, Indian Acad Philos; Humboldt Prize, 92., Pres, Socy Asian & Comp Philos, 93-95; Vis fel, All Souls Col, Oxford, 82. **SELECTED PUBLICATIONS** Auth, Edmund Husserl's Theory of Meaning; Phenomenology and Ontology. **CONTACT ADDRESS** Emory Univ, Atlanta, GA, 30322-1950.

MOHLER, R. ALBERT, JR.
DISCIPLINE CHRISTIAN THEOLOGY **EDUCATION** Samford Univ, BA; S Baptist Theol Sem, MDiv, PhD. **CAREER** Prof, pres, S Baptist Theol Sem, 93-. **HONORS AND AWARDS** Listed, Time mag, fifty outstanding young leaders US, 94. **SELECTED PUBLICATIONS** Ed, Christian Index. **CONTACT ADDRESS** Christian Theol Dept, Southern Baptist Theol Sem, 2825 Lexington Rd, Louisville, KY, 40280. **EMAIL** mohler@sbts.edu

MOHR, RICHARD
DISCIPLINE PHILOSOPHY **EDUCATION** Univ Toronto, PhD, 77. **CAREER** Prof, Univ Ill Urbana Champaign. **RESEARCH** Ancient philosophy ; social philosophy; arts. **SELECTED PUBLICATIONS** Auth, The Platonic Cosmology, 85; Gays/Justice: A Study of Ethics, Society and Law, 88; Gay Ideas: Outing and Other Controversies, 92; A More Perfect Union: Why Straight Americans Must Stand Up For Gay Rights, 94. **CONTACT ADDRESS** Philosophy Dept, Univ Ill Urbana Champaign, 52 E Gregory Dr, Champaign, IL, 61820. **EMAIL** r-mohr@uiuc.edu

MOHRLANG, ROGER L.
PERSONAL Born 12/05/1941, Hastings, NB, m, 1976 **DISCIPLINE** THEOLOGY **EDUCATION** Carnegie Inst Tech, BS, 63; Fuller Theol Sem, MA, 76; Univ Oxford, D Phil, 80. **CAREER** Consul ling & Bible transl, 68-74, Wycliffe Bible Translators; prof, 78-, Whitworth Col. **RESEARCH** Pauline Theology, Bible transl. **SELECTED PUBLICATIONS** Auth, Matthew and Paul: a Comparison of Ethical Perspectives; Vece Yesu Kristi, The New Testament in the Kamwe language; rev ed, Melifyi Alekawale Yesu Kristi, The New Testament in the Kamwe language. **CONTACT ADDRESS** Whitworth Col, Spokane, WA, 99251. **EMAIL** rmohrlang@whitworth.edu

MOMEYER, RICK
DISCIPLINE BIOETHICS, ETHICS, POLITICAL PHILOSOPHY, JUSTICE AND HEALTH CARE **EDUCATION** Allegheny, BA; Univ Chicago, MA; Univ Wash, PhD. **CAREER** Dept Philos, Miami Univ **RESEARCH** Traditional and contemporary views on the value of life, both human and that of animals. **SELECTED PUBLICATIONS** Auth, Confronting Death, Ind UP, 88. **CONTACT ADDRESS** Dept of Philosophy, Miami Univ, Oxford, OH, 45056. **EMAIL** momeyerw@muohio.edu

MONAN, JAMES DONALD
PERSONAL Born 12/31/1924, Blasdell, NY **DISCIPLINE** PHILOSOPHY **EDUCATION** Woodstock Col, AB, 48, PHL, 49, STL, 56; Cath Univ Louvain, PhD(philos), 59. **CAREER** Instr philos, St Peter's Col, 49-52; from instr to assoc prof, Le Moyne Col, NY, 60-68, chemn dept, 61-68, acad den, 68-72; pres, 72-76, chancellor, Boston Col, 96-; Trustee, Fordham Univ, 69-75 & Boston Col, 72-96, Le Moyne Col, 61-69, 95-. **HONORS AND AWARDS** LHD, Le Moyne Col, 73, St. Joseph's Col, 73, New England School of Law, 75, Northeastern Univ, 75, Univ Mass, 84; LLD, Harvard Univ, 82, Loyola Univ Chicago, 87, Nat Univ Ireland, 91, Boston Col, 96, Univ Mass, 97., LHD, Le Moyne Col, 73. **MEMBERSHIPS** Metaphys Soc Am; Jesuit Philos Asn US & Can; Mass Historical Soc. **RESEARCH** Metaphysics; ethics; epistemology. **SELECTED PUBLICATIONS** Coauth, Philosophy of Human Knowing, Newman, 53; auth, La connaissance morale, Rev Philos de Louvain, 5/60; Moral knowledge in the Nicomachaen ethics, Aritotle et les Ptoblemes de Methode, 61; coauth, Prelude to Metaphysics, Prentice-Hall, 67; auth, Moral Knowledge and its Methodology in Aristotle, Clarendon Press, Oxford, 68. **CONTACT ADDRESS** Off of the Pres, Boston Col, 140 Commonwealth Ave, Chestnut Hill, MA, 02167-3800. **EMAIL** monan@bc.edu

MONASTERIO, XAVIER O.
DISCIPLINE EXISTENTIALISM **EDUCATION** Univ Paris, PhD, 64. **CAREER** Dept Philos, Univ Dayton **RESEARCH** Sartre and Camus; faith and reason. **SELECTED PUBLICATIONS** Auth, The Body in Being and Nothingness, Jean-Paul Sartre: Contemporary Approaches to His Philosophy, Duquesne UP, 80; On MacIntyre, Rationality, and Dramatic Space, Practical Reasoning: Proc Amer Cath Assn, 84; Sartre and the Existential Approach, Sartre and Existentialism, Garland Publ Co, 96. **CONTACT ADDRESS** Dept of Philos, Univ Dayton, 300 Col Park, Dayton, OH, 75062. **EMAIL** monaster@checkov.hm.udayton.edu

MONGOVEN, ANN
DISCIPLINE RELIGIOUS STUDIES **EDUCATION** Univ Va, PhD, 96. **CAREER** Asst prof. **RESEARCH** History of Christian ethics; methods in religious and philosophical ethics; comparative ethics. **SELECTED PUBLICATIONS** Auth, **CONTACT ADDRESS** Dept of Religious Studies, Indiana Univ, Bloomington, 300 N Jordan Ave, Bloomington, IN, 47405.

MONTGOMERY, JOHN E.
DISCIPLINE TORTS AND PRODUCTS LIABILITY **EDUCATION** Univ Louisville, BChE, 64, JD, 69; Univ MI, LLM, 71. **CAREER** Dean & prof, Univ of SC. **SELECTED PUBLICATIONS** Coauth, casebk on products liability law. **CONTACT ADDRESS** School of Law, Univ of S. Carolina, Law Center, Columbia, SC, 29208. **EMAIL** Johnm@law.law.sc.edu

MONTGOMERY, SHARON BURKE
PERSONAL Born 11/01/1937, Wilkes-Barre, PA **DISCIPLINE** PHILOSOPHY **EDUCATION** Univ Pa, BA, 59, MA, 62, PhD, 72. **CAREER** Inst philos, Ohio Univ, 64-65; asst prof, Fresno State Col, 67-69; teaching fel, Univ Pa, 69; actg chair & asst prof, Del State Col, 70-71; PROF PHILOS, IND UNIV PA, 71-, chmn, Dept Philos, 85-90. **HONORS AND AWARDS** Univ of Pa Scholarship, 55-59; NSF grant, Summer Ling Inst, 60; Woodrow Wilson Nat Fel, 60-62 **MEMBERSHIPS** Am Philos Asn **RESEARCH** Value theory; philosophy of language; logic; pragmatism **CONTACT ADDRESS** Dept of Philos, Indiana Univ of Pennsylvania, Indiana, PA, 15705-0001. **EMAIL** smonty@grove.iup.edu

MOODY, LINDA A.
DISCIPLINE SYSTEMATIC & PHILOSOPHICAL THEOLOGY; PHILOSOPHY OF RELIGION **EDUCATION** Univ Mich, AB, 75, AM, 76; S Baptist Theol Sem, MDiv, 80; Grad Theol Union, PhD, 93. **CAREER** Sr chaplain, Brookville Lake Min, 79-80; Dir Curric English Ctr Int Women, 81-89, Robert F. Leavens Col chaplain & lectr, women' studies dept, Mills Col, 85-. **HONORS AND AWARDS** Quigley Summer Fel Womens Studies, 96; Stephen Bufton Nat Scholar Am Bus & Prof Women, 88; Amer Asn Univ Women Res Proj Grant. **MEMBERSHIPS** Amer Acad Relig; Soc Bibl Lit; Nat Women's Studies Asn; Nat Asn Col-Univ Chaplins. **RESEARCH** 19th and 20th Century theology; Women's Studies and Religion **SELECTED PUBLICATIONS** Auth, Paul Tillich and Feminist Theology: Echoes From the Boundary, Papers From the Annual Meeting of the North American Paul Tillich Society, 93; Your People Will Be My People, Songs of Miriam: A Women's Book of Devotions, Judson Press, 94; Constructive Theological Understandings of God: Methodological and Epistemological Contributions of Sallie McFague, New Theology Review, 95; Mills--For Women Agin: The Role of Women's Spirituality in the Effort to Remain a Women's College, Nat Womens Studiess Asn Jour, 95; Women Encounter God: Theology Across the Boundaries of Difference, Orbis Books, 96; Ties That Bind: A Response to Maria Archuleta's Review of Women Encounter God, Ctr for Women and Relig Mem Newsl, Grad Theol Union, 97; Designing A Mentoring Program for Students Interested in Graduate Studies in Religion, Women's Caucus--Religious Studies, 97; Priests, Pastors, Prophets, Preachers, and Professors of Religions: Women in Ecclesia and Academia, Jour Women and Relig, 98. **CONTACT ADDRESS** Mills Col, 5000 MacArthur Blvd, Oakland, CA, 94613.

MOOR, JAMES H.
DISCIPLINE PHILOSOPHY **EDUCATION** IN Univ, PhD. **CAREER** Prof, Dartmouth Col. **MEMBERSHIPS** Soc Machines and Mentality. **RESEARCH** Logic, philos of artificial intelligence, philos of mind, and computer ethics. **SELECTED PUBLICATIONS** Auth, Towards a Theory of Privacy for the Information Age, Comput & Soc, 97; The Logic Book, 3rd ed, McGraw-Hill, 98; Reason, Relativity, and Responsibility in Computer Ethics, Comput & Soc, 98; co-ed, The Digital Phoenix: How Computers Are Changing Philosophy Basil Blackwell, 98. **CONTACT ADDRESS** Dartmouth Col, 6035 Thornton, Hanover, NH, 03755-3592. **EMAIL** James.H.Moor@Dartmouth.edu

MOORE, BROOKE N.
PERSONAL Born 02/12/1943, Palo Alto, CA, m, 1970, 2 children **DISCIPLINE** PHILOSOPHY **EDUCATION** Antioch, BA, 66; Univ Cinn, PhD, 71. **CAREER** Asst prof, 70-74, assoc prof, 74-79, PROF, 80- , Calif State Univ Chico. **HONORS AND AWARDS** Master Tchr, 96-98; Outstanding prof, 97. **MEMBERSHIPS** Am Philos Asn; editl bd Teaching Philosophy. **RESEARCH** Critical thinking; epistemology **SELECTED PUBLICATIONS** Auth, Philosophical Possibilities Beyond Death, 81; coauth Critical Thinking, 87; The Power of Ideas, 90; The Cosmos, God and Philosophy, 92; Moral Philosophy, 93; The Power of Ideas: A Brief Edition, 95; Making Your Case, 95. **CONTACT ADDRESS** Dept of Philosophy, California State Univ, Chico, Chico, CA, 95929. **EMAIL** bmoore@csuchico.edu

MOORE, CECILIA
PERSONAL Born 01/18/1966, Danville, VA, s **DISCIPLINE** RELIGIOUS STUDIES **EDUCATION** Sweet Briar Col, AB, 88; Univ VA, MA, 91, PhD, 97. **CAREER** ASST PROF RELIG STUDIES, UNIV DAYTON, 96-. **HONORS AND AWARDS** Phi Beta Kappa; Anne Gary Punell Scholar; State Council of Higher Education in VA Scholar; Fund for Theological Education Scholar. **MEMBERSHIPS** Amer Academy Relig; Amer Cath Hist Assoc; Soc Church Hist; Black Cath Theological Symposium. **RESEARCH** Amer rel hist; US Cath hist; African Amer Cath hist. **CONTACT ADDRESS** 2615 Shroyer Rd., #4, Dayton, OH, 45419. **EMAIL** moore@chekov.hm.udayton.edu

MOORE, FRED HENDERSON
PERSONAL Born 07/25/1934, Charleston County, SC, m **DISCIPLINE** LAW **EDUCATION** SC State Coll 1952-56; Roosevelt Univ Chicago 1956; Allen U, BS 1956-57; Howard Episcopal, JD 1957-60; Teamers Sch of Religion, DD 1976; Stephens Christian Inst 1976; Reform Episcapal Seminary. **CAREER** Atty self-employed 1977. **HONORS AND AWARDS** Youth award NAACP 1957; memorial award Charles Drew 1957; Youth March for Integrated Schs 1958; stud body pres SC State Coll. **MEMBERSHIPS** Corp cncl NAACP 1960; mem Black Rep Party; mem Silver Elephant Club; 1st Dist Coun SC Conf of NAACP; asso pstr Payne RMUE Ch; asso cncl NC Mutual Ins Co; Mem Omega Psi Phy Frat. **SELECTED PUBLICATIONS** Co-auth, "Angry Black South" 1960. **CONTACT ADDRESS** 39 Spring St, Charleston, SC, 29403.

MOORE, JOSEPH G.
PERSONAL Born 10/03/1963, Boston, MA, s **DISCIPLINE** PHILOSOPHY **EDUCATION** Cornell Univ, PhD, 94. **CAREER** Asst Prof, 93-, Amherst Col. **MEMBERSHIPS** APA **RESEARCH** Philosophy of mind; philosophy of language; metaphysics; environmental ethics. **CONTACT ADDRESS** Amherst Col, Philosophy, PO Box 5000, Amherst, MA, 01002-5000. **EMAIL** jgmoore@amherst.edu

MOORE, KATHLEEN DEAN
PERSONAL Born 07/06/1947, Cleveland, OH, m, 1968, 2 children **DISCIPLINE** PHILOSOPHY **EDUCATION** Col Wooster, Oh, BA, 69; Univ Co, MA, 72, PhD, 77. **CAREER** Prof, chair, 92-, Or St Univ. **HONORS AND AWARDS** Prof of Term Award, 86; Thomas L Meehan Excellence in Teaching Award, 88; Faculty Teaching Excellence Award, 89; Pan-Hellenic All-Univ Outstanding Faculty Award, 90; Col Liberal Arts Excellence Award, 91; Phi Kappa Phi Honorary, 95; Pacific NW Booksellers Assoc Book Award, 96. **RESEARCH** Philos & nature; nature writing; critical thinking. **SELECTED PUBLICATIONS** Auth, Pardons: Justice, Mercy, and the Public Interest, Oxford Univ Press, 89; auth, Reasoning and Writing, Macmillan, 93; auth, Riverwalking: Reflections on Moving Water, Lyons & Burford, 95; auth, Holdfast: At Home in the Natural World, Lyons Press, 99; coauth, Writing Philosophy Papers: A Student Guide, Kendall/Hunt, 97. **CONTACT ADDRESS** Dept of Philosophy, Oregon State Univ, Corvallis, OR, 97331. **EMAIL** kmoore@arst.edu

MOORE, MARGARET
DISCIPLINE PHILOSOPHY **EDUCATION** London Sch Econ, Polit Sci, PhD, 89. **RESEARCH** Contemporary political philos; liberal-communitarian debate; philos of nationalism; ethics of secession; citizenship in diverse societies. **SELECTED PUBLICATIONS** Auth, Foundations of Liberalism, Oxford, 93; ed, National Self-Determination and Secession, Oxford, 98. **CONTACT ADDRESS** Dept of Philosophy, Waterloo Univ, 200 University Ave W, Waterloo, ON, N2L 3G1. **EMAIL** mrmoore@uwaterloo.ca

MOORE, MAX
PERSONAL Born 01/29/1964, Bristol, England, m, 1996 **DISCIPLINE** PHILOSOPHY, POLITICS AND ECONOMICS **EDUCATION** St. Anne's Col, Oxford Univ, BA, 84-87; Univ Southern Calif, PhD, philos, 95. **CAREER** Pres, Extropy Inst, 91-. **RESEARCH** The consequences & implications of advanced technologies. **SELECTED PUBLICATIONS** Auth, Beyond the Machine: Technology and Posthuman Freedom, Proceedings of the Fleshfactor symposium of Ars Electronica, 97; auth, Virtue and Virtuality: From Enhanced Reality to Experience Machines, Proceedings from Sense of the Senses conference, 97; auth, Ways and Memes, Rage, 97; auth, Thinking About Thinking, Wired, 96; auth, Is God a Computer Nerd?, Rage, 96; auth, Live Freely, Live Longer, The Freeman: Ideas on Liberty, 95; auth, On Becoming Posthuman, Free Inquiry, 94; auth, Extropy: Death and Taxes Must Go, Calif Liberty, 94. **CONTACT ADDRESS** 13428 Maxella Ave,, #273, Marina del Rey, CA, 90292. **EMAIL** max@maxmore.com

MOORE, RICKIE D.
PERSONAL Born 10/08/1953, Sikeston, MD, m, 1976, 2 children **DISCIPLINE** THEOLOGY **EDUCATION** Lee Col, BA, 76; Vanderbilt Univ, MA, 81, PhD, 88. **CAREER** Ed, Lee Col, 73-76; Old Testament Bibliographer, Vanderbilt Divinity Libry, 80-82; prof, Church of God Theolog Sem, 82-. **HONORS AND AWARDS** Asn Theolog Sch Grant, 92-93., Lee Col Dept Award, Rel, 76; Vanderbilt Univ Tchg Assistantship, 79-80. **MEMBERSHIPS** Soc Biblical Lit; Soc Pentecostal Stud. **RESEARCH** Old Testament Prophets. **SELECTED PUBLICATIONS** Auth, Didactic Salvation Stories in the Elisha Cycle: An Analysis of 2 Kings 5; 6:8-23: and 6:24-7:20, 88; auth, God Saves: Lessons from the Elisha Stories, 90; auth, art, Deuteronomy and the Fire of God, 95; auth, art, And Also Much Cattle?!': Prophetic Passions and the End of Jonah, 97; auth, art, Futile Labor Vs Fertile Labor: Observing the Sabbath in Psalm 127, 98. **CONTACT ADDRESS** Church of God Sch of Theol, 900 Walker St NE, Cleveland, TN, 37311. **EMAIL** rdmoore777@aol.com

MOORE, RONALD
PERSONAL Born 05/04/1943, Framingham, MA, m, 1968 **DISCIPLINE** PHILOSOPHY **EDUCATION** Stanford Univ, AB, 64; Columbia Univ, PhD, 71. **CAREER** Preceptor, Columbia Col, Columbia Univ, 66-68; asst prof to assoc prof, Univ Hawaii, 69-79; assoc prof, Univ Wash, 79- ; Dir, Univ Wash Ctr for Hum, 87-94; **HONORS AND AWARDS** Phi Beta Kappa; Harvard Lib Arts fel Law & Philos, Univ Wash Distinguished Tchg Award; Charles E Odegaard Award. **MEMBERSHIPS** Am Philos Asn; Am Asn Univ Prof; Am Soc Aesthet; Am Soc Polit & Legal Philos; Int Soc Philos Law. **RESEARCH** Philosophy of law; aesthetics and philosophy of art. **SELECTED PUBLICATIONS** Auth, Kelsens Puzzling Descriptive Ought, UCLA Law Rev, 73; The Deontic Status of Legal Norms, Ethics, 73; Legal Norms and Legal Science, Univ Press Hawaii, 78; Puzzles About Art: A Casebook in Aesthetics, St Martin's Press, 89; The Aesthetic and the Moral, Jour of Aesthet Education, 95; ed Aesthetics for Young People, Nat Aret Education Asn, 95; auth, The Nightmare Science and its Daytime Uses, Jour of Aesthet Education, 96; Ugliness, Moral Rights of Art, History of Aesthetic Education, Encyclo Aesthet, Oxford Univ Press, 98. **CONTACT ADDRESS** Dept of Philosophy, Univ Wash, Box 353350, Seattle, WA, 98195-3350. **EMAIL** ronmoore@u.washington.edu

MOORE, T.J.
PERSONAL Born 12/11/1959, Bristol, PA **DISCIPLINE** RELIGION **EDUCATION** Millerville Univ BA 81; Univ North Carolina PhD 86. **CAREER** Univ Texas, assoc and assist prof 91 to 98-; Texas A M Univ, asst prof 86 to 91. **HONORS AND AWARDS** Mellon Fel Harvard; Rome Prize Fel 98 **MEMBERSHIPS** APA; AIA; ACC; TCA; Classical Assoc Middle West and South **RESEARCH** Roman comedy and historiography. **SELECTED PUBLICATIONS** Auth, The Theater of Plautus: Playing to the Audience, Univ TX 98; Music and Structure in Roman Comedy, Amer Jour of Philology 98; Seats and Social Status in the Plautine Theater, Class Jour 94; Morality, History and Livy's Wronged Woman, Eranos 93; reviews, A Latin Course for Colleges Based on Ancient Authors, Texas Classics in Action, Kathryn Argetsinger, 98. **CONTACT ADDRESS** Dept of Classics, Texas Univ, Austin, TX, 78712-1101.

MOORE, TERRENCE L.
PERSONAL Born 04/27/1950, Hanover, PA, m, 1973, 2 children **DISCIPLINE** PHILOSOPHY **EDUCATION** Univ Pittsburgh, PhD, 87. **CAREER** USAF Acad, 81-96; Univ Colo, Colo Springs, 96-. **HONORS AND AWARDS** Fel, Harvard Ctr for Ethics and the Professions, 91-92. **MEMBERSHIPS** APA. **RESEARCH** Ethics; philosophy of religion; political theory. **CONTACT ADDRESS** Dept of Philosophy, Univ of Colorado, PO Box 7150, Colorado Springs, CO, 80930. **EMAIL** tmoore@brain.uccs.edu

MOORHEAD, JAMES HOWELL
PERSONAL Born 01/16/1947, Harrisburg, PA, m, 1969, 2 children **DISCIPLINE** AMERICAN RELIGIOUS HISTORY **EDUCATION** Westminster Col, PA, BA, 68; Princeton Theol Sem, MDiv, 71; Yale Univ, MPhil, 73, PhD(relig studies), 75. **CAREER** Asst prof, 75-80, Assoc Prof Relig, NC State Univ, 80-, Fel independent study & res, Nat Endowment for Humanities, 81-82. **HONORS AND AWARDS** Brewer Prize, Am Soc Church Hist, 76. **MEMBERSHIPS** Am Soc Church Hist; Am Acad Relig; Am Hist Asn. **RESEARCH** Nineteenth century and early twentieth century American Protestantism; Millennialism; views of death and after life. **SELECTED PUBLICATIONS** Auth, Joseph Addison Alexander: Common sense, romanticism and Biblical criticism at Princeton, J Presbyterian Hist, spring 75; American Apocalypse: Yankee Protestants and the Civil War, 1860-1869, Yale Univ Press, 78; Social reform and the divided conscience of antebellum Protestantism, Church Hist, 79; Softly And Tenderly Jesus Is Calling - Heaven And Hell In American Revivalism, 1870-1920 - Butler,Jm, Church History, Vol 0062, 1993; Glorious Contentment - The Grand Army Of The Republic, 1865-1900 - Mcconnell,S, J Of American History, Vol 0080, 1993; A Field Of Divine Wonders - The New-Divinity And Village Revivals In Northwestern Connecticut, 1792-1822 - Kling,Dw, Theology Today, Vol 0051, 1994; A Friend To Gods Poor - Smith,Edward,Parmalee - Armstrong,Wh, J Of American History, Vol 0081, 1995; Church People In The Struggle - The National- Council-Of-Churches And The Black-Freedom Movement, 1950-1970 - Findlay,JF, J Of Interdisciplinary History, Vol 0026, 95; Peddler In Divinity - Whitefield, George And The Transatlantic-Revivals, 1737-1770 - Lambert,F, Theology Today, Vol 0051, 1995; Arguing The Apocalypse - A Theory Of Millennial Rhetoric - Oleary,Sd, Theology Today, Vol 0051, 1994; No Sorrow Like Our Sorrow Northern Protestant Ministers And The Assassination Of Lincoln - Chesebrough,Db, American Historical Review, Vol 0100, 1995; auth, Consumer Rites - The Buying And Selling Of American Holidays - Schmidt,LE, Theology Today, Vol 0053, 1996; The Myth Of American Individualism - The Protestant Origins Of American Political-Thought - Shain,BA, J Of Religion, Vol 0076, 1996; Our Southern Zion - A History Of Calvinism In The South-Carolina Low Country, 1690-1990 - Clarke,E, J Of Presbyterian History, Vol 0075, 1997; Law And Providence In Bellamy, Joseph New-England - Valeri,M, American Presbyterians-J Of Presbyterian History, Vol 0074, 1996; Spreading The Word - The Bible Business In 19th- Century America - Wosh,PJ, American Presbyterians, J Of Presbyterian History, Vol 0074, 1996. **CONTACT ADDRESS** Dept of Philos & Relig, No Carolina State Univ, PO Box 5688, Raleigh, NC, 27650.

MORALES, MARIA H.
DISCIPLINE PHILOSOPHY **EDUCATION** Univ Md, BA, 87; Univ Pa, PhD, 92. **CAREER** Assoc prof. **MEMBERSHIPS** Am Philos Asn; Soc Women Philos; Fla Philos Asn. **RESEARCH** Political and social philosophy; philosophy of law; ethics; competence in ancient philosophy and feminism. **SELECTED PUBLICATIONS** Auth, Perfect Equality (rev), Rowman & Littlefield, 96; The Corrupting Influence of Power, Rodopi, 96; pubs on Jeremy Bentham, Thomas Hobbes, and John Stuart Mill. **CONTACT ADDRESS** Dept of Philosophy, Florida State Univ, 211 Wescott Bldg, Tallahassee, FL, 32306. **EMAIL** mmorales@garnet.acns.fsu.edu

MORAN, GERALD P.
DISCIPLINE LAW **EDUCATION** Univ Scranton, BS; Cath Univ Am, JD; George Wash Univ, LLM. **CAREER** Prof. **SELECTED PUBLICATIONS** Auth, A Radical Theory of Jurisprudence: The 'Decisionmaker' as the Source of Law, Akron Law Rev, 96; Tax Amnesty: An Old Debate as Viewed From Current Public Choices, Univ Fla Tax Law Rev, 93; co-auth, Ohio Joins With Other Jurisdictions in the Adoption of Spousal Election of UPC, Toledo Transcript, 97; The Rule Against Perpetuity: The Case for Exemption of Trusts or the Repeal of the Rule, Law J, 95. **CONTACT ADDRESS** Col Law, Univ of Toledo, Toledo, OH, 43606. **EMAIL** gmoran@pop3.utoledo.edu

MORAN, JON S.
PERSONAL Born 11/21/1941, Rock Island, IL, m, 1965, 3 children **DISCIPLINE** PHILOSOPHY **EDUCATION** St Louis Univ, BS, 63; Tulane Univ, PhD, 72. **CAREER** Asst prof, St Ambrose Coll, 68-73; prof, Southwest MO State Univ, 73-. **HONORS AND AWARDS** Woodrow Willion Fel, 63. **MEMBERSHIPS** Am Philos Soc; Soc of Christain Philos. **RESEARCH** Philosophy of Religion; American Philosophy. **SELECTED PUBLICATIONS** Auth, Mead on the Self and Moral Situations, Tulane Studies in Philos, 73; divine Commands and Moral Autonomy, Philos In Context: Moral Truth, 86; Mead, Gadamer, and Hermeneutics, Frontiers in Am Philos, 92; Bergsonian Sources of Mead's Philosophy, Transactions of the Charles S Peirce Soc, 96. **CONTACT ADDRESS** Dept of Philosophy, Southwest Mo State Univ, Springfield, MO, 65804-0094. **EMAIL** jsm174f@mail.smsu.edu

MORAN, RICHARD
DISCIPLINE PHILOSOPHY **EDUCATION** Cornell, PhD, 89. **CAREER** Prof; Harvard Univ, 95-; taught at, Princeton. **RESEARCH** Philosophy of mind and moral psychology; aesthetics and the philosophy of literature; Wittgenstein. **SELECTED PUBLICATIONS** Publ on, metaphor, imagination and emotional engagement with art & nature of self-knowledge. **CONTACT ADDRESS** Dept of Philosophy, Harvard Univ, 8 Garden St, Cambridge, MA, 02138. **EMAIL** moran@fas.harvard.edu

MORAN, ROBERT E., SR.
PERSONAL Born 07/24/1921, Columbus, OH, m **DISCIPLINE** THEOLOGY **EDUCATION** Ohio State Univ, BS 1944; Ohio State Univ, MA 1947; Ohio State Univ, PhD 1968; Harvard Summer School, Certificate 1971. **CAREER** Palmer Memrl Inst, teacher 1944-46; Xenia E High, teacher 1947; Allen Univ, teacher dir student teaching 1948-59; Southern Univ, prof dean 1959-87; Southern Univ, dean coll of arts & humanities, retired; Bethel AME Church, asst pastor, 1989-. **HONORS AND AWARDS** One Hundred Yrs of Child Welfare in LA 1980. **MEMBERSHIPS** Historian Assn of Soc & Behavrl Science 1981; edtr br jrnl of Negro history Assn for the Study of Negro Life & History 1982-; Omega Psi Phi Frat.

MORAVCSIK, JULIUS M.
DISCIPLINE PHILOSOPHY **EDUCATION** BA, 53; Harvard Univ, PhD, 59. **CAREER** Prof, Stanford Univ. **RESEARCH** Pre-Socratics; Plato; Aristotle. **SELECTED PUBLICATIONS** Auth, Forms, Nature and the Good in the Philebus, Phronesis, 79; Plato and Platonism, 92; The Philosophic Background of Aristotle's AITIA, 95; ed/contrib, Plato's Theory of Art and Beauty, 81. **CONTACT ADDRESS** Stanford Univ, Bldg 20, Main Quad, Stanford, CA, 94305.

MORELAND, RAYMOND T., JR.
PERSONAL Born 03/12/1944, Baltimore, MD, m, 1980 **DISCIPLINE** PASTORAL THEOLOGY AND PSYCHOLOGY **EDUCATION** Randolph-Macon Col, BA, 66; Wesley Theological Sem, M Div, 70, D Min, 73; St Mary's Sem & Univ-Ecumenical Inst, MA, 91; Graduate Theol Found, PhD, 97. **CAREER** Pastor for 29 years in MD and WV; taught course of study at Wesley Theol Sem for 3 years; Academic Policy Committee, Ecumenical Inst of Theol, St Mary's Sem and Univ; currently exec dir, MD Bible Soc. **HONORS AND AWARDS** Who's Who in Am Colleges and Universities; Nat Preaching fel, 71. **MEMBERSHIPS** AAR; Soc of Biblical Lit; Academy

of Parish Clergyman; Alban Inst, AGO; Asn for Relig and Intellectual Life. **RESEARCH** Carl Jung's influence on Biblical hermeneutics; the thinking of Joseph Campbell on myth and the Bible. **SELECTED PUBLICATIONS** Auth, thesis abstract on The Beloved Journay-Psychospiritual Study of Persons Living, Struggling and Dying of HIV-AIDS-Sharing the Practice, J of the Academy of Parish Clegy; several book reviews for the Academy. **CONTACT ADDRESS** 9731 Hall Rd, Frederick, MD, 21701-6736. **EMAIL** mdbibles@erols.com (MD Bible Soc); agape@erols.com

MORELLI, MARIO FRANK
PERSONAL Born 02/03/1945, Poughkeepsie, NY, m, 1966, 3 children **DISCIPLINE** PHILOSOPHY **EDUCATION** Johns Hopkins Univ, BA, 66; Wash Univ, MA, 68, PhD(philos), 71. **CAREER** Instr philos, Univ Mo-St Louis, 68-70 & Kent State Univ, 70-72; from Asst Prof to Assoc Prof, 72-83, Prof Philos, Western Ill Univ, 83-. **MEMBERSHIPS** Am Philos Asn;. **RESEARCH** Moral philosophy; social philosophy; philosophy of law. **SELECTED PUBLICATIONS** Coauth, Beyond Wittgensteinian fideism: An examination of John Hick's Analysis of Religious Faith, Int J Philos Relig, Vol VIII, No 4, 77; Stanley Milgram and the obedience experiment: Authority, legitimacy, and human action, Polit Theory, Vol 7, No 3, 8/79; auth, The constitutional right of privacy: Autonomy and intrusion, In: Values in the law: Proceedings of the Fourteenth Conference on Value Inquiry, State Univ NY, Geneseo, 80; coauth, Inner Judgements and Blame, Southern J Philos, Fall 82; auth, Milgram's Dilemna of Obedience, Metaphilosophy, 85; coauth, Obedience to Authority in a Laboratory Setting: Generalizability and Context Dependency, Polit Studies, 85; auth, Eduction as a Right, In: Communitarianism, Liberalism, and Social Rsponsibility, Mellen Press, 91; Equal Educational Opportunity: Rodriguez Revisited, In: The Bill of Rights: Bicentennial Reflections, Mellen Press, 93; Race-Conscious Admissions and Individual Treatment, In: Rending and Renewing the Social Order, Mellen Press, 96. **CONTACT ADDRESS** Dept of Philosophy, Western Illinois Univ, 1 University Cir, Macomb, IL, 61455-1390. **EMAIL** mario-morelli@ccmail.wiu.edu

MOREY, ANN-JANINE
PERSONAL Born 10/31/1951, Atlanta, GA, m, 1986, 2 children **DISCIPLINE** RELIGION, ETHICS **EDUCATION** Grinnell Coll, BA, 73; USC, PhD, Relig & Ethics, 79. **CAREER** Asst/assoc prof, Southern Ill Univ-Carbondale, Relig Stud, 79-89; assoc prof, SIUC, Eng, 89-93; dir, SIUC, Univ Core Curric, 93-; PROF, SIUC, ENG, 93-. **MEMBERSHIPS** MLA; ALA; Am Relig & Lit Soc; AAR **RESEARCH** Religion & Literature **SELECTED PUBLICATIONS** Religion and Sexuality in American Literature, Cambridge UP, 92; "In Memory of Cassie: Child Death and Religious Vision in American Women's Novels," Religion and American Culture, 96; "Margaret Atwood and Toni Morrison: Reflections on Postmodernism and the Study of Religion and Literature," The Fiction of Toni Morrison, Garland Publ, 96; "The Literary Physician," In Good Company: Essays in Honor of Robert Detweiler, 94, "Naked Ladies," Spelunker Flophouse, 97; "Balancing the Blame: Mother Images in Margaret Deland's The Iron Woman," National Women's Studies Association Jour, 98; What Happened to Christopher. An American Family's Story of Shaken Baby Syndrome, SIU Press, 98. **CONTACT ADDRESS** Dept Eng, Southern Ill Univ, Carbondale, IL, 62901-4503. **EMAIL** ajmorey@siu.edu

MORGAN, CHARLES G.
DISCIPLINE PHILOSOPHY **EDUCATION** Univ Memphis St, BS; Johns Hopkins Univ, MA, PhD; Alta Univ, MSc; Univ Victoria, MSc. **CAREER** Instr, Univ Alberta; prof, 75. **RESEARCH** Philosophy of science and logic. **SELECTED PUBLICATIONS** Pub(s), Jour Symbolic Logic; Philos of Sci; Zeitschrift fur Mathematische Logik; Artificial Intelligence. **CONTACT ADDRESS** Dept of Philosophy, Victoria Univ, PO Box 3045, Victoria, BC, V8W 3P4. **EMAIL** morgan@phastf.phys.uvic.ca

MORGAN, DONN F.
DISCIPLINE OLD TESTAMENT **EDUCATION** Oberlin Col, AB; Yale Divinity Sch, BD; Claremont Grad Sch, MA, PhD. **CAREER** Pres; dean, Church Divinity Sch Pacific. **SELECTED PUBLICATIONS** Auth, How to Make the Bible User-Friendly: Challenges for Contemporary Teachers, Rel Edu Jour Hong Kong, 97; Searching for Biblical Wisdom: Recent Studies and their Pertinence for Contemporary Ministry, Sewanee Theol Rev, 94; Religious Educators: Professionals or Sages?, Rel Edu Jour Hong Kong, 93; Between Text and Community: The 'Writings' in Canonical Context, Augsburg-Fortress, 90; Wisdom in the Old Testament Traditions, John Knox, 81. **CONTACT ADDRESS** Church Divinity Sch of the Pacific, 2451 Ridge Rd, Berkeley, CA, 94709-1217.

MORGAN, EDWARD M.
DISCIPLINE LAW **EDUCATION** Northwestern Univ, BA, 76; Univ Toronto, LLB, 84; Harvard Univ, LLM, 86. **CAREER** Law clerk, Madame Justice Bertha Wilson, Supreme Court Can, 84-85; prof. **RESEARCH** Corporate/commercial litigation; constitutional law; human rights; professional discipline defence work; conflict of laws and international litigation. **SELECTED PUBLICATIONS** Auth, International Law and the Canadian Courts, Carswell, 90; pubs on current legal issues. **CONTACT ADDRESS** Fac of Law, Univ Toronto, 78 Queen's Park, Toronto, ON.

MORGAN, GERALD
PERSONAL Born 05/08/1925, London, England, m, 1957, 2 children **DISCIPLINE** ENGLISH, PHILOSOPHY **EDUCATION** Loyola Col, Que, BA, 51; Univ Montreal, MA, 55, MA, 59, PhD(English), 62. **CAREER** Lectr lit & lang, Royal Mil Col, Que, 55-57, lectr lang & philos, 57-60, asst prof, 60-63, prof & head dept, 63-65; Prof Lit & Philos & Head Dept, Royal Roads Mil Col, Victoria, 65-, Mem exec comt, Humanities Res Coun Can, 70-72; Can Coun leave fel, 71-72; fel, Can Int Acad Humanities & Soc Sci, 74-. **MEMBERSHIPS** Humanities Asn Can (pres, 69-71); Can Asn Slavists; Mod Humanities Res Asn; Int Asn Univ Prof English. **RESEARCH** Conrad and maritime history; analogy versus metaphor in literature and science; Aristotle and general systems theory. **SELECTED PUBLICATIONS** Auth Conrad, Madach et Calderon, Etudes Slaves et Est- Europeennes, spring 61; Narcissus afloat: Myth and symbol in Conrad, autumn 64 & Harlequin Faustus: Marlowe's comedy of hell, spring 67, Humanities Asn Bull; coauth, Of Several Branches, Part III, Univ Toronto, 68; auth, Soundings: An Introduction to Philosophy, Queen's Printer, 76; co-ed, Critical Edition of The Nigger of the Narcissus, Norton, 79; ed, The Franklins Tale from Canterbury Tales, Homes & Meier, 81; Dowries For Daughters In West Wales, 1500-1700, Welsh History Review, Vol 0017, 95. **CONTACT ADDRESS** Dept of English, Royal Roads Mil Col, Victoria, BC, V0S 1B0.

MORGAN, MARTHA
DISCIPLINE LAW **EDUCATION** Univ Ala, BS, 72; George Washington Univ, JD, 77. **CAREER** Prof, Univ Ala, 79-. **MEMBERSHIPS** Order of the Coif; Bd, ACLU; bd, ACLU Ala; bd, Equal Justice Initiative of Ala. **RESEARCH** Constitutional law, civil rights legislation, and seminars on legal education and comparative constitutional law. **CONTACT ADDRESS** Law Dept, Univ of Alabama, Box 870000, Tuscaloosa, AL, 35487-0383. **EMAIL** mmorgan@law.ua.edu

MORICK, HAROLD
DISCIPLINE PHILOSOPHY **EDUCATION** Columbia Univ, PhD. **CAREER** Assoc prof, Univ Albany, State Univ NY **RESEARCH** Philosophy of the mind. **SELECTED PUBLICATIONS** Ed, Intr to the Philos of Mind. **CONTACT ADDRESS** Dept of Philosophy, Univ at Albany, SUNY, Albany, NY, 12222. **EMAIL** vanderluyd@aol.com

MORRAY JONES, CHRISTOPHER R.A.
PERSONAL Born 02/03/1952, Solihull, United Kingdom, m, 1993, 2 children **DISCIPLINE** RELIGIOUS STUDIES **EDUCATION** Univ of Manchester, BA, 80; Cambridge Univ, PhD, 88 **CAREER** Res Fel, 89-92, Gordon Milburn; Visit Sch, 92-94, Stanford Univ; Lect, 94-pres, Univ of CA **MEMBERSHIPS** Am Acad of Relig; Soc of Bibl Lit; Assoc for Jewish Stud **RESEARCH** Jewish Mysticism; Christian Origins; Comparative Mysticism **SELECTED PUBLICATIONS** Auth, The Temple Within-The Embodied Divine Image and its Worship in the Dead Sea Scrolls and Other Jewish and Christian Sources, Scholars Press, 98; Auth, Paradise Revisited-The Jewish Mystical Background of Paul's Apostolate, 93, 265-292 **CONTACT ADDRESS** 2625 Ridge Rd, Berkeley, CA, 94709. **EMAIL** cmorjon@uclink4.berkeley.edu

MORRILL, BRUCE T.
PERSONAL Born 06/02/1959, Bangor, ME, s **DISCIPLINE** THEOLOGY **EDUCATION** Emory Univ, PhD, 96. **CAREER** Asst Prof Theol, Boston Col, 96-. **HONORS AND AWARDS** Phi Beta Kappa **MEMBERSHIPS** Am Acad Relig; Cath Theol Soc Am; Col Theol Soc; NAm Acad Relig. **RESEARCH** Liturgical and sacramental theology. **SELECTED PUBLICATIONS** Co-ed, The Struggle for Tradition, Liturgy and the Moral Self: Humanity at Full Stretch Before God, Liturgical Press, 98. **CONTACT ADDRESS** IREPM, Boston Col, 31 Lawrence Ave., Chestnut Hill, MA, 02467-3931. **EMAIL** morrilb@bc.edu

MORRIS, CALVIN S.
PERSONAL Born 03/16/1941, Philadelphia, PA **DISCIPLINE** THEOLOGY **EDUCATION** Friends Select Schl, Philadelphia, PA, Diploma 1959; Lincoln Univ, AB, Amer Hist 1963; Boston Univ, AM, Amer Hist 1964; Boston Univ Schl of Theology, STB 1967; Boston Univ, PhD, Amer Hist 1982. **CAREER** SCLC Operation Breadbasket, assoc dir 1967-71; Simmons Coll, dir Afro-Amer Studies/Simmons Coll 1971-73; Urban Devel, Michigan State Univ, visitng lecturer 1973-76; Martin Luther King, Jr Ctr for Social Change, exec dir 1973-76; Howard Univ Divinity Schl, asst prof practical theology & dir min in church & soc 1976-82; Howard Univ Divinity Schl, assoc prof pastoral theology & dir Urban Ministries 1982-. **HONORS AND AWARDS** Distinguished Alumni Award, Friends Select HS 1974; Jr Chamber of Comm Award One of Chicago's Ten Outstanding Young Men 1970; Crusade Schlr United Methodist Church 1963-66; Rockefeller Protestant Fellow 1964-65; Whitney Young Fellow 1971-72; Grad Fellowship for Black Amer, The Natl Fellowship Fund 1979-80; Black Doctoral Dis The Fund for Theological Ed 1979-80; Distinguished Alumni Award, Lincoln Univ, Pennsylvania, 1988; Published Reverdy C. Ransom: Black Advocate of the Social Gospel Univ Press of America, 1990. **MEMBERSHIPS** Mem Amer Historical Assn, Amer Soc of Church History, Assn for the Study of Negro Life & History, Assn for Theological Field Educ, Soc for the Study of Black Religion, Amer Civil Lib Union, Amer Friends Serv Comm Amnesty Intl, NAACP-Life Mem, Natl Urban League; mem Omega Psi Phi; Intl Peace Research Assn 1987-; bd mem, Arts in Action, 1988; bd mem, The Churches Conference on Shelter and Housing 1988. **CONTACT ADDRESS** Sch of Divinity, Howard Univ, 1400 Shepherd Street NE, Washington, DC, 20017.

MORRIS, JEFFREY B.
DISCIPLINE LAW **EDUCATION** Princeton Univ, BA, 62; Columbia Univ, JD, 65, PhD, 72. **CAREER** Instr, CUNY, Univ PA, Brooklyn Law Schl; spec asst, Columbia Univ, 76-81; assoc prof Law, Touro Col. **RESEARCH** Hist of fed courts. **SELECTED PUBLICATIONS** Auth, Federal Justice in the Second Circuit; History of U.S. District Court for the Eastern District of New York. **CONTACT ADDRESS** Touro Col, Brooklyn, NY, 11230.

MORRIS, NORVAL
PERSONAL Born 10/01/1923, Auckland, New Zealand, m, 1947, 3 children **DISCIPLINE** LAW CRIMINOLOGY **EDUCATION** Univ Melbourne, LLB, 46, LLM, 47; London Sch Econ, PhD(criminology), 49. **CAREER** Asst lectr law, London Sch Econ, 49-50; lectr, Univ Melbourne, 50-58, assoc prof criminol, 55-58, Bonython prof law & dean law sch, 58-62; dir criminal justice, UN Inst, Tokyo, 62- 64; Julius Kreeger prof law & criminol & dir ctr studies criminal justice, 64-76, Prof Law & Dean Law Sch, Univ Chicago, 76-, Ezra Ripley Thayer teaching fel, Harvard Univ, 55-56; chmn, Ceylon Govt Comm Capital Punishment, 58-59; mem, Soc Sci Res Coun Australia, 60-62; vis prof, Harvard Law Sch, 61-62. **HONORS AND AWARDS** Hutchinson Silver Medal, Univ London, 50; Japanese Order of the Sacred Treasure, 65. **MEMBERSHIPS** Criminal law; criminology. **SELECTED PUBLICATIONS** Auth, The Habitual Criminal, Longmans, 51; coauth, Cases in Torts, Law Bk Co, Australia, 62; Studies in Criminal Law, Oxford Univ, 64; The Honest Pubisher's Guide to Crime Control, 72, The Future of Imprisonment, 75, Letters to the President on Crime Control, 78 & Madness & the Criminal Law, 82, Univ Chicago Press; Street-Level Purposes Of Punishment, Proceedings Of The American Philosophical Society, Vol 0140, 1996. **CONTACT ADDRESS** Law School, Univ of Chicago, Chicago, IL, 60637.

MORRIS, PAUL
PERSONAL m, 6 children **DISCIPLINE** THEOLOGY **EDUCATION** Univ SC; Grace Theol Sem, MDiv; Calif Grad Sch Theol, PhD. **CAREER** Exec VP, acad dean, instr, Bible Col, Pa, 94; educator/instr. **HONORS AND AWARDS** Nat fel, Grace Brethren churches., Affil, Presbyterian Church; asst dirship, Word of Life Island; dir youth ministries, First Brethren Church; pastorates, Grace Brethren Church; Cypress, Calif; Neighborhood Family Chapel; Nat Trng dir, Prison Fel; bd dir(s), YCIBI, Inc; Thesis 96, Inc; Charge, Inc; Avalon Commun Hospital; Word of Life, Inc. **RESEARCH** Redemptive therapy **SELECTED PUBLICATIONS** Auth, Love Therapy, Tyndale House Publ, 74; Shadow of Sodom, Tyndale House Publ, 78; Helping Others Grow, Tyndale House Publ, 80; Jour of Redemptive Therapy. **CONTACT ADDRESS** Sch Redemptive Stud, San Diego Theol Sem, 5580 La Jolla Blvd, #95, La Jolla, CA, 92037. **EMAIL** Dr.Morris@fishernet.com

MORRIS, WILLIAM O.
PERSONAL Born 12/02/1922, Fairmont, WV, m, 1948, 2 children **DISCIPLINE** LAW **EDUCATION** Col William & Mary, AB, 44; Univ IL, LLB, 46, JD, 68. **CAREER** Asst prof bus law, Univ IL, 46-55; assoc prof law, Stetson Univ, 55-58; PROF LAW, WV UNIV, 58-, PROF DENT JURISP, MED CTR, 59-; Law practice, Champaign, IL, 46-55; consult interim comt, WV Legis, 59; comptroller of currency, US Treasury Dept, 63-67; Fulbright prof, Univ Munster, 69, prof, 70; prof, Gutenberg Univ, 71 & 72, Stetson Univ, 71, 73 & 74 & Univ Oslo, 73. **HONORS AND AWARDS** Medel of Merit, Nicholas Copernicus Univ, Torun, Poland; MDC degree from Nicholas Copernicus Univ. **RESEARCH** Banking law; suretyship; law of dentistry. **SELECTED PUBLICATIONS** Auth, Accommodation Parties to Negotiable Instruments, Banking Law J, 59; Fictitious Payees on Checks Requiring Dual Signatures, WI Law Rev, 61; Negotiable Instruments Under Uniform Commerical Code, WV Law Rev, 62; Dental Litigation, 72 & The Law of Domestic Relations, 73, Michie; Cases and Statutes Relative to Domestic Relations, WV Univ, 74; Veterinarian in Litigation, V M Publ, 76; Dental Litigation, Michie, 2nd ed, 77; Revocation of Professional License by Governmental Agencies, 94; The Dentists' Legal Advisor, 95. **CONTACT ADDRESS** Law Bldg, West Virginia Univ, Morgantown, WV, 26506.

MORRISON, CLAYTON T.
PERSONAL Born 03/12/1970, Sierra Madre, CA, m, 1997 **DISCIPLINE** PHILOSOPHY **EDUCATION** Occidental Coll,

BA, 92; SUNY Binghamton, MA, 95, PhD, 98. **CAREER** Teacher intern, 94, J Hopkins Univ; teach Asst, 93-97, adj Lectr, 95-97, research Asst, 98-, Binghamton Univ. **HONORS AND AWARDS** Ford Fel, Disting Hon Sr Comprehensive Proj, Occidental Coll; Ringle Awd, Grad Student Awd Excellence in Teaching, Dissertation Yr Fel, Binghamton Univ. **MEMBERSHIPS** AAAI, APA, CSS, SMM, SPP. **RESEARCH** Nature of cognitive representation, artificial intelligence, philosophy, psychology, cognitive science, autonomous agent epistemology, and philosophy of mind. **SELECTED PUBLICATIONS** Co-auth, Why Connectionist Nets Are Good Models - Commentary on Green on Connectionist-Explanation, in: Psychology, 98; auth, What it means to be Situated, in: Cybernetics & Sys, 98; Conceptual Change as Change of Inner Perspective, in: Papers from the 1996 AAAI Fall Symposium, Menlo Park CA AAAI Press, 96; Structure-Mapping vs High-level Perception, the mistaken fight over the explanation of analogy, in: Proceedings of the Seventeenth Annual Conference of the Cognitive Sciences Society, 95. **CONTACT ADDRESS** Dept of Philosophy PACCS Program, SUNY, Binghamton, Hinman 129, Binghamton, NY, 13902-6000. **EMAIL** clayton@turing.paccs.binghamton.edu

MORRISON, FRED L.
PERSONAL Born 12/24/1939, Salina, KS, m, 1971, 4 children **DISCIPLINE** LAW **EDUCATION** Univ Kans, AB, 61; Oxford Univ, BA, 63; Princeton Univ, MA & PhD(polit), 66; Univ Chicago, JD, 67; Oxford Univ, MA, 68. **CAREER** Asst prof law, Univ Iowa, 67-69; assoc prof, 69-72, Prof Law, Univ Minn, Minneapolis, 72-; Fulbright vis prof, Univ Bonn, WGer, 75-76; counr, Counsel to Popham, Haik, Schnobrich, Kaufman & Doty, Minneapolis, Minn, 81-82; counr on int law, US Dept State, 82-83. **RESEARCH** Comparative public law; international law; American Constitutional law. **SELECTED PUBLICATIONS** Auth, Recognition in international law, Univ Chicago Law Rev, 67; chap, In: Frontiers of Judicial Research, Wiley, 69; Courts and the Political Process in England, 73; Limitations on alien investment in real estate, Minn Law Rev, 76; State corporate farming legislation, Univ Toledo Law Rev, 76; The right to fish for seacoast products, Supreme Court Rev, 77; The general competence of the municipality, Am J of Comp Law Suppl, 82. **CONTACT ADDRESS** Law Sch, Univ of Minnesota, 229 19th Ave S, Minneapolis, MN, 55455-0401. **EMAIL** morrison@umn.edu

MORRISON, KARL FREDERICK
PERSONAL Born 11/03/1936, Birmingham, AL, m, 1964, 2 children **DISCIPLINE** MEDIEVAL & CHURCH HISTORY **EDUCATION** Univ Miss, BA, 56; Cornell Univ, MA, 57, PhD(hist), 61. **CAREER** Actg instr hist, Stanford Univ, 60-61; from instr to asst prof, Univ Minn, 61-64; asst prof, Harvard Univ, 64-65; assoc prof, 65-68, chmn dept hist, 70-76, Prof Medieval Hist, Univ Chicago, 68-, McKnight Found award, 63; Am Coun Learned Socs fels, 63-64 & 66-67; mem, Inst Advan Study, 66-67 & 76-77; consult, Time-Life Bks, 66-68; pres, Midwest Medieval Conf, 77- 78. **MEMBERSHIPS** AHA; Mediaeval Acad Am; Midwest Asn Medieval Studies (pres, 76-78); Medieval Asn Midwest (pres, 77-78). **RESEARCH** History of political thought; church history. **SELECTED PUBLICATIONS** Auth, The Two Kingdoms, Princeton Univ, 64; Rome and the City of God, Am Philos Soc, 64; Tradition and Authority in the Western Church: 300-1140, Princeton Univ, 67; Carolingian coinage, Am Numis Soc, 68; Europe's Middle Ages: 565-1500, Scott, 70; ed, The Investiture Controversy: Issues, Ideals and Results, Holt, 71 & Ferdinand Gregorovius, Rome and Medieval Culture, Univ Chicago, 71; auth, The Mimetic Tradition of Reform in Western Culture, Princeton, 82; The Letters Of Damian,Peter, Vol 3 - Letters-91-150 - German - Reindel,K, Editor, Speculum-A J Of Medieval Studies, Vol 0068, 1993. **CONTACT ADDRESS** Dept of Hist, Univ of Chicago, Chicago, IL, 60637.

MORSE, BRADFORD W.
DISCIPLINE LAW **EDUCATION** Rutgers Univ, BA; Univ British Columbia, LLB; Osgoode Hall Law Sch, LLM. **CAREER** Prof. **SELECTED PUBLICATIONS** Auth, pubs on aboriginal legal issues. **CONTACT ADDRESS** Fac Common Law, Univ Ottawa, 550 Cumberland St, PO Box 450, Ottawa, ON, K1N 6N5.

MORSE, OLIVER
PERSONAL Born 05/17/1922, New York, NY, m **DISCIPLINE** LAW **EDUCATION** St Augustine's Coll, BS 1947; Brooklyn Law Sch, LLB 1950; NY U, LLM 1951; Brooklyn Law Sch, JSD 1952. **CAREER** Howard Univ School of Law, acting dean, 1986, asso dean, prof (retired); Hunter Coll, instr 1959; So Univ School of Law, prof 1956-59; Brooklyn Law School, prof 1968-69; Morse Enterprises Inc, chairman, board of directors, 1989-97. **HONORS AND AWARDS** Most Outstdng Law Prof Howard Law Sch 1967, 70-72 **MEMBERSHIPS** Vice-chmn HEW Reviewing Authority; Beta Lamba Sigma; Phi Alpha Delta; Omega Psi Phi; Am Assn of Law Schs; mem Nat Bar Assn; mem NY Bar Assn; 1st chmn of section on legal Educ of NBA 1971-72; sire archon, 1986-87, member, Sigma Pi Phi Fraternity, Maryland Boule, 1981-; board of trustees, St Augustine's College, 1991-. **SELECTED PUBLICATIONS** Pubs include 40 legal decisions of cases heard on appeal to HEW Reviewing Authority. **CONTACT ADDRESS** Morse Enterprises, Inc., 11120 New Hampshire Ave, Ste. 204, Silver Spring, MD, 20904-3448.

MORTON, CHARLES E.
PERSONAL Born 01/31/1926, Bessemer, AL, m **DISCIPLINE** PHILOSOPHY **EDUCATION** Morehouse College, Atlanta, GA, BA, 1946; Union Theological Seminary, New York, NY, 1949; Heidelberg University, Heidelberg, Germany, 1955; Garrett Biblical Institute, Northwestern University, 1956; Columbia University, New York, NY, PhD, 1958; Shaw College, Detroit, MI, LHD, 1970. **CAREER** Michigan Bd Edn, mem 1946-54; Div of Humanities & Philosophy Dillard Univ, former chmn; Albion Coll, assoc prof of philosophy; Ebeneze Baptist Ch Poughkeepsie, NY, minister; Metropolitan Baptist Church, Detroit, MI, pastor, 1963-; Oakland University, Rochester, MI, professor of philosophy, 1972-. **MEMBERSHIPS** President, board of directors, Metropolitan Baptist Church Non-Profit Housing Corporation, 1969-; member, board of directors, First Independence National Bank, Detroit, MI, 1970-; chairperson emeritus, Inner-City Business Improvement Forum of Detroit, 1972-; member, board of directors, Brazeal Dennard Chorale, 1988-; president, Michigan Progressive Baptist State Convention, 1990-92; board member, Gleaners Community Food Bank, 1990-; pres, Michigan Progressive Baptist Convention, Inc; chairperson, board of trustees, Wayne County Community College, 1990-93. **CONTACT ADDRESS** Metropolitan Baptist Church, 13110 14th St, Detroit, MI, 48238.

MORTON, JACQUELINE
PERSONAL Born 10/21/1934, Paris, France, 3 children **DISCIPLINE** TWENTIETH CENTURY FRENCH LITERATURE **EDUCATION** Hunter Col, BA, 54; Columbia Univ, MA, 65, PhD(French), 69. **CAREER** Instr, Smith Col, 66-67; asst prof, 75-79, Prof French, Wayne State Univ, 80-. **MEMBERSHIPS** Asn des Amis d'Andre Gide; Am Asn Teachers French; MLA. **RESEARCH** Andre Gide; Francois Mauriac; Andre Gide translator. **SELECTED PUBLICATIONS** Ed, La Correspondance d'Andre Gide et de Francois Mauriac, Gallimard, Paris, 71; coauth, La Presse Contemporary Issues in French Newspapers, Heath, 72; auth, Andre Gide and his American translator Justin O'Brien, Mich Aca, 77; coauth, La Presse II, Heath, 77; Mosaique, Van Nostrand, 77; English Grammar for Students of French, 79 & ed, English Grammar Series, 79, Olivia & Hill Press; 'Olga Per La Grande Dame A Sant-Ambrogio', Paideuma-A J Devoted To Ezra Pound Scholarship, Vol 0026, 1997. **CONTACT ADDRESS** 905 Olivia, Ann Arbor, MI, 48104.

MOSELEY, ALLAN
PERSONAL Born 11/18/1957, Montgomery, AL, m, 1979, 3 children **DISCIPLINE** OLD TESTAMENT STUDIES **EDUCATION** Samford Univ, BA, 80; New Orleans Baptist Sem, MDiv, 82, PhD, 87. **CAREER** Pastor, Big Level Baptist Church, 82-85; pastor, Bayou View Baptist Church, 85-90; pastor, First Baptist Church, Durham. 90-96; vice pres stud serv, dean stud, 96- , prof Old Testament, 98- , Southeastern Sem. **MEMBERSHIPS** Soc of Bibl Lit; Evangel Theol Soc. **SELECTED PUBLICATIONS** Auth, The Life-View of Qoheleth, Bibl Illusr, 94; auth, What in the World Should the Church Do? Preaching, 94; auth, Shadrach, Meshach, and Abednego: All We Know, Bibl Illusr, 95; auth, Christmas Greatness, Preaching, 95; auth,The Birth of the Church, Mothers Helper, and, Keep Climbing, Preaching, 96; auth, Survey of the Old Testament, SBC Sunday School Board, 96; auth, Beginnings: Thirteen Lessons in Genesis 1-26 for Explore the Bible teacher's book, 97; auth, Sermon Briefs, in Abingdon Preaching Annual, 99. **CONTACT ADDRESS** PO Box 1889, Wake Forest, NC, 27588-1889. **EMAIL** amoseley@sebts.edu

MOSELEY, JAMES G.
PERSONAL Born 03/24/1946, Atlanta, GA, m, 1968, 2 children **DISCIPLINE** RELIGION; LITERATURE **EDUCATION** Stanford Univ, BA, 68; Univ Chicago Div Sch, MA, 71, PhD, 73. **CAREER** Cord Amer stud (s) prog, 73-79, Ch Hum div, 79-86, asst, assoc, full prof, 73-86, New Col, Univ S Fla; prof Relig, 86-91, dir honors prog, 89-91, VP acad affairs, Dean fac, 86-89, Chapman Col, Calif, VP, Dean, prof Relig, Transylvania Univ, Ky, 91- . **HONORS AND AWARDS** Fel in res Col tchrs, Natl Endowment Hum, Princeton, 76-77; Ed proj grant, NEH, for curric devel, New Col, 77; summer sem Col tchrs, NEH, 79, Univ Calif, Irvine; summer sem Col tchrs, NEH, 82, Harvard Univ; res and creative scholar awd, Univ S Fla, Summer, 83; Co-dir, summer sem sch tchrs, NEH, 84, New Col; Core Fac, Revisioning Am: Relig and the Life of the Nation, series, Ind Univ, Lilly Endowment, 84-90; Proj Dir, Power and Morality conf for commun leaders and sec sch tchrs, Fla endowment Hum, New Col, 85; dir, summer sem sch tchrs, NEH, New Col, 86; dir, summer sem sch tchrs, NEH, Univ Calif Irvine, 90; dir, summer sem sch tchrs, Transylvania Univ, 92; Core fac, Cultural Diversity and Civic Responsibility, Wye High Sch fac sem, Transylvania Univ, 93; Core Fac, Pub Expressions of Rel in Amer, series, Ind Univ, Lilly Endowment, 92-94. **MEMBERSHIPS** Amer acad Relig; Amer Stud Asn; Org Amer Hist; Amer soc Church Hist; Natl Col honors coun; Amer conf acad Deans; Asn Amer Col Univ; Amer Asn higher educ. **RESEARCH** History of Religion. **SELECTED PUBLICATIONS** Auth, A Complex Inheritance: The Idea of Self-Transcendence in the Theology of Henry James, Sr, and the Novels of Henry James, Amer Acad Relig Diss Series, vol 4, Missoula, MT, AAR and Scholar Press, 75; Conversion through Vision: Puritanism and Transcendentalism in The Ambassadors, Jour Amer Acad Relig, XLIII/3, Sept 75; Religious Ethics and the Social Aspects of Imaginative Literature, Jour Amer Acad Relig, XL vol 3, Sept 77; Religion and Modernity: A Case Granted, Bull of the Couns on the Stud Relig, IX/1, Feb 78; Literature and Ethics: Some Possibilities for Religious Thought, Perspect Relig Stud (s), VI/1, Spring 79; The Social Organization of Religion in America: Then and Now, SEASA '79 Proceedings, Tampa, Fla, Amer Stud (s) Press, 79; Culture, Religion, and Theology, Theol Today, XXXVII/3, Oct 80; auth, A Cultural History of Religion in America, Westport, Conn, Greenwood Press, 81; From Conversion to Self-Transcendence: Religious Experience in American Literature, SEASA '83 Proceedings, Tampa, Fla, Amer Stud (s) Press, 83; Inerrantism as Narcissism: Biblical Authority as a Cultural Problem, Perspectives in Relig Stud (s), Fall 83; An Occasion for Changing One's Mind: A Response to Charles Long, Relig Studs and Theol, vol 3, Sept 85; Winthrop's Journal: Religion, Politics, and Narrative in Early America, in Religion and the Life of the Nation: American Recoveries, Sherrill, Illinois UP, 90, reprinted in Literature Criticism from 1400-1800, LC, vol 31, Bostrom, Detroit, Gale, 95; auth, John Winthrop's World: History as a Story as History, Madison, U of Wisconsin P, 92; Civil Religion Revisited, Relig and Amer Cult: A Jour of Interpretation, 4/1, Winter, 94; rev essay: Jenny Franchot's Roads to Rome: The Antebellum Protestant Encounter with Catholicism, Relig Stud (s) Rev, 23/3, July 97. **CONTACT ADDRESS** Dept of Dean, Transylvania Univ, Lexington, KY, 40508.

MOSER, PAUL K.
PERSONAL Born 10/29/1957, Bismarck, ND, m, 1980, 2 children **DISCIPLINE** PHILOSOPHY **EDUCATION** Vanderbilt Univ, PhD, 82. **CAREER** Asst prof to assoc prof Philosophy, 83-89, PROF PHILOSOPHY, 89, CHR PHILOSOPHY DEPT, 97-, LOYOLA UNIV CHICAGO. **MEMBERSHIPS** Am Philos Asn **RESEARCH** Philosophy of Religion; Theory of Knowledge. **SELECTED PUBLICATIONS** auth Empirical Justification, Philosophical Studies Series in Philosophy, 85; Knowledge and Evidence, Cambridge Univ Press, 89; Philosophy After Objectivity, Oxford Univ Press, 93; The Theory of Knowledge: A Thematic Introduction, Oxford Univ Press, 97; ed Contemporary Approaches to Philosophy, Macmillan Publ Co, 93; Contemporary Materialism, Routledge Ltd, 95; Morality and the Good Life, Oxford Univ Press, 97. **CONTACT ADDRESS** Dept of Philosophy, Loyola Univ, Chicago, 6525 N Sheridan Rd, Crown Ctr , Chicago, IL, 60626-5385. **EMAIL** PMOSER@LUC.EDU

MOSHER LOCKWOOD, KIMBERLY
DISCIPLINE PHILOSOPHY **EDUCATION** Univ Dayton, BA, 91; Univ Cincinnati, MA, 95. **CAREER** Part-time Instr, Univ Cincinnati, Wittenberg Univ, Univ Dayton. **HONORS AND AWARDS** Charles P. Taft Fel, 97-98 **MEMBERSHIPS** Amer Phil Assoc; Amer Soc for Aesthetics **RESEARCH** Art; metaphor; language **CONTACT ADDRESS** 1150 Epworth Ave., Dayton, OH, 45410. **EMAIL** mosherlockwood@yahoo.com

MOSKOP, JOHN C.
PERSONAL Born 10/19/1951, IL, m, 1977, 2 children **DISCIPLINE** PHILOSOPHY **EDUCATION** Univ Notre Dame, BA, 73; Univ Texas at Austin, PhD, 79. **CAREER** Asst Prof, 79-84, Assoc Prof, 84-89, Prof, 89-, East Carolina Univ School of Medicine; Dir, 95-, Bioethics Ctr, Univ Health Systems of Eastern Carolina. **HONORS AND AWARDS** Fel, Inst on Human Values in Medicine, 77; Basic Science Service Award, East Carolina Univ School of Medicine, 89. **MEMBERSHIPS** Amer Soc for Bioethics and Humanities; Amer Phil Assoc; Amer Soc of Law, Medicine, and Ethics **RESEARCH** Bioethics, especially ethical issues in death and dying; allocation of healthcare; emergency medicine ethics **SELECTED PUBLICATIONS** Auth, Informed Consent and the Limits of Disclosure: A Response to Joel M. Zinburg, Current Surgery; Coauth, Knowing the Score: Using Predictive Scoring Systems in Clinical Practice, American Journal of Critical Care, 96, Auth, End-of-Life Decisions in Dutch Neonatal Intensive Care Units, Journal of Pediatrics, 96; Physician Assisted Suicide: What's the Answer, Medical Center Review, 96; Not Sanctity of Dignity, But Justice and Autonomy: Key Morla Concepts in the Allocation of Critical Care, The Concepts of Human Dignity and Sanctity of Life and Their Significance for Ethical Conflicts in Modern Medicine, 96; Persons, Property or Both: Engelhardt on the Moral Status of Young Children, Reading Engelhardt, 97; Coauth, Ethical and Legal Aspects of Teratogenic Medications: The Case of Isotretinoin, Journal of Clinical Ethics, 97; Auth, A Moral Analysis of Military Medicine, Military Medicine, 98. **CONTACT ADDRESS** Dept of Medical Humanities, East Carolina Univ, Greenville, NC, 27858. **EMAIL** moskop@brody.med.ecu.edu

MOSOFF, JUDITH
DISCIPLINE LAW **EDUCATION** Univ Toronto, BA, 69; York Univ, MA, 70; Univ British Columbia, LLB, 83; LLM,

94. **CAREER** Prof, 91- **RESEARCH** Disability; mental health; public interest law. **SELECTED PUBLICATIONS** Auth, pubs about administrative law, clinical legal education and law and psychiatry. **CONTACT ADDRESS** Fac of Law, Univ British Columbia, 1822 East Mall, Vancouver, BC, V6T 1Z1. **EMAIL** mosoff@law.ubc.ca

MOSS, ALFRED A., JR.
PERSONAL Born 03/02/1943, Chicago, Illinois, d **DISCIPLINE** THEOLOGY **EDUCATION** Lake Forest College, Lake Forest, IL, BA, with honors, 1961-65; Episcopal Divinity School, Cambridge, MA, MA, divinity, 1965-68; University of Chicago, Chicago, IL, MA, 1972, PhD, 1977. **CAREER** Episcopal Church of the Holy Spirit, Lake Forest, IL, assistant minister for urban ministry, 1968-70; University of Chicago, Episcopal Chaplaincy, Chicago, IL, associate chaplain, 1970-75; Univ of Maryland, Dept of History, College Park, MD, lecturer, 1975-77, assistant professor, 1977-83, associate professor, 1983-. **SELECTED PUBLICATIONS** The American Negro Academy, Louisiana State Univ Press, 1981; Looking at History, People for the American Way, 1986; From Slavery to Freedom, Alfred A Knopf, 1988; The Facts of Reconstruction, Louisiana State Univ Press, 1991. **CONTACT ADDRESS** Professor, Dept of History, Univ of Maryland, College Park, MD, 20742-7315.

MOSS, C. MICHAEL
PERSONAL Born 02/10/1950, Danville, IL, m, 1972, 3 children **DISCIPLINE** NEW TESTAMENT & GREEK **EDUCATION** Lipscomb Univ, BA; Harding Univ Grad Sch of Relig, MA; Southern Bapt Theol Sem, M Div, PhD. **CAREER** Prof and assoc dean, col of bible and ministry, Lipscomb Univ, 83-. **MEMBERSHIPS** Soc of Bibl Lit; Amer Acad of Relig; Evang Theol Soc. **RESEARCH** New Testament backgrounds; Greek; Hermeneutics; Johannine literature. **SELECTED PUBLICATIONS** Auth, The Exposition of Scripture, Man of God, Nashville, Gospel Advocate, 96; auth, 1, 2, Timothy and Titus, Col Press New Intl Commentary, Joplin, Col Press, 94; transl, The NKSV Greek English Interlinear New Testament, Nashville, Word, 94. **CONTACT ADDRESS** 508 Adamwood Dr., Nashville, TN, 37211. **EMAIL** mosscm@dlu.edu

MOSS, LENNY
PERSONAL Born 04/24/1952, Brooklyn, NY, d, 2 children **DISCIPLINE** PHILOSOPHY AND BIOCHEMISTRY **EDUCATION** San Francisco State Univ, BA, 81; Univ Calif Berkeley, PhD, 89; Northwestern Univ, PhD, 98. **CAREER** Genetic sci in soc fel, Univ Utah, 96-97; vis asst prof, philos, Univ Utah, 97-98; instr, philos, Northwestern Univ, 98-99. **HONORS AND AWARDS** Genesis fel, Utah Ctr for Human Genome Res, Univ Utah, 96; Univ fel, Northwestern Univ, 90; Regents fel, Univ Calif Berkeley, 81. **MEMBERSHIPS** Amer Asn for the Advan of Sci; Amer Asn of Bioethics; Amer Philos Asn; Amer Soc for Cell Bio; Critical Theory Roundtable; Hist of Sci Soc; Intl Asn of Bioethics; Intl Soc for the Hist, Philos, and Social Studies of Bio; Philos of Sci Asn; Soc for Phenomenol and Existential Philos; Soc for Philos and Psychol. **SELECTED PUBLICATIONS** Auth, Life, Origins of, Routledge Encycl of Philos, 98; auth, Ethical Challenges of the New Genetic Technologies, Ethics Grand Rounds, Med Col of Wisc, 98; auth, What Genes Can't Do or Prolegomenon to a Dynamically-Relational, Developmentally-Embodying Life-Philosophy, dept of philos, Univ Utah, 97; auth, What is Selecting What?, Intl Soc for the Hist, Philos, and Social Studies of Bio, Univ Wash, 97; auth, Critical Reflections on the Gene Concept, Genetic Sci in Soc Prog, Utah Ctr for Human Genome Res, Univ Utah, 96; auth, Understanding Life: From Ontogenesis and Final Cause to Genetic Information and Back, Philos Colloquium, City Col/CUNY, 96; auth, Epigenesis, Dynamic Developmental Systems and Cancer, Workshop on the Logic and Dynamics of the Higher Level Formations in Biology, 96; auth, Post-Mendelian Biology and the Theory of Evolving Developmental Systems, The Prog in Hist and Philos of Sci at Northwestern Univ, 96; auth, Timeley Mediations: Martin Heidegger and Postmodern Politics, ETHICS, 97; auth, Gene and Generalizations: Darden's Strategies and the Question of Context, Bio and Philos, 95; **CONTACT ADDRESS** Dept. of Philosophy, Northwestern Univ, 1818 Hinman Ave, Evanston, IL, 60201. **EMAIL** lennymo@nwu.edu

MOSS, MYRA ELLEN
PERSONAL Born 03/22/1937, Los Angeles, CA **DISCIPLINE** CONTEMPORARY ITALIAN PHILOSOPHY **EDUCATION** Pomona Col, BA, 58; Johns Hopkins Univ, PhD, 65. **CAREER** Asst prof, San Jose State Col, 66-68; lectr, 68-70, asst prof, 70-74, Santa Clara Univ; tutor, 75-82, adj assoc prof Philos, 82-92, prof philos, 92-, prof philos and govt, 98-, Claremont McKenna Col. **HONORS AND AWARDS** Phi Beta Kappa (hon). **MEMBERSHIPS** Am Philos Asn; Metaphysical Soc; Am Soc Aesthetics; Vico Soc. **RESEARCH** Italian philosophers: Croce, Gentile, Gramsci; philosophy and psychology. **SELECTED PUBLICATIONS** Auth, Benedetto Croce's Coherence Theory of Truth, Filos, 68; auth, Petrarch and Modern Criticism: De Sanctis and Croce, Rivista Rosminiana Filos Cult, 77; auth, Croce's Theory of Intuition Reconsidered, Rivista Studi Crociani, 78; auth, Croce's Categorial Theory of Truth, Idealistic Studies, 80; auth, Benedetto Croce Reconsid-

ered, 87; transl, Benedetto Croce's Essays on Literature and Literary Criticism, 90. **CONTACT ADDRESS** Dept of Philosophy, Claremont McKenna Col, 500 E 9th St, Claremont, CA, 91711-6400. **EMAIL** myra_moss@mckenna.edu

MOSS, ROGER W.
PERSONAL Born 01/31/1940, Zanesville, OH, m, 1981, 2 children **DISCIPLINE** SOCIAL; CULTURAL HISTORY **EDUCATION** Univ Delaware, PhD 72; Ohio Univ, MA 66, BSed 63. **CAREER** Athenaeum of Philadelphia, exec dir 69 to 98-; Univ Penn, adj assoc prof 81 to 98-; Univ Maryland, lectr 67-68; Univ Delaware, lectr 66-68. **HONORS AND AWARDS** NEH; NEA **MEMBERSHIPS** RSA; SAH; HSP; SPNEA; Rushlight Club. **RESEARCH** American architecture and hist preservation. **SELECTED PUBLICATIONS** Auth, Historic Houses of Philadelphia, Phil, UPP, 98; Philadelphia Victorian: The Building of the Athenaeum, Phil, The Athenaeum, 98; Paint in America, ed, NY, John Wiley & Son, 94; The American Country House, NY, Henry Holt & Co, 90. **CONTACT ADDRESS** The Athenaeum of Philadelphia, 219 S. Sixth St, Philadelphia, PA, 19106. **EMAIL** rwmoss@pobox.upenn.edu

MOSSER, KURT
DISCIPLINE PHILOSOPHY OF LOGIC AND LANGUAGE **EDUCATION** Univ Chicago, PhD, 90. **CAREER** Dept Philos, Univ Dayton **RESEARCH** Kant, epistemology and metaphysics. **SELECTED PUBLICATIONS** Auth, Stoff and Nonsense in Kant's First Critique, Hist Philos Quart, 93; Was Wittgenstein a neo-Kantian? A Response to Prof Haller, Grazer Philos Stud, 93; Kant's Critical Model of the Experiencing Subject, Idealistic Stud, 95. **CONTACT ADDRESS** Dept of Philos, Univ Dayton, 300 Col Park, Dayton, OH, 75062. **EMAIL** mosser@checkov.hm.udayton.edu

MOSTAGHEL, DEBORAH M.
DISCIPLINE LAW **EDUCATION** Univ Calif Berkeley, BA; Shiraz Univ, MA; Univ Utah, JD. **CAREER** Instr. **SELECTED PUBLICATIONS** Auth, Mediating Status Offender Cases-A Successful Approach, Mediation Quarterly, 96; The Low-Level Radioactive Waste Policy Amendment Act-An Overview, DePaul, 94; Who Regulates the Disposal of Low-Level Radioactive Waste Under the Low-level Radioactive Waste Policy Act?, 88; co-auth, State Reactions to the Trading of Emissions Allowances Under Title IV of the Clean Air Act Amendments of 1990, Boston Col, 95. **CONTACT ADDRESS** Col Law, Univ of Toledo, Toledo, OH, 43606. **EMAIL** dmostag@utnet.utoledo.edu

MOTHERSILL, MARY
PERSONAL Born 05/27/1923, Edmonton, AB, Canada **DISCIPLINE** PHILOSOPHY **EDUCATION** Univ Toronto, BA, 44; Harvard Univ, PhD(philos), 54. **CAREER** Instr philos, Vassar Col, 47-51; instr, Sch Gen Studies, Columbia Univ, 51-53 & Univ Conn, 53-57; lectr, Univ Mich, 57- 58; asst prof, Univ Chicago, 58-61; assoc prof, City Col NY, 61- 64; Prof Philos, Barnard Col, Columbia Univ, 64-. **MEMBERSHIPS** Am Philos Asn. **SELECTED PUBLICATIONS** Auth, Agents, critics and philosophers, Mind, 1060; Is art a language?, J Philos, 1065; ed, Ethics, Macmillan, 67; The Moral Sense - Wilson,Jq, American Scholar, Vol 0063, 1994. **CONTACT ADDRESS** Dept of Philosophy Barnard College, Columbia Univ, New York, NY, 10027.

MOULDER, WILLIAM J.
DISCIPLINE BIBLE INTERPRETATION **EDUCATION** Columbia Bible Col, BA, 66; Trinity Evangelical Divinity Sch, Mdiv, 69; St. Andrews Univ, PhD, 74. **CAREER** Relig, Trinity Int Univ. **SELECTED PUBLICATIONS** Areas: the Old Testament and the New Testament. **CONTACT ADDRESS** Trinity Int Univ, 2065 Half Day Road, Deerfield, IL, 60015.

MOULTON, JANICE
DISCIPLINE ENGLISH, PHILOSOPHY **EDUCATION** Cornell Univ, BA, 63; Univ Chicago, MA, 68; PhD, 71. **CAREER** Asst prof, Univ Ky, 79-81; prof, Central China Tchrs Univ, 86-87; res fac, Smith Coll, 81-. **HONORS AND AWARDS** Executive Comm, Am Philos Asn, 78; Bd of Dir, Sino-Am Network for Educ Exchange. **MEMBERSHIPS** Am Philos Asn; Sino-Am Network for Educ Exchange; Soc for Women in Philos. **RESEARCH** Philosophy; Methodology; Ethics; Feminism; Philosophy Language; Research Methodology; Fraud. **SELECTED PUBLICATIONS** Auth, Plagiarism; Academic Freedom, Encycl of Ethics, 98; coauth, Scaling the Dragon, 94 **CONTACT ADDRESS** Dept of Philosophy, Smith Col, Northampton, MA, 01063. **EMAIL** jmoulton@sophia.smith.edu

MOUNCE, WILLIAM D.
DISCIPLINE NEW TESTAMENT **EDUCATION** Bethel Col, BA; Fuller Theol Sem, MA; Aberdeen Univ, Scotland, PhD. **CAREER** Instr, Azuza Pacific Univ; prof, Gordon-Conwell Theol Sem, 97-; adv, Courseware Devel. **HONORS AND AWARDS** Producer, FlashWorks and ParseWorks, integrative cmpt prog(s) for lrng lang(s). **MEMBERSHIPS** Mem, Evangel Theol Soc; Soc Biblical Lit; Inst Biblical Res; Tyndale

House. **RESEARCH** Greek and exegesis. **SELECTED PUBLICATIONS** Auth, The Basics of Biblical Greek; The Analytical Lexicon to the Greek New Testament; Profiles in Faith. **CONTACT ADDRESS** Gordon-Conwell Theol Sem, 130 Essex St, South Hamilton, MA, 01982.

MOUNT, CHARLES ERIC, JR.
DISCIPLINE RELIGION **EDUCATION** Southwestern Memphis, BA; Union Theol Sem Va, Bdiv; Yale Div Schl, MTh; Duke Univ, PhD. **CAREER** Fac, 66; dean stu; col chapl; vice pres; Nelson D. and Mary McDowell Rodes Prof Relig, current. **HONORS AND AWARDS** John E. Haycraft Awd, NAACP, 85., Chr, Boyle Co Human Rts Comm; chr, United Way; Inst Rev Bd, Ephraim McDowell Reg Med Ctr; Nursing Home Ombudsman Agency Bd. **RESEARCH** Ethics and health care; business ethics; contemporary theology. **SELECTED PUBLICATIONS** Auth, Conscience and Responsibility, John Knox, 64/71; The Feminine Factor John Knox 73; Professional Ethics in Context: Institutions, Images, and Empathy Westminster/John Knox, 90). **CONTACT ADDRESS** Centre Col, 600 W Walnut St, Danville, KY, 40422. **EMAIL** mounte@centre.edu

MOUNT, ERIC, JR.
PERSONAL Born 12/07/1935, Versailles, KY, m, 1958, 4 children **DISCIPLINE** ENGLISH, CHRISTIAN ETHICS AND RELIGION **EDUCATION** Rhodes Col, BA, 57; Union Theol Sem in Va, BD, 60; Yale Divinity Sch, STM, 61; Duke Univ, PhD, 66. **CAREER** Asst prof, 66-70, assoc prof, 70-75, prof, 75-96, Rodes prof, 96-, relig, Centre Col; dir, Centre-in-Europe, 92-93; vpres and dean of students, Centre Col, 83-88; social studies div chair, 80-83, relig prog chair, 84-88, Centre Col. **HONORS AND AWARDS** BA with distinction; Phi Beta Kappa; Omicron Delta Kappa; NEH summer seminars, 76, 81; BD, second in class; Alsop fel; PhD two univ fel; one Kearns fel; Theologian-in-residence, Amer Church in Paris, 74-75; pres, southeast region, Amer Acad of Relig, 87-88; David Hughes distinguished svc award, Centre Col, 77. **MEMBERSHIPS** Soc of Christ Ethics; Amer Acad of Relig; Soc for Values in Higher Educ; Soc of Bus Ethics; Asn for Practical and Professional Ethics. **RESEARCH** Theological ethics; Social ethics; Contemporary theology; Medical ethics; Business ethics; Professional ethics. **SELECTED PUBLICATIONS** Articles, Homing in on Family Values, The Family, Religion and Culture Series, Theol Today, 98; article, European Community and Global Community: A View from Alsace and Beyond, Soundings, 96; article, The Currency of Covenant, Annual of the Soc of Christ Ethics, 96; article, Metaphors, Morals and AIDS, Jour of Ethical Studies, 93; article, Can We Talk? Contexts of Meaning for Interpreting Illness, Jour of Med Humanities, vol 14, no 2, 93; auth, Professional Ethics in Context: Institutions, Images and Empathy, John Knox Press, 90; auth, The Feminine Factor, John Knox Press, 73; auth, Conscience and Responsibility, John Knox Press, 69. **CONTACT ADDRESS** Centre Col, 600 W. Walnut St., Danville, KY, 40422. **EMAIL** mounte@centre.edu

MOURELATOS, ALEXANDER PHOEBUS DIONYSIOU
PERSONAL Born 07/19/1936, Athens, Greece, m, 1962 **DISCIPLINE** PHILOSOPHY, CLASSICAL PHILOLOGY **EDUCATION** Yale Univ, BA, 58, MA, 61, PhD(philos), 64. **CAREER** Instr, Yale Univ, 62-64; from asst prof to assoc prof, 65-71, Prof Philos, Univ Tex Austin, 71-, Jr fel, Inst Res Humanities, Univ Wis, 64-65; mem, Inst Advan Study, Princeton, NJ, 67-68; Nat Endowment for Humanities fel, 68 & 82-83; jr fel, Ctr Hellenic Studies, Washington, DC, 73-74; Am Coun Learned Soc fel, 73-74; vis fel, Humanities Res Ctr, Australian Nat Univ, Canberra, 78. **MEMBERSHIPS** Am Philos Asn; Am Philol Asn; Can Philos Asn. **RESEARCH** Pre-Socratic philosophy; Plato; Aristotle. **SELECTED PUBLICATIONS** Auth, Aristotle's Powers and Modern Empiricism, Ratio, 67; The Route of Parmenides, Yale Univ, 70; co-ed, Exegesis and Argument: Studies Presented to Gregory Vlastos, Van Gorcum, Assen, Neth, 73; ed, The Pre-Socratics: A Collection of Critical Essays, Doubleday, 74; Events, processes, and states, Ling & Philos, 78; Astronomy and kinematics in Plato's project of rationalist explanation, Study Hist & Philos of Sci, 80; Vlastos,Gregory - In-Memoriam, Gnomon-Kritische Zeitschrift Fur Die Gesamte Klassische Altertumswissenschaft, Vol 0065, 1993. **CONTACT ADDRESS** Dept of Philos, Univ of Tex, Austin, TX, 78712-1026.

MOUSTAKAS, CLARK
DISCIPLINE PHILOSOPHY **EDUCATION** Wayne State Univ, BS, MS; Union Inst, PhD. **CAREER** Philos, Union Inst. **RESEARCH** Clinical psychology and education; phenomenological existential humanistic psychology and psychotherapy; dream psychology; philosophy; human science; jurisprudence. **SELECTED PUBLICATIONS** Auth, Creativity and Conformity; Creative Life; Existential Child Therapy; Loneliness and Love; Phenomenology, Science, and Psychotherapy; Psychotherapy with Children; Rhythms, Rituals, and Relationships; The Touch of Loneliness; Turning Points; Phenomenological Research Methods. **CONTACT ADDRESS** Union Inst, 440 E McMillan St., Cincinnati, OH, 45206-1925. **EMAIL** chs40e@aol.com

MOYER, JAMES CARROLL
PERSONAL Born 11/30/1941, Norristown, PA, m, 1965, 3 children **DISCIPLINE** OLD TESTAMENT, ANCIENT HISTORY **EDUCATION** Wheaton Col, BA, 63; Gordon Divinity Sch, MDiv, 66; Brandeis Univ, MA, 68, PhD(Mediter studies), 69. **CAREER** Sachar Int fel, Brandeis Univ, 69-70; asst prof, 70-75, assoc prof hist, 75-78, assoc prof religious studies, 78-79, Prof Relig Studies, Southwest MO State Univ, 79-, Fel archaeol, Hebrew Union Col Bibl & Archaeol Sch, Jerusalem, 69-70. **MEMBERSHIPS** Soc Bibl Lit; Am Orient Soc; Am Schs Orient Res; Cath Bibl Asn. **RESEARCH** Old Testament; Israelite historiography and chronology; Hittitology. **SELECTED PUBLICATIONS** Auth, Philistines and Samson, In: Zondervan Pictorial Encyclopedia of the Bible, 75; Review of Edwin Yamauchi, Pre Christian Gnosticism: a survey of the proposed evidences, Fides et Historia, VIII No 2, 76; contribr 14 articles for the revision of Eerdman's Int Standard Bible Encycl, Vol I, 79, Vol II, 82; co-ed, Hittite and Israelite cultic practices: A selected comparison, In: Scripture in Context II, 82; Ashkelon Discovered - From Canaanites And Philistines To Romans And Moslems - Stager,Le, J Of Biblical Literature, Vol 0112, 1993; History And Technology Of Olive-Oil In The Holy-Land - Frankel,R, Avitsur,S, Ayalon,E, Jacobson,J, Biblical Archaeologist, Vol 0059, 1996; Through The Ages In Palestinian Archaeology - An Introductory Handbook - Rast,We, Biblical Archaeologist, Vol 0057, 1994; Scripture And Other Artifacts - Essays On The Bible And Archaeology In Honor Of King,Philip,J. - Coogan,Md, Exum,Jc, Stager,Le, Biblical Archaeologist, Vol 0058, 1995. **CONTACT ADDRESS** Dept of Hist, Southwest MO State Univ, Springfield, MO, 65802.

MOZUR, GERALD E.
PERSONAL Born 11/23/1956, Birmingham, AL, m, 1984 **DISCIPLINE** PHILOSOPHY **EDUCATION** Center Col of Kentucky, BA, 79; Univ of Kentucky, MA, 83; Washington Univ, St Louis, PhD, 90. **CAREER** Millsaps Col, asst prof, 89-90; SW Missouri State Univ, asst prof, 90-94; Webster Univ, adj prof, 94-97; Lewis & Clark Comm Col, asst prof, 97-. **HONORS AND AWARDS** SWMSU FSR Fel. **MEMBERSHIPS** APA, SAAP **RESEARCH** Philo of John Dewey; pragmatism; naturalism. **SELECTED PUBLICATIONS** Auth, Argument and Abstraction: An Introduction to Formal Logic, McGraw-Hill, 98, art, Sex, Race and the Privacy of Experience, in: Becoming Persons, Applied Theo Press, 94; Half-Hearted Pragmatism, in: Jour of Spec Philo, 94; Dewey on Time and Individuality, in: Transactions of the Charles S. Pierce Society, 91. **CONTACT ADDRESS** Dept of Philosophy, Lewis and Clark Comm Col, 5800 Godfrey Rd, Godfrey, IL, 62035. **EMAIL** gmozur@lc.cc.il.us

MUELLER, DAVID L.
PERSONAL Born 10/05/1929, Buffalo, NY, m, 1959, 1 child **DISCIPLINE** RELIGION **EDUCATION** Baylor Univ, BA, 51; Southern Baptist Theol Sem, BD, 54; Duke Univ, PhD, 58. **CAREER** From asst prof to assoc prof relig, Baylor Univ, 57-61; asst prof theol, 61-62, assoc prof, 62-75, Prof Theol, Southern Baptist Theol Sem, 75-. **MEMBERSHIPS** Am Acad Relig; Am Soc Church Hist. **RESEARCH** Systematic theology; 19th and 20th century Protestant theology. **SELECTED PUBLICATIONS** Auth, Karl Barth's critique of the antrhopoligical starting point in theology, Diss Abstr, 58; Roger William's view of the church and ministry, Rev & Expositor, 58; The theology of Karl Barth and the 19th century, Relig in Life, 64-65; An Introd to the Theology of Albrecht Ritschl, Westminster, 69; Karl Barth, Word Bks, 72; Bonhoeffer,Dietrich - A Spoke In The Wheel - Wind,R, J Of Church And State, Vol 0035, 1993. **CONTACT ADDRESS** 4908 Crofton Rd, Louisville, KY, 40207.

MUELLER, HOWARD ERNEST
PERSONAL Born 08/04/1936, Danube, MN, m, 1959, 2 children **DISCIPLINE** HISTORY OF RELIGIONS **EDUCATION** NCent Col, BA, 58; Evangel Theol Sem, BD, 61; Yale Univ, Stm, 62; Northwestern Univ, PhD(relig), 73. **CAREER** Asst prof relig, Carleton Col, 73-76; asst prof Relig, 76-80, assoc prof, 81-85, PROF RELIG, NCENT COL, 85-, CHMN DEPT, 90-. **HONORS AND AWARDS** Toenniges Prof of Religious Studies, 92. **MEMBERSHIPS** Am Acad Relig. **RESEARCH** African traditional religions; death and dying; biblical studies. **CONTACT ADDRESS** Dept of Religious Studies, No Central Col, 30 N Brainard St, Naperville, IL, 60566. **EMAIL** hem@noctrl.edu

MUELLER, IAN
PERSONAL Born 02/05/1938, Andover, MA, m, 1960, 2 children **DISCIPLINE** PHILOSOPHY **EDUCATION** Princeton Univ, AB, 59; Harvard Univ, PhD(philos), 64. **CAREER** Instr philos, Harvard Univ, 63-65; asst prof, Univ Ill, Urbana, 65-67; asst prof, 67-70, assoc prof, 70-79, prof philos, Univ Chicago, 79-, Am Coun Learned Soc fel, 72-73; fel, Ctr for Hellenic Studies, 77-78; fel, Fondation des Treilles, 82; NEH fel, 84-85; Guggenheim fel, 91-92; Am Coun Learned Soc fel, 91-92; Exchange fel, CNRS, Paris, 98-99. **HONORS AND AWARDS** Exc in grad teaching, Univ Chicago, 98. **MEMBERSHIPS** Am Philos Asn; Soc Anc Grk Philos; Comite Scientifique, Sciences et Techniques en Perspective, Academie internationale d'histoire des sciences. **RESEARCH** Ancient philosophy and science. **SELECTED PUBLICATIONS** Philosophy of Mathematics & Deductive Structure in Euclid's Elements, Mass Inst Technol, 81. **CONTACT ADDRESS** Dept of Philosophy, Univ of Chicago, 1010 E 59th St, Chicago, IL, 60637-1512. **EMAIL** i-mueller@uchicago.edu

MUESSE, MARK WILLIAM
PERSONAL Born 06/01/1957, Waco, TX, s **DISCIPLINE** RELIGION **EDUCATION** Baylor Univ, BA (English), 79; Harvard Divinity School, MTS (theol), 81; Harvard Univ, AM (The Study of Relig), 83, PhD (The Study of Relig), 87. **CAREER** Assoc dean, Col Of Arts and Sciences, Univ Southern ME, 87-88; asst prof, relig studies, Rhodes Col, 88-95; vis prof, Tamilnadu Theological Sem of South India, 90; ASSOC PROF, RELIG STUDIES, RHODES COL, 95-98. **HONORS AND AWARDS** Phi Beta Kappa, 79; Roothbert fel, 85; Charlotte W. Newcombe fel, 86. **MEMBERSHIPS** Am Academy of Relig; Soc for Values in Higher Ed; Am Men's Studies Asn; Soc for Indian Philos and Relig. **RESEARCH** Asian relig and philos; gender studies; religion and sexuality. **SELECTED PUBLICATIONS** Auth, Redeeming Men: Religion and Masculinities, 96. **CONTACT ADDRESS** Rhodes Col, 2000 North Parkway, Memphis, TN, 38112-1690. **EMAIL** muesse@rhodes.edu

MULLER, RALF
DISCIPLINE PHILOSOPHY **EDUCATION** ME Univ, PhD. **CAREER** Asst prof, Fordham Univ. **RESEARCH** Pragmatism, Peirce philos of mind, logic. **SELECTED PUBLICATIONS** On the Principles of Construction and the Order of Peirce's Trichotomies of Signs, Transactions of the Charles Sanders Peirce Society, 94; Peirce and Israel/Perry on the Conditions of Informational Flow, Proceedings of the Fifth Congress on the International Association for Semiotic Studies, Berkeley, 94. **CONTACT ADDRESS** Dept of Philos, Fordham Univ, 113 W 60th St, New York, NY, 10023.

MULLIN, ROBERT BRUCE
PERSONAL Born 10/24/1953, Plainfield, NJ, m, 1960, 1 child **DISCIPLINE** RELIGIOUS HISTORY **EDUCATION** Col of William & Mary, AB, 75; Yale Divinity School, MAR, 79; Yale Univ, PhD. **CAREER** Instr, Yale Univ, 84-85; asst prof to prof, North Carolina State Univ, 85-98; LEARNING PROF OF HIST & WORLD MISSION, GENERAL THEOLOGICAL SEMINARY, 98-. **MEMBERSHIPS** Soc for the Promotion of Religion, General Theological Seminary; AAR; ASCH; Hist Soc of the Episcopal Church. **RESEARCH** American religious history; modern intellectual history; Anglicanism. **SELECTED PUBLICATIONS** Auth, Episcopal Vision/American Reality: High Church Theology and Social Thought in Evangelical America, Yale Univ Press, 86; The Scientific Theist: A Life of Francis Ellingwood Abbot, Mercer Univ Press, 87; Moneygripe's Apprentice: The Personal Narrative of Samuel Seabury III, Yale Univ Press, 89; Reimagining Denominationalism: Interpretive Essays, Oxford Univ Press, 94; Miracles and the Modern Religious Imagination, Yale Univ Press, 96. **CONTACT ADDRESS** The General Theological Sem, 175 Ninth Ave, New York, NY, 10011-4977.

MULRONEY, MICHAEL
DISCIPLINE TAX LAW **EDUCATION** State Univ Iowa, BSC, 54; Harvard Law Sch, JD, 59. **CAREER** Prof & dir, Grad Tax Prog,adj prof, Georgetown's grad tax prog; fac, Villanova Univ, 88-. **MEMBERSHIPS** ABA; DC Bar; Iowa Bar; Fed Bar Asn; Amer Asn Law Sch; Philadelphia Tax Conf; Int Fiscal Asn's USA Branch; Int Fiscal Res Inst Coun Experts & J. Edgar Murdock Inn Ct. **RESEARCH** Taxation. **SELECTED PUBLICATIONS** Publ on, Fed Tax Examinations Manual and For Taxation. **CONTACT ADDRESS** Law School, Villanova Univ, 800 Lancaster Ave, Villanova, PA, 19085-1692. **EMAIL** mulroney@law.vill.edu

MULVEY, BEN
PERSONAL Born 05/04/1954, Freeport, NY, m, 1995, 1 child **DISCIPLINE** PHILOSOPHY **EDUCATION** Mich State Univ, PhD, 93. **CAREER** Assoc prof, philos, Nova Southeastern Univ, 88-; dir, liberal arts, Nova Southeastern Univ, 97-. **MEMBERSHIPS** Amer Philos Asn; Fla Bioethics Network. **RESEARCH** Moral development; Bioethics. **SELECTED PUBLICATIONS** Auth, Response to The Case of Mr. B, Network News: The Newsletter of the Fla Bioethics Network, 98, 2, apr, 98; auth, Synopsis of a Practical Guide: Guidelines for Ethics Comittees, Jour of Fla Med Asn, v 84, n 8, nov, 97; auth, Autonomy and the Moral Tradition: The Foundation of the Patient Self-Determination Act of 1990, The Record, v 43, n 10, nov, 91; auth, Needs versus Rights: State Subsidized Abortions, The Mich Acad, v 18, n 3, jul, 86; co-auth, Guidelines for Ethics Committees, Fla Med Asn, 96. **CONTACT ADDRESS** Dept. of Liberal Arts, Nova Southeastern Univ, 3301 College Ave, Ft. Lauderdale, FL, 33314. **EMAIL** mulvey@polaris.acast.nova.edu

MUMBY, DENNIS K.
DISCIPLINE ORGANIZATIONAL COMMUNICATION, PHILOSOPHY OF COMMUNICATION **EDUCATION** Southern Ill Univ, PhD, 84. **CAREER** Assoc prof, Purdue Univ. **SELECTED PUBLICATIONS** Auth, The Political Function of Narrative in Organizations, Commun Monogr, 87; Communication & Power in Organizations, Ablex, 88; ed, Narrative & Social Control, Sage, 93. **CONTACT ADDRESS** Dept of Commun, Purdue Univ, 1080 Schleman Hall, West Lafayette, IN, 47907-1080. **EMAIL** dmumby@purdue.edu

MUNEVAR, GONZALO
PERSONAL Barranquilla, Colombia, d, 1 child **DISCIPLINE** PHILOSOPHY OF SCIENCE **EDUCATION** Calif State Univ, BA, 70; MA, 71; Univ Calif Berkeley, PhD, 75. **CAREER** Lectr, San Francisco State Univ, 75-76; asst to prof, Univ Nebr Omaha, 76-85; prof, 85-89; vis assoc prof, Stanford Univ, 83-84; vis res prof, Univ Newcastle, 86; vis res prof, Instituto de Filosofia, Madrid, 87; vis res prof, Univ Barcelona, 88; vis res prof, Univ de Santiago de Compostel a, 88; vis prof, Kobe Univ of Commerce, 93; vis prof, Univ Wash, 94; prof, The Evergreen State Coll, 89-97; vis prof Univ Calif Irvine, 97-. **HONORS AND AWARDS** Distinguished Res Award, Univ Nebr Omaha, 86; Nebr Found Professorship, Univ Nebr Omaha, 86-89. **MEMBERSHIPS** Am Philos Asn; Philos of Sci Asn; Am Asn for the Advan of Sci. **RESEARCH** Philosophy of sciences; Philosophy of Space Sciences; Philosophy of Technology; Philosophy of Mind; Ethics. **SELECTED PUBLICATIONS** Auth, Evolution and the Naked Truth, 98; The Master of Fate, 99; ed, Beyond Reason: Essays on the Philosophy of Paul K Feyerabend, 91; Spanish Studies in the Philosophy of Science, 96; co-ed, The Worst Enemy of Science? Essays on the Life and Thought of Paul Feyerabend, 99. **CONTACT ADDRESS** Dept of Philosphy, Univ of Calif, Irvine, CA, 92697. **EMAIL** munevarg@aol.com

MUNSON, RONALD
PERSONAL Born 10/19/1939, Jasper, TX, m, 1966 **DISCIPLINE** PHILOSOPHY **EDUCATION** Southern Methodist Univ, BA, 61; Columbia Univ, PhD(philos), 67. **CAREER** Preceptor contemp, civilization, Columbia Col, 64-67; from asst prof to assoc prof philos, 67-77, Prof Philos, Univ MO-ST Louis, 77-, Nat Endowment for Humanities younger humanist fel, Dept Biol, Harvard Univ, 72-73, vis prof, 77-78. **MEMBERSHIPS** Philos Sci Asn; Am Philos Asn; AAAS. **RESEARCH** Philosophy of science; philosophy of biology; philosophy of medicine. **SELECTED PUBLICATIONS** Ed, Man and Nature: Philosophical Issues in Biology, Dell, 71; auth, Biological Adaptation, Philos Sci, 71; Essay review: Ruse's philosophy of biology, Hist & Philos Sci, 75; Is biology a provincial science?, Philos Sci, 75; The Way of Words, Houghton-Mifflin, 76; Mechanism, vitalism, reductionism and organismic biology, Encycl del Novenciento, Rome, 76; coauth, Philosophy of biology, Encycl Britannica, 76; auth, Intervention and Reflection: Basic Issues in Medical Ethics, Wadsworth, 78; Testing Normative Naturalism - The Problem Of Scientific Medicine, British J For The Philosophy Of Science, Vol 0045, 1994. **CONTACT ADDRESS** Dept of Philosophy, Univ of Missouri, 8001 Natural Bridge, Saint Louis, MO, 63121-4499.

MUNZER, STEPHEN ROGER
PERSONAL Born 02/02/1944, Topeka, KS, m, 1967, 1 child **DISCIPLINE** LAW, PHILOSOPHY **EDUCATION** Univ Kans, BA, 66; Oxford Univ, BPhil, 69; Yale Univ Law Sch, JD, 72. **CAREER** Lawyer, Covington & Burling, Washington, DC, 72-73; staff atty, Legis Drafting res fund, Columbia Univ, 73-74; asst prof philos, Rutgers Col, Rutgers Univ, 74-77; assoc prof law, Univ Minn Law Sch, 77-80; Prof Law, Law Sch, Univ Calif, Los Angeles, 81-. **MEMBERSHIPS** Am Soc Polit & Legal Philos. **RESEARCH** Jurisprudence; property; legal and political philosophy. **SELECTED PUBLICATIONS** Auth, Legal Validity, Martinus Nijhoff, 72; Validity and legal conflicts, Yale Law J, 73; Retroactive law, J of Legal Studies, 77; Right answers, preexisting rights, and fairness, GA Law Rev, 77; coauth, Does the Constitution mean what it always meant?, Columbia Law Rev, 77; Aristotle Biology And The Transplantation Of Organs, J Of The History Of Biology, Vol 0026, 1993; Transplantation, Chemical Inheritance, And The Identity Of Organs, British J For The Philosophy Of Science, Vol 0045, 1994; Ellickson On Chronic Misconduct In Urban Spaces - Of Panhandlers, Bench Squatters, And Day Laborers, Harvard Civil Rights-Civil Liberties Law Review, Vol 0032, 1997. **CONTACT ADDRESS** Law Sch, Univ of California, 405 Hilgard Ave, Los Angeles, CA, 90024.

MURDOCK, JONAH
PERSONAL Born 04/28/1969, New York, NY, m, 1998 **DISCIPLINE** PHILOSOPHY **EDUCATION** Northwestern Univ, PhD, 98 **CAREER** Research Asst, Northwestern Univ, present **MEMBERSHIPS** Amer Phil Assoc. **RESEARCH** Political philosophy; ethics; health care policy **CONTACT ADDRESS** Inst for Health Services Research and Policy Studi, Northwestern Univ, 629 Noyes St, Evanston, IL, 60208-4170. **EMAIL** jmurdock@nwu.edu

MURNION, WILLIAM E.
PERSONAL Born 01/27/1933, New York, NY, m, 1969, 2 children **DISCIPLINE** PHILOSOPHY; THEOLOGY **EDUCATION** St Joseph's Sem, BA, 54; Gregorian Univ, STB, 56, STL, 58, PhD, 70. **CAREER** Instr, St John's Sem, 66-67; asst prof, Duquesne Univ, 67-68; fac fel, Boston Col, 68-69; asst prof, Newton Col, 69-72; PROF, RAMAPO COL OF NJ, 72-.

HONORS AND AWARDS Fel, Inst for Ecumenical and Cultural Res, 74-75; dir, NEH Summer seminars for school teachers, 92, 95. **MEMBERSHIPS** Amer Philos Assoc; Amer Academy Relig; Soc for Ancient Greek Philos; Soc for Medieval Philos. **RESEARCH** Aquinas; philos of mind; philos of hist; philos of relig. **SELECTED PUBLICATIONS** Auth, Questions About the Family, in M. D. Bayles, R. C. Moffat, and J. Grcic, eds, Perspectives on the Family, Lewiston, NY: Edwin Mellon Press, 90; Aquinas on Revolution, in Werner Maihofer and Gerhard Sprenger, eds, Revolution and Human Rights, Archiv fur Rechts-und Sozialphilosophie, Beiheft 41, Stuttgart: Steiner Verlag, 90; The Foundations of Rights, in J. K. Roth and C. Peden, eds, Rights, Justice, and Community, Lewiston, NY: EDwin Mellon Press, 92; Multiculturalism and the Transformation of World History, J of Multicultural Ed of NJ 1, 93; The Phenomenology of Hegel's Concept of Religion, in Ugo Bianchi, ed, The Notion of Religion in Comparative Research: Selected Proceedings of the XVI IAHR Congress, Rome: L'Erma di Bretschneider, 94; Natural Law or Social Contract? The Foundation of Rights in Hobbes and Locke, in J. Ralph Lindgren, ed, Horizons of Justice: Critic of Institutions 8, NY: Peter Lang, 96; Aquinas's Earliest Philosophy of Mind: Mens in the Commentary on the Sentences and Other Contemporaneous Writings, in Jeremiah Hackett, ed, Aquinas on Mind and Intellect: New Essays, NY: Dowling Col Press, 96. **CONTACT ADDRESS** Ramapo Col, New Jersey, Mahwah, NJ, 07430. **EMAIL** wmurnion@ramapo.edu

MURPHY, EDWARD JOSEPH
PERSONAL Born 07/16/1927, Springfield, IL, m, 1954, 9 children **DISCIPLINE** LAW **EDUCATION** Univ Ill, BS, 49, LLB, 51. **CAREER** From asst prof to assoc prof, 57-64, prof, 65-80, John N Matthews Prof Law, Univ Notre Dame, 80-. **RESEARCH** Contracts; commercial law; education. **SELECTED PUBLICATIONS** Auth, Contracts Casebook: Cases and Materials on the Law of Contracts and Sales (temp ed), 63; Facilitation and regulation in the uniform commercial code, Notre Dame Lawyer, 66; Another assault upon the Citadel: Limiting the use of negotiable notes and waiver-of-defense clauses in consumer sales, Ohio State Law J, 68; The Sign Of The Cross And Jurisprudence, Notre Dame Law Review, Vol 0069, 1994; The Sign Of The Cross And Jurisprudence, Notre Dame Law Review, Vol 0071, 1996. **CONTACT ADDRESS** Law Sch, Univ of Notre Dame, Notre Dame, IN, 46556.

MURPHY, FREDERICK J.
DISCIPLINE RELIGIOUS STUDIES **EDUCATION** Harvard Univ, BA, 71, PhD, 84; Univ London, BD, 77. **CAREER** Tchg asst, Harvard Univ, 81-83; asst prof, 83-89; assoc prof, 89-94; prof, 94-. **MEMBERSHIPS** Soc Jesuit Col and Univ. **SELECTED PUBLICATIONS** Auth, The Structure and Meaning of Second Baruch, Scholars, 85; The Religious World of Jesus: An Introduction to Second Temple Palestinian Judaism, Abingdon, 91; Pseudo-Philo: Rewriting the Bible, Oxford, 93; The Book of Revelation, 94; Apocalypses and Apocalypticism: The State of the Question, 94; The Martial Option in Pseudo-Philo, 95. **CONTACT ADDRESS** Religious Dept, Col of the Holy Cross, Worcester, MA, 01610-2395. **EMAIL** fmurphy@holycross.edu

MURPHY, JOHN F.
DISCIPLINE INTERNATIONAL LAW **EDUCATION** Cornell Univ, BA, 59; Cornell Law Sch, LLB, 62. **CAREER** Prof, Villanova Univ; taught, Aix-en Provence, London, Mexico City & Paris; past fel in the Afro-Asian Public serv Fel Prog, Govt India; past consult, Coun for Int Exchange Scholars; US Dept Justice; UN Crime Prevention Unit, Vienna, Austria; ABA Standing Comt on Law and Nat Security; US Dept State; UN Asn US Am; Comn on the Orgn Govt for the Conduct of For Policy; Int Task Force on Prevention of Nuclear Terrorism & Univ Microfilms Int. **HONORS AND AWARDS** Certificate of Merit, Amer Soc Int Law. **MEMBERSHIPS** ABA's Alternate Observer, US Mission to the UN; Coun ABA's Section Int Law and Practice, 94-96; exec coun, Amer Soc Int Law, 89-92; exec comt, Amer Branch Int Law Asn; Panel of Arbitrators for the NY Stock Exchange. **RESEARCH** International law, international business transactions, international terrorism. **SELECTED PUBLICATIONS** Auth, Report of the Task Force on an International Criminal Court of the American Bar Association, 95; State Support of International Terrorism: Legal, Political, and Economic Dimensions, 89; Punishing International Terrorists: The Legal Framework for Policy Initiatives, 85; The United Nations and the Control of International Violence: A Legal and Political Analysis, 83 & Legal Aspects of International Terrorism: Summary Report of an International Conference, 80; coauth, The Constitutional Law of the European Union, 96; Instructor's Manual for the Constitutional Law of the European Union, 96; Teacher's Guide for the Regulation of International Business and Economic Relations, 92; The Regulation of International Business and Economic Relations, 91; & Legal Aspects of International Terrorism, 78. **CONTACT ADDRESS** Law School, Villanova Univ, 800 Lancaster Ave, Villanova, PA, 19085-1692. **EMAIL** murphy@law.vill.edu

MURPHY, JULIEN
DISCIPLINE PHILOSOPHY **EDUCATION** DePaul Univ, PhD, 82. **CAREER** Prof and assoc dean, Col of Arts and Sci;

teaches in, women's stud prog and Honors prog. **RESEARCH** Contemporary continental philosophy; medical ethics; feminist theory. **SELECTED PUBLICATIONS** Publ chap, in 12 bk(s) on phenomenol, med, and recent French philosophy, unluding Feminist Interpretations of Simone de Beauvoir, Penn State UP, 95; auth, The Constructed Body: AIDS, Reproductive Technology, and Ethics, SUNY Press, 95; ed, Feminist Reinterpretations of Jean-Paul Sartre. **CONTACT ADDRESS** Dept of Philosophy, Univ of Southern Maine, 96 Falmouth St, PO Box 9300, Portland, ME, 04104-9300. **EMAIL** jmurphy@usm.maine.edu

MURPHY, LAURENCE LYONS
PERSONAL Born 08/23/1948, New York, NY **DISCIPLINE** COMPARATIVE LITERATURE, PHILOSOPHY **EDUCATION** Rugers Univ, PhD, 90 **CAREER** Asst prof Intellectual Heritage, Philos, Temple Univ, Tyler Sch Art, 91- . **HONORS AND AWARDS** Merit Hons; Violet Keters awd for disting Srv and tchg. **MEMBERSHIPS** Amer Philos Asn **RESEARCH** Phenomenology, Hermeneutics. **SELECTED PUBLICATIONS** Exec ed, Ellipses, Jour Arts and Ideas. **CONTACT ADDRESS** Dept of Art, Temple Univ, 7900 Old York Rd, No 308A, Elkins Park, PA, 19027. **EMAIL** lmurphy@erols.com

MURPHY, MARK CHRISTOPHER
PERSONAL Born 10/14/1968, Coral Gables, FL, m, 1992, 1 child **DISCIPLINE** PHILOSOPHY **EDUCATION** Univ Texas, BA, 88; Univ Notre Dame, MA, 92, PhD, 93. **CAREER** Asst prof Philos, Univ Hawaii, 93-95; asst prof Philos, Georgetown Univ, 95-; Erasmus fel, 98-99. **MEMBERSHIPS** APA; Soc Christian Philos; ACPA. **RESEARCH** Ethics; Political philosophy; Philosophy of law; History of early modern philosophy. **SELECTED PUBLICATIONS** Auth Deviant Uses of Obligation in Hobbes Leviathan, Hist of Philos Quart, 94; Acceptance of Authority and the Requirement to Comply with Just Institutions: A Comment on Waldron, Philos & Pub Affairs, 94; Philosophical Anarchism and Legal Indifference, Am Philos Quart, 95; Was Hobbes a Legal Positivist? Ethics, 95; Self-Evidence, Human Nature, and Natural Law, Am Cath Philos Quart, 95; Hobbes on Conscientious Disobedience, Archiv fur Geschichte der Philos, 95; Natural Law, Impartialism, and Others Good, Thomist, 96; Consent, Custon, and the Common Good in Aquinas Theory of Political Authority, Rev Politics, 97; Surrender of Judgment and the Consent Theory of Political Authority, Law and Philos, 97; Divine Command, Divine Will, and Moral Obligation, Faith and Philos, 98. **CONTACT ADDRESS** Philosophy Dept, Georgetown Univ, 215 New North, Washington, DC, 20057. **EMAIL** murphym@gunet.georgetown.edu

MURPHY, NANCEY
PERSONAL Born 06/12/1951, Alliance, NE **DISCIPLINE** PHILOSOPHY; THEOLOGY **EDUCATION** Creighton Univ, BA, 73; Univ Calif Berkeley, PhD, 80; Graduate Theological Union, ThD, 87. **CAREER** Lecturer, Dominican School of Philosophy and Theology, 87-88; visiting asst prof of religion, Whittier Coll, 88-89; asst prof, 89-91, assoc prof, 91-98, prof, 98-, Christian philosophy, Fuller Theological Seminary. **HONORS AND AWARDS** Creighton Univ Alumni Achievement Award, 98; Templeton Award, for Theology in the Age of Scientific Reasoning; American Acad of Religion Book Award for Excellence in the Constructive-Reflective Category, for Theology in the Age of Scientific Reasoning; National Science Found Fellow, 3 years; President's Scholar, Creighton Univ. **MEMBERSHIPS** Amer Philos Assn; Amer Acad Religion; Soc Christian Philosophers; Center Theology Natural Scis. **RESEARCH** Current Anglo-American philosophy; philosophy of religion; relation between science and religion. **SELECTED PUBLICATIONS** Coauth, On the Moral Nature of the Universe: Theology, Cosmology, and Ethics, 96; auth, Anglo-American Postmodernity: Philosophical Perspectives on Science, Religion, and Ethics, 97; auth, Reconciling Theology and Science: A Radical Reformation Perspective, 97; coauth, Virtues and Practices in the Christian Tradition: Christian Ethics after MacIntyre, 97; coauth, Whatever Happened to the Soul? Scientific and Theological Portraits of Human Nature, 98 **CONTACT ADDRESS** Fuller Theol Sem, 135 N Oakland Ave, Pasadena, CA, 91182.

MURPHY, ROMALLUS O.
PERSONAL Born 12/18/1928, Oakdale, LA, m **DISCIPLINE** LAW **EDUCATION** Howard Univ, BA 1951; Univ NC, JD 1956. **CAREER** Pvt law prac 1956-62; Erie Human Rel Commn, exec dir 1962-65; Mitchell & Murphy, 1965-70; Mayor's Comm Rel Committee, exec secr 1968; Shaw Univ, spec asst to pres 1968-70; Shaw Coll at Detroit, pres 1970-82; Gen Counsel NC State Conf of Branches NAACP; gen practice emphasis on civil rights; private practice, atty 1983-. **HONORS AND AWARDS** Omega Man of the Year 1968; Detroit Howardite for Year Howard Univ Alumni 1974; Key to City Positive Futures Inc New Orleans 1974; Citizen of the Year Awd Omega Psi Phi 1977; Community Serv Awd Greensboro Br NAACP 1985; Tar Heel of the Week NC; Educator of the Year, Gamma Phi Delta Sorority, 1975; William Robert Ming Advocacy Award, NAACP, 1990. **MEMBERSHIPS** Mem Intermittent consult conciliator 1966-69; Amer Arbitration Assoc, Arbitrators & Community Dispute Settlement Panel, ACE, AAHE,

NBL, NEA, Positive Futures Inc, Task Force Detroit Urban League Inc, NAACP; bd mem Metro Fund Inc; mem Central Governing Bd & Educ Com Model Neighborhood Agency; charter mem Regional Citizens Inc; mem Greensboro Task Force One; bd mem Good News Jail & Prison Ministry; trustee, sec trust bd Shiloh Baptist Church; pres Laymen's League Shiloh Baptist Church; mem Omega Psi Phi; bd mem Greensboro Br NAACP; mem Foreign Travel for Intl Commun Agency & other govt agencies in South Africa, Zambia, Nigeria & Kenya; partic Smithsonian InstTravel Seminar in India; mem NC Assn Amer Bar Assn, NC Black Lawyers Assn. **CONTACT ADDRESS** PO Box 20383, Greensboro, NC, 27420.

MURPHY, TIM
PERSONAL Kileen, TX **DISCIPLINE** RELIGIOUS STUDIES **EDUCATION** Wichita State Univ, BA, 84; Univ Calif Santa Cruz, PhD, 97. **CAREER** Instr, Univ Calif Santa Cruz, 91-96; adjunct prof, San Jose State Univ, 96-97; fellow, Case Western Reserve Univ, 97-. **HONORS AND AWARDS** Mellon Postdoctoral Fel. **MEMBERSHIPS** North Am Asn for the Study of Relig; Am Acad of Relig; North Am Nietzsche Soc **RESEARCH** Nineteenth-century German religious thought; Philosophy of religion; Religious theory; Postmodern cultural theory. **SELECTED PUBLICATIONS** Ed, Postmodernism and the Study of Religion: A Reader, 99; "Nietzsche's 'Jesus'" in Epoche, 98; "The Concept of Entwicklung in German Religionswissenschaft Before and After Darwin," 98. **CONTACT ADDRESS** Dept of Religion, Case Western Reserve Univ, 10900 Euclid Ave, Cleveland, OH, 44106-7112. **EMAIL** txm55@po.cwru.edu

MURRAY, J-GLENN
PERSONAL Born 04/22/1950, Philadelphia, Pennsylvania, s **DISCIPLINE** THEOLOGY **EDUCATION** St Louis University, BA, 1974; Jesuit School of Theology at Berkeley, MDiv, 1979; Aquinas Institute, MA, 1996; Catholic Theological Union of Chicago, DMin, 1996. **CAREER** St Frances Academy, asst principal, 1981-88; Office for Pastoral Liturgy, asst dir, 1989-; St Mary Seminary, homiletics professor, 1992-. **HONORS AND AWARDS** Archdiocese of Baltimore, Youth Ministry Medal of Honor, 1988. **MEMBERSHIPS** National Black Catholic Clergy Caucus, 1979-; Catholic Assn of Teachers of Homiletics, 1992-; Academy of Homiletics, 1992-; North American Academy of Liturgy, 1993-; Black Catholic Theological Symposium, 1994-. **CONTACT ADDRESS** Office for Pastoral Liturgy, 1031 Superior Ave., Ste 361, Cleveland, OH, 44114.

MURRAY, PIUS
PERSONAL Born 07/24/1957, Worcester, MA **DISCIPLINE** RELIGION **EDUCATION** Col of the Holy Cross, AB, 79; Univ Rhode Island, MLS, 82; Holy Apostles Col and Sem, MA, 90; Holy Apostles Col and Sem, MDiv, 91; Pontifical Bibl Inst, SSL, 95. **CAREER** Libr 1, Business Office, Worcester Publ Libr, 80-82; libr dir, Greenfield, MA Publ Libr, 82-83; Libr Superv, Dinand Libr, Col Holy Cross, 80-86; Town Libr, West Springfield, MA Publ Libr, 85-86; Stud Asst Libr, Holy Apostles Col and Sem, 88-90; Assoc Dir Libr Svcs and Instr in Sacred Scripture, Apostles Col and Sem, 95-96; Adj Prof Old Test, Pope John XXIII Natl Sem, 95-96; Prof Old Test and Libr Dir, Pope John XXIII Natl Sem, 96- . **HONORS AND AWARDS** Invested as priest-knight in the Equestrian Order of the Holy Sepulchre in Jerusalem, Nov 96; Mem, Ancient Order of the Hiberians, div no14, Watertown, MA; Member, Knights of Columbus; Marquis Who's Who in the East, 96; Marquis Who's Who in Am, 97; Marquis Who's Who in the World, 98; The Dictionary of International Biography, 98; Intl Biographical Ctr's 2000 Outstanding People of the 20th Century; IBC's International Who's Who of Intellectuals, 98; Mem, IBC's Order of International Fellowship; Amer Biographical Institute's 500 Leaders of Influence, 98; Nominated for inclusion in ABI's International Book of Honor, 99. **MEMBERSHIPS** Amer Acad Rel; Amer Libr Assn; Amer Theol Libr Assn; Cath Bibl Assn; Cath Libr Assn; Ctr Bus Ethics; Col Theol Soc; Inst Rel in an Age of Sci; Phi Beta Kappa; Soc Bibl Lit; Soc Christian Ethics; World Affairs Coun Boston. **RESEARCH** Old Testament Theology; Pentateuch; Deutero-Isaiah. **SELECTED PUBLICATIONS** Auth, Proposition 2 1/2 and the Message from Massachusetts Taxpayers: No Taxation Without Limitation, Current Studies in Librarianship, 2, Spring/Fall 81, 21-31; Finantial Management, in Current Studies in Librarianship, 3, Spring/Fall 82, 25-31; You Shall Know the Truth: The New Christian Right and Censorship, Drexel Library Quart, 18, Winter 82, 4-25; The Watergate Scandals; Government Publications, Current Studies in Librarianship, 4, Spring/Fall 84, 39-51; In His Own Image and Likeness:' A Review Article on Bioethics and Artificial Procreation, The Priest, Oct 89, 35-43; A Spirit of Humility, Abandonment, and Love: The Charism of the Stigmatine Fathers and Brothers, Rev for Religious, Sept/Oct 89, 774-776; Mary, The Obedient Woman of Faith, Our Lady's Dig, Summer 90, 17-23; A Pool Called Bethzatha (JN 5:2): Archaeological Evidence and the New Testament, The Holy Land Rev, 13, Summer 93, 80-90; Religion in the Secular City: The Role of the Laity in Today's Church, Emmanuel, Jan/Feb 92, 4-9, 48; The Challenge of Peace-Revisited, Emmanuel, July/Aug 93, 314-317; Rev of Eyewitness to Jesus: Amazing New manuscript Evidence About the Origins of the Gospels, by Carsten Peter Thiede and Matthew D'Ancona, Doubleday, 96, Cath Libr World, 67, Dec 96, 46; Rev of Cracking the Bible Code:

The Real Story of the Stunning Discovery of Hidden Knowledge in the First Five Books of the Bible, by Jaffrey Satinover, William Morrow, 97, Cath Libr World, 68, 42, June 98; Rev of The Convergence of Science and Faith: A Review of God & the Big Bang: Discovering Harmony Between Science and Spirituality, by Daniel C. Matt, Woodstock, VT, Jewish Lights Publ, 96, The Natl Catholic Register, 72, Nov 3-9, 96, 6; The Community of Religions: Voices and Images of the Parliament of the World's Religions, ed Wayne Teasdale and George F. Cairn, Continuum, 96, Cath Libr World, 67, Sept 96, 39-40; The Community of Religions: Voices and Images of the Parliament of the World's Religions, ed, Teasdale, Wayne, and George F. Cairns, New York, Continuum, Aug 96, Libr Jour, 121, July 96, 121; Celebrating an Authentic Passover Seder: A Haggadah for Home and Church, by Joseph M. Stallings, Resource Publ, 94, in Cath Libr World, 67, Dec 96, 54; Carmichael, Calum M., Law Legend, and incest in the Bible: Leviticus 18-20, Cornell, 97, Choice, 35, Feb 98, 1003-4; Can You Drink the Cup? by Henri J.M. Nouwen, Ave Maria Press, 96, Cath Libr World, 68, dec 97, 61; The Bible: A Soothsayer's Stock-in-Trade? A Review of The Bible Code by Michael Drosnin, The Nat Cath Reg, 73, Nov 30-Dec 6, 97, 8; Beyond the Comos: The Extra-Dimensionality of God, by Hugh Ross, NavPress, 96, Cath Libr World, 67, Sept 96, 34; America's Finest Authors on Reading, Writing and the Power of Ideas ¤Booknotesl by Brian Lamb, Random House, 97, Cath Libr World, 68, Dec 97, 76; Alternative in Jewish Bioethics, by Noam J. Zohar, State U of New York P (SUNY Series in Jewish Philosophy), 1997, Cath Libr World, 68, Sept 97, 61; Alexandria and Alexandrianism: Papers Delivered at a Symposium Organized by the J. Paul Getty Museum and the Getty Center for the History of Art and the Humanities and Held at the Museum April 22-25, 93, The J. Paul Getty Museum, 96, Cath Libr World, 68, Dec 97, 75-76. **CONTACT ADDRESS** Stigmatine Fathers and Brothers, Bertoni Hall, 554 Lexington St, Waltham, MA, 02154. **EMAIL** seminary@ziplink.net

MURRELL, NATHANIEL S.
PERSONAL Born 02/20/1945, Grenada, m, 1981, 3 children **DISCIPLINE** BIBLICAL STUDIES **EDUCATION** Drew Univ, PhD; Rutgers Univ, M Ed 90; Wheaton Grad Sch, MA 81. **CAREER** Univ N Carolina, asst prof 95-; Col of Wooster, asst prof 91-95; Univ West Indies, exam reader. **HONORS AND AWARDS** Waterman Awd; AAR Res. **MEMBERSHIPS** AAR; SBL. **RESEARCH** Hebrew Bible; Religions in the African Diaspora and Africa. **SELECTED PUBLICATIONS** Auth, Chanting Down Babylon: The Rastafari Reader, Temple Univ Press, 98; auth, Introduction to Afro-Caribbean Religions, Temple Univ Press, forthcoming 2000. **CONTACT ADDRESS** Dept Philosophy and Religion, Univ of No Carolina, 601 South College Rd, Wilmington, NC, 28409. **EMAIL** murrells@uncwil.edu

MURZAKU, INES A.
PERSONAL Born 06/02/1964, Tirana, Albania, m, 1987, 1 child **DISCIPLINE** ORIENTAL CHURCH HISTORY **EDUCATION** Ponitfical Oriental Institute, PhD, 95. **CAREER** Asst prof, Acad Arts, Tirana-Albania, 86-91; journalist, East Europe - Vatican Radio, 92-94; ADJ PROF, ST. JOHN FISHER COL, 96- . **MEMBERSHIPS** AAR; AHA; ACHA; AAASS; ASN. **RESEARCH** East Europe: religion, history and culture; Jesuit history; Albanian history; religious values and contemporary society; women in the church. **SELECTED PUBLICATIONS** Auth, Angazhimi yne Shoqeror, 94; auth, Religion in Post-Communist Albania, Missioni e Popoli, 94; auth, The Activity and the Role of the Jesuits in the Albanian History and Culture 1841-1946, 96; The Flying Mission (Missione Volante), Diakonia; The Beginning of the Jesuit Albanian Mission, Diakonia. **CONTACT ADDRESS** 3242 Leeward Cir., Walworth, NY, 14568. **EMAIL** murzaku@sjfc.edu

MUSCARI, PAUL G.
PERSONAL Born 11/09/1940, Brooklyn, NY, m, 1974, 2 children **DISCIPLINE** PHILOSOPHY **EDUCATION** NY Univ, PhD, 73. **CAREER** Prof, Humanities chmn, 73-, Adirondack Comm Coll, Queensbury. **HONORS AND AWARDS** Disting Prof Awd, Chancellors Awd Teaching Excellence, Teacher of the Yr, IAPR Awd. **MEMBERSHIPS** APA, P&PEA. **RESEARCH** Biomedical ethics, philosophy of mind. **SELECTED PUBLICATIONS** Auth, Subjective Experience, in: Philo Inquiry, 92, Plea for the Poetic Metaphor, in: J of Mind & Behavior, 92; The Depersonalization of Creativity, in: J of Mind & Behavior, 94; Science and Creativity, in: Contemp Philo, 95; A Critique of Changing the World, in: J of Mind & Behavior, 95. **CONTACT ADDRESS** 28 Broadacres Rd, Queensbury, NY, 12804.

MUUSS, ROLF EDUARD HELMUT
PERSONAL Born 09/26/1924, Tating, Germany, m, 1953, 2 children **DISCIPLINE** EDUCATIONAL PSYCHOLOGY, MINOR CLINICAL PSYCHOLOGY **EDUCATION** Univ Maryland Law School and Anne Arundel Community Col, State Level Hearing Officer Training Prog, 80; Univ IL, Urbana, PhD, 57; Western Maryland Col, Westminster, MD, Med, 53-54; Teachers Col, Columbia Univ, NY, 52; Central Missouri State Col, Warrensburg, MO, 51-52; Univ Hamburg, Germany, 51; Padagogische Hochschule, Flensburg, Teaching Diploma, 49-51; People's High School, Sigtuna, Sweden, 48-49. **CAREER** Prof Emer, Goucher Col, Towson, MD, 95-; State Level Hearing Officer (Spec Edu Hearings) for the State of Maryland, 80-85; Chair, Sociology and Anthropology, Goucher Col, Towson, MD, 83-85; Dir Spec Edu, Goucher Col, Towson,MD, 77-92; Chair, Dept edu, Goucher Col, Towson, MD, 72-75; Full Prof, Goucher Col, Towson, MD, 64-95; Assoc Prof, Goucher Col, Towson, MD, 59-64; Research Asst Prof, State Univ Iowa, IA, 57-59; Grad Asst, Univ Illinois, Urbana, IL, 54-57; Houseparent, Child Study Cen, Baltimore, MD, 53; Sub Principal and Teacher, Flensburg, Germany, 52-53; Teacher Trainee, Office of Edu, Washington, DC, 51-52; Public School Teacher, Sudtondern, Germany, 45-46. **HONORS AND AWARDS** Holder of the Elizabeth C Todd Distinguished Professorship, (honorary chair with fin support for research), 80-85; Goucher Col Award for Distinguished Scholarship, 79; Andrew Mellon Foundation Grant for Faculty Development, 76-77; Mary Williams Fellowship in the Social Services, 72, 73. **MEMBERSHIPS** Soc for Research on Adolescence; Soc for Research in Child Development; Am Psychol Asn, (Fellow in div 7 and 15); Am Psychol Soc (Fellow); Maryland Psychol Asn (Treasurer 71-73); Baltimore Psychol Asn (VP 70-71); Phi Delta Kappa; Kappa Delta Pi (chapter VP 56-57). **RESEARCH** Adolescent development; Theories of Adolescence; Adolescent Problem Behavior. **SELECTED PUBLICATIONS** Theories of Adolescence, Random House, NY, 1st ed 62, 2d ed 68, 3d ed 75, 4th ed 82, 5th ed 88, 6th ed with McGraw-Hill, 96, trans into Dutch, German, Hebrew, Italian, Japanese, Portuguese, Spanish; Adolescent Behavior and Society: A Book of Readings, Random House, NY, 1st ed 71, 2d ed 75, 3d ed 80, 4th ed 80, 4th and 5th eds, with McGraw-Hill, NY, 5th ed 99; First Aid for Classroom Discipline Problems, Holt Rinehart & Winston, 62, trans Portuguese; Grundlagen der Jugendpsychologie, Hansiche Verlagsanstalt, Lubeck, Germany; More than 100 scientific papers and research articles in medical, psychol, edu, journals in USA, Eng, Ger, Switz, Swed. **CONTACT ADDRESS** 1540 Pickett Rd, Lutherville, MD, 21093-5822. **EMAIL** rmuuss@goucher.edu

MUZOREWA, GWINYAL
PERSONAL Zimbabwe, m, 1976, 4 children **DISCIPLINE** THEOLOGY **EDUCATION** Union Theol Sem, PhD, 83. **CAREER** Lectr, 81-84, acad dean, 85-85, 91-94, United Theol Col, Harare; assoc prof, United Theol Sem, 88-90; prof relig, Lincoln Univ, 98- . **HONORS AND AWARDS** Phi Theta Capa; Maslow Fel, 77-78. **MEMBERSHIPS** Clergy of the United Methodist Church; Ecumenical Asn of Third World Theol; Acad Am Relig. **RESEARCH** African and African American religion and theology. **SELECTED PUBLICATIONS** Auth, The Origin and Development of African Theology, Orbis; auth, An African Theology of Mission, Mellen. **CONTACT ADDRESS** PO Box 4, Lincoln University, PA, 19352-0004. **EMAIL** GMuzorewa@lincoln.edu

MYERS, CHARLES EDWARD
PERSONAL Born 02/01/1955, Pasadena, CA **DISCIPLINE** THEOLOGY **EDUCATION** Univ Calif, Berkley, BA, 78; Grad Theol Union, Berkeley, MA, 84. **CAREER** Lectr, nonviolence, Sch of Applied Theol, 80; adj fac, liberation theol, Immaculate Heart Col, 86, 88; adj fac, ethics and New Testament, Sch Theol, Claremont, CA, 93; adj fac, ethics and New Testament, Fuller Sch Theol, Pasadena, 93-96; lect, Churches of Christ Theol Col, Melbourne, Australia, 97. **HONORS AND AWARDS** Phi Beta Kappa, 78. **MEMBERSHIPS** Soc for Bibl Lit. **RESEARCH** Ethics and the Bible. **SELECTED PUBLICATIONS** Auth, The Ideology and Social Strategy of Mark's Gospel, in Gottwald, ed, The Bible and Liberation: Political and Social Hermeneutics, Orbis, 93; auth, The Wilderness Temptations and the American Journey, in Ebert, ed, Richard Rohr: Illuminations of His Life and Work, Crossroads, 93; auth, Who Will Roll Away the Stone: Discipleship Queries for First World Christians, Orbis, 94; auth, I Will Ask You A Question: Interrogatory Theology, in Hauerwas, ed, Theology Without Foundations: Religions Practice and the Future of Theological Truth, Abingdon, 94; auth, Proclamation 6, Year B, Pentecost 1, Fortress, 96; coauth, Say to This Mountain: Mark's Story of Discipleship, Orbis, 96; auth, Forward, in Beck, ed, Nonviolent Story; Narrative Conflict Resolution in the Gospel of Mark, Orbis, 96; auth, Beyond the Addict's Excuse: Public Addiction and Ecclesial Recovery, in Nelson, ed, Sin and Alienation, Abingdon, 98; **CONTACT ADDRESS** 706 Burwood Terr, Los Angeles, CA, 90042. **EMAIL** chedmyers@igc.apc.org

MYERS, DAVID
DISCIPLINE RELIGIOUS HISTORY **EDUCATION** Yale Univ, PhD. **CAREER** Assoc prof, Fordham Univ. **HONORS AND AWARDS** Reviewer, Chicago Tribune Bk Rev. **RESEARCH** Hist of sin and crime in early mod Europe. **SELECTED PUBLICATIONS** Auth, Poor, Sinning Folk: Confession and the Making of Consciences in Counter-Reformation Germany, Cornell UP, 96; Die Jesuiten die Beichte, und die katholische Reformation in Bayern, Beitge zur altbayerischen Kirchengeschichte 96; Ritual, Confession, and Religion in Early Sixteenth-Century Germany, Arch fur Reformationsgeschichte, 97. **CONTACT ADDRESS** Dept of Hist, Fordham Univ, 113 W 60th St, New York, NY, 10023.

MYERS, GERALD E.
PERSONAL Born 06/19/1923, Central City, NE, m, 1948, 1 child **DISCIPLINE** PHILOSOPHY **EDUCATION** Haveland Col, AB, 47; Brown Univ, MA, 49, PhD, 54. **CAREER** Inst/Asst Prof, Williams Col, 52-61; Assoc Prof, Chmn Phil Dept, Kerry Col, 61-65; Prof, LIU, 65-67; Prof, Deputy Exec Off, Queens Col, CUNY, 67-91; Phil in Residence, Hon Dir, Amer Dance Festival, Durham, NC, 77-; Retired Emeritus Prof, 91. **HONORS AND AWARDS** NEH fel, 82-83. **MEMBERSHIPS** APA, Phi Beta Kappa **RESEARCH** Philosophy of psychology; american philosophy; aesthetics. **SELECTED PUBLICATIONS** Echoes From the Holocaust; Phil Reflect on a Dark Time, 88; The Black Tradition in American Modern Dance, 88-90; Reflections on the Home of An Art Form, Amer Dance Fest 65th Ann, 98. **CONTACT ADDRESS** 36 Gardner Ave, New London, CT, 06320.

MYERS, WILLIAM R.
DISCIPLINE THEOLOGY **EDUCATION** Westminster Col, BA, 64; Pittsburgh Theological Sem, Mdiv, 67; MA.ed, Rhode Island Col; Ed.d, 81, Loyola Univ. **CAREER** Academic Dean and Prof, Religious Education, 81-, Chicago Theological Sem. **CONTACT ADDRESS** Chicago Theol Sem, 5757 S University, Chicago, IL, 60637. **EMAIL** wmyers@chgosem.edu

MYRICKS, NOEL
PERSONAL Born 12/22/1935, Chicago, IL, w **DISCIPLINE** LAW **EDUCATION** San Francisco State Univ, BA 1965, MS 1967; Howard Univ, JD 1970; The American Univ, EdD 1974. **CAREER** Howard Univ, prof 1967-69; Univ of Dist of Columbia, educ administrator 1969-72; Private Practice, attorney 1973-; (admitted to practice before US Supreme Court); UNIV OF MARYLAND, prof beginning 1972, ASSOCIATE PROFESSOR, currently. **HONORS AND AWARDS** Appointed by Pres Jimmy Carter Natl Adv Council on Extension and Cont Educ 1978-81; Outstanding & Dedicated Serv to Youth & Community Easton, PA NAACP 1984; Outstanding Citizen of the Year Omega Psi Phi Frat Columbia, MD 1979; Faculty Minority Achievement Award, President's Commission on Ethnic Minority Issues, Univ of Maryland, 1990; Outstanding Advisor for a Student Organization, Campus Activities Office of Maryland, 1990; Superior Teaching Award, Office of the Dean for Undergraduate Studies, Univ of Maryland, 1990; Outstanding Mentor, UMCP, 1992; Outstanding Teacher of the Year, UMCP, 1992; Univ of MD at Coll Park Natl Championship Intercollegiate Mock Trial Team, coach/dir, 1992, 1993, 1996, 1998; Outstanding Teacher, Coll of Health & Human Performance, 1998; Outstanding Mentor, Omicron Delta Kappa, 1998. **MEMBERSHIPS** Certified agent NFL Players Assn 1984-; assoc editor Family Relations Journal 1978-82; mem, Kappa Upsilon Lambda, Alpha Phi Alpha, Reston, MD, 1984-; mem, American Bar Assn; mem, Groves Assn; educator, attorney coach, National Intercollegiate Mock Trial Champions, UMCP, 1992; Omicron Delta Kappa Honor Society, 1992. **CONTACT ADDRESS** Law Firm of Noel & Myricks, Reston, VA, 20191.

MYRVOLD, WAYNE C.
DISCIPLINE PHILOSOPHY **EDUCATION** McGill Univ, BS, 84; Boston Univ, PhD, 94. **CAREER** Asst prof **RESEARCH** Philosophy of physics; philosophy of mathematics; philosophy of biology. **SELECTED PUBLICATIONS** Auth, The Decision Problem for Entanglement, Kluwer, 97; Bayesianism and Diverse Evidence: A Reply to Andrew Wayne, Philos Sci, 96; Computability in Quantum Mechanics, Kluwer, 95; Peirce on Cantor's Paradox and the Continuum, 95; Tractatus 4.04: (Compare Hertz' Mechanics, on Dynamical Models, Verlag Holder-Pichler-Tempsky, 90. **CONTACT ADDRESS** Dept of Philosophy, Western Ontario Univ, London, ON, N6A 5B8. **EMAIL** wmyrvold@julian.uwo.ca

N

NADEAU, RANDALL
PERSONAL Born 04/30/1956, Lancaster, PA, m, 1987, 2 children **DISCIPLINE** RELIGION **EDUCATION** Oberlin Col, BA, 78; Princeton Univ, MA, 80; Univ British Columbia, PhD, 90. **CAREER** Assoc prof East Asian Relig, Trinity Univ, 90-. **MEMBERSHIPS** Asn Asian Studies; Am Acad Relig. **RESEARCH** Chinese religions; Buddhism; comparative religion. **SELECTED PUBLICATIONS** Auth, Dimensions of Sacred Space in Japanese Popular Culture, Intercultural Commun Studies, 97; auth, Frederick Streng, Madhyamika, and the Comparative Study of Religion, Buddhist-Christian Studies, 96; auth, Xunzi, Wang Chong, Wang Yang-ming, Great Thinkers of the Eastern World, 95; auth, The Domestication of Precious Scrolls: The Ssu-ming Tsao-chun pao-chuan, Jour Chinese Relig, 94; auth, Genre Classifications of Chinese Popular Religious Literature: Pao-chuan, Jour Chinese Relig, 93. **CONTACT ADDRESS** Dept of Religion, Trinity Univ, 715 Stadium Dr., San Antonio, TX, 78212-3422. **EMAIL** rnadeau@trinity.edu

NADIN, MIHAI
PERSONAL Born 02/02/1938, Brasov, Romania, m, 1971, 3 children **DISCIPLINE** AESTHETICS, SEMIOTICS **EDUCATION** Polytech Inst Bucharest, MS, 60; Univ Bucharest, MA, 68, PhD(aesthetics), 71; Univ Munich, Dr Phil habil (semiotics, value), 80. **CAREER** Prof philos & aesthetics, Univ Brasov, Romania, 69-75; sr philosopher, Inst Philos, Univ Bucharest, 75-77; prof aesthetics, Carolo-Wilhelmina Univ, 77-78; prof semiotics & aesthetics, Univ Munich, 78-80; assoc prof, 80-82, Prof Aesthetics & Semiotics, RI Sch of Design, 82-, Ed, ASTRA, Romania, 65-75; researcher, DAAD grant, WGer, 74-75 & Alexander von Humboldt Stiftung, Munich, 78-81; prof, Univ Essen, WGer, 79-80; ed, Kodikas Code, 80; adj prof, Ctr Res in Semiotics, Brown Univ, 81; dir, Inst for the Semiotics of the Visual, 81; consult, Semion Inc. **HONORS AND AWARDS** I L Caragiale Award, Romanian Award, 75; Richard Merton Award, Carolo-Wilhelmina Univ, 77. **MEMBERSHIPS** Semiotic Soc Am; Am Soc Aesthetics; Deutsche Gesellschaft Semiotik; Am Philos Asn. **RESEARCH** Semiotics of the visual: developing a methodological framework for visual communication; the civilization of illiteracy; value: research in artificial intelligence to model value decisions in the arts, society, market, economy, etc. **SELECTED PUBLICATIONS** Auth, A Day for Jewels, 71 & To Live Art--Elements of Metaesthetics, 72, Editura Eminescu; Mut fur den Alltag, SOI Verlag, 78; The logic of vagueness and the category of synechism, The Monist, 80; Sign and value in the energy crisis, KodikasCode, 81; Zeichen und Wert (sign and value), 81 & ed, New Elements in the Semiotics of Communication, 82, G Narr Verlag; auth, Consistency, completeness and meaning of sign theories, Am J of Semiotics, 82; 'On The Composition of Images, Signs And Ideas' - Bruno,g, Doria,c, Editor-translator, American J of Semiotics, Vol 0010, 1993; Understanding Prehistoric Images in The Post-historic Age - a Cognitive Project, Semiotica, Vol 0100, 1994. **CONTACT ADDRESS** Rhode Island Sch of Design, 2 College St, Providence, RI, 02903.

NAFZIGER, JAMES A.R.
PERSONAL Born 09/24/1940, Minneapolis, MN **DISCIPLINE** INTERNATIONAL LAW **EDUCATION** Univ Wis, BA, 62, MA, 69; Harvard Univ, JD, 67. **CAREER** Clerk, US District Ct, 67-69; fel, Am Soc Int Law, 69-70 & admin dir, 70-74; vis assoc prof law, Univ Ore, 74-77; Prof Law, Willamette Univ, Ore, 77-, lectr, Sch Law, Cath Univ, 70-74; Fulbright vis prof, Nat Univ Mex, 78; lectr & tutor, Inst Pub Int Law & Int Relations, Univ Thessaloniki, Greece, 82; Thomas B Stoel prof law & dir intl progs, Willamette University Coll of Law, 98. **MEMBERSHIPS** Assn Am Law Schs; Am Soc Int Law; Int Law Assn. **RESEARCH** Public international law; immigration law and policy; conflict of laws, private international law. **SELECTED PUBLICATIONS** auth, Law and Amateur Sports, Ind Univ Press, 82; auth, Conflict of Laws 85; auth, International Sports Law, 88. **CONTACT ADDRESS** Col of Law, Willamette Univ, 245 Winter St, SE, Salem, OR, 97301-3900.

NAGAN, WINSTON P.
PERSONAL South Africa **DISCIPLINE** LAW **EDUCATION** Univ S Africa, BA; Oxford Univ, BA, MA; Duke Univ, LLM, MCL; Yale Univ, JSD. **CAREER** Trustee res fel, prof Law,aff prof Anthrop, Univ Fla 75-. **HONORS AND AWARDS** Co-founded, 1st Human Rights & Peace Ctr in Uganda; jointly organizing int conf in Sarajevo that produced the Sarajevo Declaration. **MEMBERSHIPS** Amer Soc Int Law. **RESEARCH** Conflict of laws, international law, human rights, jurisprudence. **CONTACT ADDRESS** School of Law, Univ of Florida, PO Box 117625, Gainesville, FL, 32611-7625. **EMAIL** nagan@law.ufl.edu

NAGEL, MECHTHILD E.
PERSONAL Born 06/08/1966, Germany **DISCIPLINE** PHILOSOPHY **EDUCATION** Albert-Ludwigs-Univ, Germany, BA, 87; Univ of Mass-Amherst, PhD, 96. **CAREER** Tchg Asst, Univ Mass-Amherst, 88-96; Inst, 96-97, Asst Prof, 97-99, Mankato St Univ. **HONORS AND AWARDS** Fac Res Grant, 98-99. **MEMBERSHIPS** Rad Phil Assn; APA; AAUW; Soc Women in Phil; Natl Women Stud Asn; ASA; TASP **RESEARCH** Feminist; postmodernism **SELECTED PUBLICATIONS** Of Monsters and Transgression, Alterity, Excess, Community, Toronto, 93; Critical Theory Meets the Ethic of Care: Engendering social Justice and Social Identities, Soc Theo and Prac, 97; Play in Culture and the Jargon of Primordiality: A Critique of Huizinga's Homo Ludens, Play Writes: Diversions & Divergences in Fields of Play, 98; Reclaiming Affirmative Action, E Wind, W Wind, MSU Quart Jour, 98. **CONTACT ADDRESS** Mankato State Univ, MSU box 64, Mankato, MN, 56002-8400. **EMAIL** mecke.nagel@mankato.msus.edu

NAGEL, NORMAN E.
PERSONAL Born 09/30/1925, Kuling, China, m, 1953, 3 children **DISCIPLINE** SYSTEMATIC THEOLOGY **EDUCATION** Univ Adelaide, S Australia, BA, 45; Concordia Sem, BA, 49, MDiv, 53; Univ Cambridge, England, PhD, 62. **CAREER** Instr, Concordia Col, 47; pastor, Luther-Tyndale, London, 54-57; pastor and preceptor, Westfield House, Cambridge England, 57-68; vis prof, Concordia Sem, 62-63, summers 81-83; univ preacher and dean, prof of theol, 68-83, Valparaiso Univ; vis prof Martin Luther Sem, Papua New Guines, 75; prof systematic theology, 83-92, graduate prof, 92- chemn dept, 86-92, 94-95, Concordia Sem. **RESEARCH** Office of the Ministry; Lutheran confessions. **SELECTED PUBLICATIONS** Auth, Externum Verbum: Testing Augustana on the Doctrine of the Holy Ministry, Lutheran Theol J, 96; auth, Consubstantiation, in, Stephenson, ed, Hermann Sasse: A Man for Our Times? Concordia, 98. **CONTACT ADDRESS** Concordia Sem, 801 DeMun Ave, St. Louis, MO, 63105. **EMAIL** nageln@csl.edu

NAGEL, THOMAS
PERSONAL Born 07/04/1937, Belgrade, Yugoslavia **DISCIPLINE** PHILOSOPHY **EDUCATION** Cornell Univ, BA, 58; Oxford Univ, BPhil, 60; Harvard Univ, PhD, 63. **CAREER** Asst prof philos, Univ CA, Berkeley, 63-66; from asst prof to assoc prof, Princeton Univ, 66-72, prof philos, 72-80; chmn dept, 81-86, PROF PHILOS, NY UNIV, 80-, PROF OF PHILOS AND LAW, 86-; Fels, Guggenheim, 66-67, Nat Sci Found, 68-70 & NEH, 78-79, 84-85; Am Academy of Art and Sciences, 80-, British Academy, 88-, Honorary Fel Corpus Christi Col, Oxford, 92-; Assoc ed, Philosophy & Public Affairs, 70-82. **HONORS AND AWARDS** Tanner Lecturer, Stanford Univ, 77; Tanner Lecturer, Oxford Univ, 79; Howison Lecturer, Johns Hopkins Univ, 87; Thalheimer Lecturer, Johns Hopkins Univ, 89; John Locke Lecturer, Oxford Unv, 90; Hempel Lecturer, Priceton Univ, 95; Whitehead Lecturer, Harvard Univ, 95; Immanuel Kant Lecturer, Stanford Univ, 95. **MEMBERSHIPS** Am Philos Asn; Am Acad Arts & Sci; Soc Philos & Pub Affairs. **RESEARCH** Ethics; philos of mind; ancient philos. **SELECTED PUBLICATIONS** Auth, The Possibility of Altruism, Oxford Univ, 70 (translated into Italian); Mortal Questions, Cambridge Univ, 79 (trans into Spanish, French, German, Italian, Japanese, Romanian, Danish, and Polish); The View From Nowhere, 86 (trans into Italian, German, Spanish, Swedish, Greek, Polish, and Korean); What Does It All Mean?, 87 (trans into Greek, Italian, German, Dutch, Danish, Swedish, Slovak, French, Chinese, Japanese, Polish, Hebrew, Spanish, Slovenian, Portuguese, Korean, and Indonesian); Equality and Partiality, 91 (trans into Italian, French, German, and Spanish); Other Minds: Critical Essays, 1969-1994, 95; The Last Word, 97. **CONTACT ADDRESS** Dept of Philos, New York Univ, 100 Washington Sq E, New York, NY, 10003-6688. **EMAIL** NAGELT@TURING.LAW.NYU.EDU

NAGIN, DANIEL S.
DISCIPLINE PUBLIC POLICY **EDUCATION** Carnegie Mellon Univ, PhD, 76. **HONORS AND AWARDS** Sigma Xi; Honorable mention, Psychology Today's 1976 Social Issues Dissertation Contets; North Eastern State Tax Officials Asn Award for Excellence in Tax Admin, 85; fourteen grants from the following: Nat Sci Found, Nat Inst of Justice; Nat Consortium on Violence Res; and the Urban Mass Transit Authority. **MEMBERSHIPS** Editorial boards: Criminology, 92-; Evaluation Rev, 95-; J of Criminal Law and Criminology, 96-; Policy Sciences, 96-; J of Quantitative Criminology, 97-; Member of Committee on Law and Justice, Nat Res Coun, Nat Academy of Sciences, 97-; Brd of the PA Governor's Energy Coun, 86-90; Bd Pittsburgh Filmakers, 88-91. **RESEARCH** Crime; statistical methodology. **SELECTED PUBLICATIONS** Auth, Life-Course Trajectories of Different Types of Offenders, with D Farrington and T Moffitt, Criminology, 95; The Effects of Criminality and Conviction on the Labor Market Status of Young British Offenders, with J Waldfogel, Int Rev of Law and Economics, 95; A Comparison of Poisson, Negative Binomial, and Semiparametric Mixed Poisson Regression Models With Empirical Applications to Criminal Careers Data, with K Land and P McCall, Sociol Methods and Res, 96; Micro-Models of Criminal Careers: A Synthesis of the Criminal Careers and Life Course Approaches via Semiparametric Mixed Poisson Models with Empirical Applications, J of Quantitative Criminology, 96; The Effect of Sexual Arousal on Expectations of Sexual Forcefulness, with G Loewenstein and R Paternoster, J of Res in Crime and Delinquency, 97; Adolescent Mothers & the Criminal Behavior of Their Children, with G Pogarsky and D Farrington, Law and Soc Rev, 97; Do Right-to-Carry Laws Deter Violent Crime?, with Dan Black, J of Legal Studies, 98; Trajectories of Change in Criminal Offending: Good Marriages and the Desistance Process, with John Laub and Robert Sampson, Am Sociol Rev, 98; numerous other publications, several forthcoming. **CONTACT ADDRESS** Carnegie Mellon Univ, 2105 Hamburg Hall, Pittsburgh, PA, 15213.

NAGY, PAUL
PERSONAL Born 01/02/1937, Shelton, CT, m, 1965, 4 children **DISCIPLINE** PHILOSOPHY **EDUCATION** Fairfield Univ, BS, cum laude, 58; Boston Col, MA, 60; Fordham Univ, PhD, 68. **CAREER** Otto Salgo Prof Am Studs, Univ Budapest, 84-86; vis prof Am studs, Warsaw Univ, 77-78; prof Philos, prof Am studs, adj prof Philanthropic stud, Indiana Univ, 67-98. **MEMBERSHIPS** Amer Philos Asn; Amer Studs Asn; Soc Advance Amer Philos; Soc Values in Higher Educ; Polanyi Soc N Amer and Eng; Amer Asn Univ prof. **RESEARCH** Classical American philosophy; Ethics; Michael Polanyi. **SELECTED PUBLICATIONS** Auth, Cultural Origins of Pragmatism, Amer Studs, vol 3, Warsaw Univ, 81, 5-14; George Santayana and the American National Character, Atlantis, vol 4, Madrid, Asn Espanola de Estudios Anglo-Nortamericanos, 82, 81-91; Pragmatism and the American Frontier Experience, Annales Univ Sci Budapest de Rolando Eotvos Nominatae Sectic Philologia Moderna, vol XVI, Budapest, Eotvos Lorand Univ, 85, 89-99; Television: A Pervasive Presence in the American Cultural Landscape, USA Mag, Vienna and Budapest, US Info Agency, 86, 86-93; Some Traces of Pragmatism and Humanism in Michael Polanyi's Personal Knowledge, Polanyiana: The Periodical of the Michael Ploanyi Lib Philos Assn, vol 1, no 2, Budapest, 93, 137-147; Philosophy in a Different Voice: Michael Polanyi on Liberty and Liberalism, Tradition and Discovery, vol XXII, no 3, 96, 17-27; **CONTACT ADDRESS** Dept of Philosophy, Indiana Univ-Purdue Univ, Indianapolis, 425 University Blvd, Indianapolis, IN, 46202. **EMAIL** pnagy@iupui.edu

NAILS, DEBRA
PERSONAL Born 11/15/1950, Shreveport, LA, w **DISCIPLINE** PHILOSOPHY **EDUCATION** Univ of the Witwatersrand, S Africa, PhD, 93. **CAREER** Lect/researcher, 86-92, Univ Witwatersrand; Assoc Prof Philo, 94-, Mary Wash Coll. **HONORS AND AWARDS** Univ P-DR Fel, Univ Witwatersrand. **MEMBERSHIPS** APA, SAGP, Intl Plato Soc, NA Spinoza Soc. **RESEARCH** Plato, Spinoza, rationalism **SELECTED PUBLICATIONS** Auth, Agora Academy and the Conduct of Philosophy, Philo Stud Series, Dordrecht, Kluwer Acad Pub, 95; Mouthpiece Schmouthpiece, in: Who Speaks for Plato, ed, G A Press, Lanham Rowman & Littlefield, 98; The Dramatic Date of Plato's Republic, in: Classical J, 98; Tidying the Socratic Mess of a Method, in: SW Philo Review, 97; Socrates and Plato, Understanding the World and Changing It, in: Sci, Mind & Art, eds K Gavroglu, J Stachel & M W Wartofsky, Boston Kluwer, 95; Plato's Middle Cluster, in: Phoenix, 94; Problems with Vlastos's Platonic Developmentalism, in: Ancient Philo, 93; Platonic Chronology Reconsidered, in: Bryn Mawr Classical Review, 92. **CONTACT ADDRESS** Dept of Classics, Philosophy & Religion, Mary Washington Col, Fredericksburg, VA, 22401. **EMAIL** nails@mwc.edu

NAIM, ELISSA BEN
PERSONAL Born 11/03/1969, Chicago, IL, m, 1996 **DISCIPLINE** RELIGIOUS STUDIES **EDUCATION** Hebrew Union Col, MA, 96. **CAREER** Instr, Temple Beth El, San Pedro, CA, 98-. **HONORS AND AWARDS** Fulbright Scholar. **MEMBERSHIPS** Fulbright Asn; Nat Asn of Temple Educators. **RESEARCH** Religious studies; Hebrew; Education. **CONTACT ADDRESS** 1055 S Sherbourne Dr, Los Angeles, CA, 90035.

NAIRN, CHARLES E.
PERSONAL Born 08/26/1926, Columbus, OH, m, 1952, 5 children **DISCIPLINE** PHILOSOPHY **EDUCATION** Kent State Univ, BA, 51, MA, 52; Oberlin Coll, BD, 58; Vanderbilt Univ, MA, 72. **CAREER** Librarian Philo & Relig Div, 51-53, Cleveland Pub Library; Head Lib & teach, 60-64, Upper Iowa Univ; Hd Lib & teach, 64-68, Findlay Coll; Dir of Lib, teach & Ref/DLL librarian, 68-88, Lake Superior State Univ, Sault Ste Marie. **MEMBERSHIPS** SBL, AAR, APA, ALA, MLA, SCP, MSA. **RESEARCH** Mysticism, history of philosophy & religion, ethics, Christology as related to theology, poetry, painting & the Arts. **SELECTED PUBLICATIONS** Book review, Man as the Christian Problem, review of Dumery's Problem of God, in: Pacific Philo Forum, 67; auth, Absolutism, the Theistic Dilemma, in: Humanist's Speak, ed by S V Pehl, 74. **CONTACT ADDRESS** 903 Prospect Ave, Sault Ste. Marie, MI, 49783-1725.

NAKAMURA, C. LYNN
DISCIPLINE OLD TESTAMENT **EDUCATION** Susquehanna Univ, BA, 78; Lutheran Theol Sem, MDiv, 83; Princeton Theol Sem, PhD, 92. **CAREER** Asst prof, 88-93; assoc prof, Trinity Lutheran Sem, 93-; sec fac, 94-96; dir, Learning Tech, 96-; act mgr, Cmpt Svc, 96-. **SELECTED PUBLICATIONS** Co-auth, A Nation Turns to God, Augsburg Adult Bible Stud, 95; Mission90 Bible Study/Witness: Witnesses to the Word, Augsburg, 91; auth, Monarch, Mountain, and Meal: A Traditio-Historical Investigation of the Eschatological Banquet of Isaiah 24:21-23, PhD dissertation, Princeton Theol Sem, 92; co-ed, Lutherans and the Challenge of Religious Pluralism, Augsburg, 90. **CONTACT ADDRESS** Bible Dept, Trinity Lutheran Sem, 2199 E Main St, Columbus, OH, 43209-2334. **EMAIL** lnakamur@trinity.capital.edu

NAKASONE, RONALD
PERSONAL Born 07/13/1969, HI, m, 1998, 1 child **DISCIPLINE** BUDDHIST STUDIES **EDUCATION** Univ of WI, PhD, 80; Ryuoka Univ, MA, 75 **CAREER** Grad Theol Un, 89-98; Inst of Buddhist Stud, 87-89 **HONORS AND AWARDS** Fulbright, 78-79 **MEMBERSHIPS** Am Acad of Relig; Am Soc for Bioethics & Humanities; Japan Assoc for Bioethics; Assoc for Asian Amer Studies; Amer Soc on Aging **RESEARCH** Buddhist Studies, Aging; Asian American Religious Experience; Okinawan Spirituality **SELECTED PUBLICATIONS** Auth, Buddhist view on Biotechnology, Encyclopedia of Ethical, Legal and Policy Issues in Biotechnology, 99; Auth, Buddhist Issues in End of Life Decision Making, Sage Publications, 99 **CONTACT ADDRESS** Ronald Y Nakasone, 43109 Gallegos Ave, Fremont, CA, 94539. **EMAIL** rynakasone@aol.com

NAKHAI, BETH ALPERT
PERSONAL Born 07/05/1951, New York, NY, m, 1986, 1 child **DISCIPLINE** NEAR EASTERN ARCHAEOLOGY, BIBLICAL STUDIES **EDUCATION** Conn Col, BA, 72; Harvard Div Sch, MTS, 79; Univ Ariz, MA, 85, PhD, 93. **CAREER** Tchg asst, Univ Ariz, 83-86, 88-89; adj instr, Prescott Col, 95; Lectr, Univ Ariz, 94- . **HONORS AND AWARDS** Robert H. Pfeiffer Found Trust, 78; Zion Res Found Travel Scholar, 79; Univ Ariz Grad Tuition Scholar, 82-83; Maurice Cohen Awd in Judaic Stud, 83; Bernard Ivan Amster Mem Awd, 83; tchg asst, Dept Oriental Stud, 1st yr Hebrew, 83-87; Samuel H. Kress found fel, 86-87; Univ Ariz Grad Acad Scholar, 87-89; Dorot Found doctoral fel, 88-89; Tchg asst, Dept Near East Stud, Ancient Civilizations Near East, 88-89; Res Asst, Dept Near East Stud, 90; Mem found Jewish Cult Doctoral Scholar, 86-91; Amer Sch Oriental Res Comm Archaeol Policy Endow Bibl Archaeol grant, 97; Amer Sch Oriental Res Comm Archaelo Policy Endow Bibl Archael grant, 97; Assoc Women fac travel grant, Univ Ariz, 97-98. **MEMBERSHIPS** Amer Sch Oriental Res; Soc Bibl Lit; Ctr Middle East Stud; Assn Women Fac, Univ Ariz. **RESEARCH** Canaanite and Israelite Religion; women's issues. **SELECTED PUBLICATIONS** Auth, Tell el-Wawiyat, Israel Exploration Jour, 37, 2-3, 87, 181-185; Tell el-Wawiyat, 1986, in Excavations and Surveys in Israel 1987-1988 vol 6, Jerusalem, Hadashot Archaeologiyot, 88, 100-102; Tell el-Wawiyat, Revue biblique, 95/2, 88, 247-251; Tell el-Wawiyat, 1987 Israel Exploration Jour, 39.1-2, 102-104, 89; Tell el-wawiyat (Bet Netofa Valley)-1987, in Excavations and Surveys in Israel 1988/89 vol 7-8, Jerusalem, Hadashot Archaelolgiyot, 90; Tell el-Wawiyat, Encyclopedia of Archaelolgical Excavations in the Holy Land, 2nd ed, E. Stern, ed, Jerusalem, Israel Exploration Soc, 92; What's a Bamah? How Sacred Space Functioned in Ancient Israel, Bibl Archaeol Rev, 20, 18-19, 77-78; Wawiyat, Jell el-, Encyclopedia of Archaeology in the Bibl World, vol 5, 333-334, Eric M. Meyers, ed, New York, Oxford UP, 97; Syro-Palestinian Temples, Encyclopedia of Near Eastern Archaelolgy, vol 5, E.M. Meyers, ed, New York, Oxford UP, 169-174, 97; Locus, Encyclopedia of Near Eastern Archaeology, vol 3, E.M. Meyers, ed, NY, Oxford UP, 97, 383-384; Kitan, Tel., Encycolpedia of Near Eastern Archaeology, vol 3, E.M. Meyers, ed, New York, Oxford Univ Press, 97, 300; Furniture and Furnishings: Furnishings of the Bronze and Iron Ages, Encyclopedia of Near eastern Archaeology, vol 2, E.M. Meyers, ed, NY, Oxford UP, 97, 354-356; Beth Zur, Encyclopedia of near Eastern Archaeology vol 1, E.M. Meyers, ed, NY, Oxford UP, 97, 314; Featured in Written in Stones, People, Places and Society: A Publication for Alumni and Friends of the College of Social and Behavioral Sciences, Univ Ariz, Spring, 3, 98; Rev article, Jerusalem: An Archaeological Biography, Shofar, 16,3, 98, 174-176. **CONTACT ADDRESS** Univ of Arizona, 905 N Tenth Ave, Tucson, AZ, 85705-7623. **EMAIL** bnakhai@u.arizona.edu

NAKHNIKION, GEORGE
PERSONAL Born 11/12/1920, Varna, Bulgaria, m, 1983, 4 children **DISCIPLINE** PHILOSOPHY **EDUCATION** Harvard, AB, 44, MA, 48, PhD, 49. **CAREER** Instr to Prof, 49-68, Departmental Chr, 57-68, Wayne State Univ; Chr, 68-, Indiana Univ, Bloomington. **HONORS AND AWARDS** Vis Asst Prof, Brown Univ; Fulbright Lectr, Univ St., Andrews **MEMBERSHIPS** APA **RESEARCH** Epistemology & Epistemology of Theism. **SELECTED PUBLICATIONS** Co-ed, Readings in Twentieth Century Philosophy, W.P. Alston, 63; co-ed, Morality and the Language of Conduct, 63; auth, An Introduction to Philosophy, 67; Bertrand Russell's Philosophy, 74. **CONTACT ADDRESS** Dept of Philosophy, Indiana Univ, Bloomington, Bloomington, IN, 47401. **EMAIL** LHARL@Indiana.edu

NANCARROW, PAUL S.
PERSONAL Born 09/09/1956, Ontonagon, MI, m, 1982, 2 children **DISCIPLINE** THEOLOGY **EDUCATION** Seabury-Western Theol Sem, MDiv, 86; Univ Minn, MA, 84. **MEMBERSHIPS** AAR **RESEARCH** Sacramental theology; process theology; theology and science. **SELECTED PUBLICATIONS** Auth, Wisdom's Information: Rereading a Biblical Image in the Light of Some Contemporary Science and Speculation, Zygon: Jour Relig Sci, March, 97; auth, Realism and Anti-Realism: A Whiteheadian Response to Richard Rorty Concerning Truth, Propositions, and Practice, Process Studies, 95. **CONTACT ADDRESS** 4810 Belmont Park Terrace, Nashville, TN, 37215. **EMAIL** psnancarrow@mindspring.com

NANDA, VED P.
PERSONAL Born 11/20/1934, Gujranwala, India **DISCIPLINE** LAW **EDUCATION** Panjab Univ, India, BA, 52, MA, 53; Univ Delhi, LLB, 55, LLM, 56; Northwestern Univ, LLM, 62. **CAREER** From asst prof to assoc prof, 65-70, Prof Law, Col Law, Univ Denver, 70, Dir Int Legal Studies Prog, 72-, Chairperson, sect int legal exchange, Asn Am Law Schs; vis prof law, Col Law, Univ Iowa, 74-75, Col Law, Fla State Univ, summer, 73 & Int Law Inst, Paris, summers, 79, 80 & 81; distinguished vis prof int law, Ill Inst Technol, Chicago-Kent Col Law, 81; dir & mem exec coun, Asn US Mem Int Inst Space Law; mem adv coun, US Inst Human Rights. **MEMBERSHIPS** Am Asn Law Schs; Am Soc Int Law; Asn US Mem Int Inst Space Law; Int Law Asn; World Asn Law Professors (secygen, 79-). **SELECTED PUBLICATIONS** Auth, The Pubic Trust Doctrine: A viable approach to international environmental protection, Ecol Law Quart, 76; The world food crisis and the role of law in combating hunger and malnutrition, JInt Law & Econ, 76; Emerging trends in the use of international law and institutions for the management of international water resources, Int Law & Policy, 77; ed, Water Needs for the Future, Westview, 77; Ocean Thermal Energy Conversion (OTEC) development, Denver Law J, 79; ed, The Law of Transnational Business Transactions, Clark Boardman, 81; co-ed, Global Human Rights, 81 & ed, Global Climate Change, 82, Westview; Ethnic-conflict in Fiji And International Human-rights Law, Cornell International Law J, Vol 0025, 1992; New Legal Foundations For Global Survival - Security Through The Security Council - Ferencz,bb, American J of International Law, Vol 0089, 1995. **CONTACT ADDRESS** Col of Law, Univ of Denver, 200 W 14th Ave, Denver, CO, 80204.

NANOS, MARK D.
PERSONAL Born 07/31/1954, Corpus Christi, TX, m, 1974, 2 children **DISCIPLINE** RELIGION **EDUCATION** Univ of Missouri, BA, 81; Univ of St Andrews, Scotland, PhD cand. **CAREER** Vis lect, 97, Central Baptist Sem, KS; Vis Schol, 94, Westhill Col, UK; Co-Founder/Pres, 74-, Nanos & Gray Inc. **HONORS AND AWARDS** Nat Jewish Book Award for Jewish-Christian Relations, 96. **MEMBERSHIPS** Soc of Bibl Lit **RESEARCH** Greek, Roman, Jewish and Christian Studies of 200 bce-200ce. **SELECTED PUBLICATIONS** The Mystery of Romans The Jewish Context of Pauls Letter, Fortress Press, 96. **CONTACT ADDRESS** 313 NE Landings Dr, Lees Summit, MO, 64064.

NARDIN, TERRY
PERSONAL Born 01/19/1942, New York, NY, m, 1962, 2 children **DISCIPLINE** PHILOSOPHY **EDUCATION** NYU, BA, 63; Northwestern Univ, PhD, 67. **CAREER** State Univ of NY Buffalo, prof, 67-85; Univ of Wisconsin, Milwaukee, prof, 85-. **HONORS AND AWARDS** Rockefeller Foun Human Fel, 78-79; Princeton, IAS, visitor, 91-92, Harvard Univ, vis scholar, 98-99. **MEMBERSHIPS** ASPLP, CSPT, Collingwood Soc **RESEARCH** Polit philo; hist of polit thought; ethics and intl relations. **SELECTED PUBLICATIONS** Auth, Michael Oakeshott's World of Ideas, In: Studies in Political Thought, 93; Private and Public Roles in Civil Society, in Toward a Global Civil Society, ed by M. Walzer, Berghahn Books, 95; The Philosophy of War and Peace, Routledge Encycl of Philosophy, Routledge, 98; Law, Morality, and the Relations of States, Princeton Univ Press, 83, Portuguese trans, 87; Traditions of International Ethics, co-ed, Cambridge Univ Press, 92; The Ethics of War and Peace: Religious and Secular Perspectives, Ethikon Series, Princeton Univ Press, 96; co-ed, International Society: Diverse Ethical Perspectives, Ethikon Series, Princeton Univ Press, 98. **CONTACT ADDRESS** Dept of Political Science, Univ of Wisconsin, Milwaukee, PO Box 413, Milwaukee, WI, 53201.

NARDONE, RICHARD MORTON
PERSONAL Born 06/21/1929, Orange, NJ **DISCIPLINE** HISTORICAL THEOLOGY **EDUCATION** Seton Hall Univ, BA, 50; Cath Univ Am, STL, 54; Univ St Michael's Col, PhD(-theol), 72. **CAREER** Assoc Prof Relig Studies, Seton Hall Univ, 68-, Judge, Matrimonial Tribunal-Archdiocese of Newark, NJ, 77-. **MEMBERSHIPS** Cath Theol Soc Am; Am Acad Relig. **RESEARCH** Patristics; liturgical studies; ecumenical studies. **SELECTED PUBLICATIONS** Auth, The Roman calender in ecumenical perspective, Worship, 5/76; coauth, The Church of Jerusalem and the Christian Calender, Standing Before God, KTAV Publ House, 81; auth, Liturgical change: A reappraisal, Homiletic & Pastoral Rev, 11/81; The Story of the Christian Year, Paulist Press, 91. **CONTACT ADDRESS** Dept of Relig Studies, Seton Hall Univ, 400 S Orange Ave., South Orange, NJ, 07079-2697.

NARVESON, JAN
PERSONAL Born 06/15/1936, Erskine, MN **DISCIPLINE** PHILOSOPHY **EDUCATION** Univ Chicago, BA, 55; Harvard Univ, PhD, 61. **CAREER** PROF PHILOSOPHY, UNIV WATERLOO, 63-; vis prof, Johns Hopkins Univ, 66; vis prof, Stanford Univ, 68; vis prof, Univ Calgary, 76; vis prof, Bowling Green State Univ, 90. **HONORS AND AWARDS** Fel, Royal Soc Can; DLitt(hon), Wilfrid Laurier Univ, 89. **MEMBERSHIPS** Can Philos Asn; Am Philos Asn; Can Asn Publ Philos. **SELECTED PUBLICATIONS** Auth, Morality and Utility, 67; auth, The Libertarian Idea, 89; auth, Moral Matters, 93; coauth, Political Correctness, 94; ed, Moral Issues, 83; co-ed, For and Against the State-New Essays in Political Justification, 96; ed bd, Ethics; ed bd, Dialogue; ed bd, J Soc Philos; ed bd, Res Arch; ed bd, Int J Applied Philos; ed bd, Soc Philos & Policy; ed bd, J Value Inquiry. **CONTACT ADDRESS** Dept of Philosophy, Univ of Waterloo, Waterloo, ON, N2L 3G1. **EMAIL** jnarveso@uwaterloo.ca

NASER, CURTIS R.
DISCIPLINE PHILOSOPHY **EDUCATION** Univ Pittsburgh, BA, 86; SUNY Stony Brook, PhD, 93. **CAREER** Assoc dir, Inst Med Contemp Soc, SUNY Stony Brook, 91-95; to assoc course dir Med in Contemp Soc, 93-95; asst prof philos, Fairfield Univ, 95-. **HONORS AND AWARDS** Fellow, Univ IA Col Med, 96; Human Inst Fellow, SUNY Stony Brook, 88-89. **RESEARCH** Biomedical ethics; philos of sci; biology; Ger Idealism; Hegel; Kant; hist of philos. **SELECTED PUBLICATIONS** Auth, Patient Dignity--Physician Dignity, Trends Health Care Law Ethics, 94; The Dialectics of Self-organization and Nonlinear Systems, Dialectic, Cosmos and Soc, 95; coauth, The First Patient: Reflections and Stories about the Anatomy Cadaver, Tchg Lrng Med, 94. **CONTACT ADDRESS** Dept Philos & Prog in Applied Ethics, Fairfield Univ, 1073 N Benson Rd, 315 Donnar, Fairfield, CT, 06430. **EMAIL** cnaser@funrsc.fairfield.edu

NASH, ROBERT N.
DISCIPLINE RELIGION **EDUCATION** GA Col, BA, MA; Southern Baptist Theol Sem, MDiv, PhD. **CAREER** Asst prof; Shorter's dir, Rel Act. **SELECTED PUBLICATIONS** Auth, An 8-Track Church in a CD World: The Modern Church in the Postmodern World, Smyth & Helwys; written on, hist of Christianity and on postmodernism. **CONTACT ADDRESS** Div of Relig and Philos, Shorter Col, 315 Shorter Ave., Rome, GA, 30165-4267.

NASH, ROBERT N., JR.
DISCIPLINE CHURCH HISTORY, THEOLOGY, WORLD RELIGIONS **EDUCATION** GA Col, BA, MA; Southern Baptist Theol Sem, MDiv, PhD. **CAREER** Asst prof, dir, Relig Act, Shorter Col. **SELECTED PUBLICATIONS** Auth, An 8-Track Church in a CD World: The Modern Church in the Postmodern World, Smyth & Helwys. **CONTACT ADDRESS** Shorter Col, Rome, GA, 30165-9901.

NASH, ROGER
DISCIPLINE PHILOSOPHY **EDUCATION** Exeter Univ, PhD. **RESEARCH** Nature of creativity and imagination in the arts; relation between ethics, religion and the arts. **SELECTED PUBLICATIONS** Auth, The Poetry of Prayer, 94; auth, Ethics, Science, Technology and the Environment: A Study Guide, 93; auth, Ethics, Science, Technology and the Environment: a Reader, 93; auth, Night Flying, 90; auth, Psalms from the Suburbs, 86; auth, Settlement in a School of Whales, 83. **CONTACT ADDRESS** Philosophy Dept, Laurentian Univ, 935 Ramsey Lake Rd, Sudbury, ON, P3E 2C6.

NASH, RONALD
DISCIPLINE PHILOSOPHY; RELIGION **EDUCATION** Barrington Col, BA; Brown Univ, MA; Syracuse Univ, PhD. **CAREER** Ch, dept Philos and Rel; dir, Grad Stud, W Ky Univ; prof-. **HONORS AND AWARDS** Fel, Christianity Today Inst., Contrib ed, The Freeman; adv, US Civil Rights Commn; consult, Conservative Bk Club. **SELECTED PUBLICATIONS** Auth, 25 bk(s) on philosophical theology. **CONTACT ADDRESS** Dept of Philosophy and Religion, Reformed Theol Sem, 1015 Maitland Ctr Commons, Maitland, FL, 32751.

NASU, EISHO
PERSONAL Born 02/14/1961, Japan, m, 1996 **DISCIPLINE** CULTURAL AND HISTORICAL STUDY OF RELIGIONS; BUDDHIST STUDIES; JAPANESE RELI **EDUCATION** Kobe City Univ For Studies, BA, 83; Ryukoku Univ, MA, 86; Grad Theol Union, MA, 90, PhD, 96. **CAREER** Asst res, Jodo Shinshu Seiten Hensan Iinkaa, Jodo Shinshu Hongwanji, 85-88; adj prof, Inst of Buddhist Studies, Grad Theol union, 96-97; res fel, dept e asian lang, Univ Calif Berkeley, 96-98; acad ed, numata ctr buddhist transl res, 97-; asst prof, shin buddhism, inst buddhist studies, grad theol union; Henry Mayo Newhall Res Fel, 92-93. **HONORS AND AWARDS** Int Asn Buddhist Cult Scholar, 88-92; Horai Asn Scholar, 93-96. W E Friends Award Outstanding Res Encounters W/E Cult, 90. **SELECTED PUBLICATIONS** Auth, A Critical Review of Joseph Kitagawa's Methodology of History of Religions in the Field of Japanese Religious Studies, Pacific World, 94; Popular Pure Land Teachings of the Zenkoji Nyorai and Shinran, The Pure Land, 95; Ocean of the One Vehicle: Shinran's View of the ekayana Ideal, Watanabe Takao kyoju kanreki kinen ronshu: Bukkyoshiso bunkashi ronso, Nagata bunshodo, 97; coed, Engaged Pure Land Buddhism: Challenges Facing Jodo Shinshu in the Contemporary World, Studies in Honor of Prof Alfred Bloom, WisdomOncean Publ, 98; auth, Ordination Ceremony of the Honganji Priests in Premodern Japanese Society, Engaged Pure Land Buddhism: Challenges Facing Jodo Shinshu in the Contemporary World, 98. **CONTACT ADDRESS** 1821 Carleton St, Berkeley, CA, 94703. **EMAIL** nasu_ibs@msn.com

NATHAN, DANIEL O.
DISCIPLINE PHILOSOPHY **EDUCATION** Univ MI, AB; Univ IL, Chicago, MA, PhD. **CAREER** Assoc prof, chp, dept Philos, TX Tech Univ. **RESEARCH** Aesthetics; ethics; philos of law. **SELECTED PUBLICATIONS** His work has appeared in the Australasian J of Philos, The J of Aesthet and Art Criticism, Public Aff Quart, Erkenntnis and The Brit J of Aesthet. **CONTACT ADDRESS** Texas Tech Univ, Lubbock, TX, 79409-5015. **EMAIL** dnathan@ttu.edu

NATHANSON, STEPHEN LEWIS
PERSONAL Born 08/19/1943, Port Chester, NY, m, 1966, 2 children **DISCIPLINE** PHILOSOPHY **EDUCATION** Swarthmore Col, BA, 65; Johns Hopkins Univ, PhD(philos), 69. **CAREER** Asst prof philos, State Univ NY, Fredonia, 69-72; from Asst Prof to Assoc Prof,Northeastern Univ, 72-86, Prof, Dept Philos & Relig, 86-, chairperson, Dept of Philos & Rel, 75-81, Dir, Ctr for Effective Teaching, 96-. **HONORS AND AWARDS** Woodrow Wilson Dissertation Fel, 68-69; Phi Beta Kappa, 69. **MEMBERSHIPS** Am Philos Asn. **RESEARCH** Epistemology; value theory; history of philosophy. **SELECTED PUBLICATIONS** Auth, Nihilism, reason and the value of life, In: Infanticide and the Value of Life, Prometheus 78; Nihilism, reason and death: Reflection of John Barth's The Floating Opera, The Philosophical Reflection of Man in Literature, Reidel, 82; The Ideal of Rationality, Humanities Press Int, 85, rev ed, The Ideal of Rationality: A Defense Within Reason, Open Court, 94; An Eye for an Eye? -- The Immorality of Punishing by Death, Rowman & Littlefield, 87; Should We Consent to be Governed? -- A Short Introduction to Political Philosophy, Wadsworth, 92; Patriotism, Morality, and Peace, Rowman & Littlefield, 93; Economic Justice, Prentice-Hall, 97; author of numerous articles and reviews. **CONTACT ADDRESS** Philos Dept, Northeastern Univ, 373 Holmes Hall, Boston, MA, 02115-5000. **EMAIL** stnathan@neu.edu

NAUCKHOFF, JOSEFINE C.
PERSONAL Born 04/07/1965, Stockholm, Sweden **DISCIPLINE** PHILOSOPHY **EDUCATION** Stanford Univ, BA, 87; Univ of Penn, PhD, 94. **CAREER** Asst prof, Wake Forest Univ, 94-98. **MEMBERSHIPS** APA. **RESEARCH** Kant; history of ethics and aesthetics. **SELECTED PUBLICATIONS** "Objectivity and Expression in Thomas Reid's Aesthetics," JAA, 94. **CONTACT ADDRESS** Wake Forest Univ, PO Box 7332, Winston-Salem, NC, 27127. **EMAIL** nauckhjc@wfu.edu

NAUENBERG, M.
PERSONAL Born 12/19/1934, Berlin, Germany **DISCIPLINE** PHYSICS **EDUCATION** Cornell Univ, PhD, 59. **CAREER** Prof, Univ Cal Santa Cruz, 66-94. **HONORS AND AWARDS** A.P. Sloan fel; Guggenheim fel; Alexandre von Humboldt fel. **MEMBERSHIPS** Am Phys Soc; Hist of Sci Soc. **RESEARCH** Theoretical physics; history of science. **SELECTED PUBLICATIONS** Auth, Newton's Principia and Inverse Square Orbits, The Col Math Jour, 94; auth, Huygens and Newton on Curvature and it's Applications to Dynamics, DE Zeventiende Eeeuw, 96; auth, On Hooke's 1685 Manuscript on Orbital Mechanics, Hist Math, 98; auth, Essay Review: The Mathemeatical Principles Underlying the Principia, Revisited, Jour for the Hist of Astron, 98; auth, Newton's Unpublished Perturbation Method for the Lunar Motion, Int Jour of Engineering Sci, 98; auth, Newton's Portsmouth Perturbation Method for the Three-Body Problem and its Application to Lunar Motion, 98. **CONTACT ADDRESS** Physics Dept, Univ Calif Santa Cruz, Santa Cruz, CA, 95064.

NAYLOR, ANDREW
PERSONAL Des Moines, IA, m, 1964, 2 children **DISCIPLINE** PHILOSOPHY **EDUCATION** Yale Univ, BA, 62; Univ Chicago, MA, 63, PhD, 66. **CAREER** Asst prof, San Fernando Valley State Col, 66-71; from asst prof philos to prof, 71-, chemn dept, 71-77, 90-91, 92- , Indiana Univ, South Bend. **HONORS AND AWARDS** NEH summer sem, 75, 83; NEH summer Inst on Theory of Knowledge, 86; pres, Indiana Philos Asn, 87-88. **MEMBERSHIPS** APA; Philos Sci Asn; Soc Business Ethics; AAUP. **RESEARCH** Theory of knowledge; metaphysics; philosophy of mind. **SELECTED PUBLICATIONS** Auth, B Remembers that P from Time T, J of Philos, 81; auth, On the Evidence of One's Memories, Analysis, 73; auth, Justification in Memory Knowledge, Synthese, 83; auth, In Defense of a Nontraditional Theory of Memory, The Monist, 85; auth, Remembering without Knowing--Not without Justification, Philos Stud, 86. **CONTACT ADDRESS** Dept of Philosophy, Indiana Univ, South Bend, PO Box 7111, South Bend, IN, 46634-7111. **EMAIL** ANaylor@iusb.edu

NEALE, DAVID
PERSONAL Born 07/05/1953, Twin Falls, ID, m, 1974, 2 children **DISCIPLINE** THEOLOGY **EDUCATION** Univ Sheffield, PhD, 91. **CAREER** Canadian Nazarene Col, prof, acad dean, 90-. **HONORS AND AWARDS** Tyndale fel, Overseas res award. **MEMBERSHIPS** SBL. **RESEARCH** Gospels. **SELECTED PUBLICATIONS** Auth, None But the Sinners, Sheffield Acad Pr, 92; auth, Was Jesus a Mesith?, Tyndale Bulletin, 93. **CONTACT ADDRESS** Dept of biblical Literature, Canadian Nazarene Col, 610 833 4th Ave SW, Calgary, AB, T2P 3T5. **EMAIL** dave.neale@cnaz.ab.ca

NEALE, PHILIP WHITBY
PERSONAL Born 02/10/1945, Brooklyn, NY, m, 1973, 1 child **DISCIPLINE** PHILOSOPHY, RELIGION **EDUCATION** Col Wooster, BA, 67; Union Theol Sem, NY, BD, 70; Vanderbilt Univ, MA, 73, PhD, 75. **CAREER** Instr philos, Columbia State Community Col, 72-74; from asst prof to assoc prof to prof of philos, McKendree Col, 74-. **HONORS AND AWARDS** Assoc, Danforth Found, 78; Phi Beta Kappa, 67; Grandy Scholar Award, 82 **MEMBERSHIPS** Am Philos Assn; Soc Study Process Philos; Ill Philo Assoc Central States Philo Assoc. **RESEARCH** Whiteheadian metaphysics; theories of the self; ethics. **CONTACT ADDRESS** Dept of Philosophy, McKendree Col, 701 College Rd, Lebanon, IL, 62254-1299.

NEANDÈR, K.
DISCIPLINE PHILOSOPHY **EDUCATION** LaTrobe Univ, PhD, 84. **CAREER** Assoc Prof, Dept philo, John Hopkins Univ. **RESEARCH** Philosophy of Mind; Philo of Biology. **CONTACT ADDRESS** Dept of Philosophy, Johns Hopkins Univ, 3400 N Charles St, Baltimore, MD, 21218. **EMAIL** neander@jhunix.hcf.jhu.edu

NEEDLEMAN, JACOB
PERSONAL Born 10/06/1934, Philadelphia, PA, m, 1959, 1 child **DISCIPLINE** PHILOSOPHY; RELIGION **EDUCATION** Harvard Univ, BA, 56; Yale Univ, PhD, 61. **CAREER** Res assoc philos, Rockefeller Inst, 61-62; from asst prof to assoc prof, 62-70, chmn dept, 68-69, Prof Philos, San Francisco State Univ, 70-, Clin assoc gen med, med sch, Univ Calif, 67; vis scholar & Soc Relig Higher Educ cross-disciplinary grant, Union Theol Sem, 67-68, ed, Penguin Metaphys Libr, 71-; Rockefeller fel humanities, 77; dir, Ctr Study New Relig Movements, Grad Theol Union, Berkeley, 77- **MEMBERSHIPS** Am Philos Asn; Am Acad Relig. **RESEARCH** Comparative religion; philosophy of religion; philosophy of science. **SELECTED PUBLICATIONS** Auth, The New Religions, Doubleday, 70; ed, Religion for a New Generation, Macmillan, 73; The Sword of Gnosis, Penquin, 73; auth, On the Way to Self Knowledge, Knopf, 75; A Sense of the Cosmos, 75 & Lost Christianity, 80, Doubleday; Consciousness and Tradition, Crossroads, 82; The Heart of Philosophy, Knopf, 82; Sorcerer, 86; Sin and Sciantism, 86; Money and the Meaning of Life, 91; Modern Esoteric Spirituality, 92; The Way of the Physician, 93; The Indestructible Question, 94; A Little Book on Love, 96; Gurdjieff: Essays and Relections, 97; Time and the Soul, 98. **CONTACT ADDRESS** Dept of Philos, San Francisco State Univ, 1600 Holloway Ave, San Francisco, CA, 94132-1740. **EMAIL** jneedle@sfsu.edu

NEEL, JAMES V.
PERSONAL Born 03/22/1915, Hamilton, OH, m, 1943, 3 children **DISCIPLINE** GENETICS **EDUCATION** AB, Col of Wooster, AB, 35; PhD, 39; Univ Rochester, MD, 44,. **CAREER** Distinguished univ prof, human genetics, 66-85, prof emer, 85-, Univ Mich. **HONORS AND AWARDS** Nat Medal of Sci; Lasker Award; Amer Pub Hea Asn; Allan Award, Amer Soc Human Genetics; James D. Bruce Award, Amer Col Physicians. **MEMBERSHIPS** Nat Acad of Sci; Inst of Med; Amer Philos Soc; Amer Acad of Arts & Sci; Amer Soc of Human Genetics. **RESEARCH** Human genetics. **SELECTED PUBLICATIONS** Auth, Genetic studies at the Atomic Bomb Casualty Commission--Radiation Effects Res Found 1946-1997, Proc Nat Acad Sci, USA, 95, 5432-5436, 98; caauth, with S. Julius, A. Weder, M. Yamada, S. L. R. Kardia and M. B. Haviland, Syndrome X: Is it for real?, Genetic Epidemiology, 15, 19-32, 98; Reappraisal of studies concerning the genetic effects of the radiation of humans, mice and Drosophila, Environ, Mol Mutagen, 31, 4-10, 98; Looking ahead: Some genetic issues of the future. Perspect Bio Med, 40, 328-347, 97; coauth, with E. A. Thompson, Allelic disequilibrium and allele frequency distribution as a function of social and demographic history, Amer Jour Human Genetics, 60, 197-204, 97; with J. R. Lazutka, E. O. Major, V. Dedonyte, J. Mierquskine, G. Slapsyte and A. Kesminiene, Hight titers of antibodies to two human polyomaviruses, JCV and BKV, correlate with increased frequency of chromosomal damage in human lymphocytes, Cancer Lett, 109, 177-183, 96; with R. Kuick, J. Asakawa, M. Kodaira, C. Satoh, D. Thoraval, I. L. Gonzalez and S. M. Hanash, Studies of the inheritance of human ribosomal DNA variants detected in two-dimensional separations of genomic restriction fragments, Genetics, 144, 307-316, 96; with R. Kuick, J. Awakawa, C. Satoh and S. M. Hanash, High yield of restriction fragment length polymorphisms in two-dimensional separations of human genomic DNA, Genomics, 25, 345-353, 95; Physician to the Gene Pool, NY, John Wiley & Sons, pp ix and 457, 94; with J. Asakawa, R. Kuick, M. Kodaira, C. Satoh and S. M. Hanash, Genetic variation detected by quantitative anaysis of end-labled genomic DNA fragments, Proc Nat Acad Sci, US, 91, 9052-9056, 94. **CONTACT ADDRESS** 2235 Belmont, Ann Arbor, MI, 48104.

NEELEY, G. STEVEN
PERSONAL Born 11/08/1957, Cincinnati, OH **DISCIPLINE** PHILOSOPHY **EDUCATION** Xavier Univ, BSBA; Univ Cincinnati, MA, PhD, JD. **CAREER** Assoc prof Philos, Saint Francis Col, 97-; Philos psychotherapist, 97-; adj prof, Union Inst, 89-; atty, 85-; asst prof Philos, Saint Francis Col, 92-97; adj prof Philos, Col Mt St. Joseph, 92-93; vis asst prof Philos, Xavier Univ, 89-92; law clk, Law Off TD Shackleford, 82-84. **HONORS AND AWARDS** Who's Who Among Am Tchrs, 98, 96; Swatsworth Fac Award, 97; Saint Francis Hon Soc Distinguished Fac Award, 94; Am Philos Asn Excellence Tchg Award, 94; Bishop Fenwick Tchr Yr Award, 91; Greater Cincinnati Consortium Col Univ Celebration Tchg Award, 91; Charles Phelps Taft Mem Fel, 87-88, 88-89; Univ Res Coun Fel, 87. **MEMBERSHIPS** Am Philos Asn; Am Cath Philos Asn; AMINTAPHIL; APA Sartre Cir; Am Soc Philos, Couns, Psychotherapy; Asn Death Educ Couns; Ill Philos Asn; Ind Philos Asn; Int Asn Philos Law Soc Philos; Ky Philos Asn; N Am Nietzsche Soc; N Am Schopenhauer Soc; Ohio Philos Asn; Ohio State Bar Asn; Post-Socratic Soc; Soc Philos Psychic Res; Soc Rt Die/Choice Dying; WVa Philos Soc. **RESEARCH** Philosophy of Law; Modern Philosophy; 19th Century European Philosophy; Constitutional Privacy; Health Care Ethics; Philosophical Thanatology; Philosophical Psychotherapy; Epistemology; Logic; Political Philosophy; History of Philosophy; Theoretical Ethics; Applied Ethics; Metaphysics; Philosophy of Religion; Critical Thinking; Existentialism; Death and Dying; Constitutional Law; Criminal Law; American Legal History; The Law of Torts; Philosophy of the Paranormal. **SELECTED PUBLICATIONS** Auth, Constitutional Right to Suicide, 94; auth, Patient Autonomy and State Intervention: Re-examining the State's Purported Interest, Northern Kentucky Law Review, vol 19; auth, A Critical Examination of Schopenhauer's Concept of Human Salvation, Schopenhauer-Jahrbuch, vol 75; auth, A Re-examination of Schopenhauer's Analysis of Bodily Agency: The Ego as Microcosm, Idealistic Studies, vol 22; auth, The Death of God in Nietzsche: Pity, Revenge and Laughter, Dialogos, vol 64; auth, The Knowledge and Nature of Schopenhauer's Will, Schopenhauer-Jahrbuch, vol 77; auth, The Constitutionality of Elective and Physician Assisted Death, Physician-Assisted Death, 1994; auth, Self-Directed Death, Euthanasia, and the Termination of Life-Support: Reasonable Decisions to Die, Campbell Law Review, vol 16; auth, The Right to Self-Directed Death: Reconsidering an Ancient Proscription, The Catholic Lawyer, vol 36; auth, The Constitutional Right to Suicide, The Quality of Life, and the Slippery Slope': An Explicit Reply to Lingering Concerns, Akron Law Review, vol 28; auth, Chaos in the Laboratory of the States': The Mounting Urgency in the Call for Judicial Recognition of a Constitutional Right to Self-Directed Death, Toledo Law Review, vol 26; auth, Dworkin, Vague Constitutional Clauses, and the Eighth Amendment?s Admonition Against Cruel and Unusual' Punishment, Contemporary Philosophy, vol 16; auth, The Absurd, the Self, the Future, My Death: A Reexamination of Sartre's Views on Suicide, Phenomenological Inquiry, forthcoming; auth, The Constitutional Right to Self-Directed Death and Reciprocal Responsibilities of Health Care Personnel, Contemporary Philosophy, vol 17; auth, Schopenhauer and the Limits of Language, Idealistic Studies, forthcoming; auth, Legal and Ethical Dilemmas Surrounding Prayer as a Method of Alternative Healing for Children, Alternate Medicine and Ethics, 98; auth, Nietzsche On Apostates' and Divine Laughter, Contemporary Philosophy, vol 18. **CONTACT ADDRESS** Department of Philosophical and Religious Studies, Saint Francis Col, PO Box 600, Loretto, PA, 15940. **EMAIL** lakline@sfcpa.edu

NEELY, DAVID E.
PERSONAL Chicago, IL **DISCIPLINE** LAW **EDUCATION** Fayetteville State Univ, BA Sociology 1975; Univ of ID, MA Sociology 1978; Univ of IA School of Law, JD 1981; Univ of IL at Chicago, PhD in Education, 1997. **CAREER** Univ of IA, univ ombudsman 1979-81; IL State Univ, assoc prof pol sci 1981-83, dir of affirm action 1981-83; Natl Bar Assoc, reg dir; John Marshall Law School, asst dean; JOHN MARSHALL LAW SCHOOL, PRACTICING ATTY, PROF OF LAW, CONSULTANT, K-12, COLLEGES AND UNIVERSITIES. **MEMBERSHIPS** Legal counsel IL Affirm Action Officer Assoc, IL Human Relations Assoc, IL Comm on Black Concern in Higher Ed, Chicago Southside Branch NAACP. **SELECTED PUBLICATIONS** Capital punishment discrimination An Indicator of Inst Western Jrnl of Black Studies 1979; innovative approach to recruiting minority employees in higher ed EEO Today 1982; Blacks in IL Higher Ed A Status Report Jrnl for the Soc of Soc & Ethnic Studies 1983; The Social Reality of Blacks Underrepresentation in Legal Ed Approach Toward Racial Parity 1985. Author of articles, "Pedagogy of Culturally Biased Curriculm in Public Education," 1994; "Social Reality of African American Street Gangs," 1997. Capital punishment discrimination An Indicator of Inst Western Jrnl of Black Studies 1979; innovative approach to recruiting minority employees in higher ed EEO Today 1982; Blacks in IL Higher Ed A Status Report Jrnl for the Soc of Soc & Ethnic Studies 1983; The Social Reality of Blacks Underrepresentation in Legal Ed Approach Toward Racial Parity 1985. **CONTACT ADDRESS** John Marshall Law School, 315 S Plymouth Ct, Chicago, IL, 60604.

NEELY, WRIGHT
DISCIPLINE PHILOSOPHY **EDUCATION** Yale Univ, PhD, 67. **CAREER** Assoc prof, Univ Ill Urbana Champaign. **RESEARCH** Philosophy of mind; philosophy of action; American pragmatism; history of modern philosophy. **SELECTED PUBLICATIONS** Auth, Transitive Action, Intervention, and Prevention; Freedom and Desire. **CONTACT ADDRESS** Philosophy Dept, Univ Ill Urbana Champaign, 52 E Gregory Dr, Champaign, IL, 61820. **EMAIL** w-neely@uiuc.edu

NEILL, WARREN
PERSONAL Born 10/27/1962, Montreal, PQ, Canada, s **DISCIPLINE** PHILOSOPHY **EDUCATION** McGill Univ, MA, 92; Univ of GA, PhD, 97. **CAREER** Vis asst prof, State Univ of W GA, 97-98; asst prof, Marist Col, 98-. **MEMBERSHIPS** APA; Amer Assn of Philo Tchrs **RESEARCH** Ethics; environ-

mental ethics; philosophy of law **SELECTED PUBLICATIONS** Auth, An Interest-Satisfaction Theory of Value, Ethics & the Environ; auth, An Emotocentric Theory of Interests, Environ Ethics, 98. **CONTACT ADDRESS** 113A Jackman Dr., Poughkeepsie, NY, 12603. **EMAIL** wneill@netcom.ca

NEILSON, WILLIAM A.W.
DISCIPLINE LAW **EDUCATION** Univ Toronto, BC, 60; Univ British Columbia, LLB, 64; Harvard Univ, LLM, 65. **CAREER** Prof, 71-. **RESEARCH** International trade and business law; competition policy; regulatory modeling. **SELECTED PUBLICATIONS** Auth, Law & Economic Development: Cases and Materials from Southeast Asia; The Vietnam Investment Manual. **CONTACT ADDRESS** Fac of Law, Univ Victoria, PO Box 2400, Victoria, BC, V8W 3H7. **EMAIL** wneilson@uvic.ca

NELKIN, DOROTHY
PERSONAL Born 07/30/1933, Boston, MA, m, 1952, 3 children **DISCIPLINE** PHILOSOPHY **EDUCATION** Cornell Univ, BA, 54. **CAREER** New York Univ, Prof 88; Prof, 64-88, Cornell Univ. **HONORS AND AWARDS** Bernal Prize; Guggenheim Fel; AAAS Fel. **RESEARCH** Science and society; Biotechnical, genetics, law. **SELECTED PUBLICATIONS** Auth, Controversy: The Politics of Technical Decisions; Science as Intellectual Property; The Creation Controversy; Workers at Risk; Selling Science:" How the Press Covers Science and Technology; coauth; A Disease of Society: The Cultural Impact of AIDS, coauth; Dangerous Diagnostics: The Social Power of Biological Information, The DNA Mystic: coauth, The Gene as a Cultural Icon. **CONTACT ADDRESS** 269 Mercer St Room 440, New York, NY, 10003. **EMAIL** dorothy.nelkin@nyu.edu

NELSON, HERBERT JAMES
PERSONAL Born 08/26/1938, Grand Forks, ND, m, 1964, 2 children **DISCIPLINE** PHILOSOPHY **EDUCATION** Gregorian Univ, PhB, 60, PhL, 61; State Univ NY, Buffalo, PhD, 69. **CAREER** Instr philos, Niagara Univ, 63-66; asst prof, 68-74, assoc prof, 74-82, Prof Philos, Canisius Col, 82-, Chmn Dept, 76-90, Vice-Pres Acad Affairs, 96-. **MEMBERSHIPS** Am Philos Asn; Am Cath Philos Asn. **RESEARCH** Philosophy of religion; 17th and 18th century philosophy; American philosophy. **SELECTED PUBLICATIONS** Auth, The resting place of process theology, Harvard Theol Rev, 79; The epistemic availability of Hartshorne's Experience, Int Philos Quart, 81; Experience, Dialect, and God, Proces Studies, 82; Time(s), Eternity, and Duration, Int J Philos Relig, 87; Kant on Arguments Cosmological and Ontological, Am Cath Philos Quart, 93. **CONTACT ADDRESS** Acad Affairs, Canisius Col, 2001 Main St, Buffalo, NY, 14208-1098. **EMAIL** nelson@canisius.edu

NELSON, JAMES DAVID
PERSONAL Born 02/13/1930, Luray, KS, m, 1957, 2 children **DISCIPLINE** HISTORY OF CHRISTIAN THOUGHT **EDUCATION** Westmar Col, AB, 52; United Theol Sem, BD, 59; Univ Chicago, MA, 61, PhD(church hist), 63. **CAREER** Asst prof & librn, 63-65, from asst prof to prof hist theol, 65-77, Prof Church Hist, United Theol Sem, 77-, Mem comn arch & hist, United Methodist Church, 72-78. **MEMBERSHIPS** Am Acad Relig; Am Hist Asn; Am Soc Church Hist. **RESEARCH** German Lutehran Pietism; theological enlightenment in Germany; German romanticism. **SELECTED PUBLICATIONS** Auth, Piety and invention, In: The Impact of Christianity on its Environment, Univ Chicago, 68; Responsible Grace - Wesley,john Practical Theology - Maddox,rl, Theological Studies, Vol 0056, 1995. **CONTACT ADDRESS** 20 Greenmount Blvd, Dayton, OH, 45419.

NELSON, JAMES L.
PERSONAL Born 04/02/1954, Williamsport, PA, m, 1986, 6 children **DISCIPLINE** PHILOSOPHY **EDUCATION** Canisius Col, BA, 74; State Univ NY, PhD, 80. **CAREER** Assoc prof, Mich State Univ, 89-90; asst prof, 80-87; assoc prof, St. John's Univ, 87-90; prof, 90-. **HONORS AND AWARDS** Sr Res & Creative Achievement Award, Univ Tenn, 97. **MEMBERSHIPS** Am Philos Asn; Am Asn Univ Prof; Am Soc Bioethics Hum; British Soc Ethics Theory. **RESEARCH** Contemporary moral theory; bioethics. **SELECTED PUBLICATIONS** Auth, Alzheimer's Answers to Hard Questions for Families, 96; auth, The Patient in the Family, 95; auth, Meaning and Medicine: A Reader in the Philosophy of Health Care, 98; auth, The Meaning of the Act: Reflections on the Expressive Meaning of Prenatal Screening, Kennedy Inst Ethics Jour, 98; auth, Unlike Calculating Rules? Clinical Judgement, Formalized Decisionmaking and Wittgenstein, Slow Cures and Bad Philos: Wittgenstein and Bioethics, 98; auth, The Silence of the Bioethicists: Ethical and Political Aspects of Managing Gender Dysphoria, Gay & Lesbian Quart, April, 98; auth, Everything Includes Itself in Power: Power and Coherence in Englehardt's Foundations of Bioethics, Reading Englehardt, 97; auth, Measured Fairness, Situated Justice: Feminist Reflections on Health Care Rationing, Kennedy Inst Ethics Jour, March, 96; auth, Other Isms Aren't Enough: Feminism, Social Policy, and Long-Acting Contraception, Coerced Contraception: The Ethics of Long-Term Contraception, 96; auth, Critical Interests and Sources of Familial Decisionmaking Authority for Incapacitated Patients, Jour Law, Med, & Ethics, Summer, 95; auth, Publicity and Pricelessness: Grassroots Decisionmaking and Justice in Rationing, Jour Med & Philos, Aug, 94; auth, Moral Sensibilities and Moral Standing, Bioethics, July, 93. **CONTACT ADDRESS** Dept of Philosophy, Tennessee Univ, 801 McClung Tower, Knoxville, TN, 37996-0480. **EMAIL** jnelson@utkux.utcc.utk.edu

NELSON, LANCE E.
DISCIPLINE THEOLOGICAL AND RELIGIOUS STUDIES **EDUCATION** McMaster Univ, PhD. **CAREER** Dept Theo, Univ San Diego **RESEARCH** Vedanta and devotional traditions of Hinduism; relig and ecology in South Asia; Hindu-Christian dialogue. **SELECTED PUBLICATIONS** Publ on, res interest. **CONTACT ADDRESS** Dept of Theological and Relig Studies, Univ of San Diego, 5998 Alcal Park, Maher 282, San Diego, CA, 92110-2492. **EMAIL** lnelson@acusd.edu

NELSON, LONNIE R.
PERSONAL Born 01/17/1961, Kirkville, MO, m, 1981, 2 children **DISCIPLINE** PHILOSOPHY; THEOLOGY **EDUCATION** New Orleans Baptist Theological Seminary, MDiv, 89; Tulane Univ, MA, 91, PhD, 98. **CAREER** Author **MEMBERSHIPS** APA; Soc of Christian Philosophers; Baptist Assn of Philosophy Teachers **RESEARCH** Philosophy of Religion **CONTACT ADDRESS** 611 Cleveland Ave SW, Cullman, AL, 35055. **EMAIL** l&knelson@pobox.com

NELSON, LYNN HANKINSON
PERSONAL Born 01/07/1948, Brooklyn, NY **DISCIPLINE** PHILOSOPHY **EDUCATION** Temple Univ, PhD, 87. **CAREER** Asst, assoc and prof, Rowan Univ, 89-97; prof, Univ Missouri, St Louis, 98- . **MEMBERSHIPS** APA; Philos of Sci Asn; Soc for Women in Philos. **RESEARCH** Philosophy of science; history and philosophy of biology; feminist philosophy of science. **SELECTED PUBLICATIONS** Auth, Who Knows: From Quine to a Feminist Empiricism, Temple, 90; auth, A Question of Evidence, Hypatia 8, 93; auth, Epistemological Communities, in Alcoff, ed, Feminist Epistemologies, Routledge, 93; coauth, No Rush to Judgment, The Monist, 94; auth, The Very IDea of Feminist Epistemology, Hypatia, 95; coauth, Feminist Values and Cognitive Virtues, PSA, 95; auth, Feminist Naturalized Philosophy of Science, Synthese, 95; ed, Synthese, Special Issue on Feminism and Science, 95; co-ed and contribur, Feminism, Science, and the Philosophy of Science, Kluwer Academic, 96; auth, Who Knows? in Garry, ed, Women, Knowledge, and Reality, 2d ed, Routledge, 96; auth, Empiricism, in Jaggar, ed, Blackwell Companion to Feminist Philosophy, Oxford, 97; co-ed and contribur, Re-Reading the Canon: Feminist and Other Contemporary Interpretations of Quine, Penn State, 98. **CONTACT ADDRESS** Philosophy Dept, Univ of Missouri, St Louis, St Louis, MO, 63121. **EMAIL** hankinson-nelson@umsl.edu

NELSON, MICHAEL P.
PERSONAL Born 06/15/1966, Richland Center, WI **DISCIPLINE** PHILOSOPHY **EDUCATION** Univ Wisc, BA 86; Mich State Univ, MA, 90; Lancaster Univ, UK, PhD, 98. **CAREER** Assoc lectr, asst prof, Univ Wisc, Stevens Point, 93- . **HONORS AND AWARDS** Vice Chancellor's Merit for Tchg Excellence. **MEMBERSHIPS** APA; Int Soc for Environ Ethics; Soc for Philos in the Contemp World; Forest Service Employees for Environ Ethics; Int Asn of Environ Philos. **RESEARCH** Environmental philosophy. **SELECTED PUBLICATIONS** Auth, A Defense of Environmental Ethics, Environ Ethics, 93; auth, Rethinking Wilderness: The Need for a New Idea of Wilderness, Philos in the Contemp World, 96; auth, Holists and Fascists and Paper Tigers...Oh My! Ethics and the Environ, 96; co-ed, The Great New Wilderness Debate, Univ Georgia, 98. **CONTACT ADDRESS** Dept of Philosophy, Univ of Wisconsin, Stevens Point, WI, 54481. **EMAIL** m2nelson@uwsp.edu

NELSON, PAUL T.
PERSONAL Born 11/29/1952, Hinsdale, IL, m, 1977, 2 children **DISCIPLINE** RELIGIOUS STUDIES **EDUCATION** Princeton Univ, AB, 74; Yale Univ, M Div, 77, MA, 79, M Phil, 81, PhD, 84. **CAREER** Res assoc, Lutheran Church in Amer, NY, 82-84; visiting asst prof, theol, Univ Notre Dame, 84 85; asst prof, relig, Wittenberg Univ, 85-91; assoc prof and chair, relig, Wittenberg Univ, 91-97; prof and chair, relig, Wittenberg Univ, 97-. **MEMBERSHIPS** Amer Acad of Relig; Soc of Christ Ethics. **RESEARCH** Religious ethics; Bioethics. **SELECTED PUBLICATIONS** Articles, Lutheran Bioethics, Bioethics Yearbook, vol I, 91; vol III, 93; vol V, 97, Kluwer Acad Publ; auth, Narrative and Morality, Penn State Press, 87. **CONTACT ADDRESS** Wittenberg Univ, PO Box 720, Springfield, OH, 45501. **EMAIL** pnelson@wittenberg.edu

NELSON, STANLEY A.
PERSONAL m, 2 children **DISCIPLINE** THEOLOGY **EDUCATION** Va Commonwealth Univ, BA; Southwestern Baptist Theol Sem, MDiv, PhD; advan grad stud, Union Theol Sem; Grad Theol Union; Univ Nigeria; dan; sabbatical leaves, Oxford Univ; Regent's Park Col; Spiritual Dirs' Inst, prog spiritual direction, Mercy Ctr Burlingame, 95. **CAREER** Instr, Nigerian Baptist Theol Sem; prof, 84-; sr prof, Golden Gate Baptist Theol Sem. **HONORS AND AWARDS** Assoc, Personnel Selection Dept, S Baptist For Mission Bd; dir, Missionary Journeyman Prog, S Baptist For Mission Bd; pastor, pastor of Benicia Fel. **SELECTED PUBLICATIONS** Contrib, Baptist Prog; Student; World Mission Jour; Baptist Faith and Heritage; auth, Journey in Becoming, Broadman, 83; A Believer's Church Theology, re-pub, 96. **CONTACT ADDRESS** Golden Gate Baptist Theol Sem, 201 Sem Dr, Mill Valley, CA, 94941-3197. **EMAIL** StanNelson@aol.com

NELSON, WILLIAM N.
PERSONAL Born 02/18/1945, Oakland, CA, m, 1968, 2 children **DISCIPLINE** PHILOSOPHY **EDUCATION** Harvard Col, AB, 67; Cornell, PhD, 72. **CAREER** Prof, 71-, Univ Houston. **MEMBERSHIPS** APA; AAUP; Amintaphil. **RESEARCH** Moral & political phil. **SELECTED PUBLICATIONS** Auth, On Justifying Democracy, Routledge & Kegan Paul, 80; art, Equal Opportunity, Soc Theory & Prac, 84; art, Evaluating the Institutions of Liberal Democracy, Pol & Process, Cambridge, 89; auth, Morality: What's in it for Me? A Historical Introduction t **CONTACT ADDRESS** Dept of Philosophy, Univ of Houston, Houston, TX, 77204-3785. **EMAIL** wnelson@uh.edu

NEMEC-IGNASHEV, DIANE
DISCIPLINE EAST ASIAN RELIGIONS **EDUCATION** Univ Chicago, PhD. **CAREER** Religion, Carleton Univ. **MEMBERSHIPS** Areas: Elizaveta Goreva, Ariadna Efron. **CONTACT ADDRESS** Carleton Col, 100 S College St., Northfield, MN, 55057-4016.

NENON, THOMAS J.
DISCIPLINE PHILOSOPHY **EDUCATION** Regis Col, BA, 72; Boston Col, MA; Univ Freiburg, Germany, PhD, 83. **CAREER** ASST VPROVOST ACAD AFF, 97-, PROF PHILOS, 97-, UNIV MEMPHIS. **CONTACT ADDRESS** Dept Philosophy, Univ of Memphis, Memphis, TN, 38152. **EMAIL** tnenon@memphis.edu

NERENBERG, BRUCE EDWARD
PERSONAL Born 06/05/1948, Cincinnati, OH, m, 1989, 1 child **DISCIPLINE** PHILOSOPHY **EDUCATION** Mich State Univ, BA, 70; New Sch for Social Res, grad fac, PhD, 83; Univ Wisc Milwaukee, PhD, 93. **CAREER** Attending psychol, clinical dir, adolescent sex offender prog, Charter Behavioral Health System Wisconsin, 95-; ad hoc fac, Univ Wisc Milwaukee, fall, 98. **MEMBERSHIPS** Amer Philos Asn; Amer Psychol Asn; North Amer Kant Soc. **SELECTED PUBLICATIONS** Auth, Extraneous Reason(s): A Critical Social-Psychological and Historical Analysis of Radical Behaviorism, 93; auth, The Phantom of the Opera: Subjectivity and Antimentalism in Radical Behaviorism, 90; auth, An Enquiry into the Structure of Kant's First Two Critiques: Ethics Within the Bounds of the Idea of Technology Alone, 83; transl, Why We Can Only Use Natural Language to Talk about Principles of the Political Realm, 78; article, The Logic of Parts and Wholes: Husserl and Gurwitsch, Grad Fac Philos Jour, 4, 1, 74. **CONTACT ADDRESS** 1910 E. Menlo Blvd., Shorewood, WI, 53211-2518. **EMAIL** nerenbrg@execpc.com

NESSON, CHARLES ROTHWELL
PERSONAL Born 02/11/1939, Boston, MA, m, 1961 **DISCIPLINE** LAW **EDUCATION** Harvard Univ, AB, 60, LLB, 63. **CAREER** Prof Law, Harvard Law Sch, 66, Assoc Dean, 80-. **SELECTED PUBLICATIONS** Auth, Earnings and profits discontinuities, Harvard Law Rev, 64; Constitutional Hearsay - Requiring Foundational Testing And Corroboration Under The Confrontation Clause, Virginia Law Review, Vol 0081, 1995; The 5th-amendment Privilege Against Cross-examination, Georgetown Law J, Vol 0085, 1997. **CONTACT ADDRESS** 1525 Massachusetts, Cambridge, MA, 02138-2903.

NESTINGEN, JAMES A.
DISCIPLINE CHURCH HISTORY **EDUCATION** Concordia Col, BA, 67; Luther Sem, MDiv, 71; MTh, 78; St. Michael's Col, Univ Toronto, ThD, 84. **CAREER** Instr, 76-78; asst prof, 80; prof, 92-. **HONORS AND AWARDS** Bruce prize in New Testament, 71., Pastor, Faith Lutheran Church, 71-74; curriculum ed, Augsburg Publ House, 74-76; asst to the pastor, St. Ansgar Lutheran Church, Can, 78-80. **SELECTED PUBLICATIONS** Auth, The Faith We Hold, 83; Martin Luther: His Life and His Writings, 82; Roots of Our Faith, 78; coauth, Free to Be, 75. **CONTACT ADDRESS** Dept of Church History, Luther Sem, 2481 Como Ave, St. Paul, MN, 55108. **EMAIL** jnesting@luthersem.edu

NETA, RAM
PERSONAL Born 07/15/1966, Tel Aviv, Israel **DISCIPLINE** PHILOSOPHY **EDUCATION** Harvard Univ, BA, 88; Univ Pittsburgh, PhD, 97. **CAREER** Asst prof, Univ Utah, 98- . **HONORS AND AWARDS** Mellon predoctoral fel, 88-89; NSF grad fel, 90-93; Southwest Philos Soc prize, 98; NEH summer sem, 98. **MEMBERSHIPS** APA. **RESEARCH** Epistemology; philosophy of language; philosophy of mind. **SELECTED PUBLICATIONS** Auth, Stroud and Moore on

Skepticism, Southwest Philos Rev, 97; auth, How Can There be Semantic Facts? Southwest Philos Rev, 98. **CONTACT ADDRESS** Dept of Philosophy, Univ of Utah, Salt Lake City, UT, 84112. **EMAIL** ramneta@yahoo.com

NEU, JEROME
PERSONAL Born 06/23/1947, New York, NY **DISCIPLINE** PHILOSOPHY **EDUCATION** Princeton Univ, AB, 67; Oxford Univ, DPhil, 73. **CAREER** Assoc Prof Philos, Univ CA, Santa Cruz, 72-, Fel law & philos, Harvard Law Sch, 75-76; vis prof law, Univ TX Sch Law, 76; Soc Sci Res Coun res training fel, 75-76; Rockefeller hum fel, 78-79; NEH Fel 94-95; ACLS fel 95-96. **MEMBERSHIPS** Am Philos Asn. **RESEARCH** Philos of law; philos of mind; psychoanalytic theory. **SELECTED PUBLICATIONS** Auth, Jealous thoughts, In: Explaining Emotions, Univ CA, 80; Ed, Cambridge Companion to Freud, 91. **CONTACT ADDRESS** Philos Bd, Univ of California, 1156 High St, Santa Cruz, CA, 95064-0001. **EMAIL** neu8@hotmail.com

NEUFELD, DIETMAR
PERSONAL Born 05/03/1949, m, 1977, 4 children **DISCIPLINE** CHRISTIAN ORGINS; RELIGIOUS STUDIES **EDUCATION** Univ Winnipeg, BA; Mennonite Biblical Seminary, MA; McGill Univ, PhD. **CAREER** Asst prof, Univ of British Columbia, 94- . **MEMBERSHIPS** CBA; CSBS; AAR/SBL; Context Group. **RESEARCH** Religious Rivalry - Pagans, Jews, Christians in Ancient Sardis and Smynna; States of Ecstasy in the Ancient Near East; The Social Sciences and the New Testament. **SELECTED PUBLICATIONS** Auth, Eating, Ecstasy and Exorcism, Biblical Theology Bulletin, 96; auth, Apocalypticsm: Context, Whose Historical Jesus, 97; auth, And When That One Comes: Aspects of Johannine Messianism, Eschatology, Messianism, and the Dead Sea Scrolls, 97. **CONTACT ADDRESS** Dept of Classical, Near East, and Religious Studie, Univ of British Columbia, 1866 Main Mall Buch C 270, Vancouver, BC, V6T 1Z1. **EMAIL** dneufeld@unixg.ubc.ca

NEUHOUSER, FREDERICK
DISCIPLINE 19TH CENTURY GERMAN PHILOSOPHY **EDUCATION** Columbia Univ, PhD, 88. **CAREER** Instr, Harvard Univ; PROF, PHILOS, UNIV CALIF, SAN DIEGO. **HONORS AND AWARDS** Humboldt fel. **RESEARCH** Philosophical foundations of Hegel's social theory. **SELECTED PUBLICATIONS** Auth, Fichte's Theory of Subjectivity, Cambridge Univ Press, 90; "Freedom, Dependence, and the General Will," The Philos Rev, 93; "Fichte and the Relation between Right and Morality," Fichte: Historical Context/Contemporary Controverseries, Hum Press, 94; "The First Presentation of Fichte's Wissenschaftslehre (94/95)," The Cambridge Companion to Fichte, Cambridge Univ Press, 96. **CONTACT ADDRESS** Dept of Philos, Univ Calif, San Diego, 9500 Gilman Dr, La Jolla, CA, 92093.

NEUJAHR, PHILIP JOSEPH
PERSONAL Born 01/24/1944, San Jose, CA, 1 child **DISCIPLINE** PHILOSOPHY **EDUCATION** Stanford Univ, BA, 65; Yale Univ, MPhil, 72, PhD(philos), 73. **CAREER** Asst prof, 73-77, Assoc Prof Philos, Oglethorpe Univ, 77-. **MEMBERSHIPS** Am Philos Asn. **RESEARCH** Metaphysics, personal identity; histor of philosophy. **SELECTED PUBLICATIONS** Auth, Subjectivity, Philos Res y Arch, 12/76; Hume on identity, Hume Studies, 4/78; Kant's Idealism, Mercer Univ Press, 96. **CONTACT ADDRESS** Dept of Philosophy, Oglethorpe Univ, 4484 Peach Tree Rd, Atlanta, GA, 30319-2797.

NEUMANN, HARRY
PERSONAL Born 10/10/1930, Dormoschel, Germany, m, 1959 **DISCIPLINE** POLITICAL PHILOSOPHY, ETHICS **EDUCATION** St Johns Col, Md, BA, 52; Univ Chicago, MA, 54; Johns Hopkins Univ, PhD, 62. **CAREER** Asst prof philos, Mich State Univ, 62-63 & Lake Forest Col, 63-65; fel, Ctr Hellenic Studies, 65-66; assoc prof philos & govt, 66-69, Prof Philos & Govt, Scripps Col & Claremont Grad Sch, 69-, Res assoc, Rockefeller Inst, 62; res fel, Henry Salvatori Ctr Studies Individual Freedom in Mod World, 70-71, Earhart Found, 73-74, 78, 82, 86-90-94; adv, Scripps Asn Study Freedom, 75-. **MEMBERSHIPS** AAUP **RESEARCH** Political philosophy and humanities; classical philosophy; religion and philosophy. **SELECTED PUBLICATIONS** Auth, Liberalism, Carolina Acad Press, 91; Eternal and Temporal Enemies, Polit Commun, vol 9, 92; Political Theology?, Interpretation, Fall 95; Political Philosophy or Self-Knowledge, Interpretation, Fall 96. **CONTACT ADDRESS** Dept of Philos, Scripps Col, 1030 Columbia Ave, Claremont, CA, 91711-3948.

NEUSNER, JACOB
PERSONAL Born 07/28/1932, Hartford, CT, m, 1964, 4 children **DISCIPLINE** RELIGIOUS STUDIES **EDUCATION** Harvard College, BA magna cum laude 53; Jewish Theol Sem, Master Hebrew Letters, 60; Columbia Univ, PhD 60. **CAREER** Uppsala Univ Swed, vis prof 96; Univ Gottingen Ger, Von Humboldt res prof, 95; Inst Judaicum Aboense Finland, vis prof 93; Cambridge Univ Eng, vis fel 92; Univ Frankfurt Ger, Von Humboldt fel 90-91; Bard Col NY, prof 94 to 2003; Univ S FL, Dist res prof 90-; Princeton Univ Inst Adv Stud, mem 90-; Univ Minn, vis prof 78-79; Jewish Theol Sch, vis prof 76; Brown Univ, prof, Ungerleider Dist Sch, 68-90; Dartmouth Col, asst prof, assoc prof, 64-68; Brandeis Univ, res assoc 62-64; Univ WI Milwaukee, asst prof 61-62; Columbia Univ, instr, 60-61. **HONORS AND AWARDS** Phi Beta Kappa; Abraham Berliner Awd; LDH; Fellner Prize; Medal of Col de France; Ecumenical Medal; Comm Medal of the Cardinal of Milano; Ambassador for the Arts; Queen Christina of Sweden Medal; Guggenheim fel; Fulbright fel; Lown fel; NEH. **SELECTED PUBLICATIONS** Auth, The Encyclopaedia of Judaism, two volumes, organizer and Editor-in-Chief, E. J. Brill, forthcoming, 1999; The Talmud of Babylonia, An American Translation, Chico, Atlanta, Scholars Press for Brown Judiaic Studies, 84-95; Invitation to the Talmud: A Teaching Book, NY Harper & Row, 2nd printing of 2nd edition, Atlanta, Scholars Press for S FL Studies in the History of Judaism, 98; The Talmud: Close Encounters, Minneapolis, 91, Fortress Press, 2nd printing, 96; The Transformation of Judaism, From Philosophy to Religion, Champaign, 92, Univ IL Press, pbk ed, Baltimore, John Hopkins Univ Press, 99; Rabbinic Judaism, Structure and System, Minneapolis, Fortress Press, 96; The Theology of the Oral Torah, Revealing the Justice of God, Kingston and Montreal, McGill-Queens Univ Press, 98; Judaism in the Mainstream: Interpreting the History of a Religion, London, Routledge, 99; Religious Norms of the Oral Torah in Practice: Sanctifying the Social Order, Atlanta, Scholars Press S FL St in the Hist of Judaism, 2001, Summary of The Religious Commentary; Judaism and Islam, Comparing Religions Through Law, with Tamara Sonn, London, Routledge, forthcoming, 2000. **CONTACT ADDRESS** Dept of Religious Studies, SFlorida Univ, 735 Fourteenth Ave., North East, St Petersburg, FL, 33701-1413. **EMAIL** jneusner@luna.cas.usf.edu

NEVILLE, ROBERT C.
PERSONAL Born 05/01/1934, St. Louis, MO, m, 1963, 3 children **DISCIPLINE** PHILOSOPHY; THEOLOGY **EDUCATION** Yale, BA (magna cum laude), 60, MA, 62, PhD, 63. **CAREER** DEAN, PROF OF PHILOS, RELIG, AND PHILOS, BOSTON UNIV SCHOOL OF THEOLOGY. **HONORS AND AWARDS** DD, Lehigh Univ, 93; Doctoris honoris causa, Russian Academy of Sciences, Inst of Far Eastern Studies, 96. **MEMBERSHIPS** Am Academy Relig, pres 92; Am Theol Soc; Metaphysical Soc Am; Asn of Theol Schools. **RESEARCH** Chinese religion & philos; pragmatism; metaphysics. **SELECTED PUBLICATIONS** Auth, A Theology Primer, SUNY, 91; The High Road Around Modernism, SUNY, 92; Eternity X Time's Flow, SUNY, 93; Normative Culture, SUNY, 95; The Truth of Broken Symbols, SUNY, 95. **CONTACT ADDRESS** Boston Univ, 745 Commonwealth Ave., Boston, MA, 02215. **EMAIL** rneville@bu.edu

NEWELL, ROGER
PERSONAL Born 05/30/1952, Erie, PA, m, 1975, 2 children **DISCIPLINE** SYSTEMATIC THEOLOGY **EDUCATION** Westmont Col, BA, 74; Fuller Sem, MDiv, 77; Univ Aberdeen, PhD, 83. **CAREER** Pastor, Claypath United Reformed Church, Durham, UK, 84-92; assoc pastor, Lake Grove Presby Ch, Ore, 92-97; asst prof, George Fox Univ, 97- . **RESEARCH** Theology and science; theological epistemology; Christian education; pastoral theology. **SELECTED PUBLICATIONS** Auth, Passion's Progress: The Meanings of Love, SPCK, 94. **CONTACT ADDRESS** 104 Pinehurst Dr, Newberg, OR, 97132. **EMAIL** rnewell@georgefox.edu

NEWMAN, ANDREW
PERSONAL Born 12/24/1948, Bournemouth Dorset, m, 4 children **DISCIPLINE** PHILOSOPHY **EDUCATION** King's Coll, London, BS Physics; PhD Theoretical Physics,76; PhD, Philos, 84. **CAREER** Asst prof Univ Tulsa, 85-90; asst prof, Univ Nebr, 90-92; assoc prof, Univ Nebr, 92-. **RESEARCH** Metaphysics; Philosophy of Science. **CONTACT ADDRESS** Philosophy and Religion, Univ of Nebr Omaha, Omaha, NE, 88182-0285. **EMAIL** anewman@unomaha.edu

NEWMAN, BARBARA
DISCIPLINE RELIGION AND ENGLISH **EDUCATION** Yale Univ, PhD. **CAREER** Prof, Northwestern Univ. **RESEARCH** Repression of Heloise; child sacrifice and maternal matyrdom in saints' lives and romances; mystical womens' attitudes toward Hell and Purgatory. **SELECTED PUBLICATIONS** Auth, Sister of Wisdom: St Hildegard's Theology of the Feminine, Univ Calif Press, 87; ed, and transl, Symphonia Armonie Celestium Revelationum, Cornell UP, 88; From Virile Woman to WomanChrist: Studies in Medieval Religion and Literature, Univ Pa Press, 95; Sister of Wisdom: St Hildegard's Theology of the Feminine, 89. **CONTACT ADDRESS** Dept of Religion, Northwestern Univ, 1801 Hinman, Evanston, IL, 60208. **EMAIL** bjnewman@nwu.edu 9

NEWMAN, DAVID
DISCIPLINE PHILOSOPHY OF MIND **EDUCATION** Univ Tex, PhD. **CAREER** Asst prof, WMich Univ. **RESEARCH** Congitive science. **SELECTED PUBLICATIONS** Articles, Philos Sci; New Ideas Psychol **CONTACT ADDRESS** Kalamazoo, MI, 49008. **EMAIL** newmand@wmich.edu

NEWMAN, JOEL S.
PERSONAL Born 10/21/1946, Oceanside, NY, m, 1970, 2 children **DISCIPLINE** LAW **EDUCATION** Brown Univ, 68; Univ Chicago, JD, 71. **CAREER** Assoc, Shearman & Sterling, 71-73 & Fredrickson Law Firm, 73-76; asst prof, 76-78, assoc prof tax & ethics, law sch, Wake Forest Univ, 78-. **HONORS AND AWARDS** Nat Endowment for Humanities fel, summer 80. **RESEARCH** Personal tax deductions; estate and gift taxation; legal ethics. **SELECTED PUBLICATIONS** Auth, Research and Development Allocations Under Sections 861 and 864: An Author's Query, 60 Tax Notes, 93; art, On Section 107's Worst Feature: The Teacher-Preacher, 61 Tax notes 1505, 93; art, A Truly Moving Experience, 64 Tax Notes 261, 94; art, A Comparative Look at Three British Tax Cases, 67 Tax Notes 1509, 95; art, Legal Advice Toward Illegal Ends, 28 University of Richmond Law Review, 94; auth, Federal Income Taxation: Cases, Problems and Materials, West Publishing Company, 98 **CONTACT ADDRESS** Box 7206, Winston Salem, NC, 27109-7206. **EMAIL** jnewman@law.wfu.edu

NEWMAN, LEX
DISCIPLINE THE HISTORY OF MODERN PHILOSOPHY **EDUCATION** Irvine, PhD, 94. **CAREER** Asst prof, Univ Nebr, Lincoln, 94-; vis asst prof, Univ Pittsburgh, 96. **SELECTED PUBLICATIONS** Auth, Descartes on Unknown Faculties and Our Knowledge of the External World, Philos Rev 103, 94; Descartes' epistemology, in The Stanford Encyclopedia of Philosophy, ed, Edward N Zalta, an online publication of Ctr for Stud of Lang and Infor, Stanford Univ, http://plato.stanford.edu/entries/descartes-epistemology, 97. **CONTACT ADDRESS** Univ Nebr, Lincoln, Lincoln, NE, 68588-0417.

NEWMAN, LOUIS E.
DISCIPLINE JEWISH ETHICS **CAREER** Religion, Carleton Univ. **SELECTED PUBLICATIONS** Auth, The Sanctity of the Seventh Year: A Study of Mishnah Tractate Shebiit, 83; Coed, Contemporary Jewish Ethics and Morality, 95. **CONTACT ADDRESS** Carleton Col, 100 S College St., Northfield, MN, 55057-4016.

NEWMAN, MURRAY L.
PERSONAL Born 07/22/1924, Checotah, OK, m, 1946, 4 children **DISCIPLINE** OLD TESTAMENT **EDUCATION** Phillips Univ, AB, 45, MA, 47; Union Theol Sem, NY, BD, 51, ThD, 60. **CAREER** Tutor asst Old Testament, Union Theol Sem, NY, 50-51, instr, 53-54; instr refig, Vassar Col, 52-53; asst prof, Smith Col, 54-55; from asst prof to assoc prof Old Testament, 55-63, prof, 63-96, Catherine McBurney Prof of Old Testament, Protestant Episcopal Theol Sem, 80-; adjunct prof of Old Testament, Howard Divinity School, Howard Univ, Washington, D.C.; adjunct prof of Old Testament, Trinity School for Ministry, Ambridge, Pa. **MEMBERSHIPS** Soc Bibl Lit; Cath Bibl Soc; Soc Bibl Theol. **RESEARCH** Old Testament; Biblical archaeology. **SELECTED PUBLICATIONS** Auth, The People of the Covenant, 62 & contribr, The Interpreter's Dictionary of the Bible, 62, Abingdon; The Prophetic Call of Samuel, In: Israel's Prophetic Heritage, Harper, 62; Rahab and the Conquest; The Continuing Quest for the Historical Covenant, 90; The Pentateuch, The Psalms, and other articles in the Encyclopedia of the Episcopal Church, 98. **CONTACT ADDRESS** 3812 King St, Alexandria, VA, 22302-1906. **EMAIL** mlnewman@aol.com

NEWMAN, MURRAY L., JR.
DISCIPLINE OLD TESTAMENT LANGUAGES AND LITERATURE **EDUCATION** Phillips Univ, BA, 45; Phillips Univ, MA, 47; Union Theol Sem, BD, 51, ThD, 60; Univ Basel, Switzerland, 51-52; Univ Heidelberg, Ger, 59, 67; Univ Fribourg, Switzerland, 71-72; Inst Advan Theol Stud, Jerusalem, 80-81; St George's Col, Jerusalem, 78, 84; Inst Cath de Paris, 92. **CAREER** Instr, Phillips Univ; Vassar Col; Union Theol Sem; Smith Col; G Wash Univ; St Luke's, Univ South; St Paul's Theol Col; Cath Univ Am; Howard Univ; Catherine N. McBurney prof emeri, Va Theol, Sem, 55-.. Va Theol Sem, 55-. **SELECTED PUBLICATIONS** Auth, The People of the Covenant, Studies in Dueteronomy; Rahab and Conquest, Interpretater's Dictionary of the Bible; The Continuing Quest for the Historical Covenant. **CONTACT ADDRESS** Va Theol Sem, 3737 Seminary Rd, Alexandria, VA, 22304.

NEWMAN, ROBERT CHAPMAN
PERSONAL Born 04/02/1941, Washington, DC **DISCIPLINE** NEW TESTAMENT **EDUCATION** Duke Univ, BS, 63; Cornell Univ, PhD, 67; Faith Theol Sem, MDiv, 70; Bibl Theol Sem, Pa, STM, 75. **CAREER** Assoc prof math & phys sci, Shelton Col, 68-71; assoc prof New Testament, 71-77, prof New Testament, Bibl Theol Sem, 77-; fel, Barton Res Found, Franklin Inst, 67-68. **HONORS AND AWARDS** Pres, Evangelical Theological Society, 95-96. **MEMBERSHIPS** Evangel Theol Soc; Am Sci Affil. **RESEARCH** Interaction of science and theology. **SELECTED PUBLICATIONS** Auth, Scientific and Religious Aspects of the Origins Debate, Perspectives on Science and Christian Faith 47, September, 95; art, Scientific Problems for Scientism, Presbyterion 21/2, 95; auth, Fulfilled Prophecy as Miracle, In Defense of Miracles: A Comprehensive Case for God's Action in History, Downers Grove, IL: Inter-

Varsity, 97. **CONTACT ADDRESS** Biblical Theol Sem, 200 N Main St, Hatfield, PA, 19440-2421. **EMAIL** cnewman@erols.com; rnewman@biblical.edu

NEWSOME, CLARENCE GENO
PERSONAL Born 03/22/1950, Ahoskie, NC, m, 1972 **DISCIPLINE** THEOLOGY **EDUCATION** Duke Univ, BA 1971; Duke Divinity School, M Div 1975; Duke U, PhD 1982. **CAREER** Duke U, asst pro & dean of minority affairs 1973-74; Mt Level Baptist Church, Durham, NC Dem Nat'l Comm, asst staff dir demo charter comm 1974-75; Duke Divinity School, instructor 1978-82, asst prof 1982; Mt Level Baptist Church, Durham, NC Democratic Nat'l Comm 1974-75; Duke Univ, asst prof of Amer religious thought; Howard Univ DC Assistant Dean School of Divinity 1986-89, assoc dean, School of Divinity, l989-. **HONORS AND AWARDS** 1st Black to receive Athletic Grant-in-Aid (Scholarship) Duke Univ 1968-72; 1st Black to be named to the All Atlantic Coast Conf Acad Team Duke Univ 1970-71; 1st Black stud Comm Speaker Walter Cronkite was the Keynote Duke Univ 1972; Rockfellow Doct Fellowship, Natl Fellowship, James B Duke Dissertation Fellowship, 1975-78. **MEMBERSHIPS** Mem American Society of Church History 1980-; mem of finance comm Creative Ministries Assoc 1981; chrmn of the brd NC Gen Baptist Found, Inc 1982; mem of comm on educ Durham Comm on the Affairsof Black People 1983; co-chairman of comm on educ Durham Interdenominational Ministerial Alliance 1983-84; Planning Coordinator, Euro-American Theology Consultation Group, American Academy of Religion 1987-; pres Society for the Study of Black Religion 1989-. **SELECTED PUBLICATIONS** Number of articles and completed book length manuscript on Mary McLeod Bethund, A Religious Biography **CONTACT ADDRESS** Dean of Theology, Howard Univ, 1400 Sheperd St., NE, Washington, DC, 20017.

NEWTON, LISA HAENLEIN
PERSONAL Born 09/17/1939, Orange, NJ, m, 1972, 5 children **DISCIPLINE** PHILOSOPHY **EDUCATION** Columbia Univ, BS, 62, PhD(philos), 67. **CAREER** Asst Prof Philos, Hofstra Univ, 67-69; from Asst Prof to Assoc Prof, 69-77, Prof Philos, Fairfield Univ, 77-, Dir, Prog Applied Ethics, 82-, Dir, Prog Environmental Studies, 86-; Lectr Medicine, Yale Medical Sch, 83-. **MEMBERSHIPS** Am Philos Asn; Am Soc Polit & Legal Philos; Soc Values Higher Educ; Soc Study Prof Ethics; Am Soc Bioethics & Humanities; Soc Business Ethics. **RESEARCH** Foundations of law and concept of the state; business and professional ethics; medical ethics; environmental ethics & policy. **SELECTED PUBLICATIONS** Auth, Ethics in America: Study Guide, Prentice Hall, 89; ed, Ethics in America: Source Reader, Prentice Hall, 89; co-ed, Taking Sides: Clashing Views on Controversial Issues in Business Ethics, Dushkin Publ Group, 90, 4th ed, 96; coauth, Wake-up Calls: Classic Cases in Business Ethics, Wadsworth, 95; auth, A Passport for the Corporate Code, In: A Companion to Business Ethics, Backwell Publ 98; author of numerous articles. **CONTACT ADDRESS** Dept of Philos, Fairfield Univ, 1073 N Benson Rd, Fairfield, CT, 06430-5195. **EMAIL** lhnewton@fair1.fairfield.edu

NEYREY, JEROME H.
PERSONAL Born 01/05/1940, New Orleans, LA **DISCIPLINE** NEW TESTAMENT STUDIES **EDUCATION** Yale Univ, PhD, 77. **CAREER** Asst prof, assoc prof, prof, Weston Sch of Theol, 77-92; prof, Univ Notre Dame, 92- . **HONORS AND AWARDS** Pres, New England region, SBL. **MEMBERSHIPS** Catholic Bibl Asn; Soc of Bibl Lit; The Context Gp. **RESEARCH** Rhetoric; social-scientific criticism; prayer and sacrifice; God in the New Testament; Gospel of John. **SELECTED PUBLICATIONS** Auth, Paul, In Other Words: A Cultural Reading of His Letters, Westminster, 90; auth, The Social World of Luke-Acts: Models for Interpretation, Hendrickson, 91; auth, 2 Peter and Jude, Doubleday, 93; auth, What's Wrong With This Picture? John 4, Cultural Stereotypes of Women, and Public and Private Space, Bibl Theol Bull, 94; auth, Josephus' Vita and the Encomium: A Native Model of Personality, J for the Stud of Judaism, 94; auth, The Footwashing in John 13:6-11: Transformation Ritual or Ceremony? in White, ed, The Social World of the First Christians: Essays in Honor of Wayne A. Meeks, Fortress, 95; auth, Loss of Wealth, Loss of Family and Loss of Honor: A Cultural Interpretation of the Original Four Makarisms, in Esler, ed, Modelling Early Christianity: Social-Scientific Studies of the New Testament in Its Context, Routledge, 95; coauth, Portraits of Paul: An Archaeology of Ancient Personality, Westminster, 96; auth, Luke's Social Location of Paul: Cultural Anthropology and the Status of Paul in Acts, in Witherinton, ed, History, Literature, and Society in the Book of Acts, Cambridge, 96; auth, Despising the Shame of the Cross: Honor and Shame in the Johannine Passion Narrative, Semeia, 96; auth, The Trials (Forensic) and Tribulations (Honor Challenges) of Jesus: John 7 in Social Science Perspective, Bibl Theol Bull, 96; auth, Meals, Food and Table Fellowship, in Rohrbaugh, ed, The Social Sciences and New Testament Interpretation, Hendrickson, 96; auth, Clean/Unclean, Pure/Polluted and Holy/Profane, in Rorhbaugh, ed, The Social Sciences and New Testament Interpretation, Hendrickson, 96; coauth, It Was Out of Envy that They Handed Jesus Over (Mark 15:10): The Anatomy of Envy and the Gospel of Mark, JSNT, 98; auth, Honor and Shame: Matthew and the Great Code, Westminster, 98. **CONTACT ADDRESS** Dept of Theology, 163 Decio Faculty Hall, Notre Dame, IN, 46556. **EMAIL** neyrey.1@nd.edu

NG, ON-CHO
PERSONAL Born 01/29/1953, Hong Kong, m, 1995 **DISCIPLINE** HISTORY, RELIGIOUS STUDIES **EDUCATION** Univ HI, PhD, 86. **CAREER** Vis asst prof, Univ CA, Riverside, 86-89; asst prof, 89-95, assoc prof, PA State Univ, 95-. **MEMBERSHIPS** Am Academy of Relig; Asn for Asian Studies; Soc for Comparative and Asian Philos; Soc of Chinese Religions. **RESEARCH** Intellectual hist of late Imperial China; 16th-18th centuries; Confucian tradition. **SELECTED PUBLICATIONS** Auth, Revisiting Kung Tzu-chen's (1792-1841) Chinwen (New Text) Precepts: An Excursion in the History of Ideas, J of Oriental Studies, 31-2, fall 93; A Tension in Ch'ing Thought: Historicism in Seventeenth and Eighteenth Century Chinese Thought, J of the History of Ideas, 54-4, Oct 93; Hsing (Nature) as the Ontological Basis of Practicality in Early Ch'ing Ch'eng-Chu Confucianism: Li Kuang-ti's (1642-1718) Philosophy, Philos East and West 44-1, Jan 94; Mystical Oneness and Meditational Praxis: Religiousness in Li Yong's (1627-1703) Confucian Thought, J of Chinese Religions, no 22, fall 94; Mid-Ch'ing New Text (Chin-wen) Classical Learning and Its Han Provenance: The Dynamics of a Tradition of Ideas, East Asian History, no 8, Dec 94; Interpreting Qing Thought in China as a Period Concept: On the Construction of an Epochal System of Ideas, Semiotica: J of the Int Asn for Semiotic Studies, 107-3/4, 95; Is Emotion (Qing) the Source of a Confucian Antimony?, J of Chinese Philos, 98; Imagining Boundaries: Changing Confucian Doctrines, Texts, and Hermeneutics, co-ed with Kai-wing Chow and John Henderson, SUNY, March 99; and two book chapters. **CONTACT ADDRESS** History Dept, Pennsylvania State Univ, University Park, PA, 16802. **EMAIL** oxn1@psu.edu

NGAN, LAI LING E.
PERSONAL Hong Kong, s **DISCIPLINE** THEOLOGY **EDUCATION** California Baptist Col, BS, 76; Loma Linda Univ, MA, 79; MDiv, 82, PhD, 91, Golden Gate Baptist Theological Seminary. **CAREER** Assoc Minister, 91-93, Stockton Chinese Baptist Church; Instr, 87-89, Asst Prof, 93-95, Assoc Prof, 95-96, Golden Gate Baptist Theological Seminary; Assoc Prof, 96-, George W. Truett Seminary, Baylor Univ. **HONORS AND AWARDS** Selected for participation in NEH Summer Seminar and ATS Seminar; Intl Who's Who among professional and business women **MEMBERSHIPS** Amer Schools of Oriental Religion; Soc of Biblical Lit; Natl Assoc of Professors of Hebrew; Ethnic Chinese Biblical Colloquim **RESEARCH** Literary study of Biblical narratives **SELECTED PUBLICATIONS** Auth, 2 Kings 5, Review and Exposition, 94; A Teaching Outline of the Book of Joshua, Review and Exposition, 98. **CONTACT ADDRESS** George W. Truett Theological Seminary, Baylor Univ, Waco, TX, 76798-7126. **EMAIL** lai_ngan@baylor.edu

NI, PEIMIN
PERSONAL Born 10/22/1954, Shanghai, China, m, 1984, 1 child **DISCIPLINE** PHILOSOPHY **EDUCATION** Univ Conn, PhD, 91. **CAREER** Vis asst prof, Mont State Univ, 91-92; asst prof, Mont State Univ, 92-97; assoc prof, Grand Valley State Univ, 97-. **HONORS AND AWARDS** Outstanding Teaching Award, Mont State Univ, 92. **MEMBERSHIPS** Asn of Chinese Philosophers in Am; Am Philos Asn. **RESEARCH** East-West comparative philosophy; Philosophy of causation. **SELECTED PUBLICATIONS** Auth, "Changing the Past," 92; "Taoist Concept of Freedom," 96; "A Qigong Interpretation of Confucianism," 96; Thomas Reid, 96. **CONTACT ADDRESS** 600 Prestwick Dr SE, Grand Rapids, MI, 49546-2252. **EMAIL** NIP@GVSU.edu

NICHOL, TODD W.
DISCIPLINE CHURCH HISTORY **EDUCATION** St. Olaf Col, BA, 74; Luther Sem, MDiv, 78; Grad Theol Union, ThD, 88. **CAREER** Instr, 83; assoc prof, 91-; dir grad stud (s), 91-93. **HONORS AND AWARDS** Grad fel, Univ Minn; awd of commendation, Concordia Hist Inst., Asst pastor, Christ Eng Lutheran Church, 79-80; assoc pastor, interim sr pastor, St. Philip's Lutheran Church, 84-86. **SELECTED PUBLICATIONS** Ed, transl, Vivacious Daughter: Seven Lectures on the Religious Situation Among the Norwegians in America, by H.A. Preus, 90; co-ed, Called and Ordained: Lutheran Perspectives on the Office of the Ministry, 90. **CONTACT ADDRESS** Dept of Church History, Luther Sem, 2481 Como Ave, St. Paul, MN, 55108. **EMAIL** tnichol@luthersem.edu

NICHOLAS, JAMES C.
DISCIPLINE LAW **EDUCATION** Univ Miami, BBA, MA; Univ Ill, PhD. **CAREER** Prof, Univ Fla, 85-. **MEMBERSHIPS** Amer Econ Asn; Amer Planning Asn; Urban Land Inste Exec Coun; Southern Econ Asn; Amer Real Estate Urban Econ Asn; Omicron Delta Epsilon; Pi Mu Epsilon. **CONTACT ADDRESS** School of Law, Univ of Florida, PO Box 117625, Gainesville, FL, 32611-7625. **EMAIL** nicholas@law.ufl.edu

NICHOLAS, JOHN M.
DISCIPLINE PHILOSOPHY **EDUCATION** Sussex Univ, BS; MS; Univ Pittsburgh, PhD. **CAREER** Assoc prof **SELECTED PUBLICATIONS** Auth, pub(s) on Descartes' theory of science. **CONTACT ADDRESS** Dept of Philosophy, Western Ontario Univ, London, ON, N6A 5B8. **EMAIL** jnichola@julian.uwo.ca

NICHOLS, P.M
PERSONAL Born 09/16/1960, OR, m, 1990, 3 children **DISCIPLINE** INTERNATIONAL LAW **EDUCATION** Harvard Univ, BA, 82; Duke Univ, JD, 88, LLM, 88. **CAREER** Asst Prof, Assoc Prof, 92 to 98-, Univ Penn Wharton Sch. **HONORS AND AWARDS** 5 Teach Awds. **MEMBERSHIPS** ALSB; ACG; ASIL. **RESEARCH** Emerging Economies; Intl Trade and Investment. **SELECTED PUBLICATIONS** Auth, A Legal Theory of Emerging Economies, VA J Intl L, forthcoming; auth, Forgotten Linkages-Historical Institutionalism and Sociological Institutionalism and Analysis of the World Trade Organization, U of Penn J Intl Econ L, 98; auth, Creating a Market Along the Silk Road: A Comparison of Privatization Techniques in Central Asia, NY U J Intl L and Politics, 98; auth, The Viability of Transplanted Law: Kazakhstani Reception of A Transplanted Foreign Investment Code, U of Penn J Intl Econ L, 97; auth, Trade Without Values and the World Trade Organization, U of Penn J Intl Econ L, 96; GATT Doctrine, VA J Intl L, 96; auth, Swapping Debt for Development: A Theoretical Application of Swaps to the Creation of Microenterprise Lending Institutions in Sub-Saharan Africa, NY U J Intl L and Politics. **CONTACT ADDRESS** Dept of Legal Studies, Univ Penn, 2100 SH-DH, Philadelphia, PA, 19104-6369. **EMAIL** nicholsp@wharton.upenn.edu

NICHOLSON, L.
PERSONAL Born 01/13/1947, Philadelphia, PA **DISCIPLINE** PHILOSOPHY **EDUCATION** Univ Penn, BA 68; Brandais Univ, MA 70, PhD 75. **CAREER** Lectr, asst prof, assoc prof, prof. **HONORS AND AWARDS** Rockefeller Fel; SVPL Fel; **MEMBERSHIPS** APS; SWP; APSA **RESEARCH** Political philosophy; social theory; feminist theory. **SELECTED PUBLICATIONS** Auth, Gender and History: The Limits of Social Theory in the Age of the Family, CUP, 86; The Play of Reason: From the Modern to the Postmodern, Ithaca NY, CUP, 98; Feminism and Postmodernism, ed, NY, Routledge, 90; The Second Wave, NY, ed, Routledge, 97; Social Postmodernism, co-ed, Cambridge Eng, CUP, 95; Thinking Gender, ed, Routledge Press, 98. **CONTACT ADDRESS** Dept of Philosophy, SUNY Albany, Albany, NY, 12222. **EMAIL** ljn84@cnsuny.albany.edu

NICKELSBURG, GEORGE WILLIAM ELMER
PERSONAL Born 03/15/1934, San Jose, CA, m, 1965, 2 children **DISCIPLINE** NEW TESTAMENT & CHRISTIAN ORIGINS, EARLY JUDAISM **EDUCATION** Valparaiso Univ, BA, 55; Concordia Sem, St Louis, BD, 60, STM, 62; Harvard Div Sch, ThD, 68. **CAREER** From Asst Prof to Prof Relig, 69-98, Daniel J. Krumm Distinguished Prof New Testament and Reformation Studies, Univ Iowa, 98-; Guest lectr, Concordia Sem, St Louis, 68, instr, 69; guest prof, Christ-Sem-Seminex, 79; vis scholar, Univ Munster, 74; assoc ed, Cath Bibl Quart, 79-. **HONORS AND AWARDS** Fel, John Simon Guggenheim Mem Found, 77-78; Fel, Netherlands Inst Advan Study, 80-81; Fel, Human Sci Res Coun of SAfrica, 93. **MEMBERSHIPS** Soc Bibl Lit; Studiorum Novi Testamenti Societas; Cath Bibl Asn. **RESEARCH** The synoptic gospels; New Testament christology; history and literature of early post-biblical Judaism. **SELECTED PUBLICATIONS** Auth, Resurrection, Immortality and Eternal Life in Intertestamental Judaism, Harvard/Oxford, 72; ed, Studies on the Testament of Abraham, Scholars Press, 76; auth, Apocalyptic and myth in 1 Enoch 6-11, J Bibl Lit, 77; collabr, A Complete Concordance to Flavius Josephus, Vol 3, Brill, 79; auth, The genre and function of the markan passion narrative, Harvard Theol Rev, 80; Jewish Literature between the Bible and the Mishnah, Fortress, 81; Enoch, Levi and Peter, recipients of revelation in Upper Galilee, J Bibl Lit, 81; coauth, Faith and Piety in Early Judaism, Fortress, 83. **CONTACT ADDRESS** Sch of Relig, Univ of Iowa, Gilmore Hall, Iowa City, IA, 52242-1376. **EMAIL** george-nickelsburg@uiowa.edu

NICKLES, THOMAS
DISCIPLINE HISTORY AND PHILOSOPHY OF SCIENCE **EDUCATION** Princeton Univ, PhD, 69. **CAREER** Prof, Univ Nev, Reno. **RESEARCH** Knowledge pollution; historicism. **SELECTED PUBLICATIONS** Contributed to How to Take the Naturalistic Turn, Univ Chicago, 93; recent publications in Soc Stud of Sci; Isis; Brit J for the Philos of Sci; Biol and Philos. **CONTACT ADDRESS** Univ Nev, Reno, Reno, NV, 89557. **EMAIL** nickles@unr.edu

NICOLE, ROGER
PERSONAL Switzerland **DISCIPLINE** THEOLOGY **EDUCATION** Sorbonne, MA; Gordon Divinity Sch, ThD; Harvard Univ, PhD. **CAREER** Prof. **HONORS AND AWARDS** Assoc ed, New Geneva Study Bible; correspond ed, Christianity Today; pres, Evangel Theol Soc. **MEMBERSHIPS** Founding mem, Intl Coun on Bibl Inerrancy. **SELECTED PUBLICA-**

TIONS Auth, Calvin's Commentaries on the Gospels and Acts. **CONTACT ADDRESS** Dept of Theology, Reformed Theol Sem, 1015 Maitland Ctr Commons, Maitland, FL, 32751.

NIDITCH, SUSAN
PERSONAL Born 07/10/1950, Boston, MA, m, 1974, 2 children **DISCIPLINE** RELIGIOUS STUDIES **EDUCATION** Radcliffe Coll, AB, 72; Harvard Univ, PhD, 77. **CAREER** Asst Sr Tutor, Harvard Univ, 74-77; asst prof, Univ Cincinnati, 77-78; asst prof, Amherst Coll, 78-84; vis prof, Williams Coll, 80-81; assoc prof, Amherst Coll, 84-90; Chair Dept Rel, Amherst Coll, 86-87 and 91-93; Elizabeth Bruss Readership, 87-90; prof, Amherst Coll, 90-; Samuel Green prof, Amherst Coll, 92-. **HONORS AND AWARDS** Phi Beta Kappa; Briggs Fel for Grad Study, 72-73; NEH Fel, 85-86, 90-91, 95. **SELECTED PUBLICATIONS** Auth, Short Stories: The Book of Esther and the Theme of Women as a Civilizing Force, in Old Testament Interpretation, Past, Present, and Future, 95; War in the Hebrew Bible and Contemporary Parallels, in Word and World, 95; Oral World and Written Word, Ancient Israelite Literature, 96; Ancient Israelite Religion, 97. **CONTACT ADDRESS** Religion Dept, Amherst Col, Amherst, MA, 01002.

NIEDNER, FREDERICK A.
PERSONAL Born 05/05/1945, Lander, WY, m, 1986, 3 children **DISCIPLINE** THEOLOGY, HEBREW BIBLE AND LANGUAGE **EDUCATION** Christ Sem, ThD, 79. **CAREER** Visiting instr, Christ Sem, 76-77; instr to asst prof to assoc prof to prof, dept theol, Valparaiso Univ, 73-. **HONORS AND AWARDS** Caterpillar Award for Excellence in Teaching, 96. **MEMBERSHIPS** Soc of Bibl Lit. **RESEARCH** Hatred and war in the biblical world; Rhetoric of polarization. **SELECTED PUBLICATIONS** Auth, Keeping the Faith, Fortress, 81. **CONTACT ADDRESS** Dept. of Theology, Valparaiso Univ, Valparaiso, IN, 46383-6493. **EMAIL** fred.niedner@valpo.edu

NIEHAUS, JEFFREY J.
DISCIPLINE OLD TESTAMENT **EDUCATION** Yale Univ, BA; Harvard Univ, AM, PhD; Gordon-Conwell Theol Sem, MDiv. **CAREER** Prof, Gordon-Conwell Theol Sem, 82-. **SELECTED PUBLICATIONS** Pub(s), Jour Biblical Lit; Vetus Testamentum; Jour Evangel Theol Soc; Tyndale Bulletin; auth, Amos, Obadiah; God at Sinai; No Other Gods, forthcoming. **CONTACT ADDRESS** Gordon-Conwell Theol Sem, 130 Essex St, South Hamilton, MA, 01982.

NIELSEN, HARRY A.
DISCIPLINE PHILOSOPHY **EDUCATION** Rutgers, AB; Univ Conn, MA; Univ Nebr, PhD. **CAREER** Prof emer **SELECTED PUBLICATIONS** Pub (s), Kierkegaard; Ethics & Philosophy of Science. **CONTACT ADDRESS** Dept of Philosophy, Univ of Windsor, 401 Sunset Ave, Windsor, ON, N9B 3P4. **EMAIL** dumala@uwindsor.ca

NIELSEN, KAI
DISCIPLINE PHILOSOPHY **EDUCATION** Univ Duke, PhD. **CAREER** Adj prof. **RESEARCH** Metaphilosophy, contemporary ethical and political theory, and marxism. **SELECTED PUBLICATIONS** Auth, 22 bk(s) and 415 articles; Transforming Philosophy, 95; Naturalism Without Foundations, 96. **CONTACT ADDRESS** Dept of Philos, Concordia Univ, Montreal, 1455 de Maisonneuve W, Montreal, PQ, H3G 1M8. **EMAIL** eud@vax2.concordia.ca

NIETO, JOSE CONSTANTINO
PERSONAL Born 04/07/1929, El Ferrol, Spain, m, 1959, 2 children **DISCIPLINE** HISTORY OF RELIGIOUS THOUGHT **EDUCATION** Univ Santiago, BS, 49; United Evangel Sem, Madrid, BD, 56; Princeton Theol Sem, ThM, 62, PhD(relig), 67. **CAREER** Pastor, Span Evangel Church, 58-61; from asst prof to assoc prof, 67-78, prof relig, 78-82, Mary S Geiger Prof Relig & Hist, Juniata Col, 82-. **MEMBERSHIPS** Am Soc Reformation Res; Sixteenth Century Studies Conf; Am Acad Relig; AAUP. **RESEARCH** Spanish 16th century religious thought, particularly reformation, humanism and mysticism. **SELECTED PUBLICATIONS** Auth, Juan de Valdes and the Origins of the Spanish and Italian Reformation, Librairie Droz, Geneva, 70 & transl, Madrid-Mexico, Fondo de Cultura Economica, 79; Mystic, Rebel, Saint: A study of St John of the Cross, Geneva, Droz, 79 & Spanish ed, Mistico, poeta, rebelde, Santo, En torno a San Juan de Cruz, Marid-Mexico, Fondo de Cultura Economica, 82; ed and auth introd notes, Valdes Two Catechisms, The Dialogue on Christian Doctrine and the Christian Instruction for Children, Coronado Press, 81; Sexuality And Confession - Sexual Solicitation on Trial Before The Holy-office 16th-century to The 19th-century - Spanish - Sarrionmora,a, Sixteenth Century J, Vol 0026, 1995; Correspondence of Enzinas,francisco,de - Spanish, Latin - Enzinas,fd, Garciapinilla,ij, Sixteenth Century J, Vol 0027, 1996. **CONTACT ADDRESS** Dept History, Juniata Col, 1700 Moore St, Huntingdon, PA, 16652-2196.

NIGOSIAN, SOLOMON ALEXANDER
PERSONAL Born 04/23/1932, Alexandria, Egypt **DISCIPLINE** HISTORY OF RELIGION **EDUCATION** Univ Toronto, BA, 68; McMaster Univ, MA, 70, PhD(relig), 75. **CAREER** Teaching asst relig, McMaster Univ, 69-71; lectr, 72-75, Asst Prof Relig, Univ Toronto, 75-, Lectr relig, Ctr Christian Studies, Toronto, 71-74 & York Univ, 71-73; consult films relig, Ont Educ Commun Authority, Toronto, 72-73; assoc ed, Armenian Missionary Asn Am, Inc, Paramus, NJ, 72-76; asst prof, Ont Col Art, Toronto, 78-79. **MEMBERSHIPS** Int Asn Hist Relig; Can Soc Study Relig; Am Acad Relig. **RESEARCH** History of interreligious interactions with specialization in the Near East. **SELECTED PUBLICATIONS** Auth, World Religions, Clark, Can, 74, Arnold, England, 75 & McDougall, Littel, 76; World Religions: An Idea Book for Teachers, Clark, Can, 74; The religions in Achaemenid Persia, 74-75 & Zoroastrianism in Fifth Century Armenia, 78, Studies Relig; Occultism in the Old Testament, Dorrance, 78; The challenge of religious pluralism, Ecumenist, 78; Dialoguing For Differences, al Mushin, 79; Modes of Worship, Bk Soc, Can, 81; What Is Scripture - Cantwellsmith,w, Studies in Religion- sciences Religieuses, Vol 0023, 1994. **CONTACT ADDRESS** Dept of Relig Studies, Univ of Toronto, Toronto, ON, M5S 1A1.

NIKULIN, DMITRI
DISCIPLINE PHILOSOPHY **EDUCATION** Univ Moscow, PhD, 90. **CAREER** Asst prof, Eugene Lang Col. **RESEARCH** Ethics; metaphysics; philos of sci; theology; hist of philos. **SELECTED PUBLICATIONS** Auth, Metaphysics and Ethics, 96. **CONTACT ADDRESS** Eugene Lang Col, New Sch for Social Research, 66 West 12th St, New York, NY, 10011.

NILSON, JON
PERSONAL Born 09/03/1943, Chicago, IL, m, 1968, 3 children **DISCIPLINE** THEOLOGY **EDUCATION** St Mary of the Lake Sem, AB, 65, STB, 67; Univ Notre Dame, MA, 68, PhD(theol), 75. **CAREER** Asst prof theol, Ill Benedictine Col, 70-74 & Univ Dallas, 74-75; asst prof, 75-80, Assoc Prof Theol, Loyola Univ Chicago, 80-, Lonergan Trust Fund Pub subsidy, 77. **HONORS AND AWARDS** Best First Article in Patristics, NAm Patristic Soc, 77. **MEMBERSHIPS** Cath Theol Soc Am. **RESEARCH** Theological method; political theology; psychology and theology. **SELECTED PUBLICATIONS** Auth, Transcendent knowledge in insight: A closer look, Thomist, 73; To whom is Justin's dialogue with Trypho addressed?, Theol Studies, 77; Hegel's Phenomenology and Lonergan's Insight, Verlag Anton Hain, 78; Receiving the Vision - the Anglican Roman-catholic Reality Today - Bird,d, Theological Studies, Vol 0057, 1996; Progress in Unity - 50 Years of Theology Within the World-council-of-churches, 1945- 1995 - a Study Guide - Brinkman,me, Theological Studies, Vol 0057, 1996; Gods Spirit - Transforming a World in Crisis - Mullerfahrenholz,g, Horizons, Vol 0024, 1997. **CONTACT ADDRESS** Dept of Theol, Loyola Univ, Chicago, 6525 N Sheridan Rd, Chicago, IL, 60626-5385.

NILSSON, DONAL E.
PERSONAL Born 11/20/1936, Newton, MA, m, 1960, 3 children **DISCIPLINE** RELIGION **EDUCATION** Wheaton Collm BA, 60; Westminster Theol Sem, MDiv , 64; Univ Penna, PhD, 97. **CAREER** Prof, Nyack Coll, 67-. **HONORS AND AWARDS** Service Awards, Nyack Coll; Alumnus of the Year, 97-98. **MEMBERSHIPS** Soc of Bibl Lit; Evangel Theol Soc. **RESEARCH** Philosophy of Religion; Hermeneutics; Patristics. **CONTACT ADDRESS** Nyack Col, 11 College Ave, Nyack, NY. **EMAIL** nillsond@nyack.com

NISSEN, LOWELL
DISCIPLINE PHILOSOPHY OF SCIENCE **EDUCATION** Univ Nebr, PhD. **CAREER** Philos, Univ Ark **SELECTED PUBLICATIONS** Coauth, Reflective Thinking: The Fundamentals of Logic, 68, 76. **CONTACT ADDRESS** Univ Ark, Fayetteville, AR, 72701. **EMAIL** lnissen@comp.uark.edus

NISSIM-SABAT, MARILYN
PERSONAL Born 07/30/1938, Brooklyn, NY, m, 1967, 1 child **DISCIPLINE** PHILOSOPHY **EDUCATION** Brooklyn Col, BA, 59; DePaul Univ, PhD, 77; Univ Illinois, Chicago, MSW, 93. **CAREER** Prof philos, Lewis Univ, 79-. **MEMBERSHIPS** APA; Husserl Circle; Soc for Phenomenology and Existential Psych; Soc for Women's Philos. **RESEARCH** Integration of Husserlian phenomenology; psychoanalysis; Marxism; feminism. **SELECTED PUBLICATIONS** Auth, Freud, Feminism, and Faith, Listening, 85; auth, Psychoanalysis and Phenomenology: A New Synthesis, Psychoanalytic Rev, 96; auth, Kohut and Husserl: The Emphatic Bond, in, Self Psychology: Comparisons and Contrasts, Analytic, 89; auth, Autonomy, Empathy, and Transcendence in Sophocles' Antigone: A Phenomenological Perspective, Listening, 90; auth, The Crisis in Psychoanalysis: Resolution Through Husserlian Phenomenology and Feminism, Human Stud, 91; auth, Towards a Phenomenology of Empathy, Am Jour of Psychotherapy, 95; auth, An Appreciation and Interpretation of the Work of Lewis Gordon, C L R James Jour, 97; auth, Victims No More, Radical Philos Rev, 98. **CONTACT ADDRESS** Dept of Philosophy, Lewis Univ, Romeoville, IL, 60446. **EMAIL** nissimma@lewisu.edu

NNORUKA, SYLVANUS I.
PERSONAL Born 06/16/1953, Enugu, Nigeria **DISCIPLINE** PHILOSOPHY **EDUCATION** Urban Univ, Rome, BA, 78, BD, 82; Univ Catholique de Louvain, Belgium, MA philos, 87, MA lit, 88, PhD, 90; Katholieke Univ Leuven, Belgium, STL, 91. **CAREER** Lectr, dean of philos, St. Joseph Major Sem, Nigeria (on sabbatical). **MEMBERSHIPS** Nigeria Philos Assoc; APA. **RESEARCH** Phenomenological-Hermeneutical analysis of African values; human personality. **SELECTED PUBLICATIONS** Auth, Have Women a Voice in the Church, The Times, J of St. Augustine's School of Mass Commun, 93; auth, Personal Identity: A Philosophical Survey, 95; auth, Alfred Schutz on the Social Distribution of Knowledge, Darshana Int, 96; auth, Multiplicity of Ethnic Groups in Nigeria: A Challenge to the Nigerian Church, in Oguejiofor, ed, Ecclesia in Africa, The Nigerian Repsonse, Fulladu, Nigeria, 97. **CONTACT ADDRESS** 117 Valley Rd, Katonah, NY, 10536. **EMAIL** ifeanyinno@aol.com

NOAH, LARS
DISCIPLINE LAW **EDUCATION** Harvard Univ, AB, JD. **CAREER** Assoc prof, Univ Fla, 94-; past assoc, Covington Burling, Wash, DC. clerk, Ch Judge Abner J. Mikva, US Ct Appeals, DC Circuit; ed, Harvard Law Rev. **MEMBERSHIPS** DC Bar; Pa Bar; Food and Drug Law Inst. **RESEARCH** Administrative law, conflict of laws, food and drug law, products liability, torts. **CONTACT ADDRESS** School of Law, Univ of Florida, PO Box 117625, Gainesville, FL, 32611-7625. **EMAIL** noah@law.ufl.edu

NOBLE, WILLIAM P.
PERSONAL Born 01/25/1932, New York, NY, m, 1998, 2 children **DISCIPLINE** LAW & HISTORY **EDUCATION** Lehigh Univ, BA, 54; Univ Penn, JD, 61. **CAREER** Instr, 86- , writing assessment mentor, 94- , Commun Col of Vermont; Ver Hum Scholar, Ver Coun on Hum, 91- ; adj fac, external degree prog, Johnson State Col, 93- . **HONORS AND AWARDS** Nominated for Eli Oboler Award, ALA Intellectual Freedom Roundtable, 92. **MEMBERSHIPS** Authors Guild; Freedom to Read Comt. **RESEARCH** Law; history; writing. **SELECTED PUBLICATIONS** Auth, Bookbanning in America, Eriksson, 90; auth, Show Don't Tell, Eriksson, 91; auth, Twenty-Eight Most Common Writing Blunders, Writer's Digest, 92; auth, Conflict, Action & Suspense, Writer's Digest, 94; auth, The Complete Guide to Writers' Conferences and Workshops, Eriksson, 95; auth, Three Rules for Writing a Novel, Eriksson, 97. **CONTACT ADDRESS** PO Box 57, Salisbury, VT, 05769.

NOBLES, PATRICIA JOYCE
PERSONAL Born 06/16/1955, St. Louis, MO **DISCIPLINE** LAW **EDUCATION** Southwest Baptist Coll, BA, 1976; Univ of AK, JD, 1981. **CAREER** US District Judge, law clerk, 1981-83; Southwestern Bell Telephone Co, Attorney, 1983-. **HONORS AND AWARDS** Mem of UALR Law Review 1980-81; mem of 1988 Class of Leadership America; author with Alexander C. Larson, Calvin Manson. **MEMBERSHIPS** Mem of the executive bd, Urban League 1981-84; mem Amer Assoc of Trial Attorneys 1983-87; mem AK Bar Assn 1983-87; pres AK Assn of Women Lawyers 1985-86; mem of bd KLRE Public Radio Station 1986-87; mem NAACP 1989-; mem, Missouri Bar Assn, 1981-. **SELECTED PUBLICATIONS** "Competitive Necessity and Pricing In Telecommunications Regulation," Federal Communications Law Journal, 1989. **CONTACT ADDRESS** Southwestern Bell Telephone Co, 201 S Arkard, Rm 2925, Dallas, TX, 75202.

NODA, KEISUKE
PERSONAL Japan, m, 2 children **DISCIPLINE** PHILOSOPHY **EDUCATION** New School for Soc Res, PhD, 96. **CAREER** Adj prof, philos, SUNY Westchester Commun Col, 96- . **MEMBERSHIPS** APA. **RESEARCH** Phenomenology; Eastern thoughts. **CONTACT ADDRESS** 142 Lyons Rd, Scarsdale, NY, 10583.

NOGALES, PATTI
PERSONAL Born 02/08/1961, Caracas, Venezuela, m, 1991, 2 children **DISCIPLINE** PHILOSOPHY OF LANGUAGE **EDUCATION** St Johns Col, BA, 82; N Arizona Univ, MA, 98; Stanford, PhD, 93. **CAREER** Tchr, ORHE School, 82-84; writing lab instr, 84-85, instr spec lrng asst ctr, 85-88, N Arizona Univ; tchg asst, Stanford Univ, 89-91; instr, Col Dupage, 95-96. **MEMBERSHIPS** Asn Am Philos **RESEARCH** Philosophy of language; psycholinguistics. **SELECTED PUBLICATIONS** Auth, adj workshop prog critical classes, Jour Reading & Lrng, 87; Appleworks for Tchrs, 97; Appleworks for Stud, 91; Works for Stud, 91; Metaphorically Speaking, CSLI Press. **CONTACT ADDRESS** 270 Vereda Pradera, Goleta, CA, 93117. **EMAIL** pno@juno.com

NOHRNBERG, JAMES CARSON
PERSONAL Born 03/19/1941, Berkeley, CA, m, 1964, 2 children **DISCIPLINE** RENAISSANCE & MEDIEVAL LITERATURE, BIBLE STUDIES **EDUCATION** Harvard Col, BA, 62; Univ Toronto, PhD, 70. **CAREER** Tch fel Eng, Univ Toronto, 63-64; Jr fel, Soc of Fel, Harvard Univ, 65-68; adj Eng, Harvard Univ, 67-68; Actg instr Eng, Yale Univ, 68-69, lectr,

69-70, asst prof, 70-75; Prof Eng, Univ VA, 75-; Woodrow Wilson fel, Toronto, 62-63, Morse fel Eng, Yale Univ, 74-75; Ctr for Advan Studies fel, Univ VA, 75-78; Guggenheim fel, 81-82; Gauss Seminars in Criticism lctr, Princeton Univ, 87; Inst Adv Study fel, IN Univ, 91; lectr, 74-97, Yale, Princeton, MLA, Columbia, Hopkins, Kenyon, NEH Seminars, Cornell, Univ VA, Georgetown, Emory, Univ Calif Irvine, Ind Univ, Newberry Libr, Loyola Balitmore, Univ South. **HONORS AND AWARDS** Robert Frost Poetry Prize, Kenyon Col 60; Acad of Am Poets, harvard Col, 62. **MEMBERSHIPS** MLA; Spenser Soc. **RESEARCH** Bible; Dante; Shakespeare; Milton. **SELECTED PUBLICATIONS** Auth, On literature and the Bible, Centrum, fall 74; The Analogy of The Faerie Queene, Princeton Univ, 76, 1st cor ed, 81; The Tale Told by Twice-Told Tales, Yearbook of Comp and Gen Lit, Ind Univ, 90; Allegories of scripture, Shofar, winter 93; Like unto Moses: The Constituting of an Interruption, Ind Univ, 95; The Descent of Geryon: the Moral System of Inferno XVI-XXXI, Dante Studies, 98; Allegory D-Veiled: A New Theory for Construing Allegory's Two Bodies, Modern Philol, 11/98; contribr, Homer to Brecht: The European epic and dramatic traditions, In: The Iliad & In: The Inferno, Yale Univ, 77; contribr, Pynchon: A collection of critical essays, In: Pynchon's Paraclete, Prentice-Hall, 77; Moses, In: Images of Man and God: Old Testament Short Stories in LIterary Focus, Almond Press, 81; Centre and labryrinth: Essays in honour of Northrop Frye, In: Paradise Regained by One Greater Man: Milton's Wisdom Epic as a Fable of Identiry, Univ Toronto, 83; Spenser Encyclopedia, In: Acidale, & In: The Faerie Queene Book IV, Univ Toronto, 90; The Book and the text: the Bible and literary theory, In: The Keeping of Nahor: The Etiology of Biblical Election in Genesis, Blackwell, 90; Annotation and its texts, In: Justifying Narrative: Commentary in Biblical Storytelling, Oxford Univ, 91; Not in heaven: Coherence and complexity in Biblical narrative, In: Princely Characters, Ind Univ, 91; Fortune and romance: Boiardo in America, In: Orlando's Opportunity: Chance, Luck, Fortune, Occasion, Boats, and Blows in Boiardo's Orlando Innamorato, Ariz State Univ, 98; Lectura Dantis, Inferno, In: Inferno XVIII: Introduction to Malebolge, Univ CA, 98. **CONTACT ADDRESS** Dept of Eng, Univ of Virginia, 219 Bryan Hall, Charlottesville, VA, 22903. **EMAIL** jnc@j1.mail.virginia.edu

NOLAN, DENNIS R.
DISCIPLINE LABOR LAW **EDUCATION** Georgetown Univ, AB, 67, Additional Grad Stud, 71-73; Univ WI--Milwaukee, MA, 74; Harvard Law Sch, JD, 70. **CAREER** Webster prof, 89-, prof, 80-89, assoc prof, 77-80 & asst prof, 74-77, Univ SC; vis prof, Univ Sydney, New S Wales, Australia, 96; Fulbright res scholsr, Univ Otago, Dunedin, New Zealand, 89; vis prof, George Wash Univ, 87-88; Fulbright vis prof, Univ Col Galway, Ireland, 81-82; vis assoc prof, Univ WA, Seattle, 79-80; assoc atty, Foley & Lardner, Milwaukee, WI, 70-71, 73-74; legal adv to the Dep Under Sec Int Aff, Dept Army, WA, 71-73. Wis & SC Bars. **HONORS AND AWARDS** Founder & 1st ch, Sect on Labor and Employt Law, Soc Fed Labor Rel Prof. **MEMBERSHIPS** Am Arbitr Asn and Fed Mediation and Conciliation Serv Panels of Arbitrators; Am Soc Legal Hist; ch, Asn Am Law Sch Sect on Labor Rel and Employ Law, 90-91; VP S Atlantic Chap, Indus Rel Res Asn, 86-87;Nat Exec BD, Int Soc for Labor Law and Socl Security, 95-99; Labor Law Group Trust; Nat Acad Arbitrators, ch, Comt on Acad Hist, 90-93 & 94 Prog Comt, 92-94 & Bd Governors, 93-96. **RESEARCH** Labor and employ arbitration. **SELECTED PUBLICATIONS** Auth, Labor Arbitration Law and Practice in a Nutshell, West Publ Co, 79; Regulation of Industrial Disputes in Australia, New Zealand and the United States, 11 Whittier Law Rev 761, 90; Does American Labour Arbitration Provide a Model for Australia, 16 Monash Univ Law Rev, Australia 21, 90 & RIP: Compulsory Labour Arbitration in New Zealand, 12 Comparative Labor Law J, 411, 91; coauth, Labor Arbitration: A Coursebook, West Publ Co, 94; AIDS in Labor Arbitration, 25, Univ San Francisco Law Rev 67, 90; The United States, in Workplace Justice: Employment Obligations in International Perspective 334, Univ SC Press, 92; Arbitral Therapy, 46 Proc Nat Acad Arbitrators 269, 94; Traditional Labor Arbitration: Yesterday, Today, and Tomorrow, in The Past, Present, and Future of Labor Arbitration, Cornell UP, 96 & Arbitral Therapy, 46 Rutgers Law Rev 1751, 94; ed & contrib auth, Readings in the History of the American Legal Profession, Michie Bobbs-Merrill Co, Inc, 80. **CONTACT ADDRESS** School of Law, Univ of S. Carolina, Law Center, Columbia, SC. **EMAIL** drnolan@sc.edu

NOLAN, JOHN JOSEPH
PERSONAL Born 11/01/1928, Derby, CT, d, 2 children **DISCIPLINE** LAW **EDUCATION** Holy Cross Col, BS, 50; Suffolk Univ, LLB, 55; Harvard Univ, LLM, 62. **CAREER** From asst prof to assoc prof, 57-62, prof law, 62-75, partner, Vinci & Nolan, 75-78, Prof Law, Suffolk Univ, 78-, Ford Found teaching fel, Law Sch, Harvard Univ, 62; lectr, Boston Univ Law Sch, 77. **MEMBERSHIPS** Am Bar Asn. **RESEARCH** Administrative law; workman's compensation. **CONTACT ADDRESS** Sch of Law, Suffolk Univ, 41 Temple St, Boston, MA, 02114-4241.

NOLAN, RICHARD T.
PERSONAL Born 05/30/1937, Waltham, MA **DISCIPLINE** PHILOSOPHY OF RELIGION **EDUCATION** Trinity Col, BA, 60; Hartford Sem, MDiv, 63; Yale Univ, MA, 67; NY Univ, PhD, 73. **CAREER** Instr, Latin and English, Watkinson Sch, 61-62; instr Math, Cathedral Choir School, 62-64; instr, math and religion, Chechire Acad, 65-67; instr, philos and educ, 67-68, asst acad dean, 68-70, Hartford Sem; prof philos and soc sci, Mattatuck Commun Col, 69-92; adj lectr philos and theology, 73, 89-92, 97- , Barry Univ; adj prof philos, Florida Atlantic Univ, 98- . **HONORS AND AWARDS** Hon Canon, Christ Church Cathedral, Hartford Conn. **MEMBERSHIPS** APA; Authors Guild; Interfaith Alliance; Anglican Asn of Bibl Scholars; AAUP; Am Acad of Relig; Hemlock Soc; Integrity; English-Speaking Union. **RESEARCH** Philosophical theology; systematic theology; ethics. **SELECTED PUBLICATIONS** Ed and contribur, The Diaconate Now, 68; auth, The Significance of the Religious Thought of Edmond La B. Cherbonnier for a Basic Objective of Religious Education, NYU, 73; coauth, Living Issus in Ethics, Wadsworth, 82; ed, Occasional Papers from Christ Church Cathedral, 91-94; coauth, Living Issues in Philosophy, 9th ed, Wadsworth, 95. **CONTACT ADDRESS** 2527 Egret Lake Dr, West Palm Beach, FL, 33413-2181. **EMAIL** canonn@adelphia.net

NOLAN, RITA
DISCIPLINE PHILOSOPHY **EDUCATION** Univ Penn, PhD 65; Boston College, MA 60, BSc 58. **CAREER** Assoc Prof, Prof, 79 to 93-, SUNY Stony Brook; vis acad, 87-88, Oxford Univ; G. Santayana fel, 80, Harvard Univ; vis Assoc Prof, 78-79, Columbia Univ; Assoc Prof, 73-78, Univ N C Chapel Hill; vi Prof, 75, Univ Warwick Eng; ten Assoc Prof, act head, Asst Prof, vis Prof, 70-73, Univ N C Greensboro; vis Asst Prof, 68-70, Univ IL; Asst Prof, 65-68, Univ Wisc Madison; vis Asst Prof, 66-67, Univ Wisc Milwaukee; Instr, 63-65, Chestnut Hill College; vis Lectr, teach fel ed Asst, res Asst, teach Asst, 61-64, Univ Penn. **MEMBERSHIPS** APA; SPP; ESPP. **SELECTED PUBLICATIONS** Auth, Cognitive Practices: human language and human knowledge, Oxford UK, Cambridge, USA, Blackwell, 94; Distinguishing Perceptual from Conceptual Categories, in: Philo and the Cognitive Sciences, eds, R Casati, B Smith, G White, Wein, Verlag, Holder-Pichler-Temsky, 94; The Unnaturalness of Grue, in: Lang Art and Mind, ed, Dale Jamison, Dordrecht, Kluwer, 94; Anticipatory Themes in the Writings of Lady Welby, in: Essays on Significs, ed, H Walter Schmitz, FSS, Amsterdam/Philadelphia, John Benjamin, 90; rev, Philosophy of Mind: An Introduction, George Graham, Oxford and Cambridge MA, 92, Blackwells, in: Philo Books 94; Communicative Processes in Human Development: One Philo Perspective, in: Perspective Comments and Background Articles, Durham NC, Inst for Hum Comm Res, 95. **CONTACT ADDRESS** Philosophy Dept, SUNY Stony Brook, Stony Brook, NY, 11794-3750. **EMAIL** RDNOLAN@ccmail.sunysb.edu

NOLL, MARK ALLAN
PERSONAL Born 07/18/1946, Iowa City, IA, m, 1969, 3 children **DISCIPLINE** HISTORY OF CHRISTIANITY (NORTH AMERICAN) **EDUCATION** Wheaton Col, Ill, BA, 68; Univ Iowa, MA, 70, Trinity Evangel Divinity Sch, MA, 72; Vanderbilt Univ, PhD(church hist), 75. **CAREER** Asst prof hist, Trinity Col, Ill, 75-78; from assoc prof hist to McManis prof of Christian Thought, Wheaton Col, Ill, 78-, vis prof Regent Col, Vancouver, 90, 95, 97; vis prof Harvard Divinity School, spring 98. **HONORS AND AWARDS** Fels, Nat Endowment for Humanities 78-79, 87-88, Pew Charitable Trusts, 93-94. **MEMBERSHIPS** Am Cath Hist Asn; AHA; Am Soc Church Hist; Canadian Soc of Church Hist; Conf Faith & Hist; OAH. **RESEARCH** Theology, politics, society in America 1730-1860; Protestants in the North Atlantic region; cultural history of the Bible. **SELECTED PUBLICATIONS** Auth, Christians in the American Revolution, Eerdmans, 77; Between Faith and Criticism: Evangelicals, Scholarship, and the Bible in America, Harper & Row, 86; One Nation Under God? Christian Faith and Political Action in America, Harper & Row, 88; Princeton and the Republic, 1768-1822, Princeton Univ Press, 89; A History of Christianity in the United States and Canada, Eerdmans, 92; The Scandal of the Evangelical Mind, Eerdmans, 92; Turnung Points: Decisive Moments in the History of Christianity, Baker Books, 98. Co-ed and contrib, The Bible in America, Oxford Univ Press, 82; Religion and American Politics, Oxford Univ Press, 89; Evangelicalism: Comparative Studies of Popular Protestantism in North America, the British Isles, and Beyond, Oxford Univ Press, 93; Evangelicals and Science in Historical Perspective, Oxford Univ Press, 98; co-auth, The Search for Christian America, 2nd ed, Helmers & Howard, 89. **CONTACT ADDRESS** Hist Dept, Wheaton Col, Wheaton, IL, 60187-5593. **EMAIL** Mark.Noll@wheaton.edu

NORDBY, JON JORGEN
PERSONAL Born 11/14/1948, Madison, WI **DISCIPLINE** PHILOSOPHY, LOGIC **EDUCATION** St Olaf Col, BA, 70; Univ Mass, Amherst, MA, 76, PhD philos, 77. **CAREER** Assoc prof, Pacific Jutheran Univ, Tacoma, WA, 77-present; former dept chmn, Philos, 95-98; med investigator, Pierce County Med Examiner, 88-92; consult, Coroner's Serv Forensic Unit, BC Canada, 88-; cons, King County Medical Examiner, Seattle, WA, 93-; cons, Pierce County Medical Examiner, 92-97; cons, Puyallup Police Dept, Pullayup, WA, 95-; cons, Final Analysis, Tacoma, WA, 85-; sr res fel, Dept Forensic Med, Guy's Hosp, London, 94; Metorius Serv Award, Amer Acad of Forensic Sciences, Boston, 94; Presentations Serv Award, Intl Assoc of Bloodstain Pattern Analysts, Seattle, 97. **MEMBERSHIPS** Am Philos Asn; Am Lutheran Church; Philos Sci Asn. **RESEARCH** Philosophy of science, evidence, logic. **CONTACT ADDRESS** Dept of Philosophy, Pac Lutheran Univ, 12180 Park Ave S, Tacoma, WA, 98447-0014. **EMAIL** finalanalysis@msn.com

NOREN, STEPHEN J.
PERSONAL Born 12/16/1938, New York, NY, m, 1972, 2 children **DISCIPLINE** PHILOSOPHY **EDUCATION** Ohio Univ, BS; Univ Mass, MA, PhD. **CAREER** Assoc prof, Calif State Univ, Long Beach, 68-77; assoc prof, Univ Wisc, 75-77. **HONORS AND AWARDS** ACLS fel, 75; Gugenheim fel, 75. **MEMBERSHIPS** APA. **RESEARCH** Philosophy of the mind; philosophical sciences. **CONTACT ADDRESS** 469 Hampstead Way, Santa Cruz, CA, 95062. **EMAIL** snoren@got.net

NORMAN, ANDREW
PERSONAL Born 09/03/1963, Washington, DC, m, 1992, 1 child **DISCIPLINE** PHILOSOPHY **EDUCATION** Wesleyan Univ, BA, 86; Northwestern Univ, PhD, 92. **CAREER** Asst prof, 93-98, Hamilton Col, vis asst, 92-93, Purdue Univ. **MEMBERSHIPS** APA; DSA. **RESEARCH** The narrative structure of dialogue; the hist of science; complexity theory. **SELECTED PUBLICATIONS** Auth, Teaching Wisdom, Knowledge, Teaching and Wisdom, Kluwer, 96; Regress and the Doctrine of Epistemic Original Sin, The Philosophical Quarterly, 97. **CONTACT ADDRESS** 198 College Hill rd, Clinton, NY, 13323. **EMAIL** anorman@hamilton.ed

NORMAN, JUDITH
DISCIPLINE PHILOSOPHY **EDUCATION** Univ Wisc, Madison, PhD, 95. **CAREER** Asst prof, Trinity Univ, 97-. **RESEARCH** Nineteenth century human philosophy. **SELECTED PUBLICATIONS** Transl, "Ages of the World," by F.W.J. Schelling, Univ Mich, 97; auth, "Schelling," A Companion to the Philosophers, Blackwell, 98; "Utilitarianism," Living Well, Harcourt Brace, 99; "Ages of the World," Schelling: Between Fichte and Hegel, Gruner Verlag, 99; "Squaring the romantic Circle," Hegel and Aesthetics, SUNY, forthcoming. **CONTACT ADDRESS** Dept of Philosophy, Trinity Univ, San Antonio, TX, 78212-7200. **EMAIL** jnorman@trinity.edu

NORMAN, KEN
DISCIPLINE LAW **EDUCATION** Univ Saskatchewan, BA, 63, LLB, 65; Oxford Univ, BCL, 67. **CAREER** Prof, 68- **HONORS AND AWARDS** Dir, Int Comn Jurists. **MEMBERSHIPS** Law Soc Saskatchewan. **SELECTED PUBLICATIONS** Auth, Your Clients and The Charter: Liberty and Equality, 88; Equality and Judicial Neutrality, 87. **CONTACT ADDRESS** Col of Law, Univ Saskatchewan, 15 Campus Dr, Saskatoon, SK, S7N 5A6. **EMAIL** Norman@law.usask.ca

NORMORE, CALVIN GERARD
PERSONAL Corner Brook, NF, Canada **DISCIPLINE** PHILOSOPHY, MEDIEVAL STUDIES **EDUCATION** McGill Univ, BA, 68; Univ Toronto, MA, 69, PhD(philos), 76. **CAREER** Lectr philos, York Univ, 72-74; Killam fel, Univ Alta, 76- 77; Mellon Asst Prof Philos, Princeton Univ, 77-. **MEMBERSHIPS** Am Philos Asn; Can Medieval Acad Am; Soc Medieval & Renaissance Philos. **RESEARCH** Medieval philosophy; social and political philosophy; philosophy of time. **SELECTED PUBLICATIONS** Auth, Future contingents, In: Cambridge History of Later Medieval Philosophy, 82; Walter Burley on continuity, In: Infinity & Continuity in Ancient & Medieval Thought, 82; the Necessity in Deduction - Cartesian Inference and its Medieval Background, Synthese, Vol 0096, 1993. **CONTACT ADDRESS** Dept Philosophy, Univ Toronto, Toronto, ON, M5S 1A1.

NORRIS, JOHN
DISCIPLINE LAW **EDUCATION** Carleton Univ, BA, 82; Univ Western Ontario, MA, 84; Univ Toronto, LLB, 91. **CAREER** Associate, Ruby & Edwardh **RESEARCH** Criminal and constitutional law. **SELECTED PUBLICATIONS** Auth, Sentencing for Second-Degree Murder: R v. Shropshire, 96; co-auth, Myths, Hidden Facts and Common Sense: Expert Opinion Evidence and the Assessment of Credibility, 95. **CONTACT ADDRESS** Fac of Law, Univ Toronto, 78 Queen's Park, Toronto, ON.

NORRIS, JOHN MARTIN
PERSONAL Born 04/04/1962, Albuquerque, MN, s **DISCIPLINE** THEOLOGY **EDUCATION** Univ Dallas, BA (theol), 84; Marquette Univ, PhD, (Hist Theol), 90. **CAREER** Dir, Rome prog, Univ Dallas, 93-95; ASST PROF THEOLOGY, UNIV DALLAS, 93-. **HONORS AND AWARDS** Schmitt fel, 88-90. **MEMBERSHIPS** AAR; NAPS. **RESEARCH** Augustine; patristic exegesis. **SELECTED PUBLICATIONS** Auth, The Theological Structure of Augustine's Exegesis in the Tractatus in Iohannis Euangelium, in Collectanea Augustiniana III: Augustine, Presbyter Factus Sum, ed Joseph Lienhard et al, NY: Peter Lang, 93; Macribius: A Classical Contrast to Christian

Exegesis, Augustinian Studies, 97; Augustine and Sign in the Tractates on John, Collectanea Augustiniana V, forthcoming. **CONTACT ADDRESS** Theol Dept, Univ Dallas, 1845 E Northgate Dr., Irving, TX, 75062. **EMAIL** jmorris@acad.udallas.edu

NORRIS, ROBERT
DISCIPLINE THEOLOGY **EDUCATION** Kings Col, London, BA; Univ St Andrews, MTh, PhD. **CAREER** Adj prof **HONORS AND AWARDS** Sr pastor, Fourth Presbyterian Church, Md; exec pastor, First Presbyterian Church, Hollywood. **SELECTED PUBLICATIONS** Ed, Themelios. **CONTACT ADDRESS** Dept of Theology, Reformed Theol Sem, 2101 Carmel Rd, Charlotte, NC, 28226.

NORTH, ROBERT
PERSONAL Born 03/25/1916, Iowa City, IA **DISCIPLINE** BIBLICAL ARCHEOLOGY **EDUCATION** St Louis Univ, MA, 39; Pontif Bibl Inst, Rome, SSD, 54. **CAREER** Instr Greek, Marquette Univ High Sch, 39-41; prof archaeol & Arabic, Pontif Bibl Inst, Rome, 51-56; prof archaeol, Arabic & Hebrew & dir, Pontif Bibl Inst, Jerusalem, 56-59; dir, Excavation of Ghassul, Jericho, 59-60; from assoc prof to prof theol, Marquette Univ, 61-72; Prof Old Testament & Archaeol, Pontif Bibl Inst, Rome, 63-, Cath Bibl Asn Am scholar, 46-51; vis prof theol, Sch Divinity, St Louis Univ, 60-64 & Gonzaga Univ, 74; assoc in coun, Soc Bibl Lit, 63-66. **MEMBERSHIPS** Cath Bibl Asn Am (vp, 68-69); Soc Old Testament Studies; Soc Bibl Lit. **SELECTED PUBLICATIONS** Auth, Ghassul 1960 Excavation Report, Pontif Bibl Inst, Rome, 61; Leviticus, In: Encycl Britannica, 65; Archeo-Biblical Egypt, Pontif Bibl Inst, Rome, 67; Teilhard and the Creation of the Soul, Bruce, 67; Byblos . . ., In: New Catholic Encyclopedia, McGraw, 67; The chronicler: geography, In: Jerome Catholic Commentary, Prentice-Hall, 68; In Search of the Human Jesus, Corpus Bks, 70; Yobel etc, In: Theological Dictionary to the Old Testament, 74; Umm-al-rasas-mayfaah, Vol 1 - Excavation of the Church-of-saint-stephen - Italian - Piccirillo,m, Alliata,e, Biblica, Vol 0077, 1996; The Anchor Bible Dictionary, Vols-1-6 - Freedman,dn, Biblica, Vol 0075, 1994; One and Many - Essays on Change and Variety in Late Norse Heathenism - Mckinnell,j, Medium Aevum, Vol 0066, 1997. **CONTACT ADDRESS** Pontifical Biblical Inst, Via Pilotta 25, Rome, ..

NORTHEY, RODNEY
DISCIPLINE LAW **EDUCATION** Queen's Univ, BA, 83; Dalhousie Univ, LLB, 87; York Univ, MA, 88; Osgoode Hall Law Sch, LLM, 88. **CAREER** Partner, Birchall Northey **RESEARCH** Environmental law. **SELECTED PUBLICATIONS** Auth, Annotated Canadian Environmental Assessment Act and EARP Guidelines Order, Carswell, 94; pubs on constitutional environmental law and environmental law and policy. **CONTACT ADDRESS** Fac of Law, Univ Toronto, 78 Queen's Park, Toronto, ON.

NORTHUP, LESLEY A.
PERSONAL Born 12/02/1947, New York, NY, 1 child **DISCIPLINE** RELIGION STUDIES **EDUCATION** Catholic Univ of Amer, PhD, 91, MA, 84; Episcopal Divinity School, Mdiv, 80; Univ of Wisconsin, BA, 70. **CAREER** Assoc Prof, 98-, Asst Prof, 93-98, Dept of Rel Studies, Film de Intl Univ; Inst, Dept of English, 87-93, Univ of MD. **HONORS AND AWARDS** Florida Hum Council Master Scholar, 98; State of Florida Tchg Incentive Prog Award, 97. **MEMBERSHIPS** Amer Acad of Rel; MO Amer Acad of Lit; Societas Litwgira. **RESEARCH** Ritual Studies, Women's Ritualizing, 20th century American Religion, Episcopal Prayer Book Studies. **SELECTED PUBLICATIONS** Auth, Ritualizing Women: Patterns and Practices, Pilgrim Press, 97; coed, Leaps and Boundaries, Liturgical Revision in the Twenty-first Century, Morehouse Pub Co, 97; Women and Religious Ritual, Pastoral Press, 93; The 1892 Book of Common Prayer, Edwin Mellen Press, 93; Liturgy in The Encyclopedia of Women and World Religions, Macmillan, forthcoming 98; Bitten from Behind: Babies, Bishops and Backlash, in Feminist Theology, 98; Access without Excess, in: Leaps and Boundaries, Morehouse Pub, 97. **CONTACT ADDRESS** Florida Intl Univ, Miami, FL, 33199. **EMAIL** northupl@fiu.edu

NORTON, BRYAN G.
PERSONAL Born 07/19/1944, Marshall, MI, s **DISCIPLINE** PHILOSOPHY **EDUCATION** Univ Mich, BA, 66; PhD, 70. **CAREER** Prof, New Col of Univ S Flor, 70-87. **HONORS AND AWARDS** Pi Sigma Alpha; BA with Distinction in Pol Sci; Gilbert White Fel **MEMBERSHIPS** Amer Philos Assoc; Int Soc Ecol Econ; Int Soc Environ Ethics; Hastings Center Fel **RESEARCH** Environmental Ethics; Sustainability Concepts and Measures; Environmental Valuation. **SELECTED PUBLICATIONS** Improving Ecological Communication: The Role of Ecologists in Environmental Policy Formation, Ecol Applications, 98; coauth, Sustainability: Ecological and Economic Perspectives, Land Econ, 97; coauth, Environmental Values: A Place-Based Theory, Environ Ethics, 97; coauth, Ethics on the Ark: Zoos, Animal Welfare, and Wildlife Conservation, Smithsonian Pr, 95. **CONTACT ADDRESS** School of Public Policy, Georgia Inst of Tech, Atlanta, GA, 30332. **EMAIL** bryan.norton@pubpolicy.gatech.edu

NORTON, ELEANOR HOLMES
PERSONAL Born 06/13/1937, Washington, DC, d **DISCIPLINE** LAW **EDUCATION** Antioch Coll, attended; Yale Univ, MA 1963; Yale Law School, JD 1964. **CAREER** American Civil Liberties Union, assistant legal director, 1965-70; New York University Law School, adjunct assistant professor of law, 1970-71; New York City Commission on Human Rights, chair, 1970-77; US Equal Employment Opportunity Commission, chair, 1977-81; The Urban Institute, senior fellow, 1981-82; Georgetown University Law Center, professor of law beginning 1982; US House of Representatives, Washington, DC, nonvoting member, currently. **HONORS AND AWARDS** One Hundred Most Important Women, Ladies Home Journal, 1988; One Hundred Most Powerful Women in Washington, The Washingtonian Magazine, 1989; Distinguished Public Service Award, Center for National Policy, 1985. **SELECTED PUBLICATIONS** "Equal Employment Law: Crisis in Interpretation, Survival against the Odds," Tulane Law Review, v. 62, 1988; "The Private Bar and Public Confusion: A New Civil Rights Challenge," Howard Law Journal, 1984; "Public Assistance, Post New-Deal Bureaucracy, and the Law: Learning from Negative Models," Yale Law Journal, 1983; author, Sex Discrimination and the Law: Causes and Remedies. **CONTACT ADDRESS** US House of Representatives, 1424 Longworth House Office Bldg, Washington, DC, 20515.

NORTON, H. WILBERT, SR.
DISCIPLINE MISSIONS **EDUCATION** Wheaton Col, BA; Columbia Bible Col, MA, ThM; N Baptist Theol Sem, ThD. **CAREER** Dean, Wheaton Col Grad Sch, 72-80; prof. **HONORS AND AWARDS** Dir, Doctor of Missiology prog at RTS/Jackson, 89-93; interim dir, Stud Foreign Missions Fel-Intervarsity Christian Fel Missions Dept, 45; founder, Bible Inst Ubangi, Zaire; missions prog, Trinity Col/Evangel Divinity Sch, 50; pres, TEDS, 57-64; founding principal, JOS, ECWA Theol Sem, Nigeria; Dir, Comm to Assist Ministry Edu Overseas, 83-89; founding pres, Evangel Missiological Soc. **MEMBERSHIPS** Mem, Amer Missiological Soc. **SELECTED PUBLICATIONS** Auth, The European Background and History of the Free Church of America Missions; Twenty-five Years in the Ubangi; To Stir the Church; coauth, What's Gone Wrong with the Harvest?; ed, The Jubliee Story. **CONTACT ADDRESS** Dept of Missions, Reformed Theol Sem, 2101 Carmel Rd, Charlotte, NC, 28226.

NORWOOD, KIMBERLY JADE
PERSONAL Born 08/18/1960, New York, New York, m, 1988 **DISCIPLINE** LAW **EDUCATION** Fordham Univ, BA, 1982; Univ of Missouri-Columbia, JD, 1985. **CAREER** Hon. Clifford Scott Green, law clerk, 1985-86; Bryan Cave et al, litigation assoc, 1986-90; Univ of MO-Columbia, visiting lecturer, Cleo Program, 1990; Washington Univ School of Law, prof of law, 1990-. **HONORS AND AWARDS** American Jurisprudence Award, 1983; Bernard T Hurwitz Prize, 1984; Judge Shepard Barclay Prize, 1984-85. **MEMBERSHIPS** Greeley Comm Assn, bd mem, 1993-94; St Louis Women Lawyers Assn, bd mem, 1993-94; Mound City Bar Assn, 1986-; Jack & Jill of America, 1994-96; Girls, Inc, bd mem, 1994; Bar Assn of Metro St Louis, 1986-; Illinois Bar Assn, 1987-; American Bar Assn, 1986-; American Assn of Law Schools, 1993-. **SELECTED PUBLICATIONS** "Shopping for a Venue: The Need for More Limits on Choice," Miami Law Review, v 50, p 267, 1996. **CONTACT ADDRESS** Prof of Law, Washington Univ Sch of Law, 1 Brookings Dr, Box 1120, St Louis, MO, 63130.

NOTZ, JOHN K.
PERSONAL Born 01/05/1932, Chicago, IL, m, 1966, 2 children **DISCIPLINE** MATHEMATICS, LAW **EDUCATION** Williams Col, BA, 53; Northwestern Univ, JD, 56. **CAREER** United States Air Force, 57-60; LAWYER, 60-95; ARBITRATOR/MEDIATOR, 96-. **MEMBERSHIPS** Am Law Inst; many other memberships in legal organizations. **RESEARCH** Chicago/Milwaukee history, 1885-1915. **SELECTED PUBLICATIONS** Auth, Edward G. Uihlein, Advocate for Landscape Architect Jens Jensen, Wis Acad Rev, 98; several other publications in numerous legal journals. **CONTACT ADDRESS** 399 Fullerton Pkwy, Chicago, IL, 60614-2810. **EMAIL** jnotz@gcd.com

NOVAK, DAVID
DISCIPLINE LAW **EDUCATION** Univ Chicago, BA, 61, MHL, 64; Georgetown Univ, PhD, 71. **CAREER** Prof, Univ Toronto **SELECTED PUBLICATIONS** Auth, The Election of Israel: The Idea of the Chosen People, Cambridge, 95. **CONTACT ADDRESS** Fac of Law, Univ Toronto, 78 Queen's Park, Toronto, ON.

NOVAK, JOSEPH A.
DISCIPLINE PHILOSOPHY **EDUCATION** Univ Notre Dame, PhD, 77. **RESEARCH** Ancient philos; medieval philos. **SELECTED PUBLICATIONS** Auth, pub(s) on ancient philosophy, Greek mathematics and method, Greek ethics and New Testament, and concept of immateriality. **CONTACT ADDRESS** Dept of Philosophy, Waterloo Univ, 200 University Ave W, Waterloo, ON, N2L 3G1. **EMAIL** jnovak@uwaterloo.ca

NOVAK, PHILIP CHARLES
DISCIPLINE RELIGIOUS STUDIES **EDUCATION** Univ Notre Dame, BA, 72; Syracuse Univ, MA, 75, PhD, 81. **CAREER** Instr to PROF, PHILOS & RELIG, 80-, CHAIR, 83-, DOMINICAN COL. **CONTACT ADDRESS** Dept of Philos, Relig, Dominican Col, San Rafael, 50 Acacia Ave, San Rafael, CA, 94901.

NOWAK, JOHN E.
DISCIPLINE LAW **EDUCATION** Marquette Univ, BA; Univ Ill, JD. **CAREER** Prof, Univ Ill Urbana Champaign. **HONORS AND AWARDS** Ed, Univ Ill Law Forum. **MEMBERSHIPS** Nat Collegiate Athletic Asn. **SELECTED PUBLICATIONS** Auth, pubs on constitutional law. **CONTACT ADDRESS** Law Dept, Univ Ill Urbana Champaign, 52 E Gregory Dr, Champaign, IL, 61820. **EMAIL** jnowak@law.uiuc.edu

NOWELL, IRENE
PERSONAL Born 06/08/1940, Dallas, TX, s **DISCIPLINE** BIBLICAL STUDIES; OLD TESTAMENT **EDUCATION** Mount St Scholastica, BA, 61; Cath Univ, MA, 64, PhD, 83; St John's, MA, 78. **CAREER** Prof, Dean Acad Aff, 87-88, Dean Students, 70-71, Mount St Scholastica/Benedictine Col, 64-72, 75-78, 83-94; adj prof, St John's Univ, 83-. **MEMBERSHIPS** SBL; CBA **RESEARCH** Biblical women; Psalms; Old Testament wisdom; Monasticism. **SELECTED PUBLICATIONS** Auth Sing A New Song: Responsorial Psalm in the Sunday Lectionary, Liturgical Press, 93; Women in the Old Testament, Liturgical Press, 97. **CONTACT ADDRESS** 801 S 8th, Atchison, KS, 66002. **EMAIL** nowell@benedictine.edu

NOZICK, ROBERT
PERSONAL Born 11/16/1938, Brooklyn, NY, m, 1987, 2 children **DISCIPLINE** PHILOSOPHY **EDUCATION** Columbia Col, AB, 59; Princeton Univ, AM, 61, PhD(philos), 63; AM (honorary), Harvard Univ, 69; DHL (honorary), Knox Col, 83. **CAREER** Instr philos, Princeton Univ, 62-63, asst prof, 64-65; asst prof, Harvard Univ, 65-67; assoc prof, Rockefeller Univ, 67-69; Prof Philos, Harvard Univ, 69-, chmn dept, 81-84, Arthur Kingsley Porter Prof, 85-98, PELLEGRINO UNIV PROF, 98-; Fulbright scholar, Oxford Univ, 63-64; fel, Ctr Advan Studies Behav Sci, 71-72; Rockefeller Foundation humanities fel, 79-80; NEH fel, 87-88; Guggenheim fel, 96-97. **MEMBERSHIPS** Am Philos Asn, pres, eastern div, 97-98; Am Acad Arts and Sciences; Council of Scholars, Library of Congress; Corresponding fel, British Academy. **RESEARCH** Philosophical explanations. **SELECTED PUBLICATIONS** Auth, Anarchy, State, and Utopia, Basic Books, 74 (Nat Book Award, 75); Philosophical Explanations, Harvard Univ Press, 81 (Ralph Waldo Emerson Award, Phi Beta Kappa, 82); The Examined Life, Simon & Schuster, 89; The Nature of Rationality, Princeton Univ Press, 93; Socratic Puzzles, Harvard Univ Press, 97. **CONTACT ADDRESS** Dept of Philos, Harvard Univ, Emerson Hall, Cambridge, MA, 02138-3800. **EMAIL** nozick@fas.harvard.edu

NUGENT, DONALD CHROSTOPHER
PERSONAL Born 12/31/1930, Lousiville, KY, s **DISCIPLINE** HISTORY/THEOLOGY **EDUCATION** PhD Univ of IA, 65; MA Theol, Univ of San Francisco, 82. **CAREER** Asst Prof, Univ KY, 66-95; Vis Prof, Univ Col Dublin, 72-73; Univ Alberta, 61-62. **RESEARCH** Msyticism; Spirituality, esp St John of the Cross. **SELECTED PUBLICATIONS** Ecummenism in the Age of the Reformation, Harvard, 74; Masks of Satan: The Demonic in History, Sheed & Ward, 83; Mysticism, Deathe and Dying, Albany: SUNY, 94; Satori in St John of the Cross: The Eastern Buddhist, Kyoto, 95; Pax Sexuals: The Month, London, 98. **CONTACT ADDRESS** Dept Hist, Univ Kentucky, Lexington, KY, 40506.

NUNN, KENNETH B.
DISCIPLINE LAW **EDUCATION** Stanford Univ, AB; Univ Calif, Berkeley, JD. **CAREER** Prof, Univ Fla, 90-. **MEMBERSHIPS** Exec Comt, Nat Asn Public Interest Law; Calif Bar; DC Bar. **CONTACT ADDRESS** School of Law, Univ of Florida, PO Box 117625, Gainesville, FL, 32611-7625. **EMAIL** Nunn@law.ufl.edu

NUTBROWN, RICHARD A.
DISCIPLINE PHILOSOPHY **EDUCATION** Carleton Univ, PhD, 85. **CAREER** Assoc prof **RESEARCH** Political philosophy. **SELECTED PUBLICATIONS** Auth, History, Language and Time; pub(s) on political philosophy. **CONTACT ADDRESS** Dept of Philosophy, Waterloo Univ, 200 University Ave W, Waterloo, ON, N2L 3G1. **EMAIL** nutbrown@uwaterloo.ca

NUZZO, ANGELICA
PERSONAL Born 04/02/1964, Firenze, Italy **DISCIPLINE** PHILOSOPHY **EDUCATION** Heidelberg Univ, PhD, 91. **CAREER** Asst prof, DePaul Univ, 95-. **MEMBERSHIPS** APA; North Amer Kant Soc; Hegel Soc of Amer; North Amer Spinora Soc. **RESEARCH** German idealism; Spinoza; Political philosophy; Ethics; Logic; Metaphysics. **SELECTED PUBLICATIONS** Auth, An Outline of Italian Hegelianism, The Owl of

Minerva, 98; auth, Die Differenz zwischen dialektischer Logik und realphilosophischer Dialektik, Das Problem der Dialektik, Bouvier, 97; auth, Natur und Freiheit in Hegels Philosophie der Jenaer Zeit (bis 1803), Hegels Jenaer Naturphilosophie, Fink Verlag, 97; auth, Chap, Logica, Hegel, Laterza, 97; auth, Per una metodologia della storia della filosofia secondo Hegel - Le introduzioni berlinesi alle lezioni sulla storia della filosofia (1819-1831), Il Cannocchiale, 97; auth, Absolute Methode und Erkenntnis der Wirklichkeit in der Philosophie Hegels, Deutsche Zeitschrift f. Philosophie, 96; auth, Das Verhaltnis von Logik und Zeit bei Kant und Cassirer, Einheit des Geistes. Probleme ihrer Grundlegung in der Philosophie Ernst Cassirers, Lang, 96; auth, Zur logischen Bestimmung des ontologischen Gottesbeweises. Bemerkungen zum Begriff der Existenz im Anschlus an Hegel, Hegel-Studien, 95; auth, Pensiero e realta nell'idea hegeliana della Logica come fondazione del sistema della filosofia, Discipline Filosofiche, 95; auth, L'idea kantiana della pace perpetua tra morale, diritto e politica, Teoria Politica, 95; auth, Idee bei Kant und Hegel, Das Recht der Vernunft. Kant und Hegel uber Denken, Erkennen und Handeln, 95; auth, Metamorphosen der Freiheit in der Jenenser Kant-Rezeption (1785-1794), Evolution des Geistes: Jena um 1800, Klett-Cotta, 94. **CONTACT ADDRESS** Philosophy Dept., DePaul Univ, 1150 W Fullerton Ave, Chicago, IL, 60614. **EMAIL** anuzzo@wppost.depaul.edu

NYSSE, RICHARD W.
DISCIPLINE OLD TESTAMENT **EDUCATION** Concordia Senior Col, BA, 68; Concordia Sem, MDiv, 72; Harvard Divinity Sch, ThD, 84. **CAREER** Fac mem, Pacific Lutheran Sem; asst prof, 78; prof, 93-. **HONORS AND AWARDS** Asst pastor, Christ Lutheran Church, 74-76; bk ed, World & World, 80-84, 84-91. **SELECTED PUBLICATIONS** Auth, An Analysis of the Greek Witnesses to the Text of the Lament of David, The Hebrew and Greek Texts of Samuel, 80. **CONTACT ADDRESS** Dept of Old Testament, Luther Sem, 2481 Como Ave, St. Paul, MN, 55108. **EMAIL** rnysee@luthersem.edu

O

O'CONNELL, ROBERT H.
PERSONAL Born 12/04/1955, Kitchener, ON, Canada, m, 1982, 2 children **DISCIPLINE** RELIGION **EDUCATION** Univ of Western Ontario, BA, 78; Dallas Theol Sem, ThM, 82, DTS, ThD, 89; Univ of Cambridge UK, PhD 93. **CAREER** Co Christian Univ, prof, 91-95; US West Inc, Web Developer, 96-98. **HONORS AND AWARDS** ORS AWARD, 88-91; Lamb Foundation Shipley Award, 88-89; Fitzwilliam Col Cambridge UK Crosse Award 89-91 **MEMBERSHIPS** AAR, NAPH, SBL, SOTS **RESEARCH** Hebrew Bib; Anc Mid-East Stud; Philo Lang; Cosmology. **SELECTED PUBLICATIONS** Auth, Concentricity and Continuity: The Literary Structure of Isaiah, Jour for Stud OT, Sheffield Acad Press, 94; The Rhetoric of the Book of Judges, Vetus Testamentum 96; Telescoping N+1 Patterns in the Book of Amos, Vetus Test, 96; Deuteronomy ix 7-x7,10-11: Paneled Structure, Double Rehearsal and the Rhetoric of Covenant Rebuke, Vetus Test, 92; Proverbs vii 16-17: A Case of Fatal Deception in a 'Woman and the Window' Type Scene, Vetus Test, 91. **CONTACT ADDRESS** 3250 S Lafayette St, Englewood, CO, 80110-2924. **EMAIL** rhoconnell@wordsmyth.com

O'CONNELL KILLEN, PATRICIA
PERSONAL Born 11/30/1951, Portland, OR, m, 1975 **DISCIPLINE** RELIGION **EDUCATION** Gonzaga Univ, BA, 70; Stanford Univ, MA, 76, PhD, 87. **CAREER** Instr, 78-85, School of Theo, Univ of the South; vis Asst Prof & Asst Prof, 85-89, Univ of Chicago Loyola; Asst Prof, 89-92, Assoc Prof, 92-, Pacific Lutheran Univ. **HONORS AND AWARDS** Arnold & Lois Graves Awd, Outstanding Humanities Prof; Burlington Northern Fac Achievement Awd. **MEMBERSHIPS** AAR, ASCH, AHA, Cath Theo Soc of Amer. **RESEARCH** Religion in the American west, Roman Catholicism in the United States. **SELECTED PUBLICATIONS** Auth, The Irish in Washington State, in: The Encyclopedia of the Irish in America, ed, M Glazier, Univ Notre Dame Press, forthcoming; Finding Our Voices, Women's Wisdom and Faith, NY Crossroad Pub Co, 97; Geography Denominations and the Human Spirit, A Decade of Studies on Religion the Western United States, in: Religious Stud Rev, 95; co-auth, The Art of Theological Reflection, NY Crossroads Pub, 94; auth, An Historians Perspective, Then Now and Then? in: Sewanee Theo Review, 92. **CONTACT ADDRESS** Dept of Religion, Pacific Lutheran Univ, Tacoma, WA, 98447. **EMAIL** killenpo@plu.edu

O'CONNOR, DANIEL D.
PERSONAL Born 03/26/1931, Detroit, MI, m, 1959, 2 children **DISCIPLINE** PHILOSOPHY **EDUCATION** Univ Detroit, BA, 55; Univ Toronto, MA, 58; Yale Univ, PhD, 61. **CAREER** From asst prof to assoc prof, 61-76, PROF PHILOS, WILLIAMS COL, 76-, DEAN OF COL, 80-. **MEMBERSHIPS** Am Philos Asn; Soc Phenomenol & Existential Philos. **RESEARCH** Phenomenology; history of philosophy. **SELECTED PUBLICATIONS** Coauth, Readings in Existential Phenomenology, Prentice-Hall, 67 & Creation: Impact of an Idea, Scribner's, 69. **CONTACT ADDRESS** Dept of Philos, Williams Col, 880 Main St, Williamstown, MA, 01267-2600.

O'CONNOR, DAVID
PERSONAL Born 07/02/1949, Cork, Ireland, m, 1971, 3 children **DISCIPLINE** ANALYTIC PHYLOSOPHY, PHILOSOPHY OF RELIGION **EDUCATION** Nat Univ Ireland, BA, 71, MA, 73; Marquette Univ, PhD, 79. **CAREER** Asst philos, Villanova Univ, 79-80; Prof Philos, Seton Hall Univ, NJ, 80. **MEMBERSHIPS** Am Philos Asn. **RESEARCH** Analytical philos of relig; Hume. **SELECTED PUBLICATIONS** Auth, On the viability of Macquarrie's God-talk, Philos Studies Vol 23, 75; Remarks of Macquarrie's philosophy of death, Expository Times, Vol 88, 77; Identification and description in Ayer's sense-datum theory, Mod Schoolman, Vol 57, 80; Moore and the Paradox of analysis, Philosophy, Vol 57, 82; The Metaphysics of G E Moore, Reidel, 82; contribr, Etienne Gilson, Nelson Goodman, Charles Morris, In: Twentieth Century Thinkers, Macmillan & Gale Res; God and Inscrutable Evil, Rowman & Littlefield, 98; Hume on Religion, Routledge. **CONTACT ADDRESS** Dept of Philos, Seton Hall Univ, 400 S Orange Ave, South Orange, NJ, 07079-2696. **EMAIL** Oconnoda@lanmail.shu.edu

O'CONNOR, DAVID
DISCIPLINE PHILOSOPHY **EDUCATION** Univ Notre Dame, BA, 80; Stanford Univ, PhD, 86. **CAREER** Assoc prof. **RESEARCH** Ancient philosophy; ethics. **SELECTED PUBLICATIONS** Auth, Socrates and the Socratics, Columbia Hist W Philos, 97; Aristotle's Audience and Political Ambition, 98; Socrates and Political Ambition, Ancient Philos, 98; co-ed, Essays on the Foundations of Aristotelian Political Science, 91. **CONTACT ADDRESS** Philosophy Dept, Univ of Notre Dame, 336/7 O'Shaughnessy, Notre Dame, IN, 46556. **EMAIL** o'connor.2@nd.edu

O'CONNOR, DENNIS
DISCIPLINE PHILOSOPHY **EDUCATION** Univ St. Louis, PhD. **CAREER** Prof. **RESEARCH** Phenomenology, hermeneutics and philosophy of the social sciences. **SELECTED PUBLICATIONS** Auth, Ecart and Difference: Seeing and Writing in Merleau-Ponty and Derrida. **CONTACT ADDRESS** Dept of Philos, Concordia Univ, Montreal, 1455 de Maisonneuve W, Montreal, PQ, H3G 1M8. **EMAIL** eud@vax2.concordia.ca

O'CONNOR, JUNE ELIZABETH
PERSONAL Chicago, IL **DISCIPLINE** RELIGIOUS ETHICS **EDUCATION** Mundelein col, BA, 64; Marquette Univ, MA, 66; Temple Univ, MA, 72, PhD, 73. **CAREER** Instr theol, Mundelein Col, 65-69; asst prof, 73-79, assoc prof, 79-90, PROF RELIG STUDIES, UNIV CALIF, RIVERSIDE, 90-. **HONORS AND AWARDS** Distinguished Teaching Award, Univ Calif, Riverside, 79; Fac Public Serv Award, Univ Calif, Riverside, 93. **MEMBERSHIPS** Col Theol Soc; Am Acad Relig; Soc Christian Ethics; Pac Coast Theol Soc. **RESEARCH** Religious ethics; theology of liberation; women and religion. **SELECTED PUBLICATIONS** Auth, The Quest for Political and Spiritual Liberation: A Study in the Thought of Sri Aurobindo Ghose, Farleigh Dickinson Univ Press, 77; On Doing Religious Ethics, J Relig Ethics, spring 79; The Moral Vision of Dorothy Day, Crossroad Ppubl, 91; Does a Global Village Warrant a Global Ethic?, Relig, 94; On Being Bi-Religious in Efroymson and Rainer, The Open Church; Ritual Recognition of Abortion: Japanese Buddhist Practices and U S Jewish and Christian Proposals in Cahill and Farley, Embodiment, Morality, and Medicine. **CONTACT ADDRESS** Prog in Relig Studies, Univ of Calif, 900 University Ave, Riverside, CA, 92521-0001. **EMAIL** joconnor@ucr.ac1.ucr.edu

O'DEA, JANE
DISCIPLINE PHILOSOPHY **EDUCATION** Univ Alberta, PhD, 90. **SELECTED PUBLICATIONS** Auth, pubs on music, aesthetics, education and feminism. **CONTACT ADDRESS** Dept of Philosophy, Lethbridge Univ, 4401 University Dr W, Lethbridge, AB, T1K 3M4.

O'DONNELL, LORENA MAE
PERSONAL Born 05/01/1929, Cincinnati, OH **DISCIPLINE** THEOLOGY **EDUCATION** Univ of Cincinnati, BS Ed 1951; Miami Univ, ME 1960; Yale Univ, Post Grad 1972; Nova Univ, EdD 1976. **CAREER** Cincinnati Publ Schools, teacher 1951-61, personnel assoc 1961-65, suprv 1965-69; North Avondale School, principal 1969-72; Cincinnati Public Schools, dir of staff devel 1972-81; Hillcrest School, chaplain, beginning 1982; University of Cincinnati, Cincinnati, OH, assoc dean, 1989; educ consultant, 1990; Wyoming Baptist Church, Wyoming, OH, dir of Christian educ, beginning 1987; Northern Kentucky University, coordinator of alternative teacher certification prog, beginning 1993. **HONORS AND AWARDS** Kellogg Found Grant Yale Univ 1972; Grand Deputy Dist 6 State of OH, OES Amaranth Grand Chap 1985; One of Ten 1986 Enquirer's Women of the Year. **MEMBERSHIPS** Ed consult, beginning 1960; dir Hamilton Cty State Bank beginning 1976; 1st black female mem Cincinnati Bd of Ed, beginning 1980; dir Franchise Devel Inc, beginning 1980; partner Loram Entr 1981-83; dir Red Cross Adv Bd, beginning 1981; mem Juvenile Court Review Bd 1981-86; director, Ham County State Bank, 1976-86; director, Red Cross, 1981-87; president, Church Women United, Cincinnati Chapter, 1995-97. **SELECTED PUBLICATIONS** God in the Inner City Juv Religious Book 1970; God is Soul Juv Religious Book 1971; author, Joy In Contemplation, 1991.

O'DONOVAN-ANDERSON, MICHAEL
PERSONAL Born 08/07/1968, m, 1992 **DISCIPLINE** PHILOSOPHY; SCIENCE **EDUCATION** Yale Univ, PhD, 96; Univ Notre Dame, BS, 90. **CAREER** Tutor, St John's Col, 96-98; Biomedical Systems Scientist, Digene Res & Develop, 98-. **MEMBERSHIPS** Amer Philos Assoc; Amer Assoc for Advancement of Sci. **RESEARCH** History of Philosophy; Cognition & Embodiment. **SELECTED PUBLICATIONS** Auth, Content and Comportment: On Embodiment and the Epistemic Availability of the World, Rowman & Littlefield, 97; ed, The Incorporated Self: Interdisciplinary Perspectives on Embodiment, Rowman & Littlefield, 96. **CONTACT ADDRESS** Dept of Research and Development, Saint John's Col, 1624 Woodtree Ct West, Annapolis, MD, 21401. **EMAIL** m_o'donovan-anderson@post.harvard.edu

O'HARA, MARY L.
DISCIPLINE PHILOSOPHY **EDUCATION** Col of St. Catherine, BA, 46; Catholic Univ of Amer, MA, 48, PhD. **CAREER** Col of St. Catherine, Col of St. Mary, prof, 48-91. **HONORS AND AWARDS** Phi Beta Kappa **MEMBERSHIPS** APA **RESEARCH** The human person; wisdom. **SELECTED PUBLICATIONS** Auth, The Logic of Human Personality, Humanities, 97; Substances and Things, Univ Press of Amer. **CONTACT ADDRESS** 1870 Randolph Ave, St Paul, MN, 55105-1796. **EMAIL** mlo'hara@stkate.edu

O'HYUN, PARK
PERSONAL Born 03/15/1940, Taegu, South Korea, 3 children **DISCIPLINE** RELIGION **EDUCATION** Educ: Yonsei Univ, Korea, BTh, 64; Knox Col, NZ, dipl, 65; Bible Col, dipl, 65; Temple Univ, PhD(relig), 72. **CAREER** From asst prof to assoc prof, 71-81, Prof Orient Relig & Philos, Appalachian State Univ, 81-. **MEMBERSHIPS** Am Acad Relig. **RESEARCH** Buddhism, Zen Buddhism and Chinese religions. **SELECTED PUBLICATIONS** Auth, The World of Nothingness, Knox Collegian, 64; Paul van Buren and Theology, Theol Rev, 65; Oriental Ideas in Recent Religious Nought, 74 & Religion and the Life of Man, CSA Press; Zen as the Cosmic Psychotherapy, Pastoral Coun, 77; Invitation to Dialogue between East and West, 97. **CONTACT ADDRESS** Dept of Philos & Relig, Appalachian State Univ, 1 Appalachian State, Boone, NC, 28608-0001. **EMAIL** parko@appstate.edu

O'NEILL, WILLIAM GEORGE
PERSONAL Born 07/03/1943, Evergreen Park, IL, m, 1972, 2 children **DISCIPLINE** PHILOSOPHY OF SCIENCE; BUSINESS ETHICS **EDUCATION** Iona Col, BA, 64; Boston Col, MA, 67, PhD(philos), 70. **CAREER** Instr, 68-71, asst prof, 71-78, Assoc Prof Philos, Iona Col, 78- **MEMBERSHIPS** Am Philos Asn; Metaphys Soc Am; Am Cath Philos Asn. **RESEARCH** History of science; business ethics; theory of knowledge; moral theory. **CONTACT ADDRESS** Dept of Philosophy, Iona Col, 715 North Ave, New Rochelle, NY, 10801-1890. **EMAIL** woneill@iona.edu

O'SULLIVAN, MICHAEL
PERSONAL Born 04/10/1948, Ft. Wayne, IN, m, 1 child **DISCIPLINE** RELIGION; SOCIAL ETHICS **EDUCATION** Univ Southern Cal, PhD, 81. **MEMBERSHIPS** Amer Acad Religion **RESEARCH** New Religious Movements; Popular Religion **CONTACT ADDRESS** 4717 Lowell Ave., La Crescenta, CA, 91214-1636. **EMAIL** seanbaby@aol.com

OAKES, EDWARD T.
DISCIPLINE RELIGION **EDUCATION** St Louis Univ, BA, 71, MA, 76; Jesuit School Theol, MDiv, 79; Union Theol Sem, MPhil, 84, PhD, 87. **CAREER** Adj instr, Fordham Univ, 85-87; vis asst prof, 87-90 & 93-94, adj asst prof, 90-92, NYU; res fel, Deutscher Akademischer Austauschdienst, 92-93; scholar res, Cambridge Univ, 95 & Immaculate Conception Sem, Seton Hall Univ, 96; Assoc Prof, Regis Univ, 96-. **HONORS AND AWARDS** Res grant Marguerite Eyer Wilbur Found, 92-93; Bakers Dozen Distinguished Tchr Award 1989 Stud Coun, NYU. **SELECTED PUBLICATIONS** Auth, Discovering the American Aristotle, First Things, 93; Cardinal Newman on the Season of Lent, America, 93; Jewish Ethics Engaged, First Things, 93; The Paradox of the Literal: Protestant and Roman Catholic Confrontations with the Biblical Canon in the Sixteenth and Seventeenth Centuries, Reform and Counter-Reform: Dialectics of the Word in Western Christianity Since Luther, Mouton de Gruyter, 94; A Life of Allegory: Type and Pattern in Historical Narratives, Through a Glass Darkly: Essays in the Religious Imagination, Fordham Univ Press, 96; German Essays on Religion, Continuum, 94; The Achievement of Alasdair MacIntyre, First Things, 96; Pattern of Redemption: The Theology of Hans Urs von Balthasar, Continuum; 97; Exposed Being, Jour of Relig, 98; The Blind Programmer, First Things, 98. **CONTACT ADDRESS** Jesuit Commun, Regis Univ, 3333 Regis Blvd., Denver, CO, 80221. **EMAIL** oakesedw@regis.edu

OAKES, JAMES L.
PERSONAL Born 02/21/1924, w, 1973, 3 children **DISCIPLINE** LAW **EDUCATION** Harvard Col, AB, 45; Harvard Law School, LLB, 47. **CAREER** Atty Gen VT, 67-69; US Dist Judge, VT, 70-71; Chief judge, 89-92, Sr Status, 92- , US Circuit Judge, Second Circuit, 71- ; Adj prof, Duke Univ Law School, 85-90, 92-96; adj prof Iowa Univ Col Law, 93-97; **HONORS AND AWARDS** Hon LLD New Eng Col, 76, Suffolk Univ, 80, Vermont Law School, 95; Learned Hand Award Excellence Jurisp, 83; Environ Law Inst Award, 89; Louis Dembitz Brandeis Medal Distinguished Legal Serv; 91; William J Brennan Award for Commitment to Indiv Right & Civil Liberties, 92; Gold Medal Award Distinguished Serv In Law, NY State Bar Asn, 92; Edward Weinfeld Award for distinguished contrib to Admin Justice, 92 & Distinguished Publ Serv Award, 94 both from NY Cty Law Asn. **SELECTED PUBLICATIONS** Auth, commentary on Judge Edwards Growing Disjunction Between Legal Education and the Legal Profession, Mich Law Rev, 93; rev Teh Tenth Justice, Learned Hand: The Man and the Judge, Brooklyn Law Rev, 94; Personal Reflections on Learned Hand and the Second Circuit, Stanford Law Rev, 95; Tribute to Thomas Debevoise, VT Law Rev, 95; On Appeal: Courts, Lawyering, and Judging, Yale Law Jour, 95; Developments in Environmental Law: What to Watch, 95; rev Intellect and Craft: The Contributions of Justice Hans Linde to American Constitutionalism, Oregon Law Rev, 96. **CONTACT ADDRESS** US Court of Appeals, Second Circuit, PO Box 696, Brattleboro, VT, 05302-0696.

OAKLANDER, L. NATHAN
PERSONAL Bronx, NY, m, 3 children **DISCIPLINE** METAPHYSICS **EDUCATION** Univ Iowa, AB, 67, MA, 70, PhD, 73. **CAREER** Instr, philos, Univ Mich Flint, 72-73; asst prof, 73-77, assoc prof, 77-78, assoc prof, philos and chair dept of philos, 78-82, prof, philos, 82-85, prof, philos and chair dept of philos, 85-90, David M. French prof and prof of philos, 90-92, prof, philos and chair dept of philos, 92-95, prof, philos, 95-, Univ Mich Flint. **HONORS AND AWARDS** Special Merit award for scholarship, 82-85; facul develop comt grant, 88-89; res initiative fel for res, 90; David M. French prof award for res and teaching, Univ Mich Flint, 90-92; res initiative fel for res, 92; special merit award for scholar, 90-94; res initiative fel for res, 95. **MEMBERSHIPS** Philos of Time Soc; Amer Philos Asn; The Mind Asn. **RESEARCH** Time. **SELECTED PUBLICATIONS** Auth, Existentialist Philosophy: An Introduction, Prentice-Hall, 92, 2nd ed, 96; co-auth, Time, Change and Freedom: An Introduction to Metaphysics, Routledge; co-ed, The New Theory of Time, Yale Univ Press, 94; co-ed, Metaphysics: Classic and Contemporary Readings, Wadsworth Publ Co; auth, Temporal Relations and Temporal Becoming: A Defense of a Russellian Theory of Time, Univ Press of Amer. **CONTACT ADDRESS** Philosophy Dept., Univ of Michigan Flint, 544 CROB, Flint, MI, 48502-1950. **EMAIL** lno@umich.edu

OAKLEY, JOHN BILYEU
PERSONAL Born 06/18/1947, San Francisco, CA, m, 1974, 2 children **DISCIPLINE** LAW & PHILOSOPHY **EDUCATION** Univ Calif, Berkeley, BA, 69; Yale Univ, JD, 72. **CAREER** Law clerk, Supreme Ct Calif, 72-73; sr law clerk, US Dist Ct, Conn, 73-74 & Supreme Ct Calif, 74-75; actg prof, 75-79, PROF LAW, UNIV CALIF DAVIS, 79-; Pub mem, New Motor Vehicle Bd Calif, 76-82; Federal Judicial Code Revision Project, Am Law Ins, 95-; reporter, Comt on Federal-State Jurisdiction, U S Judicial Conf, 91-96; reporter, Civil Justice Reform Act Ad Group, U S Dist Ct, Ed Calif, 91-94; reporter, Speedy Trial Planning Group, US Dist Ct, Ed Calif, 78-82; scholar-in-residence, Civil Rights Div, US Dept Justice, 79-80; mem, Duke Univ Primate Center Bd of Visitors, 98-; mem, Calif Judicial Counc Appellate Process Task Force, 97. **MEMBERSHIPS** Am Law Ins; Amintaphil; Phi Beta Kappa **RESEARCH** Legal philosophy; anthropology; law. **SELECTED PUBLICATIONS** Coauth (with Edgar Bodenheimer and Jean C Love), An Introduction to the Anglo-American Legal System, West Publ Co, 80; (with Robert S Thompson), Law Clerks and the Judicial Process, Univ Calif Press, 80; fac visitor, Oxford Univ, 82-83. **CONTACT ADDRESS** Sch of Law, Univ of Calif, King Hall, Davis, CA, 95616-5201. **EMAIL** jboakley@ucdavis.edu

OAKMAN, DOUGLAS
PERSONAL Born 02/11/1953, Des Moines, IA, m, 1976, 2 children **DISCIPLINE** NEW TESTAMENT **EDUCATION** Grad Theol Union, PhD, 86; Christ Sem, MA, 79; U of IA, BA, 75 **CAREER** Assoc Prof of Relig, 88-pres, Pac Lutheran Univ; Visit Asst Prof, 86-87, Santa Clara Univ **HONORS AND AWARDS** Who's Who in the West; Who's Who in Am Edu; Who's Who in Relig **MEMBERSHIPS** Soc of Bibl Lit; Cath Bibl Assoc; Context Group **RESEARCH** Historical Jesus; Social Sciences and Biblical Interpretation, Hermeneutics **SELECTED PUBLICATIONS** Auth, Jesus and the Economic Questions of His Day, Edwin Mellen Press, 86; Coauth, Palestine in the Time of Jesus, Fortress Press, 98 **CONTACT ADDRESS** Dept of Religion, Pac Lutheran Univ, Tacoma, WA, 98447. **EMAIL** oakmande@plu.edu

OBAYASHI, HIROSHI
PERSONAL Born 12/03/1934, Osaka, Japan, m, 1960, 3 children **DISCIPLINE** THEOLOGY, PHILOSOPHY OF RELIGION **EDUCATION** Doshisha Univ Col, Japan, BA, 57, BD, 59; Andover Newton Theol Sch, STM, 63; Univ Pa, PhD(relig), 67. **CAREER** Minister, United Church of Christ, Japan, 59-62; from instr to asst prof relig, 67-73, assoc prof, 73-82, Prof Relig, Rutgers Univ, New Brunswick, 82- **MEMBERSHIPS** Am Acad Relig; Coun Relig & Int Affairs; AAUP. **RESEARCH** Contemporary theology; religion and politics; history of religion. **SELECTED PUBLICATIONS** Auth, Ernst Troeltsch and Contemporary Theology, Kyodan Press, Tokyo, 72; Agape and history: A theological essay on historical consciousness, Univ Press Am, 81; Towards a Trinitarian Theology of Religions - a Study of Tillich,paul Thought - Lai,pc, J of Ecumenical Studies, Vol 0033, 1996; Out of Silence - Emerging Themes in Asian-American Churches - Matsuoka,f, J of Ecumenical Studies, Vol 0034, 1997. **CONTACT ADDRESS** Dept of Religion Douglass College, Rutgers Univ, P O Box 270, New Brunswick, NJ, 08903-0270.

OBERDIEK, HANS FREDRICK
PERSONAL Born 08/04/1937, Portage, WI, 4 children **DISCIPLINE** PHILOSOPHY **EDUCATION** Univ Wis-Madison, BS, 59, PhD, 65. **CAREER** Teaching asst philos, 61-63, lectr, 64-65, Univ Wis-Madison; asst prof, 65-69, assoc prof, 70-80, prof philos, 80-, Swarthmore Cor; Old Dom res fel, 68-69; Nat Endowment Humanities fel, 72-73; vis lectr philos, 72-73, Balliol Col, Oxford, England; vis Ring prof social ethics, 76-77, Univ Fla. **HONORS AND AWARDS** Henry C & Charlotte Turner Professor, 98-. **MEMBERSHIPS** Am Philos Soc. **RESEARCH** Moral philosophy; philosophy of law; political philosophy. **SELECTED PUBLICATIONS** Art, Foresight and Intention in Criminal Law, Mind, 7/72; art, John Rawl's Theory of Justice, NY Law J, 11/73; art, Who is to judge?, Ethics, 10/76; art, The Role of Sanctions and Coercion in Understanding Law and Legal Systems, Am J Jurisp, 76; co-auth, Living in a Technological Age, Routledge, 95. **CONTACT ADDRESS** Dept of Philosophy, Swarthmore Col, 500 College Ave, Swarthmore, PA, 19081-1306. **EMAIL** hoberdi1@swarthmore.edu

OBERST, MICHAEL A.
DISCIPLINE LAW **EDUCATION** Univ Fla, BSBA, JD. **CAREER** Prof, Univ Fla, 79-; vis prof, Leiden Univ, Neth; past legislative counl, US Cong Joint Comt on Taxatiabout Wash, DC; past assoc, Buchalter, Nemer, Fields Chrystie, Los Angeles; past assoc, Ervin, Cohen Jessup, Los Angeles; past atty adv, US Tax Ct, Wash, DC. **MEMBERSHIPS** DC Bar; Calif Bar. **RESEARCH** Taxation. **SELECTED PUBLICATIONS** Auth, Florida Tax Review: Tax Analysts, Arlington, Va. **CONTACT ADDRESS** School of Law, Univ of Florida, PO Box 117625, Gainesville, FL, 32611-7625. **EMAIL** oberst@law.ufl.edu

OBITTS, STANLEY RALPH
PERSONAL Born 09/04/1933, Denver, CO, m, 1960, 3 children **DISCIPLINE** PHILOSOPHY, PHILOSOPHICAL THEOLOGY **EDUCATION** Wheaton Col, AB, 55, BD, 58; Univ Edinburgh, PhD(philos), 62. **CAREER** Instr Bible, Wheaton Col, 56-57; asst prof philos, Nyack Col, 62-65; from asst prof to assoc prof, 65-72, prof philos, Westmont Col, 72-, prof philos of relig, Trinity Evangel Divinity Sch, 69-70; exchange prof philos, Wheaton Col, 75-76; vis prof theol, Denver Theol Sem, 79-80. **MEMBERSHIPS** Evangel Philos Soc (secy-treas, 78-79, pres 79-80); Am Philos Asn; Am Sci Affil; Evangel Theol Soc; Soc Christian Philosophers. **RESEARCH** Religious epistemology; 18th century philosophy; attributes of God. **SELECTED PUBLICATIONS** Auth, The Plight of the Christian Liberal-Arts College, Christianity Today, 4/70; contribr, Toward a Theology For the Future, Creation House, 71; auth, The Scientist and Ethical Decision, Intervarsity, 73; Current Issues in Biblical and Patristic Interpretation, Eerdmans, 75; Tensions in Contemporary Theology, Moody, 76. **CONTACT ADDRESS** Dept of Philos, Westmont Col, 955 La Paz Rd, Santa Barbara, CA, 93108-1099. **EMAIL** obitts@westmont.edu

ODDIE, GRAHAM JAMES
PERSONAL Born 03/24/1954, Timaru, New Zealand, m, 1975, 3 children **DISCIPLINE** PHILOSOPHY **EDUCATION** Univ Otago, BA, 76; London Univ, PhD, 79. **CAREER** Prof Philos, Otego Univ, 79-87, Massey Univ, 88-96, Univ Co-Boulder, 94-96, Univ Canterbury, 96-97; PROF & CHR OF PHILOS, UNIV CO-BOULDER, 97-; Imre Lakatos vis fel Univ London, 86; Claude McCarty fel Prague Acad Sci ci, 92; vis fel Australian Nat Univ, 90; vis prof Univ Sydney, 93. **MEMBERSHIPS** Australian Asn Philos (pres 90); New Zealand Acad Hum (vpres 93). **RESEARCH** Metaphysics; Ethics; Logic. **CONTACT ADDRESS** Philosophy Dept, Univ Co-Boulder, Campus Box 232, Boulder, CO, 20309-0232. **EMAIL** oddie@spot.colorado.edu

ODELL, MARGARET S.
PERSONAL Born 01/18/1955, Norfolk, VA **DISCIPLINE** BIBLICAL STUDIES **EDUCATION** Meredith Col, BA, 77; Yale Univ Divinity School, MAR, 79; Univ Pittsburgh, PhD, 88. **CAREER** Asst prof, Hollins Col, 88-89; asst prof, Converse Col, 89-94; asst prof, 94-. **MEMBERSHIPS** Soc of Bibl Lit. **RESEARCH** Ancient Israelite prophecy; Book of Ezekiel. **SELECTED PUBLICATIONS** Auth, "Zephaniah," in HarperCollins Bible Commentary, 99; "History or Metaphor: Contributions to Old Testament Theology in the Works of Leo G. Perdue," in Relig Studies Review, 98; "The Particle and the Prophet: Observations on Ezekiel II 6," in Vetus Testamentum, 98; "You Are What You Eat: Ezekiel and the Scroll, in JBL, 98; "The Prophets and the End of Hosea," 96; "Who Were the Prophets in Hosea?," 96; "I Will Destroy Your Mother: The Obliteration of a Cultic Role in Hosea 4:4-6," 95; "The City of Hamoniah in Ezekiel 39: 11-16," in CBQ, 94. **CONTACT ADDRESS** 1134 Highland Ave, Northfield, MN, 55057. **EMAIL** odell@stolaf.edu

OGDEN, GREGORY L.
DISCIPLINE LAW **EDUCATION** Univ CA, LA, BA, 70; Univ CA, Davis, JD, 73; Temple Univ, LLM, 78; Columbia Univ, LLM, 81. **CAREER** Sr res ed, Univ CA; private practice, 75-76; lectr, Assoc Prof, Pepperdine Univ Sch of Law, 78-82; Prof, 82-present; vis prof, Notre Dame Law Sch, 88-89; Valparaiso Univ Sch Law, 89-90; Univ CA, 90; USC Law Ctr, 96; consult, Admin Conf US, 82-84, 87-89; fac dir, Ira Sherman ctr ethical awareness; prof, 82-. **HONORS AND AWARDS** Reginald Heber Smith fel, San Mateo Legal Aid Soc, 73-75; Law and Hum tchg fel, Temple Univ, 76-78; Chamberlain fel Legis, Columbia Univ, 80-81. **MEMBERSHIPS** Mem, Phi Kappa Phi; CA State Bar; Am Bar Assn; Christian Legal Soc. **SELECTED PUBLICATIONS** Co-auth, West's California Code Forms, Civil Procedure, 3rd ed, 81, 4th ed, 88; ed, contrib auth, Calif Public Agency. **CONTACT ADDRESS** Sch of Law, Pepperdine Univ, 24255 Pacific Coast Hwy, Malibu, CA, 90263.

OGDEN, SCHUBERT MILES
PERSONAL Born 03/02/1928, Cincinnati, OH, m, 1950, 2 children **DISCIPLINE** SYSTEMATIC THEOLOGY **EDUCATION** Ohio Wesleyan Univ, AB, 50; Univ Chicago, DB, 54, PhD, 58. **CAREER** From instr to prof theol, Perkins Sch Theol, Southern Methodist Univ, 56-69; univ prof, Divinity Sch, Univ Chicago, 69-72; Prof Theol Perkins Sch Theol, Southern Methodist Univ, 72-, Dir Grad Prof Relig Studies, 74-, Soc Values Higher Educ Kent fel, 51-; Fulbright res fel & Guggenheim Mem fel, Univ Marburg, 62-63; vis fel, Coun of Humanities, Princeton Univ, 77- 78. **HONORS AND AWARDS** Merrick lectr, Ohio Wesleyan Univ, 65; Sarum lectr, Univ Oxford, 80-81., LittD, Ohio Wesleyan Univ, 65. **MEMBERSHIPS** Am Philos Asn; Am Acad Relig (pres, 76-77); Am Theol Soc. **RESEARCH** Philosophical theology. **SELECTED PUBLICATIONS** Transl, Existence and Faith: Shorter Writings of Rudolf Bultmann, Meridian, 60; auth, Christ Without Myth: A Study Based on the Theology of Rudolf Bultmann, Harper, 61, 2nd ed, Southern Methodist Univ Press, 79; The Reality of God and Other Essays, Harper, 66, 2nd ed, 77; What is theology?, JRelig, 72; The authority of scripture for theology, Interpretation, 76; Faith and Freedom: Toward a Theology of Liberation, Abingdon, 79; The concept of a theology of liberation, In: The Challenge of Liberation Theology, Orbij, 81; The Point of Christology, Harper, 82; Theology and Biblical Interpretation + Understanding the Normative Meaning of Critical Reflection Mediated by Christian Religion and Scholarship, J of Religion, Vol 0076, 1996; Toward Doing Theology, J of Religion, Vol 0075, 1995. **CONTACT ADDRESS** Perkins Sch of Theol, Southern Methodist Univ, Dallas, TX, 75275.

OGLETREE, CHARLES J., JR.
PERSONAL Born 12/31/1952, Merced, California, m, 1975 **DISCIPLINE** LAW **EDUCATION** Stanford University, Stanford, CA, BA, 1974, MA, 1975; Harvard Law School, Cambridge, MA, JD, 1978. **CAREER** District of Columbia Public Defender Service, Washington, DC, staff attorney, 1978-82, director of staff training, 1982-83; American University/Washington College of Law, Washington, DC, adjunct professor, 1982-84; Antioch Law School, Washington, DC, adjunct professor, 1983-84; District of Columbia Public Defender Service, Washington, DC, deputy director, 1984-85; Jessamy, Fort & Ogletree, Washington, DC, partner, 1985-89; Harvard Law School, Cambridge, MA, visiting professor, 1985-89, director, introduction to trial advocacy workshop, 1986-, assistant professor, 1989-93, professor of law, 1993-; Jessamy, Fort & Botts, Washington, DC, of counsel, 1989-; Harvard Law School, Criminal Justice Institute, Cambridge, MA, director, Jesse Climenko Professor of Law, currently. **HONORS AND AWARDS** Hall of Fame, California School Boards Foundation, 1990; Nelson Mandela Service Award, National Black Law Students Association, 1991; Richard S Jacobsen Certificate of Excellence in Teaching Trial Advocacy, 1990; Honoree, Charles Hamilton Houston Institute, 1990; Award of Merit, Public Defender Service Associaton, 1990; Personal Achievement Award, NAACP and The Black Network, 1990; "Supreme Court Jury Discrimination Cases and State Court Compliance, Resistance and Innovation," Toward a Usable Past, 1990; "Justice Marshall's Criminal Justice Jurisprudence: The Right Thing to Do, the Right Time to Do It, The Right Man and the Right Place," The Harvard Blackletter Journal, Spring 1989; Boston Museum of Afro-American History, Man of Vision Award, 1992; Harvard Law School, Albert M Sacks-Paul A Freund Award for Excellence in Teaching, 1993; Criminal Practice Inst, A Champion of Liberty Award, 1994; NY State

Bar Assn-Criminal Justice Sect, honoree, Award for Outstanding Contribution in Criminal Law Education, 1992; Transafrica-Boston Chapter, Outstanding Service Award, 1992; co-author: Beyond the Rodney King Story; "Just Say No! A Proposal to Eliminate Racially Discriminatory Uses of Peremptory Challenges," 31 American Criminal Law Review 1099, 1994; "The Quiet Storm: The Rebellious Influence of Cesar Chavez," Harvard Latino Review, vol 1, 1995. **MEMBERSHIPS** Member, American Bar Association; member, National Conference of Black Lawyers; member, National Bar Association; member, American Civil Liberties Union; member, Bar Association of DC; member, Washington Bar Association; defender committee member, National Legal Aid and Defender Association; Assn of American Law Schools; DC Bar; Southern Ctr for Human Rights Committee, chairperson. **SELECTED PUBLICATIONS** Moderator of television programs including: "Surviving the Odds: To Be a Young Black Male in America," Public Broadcasting System, 1994; "Political Correctness and the Media," C-Span, 1994; "Don't Say What You Think!; Limits to Free Speech," C-Span, 1994. **CONTACT ADDRESS** Sch of Law, Harvard Univ, 1575 Massachusetts Ave., Cambridge, MA, 02138.

OH, KANG-NAM
DISCIPLINE RELIGIOUS STUDIES **EDUCATION** BA, 65, MA, 67, Seoul Natl Univ; McMaster Univ, PhD, 76. **CAREER** Prof, Religious Studies, 80-, Univ Regina **CONTACT ADDRESS** Religious Studies, Univ Regina, Regina, SK, S4S 0A2. **EMAIL** ohken@meena.cc.uregina.ca

OHNUMA, REIKO
PERSONAL Born 04/10/1963, New Haven, CT, m, 1993, 1 child **DISCIPLINE** ASIAN STUDIES, BUDDHIST STUDIES **EDUCATION** Univ of Michigan, Ann Arbor, PhD, 97. **CAREER** Vis lectr, 96-98, Univ of TX, Austin; Asst Prof, 98-99, Univ of AL, Tuscaloosa. **HONORS AND AWARDS** Charlotte Newcombe Doctoral Dissertation Fellowship. **MEMBERSHIPS** Intl Assoc of Buddhist Stud; Amer Acad of Rel. **RESEARCH** Indian Buddhist Literature, especially narrative literature; Women and Literature. **SELECTED PUBLICATIONS** Auth, The Gift of the Body and the Gift of Dharma, History of Religions, 98. **CONTACT ADDRESS** 11 Dubois Terrace, Tuscaloosa, AL, 35401. **EMAIL** rohnuma@bama.ua.edu

OKHAMAFE, IMAFEDIA
PERSONAL s **DISCIPLINE** PHILOSOPHY,. ENGLISH **EDUCATION** Purdue Univ, PhD, Philosophy and English, 1984. **CAREER** Univ of NE at Omaha, prof of philosophy & English 1993-. **MEMBERSHIPS** Modern Language Association of America; American Philosophical Association. **SELECTED PUBLICATIONS** Articles have appeared in periodicals such as Black Scholar, Journal of the British Soc for Phenomenology, UMOJA, Intl Journal of Social Educ, Auslegung, Rsch in African Literatures, Soundings, Philosophy Today, and Africa Today. **CONTACT ADDRESS** Prof of Philosophy & English, Univ of Nebraska-Omaha, Annex 39, Omaha, NE, 68182-0208.

OLBRICHT, THOMAS H.
PERSONAL Born 11/03/1929, Thayer, MO, m, 1951, 5 children **DISCIPLINE** RHETORIC, BIBLICAL THEOLOGY **EDUCATION** Northern IL, BS, 51; Univ IA, MA 53, PhD, 59; Harvard Divinity School, STB, 62. **CAREER** Chair speech, Univ Dubuque, 55-59; PA State Asn Prof speech and humanities, 62-67; Prof Biblical Theol, Abilene Christian Univ, 67-86, Dean, Col of Liberal and Fine Arts, 81-85; Distinguished Prof Relig, 94-97, chair, Relig div, 86-96, Pepperdine Univ, Distinguished Prod Relig, Emeritus, 97-. **MEMBERSHIPS** Soc of Biblical lit; Nat Commun Asn; Am Academy Relig. **RESEARCH** Rhetorical analysis of scripture; history of Biblical interpretation. **SELECTED PUBLICATIONS** Co-auth, with Stanley E Porter, Rhetoric and the New Testament 1991 Heidelberg Conference, Sheffield Academic Press, 93; auth, Hearing God's Voice: My Life with Scriptures in Churches of Christ, ACU Press, 96; co-auth, with Stanley E Porter, Rhetoric, Theology and the Scriptures, Pretoria Conf, Sheffield Academic Press, 96; with Stanley E Porter, The Rhetorical Analysis of Scripture: Essays from the 1995 London Conference, Univ of Sheffield, 97. **CONTACT ADDRESS** 14 Beaver Dam Rd, South Berwick, ME, 03908-1818. **EMAIL** Tolbrich@gw1.net

OLIKER, MICHAEL A.
PERSONAL Born 01/09/1946, Philadelphia, PA, m, 1982 **DISCIPLINE** PHILOSOPHY OF EDUCATION, LIBRARY AND INFROMATION SCIENCE, ENGLISH **EDUCATION** Kutztown Univ of Penn, BA, 67; Temple Univ, EdM, 69; Univ Ill-Urbana, PhD, 76; Drexel Univ, MS, 80. **CAREER** Tchg asst, Syracuse Univ, 69-70; adj fac, Phila Commun Col, 70; vis fac, 70-71, adj fac, 83-84, Glassboro State Col; adj fac, Bloomsburg State Col, 74; tchg asst, 71-72, 73-75, adj fac, 76, Univ Ill-Urbana; vis fac, 76-77, adj fac, 80, 89-91, Loyola Univ Chicago; adj fac, 80 & 83, Temple Univ; adj fac, Ill State Univ, 84; asst prof, E Ill Univ, 95-97; adj fac, NE Ill Univ, 97-. **MEMBERSHIPS** Midwest Philos Educ Soc; Am Educ Stud Asn; Am Libr Asn; Am Philos Asn; Mod Lang Asn; Philos Educ Soc; Popular Cult Asn. **RESEARCH** Applied of critical thinking to: (1) Popular culture, (2) Educational administration and policy; Douglas McGregors 'Theory Y' approach to administration; Philosophy of Plato and John Dewey; History of American educational thought. **SELECTED PUBLICATIONS** Auth On the Images of Education in Popular Film, Educ Horizons, 93; Analytical Philosophy and the Discourse of Institutional Democracy, Proceedings of the Midwest Philosophy of Education Society 1991-92, The Society, 93; Popula Film as Educational Ideology: A Framework for Critical Analysis, Proceedings of the Midwest Philosophy of Education Society 1993-94, The Society, 95; Educational Policy and Administration, 96; Censorship, Philosophy of Education, Garland, 96; Superman, Adolescents, and the Metaphysics of Popular Culture, 97; The Language of Educational Policy and Administration, Proceedings of the Midwest Philosophy of Education Society, The Society, 97; Toward an Intellectual Understanding of Anti-Intellectual Popular Culture, Jour of Thought, 98. **CONTACT ADDRESS** 5006 W Grace St, Chicago, IL, 60641. **EMAIL** moliker@sprynet.com

OLIPHINT, K. SCOTT
DISCIPLINE APOLOGETICS **EDUCATION** W Tex State Univ, BA, 78; Westminster Theol Sem, ThM; Westminster Theol Sem, PhD, 94. **CAREER** Assoc prof , Westminster Theol Sem. **SELECTED PUBLICATIONS** Co-auth, If I Should Die Before I Wake: Help for Those who Hope for Heaven; auth, Jonathan Edwards: Reformed Apologist, Westminster Theol Jour, 95; Plantinga on Warrant, Westminster Theol Jour, 95. **CONTACT ADDRESS** Westminster Theol Sem, PO Box 27009, Philadelphia, PA, 19118. **EMAIL** soliphint@wts.edu.

OLITZKY, KERRY M.
PERSONAL Born 12/22/1954, Pittsburgh, PA, m, 1977, 2 children **DISCIPLINE** EDUCATIONAL DEVELOPMENT **EDUCATION** Hebrew Union Col, DHL, 85; Hebrew Union Col, MAHL, 80; Univ S Fla, BA, 74; MA, 75. **CAREER** Vpres, Wexner Heritage Found, 98-; Ntl Dean of Adult Jewish Learning, Hebrew Union Col, 96-98; Ntl Dir of Res & Educ Development, Hebrew Union Col, 84-97; Dir Grad Studies Prog, Hebrew Union Col, 84-97. **HONORS AND AWARDS** Listed in: Dir of Amer Scholars, Man of the Year, Intl Dir of Distinguished Leadership, Contemporary Auths, Intl Man of Year, Intl Who's Who of Intellectuals, Dict of Intl Biography, Men of Achievement, Who's Who in Relig, Who's Who Among Young American Prof, Who's Who Among Human Services Prof, Who's Who in the East, Who's Who in Amer Educ; Amer Jewish Archives Res & Travel Grant. **MEMBERSHIPS** Advisor, Jewish Alcoholics, Chemically Dependent Persons, and Significant Others Council; Inter-Relig Proj Advisory Council Member, Felician Col; Jrnl of Psychology and Judaism former Special Ed; Shofar Magazine former Exec Ed; Jrnl of Ministry in Addiction and Recovery Ed Board; Jewish Educ News Ed Board; Assoc of Reform Zionist of Amer; Ntl Assoc Temple Educ; Central Conf of Amer Rabbis; UAHC Older Adults Committee; Gerontology Soc of Amer; Committee on Jewish Fam; Joint Commission on Jewish Educ; Assoc for Supervision and Curriculum Develop; Ntl Interfaith Coalition on Aging; Amer Soc on Aging; Assoc of Jewish Studies. **SELECTED PUBLICATIONS** Grief in Our Seasons: A Mourner's Companion for Kaddish, Jewish Lights Pub, 98; Jewish Spiritual Guidance, Jossey-Bass Pub, 97; Rediscovering Judaism: A Course of Study for Adult Bar/Bat Mitzvah, KTAV Pub, 97; The American Synagogue: A Historical Dictionary, Greenwood Pr, 96. **CONTACT ADDRESS** Dept. of Alumni Programs, Wexner Heritage Foundation, 551 Madison, New York, NY, 10022. **EMAIL** shia@Wexner.org

OLIVER, HAROLD HUNTER
PERSONAL Born 10/09/1930, Mobile, AL, m, 1951 **DISCIPLINE** RELIGION, PHILOSOPHY **EDUCATION** Samford Univ, AB, 52; Southern Baptist Theol Sem, BD, 54; Princeton Theol Sem, ThM, 55; Emory Univ, PhD, 61. **CAREER** From instr to assoc prof New Testament, Southeastern Baptist Theol Sem, 57-65; assoc prof theol, 65-70, Prof New Testament & Theol, Sch Theol, Boston Univ, 70-, Res asst, Int Greek New Testament Proj, 55-57; Christian Res Found award, 56; Am Asn Theol Schs fac fel, 63-64; res ed New Testament, J Bible & Relig, 65-67 & J Am Acad Relig, 68-; chmn Am Textual Criticism Sem, 67; fel cross-disciplinary studies, 71-72; vis fel, Inst Theoret Astron, Cambridge Univ, 71-72; consult & panelist, Nat Endowment for Humanities, 76-; Chavanne vis prof relig studies, Rice Univ, 80-81. **MEMBERSHIPS** Am Acad Relig; Soc Values Higher Educ; fel, Royal Astron Soc; Am Philos Asn; Metaphys Soc Am. **RESEARCH** Philosophy of religion; cosmology. **SELECTED PUBLICATIONS** Transl, Theory of Existence, Attic, 65; Thinking Faith, 68; auth, Hope and knowledge: The epistemic status of religious language, Cult Hermeneutics, 74; The impact of 19th century philosophy on Biblical authority, Perspectives Relig Studies, 74; Theses on the relational self and the genesis of the Western ego, Theol Z, 77; The complementarity of theology and cosmology, Zygon: JRelig & Sci, 78; Relational metaphysics and the human future, In: The Sources of Hope, Pergamm, 79; A Relational Metaphysic, Nijhoff, 81; The Neglect And Recovery of Nature in 20th-century Protestant Thought, J of The American Academy of Religion, Vol 0060, 1992. **CONTACT ADDRESS** Sch Theol, Boston Univ, Boston, MA, 02215.

OLSHEWSKY, THOMAS MACK
PERSONAL Born 11/20/1934, Springfield, MO, m, 1956, 4 children **DISCIPLINE** PHILOSOPHY **EDUCATION** Wabash Col, AB, 56; McCormick Theol Sem, BD, 60; Emory Univ, PhD(philos), 65. **CAREER** Asst prof philos, Parsons Coll 62-63 & Coe Col, 63-66; asst prof, 66-69, Assoc Prof Philos, Univ KY, 69-. **MEMBERSHIPS** Am Philos Asn; Am Soc Value Inquiry; Soc Ancient Greek Philos; Soc Advan Am Philos; Ling Soc Am. **RESEARCH** Ancient Greek philosophy; philosophy of language; philosophy of mind. **SELECTED PUBLICATIONS** Auth, Problems in the Philosophy of Language, Holt, 69; Deep structure: Essential, transcendental, or pragmatic?, Monist, 73; The analogical argument ... revisited, Am Philos Quart, 74; On competence and performance, Linguistics, 74; Depositions and reductionism in psychology, J Theory Social Behav, 75; On the notion of a rule, Philosophia, 76; On the relations of soul to body in Plato and Aristotle, J Hist Philos, 76; Self-movers And Unmoved Movers in Aristotle 'Physics Vii', Classical Quarterly, Vol 0045, 1995. **CONTACT ADDRESS** Dept of Philos, Univ of Ky, 500 S Limestone St, Lexington, KY, 40506-0003.

OLSON, CARL
PERSONAL Born 11/12/1941, Newark, NJ, m, 1968, 2 children **DISCIPLINE** RELIGIOUS STUDIES **EDUCATION** Penn State Univ, BA, 67; Drew Theol School, M Div, 70; Drew Univ, PhD, 77. **CAREER** Instr Philosophy, 78, Union Col; Instr Philosophy and religion, 76-78, Trenton State Col; vis asst prof Religious Studies, 78-79, S Ill Univ; vis asst prof Religious Studies, 79-80, Univ ND; PROF RELIGIOUS STUDIES, 81-, chr Nat Endowment Humanities, 91-94, chr Dept Religions Studies, 94-96, Allegheny Col, 81-. **MEMBERSHIPS** Am Asian Soc; Am Oriental Soc; Am Acad Relig; Soc Asian Comp Philos. **RESEARCH** Religion and philosophy of Hinduism; Theory of religion and its methods; Early Buddhism. **SELECTED PUBLICATIONS** Auth The Book of the Goddess Past and Present: An Introduction to Her Religion, Crossroads Publ Co, 83; The Mysteriousd Play of Kali: An Interpretive Study of Ramakrishna, Scholars Press, 90; The Theology and Philosophy of Eliade: A Search for the Centre, Macmillan Publ Co, 92; The Indian Renouncer and Postmodern Poison: A Cross-Cultural Encounter, Peter Lang Publ, 97. **CONTACT ADDRESS** Religious Studies Dept, Allegheny Col, Meadville, PA, 16335. **EMAIL** colson@alleg.edu

OLSON, RICHARD P.
PERSONAL Born 07/19/1934, Rapid City, SD, m, 1957, 3 children **DISCIPLINE** RELIGION **EDUCATION** Sioux Falls Col, BA, 56; Andover Newton Theol Sch, BD, 59, STM, 60; Boston Univ, PhD, 72. **CAREER** Christian minister, 59-98; Adjunct Tchr, Sioux Falls Col, Holy Redeemer Col, Col of Racine, Cent Baptist Theol Seminary; Vis Prof, Cent Baptist Seminary, 98-99. **HONORS AND AWARDS** Ten most important books for clergy, Am Acad of Parish Clergy, 91. **MEMBERSHIPS** Am Asn of Pastoral Counselors. **RESEARCH** The changing family; the changing American religious consciousness. **SELECTED PUBLICATIONS** Co-auth, Discoveries: Expanding Your Child's Vocational Horizon, United Church Press, 95; auth, Privileged Conversations: Dramatic Stories for Christmas, United Church Press, 96; co-auth, A New Day for Family Ministry, Alban, 96; auth, Midlife Journeys: A Traveler's Guide, Pilgrim Press, 96; auth, A Different Kind of Man, Judson, 98. **CONTACT ADDRESS** 9112 Slator Dr, Overland Park, KS, 66212.

OLSON, ROGER E.
PERSONAL Born 02/02/1952, Des Moines, IA, m, 1973, 2 children **DISCIPLINE** CHRISTIAN HISTORICAL THEOLOGY **EDUCATION** Open Bible Coll, BA, 74; North Amer Baptist Sem, MA, 78; Rice Univ, MA, 82, PhD, 84; Stud Univ of Munich, Germany, 81-82. **CAREER** Asst Prof, Theol, 82-84, Oral Robert Univ; Prof Theol, 84-, Bethel Coll & Sem; Ed, Christian Scholar's Review, 94-. **HONORS AND AWARDS** Bethel Coll Faculty Scholarship Award. **MEMBERSHIPS** ATS, AAR. **RESEARCH** History of Christian Theology and Contemporary Christian Thought. **SELECTED PUBLICATIONS** Co-auth, 20th Century Theology: God and the World in a Transitional Age, InterVarsity Press, 92; Who Needs Theology? An Invitation to the Study of God, InterVarsity Press, 96; auth, The Story of Christian Theology, Twenty Centuries of Tradition and Reform, forthcoming, 99. **CONTACT ADDRESS** Bethel Col, 3900 Bethel Dr, St. Paul, MN, 55112. **EMAIL** olsrog@bethel.edu

OOSTERHUIS, TOM
PERSONAL Born 03/11/1943, Bradford, ON, Canada, m, 1968, 2 children **DISCIPLINE** THEOLOGY; NEW TESTAMENT; PAULINE STUDIES **EDUCATION** Free Univ of Amsterdam, Doctor of Theology, 92. **CAREER** Campus Minister, Univ Alberta, 75-. **MEMBERSHIPS** Soc of Biblical Lit **RESEARCH** New Testament; Pauline studies; Jewish-Christian relationships **SELECTED PUBLICATIONS** The Strong and the Weak: An Exegetical Study of the Romans **CONTACT ADDRESS** Univ of Alberta, Sub 158f, Edmonton, AB, T6G 2J7. **EMAIL** toosterh@ualberta.ca

OPHARDT, MICHAEL
DISCIPLINE PHILOSOPHY **EDUCATION** Duquesne Univ, PhD, 92. **CAREER** Lectr, Malone Col, 96- . **MEMBERSHIPS** APA; Am Cath Philos Asn; Soc of Christian Philos. **RESEARCH** Ethics; aesthetics. **CONTACT ADDRESS** 3849 Silverwood Dr, Stow, OH, 44224. **EMAIL** mophardt@malone.edu

OPPENHAIM, MICHAEL
DISCIPLINE RELIGION **EDUCATION** Univ Calif, Santa Barbara, PhD, 76. **CAREER** Assoc prof. **RESEARCH** Modern Jewish philosophy and identity. **SELECTED PUBLICATIONS** Auth, What Does Revelation Mean to the Modern Jew?, 85; Mutual Upholding: Fashioning Jewish Philosophy Through Letters, 92; Feminist Judaism, Philosophy, and Religious Pluralism, Modern Judaism, 96. **CONTACT ADDRESS** Dept of Rel, Concordia Univ, Montreal, 1455 de Maisonneuve W, Montreal, PQ, H3G 1M8.

OPPENHEIM, FRANK M.
PERSONAL Born 05/18/1925, Coldwater, OH **DISCIPLINE** PHILOSOPHY **EDUCATION** Loyola Univ, AB, 47, MA, 52; St Louis Univ, PhD, 62; Loyola Univ, PhL, 49, STL, 56. **CAREER** Prof, Xavier Univ, 57- . **HONORS AND AWARDS** Exec Comm, Soc Advancement of Amer Philos. **MEMBERSHIPS** Amer Philos Assn, Eastern Div; Soc Advance Amer Philos; **RESEARCH** Josiah Royce (1855-1916); Classic American Philsophy. **SELECTED PUBLICATIONS** Auth, A Critical Annotated Bibliography of the Published Works of Josiah Royce, Revue Internationale de Philosophie, Bruxelles, 79-80, 67, 138-158; Royce's Appreciative Interest in the More Vital, The modern Schoolman, 44, March 67, 223-229; Two New Documents on Royce's Early Life, The Jour Hist Philos, 6, Oct 68, 381-385; A Roycean Road to Community, International Philosophical Quart, 10, Sept, 70, 341-377; Foreword to Edward Jarvis's The Conception of God in the Later Royce, The Hague: Nijhoff, 75, vii-xvii; Josiah Royce as Teacher, Educational Theory, 25, Spring 75, 168-185; Josiah Royce;s Intellectual Development: An Hypothesis, Idealistic Stud, 6, Jan 76, 85-102; Royce's Community: A Dimension Missing in Freud and James?, Jour Hist Behavioral Sci, 13, 77, 173-190; Graced Communities: A Problem in Loving, Theol Stud, 44, Dec 83, 605-624; Royce's Voyage Down Under: A Journey of the Mind, Lexington, UP of Kentucky, 80; The Idea of Spirit in the Mature Royce Transactions of the Charles S. Peirce Soc, 19, Fall 83, 381-395; The Mature Royce's Idea of God, Papers in Nineteenth Century Theology Working Group, Amer Acad Rel, 85, I, 12-22; Hermeneutics and the Mature Royce, Proceedings of the Ohio Philos Assn, 86, 43-56; ed, The Reasoning Heart: Towards a North American Theology, Wash DC, Georgetown UP, 86; A Report on Nicarague, Am, 154, March 8, 86, 183-185; Gullible Media Swallow Reagan's Whoppers, Nat Cath Reporter, June 6, 86, 9; Philosophy Royce's Mature of Religion, U of Notre Dame P, 87; coauth, The Mustard Seed Process: Twelve Practical Exercises on Social Justice, for Groups and Individuals, New York, Paulist, 87; None Dare Call it Disobedience-Not Even the Author, LANDAS, 11, Jan 97, 64-81; A Roycean Response to the Challenge of Individualism, in Beyond Individualism: Toward a Retrieval of Moral Discourse in America, ed Donald L. Gelpi, SJ, U of Notre Dame P, 87, 87-119; coauth, New Documents on Josiah Royce, Transactions of the Charles S. Peirce Soc, 26, Winter 90, 131-145; Josiah Royce and Rudolph Steiner: A Comparison and Contrast, Revision, 13-14, Spring-Summer 91; Major Developments in Royce's Ethics after the Problem, in Frontiers in American Philosophy, College Station, TX, Texan A&M Univ Press, 92, I, 346-356; How Can a Philosopher's Specialization Inerdigitate with his or her Teaching of Philosophy?, Proceedings of the Fifty-Fourth Jesuit Philosophical Assn Mtg, San Diego, March 92; Royce's Mature Ethics, U of Notre Dame P, 93; Royce Project Report, Newsl no 78 of the Soc for the Advancement of Amer Philos, Oct 97, 10-11; The Peirce-Royce Relationship-Part I, The Jour Speculative Philos, 11, 97, 256-279; The Peirce-Royce Relationship-Part II, The Jour Speculative Philos, 12, 98, 35-46; **CONTACT ADDRESS** Xavier Univ, 5361 S Milford Rd, Milford, OH, 45150-9746. **EMAIL** oppenhei@xavier.xu.edu

ORDOWER, HENRY M.
PERSONAL Chicago, IL, 3 children **DISCIPLINE** TAXATION LAW, MEDIEVAL LITERATURE **EDUCATION** Washington Univ, St Louis, AB, 67; Univ Chicago, MA, 70, JD, 75. **CAREER** Instr law, Univ Chicago Law Sch, 75-76; assoc atty, Sonnenschein, Calin, Nath & Rosenthal, 75-77; asst prof, 77-80, assoc prof Law, St Louis Univ Law Sch, 80-83. **MEMBERSHIPS** Soc Advan Scand Studies. **RESEARCH** United States taxation of income, estates and gifts; the Icelandic family saga. **SELECTED PUBLICATIONS** Art, Separating Statutory Frameworks: Incompatibility of the Complete Liquidation & Reorganization Provisions of the Internal Revenue Code, St Louis Univ Law J, 81; auth, Tax Act Offers New Choices: Planning the Large Estate, Trusts & Estates, 82. **CONTACT ADDRESS** Law School, St. Louis Univ, 3700 Lindell Blvd, St. Louis, MO, 63108-3412. **EMAIL** ordoweh@slu.edu

OREND, BRIAN
DISCIPLINE PHILOSOPHY **EDUCATION** Univ NY, PhD, 98. **RESEARCH** Moral and political theory. **SELECTED PUBLICATIONS** Auth, pub(s) on intl law, foreign policy and intl relations theory. **CONTACT ADDRESS** Dept of Philosophy, Waterloo Univ, 200 University Ave W, Waterloo, ON, N2L 3G1. **EMAIL** bdorend@uwaterloo.ca

ORGAN, BARBARA
DISCIPLINE RELIGIOUS STUDIES **EDUCATION** St Michael's Coll, PhD. **RESEARCH** Literary composition of the Hebrew Bible. **SELECTED PUBLICATIONS** Auth, Text and Translation, Can Cath Rev, 93; auth, Judaism for Gentiles, BIBAL, 96. **CONTACT ADDRESS** Religious Studies Dept, Laurentian Univ, 935 Ramsey Lake Rd, Sudbury, ON, P3E 2C6.

ORLANS, F. BARBARA
PERSONAL Born 01/14/1928, Birmingham, England, m, 1982, 2 children **DISCIPLINE** PHYSIOLOGY **EDUCATION** Birmingham Univ, BSc 49; London Univ, MSc 54, PhD, 56. **CAREER** Sr res fel, 89-, Georgetown Univ; Dir, 84-88, Sci Cen Anim Wel, MD; staff scientist, 79-84, Ntl Inst Hlth, MD; exec sec, 77-79, NIH; sci admin, 75-77, NIH. **HONORS AND AWARDS** Rockefeller Schl Res; ALA Outstanding Acad Book Awd. **MEMBERSHIPS** ASP; NABT. **RESEARCH** Ethical Issues Regarding the Human Use of Animals. **SELECTED PUBLICATIONS** Coauth, The Human Use of Animals: Case Studies in Ethical Choice, NY, Oxford Univ Press, 98; auth, In the Name of Science: Issues in Responsible Animal Experimentation, NY, Oxford Univ Press, 93; Regulation and Ethics of Animal Experiments: An Intl Comparison, in: Helga Kuhse, Peter Singer, eds, Companion to Bioethics, London, Blackwells, forthcoming; various entries in: Encyc of Animal Rights and Animal Welfare, eds, M Bekoff, C Meany, Westport CT, Greenwood Pub, 98; coauth, Institutional Animal Care and Use Committees: A Flawed Paradigm or Work in Progress?, Ethics and Behavior, 97; auth, Invasiveness Scales for Animal Pain and Distress, Lab Animal, 96; The Three R Alternatives in Res and Edu, in: A Long Road Ahead in the US, ATLA, 96; Suggestions from a Study Group on Teaching the Ethics of Animal Experimentation, 95. **CONTACT ADDRESS** Kennedy Inst of Ethics, Georgetown Univ, 37th and O St NW, 4th Fl Healy Hall, Washington, DC, 20057. **EMAIL** orlansfb@gunet.georgetown.edu

ORNSTEIN, JACK
DISCIPLINE BIOMEDICAL ETHICS AND PHILOSOPHY OF MIND **EDUCATION** Univ Calif, San Diego, PhD. **CAREER** Prof; undergrad adv. **SELECTED PUBLICATIONS** Auth, The Mind and the Brain. **CONTACT ADDRESS** Dept of Philos, Concordia Univ, Montreal, 1455 de Maisonneuve W, Montreal, PQ, H3G 1M8. **EMAIL** jackorn@alcor.concordia.ca

OROPEZA, B.J.
PERSONAL Born 12/21/1961, Oakland, CA, m, 1986, 1 child **DISCIPLINE** NEW TESTAMENT **EDUCATION** Univ Durham England, PhD 98. **CAREER** Victory Outreach Sch, lectr 89-97; George Fox Univ, vis asst prof, 98-99. **MEMBERSHIPS** SBL; BNTS. **RESEARCH** Pauline studies; Apostasy and Perseverance; Christian Use of Jewish Traditions. **SELECTED PUBLICATIONS** Auth, Apostasy in the Wilderness: Paul's Eschatological Warning to the Corinthians, Tubingen, JCB, Paul Siebeck, forthcoming; Sitvational Immortality: Paul's Vice Lists at Corinth, Expository Times, 98; auth, Laying to Rest the Midrash: Paul's Message on Meat Sacrificed to Idols in Light of the Deuteronomic Tradition, Biblica 98; auth, 99 Answers to Questions About Angels, Eastbourne UK, Kingsway, 98. Auth, Downers Grove, IVP, 97; auth, A Time to Laugh: The Holy Laughter Phenomenon Examined, Peabody, Hendrickson, 95. **CONTACT ADDRESS** Dept of Religion, George Fox Univ, 414 North Meridian St, Newberg, OR, 97132. **EMAIL** boropeza@georgefox.edu

ORR, JANICE
PERSONAL Born 08/10/1944, St. Louis, MO, s **DISCIPLINE** LAW **EDUCATION** Roosevelt Univ, BA, 1966; Boston Univ School of Law, JD, 1972. **CAREER** Chicago Bd of Educ, teacher, 1966-69; US Dept of Labor, law clerk, 1972-73; US Dept of Housing & Urban Development, Attorney, 1973-74; International Communication Group, general counsel, 1974-75; Natl labor Relations Bd, LAW, 1975-76; Equal Employment Opportunity Commission, 1976-83; US Dept Health & Human Services, 1983-; Self Employed, LAW, entertainment, visual arts law, 1975-. **HONORS AND AWARDS** Natl Bar Assn, Best Section, 1993, Outstanding Achievement, 1987, 1991; US Dept Health & Human Services, Outstanding Achievement, 1993, 1995. **MEMBERSHIPS** Natl Bar Assn, bd of dirs, 1973-79, 1986-, chair, Legislation Comm, 1994-, chair, International Law Section, 1989-94, chair, Committee on Southern Africa, 1986-89; Emarrons, general counsel, 1989-; DC Music Ctr, general counsel, 1982-90; Ctr for Independent Living, bd mem, 1995-; GWAC Women Lawyers Assn, NBA, bd mem, 1990-92. **CONTACT ADDRESS** Orr & Associates, 1815 E St NE, Washington, DC, 20002.

ORR, LESLIE
PERSONAL Born 04/29/1948, Ann Arbor, MI **DISCIPLINE** HISTORY OF RELIGIONS, ASIAN RELIGIONS **EDUCATION** McGill Univ, BS, 70, MA, 81-82, PhD, 93. **CAREER** Full-time lectr, asst, assoc prof, 91-; full-time lect, McGill Univ, 89-91; part-time lectr, McGill Univ, 84-89; tchg asst, McGill Univ, 82-83. **RESEARCH** Women in the religions of India (Hinduism, Buddhism, and Jainism). **SELECTED PUBLICATIONS** Auth, "Jain Worship in Medieval Tamilnadu," Proc Intl Conf on Approaches to Jaina Stud: Philosophy, Logic, Rituals and Symbols, Ctr S Asian Stud, Univ Toronto, 97; "The Vaisnava Community at Srirangam: The Testimony of the Early Medieval Inscriptions," Jour of Vaisnava Stud, 95; The Concept of Time in Sankara's Brahma-sutra-bhasya, Hermeneutical Paths to the Sacred Worlds of India, Scholar's Press, 94; Women of Medieval South India in Hindu Temple Ritual: Text and Practice, Annual Rev of Women in World Religions 3, 94. **CONTACT ADDRESS** Dept of Rel, Concordia Univ, Montreal, 1455 de Maisonneuve W, Montreal, PQ, H3G 1M8.

ORR, MARY C.
PERSONAL Born 06/01/1956, Pittsburgh, PA, 1 child **DISCIPLINE** NEW TESTAMENT **EDUCATION** Hanover Coll, BA, 78; Harvard Divinity School, MDiv, 81; Univ Virginia, PhD, 95. **CAREER** Adjunct prof, Union-PSCE, Richmond, currently. **MEMBERSHIPS** SBL. **RESEARCH** Synoptic Gospels; Paul the Apostle. **SELECTED PUBLICATIONS** Book reviews in Interpretation and JBL. **CONTACT ADDRESS** 5924 Heards Mt Rd, Covesville, VA, 22931. **EMAIL** marcy@cfw.com

ORSI, ROBERT A.
DISCIPLINE RELIGIOUS STUDIES **EDUCATION** Yale Univ, PhD, 82. **CAREER** Assoc prof. **RESEARCH** Religion and society; social theory; history of religions in America; field methods in religion. **SELECTED PUBLICATIONS** Auth, The Madonna of 115th Street: Faith and Community in Italian Harlem 1880-1950, Yale, 85; The Cult of Saints and the Reimagination of the Space and Time of Sickness in Twentieth Century American Catholicism, Johns Hopkins, 89; 'He Keeps Me Going': Women's Devotion to Saint Jude and the Dialectics of Gender in American Catholicism 1929-1965, Univ Notre Dame, 90. **CONTACT ADDRESS** Dept of Religious Studies, Indiana Univ, Bloomington, 300 N Jordan Ave, Bloomington, IN, 47405.

ORT, LARRY V.
PERSONAL Born 08/13/1947, Wauseon, OH, m, 1995, 2 children **DISCIPLINE** PHILOSOPHY **EDUCATION** Spring Arbor Col, BA, 69; Mich St Univ, MA, 76, PhD, 97. **CAREER** Assoc prof, adult stud and phil, 83-, Spring Arbor Col. **HONORS AND AWARDS** Fac Merit Award, Spring Arbor Col, 98; Honorary Prof, St Petersburg St Techn Univ of Plant Polymers, St Petersburg Russia. **MEMBERSHIPS** Soren Kierkegaard Soc; Amer Phil Asn. **RESEARCH** Kierkegaardian and Wittgensteinian studies; justice and righteousness. **SELECTED PUBLICATIONS** Wittgenstein's Kierkegaardian Heritage, Univ Micro Dis. **CONTACT ADDRESS** 244 Honey Lane, Battle Creek, MI, 49015. **EMAIL** larryort@admin.arbor.edu

ORTH, JOHN VICTOR
PERSONAL Born 02/07/1947, Lancaster, PA, m, 1972, 2 children **DISCIPLINE** HISTORY OF LAW, PROPERTY LAW **EDUCATION** Oberlin Col, AB, 69; Harvard Univ, JD, 74, PhD(hist), 77. **CAREER** Law clerk, US Ct Appeals, 77-78; asst prof, 78-81, Assoc Prof Law, Univ NC, 81-. **MEMBERSHIPS** AAUP; Am Soc Legal Hist; Am Bar Asn; Selden Soc; Conf Brit Studies. **RESEARCH** American constitutional history; history of labor law. **SELECTED PUBLICATIONS** Auth, Doing legal history, Irish Jurist, 79; The fair fame and name of Louisiana: The Eleventh Amendment and the end of reconstruction, Tulane Lawyer, 80; Sir William Blackstone: Hero of the common law, Am Bar Asn J, 80; contribr, Law-Making and Law-Makers in British History, Royal Hist Soc, 80; auth, English law and striking workmen: The Molestation of Workmen Act, 1859, J Legal Hist, 81; The Eleventh Amendment and the North Carolina state debt, NC Law Rev, 81; Jeremy Bentham: The common law's severest critic, Am Bar Asn J, 82; On the relation between the rule of law and Pubic opinion, Mich Law Rev, 82; a Bibliography of 19th-century Legal Literature - Adams,jn, Davies,mj, American J of Legal History, Vol 0038, 1994; Currents of Radicalism - Popular Radicalism, Organized-labor And Party Politics in Britain 1850-1914 - Biagini,ef, Reid,aj, American J of Legal History, Vol 0037, 1993; Law, Politics And The Church-of- england, The Career of Lushington,stephen, 1782-1873 - Waddams,sm, Albion, Vol 0025, 1993; The Independence of The Judiciary, The View From The Lord-chancellor Office - Stevens,r, Albion, Vol 0026, 1994; Judicial Enigma - The First Justice Harlan - Yarbrough,te, American J of Legal History, Vol 0040, 1996; The Republican Crown - Lawyers And The Making of The State in 20th-century Britain - Jacob,jm, Albion, Vol 0029, 1997; Leading Cases in The Common-law - Simpson,awb, American Historical Review, Vol 0102, 1997. **CONTACT ADDRESS** Sch of Law, Univ of NC, Chapel Hill, NC, 27514.

ORTIZ, MANUEL
DISCIPLINE MINISTRY AND URBAN MISSION **EDUCATION** Philadelphia Col Bible, BS, 71; Wheaton Grad Sch Theol, MA, 75; Westminster Theol Sem, DMin, 89. **CAREER**

Tchr, Philadelphia Assn for Christian Sch(s); headmaster, Humboldt Community Christian Sch, 79-87; founder, dir, Apprenticeship Sch for Urban Ministry, 81-87; bd mem, fac, Sem Consortium for Urban Pastoral Edu, 82-; bd mem, InterVarsity Fel and World Relief, 94; vis prof, E Baptist Sem, 94; instr, 86; prof, Westminster Theol Sem, 95-. **SELECTED PUBLICATIONS** Auth, The Hispanic Challenge: Opportunities Confronting the Church; One New People: Models for Developing a Multiethnic Church; My Commitment to Intercultural Christian Community: An Hispanic Pilgrimage, Urban Mission, 94. **CONTACT ADDRESS** Westminister Theol Sem, PO Box 27009, Philadelphia, PA, 19118.

ORTIZ, VICTOR
PERSONAL Born 12/12/1946, New York, NY, s **DISCIPLINE** LAW **EDUCATION** BBA, marketing, 1970; JD, 1973. **CAREER** Private practice, civil & criminal law, 1977-78, 1981-85; Office of District Attorney, Dallas County, TX, asst district attorney, 1978-81; Dallas County Mental Health Center, hearing officer, 1984-85; City of Dallas, TX, asst city attorney, 1974-77, associate municipal judge, 1977-78, 1984-85, municipal judge, 1985-. **HONORS AND AWARDS** Natl Council of Negro Women, Man of the Year, 1986; Bancroft Witney Co., American Jurisprudence Award/Trusts, 1972; St Paul AME Church, Usher Board #2, Extra Mile Award, 1985; United Negro College Fund, Community Service Award, 1975; Natl Council of Negro Women, Man of the Year; St Paul AME Church, Man of the Year, 1997. **MEMBERSHIPS** Dallas Minority Repertory Theatre, board of directors, 1976-81; Committee of 100, vice pres, membership director, 1976-82; Dallas Black Chamber of Commerce, board of directors, 1979-81; Park South YMCA, board of directors, 1978-81; Progressive Voters League, 1975-86; Natl Bar Assn, 1982-; J L Turner Legal Assn, 1974-; St Paul AME Church, stewards board, 1978-. **CONTACT ADDRESS** Municipal Judge, City of Dallas, 2014 Main St, Suite 210, Dallas, TX, 75201.

ORTS, ERIC W.
PERSONAL Born 01/11/1960, m, 1 child **DISCIPLINE** LAW **EDUCATION** Oberlin Col, BA, 82; New Schl for Soc Res, MA, 85; Univ Mich Law Schl, JD, 88; Columbia Law Schl, JSD, 94. **CAREER** Assoc, 88-90, Paul, Weiss, Rifkind, Wharton & Garrison, NY; Chem Bank Fel, Corp Soc Respon, 90-91, Columbia Law Schl; adj asst prof, law, 95, Univ Penn Law Schl; vis prof, law, 97, Univ Mich Law Schl; vis prof, law, Fulbright res schlr, 98, Univ Leuven, Belgium; fac mem, ethic prog, 94-, Nelson Peltz Term asst prof, 91-96, dir, environ manag prog, 98, assoc prof, 96-, Univ Penn, Wharton Schl, Legal Stud Dept. **MEMBERSHIPS** Amer Bar Assn; Amer Law Inst; Amer Soc for Pol and Legal Phil; Carnegie Coun on Ethics & Intl Affairs; Environ Law Inst; Intl Assn for Phil of La and Soc Phil. **SELECTED PUBLICATIONS** Art, Positive Law and Systemic Legitimacy: A Comment on Hart and Habermas, Ratio Juris, vol 6, 93; art, The Complexity and Legitimacy of Corporate Law, Wash & Lee Law Rev Vol 50, 93; auth, The Legitimacy of Multinational Corporations, Progress Corp Law, Westview Press, 95; art, A Model of Reflexive Environmental Regulation, Bus Ethics Quart, vol 5, 95; art, Reflexive Environmental Law, Nwestern Univ Law Rev, vol 89, 95; auth, A North American Legal Perspective on Stakeholder Management Theory, Persp on Co Law: 2, 97; coauth, Environmental Disclosure and Evidentiary Privilege, Univ IL law Rev, vol 1997, 97; art, Quality Circles in Law Teaching, J of Legal Ed, vol 47, 97; coauth, Informational Regulation of Environmental Risks, Risk Analysis, vol 18, 98; art, Shirking and Sharking: A Legal Theory of the Firm, Yale Law & Policy Rev, vol 16, 98. **CONTACT ADDRESS** Legal Studies Dept, Univ of Penn, The Wharton School, Philadelphia, PA, 19104. **EMAIL** ortse@wharton.upenn.edu

OSBORN, RONALD EDWIN
PERSONAL Born 09/05/1917, Chicago, IL, m, 1940, 1 child **DISCIPLINE** CHURCH HISTORY **EDUCATION** Phillips Univ, BA, 38, MA, 39, BD, 42; Univ Ore, PhD(hist), 55. **CAREER** Ed youth Pub, Christian Bd of Pub, St Louis, Mo, 43-45; prof church hist & relig, educ, NW Christian Col, 46-50; from asst prof to prof church hist, Christian Theol Sem, 50-73, dean, 59-70; Prof Church Hist, Disciples Found Chair, Sch Theol & Claremont Grad Sch & Univ Ctr, 73-, Deleg, World Conf Faith & Order, Lund, Sweden, 52 & Montreal, Can, 63; vis lectr, Grad Sch Ecumenical Studies, Celigny, Vaud, Switz, 54-55; mem, Consultation Church Union, 63-79; vis prof church hist & ecumenics, Union Theol Sem Philippines, 65; pres, Int Convention Christian Churches, 67-68; moderator, Christian Church, 68. **HONORS AND AWARDS** LittD, Phillips Univ, 69. **MEMBERSHIPS** AHA; Am Soc Church Hist; Disciples Christ Hist Soc (pres, 50-53). **RESEARCH** History of preaching; religion in Western America. **SELECTED PUBLICATIONS** Auth, The Spirit of American Christianity, Harper, 57; coauth & ed, The Reformation of Tradition, Bethany, 63; auth, A Church for These Times, Abingdon, 65; In Christ's Place: Christian Ministry in Today's World, Bethany, 67; coauth, Disciples and the Church Universal, Disciples of Christ Hist Soc, 67; auth, Religious freedom and the form of the church, Lexington Theol Quart, 76; Experiment in Liberty, 78 & The Faith We Affirm, 79, Bethany; a Case-study of Mainstream Protestantism - The Disciples Relation to American Culture, 1880-1989 - Williams,dn, Ecumenical Review, Vol 0045, 1993. **CONTACT ADDRESS** Dept of Church Hist, Sch of Theol Claremont Grad Sch, 1325 N College, Claremont, CA, 91711.

OSBORNE, KENAN BERNARD
PERSONAL Born 05/29/1930, Santa Barbara, CA **DISCIPLINE** RELIGION, THEOLOGY **EDUCATION** San Luis Rey Col, BA, 52; Old Mission Theol Sem, STB, 56; Cath Univ Am, STL, 65; Ludwig Maximilians-Univ, Munich, Dr theol, 67. **CAREER** Instr Greek & hist, St Anthony's High Sch, Santa Barbara, 56-57; asst dir, Hour of St Francis Radio & TV, Los Angeles, 57- 58; dir admin, Cent Off, Franciscan Prov, Calif, 58-64; acting pres, 69-71, Prof Theol & Dean, Franciscan Sch Theol, 68, Pres, 71-; Prof Theol, Grad Theol Union, 68-. **MEMBERSHIPS** Western Am Acad Relig (pres, 73-74); Pac Coast Theol Soc; Cath Theol Soc Am (vp, 77-78, pres, 78-79). **RESEARCH** Phenomenology, Heidegger, Merleau-Ponty & Ricoeur; Sacramental theology and christology. **SELECTED PUBLICATIONS** Auth, New Being: A Study of Paul Tillich, Martinus Nijhoff, The Hague, 69; Methodology and the Christian Sacraments, Worship, 74; coauth, The renewal of the Sacrament of Penance, Cath Theol Soc Am, 75; auth, Theology in 1977 and beyond, Christian Century, 77; Ministry as Sacrament Ministerium Ecclesia, Leiturgia, Luther- Agricol Soc, 77; Sacramental theology & Theology of the Sacraments, In: New Cath Encycl, Vol XVII, 79; The Laity in The Middle-ages - Religious Beliefs And Devotional Practices - Vauchez,a, Theological Studies, Vol 0055, 1994; The Lay-person in The Church - Focus on Damian,peter, Anselm-of-canterbury, Ivo-of-chartres - French - Grandjean,m, Theological Studies, Vol 0056, 1995; Ecumenical Wedding Celebration - German - Candolfi,bj, Editor, J of Ecumenical Studies, Vol 0033, 1996; b Hear What The Spirit Says to The Churches - Towards Missionary Congregations in Europe - Linn,g, Editor, J of Ecumenical Studies, Vol 0033, 1996; Imago-dei - Approaches to The Theological Anthropology of Bonaventure,saint - Spanish - Chaveroblanco,fda, Speculum-a J of Medieval Studies, Vol 0072, 1997; Imago-dei - Approaches to The Theological Anthropology of Bonaventure,saint - Spanish - Chaveroblanco,fda, Speculum-a J of Medieval Studies, Vol 0072, 1997. **CONTACT ADDRESS** Franciscan Sch of Theol, 1712 Euclid Ave, Berkeley, CA, 94709-1294.

OSBORNE, ROBERT E.
PERSONAL Born 06/26/1920, Sherbrooke, PQ, Canada, m, 1947, 4 children **DISCIPLINE** RELIGION **EDUCATION** Sir George Williams Univ, BA, 50; McGill Univ, BD, 53, STM, 54; Univ Edinburgh, PhD(divinity), 66. **CAREER** Assoc prof New Testament, Emmanuel Col, Victoria Univ, Ont, 61-68; assoc prof Bibl studies, 68-75, Prof Bibl Studies, Carleton Univ, 74-. **HONORS AND AWARDS** Teaching Award, OCUFA, 78. **MEMBERSHIPS** Can Soc Bibl Studies; Soc New Testament Studies; Soc Bibl Lit. **RESEARCH** St Paul; New Testament archeology. **SELECTED PUBLICATIONS** Auth, St Paul's silent years, 65 & Paul and the wild beasts, 66, J Bibl Lit; coauth, Forgar: The occurrence of Gar as one of the first four words in sentences: A test of authorship for Greek writers, Sci & Archaeol, 1-371. **CONTACT ADDRESS** Dept of Religion, Carleton Univ, 1125 Colonel By Dr, Ottawa, ON, K1S 5B6.

OSBURN, CARROLL D.
PERSONAL Born 09/02/1941, Arkansas City, KS, m, 1966, 2 children **DISCIPLINE** BIBLICAL CRITICISM **EDUCATION** Vanderbilt Univ, D Min, 70; Univ St Andrews Scotland, PhD, 74. **CAREER** Prof, Harding Grad School of Rel; 73-83; prof, Pepperdine Univ; 83-87; Carmichael-Walling Distinguished prof, Abilene Christian Univ, 87-. **HONORS AND AWARDS** 20th Century Christian Educator of the Year, 83; Abilene Christian Univ, Honors Prof of the Year, 92, 96. **MEMBERSHIPS** Soc of Bibl Lit; Asn Internationale d'etudes patristiques; Int Asn of Coptic Studies. **RESEARCH** New Testament textual criticism. **SELECTED PUBLICATIONS** Auth, Women in the Church: Refocusing the Discussion, 94; The Greek Lectionaries of the New Testament, the Text of the New Testament in Contemporary Res: Essays on the Status Quaestionis-A Volume in Honor of Bruce M Metzger, 95; 1 Cor 11:2-16 - Public or Private?, Essays on Women in Earliest Christianity, 95; The Search for the Original Text of Acts, New Testament Text and Language, 96; The Epistle of Jude; The Epistle of Second Peter, Codex Alexandrinus; Codex Claromontanus; Gothic Version; Old Latin Versions; Oxyrhynchus Frgaments; Textus Receptus; Vulgate, Eerdmans Dictionary of the Bible, 98; coauth, A Note on Luke 18: 29-30; Essays on Women in Earliest Christianity, 95; ed, Essays on Women in Earliest Christianity, 95. **CONTACT ADDRESS** Abilene Christian Univ, ACU Station, PO Box 29425, Abilene, TX, 79699.

OSLER, MARGARET JO
PERSONAL Born 11/27/1942, New York, NY **DISCIPLINE** HISTORY & PHILOSOPHY OF SCIENCE **EDUCATION** Swarthmore Col, BA, 63; Ind Univ, MA, 66, PhD(hist & philos of sci), 68. **CAREER** Asst prof hist of sci, Ore State Univ, 68-70; asst prof hist, Harvey Mudd Col, 70-74; asst prof, Wake Forest Univ, 74- 75; Assoc Prof Hist, Univ Calgary, 75-. **MEMBERSHIPS** Hist of Sci Soc; West Coast Hist Sci Soc; Can Soc Hist & Philos of Sci. **RESEARCH** Locke's relation to 17th century science; philosophical problems of 17th century science; theories of matter and scientific method in the 17th century. **SELECTED PUBLICATIONS** Auth, John Locke and the ideal certainty in 17th century science, J Hist Ideas, 70; Galileo, motion, and essences, Isis, 74; coauth, Physical sciences, history of, In: Encycl Britannica; Certainty, scepticism, and scientific optimism, In: Probability, Time, and Space, AMS Press, 78; Descartes and Charleton on nature, God, and the mechanical philosophy, J Hist of Ideas, 79; Renaissance And Revolution - Humanists, Scholars, Craftsmen, And Natural Philosophers in Early Modern Europe - Field,jv, J Ames,fajl, Isis, Vol 0086, 1995; Gassendi - Scientific Explorer - a Catalog of The Exhibition on The Occasion of Gassendi,pierre 400th Birthday at The Musee-de- digne, May 19 to October 18, 1992 - French - Turner,a, Gomez,n, Annals of Science, Vol 0051, 1994; Gassendi - Scientific Explorer - a Catalog of The Exhibition on The Occasion of Gassendi,pierre 400th Birthday at The Musee-de-digne, May 19 to October 18, 1992 - French - Turner,a, Gomez,n, Annals of Science, Vol 0051, 1994; an Overview of Gassendi Philosophy - French - Bernier,f, Annals of Science, Vol 0051, 1994; An Overview of Gassendi Philosophy - French - Bernier,f, Annals of Science, Vol 0051, 1994; Providence and divine will in Gassendi's views on scientific knowledge, J Hist Ideas (in prep); The Matter of Revolution - Science, Poetry And Politics in The Age of Milton - Rogers,j, Isis, Vol 0088, 1997; The Matter of Revolution - Science, Poetry And Politics in The Age of Milton - Rogers,j, Isis, Vol 0088, 1997; Westfall,richard,s., 22 April 1924-21 August 1996, Isis, Vol 0088, 1997. **CONTACT ADDRESS** Dept of Hist, Univ of Calgary, Calgary, AB, T2N 1N4.

OSTERTAG, GARY
PERSONAL Born 01/06/1960, New York, NY **DISCIPLINE** PHILOSOPHY **EDUCATION** Graduate School of the City Univ of NY, PhD, 94. **CAREER** Vis Scholar to Adj Asst Prof, Dept of Philo, 96-98, NY Univ. **HONORS AND AWARDS** CUNY Res Found Fellowships; Best Masters Thesis; Hum; Northeast Assoc of Grad Schools Award. **MEMBERSHIPS** APA **RESEARCH** Philosophy of Language; Philosophy of Mind. **SELECTED PUBLICATIONS** Auth, A Scorekeeping Error, Philosophical Studies, 99; Definite Descriptions: A Reader, Cambridge: Bradford Books, MIT Press, 98. **CONTACT ADDRESS** 666 West End Ave, Apt 18X, New York, NY, 10025. **EMAIL** go2@is6.nyu.edu

OTTATI, DOUGLAS FERNANDO
PERSONAL Born 06/17/1950, Indianapolis, IN, m, 1979 **DISCIPLINE** THEOLOGY **EDUCATION** Univ PA, AB, 72; Univ Chicago, MA, 74, PhD(theol), 80. **CAREER** Instr relig, Concordia Col, MN, 77; instr, 77-81, asst to PROF THEOL AND ETHICS, UNION THEOL SEM, VA, 81-. **HONORS AND AWARDS** Theological Ethics Sem, VA, 89-; Louisville Inst, summer stipend, 93. **MEMBERSHIPS** Union Theol Soc Christian Ethics; Academy of Relig Theol and Ethics. **RESEARCH** Am contemporary theology. **SELECTED PUBLICATIONS** Auth, Meaning and Method in H Richard Niebuhr's Theology, Univ Press Am, 82; Jesus Christ and Christian Vision, Westminster John Knox Press, 95; Reforming Protestantism: Christian Commitment in Today's World. Westminster John Knox Press, 95. **CONTACT ADDRESS** Union Theol Sem, 3401 Brook Rd, Richmond, VA, 23227-4514. **EMAIL** dottati@utsva.edu

OTTESON, JAMES R.
DISCIPLINE PHILOSOPHY **EDUCATION** Univ Chicago, PhD, 97. **CAREER** Asst prof philos, Univ Ala, 97-. **RESEARCH** Modern philosophy; Scottish Enlightenment; political philosophy. **CONTACT ADDRESS** Dept of Philosophy, Tuscaloosa, AL, 35487. **EMAIL** jotteson@tenhoor.as.ua.edu

OTTO, DAVID
PERSONAL Born 06/14/1961, Denver, CO **DISCIPLINE** THEOLOGY **EDUCATION** Centenary Col, BA, 83; Scarritt Grad School, MA, 85; Vandervilt Univ, EdD, 93. **CAREER** Assoc prof, 90-; chm, 96-. **MEMBERSHIPS** Asn of Prof and Res in Relig Educ; Relig Educ Asn. **RESEARCH** Practical theology; Religious education. **CONTACT ADDRESS** Dept of Religion, Centenary Col of Louisiana, PO Box 41188, Shreveport, LA, 71134-1188. **EMAIL** dotto@centenary.edu

OUDERKIRK, WAYNE
PERSONAL Born 01/08/1947, Albany, NY, d, 2 children **DISCIPLINE** PHILOSOPHY **EDUCATION** Univ of Albany (SUNY), PhD, 84. **CAREER** Mentor and Unit Coordinator, Assoc prof, 85- , SUNY Empire State Col. **MEMBERSHIPS** Intl Soc for Environmental Ethics; APA; Adirondack Mountain Club. **RESEARCH** Environmental Ethics and Philosophy; Pragmatism. **SELECTED PUBLICATIONS** Auth, Earthly Thoughts: An Essay on Environmental Philosophy, Choice: Current Reviews for Academic Libraries, 97; auth, Review of Kate Soper, What Is Nature? Culture, Politics and the non-Human, Environmental Ethics, 98; auth, Mindful of the Earth: A Bibliographical Essay on Environment Philosphy, Centennial Review, 98; auth, Review of Val Plumwood, Feminism and the Mystery of Nature, Ethics, Place, and Environment, forthcoming; auth, Can Nature Be Evil? Rolson, Disvalue, and Theodicy, Environment Ethics, forthcoming. **CONTACT ADDRESS** SUNY Empire State Col, Cobelskill, NY, 12043. **EMAIL** wouderkirk@sescua.esc.edu

OUREN, DALLAS
PERSONAL Born 11/13/1940, Pope Co, MN, s **DISCIPLINE** PHILOSOPHY **EDUCATION** Univ Minn, PhD, 73. **CAREER** Lect, Univ Minn, 73-. **MEMBERSHIPS** APA. **RESEARCH** Philosophy, genealogy. **SELECTED PUBLICATIONS** Auth, Mill on Hamilton, Mellon, 92. **CONTACT ADDRESS** PO Box 275, Glenwood, MN, 56334.

OUTKA, GENE HAROLD
PERSONAL Born 02/24/1937, Sioux Falls, SD, m, 3 children **DISCIPLINE** RELIGION **EDUCATION** Univ Redlands, BA, 59; Yale Univ, BD, 62, MA, 64, PhD, 67. **CAREER** From instr to assoc prof relig, Princeton Univ, 65-75; assoc prof, 75-81, Dwight Prof of Philos & Christian Ethics, Yale Univ, 80-; Am Coun Learned Soc fel, Oxford Univ, 68-69; Soc Values Higher Educ cross-disciplinary studies fel; serv fel, Off Spec Proj, Health Serv & Ment Health Admin, US Dept Health, Educ & Welfare, 72-73; vis scholar, Kennedy Ctr Bioethics, Georgetown Univ, 72-73; dir sem for col teachers, NEH, 77-78; fel, Woodrow Wilson Int Center for Scholars, DC, 83; Honorary member of the High Table, Queens' Col, Cambridge, England, 91. **HONORS AND AWARDS** LHD, Univ Redlands, 78. **MEMBERSHIPS** Soc Values Higher Educ; Am Theol Soc; Am Soc Christian Ethics; Am Acad Relig. **RESEARCH** Theological, philosophical, and social ethics. **SELECTED PUBLICATIONS** Co-ed, with Paul Rawley, Normand Context in Christian Ethics, Scribner, 68; co-ed,with John P Reeder, Jr, Religion and Morality, Doubleday Anchor, 73; auth, Care Settings and Values: A Response, In: Ethics of Health Care, Inst Med, Nat Acad Sci, 74; Respite for Hallowing, Reflection, 1/78; Agape: An Ethical Analysis, Yale Univ Press, New Haven & London, 72; Character, Vision, and Narrative, Religious Studies Rev, 4/80; Discontinuity in the Ethics of Jacques Ellul, In: Jacques Ellul: Interpretive Essays, Univ IL Press, 80; On Harming Others, Interpretation, 10/80; Social Justice and Equal Access to Health Care, In: Biomedical Ethics, McGraw-Hill, 81; Universal Love and Impartiality, in The Love Comandments, Georgetown Univ Press, 92; co-ed, with John P Reeder, Jr, Prospects for a Common Morality, Princeton Univ Press, 93. **CONTACT ADDRESS** Dept Relig Studies, Yale Univ, PO Box 208287, New Haven, CT, 06520-8287. **EMAIL** gene.outka@yale.edu

OVERALL, CHRISTINE D.
DISCIPLINE PHILOSOPHY **EDUCATION** Univ Toronto, BA; MA; PhD. **CAREER** Dept Philos, Queen's Univ **RESEARCH** Feminist theory; applied ethics; philosophy of religion; philosophy of education. **SELECTED PUBLICATIONS** Auth, What's Wrong With Prostitution? Evaluating Sex Work, J Women Cult Soc, 92; Human Reproduction: Principles, Practices, Policies, Oxford, 93; Paradox of Free Speech, 93; Reply to Shrage, 94; Frozen Embryos and 'Fathers' Rights': Parenthood and Decision¤Making in the Cryopreservation of Embryos, Univ Ind, 95; Reflections of a Sceptical Bioethicist, Univ Toronto, 96; Feeling Fraudulent: Some Moral Quandaries of a Feminist Instructor, 97; co-ed, Perspectives on AIDS: Ethical and Social Issues, Oxford, 92. **CONTACT ADDRESS** Philosophy Dept, Queen's Univ, Kingston, ON, K7L 3N6. **EMAIL** cdo@post.queensu.ca

OVERBECK, JAMES A.
PERSONAL Born 09/11/1940, Eau Claire, WI, m, 1966, 3 children **DISCIPLINE** ECCLESIASTICAL HISTORY **EDUCATION** Univ of Chicago, MA, PhD, Grad Library Sch, MALS. **CAREER** Librarian, professor. **MEMBERSHIPS** Amer Library Assn, Amer Acad of Religion. **RESEARCH** History of Religious Journalism **SELECTED PUBLICATIONS** Auth, The Rise and Fall of Presbyterian Official Journals 1925-1985, Diversity of Fellowship, Westminister Press, 91. **CONTACT ADDRESS** 517 Ridgecrest Rd, NE, Atlanta, GA, 30307-1845. **EMAIL** Joverbec@ce1.af.public.lib.ga.us

OVERHOLT, THOMAS WILLIAM
PERSONAL Born 08/09/1935, Bucyrus, OH, m, 1957, 2 children **DISCIPLINE** BIBLICAL STUDIES, HISTORY OF RELIGIONS **EDUCATION** Heidelberg Col, BA 57; Chicago Theol Sem, BD, 61; Univ Chicago, MA, 63, PhD, 67. **CAREER** Prof relig studies, Yankton Col, 64-75; assoc prof, 75-80, prof relig studies, Univ Wis-Stevens Point, 80-99. **HONORS AND AWARDS** Soc Values Higher Educ fel anthrop, Univ Ariz, 73-74. **MEMBERSHIPS** Am Acad Relig; Soc Bibl Lit; Soc Values Higher Educ. **RESEARCH** Old Testament; American Indian religions. **SELECTED PUBLICATIONS** Auth, Prophecy in Cross-Cultural Perspective: A Sourcebook for Biblical Researchers, Atlanta: Scholars Press, 86; auth, Jeremiah, Harper's Bible Commentary, San Francisco: Harper and Row, 88; auth, Channels of Prophecy: The Social Dynamics of Prophetic Activity, Minneapolis: Fortress Press, 89; auth, Cultural Anthropology and the Old Testament, Minneapolis: Fortress Press, 96. **CONTACT ADDRESS** Dept of Philosophy, Univ of Wisconsin, Stevens Point, 2100 Main St, Stevens Point, WI, 54481-3897. **EMAIL** toverhol@uwsp.edu

OWEN, DAVID G.
DISCIPLINE TORTS AND PRODUCTS LIABILITY **EDUCATION** Univ PA, BS, 67, JD, 71. **CAREER** Byrnes res scholar & prof, Univ of SC. **RESEARCH** Aviation. **SELECTED PUBLICATIONS** Coauth, a casebk on products liability law, a treatise on tort law; ed, bk on tort law theory; publ on, tort law, products liability & punitive damages. **CONTACT ADDRESS** School of Law, Univ of S. Carolina, Law Center, Columbia, SC, 29208. **EMAIL** Owen@law.law.sc.edu

OWENS, DOROTHY M.
PERSONAL Born 12/02/1943, Atlanta, GA, d, 2 children **DISCIPLINE** THEOLOGY **EDUCATION** Emory Univ, BA,, 66, MDiv, 91; Vanderbilt Univ, MA, 94; PhD, 96. **CAREER** Pastoral psychotherapist, 92-, Pastoral Coun Ctr,TX; res instr, med, 96-, Vanderbilt Univ; parish assoc, 96-, Westminster Presbyterian Church, TN. **HONORS AND AWARDS** Intl Soc of Theta Phi **MEMBERSHIPS** Am Acad on Phys & Patient; AAR; Am Asn of Pastoral Coun; Soc of Pastoral Theol; Amer Coun Asn; Mental Health Asn; Nashville Phsychotherapy Inst; TN Asn of Pastoral Therapists; TN Health Decisions; Am Soc for Bioethics & Hum; Functional Brain-Gut Res Group; Emory Univ Comm on Biomed Ethics, 88-90. **RESEARCH** Interface of relig/psycho/med; quality of life issues; physician/patient relationship **SELECTED PUBLICATIONS** Auth, Hospitality to Strangers: Communicating Empathy in the Physician-Patient Relationship, Scholars Press, 98; coauth, The Irritable Bowel Syndrome: Long term prognosis an th Physician-Patient Interaction, Ann Int Med vol 122, 95; auth, Emotional Stress and the Holiday Season, Peachtree Papers, 80. **CONTACT ADDRESS** 807 Huntington Cir, Nashville, TN, 37215-6112. **EMAIL** dorothy.owens@mcmail.vanderbilt.edu

OWENS, FATHER JOSEPH
PERSONAL Born 04/17/1908, Saint John, NB, Canada **DISCIPLINE** THEOLOGY/PHILOSOPHY **EDUCATION** St Anne's, Que, 28-30; St Alphonsus Sem, Ont, 30-34; Pontif Inst Medieval Stud, Toronto, 44-48, MSD, 51. **CAREER** Parish asst, St Joseph's, Moose Jaw, 34-35; parish asst, St Patrick's, Toronto, 35-36; lectr philos, St Alphonsus Sem, 36-40, 48-51, 53; missionary, Dawson's Creek, BC, 40-44; lectr, Accademia Alfonsiana, Rome, 52-53; vis lectr, Assumption Univ, Windsor, 54; asst prof to assoc prof, 54-61, prof grad stud, 61-77, PROF EMER, UNIV TORONTO. **HONORS AND AWARDS** DLitt(hon), Mt Allison Univ, 75; DHumLitt(hon), Cath Univ, 84; LLD(hon), St Francis Xavier Univ, 88. **MEMBERSHIPS** Metaphysical Soc Am; Am Cath Philos Asn; Can Philos Asn; Soc Ancient Greek Philos; Am Philos Asn. **SELECTED PUBLICATIONS** Auth, St Thomas and the Future of Metaphysics, 57; auth, A History of Ancient Western Philosophy, 59; auth, An Elementary Christian Metaphysics, 63; auth, An Interpretation of Existence, 68; auth, The Doctrine of Being in the Aristotelian Metaphysics, 3rd ed, 78; auth, The Philosophical Tradition of St Michael's College, Toronto, 79; auth, St. Thomas Aquinas on the Existence of God, 80; auth, Human Destiny, 85; auth, Towards a Christian Philosophy, 90; coauth, The Wisdom and Ideas of St Thomas Aquinas, 68. **CONTACT ADDRESS** St. Patrick's Rectory, 141 McCaul St, Toronto, ON, M5T 1W3.

OWENS, JOSEPH
PERSONAL Born 04/17/1908, St. John, NB, Canada **DISCIPLINE** PHILOSOPHY **EDUCATION** Pontif Inst Mediaeval Studies, MSD(philos), 51. **CAREER** From assoc prof to prof, 54-73, Emer Prof Philos, Pontif Inst Mediaeval Studies, 73-, Vis prof, Purdue Univ, 68-69. **HONORS AND AWARDS** Can Philos Asn (pres, 81-82)., DLitt, Mt Allison Univ, NB, 75. **MEMBERSHIPS** Am Cath Philos Asn; Metaphys Soc Am; Royal Soc Can. **RESEARCH** Thomistic metaphysics; Greek philosophy. **SELECTED PUBLICATIONS** Auth, A History of Ancient Western Philosophy, Appleton, 59; The Doctrine of Being in the Aristotelian Metaphysics, Pontif Inst Mediaeval Studies, 2nd ed, 63; An Elementary Christian Metaphysics, 63 & An Interpretation of Existence, 68, Bruce; coauth, The Wisdom and Ideas of St Thomas Aquinas, Fawcett, 68. **CONTACT ADDRESS** 59 Queen's Park, Crescent Toronto, ON, M5S 2C4.

OWENS, JOSEPH
DISCIPLINE PHILOSOPHY **EDUCATION** Univ Calif Los Angeles, PhD. **RESEARCH** Philosophy of the mind; mental state; philosophy of language. **SELECTED PUBLICATIONS** Auth, Pierre and the Fundamental Assumption, Mind Lang, 95; Contradictory Belief and Cognitive Access, Midwest Studies Philos, 89; The Failure of Lewis' Functionalism, Philos Quarterly, 87; In Defense of a Different Doppelganger, Philos Rev, 87; Synonymy and the Non-Individualistic Model of the Mental, Synthese, 86; Functionalism and Propositional Attitudes, 83; ed, Propositional Attitudes: The Role of Content in Logic, Lang Mind, 90. **CONTACT ADDRESS** Philosophy Dept, Univ of Minnesota, Twin Cities, 355 Ford Hall, 224 Church St SE, Minneapolis, MN, 55455. **EMAIL** owens002@tc.umn.edu

OWENS, KATHLEEN MARIE
PERSONAL Born 05/05/1948, Detroit, MI **DISCIPLINE** PHILOSOPHY **EDUCATION** Ohio State Univ, BA, 70; Univ Pittsburgh, MA, 71; PhD, 77. **CAREER** Instr, Southern Ill Univ, 75-76; asst, assoc prof, Canisius Coll, Buffalo, NY, 77-. **HONORS AND AWARDS** Tenure: Canisius Coll Philo Dept, 82. **MEMBERSHIPS** Am Philos Asn; Am Asoc of Univ Prof. **RESEARCH** Epistemology; Philosophy of Social Sciences; Informal Logic; Feminism. **CONTACT ADDRESS** Ellicott Sta, PO Box 305, Buffalo, NY, 14205-0305.

OWENS, RICHARD C.
DISCIPLINE LAW **EDUCATION** McGill Univ, BA, 77; Univ Toronto, LLB, 87. **CAREER** Partner, Smith Lyons, Barristers and Solicitors **MEMBERSHIPS** Int Bar Asn; Comput Law Asn; Toronto Comput Lawyers Group. **SELECTED PUBLICATIONS** Auth, pubs on provision of on-line services, electronic data interchange, opinions in copyright matters, and law and the Internet. **CONTACT ADDRESS** Fac of Law, Univ Toronto, 78 Queen's Park, Toronto, ON.

OZAR, DAVID T.
DISCIPLINE PHILOSOPHY **EDUCATION** Loyola Uniov, BA, MA; Yale Univ, PhD. **CAREER** Prof & dir, Center for Ethics; fac, Loyola Univ, 72-; co-dir, Grad Stud in Health Care Ethics, dept Philos at Loyola Univ Chicago; adj prof, Med Humanities in Loyola's Stritch Sch of Med; actg dir, Medical Humanities at Loyola, 84; lectr, Loyola's sch of law, dent, nursing, & soc work; initiated & tchg, Loyola Philos Dept's undergrad course in health care ethics,75; 7 yrs dir & designer now co-dir, Philos Dept's Grad Prog in Health Care Ethics; assoc member, Professional Staff & assoc dir, Medical Ethics Program; member, Instnl Ethics Comt; consult ethicist, Evanston Hospital, Ill; served on, Res Rev Comt, Chicago Dept of Health, 86-93; consult ethicist, Palliative Care Center of the North Shore; member, Ethics Bd of the Ill Dept of Children and Family Services; dir, Soc for Health and Human Values & Am Philos Asn. **HONORS AND AWARDS** Founder & first pres, Prof Ethics in Dent Network. **RESEARCH** Health care ethics; professional ethics; metaethics; normative ethics; history of ethics; soc contract theory; soc-Polit philosophy; philosophy of law. **SELECTED PUBLICATIONS** coauth, Dental Ethics at Chairside: Professional Principles and Practical Applications, Mosby-Yearbk, 94; co-ed, Philosophical Issues in Human Rights: Theories and Applications, Random House, 85. **CONTACT ADDRESS** Dept of Philosophy, Loyola Univ, Chicago, 820 N. Michigan Ave., Chicago, IL, 60611.

P

PACHOW, WANG
PERSONAL Born 06/01/1918, Chungking, China, m, 1956, 1 child **DISCIPLINE** ASIAN CIVILIZATION, BUDDHIST STUDIES **EDUCATION** Mengtsang Col, BA, 36; Visva-Bharati Univ, MA, 42; Univ Bombay, PhD(Buddhist studies), 48. **CAREER** Lectr Chinese, Visva-Bharati Univ, 41-47; lect & head dept, Univ Allahabad, 47-53; sr lectr Buddhist & Chinese studies, Univ Ceylon, 54-65, reader Pali & Buddhist civilization, 66-68; assoc prof world relig, 68-75, Prof World Relig, Sch Relig, Univ Iowa, 75-, Res fel, Yale Univ, 61; Acad Hospitality Award, Univ London, 61-62; vis prof, Visva-Bharati Univ, 62; hon consult for the Humanities, Washington, 77; external examr, Univ Delhi, India, 78- **MEMBERSHIPS** Am Acad Relig; Am Orient Soc; Asn Asian Studies; Maha-Bodhi Soc; Soc Study Chinese Relig. **RESEARCH** Chinese thought and literature; Sino-India culture. **SELECTED PUBLICATIONS** Auth, A Comparative Study of Pratimoksa, On the Basis of Its Chinese, Tibetan, Sanskrit and Pali Versions, Comp Sino- Indian Cult Soc, 55; A study of the Dotted Record, J Am Orient Soc, 7-965; Tripitaka, Encycl Britannica, 68; Gautama Buddha: Man or superman?, In: Malalasekera Commemoration Volume, Colombo, Ceylon, 76; The controversy over the immortality of the soul in Chinese Buddhism, J Orient Studies, Univ Hong Kong, 1278; A Study of the Twenty-Two Dialogues on Mahayana Buddhism, The Chinese Culture, 79; Chinese Buddhism: Aspects of Interaction and Reinterpretation, Univ Am Press, 80; Arahant, Bhavacakra, Paticcasamuppada, In: Abingdon Dict of Living Religions, 81; Tan,yun-shan And Cultural-relations Between China And India, Indian Horizons, Vol 0043, 1994; Tan,yun-shan And Cultural-relations Between China And India, Indian Horizons, Vol 0043, 1994. **CONTACT ADDRESS** Sch of Relig, Univ of Iowa, Iowa City, IA, 52242.

PACIOCCO, DAVID
DISCIPLINE LAW **EDUCATION** Univ Western Ontario, LLB. **CAREER** Prof. **RESEARCH** Criminal law; evidence; law of trusts. **SELECTED PUBLICATIONS** Auth, Charter Principle and Proof in Criminal Cases, 87; Getting Away with Murder: The Canadian Criminal Justice System, 98; pubs on law of evidence, criminal law, Charter and law of trusts; coauth, The Law of Evidence, Univ Manitoba, 95; Jury Selection in Criminal Cases: Skills, Science and the Law, 97. **CONTACT ADDRESS** Fac Common Law, Univ Ottawa, 550 Cumberland St, PO Box 450, Ottawa, ON, K1N 6N5.

PACKEL, LEONARD
DISCIPLINE CRIMINAL LAW **EDUCATION** Univ Pa, BS, 57; Harvard Law Sch, JD, 60. **CAREER** Prof; Villanova Univ, 73-. **RESEARCH** Evidence, trial pract. **SELECTED PUBLICATIONS** Coauth, Pennsylvania Evidence, 95; Trial Advocacy: A Systematic Approach, 84 & Trial Practice For The General Practitioner, 80. **CONTACT ADDRESS** Law School, Villanova Univ, 800 Lancaster Ave, Villanova, PA, 19085-1692. **EMAIL** packel@law.vill.edu

PACWA, MITCH
DISCIPLINE SCRIPTURE, SPIRITUALITY **EDUCATION** Vanderbilt Univ, PhD. **CAREER** Prof, Dallas Univ; Entered Soc of Jesus, 68; ordained, 76. **SELECTED PUBLICATIONS** Auth, Catholics and the New Age, 92; Father Forgive Me, For I Am Frustrated, 97. **CONTACT ADDRESS** Instit for Religious and Pastoral Studies, Univ of Dallas, 1845 E Northgate Dr, Irving, TX, 75062. **EMAIL** mdean@acad.udallas.edu

PADGETT, ALAN G.
PERSONAL Born 09/23/1955, Washington, DC, m, 1977, 1 child **DISCIPLINE** THEOLOGY & PHILOSOPHY **EDUCATION** S CA Col, BA, 77; Drew Univ, MDiv, 81; Oxford Univ, Dphil, 90 **CAREER** Asst Prof, Bethel Col; Prof, Azusa Pac Univ **HONORS AND AWARDS** John Wesley Scholar; Christian Theolog Res Fel **MEMBERSHIPS** AAR, SBL, Am Philos Assoc; Philos of Sci Assoc **RESEARCH** Christian philosophy; systemmatic Theology; Philosophy of Science **SELECTED PUBLICATIONS** Auth, God, Eternity and the Nature of Time, MacMillan, 92; Coauth, Christianity and Western Thought, Intervarsity Press, 99 **CONTACT ADDRESS** Dept of Relig & Philos, Azusa Pacific Univ, PO Box 7000, Azusa, CA, 91702-7000. **EMAIL** padgett@apu.edu

PADILLA, ALVIN
PERSONAL Born 03/11/1954, Ponce, PR, m, 1983, 4 children **DISCIPLINE** NEW TESTAMENT **EDUCATION** Drew Univ, PhD, 96. **CAREER** ACADEMIC DEAN, GORDON-CONWELL THEOL SEM, BOSTON. **MEMBERSHIPS** AAP/SBL. **CONTACT ADDRESS** Gordon-Conwell Theol Sem, 130 Essex St., South Hamilton, MA, 01982. **EMAIL** apadilla@gcts.edu

PADOVANO, ANTHONY T.
PERSONAL Born 09/18/1934, Harrison, NJ **DISCIPLINE** THEOLOGY, LITERATURE **EDUCATION** Seton Hall Univ, AB, 56; Gregorian Univ, STD(theol), 62; Pontiff Univ St Thomas Aquinas, PhL, 62; NY Univ, MA, 71; Fordham Univ, PhD, 80. **CAREER** Prof syst theol, Darlington Sem, 62-74; Prof AM Lit & Relig Studies, Ramapo Col, 71-, Consultor, Nat Cath Off Radio & TV, 67; vis prof, Villanova Univ, 68, St Mary's Col, Ind, 69, Univ St Thomas, 69, Univ Wyo, 70, Barry Col, Fla, 71, Seattle Univ, 72, Fordham Univ, 73, Univ San Francisco, 73, Boston Col, 73, Assumption Col, Worcester, Mass 73 & Georgetown Univ, Washington, DC, 73; prof, Ramapo Col, NJ, 71-; rep US dialogue group, Lutheran-Roman Cath Theol Conversations, 70-72. **HONORS AND AWARDS** Nat Cath Press Asn Bk Award, 70. **MEMBERSHIPS** Cath Theol Soc Am. **RESEARCH** Systematic theology; American literature; contemporary philosophy. **SELECTED PUBLICATIONS** Auth, Dawn Without Darkness, 71, Free to be Faithful, 72 & Eden & Easter, 74, Paulist Press; A Case for Worship, Silver Burdett, 75; America, Its People, Its Promise, St Anthony Messenger Press, 75; Presence and Structure, Paulist Press, 75; The Human Journey, 82 & Trilogy, 82, Doubleday; Ace of Freedoms - Merton,thomas Christ - Kilcourse,g, Horizons, Vol 0021, 1994. **CONTACT ADDRESS** 9 Millstone Dr, Morris Plains, NJ, 07950.

PAFFENROTH, KIM
PERSONAL Born 03/07/1966, Manhasset, NY, m, 1986, 2 children **DISCIPLINE** THEOLOGY **EDUCATION** St John's Col, BA, 88; Harvard Divinity Sch, MTS, 90; Univ of Notre Dame, PhD, 95. **CAREER** Instr, 93, Southwestern Michigan Col; tutor, 93-95, teaching fel, 94-95, adjunct asst prof, 95-96, visiting asst prof, 96-97, Univ of Notre Dame; teaching fel, 97-99, Villanova Univ. **HONORS AND AWARDS** St. John's Col Mathematics Prize, 85 and 88; NEH Summer Seminar Participant, Yale Univ, 96; Salvatori Fel, The Heritage Found, 97; Arthur Ennis Fel, Villanova Univ, 97-99; Research Fel, The Acton Institute, 98. **MEMBERSHIPS** Soc of Biblical Literature; Amer Acad of Relig; Catholic Biblical Assn of Amer; North Amer Patristic Soc **SELECTED PUBLICATIONS** Auth, The Story of Jesus according to L, Journal for the Study of the New Testament Supplement Series 147. Sheffield: Sheffield Academic Press, 97; auth, Tears of Grief and Joy, Confessions, Book 9: Chronological Sequence and Structure, Augustinian Studies, 97; auth, The Testing of the Sage: 1 Kings 10:1-13 and Q 4:1-13, The Expository Times, 96. **CONTACT ADDRESS** Villanova, Villanova, PA, 19085. **EMAIL** kpaffenr@email.vill.edu

PAGAN, CARMEN J.
PERSONAL San Juan, PR **DISCIPLINE** PHILOSOPHY **EDUCATION** Columbia Univ, Ed.D, 95. **CAREER** Prof, Evangel Sem PR, 93; prof, Inter Am Univ PR, 94-; prof, Pentecostal Inst PR, 95-; pastor, Baptist Churches PR, 98-. **MEMBERSHIPS** NAPCE, REA, APRRE, CELADEC, FTL, AETH. **RESEARCH** Social sciences of education; theological education. **SELECTED PUBLICATIONS** Coauth, Faith in Seeking of Understanding. **CONTACT ADDRESS** Dept of Religious Education, Inter American Univ of Puerto Rico, Ext Villa Rica, Bayamon, PR, 00959. **EMAIL** cjpagan@inter.edu

PAGAN, SAMUEL
PERSONAL Born 07/29/1950, San Juan, PR, m, 1973, 2 children **DISCIPLINE** HEBREW LITERATURE; HEBREW BIBLE **EDUCATION** The Jewish Theol Sem, Doctor in Hebrew Lit, 88. **CAREER** Regional coordinator, Translation of the Bible Dept, United Bible Societies, 85-95; PRES, EVANGELICAL SEM OF PUERTO RICO, 95-. **RESEARCH** Translation of the Bible and sociological exegesis. **SELECTED PUBLICATIONS** Auth, Ester, Nehemias Ester, Miami: Editorial caribe, 93; Palama viva, Miami: Editorial Caribe, 96; Obadiah, NIB, Nashville: Alsing Conn Press, 97; Isaias, Miami: Editorial Caribe, 97; Yose quien soy, San Juan: Pulsicaciones Puertorri guertas, 97; Ester, Dallas: Univ Dallas, 99. **CONTACT ADDRESS** 776 Ponce de Leon, San Juan, PR, 00925. **EMAIL** drspagan@icepr.com

PAGE, BENJAMIN BAKEWELL
PERSONAL Born 06/16/1939, Pittsburgh, PA, m, 1965, 4 children **DISCIPLINE** PHILOSOPHY, HEALTH PLANNING **EDUCATION** Harvard Univ, BA, 62; Fla State Univ, MA, 69, PhD, 70, MS, 72. **CAREER** Teacher English, Col St Pierre, Haiti, 60-61; internship, Tenn Off Comprehensive Health Planning, Nashville, 71; asst prof health planning & ethics, Meharry Med Col, 71-72; asst prof, 72-80, ASSOC PROF PHILOS & HEALTH SERV, QUINNIPIAC COL, 80-; Dir, Sleeping Giant Health Group Study Proj, Conn, 73-74; Int Res & Exchange Bd fel, Inst Philos & Sociol, Czech Acad Soc Sci, 75-76; secy, Quinnipiac fac fed, 76-80; hon vis fac mem, Univ Manchester, England, 80-81. **MEMBERSHIPS** Am Philos Asn; Christians Asn Rel East Europe; Am-Korean Friendship & Info Ctr; Inst Soc, Ethics & Life Sci; Soc Health & Human Values. **RESEARCH** Socialism and technological civilization; ethics in biomedical research and health care delivery; philosophy of health healing and medicine. **SELECTED PUBLICATIONS** Transl, Thoughts of a Czech Pastor, SCM Press, 71; auth, The Czechoslovak Reform Movement, 1963-68; A Study in the Theory of Socialism, Gruner, 73; Who owns the professions, Hastings Ctr Report, 10/76; Scientific medicine and health: The case for a reappraisal, World Outlook, summer 77; Biomedical ethics in East Europe, in Encycl Biocthics, 78; ed & auth, Marxism & Spirituality: An International Anthology, Bergin & Garvey, 93; Four Summers: A Czech Kaliedoscope, IREX Res papers, 93; Conversations with Bondy, in Monthly Rev; Tiger Still at the Gates, or The Cold War Is Not Yet Over, in Rethinking Marxism. **CONTACT ADDRESS** Dept of Fine Arts Lang & Philos, Quinnipiac Col, 275 Mt Carmel Ave, Hamden, CT, 06518-1908. **EMAIL** page@quinnipiac.edu

PAGE, JEAN-GUY
PERSONAL Born 01/17/1926, Montreal, PQ, Canada **DISCIPLINE** ECCLESIOLOGY, PASTORAL THEOLOGY **EDUCATION** Laval Univ, BA, 48; Inst Int Lumen Vitae, Brussels, dipl, 65; Pontif Gregorian Univ, Doct, 67. **CAREER** Asst priest pastoral care, N D du Chemin Parish, 52-55; chaplain, Montcalm Sch, Que, 56-59; moral adv, Young Students Cath Action, 59-63; Prof Theol, Laval Univ, 67-, Mem, Pastoral Coun, 68-74; super pastoral care, Major Sem of Diocese of Que, 69-72; mem, Presbyteral Council, Diocese of Que, 69-73. **MEMBERSHIPS** Can Corp for Studies Refig; Soc Can Theol. **RESEARCH** Church Dogmatic; ecclesiastical ministries; pastoral theology in general, as a science. **SELECTED PUBLICATIONS** Auth, Qui est l'Eglise? Vol III--Le Peuple de Dieu, 79 & Une Eglise sans laics?, 80, Bellarmin; L'appropriation, Jeu de l'esprit ou realisme?, Vol 33, No 3 & Dieu et l'Etre, Vol 37, No 1, Laval theol et philos; La theologie du laicat de 1945 a 1962, Vol 4, No 2, L'Eglise, Corps du Christ, Vol V, No 6, L'eveque, l'Eglise Particuliere et l'Eucharistie, Vol VI, No 1 & L'hommed Dieu, Vol VI, No 6, Rev Cath int Communio; God in Action - Apostolic Mysticism According to Teresa-of-avila - French - Wilhelem,fr, Laval Theologique et Philosophique, Vol 0053, 1997. **CONTACT ADDRESS** Dept of Theol, Laval Univ, Tour des Arts, Ste-Foy, PQ, G1K 7P4.

PAGE, JOSEPH ANTHONY
PERSONAL Born 04/13/1934, Boston, MA **DISCIPLINE** LAW **EDUCATION** Harvard Univ, AB, 55, LLB, 58, LLM, 64. **CAREER** From asst prof to assoc prof law, Lat Ctr, Univ Denver, 64-68; assoc prof, 68-73, Prof Law, Law Ctr, Georgetown Univ, 73, Chmn, Torts Round Table Coun, Am Asn Law Schs, 68-69; mem, Adverse Drug Effect Study Adv Panel. Off Technol Assessment, US Cong, 76; dir, Pub Citizen, Inc, 77-; dir, Nat Comt Citizen Broadcasting, 81-; Dir, Am Mus Tort Law, 98-. **RESEARCH** Tort law; government regulation of food, drugs, cosmetics, automobiles and household products. **SELECTED PUBLICATIONS** Auth, State law and the damages remedy under the Civil Rights Act, Denver Law J, fall 66; coauth, Automobile design and the judicial process, Calif Law Rev, 8/67; auth, Of mace and men: Tort law as a means of controlling domestic chemical warfare, Georgetown Law J, 6/69; The Revolution That Never Was: Northeast Brazil, 1955-1964, 72 & coauth, Bitter Wages: The Nader Report on Disease and Injury on the Job, 73, Grossman; Occupational health and the Federal Government, Law & Contemp Problems, summer-autumn 74; auth, Law of Premises Liability, Anderson, 76; coauth, Behind the looking glass: Administrative, legislative and private approaches to cosmetics safety substantiation, Univ Calif, Los Angeles Law Rev, 4/77; auth, Peron: A Biography, Random House, 83; auth, The Brazilians, Addison-Wesley, 95; co-auth, Automobile-Design Liability and Compliance with Federal Standards, George Wash Law Rev, 3/96; auth, Liability for Unreasonably and Unavoidably Unsafe Products: Does Negligence Doctrine Have a Role to Play? Chi-Kent Law Rev, 96; auth, Federal Regulation of Tobacco Products and Products that Treat Tobacco Dependence: Are the Playing Fields Level? Food & Drug Law J, Supp 98. **CONTACT ADDRESS** Law Ctr, Georgetown Univ, 600 New Jersey NW, Washington, DC, 20001-2075. **EMAIL** page@law.georgetown.edu

PAGE, PATRICIA
PERSONAL Born 11/11/1923, Melrose, MA **DISCIPLINE** SOCIOLOGY; RELIGIOUS EDUCATION **EDUCATION** Smith Coll, AB 45; Harvard Graduate School of Education, EdM, 74; NY Univ, PhD, 86 **CAREER** Dir of Christian Education Episcopal Church Parish in North Carolina and Maine 46-55; Chaplin, Episcopal Church Lay Coll, 55-63; Advisor in Christian Diocess of Zamia, 63-73; Dir, Natl Inst Lay Training New York, 75-80; Prof Educ and Dir of continuing educ, Church Divinity Sch of the Principle, 80-89; Church Divinity Sch of the Pacific, 89- **MEMBERSHIPS** Assoc of Profs and Researchers in Religious Educ; Network of Lay Profs of the Episopal Church; Ministry in Daily Life **RESEARCH** Adult Religions Educ; History of Episcopal Church Women; Theology and practice of ministry. **SELECTED PUBLICATIONS** All God's People Are Ministers, Augsburg Press, 93. **CONTACT ADDRESS** 715 Shepherd St., Durham, NC, 27701. **EMAIL** papage@juno.com

PAGE, SYDNEY
PERSONAL Born 11/27/1944, London, ON, Canada, m, 1968, 2 children **DISCIPLINE** NEW TESTAMENT **CAREER** Asst Prof, New Testament, 77-79, Assoc Prof, 79-80, N Amer Baptist Coll; Assoc Prof, 80-86, Prof, 86-, Acad Vice Pres, 81-, New Testament, Edmonton Baptist Seminary. **MEMBERSHIPS** Soc of Biblical Lit; Canadian Soc of Biblical Studies; Inst for Biblical Res; Evangelical Theol Soc; Canadian Evangelical Theol Assoc. **RESEARCH** Biblical Demonology. **SELECTED PUBLICATIONS** Auth, Powers of Evil: A Biblical Study of Satan and Demons, Grand Rapids, Baker, 95; Marital Expectations of Church Leaders in the Pastoral Epistles, J Study of the New Testament, 93; review, Dictionary of the New Testament, by X Leon-Defour, in: Westminster Theo J; Reading the Corinthian Correspondence, by K Quast, in: Christian Week, 95; Worship: Then and Now, Baptist Herald, 89. **CONTACT ADDRESS** Edmonton Baptist Sem, 11525 23 Ave, Edmonton, AB, T6J 4T3. **EMAIL** spage@nabcebs.ab.ca

PAGEL, ULRICH
PERSONAL Born 06/02/1963, Bonn, Germany, 1 child **DISCIPLINE** BUDDHIST STUDIES **EDUCATION** SOAS-London, BA, 88, PhD, 92. **CAREER** Curator Tibetan Collection, 93-97, British Library; Asst Prof, 97-, Univ of Washington. **MEMBERSHIPS** PTS, AOS, IABS, Royal Asiatic Society. **RESEARCH** Mahayana Buddhism **SELECTED PUBLICATIONS** Auth, The Bodhisattvapitaka, Its Doctrines, Practices and their Postion in Mahayana Literature, The Institute of Buddhist Stud, Tring, 95; co-auth, The Buddhist Forum III, School of Oriental & African Stud, 94; co-auth, Location List of the Shel dkar, London, Manuscript Kanur, The British Library, London, 96; auth, The Bodhisattvapitaka and Aksayamatinirdesa, Continuity and Change in Buddhist Sutras, in: The Buddhist Forum, School of Oriental and African Stud, 94; Buddhist Scriptures, Themes in Religious Studies, Cambridge, 94. **CONTACT ADDRESS** Dept of Asian Lang and Lit, Univ of Wash, Box 353521, Seattle, WA, 98195-3521. **EMAIL** pagel@u.washington.edu

PAINCHAUD, LOUIS
PERSONAL Born 03/10/1950, Quebec, PQ, Canada, m, 1975, 4 children **DISCIPLINE** THEOLOGY **EDUCATION** Laval Univ, PhD, 79. **CAREER** Prof, Ste-Foy Coll, 77-; Assoc Prof, Laval Univ, 88-. **MEMBERSHIPS** Canadian Soc of Patriotic Studies; Societe quebecoise l'eterde de la religion; Intl Assoc for Coptic Studies; Assoc internationale de esterdes patristiques; SBL. **RESEARCH** Early Christianity **SELECTED PUBLICATIONS** Auth, The Literary Contacts Between the Writing Without Title, On the Origin of the World and Eugnostos the Blessed, 95; The Use of Scripture in Gnostic Literature, Journal of Early Christian Studies 4, 96; coauth, The Kingless Generation and the Polemical Rewriting of Certain Nag Hammadi Texts, The Nag Hammadi Library after 50 Years: Papers from the 1995 Society of Biblical Literature Commemoration of the 50th Anniversary of the Discovery of the Nag Hammadi Library, 97. **CONTACT ADDRESS** Faculte De Theology, Cite Universitaire, Sainte-Foy, PQ, G1K 7P4. **EMAIL** louis.painchaud@ftsr.ulaval.ca

PAINTER, MARK A.
PERSONAL Born 02/11/1959, Huntsville, TX, m, 1984, 2 children **DISCIPLINE** PHILOSOPHY **EDUCATION** Evergreen State College, BA, 81; Univ N Texas, MA, 88; Univ Missouri, PhD, 93. **CAREER** Asst Prof, 93-, College Misericordia PA. **MEMBERSHIPS** APA; SWPS; HAS; EPPA. **RESEARCH** Ethics; History of Philosophy; Kant; Hegel. **SELECTED PUBLICATIONS** Auth, The Depravity of Wisdom: The Protestant Reformation and the Disengagement of Knowl-

edge from Virtue in Modern Philosophy, Ashgate Pub, 98; The Profane Became Sacred: The Protestant Ethics of Kant and Sarte, Southwest Philo Rev, 99; Language and Moral Justification in Pre-Reformation Philosophy, J of Philo Res, 98; Phaedo 99d-101d: Gadamer's and Socrates Second Way, SW Philo Rev, 98; Virtue Depravity and Another Disquieting Suggestion About Contemporary Moral Reasoning, SW Philo Rev, 96; The Loss of Practical Reason and Some Consequences for the Idea of Post-Modernism, SW Philo Rev, 97. **CONTACT ADDRESS** Dept of Philosophy, Col Misericordia, 301 Lake St, Dallas, PA, 18612. **EMAIL** mpainter@miseri.edu

PAINTER, RICHARD W.
PERSONAL Born 10/03/1961, Philadelphia, PA, m, 1987 **DISCIPLINE** LAW **EDUCATION** Harvard Univ, BA, 84; Yale, JD, 87. **CAREER** Vis prof, Cornell Univ; Vis prof, Boston Univ; assoc prof, Univ Ore, 93-97; assoc prof, Univ Ill, 98-. **HONORS AND AWARDS** Phi Beta Kappa. **RESEARCH** Legal Ethics; Security Regulation. **SELECTED PUBLICATIONS** Auth, The Moral Interdependence of Corporate Lawyers and Their Clients, Southern Calif Law Rev, 94;Toward A Market for Lawyer Disclosure Services: In Search of Optimal Whistleblowing Rules, George Washington Law Rev, 95; Litigating on a Contingency: A Monopoly of Champions or a Market for Champerty?, Chicago Kent Law Rev, 95; Game Theoretic and Contractarian Paradigms in the Uneasy Relationship Between Regulators and Regulatory Lawyers, Fordham Law Rev, 96; Proposal to Amend Model Rule 1.13, The Professional Lawyer, 98; rev, Open Chambers?, Michigan Law Rev, forthcoming; Sounding a False Alarm: The Congressional Initiative to Preempt State Securities Fraud Causes of Action, Cornell Law Rev, forthcoming and other numerous articles on law. **CONTACT ADDRESS** Univ of Ill Col of Law, 504 E Pennsylvania Ave, Champaign, IL, 61820.

PALECZNY, BARBARA
PERSONAL Hamilton, ON, Canada **DISCIPLINE** THEOLOGY **EDUCATION** St Jerome's Univ, BA, 71; Univ Windsor, MA, 72; Regis Col, MDiv, Bach Sacred Theol, Lic, Sacred Theol, 89, MA, 89, PhD, 94. **MEMBERSHIPS** AAR; Can Assn for Res in Home Econ; Can Soc for the Stud of Practical Ethics; Can Soc for the Stud of Relig; Can Res Inst for the Advan of Women; Can Theol Soc; Can Women's Stud Assn; Catholic Theol Soc of Amer; Col Theol Soc; Soc for Intl Devel; Soc of Bibl Lit. **RESEARCH** Religion & socio-economic transformation; eco-feminist advan in econ & ecology; new spiritual sensitivities; cultural transformation; cross-cultural communication, images, symbols, religious practice; Democratization of knowledge, social movements and faith communities; Eucharistic living & celebrating, linked with ecology, inclusive communities, economics. **SELECTED PUBLICATIONS** Coauth, Becoming Followers of Jesus, Burlington, Trinity Press, 83; coauth, From the Double Day to the Endless Day, Can Ctr for Policy Altern, 94; coauth, Justice-seeking-Faith, Jesuit Ctr for Soc Faith & Justice, 96; auth, Teaching Ethical Foundations in a Postmodern Era: Context, Meaning and Applications, Proceed of Laurier Conf on Bus & Prof Ethics, Wilfrid Laurier Univ, ON, 98; art, Systemic Wealth and Debt Accumulation and Jubilee 2000, Prof Ethics J, 98; art, Waves of Globalization and the New Millennium, Univ Incarnate Word, San Antonio TX, 98. **CONTACT ADDRESS** Univ of the Incarnate Word, 4301 Broadway, AD 255, San Antonio, TX, 78209. **EMAIL** paleczny@universe.uiwtx.edu

PALLARD, HENRI
DISCIPLINE LAW **EDUCATION** Univ Alberta, BA, 72; Univ Ottawa, BA, 75, MA, 76; McGill Univ, LLB, 84. **CAREER** Prof. **RESEARCH** Philos of law; legal theory. **CONTACT ADDRESS** Law and Justice Dept, Laurentian Univ, 935 Ramsey Lake Rd, Sudbury, ON, P3E 2C6.

PALM, CRAIG W.
DISCIPLINE BUSINESS TORTS, CONTRACTS, CORPORATIONS **EDUCATION** Univ Vermont, BA, 78; Cornell Law Sch, JD, 81. **CAREER** Prof, Villanova Univ, 87-; coordr, Villanova Law Sch Minority Stud Orientation Prog, 94-; fac, Villanova Univ Grade Sch Educ. **MEMBERSHIPS** Order of the Coif; Colorado and the ABA Litigation, Bus Law, Criminal Justice & Alternative Dispute Resolution sect. **RESEARCH** Corporations and securities. **SELECTED PUBLICATIONS** Coauth, The Informative Process in Medical Care: Preliminary Multivariate Analysis for the Nat Center for Health servs Research; publ on, corporate, securities and constitutional law, in Cornell Law Rev, Pittsburgh Law Rev & Villanova Law Rev. **CONTACT ADDRESS** Law School, Villanova Univ, 800 Lancaster Ave, Villanova, PA, 19085-1692. **EMAIL** palm@law.vill.edu

PALMER, LARRY ISAAC
PERSONAL Born 06/18/1944, St. Louis, MO, m, 1976, 3 children **DISCIPLINE** LAW **EDUCATION** Harvard Univ, AB, 66; Yale Univ, LLB, 69. **CAREER** Asst prof, Rutgers Univ, Camden, 70-73; from Assoc Prof to Assoc Prof, 73-79, Prof Law, Cornell Univ, 79-, Vice-Provost, 79-84, Vice-Pres, 87-94; Consult, Ctr Rape Concern, Philadelphia, 73-75 & Nat Inst Educ, 79-81; vis prof law, Univ Va, 79; Vis Fel, Cambridge Univ, 84-85. **MEMBERSHIPS** Am Law Inst. **RESEARCH** Law and medicine; health policy; legislation. **SELECTED PUBLICATIONS** Auth, Ethical and Legal Implications of Diabetes Self-Management, Practical Diabetology 8, 89; Law, Medicine, and Social Justice, Westminster/John Knox Press, 89; Who Are the Parents of Biotechnological Children?, Jurimetrics 35, Fall 94; Paying for Suffering: The Problem of Human Experimentation, Md Law Rev 56, 97; In Vitro Fertilization as a Social Experiment, Human Reproduction 12, 97; Institutional Analysis and Physicians' Rights after Vacco v Quill, Cornell J Law and Public Policy 7, 98. **CONTACT ADDRESS** Law Sch, Cornell Univ, Myron Taylor Hall, Ithaca, NY, 14853-4901. **EMAIL** lip1@cornell.edu

PALMER, RICHARD E.
PERSONAL Born 11/06/1933, Phoenix, AZ, m, 1956, 3 children **DISCIPLINE** PHILOSOPHY & RELIGION **EDUCATION** Univ Redlands, BA, 55, MA, 56, PhD, 59. **CAREER** Asst prof humanities, 59-64, assoc prof humanities & world lit, 64-69, dir humanities core lit prog, 65-76, prof humanities & world lit, 69-71, prof philos & lit, 72-80, CHMN DEPT PHILOS & RELIG, MACMURRAY COL, 80-. **HONORS AND AWARDS** Am Coun Learned Soc fel, 64-65; NEH younger humanist fel philos, Univ Heidelberg, 71-72, and grant, summer 78; Fulbright res grants, Germany, 91-92, 95-96; Awards for excellence in teaching, 89, 92; Jospeh R Harker Prof Philos, 93. **MEMBERSHIPS** Am Philos Asn; Soc Phenomenol & Existential Philos; Heidegger Conf Scholars; Intl Asn Philos & Lit. **RESEARCH** Philosophical hermeneutics, existentialism and phenomenology. **SELECTED PUBLICATIONS** Auth, Hermeneutics: Interpretation Theory in Schleiermacher, Dilthey, Heidegger, and Gadamer, Northwestern Univ, 69; Husserl's Brittanica article: A retranslation, J Brit Soc Phenomenol, 5/71; Toward a postmodern interpretive self-awareness, J Relig, 7/75; The postmodernity of Heidegger, winter 76 & Postmodernity and hermeneutics, winter 77, Boundary 2; contribr, Toward a postmodern hermeneutics of performance, in Performance in Postmodern Culture, Coda, 78; Allegorical, philological, and philosophical hermeneutics, Univ Ottawa Quart, 5/81; contribr, Hermeneutics 1966-78 - Review of research, in Vol 2, Contemporary Philosophy: A New Survey, Nijhoff, 82; co-ed & co-transl, Dialogue and Deconstruction: The Gadamer-Derrida Debate, SUNY, 89; co-transl, Edmund Husserl, Psychological and Transcendental Phenomenology and the Confrontation with Heidegger (1927-1931), Kluwer Acad Publ, 97; Husserl's debate with Heidegger in the margins of Kant and the Problem with Metaphysics, Man and World, 4/97; contrib, Two Late Essays of Gadamer, in The Philosophy of Hans-Georg Gadamer, Open Court Press, 97; transl, Reflections on a Philosophical Journey, and compiled bibliography. **CONTACT ADDRESS** Dept of Philos & Relig, MacMurray Col, 477 E College Ave, Jacksonville, IL, 62650-2590. **EMAIL** rpalmer@highlanders.mac.edu

PALMER, RUSS
PERSONAL Detroit, MI **DISCIPLINE** BIBLICAL STUDIES, THE HISTORY OF CHRISTIAN THOUGHT, AND CHRISTIAN ETHICS **EDUCATION** Wayne State Univ, BA; Dallas Theol Sem, MA; Univ Iowa, PhD. **CAREER** Instr, Univ Nebr, Omaha, 65-; ed, Karl Barth Soc Newsl. **MEMBERSHIPS** Exec bd, Karl Barth Soc of N Am; steering comt, Reformed Theol and Hist Consultation, Am Acad of Relig. **SELECTED PUBLICATIONS** Auth, Introduction to World Religions Study Guide, Kendall-Hunt Publ. **CONTACT ADDRESS** Univ Nebr, Omaha, Omaha, NE, 68182.

PALMER, RUSSELL W
PERSONAL Born 05/04/1936, Detroit, MI, m, 1960, 2 children **DISCIPLINE** RELIGION **EDUCATION** Wayne State Univ, BA, 57; Dallas Theol Sem, ThM, 61; Univ Iowa, PhD(relig), 66. **CAREER** From asst prof to assoc prof, 65-74, Prof Philos & Relig, Univ Nebr at Omaha, 74- **MEMBERSHIPS** Am Acad Relig. **RESEARCH** History of Christian thought; contemporary theology. **SELECTED PUBLICATIONS** Barth,karl Critically Realistic Dialectical Theology - Its Genesis And Development 1909-1936 - Mccormack,bl, Theological Studies, Vol 0057, 1996. **CONTACT ADDRESS** Dept Philos & Relig, Univ Nebr, Omaha, NE, 68101.

PANDHARIPANDE, RAJESHWARI
DISCIPLINE RELIGIOUS STUDIES **EDUCATION** Univ Ill Urbana Champaign, PhD. **CAREER** Prof, Univ Ill Urbana Champaign. **RESEARCH** Asian mythology; Hinduism; Hinduism in the United States; language of religion; language variation; Sanskrit; Hindi literature. **SELECTED PUBLICATIONS** Auth, The Eternal Self & the Cycle of Samsara: Introduction to Asian Mythology and Religion, Ginn; Intermediate Hindi, Motilal Banarsidass; Never is a Long Time Aur Anya Kavitayen: A Collection of her Original Hindi Poems, Banahatti. **CONTACT ADDRESS** Religious Studies Dept, Univ Ill Urbana Champaign, 52 E Gregory Dr, Champaign, IL, 61820. **EMAIL** raj-pan@uiuc.edu

PANICCIA, PATRICIA L.
DISCIPLINE ADMINISTRATIVE LAW **EDUCATION** Univ HI, BA, 77; Pepperdine Univ Sch Law, JD, 81. **CAREER** Reporter, weekend anchor, KEYT-ABC, 83-85; reporter, KCOP, 85-88; reporter CNN 89-93; media consult, 88-present; ABA Nat Conf Lawyer and Rep(s) Media, 88-91; vchmn Affairs Comm, 85-87; CA State Bar Fair Trial Free Press Comm, 84-85; Acad Television Arts and Sci, 87; contrib ed, consult, preview U.S. Supreme Court Cases, Public edu div, ABA, 85-95; adj prof. **HONORS AND AWARDS** Women in commun nat Clarion award., Emmy nomination for mini-doc invest ser, 87. **MEMBERSHIPS** Mem, CA State Bar; HI State Bar; Am Bar Assoc. **SELECTED PUBLICATIONS** Auth, Gender and the Law, Communications LawPractice, Matthew Bender, 88. **CONTACT ADDRESS** Sch of Law, Pepperdine Univ, 24255 Pacific Coast Hwy, Malibu, CA, 90263.

PANIKKAR, RAIMUNDO
PERSONAL Born 11/03/1918, Barcelona, Spain **DISCIPLINE** COMPARATIVE PHILOSOPHY & RELIGION **EDUCATION** Univ Barcelona, MSc, 41; Univ Madrid, MA, 42, PhD (philos), 46, DSc(chem), 58; Pontif Lateran Univ, ThL, 54, ThD(theol), 61. **CAREER** Prof Indian cult, Theol Sem, Madrid, 46-51 & Int Univ Social Studies, Rome, 62-63; vis prof compt relig, Harvard Univ, 67-71; Prof Relig Studies, Univ Calif, Santa Barbara, 71-, Fel, Inst Philos Luis Vives, Coun Sci Res, Madrid, 42-57; prof, Inst Leon XIII, 50-51; docent, Univ Rome, 63-; mem acad coun, Ecumenical Inst Advan Theol Studies, Jerusalem, 65-; Henry Luce vis prof, Union Theol Sem, NY, 70. **HONORS AND AWARDS** Teape lectr, Cambridge Univ, 66. **MEMBERSHIPS** Forsch fur Symbolic, Heidelberg; Am Soc Studies Relig; Int Soc Medieval Philos; Inst Int Philos, Paris; Am Acad Relig; UNESCO. **RESEARCH** Philosophy of science. **SELECTED PUBLICATIONS** Auth, Kerygma und Indien, Reich, Hamburg, 67; El silencio del Dios, Guadiana, Madrid, 70; Worship and Secular Man, 73 & Trinity and the Religious Experience of Man, 73, DLT, London; The Vedic Experience, Univ Calif, Berkeley, 77; Myth, Faith and Hermeneutics, 78, 79 & The Intrareligious Dialogue, 78, Paulist; The Unknown Christ of Hinduism, Orbis Bks, rev ed, 81; The Defiance of Pluralism, Soundings, Vol 0079, 1996. **CONTACT ADDRESS** Dept of Relig Studies, Univ of Calif, Santa Barbara, CA, 93106.

PANKEY, WILLIAM J.
DISCIPLINE THEOLOGY **EDUCATION** Central Bible Col, BA, 82; Assem God Theol Sem, MA, 98; Trinity Int Univ, MDiv, 96, DMin, 94; Dominican Univ, MILS, 97. **CAREER** DIR, COL LIBR, CHRISTIAN LIFE COL **MEMBERSHIPS** ALA, ACRL **RESEARCH** Hermeneutics, philosophy of religion, Buddhism **SELECTED PUBLICATIONS** Auth, Role of the Holy Spirit in the Exegetical Process, The Pneuma Rev, 2:1, winter 99. **CONTACT ADDRESS** Christian Life Col, 400 E Gregory St, Mt. Prospect, IL, 60056. **EMAIL** wpankey@christianlifecollege.edu

PAPAZIAN, MICHAEL
PERSONAL Born 03/13/1965, Englewood, NJ, s **DISCIPLINE** PHILOSOPHY **EDUCATION** Johns Hopkins Univ, BA, 87; Oxford Univ, MST, 95; Univ of VA, MA 91; Univ of VA, PhD, 95 **CAREER** Lect, 96, Univ of VA; Visit Ast Prof, 97, Hampden Sydney Col; Asst Prof, 98-pres, Berry Col **MEMBERSHIPS** Am Philos Assoc; Soc for Armenian Studies; Soc for Ancient Greek Philos **RESEARCH** Ancient Philosophy; Metaphysics; Philosophy of Logic **CONTACT ADDRESS** Dept Relig & Philos, Berry Col, Mt Berry, GA, 30149. **EMAIL** mpapazian@berry.edu

PAPER, JORDAN
PERSONAL Born 12/03/1938, Baltimore, MD **DISCIPLINE** HISTORY OF RELIGIONS, EAST ASIA **EDUCATION** Univ Chicago, AB, 60; Univ Wis-Madison, MA, 65, PhD(Chinese), 71. **CAREER** Asst prof hist, Ind State Univ, 67-72; asst prof, 72-78, Assoc Prof Humanities, York Univ, 78-, Vis prof Am lit, Ching I Col, Taiwan, 73-74. **MEMBERSHIPS** Asn Asian Studies; Am Orient Soc; Soc Studies Pre-Han China; Soc Study Chinese Relig; Can Soc Study Relig. **RESEARCH** East Asian aesthetics; Chinese intellectual history; East Asian and Amerindian religion. **SELECTED PUBLICATIONS** Auth, The Ch'un meng so yen, an erotic Chinese literary tale, Nachrichten, Hamburg, 71; Index to Short Stories in the Fa Yuan Chu Lin, CMRASC, Inc, Taipei, 72; Guide to Chinese Prose, Twayne, 73; Confucianism in the Post-Han Era, Chinese Cult, 75; A Shaman in contemporary Toronto, Relig & Cult Can, 77; The meaning of the T'ao-t'ieh, Hist Relig, 78; From Shaman to mystic in Ojibwa religion, Studies Relig, 80; From Shaman to mystic in the Chuang-Tzu, Scottish J Relig Studies, 82; Methodological Controversies in The Study of Native-american Religions + Authors Response to Review of His Book 'Offering Smoke - The Sacred Pipe And Native American Religion' by Parkhill,thom, Studies in Religion-sciences Religieuses, Vol 0022, 1993; Ethnophilosophical And Ethnolinguistic Perspectives on The Huron Indian Soul - Pomedli,mm, Studies in Religion-sciences Religieuses, Vol 0022, 1994; Mystic Endowment - Religious Ethnography of The Warao Indians - Wilbert,j, Studies in Religion-sciences Religieuses, Vol 0024, 1995; Prophecy And Power Among The Dogrib Indians - Helm,j, J of Religion, Vol 0076, 1996. **CONTACT ADDRESS** Div of Humanities, York Univ, 4700 Keele St, Downsview, ON, M3J1P3.

PAPPAS, GEORGE SOTIROS
PERSONAL Born 05/04/1942, Philadelphia, PA, m, 1963, 2 children **DISCIPLINE** PHILOSOPHY **EDUCATION** Gettysburg Col, BA, 63; Univ Pa, MA, 66, PhD(philos), 74. **CAREER** Asst prof philos, Univ Western Ont, 68-69; asst prof, 69-75, assoc prof, 75-80, prof philos, Ohio State Univ, 81-. **MEMBERSHIPS** Can Philos Asn; Am Philos Asn. **RESEARCH** Epistemology; metaphysics; philosophy of Berkeley. **SELECTED PUBLICATIONS** Auth, Seeinge and Seeingn, Mind, 4/76; coauth, Quine's Materialism, Philosophia, 3/76; auth, Armstrong's materialism, Can J Philos, 9/77; co-ed, Essays on Knowledge and Justification, Cornell Univ Press, 78; ed, Justification and Knowledge, Reidel Press, 79; auth, Ideas, minds and Berkeley, Am Philos Quart, 7/80. **CONTACT ADDRESS** Dept of Philos, Ohio State Univ, 230 N Oval Mall, Columbus, OH, 43210-1335.

PAPPAS, GREGORY F.
PERSONAL Born 02/09/1960 **DISCIPLINE** PRAGMATISM, ETHICS **EDUCATION** Univ PR, BA, 81; Univ Wyo, MA, 83; Univ Tex at Austin, PhD, 90. **CAREER** Asst prof, Tex A & M Univ; lectr and asst instr, Univ Tex. **HONORS AND AWARDS** Ford Foun postdoc fel, National Res Coun, 91-92; Douglas Greenlee Prize, 92; William James Prize, 90. **RESEARCH** American philosophy. **SELECTED PUBLICATIONS** Auth, Dewey's Philosophical Approach to Racial Prejudice, Journal of Social Philosophy, 96; William James Virtuous Believer, Transactions of the Charles Peirce Society, 94; Dewey and Feminism: The Affective and Relationships in Dewey's Ethics, Hypatia vol.8, 93; William James and The Logic of Faith, Transactions of the Charles Peirce Society, 92; rev, The Community Reconstructs: The Meaning of Pragmatic Social Thought, Vol.8, J Speculative Philos. **CONTACT ADDRESS** Dept of Philosophy, Texas A&M Univ, 309E Bolton Hall, College Station, TX, 77843-4237.

PAPPU, RAMA RAO
DISCIPLINE ORIENTAL PHILOSOPHY, PHILOSOPHY OF LAW, ETHICS **EDUCATION** Punjab, BA; Delhi, MA; Southern Ill Univ at Carbondale, PhD. **CAREER** Prof, Miami Univ **MEMBERSHIPS** Conf dir, 9th Int Cong of Vedanta, Rishikesh UP India, 97. **RESEARCH** Philosophy of law; ethics; Indian and Comparative Philosophy. **SELECTED PUBLICATIONS** Ed, Indian Philosophy: Past and Future; Dimensions of Karma & Perspectives on Vedanta. **CONTACT ADDRESS** Dept of Philosophy, Miami Univ, Oxford, OH, 45056. **EMAIL** pappuss@muohio.edu

PAPRZYCKA, KATARZYNA
PERSONAL Born 01/15/1967, Poznan, Poland, m, 1988, 1 child **DISCIPLINE** PHILOSOPHY **EDUCATION** Harvard, BA, 89; Univ Pittsburg, PhD, 97. **CAREER** Teaching asst, 90-93, teaching fel, 94-95, Univ of Pittsburg; adjunct faculty member, 96, 97, Univ TX of the Permian Basin; adjunct faculty member, 98, Univ of Southern Mississippi. **HONORS AND AWARDS** Honorary Immatriculation, 85; Merit Scholarship, 85-86; Open Society Found Scholarhsip, Oxford Univ, 86-87; Harvard Col Scholarship, Harvard University, 87-88; Graduated Magna Cum Laude from Radcliffe Col, 89; Andrew Mellon Predoctoral Fel, University of Pittsburgh, 89-90; Sloan Fel, Univ of Pittsburgh, 93-94; Andrew Mellon Predoctoral Fel, Univ of Pittsburgh, 94-95; **MEMBERSHIPS** Amer Philosophical Assn, 87-; Assoc member of The Southern Soc for Philosophy and Psychology, 92-. **RESEARCH** Philosophy of actions, mind, psychology and social sciences. **SELECTED PUBLICATIONS** Auth, A Note on von Bretzel's Solution to an Alleged Problem with Reichenbach's Definition of Time Direction, Epistemologia, 94; How Carnap Should Bite Goodman's Bullet, Philosophia, 94; Must False Consciousness Be Rationally Caused?, Philosophia of the Social Sciences, 98; Collectivism on the Horizon: A challenge to Pettit's Critque of Collectivism, Australasian Journal of Philosophy, 98; Idealization in Unitarian Metaphysics, forthcoming in a volume on Idealization and Abstraction; Socrates Meets Carnap: Explication in the Theaetetus, forthcoming in Logical Analysis and History of Philosophy. **CONTACT ADDRESS** 200 Foxgate Ave., #20-g, Hattiesburg, MS, 39402. **EMAIL** paprzyck@pitt.edu

PARCHMENT, STEVEN
DISCIPLINE HISTORY OF MODERN PHILOSOPHY, SPINOZA, ANCIENT AND MEDIEVAL PHILOSOPHY, MET **EDUCATION** Emory Univ, PhD, 96. **CAREER** Lectr, Ga State Univ. **SELECTED PUBLICATIONS** Published an article on Spinoza in Hist of Philos Quart. **CONTACT ADDRESS** Georgia State Univ, Atlanta, GA, 30303. **EMAIL** phlsgp@panther.gsu.edu

PARENS, JOSHUA
DISCIPLINE PHILOSOPHY OF BEING **EDUCATION** St John's Col, BA; Univ Chicago, MA, PhD. **CAREER** Dept Philos, Univ Dallas **SELECTED PUBLICATIONS** Auth, Theory and Practice in Medieval Aristotelianism, Polity,93; Multiculturalism and the Problem of Particularism, Amer Polit Sci Rev, 94; Whose Liberalism, Which Islam? Leonard Binder's Islamic Liberalism, PS, 94; Metaphysics as Rhetoric: Alfarabi's Summary of Plato's Laws, SUNY Press,95. **CONTACT ADDRESS** Dept of Philos, Univ Dallas, 1845 E Northgate Dr, Irving, TX, 75062. **EMAIL** parens@acad.udallas.edu

PARENT, MARK
PERSONAL Born 08/25/1954, Halifax, NS, Canada, m, 1974, 3 children **DISCIPLINE** RELIGIOUS STUDIES **EDUCATION** York Univ, BA, 76; Acadia Div Col, MDiv, 79; McGill Univ, PhD, 91. **CAREER** Fac, MTh sem, 84-85, instr, Queen's Theol Col, 89; lectr Atlantic Baptist Col, 92; fel, relig stud, Mount Allison Univ, 92-93; instr, New Brunswick Commun Col, 94; instr, Mount Allizon Univ 92- , hon res assoc, Acadia Univ, 94-96; asst prof, Mount Allizon Univ, 98- . **HONORS AND AWARDS** Edward Manning Saunders Prize, Diefenbaker Awd, Acadia Univ. **MEMBERSHIPS** Can Evangel Theol Asn; Can Theolog Soc; Faith and Hist Soc. **RESEARCH** Christianity and culture; fundamentalism; liberation theology. **SELECTED PUBLICATIONS** Auth, Enigmatic Answers, Church Leadership Unltd, 93; auth, Strange New Movements, Atlantic Baptist, 94; auth, T T Shields and the Irony of Fundamentalism, in Fides et Historia, 94; auth, Religion at Three Maritime Universities, in Aspects of Education in the Small University, McGill-Queens, 96; auth, Spiritscapes: Mapping the Spiritual and Scientific Terrain at the Dawn of the New Millennium, Northstone, 98. **CONTACT ADDRESS** RR #1, Canning, NS, B0P 1H0. **EMAIL** mparent@glinx.com

PARK, EUNG CHUN
PERSONAL Born 07/21/1958, Seoul, Korea, m, 1982, 2 children **DISCIPLINE** BIBLICAL STUDIES **EDUCATION** Seoul Natl Univ, BA, 81; Presbyterian Theol Sem, MDiv, 84; Yale Univ Div, STM, 86; Univ Chicago, PhD, 91. **CAREER** Ast prof, 96-99, asoc prof, 99- , San Francisco Theol Sem. **MEMBERSHIPS** Soc of Bibl Lit. **RESEARCH** Biblical hermeneuties; Gospel of Matthew; universalism in the New Testament. **SELECTED PUBLICATIONS** Auth, "The Nicene Creed and the New Testament," Church and Theol, 93; "The Pentecost Event Through Luke's Eyes," Bibl Ground, 93; "The Image of the Rabbi in New Testament Times," Educ and Church, 93; "Paul's Philosophy of Ministry," Bible and Ministry, Korean Inst Bibl Stud, 94; "Jewish Particularism and Universalism in New Testament Churches," Church and Theol, 94; "Paul's Appropriation and Transformation of Culture, Christian Culture and Female Leadership in the Church," Inst of the Stud of Women in Korean Church, 94; "Fruit Worthy of Repentance," Bibl Stud for Preachers and Lay Persons, 94; "The Terms of Defining Self-identity of the Early Christianity Reflected in the Areopagus Address in Acts 17:22-31," Church and Theol, 95; The Mission Discourse in Matthew's Interpretation. JCB Mohr, 95; The Gospel for the World, Inst Bibl Stud, 97; "Savior," Encyclopedia of Theology, Korean Inst for Catholic Stud, forthcoming; "Book Note on Mitzi Minor, The Spirituality of Mark: Responding to God," Theol Tod, forthcoming; "The Lord's Supper Turned into Disaster," Jrnl Case Tchg, 98. **CONTACT ADDRESS** San Francisco Theol Sem, 2 Kensington Rd, San Anselmo, CA, 94960-2905. **EMAIL** ecpark@sfts.edu

PARK, ROGER COOK
PERSONAL Born 01/01/1942, Atlanta, GA **DISCIPLINE** LAW **EDUCATION** Harvard Univ, BA, 64, JD, 69. **CAREER** Prof Law, Univ Minn Law Sch, 73-. **HONORS AND AWARDS** Julius E Davis prof, Univ Minn Law Sch, 81. **RESEARCH** Evidence; computer aided instruction; legal education. **SELECTED PUBLICATIONS** Auth, The entrapment controversy, J Minn Law Rev, 76; Computer Aided Instruction in Law, West Pub Co, 76; Computer aided instruction in law: Theories, techniques and trepidations, J Am Bar Found, 78; coauth, Teaching Law with Computers, West View Press, 80; auth, McCormick on evidence and the concept of hearsay, J Minn Law Rev, 81; the 22nd Annual Hodson,kenneth,j. Lecture - Uncharged Misconduct Evidence in Sex Crime Cases - Reassessing the Rule of Exclusion, Military Law Review, Vol 0141, 1993. **CONTACT ADDRESS** Law Sch, Univ of Minn, Minneapolis, MN, 55454.

PARK, WILLIAM WYNNEWOOD
PERSONAL Born 07/02/1947, Philadelphia, PA **DISCIPLINE** LAW **EDUCATION** Yale Univ, BA, 69; Columbia Univ, JD, 72; Cambridge Univ, England, MA, 75. **CAREER** Atty, Coudert Freres, Paris, 72-75 & Hughes, Hubbard & Reed, Paris, 77-79; fel, Selwyn Col, Cambridge Univ, England, 75-77; prof Law, Boston Univ, 79-, adjunct prof Int Law, Fletcher Sch Law & Diplomacy, 80-86; vis prof, Inst Universitaire de Hautes Etudes Int Geneva, 83; vis prof, Univ Dijon, 84; vis prof, Univ Hong Kong, 90. **HONORS AND AWARDS** Vice pres, London Court of Int Arbitration; Arbitrator; Claims Resolution Tribunal for Dormant Accounts in Switzerland. **MEMBERSHIPS** Am Soc Int Law; Int Fiscal Asn; British Inst Int & Comp Law; Brit Chartered Inst Abitrators. **RESEARCH** International business transactions; taxation; arbitration. **SELECTED PUBLICATIONS** Auth, Fiscal jurisdiction and accrual basis taxation, Columbia Law Rev, 12/78; Le nouveau statut des banques etrangeres aux Etats-Unis, Rev Int de Droit Compare, 1/80; Tax characterization of international leases, Cornell Law Rev, 11/81; coauth, French codification of a legal framework for international commercial arbitration, Georgetown J Law & Policy in Int Bus, 11/81; International Forum Selection, 95; International Commercial Arbitration with W M Reisman, 97; Arbitration in Banking & Finance, 17 Ann Rev, Banking Law 213, 98. **CONTACT ADDRESS** Law Sch, Boston Univ, 765 Commonwealth Ave, Boston, MA, 02215-1401.

PARKER, FRED LEE CECIL
PERSONAL Born 06/16/1923, Calvert, TX, m **DISCIPLINE** THEOLOGY **EDUCATION** Southwestern Baptist Theological Seminary, Ft Worth, Diploma 1956; Bishop Coll Dallas, BA 1968; E TX State Univ Commerce, MEd 1975; S Bible Sem Burnwsick GA, ThD 1978. **CAREER** Geochem Surveys, lab tech 1944-70; Dallas Independent Sch Dist, tchr 1969-84; Goodwill Baptist Ch, assoc minister, 1977-94; D Edwin Johnson Baptist Inst, seminary & ext teacher 1979-91, administrative dean 1984-91; Tabernacle of Praise Baptist Church, pastor's asst, 1994-. **HONORS AND AWARDS** Panalist Radio Sta KNOK Dallas-Ft Worth 1954-71; hon DD Universal Bible Inst Inc Brunswick GA 1977; cert Pastoral Cnsl Birmingham AL 1977. **MEMBERSHIPS** Mem GT Dallas Math Tchrs TSTA NEA 1970-; mem Classroom Tchrs of Dallas 1970-84; local & state chaplain Phi Beta Sigma Frat Inc 1970-84; Elem Math Tchrs Dev, US Off of Ed Bishop Coll Dallas 1971; Nat Sci Found, Math Bishop Coll Dallas 1972-73; Professional Growth in Ed Dallas Independent Sch Dist 1973-74; regvp, natl dean Universal Bible Inst Inc 1978-79; reg dir, dean S Bible Sem Inc 1978-79; fld rep, cnslr World-Wide Bible Inst Inc 1979-84.

PARKER, JOSEPH CAIAPHAS, JR.
PERSONAL Born 09/25/1952, Anniston, Alabama, m, 1975 **DISCIPLINE** LAW **EDUCATION** Morehouse Coll, BA 1974; Univ of Georgia, M Public Admin 1976; Univ of TX at Austin, JD 1982. **CAREER** City of Dallas, admin asst mgmt serv 1976-77, admin asst office of the city mgr 1977-79, mgr summer youth employment program 1979; Travis Co Attorney Office, trial attorney 1983-84, chief trial div 1985-86; David Chapel Missionary Baptist Church, assoc pastor 1984-; Long, Burner, Parks & Sealy PC, attorney, dir, vice pres, 1986-; Univ of TX at Austin, instructor in trial advocacy, 1991-. **HONORS AND AWARDS** Man of the Year Spelman College Student Govt Assn 1973-74; Univ of GA Fellowship 1974-76; Pi Sigma Alpha Honor Soc 1976; Dallas Jaycees Rookie of the Yr 1978-79, Presidential Awd 1978-79; Outstanding Achievement Awd Natl Conf of Minority Public Administrators 1979; Gene Woodfin Awd Univ of TX 1982; Leadership Austin 1984-85; Distinguished Morehouse Coll Alumni Citation of the Year 1986; Baptist General Convention of TX Theological Scholarship 1986-87; Benjamin E Mays Fellowship in Ministry, Fund for Theological Studies; publication "Prosecuting the DWI", True Bill Vol 6 No 4 TX Prosecutor Council. **MEMBERSHIPS** Mem Natl Conf of Minority Public Administrators 1974-80; mem Amer Soc for Public Admin; bd dirs Morehouse Coll Natl Alumni Assn; bd dirs Austin Child Guidance and Evaluation Ctr; mem Conference of Christians and Jews; mem Black Austin Democrats; mem Urban League, NAACP, Austin Jaycees; mem Travis County Public Defender Task Force; mem State Bar of TX, TX and Austin Young Lawyers Assns, Natl Bar Assns; mem Austin Black Lawyers Assn and Federal Bar Assn; mem Association of Trial Lawyers of America. **CONTACT ADDRESS** Trial Attorney, Long, Burner, Parks and Sealy, PC, PO Box 2212, Austin, TX, 78768.

PARKER, KELLIS E.
PERSONAL Born 01/13/1942, Kinston, NC **DISCIPLINE** LAW **EDUCATION** University of North Carolina, BA, 1960; Howard Univ School of Law, JD, cum laude, 1968. **CAREER** Columbia University, law professor, 1975-; Columbia University, associate professor of law, 1972-75; Univ of California, acting professor of law, 1969-72; Judge Spottswood W Robinson III, law clerk, 1968-69. **MEMBERSHIPS** NAACP, Legal Def Fund, consultant; New World Found; Comm Action Legal Serv, chairperson, 1977-79; Nat Conf on Black Lawyers; Minority Groups Com, chairperson; Assn of Am Law Schs, 1976-77; Nat Com on Legal & Ethical Implications of Sickle Cell Anemia; Comm Action for Legal Svcs, board member. **SELECTED PUBLICATIONS** Publ, "Modern Judicial Remedies", Little Brown & Co, 1975; editor in chf, Howard Law Journal, 1967-68. **CONTACT ADDRESS** Sch of Law, Columbia Univ, 435 W 116th St, New York, NY, 10027-7279.

PARKER, KELLIS E.
PERSONAL Born 01/13/1942, Kinston, NC **DISCIPLINE** LAW **EDUCATION** University of North Carolina, BA, 1960; Howard Univ School of Law, JD, cum laude, 1968. **CAREER** Columbia University, law professor, 1975-; Columbia University, associate professor of law, 1972-75; Univ of California, acting professor of law, 1969-72; Judge Spottswood W Robinson III, law clerk, 1968-69. **MEMBERSHIPS** NAACP, Legal Def Fund, consultant; New World Found; Comm Action Legal Serv, chairperson, 1977-79; Nat Conf on Black Lawyers; Minority Groups Com, chairperson; Assn of Am Law Schs, 1976-77; Nat Com on Legal & Ethical Implications of Sickle Cell Anemia; Comm Action for Legal Svcs, board member. **SELECTED PUBLICATIONS** "Modern Judicial Remedies", Little Brown & Co, 1975; editor in chf, Howard Law Journal, 1967-68. **CONTACT ADDRESS** Sch of Law, Columbia Univ, 435 W 116th St, New York, NY, 10027-7279.

PARKER, KELLY A.
PERSONAL Born 10/22/1963, Osborne, KS, m, 1984, 2 children **DISCIPLINE** PHILOSOPHY **EDUCATION** Vanderbilt Univ, PhD, 92. **CAREER** Asst prof, 92-98, assoc prof, 98-,

Grand Valley St Univ. **HONORS AND AWARDS** Vanderbilt Grad Stud Res Day, First Prize, 89; Diss Enhancement Award, Vanderbilt Grad School, 90; Harold Stirling Vanderbilt Fel, 87-91; Mellon Diss Yr Fel, 91-92; Charles S. Pierce Soc Essay Contest Winner, 91; Soc for the Advancement of Am Philos, Douglas Greenlee Essay Prize, 94; GVSU Center on Philanthropy and Non-Profit Leadership Curriculum Development Grant (Ethics and Professions), 96. **MEMBERSHIPS** APA; Charles S. Pierce Soc; Soc for the Advancement of Am Philos; The Metaphysical Soc of Am; Int Soc for Environ Ethics; Asn for Pract & Profes Ethics; North Am Merleau-Ponty Cir; Am Asn of Univ Profs, GVSU Chap; Ctr for Acad Integrity. **SELECTED PUBLICATIONS** Auth, Economics, Sustainable Growth, and Community, Environmental Values vol 2, 93; autn, Pierce's Semeiotic and Ontology, Transactions of the Charles S. Pierce Soc, vol 30, 94; auth, Pragmatism and Environmental Thought, Chap 1 Environ Pragmatism, Routledge Press, 96; auth, The Ascent of Soul to Nous: Charles S. Pierce as Neoplatonist, in Neoplatonism and Contemporary Thought, SUNY Press, forthcoming; auth, The Ethics Committee: A Concensus-Recommendation Model, in Pragmatic Bioethics, Vanderbilt Univ Press; The Continuity of Pierce's Thought, The Lib of Am Philos, Vanderbilt Univ Press, 98; auth, William James: Experience and Creative Growth, in Classical American Philosophy: Its Contemporary Vitality, Univ IL Press, 98. **CONTACT ADDRESS** Dept of Philosophy, Grand Valley State Univ, 210 Lake Superior Hall, Allendale, MI, 49401-9403. **EMAIL** parkerk@gvsu.edu

PARKER, PAUL P.
PERSONAL Born 08/25/1953, Louisville, KY, m, 1993, 3 children **DISCIPLINE** THEOLOGY **EDUCATION** Univ F, BS, 75; SBTS, MDiv, 81, PhD, 86. **CAREER** Relig, Elmhurst **RESEARCH** Theology; social ethics. **CONTACT ADDRESS** Elmhurst Col, 190 Prospect Ave., Elmhurst, IL, 60126. **EMAIL** paulp@elmhurst.edu

PARKER, THOMAS D.
PERSONAL Born 12/22/1931, Los Angeles, CA, m, 1978, 5 children **DISCIPLINE** THEOLOGY **EDUCATION** Calif State Col, Los Angeles, BA, 54; San Francisco Theol Sem, BD, 57; Princeton Theol Sem, PhD, 65. **CAREER** Asst prof, 68-71, Assoc prof, 71-74, prof, 74-94, Cyrus McCormick prof, 94-98, emer prof, 98- , McCormick Theol Sem. **HONORS AND AWARDS** Cum laude, 57; summa cum laude, 65; Rockefeller Doctoral Fel, 64-65; AATS Fac Fel, 70-71. **MEMBERSHIPS** Am Theol Soc; Am Acad of Relig; Sof for the Sci Stud of Relig; Soc of Christian Philos. **RESEARCH** Religious experience and belief; Christology; religion and science. **SELECTED PUBLICATIONS** Auth, "Promise," McCormick Q, 70; "On Doing Theology," Teachers Guide: Christian Faith and Action, 71; ed, Christian Theology, 76; auth, "The Political Meaning of the Trinity," J of Relig, 80; "Can There be a Covenant Community that is Genuinely Inclusive," Miller, ed, A Covenant Challenge to a Broken World, 82; "Spirituality and Peacemaking," Peace, War and God's Justice, 89; "Immediacy and Interpretation," Am J of Theol and Philos, 91. **CONTACT ADDRESS** PO Box 1778, Hendersonville, NC, 28793. **EMAIL** ktparker@aol.com

PARKER, VERNON B.
PERSONAL Born 11/16/1959, Houston, TX, m, 1991 **DISCIPLINE** LAW **EDUCATION** Bilingual and Cultural Institute of Cuernavaca, Mexico, 1980; California State Univ at Long Beach, BS, 1980-83; Georgetown Univ, JD, 1988. **CAREER** Rockwell International, financial analyst, 1983-85; US Office of Personnel Management, counselor to the dir/dir of policy, 1989-91, general counsel, 1992; White House, special asst to the pres, 1992-93; Kenny Rogers Roasters of Chicago, vice pres, 1993-94; Multinational Legal Services, partner, 1994-; Parian International, president & CEO; Parker, Farringer, Parker, Attorney, currently; Belsante International, pres and ceo, co-founder, currently. **HONORS AND AWARDS** Georgetown Univ Law Center, Outstanding Leader, 1988; Georgetown Univ Law Center, Outstanding Tutor, 1988, Foreign Language Scholarship recipient, 1980. **MEMBERSHIPS** National Bar Association, 1991-; District of Columbia Bar, 1989-; Virginia Bar Association, 1995; Student Bar Association, Georgetown Univ Law Center, vice pres, 1986-87. **SELECTED PUBLICATIONS** Editor-in-chief, Georgetown American Criminal Law Review; Author, "Annual Survey of White-Collar Crime Attorney Client Privilege," American Criminal Law Review, Winter 1986-1987. **CONTACT ADDRESS** Parker, Farringer, Parker, 1825 I St NW, Ste 400, Washington, DC, 20006.

PARKS, EDWARD Y.
PERSONAL Born 02/05/1951, Thomson, GA, m, 1975 **DISCIPLINE** LAW **EDUCATION** Otterbein College, BA, 1973; Howard Univ, JD, 1979. **CAREER** Ohio Public Interest campaign, assoc dir, 1979-81; Legal Aid Society, Attorney, 1981-83; Public Utilities Commission, Attorney examiner, 1983-86; Ohio Dept Health, legal counsel, 1986-89; Law Office, Edward YA Parks, president, 1989-. **HONORS AND AWARDS** Welfare Rights, Outstanding Legal Advocate, 1983; NAACP, Community Service Award, 1985; Shiloh Baptist Church, Outstanding Service-Softball Program, 1987 & 1988. **MEMBERSHIPS** Assoc Juvenile Laws, presiding officer, 1989-; NAACP, 1979-; Urban League, 1991-; Columbus Bar Assoc, 1980-; Natl Conference Black Lawyers, 1980-; Shiloh Baptist Church, trustee, 1993; Legal Aid Society Lawyer Referral, 1989-; Natl Bar Assn, 1993-. **SELECTED PUBLICATIONS** Shiloh Baptist Church Plan, 1990; Book of Poems. **CONTACT ADDRESS** Law Office, Edward Y A Parks, 8 E Long St, Ste 225, Columbus, OH, 43215.

PARKS, JENNIFER
DISCIPLINE PHILOSOPHY **EDUCATION** Queen's Univ Kingston, Ont, Can, BA, MA; McMaster Univ, Can, PhD, 96. **CAREER** Asst prof; fac, McMaster Univ, Hamilton, Ont, Can, 96; adv, MA prog in Health Care Ethics; ethics consult, Loyola's Ethics Consultation Serv. **RESEARCH** Health care ethics; ethical theory; feminism; soc philosophy. **SELECTED PUBLICATIONS** Articles in, J Med Humanities, Rsr(s) for Feminist Res & The Can Med Asn J. **CONTACT ADDRESS** Dept of Philosophy, Loyola Univ, Chicago, 820 N. Michigan Ave., Chicago, IL, 60611.

PARKS, SHARON
DISCIPLINE THEOLOGY, HUMAN DEVELOPMENT **EDUCATION** Harvard, ThD, 80 **CAREER** Assoc dir, fac, The Whidbey Inst. **RESEARCH** Leadership and ethics. **SELECTED PUBLICATIONS** Auth, The Critical Years, 86; auth, Common Fire: Leading Lives of Commitment in a Complex World, 96. **CONTACT ADDRESS** The Whidbey Inst, PO Box 57, Clinton, WA, 98236-9520.

PAROT, JOSEPH JOHN
PERSONAL Born 06/04/1940, Hammond, IN, m, 1962, 2 children **DISCIPLINE** AMERICAN RELIGIOUS & URBAN/ ETHNIC HISTORY **EDUCATION** Maryknoll College, 58; IN Univ, 59-60; St Joseph's Col, Ind, BA, 63; DePaul Univ, MA, 67; Northern IL Univ, PhD, 71. **CAREER** Instr hist, St Augustine High Sch, Chicago, 63-67; from instr to asst prof hist & bibliog, 67-74, assoc prof, 75-82, prof hist & head hist ctr, Northern IL Univ, 82-, prof hist & head soc sci dept, 84; Instr soc sci, Chicago Comt Urban Opportunity Prog, 66-67; vis prof urban/ethnic studies, George Williams Col, 72-73; assoc ed, Polish-Am Studies, 73. **HONORS AND AWARDS** Ed Emer Award, St Joseph's Col, 63; Lions Int, Outstanding Teacher Award, Chicago rea, 66; Pi Gamma Mu, DePaul Univ, 67; Oscar Halecki Award from Polish Am Hist Asn for outstanding book, 83; grants from Am Philos Soc, NEH; Honorariums from Multicultural Hist Soc of Ontario, 78; Pa Hist Comm, 76; Univ Notre Dame 82; Multicultural Curr Trnasformation Ins, 95. **MEMBERSHIPS** AHA; Polish-Am Hist Asn. **RESEARCH** Immigration hist; urban hist; religious hist in Am. **SELECTED PUBLICATIONS** Auth, Ethnic versus Black metropolis: Origins of Polish Black housing tensions in Chicago, 71, Unthinkable thoughts on unmeltable ethnics, 74 & Racial dilemma in Chicago's Polish neighborhoods, 1920-1970, 75, Polish Am Studies; contribr, Bishop Francis Hodur, suppl five, In: Dict of American Biography, 77; Strangers in the city: Immigrant Catholics and the black community in Twentieth century Chicago, Black History Conference, Lincoln Univ Press, 4/78; Immigrant Labor and the Paradox of Pluralism in American Urban Society, 1860-1930: A Comparative Study and Census Analysis of Polish, German, Irish, Bohemian, Italian and Jewish Workers in Chicago, Polish Res Inst of the Jagiellonian Univ, Cracow, 79; Sources of community conflict in Chicago Polonia: A comparative analysis and historigraphical appraisal, Ethnicity, vol 7, winter 80; Polish Catholics in Chicago, 1850-1920: A Religious History, Northern Ill Univ Press, 81; The Serdeczna Matko of the sweatshops: Marital and family crises of immigrant working-class women in late nineteenth century Chicago, Poles in North America Conference, Multicult Hist Soc of Ont, 82; Steelmills, sweatshops, stockyards, and slums: The social fabric of the immigrant Catholic working class in Chicago, 1870-1930, Perspectives in American Catholicism, Univ Notre Dame, 11/82; Catholic manuscript and archival sources in the Greater Chicago area, Mdwest Archives Conf, Chicago 5/83; The urbanization and suburbanization of the ethnic working class in Chicago, 1870-1980, Celebrate Illinois: Its Cultural Heritage, Ill Humantities Counc, 4/85; Family and social history in the immigrant community, Polish Genealogical Soc, 11/ 88; co-ed (with James Pula, et al), Polish History in America to 1908, vol 1-4; Catholic Univ of Am Press, 94-98, Kruszka Transl Proj; ed board of Ill Hist Jour, 95-98; The German immigrant in Illinois, 1840-1930, Elmhurst Hist Soc, 3/98; Reverend Vincent Barzynski, In: American National Biography, 99; Multicultural difficulties in the Polish Catholic community in Chicago, Ill Hist Teacher, 99. **CONTACT ADDRESS** Founders Libr, No Illinois Univ, Soc Sci Dept, De Kalb, IL, 60115-2825.

PARR, CHRIS
DISCIPLINE RELIGION **EDUCATION** Univ Canterbury, NZ, BA, 77, MA, 80; Boston Univ, PhD, 92. **CAREER** Tchg fel, 84-90, gallery asst, 87, assoc dir, Video Icons & Values Conf, 87, lectr and instr, Boston Univ, 89-92; asst prof, Webster Univ, 92-; steering comt, 90-92, co-ch Arts, Lit and Relig sect, Am Acad Relig, 92-95; gallery asst, Inst Contemp Art, Boston, 87-89. **HONORS AND AWARDS** Wilma and Roswell Messing, Jr, fac Award. **MEMBERSHIPS** Am Acad Relig, 87-; MLA, 88-90. **SELECTED PUBLICATIONS** Auth, Introducing James K. Baxter, Longman Paul, 83; Cars are Part of Nature Too, Illeagle Press, 92; Taking Boston as Given, & Giving Back: Bill Corbett's Quality of Attention, lift 15/16, 94; coauth, Ecologic and Symbiotic Approaches to Animal Welfare, Animal Rights, and Human Responsibility,' J of Am Vet Med Asn, 191, 6, 87; coed, Video Icons & Values, State Univ NY Press, 91. **CONTACT ADDRESS** Webster Univ, St. Louis, MO, 63119. **EMAIL** parrch@websteruniv.edu

PARRENT, ALLAN MITCHELL
DISCIPLINE CHRISTIAN ETHICS **EDUCATION** Georgetown Col, BA, 52; Vanderbilt Univ, MA, 55; Vanderbilt Univ, MDiv, 61; Duke Univ, PhD, 69. **CAREER** Lt, US Naval Reserve, 56-59; for svc off, Dept of State, 62-64; asst coord, stud act, asst dir, Stud Union, Duke Univ, 64-67; dir, Prog in Wash, Dept Intl Aff, Nat Coun of Churches, 67-72; prof, 72-83; assoc dean for acad aff, VP, Clinton S. Quin prof, Va Theol Sem, 83-97. **HONORS AND AWARDS** Fulbright scholar, Durham Univ, 52-53; Danforth Grad Fel, 52-62; Rockefeller Theol Fel, 59-60; Gurney Harriss Kearns Fel, Duke Univ, 66-67. **SELECTED PUBLICATIONS** Auth, Jesus' Messiahship and Our Discipleship, Best Sermons II, Harper and Row, 89; The War in the Persian Gulf and the Episcopal Church, Sewanee Theol Rev, 91; The Distorted and the Natural, Best Sermons IV, Harper and Row; On War, Peace and the Use of Force, The Crisis in Moral Teaching in the Episcopal Church, Morehouse Publ, 92. **CONTACT ADDRESS** Va Theol Sem, 3737 Seminary Rd, Alexandria, VA, 22304.

PARRISH, STEPHEN E.
PERSONAL Born 03/22/1952, Detroit, MI, m, 1981, 3 children **DISCIPLINE** PHILOSOPHY **EDUCATION** Schoolcraft Col, AA, 72; Eastern Mich Univ, BS, 75; Univ Mich, MLS, 79; Wayne State, MA, 84, PhD, 91. **CAREER** Instr, Wayne State Univ, 88-; William Tyndale Col Libr and asst prof Philos, 91- . **MEMBERSHIPS** Amer Philos Asn; Soc Christian Philos; Evangel Philos Soc. **RESEARCH** Philosophy of Religion; Nietzsche; Philosophy of mind; objectivism. **SELECTED PUBLICATIONS** Auth, The Mormon God, Omniscience, and eternal progression: A Philosophical Analysis, Trinity Jour 12NS, Fall, 91, 127-138; Mormon Theism and the Argument from Design: Philosophical Analysis, Criswell Theol Rev, spring 91; Yandell on Temptation and Necessity, Philosophia Christi, Jour of the Evangelical Philos Soc, vol 20:2, winter 97, 57-62; coauth, See the Gods Fall, The Col Press, Fall 97; Fod and Necessity, UP of Am, May 97; Auth, The Mormon Concept of God: A Philosophical Analysis, Mellen, 91. **CONTACT ADDRESS** Dept of Philosophy, William Tyndale Col, 35700 W Twelve Mile Rd, Farmington Hills, MI, 48331.

PARROT, ROD
PERSONAL Born 03/26/1942, Ontario, OR, m, 1964, 1 child **DISCIPLINE** RELIGION **EDUCATION** Northwest Christ Col, BTh, 65; Phillips Univ Grad Sem, MDiv, 69, MTh, 70; Clarmont Grad School, 80. **CAREER** Disciples Sem Found, asst dean, 79-89, assoc dean, 89-. **HONORS AND AWARDS** Ecumenical Serv Award, 84 **MEMBERSHIPS** SBL, SACEM, CCU, DCHS **RESEARCH** Adult learn theol; congreg stud and lead; soc formations; soclgy of relig; soclgy of conflict in Pauline churches. **SELECTED PUBLICATIONS** Auth, Impact, Semeia and Forum, revs: The Disciple, Encounter and Midstream, coauth the Ministry of Elders, Oikodome Pub, 90. **CONTACT ADDRESS** Disciples Sem Foundation, 398 W Foothill Blvd, Claremont, CA, 91711-2709. **EMAIL** rparrott@dsf.edu

PARRY, RICHARD D.
PERSONAL Born 06/30/1939, Easton, PA, m, 1967, 2 children **DISCIPLINE** PHILOSOPHY **EDUCATION** Georgetown Univ, BA, cum laude, 61; Yale Univ, MA, 63; Univ NC, PhD, 68. **CAREER** Instr philos, Univ SC, 64-65; AGNES SCOTT COL, 67-, FULLER E. CALLOWAY PROF PHILOS, 86-; Humanities Admin, Nat Endowment for the Humanities, 87-88. **HONORS AND AWARDS** Richard M. Griffin Memorial Junior Award, Southern Soc for Philos and Psychol, 70; Dir of Summer Seminar for School Teachers, Nat Endowment for the Humanities, 86, 91, 93, 94, 96; President's award for Excellence in Teaching, Agnes Scott Col, 90. **MEMBERSHIPS** Amer Philos Assoc; Amer Cath Philos Assoc; Soc for Ancient Greek Philos; Int Plato Soc; Southern Soc for Philos and Psychol. **RESEARCH** Ancient Greek philosophy; Plato's moral theory. **SELECTED PUBLICATIONS** Auth, The Gulf War and the Just War Doctrine, America, 91; The Intelligible World-Animal in Plato's Timaeus, J of the Hist of Philos, 91; Dialogue with the Text, Amer Philos Assoc Newsletter on Teaching Philos, 91; Eudaimonism, -ism, Encyclopedia of Ethics, 92; Morality and Happiness, J of Ed, 96; Plato's Craft of Justice, State Univ NY Press, 96; Philosopher Kings and Forms, Plato's Political Philosophy, 97; The Uniqueness of Forms, Great Political Thinkers: Plato, 97. **CONTACT ADDRESS** Dept of Philos, Agnes Scott Col, Decatur, GA, 30030. **EMAIL** rparry@agnesscott.edu

PARSONS, CHARLES D.
PERSONAL Born 04/13/1933, Cambridge, MA, m, 1968, 2 children **DISCIPLINE** PHILOSOPHY; MATHEMATICS **EDUCATION** AB, 54, AM, 56, Harvard Univ; Kings College, Cambridge, PhD, 61. **CAREER** Asst Prof, 61-62, Cornell Univ; Assoc Prof, 65-69, Prof, 69-89, Columbia Univ; Asst

Prof, 62-65, Prof, 89-91, Edgar Pierce Prof, 91-, Harvard Univ. **HONORS AND AWARDS** Henry Fel, 54-55; NEH Fel, 79-80; Guggenheim Fel, 86-87; Fel, NAIS, 87; Fel, Ctr for Advanced Study in Behavioral Sciences, 94-95; Fel, Amer Acad of Arts and Sciences, 82-. **MEMBERSHIPS** Assoc for Symblic Logic; Amer Phil Assoc. **RESEARCH** Logic; philosophy of logic and mathematics; Kant **SELECTED PUBLICATIONS** Auth, The Structuralist View of Mathematical Objects, Synthese 84, 90; The Uniqueness of the Natural Numbers, Iyyun 39, 90; The Transcendental Aesthetic, The Cambridge Companion to Kant, 92; On Some Difficulties Concerning Intuition and Intuitive Knowledge, Mind N.S. 102, 93; Intuition and Number, Mathematics and Mind, 94; Structuralism and the Concept of Set, Modality, Morality, and Belief: Essays in Honor of Ruth Barcan Marcus, 95; Platonism and Mahematical Intuition in Kurt Godel's Thought, The Bulletin of Symbolic Knowledge, 95; What Can We Do in Principle, Logic and Scientific Mehtods, 97; Finitism and Intuitive Knowledge, The Philosophy of Mathematics Today, 98. **CONTACT ADDRESS** Dept of Philosophy-Emerson Hall, Harvard Univ, Cambridge, MA, 02138. **EMAIL** parsons2@fas.harvard.edu

PARSONS, HOWARD L.
PERSONAL Born 07/09/1918, Jacksonville, FL, d, 3 children **DISCIPLINE** PHILOSOPHY **EDUCATION** Univ of Chicago, BA, 42; PhD, 46. **CAREER** Ast Prof, Univ of South CA, 46-47; Inst, Univ Ill, 47-49; Asst Prof, Univ of TN, 57-65; Assoc Prof; Coe Col, 65-88; Prof, Univ of Bridgeport, 80, 90; Prof, Moscow St Univ. **HONORS AND AWARDS** William Rainey Harper Fel, Univ of Chicago, 45-46; Res Grant Wenner-Gren Found, 56; Res Grant Kavir Ins, 63-64; Amer Coun of Learned Soc, 75-76; Intl Res and Exchanges Bd, 77-78 & 80; Mellon Res Fel, 85 & 88. **MEMBERSHIPS** APA; Soc for Values in Higher Ed; Soc for the Philos Stud of Marxism; Found for Philos of Creativity **RESEARCH** Philosophy of religion; ethics; marxism. **SELECTED PUBLICATIONS** Buddhism as Humanism, Tokyo, 82; Man in the Contemporary World, Moscow, 85; Christianity Today in the USSR, Intl, 87; Diverse Perspectives on Marxist Philosophy East and West, Greenwood, 95. **CONTACT ADDRESS** 232 Dunnlea Rd, Fairfield, CT, 06430-2815.

PARSONS, KEITH M.
PERSONAL Born 08/31/1952, Macon, GA, s **DISCIPLINE** HISTORY & PHILOSOPHY OF SCIENCE; PHILOSOPHY OF RELIGION **EDUCATION** Queens Univ, PhD, 86; Univ Pitts, PhD, 96. **CAREER** Asst Prof Univ Houston-Clear Lake; Ed, Philo, Jour Soc Humanist Phil **MEMBERSHIPS** Philos Sci Asn; Am Philos Asn. **RESEARCH** Rationality & theory change in science; history of the earth sciences; Darwinism; science and religion. **SELECTED PUBLICATIONS** Auth, God and the Burden of Proof, Prometheus Books, 89; Drawing Out Leviathan: What do we Really Know About Dinosaurs? Ind Univ Press. **CONTACT ADDRESS** Univ Houston-Clear Lake, 2700 Bay Area Blvd., Houston, TX, 77058-1098. **EMAIL** parsons@cl.uh.edu

PARTAN, DANIEL GORDON
PERSONAL Born 08/02/1933, Gardner, MA, m, 1957, 5 children **DISCIPLINE** LAW **EDUCATION** Cornell Univ, AB, 55; Harvard Univ, LLB, 58, LLM, 61. **CAREER** Fac asst law, Harvard Univ, 59-61; res assoc, 61-62; res assoc rule of law res ctr, Duke Univ, 62-67; assoc prof, 65-68, Prof Law, Boston Univ, 68-; Fulbright fel, Law Fac, Univ Cologne, 58-59; assoc prof law, Univ NDak, 64-65; chmn, Comt Charter UN, Am Br Int Law Asn, 71-75; consult, Law & Pop Prog, Fletcher Sch Law, Tufts Univ, 71-75; consult, Am Acad Arts & Sci, 74-75, US Dept State, 76-77 & UN Develop Prog, 77-78. **HONORS AND AWARDS** App Chpt 19 Binat Panel Roster, U S-Canada Free Trade Agreement & NAFTA, 92-; App Dispute Settlement Roster, WTO, 97-. **MEMBERSHIPS** Am Soc Int Law; Int Law Asn; Am Law Inst; UN Asn; Comn Study Orgn Peace; Acad Counc UN System; European Community Studies Asn. **RESEARCH** International law and organization; international trade law; admiralty and maritime law; arms control and legal problems in the development of world order. **SELECTED PUBLICATIONS** Auth, Individual responsibility under a disarmament agreement in American law, Minn Law Rev, 4/65; Peaceful settlement of peripheral conflict, in The Vietnam War and International Law, Princeton Univ, 68; coauth, Legal Problems in International Administration, Harvard Law Sch, 68; auth, Population in the United Nations System, Sijthoff, The Netherlands, 73; Documentary Study of the Politicization of UNESCO, (2 vols), Am Acad Arts & Sci, 75; Increasing the effectiveness of the international court, Harvard Int Law J, 77; The United States and the International Labor Organization, Comn Study Orgn Peace, 79; International Administrative Law, Am J Int Law, 80; Increasing the effectiveness of the international court, in International Law: A Contemporary Perspective, 85; The duty to inform in international environmental law, Boston Univ Intl Law J, 88; Retaliation in United States and European community trade law, Boston Univ Intl Law J, 90; co-ed, Corporate Disclosure of Environmental Risks: US and European Law, Butterworth Legal Publ, 90; The International Law Process: Cases and Materials, Carolina Acad Press, 92; Merger control in the European community: Federalism with a European flavor, in The State of the European Community, 93; Report on improving the effectiveness of the United Nations in advancing the rule of law in the world, Rapporteur, 8/94, Intl Lawyer, summer 95; The justiciability of subsidarity, in The State of the European Union, 95. **CONTACT ADDRESS** Sch of Law, Boston Univ, 765 Commonwealth Ave, Boston, MA, 02215-1401. **EMAIL** partan@bu.edu

PASCH, ALAN
PERSONAL Born 12/01/1925, Cleveland, OH, m, 1950, 1 child **DISCIPLINE** PHILOSOPHY **EDUCATION** Univ Mich, BA, 49; New Sch Soc Res, MA, 52; Princeton Univ, PhD, 55. **CAREER** Bamford fel, Princeton Univ, 55-56; from instr to asst prof philos, Ohio State Univ, 56-60; assoc prof, 60-67, prof philos, prof emer, 97- , Univ Md-College Park, 67-. **MEMBERSHIPS** Am Philos Asn (exec dir, 69-72); Metaphys Soc Am; Soc Philos & Pub Affairs; Wash Philos Club (pres, 78-79); Eastern Div Am Philos Asn (secy-treas, 65-68); Wash Rare Book Gp. **RESEARCH** Metaphysics of human sexuality; philosophy of logic. **SELECTED PUBLICATIONS** Auth, Experience and the Analytic, Univ Chicago, 58. **CONTACT ADDRESS** Dept of Philosophy, Univ of Maryland, College Park, MD, 20742-7615. **EMAIL** ap3@umail.umd.edu

PASCUZZI, MARIE
PERSONAL Born 07/18/1951, Brooklyn, NY **DISCIPLINE** BIBLICAL STUDIES **EDUCATION** Pontifical Bibl Inst, Rome, SSL, 87; Gregorian Univ, Rome, STD, 97. **CAREER** Asst prof, St. Joseph's Sem & Grad Sch of Theology, Yonkers NY, 87-92; asst prof, Immaculate Conception Sem & Graduate Sch of Tehology, Huntington NY, 92-96; assoc prof theol, St. Peter's Col, Jersey City, NJ, 98- . **MEMBERSHIPS** AAR/SBL; CBA. **RESEARCH** New Testament; Paul; Greco-Roman rhetoric. **SELECTED PUBLICATIONS** Auth, Ethics, Ecclesiology and Church Discipline: A Rhetorical Analysis of 1 Corinthians 5, Gregorian Univ Pr, 97. **CONTACT ADDRESS** 576 Prospect Ave, Brooklyn, NY, 11215-6012. **EMAIL** pascuzzi_m@spcvxa.spc.edu

PASKOW, ALAN
PERSONAL Born 06/11/1939, Elizabeth, NJ, m, 1967, 1 child **DISCIPLINE** PHILOSOPHY **EDUCATION** Haverford Col, BA, 61; Northwestern Univ, MA, 63; Yale Univ, PhD(philos), 71. **CAREER** Instr philos, Antioch Col, 67-68; from instr to asst prof, Univ Vt, 68-74; asst prof, Prescott Col, 74, mem fac, Prescott Ctr Col, 75-76; mem fac, Deep Springs Col, 76-80, Assoc Prof Philos, St Mary's Col, Md, 81-, Danforth teaching assoc humanities, 67-68; Nat Endowment Humanities grant spec humanities prog, 73; vis assoc prof philos, Haverford Col, 80-81. **HONORS AND AWARDS** Sr Res Fulbright Grant. **MEMBERSHIPS** Am Philos Asn. **RESEARCH** Phenomenology and existentialism, philosophy of art. **SELECTED PUBLICATIONS** Auth, Are College Students Educable?, J Higher Educ, 3/74; auth, "The Meaning of my Own Death," Int Philos Quart, 3/74; "A Phenomenological View of the Beetle in my Box," New Scholasticism, summer 74; auth, What do I Fear in Facing my Death?, 5/75 & Towards a Theory of Self-deception, Vol 12, No 2, Continental Philosophical Review. **CONTACT ADDRESS** Div Human Develop, St. Mary's Col, Saint Marys City, MD, 20686-0222. **EMAIL** apaskow@osprey.smcm.edu

PASKOW, SHIMON
PERSONAL Born 06/21/1932, Newark, NJ, m, 1962, 1 child **DISCIPLINE** RELIGIOUS STUDIES **EDUCATION** Brooklyn Col, BA; Hebrew Union Col, MA, 59. **CAREER** Instr, Hebrew Union Col; instr, Univ of Judaism. **HONORS AND AWARDS** Hebrew Union Col, fel, 59-60. **MEMBERSHIPS** Cent Conf of Am Rabbis; Military Chaplains Asn; Asn of Jewish Chaplains; Soc of Bibl Lit; Am Jewish Hist Soc. **RESEARCH** Religious studies; Hebrew; Judaism. **CONTACT ADDRESS** 1080 Janss Rd, Thousand Oaks, CA, 91360.

PASSAMANECK, STEPHEN MAURICE
PERSONAL Born 12/07/1933, Pittsburgh, PA, m, 1962, 2 children **DISCIPLINE** RABBINIC LITERATURE **EDUCATION** Univ Pittsburgh, BA, 55; Hebrew Union Col, MA, 60, PhD, 64; Oxford Univ, dipl law, 63. **CAREER** From instr to assoc prof, 63-72, Prof Rabbinics, Hebrew Union Col, Calif, 72-. **MEMBERSHIPS** Cent Conf Am Rabbis. **RESEARCH** Rabbinic law; comparative law; rabbinic jurisprudence. **SELECTED PUBLICATIONS** Auth, Caravan custom in early rabbinic sources, Tijdschrift voor Rechtsgeschiedenis, 68; A case of piracy, Hebrew Union Col Ann, 70; Two aspects of rabbinic maritime law, J Jewish Studies, 71; Insurance in Rabbinic Law, Edinburgh Univ, 74; ed, Jewish Law and Jewish Life, Union Am Hebrew Congregations, 77; Goldsmith,morris + Commentary And Analysis of The Career of a Jewish Immigrant And Law-enforcement Officer in 19th-century America - Deputy-united-states-marshal, American Jewish Archives, Vol 0046, 1994 **CONTACT ADDRESS** Hebrew Union Col, 3077 University Mall, Los Angeles, CA, 90007.

PASSELL, DAN
PERSONAL Born 10/08/1928, Cleveland, OH, m, 1954, 4 children **DISCIPLINE** PHILOSOPHY **EDUCATION** Univ Chicago, PhB, 49, MA, 54; Stanford Univ, PhD, 64. **CAREER** Instr philos, Fresno State Col, 61-63; asst prof, 64-72, prof philos, Portland State Univ, 72-. **RESEARCH** Theory of meaning. **CONTACT ADDRESS** Dept of Philosophy, Portland State Univ, PO Box 751, Portland, OR, 97207-0751. **EMAIL** dan@nh1.nh.pdx.edu

PATEL, RAMESH
DISCIPLINE EASTERN AND WESTERN PHILOSOPHY, WORLD RELIGIONS **EDUCATION** St Xavier Col, BA, MA; Govt Law Col, LLB; Univ NM, MA, PhD. **CAREER** Prof, Antioch Col. **RESEARCH** The philos of Mahatma Gandhi. **SELECTED PUBLICATIONS** Auth, Philosophy of the Gita, Peter Lang Publ, 91; The Numinous and the Mystical; Gandhi's Dual Concept of Truth; Brahma's Philosophical Synthesis According to Ojha. **CONTACT ADDRESS** Antioch Col, Yellow Springs, OH, 45387.

PATERSON, ROBERT
DISCIPLINE LAW **EDUCATION** Univ New Zeland, LLB, 69; Stanford Univ, JSM, 72. **CAREER** Prof, 81-. **RESEARCH** Corporations; securities regulation; international trade and investment; international commercial arbitration; cultural property and law. **SELECTED PUBLICATIONS** Auth, International Trade and Investment Law in Canada, 94; pubs about corporations, securities regulation, international trade, international arbitration and cultural property; co-ed, UNCITRAL Model Law in Canada, 89. **CONTACT ADDRESS** Fac of Law, Univ British Columbia, 1822 East Mall, Vancouver, BC, V6T 1Z1. **EMAIL** paterson@law.ubc.ca

PATRICK, ANNE E.
PERSONAL Born 04/05/1941, Washington, DC **DISCIPLINE** RELIGION **EDUCATION** Medaille Col, BA, 69; Univ Maryland, MA, 72; Univ Chicago, MA, 76, PhD, 82. **CAREER** Lectr, religion & lit, 78-80, Univ Chicago Divinity School; Warren Dist Vis Prof, 89, Univ Tulsa; Paul E McKeever vis prof, moral theology, 97-98, St John's Univ, NY; instr, 80-82, asst prof, 82-86, assoc prof, 86-91, dept chmn, 86-88, 90-91, prof, 91-, Carleton Col. **MEMBERSHIPS** AAR; Amer Asn Univ Prof; CTSA, Pres, 89-90; Col Theology Soc; Intl Network of Soc for Catholic Theology; Soc of Christian Ethics. **RESEARCH** Christian feminist ethics; moral theology; George Eliot; fiction and ethics. **SELECTED PUBLICATIONS** Art, Publications of the Park Ridge Center for Health, Faith, and Ethics, Religious Stud Rev, 93; art, Veritatis Splendor, Commonwealth, 93; art, Mass Media and the Enlargement of Moral Sensibility: Insights from Theology and Literary History, Mass Media and the Moral Imagination, Sheed & Ward, 94; art, Is Theodicy an Evil? Response to The Evils of Theodicy, Proceedings of the Catholic Theological Soc of Amer Vol 50, 95; art, From Hearing to Collaboration: Some Steps for the Privileged Toward a Praxis of Solidarity, Women and Theology, Maryknoll, Orbis, 95; auth, Liberating Conscience: Feminist Explorations in Catholic Moral Theology, NY Continuum 96; art, Creative Fiction and Theological Ethics: The Contributions of James M. Gustafson, Ann of the Soc of Christian Ethics 17, 97; art, Markers, Barriers, and Frontiers: Theology in the Borderlands, Theology: Expanding the Borders, 23rd Pub, 98; art, Imaginative Literature and the Renewal o Moral Theology, New Theology Review, 5/98. **CONTACT ADDRESS** Carleton Col, Dept of Religion, Northfield, MN, 55057-4228. **EMAIL** apatrick@carleton.edu

PATRICK, DALE
PERSONAL Born 10/10/1938, Eugene, OR, m, 1961, 1 child **DISCIPLINE** THEOLOGY **EDUCATION** Lewis & Clark Col, BS, 60; Union Theol Sem, 61; School of Theol, Drew Univ, BD, 63; Grad Theol Union/San Francisco Sem, ThD, 71. **CAREER** Asst to assoc prof, Mo Sch of Rel, 68-81; vis assoc prof, Univ Mo, 81-82; assoc prof to PROF, ENDOWED HUM CHAIR, DRAKE UNIV, 1982-. **HONORS AND AWARDS** RockeFeler Fel, 60-61. **MEMBERSHIPS** Soc Bibl Lit; Am Acad Rel. **RESEARCH** Bibl law, rhetoric, Bibl Theol. **SELECTED PUBLICATIONS** Co-auth, Rhetoric and Biblical Interpretation, 90; auth, "God's Commandment," in God in the Fray: A Tribute to Walter Brueggemann, 98; "The First Commandment in the Structure of the Pentateuch," in Vetus Testamentum XLV/1, 95; "The Rhetoric of Colective Responsibility in Deuteronomic Law," in Pomegranates and Golden Bells: Studies in Biblical, Jewish and Near Eastern Ritual, Law, and Literature in Honor of Jacob Milgrom, 95. **CONTACT ADDRESS** Dept of Philos/Rel, Drake Univ, Des Moines, IA, 50311. **EMAIL** dale.patrick@drake.edu

PATRICK, DARRYL L.
PERSONAL Born 10/05/1936, Havre, MT, m, 1966, 2 children **DISCIPLINE** MORAL THEORY **EDUCATION** Univ WA, MA, 70; N TX State Univ, PhD, 72. **CAREER** Tchg Asst, N TX State Univ, 75-. **SELECTED PUBLICATIONS** Auth, Venetian Palaces, Educl Filmstrips, 73; Times and Places Gone By Historic Photographic Exhib, Sam Houston Memorial Mus, 79; Pop Art, Popular Culture and Libraries, Shoe String Press, 84. **CONTACT ADDRESS** Sam Houston State Univ, Huntsville, TX, 77341. **EMAIL** art_dlp@shsu.eduss

PATRICK DOWNEY, JAMES
PERSONAL Waynesboro, VA **DISCIPLINE** METAPHYSICS, CONTEMPORARY MORAL ISSUES, PHILOSOPHY OF RELIGION, AND LOGIC **EDUCATION** Univ VA, PhD. **CAREER** Instr, Hollins Col. **SELECTED PUBLICATIONS** Auth, A Primordial Reply to Modern Gaunilos, Relig Stud, 86; On Omniscience, Faith and Philos, 93. **CONTACT ADDRESS** Hollins Col, Roanoke, VA, 24020.

PATRY, WILLIAM F.
DISCIPLINE LAW **EDUCATION** SF State Univ, BA, 74; MA, 76; Univ Houston, JD 80. **CAREER** Assoc prof, Yeshiva Univ. **HONORS AND AWARDS** Asst coun, House Judiciary Subcomt, 92-95; advisor, US Copyright Off.. **SELECTED PUBLICATIONS** Auth, The Fair Use Privilege and Copyright Law. **CONTACT ADDRESS** Yeshiva Univ, 55 Fifth Ave, NY, NY, 10003-4301. **EMAIL** patry@ymail.yu.edu

PATTE, DANIEL
PERSONAL Born 01/17/1939, France, m, 1960, 3 children **DISCIPLINE** PHILOSOPHY **EDUCATION** Univ Grenoble, France, BA, 58; Faculte de Theol Protestante, France, BD, 60; Univ Geneva, M Th, 64; Chicago Theol Sem, ThD, 71. **CAREER** Asst min, 63-64, Reformed Church of Meyrin, Switzerland; prof, 64-66, Col Hammar, Rep of Congo; instr, 68-71, Syracuse Univ; assoc prof, 74-80, chmn, dept relig stud, 77-98, prof, relig stud, 80-, Vanderbilt Univ. **RESEARCH** Comparative stud of interpretations of the Bible through hist & cultures. **CONTACT ADDRESS** Vanderbilt Univ, Box 1585, Station B, Nashville, TN, 37235. **EMAIL** Daniel.M.Patte@Vanderbilt.edu

PATTEN, PRISCILLA C.
PERSONAL Born 01/30/1950, Berkeley, CA, m, 1986, 1 child **DISCIPLINE** RELIGION **EDUCATION** Patten Col, BS bible 69; Holy Names Col, BA psychol 70; Wheaton Col, MA New Test 72; Drew Univ, PhD New Test 76. **CAREER** Patten Col, Pres 83, prof 75. **SELECTED PUBLICATIONS** Before the Times, co auth, Strawberry Hill Press, 80;The World of the Early Church, co auth, Edwin Mellon Press, 90; many articles. **CONTACT ADDRESS** Dept of New Testament, Patten Col, 2433 Collidge Av, Oakland, CA, 94601.

PATTERSON, BOB E.
PERSONAL Born 08/29/1931, Kings Mountain, NC, m, 1953, 2 children **DISCIPLINE** LITERATURE AND THEOLOGY **EDUCATION** Gardner-Webb Univ, AA, 50; Baylor Univ, BA, 52, MA, 57; Southern Baptist Theol Seminary, Mdiv, 56, PhD, 60. **CAREER** Distinguished Prof of Rel, Dept of Rel, 61-, Baylor Univ. **HONORS AND AWARDS** Alpha Chi Scholastic Fraternity; Outstanding Educ Of Amer; Outstanding Faculty Member; Permanent Distinguished Prof of Rel; Regional Pres of AAR; Natl Pres of N.A.B.P.R. **MEMBERSHIPS** AAR, A. A.U.D., NABPR. **RESEARCH** Theology, Faith and Science, Biblical Studies, Philosophy of Religion. **SELECTED PUBLICATIONS** Auth, Science, Faith and Revelation; Perspectives on Theology; Discovering Ezekiel and Daniel; Discovering Matthew; Discovering Revelation; Theologians, Carl F. H. Henry, Reinhold Niebuhr; Who is Jesus Christ?, ed, 18 vol series, Makers of Modern Theological Mind. **CONTACT ADDRESS** Dept of Religion, Baylor Univ, Waco, TX, 76798. **EMAIL** Bob_Patterson@baylor.edu

PATTERSON, D.
PERSONAL Born 09/29/1955, New York, NY, m, 1978, 2 children **DISCIPLINE** PHILOSOPHY LAW **EDUCATION** SUNY Buffalo, PhD, JD, 80, MA 78, BA 76. **CAREER** Rutgers Univ, assoc prof, prof, dist prof, 90 to 95-; Western New Eng College, asst prof, 87-90; Univ Maine, lect, 85-86; Loyd Bumgardner Field and Patterson, att, partner, 82-87; Preti Flaherty Beliveau, assoc, 81-82. **HONORS AND AWARDS** RUBT Awd for Excell; ACLS Sr Res Awd; Fulbright Sr Lect Gnt; Alexander von Humbolt Stifung Sr Res Gnt; Dean's Sch Rutgers; Phi Beta Kappa., Visiting Prof at: Univ Vienna 95; Georgetown Univ Law Cen 94-95; Univ Texas 93; Karl-franzens-Univ 92; Bar Admissions to: NJ 96, Supreme Court USA 84, USDC MA 82, Maine 81, NY 81. **MEMBERSHIPS** ABA; AALS; APA. **SELECTED PUBLICATIONS** Auth, The Philosophy of Law: An Introduction, with Jeffery White, Oxford Univ Press, in production; Recht and Wahrheit, translation of Law and Truth, Nomos Verlag, in preparation; Introduction to Commercial Law, with Richard Hyland, West Pub, in prep; Introduction to Contemporary Jurisprudence, Blackwell, in prep; Blackwell Anthology for Philosophy of Law and Legal Theory, Blackwell ed, in prep; Post Modern Law, Dartmouth and NY Univ Press, 94; Theory Practice and Jurisprudence: Reflections on the Work of Frederick Schauer, Hart Pub, forthcoming; Response to Critics: Symposium on Law and Truth, SMU Law Rev, forthcoming; Karl Llewellyn, in: The Philosophy of Law: An Encycl, ed, Christopher Gray, NY, NY Garland Pub, 97; Postmodernism, in: Blackwell Companion to the Philo of Law and Legal Theory, ed, 96; Law as a Social Fact: A Reply to Professor Martinez, Loyola LA, L Rev 96; Uniform Commercial Code, rev sec 1-205, Auth, pending public comment; Legality and Legitimacy: Carl Schmitt, Hans Kelsen and Hermann Heller, in: Wiemar, Jurist, forthcoming; Jorge J. E. Gracia, A. Theory of Textuality: The Logic and Epistemology, Rev of Metaphysics, 97. **CONTACT ADDRESS** Dept of Law, Rutgers State Univ, 40 Regan Lane, Voorhees, NJ, 08043. **EMAIL** dpatters@crab.rutgers.edu

PATTERSON, ELIZABETH G.
DISCIPLINE PROPERTY, HEALTH LAW, AND FAMILY LAW **EDUCATION** Agnes Scott Col, BA, 68; Univ AZ, JD, 76. **CAREER** Prof, Univ of SC. **RESEARCH** Health law; children and the law. **SELECTED PUBLICATIONS** Publ on, res interest. **CONTACT ADDRESS** School of Law, Univ of S. Carolina, Law Center, Columbia, SC, 29208. **EMAIL** Libba@law.law.sc.edu

PATTERSON, ELIZABETH HAYES
PERSONAL Born 06/25/1945, Boston, MA, m **DISCIPLINE** LAW **EDUCATION** Sorbonne Univ of Paris, diploma with honors 1966; Emmanuel Coll, AB with distinction in French 1967; Stanford U, 1967-68; Columbus Sch of Law Cath Univ of Am, JD 1973. **CAREER** Georgetown Ul Law Cntr, assoc dean JD & graduate programs, 1993-97, asso prof 1980-; DC Pub Sev Commn, chmn 1978-80; DC Pub Serv Commn, commr 1977-80 Columbus Sch of Law Cath U, adj prof 1976; Hogan & Hartson Law Firm, asso 1974-77; Hon Ruggero Aldisert US Ct of Appeals, law clk 1973-74. **HONORS AND AWARDS** Woodrow Wilson Fellow Woodrow Wilson Soc 1967; A Salute to Black Women in Gov Iota Phi Lambda Sor Gamma Cht 1978; **MEMBERSHIPS** National Florence Crittenton Mission Foundation Board, trustee, 1995-; bd of dirs, Child Welfare League of America, 1997; Amer Law Institute, 1995-; Trst Family & Child Sev Wash DC 1977-; bd of dirs, Frederick B Abramson Foundation, 1992-; trst, Emmanuel Coll, 1994-; ACLU Litigation Screening Com 1977-80; DC Bar Div I Steering Com 1980-82, DC Bar Screening Comm 1985-86; bd editors Washington Lawyer 1986-91; Sec of State's Adv Comm on Private Intl Law; study group on the Law Applicable to the Intl Sale of Goods 1983-85; adv comm Procedures Judicial Council of the DC Circuit 1981-84; DC Law Revision Comm, 1990-93; treas, District of Columbia Bar, 1987-88. **SELECTED PUBLICATIONS** "UCC 2-612(3): Breach of an Installment Contract and a Hobson's Choice for the Aggrieved Party," 48 Ohio State Law Journal 227, 1987; "UN Convention on Contracts for the Intl Sale of Goods: Unification and the Tension Between Compromise and Domination," 22 Stanford Journal of Intl Law 263, 1986. **CONTACT ADDRESS** Law Ctr, Georgetown Univ, 600 New Jersey Ave NW, Washington, DC, 20001.

PATTERSON, MARK R.
DISCIPLINE ANTITRUST LAW **EDUCATION** OH State Univ, BSEE, 78, MS, 80; Stanford Law Sch, JD, 91. **CAREER** Assoc, Choate, Hall & Stewart, Boston, 91-93; clk, Sup Judicial Court of Mass, 93-94; Bigelow tchg fel, lectr, Univ Chicago Law Sch, 94-95; assoc prof, 95-. **RESEARCH** Law and sci research. **SELECTED PUBLICATIONS** Auth, Antitrust Liability for Collective Speech: Medical Society Practice Standards, 27 Ind Law Rev 51, 93; Product Definition, Product Information, and Market Power: Kodak in Perspective, 73 NC Law Rev 185, 94; Is Unlimited Liability Really Unattainable?: Of Long Arms and Short Sales, 56 Ohio State Law Jour 815, 95; Coercion, Deception, and Other Demand-Increasing Practices in Antitrust Law, 66 Antitrust Law Jour 1, 97. **CONTACT ADDRESS** Law Sch, Fordham Univ, 113 W 60th St, New York, NY, 10023. **EMAIL** mpatterson@mail.lawnet.fordham.edu

PATTON, CORRINE
PERSONAL Born 01/19/1958, Sacramento, CA, m, 1986, 2 children **DISCIPLINE** THEOLOGY **EDUCATION** Univ San Francisco, BA, 80; Grad Theol Union, Berkeley, MA, 84; Yale Univ, PhD, 91. **CAREER** Asst Prof, Florida State Univ, 91-96; Asst Prof, Univ of St Thomas, 96-. **MEMBERSHIPS** SBL, CBA. **RESEARCH** Ezekiel, Prophets, History of Biblical Interpretation. **SELECTED PUBLICATIONS** Auth, Contribute to Chronicles and Its Synoptic Parallels in Samuel, Kings and Related Biblical Texts, Liturgical Press, 98; The Old Testament Canon in Catholic Tradition, For Theological Exegesis: Essays in Conversation with Brevard S Childs, ed C Seitz and K Greene-McCreight, in press, 1999; Hugh and Andrew of St Victor and Nicholas of Lyra, Historical Handbook of Major Biblical Interpreters, ed, K K McKim, InterVarsity Press, 98; Psalm 132, A Methodological Inquiry, Catholic Biblical Quarterly, 95. **CONTACT ADDRESS** Univ St Thomas, 2115 Summit Ave, St. Paul, MN, 55105. **EMAIL** clpatton@stthomas.edu

PATTY, STACY L.
PERSONAL 4 children **DISCIPLINE** THEOLOGICAL ETHICS **EDUCATION** Lubbock Christian Univ, Lubbock, Tex, BA, 79; Harding Univ Grad Sch Rel, Memphis, Tenn, MTh, 83; Union Theol Sem, NYork, STM, 88; Baylor Univ,Waco, Tex, PhD, 94. **CAREER** Assoc prof rel stud, Lubbock Christian Univ, 95-; ch, Southern Asn Accreditation Rev-Fac Issues, 96-98; Tenure Policy Rev, 96-97; Core Curr Rev, 95-97; Fac Senate, 95-98; asst prof Bible, 92-94; ch, Chapel, 94-95; Liberal Arts Curr Rev, 93-94; Acad Policy, 92-93; grad asst, Baylor Univ, Waco, Tex, 89-92; res asst, grader exams & papers, Hill Col, Hillsboro, Tex; instr, 83-85; Lilly Found, Inc. & Rhodes Col, fel, 98-99; Amer Acad Rel, consult fel, 96-97; Lilly fel, 96; Amer Acad Rel-Lilly Endowment-Nat Endowment for the Humanities, Lilly fel, 95-96; Lubbock Christian Univ grad fel, 91-92; Baylor Univ grad fel, 90-92; Christian Scholar Found, Atlanta, GA, Who's Who Among Stud in Amer Col(s) & Univ(s), listed for the acad yrs 90-91, 81-82, 78-79, & 77-78 Alpha Chi Honor Soc Elected to membership, 78; ch, Philos Relig & Theol Sect, Amer Acad Relig, sw region, 96-98; member, bd dir Christian Scholars' Confe, 96- & Corp Bd, Restoration Quart jour, 96-; lect, Abilene Christian Univ, Abilene, Tex, Jl 97; Lubbock Christian Univ, Lubbock, Tex), Aug 97; Amer Acad Relig-sw Region Meeting, Dallas, Tex, Mar 97; David Lipscomb Univ, Nashville, Tenn, Jl 96; Lubbock Christian Univ, Lubbock, Tex), Jl 95; church related presentations, Lubbock Christian Univ, Oct,97; Nat Youth Min Sem, Lubbock, Tex, Oct 94; Ann Lectureship, Lubbock Christian Univ, Oct 93; Ann Lectureship, Pepperdine Univ, Malibu, Calif, Apr 93; church activ, adult Bible class tchr, Vandelia Church of Christ, Lubbock, Tex, 97; col Min, Monterey Church of Christ, Lubbock, Tex, 93-95; Min, Elm Mott Church of Christ, Elm Mott, Tex, 89-92. **HONORS AND AWARDS** Trinity Univ L.R. Wilson ,sr tchg awd, 96. **MEMBERSHIPS** Amer Acad Relig; Soc Christian Ethics. **RESEARCH** Pedagogy in Religion and Theology; contemporary and Postmodern Philosophy and Theology; World Religions; Religion and Society; Religion and Science; Environmental Ethics; Medical Ethics & Business Ethics. **SELECTED PUBLICATIONS** Rev, Leonardo and Clodovis Boff's Introducing Liberation Theology and Robert McAfee Brown's Gustavo Gutierrez: An Introduction to Liberation Theology, Restoration Quart 33, 91. **CONTACT ADDRESS** Bible Dept, Lubbock Christian Univ, 5601 19th St, Lubbock, TX, 79407-2099. **EMAIL** stacypat@lcu.edu

PATZIA, ARTHUR G.
DISCIPLINE NEW TESTAMENT **EDUCATION** Univ of Manitoba, BA, 59; North Amer Baptist Sem, BO, 62; Princeton Theol Sem, ThM, 63; McMaster Univ, PhD, 70. **CAREER** Assoc Prof, 70-74, Biblical Lit, North Amer Baptist Sem; Assoc Prof NT, 79-82, Bethel Theol Sem; Temp App, 82-84, Dept Class, Univ of Minnesota; Assoc Prof, NT, 85-, Fuller Theol Sem. **HONORS AND AWARDS** Ontario Grad Fellowships; Canada Council Doctoral Fellowship. **MEMBERSHIPS** Soc of Biblical Lit; Inst of Biblical Res. **RESEARCH** Pauline Studies; Intertestamental; New Testament Church. **SELECTED PUBLICATIONS** Auth, Knowledge, Mystery, and Wisdom, Dictionary of the Later New Testament and Its Developments, ed, Ralph P. Martin and P. Davids. Downers Grove, IVP, 97; The Making of the New Testament, Origin, Collection, Text and Canon, Downers Grove, IVP, 95; Canon and Philemon, Epistle to, in Dictionary of Paul and His Letters, ed, Gerald Hawthorne, Ralph Martin and Daniel Reid, Downers Grove, IVP Press, 93; Ephesians, Colossians, Philemon, NIB Commentary, Hendrickson, 91. **CONTACT ADDRESS** 320 Middlefield Rd, Box 906, Menlo Park, CA, 94026-0906. **EMAIL** apatzia@fuller.edu

PAUL, GARRETT E.
PERSONAL Born 11/10/1949, Chicago Heights, IL, m, 3 children **DISCIPLINE** CHRISTIAN THEOLOGY **EDUCATION** Wabash Col, AB, 71; Univ Chicago, MA, 73, PhD, 80. **CAREER** Asst prof Relig, St Andrews Presbyterian Col, 76-83; REGENT PROF RELIG, GUSTAVUS ADOLPHUS COL, 83-. **MEMBERSHIPS** Am Academy Relig; Soc of Christian Ethics; Ernst Troeltsch Gesellschaft; Paul Tillich Soc. **RESEARCH** 19th and 20th century theology; philosophy, sociology, and history of religion; Ernst Troeltsch; religion and politics. **SELECTED PUBLICATIONS** Auth, Translation of Ernst Troeltsch, The Christian Faith, Glaubenslehre, Fortress, 91; Forming an Emphatic Christian Center: A Call to Political Responsibility, with Kyle Pasewark, in Christian Century 111, Aug 94, forthcoming, Abingdon Press, July 99; Theological Themes, in Lectionary Homiletics 6, no 7, June 95; Taste, Natural Law, and Biology: Connections and Separations between Ethics and Biology, in James Hurd, ed The Biology of Morality, Lewiston, NY: Edwin Mellon Press, 96; Jesus' Ethics of Perfection, review of Hans Dieter Betz, The Sermon on the Mount, in Christian Century 113, March 96; History and Ontology in Tension: Troeltsch's Glaubenslehre and Tillich's Dogmatik of 1925, forthcoming in a volume of papers on Troeltsch and Tillich, ed by Jean Richard and Robert Scharleman, to be published by Editions du Cerf, Paris; Translation of Ernst Troeltsch, Der Historismus und seine Probleme, with David Reid, Scholars Press, USA, Seigakuin Univ Press, Japan. **CONTACT ADDRESS** Dept of Relig, Gustavus Adolphus Col, 800 W College Ave, St Peter, MN, 56082-1498. **EMAIL** gpaul@gac.edu

PAULIEN, JON
PERSONAL Born 06/05/1949, New York, NY, m, 1973, 3 children **DISCIPLINE** NEW TESTAMENT **EDUCATION** Andrews Univ, M Div, 76, PhD, 87. **CAREER** Pastor, NY City, 72-81; prof, Andrews Univ, 84-. **HONORS AND AWARDS** Scholarly Publ Award, Andrews Univ, 92, 97. **MEMBERSHIPS** Soc of Bibl Lit; Chicago Soc for Bibl Res. **RESEARCH** The Apocalypse; Gospel of John; Contemporary culture issues. **SELECTED PUBLICATIONS** Auth, John, Bible Amplifier Series, Pacific Press Publ Asn, 95; auth, What the Bible Says About the End-Time, Review and Herald Publ Asn, 94; auth, Decoding Revelation's Trumpets, Andrews Univ Sem Doctoral Dissertation Series, vol 11, Andrews Univ Press, 88; article, The Role of the Hebrew Cultus, Sanctuary, and Temple in the Plot and Structure of the Book of Revelation, Andrews Univ Sem Studies, 33, 2, 245-264, 95; articles, The Anchor Bible Dict, NY, Doubleday, 92; article, The Seven Seals, Symposium on Revelation--Book I, 199-243, Bibl Res Inst, 92; article, Interpreting Revelation's Symbolism, Symposium on Revelation--Book I, 73-97, Bibl Res Inst, 92; Elusive Allusions: The Problematic Use of the OT in Revelation, Bibl Res, 33, 37-53, 88; article, Recent Developments in the Study of the Book of Revelation, Andrews Univ Sem Studies, 26, 2, 159-170, 88. **CONTACT ADDRESS** Andrews Univ, Berrien Springs, MI, 49104-1500. **EMAIL** jonp@andrews.edu

PAULO, CRAIG N.
PERSONAL Born 01/01/1968, Philadelphia, PA **DISCIPLINE** PHILOSOPHY **EDUCATION** LaSalle Univ, BA; Villanova Univ, MA; Pontifical Gregorian Univ, PhD, PhL. **CAREER** Asst prof philos, Pontifical Gregorian Univ, Rome. **HONORS AND AWARDS** Scholar in residence, Augustinianum, Rome. **MEMBERSHIPS** APA; ACPA. **RESEARCH** History of philosophy; Augustine; Heidegger; phenomenology. **SELECTED PUBLICATIONS** Auth, Being and Conversion, UMI, 97; auth, Out of the Garden: A Collection of Poetry, Spruce St Press, 98. **CONTACT ADDRESS** 1946 Durfor St, Philadelphia, PA, 19145.

PAULSEN, DAVID L.
PERSONAL Born 11/13/1936, Ephraim, UT, m, 1967, 6 children **DISCIPLINE** PHILOSOPHY, LAW **EDUCATION** Brigham Young Univ, BS, 61; Univ Chicago, JD, 64; Univ Mich, PhD(philos), 75. **CAREER** Atty, Kirton & Bettilyon, 65-68; instr, 72-75, asst prof, 75-78, Assoc Prof Philos, Brigham Young Univ, 78-. **RESEARCH** Thought of Soren Kierkegaard; philosophy of religion; William J Ames. **SELECTED PUBLICATIONS** Auth, Divine determinateness and the free will defense, Analysis, 81; a Reply to Paffenroth,kim Comment + Paulsen on Augustine, an Incorporeal or Non-anthropomorphic God - Notes And Observations, Harvard Theological Review, Vol 0086, 1993; The Mormon Concept of God - a Philosophical-analysis - Beckwith,fj, Parrish,se, International J For Philosophy of Religion, Vol 0035, 1994; The Doctrine of Divine-embodiment + The Historical Development of Classic Latter-day-saints Mormon Creeds And Covenants - Restoration, Judeo-christian, And Philosophical- perspectives, Brigham Young University Studies, Vol 0035, 1996. **CONTACT ADDRESS** 225 East 300 North, Orem, UT, 84057.

PAULSON, STANLEY LOWELL
PERSONAL Born 05/16/1941, Fergus Falls, MN, m, 1965 **DISCIPLINE** PHILOSOPHY **EDUCATION** Univ Minn, Minneapolis, BA, 64; Univ Wis-Madison, MA, 66, PhD(philos), 68; Harvard Univ, JD, 72. **CAREER** Instr philos, Univ Wis-Madison, 68-69; vis lectr, 72-73, asst prof, 74-78, Assoc Prof Philos, Wash Univ, 78-, Fels, Nat Endowment Humanities, Harvard Law Sch, 73-74 & Alexander von Humboldt Found, Law Fac, Free Univ Berlin, 76-77. **MEMBERSHIPS** Am Philos Asn; Am Soc Polit & Legal Philos; Int Asn Philos Law & Soc Philos. **RESEARCH** Philosophy of law **SELECTED PUBLICATIONS** Auth, Two types of motive explanation, Am Philos Quart, 472; Classical legal positivism at Nuremburg, Philos & Pub Affairs, winter 75; Jus Non Scriptum and the reliance principle, Mich Law Rev, 76; Neue grundlagen fuer einen begriff der rechtsgeltung, Arch Fuer Rechts--und Sozialphilos, 79; Material and formal authorisation in Kelsen's Pure Theory, Cambridge Law J, 80; Zum problem der Normenkonflikte, Arch fuer Rechtsund Sozialphilos, 80; Naturgesetze und die rechte Vernunft in Hobbes Rechtsphilosophie, Rechtstheorie, 81; Subsumption, derogation and noncontradiction in Legal Science, Univ Chicago Law Rev, summer 81; Fuller,lon,l., Radbruch,gustav, And The Positivist Theses, Law And Philosophy, Vol 0013, 1994. **CONTACT ADDRESS** Dept of Philos, Washington Univ, 1 Brookings Dr, Saint Louis, MO, 63130-4899.

PAULSON, STEVEN
DISCIPLINE SYSTEMATIC THEOLOGY **EDUCATION** St. Luther Sem, BA, 84; Lutheran Sch Theol, ThM, 88, ThD, 92. **CAREER** Res librarian, JKM Library; psychiatric counselor, Fairview Hospitals, Minn; asst prof, Concordia Col, 93-; assoc prof, 98-. **HONORS AND AWARDS** Goethe Inst scholar, 85; N Amer Ministerial fel, 80-84., Pastor, Trinity Lutheran Church, 90-93. **SELECTED PUBLICATIONS** Pub(s), ed bd, Lutheran Quart. **CONTACT ADDRESS** Dept of Systematic Theology, Luther Sem, 2481 Como Ave, St. Paul, MN, 55108. **EMAIL** spaulson@luthersem.edu

PAVESICH, VIDA
PERSONAL San Diego, CA **DISCIPLINE** PHILOSOPHY **EDUCATION** USCD, MA, 73. **CAREER** Diablo Valley Col, 92-. **MEMBERSHIPS** Am Philos Asn; Col Art Asn. **RESEARCH** Continental philosophy; History of skepticism. **SELECTED PUBLICATIONS** Gender and Hans Blumenbergs Theory of Myth, Int Stud Philos. **CONTACT ADDRESS** 2934 Ford St, #24, Oakland, CA, 94601. **EMAIL** vpavesic@viking.dvc.edu

PAVLICH, DENNIS
DISCIPLINE LAW **EDUCATION** Witwatersrand Univ, BA, 68; Yale Univ, LLM, 75. **CAREER** Asst prof, 75-78; assoc prof, 78-84; prof, 84-. **HONORS AND AWARDS** Tchg Excellence Awd. **SELECTED PUBLICATIONS** Auth, pubs about condominium law. **CONTACT ADDRESS** Fac of Law, Univ British Columbia, 1822 East Mall, Vancouver, BC, V6T 1Z1. **EMAIL** pavlich@law.ubc.ca

PAWELSKI, JAMES
PERSONAL Born 09/01/1967, Greenville, OH **DISCIPLINE** PHILOSOPHY **EDUCATION** Cedarville Coll, BA, 89; Penn State, MA, 91; PhD, 97. **CAREER** Asst prof Albright Coll, 97-; co-dir of Honors Program, 98-. **HONORS AND AWARDS** Phi Kappa Phi Honor Soc, Penn State, 91; Edwin Erle Sparks Grad Fel, Penn State, 92-93; Fulbright Grant Germany, 94-95. **MEMBERSHIPS** Am Philos Asn; Soc for the Advancement of Am Philos; Metaphysics of Am. **RESEARCH** American Philosophy; Pragmatism; Philosophy of Religion. **SELECTED PUBLICATIONS** Auth, Attention, Extension and Ecstasies in Augustine's Account of Time, J of Contemporary Philos, 93; Rev of Heaven's Champion: William James's Philosophy of Religion, J of Speculative Philos, forthcoming. **CONTACT ADDRESS** Albright Col, Box 15234, Reading, PA, 19612. **EMAIL** jamesp@joe.alb.edu

PAWLIKOWSKI, JOHN
PERSONAL Born 11/02/1940, Chicago, IL **DISCIPLINE** SOCIAL ETHICS, JEWISH-CHRISTIAN RELATIONS **EDUCATION** Loyola Univ Chicago, AB, 63; Wheeling Col, dipl Jewish studies, 67; Oxford Univ, cert ecumenical studies, 68; Univ Chicago, PhD, 70. **CAREER** From asst prof to assoc prof, 68-76, actg pres, 75-76, Prof Social Ethics, Cath Theol Union, Chicago Cluster Theol Schs, 76-, Mem adv comt, Secretariat for Cath-Jewish Rels, Nat Conf Cath Bishops, 71-73; bd dirs, Nat Cath Conf Interracial Justice, 72-73; chmn, Nat Coun Churches Faith & Order Study Comn on Israel, 72-73 & Chicago Inst Interrelig Res, 73; mem staff, Nat Cath Coalition for Responsible Investment, 73-75; bd mem, Nat Inst on Holocaust, 77-; US Holocaust Mem Coun, 80-. **HONORS AND AWARDS** Interfaith Award, Am Jewish Comt, 72; Founders' Citation, Nat Cath Conf Interracial Justice, 73; Off Cross of Merit, Govt Poland, 95; Person of Year Award, 94; Polish Coun of Christians and Jews, Warsaw. **MEMBERSHIPS** Am Soc Christian Ethics; Cath Theol Soc Am; Am Acad Relig. **RESEARCH** Christian-Jewish relations in Second Temple Period and in modern times; theology of revolution; foundations of social ethics. **SELECTED PUBLICATIONS** Auth, On renewing the revolution of the Pharisees, Cross Currents, fall 70; Jesus and the revolutionaries, Christian Century, 12/72; Catechetics and Prejudice, Paulist Press, 73; Sinai and Calvary: The Meeting of Two Peoples, Bruce, 76; Christ and the Jewish-Christian dialogue, Chicago Studies, fall 77; Judaism in Christian education and liturgy, Auschwitz: Beginning of a New Era, 77; What Are They Saying About Christian-Jewish Relations, 78 & Christ in Light of the Christian-Jewish Dialogue, 82, Paulist; Jesus and the Theology of Israel, 89. **CONTACT ADDRESS** Catholic Theol Union at Chicago, 5401 S Cornell Ave, Chicago, IL, 60615-6200. **EMAIL** jtmp@ctu.edu

PAYNE, JULIEN
DISCIPLINE LAW **EDUCATION** London Univ, LLD. **CAREER** Prof. **SELECTED PUBLICATIONS** Auth, pubs on family law, children and the law, dispute resolution processes, and family conflict resolution. **CONTACT ADDRESS** Fac Common Law, Univ Ottawa, 550 Cumberland St, PO Box 450, Ottawa, ON, K1N 6N5.

PAYNE, PHILIP B.
PERSONAL Born 07/02/1948, Rockville Center LI, NY, m, 1976, 3 children **DISCIPLINE** NEW TESTAMENT STUDIES **EDUCATION** Cambridge Univ UK, PhD 76; Trinity Evange Div Sch, Mdiv summa cum laude, 73, MA summa cum laude, 72. **CAREER** Cambridge Univ, suprv New T stud, 74-75; Trinity Evange Div Sch, vis prof, 76; Gordon Conwell Theol Sem, vis prof, 85-87; Fuller Theol Sem, adj prof, 88-. **HONORS AND AWARDS** Higgins Schshp. **MEMBERSHIPS** SBL; TF; IBR; ETS. **RESEARCH** Man and woman in the Bible; The Parable of Jesus; Christology. **SELECTED PUBLICATIONS** Auth, Man & Woman One in Christ, Grand Rapids, Zondervan, 99, forthcoming; LaserANSEL for Macintosh, Edmonds, Linguist's Software, 98; auth, LaserANSEL for Windows 95 and 3.1, Edmonds Linguist's Software, 98; auth, LaserHieroglyphics for Windows 95 and 3.1. Edmonds, Linguist's Software, 98; J. Barton Payne, Handbook for Evangelical Theologians, ed, Walter Elwell, Grand Rapids, Baker, 98; auth, New American Standard Bible for Windows, Edmonds, Linguist's Software, 97; auth, New American Standard Bible for Macintosh, Edmonds, Linguist's Software, 97; auth, Scripting for Non-English Languages, coauth, Techflow, Sydney, 95; Computer Aided Biblical Research, Twentieth Century Encycl of Religious Knowledge, 2nd edition, ed, J.D. Douglas, Grand Rapids, 95; auth, Heaven Ahead! John Fourteen, in: Encouragement in the Word, ed, Claes VS Wyckoff, El Cajon CA, CSN, 95; Ask Seek Knock Matthew Seven, in: Encouragement in the Word, ed, Claes VS Wyckoff, El Cajon CA, CSN, 95. **CONTACT ADDRESS** Dept of New Testament, Fuller Theol Sem, PO Box 580, Edmonds, WA, 98020. **EMAIL** phil@linguistsoftware.com

PAYNE, RODGER M.
PERSONAL Born 06/14/1955, Morganton, NC, m, 1974, 2 children **DISCIPLINE** AMERICAN RELIGION AND CULTURE **EDUCATION** Univ North Carolina, BA, 80; Harvard Div Sch, MTS, 83; Univ Va, PhD, 89. **CAREER** Instr, 86, lectr, 89-91 Univ Va; lectr, Hampden-Sydney Col, Va, 88; asst prof, 91-97, assoc prof, 97- , Louisiana State Univ. **HONORS AND AWARDS** Young Scholars in Am Relig, Ctr for Stud of Relig and Am Cult, Indianapolis. **MEMBERSHIPS** Am Acad Relig; Am Soc of Church Hist. **RESEARCH** Religion in American culture; religion in Louisiana and the South; American Catholicism. **SELECTED PUBLICATIONS** Auth, Metaphors of the Self and the Sacred: The Spiritual Autobiography of the Reverend Freeborn Garrettson, Early Am Lit, 92; auth, Baptist Missionary Mag, in Fackler, ed, Popular Religious Magazines of the United States, Greenwood, 95; auth, New Light in Hanover County: Evangelical Dissent in Piedmont Virginia, 1740-1755, Jour of Southern Hist, 95; auth, On Teaching Religion: A Symposium, Jour of the Am Acad of Relig, 97; auth, The Self and the Sacred: Conversion and Autobiography in Early American Protestantism, Tennessee, 98. **CONTACT ADDRESS** Dept of Philosophy and Religious Studies, Louisiana State Univ, Baton Rouge, LA, 70803. **EMAIL** rmpayne@lsu.edu

PAYNE, STEVEN
DISCIPLINE PHILOSOPHY, THEOLOGY **CAREER** Instr, Washington Theol Univ, 96-. **CONTACT ADDRESS** ICS Publications, 2131 Lincoln Rd NE, Washington, DC, 20002-1199.

PAZMINO, ROBERT W.
PERSONAL Born 06/15/1948, Brooklyn, NY, m, 1969, 2 children **DISCIPLINE** RELIGIOUS EDUCATION: CURRICULUM AND TEACHING **EDUCATION** Gordon-Conwell Theol Sem, M Div; Teachers Col, Columbia Univ in coop with Union Sem, Ed D. **CAREER** Asst prof of Christian Education, Gordon-Conwell Theol Sem, 81-86; assoc prof, 86-90, prof of relig ed, 90-96, Valeria Stone prof of Christian Education, Andover Newton Theol School, 96-. **HONORS AND AWARDS** Phi Beta Kappa; Psi Chi; Phi Eta Sigma; Phi Alpha Chi; Nat Dean's List; Hispanic Doctoral fel of the Fund for Theol Ed. **MEMBERSHIPS** North Am Professors of Christian Education. **RESEARCH** Theol foundations of Christian education. **SELECTED PUBLICATIONS** Auth, Principles and Practices of Christian Education: An Evangelical Perspective, Baker, 92, trans, Editorial Caribe, 95; Foundational Issues in Christian Education: An Introduction in Evangelical Perspective, Baker, 88, 2nd ed, Baker, 97; Latin American Journey: Insights for Christian Education in North America, United Church Press, 94; By What Authority Do We Teach? Sources for Empowering Christian Educators, Baker, 94; Nurturing the Spiritual Lives of Teachers, in The Christian Educator's Handbook on Spiritual Formation, eds Kenneth O Gangel and James C Wilhoit, Victor Books, 94; Designing the Urban Theological Education Curriculum, in The Urban Theological Education Curriculum: Occasional Papers, eds, Eldin Villafane and Bruce Jackson, CUTEEP, 96, Christian Ed J, fall 97; review of Jesuit Education and Social Change in El Salvador by Charles D Beirne in J of Res on Christian Ed 5, fall 96; Basics of Teaching for Christians: Preparation Instruction and Evaluation, Baker, 98; numerous other publications. **CONTACT ADDRESS** Andover Newton Theol Sch, 210 Herrick Rd, Newton Center, MA, 02459-2243. **EMAIL** rpazmino@arts.edu

PEACOCK, KENT
DISCIPLINE PHILOSOPHY **EDUCATION** Univ Toronto, PhD, 91. **RESEARCH** Philosophy of science; environmental and professional ethics. **SELECTED PUBLICATIONS** Auth, Living with the Earth: An Introduction to Environmental Philosophy, Harcourt Can, 96. **CONTACT ADDRESS** Dept of Philosophy, Lethbridge Univ, 4401 University Dr W, Lethbridge, AB, T1K 3M4. **EMAIL** peack000@hg.uleth.ca

PEACOCK, KEVIN
PERSONAL Born 03/28/1962, Natchez, MS, m, 1988, 2 children **DISCIPLINE** OLD TESTAMENT **EDUCATION** Southwestrn Baptist Theol Sem, PhD, 95 **CAREER** Prof, 97-pres, Can Southern Baptist Sem **HONORS AND AWARDS** Am Bibl Soc Award, 95 **MEMBERSHIPS** Soc of Bibl Lit; Am Acad of Relig; Ntl Assoc of Baptist Professors of Relig; In-Service Guidance Assoc **RESEARCH** Pentateuch; Prophets **SELECTED PUBLICATIONS** Auth, "Vanity; The Meaning," Biblical Illustrator, 98, 27-29 **CONTACT ADDRESS** PO Box 512, Cochrane, AB, T0L 0W0. **EMAIL** kpeacock@csbs.ca

PEARCE, RUSSELL G.
DISCIPLINE CONTRACTS **EDUCATION** Cornell Univ, AB, 53, JD, 55 **CAREER** Pvt practice, 57-60; former dir, Louis Stein Inst on Law and Ethics; prof, 63-. **HONORS AND AWARDS** Fulbright scholar, Univ Florence, 60-62. **SELECTED PUBLICATIONS** Auth, Hardship and its Impact on Contractual Obligations: A Comparative Analysis, Saggi, Conferenze E Seminari #20, 96; Force Majeure and Hardship Under the UNIDROIT Principles of International Commercial Contracts, 5 Tulane Jour Intl and Comp Law 1, 96. **CONTACT ADDRESS** Law Sch, Fordham Univ, 113 W 60th St, New York, NY, 10023. **EMAIL** jperillo@mail.lawnet.fordham.edu

PEARL, LEON
PERSONAL Born 07/21/1922, Dombrova, Poland, m, 1953, 4 children **DISCIPLINE** ETHICS, PHILOSOPHY OF MIND **EDUCATION** NY Univ, BA, 47, MA, 52, PhD(philos), 57. **CAREER** From asst prof to assoc prof, 60-77, Prof Philos, Hofstra Univ, 77-. **MEMBERSHIPS** Eastern Div Am Philos Asn. **RESEARCH** Theory of knowledge. **SELECTED PUB-**

LICATIONS Auth, Religious and secular beliefs, Mind, 60; Four Philosophical Problems, Harper, 63; God Had to Create The World + a Criticism of Chappell,t.d.j., Religious Studies, Vol 0030, 1994; Reported Miracles - a Critique of Hume - Houston,j, J of Religion, Vol 0077, 1997. **CONTACT ADDRESS** Dept of Philos, Hofstra Univ, Hempstead, NY, 11550.

PEARSON, ANNE
PERSONAL Born 07/23/1957, London, ON, Canada, m, 1987, 3 children **DISCIPLINE** RELIGIOUS STUDIES **EDUCATION** McMaster Univ, PhD, 93 **CAREER** Inst, 87, McMaster Univ; Inst, 94 Wilfrid Laurier Univ; Inst, 97, Univ of Waterloo **MEMBERSHIPS** Am Acad of Relig; Can Soc for Study of Relig **RESEARCH** Hinduism; Faith; Women in Hinduism; Diaspora Hinduism; Religion & Popular Culture **SELECTED PUBLICATIONS** Auth, Because it gives me peace of mind Ritual Fasts in the Religioius Lives of Hindu Women, State Univ of NY Press, 96; Auth, Aspects of Hindu Women's Vrat Tradition as Constitutive for an Eco spirituality, Journal of Dharma, 98, 228-236 **CONTACT ADDRESS** 107 Victoria St, Dundas, ON, L9H 2C1. **EMAIL** apearson@worldchat.com

PEARSON, BIRGER ALBERT
PERSONAL Born 09/17/1934, Turlock, CA, m, 1966, 5 children **DISCIPLINE** HISTORY OF RELIGION **EDUCATION** Upsala Col, BA, 57; Univ Calif, Berkeley, MA, 59; Pac Lutheran Sem, BDiv, 62; Harvard Univ, PhD(Christian origins), 68. **CAREER** Instr Greek, chmn dept, 76-79, Pac Lutheran Sem, 59-62; lectr New Testament, Episcopal Theol Sch, 65-66; from instr to asst prof relig, Duke Univ, 66-69; from asst prof to assoc prof relig studies, 69-75, assoc dir, Educ Abroad Prog, 74-76, chmn dept, 76-80, Prof Relig Studies, Univ Calif, Santa Barbara, 75-, Fel, Humanities Inst, Univ Calif, 70-71, 72-73; Am Philos Asn grant, 72; dir, Univ Calif Study Ctr, Lund, Sweden,79-81. **MEMBERSHIPS** Soc Bibl Lit; Am Acad Relig; Archaeol Inst Arn; Soc New Testament Studies; Soc Coptic Archaeol. **RESEARCH** Gnosticism; Early Christianity; Hellenistic religions. **SELECTED PUBLICATIONS** Auth, I Thessalonians 2:13-16: A Deutero-Pauline interpretation, Harvard Theol Rev, 71; Jewish Haggadic traditions in The Testimony of Truth From Nag Hammandi, In: Ex Orbe Religionum, Brill, 72; The Pneumatikos-Psychikos Terminology in I Corinthians, Soc Bibl Lit, 73, Scholars, 76; ed & transl, The Gnostic Attitude, Univ Calif Inst Relig Studies, 73; ed & contribr, Religious Syncretism in Antiquity, Scholars, 75; contribr, The Nag Hammadi Library in English, BrillHarper, 77; auth, The figure of Norea in Gnostic literature, In: Proceedings of the International Colloquium on Gnosticism, Stockholm, 1973, Almqvist & Wiksell, 77; Nag Hammadi Codices IX and X, Brill, 81; The New Alexandria Library - Promise or Threat, Biblical Archaeologist, Vol 0056, 1993; The New Alexandria Library - an Update, Biblical Archaeologist, Vol 0056, 1993; The Gospel According to The Jesus-seminar + a Methodological Assessment of The Quest For The Historical Jesus, Religion, Vol 0025, 1995; 2-peter, Jude - a New Translation With Introduction And Commentary - Neyrey,jh, J of Biblical Literature, Vol 0114, 1995. **CONTACT ADDRESS** Dept of Relig Studies, Univ of Calif, Santa Barbara, CA, 93106.

PEARSON, ERIC
PERSONAL Born 02/24/1960, Washington, DC, m, 1994, 1 child **DISCIPLINE** PHILOSOPHY **EDUCATION** Cornell Col, BPh, 82; Syracuse Univ, PhD, 89. **CAREER** Instr, 90-91, Ithaca Col; asst prof, 91-99, Berea Col. **MEMBERSHIPS** Amer Philos Soc **RESEARCH** Philos of lang **CONTACT ADDRESS** Berea Col, CPD 1569, Berea, KY, 40404. **EMAIL** eric-pearson@berea.edu

PEARSON, SAMUEL C.
PERSONAL Born 12/10/1931, Dallas, TX, m, 1955, 2 children **DISCIPLINE** HISTORY OF CHRISTIANITY **EDUCATION** TX Christian Univ, AB, 51; Univ Chicago, DB, 53, MA, 60, PhD, 64. **CAREER** Asst prof, 64-69, assoc prof, 69-74, prof, hist stud, 74-, dept chmn, 72-77 & 81-83, act dir, 86-87, Reg Res & Develop Serv, Dean, Sch of Soc Sci, 83-95, dean emeritus, 95-, Southern Ill Univ. **HONORS AND AWARDS** Phi Eta Sigma; Phi Kappa Phi (Emeritus Lifetime Member); Phi Alpha Theta; Outstanding Foreign Expert Northeast Normal Univ, 95, appointed vis prof, 96; Nat Endowment for the Hum Sum Sem grants to Yale Univ, 76, and Univ Hawaii, 98. **MEMBERSHIPS** Am Soc Church Hist; Am Hist Asn; Org of Am Hist; Am Academy of Relig. **RESEARCH** Religions in the modern world. **SELECTED PUBLICATIONS** Auth, From Church to Denomination: American Congregationalism in the Nineteenth Century, Church Hist, XXXVIII, 69; auth, Enlightenment Influence on Protestant Thought in Early National America, Encounter, XXXVII, 77; auth, The Great Awakening and Its Impact on American History, Forum Press, 78; auth, The Campbell Institute: Herald of the Transformation of an American Religious Tradition, The Scroll, LXII, 78; auth, Rationalism in an Age of Enthusiasm: The Anomalous Career of Robert Cave, The Bul of MO Hist Soc, XXXV, 79; auth, The Cave Affair: Protestant Thought in the Guilded Age, Encounter, XLI, 80; auth, The Religion of John Locke and the Character of His Thought, John Locke: Critical Assessments, 4 vols, Routledge, 91; Alexander Campbell, 1788-1866, Makers of Christian Theology in America, Abingdon Press, 97. **CONTACT ADDRESS** Dept of Historical Studies, Southern Illinois Univ, Edwardsville, IL, 62026-1454. **EMAIL** spearso@siue.edu

PECK, WILLIAM DAYTON
PERSONAL Born 07/12/1934, New York, NY, m, 1961, 2 children **DISCIPLINE** PHILOSOPHY **EDUCATION** Yale Univ, BA, 56, PhD, 74. **CAREER** From instr to asst prof, 61-67, assoc prof philos & humanities, 67-75, Prof 75-, Reed Coll. **RESEARCH** Modern European philosophy. **CONTACT ADDRESS** Dept of Philosophy, Reed Col, 3203 SE Woodstock Blvd, Portland, OR, 97202-8199. **EMAIL** william.peck@reed.edu

PECORINO, PHILIP ANTHONY
PERSONAL Born 10/10/1947, New York, NY, m, 1968, 1 child **DISCIPLINE** PHILOSOPHY, PSYCHOLOGY **EDUCATION** Boston Col, BA, 69; Fordham Univ, MA, 70, PhD, 80. **CAREER** From Instr to Assoc Prof, 72-88, Prof Philos, City Univ New York, 88-. **MEMBERSHIPS** Am Asn Philos Teachers (vpres, 80-82, pres, 82-84); Community Col Humanities Asn (Eastern vpres, 81-83); Am Philos Asn; Soc Study Process Philos; AILACT. **RESEARCH** Critical reasoning; applied ethics; metaphysics and scientific inquiry. **SELECTED PUBLICATIONS** Auth, The midwife's trickery, Vol 3, No 2 & Philosophy and interdisciplinary studies, Vol 4, No 3, Aitia; Nursing ethics, technical training and values, Process, Vol VI, No 2; Evil as direction in Plotinus, Philos Res Arch, 82; ed, Perspectives on Death and Dying, Ginn Publ Co, 2nd ed, 82; coauth, Philosophy and science fiction, in The Intersection of Philosophy and Science Fiction, Greenwood Press (in prep). **CONTACT ADDRESS** Social Sci Dept, Queensborough Comm Col, CUNY, 22205 56th Ave, Flushing, NY, 11364-1497. **EMAIL** papqcccuny@aol.com

PEDEN, WILLIAM CREIGHTON
PERSONAL Born 07/25/1935, Concord, NC, m, 1961, 2 children **DISCIPLINE** PHILOSOPHY, RELIGION **EDUCATION** Davidson Col, BA, 57; Univ Chicago, MA, 60, BD, 62; Univ St Andrews, PhD(philos relig), 65. **CAREER** Asst prof philos, St Andrews Presby Col, 64-65; prof & chmn dept, Radford Col, 65-68; prof & chmn dept, Millikin Univ, 68- 69; Fuller E Callaway Prof Philos, Augusta Col, 69-, Ed, J Social Philos, 70; assoc mem, Inst Social Philos, 72-; assoc, Danforth Found, 73-. **MEMBERSHIPS** Am Philos Asn; Am Acad Relig; Soc Studies Process Philos; Soc Social Philos; Am Asn Higher Educ. **RESEARCH** Social philosophy; process philosophy; American philosophy. **SELECTED PUBLICATIONS** Rights In a Changing Society, 81, Values In Our Developing World, 81 & Women's Liberation, 81, In: Philosophy for a Changing Society, Advocate Press; coauth (with Charles Hartshorne), Whitehead's View of Reality, Pilgrim Press, 81; auth, Immature Liberalism, Vol 3, No 1 & Liberal Religion and Education, Vol 3, No 1, Am J Theol & Philos; Philosophy for a Changing Society, Advocate Press, 82; Creative Freedom: Vocation of Liberal Religion, Pilgrim Press, 82; The Foundations of Potter,William, Religion of Humanity, Religious Humanism, Vol 0027, 1993. **CONTACT ADDRESS** Dept of Philos, Augusta State Univ, Augusta, GA, 30904.

PEDRICK, WILLARD HIRAM
PERSONAL Born 10/01/1914, Ottumwa, IA, m, 1939, 4 children **DISCIPLINE** LAW **EDUCATION** Parsons Col, BA, 36; Northwestern Univ, JD, 39. **CAREER** Instr law, Univ Cincinnati, 40-42; asst prof, Sch Law, Univ Tex, 41-42; from assoc prof to prof, Sch Law, Northwestern Univ, 46-66; dean, 66-75, Prof Law, Col Law, Ariz State Univ, 66-, Carnegie grant, Australia & Fulbright prof, Univ Western Australia, 56-57; Ford grant, Australia & George Turner vis prof, Univ Melbourne, 62; J DuPratt White vis prof, Cornell Univ, 64; consult, Am Acad Arbit & Am Law Inst; Fulbright vis prof, Univ Western Australia, 73. **HONORS AND AWARDS** LLD, Parsons Col, 64 & Calif Western Law Sch, 82. **MEMBERSHIPS** Am Bar Asn; Am Law Inst. **RESEARCH** Law of torts; federal taxation; international business investments. **SELECTED PUBLICATIONS** Coauth, Cases on Torts, 68 & Injuries to Relations, 68, West Pub; auth, Estate and Gift Taxation, 77 & Death, Taxes & the Living, 80, Commerce Clearing House; Aals Musical - Time For Revival, J of Legal Education, Vol 0043, 1993. **CONTACT ADDRESS** Col of Law, Arizona State Univ, Tempe, Tempe, AZ, 85287.

PEEBLES, I.HALL
PERSONAL Born 01/09/1930, Augusta, GA, m, 1962, 3 children **DISCIPLINE** RELIGION **EDUCATION** Univ Ga, AB, 50; Yale Univ, BD, 53, MA, 55, PhD(relig), 59. **CAREER** From instr to assoc prof, 58-77, prof, 77-80, Evans Prog Relig, Wabash Col, 80-, Ford Found fac fel non-western studies & res fel, Divinity Sch, Yale Univ, 63-64. **MEMBERSHIPS** Am Theol Soc Midwest Div; AAUP; Soc Bibl Lit; Am Acad Relig. **RESEARCH** Contemporary Christian theology; history of religions. **CONTACT ADDRESS** Dept of Relig, Wabash Col, PO Box 352, Crawfordsville, IN, 47933-0352.

PEITZ-HILLENBRAND, DARLENE
PERSONAL Born 02/04/1947, Yankton, SD, m, 1984, 2 children **DISCIPLINE** THEOLOGY **EDUCATION** Notre Dame, MA, 79; St. John's Sem, MDiv, 83; St. Michael's Col-Univ Toronto, PhD, 90. **MEMBERSHIPS** Cath Theol Soc; Am Asn of Relig. **RESEARCH** Political theology; American religion. **SELECTED PUBLICATIONS** Auth, Solidarity as Hermeneutic: A Revisionist Reading of the Social Theology of Walter Rauschenbusch," 92. **CONTACT ADDRESS** 9309 Edenberry Ct, Elk Court, CA, 95758.

PELCHAT, MARC
PERSONAL Born 05/03/1950, PQ, Canada, s **DISCIPLINE** ECCLESIOLOGY **EDUCATION** Univ Gregorienne, Rome, doctorate in theol, 86. **CAREER** Asst prof, 87, full prof, 92, dean of fac, 98, Univ Laval, Quebec. **MEMBERSHIPS** AAR; Can Soc of Theol; Acad of Practical Theol; Soc Intl de Theol Pratique. **RESEARCH** Practical theology; Ministry; Church. **SELECTED PUBLICATIONS** Co-auth, La Ville. Defis Ethiques, Ecclesiaux et Theologiques, Novalis, 98; co-auth, Gesti d'Amore. Sacramenti e Riti, Preghiera e Contemplazione, Edizioni Messaggero Padova, 94; chap, Les Implantations Ecclesiales Dans l'Espace Urbain: Nouvelles Frontieres, La Ville. Defis Ethiques, Ecclesiaux et Theologiques, Novalis, 98; chap, Les Revues Canadiennes-Francaises de Devotion et le Concile Vatican II, L'Eglise Canadienne et Vatican II, Fides, 165-188, 97; chap, Qu'est-ce Donc au Juste Que l'Education de la foi des Adultes?, L'Education de la foi des Adultes, L'Experience du Quebec, Mediaspaul, 229-249, 96; chap, Etapes de la Vie Adulte et Cheminement de Foi, L'Education de la Foi des Adultes, L'Experience du Quebec, Mediaspaul, 273-314, 96; chap, La Pastorale des Vocations: une Lecture Theolgique, La Pastorale des Vocations, Situation Actuelle, Enjeux et Defis, Diocese de Quebec, 11-13, 96; chap, La Paroisse, une Realite Deplacee? La Paroisse en Eclats, Novalis, 119-120, 95; chap, Les Priorites Pastorales du Diocese de Quebec: un Probleme de Communication? La Communication et le Monde de la Foi, Ed Pastor, 241-284, 94; chap, Le Magistere et la Loi, Loi et Autonomie Dans la Bible et la Tradition Chretienne, Fides, 249-285, 94. **CONTACT ADDRESS** Faculte de theologie, Univ Laval, Quebec, PQ, G1K7P4. **EMAIL** marc.pelchat@ftsr.ulaval.ca

PELLEGRINO, EDMUND DANIEL
PERSONAL Born 06/22/1920, Newark, NJ, 7 children **DISCIPLINE** PHILOSOPHY OF MEDICINE **EDUCATION** St John's Univ (NY), BS, 41; NY Univ, MD, 44. **CAREER** Prof & chmn, Dept Med, & dir med serv, Col Med, Univ Ky, 59-66; prof & chmn, Dept Med & dean, Sch Med, Health Sci Ctr, State Univ NY, Stony Brook, 66-73; chancellor, Ctr Health Sci, vpres health affairs & prof med & humanities in med, Univ Tenn, 73-75; pres & chmn, Med Ctr & prof med, Sch of Med, Yale Univ, 75-78; prof philos & biol & pres, Cath Univ Am, 78-82; prof clinical & community med, Sch of Med, 78-82, John Carroll Prof Med & Med Humanities, Med Ctr, Georgetown Univ, 82-, Consult & panelist, Nat Found Arts & Humanities & Nat Endowment for Humanities, 74-; nat bd consult, Nat Endowment for Humanities, 74-; nat adv comt, trial Humanities in Med, Univ Tex, 74-; chmn, Successor Generation Comt, Atlantic Coun US, 79-; mem int bd adv, Ctr Advan Res Phenomenol, 80-; mem coun adv, Inst Humanities Salado, 80-; mem coun scholars, Libr Cong, 82-84. **HONORS AND AWARDS** St John's Pres Medal, 79; Walter C Alvarez Award, Am Med Writer's Asn, 81; Encycl Brittanica Achievement in Life Award, 79; recipient of 41 honorary doctorates., Numerous from Am Cols & Univs. **MEMBERSHIPS** Soc Health & Human Values (pres, 69-70); Am Asn Advan Humanities; Am Philos Asn; Inst Med, Nat Acad Sci; Medieval Acad Am. **RESEARCH** Philosophy and ethics of medicine; mineral metabolism. **SELECTED PUBLICATIONS** Auth, Philosophy of medicine: Problematic and potential, J Med & Philos 1: 5-31; Toward a reconstruction of medical morality: The primacy of the act of profession and the fact of illness, J Med & Philos, Univ Chicago Press, 3/79; The anatomy of clinical judgments: Some notes on right reason and right action, in Philosophy and Medicine, Vol VI, D Reidel, Dordrecht, Netherlands, 77; Humanism and the Physician, Univ Tenn Press, 79; coauth (with D C Thomasma), A Philosophical Basis of Medical Practice, Toward a Philosopohy and Ethic of the Healing Professions, Oxford Univ Press, 81. **CONTACT ADDRESS** Med Ctr, Georgetown Univ, 4000 Reservoir Rd NW, Washington, DC, 20007-2195.

PELLETIER, LUCIEN
DISCIPLINE PHILOSOPHY **EDUCATION** Univ Montreal, PhD. **RESEARCH** Philos anthropology; social and political philos; philos of relig. **SELECTED PUBLICATIONS** Auth, Socialisme religieux et communaut chez Martin Buber, 93; auth, L'imergence du concept de totalit chez Lukas, 92; auth, Bloch lecteur de Schelling, 91. **CONTACT ADDRESS** Philosophy Dept, Laurentian Univ, 935 Ramsey Lake Rd, Sudbury, ON, P3E 2C6.

PELLETIER, SAMUEL R.
PERSONAL Born 06/20/1965, Philadelphia, PA, 1 child **DISCIPLINE** NEW TESTAMENT **EDUCATION** Hannibal-LaGrange Col, BA, 88; Westminster Theol Sem, MAR, 90; Univ MO-Columbia, MA, 92; Southern Baptist Theol Sem, PhD, 97. **CAREER** Adj Inst, Hannibal-LaGrange Col, 90-92; Garrett Tchg Fel, 93-95; Adj Inst/Prof, 95-98, Asst Prof, Southern Baptist Theol Sem, 98-. **MEMBERSHIPS** IBR, SBL, AAR **RESEARCH** Luke-Acts, New Testament Backgrounds, Hermenuetics **CONTACT ADDRESS** 107 Fenley Ave, Apt S-10, Louisville, KY, 40207. **EMAIL** spelletier@sbts.edu

PENASKOVIC, RICHARD
PERSONAL Born 02/11/1941, Bayone, NJ, m, 1974, 3 children **DISCIPLINE** RELIGIOUS STUDIES **EDUCATION** Univ Wurzburg, BA, 66, MA, 67; Ludwig Maximilians Univ, Munchen, PhD, 73. **CAREER** Asst prof, assoc prof, Col Saint Rose; prof, dept head, 84-94, prog dir, 94-, Auburn Univ. **HONORS AND AWARDS** Phi Kappa Phi; Delta Epsilon Sigma; Nat Scholastic Honor Soc, 96-97; Alumni Undergrad Tchg Excellence Award, Mortar Board Favorite Educator Award, Auburn Univ. **MEMBERSHIPS** Am Acad Reg; Col Theolog Soc; Catholic Theolog Soc Am. **RESEARCH** Critical thinking and the academy society of religion; spirituality; Augustine & Newman studies. **SELECTED PUBLICATIONS** Auth, art, Writing from Scratch, 91; auth, art, The Nexus Between Creativity and Critical Thinking, 92; auth, art, Nurturing Faculty Publication: The Chair's Role, 94; auth, art, Newman Studies: Present and Future, 94; auth, Critical Thinking and the Academic Study of Religion, 97. **CONTACT ADDRESS** Program Director for Religious Studies, Auburn Univ, Auburn, AL, 36849-5205. **EMAIL** penasri@mail.auburn.edu

PENCE, GREGORY E.
DISCIPLINE PHILOSOPHY **EDUCATION** Col William and Mary, MA, 70; NY Univ, PhD, 74. **CAREER** Prof, Univ Ala Birmingham, 76-; joint app, UAB Sch Med; dir, Early Med Sch Acceptance Prog, Univ Ala at Birmingham. **HONORS AND AWARDS** Ingalls awd for Best Teaching, 94. **RESEARCH** Bioethics **SELECTED PUBLICATIONS** Auth, Classic Cases in Medical Ethics: Accounts of the Cases that Shaped Medical Ethics, McGraw-Hill, 2nd ed, 95; Who's Afraid of Human Cloning, Rowman & Littlefield, 97; Flesh of My Flesh: The Ethics of Cloning Humans, Rowman & Littlefield, 98; coauth, Seven Dilemmas in World Religions, Paragon House, 94; ed, Classic Works in Medical Ethics: Core Philosophical Readings, McGraw-Hill, 97. **CONTACT ADDRESS** Dept of Philosophy, Univ of Alabama, Birmingham, 1400 University Blvd, Birmingham, AL, 35294-1150. **EMAIL** pence@uab.edu

PENCHANSKY, DAVID
PERSONAL Born 12/03/1951, Brooklyn, NY, d, 2 children **DISCIPLINE** HEBREW BIBLE **EDUCATION** Vanderbilt Univ, PhD, 88. **CAREER** Instr, Evangel Col, 79-84; instr, Western Ky Univ, 85-89; assoc prof, Univ of St. Thomas, 89-. **MEMBERSHIPS** Soc of Bibl Lit; Cath Bibl Asn; Amer Asn of Univ Prof. **RESEARCH** Wisdom literature; Hermeneutics; Literary criticism. **SELECTED PUBLICATIONS** Auth, God the Monster, The Monstrous and the Unspeakable, Sheffield Acad Press, 97; auth, The Politics of Biblical Theology, Studies in American Biblical Hermeneutics Series, Mercer Press, 95; auth, Proverbs, The Mercer Bible Commentary, Mercer Press, 94; auth, Storyteller's Companion, vol III, Abingdon Press, 92; auth, Up for Grabs: A Tentative Proposal for Ideological Criticism, Semeia, 59, 92; auth, Staying the Night, Reading Between Texts, Westminster/John Knox, 92; auth, The Betrayal of God, Westminster/John Knox, 90. **CONTACT ADDRESS** Mail #4328, 2115 Summi, St. Paul, MN, 55105. **EMAIL** d9penchansky@stthomas.edu

PENCZEK, ALAN
PERSONAL Born 06/23/1956, Chicago, IL, s **DISCIPLINE** PHILOSOPHY **EDUCATION** Johns Hopkins Univ, PhD, 98. **CAREER** Asst prof, philos, Villa Julie Col, 98-. **MEMBERSHIPS** Amer Philos Asn. **RESEARCH** Metaphysics; Philosophy of mind. **SELECTED PUBLICATIONS** Auth, Disjunctive Properties and Causal Efficacy, Philos Studies, 97; auth, Counterfactuals with True Components, Erkenntnis, 97; auth, Introductory Logic: First Day, Teaching Philos, 96. **CONTACT ADDRESS** Philosophy Dept., Villa Julie Col, Stevenson, MD, 21153. **EMAIL** f-pencze@mail.vjc.edu

PENELHUM, TERENCE M.
PERSONAL Born 04/26/1929, Bradford-on-Avon, England **DISCIPLINE** RELIGIOUS STUDIES **EDUCATION** Univ Edinburgh, MA, 50; Oriel Col Oxford, BPhil, 52; Univ Lethbridge, DHu, 82; Univ Waterloo, DLitt, 90; Univ Calgary, LLD, 91. **CAREER** Lectr to assoc prof philos, Univ Alta, 53-63; prof philos, 63-78, head philos, 63-70, dean arts & sci, 64-67, PROF EMER, RELIGIOUS STUDIES, UNIV CALGARY, 88-. **HONORS AND AWARDS** Can Coun Molson Prize Hum, 88 **SELECTED PUBLICATIONS** Auth, Survival and Disembodied Existence, 70; auth, Religion and Rationality, 71; auth, Problems of Religious Knowledge, 71; auth, Hume, 75; auth, God and Skepticism, 83; auth, Butler, 85; auth, David Hume: an Introduction to his Philosophical System, 92; auth, Reason and Religious Faith, 95; ed, Immortality, 73; ed, Faith, 89; co-ed, The First Critique, 69. **CONTACT ADDRESS** Dept Rel Stud, Univ Calgary, Calgary, AB, T2N 1N4.

PENNER, HANS HENRY
PERSONAL Born 01/29/1934, Sacramento, CA, m, 1959 **DISCIPLINE** HISTORY OF RELIGIONS **EDUCATION** Univ Chicago, DB, 58, MA, 62, PhD, 65. **CAREER** Instr hist of relig, Univ VT, 62-65; asst prof, 65-72, assoc prof relig, 72-74, John Phillips prof, & chmn dept, 74-79, Dean Fac, Dartmouth Col, 81-, Fulbright res scholar, India, 66; Soc Relig Higher Educ-Danforth Cross-disciplinary fel, 68-69; Dartmouth fac fel, 68-69. **MEMBERSHIPS** Asn Asian Studies; Soc Sci Studies Relig; Am Acad Relig; Int Asn Hist Relig. **RESEARCH** Methodological approaches to understanding relig; myth and ritual-phenomenology; relig traditions of India. **SELECTED PUBLICATIONS** Auth, Cosmogony as Myth in Vishnu Purana, Hist Relig, 66; The Study of Religion According to Jan de Vries, J Relig, 1/69; Myth and Ritual: Wasteland or Forest of Symbols, Hist & Theory, 69; The poverty of functionalism, Hist Relig, 71; Ritual, In: Encyl Britannica; Creating a Brahman & The problem of semantics in the study of religion, Method Issues Relig Studies, 75; Impasse & Resolution: A Critique of the Study of Religion, 89; Why Does Semantics Matter to the Study of Religion, Method and Theory in the Study of Religion, 7/95. **CONTACT ADDRESS** Dept Relig, Dartmouth Col, 6036 Thornton Hall, Hanover, NH, 03755-3592. **EMAIL** Hans.Penner@Dartmouth.edu

PENNER, MERRILYNN J.
PERSONAL Born 12/09/1944, New York, NY, s **DISCIPLINE** MATH; PSYCHOLOGY **EDUCATION** Harvard Univ, BA, 66; Univ Calif San Diego, PhD, 70. **CAREER** Adjunct prof Dept Surgery, Univ Md Med School, 95-; adjunct prof, Univ Md, 81-; prof, Univ Md, 80-; assoc prof, Univ Md, 76-80; asst prof, Hunter Col NY, 74-76; res Psychologist, Bell Telephone Lab, 73-74. **HONORS AND AWARDS** Ntl Inst of Health, Tinnitus, idiotones and spontaneous otoacoustic emissions Grant, 2000; Ntl Inst of Health, Tinnitus in patients with sensorineural hearing loss Grant, 85, 90, 96; Ntl Inst of Health, Res and Career Devop Grant, 77-82; Ntl Inst of Health & Ntl Sci Found Grant, 78-83; Ntl Inst Health, Temporal processing of auditory stimuli Grant, 75-78; Univ Md Distinguished Fac Res Fel Award, 92-93; Univ Md Semester Res Award, 90-91; Burroughs-Wellcome Res Travel Grant, 90. **MEMBERSHIPS** Psychonomic Soc; Ntl Acad Sci Committee on Hearing & Bioacoustics; Amer Specch & Hearing Assoc; Acoustical Soc Amer; Amer Psycholog Soc; Amer Assoc Advancement Sci. **RESEARCH** Auditory Perception; Auditory Psychophysics; Temporal Factors in Information Processing; Acoustic Emissions; Mathematical Models of Human Information Processing; Speech Perception; Tinnitus. **SELECTED PUBLICATIONS** Coauth, Prevalence of spontaneous otoacoustic emissions in adults revisited, Hearing Res, 97; auth, Rating the annoyance of synthesized tinnitus, Intl Tinnitus Jrnl, 96; auth, The emergence and disappearance of one subject's spontaneous otoacoustic emissions, Ear & Hearing, 96 **CONTACT ADDRESS** Dept Psychology, Univ of Maryland, College Park, MD, 20742. **EMAIL** oceanvac@cts.com

PENNER, ROLAND
DISCIPLINE LAW **EDUCATION** Univ Manitoba, BA, 49, LLB. **CAREER** Lectr, 68-72; assoc prof, 68-72; dean, 89-94; prof, 72-. **MEMBERSHIPS** Pres, C.A.U.T., 79-80; Chair, Legal Aid Manitoba, 72-78 **RESEARCH** Constitutional law; criminal law; labour law; evidence; charter of rights. **SELECTED PUBLICATIONS** Auth, Illegally Obtained Evidence and the Right to Privacy: Some Policy Considerations, Butterworths, 80; Law in a Cynical Society, Carswell, 85; Constraints on the Political Will, 84. **CONTACT ADDRESS** Fac of Law, Univ Manitoba, Robson Hall, Winnipeg, MB, R3T 2N2. **EMAIL** roland_penner@umanitoba.ca

PENNICK, AURIE ALMA
PERSONAL Born 12/22/1947, Chicago, IL, s **DISCIPLINE** LAW, CIVIL RIGHTS **EDUCATION** Univ of IL, BA 1971, MA 1981; John Marshall Law Sch, JD 1986. **CAREER** Coalition of Concerned Women Inc, exec dir 1976-78; Chicago Abused Women Coalition, exec dir 1978-81; Citizens Alert, exec dir 1981-82; Chicago Comm Trust Fellowship, staff assoc 1982-84; John D & Catherine T MacArthur Foundation, asst dir spec grant; Chicago Transit Authority Chief Adminstrative Atty; managing attorney/administration; LEADERSHIP COUNCIL FOR METROPOLITAN OPEN COMMUNITIES, PRESIDENT, CHIEF EXECUTIVE OFFICER, currently; part time FACULTY ROOSEVELT UNIV 1986-; **HONORS AND AWARDS** Ten Outstanding Young Citizens Chicago Jr Assoc of Commerce & Industry 1984; Kizzy Image & Achievement Awd 1985; Natl Council of Negro Women, Chicago Midwest Section, Ida B Wells Education Award, 1992. **MEMBERSHIPS** Part time trainer Vista/Action Region V 1980-81; mem Chicago Police Bd, Chicago Women in Philanthropy, Chicago Blacks in Philanthropy, Phi Alpha Delta Legal Frat; mem Cook County Bar Assoc 1988-; mem American Bar Assoc 1988-. **CONTACT ADDRESS** Leadership Council for Metropolitan Open Communities, 401 S State St, Ste 860, Chicago, IL, 60605.

PENNOCK, ROBERT T.
PERSONAL Born 05/07/1958, Ithaca, NY, m, 1998 **DISCIPLINE** PHILOSOPHY **EDUCATION** Earlham Col, BA, 80; Univ Pittsburgh, PhD, 91. **CAREER** Asst prof, Univ Texas at Austin, 91- . **HONORS AND AWARDS** Mellon fel, 85, 88; NEH summer fel, 93; Templeton Found prize, 97; NSF/NEH fel, 96. **MEMBERSHIPS** APA; Philos of Sci Asn; Sigma Xi; AAAS. **RESEARCH** Philosophy of biology; science and values; scientific explanation and evidence. **SELECTED PUBLICATIONS** Auth, Moral Darwinism: Ethical Evidence for the Descent of Man, Biol and Philos, 95; auth, Death of the Self: Changing Medical Definitions in Japan and the US, Obirin Rev of Int Stud, 95; auth, Epistemic and Ontic Theories of Explanation and Confirmation, Philos of Sci-Japan, 95; auth, Naturalism, Evidence and Creationism: The Case of Phillip Johnson, Biol and Philos, 96; auth, Inappropriate Authorship in Collaborative Scientific Research, Public Affairs Q, 96; auth, Naturalism, Creationism and the Meaning of Life: The Case of Phillip Johnson Revisited, Creation/Evolution, 96; auth, Is a Necessity-and-Sufficiency Account of Causation Contradictory? in Weingartner, ed, The Roles of Pragmatics in Contemporary Philosophy, Austrian Wittgenstein Soc, 97; auth, Pre-Existing Conditions: Disease Genes, Causation and the Future of Medical Insurance, in Magnus, ed, Contemporary Genetic Technology: Scientific, Ethical, and Social Challenges, Krieger, 98; auth, Creationism's War on Science, Environ Rev, 98; auth, Death and Taxes: On the Justice of Conscientious Objection to War Taxes, J of Acct, Ethics & Public Policy, 98; auth, Evidential Relevance and the Grue Paradox, Philos of Sci-Japan, 98; auth, The Prospects for a Theistic Science, Perspectives on Sci and Christian Faith, 98; auth, Tower of Babel: The Evidence Against the New Creationism, MIT, 99; auth, Ruts, Roots and Branches: On Learning and Teaching an Environmental Ethic With Help from Thoreau, in Aleksiuk, ed, Nature, Environment & Me: Explorations of Self in a Deteriorating World, in press. **CONTACT ADDRESS** Dept of Philosophy, Univ of Texas at Austin, Waggener Hall 316, Austin, TX, 78712-1180. **EMAIL** pennock@uts.cc.utexas.edu

PENROD, STEVEN D.
DISCIPLINE LAW **EDUCATION** Harvard Univ, BA, JD. **RESEARCH** Alternative dispute resolution. **SELECTED PUBLICATIONS** Auth, pubs on eyewitness reliability and jury decisionmaking. **CONTACT ADDRESS** Law Dept, Univ of Nebraska, Lincoln, 103 Ross McCollum Hall, PO Box 830902, Lincoln, NE, 68588-0420. **EMAIL** spenrod@unlinfo.unl.edu

PENTIUC, EUGENE
PERSONAL Born 12/08/1955, Romania, m, 1977, 2 children **DISCIPLINE** SEMITIC PHILOSOPHY **EDUCATION** Harvard Univ, PhD, 98. **CAREER** Tchng Fel, Harvard Univ, 94-96; Inst, Holy Cross Greek Orthodox Schl of Theol, 98. **MEMBERSHIPS** SBL, AOS, CBA **RESEARCH** Old Testament and Semitic Philology **CONTACT ADDRESS** 16 Romanian Ave, Southbridge, MA, 01550. **EMAIL** epentiuc@aol.com

PEPERZAK, ADRIAAN THEODOOR
PERSONAL Indonesia **DISCIPLINE** PHILOSOPHY **EDUCATION** Licenciate in philos, Higher Inst Philos, Louvain Univ, Belgium; Univ Paris-Sorbonne, PhD. **CAREER** Arthur J. Schmitt prof; fac, Amsterdam Univ, Utrecht Univ & Nijmegen Univ; vis prof, Bandung Univ, Indonesia, Mallorca Univ, Spain, Scuola Normale of Pisa, Italy, Istituto Superiore di Filosofia of Naples, Italy, Nice Univ, France, Dusquesne Univ, (ittsburgh, Pa State Univ at State Col, Boston Col & Loyola Univ Chicago. **RESEARCH** Ethics and Polit philosophy; philosophy of religion; metaphilosophy; Hegel; French phenomenology; Levinas. **SELECTED PUBLICATIONS** Auth, Le jeune Hegel et la vision morale du monde; Selbsterkenntnis des Absoluten; Hegels praktische Philosophie; To the Other; Ethics as First Philosophy; Before Ethics; Beyond: The Philosophy of Emmanuel Levinas; Platonic Transformations; and Selbsterkenntnis des Absoluten: Grundlinien der Hegelschen Philosophie des Geistes. **CONTACT ADDRESS** Dept of Philosophy, Loyola Univ, Chicago, 820 N. Michigan Ave., Chicago, IL, 60611. **EMAIL** apeperz@wpo.it.luc.edu

PEPPER, GEORGE B.
PERSONAL Born 06/17/1926, Jersey City, NJ, s **DISCIPLINE** PHILOSOPHY **EDUCATION** Fordham Univ, MA, 48, PhD, 58. **CAREER** Lectr, Fordham Univ & Col New Rochelle & Cape Cod Commun Col; vis prof, Talladega Col, 68-89; prof emer, 93-, Iona Col, 50-93; NEH Summer Inst Columbia Univ, 86; Roberta C Rudin Fel Jewish Christian Rel, 89-90; vis scholar, Columbia Univ, 89-90. **MEMBERSHIPS** Amer Asn Univ Prof; Amer Philos Asn; Karl Jaspers Soc N Amer; Soc Advan Amer Philos. **RESEARCH** Philosophy of religion; Ethics; Political philosophy; M Heidegger. **SELECTED PUBLICATIONS** Auth, Peter Berger on Modernization and Religion, Cross Currents, 88-89; Die Relevanz von Jasper's Achenzeit fur interkulterelle Studien, Karl Jaspers: Zur Aktualitat Seines Denkens, Verlag; 91; rev, The Architecture of Meaning, Philosophy East and West, 88; coauth, Jewish-Christian Dialogue: A Jewish Justification, and Beyond Occupation: American Jewish, Christian and Palestinian Voices for Peace, Cross Currents, 90-91; auth, Karl Jaspers: Basic Philosophical Writings, Humanities Press, 94; The Boston Heresy Case in View of the Secularization of Religion, Edwin Mellen Press, 88. **CONTACT ADDRESS** 470 Halstead Ave, Apt 2-P, Harrison, NY, 10528. **EMAIL** GPEPPER@gis.net

PEPPER, STEPHEN L.
DISCIPLINE LAW **EDUCATION** Stanford Univ, AB, 69; Yale Law School, JD, 73. **CAREER** Prof of law, Col of Law, Univ Denver. **RESEARCH** Professional ethics **SELECTED PUBLICATIONS** Auth, The Lawyers Amoral Ethical Role: A Defense, A Problem, and Some Possibilities, Am Bar Found Res Jour, 86; Autonomy, Community, and Lawyers Ethics, Cap

Univ Law Rev, 90; Conflicting Paradigms of Religious Freedom: Liberty Versus Equality, Brigham Young Univ Law Rev, 93; Counseling at the Limits of the Law: An Exercise in the Jurisprudence and Ethics of Lawyering, Yale Law Jour 1545, 95. **CONTACT ADDRESS** 1900 Olive St, Denver, CO, 80222. **EMAIL** SPepper@mail.law.du.edu

PERHAC., RALPH M.
PERSONAL Born 12/17/1953, Albuquerque, NM, m, 1978, 3 children **DISCIPLINE** PHILOSOPHY **EDUCATION** Univ MN, PhD, 89. **CAREER** Asst prof, Univ AL, 89-92; RES ASSOC, UNIV TN, 93-. **MEMBERSHIPS** Am Philos Asn. **RESEARCH** Environmental risk policy; environmental philos. **SELECTED PUBLICATIONS** Auth, Defining Risk: Normative Considerations, Human and Ecological Risk Assessment, June 96; Does Risk Aversion Make a Case for Conservatism?, Risk--Health, Safety & Environment, fall 96; Comparative Risk Assessment: Where Does the Public Fit In?, Science, Technology, & Human Values, spring 98; Environmental Justice: The Issues of Disproportionality, Environmental Ethics, forthcoming; Medical Costs and Lost Productivity from Health Conditions at Volatile Organic Compound Superfund Sites, with J. Lybarger, R. Lee, D. Vogt, R. Spengler, and D. Brown, Environmental Res, forthcoming. **CONTACT ADDRESS** 11316 Silver Springs Dr., Knoxville, TN, 37932. **EMAIL** rperhac@utk.edu

PERILLO, JOSEPH M.
PERSONAL Born 01/02/1933, New York, NY, m, 1963, 3 children **DISCIPLINE** CONTRACT LAW **EDUCATION** Cornell Univ, AB, 53, JD, 55. **CAREER** Assoc, Proj Int Procedures, Columbia Univ, 60-63; asst prof, 63-66, assoc prof, 66-68, actg dean, 81-82, Prof Contracts, Law Sch, Fordham Univ, 68-, Fulbright grant, Univ Florence, 60-61. **RESEARCH** Law of remedies. **SELECTED PUBLICATIONS** Coauth, Civil Procedure in Italy, Mortinus Nijhoff, 65; The Italian Legal System, Stanford Univ Press, 67; The Law of Contracts, 70, 4th ed, 98 & co-ed, Cases and Problems on Contracts, 78, 2nd ed, 89, West Publ Co. **CONTACT ADDRESS** Law Sch, Fordham Univ, 140 W 62nd St, New York, NY, 10023-7407. **EMAIL** JPerillo@mail.lawnet.fordham.edu

PERKINS, DOROTHY
DISCIPLINE RELIGION **EDUCATION** Gettysburg Col, BA, 68; Temple Univ, PHD, 82. **CAREER** Teach asst, Temple Univ, 71-74; lectr, La Salle Univ, 74-77; Commonwealth Speakers Prog, Pa Hum Counc, 84-85, 86; INDEPENDENT SCHOLAR, WRITER, 77-. **CONTACT ADDRESS** 220 Locust St, Apt 29-A, Philadelphia, PA, 19106.

PERKINS, MORELAND
PERSONAL Born 04/16/1927, Richmond, VA, 2 children **DISCIPLINE** PHILOSOPHY **EDUCATION** Harvard Univ, AB, 48, AM, 49, PhD, 53. **CAREER** PROF EMERITUS OF PHILOS, UNIV MD, COLLGE PARK. **HONORS AND AWARDS** Johnsonian Prize in Philosophy for Sensing the World, 82. **MEMBERSHIPS** Amer Philos Assoc. **SELECTED PUBLICATIONS** Auth, Sensing the World, Hackett Pub Co, 83; Reshaping the Sexes in Sense and Sensibility, Univ Press VA, 98. **CONTACT ADDRESS** 410 Auburn Dr., Daytona Beach, FL, 32118.

PERLIN, MARC G.
PERSONAL Born 07/15/1948, Brookline, MA, m, 1970, 2 children **DISCIPLINE** LAW **EDUCATION** Boston Univ, BA, 70; Northeastern Univ, JD, 73. **CAREER** Law clerk, Super Ct of Mass, 73-74; legal asst to Chief Justice, Boston Munic Ct, 74-75; instr legal writing & res, 75-77, asst prof to prof, Law Sch, Suffolk Univ, 77-; lectr, Sch of Law, Northeastern Univ, 74-76; speaker & panelist, Mass Continuing Legal Educ, Inc, 75; ed, Mass Rules Serv, 80-; reporter, Standing Adv Comt on Rules of Civil Proc of Supreme Judicial Ct of Mass, 94-. **MEMBERSHIPS** Am Bar Asn. **RESEARCH** Family law; civil practice and procedure; constitutional law. **SELECTED PUBLICATIONS** Coauth, Handbook of Civil Procedure in the Massachusetts District Courts, Lawyers Weekly Publ, 80; auth, Sum and Substance Quick Review of Family Law, 92, 97; auth, Mottla's Proof of Cases in Massachusetts, 3rd ed, vol 1, 92, vol 2, 93, coauth, vol 3, 95; auth, Handbook of Civil Procedure in the Massachusetts District Court, 80, 90; Massachusetts Collection Law, 84, 92. **CONTACT ADDRESS** Law Sch, Suffolk Univ, 41 Temple St, Boston, MA, 02114-4241. **EMAIL** mperlin@acad.suffolk.edu

PERLMAN, HARVEY
DISCIPLINE LAW **EDUCATION** Univ Nebr, BA, JD. **CAREER** Prof **RESEARCH** Torts; unfair business practices. **SELECTED PUBLICATIONS** Co-auth, Legal Regulation of the Competitive Process; Federal Criminal Jury Instructions. **CONTACT ADDRESS** Law Dept, Univ of Nebraska, Lincoln, 103 Ross McCollum Hall, PO Box 830902, Lincoln, NE, 68588-0420. **EMAIL** hperlman@unlinfo.enl.edu

PERLMAN, MARK
PERSONAL New York, NY, m **DISCIPLINE** PHILOSOPHY **EDUCATION** Ohio St Univ, BA, 87, MA, 89; Univ Ariz, PhD, 94. **CAREER** Grad tchng asst, 88-89, Ohio St Univ; grad tchng assoc, 89-93, Univ AZ; lectr, phil, 93-97, vis asst prof, 97-98, Ariz St Univ; asst prof, 98-, Western Oregon Univ. **RESEARCH** Phil of mind; metaphysics; phil of law. **SELECTED PUBLICATIONS** Art, Punishing Acts and Counting Consequences, AZ Law Rev, Vol 37, 95; art, The Trouble with Two-Factor Conceptual Role Theories, Minds and Machines, 97. **CONTACT ADDRESS** Dept of Philosophy and Religious Studies, Western Oregon Univ, 345 N. Monmouth Ave, Dept of Phil and Religious Studies, Humanities Div, Monmouth, OR, 97361. **EMAIL** perlman@wou.edu

PERLMUTTER, RICHARD MARK
PERSONAL Born 12/03/1942, Cambridge, MA, m, 1966, 2 children **DISCIPLINE** LAW **EDUCATION** Tufts Univ, AB, 64; Harvard Univ, LLB, 67. **CAREER** Prof Law, Suffolk Univ Law Sch, 75-, pvt pract Law, Boston, 68-; vis prof Law, Boston Univ Law Sch, 82-. **MEMBERSHIPS** AAUP; Am Asn Law Schs. **RESEARCH** General contracts. **SELECTED PUBLICATIONS** Coauth, Contracts: Contemporary Cases & Materials, Callaghan & Co, 80. **CONTACT ADDRESS** Law Sch, Suffolk Univ, 41 Temple St, Boston, MA, 02114-4241. **EMAIL** rperlmut@acad.suffolk.edu

PERO, ALBERT
PERSONAL Born 12/14/1935, St. Louis, MO, m, 1988 **DISCIPLINE** SYSTEMATIC THEOLOGY AND CULTURE **EDUCATION** St. Paul Col, BA, 57; Concordia Sem, B Th, 62; Univ of Det, Grad, 68; Lutheran Sch of Theol, ThD, 75; Univ of Chicago, Post Doc Study, 85; Univ of Zimbabwe, Post Doc Study, 86 **CAREER** Prof, Lutheran School of Theology, 95-pres **HONORS AND AWARDS** Ach Award, Afr Am Lutheran Assoc; Staley Distinguished Christian Scholar, St. Olaf Col; Disciple for Justice Award, Commission for Multicultural Ministries-Evangelical Lutheran Church in Amer; Milwaukee Theolog Inst **MEMBERSHIPS** Intl Afro-Am Museum; Assoc for Study of Negro Life & History; Lutheran Human Relation Assoc of Am; Ntl Committee of Black Churchmen; Lutheran Council in USA; Assoc of Black Lutheran Churchmen; Theology of the Americas; Amer Acad Relig **SELECTED PUBLICATIONS** Auth, Cultural/Self Transcendence, Lutheran School of Theology, 93; Auth, Black and Lutheran, Trinity Lutheran Sem, 90 **CONTACT ADDRESS** Lutheran Sch of Theol, 1100 E 55th St, Chicago, IL, 60615. **EMAIL** apero@lstc.edu

PERREIAH, ALAN RICHARD
PERSONAL Born 04/11/1937, Los Angeles, CA, m, 1958, 5 children **DISCIPLINE** LOGIC, HISTORY OF PHILOSOPHY **EDUCATION** Loyola Univ, Los Angeles, BA, 59; Marquette Univ, MA, 61; Ind Univ, Bloomington, PhD(philos), 67. **CAREER** Asst prof philos, Univ Wis-Whitewater, 66-67; asst prof, 67-69, Assoc Prof Philos, Univ Ky, 69-, Fel, Inst Advan Studies, Princeton Univ, 73-74; fel, Villa i Tatti, Harvard Univ Ctr Ital Renaissance Studies, 80-81; Nat Endowment for Humanities Awards, 74, 78, 79, 80-81. **HONORS AND AWARDS** Nat Endowment for Humanities Award, 74. **MEMBERSHIPS** Am Philos Asn; Southeastern Medieval Asn; Soc Int Pour L'Etude Philos Medievale. **RESEARCH** History of logic, particularly 14th and 15th century; history of science; Paul of Venice. **SELECTED PUBLICATIONS** Auth, George Santayana and recent theories of man, Philos Today, 69; Approaches to supposition-theory, New Scholasticism, 71; ed, Treatise on Suppositions From the Logica Magna by Paul of Venice, Text Ser 15, Franciscan Inst, 71; auth, Buridan and the definite description, J Hist Philos, 72; transl, Paul of Venice: Logics Parva Philosophia Verlag, Munich, 82; Paul-of- venice, 'Logica Magna', Vol 2 Pt 4 - Capitula-de-conditionali- et-de-rationali - Latin And English - Hughes,ge, Editor And Translator, Speculum-a J of Medieval Studies, Vol 0068, 1993; Medieval Mereology - Henry,dp, History And Philosophy of Logic, Vol 0014, 1993; Aristotle Axiomatic Science, Peripatetic Notation or Pedagogical Plan, History And Philosophy of Logic, Vol 0014, 1993; Sophisms in Medieval Logic And Grammar - Read,s, History And Philosophy of Logic, Vol 0015, 1994; Buridanus,iohannes Summulae in Praedicamenta - Latin - Bos,ep, History And Philosophy of Logic, Vol 0017, 1996; Semantics And Speculative Grammar in Scholarly Discourse - Paris, Bologna, And Erfurt, 1270-1330 - The Modist Semiotics - Italian - Marmo,c, Speculum-a J of Medieval Studies, Vol 0071, 1996; Buridanus,iohannes Questiones-elencorum - Latin - Vanderlecq,r, Braakhuis,hag, History And Philosophy of Logic, Vol 0017, 1996; Buridanus,iohannes Summulae-de-praedicabilibus - Latin - Derijk,lm, History And Philosophy of Logic, Vol 0017, 1996; Semantics And Speculative Grammar in Scholarly Discourse - Paris, Bologna, And Erfurt, 1270-1330 - The Modist Semiotics - Italian - Marmo,c, Speculum-a J of Medieval Studies, Vol 0071, 1996. **CONTACT ADDRESS** Dept of Philos, Univ of Ky, 500 S Limestone St, Lexington, KY, 40506-0003.

PERRIN, DAVID
PERSONAL Born 09/26/1956, Chiliwack, BC, Canada, s **DISCIPLINE** THEOLOGY **EDUCATION** Univ Ottawa/St Paul Univ, PhD, 95; Pontifical Gregorian Univ, Rome, STL, 87; Pontifical Gregorian Univ, Rome, STB, 85; W Ontario Univ, B.Sc, 78. **CAREER** Interim Dean Theology, St Paul Univ, Ottawa, 98-; asst prof Theology, St Paul Univ, Ottawa, 96-; lctr Theology, St Paul Univ, Ottawa, 94-96; Distance Educ Coord, St Paul Univ, Ottawa, 94-96; part-time lctr Theology, St Paul Univ, 91-94; Pastor, St Agnes Parish, Thunder Bay, Ontario, 89-90; asst pastor, St Mary's Parish, Fort Frances, Ontario, 87-89; part-time lctr, Ontario Eastern Cath Tchrs Assoc, 87-96. **MEMBERSHIPS** Ed, Between the Lines, 93-96; Amer Acad Relig. **SELECTED PUBLICATIONS** The Sacrament of Reconciliation: An Existential Appproach, Edwin Mellon Pr, 98; For Love of the World: The Old and New Self of John of the Cross, Intl Scholars Publ, 97; Canciones entre el alma y el esposo of Juan de la Cruz: A Hermeneutical Interpretation, Intl Scholars Publ, 96. **CONTACT ADDRESS** Dept of Theology, St Paul Univ, 223 Main St, Ottawa, ON, K1S 1C4. **EMAIL** dperrin@ustpaul.uottawa.ca

PERRITT, HENRY H., JR.
DISCIPLINE COMPUTER LAW, CIVIL PROCEDURE, ADMINISTRATIVE LAW **EDUCATION** Mass Inst Technol, BS, 66, MS, 70; Georgetown Univ Law Ctr, JD, 75. **CAREER** Prof, Villanova Univ; White House Staff; past Dep Under Sec Labor in the Ford Admin; past mem, Pres Clinton's Transition Team; past adv, Europ Comn and OECD. **HONORS AND AWARDS** Founder, Villanova Ctr for Inf Law and Policy; dir, Proj Bosnia, effort to extend the Rule of Law in Ctrl Europe by tying civic inst together through the Internet. **MEMBERSHIPS** Bars mem, Va, Pa, Dist Columbia, Md & US Supreme Ct; Past chem Sec on Law and Comput, Assoc Amer Law Sch; Nat Acad Public Admin; chem Comt on Regulatory Initiatives and Information Technol, ABA Sec on Admin Law and Regulatory Practice; VP and mem bd dir, Ctr for Comput Aided Legal Instr; Adv Comt on Internet Dissemination, SEC EDGAR data under an NSF grant to NYU and IMS. **RESEARCH** Law and the information superhighway; fed electronic information policy,international legal issues arising from internet use, reforming legal institutions through the internet. **SELECTED PUBLICATIONS** Auth, Law and the Information Superhighway, 96; Trade Secrets: A Practitioner's Guide; How to Practice Law With Computers & Electronic Contracting, Publishing and EDI Law, 91. **CONTACT ADDRESS** Law School, Villanova Univ, 800 Lancaster Ave, Villanova, PA, 19085-1692. **EMAIL** perritt@law.vill.edu

PERRY, CONSTANCE K.
PERSONAL Born 05/15/1965, Huntington, NY, m, 1990 **DISCIPLINE** PHILOSOPHY **EDUCATION** Univ Buffalo, PhD, 94. **CAREER** Sr instr, 92-93, Hahnemann Univ; asst prof, 94-, Allegheny Univ of The Health Professions **HONORS AND AWARDS** Member of Alpha Eta, nat honor soc for allied health profes. **MEMBERSHIPS** Am Philos Asn; Am Soc for Bioethics and Humanities. **RESEARCH** Ethical issues in pregnancy; feminist ethics; personhood and its connection to care of animals and incompetent humans; clinical and research ethics. **SELECTED PUBLICATIONS** Auth, Maternal-Fetal Conflict and Principles of Biomedical Ethics, Fostering a Relationship Between Flexibility & Stability, Univ Microfilms Int, 93; auth, Unreliable Results, Commentary to Protocol Review: An Investigator Considers an Animal's Experience, Lab Animal, 24:10, 95. **CONTACT ADDRESS** Dept of Liberal Arts and Applied Science, Allegheny Col, Mail stop 503, Philadelphia, PA, 19102-1192. **EMAIL** perryc@auhs.edu

PERRY, EDMUND
PERSONAL Born 05/18/1923, GA, m, 3 children **DISCIPLINE** HISTORY OF RELIGIONS **EDUCATION** Univ Ga, AB, 44; Emory Univ, BD, 46; Northwestern Univ, PhD(bibl theol, hist of relig), 50. **CAREER** Dir Wesley Found, GA State Col Women, 46-48; from instr to asst prof Bible & hist of relig, Duke Univ, 50-54; assoc prof, 54-62, Prof Hist Of Relig, Northwestern Univ, 62-, Chmn Dept, 54-, Mem univ senate, Methodist Church, 54-60; educ consult, Am Tel & Tel Co, 60-62; Fulbright prof, Vidyodaya Univ Ceylon, 67- 68. **HONORS AND AWARDS** DLitt, Vidyodaya Univ Ceylon, 68. **MEMBERSHIPS** Am Orient Soc; Am Theol Soc; Am Acad Relig; Soc Bibl Lit; Int Soc Buddhist-Christian Friends (exec secy, 68-). **RESEARCH** History and methods of studying religions; history and the history of religions; a Christian theology of religion. **SELECTED PUBLICATIONS** Coauth, Jews and Christians in North America, Westminster, 65; auth, The Study and Practice of Religion Today, Vidyodaya Univ Ceylon, 68; Buddhist Studies in Honour of Walpola Rahula, Fraser, London, 80; Theravada Buddhism - a Social-history From Ancient Benares to Modern Colombo - Gombrich,rf, J of The American Oriental Society, Vol 0117, 1997. **CONTACT ADDRESS** Dept of Hist & Relig, Northwestern Univ, Evanston, IL, 60201.

PERRY, RICHARD J., JR.
DISCIPLINE CHURCH; SOCIETY **EDUCATION** Lutheran Sch Theol at Chicago, ThD. **CAREER** Asst prof-. **HONORS AND AWARDS** Mem, treasurer, LSTC Alumni Senate; dir, Black Ministries for the ELCA; Inclusive Ministries for the North Carolina Synod of the LCA; ch, Working Group on Racism in Church and Society at the 7th Assembly in Budapest, Hungary. **RESEARCH** Urban and cross-cultural ministry. **SELECTED PUBLICATIONS** Auth, Justification by Grace and Its Social Implications, Theol and the Black Experience, Fortress Press, 88. **CONTACT ADDRESS** Dept of Church and Society, Lutheran Sch of Theol, 1100 E 55th St, Chicago, IL, 60615. **EMAIL** rperry@lstc.edu

PERRY, TIM
PERSONAL Born 04/06/1969, Ottawa, ON, Canada, s **DISCIPLINE** THEOLOGY **EDUCATION** Univ of Durham, PhD, 96 **CAREER** Asst Prof, Providence Col, 98-pres **MEMBERSHIPS** Soc of Christian Philos; Am Acad of Relig **RESEARCH** Development of Doctring; John Hick's Philosophy of Religion **SELECTED PUBLICATIONS** Auth, Anti Judaism, The Historical Jesus and the Christology of Hebrews A Theological Reflection, Didaskalia, forthcoming; Auth, The Significance of Hendrik Kraemers Theology of Religions, Didaskalia, 98, 37-59; Auth, Beyond the Threefold Typology, Canadian Evangelical Review, 97, 1-8 **CONTACT ADDRESS** Dept Bibl and Theol Studies, Providence Col, Division of Bibl & Theolog Studies, Otterburne, MB, R0A 1G0.

PERSONS, W. RAY
PERSONAL Born 07/22/1953, Talbottan, GA, m, 1977 **DISCIPLINE** LAW **EDUCATION** OH State Univ, 1971-72; Armstrong State Coll, BS 1975; OH State Univ, JD 1978. **CAREER** Armstrong State Coll, coll prof 1979-80; Natl Labor Rel Bd, attny 1980-82; Wells Braun Persons Law Firm, partner/owner 1982-; Cong Lindsay Thomas, legislative counsel; Arrington & Hollowell, PC, attorney 1986-; GEORGIA STATE UNIV COLLEGE OF LAW, ADJUNCT PROFESSOR OF LITIGATION, 1989-; State of Georgia, special asst attorney general, 1989-. **HONORS AND AWARDS** Regents Scholar Armstrong State Coll 1973-75; Silver "A" Awd Armstrong State College 1975. **MEMBERSHIPS** State Bar of GA 1979-; treas Riceboro Comm Improvement Found 1982-83; gen counsel Congressional Black Assoc 1984-85; Fed Bar Assoc 1984-85, Leadership GA Foundation 1985-; Legal Advisor to Brook Glen Neighborhood Assn 1986-; Ohio State Univ Alumni Assn 1981-; Georgia Defense Lawyers Association; Lawyers Club of Atlanta; American Bar Association; Emory University Law School, Master Lamar Inn of Court; State Bar Disciplinary Board. **SELECTED PUBLICATIONS** Co-author, Ohio Civil Rules Supplement, 1978. **CONTACT ADDRESS** Arrington & Hollowell, PC, 191 Peachtree St NE, Ste 3550, Atlanta, GA, 30303-1735.

PESANTUBBEE, MICHELENE
DISCIPLINE RELIGIOUS STUDIES **EDUCATION** Univ Calif Santa Barbara, PhD. **CAREER** Asst prof. **SELECTED PUBLICATIONS** Auth, When the Earth Shakes: The Cherokee Prophecies of 1811-1812. **CONTACT ADDRESS** Religious Studies Dept, Univ of Colorado, Boulder, Boulder, CO, 80309. **EMAIL** Michelene.Pesantubbee@Colorado.edu

PESSIN, SARAH
PERSONAL Born 07/23/1970, New York, NY **DISCIPLINE** MEDIEVAL PHILOSOPHY **EDUCATION** Yeshiva Univ, BA, 91; Columbia Univ, MA, 94; OH State Univ, doctoral candidate, 2000. **CAREER** Graduate student/fellow, OH State Univ. **HONORS AND AWARDS** Melton Center for Jewish Studies Graduate Fellowship. **RESEARCH** Neoplatonism; Jewish and Islamic Medieval Philosophy. **CONTACT ADDRESS** Dept of Philos, Ohio State Univ, 230 N. Oval Mall, 350 Univ H, Columbus, OH, 43209. **EMAIL** pessin.4@osu.edu

PESTANA, MARK
PERSONAL Born 02/14/1953, Fresno, CA, m, 1994, 2 children **DISCIPLINE** PHILOSOPHY **EDUCATION** Univ Chicago, PhD, 86. **CAREER** Asst prof; assoc prof, Grand Valley State Univ. **MEMBERSHIPS** Am Philos Asn; Am Cath Philos Asn. **RESEARCH** Philosophical Psychology; Theory of Mind. **SELECTED PUBLICATIONS** Auth, Conscience; Guilt and Shame; Envy; Self Deception, Magill's Ready Reference: Ethics, 94; Second Order Desires and Strength of Will, The Modern Schoolman, 96; The Three Species of Freedom a nd the Six Species of will Acts; The Modern Schoolman, 96; Moral Virtue or Mental Health, 98. **CONTACT ADDRESS** Dept of Philosophy, Grand Valley State Univ, Allendale, MI, 49401. **EMAIL** PestanaM@gvsu.edu

PETERS, AULANA LOUISE
PERSONAL Born 11/30/1941, Shreveport, LA, m **DISCIPLINE** LAW **EDUCATION** Notre Dame School for Girls, diploma 1959; College of New Rochelle, BA Philosophy 1963; Univ of S CA, JD 1973. **CAREER** Publimondial Spa, secty/English corres 1963; Fibramianto Spa, secty/English corres 1963-64; Turkish Delegation to Org for Economic Coop and Develop, English corres 1965; Cabinet Braconnier AAA Translation Agency, translator/interpreter 1966; Organ for Economic Coop and Develop Scientific Rsch Div, admin asst 1966-67; Gibson Dunn & Crutcher, Attorney 1973-84; US Securities and Exchange Comm, comm 1984-88; Gibson, Dunn & Crutcher, partner, 1988-. **HONORS AND AWARDS** Natl Assoc of Bank Women Inc Washington Achiever Awd 1986; Natl Women's Economic Alliance Foundation, Director's Clt Award, 1994; Hollywood Chamber of Commerce, Women in Business Award, 1995; Natl Law Journal one of the 50 most influential women attorneys in USA. **MEMBERSHIPS** Los Angeles Co Bar Assn, State of CA Bar Assn, Langston Hughes Assn; Black Women Lawyers Assn, Amer Bar Assoc; mem Univ of S CA Law Sch Law Alumni Assn; Council on Foreign Relations Inc NY; Bd of Dirs: Mobil, Merrill Lynch, 3M, Northrop Grumman Corp. **CONTACT ADDRESS** Gibson, Dunn & Crutcher, 333 S Grand Ave, Los Angeles, CA, 90071-1504.

PETERS, ELLEN ASH
PERSONAL Born 03/21/1930, Berlin, Germany, m, 1952, 3 children **DISCIPLINE** LAW **EDUCATION** Swarthmore Col, BA, 51; Yale Univ, LLB, 54. **CAREER** Law clerk, US Court of Appeals, 54-55; assoc law, Univ Calif, Berkeley, 55-56; from asst prof to prof, Yale Univ, 56- 75, Southmayd prof, 75-78; Assoc Justice, Conn Supreme Court, 78-, Adv, Am Law Inst Restatement of Restitution, 63-; mem bd managers, Swarthmore Col, 70-81; adj prof law, Yale Univ, 78-; trustee, Yale New Haven Hosp, 81-. **HONORS AND AWARDS** Conn Law Rev Award, Univ Conn Sch Law, 78; Distinguished Achievement Award, Conn Bar Asn, 81; Ella Grasso Distinguished Serv Medal, 82., MA, Yale Univ, 64. **MEMBERSHIPS** Am Law Inst. **RESEARCH** Contracts; commercial transactions; government contracts. **SELECTED PUBLICATIONS** Auth, Remedies for breach of contracts relating to the sale of goods under the Uniform Commercial Code, 1263, Suretyship under Article 3 of the Uniform Commercial Code, 468 & Quest for uncertainty, 478, Yale Law J; Commercial Transactions, Cases Text and Problems, Bobbs, 71; Reconsidering Gilmore,grant The Death-of-contract - Symposium - Foreword, Northwestern University Law Review, Vol 0090, 1995; The William-b-lockhart- lecture - Getting Away From The Federal Paradigm - Separation of Powers in State Courts, Minnesota Law Review, Vol 0081, 1997. **CONTACT ADDRESS** Supreme Court Conn Drawer N Sta A, Hartford, CT, 06106.

PETERS, THEODORE FRANK
PERSONAL Born 04/03/1941, Wayne, MI, m, 1964, 3 children **DISCIPLINE** PHILOSOPHY, RELIGION **EDUCATION** MI State Univ, BA, 63; Capital Sem, BD, 67; Univ Chicago, MA, 70, PhD, 73. **CAREER** Pastor, Trinity Lutheran Church, Chicago, 70-72; asst prof relig & philos, Newberry Col, 72-76; assoc prof relig, Loyola Univ of the South, 76-78; Prof Syst Theol, Pac Lutheran Sem & Grad Theol Union. **HONORS AND AWARDS** Prof of the Year Award, Newberry Col, 75. **MEMBERSHIPS** Am Acad Relig; SC Soc Philos (pres, 75-76); World Future Soc; Mutual UFO Network. **RESEARCH** Philosophical theol; sci and relig. **SELECTED PUBLICATIONS** Auth, God - The World's Future, Fortress, 92; For the Love of Children, Westminster/John Knox, 96; Playing God? Genetic Determinism and Human Freedom, Routledge, 97. **CONTACT ADDRESS** Pacific Lutheran Theol Sem, 2770 Marin Ave, Berkeley, CA, 94708-1530. **EMAIL** tpeters2ct@aol.com

PETERSEN, CYNTHIA
DISCIPLINE LAW **EDUCATION** Queen's Univ, Ba, LLB; Harvard Univ, LLM. **CAREER** Assoc prof. **RESEARCH** Property law; family law; consititutional law; lesbian and gay legal issues. **SELECTED PUBLICATIONS** Auth, pubs on human rights, anti-discrimination law, and lesbian and gay equality rights. **CONTACT ADDRESS** Fac Common Law, Univ Ottawa, 550 Cumberland St, PO Box 450, Ottawa, ON, K1N 6N5.

PETERSON, BRIAN
DISCIPLINE NEW TESTAMENT STUDIES **EDUCATION** Union Theological Seminary in Virginia, 97 **CAREER** Instr, 84, 86, Luther Theological Seminary; visiting instr, 91-94, Union Theological Seminary in Virginia; asst prof, 98-, Lutheran Theological Southern Seminary. **HONORS AND AWARDS** Bruce Prize, Luther Theological Seminary, 96 **MEMBERSHIPS** Soc of Biblical Lit **RESEARCH** Pauline epistles; rhetorical analysis **SELECTED PUBLICATIONS** Auth, Review of David L. Barlett's Romans (Westminister Bible Companion), Interpretation, 97; Between Text and Sermon: 2 Corinthians 6:1-13, Interpretation, 97; Conquest, Control, and the Cross: Paul's Self-Portrayal in 2 Corinthians 10-13, Interpretation, 98; Eloquence and the Proclamation of the Gospel in Corinth, Society of Biblical Literature Dissertation Series #163, 98; Review of Paul Barnett's The Second Epistle to the Corinthians (NICNT), Catholic Biblical Quarterly, Oct 98. **CONTACT ADDRESS** 4201 N. Main St., Columbia, SC, 29203. **EMAIL** bpeterson@ltss.edu

PETERSON, COURTLAND H.
PERSONAL Born 06/28/1930, Denver, CO, m, 1966, 3 children **DISCIPLINE** LAW **EDUCATION** Univ CO, BA, 51, LLB, 53; Univ Chicago, MCL, 59; Univ Freiburg, DJur, 63. **CAREER** From asst prof to assoc prof, 59-63, actg dean sch law, 73-74, dean sch law, 74-79, Prof Law, Univ Colo, Boulder, 63-96, Nicholas Doman Prof Int Law Emer, 96-; Vis prof, UCLA, 65, Max Planck Inst, Ger, 69-70, Univ TX, 73-74. **HONORS AND AWARDS** Robert L Stearns Award; William Lee Knous Award. **MEMBERSHIPS** Am Asn Comp, Studies Law (treas, 79-90, hon pres, 96-98); Am Law Inst. **RESEARCH** Comp law; for judgments; conflict of law theory. **SELECTED PUBLICATIONS** Auth, Die Anerkennung Auslindischer Urteile, Frankfurt, 64; An introduction of the history of continental civil procedure, Colo Law Rev, 69; Developments in American conflicts law: Torts, Ill Law Forum, 69; Foreign country judgments and the second restatement of conflict of law, Columbia Law Rev, 72; Particularism in conflict of laws, Hofstra Law Rev, 82. **CONTACT ADDRESS** Sch of Law, Univ of Colorado, PO Box 401, Boulder, CO, 80309-0401. **EMAIL** court.peterson@worldnet.att.net

PETERSON, GREG
PERSONAL Born 05/06/1966, MN, m, 1986, 1 child **DISCIPLINE** PHILOSOPHY OF RELIGION **EDUCATION** Univ Minnesota, BA; Luther Sem, Ma; Denver Univ, PhD. **CAREER** Univ Minnesota, asst prof, 96-97; Thiel Col, asst prof, 97-. **HONORS AND AWARDS** Templeton Sci Rel Cours Awd. **MEMBERSHIPS** AAR; APA; IRAS; PSA; AAAS. **RESEARCH** Science and religion; Philos of Mind and of Sci; Philosophical Theology. **SELECTED PUBLICATIONS** Auth, The Scientific Status of Theology: Imre Lakatos Method and Demarcation, Perspectives in Sci and Christ Faith, 98; Cognitive Science: What One Needs to Know, Zygon 97; Mind and Bodies: Human and Divine, Zygon, 97. **CONTACT ADDRESS** Dept of Religion, Thiel Col, Greenville, PA, 16125. **EMAIL** gpeterso@thiel.edu

PETERSON, MICHAEL LYNN
PERSONAL Born 01/07/1950, Linton, IN, m, 1970, 2 children **DISCIPLINE** PHILOSOPHY **EDUCATION** Asbury Col, BA, 72; Univ Ky, MA, 74; State Univ NY, Buffalo, PhD, 76. **CAREER** From instr to asst prof philos, Roberts Wesleyan Col, 74-78; Assoc Prof Philos, Asbury Col, 78, Head Philos Deft, 80-, Nat Endowment Humanities fel philos, 78; mem adv & ref bd, John Witherspoon Inst, Princeton Univ, 78-; fel philos, Inst Advan Christian Studies, 79 & 80; lectr, Univ Ky & Georgetown Col, 81-82; managing ed, J Soc Christian Philosophers, 82- **HONORS AND AWARDS** Pew Found Fel, 92-93; Distinguished Schol in Residence, Greenville Col, 96-97. **MEMBERSHIPS** Am Philos Asn; Soc Christian Philosophers; Wesleyan Theol Soc; Am Sci Affil. **RESEARCH** Philosophy of science; philosophy of religion; modern philosophy. **SELECTED PUBLICATIONS** Coauth, Reason and Religious Belief: An Introduction to the Philosophy of Religion, Oxford Univ Press, 2nd ed, 98; co-ed, Philosophy of Religion: Selected Readings, Oxford Univ Press, 96; auth, The Problem of Evil, in Companion to the Philosophy of Religion, Blackwell Publ, 97; God and Evil: An Introduction to the Issues, HarperCollins/Westview, 98; author of numerous other articles and book chapters. **CONTACT ADDRESS** Asbury Col, 1 Macklem Dr, Wilmore, KY, 40390-1198. **EMAIL** myphilos@aol.com

PETERSON, PHILIP LESLIE
PERSONAL Born 03/12/1937, San Francisco, CA, m, 1967, 2 children **DISCIPLINE** PHILOSOPHY, LINGUISTICS **EDUCATION** Col William & Mary, AB, 59; Duke Univ, PhD (philos), 63. **CAREER** From asst prof to assoc prof, 63-76, Prof Philos, Syracuse Univ, 76-, Res assoc, Century Res Corp, 59-63, consult, 63-; Woodrow Wilson fel, 60-63; proj leader ling, Info Processing Systs Res, US Air Force Contracts, 66-71; partic, Early Mod Philos Inst, R Williams Col, 74. **MEMBERSHIPS** Am Philos Asn; AAAS; AAUP; Ling Soc Am. **RESEARCH** Philosophy of language; semantics; epistemology. **SELECTED PUBLICATIONS** Auth, Concepts and Language, Mouton, The Hague, 73; An abuse of terminology, Found Lang, 76; On specific reference, Semantikos, 76; How to infer belief from knowledge, Philos Studies, 77; On representing event reference, In: Presupposition, Acad Press, 79; On the logic of few, many, and most, Notre Dame J Formal Logic, 79; What causes effects?, Philos Studies, 81; Philosophy of Language, Social Res, 81. **CONTACT ADDRESS** 222 Buckingham Ave, Syracuse, NY, 13210.

PETERSON, SANDRA
DISCIPLINE PHILOSOPHY **EDUCATION** Princeton Univ, PhD. **RESEARCH** Aristotle's ethics and metaphysics; Plato's metaphysics and philosophy of language. **SELECTED PUBLICATIONS** Auth, Plato's Parmenides: A Principle of Interpretation and Seven Arguments, J Hist Philos, 96; Apparent Circularity in Aristotle's Account of Right Action in the Nicomachean Ethics, Apeiron, 92; Horos (Limit) in Aristotle's Nicomachean Ethics, Phronesis, 88; Substitution in Aristotelian Technical Contexts, Philos Studies, 85; Remarks on Three Formulations of Ethical Relativism, Ethics, 85; Zeno's Second Argument against Plurality, J Hist Philos, 78. **CONTACT ADDRESS** Philosophy Dept, Univ of Minnesota, Twin Cities, 355 Ford Hall, 224 Church St SE, Minneapolis, MN, 55455. **EMAIL** peter009@maroon.tc.umn.edu

PETERSON, THOMAS V.
PERSONAL Born 04/14/1943, Everett, WA, m, 1980, 1 child **DISCIPLINE** RELIGIOUS STUDIES **EDUCATION** Stanford Univ BA, 65, PhD, 75; Harvard Div Sch, MTS, 69. **CAREER** Prof rel stud, 75-, Alfred Univ. **HONORS AND AWARDS** 3 NEH Fel. **MEMBERSHIPS** AAR; SCTL. **RESEARCH** Ritual Studies; Religion and the Arts. **SELECTED PUBLICATIONS** Auth, Ham and Japheth: The Mythic World of Whites in the Antebellum South, Metuchen NJ, Scarecrow Press, 78; editor of spec issue, Historical Reflections/Reflexions Historiques, 97; auth, The Prophetic Challenge of Cherokee Artist Jimmie Durham: Colonialism and Dehumanizing Images of Native Americans, in: The Future of Prophetic Christianity: Essays in Honor of Robert Mcafee Brown, ed, John Carmody, Denise Carmody, NY, Orbis, 93. **CONTACT ADDRESS** Division of Human Studies, Alfred Univ, Alfred, NY, 14802. **EMAIL** FPETT@bigvay.alfred.edu

PETTER, ANDREW J.
DISCIPLINE LAW **EDUCATION** Univ Victoria, LLB, 81; Cambridge Univ, LLM, 82. **CAREER** Asst prof, 86-88; assoc prof, 88-. **SELECTED PUBLICATIONS** Auth, pubs on constitutional law, legal and political theory, legislative and regulatory processes, contracts, and legal education. **CONTACT ADDRESS** Fac of Law, Univ Victoria, PO Box 2400, Victoria, BC, V8W 3H7. **EMAIL** lawadmss@uvic.ca

PETUCHOWSKI, JAKOB JOSEF
PERSONAL Born 07/30/1925, Berlin, Germany, m, 1946, 3 children **DISCIPLINE** THEOLOGY, LITURGY **EDUCATION** Univ London, England, BA, 47; Hebrew Union Col, Ohio, MA, 52, PhD(theol), 55. **CAREER** Rabbi, Beth Israel Congregation, Pa, 55-56; asst prof rabbinics, 56-59, assoc prof, 59-63, prof, 63-65, prof rabbinics & theol, 65-74, res prof theol & liturgy, 74-81, Res Prof Judeo- Christian Studies, Hebrew Union Col, Ohio, 81-, US citizen Vis prof, Antioch Col, 6 1; dir Jewish studies, Hebrew Union Col, Israel, 63-64; vis prof, Tel-Aviv Univ, Israel, 71. **HONORS AND AWARDS** Dr phil, Univ Cologne, West Ger, 78. **MEMBERSHIPS** Am Acad Relig; fel Am Acad Jewish Res. **RESEARCH** Jewish theology in the classical Rabbinic and in the modern periods; Jewish liturgy; the Christian-Jewish dialogue on a theological level. **SELECTED PUBLICATIONS** Auth, Prayer book Reform in Europe, World Union of Progressive Judaism, 68; Heirs of the Pharisees, Basic Books, 70; The Theology of Haham David Nieto, Ktav, second ed, 70; Understanding Jewish Prayer, Ktav, 72; Theology and Poetry, Routledge & Kegan Paul, London, 78; Metchisedech-Urgestalt der Okumene, Herder, Freiburg, 79; Ever Since Sinai, B Arbit Books, third ed, 79; co-ed, Studies in Memory of Joseph Heinemann, Magnes Press, Jerusalem, 81; 100 Years of American Conservative Judaism - a Review-essay, American Jewish History, Vol 0080, 1991. **CONTACT ADDRESS** 7836 Greenland Pl, Cincinnati, OH, 45237.

PFEIFFER, RAYMOND SMITH
PERSONAL Born 10/11/1946, New York, NY, d, 3 children **DISCIPLINE** PHILOSOPHY **EDUCATION** Millbrook School, Diploma; Kenyon Col, AB, 68; WA Univ, AM, 72; PhD, 74. **CAREER** Off, USN, 68-69; Asst Prof, Alma Col, 74-75; Prof, Delta Col, 75-. **HONORS AND AWARDS** AAUP Awd for Svc, 98; Barstow-Frevel Awd, 94; Who's Who in Humanities, 92; Natl Endowment for the Humanities, Fel, 87; APA , Fel TX, 86, KS, 77; Univ Fel, WA Univ, 71-73., AB Cum Laude, Kenyon. **MEMBERSHIPS** APA; Mich Acad of Science Arts and Letters; Sigma Xi; US & Can Intl Asn Philo of Law & Soc Philo; US Bd of Ed, Phil Now, 98; Ed Bd, Tchng Phil, 87-; Manuscript Judge for Mich Acad, 86-91. **RESEARCH** Moral philosophy; applied ethics and philosophy of technology. **SELECTED PUBLICATIONS** The Central Distinction in the Theory of Corporate Moral Personhood, Jour of Bus Ethics, 90; Owing Loyalty to One's Employer, Jour of Bus Ethics, 92; Teaching Ethical Decision- Making: The Case Study Method and the Resolved Strategy, Tchng Phil, 92; CoAuth, Ethics on the Job: Cases and Strategies, Wadsworth, 93; auth, Why blame the Organization? A Pragmatic Analysis of Collective Moral Responsibility, Littlefield, 95. **CONTACT ADDRESS** Prof, Delta Col, Univ Center, MI, 48710.

PFUND, PETER H.
PERSONAL Born 10/06/1932, Bryn Mawr, PA, m, 1959, 2 children **DISCIPLINE** HISTORY, LAW **EDUCATION** Amherst Col, BA, 54; Union PA Law Sch, JD, 59. **CAREER** US Dept of St, Officer of the Legal Advisor, full-time, 59-97; asst legal advisor for private int law, 79-97; special advisor for pvt int law, 97-. **HONORS AND AWARDS** Am Bar Asn, Sect for Int Law & Pract, Leonard J. Theberge Prize for Pvt Int Law, 87. **MEMBERSHIPS** Am Law Inst; German-American Lawyers Asn, Bonn, Ger. **SELECTED PUBLICATIONS** Auth, Contributing to Professional Development of Private International Law: The International Process and the United States Approach, 249 Recusil des cours 9-144, 94-V **CONTACT ADDRESS** 10419 Pearl St, Fairfax, VA, 22032-3824. **EMAIL** pildb@his.com; lphildos@aol.com

PHELPS, TERESA GODWIN
PERSONAL Born 05/29/1944, Bournemouth, England, m, 1964, 3 children **DISCIPLINE** LEGAL WRITING **EDUCATION** Univ Notre Dame, BA, 73, MA, 75, PhD(English), 80. **CAREER** Asst Prof Legal Writing, Law Sch, Univ Notre Dame, 80-, Ed, Notre Dame English J, 78-80. **MEMBERSHIPS** MLA; Law & Humanities Inst; Asn Am Law Sch. **RESEARCH** Legal language; law and humanities. **SELECTED PUBLICATIONS** Auth, Problems and Cases for Legal Writing, Nat Inst Trial Advocacy, 82; the Power of Persuasion, University of Cincinnati Law Review, Vol 0063, 1994. **CONTACT ADDRESS** Law Sch, Univ Notre Dame, Notre Dame, IN, 46556.

PHENIX, PHILIP HENRY
PERSONAL Born 03/01/1915, Denver, CO, m, 1943, 2 children **DISCIPLINE** PHILOSOPHY, RELIGION **EDUCATION** Princeton Univ, BA, 34; Union Theol Sem, MDiv, 42; Columbia Univ, PhD, 50; LHD, Alderson-Broaddus Col, 70. **CAREER** Asst prof philos & relig, Carleton Col, 46-48; assoc prof relig, 50-53; assoc prof educ, Teachers Col, Columbia Univ 54-58; dean, Carleton Col, 58-60; prof philos & educ, 60-73, Arthur I Gates prof, 73-80, Arthur I Gated Emer Prof Philos & Educ, 80-Teachers Col, Columbia Univ; Brown & Haley lectures, Col Puget Sound, 64. **HONORS AND AWARDS** Harbison Award, 64; Butler Silver Medal, Columbia Univ, 81. **MEMBERSHIPS** Philos Educ Soc (pres, 71-72); Relig Educ Asn; Soc Values Higher Educ; NEA. **RESEARCH** Philosophy of educaton; value education; religious education. **SELECTED PUBLICATIONS** Auth, Education and the Common Good, Harper, 61; auth, Realms of Meaning, McGraw, 64; auth, Man and His Becoming, Rutgers Univ, 64; auth, Education and the Worship of God, Westminster, 66; transl, Jorge Manach, Frontiers in the Americas, Teachers Ltd Press, 75. **CONTACT ADDRESS** 127 Rosewood Cir, Bridgewater, VA, 22812.

PHILLIPS, CLARENCE MARK
PERSONAL Born 09/18/1960, Key West, FL **DISCIPLINE** PHILOSOPHY **EDUCATION** Univ Warwick, Coventry, Eng, MA, 91; Tulane Univ, PhD, 98. **CAREER** Lectr, phil, 91-, Calif St Univ; lectr, 91-92, Justus-Liedig Volkshorchschule, Germany; lectr, 94-, Tulane, Univ New Orleans, Xavier & Dillard Univ. **HONORS AND AWARDS** French Honor Soc. **MEMBERSHIPS** APA **RESEARCH** Pragmatism, evolutionary psychology, Darwinian theory. **SELECTED PUBLICATIONS** Art, Homo Natura: Influence of Emerson's Conception of Nature on Nietzche's Will to Power, Hist of Phil Quart, 97. **CONTACT ADDRESS** 802 Pine St, New Orleans, LA, 70118. **EMAIL** cphillip@mailhost.tcs.tulane.edu

PHILLIPS, CRAIG A.
PERSONAL Born 07/01/1954, Tulsa, OK, m, 1977, 2 children **DISCIPLINE** THEOLOGY; ETHICS **EDUCATION** Brown Univ, AB, 76; Harvard Univ, M Div, 79; Duke Univ, PhD, 93. **CAREER** Visiting lectr, Univ NC Chapel Hill, 93; visiting instr, Duke Univ, 94; asst prof, Temple Univ, 94-97; rector, Incarnation/Holy Sacrament Episcopal Church, 97-; instr, Rosemont Col, 98-. **HONORS AND AWARDS** Amer Asn of Col Jr Teaching fel, 91-92; Outstanding Young Men of Amer, 86. **MEMBERSHIPS** Amer Acad of Relig; Soc of Bibl Lit. **RESEARCH** Methodology of the study of relig; Colonial and postcolonial theory; Critical social theory; Modern Christian traditions. **SELECTED PUBLICATIONS** Auth, From Aesthetics to Redemptive Politics: A Political Reading of the Theological Aesthetics of Hans Urs von Balthasar and the Materialist Aesthetics of Walter Benjamin, Univ Mich, 93. **CONTACT ADDRESS** 317 Grayling Av., Narberth, PA, 19072-1905. **EMAIL** craigphi@voicenet.com

PHILLIPS, DEWI ZEPHANIAH
PERSONAL Born 11/24/1934, Wales, m, 1959, 3 children **DISCIPLINE** PHILOSOPHY **EDUCATION** Univ Col of Swansea, BA, MA; St Catherine's Col, Oxford, BLitt. **CAREER** Asst lectr & lectr, Queen's Col Dundee, 61-63; lectr, Univ Col N Wales, 63-65; from lectr to prof, philos, 65-96, Univ Wales, Swansea; Danforth Prof Philos of Relig, 92- , Claremont Grad Univ; Rush Rhees Res Prof, Univ Wales, Swansea, 96- . **HONORS AND AWARDS** Hon PhD, Abo Akademi, Finland, 98. **MEMBERSHIPS** Aristotelian Soc; APA; AAR. **RESEARCH** Philosophy of religion; ethics; literature; Wittgenstein; metaphilosophy. **SELECTED PUBLICATIONS** Auth, Through a Darkening Glass, 82; Dramau Gwenlyn Parry, 82; auth, Belief Change and Forms of Life, 86; auth, R.S. Thomas: Poet of the Hidden God, 86; auth, Faith After Foundationalism, 88; auth, From Fantasy to Faith, 91; auth, Interventions in Ethics, 92; auth, Wittgenstein and Religion, 93; auth, Writers of Wales: J.R. Jones, 95; auth, Introducing Philosophy, 96; auth, Recovering Religious Concepts, 99; auth, Philosophy's Cool Place, 99. **CONTACT ADDRESS** Dept of Religion, Claremont Graduate Sch, Claremont, CA, 91711. **EMAIL** Jacquelyn.Huntzinger@cgu.edu

PHILLIPS, L. EDWARD
PERSONAL Born 09/24/1954, Jackson, TN, m, 1976, 3 children **DISCIPLINE** RELIGION **EDUCATION** Univ Tenn, BS; Emory Univ, MDiv; Univ Notre Dame, PhD. **CAREER** Asst prof religion, 91-94, assoc prof religion, 94-97, chair hum, 95-97, Union Col; assoc prof hist theol, Garrett Evangel Theol Sem, 97-. **HONORS AND AWARDS** James Still Fel, 94; Fac Scholars Fel, Appalachain Col Asn, 95. **MEMBERSHIPS** N Am Acad Liturgy; Am Acad Relig; Soc Liturgica. **RESEARCH** History of liturgy. **SELECTED PUBLICATIONS** Auth, Ritual Kiss in Early Christian Worship, 96. **CONTACT ADDRESS** Dept of Theology, Garrett-Evangelical Theol Sem, 2121 Sheridan Rd., Evanston, IL, 60201. **EMAIL** lephillips@nwu.edu

PHILLIPS, RANDALL R.
PERSONAL Born 01/13/1957, Detroit, MI, s **DISCIPLINE** THEOLOGY **EDUCATION** Pontifical Gregorian Univ, PhD, 88. **CAREER** St. Ephrem Church, assoc pastor, 89-92; Sacred Heart Sem, adj prof, 89-92; Our Lady of Victory Church, Pastor, 92-95; St. Linus Church, 95-. **MEMBERSHIPS** AAR, CTS **RESEARCH** Liberation theology **CONTACT ADDRESS** St. Linus Church, 6466 N Evangeline St, Dearborn Hts, MI, 48127-2029.

PHILLIPS, ROBERT L.
DISCIPLINE PHILOSOPHY **EDUCATION** Queen's Univ, MA; Oxford Univ, PhD. **CAREER** Sr instr, Queen's Univ at Kingston, Canada, 64-65; col lectr, Lincoln Col, Oxford, 65-67; asst prof, Wesleyan Univ, 67-74; dir, Prog War and Ethics, Univ Conn; prof-. **SELECTED PUBLICATIONS** Auth, Jus In Bello: Combatancy, Non-Combatancy, and Non-Combatant Immunity, Johnson and Kelsay, The Justification and Limitation of War in Western and Islamic Cultural Traditions, Greenwood Press, 90; Terrorism: Historical Roots and Moral Justifications, Crisp and Warner, Terrorism, Protest, and Power, Pergamon Press: 90; Ethics and Grand Strategy in the Gorbachov Era, Ethics and Intl Aff Annual, 90. **CONTACT ADDRESS** Dept of Philos, Univ Conn, 85 Lawlor Rd, West Hartford, CT, 06117.

PHILPOTT, MARK
PERSONAL Born 11/29/1968, London, England **DISCIPLINE** PHILOSOPHY **EDUCATION** Univ Bristol, B V Sc, 90; Univ Hull, MA, 94; Univ Bristol, M Litt, 96. **HONORS AND AWARDS** Univ Bristol scholar, 94; Brit Acad fel, 95; Stanford Univ fel, 96. **MEMBERSHIPS** APA. **RESEARCH** Genetics and identity; medical ethics; philos of lang; metaphysics. **SELECTED PUBLICATIONS** Auth, Not Guilty by Reason of Genetic Determinism, Punishment, Excuses & Moral Develop, Henry Tam, 96. **CONTACT ADDRESS** Dept of Philosophy, Stanford Univ, Stanford, CA, 94305-2155. **EMAIL** mark.philpott@stanford.edu

PHIPPS, WILLIAM EUGENE
PERSONAL Born 01/28/1930, Waynesboro, VA, m, 1954, 3 children **DISCIPLINE** RELIGION, PHILOSOPHY **EDUCATION** Davidson Col, BS, 49; Union Theol Sem, Va, MDiv, 52; Univ St Andrews, PhD(Bibl criticism), 54; Univ Hawaii, MA, 63. **CAREER** Prof Bible, Peace Col, 54-56; Prof Relig & Philos & Chmn Dept, Davis & Elkins Col, 56-, Minister, Presby US Church, 52-; vis fel, Princeton Theol Sem, 69-70; vis scholar, Emory Univ, 77-78. **HONORS AND AWARDS** MLitt, Davis and Elkins Col, WV, 72. **MEMBERSHIPS** Am Acad Relig. **RESEARCH** Bibical interpretation; religion and sexuality; thanatology. **SELECTED PUBLICATIONS** Auth, Was Jesus Married, Harper, 70; The Sexuality of Jesus, Harper, 73; The plight of the Song of Songs, J Am Acad Relig, 3/74; Did ancient Indian celibacy influence Christianity?, Studies Relig, 7/74; Recovering Biblical Sensuousness, Westminster, 75; Jesus, the prophetic Pharisee, J Ecumemical Studies, 1/77; Influential Theologians on Woman, Univ Press Am, 80; Marktwain, the Calvinist + an Analysis of His Theological Commitment to Challenge Popular Piety and Social Exploitation - Critics Corner/, Theology Today, Vol 0051, 1994; a Rabbi Talks with Jesus - Neusner,j/, Interpretation-a J of Bible and Theology, Vol 0049, 1995; Cremation is Gaining, NY Times, 2/4/81; in Our Own Voices - 4 Centuries of American Womens Religious Writing - Keller,rs, Ruether,rr/, J of Ecumenical Studies, Vol 0034, 1997. **CONTACT ADDRESS** Dept of Relig & Philos, Davis & Elkins Col, Elkins, WV, 26241.

PIAR, CARLOS R.
PERSONAL Born 06/05/1956, Santurce, Puerto Rico, m, 1986, 2 children **DISCIPLINE** RELIGION **EDUCATION** Biola Col, BA, 77; Talbot Theol Sem, MDiv, 80, ThM, 82; Univ S Cal, PhD, 91. **CAREER** Assoc prof, Cal State Univ, 90-. **MEMBERSHIPS** Am Acad Relig; Soc Christian Ethics; Pac Coast Theol Soc. **RESEARCH** Ethnicity & religion; Christian social ethics. **SELECTED PUBLICATIONS** Auth Jesus and Liberation, Peter Lang, 94; Cesar Chavez and La Causa: Toward a Hispanic Christian Social Ethic, Ann Soc Christian Ethics, 96. **CONTACT ADDRESS** 11405 Harrisburg Rd, Los Alamitos, CA, 90720. **EMAIL** crpiar@csulb.edu

PICART, CAROLINE JOAN KAY S.
PERSONAL Born 01/31/1966, Philippines, m, 1995 **DISCIPLINE** PHILOSOPHY & RELIGIOUS STUDY **EDUCATION** Ateneo de Manila Univ, Philippines, BS, 87, MA, 89; Cambridge Univ, England, MPhil, 91; Pa St Univ, PhD, 96. **CAREER** Instr, 87-89, Ateneo de Manila Univ; instr, 92-93, Yonsei Univ, Korea; instr, teaching asst, 93-96, Pa St Univ; instr, 96-97, Fl Atlantic Univ; instr, 97-, Univ We Eau Claire. **HONORS AND AWARDS** Ateneo de Manila Univ Merit Schol, 84-87; Ateneo Scholar Found Grant, 84-87; Acad Excellence & Extra-Acad Involvement Award, 87; Magna Cum Laude, 87; Univ Scholar, 87-89; Overseas Res Student Award, 89-90; Sir Run Run Shaw Award, 89-91; Rueben Levy Travel Awards Scheme award, 89, 91; Wolfson Prize for Acad Excellence, 91; XIIIth Int Cong on Logic, Methodology & Philos of Sci Award, 95; Grad Res Exhib, 96; Vis Minority Scholar/Artist, 97; Network for Excellence in Teaching Award, 97, 98; Faculty-Student Res Collaboration Grant, 97; Internal Res Grant, 97; Off of Univ Travel Award, 98; Univ Res & Creative Activity Award, 98; Inst on Race & Ethnicity Reading Sem Grant, 98. **MEMBERSHIPS** Nietzsche Soc; Amer Philos Assoc; Soc for Phenomenology & Existential Philos; NA Soc for Soc Philos; Int Assoc for Philos & Lit; Pa St Filipino Stud Assoc; Amer Conf on Romanticism; Int Group of Poets & Artists, Int Writers' Group; Pa St Ballroom Dance Club; Int Dance Club. **RESEARCH** Aesthetics; philos/sociology of sci; soc & polit philos/ethics; feminist philos; nineteenth & twentieth cen-

tury continental philos. **SELECTED PUBLICATIONS** Auth, Scientific Controversy as Farce: The Benveniste-Maddox Counter-Trials, Soc Stud of Sci, 94; art, Metaphysics in Gaston Bachelard's Reverie, Human Stud: A J for Philos & Soc Sci, 97; auth, The Darwinian Shift: Kuhn vs. Laudan, 97; Resentment and 'the Feminine' in Nietzsche's Politico-Aesthetics, Pa St Univ Press, 99. **CONTACT ADDRESS** Dept of Philos & Relig Stud, Univ Wi Eau Claire, Eau Claire, WI, 54702-4004. **EMAIL** picartcj@uwec.edu

PICIRILLI, ROBERT EUGENE
PERSONAL Born 10/06/1932, High Point, NC, m, 1953, 5 children **DISCIPLINE** BIBLICAL STUDIES, THEOLOGY **EDUCATION** Free Will Baptist Bible Col, BA, 53; Bob Jones Univ, MA, 55, PhD, 63. **CAREER** Registrar, 60-79, teacher Bible & Greek, Free Will Baptist Bible Col, 55-, acad dean, 79-, dean Grad Sch, 82-84, writer, Sunday Sch Dept, Nat Asn Free Will Baptists, 61-81; pastor, Cofer's Chapel, Free Will Baptist Church, 62-64; gen ed, Randall House Commentary, 86-. **HONORS AND AWARDS** DD, Bob Jones Univ, 67. **MEMBERSHIPS** Evangel Theol Soc; Inst Bibl Res. **RESEARCH** Biblical studies; Free Will Baptist history. **SELECTED PUBLICATIONS** Auth, By what authority?, in Presby J, 66; He Emptied Himself: Philippians 2: 5-11, in Bibl Viewpoint, 69; The Book of Galatians, Randall House Publ, 73; The Book of Romans, Randall House Publ, 75; The Meaning of Epignosis, in Evangel Quart, 75; ed & contribr, History of Free Will Baptist State Associations, Randall House Publ, 76; auth, A Study of Separate Free Will Baptist Origins in Middle Tennessee, in Quart Rev Southern Baptists, 77; contribr, Christian Education: An Introduction to Its Scope, Randall House Publ, 78; 1,2 Corinthians, Randall House Publ, 87; Ephesians and Phillipians, Randall House Publ, 88; 1,2 Thessalonians, Randall House Publ, 90; 1,2 Peter, Randall House Publ, 92; coauth, The NKJV Greek English Interlinear New Testament, Thomas Nelson Publ, 94; auth, Arminius and the Deity of Christ, in Evangel Quart, 97. **CONTACT ADDRESS** 3606 West End Ave, Nashville, TN, 37205-2403. **EMAIL** repic@fwbbc.edu

PICKARD, DEAN
PERSONAL Born 03/12/1947, Geneva, NY **DISCIPLINE** PHILOSOPHY **EDUCATION** Univ Calif, Riverside, BA, 73; Calif State Univ, Long Beach, MA, 77; Claremont Grad Univ, PhD, 92. **CAREER** Phys educ dept, Pomona Col, 75-82; philos, phys educ, Moorpark & Ventura Col, 78-82; prof, philos, hum, phys educ, Los Angeles Mission Col, 79-83; philos, Calif State Univ, 88-94; prof philos, Los Angeles Pierce Col, 83-98. **HONORS AND AWARDS** Phi Beta Kappa, cum laude, 73; fel Claremont Grad Univ, 88-89; Golden Apple Award tchg, 86, 88, 92, 95, 96, 97; Who's Who Among America's Teachers, 96, 98; NEH grant, 95; Liberty Fund Grant, 98. **MEMBERSHIPS** Los Angeles Ara Nietzsche Soc, APA; North Am Nietzsche Soc; Nietzsche Soc. **RESEARCH** Nietzsche; Kant; nineteenth and twentieth century continental philosophy; interdisciplinary humanities; philosophy and literature; contemporary philosophy; Heidegger; Wittgenstein; philosophy of martial arts; Asian/Buddhist philosophy; world religions. **SELECTED PUBLICATIONS** Auth, Martial Arts and Meditative Disciplines, Black Belt Mag, 79; auth, Mystical Experience, Language & Ontological Claims, Jour of the Los Angelés Commun Col, 82; auth, The Problem of Reflexivity in Habermasian Universalism, Auslegung, 93; auth, Logic, Truth, and Reasoning: A Textbook in Critical Thinking, Pierce Col, 97; auth, Nietzsche, Emancipation, & Truth, in Babich, ed, New Nietzsche Studies, 97. **CONTACT ADDRESS** Dept of Philosophy, Pierce Col, 6201 Winnatka Ave, Woodland Hills, CA, 91371. **EMAIL** pickard@laccd.cc.ca.us

PICKENS, GEORGE F.
PERSONAL Born 02/26/1958, Parkersburg, WV, m, 1980, 2 children **DISCIPLINE** INTERCULTURAL STUDIES, MISSION STUDIES **EDUCATION** Ky Christian Col, BA, 80; Ohio Univ, MA, 84; Univ Birmingham, Eng, PhD, 97. **CAREER** Lectr, Daystar Univ, Nairobi, Kenya; prof Intercult Studs, Ky Christian Col, 97- . **HONORS AND AWARDS** Overseas Studs Res Scheme, UK, 94-97, Neville Chamberlain prize, Univ Birmingham, UK, 94-95. **MEMBERSHIPS** Amer Acad Rel; Amer Soc Missiology. **RESEARCH** Oral history, African religion and Historical studies. **CONTACT ADDRESS** Dept of Intercultural Studies, Kentucky Christian Col, 100 Academic Pkwy, PO Box 2050, Grayson, KY, 41143-2205. **EMAIL** gpickens@email.kcc.edu

PICKENS, RUPERT TARPLEY
PERSONAL Born 02/20/1940, High Point, NC, m, 1963, 2 children **DISCIPLINE** ROMANCE PHILOLOGY, MEDIEVAL FRENCH **EDUCATION** Univ NC, Chapel Hill, AB, 61, MA, 64, PhD(Romance philol), 66. **CAREER** Asst prof French, Univ NC, Chapel Hill, 66-69; from asst prof to assoc prof, 69-78, Prof French, Univ KY, 78-, Managing ed, Fr Forum, 75-. **MEMBERSHIPS** MLA; Soc Rencesvals; Am Asn Teachers Fr.. **RESEARCH** The Bestiaire and Cumpot of Philippe de Thaun; Old French courtly literature; medieval lyric poetry. **SELECTED PUBLICATIONS** Auth, The concept of the feminine ideal in Villon's Testament: Huitain 89, Studies Philol, 73; Thematic Structure of Marie de France's Guigemar, Romania, 74; Somnium and Interpretation in Guillaume de Lorris, Symposium, 74; Estoire, Lai and romance: Chretien's Erec et Enide and Cliges, Romanic Rev, 75; The Welsh Knight: Paradoxicality in Chretien's Conte del Graal, FS Forum, 77; Jafure Rudel et la poetique de la mouvance, Cahiers Civilisation Medievale, 77; The Songs of Jaufre Rudel, Pontif Inst Mediaeval Studies, 78; the French Canon - What Should We Teach - Introduction/, Romance Quarterly, Vol 0041, 1994; La Poetique de Marie de France d'apres les prologues des Lais, Les Lett Romanes, 78; Women Readers and the Ideology of Gender in Old French Verse Romance - Krueger,rl/, Romance Quarterly, Vol 0043, 1996; the Fall of Kings and Princes - Structure and Destruction in Arthurian Tragedy - Guerin,mv/, Esprit Createur, Vol 0037, 1997; The Faces of Time - Portrayal of the past in Old French and Latin Historical Narrative of the Anglo-norman Regnum - Blacker,j/, Romance Quarterly, Vol 0044, 1997. **CONTACT ADDRESS** Dept of French, Univ of Ky, 500 S Limestone St, Lexington, KY, 40506-0003.

PICKERING, GEORGE W.
DISCIPLINE RELIGIOUS STUDIES **EDUCATION** Bates Col, AB; Univ Chicago, BD, MA, PhD. **CAREER** Prof, Univ Detroit Mercy, 70-. **MEMBERSHIPS** Amer Soc Christian Ethics; Amer Acad Rel. **RESEARCH** American civil rights movement, development of American religious liberalism, ethical issues in contemporary society. **CONTACT ADDRESS** Dept of Religious Studies, Univ of Detroit Mercy, 4001 W McNichols Rd, PO Box 19900, Detroit, MI, 48219-0900. **EMAIL** PICKERGW@udmercy.edu

PIECK, MANFRED
DISCIPLINE PUBLIC INTERNATIONAL LAW **EDUCATION** NY Univ, BS, 52; Columbia Univ, JD, 55, LLM, 58. **CAREER** Prof, Creighton Univ; pvt pract NY City, 55-57; fac adv, Int Moot Ct bd; Jessup Int Moot Ct team; Int Law Soc; Ger transl for Vera Lex. **MEMBERSHIPS** US and Int Asn(s), Semiotics Law; Int Soc Legal Philos; Ger-Amer Lawyers Asn; Omaha Comt Coun on For Relations. **SELECTED PUBLICATIONS** Pub(s), Rev Socialist Law; Nebr Law Rev; Amer J Comp Law; Villanova Law Rev; Amer J Int Law; Critic of Institutions, Vol 1, Codes and Customs, Lang, 94. **CONTACT ADDRESS** School of Law, Creighton Univ, 2500 California Plaza, Omaha, NE, 68178.

PIETSCH, PAUL ANDREW
PERSONAL Born 08/08/1929, New York, NY, m, 1950, 4 children **DISCIPLINE** ANATOMY, BIOLOGY, & PHILOSOPHY **EDUCATION** Syracuse Univ, AB, 54; Univ of Pa, PhD, 60. **CAREER** Instr in nursing, School of Nursing, Univ of Pa, 59; instr in anatomy, The Bowman Gray School of Medicine, Wake Forest Col, 60-61; asst prof of anatomy, School of Medicine, School of Dentistry and the Grad School, SUNY, 61-64; senior res molecular biologist, Biochemical Res Lab, The Dow Chemical Co, 64-70; ASSOC PROF, 70-78, CHAIR, DEPT OF BASIC HEALTH SCI, SCHOOL OF OPTOMETRY, 75-83, PROF, 78-94, PROF EMERITUS, 94-, IND UNIV. **HONORS AND AWARDS** Medical Journalism Award, AMA, 72; res featured on 60 Minutes, 73; 14 teaching awards, 73-94. **MEMBERSHIPS** Am Asn of Anatomists; AAAS; Soc Dev Biol (emeritus); Am Federation of Teachers; Am Asn of Univ Profs; Sci Handicapped Asn. **RESEARCH** Neurosciences: memory; developmental biology: regeneration; science journalism: publishing on the World Wide Web. **SELECTED PUBLICATIONS** Auth, Shufflebrain, Houghton-Mifflin, 81; auth, The Mind of a Microbe, Sci Digest, 83; auth, The Effects of Retinoic Acid on Mitosis During Tail and Limb Regeneration in the Axolotl Larva, Ambystoma mexicanum, Roux's Arch Dev Biol, 87; coauth, C.W. Vision and the Skin Camouflage Reactions of Ambystoma Larvae: the Effects of Eye Transplants and Brain Lesions, Brain Res, 85; coauth, The Dermal Melanophore of the Larval Salamander, Ambystoma tigrinum, Cytobios, 92; coauth, Phototaxic Behavior and the Retinotectal Transport of Horseradish Perxidase (HRP) in Surgically Created Cyclopean Salamander Larvae (Ambystoma), Neuroscience Res, 93. **CONTACT ADDRESS** School of Optometry, Indiana Univ, Bloomington, Bloomington, IN, 47405-3680. **EMAIL** pietsch@indiana.edu

PILANT, CRAIG WESLEY
PERSONAL Born 08/26/1952, San Francisco, CA **DISCIPLINE** THEOLOGY, AMERICAN RELIGIOUS STUDIES, HISTORICAL THEOLOGY **EDUCATION** Loyola Univ, Chicago, BA, 74; Univ Ill, Chicago, MA, 83; Fordham Univ, MSEd, 87, PhD, 97. **CAREER** Dir of admissions, GSAS, 90-97, asst dean, GSAS, 97-, Fordham Univ. **MEMBERSHIPS** AAR; CHS; NAGAP. **RESEARCH** American religious history; hagiography; music and theology; Social Gospel; Orestes A. Brownson. **SELECTED PUBLICATIONS** Auth, Inward Promptings: Orestes A. Brownson, Outsidership and Roman Catholicism in the United States, 96. **CONTACT ADDRESS** 838 Wesley Ave., 1-K, New Rochelle, NY, 10801. **EMAIL** cwphd@aol.com

PILCH, JOHN J.
PERSONAL Born 08/07/1936, Brooklyn, NY, w, 1975 **DISCIPLINE** THEOLOGY **EDUCATION** St. Francis Col, BA (summa cum laude), 59; Marquette Univ, MA, 67, PhD, 72. **CAREER** Inst, Bishop Neuman High School, 64-65; visiting prof of Liturgy, Sisters of Saint Casimir, Marymount Col, 65; acting chair and inst, St. Francis Col, 65-68; visiting prof of Theology and New Testament, Mount Saint Scholastica Col, 69 & 70; visiting prof of Hebrew Scriptures, Marquette Univ, 71; visiting prof of New Testament, 71-72, asst prof of Hebrew Scriptures, Univ of Saint Mary of the Lake, 72-74; New Testament Renewal Prog for the Sisters of Providence, Col of Great Falls, 73; visiting prof, St. John's Univ; lectr, Milwaukee Area Tech Col, 74-76; prog coord, Uni of Wis, 77-79; adjunct prof, Univ of Wis-Platteville, 78; visiting prof, Old St. Mary's Seminary and Univ, 84; visiting prof, Theological Inst at the Univ of Albuquerque, 86; speaker, Sinsinawa Biblical Inst, 87; speaker, 19th Annual Scripture Inst, Col Misericordia, 87; visiting prof, Pacific Lutheran Univ, 91; visiting prof, Ecumenical Inst of St. Mary's Seminary and Univ, 93; visiting prof of Bible, Univ of San Francisco, 95; adjunct asst prof, 93-94, visiting asst prof, 94-97, adjunct asst prof of biblical lit, Georgetown Univ, 97-; visiting prof of Old Testament, Loyola Univ, 98. **HONORS AND AWARDS** St. Francis Col Scholar, 55-59; Teaching fel, Christ the King Seminary, 59-64; Franciscan Scholar, 66-70; Marquette Univ Scholar, 70-71. **MEMBERSHIPS** Catholic Biblical Asn of Am; Soc of Biblical Lit; Am Acad of Religion; Soc for Ancient Medicine; Soc for Cross-Cultural Res; The Context Group. **RESEARCH** Utilizing social scientific methods and sources to analyze ancient documents; health, sickness and healing in antiquity; secrecy, deception, and lying in the ANE; experiences in alternate reality/altered states of consciousness; aspects of ancient, Eastern Mediterranean cultures. **SELECTED PUBLICATIONS** Auth, Cultural Dictionary of the Bible, Liturgical Press, 99; auth, Healing in the New Testament: Insights from Medical and Mediterranean Anthropology, Fortress Press, 99; auth, The Cultural World of Jesus Sunday by Sunday: Cycle C: Luke, Liturgical Press, 97; auth, The Cultural World of Jesus Sunday by Sunday: Cycle B: Mark, Liturgical Press, 96; auth, The Cultural World of Jesus Sunday by Sunday: Cycle A: Matthew, Liturgical Press, 95; auth, Appearances of the Risen Jesus in Cultural Context: Experiences of Alternate Reality, Biblical Thology Bulletin, 98; auth, A Window into the Biblical World: Caves, The Bible Today, 98; A Window into the Biblical World: Walking on the Sea, The Bible Today, 98; auth, A Window into the Biblical World: The Art of Insult, The Bible Today, 98; auth, A Window into the Biblical World: Games, Amusement, and Sport, The Bible Today, 98; co-ed & contribur, Handbook of Biblical Social Values, Hendrickson Pub, 98. **CONTACT ADDRESS** 1318 Black Friars Rd., Cantonsville, MD, 21228. **EMAIL** pilchjj@gusun.georgetown.edu

PILGRIM, WALTER E.
PERSONAL Born 03/26/1934, St. Paul, MN, m, 1957, 3 children **DISCIPLINE** NEW TESTAMENT **EDUCATION** Princeton Theol Seminary, PhD, 1971. **CAREER** Prof, Pacific Lutheran Univ, 71-; Dir, Lutheran Inst of Theol Educ, 73-93. **MEMBERSHIPS** Soc of Biblical Lit. **RESEARCH** New Testament Ethics; apocalyptic lit; Luke-Acts. **SELECTED PUBLICATIONS** Auth, Good News to the Poor, Augsburg, 81; auth, Revelation: Vision of Hope, Augsburg, 89; Uneasy Neighbors: Church and State in the New Testament, Fortress, 99. **CONTACT ADDRESS** 2410 Western Rd, Steilacoom, WA, 98388. **EMAIL** pilgriwe@aol.com

PILLSBURY, SAMUEL H.
DISCIPLINE CRIMINAL LAW **EDUCATION** Harvard Univ, AB, 76; Univ Southern Calif, JD, 83. **CAREER** Prof & William M. Rains fel; clerk, hon William Matthew Byrne, Jr, US Dist Ct, Los Angeles; Loyola Law Sch, 86-; asst US Atty, Criminal Div, Los Angeles. **HONORS AND AWARDS** USC Law Alumni Awd. **MEMBERSHIPS** Southern Calif Law Rev; **SELECTED PUBLICATIONS** Writes on, criminal law. **CONTACT ADDRESS** Law School, Loyola Marymount Univ, 7900 Loyola Blvd, Burns 417, Los Angeles, CA, 90045. **EMAIL** spillsbu@lmulaw.lmu.edu

PINCH, TREVOR J.
DISCIPLINE SOCIOLOGY, SCIENCE AND TECHNOLOGY **EDUCATION** Bath Univ, UK, PhD, 82. **CAREER** Lectr, Dept of Sociology, York Univ, UK, 83-90; prof, Dept of Sci and Technol Stud, Cornell Univ, 90- . **HONORS AND AWARDS** Merton Prize, Am Sociol Asn, 95. **MEMBERSHIPS** ASA; SHOT; HSS; CASST. **RESEARCH** Sociology of science and technology, sound technologies and the synthesizer. **SELECTED PUBLICATIONS** Coauth, The Golem: What Everyone Should Know about Science, Cambridge, 94, 2d ed,98; co-ed, The Handbook of Science and Technology Studies, Sage, 95; coauth, The Golem at Large: What You Should Know about Technology, Cambridge, 98; auth, The Hard Sell: The Language and Lessons of Street-Wise Marketing, HarperCollins, 96. **CONTACT ADDRESS** Dept of Science and Technology Studies, Cornell Univ, Clark Hall 622, Ithaca, NY, 14853. **EMAIL** TJP2@cornell.edu

PINKARD, TERRY
DISCIPLINE PHILOSOPHY **EDUCATION** Univ Tex, BA; Tobingen Univ, PhD, 74. **CAREER** Prof. **RESEARCH** Ethics, political philosophy; philosophy of history; German idealism. **SELECTED PUBLICATIONS** Auth, Hegel's Phenomenology: The Sociality of Reason, Cambridge, 94. **CONTACT ADDRESS** Dept of Philosophy, Georgetown Univ, 37th and O St, Washington, DC, 20057.

PINN, ANTHONY B.
PERSONAL Born 05/12/1964, Buffalo, NY **DISCIPLINE** RELIGIOUS STUDIES **EDUCATION** Columbia Univ, BA, 86; Harvard Divinity School, Mdiv, 89; Harvard Univ, MA, PhD, 94. **CAREER** McAlester Coll, 94-present. **MEMBERSHIPS** AAR, Soc for the study of Black Rel. **RESEARCH** Liberation Theology, Humanism, Popular Culture, non Christian Religions. **SELECTED PUBLICATIONS** Auth, Why Lord?, Suffering and Evil in Black Theology, Continuum Publishing Group, 95; Varieties of African American Religious Experience, Fortress Press, 98; coed, Studies in African-American Religious Thought and Life, Trinity Press International, forthcoming, 99; Studies in The History of African-American Religions, Univ Press of Florida, forthcoming, 2000; Protest Thought in The African Methodist Episcopal Church, 1863-1939, Vol 1, Univ Of Tennessee Press, spring, 99; Anybody There?: Reflections on African American Humanism, Religious Humanism, vol xxxi, 97. **CONTACT ADDRESS** Dept of Religious Studies, Macalester Col, 1600 Grand Ave, St. Paul, MN, 55105. **EMAIL** pinn@macalester.edu

PINTADO-CASAS, PABLO
PERSONAL Born 07/09/1966, Madrid, Spain, m, 1996, 1 child **DISCIPLINE** PHILOSOPHY OF LANGUAGE **EDUCATION** Univ of Madrid, BA, 89, Certificate in Education, 90, PhD, 96. **CAREER** Teaching asst, 92-93, Skidmore Col; teaching asst, 95, Univ of Maryland; adjunct asst prof, 97-98, adjunct asst prof, 97-present, Long Island Univ; prof, 97-present, Cervantes Institute; lectr, 98-present, Columbia Univ; The Cooper Union; adjunct asst prof, 98, Wagner Col. **HONORS AND AWARDS** Academic Scholarship, Ministry of Public Administration, 88-89; research fel, 90-92, dept of logic and linguistics, Univ of Madrid; research fel, 92-93, dept of language and literatures, Skidmore Col; research fel, 95, dept of linguistics, Univ of Maryland. **MEMBERSHIPS** APA **RESEARCH** Philosophy of language; logic; linguistics; Spanish language. **SELECTED PUBLICATIONS** Auth, Book Review: Wittgenstein on Mind and Language (David Stern), Teorema, 97; auth, Book Review: Wittegensteinian Themes (Norman Malcom), Teorema, 97; auth, Libros al aire libre: La Feria del Libro en el Parque del Retiro de Madrid, Hispania, March 98; auth, The Antecedents of Situation Semantics: Boguslaw Wolniewicz's Interpretation of the Notion of Situation in Wittgenstein, Teorema, forthcoming; Differences and Similarities Between Situation Semantics and Possile Worlds, Teorema, forthcoming. **CONTACT ADDRESS** 44 Bay St. Landing, #Q2E, Staten Island, NY, 10301. **EMAIL** pp171@columbia.edu

PINTCHMAN, TRACY
PERSONAL Born 09/21/1962, White Plains, NY, m, 1995 **DISCIPLINE** RELIGIOUS STUDIES **EDUCATION** Cornell Univ, BA, 84; Boston Univ, MA, 87; Univ CA, Santa Barbara, PhD, 92. **CAREER** Teaching fel and lectr, 85-87, Boston Univ; teaching asst and lectr, 87-91, Univ CA, Santa Barbara; vis prof, 96, Northwestern Univ; dir, Religion, Culture, and Society Minor Program, Loyola Univ Chicago, 97- . **HONORS AND AWARDS** Graduation Magna Cum Laude with distinction in all subjects, Cornell Univ, 84; Loyola Endowment for the Humanities Faculty Development Award, 94; Loyola Summer Research Fel, 97; Sujack Award for Teaching Excellence, Loyola Univ Chicago, 97; Amer Insti of Indian Studies Senior Research Fel, 97; Natl Endowment for the Humanities Fel, 98. **MEMBERSHIPS** Amer Acad of Religion, Assn for Asian Studies. **RESEARCH** Hindu Studies **SELECTED PUBLICATIONS** Auth, The Ambiguous Female: The Conception of Female Gender in the Brahmanical Tradition and the Roles of Women in India, Ethical and Political Dilemmas of Modern India, 93; auth, The Rise of the Goddess in the Hindu Tradition, 94; auth, Gender Complementarity and Gender Hierarchy in Puranic Accounts of Creation, Journal of the American Academy of Religion, 98; auth, contributions to this volume include two chapters, Seeking Mahadevi: Constructing the Identities of the Hindu Great Goddess, forthcoming; auth, Is The Hindu Goddess Tradition a Good Resource for Western Feminism? Working Goddesses, forthcoming. **CONTACT ADDRESS** 5846 N Drake Ave, Chicago, IL, 60659. **EMAIL** tpintd@luc.edu

PINZINO, JANE M.
PERSONAL Born 04/27/1958, Chicago, IL, s **DISCIPLINE** CHRISTIANITY, BUDDHISM **EDUCATION** Colgate Univ, BA, 81; Duke Univ, MDiv, 86; Univ Pa, PhD, 96. **CAREER** Instr Bibl Stud, 88-91 & 92-94 & 95-96, tchg asst, 90-92, tchg & res asst, Univ Pa, 94-96; peer evaluator, Thomas Jefferson Univ, 92-96; vis asst prof Relig Stud, Grinnell Col, 96-97; asst prof Relig, Univ Puget Sound, 97-. **HONORS AND AWARDS** Merit Scholar, Duke Univ, 84-86; Boardman fel, Univ Pa, 92-95; Dean's Scholar, Univ Pa, 94-95. **MEMBERSHIPS** Am Acad of Relig; exec comt bd-mem, Mid-Atlantic Region, 92-95; women's caucus co-moderator, Mid-Atlantic Region, 94-96. **RESEARCH** Medieval canon law; religions of Near Eastern origin and women and religion. **SELECTED PUBLICATIONS** Auth, Speaking of Angels: A 15th-Century Bishop in Defense of Joan of Arc's Mystical Voices, Fresh Verdicts on Joan of Arc, Garland Press, 96; Valerie Hotchkiss, Clothes Make the Man: Female Cross-Dressing in Medieval Europe, Arthuriana, vol 7.4, 98; ed, Some Skeptical Thoughts About Active Euthanasia and Assisted Suicide, Relig Stud Dept of Univ Pa; co-ed, The Culture of Disbelief, Relig Stud Dept of Univ Pa. **CONTACT ADDRESS** Dept of Relig Stud, Univ Puget Sound, 1500 North Warner, Tacoma, WA, 98416. **EMAIL** jpinzino@ups.edu

PIPER, ADRIAN MARGARET SMITH
PERSONAL Born 09/20/1948, New York, New York, s **DISCIPLINE** PHILOSOPHY **EDUCATION** School of Visual Arts, New York, NY, AA, fine arts, 1969; City College of New York, New York, NY, BA, philosophy, 1974; Harvard University, Cambridge, MA, philosophy, 1977, PhD, philosophy, 1981. **CAREER** Harvard University, graduate teaching assistant, 1976-77; University of Michigan, assistant professor, 1979-86; Georgetown University, associate professor, 1986-88; University of California, San Diego, associate professor, 1988-90; Wellesley College, professor, 1990-. **HONORS AND AWARDS** Sperling Prize for Excellence in Philosophy, 1974, Phi Beta Kappa Medal for the Best Honors Essay in the Social Sciences, 1974, Research Honors in Philosophy, 1974, City College of New York; First Prize in Drawing, Annual Student Exhibition, 1968, School of the Visual Arts; Stanford University, Mellon Post-Doctoral Research Fellowship, 1982-84; Woodrow Wilson International Scholars' Fellowship, 1989-90; NEA, Visual Artists' Fellowship, 1979, 1982; Guggenheim Fellowship, 1988-89; Awards in the Visual Arts Fellowship, 1990; California Institute of the Arts, Honorary Doctorate of Arts, 1991; NEH Coll Teacher's Research, Fellowship, 1998; Getty Research Inst, Distinguished Scholar, 1998-99. **MEMBERSHIPS** American Philosophical Association, 1979-; AAUP, 1979-; Association for Legal and Political Philosophy, 1979-; College Art Association, 1983-; North American Kant Society, 1979-. **CONTACT ADDRESS** Professor of Philosophy, Wellesley Col, 106 Central St, Wellesley, MA, 02181-8249.

PIPKIN, HARRY WAYNE
PERSONAL Born 08/10/1939, Houston, TX, m, 1965, 2 children **DISCIPLINE** HISTORY OF CHRISTIANITY **EDUCATION** Baylor Univ, BA, 61; Univ Conn, MA, 63; Hartford Sem Found, PhD(hist Christianity), 68. **CAREER** Asst in instr church hist, Hartford Sem Found, 67-68; Fulbright scholar Renaissance hist, Univ Vienna, 68-69; asst prof church hist, Baylor Univ, 69-74; assoc dir consortium higher educ relig studies, Pontif Col Josephinum, 74-76; dir, Univ Without Walls, Ohio, 76-78; Assoc Prof Church Hist, Baptist Theol Sem, Switz, 78-, Dir, Inst Baptist & Anabaptist Studies; Reporter & coordr, The Primary Source: Int Newslett Baptist Hist. **MEMBERSHIPS** Am Soc Church Hist; Zwingli Verein; Am Soc Reformation Res. **RESEARCH** Reformation studies and theology; Huldrych Zwingli; Balthasar Hubmaier. **SELECTED PUBLICATIONS** Auth, Zwingli, The Laity and the Orders: From the Cloister Into the World, Hartford Quart, winter 68; The Preaching and Sermons of Huldrych Zwingli, In: 20 Centuries of Great Preaching, Word Bks, 71; A Zwingli Bibliography: Bibliographia Tripotamopolitana, Clifford E Barbour Libr, 72; transl, The Gospel of Liberation by Jurgen Moltmann, Word Bks, 73; auth, Huldrych Zwingli and True Religion, AD 1974, 10/74; Christian Meditation, Its Art and Practice, Hawthorn, 77; Marpeck,pilgram - His Life and Theology - Boyd,sb/, Sixteenth Century J, Vol 0024, 1993; Spiritual Legacy of Denck,hans - Interpretation and Translation of Key Texts - Bauman,c/, Sixteenth Century J, Vol 0024, 1993. **CONTACT ADDRESS** Dept Church Hist, Baptist Theol Sem, Ruschlikon, ..

PIPPIN, TINA
PERSONAL Born 09/10/1956, Kinston, NC, m, 1984, 1 child **DISCIPLINE** RELIGIOUS STUDIES **EDUCATION** Marshill Col, BA, 78; Candler School of Theol, MDiv, 80; S Baptist Theol Sem, ThM, 82, PhD, 87. **CAREER** Asst prof to assoc prof, chair, Agnes Scott Col, 89- **RESEARCH** Bible & culture; critical theory & ethics **SELECTED PUBLICATIONS** Auth, The Bible and Culture Collective, The Postmodern Bible, Yale Univ Press, 95; Death and Desire: The Rhetoric of Gender in the Apocalypse of John, John Knox Press, 92; coed, The Monstrous and the Unspeakable: The Bible as Fantastic Literature, Sheffield Acad Press, 97; Violence, Utopia, and the Kingdom of god, Routledge Press, 98; auth, Apocalyptic bodies: The Biblical End of the World in Text and Image, Routledge, 99. **CONTACT ADDRESS** Agnes Scott Col, 141 E College Ave, Decatur, GA, 30030-3797. **EMAIL** tpippin@agnesscott.edu

PIRAU, VASILE
PERSONAL Born 02/20/1955, Fagaras, Romania, m, 1989, 3 children **DISCIPLINE** PHILOSOPHY **EDUCATION** Univ of Bucharest, ABD, MA, 80; Michigan State Univ, PhD, 98. **CAREER** Prof, philos, Caragiale Col, Bucharest, 80-85; lectr, hum, Norwalk Commun Col, 91; adj prof, hum, Lansing Commun Col, 93; tchg asst, instr, philos, Michigan State Univ, 92, 93, 94, 95, 97; adj prof, hum, Mott Commun Col, 98-. **HONORS AND AWARDS** Magna Cum Laude, 80; Michigan State Col of Arts and LettsVarg-Sullivan Award, outstanding grad stud, Dean's Award. **MEMBERSHIPS** APA. **RESEARCH** Philosophy of social sciences; continental philosophy; philosophy of science. **SELECTED PUBLICATIONS** Auth, Ways of Understanding in Social Sciences, Cultura Militans, 86; auth, The Relationship between Age and Creativity from Cognitive Sociology of Science Perspective, Youth Problems, 87; auth, Social and Behavioral Factors Responsible for the Idiosyncrasy toward the Implementation of Technological Innovations, Youth and Educ, 88; auth, Are There Irrational People or Only Mistranslated Ones?, Sci Bull of Baia Mare Univ, 96. **CONTACT ADDRESS** Dept of Humanities, Mott Comm Col, 813 Cherry Ln, Apt 1, East Lansing, MI, 48823. **EMAIL** pirauvas@pilot.msu.edu

PISON, RAMON MARTINEZ DE
PERSONAL Born 09/17/1953, Jaen, Spain, s **DISCIPLINE** THEOLOGY **EDUCATION** Comillas Univ, BA, 79; Gregorian Univ, Rome, Italy, Lic Th, 81; Ottawa Univ & St Paul Univ, PhD, 888; St Paul Univ, D.Th, 89; Calif Coast Univ, MSc. **CAREER** Prof, St Paul Univ, 98-; assoc prof, St Paul Univ, 95-98; asst prof, St Paul Univ, 90-95; lctr, St Paul Univ, 89-90. **MEMBERSHIPS** Amer Acad Relig; Societe canadienne de theologie. **RESEARCH** Relationship between Philosophy, Theology and Psychology. **SELECTED PUBLICATIONS** The Religion of Life: The Spirituality of Maurice Zundel, Mediaspaul, 97; Creation et liberte; essai d'anthropologie chretienne, Mediaspaul, 97; La apertura a la transcendencia, Communio, 97. **CONTACT ADDRESS** Dept of Theology, Saint Paul Univ, 223 Main St, Ottawa, ON, K1S 1C4.

PITCHER, GEORGE WILLARD
PERSONAL Born 05/19/1925, Newark, NJ **DISCIPLINE** PHILOSOPHY **EDUCATION** US Naval Acad, BS, 46; Harvard Univ, MA, 54, PhD, 57. **CAREER** From instr to assoc prof, 56-70, Prof Philos, Princeton Univ, 70-81, Guggenheim fel, 65-66, Emer Prof Philos, Princeton Univ 81-. **MEMBERSHIPS** Am Philos Asn. **RESEARCH** Epistemology; Wittgenstein; philos of mind. **SELECTED PUBLICATIONS** Auth, The Philosophy of Wittgenstein, 64 & ed, Truth, 64, Prentice-Hall; ed, Wittgenstein: A Collection of Critical Essays, 66 & co-ed, Ryle, 70, Doubleday; auth, A Theory of Perception, Princeton Univ, 71; Berkeley, Routledge & Kegan, 77. **CONTACT ADDRESS** Dept of Philosophy, Princeton Univ, Princeton, NJ, 08544.

PITOFSKY, ROBERT
PERSONAL Born 12/27/1929, Paterson, NJ, m, 1961, 3 children **DISCIPLINE** LAW **EDUCATION** NY Univ, BA, 51; Columbia Univ, LLB, 54. **CAREER** Prof law, NY Univ, 64-70; dir, Bur Consumer Protection, Fed Trade Comn, 70-73 ; prof law, Georgetown Univ, 73-77; comnr, Fed Trade Comn, 78-81; Prof Law, Georgetown Univ, 81-. **RESEARCH** Antitrust and economic regulation. **SELECTED PUBLICATIONS** Coauth, Antitrust Law: Cases and Materials, Found Press, 67; auth, Joint ventures under the antitrust laws, Harvard Law Rev, 3/69; coauth, Trade Regulation: Cases and Materials, Found Press, 75; Beyond Nader: Consumer protection and the regulation of advertising, Harvard Law Rev, 2/77; Proposals for Revised United-states Merger Enforcement in a Global Economy, Georgetown Law J, Vol 0081, 1992; the Scholar as Advocate - Comment/, J of Legal Education, Vol 0043, 1993; Healy,timothy,s. - In-memoriam, Georgetown Law J, Vol 0081, 1993. **CONTACT ADDRESS** Law Sch, Georgetown Univ, 600 New Jersey N W, Washington, DC, 20001-2022.

PITT, DAVID
DISCIPLINE PHILOSOPHY OF LANGUAGE, FORMAL SEMANTICS, AND THE PHILOSOPHY OF MIND **EDUCATION** CUNY, PhD, 94. **CAREER** Vis asst prof, Univ Nebr, Lincoln. **SELECTED PUBLICATIONS** Published in music and the philosophy of mind. **CONTACT ADDRESS** Univ Nebr, Lincoln, Lincoln, NE, 68588-0417.

PITT, JACK
PERSONAL Born 09/14/1928, Montreal, PQ, Canada, m, 1953, 2 children **DISCIPLINE** PHILOSOPHY **EDUCATION** Sir George Williams, NS, 50; McGill, BA, 52, MA, 53; Yale Univ, PhD, 57. **CAREER** Cal State Univ-Fresno, 57-97. **MEMBERSHIPS** Am Philos Asn. **RESEARCH** Analytical Marxism; Logical atomican. **SELECTED PUBLICATIONS** Russell on Religion, Critical Essays, Routledge. **CONTACT ADDRESS** 1135 E Santa Ana, Fresno, CA, 93704. **EMAIL** jpitt@csufresno.edu

PITT, JOSEPH C.
PERSONAL Born 09/12/1944, Hampstead, NY, m, 1966 **DISCIPLINE** PHILOSOPHY **EDUCATION** Col of William & Mary, AB, 66; Univ Western Ontario, MA, 70, PhD, 72. **CAREER** Tchng fel, 70-71, Univ Western Ontario; instr, 71-72, asst prof, 72-78, assoc prof, 78-83, prof, 83-, dir, grad stud, dept of philos, 98-, Virginia Polytech Inst & St Univ; vis asst prof, 74, Univ Pitts; founding dir, 79-80, adj prof, 81-, Ctr for Study of Sci in Soc; dir, Human, Sci & Tech prog, 79-89, actng dept head, philos, 91-92, dept head, 92-98, admin fel, office of dean, 98-99, Virginia Tech **RESEARCH** History & Philosophy of sci and technology. **CONTACT ADDRESS** Dept of Philosophy, Virginia Polytech Inst & State Univ, Blacksburg, VA, 24601. **EMAIL** jcpitt@vt.edu

PITT, JOSEPH C.
PERSONAL Born 09/12/1944, Hempstead, NY, m, 1966 **DISCIPLINE** PHILOSOPHY **EDUCATION** Col of William and Mary, AB, 66; Duke Univ, advan study, 96-98; Univ Western

Ontario, MA, 70, PhD, 72. **CAREER** Teaching fel, Univ Western Ontario, 70-71; instr, Va Polytech Inst & State Univ, 71-72; asst prof, philos, Va Polytechnic Inst & State Univ, 72-78; vis asst prof, Univ Pittsburgh, 74; assoc prof, philos, Va Polytechnic Inst & State Univ, 78-83; adjunct prof, Ctr for the Study of Sci in Soc, 81-; prof, philos, Va Polytech Inst & State Univ, 83-. **HONORS AND AWARDS** Eta Sigma Phi, 66; Can Cound Doctoral fel, 70, 71; teaching excellence award, Va Polytech Inst & State Univ, 74, 75, 76, 77, 85; acad of teaching excellence, Va Polytech Inst & State Univ, 78, 85; sr vis fel, Ctr for Philos of Sci, Univ Pittsburgh, 84; alumni teaching award, Va Polytech Inst & State Univ, 85; acad of univ svc, Va Polytech Inst & State Univ, 86; Sigma Xi, 88; res assignment, Va Polytech Inst & State Univ, 91; trustee, Amer Philos Inst, 97; Who's Who Amer Men & Women of Sci; Who's Who in Tech. **MEMBERSHIPS** Amer Philos Asn; Amer Asn for the Advan of Sci; Can Soc for Hist and Philos of Sci; Hist of Sci Asn; Intl Soc for Hist, Philos, and Social Studies of Bio; Philos of Sci Asn; Sigma Xi; Soc for Philos and Tech; Soc for Hist of Tech; Southern Soc for Philos and Psychol. **SELECTED PUBLICATIONS** Auth, Philosophical Methodologies and the Philosophy of Technology, Soc for Philos and Tech Quart Elec Jour, 97; rev, Galilio Courtier, Physis, Nuova Serie, 97; auth, Developments in the Philosophy of Science 1965-1995, The Encycl of Philos, suppl vol, Macmillan, 97; auth, On the Philosophy of Technology, Past and Future, Soc for Philos and Tech, 96; rev, The Invisible World, Jour of Hist of Bio, vol 29, 466-468, 96; auth, Discovery, Telescopes and Progress, New Directions in the Philosophy of Technology, Philos & Tech, 95; rev, The Discovery of Kepler's Laws; The Interaction of Science, Philosophy, and Religion, Isis, 95; ed, New Directions in the Philosophy of Technology, Philos & Tech, Kluwer, 95. **CONTACT ADDRESS** Dept. of Philosophy, Virginia Polytechnic Institute & State Univ, Blacksburg, VA, 24061-0126. **EMAIL** jcpitt@vt.edu

PITTS, BILL
PERSONAL Born 12/27/1937, Winfield, KS, m, 1961, 2 children **DISCIPLINE** RELIGION; CHURCH HISTORY **EDUCATION** Baylor Univ, BA, 60; Vanderbilt Divinity School, MD, 63; Vanderbilt, PhD, 69. **CAREER** Instr, Mercer Univ, 66-69; asst prof, Houston Baptist Univ, 69-70; assoc prof, Dallas Baptist Univ, 70-75; assoc prof & prof, Baylor Univ, 75- . **HONORS AND AWARDS** Luke Acts Prize & Hist Prize, Vanderbilt, 73; Lilly Scholar, 64-65; Piper Prof Nominee, 74; Mortar Bd Distinguished Prof, 93. **MEMBERSHIPS** Soc Study Christian Spirituality; Am Acad Relig; Am Soc Church Hist; Nat Asn Baptist Prof Relig; Conf Faith & Hist. **RESEARCH** New religious movements; historiography; spirituality; Baptist history. **SELECTED PUBLICATIONS** Auth, Millennial Spirituality of the Branch Davidians, Christian Spirituality Bull, 93; The Mount Carmel Davidians: Adventist Reformers, 1935-1959, Syzgy, 93; The Davidian Tradition, The Coun Soc for Study Relig Bull, 93; The Davidian Tradition, From the Ashes: Making Sense of Waco, Rowman & Littlefield Publ, 94; Davidians and Branch Dividians: 1929-1987, Armageddon in Waco, Univ Chicago Press, 95; Davidians and Branch Davidians, New Cath Encycl, Cath Univ Press, 95; The Persistence of the Millennium, Medieval Perspectives, 97. **CONTACT ADDRESS** Religion Dept, Baylor Univ, Waco, TX, 76798. **EMAIL** william_pitts@baylor.edu

PLACHER, WILLIAM C.
PERSONAL Born 04/28/1948, Peoria, IL **DISCIPLINE** THEOLOGY **EDUCATION** Wabash Col, BA, 70; Yale Univ, MA, 74, PhD, 75. **CAREER** Wabash Col, inst, asst prof, assoc prof, prof, dept ch, 72-. **HONORS AND AWARDS** Danforth Grad Fellow. **MEMBERSHIPS** APA, AAR. **RESEARCH** Christian Theology. **SELECTED PUBLICATIONS** Auth, A History of Christian Theology, Westminster, 83; auth, Readings in the History of Christian Theology, Westminster, 88; auth, Unapologetic Theology, Westminster John Knox, 89; Belonging to God, coauth, Westminster John Knox, 92; auth, Narratives of a Vulnerable God, Westminster John Knox, 94; auth, The Domestication of Transcendence, Westminster John Knox, 96; Why Are We Here?, coauth, Trinity Press Intl, 98. **CONTACT ADDRESS** Dept of Philosophy, Wabash Col, Crawfordsville, IN, 47933. **EMAIL** placherw@wabash.edu

PLANEAUX, CHRISTOPHER
PERSONAL Born 04/10/1967, Atlanta, GA, m, 1996 **DISCIPLINE** PHILOSOPHY; HISTORY; CLASSICS GREEK **EDUCATION** Ind Univ, AB, 93, AB, 94; Univ Cambridge, MPhil, 97. **CAREER** Dept For Lang, Purdue Univ **HONORS AND AWARDS** Fac Develop Mentorship grant, Ind Univ, 94; Univ Cambridge res grant, 94. Thelander Mem Award, Ind Univ, 94. **MEMBERSHIPS** Amer Philol Asn; Class Asn Mid W & S; Asn Ancient Hist; Soc Greek Philos; Univ London Inst Class Studies; Cambridge Philol Soc; Darwin Col Soc. **RESEARCH** Dramatic settings of Platos Dialogues; Athens (ca. 470-40413 BCE); Peloponnesioan War; Thirty tyrants; Greek poets; Athenian calendar; AtticCultic societies; Philosophical schools; Alcibiades. **SELECTED PUBLICATIONS** Auth, Socrates, Alcibiades, and Plato's: Does the Charmides Have an Historical setting?, Mnemosyne, 99. **CONTACT ADDRESS** Dept of Foreign Languages & Cultures, Indiana Univ-Purdue Univ, Indianapolis, 425 Univ Blvd, Indianapolis, IN, 46202. **EMAIL** cplaneau@iupui.edu

PLANK, KARL A.
PERSONAL Born 11/18/1951, Raleigh, NC, m, 1989, 1 child **DISCIPLINE** RELIGION **EDUCATION** Hanover Col, BA, 74; Vanderbilt Univ, M.Div, 77, MA, 80, PhD, 83. **CAREER** From instr to asst prof to assoc prof to prof to JW Cannon prof, 92-, Davidson Col. **HONORS AND AWARDS** Thomas Carter Prize for Non Fiction Prose, 93. **MEMBERSHIPS** Soc Biblical Lit; Am Acad Relig. **RESEARCH** Biblical intertextuality and hermeneutics; modern Jewish lit. **SELECTED PUBLICATIONS** Auth, Paul and The Irony of Affliction, 87; "Thomas Merton and Hannah Arendt: Contemplation after Eichmann," Merton Annual, 90; "The Eclipse of Difference: Merton's Encounter with Judaism," Cistercian Studies, 93; Mother of the Wire Fence, 94; Inside and Outside the Holocaust, 94; "Ascent to Darker Hills: Psalm 121 and its Poetic Revision," Lit and Theol, 97. **CONTACT ADDRESS** Dept of Religion, Davidson Col, Davidson, NC, 28036. **EMAIL** kaplank@davidson.edu

PLANTINGA, ALVIN
DISCIPLINE PHILOSOPHY **EDUCATION** Calvin Col, AB, 54; Univ Mich, MA, 55; Yale Univ, PhD, 58. **CAREER** Prof. **RESEARCH** Epistemology; metaphysics; philosophy of religion. **SELECTED PUBLICATIONS** Auth, Justification in the 20th Century, 90; Warrant: the Current Debate, 93; Warrant and Proper Function, 93; Methodological Naturalism?, 95. **CONTACT ADDRESS** Philosophy Dept, Univ of Notre Dame, 336/7 O'Shaughnessy, Notre Dame, IN, 46556. **EMAIL** plantinga.1@nd.edu

PLATA, FERNANDO
DISCIPLINE RENAISSANCE AND BAROQUE SPANISH LITERATURE **EDUCATION** Univ de Navarra, Pamplona, Spain, licenciado, 87; Univ MI, MA, 89, PhD, 94. **CAREER** Asst prof, Colgate Univ. **HONORS AND AWARDS** Rackham predoctoral fel, Univ MI, 92-93; dissertation scholar, prog for cult coop, Spain Ministry of Cult and US Univ(s), 92; Tercer Premio Nacional de Terminacion de Estudios de Filologia, 87; scholar, Universidad Internacional Menendez Pelayo, Santander, 86. **MEMBERSHIPS** Mem, Univ student disciplinary syst. **SELECTED PUBLICATIONS** Auth, Ocho poemas satericos de Quevedo, EUNSA, 97; Inquisicion y censura en el siglo XVIII: El Parnaso espanol de Quevedo, La Perinola. Revista de investigacion quevediana, 97; rev, Robert L. Hathaway, Not Necessarily Cervantes: Readings of the 'Quixote', Juan de la Cuesta, 95; Una nota sobre Lope de Vega y las 'leneas del amor' de Terencio, Romance Notes 32, 92; Hacia una edicion cretica de la comedia La inclinacion espanola de Bances Candamo, RILCE, Revista de Filologea Hispanica 8, 92. **CONTACT ADDRESS** Dept of Romance Lang, Colgate Univ, 13 Oak Drive, Hamilton, NY, 13346. **EMAIL** fplata@center.colgate.edu

PLATT, DAVID S.
PERSONAL Born 04/22/1924, China, m, 1969 **DISCIPLINE** PHILOSOPHY **EDUCATION** Univ Penn, PhD, 58. **CAREER** Prof Emeritus Philos, Wilson Col, 33 years. **HONORS AND AWARDS** Lindback disting tchg awd, 69. **MEMBERSHIPS** APA; Metaphysical Soc; N Am Nietzsche Soc; Hegel Soc. **RESEARCH** Philosophy of Religion. **SELECTED PUBLICATIONS** Auth, Intimations of Divinity, 89; The Gift of Contingency, 91. **CONTACT ADDRESS** Dept of Philosophy, Wilson Col, 914 Wallace Ave, Chambersburg, PA, 17201.

PLATT, ELIZABETH ELLAN
PERSONAL Born 02/11/1936, Orange, NJ, s **DISCIPLINE** THEOLOGY **EDUCATION** College of Wooster, Ohio, BA, 57; Columbia Univ and Union Theol Sem, MA, 61; Harvard Univ, PhD, 73. **CAREER** Asst prof Bibl Stud, Rutgers Col, State Univ NJ, 73-80; assoc pastor, Presbyterian Church, Westfield, NJ, 81-88; assoc prof, Bibl Stud, 88-98, Prof of Old Testament, 98- , Univ Dubuque Theol Sem. **HONORS AND AWARDS** Vis prof in archaeol res, Andrews Univ, Mich, 76-83. **MEMBERSHIPS** Am Acad Relig; Am Schools of Oriental Res. **RESEARCH** Biblical archaeology; ancient Near Eastern jewelry; Old and New Testament studies; women in ancient Near East; Object Registry for Madaba Plains project, Jordan. **SELECTED PUBLICATIONS** Auth, The Ministry of Mary of Bethany, Theol Today, 74; auth, Jewelry, Anchor Bible Dictionary, 95; Madaba Plains Project, Jordan publications in jewelry and objects. **CONTACT ADDRESS** Div of Biblical Studies, Univ of Dubuque Theol Sem, 2000 University Ave, Dubuque, IA, 52001-5099.

PLOTKIN, HOWARD
DISCIPLINE PHILOSOPHY **EDUCATION** Univ Mich, BA, 64; Univ Wis, MA, 66; Johns Hopkins Univ, PhD, 72. **CAREER** Prof **RESEARCH** History of Science; history of astronomy and astrophysics; history of meteoritics; history of American science; institutional history. **SELECTED PUBLICATIONS** Auth, The Henderson Network vs the Prairie Network: The Dispute Between the Smithsonian's National Museum and the Smithsonian Astrophysical Observatory Over the Acquisition and Control of Meteorites 1960-1970, Jour Royal Astronomical Soc Can, 97; The Port Orford Meteorite Hoax, Sky Telescope, 93; William H. Pickering in Jamaica: The Founding of Woodlawn and Studies of Mars, Jour Hist Astronomy, 93; Harvard Col Observatory's Boyden Station in Peru: Origin and Formative Years 1879-1898, 93; Edward C. Pickering, Jour Hist Astronomy, 90. **CONTACT ADDRESS** Dept of Philosophy, Western Ontario Univ, London, ON, N6A 5B8. **EMAIL** hplotkin@julian.uwo.ca

PLUHAR, EVELYN BEGLEY
PERSONAL Born 07/08/1947, Harlan, KY, m, 1971 **DISCIPLINE** PHILOSOPHY **EDUCATION** Univ Denver, BA, 69; Univ Mich, PhD(philos), 76. **CAREER** Teaching asst philos, Univ Mich, 70-73; instr, Grinnell Col, 73-76, asst prof, 76-78; Asst Prof Philos, PA State Univ, Fayette, 78-. **HONORS AND AWARDS** Horan H Rackham Prize, Univ Mich, 71. **MEMBERSHIPS** Am Philos Asn; Soc Study Ethics & Animals; Am Soc Aesthetics; Am Asn Univ Women. **RESEARCH** Ethics; philosophy of science; philosophy of mind; philosophy of mind; ethics. **SELECTED PUBLICATIONS** Auth, Emergence and Reduction, Studies in the History and Philosophy of Science, 78; Physicalism and the identity theory, J Critical Analysis, 79; Preferential hiring and unjust sacrifice, Philos Forum, Vol XII, 81; Must an opponent of Animal Rights also be an opponent of Human Rights?, Inquiry, 81; On Replaceability, Ethics and Animals, 82; The Justification of an Environmental Ethic, Environmental Ethics; On Vegetarianism, Morality, and Science - a Counter Reply, J of Agricultural & Environmental Ethics, Vol 0006, 1993. **CONTACT ADDRESS** Dept of Philos, Pennsylvania State Univ, P O Box 519, Uniontown, PA, 15401-0519.

PLUHAR, WERNER S.
PERSONAL Born 05/29/1940, Berlin, Germany, m, 1971 **DISCIPLINE** PHILOSOPHY **EDUCATION** Univ of Calif Berk, BA, 68; Univ Mich, Ann Arbor, PhD, 73. **CAREER** Grinnell Col, asst prof, 73-78; Penn State Univ, lectr, asst prof, affil prof, 78-. **HONORS AND AWARDS** Horace H. Rackman Prize, Eleanor L. Coldern Award, PSU Res and Scholarly Excellence Award. **MEMBERSHIPS** APA, Phi Beta Kappa, ASA. **RESEARCH** Immanuel Kant; ethics; aesthetics. **SELECTED PUBLICATIONS** Auth, Translation of Immanuel Kant's Critique of Pure Reason of 1781,1787, Indianapolis & Cambridge MA: Hacket Pub Co, 96; auth, Translation of Immanuel Kant's Critique of Judgement, Indianapolis and Cambridge MA, Hacket Pub Co, 87. **CONTACT ADDRESS** Dept of Philosophy, Pennsylvania State Univ, 119 Brownfield Lane, Uniontown, PA, 15401-5603. **EMAIL** WPluhar@psu.edu

POETHIG, EUNICE BLANCHARD
PERSONAL Born 01/16/1930, Hempstead, NY, m, 1952, 5 children **DISCIPLINE** OLD TESTAMENT **EDUCATION** DePauw Univ, BA, 51; Union Theol Sem, MA, 52m Phd, 85; McCormick Theol Sem, MDiv, 75, STM, 77. **CAREER** Missionary with United Church of Christ (Philippines), Philippine Womens Univ, 56-72; assoc exec, Presby of Chicago, 79-85; ex presbyter, Presby of W NY, 86-93; DIR, CONGREGATIONAL MIN DIV, GEN ASSEMBLY COUN, 94-; Nettie F McCormick fel Old Testament Hebrew, McCormick Sem. **MEMBERSHIPS** SBL; AAR; Int Assn Women Min. **RESEARCH** Early Osraelite history; Womens history-Biblical, mission, contemporary; Music, especially Biblical traditions. **SELECTED PUBLICATIONS** Auth Sing, Shout, and Clap for Joy, United Meth Womens Bd, 85; Good News Women, Presby Women, 87; many Bible studies and curricula and articles for church publ. **CONTACT ADDRESS** 3606 Trail Ridge Rd, Louisville, KY, 40241. **EMAIL** ebpoethig@unidial.com

POHLHAUS, GAILE
PERSONAL Born 11/04/1938, Jamaica, NY, m, 1969, 2 children **DISCIPLINE** RELIGIOUS STUDIES **EDUCATION** Col of St. Elizabeth, BA, 61; Boston col, MA, 65, Villanova Univ, MA, 77; Temple Univ, PhD, 87 **CAREER** Tchr, 61-71; Adj Inst, 77-87, Villanova Univ; Asst Prof, 87-pres, Villanova Univ **MEMBERSHIPS** AAR/SBL, CTS, NWSA; AAUP; CTSA **RESEARCH** Marriage; Sexuality; Feminist Ethics **SELECTED PUBLICATIONS** Auth, Readings on Christian Marriage, Ginn Press, 93 **CONTACT ADDRESS** Theology and Relig Studies Dept, Villanova Univ, 800 Lancaster Ave, Villanova, PA, 19080. **EMAIL** gpohlhau@email.vill.edu

POLAND, LYNN
DISCIPLINE RELIGION **EDUCATION** Bates College, AB, Univ Chicago, AM and PhD. **CAREER** Fac, 91-; assoc prof, Davidson Col. **HONORS AND AWARDS** Ed bd, Lit and Theol and Bibl Interpretation. **RESEARCH** Hist of bibl interpretation, gender, and ecology. **SELECTED PUBLICATIONS** Auth, Literary Criticism and Biblical Hermeneutics, 85; numerous essays on Augustine, biblical interpretation, and the sublime. **CONTACT ADDRESS** Davidson Col, 102 N Main St, PO Box 1719, Davidson, NC, 28036.

POLANSKY, RONALD M.
PERSONAL Born 08/06/1948, Okinawa, RI, m, 1971, 2 children **DISCIPLINE** PHILOSOPHY **EDUCATION** Yale Univ, BA, 70; Boston Col, PhD, 74. **CAREER** Asst prof, Purdue Univ, 74-75; asst to full prof , Duquesne Univ, 74-; Ed of Ancient Philos, 79-. **MEMBERSHIPS** Am Philos Soc; Soc for Ancient Greek Philos; Int Plato Soc. **RESEARCH** Ancient philosophy; political philosophy. **SELECTED PUBLICATIONS** Auth, Philosophy and Knowledge: A Commentary on Plato's

Theaetetus, Bucknell Univ Press, 92; The Unity of Plato's Crito, Scholia, 97; Foundationalism in Plato?, Foundationalism Old and New, Temple Univ Press, 92; coauth, The Viability of Virtue in the Mean, Apeiron, 96; Locating Justice through Process of Elimination on Plato's Republic, forthcoming. **CONTACT ADDRESS** Dept of Philososphy, Duquesne Univ, Pittsburgh, PA, 15282. **EMAIL** polansky@duq3.cc.duq.edu

POLASKI, SANDRA HACK
PERSONAL Born 11/26/1964, Louisville, KY, m, 1991 **DISCIPLINE** RELIGION **EDUCATION** Furman Univ, BA summa cum laude, 87; Vanderbilt, MDiv 90; Duke Univ, PhD 95. **CAREER** St. Mary's Col NC, instr 94; Elon Col NC, instr 94; Furman Univ, asst prof, 95-96; Baptist Theol Sem, asst prof, 96-. **HONORS AND AWARDS** Wabash Cen Prog Gnt. **MEMBERSHIPS** AAR; SBL; NABPR. **RESEARCH** New Testament Interpretation; Pauline Studies; Feminist Biblical Interpretation. **SELECTED PUBLICATIONS** Auth, Paul and the Discourse of Power, Sheffield Eng, Sheffield Acad Press, forthcoming; 2 Corinthians, IVP Women's Bible Commentary, Inter-Varsity Press, forthcoming. **CONTACT ADDRESS** Dept of New Testament, Baptist Theol Sem, 3400 Brook Rd, Richmond, VA, 23227. **EMAIL** sandra.hack.polaski@btsr.edu

POLE, NELSON
PERSONAL Born 10/13/1941, Detroit, MI, m, 1963, 4 children **DISCIPLINE** PHILOSOPHY OF SCIENCE, LOGIC **EDUCATION** Wayne State Univ, BPhil, 63; Ohio State Univ, PhD(philos), 71. **CAREER** From instr to assoc prof, 68-92, Prof Philos, Cleveland State Univ, 93-. **MEMBERSHIPS** Am Philos Asn; Philos Sci Asn; AAAS; Am Asn Philos Teachers (pres, 86-88). **RESEARCH** Logic; philosophy of religion and technology. **SELECTED PUBLICATIONS** Auth, Logic-Coach Software. **CONTACT ADDRESS** Dept of Philos, Cleveland State Univ, 1983 E 24th St., Cleveland, OH, 44115-2440. **EMAIL** n.pole@csuohio.edu

POLHILL, JOHN B.
PERSONAL Born 01/06/1939, Americus, GA, m, 1966, 2 children **DISCIPLINE** THEOLOGY **EDUCATION** Univ Richmond, BA, 60; Southern Baptist Theolog Sem, Mdiv, 63, PhD, 69. **CAREER** James B. Harrison chemn; assoc dean, 90-, dir, 95-, fac mem, 69-, Southern Baptist Theological Sem. **MEMBERSHIPS** Society Biblical Lit; Asn Baptists Prof of Relig; Evangelical Theolog Society. **RESEARCH** Greek language and literature; pawline studies; Acts. **SELECTED PUBLICATIONS** Auth, Acts, New American Commentary, 92; auth, Paul and His Letters, 99. **CONTACT ADDRESS** Southern Baptist Theological Seminary, 2825 Lexington Rd, Louisville, KY, 40280. **EMAIL** thmphd@sbts.edu

POLISCHUK, PABLO
DISCIPLINE PASTORAL COUNSELING, PSYCHOLOGY **EDUCATION** Univ Calif, BA; SF State Univ, MA; Fuller Theol Sem, MA, PhD. **CAREER** Adj prof, S Calif Col; Fuller Theol Sem; instr, Harvard Med Sch; prof, Gordon-Conwell Theol Sem, 80-. **HONORS AND AWARDS** Ch psychologist, Chelsea Health Ctr; dir, Willowdale Ctr for Psychol Svc. **SELECTED PUBLICATIONS** Auth, Depression and its Treatment; The Therapeutic Counseling; Dotting the I's. **CONTACT ADDRESS** Gordon-Conwell Theol Sem, 130 Essex St, South Hamilton, MA, 01982.

POLK, ELMER
DISCIPLINE CRIMINOLOGY AND CRIMINAL JUSTICE **EDUCATION** Sam Houston Sate Univ, PhD. **CAREER** Asst prof, Univ of TX at Arlington. **RESEARCH** Juvenile justice; probation; correctional issues. **SELECTED PUBLICATIONS** Auth, Police Training and Violence, Contemp J of Criminal Justice, 96; The Effects of Ethnicity on Career Paths of Advanced/Specialized Law Enforcement Officers, Police Stud, 95; coauth, Intensive Supervision Probation--Fad or For Keeps, in Correctional Theory and Practice, 92. **CONTACT ADDRESS** Criminology and Criminal Justice Prog, Univ of Texas at Arlington, 303 Univ Hall, PO Box 19595, Arlington, TX, 76019-0595. **EMAIL** epolk@uta.edu

POLK, TIMOTHY H.
PERSONAL Born 04/22/1946, Harrisburg, PA, m, 1970, 3 children **DISCIPLINE** OLD TESTAMENT STUDIES **EDUCATION** Wesleyan Univ, BA, 68; Yale Divinity Sch, MDiv, 74; Yale Univ, PhD, 82. **CAREER** Prof, Hamline Univ, 82- . **HONORS AND AWARDS** Agnes Conger Award for Scholar in Hum, 84; Master of Arts in Liberal Stud Tchg Award, 92; Burton Teaching Prize, 92. **MEMBERSHIPS** AAR; SBL; Kierkegaard Soc; Karl Barth Soc of North Am. **RESEARCH** Kierkegaard and Barth's use of scripture. **SELECTED PUBLICATIONS** Auth, The Biblical Kierkegaard: Reading by the Rule of Faith, Mercer, 97. **CONTACT ADDRESS** 1388 Englewood Ave, St Paul, MN, 55104-1903. **EMAIL** tpolk@gw.hamline.edu

POLLAK, LOUIS HEILPRIN
PERSONAL Born 12/07/1922, New York, NY, m, 1952, 5 children **DISCIPLINE** LAW **EDUCATION** Harvard Univ, AB, 43; Yale Univ, LLB, 48. **CAREER** Vis lectr law, Law Sch, Howard Univ, 53; from asst prof to prof, Law Sch, Yale Univ, 55-74, dean, 65-70; Greenfield prof law, 74-78, dean law sch, 75-78, Lectr Law, Univ Pa, 79-; Judge, US Dist Ct, Pa, 78-. **RESEARCH** Constitutional law; civil liberties. **SELECTED PUBLICATIONS** Ed, The Constitution and the Supreme Court: A Documentary History, World Pub, 66; The Disjunction Between Edwards and Priest, Michigan Law Review, Vol 0091, 1993. **CONTACT ADDRESS** US Courthouse, 601 Mkt St, Philadelphia, PA, 19106.

POLLARD, ALTON BROOKS, III
PERSONAL Born 05/05/1956, St Paul, Minnesota, m **DISCIPLINE** THEOLOGY **EDUCATION** Fisk Univ, BA 1978; Harvard Univ Divinity School, MDiv 1981; Duke Univ, PhD 1987. **CAREER** John St Baptist Church, pastor 1979-82; Clark Univ, dir 1981-82; New Red Mountain Baptist Church, pastor 1984-86; St Olaf Coll, asst prof 1987-88; Wake Forest Univ, asst prof, beginning 1988, assoc prof, 1992-98; Emory Univ, Candler School of Theology, Black Church Studies, dir, assoc prof of religion and culture currently. **HONORS AND AWARDS** Thomas J Watson Fellowship Fisk Univ 1978; Fund for Theological Educ Fellowships Princeton NJ 1978-81, 1983-86; Andrew Mellon Fellowship Duke Univ 1986-87; article "Religion, Rock, & Eroticism," The Journal of Black Sacred Music 1987; "The Last Soul Singer in Amer," Black Sacred Music 1989. **MEMBERSHIPS** Mem Soc for the Scientific Study of Religion 1984-, Assoc for the Sociology of Religion 1985-; mem (clergy) Amer Baptist Convention; mem NAACP, Amer Acad of Religion 1987; Religious Research Assn 1988-; member, Society for the Study of Black Religion, 1989-. **SELECTED PUBLICATIONS** review of "The Color of God" and "Black Theology in Dialogue," Perspectives in Religious Studies 1989; "Howard Thurman and the Experience of Encounter," Journal of Religious Thought, 1990; "Of Movements and Motivations," AME Zion Quarterly Review, 1991; "The Promise and Peril of Common Ground," BRIDGES, 1991; Mysticism and Social Change, Peter Lang, 1992. **CONTACT ADDRESS** Director of Black Church Studies, Emory Univ, Atlanta, GA, 30322. **EMAIL** abpolla@emory.edu

POLLEY, MAX EUGENE
PERSONAL Born 06/03/1928, South Bend, IN, m, 1950 **DISCIPLINE** RELIGION **EDUCATION** Albion Col, AB, 50; Duke Univ, BD, 53, PhD(Old Testament), 57. **CAREER** Asst prof Bible & relig, 56-66, Prof Relig, Davidson Col, 66-. **MEMBERSHIPS** Soc Bibl Lit; Am Acad Relig. **RESEARCH** Biblical theology. **SELECTED PUBLICATIONS** Auth, Bibliography of H Wheeler Robinson's Writings, 472 & The Place of Henry Wheeler Robinson Among Old Testament Scholars, 472, Baptist Quart; H Wheeler Robinson and the Problem of Organizing an Old Testament Theology, In: The Use of the Old Testament in the New and Other Essays: Studies in Honor of William Franklin Stinespring, Duke Univ, 72; Revelation in the writings of H Wheeler Robinson and Eric Rust: A comparative study, In: Science, Faith, and Revelation, Broadman press, 79; Hebrew prophecy within the council of Yahweh, examined in its ancient Near Eastern setting, In: Scriptures in Context: Essays on the Comparative Method, Pickwick Press, 80; Amos - a Commentary on the Book of Amos - Paul,sm, J of Biblical Literature, Vol 0112, 1993; Isaiah-xlvi, Isaiah-xlvii, and Isaiah-xlviii - a New Literary-critical Reading - Franke,C, J of Biblical Literature, Vol 0115, 1996. **CONTACT ADDRESS** Dept Relig, Davidson Col, Davidson, NC, 28036.

POLLOCK, JOHN LESLIE
PERSONAL Born 01/28/1940, Atchison, KS **DISCIPLINE** PHILOSOPHY **EDUCATION** Univ MN, BA, 61; Univ CA, Berkeley, PhD, 65. **CAREER** From asst prof to assoc prof philos, State Univ NY Buffalo, 65-71; from assoc prof to prof, Univ Rochester, 71-78; PROF PHILOS, UNIV AZ, 78-, ed-in-chief, Philosophical Studies, 80-87. **RESEARCH** Artificial intelligence; epistemology; logic; philosophical logic. **SELECTED PUBLICATIONS** Auth, Introduction to Symbolic Logic, Holt, 69; Knowledge and Justification, Princeton Univ, 74; Subjunctive Reasoning, D Reidel, 76; Language and Thought, Princeton Univ, 82; The Foundations of Philosophical Semantics, Princeton Univ, 84; Contemporary Theories of Knowledge, Rowman and Littlefield, 86; How to Build a Person, MIT, 90; Nomic Probability and the Foundations of Induction, Oxford, 90; Technical Methods in Philosophy, Westview, 90; Cognitive Carpentry, MIT, 95. **CONTACT ADDRESS** Dept of Philos, Univ AZ, Tucson, AZ, 85721-0001. **EMAIL** pollock@arizona.edu

POLS, EDWARD
PERSONAL Born 02/01/1919, Newark, NJ, m, 1942, 6 children **DISCIPLINE** PHILOSOPHY **EDUCATION** Harvard Univ, AB, 40, AM, 47, PhD, 49. **CAREER** Asst philos, Harvard Univ, 47-48; instr, Princeton Univ, 48-49; from asst prof to assoc prof, 49-62, chmn dept, 55-75, Prof Philos, 62- , Kenan Prof Humanities, 75-84, res prof, 84-94, Kenan Prof Philos & Hum Emeritus, 94- , Bowdoin Col **MEMBERSHIPS** Am Philos Asn. **RESEARCH** Metaphysics; epistemology. **SELECTED PUBLICATIONS** Auth, To live at east ever after, Sewanee Rev, 58; The Recognition of Reason, Southern Ill Univ, Carbondale, 63; Whitehead's Metaphysics: A Critical Examination of Process and Reality, Southern Ill Univ, Carbondale & Edwardsville, 67; Consciousness-makers and the autonomy of consciousness, Yale Rev, 71; Meditation on a Prisoner: Towards Understanding Actiona and Mind, Southern Ill Univ, Carbondale & Edwardsville, 75; The Acts of Our Being: A Reflection on Agency and Responsibility, Univ Mass, Amherst, 82; auth, Radical Realism: Direct Knowing in Science and Philosophy, Cornell, 92; auth, Mind Regained, Cornell, 98. **CONTACT ADDRESS** Dept of Philosophy, Bowdoin Col, Brunswick, ME, 04011. **EMAIL** epols@polar.bowdoin.edu

POLYTHRESS, N.G.
PERSONAL Born 04/01/1947, Birmingham, AL, d **DISCIPLINE** CLINICAL PSYCHOLOGY **EDUCATION** Univ TX at Austin, PhD, 77. **CAREER** Psychologist, Center for Forensic Psychiatry, 77-82; Psychologist, Taylor Hardin Secure Medical Facility, 82-90; prof, Univ South FL, 90-. **MEMBERSHIPS** Fel, Am Psychological Asn. **RESEARCH** Psychology and law. **SELECTED PUBLICATIONS** Auth, with R Wiener, Reforming Medical Malpractice Torts: Accuracy, Procedural Justice, and the Law as Moral Educator, The Litigator, 95; review, Back to the Asylum: The Future of Mental Health Law and Policy in the United States, by John Q LaFond and Mary Durham, J of Mental Health and Aging, 96; co-auth with T Y Boyd and M A Cascardi, The Factor Structure and Convergent Validity of the Agression Questionnaire in an Offender Population, Psychological Assessment, 96; with R J Bonnie, S K Hoge, H Monahan, and M M Eisenberg, Decision-Making in Criminal Defense: An Empirical Study of Insanity Pleas and the Impact of Doubted Client Competence, J of Criminal Law and Criminology, 96; with Christopher Slobogin, Psychological Constructs Relevant to Defenses of Insanity and Diminished Capacity, in David L Faigman, David Kaye, Michael J Saks, & Joseph Sanders, eds, Scientific Evidence Reference Manual, West, 97; with G B Melton, J Petrila, and C Slobogin, Psychological Evaluations for the Courts: A Handbook for Mental Health Professionals and Lawers, 2nd ed, Guilford, 97; with S J Sydeman, M Cascardi, and L M Ritterband, Procedural Justice in the Context of Civil Commitment: A Critique of Tyler's Analysis, Psychology, Public Policy and Law, 97; with M Cascardi and L Ritterband, Stability of Psychiatric Patients' Perceptions of Their Admission Experience, J of Clinical Psychology, 97; with R Bonnie, S Hoge, J Monahan, M Eisenberg, & T Feucht-Haviar, The MacArthur Adjudicative Competence Study: A Comparison of Criteria for Assessing the Competence of Criminal Defendants, J of the Am Academy of Psychiatry and the Law, 97; with M Cascardi, Correlates of Perceived Coersion During Psychiatric Hospital Admission, Int J of Law & Psychiatry, 97; with S K Hoge, R J Bonnie, J Monahan, M Eisenberg, & T Feucht-Haviar, The Competence-Related Abilities of Woman Criminal Defendents, J of the Am Academy of Psychiatry and the Law, 98; numerous other publications including many in: Law and Human Behavior, the Criminal Justice Review, Behavioral Sciences and the Law, the Bul of the Am Academy of Psychiatry and the Law; and the American Psychologist. **CONTACT ADDRESS** Dept of Mental Health Law and Policy, Univ of South Florida, 13301 Bruce B Downs Blvd, Tampa, FL, 33612-3899.

POMERLEAU, WAYNE PAUL
PERSONAL Born 12/19/1946, Shreveport, LA, m, 1968, 1 child **DISCIPLINE** PHILOSOPHY **EDUCATION** Georgetown Univ, AB, 68; Northwestern Univ, MA, 72, PhD(philos), 77. **CAREER** Instr philos, Evening Div, Northwestern Univ, 73-77 & Ill Inst Tech, 76-77; asst prof, 77-82, assoc prof Philos, Gonzaga Univ, 82-98, prof, 98, chmn Dept, 80-85. **RESEARCH** History of modern philosophy; philosophy of religion, philosophy of human nature. **SELECTED PUBLICATIONS** Auth, The accession and dismissal of an upstart handmaid, Monist, 5/77; Twelve Great Philosophers, 97, Western Philosophies of Religion, 98. **CONTACT ADDRESS** Dept of Philosophy, Gonzaga Univ, 502 E Boone Ave, Spokane, WA, 99258 0001. **EMAIL** pomerleau@gonzaga.edu

PONTON, LIONEL
PERSONAL Born 06/14/1930, East Angus, PQ, Canada **DISCIPLINE** PHILOSOPHY **EDUCATION** Univ Montreal, BA, 50; Univ Laval, BPh, 51, LPh, 53; Angelicum, Rome, PhD(-philos), 70. **CAREER** Prof philos, Ecole Normale Laval, 59-70; assoc prof, 70-78, vdean, 77-78, Prof Philos, Fac Philos, Univ Laval, 78-, Co-ed, Laval Theol Philos, 82-. **MEMBERSHIPS** Can Philos Asn. **RESEARCH** Aristotle and Hegel. **SELECTED PUBLICATIONS** Auth, A propos de Metaphysique Z.3,74 & L'Etat hegelien, le Christianisme st la pensee grecque, 81, Observations on Art - French - Rodislewis,g, Laval Theologique et Philosophique, Vol 0049, 1993; Laval Theol Philos; Man and Animal God Created Them - the Animals of the Old-testament - French - Pury,ad, Laval Theologique et Philosophique, Vol 0050, 1994; Hegel Opposition to the Conservatism of Haller,louis,charles,de, Laval Theologique et Philosophique, Vol 0051, 1995; The Politics of Friendship Followed by Heidegger Ear - French - Derrida,j, Laval Theologique et Philosophique, Vol 0051, 1995; Ricoeur,paul Political Anti-hegelianism in 'Soi-meme Comme Un Autre', Laval Theologique et Philosophique, Vol 0052, 1996; Hegel,gwf and Aristotle - the Sovereignty of the State, Laval Theologique et Philosophique, Vol 0052, 1996; In-memoriam Levinas,emmanuel, Laval Theologique et Philosophique, Vol

0052, 1996; The Future of Human-rights - Theological Approach of the Christian Middle- ages and Divine Law - Rational Approach of Modernity and the Rights of Man - Human Approach of the Postmodern Era and Human- rights - French - Rousseau,, Laval Theologique et ph. **CONTACT ADDRESS** Fac Philos Tour des Arts, Univ Laval, Laval, PQ, G1K 7P4.

POPE, STEPHEN J.
PERSONAL Born 05/26/1955, San Francisco, CA, m, 1980, 3 children **DISCIPLINE** THEOLOGICAL ETHICS **EDUCATION** Univ Chicago, PhD, 98. **CAREER** Assoc Prof, Boston Col. **MEMBERSHIPS** Soc Christian Ethics. **RESEARCH** Evolution of theological ethics; charity in Thomas Aquinas. **SELECTED PUBLICATIONS** Auth, The Evolution of Altruism and the Ordering of Love, Georgetown Univ Press, 94; Love in Contemporary Christian Ethics, J of Relig Ethics 23, 95; Finding God in All Things: Essays in Honor of Michael J Buckley, S J, co-ed with Fr Michael J Himes, Crossroad Pubs, 96; Knowability of the Natural Law: A Foundation for the Ethics of the Common Good, Religion, Ethics, and the Common Good, ed James Donahue and M Theresa Moser, RSCJ, Twenty-Third Pubs, 96; Descriptive and Normative Uses of Evolutionary Theory, in Christian Ethics: Problems and Prospects, ed Lisa Sowle Cahill and James Childress, Pilgrim Press, 96; Neither Enemy nor Friend: Nature as Creation in the Theology of St Thomas, Zygon: J of Relig and Science 32, spring 97; Scientific and Natural Law Assessments of Homosexuality, J of Relig Ethics 2 5 spring 97; 'Equal Regard' vs 'Special Relations'? Reaffirming the Inclusiveness of Agape, J of Relig 77 3, July 97; Sociobiology and Human Nature: A Perspective from Catholic Theology, Zygon: J of Relig and Science 33, June 98; Response to Outka, J of Relig Ethics 78, Dec 98; Essays on the Ethics of St Thomas Aquinas, ed, Georgetown Univ Press, forthcoming; Christian Ethics and Evolutionary Theory, Cambridge Univ Press, forthcoming; numerous scholarly articles and other publications. **CONTACT ADDRESS** Theology Dept, Boston Col, Chestnut Hill, MA, 02167-3806. **EMAIL** stephen.pope.1@bc.edu

POPIDEN, JOHN ROBERT
PERSONAL Born 11/02/1949, Pittsburgh, PA, m, 1972, 2 children **DISCIPLINE** THEOLOGY, MORAL THEOLOGY **EDUCATION** Rice Univ, BA, 72; Univ Notre Dame du Lac, MA, 77, PhD, 80. **CAREER** Assoc prof Theological Stud, Loyola Marymount Univ, 77-. **MEMBERSHIPS** Soc Christian Ethics; Cath Theol Soc Am; Col Theol Soc; Soc Christian Ethics. **RESEARCH** Christian social ethics; constructive moral theology; war and peace; marriage and sexuality. **SELECTED PUBLICATIONS** Auth, Choice and Conscience: Abortion in Perspective, Choice and Conscience Comt, 80; An American Catholic Moralist and World War II: John Ford on Obliteration Bombing, Irish Theol Quart, 90; Saturdays of Competition and Christianity; Reformed Rev, 94. **CONTACT ADDRESS** Dept of Theol Stud, Loyola Marymount Univ, 7900 Loyola Blvd, Los Angeles, CA, 90045-8400. **EMAIL** jpopiden@popmail.lmu.edu

POPKIN, RICHARD
DISCIPLINE PHILOSOPHY **EDUCATION** Columbia Univ, Ba, 43, MA, 47, PhD, 50. **CAREER** Instr, Univ Conn, 46-47; prof, Univ Iowa, 47-60; prof, Harvey Mudd Col, 60-63; prof, Univ Calif, San Diego, 63-73; prof, 73-86, PROF EMER, 86-, WASH UNIV; ADJ PROF, PHILOS, HIST, UNIV CALIF, LOS ANGELES, 85-. **SELECTED PUBLICATIONS** Auth, History of Scepticism, 60, 4th ed, 80; ed, Readings in the History of Philosophy, 16th and 17th Century, Free, 66; The Second Oswald, Avon, 66, rev ed, Andre Deutsch & Sphere, 67 & Lisbon, 68; Les assassins de Kennedy, Gallimard, Paris, 67; coauth, Introductory Readings in Philosophy, Holt, 72; auth, High Road to Pyrrhorism, 80; over 200 articles on history of philosophy and Jewish intellectual history; New Views on the Role of Skepticism in the Enlightenment, Modern Language Quarterly, Vol 0053, 1992; The Olympian Dreams and Youthful Rebellion of Descartes,rene - Cole,JR, American Historical Review, Vol 0098, 1993; Sources of Knowledge of Sextus-empiricus in Hume Time, J of the History of Ideas, Vol 0054, 1993; Defenders of the Text - the Tradition of Scholarship in an Age of Science, 1450-1800 - Grafton,A, J of Interdisciplinary History, Vol 0024, 1993. **CONTACT ADDRESS** 15340 Albright St, #204, Pacific Palisades, CA, 90272. **EMAIL** rpopkin@humnet.ucla.com

POPPE, SUSAN
DISCIPLINE PHILOSOPHY **EDUCATION** Univ Notre Dame, PhD, 95. **CAREER** Asst Prof, Philosophy, 95-, Concordia Col. **CONTACT ADDRESS** Concordia Col, Minnesota, 901 S. Eight St., Moorhead, MN, 56562. **EMAIL** poppe@cord.edu

POPPER, ROBERT
DISCIPLINE LAW **EDUCATION** Univ Wis, BA; Harvard Univ, LLB; Univ NY, LLM. **CAREER** Prof emer. **MEMBERSHIPS** Legal Aid Soc. **RESEARCH** Criminal law and procedure; constitutional law. **SELECTED PUBLICATIONS** Auth, Post Conviction Remedies in a Nutshell, W, 78; pubs on professional responsibility, law and mental illness, and criminal, juvenile and prisoners' rights. **CONTACT ADDRESS** Law Dept, Univ of Missouri, St. Louis, 5100 Rockhill Rd, Kansas City, MO, 64110-2499. **EMAIL** popperr@umkc.edu

PORTEN, BEZALEL
PERSONAL Born 02/14/1931, Philadelphia, PA, m, 1956, 4 children **DISCIPLINE** BIBLE, ARAMAIC PAPYROLOGY **EDUCATION** Temple Univ, BA, 52; Columbia Univ, MA, 54, PhD(hist), 64; Jewish Theol Sem Am, MHL, 57. **CAREER** Teacher Bible & Jewish hist, Teachers' Inst, Jewish Theol Sem Am, 58; vis lectr, Spertus Col of Judaica, 59-60, lectr, 60- 61 & 62-64; lectr hist, Roosevelt Univ, 63-64; vis asst prof Hebrew & Bible, Univ Calif, Berkeley, 64-65; from asst prof to assoc prof, Univ Calif, Davis, 65-70; teaching fel, 69-72, Sr Lectr Jewish Hist, Hebrew Univ, Jerusalem, 72-, Univ Calif, Los Angeles Near Eastern Ctr res grant, 68-70; teaching fel Bible, Haifa Univ, 68-71, sr lectr, 71-72: teaching fel Bible, Tel Aviv Univ, 70; vis assoc prof Bible, York Univ, 75-76; sr fel, Univ Pa, 79-81; Nat Endowment for Humanities fel, 79-80; Am Coun Learned Soc grant, 79-80. **MEMBERSHIPS** Am Schs Orient Res; Rabbinical Assembly; Soc Bibl Lit; Israel Explor Soc. **RESEARCH** Aramaic texts; papyri; Biblical narrative. **SELECTED PUBLICATIONS** Auth, The period of the restoration in light of the Elephantine papyri, Beth Mikra, 63; The structure and theme of the Solomon narrative, Hebrew Union Col Annual, 67; Archives from Elephantine: Life of an Ancient Jewish Military Colony, Univ Calif, Berkeley, 68; Jews of Elephantine and Arameans of Syene, Dept Jewish Hist, Hebrew Univ, 74; The return to Zion in vision and reality, Cathedra, 77; Theme and historiosophic background of the Scroll of Ruth, Gratz Col Annual Jewish Studies, 77; Aramaic papyri and parchments: A new look, 79 & The identity of King Adon, 81, Biblical Archeol; Ostracon Clermontganneau N-125, a Case of Ritual Purity, J of the American Oriental Society, Vol 0113, 1993. **CONTACT ADDRESS** Dept of Jewish Hist, Hebrew Univ, Jerusalem, ..

PORTER, ANDREW P.
PERSONAL Born 10/05/1946, Boston, MA, s **DISCIPLINE** APPLIED SCIENCE; PHILOSOPHICAL THEOLOGY **EDUCATION** Harvard Col, BA, 68; MS, 68, PhD, 76, Univ California-Davis; Church Divinity School, Berkeley, MTS, 80; Graduate Theological Union, PhD, 91. **CAREER** Teaching Asst, 83, Church Divinity School of the Pacific; Instr, 80-87, The School for Deacons of the Episcopal Church; Instr, 92, Los Medanos Col; Physicist, 68-94, Special Studies Group, Lawrence Livermore Natl Lab; Physicist, 94-, Physics and Space Div, Lawrence Livermore Natl Lab; Instr, 96-, Las Positas Col. **MEMBERSHIPS** Amer Acad of Religion; Mathematical Assoc of Amer. **RESEARCH** Theology and religious studies; philosophy of religion; phenomenological philosphy; Bible introduction; history of philosophy; Martin Heidegger; H. Richard Niebuhr **SELECTED PUBLICATIONS** Science, Religious Language and Analogy, Faith and Philosophy, 96; When Failure is Success: Counter-Performative Speech Acts, Amer Acad of Religion Western Regional Meeting, 94; The Fertility of Niebuhr's Idea of Monotheism, Pacific Coast Theological Soc, 94; Extending Merold Westphal's Typology of Basic Religious Options, Soc of Christian Philosophers Meeting, 95; The Logic of Confessional Speech Acts, Amer Acad of Religion Western Regional Meeting, 96; Critical and Confessional Responsibility in Theology, Pacific Coast Theological Soc, 96. **CONTACT ADDRESS** 774 Joyce St., Livermore, CA, 94550. **EMAIL** app@jedp.com

PORTER, BURTON F.
PERSONAL Born 06/22/1936, m, 1980, 3 children **DISCIPLINE** PHILOSOPHY **EDUCATION** Univ Maryland, BA, 59; Univ St Andrews, PhD, 64. **CAREER** Lectr, Europ Div, Univ Maryland, 66-69; asst prof, Kings Col, 69-71; assoc & full prof, Russell Sage Col, 71-87; prof of Philosophy & Dept chr, Drexel Univ, 87-91; Dean Arts & Sciences, W New England Col, 91- . **HONORS AND AWARDS** Outstanding Educ Am, 74-75; Award for Tchg Excellence, Kings Col. **MEMBERSHIPS** Am Philos Asn; Mod Lang Asn; Am Asn Higher Educ; Am Conf Acad Deans. **RESEARCH** Ethical theory; contemporary moral issues, critical thinking; philosophy in literature; philosophy of religion. **SELECTED PUBLICATIONS** Auth. Deity and Morality: With Regard to the Naturalistic Fallacy, Hum Press, 68; Philosophy, A Literary and Conceptual Approach, Harcourt Brace, 95; Personal Philosophy, Perspectives on Living, Harcourt Brace, 76; The Good Life, Alternatives in Ethics, Ardsley House, 91, rev ed, 94; Reasons for Living. A Basic Ethics, Macmillan Publ, 88; Religion and Reason, St Martin's Press, 92. **CONTACT ADDRESS** School of Arts and Sciences, W New England Col, Off of the Dean, Springfield, MA, 01002. **EMAIL** bporter@wnec.com

PORTER, KWAME JOHN R.
PERSONAL Born 04/02/1932, Mineral Springs, AR, m **DISCIPLINE** THEOLOGY **EDUCATION** IO Wesleyan Coll, BA 1959; Garrett Evan Theol Sem, MDiv 1962; Union Grad Sch, PhD 1975. **CAREER** Christ United Meth Ch, pastor 1962-71 & 1979-95; Urban Young Life, vice pres 1974-79; Chicago Cntr Black Religious Studies, dir 1971-74; Sch of Human Dignity, dir, 1967-70; Fellowship United Methodist Church, pastor, 1996-; National Urban Black Church Growth Institute, Chicago, dean. **HONORS AND AWARDS** Three awards for work in 7th District's CAPS projects; Alumnus of the year, 1996 Iowa Wesleyan College, 1994-95. **MEMBERSHIPS** Adj prof Garrett Theol Sem; mem Intl Black Writers 1980; pres Student Assn Garrett Theol Sem 1961; community trainer, JCPT/CAPS, Chicago Alliance for Neighborhood Safety, 1995-96; founding mem, Operation Breadbasket PUSH, 1966. **SELECTED PUBLICATIONS** Research writer, proposal developer, chair, Englewood's New Village, EZEC project, 1994-95; author, "The Dating Habits of Young Black Americans," 1979; Pending publications "Black Male Violence," 1997; "How Blackfolk and Others Die," 1997; "Basic Training Manual for 21st Century Christians." Pub book "Dating Habits of Young Black Ams" 1979; pub articles best black sermons Vol II Judson Press 1979; pub articles Metro Ministry David C Cook Pub 1979. **CONTACT ADDRESS** Fellowship United Methodist Church, 447 W 120th St, Chicago, IL, 60628.

PORTER, SAMUEL C.
PERSONAL Born 09/25/1952, Eugene, OR, d, 1 child **DISCIPLINE** RELIGION; SOCIOLOGY OF RELIGION AND CULTURE IN THE US **EDUCATION** Emory Univ, PhD, 96. **CAREER** INSTR, UNIV OR, 98-. **HONORS AND AWARDS** Graduate fellowships, tuition scholarships, Emory Univ. **MEMBERSHIPS** Am Academy of Relig; Asn for the Sociology of Relig; Soc for the Scientific Study of Relig; Asn of Religious Res. **RESEARCH** Sociology of religion and culture; religion in the US; history and theory of religion; morality and society; ecological politics of religion. **SELECTED PUBLICATIONS** Auth, Review, The Future of Religion: Secularization, Revival, and Cult Formation, by Rodney Stark and William Sims Bainbridge, in the J for the Am Academy of Relig 54, 86; submission under review, The Paufre Northwest Forest Debate: Bringing Religion Back In?, Worldviews: Environment, Culture, and Religion, ed, Clare Palmer, Univ Greenwich, 98. **CONTACT ADDRESS** 2680 Baker Blvd., Eugene, OR, 97403-1626. **EMAIL** PorterSamC@aol.com

PORTERFIELD, AMANDA
PERSONAL Born 02/06/1947, Bronxville, NY, m, 1979, 1 child **DISCIPLINE** RELIGIOUS STUDIES **EDUCATION** Mt. Holyoke Col, BA, 69; Columbia Univ, MA, 71; Stanford Univ, PhD, 75. **CAREER** Asst Prof, 75-81, Assoc Prof, 81-90, Prof, 91-94, Syracuse Univ; Prof, 94-98, IUPUI; Prof, 98-, Univ Wyoming. **HONORS AND AWARDS** Phi Betta Kappa; Sarah Willington Scholar **MEMBERSHIPS** AAR; ASCH; ASA; SSSR **RESEARCH** American religious history **SELECTED PUBLICATIONS** Auth, Female Piety in Puritan New England, 92; Mary Lyon and the Mt Holyoke Missionaries, 97; The Power of Religion, 97. **CONTACT ADDRESS** Religious Studies Program, Univ of Wyoming, Hoyt Hall 201, Laramie, WY, 82071. **EMAIL** ap@uwyo.edu

PORTIER, WILLIAM L.
PERSONAL Born 07/08/1945, Englewood, NJ, m, 1971, 3 children **DISCIPLINE** THEOLOGY **EDUCATION** Loyola Univ, BA, 69; Washington Theological Union, MA, 72; Faculty of Theology, St. Michael's Col, PhD, 80 **CAREER** Henry J Knott Prof of Theol, Mt Saint Mary's Col, 97-; prof, Mt Saint Mary's Col 89-; assoc prof, Mt Saint Mary's Col, 86- **MEMBERSHIPS** Amer Acad Relig; Cath Theol Soc Amer; Col Theol Soc; Amer Cath Hist Assoc **RESEARCH** Historical Theology, Nineteen-Century American Catholic History, US-Vatican Relations **SELECTED PUBLICATIONS** Tradition and Incarnation, Foundations of Christian Theology, 94; Isaac Hecker and The First Vatican Council, 85; co-ed, American Catholic Traditions, Resources for Renewal, 97 **CONTACT ADDRESS** Dept of Theology, Mount St. Mary's Col, Emmitsburg, MD, 21727. **EMAIL** wportier@msmary.edu

POSPESEL, HOWARD
PERSONAL Born 01/25/1937, Dayton, OH, m, 1960, 3 children **DISCIPLINE** PHILOSOPHY **EDUCATION** Wittenberg Univ, BA, 59; Univ FL, MA, 61; Univ NC at Chapel Hill, 67. **CAREER** Asst prof, 65-71, assoc prof 71-77, prof, 77- , Univ Miami. **HONORS AND AWARDS** Phi Eta Sigma; Alpha Lambda Delta; Phi Kappa Phi; Phi Beta Kappa; Phi Sigma Tau; James W. Mchamore Outstanding Service Award. **MEMBERSHIPS** FL Philosophical Assn; Southern Soc for Philosphy and Psychology; APA. **RESEARCH** Logic; Plato; Continental Rationalism. **SELECTED PUBLICATIONS** Auth, Arguments: Deductive Logic Exercises, Prentice-Hall, 71; auth, Propositional Logic, Prentice-Hall, 74; auth, Predicate Logic, Prentice-Hall, 76; auth, The Method of Propositional Analogues, Teaching Philosophy, Prentice-Hall, 93; coauth, Premises and Conclusions: Symbolic Logic for Legal Analysis, 97; auth, Toward a Legal Deontic Logic, Notre Dame Law Review, 98. **CONTACT ADDRESS** Dept of Philosophy, Univ of Miami, Coral Gables, FL, 33124. **EMAIL** pospesel@miami.edu

POST, DEBORAH W.
DISCIPLINE LAW **EDUCATION** Hofstra Univ, BA (Cum Laude), 71; Harvard Univ, JD, 78. **CAREER** Assoc, Bracewell & Patterson, Houston, TX; asst prof, Univ Houston; prof Law, Touro Col. **SELECTED PUBLICATIONS** Auth, Continuity and Change: Partnership Formation Under the Common Law, Villanova Law Rev, 87; Reflections on Identity, Diversity, and Morality, Berkeley Women's Law J, 90-91; Race, Riots and the Rule of Law, Denver Law Rev, 93; Profit, Progress and Moral Imperatives, Touro Law Rev, 93; Critical Thoughts About Race, Exclusion, Oppression and Tenure, Pace Law Rev, 94; Power and Morality of Grading: A Case Study and a Few Criti-

cal Thoughts on Grade Normalization, Univ Mo, Kansas City Law Rev, 97; coauth, Cultivating Intelligence: Power, Law and the Politics of Teaching, NY UP; Contracting Law, Carolina Acad Press. **CONTACT ADDRESS** Touro Col, Brooklyn, NY, 11230. **EMAIL** DeborahP@tourolaw.edu

POSTEMA, GERALD JAY
PERSONAL Born 11/26/1948, Chicago, IL, m, 1969, 1 child **DISCIPLINE** LEGAL & MORAL PHILOSOPHY **EDUCATION** Calvin Col, AB, 70; Cornell Univ, MA, 73, PhD(philos), 76. **CAREER** Tutor jurisp, Queen's Col, Oxford, England, spring, 74; instr philos, Cornell Univ, 74-75; asst prof, Johns Hopkins Univ, 75-80; Assoc Prof Philos, Univ Nc, Chapel Hill, 80-, Fel, Am Coun Learned Soc & Nat Endowment for Humanities, 78; hon res assoc, Dept Philos, Univ Col, London, 78; vis asst prof, Sch Law, Univ Calif, Berkeley, 79; vis assoc prof, Univ Mich, 82. **MEMBERSHIPS** Am Philos Asn; Am Soc Polit & Legal Philos; Soc Legal & Social Philos. **RESEARCH** Philosophy of law, Bentham, positivism, and judicial reasoning; professional ethics, law and medicine; moral and political philosophy, international justice and Marxism. **SELECTED PUBLICATIONS** Auth, The Principle Of Utility And The Law Of Procedure: Bentham's Theory Of Adjudication, Ga Law Rev, 77; The Expositor, The Censor And The Common Law, Can J Philos, 79; Bentham And Dworkin On Positivism And Adjudication, & Nozick On Liberty, Compensation And The Individual's Right To Punish, Social Theory; Moral Responsibility And Professional Ethics, NY Univ Law Rev, 80; Coordination And Convention At The Foundations Of Law, J Legal Studies, 82; Bentham's Early Reflections On Law, Justice And Adjudication, Rev Int Philos, 82; Facts, Fictions And Law: Bentham On The Foundations Of Evidence, Arch Legal & Social Philos; Risks And Wrongs - Coleman,Jl/, Yale Law Journal, Vol 0103, 1993. **CONTACT ADDRESS** Dept of Philos, Univ of NC, Chapel Hill, NC, 27514.

POSTLEWAITE, PHILIP F.
PERSONAL Born 06/30/1945, Modesto, CA, 2 children **DISCIPLINE** LAW **EDUCATION** Univ Calif, Berkeley, JD, 70; New York Univ, LLM, 71. **CAREER** Instr law, New York Univ, 71-73; assoc prof law, Notre Dame Univ, 76-81; assoc prof, 81-82, Prof Law, Northwestern Univ, 82-; Mem, Tax Adv Group, Am Law Inst, 82, 98. **RESEARCH** Law taxation, federal individual, partnerships, international. **SELECTED PUBLICATIONS** Auth, Partnership Taxation, 6th ed, Warren, gorham, and Lamont, 97; International Taxation: Corporate and Individual, 3rd ed, Carolina Acad Press, 98; Taxation of Intellectual Property and Intangible Assets, Warren, Gorham, amd Lamont, 97. **CONTACT ADDRESS** Sch of Law, Northwestern Univ, 357 E Chicago Ave, Chicago, IL, 60611-3069.

POSY, CARL J.
DISCIPLINE PHILOSOPHY **EDUCATION** Yale Univ, PhD, 71. **CAREER** Prof, 81-, Duke Univ. **RESEARCH** Philos of mathematics; logic; hist of philos; contemp metaphysics. **SELECTED PUBLICATIONS** Ed, Kant's Philosophy of Mathematics: Modern Essays, Kluwer, 92; Autonomy, Omniscience and the Ethical Imagination, Kluwer, 89; pubs on math intuitionism. **CONTACT ADDRESS** Philos Dept, Duke Univ, West Duke Bldg, Durham, NC, 27706. **EMAIL** cpo@acpub.duke.edu

POTESTA, WOODROW A.
DISCIPLINE TRIAL ADVOCACY **EDUCATION** St John Fisher Col, BA, 70; Claremont Grad Sch, MA, 71; Univ S Calif, JD, 74. **CAREER** Atty and Smith Poverty law fel, Appalachian res and defense fund, 74-78; Bigelow tchg fel, Univ Chicago Law Sch, 78-79; prof, 79-. **HONORS AND AWARDS** Prof yr, 86, 90, 94; outstanding tch, WVU Found; Hale Posten award; Roscoe Pound found, 95; Richard S Jacobson award., Founder, W Va Fund for law in the public interest. **SELECTED PUBLICATIONS** Auth, articles on civil disobedience, jury selection, faith and the law, bioethics and technology. **CONTACT ADDRESS** Law Sch, W Va Univ, PO Box 6009, Morgantown, WV, 26506-6009.

POTTER, KARL HARRINGTON
PERSONAL Born 08/19/1927, Oakland, CA **DISCIPLINE** PHILOSOPHY **EDUCATION** Univ Calif, BA, 50; Harvard Univ, MA, 52, PhD(philos), 55. **CAREER** Instr philos, Carleton Col, 55-56; from instr to prof, Univ Minn, Minneapolis, 56-71, chmn dept, 64-67; Prof Philos & S Asia Studies, Univ Wash, 71-, Fulbright res fel, India, 59-60; res fel, Am Inst Indian Studies, 63-64; vis prof, Univ Hawaii, 78 & Jadavpur Univ, 81. **MEMBERSHIPS** Am Philos Asn; Western Div Am Philos Asn; Asn Asian Studies; Am Orient Soc. **RESEARCH** Indian philosophy; Sanskrit. **SELECTED PUBLICATIONS** Auth, The Padarthatattvanirupanam Of Reghunatha Siromani, Harvard Univ, 57; Presuppositions Of India's Philosophies, Prentice-Hall, 63; Bibliography Of Indian Philosophies, Motilal Banarsidass, Delhi, 70; Indian Metaphysics And Epistemology, 77 & Advaita Vedanta To Samkara And His Pupils, 81, Motilal Banarsidass, Princeton Univ; Reason And Tradition In Indian Thought--An Essay On The Nature Of Indian Philosophical Thinking, J Of The Am Oriental Soc, Vol 114, 94; Language, Reality And Analysis--Essays On Indian Philosophy, J Of The Am Oriental Soc, Vol 112, 92; Meaning, Truth And Predication, Philosophy East & West, Vol 46, 96. **CONTACT ADDRESS** Dept of Philos, Univ of Wash, Seattle, WA, 98195.

POTTER, NANCY
DISCIPLINE ETHICS **EDUCATION** Univ MN, PhD. **CAREER** Dept Philos, Univ Louisville **RESEARCH** Philosophical analysis of trust. **SELECTED PUBLICATIONS** Auth, The Severed Head and Existential Dread: The Classroom as Epistemic Community and Student Survivors of Incest. **CONTACT ADDRESS** Dept of Philos, Univ Louisville, 2301 S 3rd St, Louisville, KY, 40292. **EMAIL** nlpott01@ulkyvm.louisville.edu

POTTER, NELSON
DISCIPLINE ETHICS AND KANT **EDUCATION** Johns Hopkins Univ, PhD, 69. **CAREER** Assoc prof, Univ Nebr, Lincoln. **RESEARCH** Kant's philosophy. **SELECTED PUBLICATIONS** Auth, What is Wrong with Kant's Four Examples, J of Philos Res 43, 93; Kant on Obligation and Motivation in Law and Ethics, Jahrbuch fur Recht and Ethik 2, 94; Kant and the Moral Worth of Actions, Southern J of Philos 34, 96. **CONTACT ADDRESS** Univ Nebr, Lincoln, Lincoln, NE, 68588-0417.

POTTER, PITMAN
DISCIPLINE LAW **EDUCATION** Univ Wash, BA, 78; MA, 75; JD, 85; PhD, 86. **CAREER** Assoc prof, 86-; assoc dean, 97-. **RESEARCH** Chinese law; comparative law; international law; international business transactions; law and society. **SELECTED PUBLICATIONS** Auth, pubs about Chinese law. **CONTACT ADDRESS** Fac of Law, Univ British Columbia, 1822 East Mall, Vancouver, BC, V6T 1Z1. **EMAIL** potter@law.ubc.ca

POTTS, DONALD R.
PERSONAL Born 06/10/1930, St. Louis, MO, m, 1951, 2 children **DISCIPLINE** THEOLOGY **EDUCATION** OK Baptist Univ, BA, 50; Southwestern Baptist Theol Sem, BD, 55, ThD, 59, M Div, 73. **CAREER** Instr, Homiletics, Southwestern Baptist Theol Sem, 59-60; prof, Humanities, Cameron Col, 60-64; adjunct prof and Pastor, 60-75; PROF/CHAIRMAN, RELIGION DEPT, EAST TX BAPTIST UNIV, 76-. **HONORS AND AWARDS** Postdoctoral study grant at Oxford, England, 85; Most Scholarly Prof, ETBU, 85; Eleventh Annual Andy Reavis Lecturer at Marshall Memorial Hospital, 92., Guest prof, Fosham Education Col, Fosham, China, 92; guest prof, Ecole Baptiste de Theologie, Lome, Togo, 94. **MEMBERSHIPS** Am Academy of Relig; Biblical Archaeology Soc; Asn of Baptist Teachers of Relig. **RESEARCH** Theology; ethics; homiletics; archaeology. **SELECTED PUBLICATIONS** Auth, articles for various periodicals, 76-98; articles for Holman Bible Dictionary, 95; articles for Eerdman Bible Dictionary, 97; Biblical Stewardship Studies for Baptist Conventions in MS. AR, and MO, 98; Bible Studies for Baptist Standard, May-Nov, 98. **CONTACT ADDRESS** Dept of Relig, East Texas Baptist Univ, 1109 N. Grove, Marshall, TX, 75670. **EMAIL** dpotts@etbu.edu

POTUTO, JOSEPHINE R.
DISCIPLINE LAW **EDUCATION** Douglass Univ, BA; Seton Hall Univ, MA; Rutgers Univ, JD. **CAREER** Prof **RESEARCH** Constitutional law; federal jurisdiction; criminal procedure. **SELECTED PUBLICATIONS** Auth, Prisoner Collateral Attacks: Habeas Corpus; Federal Prisoner Motion Practice, Clark Boardman; Winning Appeals; co-auth, Federal Criminal Jury Instructions, Michie. **CONTACT ADDRESS** Law Dept, Univ of Nebraska, Lincoln, 103 Ross McCollum Hall, PO Box 830902, Lincoln, NE, 68588-0420. **EMAIL** jpotuto@unlinfo.unl.edu

POTVIN, THOMAS R.
PERSONAL Born 09/22/1934, Worcester, MA **DISCIPLINE** THEOLOGY **EDUCATION** Univ Montreal, BPh, 54; Univ Ottawa, MTh, 64; Fribourg (Suisse) DTh, 75. **CAREER** Secy treas, 67-88, Prior, St-Jean-Baptiste Priory, 87-93; prof, 74, prof titulaire, 84, doyen, fac theol, College Dominicain de Philosophie et de Theologie, 93; Provincial Prior, Dominicans of Canada, 93-97. **MEMBERSHIPS** Soc can Theologie; Can soc theol; Cath Theol Soc Am; Relig Educ Asn; Societas Liturgica. **SELECTED PUBLICATIONS** Auth, The Theology of the Primacy of Christ According to St. Thomas and its Scriptural Foundations, 73; coauth, L'experience comme lieu theologie, 83; coauth, Questions actuelles sur la foi, 84. **CONTACT ADDRESS** 96 Empress Ave, Ottawa, ON, K1R 7G3. **EMAIL** thomasraymond.potvin@sympatico.ca

POULIN, ANNE BOWEN
DISCIPLINE CRIMINAL LAW **EDUCATION** Radcliffe Col, Harvard Univ, BA, 69; Univ Maine Sch Law, JD, 73; Univ Mich Law Sch, LLM, 75. **CAREER** Prof, Villanova Univ, 81-. **RESEARCH** Evidence, criminal procedure. **SELECTED PUBLICATIONS** Auth, Female Delinquents: Defining Their Place in the Justice System, Wisc. L. Rev 543, 96; Double Jeopardy and Judicial Accountability: When is an Acquittal not an Acquittal, 27 Ariz St L. J 953, 95; The Jury: The Criminal Justice System's Different Voice, 62 U Cin. L. Rev 1377, 94 & The Fourth Amendment: Elusive Standards, Elusive Review, 67 Chi.-Kent L. Rev 127, 92; coauth, Pennsylvania Evidence, 87. **CONTACT ADDRESS** Law School, Villanova Univ, 800 Lancaster Ave, Villanova, PA, 19085-1692. **EMAIL** poulin@law.vill.edu

POVARSKY, CHAIM
DISCIPLINE JEWISH AND AMERICAN LAW **EDUCATION** Hebrew Univ, LLB, 66; Tel Aviv Univ, LLM, 78, JSD, 86. **CAREER** Pvt pract, Israel; instr, Tel Aviv Univ; instr, dir, Inst of Jewish Law, Touro Col. **MEMBERSHIPS** Dir, Jewish Law Asn **SELECTED PUBLICATIONS** Author of scholarly articles in the field of Jewish law and philos; ed of the Institute's Jewish Law Rpt, co-editor of the Dine-Israel J. **CONTACT ADDRESS** Touro Col, Brooklyn, NY, 11230. **EMAIL** ChaimP@tourolaw.edu

POWELL, JOUETT L.
PERSONAL Born 12/02/1941, Dallas, TX, m, 1964, 1 child **DISCIPLINE** PHILOSOPHICAL THEOLOGY; PHILOSOPHY OF RELIGION **EDUCATION** Baylor Univ, BA 64; S Baptist Theo Sem, BD 67; Yale Univ, MPhil 70, PhD 72. **CAREER** Univ N Carolina Chapel Hill, instr 71-72; UNC Chapel Hill, asst prof, 72-78; Christopher NP Univ, asst prof, 78-80; CNU, assoc prof, 80-89, prof 89-; CNU, Dean Sch Letters, 83-92, College Arts Hum, Dean, 92-95, dir grad stud, 92-95, act prov, 95-96, College Lib Arts, dean, 96-; College of William and Mary, vis assoc prof, 84-85, 87-90. **HONORS AND AWARDS** 2 NEH; Rockefeller Doc Fel. **MEMBERSHIPS** AAR; APA; AAHE; AAUP. **RESEARCH** John Henry Newman; Other Philos and Theol Figures and Trends in Vict England; Philo of Religion. **SELECTED PUBLICATIONS** Auth, rev, Pricilla Pope-Levison, John R. Levison, Jesus in Global Contexts, and Andrew D. Clarke, Bruce W. Winter, One God One Lord: Christianity in a World of Rel Pluralism, Jour of Ecumen Stud, 94; rev, Mircea Eliade, Ioan P. Couliano with Hillary S. Wiesner, The Eliade Guide to World Rel, Jour of Ecumen Stud, 92. **CONTACT ADDRESS** Office of the Dean, One University Place, 104 Gosnold Hall, Newport News, VA, 23606-2998. **EMAIL** jpowell@cnu.edu

POWELL, MARK ALLAN
DISCIPLINE NEW TESTAMENT **EDUCATION** Tex Lutheran Col, BA, 75; Trinity Lutheran Sem, MDiv, 80; Union Theol Sem, PhD, 88. **CAREER** Asst prof, 87-92; dir, Cont Edu, Post-Grad Stud, 89-92; assoc prof, 92-; Robert and Phyllis Leatherman prof. **HONORS AND AWARDS** Prog ch, Soc Biblical Lit. **MEMBERSHIPS** E Great Lakes Biblical Soc; Cath Biblical Assn. **SELECTED PUBLICATIONS** Ed, Reading the New Testament in the 21st Century, Westminster/John Knox, 98; auth, Jesus As A Figure in History, Westminster/John Knox, 98; A Fortress Introduction to The Four Gospels, Fortress, 97; Mark: God's Grace in Action, Inspire Series, Augsburg, 97; Epiphany, Proclamation 6-Series B, Fortress, 96; co-ed, auth, Treasures Old and New: Recent Contributions to Matthean Studies, Scholars, 96. **CONTACT ADDRESS** Bible Dept, Trinity Lutheran Sem, 2199 E Main St, Columbus, OH, 43209-2334. **EMAIL** mapowell@trinity.capital.edu

POWELL, SAM
PERSONAL Born 02/23/1956, San Bernardino, CA, m, 1976, 2 children **DISCIPLINE** PHILOSOPHY AND RELIGION **EDUCATION** Point Loma Nazarene Univ, BA, 78; Nazarene Theol Sem, MDiv, 81; Claremont Grad Univ, PhD, 87. **CAREER** Lectr Theol, Nazarene Theol Col, 94-95; Prof Philos & Relig, Point Loma Nazarene Univ, 86-. **HONORS AND AWARDS** Templeton Found Sci-Relig Course Prog Award, 96-97; Wesley Ctr Fel 21st Century Stud, 98-99. **MEMBERSHIPS** Am Acad Relig; Soc Bibl Lit. **RESEARCH** German philosophy and religious thought; the doctrine of the Trinity. **SELECTED PUBLICATIONS** Auth, The Doctrine of the Trinity in 19th Century American Wesleyan Theology, Wesleyan Theol Jour, 83; Religious Experience and Myth: The Philosophy of C H Weisse, Annals of Scholar, 89; Thinking About Economics and Ethics as a Wesleyan, Grace in the Academic Community, Festschrift for Dr Cecil Paul, Point Loma Press, 96; Committing Christianity in Public, Maps and Models for Ministry, Point Loma Press, 96; The Fear of the Lord is the Beginning of Wisdom: Thoughts on the Relation between Holiness and Ethics, 99; Holiness and Community, Intervarsity Press, 99. **CONTACT ADDRESS** Point Loma Nazarene Col, 3900 Lomaland Dr, San Diego, CA, 92106. **EMAIL** spowell@ptloma.edu

POWER, GARRETT
PERSONAL Born 10/16/1938, Baltimore, MD, m, 1960, 3 children **DISCIPLINE** LAW **EDUCATION** Duke Univ, AB, 60, LLB, 62; Univ Ill, LLM, 65. **CAREER** Prof Law, Univ Md, Baltimore City, 63-, Prin investr, Chesapeake Res Consortium, 71-; assoc ed, Coastal Zone Mgt J, 72- **RESEARCH** Environmental law; coastal zone planning. **SELECTED PUBLICATIONS** Coauth, Chesapeake Bay In Legal Perspective, 70 & Legal Problems Of Coal Mine Reclamation, 72, US Govt Printing Off; contribur, Federal Environmental Law, West Pub, 74; The Case Of The 1989 Bordeaux, J Of Legal Ed, Vol 44, 94. **CONTACT ADDRESS** 107 Longwood Rd, Baltimore, MD, 21210.

POWER, WILLIAM L.
PERSONAL Born 08/02/1934, Biloxi, MS, m, 1970, 4 children **DISCIPLINE** RELIGION **EDUCATION** Univ Mississippi, BAE 56; Emory Univ, Mdiv 59, PhD 65. **CAREER** Lambuth Col, asst prof 65-67; Univ Georgia, assoc prof, prof, 67 to 98-.

HONORS AND AWARDS VP & Pres of Amer Acad of Rel, and Soc for Philo of Rel. **MEMBERSHIPS** AAR; SPR; SSPP; HIART **RESEARCH** Philos theology, religion. **SELECTED PUBLICATIONS** Imago Dei-Imatito Dei, Intl Jour for Philo of Religion, 97; Divine Poeisis and Abstract Entities, Religious Stud, 94; Our Knowledge of God, Perspectives in Religious Stud, 94; On Divine Perfection, Anglican Theological Rev, 93; Peircean Semiotics, Religion and Theological Realism, New Essays in Religious Naturalism, ed, Creighton Peden, Macon G.A., Mercer Univ Press, 94; On Divine Perfection, Logic God and Metaphysics, ed, J. F. Harris, Netherlands, Kluwer Acad Pub, 92. **CONTACT ADDRESS** Dept of Religion, Univ of Georgia, Athens, GA, 30602-1625. **EMAIL** power@arches.uga.edu

POWERS, BRUCE P.
PERSONAL Born 05/25/1940, Savannah, GA, m, 2 children **DISCIPLINE** RELIGION **EDUCATION** Mercer Univ, BA, 64; Southern Baptist Sem, MRE, 67, PhD, 71. **CAREER** Dir, Church Prog Training Center, Sunday Sch Bd, Nashville TN, 71-77; prof, Southeastern Baptist Theol Sem, Wake Forest, NC, 78-95; assoc dean, Campbell Univ, 96- . **HONORS AND AWARDS** Award for Fac Excellence, 89; Dean's Excellence Award, 96. **MEMBERSHIPS** Intl Relig Educ Asn; North Am Prof of Christian Educ; World Future Soc. **SELECTED PUBLICATIONS** Auth, "How to Handle Conflict in the Church," Convention, 91; "Christian Education Handbook," rev, "Broadman & Holman," 96; "Church Administration Handbook," rev ed, Broadman & Holman, 97. **CONTACT ADDRESS** Divinity Sch, Campbell Univ, Bluies Creek, NC, 27506-4050.

POWERS, DAVID STEPHEN
PERSONAL Born 07/23/1951, Cleveland, OH, 3 children **DISCIPLINE** ISLAMIC HISTORY, LAW **EDUCATION** Yale Univ, BA, 73; Princeton Univ, MA & PhD(Islamic hist), 79. **CAREER** Prof Arabic & Islamics, Cornell Univ, 79-. **MEMBERSHIPS** Am Oriental Soc; Mid Eastern Studies Asn. **RESEARCH** Islamic law; Islamic history; medieval social history. **SELECTED PUBLICATIONS** Auth, Studies in Quran and Hadith: The Formation of the Islamic Law of Inheritance, Berkeley, 86; Islamic Legal Interpretation: Muftis and Their Fatwas, Harvard, 86; The History of al-Tabari, volume XXIV The Empire in Transition, tras, David Stephen Powers, Suny Press, 89. **CONTACT ADDRESS** Cornell Univ, Rockefeller Hall, Ithaca, NY, 14853-0001. **EMAIL** dsp4@cornell.edu

POWERS, MADISON
DISCIPLINE PHILOSOPHY **EDUCATION** Oxford Univ, PhD. **CAREER** Assoc prof. **RESEARCH** Political, legal, and moral philosophy; genetics and reproductive ethics. **SELECTED PUBLICATIONS** Co-auth, Aids, Women and the Next Generation. **CONTACT ADDRESS** Dept of Philosophy, Georgetown Univ, 37th and O St, Washington, DC, 20057.

POYTHRESS, VERN S.
PERSONAL Born 03/29/1946, Madera, CA, m, 1983, 2 children **DISCIPLINE** THEOLOGY, MATHEMATICS **EDUCATION** Cal Tech, BS, 66; Harvard Univ, PhD, 70; Westminster Theological Seminary, MDiv, 74, ThM, 74; Cambirdge Univ, MLitt, 77; Univ of Stellenbosch, ThD, 81. **CAREER** Tchg asst, 69, asst prof, Fresno State Col, 70-71; tchg fel, Harvard Univ, 70-71; lectr, summer 74, adjunct asst prof, Univ of Okla, 77; ASST PROF, 76-81, ASSOC PROF, 81-87, PROF, WESTMINSTER THEOLOGICAL SEMINARY, 87-. **MEMBERSHIPS** Evangelica Theol Soc; Ling Asn of Can and U.S. **RESEARCH** Hermeneutics; New Testament. **SELECTED PUBLICATIONS** Auth, Symphonic Theology, Korean Lang, Compass House Pub, 93; Divine Meaning of Scripture, The Right Doctrine from the Wrong Texts? Essays on the Use of the Old Testament in the New, Baker, 94; Understanding Dispensationalists, Presbyterian and Reformed, 94; Reforming Ontology and Logic in the Light of the Trinity: An Application of Van Til's Idea of Analogy, Westminster Theological J, 95; Indifferentism and Rigorism in the Church: With Implications for Baptizing Small Children, Westminster Theological J, 97; Linking Small Children with Infants in the Theology of Baptizing, Westminster Theological J, 97; Gender in Bible Translation. Exploring a Connection with Male Representatives, Westminster Theological J, 98; Keep On Praying!, Decision, 98; contribur, Notes on Revelation, New Geneva Study Bible, Thomas Nelson, 95. **CONTACT ADDRESS** Westminster Theol Sem, PO Box 27009, Philadelphia, PA, 19118-0009.

POZZO, RICCARDO
DISCIPLINE KANT AND HEGEL **EDUCATION** Univ Trier, PhD. **CAREER** Philos, Catholic Univ Am. **SELECTED PUBLICATIONS** Auth, Karl-Heinz Iltings Edition und Interpretation der Hegelschen Rechtsphilosophie, Hegel-Jahrbuch, 94; Philosophische Terminologie zwischen Leibniz und Meier, In VI. Internationaler Leibniz-Kongress, Vortrage, Hannover, Leibniz-Gesellschaft, 94, Coed, Norbert Hinske, Kant-Index. Bd. 6: Stellenindex und Konkordanz zur 'Logik; Transl, Henry S. Harris, La fenomenologia dell'autocoscienza in Hegel, 95; Wissenschaft und Reformation. Die Beispiele der Universitaten Konigsberg und Helmstedt, 95; Tracce zabarelliane nella logica kantiana, 95; Formal Logic versus Epistemic Logic between 1500 and 1800, 95; Coed, John Locke, Anleitung des menschlichen Verstandes. Eine Abhandlung von den Wunderwerken. In der ubersetzung Konigsberg 1755 von Georg David Kypke - Of the Conduct of the Understanding. A Discourse of Miracles. Nach der ersten Werkausgabe London 1714. Festgabe fur Norbert Hinske zum 65. Geburstag, 96; Theodor F. Geraets, La logica di Hegel fra religione e storia, 96; Vorlesungsverzeichnisse als Quelle der Universitatsgeschichte Preussens, 97; 18 Seiki Kenihisuberuku Daigakushi (The History of the University of Konigsberg in the 18th Century), 97; 18 Seiki Kenihisuberuku Daigaku no Kougiyoukou (Course Announcments at the University of Konigsberg in the 18th Century), 97. **CONTACT ADDRESS** Catholic Univ of America, 620 Michigan Ave Northeast, Washington, DC, 20064. **EMAIL** pozzo@cua.edu

PRADES, JOSE ALBERT
PERSONAL Born 11/01/1929, Valencia, Spain, m, 1971 **DISCIPLINE** SOCIOLOGY OF RELIGION **EDUCATION** Cath Univ Louvain, lic econ, 57, lic soc sci, 63, PhD(soc sci), 65. **CAREER** Asst soc sci, Cath Univ Louvain, 65-70; asst prof social relig, Cath Inst Paris, 70-71; vis prof, 71-74, Prof Sociol Relig, Univ Que, Montreal, 74-, Dir Dept Relig, 78-, Mem, Coun Sci Res, Spain, 65-; Conf Learned Socs, Can, 71- **MEMBERSHIPS** Fr-Can Asn Advan Sci. **RESEARCH** Contemporary industrial society; ultimate concerns and social class in Canada today. **SELECTED PUBLICATIONS** Auth, Valeurs Religieuses En Milieu Urbain, Social Compass, 66; La Cociologie De La Religion Chez Max Weber, Nauwelaerts, Louvain, 69; Sur Le Concept De Religion, Relig Studies, 73; Renouveau Communantaire Et Utopie Autogestionnaire, In: Renouveau Communantaire Au Quebec, Ed Fides, 74; Ethics And Sociology--Development Of Human Solidarities In The Philosophy Of Emile Durkheim, Studies In Religion-Sciences Religieuses, Vol 22, 93; Durkheim--The Sacred And Society--Introduction, Social Compass, Vol 40, 93; Civil Religion And Humanitarian Religion--Return To Durkheimian Anthropocentrism, Social Compass, Vol 40, 93; Ecology, Ethics And Creation--From The Green-Movement To Ecological Ethics, Studies In Religion-Sciences Religieuses, Vol 24, 95; Introduction To Environmental Ethics, Studies In Religion-Sciences Religieuses, Vol 23, 94. **CONTACT ADDRESS** Dept of Relig, Univ of Que, C P 8888, Montreal, PQ, H3C 3P8.

PRADO, C.G.
DISCIPLINE PHILOSOPHY **EDUCATION** Univ Berkeley, BA; MA; Queen's Univ, PhD. **CAREER** Dept Philos, Queen's Univ **RESEARCH** Epistemology; philosophy of religion. **SELECTED PUBLICATIONS** Auth, Starting With Foucault: An Introduction to Genealogy; Descartes and Foucault: A Contrastive Introduction to Philosophy; The Last Choice: Preemptive Suicide in Advanced Age; The Limits of Pragmatism; Rethinking How We Age: A New View of the Aging Mind; Making Believe: Philosophical Reflections on Fiction; Illusions of Faith: A Critique of Noncredal Religion. **CONTACT ADDRESS** Philosophy Dept, Queen's Univ, Kingston, ON, K7L 3N6. **EMAIL** pradocg@post.queensu.ca

PRATICO, GARY D.
DISCIPLINE OLD TESTAMENT **EDUCATION** Berkshire Christian Col, BA; Gordon-Conwell Theol Sem, MDiv; Harvard Divinity Sch, ThD. **CAREER** Assoc prof, Gordon-Conwell Theol Sem, 82-; dir, Hebrew Lang Prog. **HONORS AND AWARDS** Cur, Harvard Semitic Mus, 82-93. **SELECTED PUBLICATIONS** Auth, Nelson Glueck's 1938-1940 Excavations at Tell el-Kheleifeh: A Reappraisal; pub(s), on topics concerning biblical and ancient Near Eastern studies. **CONTACT ADDRESS** Gordon-Conwell Theol Sem, 130 Essex St, South Hamilton, MA, 01982.

PRATT, RICHARD L., JR.
PERSONAL Born 10/17/1953, Roanoke, VA, m **DISCIPLINE** RELIGION **EDUCATION** Covenant Col, 73; Roanoke Col, BA, 77; Westminster Theol Sem, 79; Union Theol Sem, MDiv, 81; Harvard Univ, ThD, 87. **CAREER** Pulpit supply & conf speaker, 84-; from asst prof to assoc prof to prof, Reformed Theol Sem, 84-; instr, Chesapeake Theol Sem, 83-84. **SELECTED PUBLICATIONS** Auth, 1 and 2 Chronicles, New Geneva Study Bibl, 95; auth, Designed for Dignitym 93. **CONTACT ADDRESS** Dept of OT, Reformed Theol Sem, PO Box 945120, Maitland, FL, 32751. **EMAIL** RichPratt@aol.com

PREBISH, CHARLES STUART
PERSONAL Born 10/11/1944, Chicago, IL, m, 2 children **DISCIPLINE** BUDDHIST STUDIES **EDUCATION** Case Western Reserve Univ, BA, 66, MA, 68; Univ WI, PhD, 71. **CAREER** Asst prof, 71-77, Assoc Prof Relig Studies, Pa State Univ, University Park, 77-; ed, J Buddhist Ethics, 94-; ed, Critical Rev Bks Relig, 94-98; series ed, Critical Studies in Buddhism, 96. **HONORS AND AWARDS** Nat Sci Found grant, 72-73; Yehan Numata (visiting) Chair in Buddhist Studies, Univ Calgary, Fall 93; Am Acad Relig grant, 94; Rockefeller Found Hum Fel, 97-98. **MEMBERSHIPS** Am Acad Relig; Asn Asian Studies; Am Orient Soc; Int Asn Buddhist Studies. **RESEARCH** Buddhist monastic lit; early Buddhist hist and doctrine; Buddhism in Am. **SELECTED PUBLICATIONS** Auth, Theories concerning the Skandhaka: An appraisal, 8/73 & A review of scholarship on the Buddhist councils, 2/74, J Asian Studies; The Pratimoksa puzzle: Fact versus fantasy, J Am Orient Soc, 74; Co-ed & contribr, Introduction to the Religions of the East: Reader, 74, Kendall/Hunt; ed & contribr, Buddhism: A Modern Perspective, 75 & transl, Buddhist Monastic Discipline, 75, Pa State Univ Press; auth, American Buddhism, Duxbury Press, 79; Religion and Sport, Greenwood Press, 92; Historical Dictionary of Buddhism, Scarecrow Press, 93; A Survey of Vinaya Literature, Curzon Press, 94; co-ed, The Faces of Buddhism in America, Univ CA Press, 98; auth, Luminous Passage: The Practice and Study of Buddhism in America, Univ CA Press, 99. **CONTACT ADDRESS** Relig Studies Program, Pennsylvania State Univ, 216 Weaver Bldg, University Park, PA, 16802-5503. **EMAIL** csp1@psu.edu

PRENTISS, KAREN PECHILIS
DISCIPLINE RELIGIOUS STUDIES **EDUCATION** Bowdoin Col, AB, 84; Univ Chicago, AM, 86, PhD, 93. **CAREER** ASST PROF, DREW UNIV, 94-. **CONTACT ADDRESS** Relig Stud, Drew Univ, 36 Madison Ave, Madison, NJ, 07940.

PRESSEAU, JACK R.
PERSONAL Born 11/16/1933, Curtisville, PA, m, 1955, 4 children **DISCIPLINE** RELIGIOUS EDUCATION **EDUCATION** IN State Tchr(s), Col PA, BS, 55; Pittsburgh-Xenia Sem, MDiv, 58; Presby Sch Christian Educ, MCE, 59; Univ Pittsburgh, PhD, 65. **CAREER** Assoc pastor, North Presby Church, Elmira, NY, 59-62; studies asst relig educ, Univ Pittsburgh, 63-65; assoc prof relig & psychol, 65-69, prof psychol, 69-75, counselor, 72-75, Prof Relig, Presby Col, SC, 69-98, retired, 98. **RESEARCH** Faith development; recruiting and training for church vocations. **SELECTED PUBLICATIONS** Auth, I'm Saved, You're Saved--Maybe, John Knox Press, 77; Gospel illustrations: What's memorable may be irrelevant, Duke Divinity Sch Rev, winter 78; Life maps, Harvard Educ Rev, 11/80; Tradition, trends, and tomorrow, Presby Survey, 9/81; Pendulum swings and pre-ministerial preparation, The Presby Outlook, 4/12/80; Teach-niques, John Knox Press, 82. **CONTACT ADDRESS** Rt 2, Box 327, Clinton, SC, 29325-2865.

PRESSMAN, H. MARK
PERSONAL Born 07/07/1968, m, 1998 **DISCIPLINE** PHILOSOPHY **EDUCATION** U C Davis, PhD, 97. **CAREER** Adj Instr, Philosophy, Fresno City Col & Calif State Univ, Fresno. **MEMBERSHIPS** Hume Soc; Am Philos Asn **RESEARCH** Hume; philosophy of Religion **SELECTED PUBLICATIONS** Auth, Hume on Geometry, Hume Studies, 98. **CONTACT ADDRESS** 1915 E Revere, Fresno, CA, 93720. **EMAIL** jmp78@cvip.fresno.com

PRESTON, CHERYL B.
PERSONAL Born 11/23/1952, Provo, UT, m, 1976, 3 children **DISCIPLINE** LAW **EDUCATION** Brigham Young Univ, BA, summa, cum laude, 75, JD, 79. **CAREER** Assoc Prof, 89-95, Prof, 95-, BYU Rueben Clark Law Sch; VP, Sr Counl, 87-89, Fst Interstate Bank SLC; Assoc, 84-87, Holme Roberts and Owen SLC; Assoc, 81-83, O'Melveny and Myers LA; law clerk, 79-80, Hon Monroe G McKay Ct of Appeals. **HONORS AND AWARDS** Phi Delta Phi; Order of the Coif; ISR Gnt David M Kennedy Cen; BYU Women's Res Gnt; UT Court of Appeals nom. **MEMBERSHIPS** NAWJ; BYUFWA; AALS; ABA; USB; CBA. **SELECTED PUBLICATIONS** Auth, To See as We are Seen: Advertising Culture and Gender, forthcoming; Buying In: A Look at Women Consumers of Sexism, forthcoming; coed, Conflict Resolution: Come Let Us Reason Together, in: Talks Selected from the 97 LDS Women's Conf, 98; auth, Consuming Sexism: Pornography Suppression in the Larger Context of Commercial Images, GA L Rev, 97; It Moves Even if We Don't: A Reply to Arthur Austin, The Top Ten Politically Correct Law Reviews, Tenn L Rev, 96; Feminist Legal Theory: Concepts Applications and Bibliography, Utah State Bar Annual Meeting Source Book, 96; This Old House: A Blueprint for Constructive Feminism, Geo L J, 95; Joining Traditional Values and Feminist Legal Scholarship, J Legal Edu, 93. **CONTACT ADDRESS** Brigham Young Univ, 424 JRCB, Provo, UT, 84602. **EMAIL** prestonc@lawgate.byu.edu

PREUS, J. SAMUEL
DISCIPLINE RELIGIOUS STUDIES **EDUCATION** Harvard Univ, ThD, 67. **CAREER** Prof. **RESEARCH** Religious Thought and Theories of Religion in Early Modern Europe, History of Biblical Interpretation. **SELECTED PUBLICATIONS** Auth, Explaining Religion: Criticism and Theory from Bodin to Freud, Yale, 87; From Shadow to Promise: OT Interpretation from Augustine to the Young Luther, Harvard, 69; Spinoza, Vico and the Imagination of Religion, Jour Hist Ideas, 89; Secularizing Divination: Spiritual Biography and the Invention of the Novel, JAAR, 91. **CONTACT ADDRESS** Dept of Religious Studies, Indiana Univ, Bloomington, 300 N Jordan Ave, Bloomington, IN, 47405.

PRIALKOWSKI, KRISTOFF
PERSONAL Born 06/13/1958, Warsaw, Poland **DISCIPLINE** PHILOSOPHY **EDUCATION** Univ of Lublin, MA, Christian Philos; Temple Univ, MA, 91, PhD, 97. **CAREER** Lectr, CCP, 90-; Adjunct Prof, 86-94, Villanova Univ; Adjunct

Prof, 94-96, St Joseph's Univ. **HONORS AND AWARDS** Pres Scholarship, Villanova Univ; Tchg Asst, Temple Univ. **MEMBERSHIPS** APA. **RESEARCH** Epistemology/Metaphysics. **CONTACT ADDRESS** 762 Rugby Rd, Bryn Mawr, PA, 19010.

PRICE, CHARLES EUGENE
PERSONAL Apalachicola, FL, m **DISCIPLINE** LAW **EDUCATION** Johnson C Smith U, BA 1946; Howard U, AM 1949; Johns Hopkins U, further study 1951-52; Boston U, further study 1956; John Marshall Law Sch JD, 1967; Harvard Law Sch, CS, 1980. **CAREER** NC Mutual Life Ins, ins mgr 1949-50; Butler Coll, dean of coll 1950-53; FL Mem Coll, dean of coll 1953-55; NAACP (assgnd to GA), field dir 1955-57; Livingstone Coll, asst prof 1957-59; Morris Brown Coll, assoc prof/atty. **HONORS AND AWARDS** Ldrshp Awrd GA NAACP 1965-66; schlrshp Alpha Kappa Mu 1954; artcls pub Atlanta Daily Wrld & Pittsbrgh Courier 1955-57; Tchr of Yr Morris Brown Coll 1972, 1980-81. **MEMBERSHIPS** Bd dir Hemphill Food Serv 1982-; cnsltnt Thomas & Russell 1979-; atty at law State Bar of GA Fed Bars 1968-; bd dir Dekalb, GA EOA 1965-70; pres Dekalb, GA NAACP Chptr 1962-70; adv bd Sm Bsns Adm GA 1968-82. **CONTACT ADDRESS** Morris Brown Col, 643 MLK Dr NW, Atlanta, GA, 30314.

PRICE, DANIEL
PERSONAL Born 10/03/1965, Houston, TX **DISCIPLINE** PHILOSOPHY **EDUCATION** DePaul Univ, PhD, 99. **CAREER** Dept Philos, De Paul Univ **SELECTED PUBLICATIONS** Auth, Without a Woman to Read: Toward the Daughter in Post modernism, St. Univ of NY Press, 97; art, Negotiated Escape, Cimarron Review, 93; Who Owns the Lie? The Problem of Presentation in Shakespeare's Troilus and Cressida, in Man and World, 94; Stein's Audiences: Gertrude Stein and the Philosophical Exemplar, in: Jour for the Brit Soc of Phenomenology, 96. **CONTACT ADDRESS** Dept of Philosophy, DePaul Univ, 1150 W Fullerton Ave, Chicago, IL, 60614. **EMAIL** dprice@condor.depaul.edu

PRICE, MARJORIE S.
DISCIPLINE PHILOSOPHY **EDUCATION** Barnard Col, BA; NY Univ, PhD. **CAREER** Prof, Univ Ala Birmingham, 77-. **RESEARCH** Metaphysics, philosophy of mathematics, philosophy of language. **CONTACT ADDRESS** Dept of Philosophy, Univ of Alabama, Birmingham, 1400 University Blvd, Birmingham, AL, 35294-1150. **EMAIL** price@uab.edu

PRICE, MONROE E.
DISCIPLINE LAW **EDUCATION** Yale Univ, BA, 60; LLB, 64. **CAREER** Prof, UCLA, 68; Joseph and Sadie Danzinger Prof, Yeshiva Univ. **HONORS AND AWARDS** Pres, Calif Found Community Service Cable Television; dep dir, Sloan Commission Cable Comm. **RESEARCH** Communications policy; Native American land and water rights; copyright and the arts. **SELECTED PUBLICATIONS** Auth, Law and the American Indian. **CONTACT ADDRESS** Yeshiva Univ, 55 Fifth Ave, NY, NY, 10003-4301. **EMAIL** schroedr@ymail.yu.edu

PRICE, ROBERT GEORGE
PERSONAL Born 06/01/1934, New York, NY, m, 1955, 2 children **DISCIPLINE** HISTORY OF LOGIC, ETHICS **EDUCATION** Yale Univ, BA, 55, MA, 57, PhD(philos), 63. **CAREER** From instr to asst prof, 59-66, Assoc Prof Philos, PA State Univ, University Park, 66- **MEMBERSHIPS** Am Philos Asn; Asn Symbolic Logic; Mind Asn. **RESEARCH** History of logic; moral and political philosophy; Greek philosophy. **SELECTED PUBLICATIONS** Auth, Some Antistrophes To The Rhetoric, Philos & Rhet, 68; Ockham And Supposito Personalis, Franciscan Studies, 71; A Refutative Demonstration In Metaphysics Gamma, Philos And Rhetoric, Vol 29, 96. **CONTACT ADDRESS** Dept Philos, Pennsylvania State Univ, 240 Sparks Bldg, University Park, PA, 16802-5201.

PRICE, ROBERT M.
PERSONAL Born 07/07/1954, Jackson, MS, m, 1984, 2 children **DISCIPLINE** PHILOSOPHY **EDUCATION** Montclair State Coll, BA, 76; Gordon-Cromwell Theol Sem, S Hamilton, MA, Theol, 78; Drew Univ, Madison, NJ, PhM, 80, PhD, 81, PhM, 92, PhD 93. **HONORS AND AWARDS** Phi Kappa Phi; Phi Alpha Theta; Phi Alpha Chi; Who's Who in Biblical Stud and Archaeol; Dissertation Awarded Distinction. **MEMBERSHIPS** Soc of Biblical Lit; The Westar Inst; Collegium. **RESEARCH** Christian Origins; Hist Jesus; Auth of Pauline Epistles; Deconstruction. **SELECTED PUBLICATIONS** Auth, Beyond Born Again: Towards Evangelical Maturity, Hypatia Press, 93; The Widow Traditions in Luke-Acts: A Feminist-Critical Scrutiny, Scholars Press, 97; Mystic Rhythms: The Philosophical Vision of RUSH, Borgo Press, 98; Apocryphal Apparitions: 1 Corinthians 15:3-11 as a Post-Pauline Interpolation, Journal of Higher Criticism, 2, #2, 95; Protestant Hermeneutical Axiomatics: A Deconstruction, Christian New Age Quarterly 4-6, 97. **CONTACT ADDRESS** 30 Stockton St, Bloomfield, NJ, 07003-5016. **EMAIL** criticus@aol.com

PRICHARD, ROBERT W.
DISCIPLINE CHRISTIANITY **EDUCATION** Princeton Univ, AB, 71; Berkeley at Yale Divinity Sch, MDiv, 74; Emory Univ, PhD, 83. **CAREER** Asst to the rector, St George's Episcopal Church, 74-77; stud colloquy leader, Emory Univ, 77-79; rector, Clarke Episcopal Parish, 80-83; instr, 80-81; asst prof, 83-89; assoc prof, 89-94; Arthur Lee Kinsolving prof, Va Theol Sem, 94. **HONORS AND AWARDS** Interim vicar, St Martin's Episcopal Church, 79-80; La Iglesia de San Jose, 90. **SELECTED PUBLICATIONS** Auth, The Nature of Salvation: Theological Consensus in the Episcopal Church, 1801-1873, Univ Ill Press, 97; A Proposal for the Renovation of the VTS chapel, Va Sem Jour 38, 96; Handbook of Anglican Theologians, McGrath, 98; co-auth, Historical Background to the Current Seminary Policy on Sexual Behavior, Va Sem Jour 38, 96; bk rev(s), Va Sem Jour, 93, 95, 97; Anglican Theol Rev, 97, 98; Sewanee Theol Rev, 96; Anglican and Episcopal History, 92, 95 **CONTACT ADDRESS** Va Theol Sem, 3737 Seminary Rd, Alexandria, VA, 22304. **EMAIL** RPrichard@vts.edu

PRIEBE, DUANE A.
PERSONAL Born 06/29/1934, Rhinelander, WI, m, 1960, 2 children **DISCIPLINE** THEOLOGY **EDUCATION** Univ Washington, BSc, 56; Luther Sem, BD, 61; Sch of Theol at Claremont, ThD, 65. **CAREER** Pastor, St. Paul Lutheran Church, Garrison ND, 65-67; dir, Great Plains Inst of Theol, 66-70; instr, 63-64, prof, 70- , dean, 83- , Wartburg Sem. **MEMBERSHIPS** Soc of Bibl Lit. **RESEARCH** Theology and Biblical theology; Hermeneutics; the systematic power of simple structures of thought; Christian faith and relitious pluralism. **CONTACT ADDRESS** Wartburg Theological Sem, 333 Wartburg Plz, Dubuque, IA, 52003. **EMAIL** dapriebe@mwci.net

PRIMACK, MAXWELL
PERSONAL Born 06/04/1934, Brooklyn, NY, m, 1955, 4 children **DISCIPLINE** PHILOSOPHY; INTELLECTUAL HISTORY **EDUCATION** Brandeis Univ, BA, 56; John Hopkins Univ, PhD, 62. **CAREER** Erie Community Col, 26 years; Univ Buffalo (SUNYAB); Lincoln Univ in Pennsylvania; Illinois Inst Tech; Bloomsburg State College. **HONORS AND AWARDS** Cume Laude; Phi Betta Kappa **MEMBERSHIPS** Amer Phil Assoc. **RESEARCH** Marx; Lenin; The Bible **SELECTED PUBLICATIONS** Auth, A Reinterpretation of Francis Bacon's Philosophy, 68; The Last American Frontier: Education, 72. **CONTACT ADDRESS** 20 Marjann Ter., Buffalo, NY, 14223. **EMAIL** mprinted@aol.com

PRIMIANO, LEONARD NORMAN
DISCIPLINE RELIGIOUS STUDIES; FOLKLORE AND FOLKLIFE **EDUCATION** Harvard Univ, MTs; Univ Pennsylvania, PhD. **CAREER** Asst Prof, Religious Studies, 93-, Cabrini Col. **CONTACT ADDRESS** Dept of Relig, Cabrini Col, 610 King of Prussia Rd., Radnor, PA, 19087-3698. **EMAIL** primiano@cabrini.edu

PRINCE, ARTHUR
PERSONAL Born 08/30/1938, Memphis, TN, s **DISCIPLINE** PHILOSOPHY **EDUCATION** Univ of Memphis, BA, 64, MA, 70; Univ of Tenn, MS, 87; Univ of Okla, PhD, 96. **CAREER** Tchng Asst, Instr, 68-71, Univ of Memphis; Instr, 77-87, Univ of TN; Instr, 86-88, Maryville Univ; Instr, 89-91, Rhodes Col; Instr, 92-, Dyersburg St Univ, Instr, 97-, Mid-South Com Col; Adj Asst Prof, 98-, Christian Bros Univ. **HONORS AND AWARDS** Hon Sargent-At-Arms TN House of Repr; Colonel Aide de Camp Governors Staff; Community Leaders and Noteworthy Amer Awd; Personalities of Presidential Achievement Award (Ronald Reagan), The South Awd., Paper Accpt Tenth Interamerican Cong of Philos; Paper Accpt Twentieth World Cong of Philos. **MEMBERSHIPS** APA **RESEARCH** Philososphy, especially political and social philosophy, ethics. **SELECTED PUBLICATIONS** Art, Don't Forget Grace, 93; Thought Provoking, 93; Insult to Churchgoers, 93; Complacency's Results, 93; Olympics and China, 93; Let Ideas Flow, 93; Some are Overlooked, 93; Needed Conscience, 93; Believe It, 93; Coherent Education, 93; Words for Change, 93; Impersonal Teaching, 93; Unseen Scars, 94; Educators Salaries Seldom Reflect Value, 94; Midways Man, 94; Vietnams Purpose, 94; We Must Give Hope, 94; A Matter Of Freedom, 94; Know Their Minds, 94; His Best to Pepper, 95; A Deaf Ear, 95; Abusers Rampant, 95; Telling It Like It Is, 95; Third-Party Influence, 95; Overstepping Bounds, 95; Heroes Should Heed Dr. Kings Words on Violence, 95; Coach Saluted, 96; Where to Invest, 96; Right-Left Wrongs, 96; Giving Thanks, 96; Mockery of Justice, 96; Mind and Body, 96; Right Forum, 97; Cutbacks Not Worthy of A Great State, 97; Welcome Laughter, 97; Vietnam War Wasn't Pointless, 97; Building Character, 97; Games and Lessons, 97; Slamming Southerners, 98; View of Humanism, 98; School Matters, 98; Pub in The Commercial Appeal; The Philosophy of Rights of William Ernest Hocking, 96. **CONTACT ADDRESS** 1446 Snowden Ave, Memphis, TN, 38107.

PRINCE, JOHN R.
DISCIPLINE LEGAL WRITING AND APPELLATE ADVOCACY **EDUCATION** Okla Baptist Univ, BA, 79; Duke Univ Sch Law, JD, 83. **CAREER** Prof, Villanova Univ; clerked, Honorable Thomas N. O'Neill, Jr. US Dist Ct Eastern Dist Pa; past assoc, firms in Philadelphia; private pract in his own firm; taught at, Rutgers-Camden Sch Law & St Thomas Univ Sch Law. **MEMBERSHIPS** Amer, Philadelphia & Dela Co Bar Asn. **CONTACT ADDRESS** Law School, Villanova Univ, 800 Lancaster Ave, Villanova, PA, 19085-1692. **EMAIL** prince@law.vill.edu

PRITCHARD, MICHAEL
DISCIPLINE ETHICAL THEORY **EDUCATION** Univ Wis, PhD. **CAREER** Asst prof, WMich Univ. **RESEARCH** Professional ethics, philosophy for children. **SELECTED PUBLICATIONS** Ed, Responsible Communication: Ethical Issues in Business, Industry, and the Professions, Hampton Press; Co-ed, Profits and Professions; Practicing Engineering Ethics, Inst Electrical & Electronic Engineeres; Auth, On Becoming Responsible, Kans Univ Press; Reasonable Children, Univ Press of Kans; Coauth, Ethics in Engineering; Communication Ethics. **CONTACT ADDRESS** Kalamazoo, MI, 49008. **EMAIL** pritchard@wmich.edu

PRITZL, KURT
PERSONAL Milwaukee, WI **DISCIPLINE** PHILOSOPHY **EDUCATION** Marquette Univ, BA, 74; Univ Toronto, MA, 75, PhD, 82. **CAREER** Assoc prof, philos, Catholic Univ, 80- . **MEMBERSHIPS** APA; Am Catholic Philos Asn; Soc for Ancient Greek Philos; Metaphysical Soc of Am. **RESEARCH** Ancient philosophy; theory of knowledge. **SELECTED PUBLICATIONS** Auth, Ways of Truth and Ways of Opinion in Aristotle, The Importance of Truth: Proceedings of the American Catholic Philosophical Association, 93; auth, Opinions as Appearances: Endoxa in Aristotle, Ancient Philos, 94; auth, The Significance of Some Structural Features of Plato's Crito, in van Ophuijsen, Plato and Platonism, Washington DC, 98; auth, Being True in Aristotle's Thinking, Proceedings of the Boston Area Colloquium in Ancient Philosophy, forthcoming. **CONTACT ADDRESS** School of Philosophy, Catholic Univ of America, Washington, DC, 20064. **EMAIL** pritzl@cua.edu

PROCTER, HARVEY THORNTON, JR.
PERSONAL Born 12/29/1945, Monongahela, PA, d **DISCIPLINE** LAW **EDUCATION** Southern IL Univ, BA 1967; Roosevelt Univ, MA 1970; Wayne State Univ, JD 1976. **CAREER** Chicago Comm on Youth Welfare, asst zone dir 1966, dir special events 1967; FORD MOTOR COMPANY, HUMAN RES 1968-; UNIVERSITY OF MICHIGAN, SCHOOL OF BUSINESS, LEAD PROGRAM, LECTURER, 1986-; NATIONAL URBAN LEQGUE, BLACK EXECUTIVE EXCHANGE PROGRAM, VISITING PROFESSOR, 1988-. **HONORS AND AWARDS** Univ of IL Law Fellowship; IL General Assembly Scholarship; Vice President's Award - Youth Motivation, Vice President of the United States, 1970; Citation of Merit, City of Detroit Police Dept, 1990, 1991; Award of Merit, Jarvis Christian College, 1990, 1992. **MEMBERSHIPS** Mem Amer, MI State, Detroit Bar Assocs, Assoc of Trial Lawyers of Amer; mem Amer Mgmt Assoc; Society of Human Resource Management; Midwest Co-op Educ Assoc, Employer Management Assoc; life mem Alpha Phi Alpha Inc, NAACP; parish council St Thomas the Apostle Church; assy & comm chmn Midwest Coll Placement Assoc 1983-; pres bd of dirs Earhart Village Homes; pres, exec bd, Midwest College Placement Assoc 1988-; mem Business Advisory Council Univ of MI Comprehensive Studies Program 1989-; mem Business Advisory Council Clark-Atlanta University Center 1988-89; mem Business Advisory Council GMI Mgt Instit 1987-90; president, National Association of Colleges & Employers, 1997-; vp, employer relations, board of governors, College Placement Council, 1991-; task force mem, National Governor's Assn, 1990-. **CONTACT ADDRESS** Ford Motor Co, The American Rd, Rm 367, Dearborn, MI, 48121.

PROFFITT, ANABEL C.
PERSONAL Born 12/18/1956, Yonkers, NY, m, 1984, 1 child **DISCIPLINE** RELIGION **EDUCATION** Hood Col, BA, 79; Presbyterian Sch of Christ Ed, MA, 81; Princeton Theol Sem, PhD, 90. **CAREER** Vis Inst, Presbyterian Schl of Christ Ed, 86; Adj Prof, United Theol Sem, 92; Hon Sr Res Fel, Univ, Birmingham UK, 97; Dean, Assoc Prof, Lancaster Theol Sem, 89-. **MEMBERSHIPS** Assoc of Prof and Res in Relig Ed, Assoc for Supvr and Curric Dev, Intl Sem on Rel Ed and Values, Rel Ed Assoc **RESEARCH** The role of wonder in education and religion, teaching and learning, theological education. **SELECTED PUBLICATIONS** A Sense of Wonder, In Season, 95; Mystery Metaphor and Religious Education: The Challenge of Teaching in a Postmodern World, Salt Jour of the Rel and Moral Ed Coun, 95; Reclaiming Piety as a Goal of Religious Education, 95; Wonder as an Attitude, 96; Playing in the Presence of God: Wonder, Wisdom and Education, Intl Jour of Child Spirit, 98. **CONTACT ADDRESS** Lancaster Theol Sem, 555 W James St, Lancaster, PA, 17603. **EMAIL** aproffitt@lts.org

PROOPS, IAN
DISCIPLINE PHILOSOPHY **EDUCATION** Oxford Univ, BA, 89; Harvard Univ, PhD, 98. **CAREER** Asst prof, Univ Mich, 98-. **HONORS AND AWARDS** Rm. Martin Prize Fel, Harvard Univ, 96-97. **MEMBERSHIPS** Am Philos Asn. **RESEARCH** Philosophy of language; metaphysics; analytical philosophy; Wittgenstein; Kant. **SELECTED PUBLICATIONS**

Auth, The Early Wittgenstein on Logical Assertion, Philos Topics, Fall, 97. **CONTACT ADDRESS** Dept of Philosophy-2215 Angell Hall, 435 S State St., Ann Arbor, MI, 48109-1003. **EMAIL** iproops@umich.edu

PROSSER, PETER E.
PERSONAL Born 12/16/1946, Birmingham, England, m, 1970, 2 children **DISCIPLINE** CHURCH HISTORY **EDUCATION** Univ Montreal, MDiv, 75, MA, 78, PhD, 89. **CAREER** Lectr, Inst Biblione Beree, Montreal, 72-75; fel, Univ Montreal, 82-83; asst prof, Church Hist, Regent Univ, 83-90; prof, 98- . **HONORS AND AWARDS** Who's Who in Am, 79, 84, 90-92, 98; Int Men of Distinction, 79. **MEMBERSHIPS** AAR/SBL; SPS; ETS. **RESEARCH** Millennialism; Reformation; apocalypticism; Methodist history. **SELECTED PUBLICATIONS** Auth, Prophecy: A Vital Gift to the Church, Including Yours, Acts 29 Mag, 92; Spirit-Filled Life Bible, Sections on 1 and 2 John, Thomas Nelson publ. **CONTACT ADDRESS** School of Divinity, Regent Univ, 1000 Regent Dr, Virginia Beach, VA, 23464-9800. **EMAIL** petepro@regent.edu

PROSTERMAN, ROY L.
PERSONAL Chicago, Ill **DISCIPLINE** LAW **EDUCATION** Univ Chicago, AB, 54; Harvard Univ, LLB, 58. **CAREER** Assoc, Sullivan & Cromwell, 59-65; from asst prof to assoc prof law, 65-70, Prof Law, Univ Wash, 70-, Mem bd dirs, World Without War Coun, US, 71-; consult, Stanford Res Inst, 67; adv, Ctr War/Peace Studies, 67- **HONORS AND AWARDS** Ralph Bunche Award, Seattle-King County Bar Asn, 73. **RESEARCH** Land tenure reform; lethal violence; international legal order. **SELECTED PUBLICATIONS** Auth, Land-to-the-tiller in South Vietnam: The tables turn, Asian Survey, 8/70; Land reform as foreign aid, Foreign Policy, spring 72; Land reform in Vietnam, In: Focus Southeast Asia, Praeger, 72; Surviving to 3000, Duxbury, 72; IRI: A Simplified Predictive Index of Rural Instability, Comp Polit, 4/76; Land Reform and the El Salvador Crisis, Int Security, summer 81; Land Reform in El Salvador: The Democratic Alternative, World Affairs, summer 81; contribr, Freedom in the World, Freedom House, 82. **CONTACT ADDRESS** Sch of Law, Univ of Wash, Seattle, WA, 98195. **EMAIL** laura.purdy@utoronto.ca

PROUDFOOT, WAYNE
DISCIPLINE RELIGION **EDUCATION** Yale Univ, BS, 61; Harvard Univ, PhD, 66. **CAREER** Prof. **HONORS AND AWARDS** Am Acad Relig Awd, 86. **SELECTED PUBLICATIONS** Auth, God and Self, Bucknell, 76; Religious Experience, Berkeley, 85. **CONTACT ADDRESS** Dept of Religion, Columbia Col, New York, 2960 Broadway, New York, NY, 10027-6902. **EMAIL** wlp2@columbia.edu

PRUETT, GORDON EARL
PERSONAL Born 10/16/1941, Raton, NM, m, 1966, 1 child **DISCIPLINE** HISTORY OF RELIGION **EDUCATION** Yale Univ, BA, 63; Oxford Univ, BA & MA, 65; Princeton Univ, PhD, 68. **CAREER** Asst prof relig, Lehigh Univ, 68-69; asst prof, 69-74; acting chmn dept eng, 76-80; assoc prof philos & relig, Northeastern Univ, 74- . **RESEARCH** History of Christianity; Sociology of religion; Mysticism and psychoanalysis. **SELECTED PUBLICATIONS** Auth, A note on Robert Bellah's theory of religious evolution: The early modern period, Sociol Analysis, 73; History, transcendence, and world community in the work of Wilfred Cantwell Smith, Jour Am Acad Relig, 73; Christianity, history and culture in Nagaland, Contribs to Indian Sociol, 74; A Protestant doctrine of the Eucharistic presence, Calvin Theol Jour, 75; Thomas Cranmer's progress in the doctrine of the Eucharist, 1535-1548, Hist Mag Protestant Episcopal Church, 76; Will and freedom: Psychoanalytic themes in the work of Jacob Boehme, Studies Relig & Sci Relig, 77; Religion in higher education, Int Encycl Higher Educ, 78; The escape from the Seraglio: Anti-orientalist trends in modern religious studies, Arab Studies Quart, 80; Preparatio Evangelii: Religious Studies and Secondary Education, Nat Asn of Episcopal Schools Jour 1:1, 84; Islam and Orientalism, Orientalism, Islamists and Islam, ed Asaf Hussain, Robert Olson, and Jamil Qureshi, Amana, 84; Through a Glass Darkly: Knowledge of the Self in Dreams in Ibn Khaldun's Mugaddima, The Muslim World LXXV:1, 85; The Meaning and End of Suffering for Freud and the Buddhist Tradition, 87; World Theology and World Community: The Vision of Wilfred Cantwell Smith, Studies in Religion 19:4, 1990; Theravadin Buddhist Commentary on the Current State of Western Epistemology, Buddhist-Christian Studies 10, 1990; As a Father Loves His Children: The Image of the Supreme Being as Loving Father in Judaism, Christianity and Islam, 94. **CONTACT ADDRESS** Dept of Philosophy and Religion, Northeastern Univ, 360 Huntington Ave, Boston, MA, 02115-5000.

PRUST, RICHARD CHARLES
PERSONAL Born 04/21/1939, Milwaukee, WI **DISCIPLINE** PHILOSOPHY; RELIGION **EDUCATION** Univ Wis, BA, 61; Yale Univ, BD, 64; Duke Univ, PhD, 70. **CAREER** Assoc prof Philos, St Andrews Presby Col, 67-. **HONORS AND AWARDS** Sears Award for Excellence in Tchg, 91. **MEMBERSHIPS** Am Acad Relig; Am Philos Asn; N.C. Philos Soc; Am Assoc of Univ. Profs; Intl. Personalist Assoc. **SELECTED PUBLICATIONS** Auth, Was Calvin a Biblical literalist, Scottish J Theol, 9/67; The self as saved, Personalist, 7/78; Personal Integrity and Moral Value, The Personalist Forum, 12/96; When She Comes into a Room: Reflections on Wholeness and Personal Presence, Soundings, 80/97; Soul Talk and Bowne's Ontology of Personhood, The Personalist Forum, 13/97. **CONTACT ADDRESS** 1700 Dogwood Mile, Laurinburg, NC, 28352-5521. **EMAIL** rcp@tartan,sapc.edu

PUCKETT, PAULINE N.
PERSONAL Born 03/18/1928, Dayton, OH, s **DISCIPLINE** PASTORAL SUPERVISION **EDUCATION** United Theological Sem, D.Min, 95; United Theological Sem, MARE, 85; Wright St Univ, Med, 74; Miami Univ of Ohio, BS Ed, 66. **CAREER** Air Force, Logistics Command, Wright-Patterson AFB, 33 years. **MEMBERSHIPS** Amer Bus Women's Assoc; League of Women Voters; Church Women United. **CONTACT ADDRESS** Dept of The Air Force, Wright Patterson AFB, 5838 Troy Villa Blvd, Huber Heights, OH, 45424-2650.

PUE, WESLEY W.
DISCIPLINE LAW **EDUCATION** Oxford Univ, BA, 77; BA, 79; Univ Alberta, LLM, 80; Osgoode, JD, 89. **CAREER** Prof, 93-. **HONORS AND AWARDS** Pres, Can Law Soc Asn. **MEMBERSHIPS** Pres, Can Law Soc Asn. **RESEARCH** Legal pluralism; cultural history approaches to the history of law. **SELECTED PUBLICATIONS** Auth, pubs about English and Canadian legal history, history of the legal profession, administrative law, law and geography and law and society. **CONTACT ADDRESS** Fac of Law, Univ British Columbia, 1822 East Mall, Vancouver, BC, V6T 1Z1. **EMAIL** pue@law.ubc.ca

PUGSLEY, ROBERT ADRIAN
PERSONAL Born 12/27/1946, Mineola, NY, m, 1978 **DISCIPLINE** LAW **EDUCATION** State Univ NY, Stony Brook, BA, 68; NY Univ, JD, 75, LLM, 77. **CAREER** Coordr, Peace Educ Prog, The Christophers, 71-78; assoc prof, 78-81, PROF LAW, SCH OF LAW, SOUTHWESTERN UNIV, 81-; Lectr sociol, New Sch Social Res, 71; res asst, Crime Deterrence & Offender Career Proj, 74; adj asst prof criminal justice, Southhampton Col, Long Island Univ, 75-76; mem exec comt, Non-Govt Orgn, Off Pub Info, UN, 75; Robert Marshall fel civil liberties, Criminal Law Educ & Res Ctr, Sch Law, NY Univ, 76-78 & actg dep dir, 77-78; producer, Inside LA, KPFK, Los Angeles, 79-; mem bd adv, Ctr Legal Educ, City Col, City Univ New York, 78-. **MEMBERSHIPS** Am Legal Studies Asn; Am Soc Polit St Legal Philos; Inst Study Bioethics & Life Sci; Am Soc Criminol. **RESEARCH** The rationales for and practice of criminal punishment and sentencing; moral, constitutional, and practical questions raised by capital punishment; the education, organization, and discipline of the legal profession. **SELECTED PUBLICATIONS** Auth, Kill for peace?, Cath Worker, 3-4/71; Embattled prelate: Review of Cardinal Mindszenty's memoirs, New Leader, 3/3/75; Capital punishment: Bringing back death, Commonweal, 8/13/76; Reflections on January 17, 1977, Christianity & Crisis, 2/7/77; coauth, Peace--Justice Curriculum Unit for Grade 12, Arcdiocese of NY, 78; auth, Retributivism: A just basis for criminal sentences, 7:379-405 & A retributivist argument against capital punishment, 9: 1501-1523, Hofstra Law Rev; coauth, Current leading issues in criminal law: A panel, Southwestern Univ Law Rev, 12:431-448. **CONTACT ADDRESS** Sch of Law, Southwestern Univ, 675 S Westmoreland Ave, Los Angeles, CA, 90005-3905. **EMAIL** rpugsley@swlaw.edu

PULCINI, THEODORE
PERSONAL Born 05/11/1954, Sewickley, PA **DISCIPLINE** RELIGIOUS STUDIES **EDUCATION** Harvard Coll, BA, 76; Univ Notre Dame, MA, 79; Harvard Divinity School, ThM, 82; Cath Univ Am, DMin, 85; Univ Pittsburgh, PhD, 94. **CAREER** Tchg asst, Univ Notre Dame, 78; Jr Tutorial Instr, Harvard Univ, 82; tchg fel, Univ Pittsburgh, 92-94; instr, Chatham Coll, 93-94; vis prof, St Vladimir's Orthodox Theol Sem NY, 94-95; asst prof, Dickinson Coll Carlisle PA, 95-. **MEMBERSHIPS** Am Acad of Rel; Soc of Bibl Lit; Middle East Studies Asn. **RESEARCH** Eastern Orthodoxy; Islam; Interreligious Dialogue; Religious Polemic. **SELECTED PUBLICATIONS** Auth, Orthodoxy and Catholicism: What Are the Differences?, 95; Appreciating Islam, New Theol Rev, 96; Eastern Orthodox-Oriental Orthodox relations: Practical Steps Toward Unity, St Nerses Theol Rev, 96; Of Flesh and Faith: Abraham as a Principle of Inclusion and Exclusion in Christian Thought, Abrahamic Faith, Ethnicity, and Ethics Conflicts, 97; Reasserting Boundaries: Another View of 'Ecumenical Jihad', in Reclaiming the Great Tradition: Evangelicals, Catholics, and Orthodox in Dialogue; Exergesis as Polemic Discourse: Ibn Hazm on Jewish and Christian Scriptures, 98; Cultivating Christian Anger: A Warning from the Fifth Century, Touchstone, 98. **CONTACT ADDRESS** Dept of Religion, Dickinson Col, Box 1773, Carlisle, PA, 17013. **EMAIL** pulcini@dickinson.edu

PULIGANDLA, RAMAKRISHNA
PERSONAL Born 09/08/1930, Nellore, India, m, 1949, 5 children **DISCIPLINE** PHILOSOPHY **EDUCATION** Rice Univ, PhD, 66. **CAREER** Prof, Univ of Toledo,Ohio, 70-. **HONORS AND AWARDS** Fulbright Lecturing Fel, 92 (India), 97 (Russia). **MEMBERSHIPS** APA; Soc for Asian and Comparative Philo **RESEARCH** Logic; phil of science; comprehensive philo and religion. **SELECTED PUBLICATIONS** Coed, Buddhism and th Emerging World Civilization: Essays in Honor of Nolan Pliny Jacobson, 96; Fundamentals of Indian Philosophy, 97; Jnana-Yoga (The Way of Knowledge): An Analytical Interpretation, 97; Reality and Mysticism: Perspectives in the Upanishads, 97. **CONTACT ADDRESS** 4138 Beverly Dr, Toledo, OH, 43614. **EMAIL** Rpuliga@aol.com

PURTILL, RICHARD L.
PERSONAL Born 03/12/1931, Chicago, IL, m, 1959, 3 children **DISCIPLINE** PHILOSOPHY **EDUCATION** Univ Chicago, BA, 58, MA, 60, PhD(philos), 65. **CAREER** Assoc prof, 62-72, actg chmn dept, 70-71, Prof Philos, Western Wash Univ, 72-96, Prof Emeritus, 96-; Vis lectr philos, San Francisco State Col, 68-69. **HONORS AND AWARDS** Western Wash Univ res off res grants. **MEMBERSHIPS** Am Philos Asn. **RESEARCH** Logic, metaphysics, ethics and aesthetics; Modal logic; arguments for God's existence. **SELECTED PUBLICATIONS** Auth, Logic for Philosophers, 71 & Logical Thinking, 72, Harper; Lord of the Elves and Eldils, Zondervan, 74; Reason to Believe, Eerdmans, 74; Philosophically Speaking, 75, Thinking About Ethics, 76 & Thinking About Religion, 78, Prentice Hall; Logic: Argument, Refutation and Proof, Harper, 79; C.S. Lewis' Case for the Christian Faith, Harper, 81; A Logical Introduction to Philosophy, Prentice Hall, 88; author of 6 novels, 8 short stories, and over 30 journal articles. **CONTACT ADDRESS** 1708 Douglas Ave, Bellingham, WA, 98225-6709. **EMAIL** purtill@cc.wwu.edu

PUTNAM, HILARY
PERSONAL Born 07/31/1926, Chicago, IL, m, 1962, 4 children **DISCIPLINE** PHILOSOPHY **EDUCATION** Univ Pa, AB, 48; Univ Calif, Los Angeles, PhD, 51. **CAREER** Rockefeller fel, 51-52; instr philos, Northwestern Univ, 52-53; from asst prof to assoc prof, 53-61, Princeton Univ; prof, Mass Inst Technol, 61-65; prof philos, 65-, Walter Beverly Pearson Prof mod math & math logic, 76, Harvard Univ; Nat Sci Found fel, Minn Ctr Philos Sci, 57; Guggenheim fel, 60-61; Nat Sci Found fel, 68-69; NEH fel, 75-76; John Locke lectr, Oxford Univ, 76; Cogan Univ Prof, 95. **HONORS AND AWARDS** Fel Acad Arts & Sciences; Fel of Brit Acad. **MEMBERSHIPS** Am Math Soc; Am Philos Assn; Assn Symbolic Logic; Philos Sci Assn. **RESEARCH** Mathematical logic. **SELECTED PUBLICATIONS** Auth, Renewing Philosophy, Harvard University, 92; auth, Pragmatism, Blackwell, 94; auth, Words and Life, Harvard University, 94. **CONTACT ADDRESS** Dept of Philosophy, Harvard Univ, Emerson Hall, Cambridge, MA, 02138-3800. **EMAIL** hputnam@fas.harvard.edu

PUTNEY, DAVID P.
DISCIPLINE ASIAN PHILOSOPHY AND RELIGION **EDUCATION** Univ Hawaii, PhD, 90. **CAREER** Philos, Old Dominion Univ. **SELECTED PUBLICATIONS** Area; Buddhist philosophy. **CONTACT ADDRESS** Old Dominion Univ, 4100 Powhatan Ave, Norfolk, VA, 23058. **EMAIL** DPutney@odu.edu

PYLES, JOHN E.
PERSONAL Born 01/11/1927, Memphis, TN, m **DISCIPLINE** LAW **EDUCATION** BCL 1951; JD 1968. **CAREER** Office of John E Pyles, Attorney 1968-; municipal judge 1979-81. **MEMBERSHIPS** Mem Wichita Bar Assn; Sedgwick County Bar Assn; Wichita Bd of Realtors 1960-; Multilist Serv of Wichita 1967-; MS Trial Lawyer Assn 1967-. **CONTACT ADDRESS** 2703 E 13th, Wichita, KS, 67214.

Q

QUANDER, ROHULAMIN
PERSONAL Born 12/04/1943, Washington, DC, m **DISCIPLINE** LAW **EDUCATION** Howard Univ, BA 1966, JD 1969. **CAREER** Neighborhood Legal Serv, 1969-71; Geo Wash Univ, 1970-72; Intl Investors, Inc, market cons, Attorney, state dir 1973-; private practice 1975-; Office of Adjudication DC Govt 1986-; geneological hist and researcher for private groups; DC Dept of Consumer & Regulatory Affairs, administrative law, 1986-. **HONORS AND AWARDS** Man of Yr Award Omega Psi Phi Frat 1965 & 1968; Spl Award Howard Univ Outstdg Serv to Law Sch, the Community and the Univ 1969; Dean's List Howard Univ 1964, 1965, 1968; Travel Fellowship to 13 foreign countries 1964; Outstanding Service Award, Quanders United, Inc, 1991; author, The History of the Quander Family, 1984; have published numerous articles for Howard Univ Alumni newspaper. **MEMBERSHIPS** Mem Superior Ct of DC 1975; US dist Ct of DC 1976; mem Amer Bar Assn; Natl Bar Assn; DC Bar Assn; Bar of Supreme Ct of PA; US Dist Ct for Eastern PA; Ct of Appeals DC; Phi Alpha Delta Law Frat 1967; Phi Alpha Theta His Soc; founder Howard Univ Chap of Black Amer Law Students Assn 1968; mem Omega Psi Phi Frat 1964-; pres Student Bar Assn 1968-69, vice pres 1967-68; mem bd of dir The Wash DC Parent & Child Center 1977-81; chief archivist Quander Family History 1977-; reg chmn Howard Univ Alumni 1979-87; chmn Educ Inst Licensure

Commn of DC 1979-; bd dir Wash Urban League 1969-70; pres Howard Univ Alumni Club for Wash DC 1970-71; guest lecturer on the geneology hist & contributions of the Quander Family (America's oldest documntd black fam); member, MLK Holiday Commission for DC, 1987-89;s Quanders United, Inc 1983-; mem of, Columbia Hist Soc, Int'l Platform Speakers Assoc 1985-, Republican Party of DC; bd of dir Pigskin Club 1986-; pres, founder, Quanders Historical Society, Inc, 1985-; co-chair, founder, Benjamin Banneker Memorial Comm, Inc, 1991; dir and vp, Torruella-Quander Gallery, Ltd, 1988-; founder and pres, IliRoFa International, Inc, 1991-. **CONTACT ADDRESS** 1703 Lawrence St NE, Washington, DC, 20018.

QUEEN, EVELYN E. CRAWFORD
PERSONAL Born 04/06/1945, Albany, NY, m, 1971 **DISCIPLINE** LAW **EDUCATION** Howard University, BS, 1963-68, JD, 1972-75. **CAREER** National Institute of Health, support staff, 1968-75; Metropolitan Life Insurance Co, attorney, 1975-77; United States Department of Commerce, Maritime Adm, attorney-advisor, 1977-79; United States Attorneys Office, assistant United States attorney, 1979-81; DC Superior Court, commissioner, 1981-86; judge, 1986-; DC School of Law, adjunct professor, 1991-92. **HONORS AND AWARDS** Hudson Valley Girl Scout, Trefoil Award, 1988; Director of Distinguished Americans, Achievement in Law, 1985; Personalities of America, Contributions to Government and Justice, 1986; Department of Justice, Special Achievement Award, 1981; Department of HEW, Special Achievement Award, 1975. **MEMBERSHIPS** ABA, 1975-; NBA, 1975-. **CONTACT ADDRESS** Judge, DC Superior Court, 500 Indiana Ave NW, H Carl Moultne I Courthouse, Ste 1510, Washington, DC, 20001.

QUERE, RALPH WALTER
PERSONAL Born 09/26/1935, Cleveland, OH, m, 1957, 3 children **DISCIPLINE** HISTORY OF CHRISTIAN THOUGHT **EDUCATION** Princeton Univ, AB, 57; Trinity Sem, Columbus Ohio, BD, 64; Princeton Theol Sem,, 70. **CAREER** From instr to assoc prof, 69-84, Prof Hist & Theol, Wartburg Theol Sem, 84-. **MEMBERSHIPS** Am Soc Reformation Res; Am Soc Church Hist; Acad Evangel Theol Educ; Sixteenth Century Cong; Concordia Acad. **RESEARCH** Melanchthon's eucharistic thought; history of Christological thought; history of worship. **SELECTED PUBLICATIONS** Auth, Confrontation at Marburg, Harvard Case Study Inst, 73; Superstar and Godspell, Dialogue, summer 73; Evangelical Witness, Augsburg, 75; The spirit and the gifts are ours..., ordination rites, Lutheran Quart, 11/75; Melanchthonian motifs in the formula, in Dialogue, Discord and Concord, Fortress, 77; Melanchthon's Christum Cognoscere, DeGraaf, 77; Christ's efficacious presence in The Lord's Supper, Lutheran Quart, 2/77. **CONTACT ADDRESS** Wartburg Theol Sem, 333 Wartburg Pl, Dubuque, IA, 52004-5004. **EMAIL** quere@mwci.com

QUICK, ALBERT T.
DISCIPLINE LAW **EDUCATION** Univ Ariz, BA; Central Mich Univ, MA; Wayne State Univ, JD; Tulane Univ, LLM. **SELECTED PUBLICATIONS** Auth, 'Against the Framers' Intent: The Court's Fourth Amendment Jurisprudence, 91; co-auth, Federal Rules of Criminal Procedure, New York, Clark Boardman Callaghan, 94; Retention of Minority Professors: Dealing with the Failure to Presume Competence, 91. **CONTACT ADDRESS** Col Law, Univ of Toledo, Toledo, OH, 43606. **EMAIL** aquick@uoft02.utoledo.edu

QUIGLEY, TIM
DISCIPLINE LAW **EDUCATION** Univ Saskatchewan, BS, 70, LLB, 74, LLM, 86. **CAREER** Prof, 85- **HONORS AND AWARDS** Ed, Can Criminal Law Rev. **MEMBERSHIPS** Law Soc Saskatchewan. **SELECTED PUBLICATIONS** Auth, Some Issues in Sentencing of Aboriginal Offenders, 94; Battered Women and the Defence of Provocation, 91; Reform of the Intoxication Defence, 87; Specific and General Nonsense, 87; Procedure in Canadian Criminal Law, Carswell, 97. **CONTACT ADDRESS** Col of Law, Univ Saskatchewan, 15 Campus Dr, Saskatoon, SK, S7N 5A6. **EMAIL** Quigley@law.usask.ca

QUIGLEY, TIMOTHY R.
DISCIPLINE PHILOSOPHY; PAINTING **EDUCATION** Univ of Wisconsin-Madison, BS ART, 80, MFA ART, 83, MA Philosophy, 84; PhD Philsophy, 91. **CAREER** Instr, 80-83, Univ of Wisconsin-Extension; lectr, 83-84, teaching asst, 84-86, Univ of Wisconsin-Madison; adjunct instr, 87-88, Kenyon Col; vis asst prof, 88-91, Oakland Univ; special instr, 88-91, instr, 91-95, Wayne State Univ; instr, 91-95, College of Art and Design; adjunct asst prof, 96-98, New York Univ; instr, 95-98, School of Visual Arts; core faculty, 95- , acting academic coordinator, 98- , New School for Social Research. **HONORS AND AWARDS** Univ of Wisconsin Graduate Sch Research Grant, 81; European Foreign Travel Fel, Univ of Wisconsin Graduate Sch, 86; Mellon Found Grant, The Postmodern Perspective, 88, Kenyon Col. **MEMBERSHIPS** Amer Philosophical Assn; College Art Assn of Amer; Radical Philosophy Assn. **SELECTED PUBLICATIONS** Auth, The Ethical and the Narrative Self, Philosophy Today, 94; auth, Shooting at the Father's Corpse: The Feminist Art Historian as Producer, Journal of Aesthetics and Art Criticism, fall 94; auth, Review of Alain Finkielkraut, The Defeat of the Mind, Canadian Philosophical Reviews, 95. **CONTACT ADDRESS** 25 E 10th St, #11B, New York, NY, 10003. **EMAIL** quigleyt@newschool.edu

QUILLIAN, WILLIAM F.
PERSONAL Born 04/13/1913, Nashville, TN, m, 1940, 4 children **DISCIPLINE** PHILOSOPHY **EDUCATION** Emory Univ, AB, 35; Yale Univ, BD, 38, PhD, 43. **CAREER** Asst Prof, 41-45, Gettysburg Col; Prof, 45-52, Ohio Wesleyan Univ; Pres, 52-78, Randolph-Macon Womans Col. **HONORS AND AWARDS** LLD Ohio-Wesleyan Univ, 52; Hampden-Sydney Col, 78; Randolph-Macon Col, 67; LTTD Emory Univ, 59; LHD Randolph-Macon Womans Col. **MEMBERSHIPS** APA; Amer Acad of Religion **RESEARCH** The nature of moral obligation; what and where is God. **SELECTED PUBLICATIONS** The Moral Theory of Evolution Naturalism, Yale Univ Press, 45; Evolution and Moral Theory in America, Evolutionary Thought in America, Yale Univ Press, 50. **CONTACT ADDRESS** Pres, 1407 Club Dr, Lynchburg, VA, 24503.

QUINN, JOHN F.
DISCIPLINE BUSINESS ETHICS, PHILOSOPHY OF LAW, MEDIEVAL PHILOSOPHY **EDUCATION** Univ Dayton, JD, 82. **CAREER** Dept Philos, Univ Dayton **SELECTED PUBLICATIONS** Co-auth, Indonesian Deforestation: A Policy Framework for Sustainable Development, Jour of Asian Bus, 94; Development in the Underdeveloped World: A New Challenge for Business Ethics, Who's Business Values?: Some Asian and Cross-Cultural Perspectives, Hong Kong UP, 95; Anthropocentric Modernism and the Search for a Universal Environmental Philosophy, Dialogue and Universalism, 95. **CONTACT ADDRESS** Dept of Philos, Univ Dayton, 300 Col Park, Dayton, OH, 75062. **EMAIL** quinn@checkov.hm.udayton.edu

QUINN, PHILIP L.
DISCIPLINE PHILOSOPHY OF SCIENCE **EDUCATION** Georgetown Univ, AB, 62; Univ Del, MS, 66; Univ Pittsburgh, PhD, 69. **CAREER** Prof. **RESEARCH** Philosophy of space and time; issues in ethics and science. **SELECTED PUBLICATIONS** Auth, Creation, Conservation and the Big Bang, 93; Moral Objections to Pascalian Wagering, 94; Religious Pluralism and Religious Relativism, 95; Political Liberalisms and Their Exclusions of the Religious, 95; The Divine Command Ethics in Kierkegaard's Works of Love, 96; Relativism About Torture: Religious and Secular Responses, 96; Tiny Selves: Chisholm on the Simplicity of the Soul, 97; Augustinian Learning, 98. **CONTACT ADDRESS** History and Philosophy of Science Dept, Univ of Notre Dame, Notre Dame, IN, 46556.

QUINN, THOMAS MICHAEL
PERSONAL Born 08/05/1924, New York, NY, m, 1972, 2 children **DISCIPLINE** LAW **EDUCATION** Holy Cross Col, AB, 47; Harvard Univ, LLB, 50 & LLM, 56; Bellarmine Col, PhL, 55; Woodstock Col, STL, 62. **CAREER** Assoc prof, 63-66, asst prof, 66-70, PROF LAW, LAW SCH, FORDHAM UNIV, 70-; Lectr, Practising Law Inst, 64-70; auth, Uniform commercial code law letter, monthly, 67- & auth, coauth & ed, The banker's letter of the law, monthly, 75-80; chmn, Community Serv Comt, Asn Am Law Sch, 69-70 & Paralegal Comt, 73-75; dir, NY City Legal Serv Corp, 68-70 & chmn of bd, 70-71. **RESEARCH** Commercial law; banking law; consumer law. **SELECTED PUBLICATIONS** Coauth, Modern Banking Forms, 2 vols, 70 & Uniform Commercial Code Commentary & Law Digest, 1 vol supplemented 2 times per yr, 78, Warren, Gorham & Lamont. **CONTACT ADDRESS** Law Sch, Fordham Univ, 140 W 62nd St, New York, NY, 10023-7407.

QUIRK, WILLIAM J.
DISCIPLINE LEGAL RESEARCH **EDUCATION** Princeton Univ, AB, 56; Univ VA, LLB, 59. **CAREER** Prof, Univ of SC. **SELECTED PUBLICATIONS** Publ on, tax and financial policy. **CONTACT ADDRESS** School of Law, Univ of S. Carolina, Law Center, Columbia, SC, 29208. **EMAIL** law0159@univscvm.csd.scarolina.edu

QUITSLUND, SONYA ANTOINETTE
PERSONAL Born 03/08/1935, Portland, OR **DISCIPLINE** RELIGION **EDUCATION** Seattle Univ, BA, 58; Cath Univ Am, MA, 64, PhD(relig), 67. **CAREER** From grad asst to instr relig, Cath Univ Am, 64-67; Asst Prof Relig, George Washington Univ, 67-, Mem nat bd, Col Theol Soc, 77-79; mem subcomt discriminatory lang, Inst Comn English in Liturgy 77-8-. **MEMBERSHIPS** Am Acad Relig; Cath Bibl Asn; Col Theol Soc; AAUP. **RESEARCH** Modern Roman Catholicism, especially Lambert Beauduin; Bible and religious thought; woman in Western religious tradition. **SELECTED PUBLICATIONS** Auth, The Women's Bible Commentary , Theological Studies, Vol 54, 93; The Annual-Rev Of Women In World Religions, Vol 2--Heroic Women, J Of Ecumenical Studies, Vol 31, 94; Mary Magdalene And Many Others--Women Who Followed Jesus, Theological Studies, Vol 56, 95; Lev Gillet--A Monk Of The Eastern Church--A Free Universalist, Evangelical And Mystical Believer, J Of Ecumenical Studies, Vol 33, 96; Church In The Round--Feminist Interpretation Of The Church, J Of Ecumenical Studies, Vol 31, 94; An Anthology Of Sacred Texts By And About Women, J Of Ecumenical Studies, Vol 31, 94. **CONTACT ADDRESS** Dept of Relig, George Washington Univ, Washington, DC, 20052.

R

RAABE, PAUL R.
PERSONAL Born 04/09/1953, Fairview, KS, m, 1996 **DISCIPLINE** EXEGETICAL THEOLOGY **EDUCATION** Concordia Tchrs Col, BS, 75; Concordia Sem, MDiv, 79; Washington Univ, MA, 79; Univ Michigan, PhD, 89. **CAREER** Instr, Concordia Col, 79-83; from asst prof to assoc prof, 83-97, prof exegetical theol, 97- , chemn dept, 98- , Concordia Sem. **MEMBERSHIPS** Am Schs of Oriental Res; Bibl Archeol Soc; Soc of Bibl Lit; Cath Bibl Asn. **RESEARCH** Prophecy; Psalms; eschatology; Old Testament theology. **SELECTED PUBLICATIONS** Auth, Psalm Structure: A Study of Psalms with Refrains, Sheffield Academic, 90; auth, Obadiah, Doubleday, 96. **CONTACT ADDRESS** Concordia Sem, 801 DeMun Ave, St. Louis, MO, 63105. **EMAIL** raabep@csl.edu

RABIN, ROBERT LEONARD
PERSONAL Born 08/09/1939, Chicago, IL, m, 1966, 3 children **DISCIPLINE** LAW, SOCIAL SCIENCE **EDUCATION** Northwestern Univ, BS, 60, JD, 63, PhD (polit sci), 67. **CAREER** Asst prof law, Univ Wis-Madison, 66-69; assoc prof, 70-73, Prof Law, Stanford Univ, 73-, Consult, Div Resources & Environ, Ford Found & Admin Conf of US, 70- **RESEARCH** Empirical research on the administrative process. **SELECTED PUBLICATIONS** Auth, Do You Believe In A Supreme Being--The Administration Of The Conscientious Objector Exemption, 67 & Some Thoughts On Tort Law From A Sociopolitical Perspective, 69, Wis Law Rev; Implementation Of The Cost Of Living Adjustment For AFDC Recipients: A Case Study In Welfare Administration, Univ Pa Law Rev, 70; Agency Criminal Referrals In The Federal System: An Empirical Study Of Prosecutorial Discretion, 72 & Lawyers For Social Change: Perspectives On Public Interest Law, 76, Stanford Law Rev; Job Security And Due Process: Monitoring Administrative Discretion Through A Reasons Requirements, Univ Chicago Law Rev, 76; Perspectives On Tort Law, Little Brown, 76; Administrative Law In Transition: A Discipline In Search Of An Organizing Principle, Northwestern Law Rev, 77; The Idea Of Private Law, Yale Law J, Vol 105, 96. **CONTACT ADDRESS** Sch of Law, Stanford Univ, Stanford, CA, 94305-1926.

RABINOWITZ, MAYER E.
DISCIPLINE TALMUHD AND RABBINICS **EDUCATION** Yeshiva Univ, BA, BHL, MA; Jewish Theol Sem Am, MHL, PhD. **CAREER** Libn, assoc prof, assoc dean grad schl, dir Saul Lieberman Inst Talmudic Res, 93-97, Jewish Theol Sem. **HONORS AND AWARDS** Nat Def Foreign Lang Fel; grant, Mem Found; fel, Herbert Lehman Inst Talmudic Ethics., Chmn, Joint Bet Din Conser Mvmt; secy and res consult, Comm Jewish Law and Stds Rabbinical Assembly. **MEMBERSHIPS** Comm Jewish Law and Stds Rabbinical Assembly. **SELECTED PUBLICATIONS** Auth, On the Ordination of Women--An Advocate's Halakhic Response, Judaism Mag, 84; critical editions of medieval halakhic works and articles in Conservative Judaism, Reconstructionist Magazine, Sinai; responsa, Comm on Jewish Law and Stds, Proceedings Comm Jewish Law and Stds, 80-85; ed/transl, Jewish Law in the State of Israel, Proceedings Rabbinical Assembly, 74. **CONTACT ADDRESS** Jewish Theol Sem of America, 3080 Broadway, New York, NY, 10027. **EMAIL** marabinowitz@jtsa.edu

RABOUIN, E. MICHELLE
PERSONAL Born 11/07/1956, Denver, CO, d **DISCIPLINE** LAW **EDUCATION** University of Colorado, BS, 1977; University of Denver, MBA, 1984, JD, 1984. **CAREER** Coal Employment Project, assistant director, 1983-85; Colorado Office of Attorney General, assistant attorney general, 1986-89; Colorado Education Association, legal counsel, 1989-90; Community College of Denver, management chair, faculty, 1991-94; Texas Southern Univ, visiting prof of law, 1994-95; Washburn Univ School of Law, assoc prof of law, 1994-. **HONORS AND AWARDS** Colorado Energy Research Fellow, 1983; Colorado Black Women for Political Action, Community Service Award, 1981; University of Colorado, President's Academic Scholarship, 1974-77. **MEMBERSHIPS** Colorado Coalition of Mediators & Mediation Organization. 1990-; Colorado Bar Association, 1984-; Colorado Women's Bar Association, 1988- ;Colorado Chapter, National Association of Black Women Attorney, Founding Member, 1987-; American Civil Liberties Union, board member, 1991-92; Junior League of Denver, 1988-1991; Northeast Women's Center, board member, 1980-82; Colorado Black Women for Political Action, board member, editor, 1979-. **SELECTED PUBLICATIONS** Co-author with Anthony Leo, "1992 Tenth Circuit Court of Appeals Survey of Corporate and Commercial Law", Denver University Law Review, 1601; author, Valuing Diversity: Train the Trainer Manual, Mahogany Mountain Press, 1992; author, "The Legal Dimensions of Diversity: the Civil Rights Act of 1991, and the ADA," City of Boulder, Department of Social Services, 1992; lecturer, "Pro Bono: Enforceable Duty of Voluntary Obligation," "Intersection of Race and Poverty, Common Issues," Statewide Legal Services Conference, 1992. **CONTACT ADDRESS** Assoc Professor, Washburn Univ, School of Law, 1700 College, Topeka, KS, 66621.

RACHELS, JAMES
DISCIPLINE PHILOSOPHY **EDUCATION** Mercer Univ, BA; Univ NC at Chapel Hill, PhD. **CAREER** Prof, Univ Ala at Birmingham, 77-; dean, Univ Ala at Birmingham Sch of Arts and Humanities, 78-83; instr, Univ Richmond, NY Univ & Univ Miami. **SELECTED PUBLICATIONS** Auth, The End of Life: Euthanasia and Morality, Oxford UP, 86; Created from Animals: The Moral Implications of Darwinism, Oxford UP, 91; The Elements of Moral Philosophy, McGraw-Hill, 3rd ed, 98; Can Ethics Provide Answers? And Other Essays in Moral Philosophy, Rowman and Littlefield, 97. **CONTACT ADDRESS** Dept of Philosophy, Univ of Alabama, Birmingham, 1400 University Blvd, Birmingham, AL, 35294-1150. **EMAIL** rachels@uab.edu

RACHELS, STUART
PERSONAL Born 09/26/1969, s **DISCIPLINE** PHILOSOPHY **EDUCATION** Syracuse Univ, PhD, 98 **CAREER** Instr, Univ Colorado at Boulder, 98-99 **HONORS AND AWARDS** Marshall Scholar, Oxford Univ, 91-93 **MEMBERSHIPS** Amer Phil Assoc. **RESEARCH** Ethics **SELECTED PUBLICATIONS** Auth, Counterexamples to the Transitivity of Better Than, Australasian Journal of Philosophy, 98; Intrasitivity, Encyclopedia of Ethics, 2nd ed, 98; Is Unpleasantness Intrinsic to Experience, Philosophical Studies, forthcoming. **CONTACT ADDRESS** Dept of Philosophy, Univ of Colorado at Boulder, Campus Box 232, Boulder, CO, 80309-0232. **EMAIL** rachels@stripe.colorado.edu

RACHLINSKI, J.J.
PERSONAL Born 06/22/1966, Buffalo, NY, m, 1991 **DISCIPLINE** LAW **EDUCATION** Stanford Univ, JD 93, PhD 94. **CAREER** Cornell Law Sch, asst prof, assoc prof, 94 to 96-. **CONTACT ADDRESS** Law School, Cornell Univ, Ithaca, NY, 14853-4901.

RADDEN, JENNIFER
PERSONAL Born 09/10/1943, Melbourne, Australia, m, 1971, 3 children **DISCIPLINE** PHILOSOPHY **EDUCATION** Univ Melbourne, BA, 68; Oxford Univ, B Phil, 71, D Phil, 76. **CAREER** Lectr, 72-74, Tufts Univ; lectr, 75-84, asst prof, 84-89, assoc prof, 90-97, prof, 97-, Univ Mass. **RESEARCH** Philosophical issues in the theory and practice of psychiatry, philosophy of mind, moral philosophy and professional ethics. **CONTACT ADDRESS** Dept Philosophy, Univ of Massachusetts, Boston, MA, 02125. **EMAIL** radden@umbsky.cc.umb.edu

RADER, ROSEMARY
DISCIPLINE HISTORY OF CHRISTIANITY **EDUCATION** Col St Catherine, BA; Univ Minn, MA; Stanford Univ, PhD. **CAREER** Religion, Carleton Univ. **SELECTED PUBLICATIONS** Auth, Breaking Boundaries: Male/Female Friendship in Early Christian Communities; Coauth, Women Writers of the Early Church. **CONTACT ADDRESS** Carleton Col, 100 S College St., Northfield, MN, 55057-4016.

RADIC, RANDALL
PERSONAL Born 12/20/1952, NM, s **DISCIPLINE** THEOLOGY **EDUCATION** Agape Sem, STD, 95. **CAREER** First Congregational Church, Pastor; Grace Notes, writer. **MEMBERSHIPS** SBL **RESEARCH** Old and New Testament word studies. **CONTACT ADDRESS** First Congregational Church, 137 N Elm Ave, Ripon, CA, 95366. **EMAIL** drradic@sprynet.com

RADOMSKI, HARRY B.
DISCIPLINE LAW **EDUCATION** Univ Toronto, BC, 72, LLB, 75; Univ Ca, LLM, 76. **CAREER** Lectr, 88-. **RESEARCH** General commercial and insurance related litigation; administrative law practice. **SELECTED PUBLICATIONS** Co-auth, The Insurance Act of Ontario; pubs on insurance policy. **CONTACT ADDRESS** Fac of Law, Univ Toronto, 78 Queen's Park, Toronto, ON.

RADZIK, LINDA
DISCIPLINE ETHICS, EPISTEMOLOGY **EDUCATION** Univ NC at Chapel Hill, BA, 92; Univ Ariz, MA, 96, PhD, 97. **CAREER** Asst prof, Tex A&M Univ, 97-. **HONORS AND AWARDS** Univ Fel, Univ Ariz, 96; Fink Prize for Outstanding Grad Stud in Philos, Univ Ariz, 96; Univ Fel, Univ Ariz, 92-93; Phi Beta Kappa, Univ NC, 91. **RESEARCH** Political philosophy, history of ethics, applied ethics. **SELECTED PUBLICATIONS** Coauth, Contested Commodities, Law & Philosophy 16 6, 97. **CONTACT ADDRESS** Dept of Philosophy, Texas A&M Univ, College Station, TX, 77843-4237. **EMAIL** lradzik@snaefell.tamu.edu

RAE, BOB
DISCIPLINE LAW **EDUCATION** Univ Toronto, BA, 69, LLB, 77; Oxford Univ, BPhill, 71. **CAREER** Partner, Goodman Phillips & Vineberg **SELECTED PUBLICATIONS** Auth, From Protest to Power. **CONTACT ADDRESS** Fac of Law, Univ Toronto, 78 Queen's Park, Toronto, ON.

RAE BAXTER, LAURIE
DISCIPLINE EDUCATIONAL PHILOSOPHY **EDUCATION** Holland Col Sch Art & Design, AA; Fairhaven Col, BA; W Wash Univ, Med; Ohio State Univ, PhD. **CAREER** Instr, Univ Brit Columbia; Univ Ariz; Ohio State Univ; prof. **RESEARCH** Cross-cultural aesthetics media and film studies. **SELECTED PUBLICATIONS** Past sr ed, contrib, Can Rev of Art Edu: Research and Issues; pub(s), Jour Aesthetic Edu; Stud in Edu; Jour Multi-Cult and Cross-Cult Res in Art Edu. **CONTACT ADDRESS** Dept of Commun and Soc Found(s), Victoria Univ, PO Box 3045, Victoria, BC, V8W 3P4. **EMAIL** lbaxter@uvic.ca

RAINBOLT, GEORGE
DISCIPLINE ETHICS, PHILOSOPHY OF LAW, SOCIAL AND POLITICAL PHILOSOPHY, HISTORY OF ETHI **EDUCATION** Univ Ariz, PhD, 90. **CAREER** Asst prof, Ga State Univ. **SELECTED PUBLICATIONS** Coauth, Ethics; author of ten articles in journals such as Nous, Am Philos Quart and Philos and Phenomenol Res. **CONTACT ADDRESS** Georgia State Univ, Atlanta, GA, 30303. **EMAIL** grainbolt@gsu.edu

RAINER, THOM S.
DISCIPLINE EVANGELISM AND CHURCH GROWTH **EDUCATION** Univ Ala, BS; S Baptist Theol Sem, MDiv, PhD. **CAREER** Dean, Billy Graham Sch Missions, Evangel and Church Growth, S Baptist Theol Sem. **MEMBERSHIPS** Mem, Acad Evangel in Theol Edu; Amer Soc for Church Growth. **SELECTED PUBLICATIONS** Auth, The Bridger Generation; The Book of Church Growth: History, Theology, and Principles; Eating the Elephant; Giant Awakenings. **CONTACT ADDRESS** Billy Graham Sch Missions, Evangel and Church Growth, Southern Baptist Theol Sem, 2825 Lexington Rd, Louisville, KY, 40280. **EMAIL** trainer@sbts.edu

RAITT, JILL
DISCIPLINE THEOLOGY **EDUCATION** Radcliffe Col, Latin/Eng, 49-51; Inst Hist, Rome, Italy, Philos/Theol, 51-52; San Francisco Col for Women, BA, Philos, 53; San Francisco Col for Women, Eng, 64; Inst Pontificum, Rome, Italy, Theol; Marquette Univ, Theol, MA, 67; Univ Chicago, theol, MA, 67; Univ Chicago, theol, PhD, 70. **CAREER** Instr and asst prof, San Francisco Col for Women, 63-64; Marywood Col, theol dept, summer, 66; Immaculate Heart Col, theol and eng, summer, 67; instr and asst prof, theol dept, St Xavier Col, 66-68; asst prof, Univ Calif Riverside, 69-73; assoc prof and mem grad facul, hist theol, Duke Univ, Divinity Sch, 73-81; Iliff Sch of Theol, summer, 79, 80; prof and chair, dept relig studies, Univ Mo Columbia, 81-87, 90-95. **HONORS AND AWARDS** Radcliffe Scholar, 49-51; scholar, San Francisco Col for Women, 52-53; tuition grant, Marquette Univ, 64-65; DAAD scholar, Goethe Inst, Germany, summer, 65; full tuition grant, Univ Chicago, 65-68; jr fel, Foun for Reformation Res, summer, 68; univ fel, Univ Chicago, 68-69; facul fel, Univ Calif Riverside, summer, 70; SRHE for Lilly-Johnson project, 72-73; Humanities Inst fel, Univ Calif, 72-73; ACLS grant-in-aid, res, summer, 74; Duke Res Coun Grant, 74-76; ACLS and ATS fel, 75-76; Radcliffe Inst fel, 75-76; NEH fel, 75-76; Alumna of the Year, Divinity Sch of Univ Chicago, 80; ACLS grant-in-aid, summer, 81; NEH fel, 81-82; Fel of Nat Humanities Ctr, 81-82; Fleming Scholar, Southwestern Univ, fall, 81; UMC Res Coun res grant and travel grant; Amer Coun of Learned Soc grant, Intl Congress for Calvin Studies, sep 6-9, 82; Comt for Fulbright Scholar, relig, jul 84-jun 87, chair, 85-87; Nat Endow for the Humanities grant, 83-85; Alpha Sigma Nu, Nat Jesuit Honor Soc, 84; Exxon Educ Foun grant, 85-87; Alexander Robertson lectr, Univ Glasgow, apr-jun, 85; Univ Mo Columbia res coun leave, 87-88; fel, Nat Humanities Ctr, 87-88; outstanding teacher, Sect of Acad Teaching and Study of Relig, Amer Acad Relig, 90; NEH speaker, Whittier Col, feb 25-28, 92; key note address, Central States Reg Mtg, apr, 93; Plenary address, Col Theol Teachers Annual Mtg, jun, 93; fel, East-West Ctr, jan and jun, 91-93; commencement speaker, Col of Arts and Sci, MU, aug 6, 93; Catherine Paine Middlebush Prof in the Humanities, 90-95; respondent to keynote, Calvin Studies Soc, mar, 95; visiting scholar, Grad Theol Union, mar, 96; facul intl travel award, jul, 96; summer stipend, Lilly Foun for the Valparaiso Project, summer, 96; renewal 97 participant, Fairfield Univ, sumer, 97; Collegium Mentor, Univ San Diego, jun, 98. **MEMBERSHIPS** Amer Acad of Relig; Amer Soc of Church Hist; Amer Soc for Reformation Res; Bishops Comm for Inter-Relig and Ecumenical Affairs; Duke Univ Comt on Medieval Renaissance Studies; Soc for Calvin Studies; Univ Chicago Nat Alumni Cabinet; Univ Chicago Divinity Sch Alumni Asn; Univ Mo Columbia Mus of Art and Archeol; Univ Mo Columbia Sinclair Comparative Med Res Farm; Univ Mo Columbia. **SELECTED PUBLICATIONS** Auth, The Colloquy of Montbeliard: Religion and Politics in the Sixteenth Century, NY, Oxford Univ Press, mar, 93; ed and contrib, Saints and Sinners, Christian Spirituality: High Middle Ages and Reformation, vol 17, World Spirituality Series, NY, Crossroad/Continuum Publ Co, jun, 87; ed, Theodore Beza, transl, Lambert Daneau, Shapers of Traditions in Germany, Switzerland and Poland, 1560-1600, New Haven, Yale Univ Press, 81; auth, The Eucharistic Theol of Theodore Beza: The Development of the Reformed Tradition, AAR Studies in Relig, no 4, 72; article, Two Spiritual Directors of Women in the Sixteenth Century: St. Ignatius Loyola and St. Teresa of Avil, In Laudem Caroli: Renaissance and Reformation Studies for Charles G. Nauert, Sixteenth Century Studies, 98; article, Contemplatives in Action, the World Christian Life Community, Doors of Understanding: Conversations in Global Spirituality, Franciscan Press, 98; article, Transformations and Traditions: Augustine's Teaching on the Transformation of Christians in the Liturgy and the Use of these Teachings in the Sixteenth Century, The Australasian Cath Record, apr, 97. **CONTACT ADDRESS** Dept. of Religious Studies, Univ of Missouri, 405 GCB, Columbia, MO, 65211-4140.

RAITT, RONALD D.
DISCIPLINE LAW **EDUCATION** Univ Nebr, BS, JD. **CAREER** Prof. **SELECTED PUBLICATIONS** Auth, Evidence Cases and Problems, Harrison, 95; The Preemption and Economic Loss Provisions of the Ohio Product Liability Code, Univ Dayton Law Rev, 91; The Ohio Product Liability Code: The Mechanical Problems Involved in Applying Strict Tort Remedies to Economic Loss in Commercial Cases, Univ Dayton Law Rev, 91; Personal Knowledge Under the Federal Rules of Evidence: A Three-Legged Stool, Rutgers Law J, 87. **CONTACT ADDRESS** Col Law, Univ of Toledo, Toledo, OH, 43606. **EMAIL** rraitt@pop3.utoledo.edu

RAJ, VICTOR A.R.
PERSONAL Born 03/22/1948, Trivandrum, India, m, 1976, 3 children **DISCIPLINE** EXEGETICAL THEOLOGY **EDUCATION** Kerala Univ, India, BSc, 67; Gurukul Col, India, BD, 71; Concordia Sem, STM, 76, ThD, 81. **CAREER** Pastor, Cochin, India, 71-74; pastor, Trivandrum, India, 75-78; pastor, Gospel, Trivandrum, India, 81-84; dir, Renewal Prog, India Evangel Lutheran Church, 84-88; pres, 88-90, Concordia Theol Sem, Nagercoil, India; prof, chemn div theol, 90-95, Concordia Univ, Mequon, Wisc; mission prof of exegetical theol, asst dir of Inst for Mission Stud, Concordia Sem, 95- . **RESEARCH** Missions; world religions and their influence on Christian theology and culture; New Testament studies. **SELECTED PUBLICATIONS** Auth, The Hindu Connection: Roots of the New Age, Concordia, 95. **CONTACT ADDRESS** Concordia Sem, 801 DeMun Ave, St. Louis, MO, 63105. **EMAIL** rajv@csl.edu

RAJASHEKAR, J. PAUL
DISCIPLINE SYSTEMATIC THEOLOGY **EDUCATION** Univ Mysore, BA, 68; United Theol Col, BD, 71; Concordia Sem-Seminex, STM, 74; Univ Iowa, PhD, 81. **CAREER** Prof **RESEARCH** Christian ecumenism, cross-cultural dialogue, social and political ethics. **SELECTED PUBLICATIONS** Pub(s), on authentic forms of Christian witness/mission in a multi-religious world. **CONTACT ADDRESS** Dept of History and Systematic Theology, Lutheran Theol Sem, 7301 Germantown Ave, Philadelphia, PA, 19119 1794. **EMAIL** Rajashekar@ltsp.edu

RAKUS, DANIEL T.
PERSONAL Born 03/05/1958, Philadelphia, PA, s **DISCIPLINE** PHILOSOPHY **EDUCATION** La Salle Col, BA, 80; St. Charles Borromeo Sem, MA, 85; Villanova Univ, MA, 90; Univ of Toronto, PhD, 97. **CAREER** Unaffiliated Scholar. **MEMBERSHIPS** APA **RESEARCH** Medieval philo; philo of religion; ethics and social philo. **SELECTED PUBLICATIONS** Auth, Towards an Anselmian Theodicy, Ottawa: Nat Lib of Can, 97; Augustinian Libertas: The Foundations of an Ethics of Being, in: Downside Review, 97; Alter Augustinus and the Question of Moral Knowledge: Answering Philosophically as an Anselmian, in: Revue des Etudes Augustiniennes, fc 98. **CONTACT ADDRESS** 1512 Spruce St, PO Box 196, Philadelphia, PA, 19102.

RAMEY, GEORGE
PERSONAL Born 08/17/1938, Dixon, MO, m, 1959, 2 children **DISCIPLINE** THEOLOGY **EDUCATION** Southwest Baptist Col, AA, 58; William Jewel Col, BA, 60; Midwestern Baptist Theo Seminary, BD, 63; Southern Baptist Theo Seminary, ThM, 65, Phd, 68. **CAREER** Prof, 68-98, vice president, 75-98, Cumberland Col. **MEMBERSHIPS** Soc of Biblical Literature; Amer Acad of Relig; Internation Organization for Study of Old Testament; Amer Schs of Oriental Research; Natl Assn of Col & Univ Business Officers; Southern Assn of Col & Univ Business Officers; Council of Independent Kentucky Col & Univ Business Officers. **CONTACT ADDRESS** Cumberland Col, 75 Hemlook St., Williamsburg, KY, 40769-1793. **EMAIL** gramey@cc.cumber.edu

RAMOS-GONZALEZ, CARLOS
PERSONAL Born 10/20/1952, Caguas, PR, m, 1988, 3 children **DISCIPLINE** LAW **EDUCATION** Univ of Puerto Rico, BA, 74; Univ of Stockholm, Sweden, Dipl, 75; Univ of Puerto Rico, JD, 78; Univ of Calif, LLM, 87. **CAREER** Atty, PR Legal Servs, 78-80; exec dir, Santurce Law Off, 84-87; assoc dean, Interamerican Univ of PR, Sch of Law, 87-92; prof, Interamerican Univ of PR, Sch of Law, 80-92; prof and dean, Interamerican Univ of PR, Sch of Law, 92-. **MEMBERSHIPS** PR Bar Asn; Am Bar Asn; Asn of Trial Lawyers of Am; Judicature. **RESEARCH** Civil rights; correctional systems. **SELECTED PUBLICATIONS** Coauth, Derecho Constitucional de E.U. y Puerto Rico, Vol. II, 88; Litigation Theory and Practice, 96. **CONTACT ADDRESS** Sch of Law, Inter American Univ of Puerto Rico, Box 70351, San Juan, PR, 00936-8351. **EMAIL** ceramos@ns.inter.edu

RAMOS-MATTEI, CARLOS J.
PERSONAL Born 03/01/1947, Ponce, PR, m, 1974, 1 child **DISCIPLINE** PHILOSOPHY **EDUCATION** Cath Univ Louvain, PhD, 79. **CAREER** Prof, Univ PR, 73-. **MEMBERSHIPS** Am Philos Asn; Soc for Medieval and Renaissance Philos; PR Philos Asn. **RESEARCH** Philosophy; Ethics. **SELECTED PUBLICATIONS** Auth, Annotations on the Philosophy of Values, 99; Apuntes Sobre el Tema de los Valores, 98; Ethical Self-Determination in Don Jose Ortega y Gasset, 87; "Value Orientation and Human Creativity" in Analecta Husserliana, 98; "Pluralism: Another Characteristic of General Studies" in J of the Col of General Studies, 96-97; "Umberto Eco: Rhetorical Truth and the Police Novel" in J of the Col of General Studies, 92-93. **CONTACT ADDRESS** 311 Coll y Toste, San Juan, PR, 00918. **EMAIL** cramos@rr.pac.upr.elu.edu

RAMSEY, JEFF
DISCIPLINE HISTORY AND PHILOSOPHY OF SCIENCE **EDUCATION** Kans State Univ, BA; Univ Chicago, MS (chem), PhD (hist & plilos science). **CAREER** Philos, Oregon St Univ. **RESEARCH** Three-dimensional molecular shape. **SELECTED PUBLICATIONS** Area: how approximations and idealizations affect our notions of justification and reduction. **CONTACT ADDRESS** Dept Philos, Oregon State Univ, Corvallis, OR, 97331-4501. **EMAIL** jramsey@orst.edu

RAMSEY, WILLIAM M.
DISCIPLINE PHILOSOPHY OF SCIENCE **EDUCATION** Univ Ore, BS, 82; Univ Calif San Diego, PhD, 89. **CAREER** Assoc prof. **RESEARCH** Cognitive science; philosophy of psychology. **SELECTED PUBLICATIONS** Auth, Parallelism and Functionalism, 89; Connectionism, Eliminativism and the Future of Folk Psychology, 90; Where Does the Self-refutation Objection Take Us?, 91; Prototypes and Conceptual Analysis, 92; Connectionism and the Philosophy of Mental Representation, 93; Prototypes and Conceptual Analysis, 94; Investigating Common Sense Psychology, 96; co-auth, Connectionism and Three Levels of Nativism, 90; co-ed, Philosophy and Connectionist Theory, 91. **CONTACT ADDRESS** History and Philosophy of Science Dept, Univ of Notre Dame, Notre Dame, IN, 46556. **EMAIL** William.M.Ramsey.1@nd.edu

RAMSHAW, ELAINE JULIAN
DISCIPLINE PASTORAL CARE **EDUCATION** Valparaiso Univ, BA, 78; Univ Chicago Divinity Sch, MA, 79, PhD, 89. **CAREER** Fac mem, Methodist Theol Sch, 86; assoc prof, 95-. **HONORS AND AWARDS** Danforth fel, 78-82; Theol scholar, Assn Theol Sch(s); res grant for younger scholars, 93-95., Intern in pastoral psychotherapy, Ctr Rel and Psychotherapy, 82-85. **MEMBERSHIPS** Mem, Soc Pastoral Theol; Evangel Lutheran Church, Confirmation Ministry Task Force, 89-93; Consult Comm S Ohio Synod of the ELCA, 88-94; Family Violence Policy Panel, Ohio State Univ, 86-89. **RESEARCH** Religion and psychological studies. **SELECTED PUBLICATIONS** Auth, Ritual and Pastoral Care, 87. **CONTACT ADDRESS** Dept of Pastoral Care, Luther Sem, 2481 Como Ave, St. Paul, MN, 55108. **EMAIL** eramshaw@luthersem.edu

RANDALL, KENNETH C.
DISCIPLINE LAW **EDUCATION** Hofstra Univ, JD, 81; Yale Univ, MA, 82; Columbia Univ Sch Law, MA, 85, SJD, 88. **CAREER** Prof, Univ Ala, 85. **HONORS AND AWARDS** Outstanding fac mem, Univ Ala, 87-88; outstanding law grad, Hofstra Univ. **RESEARCH** Public international law, international business transactions,and constitutional law. **SELECTED PUBLICATIONS** Auth, Int Law Bk, Duke UP. **CONTACT ADDRESS** Law Dept, Univ of Alabama, Box 870000, Tuscaloosa, AL, 35487-0383. **EMAIL** kcrandal@law.ua.edu

RANDALL, SUSAN LYONS
DISCIPLINE LAW **EDUCATION** Univ NC-Chapel Hill, BA, 78; Columbia Univ Sch Law, JD, 82. **CAREER** Prof, Univ Ala, 92-. **MEMBERSHIPS** Phi Beta Kappa. **RESEARCH** Torts I and II, insurance, and jurisprudence. **CONTACT ADDRESS** Law Dept, Univ of Alabama, Box 870000, Tuscaloosa, AL, 35487-0383. **EMAIL** srandall@law.ua.edu

RANKIN, DUNCAN
DISCIPLINE THEOLOGY **EDUCATION** Clemson Univ, BS; Reformed Theol Sem, MDiv; Univ Edinburgh, PhD. **CAREER** Prof **SELECTED PUBLICATIONS** Auth, articles in the Jour Amer Ceramic Soc; Christian Observer; contrib, James Henley Thornwell; Westminster Confession of Faith. **CONTACT ADDRESS** Dept of Theology, Reformed Theol Sem, 5422 Clinton Blvd, Jackson, MS, 39209-3099.

RANSDELL, JOSEPH M.
DISCIPLINE PHILOSOPHY **EDUCATION** San Francisco State Univ, BA, 61; Columbia Univ, PhD, 66. **CAREER** Assoc prof, TX Tech Univ. **RESEARCH** Socrates and Plato; early mod philos. **SELECTED PUBLICATIONS** Publ(s) are chiefly on var aspects of the philos of the Am philosopher Charles Peirce, espec his semiotic or theory of representation; Ransdell has also authored an introductory work on the hist of philos. **CONTACT ADDRESS** Texas Tech Univ, Lubbock, TX, 79409-5015. **EMAIL** ransdell@hub.ofthe.net

RAPAPORT, WILLIAM J.
PERSONAL Born 09/30/1946, Brooklyn, NY, m, 1993, 4 children **DISCIPLINE** PHILOSOPHY **EDUCATION** Univ of Rochester, BA, 68; Indiana Univ, AM, 74, PhD, 76; SUNY Buffalo, MS, 84. **CAREER** Inst, Inwood Jr High Sch, 68-69; Dir, Math Prog, Walden Schl, 69-71; Assoc Inst Phil, 71-72, Assoc Inst Math, 75, Res Ass Phil, 72-75, Indiana Univ; Asst Prof, 76-83, Assoc Prof 83-84, SUNY Fredonia; Vis Asst Prof, 84-86, Asst Prof, 86-88, Assoc Prof 88-98, Computer Science, Adj Prof, Phil, 94-, Assoc Prof, Computer Science & Eng, 98-, SUNY Buffalo. **HONORS AND AWARDS** Dist Alumnus, Indiana Univ, 90; Steelman Vis Scientist Dist Let, Lenoir-Rhyne Col, 89; Northeastern Assoc of Grad Schl Masters Scholar Awd, 87; APA Quarterly Essay Prize, 92; SUNY Chancellor's Awd for Exc in Tchg, 81. **MEMBERSHIPS** Amer Assoc for Artificial Intel; APA; Assoc for Comutational Linguistics; Assoc for Computing Machinery; Assoc for Symbolic Logic; Congnitive Science Soc **RESEARCH** Artificial inelligence, cognitive science; computational linguistics; knowledge representation; logic philosophy of mind; philosophy of language; critical thinking; cognitive development. **SELECTED PUBLICATIONS** Understanding Understanding Syntactic Semantics and Computational Cognition, Philo Persp, Conn and Philo Psychol, 95; Cognition and Fiction, & An Introduction to a Computational Reader of Narratives, Deixis in Narrative A Cogn Science Persp, 95; Quasi-Indexicals and Knowledge Reports, Cognitive Science, 97; Thought Language and Ontology Essays in Memory of Hector-Neri Castaneda, Philo Stud Series, 98. **CONTACT ADDRESS** SUNY Buffalo, Dept of Computer Science, 226 Bell H, Box 602000, Buffalo, NY, 14260-2000. **EMAIL** rapaport@cs.buffalo.edu

RAPPAPORT, STEVEN D.
PERSONAL Born 08/09/1945, New York, NY, m, 1983 **DISCIPLINE** PHILOSOPHY **EDUCATION** Univ Calif, Berkeley, BA, 67; Sãn Jose State Univ, MA, 83; Univ Toronto, PhD, 72. **CAREER** Vis asst prof, McGill Univ, 72-73; vis asst prof, Ryerson Polytechnical Inst, 73-74; prof, De Anza Col, 74-. **MEMBERSHIPS** APA; Philos of Sci Assoc. **RESEARCH** Philosophy of economics; philosophy of social science; epistemology. **SELECTED PUBLICATIONS** Auth, Must a Metaphysical Relativist be a Truth Relativist? Philosophia, 93; auth, Basic Beliefs and the Regress of Justification: A Reply to Yalcin, Southern Jour of Philos, 93; auth, Is Economics Empirical Knowledge? Econ and Philos, 95; auth, Economic Models and Historical Explanation, Philos of Soc Sci, 95; auth, Inference to the Best Explanation: Is It Really Different from Mill's Methods? Philos of Sci, 96; auth, Abstraction and Unrealistic Assumptions in Economics, Jour of Econ Methodology, 96; auth, Relativism and Truth: A Rejoinder to Lynch, Philosophia, 97; auth, Relativism and Truth: A Reply to Davson-Galle, Philosophia, 98; auth, Models and Reality in Economics, Elgar, 98. **CONTACT ADDRESS** Dept of Philosophy, De Anza Col, Cupertino, CA, 95014.

RAPPLE, EVA MARIE
PERSONAL Born 02/19/1959, Frankfurt, Germany, m, 1986, 2 children **DISCIPLINE** THEOLOGY **EDUCATION** Univ Frankfurt, 83; Cath Theol Union, MA, 95. **CAREER** Instr, Col Du Page, 98-; instr, Tepeyac Inst, 95-98; instr, Bible Inst, 85-87. **MEMBERSHIPS** Soc Bibl Lit. **RESEARCH** Biblical literature; religious studies. **CONTACT ADDRESS** Dept of Theology, Col of DuPage, 6737 Greene Rd., Woodridge, IL, 60517-1470. **EMAIL** rapple@ix.netcom.com

RASER, HAROLD E.
PERSONAL Born 03/09/1947, Altadena, CA, m, 1968, 2 children **DISCIPLINE** RELIGION **EDUCATION** Pasadena Col, BA, 68, MA, 70; Nazarene Theol Sem, MDiv, 74; Penn State Univ, PhD, 87. **CAREER** Adj grad prof relig studies, Univ Mo, 96-; adj lectr, S Nazarene Univ, 96-97; adj lectr, Point Loma Nazarene Univ, 93-94; adj lectr, Fuller Theol Sem, 89; vis prof, Europ Nazarene Bibl Col, 86-87; adj lectr, St. Paul Sch Theol, 84-87; from asst prof to assoc prof to prof, Nazarene Theol Sem, 80-. **MEMBERSHIPS** Am Acad Relig; Am Soc Church Hist; Wesleyan Theol Soc. **RESEARCH** History of the American Holiness Movement; American revivalism and evangelicalism; 19th century American religion; new religious movements in America. **SELECTED PUBLICATIONS** Auth, Phoebe Palmer: Her Life and Thought, 87; auth, More Preachers and Better Preachers: The First Fifty Years of Nazarene Theological Seminary, 95; Views of Last Things in the American Holiness Movement, Second Coming: Wesleyan Perspective on Eschatology, 95; auth, Forming and Reforming Worship, Worshipping God: The Church's First Call, 96; auth, Worship Since the Reformation, Worshipping God: The Church's First Call, 96. **CONTACT ADDRESS** Dept of Religious Studies, Nazarene Theol Sem, 1700 E Meyer Blvd, Kansas City, MO, 64131. **EMAIL** heraser@nts.edu

RASKIN, JAMIN
DISCIPLINE CONSTITUTIONAL LAW; CRIMINAL LAW **EDUCATION** Harvard Col, BA, 83; Harvard Law Sch, JD, 87; **CAREER** Prof, Am Univ; Benjamin Trustman Fel; Harvard Univ Carnochan Nat Scholar, Presidential Scholar WCL Pauline Ruyle Moore Scholar, 96; Tchg fel, Harvard Univ. **HONORS AND AWARDS** First Circuit Court Appeals Prize., Asst atty gen, Commonwealth Mass, 87-89; Gen counsel, Natl Rainbow Coalition, 89-90; Mem, Clinton-Gore Justice Dept Transition Team, 92; Codir WCL Prog Law & Government; Ed, Harvard Law Rev. **SELECTED PUBLICATIONS** Ed, Harvard Law Rev; Contrib, Columbia Law Rev; Univ Pa Law Rev; American Univ Jour Gender & the Law; Yale Law & Policy Rev; Hastings Law Jour; Howard Law Jour; Catholic Univ Law Rev **CONTACT ADDRESS** American Univ, 4400 Massachusetts Ave, Washington, DC, 20016.

RASKIN, JAY
PERSONAL Born 08/16/1953, New York, NY, m, 1987, 1 child **DISCIPLINE** PHILOSOPHY **EDUCATION** School of Visual Arts, BFA Filmmaking, 76; Univ S Fla, MA, 95, PhD, 97. **CAREER** Adj prof, Rollins Col. **MEMBERSHIPS** Amer Philos Asn; Fla Philos Asn. **RESEARCH** Film; Marxism; Technology; Classical History. **CONTACT ADDRESS** Dept of Philosophy, Rollins Col, 1477 Hastings Rd, Spring Hill, FL, 34608. **EMAIL** jraskin@rollins.edu

RAST, WALTER EMIL
PERSONAL Born 07/03/1930, San Antonio, TX, m, 1955, 4 children **DISCIPLINE** OLD TESTAMENT, ARCHEOLOGY **EDUCATION** St John's Col, BA, 52; Concordia Theol Sem, MDiv, 55, STM, 56; Univ Chicago, MA, 64, PhD(Old Testament), 66. **CAREER** From asst prof to assoc prof, 61-73; Prof Old Testament & Archaeol, Valparaiso Univ, 73-, James Alan Montgomery fel, Am Schs Orient Res, Jerusalem, 66-67; res prof, Albright Inst Archaeol Res, Jerusalem, 71-72; Danforth assoc, 73-; co-dir, Excavations at Bab edh-Dhra & Numeira, 75-; Nat Endowment for Humanities res grants, 75, 77, 79 & 81; Univ Chicago fel, 76; vis prof Old Testament, Univ Notre Dame, 77-78 & 82; pres, Am Ctr of Orental Res Amman, 78-82; prof, Albright Inst Archaeol Res, Jerusalem, 82-83; Am Coun Learned Soc fel, 71-72; Nat Endowment for Humanities fel, 82. **MEMBERSHIPS** Archaeol Inst Am; Am Schs Orient Res; Soc Bibl Lit; Israel Explor Soc. **RESEARCH** Old Testament; Syro-Palestinian archeology; Semitic languages. **SELECTED PUBLICATIONS** Auth, Tradition History and the Old Testament, Fortress, 72; coauth, Survey of the Southeastern plain of the Dead Sea, Ann Dept Antiq Jordan, 74; A preliminary report of excavations at Bab edh, Dhra, 1975, Ann Am Schs Orient Res, 76; auth, Tannach I: Studies in the Iron Age Pottery, Am Scholars Orient Res, 78; Joshua, Judges, Samuel and Kings, Fortress, 78; An Ostracon from Tell el-Ful, 78 &; co-ed, The Southeastern Dead Sea Plain Expedition: An Interim Report of the 1977 Season, 79, Annals Am Scholars Orient Res; coauth, Preliminary Report of the 1979 Expedition to the Dead Sea Plain, Jordan, Bull Am Scholars Orient Res, 240; Studies In The Archaeology And History Of Ancient-Israel In Honor Of Moshe Dothan--English, French, German, Italian, Hebrew, J Of Near Eastern Studies, Vol 56, 97; The Archaeology Of The Israelite Settlement, J Of Near Eastern Studies, Vol 52, 93. **CONTACT ADDRESS** Dept of Theol, Valparaiso Univ, Valparaiso, IN, 46383.

RATES, NORMAN M.
PERSONAL Born 01/01/1924, Owensboro, KY, m **DISCIPLINE** THEOLOGY **EDUCATION** KY State Coll, AB 1947; Lincoln Univ, BD 1950; Oberlin Coll, MDiv 1952; Yale Univ, MAR 1961; Vanderbilt Univ, DMin 1974; Oberlin Coll, STM 1953; Harvard Univ, independent study 1968-69. **CAREER** Camac Comm Ctr Phila, student counselor 1947-48; Philadelphia Gen Hosp, asst to protestant chaplain 1948-49; St Paul Bapt Ch W Chester PA, asst to pastor 1949-50; Div of Home Missions Natl Council for Ch of Christ in USA NY FL DE, missionary to agricultural migrants 1948-56; Morris Coll, minister dean of men tchr 1953-54; Morehouse Spelman Coll Pre-Coll Prog summers, counselor & minister 1966-67; Central Brooklyn Model Cities Summer Acad Spelman Coll summer, couns 1972; Interdenom Theol Ctr, guest lectr & part-time tchr 1971; Westhills Presb Ch GA summer, interim pastor 1963; SPELMAN COLL GA DEPT OF RELIGION, COLL MINISTER & CHMN 1954-. **HONORS AND AWARDS** C Morris Cain Prize in Bible Lincoln Univ 1949; Samuel Dickey Prize in New Testament Lincoln Univ 1949; Campus Christian Worker Grant Danforth Found 1960-61; Atlanta Univ Ctr Non-Western Studies Prog Grant for Travel & Study Ford Found 1968-69. **MEMBERSHIPS** Mem Natl Assn of Coll & Univ Chaplains; mem Ministry to Blacks in Higher Educ; mem Amer Assn of Univ Profs; mem Natl Assn of Biblical Instr; mem Univ Ctr in GA Div of Tchr of Religion; Petit Juror Fulton Co Superior Ct 1971, 1973; grand juror Fulton Co Superior Ct 1972; ministerial standing The United Ch of Christ; Fellow Conf on African & African-Amer Studies Atlanta Univ Campus; bd mem Camping Unlimited Blue Star Camps Inc; bd dir Planned Parenthood Assn of Atlanta; chmn Religious Affairs Com Planned Parenthood Assn of Atlanta; mem Com on the Ministry The United Ch of Christ; mem The Metro Atlanta Christian Council; mem GA-SC Assn of the United Ch of Christ SE Conf; mem Alpha Phi Alpha Frat. **CONTACT ADDRESS** Dept Religion, Spelman Col, 350 Spelman Lane SW, Atlanta, GA, 30314.

RATNER, STEVEN RICHARD
PERSONAL Born 12/09/1959, New York, NY, m, 1995, 1 child **DISCIPLINE** INTERNATIONAL LAW **EDUCATION** Princeton Univ, AB, 82; Yale Law School, JD, 86; Institut Un-

iversitaire de Hautes Etudes Internationales Geneva, MA, 93. **CAREER** Atty adv, Off of Legal Advs, US Dept of State, 86-93; Int Affairs Fel, Council of Foreign Rels, 92-93; asst prof Univ Tex School Law, 93-97; prof, Univ Tex School Law, 97-. **HONORS AND AWARDS** Certificate of Merit for Best Scholarly book, Am Soc of Int Law, 97; Bd of Ed of Am J of Int Law; Fulbright Scholar, 98-99. **MEMBERSHIPS** Am Soc of Int Law; Council for Foreign Rel; Acad Council of the UN Syst; Asn of Am Law Schools. **RESEARCH** International Law; Human Rights; United Nations; Foreign Investment. **SELECTED PUBLICATIONS** Auth, The New Un Peacekeeping: Building Peace in Lands of Conflict After the Cold War, 95; Accountability for Human Rights Atrocities In International Law: Beyond the Nuremberg Legacy, 97; numerous articles in law journals, 84-98. **CONTACT ADDRESS** Univ of Tex School of Law, 727 E 26th St, Austin, TX, 78705. **EMAIL** sratner@mail.law.utexas.edu

RATUSHNY, EDWARD J.
DISCIPLINE LAW **EDUCATION** Univ Saskatchewan, BA, LLB; London Univ, LLM; Univ Mich, LLM. **CAREER** Prof. **RESEARCH** Sports and entertainment law. **SELECTED PUBLICATIONS** Auth, pubs on transportation, environmental, labour, competition, immigration, refugee and human rights law. **CONTACT ADDRESS** Fac Common Law, Univ Ottawa, 550 Cumberland St, PO Box 450, Ottawa, ON, K1N 6N5.

RAUCH, DOREEN E.
PERSONAL Born 07/17/1947, Port of Spain, Trinidad and Tobago, m, 1969 **DISCIPLINE** LAW **EDUCATION** Univ of Cincinnati, BA, 1976; Howard Univ School of Law, JD, 1984. **CAREER** Emerson Law School, faculty, 1984-89; Univ of Massachusetts-Boston, instructor, 1985-86; Massachusetts Bay Comm College, instructor, 1985-86; Murray State Univ, dir of equal opportunity & affirm action, 1991-93; Northern Michigan Univ, afirmative action officer, 1993-. **HONORS AND AWARDS** Howard Univ, Amer Jurisprudence Award in Commercial Paper, 1983; Amer Jurisprudence Award in Criminal Law, 1982; Amer Jurisprudence Award in Contracts, 1983; Amer Jurisprudence Award in Municipal Law, 1982; Univ of Cincinnati, Dean's List, 1974-76. **MEMBERSHIPS** Natl Organization of Women, 1990-; Amer Assn of Univ Women, 1990-; Amer Assn of Univ administrators, 1995; Amer Assn of Affirmative Action, 1990-. **CONTACT ADDRESS** Affirmative Action Officer, Northern Michigan Univ, 1401 Presque Isle Avenue, Marquette, MI, 49855.

RAUHUT, NILS
PERSONAL Born 10/05/1965 **DISCIPLINE** PHILOSOPHY **EDUCATION** Univ Colo, MA, 90; Univ Wash, PhD, 97. **CAREER** Vis asst prof, Webster State Univ, 97-98; asst prof Coastal Carolina Univ, 98-. **MEMBERSHIPS** Am Philos Asn. **RESEARCH** Ancient Philosophy; Plato. **CONTACT ADDRESS** Dept of Philosophy, 3782-H Cape Landing Circle, Myrtle Beach, SC, 29577. **EMAIL** nrauhut@cpastal.edu

RAUSCH, THOMAS P.
PERSONAL Born 02/12/1941, Chicago, IL **DISCIPLINE** THEOLOGY **EDUCATION** Gonzaga, BA, 66; MA, 67; Jesuit School of Theol Berkeley, STM, 72; Duke Univ, PhD, 76. **CAREER** Prof and Chair, Dept of Theol Studies, Loyola Marymount Univ. **MEMBERSHIPS** Cath Theol Soc of Am; Am Acad of Rel; N Am Acad of Ecumenists; Cath/ Southern Baptist Conversation. **RESEARCH** Contemporary theological issues; ecclesiology; authority; priesthood; ecumenism. **SELECTED PUBLICATIONS** Auth, The Roots of Catholic Tradition, 86; Authority and Leadership in the Church: Past Directions and Future Possibilities, 89; Radical Christian Communities, 90; Priesthood Today: An Appraisal, 92; Wspotczesne Kaptastwo, 96; Catholicism at the Dawn of the Third Millenium, 96; ed, The College Student's Introduction to Theology, 92. **CONTACT ADDRESS** Jesuit Comm, Loyola Marymount Univ, 7900 Loyola Blvd, Box 45041, Los Angeles, CA, 90045-0041. **EMAIL** trausch@lmumail.lmu.edu

RAVEN-HANSEN, PETE
PERSONAL Born 06/05/1946, Copenhagen, Denmark, m, 1974, 2 children **DISCIPLINE** LAW **EDUCATION** Harvard Col, BA, 68; Harvard Law Sch, JD, 74. **CAREER** Assoc prof of law, George Wash Univ Law Sch, 80-85; prof of law, George Wash Univ Law Sch, 85-96; Glenn Earl Weston res prof of law, George Wash Univ Law Sch, 92-. **HONORS AND AWARDS** Phi Beta Kappa. **MEMBERSHIPS** Civil Procedure Sect; Asn Amer Law Sch. **RESEARCH** Law of the Presidency; National security; Civil procedure. **SELECTED PUBLICATIONS** Coauth with W. Banks, A Berney & S. Dycus, National Security Law, Little Brown, 2nd ed, 97; coauth with G. Shreve, Understanding Civil Procedure, Matthew Bender, 2nd ed, 94; Coauth with W. Banks, National Security Law and the Power of the Purse, Oxford Univ Press, 94. **CONTACT ADDRESS** Law Sch, George Washington Univ, Washington, DC, 20052. **EMAIL** praven@main.nlc.gwu.edu

RAVENELL, MILDRED
PERSONAL Born 12/01/1944, Charleston, SC, m **DISCIPLINE** LAW **EDUCATION** Fisk Univ, BA 1965; Howard Univ, JD 1968; Harvard Univ, LLM 1971. **CAREER** IBM, systems engr 1968-70, marketing rep 1970; Boston Univ, asst dean for admissions & financial aid 1971-72; FL State Univ, assoc prof of law 1976-84; Univ of VA, visiting assoc prof of law 1984-85. **MEMBERSHIPS** Mem Phi Beta Kappa; mem Amer Bar Assn; mem MA Bar Assn; mem Bethel AME Church; mem Delta Sigma Theta Sor; mem Jack & Jill of Amer Inc; former mem bd of dirs Terrell House at Tallahassee; mem bd of trustees Law Sch Admission council; former mem Bd of Bus Regulation FL. **CONTACT ADDRESS** Sch of Law, Univ of Virginia.

RAVENELL, WILLIAM HUDSON
PERSONAL Born 05/31/1942, Boston, MA **DISCIPLINE** LAW **EDUCATION** Lincoln Univ PA, BA 1963; State Coll at Boston, MEd 1965; Howard Univ Sch of Law, JD 1968. **CAREER** John Hancock Ins Co, analyst 1968-71; Housing Inspection Dept, admin 1971-72; State Dept of Comm Affairs, dep sec 1972-75; FL Dept of Comm Affairs, sec 1975-79; FL A&M Univ, prof 1979; FL Office of the Atty Gen, special asst 1979-80; US Dept of Transportation Fed Hwy Admin, chief counsel 1980-81; State of FL, asst attorney general 1982-85; FLORIDA A&M UNIV, ATTORNEY, PROFESSOR 1985-. **MEMBERSHIPS** Chmn FL Commn on Human Relations 1975-77; chmn FL Manpower Serv Council 1975-80; FL, DC, VA, Natl, Amer Bar Assns; mem Phi Alpha Delta, Omega Psi Phi, FL Council of 100; First Union Bank, board of directors, 1990-; NAACP, life member. **CONTACT ADDRESS** Florida A&M Univ, Tallahassee, FL, 32303.

RAVVEN, HEIDI
PERSONAL Born 04/28/1952, Boston, MA, m, 1988, 1 child **DISCIPLINE** PHILOSOPHY **EDUCATION** Brandeis Univ, BA, 74, PhD, 84. **CAREER** Jewish Chaplain, Wellesley Col, 79-82; assoc prof, Hamilton Col, 83-; Stroum vis prof Jewish studies, Univ Wash, 97. **MEMBERSHIPS** Am Philos Asn; Acad Jewish Philos; N Am Spinoza Soc; Hegel Soc Am. **RESEARCH** Spinoza; feminist philosophy; Hegel; Jewish philosophy. **SELECTED PUBLICATIONS** Auth, Has Hegel Anything to Say to Feminists?, Int Libr Critical Essays Hist Philos Ser: Vol II Hegel, 98; co-ed & contribur, Spinoza and Judaism: A Collection of Essays, 99; auth, Spinoza's Rupture with Tradition, Spinoza & Jewish Philos: A Collection of Essays, 99; auth, Observations on Jewish Philosophy and Feminist Thought, Judaism: Quart Jour Jewish Life & Thought, Fall, 97; auth, Spinoza's Individualism Reconsidered: Some Lessons from the Short Treatise on God, Man, and His Well-Being, Iyyun: Jerusalem Philos Quart, July, 98; auth, Response to James Pinkerton: Hegel and Nazism, The Owl of Minerva: Jour Hegel Soc Am. **CONTACT ADDRESS** Dept of Religious Studies, Hamilton Col, Clinton, NY, 13323. **EMAIL** hravven@hamilton.edu

RAWLING, J. PIERS
DISCIPLINE DECISION THEORY, LOGIC, ETHICAL THEORY, PHILOSOPHY OF MATHEMATICS **EDUCATION** Cambridge Univ, Eng, BA, 81; Cornell Univ, MS, 86; Univ Calif, Berkeley, PhD, 89. **CAREER** Asst prof, Univ Ga, 89-91; invited vis lectr, Keele Univ, Eng, 93-94; asst prof, Univ Mo, St Louis; bd of counsult ed, Theory and Decision, 96. **HONORS AND AWARDS** Richard M Griffith Mem Award in Philos, Southern Soc for Philos and Psychol, 90; NEH summer inst, 90; summer res grant, Univ Ga, 90; summer res grant, Univ Mo, St Louis, 91; NEH summer inst, 92; NEH summer sem, 93; NEH summer fel, 93; Univ Mo Syst Res Bd Award, 95; Univ Mo Syst Inst for Instruct Develop Award, 96-97. **SELECTED PUBLICATIONS** Auth, A Note on the Two Envelopes Problem, Theory and Decision 36, 94; Psychology and Newtonian Methodology, J of Mind and Behav 16(1), 95; coauth, Value and Agent-Relative Reasons, Utilitas 7(1), 95; Agent-Relativity and Terminological Inexactitudes, Utilitas 7(2), 95. **CONTACT ADDRESS** Univ Mo, St Louis, St Louis, MO, 63121.

RAWLS, JOHN
PERSONAL Born 02/21/1921, Baltimore, MD, m, 1949, 3 children **DISCIPLINE** PHILOSOPHY **EDUCATION** Princeton Univ, PhD, 50. **CAREER** Instr philos, Princeton Univ, 50-52; asst prof, Cornell Univ, 53-62; prof, 62-76, John Cowles Prof Philos, Harvard Univ, 76-, Fulbright fel, Oxford Univ, 52-53. **MEMBERSHIPS** Am Philos Asn. **RESEARCH** Moral and political philosophy; philosophical analysis. **SELECTED PUBLICATIONS** Auth, Outline Of A Decision Procedure For Ethics & Two Concepts Of Rules, Philos Rev; The Law Of Peoples + International-Law, Justice, And Political Liberalism, Critical Inquiry, Vol 20, 93. **CONTACT ADDRESS** Dept of Philos, Harvard Univ, Cambridge, MA, 02138.

RAY, DOUGLAS E.
DISCIPLINE LAW **EDUCATION** Univ Minn, BA; Harvard Univ, JD. **CAREER** Prof. **SELECTED PUBLICATIONS** Auth, Sexual Harassment, Labor Arbitration and National Labor Policy, Nebr Law Rev, 94; Some Overlooked Aspects of the Strike Replacement Issue, Kansas Law Rev, 92; Labor Management Relations: Strikes, Lockouts and Boycotts, Clark Boardman Callaghan, 92. **CONTACT ADDRESS** Col Law, Univ of Toledo, Toledo, OH, 43606. **EMAIL** dray@uoft02.utoledo.edu

RAY, GREG
DISCIPLINE PHILOSOPHY **EDUCATION** Univ of Calif, Berkley, PhD, 92. **CAREER** Asst Prof, Univ Florida, 92-97; Vis Assoc Prof, Univ of MI, 98; Assoc Prof, Univ of FL, 98-. **MEMBERSHIPS** Amer Philo Asn; Asn for Symbolic Logic; Soc for Exact Phil; Florida Philo Asn **RESEARCH** Philosophical logic; metaphysics; philosophy of language. **CONTACT ADDRESS** Prof, Univ of Florida, Dept of Philosophy, Gainesville, FL, 32611-8545. **EMAIL** gray@phil.ufl.edu

RAY, REGINALD
DISCIPLINE RELIGIOUS STUDIES **EDUCATION** Univ Chicago, PhD. **CAREER** Senior instr. **RESEARCH** Buddhist saints; Tantric Buddhism; Tibetan Buddhism; Vajrayana. **SELECTED PUBLICATIONS** Auth, Buddhist Saints in India. **CONTACT ADDRESS** Religious Studies Dept, Univ of Colorado, Boulder, Boulder, CO, 80309. **EMAIL** Reginald.Ray@Colorado.edu

RAYE, VANCE WALLACE
PERSONAL Born 09/06/1946, Hugo, OK, m **DISCIPLINE** LAW **EDUCATION** Univ of OK, BA 1967, JD 1970. **CAREER** Bulla and Horning, attorney; US Air Force, asst staff judge advocate, Beale AFB chief of military justice, chief of civil law, judge advocate, 1970-74; CA Attorney General, civil division, deputy atty general 1974-80, sr asst atty general 1980-82, deputy legislative scty 1982-83; Governor of CA, legal affairs secretary, advisor, legal counsel, 1983-89; Sacramento County Superior Court, judge, 1989-90; CALIFORNIA COURT OF APPEAL, THIRD DISTRICT, ASSOCIATE JUSTICE, 1991-; LINCOLN LAW SCHOOL, PROFESSOR. **MEMBERSHIPS** State Bar of CA 1972-; vice chair CA Exec Emergency Council 1984-; CA Assn of Black Lawyers; NAACP; Urban League; CA State Bar Commn on Malpractice Insurance; chmn Staff Adv Council Natl Governors Assn Comm on Criminal Justice and Public Safety; Government's Emergency Operations Executive Council, vice chairman; National Institute of Justice, peer reviewer; Martin Luther King Holiday Commission, vice chairman; California Health Decisions; 100 Black Men of Sacramento; National Bar Association; Wiley Manuel Bar Association; California Judges Association; Judicial Council Committee on Family Law, chairman; Amer Bar Assn, criminal justice standards comm; CA Commission on the Future of the Courts, Family Relations Comm, chair; Judicial Council Appellate Standards Committee, chair legislative subcommittee; CA Commission on the Status of the African American Male; Univ of CA, Davis Med School Leadership Council. **SELECTED PUBLICATIONS** Publications: Contributor, "California Public Contract Law;" co-author: California Family Law Litigation, 3 volumes. **CONTACT ADDRESS** California Court of Appeal, 3rd Appellate District, 914 Capitol Mall, Sacramento, CA, 95814.

RAYFIELD, DAVID
PERSONAL Born 04/10/1940, Miami, FL **DISCIPLINE** PHILOSOPHY **EDUCATION** Earlham Col, AB, 62; Duke Univ, PhD(philos), 66. **CAREER** Asst prof philos, Univ Akron, 66-68; mem fac, Univ Nfld, 68-70; assoc prof, 70-77, PROF PHILOS, SAGINAW VALLEY STATE COL, 77-, CHMN DEPT, 70-. **RESEARCH** Philosophy of action. **SELECTED PUBLICATIONS** Auth, Action, Nous, 5/68; On describing actions, Inquiry, 70; Action: An Analysis of the Concept, Nijhoff, The Hague, 72; Cody's categories, 74 & On Miller's paradoxes and circles, winter 74, Inquiry. **CONTACT ADDRESS** Saginaw Valley State Col, Univ Center, 7400 Bay Rd, Univ Center, MI, 48710-0001.

RAYMOND, DIANE
DISCIPLINE PHILOSOPHY **EDUCATION** Vassar Col, BA; NY Univ, PhD. **CAREER** Prof; dir, Women's Stud Prog; mem, GALA & Curric Comt. **MEMBERSHIPS** Am Philos Asn; Socr Women in Philos. **RESEARCH** Feminist theory; critical race theory; applied ethics; cult studies. **SELECTED PUBLICATIONS** Auth, Existentialism and the Philosophical Tradition, Prentice Hall; coauth, Looking at Gay and Lesbian Life, Beacon Press; ed, Sexual Politics and Popular Culture, Bowling Green UP; articles in, feminist theory, app ethics & popular cult theory. **CONTACT ADDRESS** Dept of Philos, Simmons Col, 300 The Fenway, Boston, MA, 02115. **EMAIL** draymond@simmons.edu

REA, MICHAEL C.
DISCIPLINE PHILOSOPHY **EDUCATION** UCLA, BA, 91; Univ Notre Dame, MA, 94, PhD, 96. **CAREER** Asst Prof, 96 to 98-, Univ Delaware. **HONORS AND AWARDS** Vis Schl, 99, Univ Notre Dame; Pew Evan Fel; UD U Gnt; Diss Yr Fel; John A O'Brien Fel; Robert E Gordon Gnt; Phi Beta Kappa; Magna Cum Laude. **MEMBERSHIPS** SCP; APQ; PPR. **RESEARCH** Metaphysics, Philosophy of Religion, Ancient Philosophy. **SELECTED PUBLICATIONS** Ed, Material Constitution: A Reader, Lanham MD, Rowman and Littlefield, 97; coauth, Personal Identity and Psychological Continuity, Philo and Phenomenological Res, forthcoming; auth, Temporal Parts Unmotivated, Philo Rev, forthcoming; In Defense of Mereological Universalism, Philo and Phenom Res, 98; Supervenience and Co-location, Amer Philo Qtly, 97; ed, Introduction, in Material Constitution: A Reader, Lanham MD, Rowman

and Littlefield, 97; auth, The Problem of Material Constitution, Philo Rev, 95. **CONTACT ADDRESS** Dept of Philosophy, Univ Delaware, Newark, DE, 19718. **EMAIL** mcrea@udel.edu

REATH, ANDREWS
DISCIPLINE SOCIAL AND POLITICAL PHILOSOPHY **EDUCATION** Harvard Univ, PhD. **CAREER** PROF, CH, UNIV CALIF, RIVERSIDE. **RESEARCH** Kant's moral and political philosophy; Contemporary moral theory; History of ethics. **SELECTED PUBLICATIONS** Auth, "Legislating the Moral Law," Nous, 94; "Agency and the Imputation of Consequences in Kant's Ethics," Jahrbuch for Recht und Ethik, Vol 2, 94; "Autonomy and Practical Reason: Thomas Hill's Kantianism," Jahrbuch for Recht und Ethik, Vol 3, 95; Reclaiming the History of Ethics: Essays for John Rawls, Cambridge Univ Press, 97; "Introduction to the Critique of Practical Reason," Kant, Critique of Practical Reason, Cambridge Univ Press, 97; "Legislating for a Realm of Ends: the Social Dimensions of Autonomy," Reath, Herman & Korsgaard, 97. **CONTACT ADDRESS** Dept of Philos, Univ Calif, 1156 Hinderaker Hall, Riverside, CA, 92521-0209. **EMAIL** reath@citrus.ucr.edu

RECK, ANDREW JOSEPH
PERSONAL Born 10/29/1927, New Orleans, LA, m, 1987 **DISCIPLINE** PHILOSOPHY **EDUCATION** Tulane Univ, BA, 47, MA, 49; Yale Univ, PhD, 54. **CAREER** Reader econ, Tulane Univ, 45-47; instr, Univ Conn, 49-50; asst instr philos, Yale Univ, 50-51, part-time instr, 51-52, instr, 55-58; from asst prof to assoc prof, 58-64, Prof Philos, Tulane Univ, 64-, Chmn Dept, 69-89, Dir, Master Liberal Arts Prog, 83-; mem adv comt Am Studies, 71-; Howard Found fel, 62-63; Am Philos Soc grantee, 72; vis fel, Huntington Libr, San Marino, Calif, 73; adv ed, Southwestern J Philos, 72 & Southern J Philos, 78; vis prof, Fordham Univ, 79; vis scholar, Inst Soc, Ethics and the Life Sci, Hastings on the Hudson, New York, 81; sr scholar, Inst Humane Studies, 82; Ed, Hist Philos Quart, 93-98; Acad Specialist, U.S. Information Agency (Brazil), 93. **HONORS AND AWARDS** Am Coun Learned Soc grant, 61-62; LEQSF grant, 94-96; The Outstanding Graduate of the Class of 1947, Emeritus Club, Tulane Univ, 97. **MEMBERSHIPS** Western Div Am Philos Asn; Metaphys Soc Am (pres, 77-78); Southwestern Philos Soc (vpres, 71-72, pres, 72-73); Southern Soc Philos & Psychol (treas, 68-71, pres, 76-77); Soc Adv Am Philos (exec coun, 80-83, pres, 98-); Charles S. Peirce Soc (secy-treas, 85-86, vpres, 86-87, pres, 87-88). **RESEARCH** American philosophy; metaphysics; history of philosophy. **SELECTED PUBLICATIONS** Auth, Recent American Philosophy, Pantheon, 64; Introduction to William James, Ind Univ, 67; The New American Philosophers, La State Univ, 68; Speculative Philosophy, Univ NMex, 72; ed, Knowledge and Value, Essays in Honor of H N Lee, M Nijhoff, 72; co-ed, Studies on Santayana, Southern J Philos, 72; ed, George Herbert Mead, Selected Writings, Univ Chicago Press, 81; co-ed, American Philosophers' Ideas of Ultimate Reality and Meaning, Univ Toronto Press, 93. **CONTACT ADDRESS** Dept of Philos, Tulane Univ, 6823 St Charles Ave, New Orleans, LA, 70118-5698.

RECK, ERICH H.
PERSONAL Born 05/01/1959, Riedlingen, Germany **DISCIPLINE** PHILOSOPHY **EDUCATION** Univ Chicago, MA, 97; PhD, 92. **CAREER** Postdoctoral Res Fel, Univ Minn, 92-93; instr, Univ Chicago, 93-95; asst prof, Univ Calif Riverside, 95-. **MEMBERSHIPS** APA; PSA; ASL; GAP. **RESEARCH** Philosophy of Mathematics; Logic; History of Analytical Philosophy. **SELECTED PUBLICATIONS** Auth, Frege's Influence on Wittgenstein: Reversing Metaphysics via the Context principle, 97. **CONTACT ADDRESS** Dept of Philosophy, Univ of Calif, Riverside, CA, 92521-0201. **EMAIL** reck@citrus.ucr.edu

REDDISH, MITCHELL GLENN
PERSONAL Born 08/13/1953, Jessup, GA, m, 1975, 3 children **DISCIPLINE** RELIGIOUS STUDIES **EDUCATION** Univ Georgia, BA, 75; Southern Baptist Theol Sem, MA, 78, PhD, 82. **CAREER** Instr, 80-83, New Testament, adj prof, 82-83, Southern Baptist Theol Sem and Sem Evening School; asst prof, 83-89, assoc prof, 89-95, prof, 95- , relig, chemn, 92-, Stetson Univ. **HONORS AND AWARDS** Phi Beta Kappa, Magna Cum Laude, 75; Fac summer res grant, 86; listed, Who's Who in Religion, 92-93; listed, Who's Who in Bibl Stud and Archaeol, 93; Homer and Dolly Hand Fac Res Award, 98. **MEMBERSHIPS** Am Acad Relig; Soc of Bibl Lit; Natl Assoc Baptist Prof of Relig. **RESEARCH** New Testament studies; apocalyptic literature. **SELECTED PUBLICATIONS** Auth, Apocalyptic Literature: A Reader, Abingdon, 90; coauth, An Introduction to The Bible, Abingdon, 91; auth, Daniel, Revelation, in Mercer Commentary on The Bible, Mercer, 94; auth, Reclaiming the Apocalypse, Perspectives in Relig Stud, 97; auth, An Introduction to the Gospels, Abingdon, 97; auth, Apocalyptic Literature and Western Culture, Tchg Apocalypse, Scholars, forthcoming; auth, Revelation, Smyth & Helwys, forthcoming. **CONTACT ADDRESS** Dept of Religious Studies, Stetson Univ, 421 N Woodland Blvd, Unit 8354, DeLand, FL, 32720. **EMAIL** mreddish@stetson.edu

REDDITT, PAUL L.
PERSONAL Born 08/08/1942, Little Rock, AR, m, 1965, 2 children **DISCIPLINE** RELIGION, BIBLICAL STUDIES **EDUCATION** Ouachita Bapt Univ, BA, 63; So Bapt Theol Sem, Mdiv, 67; Vanderbilt Univ, MA, 71, PhD, 72 **CAREER** Prof, 72-86, Otterbein Col; Prof, 86-, Georgetown Col **HONORS AND AWARDS** NEH, Yale Univ, 81 **MEMBERSHIPS** Soc of Bibl Lit; Cath Bibl Asn **SELECTED PUBLICATIONS** Auth, Haggai, Zechariah, Malachi, New Century Bible, 1995; Daniel, New Century Bible, forthcom **CONTACT ADDRESS** Dept of Relig, Georgetown Col, Georgetown, KY, 40324. **EMAIL** predditt@georgetowncollege.edu

REDENBARGER, WAYNE JACOB
PERSONAL Born 11/27/1945, Alton, IL, m, 1993, 2 children **DISCIPLINE** ROMANCE LINGUISTICS, PORTUGUESE **EDUCATION** Ind Univ, BA, 71; Harvard Univ, MA, 75, PhD, 76. **CAREER** Lectr Port, Boston Univ, 74-76; asst prof, 76-82, Assoc Prof Port & Romance Ling, 82- , asst dean, Col of Human, dir comput, 86-90, Ohio State Univ. **HONORS AND AWARDS** Pres, Omicron Chap Phi Beta Kappa; Woodrow Wilson Fel; vis sci, MIT RLE speech grp. **MEMBERSHIPS** Ling Soc Am. **RESEARCH** Morphology of Latin, Portuguese, and Western Romance. **SELECTED PUBLICATIONS** Auth, Vowel lowering and i-epenthesis in Classical Latin, In: Current Studies in Romance Linguistics, Georgetown Univ, 76; Lusitanian Portuguese a is advanced tongue root and constricted pharynx, In: Studies in Romance Linguistics, Newbury House, 77; Portuguese vowel harmony and the elsewhere condition, In: Contemporary Studies in Romance Linguistics, Georgetown Univ, 78; Portuguese evidence for the non-unitary nature of syllable phrasing, Georgetown Univ, 81; Articulator Features and Portuguese Vowel Height, Harvard Univ, 81; auth, Apocopy and Lenition in Portuguese, Issues in the Phonology and Morphology of the Major Iberian Languages, Georgetown U, 97. **CONTACT ADDRESS** Dept of Spanish and Portuguese, Ohio State Univ, 1841 Millikin Rd, Columbus, OH, 43210-1229. **EMAIL** redenbarger.2@osu.edu

REED, GREGORY J.
PERSONAL Born 05/21/1948, MI, m **DISCIPLINE** LAW **EDUCATION** MI State Univ, BS 1970, MS 1971; Wayne State Univ, JD 1974, LLM 1978. **CAREER** Gregory J Reed & Assocs PC, Attorney specializing in corporate, taxation and entertainment law, currently; Wayne State Univ, Detroit MI, prof 1988-89; AHR Packaging Consultant Corp, Detroit MI, pres/developer 1987-. **HONORS AND AWARDS** Graduate Professional Scholarship 3 consecutive years; Distinguished Alumni of the Yr Awd MI State Univ 1980; Resolution for Achievement State of MI Senate, City of Detroit; one of the top ten blacks in the law profession, Detroit News 1985; implemented Gregory J Reed Scholarship Foundation 1986; Award for Contributions to the arts Black Music Month State of MI House of Rep 1987; govt appointment Martin Luther KingCommn of Michigan 1989-; 1992 Hall of Fame inductee by BESLA. **MEMBERSHIPS** Chairperson, Martin Luther King Statue Committee; bd of dirs MI Assn of Community Arts Agencies; mem Natl Bar Assn; MSU Foundation, board of directors; comm mem of entertainment sports, taxation, corp and real estate sects Amer Bar Assn; mem Amer Bar Assn; mem Accounting Aide Soc of Metro Detroit; bd comm New Detroit Inc; tax and corp advisor BUF; mem MI State Bar Taxation and Corporate Div; mem Amer Arbitration Assn; bd of dir BESLA Entertainment Law Assn; bd of dirs MI Assn of Community Arts Agencies; mem State Bar Law Media Comm; first black Attorney adv bd mem US Internal Revenue Serv; founder Advancement Amateur Athletics Inc 1986; first black chmn in US State Bar of MI Arts Communication Sports and Entertainment Sect 1987; speaker, lecturer US & foreign countries; MSU Foundation, vice chairperson, 1996-97. **SELECTED PUBLICATIONS** Author: Tax Planning and Contract Negotiating Techniques for Creative Persons; Professional Athletes and Entertainers (first book of its kind cited by American Bar Association); This Business of Boxing & Its Secrets, 1981; This Business of Entertainment and Its Secrets, 1985; Negotiations Behind Closed Doors, 1987; Economic Empowerment through the church, American Book Award, 1994; "Quiet Strength," co-author with Rosa Parks; "Dear Mrs Parks," co-author with Rosa Parks. **CONTACT ADDRESS** Gregory J. Reed & Associates, PC, 1201 Bagley, Detroit, MI, 48226.

REED, ROSS CHANNING
PERSONAL Born 11/23/1961, Lancaster, PA, s **DISCIPLINE** PHILOSOPHY **EDUCATION** Millersville Univ, BA, 83; Baylor Univ, MA, 86; Loyola Univ Chicago, PhD, 94. **CAREER** Sr Lect, 86-97, Loyola Univ of Chicago; Vis Fac, 94-97, Schl of the Art Inst of Chicago; Instr, 94-97, Columbia Col Chicago; Instr, 970, Univ of Memphis. **MEMBERSHIPS** APA; Amer Soc for Philos; Counseling and Psychotherapy; Amer Fed of Musicians; Soc for the Advancement of Amer Philos **RESEARCH** Philosophical psychology, existentialism, phenomenology, phil of religion, ethics, history and theor of jazz/comercial music. **CONTACT ADDRESS** 3778 Friar Tuck Rd, Memphis, TN, 38111.

REEDER, JOHN P.
PERSONAL Born 07/11/1937, Charlotte, NC, m, 1965, 2 children **DISCIPLINE** RELIGIOUS STUDIES **EDUCATION** Yale Univ, PhD, 68. **CAREER** PROF, BROWN UNIV. **RESEARCH** Ethics & religious thought. **SELECTED PUBLICATIONS** Killing and Saving: Abortion, Hunger and War, Penn State Press, 96. **CONTACT ADDRESS** Dept Relig Stud, Brown Univ, PO Box 1927, Providence, RI, 02912.

REESE, THOMAS
PERSONAL Born 01/11/1945, Altadena, CA **DISCIPLINE** POLITICAL SCIENCE; RELIGION **EDUCATION** St. Louis Univ, MA, 68; Jesuit Sch of Theology, Mdiv, 74; Univ CA, Berkeley, PhD, 76. **CAREER** Instr, 68-70, St. Ignatius Coll Prep; Univ San Francisco, spring 69; asst to the president, 70-71, Univ Santa Clara; assoc ed, 78-85, sr fel, 85-98, Woodstock Theological Ctr at Georgetown Univ, ed-in-chief, June 98, at America magazine. **SELECTED PUBLICATIONS** Auth, The Politics of Taxation, 80; Archbishop: Inside the Power Structure of the American Catholic Church, 89; A Flock of Shepherds: The National Conf of Catholic Bishops, 92; Inside the Vatican: The Politics and Organization of the Catholic Church, 97; 2001 and Beyond: Preparing the Church for the Next Millenium, 97, America; Synod of America, America, 97; Synod for America Ends, 98, America. **CONTACT ADDRESS** America Magazine, 106 W 56th St, New York, NY, 10019.

REESE, WILLIAM LEWIS
PERSONAL Born 02/15/1921, Jefferson City, MO, m, 1945, 3 children **DISCIPLINE** PHILOSOPHY **EDUCATION** Drury Col, AB, 42; Univ Chicago, BD, 45, PhD(philos of relig), 47. **CAREER** From asst prof to assoc prof philos, Drake Univ, 47-57, head dept, 54-57; assoc prof, Grinnell Col, 57-60; prof & chmn dept, Univ Del, 60-67; chmn dept, 68-74,84, Prof Philos, State Univ NY Albany, 67-, Ford Found grant, Yale Univ, 55-56; vis prof, IA State Univ, 58; Ford Found grant, Status of the Hum, Argentina & Latin Am, 67-68; co-ed, Metaphilosophy, 68-76. **HONORS AND AWARDS** Tully Cleon Knoles lectr, Univ of the Pac, 62, Chancellor's Award for Lulti-Campus Seminar in Philos of the Soc Sci, 68-74; NEH Grant for Philos of the Hum, 69-74; Fulbright lctr, Argentina, Summer 1971. **MEMBERSHIPS** Am Philos Soc; Charles S Peirce Soc; Metaphys Soc Am (secy-treas, 62-65); Latin Am Studies Asn; Soc for Iberian and Latin Am Thought. **RESEARCH** Metaphysics; philos of relig; Latin Am philos. **SELECTED PUBLICATIONS** Auth, The Ascent From Below, Houghton, 59; gen ed, Philosophy of Science, the Delaware Seminar, Intersci Publ, Vols I & II, 63 & Springer Verlag, Vol III, 67; coauth, Process and Divinity, Open Ct Publ, 64; contribr ed, Philosophical Investigations, Colloquium on Paul Tillich, Reinhart and Winston, 64; contribr, The Future of Metaphysics, Quadrangle, 70; auth, Pantheism and panentheism, In: Encyclopaedia Britannica, 74; Religious seeing-as, Relig Studies, 9/77; Dictionary of Philosophy and Religion, Humanities Press, 80; 2nd ed, new and enlarged, 96; Language games, seeing-as and metaphorical experience, In Holer Pichler, 81; Dipolarity and Monopolarity in the idea of God, Dialogos, 83; Metaphilosophy and the Philosophy of Sciences, Holder-Pichler-Tempsky, 83; Introduction to Philosophy as a Large Class Tutorial, Teach Philo, 84; Christianity and the Final Solution, The Phil Forum, 84-85; co-auth, Systems of Religious Belief, The New Encyclopaedia Britannica, 88; ed, The Reader's Advisor, 13th ed, 88; Morris Lazerowitz and Metaphilosophy, Metaphilosophy, 90; Prospecting Across the Idealogical Divide, 90; The Trouble with Panentheism-and the Divine Event, Open Court, 91; Process Philosophy in Whitehead and Chu His, Journal of Chinese Philosophy, 93; contribr auth Biographical Dictionary of 20th Century Philosophers, Routledge, 96. **CONTACT ADDRESS** Font Grove Rd, Slingerlands, NY, 12159. **EMAIL** wlr@cnsunix.albany.edu

REGNISTER, BERNARD
PERSONAL Born 07/16/1961, Belgium, s **DISCIPLINE** PHILOSOPHY **EDUCATION** Univ Penn, PhD, 92. **CAREER** Loyola Marymont Univ, asst prof, 92-94; Brown Univ, asst prof, 94-. **HONORS AND AWARDS** L. S. Rockefeller fel, J. R. Workman Award for tchg Excellence. **MEMBERSHIPS** APA, NANS, NAKS. **RESEARCH** Ethical issues in Kant; Existentialism; 19th century German Philosophy. **CONTACT ADDRESS** Dept of Philosophy, Brown Univ, PO Box 1918, Providence, RI, 02912. **EMAIL** bernard_reginster@brown.edu

REHER, MARGARET MARY
PERSONAL Reading, PA **DISCIPLINE** HISTORICAL THEOLOGY, CHURCH HISTORY **EDUCATION** Immaculata Col, BA, 60; Providence Col, MA, 64; Fordham Univ, PhD, 72. **CAREER** Asst prof theol, Immaculata Col, 60-64; asst prof, 73-76, assoc prof, 76-80, Prof Relig, Cabrini Col, 80-93, Prof Emerita, 93. **MEMBERSHIPS** Col Theol Soc Am; Cath Hist Soc; Am Cath Hist Asn. **RESEARCH** Domestic and for outreach of communities of women relig established in Philadelphia. **SELECTED PUBLICATIONS** Auth, Pope Leo XIII and Americanism, In: The Inculcation of American Catholicism 1820-1900, Garland Publ Inc, 88; Americanism and Modernism -- Continuity or Discontinuity?, In: Modern American Catholicism, 1900-1965, Garland Publ Inc 88; Catholic Intellectual Life in America: A History of Persons and Movements, Macmillan Co, 89; Den¤nlis J Dougherty and Anna M Dengle: The

Missionary Alliance, Records Am Cath Hist Soc of Philadelphia, spring 90; Bishop John Carroll and Women, Archbishop Gerety Lectures, 1988-89, Seton Hall Univ, 89; Get Thee to a ¤Peruvianl Nunnery: Cardinal Dougherty and the Philadelpha IHM's, Records Am Cath Hist Soc of Philadelphia, winter 92; Phantom Heresy: A Twice-Told Tale, U S Cath Hist, summer 93; Review Symposium on Begin Catholic: Commonweal from the Seventies to the Nineties, Loyola Univ Press, 93, Horizons, spring 94; co-auth, From St Edward's School to Providence Center: A Story of Commitment, Records Am Cath Hist Soc of Philadelphia, spring-summer, 96; Mission of America: John J Burke in Peru, U S Cath His, fall 97. **CONTACT ADDRESS** Dept of Relig, Cabrini Col, 610 King of Prussia, Radnor, PA, 19087-3698. **EMAIL** margaret.mcguinness@cabrini.edu

REHNQUIST, WILLIAM HUBBS

PERSONAL Born 10/01/1924, Milwaukee, WI, m, 3 children **DISCIPLINE** LAW **EDUCATION** Stanford Univ, BA & MA, 48, LLB, 52; Harvard Univ, MA, 50. **CAREER** Law clerk, US Supreme Court Justice Robert H Jackson, 52-53; pvt pract law, Phoenix, Ariz, 53-69; asst atty gen, Off Legal Coun, 69-72; Assoc Justice, US Supreme Court, 72-86; Chief Justice of US, 86-. **RESEARCH** General practice of law, especially civil litigation. **CONTACT ADDRESS** US Supreme Court, One First St NE, Washington, DC, 20543.

REIBETANZ, S. SOPHIA

PERSONAL Born 11/27/1972, Toronto, ON, Canada **DISCIPLINE** PHILOSOPHY **EDUCATION** Univ Toronto, BA, 94; Oxford Unic, BPhil, 96; Harvard Univ, PhD, 96- . **CAREER** Grad stud, philos, Harvard Univ, 96- . **HONORS AND AWARDS** Frank Knox Mem Fel, 96-97, 97-98; Commonwealth Scholar, Balliol Col, Oxford Univ, 94-96. **RESEARCH** Ethics; metaphysics; philosophy of mind. **SELECTED PUBLICATIONS** Auth, Contractualism and Aggregation, Ethics, 98; auth, A Problem for the Doctrine of Double Effect, Proc of the Aristotelian Soc, 98. **CONTACT ADDRESS** Emerson Hall, Harvard Univ, Cambridge, MA, 02138. **EMAIL** reibetan@fas.harvard.edu

REICH, LOUIS JOHN

PERSONAL Born 11/30/1947, Jersey City, NJ, s **DISCIPLINE** PHILOSOPHY **EDUCATION** Univ Calif, Riverside, MA, 86, PhD, 93. **CAREER** Lectr, CSUSB, 8 years. **MEMBERSHIPS** APA; Hume Soc. **SELECTED PUBLICATIONS** Auth, Hume's Religious Naturalism, University Press of America, 98. **CONTACT ADDRESS** 137 S Princeton, #3, Fullerton, CA, 92831.

REICH, PETER L.

PERSONAL Born 03/20/1955, Los Angeles, CA, m, 1985, 2 children **DISCIPLINE** LAW **EDUCATION** UCLA, BA, 76; UCLA, MA, 77, PhD, 91; UC Berkeley, JD, 85. **CAREER** Vis lectr, UC Riverside, 81; asst prof, 88-91, assoc prof, 91-93; prof, Whittier Law Sch 93-. **HONORS AND AWARDS** Hubert Herring Mem Award, Pacific Coast Coun on Latin Am Studies, 91; Ray Allen Billington Award, Western Hist Asn, 95; Huntington Library Res Fel, 97. **MEMBERSHIPS** Am Soc Legal Hist; Calif Bar Asn. **RESEARCH** Legal history of U.S. Southwest, Mexico; environmental and natural resource policy. **SELECTED PUBLICATIONS** Auth, Mexico's Hidden Revolution: Catholic Church in Law & Politics Since 1929, Univ Notre Dame Press, 95; auth, Mission Revival Jurisprudence: State Courts and Hispanic Water Law Since 1950, Washington Law Review, Vol 69: 869, 95; auth, Western Courts and the Privatization of Hispanic Mineral Rights Since 1850: An Alchemy of Title, Columbia Jour of Environ Law, Vol 23: 57, 98. **CONTACT ADDRESS** Law Sch, Whittier Col, 3333 Harbor Blvd, Costa Mesa, CA, 92626. **EMAIL** preich@law.whittier.edu

REICH, WARREN T.

PERSONAL Born 12/21/1931, Paterson, NJ, m, 1995, 2 children **DISCIPLINE** BIOETHICS **EDUCATION** St Joseph Coll, Holy Trinity, AL, BA, 54; Catholic Univ Amer, Washington, DC, STB, 58, STL, 59; Gregorian Univ, Rome, Italy, STD, 62. **CAREER** Res Assoc Prof, Assoc Prof, Prof, 71-, Sr Res Scholar, Kennedy Inst, 71-, Sr Res Scholar, Center for Clin Bioethics, 71-, Dir, Div of Health and Hum, Dept Family Med, 77-97, Georgetown Univ; Lectr to Assoc Prof, Sch Theol, 66-71, Catholic Univ Amer, Washington, DC; Asst Prof, 62-68, Holy Trinity Mission Sem, Silver Spring, MD. **HONORS AND AWARDS** Royal Natl Acad Med of Spain, Honorary Foreign Member; Amer Lib Assoc; Soc Health and Hum Values; Georgetown Univ The Vicennial Medal; Natl Hum Center, Fellow; Acad of Med of Washington, DC, Dir; Amer Lib Assoc, Dartmouth Medal, 1st ed of Encyclopedia of Bioethics; Univ Wurzburg, Post-doctoral Fellow. **MEMBERSHIPS** Amer Assoc Bioethics and Hum; Alexander von Humboldt Assoc Amer; Amer Philos Assoc; Acad Med of Washington, DC; Soc Health and Hum Values; Inst Soc, Ethics and the Life Sci; Amer Acad Rel; Council on the Stud of Rel; Soc of Christian Ethics; Catholic Theol Soc Amer. **RESEARCH** Ethics Methodology; Philosophy and History of care; Applied ethics: assisted suicide. **SELECTED PUBLICATIONS** Ed in Chief, The Ethics of Sex and Genetics, Encyclopedia of Bioethics, NY, Simon & Schuster Macmillan, 97; ed Chief, Bioethics, Sex, Genetics and Human Reproduction, Macmillan Compendium, Sel from the 5 vol Encyclopedia of Bioethics, NY, Simon & Schuster Macmillan, 97; Encyclopedia of Bioethics, ed Chief, rev ed, 5 vol, NY, Simon & Schuster Macmillan, 95; Encyclopedia of Bioethics, ed Chief, 4 vol, NY, The Macmillan Co., The Free Press, 78. **CONTACT ADDRESS** Georgetown Univ, 415 Kober-Cogan, Washington, DC, 20007.

REICHBERG, GREGORY M.

DISCIPLINE PHILOSOPHY **EDUCATION** Emory Univ, PhD. **CAREER** Assoc prof, Fordham Univ. **RESEARCH** Metaphysics, theories of knowledge, and ethics. **SELECTED PUBLICATIONS** Auth, La Communication de la Nature Divine en Dieu Selon Thomas d'Aquin, Revue Thomiste 93, 93; Thomas Aquinas on Moral Responsibility in the Pursuit of Knowledge, Thomas Aquinas and his Legacy, Cath UP, 94; Contextualizing Theoretical Reason: Thomas Aquinas and Postmodern Thought, Aquinas 38, 95. **CONTACT ADDRESS** Dept of Philos, Fordham Univ, 113 W 60th St, New York, NY, 10023.

REICHENBACH, BRUCE ROBERT

PERSONAL Born 12/13/1943, Staten Island, NY, m, 1965, 2 children **DISCIPLINE** PHILOSOPHY **EDUCATION** Wheaton Col, Ill, AB, 65; Northwestern Univ, MA, 67, PhD, 68. **CAREER** Assoc prof, 68-80, prof philos, Augsburg Col, 80-, vis prof New Testament, Morija Theol Sem, Lesotho, 76-77; summer sem, Nat Endowment for Humanities, 78; vis distinguished prof Evangelical Christianity, Juniata Col, 85-86. **HONORS AND AWARDS** NEH Summer Sem, 78; NEH Summer Inst, 84; Res Grant Inst Advan Christian Study, 84; Fulbright-Hays Sem India, 86; Fulbright-Hays Sem Pakistan, 91; John Templeton Found Grant, 95. **MEMBERSHIPS** Am Philos Asn **RESEARCH** Philosophical theology; philosophy of religion. **SELECTED PUBLICATIONS** Auth, The Cosmological Argument: A Reassessment, CC Thomas, 72; The cosmological argument and the causal principle, Int J Philos Relig, 75; Natural evils and natural laws, Int Philos Quart, 76; Is Man the Phoenix: A Study of Immortaility, Eerdmans, 78; Why is God Good, J Religion, 80; The inductive argument from evil, Am Philos Quart, 80; CS Lewis on the desolation of de-valued science, Christian Scholar's Rev, 82; Evil and a Good God, Fordham Univ, 82; The Law of Karma: A Philosophical Study, MacMillan, 90; coauth, Reason and Religious Belief: An Introduction to the Philosophy of Religion, Oxford Univ, 91, 2 ed, 98; On Behalf of God: A Christian Ethic for Biology, Wm B Eerdmans, 95; Philosophy of Religion: Selected Readings, Oxford Univ, 96; An Introduction to Critical Thinking: A Text for Beginners, McGraw Hill, 99. **CONTACT ADDRESS** Dept of Philos, Augsburg Col, 2211 Riverside Ave, Minneapolis, MN, 55454-1350. **EMAIL** reichen@augsburg.edu

REICHENBACH, MARIA

PERSONAL Born 03/30/1909, Berlin, Germany, w, 1946, 1 child **DISCIPLINE** PHILOSOPHY **EDUCATION** Freiburg, PhD. **CAREER** Univ Calif Los Angeles City Col, 48-74. **HONORS AND AWARDS** Nat Sci Found fel, 65. **MEMBERSHIPS** Amer Philos Asn. **RESEARCH** Science. **SELECTED PUBLICATIONS** Auth, Ger ed, Collected Works in Wiesbaden, Germany. **CONTACT ADDRESS** 456 Puerto del Mar, Pacific Palisades, CA, 90272.

REICHMANN, JAMES B.

PERSONAL Born 01/14/1923, Everett, WA **DISCIPLINE** PHILOSOPHY **EDUCATION** Gonzaga Univ, BA, 46, MA, 47; Gregorian Univ, STL, 54, PhD, 60. **CAREER** From instr to asst prof Philos, Seattle Univ, 55-62; assoc prof Mt St Michael's Sem, 64-65; assoc prof, 65-71, chmn dept, 69-79, prof Philos, Seattle Univ, 71-. **MEMBERSHIPS** Northwestern Philos Asn (pres, 64-65); Am Cath Philos Asn. **RESEARCH** Philosophical psychology; Aristotle's philosophy of God; immanent and subsistent esse in Aquinas. **SELECTED PUBLICATIONS** Auth, St Thomas, Capreolus, Cajetan and the Created Person, New Scholasticism, 1-2/59; Logic and the method of metaphysics, 10/65, The transcendental method and the psychogenesis of being, 10/68 & Immanently transcendent and subsistent esse: A comparison, 4/74, Thomist; Hegel's ethics of the epochal situation, Proc Am Cath Philos Asn, 75; The Philosophy of the Human Person, 80; Evolution, Animal Rights and the Environment, The Catholic Univ of America Pres, 99. **CONTACT ADDRESS** Dept of Philosophy, Seattle Univ, 901 12th Ave, Seattle, WA, 98122-4340.

REID, BENJAMIN F.

PERSONAL Born 10/05/1937, New York, NY, m **DISCIPLINE** THEOLOGY **EDUCATION** Univ of Pittsburgh, attended; No Bapt Theol Sem, attended; Amer Bible Inst, DD 1971; CA Western Univ, PhD 1975; Ctr for Pastoral Studies Anderson IN School of Theol, 1980; CA Grad School of Theol, LD 1981; Anderson Coll, DD 1982; Univ of So CA, Diploma Continuing Educ Ctr 1982-86; World University, DTheol 1988; DD Pacific Christian Coll, 1996. **CAREER** Springfield IL, pastor 1958-59; Junction City KS, pastor 1959-63; Detroit MI, pastor 1963-70; LA 1st Church of God, pastor 1971-96. **HONORS AND AWARDS** Mayor's Awd (LA) for community serv 1986, 1996; Outstanding Bishop's Awd LA Awds Dinner; Inglewood Mayor's Awd 1987, 1996; CA Senate Awd 1987, 1996; Los Angeles City Council Awd 1987, 1996; Compton Mayor's Awd 1987; Los Angeles County Supervisor's Awd 1987, 1996; named by Los Angeles Times as "One of Southern California's Twenty Outstanding Preachers"; Los Angeles Mayor's Award 1988, 1996; Honored Service Award City of Inglewood CA 1988; Ebony Mag, List of Great Black Preachers, 1997. **MEMBERSHIPS** Mem Natl Bd of Ch Ext & Home Missions of the Church of God 1968-80; police chpln Inglewood CA 1973-84; founder, pres So CA Assoc of Holiness Chs 1977-79; dir West Coast Effective Ministries Workshop 1975, 1977-84; vice-chmn General Assembly of the Ch of God 1977-79; pres Partners in Ecumenism SW USA Reg 1979; pres LA Council of Chs 1980; presiding bishop 1st Ch of God Nigerian Conf Africa 1980-95; mem bd of trustees Anderson College 1982-92; pres So CA School of Ministry LA 1984-; elected Sr Bishop The Interstate Assoc of the Ch of God 1985; pres Natl Assoc of the Ch of God 1996; chmn Ministerial Assembly of the So CA Assoc of the Ch of God 1986; mem Natl Black Evangelical Assoc 1988-; founding mem Black Ecumenical Task Force Los Angeles CA 1988-; mem bd dir LA Urban League; gen chmn Interstate WestCoast Assoc of the Ch of God;m Council of Churchmen School of Theol Azusa Pacific Univ; mem bd of trustees, Hope Intl Univ, 1997-; mem LA Council of Chs, So Christian Leadership Conf, LA Met Learning Ctr, Ecumenical Ctr for Black Ch Studies of LA, USC Comm Advs Bd; elected pres; Nat Assn of the Church of God, 1996-. **SELECTED PUBLICATIONS** Author "Confessions of a Happy Preacher" 1971, "Black Preacher Black Church" 1975, "Another Look at Glossalalia" 1977, "Another Look at Other Tongues" rev ed 1982, "Glory to the Spirit" 1989; "Glory to The Spirit" Pastor's WorkbooKed, 1998; "Excellence in Preaching Awd Disciples of Christ." Indianapolis IN 1986. **CONTACT ADDRESS** LA 1st Church of God, 9550 S Crenshaw Blvd, Inglewood, CA, 90305.

REID, GARNETT

PERSONAL Born 12/15/1955, Nashville, TN, m, 1976, 2 children **DISCIPLINE** OLD TESTAMENT INTERPRETATION **EDUCATION** Bob Jones Univ, PhD, 91. **CAREER** Prof of Bible, Free Will Baptist Bible Col, 82- . **MEMBERSHIPS** Soc Bibl Lit; Evangelical Theol Soc; Near E Archaeol Soc; Nat Asn Prof of Hebrew. **RESEARCH** Bible, primarily Old Testament; history. **SELECTED PUBLICATIONS** Auth, articles for the Greek-English Dictionary, Complete Biblical Library, 90, the Hebrew-English Dictionary, 94-98, The Complete Biblical Library, 90; Jeremiah30-33: Heart of Jeremiah's Covenantal Message, Bibl Viewpoint, 91; Defending Christianity in a Pluralistic Society, Contact, 92; Minimalism & Biblical History; Bibliotheca Sacra, 98. **CONTACT ADDRESS** Free Will Baptist Bible Col, 3606 West End Ave, Nashville, TN, 37205. **EMAIL** greid@fwbbc.edu

REID, INEZ SMITH

PERSONAL Born 04/07/1937, New Orleans, LA **DISCIPLINE** LAW **EDUCATION** Tufts Univ, BA 1959; Yale Univ Law Sch, LLB 1962; UCLA, MA 1963; Columbia Univ, PhD 1968. **CAREER** Barnard Coll Columbia Univ, assoc prof 1969-76; NY State Div for Youth, genl counsel 1976-77; Dept of Health Educ & Welfare, deputy genl counsel 1977-79; Environmental Protection Agency, inspector genl 1979-80; Dist of Columbia Govt, corp counsel. **HONORS AND AWARDS** Numerous articles published; numerous awds. **MEMBERSHIPS** Past bds Antioch Univ Bd of Trustees, United Ch of Christ Bd for Homeland Ministries. **CONTACT ADDRESS** Corporation Counsel, Dist of Columbia Govt, Dist Bldg Ofc of Corp Coun, Rm 329, Washington, DC, 20004.

REID, JOHN PHILLIP

PERSONAL Born 05/17/1930, Weehawken, NJ **DISCIPLINE** HISTORY, LAW **EDUCATION** Georgetown Univ, BSS, 52; Harvard Univ, LLB, 55; Univ NH, MA, 57; New York Univ, LLM, 60, JSD, 62. **CAREER** From instr to assoc prof, 60-66, Prof legal hist, NY Univ, 66-, Guggenheim Found fel, 80; fel, Henry E. Huntington Libr, 80. **RESEARCH** Am legal hist. **SELECTED PUBLICATIONS** Auth, Chief Justice: Judicial World of Charles Doe, Harvard Univ, 67; A Law of Blood: The Primitive Law of the Cherokee Nation, New York Univ, 70; A Better Kind of Hatchet: Law, Trade and Diplomacy in the Cherokee Nation During the Early Years of European Contact, 76, In a Defiant Stance: The Conditions of Law in Massachusetts Bay, The Irish Comparison and the Coming of the American Revolution, 77 & In a Rebellious Spirit: The Argument of Facts, the Liberty Riot, and the Coming of the American Revolution, 78, Pa State Univ; Law for the Elephant: Property and Social Behavior on the Overland Trail, Huntington Libr, 80; In Defiance of the Law: The Standing-Army Controversy, the Two Constitutions, and the Coming of the American Revolution, Univ NC, 81; The Briefs of the American Revolution: Constitutional Arguments between Thomas Hutchinson, Governor of Massachusetts Bay, and James Bowdoin for the Council, and John Adams for the House of Representatives, NY Univ, 81. **CONTACT ADDRESS** Sch of Law, New York Univ, New York, NY, 10003. **EMAIL** reidj@tuving.law.nyu.edu

REIDE, JEROME L.

PERSONAL Born 04/23/1954, New York, New York, s **DISCIPLINE** LAW **EDUCATION** SUNY, New Paltz, BA, 1977;

Hofstra University Law School, JD, 1981; Columbia University Graduate Journalism School, MS, 1982; Michigan State University, PhD, 1991. **CAREER** American Civil Liberties Union, Access to Justice, coordinator, 1986-87; Center for Labor Studies, SUNY, political science lecturer, 1986-87; Eastern Michigan University, African-American studies lecturer, 1987-88; Detroit City Council, special projects assistant, 1987-88; Michigan State University, Dean of Urban Studies, research assistant, 1988-90; Wayne State University, School of Education, lecturer, 1992-93; NAACP, Special Contribution Fund Midwest, development director, 1990-93; Wayne County Commission, Chair of Ways and Means, legislative aide, 1993-94; Wayne State Univ, Interdisciplinary Studies, asst prof, 1994-; Raheem Fuckemeyer & Reide PLLC. **HONORS AND AWARDS** NAACP, Religious Affairs, Back to School/Stay in School, 1992; University of Michigan, Flint, College Bound, Most Inspirational Teacher, 1992; Jackson Fair Housing Commission, Fair Housing Award, 1992; Governor of Kentucky, Order of the Kentucky Colonels, 1991; Committee on Institutional Cooperation, Social Science Fellow, 1988; State Legislature of Michigan, Special Tribute, 1994; Wayne State Univ, ISP, CLL Teaching Excellence Award, 1997. **MEMBERSHIPS** Urban League, Michigan, 1988-; Dispute Resolution Coordination Council, board of directors, 1991-95; NAACP, life member, 1975-; Boniface Community Action, board of directors, 1991-95; Urban Affairs Graduate Studies Association, president, 1989-90; National Conference of Black Lawyers, press secretary, 1986-87; Black Law Students Association, national press secretary, 1980-81; Sutton for Mayor, press aide, 1977; Global Economic Development Conf, pres, 1993; Wayne State Univ, Ctr for Peace & Conflict Studies, Exec Committee, 1994; State Bar of Michigan, 1996; American Bar Assn, 1997-; Wolverine Bar Assn, 1997-; Team Justice, 1997. **SELECTED PUBLICATIONS** Author, Justice Evicted, American Civil Liberties Union, 1987; executive producer/moderator, "The State of Black Michigan," 1989-; editor, Mulitcultural Education Resource Guide, Michigan State Board of Education, 1990; executive producer, "Human Rights and Civil Wrongs," Museum of African-American History, 1991; writer, "NAACP Community Economic Development," The Crisis Magazine, 1992. **CONTACT ADDRESS** Wayne State Univ, 2220 Academic/ Administrative Bldg, Detroit, MI, 48202.

REIDENBERG, JOEL R.
DISCIPLINE INFORMATION TECHNOLOGY LAW, COMPARATIVE LAW **EDUCATION** Dartmouth, AB, 83; Columbia, JD, 86; Univ de Paris, DEA, 87. **CAREER** Assoc, Debevoise and Plimpton, Wash DC, 87-90; vis prof, AT&T Lab(s) Pub Policy Res, 96; guest lectr, Univ de Paris, 97; vis prof, Univ de Paris I (Panth,on-Sorbonne), 96-97; ch, Assn Am Law Sch, 96; ch, sect defamation and privacy, Assn Amer Law Sch, 98; prof, 90-. **HONORS AND AWARDS** Friedmannfel, Promethee, Paris, 86-87; **SELECTED PUBLICATIONS** Auth, Rules of the Road on Global Electronic Highways: Merging the Trade and Technical Paradigms, 6 Harvard J Law & Tech 287, 93; Information Flows on the Global Infobahn, New Information Infrastructure: Strategies for US Policy, Twentieth Century Fund Press, 95; Setting Standards for Fair Information Practice in the US Private Sector, 80 Iowa L Rev 497, 95; Governing Networks and Rule-Making in Cyberspace, 45 Emory L Jour 911, 96; Multimedia as a New Challenge and Opportunity in Privacy, 22 Materialien Zum Datenschutz 9, 96; The Use of Technology to Assure Internet Privacy: Adapting Labels and Filters for Data Protection, Lex Electronica, 97; Lex Informatica: The Formulation of Information Policy Rules through Technology, 76 Texas L Rev 553, 98; co-auth, The Fundamental Role of Privacy and Confidence in Networks, 30 Wake Forest L Rev 105, 95. **CONTACT ADDRESS** Law Sch, Fordham Univ, 113 W 60th St, New York, NY, 10023. **EMAIL** reidenberg@sprynet.com

REIDY, DAVID
DISCIPLINE PHILOSOPHY **EDUCATION** Depauw Univ, BA, 84; Indiana Univ, JD, 87; Univ of Kansas, MA, 92, PhD, 97. **CAREER** Asst Inst, Lect, 86-90, Indiana Univ Sch of Law; Inst, 90-96, Univ of Kansas; Vis Asst Prof, Depauw Univ, 97-99; Vis Asst Prof, 98, Post Doct Fel, Indiana Univ, 97-. **MEMBERSHIPS** Intl Assoc for Philo of Law and Soc and Philo; Amer Soc for Political and Legal Philo; North Amer Soc for Social Philo; APA **RESEARCH** Political and social philosophy; philosophy of law. **SELECTED PUBLICATIONS** Art, Law, Dominant Paradigms and Legal Education, Kansas Law Rev, 91; art, Eastern Europe, Civil Society and the Real Revolution, Praxis Intl, 92; art, Does Hume Have a Theory of Justice, Auslegung, 93; art, Antigone, Hegel, and the Law, Legal Stud Forum, 95; art, Education for Citizenship in a Just and Stable Pluralist Democracy, Jour of Value Inquiry, 96; art,Citizenship and Educational Institutions, Arch for Phil of Law and Soc Phil, 97. **CONTACT ADDRESS** Indiana Univ-Purdue Univ, Indianapolis, Dept of Philo, Indianapolis, IN, 46202-5140. **EMAIL** dreidy@iupui.edu

REILLY, BERNARD F
PERSONAL Born 06/08/1925, Audubon, NJ, m, 1948, 9 children **DISCIPLINE** MEDIEVAL HISPANIC & CHURCH HISTORY **EDUCATION** Villanova Univ, BA, 50; Univ Pa, MA, 55; Bryn Mawr Col, PhD(medieval hist), 66. **CAREER** From instr to assoc prof, 55-71, PROF HIST, VILLANOVA UNIV, 72- **MEMBERSHIPS** Mediaeval Acad Am; AHA; Am Cath Hist Asn. **RESEARCH** French influence in eleventh and twelfth century Spain; Leon-Castile in the eleventh and twelfth centuries; medieval Spanish historiography. **SELECTED PUBLICATIONS** Auth, Santiago and Saint Denis: The French Presence in twelfth-century Spain, Cath Hist Rev, 10/68; The Historia Compostelana: The genesis and composition of a twelfth-century Spanish Gesta, Speculum, 1/69; Existing manuscripts of the Historia Compostelana, notes toward a critical edition, Manuscripta, 7/71; The Court Bishops of Alfonso VII of Leon-Castilla, Medieval Studies, 7/74; The Chancery of Alfonso VII of Leon-Castilla: The period 1115-1135 reconsidered, Speculum, 4/76; Sources of the fourth book of Lucas of Tuy's Chronicon Mundi, Classical Folia, 12/76; On getting to be a bishop in Leon-Castilla: The emperor Alfonso VII and the post-Gregorian church, Studies in Medieval and Renaissance History, Vol 1, 78; The kingdom of Leon-Castilla under Queen Urraca: 1109-1126, Princeton Univ Press, 82; History Of The Iberian Peninsula In The Middle-Ages: 711-1480 Kingdoms, Crowns, Regions, Catholic Hist Rev, Vol 80, 94. **CONTACT ADDRESS** Dept of Hist, Villanova Univ, 845 E Lancaster Ave, Villanova, PA, 19085.

REIMER, JAMES A.
DISCIPLINE RELIGIOUS STUDIES **EDUCATION** University Toronto, MA, 74; Univ St. Michael's Col, PhD, 83. **CAREER** Prof **SELECTED PUBLICATIONS** Auth, pub(s) on nineteenth century European intellectual history and modem theology, and German theology in the Hitler era. **CONTACT ADDRESS** Dept of Religious Studies, Conrad Grebel Col, 200 Westmount Rd, Waterloo, ON, N2L 3G6. **EMAIL** ajreimer@uwaterloo.ca

REINHARTZ, ADELE
PERSONAL Born 05/06/1953 **DISCIPLINE** RELIGION **EDUCATION** Univ Toronto, BA, 75; McMaster Univ, MA, 77; PhD, 83. **CAREER** Asst prof, 81-87, Univ Toronto; asst prof, 87-, tenure, 90-, prof, 97-, dept relig, McMaster Univ; vis prof, 99-, Harvard Div Schl. **MEMBERSHIPS** AAR; Soc of Bibl Lit; Canadian Soc of Bibl Stud; Assn of Jewish Stud. **RESEARCH** Early Christianity; second Temple Judaism; Hebrew Bible; lit & feminist criticism. **SELECTED PUBLICATIONS** Auth, The Word in the World: The Cosmological Tale in the Fourth Gospel, SBL Mono Ser 45, Scholars Press, 92; auth, Parents and Children: A Philonic Perspective, Jewish Family in Antiq, Scholars Press, 93; art, Anonymity and characterization in the Books of Samuel, Semeia 63: Character in Biblical Narrative, 93; art, Samson's Mother: An Unnamed Protagonist, Fem Companion to Judges, Sheffield Acad Press, 93; auth, A Feminist Commentary on the Gospel of John, Searching the Scriptures, vol 2, Crossroad, 94; auth, Anonymous Female Characters in the Books of Kings, Fem Comp to Samuel & Kings, JSOT Press, 94; art, Jewish Feminist Discourse, Concilium 263, 96; auth, Feminist Criticism and Biblical Studies on the Verge of the Twenty-First Century, Fem Comp to Reading the Bible: Approaches, Methods & Strategies, Sheffield Acad Press, 97; auth, Why Ask My Name? Anonymity & Identity in Biblical Narratives, Oxford Univ Press, 98; auth, The Greek Book of Esther, Women's Bible Comm 2nd ed, Westminster/John Knox, 98; auth, On Travel, Translation and Ethnography: the Gospel of John at the Turn of the Century, What is John? Vol 2 Lit & Soc Readings of the 4th Gospel, Scholars Press, 98; auth, The Johannine Community and its Jewish Neighbors: A Reappraisal, What is John? Vol 2 Lit & Social Readings of the 4th Gospel, Scholars Press, 98; art, A Nice Jewish Girl Reads the Gospel of John, Semeia 77, Ethics & Reading the Bible, Scholars Press, 98; art, Midrash She Wrote: Jewish Women's Writing on the Bible, Shofar 16/4, 98. **CONTACT ADDRESS** Dept of Religious Studies, McMaster Univ, 1280 Main St W, Hamilton, ON, L8S 4K1. **EMAIL** reinhart@mcmaster.ca

REISCH, GEORGE
PERSONAL Born 12/25/1962, NJ **DISCIPLINE** HISTORY AND PHILOSOPHY OF SCIENCE **EDUCATION** Univ Chicago, MA, 90, PhD, 95. **CAREER** Vis asst prof, Il Inst Tech, 96-97; res fel, Northwestern Univ, 95-96. **MEMBERSHIPS** Philos of Sci Assoc. **SELECTED PUBLICATIONS** Auth, "Planning Science: Otto Neurath and the International Encyclopedia of Unified Science," Brit Jrnl for the Hist of Sci, 94; "Scientism Without Tears," Hist and Theory, 95; "Terminology in Action," in Encyclopedia and Utopia, Kluwer, 96; "How Postmodern was Neurath's Idea of Unified Science," Stud in Hist and Philos of Sci, 97; "Epistemologist, Economist...and Censor: On Otto Neurath's Infamous Index Verborum Prhibitorum," Perspectives on Sci, 97. **CONTACT ADDRESS** 5246 N. Kenmore Ave., 1N, Chicago, IL, 60640. **EMAIL** greisch@tezcat.com

REISMAN, W. MICHAEL
PERSONAL Born 04/23/1939, Philadelphia, PA **DISCIPLINE** INTERNATIONAL LAW, JURISPRUDENCE **EDUCATION** Johns Hopkins Univ, BA, 60; Hebrew Univ, LLB, 63; Yale Univ, LLM, 64, JSD, 65. **CAREER** Prof Law, Yale Univ, 68-, Fulbright fel, Netherlands, 66-67. **HONORS AND AWARDS** Gherini Prize, Yale Univ, 64; World Acad Arts & Sci Award, 81. **MEMBERSHIPS** Int Law Asn; Coun Foreign Rel. **SELECTED PUBLICATIONS** Auth, Nullity and Revision, Yale Univ Press, 71; Art of the Possible, Princeton Univ, 71; Puerto Rico and the International Process, West Publ Co, 75; co-ed, Toward World Order and Human Dignity, Free Press, 75; auth, Folded Lies, Free Press, 75 & Span tranal, Fundo Cult Econ, Mex, 82; coauth, International law in contemporary perspective, 81 & International Law Essays, 81, Found; Autonomy, Interdependence, And Responsibility, Yale Law J, Vol 103, 93. **CONTACT ADDRESS** P O Box 208215, New Haven, CT, 06520-8215.

REISS, LESTER JOSEPH
PERSONAL Born 09/27/1933, Brooklyn, NY, m, 1961, 2 children **DISCIPLINE** PHILOSOPHY **EDUCATION** Yale Univ, BA, 55; Boston Univ, MA, 58, PhD(philos), 67. **CAREER** From instr to assoc prof, 61-76, co-chmn dept, 73-75 & 76-77, chmn dept, 85-94, Prof Philos, Conn Col, 76- **RESEARCH** History of philosophy. **SELECTED PUBLICATIONS** Auth, What is metaphysics?, 59 & St Anselm's arguments and the double-edged sword, 72, Philos Forum. **CONTACT ADDRESS** Dept of Philos, Connecticut Col, 270 Mohegan Ave, New London, CT, 06320-4125. **EMAIL** ljrei@conncoll.edu

REITER, DAVID DEAN
DISCIPLINE PHILOSOPHY **EDUCATION** Univ Nebraska, PhD. **CONTACT ADDRESS** Philosophy Dept, Univ St Thomas, St. Paul, MN, 55105. **EMAIL** davidreiter@juno.com

REITZ, CHARLES
PERSONAL Born 03/10/1946, Buffalo, NY, m, 1987, 2 children **DISCIPLINE** PHILOSOPHY OF EDUCATION **EDUCATION** Canisius Col, BA, 68; SUNY Buffalo, PhD, 83. **CAREER** Assoc prof philos, Kansas City Commun Col, 87- . **HONORS AND AWARDS** Tchg award, 90. **MEMBERSHIPS** APA; Soc for Ger-Am Stud. **RESEARCH** Critical theory of society and education. **SELECTED PUBLICATIONS** Auth, Art, Alienation and the Humanities: A Critical Engagement with Herbert Marcuse, SUNY, 99. **CONTACT ADDRESS** 2 East 58th St, Kansas City, MO, 64113. **EMAIL** creitz@toto.net

REITZ, CURTIS R.
PERSONAL Born 11/20/1929, Reading, PA, m, 1983, 3 children **DISCIPLINE** LAW **EDUCATION** Univ PA, AB, LLB, 56. **CAREER** From asst prof to assoc prof, 57-63, prof law, Univ PA, 63-; Frances Lewis Schol-in-Res, Sch Law, Washington & Lee Univ, 82. **MEMBERSHIPS** Am Law Inst; Nat Conf Comnr Uniform State Laws. **RESEARCH** International trade and investment; commercial law; commercial credit; construction contracts. **SELECTED PUBLICATIONS** Ed, Cases and Materials on Contracts as Basic Commercial Law, West Publ, 75; auth, Consumer Protection Under the Magnuson-Moss Warranty Act, Am Law Inst, 78; Cases, Problems and Materials on Sales Transactions: Domestic and International Law, 92. **CONTACT ADDRESS** Sch Law, Univ PA, 3400 Chestnut St, Philadelphia, PA, 19104-6204. **EMAIL** creitz@oyez.law.upenn.edu

RENDSBURG, G.A.
PERSONAL Born 02/13/1954, Baltimore, MD, m, 1977, 3 children **DISCIPLINE** BIBLICAL STUDIES **EDUCATION** New York Univ, PhD 80, MA 77; Univ North Carolina, BA 75. **CAREER** Cornell Univ, asst prof, assoc prof, prof, 86-; Canisius College, asst prof 80-86. **HONORS AND AWARDS** NEH; Vis fel, U of Penn Judaic Stud. **MEMBERSHIPS** SBL; AOS; AJS. **RESEARCH** Bible; history of the Hebrew language; Semitic lang; Egyptology. **SELECTED PUBLICATIONS** Auth, The Bible and the Ancient Near East, coauth, NY, W. W. Norton, 97; Ancient Hebrew Phonology, in: A. S. Kaye, ed, The Phonologies of Asia and Africa, Winona Lake, IN, Eisenbrauns, 97; The Early History of Israel, in: G D Young, M W Chavalas, R E Averback, eds, Crossing Boundaries and Linking Horizons: Studies in Honor of Michael C. Astour on His 80th Birthday, Bethesda, MD, CDL Press, 97; Biblical Literature as Politics: The Case of Genesis, in: A Berlin, ed, Religion and Politics in the Ancient Near East, Bethesda MD, UPMD, 96; Linguistic Variation and the Foreign Factor in the Hebrew Bible, Israel Oriental Studies, 96. **CONTACT ADDRESS** Dept of Near Eastern Studies, Cornell Univ, 360 Rockefeller Hall, Ithaca, NY, 14853. **EMAIL** gar4@cornell.edu

RENICK, TIMOTHY M.
DISCIPLINE RELIGION **EDUCATION** Princeton Univ, PhD, 86; Princeton Univ, MA, 84; Dartmouth Col, BA, 82 **CAREER** Asst prof, Georgia State Univ, 86-92; assoc prof, Georgia State Univ, 92- **HONORS AND AWARDS** Distinguished Honors Prof, Georgia State Univ, 93; Blue Key National Honor Soc Outstanding Teacher Award, 93; Outstanding Teacher Award, Georgia State Univ, 91; Phi Beta Kappa, 82 **MEMBERSHIPS** Amer Acad Relig; Soc Christian Ethics **RESEARCH** Religion and Ethics; Issues of War and Peace; Religious Pluralism; Cloning **SELECTED PUBLICATIONS** "A Rabbit in Sheep's Clothing: Exploring the Sources of Our Moral Disquiet About Cloning," Annual Soc Christian Ethics, 98; "The Time is Now: The Living Eschaton as Unifying Theme in Contemporary Christian Thought," Texts and Translators, 98; "Charity Lost: The Secularization of the Principle of

Double Effect in the Just-War Tradition," Thomist, 94 **CONTACT ADDRESS** Philosophy Dept, Georgia State Univ, PO Box 4089, Atlanta, GA, 30302-4089. **EMAIL** phltmr@panther.gsu.edu

RENNIE, BRYAN S.
PERSONAL Born 12/13/1954, Ayr, Scotland, m **DISCIPLINE** HISTORY; PHILOSOPHY OF RELIGION **EDUCATION** Edinburgh Univ, Scotland, BA, 77, MA, 88, PhD, 91. **CAREER** Instr, Youngstown S Univ, 91; instr, Allegheny Col, 92; instr, Westminster Col, 92-93; asst prof, Westminster Col, 93- . **MEMBERSHIPS** AAR; Amer Philos Asn; SSSR; NASR. **RESEARCH** Mircea Eliade; Theory and method in the study of religion; The broad application of philosophy to the study of religion. **SELECTED PUBLICATIONS** Auth, Kali: the Terrible Goddess of Hindu Tantra, The Jour Rel Stud (s), Patiala, Univ Punjab, 12, 2, Autumn 89, 27-34; Rev of Other Peoples' Myths by Wendy Doniger and Metaphorical Worlds by Samuel R. Levin, 24, 4, Winter 90; The Diplomatic Career of mircea Eliade: a Response to Adriana Berger, Rel, 22, 4, 92, 375-392; The Religious Creativity of Modern Humanity: Some Observations on Eliade's Unfinished Thought, Rel Stud (s), June 95; Mircea Eliade: coupable jusqu'a preuve du contraire? Jurnalul Literar, 13-16, May-June 94, 2; Reconstructing Eliade: Making Sense of Religion, New York, State U of New York P, 96; Memory, Identity, and Imagination: Imagining the Past and Remembering Destiny, in Memory, History, and Critique, European Identity at the Millenium, Proceedings of the 6th International ISSEI Conference at the University for Humanist Studies, Utrecht, The Netherlands, Aug 96; Actualitatea lui Mircea Eliade, Origini: A Review of Literature, Ideas, and the Arts, vol, 5-6, Nov-Dec 97, vii, ix; Mircea Eliade in The Routledge Encycl of Philos, ed Edward Craig, Routledge, 98. **CONTACT ADDRESS** Dept of Religion and Philosophy, Westminster Col, New Wilmington, PA, 16172. **EMAIL** brennie@westminster.edu

RESCHER, NICHOLAS
PERSONAL Born 07/15/1928, Hagen, Germany, m, 1968, 4 children **DISCIPLINE** PHILOSOPHY **EDUCATION** Queens Col, NY, BS, 49; Princeton Univ, MA, 50, PhD(philos), 51. **CAREER** Instr philos, Princeton Univ, 51-52; mathematician, Rand Corp, Calif, 54-57; assoc prof philos, Lehigh Univ, 57-61; prof, 61-70, univ prof philos, Univ Pittsburgh, 70, dir, Ctr Philos Sci, 81-88; secy gen, Int Union Hist & Philos Sci, 71-75; mem, Int Inst Philos, 70-; Guggenheim Found fel, 71-72. **HONORS AND AWARDS** LHD, Loyola Univ Chicago, 70, Lehigh Univ, 93; Dr honoris causa, Cordoba (Argentina), 92, Konstanz (Germany), 96; Alexander von Humboldt Prize, 83; Academia Europaea, 97. **MEMBERSHIPS** Am Philos Asn; Royal Asiatic Soc; Philos Sci Asn; pres, Charles S. Peirce Soc, 83; pres, Leibniz Soc of Am, 83-86; pres, Am Philos Asn (Eastern Div), 89-90. **RESEARCH** Metaphysics; theory of knowledge; philosophy of science. **SELECTED PUBLICATIONS** Auth, Many-Valued Logic, McGraw, 69; Coherence Theory of Truth, Clarendon, 73; Conceptual Idealism, 73; Methodological Pragmatism, 77; Scientific Progress, 78, Basil Blackwell; Limits of Science, Calif, 85; Predicting the Future, SUNY, 98. **CONTACT ADDRESS** Dept of Philos, Univ of Pittsburgh, 1012 Cathedral/Learning, Pittsburgh, PA, 15260-0001. **EMAIL** Rescher@vms.cis.pitt.edu

RESNICK, IRVEN M.
PERSONAL Born 11/22/1952, Rochester, NY, m, 1989, 3 children **DISCIPLINE** RELIGION **EDUCATION** Tulane Univ, BA, 74; Catholic Univ Amer, MA, 80; Univ Va, PhD, 83. **CAREER** Acting asst prof, 82-83, Univ Va Charlottesville; lectr, 84, Smith Col; asst prof, 83-84, Mt Holyoke Col; asst prof, 87-90, Va Polytechnic Inst & St Univ; assoc prof to prof, chair, , 90- Univ Tn Chattanooga. **HONORS AND AWARDS** NEH Summer Sem, 85; NEH Summer Stipend, 88; NEH Travel to Collections Grant, 89; NEH Summer Inst, Univ Notre Dame, 89; Summer Res Coun Grant, La St Univ, 89; DAAD, Res Visit Grant, Germany, 92; Jerusalem Trust Fel, Oxford Univ, 95; co-dir, Nat Endow for the Humanities, 96; Corresponding Fel, Bar-Ilan Univ, Israel., Knights of Columbus Fel, 79-80; DuPont Fel, 77-79, 80-81; Andrew W. Mellon Fel, 81-82; Summer Fel, Harvard Univ, 82. **MEMBERSHIPS** Midwest Jewish Stud Assoc; Soc for Medieval & Renaissance Philos; Assoc for Jewish Stud. **RESEARCH** Medieval Judaism & Christianity; Jewish-Christian polemics. **CONTACT ADDRESS** Dept of Philos & Relig, Univ Tn Chattanooga, 615 McCallie Ave, Chattanooga, TN, 37403-2598. **EMAIL** Irven-Resnick@UTC.EDU

RESNIK, JUDITH
PERSONAL Born 06/27/1950, Orange, NJ **DISCIPLINE** LAW **EDUCATION** Bryn Mawr Col, AB, 72; New York Univ, JD, 75. **CAREER** Lectr & supvy atty, Yale Univ, 77-79, actg dir, Guggenheim Prog Criminal Justice, 79-80; asst prof, 80-82, Assoc Prof Law, Univ Southern Calif, 82-, Lectr, Nat Inst Corrections, 80-; consult, Inst Civil Justice, Rand Corp, 81- **RESEARCH** Courts in the United States; procedure and process of dispute resolution; women prisoners. **SELECTED PUBLICATIONS** Coauth, Prisoners of their sex: Women's health in jails and prisons, In: Prisoners' Rights Sourcebook, Vol II, Clark Boardman, 80; auth, Women's prisoners, men's prisons: Should prisoners be segregated by sex?, In: Criminal Corrections: Ideals and Realities, Lexington Bks, 82; Managerial Judges, Harvard Law Rev, 12/82; Gender Bias--From Classes To Courts, Stanford Law Rev, Vol 45, 93; Aggregation, Settlement, And Dismay, Cornell Law Rev, Vol 80, 95; Procedural Innovations, Sloshing Over--A Comment On Hensler,Deborah, A Glass Half Full, A Glass Half Empty--The Use Of Alternative Dispute Resolution In Mass Personal-Injury Litigation, Texas Law Rev, Vol 73, 95; Multiple Sovereignties--Indian Tribes, States, And The Federal-Government, Judicature, Vol 79, 95; Whose Judgment--Vacating Judgments, Preferences For Settlement, And The Role Of Adjudication At The Close Of The 20th-Century, UCLA Law Rev, Vol 41, 94. **CONTACT ADDRESS** Law Ctr, Univ Southern Calif, Los Angeles, CA, 90007.

RESNIK, MICHAEL D.
PERSONAL Born 03/20/1938, New Haven, CT, m, 1960, 3 children **DISCIPLINE** PHILOSOPHY, LOGIC **EDUCATION** Yale Univ, BA, 60; Harvard Univ, AM, 62, PhD(philos), 64. **CAREER** Mathematician, US Air Force Cambridge Res Labs, 61-63; asst prof philos, Univ Hawaii, 64-67; assoc prof, 67-75, Prof Philos & Chmn Dept, Univ NC, Chapel Hill, 75-, Vis asst prof, Wash Univ, 66-67; dir summer sem for col teachers, Nat Endowment for Humanities, 80; pres, NC Philos Soc, 80-81. **MEMBERSHIPS** Asn Symbolic Logic; Am Philos Asn. **RESEARCH** Philosophy of mathematics; decision theory. **SELECTED PUBLICATIONS** Auth, The role of the context principle in Frege's philosophy, Philos & Phenomenol Res, 67; More on Skolem's paradox, NOUS, 69; Elementary Logic, McGraw, 70; The Frege-Hilbert controversy, Philos & Phenomenol Res, 74; Frege's context principle revisited, Studien zu Frege, 75; Mathematical knowledge and pattern cognition, Can J Philos, 75; Frege and the Philosophy of Mathematics, Cornell, 80; Mathematics as a science of patterns, Nous, 81 & 82; Foundations Without Foundationalism--A Case For 2nd-Order Logic, Hist And Philosophy Of Logic, Vol 14, 93. **CONTACT ADDRESS** Dept of Philos, Univ of NC, Chapel Hill, NC, 27514.

RESSEGUIE, JAMES L.
PERSONAL Born 01/01/1945, Buffalo, NY, m, 1970, 3 children **DISCIPLINE** THEOLOGY **EDUCATION** Univ California-Berkeley, AB, 76; Princeton Theological Seminary, MDiv, 72; Fuller Theological Seminary, PhD, 78. **CAREER** Asst Prof, 76-78, Assoc Prof, 79-83, Dean of Academic & Student Affairs and Registrar, 90-97, J. Russell Bucher Prof, 84-, Winebrenner Theological Seminary. **HONORS AND AWARDS** Natl Endowment for Humanities Fel, Indiana Univ, 79; Fel, Case Method Inst, 81; Natl Endowment for Humanities Fel, Stanford Univ, 82; Fel, Inst for Ecumenical & Cultural Research, Collegeville, MN, 83; Natl Endowment for Humanities Fel, Univ Florida, 85; Coolidge Research Fel, Episcopal Divinity School, Cambridge, 87; Natl Endowment for Humanities Fel, Univ California-Berkeley, 88; Fulbright Scholar, Univ Iceland, 90; Natl Endowment for Humanities Fel, Ohio State Univ, 91. **MEMBERSHIPS** SBL; Maumee Valley Presbytery **RESEARCH** New Testament **SELECTED PUBLICATIONS** Auth, Defamiliarization and the Gospels, Biblical Theology Bulletin, 90; Automatization and Defamiliarization in Luke 7: 36-50, Literature and Theology: An Interdisciplinary Journal of Theory and Criticism, 91; Making the Familiar Strange, Interpretation: A Journal of Bible and Theology, 92; Revelation Unsealed: A Narrative Critical Approach to John's Apocalypse, 98. **CONTACT ADDRESS** Winebrenner Theol Sem, 701 E. Melrose Ave., Findlay, OH, 45839.

REUMANN, JOHN HENRY PAUL
PERSONAL Born 04/21/1927, Easton, PA, m, 1958, 3 children **DISCIPLINE** THEOLOGY **EDUCATION** Univ PA, MA, 50, PhD, 57; Lutheran Theol sem, STM, 51. **CAREER** Asst prof New testament, 55-59, dean, 74-78, acting pres, 75-76, Prof New Testament, Lutheran Theol Sem, Philadelphia, 59-, res assoc, sem New Testament studies, Columbia Univ, 60-; mem bd trustees, Muhlenberg Col, 60-78, 95-; assoc ed, J Bibl Lit, 61-69, ed, 70; ed, Facet Bks Bibl ser, Fortress, 63-72; mem, Lutheran Coun in USA, 66-78; guest lectr, Princeton Theol Sem, 70, La Salle Col, 71 & United Theol Col, India, 72; mem adv coun, Interpretation, 71-78, 84-89; Fry fel, Lutheran Church in America, 72-73; mem bd, Inst Ecumenical Res, France, 74-86, U.S. Lutheran-Roman Catholic dialogue, 65-95, 98-. **HONORS AND AWARDS** Am Asn Theol Sem fac fel, Cambridge Univ, 59-60; Guggenheim fel, Univ Gottingen, 65-66. **MEMBERSHIPS** Soc Study New Testament; Soc Bibl Lit. **RESEARCH** New Testament; Greek; patristics. **SELECTED PUBLICATIONS** Coauth, Righteousness and Society, 67 & auth, Jesus in the Church's Gospels, 68, Fortress; ed & contribr, Understanding the Sacred Text, Judson, 71; Peter in the New Testament, Augsburg & Paulist, 73; auth, Creation and New Creation, Augsburg, 73; ed & contribr, The Church Emerging, Fortress, 77; coauth, Witness of the Word, Fortress, 86; co-ed & contribr, Peter in the New Testament, Fortress & Paulist, 73; Mary in the New Testament, Fortress & Paulist, 78; Ministries Examined, Augsburg, 87-, Variety and Unity in the New Testament, Oxford, 91. **CONTACT ADDRESS** Lutheran Theol Sem, 7301 Germantown Ave, Philadelphia, PA, 19119.

REUSCHER, JOHN
DISCIPLINE PHILOSOPHY **EDUCATION** Fordham Univ, PhD. **CAREER** Assoc prof. **RESEARCH** Development of Kant's thought. **SELECTED PUBLICATIONS** Auth, A Concordance to the Critique of Pure Reason. **CONTACT ADDRESS** Dept of Philosophy, Georgetown Univ, 37th and O St, Washington, DC, 20057.

REYMOND, ROBERT L.
DISCIPLINE SYSTEMATIC THEOLOGY **EDUCATION** Bob Jones Univ, BA, MA, PhD. **CAREER** Prof, Knox Theol Sem. **SELECTED PUBLICATIONS** Auth, A New Systematic of the Christian Faith. **CONTACT ADDRESS** Knox Theol Sem, 5554 N Federal Hwy, Ft. Lauderdale, FL, 33308.

REYNOLDS, CLARK WINTON
PERSONAL Born 03/13/1934, Chicago, IL, m, 1977, 4 children **DISCIPLINE** ECONOMICS, HUMANITIES **EDUCATION** Claremont Men's Col, AB (magna cum laude), 56; MIT, Danforth fel, 58; Harvard Divinity School, Rockefeller Brothers Theological fel, 57-58; Univ of Calif at Berkeley, MA, PhD, 62. **CAREER** Asst prof, Occidental Col, 61-62; asst prof to assoc prof, Yale Univ, 62-67; ASSOC PROF TO FULL PROF, FOOD RES INST, 67-96, PROF EMERITUS, SENIOR FEL, INST FOR INTERNATIONAL STUDIES, STANFORD UNIV, 90-. **HONORS AND AWARDS** Ford Foundation Grant, 92-96; Canadian Consular Grants, 1980s & 92; Mellon Found Grants, US-Mex Project, 1980s & 92-96; MacArthur Found Grant, 88; Tinker Found Grant, 86-87; Hewlett Found Grants, 1980s & 90; Rockefeller Found Grants, 79-1980s; Inter-Am Development Bank res grant, 1970s; Org of Am States res grants, 1970s; Soc Sci Res Coun Collaborative Res Grant, 70-72; Norman Buchanan Award, 64; Doherty Found Fel, 60-61; Rockefeller Brothers Theological Fel, 57-58; Danforth Found Grad Fel, 56-60; Woodrow Wilson Grad Fel, 56-67. **MEMBERSHIPS** U.S.-Mex Consultative Group, Carnegie Endowment for Int Peace; North Am Economics and Finance Asn; Am Economics Asn. **RESEARCH** Economic development, particularly in Latin America; international trade, finance, and development; regional economics; labor economics; corporate finance. **SELECTED PUBLICATIONS** Auth, The Political Economy of Open Regionalism, in Integrating Cities and Regions: North Am Faces Globalization, forthcoming; auth, Regionalismo abierto y aceso social: nuevos enfoques hacia la integracion en las Americas, in El Ecuador en el Mercado Mundial, 97; auth, Efficiency, Control, and Convergence: Lessons from Privatization of the Mexican Banking System, Quaderni di economia e finanza, 96; auth, Open Regionalism, Lessons from Latin America for East Asia, working paper, 97; auth, Open Regionalism and Social Access: Approaches to Integration in the Americas, Growth, Trade, and Integration in Latin America, 96; auth, The NAFTA and Wage Convergence: a Case of Winners and Losers, NAFTA as a Model of Development: the Benefits and Costs of Merging High and Low Wage Areas, 95; coauth, Japanese Investment in Mexico: A New Industrial Nexus?, The Effect of Japanese Investment on the World Economy, 96; auth, A Case for Open Regionalism in the Andes, forthcoming. **CONTACT ADDRESS** Food Research Inst, Standford Univ, Stanford, CA, 94305. **EMAIL** reynolds@leland.stanford.edu

REYNOLDS, EDWARD
PERSONAL Born 01/23/1942, s **DISCIPLINE** THEOLOGY **EDUCATION** Wake Forest Univ, BA 1964; OH Univ, MA 1965; Yale Univ, MDiv 1968; London Univ PhD 1972. **CAREER** Christ United Presby, assoc pastor 1982-; Univ of CA San Diego, asst prof 1971-74, assoc prof 1974-83, prof 1983-; City of San Diego, planning commissioner, 1989-93. **HONORS AND AWARDS** Books-Trade and Economic Change on the Gold Coast 1974; Stand the Storm A History of the Atlantic Slave Trade 1985; Focus on Africa, 1994; vice moderator Presbytery of San Diego, 1993; Excellence in Teaching Award, University of California, San Diego, 1990-91; Moderator, Presbytery of San Diego, 1994; Director Univ of CA Study Center, 1994-96. **CONTACT ADDRESS** Dept of History 0104, 9500 Gilman Dr, La Jolla, CA, 92093-0104.

REYNOLDS, FRANK E.
PERSONAL Born 11/13/1930, Hartford, CT, m, 1997, 3 children **DISCIPLINE** HISTORY OF RELIGION, BUDDHIST STUDIES **EDUCATION** Oberlin Col, BA, 52; Yale Univ, BD, 55; Univ Chicago, MA, 64, PhD, 71. **CAREER** Prog dir, Student Christian Ctr, Bangkok, 56-59; minister to foreign students, Univ Chicago, 62-65, from instr to asst prof, 67-71, assoc prof, 72-79, PROF HIST RELIG & BUDDHIST STUDIES, UNIV CHICAGO, 79-, chmn, Comt Asian Southern Asian Studies, 78-83, prog dir, Inst Advan Studies Relig, 92-98; Lectr hist, Chulalonkorn Univ, 57-59; vis prof, Stanford Univ, 70-71; ed, Hist Relig J, 76-; Asn Asian Studies Monograph Series, 77-83; Fulbright sr fel, 73-74; NEH res fel, 78-79; assoc ed, J Relig Ethics, 90-, assoc ed, J Relig, 88-. **MEMBERSHIPS** Am Soc Study Relig; Am Acad Relig; Asn Asian Studies; NAm Soc Buddhist Studies; Int Asn Buddhist Studies; Law & Soc. **RESEARCH** Therauada Buddhism; Thailand; comparative ethics. **SELECTED PUBLICATIONS** Coauth, Two Wheels of Dhamma, Am Acad Relig, 72; co-ed, Religious Encounters with Death, Pa State Univ, 77; co-ed & contribr, The Biographi-

cal Process, Mouton, 76; Transitions and Transformations in the History of Religion, E J Brill, 80; auth, Guide to Buddhist Religion, 80; co-ed & transl, Those Worlds according to King Buang: A Thai Buddhists Cosmology, Asian Humanities Press, 82; co-ed, Cosmogony and Ethical Order, Chicago, 85; co-ed, Myth and Philosophy, SUNY, 90; co-ed, Discourse and Practice, SUNY, 92; co-ed, Religion and Practical Reason, 94. **CONTACT ADDRESS** Swift Hall, Univ of Chicago, 1025-35 E 58th St, Chicago, IL, 60637-1577. **EMAIL** mgp2@midway.uchicago.edu

REYNOLDS, J. ALVIN
PERSONAL Born 10/03/1929, Gaston, SC, m, 1961, 2 children **DISCIPLINE** RELIGION **EDUCATION** Univ SC, AB, 54; New Orleans Baptist Theol Sem, BD, 57, ThD, 62. **CAREER** Assoc prof relig & head dept, 62-72, Prof Relig & dept head, Univ Mary Hardin-Baylor, 72-97, Dir, In-Serv Guide, 75-88; Janey S Briscoe Chair Relig and Life, 97. **HONORS AND AWARDS** Honoray alumnus, UMHB, 85. **MEMBERSHIPS** Southwestern Asn Baptist Tchr(s) Relig (vpres, 72-73, pres, 73-74); Southern Baptist In-Serv Guidance Conf (charter mem, vpres, 83-84, pres, 84-85); Southern Baptist Hist Soc; Nat Asn Baptist Prof Relig; TX Baptist Hist Assoc. **RESEARCH** Church hist; Bible. **SELECTED PUBLICATIONS** Contribr, Wycliffe Bible Encyclopedia, Moody, 75; Mercer Dictionary of the Bible, Mercer Univ, 90; Holman Bible Dictionary, Holman, 91; Baptists Working Together, Baptist Gen Conv TX, 76; auth, Richard Furman: Denominational Architect, Quart Rev, 10-12/76. **CONTACT ADDRESS** Dept of Relig, Univ of Mary Hardin-Baylor, 900 College St, Belton, TX, 76513-2599.

REYNOLDS, LAURIE A.
DISCIPLINE LAW **EDUCATION** Georgetown Univ, BA; Univ Ill, MA; JD. **CAREER** Prof, Univ Ill Urbana Champaign. **HONORS AND AWARDS** Ed, Univ Ill Law Forum. **RESEARCH** Property, state and local government; land use; and American Indian law. **SELECTED PUBLICATIONS** Auth, pubs about municipal annexation law. **CONTACT ADDRESS** Law Dept, Univ Ill Urbana Champaign, 52 E Gregory Dr, Champaign, IL, 61820. **EMAIL** lreynold@law.uiuc.edu

REYNOLDS, NOEL BELDON
PERSONAL Born 02/26/1942, Los Angeles, CA, m, 1965, 11 children **DISCIPLINE** POLITICAL & LEGAL PHILOSOPHY **EDUCATION** Brigham Young Univ, AB, 67; Harvard Univ, AM, 68, PhD, 71. **CAREER** Chmn dept Philos, 71-76, assoc prof, 74-78, dir Gen Educ, 80, prof Govt & Philos, Brigham Young Univ, 80, assoc Acad VPres, 81-, Vis fac philos Law, J Reuben Clark Law School, 74, 75 & 79; fel Law & Philos, Harvard, 76-77 & Lib Arts fel, Law Sch, 76-77. **MEMBERSHIPS** Int Asn Philos Law & Social Philos; Mont Pelerin Soc. **RESEARCH** Constitutionalism; Plato; philosophy of law. **SELECTED PUBLICATIONS** Auth, A formal model for judicial discretion, Proc World Cong Legal & Social Philos, 71; Empirical science and the future of epistemology, Proc World Cong Philos, 73; The concept of objectivity in judicial reasoning, 14 Western Ont Law Rev 1, 75; Dworkin as Quixote, 123 Univ Penn Law Rev 574, 75; Mormonism, capitalism, and the rule of law, Proc Mormon Economists Conf, 10/75; The enforcement of morals and the rule of law, 11 Ga Law Rev 1325, 9/77; Public virtue and the rule of law in America 's third century, In: Bicentennial Lectures on Public Ethics, Utah Endowment for Humanities. **CONTACT ADDRESS** Dept of Philosophy, Brigham Young Univ, 745 Swkt, Provo, UT, 84602-0002. **EMAIL** nbr@email.byu.edu

REYNOLDS, STEVEN
PERSONAL Born 04/12/1956, UT, m, 1985, 3 children **DISCIPLINE** PHILOSOPHY **EDUCATION** UCLA, PhD, 88. **CAREER** Assoc prof, Ariz State Univ, 88-. **MEMBERSHIPS** Am Philso Asn. **RESEARCH** Epistemology; Perception; Metaphysics. **SELECTED PUBLICATIONS** Auth, Skeptical Hypotheses and 'Omniscient' Interpreters, Australasian J of Philos, 93; proxy Functions and Inscrutability of Reference, Analysis, 94; Evaluation Illusions and Skeptical Arguments, Philos and Phenomenol Res, forthcoming; Skills and Perceptual Justification, forthcoming. **CONTACT ADDRESS** Dept of Philosophy, Arizona State Univ, Tempe, Tempe, AZ, 85287-2004. **EMAIL** steven.reynolds@asu.edu

RHOADS, DAVID
PERSONAL Born 11/17/1941, Altoona, PA, m, 2 children **DISCIPLINE** RELIGION, BIBLICAL STUDIES **EDUCATION** Gettysburg Col, BA, 63; Oxford Univ, MA, 65; Gettysburg Luth Sem, BD, 66; Duke Univ, PhD, 73 **CAREER** Prof, 88-, Luth Sch of Theol; Prof, 73-88, Carthage Col; Pastor, 68-70, St John Luth Church **MEMBERSHIPS** Cath Bibl Asc; Chicago Soc for Bibl Res; The Context Group **SELECTED PUBLICATIONS** Auth, Israel in Revolution: 6-74 C.E. A Political History Based on the Writings of Josephus, Fortress, 76; Coauth, Mark as Story: An Introduction to the Narrative of a Gospel, Fortress, 99 **CONTACT ADDRESS** Lutheran Sch of Theol, Chicago, Chicago, IL, 60615. **EMAIL** drhoads@lstc.edu

RHODE, DEBORAH L.
DISCIPLINE LAW **EDUCATION** Yale Univ, BA, 74; Yale Law School, 77. **CAREER** Law Clerk, 78-79, Justice Thurgood Marshall, Supreme Court of the US; Dir, 86-90, Inst for Research on Women and Gender, Prof, 86-97, Dir, 94-, Keck Ctr on Legal Ethics and the Legal Profession, Ernest W. McFarland Prof of Law, 97-, Stanford Law School and Stanford Univ. **MEMBERSHIPS** Assoc of Amer Law Schools (Pres); Trustee, Yale Univ. **RESEARCH** Legal ethics and the legal professor; gender law; public policy **SELECTED PUBLICATIONS** Ed, Theoretical Perspectives on Sexual Difference, 90; Coauth, Legal Ethics, 95; Coed, The Politics of Pregnancy: Adolescent Sexuality and the Public Policy, 93; Auth, Speaking of Sex, 97; Professional Responsibility: Ethics by the Pervasive Method, 98. **CONTACT ADDRESS** Stanford Univ School of Law.

RHODES, PAULA R.
PERSONAL Born 07/18/1949, New Orleans, Louisiana, s **DISCIPLINE** LAW **EDUCATION** Amer Univ, BA 1971; Harvard Univ, JD 1974. **CAREER** Legal Serv Corp, atty 1977-79; Mid Atlantic Legal Educ, prof 1980; Univ of San Diego Law School, visiting prof 1983-84; Howard Univ School of Law, assoc prof 1979-90; Univ of Bridgeport, adjunct prof 1985; Univ of Denver College of Law, Denver, CO, visiting prof, 1989-90, professor, dir, LLM in Amer & Comparative Law Program, 1990-. **HONORS AND AWARDS** Various conferences including Amer Friends Serv Committee Consultation on Korea, Los Angeles, CA 1983, Inst for Policy Studies/Transnatl Inst Intl Conf on "Meeting the Corporate Challenge" Washington DC 1984; Brown Univ, ACUNS/ASIL Summer Workshop on Intl Organization Studies, 1994; African American Leaders Meetings with Mexican Leaders, Mexico City, Mexico, delegation spokesperson, 1992; featured in Lisa Jones, The Path, Six Women Talk About Their Religious Faith Essence vol16 #9 Jan 1986; Phi Delta Phi Legal Fraternity; panelist, moderator, v of Denver Consortium on Rights Development, seminar, international debt, structural adjustment, development and human rights, 1990; panelist, Human Rights and the Underclass, CORD, 1990. **MEMBERSHIPS** Dist of Columbia Bas Assn; LA Bar Assn; American Bar Assn; Inter Wolsa; American Soc of Intl Law; Academic Council on United Nations Studies; vice chair, American Friends Serv Committee; Afr Amer United Nations Comm; Transafrica; Mountainview Friends Meetings, bd of trustees. **SELECTED PUBLICATIONS** Auth, "Expanding NGO Participation in Intl Decision Making," World Debt and the Human Condition: Structural Adjustment and the Right to Development, 1993; "Devel of New Business Opportunities for Minorities in the Synthetic Fuels Program", Rsch & Legislative Narrative 1981; "Energy Security Act and its Implications for Economic Devel", Howard Law Journal 1981, "We the People and the Struggle for a New World," WSA Constitution on Human Rights 1987; Assoc Ed Fed Bar Assn Forum 1982-83. **CONTACT ADDRESS** Professor, Univ of Denver Col of Law, 1900 Olive St, Denver, CO, 80220.

RHODES, RON
DISCIPLINE APOLOGETICS **EDUCATION** Houston Baptist Univ, BA; Dallas Theol Sem, ThM, ThD. **CAREER** Adj prof. **SELECTED PUBLICATIONS** Auth, New Age Movement, Zondervan Publ House, 95. **CONTACT ADDRESS** Southern Evangel Sem, 4298 McKee Rd, Charlotte, NC, 28270. **EMAIL** ses@perigee.net

RHODES BAILLY, CONSTANTINA
DISCIPLINE RELIGIOUS STUDIES **EDUCATION** Columbia Univ, PhD. **CAREER** Asst prof. **RESEARCH** Kashmir Shaiva Hinduism; Goddess traditions of India. **SELECTED PUBLICATIONS** Auth, Shaiva Devotional Songs of Kashmir: The Shivastotravali of Utpaladeva; co-auth, God Dwells within You As You. **CONTACT ADDRESS** Religious Studies Dept, Eckerd Col, 54th Ave S, PO Box 4200, St Petersburg, FL, 33711. **EMAIL** baillycr@eckerd.edu

RHYS, J HOWARD W.
PERSONAL Born 10/25/1917, Montreal, Canada, m, 1954 **DISCIPLINE** THEOLOGY **EDUCATION** McGill Univ, BA, 39; Gen Theol Sem, STM, 49, ThD, 53. **CAREER** Asst prof, 53-61, prof, 61-83, Schl of Theol Univ of S Sewanee TN. **CONTACT ADDRESS** 75 Louisiana Circle, Sewanee, TN, 37375.

RICCI, PAUL O.
PERSONAL Born 08/15/1932, Bristol, CT, m, 1963, 2 children **DISCIPLINE** PHILOSOPHY **EDUCATION** Univ Conn, BA, 54; Univ Ariz, MA, 62; Univ So Calif, grad study, 70-73. **CAREER** Pueblo Col, 59-61; Fullerton Col, 63-66; Cypress Col, 66-93. **MEMBERSHIPS** Sigma Pi Sigma. **RESEARCH** Philosophy of religion; philosophy of science; epistemology. **SELECTED PUBLICATIONS** Auth, Humanism and Religion: Independent Thinking Review; Resources for Independent Thinking, 96. **CONTACT ADDRESS** 6157 James Alan St, Cypress, CA, 90630.

RICCIARDELLI, ANGELA R.
DISCIPLINE PHILOSOPHY **EDUCATION** Georgetown Univ, PhD, 86. **CAREER** Adj fac, , 89-, Notre Dame, Md; dir, devel, 97-, Mcauley Inst **MEMBERSHIPS** APA; Zorta Int; ASAE; NSFRE. **RESEARCH** Ethics and philos of relig. **SELECTED PUBLICATIONS** Auth, Reason and Faith in the Philosophy of Sacred Kwikegaard; auth, A Comparison of Wilfrid Desan's and Pierre L'eilkards de Chaudia's Concept of United World. **CONTACT ADDRESS** 4601 Park Ave, #404, Chevy Chase, MD, 20815. **EMAIL** angela218@aol.com

RICE, BERRY
PERSONAL Born 03/23/1940, Birmingham, AL, m, 1962, 2 children **DISCIPLINE** ELEMENTARY EDUCATION, NURSING; DIVINITY **EDUCATION** Univ Ala, BSED, 61; Med Col Ga, BNursing, 89; Interdenominational Theol Ctr, MDiv, 96. **CAREER** Reg Nurse, Athens Reg Med Ctr, 89- . **HONORS AND AWARDS** Theta Phi; Briggs NT scholar awd; nurs hon soc. **MEMBERSHIPS** Ga Nurses Asn; Soc Bibl Studs. **RESEARCH** Prayer, Judaic and Christian; Healing. **CONTACT ADDRESS** Athens Regional Medical Ctr, 386 Milledge Cir, Athens, GA, 30606. **EMAIL** price@negia.net

RICE, CHARLES E.
PERSONAL Born 08/07/1931, New York, NY, m, 1956, 10 children **DISCIPLINE** LAW, POLITICAL SCIENCE **EDUCATION** Col Holy Cross, AB, 53; Boston Col, JD, 56; NY Univ, LLM, 59, JSD, 62. **CAREER** Prof law, Fordham Univ, 60-69; prof law, 69-, Univ Notre Dame, 69-; co-ed, American Journal of Jurisprudence; pres, Wanderer Forum Found. **SELECTED PUBLICATIONS** Auth, Freedom of Association, NY Univ, 62; The Supreme Court and Public Prayer, Fordham Univ, 64; The Vanishing Right to Live, 69 & Authority and Rebellion, Doubleday, 71; Beyond Abortion: The Theory and Practice of The Secular State, Franciscan Herald Press, 79; 50 Questions on the Natural Law, Ignatius Press, 93. **CONTACT ADDRESS** Sch of Law, Univ of Notre Dame, Notre Dame, IN, 46556.

RICE, CHARLES L.
PERSONAL Born 12/12/1936, Chandler, OK, s **DISCIPLINE** THEOLOGY **EDUCATION** Baylor Univ, BA, 59; Southern Bapt. Theol Sem, BD, 62; Union Theol Sem, STM, 63; Duke Univ, PhD, 67. **CAREER** Prof, Drew Univ, 70- . **MEMBERSHIPS** Acad of Homiletics. **RESEARCH** Hist of preaching; Preaching and the arts . **SELECTED PUBLICATIONS** Auth, Interpretational Imagination, 70; Preaching the Story, 80; The Embodied World, 91. **CONTACT ADDRESS** Dept of Theology, Drew Univ, Madison, NJ, 07940.

RICE, HORACE WARREN
PERSONAL Born 02/14/1944, Huntsville, AL, d **DISCIPLINE** LAW **EDUCATION** Chicago City College, AA, 1964; Alabama A&M University, BS, 1966; University of Toledo, JD, 1972. **CAREER** Chicago Legal Assistance Foundation, attorney, 1972-75; University of Alabama-Huntsville, professor, 1976-82; self-employed, player representative, sports agent, 1977-84; ALABAMA A&M UNIV, PROF, 1976-; SELF-EMPOLYED, ARBITRATOR/MEDIATOR, 1977-. **HONORS AND AWARDS** Ohio State Impass Panel, appointed to Arbitration Panel, 1985; American Arbitration Association, National Panel, 1980; Federal Mediation & Conciliation Service, National Panel, 1982; United States Postal Service, National Panel, 1983; Citizens Ambassador Program, US State Department, educator, Europe, Russia, Africa, 1988-89. **MEMBERSHIPS** American Arbitration Association; Academy for Legal Studies in Business; American Management Association; Society of Professionals in Dispute Resolution. **SELECTED PUBLICATIONS** "Zoning: A Substantive Analysis," AAMU Faculty Research Journal, 1978; "Labor Arbitration: A Viable Method of Dispute Resolution," American Business Law Assn Journal, 1983; "Class Actions Under the 1964 Civil Rights Act," AAMU Faculty Res Journal, 1989; "What Consumers Should Know About Installment Buying," Business Newsletter, 1980; published 23 arbitration cases in Bureau of National Affairs, Commerce Clearinghouse, Labor Relations Reporter, Labor Arbitration In Government. **CONTACT ADDRESS** Department of Business Administration, Alabama A&M Univ, Normal, AL, 35762.

RICE, PAUL R.
DISCIPLINE PUBLIC LAW **EDUCATION** Marshall Univ, BBA, 65; W Va Col Law, JD, 68; Yale Law Sch, LLM, 72. **CAREER** Prof, Am Univ; Lect, Practicing law Inst. **HONORS AND AWARDS** Fel, Am Bar Found; Pauline Ruyle Moore Scholar, 87-88; Reporter;DC; Law Revision Comn, Consultant: Fed Trade Comn; DC. **MEMBERSHIPS** Finnegan,Henderson, Farabow, Garrett and Dunner; Bar Asn Comn Court Improvement; Instit Advan Studies Justice. **RESEARCH** Evidence, civil procedure. **SELECTED PUBLICATIONS** Auth, Attorney-Client Privilege: State law, 96; Evidence, Common law and Federal Rules, 96; Attorney Clien Privilege in the U. S., 93; contribur, Am Univ Law Rev; Univ of Conn Law Rev; Duquesne Law Rev; Mercer Law Rev; Miss Law Jour; Northwestern Univ Law Rev; Temple Law Rev; Vanderbilt Law Rev; W Va Univ Law Rev. **CONTACT ADDRESS** American Univ, 4400 Massachusetts Ave, Washington, DC, 20016.

RICH, ROBERT F.
DISCIPLINE LAW **EDUCATION** Oberlin Col, BA; Univ Chicago, MA; Ph.D. **CAREER** Prof, Univ Ill Urbana Champaign. **RESEARCH** Health law and policy; federalism and the role of the states; environmental policy; and science policy **SELECTED PUBLICATIONS** Auth, pubs on health law and policy, federalism and the role of the states, environmental policy, and science policy. **CONTACT ADDRESS** Law Dept, Univ Ill Urbana Champaign, 52 E Gregory Dr, Champaign, IL, 61820. **EMAIL** rrich@law.uiuc.edu

RICHARDS, EDWARD P.
DISCIPLINE LAW **EDUCATION** Rice Univ, BA; Univ Houston, JD. **CAREER** Prof **RESEARCH** Public health; communicable diseases control; bioengineering; legal problems in health care delivery. **SELECTED PUBLICATIONS** Auth, Law and the Physician: A Practical Guide; pubs on medical and scientific issues, public health and communicable disease control, bioengineering, and legal problems in health care delivery. **CONTACT ADDRESS** Law Dept, Univ of Missouri, Kansas City, 5100 Rockhill Rd, Kansas City, MO, 64110-2499. **EMAIL** richardse@umkc.edu

RICHARDS, JEFFERY JON
PERSONAL Born 07/12/1949, Columbus, OH, m, 1972, 2 children **DISCIPLINE** THEOLOGY **EDUCATION** Pfeiffer Univ, BA, 72; Dallas Theol Sem, ThM, 78; Drew Univ, MA, 83, PhD, 85; Mellen Univ, D. Habil, 96. **CAREER** Univ of NC Charlotte, vis prof, 87-97; Hood Theo Sem, prof, ch of Theol & ethics, 87-, adj prof at Houston Grad Sch of Theol, 96-, Columbia Int Univ, 92-. **HONORS AND AWARDS** Pfeiffer Univ & Drew Univ Hon Grad. **MEMBERSHIPS** AAR, ETS, SBL. **RESEARCH** American Religious History; Reformation Studies; patrology; contemporary theology; Biblical studies. **SELECTED PUBLICATIONS** Auth, The Promise of Dawn, Univ Press Am, 91; auth, The Cry at Salem, Paladin House, 92; auth, Twenty-one Who Speak: Powerful Voices of Christianity from the First through the Twentieth Centuries, Paladin House, 93; auth, Contemporary Christians Options of the World's End, Edwin Mellen Press, 94. **CONTACT ADDRESS** Dept of Theology, Columbia Intl Univ, 237 Richmond Rd, Salisbury, NC, 28144. **EMAIL** jjrich@cbiinternet.com

RICHARDS, JERALD H.
PERSONAL Born 01/22/1933, Pittsburgh, PA, m, 4 children **DISCIPLINE** PHILOSOPHY **EDUCATION** Univ TX at Arlington, 56-58; Univ KY, BA, philos, 61; Harvard Univ, philos, 61-62; Boston Univ, AM, 62-65, PhD, 66; Harvard Univ, postdoctoral scholar, relig studies, 67-68. **CAREER** Asst prof philos, Western KY Univ, 65-69, assoc prof philos, 69-72; assoc prof philos, Northern NY Univ, 72-76, PROF PHILOS, 76-. **HONORS AND AWARDS** Phi Beta Kappa; BA "with high distinction" and "honors in philos;" Danforth grad fel, 61-65; grant from Soc for Values in Higher Ed to study at Harvard Univ, 67-68. **MEMBERSHIPS** Amer Soc Social Philos; Amer Philos Assoc; Concerned Philos for Peace. **RESEARCH** Ethics and int relations; value theory; social and political philos; peace studies; philos of war and peace; war and morality. **SELECTED PUBLICATIONS** Auth, Alan Donagan, Hebrew-Christian Morality, and Capital Punishment, The J of Relig Ethics, vol 8, no 2, fall 90; Raymond Moody, Near-Death Experiences, and Life After Death, Essence, vol 5, no 3, 82; Walzer's Just War Theory and Limited Nuclear First Strikes, Peace Res, vol 15, no 3, Sept 83; C. S. Lewis, Retributive Punishment, and the Worth of Persons, Christian Scholar's Rev, vol XIV, no 4, 85; Harmful Psychological and Moral Effects of US Nuclear Weapons Policy, Peace Res, vol 19. no 2, May 87; Limited Nuclear First Strikes and Just War Theory, Philosophy and Culture: Proceedings of the XVIIth World Congress of Philosophy, vol III, Montreal: Editions Montmorency, 88; On Saving the Bishops: Deterrence without Deterrence Doctrine, Philosophy in Context, vol 18, 88; Radhakrishan, Religion, and World Peace, Darshana International, vol XXVII, no 4, 89; Gene Sharp's Pragmatic Defense of Nonviolence, The Int J of Applied Philos, vol 6, no 1, summer 91; Gene Sharp, Nonviolence, and the Western Moral Tradition, in Werner, Richard, and Duane Cady, eds, Just War, Nonviolence and Nuclear Deterrence: Philosophers on War and Peace, Wakefield, NH: Longwood Academic, 91; George Bush, Justified War Morality, and the Gulf War, in Bove, Laurence, and Laura Duhan Kaplan, eds, In the Eye of the Storm: Philosophers Reflect on Militarism and Regional Conflict, Amsterdam/Atlanta: Rodopi Press, 95; Radhakrishnan, Religion, and World Peace, in Pappu, S.S. Rama Rao, ed, New Essays in the Philosophy of Sarvepalli Radhakrishnan, Delhi: Sri Satguru Pubs, 95; Gandhi's Qualified Acceptance of Violence, The Acorn, vol VII, no 2, fall 95; Power Imbalance and Human Worth, in Kaplan, Laura, and Laurence F. Bove, eds, Philosophical Perspectives on Power and Domination: Theory and Practice, Rodopi Press, 97; Ideological Intolerance: Causes, Consequences, and Alternatives, in Curtin, Deane, and Robert Litke, eds, Institutional Violence, Rodopi Press, forthcoming; Common Morality and Peacemaking, in Presler, Judith, and Sally J. Scholz, eds, Peacemaking: Lessons from the Past, Visions from the Future, Rodopi Press, forthcoming; Hiroshima, Morality, and Democracy, in Kultgen, John, and Mary Lenzi, eds, Problems for Democracy, Rodopi Press, forthcoming. **CONTACT ADDRESS** Philos Program, No Kentucky Univ, Highland Heights, KY, 41076. **EMAIL** RichardsJ@nku.edu

RICHARDS, KENT HAROLD
PERSONAL Born 07/06/1939, Midland, TX, m, 1960, 2 children **DISCIPLINE** OLD TESTAMENT **EDUCATION** Fresno State Col, BA, 61; Sch Theol Claremont, MTh, 64; Claremont Grad Sch, PhD(Old Testament), 70. **CAREER** Res assoc Old Testament, Inst Antiq & Christianity, 68-69; asst prof, Univ Dayton, 69-72; asst prof, 72-75, Assoc Prof Old Testament, Iliff Sch Theol, 75-, Researcher, Univ Heidelberg, 71; Asn Theol Schs Basic Theol Scholar & Res Award, 75-76; exec secy, Soc Bibl Lit, 81-; chmn bd of trustees, Scholars Press, 80- **MEMBERSHIPS** Soc Bibl Lit (tress, 76-); Cath Bibl Asn Am; Am Acad Relig; AAUP; Am Sch Orient Res. **RESEARCH** Old Testament form criticism; I and II Chronicles; Ezra and Nehemiah. **SELECTED PUBLICATIONS** Auth, A note on the bisection of Isaiah, Rev Qumran, 65; Correlating methods in the interpretation of the Old Testament, Univ Dayton Rev, 70; Changing contexts for Biblical interpretation, Christian Century, 73; Lament and praise in the Old Testament, 75 & Can we discover fire?, 76, Cross-Talk; Beyond Bruxism, Soc Bibl Lit, 76; Ed, Society Of Biblical Literature Seminar Papers, 81 & 82; The Poems And Psalms Of The Hebrew Bible, J of Religion, Vol 76, 96. **CONTACT ADDRESS** Iliff Sch of Theol, 2201 S University Blvd, Denver, CO, 80210.

RICHARDS, RANDY
PERSONAL Born 06/20/1958, Altus, OK, m, 1980, 2 children **DISCIPLINE** NEW TESTAMENT STUDIES **EDUCATION** Texas Wesleyan Col, BA, 80; Southwestern Baptist Theol Sem, MDiv, 83, PhD, 88. **CAREER** Tchg fel, New Testament Greek, Southwestern Baptist Theol Sem, 84-85; instr Latin, Sch for Sci and Engg Professions, 85-86; instr relig stud, Tarrant Co Jr Col, 86-88; prof New Testament, Bibl Theol, Indonesia Theol Col, 89-92; guest prof New Testament, Asia Baptist Grad Theol Sem, 92-94; missionary guest prof New Testament, SW Baptist Theol Sem, 93; prof New Testament and Bibl Theol, dean Grad Stud, Indonesia Grad Sch Theol, 93-96; guest lect ser, Indonesia, 94, 95; asst prof 96-98, assoc prof and chemn Dept of Relig and Philos, 98- , Williams Baptist Col. **MEMBERSHIPS** Soc of Bibl Lit; Inst for Bibl Res. **SELECTED PUBLICATIONS** Auth, Judgment Seat in the Theology of Paul, Bibl Illusr, 94; auth, Patience in Pauline Theology, Bibl Illusr, 95; auth, Peter, Babylon and Rome, Bibl Illusr, 98; auth, The Codex and the Early Collection of Paul's Letters, Bull for Bibl Res, 98; auth, Stop Lying, Bibl Illusr, 99; auth, The Greek Gymnasium and 1 Tim 4:8, Bibl Illusr, forthcoming. **CONTACT ADDRESS** Williams Baptist Col, PO Box 3426, Walnut Ridge, AR, 72476. **EMAIL** RRichards@wbcoll.edu

RICHARDS, WILLIAM M.
DISCIPLINE PHILOSOPHY **EDUCATION** Georgetown Univ, PhD, 70. **CAREER** Dept Philos, Univ Dayton **RESEARCH** Buddhist doctrine of annata; antirealism in ethics. **SELECTED PUBLICATIONS** Auth, A Case for Non-rigid Proper Names, Proc Ohio Philos Assn, 75; Self-Consciousness and Agency, Synthese, 84. **CONTACT ADDRESS** Dept of Philos, Univ Dayton, 300 Col Park, Dayton, OH, 75062. **EMAIL** richards@checkov.hm.udayton.edu

RICHARDSON, ANDRA VIRGINIA
PERSONAL Born 04/16/1954, Detroit, MI, m, 1984 **DISCIPLINE** LAW **EDUCATION** Wayne State Univ, BS, 1984; Wayne State Univ Law School, JD, 1987. **CAREER** Delta Airlines, reservation sales agent, 1977-86; Oakland County Prosecutor, asst prosecuting atty, 1988-90; 52ND-1ST DISTRICT COURT, MAGISTRATE, 1990-; EASTERN MICHIGAN UNIV, ADJUNCT PROF, 1998-. **HONORS AND AWARDS** Dollars and Sense Magazine, Outstanding Business and Professional Award, 1993; National Assn of Negro Business and Professional Women Club, Inc, Professional Woman of the Year, 1993. **MEMBERSHIPS** Top Ladies of Distinction, Inc, exec board, recording secretary, 1993-95; Top Ladies, president, 1995-97; Jack & Jill of America, Inc, exec board, parlimentarian, 1993-95; Oakland County Chap Child Abuse and Neglect Council, executive bd/chair, 1990-94; Girl Scouts of America, board of directors, 1991-94; The Doll League, 1998-. **CONTACT ADDRESS** Magistrate Andra V Richardson, 52nd 1st District Court, 48150 Grand River Ave, Novi, MI, 48374.

RICHARDSON, BRIAN C.
DISCIPLINE CHRISTIAN EDUCATION **EDUCATION** Campbell Univ, BA; Southwestern Baptist Theol Sem, MA, PhD. **CAREER** Prof, ch, Biblical Stud Div, Bryan Col; Basil Manly, Jr. prof, S Baptist Theol Sem. **SELECTED PUBLICATIONS** Auth, Christian Education: Foundations for the Future, Moody Press. **CONTACT ADDRESS** Sch Christian Edu and Leadership, Southern Baptist Theol Sem, 2825 Lexington Rd, Louisville, KY, 40280. **EMAIL** brichardson@sbts.edu

RICHARDSON, DAVID M.
DISCIPLINE LAW **EDUCATION** Rensselaer Polytech Inst, BS; Columbia Univ, LLB; NY Univ, LLM. **CAREER** Prof, Univ Fla, 84-. **HONORS AND AWARDS** Founding ed, Fla Tax Rev. **MEMBERSHIPS** Fla Bar. **RESEARCH** Taxation. **CONTACT ADDRESS** School of Law, Univ of Florida, PO Box 117625, Gainesville, FL, 32611-7625. **EMAIL** richards@law.ufl.edu

RICHARDSON, DEAN M.
DISCIPLINE AMERICAN INDIAN LAW, CIVIL RIGHTS, PRODUCTS LIABILITY **EDUCATION** Univ Rochester, BA, 66; Syracuse Univ, JD, 69. **CAREER** Willamette Univ, Sch Law **HONORS AND AWARDS** NEH fel, Harvard Univ, 80., Ch, Northwest Afrikan Amer Ballet, Portland, Oregon, 94. **MEMBERSHIPS** Mem, Justinian Hon Law Soc. **SELECTED PUBLICATIONS** articles ed, Syracuse Law Rev. **CONTACT ADDRESS** Sch of Law, Willamette Univ, 900 State St, Salem, OR, 97301. **EMAIL** drichard@willamette.edu

RICHARDSON, HENRY
DISCIPLINE PHILOSOPHY **EDUCATION** Harvard Univ, BA, PhD, 86. **CAREER** Prof. **SELECTED PUBLICATIONS** Auth, Practical Reasoning about Final Ends, Cambridge, 94; pubs on history of ethics, ethical theory, political philosophy, and practical reasoning. **CONTACT ADDRESS** Dept of Philosophy, Georgetown Univ, 37th and O St, Washington, DC, 20057.

RICHARDSON, KURT A.
PERSONAL Born 04/04/1957, m, 1983, 4 children **DISCIPLINE** SYSTEMATIC THEOLOGY AND ETHICS **EDUCATION** D Theo, 91. **CAREER** Assoc Prof, Theo and Ethics, 11 years, Gordon-Cromwell Theo Sem; Continuing Vis Prof of Theo, Theologische Fabuultat, Unive of Marburg. **HONORS AND AWARDS** Sci and Rel Scholar. **MEMBERSHIPS** AAR; ETS; CTWS. **RESEARCH** Theology of culture & Technology, Theology of Religion. **SELECTED PUBLICATIONS** Auth, The Epistle of James, NAC Broadman, 97. **CONTACT ADDRESS** Gordon-Conwell Theol Sem, 130 Essex St, South Hamilton, MA, 01982.

RICHARDSON, PETER
PERSONAL Born 01/06/1935, Toronto, ON, Canada, m, 1959, 4 children **DISCIPLINE** PHILOSOPHY, ARCHITECTURE **EDUCATION** Univ Toronto, B Archit, 57; B Divinity, 62; Cambridge Univ, PhD Philos, 65. **CAREER** Asst/assoc prof, Loyola Montreal, 69-74; asst to the dean of arts, 71-72; asst to the acad vice-pres, 72-73; coordr,73-74; chemn, Univ of Toronto Scarborough Coll Div of Humanities, 74-77; prin, Univ Coll Univ Toronto, 77-89; prof, Univ Toronto, 80-. **HONORS AND AWARDS** Honorary Mem, Ontario Asn of Archits, 87. **MEMBERSHIPS** Studiorum Novi Testamenti Societas; Can Soc of Bibl Studies; Soc of Bibl Lit; Am Soc for Oriental Res; Am Inst of Archeol, Can Soc for Patristic Study; Am Soc for Greek and Latin Epigraphy. **RESEARCH** Second Temple Judaism; Early Christian history and literature; Architecture in the late Hellenistic and Roman periods. **SELECTED PUBLICATIONS** Auth, Herod, Friend of Romans and King of Jews, 96; co-ed, Gospel in Paul: Studies on Corinthians, Galatians and Romans in Honour of Richard N Longencker, 94; Judaism and Christianity in First-Century Rome, 98. **CONTACT ADDRESS** Univ of Toronto, 15 Kings College, Rm 173, Toronto, ON, M5S 1A1.

RICHARDSON, ROBERT CALVIN
PERSONAL Born 04/22/1949, Pueblo, CO, m, 1972, 1 child **DISCIPLINE** PHILOSOPHY **EDUCATION** Univ Colo, BA, 71; Univ Chicago, MA, 72, PhD(philos), 76. **CAREER** Asst prof, 75-82, Assoc Prof Philos, Univ Cincinnati, 83-, Vis assoc prof philos, Ohio State Univ, 83. **MEMBERSHIPS** Am Philos Asn; Philos Sci Asn; Soc Philos & Psychol; Soc Interdisciplinary Study of Mind. **RESEARCH** Philosophy of mind/psychology; philosophy of science; epistemology. **SELECTED PUBLICATIONS** Auth, Functionalism and reductionism, Philos Sci, 79; Reductionist Research Programs in Psychology, Philos Sci Asn, 80; Internal representations: Prologue to a theory of intentionality, Philos Topics, 81; The scandal of Cartesian Interactionism, Mind, 82; How not to reduce a functional psychology, Philos Sci, 82; coauth (with G Muilenburg), Sellars and Sense Impressions, Ekenntnis, 82; auth, Grades of Organization and Units of Selection, Philos Sci Asn, 82; The Structure Of Biological Theories , Hist And Philosophy Of The Life Sciences, Vol 14, 92; William Whewell Philosopher Of Science, History And Philos Of The Life Sci, Vol 16, 94; The Structure Of Biological Theories, Hist And Philosophy Of The Life Sciences, Vol 14, 92; Whewell,William Philosopher Of Science, Hist And Philos Of The Life Sciences, Vol 16, 94; Adaptation And Environment, Philos Of Sci, Vol 63, 96. **CONTACT ADDRESS** Dept of Philos, Univ of Cincinnati, P O Box 210374, Cincinnati, OH, 45221-0374.

RICHARDSON, STEPHEN R.
DISCIPLINE LAW **EDUCATION** Wayne State Univ, BA, 68; Univ Mich, MA, 70; Univ Toronto, LLB, 73. **CAREER** Lawyer, Tory Tory DesLauriers & Binnington **HONORS AND AWARDS** Dir, Tax Policy Legislation, 83-85. **SELECTED PUBLICATIONS** Auth, pubs on various aspects of taxation. **CONTACT ADDRESS** Fac of Law, Univ Toronto, 78 Queen's Park, Toronto, ON.

RICHEY, RUSSELL EARLE
PERSONAL Born 10/19/1941, Asheville, NC, m, 1965, 2 children **DISCIPLINE** CHURCH HISTORY **EDUCATION** Wesleyan Univ, BA (high honors), 63; Union Theol Sem, BD (M

Div), 66; Princeton Univ, MA, 68, PhD, 70. **CAREER** Instr, asst prof, assoc prof, prof of church history, Drew Univ Theol and Graduate Schools, 69-86; assoc dean for academic progs and res prof of church hist, The Divinity School, Duke Univ, 86-92, assoc dean for Academic Progs and prof Church Hist, 92-, prof Church Hist, Duke Univ, 97-. **HONORS AND AWARDS** Wesleyan: High Honors, Distinction in Hist, Phi Beta Kappa, Sophomore, Junior, and Senior Honor Societies, French Prize in Relig, Honorary Woodrow Wilson; Union Theol Sem: Int Fels Prog, Columbia, Prize in Church Hist, Senior Honor Society; Princeton: Rockefeller Doctoral Fel (withdrew to be Univ Teaching Fel, 68-69), Frelinghuysen Fel, dissertation received with distinction; Ecumenical fac assoc grant, Gen Comm on Christian Unity and Interreligious Concerns, for Bossey conf on Teaching Ecumenics and subsequent three-year service as liason from Commision to United Methodist seminaries, ended 92; Lilly Endowment grant, 91; planning and implementation grant from the Lilly Endowment for a major study of US United Methodism. **MEMBERSHIPS** Am Soc of Church Hist (member, Council 76-78, 95-97); Am Academy of Relig; Hist Soc of the United Methodist Church; adv bd: Quart Rev, Christian Hist, Church Hist, and J of Southern Relig. **SELECTED PUBLICATIONS** Co-ed with Donald Jones, American Civil Religion, Harper & Row, 74, Mellon Res Univ Press, 90; ed and co-auth, Denominationalism, Abingdon Press, 77; co-ed with Kenneth E Rowe, Rethinking Methodist History, United Methodist Pub House, 85; auth, Early American Methodism, IN Univ Press, 91; co-auth and ed, Ecumenical and Interreligious Perspectives: Globalization in Theological Education, Quart Rev Imprint, 92; co-ed with Kenneth E Rowe and Jean Miller Schmidt, Perspectives on American Methodism, IN Univ Press, Kingswood/Abingdon, 93; co-ed and co-auth with R Bruce Mullin, Reimagining Denominationalism, Oxford Univ Press, 94; auth, The Methodist Conference in America: A History, Kingswood/Abingdon, 96; The Methodists, with James Kirby and Kenneth Rowe, Greenwood, 96; Connectionalism: Ecclesiology, Mission, and Identity, primary co-ed with Dennis M Campbell and William B Lawrence, UMAC, I, Abingdon, 97; The People(s) Called Methodist: Forms and Reforms of Their Life, co-ed with Dennis M Campbell and William B Lawrence, UMAC, II, Abingdon, 98; Doctrines and Discipline, co-ed with Dennis M Campbell and William B Lawrence, UMAC, III, Abingdon, forthcoming 99; Questions for the Twenty-First Century Church, co-auth and primary co-ed with Dennis M Campbell and William B Lawrence, UMAC, IV, forthcoming 99. **CONTACT ADDRESS** Divinity School, Duke Univ, Durham, NC, 27708-0968. **EMAIL** rrichey@mail.duke.edu

RICHMAN, PAULA
DISCIPLINE SOUTH ASIAN RELIGIONS **EDUCATION** Oberlin Col, BA, 74; Princeton Univ, MA, 77; Univ Chicago, MA, 80, PhD, 83. **CAREER** Irvin E. Houck prof, 85. **RESEARCH** Tamil religious literature; Ramayana. **SELECTED PUBLICATIONS** Au, Many Ramayanas: The Diversity of a Narrative Tradition in South Asia; A Gift of Tamil; transl from Tamil literature, Women, Branch Stories, and Relig Rhetoric in a Tamil Buddhist Text. **CONTACT ADDRESS** Dept of Relig, Oberlin Col, Oberlin, OH, 44074.

RICHMAN, WILLIAM M.
DISCIPLINE LAW **EDUCATION** Univ Pa, BA; Univ Md, JD. **CAREER** Prof. **SELECTED PUBLICATIONS** Co-auth, Cases and Materials on Conflict of Laws, Matthew Bender, 90; Understanding Conflict of Laws, Matthew Bender, 93; Elitism, Expediency and the New Certiorari, Cornell Law Rev, 96. **CONTACT ADDRESS** Col Law, Univ of Toledo, Toledo, OH, 43606. **EMAIL** wrichma@uoft02.utoledo.edu

RICHTER, DUNCAN J.
PERSONAL Born 12/26/1966, Chester, England, m, 1994, 1 child **DISCIPLINE** PHILOSOPHY **EDUCATION** Univ of Virginia, PhD, 95; Univ Coll of Swansea, Wales, Mphilo, 89; Oxford UnivBA, 88. **CAREER** Asst Prof, 95-, Virgina Military Inst. **HONORS AND AWARDS** Thomas Jefferson Tchg Award, 98; V.M.I. **MEMBERSHIPS** Amer Philo Assoc, Southern Soc for Philo and Psych, VA Philos Assoc, Soc for Philo and Public Affairs. **RESEARCH** Wittgenstein, Anti-Theory in Ethics, Virtue, Theory of Applied Ethics. **SELECTED PUBLICATIONS** Auth, The Incoherence of the Moral Ought, Philosophy, 95; Nothing to be Said, Wittgenstein and Wittgensteinian Ethics, Southern Journal of Philosophy, 96; Is Abortion Vicious?, Journal of Value Inquiry, forthcoming. **CONTACT ADDRESS** Dept of Psychology & Philosophy, Va Military Inst, Lexington, VA, 24450. **EMAIL** richterdj@vmi.edu

RICKETTS, THOMAS G.
PERSONAL Born 02/02/1949, Cleveland, OH **DISCIPLINE** PHILOSOPHY **EDUCATION** Oberlin Col, BA, 71; Univ Mich, MA, 74, PhD, 77. **CAREER** Instr & asst prof, Harvard Univ, 76-69; asst prof, 79-85, assoc prof, 85- , dept chemn, 89-92, Univ Penn. **HONORS AND AWARDS** ACLS fel, 83-84. **MEMBERSHIPS** APA; AAUP. **RESEARCH** History of analytic philosophy; Frege; Russell; Wittgenstein; Carnap; Quine. **SELECTED PUBLICATIONS** Auth, Carnap's Principle of Tolerance, Empiricism and Conventionalism, in Clark, ed, Reading Putnam, Blackwell, 94; auth, Logic and Truth in Grege, Aristotelian Soc Suppl, 96; auth, Pictures, Logic, and the Limits of Sense in Wittgenstein's Tractatus, in Sluga, ed, Cambridge Wittgenstein Companion, Cambridge, 96; auth, Carnap: From Logical Syntax to Semantics, in Giere, ed, Origins of Logical Empiricism: Minnesota Studies in Philosophy of Science, Univ Minneapolis, 96; auth, Truth-Values and Courses-of-Values in Frege's Grundgesetze, in Tait, ed, Early Analytic Philosophy: Essays in Honor of Leonard Linsky, Open Court, 97; auth, Frege's 1906 Foray into Metalogic, Philos Topics, 97; auth, Truth and Propositional Unity in Early Russell, in Floyd, ed, Future Pasts; Reflections on the History and Nature of Analytic Philosophy, Harvard, 99. **CONTACT ADDRESS** Logan Hall, Univ of Pennsylvania, Philadelphia, PA, 19104. **EMAIL** ricketts@sas.upenn.edu

RICKLESS, SAMUEL
DISCIPLINE PHILOSOPHY **EDUCATION** Harvard Univ, BA, 86; Univ Ca, PhD, 96. **CAREER** Asst prof. **MEMBERSHIPS** Am Philos Asn, 94-; Soc Ancient Greek Philos, 98-. **RESEARCH** Philosophy of language; metaphysics; ethics; history of Plato, Descartes, Locke, Kant, and Frege. **SELECTED PUBLICATIONS** Auth, Locke on Primary and Secondary Qualities, Pacific Philos Quarterly, 97. **CONTACT ADDRESS** Dept of Philosophy, Florida State Univ, 211 Wescott Bldg, Tallahassee, FL, 32306. **EMAIL** srickles@mailer.fsu.edu

RICOEUR, PAUL
PERSONAL Born 02/27/1913, m, 1935, 5 children **DISCIPLINE** PHILOSOPHY **EDUCATION** Univ Paris, Agregation, 35, D es Lett, 50. **CAREER** Prof hist of philos, Univ Strasbourg, 48-56; prof, Univ Paris, 56-65; prof, 65-76, John Nuveen Prof Philos Theol & Prof Philos, Univ Chicago, 76-. **HONORS AND AWARDS** Hon degrees from Univs Basil, Chicago, Montreal, Nijmegen, Zurich, Ohio State & DePaul. **RESEARCH** Philosophy of language; philosophy of action; hermeneutics. **SELECTED PUBLICATIONS** Auth, Fallible Man, Henry Regnery, 65; History and Truth, 65 & Freedom and Nature: The Voluntary and the Unvoluntary, 66, Northwestern Univ; The Symbolism of Evil, Harper, 67; Freud and Philosophy, Yale Univ, 70; Interpretation Theory, Tex Christian Univ Press, 76; The Crisis Of The Cogito, Synthese, Vol 106, 96. **CONTACT ADDRESS** Dept of Philos, Univ of Chicago, Chicago, IL, 60637.

RIDGE, MICHAEL
PERSONAL Born 07/21/1970, Dover, DE, m, 1993 **DISCIPLINE** PHILOSOPHY **EDUCATION** Wake Forest, BA, 92; Tufts Univ, MA, 95; Univ North Carolina, MA 97, PHd cand. **CAREER** Author **MEMBERSHIPS** APA. **RESEARCH** Moral theory; action theory; philosophy of mind. **SELECTED PUBLICATIONS** Auth, "How to avoid being driven to consequentialism," Philos & Pub Aff, 98; "Human Intentions," Am Philos Q, 98; "Hobbesian Public Reason," Ethics, 98. **CONTACT ADDRESS** 121 Westview Dr, #102, Carrboro, NC, 27510. **EMAIL** mridge@email.unc.edu

RIDGWAY, JOHN KARL
PERSONAL Born 12/13/1949, Seattle, WA **DISCIPLINE** RELIGION **EDUCATION** Marquette Univ, PhD, 95. **CAREER** Asst prof, Dept Relig Studies, Regis Univ. **MEMBERSHIPS** Cath Bibl Asn; Soc Bibl Lit. **RESEARCH** Gospel of Matthew; the Concepts of Healing and Peace in the Old and New Testaments; Johannine literature. **SELECTED PUBLICATIONS** Auth, Let Your Peace Come Upon It: Healing and Peace in Matthew 10:1-15, forthcoming. **CONTACT ADDRESS** Dept of Religious Studies, Regis Univ, 3333 Regis Blvd., Denver, CO, 80221-1099. **EMAIL** jridgway@regis.edu

RIEBER, STEVEN
DISCIPLINE PHILOSOPHY OF LANGUAGE, PHILOSOPHY OF MIND, METAPHYSICS, EPISTEMOLOGY, ETHI **EDUCATION** Princeton Univ, PhD, 91. **CAREER** Assoc prof, Ga State Univ. **SELECTED PUBLICATIONS** Author of eight recent articles in journals such as Analysis, Nous and Philos Stud. **CONTACT ADDRESS** Georgia State Univ, Atlanta, GA, 30303. **EMAIL** phlsdr@panther.gsu.edu

RIESENFELD, STEFAN ALBRECHT
PERSONAL Born 06/08/1908, Breslau, Germany, m, 1943, 2 children **DISCIPLINE** LAW **EDUCATION** Breslau Univ, JUD, 32; Univ Calif, LLB, 37; Harvard Univ, SJD, 40; Univ Minn, BS, 40. **CAREER** Prof law, Univ Minn, 38-42; from prof to Emanuel S Heller prof, 52-76, Emer Emanuel S Heller Prof Law, Univ Calif, Berkeley, 76-, Consult, comt restrictive bus practices, UN; US Dept Defense; workman's compensation, Minn Legis; Fulbright lectr, Ger, 56, Australia, 59 & Univ Auckland, 68; fel, Ctr Advan Studies Behav Sci, 62; consult, legis-ref bur, Univ Hawaii, 67-; mem adv comt bankruptcy rules, Nat Bankruptcy Conf; vis prof law, Univ Mich, 72. **HONORS AND AWARDS** Dr jur, Univ Cologne, 70. **MEMBERSHIPS** Am Bar Asn; Am Soc Int Law; Am Soc Legal Hist; Int Law Asn. **RESEARCH** International law; modern social legislation; commercial law. **SELECTED PUBLICATIONS** Auth, Protection of Fisheries Under International Law; California Security Transactions; Creditors Remedies and Debtors Protection Wes, 67; Prepaid Health Care in Hawaii, Univ Hawaii, 71; European Administrative-Law, Am J Of Comparative Law, Vol 0042, 1994. **CONTACT ADDRESS** 1129 Amador Ave, Berkeley, CA, 94707.

RIESER, ALISON
DISCIPLINE LAW **EDUCATION** Cornell Univ, BS; George Washington Univ, JD; Yale Law Sch, LLM. **CAREER** Prof and dir, Marine Law Inst; res fel, Woods Hole Oceanographic Inst, 2 yrs; fac law sch, Louisiana Tech Univ, 80-; app prof, Maine Law, 93-; consult to state and fed agencies; fac adv, law student-edited Ocean and Coastal Law J; **MEMBERSHIPS** US Env Protection Agency; Nat Oceanic and Atmospheric Admin. **RESEARCH** World's oceans. **SELECTED PUBLICATIONS** Coauth, leading casebk in ocean and coastal law. **CONTACT ADDRESS** School of Law, Univ of Southern Maine, 96 Falmouth St, PO Box 9300, Portland, ME, 04104-9300.

RIGALI, NORBERT JEROME
PERSONAL Born 12/29/1928, Los Angeles, CA **DISCIPLINE** MORAL THEOLOGY **EDUCATION** Gonzaga Univ, AB, 52, MA, 53; Innsbruck Pontif Col, STL, 60; Univ Munich, PhD(philos), 65. **CAREER** Asst prof philos, Mt St Michael Col Philos & Sci, Gonzaga Univ, 64-65 & Loyola Univ, Calif, 65-68; res assoc ethics & moral theol, Cambridge Ctr Soc Studies, 68-69; asst prof, 72-75, chmn dept relig studies, 74-78, assoc prof, 75-81, prof Moral Theol, Univ San Diego, 81-. **MEMBERSHIPS** Col Theol Soc; Catholic Theol Soc Am. **RESEARCH** Moral theology. **SELECTED PUBLICATIONS** Auth, Die Selbstkonstitution der Geschichte im Denken von Karl Jaspers, Anton Hain, Meisenheim, 68; Moral theology: Old and new, Chicago Studies, spring 69; A new axis of history, Int Philos Guart, 70; Toward a Moral Theology of Social Consciousness, fall 77 & Evil and Models of Christian Ethics, spring 81, Horizons; Reimaging Morality: A Matter of Metaphors, The Heythrop J, Jan 94; Christian Morality and Universal Morality: The One and the Many, Louvain Studies, Spring 94; Church Responses to Pedophilia, Theol Studies, March 94. **CONTACT ADDRESS** Dept of Theol and Relig Studies, Univ of San Diego, San Diego, CA, 92110.

RIGBY, KENNETH
PERSONAL Born 10/20/1925, Shreveport, LA, m, 1951, 3 children **DISCIPLINE** LAW **EDUCATION** La State Univ, BA, JD. **CAREER** Adj prof Law, La State Univ Law Center, 90- , lect La State Univ annual bar review course. **HONORS AND AWARDS** Magna Cum Laude; Summa Cum Laude; Order of the Coif; Phi Delta Phi; Omicron Delta Kappa; listed in Best Lawyers of Am, Who's Who in the South and Southwest, Who's Who in American Law and Who's Who in the World; Am Acad of Matrimonial Lawyers Fel; Am Col of Trial Lawyers Fel **MEMBERSHIPS** Am Acad of Matrimonial Lawyers; Am Col of Trial Lawyers; La St Law Inst; La State Bar Asn. **RESEARCH** Family law; matrimonial regimes. **SELECTED PUBLICATIONS** Auth, Some Views, Old and New on Recent Developments in Family Law, in La Bar J, 82; auth, Alternate Dispute Resolution, in La Law Rev, 84; coauth, Louisiana's New Divorce Legislation: Background and Commentary, La Law R, 93; auth, The 1993 Custody and Child Support Legislation, La Law Rev, 94; auth, The 1997 Spousal Support Act, La Law Review, 98; auth, Divorce Forms, West LSA Civil Procedure, West, 96, 98. **CONTACT ADDRESS** 8916 Creswell Rd, Shreveport, LA, 71106.

RIGDON, V. BRUCE
PERSONAL Born 02/23/1936, Philadelphia, PA, m, 1959, 3 children **DISCIPLINE** RELIGION **EDUCATION** Wooster, BA, 58; Yale Divinity Sch, BD, 62; Yale Univ, MA, 63, PhD, 68. **CAREER** Asst prof/prof, McCormicle Theol Sem, 65-88; pastor, Grosse Pointe Mem Church, 88-; prof church hist, 89-, pres, 97-, Ecumenical Theol Sem. **CONTACT ADDRESS** Dept of Theology, Ecumencial Theol Sem, 1028 Yorkshire Rd., Grosse Pointe, MI, 48230.

RIGGINS, THOMAS
PERSONAL Born 02/17/1942, West Palm Beach, FL, d, 2 children **DISCIPLINE** PHILOSOPHY **EDUCATION** FL State Univ, BA, MA; CUNY, MPhil, PhD. **CAREER** Adjunct Asst Prof, NYU; faculty, New Sch for Social Research **MEMBERSHIPS** APA **RESEARCH** Comparative philosophy; hist of philosophy; Marxism **SELECTED PUBLICATIONS** Various reviews in Philosophy East and West; International Journal of Philosophy; Korea Focus. **CONTACT ADDRESS** 150 E 2 St, #3B, New York, NY, 10009. **EMAIL** jtr2@is6.nyu.edu

RIKE, JENNIFER L.
DISCIPLINE RELIGIOUS STUDIES **EDUCATION** Univ Mich, BA; Univ Chicago Divinity Sch, MA, PhD. **CAREER** Ordained minister, Presbyterian Chruch, USA; asst prof, Univ Detroit Mercy, 95-. **RESEARCH** Paradoxical relationship between violence and religion. **CONTACT ADDRESS** Dept of Religious Studies, Univ of Detroit Mercy, 4001 W McNichols Rd, PO Box 19900, Detroit, MI, 48219-0900. **EMAIL** RIKEJL@udmercy.edu

RIND, MILES
PERSONAL Seattle, WA **DISCIPLINE** PHILOSOPHY **EDUCATION** Univ Chicago, PhD, 98. **CAREER** Author **MEMBERSHIPS** APA; Am Soc for Aesthet; North Am Kant Soc. **RESEARCH** Kant; aesthetics; philosophy of music. **CONTACT ADDRESS** 5851 South Blackstone Ave, Apt 113, Chicago, IL, 60637.

RINDERLE, WALTER
PERSONAL Born 08/31/1940, Vincennes, IN, m, 1974, 2 children **DISCIPLINE** CHURCH HISTORY, THEOLOGY, EURO HISTORY **EDUCATION** St Meinrad Col, AB 62; State Univ Innsbruck, Austria, STL 66, MA 67; Univ Notre Dame, MA 73, PhD 76. **CAREER** Vincennes Univ, asst prof 90-94; Univ Southern IN, asst prof 94-97; Univ St Francis, instr 98. **HONORS AND AWARDS** 2 NEH awds. **MEMBERSHIPS** Indiana Hist Soc; Catholic Hist Soc. **RESEARCH** Role of the Lutheran Church in the collapse of East Germany; Medical hist; Nazi Germany. **SELECTED PUBLICATIONS** Nazi Impact on a German Village; 200 Years of Catholic Education; Permanent Pastors in Knox County. **CONTACT ADDRESS** RR 6, E-2, Vincennes, IN, 47591. **EMAIL** rinderle@bestonline.net

RING, NANCY C.
PERSONAL Born 08/26/1937, Memphis, TN, s **DISCIPLINE** THEOLOGY **EDUCATION** Marquette Univ, PhD, 80. **CAREER** Prof, Dept Chr, LeMoyne Coll, 79-. **MEMBERSHIPS** Catholic Theol Soc of Amer; Amer Acad of Relig; Coll Theol Soc **RESEARCH** Theol Method; feminist studies, spirituality **SELECTED PUBLICATIONS** An Introduction to the Study of Religion **CONTACT ADDRESS** LeMoyne Col, Syracuse, NY, 13214. **EMAIL** Ring@Maple.Lemoyne.edu

RIPPLE, KENNETH FRANCIS
PERSONAL Born 05/19/1943, Pittsburgh, PA, m, 1968, 3 children **DISCIPLINE** LAW **EDUCATION** Fordham Univ, AB, 65; Univ Va, JD, 68; George Washington Univ, LLM, 72. **CAREER** Atty, IBM Corp, 68 & Judge Advocate General's Corps, US Navy, 68-72; legal officer, Supreme Ct US, 72-73, special asst to Chief Justice Burger, 73-77; PROF LAW, UNIV NOTRE DAME, 77-, Reporter, Adv Comt Fed Appellate Rules, 78-; mem, Nat Adv Comt to Chief Justice on Law Clerk Selection, 78 & Anglo Am Judicial Exchange, 80; United States Circuit Court Judge, South Bend, Ind, 85-. **HONORS AND AWARDS** Teacher of Year, Law Sch, Univ Notre Dame, 78-80, 84 & 85; Special Pres Award, 85. **MEMBERSHIPS** Am Law Inst; Am Bar Asn; Fed Bar Asn; NY State Bar Asn; Phi Beta Kappa; Supreme Court Hist Soc. **RESEARCH** Constitutional law; conflicts of law; Supreme Court of the United States. **SELECTED PUBLICATIONS** Coauth, Extralegal standards in the process of constitutional adjudication in the Supreme Court of the United States, Zeitschrift fur Politik, 79; State sovereignty--A polished but slippery crown, 79 & World Wide Volkswagon Corporation versus Woodson: Relfections on the road ahead, 80, Notre Dame Lawyer; auth, The Supreme Court's workload: Some thoughts for the practitioner, Am Bar Asn J, 80; The entanglement test of the religion clauses: A ten year assessment, Univ Calif Los Angeles Law Rev, 80; coauth, The separate appendix in federal appellate practice: Necessary tool or costly luxury?, Southwestern Law J, 81; American constitutional law 1976-1981, Jahrbuch Des Offentlichen Rechts Der Gegenwart, 81; Sanctions Imposable for Violations of the Federal Rules of Civil Procedure, Fed Judicial Ctr, 81. **CONTACT ADDRESS** Sch of Law, Univ of Notre Dame, Notre Dame, IN, 46556.

RISJORD, MARK
DISCIPLINE PHILOSOPHY OF LANGUAGE **EDUCATION** Univ NC, PhD, 90. **CAREER** Philos, Emory Univ. **SELECTED PUBLICATIONS** Articles, Am Philos Quart, Jour Med & Philos, Canadian Jour Philos, Studies Hist & Philos Science. **CONTACT ADDRESS** Emory Univ, Atlanta, GA, 30322-1950.

RISSER, JAMES C.
PERSONAL Born 08/23/1946, Allentown, PA, m, 2 children **DISCIPLINE** PHILOSOPHY **EDUCATION** Calif State Univ-Long Bch, BA, 71; Duquesne Univ, PhD, 78. **CAREER** Vis asst prof, Villanova Univ, 78-79; asst prof, 79-85, prof, 96-, Seattle Univ, 79-; Pigott McCone Chr Hum, 91-94. **MEMBERSHIPS** Am Philos Asn; Soc Phenomenol & Existential Philos. **RESEARCH** Hermeneutics; Aesthetics. **SELECTED PUBLICATIONS** Hermeneutics and the Voice of the Other, SUNY Press, 97. **CONTACT ADDRESS** Dept of Philosophy, Seattle Univ, Seattle, WA, 98122. **EMAIL** jrisser@seattleu.ed

RISSI, MATHIAS
PERSONAL Born 09/29/1920, Wienacht, Switzerland, m, 1945, 4 children **DISCIPLINE** RELIGION **EDUCATION** Univ Basel, ThD, 52. **CAREER** Minister, Sargans, Hauptwil, Rheineck & Basel, Switz, 44-63; Prof New Testament, Union Theol Sem, Va, 63-, Privat docent, Univ Basel, 56-63; guest lectr, Univ Hamburg, 67; dean studies, Ecumenical Sem, Vienna, Austria, 77- **MEMBERSHIPS** Soc Studies New Testament; Soc Bibl Lit. **RESEARCH** New Testament. **SELECTED PUBLICATIONS** Auth, The Kerygma Of The Revelation To John, Interpretation, 68; Studies Zum 2 Korintherbrief, Zwingli Verlag, 69; Die Logoslieder Im Prolog Des Vierten Evangeliums, Theol Zeitschrift, 75; The Eternal Word, Interpretation, 77; Voll Grosser Fische, Theoll Zcitschrift, 79; Coauth, Biblisch-Historisches Worterbuch, Vandenhoeck-Ruprecht, Gottingen, 62-79; Der Aufgau Des Johanmesevangeliums, New Testament Studies, 82; Exegetisches Worterbuch Zum Neven Testament, Kohlhammer, 81-82; The Theology Of The Book Of Revelation, Interpretation-A J Of Bible And Theology, Vol 49, 95; Revelation--A Continental Commentary, Interpretation-A J Of Bible And Theology, Vol 49, 95; After The 1000 Years--Resurrection And Judgment In Revelation-XX, Interpretation-A J Of Bible And Theology, Vol 48, 94. **CONTACT ADDRESS** Union Theol Sem, Richmond, VA, 23227.

RITSON, G. JOY
PERSONAL Born 12/18/1945, Highworth, England **DISCIPLINE** HISTORICAL THEOLOGY **EDUCATION** Graduate Theo Union, PhD, 97. **CAREER** Seeking first position. **MEMBERSHIPS** AAR/SBL, APA, SSSR. **RESEARCH** History of Christian Spirituality; Early and Medieval Church; Linguistic Issues involving Latin and Greek Text. **SELECTED PUBLICATIONS** Auth, Eros, Allegory and Spirituality, in preparation, based on PhD Dissertation; Shame in the Developing Though of Augustine, in preparation. **CONTACT ADDRESS** 1277 Sun Cir E, Melbourne, FL, 32935. **EMAIL** MINDOX@ix.NETCOM.COM

RIVERS, CLARENCE JOSEPH
PERSONAL Born 09/09/1931, Selma, AL **DISCIPLINE** RELIGION **EDUCATION** BA 1952; MA 1956; St Mary's Sem, Cincinnati; English Lit Xavier U; Cath Univ of Am; Union Grad Sch, PhD; Institut Catholique, Paris. **CAREER** Archdiocese of Cincinnati, priest 1956-; Purcell HS, tchr, English Lit 1956-66; St Joseph's & Assumption Parishes, asso pastor 1956-66; Dept of Culture & Worship Nat Ofc of Black Cath, founder first dir 1972, spl cons; Stimuli Inc, "Newborn Again", pres. **HONORS AND AWARDS** Recipient pub serv awards; 1966 Gold Medal of Cath Art Assn for "An Am Mass Prog". **MEMBERSHIPS** Mem bd dir Nat Liturgical Conf; N Am Academy of Liturgy; Martin Luther Kings Fellows; pub "Turn Me Loose"; mem worship comm Archdiocese of Cincinnati. **SELECTED PUBLICATIONS** Rec, "An Am Mass Prog," 1963; auth, books on worship; CBS Network, scripted/co-prod/starred "Freeing the Spirit" 1971; CBS Network Easter Special, prod cons/narrator/composer "The Feast of Life." **CONTACT ADDRESS** PO Box 20066, Cincinnati, OH, 45220.

ROACH, KENT
DISCIPLINE LAW **EDUCATION** Univ Toronto, BA, 84, LLB, 87; Yale Univ, LLM, 87. **CAREER** Law clerk, Justice Bertha Wilson, Supreme Court Can, 88-89; prof, 98- **HONORS AND AWARDS** Walter Owen Prize, 84., Ed, Criminal Law Quarterly; assoc ed, Dominion Law Reports. **MEMBERSHIPS** Law Soc Saskatchewan; Law Found Saskatchewan; Law Soc Upper Can. **SELECTED PUBLICATIONS** Auth, Constitutional Remedies in Canada, Can Law Bk, Criminal Law, Irwin Law, 96. **CONTACT ADDRESS** Col of Law, Univ Saskatchewan, 15 Campus Dr, Saskatoon, SK, S7N 5A6. **EMAIL** Roach@law.usask.ca

ROARK, DALLAS MORGAN
PERSONAL Born 12/15/1931, Birchwood, TN, m, 1955, 2 children **DISCIPLINE** PHILOSOPHY, RELIGION **EDUCATION** Northern Baptist Theol Sem, ThB, 54; Univ Iowa, MA, 58, PhD, 63. **CAREER** Pastor, Harrisburg & Downey Baptist Churches, 55-60; assoc prof relig, Wayland Baptist Col, 60-66; assoc prof Soc Sci, 66-80, PROF PHILOS & CHMN, DIV SOC SCI, EMPORIA STATE UNIV, 80-. **MEMBERSHIPS** Am Soc Church Hist; Am Acad Relig; Southwestern Philos Soc. **RESEARCH** History of doctrine; American theological thought; theology. **SELECTED PUBLICATIONS** Ed, Wayland Lectures, Wayland Press, 62; auth, The Christian Faith, Broadman, 69; Dietrich Bonhoeffer, Word Publ, 72; Introduction to Philosophy, Ginn, 82. **CONTACT ADDRESS** Dept of Soc Sci, Emporia State Univ, 1200 Commercial St, Emporia, KS, 66801-5087. **EMAIL** roarkdal@esuvm.emporia.edu

ROBANA, ABDERRAHMAN
PERSONAL Born 01/29/1938, Tunis, Tunisia, m, 1975, 2 children **DISCIPLINE** CORPORATE FINANCE, INTERNATIONAL BUSINESS & ECONOMICS **EDUCATION** Washington Univ, St Louis, BSBA, 62, MBA, 64; NY Univ, PhD, 72. **CAREER** Prof of Business Administration, Alfred Univ, NY, 71-98; vis scholar, Harvard Univ, Middle East Inst, 98. **HONORS AND AWARDS** Sam Walton Fellow in Free Enterprise. **MEMBERSHIPS** Eastern Finance Asn; Small Business Directors Asn; The Financial Executive Inst. **RESEARCH** Privatization in emerging countries; country risk assesments and financial markets (global). **CONTACT ADDRESS** Harvard Univ, Prescott St, Apt #17, Cambridge, MA. **EMAIL** FRobana@Bigvax.alfred.edu

ROBBINS, IRA PAUL
PERSONAL Born 01/02/1949, Brooklyn, NY, m, 1970, 2 children **DISCIPLINE** LAW **EDUCATION** Univ PA, AB, 70; Harvard Univ, JD, 73. **CAREER** Law clerk, US Ct Appeals Second Circuit, 73-75; assoc prof law & dir, KS Defender Proj, Univ KS, 75-79; Prof Law & Justice, Am Univ, 79, Vis prof law, Georgetown Univ, 82, 90. **HONORS AND AWARDS** Ethel & Raymond F. Rice Prize Fac Scholar, Sch Law, Univ KS, 78; Pauline Ruyle Moore Scholar, WA Col Law, Am Univ, 80, 89, Outstanding Scholar, 81 & Outstanding Tchr, 82-85, 94, 97, Tchr/Sch of the Year, 87. **MEMBERSHIPS** Am Law Inst **RESEARCH** Criminal law; penology; judicial process. **SELECTED PUBLICATIONS** Auth, Comparative Postconviction Remedies, DC Heath/Lexington Bks, 80; Prisoners' Rights Sourcebook: Theory, Litigation, Practice, Vol II, Clark Boardman Co Ltd, 80; The Law and Processes of Post-Conviction Remedies: Cases and Materials, West Publ Co, 82; Judicial Sabbaticals, Fed Judicial Ctr, 87; The Legal Dimensions of Private Incarceration, Am Bar Asn, 88; Rationalizing Federal Habeas Corpus Review of State Court Criminal Convictions in Capital Cases, Background and Issues Paper, Am Bar Asn, 89; Toward a More Just and Effective System of Review in State Death Penalty Cases, Am Bar Asn, 90; Prisoners and the Law, West Group (4 vols), 98; Habeas Corpus Checklists, West Group, 98; auth of numerous articles. **CONTACT ADDRESS** WA Col of Law, American Univ, 4801 Massachusetts Ave NW, Washington, DC, 20016-8181. **EMAIL** robbins@wcl.american.edu

ROBERGE, RENE-MICHEL
PERSONAL Born 07/08/1944, Charny, PQ, Canada **DISCIPLINE** THEOLOGY/HISTORY **EDUCATION** Univ Laval, BA, 65, BTh, 67, LTh, 69, DTh, 71. **CAREER** PROF THEOLOGIE FONDAMENTALE ET D'HISTOIRE DE LA THEOLOGIE, UNIV LAVAL, 71-, prof titulaire, 83-, vice-doyen theol, 88-89, doyen, 89-97; dir de la revue Laval theologique et philosophique, 87-92. **MEMBERSHIPS** Int Asn Patristic Stud; Can Soc Patristic Stud; N Am Patristic Soc; Soc can de theologie. **SELECTED PUBLICATIONS** Auteur d'une cinquantaine de pubs et de nom communications en patristique, en theol fond et system, et en documentation spec. **CONTACT ADDRESS** Fac de Theologie, Laval Univ, Laval, PQ, G1K 7P4. **EMAIL** Rene-Michel.Roberge@ftsr.ulaval.ca

ROBERSON, CHRISTOPHER
PERSONAL Binghamton, NY, m, 1991 **DISCIPLINE** PHILOSOPHY **EDUCATION** Yale Univ, BA, 86; Univ Mich, PhD, 96. **CAREER** Vis asst prof, Univ Mich, 96-97; instr, Roosevelt Univ, 98-. **MEMBERSHIPS** Am Philos Asn **RESEARCH** Political Philosophy; Ethics; 18th Century Philosophy. **SELECTED PUBLICATIONS** Auth, The State as Rational Authority, Oxford J of Legal Studies, forthcoming; philos ed, The Eighteen Century: A Current Bibliography. **CONTACT ADDRESS** 1303 Maple Ave #2-W, Evanston, IL, 60201-4329. **EMAIL** robchr@enteract.com

ROBERTS, DON
DISCIPLINE PHILOSOPHY **EDUCATION** Univ Ill, PhD, 63. **RESEARCH** Logic; theory of knowledge; American philos. **SELECTED PUBLICATIONS** Auth, Logical Fragments, Univ Waterloo, 69; The Existential Graphs of Charles S. Peirce, Mouton, 73. **CONTACT ADDRESS** Dept of Philosophy, Waterloo Univ, 200 University Ave W, Waterloo, ON, N2L 3G1. **EMAIL** ddrob@uwaterloo.ca

ROBERTS, KATHRYN L.
PERSONAL Born 12/21/1949, Grand Haven, MI, m, 1994, 2 children **DISCIPLINE** OLD TESTAMENT **EDUCATION** Hope Col, BA magna cum laude, 85; Colgate Rochester Divinity School, MDiv, 88; Princeton Theo Sem, PhD, 96. **CAREER** Adj Prof, 94-98, SUNY Rutger; Asst Prof, 98-, Austin Presbyterian Theo Sem. **MEMBERSHIPS** SBL, AAUP, AAUW. **RESEARCH** Worship in Israel, religions of Israel, the prophets. **CONTACT ADDRESS** 725 E 32nd St, Austin, TX, 78705. **EMAIL** kathlee@ix.netcom.comkroberts@austinseminary.edu

ROBERTS, LANI
PERSONAL Born 09/08/1946, The Dalles, OR **DISCIPLINE** PHILOSOPHY **EDUCATION** BA, 85, PhD, 93, Univ Oregon **CAREER** Sr. Instructor (indefinite tenure), Oregon State Univ, 89-. **HONORS AND AWARDS** Col of Liberal Arts Master Teacher, 97-99, 99-01; Col of Liberal Arts, Meehan Excellence in Teaching, 97. **MEMBERSHIPS** Soc for Phil in the Contemporary World; Soc for Women in Phil. **RESEARCH** Philosophy of oppression; ethics; social and political philosophy; feminism **SELECTED PUBLICATIONS** Auth, Chapter IX, Duty, Virtue and the Victim's Choice, Duty to Others, 94; auth, One Oppression or Many, Philosophy in the Contemporary World, 97. **CONTACT ADDRESS** Dept of Philosophy, Oregon State Univ, 102B Hovland Hall, Corvallis, OR, 97331-3902. **EMAIL** lroberts@orst.edu

ROBERTS, MELINDA
DISCIPLINE PHILOSOPHY OF LAW **EDUCATION** Univ MA, PhD, 83. **CAREER** Philos, Col NJ. **MEMBERSHIPS** Pre-Law Adv Comt; Exec Comt, Women's Studies. **SELECTED PUBLICATIONS** Auth, Human Cloning: A Case of No Harm Done?, Jour Med Philos, 96; Parent and Child in Conflict: Between Liberty and Responsibility, Notre Dame Jour Law, Ethics, & Public Policy, 96. **CONTACT ADDRESS** Col of New Jersey, PO Box 7718, Ewing, NJ, 08628-0718.

ROBERTS, RODNEY C.
DISCIPLINE PHILOSOPHY **EDUCATION** Univ Wisconsin, Madison, PhD, 97. **CAREER** Instr, Seattle Central Commun Col, 96-98; asst prof, philos, Univ Hawaii, Manoa, 98- . **MEMBERSHIPS** APA; Am Sect Int Asn for Philos of Law and Soc Philos; Soc for Ethics; AAUP. **RESEARCH** Injustice; Hume. **SELECTED PUBLICATIONS** Auth, Race, Family, and Obligation, Center for the Study of Ethics in Society, Western Michigan Univ, 95; rev, The Underclass Question by Lawson, ed, Black Scholar, 96; auth, Note on Imbo, ed, An Introduction to African Philosophy, Roman & Littlefield, 98; auth, Philos East & West, forthcoming; auth, Note on Eze, Blackwell 98; auth, ed, African Philosophy: An Anthology, Philosophy East & West, forthcoming. **CONTACT ADDRESS** Department of Philosophy, Univ of Hawaii at Manoa, 2530 Dole St, Sak B-306, Honolulu, HI, 96822-2383. **EMAIL** rodneyr@hawaii.edu

ROBERTS, SAMUEL KELTON
PERSONAL Born 09/01/1944, Muskogee, OK, m **DISCIPLINE** THEOLOGY **EDUCATION** Univ de Lyon France, Diplome 1966; Morehouse Coll, BA 1967; Union Theol Sem, MDiv 1970; Columbia Univ, PhD 1974. **CAREER** New York City Mission Soc, summer proj dir 1967-70; S Hempstead Congregational Church, pastor 1972-73; Pittsburgh Theol Sem, asst prof 1973-76; Union Theol Sem, asst prof religion & soc 1976-80; VA Union Univ, dean 1980-. **HONORS AND AWARDS** Merril Overseas Study Award Morehouse Coll 1965-66; Protestant Fellow Fund for Theol Educ 1967-70; Fellow Columbia Univ 1970-72. **MEMBERSHIPS** Mem Amer Acad of Rel; mem Soc for the Scientific Study of Rel; mem Soc for the Study of Black Relition. **SELECTED PUBLICATIONS** Auth, "George Edmund Haynes" 1978 **CONTACT ADDRESS** Dean, Virginia Union Univ, 1500 N Lombardy St, Richmond, VA, 23220.

ROBERTS, VICTOR WILLIAM
PERSONAL Born 02/22/1942, Oklahoma City, OK **DISCIPLINE** PHILOSOPHY, THEOLOGY **EDUCATION** St John's Univ, MN, BA, 65; Univ Ottawa, MA & STL, 69; Fordham Univ, PhD, 73. **CAREER** Chmn hum div, 74-77, Prof Philos, St Gregory's Univ, 73-, V Pres Acad Affairs, 77. **MEMBERSHIPS** Am Philos Asn; Am Cath Philos Asn; Hegel Soc Am. **RESEARCH** Hegel; St Anselm of Canterbury; 19th century Europe. **SELECTED PUBLICATIONS** Auth St Anselm of Canterbury's tchg on faith, 9/70 & The rel of faith and reason in St Anselm of Canterbury, 12/74, Am Benedictine Rev. **CONTACT ADDRESS** St Gregory's Col, 1900 W Macarthur, Shawnee, OK, 74804-2499. **EMAIL** vwroberts@sgc.edu

ROBERTS, WENDY HUNTER
PERSONAL Born 01/15/1948, New York, NY **DISCIPLINE** RITUAL AND THEOLOGY **CAREER** Therapist in private practice, 81-, East West Healing Arts Center, Oakland CA. **MEMBERSHIPS** AAR **RESEARCH** Moral Theology; Ancient Women's History. **SELECTED PUBLICATIONS** Auth, In Her Name, in: Women at Worship, ed, Proctor Smith and Walton, Lexington KY, WJK, 93; Celebrating Her, Cleveland, Pilgrim Press, 98. **CONTACT ADDRESS** East West Healing Arts Center, 4174 Park Blvd, Oakland, CA, 94602. **EMAIL** whr@evolution.com

ROBERTS, WESLEY A.
PERSONAL Born 01/03/1938, Jamaica, Wisconsin, m **DISCIPLINE** THEOLOGY **EDUCATION** Waterloo Lutheran Univ, BA 1965; Toronto Baptist Seminary, MDiv 1965; Westminster Theological Seminary, ThM 1967; Univ of Guelph, MA 1968, PhD 1972 **CAREER** Gordon-Conwell Theological Seminary, asst prof of black studies 1972-73, asst prof of Christian Thought 1974-75, assoc prof of Church History, 1977-84, asst dean for acad prog 1980-84, prof of Church History 1984-85; Peoples Baptist Church of Boston, MA, interim pastor, 1980-82, pastor, 1982-; Gordon College, Wenham, MA, adjunct professor of History, 1974-. **MEMBERSHIPS** Mem Soc for the Study of Black Religion, Amer Soc of Church History, Conf of Faith & History; mem exec comm The Assoc of Theological Schools in the US & Canada 1980-84; pres, Black Ministerial Alliance of Greater Boston 1994-. **SELECTED PUBLICATIONS** Articles published in Eerdman's Handbook of Amer Christianity, Eerdman's Handbook of the History of Christianity, Fides et Historia; Ontario Grad Fellowship Government of Ontario 1968-70; Canada Council Doctoral Fellowship Government of Canada 1970-72; author, Chapter on Cornelius VanTil in Reformed Theology in America, Wm B Eerdman, 1985, in Dutch Reformed Theology, Baker Bookhouse, 1988; article, Martin Luther King Jr and the March on Washington, in Christian History Magazine, 1989; article, Rejecting the "Negro Pew," in Christian History Magazine, 1995. **CONTACT ADDRESS** Senior Pastor, Peoples Baptist Church of Boston, 134 Camden Street, Boston, MA, 02118.

ROBERTSON, BENJAMIN W.
PERSONAL Born 04/06/1931, Roanoke, VI, m **DISCIPLINE** THEOLOGY **EDUCATION** VA Theol Seminary, BTh 1951; VA Union Univ, AB 1954; VA Seminary & Coll MDiv 1956, DD 1959, DMin 1968; Union Baptist Seminary, LLD 1971; Richmond VA Seminary LLD 1982; VA Union Univ, HLD 1997. **CAREER** Cedar St Memorial Bapt Ch of God, pastor 1955-; Radio Station WLEE, radio preacher 1961-; Natl Progressive Bapt Cong, tchr 1962-; Radio Station WANT, 1965-; Robertson's Kiddie Coll, pres 1968-; First Union Bapt Ch Chesterfield, pastor; Piney Grove Bapt Ch, pastor; Richmond VA Seminary, pres, 1981-; VIRGINIA THEOLOGICAL SEMINARY & COLLEGE, LYNCHBURG, VA, PRES, currently. **HONORS AND AWARDS** Afro-Amer Awd for Superior Public Serv without Thought of Gain 1981; Minister of Yr Hayes-Allen VTS&C 1975; Rich Com Hosps Humanitarian Awd 1975; Beta Gamma Lambda Chap Alpha Phi Alpha Frat Inc 1968; FOX Channel 35, television ministry. **MEMBERSHIPS** Bd dirs Commonwealth of VA Girl Scouts 1960-69, Brookland Branch YMCA 1963-75, Rich Met Blood Serv 1963-68, Rich Br NAACP 1964-68, vice pres Lott Carey Bapt Foreign Miss Conv 1976-83; treas Baptist Ministers Conf 1960-70; founder Progressive Natl Bapt Convention 1961; dean of preaching VA Theological Seminary 1965-75; pres VA Seminary & Coll 1980-81; Xi Delta Lambda Chap of Alpha Phi Alpha Frat Inc; tchr of leaders PNBC 1961-81; Founder and First Pres of Richmond VA Seminary 1981-State Board of Psychology, 1996-2000; mem VA State Board of Psychology; VA State Board of Health Professionals. **SELECTED PUBLICATIONS** Author, "Just As He Promised," Providence House Publisher. **CONTACT ADDRESS** Richmond Virginia Theol Sem, 2318-20 Cedar St, Richmond, VA, 23223.

ROBERTSON, HEIDI GOROVITZ
PERSONAL Born 04/02/1964, m, 1993, 2 children **DISCIPLINE** LAW **EDUCATION** Tufts Univ, BA (political science, cum laude), 85; Univ WI Law School, JD (cum laude), 90; Columbia Univ School of Law, LLM, 95, JSD candidate. **CAREER** Teaching asst, Univ WI-Madison, 89; instr, legal writing and res, Univ WI Law School, 88-90; assoc in law, Columbia Univ School of Law, 93-95; asst prof Law, Cleveland State Univ, Cleveland-Marshall Col of Law, 96-; clerk intern, WI Supreme Court, Madison, 89; intern, WI Dept of Justice, Madison, 90; assoc, Pillsbury Madison & Sutro, San Francisco and Washington, DC, 90-93; ed bd, CA Environmental Law Reporter, 92-93; consult attorney, World Wildlife Fund, 94-95. **HONORS AND AWARDS** Ruth B Doyle Award, Univ WI Law School, 89; George H Young Memorial Award, Univ WI Law School, 90; Teaching Enhancement Award, Center for Teaching Excellence, Cleveland State Univ, 96, 97. **SELECTED PUBLICATIONS** Auth, Commentary: The EPA Propsed Rule on Lender Liability Under CERCLA, CA Environmental Law Reporter, Sept 91; Commentary: Western World Insurance Co v Dana, CA Environmental Law Reporter, Sept 91; Commentary: Shell Oil Co v EPA, CA Environmental Law Reporter, Feb 92; Commentary: Arkansas v Oklahoma, CA Environmental Law Reporter, April 92; Commentary: The EPA Final Rule On Lender Liability Under CERCLA, CA Environmental Law Reporter, June 92; Commentary: Chemical Waste Management v Hunt and Fort Gratiot Sanitary Landfill v Michigan Dept of Natural Resources, CA Environmental Law Reporter, July 92; Commentary: People v Blech, CA Environmental Law Reporter, Nov 92; If Your Grandfather Could Pollute, So Can You: Environmental 'Grandfather Clauses' and Their Role in Environmental Inequity, 45 Cath U L Rev 131, 95; Environmental Justice: The Social and Demographic Impact of Environmental Choices 9 09 in Frank Grad, Environmental Law Treatise, Matthew Bender, 95 update; Methods for Teaching Environmental Law: Some Thoughts on Providing Access to the Environmental Law System, 23 Colum J Envtl L 237, 98; One Piece of the Puzzle: Legislative Innovation and Other Barriers to the Success of Brownfields Redevelopment Efforts, forthcoming. **CONTACT ADDRESS** Cleveland-Marshall Col of Law, Cleveland State Univ, 1801 Euclid Ave, Cleveland, OH, 44115. **EMAIL** Heidi.Robertson@law.csuohio.edu

ROBERTSON, O. PALMER
DISCIPLINE OLD TESTAMENT **EDUCATION** Belhaven Col, BA; Westminster Theol Sem, BDiv; Union Theol Sem, ThM, ThD. **CAREER** Prof, Knox Theol Sem. **SELECTED PUBLICATIONS** Auth, Psalms in Congregational Celebration. **CONTACT ADDRESS** Knox Theol Sem, 5554 N Federal Hwy, Ft. Lauderdale, FL, 33308.

ROBERTSON, TERESA
PERSONAL Born 05/23/1964, Ft. Hood, TX **DISCIPLINE** PHILOSOPHY **EDUCATION** Univ Wash, BA, 87; Princeton Univ, MA, 93. **CAREER** Reed Coll, vis asst prof of philos and humanities, 95-98 **HONORS AND AWARDS** Phi Beta Kappa. **MEMBERSHIPS** Am Philos Asn. **RESEARCH** Philosophy of Language; Metaphysics. **SELECTED PUBLICATIONS** Auth, Possibilties and the Arguments for Origin Essentialism, Mind, 98. **CONTACT ADDRESS** 8709 SW 11th Ave, Portland, OR, 97219. **EMAIL** teresa.robertson@reed.edu

ROBINSON, HADDON W.
DISCIPLINE PREACHING **EDUCATION** Dallas Theol Sem, ThM, 55; S Methodist Univ, MA, 60; Univ Ill, PhD, 64. **CAREER** Instr, Univ Ill, 60-62; Dallas Theol Sem; co-dir, DMin Prog; Harold John Ockenga Distinguished prof, Gordon-Conwell Theol Sem, 91-. **HONORS AND AWARDS** Hon degree, DD, Gordon Col., Dir, Dallas Youth for Christ, 52-55; assoc pastor, First Baptist Church, 56-58; pres, Denver Conservative Baptist Sem, 79; gen dir, Christian Med and Dental Soc, 70-79; tchr, Radio Bible Class; pres, Evangel Theol Soc, 83. **SELECTED PUBLICATIONS** Ed, Theol Annual; contrib ed, Preaching; fel and sr ed, Christianity Today; ed, Christian Medical Soc Jour, Our Daily Bread; pub(s), Christianity Today; Bibliotheca Sacra; Moody Monthly; Amer Lutheran Mag; Leadership and Decision mag; auth, Psalm 23; Grief; Biblical Preaching; Biblical Sermons; What Jesus Said About Successful Living; Decisions by the Book. **CONTACT ADDRESS** Gordon-Conwell Theol Sem, 130 Essex St, South Hamilton, MA, 01982.

ROBINSON, HOKE
PERSONAL Born 08/16/1942, Columbia, SC, 1 child **DISCIPLINE** PHILOSOPHY **EDUCATION** George Washington Univ, BA, 69; Univ Tex, MA, 71; State Univ NY, Stony Brook, PhD(Philos), 78. **CAREER** Asst prof, Southern Methodist Univ, 78, Univ Tex, Tyler, 78-79 & Rice Univ, 79-81; prof Philos, Memphis State Univ, 81-83; from assoc prof to prof, 82-95; Deutscher Akademischer Austauschdienst fel, 72 & 73; Alexander von Humboldt-Stiftung fel, 82-90. **MEMBERSHIPS** Am Philos Asn; North Am Kant Soc; Southwestern Philos Soc; Southern Soc Philos & Psychol; Centro Superiore Logica Scienze Comparate. **RESEARCH** Kantian Exegesis; foundations of logic; classical metaphysics. **SELECTED PUBLICATIONS** Auth, Anschauung und Manigfaltiges in der Transzendentalen Duduktion & Incongruent counterparts and the refutation of idealism, Kant-Studien, 81; Two Perspectives on Kant's Appearances & Things in Themselves, J Hist Phil, 94. **CONTACT ADDRESS** Dept Philosophy, Memphis State Univ, 3706 Alumni St, Memphis, TN, 38152-0001. **EMAIL** hrobinsn@latte.memphis.edu

ROBINSON, JAMES BURNELL
PERSONAL Born 09/07/1944, Indianapolis, IN, m, 1977, 1 child **DISCIPLINE** WORLD RELIGIONS, TIBETAN BUDDHISM **EDUCATION** Wabash Col, BA, 66; Univ Wis, MA, 68, PhD(Buddhist studies), 75. **CAREER** ASSOC PROF RELIG, UNIV NORTHERN IOWA, 71-, Coordr, Iowa Theol Soc, 76-82. **MEMBERSHIPS** Am Acad Relig; Am Theol Soc; Tibet Soc; Int Asn Buddhist Studies **RESEARCH** Tibetan Buddhism; the primordial tradition; religious symbolism **SELECTED PUBLICATIONS** Auth, The Buddha's Lions: The Lives of the 84 Siddhas, Dharma Publ Col, 79; The Siddhas: Saints & Sorcerers, Gesar Mag, spring 79; The Coming American Dictatorship, Humanities Newslett, 81; coauth, The Doctrine of Socialist Realism, J Social & Polit Studies, spring 81; Ahimsa: Trajectory of a Moral Ideal, In: Boeings & Bullock Carts, Canakya Publ, Delhi, 90; History of Religions & Primordial Tradition, In: Fragments of Infinity, Prism Press, Great Brit, 91; Lives of the Buddhist Saints: Biography, Hagiography & Myth, In: Tibetan Literature: Studies in Genre, Snow Lion Publ, 96. **CONTACT ADDRESS** Dept of Philos & Relig, Univ Northern Iowa, Cedar Falls, IA, 50614-0001. **EMAIL** robinson@uni.edu

ROBINSON, JOHN H.
DISCIPLINE PHILOSOPHY **EDUCATION** Boston Col, BA, 67; Univ Notre Dame, MA, 72, PhD, 75; Univ Calif Berkeley, JD, 79. **CAREER** Asst prof. **RESEARCH** Philosophy of law; legal ethics; education law. **SELECTED PUBLICATIONS** Auth, Foreword: Church, State, and Sex, Notre Dame J Law, 95; Foreword: Physician Assisted Suicide: Its Challenge to the Prevailing Constitutional Paradigm, Notre Dame J Law, 95; H. Jefferson Powell on the American Constitutional Tradition, Notre Dame Law Rev, 96; co-auth, The Law of Higher Education and the Courts: 1994 in Review, J Col Univ Law, 96. **CONTACT ADDRESS** Philosophy Dept, Univ of Notre Dame, 336/7 O'Shaughnessy, Notre Dame, IN, 46556. **EMAIL** robinson.1@nd.edu

ROBINSON, KEITH ALAN
PERSONAL Born 04/24/1963, London, England, m, 2 children **DISCIPLINE** PHILOSOPHY **EDUCATION** Univ Essex, BA, 87, MA 88; Univ Warwick, PhD, 95. **CAREER** Instr, Warwick Univ. **MEMBERSHIPS** Am Philos Asn. **RESEARCH** Continental philsophy; Twentieth-century French philosophy. **SELECTED PUBLICATIONS** Auth, "The Passion and the Pleasure: Foucault's Art of Not Being Oneself," in the J of the British Soc for Phenomenol, 99; "The Foucault/Deleuze Conjunction: Thought of the Outside" in Philos Today, 99. **CONTACT ADDRESS** 3959 Prairie SW, Grandville, MI, 49418.

ROBINSON, LYMAN R.
DISCIPLINE LAW **EDUCATION** Saskatchewan Univ, BA, 62, LLB, 63; Harvard Univ, LLM, 68. **CAREER** Law, Univ Victoria **RESEARCH** Debtor-creditor law; evidence; taxation; criminal law. **SELECTED PUBLICATIONS** Auth, British Columbia Debtor-Creditor Law and Precedents. **CONTACT ADDRESS** Fac of Law, Univ Victoria, PO Box 2400, Victoria, BC, V8W 3H7. **EMAIL** lrobinso@uvic.ca

ROBINSON, MARY ELIZABETH
PERSONAL Born 02/16/1946, Sallis, MS, d **DISCIPLINE** LAW **EDUCATION** Wartburg Coll Waverly IA, BA 1972;

Univ of IA Coll of Law Iowa City, JD 1977-78. **CAREER** Mary E Robinson Law Office, atty 1979-; Coll of Law Univ of IA Iowa City, asst to dean of law 1977-79; Coll of Law Univ of IA, dir acad asst prog 1976-77; Martin Luther King Center for Vocational & Educ Training Waterloo IA, acting dir 1972-74; Educ Opportunity Prog Univ No IA Ceader Falls, dir on campus 1972-73. **HONORS AND AWARDS** Outstanding Black Grad Student Award; AG Clark Award Water Loo 1976; Achievement Award NAACP Cedar Rapids Chap 1979; One of Top 10 Black Women Ldrs State of IA US Dept of Labor. **MEMBERSHIPS** Gov appointed bd mem IA State Dept of Pub Instr 1979-85; mem Nat Conf of Black Lawyers; mem Assn of Trial Lawyers of IA & Am; founder & pres Black Womens Civil Orgn Cedar Rapids IA 1978-; commr Human Rights Commn Cedar Rapids 1978-; dep IA-nE NAACP Legal Redress Commn; IA rep Nat Task Force to the White House Conf on Families 1980; IA del White House Conf on Families Minneapolis 1980; bd mem United Way of Linn Co Acad Ascholarship & Dean's List Wartburg Coll Waverly IA 1970-72; offered internship Washington Interns in Educ Inst for Educ Leadership Washington DC 1974-75. **CONTACT ADDRESS** Higley Bldg, Ste 315, Cedar Rapids, IA, 52401.

ROBINSON, WILLIAM SPENCER
PERSONAL Born 10/22/1940, Staten Island, NY, m, 1963, 2 children **DISCIPLINE** PHILOSOPHY **EDUCATION** Yale Univ, BA, 62; Ind Univ, PhD(Philos), 66. **CAREER** Asst prof Philos, Univ Iowa, 66-72; asst prof Philos, Iowa State Univ, 72-74; assoc prof Philos, Iowa State Univ; 74-83; prof Philos, Iowa State Univ, 83-; chmn of dept, 91. **RESEARCH** Philosophy of mind and history. **SELECTED PUBLICATIONS** Auth, Judgements involving identification, Analysis, 6/64; Brainier and People, Temple, up, 88; Computers, Minds of Robots, Temple, UP, 92. **CONTACT ADDRESS** Dept of Philosophy, Iowa State Univ of Science and Tech, Ames, IA, 50011-0002.

ROCA, ROBERT PAUL
PERSONAL Born 11/06/1952, San Francisco, CA, m, 1979, 2 children **DISCIPLINE** MEDICINE **EDUCATION** Occidental Col, BA summa cum laude 74; Univ Cal LA, MD 78, MPH 78. **CAREER** Sheppard Pratt Health Sys, Geri and Gen Hosp, med dir; John Hopkins Univ Sch of Med, assoc prof; Fallston Gen Hosp, chemn Dept Psych; Harford Mem Hosp, chmn Dept of Psych; Sheppard Pratt Health Sys, active staff; John Hopkins Hosp, assoc staff; Greater Baltimore Med Cen, assoc staff; Francis Scott Key Med Cen, ch ethics comm 87-93; Chesapeake Physicians PA, mem bd dir 87-93; John Hopkins Hosp, asst prof psych 85-92, asst prof med 86-93; Francis Scott Key Med Cen, dir consul geri psychiatry 85-93, Eldercall, team phys, psychiatric consul 85-87, GRE Nat Inst Aging, guest worker 84-85; JHU Sch of Med, inst 84-85, chief res 83-84, admin res 83, asst res Dept psychiatry 81-83; John Hopkins Hospital, Henry J. Kaiser foun fel 80-81, asst resident 79-80, intern 78-79. **HONORS AND AWARDS** Phi Beta Kappa; Alpha Omega Alpha; Lange Med Pub Awd; Smith Kline French Fel; Teacher of the Year; Baltimore Mag Top Doc Geriatrics; APA Fel. **MEMBERSHIPS** APA; GSA; AGS; AAGP; IPA; MPS; BCMA. **RESEARCH** Mental health services for the elderly; Mgmt of the behavioral complications of dementing illness; Psychiatric disorders in the mentally ill. **SELECTED PUBLICATIONS** Auth, Use of formal and informal sources of mental health care among older African-American public-housing residents, coauth, in: Psychological Medicine, 98; The prevalence of psychiatric disorder in elderly residents of public housing, coauth, in: Jour of Gerontology, 96; Profiles in Cognitive Aging, D Powell, Cambridge, Harv Univ Press, 94, rev, The Jour of Nervous and Mental Disease, 96; Physicians and guardianship: a brief commentary, coauth, MD Jour of Contemporary Legal Issues, 95; The Elderly Patient, in: Managing Care Not Dollars: The Continuum of Mental Health Services, eds, R. Schreter, S. Sharfstein, C. Schreter, Amer Psych Press, 96; Psychiatric aspects of systemic sclerosis, in: Systemic Scleroderma, coauth, eds, P.J. Clements, D.E. Furst, Baltimore, Williams and Wilkens, 96; Delirium and dementia: Management of behavioral complications, Audio Digest, Internal Med, Geriatrics and the Internist, 94; Reducing Resident Depression: Assessment and Intervention, Baltimore U of MD Sch of Med, Video Press, 93. **CONTACT ADDRESS** Geriatric Services, Sheppard Pratt Health System, 6501 North Charles St, PO Box 6815, Baltimore, MD, 21285-6815.

ROCKEFELLER, STEVEN C.
DISCIPLINE HISTORY OF RELIGION, PHILOSOPHY OF RELIGION, AND RELIGION, ETHICS, AND THE **EDUCATION** Princeton Univ, AB; Union Theol Sem, MDiv; Columbia Univ, PhD. **CAREER** Prof; Middlebury Col, 71-. **SELECTED PUBLICATIONS** Auth, John Dewey: Religious Faith and Democratic Humanism; co-ed, Spirit and Nature: Why the Environment is a Religious Issue-An Interfaith Dialogue. **CONTACT ADDRESS** Dept of Religion, Middlebury Col, Middlebury, VT, 05753.

ROCKER, STEPHEN
PERSONAL Born 09/12/1953, Lowville, NY **DISCIPLINE** PHILOSOPHY **EDUCATION** Univ Ottawa, PhD, 90. **CAREER** Prof Philos, Wadhams Hall Sem Col, 82-. **MEMBERSHIPS** Hegel Soc Am; Am Philos Asn. **RESEARCH** Philosophy of religion; ethics; metaphysics; Hegel studies. **SELECTED PUBLICATIONS** Auth, Hegel's Rational Religion, 95; auth, The Integral Relation of Religion and Philosophy in Hegel's Philosophy of Religion, New Perspectives on Hegel's Philos of Relig, 92. **CONTACT ADDRESS** Dept of Philosophy, Wadams Hall Sem Col, 6866 State Hwy. 37, Ogdensburg, NY, 13669-4420.

RODA, ANTHONY
DISCIPLINE PHILOSOPHY **EDUCATION** St Peter's Col, BA, 62; WA Univ, MA, 64; Southern IL Univ, PhD, 68. **CAREER** Instr, SUNY Oneonta, 67-69; to assoc prof, 79-91; to prof, 91-. **HONORS AND AWARDS** NEH Summer Sem, Yale Univ, 94; NEH Summer Inst, Yale Univ, 91; NEH Summer Inst, Yale Univ, 89; NEH Summer Inst, Dartmouth Col, 86; **MEMBERSHIPS** APA; Soc Asian Comp Philos; Dante Soc Am; Inst Vico Studies; NY State Found Educ Assn. **RESEARCH** Epistemology; Am philos; Giambattista Vico; Immanuel Kant. **SELECTED PUBLICATIONS** Auth, Dante's Vision and the Circle of Knowledge by Giuseppe Mazzotta (rev), Philos Lit, 95; The Demos and the Dictator, Singuliers; The Federalist Papers: Political Principles and Educational Consequences, Singuliers; ed, Educational Change, 96 and 95. **CONTACT ADDRESS** SUNY Col at Oneonta, Oneonta, NY, 13820. **EMAIL** maniscsj@oneonta.edu

RODAS, M. DANIEL CARROLL
DISCIPLINE OLD TESTAMENT THEOLOGY **EDUCATION** Dallas Theol Sem, ThM; Univ Sheffield, PhD. **CAREER** Prof, Denver Sem, 96-. **RESEARCH** Prophetic literature, Old Testament ethics, and the use of the Bible in the third world. **SELECTED PUBLICATIONS** Auth, Contexts for Amos: Prophetic Poetics, Latin Amer Perspective; co-ed, The Bible in Ethics and The Bible in Human Society: Essays in Honour of John Rogerson. **CONTACT ADDRESS** Denver Conservative Baptist Sem, PO Box 10000, Denver, CO, 80250. **EMAIL** danny@densem.edu

RODDY, NICOLE
PERSONAL Born 03/05/1954, Lincoln, NE, d, 1 child **DISCIPLINE** RELIGIOUS STUDIES **EDUCATION** Univ of Nebraska at Omaha, BA; St Vladimir's Orthodox Theol Seminary, Crestwood, NY, MA; Univ of Iowa, PhD. **CAREER** Lectr in Rel, 95-, Univ NE, Omaha; Tchg Asst, 90-94, Univ of Iowa. **HONORS AND AWARDS** Fulbright Scholar, 94-95, to Romania; Soc of Biblical Lit Regional Scholar Award, 98. **MEMBERSHIPS** AAR, SBL. **RESEARCH** Pseudoepigraphical and Apocryphal Literature. **SELECTED PUBLICATIONS** Auth, The Campaign for Catholicity in the Letters of St Ignatius of Antioch, Coptic Church Review, 91; The Form and Function of the Protevangelium of James, Coptic Church Review, 93; Two Parts: Weeks of Seven Weeks: The End of the Age as Terminus ad Quem for 2, Syriac Apocalypse of Baruch, Journal for the Study of the Pseudepigrapha, 96. **CONTACT ADDRESS** Dept of Philosophy, Univ of Nebr-Omaha, Omaha, NE, 68182. **EMAIL** nroddy@unomaha.edu

RODES, ROBERT EMMET
PERSONAL Born 05/29/1927, New York, NY, m, 1953, 7 children **DISCIPLINE** LAW **EDUCATION** Harvard, LLB (JD), 52; Brown, AB, 47. **CAREER** Attorney, Lib Mut Ins Co, 52-54; Rutgers Univ, Asst Prof, 54-56; Notre Dame, Asst prof, Assoc prof, Prof, 56-. **RESEARCH** Law and Theology **SELECTED PUBLICATIONS** Pilgrim Law, 98; Premises and Conclusions, with H Pospesel, 97. **CONTACT ADDRESS** Univ Notre Dame, School Law, Notre Dame, IN, 46556. **EMAIL** rodes.1@nd.edu

RODGERS, SANDA
DISCIPLINE LAW **EDUCATION** Univ Case Reserve, BA; McGill Univ, LLB, LLM. **CAREER** Prof. **RESEARCH** Canadian health law. **SELECTED PUBLICATIONS** Auth, pubs on health law. **CONTACT ADDRESS** Fac Common Law, Univ Ottawa, 550 Cumberland St, PO Box 450, Ottawa, ON, K1N 6N5.

RODRIGUES, HILLARY
DISCIPLINE RELIGIOUS STUDIES **EDUCATION** McMaster Univ, BA, 86; MA, 88; PhD, 93. **RESEARCH** Religions of India; anthropology of religion; philosophy and culture; medieval and modern hinduism. **SELECTED PUBLICATIONS** Auth, pubs on the contemporary religious teacher Jiddu Krishnamurti and popular Hindu goddess Durga. **CONTACT ADDRESS** Dept of Religious Studies, Lethbridge Univ, 4401 University Dr W, Lethbridge, AB, T1K 3M4. **EMAIL** rodrigues@hg.uleth.ca

RODRIGUEZ, ANGEL MANUEL
PERSONAL Born 05/06/1945, Cidra, PR, m, 1967, 2 children **DISCIPLINE** THEOLOGY **EDUCATION** Antillian Col, PR, BA, 68; Andrews Univ Theol Sem, MDiv, 70, ThD, 79. **CAREER** Dis Pastor, PR, 70-73; Acad Bible Tchr, PR, 73-75; asst prof, Antillian Col, 79-80, acad vice-pres, 81-82, pres, 83-87; prof, Southwestern Adventist Univ, 87-89, acad vice-pres, 89-92; assoc dir, Biblical Res Inst, 92- . **MEMBERSHIPS** Soc Bibl Lit; Am Acad Relig; Adventist Theol Soc. **RESEARCH** Hebrew cultus; wisdom literature. **SELECTED PUBLICATIONS** Auth, Substitution in the Hebrew Cultus, Andrews Univ, 82; auth, El rapto secreto de la iglesia, Pacific, 93; auth, Stewardship Roots, Church Ministries, 94; auth, Health and Healing in the Pentateuch, in Health 2000 and Beyond: A Study Conference of Adventist Theology, Philosophy, and Practice of Health and Healing, Home Study Int, 94; auth, Esther: A Theological Approach, Andrews Univ, 95; auth, Fin del mundo o muevo comienzo? Pacific, 96; auth, Leviticus 16: Its Literary Structure, Andrew Univ Sem Stud, 96; auth, Jewelry in the OT: A Description of Its Function, in Merling, ed, To Understand the Scriptures: Essays in Honor of William H. Shea, Inst of Archaeol, 97. **CONTACT ADDRESS** Biblical Research Inst, 12501 Old Columbia Pike, Silver Spring, MD, 20904-6600.

RODRIGUEZ, JOSE DAVID
DISCIPLINE THEOLOGY **EDUCATION** Lutheran Sch Theol at Chicago, PhD. **CAREER** Dir, Hisp Ministry Prog; vis prof, Sem Evangel de Puerto Rico; Comunidad Teologica de Mexico; assoc prof-. **HONORS AND AWARDS** Co-ch, planner of the First Encuentro of Hispanic-Latina Theologians and Ethicists, Princeton Theol Sem. **SELECTED PUBLICATIONS** Pub(s), articles on Hispanics in the church to The Lutheran. **CONTACT ADDRESS** Dept of Theology, Lutheran Sch of Theol, 1100 E 55th St, Chicago, IL, 60615. **EMAIL** jrodrigu@lstc.edu

RODRIGUEZ-HOLGUIN, JEANETTE
PERSONAL Born 01/04/1954, NY, m, 1983, 2 children **DISCIPLINE** THEOLOGY **EDUCATION** Queens Col, BA, 76; Fordham Univ, MA, 78; Univ Guam, MA, 81; Grad Theol Union, PhD, 90. **CAREER** From asst prof to assoc prof to chemn, 90-, Seattle Univ. **HONORS AND AWARDS** Who's Who Among Hispanic Am, 91-92; Nat Hispana Leadership Inst Fel, 94; Assoc Status, 98, United Holocaust Mus., Partial scholar, Grad Theol Union, 84; Nat Hispana Leadership Inst Fel, 94; Summer Fac Fel Award, 98. **MEMBERSHIPS** Am Asn Marriage and Family Therapy. **RESEARCH** US Hispanic theology; cultural memory; women's spirituality; religion and culture. **SELECTED PUBLICATIONS** Auth, Our Lady of Guadalupe: Faith and Empowerment Among Mexican-American Women, 94; auth, Stories We Live: Cuentos que Vivimos, 96; ed, Isasi-Diaz and Mujerista Theology, 96; ed, Cultural Memory: Source of Theological Insight, 96. **CONTACT ADDRESS** Dept of Theology and Religious Studies, Seattle Univ, Seattle, WA, 98122. **EMAIL** jrodrigu@seattleu.edu

ROGERS, ISABEL WOOD
PERSONAL Born 08/26/1924, Tallahassee, FL **DISCIPLINE** RELIGION **EDUCATION** Fla State Univ, AB, 45; Univ Va, MA, 47; Presby Sch Christian Educ, MRE, 49; Duke Univ, PhD, 61. **CAREER** Dir student work, First Presby Church, Milledgeville, Ga, 49-52; instr relig & chaplain, Women's Col, Ga, 52-61; Prof Appl Christianity, Presby Sch Christian Educ, 61-98, Kent fel, Soc Relig Higher Educ, 58. **HONORS AND AWARDS** DD, Austin Col; LLD, Westminster Col; DD Centre Col. **RESEARCH** Christianity and politics; church and women; reformed theology. **SELECTED PUBLICATIONS** Auth, The Christian and World Affairs, 64 & In Response to God: How Christians Make Ethical Decisions, 69, CLC Press; Sing a New Song, United Presby Church US Am, 80; Our Shared Earth, CE:SA Press, 80. **CONTACT ADDRESS** 1214 Palanyra Ave, Richmond, VA, 23227-4435.

ROGERS, KIM W.
DISCIPLINE PHILOSOPHY **EDUCATION** New Sch Soc Res, PhD. **CAREER** Prof emer, E Tenn State Univ. **RESEARCH** Contemporary continental philosophy. **SELECTED PUBLICATIONS** Auth Hegel and Fukuyama, 87; Existentialism is not Irrationalism: A Challenge to the Common Interpretation of Existentialism, J British Soc Phenomenology, 89; Ortega's Development of an Ecological Philosophy, J Hist Ideas, 94. **CONTACT ADDRESS** Philosophy Dept, East Tennesee State Univ, Box 70717, Johnson City, TN, 37614- 0717. **EMAIL** wylier@worldnet.att.net

ROHATYN, DENNIS ANTHONY
PERSONAL Born 04/21/1949, New York, NY, m **DISCIPLINE** PHILOSOPHY, HUMANITIES **EDUCATION** Queens Col, BA, 68; City Col New York, MA, 69; Fordham Univ, PhD(Philos), 72. **CAREER** Asst prof Philos, Roosevelt Univ, 72-77; assoc prof Philos, Univ San Diego, 77-; prof, 82. **HONORS AND AWARDS** Lowell Davies Award for Outstanding Faculty Achievement, 87; Class of 91 prof of the yr. **MEMBERSHIPS** Am Philos Asn; Am Cath Philos Assn; Soc for the Advancemtn of Am Philosophy; Am Soc for Value Inquiry; Phi Betta Kappa, 67-. **RESEARCH** History of philosophy; contemporary philosophy; ethics and value theory. **SELECTED PUBLICATIONS** Auth, Naturalism and Deontology: An Essay on the Problems of Ethics, Mouton, 76; Two Dogmas of Philosophy and other Essays on the Philosophy of Philosophy, Assoc Univ, 77; Bennett on Kant, Kant-Studien, 78; What are Kant's presuppositions, Brit J Phenomenol, 78; Resurrecting Peirce's Neglected Argument for God, 82 & Peirce and the Defense of Realism (in prep), Trans C S Peirce Soc; Hume's Dialectical Conceits: The Case of Dialogue XII,

Philos & Phenomenol Res (in prep); Aristotle and the Limits of Philosophic Proof, Nature & System (in prep); Philosophy/History/Sophistry, Rodopi, 97. **CONTACT ADDRESS** Dept of Philosophy, Univ of San Diego, 5998 Alcala Park, San Diego, CA, 92110-2492. **EMAIL** drohatyn@acuds.edu

ROHR, MICHAEL D.
PERSONAL Born 04/02/1940, Bronx, NY, m, 1987, 3 children **DISCIPLINE** PHILOSOPHY **EDUCATION** Harward Coll, AB, 62; Stanford Univ, PhD, 75. **CAREER** Instr, C/ W Post Coll, 66-68; instr, Univ Pittsburgh, 68-69; instr, Rutgers Univ 72-75; asst prof, 75-79; Assoc Prof, 79-. **MEMBERSHIPS** Am Philos Asn; Soc for Ancient Greek Philos; NY Ancient Philos Colloquium. **RESEARCH** Plato; Aristotle; Richard Rorty. **SELECTED PUBLICATIONS** Auth, Empty Forms in Plato, Arh for Geschichte der Philosophie, 78; Rorty Richard, Routledge Encycl of Philos, 98. **CONTACT ADDRESS** Rutgers Univ, 427 Conklin Hall, Newark, NJ, 07102. **EMAIL** rohr@alumni.stanford.orgMichael_Rohr_ab61@post.harvard.edu

ROHRBAUGH, RICHARD L.
PERSONAL Born 12/12/1936, Addis Ababa, Ethiopia, m, 1960, 2 children **DISCIPLINE** RELIGIOUS STUDIES **EDUCATION** Sterling Col, BA, 58; Pittsburgh Theol Sem, MDiv, 61; San Francisco Theol Sem, STD, 77. **CAREER** Pastor, Tri-City Presbyterian Church, Myrtle Creek, Ore, 61-68; pastor, St. Mark Presbyterian Church, Portland, Ore, 68-77; from asst prof to prof, Lewis and Clark Col, 77-. **HONORS AND AWARDS** James C. Purdy Sch, 59-60; Fund for Theol Educ Fel, 70-72; Outstanding Young Men of America, 72; Who's Who in Religion, 84; Who's Who in Biblical Studies and Archaeology, 85-. **MEMBERSHIPS** Am Acad of Relig; Soc of Bibl Lit; Cath Bibl Asn; Am Schs of Oriental Res; The Context Group. **RESEARCH** Social-scientific criticism of the New Testament; social world of early Christianity; New Testament hermeneutics. **SELECTED PUBLICATIONS** Auth, The Biblical Interpreter: An Agrarian Bible in an Industrial World, 78; Into All the World: A Basic Overview of the New Testament, 80; Methodological Considerations in the Debate over the Social Class Status of Early Christians, in J of the Am Acad of Relig, LII/3, 84; Parables: Occasions for the Unexpected, in Pacific Theol Rev, 84; Interpretation: An Introduction to the Study of the Bible, 85; Social Location of Thought as a Heuristic Device on New Testament Interpretation, in Jour for the Study of the New Testament 30, 87; Models and Muddles, in Foundations and Facets Forum 3,2, 87; Church Canon or Scholars' Canon?, in Fourth R 2,3, 89; The Patronage System in Roman Palestine, in Fourth R 3,1, 90; The City in the Second Testament: A Reader's Guide, in Bibl Theol Bull, 21/2, 91; The Social Location of the Markan Audience, in Bibl Theol Bull 23/3, 93; A Peasant Reading of the Parable of the Talents: A Text of Terror? In Bibl Theol Bull 22/4, 93; The Progress of the Gospel: From Jerusalem to Rome, in The Bible Today 31/1, 93; Social Science and Literary Criticism: What is at Stake?, in Hervormde Teologiese Studies 49/1, 93; Autobiographical Criticism: A Social-Scientific Response, in Semeia 72, 95; coauth, Social Science Commentary on the Synoptic Gospels, 92; Los evangelicos sinopticos y la cultura mediterranea del siglo I: Comentario desde las ciencias sociales, 96; Social Science Commentary on the Gospel of John, 98; ed, Using the Social Sciences in New Testament Interpretation, 96; rev, The Orphan Gospel: Mark's Perspective on Jesus, in Crit Rev of Books in Relig, 94; Feasting and Social Rhetoric in Luke 14, in Soc for New Testament Studies, Monograph Series 85, 95. **CONTACT ADDRESS** Religious Studies Dept, Lewis & Clark Col, Portland, OR, 97219. **EMAIL** rbaugh@lclark.edu

ROHRER, JAMES
PERSONAL Born 05/13/1960, Canton, OH, m, 1994, 2 children **DISCIPLINE** RELIGIOUS STUDIES **EDUCATION** Kent State Univ, BA, 82; Ohio State Univ, MA, 85, PhD, 91; Univ Dubuque Theol Sem, MDiv, 95. **CAREER** Asst prof, Presbyterian Bible Col, 93-96; asst prof, Yushan Theol Sem, 96-98; asst prof, Northwestern Col, 98-. **MEMBERSHIPS** Am Acad of Relig; Am Soc of Church Hist; Asn for Asian Studies; Conf on Faith and Hist. **RESEARCH** History of Christian mission; Christianity in the non-western world; Taiwanese Christianity; Cross-cultural theology. **SELECTED PUBLICATIONS** Auth, Keepers of the Covenant: Frontier Missions and the Decline of Congregationalism, 1774-1818; "German Presbyterians or Christian Americans? Intercollegiate Sports and the Identity Crisis at the University of Dubuque, 1902-1927," in Am Presbyterians, 96; "The Theologian as Prophet: Donald Bloesch and the Crisis of the Modern Church," in From East to West: Essays in Honor or Donald G. Bloesch, 97. **CONTACT ADDRESS** 101 7th St SW, Orange City, IA, 51041-1996. **EMAIL** rohrer@esther.nwciowa.edu

ROLLIN, BERNARD E.
DISCIPLINE PHILOSOPHY **EDUCATION** Columbia Univ, PhD, 72. **CAREER** Prof. **RESEARCH** Traditional philosophy; applied philosophy. **SELECTED PUBLICATIONS** Auth, Natural and Conventional Meaning, 76; Animal Rights and Human Morality, 81; The Unheeded Cry: Animal Consciousness, Animal Pain and Scientific Change, 88; Farm Animal Welfare, 95; The Frankenstein Syndrome, 95; ed, The Experimental Animal in Biomedical Research, 95. **CONTACT ADDRESS** Philosophy Dept, Colorado State Univ, Fort Collins, CO, 80523.

ROLLINS, RICHARD ALBERT
PERSONAL Born 11/30/1927, Philadelphia, Pennsylvania, m **DISCIPLINE** THEOLOGY **EDUCATION** Lincoln Univ, AB 1952; Union Theological Seminary, MDiv 1955; Boston Univ School of Theology, STM 1960; Claremont School of Theology, RelD 1969. **CAREER** Bishop Coll, chmn div of rel 1958-67, assoc dean/admin 1969-70, dean of the college 1970-77, vice pres for pme/prof of religion 1977-83, exec asst to pres dean of chapel 1983-. **HONORS AND AWARDS** Danforth Foundation Teacher Awd 1960-62; Ford Foundation Fellowship Awd 1967; Dallas Citizenship Awd Radio Station KNOK 1970. **MEMBERSHIPS** Mem Goals for Dallas, Natl Urban League, NAACP, Natl Campus Ministry Assoc, Acad of Religion, TX Alcohol/Narcotics Assoc; bd of dirs Dallas YMCA; chmnMoorland Branch YMCA 1969-85. **CONTACT ADDRESS** Exec Asst to the President, Bishop Col, 3837 Simpson Stuart Rd, Dallas, TX, 75241.

ROLLINS, WAYNE GILBERT
PERSONAL Born 08/24/1929, Detroit, MI, m, 1953, 3 children **DISCIPLINE** RELIGION **EDUCATION** Capital Univ, BA, 51; Yale Univ, BD, 54, MA, 56, PhD, 60. **CAREER** Instr relig, Princeton Univ, 58-59; asst prof Bibl hist, Wellesley Col, 59-66; from assoc prof to prof New Testament, Hartford Sem Found, 66-74; prof Relig Studies, dir Ecumenical Inst & coordr Grad Prog Relig Studies, Assumption Col, 74-, minister, United Church of Christ, 58-; Huber Found fel, 60-61; vis prof, Colgate Rochester Divinity Sch, 68, dept relig studies, Yale Univ, 68-69, Greater Hartford Community Col, 69, St Joseph Col, 71, Mt Holyoke Col, 72 & Col of the Holy Cross, 76-77; Am Asn Theol Schs fel, 70. **MEMBERSHIPS** Soc Bibl Lit; Am Acad Relig; AAUP; Soc New Testament Studies. **RESEARCH** Biblical theology; hermeneutics; psychology and Biblical studies. **SELECTED PUBLICATIONS** Auth, The Gospels, Portraits of Christ, Westminster, 64; God and the New Critics, Can Forum, 6/65; The New Testament and Apocalyptic, New Testament Studies, 7/71; De Pythiae Oraculis, In: Plutarch's Theological Writings and Early Christian Literature, Brill, 75; Slavery in the New Testament, In: Interpreter's Dictionary of the Bible Supplement, Abingdon, 76; Christological Tendenz in Colossians 1: 15-20: A Theologia Crucis, In: Christological Perspectives, 82; auth, Jung and the Bible, John Knox, 83; auth, Psychology, Hermeneutics, and the Bible, in, Jung and the Interpretation of the Bible, Continuum, 95; auth, The Bible and Psychology: New Directions in Biblical Scholarship, Pastoral Psychol, 97; auth, Habits of the Soul: The Bible and Its Interpretation in Psychological Perspective, Fortress, 99. **CONTACT ADDRESS** Assumption Col, 500 Salisbury St, Worcester, MA, 01609. **EMAIL** wrollins@worldnet.att.net

ROLNICK, PHILIP
PERSONAL Born 06/27/1949, Pittsburgh, PA, m, 1975, 2 children **DISCIPLINE** THEOLOGY **EDUCATION** Duke Univ, PhD, 89. **CAREER** Assoc prof, 89-, dept relig, dir, Ethics Across Cur, 95-, Greensboro Col. **MEMBERSHIPS** AAR; Soc of Christian Ethics; Michael Polany Soc **RESEARCH** Religious lang; science & religion; social ethics. **SELECTED PUBLICATIONS** Auth, Analogical Possibilities: How Words Refer to God, Atlanta Scholars Press, 93; ed, Explorations in Ethics: Readings form Across the Curriculum, Greensboro Col Press, 98. **CONTACT ADDRESS** Dept of Religion & Philosophy, Greensboro Col, 815 W Market St, Greensboro, NC, 27401-1875. **EMAIL** rolnickp@gborocollege.edu

ROLSTON, HOLMES, III
PERSONAL Born 11/19/1932, Staunton, VA, m, 1956, 2 children **DISCIPLINE** PHILOSOPHY **EDUCATION** Davidson Col, BS, 53; Union Theol Sem, BD, 56; Univ Pittsburgh, MA, 68; Univ Edinburgh, PhD, 58. **CAREER** From asst prof to assoc prof to prof philos, Colo State Univ, 68-; vis scholar, Ctr Study World Relig, Harvard Univ, 74-75. **HONORS AND AWARDS** Oliver P. Penock Distinguished Service Award, Colo State Univ, 83; Col Award for Excellence, 91; Univ Distinguished Prof, 92; Distinguished Russell Fel, Grad Theol Union, 91; Distinguished Lectr, Chinese Acad Soc Sci, 91; Gifford Lectr, Univ Edinburg, 97. **MEMBERSHIPS** AAAS; Am Acad Relig; Soc Bibl Lit; Am Philos Asn; Int Soc Environ Ethics; Phi Beta Kappa. **SELECTED PUBLICATIONS** Auth, Religious Inquiry: Participation and Detachment, 85; auth, Philosophy Gone Wild, 86; auth, Science and Religion: A Critical Survey, 87; auth, Environmental Ethics, 88; Conserving Natural Value, 94; ed, Biology, Ethics, and the Origins of Life, 94 ; auth, Genes, Genesis, and God, 99. **CONTACT ADDRESS** Philosophy Dept, Colorado State Univ, Fort Collins, CO, 80523. **EMAIL** rolston@lamar.colostate.edu

ROLWING, RICHARD J.
DISCIPLINE THEOLOGY **EDUCATION** Notre Dame Univ, BA, 55, BD, 62, MA, 64. **CAREER** Asst prof, Univ Dayton, Xavier Univ. **MEMBERSHIPS** AAR; CBA; ACPA; SCP; Mantain Soc; Rahner Soc. **RESEARCH** Political Philosophy. **SELECTED PUBLICATIONS** Auth, Israels Original Sin: A Catholic Confession, Intl Sch Publ, 94. **CONTACT ADDRESS** Dept of Theology, Xavier Univ, 7651 Burkey, Reynoldsburg, OH, 43068. **EMAIL** dicrolwing@aol.com

ROMAN, ERIC
PERSONAL Born 03/26/1926, Bekescsaba, Hungary, m, 1953, 2 children **DISCIPLINE** MODERN HISTORY, WESTERN PHILOSOPHY **EDUCATION** Hunter Col, BA, 58; NY Univ, MA, 59, PhD(Hist), 65. **CAREER** From instr to assoc prof, 65-77, prof Hist, Western Conn State Univ, 77-. **HONORS AND AWARDS** Americanism Medal, Nat Daughters Am Revolution, 70. **MEMBERSHIPS** AHA. **RESEARCH** Modern German history; immediate origins of World War II; diplomacy of interwar period. **SELECTED PUBLICATIONS** Auth, The Best Shall Die, Prentice-Hall, 61, Davies, London, 61 & Plaza & Janes, Madrid, 64; After the Trial, Citadel, 68 & Carl Scherz, Berne, 69; Munich and Hungary, Eastern Europ Quart, 74; Will, Hope and the Noumenon, J Philos, 2/75; A Year as a Lion, Stein & Day, 9/78; Hungary and the Victor Powers, New York, St Martin's Press, 96. **CONTACT ADDRESS** 181 White St, Danbury, CT, 06810-6826. **EMAIL** romane@wsu.ctstateu.edu

ROOKS, CHARLES SHELBY
PERSONAL Born 10/19/1924, Beaufort, NC, m **DISCIPLINE** THEOLOGY **EDUCATION** VA State Coll, AB 1949; Union Theol Sem, MDiv 1953; Coll of Wooster, DD 1968; Interdenominational Theol Ctr, DD 1979; VA Union Univ, DD 1980. **CAREER** Shanks Vill Protestant Church Orangeburg, pastor 1951-53; Lincoln Meml Temple United Church of Christ Washington, pastor 1953-60; Fund for Theol Educ Princeton, assoc dir 1960-67, exec dir 1967-74; Chicago Theol Sem, pres 1974-84; United Church Bd for Homeland Ministries, exec vice pres, 1984-92. **HONORS AND AWARDS** Distinguished Service Medal, Association of Theological Schools in the US and Canada, 1992; Numerous honorary degrees. **MEMBERSHIPS** Pres Commun Recruitment & Training Inc; bd of dir Office of Comm United Church of Christ; Pres, Soc for the Study of Black Religion, 1970-74, 1980-84. **SELECTED PUBLICATIONS** Author of Rainbows and Reality, Atlanta, The ITC Press 1984; The Hopeful Spirit, New York, Pilgrim Press 1987; Revolution in Zion; Reshaping African American Ministry, New York, Pilgrim Press, 1989. **CONTACT ADDRESS** United Church Board for Homeland Ministries, 700 Prospect, Cleveland, OH, 44115-1100.

ROOT, MICHAEL
DISCIPLINE SYSTEMATIC THEOLOGY **EDUCATION** Dartmouth Col, AB, 73; Yale Univ, MA, 74, MPhil, 76-77, PhD, 79. **CAREER** Instr, Davidson Col, 78-80; asst prof, Lutheran Theol S Sem, 80-84; assoc prof, Lutheran Theol S Sem, 84-88; res prof, Inst Ecumenical Res, Strasbourg, 88-98; dir, Inst Ecumenical Research, Strasbourg, 91-93, 95-98; prof, Trinity Lutheran Sem, 98-. **HONORS AND AWARDS** Consult, Lutheran-Cath Coord Comm; Anglican-Lutheran Intl Comm; ed coun, A Jour Theol. **MEMBERSHIPS** Faith and Order Commission Observer, Anglican-Roman Cath Intl Comm; ecumenical mem, Inter-Anglican Theol and Doctrinal Comm. **SELECTED PUBLICATIONS** Auth, Conditions of Communion: Bishops, the Concordat, and the Augsburg Confession, Inhabiting Unity: Theological Perspectives on the Proposed Lutheran-Episcopal Concordat, Eerdmans, 95; Full Communion between Episcopalians and Lutherans in the United States: What Would It Look Like?, Concordat of Agreement: Supporting Essays, Augsburg, Forward Movement, 95; The Immediate Ecumenical Task: A Response to William Rusch, 95; The Concordat and the Northern European Porvoo Common Statement: Different Paths to the Same Goal, A Commentary on Concordat of Agreement, Augsburg, Forward Movement, 94; The Ecumenical Identity of the Lutheran World Federation, Ecumenical Rev 46, 94; Ministry in the Lutheran-Methodist Dialogue, Lutheran Forum, 94; The Unity of the Church as a Moral Community: Some Comments on Costly Unity, Ecumenical Rev 46, 94. **CONTACT ADDRESS** Hist, Theol, Soc Dept, Trinity Lutheran Sem, 2199 E Main St, Columbus, OH, 43209-2334.

ROOT, MICHAEL
DISCIPLINE PHILOSOPHY **EDUCATION** Univ Ill Urbana Champaign, PhD. **RESEARCH** Philosophy of language; metaphysics; philosophy of social sciences. **SELECTED PUBLICATIONS** Auth, Philosophy of Social Science: The Methods, Ideals, and Politics of Social Inquiry, Blackwell, 93; Miracles and the Uniformity of Nature, Am Philos Quarterly, 89; Davidson and Social Science, Blackwell, 86; co-auth, Meaning and Interpretation, J Formal Logic, 82. **CONTACT ADDRESS** Philosophy Dept, Univ of Minnesota, Twin Cities, 355 Ford Hall, 224 Church St SE, Minneapolis, MN, 55455. **EMAIL** rootx001@maroon.tc.umn.edu

RORTY, AMELIE OKSENBERG
PERSONAL Antwerp, Belgium, 1 child **DISCIPLINE** PHILOSOPHY **EDUCATION** Univ Chicago, BA, Yale, MA, PhD. **CAREER** Rutgers Univ, instructor to Distinguished prof, Harvard Grad Sch, vis prof, Brandeis Univ, dir & prof. **HONORS AND AWARDS** Awards from Guggenheim, Woodrow Wilson Center, CASBS & IAS **MEMBERSHIPS** APA **RESEARCH** Aristotle; moral psychol; hist of polit theory; psychol anthro. **CONTACT ADDRESS** 54 Hammond St, Cambridge, MA, 02138. **EMAIL** rorty@binah.cc.brandeis.edu

RORTY, R.
PERSONAL Born 10/04/1931, New York, NY, m, 1972, 3 children **DISCIPLINE** PHILOSOPHY **EDUCATION** Univ of Chicago, BA, 49, MA, 52; Yale, PhD, 56. **CAREER** Instr/Asst Prof, 58-61, Wellesley Univ; Asst, Assoc, Prof, 61-82, Princeton Univ; Prof, 82-98, Univ of Virginia; Prof, 98-, Stanford Univ. **HONORS AND AWARDS** MacArthur Guggenheim; NEH; ACLS Fel; Amer Acad of Sciences. **MEMBERSHIPS** APA **RESEARCH** American Pragmatism **SELECTED PUBLICATIONS** Auth, Achieving Our Country, Harvard Univ Press, 98; auth, Truth and Progress, Campbridge Univ Press, 98. **CONTACT ADDRESS** Dept of Comparative Literature, Stanford, CA, 94305-2031. **EMAIL** rrorty@leland.stanford.edu

ROSE, KENNETH
DISCIPLINE PHILOSOPHY **EDUCATION** OH State Univ, BA; Harvard Univ, MDiv, MA, PhD. **CAREER** Philos, Christopher Newport Univ. **SELECTED PUBLICATIONS** Auth, Knowing the Real: John Hick on the Cognitivity of Relgions and Religious Pluralism, Peter Lang, 96. **CONTACT ADDRESS** Dept of Philos, Christopher Newport Univ, 1 University Place Newport News, Newport News, VA, 23606. **EMAIL** krose@cnu.edu

ROSELL, GARTH M.
PERSONAL m, 3 children **DISCIPLINE** CHURCH HISTORY **EDUCATION** Wheaton Col, BA; Princeton Theol Sem, MDiv, 64, ThM, 66; Univ Minn, PhD, 71. **CAREER** Instr, Bethel Theol Sem; acad dean, 78; prof, Gordon-Conwell Theol Sem -; dir, Ockenga Inst. **MEMBERSHIPS** Mem, Assn Theol Sch(s); Boston Theol Inst. **SELECTED PUBLICATIONS** Co-auth, The Memoirs of Charles G. Finney: The Complete Restored Text, Zondervan, 89; American Christianity, Eerdmans, 86; The Millionaire and The Scrublady and Other Parables by William E. Barton, Zondervan, 90; auth, Shoeleather Faith, Bruce, 62; Cases in Theological Education, ATS, 86. **CONTACT ADDRESS** Gordon-Conwell Theol Sem, 130 Essex St, South Hamilton, MA, 01982.

ROSEMANN, PHILIPP W.
PERSONAL Born 02/24/1964, Frankfurt am Main, Germany **DISCIPLINE** PHILOSOPHY **EDUCATION** Univ Hamburg,, Candidatus philos, 87; Queen's Univ, Belfast, MA, 89; Univ Catholique de Louvain, Licence en philos, 91, PhD, 95. **CAREER** Tchg fel, Queen's Univ, Belfast, 89-90; chercheur sur fonds FDS, 90-93, maitre de conferences invite, 95-96, Univ catholique de Louvain; lectr, Uganda Martyrs Univ, 96-97; asst prof, Univ Dallas, 97- . **HONORS AND AWARDS** Studienstiftung des deutschen Volkes grant, 83-87, 88-89, 93-95; Warburg scholar, Univ London, 87-88; Haggar Presidential Award, Univ Dallas, 98. **MEMBERSHIPS** Martin-Heidegger-Ges; Soc int pour l'etude de la philos; APA; Soc for the Promotion of Eriugenian Stud; Uganda Soc; Am Catholic Philos Asn; AAUP. **RESEARCH** Medieval philosophy; Thomas Aquinas; contemporary continental philosophy; African and African-American philosophy. **SELECTED PUBLICATIONS** Coauth, Alltagssprachliche Metakommunikation im Englischen und Deutschen, Peter Lang, 90; auth, Tabula, in Opera Roberti Grosseteste Lincolniensis, v 1, Brepols, 95; auth, Omne ens est Aliquid: Introduction a la Lecture du Systeme Philosophique de Saint Thomas d'Aquin, Peeters, 96; auth, Omne Agens Agit sibi Simile: A Repetition of Scholastic Metaphysics, Leuven, 96; co-ed, Business Ethics in the African Context Today, Uganda Martyrs, 96; co-ed, Editer, Traduire, Interpreter: Essais de Methodologie Philosophique, Peeters, 97. **CONTACT ADDRESS** Philosophy Department, Univ of Dallas, 1845 E Northgate Dr, Irving, TX, 75062-4736. **EMAIL** rosemann@acad.udallas.edu

ROSEMONT, HENRY
PERSONAL Born 12/20/1934, Chicago, IL, m, 1961, 5 children **DISCIPLINE** PHILOSOPHY **EDUCATION** Univ IL, AB, honors, 62; Univ Washington, PhD, 67. **CAREER** Oakland Univ, Instr, Asst Prof, philos, 65-69; MIT, post doctoral fellow in Linguistics, 69-72; Brooklyn Col, CUNY, Asst and Assoc Prof, 72 77; St Mary's Col, MD, Prof philos and rel studies, 77-, George B and Wilma Reeves Dist Prof Liberal Arts, 97-. **HONORS AND AWARDS** Post doctoral Fellowships from ACLS, NGH, NSF, Fulbright; Homer Dodge Excellence in Teaching Award, St Mary's Col MD, 91. **MEMBERSHIPS** Soc for Asian and Comparative Philos; Asn Asian Studies; Am Acad Religion. **RESEARCH** Classical Chinese philos, comparative philos, moral and political philos. **SELECTED PUBLICATIONS** A Chinese Mirror, Open Ct pub, 91; Chinese Texts and Philosophical Contexts, Open Ct Pub, 91; Leibniz: Writings on China, with Daniel J Cook, Open Ct Pub, 94; The Analects of Confucius, with Roger T Ames, Random House-Ballantine, 98; A Confucian Alternative, Univ Hawaii Press, 99. **CONTACT ADDRESS** Dept Philosophy & Religious Studies, St Mary's Col of MD, St Mary's City, MD, 20686.

ROSENBERG, ALEXANDER
PERSONAL Born 08/31/1946, Austria **DISCIPLINE** PHILOSOPHY OF SCIENCE **EDUCATION** CCNY, BA, 67; Johns Hopkins Univ, PhD, 71. **CAREER** Vis asst prof, Univ Minn, 75; assoc prof, Syracuse Univ, 76-81; vis assoc prof, Univ Calif, Santa Cruz, 78-79; prof, Syracuse Univ, 81-86; prof, Univ Calif, Riverside, 86-95; vis lectr, Oxford Univ, 94-95; prof, Univ Ga, 95- . **HONORS AND AWARDS** Phi Beta Kappa, 67; Am Coun of Learned Soc Study-Fel, 81-82; Guggenheim Found Fel, 82-83; Nat Sci Found Sr Scholar Award, 87; Lakatos Prize for Phil in Sci, 93. **MEMBERSHIPS** Am Phil Asoc; Phil of Sci Asoc. **RESEARCH** Philosophy of biology; philosophy of science. **SELECTED PUBLICATIONS** Co-auth with T.L. Beauchamp, Hume and the Problem of Causation, 81; ath, The Structure of Biological Science, 85; auth, Philosophy of Social Science; 88; auth, Economics: Mathematical Politics or Science of Diminishing Returns?, 92; auth, Instrumental Biolgoy or the Disunity of Science, 94. **CONTACT ADDRESS** Honors Program, Univ of Georgia, Athens, GA, 30602-6116. **EMAIL** alexrose@arches.ga.edu

ROSENBLUM, VICTOR GREGORY
PERSONAL Born 06/02/1925, New York, NY, m, 1946, 8 children **DISCIPLINE** LAW, POLITICAL SCIENCE **EDUCATION** Columbia Univ, AB, 45, LLB, 48; Univ Calif, Berkeley, PhD(polit sci), 53. **CAREER** Asst prof polit sci, Univ Calif, Berkeley, 53-57; assoc count, US House Rep, 56-58; from assoc prof to prof law & polit sci, Northwestern Univ, 58-68; pres, Reed Col, 68-70; prof law & polit sci, Northwestern Univ, Chicago, 70-, sr legal consult, Brookings Inst, 65-69; Fulbright prof, Sch Law, Cath Univ Louvain, 66-67 & 78; consult, Admin Conf of US, 71-; mem bd dirs, Ctr Admin Justice, 72-80; consult, Nat Inst Law Enforcement & Criminal Justice, 73-; chmn, Admin Law Sect, Am Bar Asn, 77-78. **HONORS AND AWARDS** DHL, Hebrew Union Col, 70; LittD, Siena Heights Col, 82. **MEMBERSHIPS** Am Bar Asn; Am Polit Sci Asn; Law & Soc Asn (pres, 70-72). **RESEARCH** Interactions of legal and political factors in the development of public policy and the formulation of public law. **SELECTED PUBLICATIONS** Auth, Judicial reform & Courts and judges: Power and politics, In: The Fifty States and Their Local Governments, Knopf, 67; Legal dimensions of tenure, In: Faculty Tenure, Jossey-Bass, 73; coauth, Constitutional Law: Political Roles of the Supreme Court, Dorsey, 73; auth, Handling citizen initiated complaints: An introductory study of federal agency procedures, practices, Admin Law Rev, winter 74; Schoolchildren: Yes, Policemen: No--some thoughts about the Supreme Court's priorities concerning the right to a hearing in suspension & removal cases, Northwestern Law Rev, 77; coauth, The Making of a Public Profession, Am Bar Found, 81; auth, Administrative Law and the Regulatory Process, In: Contemporary Public Administration, Harcourt Brace, 81. **CONTACT ADDRESS** Sch of Law, Northwestern Univ, 357 E Chicago Ave, Chicago, IL, 60611-3069.

ROSENFELD, MICHEL
DISCIPLINE CONSTITUTIONAL LAW **EDUCATION** Columbia Univ, BA, 69; MA, 71; MPhil, 78; PhD, 91; Northwestern Univ, JD, 74. **CAREER** Prof, Yeshiva Univ, 82-. **HONORS AND AWARDS** Asso, Skadden, Arps, Slate, Meagher & Flom, 77-80; Asso, Rosenman, Colin, Freund, Lewis & Cohen, 80-82. **RESEARCH** Comparative constitutionalism, jurisprudence, and the philosophy of human rights. **SELECTED PUBLICATIONS** Auth, Affirmative Action and Justice: A Philosophical and Constitutional Inquiry, Yale Univ Press, 91; Co-ed, Hegel and Legal Theory, Routledge Press, 91; Deconstruction and the Possibility of Justice, Routledge Press, 92; ed, Constitutionalism, Identity, Difference and Legitimacy: Theoretical Perspectives , Duke Univ Press, 94. **CONTACT ADDRESS** Yeshiva Univ, 55 Fifth Ave, NY, NY, 10003-4301.

ROSENKRANTZ, GARY SOL
PERSONAL Born 07/12/1951, New York, NY **DISCIPLINE** PHILOSOPHY **EDUCATION** City Col New York, BA, 72; Brown Univ, PhD(philos), 76. **CAREER** From Asst Prof to Assoc Prof, 76-94, Prof Philos, Univ NC, Greensboro, 94-. **HONORS AND AWARDS** Bd of Editors Philos and Phenomenol Res, 97-02. **MEMBERSHIPS** Am Philos Asn. **RESEARCH** Epistemology; metaphysics; philosophy of religion. **SELECTED PUBLICATIONS** Auth, Haecceity: An Ontological Essay, Kluwer Acad Publ, 93; Substance Among Other Categories, Cambridge Univ Press, 94; Substance: Its Nature and Existence, Routledge, 97; Exploring the Divine Attributes, Basil Blackwell (under contract); author of numerous journal articles. **CONTACT ADDRESS** Dept of Philosophy, Univ of No Carolina, PO Box 26170, Greensboro, NC, 27402-6170. **EMAIL** rosenkra@iris.uncg.edu

ROSENSTEIN, LEON
PERSONAL Born 07/04/1943, Newark, NJ, m, 1972 **DISCIPLINE** PHILOSOPHY **EDUCATION** Columbia Univ, BA, 65, PhD(philos), 72. **CAREER** Prof philos, San Diego State Unin, 69, chm Europ Studies prof, 78, chm Humanities Prog, 80-, Fulbright fel philos, US Govt, Univ Paris, 68-69. **MEMBERSHIPS** Am Philos Asn; Am Soc Aesthet; Int Asn Philos & Lit; Int Soc Comp Study Civilizations. **RESEARCH** Existentialism; aesthetics; European intellectual and artistic culture. **SELECTED PUBLICATIONS** Auth, Metaphysical foundations of Hegel and Nietzsche's theories of tragedy, J Aesthet & Art Criticism, summer 70; Some metaphysical problems of Cassirer's symbolic forms, Man & World, 9/73; The ontological integrity of the art object from the Ludic viewpoint, J Aesthet & Art Criticism, spring 76; On Aristotle and thought in the drama, Critical Inquiry, spring 77; Mysticism as pre-ontology: A note on the Heideggerian connection, Philos & Phenomenol Res, 9/78; Re-thinking Aristotle's thought, Critical Inquiry, spring 78; Heidegger and Plato and the good, Philos Today, fall 78; Hegelian sources of Freud's social and political philosophy (3 article ser), Kronos, fall 78-spring 79; The Last Word on Catharsis, Annales d'Esthetique, vol 23-24, 85; The Aesthetic of the Antique, J Aesthet and Art Criticism, summer 97. **CONTACT ADDRESS** Dept of Philos, San Diego State Univ, 5500 Campanile Dr, San Diego, CA, 92182-8142.

ROSENTHAL, DAVID M.
PERSONAL Born 04/10/1939, New York, NY, 1 child **DISCIPLINE** PHILOSOPHY **EDUCATION** Univ Chicago, AB, 61; Princeton Univ, MA, 64, PhD, 68. **CAREER** Asst prof, Rutgers Univ, 67-71; asst prof, City Univ NY, 71-. **HONORS AND AWARDS** McDonnell-Pew Vis Fel, 96. **MEMBERSHIPS** Am Philos Asn; Soc for Philos and Psych; Asn for the Sci Study of Consciousness. **RESEARCH** Philosophy of the mind; Cognitive science; Philosophy of language; Ancient philosophy; Continental rationalism. **SELECTED PUBLICATIONS** Auth, Consciousness and Mind; "Consciousness and its Expression," in Midwest Studies in Philos, 98; "Consciousness and Metacognition," 98; "The Colors and Shapes of Visual Experiences," 98; "Perceptual and Cognitive Models of Consciousness," in J of the Am Psychoanalytic Asn, 97; "Apperception, Sensation, and Dissociability," in Mind and Language, 97; "A Theory of Consciousness," 97; "Multiple Drafts and Facts of the Matter," 95; "Moore's Pradox and Consciousness," in Philos Persepctives, 95; "First-Person Operationalism and Mental Taxonomy," in Philos Topics, 95. **CONTACT ADDRESS** 425 Riverside Dr, Apt 12F, New York, NY, 10025. **EMAIL** drosenth@broadway.gc.cuny.edu

ROSENTHAL, MICHAEL A.
PERSONAL Born 06/10/1962, Anaheim, CA, m, 1996, 2 children **DISCIPLINE** PHILOSOPHY **EDUCATION** Stanford Univ, AB, 86; Univ Chicago, AM, 88, PhD, 96. **CAREER** Lectr, Univ Delaware, 94-95, from instr to asst prof, 95-, Grinnell Col. **HONORS AND AWARDS** Mellon Fel, 87-91. **MEMBERSHIPS** Am Philos Asn; N Am Spinoza Soc; Iowa Philos Soc. **RESEARCH** Spinoza; early modern philosophy; ethics and political philosophy. **CONTACT ADDRESS** Dept of Philosophy, Grinnell Col, Box 805, Grinnell, IA, 50112. **EMAIL** rosentha@ac.grin.edu

ROSENTHAL, PETER
DISCIPLINE LAW **EDUCATION** Univ Ca, BS, 62; Univ Mich, MA, 63, PhD, 67; Univ Toronto, LLB, 90. **CAREER** Law, Univ Toronto **SELECTED PUBLICATIONS** Auth, pubs on criminal law. **CONTACT ADDRESS** Fac of Law, Univ Toronto, 78 Queen's Park, Toronto, ON.

ROSIN, ROBERT L.
PERSONAL Born 02/12/1951, Lexington, MO, m, 1975 **DISCIPLINE** HISTORICAL THEOLOGY **EDUCATION** Concordia Tchrs Col, BA, 72; Concordia Sem, MDiv, 76; Stanford Univ, MA, 77, PhD, 86. **CAREER** From instr to assoc prof, 81-97, prof hist theol, 97- , chemn dept, 95- , Concordia Sem; guest instr, Martin Luther Sem, Papua New Guines, 83; actg dir lib services, 88-90, fac marshal, 89-97, ed, Concordia Sem Publ, 95- ; Exec dir Center for Reformation Res, 97- . **MEMBERSHIPS** Soc for Reformation Res; Sixteenth-Century Stud Conf; Renaissance Soc of Am; Luther-Gesellschaft; Am Soc of Church Hist; Lutheran Hist Conf; Am Friends of the Herzog August Biliothek. **RESEARCH** Reformation and education/curriculum in the sixteenth century. **SELECTED PUBLICATIONS** Auth, Christians and Culture: Finding Place in Clio's Mansions, in, Christ and Culture: The Church in Post-Christian(?) America, Concordia Sem, 96; auth, Bringing Forth Fruit: Luther on Social Welfare, in Rosin, ed, A Cup of Cold Water: A Look at Biblical Charity, Concordia Sem, 97; auth, Reformers, The Preacher, and Skepticism: Luther, Brenz, Melanchthon, and Ecclesiastes, Verlag Philipp von Zabern, 97. **CONTACT ADDRESS** Concordia Sem, 801 DeMun Ave, St. Louis, MO, 63105. **EMAIL** rosinr@csl.edu

ROSNER, JENNIFER
PERSONAL Born 04/08/1966, New York, NY, m, 1984 **DISCIPLINE** PHILOSOPHY **EDUCATION** Stanford Univ, PhD, 98. **HONORS AND AWARDS** Dept Fel Stanford Univ, 92-96; Mellon Dissertation Fel, Stanford Univ, 96-97. **MEMBERSHIPS** APA. **RESEARCH** Ethics; Moral Philosophy; Epistemology. **SELECTED PUBLICATIONS** Auth, Quine's Global Structuralism, Dialectica, 96; Reflective Endorsement and the Self: A Response to Arpaly and Schroeder, Philos Studies, forthcoming. **CONTACT ADDRESS** Dept of Philosophy, Stanford Univ, Stanford, CA, 94305-2155. **EMAIL** rosner@csli.stanfrod.edu

ROSS, CHRISTOPHER F.J.
PERSONAL Born 06/17/1946, London, England, s, 1 child **DISCIPLINE** PSYCHOLOGY OF RELIGION **EDUCATION** Univ Durham, BA, 67; Univ Edinburgh, MSc, 69; Univ Calany, PhD, 73. **CAREER** Assoc Prof **HONORS AND**

AWARDS Citation in Outstanding Young Men of Amer, 77. **MEMBERSHIPS** Clinical Psychologist, 69-71; clinical supervisor, 80-82, **RESEARCH** Jung's Personality Typology; Religious Orientations **SELECTED PUBLICATIONS** Auth, The Intuitive Function and Religious Orientation, Journal of Analytical Psychology, 92; auth, Orientation to Religion and the Feeling Function in Jung's Personality Typology, Studies in Religion, 92; auth, Type Patterns Among Members of the Anglican Church: Comparisions with Catholics, Evangelicals and Clergy, Journal of Psychological Type, 93; auth, Type Patterns among Catholics: A Study of Four Anglophone Congregations with Comparisons to Protestants, Francophone Catholics and Priests, Journal of Psychological Type, 95; co auth, Relationship of Jungian Psychological Type to Religious Orientation and Spiritual Practices, International Journal for the Psychology of Religion, 97; auth, Experiencing Mother Meera, Canadian Woman Studies, 97; coauth, The Perceiving Function and Christian Spirituality: Distinguishing between Sensing and Intuition, Pastoral Sciences, forthcoming. **CONTACT ADDRESS** Dept of Relig and Culture, Wilfrid Laurier Univ, Waterloo, ON, N2L 3C5. **EMAIL** cross@mac1.wlu.ca

ROSS, JAMES F.
DISCIPLINE OLD TESTAMENT **EDUCATION** Doane Col, BA, 49; Union Theol Sem, BD, 52, ThD, 55; Amer Sch Oriental Res, Jerusalem, Jordan, 53-54. **CAREER** Instr, Dartmouth Col, 55-57; asst prof, Dartmouth Col, 57-59; asst prof, Drew Univ, 59-63; assoc prof, Drew Univ, 63-68; vis prof, Princeton Univ, 62-63; vis prof, Swarthmore Col, 64; prof, Va Theol Sem, 68-96; emeri, 96-. **SELECTED PUBLICATIONS** Auth, Reports on excavations in Field VI, Tell el-Hesi, 83; The Vounous Jars Revisited, BASOR 296, 94. **CONTACT ADDRESS** Va Theol Sem, 3737 Seminary Rd, Alexandria, VA, 22304. **EMAIL** JRoss@vts.edu

ROSS, JAMIE
PERSONAL Born 05/10/1955, New York, NY, m, 1992, 1 child **DISCIPLINE** PHILOSOPHY **EDUCATION** Univ Ore, PhD, 95. **CAREER** Instr, Lewis and Clark Coll; asst prof, Portland State Univ. **MEMBERSHIPS** Am Philos Asn; Soc for Advancement Am Philos; Soc for Women in Philos. **RESEARCH** American Pragmatism; Feminist Theory. **CONTACT ADDRESS** 1712 SW Highland Pkwy, Portland, OR, 97221-2634. **EMAIL** d8jr@odin.cc.pdx.edu

ROSS, JEROME C.
PERSONAL Born 09/24/1953, Richmond, VA, m, 1977 **DISCIPLINE** RELIGIOUS STUDIES **EDUCATION** Randolph-Macon College, BA, 75; VA Union Univ, MDiv, 78; Univ Pitt, PhD, 97. **CAREER** Instr, Asst Prof, 82 to 84-, VA Union Univ; Pastor 83-93, Mt Olive Bap Church VA; Providence Pk Baptist Church VA, 93-. **HONORS AND AWARDS** Most Outstanding Stud of the New Testament; Asbury Christian Awd; Amer Bible Soc Awd. **MEMBERSHIPS** SBL **RESEARCH** Hebrew Law; Pentateuch; Worship; History. **SELECTED PUBLICATIONS** Coauth, Proclamation 6, Series B: Lent, Minneapolis, Fortress Press, 96; rev, Stony the Road We Trod, Interpretation, 93. **CONTACT ADDRESS** 8211 Chipplegate Dr, Richmond, VA, 23227.

ROSS, PARTICIA A.
PERSONAL Born 03/18/1961, Washington, PA, m, 1992 **DISCIPLINE** PHILOSOPHY **EDUCATION** Univ Ill, MA, 87; Univ Md, PhD, 96. **CAREER** Fel, Cent Philos Sci, Univ Minn, 96-98; vis asst prof, Univ Minn, 98-99. **MEMBERSHIPS** Philos Sci Asn; Am Philos Asn; Asn Advan Psychol Psychiat; Int Soc Theoret Psychol. **RESEARCH** Philosophy of science. **SELECTED PUBLICATIONS** Auth, The Limits of Physicalism, Philos Sci, 98; Values and Objectivity in Psychiatric Nosology, 98. **CONTACT ADDRESS** Dept of Philosophy, Univ of Minnesota, 4232 17th Ave S, Minneapolis, MN, 55407. **EMAIL** rossx035@tc.umn.edu

ROSS, PETER W.
PERSONAL Born 05/27/1963, Canton, OH, m, 1995 **DISCIPLINE** PHILOSOPHY **EDUCATION** Oberlin Col, BA, 85; Graduate Sch of CUNY, PhD, 97. **CAREER** Lectr, Calif State Polytech Univ, Pomona, 97-98. **MEMBERSHIPS** APA; Soc for Philos and Psych; Southern Soc for Philos and Psychol. **RESEARCH** Color; color perception; consciousness. **SELECTED PUBLICATIONS** Auth, Trichromacy and the Neural Basis of Color Discrimination: Commentary on B.A.C. Saunders and J. Van Brakel, Are There Nontrivial Constraints on Colour Categorization? Behav and Brain Sci, 97. **CONTACT ADDRESS** Dept of Philosophy, California State Polytech Univ, 3801 West Temple Ave, Pomona, CA, 91768-4051. **EMAIL** pross@pomona.edu

ROSS, RALPH M.
PERSONAL Born 12/23/1936, Miami, Florida, m **DISCIPLINE** THEOLOGY **EDUCATION** AB 1961; BD 1965; MDiv 1970; DMin, 1988. **CAREER** Beth Salem United Presb Ch Columbus, GA, minister 1965-66; Eastern Airlines Atlanta, ramp agt 1965-66; Mt Zion Baptist Church Miami, asso minister 1966-68; Urban League Miami, field rep 1967-68; Knoxville Coll, campus minister 1968-70; UT Knoxville, lecturer/religious dept 1969-; Knoxville Coll, dean of students; NC A&T State U, dir religious activities 1978-86, asst dean student devel 1986-90; Mount Zion Baptist Church, Miami, FL, pastor/teacher, 1990-. **HONORS AND AWARDS** YMCA Best Blocker Award Knoxville Coll 1959; Rockefeller Fellowship Award 1964; Theta Phi Hon Soc 1965. **MEMBERSHIPS** Mem bd dir Ministries to Blacks in Higher Edn Knoxville; Knoxville Interdenominational Christian Ministeral Alliance; life mem Alpha Phi Alpha; NAACP; Baptist Ministers Council & Faith In The City; ROA. **CONTACT ADDRESS** Pastor/Teacher, Mt Zion Baptist Church, 301 NE 9th St, Miami, FL, 33136.

ROSS, ROSETTA
DISCIPLINE RELIGION/CHRISTIAN SOCIAL ETHICS **EDUCATION** Emory Univ, PhD, 95 **CAREER** Asst prof of ethics and public policy interdenominational theological ctr Atlanta GA **MEMBERSHIPS** Amer Acad of Religion; Soc of Christian ethics; Soc for the Study of Black Religion **RESEARCH** Womanist/feminist theology & ethics; social theory; ethics & public policy **CONTACT ADDRESS** 426 Avery Glen, Decatur, GA, 30030. **EMAIL** rross@itc.edu

ROSS, STEPHANIE A.
DISCIPLINE AESTHETICS, FEMINISM **EDUCATION** Smith Col, BA, 71; Harvard Univ, MA, 74, PhD, 77. **CAREER** Assoc prof, Univ Mo, St Louis. **HONORS AND AWARDS** UMSL summer res fel, 78; NEH summer sem, 80; Weldon Spg grant, Univ Mo, St Louis, 81; UMSL summer res fel, 84; trustee, Am Soc for Aesthet, 86-89; Huntington Libr NEH fel, 89; fel, Yale Ctr for Brit Art, 90; Univ Mo Res Bd grant, 94; NEH summer inst, 95. **MEMBERSHIPS** Am Philos Asn; Am Soc for Aesthet; Soc for Women in Philos. **RESEARCH** Misguided marriage. **SELECTED PUBLICATIONS** Auth, Conducting and Musical Interpretation, Brit J of Aesthet, Vol 36, No 1, 96. **CONTACT ADDRESS** Univ Mo, St Louis, St Louis, MO, 63121.

ROSS, STEPHEN F.
DISCIPLINE LAW **EDUCATION** Univ Calif Berkeley, BA; JD. **CAREER** Law clerk, Judge Ruth Bader Ginsburg, US Court Appeals; prof, Univ Ill Urbana Champaign. **HONORS AND AWARDS** Ed, Calif Law Rev. **RESEARCH** Antitrust; sports law; statutory interpretation; Canadian law; and welfare law. **SELECTED PUBLICATIONS** Auth, Principles of Antitrust Law, Foundation, 93; pubs on general antitrust and competition policy in the USA and Canada, sports antitrust issues, and statutory interpretation. **CONTACT ADDRESS** Law Dept, Univ Ill Urbana Champaign, 52 E Gregory Dr, Champaign, IL, 61820. **EMAIL** sross@law.uiuc.edu

ROSS BRYANT, LYNN
DISCIPLINE RELIGIOUS STUDIES **EDUCATION** Univ Chicago, PhD. **CAREER** Assoc prof. **RESEARCH** Autobiography and religion; women and religion. **SELECTED PUBLICATIONS** Auth, Imagination and the Life of the Spirit; The Land in American Religious Experience. **CONTACT ADDRESS** Religious Studies Dept, Univ of Colorado, Boulder, Boulder, CO, 80309. **EMAIL** Lynn.Ross-Bryant@Colorado.edu

ROSSI, CHRISTOPHER
DISCIPLINE INTERNATIONAL LAW AND ORGANIZATION **EDUCATION** Wash Univ, BA, Univ Iowa, JD; Univ London, LLM; John Hopkins Univ, MA,PhD. **CAREER** Prof, Am Univ. **MEMBERSHIPS** Asso Dir, World Jurist Asn. **RESEARCH** International law and organization, human rights, international courts and tribunals. **SELECTED PUBLICATIONS** Auth, Equity and International Law: A Legal Realist Approach to International Decisionmaking,Transnational Publs, 93; coauth, Arms Control Treaties, Review and Revision, Bull Int Atomic Energy Agency. **CONTACT ADDRESS** American Univ, 4400 Massachusetts Ave, Washington, DC, 20016.

ROSTHAL, ROBERT
PERSONAL Born 10/16/1923, New York, NY, m, 1952, 1 child **DISCIPLINE** PHILOSOPHY **EDUCATION** Univ Wis Madison, BA 44; Univ Chicago, MA 54; Univ Mich, PhD 59. **CAREER** NY Univ, inst 53; Brooklyn Col, instr 54; Univ Mich, fel, instr 55-59; Ohio State Univ, vis lectr 59; Kenyon Col, asst prof 60; Univ N Carolina, asst prof, assoc prof, prof, 61-93. Retired 1993. **HONORS AND AWARDS** Hd of Philos Dept; Ford Foun Gnt; Pres NC Assoc Scholars 93-. **MEMBERSHIPS** APA; PPS; SA. **RESEARCH** Contemporary Philosophy; Aesthetics; Philosophy of mind; Value theory; Ethics. **SELECTED PUBLICATIONS** Auth, Philosophy in France Since 1945, World Philosophy: Contemporary Developments Since 1945, ed John Burr, Greenwood 80; auth, Gabriel Marcel, Creative Fidelity, translation and intro, Farrar Straus, 63; auth, Moral Weakness and Remorse, MIND, 67. **CONTACT ADDRESS** 4403 Graham Rd, Greensboro, NC, 27410. **EMAIL** rrosthal@aol.com

ROTAN, CONSTANCE S.
PERSONAL Born 04/19/1935, Baton Rouge, Louisiana, m **DISCIPLINE** LAW **EDUCATION** Southern Univ,BA (Cum Laude) 1956; Howard Univ Grad School, 36 hrs toward MA 1968; Howard Univ School of Law, JD (Hon Grad) 1967. **CAREER** US Dept of Justice, gen trial atty 1968-70; United Planning Org, asst gen counsel 1970-72; Howard Univ School of Law, asst dean, asst prof 1972-75; Howard Univ, exec asst to the vice pres for admin 1975-87, university secretary, board of trustees secretary, 1987-92, vice pres for administration, 1989-92. **HONORS AND AWARDS** Public Mem of USIA Selection Bd 1986. **MEMBERSHIPS** Mem Natl Bar Assoc 1970-, Kappa Beta Pi Intl Legal Sor 1965-, Alpha Kappa Alpha 1977-, Assoc of Amer Law Schools, Natl Assoc of Coll & Univ Attnys, US Dist Ct for DC, US Ct of Appeals for DC; dean Howard Univ Chap Kappa Beta Pi Intl Legal Sor 1963-64; co-chmn Comm on Age of Majority of DC; mem DC Bar, Phi Sigma Alpha; founding mem, officer Waring/Mitchell Law Soc; mem Public Mem Assoc of Foreign Svc.

ROTH, JEAN
PERSONAL Born 08/08/1939, Kunming, China, m, 1963, 2 children **DISCIPLINE** RELIGIOUS STUDIES **EDUCATION** Radcliffe Col, BA, 61; Union Theol Sem, MRE; Stanford Univ, PhD, 97. **CAREER** Tchg asst, 83, 85, lectr, 97-98, Stanford Univ. **HONORS AND AWARDS** Shared first prize for student papers at Am Acad of Relig W Regional Conf, 89. **MEMBERSHIPS** Am Acad Relig. **RESEARCH** Modern Western philosophy of religion, particularly the problems in the relationship between reason and faith in the Victorian period. **CONTACT ADDRESS** 12113 Foothill Ln, Los Altos Hills, CA, 94022.

ROTH, JEFFREY I.
DISCIPLINE LAW **EDUCATION** Yeshiva Univ, BA, 68; Columbia Univ, MA, 69; Yale Univ, JD, 74. **CAREER** Fac fel, Columbia Univ, 68-69; Fulbright prof, Hungary, 91; assoc prof, NY Law Schl; assoc prof, Touro Col. **HONORS AND AWARDS** Nat Sci Found grad fel. **SELECTED PUBLICATIONS** Auth, The Justification for Controversy in Jewish Law, CA Law Rev, 88; Successor Trustees of Tentative Trusts: Trust Law Phantoms, St Louis Law J, 93. **CONTACT ADDRESS** Touro Col, Brooklyn, NY, 11230.

ROTH, JOEL
PERSONAL Detroit, MI, m, 3 children **DISCIPLINE** TALMUDIC STUDIES **EDUCATION** Wayne State Univ, BA; Jewish Theol Sem Am, MA, 68; PhD, 73. **CAREER** Dean stud List Col; dir, Melton Res Ctr Jewish Educ; assoc dean and dean, Rabbinical Schl; prof 96-.. **HONORS AND AWARDS** Chmn, Comm Jewish Law and Stds Rabbinical Assembly, 78-85. **SELECTED PUBLICATIONS** Auth, The Halakhic Process: A Systemic Analysis; Sefer ha-Mordecai: Tractate Kiddushin; articles and responsa, Law Comm Jewish Law and Stud. **CONTACT ADDRESS** Jewish Theol Sem of America, 3080 Broadway, New York, NY, 10027. **EMAIL** joroth@jtsa.edu

ROTH, PAUL A.
PERSONAL Born 11/18/1948, New York, NY, m, 1989, 1 child **DISCIPLINE** PHILOSOPHY **EDUCATION** Wesleyan Univ BA, 70, Univ Chicago MA, 72, Univ Chicago PhD, 78. **CAREER** Washington Univ, St Louis MO, vis assoc prof, 86, Univ MO, vis asst prof to prof Philo, 78-; UM-St Louis, Dir Philo 92-94, UM St Louis, chemn Philo 95-. **MEMBERSHIPS** APA, PSA, CSPA, CAPA **RESEARCH** Epistemology;Theol explanation **SELECTED PUBLICATIONS** Auth, Meaning and Method in the Social Sciences: A Case for Methodological Pluralism, 87 /pb 89; The Cure of Stories: Self-Deception, Danger Situations, and the Clinical Role of Negatives in Roy Schafer's Psychoanalytic Theory, Psycho Ver of the Human Condition 98, Dubious Liaisons: Review essay of Alvin Goldman's Liaisons: Philosophy Meets the Cognitive and Social Sciences Philo Psychology 96; Microfoundations Without Foundations: Comments on D. Little's Causation in the Social Sciences The S Jour of Philo 95; Will the Real Scientists Please Stand Up? Dead Ends and Live Issues in the Explanation of Scientific Knowledge, Studies in Hist and Philo of Science, Chaos, Clio and Scientific Illusions of Understanding, Hist & Theory 95; Can Post-Newtonian Psychologists Find Happiness in a Pre-Paradigm Science?, Jour of Mind and Behavior 95; Testing Normative Naturalism: The Problem of Scientific Medicine, Brit Jour for the Philo of Science 94. **CONTACT ADDRESS** Dept of Philosophy, Univ of Missouri, 7471 Cromwell Dr, St Louis, MO, 63105. **EMAIL** roth@umsl.edu

ROTH, ROBERT J.
PERSONAL Born 11/28/1920, NJ **DISCIPLINE** PHILOSOPHY **EDUCATION** Boston Col, BA, 44; Fordham Univ, MA, 48, PhD, 61. **CAREER** From instr to assoc prof, 53-70, vice chmn dept, 60-64, chmn, 70-73, pres, fac senate, 72-74, dean, 74-79, Fordham Col; prof philos, 70-91, prof emeritus, 91-, Fordham Univ; res fel, Yale Univ, 68-69. **MEMBERSHIPS** Jesuit Philos Assn US & Can; Am Cath Philos Assn; Am Philos Assn. **RESEARCH** Philosophy of person; American pragmatism; British empiricism. **SELECTED PUBLICATIONS** Art, Locke on Ideas and the Intuition of the Self, Int Philos Quart, 90; auth, David Hume on Religion in England, Thought, 91;

auth, British Empiricism and American Pragmatism, Fordham Univ, 93; auth, Radical Pragmatism: An Alternative, Fordham Univ, 99. **CONTACT ADDRESS** Dept of Philosophy, Fordham Univ, Bronx, NY, 10458.

ROTHAUGE, ARLIN J.
DISCIPLINE RELIGION **EDUCATION** Univ Oregon, BA; Phillips Univ, BD; Univ Scotland, Glasgow, PhD; Berkeley Divinity Sch, DD. **CAREER** Prof, exec dir, Seabury-Western Theol Sem, 95-. **HONORS AND AWARDS** Nat coord, Congregational Develop on the Presiding Bishop's staff. **SELECTED PUBLICATIONS** Auth, Sizing Up a Congregation for New Member Ministry; A Church is Born: Basics for Developing a New Mission Congregation; Reshaping a Congregation for a New Future; An Overview of New Church Development; A Diocesan Strategy for New Church Development. **CONTACT ADDRESS** Seabury-Western Theol Sem, 2122 Sheridan Rd, Evanston, IL, 60201.

ROTHBART, DANIEL
PERSONAL Born 09/05/1950, Newark, NJ, m, 1973, 2 children **DISCIPLINE** PHILOSOPHY **EDUCATION** Farleigh Dickinson Univ, BA, 72; State Univ NY-Binghamton, MA, 75; Wash Univ, PhD, 79. **CAREER** Post-doctoral lectr, phil, Wash Univ, 78-79; vis asst prof to ASSOC PROF, PHIL, GEORGE MASON UNIV, 79-; vis research scholar, dept hist and phil of sci, Univ Cambridge, 90; vis research scholar, dept phil, Darmouth Col, 94. **HONORS AND AWARDS** Intensive Bioethics Course, Kennedy Inst of Ethics, 82; NEH Summer Seminiar: Agreement and Disagreement in Science, 85; Travel Grant, Am Counc of Learned Scholars, 88; Grant-in-Aid, Am Council of Learned Scholars, Univ of Cambridge, 90; Templeton Foundation Award, 97., Exec Comm, Int Soc Phil of Chem, 94-; editorial board, Foundations of Chemistry and Philosophical and Historical Studies in Chemistry, 97-; scientific board, Hyle: An International Journal in the Philosophy of Chemistry, 97-. **SELECTED PUBLICATIONS** Auth, Explaining the Growth of Scientific Knowledge: Metaphors, Models and Meanings, Edwin Mellen Press, 97; ed, Science, Reason and Reality: Issues in the Philosophy of Science, Harcourt/Brace, 97; ed, Inquiry: Critical Thinking Across the Disciplines, Summer 96; auth, "Spectometers as Analogues of Nature," in PSA: 1994, Vol One, Phil of Sci Asn, 94; auth, "The Design of Nature through Chemical Instrumentation," in Chemistry and Philosophy, Koenigshausen und Neumann, 97; auth, "Flew on Popper and Popper on Properties," in Philosophy, Theology and Justice, Kluwer Academic Press, 98; auth, "Can Nature by Excluded from the Stability of Chemical Research?" in PSA 1998 Vol Two, Phil of Sci Asn, forthcoming; auth, "The Epistemology of a Spectrometer," in Phil of Sci 61, 94; auth, "Extending Popper's Epistemology to the Laboratory," in Dialectica 51, 97; auth, "Kant's Critique of Judgment and the Scientific Investigation of Nature," in Hyle: An Int Jour in the Phil of Chemistry 3, 97. **CONTACT ADDRESS** Dept Phil & Relig Studies, George Mason Univ, Fairfax, VA, 22030.

ROTHBERG, DONALD JAY
PERSONAL Born 07/15/1950, Washington, DC **DISCIPLINE** PHILOSOPHY **EDUCATION** Yale Col, BA, 72; Boston Univ, PhD, 83. **CAREER** Vis instr philos, Bowling Green State Univ, 81-82; asst prof philos, Univ Ky, 82-86; asst prof philos, Kenyon Col, 86-89; mem exec fac, Saybrook Grad Sch, 90- . **HONORS AND AWARDS** NSF fel polit sci, Paris, 70; Magna Cum Laude, 72; Ger Acad Exchange Serv fel, Heidelberg Univ, 75-76; NEH sum sem fel, Berkeley, 85; one of twenty selected for Revisioning Philosophy, funded by L Rockefeller, 87-89. **MEMBERSHIPS** APA; Am Acad of Relig; Asn for Transpersonal Psych. **RESEARCH** Philosophy of the human sciences; spirituality and epistemology; spirituality and social action; transpersonal psychology; Buddhist philosophy and psychology; nineteenth and twentieth century continental philosophy. **SELECTED PUBLICATIONS** Auth, Toward an Integral Spirituality, ReVision, 96; auth, Structural Violence and Spirituality: Socially Engaged Buddhist Perspectives, ReVision, 97; coauth, Unlearning Oppression: Healing Racism, Healing Violence, ReVision, 97; auth, Responding to Violence: An Introduction, ReVision, 97; coauth, Directions for Transpersonal Inquiry: Reflections on the Conversation, and Ken Wilber and the Future of Transpersonal Inquiry: An Introduction to the Conversation, in Rothberg, ed, Ken Wilber in Dialogue: Conversations with Leading Transpersonal Thinkers, Quest, 98; coauth, ReVisioning ReVision: A Statement from the Executive Editors, ReVision, 98; auth, Spiritual Practice at Work: The Importance of Community: The Buddhist Peace Fellowship BASE Program, Inner Edge, 98; auth, Responding to the Cries of the World: Socially Engaged Buddhism in North America, in Prebish, ed, The Face of Buddhism in America, Univ Calif, 98; ed, Intimate Relationships and Spirituality, ReVision, 98; co-ed, Ken Wilber in Dialogue: Conversations with Leading Transpersonal Thinkers, Quest, 98. **CONTACT ADDRESS** 1507 Josephine St, Berkeley, CA, 94703. **EMAIL** drothberg@igc.org

ROTHMAN, FREDERICK P.
DISCIPLINE CORPORATIONS, DECEDENTS' ESTATES AND TRUSTS **EDUCATION** Cornell Univ, AB, 62; Cornell Law Sch, JD, 64. **CAREER** Prof, Villanova Univ, 71-. **RESEARCH** Corporate finance, probate, professional responsibility, taxation. **SELECTED PUBLICATIONS** Coauth, Probate Law and Taxation of Transfers, Trusts and Estates, Vol I and II, 80. **CONTACT ADDRESS** Law School, Villanova Univ, 800 Lancaster Ave, Villanova, PA, 19085-1692. **EMAIL** rothman@law.vill.edu

ROTHSTEIN, PAUL FREDERICK
PERSONAL Born 06/06/1938, Chicago, Ill, m, 1963, 2 children **DISCIPLINE** LAW **EDUCATION** Northwestern Univ, BS, 59, LLB, 61. **CAREER** Instr law, Univ Mich, 63-64; from asst prof to assoc prof, Univ Tex, Austin, 64-71; Prof Law, Georgetown Univ, 71-, Guest lectr, Univ Wales, 63; co-dir, Univ Tex, Fed Defender Prog, 65-67; reporter-consult, comt rev penal code, State Bar Tex, 66-68 & Dist Columbia, 77; consult, Fed Trade Comn, US Dept Treas, US Dept Health, Educ & Welfare, Nat Acad Sci, Am Acad Judicial Educ, Nat Col State Judiciary, Comnr Uniform State Laws, US Senate Judiciary Comt, 67-; atty, Surrey, Karasik, Gould & Greene, Wash, DC, 67; chmn, Fed Bar Asn federal rules evidence comt, 76 & Asn Am Law Schs evidence sect, 77; mem, Nat Coun & Continuing Legal Educ Bd, Fed Barn Asn, 77-; secy, Nat Asn Criminal Injuries compensation bds, 77- **MEMBERSHIPS** Fed Bar Asn; Am Bar Asn. **RESEARCH** Trial law; constitution and supreme court; philosophy of law. **SELECTED PUBLICATIONS** Auth, A reevaluation of the privilege against adverse spousal testimony in the light of its purpose, Int & Comp Law Quart, 10/63; The new British Resale Prices Act, parts I and II (Part II: Recent developments), Am J Comp Law, spring & autumn 64; State compensation for criminally inflicted injuries, Univ Tex Law Rev, 11/65; Evidence in a Nutshell, West Publ, 69; Understanding the federal rules of evidence, Law J Press, 75; The Federal Rules of Evidence, Clar Boardman Co, 98; auth, Evidence: Cases, Materials, and Problems, Matthew Bender Co., 2nd Ed, 98. **CONTACT ADDRESS** Law Ctr, Georgetown Univ, 600 New Jersey N W, Washington, DC, 20001-2022.

ROTTSCHAEFER, WILLIAM ANDREW
PERSONAL Born 06/20/1933, Tulsa, OK, m, 1974 **DISCIPLINE** PHILOSOPHY **EDUCATION** St Louis Univ, BA, 57, MA, 60, STL, 66; Univ IL, Urbana-Champaign, MS, 69; Boston Univ, PhD, 73. **CAREER** Asst prof philos, State Univ NY Col Oswego, 72-73 & State Univ New York Col Plattsburgh, 73-74; asst prof, 75-79, assoc prof, 79, Prof Philos, Lewis & Clark Col, 79. **MEMBERSHIPS** Am Philos Asn; Philos Sci Asn; Inst Relig in Age of Sci; Int Soc Hist, Philos, Soc Study of Biol; Hist of Sci Soc; Ore Acad Sci; Soc Philos and Psychol. **RESEARCH** Relationships between theory and observation in sci and other modes of cognition; behaviorism and cognitive behavioral theory; sci and values; sci and relig. **SELECTED PUBLICATIONS** Auth, Believing is seeing--sometimes, New Scholasticism, 75; Observation: Theory-laden, theory-neutral or theory free?, Southern J Philos, 76; Wilfrid Sellars and the demise of the manifest image, Mod Schoolman, 76; Cognitive characteristics of belief systems, Am Psychologist, 78; Ordinary knowledge and scientific realism, In: The Philosophy of Wilfrid Sellars: Queries and Extensions, Reidl, 78; coauth (with William Knowlton), A Social Learning Theory Perspective on Human Freedom, Behaviorism, 79; Is there a values expert in the house, Comtemp Philos, 82; The psychological foundations of value theory: B F Skinner's Science of Values, Zygon, 82; Religious Cognition as Interpreted Experience: An Examination of Ian barbour's Compaison of the Epistemic Structures of Science and Religion, Zygon, 85; Learning to Be a Moral Agent, Personalist Forum, 86; Wilfrid Sellars on the Nature of Though, In: Naturalistic Epistemology, Reide, 87; Roger Sperry's Science of Values, Jour Mind and Behavior, 87; The New Interactionism between Science and Religion, Relig Studies Rev, 88; The Ghost of the Given: A Case for Epistemological Ghostbusters or Ghostlovers?, Bridges, 89; Creation and Evolution: Some Epistemological Criteria for an Integration, Explorations, 90; co-auth, Really Taking Darwin Seriously: An Alternative to Michael Ruse's Darwinian Metaethics, Biol and Philos, 90; Evolutionary Naturalistic Justifications of Morality: A Matter of Faith and Works, Biol and Philos, 91; Some Philosophical Implications of Bandura's Social Cognitive Learning Theories of Personality, Zygon, 91; Social Learning Theories of Moral Agency, Behavior and Philos, 91; The Insufficiency of Supervenient Explanations of Moral Actions, Biol and Philos, 91; A Course in the History and Philosophy of Mathematics from a Naturalistic Perspective, Teaching Philos, 91; What if the Universe if Fine-Tuned for Life, Explorations, 93; The Interaction between Science and Religion: An Assessment of Polkinghorne's Amiable Interactionism, 95; Scientific Naturalistic Philosophy and Gustafason's Theocentrism: A Marriage Made in Heaven, Zygon, 95; B F Skinner and the Grand Inquisitor, Zygon, 95; Is Science Epistemically Dependent on Religious Knowledge? Center for Theol and the Natural Sci Bull, 95; Evolutionary Ethics: An Irresistibe Temptation: Some Reflections on Paul Farber's The Temptation of Evolutionary Ethics, Biol and Philos, 97; Road Runner and the Bunch of Carrots: Some Teleological Implications of Theory of Natural Selection, Bridges, 97; Adaptational Functional Ascriptions in Evolutionary Biology: A Critique of Schaffner's Views, Philos Sci, 97; Naturalizing Moral Agency: A Critical Review of Some Recent Works on the Bilogical and Psychological Bases of Human Morality, Bridges 97; The Biology and Psychology of Moral Agency, Cambridge Univ Press, 98. **CONTACT ADDRESS** Dept of Philos, Lewis & Clark Col, 0615 SW Palatine Hill, Portland, OR, 97219-7879. **EMAIL** rotts@lclark.edu

ROTUNDA, RONALD DANIEL
PERSONAL Born 02/14/1945, Blue Island, IL, m, 1969, 2 children **DISCIPLINE** LAW **EDUCATION** Harvard Univ, BA, 67, JD, 70. **CAREER** Law clerk, Second Circuit Court Appeals, 70-71; lawyer, Wilmer, Cutler & Pickering, Washington, DC, 71-73; asst coun law, Senate Watergate Comt, 73-74; asst prof, 74-77, assoc prof, 77-80, prof Law, Univ Ill, 80-. **MEMBERSHIPS** Am Law Inst; Am Bar Asn. **RESEARCH** Constitutional law; legal ethics; Federal jurisdiction. **SELECTED PUBLICATIONS** Coauth (with Morgan), Problems and Materials on Professional Responsibility, Found Press, 76; (with Nowak and Young), Constitutional Law, West Publ Co, 78; Standing, waiver, laches, and appealability in attorney disqualification cases, 3 Corp Law Rev 82, Winter 80; (with Hacker), The extraterritorial regulation of foreign business under the US Securities Laws, 59 NC Law Rev 643, 81; Cases & Materials on Modern Constitutional Law, West Publ Co, 81; (with Morgan), Problems and Materials on Professional Responsibility, Found Press, 2nd ed, 81; (with Hay), The United States Federal System: Legal Integration in the American Experience, Giuffre, 82; (with Nowak), A comment on Dames and Moores v Regan, Univ Calif, Los Angeles Law Rev, 82; Modern Constitutional Law: Cases and Notes, West Publishing Co, St Paul, Minnesota, 5th ed, 97; 1998 Selected Standards on Professional Responsibility, with Morgan, Foundation Press, Westbury NY, 98. **CONTACT ADDRESS** Col of Law, Univ of Illinois, 504 E Pennsylvania, Champaign, IL, 61820-6996. **EMAIL** rrotunda@law.uius.edu

ROUSH, SHERRILYN
DISCIPLINE PHILOSOPHY **EDUCATION** Penn St Univ, BS, 88, BA, 88; Harvard Univ, PhD, 99 **CAREER** Tch Fel, 91-98, Harvard Univ; Lect, 91-96, New Eng Conserv of Music **HONORS AND AWARDS** AAUW Dissert Fel, 95-96; Nat Sci Found Fel, 88-91; Mellon Fel in Humanities, 88 **MEMBERSHIPS** Am Philos Assoc; Philos of Sci Assoc **RESEARCH** Metaphysics and Epistemology; Kant; Philosophy of Science; Subjects & Objects; Anthropic Principle; Transcendental Arguments **SELECTED PUBLICATIONS** Auth, Alternate Possibilities and their Entertainment, Philosophy, 98 **CONTACT ADDRESS** Dept Philos, Harvard Univ, 208 Emerson Hall, Cambridge, MA, 02138. **EMAIL** roush@fas.harvard.edu

ROWAN, ALBERT T.
PERSONAL Born 05/15/1927, Kansas City, MO, m, 1948 **DISCIPLINE** THEOLOGY **EDUCATION** MI State U, 1946; Western Baptist Bible Coll, BRE, BTh 1955-59; Ashland Theological Sem, MDiv 1976; Trinity Theol Sem, DMin 1987. **CAREER** First Baptist, Quincy IL, pastor 1955-60; Zion Baptist, Springfield IL, pastor 1960-61; Salem Baptist, Champaign IL, pastor 1961-64; Bethany Baptist, Cleveland OH, pastor 1964-; TRINITY THEOLOGICAL SEMINARY, adjunct professor, 1990-95, COURSE ASSESSOR, 1995-. **HONORS AND AWARDS** Proclamation "Rev Albert T Rowan Day" Mayor Carl B Stokes 1970; Certificate of Appreciation Champaign County Urban League 1963; elected to Lincoln High School Hall of Fame 1981; Hon Dr of Div Am Bible Inst 1969; Hon Dr of Div VA Seminary & Coll 1975; Outstanding Pastor of the Year, Baptist Ministers Conference of Cleveland, 1983; Hall of Fame, Lincoln High School, Kansas City, MO, 1981. **MEMBERSHIPS** 1st vice pres Baptist Minister's Conf of Cleveland; pres Northern OH Dist Congress 1955-60; past pres Cleveland Baptist Assn 1983-; mem exec bd OH General Baptist State Convention; mem Cleveland Library Bd of Trustees 1976-78; first vice moderator, Northern Ohio Baptist District Assn, 1987-; City Planning Commission of Cleveland, Ohio, chairman, mem, 1976-. **CONTACT ADDRESS** Bethany Baptist Church, 1201-1225 E 105th St, Cleveland, OH, 44108.

ROWAN, JOHN R.
PERSONAL Born 03/06/1967, Philadelphia, PA, m **DISCIPLINE** PHILOSOPHY **EDUCATION** Univ of Virginia, PhD, 97. **CAREER** Asst Prof, Purdue Univ, Calumet, 97-. **MEMBERSHIPS** Amer Phil Assoc; Soc for Business Ethics; Assoc for Practical and Professional Ethics; Intl Assoc of Business and Soc; Intl Economics and Phil Soc; North Amer Soc for Social Phil. **RESEARCH** Business and professional ethics; ethical theory; issues in applied ethics; political and social philosophy; legal philosophy **SELECTED PUBLICATIONS** Auth, Philosophy on Messick and Social Conflict: Resolving the Reolution Conflict, 97; Grounding Hypernorms: Toward a Contractarian Theory of Business Ethics, 97; State Sponsored Abortion in a Property Rights Framework, 98; Moral Rights and Social Policy, 99. **CONTACT ADDRESS** Dept of Philosophy, Purdue Univ, Calumet, 2200 169th St, Hammond, IN, 46323-2094. **EMAIL** jrowan@calumet.purdue.edu

ROWE, STEPHEN C.
PERSONAL Born 02/25/1945, Cincinnati, OH, m **DISCIPLINE** ETHICS AND SOCIETY **EDUCATION** Colgate Univ, BA, 67; Univ Chicago Divinity Sch, MTh, 69, PhD, 74. **CAREER** Chemn Philos Dept, 88- , coordr Liberal Studies Prog, 95- , Grand Vallet State Univ. **HONORS AND AWARDS** Univ Fel, 71-72; Danforth Assoc, 77-84; Phi Kappa Phi; Distinguished Fac Award, 83; Mich Hum Fac, 84- ; Outstanding Educr Award, 97. **MEMBERSHIPS** Am Acad Relig; APA; Asn for General and Liberal Stud; Ctr for Process Stud;

Chicago Social Ethics Sem; Soc for the Advanc of Am Philos; Soc for Buddhist-Christian Stud; Soc for Values in Higher Educ. **RESEARCH** Philosophy of religion; ethics. **SELECTED PUBLICATIONS** Auth, Living Beyond Crisis: Essays on Discovery and Being in the World, Pilgrim, 80; auth, Leaving and Returning: On America's Contribution to a World Ethic, Bucknell, 89; auth, Claiming a Liberal Education: Resources for Realizing the College Experience, Ginn, 90; auth, Rediscovering the West: An Inquiry into Nothingness and Relatedness, SUNY, 94; auth, The Vision of William James, Element/Penguin, 96; auth, Toward a Postliberal Liberalism: James Luther Adams and the Need for a Theory of Relational Meaning, Am J of Theol & Philos, 96; auth, A Zen Presence in America: Dialogue As Religious Practice, in Mitchell, ed, Masao Abe: Zen Life in Dialogue, Tuttle, 98. **CONTACT ADDRESS** Philosophy Dept, Grand Valley State Univ, 1 Campus Dr, Allendale, MI, 49401. **EMAIL** rowes@gvsu.edu

ROWE, WILLIAM L.
PERSONAL Born 07/26/1931, Detroit, MI, m, 1952, 3 children **DISCIPLINE** PHILOSOPHY **EDUCATION** Wayne State Univ, AB, 54; Chicago Theol Sem, BD, 57; Univ Mich, PhD, 62. **CAREER** Instr philos, Univ Ill, 60-62; from asst prof to assoc prof, 62-69, Prof Philos, Purdue Univ, W Lafayette, 69-. **HONORS AND AWARDS** Guggenheim Fel, 84-85; Nat Humanities Ctr Fel, 84-85. **MEMBERSHIPS** Soc Relig Higher Educ. **RESEARCH** Philosophy of religion; metaphysics. **SELECTED PUBLICATIONS** Auth, Religious Symbols and God: A Philosophical Study of Tillich's Theology, Univ Chicago, 68; co-ed, Philosophy of Religion: Selected Readings, Harcourt, 73; auth, The Cosmological Argument, Princeton Univ, 75; Philosophy of Religion, Dickenson, 78; Thomas Reid on Freedom and Morality, Cornell Univ, 95. **CONTACT ADDRESS** Dept of Philos, Purdue Univ, West Lafayette, IN, 47907-1968. **EMAIL** wlrowe@purdue.edu

ROWOLD, HENRY
PERSONAL Born 07/10/1939, St. Louis, MO, m, 1962, 3 children **DISCIPLINE** THEOLOGY **EDUCATION** Concordia Sem, MDiv, 64, STM, 65; Christ Sem, ThD, 77. **CAREER** Dir res and plan, Lutheran Church, South Asia, 83-87; dir, Lutheran Church, China Coordinating Ctr, 87-95; prof, Concordia Sem, 95- . **HONORS AND AWARDS** Listed, Who's Who in Biblical Archaeology; listed, Who's Who in the Midwest. **MEMBERSHIPS** Cath Bibl Asn; Soc of Bibl Lit; Am Soc of Missiology; Lutheran Soc for Missiology. **RESEARCH** Wisdom and wisdom literature; history of Christianity in China. **SELECTED PUBLICATIONS** Auth, Educating for World Missions: A Missionary Perspective, Issues in Chr Educ, 93; auth, Lord of the Reach, Missio Apstolica, 94; auth, Arresting Developments in China's Religious Policies, Concordia J, 95; auth, Reflections on Leaving the Mission Field, Missio Apostolica, 96; auth, Teaching English as Ministry, Missio Apostolica, 97; auth, The Reunification of Hong Kong with China: Why? What's at Stake? What about the Church? Concordia J, 98; auth, Ministry at the Fringes: The Missionary as Marginal Person, Missio Apostolica, 98. **CONTACT ADDRESS** 801 DeMun Ave, St Louis, MO, 63105-3199. **EMAIL** rowoldh@csl.edu

RUBARTH, SCOTT M.
PERSONAL Born 07/21/1962 **DISCIPLINE** PHILOSOPHY **EDUCATION** Univ of Toronto, PhD, 97. **CAREER** Vis Asst Prof, Rollins Col. **HONORS AND AWARDS** Cornell Scholar in Classical Philos. **MEMBERSHIPS** Amer Philos Asn; Amer Philol Asn **RESEARCH** Hellenistic philosophy; Greek moral theory. **CONTACT ADDRESS** Rollins Col, 1000 Holt Ave, Philosophy, Winter Park, FL, 32789-4499. **EMAIL** srubarth@rollins.edu

RUBENSTEIN, ERIC M.
DISCIPLINE CONTEMPORARY ANGLO-AMERICAN PHILOSOPHY, MODERN PHILOSOPHY **EDUCATION** Univ NC, Chapel Hill, PhD, 96. **CAREER** Vis asst prof, Colgate Univ. **SELECTED PUBLICATIONS** Auth, Absolute Processes: A Nominalist Alternative, The S Jour Philos; Color as Simple: Reply to Westphal, Philos. **CONTACT ADDRESS** Dept of Philos and Relig, Colgate Univ, 13 Oak Drive, Hamilton, NY, 13346. **EMAIL** erubenstein@mail.colgate.edu

RUBENSTEIN, RICHARD LOWELL
PERSONAL Born 01/08/1924, New York, NY, m, 3 children **DISCIPLINE** RELIGIOUS STUDIES, HUMANITIES **EDUCATION** Univ Cincinnati, AB, 46; Jewish Theol Sem, MHL, 52; Harvard Univ, STM, 55, PhD(hist & philos relig), 60. **CAREER** Prof, 70-77, Distinguished prof Relig, 77-95, prof emer, 95- , Fla State Univ; dir, Ctr Study Southern Cult & Relig, 73-95; pres, Univ of Bridgeport, 95- . **HONORS AND AWARDS** Nat Humanities Inst fel, Yale Univ, 76-77; Portico d'Ottavia Lit Prize, 77; Doctor of Hebrew Letters, honoris causa, Jewish Theol Sem of Am, 87. **MEMBERSHIPS** Am Acad Relig; Soc Bibl Lit; Soc Values Higher Edue; Soc Arts, Relig & Contemp Cult. **RESEARCH** Contemporary religious thought; Holocaust studies; values in contemporary society. **SELECTED PUBLICATIONS** Auth, After Auschwitz, Bobbs-Merrill, 68; The Religious Imagination, Beacon Paperbk, 68; Morality and Eros, McGraw Hill, 70; My Brother Paul, Harper & Row, 72; Power Struggle, Scribners, 74; The Cunning of History, Harper & Row, 75; auth, The Aft of Triage, Beacon, 83; ed, Modernization: The Humanist Response to Its Promise and Problems, Paragon, 84; coauth, Approaches to Auschwitz: The Holocaust and Its Legacy, Westminster, 87; ed, Spirit Matters: The World Wide Impact of Religion on Contemporary Politics, Paragon, 87; ed, The Dissolving Alliance: The United States and the NATO Alliance, Paragon, 87; co-ed, the Politics of Liberation Theology: North American and Latin American Views, Paragon, 88; auth, After Auschwitz: History, Theology and Contemporary Judaism, 2d ed, Johns Hopkins, 92; **CONTACT ADDRESS** Office of the President, Univ Bridgeport, Bridgeport, CT, 32306-6601.

RUBIN, ALFRED P.
PERSONAL Born 10/13/1931, New York, NY, m, 1960, 3 children **DISCIPLINE** INTERNATIONAL LAW **EDUCATION** Columbia Univ, BA, 52, JD, 57; Univ Cambridge, MLitt, 63. **CAREER** Atty, adv, 61-66, dir trade control, 66-67, US Dept Defense; prof law, Univ Oregon, 67-75; prof, distinguished prof, int law, Fletcher Sch of Law and Diplomacy, Tufts Univ, 75-. **HONORS AND AWARDS** Pres, Am branch, Int Law Assoc; Charles H. Stockton Prof of Int Law, US Naval War College, 81-82. **MEMBERSHIPS** Am Soc of Int Law; Int Law Asn. **RESEARCH** Public international law. **SELECTED PUBLICATIONS** Auth, Ethics and Authority on International Law, Cambridge, 71; auth, Enforcing the Rules of International Law, Harvard Int Law Jour, 93; auth, Dayton and the Limits of Law, 97; auth, The Law of Piracy, 2d, Transnational, 98. **CONTACT ADDRESS** Fletcher School of Law and Diplomacy, Tufts Univ, Medford, MA, 02155. **EMAIL** arubin@emerald.tufts.edu

RUBIN, PAUL H.
PERSONAL Born 08/09/1942, Boston, MA, m, 2 children **DISCIPLINE** LAW & ECONOMICS **EDUCATION** Univ Cinn, BA, 63; Purdue Univ, PhD, 70. **CAREER** Asst, assoc, & full prof of Econ, Univ Georgia, 68-82; prof, Baruch Col & Grad Ctr CUNY, 82-83; adj prof, VPI, 84, Goerge Wash Law Ctr, 85-89; Prof Econ, 91- , actg chr, 93-94, Emory Univ; adj scholar, Am Enterprise Inst, Cato Inst, 92-98; **HONORS AND AWARDS** Chemn Award, Consumer Prod Safety Comn, 87; grants & fel: William H Donner Found, 97-98, Pfizer, 97, IRIS, 92-93, Paul Oreffice Fund, 93, Liberty Fund, 79, CUNY, 83. **MEMBERSHIPS** Am Econ Asn; Allied Soc Sci Asn; Am Law & Econ Asn; Int Soc New Inst Econ; Publ Choice Soc; S Econ Asn; W Econ Asn. **RESEARCH** Law and economics, industrial organization and antitrust; transactions cost economice, economics of advertising and safety, price theory, law in post-Communist economies. **SELECTED PUBLICATIONS** Auth, Managing Business Transactions: Controlling the Costs of Coordinating, Communicating, and Decision Making, Free Press, 93; Tort Reform by Contract, Am Enterprise Inst, 93; ed, Deregulating Telecommunications: The Baby Bells Case for Competition, Wiley, 95; Promises, Promises: Contrcts in Russia and Other Post-Communist Economies, Shaftesbury Papers, 98; Indicting Liability: How the Liability System Has Turned Against Itself, Am Enterprise Inst, 98; Lives Saved or Lives Lost: The Effect of Concealed Handgun Laws on Crime, Am Econ Rev, 98. **CONTACT ADDRESS** Dept of Economics, Emory Univ, 1635 N Decatur Rd., Atlanta, GA, 30322-2240. **EMAIL** prubin@emory.edu

RUBIN SCHWARTZ, SHULY
DISCIPLINE RELIGION **EDUCATION** Barnard Col, BA, MA, PhD. **CAREER** Asst prof, Jewish Theol Sem Am. **RESEARCH** Image and role of the Rebbetzin in Am Jewish life; women in Jewish hist. **SELECTED PUBLICATIONS** Auth, The Emergence of Jewish Scholarship in America: The Publication of the Jewish Encyclopedia, Hebrew Union, 91; Camp Ramah: The Early Years, 1947-1952, Conservative Judaism, 87; Ramah Philosophy and the Newman Revolution, Jewish Education and Judaica; pubs on modern Jewish life. **CONTACT ADDRESS** Dept of Jewish Hist, Jewish Theol Sem of America, 3080 Broadway, PO Box 3080, New York, NY, 10027. **EMAIL** shschwartz@jtsa.edu

RUBINSTEIN, ERNEST
PERSONAL Born 07/11/1952, New York, NY **DISCIPLINE** RELIGION **EDUCATION** Northwestern Univ, PhD, 95. **CAREER** LECTR, NY UNIV SCHOOL OF CONTINUING ED, 96-; LIBRN, THE INTERCHURCH CENTER, 95-; BOOK REVIEWER, KIRKUS REV, 97-. **MEMBERSHIPS** Am Acad of Relig. **RESEARCH** Jewish Theology; German Judaism; philosophy. **SELECTED PUBLICATIONS** Auth, A New German Jewish Identity, Aufbau, 98; auth, An Episode of Jewish Romanticism: Franz Rosenzweig's Star of Redemption, SUNY Press, forthcoming. **CONTACT ADDRESS** 116 Pinehurst Ave., New York, NY, 10033. **EMAIL** ehr3@is6.nyu.edu

RUBSYS, ANTHONY L.
PERSONAL Born 11/05/1923, Lithuania **DISCIPLINE** THEOLOGY **EDUCATION** Universita Gregoriana, Rome, STL, 49; Pontifical Bibl Inst, Rome, CD, 78. **CAREER** Prof Old Testament & New Testament, Immaculate Heart Sem, 53-57; prof relig stud, Manhattan Col, 59-92, prof emer, 93- ; vis prof sacred scripture, St Joseph's Sem, 69-82. **HONORS AND AWARDS** Nat award by Educ Dept of Lithuania for transl Old Testament into Lithuanian, 95; STD, Vytantas Magnus Univ. **MEMBERSHIPS** SBL; CBQ; ASOR; Lithuanian Catholic Acad of Sci. **RESEARCH** Pentateuchal studies; archaeology. **SELECTED PUBLICATIONS** Auth, Key to the Old Testament (in Lithuanian), 3 v, Vilnius, Kataliku Pasaulis, 95; auth, Key to the New Testament (in Lithuanian) 2 v, Vilnius, Kataliku Pasaulis, 97; auth, Sventojo Rasto Krastuose, 3 v, Vilnius, Kataliku Pasaulis, 98; transl and contribur to two ed of Bible (in Lithuanian) to be published by The Bible Soc, ecumenical ed, and The Bishop's Conf, Catholic ed. **CONTACT ADDRESS** Manhattan Col, Riverdale, NY, 10471-4098.

RUDENSTINE, DAVID
DISCIPLINE CONSTITUTIONAL LAW **EDUCATION** Yale Univ, BA, 63; MAT, 65; NY Univ, JD, 69. **CAREER** Prof, Yeshiva Univ, 82-. **HONORS AND AWARDS** Staff atty, NY City Legal Services Prop, 69-72; Dir Citizen's Inquiry Parole & Criminal Justice, Inc, 72-74; counl Nat News Coun; Proj dir, assoc dir, acting exec dir, NY Civil Liberties Union; Guggenheim vis fel. **RESEARCH** The First Amendment, and labor arbitration. **SELECTED PUBLICATIONS** Auth, Prison Without Walls: Report on New York Parole; Rights of Ex-Offenders **CONTACT ADDRESS** Yeshiva Univ, 55 Fifth Ave, NY, NY, 10003-4301.

RUDGE, DAVID W.
PERSONAL Born 11/29/1962, Syracuse, NY, s **DISCIPLINE** HISTORY AND PHILOSOPHY OF SCIENCE **EDUCATION** Duke Univ, BS, 86; Univ Pittsburgh, MS, 90; Univ Pittsburgh, MA, 92; Univ Pittsburgh, PhD, 96. **CAREER** Lectr, philos, Tex A&M Univ, 96-97; temp asst prof, philos, Iowa State Univ, 97-. **HONORS AND AWARDS** London Visiting Scholars fel, Centre for the Philos of the Natural and Soc Sci, London Sch of Econ and Polit Sci, summer, 97; Intl Res Travel Assistance grant, Office of the Asst Provost for Intl Prog, Tex A&M Univ, spring, 97; Pew teaching leadership award, fall, 93. **MEMBERSHIPS** Amer Asn of Philos Teachers; Amer Philos Asn; Central States Philos Asn; Hist of Sci Soc; Intl Soc for the Hist, Philos & Soc Studies of Bio; Philos of Sci Asn; Sigma Xi. **RESEARCH** Experiments in evolutionary biology; H. B. D. Kettlewell. **SELECTED PUBLICATIONS** Article, Classroom Videotaping: A Protocol for Camera Operators and Consultants, Jour of Grad Teaching Asst Develop, 2, 3, 113-123, 95; co-auth, article, Structure, Function and Variation in the Hindlimb Muscles of the Margarornis Assemblage, Annals of the Carnegie Mus, 61, 207-237, 92; co-auth, article, The Phylogenetic Relationships of the Margarornis Assemblage, Condor, 94, 760-766, 92; book rev, Scientific Thinking by Robert M. Martin, Philos in Rev/Comptes rendus philos, 17, 5, 350-352, 97. **CONTACT ADDRESS** Department of Philosophy, Iowa State Univ of Science and Tech, Rm. 435 Catt Hall, Ames, IA, 50011-1036. **EMAIL** rudge@iastate.edu

RUEDA, ANA
DISCIPLINE ROMANCE LANGS & LITS **EDUCATION** Vanderbilt Univ, PhD, 85. **CAREER** ASSOC PROF, SPAN, UNIV MO, 92-. **CONTACT ADDRESS** Dept of Romance Langs, Lit, Univ of Missouri, Columbus, 143 Arts & Scis, Columbus, MO, 65211. **EMAIL** RuedaA@missouri.edu

RUFFING, JANET
PERSONAL Born 07/17/1945, Spokane, WA, s **DISCIPLINE** CHRISTIAN SPIRITUALITY AND SPIRITUAL DIRECTION **EDUCATION** Russell Col, BA, 68; Univ San Fran, MAS, 78; Jesuit Sch of Theol, Berkley, 84; Grad Theol Union, PhD, 86. **CAREER** Tchr, Sec Ed Mercy HS, Burlingame & San Fran, Marian HS, San Diego, 68-80; Assoc Prof, Fordham Univ, 86-. **HONORS AND AWARDS** Comprehensive Exams with Distinction, GTU. **MEMBERSHIPS** Amer Acad of Religion, Cath Theol Soc of Amer, Spiritual Dir Intl. **RESEARCH** Spiritual direction, Mysticism, religious life, spirituality. **SELECTED PUBLICATIONS** Enkindling the Embers: The Challenge of Recent Research on Religious Life, Mast Jour 4, 94; Physical Illness: A Mystically Transformative Element in the Life of Elizabeth Leseur, Spiritual Life, 94; Leadership a New Way Part 1: Women, Power, and Authority, Rev for Religious, 94; The Burning of the Heart for All Creation: The Challenges to Religious Life, Mast Jour, 95; Look at Every Path Closely and Deliberately: What's On Offer?, The Way Sup 84, 95; Encountering Love Mysticism: Issues in Supervision, Presence: Intl Jour in Spirit Dir 1, 95; The World Transfigured: Kataphatic Experience Explored through Qualitative Research Methodology, Stud in Spirit, 95; You Fill Up My Senses: God and the Senses, The Way, 95; On Resisting the Demon of Busyness, Spirit Life, 95; As Refined by Fire, Living Prayer, 95; The Passage of Mercy Life into the Third Millennium, Mast Jour, 96; Leadership a New Way Part II: The Religious Dimensions of Leadership, The Church and Cons Life, 96; The Human Experience of Prayer: East and West, Teach us to Pray, Villanova Univ Press, 96; Visiting a Scene of Election, Rev for Rel 56, 97; Celibacy and Contemplation, InFormation, 97; Supervision and Spiritual Development: the Conventional Post Conventional Divide, Jour of Supv and Trng in Ministry, 97; Knitting Together the Mind and the Body, and the Spirit: The Experience of Contemporary Christian Women, Stud in Spirit, 97; To Have Been One With The Earth: Nature in Contemporary Christian Mystical Experience, Presence 3, 97; Unacknowledged Con-

flicts: Prayer and Morality, The Way Sup 88, 97; Catherine McAuley's Quaker Connection: What Can We Know? What Do We Imagine?, Mast Jour, 97; Going Up Into the Gaps: Prophetic Life and Vision, InFormation, 98. **CONTACT ADDRESS** Fordham Univ, Grad Sch of Religious Ed., Bronx, NY, 10458. **EMAIL** Ruffing@murray.fordham.edu

RUJA, HARRY
PERSONAL Born 02/26/1912, Paterson, NJ, m, 1940, 3 children **DISCIPLINE** PHILOSOPHY **EDUCATION** Univ Calif, Los Angeles, BA, 33; Univ Chicago, MA, 34; Princeton Univ, PhD, 36; San Diego State Col, MA, 53. **CAREER** Instr, psych and philos, Compton Col, 39-47; asst prof, assoc prof, prof, philos, San Diego State Col, 47-79; prof emer philos, San Diego State Univ, 79- ; vis prof philos, Univ Minnesota, 59, C W Post Col, 65, Penn State Univ, 64-65, Haifa Univ, 81. **HONORS AND AWARDS** Russell Scholar of the Year, 93, Bertrand Russell Soc. **MEMBERSHIPS** APA. **RESEARCH** Bertrand Russell; Zionism; Judaica; civil liberties. **SELECTED PUBLICATIONS** Auth, Floral Lewis, Russell Soc News, 93; coauth, A Bibliography of Bertrand Russell, Routledge, 94; auth, Arab Terrorism, Russell Soc News, 94; auth, Visitor's Day Revisited, UCLA Mag, 95; auth, Bertrand Russell's Life in Pictures, Russell: The Journal of the Bertrand Russell Archives, 95-96; auth, Arab Aggression Spawned the Mythical East Jerusalem, San Diego Union-Tribune, 97; auth, Philosophically speaking, UCLA Alumni News, 98; ed, Russell, Mortals and Others, Routledge, 2 vols, 96, 98. **CONTACT ADDRESS** 4664 Troy Ln, La Mesa, CA, 91941.

RUKMANI, T.S.
DISCIPLINE RELIGION **EDUCATION** Delhi Univ, PhD, 58, Dlitt, 91. **CAREER** Prof; ch, Hindu Stud. **HONORS AND AWARDS** Ed, Jour Indological Soc, S Africa, 95; mem, Consult Comm Intl Asson for Sanskrit Stud, 94; Adv Bd for the Xth World Sanskrit Conf, 97. **SELECTED PUBLICATIONS** Auth, Sankara; The Man and His Philosophy, Shimla, India, Indian Inst Adv Stud, 91; Yogavartikka of Vijnanabhiksu, Delhi, India: Munshiram Manohariai Publ, 81-89 A Critical Study of the Bhagavata Purana, Varanasi, India: Chowkhamba Sanskrit Press, 71; "Vitanda as a Method of debate in the Khandanakhandakhadya of Sri Harsa," Adyar Library Bulletin, 94; "Bhakti as a Means of Empowerment of Women," Jour for the Stud of Rel, 95; ed, Colloquium on Religious Consciousness and Life Worlds, Shimla, India: Indian Inst Adv Stud, 91. **CONTACT ADDRESS** Dept of Rel, Concordia Univ, Montreal, 1455 de Maisonneuve W, Montreal, PQ, H3G 1M8.

RUNKEL, ROSS R.
DISCIPLINE ARBITRATION, CONTRACTS, DISPUTE RESOLUTION, EMPLOYMENT DISCRIMINATION **EDUCATION** Univ Wash, BS, 61; JD, 65. **CAREER** Tchg fel, Stanford Univ, 65-66; private practice, Seattle, 66-67; asst prof, 67-70; assoc prof, 70-74; prof, 74-; vis prof, Univ Wash, 85; dir, Ctr Dispute Resolution, 89-92. **HONORS AND AWARDS** Co-pres, Pacific Northwest Chapter, 92-93; v ch, Ore Dispute Resolution Comm, 89-93; dir, Portland Branch of the Fed Reserve Bank, 91-. **MEMBERSHIPS** Mem, Order of the Coif; IRRA; Soc Prof in Dispute Resolution. **SELECTED PUBLICATIONS** Assoc ed, Wash Law Rev. **CONTACT ADDRESS** Sch of Law, Willamette Univ, 900 State St, Salem, OR, 97301. **EMAIL** rrunkel@willamette.edu

RUPRECHT, LOUIS A., JR.
PERSONAL Born 03/24/1961, Elizabeth, NJ, s **DISCIPLINE** ETHICS; COMPARATIVE RELIGION **EDUCATION** Duke Univ, AB, 83, MA, 85; Emory Univ, PhD, 90. **CAREER** Vis prof, 92-96, relig and classics, Emory Univ; vis prof, 96-97, relig department, Barnard Col; visiting prof, 97-98, Mercer Univ & GA State Univ; vis prof, 98, Princeton Univ. **HONORS AND AWARDS** Charlotte W. Newcombe Dissertation Fel; New Summer Institute Fels (twice). **MEMBERSHIPS** Amer Academy of Relig; Soc of Biblical Lit; Soc for Values in Higher Education; Woodrow Wilson Found; Amer Sch of Classical Studies in Athens. **RESEARCH** Comparative relig; classical antiquity; modern Greek studies; ethics **SELECTED PUBLICATIONS** Auth, Afterwards: Hellenism, Modernism, and the Myth of Decadence, 96; auth, Symposia: Plato, the Erotic and Moral Value, Homeric Wisdom and Heroic Friendship, South Atlantic Quarterly, 98; auth, The Virtue of Courage: The Penultimacy of the Political, forthcoming in Soundings, forthcoming; auth, Panamanian Peregrinations, recently submitted for review by Farrar; God Gardened in the East, forthcoming in South Atlantic Quarterly, Spring 99; auth, To The Gods of Hellas: A History of Greek Games at Barnard College, 1903-1968, forthcoming in Arion, Fall 99; auth, Classics at the Millennium: An Outsider's View of a Discipline, commissioned for Soundings, 99; auth, Are We Living in an Ethical Age? Instilling Ethics: The collected Papers of the Olmsted Symposium, forthcoming with Yale University Press, 99; auth, Why the Greeks? Agon" On the Democratic Future of the Classical, forthcoming 99. **CONTACT ADDRESS** Emory Univ, Atlanta, GA, 30322. **EMAIL** larupre@emory.edu

RURA, SVETLANA
PERSONAL Born 11/23/1958, Yugoslavia, m, 1992 **DISCIPLINE** PHILOSOPHY **EDUCATION** Univ Cincinnati, PhD, 97. **CAREER** Prof, part-time, Univ Cincinnati. **RESEARCH** Epistemology. **CONTACT ADDRESS** 6234 Joyce Ln, Cincinnati, OH, 45237. **EMAIL** svetlanar@juno.com

RUSH, SHARON E.
DISCIPLINE LAW **EDUCATION** Cornell Univ, BA, JD. **CAREER** Irving Cypen prof, Univ Fla, 85-. **MEMBERSHIPS** Asn Amer Law Schools Sect on Women, Minorities, and Constitutional Law; Soc Amer Law Teachers; DC Bar; Phi Kappa Phi. **RESEARCH** Constitutional law, civil procedure, federal courts, outsider jurisprudence, fourteenth amendment . **CONTACT ADDRESS** School of Law, Univ of Florida, PO Box 117625, Gainesville, FL, 32611-7625. **EMAIL** rush@law.ufl.edu

RUSSELL, BRUCE ALAN
PERSONAL Born 03/15/1945, San Francisco, CA, m, 1971, 2 children **DISCIPLINE** PHILOSOPHY **EDUCATION** Univ Calif, Davis, BS, 67, MA, 72 PhD(philos), 77. **CAREER** Sessional lectr philos, Univ Alta, 73-74; asst prof, 78-80, 80-82, assoc prof, 85-92, prof, 92- , Wayne State Univ; Andrew Mellon fel, Univ Pittsburgh, 80-81; Nat Endowment for Humanities, Princeton Univ, summer, 82; Western Wash, 86; Univ Neb 87; Univ Cal Berkeley, 93. **MEMBERSHIPS** Am Philos Asn. **RESEARCH** Ethics, epistemology, philosophy of religion. **SELECTED PUBLICATIONS** Auth, What is the ethical in fear and trembling, Inquiry, fall 75; Probability, utility and rational belief, Sophia, 3/76; On the relative strictness of negative and positive duties, Am Philos Quart, 4/77; Still a live issue, Philos & Publ Affairs, spring 78; On the relation between psychological and ethical egoism, Philos Studies, 82; auth, Two forms of Ethical Skepticism, Ethical Theory, 88; auth, Defenseless, The Evidential Argument from Evil, 96; auth, Justification and Knowledge, Knowledge, Teaching, and Wisdom, 96; auth, Critical Study of Reason, Ethics, and Society, Nous, 98. **CONTACT ADDRESS** Dept of Philosophy, Wayne State Univ, 3001 51 W Warren, Detroit, MI, 48201. **EMAIL** bruce.russell@wayne.edu

RUSSELL, C. ALLYN
PERSONAL Born 09/03/1920, Bovina Center, NY, m, 1947 **DISCIPLINE** RELIGION **EDUCATION** Houghton Col, AB, 42; Eastern Baptist Theol Sem, BD, 44, ThM, 46; Univ Buffalo, MA, 55; Boston Univ, PhD, 59. **CAREER** Clergyman, 44-56; asst prof church hist, Southern Baptist Theol Sem, 59; from lectr to assoc prof relig, 59-73, travel grant sabbatical res, 68-69, Prof Relig, 73-88, PROF EMERITUS, BOSTON UNIV; Danforth assoc, 65- **HONORS AND AWARDS** Solon J Buck Award, Minn Hist Soc, 73; Metcalf Cup and Prize, Boston Univ, 82. **MEMBERSHIPS** Am Acad Relig; Am Soc Church Hist; Am Baptist Hist Soc; AAUP. **RESEARCH** Religion in America; religious biography; fundamentalism. **SELECTED PUBLICATIONS** Auth, A History of the Fredonia Baptist Church, McClenathan, 55; Voices of American Fundamentalism: Seven Biographical Studies, Westminster, 76. **CONTACT ADDRESS** 43 Prospect St, Carlisle, MA, 01741.

RUSSELL, KATHRYN
DISCIPLINE PHILOSOPHY **EDUCATION** Univ Cincinnati, PhD. **CAREER** Prof, State Univ NY Cortland. **RESEARCH** Social and political philosophy; philosophy of science; Marxism; feminist theory. **SELECTED PUBLICATIONS** Auth, Birth, Social Reproduction and Abstract Labor, Sci Soc, 94; co-auth, Curriculum Reform Through General Education: A Requirement in Prejudice and Discrimination, 93. **CONTACT ADDRESS** Philosophy Dept, State Univ NY Cortland, Box 2000, Cortland, NY, 13045-0900. **EMAIL** russellk@snycorva.cortland.edu

RUSSELL, WILLIAM R.
PERSONAL Born 10/01/1954, Iowa City, IA, m, 1979, 3 children **DISCIPLINE** RELIGION **EDUCATION** Univ Iowa, BA, 77; Luther Sem, Master of Divinity, 81; Univ Iowa, PhD, 89. **CAREER** Adj and/or vis appointments at various inst, 89-98; Luth Campus pastor, Ndak State Univ, 95-98. **HONORS AND AWARDS** Walker award, 77; Evangelisch-lutherische kirche in Deutschland award, ger lang study, 83; NEH sumer seminar for col teachers, 92. **MEMBERSHIPS** 16th century studies conf; Amer Acad of Relig; Luther Gesellschaft. **RESEARCH** Reformation history and theology. **SELECTED PUBLICATIONS** Rev, The Reformation, vol I and II, The Book Newsletter, 98; rev, Christian Confessions: A Historical Introduction, The Jour of the Amer Acad of Relig, 98; rev, Martinus Noster, Dialog: A Jour of Theol, winter, 98; article, Dusting off The Book of Concord, Lutheran Partners, 96; auth, How to Read Luther, Inquirere Jour, 96; auth, A Neglected Key to the Theology of Martin Luther, Word and World, 96; auth, The Theological Magna Charta of Confessional Lutheranism, Church Hist, 95; auth, Ash Wednesday, Living by Faith under the Cross, Immanuel Lutheran Church, 95; auth, Luther's Theological Testament: The Schmalkald Articles, Fortress Press, 95; auth, Topical Index to Luther's Works and the Lutheran Confessional Writings, Fortress Press, 95; rev, The Early Reformation in Europe, The Lutheran Quart, 95; rev, Kommentar zu Luthers Katechismen, vol I-V, The Sixteenth Century Jour, 91-95; ed and transl, The Schmalkald Articles by Martin Luther, Fortress Press, 95; ed, Martin Luther, Theologian of the Church by George W. Forell: Collected Essays in Honor of His Seventy-Fifth Birthday, word and world suppl vol II, Luther Sem, 94; auth, Luther's Understanding of the Pope as the Antichrist, Die Archiv fuer Reformationsgeschichte/The Arch for Reform Res, 94; rev, A Cry of Absence, The Lutheran Quart, 94. **CONTACT ADDRESS** Univ Lutheran Center, 1201 13th Ave. N., Fargo, ND, 58102. **EMAIL** wrussell@prairie.kodak.edu

RUSSO, DONALD T.
PERSONAL Born 04/05/1943, New York, NY, d, 1 child **DISCIPLINE** RELIGIOUS EDUCATION AND RELIGIOUS STUDIES **EDUCATION** Cathedral Col, Brooklyn, NY, BA, Philos, 64; Gregorian Univ, Rome, theol, STB, 66, STL, 75; New York Univ, PhD, relig educ, 84. **CAREER** Tchr, relig and latin, Xaverian High Sch, Brooklyn, NY, 73-; asst prin for supv, Xaverian High Sch, Brooklyn, NY, 75-77; adjunct lectr, relig dept, Syracuse Univ, 79-; adjunct asst prof, develop reading, NY City Tech Col, Brooklyn, NY, 73-. **HONORS AND AWARDS** Who's Who among students in Amer Univ, 77-78; Educr of the Yr, Asn of Tchrs of NY, 86; Educr of the Yr, Xaverian Brothers Sponsored Sch, 95; Who's Who among Amer Tchrs, 98. **MEMBERSHIPS** Amer Acad of Relig; Amer Class Leag; Asn of Prof and Res in Relig Educ; Asn for Supv and Curric Develop; Class Asn of the Empire State; Nat Cath Educ Asn; NY Metro Asn of Develop Educ; NY State Asn of Foreign Lang Tchrs; Relig Educ Asn of the US and Can. **RESEARCH** Religion and American culture; Religious education and ecumenism. **SELECTED PUBLICATIONS** Auth, Twenty-five Years of Religious Education in Catholic High Schools, PACE 25, Professional Approaches for Christ Educ, Mar, 96; auth, A Response to Dykstra: Youth and the Language of Faith, Relig Educ, 81, 188-193, 86; book rev, Ministries, James Dunning, Relig Educ, Summer, 81. **CONTACT ADDRESS** 601 79th St., Apt B16, Brooklyn, NY, 11209. **EMAIL** drussodr@aol.com

RUSSON, JOHN EDWARD
PERSONAL Born 06/11/1960, Regina, SK, Canada **DISCIPLINE** PHILOSOPHY **EDUCATION** Univ of Toronto, PhD, 90 **CAREER** Asst Prof, 95-pres, Penn St Univ; Asst Prof, 93-95, Acadia Univ; Asst Prof, 92-93, Univ of Toronto **HONORS AND AWARDS** SSHRCC Post Doc Fel, Harvard Univ, 90-92 **MEMBERSHIPS** Am Philos Assoc; Hegel Soc of Am; Canadian Philos Assoc **RESEARCH** Hegel; Phenomenology; Ritual; Mental illness; Ancient Philosophy; Embodiment **SELECTED PUBLICATIONS** Auth, The Self and its Body in Hegel's Phenomenology, Univ of Toronto Press, 97; Coauth, Hegel and the Tradiition, Univ of Toronto Press, 97; Coauth, Retracing the Platonic Text, Northwestern Univ Press **CONTACT ADDRESS** Dept. Of Philos, Pennsylvania State Univ, University Park, PA, 18802-5201. **EMAIL** jxr36@psu.edu

RUSSOW, LILLY-MARLENE
DISCIPLINE THE PHILOSOPHY OF MIND, ETHICS **EDUCATION** Princeton Univ, PhD. **CAREER** Assoc prof, Purdue Univ. **RESEARCH** Philosophy of mind; artificial intelligence and cognitive science; Hume; Merleau-Ponty. **SELECTED PUBLICATIONS** Coauth, Principles of Reasoning. **CONTACT ADDRESS** Dept of Philos, Purdue Univ, 1080 Schleman Hall, West Lafayette, IN, 47907-1080.

RUTHERFORD, DONALD P.
DISCIPLINE HISTORY OF MODERN PHILOSOPHY **EDUCATION** Univ CA, PhD, 88. **CAREER** Philos, Emory Univ. **SELECTED PUBLICATIONS** Auth, Leibniz and the Rational Order of Nature. **CONTACT ADDRESS** Emory Univ, Atlanta, GA, 30322-1950.

RUTHVEN, JON M.
DISCIPLINE SYSTEMATIC THEOLOGY **EDUCATION** Ctr Bible Col, BA; Trinity Evangel Divinity Sch, BD; Ctr Bible Col, MA; Inst Holy Land Stud, Hebrew Univ, Jerusalem; Marquette Univ, PhD. **CAREER** Assoc prof, 88. **SELECTED PUBLICATIONS** Contrib, articles in the Bible Dictionary of The Complete Biblical, Gospel Publ House, 90; Notes on the Book of James for the King's Bible, Thomas Nelson; auth, On the Cessation of the Charismata: The Protestant Polemic of Benjamin B. Warfield, Pneuma 12/1, 90; On the Cessation of the Charismata: The Protestant Polemic on Post-Biblical Miracles, Univ Sheffield Acad Press, 93. **CONTACT ADDRESS** Dept of Systematic Theology, Regent Univ, 1000 Regent Univ Dr, Virginia Beach, VA, 23464-9831.

RUTTER, IRVIN C.
PERSONAL Born 11/08/1909, New York, NY, m, 1938, 2 children **DISCIPLINE** LAW **EDUCATION** Columbia Univ, AB, 29, JD, 31. **CAREER** Law secy, SDist NY, US Dist Ct, 31-33; asst US atty, SDist NY, US Dept Justice, 34-40, spec asst to Atty Gen US, 40-42; chief enforcement atty, Off Price Admin, 42-44, chief hearing comnr, 44-46; pvt pract, NY, 46-56; prof, 56-66, Distinguished Prof Law, Col Law, Univ Cincinnati, 66-, Lectr, Practising Law Inst, 46-50; mem curric comt, Asn Am Law Schs, 61-62, chmn, 62-63; vis prof, Sch Law, Columbia Univ, 64. **SELECTED PUBLICATIONS** Auth, Law, Language, And Thinking Like A Lawyer/, Univ Cincinnati Law Rev, 1993. **CONTACT ADDRESS** Col of Law, Univ Cincinnati, Cincinnati, OH, 45221.

RYAN, DAVID L.
DISCIPLINE ADMINISTRATIVE LAW, CONSTITUTIONAL LAW (I AND II), AND ANTITRUST **CAREER** Law, Washburn Univ. **HONORS AND AWARDS** Ch the Administrative Law Committee the Judicial Council, a mem the KS Bar Asn J Board Ed(s) and serves as Counsel to the Topeka Metropolitan Transit Authority. **SELECTED PUBLICATIONS** Auth, Kansas Administrative Law with Federal References; Vernon's Kansas Criminal Code Annotated and Code Criminal Profocedure. **CONTACT ADDRESS** Washburn Univ, 1700 SW College, Topeka, KS.

RYAN, EILISH
PERSONAL Born 05/22/1943, Birmingham, England, s **DISCIPLINE** PASTORAL THEOLOGY; CHRISTIAN SPIRTUALITY **EDUCATION** Univ of St Michael's Col, ThD, 94. **CAREER** Instr, 81-86, asst prof, 86-89, asst prof, 94-97, assoc prof, 97- , Univ of the Incarnate Word. **MEMBERSHIPS** AAR; CTSA; CTS. **RESEARCH** Contemporary Christian spirituality and theology; Practical theology **SELECTED PUBLICATIONS** Auth, Rosemary Haughton: Witness to Hope, Scheed, 97. **CONTACT ADDRESS** Univ of the Incarnate Word, 4301 Broadway, San Antonio, TX, 78209. **EMAIL** eryan@universe.uiwtx.edu

RYAN, EUGENE EDWARD
PERSONAL Born 11/27/1926, Chicago, IL, m, 1967, 2 children **DISCIPLINE** PHILOSOPHY **EDUCATION** St Mary of the Lake Sem, BA, 49; Gregorian Univ, PhL, 60, PhD(philos), 62. **CAREER** Instr philos, Marshall Univ, 67-68; from asst prof to assoc prof, 68-75, Prof Philos, East Carolina Univ, 75-, Chmn Dept, 79-, Vis fel, Inst Res Humanities, Univ Wis, 73-74; Nat Endowment of Humanities fel, 73-74. **MEMBERSHIPS** Am Philos Asn; Soc Ancient Greek Philos. **RESEARCH** Ancient Greek philosophy; Aristotle; medieval philosophy. **SELECTED PUBLICATIONS** Auth, Essays On Aristotle 'De Anima' - Nussbaum,Mc, Rorty,Ao/, Classical Bulletin, Vol 0069, 1993; 'On Ideas', Aristotle Criticism Of Plato Theory Of Forms - Fine,G/, Classical Bulletin, Vol 0070, 1994; Rhetorical Argumentation In Cavalcanti,Bartolomeo La 'Retorica' - The Enthymeme/, Rinascimento, Vol 0034, 1994. **CONTACT ADDRESS** Dept of Philos, East Carolina Univ, Greenville, NC, 27834.

RYAN, FRANK X.
PERSONAL Born 08/03/1952, Morristown, NJ, m, 1987, 3 children **DISCIPLINE** PHILOSOPHY **EDUCATION** Univ Colorado, BS, 74; Univ S Calif, BA, 83; Emory Univ, MA, 89, PhD, 96. **CAREER** Tchg assoc, Emory Univ, 88-91; instr, Georgia State Univ, 88-91; instr, Reinhardt Col, 88-91; instr, Auburn Univ, 92-97; asst prof, Kent State Univ, 97- . **HONORS AND AWARDS** Grad scholar and fel, 84-87; Outstanding Prof Award, 96; tchg award, Auburn Univ Student Govt Asn, 97; chemn Sem on Am Philos, NE Ohio Philos Consortium, 98. **MEMBERSHIPS** APA; Soc for Advan Am Philos; Charles S Peirce Soc; John Dewey Discussion List. **SELECTED PUBLICATIONS** Auth, Primary Experience as Settled Meaning, Philos Today, 94; auth, The Extreme Heresy of John Dewey and Arthur F. Bentley I: A Star-Crossed Collaboration?, Trans of the Charles S Peirce Soc, 97; auth, The Extreme Heresy of John Dewey and Arthur F. Bentley II: Knowing Knowing and the Known, Trans of the Charles S Peirce Soc, 97; auth, Affirming Dewey's Philosophy, A Rejoinder, Trans of the Charles S Peirce Soc, 97; contribur, Ginsberg, ed, Pragmatism: An Annotated Bibliography, 1898-1940, Rodopi, 98; auth, A Transactional Theory of Propositions, in Hester, ed, New Essays on Dewey's Logical Theory, Oxford, 98. **CONTACT ADDRESS** Dept of Philosophy, Kent State Univ, PO Box 5190, Kent, OH, 44242. **EMAIL** fryan@kent.edu

RYAN, HERBERT JOSEPH
PERSONAL Born 02/19/1931, Scarsdale, NY **DISCIPLINE** THEOLOGY, HISTORY **EDUCATION** Loyola Univ, Ill, AB, 54, MA, 60, PhL, 56; Woodstock Col, Md, STL, 63; Gregorian Univ, STD, 67. **CAREER** From asst prof to assoc prof hist theol, Woodstock Col, Md, 67- 74; assoc prof relig studies, 74-79, Prof Theol, Loyola Marymount Univ, 79-, Off Roman Cath observer, Lambeth Conf, 68; mem joint comn Anglican-Roman Cath relat, Roman Cath Bishops Comn Ecumenical, Affairs, 68-; convenor joint comn ministry & off observer Roman Cath Church, Gen Conv Episcopal Church, 69, 71 & 73; secretariat for promoting Christian unity, Anglican-Roman Cath Int Comn, 69-; vis lectr hist theol, Union Theol Sem, NY, 71-74; vis prof ecumenical & ascetical theol, Gen Theol Sem, 73-74. **HONORS AND AWARDS** Int Christian Unity Award, Graymoor Ecumenical Inst, 74; Medal Order St Augustine, Archbishop Canterbury, London, 81., STD, Gen Theol Sem, 73. **MEMBERSHIPS** Am Acad Relig; Cath Hist Soc; Cath Theol Soc Am; Church Hist Soc; N Am Acad Ecumenists; Mediaeval Acad Am. **RESEARCH** Anglican theological tradition; influence of St Augustine on Christian theology; methodology of ecumenical theology. **SELECTED PUBLICATIONS** Auth, Wolsey - Church, State And Art - Gunn,Sj, Lindley,Pg, Editors/, Theol Studies, Vol 0053, 1992; The Synods For The Carolingian Empire From Ad721 To Ad090 Held In France And In Italy - Ger - Hartmann,W/, Speculum-A J Of Medieval Studies, Vol 0067, 1992; The Renewal Of Anglicanism - Mcgrath,Ae/, Theol Studies, Vol 0055, 1994. **CONTACT ADDRESS** Dept of Relig Studies, Loyola Marymount Univ, 7900 Loyola Blvd, Los Angeles, CA, 90045.

RYAN, ROBERT M.
DISCIPLINE BRITISH ROMANTICISM, RELIGION IN LITERATURE **EDUCATION** Columbia Univ, PhD. **CAREER** Instr, Rutgers, State Univ NJ, Camden Col of Arts and Sci. **MEMBERSHIPS** Bd dir, Keats-Shelley Asn of Am, 19th-Century Stud Asn. **SELECTED PUBLICATIONS** Auth, Keats: The Religious Sense, Princeton Univ Press, 76; contribu, Mod Philol, keats-Shelley Jour, Wordsworth Circle, Jour of Rel. **CONTACT ADDRESS** Rutgers, State Univ NJ, Camden Col of Arts and Sci, New Brunswick, NJ, 08903-2101. **EMAIL** rmryan@camden.rutgers.edu

RYCHLAK, JOSEPH F.
DISCIPLINE CLINICAL PSYCHOLOGY **EDUCATION** OH State Univ, PhD (clinical psychology), 57. **CAREER** Asst prof psychol, FL State Univ, 57-58; asst prof psychol, WA State Univ, 58-61; assoc & full prof, St Louis Univ, 61-69; full prof, Purdue Univ, 69-83, interim head psychol dept, 79-80; Maude C Clarke prof Psychol, Loyola Univ of Chicago, 83-. **HONORS AND AWARDS** Donald Biggs-Gerald J Pine Award for Outstanding Scholarly Contribution to Counseling and Values, 88. **MEMBERSHIPS** Fel, Am Psychol Asn; fel, Am Psychol Soc. **RESEARCH** Agency in human behavior, learning, and memory. **SELECTED PUBLICATIONS** Auth, Artificial Intelligence and Human Reason: A Teleological Critique, Columbia Univ Press, 91; Logical Learning Theory: A Human Teleology and Its Empirical Support, Univ NE Press, 94; In Defense of Human Consciousness, Am Psychol Asn Press, 97. **CONTACT ADDRESS** Dept of Psychology, Loyola Univ, Chicago, 6526 N Sheridan Rd, Chicago, IL, 60626. **EMAIL** jrychla@luc.edu

RYDER, JOHN
PERSONAL Born 09/29/1951, New York, NY, m, 1985 **DISCIPLINE** PHILOSOPHY **EDUCATION** SUNY Stony Brook, PhD, 82. **CAREER** Lectr to prof, SUNY Cortland, 80-; dean of arts and sci, SUNY Cortland, 96-. **MEMBERSHIPS** Amer Philos Asn; Soc for the Adv of Amer Philos; Soc for the Philos Study of Marxism; Alliance of Univ for Democracy. **RESEARCH** History of American philosophy; Philosophy of education. **SELECTED PUBLICATIONS** Ed, American Philosophic Naturalism in the 20th Century, Prometheus Books, Jul, 94; ed, Contemporary Philosophy in Eastern Europe, Metaphilosophy, v 25, n 2&3, 94; article, Yuri K. Melvil and American Pragmatism, Trans of the Charles S. Peirce Soc, vol XXXII, no 4, 598-632, 96; article, Cadwallader, Colden, Samuel Johnson, and the Activity of Matter: Materialism and Idealism in 18th Century Colonial American Thought, Trans of the Charles S. Peirce Soc, vol XXXII, no 2, 248-272, 96; article, The Use and Abuse of Modernity: Postmodernism and the American Philosophic Tradition, Jour of Speculative Philos, vol VII, no 2, 92-102, 93, reprinted, Philos in Experience: Amer Philos in Trans, Fordham Univ Press, 97; transl, Women and Patriarchy, Women's Studies Intl Forum, vol 16, no 1, 57-63, 93; article, Contradictions in American Culture, Frontiers in Amer Philos, Tex A&M Univ Press, 92; rev, Nature and Spirit, Metaphilosophy, vol 26, no 1&2, 138-146, 95; rev, Psychology and Nihilism, Jour of Speculative Philos, vol X, no 2, 153-159, 96; rev, War and Democracy, Soc for the Adv of Amer Philos Book Rev, 93. **CONTACT ADDRESS** Dean of Arts & Sciences, SUNY Cortland, Cortland, NY, 13045. **EMAIL** ryderj@cortland.edu

RYOU, DANIEL H.
PERSONAL Born 10/12/1953, Seoul, Korea, m, 1980, 4 children **DISCIPLINE** OLD TESTAMENT **EDUCATION** Calvin Theol Sem, MDiv, 84, ThM, 86; Free Univ, Amsterdam, PhD, theol, 94. **CAREER** Assoc prof, 95-, OT & Hebrew, Christian Theol Sem, Seoul Korea. **MEMBERSHIPS** SBL **RESEARCH** Prophetic literature; Hebrew syntax (text-linguistic). **SELECTED PUBLICATIONS** Auth, Zephaniah's Oracles Against the Notions, Bibl Inter Ser 13, EJ Brill, 95. **CONTACT ADDRESS** 2223 Rowland Dr SE, Grand Rapids, MI, 49546. **EMAIL** dhryou@hotmail.com

RYSKAMP, GEORGE R.
PERSONAL Born 05/06/1950, Detroit, MI, m, 1975, 4 children **DISCIPLINE** LAW **EDUCATION** Brigham Young Univ, BA, 74, JD, 79. **CAREER** Acredited Genealogist, 75-, Spain; prvt law pract, 79-93, Riverside CA; cert estate plan & probate spec, 91-93, CA; City Attny, 82-92, Beaumont CA; asst prof, 93-, Brigham Young Univ. **RESEARCH** Family history in S Europe and Latin Amer; legal hist in the US as it relates to record creation, Spanish borderlands study. **CONTACT ADDRESS** 334 KMB BYU, Provo, UT, 84602. **EMAIL** ryskamp@byu.edu

RYZL, MILAN
PERSONAL Born 05/22/1928, Prague, Czechoslovakia, m, 1951, 3 children **DISCIPLINE** PHYSICS, CHEMISTRY **EDUCATION** Charles' Univ Prague, Czech Republic, RNDr, equiv to PhD, 92. **CAREER** Instr Biol, Czechoslovak Acad Sci, 67; Corr Res Assoc Parapsychology Lab, Duke Univ Durham NC; Tchg Psotions: San Diego State Univ, San Jose State Univ, Univ of California, Santa Barbara, CA, J F Kennedy Univ Orinda, CA, retired. **HONORS AND AWARDS** Wm McDougall Award, parasychological Res, 92. **MEMBERSHIPS** Parapsychol Assoc. **RESEARCH** Extra-sensory perception, its develo in hypnosis and its soc significance. **SELECTED PUBLICATIONS** Over 100 res papers; Parapsychologh; A scientific Approach, Hawthorn, NY 70; Das grosse Handbuch der Parapsychologie, Ariston Verlag, Munchen Germany, 97; as of Agust 98: total of 15 books(including 3 text books) on experimental parapsycholog and its relation to religion; published in 15 languages. **CONTACT ADDRESS** Westgate Station, PO Box 9459, San Jose, CA, 95157.

S

SAATKAMP, HERMAN J.
PERSONAL Born 09/29/1942, Knoxville, IN, m, 1964, 2 children **DISCIPLINE** PHILOSOPHY **EDUCATION** Vanderbilt Univ, PhD, 72. **CAREER** Dana Prof, 81-85, Chmn Humanities Div, 83-85, Univ of Tampa FL; Dept Head, Phil & Human, 85-94, Dept Head, Human in Med, 96-98, Texas A&M Univ; Dean, Prof, Indiana Univ, 98-. **HONORS AND AWARDS** NEH; faculty development grant, Univ of Tampa, 81; General Electric grant, 76; NDEA fel, 68-70; Vanderbilt Univ fel, 67-68; Phi Kappa Phi, 88; Phi Beta Delta, 87; Outstanding Educators of Amer, 73; Outstanding Fac Mem, 72. **MEMBERSHIPS** APA; Arts Coun of Brazos Valley; Assoc for Comp and the Human; Assoc for Documentary Editing; Assoc for Lit and Ling Comput; The Bibliographical Soc of the Univ of Virginia; Bryan-College Station Sister City Asn; Inst for the Humanities at Salado; Interdisciplinary Group for Hist Lit Stud Texas A&M Univ. **RESEARCH** American philosophy; genetics **SELECTED PUBLICATIONS** Coauth, Frontiers in American Philosophy, Vol I, Texas A&M Press, 92; The Works of George Santayana, InteLex, 96; Coauth, Frontiers in American Philosophy, Vol II, Texas A&M Press, 96. **CONTACT ADDRESS** Dean, School of Liberal Arts/IUPUI, 425 University Blvd, Rm 441, Indianapolis, IN, 46202-5140. **EMAIL** hsaatkam@iupui.edu

SABLE, THOMAS F.
PERSONAL Born 08/16/1945, Rochester, NY **DISCIPLINE** THEOLOGY **EDUCATION** Boston Col, BA, 69; Georgetown Univ, MS, 73; Jesuit Sch Theol, MDiv, 75; Graduate Theol Union, PhD, 83. **CAREER** Adj faculty, Fordham Univ, 82-85; assoc prof, Univ Scranton, 85- . **MEMBERSHIPS** Amer Cath Hist Assoc. **RESEARCH** American Catholic history; Byzantine theology. **SELECTED PUBLICATIONS** Auth, Uniate Churches, The Encyclopedia of Relig, Macmillan & Co, 85; Eastern-Rite Catholics, Kenrick, Peter Richard, Knights of Labor, McCloskey, John, McMaster, James Alphonsus, Satolli, Francesco, & Wimmer, Bonifact, in dictionary of Christianity in American, InterVarsity Press, 90; The Spirituality of the Christian East: A Systematic Handbook, rev, Diakonia, 94-95. **CONTACT ADDRESS** Univ of Scranton, T-362A, Scranton, PA, 18510. **EMAIL** sable@uofs.edu

SACHS, JOHN R.
PERSONAL Born 12/09/1948, Chicago, IL **DISCIPLINE** SYSTEMATIC THEOLOGY **EDUCATION** Boston Col, AB, 69, MA, 73; Weston Jesuit School Theol, MDiv, 76; Tubingen, ThD, 84. **CAREER** Asst prof, Fairfield Univ, 84-86; asst prof, 86-93, assoc prof, 94-, adac dean, 99-, Weston Jesuit School Theol. **MEMBERSHIPS** AAR; CTSA. **RESEARCH** Trinity; Creation; Eschatology; Spirituality. **SELECTED PUBLICATIONS** Auth The Christian Vision of Humanity: Basic Christian Anthropology, Liturgical Press, 91; And God saw it was good: Spirituality for an Ecological Age, Handbook of Spirituality for Ministers, Paulist Press, 95; Ignatian Mysticism, The Supplement to The Way, 95; Do not Stifle the Spirit: Karl Rahner, The Legacy of Vatican II, and its Urgency for Theology Today, CTSA Proceedings, 96; Trinity and Communications: the Mystery and Task of Self-Communication, Budhi, 97. **CONTACT ADDRESS** 3 Phillips Pl, Cambridge, MA, 02138. **EMAIL** sachser@aol.com

SACHS, MENDEL
PERSONAL Born 04/13/1927, Portland, OR, m, 1952, 4 children **DISCIPLINE** PHYSICS **EDUCATION** Univ Calif, AB, 49, MA, 50, PhD, 54. **CAREER** Theoretical physicist, Univ Calif Rad Lab, 54-56; asst prof, San Jose State Col, 56-61; assoc prof, Boston Univ, 62-66; prof physics, 66-97, emeritus prof physics, State Univ New York-Buffalo, 97-. **RESEARCH** Theoretical physics (general relativity, astrophysics, particle physics); philosophy of physics. **SELECTED PUBLICATIONS** Auth, General Relativity and Matter, Reidel, 82; auth, Quantum Mechanics from General Relativity, Reidel, 86; auth, Einstein Versus Bohr, Open Court, 88; auth, Relativity in Our Time, Francis and Taylor, 93; auth, Dialogues on Modern Physics, World Scientific, 98. **CONTACT ADDRESS** Dept Physics, SUNY/Buffalo, Buffalo, NY, 14260. **EMAIL** msachs@acsu.buffalo.edu

SACHS, WILLIAM L.
PERSONAL Born 08/23/1947, Richmond, VA, m, 1986, 1 child **DISCIPLINE** HISTORY OF CHRISTIANITY **EDUCATION** Baylor, BA, 69; Vanderbilt Univ, MDiv, 72; Yale Univ, STM, 73; Univ Chicago, PhD, 81. **CAREER** Adj fac of Union Sem and Univ Richmond; consult for Lilly Endowment and Episcopal Church Found; Episcopal parish priest, 73- . **RESEARCH** English and American evangelicism; religious leadership; Anglican communion. **SELECTED PUBLICATIONS** Auth, The Transformation of Anglicanism, Cambridge; auth, Of One Body, John Knox. **CONTACT ADDRESS** 36 New Canaan Rd, Wilton, CT, 06897. **EMAIL** wls@aol.com

SACKSTEDER, WILLIAM
PERSONAL Born 05/30/1925, Muncie, IN, m, 3 children **DISCIPLINE** PHILOSOPHY **EDUCATION** Univ Chicago, PhB, 46, MA, 49, PhD, 53. **CAREER** Instr in philos, 49-50, IL Inst Technology; asst in philos, 49-52, Univ Chicago; instr, asst prof, assoc prof, full prof, 52-90, prof emeritus, 90-, Univ Co; vis lect, 57, Univ CA, Berkeley; asst prof, 77, Univ Graz, Austria **HONORS AND AWARDS** Phi Beta Kappa, 49. **MEMBERSHIPS** APA; Mt/Plains Philos Asn. **RESEARCH** Hist of philos; ethics; major philosophers. **SELECTED PUBLICATIONS** Auth, Hobbes Bibliography, 1879-1979; auth, The Philosopher in the Community. **CONTACT ADDRESS** 325 Hopi Pl, Boulder, CO, 80303.

SADE, ROBERT
PERSONAL Born 09/23/1938, MA, m **DISCIPLINE** MEDICINE **EDUCATION** Wesleyan Univ, BA, 59; Columbia Univ, MD, 63 **CAREER** Asst Prof of Surgery, 73-75, Harvard Med Sch; Assoc Prof of Surgery, 75-81, Med Univ of SC; Prof of Surgery, 81-pres; Med Univ of SC; dir, 94-, Inst of Human Values in Health Care **HONORS AND AWARDS** Alpha Omega Alpha; 82 **MEMBERSHIPS** Am Assoc for Theor Surgery; Soc of Theor Surgeons; Soc of Univ Surgeons **RESEARCH** Health Policy and Bioethics; Cardiac Surgery **SELECTED PUBLICATIONS** Auth, Blackstone EH, 93; Auth, Freedom RM, Blackstone EH, 93; Auth, Pediatric Cardiac Surgery, Mosby Year Book Inc, 94, 512-15 **CONTACT ADDRESS** 171 Ashley Ave, Charleston, SC, 29401. **EMAIL** sader@musc.edu

SAENZ, MARIO
PERSONAL Born 04/01/1956, Cali, Colombia, m, 1983, 1 child **DISCIPLINE** PHILOSOPHY **EDUCATION** Southern Ill Univ, PhD, 85 **CAREER** Instr, St Augustine Comm Col, 86-87; lctr, Loyola Univ, 87; visiting asst prof, Earlham Col, 87-89; assoc prof, Le Moyne Col, 89- **MEMBERSHIPS** Amer Philos Assoc; Amer Acad Relig **RESEARCH** Latin American Philosophy **SELECTED PUBLICATIONS** Auth, "Dussel on Marx: Dussel's Conceptualization of Living Labor and the Materiality of Life," Thinking from the Underside of History: Enrique Dussel's Philosophy of Liberation, Rowman & Littlefield, forthcoming; "Rigoberta Menchu: "A quien muy pronto le nacio la conciencia," Las desobedientes: biografias sobre mujeres Latinoamericanas, Editorial Panamericana, 97; auth, "Philosophy of Liberation and Modernity: The Case of Latin America," Philos Today, 94 **CONTACT ADDRESS** Dept Philos, LeMoyne Col, Syracuse, NY, 13214. **EMAIL** saenz@maple.lemoyne.edu

SAFFIRE, PAULA REINER
PERSONAL Born 09/05/1943, NJ, s, 2 children **DISCIPLINE** CLASSICS AND PHILOSOPHY **EDUCATION** Mount Holyoke Col, BA, 65; Harvard, PhD, 76. **CAREER** Assoc Prof, Butler Univ, 89-. **HONORS AND AWARDS** Writing Across the Curriculum Awd, Butler Univ; Creative Tchr Awd; Indiana Classical Conference. **MEMBERSHIPS** APA, CAMUS, ICC **RESEARCH** Sappho; tragedy; mythology; pedagogy; performance. **SELECTED PUBLICATIONS** Auth, Aristotle on Personality and Some Implications for Friendship, in: Ancient Phil, 91; auth, Ancient Greek Alive, Aldine Press, 92; Coauth, Deduke men a Selanna: The Pleiades Mid-Sky, Mnemosyne, 93; auth, Whip, Whipped and Doctors: Homers Iliad and Camus the Plague, Interpretations, 94. **CONTACT ADDRESS** Dept of Classics, Butler Univ, 4600 Sunset Ave, Indianapolis, IN, 46208. **EMAIL** psaffire@butler.edu

SAGER, ALLAN HENRY
PERSONAL Born 08/29/1934, Boerne, TX, m, 1959, 2 children **DISCIPLINE** THEOLOGY, SPEECH COMMUNICATIONS, SPIRITUALITY **EDUCATION** Tex Lutheran Univ, BA, 55; Wartburg Theol Seminary, BD, 59; Northwestern Univ, Evanston, MA, 60, PhD, 63. **CAREER** Assoc pastor, Trinity Lutheran Church, Ft Worth, Tex, 63-65, sr pastor, 65-72; prof contextual educ, Trinity Lutheran Sem, 72- **MEMBERSHIPS** Speech Commun Asn; Lutheran Acad Scholar; Asn Theol Field Educ; Enneagram Asn. **RESEARCH** Contextual education; homiletics; communications; spirituality. **SELECTED PUBLICATIONS** Auth, The fundamentalist-modernist controversy, 1918-1930, in Preaching in American History, 69 & Sermons in American History, 71, Abingdon; Modernists and fundamentalists debate restraints on freedom, in America in Controversy: History of American Public Address, W C Brown, 73; Augsburg Sermons: Epistles, Series A, 77, Old Testament, Series C, 79, Old Testament, Series A, 80 & Old Testament, Series B, 81, Augsburg Publ House; Gospel-Centered Spirituality, Augsberg, 90. **CONTACT ADDRESS** Trinity Lutheran Sem, 2199 E Main St, Columbus, OH, 43209-2334. **EMAIL** asager@trinity.capital.edu

SAGOFF, MARK
PERSONAL Born 11/29/1941, Boston, MA, m, 1984, 2 children **DISCIPLINE** PHILOSOPHY **EDUCATION** Harvard Univ, BA, 63; Columbia Univ, MA, 65; Univ of Rochester, PhD, 70. **CAREER** Princeton Univ, lectr, 68-69; Univ of Pennsylvania, asst prof, 69-75; Univ of Wisconsin Madison, vis asst prof, 75-76; Cornell Univ, asst prof, 76-78; Center for Philos and Pub Policy, res scholar, 79-88; Maryland Law Sch, lectr, 82-84 & 89; Inst for Philos and Pub Policy, dir, sr res scholar, 88-95, 88-. **HONORS AND AWARDS** Pew Scholars Award, Woodrow Wilson Center fel. **MEMBERSHIPS** ISEE, Hastings Center Fellow. **RESEARCH** International environmental ethics; philosophy; law and technology. **SELECTED PUBLICATIONS** Auth, The Economy of the Earth: Philosophy, Law and the Environment, New York: Cambridge Univ Press, 88; auth, On the Value of Endangered and other Species, Environmental Management, 96; auth, Patented Genes: An Ethical Appraisal, Issues in Science and Technology, 98; auth, Aggregation and Deliberation in Valuing Environmental Public Goods: A Look Beyond Contingent Pricing, Ecological Economics, 98; auth, Is the Economy Too Big for the Environment? Environmental Ethics and the Global Marketplace, eds. D. Dallmeyer and A. Ike, Athens GA: Univ of Georgia Press, 98. **CONTACT ADDRESS** Inst for Philosophy and Public Policy, College Park, MD, 20742. **EMAIL** msagoff@puafmail.umd.edu

SAHADAT, JOHN
PERSONAL Born 02/22/1936, Trinidad and Tobago, m, 1987 **DISCIPLINE** THEOLOGY **EDUCATION** Laurentian Univ, BA, 66; Banaras Hindu Univ (India), MA, 69; Univ of Lancaster (UK), PhD, 75. **CAREER** Prof, 70-, Univ Sudbury Col in Laurentian Univ. **HONORS AND AWARDS** The Thorneloe Univ Mitre Award for Teaching Excellence, 97. **MEMBERSHIPS** Canadian Soc for the Study of Religion; Amer Acad of Religion **RESEARCH** Cross Cultural study of Salvation; interreligious dialogue **SELECTED PUBLICATIONS** Auth, Religion and the Metaphysics of One, Vidyajyoti 58, 94; The Ontological and Functional in Islam, Islamic Univ, 95; Religious Influence in the Rise of Indian Nationalism, Asian Thought and Society, 95; The Indian Contribution to Harmony in Diversity, Indo Caribbean Review, 96; Divine Revelation and the Status of the Qur'an, Muslim Educational Quarterly, 96; Swidlerian and Jain Prolegomenon to Dialogue, Journal of Ecumenical Studies, 97; Islamic Education: A Challenge to Conscience, The American Journal of Islamic Social Sciences, 97. **CONTACT ADDRESS** Dept of Religious Studies, Sudbury Col, Laurentian Univ, Sudbury, ON, P3E 2C6. **EMAIL** jsahadat@nickel.laurentian.ca

SAHADAT, JOHN
DISCIPLINE RELIGIOUS STUDIES **EDUCATION** Lancaster Univ, PhD. **RESEARCH** Comparative study of religions; comparative mystical philosophies. **SELECTED PUBLICATIONS** Auth, Religion and the Metaphysics of the One, Vidyajyoti, 94; art, Tawhid: The Affirmation of Affirmations and the Negation of Affirmations, Muslim Edu Quarterly, 93. **CONTACT ADDRESS** Religious Studies Dept, Laurentian Univ, 935 Ramsey Lake Rd, Sudbury, ON, P3E 2C6.

SAKEZLES, PRISCILLA
PERSONAL Born 04/12/1962, Tampa, FL **DISCIPLINE** PHILOSOPHY **EDUCATION** Univ S Fla, BA, 86, MA, 89; Fla State Univ, PhD, 93. **CAREER** Asst prof, Mich State Univ, 93-94; asst prof, Millsaps Col, 94-95; asst prof, Univ Akron, 95-; Univ Akron Fac Res grant, 97 & 98. **MEMBERSHIPS** Am Philos Asn; Soc Ancient Greek Philos; Soc Women Philos. **RESEARCH** Ancient philosophy **SELECTED PUBLICATIONS** Auth Pyrrhonian Indeterminacy: A Pragmatic Interpretation, Apeiron, 93; Bringing Ancient Philosophy to Life: Teaching Aristotelian and Stoic Theories of Responsibility, Teaching Philosophy, 97; rev Stoics, Epicureans and Sceptics, Rphilos in Rev, 97; rev The Sceptics, Ancient Philos, 98; auth Aristotle and Chrysippus on the Physiology of Human Action, Apeiron, 98. **CONTACT ADDRESS** Dept of Philosophy, Univ Akron, Akron, OH, 44325-1903. **EMAIL** psakezles@uakron.edu

SAKS, ELYN R.
DISCIPLINE FAMILY LAW **EDUCATION** Vanderbilt Univ, BA,77; Oxford Univ, MLitt,81; Yale Univ, JD,86.. **CAREER** Orrin B. Evans prof Law, Univ Southern Calif; Psychiatry & Behavioral Sci; Marshall Scholar, Oxford Univ; practd family law with Conn Legal Serv; fac, Inst Psychiatry and the Law, USC Sch Med. **SELECTED PUBLICATIONS** Auth, Multiple Personality Disorder and Criminal Responsibility & Competency to Refuse Psychotropic Medication: Three Alternatives to the Law's Cognitive Standard; coauth, Jekyll on Trial: Multiple Personality Disorder and Criminal Law. **CONTACT ADDRESS** School of Law, Univ Southern Calif, University Park Campus, Los Angeles, CA, 90089. **EMAIL** esaks@law.usc.edu.

SALE, MARY
PERSONAL Born 11/27/1929, New Haven, CT **DISCIPLINE** PHILOSOPHY; CLASSICS **EDUCATION** BA, 51, MA, 54, PhD, 58, Cornell Univ. **CAREER** Instr, Yale Univ, 57-58; Instr, 58-59, Asst Prof, 59-64, Assoc Prof, 64-75, Prof, 75-, Washington Univ. **MEMBERSHIPS** London Inst of Classical Studies; Honorary Fel, Univ Wales, Univ College Cardiff. **RESEARCH** Philosophy; Classics **SELECTED PUBLICATIONS** Auth, Homer, Iliad, Odyssey, Reader's Guide to World Literature, 93; Homer and the Roland: the Shared Formulary Technique, Oral Tradition, 93; The Government of Troy: Politics in the Illiad, Greek, Roman and Byzantine Studies, 94; Homer and Avdo: Investigating Orality through External Consistency, Voice into Text, 96; In Defense of Milman Parry, Oral Tradition, 96; Virgil's Formularity and Pius Aeneas, Epos and Logos, 98. **CONTACT ADDRESS** 2342 Albion Pl, St. Louis, MO, 63104. **EMAIL** Aperkins@midwest.net

SALIBA, JOHN A.
PERSONAL Born 04/16/1937, Valletta, Malta **DISCIPLINE** RELIGION **EDUCATION** Heythrop Col, licentiates philos, 60, theol, 66; Oxford Univ, dipl anthrop, 62; Cath Univ Am, PhD relig educ, 71. **CAREER** From asst prof to prof relig studies, Univ Detroit Mercy. **MEMBERSHIPS** Am Acad Relig; Soc Sci Study Relig; Asn Sociol Relig; Soc Hindu-Christian Studies. **RESEARCH** Contemporary religious movements; religious education; anthropology of religion. **SELECTED PUBLICATIONS** Auth, Au Carrefour des Verites: Un Approach Chretienne des Nouvelles Religions, 94; auth, Perspectives on New Religious Movement, 95; auth, Signs of the Times: The New Religious Movements in Theological Perspective, 96; auth, Christian Responses to the New Age Movement: A Critical Assessment, 98; auth, The New Religions and Mental Health, Relig & Soc Order, 93; auth, Dialogue with the New Religious Movements: Issues and Prospects, Jour Ecumenical Studies, Winter, 93; auth, Magical Thinking in Contemporary Western Societies: A Psychological View, Le Defi Magique: Esoterisme, Occultisme, Spiritism, 94; auth, Official Catholic Responses to the New Religious Movements, Anti-Cult Movements in Cross-Cultural Perspective, 94; auth, Religious Dimensions of UFO Phenomena and The UFO Contactee Phenomenon from a Sociopsychological Perspective: A Review, The Gods Have Landed, 95; auth, Scholarly Studies on the Children of God/The Family: A Comprehensive Survey, Sex, Sin & Salvation: Investigating the Family/Children of God, 95; auth, Dialogue with the International Society for Krishna Consciousness (ISKCON): A Roman Catholic Perspectives, Croyances et Societes, 98. **CONTACT ADDRESS** Dept of Religious Studies, Univ of Detroit Mercy, 4001 W McNichols Rd., Detroit, MI, 48219-3599. **EMAIL** salibaja@udmercy.edu

SALIBA, JOHN A.
DISCIPLINE RELIGIOUS STUDIES **EDUCATION** Cath Univ Am, PhD. **CAREER** Prof; Univ Detroit Mercy, 70-. **RESEARCH** World religions, anthropology of religion, and new religious movements. **CONTACT ADDRESS** Dept of Religious Studies, Univ of Detroit Mercy, 4001 W McNichols Rd, PO Box 19900, Detroit, MI, 48219-0900. **EMAIL** SALIBAJA@udmercy.edu

SALIERS, DON E.
PERSONAL Born 08/11/1937, Fostoria, OH, m, 1959, 4 children **DISCIPLINE** PHILOSOPHICAL THEOLOGY **EDUCATION** Ohio Wesleyan Univ, BA, 59; Yale Divinity Schl, BD, 62; St Johns Cambridge Univ, grad fel, 64-65; Yale Univ, PhD, 67 **CAREER** Instr, asst, assoc prof, 66-74, Yale Divinity Schl; prof, theol & worship, 74-, Franklin Parker Chmn, 96-, dir MSM prog, Emory Univ, Chandler Schl of Theol; vis prof, liturgy, St Johns Univ, Notre Dame. **HONORS AND AWARDS** Phi Beta Kappa; Fulbright Fel, Emory Williams Tchng Award; Berakah Award (NAAL), Dist Alumnus (OWU); Henry Luce III Fel. **MEMBERSHIPS** N Amer Acad of Liturgy; Soc for Stud of Christian Spirituality; AAR; Societas Liturgica; Charles Wesley Soc; Assn of Anglican Musicians. **RESEARCH** Contemporary issues in liturgical theology; relig discourse and human emotion; theology and aesthetics: doxa, beauty, holiness. **SELECTED PUBLICATIONS** Auth, The Soul In Paraphrase: Prayer and the Religious Affections, OSL Pub, 92; auth, Worship as Theology: Foretaste of Glory Divine, Abingdon, 94; auth, Liturgy As Holy Play, Communion, Community, Commonweal, Upper RmBks, 95; auth, Worship and Spirituality, OSL Pub, 96; auth, Worship Come To Its Senses, Abingdon Press, 96; art, Divine Grace, Diverse Means: Sunday Worship in Unite Methodist Congregations, Sunday Svcs of the Methodists: 20th Century Worship in Worldwide Methodism, Abingdon: Kingswood Bks, 96; art, Singing Our Lives, Practicing Our Faith: A Way of Life for a Searching People, Jossey-Bass Pub, 96; art, Liturgy As Art, & David's Song In Our Land, Landscape of Praise: Readings in Liturgical Renewal, Trinity Press Intl, 96; art, Musique Liturgique et Techniques Electroniques, La Maison-dieu, 212, 97; coauth, Human Disability and the Service of God: Reassessing Religious Practice, Abingdon, 98; art, Afterword: Liturgy and Ethics Revisited, Liturgy and the Moral Self: Humanity at Full Stretch Before God, Liturgical Press 98. **CONTACT ADDRESS** Chandler Sch of Theology, Emory Univ, 302 Cannon Chapel Bldg, Atlanta, GA, 30322. **EMAIL** dsalier@emory.edu

SALLA, MICHAEL
DISCIPLINE INTERNATIONAL LAW AND ORGANIZATION **EDUCATION** Univ Melbourne, BA, BS, MA; Univ

Queensland, PhD. **CAREER** Prof, Am Univ. **RESEARCH** Peace and conflict studies; religious nationalism, and politics of nonviolent action. **SELECTED PUBLICATIONS** Auth, Islamic Radicalism, Muslim Nations and the West; Co-ed, Why the Cold War Ended; Essays on Peace:Paradigms for a New World Order. **CONTACT ADDRESS** American Univ, 4400 Massachusetts Ave, Washington, DC, 20016.

SALLIS, JOHN C.
PERSONAL Born 06/08/1938, Poplar Grove, AK, m, 1959, 2 children **DISCIPLINE** PHILOSOPHY **EDUCATION** Univ Arkansas, BA, 59; Tulane Univ, MA, 62, PhD, 64. **CAREER** Instr, phil, 64-66, Univ South; assoc prof, 66-70, prof, 70-83, chmn, phil, 78-83, Duquesne Univ; Arthur J. Schmitt Prof, phil, 83-90, Loyola Univ; W. Alton Jones Prof, phil, 90-95, Vanderbilt Univ; prof, liberal arts, 96-, Penn St Univ. **HONORS AND AWARDS** Alexander von Humboldt-Stiftung grant, res Hegel Archiv, Ruhr-Univ Bochum, Germany; Amer Council of Learned Soc Fel, 82-83; Fritz Thyssen-Stiftung Res Grant, 79; Alexander von Humboldt-Stiftung Dozentenstipendium, 74-75. **MEMBERSHIPS** APA; Hegel Soc of Amer; Heidegger Conf; Metaphysical soc; Soc for Phenomenology & Existential Phil. **RESEARCH** Ancient phil; German idealism; contemp continental phil; phil of art. **SELECTED PUBLICATIONS** Auth, Echoes: After Heidegger, IN Univ Press, 90; auth, Crossings: Nietzsche and the Space of Tragedy, Univ Chicago Press, 91; ed, Reading Heidegger: Commemorations, IN Univ Press, 93; auth, Stone, IN Univ Press, 94; auth, Delimitations: Phenomenology and the End of Metaphysics, IN Univ Press, 95; auth, Double Truth, Albany SUNY Press, 95; auth, Being and Logos: The Way of Platonic Dialogue, IN Univ Press, 96; auth, Shades: Of Painting at the Limit, IN Univ Press, 98. **CONTACT ADDRESS** Dept of Philosophy, Pennsylvania State Univ, 240 Sparks Bldg, University Park, PA, 16802. **EMAIL** jcs29@psu.edu

SALLSTROM, JOHN EMERY
PERSONAL Born 04/28/1939, Quincy, IL, m, 1969, 2 children **DISCIPLINE** PHILOSOPHY, RELIGION **EDUCATION** Elmhurst Col, BA, 61; Union Theol Sem, NY, MDiv, 64; Duke Univ, PhD(relig), 68. **CAREER** PROF & CHMN PHILOS & RELIG, GA COL & STATE UNIV, 67-, Minister, United Church Christ, 67-. **MEMBERSHIPS** Am Acad Relig, Am Philos Asn; Soc Christian Philosophers **CONTACT ADDRESS** Dept of Philos & Relig, Georgia Col, Campus Box 029, Milledgeville, GA, 31061-0490. **EMAIL** jsalstr@mail.gac.peachnet.edu

SALMON, NATHAN
PERSONAL Born 01/02/1951, Los Angeles, CA, m, 1980, 1 child **DISCIPLINE** PHILOSOPHY **EDUCATION** UCLA, MA, 73, MA, 74, CPhil, 77, PhD, 79. **CAREER** Instr, UCLA, 76 & 77; instr, 76-77, lectr, 77-78, Cal State Univ; asst prof, 78-82, vis sr res philos, 82, Princeton Univ; assoc prof UCLA-Riverside 82-84 & -Santa Barbara 84-85, Prof, 85-. **HONORS AND AWARDS** Univ Calif-Santa Barbara; Gustave O Arlt Award in Hum, 84; Fulbright Distinguished prof grant Yugoslavia, 86; Am Coun Learned Soc Travel grant, 90; res grants Princton Univ, 79-80 & Univ Cal, 82-92; Philos Perspectives lectr, Cal State Univ, 96. Aristotelian Soc Speaker, London, 88. **MEMBERSHIPS** Am Philos Asn; Hon Life Mem Royal Inst Philos. **RESEARCH** Analytic metaphysics; philosophy of language. **SELECTED PUBLICATIONS** Auth, A Problem in the Frege-Church Theory of Sense and Denotation, Nous, 93; Wholes, Parts, and Numbers, Philos Perspectives, Ridgeview Press, 97; Nonexistence, Nous, 98. **CONTACT ADDRESS** Dept of Philososphy, Univ Cal, Santa Barbara, CA, 93106. **EMAIL** nsalmon@humanitas.ucsb.edu

SALMON, WESLEY CHARLES
PERSONAL Born 08/09/1925, Detroit, MI, 1 child **DISCIPLINE** PHILOSOPHY OF SCIENCE **EDUCATION** Univ Chicago, MA, 47; Univ Calif, Los Angeles, PhD(philos), 50. **CAREER** Instr philos, Univ Calif, Los Angeles, 50-51; State Col Wash, 51-53, asst prof, 53-54; vis asst prof, Northwestern Univ, 54-55; asst prof, Brown Univ, 55-59, assoc prof, 59-63; prof philos sci & hist, Ind Univ, Bloomington, 63-67, Norwood Russell Hanson prof, 67-73; prof, Univ Ariz, 73-81; prof to univ prof philos, Univ Pittsburgh, 81-, Fund Advan Educ fac fel, 53-54; vis lectr, Univ Bristol, 59; mem Us Nat Comt, Int Union Hist & Philos Sci, 62-67, chmn, 66-67; vis res prof, Univ Minn, 63; vis prof, Univ Pittsburgh, 68-69 & Univ Melbourne, 78; fel, Am Acad Arts & Sci, 79, Am Asn Advan Sci, 81. **HONORS AND AWARDS** MA, Brown Univ, 59. **MEMBERSHIPS** Am Philos Asn; Philos Sci Asn (vpres, 67-69, pres, 71-72); Pac Div Am Philos Asn (vpres, 76-77, pres, 77-78); Int Union Hist & Philos Sci (vice-pres, 96-97; pres, 98-99), (Div of Logic, Methodology, and Philos of Sci, 1st vice-pres, 80-83; pres, 96-99). **RESEARCH** Probability, induction and confirmation; causality and scientific explanation. **SELECTED PUBLICATIONS** Auth, Logic, Prentice-Hall, 63, 3rd ed, 84; Foundations of Scientific Inference, Univ Pittsburgh, 67; ed, Zeno's Paradoxes, Bobbs-Merrill, 70; coauth, Statistical Explanation and Statistical Relevance, Univ Pittsburgh, 71; auth, Space, Time and Motion, Dickenson, 75, 2nd ed, 81; ed, Hans Reichenbach, Logical Empiricist, D Reidel Publ, 79; auth, Scientific Explanation and the Causal Structure of the World, Princeton, 84; co-ed, The Limitations of Deductivism, Calif, 88; auth, Four Decades of Scientific Explanation, Minn, 90; co-ed, Logic, Language, and the Structure of Scientific Theories, Konstanz, 94; co-ed, Scientific Explanation, Minn, 89; auth, Causality and Explanation, Oxford, 98. **CONTACT ADDRESS** Dept of Philos, Univ Pittsburgh, 1001 Cathedral/Learn, Pittsburgh, PA, 15260-0001. **EMAIL** wsalmont@pitt.edu

SALTZMAN, JUDY DEANE
PERSONAL Born 02/02/1942, San Jose, CA, m **DISCIPLINE** RELIGIOUS STUDIES, PHILOSOPHY OF RELIGION **EDUCATION** San Jose State Univ, BA, 63; Univ Calif, Berkeley, MA, 65; Univ Calif, Santa Barbara, MA & PhD, 77. **CAREER** Teaching asst social sci, Univ Calif, Berkeley, 65-66; Instr philos & sociol, Santa Barbara City Col, 66-67 & philos, 68-70; instr philos & relig, Ventura Community Col, 73-75; from Asst Prof to Assoc Prof, 75-85, Prof Philos, Calif Polytech State Univ, 85-. **HONORS AND AWARDS** Fulbright Schol, Freie Universitat, Berlin. **MEMBERSHIPS** Am Acad Relig; Soc Values Higher Educ; Soc Sci Study Relig; Western Asn Ger Studies; AAUP; Soc Asian and Comparative Philos. **RESEARCH** Neo-Kantian philosophy; German philosophy of religion and theology; sociology of religion; philosophies of India. **SELECTED PUBLICATIONS** Auth, The Young, Center Mag, 1/69; Simulation Gesellshaft Realitat, in Prioritaten Fur die Gesellshaft Politik, Verlag, 70; Paul Natorps philosophy of religion within the Marburg Neo-Kantian tradition, Olms Verlag, 81; The Individual and the Avatara in the Thought of Radhakrishman, India Books Centre, 95; Karma and Reincarnation in the West, 94, Transaction # 94 Indian Institute of World Culture; Plato and Vedanta: Tradition or Imagination? in Facets of Humanism, Indian Inst World Culture, Bangalore, 95. **CONTACT ADDRESS** Philos Dept, California Polytech State Univ, 1 Grand Ave, San Luis Obispo, CA, 93407-0001. **EMAIL** jsaltzma@calpoly.edu

SALTZMAN, ROBERT M.
DISCIPLINE LAW **EDUCATION** Dartmouth Col, BA,83; Harvard Univ, JD,87. **CAREER** Assoc dean and adj prof, Univ Southern Calif; private practice, Colorado law firm; past legal coun, Los Angeles Co; past supvr and spec coun, Los Angeles Co Dept Health Serv; responsible for stud serv at, Law Sch. **MEMBERSHIPS** Past mem, bd Trustees, Law Sch Admission Coun; bd Visitors, Rockefeller Ctr for Soc Sci at Dartmouth Col & ch, Section on Pre-Legal Educ & Admission to Law Sch Amer Asn Law Sch. **RESEARCH** Academic administration. He teaches Family Law, Property, Jurisprudence, and Community Property. **SELECTED PUBLICATIONS** Auth, Affirmative Action in Law School Admissions and Legal Employment: Facts, Observations, &Suggestions for Gatekeepers. **CONTACT ADDRESS** School of Law, Univ Southern Calif, University Park Campus, Los Angeles, CA, 90089. **EMAIL** esaks@law.usc.edu

SALZBERG, STEPHAN
DISCIPLINE LAW **EDUCATION** Rochester Univ, BA, 74; Univ British Columbia, MA, 83; Univ Wash, JD, 85. **CAREER** Prof. **HONORS AND AWARDS** Japanese Ministry of Education Graduate Research Fel, Kyoto Univ, 77-78, 1978-80 **RESEARCH** Comparative medical and mental health law; Japanese constitutional law; Japanese law and society. **SELECTED PUBLICATIONS** Auth, pubs about mental health law of Japan and Taiwan. **CONTACT ADDRESS** Fac of Law, Univ British Columbia, 1822 East Mall, Vancouver, BC, V6T 1Z1. **EMAIL** salzberg@law.ubc.ca

SALZMAN, JIM
DISCIPLINE U.S. AND INTERNATIONAL ENVIRONMENTAL LAW **EDUCATION** Yale Col, BA, 85; Harvard Law Sch, 89; Harvard Univ, Msc, JD, 90. **CAREER** Prof, Am Univ. **HONORS AND AWARDS** Fel, Royal Geog Soc, 95; Europ environ mgr, S.C. Johnson, 92-95; environ dir, OECD, 90-92; consult, UN Environment Program. **RESEARCH** Environmental law and policy. **SELECTED PUBLICATIONS** Auth, Environmental Labeling in OECD Countries, OECD, 91; Greener Product policy in Practice, Swedish Ministry Environ, 95; Setting Environmental Goals, Environmental Management, Croner Publ Ltd, 94. **CONTACT ADDRESS** American Univ, 4400 Massachusetts Ave, Washington, DC, 20016.

SAMAR, VINCENT J.
PERSONAL Born 02/12/1953, Syracuse, NY **DISCIPLINE** PHILOSOPHY **EDUCATION** Syracuse Univ, BA, 75, JD, MPA, 78; Univ Chicago, PhD, 86. **CAREER** Adj prof philos, Loyola Univ, 84- ; adj prof law, Ill Inst Technol, Chicago/Kent Col of Law, 90-. **HONORS AND AWARDS** BA, cum laude; ACLU for service as director. **MEMBERSHIPS** NY State Bar; Ill State Bar. **RESEARCH** Philosophy of law; political philosophy; ethics and constitutional law. **SELECTED PUBLICATIONS** Auth, the Right to Privacy: Gays, Lesbians, and the Constitution, Temple, 91; auth, Privacy and AIDS, Univ of West Los Angeles Law Rev, 91; auth, AIDS and the Politician's Right to Privacy, in Cohen, ed, AIDS: Crisis in Professional Ethics, Temple, 94; auth, A Moral Justification for Gay and Lesbian Civil Rights Legislation, Jour of Homosexuality, 94; auth, Justifying Judgment: Practicing Law and Philosophy. Kansas, 98. **CONTACT ADDRESS** Dept of Philosophy, Loyola Univ, 820 N Michigan Ave, Chicago, IL, 60611. **EMAIL** vsamar@luc.edu

SAMPLE, RUTH
PERSONAL Born 05/28/1964, Washington, DC, m, 1991 **DISCIPLINE** PHILOSOPHY **EDUCATION** Oberlin, BA; PhD. **CAREER** Asst prof, 3 yrs. **HONORS AND AWARDS** DAAD scholar; Mellon fel. **MEMBERSHIPS** APA. **RESEARCH** Social philosophy. **CONTACT ADDRESS** Dept of Philosophy, Univ of New Hampshire, Durham, NH, 03824.

SANDALOW, TERRANCE
PERSONAL Born 09/08/1934, Chicago, IL, m, 1955, 3 children **DISCIPLINE** LAW **EDUCATION** Univ Chicago, AB, 54, JD, 57. **CAREER** Prof law, Univ Minn, 61-66; prof, 66-78, Dean Law Sch, Univ Mich, Ann Arbor, 78-, Ctr Advan Studies Behav Sci fel, 72-73. **RESEARCH** Local government law; constitutional law; federal courts and the federal system. **SELECTED PUBLICATIONS** Auth, Soc-Justice And Fundamental Law - A Comment On Sager Constitution/, Northwestern Univ Law Rev, Vol 0088, 1993. **CONTACT ADDRESS** Law Sch, Univ of Michigan, 922 Legal Res Bldg, Ann Arbor, MI, 48104.

SANDER, FRANK E A
PERSONAL Born 07/22/1927, Stuttgart, Germany, m, 1958, 3 children **DISCIPLINE** LAW **EDUCATION** Harvard Univ, BA, 49, LLB, 52. **CAREER** Law clerk, US Ct of Appeals, 52-53; US Supreme Ct, 53-54; atty, Tax Div, US Dept Justice, 54-56; assoc, Hill & Harlow, Boston, 56; asst prof, 59-62, prof, 62-80, BUSSEY PROF LAW, HARVARD UNIV, 80-; Mem tax mission, Rep Colombia, 59; mem labor panel, Am Arbit Asn & Fed Mediation & Conciliation Serv, 60-; mem comt civil & polit rights, President's Comn Status Women, 61-63; consult, US Treas Dept, 67-68; chmn spec subcomt domestic relation probs, Am Bar Asn, 63-64; chmn, State Adv Bd Mass Dept Pub Welfare, 75-. **HONORS AND AWARDS** Phi Beta Kappa; Kutau Medal, ABA; CPR Int of Dep Res Prize. **MEMBERSHIPS** Am Bar Asn. **RESEARCH** Family law; welfare law; taxation. **SELECTED PUBLICATIONS** Co-ed, Readings in Federal Taxation, Foundation, 70; auth, Tax Aspects of Divorce, Bur Nat Affairs, 75; coauth, Cases and Materials in Family Law, Little, 76; Varieties of dispute processing, 70, Fed Rules Decision, III, 76; Report of Conference on minor disputes resolution, Am Bar Asn, 77; co-auth, Dispute Resolution, Little Brown, 92. **CONTACT ADDRESS** Law Sch, Harvard Univ, 1525 Massachusetts, Cambridge, MA, 02138-2903.

SANDERS, CHERYL J.
PERSONAL Washington, DC, m, 1982, 2 children **DISCIPLINE** APPLIED THEOLOGY **EDUCATION** Harvard Divinity School, M Div (cum laude), 80, ThD, 85. **CAREER** Asst prof to prof Christian Ethics, Howard Univ School of Divinity, 84-. **HONORS AND AWARDS** Minister of the Year Award, Nat Asn of Negro Business and Professional Women's Clubs, 94; Outstanding Author award, Howard Univ, 95. **MEMBERSHIPS** Am Academy Relig; Soc Christian Ethics. **RESEARCH** Christian ethics; African Am relig studies; wananist studies; biamedical ethics. **SELECTED PUBLICATIONS** Auth, Living the Intersection, Fortress Press, 95; Empowerment Ethics for a Liberated People, Fortress Press, 95; Saints in Exile, Oxford Univ Press, 96; Ministry at the Margins, Intervarsity Press, 97. **CONTACT ADDRESS** 7704 Morningside Dr NW, Washington, DC, 20012. **EMAIL** csanders@fac.howard.edu

SANDERS, DOUGLAS
DISCIPLINE LAW **EDUCATION** Univ Alberta, BA, 60; LLB, 61; Univ Ca, LLM, 63. **CAREER** Assoc prof, Windsor Univ, 69-72; assoc prof, 72-77; prof, 77-. **RESEARCH** Indigenous peoples; international human rights law; lesbian and gay issues; canadian feberalism. **SELECTED PUBLICATIONS** Auth, pubs about constitutional law, First Nation's legal issues, gays/lesbians and the law, and international human rights law. **CONTACT ADDRESS** Fac of Law, Univ British Columbia, 1822 East Mall, Vancouver, BC, V6T 1Z1. **EMAIL** sanders@law.ubc.ca

SANDERS, JACK THOMAS
PERSONAL Born 02/28/1935, Grand Prairie, TX, m, 1959, 1 child **DISCIPLINE** RELIGION **EDUCATION** Tex Wesleyan Col, BA, 56; Emory Univ, MDiv, 60; Claremont Grad Sch & Univ Ctr, PhD(relig), 63. **CAREER** Asst prof New Testament, Emory Univ, 64-67, Garrett Theol Sem, 67-68 & McCormick Theol Sem, 68-69; assoc prof, 69-75, chmn dept, 73-76 & 77-80, Prof Relig Studies, Univ Ore, 75-, Fulbright fel, Univ Tubingen, 63-64; corresp mem Inst Antiq & Christianity, Claremont Grad Sch, 69-73; mem policy bd, Dept Higher Educ, Nat Coun Churches of Christ, USA, 71-73; Danforth assoc, 71-76; res grant, Ctr Bibl Res & Archives, Soc Bibl Lit, 76-77. **MEMBERSHIPS** Soc Bibl Lit; Studiorum Novi Testament Soc; AAUP. **RESEARCH** New Testament; Judaism of second temple period. **SELECTED PUBLICATIONS** Auth, Between Synagogue And Government - Historical Situation Of Lukan Christians - Ger - Stegemann,W/, J Of Ecumenical Studies, Vol 0029, 1992; Christians And Jews In The Roman-Empire - A Conversation With Stark,Rodney/, Sociol Analysis, Vol 0053, 1992; Encounters Between Christianity And Judaism In Antiquity And In The Middle-Ages - Festschrift In Honor Of Schreckenberg,Heinz - Ger - Koch,Da, Lichtenberger,H, Editors/,

J Of Ecumenical Studies, Vol 0031, 1994; Jewish Responses To Early Christians - Hist And Polemics, 30-150ce - Setzer,Cj/, J Of Bibl Lit, Vol 0115, 1996; Pagans - Jews, Christians And The Issue Of The Stranger - Ger - Feldmeier,R, Heckel,U, Hengel,M/, J Of Ecumenical Studies, Vol 0033, 1996; Related Strangers - Jews And Christians 70-170ce - Wilson,Sg/, J Of Bibl Lit, Vol 0116, 1997. **CONTACT ADDRESS** Dept of Relig Studies, Univ of Ore, Eugene, OR, 97403-1205.

SANDERS, JAMES ALVIN
PERSONAL Born 11/28/1927, Memphis, TN, m, 1951, 1 child **DISCIPLINE** BIBLICAL STUDIES **EDUCATION** Vanderbilt Univ, BA, 48, BD, 51; Hebrew Union Col, PhD, 55. **CAREER** Hoyt prof Old Testament interpretation, Colgate Rochester Divinity Sch, 54-65; Auburn prof Bibl studies, Union Theol Sem, NY, 65-77; E H Bechtel Prof Intertestamemtal & Bible Studies, Sch Theol & Prof Relig, Claremont Grad Sch, 77-, Guggenheim Found fel & ann prof, Am Sch Orient Res, Jerusalem, 61-62; mem Dead Sea Scroll fund comt, Am Schs Orient Res, 62-; adj prof, Columbia Univ, 65-77; Guggenheim Found fel, 72-73; Ecumencial Inst Jerusalem fel, 72-73; trustee, Am Sch Orient Res, 77-80; pres, Ancient Bibl Manuscript Ctr for Preserv & Res, Claremont, 80-; Hebrew Old Testament Text Critical Proj United Bible Soc, Stuttgart, 69- **HONORS AND AWARDS** DLitt, Acadia Univ, 73; STD, Univ Glasgow, 75. **MEMBERSHIPS** Soc Bibl Lit (pres, 78). **RESEARCH** Old Testament texts and canon; Hellenistic Judaism and New Testament; Biblical history, literature and theology. **SELECTED PUBLICATIONS** Auth, Jesus, Qumran, And The Vatican - Clarifications - Betz,O, Riesner,R/, Interpretation-A J Of Bible And Theol, Vol 0049, 1995; Clio Confronts Conformity - The Univ-Of-Wash Hist-Department During The Cold-War Era/, Pac Northwest Quart, Vol 0088, 1997; Canon And Theol - Overtures To An Old-Testament Theol - Rendtorff,R/, J Of Semitic Studies, Vol 0042, 1997. **CONTACT ADDRESS** PO Box 593, Claremont, CA, 91711.

SANDERS, JOHN
PERSONAL Born 07/16/1956, Danville, IL, m, 5 children **DISCIPLINE** THEOLOGY **EDUCATION** Univ South Africa, ThD, 96. **CAREER** Chair, relig studies, Oak Hills Col, 81-98; ASSOC PROF PHILOS & RELIG, HUNTINGTON COL, 98. **HONORS AND AWARDS** Extraordinary fel, Center of Philosophy of Relig, Univ Notre Dame, 97-98. **MEMBERSHIPS** AAR; Christian Theol Res Fel; Soc of Christian Philos. **RESEARCH** Religious pluralism; doctrine of God. **SELECTED PUBLICATIONS** Auth, No Other Name, Eerdmans, 92; co-auth, The Openness of God, Inter Varsity Press, 94; ed, What About Those Who Have Never Heard?, Inter Varsity Press, 95; The God Who Risks: A Theology of Providence, Inter Varsity Press, 98. **CONTACT ADDRESS** Dept of Philos & Relig, Huntington Col, 2203 College Ave, Huntington, IN, 46750. **EMAIL** jsanders@huntington.edu

SANDERS, JOHN E.
DISCIPLINE PHILOSOPHY AND RELIGION **EDUCATION** Wartburg Theol Sem, MA, 87; Trinity Col, BA, 79; Univ Safrica, ThD, 96. **CAREER** Assoc prof; assoc prof, Oak Hills Col, Minn, 81- & past dir, gen educ and ch, relig stud dept. **HONORS AND AWARDS** Extraordinary fel, Univ Notre Dame Ctr Philos Relig; Soc Christian Philosophers Amer Acad Relig & Christian Theol Res fel. **SELECTED PUBLICATIONS** Auth, Idolater Indeed! Response to Paul Knitter's Christology, in The Uniqueness of Jesus: A Dialogue with Paul Knitter; Why Simple Foreknowledge Offers No More Providential Control Than the Openness of God, in Faith and Philosophy; Evangelical Responses to Salvation Outside the Church, in Christian Scholars Review; Mercy to All: Romans 1-3 and the Destiny of the Unevangelized, in Proceedings of the Wheaton College Theology Conference; The Perennial Debate, in Christianity Today; God as Personal in The Grace of God, the Will of Man & Is Knowledge of Christ Necessary for Salvation, in Evangelical Quart; coauth & ed, The Openness of God; contrib chap, Historical Considerations on the Open View of God; ed, No Other Name! An Investigation into the Destiny of the Unevangelized & What About Those Who Have Never Heard? Three Views; **CONTACT ADDRESS** Dept of Philosophy, Hunter Col, CUNY, 695 Park Ave, New York, NY, 10021.

SANDERS, JOHN T.
PERSONAL m, 3 children **DISCIPLINE** PHILOSOPHY **EDUCATION** Purdue Univ, BA, 68; Boston Univ, MA, 72, PhD, 77. **CAREER** Social work/Psychology specialist, U.S. Army, 68-70; from asst prof to prof, Rochester Inst of Technol, 76-; consult to the Instruct Telecommunications Consortium Course Develop Proj of The Corp for Community Col Television in Cypress, Calif, 88-89; consult to the City Col of Loyola Univ, New Orleans, 95; vis prof, Univ of Helsinki, 95; vis prof, Polish Acad of Scis, 95-96; prof, U.S. Bus Sch in Prague, 97-. **HONORS AND AWARDS** Bronze Star for meritorious service, U.S. Army, 70; Eisenhart Annual Award for Outstanding Teaching, Rochester Inst of Technol, 79-80. **MEMBERSHIPS** Am Philos Inst. **SELECTED PUBLICATIONS** Auth, The Ethical Argument Against Government, 80; The Attractiveness of Risk, in Am Soc for Value Inquiry Newsletter, fall, 94; An Ecological Approach to Cognitive Science, in The Electronic J of Analytic Philos, issue 4, 96; Risk and Value, in A.S.V.I. News: The Newsletter of the Am Soc for Value Inquiry, spring, 96; The State of Statelessness, in For and Against the State: New Philosophical Readings, eds. J.T. Sanders and J. Narveson, 96; Comments on the Habermas/Rorty Debate, Comments on Philosophy and the Dilemmas of the Contemporary World, in Debating the State of Philosophy: Habermas, Rorty, and Kolakowski, eds. J.T. Sanders and J. Niznik, 96; Stanislaw Lesniewski's Logical Systems, in Axiomathes, vol. vii, no. 3, 96; An Ontology of Affordances, in Ecological Psychology, vol. 9, no. 1, 97; Reflections on the Value of Freedom, in Taking the Liberal Challenge Seriously: Essays on Contemp Liberalism at the Turn of the 21st Century, eds. S. Hellsten, M. Kopperi and O. Loukola, 97; A Mixed Bag: Political Change in Central and Eastern Europe and its Impact on Philosophical Thought, in Philosophy in Post-Communist Europe, ed. D.R. Gordon, 98; Incommensurability and Demarcation, in Criticism and Defense of Rationality in Contemp Philos, eds. D.R. Gordon and J. Niznik, 98; Contra Leviathan: On the Legitimacy and Propriety of the State, 99; ed, Niels Bohr: Essays and Papers, two vols., Manuscript archive, 87; coed, The Philosopher's Annual, vols. I-IV, 78-81; The Philosopher's Annual, vol. V, 84; For and Against the State: New Philosophical Readings, 96; Debating the State of Philosophy: Habermas, Rorty, and Kolakowski, 96. **CONTACT ADDRESS** Dept of Philosophy, Rochester Inst of Tech, 92 Lomb Memorial Dr, Rochester, NY, 14623-5604. **EMAIL** jtsgsh@rit.edu

SANDS, KATHLEEN M.
PERSONAL Born 09/12/1954, New York, NY, s **DISCIPLINE** THEOLOGY **EDUCATION** Boston Univ, BA, 76; Harvard Div Sch, MTS; Boston Col, PhD. **CAREER** Assoc prof, relig stud, Univ Mass, Boston, 96- . **HONORS AND AWARDS** Summa Cum Laude; Harvard Univ res fel, 98. **MEMBERSHIPS** Am Acad Relig. **RESEARCH** Evil and tragedy; religion in American public life; religion and culture. **SELECTED PUBLICATIONS** Auth, Escape from Paradise: Evil and Tragedy in Feminist Theology, Augsberg/Fortress, 99; ed, contribur, Religion and Sex in American Public Life, Oxford, 99. **CONTACT ADDRESS** 89 Rossmore Rd, Jamaica Plain, MA, 02130-3666. **EMAIL** sands@umbsky.cc.umb.edu

SANFORD, DAVID HAWLEY
PERSONAL Born 12/13/1937, Detroit, MI, m, 1965, 2 children **DISCIPLINE** PHILOSOPHY **EDUCATION** Wayne State Univ, BA, 60; Cornell Univ, PhD(philos), 66. **CAREER** From instr to asst prof philos, Dartmouth Col, 63-70; assoc prof, 70-78, prof philos, Duke Univ, 78-, vis assoc prof philos, Univ Mich, 70; Nat Endowment Humanities fel selected fields, 74-75, fel, 82-83, 89-90; Nat Humanities Center, fel, 89-90. **MEMBERSHIPS** Mind Asn; Am Philos Asn; Soc Philos Psychol. **RESEARCH** Philosophical logic; metaphysics; theory of knowledge. **SELECTED PUBLICATIONS** Auth, The Direction of Causation and the Direction of Conditionship, J Philos, 76; Where was I?, Hofstadter and Dennett, eds, The Mind's I, 81; The Perception of Shape, Ginet and Shoemaker, eds, Knowledge and Mind, 83; Infinite Regress Arguments, Fetzer, ed, Principles of Philosophical Reasonong, 84; Self-Deception as Rationalism, A.O. Rorty and McLaughlin, eds, Perspectives on Self-Deception, 88; If P, then Q: Conditionals and the Foundations of Reasoning, Routledge, 89; paperback ed, 92; Causation and Intelligibility, Philosophy, 94; Temporal Parts, Temporal Portions, and Temporal Slices: An Exercise in Naive Mereology, Acta analytica, 96. **CONTACT ADDRESS** Dept of Philos, Duke Univ, P O Box 90743, Durham, NC, 27708-0743. **EMAIL** dhs@acpub.duke.edu

SANTA MARIA, DARIO ATEHORTUA
PERSONAL Born 06/19/1943, Medellin, Colombia **DISCIPLINE** RELIGION **EDUCATION** Univ St. Thomas Bogota, BD, BPh 65; Ashbury Sem, ThM 67; Univ Madrid, Lic comunicaciones 69; Episcopal Sem VA, cert theol, palaeography 71-74; Univ Lateranense Rome, ThD 75; Ecole Biblique Francaise Jerusalem, post grad 76; Oxford Univ, 82-84. **CAREER** NT Union Theol Sem Madrid, prof 67-70; Prot Theol Inst Fe y Secularidad Madrid, prof 67-70; Iglesia De Camillejas Madrid, pastor 68-70; Oikoumenikon Vatican City Italy, asst editor 72-76; Ed Clie Spain, ed 76-81; St. James Piccadilly Inst London, prof 81-84; United Bible Soc London, 76-85; Ch World Svc Geneva, 80-; British Lib London, man dept 81-; Inst Contemp Christianity, prof 95-; German Seamen's Mission NY, assoc pastor 96-. **HONORS AND AWARDS** Sion Col Fel; Dr. of Letters recp., Ordained Priest, Roman Catholic Church. **MEMBERSHIPS** APC; ACL; ATE; AAH **SELECTED PUBLICATIONS** Auth, Diccionario Biblico Ilustrado, 82, revised ed 98; Los Manuscriptos Del Mar Muerto y su impacto En Los Estudios Biblicos, Madrid 97; La Reforma En La Iglesia Hoy, Barcelona 97; Yel Texto Griego Delabiblia, 83; The World After Columbus, 1492-1992, 91. **CONTACT ADDRESS** Dept of Theology, Inst for Contemporary Christianity, Wall Street Station, PO Box 87, New York, NY, 10268.

SANTAS, GERASIMOS
PERSONAL Born 03/23/1931, Greece, m, 1979, 5 children **DISCIPLINE** PHILOSOPHY **EDUCATION** Cornell Univ, PhD. **CAREER** Prof, philos, Univ Calif Irvine. **HONORS AND AWARDS** Doctorate, Honoris Causa, Univ Athens, 94. **MEMBERSHIPS** Amer Philos Asn; Intl Asn of Greek Philos. **RESEARCH** Ancient Greek philosophy; History of ethics. **SELECTED PUBLICATIONS** Auth, Socrates, Greek ed, 97, new ed, 99, Routledge; auth, Pluto and Focero, Blackwell. **CONTACT ADDRESS** Philosophy, Univ of California, Irvine, CA, 92664. **EMAIL** gxsantas@uci.edu

SANTILLANA, FERNANDO
PERSONAL Born 02/09/1940, Lima, Peru, m, 1965, 3 children **DISCIPLINE** THEOLOGY **EDUCATION** Claremont Schl Theol, MDiv, DMin, 83; LaSalle Univ, PhD, 87. **CAREER** Rector, 87-90, Comunidad Biblico-Theologica, Peru; prof, 90-94, Sem Metodista, Brazil; coordr, 94-97, Mission Ed, Univ Methodist Church, S Cent Jurisdiction, USA; coordr, 98-, MDiv prog, Seminario Metodista, Mexico. **HONORS AND AWARDS** Magna Cum Laude, PhD, LaSalle Univ **MEMBERSHIPS** AAR; OEF. **RESEARCH** Misticism, liberation theology, liturgy. **SELECTED PUBLICATIONS** Auth, Modulo de Liturgia, Porto Alegre, ITJW, 93; auth, Miquras: Profita para Latinoamerica, Maryland Intl Scholars Pub, 98. **CONTACT ADDRESS** 10014 Goodyear Dr., Dallas, TX, 75229-5819. **EMAIL** ferdyS@worldnet.att.net

SANTONI, ROLAND J.
DISCIPLINE BUSINESS LAW **EDUCATION** Univ Penn, BS, 63, JD, 66. **CAREER** Prof, Creighton Univ; pvt pract, Philadelphia, 66-77; ed, Annual Inst on Sec Reg for Practicing Law Inst, 81-87; arbitrator, National Asn Securities Dealers. **HONORS AND AWARDS** Creighton Univ Robert F. Kennedy Mem Outstanding Prof awd. **MEMBERSHIPS** Order of the Coif. **SELECTED PUBLICATIONS** Pub(s), Creighton Law Rev; Employee Relations Law J; J Corp Law. **CONTACT ADDRESS** School of Law, Creighton Univ, 2500 California Plaza, Omaha, NE, 68178. **EMAIL** santoni@culaw.creighton.edu

SANTONI, RONALD ERNEST
PERSONAL Born 12/19/1931, Arvida, Que, m, 1955, 6 children **DISCIPLINE** PHILOSOPHY **EDUCATION** Bishop's Univ, BA, 52; Brown Univ, MA, 54; Boston Univ, PhD(philos), 61. **CAREER** Asst prof philos, Univ of the Pac, 58-61; Wabash Col, 62-64; assoc prof, 64-68, chmn dept, 71-73, Prof Philos, Denison Univ, 68- & Maria Theresa Barney Chair, 78-, Church Soc Col Work fel, 61-62; res fel, Yale Univ, 61-62 mem nat exec comt, Episcopal Peace fel, 69-79; Soc Relig Higher Educ fel, 71-; trustee, Margaret Hall Sch, 72-74; res fel, Yale Univ, 75; vis fel, Berkeley Col, Yale Univ, 75 & 81, 93-94, 97; vis fel, Cambridge Univ, 86; vis schol, Cambridge Univ, 86,90,94,97; vis lectr, Cambridge, 90; Robert C. Good fel, 86. **HONORS AND AWARDS** Mellon Award for distinguished faculty, 72. **MEMBERSHIPS** Am Philos Asn; Int Phenomenol Soc; Soc Phenomenology & Existential Philos; Sarte Soc of N Am; Sarte Circ; Concerned Philos for Peace; Int Philos for Prev of Nuc Omnicide **RESEARCH** Philosophy of Jean-Paul Sartre; existentialism; social and political philosophy. **SELECTED PUBLICATIONS** Co-ed, Social and Political Philosophy, Doubleday, 63; ed & contribr, Religious Language and The Problem of Religious Knowledge, Ind Univ, 68; auth, Sartre on sincerity: Bad faith? or equivocation? spring 72 & Ducasse's criterion of morality: An exploration and critique, fall 72, Personalist; Ducasse on cause: Another look, Current Philos Issues, 66; Marjorie Grene's Sartre, Int Philos Quart, 75; Quebec's language problem, The Progressive, 77; Bad faith and lying to oneself, Philos & Phenomenol Res, 78; Sartre and morality: Jeanson's classic revisited, In Philos Quart, 81; Omnicide and the problem of belief, Churchman, 8-9/80; auth, Nurturing the Institution of War: Just War Theory's Justifications and Accomodations, 91; auth, On the Existential Meaning of Violence, 91; auth, Dialogue and Humanism, 98. **CONTACT ADDRESS** Dept of Philos, Denison Univ, 1 Denison University, Granville, OH, 43023-1359. **EMAIL** santoni@denison.edu

SANTONI, RONALD ERNEST
PERSONAL Born 12/19/1931, Arvida, PQ, Canada, m, 1955, 6 children **DISCIPLINE** PHILOSOPHY **EDUCATION** Bishop's Univ, BA, 52; Brown Univ, MA, 54; Univ of Paris, Sorbonne, Boston Univ, PhD(philos), 61. **CAREER** Asst prof philos, Univ of the Pac, 58-61; Wabash Col, 62-64; assoc prof, 64-68, chmn dept, 71-73, prof philos, Denison Univ, 68- & Maria Theresa Barney Chair, 78-, Church Soc Col Work fel, 61-62; res fel, Yale Univ, 61-62 mem nat exec comt, Episcopal Peace fel, 69-79; Soc Relig Higher Educ fel, 71-; trustee, Margaret Hall Sch, 72-74; res fel, Yale Univ, 75; vis fel, Berkeley Col, Yale Univ, 75 & 81, 93-94, 97; vis fel, Clare Hall, Cambridge Univ, UK, 86; vis scholar in philos, Cambridge Univ, 86, 90, 94, 97; vis lecturer on Sartre'sphilosophy, Cambridge, 90; life member Clare Hall, Cambridge; Robert C. Good Fellow (for research and writing at Cambridge), 86, 94. **HONORS AND AWARDS** Mellon Award for distinguished faculty, 72. **MEMBERSHIPS** Am Philos Asn; Int Phenomenol Soc; Soc Phenomonology & Existential Philos; Sartre Soc of North Am (exec comm95-); Sartre Circle, co-ord, 97; Concerned Philosophers for Peace, Pres, 96-97; Int Philosophers for Prevention of Nuclear Omnicide, Pres, 91-96. **RESEARCH** Philosophy of Jean-Paul Sartre; existentualism; philosophy of violence and nonviolence; social and political philosophy. **SELECTED PUBLICATIONS** Co-ed, Social and Political Philosophy, Doubleday, 63; ed & contribr, Religious Language and The Problem of Religious Knowledge, Ind Univ, 68; auth, Sartre on Sincerity: Bad

Faith? or Equivocation? spring 72 & Ducasse's Criterion of Morality: An Exploration and Critique, fall 72, Personalist; Ducasse on cause: Another look, Current Philos Issues, 66; Marjorie Grene's Sartre, Int Philos Quart, 75; ; Bad Faith and Lying to Oneself, Philos & Phenomenol Res, 78; Sartre and Morality: Jeanson's Classic Revisited, Int Philos Quart, 81; Omnicide and the problem of belief, Churchman, 8-9/80; Nurturing the Institution of War: Just War Theory's Justifications and Accomodations, 91; On the Existential Meaning of Violence, 91; Bad Faith, Good Faith, and Authenticity, Temple Univ, 95; Dialogue and Humanism, On the Existential Meaning of War, 98; and over 100 additional articles, commentaries, and reviews. **CONTACT ADDRESS** Dept of Philos, Denison Univ, 1 Denison University, Granville, OH, 43023-1359. **EMAIL** santoni@denison.edu

SANTOS, SHEROD
PERSONAL Born 09/09/1948, Greenville, SC, m, 1975, 2 children **DISCIPLINE** ENGLISH, PHILOSOPHY **EDUCATION** San Diego State Univ, BA, 71; MA, 74;, MFA, 78; Univ Utah, PhD, 82. **CAREER** Asst prof, Calif State Univ San Bernardino, 82-83; asst prof, Univ Mo Columbia, 83-86; vis prof, Univ Calif Irvine, 89-90; assoc prof, Univ Mo Columbia, 86-92; prof, Univ MO Columbia, 93-. **HONORS AND AWARDS** Utah Arts Council Award in Lit, 80; Discovery The Nation award, 78; Pushcart Prize in Poetry, 80; Oscar Blumenthal Prize, 81; Nat Poetry Series Selection, 82; Meralmikjen Fel in Poetry, Bread Loaf Writers' Conference, 82; Ingram Merrill Found Grant, 82; The Robert Frost Poet, 84; Mo Arts Council Award in Lit, 87; Fel to the Yaddo Center fort he Arts, 87; NBC Today Show Appearance, 87; Nat Endowment for the Arts Grant, 87; Weldon Springs Res Grant, Univ Mo, 91-92; Chancellor's Award for Outstanding Fac Res, Univ Mo, 93; Pushcart Prize in the Essay, 94; British Arts Council Int Travel Grant, 95; Appointed Mem, Nat Endowment for the Arts Lit Panel, 95; BF Conners Award in Poetry, 98. **MEMBERSHIPS** Acad Am Poets; Poetry Soc of Am; PEN Am Center; Robinson Jeffers Soc; Poets and Writers; Associated Writing Programs. **RESEARCH** Poetry and Poetics. **SELECTED PUBLICATIONS** Auth, The City of Women, 93; The Pilot Star Elegies, 98; numerous chapbooks, screenplay, poetry in journals and magazines. **CONTACT ADDRESS** Dept of English, Univ of Mo, 107 Tate Hall, Columbia, MO, 65211. **EMAIL** engss@showme.missouri.edu

SAPONTZIS, STEVE FREDERIC
PERSONAL Born 02/09/1945, New York, NY **DISCIPLINE** PHILOSOPHY **EDUCATION** Rice Univ, BA, 67; Yale Univ, MPhil, 70, PhD(philos), 71. **CAREER** Asst prof, 71-76, assoc prof, 76-81, Prof Philos, Calif State Univ, Hayward, 81- **MEMBERSHIPS** Am Soc Value Inquiry; Am Philos Asn; Soc Study of Ethics & Animals. **RESEARCH** Ethics; animal rights; philosophical psychology. **SELECTED PUBLICATIONS** Auth, Anatomy Of A Defeat In Renaissance Italy - The Battle Of Fornovo In 1495/, Int Hist Rev, Vol 0016, 1994. **CONTACT ADDRESS** Dept of Philos, California State Univ, Hayward, 25800 Carlos Bee Bvd, Hayward, CA, 94542-3001.

SARAO, KARAM TEJ S
PERSONAL Born 04/01/1955, Sangrur, India, m, 1981, 2 children **DISCIPLINE** RELIGION **EDUCATION** Univ Delhi, PhD, 85; Univ Canfab, PhD, 89. **CAREER** Cambridge Univ, Commonwealth Fel, 85-89; Delhi Univ, prof, dept chemn, 93-. **HONORS AND AWARDS** Delhi Univ, Gold Medal, Commonwealth Fel. **MEMBERSHIPS** RAS London, IABS, Indian Hist Congress. **RESEARCH** Animal rights; thesavada Buddhism. **SELECTED PUBLICATIONS** Auth, Urbanization and Urban Centers as Reflected in the Sali Vinaya and Sutta Pitakas, Delhi: Vidyanidhi, 89; auth, Origin and Nature of Early Indian Buddhism, Delhi: Eastern Book Linkess, 89; auth, A Text Book of the History of Thesavada Buddhism, Delhi Univ, Delhi, 93. **CONTACT ADDRESS** Dept of Buddhist Studies, Delhi Univ, 1701-17 Knightsbridge Rd, Brampton, ON, L6T 3X9. **EMAIL** ktsarao@hotmail.com

SARASON, RICHARD SAMUEL
PERSONAL Born 02/12/1948, Detroit, MI **DISCIPLINE** RELIGIOUS STUDIES, HISTORY OF RELIGIONS **EDUCATION** Brandeis Univ, AB, 69; Hebrew Union Col, MAHL, 74; Brown Univ, PhD(relig studies), 77. **CAREER** Instr relig studies, Brown Univ, 76-77, asst prof, 77-79; asst prof, 79-81, Assoc Prof Rabbinic Lit & Thought, Hebrew Union Col, 81- **MEMBERSHIPS** Am Acad Relig; Soc Bibl Lit; Asn Jewish Studies; Am Sch Orient Res; Soc Values Higher Educ. **RESEARCH** Judaism in late antiquity; early rabbinic Judaism, Mishnah-Tosefta, rabbinic midrash and liturgy. **SELECTED PUBLICATIONS** Auth, Intertextuality And The Reading Of Midrash - Boyarin,D/, J Of Rel, Vol 0074, 1994. **CONTACT ADDRESS** Hebrew Union Col, 3101 Clifton Ave, Cincinnati, OH, 45220.

SARGENTICH, THOMAS O.
DISCIPLINE ADMINISTRATIVE LAW. CONSTITUTIONAL LAW **EDUCATION** Harvard Univ, AB, 72; Oxford Univ, M Phil, 74; Harvard Law Sch, JD, 77. **CAREER** Prof, Am Univ. **HONORS AND AWARDS** Award for Outstanding Res Scholar, 90;, Pauline Ruyle Moore Scholar, 89; Comt Government Org Separation Powers, ABA section Admin Law Regulatory Policy, 90-; U.S. Dept Justice; Law clerk, Judge Arlin M. Adams, U.S. Court Appeals. **RESEARCH** Separation of Powers; constitutional interpretation. **SELECTED PUBLICATIONS** Contribur, Admin Law Rev; Cornell Law Rev; Harvard Law Rev; Trial Mag; William; Mary Law Rev; Wisconsin Law Rev. **CONTACT ADDRESS** American Univ, 4400 Massachusetts Ave, Washington, DC, 20016.

SARNA, NAHUM M.
PERSONAL Born 03/27/1923, London, England, m, 1947, 2 children **DISCIPLINE** BIBLICAL & SEMITIC STUDIES **EDUCATION** Univ London, BA, 44, MA, 46; Dropsie Col, PhD(Bibl studies & Semitics), 55. **CAREER** Asst lectr Hebrew, Univ Col, Univ London, 46-49; lectr Bible, Gratz Col, 51-57; librn & asst prof, Jewish Theol Sem, 57-63, assoc prof, 63-65; assoc prof, 65-67, chmn Dept Near Eastern & Judaic Studies, 69-75, Dora Golding Prof Bibl Studies, Brandeis Univ, 67-, Vis assoc prof relig, Columbia Univ, 64-65; assoc trustee, Am Schs Orient Res, 65-67; ed & translr, Bible Transl Comt, Jewish Publ Soc Am, 65, ed-in-chief, Bible Commentary, 73-; vis prof Bible studies, Andover Newton Theol Sch, 66-67 & Dropsie Col, 67-68; mem B'nai B'rith Adv Bd Adult Jewish Educ, 67-; dept ed, Bible Div, Encycl Judaica, 68-72; trustee, Boston Hebrew Col, 68-75, mem exec comt, 70-75; Am Coun Learned Soc sr fel, 71-72; mem acad adv coun, Nat Found Jewish Cult, 73-; Inst for Advan Studies fel, Hebrew Univ, Jerusalem, 82-83. **HONORS AND AWARDS** Jewish Bk Coun Award, 67. **MEMBERSHIPS** Fel Am Acad Jewish Res; Am Orient Soc; Soc Bibl Lit; Asn Jewish Studies (hon secy-trcas, 72-); fel Royal Asiatic Soc. **RESEARCH** History of the ancient Near East; Semitic literature and languages. **SELECTED PUBLICATIONS** Auth, Students Of The Covenant - A Hist Of Jewish Biblical Scholarship In N-Am - Sperling,Sd/, J Of Rel, Vol 0074, 1994. **CONTACT ADDRESS** Dept of Near Eastern Studies, Brandeis Univ, Waltham, MA, 02154.

SARRA, JANIS
DISCIPLINE LAW **EDUCATION** Univ Toronto, BA, MA, LLB. **CAREER** Labour arbitrator, Social Assistance Review Board **SELECTED PUBLICATIONS** Auth, pubs on labour law, equality law and diversity management, and corporate governance. **CONTACT ADDRESS** Fac of Law, Univ Toronto, 78 Queen's Park, Toronto, ON.

SARVER, VERNON T.
PERSONAL Born 12/17/1943, Bluefield, WV, m, 1970, 2 children **DISCIPLINE** PHILOSOPHY **EDUCATION** Fla State Univ, BA, 66; Tufts Univ, Mdiv, 69; Boston Univ, STM, 71; Ohio State Univ, MA, 71; Univ Fla, PhD, 94. **CAREER** Adj instr, Fla Community Coll Jacksonville, 79-81; adj instr, Lake City Community Coll, 81-83; grad res asst, Univ Fla, 82-85; tchr of emotionally handicapped, Bradford County Schools Starke Fla, 85-86; tchr of gifted, Marion County Schools Ocala Fla, 86-; adj prof, Saint Leo Coll, 94-. **HONORS AND AWARDS** Rockefeller Prize, Am Philos Asn, 96; Who's Who in Am Educ, 96-97. **MEMBERSHIPS** Am Philos Asn; Am Soc for Value Inquiry; Int Soc for Value Inquiry. **RESEARCH** Political Philosophy; Ethics. **SELECTED PUBLICATIONS** Auth, Ajzen and Fishbein's 'Theory of Reasoned Action': A Critical Assessment, J for the Theory of Soc Behavior, 83; Kant's Purported Social Contract and the Death Penalty, J of Value Inquiry, 97. **CONTACT ADDRESS** Box 605, Archer, FL, 32618.

SASSON, VICTOR
PERSONAL Born 12/20/1937, Baghdad, Iraq, d, 1 child **DISCIPLINE** RELIGION; ENGLISH LITERATURE **EDUCATION** Univ London, BA honors, 73; New York Univ, PhD, 79. **CAREER** Univ S Africa, sr lectr, 81-85; Long Island Univ, asst prof, 90-91; Touro Col NY, asst prof, 90-96. **HONORS AND AWARDS** Thayer fel; AAR. **MEMBERSHIPS** Colum Univ Sem Hebrew Bible and Shakespeare; SOTS. **RESEARCH** Text and language of Hebrew bible; N W Semitic Epigraphy; tense and aspect in Biblical Hebrew and old Aramaic; ancient near east. **SELECTED PUBLICATIONS** Auth, The Literary and Theological Function of Job's Wife in the Book of Job, Biblica, 98; Some Observations on the Use and Original Purpose of the Waw Consecutive in Old Aramaic and Biblical Hebrew, VT, 97; The Inscription of Achish Governor of Eqron and Philistine Dialect, Cult and Culture, UF, 97; The Old Aramaic Inscription for Tell Dan: Philological Literary and Historical Aspects, JSS, 95; The Book of Oraccular Visions of Balaam from Deir Alla, UF, 86. **CONTACT ADDRESS** Brighton 3F, Brooklyn, NY, 11235.

SASSOWER, RAPHAEL
PERSONAL Born 09/26/1955, Israel, d, 2 children **DISCIPLINE** PHILOSOPHY **EDUCATION** Boston Univ, PhD, 85. **CAREER** Asst prof, assoc prof, prof, 86-, chemn 91-97, Univ Colorado, Colorado Springs. **RESEARCH** Philosophy of science and technology; postmodernism; aesthetics. **SELECTED PUBLICATIONS** Auth, Knowledge Without Expertise: On The Social Status of Scientists, SUNY, 93; auth, Cultural Collisions: Postmodern Technoscience, Routledge, 95; auth, Technoscientific Angst: Ethics and Responsibility, Univ Minn, 97. **CONTACT ADDRESS** Dept of Philosophy, Univ of Colorado, Colorado Springs, CO, 80933. **EMAIL** rsassowe@brain.uccs.edu

SATRIS, STEPHEN A.
PERSONAL Born 05/05/1947, New York, NY, m, 1975, 2 children **DISCIPLINE** PHILOSOPHY **EDUCATION** Univ Calif, BA, 69; Univ Hawaii, MA, 71; Cambridge Univ, PhD, 84. **CAREER** Vis instr Philos, Gustavus Adolphus Col, 78-80; from instr to assoc prof Philos, SE Mo State Univ, 80-86; from asst to assoc prof, Clemson Univ, 86-. **MEMBERSHIPS** Am Philos Asn; SC Soc Philos. **RESEARCH** Ethics; Wittgenstein. **SELECTED PUBLICATIONS** Ed, Taking Sides: Clashing Views on Controversial Moral Issues, 98. **CONTACT ADDRESS** Dept of Philosophy and Religion, Clemson Univ, Clemson, SC, 29634-1508. **EMAIL** stephen@clemson.edu

SATTERFIELD, PATRICIA POLSON
PERSONAL Born 07/10/1942, Christchurch, VA, m, 1966 **DISCIPLINE** LAW **EDUCATION** Howard University, BME, 1964; Indiana University, MM, 1967; St Johns University, School of Law, JD, 1977. **CAREER** Sewanhaka High School District, vocal music teacher, 1968-77; UCS Counsels Office of Court Administration, assistant deputy counsel, senior counsel, 1978-90; Unified Court System of State of New York, judge, 1991-94, acting supreme court justice, 1994-98, supreme court justice, 1998-. **HONORS AND AWARDS** Alpha Kappa Alpha, Epsilon Omega Chapter, Outstanding Community Leader of the Year, 1991; Queens County Women's Bar Association, Ascension to Bench, 1991; Alva T Starforth, Outstanding Teacher of the Year, 1976. **MEMBERSHIPS** St John's University, cultural diversity committee, School of Law, 1991-, board of directors, law alumni, 1991-; Queens Women's Network, co-chair, board of directors, 1983-90; Human Resources Center of St Albans, board of directors, 1990-; Association of Women Judges, 1991-; Metropolitan Black Lawyers Association, 1988-; Queens County Bar Association, 1989-; Jack and Jill of America Inc Queens Co, president, 1978-87; St Albans Congregational Church, United Church of Christ, moderator, 1996-; Greater Queens Chapt of the Links, Inc, pres, 1998-. **CONTACT ADDRESS** Supreme Court of the State of New York, 88-11 Sutphin Blvd, Jamaica, NY, 11435.

SAUER, JAMES B.
PERSONAL Born 12/31/1948, Richmond, VA, m, 1968, 3 children **DISCIPLINE** PHILOSOPHY **EDUCATION** Univ Richmond, BA, 66; Union Theol Sem, MDiv, 74, DMin, 79; St Paul's Univ, MA, 90, PhD, 92. **CAREER** Prof, theol, Inst Superieur de Theol, 74-79; minister, Presby Church, 79-91; vis prof ethics, St Paul's Univ, 91-93; assoc prof philos, St. Mary's Univ, 93- . **HONORS AND AWARDS** Centennial mem fel, 80; distinguished fac award, 97; listed, Who's Who Among American Teachers, 98. **MEMBERSHIPS** APA. **RESEARCH** Ethics; applied ethics; economic philosophy; environmental philosophy. **SELECTED PUBLICATIONS** Auth, Conscience and Deliberation: Notes for A Critical Realist Ethics, St Mary's, 93; auth, Method in Theology: A Commentary, St Mary's, 95; auth, Faithful Ethics According to John Calvin: The Teachability of the Heart, Edwin Mellin, 97. **CONTACT ADDRESS** One Camino Santa Maria, San Antonio, TX, 78228-8566. **EMAIL** philjim@stmarytx.edu

SAUNDERS, KURT M.
PERSONAL McKeesport, PA **DISCIPLINE** BUSINESS LAW, ECONOMICS **EDUCATION** Carnegie Mellon Univ, BS, 82; Univ Pittsburgh, JD, 85. **CAREER** Instr, 88-89, Dickinson Sch of Law; instr, 89-94, Univ of Pitts Sch of Law; adj prof of law,94-97,; clin prof of law, 97-98, Duquesne Univ Sch of Law; asst prof, law, 98-, Calif St Univ, Northridge, School of Bus Admin & Econ **MEMBERSHIPS** PA Bar Asn; Allegheny Co Bar Asn, 92-94, ed staff, Pitts Legal J, 87-93; Clin Legal Ed Asn; Acad of Legal Stud in Bus; Asn for Pract & Profes Ethics; The Federalist Soc for Law & Pub Pol Stud; Int Coun for Innovation in Higher Ed. **RESEARCH** Computer and internet law; advanced technology law; legal education; rhetoric. **CONTACT ADDRESS** Col of Business Administration and Economics, Dept of Business Law, California State Univ, Northridge, 18111 Nordhoff St, Northridge, CA, 91330-8245. **EMAIL** kurt.saunders@csun.edu

SAVAGE, C. WADE
PERSONAL Born 09/01/1932, Tuscaloosa, AL, m, 1955, 3 children **DISCIPLINE** PHILOSOPHY **EDUCATION** Cornell Univ, PhD, 63. **CAREER** Asst prof, Harpur Col, 59-64; asst prof, Univ Calif, 64-71; assoc prof, 71-80, prof, 80-, Univ Minn. **MEMBERSHIPS** Am Philos Asn; Philos Sci Asn; British Asn Philos Sci; Soc Philos Psychol; Am Asn Univ Prof. **RESEARCH** Epistemology; philosophy of psychology; measurement. **SELECTED PUBLICATIONS** Auth, Introspectionist and Behaviorist Interpretations of Ratio Scales of Perceptual Magnitudes, Psychol Monogr, 66; auth, The Measurement of Sensation: A Critique of Perceptual Psychophysics, 70; auth, The Continuity of Perceptual and Cognitive Experiences, Hallucinations: Behavior, Experience, and Theory, 75; auth, An Old Ghost in a New Body, Consciousness and the Brain: A Sci and Philos Inquiry, 76; auth, Sense-Data in Russell's Theories of Knowledge, Rereading Russell: Essays on Bertrand Russell's Metaphysics and Epistemology, 89; auth, Epistemological Advantages of a Cognitivist Analysis of Sensation and Perception, Sci, Mind, and Psychol: Essays in Honor of Grover Maxwell; auth, A Brief Introduction to Measurement Theory, Philos and

Foundational Issues in Measurement Theory, 92; auth, Foundationalism Naturalized, Cognitive Models of Sci, 92. **CONTACT ADDRESS** Dept of Philosophy, 224 Church St. SE, Minneapolis, MN, 55455. **EMAIL** savag001@maroon.tc.umn.edu

SAVAGE, WADE S.
DISCIPLINE PHILOSOPHY **EDUCATION** Cornell Univ, PhD. **RESEARCH** Epistemology; philosophy of cognitive sciences; philosophy of science. **SELECTED PUBLICATIONS** Auth, Foundationalism Naturalized, Univ Minn, 91; Epistemological Advantages of a Cognitivist Analysis of Sensation and Perception, Univ Am, 91; Sense-Data in Russell's Theories of Knowledge, Univ Minn, 89; An Old Ghost in a New Body, Plenum, 76; The Measurement of Sensation, Univ Calif, 70; ed, Perception and Cognition, Univ Minn. 78; Reading Russell, Univ Minn, 89. **CONTACT ADDRESS** Philosophy Dept, Univ of Minnesota, Twin Cities, 355 Ford Hall, 224 Church St SE, Minneapolis, MN, 55455. **EMAIL** savag001@maroon.tc.umn.edu

SAWATSKY, RODNEY JAMES
PERSONAL Born 12/05/1943, Altona, MB, Canada, m, 1965, 3 children **DISCIPLINE** RELIGION, HISTORY **EDUCATION** Can Mennonite Bible Col, Winnipeg, B Christian Ed, 64; Bethel Col, Kans, BA, 65; Univ Minn, MA, 72; Princeton Univ, MA, 73 & Phd(relig), 77. **CAREER** Instr hist, Can Mennonite Bible Col, Winnipeg, 67-70; asst prof relig, 74-80, Dir Acad Affairs, Conrad Grabel Col, Univ Waterloo, 74, Assoc Prof Relig, 81- **MEMBERSHIPS** Am Soc Church Hist; Am Acad Relig; Can Soc Study Relig; Can Protection Relig Freedom (pres, 78-). **RESEARCH** Mennonite history; evangelical and new religions; Canadian religious history. **SELECTED PUBLICATIONS** Auth, Limits On Liberty, The Experience Of Mennonite, Hutterite And Doukhobor Communities In Can - Janzen,W/, Studies In Rel-Sciences Religieuses, Vol 0021, 1992. **CONTACT ADDRESS** 55 Menno, Waterloo, ON, N2L 2A6.

SAYRE, KENNETH MALCOLM
PERSONAL Born 08/13/1928, Scottsbluff, NE, m, 1958, 3 children **DISCIPLINE** PHILOSOPHY **EDUCATION** Grinnell Col, AB, 52; Harvard Univ, MA, 54, PhD, 58. **CAREER** Asst dean grad sch arts & lett, Harvard Univ, 53-56; mem staff syst anal, Lincoln Lab, 56-58; from instr to assoc prof, 58-71, prof philos, Univ Notre Dame, 71-, dir philos inst, 66-, vis scientist, Sylvania Elec Prod, Inc, 59; consult, Lincoln Lab, 61; vis fel, Princeton Univ, 67-68; vis prof, Bowling Green Univ, 81; vis fel, Merton Col, Oxford, 86; senior res fel, St. Edward's Col, Cambridge, 96. **RESEARCH** Plato; cybernetics; philosophy of mind. **SELECTED PUBLICATIONS** Auth, Recognition: A Study in the Philosophy of Artificial Intelligence, 65 & coauth, Philosophy and Cybernetics, 67, Univ Notre Dame; auth, Plato's Analytic Method, 69 & Consciousness: A Philosophic Study of Minds and Machines, 69, Random; Cybernetics and the Philosophy of Mind, Routledge & Kegan Paul, 76; Moonflight, 77 & Starburst, 77, Univ Notre Dame; auth, Plato's Literary Garden: How to Read a Platonic Dialogue, Univ Notre Dame, 95; Parmenides' Question: Translation and Explication of Plato's Parmenides, Univ Notre Dame, 96; Belief and Knowledge: Mapping the Cognitive Landscape, Ronmau and Littlefield, 97. **CONTACT ADDRESS** Dept of Philos, Univ of Notre Dame, 337 Oshaugnessy Hall, Notre Dame, IN, 46556.

SAYRE, PATRICIA
PERSONAL Born 05/27/1958, Mt. Holly, NJ, m, 1983, 1 child **DISCIPLINE** PHILOSOPHY **EDUCATION** Wheaton Col, BA, 80; Univ Notre Dame, PhD, 87. **CAREER** Tutor, instr, Saint Olaf Col, 85-87; assoc prof, chair, Saint Marys Col, 87-. **HONORS AND AWARDS** Maria Piena Award; vis scholar, St Edmunds Col, Cambridge; Executive Committee, Soc Christian Philosophers; Coolidge Res Fel; ed board, Personalist Forum. **MEMBERSHIPS** Am Philos Soc; Soc Christian Philosophers; Austrian Ludwig Wittgenstein Soc; Int Forum on Persons. **RESEARCH** Wittgenstein; metaphysics; moral psychology. **SELECTED PUBLICATIONS** Auth, "The Philosophical Life as Literature: Fictional Renditions of Wittgenstein," The Cresset, 93; "The Dialectics of Trust and Suspicion," Faith and Philosophy, 93; "Moral Psychology and Persons," Becoming Persons: Proceedings of the Second Conf on Persons, 96; "Personalism," in The Companion to the Philos of Rel, 97; "Socrates is Mortal: Formal Logic and the Pre-Law Undergraduate," Notre Dame Law Rev, 98. **CONTACT ADDRESS** Dept of Philosophy, St. Mary's Col, Notre Dame, IN, 46556. **EMAIL** psayre@saintmarys.edu

SAYWARD, CHARLES
DISCIPLINE PHILOSOPHY OF LOGIC, PHILOSOPHY OF LANGUAGE, AND POLITICAL PHILOSOPHY **EDUCATION** Cornell Univ, PhD, 64. **CAREER** Prof, Univ Nebr, Lincoln. **RESEARCH** The philosophy of mathematics. **SELECTED PUBLICATIONS** Auth, Definite Descriptions, Negation and Necessitation, Russell 13, 93; coauth, Two Concepts of Truth, Philos Stud 70, 93; The Internal/External Question, Grazer Philosophische Studien 47, 94; Intentionality and truth: an essay on the philosophy of Arthur Prior. **CONTACT ADDRESS** Univ Nebr, Lincoln, Lincoln, NE, 68588-0417.

SCAER, DAVID P.
PERSONAL Born 03/13/1936, Brooklyn, NY, m, 1960, 3 children **DISCIPLINE** THEOLOGY **EDUCATION** Concordia Sem, BA, 57, BD, 60, ThD(baptism), 63. **CAREER** From asst prof to assoc prof, 66-77, prof syst theol, Concordia Theol Sem, 77-, instr relig, Univ Ill, 66-76; John W Behnken fel, Univ Heidelberg, 69-70, 86-87; ed, Springfielder, 69-76; mem subcomt ordination, Inter-Lutheran Worship Comn, 73-76; ed, Concordia Theol Quart, 76-93;member, comm on Theology and Church Relations, The Lutheran Church-Missouri Synod, 98-; contrib ed, Christianity Today, 81-, Modern Reformation, and Logia. **MEMBERSHIPS** Evangel Theol Soc; Concordia Hist Inst; Soc Bibl Lit. **RESEARCH** Lutheran confessional theology; contemporary theology; quest for the historical Jesus studies. **SELECTED PUBLICATIONS** Auth, Lutheran World Federation Today, 71, The Apostolic Scriptures, 71; What Do You Think of Jesus?, 73 & Getting Into the Story of Concord, 77, Concordia; contribr, Tensions in Contemporary Theology, Moody, 76; History of Christian Doctrine, Baker, 79; auth, James the Apostle of Faith, Concordia Pub House, 83; Christology, Confessional Lutheran Dogmatics: The Int Foundation for Lutheran Confessional Research, 89; contrib, Evangelical Affirmations, Academie Books, 90; Doing Theology in Today's World, Harper and Row, 91; Handbook of Evangelical Theologians, Baker, 93; Evangelical Dictionary of Biblical Theology, Baker, 95; Eintraechtig Lehren, Verlag der Lutherischen Buchhandlung Heinrich Harms, Gross Oesingen, Germany, 97; The Pieper Lectures: The Office of the Ministry, Concordia Hist Institute, 97; auth, Baptism, Confessional Lutheran Dogmatics, The Int Found for Lutheran Confessional Research, 98; and articles in: The Lutheran Witness, Lutheran Forum, Forum Letter, Lutheran Quart, Modern Reformation, Logia, Concordia Journal, Grace Theological Journal, Lutheran Worship Notes, Journal of the Evangelical Theological Society, and Issues in Christian Education. **CONTACT ADDRESS** Dept of Syst, Theol Concordia Theol Sem, 6600 N Clinton St, Fort Wayne, IN, 46825-4996. **EMAIL** dpscaer@juno.com

SCALES-TRENT, JUDY
PERSONAL Born 10/01/1940, Winston-Salem, NC **DISCIPLINE** LAW **EDUCATION** Oberlin Coll, BA 1962; Middlebury Coll, MA 1967; Northwestern Univ Sch of Law, JD 1973. **CAREER** Equal Empl Opp Commn, spec asst to vice chmn 1977-79, spec asst to gen counsel 1979-80, appellate Attorney 1980-84; SUNY Buffalo Law Sch, assoc prof of law 1984-90, professor of law, 1990-. **MEMBERSHIPS** mem DC Bar; mem NY State Bar; US Ct of Appeals for the Fourth, Fifth, Sixth, Seventh, Ninth and Eleventh Circuits; mem Amer Bar Assn; mem bd dir Park School of Buffalo (1985-88 term); mem, bd of dirs, National Women and the Law Assn 1987-91; mem, bd of visitors, Roswell Park Memorial Cancer Institute, 1991-96; mem, bd of governors, Society of American Law Teachers, 1992-95. **SELECTED PUBLICATIONS** Auth, "Comparable Worth: Is This a Theory for Black Workers" 8 Women's Rights L Rptr 51 (Winter 1984); "Sexual Harassment and Race, A Legal Analysis of Discrimination," 8 Notre Dame J Legis 30 (1981); "A Judge Shapes and Manages Institutional Reform: School Desegregation in Buffalo," 12 NYU Review of Law and Social Change 19 (1989); "Black Women and the Constitution: Finding our Place, Asserting our Rights," 24 Harvard Civil Rights-Civil Liberties Law Review 9 (1989); "Women of Color and Health: Issues of Gender, Power and Community," 43 Stanford Law Review 1357, 1991; "The Law as an Instrument of Oppression and the Culture of Resistance," in Black Women in America: An Historical Encyclopedia 701, 1993; "On Turning Fifty," in Patricia Bell-Scott, ed, Life Notes 336, 1994; Notes of a White Black Woman: Race, Color, Community, 1995. **CONTACT ADDRESS** Law Sch, SUNY, Buffalo, O'Brian Hall, Buffalo, NY, 14260.

SCALISE, CHARLES J.
PERSONAL Born 07/25/1950, Baltimore, MD, m, 1980, 2 children **DISCIPLINE** CHURCH HISTORY, CHRISTIAN THEOLOGY **EDUCATION** Princeton Univ, AB, summa cum laude, 72; Yale Div Sch, MDiv, magna cum laude, 75; S Baptist Theol Sem, PhD, 87; Univ Oxford, postgrad, 90-91. **CAREER** Baptist Chaplain, Yale, 75-82; lectr, Pastoral Theol, Yale Div Sch, 76-80; dir, dept Christian higher educ, Baptist Conven New Eng, 82-84; asst prof, S Baptist Theol Sem, 87-94; assoc and mang ed, Rev and expositor, 91-94. **HONORS AND AWARDS** Sloan Scholar, 68-72; Ger bk prize, 71; Albert G. Milband mem scholar prize, 71; Phi Beta Kappa, 72; Tew prize, 73; Oliver Ellsworth Daggett prize, 74; Julia A. Archibald high scholar prize, 75; Outstanding young men Am, 75; Who's Who S and SW, 93-94. **RESEARCH** Theological hermeneutics; History of exegesis; History of doctrine; pastoral Theology. **SELECTED PUBLICATIONS** Auth, Allegorical Flights of Fancy: The Problem of Origen's Exegesis, The Greek Orthodox Theol Rev, 32, 87, 69-88; Origen and the Sensus Literalis, in Origen of Alexandria, Notre Dame, 88, 117-129; Developing a Theological Rationale for Ministry: Some Reflections on the Process of Teaching Pastoral Theology to MDiv Students, Jour Pastoral Theol, 1, 91, 53-68; Hermeneutics as Theological Prolegomena: A Canonical Approach, Mercer UP, 94; Canonical Hermeneutics: Childs and Barth, Scotish Jour Theol, 47, 94, 61-88; Teresa of Avila: Teacher of Evangelical Women? Cross Currents: The Jour of the Asn for Rel and Intel Life, 46, 96, 244-249; From Scripture to Theology: A Canonical Journey

into Hermeneutics, InterVarsity Press, 96; Agreeing on where We Disagree: Lindbeck's Postliberalism and Pastoral Theology, Jour Pastoral Theol, 8, 98, 43-51. **CONTACT ADDRESS** Fuller Theol Sem, 101 Nickerson St, Ste 330, Seattle, WA, 98109-1621. **EMAIL** cscalise@fuller.edu

SCANLAN, J.T.
DISCIPLINE EIGHTEENTH-CENTURY ENGLISH LITERATURE, LEGAL HISTORY **EDUCATION** Univ Mich, PhD. **CAREER** Vis asst prof, Vassar Col; asst prof Eng, Providence Col. **RESEARCH** The spirit of contradiction in 18th-century London; legal history, contemporary non-fiction. **SELECTED PUBLICATIONS** Writes on eighteenth-century English literature, legal history, and contemporary non-fiction. **CONTACT ADDRESS** Dept of Eng, Providence Col, EH 215, Providence, RI, 02918-0001. **EMAIL** hambone@providence.edu

SCANLAN, JAMES P.
PERSONAL Born 02/22/1927, Chicago, IL, m, 1948 **DISCIPLINE** PHILOSOPHY **EDUCATION** BA, 48, MA, 50, PhD, 56, Univ Chicago. **CAREER** Research Fel, Inst for Phil Research, 53-55; Ford Fdn Teaching Fel and Instr, Case Inst of Tech, 55-56; Instr to Assoc Prof, Goucher Col, 56-68; Prof and Dir, Ctr for Soviet and Eastern European Studies, Univ Kansas, 68-70; Dir, Ctr for Slavic and Eastern European Studies, 88-91, Prof, 71-. Ohio State Univ. **HONORS AND AWARDS** Resident Fel, Woodrow Wilson Intl Ctr for Scholars, 82; Fulbright-Hays Faculty Research Award, 82-83; Visiting Research Scholar, Univ Fribourg, Switzerland, 82-83; Resident Scholar, Bellagio Study Ctr of Rockefeller Fdn, Ballagio Italy, 83; Foreign Visiting Fel, Sapporo Japan, 87-88; Visiting Research Scholar, Moscow State Univ, 93; Visiting Research Scholar, Russian State Univ for the Humanities, 95. **MEMBERSHIPS** Amer Phil Assoc; Amer Assoc for the Advancement of Slavic Studies **RESEARCH** Russian philosophy; Soviet Marxism; social and political philosophy **SELECTED PUBLICATIONS** Auth, Marxism in the USSR: A Critical Survey of Current Soviet Thought, 85; ed, A History of Young Russia, 86; Technology, Culture, and Development: The Experience of the Soviet Model, 92; Russian Thought after Communism: The Recovery of a Philosophical Heritage, 94. **CONTACT ADDRESS** 1000 Urlin Ave., Apt. 206, Columbus, OH, 43212. **EMAIL** scanlan.1@osu.edu

SCANLAN, MICHAEL
DISCIPLINE PHILOSOPHY OF SCIENCE **EDUCATION** SUNY-Buffalo, PhD. **CAREER** Philos, Oregon St Univ. **RESEARCH** Logic; artificial intelligence; Bertrand Russell; F.P. Ramsey. **SELECTED PUBLICATIONS** Area: Aristotle's logic; the American Postulate Theorists, and Wittgenstein's Tractatus. **CONTACT ADDRESS** Dept Philos, Oregon State Univ, Corvallis, OR, 97331-4501. **EMAIL** scanlanm@ucs.orst.edu

SCANLON, T.M.
DISCIPLINE PHILOSOPHY **EDUCATION** Princeton, BA, 62; Harvard Univ, PhD. **CAREER** Prof; Harvard Univ, 84-; taught at, Princeton Univ, 66-84; Fulbright fel, Oxford. **SELECTED PUBLICATIONS** Auth, What We Owe to Each Other, Harvard UP, 98; publd papers, on freedom of expression, nature of rights, conceptions of welfare, theories of justice & foundational questions in moral theory. **CONTACT ADDRESS** Dept of Philosophy, Harvard Univ, 8 Garden St, Cambridge, MA, 02138. **EMAIL** scanlon@fas.harvard.edu

SCAPERLANDA, MICHAEL
PERSONAL Born 04/29/1960, Austin, TX, m, 1981, 4 children **DISCIPLINE** LAW **EDUCATION** Univ TX, Austin, BA, 81, JD, 84. **CAREER** Judicial clerk, Chief Justice to Supreme Court, 84-85; assoc, Hogan & Hartson, DC, 85-86; assoc, Hughes & Luce, Austin, TX, 86-89; assoc prof, 89-95, prof, Univ OK, College of Law, 95-. **HONORS AND AWARDS** James D Feller Award for Outstanding Scholarship; Outstanding Young Man of America, 82, 88. **MEMBERSHIPS** Order of the COIF; Asn of Am Law Schools. **RESEARCH** Religious influence on law and society; The Constitution and the Am people; immigration. **SELECTED PUBLICATIONS** Auth, Judicial Solecism Repeated: An Analysis of the Oklahoma Supreme Court's Refusal to Recognize the Adjudicative Nature of Particularized Ratemaking, 47 OK Law Rev 601, 94; Justice Thurgood Marshall and the Legacy of Dissent in Federal Alienage Cases, 8 Georgetown Immigration Law J 1, 94; Are We That Far Gone?: Due Process and Secret Deportation Proceedings, 7 Stanford Law and Policy Rev 23, 96; A Godless Constitution?, Our Sunday Visitor, Nov 10, 96; Partial Membership: Aliens and the Constitutional Community, 81 IA Law Rev 707, 96; Who is My Neighbor?: An Essay on Immigrants, Welfare Reform, and the Constitution, 29 CT Law Rev 1587, 97; Church & Nation are Poorer Sans Religious Freedom Restoration Act, Nat Cath Register, July 20, 97; Kiryas Joel and the Need for Religious Accommodation, Nat Cath Register, Sept 21, 97; To Bind Up the Nation's Wounds: Lessons from Abraham Lincoln, Our Sunday Visitor, Nov 9, 97; Louisiana's Covenant Marriage Law Misses the Mark, Cath Parent, forthcoming. **CONTACT ADDRESS** College of Law, Univ of Oklahoma, 300 W Timberdell, Norman, OK, 73019. **EMAIL** mscaperlanda@ou.edu

SCARBOROUGH, MILTON R.
PERSONAL Born 06/02/1940, Gulfport, MS, d, 2 children **DISCIPLINE** RELIGION **EDUCATION** Univ Miss, BA, eng, 62; New Orleans Bapt Theol Sem, BD, theol, 65; Duke Univ, PhD, relig, 72. **CAREER** Prof, philos and relig, Centre Col, 69-. **HONORS AND AWARDS** Nat Endow of Humanities Distinguished Prof of Humanities; Dana fel, Emory Univ, 91-92. **MEMBERSHIPS** Amer Acad of Relig. **RESEARCH** Myth; Phenomenology; Buddhism. **SELECTED PUBLICATIONS** Auth, Myth & Modernity: Postcritical Reflections, SUNY, 94. **CONTACT ADDRESS** Centre Col, 600 W Walnut St., Danville, KY, 40422. **EMAIL** mscarb@centre.edu

SCARLETT, JAMES D.
DISCIPLINE LAW **EDUCATION** McGill Univ, BC, 75; Univ Toronto, LLB, 81. **CAREER** Partner, McMillan Binch **HONORS AND AWARDS** Dir, Capital Markets Branch. **RESEARCH** Corporate and securities law. **SELECTED PUBLICATIONS** Auth, pubs on public finance, mergers and acquisitions, and providing regulatory advice. **CONTACT ADDRESS** Fac of Law, Univ Toronto, 78 Queen's Park, Toronto, ON.

SCERRI, ERIC R.
DISCIPLINE PHILOSOPHY **EDUCATION** London Univ, BS, 74; Southampton Univ, M Phil; King's Col, London, hist of philos of sci, PhD, 92. **CAREER** Postdoctoral fel, Caltech, 95-97; asst prof, Bradley Univ, 97-98; asst prof, Purdue Univ, 98-. **MEMBERSHIPS** Amer Philos Asn; Philos of Sci Asn; Amer Chem Soc. **RESEARCH** History and philosophy of chemistry; Chemical education. **SELECTED PUBLICATIONS** Article, The Evolution of the Periodic System, Sci Amer, 78-83, Sept, 98; article, Popper's Naturalized Approach to the Reduction of Chemistry, Intl Studies in Philos of Sci, 12, 33-44, 98; article, Has the Periodic Table Been Successfully Axiomatized?, Erkentnnis, 47, 229-243, 97; article, The Periodic Table and the Electron, Amer Sci, 85, 546-553, 97; article, Interdisciplinary Research at the Beckman Institutes, Interdisciplinary Sci Rev, 22, 131-137, 97; article, Chemical Periodicity, Macmillan Encycl of Chem, Macmillan, vol 3, 23-33, 97; article, The Case for Philosophy of Chemistry, Synthese, 111, 213-232, 97; article, A Bibliography for the Philosophy of Chemistry, Synthese, 111, 305-324, 97; article, It All Depends What You Mean By Reduction, From Simplicity to Complexity, Information, Interaction, Emergence, Vieweg-Verlag, 97; article, Are Chemistry and Philosophy Miscible?, Chem Intelligencer, 3, 44-46, 97; article, Reduktion und Erklarung in der Chemie, Philosophie der Chemie - Bestandsaufnahme und Ausblik, Wurtzburg, Koningshausen & Neumann, 77-93, 96; article, Why the 4s Orbital Is Occupied before the 3d, Jour of Chem Educ, 73, 6, 498-503, 96; article, Stephen Brush, The Periodic Table and the Nature of Chemistry, Die Sprache der Chemie, Wurtzburg, Koningshausen & Neumann, 96; article, Why is There (Almost) No Philosophy of Chemistry?, Hist Grp of Royal Soc of Chem Newsletter and Summary of Papers, 19-24, Feb, 96; article, Philosophy of Chemistry Resurgens, Chem Heritage, 13, no 1, 33, Winter, 95-96; article, The Exclusion Principle, Chemistry and Hidden Variables, Synthese, 102, 165-169, 95; article, Has Chemistry Been at Least Approximately Reduced to Quantum Mechanics?, PSA, 1, 160-170, 94; article, Please Change (The Periodic Table), Chem in Britain, 30, no 5, 379-381, 94; article, Prediction of the Nature of Hafnium from Chemistry, Bohr's Theory and Quantum Theory, Annals of Sci, 51, 137-150, 94. **CONTACT ADDRESS** Dept. of Chemistry, Purdue Univ, W. Lafayette, IN, 47907. **EMAIL** scerri@bradley.edu

SCHABERG, JANE D.
DISCIPLINE RELIGIOUS STUDIES AND WOMEN'S STUDIES **EDUCATION** Manhattanville Col, BA; Columbia Univ, MA; Union Theol Sem NYC, PhD. **CAREER** Prof; Univ Detroit Mercy, 77-. **RESEARCH** Feminist interpretation, biblical studies, introductions to RS and WS **CONTACT ADDRESS** Dept of Religious Studies, Univ of Detroit Mercy, 4001 W McNichols Rd, PO Box 19900, Detroit, MI, 48219-0900. **EMAIL** SCHABEJD@udmercy.edu

SCHACHT, RICHARD
DISCIPLINE PHILOSOPHY **EDUCATION** Princeton Univ, PhD, 67. **CAREER** Prof, Univ Ill Urbana Champaign. **RESEARCH** Post-Kantian continental philosophy; philosophical anthropology; social theory; value theory. **SELECTED PUBLICATIONS** Auth, Alienation, Hegel and After, Nietzsche; Classical Modern Philosophers: Descartes to Kant; The Future of Alienation and Making Sense of Nietzsche; ed, Nietzsche: Selections and Nietzsche, Genealogy, Morality. **CONTACT ADDRESS** Philosophy Dept, Univ Ill Urbana Champaign, 52 E Gregory Dr, Champaign, IL, 61820. **EMAIL** rschacht@uiuc.edu

SCHACK, HAIMO
DISCIPLINE LAW **EDUCATION** Univ Calif Berkeley, LL.M. **CAREER** Prof, Univ Ill Urbana Champaign. **SELECTED PUBLICATIONS** Auth, Copyright Law, 97; International Civil Litigation, 96; Jurisdictional Minimum Contacts Scrutinized, Heidelberg, 83. **CONTACT ADDRESS** Law Dept, Univ Ill Urbana Champaign, 52 E Gregory Dr, Champaign, IL, 61820. **EMAIL** hschack@law.uiuc.edu

SCHAEFER, JAME
PERSONAL Born 01/07/1940, Syracuse, NY, m, 1962, 4 children **DISCIPLINE** SYSTEMATIC THEOLOGY, ETHICS **EDUCATION** PhD **CAREER** Asst prof/vis, Marquette Univ, 95-; John Templeton Found Relig & Sci Award. **MEMBERSHIPS** Am Acad Relig; Soc Christian Ethics; Nat Asn Environ Ethics; Col Theol Soc; Int Soc Environ Ethics; Cath Theol Soc Am. **RESEARCH** Theological/Theistic Foundation for environmental ethics; Theological discourse informed by the natural sciences. **SELECTED PUBLICATIONS** Auth Theistic Foundations for Environmental Ethics: Promising Patristic and Medieval Sources. **CONTACT ADDRESS** Theology Dept, Marquette Univ, 207 Coughlin Hall, Milwaukee, WI, 53201-1881. **EMAIL** jame.schaefer@marquette.edu

SCHAEFFER, PETER MORITZ-FRIEDRICH
PERSONAL Born 05/14/1930, Breslau, Germany, m, 1968 **DISCIPLINE** GERMANIC STUDIES, CLASSICS, RELIGIOUS STUDIES. **EDUCATION** Univ Ottawa, Lic Theol, 59; Princeton Univ, PhD(Germanic studies), 71. **CAREER** From lectr to asst prof Germanic studies, Princeton Univ, 70-74; vis lectr Ger & comp lit, Univ CA, Berkeley, 74-76; ASSOC PROF TO PROF GER, UNIV CA, DAVIS, 76-. **MEMBERSHIPS** ALSC; Renaissance Soc Am; Erasmus Soc; Tyndale Soc. **RESEARCH** Renaissance; Neo-Latin literature; Classical tradition. **SELECTED PUBLICATIONS** Auth, Joachim Vadianus, De poetica, Text, Translation & Commentary, Wilhelm Fink, Munich, 73; Hoffmannswaldau, De curriculo studiorum, Peter Lano, Bern, 91; Sapidus Consulator, Annvaire de Selestat, 96. **CONTACT ADDRESS** German Dept, Univ of California, Davis, One Shields Ave, Davis, CA, 95616-5200. **EMAIL** pmschaeffer@ucdavis.edu

SCHALL, JAMES VINCENT
PERSONAL Born 01/20/1928, Pocahontas, IA, m **DISCIPLINE** POLITICAL PHILOSOPHY **EDUCATION** MA Philos, Fon309A Univ, 55; PhD Political Philos, Georgetown Univ, 60; MST Theol, Univ of Santa Clara, 64. **CAREER** Inst Soc, Georgian Univ, Rome, Italy, 65-77; Univ of San Francisco, 69-77; Georgetown Univ, 78-. **MEMBERSHIPS** Amer Political Sci Assoc. **SELECTED PUBLICATIONS** At Thee Limits of Political Philosophy(Was): The Catholic Univ of Amer Press, 96; Jacques Maritain: A Philosopher in Society, Lanham, Rowman and Littlefield, 98; The Death of Plato, The American Scholar, 65, pp 401-415, 96; On the Uniqueness of Socrates, Gregorianum, 76(#2 95); In the Place of Augustine in Political Philosophy, The Political Science Reviewer XXIII, 94; Post-Aristotelian Political Philosophy and Modernity, Aufstieg und Niedergang der Romischen Welt, Berlin: Gruyter 11 36.7, 94; Friendship and Political Philosophy, The Review of Metaphysics, L pp121-141, 96; The Role of Christian Philosophy in Politics, American Catholic Philosophical Quarterly (#1,95) 1-14. **CONTACT ADDRESS** Dept of Government, Georgetown Univ, 37th and 0 Sts NW, WA, DC, 20057. **EMAIL** schallsj@gusun.georgetown.edu

SCHALLER, WALTER E.
DISCIPLINE PHILOSOPHY **EDUCATION** Univ CA, Berkeley, MA; Univ WI, PhD, 84. **CAREER** Instr, Wheaton Col; instr, Univ KY; assoc prof, TX Tech Univ. **RESEARCH** Ethics; polit philos; the philos of law. **SELECTED PUBLICATIONS** Publ articles on Kant's ethics, utilitarianism, and the relationship between virtues and duties in Philos and Phenomenol Res, Ratio, Southern J of Philos, Dialogue and Hist of Philos Quart. **CONTACT ADDRESS** Texas Tech Univ, Lubbock, TX, 79409-5015. **EMAIL** a4wes@ttacs.ttu.edu

SCHALOW, FRANK
PERSONAL Born 02/23/1956, Denver, CO, s **DISCIPLINE** PHILOSOPHY **EDUCATION** Univ Denver, BA, 78; Tulane Univ, PhD, 84. **CAREER** Assoc prof, Loyola Univ New Orleans, 86-92; lectr, Dillard Univ, 93-95; vis assoc prof, Univ New Orleans, 95-. **HONORS AND AWARDS** Phi Beta Kappa. **MEMBERSHIPS** North Amer Heidegger Conf; Amer Philos Asn. **RESEARCH** History of philosophy; Kant; Heidegger. **SELECTED PUBLICATIONS** Auth, Language and Deed: Rediscovering Politics through Heidegger's Encounter with German Idealism, Editions Rodopi, 98; auth, The Renewal of the Heidegger-Kant Dialogue: Action, Thought, and Responsibility, State Univ of NY Press, 92; co-auth, Traces of Understanding: A Profile of Heidegger's and Ricoeur's Hermeneutics, Editions Rodopi, 90; auth, Imagination and Existence: Heidegger's Retrieval of the Kantian Ethic, Univ Press of Amer, 86. **CONTACT ADDRESS** 7422 Maple St., New Orleans, LA, 70118. **EMAIL** fhs@uno.edu

SCHARLEMANN, ROBERT PAUL
PERSONAL Born 04/04/1929, Lake City, MN **DISCIPLINE** THEOLOGY **EDUCATION** Concordia Col & Sem, Mo, BA, 52, BD, 55; Heidelberg Univ, DrTheol, 57. **CAREER** Instr philos, Valparaiso Univ, 57-59; pastor, Bethlehem Lutheran Church, Carlyle, Ill, 60-61, Grace Lutheran Church, Durham, NC, 62-63; asst prof theol, Grad Sch Relig, Univ Southern Calif, 63-66; assoc prof theol, Univ Iowa, 66-68, prof, 68-81; Commonwealth Prof Philos Theol, Univ Va, 81-, Res fel, Yale Univ, 59-60; assoc ed, Dialog, 60-; Coun Int Exchange Scholars Fulbright sr res grant, 75-76; ed, J Am Acad Relig, 80- **MEMBERSHIPS** Am Acad Relig; NAm Paul Tillich Soc (vpres, 77, pres, 78); Am Theol Soc. **RESEARCH** History of thought; constructive theology; theology and science. **SELECTED PUBLICATIONS** Auth, From Text To Action - Essays In Hermeneutics, Vol 2 - Ricoeur,P/, Lang In Soc, Vol 0022, 1993; Can Religion Be Understood Philosophically/, Int J For Philos Of Rel, Vol 0038, 1995; The Quadrilog - Tradition And The Future Of Ecumenism - Essays In Honor Of Tavard,George,H. - Hagan,K, Editor/, J Of Ecumenical Studies, Vol 0033, 1996; The Royal Priesthood - Essays Ecclesiological And Ecumenical - Yoder,Jh, Cartwright,Mg/, J Of Ecumenical Studies, Vol 0033, 1996. **CONTACT ADDRESS** Dept Relig Studies, Univ Va, Charlottesville, VA, 22903.

SCHARPER, STEPHEN B.
PERSONAL Born 09/05/1960, Port Chester, NY, m, 1994, 1 child **DISCIPLINE** THEOLOGY **EDUCATION** Univ Toronto, BA, 82; Univ St. Michael's Col, MA, 88; McGill Univ, PhD, 97. **CAREER** The John A. O' Brien Chr, Univ Notre Dame, Visiting Instr, 94-97; Dir, English Publications, Novalis Publications, 97-. **HONORS AND AWARDS** Fel, Joan B. Kroc Inst for Intl Peace Studies **MEMBERSHIPS** Amer Acad of Religion; Catholic Theological Soc of Amer; College Theology Soc. **RESEARCH** Globalization; religion and environment; economic disparity **SELECTED PUBLICATIONS** Coauth, The Green Bible, 93; Auth, Four Books about Saving the Planet God Loves, National Catholic Reporter, 95; We are the World's Most Dangerous Animals, National Catholic Reporter, 95; And God Saw That it was Good: Catholic Theology and the Environment, Catholic New Times, 97; Redeeming the Time: A Political Theology of the Environment, 97. **CONTACT ADDRESS** Massey Col, 4 Devonshire Pl., Gatehouse , Toronto, ON, M5S 2E1. **EMAIL** scharper@spu.stpaul.uottawa.ca

SCHAUB, MARILYN MCNAMARA
PERSONAL Born 03/24/1928, Chicago, IL, m, 1969, 1 child **DISCIPLINE** RELIGIOUS STUDIES, CLASSICAL LANGUAGES **EDUCATION** Rosary Col, BA, 53; Univ Fribourg, PhD(class philos), 57. **CAREER** Asst prof class lang, 57-62, assoc prof relig studies & class lang, 62-69, Rosary Col; assoc prof, 73-80, prof theol, 80-, Duquesne Univ; hon assoc, Am Schs Orient Res, Jerusalem, 66-67; admin dir, expedition to the southeast end of the Dead Sea, Jordan, 77, 79, 81. **HONORS AND AWARDS** Pres Award for Faculty Excellence in Teaching, Duquesne Univ, 90. **MEMBERSHIPS** Soc Bibl Lit; Cath Bibl Asn; Am Acad Relig; Archaeol Inst Am. **RESEARCH** Old Testament; New Testament; early Bronze Age settlements at the southeast end of the Dead Sea, Jordan. **SELECTED PUBLICATIONS** Co-translr, Agape in the New Testament, Herder, 63-67; auth, Friends and Friendship in St Augustine, Alba, 65; contribr, Encyclopedic Dictionary of Religion, Corpus, 78; ed, Harper Collins Bible Dictionary, 96; auth, Collegeville Pastoral Dictionary of Biblical Theology, 96. **CONTACT ADDRESS** Theol Dept, Duquesne Univ, Pittsburgh, PA, 15282. **EMAIL** schaub@duq3.cc.duq.edu

SCHAUB, R. THOMAS
PERSONAL Born 03/26/1933, South Bend, IN, m, 1959, 1 child **DISCIPLINE** RELIGIOUS STUDIES (BIBLICAL), HISTORY & ARCHAEOLOGY OF ANCIENT NEAR EAST **EDUCATION** Architecture, Univ Notre Dame, 49-52; MIT, construction & engineering, 52-53; Aquinas Inst of Philos, BA (madna cum laude), 57, MA (summa cum laude), 58; Aquinas Inst of Theol, MA (cum laude), 61, STD cand, 63; Cath Univ AM, Semitic Studies; Harvard Divinity School, Old Testament and Semitic Studies, 64-65; Ecole Biblique et Archeologique, SSB, 65, SSL, 67 (Pontifical Biblical Commission); Univ Pittsburgh, Pittsburgh Theol Sem, PhD, 73. **CAREER** Asst prof, Aquinas Inst Theol, 68-69; vis lect, Pittsburgh Theol Sem, 70-71; asst Prof, relig Studies, Indiana Univ of PA, 69-71, 73-76, asoc prof, 76-79; prof, Religious Studies, Indiana Univ of PA, 79-. **HONORS AND AWARDS** Teaching fel, Pittsburgh Theol Sem, 69-70; Thayer fel, Am Schools of Oriental Res, 71-72; Ed Counsellor, Old Master, Purdue Univ, 75; Danforth Assoc, 75-; res assoc, Carnegie Museum Nat Hist, 79-; fel, Explorer's Club, 79-; NEH fel, 82-83; Distinguished Fac Award for Res, Indiana Univ PA, 85; Fac Res Assoc, Inst of Applied Res and Public Policy, IUP, 88-89; Fulbright res fel, 89, 91; numerous res grants from the following: Indiana Univ PA, NEH, Nat Geographic Soc, Fulbright. **MEMBERSHIPS** Soc of Biblical Lit; Cath Biblical Asn; Am Schools of Oriental Res; Am Academy of Relig; Am Inst of Archaeology; Am Assn for Field Archaeology. **RESEARCH** Early Bronze Age, Near East. **SELECTED PUBLICATIONS** Auth, Review of the Jordan Valley Survey, 1953: Some Unpublished Soundings Conducted by James Mellaart, by Albert Leonard, Jr, Annual of the American Schools of Oriental Res, 50, Bul of the Am Schools of Oriental Res, 95; Pots as Containers, in Retrieving the Past, Essays on Archaeological Research and Methodology, in Honor of Gus W Van Beek, ed Joe D Seger, Cobb Inst of Archaeol, MS State Univ, Eisenbraun, 96; Southeast Dead Sea Plain, in The Oxford Encyclopedia of Archaeology in the Near East, ed Eric Meyers, Oxford Univ Press, vol 5, 97; Bab edh-Dhra' in the Oxford Encyclopedia of Archaeology in the Near East, ed Eric M Meyers, Oxford Univ Press, 97; The Southeastern Dead Sea Plain: Changing Shorelines and their Impact on Settlement Patterns of the Major Historical Periods of the Region, with Jack Donahue and Brian Peer, in Studies in the History and Archaeology of

Jorgdan, 98; two books and numerous other publications. **CONTACT ADDRESS** Indiana Univ of Pennsylvania, 442 Sutton Hall, Indiana, PA, 15705. **EMAIL** rtschaub@grove.iup.edu

SCHAUBER, NANCY E.
PERSONAL Born 03/25/1960, White Plains, NY, m, 1987, 1 child **DISCIPLINE** PHILOSOPHY **EDUCATION** St. John's Col, BA, 81; UVA, MA, 87; Yale Univ, PhD, 93. **CAREER** Asst prof, 93, Univ Richmond. **RESEARCH** APA; Ethics; Aristotle. **SELECTED PUBLICATIONS** Auth, Integrity, Commitment & the Concept of a Person. **CONTACT ADDRESS** Department of Philosophy, Univ of Richmond, Richmond, VA, 23173. **EMAIL** nschaube@richmond.edu

SCHECHTMAN, MARYA
DISCIPLINE PHILOSOPHY **EDUCATION** Harvard Univ, PhD, 88. **CAREER** Assoc prof, Univ IL at Chicago. **RESEARCH** Philos of psychology; existentialism; philos of lit; Am philos. **SELECTED PUBLICATIONS** Auth, Personhood and Personal Identity, Jour Philos, 90; Consciousness, Concern, and Personal Identity, Logos, 91. **CONTACT ADDRESS** Philos Dept, Univ Illinois Chicago, S Halsted St, PO Box 705, Chicago, IL, 60607.

SCHEDLER, GEORGE EDWARD
PERSONAL Born 12/22/1945, Fresno, CA, m, 1970, 3 children **DISCIPLINE** PHILOSOPHY **EDUCATION** St Mary's Col, Calif, BA, 67; Univ Calif, San Diego, MA, 70, PhD(philos), 73; South Ill Univ, JD, 87. **CAREER** Asst prof to assoc prof, 73-84, prof philos, Southern Ill Univ, Carbondale, 84-. **MEMBERSHIPS** Am Philos Asn; Am Cath Philos Asn; SW Philos Soc. **RESEARCH** Political philosophy; legal philosophy; ethics. **SELECTED PUBLICATIONS** Auth, On Punishing the Guilty, Ethics, 4/76; Capital Punishment and its Deterrent Effect, Social Theory & Pract, 12/76; Behavior Modification and Punishment of the Innocent, Gruner, 77; Justice in Marx, Engels and Lenin, Studies Soviet Thought, 8/78; Does Society Have the Right to Force Pregnant Drug Addicts to Abort their Fetuses?, Soc Theory and Pract, 11/91; Racist Symbols and Reparations, Rowman and Littlefield, 98. **CONTACT ADDRESS** Dept of Philos, Southern Ill Univ, Carbondale, IL, 62901-4505. **EMAIL** geosched@siu.edu

SCHEFFLER, ISRAEL
PERSONAL Born 11/25/1923, New York, NY, m, 1949, 2 children **DISCIPLINE** PHILOSOPHY **EDUCATION** Brooklyn COl, BA, 45, MA, 48; Jewish Theol Sem, MHL, 49; Univ Pa, PhD(philos), 52. **CAREER** From instr to asst prof educ, 52-57, lectr, 57-59, from assoc prof to prof, 60-62, prof educ & philos, 62-64, Victors Thomas Prof Educ & Philos, Harvard Univ, 64-, Guggenheim fel, 58-59 & 72-73; NSF res grants, 62 & 65-66; chmn gen probs sect, Int Cong Logic; Methodol & Philos Sci, 64; hon res fel cognitives studies, Harvard Univ, 65-66; fel, Ctr Advan Studies Behav Sci, 72-73. **HONORS AND AWARDS** Distinguished Serv Medal, Teachers Col Columbia, 80., AM, Harvard Univ, 60. **MEMBERSHIPS** Eastern Div Am Philos Asn; Aristotelian Soc; Philos Sci Asn(pres, 73-75); Nat Acad Educ; Am Acad Arts & Sci. **RESEARCH** Philosophy of science, language and education. **SELECTED PUBLICATIONS** Auth, Responses/, Synthese, Vol 0094, 1993; Responses To Pekarsky, Yob, And Brown/, Rel Educ, Vol 0090, 1995. **CONTACT ADDRESS** Dept of Philos, Harvard Univ, Cambridge, MA, 02138.

SCHEJBAL, DAVID
PERSONAL Born 02/12/1961, Prague, Czechoslovakia, d **DISCIPLINE** PHILOSOPHY **EDUCATION** Univ Conn, PhD, 92 **CAREER** Assoc dean cont educ & dir summer sessions spec prog, Northwestern Univ. **HONORS AND AWARDS** Award Merit Credit Prog; N Amer Asn Summer Sessions **MEMBERSHIPS** Amer Philos Asn; Asn Univ Summer Sessions; N Amer Asn Summer Sessions **RESEARCH** Environmental ethics; Philosophy of education. **SELECTED PUBLICATIONS** Auth, On the Notion of Following a Rule Privately, Ludwig Wittgenstein: A Symposium on the Centennial of His Birth, Longwood Acad, 90; The Aesthetics of Summer Session Administration, Summer Acad: A Jour of Higher Educ, 97-98; Summer Sessions: A Time in Change, Adv Quart, 98; Summer Session Homeostasis, Proceedings: 34th Annual Conference of the North American Association of Summer Sessions, 98; Summer Language Instruction, International Study Guides: Studying Abroad, 98. **CONTACT ADDRESS** Northwestern Univ, 2115 N Campus Dr, Evanston, IL, 60208-2650. **EMAIL** schejbal@merle.acns.nwu.edu

SCHEMAN, NAOMI
DISCIPLINE PHILOSOPHY **EDUCATION** Harvard Univ, PhD. **RESEARCH** Politics of epistemology. **SELECTED PUBLICATIONS** Auth, Feeling Our Way Toward Moral Objectivity, Mind Morals, 96. **CONTACT ADDRESS** Philosophy Dept, Univ of Minnesota, Twin Cities, 355 Ford Hall, 224 Church St SE, Minneapolis, MN, 55455. **EMAIL** nschema@maroon.tc.umn.edu

SCHERER, IMGARD S.
PERSONAL Born 01/14/1937, Berlin, Germany, m, 1958, 4 children **DISCIPLINE** HISTORY OF PHILOSOPHY **EDUCATION** Amer Univ, PhD, 91. **CAREER** Asst Prof, 92-, Loyola Coll, MD; Vis Prof, 92, Amer Univ; Vis Prof, 88-91, George Mason Univ. **HONORS AND AWARDS** Amer Philos Assoc; North Amer Kent Soc. **MEMBERSHIPS** ASA, Phi Sigma Tan, IHSP. **RESEARCH** Science of Aesthetics, Theory of Judgement applied to Science, Morality and Art. **SELECTED PUBLICATIONS** Auth, The Crisis of Judgement in Kant's Three Critiques, In Search of a Science of Aesthetics, NY, Peter Lang Pub Co, 95; The Problem of the A Priori in Sensibility, Revisiting Kant's and Hegel's Theories of the Senses, forthcoming, The Review of Metaphysics; co-auth, Kant's Critique of Judgement and the Scientific Investigation of Matter, Universitat Karlsruhe, Germany, Inst Of Philos, Vol 3, 97; Kant's Eschatology in Zum ewigen Frieden: The Concept of Purposiveness to Guarantee Perpetual Peace, Proceedings of the 8th International Kant Congress, Memphis, 95. **CONTACT ADDRESS** Dept of Philosophy, Loyola Col, 4501 N Charles St, Baltimore, MD, 21210-2699. **EMAIL** ischerer@loyola.edu

SCHIAVONA, CHRISTOPHER F.
PERSONAL Born 09/08/1958, Boston, MA, s **DISCIPLINE** PHILOSOPHY **EDUCATION** Georgetown Univ, MA, PhD, 92; St John's Seminary, BA, MA, M.Div. **CAREER** Asst prof, St John's Sem; Dean of Students, St John's Sem; Senior Consultant, Taylor Res Consulting Group; Pres, City Square Assoc. **MEMBERSHIPS** Amer Philos Assoc; Greater Boston Bus Council; Soc for Bus & Prof Ethics. **RESEARCH** Business Ethics; Philosophy of Religion; Media Studies; Popular Culture. **CONTACT ADDRESS** City Square Associates, 26 Prospect St, Charlestown, MA, 02129. **EMAIL** cschiavone@citysquareassociates.com

SCHICK, FREDERIC
PERSONAL Born 08/27/1929, Brunn, Czechoslovakia, m **DISCIPLINE** PHILOSOPHY **EDUCATION** Columbia Univ, BA, 51, MA, 52, PhD, 58. **CAREER** Instr philos, CT Col, 54-57; lectr, City Col NY, 57-58; insts, Columbia Univ, 58-60; asst prof, Brandeis Univ, 60-62; from asst prof to assoc prof, 62-69, chmn dept, 65-68, 79-82, Prof Philos, Rutgers Univ, 69-, Lectr, New Sch Social Res, 57-59; Coun Res Humanities grant, 59; Nat Sci Found res grants, 63-64 & 73-74; ed, Theory & Decision, 74-82, adv ed, Theory & Decision Libr, 77-; adv ed, Econ & Philos, 87-; vis scholar, Corpus Christi Col, Cambridge Univ, 75; vis fel, Clare Hall, Cambridge Univ, 94. **MEMBERSHIPS** Am Philos Asn (life mem 95). **RESEARCH** Philos of sci; inductive logic; decision theory. **SELECTED PUBLICATIONS** Auth, Beyond utilitarianism, 71 & A justification of reason, 72, J Philos; Democracy and interdependent preferences, Theory & Decision, 72; Some notes on thinking ahead, Social Res, 77; Self-knowledge, uncertainty and choice, British J Philos Sci, 79; Toward a logic of liberalism, J Philos, 80; Welfare, Rights and Fairness, In: Science, Belief and Behavior, 80 & Under Which Description? In: Beyond Utilitarianism, Cambridge Univ, 82; Having Reason, Princeton Univ Press, 82; Understanding Action, Cambridge Univ Press, 91; Making Choices, Cambridge Univ Pres, 97. **CONTACT ADDRESS** Dept of Philos, Rutgers Univ, PO Box 270, New Brunswick, NJ, 08903-0270. **EMAIL** fschick@rci.rugers.edu

SCHIEFEN, RICHARD JOHN
PERSONAL Born 05/09/1932, Rochester, NY **DISCIPLINE** MODERN CHURCH HISTORY, HISTORY OF RELIGION **EDUCATION** Univ Toronto, BA, 56, MA, 62; Univ St Michael's Col, STB, 61; Univ Rochester, MEd, 58; Univ London, PhD, 70. **CAREER** From asst prof to assoc prof hist, Univ St Thomas, Tex, 65-72, chmn dept, 70-72; assoc prof church hist, St Michael's Col, Univ Toronto, 72-81; DEAN SCH THEOL, UNIV ST THOMAS, 81- **MEMBERSHIPS** AHA; Am Cath Hist Asn; Can Cath Hist Asn; Ecclesiastical Hist Soc. **RESEARCH** Victorian religion; 19th century Roman Catholicism. **SELECTED PUBLICATIONS** Auth, A Hist Commentary On The Major Catholic Works Of Newman,Cardinal - Griffin,Jr/, Cath Hist Rev, Vol 0080, 1994; Trial Of Strength, Furtwangler,Wilhelm In The Third-Reich - Prieberg,Fk/, Biog-An Interdisciplinary Quart, Vol 0018, 1995; Cath Devotion In Victorian Eng - Heimann,M/, Cath Hist Rev, Vol 0083, 1997. **CONTACT ADDRESS** Sch of Theol, Univ of St Thomas, Houston, TX, 77024.

SCHIEVELLA, P.S.
PERSONAL Born 03/13/1914, Bayonne, NJ, m, 1965, 4 children **DISCIPLINE** PHILOSOPHY **EDUCATION** Columbia Univ, BS, 50, MA, 51, PhD, 67. **CAREER** Tchr, Brooklyn Acad, 54, E Islip, 54-55, Earl L Vandermeulen High School, 55-68; prof of Philosophy, Bemidji Univ, 68-70; prof philosophy & chr, Jersey City State Univ, 70-78; adj prof of philosophy, Suffolk Community Col, 78-. **HONORS AND AWARDS** Wall of Fame, Earl L Vandermeulen High School, 98. **MEMBERSHIPS** Amer Philos Asn; Nat Coun Critical Anal; Long Island Philos Asn; NJ Reg Philos Soc. **RESEARCH** Clear, critical and analytical thinking. **SELECTED PUBLICATIONS** Auth, Critical Analysis: Language and Its Functions, Hum Press, 66; The Philosophy of Conwy Lloyd Morgan, Univ Microfilms, 67; ed, The Jour of Critical Analysis, 68; The Jour of Pre-Col Philos, 75; Emergent Evolution and Reductionism, Scientia, 73; auth, Hey! Is That You, God?, Sebastian Publ Co, 87. **CONTACT ADDRESS** Box 137, Port Jefferson, NY, 11777. **EMAIL** passch@li.net

SCHINE, ROBERT S.
DISCIPLINE JEWISH STUDIES AND BIBLICAL HEBREW **EDUCATION** Kenyon Col, AB; Univ Freiburg, MA; Jewish Theol Sem Am, PhD. **CAREER** Prof, Relig dept & Class dept; coordr, annual Hannah A. Quint Lect in Jewish Stud; Middlebury Col, 85-. **RESEARCH** 19th- and 20th-century European Jewish thought. **SELECTED PUBLICATIONS** Auth, Jewish Thought Adrift: Max Wiener 1882-1950. **CONTACT ADDRESS** Dept of Religion, Middlebury Col, Middlebury, VT, 05753.

SCHLAGEL, RICHARD H.
PERSONAL Born 11/22/1925, Springfield, MA, m, 1962 **DISCIPLINE** PHILOSOPHY **EDUCATION** Springfield Col, BS, 49; Boston Univ , MA, 53, PhD, 55. **HONORS AND AWARDS** Borden Parker Bowne fel, Boston Univ, 54-55; Res Award, George Wash Univ, 96. **MEMBERSHIPS** AAUP; Am Philos Asn. **RESEARCH** Epistemology; hist and philos of science; philos of mind. **CONTACT ADDRESS** Dept of Philosophy, George Washington Univ, Washington, DC, 20052. **EMAIL** schlagel@wis2

SCHMALENBERGER, JERRY L.
DISCIPLINE PARISH MINISTRY **EDUCATION** Wittenberg Univ, BA; Hamma Sch Theol, MDiv; Consortium for Higher Edu Rel Stud, Dmin; Wittenberg Univ, DD. **CAREER** Roland Payne lectr, Gbarnga Sch Theol; lectur, Lutheran Theol Sem, Hong Kong; Theol Col of the West Indies, Jamaica; Belgum Memorial lectr, Calif Lutheran Univ, 89; prof, 88-. **HONORS AND AWARDS** Pastor, dir, consult, Evangel Outreach; co-dir, PLTS Ctr for Lutheran Church Growth and Mission; bd(s) of dir(s), Hamma Sch Theol; Wittenberg Univ; Lutheran Soc Serv Iowa; Grand View Col; pres, Downtown Revitalization Comm; **SELECTED PUBLICATIONS** Auth, Preparation for Discipleship: A Handbook for New Christians, C.S.S. Publ, 98; The Preacher's Edge, C.S.S. Publ, 96; Plane Thoughts on Parish Ministry, C. S. S. Publ, 94; Called to Witness, C.S.S. Publ, 93. **CONTACT ADDRESS** Dept of Parish Ministry, Pacific Lutheran Theol Sem, 2770 Marin Ave, Berkeley, CA, 94708-1597. **EMAIL** 102567.3522@compuserve.com

SCHMALTZ, TED M.
PERSONAL Born 12/17/1960, Ft Wayne, IN, m, 1983, 2 children **DISCIPLINE** PHILOSOPHY **EDUCATION** Kalamazoo Col, BA, 83; Univ Notre Dame, PhD, 88. **CAREER** Tchg asst and grad asst, 83-88, adj asst prof, 88-89, Univ Notre Dame; asst prof, 89-96, assoc prof, 96- , Duke Univ. **HONORS AND AWARDS** Benjamin N. Duke Fellow, Natl Human Ctr, 97-98; Andrew W. Mellon Asst Prof Philos, Duke Univ 94-95; Fel for Univ Tchrs, NEH, 93-94; Univ Res Coun Fac Res Grant, 90-97; Univ Res Counc Travel Grant, Duke Univ, 91, 94-97. **RESEARCH** The Development of Early Modern (ie 17th to mid-18th century)Philosophy (with emphasis on the history of French Cartesianism as well as the relations among philosophy, theology, science and politics I the Ancien Regime); Historiography of Modern Philosophy; Early Modern Metaphysics and Epistemology (with emphasis on cartesianism and reactions to Cartesianism, Spinoza's metaphysics, early modern philosophy of mind, and modern theories of substance). **SELECTED PUBLICATIONS** Auth, Platonism and Descartes' View of Immutable Essences, Archiv fur Geschichte der Philosophie, 73, Bd, Heft 2, 91, 129-70; Sensation, Occasionalism, and Descartes' Causal Principles, in Minds, Ideas, and Objects: Essays on the Theory of Representation in Modern Philosophy, ed, P. Cummins and G. Zoeller, 33-55, N Amer Kant Soc Stud in Philos, vol 2, Atascadero, CA, Ridgeview Publ, 92; Descartes and Malebranche on Mind and Mind-Body Union, Philos Rev, 101, 2, 92, 281-325; Human Freedom and Divine Creation in Malebranche, Descartes and the Cartesians, British Jour Hist Philos, 2, 2, 94, 3-50; Malebranche on Descartes on Mind-Body Distinctness, Jour Hist of Philos, 32, 4, 94, 573-603; Malebranche's Cartesianism and Lockean Colors, Hist of Philos Quart, 12, 4, 95, 387-403; Malebranche's Theory of the Soul: A Cartesian Interpretation, New York, Oxford Univ Press, 96; Spinoza's Mediate Infinite Mode, Jour Hist Philos, 35, 2, 97, 199-235; Descartes on Innate Ideas, Sensation, and Scholasticism: The Response to Regius, in Studies in Seventeenth-Century European Philosophy, ed MA Stewart, 33-73, Oxford Studies in the History of Philosophy, 2, Oxford, Clarendon Press, 97; Rev of Ch. J. McCracken, Archiv fur Geschichte der Philosophie, 79, Bd, Heft 3, 97. **CONTACT ADDRESS** Dept of Philosophy, Duke Univ, PO Box 90734, Durham, NC, 27708. **EMAIL** tad.schmaltz@duke.edu

SCHMANDT, JORGEN
DISCIPLINE PHILOSOPHY **EDUCATION** Univ Bonn, PhD, 56. **CAREER** Org Econ Coop & Dev, Paris, 58-65; Harvard Univ, 65, 71; HOUSTON ADV RES CTR, 87-; UNIV TEX, AUSTIN, 71-. **CONTACT ADDRESS** Ctr for Global Studies, Houston Advanced Research Ctr, 4800 Research Forest Dr, Woodlands, TX, 77381. **EMAIL** jas@harc.edu

SCHMAUS, WARREN STANLEY
PERSONAL Born 04/02/1952, Staten Island, NY, m, 1979, 2 children **DISCIPLINE** PHILOSOPHY & HISTORY OF SCIENCE **EDUCATION** Princeton Univ, AB, 74; Univ Pittsburgh, MA, 75, PhD(Hist & Philos of Sci), 80. **CAREER** Asst prof Philos, Ill Inst Technol, 80-, res assoc, Study Ethics in Professions, Ill Inst Technol, 80-; asst prof Phil, Ill Inst Technol, 80-85; from assoc prof to prof, 85-95. **HONORS AND AWARDS** Vis fel, Center for Philosophy of Science, Univ of Pittsburgh, 96-97; vis scholar, Univ Chicago, 87-88. **MEMBERSHIPS** Am Philos Asn; Philos Sci Asn; Hist Sci Soc; Cheiron; Soc Social Studies Sci. **RESEARCH** History and philosophy of the social sciences; philosophy of history; ethics of research. **SELECTED PUBLICATIONS** Auth, Fraud and sloppiness in science, Perspectives on Professions, 9 & 12/81; A reappraisal of Comte's three-state law, Hist & Theory, 5/82; Durkheim's Philosophy of Science and the Cosiology of Knowledge, Univ of Chicago Press, 94; some 30 articles. **CONTACT ADDRESS** Dept of Humanities, Illinois Inst of Tech, 3300 S Federal St, Chicago, IL, 60616-3793. **EMAIL** schmaus@charlie.iit.edu

SCHMID, WALTER T.
DISCIPLINE PHILOSOPHY **EDUCATION** Yale Univ, PhD, 76. **CAREER** Univ of Hartford, 77-78; Valparaiso, 78; Grinnell, 79; Univ of NC at Wilmington, 79-. **MEMBERSHIPS** SAGP. **RESEARCH** History of philosophy; contemporary political philosophy, especially race & justice. **SELECTED PUBLICATIONS** Auth, On Manly Courage: A Study of Plato's Laches, S Ill Univ Press 92; Plato's Charmides and the Socratic Ideal of Rationality, SUNY, 98. **CONTACT ADDRESS** Dept of Philososphy and Religion, Univ of N. Carolina at Wilmington, Wilmington, NC, 28403. **EMAIL** schmidt@uncwil.edu

SCHMIDT, DARYL DEAN
PERSONAL Born 08/12/1944, Sioux Falls, SD, m, 1977 **DISCIPLINE** NEW TESTAMENT STUDIES, LINGUISTICS **EDUCATION** Bethel Col, BA, 66; Assoc Mennonite Bibl Sem, MDiv, 70; Grad Theol Union, PhD(bibl studies), 79. **CAREER** Instr New Testament, Pac Sch Relig, 77-78; Asst Prof Relig, Tex Christian Univ, 79- **MEMBERSHIPS** Soc Bibl Lit. **RESEARCH** Synoptic gospels; Hellenistic Greek syntax; second language acquisition. **SELECTED PUBLICATIONS** Auth, A Morphology Of New-Testament Greek - A Rev And Reference Grammar - Brooks,Ja, Winbery,Cl/, J Of Bibl Lit, Vol 0115, 1996. **CONTACT ADDRESS** Dept of Relig Studies, Tex Christian Univ, Fort Worth, TX, 76129-0002.

SCHMIDT, DENNIS
DISCIPLINE PHILOSOPHY **EDUCATION** Bucknell Univ, BA, 74; Boston Col, MA, 76, PhD, 80. **CAREER** Prof, Villanova Univ. **HONORS AND AWARDS** Univ Fac Res awd, 95; PDQWL awd, 93; Univ Res Semester awd; 88; Univ awd for Excellence in Undergrad Tchg, SUNY, 87; Chancellor's awd for Excellence in Tchg, NY State Univ, 87; SUNY Fac Summer Res grant, 87; Experienced Fac Travel grant, 87; New Fac Develop awd, 85; SUNY Fac Summer Res grant, 84; Phi Beta Kappa, Bucknell Univ, 84; Fulbright-Hays Full Fel, Univ Freiburg, 78; Univ Dissertation awd, Boston Col, 78. **SELECTED PUBLICATIONS** Auth, The Ubiquity of the Finite: Hegel, Heidegger and the Entitlements of Philosophy, MIT Press: Cambridge, MA, 88; What We Owe the Dead, in Revue Philos, 96; Beauty, Encycl Philos Supp, Macmillian Publ Co, 96; The Ordeal of the For, Philos Today, Caputo and Berghofen, 96; What We Didn't See, in The Silverman Lectures, Duquesne UP, 95, rep in The Presocratics After Heidegger, SUNY Press, 96; Putting Oneself in Words..., in Library of Living Philosophers, Open Ct Press, 95; Heidegger and the Greeks / History, Catastrophe and Community, in Heidegger Toward the Turn: Essays on Texts of the 1930's, SUNY Press, 95 & Ruins and Roses: Hegel and Heidegger on Mourning, Sacrifice and History, in Endings: The Question of Memory in Hegel and Heidegger, Northwestern UP, 95; transl, Natural Law and Human Dignity, by Ernst Bloch, MIT Press: Cambridge, MA, 86; ed, Hermeneutics and the Poetic Motion, SUNY/CRIT, 90. **CONTACT ADDRESS** Dept of Philosophy, Villanova Univ, 800 Lancaster Ave, Villanova, PA, 19085-1692.

SCHMIDT, FREDERICK W.
PERSONAL Born 06/20/1953, Louisville, KY, m, 1975, 1 child **DISCIPLINE** NEW TESTAMENT STUDIES **EDUCATION** Asbury Coll, BA, 75; Asbury Theo Seminary, MDiv, 78; Oxford Univ, DPhil, 86. **CAREER** Teaching fel, New Testament Greek, Biblical Studies Dept, Asbury Theological Seminary, 78-80; instr in New Testament Theology, Oxford Univ, 84-86; tutor New Testament Studies, Keble Coll, 86; assoc prof, New Testament Studies, Dept Religion and Philosophy, Messiah Coll, 87-94; dean, Saint George's Coll, 94-95; special asst to the pres, La Salle Univ, 95-96; canon edu, dir, Programs Spirituality and Religious Educ, Washington Natl Cathedral, 97-. **HONORS AND AWARDS** Amer Coun Educ Fel, Center Leadership Development, 96; sr fel, W. F. Albright Inst Arch Research, 95; Young Scholars Fel, Catholic Biblical Assn, Catholic Univ, 93; Who's Who in Biblical Studies in Arch, Biblical Arch Soc, 93. **MEMBERSHIPS** Amer Acad Religion; mem, sec-treas, Anglican Assn Biblical Studies; Soc Biblical Literature; Soc Scientific Study Religion. **RESEARCH** Historical Jesus; early Jewish apocalyptic literature; other theological topics. **SELECTED PUBLICATIONS** Auth, "Jesus: Prophet, Teacher, Messiah, Lord. An Interview with N.T. Wright," Cathedral Age, fall 97; auth, "A Still Small Voice: Women, Ordination and the Church," Women and Gender in North American Religions, 96; auth, "Beyond a Biblicistic Feminism: H **CONTACT ADDRESS** Washington National Cathedral, Massachusetts and Wisconsin Aves, NW, Washington, DC, 20016. **EMAIL** fschmidt@cathedral.org

SCHMIDT, PAUL F.
PERSONAL Born 09/14/1925, Rochester, NY, m, 1964 **DISCIPLINE** PHILOSOPHY **EDUCATION** Univ Rochester, BA, 47; Yale Univ, PhD, 51. **CAREER** Instr, Oberlin Col, 51-53; asst prof to prof, philos, chemn 65-76, Univ New Mexico, 53-89. **HONORS AND AWARDS** Phi Beta Kappa, 47. **MEMBERSHIPS** APA; AAUP. **RESEARCH** Whitehead; American philosophy; philosophy of science; Buddhism. **SELECTED PUBLICATIONS** Auth, Religious Knowledge, Free Press, 61; auth, Perception and Cosmology in Whitehead's Philosophy, Rutgers, 67; auth, Rebelling, Loving & Liberation, Hummingbird Press, 71; auth, Temple Reflections, Humanities Press, 80; auth, Buddhist Meditation on China, Hummingbird Press, 84. **CONTACT ADDRESS** 2400 Hannett NE, Albuquerque, NM, 87106.

SCHMIDT, WILLIAM JOHN
PERSONAL Born 05/22/1926, Green Bay, WI, m, 1949 **DISCIPLINE** CHURCH HISTORY **EDUCATION** N Cent Col, BA, 51; Evangel Theol Sem, BD, 54; Columbia Univ, PhD (church hist), 66. **CAREER** Pastor, Wis Conf Evangel United Brethren Church, 52-62; tutor, Union Theol Sem, 62-65; from asst prof to assoc prof church hist, NY Theol Sem, 67-70; adj assoc prof church hist, 67-70, assoc prof, 70-78, Prof Theol, St Peter's Col, NJ, 78-, Res writer with Samuel McCrea Cavert on The American Churches in the Ecumenical Movement, 1900-1968, 65-67; mem Gen Prog Coun, Reformed Church Am, 70-76. **MEMBERSHIPS** Am Soc Church Hist; N Am Acad Ecumenists (secy-treas, 68-72). **RESEARCH** American church history; history of the ecumenical movement; religous syncretism. **SELECTED PUBLICATIONS** Auth, Weigel,Gustave - A Pioneer Of Reform - Collins,Pw/, J Of Ecumenical Studies, Vol 0030, 1993; Between The Flood And The Rainbow - Interpreting The Conciliar Process Of Mutual Commitment Covenant To Justice, Peace, And The Integrity Of Creation - Niles,Dp, Editor/, J Of Ecumenical Studies, Vol 0030, 1993; The Cath-Church In Mission - Highlights Of Church Teaching Since 1891 - Daniels,E/, J Of Ecumenical Studies, Vol 0031, 1994; Directory For The Application Of Principles And Norms On Ecumenism - United-States-Cath-Conference/, J Of Ecumenical Studies, Vol 0031, 1994. **CONTACT ADDRESS** Dept of Theol, St Peter's Col, Kennedy Blvd, Jersey City, NJ, 07306.

SCHMITT, FREDERICK FRANCIS
PERSONAL Born 04/20/1951, Indianapolis, IN, m, 1981, 1 child **DISCIPLINE** PHILOSOPHY **EDUCATION** Syracuse Univ, BS, 73; Univ Mich, MA, 76, PhD, 80. **CAREER** Vis instr, Univ Southern Calif, 77-78; vis lectr, Univ NC, Chapel Hill, 78-80; from Asst Prof to Assoc Prof, 80-92, Prof Philos, Univ IL, Urbana-Champaign, 92. **HONORS AND AWARDS** Fel, Ohio State Univ, 82; Fel, Ctr for Advanced Study, Urbana, 84; Fel, Univ Melbourne, 95. **MEMBERSHIPS** Am Philos Asn. **RESEARCH** Epistemology; metaphysics; hist of 17th and 18th century philos. **SELECTED PUBLICATIONS** Auth, Change, 78 & Justification as reliable indication or reliable process?, 81, Philos Studies; Knowledge justification and reliability, Synthese, 83; Against epistemic indolence, Mind, 84; Knowledge and Belief, Routledge, 92; ed, Socializing Epistemology: The Social Dimensions of Knowledge, Rowan & Littlefield, 94; auth, Truth: A Primer, Westview Press, 95. **CONTACT ADDRESS** Dept of Philos, Univ of Illinois, 105 Gregory Hall, Urbana, IL, 61801-3611. **EMAIL** fschmitt@uiuc.edu

SCHMITT, RICHARD GEORGE
PERSONAL Born 05/05/1927, Frankfurt, Germany, m, 1961 **DISCIPLINE** PHILOSOPHY **EDUCATION** Univ Chicago, AB, 49, MA, 52; Yale Univ, PhD, 56. **CAREER** Instr, Yale Univ, 56-58; from asst prof to full prof, Brown Univ, 58-, vis assoc prof, Stanford Univ, 67-68; vis prof, Univ Calif, Santa Barbara, 71-72. **HONORS AND AWARDS** Alfred Hodder fel, Princeton Univ, 62-63; Guggenheim fel, 65-66; MA, Brown Univ, 66. **MEMBERSHIPS** Am Philos Asn, Rad Philos Asn. **RESEARCH** Phenomenology; existentialism. **SELECTED PUBLICATIONS** Auth, Maurice Meleau-Ponty, Rev Metaphys, 66; Phenomenology, In: Encycl of Philosophy, Collier-Macmillan, 67; Can Heidegger Be Understood?, Inquiry, 67; Martin Heidegger on Being Human, Random, 69; Alienation and Class, Schenkman, 82; Introduction to Marx and Engels, Westview, 87, 2nd ed, 97; with Tom Moody, Alienation and Social Criticism, Humanities, 94; Beyond Separateness, Westview, 95. **CONTACT ADDRESS** Dept of Philos, Brown Univ, Providence, RI, 02912-9127. **EMAIL** rschmitt@famtree.com

SCHMITTER, AMY
DISCIPLINE HISTORY OF EARLY MODERN PHILOSOPHY, HISTORY OF METAPHYSICS, PHILOSOPHY OF A **EDUCATION** Bryn Mawr Col, AB, 84; grad work, Univ Bonn, 88-89; Univ Pittsburgh, PhD, 93. **CAREER** Asst prof, Univ NMex. **SELECTED PUBLICATIONS** Auth, Representation, Self-Representation, and the Passions in Descartes, Rev of Metaphysics, Vol XVII, No 2, Dec 94; Formal Causation and the Explanation of Intentionality in Descartes, The Monist, Jl 96. **CONTACT ADDRESS** Univ NMex, Albuquerque, NM, 87131.

SCHNABEL, ECKHARD J.
PERSONAL Born 05/09/1955, Stuttgart, Germany, m, 1981, 2 children **DISCIPLINE** NEW TESTAMENT LITERATURE & THEOLOGY **EDUCATION** Staatsunabhaengige Hochschule Basel, Th M, 79; Aberdeen Univ, PhD, 83. **CAREER** Asst prof, new testament, Asian Theol Sem, Manila, Philippines, 85-88; lectr, new testament, Wiedenest Bible Col, Ger, 89-94; head of dept, new testament, Ger Theol Sem, Giessen, Ger, 94-98; assoc prof, new testament, Trinity Evang Divinity Sch, Deerfield, Ill, 98-. **MEMBERSHIPS** Soc of New Testament Studies; Tyndale Fel; Evang Theol Soc; Inst for Bibl Res; Fel of Europ Evang Theol. **RESEARCH** Early Christian history; New Testament theology; Pauline literature. **SELECTED PUBLICATIONS** Auth, Sind Evangelikale Fundamentalisten?, TVG-Orientierung, Wuppertal, R. Brockhaus, 95; auth, Das Reich Gottes als Wirklichkeit und Hoffnung. Neuere Entwicklungen in der evangelikalen Theologie, Wuppertal, R. Brockhaus, 93; auth, Inspiration und Offenbarung: Die Lehre vom Ursprung und Wesen der Bibel, TVG Allgemeine Reihe, Wuppertal, R. Brockhaus, 86; auth, Law and Wisdom from Ben Sira to Paul: A Tradition Historical Enquiry into the Relation of Law, Wisdom, and Ethics, WUNT, 2/16, Tubingen ,Mohr-Siebeck, 85; article, Theologisches Begriffslexikon zum Neuen Testament, Wuppertal/Neukirchen-Vluyn, R. Brockhaus/ Neukirchener Verlag, 97; article, Mission, Early Non-Pauline, Dict of the Later New Testament and Its Develop, Downers Grove/Leicester, InterVarsity Press, 97; Die urchristliche Heidenmission als endzeitliches Phanomen, Werdet meine Zeugen. Welmission im Horizont von Theologie und Geschichte, Neuhausen-Stuttgart, Hanssler, 81-104, 96; article, Die Gemeinde des Neuen Bundes in Kontinuitat und Diskontinuitat zur Gemeinde des Alten Bundes, Israel in Geschichte und Gegenwart. Beitrage zur Geschichte Israels und zum judsich-christlichen Dialog, Wuppertal, R. Brockhaus, 147-213, 96; article, History, Theology and the Bibilical Canon: An Introduction to Basic Issues, Themelios, 20, 2, 16-24, 95; article, How Paul Developed His Ethics, Understanding Paul's Ethics. Twentieth Century Approaches, Exeter/Grand Rapids, Paternoster/Eerdmans, 267-297, 95; article, Jesus and the Beginnings of the Mission to the Gentiles, Jesus of Nazareth: Lord and Christ, FS, Grand Rapids/Carlisle, Eerdmans/Paternoster, 37-58, 94; article, Wisdom, Dict of Paul and His Letters, Downers Grove, Inter-Varsity Press, 967-973, 93; article, Die Entwurfe von B. S. Childs und H. Gese bezuglich des Kanons, Der Kanon der Bibel, Wuppertal/Giesen, R. Brockhaus, Brunnen, 102-152, 90. **CONTACT ADDRESS** 216 Tanglewood Dr., Gurnee, IL, 60031. **EMAIL** eschnabe@trin.edu

SCHNEEWIND, JEROME B.
PERSONAL Born 05/17/1930, m, 3 children **DISCIPLINE** PHILOSOPHY **EDUCATION** Cornell Univ, BA, 51; Princeton Univ, MA, 53, PhD, 57. **CAREER** Prof, Johns Hopkins Univ, 81-. **MEMBERSHIPS** APA, Am Acad of Arts and Sci. **RESEARCH** Philosophy; Victorian literature; Victorian morality. **SELECTED PUBLICATIONS** Auth, Backgrounds of English Victorian Literature, 70; "Moral Problems and Moral Philosophy in the Victorian Period," 71; "Moral Knowledge and Moral Principles," 70; Sidgwick's Ethics and Victorian Moral Philosophy, 86; Moral Philosophy from Montaigne to Kant: An Anthology, 90; "Classical Republicanism and the History of Ethics," 93; "Locke's Moral Philosophy," 94; "Voluntarism and the Foundations of Ethics," 96; Immanuel Kant: Lectures on Ethics, 97; The Invention of Autonomy: A History of Modern Moral Philosophy, 98. **CONTACT ADDRESS** Dept of Philosophy, Johns Hopkins Univ, 3400 N Charles St, Baltimore, MD, 21218.

SCHNEIDER, CARL E.
PERSONAL Born 02/23/1948, Exeter, CT, m **DISCIPLINE** LAW **EDUCATION** Harvard Univ, BA, 72; Univ Mich Law Sch, JD, 79. **CAREER** Adv on educ policy, Mass Tchrs Asn, 72-75; law clerk, US Court of Appeals for the District of Columbia Circuit, 79-80; law clerk to Hon Potter Stewart, Assoc Justice, US Supreme Court, 80-81; prof law, Univ Mich Law School, 81- ; prof Internal Med, Univ Mich Med Sch, 98- . **MEMBERSHIPS** Fel, Hasting Ctr; Am Soc Law, Med, & Ethics; Int Asn of Bioethics; Acad Adv Bd, Inst for Am Values; Int Soc of Family Law; AALS; Order of the Coif. **RESEARCH** Moral culture of the American family; moral culture of medical decisions. **SELECTED PUBLICATIONS** Auth, The Tension Between Rules and Discretion in Family Law: A Report and a Reflection, Family Law Q, 93; auth, Bioethics with a Human Face, Indiana Law J, 94; auth, Bioethics in the Language of the Law, Hastings Ctr Rpt, 94; auth, Marriage, Morals, and the Law: No-Fault Divorce and Moral Discourse, Utah Law Rev, 94; auth, The Decision to Withdraw from Dialysis, Advan in

Renal Replacement Therapy, 94; auth, The Frail Old Age of the Socratic Method, Law Quadrangle Notes, 94; auth, Triumph and Crisis: The Autonomy Principle in the American Law of Medicine, Jurisuto, 95; auth, The Socratic Method and the Goals of Legal Education: With Some Thoughts Inspired by Travel, Hogaku Kyoshitsu, 95; auth, Medical Decisions at the End of Life: Cruzan, Advance Directives, and Individual Autonomy, Jurisuto, 95; auth, From Consumer Choice to Consumer Welfare, Hastings Ctr Rpt, 95; coauth, Medical Decisions in the Moral Lives of Patients, Bull of the Europ Soc of Philos of Med and Health Care, 95; auth, On the Duties and Rights of Parents, Va Law Rev, 95; auth, The Law and the Stability of Marriage: The Family as a Social Institution, in Popenoe, ed, Promises to Keep: Decline and Renewal of Marriage in America, Rowman & Littlefield, 96; coauth, An Invitation to Family Law: Principles, Process, and Perspectives, West, 96; auth, Moral Discourse, Bioethics, and the Law, Hastings Ctr Rpt, 96; auth, Making Sausage, Hastings Ctr Rpt, 97; auth, Testing Testing, Hastings Ctr Rpt, 97; auth, Hard Cases, Hastings Ctr Rpt, 98; auth, The Book Review Issue: An Owner's Manual, Mich Law Rev, 98; auth, The Practice of Autonomy: Patients, Doctors, and Medical Decisions, Oxford, 98. **CONTACT ADDRESS** Law School, Univ of Michigan, Ann Arbor, 625 S State St, 341 HH, Ann Arbor, MI, 48109-1215. **EMAIL** carlschn@umich.edu

SCHNEIDER, SAMUEL
PERSONAL Born 08/26/1907, Yonkers, NY, w, 1936, 3 children **DISCIPLINE** PHILOSOPHY **EDUCATION** NY Univ, PhD, 69. **CAREER** Hunter Col, tchr, adj assoc prof, 54-58. **HONORS AND AWARDS** CCNY, Phi Beta Kappa, 1930 **MEMBERSHIPS** Philo of Edu Society **RESEARCH** Philosophy of Education **SELECTED PUBLICATIONS** Auth, An Identification, Analysis and Critique of Thorstein Veblen's Philosophy of Higher Education, Edwin Mellen Press, 98; Three American Economics Professors Battle Against Monopoly and Pricing Practices, Ripley, Fetter and Commons: Three for the People, Edwin Mellen Press, 98. **CONTACT ADDRESS** Apartment 25M, NYC, NY, 10023.

SCHNEIDERS, SANDRA MARIE
PERSONAL Born 11/12/1936, Chicago, IL **DISCIPLINE** NEW TESTAMENT STUDIES, CHRISTIAN SPIRITUALITY **EDUCATION** Marygrove Col, BA, 60; Univ Detroit, MA, 67; Cath Inst, Paris, STL, 71; Gregorian Univ, Rome, STD, 75. **CAREER** Instr philos, Marygrove Col, 65-67, instr relig studies, 71-72; from asst prof to assoc prof, 76-89, prof New Testament & Spirituality, Jesuit Sch Theol, 89-. **HONORS AND AWARDS** Assoc Theol Sch res grant, 78; elected to Delta Epsilon Sigma, Nat Catholic Hon Soc, 87; Book-of-the-Year, for: New Wineskins, Human Development V.8:1, Spring 87; The Twentieth Century Award for Achievement, Int Biog Ctr, 93; Honorary Degrees from St. Mary's Col, Lafayette Col, and St. Bernard's Inst; Christian Culture Gold Medalist, Assumption Univ, 94; Teresa of Avila Award, Long Island Women's Ordination Conf, 94. **MEMBERSHIPS** Cath Bibl Asn; Soc Bibl Lit; Cath Theol Soc Am; Cath Comn on Intellectual and Cultural Affairs; Soc Study Christian Spirituality, vice-pres, 96, pres, 97; Soc New Testament Studies. **RESEARCH** Gospel of St John; Biblical hermeneutics; spirituality. **SELECTED PUBLICATIONS** Auth, Women and the Word: The Gender of God in the New Testament and the Spirituality of Women, Paulist Press, 86; New Wineskins: Re-Imagining Religious Life Today, Paulist Press, 86; Beyond Patching: Faith and Feminism in the Catholic Church, Paulist Press, 90; The Revelatory Text: Interpreting the New Testament as Sacred Scripture, HarperCollins, 91; Feminist Spirituality: Christian Alternative or Alternative to Christianity?, in Women's Spirituality: Resources for Christian Development, Paulist Press, 2nd ed, 96; A Case Study: A Feminist Interpretation of John 4:1-42, in The Interpretation of John, T&T Clark, 2nd ed, 97; Biblical Spirituality: Life, Literature, and Learning, in Doors of Understanding: Conversations in Global Spirituality in Honor of Ewert Cousins, Franciscan Press, 97; author of numerous articles and other book chapters. **CONTACT ADDRESS** Jesuit Sch of Theol, Berkeley, 1735 LeRoy Ave, Berkeley, CA, 94709-1193. **EMAIL** sschneider@jstb.edu

SCHNER, GEORGE
PERSONAL Born 05/22/1946, St. Boniface, MB, Canada, s **DISCIPLINE** PHILOSOPHY; THEOLOGY **EDUCATION** BA, 69, MA, 70, Gonzaga Univ; Mdiv, 74, Regis Col; PhD, 80, Yale Univ. **CAREER** Lectr, 69, 74, Gonzaga Univ; Lectr, 70, Concordia Univ; Prize Teach Fel, 77, Yale Univ; Lectr, 79, Asst Prof, 80, Dir of Basic Degree Studies, 81-88, Asst to the Pres of Academic Affairs, 84-85, Academic Dean, 85-89, Assoc Prof, 87, Dir of Advanced Degree Studies, 93-96, Acting Academic Dean, 94, Regis Col; Chr Basic Degree Council, 84-86, Chr Advanced Degree Council, 93-95, Chr Theology, 96, Toronto School of Theology. **MEMBERSHIPS** Amer Acad of Religion; Canadian Phil Assoc; Canadian Theological Soc; Catholic Theological Soc Amer; Jesuit Phil Assoc. **RESEARCH** Philosophy; Theology **SELECTED PUBLICATIONS** Auth, On Theology: A Speech to its Cultured Despisers, 90; Response to Issues Research Seminar, Thological Education, 90; McClelland and Buckley on Modern Athesim, Toronto Journal of Theology, 91; Hume's Dialogues and the Redefinition of the Philosophy of Religion, The Thomist, 91; The Eclipse of Biblical Narrative: Analysis and Critique, Modern Theology, 92; The Appeal to Experience, Theological Studies, 92; Education for Ministry, 93; Post Liberal Theology and Roman Catholic Theology, Religious Studies Review, 95; Christian Spirituality and the Culture of Modernity: The Thought of Louis Dupre, 98; Theological Method After Liberalism, forthcoming. **CONTACT ADDRESS** Regis Col, 15 St. Mary St., Toronto, ON, M4Y 2R5. **EMAIL** gschner@chass.utoronto.ca

SCHOEDEL, WILLIAM RICHARD
PERSONAL Born 01/10/1930, Stratford, ON, Canada, m, 1956, 3 children **DISCIPLINE** RELIGION **EDUCATION** Univ Western Ont, BA, 51, MA, 52; Univ Chicago, PhD (relig), 63. **CAREER** From instr to assoc prof relig, Brown Univ, 60-70; dir relig studies, Univ Ill, Urbana, 70-76, prof classics, 70-80. **MEMBERSHIPS** Am Acad Relig; Am Soc Church Hist; Am Soc Studies Relig; Soc Bibl Lit. **RESEARCH** Classical and early Christian literature. **SELECTED PUBLICATIONS** Auth, The Clementine Letters - Ger - Lindemann,A/, J Of Bibl Lit, Vol 0112, 1993; Gnosticism And The New-Testament - Perkins,P/, Cath Bibl Quart, Vol 0057, 1995; On Canonic Sources - The Testament Of Irenaeus - Fr - Blanchard,Ym/, Cath Bibl Quart, Vol 0057, 1995. **CONTACT ADDRESS** 1207 S Race, Urbana, IL, 61801.

SCHOEN, EDWARD LLOYD
PERSONAL Born 12/16/1949, Providence, RI **DISCIPLINE** PHILOSOPHY **EDUCATION** Wheaton Col, IL, AB, 71; Univ Southern CA, MA, 74, PhD, 76. **CAREER** From Asst Prof to Assoc Prof, 76-85, Prof Philos, Western KY Univ, 85; Contrib ed philos, J Psychol & Theol, 76-; ed consult philos, Pacific Philos Quart, 78-81. **MEMBERSHIPS** Am Philos Asn; Soc Philos Relig; Soc Christian Philos. **RESEARCH** Epistemology; hist of ancient philos. **SELECTED PUBLICATIONS** Auth, Religious Explanations: A Model from the Sciences, Duke Univ Press, 85; Galileo and the Church: An Untidy Affair, Philos in the Contemp World, Fall 95; Philosophy 310: Religion, Science, and Contemporary Life, Sci & Relig Courses (forthcoming); Between Addition and Difference: A Place for Religious Critiques of the Sciences, Zygon (forthcoming); Perceiving an Imperceptible God, Relig Studies (forthcoming); auth of numerous other articles. **CONTACT ADDRESS** Dept of Philos & Relig, Western Kentucky Univ, 1 Big Red Way St, Bowling Green, KY, 42101-3576. **EMAIL** edward.schoen@wku.edu

SCHOENFELD, MARCUS
PERSONAL Born 07/01/1933, New York, NY, 2 children **DISCIPLINE** LAW **EDUCATION** Harvard Univ, AB, 54, JD, 57; NY Univ, LLM, 62. **CAREER** From instr to asst prof law, Cleveland-Marshall Law Sch, 63-66; assoc prof, 66-69, Prof Law, Villanova Univ, 69- ; Ford fel, NYU, 63 & 65. **MEMBERSHIPS** Am Bar Asn. **RESEARCH** Taxation. **SELECTED PUBLICATIONS** Auth, Tax Management Portfolio-Moving Expenses, Bur Nat Affairs, 70-76; contribr, Non Profit Organizations, Prentice-Hall, 68. **CONTACT ADDRESS** Sch of Law, Villanova Univ, 299 N Spring Mill Rd, Villanova, PA, 19085-1597. **EMAIL** Schoenfe@law.vill.edu

SCHOENING, JEFFREY D.
PERSONAL Born 04/16/1953, Providence, RI, m, 1984 **DISCIPLINE** RELIGIOUS STUDIES **EDUCATION** Amherst Coll, BA, 76; Univ Wash, MA, 83; Univ Wash, MLS, 85; PhD, 91. **CAREER** Vis lectr, Univ Wash, 92, 94-96; DIR, virupa Ecumenical Inst, Seattle Wash, 98-. **HONORS AND AWARDS** Fulbirght-Itays Doctrinal Dissertation Fel, 87-88. **RESEARCH** Tibetan Buddhism; Mahayana Buddhism. **SELECTED PUBLICATIONS** Auth, The Salisatamba Sutra and Its Indian Commentaries, Wien, 95; Sutra Commentaries in Tibetan Translation, Tibetan Lit: Studies In Genre, 96. **CONTACT ADDRESS** 6817 27th Ave NE, Seattle, WA, 98115-7140. **EMAIL** jdschoe@juno.com

SCHOLER, DAVID M.
PERSONAL Born 07/24/1938, Rochester, MN, m, 1960, 2 children **DISCIPLINE** NEW TESTAMENT **EDUCATION** Wheaton College, BA 60, MA, 64; Gordon Divinity Sch, BD, 64; Harvard Divinity Sch, ThD, 80. **CAREER** Asst to Assoc Prof, 69-81. Gordon-Cromwell Theol Sem; Dean, Prof, 81-88, Northern Baptist Theol Sem; Distinguished Prof, 88-94, North Park Theol Sem; Prof, Assoc Dean, 94-, Fuller Theol Sem. **MEMBERSHIPS** Amer Acad of Rel; Chicago Soc of Biblical Res; Catholic Biblical assoc; Inst for Biblical Res; Natl Assoc of Baptist Prof of Rel; North Amer Patristic Soc; Soc of Biblical Lit; Studiorum Nov; Testamenti Soc. **RESEARCH** Women in the early Church; Gnosticism; Separation of Church and Judaism; Eng Trans of the New Testament. **SELECTED PUBLICATIONS** Asst ed, The Encyclopedia of Modern Christian Missions: The Agencies, Camden Thoma Nelson and Sons, 67; Auth, Nag Hammadi Bibliography 1948-1969, Leiden, E.J. Brill, 71; The Caring God: Biblical Models of Discipleship, Valley Forge, Judson, 89; Gnosticism in the Early Church, Studies in Early Christianity 14, NY and London, ed, Garland, 93; Perspectives on Ethical and Social Issues: Essays in Honor of Culbert Gerow Rutenber, NABPR Festschrift Series 11, Macon, National Assoc of Baptist Prof of Rel, 94; Nag Hammadi Bibliography 1970-1994, Nag Hamadi and Manichaean Studies 32, Leiden, E.J. Brill, 97. **CONTACT ADDRESS** 1504 Creekside Ct A, Pasadena, CA, 91107-1456. **EMAIL** dscholer@fuller.edu

SCHOLZ, DANIEL J.
PERSONAL Born 07/31/1960, Milwaukee, WI, m, 1997, 2 children **DISCIPLINE** THEOLOGY **EDUCATION** Mundelein Col, MA, 85; Marquette Univ, PhD, 97. **CAREER** Pius XI High School, dept ch, 86-. **MEMBERSHIPS** AAR, SBL, CBA. **CONTACT ADDRESS** Dept of Theology Chair, Pius XI High Sch, 2603 N 89th St, Wauwatosa, WI, 53226. **EMAIL** dbscholz@execpc.com

SCHOLZ, SALLY J.
PERSONAL Born 04/05/1968, Eugene, OR, m, 1996 **DISCIPLINE** PHILOSOPHY; ETHICS **EDUCATION** Univ Portland, BA, 89; MA, 91, PhD, 93, Purdue Univ. **CAREER** Villanova Univ. **MEMBERSHIPS** Amer Phil Assoc; North Amer Soc for Social Phil; Intl Soc for Value Inquiry; Amer Soc for Value Inquiry; Soc for Phil in Contemporary World; Concerned Philosophers for Peace; Radical Phil Assoc. **RESEARCH** Social and political philosophy; ethics; feminist theory **SELECTED PUBLICATIONS** Auth, Civil Disobedience in the Social Theory of Thomas Aquinas, The Thomist, 96; A Feminist Look at Ferdinand Schoeman's Privacy and Social Freedom Rending and Renewing the Social Order, Social Philosophy Today Book series, 96; Coauth, Seven Principles for Better Practical Ethics, Teaching Philosophy, 96; Auth, Service Learning in Ethics: A New Pedagogical Approach to Old Theory v. Practice Problem, Beyond the Tower: Philosophy in Service Learning, 98; The Dignity of Work and Economic Concerns, Visions and Values, 98; Can Opressed Groups dialogue? Self-Determination, Power, and Coercion in Iris Young's Dialogic Community, Crossing Cultural Boundaries, forthcoming; Peacemaking in Domestic Violence: From and Ethics of Care to an Ethics of Advocacy, Journal of Social Philosophy, forthcoming; The Duty of Solidarity: Catholic Social Teaching and Feminist Moral Theory, Philosophy in the Contemporary World, forthcoming; Values and Language: Toward a Theory of Translation for Alain Locke, Alain Locke and Values, forthcoming; Catcalls and Military Strategy, Peacemaking: Lessons from the Past, Visions for the Future, forthcoming. **CONTACT ADDRESS** Dept of Philosophy, Villanova Univ, Villanova, PA, 19085-1699. **EMAIL** sscholz@email.vill.edu

SCHOLZ, SUSANNE
PERSONAL Born 03/14/1963, Frankfurt/Main, Germany **DISCIPLINE** THEOLOGY **EDUCATION** Univ of Heidelberg, Germany, Erstes Kirchliches Examen, 89; Union Theo Sem NY, STM, 91, MA, 94, PhD, 97. **CAREER** Adj Prof, 97-98, Fordham Univ; Asst Prof, Biblical Studies, Coll of Wooster, Wooster OH. **HONORS AND AWARDS** WCC Scholarship. **MEMBERSHIPS** SBL, AAR, ESWTR, NAPH. **RESEARCH** Biblical cultural studies, feminist Biblical studies. **SELECTED PUBLICATIONS** Auth, Through Whose Eyes? A Right Reading of Genesis 34, in: Genesis, A Feminist Companion to the Bible, ed, A Brenner, Sheffield Univ Press Sheffield, 98; Exodus, Was Befreiung aus seiner Sicht Bedeutet, in: Kompendium Feministische Bibelauslegung, eds L Schottroff & M-T Wacker, Gutersloh, Gutersloher Verlagshaus, 98; Was It Really Reap in Genesis 34? Biblical Scholarship as a Reflection of Cultural Assumptions, in: Marking Boundaries, Essays on Feminist Theological Hermeneutics, eds H Washington S L Graham & P Thimmes, Sheffield Academic Press, Sheffield, forthcoming; Rape Plots, A Feminist Cultural Study of Genesis 34, NY, Peter Lang, 99, forthcoming. **CONTACT ADDRESS** Dept of Religious Studies, The Col of Wooster, Wooster, OH, 44691. **EMAIL** sscholz@acs.wooster.edu

SCHONFELD, MARTIN
PERSONAL Born 02/20/1963, Regensburg, Germany **DISCIPLINE** PHILOSOPHY **EDUCATION** Univ Regensburg, BA, 84; Ludwigs-Maximilian Univ, BA, 86; Univ Georgia, MA, 88; Indiana Univ, PhD, 95. **CAREER** Asst prof, Univ S Fla, 95-. **HONORS AND AWARDS** Studienstiftung fel, 85-90; MacArthur Found Fel, 91; creative scholar grants, 96, 98. **MEMBERSHIPS** APA; Fl Philos Assoc; N Am Kant Soc; Soc for Asian and Comp Philos; Int Soc for Environ Ethics; Soc for the Study of Ethics and Animals. **RESEARCH** History of philosophy and science: eighteenth century; Kant; current environmental philosophy; Chinese philosophy. **SELECTED PUBLICATIONS** Contribur, Justifying Value in Nature, Electronic J of Analytic Philos, 95; auth, Dogmatic Metaphysics and E.W. v. Tschirnhaus's methodology, J of the Hist of Philos, 98; auth, Bernard de Fontenelle, & Ehrenfried Walther von Tschirnhaus, in Craig, ed, Routledge Encyclopedia of Philosophy, Routledge, 98; auth, Was There A Western Inventor of Porcelain? Technol and Culture, 98; auth, How Much is Enough? The Limits of Interdisciplinary Openness in Environmental Ethics, Issues in Integrative Stud, 99; auth, The Philosophy of the Young Kant: The Precritical Project, Oxford, 99. **CONTACT ADDRESS** CPR 107, Univ of South Florica, Tampa, FL, 33620. **EMAIL** mschonfe@chuma.cas.usf.edu

SCHOTCH, PETER K.
PERSONAL Born 07/26/1946 **DISCIPLINE** PHILOSOPHY IN LITERATURE, INTERMEDIATE LOGIC, STOICISM.

EDUCATION Waterloo Univ, PhD, 73. **CAREER** Prof, 84-. **RESEARCH** Formal logic and its applications, philosophy of Descartes, the early Stoa. **SELECTED PUBLICATIONS** Auth, Paraconsistent Logic: The View from the Right, PSA 92; Remarks on Copenhagen Semantics, Essays in Honour of R.E. Jennings, Simon Fraser Univ, 93; Hyperdeontic Logic: An Overview, Social Rules, Westview Press, Boulder, 96; co-auth, Logic on the Track of Social Change, Oxford, Clarenden, 95. **CONTACT ADDRESS** Dept of Philos, Dalhousie Univ, Halifax, NS, B3H 3J5. **EMAIL** peter.schotch@dal.ca

SCHOUBORG, GARY
PERSONAL Born 03/02/1936, Beatrice, NB, Canada, d **DISCIPLINE** PHILOSOPHICAL PSYCHOLOGY **EDUCATION** Univ Texas, Austin, PhD, 78. **CAREER** General partner and founder, Performance Consulting, 89-. **MEMBERSHIPS** APA; Am Psychol Assoc; Am Psychol Soc. **RESEARCH** Philosophy of mind, especially consciousness. **SELECTED PUBLICATIONS** Auth, FLEX : A Flexible Tool for Continuously Improving Your Evaluation of Training Effectiveness, HRD, 93; auth, Keep Cameras in Court, SF Chronicle, 95; coauth, Crafting Personal Effectiveness, Capitol, 96; coauth, The Basic Quality Improvement Tools, CRM Films, 97; coauth, The Managing and Planning Tool System, CRM Films, 97; auth, Promoting Transfer Through a Network of Problem Solvers, in Broad, ed, Transferring Learning to the Workplace, ASTD, 97; auth, A Methodology for the Science of Consciousness, The Karl Jaspers Forum, (electronic journal) 97. **CONTACT ADDRESS** 1947 Everidge Ct, Walnut Creek, CA, 94596-2952. **EMAIL** garyscho@att.net

SCHOULS, PETER A.
PERSONAL Born 12/01/1937, Netherlands, m, 1960, 2 children **DISCIPLINE** PHILOSOPHY **EDUCATION** Univ Toronto, BA, 60, MA, 62, PhD(epistemology), 67. **CAREER** Lectr philos, Univ Toronto, 64-67; from asst prof to assoc prof, 67-76, Prof Philos, Univ Alta, 76-, Can Coun leave fel, 72-73. **MEMBERSHIPS** Can Philos Asn; Mind Asn. **RESEARCH** Epistemology; history of philosophy; methodology. **SELECTED PUBLICATIONS** Auth, Diderot Dream - Anderson,W/, Philos Of Sci, Vol 0060, 1993. **CONTACT ADDRESS** Dept of Philos, Univ of Alta, Edmonton, AB, T6G 2E5.

SCHOVILLE, KEITH NORMAN
PERSONAL Born 03/03/1928, Soldiers Grove, WI, 5 children **DISCIPLINE** HEBREW, BIBLICAL STUDIES **EDUCATION** Milligan Col, BA, 56; Univ Wis-Madison, MA, 66, PhD(Hebrcw & Semitic studies), 69. **CAREER** From instr to asst prof, 68-74, assoc prof, 74-81, chmn dept, 77-82, Prof Hebrew & Semitic Studies, Univ Wis-Madison, 81-, Ed, Hebrew Studies. **MEMBERSHIPS** Am Orient Soc; Soc Biblical Lit; Am Schs Orient Res; Nat Asn Prof Hebrew (secy); Archaeol Inst Am. **RESEARCH** The human factor in archaeology; literary and historical illumination of biblical literature; the Intertestamental Period. **SELECTED PUBLICATIONS** Auth, Bab-Edh-Dhra - Excavations In The Cemetery Directed By Lapp,Paul,W 1965-67 - Schaub,Rt, Rast,Pw/, J Of The Am Oriental Soc, Vol 0112, 1992. **CONTACT ADDRESS** Hebrew & Semitic Studies, Univ Wis, Madison, WI, 53706.

SCHRADER, DAVID E.
PERSONAL Born 10/01/1947, Northfield, MN, m, 1980, 2 children **DISCIPLINE** PHILOSOPHY **EDUCATION** Saint Olaf Col, BA, 69; Harvard Univ, MTS, 71; Univ MA, MA, 74, PhD, 75. **CAREER** Instr, Loras Col, 75-77, asst prof, 77-79; asst prof, Austin Col,, 79-84, assoc prof, 84-89; assoc prof, 89-96, PROF, WASHINGTON & JEFFERSON COL, 96-. **HONORS AND AWARDS** Vis fel, Center for Philos of Science, Univ Pittsburgh, 96. **MEMBERSHIPS** Amer Philos Assoc; Amer Soc for Value Inquiry; Int Economics and Philos Soc; Philos of Science Assoc; Soc for Business Ethics; Soc for the Philos of Relig. **RESEARCH** Applied ethics; philos of economics; philos of relig. **SELECTED PUBLICATIONS** Auth, The Corporation as Anomaly, Cambridge Univ Press, 93; The New Orleans Jazz: Basketball and Music, in Gunter Gebauer, ed, Die Aktualitat der Sportphilosophie/The Relevance of the Philosophy of Sport, Academia Verlag, 93; Review of R. Douglass Geivett, Evil and the Evidence for God: The Challenge of John Hick's Theodicy, Temple Univ Press, 93, The Review of Metaphysics, vol XLIX, no 1, Sept 95; The Oddness of Corporate Ownership, Journal of Social Philosophy, vol 27, no 2, fall 96; Simonizing James: Taking Demand Seriously, Transactions of the Charles S. Peirce Soc, vol XXXIV, no 4, fall 98; Home is Where the Heart Is: Homelessness and the Denial of Moral Personality, in John M. Abbarno, ed, The Ethics of Homelessness: A Philosophical Perspective, Editions Rodopi, 99; and several articles forthcoming. **CONTACT ADDRESS** Philos Dept, Washington & Jefferson Col, Washington, PA, 15301. **EMAIL** Dschrader@washjeff.edu

SCHRAG, CALVIN
DISCIPLINE METAPHYSICS, PHILOSOPHY OF THE HUMAN SCIENCES, PHILOSOPHY OF RELIGION **EDUCATION** Harvard Univ, PhD. **CAREER** Dept Phhilos, Purdue Univ **HONORS AND AWARDS** Ade Distinguished prof, Purdue Univ. **RESEARCH** The contributions of postmodernism; hermeneutics; critical theory. **SELECTED PUBLICATIONS** Auth, The Resources of Rationality: A Response to the Postmodern Challenge; co-ed, man and World: Int Philos Quart.. **CONTACT ADDRESS** Dept of Philos, Purdue Univ, 1080 Schleman Hall, West Lafayette, IN, 47907-1080.

SCHRAG, CALVIN ORVILLE
PERSONAL Born 05/04/1928, Marion, S Dak, m, 1964, 1 child **DISCIPLINE** PHILOSOPHY **EDUCATION** Bethel Col, Kans, BA, 50; Yale Univ, BD, 53; Harvard Univ, PhD, 57. **CAREER** From asst prof to assoc prof, 57-63, interim head dept, 72-73, Res Found grants, 59 & 61, prof, 63-81, Georg Ade Distinguished Prof Philos, Purdue Univ, West Lafayette, 82-, Vis lectr, Univ Ill, 59-60; Eli Lilly fel, 62; vis prof, Northwestern Univ, 63-64; Guggenheim fel, 65-66. **MEMBERSHIPS** Am Philos Asn; Metaphys Soc Am; Soc Phenomenol & Existential Philos. **RESEARCH** Phenomenology; existentialism; philosophy of the human sciences. **SELECTED PUBLICATIONS** Contribr, Phenomenology: The Philosophy of Edmund Husserl and Its Interpretation, Doubleday, 57; coauth, Masterpieces of World Philosophy, Salem, 61; auth, Existence and Freedom, Northwest Univ, 61; contribr, Heidegger and the Quest for Truth, Quadrangle, 68; Experience and Being, 69 & co-ed & contribr, Patterns of the Life-World, 70, Northwest Univ; auth, Radical Reflection and the Origin of the Human Sciences, Purdue Univ, 80; auth, Communicative Praxis and the Space of Subjectivity, Indiana, 86; auth, The Resources of Rationality, Indiana, 92; auth, Philosophical Papers, SUNY, 94; auth, The Self After Postmodernity, Yale, 97. **CONTACT ADDRESS** Dept of Philos, Purdue Univ, West Lafayette, IN, 47907-1968. **EMAIL** eschrag@purdue.edu

SCHRAG, OSWALD O.
PERSONAL Born 06/04/1916, Parker, SD, m, 1945 **DISCIPLINE** PHILOSOPHY **EDUCATION** Bethel CAl, AB, 42; Hartford Theol Sem, BD, 45, STM, 48; Boston Univ, PhD, 52. **CAREER** Minister, Bolton Congregational Church, Conn, 45-48; trustee scholar, Bolton Univ, 48-49, asst, 49-50; minister, W Congregational Church, 51; minister, Chicopee Congregational Church, Mass, 52; assoc prof, 52-58, chmn dept, 57-72 & 76-81, Prof Philos, PROF PHILOS & RELIG EMER, 86- , FISK UNIV, 58-. **HONORS AND AWARDS** Tyler Prize, Hartford Theol Sem, 43-44. **MEMBERSHIPS** Am Philos Asn; Am Theol Soc; Am Acad Relig; Metaphys Soc Am; Soc Philos Relig (vpres, 71-72, pres, 72-73); Jaspers Soc N Am (pres, 82-83); mem Hon Presidium elected by Jaspers Soc, Int Jaspers Conf, 88. **RESEARCH** Philosophy of religion; history of philosophy; contemporary philosophy and theology. **SELECTED PUBLICATIONS** Auth, Existentialist ethics and axiology, Southern J Philos, 63; Jaspers: Beyond traditional metaphysics and ontology, Int Philos Quart, 65; Philosophical, religious, and scientific symbols, Int J Philos Relig, Vol II, No 2; Existence, Existenz, and Transcendence, An Introduction to the Philosophy of Karl Jaspers, Duquesne Univ, 71; contrib auth Jaspers Today: Philosophy at the Threshold of the Future, Univ Press Am, 88; Karl Jaspers: Philosopher Among Philosophers, Wurtzberg, Konigshausen & Neuman, 93; Karl Jaspers Philosophy of the Way to World Philosophy, Wurtzburg, Konigshausen and Neuman, 98; A Companion to the Philosophers, Blackwell Publ, 98. **CONTACT ADDRESS** 3511 Echo Hill Rd, Nashville, TN, 37215.

SCHREINER, THOMAS R.
DISCIPLINE NEW TESTAMENT **EDUCATION** W Ore Univ, BS; W Conservative Baptist Sem, MDiv, ThM; Fuller Theol Sem, PhD. **CAREER** Instr, Bethel Theol Sem; Azusa Pacific Univ; prof, S Baptist Theol Sem. **HONORS AND AWARDS** Pauline Schol **SELECTED PUBLICATIONS** Auth, Interpreting the Pauline Letters; The Law and Its Fulfillment: A Pauline Theology of Law; co-auth, The Grace of God, The Bondage of the Will; Women in the Church: A Fresh Analysis of 1 Timothy 2:9-15. **CONTACT ADDRESS** New Testament Dept, Southern Baptist Theol Sem, 2825 Lexington Rd, Louisville, KY, 40280. **EMAIL** tschreiner@sbts.edu

SCHREITER, ROBERT JOHN
PERSONAL Born 12/14/1947, Nebraska City, NE **DISCIPLINE** RELIGION **EDUCATION** St Joseph's Col, BA, 68; Univ Nijmegen, Netherlands, Dr theol, 74. **CAREER** From Asst Prof to Assoc Prof, 74-85, Prof Theol, Cath Theol Union, Chicago, 85-, Dean, 77-86. **MEMBERSHIPS** Am Acad Relig; Cath Theol Soc Am; Am Soc Missiology. **RESEARCH** Contextual theology; Christology; hermeneutics. **SELECTED PUBLICATIONS** Auth, Constructing Local Theologies, 85; Faces of Jesus in Africa, 91; Reconciliation, 92; The New Catholicity, 97. **CONTACT ADDRESS** Catholic Theol Union at Chicago, 5401 S Cornell Ave, Chicago, IL, 60615-6200. **EMAIL** rschreit@ctu.edu

SCHRIFT, ALAN D.
PERSONAL Born 03/02/1955, Brooklyn, NY, m, 1984 **DISCIPLINE** PHILOSOPHY **EDUCATION** Brown Univ, BA, 77; Purdue Univ, MA, 80, PhD, 83. **CAREER** Vis asst prof, Clarkson Univ, 85-87; from asst prof to assoc prof to chemn to prof, 87-, Grinnell Col. **HONORS AND AWARDS** Purdue Univ Fel, 78-79; David Ross Res Fel, 81-83, Purdue Univ; Travel Grant, 84; Fel Stud, 85-86, Am Council Learned Soc; Harris Fac Fel, 90-91, Grinnell Col; External Fel, 91, Univ Or, Eugene; Nat Endowment Hum, 92, 97. **MEMBERSHIPS** Am Philos Asn; Soc Phenomenology Existential Philos; Nietzsche Soc; N Am Nietzsche Soc; Fredrick Neitzsche Soc; Int Asn Philos Lit. **RESEARCH** 20th century European philosophy: existentialism, poststructuralism, hermeneutics, Nietzche, Foucault, 19th century philosophy, philosophy of literature, aesthetics. **SELECTED PUBLICATIONS** Auth, Nietzsche and the Question of Interpretation: Between Hermeneutics and Deconstruction, 90; auth, Nietzsche's French Legacy: A Genealogy of Poststructuralism, 95; auth, art, Nietzsche's Contest: Nietzsche and the Culture Wars, 99; auth, art, Rethinking the Subject, or How One Becomes-other than What One Is, 99; auth, art, Kofman, Nietzche, and the Jews, 99. **CONTACT ADDRESS** Dept of Philosophy, Grinnell Col, Dept of Philos, Grinnell, IA, 50112. **EMAIL** schrift@ac.grin.edu

SCHROEDER, JEANNE L.
DISCIPLINE COMMERCIAL LAW **EDUCATION** Williams Col, BA, 75; Stanford Univ, JD, 75. **CAREER** Prof, Yeshiva Univ. **MEMBERSHIPS** Milgrim Thomajan & Lee, P.C. **RESEARCH** Feminist jurisprudence; Corporate finance, and securities law. **SELECTED PUBLICATIONS** Auth, Abduction From the Seraglio: Feminist Methodologies and the Logic of Imagination; Feminism Historicized; History's Challenge to Feminism; Security Interests Under Article 8 of the U.C.C. **CONTACT ADDRESS** Yeshiva Univ, 55 Fifth Ave, NY, NY, 10003-4301. **EMAIL** schroedr@ymail.yu.edu

SCHROEDER, STEVEN H.
PERSONAL Born 06/29/1954, Wichita Falls, TX **DISCIPLINE** RELIGION/PHILOSOPHY **EDUCATION** Valparaiso Univ, BA, 74; Univ Chicago, MA, 76; PhD, 82. **CAREER** Tchr, Roosevelt Univ, Univ N Iowa, & Calumet Col, 84-96; Assoc Prof, Capital Univ, 97-. **HONORS AND AWARDS** Emily Dickinson Poetry Award, 96; Samuel Ostrowsky Humanities Award, 95. **MEMBERSHIPS** APA; AAR; ASA; Intl Bonhoeffer Soc; Intl Virginia Woolf Soc; Soc for Philo in the Cont World **SELECTED PUBLICATIONS** It's the End of the World as We Know It (And I Feel Fine): The End of History, Marxist Eschatology and the New World Order, Jour of Soc Phil, 92; The End of History and Responsibility to Order the World: Dietrich Bonhoeffer and the New World Order, Union Sem Quart Rev, 92; A Community and a Perspective: Lutheran Peace Fellowship and the Edge of the Church, 1941-1991, Univ Press of Amer, 93; An Interview With Mairead Corrigan Maquire, The Christian Century, 94;The Imperialism of Our Little Senses: An Essay on the Southwest and Civilization, Cimarron Rev, 95; Eyes of Texas: Seven Songs Out of Lubbock, Jour Amer Stud Assn of TX, 95; No Goddess Was Your Mother: Western Philosophy's Abandonment of its Multicultural Matrix , Phil in Cont World, 95; The End of History and the New World Order, Theol and Prac of Res, Ess on Dietrich Bonhoeffer, Trinity Press, 94; Notes Towards a Poetics of Persons, Becoming Persons, App Theol Press, 95; Virginia Woolfs Subject and the Subject of Ethics: Notes Toward a Poetics of Persons, Ed Mellen Press, 96; Memo Re: God, Ram Rev, 93; On Measuring Coastlines, Mosaic, 94; It is Good for My Heart, Mosaic, 94; Why Sarah Laughed, Ram Rev, 94-95; Good Faith One Cannot Be Present Alone, Rhino, 95; River of My Childhood, Ram Rev, 95-96; Presence of Mind/Body of Thought, Ram Rev, 96-96; A Story About a Man I Think In New Jersey, Ram Rev, 96-97; Weather Report, Georgetown Rev, 96. **CONTACT ADDRESS** 5710 S. Kimbark #3, Chicago, IL, 60637-1615. **EMAIL** sschroed@capital.edu

SCHROEDER, WILLIAM
DISCIPLINE PHILOSOPHY **EDUCATION** Univ Mich, PhD, 79. **CAREER** Assoc prof,Univ Ill Urbana Champaign. **RESEARCH** Recent Continental philosophy; philosophy in and of literature and film. **SELECTED PUBLICATIONS** Auth, Sartre and His Predecessors: The Self and the Other; ed, Blackwell Companion to Continental Philosophy. **CONTACT ADDRESS** Philosophy Dept, Univ Ill Urbana Champaign, 52 E Gregory Dr, Champaign, IL, 61820. **EMAIL** wschroed@uiuc.edu

SCHUBERT, E.
PERSONAL Born 03/29/1945, Glendale, CA, m, 1971, 4 children **DISCIPLINE** MEDICINE; PSYCHIATRY **EDUCATION** Asbury Col, BA 66; Indiana Univ Med Sch, MD 70; Meth Hosp IN, intern 70-72; Amer Bd Family Practice, Diplom, 76; Amer Bd Emerg 81, recert 90; Amer Bd Psychiatry and Neurology, 96. **CAREER** Family Practice, 72-73; Emergency Med, 73-89; Psychiatry, 89-; Indiana Univ, clinical asst psychiatry. **HONORS AND AWARDS** IN Psych Soc Res Awd; Who's Who of American Women; Who's Who in: Health and Med, Med and Healthcare, Sci and Engineering, the World, the Midwest; Mother of the Year; Outstanding Young Women of Amer., Nominated for Chief Resident; Dir of Psychiatry Class for Occup Ther Students; Fac-Res Educ Retreat; Examiner for Oral Bd Rev. **MEMBERSHIPS** AAFP; ACEP; APA; CMDS. **RESEARCH** Cross Cultural and Missionary psychiatry. **SELECTED PUBLICATIONS** Auth, What Missionaries Need to Know About Burnout and Depression, New Castle IN, Olive Branch Pub, 93; Intl Bulletin of Missionary Research, rev, Cross-Cultural Conflict: Building Relationships for Effective Ministry, Elmer, Inter Varsity Press, 95; Even MK's Can Be-

come Depressed, Interact, 95; MMPI As a Predictive Tool for Missionary Candidates, Jour Psychology and Theology, 96; Personality Disorders in Overseas Missions: Guidelines for the Mental health care Professional, Jour of Psychol and Theol, 93; Missionary Care: Counting the Cost, ed Kelly O'Donnell, Selection and Screening Challenges: Bruising Personality Disorders and the MMPI, Carey, Pasadena, 92. **CONTACT ADDRESS** 2239 N Cadiz Pike, New Castle, IN, 47362. **EMAIL** abs@iquest.net

SCHUBERT, JUDITH
DISCIPLINE THEOLOGY **EDUCATION** Georgian Court Col, BA, 66; Providence Col, MA, 75; Ecole Biblique et Archeologique, Eleve Titulaire, 86; Fordham Univ, PhD, 92 **CAREER** Instr Music, Georgian Court Col, 78-80; instr Relig Studies, Georgian Court Col, 80-85; lectr Relig Studies, Georgian Court Col, 87-92; asst prof Relig Studies, Georgian Court Col, 92-95; assoc prof Relig Studies, Georgian Court Col, 96; dir, master arts Theol, Georgian Court Col, 97- **HONORS AND AWARDS** NEH Grant, Brown Univ; Grant, Ecole Biblique et Archeologique **MEMBERSHIPS** Col Theol Soc; Cath Bibl Assoc; Soc Bibl Lit; Cath Theol Soc Amer; Mercy Assoc Scripture Theol **RESEARCH** Luke-Acts; Women and Bible **SELECTED PUBLICATIONS** Auth, "Jesus as Prophet," Bible Today, 97; auth, "The Good Samaritan: A Reflection of the Compassion of God," Mast Jrnl, 97; auth, "Two Forgotten Disciples in John," Mast Jrnl, 95 **CONTACT ADDRESS** 900 Lakewood Ave., Lakewood, NJ, 08701. **EMAIL** schubert@georgian.edu

SCHUCHARD, BRUCE G.
PERSONAL Born 11/30/1956, Corona, CA, m, 1990, 2 children **DISCIPLINE** EXEGETICAL THEOLOGY **EDUCATION** Univ Mich, BS, 79; Concordia Theol Sem, MDiv, 84, STM, 85; Union Theol Sem, PhD, 91. **CAREER** Pastor, St. James, Iowa, 90-97; asst prof, exegetical theol, Concordia Sem, 97- . **MEMBERSHIPS** Soc of Bibl Lit. **RESEARCH** Johannine literature; New Testament use of the Old Testament. **SELECTED PUBLICATIONS** Auth, Scripture within Scripture: The Interrelationship of Form and Function in the Explicit Old Testament Citations in the Gospel of John, Scholars Press, 92. **CONTACT ADDRESS** Concordia Sem, 801 DeMun Ave, St. Louis, MO, 63105. **EMAIL** schuchardb@csl.edu

SCHUCK, PETER H.
PERSONAL Born 04/26/1940, New York, NY, m, 1966, 2 children **DISCIPLINE** LAW **EDUCATION** Cornell Univ, BA, 62; Harvard Univ, JD, 65, MA, 69; NY Univ, LLM, 66. **CAREER** Assoc, Cahill, Gordon, Reindel & Ohl, 65-67 & Wachtell, Lipton, Rosen & Katz, 67-68; teaching fel govt, Harvard Univ, 69-70; consult, Ctr Study Responsive Law, 71-72; dir, Wash Off, Consumers Union, 72-77; dep asst secy, US Dept Health, Educ & Welfare, 77-79; assoc prof Law, 78-81, Simeon E Baldwin Prof Law, 84, prof law, Yale Univ, 81-; Guggenheim Fel, 84-85. **RESEARCH** Administrative law; tort law; regulation; immigration, citizenship, and refugee law. **SELECTED PUBLICATIONS** Auth & ed, The Judiciary Committees, Viking, 75; auth, Suing Government; Citizen Remedies for Official Wrongs, Yale Univ, 83; Citizenship Without Consent: Illegal Aliens in the American Party, Yale Univ, 85; Agent Orange on Trial: Mass Toxic Disasters in the Courts, Harvard Univ, 87; Tort Law and the Public Interest: Competition, Innovation, and Consumer Welfare, Norton, 91; ed, Foundations of Administrative Law, Oxford Univ, 94; Citizens, Strangers, and In-Betweens: Essays on Immigration and Citizenship, Westview Press, 98; Paths to Inclusion: The Integration of Migrants in the United States and Germany, Berghahn Books, 98. **CONTACT ADDRESS** Law Sch, Yale Univ, PO Box 208215, New Haven, CT, 06520-8215. **EMAIL** peter.schuck@yale.edu

SCHUELER, G.F.
PERSONAL Born 08/09/1944, Columbus, OH, m, 1966, 2 children **DISCIPLINE** PHILOSOPHY **EDUCATION** Stanford Univ, AB, 66; Univ Calif, Berkeley, PhD, 73. **CAREER** Prof, 71-, chemn, 96-; Univ N Mex. **MEMBERSHIPS** Am Philos Asn **RESEARCH** Ethics, philosophy of action; philosophy of mind. **SELECTED PUBLICATIONS** Auth, art, Pro-Attitudes and Direction of Fit, 91; auth, DESIRE: It's Role in Practical Reason and the Explanation of Action, 95; auth, art, Why Ought's are Not Facts, 95; auth, art, Why Modesty is a Virtue, 97. **CONTACT ADDRESS** Dept of Philosophy, Univ of New Mexico, Albuquerque, NM, 87131. **EMAIL** schueler@unm.edu

SCHUFREIDER, GREGORY
DISCIPLINE HISTORY OF PHILOSOPHY, RECENT CONTINENTAL PHILOSOPHY, THE PHILOSOPHY OF ART **EDUCATION** Northwestern Univ, BA, 69; Univ Calif, Santa Barbara, MA, PhD, 75. **CAREER** Prof, La State Univ. **RESEARCH** Heidegger. **SELECTED PUBLICATIONS** Auth, An Introduction to Anselm's Argument, Temple UP, 78; The Metaphysician as Poet-Magician, in Metaphilosophy, 79; Art and the Problem of Truth, Man and World, 81; Heidegger on Community, Man and World, 81; The Logic of the Absurd, in Philos and Phenomenol Res, 83; Overpowering the Center: Three Compositions by Modrian, in JAAC, 85; Heidegger Contribution to a Phenomenology of Culture, 86; Confessions of a Rational Mystic: Anselm's Early Writings, Purdue Univ ser, in the Hist of Philos, 94. **CONTACT ADDRESS** Dept of Philos and Relig Stud, Louisiana State Univ, 106 Coates Hall, Baton Rouge, LA, 70803.

SCHULTENOVER, DAVID
PERSONAL Born 08/19/1938, Sauk Rapids, MN, s **DISCIPLINE** HISTORICAL THEOLOGY **EDUCATION** Spring Hill Col, BS, 63; Loyola Univ, MS, 66; St. Louis Univ, PhD, 75 **CAREER** Prof, 94-pres, Assoc Prof, 85-94, Adj Asst Prof, 78-83, Creighton Univ; Asst Prof, 75-78, Marquette Univ **HONORS AND AWARDS** Nat Endowm for the Humanities Fel; Alpha Sigma Nu Ntl Bk Award; Deutscher Akademischer Austauschdienst Fel; Alpha Sigma Nu **MEMBERSHIPS** Am Acad of Relig; Am Soc Church History; Cath Theolog Soc of Am **RESEARCH** Christology; Roman Catholic Modernism; Models and Images of the Church **SELECTED PUBLICATIONS** Auth, George Tyrrell: In Search of Catholicism, Patmos Press, 81; Auth, A View from Rome: The Eve of the Modernist Crisis, Fordham University Press, 93 **CONTACT ADDRESS** 518 N 19th St, Omaha, NE, 68102-4612. **EMAIL** dnover@creighton.edu

SCHULTZ, CARL
PERSONAL Born 09/15/1930, New Castle, PA, m, 1955, 3 children **DISCIPLINE** HEBREW BIBLE **EDUCATION** Malone Col, Canton, OH, BRE(Christian ed), 52; Houghton Col, NY, BA(Bible), 53; Wheaton Col, IL, MA(Theology), 55; Brandeis Univ, Waltham, MA(Biblical Studies), PhD, 73. **CAREER** Asst prof, Hebrew Bible, Houghton Col, 65-67; grad study leave, 67-71; assoc prof, Hebrew Bible, 74-75, prof, Hebrew Bible, Houghton Col, 75-, chair, div of relig and philos, 75-96, dean of the Buffalo Suburban Campus, 88-89. **HONORS AND AWARDS** Fac of the Year, Student Senate Excellence Award, Houghton Col, 75-76; Nat Endowment for the Humanities, grant at Yale, 78, 81, grant at Bethel Col, 83, grant at Cornell, 85; Malone Col Alumni Asn Certificate of Merit, 88; Paul Harris Fel by Fillmore Rotary Club, 88; New York State Electric and Gas Co and Independent Col Fund of New York Teaching Excellence Award, 94; Houghton Col Nominee for 1997 US Prof of the Year sponsored by the Carnegie Found. **MEMBERSHIPS** Soc of Biblical Lit; Am Academy of Relig; Nat Asn of Profs of Hebrew. **RESEARCH** Apocalyptic lit; Book of Job; Dead Sea Scrolls. **SELECTED PUBLICATIONS** Auth, Psalms 76-150 for Wesley Study Bible, Thomas Nelson, 90; Job and Ecclesiastes, Asbury Bible Commentary, Zonervan Pub House, 91; chapter, Responsible Reluctance or When a Quick Yes is Unwise, A Greater Work to Do, Wesley Press, 91; articles: Folly, Ignorance, Knowledge, Spirit, Soul, Understanding, Reason, for The Evangelical Dictionary of Theology, 92; Case Rehoboam: Vulnerable or Vicious?, J for Case Teaching, fall 92; When Reading is Difficult, J for Case Teaching, fall 93; The Cohesive Issue of Mispat in Job, Festschrift for Dr Dwight Young, Brandeis Univ, Go to the Land I will Show You, Eisenbrauns, 96; numerous other publications. **CONTACT ADDRESS** 7405 Park Dr, Houghton, NY, 14744. **EMAIL** cschultz@houghton.edu

SCHULTZ, JANICE LEE
PERSONAL Born 07/23/1945, Cleveland, OH **DISCIPLINE** PHILOSOPHY **EDUCATION** John Carroll Univ, BA, 69; State Univ NY Buffalo, MA, 72, PhD, 78. **CAREER** Instr, Ryerson Polytech Inst, 74-79; asst prof, 79-88, FULL PROF PHILOS, CANISIUS COL, 89-. **MEMBERSHIPS** Am Cath Philos Asn. **RESEARCH** Aquinas; business ethics; natural law and human rights. **SELECTED PUBLICATIONS** Auth, Adam of St Victor, Adelaid of Bath, Richard of St Victor, John of Salisbury, & Honorius Augustodunensis, In: Dict of the Middle Ages, Scribner's, summer 82; many articles on Thomas Aquinas in The New Scholasticism, Proceedings of the PMR Conference, Am Cath Philos Quart (also articles on Abelard, Boethius), 82-98. **CONTACT ADDRESS** Dept of Philos, Canisius Col, 2001 Main St, Buffalo, NY, 14208-1098. **EMAIL** SchultzJ@canisius.edu

SCHULTZ, JOSEPH P.
PERSONAL Born 12/02/1928, Chicago, IL, m, 1955, 3 children **DISCIPLINE** JEWISH STUDIES, RELIGION **EDUCATION** Yeshiva Univ, BA, 51; Jewish Theol Sem, MHL, 55; Brandeis Univ, PhD, 62. **CAREER** Lectr foreign lang, Boston Univ, 63-64, instr foreign lang, 64-68, asst prof relig, 68-73; assoc prof hist, 73-78, OPPENSTEIN BROS DISTINGUISHED PROF JUDAIC STUDIES, UNIV MO-KANSAS CITY, 78-, DIR JUDAIC STUDIES PROG, 73-, dir Center for Relig Studies, 95; Res grant, Grad Sch Arts & Sci, Boston Univ, 71-72. **HONORS AND AWARDS** Hyman G Enelow Award, Jewish Theol Sem, 76. **MEMBERSHIPS** Asn Jewish Studies; Am Acad Relig. **RESEARCH** Comparative religion; Jewish studies. **SELECTED PUBLICATIONS** Auth, Angelic opposition to the ascension of Moses and the revelation of the law, Jewish Quart Rev, 71; The religious psychology of Jonathan Edwards and the Hasidic Masters of Habad, J Ecumenical Studies, 73; The Lurianic strand in Jonathan Edwards' Concept of Progress, Judaica, 74; Reciprocity in confucian and Rabbinic ethics, J Relig Ethics, 74; contribr, Studies and Texts in Honor of Nahum Glatzer, Brill, 75; auth, From My Father's Vineyard, Vile-Goller, 78; co-ed, From Destruction to Rebirth: The Holocaust and the State of Israel, Univ Am, 78; auth, Judaism and The Gentile Faiths; Comparative Studies in Religion, Fairleigh Dickinson Univ, 78; Mid-America's Promise: A Profile of Kansas City Jewry, Am Jewish Hist Soc, 82; ed, Ze'enah U-Re'enah: Book of Genesis, Dropsie Col, 85; Sinai and Olympus: A Comarative Study with Lois S. Spatz, Univ Press of Am, 95. **CONTACT ADDRESS** Danciger Judaic Studies Prog, Univ of Mo, 5100 Rockhill Rd, Kansas City, MO, 64110-2499.

SCHULTZ, WALTER
PERSONAL Born 01/23/1950, Chicago, IL, m, 1975, 2 children **DISCIPLINE** PHILOSOPHY **EDUCATION** Univ Minnesota, PhD, 97. **CAREER** Cedarville Col, 97-. **HONORS AND AWARDS** Univ Wisconsin - Eauclaire; Sigma Gamma Zeta, Scholastic Honor Soc; Winner Bertrand Russell Competition on Logic; Cedarville College Faculty Scholarship Grant, 98. **MEMBERSHIPS** Amer Phil Assoc; Soc of Christian Philosophers; Evangelical Theological Soc; Evangelical Philosophical Soc. **RESEARCH** Ethics; welfare economics **SELECTED PUBLICATIONS** Auth, Wittgenstein and Postmodern Epistemology, Wittgenstein's Philosophy of Mathematics, 93; Towards a Communitarian Liberalism, Kinesis, 94; What is Truth, Torch, 98. **CONTACT ADDRESS** Cedarville Col, Cedarville, OH, 45314-0601. **EMAIL** schultz@cedarville.edu

SCHUMACHER, JOHN
DISCIPLINE THE NATURE OF INQUIRY IN THE SCIENCES, METAPHYSICS, THEORIES OF KNOWLEDGE, **EDUCATION** Rensselaer Polytech Inst, MA; Oxford Univ, DPhil. **CAREER** Prof, dir, undergrad prog, Rensselaer Polytech Inst. **SELECTED PUBLICATIONS** Auth, Human Posture: The Nature of Inquiry, 89. **CONTACT ADDRESS** Rensselaer Polytech Inst, Troy, NY, 12180. **EMAIL** selmer@rpi.edu

SCHUTZ, SAMUEL R.
PERSONAL m, 1 child **DISCIPLINE** EVANGELISM AND MINISTRY **EDUCATION** Calif State Univ, BA, 66; Univ Calif, PhD, 69; Andover Newton Theol Sch, MDiv; postdoctoral stud, Gordon-Conwell Theol Sem; N Park Theol Sem; Fuller Theol Sem. **CAREER** Instr, Westmont Col; Gordon Col; prof, dir, DMin prog, assoc dean, Bethel Sem, 86-90; act dean, Bethel Sem, 89-90; prof, Gordon-Conwell Theol Sem, 90-. **HONORS AND AWARDS** Res grant, US Off Edu; Nat Inst Mental Health. **MEMBERSHIPS** Mem, Amer Psychol Assn. **SELECTED PUBLICATIONS** Contrib ed, Jour Psychol and Theol. **CONTACT ADDRESS** Gordon-Conwell Theol Sem, 130 Essex St, South Hamilton, MA, 01982.

SCHWAB, STEWART J.
DISCIPLINE LAW **EDUCATION** Swarthmore Col, BA, 75; Univ Mich, MA, 78, JD, 80, PhD, 81. **CAREER** Res Asst, Fed Reserve Bank Philadelphia, 75-76; Summer Assoc, Covington & Burling, 79; Law Clerk, US Court of Appeals, 81-82; Law Clerk, US Supreme Court, 82-83; Vis Prof, Univ Mich, 88; Vis Fel, Ctr Socio-Legal Studies, Wolfson Col, Oxford Univ, 90; Olin Vis Res Prof Law & Econ, Univ Va, 91; Chapman Tripp Vis Lectr, Victoria Univ Fac Law, Wellington, New Zealand, 97; Fulbright Sr. Schol, Ctr Law & Econ, Australian Nat Univ, 97-98; Asst Prof to Prof Law, Cornell Law Sch, 83-. **HONORS AND AWARDS** Nat Sci Found Grant, 85-87; Fund for Labor Relations Studies, 89-90. **MEMBERSHIPS** Am Bar Asn; DC Bar; Am Arbitration Asn. **SELECTED PUBLICATIONS** Auth, Employment Life Cycles and the Employment-At-Will Doctrine, Cornell Law Forum, 94; coauth, Property Rules and Liability Rules: The Cathedral in Another Light, NY Univ Law Rev, 95; auth, Wrongful Discharge Law and the Search for Third-Party Effects, Tex Law Rev, 96; Legal Positivism as an Empirical Proposition, Cornell Law Rev, 97; coauth, Employment Law: Cases and Materials, Lexis Law Publ, 93, 2nd ed, 98; Employment Law: Selected Federal and State Statutes, Lexis Law Publ, 93, 2nd ed, 98; Foundations of Labor and Employment Law, Oxford Univ Press (forthcoming 99); author of numerous other articles. **CONTACT ADDRESS** Law School, Cornell Univ, Myron Taylor Hall, Ithaca, NY, 14853. **EMAIL** sjs15@cornell.edu

SCHWANAUER, FRANCIS
DISCIPLINE PHILOSOPHY **EDUCATION** Univ Stuttgart, Ger, PhD, 59. **CAREER** Prof **RESEARCH** Semiotics; workings of the mind; role of the brain. **SELECTED PUBLICATIONS** Auth, Truth is a Neighborhood, transl into Ger; The Mind is a Fact; Those Fallacies by Slight of Reason. **CONTACT ADDRESS** Dept of Philosophy, Univ of Southern Maine, 96 Falmouth St, PO Box 9300, Portland, ME, 04104-9300. **EMAIL** franz@usm.maine.edu

SCHWARTZ, BRYAN
DISCIPLINE LAW **EDUCATION** Queen's Univ, LLB, 78; Yale Univ, LLM, 78, JSD, 86. **CAREER** Asst prof, 81-84; assoc prof, 84-87; prof, 87-. **HONORS AND AWARDS** Rh Institute Award for Outstanding Scholarship in the Humanities, 89 **RESEARCH** Constitutional law; charter of rights; international law. **SELECTED PUBLICATIONS** Auth, Still Thinking, Voyageur, 92; Opting In? The New Federal Proposals on

the Constitution, Voyageur, 92; First Principles, Second Thoughts, 86; Fathoming Meech Lake, 87. **CONTACT ADDRESS** Fac of Law, Univ Manitoba, Robson Hall, Winnipeg, MB, R3T 2N2. **EMAIL** bschwar@cc.umanitoba.ca

SCHWARTZ, HERMAN
DISCIPLINE CONSTITUTIONAL LAW, CIVIL RIGHTS **EDUCATION** Harvard Univ, AB, 53; Harvard Law Sch, JD, 56; **CAREER** Prof, Am Univ. **HONORS AND AWARDS** ACLU-Niagara Frontier Award, 72; William Conable Award Civil Rights, 74; NY State Bar Asn Criminal Justice Section Award Outstanding Work,76; Medgar Evers Award, 76; Felicitation Humanitarian Work, 77; Citizens Counsel for Human Rights Award,82. **MEMBERSHIPS** U.S./Israel Civil Liberties Law prog; Human Rights Watch Committee, 87; co-dir, Wash Col Law, Human Rights Ctr.; Found, Civil Soc; Congressional Human Rights Found; Helsinki Watch; Am Civil Liberties Union, 69. ACLU; U.S. Senate comt; Dept Treasury. **RESEARCH** Civil rights and liberties. **SELECTED PUBLICATIONS** Auth, Packing the Court: the Conservative Compaign to Rewrite the Constitution; The Berger Years, 78; contribur, Harvard Law Rev, Yale Law Jour, Mich Law Rev, Univ Chicago Law Rev, NY Times. **CONTACT ADDRESS** American Univ, 4400 Massachusetts Ave, Washington, DC, 20016.

SCHWARTZ, JUSTIN
PERSONAL Born 07/19/1957, Columbus, OH, m, 1984, 2 children **DISCIPLINE** PHILOSOPHY **EDUCATION** Princeton Univ, AB, 79; Univ Mich, MA, 84, PhD, 89. **CAREER** Asst prof, Kalamazoo Col, 88-89; Ohio State Univ, 89-94. **MEMBERSHIPS** Nat Lawyers Guild; Am Philos Asn; Radial Philos Asn. **RESEARCH** Philosophy of law; Political and social philosophy; Philosophy of social science; Labor and employment law; Constitutional law and theory. **SELECTED PUBLICATIONS** Auth, "Money for Nothing: Business Location Incentives and the Law," 98; "A Not So Quite Color-Blind Constitution: Racial Discrimination and Racial Preference in Justice O'Connor's 'Newest' Equal Protection Jurisprudence" in Ohio State Law J, 97; "Relativism, Reflective Equilibrium, and Justice" in Legal Studies, 97. **CONTACT ADDRESS** 2227 Lincolnwood Dr, Evanston, IL, 60201. **EMAIL** jkschw@aol.com

SCHWARTZ, MARTIN A.
DISCIPLINE LAW **EDUCATION** City Col, BBA, cum laude, 66; Brooklyn Law Sch, JD, magna cum laude, 68; NY Univ, LLM, 73. **CAREER** Mng atty, Westchester Legal Serv; adj prof, NY Law Schl; prof Law, Touro Col. **MEMBERSHIPS** NY State Bar Asn comt on State Const Law. **SELECTED PUBLICATIONS** Auth, Public Interest Law, NY Law J; Section 1983 Litigation: Federal Evidence; coauth, Section 1983 Litigation: Claims, Defenses and Fees, 91. **CONTACT ADDRESS** Touro Col, Brooklyn, NY, 11230. **EMAIL** MartinS@tourolaw.edu

SCHWARTZ, WILLIAM
DISCIPLINE ESTATE PLANNING, PROPERTY, AND TORTS **EDUCATION** Boston Univ, JD, 55; Stanford Univ, AM, 60. **CAREER** Prof, Yeshiva Univ; vcprs, Acad Affairs. **HONORS AND AWARDS** Dir, Viacom, Inc.; vchmn, UST Corp. **MEMBERSHIPS** Asn Trial Lawyers Am; Legal Adv Comt NY Stock Exchange; Legal Adv Board; Nat Comn Medical Malpractice; NGO Section, UN. **RESEARCH** Estate planning, property, and torts. **SELECTED PUBLICATIONS** Areas of research. **CONTACT ADDRESS** Yeshiva Univ, 55 Fifth Ave, NY, NY, 10003-4301.

SCHWARZ, HANS
PERSONAL Born 01/05/1939, Schwabach, Germany, m, 1967, 2 children **DISCIPLINE** SYSTEMATIC THEOLOGY **EDUCATION** Univ Erlangen, Dr Theol, 63. **CAREER** World Coun Churches scholar & Fulbright travel grant, Oberlin Grad Sch Theol, 64-65; asst pastor, St Peter & Paul, Erlangen-Bruck, Ger, 65-66; Ger Res Soc fel, Univ Erlangen, 66-67; from instr to assoc prof syst theol, Trinity Lutheran Sem, Capital Univ, 67-78, Edward C Fendt prof syst theol, 78-80; Prof Protestant Theol, Inst Evangelische Theol, Univ Regensburg, Wger, 81-, Vis profsyst theol, Augustana Sem, Neuendetelsau, Ger, 73-74 & Pontif Gregorian Univ, Rome, 74; Am Lutheran Church rep, Nat Comn Faith & Order, 73-81. **HONORS AND AWARDS** Fredrik A Schiotz Award, Aid Asn Lutherans & Am Lutheran Church, 73. **MEMBERSHIPS** Am Acad Relig. **RESEARCH** Relationship between theology and natural science; history and philosophy of religion; Luther studies. **SELECTED PUBLICATIONS** Auth, The Interplay Between Science And Theol In Uncovering The Matrix Of Human Morality/, Zygon, Vol 0028, 1993. **CONTACT ADDRESS** Inst Evangelische Theol, Univ Regensburg, Regensburg, ., 8400.

SCHWEER, G. WILLIAM
PERSONAL m, 3 children **DISCIPLINE** EVANGELISM **EDUCATION** Univ Mo, BS; Cent Baptist Theol Sem, BD, ThM, ThD; addn stud, Trinity Evangel Sem; SF State Univ; Fuller Sem; Oxford Univ. **CAREER** Instr, Baptist Sem Indonesia, 57-70; pres, Baptist Sem Indonesia, 70; fac, 75; E. Hermond Westmoreland prof, 96; sr prof, Golden Gate Baptist Theol Sem-. **HONORS AND AWARDS** Pastor, First Baptist Church of Union Star; Calvary Baptist Church of Independence; First Baptist Church, Palatine, Ill. **SELECTED PUBLICATIONS** Auth, Personal Evangel for Today, Broadman; pub(s), Adult Teacher; Home Life; Open Windows mag(s). **CONTACT ADDRESS** Golden Gate Baptist Theol Sem, 201 Sem Dr, Mill Valley, CA, 94941-3197. **EMAIL** B 1360 Gordon-Conwell Theological Seminary URL: http://www.gcts.edu/ 130 Essex St South Hamilton, MA 01982 (978) 468-7111 (978) 468-6691 (fax) Email: info@gcts.edu

SCHWEICKART, DAVID
DISCIPLINE PHILOSOPHY **EDUCATION** Univ Dayton, BS, 64; Univ Va, PhD in math, 69; Ohio State Univ, PhD in phil, 77. **CAREER** Prof & grad prog dir; Loyola Univ, 75-; 2 times at, Loyola Rome Center, 87-88 & 94-95; vis prof of Math, Univ Ky, 69-70 & vis prof of Philos, Univ NH, 86-87; lectr in, Spain, Cuba, El Salvador, Czech Republic & US. **RESEARCH** Soc and Polit philosophy; theories of socism; feminist philosophy; critical theory. **SELECTED PUBLICATIONS** Auth, Against Capitalism, Cambridge UP, 93 & Westview Press, 96, publ in Spanish as, Masalla del capitalismo, 97; Capitalism or Worker Control An Ethical and Economic Appraisal, Praeger, 80; articles in, Theoria, Rev of Radical Polit Econ, Can Journal of Philos, Econ and Philos, Critical Rev, Sci and Soc, Soc Theory and Practice, Praxis Int & The Nat Women's Stud Asn J. **CONTACT ADDRESS** Dept of Philosophy, Loyola Univ, Chicago, 820 N. Michigan Ave., Chicago, IL, 60611.

SCHWEIGERT, FRANCIS J.
PERSONAL Born 12/29/1950, Ladysmith, WI, m, 1950, 4 children **DISCIPLINE** EDUCATIONAL POLICY AND ADMINISTRATION **EDUCATION** Macalester Col, BA, 73; Col of St. Thomas, MA, 80; Col of St. Catherine, MA, 88; Univ Minn, PhD, 97. **CAREER** Dir Relig Ed, Church of St Alphonsus, Brooklyn Center, Minn, 88-94; Dir of Adult Formation, Church of St. Joan of Arc, Minneapolis, 94-96; guest tchr, St. Paul Public Schools, 97- ; independent consult, instr, 88- ; adj fac, Col of St. Catherine, Hamline Univ, United Theol Sem, Univ Minn, Univ St. Thomas, 88- . **MEMBERSHIPS** Am Acad Relig; Am Cath Philos Asn; Am Educ Res Asn; Am Philos Asn; Asn for Moral Ed; Philos of Educ Soc. **RESEARCH** Moral education; theory and practice of restorative justice; social ethics; community organization and leadership; Church ministries and religious education; Catholic pastoral theology. **SELECTED PUBLICATIONS** Auth, Faith Formation Futures, The Living Light, 93; auth, Small Christian Communities: An Invitation to Discipleship, Evangelization Update, 98; auth, Learning the Common Good: Principles of Community- Based Moral Education in Restorative Justice, J of Moral Educ, 99; auth, Undoing Violence: Restorative Justice Versus Punitive Justice, Chicago Stud, 99. **CONTACT ADDRESS** Dept of Philosophy, Univ of St. Thomas, 300 Aquina, Saint Paul, MN, 55105. **EMAIL** schwe015@tc.umn.edu

SCHWEITZER, DON
DISCIPLINE SYSTEMATIC THEOLOGY **EDUCATION** Princeton Theol Sem, PhD, 93. **CAREER** Sessional lectr, 97-99, SIAST Prince Albert SK. **MEMBERSHIPS** AAR; CCS. **RESEARCH** Contemporary Christian Theology. **SELECTED PUBLICATIONS** Auth, Douglas Hall's Critique of Jugen Moltmann's Eschatology of the Cross, in: Studies Religion Sciences Religieuses, 98; Gregory Baum on the revelatory work of the Holy Spirit, Horizons, 97; Gregory Baum on Secularization Evangelism and Social Change, Rel Studies and Theol, 96; Curse God and Die: Was Job's Wife Completely Wrong?, Touchstone, 96; Marginality Status and Power in Asian-American Theology, The Ecumenist, 96; Interpreting Bishop Spong Literally, Touchstone, 95; Jurgen Moltmann's theology as a theology of the Cross, Stud In rel sci Religieuses, 95; The Consistency of Jurgen Moltmann's Theology, Stud Rel Sci, Religiuses, 93; Biblical Principles applied to native-white relationships, The Prince Albert Daily Herald, 93. **CONTACT ADDRESS** 65 11th St East, Prince Albert, SK, S6V 0Z8.

SCHWEITZER, THOMAS A.
DISCIPLINE LAW **EDUCATION** Col Holy Cross, AB, cum laude, 66; Univ WI, MA 68, PhD, 71; Yale Univ, JD, 77. **CAREER** Assoc, Davis Polk & Wardwell; trial atty, US Dept of Energy; assoc prof Law, Touro Col. **HONORS AND AWARDS** Ford Found fel, WI. **SELECTED PUBLICATIONS** Auth, The United Nations as a Source of Domestic Law: Can Security Council Resolutions be Enforced in American Courts?, Yale Stud in World Pub Order, 78; Federal Oil Price Controls in Bankruptcy Cases: Government Claims for Repayment of Illegal Overcharges Should Not Be Subordinated as 'Penalties' Under 11 USC 726, (a) (4), Okla Law Rev, 89; Student 'Academic Challenge' Cases: Should Judges Grade the Professors on Due Process and Respect for Students' Contract Rights?, Am Univ Law Rev, 91; Lee v. Weisman and the Establishment Clause: Are Invocations and Benedictions at Public School Graduations Constitutionally Unspeakable?, Unvi Detroit Mercy Law Rev, 92; Lee v. Weisman: Whither the Establishment Clause and the Lemon v. Kurtzman Three-Pronged Test?, Touro Law Rev, 93; The Progeny of Lee v. Weisman: Can Student-Initiated Prayer at Public School Graduations Still Be Constitutional?, Brigham Young Univ J of Pub Law, 95; Hate Speech and the First Amendment: Can They Be Reconciled?, Conn Law Rev, 95. **CONTACT ADDRESS** Touro Col, Brooklyn, NY, 11230.

SCHWERIN, ALAN
PERSONAL Born 03/16/1953, Johannesburg, South Africa, m, 1977, 2 children **DISCIPLINE** PHILOSOPHY **EDUCATION** Rhodes Univ, MA, 78; Rice Univ, PhD, 88. **CAREER** Sr Lectr, Univ of Transkei (South Africa), 80-85; Asst Prof, McNeese Univ, 88-95; Chr, Dept of Political Science and Philosophy, Monmouth Univ, 96-. **HONORS AND AWARDS** Rice Univ Fel; Stanley Travelling Fel; Human Sciences Research Grant (South Africa). **MEMBERSHIPS** Amer Phil Assoc; Hume Soc; Leibnig Soc; Soc for 18th Century Studies **RESEARCH** David Hume's philosophy; Betrand Russell's epistemology **SELECTED PUBLICATIONS** Auth, Some Thoughts on Introducing Young Minds to Science, Soaring Digest, 93; Ed, On the Assertation I am my Brain, Expanding the Universe: An Introduction to Philosophy, 93; The Expanding Universe: An Introduction to Philosophy, 93; Soaring to New Heights, The Science Teacher, 94; Auth, Hume's Paradoxical Thesis and His Critics: Some Comments, Southwest Philosophy Review, 95; The Rise of Modern Philosophy, Leibniz Society Review, 96; Some Thoughts on Thinking and Teaching Styles, Inquiry: Critical Thinking Across the Disciplines, 96; A Scorched Sole: Apartheid's Landscape and Ideas, The Mcneese Review, 97; Some Questions about Kant's Clear Question, Southwest Philosophy Review, forthcoming. **CONTACT ADDRESS** Dept of Political Science and Philosophy, Monmouth Univ, 400 Cedar Ave, West Long Branch, NJ, 07764. **EMAIL** ASCHWERI@MONDEL.MONMOUTH.EDU

SCHWITZGEBEL, ERIC
DISCIPLINE PHILOSOPHY **EDUCATION** Univ Calif-Berkeley, PhD, 97. **CAREER** ASST PROF, UNIV CALIF, RIVERSIDE. **RESEARCH** Philosophy of mind; Ancient Chinese philosophy; Philosophy of science; Epistemology; Cognitive psychology. **SELECTED PUBLICATIONS** Auth, "Zhuangzi's Attitude Toward Language and His Skepticism," Essays on Skepticism, Relativism, and Ethics, Zhuangzi, SUNY Press, 96; "Theories in Children and the Rest of Us," Philos of Sci, Supp **CONTACT ADDRESS** Dept of Philos, Univ Calif, 1156 Hinderaker Hall, Riverside, CA, 92521-0209. **EMAIL** eschwitz@ucrac1.ucr.edu

SCOLEDES, ARISTOTLE
PERSONAL Born 02/22/1929, New York, NY, m, 1977, 3 children **DISCIPLINE** PHILOSOPHY **EDUCATION** Syracuse Univ, BA, 51; Johns Hopkins Univ, MSE, 53; MIT, ScD, 57; Stanford Univ, PhD, 65. **CAREER** Res assoc, Johns Hopkins Univ, 51-53; res fel Univ Chicago, 53-54; res fel, MIT, 55-59; exec engr, project coord Apollo Mission program, Philco Western Develop Labs/Ford Aerospace, 60-62; asst prof, philos of sci, Alfred Univ, 62-63; assoc prof, philos of sci and theoretical biol, SUNY Buffalo, 63-68; prof philos sci and technol, Georgia Inst Technol, 68-72; sr consult, sponsored minorities prog Econ Opportunity Atlanta/CETA, 72-77; proj mgr, dir, Consulting Consortium, Stanford Univ, 77-95. **HONORS AND AWARDS** Hon fel, AIAA, 71; Res Serv Recognition award, Offices of Naval Res and Chief of Naval Oper, 84; Who's Who in America, 99. **MEMBERSHIPS** Nat Space Soc; Planetary Soc; AAUP; Democritus Soc; Hist of Sci Soc; Air Force Asn; Philos of Sci Asn; APA; Sigma Xi; Tau Beta Pi. **CONTACT ADDRESS** 3609 South Court, Palo Alto, CA, 94306-4258.

SCOLES, EUGENE FRANCIS
PERSONAL Born 06/12/1921, Shelby, IA, m, 1942, 2 children **DISCIPLINE** LAW **EDUCATION** State Univ Iowa, AB, 43, JD, 45; Harvard Univ, LLM, 49; Columbia Univ, JSD, 55. **CAREER** Assoc Seyfarth, Shaw & Fairweather, Chicago, Ill, 45-46; from asst prof to assoc prof law, Northeastern Univ, 46-49; from assoc prof to prof, Univ Fla, 49-56; prof, Univ Ill, Champaign, 56-68; prof & dean, 68-74, distinguished prof, Univ Ore, 74-82, Prof Emer, Sch Law, Univ Ore, 82-; Prof Law, Univ Ill, Champaign, 82-, Reporter, Uniform Probate Code, 66- **MEMBERSHIPS** Asn Am Law Schs (pres, 78). **RESEARCH** Trusts and estates; conflict of laws. **SELECTED PUBLICATIONS** Auth, The Hague Convention On Succession/, Am J Of Comparative Law, Vol 0042, 1994. **CONTACT ADDRESS** Col of Law, Univ of Ore, Urbana-Champaign, Champaign, IL, 61820.

SCORGIE, GLEN G.
PERSONAL Born 03/29/1952, Vancouver, BC, Canada, m, 1978, 3 children **DISCIPLINE** HISTORICAL THEOLOGY **EDUCATION** Univ of St Andrews, Scotland, PhD, 86. **CAREER** Data-processing marketing asst, 74-76; IBM Canada, Toronto; adjunct prof of theology, 84-91, Canadian Theological Seminary; dir of admissions, 76-79, asst prof, 84-88, acting dean of faculty, Jan-May 89, assoc prof 88-91, Canadian Bible Col; academic dean and vice-pres, 91-96, prof 95-96, North Amer Baptist Col; adjunct pastor for English Mininistries, 97, Chinese Bible Church of San Diego; prof, 96- , Bethel Theological Seminary. **HONORS AND AWARDS** Who's Who in America; British Government Overseas Research Student Scholarship; Regent College Church History Prize; Delta Epsilon Chi Honor Society. **MEMBERSHIPS** American Academy of Religion; Canadian Evangelical Theological Assn; Confer-

ence on Faith and History; Evangelical Theological Society. **RESEARCH** Key Determinants of Spirtual Resilience: An Interdisciplinary Perspective; Movie Theology: Thinking Christianly about Contemporary Film and Cinema; Asian theology and spirituality, Christology and pluralism. **SELECTED PUBLICATIONS** Auth, A Call for Continuity: The Theological Contribution of James Orr, 88; Directionary of Twentieth Century Christian Biography, 95; auth, A.B. Simpson, Holiness and Modernity, in Studies in Canadian Evangelical Renewal, Faith Today, 96; coauth, Human Life is Not Sheep: An Ethical Perspective on cloning, Journal of the Evangelical Theological Society, Dec 97; auth, Yearning for God: The Potential and Poverty of the Catholic Spirituality of Francis de Sales, Journal of the Evangelical Theological Society, Sept 98. **CONTACT ADDRESS** 6116 Arosa St, San Diego, CA, 92115-3902. **EMAIL** gscourgie@bethel.edu

SCOTT, CHARLES
PERSONAL Born 09/03/1935, Oklahoma, OK, m, 1994, 3 children **DISCIPLINE** PHILOSOPHY **EDUCATION** S. Methodist Univ, BA, 57; Eberhard-Karls Univ, Fulbright Fel, 57-58; Yale Div Sch, MDiv, 61; Yale Grad Sch, MA, 62, PhD, 65. **CAREER** Yale Univ, grad asst, 60-63; Yale Berk Col, dean, inst, 63-66; Vanderbilt, asst prof, assoc prof, prof, 66-94; Mellon Regional Fac Devel Prog, dir, 79-87; Robert Penn Warren Center, dir, 87-93; Penn State Univ, E.E. Sparks prof, 94-. **HONORS AND AWARDS** Phi Beta Kappa, Fulbright Fel, Kent-Danforth Fel, Hooker Fel, Julia A. Archibald High Sch, Chancellor's Cup, NEH Fel, Vanderbilt sr res Fel. **MEMBERSHIPS** APA, SPEP, SSPP, AAUP, MSA, NEH reviewer. **RESEARCH** 19th and 20th cent Euro philos. **SELECTED PUBLICATIONS** Auth, Boundaries in Mind: A Study of Immediate Awareness Based in Psychotherapy, Scholars Press and Crossroads Press, 82; auth, The Language of Difference, Humanities Press Intl and MacMillan 87; auth, The Question of Ethics: Nietzsche, Foucault, Heidegger, Indiana Univ Press, 90; auth, On the Advantages and Disadvantages of Ethics and Politics, Indiana Univ Press, 96; auth, The Time of Memory, in: Contemporary Continental Philosophy, forthcoming, 98. **CONTACT ADDRESS** Dept of Philosophy, Pennsylvania State Univ, 240 Sparks Building, University Park, PA, 16802. **EMAIL** ces11@psu.edu

SCOTT, DAVID ALLEN
DISCIPLINE SYSTEMATIC THEOLOGY **EDUCATION** Amherst Col, BA, 54-58; Episcopal Divinity Sch, MDiv, 59-61; Princeton Univ, MA, 63-65, PhD, 68; Goethe Inst, Ebersberg, Passed State Exam in Ger Lang, 66; Tubingen Univ, stud and res, 66-67. **CAREER** Part-time asst, part-time chaplain, Trinity Church, Princeton Univ, 63-65; grad asst, Princeton Theol Sem, 65; instr, Episcopal Divinity Sch, 68-70; asst prof, 70-73; assoc prof, 73-79; instr, Dartmouth Col, 76; prof, 79-89; William Meade prof, Va Theol Sem, 89-. **HONORS AND AWARDS** Order of the Holy Cross, missionary, Liberia, W Africa, 61-63; **SELECTED PUBLICATIONS** Auth, Episcopal Ethical Teaching: Case Study Abortion:The Crisis in Moral Teaching in the Episcopal Church, Morehouse, 92; Christian Character: Jeremy Taylor and Christian Ethics Today, Latimer House, 91; Creation as Christ: A Problematic Theme in Some Feminist Theology, Speaking the Christian God, The Holy Trinity and the Challenge of Feminism, William B. Eerdmanns Publ Comp, 91. **CONTACT ADDRESS** Va Theol Sem, 3737 Seminary Rd, Alexandria, VA, 22304. **EMAIL** DAScott@vts.edu

SCOTT, GARY ALAN
PERSONAL Long Beach, CA, m **DISCIPLINE** PHILOSOPHY **EDUCATION** Univ Calif, Santa Cruz, BA, 75; Duquesne Univ, MA, 91, PhD, 95. **CAREER** Adj instr, Duquesne Univ, 92-94; vis asst prof philos, Whittier Col, 95-96; vis asst prof philos, Sienna Col, 96-97; asst prof philos, Saint Peter's Col, 97- . **MEMBERSHIPS** APA; Soc for Ancient Greek Philos; Int Assoc for Philos and Lit. **RESEARCH** Plato; history of Plato interpretation. **SELECTED PUBLICATIONS** Auth, Limits and Liberation in Plato's Lysis, disClosure: A J of Soc Theory, 94-95; auth, Irony and Inebriation in Plato's Symposium: The Disagreement Between Socrates and Alcibiades over Truth-Telling, J of Neoplatonic Stud, 95; auth, Games of Truth: Foucault's Analysis of The Transformation in Plato from Political to Ethical Parrhesia, So J of Philos, 96; coauth, An Overlooked Motive in Alcibiades' Symposium Speech, Interpretation, 96; auth, Foucault's Analysis of Power's Methodologies, Auslegung, 96; auth, Plato's Immortalization of Socrates, in Brinkhuis, ed, Proceedings of the Fifth Conference of the International Society for the Study of European Ideas, MIT, 98; coauth, Eros as Messenger: Diotima's Symposium Speech, in, Press, ed, Who Speaks for Plato? Studies in Platonic Anonymity, Rowman and Littlefield, 99. **CONTACT ADDRESS** 1028 Kennedy Blvd, Bayonne, NJ, 07002. **EMAIL** scott_G@spcvxa.spc.edu

SCOTT, GREGORY L.
PERSONAL Washington, DC **DISCIPLINE** PHILOSOPHY **EDUCATION** Univ Of California, BA, 79; Columbia Univ, MA, 86; Univ of Toronto, PhD, 92. **CAREER** Dir of Doctoral Stud, 95-98, Dance Edu, NY Univ; Vis Res Fellow, Philo, 95-97, Princeton Univ; Asst Prof Philo, 93-95, Univ of Ottawa, Canada; Asst Prof, Philo, 92-93, St Mary's Univ, Halifax; Asst Prof Philo, 91-92, Texas Tech Univ, Lubbock. **MEMBERSHIPS** APA, Soc of Dance Hist Stud. **RESEARCH** Aesthetics, Philosophy of Sex. **SELECTED PUBLICATIONS** Auth, Banes and Carroll on Defining Dance, Dance Research Journal, 97; The Poetics of Performance, The Necessity of Performance and Spectacle in Aristotelian Tragedy, eds, Salim Kemal and Ivan Gaskell, Cambridge Univ Press, 99; Empires, Egalitarianism and the International Dance Academy, Proceedings of the Society of Dance History Scholars Conference-Border Crossings, Dance and Boundaries in Society, Politics, Gender, Education and Technology, Ryerson Polytechnic Univ, Toronto, Ontario, 95. **CONTACT ADDRESS** 83 Park Terrace W #3A, New York, NY, 10034. **EMAIL** gs30@ts3.nyu.edu

SCOTT, HUGH B.
PERSONAL Born 04/29/1949, Buffalo, NY, m, 1973 **DISCIPLINE** LAW **EDUCATION** Niagara University, Lewiston, NY, BA, 1967-71; State University of New York at Buffalo Law School, JD, 1971-74. **CAREER** County of Erie Dept of Law, assistant county attorney, 1974-75; City of Buffalo Dept of Law, assistant corporation counsel, 1975-77; Dept of Justice, Buffalo, NY, assistant US attorney, 1977-79; New York State Dept of Law, Buffalo, NY, assistant attorney general, 1979-83; UB LAW SCHOOL, AMHERST CAMPUS, LECTURER, 1980-; NY STATE OFFICE OF COURT, BUFFALO, CITY COURT JUDGE, 1983-. **MEMBERSHIPS** Board of managers, Buffalo Museum of Science, 1989-; board of directors, UB Law Alumni Association, 1988-; former vice chairman, Urban League of Buffalo, 1980; advisory council, TransAfrica Buffalo, 1990-; member, Alpha Kappa Boule, 1983-. **CONTACT ADDRESS** Buffalo City Court, 25 Delaware, Suite 600,, Buffalo, NY, 14202.

SCOTT, JAMES
DISCIPLINE PHILOSOPHY OF CULTURE **EDUCATION** Columbia Univ, PhD. **CAREER** Philos, Univ Ark **SELECTED PUBLICATIONS** Area: philosophy of art, and American philosophy. **CONTACT ADDRESS** Univ Ark, Fayetteville, AR, 72701. **EMAIL** jhscott@comp.uark.edu

SCOTT, KERMIT
DISCIPLINE MEDIEVAL PHILOSOPHY **EDUCATION** Columbia Univ, PhD. **CAREER** Assoc prof, Purdue Univ. **RESEARCH** Social and political philosophy; Marxism. **SELECTED PUBLICATIONS** Published articles, a translation, and a critical text on medieval philosophy. **CONTACT ADDRESS** Dept of Philos, Purdue Univ, 1080 Schleman Hall, West Lafayette, IN, 47907-1080.

SCOTT, KIERAN
PERSONAL Born 08/28/1942, County Cavan, Ireland, m, 1988 **DISCIPLINE** RELIGION **EDUCATION** Columbia Univ, PhD, 78. **CAREER** Fordham Univ NY. **MEMBERSHIPS** AAR, CTS, APRRE, REA **RESEARCH** Church edu; ecclesiology; adult edu. **SELECTED PUBLICATIONS** Coauth, Perspectives on Marriage, Oxford Press. **CONTACT ADDRESS** 115 Cornell Ave, Hawthorne, NJ, 07506. **EMAIL** onovrice@paterson.k12.us

SCOTT, NATHAN ALEXANDER, JR.
PERSONAL Born 04/24/1925, Cleveland, OH, m, 1946, 2 children **DISCIPLINE** THEOLOGY **EDUCATION** Univ Michigan, BA, 44; Union Theol Sem, MDiv, 46; Columbia Univ, PhD, 49. **CAREER** Instr, asst prof, assoc prof Hum and Dir General Educ Prog in Hum, Howard Univ, 48-55; asst prof, assoc prof, prof, Theol and Lit, 55-72, Sailer Methews Prof of Theol and Lit, 72-76, Univ Chicago; William R. Kennan Prof Relig Stud, Univ Va, 76-90, now William R. Kennan Prof Emer, Univ Va. **HONORS AND AWARDS** Hon LittD, Brown Univ, 81; hon LittD, Northwestern Univ; hon HumD, Univ Mich, 88; hon LHD, Wesleyan Univ, 89; hon DD, Bates Col, 90; hon STD, Univ of the South, 92; hon DD, Kenyon Col, 93; hon DD, Wabash Col, 96. **MEMBERSHIPS** Am Acad of Arts and Sci; MLA; Am Acad Relig. **RESEARCH** Modern American poetry; Victorian literature, modern literary theory; modern theology. **SELECTED PUBLICATIONS** Auth, The Broken Center: Studies in the Theological Horizon of Modern Literature, Yale, 66; auth, Negative Capability: Studies in the New Literature and the Religious Situation, Yale, 69; auth, The Wild Prayer of Longing: Poetry and the Sacred, Yale, 71; auth, The Poetics of Belief, Univ North Carolina, 85; auth, Visions of Presence in Modern Amrican Poetry, Johns Hopkins, 93. **CONTACT ADDRESS** 1419 Hilltop Rd, Charlottesville, VA, 22903.

SCOTT, TIMOTHY
PERSONAL Born 10/22/1957, Regina, SK, Canada, s **DISCIPLINE** NEW TESTAMENT **EDUCATION** SSL; STD. **CAREER** President, St Joseph's Col, Univ of Alberta. **MEMBERSHIPS** AAR-SBL; CBA; CSBS; CTSA. **RESEARCH** New Testament; Hermeneutics **CONTACT ADDRESS** St Josephs Col, Univ of Alberta, Edmonton, AB, T6G 2J5. **EMAIL** timothy.scott@ualberta.ca

SCOTT, WALTER GAYLORD
PERSONAL Born 12/22/1928, El Paso, TX, m, 1950, 2 children **DISCIPLINE** PHILOSOPHY **EDUCATION** Baylor Univ, BA, 49, MA, 58; Southwestern Baptist Theol Sem, BD, 52, ThM, 54; Johns Hopkins Univ, PhD(philos), 69. **CAREER** Instr philos, Baylor Univ, 55-56; asst prof & acting chmn philos, La Col, 56-57; jr instr philos, Johns Hopkins Univ, 59-60; asst prof philos, 60-69, acting chmn dept relig, 61-67, assoc prof philos & chmn dept, 70-76, assoc prof philos, Okla State Univ, 76-97, assoc prof emeritus, 97-. **MEMBERSHIPS** Central Div Am Philos Asn; Southwestern Philos Soc; Medieval Acad Am; Renaissance Soc Am; Soc Medieval & Renaissance Philos. **RESEARCH** Philosophy of William Ockham; medieval cosmology; medieval geomancy; oriental philosophy, philosophy of religion. **CONTACT ADDRESS** Dept of Philos, Oklahoma State Univ, Stillwater, OK, 74078-0002. **EMAIL** wscott_osu@osu.net

SEARLE, JOHN R.
PERSONAL Born 07/31/1932, Denver, CO, m, 1958, 2 children **DISCIPLINE** PHILOSOPHY **EDUCATION** Oxford Univ, BA, 55, MA & DPhil, 59. **CAREER** Lectr philos, Christ Church Col, Oxford, 56-59; from asst prof to assoc prof, 59-67, spec asst to chancellor, 65-67, Prof Philos, Univ Calif, Berkeley, 67-, Vis assoc prof, Univ Mich, 61-62; Am Coun Learned Soc res grant, 63-64; vis fel, Brasenose Col, Oxford, 67-68; panelist and moderator weekly prog, World Press, Nat Educ TV, 70-77; Mass Inst Technol Vis Comt for Ling & Philos, 71-77; Guggenheim fel, 75-76; mem bd dirs, Coun Philos Studies, 75-; mem bd trustees, Nat Humanities Ctr, 75-; mem bd dirs, Am Coun Learned Soc, 79- **MEMBERSHIPS** Aristotelin Soc; Am Acad Arts & Sci; Am Philos Asn. **RESEARCH** Philosophy of language. **SELECTED PUBLICATIONS** Auth, Is There A Crisis In Am Higher-Educ + Liberal Educ And Multiculturalism, Partisan Rev, Vol 0060, 1993; Rationality And Realism Or What Is At Stake, Merkur-Deutsche Zeitschrift Fur Europaisches Denken, Vol 0048, 1994; Structure And Intention In Lang - A Reply To Knapp And Michaels/, New Literary Hist, Vol 0025, 1994; Literary-Theory And Its Discontents/, New Literary Hist, Vol 0025, 1994; The Remembered Present - A Biological Theory Of Consciousness - Edelman,Gm, NY Rev Of Books, Vol 0042, 1995; Consciousness Explained - Dennett,Dc/, NY Rev Of Books, Vol 0042, 1995; The Astonishing Hypothesis - The Scientific Search For The Soul - Crick,F/, NY Rev Of Books, Vol 0042, 1995; The Strange, Familiar And Forgotten - An Anatomy Of Consciousness - Rosenfield,I/, NY Rev Of Books, Vol 0042, 1995; Bright Air, Brilliant Fire - On The Matter Of The Mind - Edelman,Gm/, NY Rev Of Books, Vol 0042, 1995; Shadows Of The Mind - A Search For The Missing Science Of Consciousness - Penrose,R/, NY Rev Of Books, Vol 0042, 1995; The Construction Of Soc-Reality - Reply/, Hist Of The Human Sci, Vol 0010, 1997; The Conscious Mind - In Search Of A Fundamental Theory - Chalmers,Dj/, NY Rev Of Books, Vol 0044, 1997. **CONTACT ADDRESS** 1900 Yosemite Rd, Berkeley, CA, 94707.

SEARLS, EILEEN H.
PERSONAL Born 04/27/1925, Madison, WI **DISCIPLINE** LAW **EDUCATION** Univ Wi, BA, 48, JD, 50, MS, 51 **CAREER** Instr to asst prof to assoc prof, librn, St. Louis Univ, 52-53 **MEMBERSHIPS** ABA; ALA, Wi Bar Assoc; Bar Assoc Metrop St. Louis; Amer Assoc Law Librn; Mid Amer Assoc Law Librn; SW Assoc Law Librn. **CONTACT ADDRESS** 3700 Lindell Blvd, St. Louis, MO, 63108. **EMAIL** searlseh@slu.edu

SECADA, JORGE E.K.
PERSONAL Born 03/02/1951, Lima, Peru, s **DISCIPLINE** PHILOSOPHY **EDUCATION** Univ Catolica de Peru, BA, 75; Univ of York, England, B Phil, 77; Univ Cambridge, PhD, 83. **CAREER** Fel, St. John's Col, 80-84; assoc prof, Univ Va, 84-. **HONORS AND AWARDS** Brit Coun Scholar, 75-77; Title A fel, St. John's Col, 80-84; NEH distinguished visiting prof, State Univ NY at Potsdam, 98. **MEMBERSHIPS** APA; Soc Peruana de Filosofia; Soc for Medieval and Renaissance Philos. **RESEARCH** Late medieval and early modern philosophy; Metaphysics; Political philosophy. **SELECTED PUBLICATIONS** auth, Berkeley y el idealismo, Del Renacimiento a la llustracion II, Madrid, 98; auth, Descartes y la escolastica, Arete, 96. **CONTACT ADDRESS** Dept. of Philosophy, Univ of Virginia, Cabell Hall 512, Charlottesville, VA, 22903. **EMAIL** jes2f@virginia.edu

SECKINGER, DONALD SHERMAN
PERSONAL Born 02/01/1933, New York, NY, m, 1955, 3 children **DISCIPLINE** PHILOSOPHY & HISTORY OF EDUCATION **EDUCATION** Univ Calif, Los Angeles, AB, 54, MA, 56, EdD, 65. **CAREER** From asst prof to assoc prof educ, Calif State Univ, Los Angeles, 64-70; assoc prof educ found, 70-77, Prof Educ Found, Univ Wyo, 77-, Vis lectr educ, Univ Calif, Los Angeles, 68-69. **MEMBERSHIPS** Fel Philos Educ Soc; Am Educ Studies Asn; fel Far Western Philos Educ Soc(-secy-treas, 74-77, vpres, 77 & pres, 78-). **RESEARCH** Philosophical anthropology; existential philosophy. **SELECTED PUBLICATIONS** Auth, Tombaugh,Clyde - Discoverer Of The Planet Pluto - Levy,D/, J Of The W, Vol 0032, 1993. **CONTACT ADDRESS** Dept of Educ Founds, Univ of Wyo, Laramie, WY, 82070.

SEDGWICK, TIMOTHY F.
DISCIPLINE CHRISTIAN ETHICS **EDUCATION** Albion Col, AB, 69; Vanderbilt Univ, Grad Sch Rel, MA, 74, PhD, 75. **CAREER** Asst prof, Denison Univ, 75-76; Marshall Univ, 76-77; Blackburn Col, 77-78; asst prof to prof, Seabury-Western Theol Sem, 78-97; prof, Va Theol Sem, 97-. **SELECTED PUBLICATIONS** Auth, The Making of Ministry, Cowley, 93; Sacramental Ethics: Paschal Identity and the Christian Life, Fortress, 87; co-ed, The Crisis in Moral Teaching in the Episcopal Church, Morehouse, 92. **CONTACT ADDRESS** Va Theol Sem, 3737 Seminary Rd, Alexandria, VA, 22304. **EMAIL** TSedgwick@vts.edu

SEDLER, ROBERT ALLEN
PERSONAL Born 09/11/1935, Pittsburgh, PA, m, 1960, 2 children **DISCIPLINE** LAW **EDUCATION** Univ Pittsburgh, BA, 56, JD, 59. **CAREER** Teaching assoc law, Rutgers Univ, 59-60, asst prof, 61; from asst prof to assoc prof, St Louis Univ, 61-65; from assoc prof to prof, Univ Ky, 66-77; Prof Law, Wayne State Univ, 77-, Assoc prof & asst dean, Haile Sellassic Univ, 63-66. **MEMBERSHIPS** Am Bar Asn. **RESEARCH** Conflict of laws; civil rights; constitutional law. **SELECTED PUBLICATIONS** Auth, The Complex Litigation Projects Proposal For Federally-Mandated Choice Of Law In Mass Torts Cases - Another Assault On State Sovereignty/, Louisiana Law Rev, Vol 0054, 1994. **CONTACT ADDRESS** Law Sch, Wayne State Univ, 468 Ferry Mall, Detroit, MI, 48202-3698.

SEESKIN, KENNETH
DISCIPLINE PHILOSOPHY **EDUCATION** Yale Univ, PhD. **CAREER** Prof, Northwestern Univ. **RESEARCH** Ancient philosophy, Jewish philosophy, philosophy of religion, philosophy in literature. **SELECTED PUBLICATIONS** Auth, Dialogue and Discovery: A Study in Socratic Philosophy; Jewish Philosophy in a Secular Age. **CONTACT ADDRESS** Dept of Philosophy, Northwestern Univ, 1801 Hinman, Evanston, IL, 60208.

SEGAL, ALAL FRANKLIN
PERSONAL Born 08/02/1945, Worcester, MA, m, 1970, 2 children **DISCIPLINE** JUDAICA, HISTORY OF RELIGION **EDUCATION** Amherst Col, BA, 67; Brandeis Univ, MA, 69; Hebrew Union Col, BHL, 70; Yale Univ, MPhil, 72, PhD(Judaica), 75. **CAREER** Asst prof Judaica, Princeton Univ, 74-78; assoc prof, Univ Toronto, 78-81; Assoc Prof Judaica, Barnard Col & Grad Fac, Columbia Univ, 81-, Woodrow Wilson fel, 67-68; Jewish Mem Found fel, 73 & 78; Guggenheim fel, 78; chairperson Judaica Sect IAHR, Winnipeg, 80; Mellon fel, Aspen Inst, 81; chmn relig dept, Barnard Col, 81. **MEMBERSHIPS** Soc Bibl Lit; Asn Jewish Studies; Asn Sci Study Relig. **RESEARCH** Judaica; early Christianity. **SELECTED PUBLICATIONS** Auth, Revelation And Mystery In Ancient Judaism And Pauline Christianity - Bockmuehl,Mna/, J Of Bibl Lit, Vol 0111, 1992; Disinheriting The Jews - Abraham In Early-Christian Controversy - Siker,Js/, J Of Rel, Vol 0073, 1993; Dangerous Food - 1-Corinthians 8-10 In Its Context - Gooch,Pd/, Studies In Rel-Sci Religieuses, Vol 0024, 1995. **CONTACT ADDRESS** Dept of Relig Barnard Col, Columbia Univ, New York, NY, 10027.

SEGAL, ALAN
DISCIPLINE RELIGION **EDUCATION** Amherst Col, BA, 67; Brandeis Univ, MA, 71; Yale Univ, PhD, 75. **CAREER** Prof. **SELECTED PUBLICATIONS** Auth, Two Powers in Heaven, Brill; Deus Ex Machina: Computers in the Humanities, Penn; Rebecca's Children: Judaism and Christianity in the Roman World, Harvard; The Other Judaisms of Late Antiquity, Scholars. **CONTACT ADDRESS** Dept of Religion, Columbia Col, New York, 2960 Broadway, New York, NY, 10027-6902. **EMAIL** asegal@barnard.columbia.edu

SEIDEL, ASHER M.
PERSONAL Born 06/22/1943, Philadelphia, PA, m, 1977, 2 children **DISCIPLINE** METAPHYSICS, EPISTEMOLOGY, AND PHILOSOPHICAL ASPECTS OF COGNITIVE SCIENCE **EDUCATION** Rutgers Univ, AB, philos, 65; Univ Mich, philos, MA, 67, PhD, 70. **CAREER** Teaching fel, Univ Mich, 68-70; visiting asst prof, Mich State Univ, 70-71; asst prof, Miami Univ, 71-84; assoc prof, Miami Univ, 84-. **SELECTED PUBLICATIONS** Auth, Searle's New Argument, Dialogue, 97; rev, Thinking About Logic, Teaching Philosophy, Stephen Read, 96; auth, Plato, Wittgenstein, and Artificial Intelligence, Metaphilos, 91; auth, Chinese Rooms A, B, and C, Pacific Philos Quart, 89; auth, Searle on the Biological Basis of Cognition, Analysis, 88; auth, The Probability of Free Will, Philos, 85; auth, Numbers as Qualities, Philos, 84; auth, Anti Zero-Growth: Brief for Development, Philos and Soc Action, 81; auth, The Picture Theory of Meaning, Linguistics and Philos, 77; auth, Universals and the Coextension of Qualities, New Scholasticism, 76. **CONTACT ADDRESS** Philosophy Dept., Miami Univ, 10 Oakhill Dr, Oxford, OH, 45056. **EMAIL** seidela@muohio.edu

SEIDEL, GEORGE J.
PERSONAL Born 04/25/1932, Tacoma, WA **DISCIPLINE** PHILOSOPHY **EDUCATION** St Martin's Col, BA, 55; Univ Toronto, MA, 60; PhD, 62. **CAREER** Prof, philos, St Martin's Col, 62- . **HONORS AND AWARDS** Fulbright fel, 61-62; Orgn Am States fel, 65. **MEMBERSHIPS** APA; N Am Fichte Soc; Northwest Conf on Philos. **RESEARCH** German idealism; twentieth century continental philosophy. **SELECTED PUBLICATIONS** Auth, Fichte's Wissenschaftslehre of 1794: A Commentary on Part I, Purdue, 93; auth, Minded Body/Embodied Mind, man and World, 94; auth, A Key to Heidegger's Beitrage, Gregorianum, 95; auth, The Atheism Controversy of 1799 and the Christology of Fichte's Anweisung zum seligen Leben of 1806, New Perspectives on Fichte, Humanities, 95; auth, Buddhism as Radical Religion, Darshana Int, 95; auth, Angels, Peter Lang, 95; auth, Knowledge as Sexual Metaphor, Susquehana, forthcoming; auth, Fichte and German Idealism: The Heideggerian Reading, Idealistic Stud, forthcoming; auth, Heidegger's Last God and the Schelling Connection, Laval Theologique et Philosophique, forthcoming. **CONTACT ADDRESS** St Martins Col, 5300 Pacific Ave SE, Lacey, WA, 98503. **EMAIL** gseidel@crc.stmartin.edu

SEIDENFELD, TEDDY
PERSONAL Born 05/15/1948, New York, NY, m, 1971, 2 children **DISCIPLINE** PHILOSOPHY **EDUCATION** Univ Rochester, AB, 69; Columbia Univ, PhD, 76. **CAREER** HA Simon prof Phil Stat, 97-, ch, fac sen, 95-96, head, dept Phil, 89-94, prof Phil and Stat, 87-, assoc prof, 86, assoc prof Phil, 85, Carnegie Mellon Univ; assoc prof Phil and Hea care res, 83, assoc prof Phil, 81, Washington Univ; asst prof Phil and Hist Phil of Sci, 77, asst prof Phil, 75, Univ Pittsburgh. **HONORS AND AWARDS** NSF Grant DMS-9801401; STICERD disting scholar, London sch Econ, 97; asst-PI in FIPSE awd; NSF grant; vis scholar, summer inst, Vaxjo Univ, Sweden, 92. **RESEARCH** Philosophy of Science. **SELECTED PUBLICATIONS** Coauth, A Representation of Partially Ordered Preferences, Ann Stat 23, 95, 2168-2217; Coauth, Reasoning to a Foregone Conclusion, J Am Stat Assoc 91, 96, 1228-1235; coauth, Divisive Conditioning: Further Results on Dilation, Phil Sci 64, 97, 411-444. **CONTACT ADDRESS** Dept of Philosophy, Carnegie Mellon Univ, Pittsburgh, PA, 15213. **EMAIL** Teddy@stat.cmu.edu

SEIDMAN, LOUIS MICHAEL
PERSONAL Born 02/16/1947, Washington, DC, m, 1977, 1 child **DISCIPLINE** LAW **EDUCATION** Univ Chicago, BA, 68; Harvard Univ, JD, 71. **CAREER** Law clerk, US Ct of Appeals, 71-72 & Supreme Ct Justice, 72-73; staff atty, DC Pub Defender Serv, 73-76; asst prof law, 76-79, assoc prof, 79-82, Prof Law, Georgetown Univ Law Ctr, 82- **RESEARCH** Criminal law; constitutional law. **SELECTED PUBLICATIONS** Auth, The Problems With Privacys Problem - Response/, Mich Law Rev, Vol 0093, 1995. **CONTACT ADDRESS** Law Ctr, Georgetown Univ, 600 New Jersey N W, Washington, DC, 20001-2022.

SEIGEL, MICHAEL L.
DISCIPLINE LAW **EDUCATION** Princeton Univ, AB; Harvard Univ, JD. **CAREER** Prof, Univ Fla, 90-; vis prof, Univ BC, Can; past asst US atty, Philadelphia; spec atty, US Dept Justice, Organized Crime Racketeering Sect, Philadelphia Strike Force, 85-89; clerk, Judge Edward R. Becker, US Ct Appeals, 3rd Circuit. **MEMBERSHIPS** Pa Bar; Phi Beta Kappa. **RESEARCH** Evidence, criminal law, professional responsibility, federal criminal law. **CONTACT ADDRESS** School of Law, Univ of Florida, PO Box 117625, Gainesville, FL, 32611-7625. **EMAIL** seigel@law.ufl.edu

SEIGFRIED, CHARLENE
DISCIPLINE CLASSICAL AMERICAN PHILOSOPHY, 19TH-CENTURY PHILOSOPHY, FEMINIST PHILOSOPHY **EDUCATION** Loyola Univ, Chicago, PhD. **CAREER** Prof, Purdue Univ. **RESEARCH** Pragmatism and feminism. **SELECTED PUBLICATIONS** Published works in the areas of social and political philosophy, metaphysics, and aesthetics. **CONTACT ADDRESS** Dept of Philos, Purdue Univ, 1080 Schleman Hall, West Lafayette, IN, 47907-1080.

SEIGFRIED, HANS
PERSONAL Born 12/18/1933, Karavukovo, Yugoslavia, m, 1970, 1 child **DISCIPLINE** PHILOSOPHY **EDUCATION** St Rupert Gymnasium, Bischofshofen/Salzburg, 49-55; St Gabriel Academy, Moedling/Vienna, Grad Studies, 55-60; Univ Bonn/Germany; Philosophy Germanistik Canon Law, PhD, 66. **CAREER** Asst prof, 68-69, assoc prof, 72-81, prof, 82-, Dept of Philosophy, Loyola Univ of Chicago. **HONORS AND AWARDS** Yale Univ, Dept of Phil, Postdoctoral Fel, 66-67; Univ of TX at Austin, Postdoctoral Fel, 67-68. **MEMBERSHIPS** Amer Phil Asn; Soc for Phenomenology and Existential Phil; Intl Soc for Phil and Technology; Soc for the Advancement of Amer Phil; North Amer Nietzsche Soc; North Amer Kant Soc; Heidegger Conf; Soc for the Philosophic Study of Genocide and the Holocaust. **RESEARCH** Kantian and Post-Kantian transcendental phil; phenomenology esp Heidegger; 19th century phil esp Nietzsche & Marx; contemporary German phil; phil and science/technology; Amer phil esp Dewey. **SELECTED PUBLICATIONS** Auth, Heideggers Technikkritik, Lebenswelt und Wissenschaft Studien zum Verhaltnis von Phanomenologie und Wissenschaftstheorie, Bouvier Verlag, 91; art, On the Ambivalence of Progress in Nietzsche and Heidegger Science and Technology as Mediators, Allgemeine Zeitschrift fur Philosophie 16, 91; art, Nietzsche's Natural Morality, Jour of Value Inquiry 26, 92; art, Dewey's Critique of Kant's Copernican Revolution Revisited, Kant-Studien 83, 93; art, Art as Fetish in Nietzsche and Heidegger, Intl Stud in Phil 27, 95; auth, Heidegger at the Nuremberg Trails The Letter on Humanism Revisited, Martin Heidegger and the Holocaust, Humanities Press, 96; art, Human Rights Ends-in-view & Controlled Inquiry A Response to Paul Chevigny's Dialogue Rights, Jour of Speculative Phil 12, 98; auth, The Voices of the Victims, Contemporary Portrayals of Auschwitz an Genocide: Philosophical Challenges, Humanities Press, 98. **CONTACT ADDRESS** Philosophy Dept, Loyola Univ, Chicago, 6525 North Sheridan Road, Chicago, IL, 60626-5385. **EMAIL** hseigfr@luc.edu

SEIPLE, DAVID I.
PERSONAL Born 06/03/1949, Columbus, OH, s **DISCIPLINE** PHILOSOPHY **EDUCATION** Col of Wooster, BA, 71; Drew Univ, MTS, 74; Columbia Univ, PhD, 93. **CAREER** Adj instr, Drew Univ, theol, 73-76; tchg asst, Columbia Univ, 79; adj lectr, relig, Wagner Col, 83; adj instr, philos, NY Inst Technol, 83; adj lectr, philos, LaGuardia Commun Col, 83-86; adj lectr, Drew Univ, 89; adj lectr, hum, NYU, 85-91, currently independent scholar. **HONORS AND AWARDS** Miller Prize, philos, 71; MacDaniel fel, 74; Magna Cum Laude, 74; SCE summer res grant, 90; Lina Kahn prize in metaphysics, 91. **MEMBERSHIPS** APA; Soc for the Advanc of Am Philos. **RESEARCH** Ethics; aesthetics; gay/lesbian philosophy; American philosophy/Dewey studies; social philosophy. **SELECTED PUBLICATIONS** Auth, Exemplary Ethics in the History of Moral Theory, Punishment, War, in, Ethics Applied, McGraw-hill, 93; auth, Experience and the Organic Unity of Artworks, in Kelly, ed, Encyclopedia of Aesthetics, Oxford, 98; co-ed, Dewey Reconfigured, SUNY, forthcoming; auth, Arthur C. Danto, in Dictionary of Literary Biography, Bruccoli Clark and Layman, forthcoming; auth, Philosophy's Labrynth, http://www.dsieple.com. **CONTACT ADDRESS** 204 W 108th St, #44, New York, NY, 10025. **EMAIL** dseiple@idt.net

SEITZ, BRIAN
DISCIPLINE PHILOSOPHY **EDUCATION** PhD. **CAREER** Asst Prof of Philo, Babson Coll. **MEMBERSHIPS** APA, SPEP, IAPL, ASE, SBE. **RESEARCH** Social and Political Philosophy. **SELECTED PUBLICATIONS** Auth, The Trace of Political Representation, SUNY Press; co-ed, Eating Culture, SUNY Press. **CONTACT ADDRESS** Arts and Humanities, Babson Col, Babson Park, MD, 02157-0310.

SELENGUT, CHARLES
PERSONAL New York, NY **DISCIPLINE** THEOLOGY **EDUCATION** Drew Univ, MA, 69, PhD, 83. **CAREER** Visiting Prof, Drew Univ, 85-; Prof, County Col of Morris, 70-. **HONORS AND AWARDS** Natl Endowment for the Humanities Award, 88; Eastern Sociological Soc Merit Award **MEMBERSHIPS** Soc for the Scientific Study of Religion; Amer Sociological Soc. **RESEARCH** Comparative fundamentalism; conversion to new religion **SELECTED PUBLICATIONS** Auth, Seeing Society, 92; Accounting for Fundamentalism; By Torah Alone: Yeshive Fundamentalism in Jewish Society, 94; Judaism in a Post Modern Age, 99. **CONTACT ADDRESS** 544 Rutland Ave., Teaneck, NJ, 07666-2923. **EMAIL** cselengu@ccm.edu

SELINGER, CARL MARVIN
PERSONAL Born 12/28/1934, Los Angeles, CA, m, 1959, 2 children **DISCIPLINE** LAW **EDUCATION** Univ Calif, Berkeley, BA, 55; Harvard Univ, JD, 58. **CAREER** Prof law, Albany Law Sch, Union Univ, 61-63 & Univ NMex, 63-68; acad dean, Bard Col, 68-75; prof law, Univ Hawaii, 75-79; dean & prof law, Univ Detroit, 79-82; dean & prof law, WVa Univ, 82-; consult, Nat Endowment for Humanities, 68, Legal Serv Prog, Off Econ Opportunity, 70, Curric Study Proj Comt, Asn Am Law Schs, 71, Bryn Mawr Col, 74 & Hawaii Inst Mgt & Anal Gov, 77; NIH grant dir prof communicating ethical dimension of pub policy issues through the info media, 74-75; reporter, Devitt Comt Pilot prog US Dist Court, Eastern Dist Mich, 81. **MEMBERSHIPS** Asn Am Law Schs, Chemn, section on Comparative Law; Am Soc Political & Legal Philos; Inter-Am Bar Asn, Pres, Committee XII. **RESEARCH** Law and ethics; the legal profession; reform of undergraduate education. **SELECTED PUBLICATIONS** Auth, The Public's Interest in Preserving the Dignity and Unity of the Legal Profession, 32 Wake Forest L Rev 861, 97; Dramatizing on Film the Uneasy Role of the American Criminal Defense Lawyer: True Believer, 22 Okla. City U.L. REV. 223, 97; Public Interest Lawyering in Mexico and the United States, 27 U. Miami Inter-Am. L. Rev. 343, 96; The Retention of Limitations on the Out-of-Court Practice of Law By Independent Paralegals, 9 Geo J Legal Ethics 879, 96; Inventing Billable Hours: Contract vs Fairness in Charging Attorneys' Fees, 22 Hofstra L Rev, 671, 94; The Law on Lawyer Efforts to Discredit Truthful Testimony, 46 Okla L Rev 99, 93; Robinson Crusoe Torts, 96, W Va L Rev 169, 93. **CONTACT ADDRESS** Sch of Law, West Virginia Univ, PO Box 6130, Morgantown, WV, 26506-6130. **EMAIL** cselinge@wvu.edu

SELJAK, DAVID
DISCIPLINE RELIGIOUS STUDIES **EDUCATION** Univ Toronto, BA, 82; MA, 87; McGill Univ, PhD, 96. **CAREER** Asst prof **SELECTED PUBLICATIONS** Auth, Antisemitism in Canada: History and Interpretation (rev); David M. Wulff, Psychology of Religion: Classic and Contemporary Views (rev); Is nationalism a religion?: a critique of Ninian Smart; Jacques Grand'Maison: Religion and Nationalism During Quebec's Quiet Revolution; Religion, Nationalism and the Break-Up of Canada. **CONTACT ADDRESS** Dept of Religious Studies, St. Jerome's Univ, Waterloo, ON, N2L 3G3. **EMAIL** dseljak@watarts.uwaterloo.ca

SELLERS, MORTIMER
PERSONAL Born 04/21/1959, Philadelphia, PA, m, 1984, 1 child **DISCIPLINE** JURISPRUDENCE **EDUCATION** Harvard Univ, AB, 80, JD, 88; Oxford Univ, DPhil, 86, BCL, 88. **CAREER** Prof law and dir, center for Intl and Comparative Law, Univ Baltimore Sch Law, 89- . **HONORS AND AWARDS** Rhodes Scholar, 80. **MEMBERSHIPS** Amer soc Polit and Legal Philos; Selden soc; Amer Soc Intl Law. **RESEARCH** Political and legal philosophy; Constitutional Law. **SELECTED PUBLICATIONS** Auth, American Republicanism, Macmillan and NYU Press, 94; The Sacred Fire of Liberty, Macmillan and NYU Press, 98. **CONTACT ADDRESS** School of Law, Univ of Baltimore, 1420 North Charles St, Baltimore, MD, 21201. **EMAIL** msellers@ubmail.ubalt.edu

SELNER-WRIGHT, SUSAN C.
DISCIPLINE PHILOSOPHY AND METAPHYSICS OF THOMAS AQUINAS **EDUCATION** Univ Notre Dame, BA, 83; Cath Univ Amin Wash, MA, 86, PhD, 92. **CAREER** Dept Philos, Mt Saint Mary's Col **HONORS AND AWARDS** Nat Endowment for the Humanities awd, 94. **RESEARCH** Metaphysics of the relation between charity toward God and toward neighbor. **SELECTED PUBLICATIONS** Auth, The Order of Charity in Thomas Aquinas. **CONTACT ADDRESS** Dept of Philosophy, Mount Saint Mary's Col, 16300 Old Emmitsburg Rd, Emmitsburg, MD, 21727-7799. **EMAIL** selner@msmary.edu

SELVIDGE, MARLA J.
PERSONAL Born 11/11/1948, Gross Pt, MI, m, 1982 **DISCIPLINE** BIBLICAL LANGUAGES AND LITERATURE **EDUCATION** Taylor Univ, BA, 70; Wheaton Col, MA, 73; St. Louis Univ, PhD, 80. **CAREER** Asst prof, John Wesley Col, 73-74; pers dir, Thalhimers, 74-76; res asst, Cts for Reformation Res, 76-77; dir evening div, St Louis Univ, 77-80; lect, St. Louis Univ, 78-80; asst prof, Carthage Col, 80-81; ast prof, Univ Dayton, 81-84; asst prof, Converse Col, 84-87; chemn Relig and Philos, Converse Col, 84-85; coordr grant writing, Cheshire Public Sch, 87-89; asst prof, Marist Col, 89-90; dir, assoc prof, Central Missouri St Univ, 90-94; prof, dir, Center for Relig Stud, Central Missouri St Univ, 94- . **HONORS AND AWARDS** Tenney Awd, Best Thesis, 73; Fac of the Year, 74; nominated Outstanding Women in America, 80; res grant, William R. Kenan Fund and Natl Endowment for the Hum, 84-87; res grant CMSU, 91-92; Missouri Hum Council Grant, 92-94. **MEMBERSHIPS** Soc Bibl Lit; Am Acad Relig; Missouri St Tchr Asn. **SELECTED PUBLICATIONS** Auth, "Chautauqua Revival Brings to Life Religious Figures," Relig Stud News, 93; "Mennonites and Amish," Women in American Religious History, Kathryn Kuhlman, Missouri Chautauqua, 93; "Magic and Menses," Explorations, 93; "Discovering Women," Teacher Created Materials, 95; "Notorious Voices," Continuum, 96; "Reflections on Violence and Pornography," A Feminist Companion to the Bible, Sheffield, 96; The New Testament, PrenticeHall, 98. **CONTACT ADDRESS** Center For Religious Studies, Central Missouri State Univ, Martin 118, Warrensburg, MO, 64093.

SENCERZ, STEFAN
PERSONAL Born 06/08/1954, Warsaw, Poland **DISCIPLINE** PHILOSOPHY **EDUCATION** Univ Rochester, PhD, 91. **MEMBERSHIPS** Am Philoso Asn. **RESEARCH** Ethical theory; Applied ethics; Metaphysics. **CONTACT ADDRESS** 9350 S Padre Island Dr, #11, Corpus Cristi, TX, 78418. **EMAIL** sencerz@falcon.tamucc.edu

SENNETT, JAMES
PERSONAL Born 08/04/1955, Norfolk, VA, m, 1978, 1 child **DISCIPLINE** PHILOSOPHY **EDUCATION** Atlanta Christian Col, BA, 77; Lincoln Christian Sem, MDiv, 81; Univ Nebraska, MA, 87, PhD, 90. **CAREER** Asst prof philos, Pacific Lutheran Univ, 90-92; asst prof philos, Palm Beach Atlantic Col, 92-95; asst prof philos, McNeese State Univ, 95- . **HONORS AND AWARDS** Exec Comm Soc of Christian Philos, 95-97; Pew scholar, 98. **MEMBERSHIPS** APA; Southern Soc of Philos and Psychol; Soc of Christian Philos. **RESEARCH** Philosophy of religion; philosophy of mind. **SELECTED PUBLICATIONS** Auth, Modality, Probability, and Rationality: A Critical Examination of Alvin Plantinga's Philosophy, Peter Lang, 92; auth, Toward a Compatibility Theory for Internalist and Externalist Epistemologies, Philos and Phenomenological Res, 92; auth, The Inscrutable Evil Defense Against the Inductive Argument from Evil, Faith and Philos, 93; auth, Is God Essentially God? Relig Stud, 94; auth, Theism and Other Minds: On the Falsifiability of Non-Theories, Topoi, 95; auth, Christianity, Education, and the Image of God, Christianity, Humanism, Health: Proceedings from the First International Symposium, Ukraine, 95; auth, Requiem for an Android? A Response to Lillegard, Cross Currents, 96; auth, Direct Justification and Universal Sanction, J of Philos Rev, 98; ed, The Analytic Theist: A Collection of Alvin Plantinga's Works in Philosophy of Religion, Eerdmans, 98; auth, Is There Freedom in Heaven? Faith and Philos, forthcoming. **CONTACT ADDRESS** Dept of Social Sciences, McNeese State Univ, PO Box 92335, Lake Charles, LA, 70809-2335. **EMAIL** jsennett@acc.mcneese.edu

SENOR, THOMAS
DISCIPLINE EPISTEMOLOGY **EDUCATION** Univ Ariz, PhD. **CAREER** English and Lit, Univ Ark. **SELECTED PUBLICATIONS** Ed, The Rationality of Belief and the Plurality of Faith, Cornell Univ Press, 96. **CONTACT ADDRESS** Univ Ark, Fayetteville, AR, 72701. **EMAIL** senor@comp.uark.edu

SENT, ESTHER MIRJAM
DISCIPLINE PHILOSOPHY OF SCIENCE **EDUCATION** Stanford Univ, PhD, 94. **CAREER** Prof. **RESEARCH** Philosophy of economics; history of economic thought; economics of science; science studies. **SELECTED PUBLICATIONS** Auth, Convenience: The Mother of All Rationality in Sargent, 96; What an Economist Can Teach Nancy Cartwright, 96; Sargent versus Simon: Bounded Rationality Unbound, 97. **CONTACT ADDRESS** History and Philosophy of Science Dept, Univ of Notre Dame, Notre Dame, IN, 46556. **EMAIL** Sent.2@nd.edu

SEPLOWITZ, RENA C.
DISCIPLINE LAW **EDUCATION** Barnard Col, AB, summ cum laude, 73; Columbia Law Sch, JD, 75; **CAREER** Prof Law, Touro Col; articles ed, Columbia J of Law and Soc Prob; assoc ed, Real Property Probate & Trust J; pvt prac, Kay, Scholer, Fierman, Hayes & Handler. **HONORS AND AWARDS** Harlan Fiske Stone Scholar. **MEMBERSHIPS** Am Bar Asn; Asn of the Bar of the City of NY. **SELECTED PUBLICATIONS** Auth, Transfers Before Marriage and the Uniform Probate Code's Redesigned Elective Share Why the Partnership Is Not Yet Complete, Ind Law Rev, 91; coauth, Testamentary Substitutes - A Time for Statutory Clarification, Real Property and Probate J, 88; Testamentary Substitutes: Retained Interests, Custodial Accounts, and Contractual Transactions A New Approach, Am Univ Law Rev, 88. **CONTACT ADDRESS** Touro Col, Brooklyn, NY, 11230. **EMAIL** RenaS@tourolaw.edu

SEPPER, DENNIS L.
DISCIPLINE PHILOSOPHY, ETHICS **EDUCATION** Harvard Univ, BA; Univ Chicago, MA, PhD. **CAREER** Dept Philos, Univ Dallas **SELECTED PUBLICATIONS** Auth, Showing, Doing, and the Ontology of Using Scientific Instruments, Proc Eleventh Intl Sci Instrument Symp, Bologna: Grafis Edizioni, 94; Newton's Optical Writings: A Guided Study, series Masterworks of Discovery, Rutgers Univ Press, 94; Newton's Optics as Classic: On Teaching the Texture of Science, PSA, 94; Descartes's Imagination: Proportion, Images, and the Activity of Thinking, Univ Calif Press, 96. **CONTACT ADDRESS** Dept of Philos, Univ Dallas, 1845 E Northgate Dr, Irving, TX, 75062. **EMAIL** sepper@acad.udallas.edu

SEREQUEBERHAN, TSENAY
PERSONAL Born 05/18/1952, Eritrea, m, 1979, 2 children **DISCIPLINE** PHILOSOPHY **EDUCATION** Univ Mass, BA, 79; Boston Col, MA, 82, PhD, 88. **CAREER** Instr, Boston Col, 82-83; Univ Mass at Boston, 83-88; Asst prof, Hampshire Col, 88-94; Assoc prof, Simmons Col, 94-96; Vis assoc prof, Simmons Col, 96-97; Brown Univ, 98-. **HONORS AND AWARDS** Res Grant, Simmons Col, 95; Hewlett-Mellon Fac Dev Grant, Hampshire Col, 90-92. **MEMBERSHIPS** APA; African Studies Asn. **RESEARCH** Philosophy; African-American Philosophy; Ancient Philosophy. **SELECTED PUBLICATIONS** Auth, The Hermeneutics of African Philosophy, 94; African Philosophy: The Essential Readings, 91; "Africanity at the End of the 20th Century," 98; "The Critique of Eurocentrism and the Practice of African Philosophy," 97; "Fanon and the Contemporary Discourse of African Philosophy: The Case of Immanuel Kant," 96; "Reflections on: In My Father's House," 96. **CONTACT ADDRESS** 307 Lamartine St, Apt 1, Jamaica Plain, MA, 02130.

SERGEEV, MIKHAIL YU
PERSONAL Born 04/29/1960, Moscow, Russia, m, 1980, 1 child **DISCIPLINE** RELIGION/PHILOSOPHY OF RELIGION **EDUCATION** Temple Univ, MA, 92, PhD, 97. **CAREER** Sr lect, Univ of the Arts, 97-. **HONORS AND AWARDS** Teaching assistanship, Temple Univ, 91-96; dissertation res grant, The Spalding Trust, England, 96. **MEMBERSHIPS** Am Academy of Relig; Am Philos Asn; Am Asn for the Advancement of Slavic Studies. **RESEARCH** Philosophy of religion; Russian religious thought. **SELECTED PUBLICATIONS** Auth, Postmodern Themes in the Philosophy of Nicholas Berdyaev, J of the CAREE, vol XIV, no 2, Oct 94; Religious Nationalism in Russia: A Postmodern Identity?, J of the Christians Associated for Relations with Eastern Europe (CAREE), vol XIV, no 2, April 94; Russian Orthodoxy: Renewal or Revival?, J of Ecumenical Studies, 33:1, winter 96; Sophiology of Nikolai Berdiaev, in Transactions of Russian-American Scholars in the USA, vol XXX, forthcoming, 98; Liberation from the Soviet Past: A Reflection on the Possibility of Post-Gulag Theology, in Symposion, A J of Russian Thought, vol III, 98. **CONTACT ADDRESS** 217 S Buckingham Pl, #2, Philadelphia, PA, 19104. **EMAIL** sg93d237@post.drexel.edu

SESSIONS, ROBERT
DISCIPLINE PHILOSOPHY **EDUCATION** Drake Univ, BA, 67; Univ Mich, MA, 70, PhD, 75. **CAREER** Asst prof philos, 73-77, Univ Minn; asst prof philos, 77-79, Luther Col, Decoral; asst manager, 79-84, CETA reg office, Decorah; asst prof philos, 84-85, Grinnell Col; prof, 85-, Kirkwood Community Col, Rapid Cedars, IA. **HONORS AND AWARDS** Woodrow Wilson & Danforth Graduate fels; Master Tchr Award, Nat Inst for Staff & Organ Devel, 88; Master Tchr Award, Community Col Hum Asn, 89; Asn of Comm Col Trustees Tchr of Yr Award for Midwest Reg, 91; Asn of Comm Col Trustees Nat Tchr of Yr Award, 91; NEH grants, 90-97. **SELECTED PUBLICATIONS** Auth, Working in America: A Humanities Reader, Univ Notre Dame Press, 92; auth, Work and the Environment, Community Col Hum Rev, 94; auth, Teaching Humanities Courses on the Environment, Comm Col Hum Rev, 94; auth, An Annotated Bibliography on Humanities and the Environment, Comm Col Hum Rev, 94; auth, Ecofeminism and Work, Ecological Feminism: Multidisciplinary Perspectives, IN Univ Press, 95; auth, Work, Encycl of Ed, 95 ed; auth, Education is a Gift, Not a Commodity, Comm Col Hum Rev, 96; auth, Deep Ecology versus Ecofeminism: Healthy Differences or Incompatible Philosophies?, Ecological Feminist Philosophies, Ind Univ Press, 96; auth, Work and the Environment; Toward Reconciliation, Utopian Visions of Work & Commmunity, Obermann Ctr for Advanced Stud, Univ Iowa, 96; auth, Work and Peacemaking, Institutional Violence, Ind Univ Press. **CONTACT ADDRESS** Arts & Humanities, Kirkwood Comm Col, Cedar Rapids, IA, 52406. **EMAIL** bsession@kirkwood.cc.ia.us

SESSIONS, WILLIAM LAD
PERSONAL Born 12/03/1943, Somerville, NJ, m, 1965, 2 children **DISCIPLINE** PHILOSOPHY **EDUCATION** Univ Colo, Boulder, BA, 65; Columbia Univ, MA, 67; Yale Univ, PhD, 71. **CAREER** Teaching fel, Yale Univ, 69; instr philos, Univ Conn, Waterbury, 70-71; from Asst Prof to Assoc Prof, 71-83, Prof Philos, Washington & Lee Univ, 83-, Assoc Dean of Col, 92-95, Actg Dean, 95-96. **MEMBERSHIPS** Am Philos Asn; Soc Philos Relig; Va Philos Asn; Soc Christian Philos. **RESEARCH** Philosophy of religion. **SELECTED PUBLICATIONS** Auth, Hartshorne's early philosophy, in Studies in religion, Am Acad Relig, 73; Charles Hartshorne and thirdness, summer 74 & On Inclusion: A response to Hartshorne, winter 79, Southern J Philos; Kant and Religious Belief, Kant-Studien, 4: 455-468; William James and the Right to Over-Believe, Philos Res Arch, 6: 1420; Rawls's Concept and Conception of Primary Good, Social Theory & Pract, fall 81; The Concept of Faith, Cornell Univ Press, 94. **CONTACT ADDRESS** Dept of Philos, Washington & Lee Univ, 116 N Main St, Lexington, VA, 24450-2504. **EMAIL** sessionsl@wlu.edu

SETTLE, TOM
PERSONAL Born 08/30/1931, Manchester, England, m, 1956, 3 children **DISCIPLINE** PHILOSOPHY **EDUCATION** Univ Manchester, BSc, 52, cert educ, 58; Univ Leeds, BA, 55; Univ Hong Kong, PhD(philos), 65. **CAREER** Minister, Methodist Church Gt Brit, 55-57; chaplain & head sci, Methodist Col, Hong Kong, 58-65; minister, Methodist Church Gt Brit, 65-67; asst prof, 67-70, assoc prof, 70-75, dean, Col Arts, 75-80, Prof Philos, Univ Guelph, 75- **MEMBERSHIPS** Can Philos Asn; Philos Sci Asn; Can Soc Hist & Philos Sci. **RESEARCH** Philosophy of science and of religion; political economy; ethics. **SELECTED PUBLICATIONS** Auth, How Determinism Refutes Compatibilism + Deterministic Interpretation Of Quantum-Theory And Its Implications For Theodicy/, Religious Studies, Vol 0029, 1993; Fitness And Altruism - Traps For The Unwary, Bystander And Biologist Alike/, Biology & Philos, Vol 0008, 1993; 6 Things Popper Would Like Biologists Not To Ignore - In-Memoriam, Popper,Karl,Raimund, 1902-1994/, Biology & Philos, Vol 0011, 1996. **CONTACT ADDRESS** Dept of Philos, Univ of Guelph, Guelph, ON, N1G 2W1.

SETZER, CLAUDIA
PERSONAL Born 03/11/1952, La Crosse, WI, m, 1998, 2 children **DISCIPLINE** BIBLICAL STUDIES **EDUCATION** Macalester Col, BA, 74; Jewish Theological Seminary, MA, 80; Columbia/Union, PhD, 90. **CAREER** ASST/ASSOC PROF OF RELIGIOUS STUDIES, MANHATTAN COL, 90-. **MEMBERSHIPS** AAR/SBL **RESEARCH** New Testament; Early Judaism & Christianity. **SELECTED PUBLICATIONS** Auth, Jewish Reactions to Early Christians, Fortress, 94; auth, Excellent Women: Female Witness to the Resurrection, JBL, 97. **CONTACT ADDRESS** Dept of Religious Studies, Manhattan Col, Manhattan College Pkwy, Bronx, NY, 10471. **EMAIL** csefzer@manhattan.edu

SEUNG, THOMAS KAEHAO
PERSONAL Born 09/20/1930, Jungju, Korea, m, 1965, 3 children **DISCIPLINE** PHILOSOPHY **EDUCATION** Yale Univ, BA, 58, MA, 61, PhD, 65. **CAREER** From lectr to instr, Yale Univ, 63-65; asst prof, Fordham Univ, 65-66; from asst prof to assoc prof, 66-72, Prof Philos, Univ Tex, Austin, 72-; Soc Relig Higher Educ fel, 69-70; Am Coun Learned Soc fel, 70-71; NEH fel, 77-78. **RESEARCH** Continental philosophy; philosophy of culture; philosophy of values. **SELECTED PUBLICATIONS** Auth, The fragile leaves of the Sibyl: Dante's master plan, Newman, 62; Kant's Transcendental Logic, Yale Univ, 69; Cultural Thematics, Yale Univ, 76; Structuralism and Hermeneutics & Semiotics, Columbia Univ, 82; Thematics in Hermeneutics, Columbia Univ, 82; Institution and Construction: The Foundation of Normative Theory, Yale Univ, 93; Kant's Platonic Revolution in Moral and Political Philosophy, Johns Hopkins Univ, 94; Plato Rediscovered, Rowman and Littlefield, 96. **CONTACT ADDRESS** Dept Philos, Univ Tex, Austin, TX, 78712-1180. **EMAIL** t.k.seung@mail.utexas.edu

SEYMOUR, JACK L.
PERSONAL Born 10/27/1948, Kokomo, IN, m, 1997, 2 children **DISCIPLINE** HISTORY AND PHILOSOPHY OF EDUCATION **EDUCATION** Ball State Univ, BS; Vanderbilt Divinity School, DMin & MDiv; George Peabody Col of Vanderbilt, PhD. **CAREER** Asst prof Church & Ministry, Vanderbilt Univ 74-78; Dir Field Educ, Chicago Theol Sem, 78-82; prof Christian Educ, assoc prof, asst prof, Scarritt Grad School, 82-88; prof Relig Educ, 88-, acad dean, 96-, Garrett-Evangelical Theol Sem, 88-. **RESEARCH** Theology of people of God; Ethnographic Research in education; Theological education. **SELECTED PUBLICATIONS** Coauth Educating Christians: The Intersection of Meaning, Learning, and Vocation, Abdington Press, 93; For the Life of a Child: The 'Religious' in the Education of the Public, Relig Educ, 94; Contemporary Approaches to Christian Education, Theological Perspectives on Christian Formation, W B Eerdmans, 96; The Ethnographer as Minister: Ethnographic Research in the Context of Ministry Vocations, Relig Educ, 96; Temples of Meaning: Theology and the People of God, Lib Relig Educ, 96; rev Essays on Religion and Education: An Issue in Honor of William Bean Kennedy, Relig Educ, 96; The Cry for Theology: Laity Speak about the Church, and The Cry for Theology: Laity Speak about Theology, PACE: Professional Approaches for Christian Education, 96; auth Mapping Christian Education: Approaches to Congregational Learning, Abingdon Press, 97; Thrashing in the Night: Laity Speak about Religious Knowing, Relig Educ, 97. **CONTACT ADDRESS** Garrett-Evangelical Theol Sem, 2121 Sheridan Rd, Evanston, IL, 60201. **EMAIL** Kack/Seymour@nwu.edu

SEYNAEVE, JAAK
DISCIPLINE NEW TESTAMENT STUDIES **EDUCATION** Univ Leuven/Louvain STD, 50, Magister in Theol, 55. **CAREER** Vis prof, prof Relig Stud, La State Univ. **SELECTED PUBLICATIONS** Auth, Cardinal Newman's Doctrine on Holy Scripture, Louvain, 53. **CONTACT ADDRESS** Dept of Philos and Relig Stud, Louisiana State Univ, 106 Coates Hall, Baton Rouge, LA, 70803.

SHAFER-LANDAU, RUSSELL
PERSONAL Born 02/18/1963, Paris, France, m, 1989, 2 children **DISCIPLINE** PHILOSOPHY **EDUCATION** Brown Univ, AB, 86; Oxford Univ, MS, 87; Univ Ariz, PhD, 92. **CAREER** Asst prof, Univ Kans, 92-97; assoc prof, Univ C Barkeley, 97-98; assoc prof, Univ Kans, 97-. **MEMBERSHIPS** Am Philos Asn. **RESEARCH** Ethics; Philosophy; Laward. **SELECTED PUBLICATIONS** Auth, articles, Must Punishment Morally Educate?, lAward and Philosophy, 91; Health Care and Human Values, Health Care: Myths, Values and Expectations, 94; Vegetarianism, Causation and Ethical Theory, Pub Affairs Quart, 4; Ethical Disagreement, Ethical Objectivism and Moral Indeterminacy, Philos and Phenomenol Res, 94; Supervenience and Moral Realism, Ratio, 94; Specifying Absolute Rights, Ariz LAward Rev, 95; Vagueness, Borderline Cases and Moral Realism, Am Philos Quart, 95; The Failure of Retributivism, Philos Studies, 96; Moral Rules, Ethics, 97; Ethical Subjectivsm, Reason and Responsibility, 98; Moral Judgement and Moral Motivation, Philos Quart, 98. **CONTACT ADDRESS** Philosophy Dept, Univ of Kans, Lawardrence, KS, 660045. **EMAIL** RSL@falion.cc.ukans.edu

SHAFFER, JEROME A.
PERSONAL Born 04/02/1929, Brooklyn, NY **DISCIPLINE** PHILOSOPHY **EDUCATION** Cornell Univ, BA, 50; Princeton Univ, PhD, 52; Univ Conn, MA 66. **CAREER** Assoc prof, Swarthmore Col, 55-67; Dept Head, Univ Conn, 67-94; Marital & Family Therapist, 96-. **HONORS AND AWARDS** Senior Fel; Ntl Humanities Found Fel; Woodrow Wilson Fel; Fulbright Fel **MEMBERSHIPS** Amer Philos Assoc; Amer Assoc for Marital & Family Therapy **RESEARCH** Philosophy of Mind; Philosophical Psychology. **SELECTED PUBLICATIONS** Dreaming," Amer Philos Quart, 84; An assesment of emotion, Amer Philos Quart, 82. **CONTACT ADDRESS** Dept of Philosophy, Univ of Connecticut, Philosophy/U-54, Storrs, CT, 06269-2054. **EMAIL** jshaffer@uconnvm.uconn.edu

SHAFFER, NANCY E.
PERSONAL Los Angeles, CA **DISCIPLINE** THE HISTORY AND PHILOSOPHY OF SCIENCE **EDUCATION** Graceland Col, BS, 85; Rice Univ, MA, 87; Ariz State Univ, MA, 91; Univ Calif, Davis, PhD, 96. **CAREER** Instr, Concordia Univ, Montreal, Quebec; asst prof, Univ Nebr, Omaha. **MEMBERSHIPS** Philos of Sci Asn; Am Asn of Philos Tchr. **SELECTED PUBLICATIONS** Auth, Bias in Scientific Practice, Philos of Sci. **CONTACT ADDRESS** Univ Nebr, Omaha, Omaha, NE, 68182.

SHAKOOR, ADAM ADIB
PERSONAL Born 08/06/1947, Detroit, MI, d **DISCIPLINE** LAW **EDUCATION** Wayne State Univ, Univ of MI Labor Sch, certificate 1969; Wayne State Univ, BS 1971, MEd 1974, JD 1976; King Abdul Aziz Univ Saudi Arabia, certificate 1977. **CAREER** Wayne County Comm Coll, Detroit MI, prof bus law & black studies, 1971-93; Marygrove Coll, Detroit MI, prof real estate law, 1984; 36th Dist Court, Detroit MI, chief judge, 1981-89; City of Detroit, deputy mayor, chief administrative officer, 1989-93; Reynolds, Beeby & Magnuson, partner, 1994-97; Shakoor Grubba & Miller, PLLC, 1997-. **HONORS AND AWARDS** Grnd Fellowship HUD 1971-73; Grad Fellow SE MI Council of Govt 1971-73; Wolverine Bar Assn Scholarship Natl Bar Assn 1975; Cert of Distinction Com for Student Rights 1979; Certificate of Merit for Exceptional Achievement in Govt Affairs MI State Legislature 1980; Resolution of Tribute MI State Legislature 1981; numerous others. **MEMBERSHIPS** Consult in comm affairs New Detroit Inc 1973-74; pres Black Legal Alliance 1975-76; founding mem Natl Conf of Black Lawyers Detroit Chap 1975-; com mem New Detroit Inc 1977-81; president of bd, Boysville, Inc, 1994; club pres Optimist Club of Renaissance Detroit 1982-83; pres Assoc of Black Judges of MI1985-86; life mem Kappa Alpha Phi. **CONTACT ADDRESS** Shakoor, Grubba & Miller, PLLC, 615 Griswold, Ste 1800, Detroit, MI, 48226.

SHALLECK, ANN
DISCIPLINE FAMILY LAW. CHILD WELFARE **EDUCATION** Bryn Mawr Col, AB, 71; Harvard Law Sch, JD, 78. **CAREER** Prof, Am Univ. **MEMBERSHIPS** DC Task Force on Gener Bias in Courts; Asn Am Law Sch (AALS), Comt Curric & Res; Nat Women's Law Ctr; Prog Comt, AALS 88, 91; Planning Comt, Office Coun Child Abuse & Neglect Practice Manual, Child Protection Proceedings; Adv Comt; Coun Court Excellence. **RESEARCH** Women; Law Clinic Theories of state, family and socity.. **SELECTED PUBLICATIONS** Articles, clinical education, child welfare, and women's rights. **CONTACT ADDRESS** American Univ, 4400 Massachusetts Ave, Washington, DC, 20016.

SHAMAN, JEFFREY MARC
PERSONAL Born 06/29/1941, Pittsburgh, PA, m, 1966, 2 children **DISCIPLINE** LAW **EDUCATION** Pa State Univ, BA, 64; Univ Southern Calif, JD, 67; Georgetown Univ, Llm, 71. **CAREER** Asst prof, Univ Akron, 71-73; asst prof, 73-74, assoc prof, 74-79, prof Law, DePaul Univ, 79-, coop atty, Am Civil Liberties Union, 81-; Wechlander Chems for Prof Ethics, 94-95. **HONORS AND AWARDS** Outstanding Leadership Award - ACLU of Illinois, 90-93; Excellence in Teaching Award, DePaul Univ, 93; Outstand Fac Serv, DePaul Univ, Col of Law, 98. **MEMBERSHIPS** Am Law Inst; Am Soc Legal Hist. **RESEARCH** Constitutional law; federal courts; conflict of laws. **SELECTED PUBLICATIONS** Auth, The rule of reasonableness in constitutional adjudication, Hasting Const Law Quart, 75; coauth, Huffman v Pursue: The federal courthouse door closes further, Boston Univ Law Rev, 76; auth, Revitalizing the clear and present danger test: Toward a principled interpretation of the 1st Amendment, Villanova Law Rev, 76; Persons who are mentally retarded: Their right to marry and have children, Family Law Quart, 78; The First Amendment rule against overbreadth, Temple Law Quart, 79; Legal aspects of artificial insemination, J Family Law, 79; The choice of law process: Territorialism and functionalism, William & Mary Law Rev, 80; The Constitution, the Supreme Court and creativity, Hastings Const Law Quart, 82. **CONTACT ADDRESS** Col of Law, DePaul Univ, 25 E Jackson Blvd, Chicago, IL, 60604-2287. **EMAIL** jshaman@condor.depaul.edu

SHANAB, ROBERT
PERSONAL Born 09/29/1939, Jerusalem, Palestine, s, 2 children **DISCIPLINE** PHILOSOPHY **EDUCATION** Ohio State Univ, PhD, 69. **CAREER** From Instr to Prof Philos, Cleveland State Univ, 69-70, Fla State Univ, 70-76, Univ Nev at Las Vegas, 77-87, Calif State Univ at Northridge, 88-92, Univ Nev at Las Vegas, 92-. **MEMBERSHIPS** Am Philos Asn; Amnesty Int; Libr Congress Assoc. **RESEARCH** Arabic culture; history of philosophy; logic. **SELECTED PUBLICATIONS** Co-ed and contribr, Readings in Philosophy and Literature, Kendall/Hunt, 71; Present Day Issues in Philosophy, Kendall/Hunt, 72; Social Philosphy: From Plato to Che, Kendall/Hunt, 72; auth, Misconceptions about Arabic Medieval Philosophy, Pakistan Philos J, 7/74; Historical Roots of Three Intellectual Movements, J Fac Arts, Univ Benghazi, 82; author of numerous other articles. **CONTACT ADDRESS** 4868 Benecia Way, Las Vegas, NV, 89122.

SHANAHAN, THOMAS JOSEPH
PERSONAL Born 06/10/1936, Milwaukee, WI **DISCIPLINE** THEOLOGY **EDUCATION** St Louis Univ, AB, 60, AM, 61; Fordham Univ, PhD, 75. **CAREER** Eng tchr, Creighton Prep Sch, 61-64; instr theol, Marquette Univ, 69-70; Asst Prof Theol, Creighton Univ, 73. **MEMBERSHIPS** Cath Theol Soc Am; Am Acad Relig. **RESEARCH** Eccesiology; spirituality; death and dying. **SELECTED PUBLICATIONS** Auth, Negroes in nursing education: A report on Catholic schools, Hosp progress, 7/61 & Interracial Rev, 7/61; contribr, Theology Today, Bruce, 65; co-ed, Prose and Poetry of the World, 65 & Patterns of Literature, 67, L W Singer. **CONTACT ADDRESS** Creighton Univ, 2500 California Plz, Omaha, NE, 68178-0001. **EMAIL** tshan@creighton.edu

SHANKS, HERSHEL
PERSONAL Born 03/08/1930, Sharon, PA, m, 1966, 2 children **DISCIPLINE** ENGLISH LITERATURE; SOCIOLOGY; LAW **EDUCATION** Haverford Col, BA, 52; Colombia Univ, MA, 56; Harvard Law Sch, LLB, 56. **CAREER** Ed, Biblical Archaeology Review, Bible Review, Archaeology Odyssey, and Moment. **MEMBERSHIPS** ASOR; SBL; AOS; NEAS; ABA. **RESEARCH** Archaeol; Bible; Judaism. **SELECTED PUBLICATIONS** Ed, Understanding the Dead Sea Scrolls, Random Hse, 92; co-auth, The Rise of Ancient Israel, Biblical Archaeol Soc, 92; ed, Christianity and Rabbinic Judaism: A Parallel History of Their Origins and Early Development, Biblical Archaeol Soc, 92; auth, Jerusalem: An Archaeological Biography, Random Hse, 95; auth, The Mystery and Meaning of the Dead Sea Scrolls, Random Hse, 98. **CONTACT ADDRESS** 5208 38th St, NW, Washington, DC, 20015. **EMAIL** shanks@clark.net

SHANKS, NIALL
DISCIPLINE PHILOSOPHY **EDUCATION** Univ Alberta, PhD. **CAREER** Assoc prof, E Tenn State Univ. **RESEARCH** Philosophy of biology; philosophy of science; philosophy of mind. **SELECTED PUBLICATIONS** Auth, Idealization in Contemporary Physics, Rodopi, 98; Biochemical Reductionism in Biological Context, Idealistic Studies, 97; co-auth, Mind Viruses and the Importance of Cultural Diversity, Rodopi, 98; Brute Science: The Dilemmas of AnimalExperimentation, Routledge, 97; Methodology and the Birth of Modern Cosmology, Studies Hist Philos Modern Physics, 97. **CONTACT ADDRESS** Philosophy Dept, East Tennesee State Univ, Box 70717, Johnson City, TN, 37614- 0717. **EMAIL** shanksn@etsu.edu

SHANNON, DANIEL E.
PERSONAL Born 10/30/1955, Bethesda, MD, m, 1991, 1 child **DISCIPLINE** PHILOSOPHY **EDUCATION** Loyola Univ, BA 80; Univ Toronto, MA 82, PhD 89. **CAREER** Univ Toronto, inst 86-88; McGill Univ, asst prof 89-90; DePauw Univ, asst prof, assoc prof, 90 to 97-. **MEMBERSHIPS** APA; CPA; HAS. **RESEARCH** German idealism; continental philosophy. **SELECTED PUBLICATIONS** Auth, The Journey of the Mind of God to Us, Clio, 98; Hegel: On modern Philosophy versus Faith, Philo and Theology, 96; A Criticism of a False Idealism and Onward to Hegel, The Owl of Minerva, 95. **CONTACT ADDRESS** Dept of Philosophy, DePauw Univ, 100 Center St, Greencastle, IN, 46135. **EMAIL** deshan@depauw.edu

SHANNON, THOMAS A.
PERSONAL Born 09/28/1940, Indianapolis, IN, m, 1972, 2 children **DISCIPLINE** SOCIAL ETHICS; MEDICAL ETHICS **EDUCATION** Quincy Univ, BA, 64; St Joseph Sem, STB, 68; Boston Univ School Theol, STM, 70, PhD, 73. **CAREER** Prof, religion & social ethics, dept humanities, Worcester Polytechnic Inst; Paris Fletcher Distinguished Prof Hum, 88. **HONORS AND AWARDS** WPI Trustees Award, 88; Dr Hum Letters Quincy Univ, 96. **MEMBERSHIPS** AAR; Hastings Ctr; AAAS; Amer Soc Bioethics & Hum; Soc Christian Ethics. **RESEARCH** Medical ethics; Fetal status; Genetics; Cloning. **SELECTED PUBLICATIONS** Ed, Bioethics: Selected Readings, Paulist Press, 93; auth, The Ethical Method of John Duns Scotus, Franciscan Univ Press, 95; coauth, The Context of Casuistry, Georgetown Univ Press, 95; auth, Made in Whose Image? Genetic Engineering and Christian Ethics, Hum Press, 97; coauth, An Introduction to Bioethics, Paulist Press, 97. **CONTACT ADDRESS** Dept of Humanities & Arts, Worcester Polytech Inst, 100 Institute Rd, Worcester, MA, 01609. **EMAIL** tshannon@wpi.edu

SHAPERE, DUDLEY
PERSONAL Born 05/27/1928, Harlingen, TX, m, 1974, 4 children **DISCIPLINE** PHILOSOPHY **EDUCATION** BA, 49, MA, 54, PhD, 57, Harvard Univ. **CAREER** Instr, Ohio State Univ, 57-60; Asst Prof, Prof, Univ Chicago, 60-72; Prof, Univ Illinois, 72-75; Prof, Univ Maryland, 75-84; Z. Smith Reynolds Prof (non departmental Univ professorship), Wake Forest Univ, 84-. **HONORS AND AWARDS** Quantrell Award for Excellence in Undergraduate Teaching, Univ Chicago, 68; Distinguished Scholar-Teacher Award, Univ Maryland, 79; Doctor Honoris Causa, Universidad Peruana Cayetano Heredia, Lima, Peru, 87. **MEMBERSHIPS** Amer Phil Assoc; Phil of Science Assoc; History of Science Soc; Amer Psychological Assoc;

Amer Assoc for the Advancement of Science **RESEARCH** Philosophy and history of science **SELECTED PUBLICATIONS** Auth, The Origin and Nature of Metaphysics, Philosophical Topics, 90; The Universe of Modern Science and Its Philosophical Exploration, Philosophy and the Origin and Evolution of the Universe, 91; On the Introduction of New Ideas in Science, The Creation of Ideas in Physics, 95; The Origin and Nature of Time, Philosophy Scientiae, 96; Testability and Empiricism, The Reality of the Unobservable, forthcoming. **CONTACT ADDRESS** 3125 Turkey Hill Ct., Winston-Salem, NC, 27106. **EMAIL** shapere@wfu.edu

SHAPIRO, DANIEL
PERSONAL Born 05/02/1954, New York, NY **DISCIPLINE** PHILOSOPHY **EDUCATION** Vassar Coll, BA, 76; Univ Minn, PhD, 84. **CAREER** Assoc prof philos, West Va Univ, 88-. **MEMBERSHIPS** Amer Philos Assn; Intl Econ Philos Assn. **RESEARCH** Social and political philosophy; public policy. **SELECTED PUBLICATIONS** Auth, "Can Old-Age Social Insurance Be Justified?" Social Philosophy and Policy, spring 97; auth, "Profits and Morality," Ethics, Jan 97; auth, "Why Even Egalitarians Should Favor Market Health Insurance," Social Philosophy and Policy, spring 98; auth, "A Pluralist Case for Social Security Privatization," Cato Policy Analysis, 98; auth, "Addiction and Drug Policy," Morality and Moral Controversies, 98. **CONTACT ADDRESS** Dept of Philosophy, West Virginia Univ, PO Box 6312, Morgantown, WV, 26506-6312. **EMAIL** dshapiro@wvu.edu

SHAPIRO, DAVID LOUIS
PERSONAL Born 10/12/1932, New York, NY, m, 1954, 1 child **DISCIPLINE** LAW **EDUCATION** Harvard Univ, BA, 54, Llb, 57. **CAREER** Asst prof, 63-66, assoc dean Law Sch, 71-76, Prof Law, Harvard Univ, 66-, Asst reporter, studies fed jurisdiction, Am Law Inst, 63-65; reporter, Restatement of Judgments, Am Law Inst, 70-74; Deputy solicitor general, U S Dept Justice, 88-91. **RESEARCH** Civil procedure; administrative law; labor law; federal jurisdiction. **SELECTED PUBLICATIONS** Auth, The choice of rulemaking or adjudication, 3/65 & Some thoughts on intervention, 2/68, Harvard Law Rev; ed, The Evolution of a Judicial Philosophy, Harvard Univ, 69; coauth, The Federal Courts and the Federal System, Foundation, 73; auth, Federal Habeas Corpus, 73, Mr Justice Rehnquist: A preliminary view, 76 & Federal diversity jurisdiction, 77, Harvard Law Rev; Federal diversity jurisdiction: A survey and a proposal, Harvard Law Rev, 77; The enigma of the lawyer's duty to serve, NY Univ Law Rev, 80, 7 Bar Leader, 81, The Advocate, 82; Jurisdiction and discretion, NY Univ Law Rev, 85; In defense of judicial candor, Harvard Law Rev, 87; Courts, legislatures, and paternalism, Virginia Law Rev, 88; Hart & Wechsler's The Federal Courts and the Federal System, 3rd ed, 88, 4th ed, 96; Federal Rule 16: A look at the theory and practice of rulemaking, Univ Penn Law Rev, 89; Continuity and change in statutory interpretation, NY Univ Law Rev, 92; Federalism: A Dialogue, 95; Class actions: The class as party and client, Notre Dame Law Rev, 98. **CONTACT ADDRESS** Law Sch, Harvard Univ, 1575 Massachusetts, Cambridge, MA, 02138-2903.

SHAPIRO, GARY
PERSONAL Born 06/17/1941, St. Paul, MN, d, 3 children **DISCIPLINE** PHILOSOPHY **EDUCATION** Columbia Col, BA, 63; Columbia Univ, PhD, 70. **CAREER** Univ Kansas, asst prof, assoc prof, prof, 70-91; Univ Richmond, T-B prof in the human and prof philo, 91-. **HONORS AND AWARDS** School of Crit & Theol, fellow, 76-77; ACLS 78-79; NHC, 93-94 **MEMBERSHIPS** APA, SPEP, ASA **RESEARCH** Fr and Ger philo of 19th and 20th cen; philo of art. **SELECTED PUBLICATIONS** Auth, Nietzschean Narratives, IN Univ Press, 89; Alcyone: Nietzsche on Gifts, Noise and Women, State Univ NY Press, 91; Earthwards: Robert Smithson and Art After Babel, Univ Cal Press, 95; co-ed, Hermeneutis: Questions and Prospects, Univ Mass Press, 84; ed, After the Future: Postmodern Times and Places, State Univ of NY Press, 90. **CONTACT ADDRESS** Dept of Philosophy, Richmond Univ, Richmond, VA, 23173. **EMAIL** gshapiro@richmond.edu

SHAPIRO, HENRY L.
PERSONAL New York, NY **DISCIPLINE** ANCIENT PHILOSOPHY, AESTHETICS **EDUCATION** Univ Toronto, BA, 60; Columbia Univ, PhD, 69. **CAREER** Preceptor philos, Columbia Univ, 64-66; actg asst prof, Univ Calif, Riverside, 66-68; chmn dept, 70-73, Asst Prof Philos Univ Mo-St Louis, 68-. **RESEARCH** Greek philosophy; 19th century continental philosophy; philosophy of literature. **SELECTED PUBLICATIONS** Auth, The Oxford Book Of Gothic Tales - Baldick,C/, Studies In Short Fiction, Vol 0030, 1993; 'Proofs And Three Parables' - Steiner,G/, Studies In Short Fiction, Vol 0031, 1994; The Oxford Book Of Sea Stories - Tanner,T/, Studies In Short Fiction, Vol 0032, 1995. **CONTACT ADDRESS** Dept of Philos, Univ of Mo, 8001 Natural Bridge, Saint Louis, MO, 63121-4499.

SHAPIRO, MICHAEL H.
DISCIPLINE CONSTITUTIONAL LAW **EDUCATION** Univ Calif, Los Angeles, BA,59; MA,62; Univ Chicago, JD,64. **CAREER** Dorothy W. Nelson prof;Univ Southern Calif. **MEMBERSHIPS** Order of the Coif; Phi Beta Kappa; Institutional Review Board, Los Angeles County/USC Medical Center, since 1989; Member, Pacific Council for Health Policy and Ethics; Reviewer, U.S. Department of Energy (Proposals to Study the Human Genome Project), 1990-92; Advisory Panel to the Joint Committee on Surrogate Parenting of the California Legislature **RESEARCH** Constitutional Law, Constitutional Law II, Bioethics, and Healthcare Regulation. **SELECTED PUBLICATIONS** Auth, Law, Culpability and the Neural Sciences; Bioethics and Law: Cases, Materials and Problems & Who Merits Merit? Some Problems in Distributive Justice Posed by the New Biology. **CONTACT ADDRESS** School of Law, Univ Southern Calif, University Park Campus, Los Angeles, CA, 90089.

SHAPIRO, STEWART
PERSONAL Born 06/15/1951, Youngstown, OH, m, 1975, 3 children **DISCIPLINE** PHILOSOPHY/MATH **EDUCATION** Case Western Res Univ, BA, 73; SUNY, MA, 75, PhD, 78. **CAREER** Vis lect, 82, Hebrew Univ, Jerusalem; vis fel, 87-88, Ctr for Phil of Sci, Univ Pitts; prof, 96-97, dept of Logic & Metaphysics, Univ St Andrews, Scotland; instr, 78-91, prof, 91-, dept phil, Ohio St Univ, Newark. **HONORS AND AWARDS** OSUN, Scholar Achievements, 92, 97, res grants, 90, 92. **SELECTED PUBLICATIONS** Auth, Foundations Without Foundationalism: A Case for Second-Order Logic, Oxford Logic Guides 17, Oxford Univ Press, 91; auth, Reasoning, Logic, and Computation, Philos Math 3, 95; auth, Introduction, Philos Math 3, 96; coauth, Intuitionism, Pluralism, and Cognitive Command, J Phil, 96; ed, The Limits of Logic: Second-Order Logic and the Skolem Paradox, The International Research Library of Philosophy, Dartmouth Pub Co, 96; auth, Philosophy of Mathematics: Structure and Ontology, Oxford Univ Press, 97; auth, Induction and Indefinite Extensibility: the Godel Sentence in True, But Did Someone Change the Subject?, Mind 107, 98; auth, Logical Consequence: Models and Modality, Philos of Math Today; Proceed of Intl Conf in Munich, 98. **CONTACT ADDRESS** Dept of Philosophy, Ohio State Univ, Newark, Newark, OH, 43055.

SHAPO, MARSHALL S.
PERSONAL Born 10/01/1936, Philadelphia, PA, m, 1959, 2 children **DISCIPLINE** LAW **EDUCATION** Univ Miami, AB, 58, Llb, 64; Harvard Univ, Am, 61. **CAREER** Instr hist, Univ Miami, 60-61; from asst prof to assoc prof law, Univ Tex, Austin, 65-70; prof law, 70-76, Joseph M Hartfield Prof, Law Sch, Univ Va, 76-78; Frederic P Vose Prof Law, Northwestern Univ, 78-, Mem torts round table coun Asn Am Law Sch, 67-69, chmn, 70, mem exec coun, torts-compensation syst round table, 73; vis prof, Sch of Law, Univ Va, 60-70, Univ Mich, summer 73 & Univ Gottingen, summer 76; Nat Endowment for Humanities sr fel, 74-75; sesquicentennial assoc, Univ Va, 74-75; vis fel, Ctr Socio-legal Studies, Welfson Col, Oxford Univ, 75; mem, Ctr Advan Studies, Univ Va, 76-77 & panel Food Safety Regulation & Societal Impact, Inst Med, Nat Acad Sci, 78; adv subcomt, Infringement Sci Freedom in US, Am Advan Sci, 77-78; consult, Med Malpractice & Tort Law Reform, US Dept Justice, 78-79; reporter spec comt, Tort Liability System, Am Bar Asn, 80-; consult, Pres Comn Study Ethical Prob Med & Biomed & Behavior Res, 80-81; exec comt, Torts-Compensation Systems Sect, 80-81, secy, 81-82 & chair-elect, 82-83. **MEMBERSHIPS** Am Law Inst. **RESEARCH** Legal control of products hazards and deceptive advertising; tort and compensation law; legal control of science and technology. **SELECTED PUBLICATIONS** Auth, Comparing Products-Liability - Concepts In Europ And Am Law/, Cornell Int Law J, Vol 0026, 1993; In The Looking-Glass - What Torts Scholarship Can Teach Us About The Am Experience/, Northwestern Univ Law Rev, Vol 0089, 1995; In Search Of The Law Of Products-Liability - The Ali Restatement Project/, Vanderbilt Law Rev, Vol 0048, 1995; Freud, Cocaine, And Products-Liability/, Boston Univ Law Rev, Vol 0077, 1997. **CONTACT ADDRESS** 1910 Orrington Ave, Evanston, IL, 60201.

SHARKEY, PAUL
PERSONAL Born 03/25/1945, Oakland, CA, m, 1986 **DISCIPLINE** PHILOSOPHY **EDUCATION** Univ S Mississippi, MPH, 85; Univ Notre Dame, PhD, 75. **CAREER** Univ S Mississippi, prof emeritus, 96; Am Soc Philos Counseling & Psychotherapy, Am Philos Pract Assoc, vpres; Int Jour Value Inquiry, ed. referee. **HONORS AND AWARDS** Two SUM Excellence Awards, Sigma Xi, Eta Sigma Gamma, Realia Special Commendation. **MEMBERSHIPS** APA, ASPCP, APPA, APHA, ASLME. **RESEARCH** Health ethics; law policy; Philosophical counseling; value inquiry and analysis. **SELECTED PUBLICATIONS** Auth, A Philosophical examination of the History and values of Western Medicine, Edwin Mellen Pr, 92; auth, Health Values and Professional Responsibility, Health Values, 95; auth, Bioclinical Ethics and the Mid-Level Practitioner, Advance for Physician Assistants, 95; auth, Individual Liberty vs. the Public Good: Coping with the Tuberculosis Epidemic, Clinician Rev, 93; auth, Can the Principle of Bioethics Work for Public Health, Abstracts of the American Public Health Association, 96. **CONTACT ADDRESS** Dept of Community Health, S Mississippi Univ, PO Box 222, Lancaster, CA, 93584.

SHARMA, ARVIND
PERSONAL Born 01/13/1940, Varanasi, India **DISCIPLINE** RELIGION **EDUCATION** Allahabad Univ, BA, 58; Syracuse Univ, MA, 70; Harvard Divinity School, StM, 74; Harvard Univ, PhD, 78. **CAREER** Lectr, Univ of Queensland, 76-80; Lectr, Sr Lectr, Univ of Sydney, 80-87; Assoc Prof, 86-, Mcgill Univ. **HONORS AND AWARDS** Birks Chair Comparative Religion, McGill Univ, 94. **MEMBERSHIPS** Amer Acad of Religion; Amer Oriental Soc; Assoc of Asian Studies **RESEARCH** Comparative religion; religion and human rights **SELECTED PUBLICATIONS** Ed, Religion and Women, 94; Today's Women in World Religions, 94; Our Religions, 95; Auth, The Philosophy of Religion and Advaita Vedanta, 95; The Philosophy of Religions: A Buddhist Perspective, 95; Hinduism for Our Times, 96. **CONTACT ADDRESS** McGill Univ, 3520 University St., Montreal, PQ, H3A 2A7.

SHARPE, CALVIN WILLIAM
PERSONAL Born 02/22/1945, Greensboro, North Carolina, m **DISCIPLINE** LAW **EDUCATION** Clark Coll, BA 1967; Oberlin Coll, Post-Baccalaureate 1968; Chicago Theological Seminary, attended 1969-71, MA, 1996; Northwestern Univ Law Sch, JD 1974. **CAREER** Hon Hubert L Will US District Court, law clerk 1974-76; Cotton Watt Jones King & Bowlus Law Firm, assoc 1976-77; Natl Labor Relations Bd, trial attorney 1977-81; Univ of VA Law School, asst prof 1981-84; Case Western Reserve Univ, prof of law (tenured) 1984-; Arizona State University College of Law (Tempe), scholar-in-residence, 1990; George Washington University National Law Center, DC, visiting professor, 1991; Case Western Reserve University Law School, professor/associate dean, academic affairs, 1991-92; De Paul Univ College of Law, Distinguished Visiting Professor, 1995-96; Chicago-Kent Coll of Law, visiting scholar. **MEMBERSHIPS** National Academy of Arbitrators 1991-; convener/first chair, Labor and Employment Law Section, IRRA, 1994-96; labor panel Amer Arbitration Assoc 1984-; bd of trustees Cleveland Hearing & Speech Ctr 1985-89; mem OH State Employment Relations Bd Panel of Neutrals 1985-; Phoenix Employment Relations Bd Panel of Neutrals; Los Angeles City Employee Relations Bd Panel of Neutrals; chair-evidence section Assn of Amer Law Schools 1987; Assn of Amer Law Schools Committee on Sections and Annual Meeting 1991-94; exec bd Public Sector Labor Relations Assoc 1987-89; Federal Mediation and Conciliation Serv Roster of Arbitrators 1987-; Permanent Arbitrator State of Ohio, OH Health Care Employees Assoc Dist 1199, 1987-92; AFSCME/OCSEA, 1987-92; State Council of Professional Educators OEA/NEA 1989-; Federation of Police 1988-92; Youth Services Subsidy Advisory Bd of Commissioners, Cuyahoga County Ohio 1989. **SELECTED PUBLICATIONS** Publications: "Two-Step Balancing and the Admissibility of Other Crimes Evidence, A Sliding Scale of Proof," 59 Notre Dame Law Review 556, 1984; "Proof of Non-Interest in Representation Disputes, A Burden Without Reason," 11 Univ Dayton Law Review 3, 1985; "Fact-Finding in Ohio, Advancing the Pole of Rationality in Public Sector Collective Bargaining," Univ of Toledo Law Review, 1987; "NLRB Deferral to Grievance-Arbitration, A General Theory," 48 Ohio St LJ No 3, 1987; Introduction, The Natl War Labor Bd and Critical Issues in the Development of Modern Grievance Arbitration, 39 Case W Res L Rev No 2, 1988; A Study of Coal Arbitration Under the National Bituminous Coal Wage Agreement-Between 1975 and 1991, vol 93, issue 3, National Coal Issue, West Virginia Law Review; "The Art of Being A Good Advocate," Dispute Resolution Journal, January 1995; "Judging in Good Faith -- Seeing Justice Marshall's Legacy Through A Labor Case," 26 Arizona State LJ 479 (1994); "From An Arbitrator's Point of View--The Art of Being a Good Advocate;" Dispute Resolution Journal, 1995; Book Review: Edward J Imwinkelreid, Evidentiary Distinction: Understanding the Federal Rules of Evidence, 1993; and Arthus Best, Evidence and Explanations, 1993; 46 J Legal Ed 150, 1996. **CONTACT ADDRESS** Prof of Law, Case Western Reserve Univ, 11075 East Boulevard, Cleveland, OH, 44106.

SHARPE, KEVIN J.
DISCIPLINE RELIGIOUS STUDIES **EDUCATION** Univ Canterbury, BS; La Trobe Univ, PhD; Boston Univ, PhD. **CAREER** Prof. **RESEARCH** Philosophy of religion; systematic theology; philosophy of science; mathematics; science and religion, science and society. **SELECTED PUBLICATIONS** Auth, David Bohm's World: New Physics and New Religion, 93; Religion's Response to Change, 85; From Science to an Adequate Mythology, 84; Toward an Authentic New Zealand Theology, 83; Religion and New Zealand's Future, 82; co-auth, Religion and Nature, 83. **CONTACT ADDRESS** Religious Studies Dept, Union Inst, 440 E McMillan St, Cincinnati, OH, 45206-1925.

SHARPE, VIRGINIA A.
DISCIPLINE PHILOSOPHY, MEDICAL ETHICS **EDUCATION** Smith Col, AB, 81; Georgetown Univ, MA, 86, PhD, 91. **CAREER** Asst prof, dept med, 92-96, vis asst prof, 96-97, Georgetown Univ; Assoc Biomed & Environ Ethics, 97-, The Hastings Center. **HONORS AND AWARDS** Charles E. Culpeper Scholar in Med Hum. **MEMBERSHIPS** Am Philos Asn; Int Soc for Environmental Ethics; Am Soc for Bioethics and Humanities. **SELECTED PUBLICATIONS** Auth, Justice and Care: The Implications of the Kohlberg-Gillian Debate for

Medical Ethics, Theoretical Med, 92; coauth, Appropriateness in Patient Care: A New Conceptual Framework, Milbank Quart, 96; coauth, Affiliations Between Catholic and Non-Catholic Health Care Providers and the Availability of Reproductive Health Services, Kaiser Family Found, 97; Why "Do No Harm"?, Theoretical Med, 97; coauth, Medical Ethics in the Courtroom: A Reappraisal, J of Med and Philos, 97; auth, The Politics, Economics, and Ethics of 'Appropriateness, Kennedy Inst of Ethics J, 97; coauth, Medical Harm: Historical, Conceptual and Ethical Dimensions of Iatrogenic Illness, Cambridge Univ Press, 98; auth, Taking Responsibility for Medical Mistakes, Margin of Error: The Necessity, Inevitability & Ethics of Mistakes in Med and Bioethics Consultation, Univ Pub Group, forthcoming. **CONTACT ADDRESS** The Hastings Center, RR 2, Garrison, NY, 10524-5555. **EMAIL** sharpeva@thehastingscenter.org

SHAW, CURTIS MITCHELL
PERSONAL Born 04/13/1944, Jacksonville, TX, d **DISCIPLINE** LAW **EDUCATION** Univ of NM, BS 1967; Loyola Univ of LA, JD 1975. **CAREER** Priv Prac, atty; Musical Entertainers & Motion Picture Personalities, rep; Denver Public Schools, educator; LA Unified School Dist Bd; Hollywood Chamber of Commerce; LA Co Bar Assn; Langston Law Club; Amer Bar Assn; Beverly Hills Bar Assn. **MEMBERSHIPS** Dir num motion picture & prod cos. **CONTACT ADDRESS** 6255 Sunset Blvd, Hollywood, CA, 90028.

SHAW, DANIEL
DISCIPLINE AESTHETICS, 19TH AND 20TH CENTURY CONTINENTAL PHILOSOPHY **EDUCATION** Northern Ill Univ, BA, 72, MA, 75; Ohio State Univ, PhD, 81. **CAREER** Lectr, Ohio State Univ, 79-81; asst prof, Gettysburg Col, 81-86; assoc prof, 86-, Perf Arts comt, 88-90, treas, 92-94, Prof Develop Comt, 88-91, 92-94, fac adv, WLHU Radio Station, Philos Club, ch, APSCUF Presidential Eval Comt, 89, ch, APSCUF Honors Comt, 89-90, 90-91, APSCUF Gender Issues Comt, ch, APSCUF Comt to Revise the Prom Doc, Lock Haven Univ, 95. **HONORS AND AWARDS** NEH, summer sem, Univ Calif, Riverside, 85; Deut Academisches Austauschdienst (DAAD) scholar prog, 86; NEH summer sem, Yale Univ, 94. **SELECTED PUBLICATIONS** Auth, The Survival of Tragedy: Dostoevsky's The Idiot, Dialogue: J of the Nat Honor Soc for Philos, Oct, 75; Absurdity and Suicide: A Reexamination, Philos Res Arch, Mar, 86; A Kuhnian Metatheory for Aesthetics, J of Aesthet and Art Criticism, Fall, 86; Nietzsche as Sophist: A Polemic, Int Philos Quart, Dec, 86; Rorty and Nietzsche: Some Elective Affinities, Int Stud in Philos, Nov, 89; The American Democratic Ideology, The Lock Haven Int Rev, Fall, 90; Thelma and Louise: Liberating or Regressive? in Film, Individualism and Community, Ronald Dotterer, ed, Susquehanna UP, 94; Lang Contra Vengeance: The Big Heat, J of Value Inquiry, Dec 95. **CONTACT ADDRESS** Lock Haven Univ, Pennsylvania, R.D. 2, 190A, Mill Hall, PA, 17751.

SHAW, GARY M.
DISCIPLINE LAW **EDUCATION** Univ IL, AB, 75; John Marshall Law Sch, JD, 79; Temple Univ, LLM, 83. **CAREER** Prof, Touro Col; counr, Govt of Belarus, 94; lectr, Conf on Const Law for mem of the Polish Parliament, Poland. **MEMBERSHIPS** Am Bar Assoc; Cent and E Europ Law Initiative; Assoc of Am Law Schls. **SELECTED PUBLICATIONS** Auth of the annual revisions of Evidence Laws of New York and has written sev law rev articles. **CONTACT ADDRESS** Touro Col, Brooklyn, NY, 11230. **EMAIL** GaryS@tourolaw.edu

SHAW, MARVIN C.
PERSONAL Born 03/27/1937, Los Angeles, CA, m, 1959, 2 children **DISCIPLINE** PHILOSOPHY **EDUCATION** Occidental Col, BA 59; Union Theol Sem, MA, 62; Columbia Univ, PHD, 68 **CAREER** Prof of Relig Studies, 68-99, MT St Univ **HONORS AND AWARDS** Phi Kappi Phi Nat Scholastic Hon Soc; Danforth Assoc, Danfourth Found; Fridley Distinguished Tch Award, MT St Univ **MEMBERSHIPS** Am Acad of Relig; Highlands Inst; Soc for Buddhist-Christian Studies **RESEARCH** American Pragmatism and Naturalism; Process Theology; Buddhist-Christian Dialogue **SELECTED PUBLICATIONS** Auth, The Paradox of Intention: Reaching the goal by giving up the attempt to reach it, Atlanta Scholars Press, 1988; Auth, Nature's Grace: Essays on H.N. Weiman's Finite Theism, New York, Peter Lang, 1995 **CONTACT ADDRESS** 604 S Black Ave, Bozeman, MT, 59715. **EMAIL** biodag@montana.campus.mci.net

SHAW, SUSAN J.
PERSONAL Born 09/30/1943, New York, NY, s, 2 children **DISCIPLINE** THEOLOGICAL AND RELIGIOUS STUDIES, FEMINISM **EDUCATION** Syracuse Univ, BMusEd, 65; Alliance Theological Seminary, MDiv, 84; Drew Univ, MPhil, 89, PhD, 91. **CAREER** Music teacher, Westchester County NY Schools, 66-73; commun specialist, World Relief, 81-84; instr, Berkshire Christian Col, 87-90; instr, Pace Univ, 90-91; vP & dean, Trinity Col & Seminary, 93-96; NAT ACCOUNTS COORD FOR DISTANCE ED, ED VIDEO CONFERENCING, 97-. **HONORS AND AWARDS** Drew Merit Scholar; Who's Who in Am Women. **MEMBERSHIPS** Int Ministerial Fel; Am Acad of Rel/Soc of Biblical Lit; Am Asn of Univ Women; Nat Women's Studies Asn. **SELECTED PUBLICATIONS** Contribur, International Ministerial Fellowship Pastoral Letter, Women as Ministers, Int Ministerial Fel, 96-98; auth, The Theological Handbook of Misogynist Texts, Multiple Ministries Press, 96; auth, Doing More Than Any Man Has Ever Done, Multiple Ministries Press, 95; contribur, ed, The Consultant, 95-96; coauth, Smith, Abby Hadassah and Julia Evelina Smith, Am Nat Bio, Oxford Univ Press, 94. **CONTACT ADDRESS** 80 W Grand St., Apt C6, Mount Vernon, NY, 10552-2131. **EMAIL** drsjshaw@hotmail.com

SHAW, THEODORE MICHAEL
PERSONAL Born 11/24/1954, New York, NY, m **DISCIPLINE** LAW **EDUCATION** Wesleyan Univ, BA, Honors, 1976; Columbia Univ School of Law, JD, 1979. **CAREER** US Dept of Justice, Civil Rights Div, trial attorney, 1979-82; NAACP Legal Defense Fund, asst counsel, 1982-87, western regional counsel, 1987-90, assoc dir-counsel, 1993-; Columbia Univ School of Law, anjunct prof, 1993-; Univ of MI School of Law, asst prof of law, 1990-. **HONORS AND AWARDS** US Dept of Justice, Civil Rights Div, Special Commendation, 1981; Aspen Inst Fellowship on Law & Society, 1987; Twenty-first Century Trust Fellowship on Global Interdependence, London Eng, 1989; Salzburg Seminars Fellowship, Salzburg, Austria, Summer, 1991; Langston Bar Assn, (Los Angeles, CA) Civil Trial Lawyer of the Year, 1991. **MEMBERSHIPS** Wesleyan Univ, bd of trustees, alumni elected trustee, 1986-89, charter mem, 1992-, sec of the bd, 1993-; Poverty & Race Research Action Council, bd mem, 1990-; Archbishop's Leadership Proj, bd mem, 1994-; Greater Brownsville Youth Council, bd mem, 1982-; Natl Bar Assn; Amer Bar Assn. **CONTACT ADDRESS** NAACP Legal Defense & Educational Fund Inc, 99 Hudson St, 16th Fl, New York, NY, 10013.

SHEAR, JONATHAN
PERSONAL Born 08/17/1940, Washington, DC, m, 1990 **DISCIPLINE** PHILOSOPHY **EDUCATION** Brandeis Univ, BA, 62; Univ California-Berkeley, PhD, 72. **CAREER** Instr, Lone Mountain Col, 70-71; Prof, Maharizhi Intl Univ, 72-83; Dir, Inst for Philosophy and Consciousness, 79-84; Asst Prof College of William & Mary, 88-89; Affil Assoc Prof, Virginia Commonwealth Univ, 94-; Affil Asst Prof, 90-94, Adj Prof, 87-90, Managing Editor, J. of Consciousness Studies, 94-. **HONORS AND AWARDS** Fulbright Scholar in Phil of Science, London School of Economics; Woodrow Wilson Fel in Philosophy, Univ California-Berkeley; Distinct Adjunct Faculty, Virginia Commonwealth Univ. **MEMBERSHIPS** Amer Phil Assoc **RESEARCH** The significance of deep experiences of inner awareness, especially as produced by traditional Asian experimental methodologies for traditional questions of Western Philosophy and Psychology **SELECTED PUBLICATIONS** Auth, The Inner Dimension: Philosophy and the Experience of Consciousness, 90; On Mystical Experiences as Empirical Support for Perennial Philosophy, Journal of the American Academy of Religion, 94; Mystical Knowledge, Sufi, 95; The Hard Problem: Closing the Empirical Gap, J. of Consciousness Studies, 96; On a Culture-Independent Core Component of Self, East-West Encounters in Philosophy and Religion, 96; ed, Explaining Consciousness: The Hard Problem, 97; Ethics and the Experience of Happiness, Crossing Boundaries: Ethics, Antinomianism and the History of Mysticism, forthcoming; Scientific Exploration of Meditation Techniques, J. of Consciousness, forthcoming. **CONTACT ADDRESS** Dept of Philosophy, Virginia Commonwealth Univ, Richmond, VA, 23284-2025. **EMAIL** jcs@richmond.infi.net

SHEARER, RODNEY H.
PERSONAL Born 09/21/1944, Reading, PA, m, 1966, 4 children **DISCIPLINE** BIBLICAL STUDIES, OLD TESTAMENT, HEBREW BIBLE **EDUCATION** Conrad Weiser Area Schools, high school diploma, 62; Lebanon Valley Col, BA, 66; Lutheran Theological Seminary in Gettysburg, 66-68; United Theological Seminary in Dayton, Ohio, MDiv, 69; Drew Univ, PhD, 85. **CAREER** Assoc Pastor, St. Paul's United Methodist Church, 69-72; pastor, Green Village United Methodist Church, 72-76; chaplain & adjunct asst prof of religion, Lebanon Valley Col, 76-80; pastor, Fritz Memorial UMC, 80-87; PASTOR, ONO UMC, 87-; DIR OF UNITED METHODIST STUDIES & ADJUNCT LECTR IN WORSHIP & UNITED METHODIST POLITY, EVANGELICAL SCHOOL OF THEOLOGY, 95-. **HONORS AND AWARDS** Whos Who in Religion, 85; Who's Who in Biblical Studies and Archeol, 93; Eagle Scout Community Leaders and Noteworthy Americans. **MEMBERSHIPS** Soc of Biblical Lit; ordained elder in full connection, Eastern Pa Conf of The United Methodist Church. **RESEARCH** Biblical studies in ministry and worship. **SELECTED PUBLICATIONS** Auth, A Contextual Analysis of the Phrase "Al-tira" as it Occurs in the Hebrew Bible and in Selected Related Literature, Univ Microfilms Int, 86; the following articles in The Anchor Bible Dictionary, Doubleday, 92: Ashnah; Bakbuk; Barkos; Bazlith; Besai; Bishlam; Darkon; Gahar; Habaiah; Jahaziel; Jarib; Joiarib; Josiphiah; Juel; Mahli; Meremoth; Noadiah; Ono; Sherebiah; Uthai; Zarahiah. **CONTACT ADDRESS** Jonestown & McGillstown Rds., PO Box 61, Ono, PA, 17077-0061.

SHEEHAN, THOMAS
PERSONAL Born 06/25/1941, San Francisco, CA, m, 3 children **DISCIPLINE** PHILOSOPHY **EDUCATION** St Patrick's Col, BA, 63; Fordham Univ, MA, 68, PhD(philos theol), 71. **CAREER** Adj prof philos, Loyola Univ, Rome, 70-71; asst prof, St Mary's Col, Rome, 71-72; asst prof to prof Philos, Loyola Univ Chicago, 72-; freelance journ, El Salvador, 82-89. **HONORS AND AWARDS** Mellon Found grant teaching develop, 75; Am Cath Philos Asn publ subsidy, 77; dir philos, Col Phaenomenologicum, Perugia, Italy, 77-78; Fritz Thyssen Stiftung grant, 79-80; Nat Endowment for Humantities grant, 80; Ford Found grant, 83-85. **MEMBERSHIPS** Am Philos Asn; Soc for Phenomenol & Existential Philos. **RESEARCH** Metaphysics; philosophy of religion; continental philos; Marxism. **SELECTED PUBLICATIONS** Ed, Heidegger's, The Man and the Thinker, Precedent Press, 81; Karl Rahner: The Philosophical Foundations, Ohio Univ Press, 82; auth, The First Coming: How the Kingdom of God Became Christianity, Random House, 86; Heidegger and the Nazis, NY Rev of Books, 88; Das Gewesen, In: From Phenomenology to Thought, Errancy and Desire, Kluwer, 95; ed & transl, Edmund Husserl, Psychological and Transcendental Phenomenology, Kluwer, 97; auth, Friendly Fascism, In: Fascism's Return, Univ Nebr Press, 98; Nihilism in Phenomenology, Japanese and American Perspectives, Kluwer, 98; Martin Heidegger, Routledge Encyclopaedia of Philosophy, 98; ed & transl, Heidegger, Logic: The Question of Truth, Ind Univ Press (in prep). **CONTACT ADDRESS** Dept of Philos, Loyola Univ, Chicago, 6525 N Sheridan Rd, Chicago, IL, 60626-5385. **EMAIL** tsheeha@orion.it.luc.edu

SHEEHY, ELIZABETH A.
DISCIPLINE LAW **EDUCATION** Osgoode Hall Law Sch, LLB; Univ British Columbia, LLM. **CAREER** Prof. **MEMBERSHIPS** Can Asn Elizabeth Fry Soc. **SELECTED PUBLICATIONS** Auth, pubs on criminal law as it affects women, Charter, and torts. **CONTACT ADDRESS** Fac Common Law, Univ Ottawa, 550 Cumberland St, PO Box 450, Ottawa, ON, K1N 6N5.

SHEELEY, STEVEN M.
DISCIPLINE RELIGION **EDUCATION** MO State Univ, BSEd, 79; Southwestern Baptist Theol Sem, Mdiv, 83; IN Univ, Special Stud, 84; Southern Baptist Theol Sem, PhD, 87. **CAREER** Assoc Dean of the Col, Shorter Col, 97-; ch, Effectiveness Plan Coun, 97-; assoc prof, Shorter Col, 93-; mem, 125th Anniversary Comt, 96-; ch, Enrollment Coun, 95-97 & DeLamotte Lect Ser Comt, 94-; Ga Athletic Conf Fac Athletics Rep, 94-95; mem, Technol Comt, 93-95 & Interdisciplinary Taskforce 93-94; NAIA Dist 25 Fac Athletics Repr, 92-93; mem, Gen Educ Comt, 92- & Awd(s) Comt, 91-96; 1st Asst Sponsor, Alpha Chi Nat Hon Soc, 91-97; Fac Athletic Rep to the NAIA, 89-96; ch, Retention Comt, 89-96; dir, Rel Act, 88-94; ch, Rel Act Comt, 88-94; mem, Acad Standards and Awd(s) Comt, 88-97 & Scheduling Comt, 88-94; ch, The Mrs Columbus Roberts Dept Relig & Philos, Shorter Col, 92- & act ch, 92; sponsor: Theta Alpha Kappa Nat Relig & Theol Hon Soc, 96-; mem, Provost's Coun, 92- & Curric Comt, 92-; asst prof, Shorter Col, 88-93; mem, Hon(s) Coun & Fac, 92-93; secy, Taskforce on Enrollment, 91-92; ch, Self-Stud Comt on Conditions of Eligibility, 90-92; fac adv to Alpha Gamma Omega Fraternity, 89-93; mem, Self-Stud Steering Comt, 89-92; ch, Self-Stud Comt on Intercollegiate Athleticsm, 89-92; freshman adv, 88-92; adj prof, The Southern Baptist Theol Sem, 87-88. **HONORS AND AWARDS** Outstanding Young Men of Am, 96; Sigma Tau Delta Int Engl Hon Soc, 96; Theta Alpha Kappa Nat Rel and Theol Hon Soc, 96; Vulcan Materials Tchg Excellence & Campus Leadership Awd, Shorter Col, 94; Special Person awd, Shorter Col, 90, 94, 95 & 96; Who's Who in Bibl Stud and Archaeol, 92-93; Argo Yearbk Dedication, Shorter Col, Class of 92; Who's Who Among Stud in Am Univ & Col, 85-86, 79-80, 77-78; Am Bibl Soc Awd, Southwestern Baptist Theol Sem, 83; Chosen to speak in Chapel for Sr Preaching Week, Southwestern Baptist Theol Sem, 83; Phi Kappa Phi Nat Scholastic Hon Soc, 79. **MEMBERSHIPS** Soc Bibl Lit; Nat Asn Baptist Prof Rel; Baptist Union Rel Prof. **SELECTED PUBLICATIONS** Auth, Narrative Asides in Luke-Acts, JSNTS, Sheffield: JSOT/Sheffield Acad Press, 92; Following everything closely: Narrative presence in Luke 1-2, Essays in Lit 20, 93; Lift Up Your Eyes: John 4:4-42, Rev and Expositor, 95; The Narrator in the Gospels: Developing a Model, Perspectives in Rel Stud 16, 89; Narrative Asides and Narrative Authority in Luke-Acts, Bibl Theol Bull 18, 88; The Politically Correct Church: Ephesians 2:11-22, Interpreting Ephesians for Preaching and Tchg, Macon, Smyth and Helwys Press, 92; Acts, Holman Bibl Handbk, Nashville, Broadman Press, 92; Demetrius the Chronographer 208, Elijah, Apocalypse of 244, Ezekiel the Tragedian 283, Jacob, Ladder of 425, Jacob, Prayer of 425, Jeremiah, Letter of 438, Persecution in the New Testament 668, Righteousness 765f, Shem, Treatise of 818, Shroud of Turin 822, Swine 864, Tobit 922, Zephaniah, Apocalypse of 983f, Mercer Dictionary of the Bibl, Macon, Mercer UP, 90; coauth, The Bible in English Translation: An Essential Guide Nashville, Abingdon Press, 97; rev(s), Engaging the New Testament: An Interdisciplinary Introduction. In JBL/CRBR Online Rev(s), 97; Moses or Jesus: An Essay in Johannine Christology; John, the Son of Zebedee: The Life of a Legend; John, the Maverick Gospel; and Scott Sinclair, The Road and the Truth: The Editing of John's

Gospel, Perspectives in Rel Stud 23, 96; Windows on the World of Jesus: Time Travel to Ancient Judea, Bibll Archaeologist 58, 95; Our Journey With Jesus: Discipleship according to Luke-Acts, Critical Rev of Bk(s) in Rel 92, Atlanta, Scholars Press, 93; Paul, In Other Words, Bibl Archaeologist 55, 92; Host, Guest, Enemy, and Friend, Rev and Expositor 89, 92; ed, PSYC 315: Counseling and Pastoral Care, Shorter Col, 97; RELN 380: Missions and Evangelism, Shorter Col, 97; EDUC 300: Christian Education, Shorter Col, 96; RELN 300: Spirituality and the Minister, Shorter Col, 96; RELN 350: History of Christianity, Shorter Col, 96; RELN 355: American Church History, Shorter Col, 96; RELN 360: World Religions, Shorter Col, 96; ENGL 346: Professional Communication in Ministry, Shorter Col, 96; RELN 340: Christian Theology, Shorter Col, 96; RELN 375: Church Administration, Shorter Col, 96; **CONTACT ADDRESS** Div of Relig and Philos, Shorter Col, 315 Shorter Ave, Box 345, Rome, GA, 30165-4267. **EMAIL** ssheeley@shorter.peachnet.edu

SHEETS-JOHNSTONE, MAXINE
PERSONAL Born 09/05/1930, San Francisco, CA, m, 1974, 2 children **DISCIPLINE** DANCE PHILOSOPHY **EDUCATION** Univ Calif, Berkeley, BA, 52; Univ Wisc, MS, 54, PhD, 63. **CAREER** Prof, dance, 68-84, prof, phil, 88-, Univ Ore; independent scholar, 98-. **MEMBERSHIPS** Husserl Cir; Intl Soc for hist, phil & Soc Stud of Biology. **RESEARCH** Interdisciplinary: phil of mind/body; evolutionary biology; psychol/psychiatry. **SELECTED PUBLICATIONS** Auth, The Phenomenology of Dance, Univ Wisc Press, 66, Arno Press, 80; auth, Illuminating Dance: Philosophical Explorations, Assoc Univ Press, 85; auth, The Roots of Thinking, Temple Univ Press, 90; auth, Giving the Body It's Due, SUNY Press, 92; auth, The Roots of Power: Animate form and Gendered Bodies, Open Court, 94; art, Race and Other Miscalculations, Misconceptions, and Mismeasures: Essays in Honor of Ashley Montague, General Hall Pub, 95; art, Taking Evolution Seriously: A Matter of Primate Intelligence, Etica & Animali 8, 96; art, Tribal Lore in Present-Day Paleoanthropology: A Case Study, Anthropology of Consciousness 7/4, 96; art, On the Significance of Animate Form, Analecta Husserliana, Kluwer Acad, 98; art, Consciousness: A Natural History, J Consciousness Stud 5/3, 98; art, Binary Opposition as an Ordering Principle in (Male?) Human Thought, Phenomenology & Feminism, Kluwer Acad, 99; art, The Primacy of Movement, John Benjamins Pub, 98. **CONTACT ADDRESS** Dept of Philosophy, Univ of Oregon, Eugene, OR, 97403. **EMAIL** msj@oregon.uoregon.edu

SHEHADI, FADLOU A.
PERSONAL Born 02/09/1926, Beiruit, Lebanon, m, 1954, 3 children **DISCIPLINE** PHILOSOPHY **EDUCATION** Am Univ Beirut, BA, 48; Princeton Univ, PhD, 59. **CAREER** Asst instr, Princeton Univ, 50-51; instr, Rutgers Univ, 53-57; asst prof, 57-63; assoc prof, 63-72; full prof, 72-94; prof emer, 94-. **HONORS AND AWARDS** Rockefeller fel; NEH grant. **MEMBERSHIPS** Am Philos Asn. **RESEARCH** Islamic philosophy. **SELECTED PUBLICATIONS** Auth, Philosophies of Music in Medieval Islam, 95; co-ed, Applied Ethics and Ethical Theory, 88; auth, Metaphysics in Islamic Philosophy, 82; auth, Ghazali's al-Magrad al-Asna, 71. **CONTACT ADDRESS** 220 State Rd, Princeton, NJ, 08540. **EMAIL** Fshehadi@aol.com

SHELLEY, BRUCE
DISCIPLINE HISTORICAL THEOLOGY **EDUCATION** Columbia Bible, BA; Fuller Sem, M.Div; Iowa Univ, Ph.D. **CAREER** Sr prof, Denver Sem. **HONORS AND AWARDS** Ed adv bd, Christian Hist; consult ed, InterVarsity's popular Dictionary of Christianity in Am. **SELECTED PUBLICATIONS** Auth, Church History in Plain Language; All the Saints Adore Thee; The Gospel; and the American Dream and The Consumer Church; corresponding ed, Christianity Today; pub(s), articles in Encycl Am; Evangel Dictionary of Theol; New Intl Dictionary of the Christian Church. **CONTACT ADDRESS** Denver Conservative Baptist Sem, PO Box 10000, Denver, CO, 80250. **EMAIL** bruces@densem.edu

SHELP, EARL E.
PERSONAL Born 10/28/1947, Louisville, KY **DISCIPLINE** THEOLOGY **EDUCATION** Univ Louisville, 69; So Baptist Theol Sem, Theol, 72, Theol Ethics, 76. **CAREER** Res fel, , 76-88 Inst of Relig, asst prof, 77-88, Baylor Col of Med; vis prof, 85, 89, Dept of Relig, Dartmouth Col; pres, 88-, Found For Interfaith Res and Ministry **HONORS AND AWARDS** America's Award, Postive Thinking Found at Kennedy Center, Wash, DC, 92. **MEMBERSHIPS** Soc of Christian Ethics. **RESEARCH** Medical ethics; theol ethics; pastoral theol. **SELECTED PUBLICATIONS** Co-ed, Competency: A Study of Informal Completency Determinations in Primary Care, Philos and Med Series, 36, Kluwer Acad Pubs, 91; contrib auth, The Social Impact of AIDS, Nat Acad Press, 93; ed, Secular Bioethics in Theological Perspective, Theol and Med Series, vol 8, Kluwer Acad Pubs, 96; co-auth, Prediction of Grief and HIV/AIDS-related Burnout in Volunteers, AIDS Care 8, no 2, 96; co-auth, Ministries of Sustaining Presence: Congregational Care Teams, Abingdon Press; ed, Pastoral Ministry Series, Pilgrim Press, 1 vol yr, 85-90; ed, Theology & Med Ser, Kluwer Academic Pubs, 92-97. **CONTACT ADDRESS** Foundation for Interfaith Research and Ministry, 701 N Post Oak Rd, #330, Houston, TX, 77024. **EMAIL** firm.hou@neosoft.com

SHELTON, JIM D.
DISCIPLINE PHILOSOPHY **EDUCATION** Univ Kans, PhD, 72. **CAREER** Prof, Univ Central Ark. **RESEARCH** Twentieth-century analytic philosophy; philosophy of science; modern philosophy. **SELECTED PUBLICATIONS** Auth, The Role of Obbservation and Simplicity in Einstein's Epistemology, Studies in History and Philosophy of Science; auth, Schlick and Husserl on the Foundations of Phenomenology, Philosophy and Phenomenological Research; auth, Responsibility and Freedom: A Revision of Schlick's Soft Determinism, Dialogos; auth, Contextualism: A Right Answer to the Wrong Question, Southwest Philosophical Studies; auth, Schlick's Theory of Knowledge, Synthese, 89; coauth, Husserl's Phenomenology and the Ontology of the Natural Sciences, Phenomenology of Natural Science, 92; Up From Poverty, Falling in Love With Wisdom, 93; auth, Seeing and Paradigms in the Chemical Revolution, Philosophy in Science, 94. **CONTACT ADDRESS** Univ Central Ark, 201 Donaghey Ave, Conway, AR, 72035-0001.

SHELTON, MARK
DISCIPLINE PHILOSOPHY **EDUCATION** Harvard Univ, PhD, 96 **CAREER** Visiting Instr, 94-96, Georgetown Univ; Asst Prof, 96-, Old Dominion Univ. **MEMBERSHIPS** Amer Phil Assoc **RESEARCH** Ethics; political philosophy; Hegel **CONTACT ADDRESS** Dept of Philosophy, Old Dominion Univ, 4100 Powhatan Ave, Norfolk, VA, 23529-0083.

SHEPPARD, ANTHONY
DISCIPLINE LAW **EDUCATION** Univ British Columbia, BA, 64; LLB, 67; LLM, 68. **CAREER** Asst prof, 69-72; assoc prof, 72-76; prof, 76-. **MEMBERSHIPS** UBC Fac Asn. **RESEARCH** Evidence; creditors remedies; equity law; taxation law. **SELECTED PUBLICATIONS** Auth, pubs about creditors remedies, equitable remedies, evidence and taxation. **CONTACT ADDRESS** Fac of Law, Univ British Columbia, 1822 East Mall, Vancouver, BC, V6T 1Z1. **EMAIL** sheppard@law.ubc.ca

SHER, GILA
DISCIPLINE PHILOSOPHY **EDUCATION** Columbia Univ, PhD, 89. **CAREER** ASSOC PROF, UNIV CALIF, SAN DIEGO. **RESEARCH** Truth & philosophical method; Quine's epistemology; Logic & the mind. **SELECTED PUBLICATIONS** Auth, The Bounds of Logic: A Generalized Viewpoint, The MIT Press, 91; "Did Tarski Commit Tarski's Fallacy?," Jour of Symbolic Logic 61, 96; "Semantics and Logic," Handbk of Contemp Semantic Theory, 96; "Logical Consequence," The Encycl of Philos Supplement, Macmillan, 96; "Logical Terms," The Encycl of Philos Supplement, Macmillan, 96; "On the Place of Philosophy in Quine's Early Theory," The role of Pragmatics in Contemporary Philosophy: Papers of the 20th International Wittgenstein Symposium, The Austrian Ludwig Wittgenstein Soc, 97; Partially-Ordered (Branching) Generalized Quantifiers: A General Definition, Jour Philos Logic 26, 97. **CONTACT ADDRESS** Dept of Philos, Univ Calif, San Diego, 9500 Gilman Dr, La Jolla, CA, 92093.

SHERIDAN, THOMAS L.
PERSONAL Born 12/17/1926, New York, NY **DISCIPLINE** THEOLOGY **EDUCATION** Woodstock Col, MD, AB, 50, MA, 52, STL, 58; Cath Inst Paris, STD, 65. **CAREER** Tchr, Xavier High Sch, 51-54; instr, 59-62, asst prof theol, Fordham Univ, 65-66; assoc prof, 66-75, chmn dept, 68-75, Prof Theol, St Peter's Col, NJ, 75. **MEMBERSHIPS** Cath Theol Soc Am; Col Theol Soc. **RESEARCH** Systematics. **SELECTED PUBLICATIONS** Auth, Newman on Justification, Alba, 67; articles and reviews, In: Theol Studies; America; Spiritual Life & Homiletic & Pastoral Rev. **CONTACT ADDRESS** Dept of Theol, St Peter's Col, 2641 Kennedy Blvd, Jersey City, NJ, 07306-5997. **EMAIL** sheridan_t@spcvxa.spc.edu

SHERLINE, ED
PERSONAL Born 12/04/1959, Evanston, IL, s **DISCIPLINE** PHILOSOPHY **EDUCATION** Princeton Univ, BA, 82; Univ Chicago, MA, 83; Univ IL, PhD, 90. **CAREER** Univ Wyoming, lectr, asst prof, assoc prof, 89-. **MEMBERSHIPS** APA **RESEARCH** Ethics; Political philo **SELECTED PUBLICATIONS** Auth, Confirmation Theory and Moral Justification, Philo Stud, 94. **CONTACT ADDRESS** Dept of Philosophy, Univ of Wyoming, Laramie, WY, 82071-3392. **EMAIL** sherline@uwyo.edu

SHERMAN, NANCY
DISCIPLINE PHILOSOPHY **EDUCATION** Harvard Univ, PhD. **CAREER** Prof. **MEMBERSHIPS** U.S. Naval Acad. **RESEARCH** Moral philosophy; history of moral philosophy; moral psychology and the emotions; ancient philosophy; ancient ethics; psychoanalysis; military ethics. **SELECTED PUBLICATIONS** Auth, Making a Necessity of Virtue, Cambridge, 97; The Fabric of Character, Oxford, 89. **CONTACT ADDRESS** Dept of Philosophy, Georgetown Univ, 37th and O St, Washington, DC, 20057.

SHEROVER, CHARLES M.
PERSONAL Born 01/20/1922, New York, NY, s **DISCIPLINE** PHILOSOPHY **EDUCATION** Oberlin Col, AB, 43; Northwestern Univ, MA, 47; New York Univ, PhD, 66. **CAREER** Vis Prof, 69, Duquesne; grad fac, 70-74, The New School; instr to prof, 63-93, Prof Emeritus, 93; SUNY Stony Brook, 78; Emory Univ, 89. **MEMBERSHIPS** APA; Intl Soc for the Study of Time; Metaphysical Soc of Amer; Soc for Advancement of Amer Phil; The Heidegger Conf. **RESEARCH** Philosophy of time; democratic theory; Kant Rousseau **SELECTED PUBLICATIONS** Auth, Time Freedom and the Common Good, Suny Press, 89. **CONTACT ADDRESS** PO Box 6604, Santa Fe, NM, 87505.

SHERRY, JOHN E.H.
PERSONAL Born 03/17/1932, New York, NY, m, 1960, 3 children **DISCIPLINE** LAW **EDUCATION** Yale Univ, BA, 54; Columbia Law Sch, JD, 59; NY Univ Law Sch, LLM, 68. **CAREER** Prof of Law, Cornell Univ, 72-97; Prof Emeritus, 97; Vis Prof at Canesius Col, 97-98. **HONORS AND AWARDS** US Diplomatic Representative to UNIDROIT, 79. **MEMBERSHIPS** External Collaborator to World Terrorism Organization, Madrid, Spain. **RESEARCH** Business & Hotel Law. **SELECTED PUBLICATIONS** Auth, The Laws of Innkeepers, rev ed, Cornell Univ Press, 94; auth, Legal Aspects of Hospitality Management, 2nd ed, Educ Found of Nat restaurant Asn, 94. **CONTACT ADDRESS** Cornell Univ, 548 Statler Hall, Ithaca, NY, 14853. **EMAIL** jes22@cornell.edu

SHERWIN, BYRON
PERSONAL Born 02/18/1946, New York, NY, m, 1972, 1 child **DISCIPLINE** PHILOSOPHY **CAREER** Res Asst, 66-70; Instr, Jewish theol Sem, 69; Vis Prof Chicago theol Sem, 72-74; Vis Prof, Mundelein Col, 74-82, Asst Prof, 70-74, Assoc Prof, 74-78, Prof, 78-, V Pres for Academic Affairs, 84-, Spertus Inst of Jewish Stud. **HONORS AND AWARDS** Presidential Medal, Poland, 95; Man of Dialogue Award, Warsaw, 92; Life Tenure, Spertus Inst of Jewish Studies, 72; Cytron Prize, 70; Jcob Minkin Prize, 69; Chyrus Adler Scholar, 69; Friedenwald Prize, 67. **MEMBERSHIPS** Midwest Jewish Stud Assoc; The Authors Guild; Amer Assoc of Univ Prof; APA; Assoc of Jewish Stud; Rabbinical Assembly. **RESEARCH** Philosophy, Mysticism. **SELECTED PUBLICATIONS** Auth, Duchowe Dziedzictwo Zydow Polskich (The Spiritual Heritage of Polish Jews), Vocatio Pub, 95; art, The Tower of Babel, in: Bible Today, 95; art, Toward a Just and Compassionate Society: A Jewish View, in: Cross Currents, 95; art, The Golem, Zevi Ashkenazi and Reproductive Biotechnology, in: Judaism, 95; art, Euthanasia: A Jewish View, in: Reader in Jewish Ethics, 95; art, Jewish View of Abortion, in: New Theol Rev, 96; Inward Journeys: Life as Art Form, Comm in the Midst of Pluralism, 96; auth, Sparks Amidst the Ashes: The Spiritual Legacy of Polish Jewry, Oxford Press, 97; art, Yehudah Liva Ben Betsalel, in: Oxford Dict of the Jewish Rel, Oxford Univ Press, 97; art, Jewish Views on Euthanasia, Last Rights? Assisted Suicide and Euthanasia Debated, Eerdmans, 98; art, Memories and Meanings of Being Heschels Disciple, in: Consr Judaism, 98; auth, Crafting the Soul: Creating Your Life as a Work of Art, Inner Trad, 98. **CONTACT ADDRESS** 618 S. Michigan Ave, Chicago, IL, 60605. **EMAIL** sijs@spertus.edu

SHERWIN, SUSAN
DISCIPLINE PHILOSOPHY **EDUCATION** Univ York, BA, 69; Stanford Univ, PhD, 74. **CAREER** Prof. **RESEARCH** Feminist theory, bioethics, ethics. **SELECTED PUBLICATIONS** Auth, Feminist and Medical Ethics, Hypatia, 89; No Longer Patient: Feminist Ethics and Health Care, 92; Theory vs Practice in Ethics, Philos Perspectives on Bioethics, 96; The Politics of Women's Health, Temple UP, 98. **CONTACT ADDRESS** Dept of Philos, Dalhousie Univ, Halifax, NS, B3H 3J5. **EMAIL** susan.sherwin@dal.ca

SHERWOOD, O. PETER
PERSONAL Born 02/09/1945, Kingston, Jamaica, m **DISCIPLINE** LAW **EDUCATION** Brooklyn Coll, BA 1968; NYU Sch of Law, JD 1971. **CAREER** NY Civil Court, law sec to Hon Fritz W Alexander II 1971-74; NAACP Legal Def & Educ Fund Inc, atty 1974-84; NY Univ School of Law, adj asst prof of law 1980-87; State of NY, solicitor general, 1986-91, City of New York, corporation counsel, 1991-93; Kalkines, Arky, Zall & Bernstein, partner, 1994-; NYS Ethics Commission, commissioner, 1998-2003. **MEMBERSHIPS** Trustee NY Univ Law Ctr Found; co-chmn Compliance & Enforcement Comm NY & St Bar Assn; Taskforce on NY St Div on Human Rights 1977-80; board of directors New York City Comm Action Legal Serv 1971-75; 100 Black Men; Metro Black Bar Assn; Natl Bar Assn; secretary, Bar of the City of New York Association, 1992-97. **CONTACT ADDRESS** Kalkines, Arky, Zall & Bernstein, 1675 Broadway, New York, NY, 10019.

SHERWOOD, STEPHEN K.
PERSONAL Born 05/08/1943, Hollywood, CA, s **DISCIPLINE** BIBLICAL THEOLOGY **EDUCATION** Pontifical Gregorion Univ, STD, 90. **CAREER** Assoc prof, Oblate Sch of Theology, 91- . **MEMBERSHIPS** Catholic Biblical Assn; Soc of Biblical Lit. **RESEARCH** Narrative criticism of Hebrew Bible. **SELECTED PUBLICATIONS** Auth, Mad God Not

Been on My Side, An Examination of the Narrative Technique of the Story of Jacob and Laban Genesis 29,1 -32,2, 90; auth, Psalm 112-A royal Wisdom Psalm?, CBQ, 89. **CONTACT ADDRESS** 285 Oblate Dr., San Antonio, TX, 78216-6693. **EMAIL** sksherwood@earthlink.net

SHERWOOD, WALLACE WALTER
PERSONAL Born 10/06/1944, Nassau, Bahamas **DISCIPLINE** LAW **EDUCATION** St Vincent Coll, BA 1966; Harvard Univ, LLM 1971; George Washington Univ, JD 1969. **CAREER** Legal Svcs, staff atty 1969-71; MA Comm Against Discrimination, commnr 1971-73; Roxbury Pub Def, dir 1971-73; OEO, gen counsel 1973-74; Lawyers Comm for Civil Rights under Law, exec div 1974-76; Private Practice, Attorney 1976-; NE Univ Coll of Criminal Justice, assoc prof. **HONORS AND AWARDS** Dulles Fulbright Awd Natl Law Ctr 1969; Teacher of The Year, 1987 Coll of Criminal Justice. **MEMBERSHIPS** Mem MA Bar Assn 1969-; mem Boston Bar Assn 1969-; mem MA Council for Pub Justice. **CONTACT ADDRESS** Col of Criminal Justice, Northeastern Univ, 360 Huntington Ave, Boston, MS, 02115.

SHIBLES, WARREN ALTON
PERSONAL Born 07/10/1933, Hartford, CT, m, 1977, 3 children **DISCIPLINE** PHILOSOPHY **EDUCATION** Univ Conn, BA, 58; Univ Colo, MA, 63. **CAREER** Instr philos, NTex State Univ, 66; lectr, Parsons Col, 66-67; Asst Prof Philos, Univ Wis-Whitewater, 67-, Dir, Lang Press, 71- **MEMBERSHIPS** Am Philos Asn; AAUP; Div Philos Psychol of Am Psychol Asn. **RESEARCH** Philosophy; psychology; poetry. **SELECTED PUBLICATIONS** Auth, Metaphor: An Annotated Bibliography and History, 71, Death: An Interdisciplinary Analysis, 74, Emotion: The Method of Philosophical Therapy, 74, Ethics for Children, 78, Emotion: A Critical Analysis for Children, 78, Humor: A Critical Analysis for Children, 78, Time: A Critical Analysis for Children, 78 & Rational Love, 78, Lang Press, auth Emotion in Aesthetics, Kluwer, 95, auth Unsere Gefuhlswelt, Lehrman Verlog, 95, auth Was it Zeit?, Lehrman Verlog, 97. **CONTACT ADDRESS** 800 W Main, PO Box 342, Whitewater, WI, 53190-1790. **EMAIL** shiblesw@idcnet.com

SHIELDS, BRUCE E.
PERSONAL Born 08/09/1937, PA, m, 1957, 3 children **DISCIPLINE** NEW TESTAMENT AND HOMILETICS **EDUCATION** Milligan Col, BA, 59; Princeton Theol Sem, BD, 65; Eberhard-Karls Universiteit zu Tubingen, D Theol, 81. **CAREER** Prof, 77-83, Lincoln Christian Sem; prof , 83-, Emmanuel Sch Relig. **HONORS AND AWARDS** NEH sum grant, 91. **MEMBERSHIPS** Soc of Bibl Lit; Acad of Homiletics; Societas Homiletica. **RESEARCH** Preaching in the early church. **SELECTED PUBLICATIONS** Auth, Romans, Cincinnati: Standard Pub Co, 88; auth, Campbell on Language and Revelation and Modern Approaches to Language, Building Up the Church: Scripture, Hist, & Growth, A Festschrift in Honor of Henry E. Webb, Milligan Col, 93, TN; rev, Dale B. Martin, Slavery as Salvation: The Metaphor of Slavery in Pauline Christianity, Yale Univ Press, 90, Restor Quart vol 35, 93; rev, Sidney Greidanus, The Modern Preacher and the Ancient Text: Interpreting and Preaching Biblical Literature, Eerdmans Pub Co, 88, J for Christian Stud, 93; auth, The Areopagus Sermon as a Model for Apologetic Preaching, Faith in Pract: Stud in Bk of Acts, A Festschrift in Honor of Earl and Ottie Mearl Stuckenbruck, European Evangel Soc, 95; auth, John Henry Jowett, Concise Encycl of Preaching, Westminster/John Knox Press, 95; rev, Jeffrey T. Myers, Unfinished Errand into the Wilderness: Tendenzen und Schwerpunkte der Homilitic in den USA 1960-1985, doct diss, Johannes Gutenburg Univ, Mainz, Germany, in Homiletic, XXI/1, 96; rev, H. David Schuringa, Hearing the Word in a Visual Age in Encounter, 97; auth, Integrating Ministry and Theology: One Seminary's Story, Theological Ed, vol 33, no 2, 97; auth, Preaching and Culture, Homiletic vol XXII no 2, 97; auth, Readers Guide: Literary Resources for Worship, Leaven vol 6, no 1, 98. **CONTACT ADDRESS** Emmanuel Sch of Religion, One Walker Dr, Johnson City, TN, 37601-9989. **EMAIL** shieldsb@esr.edu

SHIELDS, GEORGE W.
DISCIPLINE PHILOSOPHY **EDUCATION** Univ of Louisville, BA, 73, MA, 75; Univ of Chicago, PhD, 81. **CAREER** Lectr, Univ of Louisville, 75-55, 79-81; from asst professorial lectr to professorial lectr, Univ of Louisville, 81-; adj lectr, Ind Univ Southeast, 80-82, 83-85; vis asst prof, Ind Univ Southeast, 82-83; adj prof, Ky State Univ, 84-85; from asst prof to prof, Ky State Univ, 85-; chemn, Div of Lit, Langs, and Philos, 94-. **HONORS AND AWARDS** Nat Defense/Col of Arts and Scis Scholar Award, Univ of Louisville, 72-73; A. Flexner Honorarium for Grad Study, Univ of Louisville, 73; First Prize Award, Ky Philos Asn Essay Contest, 73; R.C. Smith Mem Award for Excellence in Philos, Univ of Louisville Honors Convocation, 74; Grad Teaching Apprentice Stipend, univ of Louisville, 74; Phi Kappa Phi Nat Honor Soc, 76; Bingham Found Grant Award, Univ of Louisville, 76; House Scholar, Disciples House of the Univ of Chicago, 77-79; Commonwealth of Ky Fac Incentive Fund Merit Salary Recipient, 86; Nat Endowment for the Hums Travel Grant, 90; Hon Order of Ky Colonels, 92; U.S. Dept of Educ Title III Grant Award, 95; Templeton Found Sci and Relig Course Prog Award, 97; numerous Ky State Univ Fac Res Fund Comt Grant Awards; numerous biographical entries in Who's Who. **MEMBERSHIPS** Am Acad of Relig; Am Philos Asn; Asn for Cult and Sci; Asn for Integrative Studies; Ctr for Process Studies; Ky Philos Asn; Soc of Christian Philos; Soc fo rPhilos of Relig; Soc for the Study of Process Philos; Southeastern Sem in Early Modern Philos. **SELECTED PUBLICATIONS** Ed, Nexus: Journal of the Association for Culture and Science; coed, Proceedings of the Institute for Liberal Studies, vols 1-8, 90-97; Foundations of Cultures: Readings, 92; The Convergence of Cultures: Readings, 93; The Search for New Forms of Culture, 94; coed and coauth, Faith and Creativity: Essays in Honor of Eugene H. Peters, 87; Science, Technology, and Religious Ideas, 94; auth, Preface, in Science, Technology, and Religious Ideas, 94; Introduction to Nietzsche, in The Search for New Forms of Culture, 94; Review of Lewis E. Hahn, ed. The Philosophy of Charles Hartshorne, Vol. 20, Library of Living Philosophers Series, in Int J for Philos of Relig 36/4, 94; Introduction, in Proceedings of the Inst for Liberal Studies 6, 95; Abstract: Donald Sherburne, 'Whitehead and Dewey on System and Experience' in Frontiers of American Philosophy, in Process Studies 24/3, 95; Design, Chance and Necessity, in Facets of Faith and Science: Vol 4, Interpreting God's Action in the World, 96; Abstract: Nicholas Rescher, 'The Promise of Process Philosophy' in Frontiers of American Philosophy, in Process Studies 24/3, 96; Introduction to Descartes: Discours de la methode and Le monde, in The Convergence of Cultures, 96; Introduction, in Proceedings of the Inst for Liberal Studies 7, 96; Critical Study: Nicholas Rescher, Process Metaphysics: An Introduction to Process Philosophy, in Process Studies 25, 96; Introduction: On the Interface of Analytic and Process Philosophy, in Process Studies 25, 96; Introduction, in Proceedings of the Institute for Liberal Studies 8, 97, Critical Study: Dorothy Emmet, The Passage of Nature, in Process Studies, 26/1-2, 97. **CONTACT ADDRESS** 4630 Shady View Dr, Floyds Knobs, IN, 47119. **EMAIL** Gshields@gwmail.kysu.edu

SHIELDS, MARY
DISCIPLINE PHILOSOPHY **EDUCATION** Emory Univ, PhD. **CAREER** Philos, Drury Col. **HONORS AND AWARDS** Neumann Prize for excellence in Hebrew and Greek. **RESEARCH** Hebrew Bible; New Testament; gender issues related to relig(s) studies; lit approaches to bibl studies; feminist theology. **SELECTED PUBLICATIONS** Auth, Circumcision of the Prostitute: Gender, Sexuality and the Call to Repentance in Jer 3:1-4:4, 95; Subverting a Man of God, Elevating a Woman: Role and Power Reversals in 2 Kgs 4, 93; Satire and the Hebrew Prophets (rev), 92; Reading Between Texts: Intertextuality in the Hebrew Bible (rev), 92; Let the Oppressed Go Free: Feminist Perspectives on the New Testament (rev), 93. **CONTACT ADDRESS** Relig and Philos Dept, Drury Col, N Benton, PO Box 900, Springfield, MO, 65802.

SHIELDS, MARY E.
PERSONAL Born 12/05/1960, Butler, PA **DISCIPLINE** RELIGION **EDUCATION** Westminster Col, BA, 82; Princeton Theol Sem, MDiv, 86; Emory Univ, PhD, 96. **CAREER** Tchg and res fel, Univ St Andrews, Scotland, 92-94; adj instr, Emory Univ, 94-95; instr, 95-96, asst prof, 96- , Dept Philos and Relig, Drury Col. **HONORS AND AWARDS** Magna cum laude; Neumann Prize, 84; Kenneth Willis Clark Student Essay Award, 91; Mellon Diss Fel, 92-93; Drury Fac Award for Leadership, 98. **MEMBERSHIPS** Soc of Bibl Lit; Am Acad Relib; Soc for OT Study; Natl Asn of Presby Clergywomen; Omicron Delta Kappa; AAUP. **RESEARCH** The marriage metaphor in the Hebrew prophets; feminist criticism of the Hebrew Bible; literary criticism of the Hebrew Bible. **SELECTED PUBLICATIONS** Auth, Subverting a Man of God, Elevating a Woman: Role and Power Reversals in 2 Kgs 4, JSOT, 93; auth, Circumcision of the Prostitute: Gender , Sexuality and the Call to Repentance in Jer 3:1-4:4, Bibl Interp, 95; auth, Multiple Exposures: Body Rhetorics and Gender Characterization in Ezekiel 16, JFSR, 98; auth, Haggai, in Hayes, ed, Dictionary of Biblical Interpretation, Abingdon, forthcoming; auth, Revelation Meets Star Trek and X-Files or A New Twist on Ancient Traditions? Teaching the Heaven's Gate Cult, in Pippin, ed, Teaching Apocalypse, AAR Tchg Ser, forthcoming. **CONTACT ADDRESS** Dept of Philosophy and Religion, Drury Col, 900 N Benton Ave, Springfield, MO, 65802. **EMAIL** mshields@lib.drury.edu

SHIELS, RICHARD DOUGLAS
PERSONAL Born 04/05/1947, Detroit, MI, m, 1972 **DISCIPLINE** AMERICAN AND RELIGIOUS HISTORY **EDUCATION** Hope Col, BA, 68; Yale Univ, MAR, 71; Boston Univ, PhD, 76. **CAREER** Asst prof, Boston Univ, 75-76; asst prof, 76-82, assoc orof hist, Ohio St Univ, Newark, 82-. **MEMBERSHIPS** Orgn Am Historians; AHA. **RESEARCH** American intellectual and social history. **SELECTED PUBLICATIONS** Auth, "Second Great Awakening in Connecticut," Church History, Vol 49, 80; Feminization of American congregationalists, 1730-1835, Am Quart, Vol 33, 81. **CONTACT ADDRESS** History Dept, Ohio State Univ, 1179 University Dr, Newark, OH, 43055-1797. **EMAIL** shiels.1@osu.edu

SHIER, DAVID
PERSONAL Born 11/19/1958, Cleveland, OH, m, 1988, 2 children **DISCIPLINE** PHILOSOPHY **EDUCATION** Wayne State Univ, PhD, 93 **CAREER** Wash State Univ, asst prof, 94-. **MEMBERSHIPS** APA, BRS **RESEARCH** Philo of language; philo of mind. **SELECTED PUBLICATIONS** Auth, Why Kant Finds Nothing Ugly, Brit Jour of Aesthetics, 98; auth, How Can Pictures Be Propositions?, Ratio, 97; co-ed The Two Envelope Paradox Resolved, Analysis, 97; auth, Direct Reference for the Narrow Minded, Pac Philo Quart, 96. **CONTACT ADDRESS** Dept of Philosophy, Washington State Univ, 13 Oak Dr., Box 645130, Pullman, WA, 99164-5130. **EMAIL** shier@wsu.edu

SHILLING, BURNETTE P.
DISCIPLINE CHRISTIAN MINISTRIES **EDUCATION** Taylor Univ, BA; Winebrenner Sem, MDiv; Trinity Evangel Divinity Sch, DMin; Bowling Green State Univ, PhD. **CAREER** Campus pastor, Bluffton Col; assoc prof, 86-; dir, DMin Dipl in Pastoral Stud, Wiinebrenner Theol Sem. **HONORS AND AWARDS** Interim writer/ed, Workman Quart; The Gem. **MEMBERSHIPS** Mem, Speech Commun Assn; Cent States Speech Commun Assn; Rel Speech Commun Assn. **SELECTED PUBLICATIONS** Pub(s), articles in The Church Advocate; Churches of God, General Conf; contrib, Life Application Bible, Tyndale House, 88. **CONTACT ADDRESS** Winebrenner Theol Sem, 701 E Melrose Ave, PO Box 478, Findlay, OH, 45839.

SHILLINGTON, V. GEORGE
PERSONAL Born 05/23/1937, Porthdown, Northern Ireland, m, 1959, 2 children **DISCIPLINE** RELIGION **EDUCATION** Cent Baptist Col, BTh; Waterloo Lutheran Univ, BA, 70; Cent Baptist Sem, Mdiv, 72; Wilfred Laurier Univ, MA, 73; McMaster Univ, PhD, 85; **CAREER** Emmanuel Bib Col, asst prof, 73-81; Concord Col Univ of Winnipeg, asst prof, 81-85, assoc prof 85-96, prof 96-. **HONORS AND AWARDS** NT Studies Award **MEMBERSHIPS** SBL **RESEARCH** Rhetoric of Silence in the letters of Paul. **SELECTED PUBLICATIONS** Auth, A New Testament Perspective on Work, CGR 90; Jesus and His Parables, T&T Clarke 97; II Corinthians, Herald Press 98; Atonement Texture in I Corinthians 5:5, JSNT 98. **CONTACT ADDRESS** Dept of Biblical Studies, Concord Col, Manitoba, 169 Riverton Ave, Winnipeg, MB, R2L 2E5. **EMAIL** georges@farlink.com

SHIN, SUN JOO
DISCIPLINE PHILOSOPHY **EDUCATION** Seoul Nat Univ, BA, 79; Stanford Univ, MA, 81, PhD, 91. **CAREER** Assoc prof. **RESEARCH** Philosophy of logic; philosophy of language; logic. **SELECTED PUBLICATIONS** Auth, Peirce and the Logical Status of Diagrams, Hist Philos Logic, 93; A Semantic Analysis of Venn Diagrams, J Symbolic Logic, 93; The Logical Status of Diagrams, 94. **CONTACT ADDRESS** Philosophy Dept, Univ of Notre Dame, 336/7 O'Shaughnessy, Notre Dame, IN, 46556. **EMAIL** shin.3@nd.edu

SHINER, ROGER ALFRED
PERSONAL Born 05/13/1940, Kidderminster, England **DISCIPLINE** PHILOSOPHY **EDUCATION** Cambridge, BA, 63, MA, 66, PhD(philos), 71; Univ Alta, MA, 65. **CAREER** Sessional lectr, 65-66, from asst prof to assoc prof, 66-77, Prof Philos, Univ Alta, 77- **MEMBERSHIPS** Mind Asn; Can Philos Asn; Class Asn Can; Royal Inst Philos; Aristotelian Soc. **RESEARCH** Greek philosophy; ethics; philosophy of religion. **SELECTED PUBLICATIONS** Auth, Sparshott And The Philos Of Philos/, J Of Aesthetic Educ, Vol 0031, 1997. **CONTACT ADDRESS** Dept of Philos, Univ of Alberta, Edmonton, AB, T6G 2E1.

SHIPKA, THOMAS A.
PERSONAL Born 02/17/1943, Youngstown, OH, m, 1967, 2 children **DISCIPLINE** PHILOSOPHY **EDUCATION** John Carroll Univ, AB, philos, 66; Boston Col, PhD, philos, 69. **CAREER** Asst prof, philos, Youngstown State Univ, 69-74; assoc prof, philos, Youngstown State Univ, 74-81; prof, philos, Youngstown State Univ, 81-; chair, dept of philos and relig, Youngstown State Univ, 86-. **HONORS AND AWARDS** Distinguished Prof award, Youngstown State Univ, 80, 84; Davenport award, Nat Educ Asn, 94; Watson Merit award, Youngstown State Univ, 91, 97. **MEMBERSHIPS** Amer Philos Asn; Nat Educ Asn. **RESEARCH** Social and political philosophy; Unions in higher education; Evaluation in higher education. **SELECTED PUBLICATIONS** Auth, Philosophy: Paradox and Discovery, 4th ed, McGraw-Hill, 96; auth, Organizing the Faculty at Youngstown State, Thought & Action, vol XII, no 2, 105-106, fall, 96; auth, Personnel Evaluation in American Higher Education: An Introduction, School Personnel Evaluation Manual, Wash, DC, Nat Educ Asn, 137-155, 87; auth, A Critique of Anarchism, Studies in Soviet Thought, 15, 219-224, 85. **CONTACT ADDRESS** Dept. of Philos, Youngstown State Univ, 1 University Plz, Youngstown, OH, 44555. **EMAIL** tashipka@cc.ysu.edu

SHIPLEY, ANTHONY J.
PERSONAL Born 05/19/1939, New York, NY, m, 1960 **DISCIPLINE** THEOLOGY **EDUCATION** Drew University, BA 1961; Garrett Seminary, DMin 1964; Adrian College, DD 1974. **CAREER** United Methodist Church, supt Detroit West Dist 1982-; Scott Church, pastor, 1987-; UMC, General Board of Global Ministry, deputy general secretary, 1992; Christ United Methodist Church, sr pastor, 1994. **MEMBERSHIPS** Consultant NCJ Urban Network; adjunct prof Garrett Evangelical Theol Sem; bd of dir Adrian Coll; chmn Devel Commn for National Black United Fund; President's Assn of the Amer Mgmt Assn; delegate, Gen Conf of the United Methodist 1980; lecturer, Church Admin at N MS Pastors School; Inst for Adv Pastoral Studies; Oppor Indus Ctr; pres Natl Fellowship Conf Council; dir Detroit Council of Churches; MI State Council of Churches; MI State United Ministries in Higher Educ; Natl Bd of Higher Educ & Min; mgmt consultant Charfoos Christenson Law Firm; bd dir Methodist Theol School in OH; founder, McKenzie High School/Adrian College Bound Program; bd of directors, Barton McFarland Neighborhood Assn; Cuvy Leadership Center, certified trainer, 7 Habits of Highly Effective People; U-Snap-Back Comm Development Corp, chair of bd; Phoenix District Boy Scouts of America, chair; Chandler Park Academy Charter Schl, founder; Finney Aspires Program, founder. **SELECTED PUBLICATIONS** Author: "The Care & Feeding of Cliques in the Church" Interpreter Magazine 1975; "The Self Winding Congregation" Interpreter Magazine 1975; "The Council on Ministries as a Support System" Letter Ctr for Parish Devel; "Everybody Wants to Go to Heaven But Nobody Wants to Die" Christian Century 1976; "Long Range Planning in the Local Church" MI Christian Advocate; "Something for Nothing" MI Christian Advocate; "Fable of Disconnection" MI Christian Advocate. **CONTACT ADDRESS** Christ Methodist Church, 15932 E Warren, Detroit, MI, 48224.

SHIRLEY, EDWARD S.
DISCIPLINE EPISTEMOLOGY **EDUCATION** Univ South, BA, 52; Va Theol Sem, MDiv, 56; Hartford Sem Found, STM; 60; Univ Mass, PhD, 69. **CAREER** Prof, La State Univ. **SELECTED PUBLICATIONS** Published articles on such topics as philosophy of language, mind-body problem, scepticism, truth, perception, and about such thinkers as Descartes, Kant, Santayana, James, Wittgenstein, Quine, Rorty, Ryle, Chisholm, Goodman, and Putnam in Philos Stud, Philos of Sci, J of Critical Anal, Erkenntnis, Southern J of Philos, J of Speculative Philos, and Philos Topics. **CONTACT ADDRESS** Dept of Philos and Relig Stud, Louisiana State Univ, 106 Coates Hall, Baton Rouge, LA, 70803.

SHKOLNICK, RODNEY
DISCIPLINE CONTRACT LAW **EDUCATION** State Univ Iowa, BA, 53; Univ Iowa, JD, 55. **CAREER** Instr, Univ Mich Law Sch, 59 and 60; dean, Creighton Law Sch, 77-88; partner, McGrath, North, 65-71; prof, Creighton Univ. **SELECTED PUBLICATIONS** Coauth, Nebraska Uniform Commercial Code Forms; pub in, Nebr and Creighton Law Rev(s). **CONTACT ADDRESS** School of Law, Creighton Univ, 2500 California Plaza, Omaha, NE, 68178. **EMAIL** shkolnic@culaw.creighton.edu

SHOBEN, ELAINE W.
DISCIPLINE LAW **EDUCATION** Barnard Col, BA; Univ Calif Hastings, JD. **CAREER** Prof, Univ Ill Urbana Champaign. **HONORS AND AWARDS** Ed, Hastings Law J; fel, Am Bar Found; ed, J Legal Edu. **MEMBERSHIPS** Asn Am Law Sch. **RESEARCH** Torts; remedies; and employment discrimination; workplace law, tort policy, and the uses and abuses of the contempt power. **SELECTED PUBLICATIONS** Auth, pubs on employment discrimination and the legal application of quantitative methods; co-auth, Remedies: Cases and Problems, Foundation, 89; Employment Discrimination Cases and Materials, West, 90; Employment Law. **CONTACT ADDRESS** Law Dept, Univ Ill Urbana Champaign, 52 E Gregory Dr, Champaign, IL, 61820. **EMAIL** eshoben@law.uiuc.edu

SHOEMAKER, DAVID W.
PERSONAL Born 07/24/1964, Ft. Wayne, IN, m, 1996, 2 children **DISCIPLINE** PHILOSOPHY **EDUCATION** Univ Cal Irvine, PhD, 96 **CAREER** Vis asst prof, Philosophy, Arkansas State Univ, 96-97; vis asst prof, Univ Memphis, 97-. **MEMBERSHIPS** Amer Philos Soc **RESEARCH** Personal identity; Ethical theory; Philosophy of law. **SELECTED PUBLICATIONS** Auth, Theoretical Persons and Practical Agents, Philos & Public Affairs, 96. **CONTACT ADDRESS** Dept of Philosophy, Univ Memphis, Memphis, TN, 38152. **EMAIL** dshoemkr@memphis.edu

SHOEMAKER, MELVIN H.
PERSONAL Born 02/11/1940, Jay County, IN, m, 1961, 3 children **DISCIPLINE** NEW TESTAMENT BIBLICAL LITERATURE; BIBLICAL THEOLOGY **EDUCATION** Indiana Wesleyan University, AB, 62; Hewbrew Seminar in Israel, Univ of Wisconsin, Graduate Studies, 66; Asbury Theological Seminary, MDiv, 67; Drew Univ, MPhil, 88; Fuller theological seminary, Pasadena, CA, D Min, 97. **CAREER** Instr, 66-67, Indiana Wesleyan Univ; prof, 79-84, Barlesville Wesleyan Col; prof, 86- , CP Haggard Sch of Theology, Dir, 95- , Azusa Pacific Univ. **HONORS AND AWARDS** Biographical listings in Dictionary of International Biography, 79; Who's Who in Religion, 92; Alphi Chi Teacher of the Year at Azusa Pacific Univ, 93; Who's Who in the West, 97; Who's Who in America, 99. **MEMBERSHIPS** Wesleyan Theological Soc, 80-82, 91-present; APU Honors Program Task Force/Council, 91-present; APU Eucation Council, 94-present; Soc of Biblical Lit, 87-present; International Soc of Theta Phi; Advisory Council for the Oxford Honors Semester of the Coalition for Christian Colleges & Universities, 97-2000; International Education Committee of the National Collegiate Honors Council 97-2000; Small College Honors Programs Committee of the National Collegiate Honors Council, 97-2000 **RESEARCH** NT Biblical Literature and theology; gospels. **SELECTED PUBLICATIONS** Auth, Good News to the Poor in Luke's Gospel, Connection, 94; King, Christ as, Lamb, Lamb of God, Life, Priest, Christ as, Baker BookHouse, 96; Discipling Generation X, Fuller Theological Seminary, 97; Jesus Used Headline News in His Preaching, Decision, Nov 98. **CONTACT ADDRESS** Azusa Pacific Univ, 901 E Alosta, Azusa, CA, 91702-7000. **EMAIL** mshoemaker@apu.edu

SHOFNER, ROBERT DANCEY
PERSONAL Born 11/22/1933, Seattle, WA **DISCIPLINE** PHILOSOPHICAL THEOLOGY **EDUCATION** Univ Puget Sound, BA, 61; Yale Univ, BD, 64; Hartford Univ, PhD(theol), 72. **CAREER** Minister, Marlborough Congregational Church, 64-67; teaching fel theol, Hartford Sem Found, 67-70; from asst prof to assoc prof, 70-78, Prof Relig Studies, Calif State Univ, Northridge, 78-, Chmn Dept, 72- **MEMBERSHIPS** Am Acad Relig; Am Philos Asn; Soc Values Higher Educ. **RESEARCH** Systematic theology; theological ethics. **SELECTED PUBLICATIONS** Auth, The Origins Of The Gods - Hans,Js/, J Of The Am Acad Of Rel, Vol 0063, 1995. **CONTACT ADDRESS** Dept of Relig Studies, California State Univ, Northridge, Northridge, CA, 91330.

SHOPSHIRE, JAMES MAYNARD
PERSONAL Born 10/07/1942, Atlanta, Georgia, m **DISCIPLINE** THEOLOGY **EDUCATION** Clark Coll, BA 1963; Interdenominational Theological Ctr Gammon Seminary, BD 1966; Northwestern Univ, PhD 1975. **CAREER** Interdenominational Theol Ctr, asst prof 1975-80, chair of church & soc dept 1978-80; Wesley Theological Seminary, assoc prof 1980-83, assoc dean 1980-85, prof 1983-. **HONORS AND AWARDS** Rockefeller Doctoral Fellowship Fund for Theol Educ 1971-72; Crusade Scholarship United Methodist Church 1973-74. **MEMBERSHIPS** Minister Bethlehem United Methodist Church 1964-66, Burns United methodist Church 1966-71, Ingleside-Whitfield United Meth Church 1974-75. **CONTACT ADDRESS** Prof of Sociology of Religion, Wesley Theol Sem, 4500 Massachusetts Ave NW, Washington, VT, 20016.

SHORES, DAVID FRANCIS
PERSONAL Born 08/28/1941, New Hampton, IA, m, 1964, 2 children **DISCIPLINE** LAW **EDUCATION** Univ Iowa, BBA, 65, JD, 67; Georgetown Univ, LLM, 69. **CAREER** Trial atty, Fed Trade Comn, Washington, DC, 67-69; assoc, Porter, Stanley, Platt and Arthur, Columbus, Ohio, 69-72; asst prof, 72-74, assoc prof, 74-77, Prof Law, Wake Forest Univ, 77-. **RESEARCH** Antitrust; taxation. **SELECTED PUBLICATIONS** Auth, Section 304 and the Limits of Statuatory Law, Tax Rev, 97; Deferential Review of Tax Court Decisions: Dobson Revisited, Tax Lawyer, 96; Law, Facts, and Market Realities in Antitrust Cases After Brooke and Kodak, SMU Law Rev, 95; Taxation of Interstate Commerce: Quill, Allied Signal and a Proposal, Neb L Rev, 93; Recovery of Unconstitutional Taxes: A New Approach, VA. Tax Rev, 92; Repeal of General Utilities and the Triple Taxation of Corporate Income, Tax Lawyer, 92; Closing the Open Transaction Loophole: Mandatory Installment Reporting, VA Tax Rev, 90; State Taxation of Gross Receipts and the Negative Commerce Clause, Mo Law Rev, 89; Narrowing the Sherman Act Through an Extension of Colgate: The Matsushita Case, Tenn. Law Rev, 88. **CONTACT ADDRESS** Sch of Law, Wake Forest Univ, PO Box 7206, Winston Salem, NC, 27109-7206.

SHOSKY, JOHN
DISCIPLINE PHILOSOPHY **EDUCATION** American Univ, PhD, 92 **CAREER** Adjunct Prof, 90-94, George Mason Univ; Adjunct Prof, Philosophy, 87-, American Univ; Visiting Prof of Phil, Chartis Univ, Prague, 98. **CONTACT ADDRESS** 1806 Rollins Dr., Alexandria, VA, 22307.

SHRADER, DOUGLAS WALL, JR.
PERSONAL Born 05/22/1953, Grundy, VA, m, 1975, 2 children **DISCIPLINE** PHILOSOPHY **EDUCATION** Virginia Tech, BA, 74; Univ Illinois, MA, 75, PhD, 79. **CAREER** Asst prof, 79-85, assoc prof, 85-92, prof, 92-, actng dean of human & fine arts, 91-93, chmn, philos, 88, 91, 93-, SUNY Oneonta. **RESEARCH** Epistemology & metaphysics, philos of sci & relig **CONTACT ADDRESS** Dept of Philosophy of Science & Religion, SUNY, Oneonta, NY, 13820-4015. **EMAIL** shraderw@oneonta.edu

SHRADER-FRECHETTE, KRISTIN
DISCIPLINE PHILOSOPHY OF SCIENCE **EDUCATION** Univ Notre Dame, PhD, 72. **CAREER** Prof. **RESEARCH** Philosophy of science; ecological methods; normative and environmental ethics; quantitative risk assessment. **SELECTED PUBLICATIONS** Auth, Burying Uncertainty: Risk and the Case Against Geological Disposal of Nuclear Waste, 93; The Ethics of Scientific Research, 94; Science, Risk Assessment, and the Frame Problem, 94; Hydrogeology and Framing Questions Having Policy Consequences, 97; Ecological Risk Assessment and Ecosystem Health, 97; co-auth, Method in Ecology, 93; Vedrification, Validation, and Confirmation of Numerical Models in the Earth Sciences, 94; Applied Ecology and the Logic of Case Studies, 94. **CONTACT ADDRESS** History and Philosophy of Science Dept, Univ of Notre Dame, Notre Dame, IN, 46556. **EMAIL** Kristin.Shrader-Frechette.1@nd.edu

SHRIVER, DONALD W.
PERSONAL Born 12/20/1927, Norfolk, VA, m, 1953, 3 children **DISCIPLINE** RELIGION **EDUCATION** Davidson College, AB 51; Union Seminary VA, BD 55; Yale Univ DS, STM 57; Harvard Univ, PhD 63. **CAREER** Presbyterian Church USA, minister, 55-; N Carolina State Univ, prof, 62-72; Emory Univ, prof 72-75; Union Theological Seminary NY, pres, Wm E Dodge Prof, Wm E Dodge Prof Emeritus, 75 to 98-; Columbia Univ schools of Bus, Journ, Law and Intl Affs, adj prof of ethics. **HONORS AND AWARDS** Six honorary degrees. **MEMBERSHIPS** SCE; CFR; SSSR. **RESEARCH** Religious ethics; influence of society and religion on each other; business ethics and intl peace, with emphasis on social recovery from massive violence. **CONTACT ADDRESS** Office of the President, Union Theology Sem, 440 Riverside Dr., #58, New York, NY, 10027-6830. **EMAIL** dwshriver@aol.com

SHTROMAS, ALEXANDER
DISCIPLINE LAW **EDUCATION** Univ Moscow, equiv MA, LLM/JD, 52; Spec Inst Adv Legal Stud, Ministry Justice, Moscow, postgrad diploma, 59; All-Union Inst Crimin, Moscow, equiv PhD, 64. **CAREER** Defense lawyer, part time lectr, Lithuania, 52-55; res, All- Union Res Inst Leg Scis, Spec Inst Adv Legal Stud, Moscow, 55-59; leg consult, KT Ltd. UK, 73-74; sen res assoc, Sch Peace Studies, UK, 74-77; lectr, politics, depts soc, pol studies, Univ Salford, UK, 78-83; reader in politics, dept politics, cont hist, Univ Salford, UK; PROF, POL SCIENCE. **CONTACT ADDRESS** Dept of Pol Sci, Hillsdale Col, 33 E College St, Hillsdale, MI, 49242. **EMAIL** shtro@ac.hillsdale.edu

SHUGRUE, RICHARD E.
DISCIPLINE CONSTITUTIONAL LAW **EDUCATION** Univ Nebr, BA, 59, JD,62, PhD, 68. **CAREER** Priv pract, Lincoln, Nebr, 62-64; spec asst dir, Nebr State Dept Agr, 64-66; asst prof and ch dept Polit Sci, Creighton Univ, 66- to assoc prof, 71-. **MEMBERSHIPS** Past ch, House Deleg, Nebr State Bar Asn; bd dir, Amer Judicature Soc. **SELECTED PUBLICATIONS** Pub(s) Creighton Law Rev; Prairie Barrister; Trial Lawyers Forum; Nebr Law Rev. **CONTACT ADDRESS** School of Law, Creighton Univ, 2500 California Plaza, Omaha, NE, 68178. **EMAIL** shugrue@culaw.creighton.edu

SHULER, PHILIP L.
PERSONAL Born 07/02/1938, Fort Worth, TX, m, 1991, 6 children **DISCIPLINE** RELIGION **EDUCATION** Calremont Grad Univ, MA, 67; McMaster Univ, PhD, 75 **CAREER** Prof, 79-pres, McMurry Univ **HONORS AND AWARDS** Societas Novi Testamentum Studiorum Member; Fulbright Res Lctr Scholar; Soc of Bibl Lit Pres, Southwest Region; Southwest Commission of Religious Studies Pres **MEMBERSHIPS** Soc of Bibl Lit; Societas Novi Testamentum Studorium; Inst for the Renewal of Gospel Studies **RESEARCH** Gospel Genre, Holocaust; Synoptic Problem; Canonical Gospels; Elie Wiesel **SELECTED PUBLICATIONS** Auth, A Genre for the Gospels: the Biographical Character of Matthew, Fortress, 82; Coauth, Beoyond the Q Impasse: Luke's Use of Matthew, Trinity International, 97 **CONTACT ADDRESS** 2501 Darrell Dr, Abilene, TX, 79606-3403. **EMAIL** pshuler@abilene.com

SHUMAN, DANIEL WAYNE
PERSONAL Born 05/04/1948, Philadelphia, PA, m, 1982, 2 children **DISCIPLINE** LAW **EDUCATION** Univ Ariz, BS, 69, JD, 72. **CAREER** Supv atty, Pima County Legal Aid Soc, 72-75; asst atty gen, State Ariz, 76-77; Assoc Prof Law, Southern Methodist Univ, 77- **MEMBERSHIPS** Am Judicature Soc; Asn Am Law Sch. **RESEARCH** Psychotherapist-patient privilege; civil commitment of mentally ill; psychological underpinnings of rules of evidence. **SELECTED PUBLICATIONS** Auth, The Problem With Empirical-Examination Of The Use Of Court-Appointed Experts - A Report Of Non-Findings/, Behavioral Scis & The Law, Vol 0014, 1996. **CONTACT ADDRESS** Sch of Law, Southern Methodist Univ, P O Box 750001, Dallas, TX, 75275-0001.

SHWAYDER, DAVID
DISCIPLINE PHILOSOPHY **EDUCATION** Oxford Univ, PhD, 54. **CAREER** Prof emer, Univ Ill Urbana Champaign. **RESEARCH** First philosophy; practical reason and philosophy

of language; theory of knowledge; philosophy of mathematics. **SELECTED PUBLICATIONS** Auth, Modes of Referring and the Problem of Universals; The Stratification of Behavior; Statement and Referent: An Enquiry into the Foundations of Our Conceptual Order. **CONTACT ADDRESS** Philosophy Dept, Univ Ill Urbana Champaign, 52 E Gregory Dr, Champaign, IL, 61820. **EMAIL** shwayder@uiuc.edu

SIBLEY, JACK RAYMOND
PERSONAL Born 06/17/1930, Arnett, OK, m, 1949, 2 children **DISCIPLINE** PHILOSOPHY, PHILOSOPHICAL THEOLOGY **EDUCATION** Phillips Univ, AB, 54; Phillips Grad Sem, DB, 57; Univ Chicago, Am, 63, PhD, 67. **CAREER** Assoc prof relig & philos, Bethany Col, WVa, 67-70; prof philos, Tex Woman's Univ, 70-. **MEMBERSHIPS** Am Acad Relig; Am Philos Assn; Southwestern Philos Soc; SCent Soc 28th Century Studies; Int Soc Metaphysics. **RESEARCH** Process philosophy; process theology; classical and humanistic studies. **SELECTED PUBLICATIONS** Auth, An Effort at a Portrait & Precious Vien, Euthanaasia, Illness, Crisis & Loss, 94; art, An Ethic of Negotiability, Lamar Journal of Humanities, 94; art, The Absence of Ethics in Scriptuaral Religions, Encounter, 94. **CONTACT ADDRESS** PO Box 425470, Denton, TX, 76204-5470.

SICHA, JEFFREY FRANKLIN
PERSONAL Cleveland, OH **DISCIPLINE** PHILOSOPHY **EDUCATION** Oberlin Col, AB, 62; Oxford Univ, DPhil, 66. **CAREER** Asst prof philos, Univ Ill, Chicago Circle, 66-68 & Amherst Col, 68-73; assoc prof, 73-79, Prof Philos, Calif State Univ, Northridge, 79-, Mellon fel philos, Univ Pittsburgh, 67-68; Nat Endowment Humanities fel, 73-74. **RESEARCH** Philosophy of language; epistemology; metaphysics. **SELECTED PUBLICATIONS** Auth, Counting and the natural numbers, Philos Sci, 9/70; A Metaphysics of Elementary Mathematics, Univ Mass, 74; Logic: The fundamentals of a Sellarsian theory, In: The Philosophy of Wilfrid Sellars: Queries & Extensions, Reidel, 78; ed, Introd to Pure Pragmatics & Possible Worlds: The Early Essays of Wilfrid Sellars, Ridgeview, 78. **CONTACT ADDRESS** Dept of Philos, California State Univ, Northridge, 18111 Nordhoff St, Northridge, CA, 91330-8200.

SIDER, ROBERT DICK
PERSONAL Born 03/10/1932, Cheapside, ON, Canada, m, 1959, 3 children **DISCIPLINE** CLASSICS, RELIGION **EDUCATION** Univ Sask, BA, 55, MA, 56; Oxford Univ, BA, 58, MA, 64, PhD, 65, DPhil, 65. **CAREER** Assoc prof bibl and class lit, Messiah Col, 62-68; from asst prof to assoc prof, 68-77, prof class studies, 77-81, Charles A Dana Prof Class Lang, 81-97, Charles A Dana prof emeritus, 97-, Dickinson Col; adj prof Col of Grad Stud, Univ Sask, 97-; Am Coun Learned Soc fel, 74-75; vis prof Greek & Latin, Cath Univ Am, 78-79; vis prof Univ Col, Univ Toronto, 82-83; fel-in-residence, Netherlands Inst for Adv Stud, 89-90; gen ed, New Testament Scholarship of Erasmus for Collected Works of Erasmus, Univ Toronto Press. **MEMBERSHIPS** Can Asn Rhodes Scholars;Asn Am Rhodes Scholars; NAm Patristic Soc (vpres, 72, pres, 73). **RESEARCH** Classical rhetoric; Christian Latin literature in antiquity and Renaissance; Christian humanism. **SELECTED PUBLICATIONS** Auth, Ancient Rhetoric and the Art of Tertullian, Oxford Univ, 71; coauth, A Decade of Patristic Studies, 2 v, Classical World, 82, 83; auth, The Gospel and its Proclamation, Michael Glazier, 83; ed, Paraphrase on Romans (CWE 42), Toronto, 84; ed, Annotations on Romans (CWE 56), Toronto, 94; transl, Paraphrase on Acts (CWE 50), Toronto, 95. **CONTACT ADDRESS** 304 Arthur Ave, Saskatoon, SK, S7N 1J3. **EMAIL** sider@skyway.usask.ca

SIDER, RONALD J.
PERSONAL m, 3 children **DISCIPLINE** THEOLOGY **EDUCATION** Waterloo Lutheran Univ, BA; Yale Univ, MA, BD, PhD. **CAREER** Prof, E Baptist Theol Sem. **HONORS AND AWARDS** Pres, Evangelicals for Soc Action. **SELECTED PUBLICATIONS** Publ, Green Cross; contrib ed, Sojourners; corresponding ed, Christianity Today; co-ed, Transformation: An International Dialogue on Evangelical Social Ethics. **CONTACT ADDRESS** Eastern Baptist Theol Sem, 6 Lancaster Ave, Wynnewood, PA, 19096.

SIDER, TED
PERSONAL Born 04/20/1967, New Haven, CT, s **DISCIPLINE** PHILOSOPHY **EDUCATION** Univ MA, PhD **CAREER** Asst prof, 92-97; Assoc prof, 97-98, Univ Rochester; Assoc prof, 98- , Syracuse **HONORS AND AWARDS** Univ Rochester Distinguished Teacher, 97/98. **MEMBERSHIPS** APA **RESEARCH** Metaphysics **SELECTED PUBLICATIONS** Auth, Naturalness and Arbitrariness, Philosophical Studies, 96; auth, Intrinsic Properties, Philosophical Studies, 96; auth, All the World's a State, Autralasian Journal of Philosophy, 96; auth, Four-Dimemsionalism, The philosophical Review, 97. **CONTACT ADDRESS** Dept of Philosophy, Syracuse Univ, Syracuse, NY, 13244. **EMAIL** trsider@syr.edu

SIEBER, JOHN HAROLD
PERSONAL Born 09/19/1935, Janesville, WI, m, 1960, 2 children **DISCIPLINE** RELIGION, CLASSICS **EDUCATION** Luther Col, BA, 58; Luther Theol Sem, BD, 62; Claremont Grad Sch, PhD(relig), 66. **CAREER** Asst prof classics, 65-67, asst prof relig, 67-72, assoc prof, 72-80, Prof Relig & Classics, Luther Col, 80-, Am Philos Soc res grant, 72. **MEMBERSHIPS** Soc Bibl Lit. **RESEARCH** Theology of Rudolf Bultman; Gnostic library from Nag-Hammdi, Egypt. **SELECTED PUBLICATIONS** Auth, Conflict And Community In Corinth - A Socio-Rhetorical Commentary On 1-Corinthians And 2-Corinthians - Witherington,B/, Interpretation-A J Of Bible And Theol, Vol 0051, 1997. **CONTACT ADDRESS** Dept of Relig, Luther Col, 700 College Dr, Decorah, IA, 52101-1045.

SIEG, WILFRIED
PERSONAL Born 07/01/1945, Germany, m, 1979, 2 children **DISCIPLINE** PHILOSOPHY AND FOUNDATIONS OF MATHEMATICS **EDUCATION** Stanford Univ, PhD, 77. **CAREER** Asst to assoc prof, dept of philos, Columbia Univ, 77-85; assoc to full prof, dept of philos, Carnegie Mellon Univ, 85-. **MEMBERSHIPS** Amer Philos Asn; Asn for Symbol Logic; Amer Math Soc. **RESEARCH** Mathematical logic; History and philosophy of modern mathematics; Foundations of cognitive science. **SELECTED PUBLICATIONS** Co-ed, Special Issue on Natural Deduction, Studia Logica, 98; auth, Step by Recursive Step: Church's analysis of effective calculability, Bull of Symbolic Logic, 97; co-auth, Godel, Turing, and K-graph machines, Logic in Florence, Kluwer Acad Publ, Studies in Epistemol, Logic, Methodol, and Philos of Sci, 97; auth, Aspects of mathematical experience, Philos of Math Today, Kluwer Acad Publ, 97; co-auth, Normal Natural Deduction Proofs, Studia Logica, 98; co-auth, K-Graph Machines: generalizing Turing's machines and arguments, Godel '96, Springer Lecture Notes in Logic, 96; co-auth, Paper Machines, Philosophia Mathematica, 95; co-auth, Lecture at Zilsel's, Collected Works of Kurt Godel, vol III, Oxford Univ Press, 95; auth, Church's Thesis, Consistency, Formalization, Proof Theory: Dictionary Entries, Cambridge Dict of Philos, Cambridge Univ Press, 95; auth, Mechanical procedures and mathematical experience, Math and Mind, Oxford Univ Press, 94; auth, Effectiveness and provability, Rendiconti di Seminario Matematico e Fisico di Milano, 94; auth, Eine neue Perspektive fur das Hilbertsche Programm, Dialektik, 94; co-auth, Computer environments for proof construction, Interactive Learning Environ, 94. **CONTACT ADDRESS** Dept. of Philosophy, Carnegie Mellon Univ, Pittsburgh, PA, 15213. **EMAIL** sieg@cmu.edu

SIEG, WILLIAM
PERSONAL Born 07/01/1945, Lunen, Germany, m, 1979, 2 children **DISCIPLINE** PHILOSOPHY **EDUCATION** Univ Munster, Germany, 71; Stanford Univ, MA, 75, PhD, 77. **CAREER** Asst to assoc prof, Columbia Univ, 77-85; assoc prof to prof, Carnegie Mellon Univ, 85- . **MEMBERSHIPS** Assoc of Symbolic Logic; Amer Philos Assoc; Amer Math Soc. **RESEARCH** Philos of math; math & logic; found of cognitive sci. **SELECTED PUBLICATIONS** Coauth, Iterated Inductive Definitions and Subsystems of Analysis, Berlin-Heidelberg-New York, 81; ed, Acting and Reflecting, Synthese Libr, 90, Logic and Computation, Contemp Math, 90; coed, Natural Deduction, Studia Logica, 98; auth, Step by Recursive Step: Church's analysis of effective calculability, Bull Symbolic Logic, 97. **CONTACT ADDRESS** Dept of Philosophy, Carnegie Mellon Univ, Pittsburgh, PA, 15213. **EMAIL** sieg@andrew.cmu.edu

SILBAUGH, KATHERINE
PERSONAL Born 02/01/1963, Corning, NY, m, 1990, 1 child **DISCIPLINE** LAW **EDUCATION** Amherst Col, BA, 85; Univ Chicago Law Sch, JD, 92. **CAREER** Assoc prof of law, Boston Univ, 93-pres. **RESEARCH** Women's household; family law. **SELECTED PUBLICATIONS** Coauth, A Guide to America's Sex Laws, 96; auth, Turning Labor Into Love: Housework and the Law, 91 Northwestern L. Rev. 1-86, 96; auth, Commodification and Women's Household Labor, 9 Yale J. Law & Fem, 97; auth, The Polygamous Heart?, a review of Arlie Hochschild's 'The Time Bind', in 1 Green Bag 2d, 97. **CONTACT ADDRESS** Sch of Law, Boston Univ, 765 Commonwealth Ave, Boston, MA, 02215. **EMAIL** silbaugh@bu.edu

SILBER, DANIEL
DISCIPLINE PHILOSOPHY **EDUCATION** George Washington Univ, BA, 89; MA, 93, PhD, 94, Vanderbilt Univ. **CAREER** Asst Prof, Philosophy, Florida Southern Col. **CONTACT ADDRESS** 111 Lake Hollingsworth Dr., Lakeland, FL, 33801. **EMAIL** dsilber@flsouthern

SILBER, JOHN ROBERT
PERSONAL Born 08/15/1926, San Antonio, TX, m, 1947, 7 children **DISCIPLINE** PHILOSOPHY **EDUCATION** Trinity Univ, BA, 47; Yale Univ, MA, 52, PhD, 56. **CAREER** Instr philos, Yale Univ, 52-55; from asst prof to prof, Univ Tex, Austin, 55-70, chm dept philos, 62-67 & comp studies, 67, univ prof arts & lett & dean col arts & sci, 67-70; Univ Prof Philos & Law & Pres, Boston Univ, 71-, Fulbright res scholar, Ger, 59-60; guest prof, Univ Bonn, 60; Guggenheim fel, Univs London & Oxford, 63-64; assoc ed, Kant-Studies, 68-; Lindley lectr, Univ Kans, 70; mem ed adv comt, New England Aquarium, 71; trustee, Col St Scholastica, 73; mem, Nat Comn United Methodist Higher Educ, 74-77; mem bd visitors, Air Univ, 74-; mem exec bd, Nat Humanities Inst, 75-78. **HONORS AND AWARDS** Wilbur Lucius Cross Medal, Yale Grad Sch, 71., LHD, Kalamazoo Col, 70 & Univ Evansville, 75; LLD, Maryville Col, 75, Col St Scholastics, 75 & Colo Col, 78; DEd, Southwestern at Memphis, 78. **MEMBERSHIPS** Soc Phenomenol & Existential Philos; Am Asn Higher Educ; Royal Inst Philos; Am Soc Polit & Legal Philos; Metaphys Soc Am. **RESEARCH** Financing of higher education. **SELECTED PUBLICATIONS** Auth, The Ethical Significance of Kant's Religion, Harper, 60; The Pollution of Time, Ctr Mag, 9-10/71; Tenure in Context, In: The Tenure Debate, Jossey-Bass, 73; Democracy: Its Counterfeits and Its Promise, Boston Univ, 76; The Flight From Excellence, Harpers Mag, 6/77; The Tuition Dilemma, Atlantic Mag, 7/78. **CONTACT ADDRESS** Off of the Chancellor, Boston Univ, 147 B S R, Boston, MA, 02215-2802.

SILLIMAN, MATTHEW R.
PERSONAL Born 08/28/1956, Hanover, NH, d **DISCIPLINE** PHILOSOPHY **EDUCATION** Purdue Univ, PhD, 86. **CAREER** Vis asst prof, Earlham Col, 85; asst prof, N Adams State Col, 86-93; assoc prof, NASC/Mass Col Lib Arts, 93-. **MEMBERSHIPS** Am Philos Asn; N Am Soc Soc Philos. **RESEARCH** Social and political philosophy; philosophy of law. **SELECTED PUBLICATIONS** Coauth, Critical Thinking and the Argumentative Essay, Inquiry: Critical Thinking Across the Disciplines, Summer, 98; auth, Law, Politics, and Tushnet's Epistemology, Rending & Renewing Soc Order, 96; auth, The Antioch Policy: A Community Experiment in Communicative Sexuality, Date Rape, Feminism, Philos & Law, 96; auth, Domestic Abuse: Locke's Liberal (mis)Treatment of Family, Is Feminist Philos Philos?, 97; auth, Freedom, Property and the Politics of Family, Freedom, Obligation and Rights, 93. **CONTACT ADDRESS** Dept of Philosophy, Massachusetts Col of Liberal Arts, North Adams, MA, 01247. **EMAIL** msillima@mcla.mass.edu

SILVA, MOISES
DISCIPLINE RELIGION **EDUCATION** Bob Jones Univ, BA; Westminster Theol Sem, BD, ThM; Dropsie Univ, grad stud; Univ Manchester, PhD. **CAREER** Instr, Westmont Col; instr, dept ch, Westminster Theol Sem; vis lectr, Fuller Theol Sem; Trinity Evangel Divinity Sch; E Baptist Theol Sem; Mary French Rockefeller Distinguished prof, Gordon-Conwell Theol Sem, 96-. **MEMBERSHIPS** Mem, Evangel Theol Soc; Intl Org Septuagint and Cognate Stud; Inst Biblical Res; Soc Biblical Lit; Studiorum Novi Testamenti Societas. **SELECTED PUBLICATIONS** Auth, Explorations in Exegetical Method: Galatians as a Test Case; An Introduction to Biblical Hermeneutics. **CONTACT ADDRESS** Gordon-Conwell Theol Sem, 130 Essex St, South Hamilton, MA, 01982.

SILVER, MARJORIE A.
DISCIPLINE LAW **EDUCATION** Brandeis Unvi, BA, summa cum laude, 70; Univ Pa, JD, magna cum laude, Order of the Coif, 73. **CAREER** Ch reg civil rights atty, US Dept of Educ, 79-83; assoc prof, NY Law Schl, 83-91; arbitrator, Better Bus Bur of Metropolitan NY, 86-89; assoc prof, Touro Col. **MEMBERSHIPS** Mem, Civil Rights Comt, 88-91; 92-, Educ and Law Comt, 91-92, Asn of the Bar of the City of NY. **SELECTED PUBLICATIONS** Auth, The Uses and Abuses of Informal Procedures in Federal Civil Rights Enforcement, George Washington Law Rev, 87; Evening the Odds: The Case for Attorneys' Fee Awards for Administrative Resolution of Title VI and Title VII Disputes, NC Law Rev, 89; In Lieu of Preclusion: Reconciling Administrative Decisionmaking and Federal Civil Rights Claims, Ind Law J, 90; Giving Notice: An Argument for Notification of Putative Plaintiffs in Complex Litigation, Washington Law Rev, 91; Fairness and Finality: Third-Party Challenges to Employment Discrimination Consent Decrees After the 1991 Civil Rights Act, 62 Fordham Law Rev 321, 93; coauth, Dissent without Opinion: The Behavior of Justice William O. Douglas in Federal Tax Cases, 75. **CONTACT ADDRESS** Touro Col, Brooklyn, NY, 11230. **EMAIL** MarjorieS@tourolaw.edu

SILVER, MITCHELL
PERSONAL Born 10/04/1950, New York, NY, m, 2 children **DISCIPLINE** PHILOSOPHY **EDUCATION** Univ of Connecticut, PhD, 80. **CAREER** Lectr, 17 yr, Philos, U MA, Boston. **HONORS AND AWARDS** Phi Beta Kappa. **MEMBERSHIPS** APA. **RESEARCH** Ethics; Political Philosophy. **SELECTED PUBLICATIONS** Auth, Respecting the Wicked Child, Univ of Mass Press, 98; A Philosophy of Secular Identity and Education. **CONTACT ADDRESS** 209 Derby St, West Newton, MA, 02165. **EMAIL** silver@umb.cc.umb.edu

SILVERS, ANITA
PERSONAL Born 11/01/1940, New York, NY **DISCIPLINE** PHILOSOPHY, AESTHETICS **EDUCATION** Sarah Lawrence Col, BA, 62; Johns Hopkins Univ, PhD(philos), 67. **CAREER** Prof Philos, San Francisco State Univ, 67-, Vis lectr philos, Sussex Univ, 72-73; assoc ed, J Aesthetics & Art Criticism, 79-; mem, Nat Coun Humanities, 80-; Exec Secy, Coun Philos Studies, 79-82. **MEMBERSHIPS** Am Philos Asn; Am Soc Aesthetics; Asn Advan Humanities. **RESEARCH** Philosophy of the arts; ethics; journalism ethics. **SELECTED PUBLICA-**

TIONS Auth, Vincent Story, The Importance Of Centextualism For Art Educ/, J Of Aesthetic Educ, Vol 0028, 1994. **CONTACT ADDRESS** 15 Otsego Ave, San Francisco, CA, 94112.

SIMCO, NANCY DAVIS
PERSONAL Born 05/09/1940, Rogers, Ark, d **DISCIPLINE** PHILOSOPHY **EDUCATION** Univ Kans, BA, 62, MA, 65, MPhil & PhD(philos), 69. **CAREER** From instr to asst prof philos, 66-73, assoc prof, 73-78, Prof Philos, Univ Memphis, 78-, Assoc Dean Res & Grad Studies, Col Arts & Sci, 75-89, Ed, Southern J Philos, 74-, dept ch, 89- **MEMBERSHIPS** Am Philos Asn; Asn Symbolic Logic; Metaphys Soc Am; Southern Soc Philos & Psychol (pres, 85-86); Asn Philos Jour Ed (pres 93-); SW Phil Soc (pres, 88-); Soc of Phil in Am; Conf of Phil Soc. **RESEARCH** Contemporary metaphysics; philosophical logic. **SELECTED PUBLICATIONS** Auth, Strawson's ontology in individuals, 71 & Note on instances of invalid elementary argument forms, 73, Southern J Philos; Transcendental arguments and ontological commitment, Proc XVth World Cong Philos, 73; Logic and ontology as normative sciences, Fifth Int Cong Logic, Methodology & Philos Sci, 75; coauth, Elementary Logic, Dickenson, 76; auth, Elementary Logic, 2nd ed, Wadsworth, 83, 3rd ed, McGraw-Hill, 96; auth, Rationality, Sci Rationality, and Philos Questions, PROC XVIth World Cong Philos, 78; auth, The Linguistic Turn Afain, SW Phil Rev, 89; auth, On Avoiding Rejection by Journals, Am Philos Assoc,. 97. **CONTACT ADDRESS** Dept of Philos, Univ of Memphis, Memphis, TN, 38152-0001. **EMAIL** nsimco@memphis.edu

SIMMELKJAER, ROBERT T.
PERSONAL New York, NY, m **DISCIPLINE** LAW **EDUCATION** CCNY, BS Pol Sci 1962, MA Pol Sci 1964; Columbia Univ Teachers Coll, EdD Ed Admin 1972; Columbia Univ Business School, MBA Bus Admin 1977; Fordham Univ School of Law, JD 1978. **CAREER** Inst for Ed Devel, exec asst to pres 1969-71; NY City Bd of Ed, principal 1971-74; CCNY, prof ed admin 1974-79, dean of gen studies and vice provost for academic administration, 1979-86; Attorney/arbitrator; Governor's Advisory Commission for Black Affairs, executive director 1986-88; New York City Transit Authority, administration law judge 1988-90; Joint Commission for Integrity in the Public Schools, deputy chief counsel 1989-90; Institute for Mediation and Conflict Resolution, president 1991-. **HONORS AND AWARDS** NY State Regents Scholarship 1957; US OE Ed Fellowship 1969-70; Great Cities Rsch Fellow 1971; **MEMBERSHIPS** PERC, OCB 1977-; minority school fin network Urban League & NAACP 1980-83; bd of dir Inst for Mediation & Conflict Resolution 1980-84; consult Ford Found, Natl School Fin Proj, NY Task Force Equity & Excellence, Urban Coalition Local School Devel 1980-83; vice chmn Personnel Appeals Bd US Acctg Office 1981-84; speaker, consult US Info Agency 1981-84; consult NY Univ School of Bus 1982-83; board of directors, Institute for Mediation and Conflict Resolution, 1980-92; board of directors, National Academy of Arbitrators, 1988-. **SELECTED PUBLICATIONS** Chap in "A Quest for Ed Oppty in a Major Urban School District, The Case of Washington DC" 1975; author, "From Partnership to Renewal, Evolution of an Urban Ed Reform," The Ed Forum, 1979; author, "State Aid to Substantially Black School Districts," Crisis and Opportunity; "Finality of Arbitration Awards, The Arbitration Forum," Fall 1989; author chapters on Representation, Collective Bargaining Impasses in Federal Civil Service Law and Procedures, BNA, 1990; "State Aid to Substantially Black School Districts," in Crisis and Opportunity Report (NY, NY); Federal Civil Service Law and Procedure, Washington, DC (BNA) 1990: two chapters on collective bargaining and arbitration. **CONTACT ADDRESS** 160 W 97th St, New York, NY, 10025.

SIMMONS, A.J.
PERSONAL Born 05/04/1950, Dover, NJ, m, 1987, 2 children **DISCIPLINE** PHILOSOPHY **EDUCATION** Princeton Univ, AB, 72; Cornell Univ, MA, 75, PhD, 77. **CAREER** Asst prof, 76-81, assoc prof, 81-89, prof, 89-, commonwealth prof of philos, 97-, Univ Va. **HONORS AND AWARDS** NEH Fel, 80-81; All-Univ Teaching Award, 92. **MEMBERSHIPS** Amer Philos Asn, Amer Soc for Polit and Legal Philos. **RESEARCH** Moral, political, legal philosophy; Philosophy of John Locke. **SELECTED PUBLICATIONS** Auth, On the Edge of Anarchy: Locke, Consent, and the Limits of Society, Studies in Moral, Political, and Legal Philosophy, Princeton Univ Press, 93; auth, The Lockean Theory of Rights, Studies in Moral, Political, and Legal Philosophy, Princeton Univ Press, 92; auth, Moral Principles and Political Obligations, Princeton Univ Press, 79; article, Makers' Rights', Jour of Ethics, 2, 1-22, 98; article, Denisons and Aliens: Locke's Problem of Political Consent, Social Theory and Practice, 24, summer, 98; article, Menchenrechte und Weltburgerrecht: die Universalitat der Menschenrechte bei Kant und Locke, Univ of Human Rights in Kent and Locke, Republik und Weltburgerrecht, Bohlau Verlag, 91-114, 98; article, Philosophical Anarchism, For & Against the State: New Philosophical Readings, Rowman & Littlefield, 19-39, 96; article, External Justifications and Institutional Roles, Jour of Philos, 93, 28-36, jan, 96; article, Associative Political Obligations, Ethics, 106, 247-273, Jan, 96; article, Historical Rights and Fair Shares, Law and Philos, 14, 149-84, may, 95; article, Locke on the Death Penalty, Philos, 69, 471-477, oct, 94; article, Original-Acquisition Justifications of Private Property, Soc Philos & Policy, 11, 63-84, summer, 94. **CONTACT ADDRESS** Univ of Virginia, 512 Cabell Hall, Charlottesville, VA, 22903. **EMAIL** ajs7m@virginia.edu

SIMMONS, ESMERALDA
PERSONAL Born 12/16/1950, Brooklyn, NY **DISCIPLINE** LAW **EDUCATION** Hunter Coll CUNY, BA 1974; Brooklyn Law School, JD 1978. **CAREER** New York City Law Dept, honors attorney, civil rights employment unit 1978-79; US Dist Ct US Dist Judge Henry Bramwell, law clerk 1979-80; US Dept of Educ Office of Civil Rights, regional civil rights atty 1980-82; NY Dept of Law Atty General's Office, asst attorney general 1982-83; NY State Div of Human Rights, first deputy commissioner 1983-85; Medgar Evers Coll Ctr for Law and Social Justice, dir 1985-. **HONORS AND AWARDS** Partner in Educ Awd NY City Bd of Educ 1981; Appreciation Awd Central Brooklyn Mobilization 1982; Lawyer of the Year Bedford Stuyvesant Lawyers Assn Inc 1984; Imani Awd Weusi Shule Parents Council 1984; Professional of the Year Natl Assn of Negro Business and Professional Womens Clubs Inc 1986; Harriet Tubman Award, Fannie Lou Hamer Collective, 1987; Woman on the Move, Concerned Women of Brooklyn, 1988; Leadership Award, Asian Americans for Equality, 1990; Leadership in Civil Rights Award, United Negro College Fund, Brooklyn Chapter, 1990; Women for Racial and Economic Equality, Fannie Lou Hamer Award, 1991; council member Annette M Robenson, Spirited Leadership Award, 1992; Community Service Society, Ellen Luriel Award, 1992; Magnolia Tree Earth Center, Magnolia Award, 1992. **MEMBERSHIPS** Natl Conf Black Lawyers 1975-; Natl Bar Assn 1979-; pres Bedford Stuyvesant Lawyers Assn 1981-84; legal committee chair, Coalition for Community Empowerment 1983-91; bd dirs Metro Black Bar Assn 1984-91; vice chair, New York City Districting Commission, 1990-92; board member, Fund for the City of New York, 1990-. **CONTACT ADDRESS** Ctr for Law & Social Justice, Medgar Evers Col, 1473 Fulton St, Brooklyn, NY, 11216.

SIMMONS, JACK R.
PERSONAL Born 12/08/1964, San Diego, CA, m, 1993, 1 child **DISCIPLINE** PHILOSOPHY **EDUCATION** La State Univ, BA, 87, 90; Tulane Univ, PhD, 97. **CAREER** Vis asst prof, Univ N Fla, 97-98; asst prof, Savannah St Univ, 98. **MEMBERSHIPS** Amer Philos Assoc **RESEARCH** Film Theory; Critical Theory; Hermeneutics. **SELECTED PUBLICATIONS** The Ontology of Perception in Cinema, Film and Philos, 98. **CONTACT ADDRESS** Dept of Humanities, Savannah State Univ, PO Box 20029, Savannah, GA, 31404. **EMAIL** simmonsj@savstate.edu

SIMMONS, LANCE
DISCIPLINE PHILOSOPHY, ETHICS **EDUCATION** Univ Calif, AB; Univ Notre Dame, MA, PhD. **CAREER** Dept Philos, Univ Dallas **SELECTED PUBLICATIONS** Auth, Kant's Highest Good: Albatross, Keystone, Achilles Heel, Hist of Philos Quart, 93; auth, Abelardian Ethics Reconstructed, Proc Amer Cath Philos Assn, 93; Three Kinds of Incommesurability Thesis, Amer Philos Quart, 94. **CONTACT ADDRESS** Dept of Philos, Univ Dallas, 1845 E Northgate Dr, Irving, TX, 75062. **EMAIL** simmons@acad.udallas.edu

SIMMONS, WILLIAM A.
PERSONAL Metairie, LA, m, 1 child **DISCIPLINE** THEOLOGY AND PHILOSOPHY **EDUCATION** Lee uUniv, BA, 78; Princeton, MA, Phd; Univ St Andrews, PhD. **CAREER** Conn Comm Col; Assoc prof, Lee Univ, 97-. **HONORS AND AWARDS** Lee Univ Excellence Res Award, 94. **RESEARCH** Galatians and Philippians Karl Barth. **SELECTED PUBLICATIONS** Areas: Different aspects of the New Testament **CONTACT ADDRESS** Lee Univ, 1120 N. Ocoee St, Cleveland, TN, 37320-3450. **EMAIL** Lcross@leeuniversity.edu

SIMON, JULIUS J.
PERSONAL m, 3 children **DISCIPLINE** PHILOSOPHY **EDUCATION** PhD **CAREER** Fac, Univ Tex at El Paso, over 4 yrs; Fulbright Scholar. **RESEARCH** Jewish Philosophy and 19th- and 20th-century German and French philosophy; philosophical roots of nationalist-inspired genocide. **SELECTED PUBLICATIONS** Rev bk on,Jewish thought and Holocaust studies. **CONTACT ADDRESS** Dept of Philosophy, Univ of Texas, El Paso, Worrell Hall, El Paso, TX, 79968. **EMAIL** jusimon@nmsu.edu

SIMON, LARRY G.
DISCIPLINE CONSTITUTIONAL LAW **EDUCATION** Hobart Col, BA,63; Yale Univ, LLB,66. **CAREER** H.W. Armstrong prof, Univ Southern Calif; clerked for, Honorable Earl Warren, Ch Justice US; taught at, Yale Law Sch. **MEMBERSHIPS** Order of the Coif. **RESEARCH** Constitutional Law, Legal Profession, and Insurance. **SELECTED PUBLICATIONS** Auth, The Authority of the Framers of the Constitution & The Authority of the Constitution and its Meaning. **CONTACT ADDRESS** School of Law, Univ Southern Calif, University Park Campus, Los Angeles, CA, 90089.

SIMON, WILLIAM HACKETT
PERSONAL Born 07/06/1947, Chicago, IL, m, 1981 **DISCIPLINE** LAW **EDUCATION** Princeton Univ, AB, 69; Harvard Univ, JD, 74. **CAREER** Assoc atty, Foley, Hoag & Eliot, 74-77; staff atty, Legal Serv Inst, 79-81; Asst Prof Law, Stanford Univ, 81- **RESEARCH** Social welfare; legal profession; jurisprudence. **SELECTED PUBLICATIONS** Auth, The Ethics Of Criminal Defense/, Mich Law Rev, Vol 0091, 1993. **CONTACT ADDRESS** Law Sch, Stanford Univ, Stanford, CA, 94305-1926.

SIMPSON, EVAN
DISCIPLINE PHILOSOPHY **EDUCATION** Duke Univ, PhD. **CAREER** Prof. **RESEARCH** Moral and political philos. **CONTACT ADDRESS** Philosophy Dept, McMaster Univ, 1280 Main St W, Hamilton, ON, L8S 4L9.

SIMPSON, GARY M.
DISCIPLINE SYSTEMATIC THEOLOGY **EDUCATION** Concordia Sr Col, BA, 72; Christ Sem-Seminex, MDiv, 76, ThD, 83. **CAREER** Adj tchr, Warner Pacific Col; Pacific Lutheran Theol Sem; Lutheran Inst Theol Edu; assoc prof, 90-. **HONORS AND AWARDS** Pastor, Immanuel Lutheran Church; chaplain, Highland-Alameda County Hospital, Oakland, 76-81; minister of edu and youth, St. Charles Christian Church, 81-83; pastor, Resurrection Lutheran Church, 83-90; ch, Jewish-Christian Assn Ore; VP, Oregon Holocaust Resource Ctr; ch, Oregon Governor's Task Force on Hunger. **MEMBERSHIPS** Mem, Amer Acad Rel; Soc Christian Ethics; Gospel and Our Culture Network. **SELECTED PUBLICATIONS** Ed bd(s), Word & World; pub(s), essays on theology and public life, Eng and Ger lang collections. **CONTACT ADDRESS** Dept of Systematic Theology, Luther Sem, 2481 Como Ave, St. Paul, MN, 55108. **EMAIL** gsimpson@luthersem.edu

SIMPSON, MARK E.
DISCIPLINE CHRISTIAN EDUCATION **EDUCATION** Spring Arbor Col, BA; Denver Conservative Baptist Sem, MACE; DePauw Univ, MA; Trinity Evangel Divinity Sch, PhD. **CAREER** Acad Doctorate Prog(s) coord, Trinity Evangel Divinity Sch; assoc dean, Nontraditional Edu, Col Liberal Arts, Trinity Intl Univ; assoc prof; assoc dean, Sch Christian Edu and Leadership. **SELECTED PUBLICATIONS** Ed, NAPCE Newsletter; contrib, With an Eye on the Future: Development and Mission in the 21st Century; pub(s), Christian Edu Jour; Key To Christian Edu. **CONTACT ADDRESS** Sch Christian Edu and Leadership, Southern Baptist Theol Sem, 2825 Lexington Rd, Louisville, KY, 40280. **EMAIL** msimpson@sbts.edu

SIMPSON, PETER
DISCIPLINE PHILOSOPHY **EDUCATION** Univ Toronto, PhD. **RESEARCH** Philos of hist; phenomenology; empiricism. **SELECTED PUBLICATIONS** Auth, Hegel's Transcendental Induction, 98; art, Out of this World: Heidegger and the Problem of Phenomenology, Strategies of Critique, 91. **CONTACT ADDRESS** Philosophy Dept, Laurentian Univ, 935 Ramsey Lake Rd, Sudbury, ON, P3E 2C6.

SIMPSON, PETER L.P.
PERSONAL England **DISCIPLINE** CLASSICS, PHILOSOPHY **EDUCATION** Victoria Univ Manchester, UK, PhD **CAREER** Asst prof, Univ Col Dublin, Ireland, 82-84; asst prof, Catholic Univ Am, DC, 84-88; Full prof, City Univ NY, 88- . **HONORS AND AWARDS** Earhart found fel, 95; Jr fel, Ctr Hellenic stud, 92. **MEMBERSHIPS** APA; ACPA; APSA; SAGP. **RESEARCH** Ancient and medieval philosophy; moral and political philosophy. **SELECTED PUBLICATIONS** Auth, The Politics of Aristotle, U of North Carolina P, 97; A Philosophical Commentary on the Politics of Aristotle, U of North Carolina P, 98. **CONTACT ADDRESS** Dept of Philosophy, Staten Island Col, 2800 Victory Blvd, 2N, Staten Island, NY, 10314. **EMAIL** simpson@postbox.csi.cuny.edu

SIMPSON, STEPHEN WHITTINGTON
PERSONAL Born 03/14/1945, Philadelphia, PA, m **DISCIPLINE** LAW **EDUCATION** Harvard Univ, AB 1966; Univ of PA, JD 1969. **CAREER** Suns Co, Inc, chief counsel, 1970-87; Goodrs Greenfield, atty 1973-77; Dechert, Price & Rhoades, atty 1970-73; PA Superior Ct, law clerk 1969-70; Vance, Jackson, Simpson & Overton, Attorney, currently. **MEMBERSHIPS** Amer Bar Assc; Philadelphia Bar Assc; Barristers Club. **CONTACT ADDRESS** Vance, Jackson, Simpson, & Overton, 1429 Walnut St, 8th Floor, Philadelphia, PA, 19107.

SIMS, GENEVIEVE CONSTANCE
PERSONAL Born 11/04/1947, Baltimore, MD, s **DISCIPLINE** LAW **EDUCATION** North Carolina State Univ, BA, 1969; Univ of Southern California, MPA, 1976; North Carolina Central Univ, JD, 1986. **CAREER** Law Offices of Genevieve C. Sims, lawyer, 1987-; Merit Sys Protection Bd, special asst, 1979-81; US Civil Serv Commn, special asst commr, 1977-78; Office of Mgmt & Budget Exec Office Pres, mgmt analyst, 1976-77; US Civil Serv Commn, personnel mgmt spec, 1972-76; Office of State Personnel, North Carolina State Govt, econ analyst 1969-72; North Carolina State Univ, Raleigh, NC, asst

professor, 1982-93; North Carolina Central Univ, Durham, NC, visiting instr, 1982-92. **HONORS AND AWARDS** Award, North Carolina Special Olympics, 1982. **MEMBERSHIPS** Former chairperson, bd of dir, Shelley School; bd of dir, North Carolina Assn Black Lawyers, 1989-92; board of directors, North Carolina Academy of Trial Lawyers, 1995-; North Carolina Bar Assn; board of directors, United Black Fund of Washington, 1976-81. **CONTACT ADDRESS** 313 S Blount St, Raleigh, NC, 27601.

SIMSON, ROSALIND S.
PERSONAL Born 04/03/1952, New York, NY, m, 1971, 2 children **DISCIPLINE** PHILOSOPHY **EDUCATION** Yale Univ, BA, 73, PhD, 79. **CAREER** Inst, Southwest Texas State Univ, 78-79; asst prof, Hobart and William Smith Col, Geneva, NY, 79- . **HONORS AND AWARDS** Phi Beta Kappa. **MEMBERSHIPS** APA. **RESEARCH** Epistemology; feminist philosophy. **SELECTED PUBLICATIONS** Auth, An Internalist View of the Epistemic Regress Problem, Philos and Phenomenol Res, 86; auth, Values, Circumstances and Epistemic Justifications, Southern J of Philos, 93. **CONTACT ADDRESS** 126 Burleigh Dr, Ithaca, NY, 14850. **EMAIL** simson@hws.edu

SIMUNDSON, DANIEL J.
DISCIPLINE OLD TESTAMENT **EDUCATION** Stanford Univ, BA, 55; Lutheran Sch Theol, BD, 59; Harvard Univ, PhD, 71. **CAREER** Hospital chaplain, Wash Univ Med Sch, 61-67; asst prof, Appalachian State Univ, 71-72; tchg fel, Harvard Univ, 70-71; prof, 81-; dean of stud (s), 74-75; dean acad aff, 76-78, 88-93, 95-96. **HONORS AND AWARDS** Graduate Prize fel, Harvard Univ, 71; Fredrik A. Schiotz fel, Cambridge Univ, 78-79., Pastor, Salem Lutheran Church, 59-61. **SELECTED PUBLICATIONS** Auth, Faith Under Fire, 80, reprint, 91; Hope for All Seasons, 88; The Message of Job, 86; Where Is God in My Praying?, 86; Where Is God in My Suffering?, 83; coauth, Chosen: The Story of God and His People, 76. **CONTACT ADDRESS** Dept of Old Testament, Luther Sem, 2481 Como Ave, St. Paul, MN, 55108. **EMAIL** dsimunds@luthersem.edu

SINCLAIR, SCOTT G.
PERSONAL Born 03/29/1950, Baltimore, MD, s **DISCIPLINE** THEOLOGY **EDUCATION** Johns Hopkins Univ, BA, 71, MA, 72; Church Div School of the Pacific, MDiv, 76; Graduate Theol Union, PhD, 86. **CAREER** Univ of Calif, Davis, lecrt, 86-87; Codrington Col, Barbados, tutor 87-91; Dominican Col, San Rafael, inst, 92-. **MEMBERSHIPS** SBL **RESEARCH** New testament. **SELECTED PUBLICATIONS** Auth, A Study Guide to Mark's Gospel, N. Richland Hills: BIBAL, 96; auth, The Road and the Truth: The Editing of John's Gospel, Vallejo: BIBAL, 94; auth, Revelation -- A Book for the Rest of Us, Berkeley: BIBAL, 92; auth, Jesus Christ According to Paul, Berkeley, BIBAL, 88. **CONTACT ADDRESS** Dept of Theology, Dominican Col, San Rafael, 663 Coventry Rd, Kensington, CA, 94707-1329.

SINGER, BETH J.
PERSONAL Born 10/27/1927, New York, NY, 2 children **DISCIPLINE** PHILOSOPHY **EDUCATION** Univ Wis, BA, 49; Columbia Univ, MA, 58, PhD, 67. **CAREER** From instr to asst prof, Manhattanville Col, 66-72; asst prof, 72-73, assoc prof social insts, ideas & philos, 74-80, prof philos, Chp, 91-95, prof emer, 96, Brooklyn Col, 80-96. **HONORS AND AWARDS** Herbert W Schneider Award Distinguished Contrib Understanding Develop Am Philos, Soc Advan Am Philos, 94. **MEMBERSHIPS** Am Philos Asn; Soc Advan Am Philos; Metaphys Soc; Charles S Peirce Soc; Concerned Philos Peace; Alain Locke Soc. **RESEARCH** History of philosophy; American philosophy; metaphysics; philosophy of human rights. **SELECTED PUBLICATIONS** Auth, The rational society: A critical study of Santayana's social thought, Case West Reserve Univ, 70; ed, Philosophy After Darwin: Chapters for the Career of Philosophy, Vol III and Other Essays by John Herman Randall, Jr, Columbia Univ, 77; Ordinal Naturalism, An Introduction to the Philosophy of Justus Buchler, Bucknell Univ, 82; ed, Antifoundationalism Old and New, Temple Univ, 92; Operative Rights, SUNY, 93; Human Nature and Community, Open Times, 97; Pragmatism, Rights, and Democracy, Fordham Univ, 98. **CONTACT ADDRESS** Dept of Philos, Brooklyn Col, CUNY, 2900 Bedford Ave, Brooklyn, NY, 11210-2889. **EMAIL** 105152.1772@compuserve.com

SINGER, IRVING
PERSONAL Born 12/24/1925, New York, NY, m, 1949, 4 children **DISCIPLINE** PHILOSOPHY **EDUCATION** Harvard Univ, AB, 48, MA, 49, PhD, 52. **CAREER** Instr philos, Sage Sch Philos, Cornell Univ, 53-56; asst prof, Univ Mich, 56-59; assoc prof, 59- 69,prof philos, Mass Inst Technol, 69-, Fulbright grant, Univ Paris, 55-56; vis lectr, Johns Hopkins Univ, 57-58; Am Coun Learned Soc award, 58, grant-in-aid, 66-67; vis lectr, Mass Inst Technol, 58- 59; Bollingen award, 58-59, grant-in-aid, 65-66 & fel, 66-67; Hudson Rev fel, 58-59; Guggenheim fel, 65-66; fel, Villa I Tatti, Harvard Ctr Ital Renaissance Studies, Florence, Italy, 65-67; Rockefeller Found res grant, 70-72; vis lectr philos, Harvard Univ, 77-81. **MEMBERSHIPS** Am Philos Asn; Am Soc Aesthetics. **RESEARCH** Aesthetics; moral philosophy; philosophy of life sciences. **SELECTED PUBLICATIONS** Auth, Santayana's Aesthetics, Harvard Univ, 57; The Nature of Love: Plato to Luther, Random, 66; The Goals of Human Sexuality, Norton, 73; Mozart & Beethoven: The Concept of Love in Their Operas, Johns Hopkins Univ, 77; The Nature of Love Trilogy, Chicago Univ, 84-87; Meaning in Life: The Creation of Value, Free Press, 92; Meaning in Life Trilogy, John Hopkins Univ, 94-96; Reality Transformed: Film as Meaning and Technique, MIT, 98. **CONTACT ADDRESS** Dept of Ling & Philos, Massachusetts Inst of Tech, 77 Massachusetts Ave, E 39-351, Cambridge, MA, 02139-4307. **EMAIL** pis@mit.edu

SINGER, MARCUS G.
PERSONAL Born 01/04/1926, New York, NY, m, 1947, 2 children **DISCIPLINE** PHILOSOPHY **EDUCATION** Univ Illinois, AB, 48; Cornell Univ, PhD, 52. **CAREER** Asst in Philosophy, 48-49, Instr, 51-52, Cornell Univ; Instr, 52-55, Asst Prof, 55-59, Assoc Prof, 59-63, Prof, 63-92, Prof Emer, 92-, Chr, Dept Phil, 63-, Univ Wisconsin (Madison). **HONORS AND AWARDS** Western Div Fel, Amer Phil Assoc, 56-57; Guggenheim Fel, 62-63; Inst for Resarch in the Humanities Fel, 84. **MEMBERSHIPS** Amer Phil Assoc (pres, 85-86); AAUP; Royal Inst Phil; Wisconsin Acad of Sciences Arts and Letters; Sidgwick Soc; Phi Betta Kappa; Phi Kappa Phi **RESEARCH** Ethics; moral philosphy; legal philosophy; political philosophy; practical logic; American philosophy, philosophy of culture; history of ethics **SELECTED PUBLICATIONS** Auth, The Context of American Philosophy, 86; Nineteenth Century British Ethics, 92; Institutional Ethics, 93; Presuppositions of Inference, 98. **CONTACT ADDRESS** Dept of Philosophy, Univ of Wisconsin, 600 N. Park St., Madison, WI, 53706.

SINKLER, GEORGETTE
DISCIPLINE PHILOSOPHY **EDUCATION** Princeton Univ, BS; Cornell Univ, PhD. **CAREER** Philos Dept, Univ IL at Chicago **RESEARCH** Medieval philos; philos of relig; early mod philos. **SELECTED PUBLICATIONS** Auth, Ockham and Ambiguity, Medieval Philosophy & Theology, 94; Causal Principles, Degrees of Reality, and the Priority of the Infinite, Can Jour Philos, 89. **CONTACT ADDRESS** Philos Dept, Univ Illinois Chicago, S Halsted St, PO Box 705, Chicago, IL, 60607.

SIPFLE, DAVID A.
PERSONAL Born 08/29/1932, Pekin, IL, m, 1954, 2 children **DISCIPLINE** PHILOSOPHY **EDUCATION** Carleton Col, BA, 53; Yale Univ, MA, 56, PhD, 58. **CAREER** Mem fac philos, Robert Col, Turkey, 57-58, Am Col Girls, Turkey, 57-60; from asst prof to assoc prof, 60-70, chmn dept, 68-71, Prof Philos, Carleton Col, 70-92; William H Laird prof Philos & Lib Arts, 92-98; prof Emeritus, 98-; Nat Endowment for Humanities younger humanist fel, 71- 72; Nat Sci Found fac fel, 75-76. **HONORS AND AWARDS** Bush Fac Develop Award, Carleton Col, 81. **MEMBERSHIPS** Western Div Am Philos Asn; Metaphys Soc Am; Philos of Sci Asn. **RESEARCH** Philosophy of science; philosophy of time and space; the problem of freedom. **SELECTED PUBLICATIONS** Auth, A wager on freedom, Int Philos Quart, 6/68; Henri Bergson and the epochal theory of time, In: Bergson and the Evolution of Physics, Univ Tenn, 69; Free action and determinism, Ratio, 6/69; On the intelligibility of the epochal theory of time, In: Basic Issues in the Philosophy of Time, Open Court, 71; trans with Mary-Alie Sipble of Emile Meyerson, The Relativistic Deduction, Boston Studies in the Philosophy of Science, D Reidel, 75; Emile Meyerson, Explanation in the Sciences, Boston Studies, Kluner Academic Publishers, 85. **CONTACT ADDRESS** Dept of Philosophy, Carleton Col, 1 N College St, Northfield, MN, 55057-4044. **EMAIL** dsipele@carleton.edu

SIRICO, LOUIS J., JR.
DISCIPLINE ADVANCED LEGAL WRITING **EDUCATION** Yale Univ, BA, 67; Univ Tex Sch Law, JD, 72. **CAREER** Prof & dir, Legal Writing Prog;Villanova Univ, 81-. **HONORS AND AWARDS** Founding Ed-in-Ch, Amer J Criminal Law; assoc ed, Texas Law Rev. **MEMBERSHIPS** Dist Columbia Bar Asn; Conn Bar; bd dir, Legal Writing Inst; Asn Legal Writing Directors; ed bd, Perspectives: Tchg Legal Res and Writing; ed bd, Casenotes Publ Co; adv bd, Villanova Univ Paralegal Prog. **RESEARCH** Legal writing, constitutional law. **SELECTED PUBLICATIONS** Coauth, Legal Research; Persuasive Legal Writing for Lawyers and the Legal Profession, 95; Introduction to Legal Writing and Oral Advocacy, 2d ed, 93 & How to Talk Back to the Telephone Company: Playing the Telephone Game to Win, 79. **CONTACT ADDRESS** Law School, Villanova Univ, 800 Lancaster Ave, Villanova, PA, 19085-1692. **EMAIL** sirico@law.vill.edu

SIRRIDGE, MARY
DISCIPLINE ANCIENT AND MEDIEVAL PHILOSOPHY, PHILOSOPHY OF ART **EDUCATION** St Mary's Col, Notre Dame, BA, 67; Ohio State Univ, MA, PhD, 72. **CAREER** Prof, La State Univ. **RESEARCH** Philosophy of language in ancient and medieval thought. **SELECTED PUBLICATIONS** Auth, Donkeys, Stars and Illocutionary Acts, J of Aesthet and Art Criticism; The Moral of the Story: Exemplification and the Literary Work, The Brit J of Aesthet; Can Est' Be Used Impersonality?, in Sophisms in Medieval Logic and Grammar. **CONTACT ADDRESS** Dept of Philos and Relig Stud, Louisiana State Univ, 106 Coates Hall, Baton Rouge, LA, 70803.

SISK, G.C.
PERSONAL Born 05/29/1960, Des Moines, IA, m, 1981, 1 child **DISCIPLINE** LAW **EDUCATION** Montana State Univ, BA, highest honors, 81; Univ Washington, JD, highest honors, 84. **CAREER** Asst Prof, Assoc Prof, Prof law, 91 to 97-, Drake Univ; appeal Att'y, 89-91, Karr Tuttle Campbell; appeal staff, 86-89, US Dept of Justice; clerk, 85-86, Judge R R Breezer US Circ; legis Asst, 84-85, US Senator Slade Gorton. **HONORS AND AWARDS** Order of the Coif. **MEMBERSHIPS** ABA; APSA. **RESEARCH** Judicial decision making, litigation with the Federal Govt, legal ethics. **SELECTED PUBLICATIONS** Coauth, Charting the Influences on the Judicial Mind: An empirical Study of Judicial Reasoning, NYU L Rev, 98; Auth, Stating the Obvious: Protecting Religion for Religion's Sake, Drake L Rev, 98; coauth, The Sun Sets On Federal Common Law: Corporate Successor Liability Under CERCLA After O'Melveny and Myers, VA Environ L J, 97; auth, The Balkanization of the Appellate Justice: The Proliferation of Local Rules in the Federal Circuits, U CO L Rev, 97; auth, The Essentials of the Equal Access to Justice Act: Court Awards of Attorney's Fees for Unreasonable Govt Conduct, part two, LA L Rev, 95, part one 94; Questioning Dialogue by Judicial Decree: A Different Theory of Constitutional Review and Moral Discourse, Rutgers L Rev, 94; Comparative Fault and Common Sense, Gonzaga L Rev, 94/95; A Primer on Awards of Attorney Fees Against the Federal Govt, AZ State L J, 94. **CONTACT ADDRESS** Law School, Drake Univ, Cartwright Hill, Des Moines, IA, 50311. **EMAIL** greg.sisk@drake.edu

SISMONDO, SERGIO
DISCIPLINE PHILOSOPHY **EDUCATION** Univ Toronto, BA; MA; Cornell Univ, PhD. **CAREER** Dept Philos, Queen's Univ **RESEARCH** Philosophy of science; history and philosophy of biology; metaphysics. **SELECTED PUBLICATIONS** Auth, Science without Myth: On Constructions, Reality and Social Knowledge, SUNY, 96; The Scientific Domains of Feminist Standpoints, 95. **CONTACT ADDRESS** Philosophy Dept, Queen's Univ, Kingston, ON, K7L 3N6. **EMAIL** sismondo@post.queensu.ca

SISSON, RUSSELL
PERSONAL Born 08/15/1959, Memphis, TN, m, 1985, 1 child **DISCIPLINE** RELIGION; PHILOSOPHY **EDUCATION** Rhodes Col, BA, 81; Yale Univ, MDiv, 84, Emory Univ, 94. **CAREER** Instr, Memphis Theological Seminary, 92; Adjunct Prof, Murray State Univ, 96-97; Asst Prof, Union Col, 97-. **HONORS AND AWARDS** Winner John Templeton Fdn Science-Religion Course Competition **MEMBERSHIPS** Soc Biblical Lit; Amer Acad of Religion **RESEARCH** Rhetoric and Hermeneutics; religion and science; philosopy of language **CONTACT ADDRESS** Dept of Religion and Philosophy, Union Col, 310 College St., Barbourville, KY, 40906. **EMAIL** rsisson@unionky.edu

SITTGER, GERALD L.
PERSONAL Born 06/14/1950, Milwaukee, WI, w, 1971, 4 children **DISCIPLINE** THEOLOGY **EDUCATION** Hope Col, BA, 72; Fuller Theol Sem, M Div, 75; Univ Chicago, PhD, 89. **CAREER** Assoc pastor, 75-79, Emmanuel Reformed Church, CA; chaplain, 79-85, Northwestern Col, IA; asst, assoc, full prof, relig & philos, 89-, Whitworth Col. **RESEARCH** Religion and WW II; relig and democracy in post war Amer. **CONTACT ADDRESS** Whitworth Col, #1502, Spokane, WA, 99251. **EMAIL** gsittger@whitworth.edu

SITTSER, GERALD
PERSONAL m, 3 children **DISCIPLINE** RELIGION **EDUCATION** Hope Col, BA; Fuller Theol Sem, Mdiv; Univ Chicago, PhD, 89. **CAREER** Assoc prof, 89-. **HONORS AND AWARDS** Javitts grad fel award, Univ Chicago., Five times, Most Influential Prof award; ch, Fac Evaluation Comm; certification for Ministry prog. **SELECTED PUBLICATIONS** Auth, The Adventure, Intervarsity Press, 85; Loving Across Our Differences, InterVarsity Press, 94; A Grace Disguised: How the Soul Grows Through Loss, Zondervan 96; Cautious Patriotism: The American Churches and the Second World War, Univ NC Press, 97. **CONTACT ADDRESS** Dept of Rel/Philos, Whitworth Col, 300 West Hawthorne Rd, Spokane, WA, 99251. **EMAIL** gsittser@whitworth.edu

SKAGGS, REBECCA
PERSONAL Born 01/30/1950, Berkeley, CA, m, 1995 **DISCIPLINE** PHILOSOPHY **EDUCATION** Patten Coll, Oakland, BS, 69; Holy Names Coll, Oakland, BA, 70; Wheaton Coll, MA, 72; Drew Univ, Madison, PhD, 76; Dominican School of Philos and Theol, Berkeley, MA, 90. **CAREER** Prof of New Testament, 75-, Academic Dean, 78-, Patten Coll. **HONORS AND AWARDS** Fellowship at Kierkegaard Library, St Olaf's Coll. **SELECTED PUBLICATIONS** Auth, Before the Times, Strawberry Hill Press, 80; The World of the Early Church, Edwin Mellen Press, 90; The Role of Reason in Faith in Kierkegaard and St Thomas, in progress, International Scholar's Press, 94; co-auth, Pentecostal Hermeneutics and Post-Modern Literary Theory, Pneuma, 94; Critical Thinking and the Christian Perspective: A Response to Baird and Soden, Faculty Dialogue, 95; The Role of Reason in Faith, paper presented at European Pentecostal-Charismatic Res Assoc, 95; Knowledge of Things

Unseen, Seminar paper at International Conference for Critical Thinking at Sonoma State Univ, 96. **CONTACT ADDRESS** 2433 Coolidge Ave, Oakland, CA, 94601.

SKELLY, BRIAN
PERSONAL Born 03/25/1960, Stamford, CT, m, 1985, 2 children **DISCIPLINE** PHILOSOPHY **EDUCATION** Mich St Univ, BA, 81; Rome Gregorian Univ, PhL, 84; Univ of Mass/ Amherst, PhD, 91. **CAREER** Univ of Hartford, 92-; St Joseph Col, 93-. **HONORS AND AWARDS** Phi Beta Kappa; Eta Sigma Phi Classics Honor Soc. **RESEARCH** Ethics, history of philos, natural theology. **CONTACT ADDRESS** 59 Crystal Brook Dr, Springfield, MA, 01118-1907. **EMAIL** brianskelly@msn.com

SKERIS, ROBERT A.
PERSONAL Born 05/11/1935, Sheboygan, WI **DISCIPLINE** THEOLOGY **EDUCATION** Rheinische Friedrich-Wilhelms Univ Bonn, PhD, 75. **CAREER** Prof, Pontifical Inst Sacred Music, 86-90; prof, Christendom Col, 90-. **HONORS AND AWARDS** Ordem Nacional dos Bandeirantes, 83; Order of Merit, 89, Republic of Austria; Knight of the Holy Sepulchre of Jerusalem, 95., Sec Head, Maria Laach, 78-86; pres, Music Asn Am, 98. **MEMBERSHIPS** Church Music Asn Am; Catholic Music Assocs; Fel Catholic Scholars. **RESEARCH** Hymnology; theology of worship and of it's music. **CONTACT ADDRESS** 134 Christendom Dr, Front Royal, VA, 22630-6534. **EMAIL** rskeris@christendom.edu

SKIBA, PAULETTE
DISCIPLINE THEOLOGY **EDUCATION** Marquette Univ, BVM. **CAREER** Asst prof, Clarke Col. **MEMBERSHIPS** Cath Theol Soc; AAR; Soc for Buddhist-Christian Stud. **RESEARCH** Karl Rahner; systematics; liberation theol; Christian-Buddhist Studies. **CONTACT ADDRESS** 1150 Carmel Dr, Dubuque, IA, 52003-7998. **EMAIL** pskiba@feller.clarke.edu

SKJOLDAL, NEIL O.
DISCIPLINE RELIGION **EDUCATION** Cedarville Col, BA, 85; Bibl Theol Sem, Mdiv, 88, STM, 91; Trinity Evangelical Div Sch, PhD, 95. **SELECTED PUBLICATIONS** Article, Jour Evangelical Theol Soc; Contrib, New Int Dictionary Old Testament Theol & Exegesis. **CONTACT ADDRESS** Trinity Int Univ, 500 NE 1st Ave, PO Box 109674, Miami, FL, 33101-9674.

SKLAR, LAWRENCE
PERSONAL Born 06/25/1938, Baltimore, MD, m, 1962, 1 child **DISCIPLINE** PHILOSOPHY **EDUCATION** Oberlin Col, BA, 58; Princeton Univ, MA, 60, PhD(philos), 64. **CAREER** From instr to asst prof philos, Swarthmore Col, 62-66; asst prof, Princeton Univ, 66-68; assoc prof, 68-74, Prof Philos, Univ Mich, Ann Arbor, 74-, Am Coun Learned Soc Study fel, 65-66; Guggenheim Found fel, 74-75. **HONORS AND AWARDS** Franklin J Matchette Prize, Am Philos Asn, 75. **MEMBERSHIPS** Am Philos Asn; Philos Sci Asn. **RESEARCH** Philosophy of physics; philosophy of science; epistemology. **SELECTED PUBLICATIONS** Auth, Time, Space, And Philos - Ray,C/, Isis, Vol 0084, 1993; Quantum Nonlocality And Relativity - Aristotelian Soc Series - Maudlin,T/, British J For The Philos Of Sc, Vol 0045, 1994; Boltzmann,Ludwig - His Later Life And Philos, 1900-1906 - Book One - A Documentary Hist - Book 2 - The Philosopher - Blackmore,J/, British J For The Philos Of Sc, Vol 0047, 1996; In The Wake Of Chaos - Unpredictable Order In Dynamic-Systems - Kellert,Sh/, Philos Of Sci, Vol 0064, 1997. **CONTACT ADDRESS** Dept of Philos, Univ of Mich, Ann Arbor, MI, 48104.

SKLOOT, ROBERT
PERSONAL Born 07/27/1942, Brooklyn, NY **DISCIPLINE** THEATRE, DRAMA, JEWISH STUDIES **EDUCATION** Union Col, NY, AB, 63; Cornell Univ, MA, 65; Univ Minn, Minneapolis, PhD, 68. **CAREER** Prof theatre & drama & Jewish studies, Univ of Wis-Madison, 68-, Assoc Vice-Chancellor Acad Affairs, 96-, Dir Ctr Jewish Studies, 99-; Fulbright prof theatre, Hebrew Univ, Jerusalem, Israel, 80-81, Univ Austria, Vienna, 88, Cath Univ Valparaiso, Chile, 96. **RESEARCH** Holocaust drama; British, classical and American drama; directing. **SELECTED PUBLICATIONS** Ed, The Theatre of the Holocaust: Four Plays, Univ Wis Press, 82, vol 2, 99; auth, The Darkness We Carry: The Drama of the Holocaust, Univ Wis Press, 88. **CONTACT ADDRESS** Dept of Theatre & Drama, Univ of Wis, 821 University Ave, Madison, WI, 53706-1497. **EMAIL** skloot@mall.wisc.edu

SKOVER, DAVID
PERSONAL Born 12/04/1951, Racine, WI, s **DISCIPLINE** LAW **EDUCATION** Princeton Univ, AB 74; Yale Univ Sch of Law, JD, 78. **CAREER** Law Clerk, Judge Jon O. Newman, United States Court of Appeals, Newark NJ, 78-79; Trademark Atty, Levi-Strauss Co., 79-82; asst prof, 82-85, assoc prof, 85-90, prof, Univ Puget Sound Sch of Law, 90-94; Prof, Seattle Univ Sch of Law, 94-. **HONORS AND AWARDS** Consult, Advisory Comn on Inter-Governmental Relations, 88-90; Consult and Presenter, The Inquiring Mind Program, Wash Comn for the Humanities, 90-91; Consult and Presenter, Political Philosophy in Teaching Seminar, Nat Endowment for the Humanities, 91, 93. **MEMBERSHIPS** Am Asn of Law Schs. **RESEARCH** Constitutional law; mass media theory and free speech jurisprudence; law and sexuality. **SELECTED PUBLICATIONS** Coauth, Tactics of Legal Reasoning, Carolina Academic Press, 86; coauth, The Future of Liberal Legal Scholarship, 87 Mich Law Rev 601, 88; coauth, The First Amendment in the Age of Paratroopers, 68 Tex Law Rev 1087, 90; coauth, Paratexts, 44 Stanford Law Rev 509, 92; coauth, Pissing in the Snow: A Cultural Approach to the First Amendment, 45 Stanford Law Rev 783, 93; coauth, Commerce & Communications, 40 Texas Law Rev 697; 93; coauth, The Pornographic State, 107 Harvard Law Rev 1374, 94; coauth, The Death of Discourse, Westview Press/HarperCollins, 96; coauth, Speech & Power, The Nation, 97. **CONTACT ADDRESS** Seattle Univ Law Sch, 950 Broadway Plz, Tacoma, WA, 98402. **EMAIL** davidskover@seanet.com

SKRUPSKELIS, IGNAS KESTUTIS
PERSONAL Born 03/15/1938, Lithuania, m, 1964, 2 children **DISCIPLINE** PHILOSOPHY **EDUCATION** Fordham Univ, BS, 59; Univ Toronto, MA, 61, PhD (philos), 67. **CAREER** From instr to assoc prof, 64-77, Prof Philos, Univ SC, 77-, Co-ed, Works of William James, Harvard Univ, 75- **MEMBERSHIPS** Am Philos Asn; Asn Advan Baltic Studies; Soc Advan Am Philos. **RESEARCH** American philosophy; post-Kantian idealism; pragmatism. **SELECTED PUBLICATIONS** Auth, Submitting To Freedom - The Religious Vision Of James,William - Ramsey,B/, Int J For Philos Of Rel, Vol 0036, 1994; Jamess Conception Of Psychol As A Natural-Sci/, Hist Of The Human Scis, Vol 0008, 1995. **CONTACT ADDRESS** Dept of Philos, Univ of SC, Columbia, SC, 29208.

SKYRMS, BRIAN
PERSONAL Born 03/11/1938, Pittsburgh, PA **DISCIPLINE** PHILOSOPHY **EDUCATION** Lehigh Univ, AB, 60; Univ Pittsburgh, MA, 62, PhD(philos), 64. **CAREER** Asst prof philos, San Fernando Valley State Col, 64-65, Univ Del, 65-66; vis asst prof, Univ Mich, 66-67; asst prof, Univ Ill, Chicago, 67-68, assoc prof, 68-70, prof, 70-80; Prof Philos, Univ Calif, Irvine, 80-, Nat Sci Found fel, summers, 68, 69 & 80; vis prof, Univ Calif, Santa Barbara, 71, Univ Calif, Berkeley, 74-75 & 78-79, Univ NC, Chapel Hill, 77, Letrobe Univ, 77, Univ Queensland, 81. **MEMBERSHIPS** Philos Sci Asn; Am Philos Asn; Asn Symbolic Logic. **RESEARCH** Philosophy of science and language; epistemology. **SELECTED PUBLICATIONS** Auth, A Mistake In Dynamic Coherence Arguments - Discussion/, Philos Of Sci, Vol 0060, 1993; Darwin Meets The Logic Of Decision - Correlation In Evolutionary Game-Theory/, Philos Of Sci, Vol 0061, 1994; Rationality And Coordination - Bicchieri,C/, British J For The Philos Of Sci, Vol 0047, 1996. **CONTACT ADDRESS** Dept of Philos, Univ of Calif, Irvine, CA, 92717.

SLATE, PHILIP
DISCIPLINE EUROPEAN MISSIONS, COMMUNICATION, HISTORICAL MISSIOLOGY **EDUCATION** David Lipscomb Univ, BA, 57; Harding Grad Sch, MA, 61; Oxford Univ, England, 68-71, Fuller Theological Seminary, Dmiss, 76. **CAREER** Instr, Harding Grad Sch Rel, 72-93; prof, Missions and Homiletics; dean, 86-92; chm; prof, 93-. **MEMBERSHIPS** Mem, Am Soc Missiology; Evangelical Missiological Soc. **SELECTED PUBLICATIONS** Auth, Perspectives on Worldwide Evangelism, Resource Publ, 88; co-auth, Reaching Russia, ACU Press, 94; articles, Culture Concept and Hermeneutics: Quest to Identify the Permanent in Early Christianity. Encounter 53, 92; The Deceiving Nature of Adaptation in E-1 Situations, J Applied Missiology 3, 95; Two Features of Irenasus' Missiology. Missiology 23, 96; numerous articles. **CONTACT ADDRESS** Dept of Missions, Abilene Christian Univ, Abilene, TX, 79699-9000. **EMAIL** slate@bible.acu.edu

SLATER, PETER
PERSONAL Born 03/24/1934, Newcastle-upon-Tyne, England **DISCIPLINE** THEOLOGY **EDUCATION** McGill Univ, BA, 54; Queen's Col Cambridge, BA, 57, MA, 61; Harvard Univ, PhD, 64. **CAREER** Asst prof relig, Haverford Col, Pa, 64-70; assoc prof relig, Sir George Williams Univ, Montreal, 70-71; assoc to full prof relig, Carleton Univ, 71-82; prof theol, Wycliffe Col, 82-85; prof theol, Toronto Sch Theol Grad Fac, 82-, prof, Centre Relig Stud, 83-, dean divinity, Trinity Col, 85-90, PROF EMER SYSTEMATIC THEOL, TRINITY COL, TORONTO SCH THEOL, UNIV TORONTO; ADJ PROF GENERAL THEOL, SEMINARY NEW YORK 95-98. **HONORS AND AWARDS** Gold Medal Philos McGill, 54; Harvard Prize Fel, 57. **MEMBERSHIPS** Can Soc Stud Relig; Am Acad Relig; Soc Values Higher Educ; Am Theol Soc; N Am Paul Tillich Soc; Am Soc Stud Relig; Can Theol Soc. **SELECTED PUBLICATIONS** Auth, The Dynamics of Religion and Culture in Canada, 77; co-ed, Traditions in Contact and Change, 83; co-ed, Toronto Journal of Theology, 85-94. **CONTACT ADDRESS** General Theol Sem, 175 9th Ave, New York, NY, 10011-4977.

SLATTERY, KENNETH F.
PERSONAL Born 06/12/1921, Brooklyn, NY **DISCIPLINE** PHILOSOPHY **EDUCATION** Cath Univ Am, MA, 50, PhD, 52. **CAREER** Instr Greek & Ger, St Joseph's Col, NJ, 48-49; instr Philos, Cath Univ Am, 49-52; assoc prof, Niagara Univ, 52-54; dean students, Mary Immaculate Sem, 54-56; asst prof Philos, St John's Univ, NY, 56-61; dean grad sch & sch educ, Niagara Univ, 61-65, pres, 65-76; vpres Commun, St John's Univ, 76-79, acad vpres, St John's Univ, Staten Island Campus, 79-, mem bd dirs, Manresa Educ Corp, 79-; mem bd trustees, Cardinal Newman Col, St Louis, 79-, Molloy Col, Hempstead, NY, 81-. **HONORS AND AWARDS** LLD, St John's Univ, NY, 69; DH, Cath Univ PR, 77. **MEMBERSHIPS** Am Cath Philos Asn; Fel Cath Scholars. **RESEARCH** Philosophical psychology. **SELECTED PUBLICATIONS** Auth, The Necessity for God for a Complete Psychological Understanding of the Nature of Man, 50 & The Virtue of Temperance & Its Relation to the Emotions, 52, Cath Univ Am Press. **CONTACT ADDRESS** St. John's Univ, 8150 Utopia Pky, Jamaica, NY, 11439-0002.

SLAUGHTER, FRED L.
PERSONAL Born 03/13/1942, Santa Cruz, California, m **DISCIPLINE** LAW **EDUCATION** UCLA, BS 1964, MBA 1966; Columbia U, JD 1969. **CAREER** Practicing atty 1970-; School of Law, UCLA, asst dean, lecturer 1971-80; real est broker 1974-; assoc campus advocate 1971-72; spec asst to chnclr 1969-71. **MEMBERSHIPS** Mem LA Co, CA St Am Bar Asn; licensed to prac law before the US Supreme Ct, US Fed Cts, CA St Cts; life mem UCLA Alumni Assn.

SLAWSON, W. DAVID
DISCIPLINE ADMINISTRATIVE LAW **EDUCATION** Amherst Col, AB,53; Princeton Univ, MA,54; Harvard Univ, LLB,59. **CAREER** Torrey H. Webb prof;Univ Southern Calif; past asst coun, Presidential Comn on the Assassination of President Kennedy; gen coun, US Price Comn; private practice, Colo. **MEMBERSHIPS** Phi Beta Kappa; Sigma Xi; Order of the Coif; Chair, Section on Contracts, American Association of Law Schools (AALS), 1989; Member, Planning Committee, AALS Conference on the Teaching of Contracts, 1988. **RESEARCH** Administrative Law, Agency, Antitrust Law, Contracts, and Insurance. . **SELECTED PUBLICATIONS** Auth, Binding Promises: The Late 20th Century Reformation of Contract Law; The New Inflation: The Collapse of Free Markets & The New Meaning of Contract: The Transformation of Contract Law by Standard Forms. **CONTACT ADDRESS** School of Law, Univ Southern Calif, University Park Campus, Los Angeles, CA, 90089.

SLEIGH, ROBERT COLLINS
PERSONAL Born 11/30/1932, Marblehead, MA, m, 1953, 3 children **DISCIPLINE** PHILOSOPHY **EDUCATION** Dartmouth Col, BA, 54; Brown Univ, MA, 57, PhD, 63. **CAREER** From instr to assoc prof, Wayne State Univ, 58-69; prof, Univ of Mass, 69- ; vis prof, Univ of Mich, 73; Univ of Ariz, 84; Univ of Calif, 89; Univ of Notre Dame, 90; Amherst Col, 97; Harvard Univ, 97-98. **HONORS AND AWARDS** Fel, Ctr for Advan Study in the Behavioral Scis, 67-68; Inst for Advan Study, 82-83, 86-87; Am Coun of Learned Socs, 75-76, 67-68; NEH, 91-92. **MEMBERSHIPS** APA; AHA; Leibniz Soc of North Am. **RESEARCH** Early Modern Philos; Leibniz. **SELECTED PUBLICATIONS** On Quantifying into Epistemic Contexts, Nous I, 67; Restricted Range in Epistemic Logic, The Jour of Philos, 72; Truth and the Principle of Sufficient Reason in the Philosophy of Leibniz, Leibniz: Critical and Interpretive Essays, ed M. Hooker, 82; Leibniz on Malebranche on Causality, Central Themes in Early Modern Philos: Essays presented to J. Bennett, 90; Leibniz and Arnauld: A Commentary on their Correspondence, 90; Leibniz on Divine Foreknowledge, Faith and Philos, vol 11, 94; coauth, Determinism and Human Freedom, The Cambridge Hist of 17th Century Philos, ed V. Chappell, 98. **CONTACT ADDRESS** Dept of Philosophy, Univ of Massachusetts, Amherst, MA, 01003.

SLINGERLAND, DIXON
DISCIPLINE NEW TESTAMENT **EDUCATION** Tufts Univ, BA, 66; Lutheran Sch Theology Chicago, MDiv, 69; Union Theol Sem, PhD, 73. **CAREER** Tutor, Union Theol Sem, 70-72; pastor, St Jacobi Lutheran Ch, Brooklyn, 73-79; instr, Wagner col, 77-78; vis prof, Brite Div Sch, 85; PROF, HIRAM COL, 79-. **CONTACT ADDRESS** Dept of Relig Stud, Hiram Col, PO Box 67, Hiram, OH, 44234. **EMAIL** slingerlandh@hiram.edu

SLOBOGIN, CHRISTOPHER
DISCIPLINE LAW **EDUCATION** Princeton Univ, AB; Univ Va, JD, LLM. **CAREER** Stephen C. O' Connell ch, assoc dean for fac develop, aff prof psychiat, Univ Fla, 82-. **HONORS AND AWARDS** Alumni res scholar, 94-. **MEMBERSHIPS** Ch, Asn Amer Law Schools Criminal Justice Sect; past ch, AALS Sect on Law Mental Disability. **RESEARCH** Law & psychiatry, criminal law & procedure, evidence, professional responsibility, social science & law. **SELECTED PUBLICATIONS** Auth, Regulation of Police Investigation and Criminal Procedure: An Analysis of Cases and Concepts; coauth, Psychological Evaluations for the Court. **CONTACT ADDRESS** School of Law, Univ of Florida, PO Box 117625, Gainesville, FL, 32611-7625. **EMAIL** slobogin@law.ufl.edu

SLOCUM, ROBERT B.
PERSONAL Born 05/21/1952, Macon, GA, m, 1982, 3 children **DISCIPLINE** THEOLOGY **EDUCATION** Marquette Univ, PhD, 97 **CAREER** Church of the Holy Communion, Lake Geneva, rector; Marquette Univ, lectr, 97-. **MEMBERSHIPS** SSCS, SALT, AAUP **RESEARCH** Spirituality and theology; narrative theology; Anglican theology. **SELECTED PUBLICATIONS** Co-ed., Documents of witness : A History of the Episcopal Church, 1782-1985, NY: Church Hymnal Corp, 94; ed. Prophet of Justice, Prophet of Life: Essays on William Stringfellow, NY: Church Pub Inc, 97; auth, Christian Assurance in the Face of Death: Anglican Witnesses, in: Sewanee Theol Rev, 95; Justification': Stumbling Block for Anglican-Roman Catholic Unity?, St. Luke's Jour of Theol, 89; The Lessons of Experience and the Theology of William Porcher DeBose, Anglican Theol Rev, 97. **CONTACT ADDRESS** Dept of Theology, Marquette Univ, 1325 Madison St, Lake Geneva, WI, 53147. **EMAIL** rob_slocum@ecunet.org

SLOVENKO, RALPH
PERSONAL Born 11/04/1926, New Orleans, LA **DISCIPLINE** PSYCHIATRY **EDUCATION** Tulane Univ, BE, 48, LLB, 53, MA, 60, PhD(Psychiat, psycho-dynamics), 65. **CAREER** Law clerk, La Supreme Court, 53; prof law, Tulane Univ, 54-64, mem fac, psychiat, 60-65; prof psychiat & law, Menninger Found & Univ Kans, 65-67; assoc, Walter Hailey Law Firm, 67-69; Prof Law, Wayne State Univ, 69-, Ed, Am Lect Set Behav Sci & Law, Tulane Law Rev; consult, Group Advan Psychiat. **MEMBERSHIPS** Order of Coif; Am Psychol-Law Soc; assoc Am Acad Psychoanal; Southern Soc Philos & Psychol; Am Orthopsychiat Asn. **RESEARCH** Psychiatry and law; behavioral science and law. **SELECTED PUBLICATIONS** Auth, Psychotherapy, Confidentiality and Privileged Communication, 65 & ed, Sexual Behavior and the Law, 65, C C Thomas; auth, Security Rights, 66 & Handbook of Criminal Procedure, 67, Claitor's; co-ed, Motivations in Play, Games and Sports, C C Thomas, 67; auth, Psychiatry and Law, Little, 73; auth numerous journal articles; Psychiatry and Criminal Anlyability, Wiley, 95; Psychotherapy and Confidentiality, cc 98. **CONTACT ADDRESS** Law School, Wayne State Univ, 468 Ferry Mall, Detroit, MI, 48202-3698.

SLUSSER, MICHAEL
DISCIPLINE THEOLOGY **EDUCATION** Catholic Univ Belgium, STB 66; Univ Oxford, D. Phil 75. **CAREER** Univ St. Thomas MN, 68-81, 85-87; Catholic Univ, 81-85; Duquesne Univ, 87-. **MEMBERSHIPS** SBL; CTSA; NAPS; AIEP; CTS. **SELECTED PUBLICATIONS** Auth, St. Gregory Thaumaturgus: Life and Works, WA, Catholic U of Amer Press 98. **CONTACT ADDRESS** Dept of Theology, Duquesne Univ, Pittsburgh, PA, 15282. **EMAIL** slusser@duq.edu

SLY, DOROTHY
PERSONAL Born 02/02/1933, Canada, m, 1955, 5 children **DISCIPLINE** RELIGIOUS STUDIES **EDUCATION** McMaster Univ, PhD, 87. **CAREER** Assoc prof, Univ Windsor, 89-98. **RESEARCH** Hellenistic Judaism; Feminist studies. **SELECTED PUBLICATIONS** Auth, Philo's Alexandria, 95. **CONTACT ADDRESS** 6-460 Schley Pl, Qualicum Beach, BC, V9K 2M5. **EMAIL** ddsly@nanaimo.ark.com

SMALLS, O'NEAL
PERSONAL Born 09/07/1941, Myrtle Beach, South Carolina **DISCIPLINE** LAW **EDUCATION** Tuskegee Inst, BS 1964; Harvard Law Sch, JD 1967; Georgetown Univ, LLM 1975. **CAREER** Amer Univ, assoc prof 1969-76; Systems & Applied Sci Corp, bd of dirs, 1974-85; George Washington Univ Sch of Law, prof law 1976-79; American Univ, prof of law 1979-88; Univ of SC School of Law, professor, 1988-. **MEMBERSHIPS** Mem Harvard Law Sch Res Com 1966-67; asst dir Harvard Law Sch Summer Prog for Minority Students 1966; dir of admissions & chmn of Com Admissions & Scholarships Amer Univ 1970-74; mem DC, Natl, Amer Bar Assns; chmn bd dir Skyanchor Corp; exec bd DC Bapt Conv; Services Com & bd trustees Law Sch Admissions Coun Princeton 1972-76; adv com Leg Serv Plan Laborers' Dist coun of Washington DC 1973-75; bd dir Systems & Applied Sci Corp 1974-85; bd chmn, Frewood Foundation, 1987-; Freedoms Foundation, pres/chair of bd, Myrtle Beach, SC, currently. **SELECTED PUBLICATIONS** Articles "Class Actions Under Title VII" Amer Univ Law Review 1976; "The Path & The Promised Land" Amer Univ Law Review 1972; booklets "New Directions, An Urban Reclamation Program for the Dist of Columbia" July 1982; "Manhood Training An Introduction to Adulthood for Inner City Boys Ages 11-13" April 1985. **CONTACT ADDRESS** Professor of Law, Univ of South Carolina, Columbia, SC, 29208.

SMART, NINIAN
PERSONAL Born 05/06/1927, Cambridge, England, m, 1954, 4 children **DISCIPLINE** PHILOSOPHY, CLASSICS **EDUCATION** Oxford, BA, 51; MA, 53; B Philos, 54. **CAREER** Lectr, Univ Wales, 52-65; lectr, Univ London, 56-61; prof, Univ Birmingham, 61-67; prof, Univ Lancaster, 67-88; prof, Univ Calif, Santa Barbara, 77-98. **HONORS AND AWARDS** Univ Chicago, 68; Glasgow, 84; Stiring Univ, 86; Lancaster Univ, 96. **MEMBERSHIPS** Am Acad of Relig; Brit Asn for the Study of Religs. **RESEARCH** History of religion; comparative religion; Indian religion; Buddhism. **SELECTED PUBLICATIONS** Auth, Worldviews: Crosscultural Explorations of Human Beliefs, 95; The Dimensions of Religion: An Analysis of the World's Beliefs, 96; Reflections in the Mirrors of Religion, 97; The Buddha and Christ: Lights of Asia, 97; World Philosophies, 98. **CONTACT ADDRESS** Dept of Religious Studies, Univ of California, Santa Barbara, CA, 93106. **EMAIL** smart@humanitas.ucsb.edu

SMAW, ERIC
PERSONAL Born 01/22/1971, Washington, DC, s **DISCIPLINE** PHILOSOPHY; ETHICS; LAW **EDUCATION** Penn State Univ, BA, 96; Ohio Univ, MA, 98; Univ KY **CAREER** Logic instr **RESEARCH** Legal ethics; Intl law. **CONTACT ADDRESS** Philosophy Dept, 1415 Patterson Office Tower, Lexington, KY, 40506-0027.

SMILLOV, MARIN S.
PERSONAL Born 01/27/1963, Targovishte, Bulgaria, m, 1997, 1 child **DISCIPLINE** PHILOSOPHY **EDUCATION** Univ FL, PhD, 97. **CAREER** VIS PROF, UNIV CENTRAL FL, 96-; VIS LECT, UNIV FL, 98-. **MEMBERSHIPS** Am Philos Asn; FL Philos Asn. **RESEARCH** Epistemology; metaphysics; philos of mind; ethics; social and political philos. **CONTACT ADDRESS** G91h SW 80th Dr., Gainesville, FL, 32608. **EMAIL** msmillov@aol.com

SMIT, HANS
PERSONAL Born 08/13/1927, Amsterdam, Netherlands, m, 1954, 2 children **DISCIPLINE** LAW **EDUCATION** Univ Amsterdam, LLB, 46, JD, 49; Columbia Univ, AM, 53, LLB, 58. **CAREER** Attorney, The Hague, Netherlands, 49-56, Sullivan & Cromwell, 59-60; prof law, 60-78, Stanley H Fuld Prof Law, Columbia Univ, 78-, Reporter, US Comt on Int Rules of Judicial Procedure, 60-68; dir proj in int procedure & proj on Europ legal insts, Columbia Univ Summer Prog in Am Law, Leyden & Amsterdam, 62-; adv, US Deleg to UN Comn on Int Trade Law, 71-; vis prof int-nat com law, Univ Paris I, Sorbonne-Pantheon, 76-77; dir, Parker Sch Foreign & Comparative Lang, 80- **MEMBERSHIPS** Am Foreigh Law Asn; Int Bar Asn; Int Fiscal Asn; Neth Bar Asn. **RESEARCH** Civil Procedure; international law; international procedure. **SELECTED PUBLICATIONS** Auth, Rosenberg,Maurice - In-Memoriam/, Columbia Law Rev, Vol 0095, 1995. **CONTACT ADDRESS** 435 W 116th St, Box 4435, New York, NY, 10027-7201.

SMITH, BARDWELL L.
DISCIPLINE RELIGIOUS TRADITIONS OF ASIA **EDUCATION** Yale Univ, BA, BD, PhD. **CAREER** Religion, Carleton Univ. **SELECTED PUBLICATIONS** Auth, Ed, The City as a Sacred Complex, 87, Warlords, Artists; Commoners: Japan in the Sixteenth Century. **CONTACT ADDRESS** Carleton Col, 100 S College St., Northfield, MN, 55057-4016.

SMITH, BARRY
PERSONAL Born 06/04/1952, Bury, England **DISCIPLINE** MATHEMATICS & PHILOSOPHY **EDUCATION** Oxford Univ, BA, 73, MA, 77; Manchester Univ, PhD, 76. **CAREER** Res fel, Univ Sheffield, 76-79; lectr, Univ Manchester, 79-89; prof, int acad philos, liechtenstein, 89-93; prof, SUNY Buffalo, 93-; Res Sci, Nat Ctr geog infor & anal, 96-. **HONORS AND AWARDS** Alexander von Humboldt fel, 84-85. **MEMBERSHIPS** Amer Philos Soc **RESEARCH** Metaphysics; Austrian philosophy; Husserl. **SELECTED PUBLICATIONS** Ed, Philosophy and Political Change in Eastern Europe, Hegeler Inst, 93; auth, Austrian Philosophy: The Legacy of Franz Brentano, Open Court, 94; ed, European Philosophy and the American Academy, The Hegeler Inst, 94; coed, The Cambridge Companion to Husserl, Cambridge Univ Press, 95; auth, Formal Ontology, Common Sense, and Cognitive Science, Int Jour Human-Computer Studies, 95; auth, More Things in Heaven and Earth, Grazer Philos Studien, 95; Mereotopology: A Theory of Parts and Boundaries, Data and Knowledge Engineering, 96; On Substances, Accidents and Universals: In Defence of a Constituent Ontology, Philos Papers, 97. **CONTACT ADDRESS** Dept of Philosophy, SUNY-Buffalo, 607 Baldy Hall, Buffalo, NY, 14260-1010. **EMAIL** phismith@acsu.buffalo.edu

SMITH, CHARLES EDISON
DISCIPLINE LAW **EDUCATION** California Polytechnic, BS, 1965; Georgetown University, Washington, DC, JD, 1972; Duke University, LLM, 1983. **CAREER** US Patent and Trademark Office, Washington, DC, Patent Examiner, 1967-69; Xerox Corp, Patent Attorney, 1972-75; Bechtel Corp, Patent Attorney, 1975-78; Golden Gate University, Assistant Professor of Law, 1977-79; Con Edison, Consultant, 1987-; North Carolina Central University School of Law, Durham, NC, Professor, currently. **HONORS AND AWARDS** Fellowship Grant, Duke University, 1982-83; American Jurisprudence Award, Lawyers Cooperative Publishers. **MEMBERSHIPS** Arbitrator, American Bar Assn, 1979-, state reporter (NC), ABA Limited Partnership Laws, 1986-; member, Delta Theta Phi Law Fraternity, 1970-; commissioner, North Carolina Statutes Commission, 1987-; attorney volunteer, AIPLA Inventor Consulting Service, 1985-; state reporter (NC), ABA Limited Liability Company Act, 1993-. **CONTACT ADDRESS** Professor of Law, North Carolina Central Univ School of Law, 1512 S Alston Ave, Durham, NC, 27707.

SMITH, D. MOODY
PERSONAL Born 11/21/1931, Murfreesboro, TN, m, 1954, 4 children **DISCIPLINE** RELIGION/NEW TESTAMENT **EDUCATION** Davidson Coll, BA, 54; Duke Univ, BD, 57; Yale Univ, MA, 58, PhD, 61. **CAREER** Asst prof, New Testament, Meth Theol Sch, 60-65; assoc prof New Testament, 65-70, prof New Testament, 70-87, dir grad stud rel, 74-80, George Washington Ivey Prof New Testament, 87-, Div Sch, Duke Univ. **HONORS AND AWARDS** Lilly fel, 63-64; Guggenheim fel, 70-71; Asn Theol Schs fel, 77-78; res mem, Ctr Theol Inquiry, 90, 91; Scholar/Teacher of the Year, Duke Univ, 93; Dist Alumni, Duke Div Sch, 93. **MEMBERSHIPS** Soc Bib Lit; Studiorum Novum Testamentum Soc, Am Theol Soc, Ctr Theol Inquiry. **RESEARCH** New Testament hist, exegesis, theol; gospels and letters of John; hist New Testament crit. **SELECTED PUBLICATIONS** Auth, The Composition and Order of the Fourth Gospel, Yale Univ Press, 65; co-auth, Anatomy of the New Testament, Prentice- Hall, 69, 95; auth, Johannine Christianity, Univ SC Press, 84; auth, John Among the Gospels, Fortress, 92; auth, The Theology of the Gospel of John, Cambridge Univ Press, 95. **CONTACT ADDRESS** Duke Univ, Box 33 Divinity, Durham, NC, 27708. **EMAIL** dmsmith@mail.duke.edu

SMITH, DANIEL L.
DISCIPLINE LAW, LIBRARY SCIENCE **EDUCATION** Univ Iowa, BS (biochemistry), 80, BA (Russian), 89, MFA (Comp lit), 93, JD, 93, MA (Libr, Info Sci), 94. **CAREER** PUBLISHER, CANONYMOUS PRESS, 92-, REF LIBRN, CURATOR, CORNELL LAW LIBRARY, 97-; asst ed, Exchanges: A Journal of Translations, Univ Iowa, 89-93. **CONTACT ADDRESS** Law Sch Library, Cornell Univ, Myron Taylor Hall, Ithaca, NY, 14853-4901. **EMAIL** smith@canonymous.com

SMITH, DAVID H.
PERSONAL Born 04/28/1939, Evanston, IL, m, 1961, 3 children **DISCIPLINE** RELIGIOUS STUDIES **EDUCATION** Carleton Col, BA, 61; Yale Div Sch, BD, 64; Princeton Univ, PhD, 67. **CAREER** Asst prof, Rel Stud, 67-70, assoc prof, 70-79, Indiana Univ; sr res scholar, Joseph and Rose Kennedy Inst for Bioethics, Georgetown Univ, 73-74; prof rel Stud, Indiana Univ, 79- ;dir, Poynter Ctr for the Stud Ehtics and Am Inst, 82; Sem dir, Liberal Education and Moral Criticism, at Workshop on the Liberal Arts, funded by Lilly Endow, 85-94; subj matter expert, Chaplain Corps, US Navy, 85-86; Ch, Exec Comm, Assn Practical and Prof Ethics, 91- . **HONORS AND AWARDS** Natl Endow human fel, Summer 69; Cross-Disciplinary fel, Soc Rel in Higher Ed, 73-74; Lilly Endow open fel, 80-81; fel, Hastings Ctr, 74-86; Amoco disting tchg awd, 78; Student Alumni Coun outstanding fac awd, 86. **RESEARCH** Professional ethics; ethics and governance; theological ethics; teaching ethics. **SELECTED PUBLICATIONS** On Being Queasy, IRB: A Review of Human Subjects Research 2, 4, April 80, 6-7; Deciding for the Death of a Baby, in Marc D. Basson, ed, Rights and Responsibilities in Modern Medicine, New York, Alan R. Liss, Inc, 81, 49-55; The American Way of Hospice, with Judith A. Granbois, Hastings Center Report, 12, 2, April 82, 8-10; A Theological Context for the Relationship Between Patient and Physician, in Earl L. Shelp, ed, The Clinical Encounter, Dordrecht, D. Reidel Publ Co, 83, 289-301; Who Counts? Jour of Rel Ethics, 12, 2, Fall 84, 240-255; Ed, Respect and Care in Medical Ethics, Lanham, MD, Univ Press Am, 84; Medical Loyalty: Dimensions and Problems of a Rich Idea, in Earl L. Shelp, ed, Theology and Bioethics, Dordrecht: D. Reidel Publ Co, 85, 267-282; Our Religious Traditions and the treatment of Infants, in Thomas H. Murray and Arthur L. Caplan, eds, Which Babies Shall Live? Humanistic Dimensions of the Care of Imperilled newborns, Clifton, NJ, Humana Press, 85; Care of the Sick, Fidelity, Hospitality, Loyalty, in The Westminster Dictionary of Christian Ethics, Philadelphia, The Westminster Press, 86; The Limits of Narrative, in Joanne Trautmann Banks, ed, Literature and Medicine: Use and Abuse of Literary Co-Concepts in Medicine, Baltimore: Johns Hopkins UP, 86; The Moral Dimension to Teaching, in David D. Dill and Patricia K. Fullager, ed, The Knowledge Most Worth Having in Teacher Education, Proceedings of the Chancellor's Invitational Conference, Chapel Hill: Univ NC, 86; Health and Medicine in the Anglican Tradition: Conscience, Community and Compromise, New York: Crossroads Publ Co, 86; McCormick and Medicine, Rel Stud Rev, 13, 1, Jan 87, 42-44; Suffering, Medicine and Christian Theology, in Stephen E. Lammers and Allen Verhey, eds, On Moral Medicine: Theological Perspectives in Medical Ethics, Grand Rapids: William B. Eerdmans Publ Co, 87; On Paul Ramsey: A Covenant-Centered Ethic for Medicine, Second Opinion, 6, Nov 87, 107-127, Reprinted in Aleen Verhey and Stephen E. Lammers, eds, Theological Voices in Medical Ethics, Grand Rapids, William B. Eerdmans Publ Co, 93, 7-29; AIDS and Aid for Patient and Healer, with Robin Levin Penslar and Judith A. Granbois, rep submit to Task Force on AIDS Ethical/Legal Working Group, Pub Health Svc, US Dept Health and Human Svcs, Dec 2, 87; Teaching Ethics in a Professional Age, in Bruce A. Kimball, ed, Teaching Undergraduates: Essays from the Lilly Endowment Workshop on the Liberal Arts, New York: Prometheus Books, 88, 151-172; Wombs for Rent, Selves for Sale, Jour Contmep Hea Law and Policy, 4, Spring 88, 23-36; Using Human Fetal Tissue for Transplantation and Research: Selected Issues, in Report of the

Human Fetal Tissue Transplantation and Research Panal, 2, F1-F43, Bethesda MD, Dept Hea and Human Svcs, Natl Inst Hea, Dec, 88; Called to Profess: Religion and Secular Theories of Vocation, The Centennial Rev, 34, 2, Spring 90, 275-294; The Anglican Communion, in Bioethics Yearbook-Vol I: Theological Developments in Bioethics, 1988-90, Dordrecht, Boston, London: Kluwer Acad Publ, 91; Quality, Not Mercy: Some Reflections on Recent Work in Medical Ethics, Medical Human Rev, 5, 2, July 91, 9-18; Trustees and Health Care Priorities, Trustee, 44, 11, Nov 91, 16-17; The Episcopal Church and Assisted Reproduction, in The Episcopal Church as Moral Teacher: A Critical Study, Harrisburg, PA, Morehouse-Barlow, 92; Seeing and Knowing Dementia, in Dementia and Aging: Ethics, Values, and Policy Choices, Baltimore, The Johns Hopkins Univ Press, 92, 44-54; Moral Responsibilities of Trustees, Jour of Non-Profit Mgt, 2, 4, 92, 351-362; The Anglical Tradition, in Bioethics Yearbook-Vol 3, Theological Developments in Bioethics, 1992-94, Dordrecht, Boston, London, Kluwer, 97; Religion and the Use of Animals in Research: Some First Thoughts, Ethics and Behavior, 72, 97, 137 Entrusted: The Moral Responsibilities of Trustees, Bloomington, Indiana UP, 95; The Social Face of Death: Confronting Mortality in Paoli, Indiana, Bloomington, Poynter Ctr, 98; Paul Ramsey, Love and Killing, in Smith and Johnson, Love and Society; Suicide, with Seymour Perlin and Warren T. Reich, ed, Encycl of Bioethics, vol 4, New York: Macmillan Publ Co, and the Free Press, 1618-1627; The Abortion of Defective Fetuses: Some Moral Considerations, in Smith, ed, No Rush to Judgment; **CONTACT ADDRESS** Poynter Center, Indiana Univ, Bloomington, 618 E 3rd St, Bloomington, IN, 47405.

SMITH, DAVID R.
PERSONAL Born 09/27/1946, Loveland, OH, 1969 **DISCIPLINE** LAW **EDUCATION** Central State Univ, Wilberforce OH, BA, 1969; DePaul Univ Coll of Law, Chicago IL, JD, 1974. **CAREER** US Dept of Energy, asst chief counsel, 1972-83; Cole & Smith, partner, 1983-85; The MAXIMA Corp, corporate senior vp, gen counsel sec, 1985-; Reed, Smith, Shaw & McClay, counsel; Alexander, Gebhardt, Aponte & Marks, partner, currently. **MEMBERSHIPS** Alpha Phi Alpha Frat, 1969; Amer Bar Assn; Maryland Bar Assn; Natl Bar Assn; Illinois Bar Assn; admitted to practice: US Supreme Court; US Claims Court; Federal Trial Bars: Illinois; Maryland; Virginia; District of Columbia. **SELECTED PUBLICATIONS** Author: "Contracting with The Federal Government: 10 Key Areas," Chicago Bar Association, 1984; Small Business and Technology Devel Contract Mgmt Magazine; Sphinx Magazine, 1983; "Exploring The Energy Frontier," Natl Bar Assn, 1982. **CONTACT ADDRESS** Alexander, Gebhardt, Aponte & Marks, 8601 Georgia Ave, Silver Spring, MD, 20910.

SMITH, DAVID T.
DISCIPLINE LAW **EDUCATION** Yale Univ, BA; Boston Univ, JD. **CAREER** Prof, Univ Fla, 68-. **MEMBERSHIPS** Mass Bar; Amer Law Inst; Order of the Coif; Omicron Delta Kappa; Fla Blue Key; adv bd, HEIRS; Title Issues and Standards Comt, Fla Bar Real Property, Probate and Trust Law Sect. **RESEARCH** Property, estates and trusts, fiduciary administration, future interests. **SELECTED PUBLICATIONS** Auth, Florida Probate Code Manual; Florida Estates Pract Guide. **CONTACT ADDRESS** School of Law, Univ of Florida, PO Box 117625, Gainesville, FL, 32611-7625. **EMAIL** smith.dt@law.ufl.edu

SMITH, DENNIS E.
PERSONAL Born 12/01/1944, Conroe, TX, m, 1966, 1 child **DISCIPLINE** NEW TESTAMENT **EDUCATION** Abilene Chr Univ, BA, 67, MA, 69; Princeton Theol Sem, MDiv, 72; Harvard Div Sch, ThD, 80. **CAREER** Asst prof, Princeton Theol Sem, 79-81; asst prof, Oklahoma State Univ, 81-86; assoc prof, 86-97, prof, 97- , Phillips Theol Sem. **MEMBERSHIPS** Sos of Bibl Lit; Westor Inst. **RESEARCH** Ancient meal customs; social history of the early Christian world. **SELECTED PUBLICATIONS** Coauth, Many Tables: The Eucharist in the New Testament and Liturgy Today, SCM & Trinity Press Int, 90; ed, How Gospels Begin, v. 52 of Semeia, 90; auth, The Storyteller's Companion to the Bible, v.10: John, Abingdon, 96; auth, The Storyteller's Companion to the Bible, v.12: Acts, Abingdon, 99; auth, The Storyteller's Companion to the Bible, v.13: Women in the New Testament, Abingdon, 99. **CONTACT ADDRESS** Phillips Theol Sem, 816 S Evanston, Tulsa, OK, 74101. **EMAIL** demcsmith@aol.com

SMITH, EDWIN M.
DISCIPLINE INTERNATIONAL LAW **EDUCATION** Harvard Univ, AB,72; JD,76. **CAREER** Leon Benwell prof Law and Int Relations,Univ Southern Calif; past atty, National Oceanic Atmospheric Admin; past spec coun for policy, US Senator Daniel Patrick Moynihan; app by pres Clinton as a sci and policy adv, US Arms Control and Disarmament Agency. **MEMBERSHIPS** Coun For Relations; past VP, Amer Soc Int Law. **RESEARCH** International law; international relations theory; foreign relations law. **SELECTED PUBLICATIONS** Auth, The Endangered Species Act and Biological Conservation; Congressional Authorization of Nuclear First Use: Problems of Implementation; The United Nations in a New World Order & Understanding Dynamic Obligations: Arms Control Agreements. **CONTACT ADDRESS** School of Law, Univ Southern Calif, University Park Campus, Los Angeles, CA, 90089. **EMAIL** esmith@law.usc.edu.

SMITH, F. LAGARD
DISCIPLINE LAW AND MORALITY SEMINAR **EDUCATION** Willamette Univ, BS, 66; Willamette Univ Sch Law, JD, 68. **CAREER** Dep dist atty, Malheur County, 68-70; dist atty, 70-71; dir, OR State Bar, 71-72; prof. **MEMBERSHIPS** Mem, OR State Bar; Am Bar Assn. **SELECTED PUBLICATIONS** Auth, Criminal Law Color Book; The Narrated Bible; The Daily Bible; ACLU-The Devil's Advocate, Marron Publ, 96; numerous Christian bk(s). **CONTACT ADDRESS** Sch of Law, Pepperdine Univ, 24255 Pacific Coast Hwy, Malibu, CA, 90263.

SMITH, GEORGE P.
PERSONAL Born 09/01/1939, Wabash, IN, s **DISCIPLINE** LAW **EDUCATION** Indiana Univ, BS, 61, JD, 64; Columbia Univ, LLM, 75. **CAREER** Instr, Univ of Mich Law School, 65-66; legal adv, U.S. Dept of State, 66-67; vis asst prof, George Washington Univ Nat Law Ctr, 67; asst prof, State Univ of NY, 67-69; spec coun to the Gov of Ark, 69-71; assoc prof, Univ of Ark, 69-71; consult, Model Legis drafting proposals concerning artificial insemination in NY and Penn, 69, 76; consult, Ark Planning Comn, 69-71; mem, Ark Gov's Inland Waterway Comt, 69-71; mem, Ark Govs Spec Comt on Disposal of Toxic Substances, 70-71; spec coun, U.S. EPA, Wash, D.C., 71-74; adj prof, Georgetown Univ, 71-75; nat co-chairman, ABA Spec Comt on Environ Quality, 71-75; lectr, Cath Univ School of Law, Wash, D.C., 73-75; consult, Univ of Pittsburgh School of Engineering, 75-77; assoc prof, Univ of Pittsburgh, 75-77; consult, Interstate Comn on the Potomac River Basin, 75-82; adj prof, Univ of Pittsburgh, 76; spec coun for Environ Legis by courtesy, Athens, Greece, 77; vis prof, Univ of Conn, 77; prof, Cath Univ of Am, 77- ; disting. vis scholar, Inst of Ethics, Georgetown Univ, 77-81; contrib ed, U.S. Supreme Ct Doc Hist Proj, 78; occas lectr, Uniformed Servs, Univ of the Hea Scis, 79-86; occas lectr, Cath Univ of Am, 81-86; spec coun, House Comt on Sci and Tech, U.S. Congress, 81-87; regional admin, Jessup Int Moot Ct Competition, 82; disting. vis lectr and scholar, Univ of New South Wales, Australia, 82; mem, The President's Pvt Sector Survey on Cost Control, Air Force Task Force, 82-83; consult, The Heritage Found, 82-83; consult, New South Wales, Australia, Law Reform Comn, 82-88; vis prof, Univ of New South Wales, Australia, 84; found ed, The Jour of Contemp Hea Law and Policy, 84-94; mem, bd of advs, Huddleston-Brown Publ House, 85-89; mem bd of dirs, Inst for Law and Publ Hea Protection, 85-89; vis prof, Notre Dame Univ, 86; coun to to the Atty Gen of Ind, 87; vis prof, Univ of New South Wales, Australia, 87; mem Standing Comt on Curriculum and Res, Asn of Am Law Schools, 87-90; contribur, World Book Encycl, 88- ; assoc, Med Inst for Law Fac, Cleveland State Univ, 91; vis prof, Univ of Auckland, New Zealand, 91; vis prof, Univ of Sydney, Australia, 91; mem, ed bd of Int Jour of Med Practice and the Law, England, 91- ; vis prof, Univ of Victoria, BC, Canada, 92; vis prof, Dublin Univ, Ireland, 92; vis prof, Ind Univ, 92; vis prof, Queensland Univ, Australia, 93; fac adv, Cath Univ, Wash, D.C., 94; vis prof, Univ of Ottago, New Zealand, 94; fac adv, Hea Law Soc, 95; consult, Int Bioethics Comt, UNESCO Declaration on The Protection of The Human Genome, France, 95-97; mem, bd of dirs, Brooks Foun for Ethics and Human Values, Tex, 96-98; mem, bd of visitors, Ind Univ, 97- ; vis prof, Ind Univ, 97; vis prof, Univ of Sydney, Australia, 98. **HONORS AND AWARDS** Ark Traveler Citation by Gov W. Rockefeller for distinguished accomplishments in pub serv, 70; Cert of Merit for Distinguished Serv, U.S. EPA, 74; Australian-Am Fulbright Found Award, 84; Distinguished Alumni Medallion and Citation for Achievements in the Legal Profession, Ind Univ, 85; Citation of Honor, Inst of Advan Study, Ind Univ, 85; Dedicatory Issue of 2 Jour of Contemporary Hea Law and Policy 1, 86; Estab of the George P. Smith, II, Distinguished Professorship and Ch of Law and Legal Res, Ind Univ, 86; inducted, The Most Venerable Order of The Hospital of St John of Jerusalem, for contribs to Med Sci, NY, 88; A 25th Anniversary of Professional Serv Tribute: 135 CONGRESSIONAL RECORD E3418, A Bibliographic Tribute, 6 Jour of Contemp Hea Law and Policy 483, 90; Raymond C. O'Brien, The World of Law, Science and Medicine According to George P. Smith, II, (a bio-bibliographic retrospective), 8 Jour of Contemp Hea Law and Policy 163, 92; elected as Law School Graduating Class Marshall, Cath Univ Law School, 96; Estab of the annual George P. Smith Award for Outstanding Service by the bd of eds of The Jour of Contemp Hea Law and Policy, 97; LLD, honoris causa, Ind Univ, 98; incl as a subject of biog record in Who's Who in the World, Who's Who in America, Who's Who in American Law, Who's Who in the East, Who's Who in American Education, Directory of American Scholars, Contemporary Authors, The Writer's Directory, International Authors and Writers Who's Who., Admitted to U.S. Supreme Ct; Indiana, District of Columbia **MEMBERSHIPS** Am Law Inst; Am Law and Economics Asn; Soc of Ind Pioneers. **RESEARCH** Health Law; Bioethics; Land Use. **SELECTED PUBLICATIONS** Selected Decisions, Legal Notes, And Commentaries Before The United States Foreign Claims Settlement Commission, United States Department Of State, 66; Restricting the Concept of Free Seas: Modern Maritime Law Re-Evaluated, 80; Genetics, Ethics and the Law, 81; Ethic, Legal and Social Challenges to a Brave New World, 82; Medical-Legal Aspects of Cryonics: Prospects for Immortality, 83; Final Choices: Autonomy in Health Care Decisions, 89; The New Biology: Law, Ethics and Biotechnology, 89; Assisted Noncoital Reproduction: A Comparative Analysis, 8 Boston Univ Int Law Jour 21, 90; Stop, in the Name of Love, 19 Anglo-Am Law Rev 55, 90; Re-thinking Euthanasia and Death with Dignity: A Transnational Challenge, 12 Adelaide Law Jour 480, 90; Toward an International Standard of Scientific Inquiry, 2 Health Matrix, Jour of Law-Med 167, 92; Market and Non Market Mechanisms for Procuring Human and Cadaveric Organs: When the Price is Right, 1 Med Law Int 17, 93; Bioethics and the Law: Medical, Socio-Legal and Philosophical Directions for a Brave New World, 93; Biological Determinism or Genetic Discrimination, 3 Proceedings, 10th World Congress on Med Law 164, 94; Restructuring the Principle of Medical Futility, 11 Jour of Palliative Care 9, 95; Legal and Healthcare Ethics for the Elderly, 96; Harnessing The Human Genome Through Legislative Constraint, 5 European Jour of Hea Law 53, 98; Family Values and the New Society: Dilemmas of the 21st Century, 98. **CONTACT ADDRESS** School of Law, Catholic Univ of America, Washington, DC, 20064.

SMITH, HAROLD TELIAFERRO, JR.
PERSONAL Born 04/10/1947, Miami, FL, d **DISCIPLINE** LAW **EDUCATION** Florida A&M University, BS, math, 1968; University of Miami, JD, 1973. **CAREER** Dade County Public Defenders, Attorney; Dade County Attorneys Office, Long and Smith PA, H T Smith PA, president, currently. **HONORS AND AWARDS** Best Lawyers in America, 1995-96; National Conference of Black Lawyers, Service Award, 1991; Miami Herald, Charles Whited Spirit of Excellence Award, 1993. **MEMBERSHIPS** National Bar Association, president, 1994-; Miami Partners for Progress, co-chair, 1993-; Inroads/Miami, secretary, 1993-; Community Partnership for the Homeless, board, 1993-94; Kappa Alpha Psi Fraternity, 1983-; Miami Dade Branch, NAACP, executive committee, 1990-; Boyscott Miami Campaign, co-spokesperson, 1990-93; Coalition fo a Free South Africa, chair, 1985-90. **SELECTED PUBLICATIONS** Wrote numerous articles for publication and gave hundreds of speeches and seminars. **CONTACT ADDRESS** H T Smith, P A, 1017 NW 9th Ct, Miami, FL, 33136.

SMITH, HEMAN BERNARD
PERSONAL Born 08/20/1929, Alexandria, LA, m, 1952 **DISCIPLINE** LAW **EDUCATION** Univ of Maryland (Far East Div), attended, 1958-60; Univ of Pacific, McGeorge School of Law, JD, 1971. **CAREER** Smith, Hanna, de Bruin & Yee, Sacto CA, partner, sr attorney, 1971-78; Smith & Yee, Sacto CA, partner, 1978-84; SMITH & ASSOC, SACTO CA, SR ATTORNEY, 1984-; UNIV OF NORTHERN CALIFORNIA, L P SCHOOL OF LAW, SACTO CA, EXEC DEAN, 1988-. **MEMBERSHIPS** Bd mem, Amer Red Cross, Sacto CA, 1980-87; mem, Minority Steering Comm California Youth Authority, 1985-87, Sacto Urban League, currently, Sacto NAACP, currently; pres, Zeta Beta Lambda, 1987-88, Wiley Man Bar Assn, 1988-. **CONTACT ADDRESS** Smith & Associates, 6700 Freeport Blvd, Ste 101, Sacramento, CA, 95822.

SMITH, J. CLAY, JR.
PERSONAL Born 04/15/1942, Omaha, NE, m **DISCIPLINE** LAW **EDUCATION** Creighton Univ Omaha, NE, AB 1964; Howard Law Sch Washington, DC, JD 1967; George Washington Law Sch Washington, DC, LLM, 1970, SJD 1977. **CAREER** US Army Judge Advocates Gen Corp, capt lyr 1967-71; Arent Fox Kintner Plotkin & Kahn Washington, DC, assc 1971-74; Fed Commctn Cmsn, deputy chf cable TV bureau 1974-76; Fed Communications Commission, assc gen cnsl 1976-77; Equal Emplymnt Opprtnty Cmsn, us cmsnr apptd by Jimmy Carter 1977-82, actng chrmn apptd by Ronald W Reagan 1981-82; HOWARD UNIV SCH OF LAW, PROF OF LAW 1982-, dean & professor of law, 1986-88. **HONORS AND AWARDS** First Governor of Boys State (NE) and Nation (1959); First African American elected as natl pres, Fed Bar Assn 1980-81; founder juris art movement Washington Bar Assn 1978; Am Bar Assn 1982-; order of the coif hon George Washington Law Sch 1978; Ollie May Cooper Award, 1986; The C Francis Stradford Award 1986; Outstanding Alumni Achievement Awards from Howard University, 1981, Creighton University, 1989, George Washington University, 1990. **MEMBERSHIPS** NE Bar Assoc 1967; mem Howard Law Sch Alumni Assc 1967-; Dist of Columbia Bar 1968; pres bd dir Washington Bar Assc 1970; US Supreme Court 1973; advsr pres Natl Bar Assc 1973-; mem NAACP 1975-; mem Urban League 1975-; natl pres mem Fed Bar Assc 1979; utlty spec Pblc Serv Cmsn 1982-84; editorial board ABA Compleat Lawyer 1984-87; Advisory Committee, DC Bar Exam; bd mem Natl Lawyers Club; planning committee for Task Force on Black Males, AM Psyh Assn 1986-90; mem Am Law Inst 1986-88; chair Natl Bar Assn Comm on History of Blk Lawyers; legal counsel for the Elderly Policy Bd 1986-88. **SELECTED PUBLICATIONS** Publications, Fed Bar Assn Natl Pres Messages, Fed Bar News, CIVICS LEAP, Law Reason & Creativity, Mgng Multi-ethnic Multi-racial Workforce Criminal, Chronic Alcoholism -- Lack of Mens Rea -- A Dfns Pblc Intoxication 13 Howard Law Journal, An Investment in a New Century, Wash Afro Am; The Black Bar Assn & Civil Rights; A Black Lawyer's Response to the Fairmont Papers; Memoriam: Clarence Clyde Ferguson, Jr,

Harvard Law Rev; Forgotten Hero: Charles H Houston, Harvard Law Rev; Justice & Jurisprudence & The Black Lawyer, Notre Dame Law Rev; Emancipation: The Making of The Black Lawyer, 1844-1944; National Book Award of the Natl Conference of Black Political Scientist, 1995; Rebels in Law: Voices in History of Black Women Lawyers, 1998; Served on the transition team of President Clinton & Vice Pres Gore, 1992. **CONTACT ADDRESS** Sch of Law, Howard Univ, 2900 Van Ness St NW, Washington, DC, 20008.

SMITH, JANET E.
DISCIPLINE BIOETHICS, PHILOSOPHY OF GOD **EDUCATION** Grinnell Col, BA; Univ NC, MA; Univ Toronto, PhD. **CAREER** Dept Philos, Univ Dallas **SELECTED PUBLICATIONS** Auth, Natural Law and Personalism in Veritatis Splendor, Veritatis Splendor: American Responses, Sheed and Ward, 95; Pope John Paul II, Feminists, Women, and the Church, Cath Dossier 1:4, 95; The Christian View of Sex: A Time for Apologetics, Not Apologies, The Family in America, Review of Turning Point, Corssroad Publ, 95; Homiletic and Pastoral Rev, 96; The Pre-Eminence of Autonomy in Bioethics, Human Lives: Critical Essays on Consequentialist Bioethics, McMillan Press, 97; Old Stuff, New Stuff, Dossier, 97; Rights, the Person and Conscience in the Catechism, Dossier, 97. **CONTACT ADDRESS** Dept of Philos, Univ Dallas, 1845 E Northgate Dr, Irving, TX, 75062.

SMITH, JERALDINE WILLIAMS
PERSONAL Born 01/14/1946, Tampa, FL, m **DISCIPLINE** LAW **EDUCATION** Univ of FL, BS Journalism 1967; Atlanta Univ, MBA 1970; FL State Law School, JD 1981. **CAREER** Freedom Savings, bank mgr 1973-75; Digital Equip Corp, admin mgr 1975-77; FL Dept of Ins, lawyer 1983-. **HONORS AND AWARDS** William Randolph Hearst Natl Newspaper Awards Winner 1967; Businesswoman of the Year Iota Phi Lambda 1971. **MEMBERSHIPS** Mem Amer Bar Assoc, FL Bar Assoc, Natl Newspaper Publ Assoc, FL Press Assoc. **SELECTED PUBLICATIONS** Capital Outlook Weekly Newspaper, publ 1983-. **CONTACT ADDRESS** Capitol Outlook Newspaper, PO Box 11335, Tallahassee, FL, 32302.

SMITH, JOHN EDWIN
PERSONAL Born 05/27/1921, Brooklyn, NY, m, 1951, 2 children **DISCIPLINE** PHILOSOPHY **EDUCATION** Columbia Univ, BA, 42, PhD, 48; Union Theol Sem, MDiv, 45. **CAREER** Instr philos and relig, Vasar Col, 45-46; from instr and asst prof to prof philos, 46-72, Barnard Col, chemn dept, 61-64; Clark Prof Philos, Yale Univ, 72-91, Clark Prof Emer, 91- . **HONORS AND AWARDS** Herbert W. Schneider Award for contributions to American Thought over an entire career, 90; Founder's Medal, MSA, 96; named Honorary Alumnus, Harvard Div Sch, 60. **MEMBERSHIPS** APA; Metaphysical Soc Am; Charles S. Peirce Soc; Hegel Soc Am. **RESEARCH** Metaphysics; philosophy of religion; American philosophy. **SELECTED PUBLICATIONS** Auth, Themes in American Philosophy, Harper, 70; auth, The Analogy of Experience, Harper, 73; auth, Purpose and Thought: The Meaning of Pragmatism, Yale, 78; auth, America's Philosophical Vision, Chicago, 92; auth, Jonathan Edwards: Puritan, Preacher, Philosopher, Notre Dame, 92; auth, Quasi-Religions, St Martin's, 95; auth, Reason, Experience, and God: John E. Smith in Dialogue, Fordham, 97. **CONTACT ADDRESS** Dept of Philosophy, Yale Univ, PO Box 201562, New Haven, CT, 06520-1562. **EMAIL** john.smith@yale.edu

SMITH, JONATHON ZITTELL
PERSONAL Born 11/21/1938, New York, NY, m, 1965 **DISCIPLINE** HISTORY OF RELIGION, HELLENISTIC RELIGIONS **EDUCATION** Haverford Col, BA, 60; Yale Univ, PhD(hist relig), 69. **CAREER** Instr relig, Dartmouth Col, 65-66; actg asst prof, Univ Calif, Santa Barbara, 66-68; asst prof, 68-73, William Benton prof relig & human sci, 74-82, dean col, 77-82, Robert O Anderson Distinguished Serv Prof Humanities, Univ Chicago, 82-, Co-ed, Hist Relig, 68-81. **MEMBERSHIPS** Soc Relig Higher Educ; Soc Bibl Lit; Am Acad Relig; Soc Study Relig. **RESEARCH** Hellenistic religions; anthropology of religion; method and theory of religion. **SELECTED PUBLICATIONS** Auth, Map is not Territory: Studies in the History of Religions, E J Brill, 78; Imagining Religion: From Babylon to Jonestown, Univ Chicago, 82; Nothing Human Is Alien To Me: Polygenesis And Human-Diversity As Characterizations Of Enlightenment Universalism In Early Anthropological Discourse, Religion, Vol 26, 96; A Matter Of Class: An Examination Of The Relationship Of Classification And Typology To Religious Thought--Taxonomies Of Religion, Harvard Theological Rev, Vol 89, 96. **CONTACT ADDRESS** Univ of Chicago, 1116 E 59th St, Chicago, IL, 60637.

SMITH, KATHRYN
PERSONAL Born 08/20/1954, Orange, CA, m, 1974, 2 children **DISCIPLINE** RELIGION **EDUCATION** Claremont Grad Univ, PhD, 97. **CAREER** Adj prof, Univ Washington, 99- . **HONORS AND AWARDS** Claremont tuition grants, 94-96. **MEMBERSHIPS** Soc of Bibl Lit. **RESEARCH** New Testament; Synoptic Gospels; early Jewish groups; early Jewish Christianity. **CONTACT ADDRESS** 6908 Pala Mesa Dr, Oak Park, CA, 91301. **EMAIL** ksills@qnet.com

SMITH, KELLY C.
PERSONAL Born 01/18/1964, Atlanta, GA, m, 1985, 2 children **DISCIPLINE** PHILOSOPHY **EDUCATION** Duke Univ, MS, 92, PhD, 94. **CAREER** Vis asst prof, Ga State Univ, 93-94; asst prof, Col NJ, 94-98; asst prof, Clemson Univ, 98-. **MEMBERSHIPS** Am Philos Asn; Philos Sci Asn; Int Soc Hist, Philos, & Soc Studies Biol; Am Asn Advan Sci; Nat Ctr Sci Educ. **RESEARCH** Philosophy of science; philosophy of biology; bioethics; genetics; evolution. **SELECTED PUBLICATIONS** Auth, Equivocal Nations of Accuracy and Genetic Screening of the General Population, Mt Sinai Jour Med, 98; coauth, The Extended Replicator, Biol & Philos, 96; coauth, Sober on Brandon on Screening-Off and the Levels of Selection, Philos Sci, 94; auth, The Effects of Temperature and Daylength on the Rosa Polyphenism in the Buckeye Butterfly Precis Coenia (Nymphalidae), Jour Res Lepidoptera, 93; auth, Neo-rationalism Vs. Neo-Darwinism: Integrating Development and Evolution, Biol & Philos, 93; auth, Marketing Structuralism: Reflections on the Process Structuralist Critique of Neo-Darwinism, Rivista di Biologia/Biol Forum, 93; auth, The New Problem of Genetics: A Response to Gifford, Biol & Philos, 92. **CONTACT ADDRESS** Dept of Philosophy and Religion, Clemson Univ, 101 Hardin Hall, Clemson, SC, 29634-1508. **EMAIL** kcs@clemson.edu

SMITH, LUTHER EDWARD, JR.
PERSONAL Born 05/29/1947, St. Louis, MO, m **DISCIPLINE** THEOLOGY **EDUCATION** WA Univ, AB 1965-69; Eden Theological Sem, MDiv 1969-72; St Louis Univ, PhD 1973-79. **CAREER** E St Louis Welfare Rgts Org, coord 1970-72; Educ for Blk Urban Mnstrs, exec coord 1972-79; Lane Tabernacle CME Church, asst pstr 1972-79; Black Church Ldrs Prog St Louis Univ, prog coord 1975-79; Candler Sch of Theology Emory Univ, prof of Church and Comm. **HONORS AND AWARDS** Distg srv awards St Louis and Mid St Louis Cty Jaycees 1975; member of Honor Society International Society of Theta Phi 1987; member, Omicron Delta Kappa 1991; Inducted into the Martin Luther King, Jr Collegium of Scholars, Morehouse College. **MEMBERSHIPS** Bd chmn Northside Team Ministries 1973-79; 1st vice pres MO Assoc Soc Welfare St Louis Div 1973-79; prog coord Metropolitan Ministerial Alliance of St Louis 1975-79, Urban Churches in Community Dev Prog 1978-79; bd mem Urban Training Org of Atlanta 1980-; bd mem Inst for World Evangelism 1982-, Eden Theological Sem; Families First 1992. **SELECTED PUBLICATIONS** Co-author, actor: "What's Black," televised KFTC, 1970, "Earth Day," televised PBS, 1970; author: "Howard Thurman, the Mystic as Prophet," 1992; author, Intimacy & Mission: Intentional Community as Crucible for Radical Discipleship. **CONTACT ADDRESS** Candler Sch of Theol, Emory Univ, Atlanta, GA, 30322.

SMITH, LYNN C.
DISCIPLINE LAW **EDUCATION** Calgary Univ, BA, 67; Univ British Columbia, LLB, 73. **CAREER** Dean, 91-; adj prof, 91-. **HONORS AND AWARDS** Dir, Women's Legal Edu Action Fund; dir, Nat Judicial Inst. **MEMBERSHIPS** Law Soc. **RESEARCH** Constitutional Law, civil litigation; evidence. **SELECTED PUBLICATIONS** Auth, Have the Equality Rights Made Any Difference?, Univ Toronto, 94; Beverly McLachlin, Greenwood, 96; co-auth, The Equality Rights, Wilson & Lafleur Ltee, 96. **CONTACT ADDRESS** Fac of Law, Univ British Columbia, 1822 East Mall, Vancouver, BC, V6T 1Z1. **EMAIL** lsmith@law.ubc.ca

SMITH, MARK STRATTON
PERSONAL Born 12/06/1955, Paris, France, m, 1983, 3 children **DISCIPLINE** THEOLOGY **EDUCATION** John Hopkins Univ, BA, 75; Catholic Univ of Am, MA, 79; Harvard Div Sch, MTS, 80; Hebrew Univ, vis res, 83-84; Yale Univ, PhD, 85. **CAREER** Albertus Magnus Col, inst, 81-82; Yale Univ, inst, 82-83; Ecole Biblique et Archaeologique Francaise, inst, 83-84; Univ of St Thomas Saint Paul Sem, asst prof, 84-86; Yale Univ, ass prof, 86-93; Univ of Penn, lectr, 94-95, 98-99; Hebrew Univ, Lady Davis vis prof, 97; Saint Joseph's Univ, assoc prof, prof, 93-. **HONORS AND AWARDS** Mary Cady Tew Prize, Mitchell Dahood Memorial Prize, Mellon Fell, Morse Fell, Dorot Dead Sea Scrolls Fel. **MEMBERSHIPS** CBA, OTC, SBL. **SELECTED PUBLICATIONS** Auth, Psalms: The Divine Journey, NY / Mahwah, NJ: Paulist Press, 87; The Early History of God: Yahweh and the Other Deities in Ancient Israel, San Fran/NY: Harper and Row, 90; auth, The Laments of Jeremiah and Their Context: A Literary and Redactional Study of Jeremiah 11-20, Society of Biblical Lit Monograph, Atlanta GA: Scholars, 90; auth, The Origins and Development of the Waw-Consecutive: Northwest Semitic Evidence From Ugarit to Qumran, Harvard Semitic Studies, Atlanta GA, Scholars Press, 91; auth, The Ugaritic Baal Cycle: vol 1, Introduction with Text, Translation and Commentary of KTU 1.1-1.2 Vetus Testamentum Supplements, Leiden: Brill, 94; auth, The Pilgrimage Pattern in Exodus, with Contributions by E. M. Bloch-Smith, Jour for the Soc of OT Supplements, Sheffield: Sheffield Acad Press, 97; ed., Probative Pontificating in Ugaritic and Biblical Studies: Collected Essays, by M. H. Pope, Munster: Ugarit-Verlag, 94; coauth, Qumran Cave 4Q XIV: Parabiblical Texts, Part 2, Discoveries in the Judaean Desert, Oxford: Clarendon, 95; auth, The Son of Man in Ugaritic, Catholic Bibl Quart, 83; auth, The Psalms as a Book for Pilgrims, Interpretation, 92; auth, Myth and Myth-making in Ugaritic and Israelite Literatures, Ugarit and the Bible: Proceedings of the International Symposium on Ugarit and the Bible, Manchester 92, Munster: Ugarit-Verlag, 94; auth, The Death of Dying and Rising Gods in the Biblical World: An Update, with Special Reference to Baal in the Baal Cycle, in: Scandinavian Jour of the OT, 99. **CONTACT ADDRESS** Dept of Theology, Saint Joseph's Univ, 5600 City Line Ave, Philadelphia, PA, 19131. **EMAIL** msmith@sju.edu

SMITH, PAMELA A.
PERSONAL Born 10/22/1947, New York, NY **DISCIPLINE** THEOLOGY **EDUCATION** Villanova Univ, MA, 71; St. Charles Borromeo Univ, MA, 83; Duquesne Univ, PhD, 95. **CAREER** Assoc dean, 96-. **MEMBERSHIPS** Col Theol Soc; Cath Theol Soc of Am; Am Acad of Relig; Soc of Christian Ethics. **RESEARCH** Environmental ethics; Creation theology; Lay spirituality. **SELECTED PUBLICATIONS** Auth, What Are They Saying About Environmental Ethics?, 97; Days of Dust and Ashes: Hope-filled Lenten Reflections, 97; Woman Gifts: Biblical Models for Forming Church, 94; Life After Waster: Mystagogia for Everyone, 93; "Sitting Still with Mark on a Non-Sick Day," 99; "The Ecospirituality of Alice Walker: Green Lap, Brown Embrace, Blue Body," 98; "Toward an Ecological Model of the Church," 98; "The Ecotheology of Annie Dillard: A Study in Ambivalence," 95. **CONTACT ADDRESS** SS Cyril & Methodius Seminary, 3535 Indian Tr, Orchard Lake, MI, 48324-0515. **EMAIL** au669@detroit.freenet.org

SMITH, PAUL
PERSONAL Born 09/20/1935, South Bend, IN, m **DISCIPLINE** THEOLOGY **EDUCATION** Talladega Clge, AB 1957; Hartford Sem, MDiv 1960; Eden Theological Sem, DMin 1977. **CAREER** WA Univ, assc vice chancellor 1974-78; Morehouse Coll, vice pres 1978-79; Columbia Theological Sem, adjunct prof 1979-; CANDLER SCHOOL OF THEOLOGY, ADJUNCT PROF 1979-; Hillside Presb Church, pastor. **HONORS AND AWARDS** NEH Recepient 1982; publ Unity, Diversity, Inclusiveness 1985; book J Knox Press Theology in a Computerized World 1985-86. **MEMBERSHIPS** Trustee Presby Schl of Christian Educ 1981-; consult Howard Thurman Educ Trust 1982; bd mem Child Srv Family Cnslng 1983-; Metro Fair Housing Srv Inc 1981-; Ldrshp Atlanta 1981; mem Council Atlanta Presb; former mem State Adv Comm US Civil Rights Comm 1977-1983. **CONTACT ADDRESS** Hillside Presb Church, 1879 Columbia Dr, Decatur, GA, 30032.

SMITH, QUENTIN
DISCIPLINE METAPHYSICS **EDUCATION** Boston Col, PhD. **CAREER** Prof, W Mich Univ. **RESEARCH** Philosophy of religion, philosophy of language. **SELECTED PUBLICATIONS** Coauth, Time, Change and Freedom: The New Theory of Time, Yale Univ Press; Theism, Atheism and Big Bang Cosmology, Oxford Univ Press; Language and Time,Oxford Univ Press; Auth, The Felt Meanings of the World, Purdue Univ Press; coauth, Uncreated Universe, Oxford Univ Press. **CONTACT ADDRESS** Kalamazoo, MI, 49008. **EMAIL** smithq@wmich.edu

SMITH, RANDALL BRIAN
PERSONAL Born 07/31/1959, Upper St. Clair, PA, s **DISCIPLINE** MEDIEVAL PHILOSOPHY; MEDIEVAL THEOLOGY **EDUCATION** Cornell Col, BA, 81; Univ Dallas, MA, 87; Univ Notre Dame, MMS, 91; PhD, 98. **CAREER** Post-Doctoral Res Assoc, Univ Notre Dame, 98-99. **HONORS AND AWARDS** Bradley Fel; Strake Found Grant. **MEMBERSHIPS** Amer Philos Assoc **RESEARCH** Thomas Aquinas; Medieval Philosophy & Theology; Natural Law; History of Biblical Exegesis. **CONTACT ADDRESS** Dept of Theology, Univ Notre Dame, Notre Dame, IN, 46556. **EMAIL** rsmith.11@nd.edu

SMITH, ROBERT HARRY
DISCIPLINE NEW TESTAMENT **EDUCATION** Concordia Sem, BA, MDiv, STM, ThD. **CAREER** Assoc prof, Concordia Sem; dean, Christ Sem-Seminex; prof, 83. **HONORS AND AWARDS** GTU Core Doctoral Fac. **MEMBERSHIPS** Memb, Bd of Dir(s), Berkeley Emergency Food Proj. **SELECTED PUBLICATIONS** Ed, Preaching Helps, Currents in Theology and Mission; auth, Easter Gospels: The Resurrection of Jesus According to the Four Evangelists, 83; Hebrews in The Augsburg Commentary Series, 84; Matthew in The Augsburg Commentary Series, 89; Easter: Proclamation 4, 92; Holy Week: Proclamations 5, 93. **CONTACT ADDRESS** Dept of New Testament, Pacific Lutheran Theol Sem, 2770 Marin Ave, Berkeley, CA, 94708-1597. **EMAIL** duensmith@aol.com

SMITH, ROBERT HOUSTON
PERSONAL Born 02/13/1931, McAlester, OK, m, 1969, 1 child **DISCIPLINE** RELIGION **EDUCATION** Univ Tulsa, BA, 52; Yale Univ, BD, 55, PhD(New Testament), 60. **CAREER** From instr to prof relig, 60-72, chmn humanities div lib studies prog, 68-69, Fox Prof Relig, Col Wooster, 72-, Chmn Dept Relig, 81-, Yale Two Bros fel, Am Sch Orient Res, Jerusalem, 58-59; mem staff, Univ Pa Mus archaeol exped, El Jib, Gibeon, 59, univ archaeol exped, Tell es-Saidiyeh, Jordan, 64;

dir, Wooster exped, Pella, Jordan, 65-; lectr Digging up the Past ser on Educ Exchange, NBC-TV, 68; Nat Endowment for Humanities grant, 79- & Nat Geog Soc grant, 79- **HONORS AND AWARDS** Christian Res Found Prize, 60. **MEMBERSHIPS** Soc Bibl Lit; Am Orient Soc; Am Schs Orient Res; Archaeol Inst Am. **RESEARCH** Biblical studies; art and archaeology; business and professional ethics. **SELECTED PUBLICATIONS** Auth, Excavations in the Cemetery at Khirbet Kufin, Palestine, Colt Archaeol Inst, 62; Pella of the Decapolis, Col Wooster, 73; New directions for ethical codes, Asn & Soc Manager, 74; coauth, Atomic absorption for the archaeologist, J Field Archaeol, 76; Inclusions in ancient ceramics, Archaeometry, 76; Patches of Godlight: The Pattern of Thought of C S Lewis, Univ Ga Press, 81; Pella in Jordan, Report on the Seasons of 1979-81, Australian Nat Gallery, Canberra, 82; Bloom-Of-Youth--A Labeled Syro-Palestinian Unguent Jar, J Of Hellenic Studies, Vol 112, 92. **CONTACT ADDRESS** Col of Wooster, Wooster, OH, 44691.

SMITH, ROBIN
DISCIPLINE PHILOSOPHY **EDUCATION** Univ Chattanooga, BA, 68; Claremont Grad Sch, PhD, 74. **CAREER** Prof & dept head, Tex A&M Univ 94-. **HONORS AND AWARDS** Franklin J. Matchette Found Conf Grant, 91; NEH Fel for Col Teachers, 92-93. **MEMBERSHIPS** Sec, KSU Chap, AAUP, 91-94; APA Central Div Prog Comt, 88 and 94; sec/Treas, APA Central Div, 96-. **RESEARCH** Logic, philosophy of language, modern philosophy, medieval philosophy. **SELECTED PUBLICATIONS** Auth, Aristotle, Topics I, VIII, and Selections, Clarendon Aristotle Series, Oxford UUP, 97; chap 2, Logic, in The Cambridge Companion to Aristotle, Cambridge UP, 95 & Aristotle's Regress Argument, in Studies on the History of Logic, de Gruyter, 96; rev, The Origins of Aristotelian Science, Can Philos Reviews 13, 93. **CONTACT ADDRESS** Dept of Philosophy, Texas A&M Univ, College Station, TX, 77843-4237. **EMAIL** rasmith@tamu.edu

SMITH, STANLEY G.
PERSONAL Born 07/21/1940, Brooklyn, NY, m **DISCIPLINE** LAW **EDUCATION** Seton Hall U, JD 1970; Rutgers U, BA Actg **CAREER** Urb Dev Res Inc, pres; Newark Hsng Dev & Rehab Corp, pres, chief exec ofcr 1980-; City Newark NJ, asst corp cncl 1972; Fed Prog Newark Hsng Dev Corp, att; Fidelity Union & Trust Co, fed asst, code enfor, fin analyst 1968-70; RCA, 1964-68; Seton Hall Univ Sch of Law, prof 1972-; Lofton Lester & Smith, att law prtnr 1985. **HONORS AND AWARDS** On dean's list Rutgers Univ 1961-62; adjunct prof Seton Hall Univ 1972-; St Schlrshp (4 yrs) Rutgers Univ 1957; Hon Soc Seton Hall Law Sch 1967; Hon Schlrshp NJ Bell Elks Club. **MEMBERSHIPS** Mem Nat Bar Assn; concerned legal asso mem, bd dirs Nghbrhd Hlth Serv Corp 1972; bd dirs Voice Nwspr 1971-72; vice pres Phi Sigma Delta 1960; member, New Jersey State Bar Assn, 1990-91. **CONTACT ADDRESS** Smith & Forbes, 1032 South Ave, Plainfield, NJ, 07062.

SMITH, STEVEN G.
DISCIPLINE HISTORY OF WESTERN PHILOSOPHY AND ABRAHAMIC RELIGIOUS THOUGHT, PHILOSOPHY O **EDUCATION** Fla State Univ, BA, 73; Vanderbilt Univ, MA, 78; Duke Univ, PhD, 80. **CAREER** Dept Philos, Millsaps Col **SELECTED PUBLICATIONS** Auth, The Argument to the Other: Reason Beyond Thought in Karl Barth and Emmanuel Levinas, 83; The Concept of the Spiritual: An Essay in First Philosophy, 88 & Gender Thinking, 92. **CONTACT ADDRESS** Dept of Philosophy, Millsaps Col, 1701 N State St, Jackson, MS, 39210. **EMAIL** smithsg@okra.millsaps.edu

SMITH, TERRY
DISCIPLINE CIVIL PROCEDURE, EMPLOYMENT SECURITY, VOTING RIGHTS AND POLITICAL PARTICIPA **EDUCATION** Brown Univ, AB, 86; NY Univ Sch Law, JD, 89. **CAREER** Law clk, US Court of Appeals, Sixth Circuit, 89-90; assoc, Kirkland & Ellis, 90-93; assoc prof, 93-. **SELECTED PUBLICATIONS** Auth, Rediscovering the Sovereignty of the People: The Case for Senate Districts, 75 NC Law Rev 1, 96. **CONTACT ADDRESS** Law Sch, Fordham Univ, 113 W 60th St, New York, NY, 10023. **EMAIL** tsmith@mail.lawnet.fordham.edu

SMITH, W. ALAN
PERSONAL Born 01/24/1949, Cleveland, TN, m, 1971, 2 children **DISCIPLINE** THEOLOGY; RELIGIOUS EDUCATION **EDUCATION** FL State Univ, BA, 72, additional grad study, 72-73; The Divinity School, Vanderbilt Univ, MDiv, 76, DMin, 83; additional grad study, School of Theology, Univ of the South, 83; School of Theology at Claremont, CA, PhD, 91. **CAREER** Pastor, First C. C. (Disciples of Christ), Greenville, KY, 76-79; Pastor, Fairhope Christian Church (Disciples of Christ), Fairhope, AL, 79-84; Assoc Minister, First Christian Church (Disciples of Christ), Pomona, CA, 84-87; asst prof relig, 87-95, assoc prof relig, 95-97, PROF RELIG, 97-, ASST DEAN FOR ACADEMIC AFFAIRS, FL SOUTHERN COL, 98-. **HONORS AND AWARDS** Phi Eta Sigma Lover of Wisdom Award, FSC, 92; Panhellenic Teacher of the Year Award, FSC, 93; Grant recipient, Jessie Ball du Post summer seminars, 96; Fac/staff Volunteer of the Year Award, FSC, 96. **MEMBERSHIPS** Amer Academy Relig; Soc Biblical Lit; Assoc Profs and Researchers in Relig Ed; Relig Ed Assoc; Disciples Assoc for The Academic Discussion of Christian Education; United Methodist Assoc for the Academic Study of Christian Education. **RESEARCH** Theology; religious ed; hermeneutical theory; Biblical studies; congregational studies; children in worship; youth ministry; Native Amer religions and philos. **SELECTED PUBLICATIONS** Auth, Children Belong in Worship: A Guide to the Children's Sermon, St Louis: CBP Press (Chalice Press), 84; Youth in the Local Congregation in Disciple Youth in the Church, St Louis: Christian Board of Pub, 85; Church Membership Curriculum, Called to Be Disciples: Worshiping, Witnessing, Serving, 4 vols, with cassette tape, St Louis: Christian Board of Pub, 88; Six articles in Harper's Encyclopedia of Religious Education, San Francisco: Harper & Row, 90; contrib, Discerning the Call: Advancing the Quality of Ordained Leadership, ed, John M. Imbler and Linda Plengemeier, St Louis: Chalice Press, 92; Intersubjectivity and Community: Some Implications from Gadamer's Philosophy for Religious Education, Relig Ed 88, no 3, summer 93; Naaman and Elisha: Healing, Wholeness, and the Task of Religious Education, Relig Ed 89, no 2, spring 94; A Cherokee Way of Knowing: Can Native American Spirituality Impact Religious Education?, Relig Ed 90, no 2, spring 95. **CONTACT ADDRESS** Florida So Col, 111 Lake Hollongsworth Dr., Lakeland, FL, 33801-5698. **EMAIL** wsmith@flsouthern.edu

SMITH, WALLACE CHARLES
PERSONAL Born 11/06/1948, Philadelphia, Pennsylvania, m **DISCIPLINE** THEOLOGY **EDUCATION** Villanova U, BA 1970; Eastern Bapt Sem, MDiv 1974; Eastern Bapt Sem, DMin 1979. **CAREER** Eastern Bapt Sem, dir alumni affairs & asst dir field educ 1979-; Calvary Bapt Church, pastor; Prog Natl Bapt, home mission bd, 1979; Shiloh Baptist Church, pastor, 1991-. **MEMBERSHIPS** Exec bd Chester Br NAACP 1974-; pres Chester Clergy Assn 1977-79; pres Chester Community Improvement Project 1979-. **CONTACT ADDRESS** Pastor, Shiloh Baptist Church, 1500 9th St, NW, Washington, VT, 20001.

SMITH, WILLIAM A.
PERSONAL Born 12/12/1929, Newburgh, NY, m, 1958, 5 children **DISCIPLINE** PHILOSOPHY **EDUCATION** Gregorian Univ, Rome, PhD, 53; St John's Univ, PhD, 67. **CAREER** Instr, Col of New Rochelle, 56-57; from instr to prof, Seton Hall Univ, 58- . **HONORS AND AWARDS** McQuald Medal, 88. **RESEARCH** Ethics; American philosophy; philosophy of death. **SELECTED PUBLICATIONS** Auth, Ethical Reflections, Simon & Schuster, 97; auth, Readings in Ethics, 3d ed, Kendall Hunt, 98. **CONTACT ADDRESS** Dept of Philosophy, Seton Hall Univ, 400 S Orange Ave, South Orange, NJ, 07079. **EMAIL** smithwia@shu.edu

SMITH, YOLANDA YVETTE
PERSONAL Born 10/01/1957, San Antonio, TX, s **DISCIPLINE** THEOLOGY **EDUCATION** Claremont School Theology, PhD, 98. **CAREER** Minister, Evangelism and Discipleship, First Institutional Baptist Church, 83-87 & 90-93; Co-Dir, Youth Discipleship Project, Admin Allen J. Moore Multicultural Resource and Research Center, 97-98, Claremont School of Theology; vis asst prof, Christian Rel Ed, Iliff School of Theology, 99-. **HONORS AND AWARDS** Pres Award for Acad Excellence, Claremont School for Theology, 98; Bishop Charles Golden Scholarship, Claremont School of Theology, 97; Willis and Dorothy Fisher Scholarship to a PhD Student Who Shows Promise as Teacher of Religion and Theological Studies, Claremont School of Theology, 97; Fund for Theological Education Black Doctoral Scholar Fel, 94-95, 95-96, 96-97; Amer Baptist Churches, USA Doctoral Grant Recipient, 94-95. **MEMBERSHIPS** Religious Ed Asn; Asn of Professors and Res in Religious Ed; Amer Acad of Religion/Soc of Biblical Lit; Asn of Pan African Doctoral Scholars; Natl Black Grad Student Asn; Natl Asn for Female Exec. **RESEARCH** Christian education from an African Amer Perspective; the use of cultural resources to inform content and process of Christian Ed. **SELECTED PUBLICATIONS** Ed, Resources for Sacred Teaching, Allen J Moore Multicultural Resource and Research Center, 95; art, Sister to Sister: Women Sharing Christ One with Another, Woman to Woman: Approaches to Witness and Outreach, USA Natl Ministries, 96; coauth, Olivia Pearl Stokes: A Living Testimony of Faith, John Knox Press, 97. **CONTACT ADDRESS** Iliff Sch of Theol, 2201 S. University Blvd, Denver, CO, 80210. **EMAIL** ysmith@Iliff.edu

SMITHBURN, JOHN ERIC
PERSONAL Born 11/21/1944, Noblesville, IN, 1 child **DISCIPLINE** LAW **EDUCATION** IN Univ, BS, 66, MA, 69, JD, 73. **CAREER** Assoc prof law, 78-82, Prof Law, Notre Dame Law Sch, 82-, Fac, Ind Judicial Ctr, 77-, Nat Judicial Col, 78, Nat Inst Trial Advocacy, 79- & Nat Col Juvenile Justice, 79. **HONORS AND AWARDS** Tchg Serv Award, Nat Judicial Col, 82. **RESEARCH** Family law; evidence; juvenile law **SELECTED PUBLICATIONS** Auth, Sentencing in Indiana: Appellate review of the trial court's discretion, Valparaiso Law Rev, winter 78; Perceived perjury as a factor in criminal sentencing, Res Gestae, 10/79; Review of Bellow and Moulton, The Lawyering Process: Materials for Clinical Instruction in Advocacy, Ariz Law J, No 1, 1980; coauth, Effective assistance of counsel: In quest of a uniform standard of review, Wake Forest Law Rev, 8/81; auth, Review of Nolan, Trial Practice: Cases and Materials, Univ Calif Los Angeles Law Rev, Vol 28, No 5; Judicial Discretion, Nat Judicial Col, 81, successor ed, 91; co-ed, Lizzie Borden: A Case Book of Family and Crime in the 1890s, Tichenor Inc, 81; auth, Criminal Trial Advocacy, NITA, 83, 2nd ed, 85; Indiana Family Law, vols 14-15, West, 91; Family Law: Problems and Documents, Aspen, 97. **CONTACT ADDRESS** Law Sch, Univ of Notre Dame, Notre Dame, IN, 46556. **EMAIL** smithburn.1@nd.edu

SMITHERMAN, CAROLE
PERSONAL m **DISCIPLINE** LAW **EDUCATION** Spelman College, BA, political science; Miles Law School, JD, 1979. **CAREER** Miles Law School, professor, 1982-; State of Alabama, circuit court judge, 1991; private practice, attorney, currently. **HONORS AND AWARDS** Recipient of numerous honors and awards for public service. **SELECTED PUBLICATIONS** First African-American woman deputy district attorney, State of Alabama, 1982; first appointed woman judge, City of Birmingham, 1986; first appointed African-American woman circuit court judge, 1991. **CONTACT ADDRESS** Law Office of Rodger & Carole Smitherman, 1919 Morris Ave, Suite 1550, Birmingham, AL, 35203.

SMURL, JAMES FREDERICK
PERSONAL Born 08/20/1934, Wilkes-Barre, PA, m, 1967, 4 children **DISCIPLINE** PHILOSOPHY, THEOLOGY **EDUCATION** St Mary's Univ, Md, BA, 55; Gregorian Univ, STL, 59; Cath Univ Am, STD, 63. **CAREER** Instr theol, Marywood Col, 59-61; asst prof, St Pius X Sem, Pa, 64-67; asst prof humanities & relig, Okla State Univ, 68-70, assoc prof, 70-73; assoc prof relig studies & chmn dept, 73-80, Prof Social & Comp Relig Ethics, Ind Univ, Indianapolis, 80-, Vis scholar, Kennedy Ctr Bioethics, 78-; vis prof, Ind Univ, Bloomington, 79; adj prof nursing, med genetics, Ind Univ, Indianapolis, 80-; Lilly open fac fel, 81. **MEMBERSHIPS** Am Acad Relig; Soc Christian Ethics; Soc Values Higher Educ. **RESEARCH** Thomistic ethics; social and comparative religious ethics; distributive justice in American culture. **SELECTED PUBLICATIONS** Auth, To Generate New Will, Cimarron Rev, 6/68; Willingness: Key To Freedom, J Thought, 69; Religious Ethics, Prentice-Hall, 72; Cross-cultural comparisons in ethics, J Relig Ethics, 76; Eligibility for legal aid: Whom to help when unable to help all, Int Law Rev, 79; Distributing the burden fairly: Ethics and national health policy, Man & Med, 80; Making ethical decisions systematically, Nursing Life, 82; Christian Ethics And Political--Economy In North-America, J Of Church And State, Vol 0038, 1996; What Does The Lord Require--How American Christians Think About Justice, J Of Church And State, Vol 35, 93. **CONTACT ADDRESS** Dept Relig, Studies Ind Univ, 1100 W Michigan St, Indianapolis, IN, 46202-2880.

SMYERS, KAREN A.
PERSONAL Born 10/31/1954, Annapolis, MD, d **DISCIPLINE** RELIGION **EDUCATION** Smith Col, BA, 76; Princeton Univ, MA, 89, PhD, 93. **CAREER** Lectr, Princeton Univ, 92; asst dir, prof anthrop, EAGLE Prog, Japan, 93; asst prof Wesleyan Univ, 93-. **HONORS AND AWARDS** Nat Rsrc Fel, 83-84; Coll Women's Asoc of Japan fel, 84-85; Princeton Univ Fel, 86-87, 87-88, 88-89, 91-92; Fulbright-Hays Diss Fel, 89-90; Japan Found Diss Fel, 90-91; A W Mellon Post-Enrollment Fel, 92; Fac Proj Grant, Wesleyan Univ, 94, 98; Pedag Develop Grant, Wesleyan Univ, 95, 96; Japan Soc for the Prom of Sci Postdoc Fel, 97-98; Japanese Ministry of Ed Grant, 97-98., Cum laude, Smith Col, 76. **MEMBERSHIPS** Am Anthrop Asoc; Am Acad of Rel; Asoc of Asian Stud; C G Jung Found for Anal Psychol; Conn Asoc for Jungian Psychol. **RESEARCH** Anthropology of religion; religions of Japan, Jungian thought. **SELECTED PUBLICATIONS** Auth, "The Japanese Altar," in Dictionary of Art, Macmillan, 96; "My Own Inari: Personalization of the Deity in Inari Worship," Japanese Jrnl of Relig Stud, 96; "Encountering the Fox in Contemporary Japan: Thoughts of an American Anthropologist," in Etudes sur les Cultes Populaires de Japon, 98; Inari Pilgrimage, Japanese Jrnl of Relig Stud, 97; "The Fox and the Jewel: Shared and Private Meanings in Japanese Inari Worship," Univ Hawaii, forthcoming **CONTACT ADDRESS** Dept of Religion, Wesleyan Univ, Middletown, CT, 06459. **EMAIL** ksmyers@wesleyan.edu

SMYTHE, THOMAS W.
PERSONAL Born 02/03/1941, Buffalo, NY, m, 1969, 1 child **DISCIPLINE** PHILOSOPHY **EDUCATION** Univ Mich, PhD, 71; Univ Calif, MA, 65; State Univ NY, BA, 63. **CAREER** Vis instr, NC Cent Univ, 96-97; vis asst prof, NC State Univ, 94-96; adj asst prof, Fayetteville State Univ, 92-94. **MEMBERSHIPS** Am Philos Asn; Triangle Ethics Discussion Group; Soc Christian Philos. **RESEARCH** Self-knowledge; problems of consciousness; philosophy of religion. **SELECTED PUBLICATIONS** Auth, The Reliability of Premise and Conclusion Indicators, Inquiry: Critical Thinking Across the Disciplines, Spring, 97; auth, Fawkes on Indicator Words, Inquiry: Critical Thinking Across the Disciplines, Fall, 96; coauth, Simplicity and Theology, Relig Studies, June, 96; coauth, Swinburne's Argument for Dualism, Faith & Philos, Jan, 94. **CONTACT ADDRESS** 213 Chesley Lane, Chapel Hill, NC, 27514. **EMAIL** twsmythe@email.unc.edu

SNEED, JOSEPH DONALD
PERSONAL Born 09/23/1938, Durant, OK, 1 child **DISCIPLINE** PHILOSOPHY OF SCIENCE **EDUCATION** Rice Univ, BS, 60; Univ Ill, MS, 62; Stanford Univ, PhD(philos), 64. **CAREER** Prof philos, Stanford Univ, 66-73; policy analyst, SRI Int, Menlo Park, Calif, 73-74; prof philos, Univ Munich, Ger, 74-76, Univ Calif, Santa Cruz, 76-77, Tech Univ Eindhoven, Netherlands, 77-78 & State Univ NY Albany, 78-80; Prof Humanities, Colo Sch Mines, 80-, Vis prof, Univ Uppsala, Sweden, 69 & Heidelberg Univ, Ger, 76. **MEMBERSHIPS** Am Philos Asn. **RESEARCH** Logical structure of empirical theories; decision theory; distributive justice. **SELECTED PUBLICATIONS** Auth, Quantum mechanics and classical probability theory, Synthese, 20: 34-64; The Logical Structure of Mathematical Physics, Reidel, Dordrecht, Holland, 71; co-ed, Restructuring the Federal System: Approaches to Accountability in Post-Categorical Programs, Crane-Russak, 75; auth, John Rawls and the liberal theory of society, Erkenntnis, 4/76; coauth, Generalized net structures for empirical theories, Part I, Studia Logics, Vol XXXVI, No 3; Patrick Suppes' contribution to the foundations of physics, In: Profile of Contemporary Philosophers: Patrick Suppes, Reidel, Dordrecht, Holland, 78; auth, A utilitarian framework for policy analysis in food and food-related foreign aid, In: Food Policy: US Responsibility in the Life and Death Choices, Free Press, 78; Theoritization and invariance principles, In: The Logic and Epistemology of Scientific Change, North-Halland, 79. **CONTACT ADDRESS** Humanities & Soc Sci Dept, Colorado Sch of Mines, 1500 Illinois St, Golden, CO, 80401-1887. **EMAIL** jsneed@mines.edu

SNEIDERMAN, BARNEY
DISCIPLINE LAW **EDUCATION** Trinity Col, BA, 59; Univ Conn, LLB, 68; Univ NY, LLM, 67. **CAREER** Prof. **RESEARCH** Criminal law; issues in law and biomedical ethics; issues in crime and punishment; the limits of law. **SELECTED PUBLICATIONS** Auth, Just Say No to the War on Drugs, Manitoba Law, 96; Euthanasia in the Netherlands, 96; co-auth, Canadian Medical Law: An Introduction for Physicians and Other Health Care Professionals, 96. **CONTACT ADDRESS** Fac of Law, Univ Manitoba, Robson Hall, Winnipeg, MB, R3T 2N2. **EMAIL** drewnia@cc.umanitoba.ca

SNODGRASS, KLYNE RYLAND
PERSONAL Born 12/28/1944, Kingsport, TN, m, 1966, 2 children **DISCIPLINE** BIBLICAL STUDIES **EDUCATION** Columbia Bible Col, BA, 66; Trinity Evangel Divinity Sch, MDiv, 69; Univ St Andrews, Scotland, DPhil, 73. **CAREER** Lectr, bibl studies, Georgetown Col, 73-74; asst prof, 74-78, assoc prof bibl lit, N Park Theol Sem, 78-84, prof, 84-89, dean of faculty, North Park Theol Sem, 88-93, Paul W. Brandel Prof of New Testament Studies, 89-; ed, Ex Auditu, consulting ed, NIV Application Commentary, trans analysis, New Living Translation. **HONORS AND AWARDS** Recipient of Asn of Theological Schools grant for sabbatical research, 81; Honorary Alumnus of North Park Col for 94; Recipient of Pew Evangelical Scholars Program grant for 95-96; Listed in Who's Who in Am Education, Who's Who in Biblical Studies and Archaeology, and Who's Who in Religion. **MEMBERSHIPS** Soc Bibl Lit; Inst Bibl Res, ex sec, 89-93, pres, 93-95; Chicago Soc Bibl Research, ex sec, 82-86, vice pres, 89-90, pres, 90-91; Studiorum Novi Testamenti Societas. **RESEARCH** The parables of Jesus; the semitic background of the New Testament; Pauline studies. **SELECTED PUBLICATIONS** Auth, Western Non-Interpolations, J Bibl Lit, 73; The Parable of the Wicked Husbandmen: Is the Gospel of Thomas Version the Original, New Testament Studies, 75; Liberty or Legality?, The Pauline Dilemma, 75, Exegesis and Preaching: The Principles and Practice of Exegesis, 76 & Paul and Women, 76, Covenant Quart; I Peter 11.1-10: Its Formation and Literary Affirmities, New Testament Studies, 78; Streams of Tradition Emerging from Isaiah 40: 1-5 and Their Adaptation in the New Testament, J Study New Testament, Vol VIII, 80; The Parable of the Wicked Tenants, Tubingen: J. C. B. Mohr (Paul Siebeck), 83; A Biblical and Theological Basis for Women in Ministry: An Occasional Paper, Chicago: Covenant Pubs, 87; Between Two Truths: Living with Biblical Tensions, Grand Rapids: Zondervan Pub House, 90; Divorce and Remarriage: An Occasional Paper, Chicago: Covenant Pubs, 92; Ephesians in The NIV Application Commentary, Grand Rapids: Zondervan Pub House, 96; and numerous articles in : Journal of Biblical Literature, New Testament Studies, Covenant Companion, Seminary Review: North Park Theological Seminary, The Covenant Quarterly, Daughters of Sarah, Journal for the Study of the New Testament, New Testament Backgrounds: A Sheffield Reader, Women, Authority and the Bible, Christianity Today, The Best in Theology, The Pauline Writings, SBL Seminar Papers, Treasures New and Old: Contributions to Matthean Studies, Baker Encylopedia of the Bible, The Second Century, Mercer Dictionary of the Bible, Perspectives on John: Method and Interpretation in the Fourth Gospel, New Testament Criticism and Interpretation, The Right Doctrine From the Wrong Texts?, Biblical Research, Dictionary of Jesus and the Gospels, Chiasmus in the New Testament, Interpretation, Gospel Interpretation: Narritive-Critical and Social-scientific Approaches, Holman Bible Handbook, A Dictionary of Biblical Tradition in English Literature, Perspectives in Religious Studies, Gospel in Paul: Studies on Corinthians, Galations and Romans for Richard N. Longenecker, Theology, News and Notes. **CONTACT ADDRESS** North Park Theol Sem, 3225 W Foster Ave, Chicago, IL, 60625-4810. **EMAIL** ksnodgr@northpark.edu

SNOEYENBOS, MILTON
DISCIPLINE PHILOSOPHY OF ART, ORGANIZATIONAL AND BUSINESS ETHICS, INFORMAL LOGIC, PHIL **EDUCATION** Univ Minn, PhD, 75. **CAREER** Assoc prof, Ga State Univ. **HONORS AND AWARDS** Several teaching awards. **SELECTED PUBLICATIONS** Coed, Business Ethics; author of over sixty articles, primarily in business ethics and philosophy of art. **CONTACT ADDRESS** Georgia State Univ, Atlanta, GA, 30303.

SNOOK, LEE E.
DISCIPLINE SYSTEMATIC THEOLOGY **EDUCATION** Gettysburg Col, BA; Lutheran Theol Sem, MDiv, 56; Union Theol Sem, STM, 67, PhD, 70. **CAREER** Instr, United Theol Col; vis prof, Univ Zimbabwe, 87-89, 92-93; asst prof, 70; prof, 77-. **HONORS AND AWARDS** Sr fel, Inst Advan Stud Rel, Univ Chicago, 84., Sr pastor, chaplain, Cornell Univ, 62-70; pastor, Good Shepherd Evangel Lutheran Church, 59-62; St Luke Evangel Lutheran Church, 55-59. **MEMBERSHIPS** Mem, ALC task force. **SELECTED PUBLICATIONS** Auth, The Anonymous Christ, Jesus as Savior in Modern Theology, 86; Preaching on National Holidays, 76; O God...Pay Attention: A Journal for Lent, 70. **CONTACT ADDRESS** Dept of Systematic Theology, Luther Sem, 2481 Como Ave, St. Paul, MN, 55108. **EMAIL** lsnook@luthersem.edu

SNYDER, LEE DANIEL
PERSONAL Born 06/04/1933, Waterbury, CT, m, 1961, 2 children **DISCIPLINE** CHURCH HISTORY **EDUCATION** Williams Col, AB, 55; Harvard Univ, AM, 56, PhD(Europ hist), 66; Union Theol Sem, BD, 61. **CAREER** Asst prof hist, Ithaca Col, 63-64 & Ohio Wesleyan Univ, 64-69; assoc prof hist, 69-80, PROF SOC SCI, NEW COL, UNIV S FLA, 80-, DIR MEDIEVAL-RENAISSANCE STUDIES, 77-, Vis prof, Methodist Theol Sch Ohio, 68. **MEMBERSHIPS** AHA; Mediaeval Acad Am; Am Soc Church Hist; Soc Values Higher Educ; Am Soc Reformation Res. **RESEARCH** Renaissance and Reformation church history; Christian devotion in 15th and 16th centuries; humanism. **SELECTED PUBLICATIONS** Auth, Seeking insight on insight, Soundings, 74; Some thoughts on a theology of resurrection, Encounter, 75; Erasmus on prayer, Renaissance & Reformation, 76; ; The Social Dimension Of Piety--Associative Life And Devotional Change In The Penitent Confraternities Of Marseilles: 1499-1792, Church Hist, Vol 65, 96; Patronage In Renaissance Italy From 1400 To The Early 16th-Century, Church Hist, Vol 66, 1997; Religion, Political-Culture And The Emergence Of Early-Modern Society --Essays In German And Dutch History, Church Hist, Vol 64, 95; translator, Macrobius,Ambrosius,Aurelius,Theodosius--Commentary On The Dream Of Scipio, Church Hist, Vol 61, 92. **CONTACT ADDRESS** Div of Soc Sci, New Col of the Univ of So Florida, Sarasota, FL, 33580.

SOBEL, LIONEL S.
DISCIPLINE LAW **EDUCATION** Univ Calif, Berkeley, BA, 66; Univ Calif, Los Angeles, JD, 69. **CAREER** Prof Loyola Univ, 82-; former partner, Freedman & Sobel, Beverly Hills; ed, Entertainment Law Reporter, 78-. **RESEARCH** Copyright; trademark; libel; privacy problems. **SELECTED PUBLICATIONS** Writes on, of copyright, entertainment and sports law. **CONTACT ADDRESS** Law School, Loyola Marymount Univ, 7900 Loyola Blvd, Burns 344, Los Angeles, CA, 90045. **EMAIL** lsobel@lmulaw.lmu.edu

SOBER, ELLIOTT REUBEN
PERSONAL Born 06/06/1948, Baltimore, MD, m, 1969, 2 children **DISCIPLINE** PHILOSOPHY **EDUCATION** Univ Pa, BA, 69, MScEd, 70; Harvard Univ, PhD, 74. **CAREER** From Asst Prof to Assoc Prof, 74-84, Prof Philos, Univ Wis, Madison 84-. **HONORS AND AWARDS** Lakatos Prize, 89; Vilas Res Prof, 93-. **MEMBERSHIPS** Am Philos Asn (Pres Central Div, 98-99); Philos Sci Asn. **RESEARCH** Philosophy of biology and psychology; metaphysics; epistemology. **SELECTED PUBLICATIONS** Auth, The Nature of Selection: Evolutionary Theory in Philosophical Focus, MIT Press, 84, 2nd ed, Univ Chicago Press, 93; Reconstructing the Past: Parsimony, Evolution, and Inference, MIT Press, 88, Japanese ed, Souju Publ, 96; coauth, Reconstructing Marxism: Essays on Explanation and the Theory of History, Verso Press, 92, Portugese ed, 93; auth, Philosophy of Biology, Westview Press, 93, UK ed, Oxford Univ Press, 93, Span ed, Alianza, 96; From a Biological Point of View: Essays in Evolutionary Philosophy, Cambridge Univ Press, 94; coauth, Unto Others: The Evolution and Psychology of Unselfish Behavior, Harvard Univ Press, 98. **CONTACT ADDRESS** Dept of Philos, Univ of Wis, 600 North Park St, Madison, WI, 53706-1403. **EMAIL** ersober@facstaff.wisc.edu

SOBLE, ALAN
DISCIPLINE PHILOSOPHY **EDUCATION** Albright Col, BS, 69; SUNY, Buffalo, MA, 72, PhD, 76. **CAREER** Prof, Univ New Orleans. **HONORS AND AWARDS** Fel, SUNY, Buffalo, 75-76; res grant, Univ Tex Res Inst, 78; NEH summer sem, Ind Univ, Bloomington, 80; NEH summer sem, Clark Col, 85; NEH summer stipend, 88; Summer Scholar and Res Counc Awards, Univ New Orleans, 88; La Endowment for Hum and GTE grant, 90; Fulbright tchg grant, Hungary, 91-92., Founder, Soc for Philos of Sex and Love. **MEMBERSHIPS** Pres, Soc for Philos of Sex and Love, 77-92. **RESEARCH** The failures of feminist scholarship. **SELECTED PUBLICATIONS** Auth, Egyesules es Joakarat (Union and Concern), Athenaeum 2, #2, 94; Gender, Objectivity, and Realism, The Monist 77, #4, 94; In Defense of Bacon, Philos of Soc Sci 25, #2, 95; La Morale Sexuelle, in Monique Canto-Sperber, ed, Dictionnaire de philosophie morale, Presses Universitaires de Fr, 96; Sexual Investigations, NY UP, 96; Union, Autonomy, and Concern, in Roger Lamb, ed, Love Analyzed, Westview Press, 97; Antioch's 'Sexual Offense Policy': A Philosophical Exploration, J of Soc Philos 28, #1, 97; articles: A Lakoma, Irreplaceability, Love At Second Sight, More on Abortion and Sexual Morality, Sexual Activity, and The Unity of Romantic Love, in Sex, Love, and Friendship, Ed Rodopi, 97; ed, Sex, Love, and Friendship, Ed Rodopi, 97 The Philosophy of Sex: Contemporary Readings, 3rd ed, Rowman and Littlefield, 97. **CONTACT ADDRESS** Dept of Philos, Univ New Orleans, New Orleans, LA, 70148. **EMAIL** AGSPL@uno.edu

SOBSTYL, EDRIE
DISCIPLINE PHILOSOPHY **EDUCATION** Univ Alberta, PhD, 95. **CAREER** Asst prof. **HONORS AND AWARDS** Ed asst, Acta Analytica. **RESEARCH** Philosophy of science; feminist theory; social and political philosophy; theory of knowledge. **SELECTED PUBLICATIONS** Coauth, Women, Madness and Special Defenses in the Law, Jour Soc Philos, 90. **CONTACT ADDRESS** Dept of History, Richardson, TX, 75083-0688. **EMAIL** esobstyl@utdallas.edu

SOCKNESS, BRENT
PERSONAL Born 03/02/1962, St. Paul, MN, m, 1989, 1 child **DISCIPLINE** THEOLOGY **EDUCATION** St Olaf Col, BA, 84; Univ Chicago, MA, 85, PhD, 96. **CAREER** Instr, relig, DePaul Univ, 88; res anal, City of Chicago Bd Ethics, 89-90; instr and tutor, relig, St Olaf Col, 92, 93-96; DAAD res grant, Germany, 92-93; asst prof relig stud, Stanford Univ, 96-. **HONORS AND AWARDS** Phi Beta Kappa, 83; Summa Cum Laude, 84; fel, Divinity Sch, Univ Chicago, 87-88, 88-89; Josephine De Karmen Fel, 88-89; jr fel, Inst for Advan Stud Relig, Univ Chicago, 89-90; Brown Fac Fel, Stanford Univ, 98-99. **MEMBERSHIPS** Am Acad Relig; Ernst-Troeltsch-Gesellschaft; Schleiermacher-Gesellschaft, Soc of Christian Ethics. **RESEARCH** Nineteenth-century German theology and ethics. **SELECTED PUBLICATIONS** Auth, Luther's Two Kingdoms Revisited: A Response to Reinhold Niebuhr's Criticism of Luther, Jour of Relig Ethics, 92; auth, The Ideal and the Historical in the Christology of Wilhelm Herrmann: The Promise and Perils of Revisionary Christology, Jour of Relig, 92; auth, Ethics as Fundamental Theology: The Function of Ethics in the Theology of Wilhelm Herrmann, Annual of Soc of Christian Ethics, 92; auth, Looking Behind the Social Teachings: Troeltsch's Methodological Reflections in Grundprobleme der Ethik, Annual Soc of Christian Ethics, 95; auth, Troeltsch's Practical Christian Ethics: The Heidelberg Lectures, Annual of Soc of Christian Ethics, 97; auth, Against False Apologetics: Wilhelm Herrmann and Ernst Troeltsch in Conflict, JCB Mohr, 98. **CONTACT ADDRESS** Dept of Religious Studies, Stanford Univ, Stanford, CA, 94305. **EMAIL** sockness@leland.stanford.edu

SODEN, RICHARD ALLAN
PERSONAL Born 02/16/1945, Brooklyn, NY, m, 1969 **DISCIPLINE** LAW **EDUCATION** Hamilton Coll, AB 1967; Boston Univ Sch of Law, JD 1970. **CAREER** Hon Geo Clifton Edwards Jr US Court of Appeals for the 6th Circuit, law clerk 1970-71; Boston Coll Sch of Law, faculty 1973-74; Goodwin Procter & Hoar LLP, assoc 1971-79, partner 1979-. **HONORS AND AWARDS** American Bar Foundation, Fellow; Boy Scouts of America, Silver Beaver Awd and Community Youth Svc Award, Heritage District; Theodore L Storer Awd; Boston University School of Law, Silver Shingle Awd; Massachusetts Bar Association, Community Service Awd; UNICEF-Boston Local Hero Awd; Camille Cosby World of Children Medallion. **MEMBERSHIPS** Amer Natl MA & Boston Bar Assns, Boston Bar Association, president, 1994-95; MA Black Lawyers Assn, pres, 1980-81; chairman, emeritus, trustee Judge Baker Guidance Ctr 1974-; chairman, Boston Municipal Rsch Bureau 1996-98; pres United South End Settlements 1977-79; adv cncl Suffolk Univ Sch of Mgmt 1980-; faculty MA Continuing Legal Educ 1980-; pres Mass Black Lawyers Assn 1980-81; Adv Task Force on Securities Regulation Sec of State of the Commonwealth of MA 1982-; pres, Greater Boston Cncl Boy Scouts of Amer 1997-99; adv comm on Legal Educ Supreme Judicial Ct of MA 1984-; Mass Minority Business Devel Commn; bd of visitors Boston Univ Goldman School of Graduate Dentistry; trustee, Boston University, 1995-; co-chairman, 1991-93, Lawyers Committee for Civil Rights Under Law; Amer Bar Assn, House of Delegates, 1995-97, chair, Standing Comm on Bar Activities and Services 1998-. **CONTACT ADDRESS** Goodwin Procter & Hoar, LLP, Exchange Pl, Boston, MS, 02109.

SOFFER, GAIL
DISCIPLINE PHILOSOPHY **EDUCATION** Columbia Univ, PhD, 89. **CAREER** Assoc prof, Eugene Lang Col. **RESEARCH** Phenomenology; hermeneutics; hist of philos; metaphysics; epistemology. **SELECTED PUBLICATIONS** Auth, Heidegger, Humanism, and the Destruction of History, Rev Metaphysics, 96; Husserl and the Question of Relativism, 91. **CONTACT ADDRESS** Eugene Lang Col, New Sch for Social Research, 66 West 12th St, New York, NY, 10011.

SOFFER, WALTER
PERSONAL Born 09/22/1941, Philadelphia, PA **DISCIPLINE** PHILOSOPHY **EDUCATION** Temple Univ, BA, 65; New Sch Social Res, MA, 70, PhD, 77. **CAREER** Asst prof philos, George Washington Univ, 73-75; asst prof to PROF, PHILOS STATE UNIV NY COL, GENESEO, 76-. **HONORS AND AWARDS** Chancellor's Award for Excellence in Teaching, 82. **RESEARCH** Descartes; philosophical anthropology; political philosophy. **SELECTED PUBLICATIONS** Auth, The Methodological Achievement of Cartesian doubt, Southern J Philos, spring 78; Descartes, Rationality and God, Thomist, 10/78; Kant on the Tutelage of God and Nature, Thomist, 1/81; Husserl's Neo-Carteianism, Res in Phenemenology, winter, 81; Descartes's Rejection of the Aristotelian Soul, Int Studies in Philos, vol XVI, no 1, 84; co-ed, The Crisis of Liberal Democracy: A Straussian Perspective, SUNY Press, 87; auth, From Science to Subjectivity: An Interpretation of Descartes's Meditations, Greenwood Press, 87; Dreaming, hyperbole, & Dogmatism, Idealistic Studies, vol XVIII, no 2, 88; reprint of Descartes's Rejection of the Aristotelian Soul, in Moyal, ed, Descartes: Critical Assessments, vol III, London, 91; Modern Rationalism, Miracles, & Revelation: Strauss's Critique of Spinoza, in Deutsch & Nicgorski, eds, Leo Strauss: Political Philosopher and Jewish Thinker, Rowman & Little, 94; Descartes' Secular Paradise: The Discourse on Method as Biblical Criticism, Philos and Theol, vol 8, no 4, summer 94; Socrates's Proposals Concerning Women: Feminism or Fantasy?, Hist of Political Thought, vol XVI, issue 2, summer 95. **CONTACT ADDRESS** NY Col, State Univ, 1 College Cir, Geneseo, NY, 14454-1401. **EMAIL** soffer@uno.cc.geneseo.edu

SOGEN HORI, G. VICTOR
DISCIPLINE RELIGIOUS STUDIES **EDUCATION** Stanford, PhD, 76 **CAREER** Asst Prof, Faculty of Religious Studies, Mcgill Univ. **CONTACT ADDRESS** Faculty of Religious Studies, McGill Univ, 3520 University St., Montreal, PQ, H3A 2A7. **EMAIL** czvh@musica.mcgill.ca

SOHN, LOUIS BRUNO
PERSONAL Born 03/01/1914, Lwow, Poland **DISCIPLINE** LAW **EDUCATION** John Casimir Univ, dipl, ScM & LLM, 35; Harvard Univ, LLM, 40, SJD, 58. **CAREER** Lectr, Harvard Univ, 47-51, asst prof, 51-53, prof law, Law Sch, 53-81; Prof Law, Law Sch, Ga Univ, 81-, Consult, Legal Dept, UN Secretariat, 48, 69, Legal Affairs Off, UN, 50-51, US Arms Control & Disarmament Agency, 61-70 & Off Int Security Affairs, US Dept Defense, 63-70; vchmn, Fed Am Scientists, 63-64; chmn, Comn Study Orgn Peace, 68-; consult int law, US Dept State, 70-71, counr law of the sea task force, 72-; dep deleg, US Deleg to UN Law of Sea Conf, 74-81; comnr-at-large, US Nat Comn Unesco. **HONORS AND AWARDS** Addison-Brown Prize Harvard Univ, 41. **MEMBERSHIPS** Am Soc Int Law; Int Law Asn. **RESEARCH** International law; United Nations; human rights. **SELECTED PUBLICATIONS** Auth, Cases on World Law, 50 & Cases on United Nations Law, 56, 2nd ed, 67, Found Press; coauth, World Peace Through World Law, Harvard Univ, 58, 2nd ed, 60, 3rd ed, 66; ed, Basic Documents of African Regional Organizations (4 vols), Oceans, 71-72; Managing The Law Of The Sea--Ambassador Pardos Forgotten 2nd Idea, Columbia J Of Transnational Law, Vol 36, 97; Important Improvements In The Functioning Of The Principal Organs Of The United-Nations That Can Be Made Without Charter-Revision, Am J Of Int Law, Vol 91, 97; coauth, International Protection of Human Rights, Bobbs, 73. **CONTACT ADDRESS** Law Sch, Harvard Univ, Cambridge, MA, 02138.

SOKOLOWSKI, ROBERT S.
PERSONAL Born 05/03/1934, New Britain, CT **DISCIPLINE** PHILOSOPHY **EDUCATION** Cath Univ Am, BA, 56, MA, 57; Cath Univ Louvain, MA, 61, PhD, 63. **CAREER** From instr to assoc prof, 63-71, prof philos, 71-, Cath Univ Am; vis assoc prof philos, grad fac, 69-70, New Sch Social Res; NEH jr fel, 71-72; vis prof philos, 78, Univ Tex, Austin; NEH fel, independent study & res, 82-83; vis prof, 84, Villanova Univ; vis prof, 92, Yale Univ. **HONORS AND AWARDS** Pres, Metaphysical Soc, 89-90; mem, Polish Acad of Sci, 96; 26th Oppenheimer Lectr, Los Alamos, NM, 96; Festschrift: The Truthful and the Good. **MEMBERSHIPS** Soc Phenomenol & Existential Psychol; Am Philos Assn; Am Cath Philos Soc; Metaphys Soc Am. **RESEARCH** Phenomenology; Aristotle; philosophy of language. **SELECTED PUBLICATIONS** Auth, Pictures, Quotations, and Distinctions, Notre Dame Univ Press, 92; auth, Eucharistic Presence, CVA Press, 94; auth, Introduction to Phenomenology, Cambridge Univ Press, forthcoming. **CONTACT ADDRESS** Sch of Philos, Catholic Univ of America, Washington, DC, 20017. **EMAIL** sokolowski@cva.edu

SOKOLOWSKI, WILLIAM R.
DISCIPLINE PHILOSOPHY **EDUCATION** MDiv, MA, PhD. **CAREER** Central Connecticut State Univ, prof. **HONORS AND AWARDS** Fulbright Scholarship, CT State Elections Enforcement Commission **RESEARCH** Semiotics; Pragmatism; Science. **CONTACT ADDRESS** 1300 Woodstick Rd, Wolcott, CT, 06716. **EMAIL** sokol@juno.com

SOLAN, LAWRENCE
PERSONAL Born 05/07/1952, New York, NY, m, 1982, 2 children **DISCIPLINE** LAW, LINGUISTICS **EDUCATION** Brandeis Univ, BA, 74; Univ Massachusetts, PhD Linguistics, 78; Harvard Law School, JD, 82. **CAREER** Law Clerk, Supreme Ct of NJ, 83-86; assoc, Orans, Elsen & Lupert, 83-86; partner, Orans, Elsen & Lupert, 89-96; Assoc Prof, Brooklyn Law School ol, 96-. **HONORS AND AWARDS** Bd Dir, Int Acad of Law and Mental health, 98-. **MEMBERSHIPS** Ling Soc of Am; Asn of the Bar of the City of New York; Law and Soc Asn; Int Asn of Forensic Ling; Int Acad of Law and Mental Health. **RESEARCH** Law; Language; Cognition. **SELECTED PUBLICATIONS** Auth, The Language of Judges, 993; When Judges Use the Dictionary, Am Speech, 93; Chomsku and Cardozo: Linguistics and the Law, 94; When All is Lost: Why it is Difficult for Judges to Write About Concepts, Graven Images, 94; Judicial Decision and Linguistic Analysis: Is There a Linguist in the Court?, Wash Univ, 95; Learning Our Limits: The Decline of Textualism in Statutory Cases, Wisconsin L Rev, 97; rev, Making Sense in Law, Forensic Ling, 97; Law, Language, and Lenity, William & Mary Rev, forthcoming; coauth, Linguists on the Witness Stand: law, Language and Cognition, forthcoming. **CONTACT ADDRESS** Brooklyn Law Sch, 250 Joralemon St, Brooklyn, NY, 11201. **EMAIL** lsolan@brooklaw.edu

SOLDAN, ANGELIKA
PERSONAL Born 02/10/1953, m, 1987, 1 child **DISCIPLINE** PHILOSOPHY **EDUCATION** Humboldt Univ, MA, 75, PhD, 90; Martin Luther Univ, PhD, 82. **CAREER** Asst prof, philos, Martin Luther Univ, 75-80; asst prof, 81-89, assoc prof, philos, 89-91, Humboldt Univ; adj prof philos, 92-97, Univ Texas, Edinburgh; adj instr, English as a Second Lang, 97-98, adj prof, philos, 92-98, Univ Texas, Brownsville; sr lectr, German, English as a Second Lang, Univ Wisconsin, Eau Claire, 98- . **HONORS AND AWARDS** Scholar for Joint Sessions of Workshops, UK, 91. **MEMBERSHIPS** Int Fromm Soc; APA; Asn for Practical and Professional Ethics; Asn of Am Teachers of German. **RESEARCH** Ethical values; Kegel; Fromm; Marx; Nietzsche; cultural history; humor and society; eighteenth, nineteenth, twentieth century philosophy. **SELECTED PUBLICATIONS** Auth, Das Sozialismusbild Erich Fromms, Erich-Fromm-Archiv, 93; auth, Lotte in Weimar, oden eine Zwischenstation Thomas Manns auf dem Wege zu sich, Orbis Litterarum, 96; auth, To Live Together, but Laugh Apart? German-German Communication Problems as Mirrored by Jokes, Int J of Humor Res, 98; auth, Im Wahren Leben: Franz Kafka Zwischen Beruf und Berufung, Mississippi Lang Crusader, 98. **CONTACT ADDRESS** 200 Santa Ana Ave, Apt 26, Rancho Viejo, TX, 78575-9753. **EMAIL** soldanah@uwec.edu

SOLHEIM, BARBARA P.
PERSONAL Evanston, IL **DISCIPLINE** PHILOSOPHY, ETHICS **EDUCATION** Univ Ill Chicago, PhD, 96. **CAREER** Adj prof, Lake Forest Coll; Wm Rainey Harper Coll. **HONORS AND AWARDS** Phi Betta Kappa; Phi Kappa Phi. **MEMBERSHIPS** Am Philos Soc. **RESEARCH** Ethics; Medical ethics; Business ethics; Environmental ethics. **CONTACT ADDRESS** 654 Warwick Rd, Deerfield, IL, 60015. **EMAIL** bpsolheim@aol.com

SOLOMON, ROBERT CHARLES
PERSONAL Born 09/14/1942, Detroit, MI **DISCIPLINE** PHILOSOPHY **EDUCATION** Univ Pa, BA, 63; Univ Mich, MA, 65, PhD(philos), 67. **CAREER** Instr philos, Princeton Univ, 66-68, vis asst prof, Univ Calif, Los Angeles, 68-69; asst prof, Univ Pittsburgh, 69-71; asst prof, City Univ New York, 71-72; assoc prof, 72-77, Prof Philos, Univ Tex, Austin, 77-, Vis asst prof, Univ Pa, 67-68; vis sr lectr, La Trobe Univ, Melbourne, 70-71; City Univ New York Res Found grant, 72; Nat Endowment for Humanities grant, 76; consult ed, J Theory Social Behav, 77- **MEMBERSHIPS** Am Philos Asn; Soc Phenomenol & Existential Philos. **RESEARCH** Existentialism and Phenomenology; 19th century German philosophy; philosophy of psychology. **SELECTED PUBLICATIONS** Auth, From Rationalism to Existentialism, 72 & ed, Phenomenology and Existentialism, 72, Harper; Nietzsche, Doubleday, 73; Existentialism, Randon, 74; auth, The Passions, Doubleday, 76; Introducing Philosophy, Harcourt, 77; History & Human Nature, Harcourt, 79; Love: Emotion Myth & Metaphor, 81; The Philosophy Of Mind, Philos East & West, Vol 46, 96; Culture And Modernity--East-West Perspectives, Philos East & West, Vol 43, 93; Some Notes On Emotion, East And West + Philosophy And Emotions, Philos East & West, Vol 45, 95. **CONTACT ADDRESS** Dept of Philos, Univ of Tex, 0 Univ of Texas, Austin, TX, 78712-1026.

SOLOMON, WILLIAM DAVID
DISCIPLINE PHILOSOPHY **EDUCATION** Baylor Univ, BA, 64; Univ Tex, PhD, 72. **CAREER** Assoc prof. **RESEARCH** Ethical theory; medical ethics. **SELECTED PUBLICATIONS** Auth, Moral Realism and Moral Dilemmas, 86; Moral Realism and the Amoralist, Midwest Studies Philos, 87; Internal Objections to Virtue Ethics, Midwest Studies Philos, 88. **CONTACT ADDRESS** Philosophy Dept, Univ of Notre Dame, 336/7 O'Shaughnessy, Notre Dame, IN, 46556. **EMAIL** solomon.1@nd.edu

SOLUM, LAWRENCE B.
DISCIPLINE LAW **EDUCATION** Univ Calif, Los Angeles, BA, 81; Harvard Univ, JD, 84. **CAREER** Prof & William M. Rains fel; clerk, hon William Norris US Ct Appeals, 9th Circuit; ch jurisp sect, Asn Amer Law Sch(s) & ch-elect, Asn's Sect on Law & Interp; fac, Loyola Law Sch, 85-; assoc dean, Acad Aff, 93-96; vis prof, Univ Southern Calif, 92; vis prof, Boston Univ, 97-98. **SELECTED PUBLICATIONS** Publ on, civil procedure; Const theory; legal philosophy. **CONTACT ADDRESS** Law School, Loyola Marymount Univ, 7900 Loyola Blvd, Burns 334, Los Angeles, CA, 90045. **EMAIL** lsolum@lmulaw.lmu.edu

SOMERVILLE, ROBERT
DISCIPLINE RELIGION **EDUCATION** Yale Univ, PhD. **CAREER** Prof. **RESEARCH** History of Christianity through the 16th century Reformation; Medieval Latin church; Medieval Latin manuscripts. **SELECTED PUBLICATIONS** Auth, Pope Alexander III and the Council of Tours; Scotia Pontifica: Papal Letters to Scotland before the Pontificate of Innocent III; Pope Urban II, the Collectio Britannica; Council of Melfi. **CONTACT ADDRESS** Dept of Religion, Columbia Col, New York, 2960 Broadway, New York, NY, 10027-6902. **EMAIL** somervil@columbia.edu

SOMMER, BENJAMIN D.
PERSONAL Born 07/06/1964, New York, NY, m, 1995, 1 child **DISCIPLINE** RELIGION **EDUCATION** Yale, BA, 86; Brandeis, MA, 91; Univ Chicago, PhD, 94. **CAREER** Asst pof, 94-, Northwestern Univ. **HONORS AND AWARDS** ACLS, 98-99; Yad Hana Div Fel, 98-99. **MEMBERSHIPS** SBL; AOS; AJS **RESEARCH** History of Israelite religion; literary study of Bible; history of biblical exegesis **SELECTED PUBLICATIONS** Art, Did Prophecy Cease? Evaluating a Reevaluation, Jour of Bible Lit, 96; art, The Scroll of Isaiah as Jewish Scripture, Or, Why Jews Don't Read Books, Soc of Bibl Lit 1996 Sem Papers, Scholars Press 96; art, Allusions and Illusion: The Unity of the Book of Isaiah in Light Of Deutero-Isaiah's Use of Prophetic Tradition, New Visions of Isaiah, Sheffield Acad Press, 96; art, Exegesis, Allusion and Intertextuality in the Hebrew Bible: A Response to Lyle Eslinger, Vetus Testamentum, 96; auth, A Prophet Reads Scripture: Allusion in Isaiah 40-66, Stanford Univ Press, 98. **CONTACT ADDRESS** Dept of Religion, Northwestern Univ, 1940 Sheridan Rd, Evanston, IL, 60208-4050. **EMAIL** b-sommer@nwu.edu

SOMMER, JOHN D.
PERSONAL Born 01/19/1929, Peoria, IL, m, 1950, 3 children **DISCIPLINE** PHILOSOPHY **EDUCATION** Univ Chicago, PhD, 65. **CAREER** Assoc prof, Miami Univ, 62-90; prof, Western Col, 72-74; lect, Univ Md, overseas, 76-77. **MEMBERSHIPS** APA. **RESEARCH** History of philosophy. **SELECTED PUBLICATIONS** Auth, Moments of Soul, Humanities, forthcoming. **CONTACT ADDRESS** PO Box 356, Oxford, OH, 45056. **EMAIL** jnsommer@erinet.com

SONDEREGGER, KATHERINE
DISCIPLINE WESTERN RELIGIOUS THOUGHT **EDUCATION** Smith Col, AB; Yale Univ, MDiv, STM; Brown Univ, PhD. **CAREER** Prof, act, Women's Stud prog; Middlebury Col, 87-. **RESEARCH** Study of theology. **SELECTED PUBLICATIONS** Auth, That Jesus Christ was Born a Jew: Karl Barth's Doctrine of Israel. **CONTACT ADDRESS** Dept of Religion, Middlebury Col, Middlebury, VT, 05753.

SONTAG, FREDERICK EARL
PERSONAL Born 10/02/1924, Long Beach, CA, m, 1950, 2 children **DISCIPLINE** PHILOSOPHY **EDUCATION** Stanford Univ, BA, 49; Yale Univ, MA, 51, PhD, 52; Col of Idaho, LLD, 71. **CAREER** Instr, Yale Univ, 51-52; prof philos, 52-, chemn dept 60-67, 76-77, 80-84, Denison Prof Philos, 72- , Pomona Col. **HONORS AND AWARDS** Phi Beta Kappa; listed Who's Who in Am, 96; Fulbright Reg Vis Prof, India, East Asia, and Pacific Areas, 77-78., LLD, Col Idaho, 71. **MEMBERSHIPS** APA; Metaphysical Soc of Am; Soc on Relig in Higher Educ; Am Acad Relig; Soc for the Sci Study of Relig; Asn for Humanistic Psych; Soc for Philos and Psychol; Soc of Christian Philos. **RESEARCH** History of philosophy; metaphysics; philosophical theology. **SELECTED PUBLICATIONS** Auth, Uncertain Truth, University Press of America, 95; auth, Wittgenstein and the Mystical: Philosophy as an Ascetic Practice, Scholar's, 95; auth, The Descent of Women, Paragon, 97; auth, Truth and Imagination, University Press of America, 98. **CONTACT ADDRESS** Department of Philosophy, Pomona Col, 551 N College Ave, Claremont, CA, 91711-6355.

SORENSEN, ROY
PERSONAL Born 02/25/1957, Brooklyn, NY, m, 1982, 1 child **DISCIPLINE** PHILOSOPHY **EDUCATION** Mich State Univ, PhD, 82. **CAREER** Asst prof, Univ Del, 84-87; asst prof, 87-90, assoc prof, 90-95, full prof, 95-, NY Univ. **MEMBERSHIPS** Amer Philos asn; Soc exact Philos. **RESEARCH** Philosophy of Language; Philosophy of Logic; Epistemology. **SELECTED PUBLICATIONS** Auth, Blindspots, Oxford: Clarendon Press, 88; Thought Experiments, NY, Oxford UP, 92; Pseudo-Problems, London: Routlege, 93. **CONTACT ADDRESS** Dept of Philosophy, New York Univ, 100 Washington Sq E, 503 Main Bldg, New York, NY, 10003-6688. **EMAIL** rs3@is2.nyu.edu

SOROKA, JACEK
PERSONAL Born 12/21/1966, Poland, m, 1995, 2 children **DISCIPLINE** THEOLOGY **EDUCATION** Pontificia Facolta Teologica, Rome, BA, MA, 91; Pontificio Atened "Antonianum," Rome, two years of advanced graduate study, 93. **CAREER** Prof Theol, St Thomas Col of Theol, Moscow, 93-95; DIR RELIG ED, ST CECILIA CHURCH, AMES, IA, 96-. **MEMBERSHIPS** NCEA **RESEARCH** Franciscan spirituality. **CONTACT ADDRESS** Dir Relig Ed, St Cecilia Parish, 2900 Hoover Ave, Ames, IA, 50010-4460. **EMAIL** DBQ003RE@impresso.com

SORRENSON, RICHARD J.
DISCIPLINE HISTORY OF PHILOSOPHY **EDUCATION** Auckland Univ, MS, 84; Princeton Univ, PhD, 93. **CAREER** Asst prof. **MEMBERSHIPS** Am Philos Soc. **SELECTED PUBLICATIONS** Auth, The ship as a scientific instrument in the eighteenth century, Osiris. 96; Towards a history of the Royal Society of London in the 18th century, 96. **CONTACT ADDRESS** Dept of History and Philosophy of Science, Indiana Univ, Bloomington, 300 N Jordan Ave, Bloomington, IN, 47405. **EMAIL** rjs@indiana.edu

SOSA, ERNEST
PERSONAL Born 06/17/1940, Cardenas, Cuba, m, 1961, 2 children **DISCIPLINE** PHILOSOPHY **EDUCATION** Univ Miami, BA, 61; Univ Pittsburgh, MA, 62, PhD(philos), 64. **CAREER** Lectr philos, Univ Western Ont, 63-64; interdisciplinary fel philos & psychol, Brown Univ, 64-66; asst prof philos, Univ Western Ont, 66-67; from asst prof to assoc prof, 67-74, chmn dept, 70-76, prof philos, 74-81, Romer Elton Prof Natural Theol, Brown Univ, 81-, Carnegie fel, 64-66; Nat Sci Found grant, 70-72; assoc ed, Philos and Phenomenol Res, 80; vis prof, Univ Western Ontario, Univ Miami, Univ Mich, Univ Tex, Univ Mex & Harvard Univ, Distinguished Visiting Prof, Rutgers Univ, 98-. **HONORS AND AWARDS** Institut International de Philosophie, 93-. **MEMBERSHIPS** Am Philos Asn. **RESEARCH** Epistemology; metaphysics; ethics. **SELECTED PUBLICATIONS** Auth, Propositional Attitudes De Dicto and De Re, J Philos, 70; How do you Know?, Am Philos Quart, 74; The Raft and the Pyramid: Coherence vs Foundations in the Theory of Knowledge, Midwest Studies in Philos, 80; Propositions and Indexical Attitudes, Believing: Epistemology and semiotics of belief, Walter de Gruyter Verlag, 82; Subjects Among Other Things, Phil Pers, 87; Surviving Matters, Nous, 90; Knowledge in Perspective: Selected Essays in Epistemology, CUP, 91; Putnam's Pragmatic Realism, J Philos, 93; Philisophical Scepticism and Externadent Epistemology, Proceeding at the Arest Sic, 94; How to Resolve the Pythagorian Problematic: A Lesson from Descartes, Philo Studies, 97; Reflective Knowledge in the Best Circles, J Philos, 97. **CONTACT ADDRESS** Dept of Philos, Brown Univ, 1 Prospect St, Providence, RI, 02912-9127. **EMAIL** Ernest_Sosa@Brown.edu

SOVERN, MICHAEL I.
PERSONAL Born 12/01/1931, New York, NY, 1952, 4 children **DISCIPLINE** LAW **EDUCATION** Columbia Univ, AB, 53, LLB 55. **CAREER** From asst prof to assoc prof, Univ Minn Law Sch, 55-58; fac, Columbia Law Sch, 57-, prof, 60-, Chancellor Kent prof, 77-, dean, Law Sch, 70-79, chmn, Exec Com Fac, 68-69, provost, exec vp, 79-80, univ pres, 80-93, pres Emeritus, 93. **HONORS AND AWARDS** Alexander Hamilton medal, Columbia Univ, Citizens Union Civic Leadership Awd, fel, Am Acad Arts and Scis, hon LLD, Columbia Univ, hon PhD, Tel Aviv Univ, hon LLD Univ S Calif. **MEMBERSHIPS** bd dirs AT&T; Warner Lambert; Sequa; Asian Cult Coun; Schibert Org; WNET-TVl Freedom Forum; NYC Chart Rev Comm, **RESEARCH** Dir legal restraints on racial discrimination in employment, 20th century fund. **SELECTED PUBLICATIONS** Auth, Lagal Restraints on Racial Discrimination in Employment, 66; auth, Law and Poverty, 69; auth, Of Boundless Domains, 94. **CONTACT ADDRESS** Sch of Law, Columbia Univ, 435 W 116th St, New York, NY, 10027-7201.

SOVERN, MICHAEL I.
PERSONAL Born 12/01/1931, New York, NY, m, 1952, 4 children **DISCIPLINE** LAW **EDUCATION** Columbia Univ, AB, 53, LLB 55. **CAREER** From asst prof to assoc prof law, Univ Minn Law Sch, 55-58; mem fac, Columbia Law Sch, 57-, prof law, 60-, CHANCELLOR KENT PROF LAW, COLUMBIA UNIV LAW SCH, 81-, Dean, 70-79, chmn, Exec Comt Fac, 68-69, provost, exec vpres, 79-80, pres, 80-93, pres emer, 93-. **HONORS AND AWARDS** LLD (hon), Columbia Univ, 80; PhD (hon), Tel Aviv Univ, 82; LLD (hon), Univ South Calif, 89; Commendatore in the Order of Merit of the Republic of Italy, 91; Alexander Hamilton Medal, Columbia Col, 93; Citizens Union Civic Leadership awared, 93; Fel, Am Acad Arts and Sci. **MEMBERSHIPS** Bd dirs AT&T, Warner Lambert, Sequa, Asian Cultural Coun, Shubert Org, Stat WNET-TV, Freedom Forum Newseum; chmn, NYC Charter Rev Comn, 82-83; co-chmn, 2nd Cir Comn on Reduction of Burdens and Costs in Civil Litigation, 77-80; chmn, Comn on Integrity in Govt, 86; pres, Ital Acad Advanced Studies in Am, 91-93, Shubert Found, 96; chmn, Japan Soc, 93; Am Acad Rome, 93; chmn, Nat Adv Coun Freedom Forum Media Studies Ctr, 93-; Pulitzer Prize bd, 80-93, chmn pro-tem, 86-87; trustee Kaiser Family Found, Presdl Legal Expense Trust, 94-98; ABA; Counc Fgn Rels; Asn Bar City NY; Am Arbitration Asn (panel arbitrators); Am Law Int; Econ Club; Nat Acad Arbirtators. **RESEARCH** Dir legal restraints on radical discrimination in employment, Twentieth Century Fund, 62-66; spl counsel to gov NJ, 74-77; cons Time mag, 65-80. **SELECTED PUBLICATIONS** Auth, Legal Restraints on Racial Discrimination in Employment, 66; Law and Poverty, 69; Of Boundless Domains, 94. **CONTACT ADDRESS** Sch of Law, Columbia Univ, 435 W 116th St, New York, NY, 10027.

SPALDING, CHRISTOPHER J.
PERSONAL Born 03/26/1964, Minneapolis, MN, m **DISCIPLINE** RELIGION **EDUCATION** Boston Univ, BA, 93; Univ Sheffield, UK, MA, 96. **CAREER** Asst head, relig, Cardigan Mountain Schl. **MEMBERSHIPS** AAR; SBL. **RESEARCH** Buddhist/Christian dialogue **CONTACT ADDRESS** Cardigan Mountain School, PO Box 58, Canaan, NH, 03741-9307. **EMAIL** cspaldin.cms@cardigan.org

SPALDING, JAMES COLWELL
PERSONAL Born 11/06/1921, Kansas City, MO, m, 1945, 5 children **DISCIPLINE** RELIGION **EDUCATION** Univ Ill, BA, 42; Hartford Theol Sem, BD, 45; Columbia Univ, PhD(-relig), 50. **CAREER** Prof relig, Mo Valley Col, 48-53; assoc prof relig & philos, Trinity Univ, 53-56; from asst prof to assoc prof relig, 56-68, Prof Relig, Univ Iowa, 68-, Dir Sch Relig, 71-. **MEMBERSHIPS** Am Acad Relig; Renaissance Soc Am; Coun Grad Studies Relig (sec-treas, 68-); Am Soc Reformation Res; Am Soc Church Hist. **RESEARCH** History of Christian thought. **SELECTED PUBLICATIONS** Auth, Ulster 1641--Aspects Of The Rising, Church Hist, Vol 66, 97; Predestination, Policy And Polemic--Conflict And Consensus In The English Church From The Reformation To The Civil-War, Sixteenth Century J, Vol 26, 95; Ulster 1641--Aspects Of The Rising, Church Hist, Vol 66, 97; Authority, Church, And Society In George Herbert--Return To The Middle-Way, Church Hist, Vol 63, 94; ed, Calvin And Calvinism, 14 Vols, Sixteenth Century J, Vol 24, 93. **CONTACT ADDRESS** Dept of Relig, Univ of Iowa, Iowa City, IA, 52242.

SPANOS, WILLIAM
PERSONAL Born 01/01/1925, Newport, NH, m, 1954, 3 children **DISCIPLINE** ENGLISH, EXISTENTIAL PHILOSOPHY **EDUCATION** Wesleyan Univ, BA, 50; Columbia Univ, MA, 54; Univ Wis, PhD (Eng), 64. **CAREER** Master Eng, Mt Hermon Sch, 51-53; asst ed, Encycl Americana, Grolier, 54-56; instr Eng, Univ KY, 60-62; asst prof, Knox Col, 62-66; Asst Prof Eng & Comp Lit, State Univ NY Binghamton, 66-, Fulbright prof Am lit, Nat Univ Athens, 69-70; founder & ed, boundary 2, 72-. **MEMBERSHIPS** MLA; Col Eng Asn; Mod Greek Studies Asn. **RESEARCH** Mod Brit and Am poetry; mod drama; redefining modernism in lit. **SELECTED PUBLICATIONS** Ed, A Casebook on Existentialism, Crowell, 66; auth, The Christian Tradition in Modern British Verse Drama: The Poetic of Sacramental Time, Rutgers Univ, 67; Modern drama and the Aristotelian tradition: The formal imperatives of absurd time, Contemp Lit, summer 71; The detective and the boundary: Some notes on the postmodern literary imagination, fall 72, Heidegger, Kierkegaard and the Hermenentic circle: Toward a postmodern theory of interpretation as dis-closure, winter 76 & Breaking the circle: Hermenentics as dis-closure, winter 77, boundary 2; ed, Existentialism 2, Random House, 77; Repititions: the Postmodern Occasion in Literature and Culture, Louisiana State Univ Press, 87; Heidegger and Criticism: Retrieving The Politics of Destruction, Univ of MN Press, 93, The End of Education, Univ of MN Press, 93; The Errant Art of Moby Dick: The Canon, the Cold War and the Struggle for American Studies, Duke Univ, 95 Philosophy and Imperialism, Thinking the Specter of Postmodernity, Univ of MN Press, forthcoming. **CONTACT ADDRESS** Dept of English, SUNY, Harpur Col, Binghamton, NY, 13901. **EMAIL** wspanose@binghampton.edu

SPARKS, KENTON L.
PERSONAL Born 07/11/1963, Flemingsburg, KY, m, 1988, 2 children **DISCIPLINE** BIBLICAL STUDIES **EDUCATION** Johnson Bible Col, Tenn, Ba, 85; Kennesaw State Univ, MBA, 87; Columbia Bibl Sem, MA, 90; Univ North Carolina, Chapel Hill, PhD, 96. **CAREER** Instr, relig, North Carolina Wesleyan Col, 92-94; tchg fel, Univ North Carolina, Chapel Hill, 93-95; resident scholar, Providence Baptist Church, Raleigh NC, 93-. **HONORS AND AWARDS** Cum laude, 85; Eta Beta Rho, 90. **MEMBERSHIPS** Soc of Bibl Lit; Inst for Bibl Res; Catholic Bibl Asn; Evangel Theol Soc. **RESEARCH** Hebrew law; Hebrew; Hebrew historiography; ethnicity. **SELECTED PUBLICATIONS** Auth, In the Footsteps of the Sages: Interpreting Wisdom for Preaching, Faith and Mission, 95; auth, Ethnicity and Identity in Ancient Israel, Eisenbrauns, 98; auth, Patriarchs, and, Semites, in Freedman, ed, Eerdmans Dictionary of the Bible, Eerdmans, forthcoming; coauth, Israelite Literature in Its Ancient Context: A Comparative Introduction to the Genres of the Hebrew Bible, Hendrickson, forthcoming. **CONTACT ADDRESS** Providence Baptist Church, 6339 Glenwood Ave, Raleigh, NC, 27612. **EMAIL** kent@pray.org

SPEIDELL, TODD
PERSONAL Born 07/31/1957, Chicago, IL, m, 1990, 1 child **DISCIPLINE** THEOLOGY/ETHICS; PSYCHOLOGY **EDUCATION** Gordon Col, BA, 79; Fuller Theological Seminary, M Div, 83, PhD,86, Fuller Theological Seminary; New College Edinburgh, postdoctoral study, July 92-95. **CAREER** Dir, of Extended Education and Adjunct prof, 87-89, Fuller Theological Seminary; assoc prof, 89-90, Knoxville Col; head of religious studies, 90- , Webb Sch of Knoxville. **MEMBERSHIPS** Karl Barth Soc of North America; Intl Bonhoeffer Soc. **RESEARCH** Theological ethics, theology and culture. **SELECTED PUBLICATIONS** Auth, The Incarnation as Theological Imperative for Human Reconciliation: A Christocentric Social Ethic, 86; Coed, Incarnational Ministry: The Presence of Christ in Church, Society, & Family, Essays in Honor of Ray S. Anderson, 90; auth, A Trinitarian Ontology of Persons in Society, Scottish Journal of Theology, 94; auth, I Want a Picture of God! The Chaplain's Craft, 94. **CONTACT ADDRESS** 1137 Farrington Dr., Knoxville, TN, 37923. **EMAIL** todd_speidell@webbschool.org

SPELLMAN, NORMAN WOODS
PERSONAL Born 05/17/1928, Robstown, TX, m, 1950, 4 children **DISCIPLINE** RELIGION **EDUCATION** Southwestern Univ, BA, 49; Perkins Sch Theol, Southern Methodist Univ, BD, 52; Yale Univ, PhD, 61. **CAREER** Instr relig, Southern Methodist Univ, 58-60; from asst prof to prof, 60-76, prof Relig & Philos, Southwestern Univ, 76-98; RETIRED 6/01/98. **MEMBERSHIPS** Am Soc Church Hist; Am Hist Asn; Am Acad Relig; Am Studies Asn. **RESEARCH** American church history; American Methodism. **SELECTED PUBLICATIONS** Coauth, History of American Methodism (3 vols), Abingdon, 64 & 66; Early Leaders in Texas Methodism, Am Methodism, 66; The early native Methodist preachers, Duke Div Sch Rev, autumn 69. **CONTACT ADDRESS** Dept of Relig & Philos, Southwestern Univ, 1001 E University, Georgetown, TX, 78626-6100.

SPENCE, JOSEPH SAMUEL, SR.
PERSONAL Born 12/20/1950, m **DISCIPLINE** LAW **EDUCATION** Pikes Peak Coll, AA; Univ of MD, BSc; Webster Univ, MA Washburn Univ Law School, Topeka, KS, JD. **CAREER** Century 21 Real Estate, realtor assoc 1978-80; United States Army, capt 1980-86; Riley County District Attorney's Office, 1987; City of Topeka Attorney's Office, 1988-89; Kansas State Senate, 1988-89; Milwaukee Area Technical College, 1991-; Spence Law Offices, Milwaukee, 1992-. **HONORS AND AWARDS** Disting Military Student 1979, Disting Military Grad 1980 Howard Univ ROTC; Earl Warren Scholar NAACP Legal Defense Fund 1986-89; various awds for public speaking; Daughters of Amer Revolution Awd; Disting Grad Air Assault School; Disting Grad Logistics Automated Mgmt Sch; Expert Shooting Qualification; Jurcyk-Royle Oral Advocacy Competition; Certificate of Commendation, Amer Bar Assn, 1989; Certificate of Merit, Washburn Law Clinic, 1988; founder & chapter pres, Lambda Alpha Epsilon Criminal Justice Fraternity, 1985. **MEMBERSHIPS** Alpha Phi Alpha; Rep-at-large Frederick Douglass Ctr Manhattan KS 1986-87, WSBA Washburn Law Sch 1986-87; Kiwanis Intl 1986-87; marshal Phi Alpha Delta Law Frat 1986-87; founder & charter pres NAACP Manhattan KS 1986; founder & legal advisor, Lex Explorer, Washburn Law School, 1988; assoc minister St. Mark AME Church; chairperson Legal Redress Comm NAACP KS 1987-89; mem Manhattan Kansas Chamber of Commerce, Manhattan KS Amer Red Cross; Commissioner-at-large, Amer Bar Assn, 1987-89; Christian Lawyers Assn, 1987-; Christian Legal Soc, 1987-; Americans United for Seperation of Church & State, 1987-; American Bar Assn, 1989-; Natl Bar Assn, 1992-; American Trial Lawyer Assn, 1993-; Wisconsin Academy of Trial Lawyers. **CONTACT ADDRESS** PO Box 26342, Milwaukee, WI, 53226.

SPENCER, AIDA BESANCON
PERSONAL Born 01/02/1947, Santo Domingo, Dominican Republic, m, 1972, 1 child **DISCIPLINE** NEW TESTAMENT **EDUCATION** Douglass Col, BA, 68; ThM, 75, MDiv, 73, Princeton Theological Seminary; Southern Baptist Theological Seminary, PhD, 82. **CAREER** Adjunct Prof, 74-76, New York Theological Seminary; Academic Dean, Prof, 76-78, Alpha-Omega Community Theological School; Asst/Assoc Prof, 82-92, Prof 92-, Gordon Conwell Theological Seminary. **HONORS AND AWARDS** Staley Distinguished Scholar, 94; Christianity Today Book Award, 96. **MEMBERSHIPS** Evangelical Theol Soc; Soc of Biblical Research; Christians for Biblical Equality; Asociacon para la educacion teologica hispana **RE-**

SEARCH Paul's letters; Luke acts; Peter; James; women's concerns **SELECTED PUBLICATIONS** Auth, The Prayer Life of Jesus, 90; The Goddess Revival, 95; God Through the Looking Glass: Glimpses from the Arts, 98; The Global God: Multicultural Evangelical Views of God, 98. **CONTACT ADDRESS** 10 Maple St., S. Hamilton, MA, 01982.

SPENDER, ROBERT D.
PERSONAL Born 11/17/1945, Waterbury, CT, m, 1970, 3 children **DISCIPLINE** BIBLICAL STUDIES **EDUCATION** Barrington Col, BA, 67; Trinity Evangel Div Sch, MA, 70; Dropsie Univ, PhD, 76. **CAREER** Prin and found, West Woods Chr Acad, Hamden, Conn, 75-78; asst and assoc prof Bibl Stud, 78-85, dept chemn 82-85, Barrington Col; prof Bibl Stud, 85-95, chemn 89-95, Briarcliff Manor; actg vpres for Acad Aff, Kings Col, 88; prof Bibl Stud, 95- , dept chemn 98- , Lancaster Bible Col. **HONORS AND AWARDS** Prof of the Year, Barrington Col, 82; Prof of the Year, Kings Col, 91. **MEMBERSHIPS** Soc of Bibl Lit; Evangel Theol Soc. **RESEARCH** Old Testament Prophets; idols and idolatry. **SELECTED PUBLICATIONS** Contribur, Baker Encyclopedia of the Bible, Baker Book House, 88; contribur, Elwell, ed, Evangelical Dictionary of Biblical Theology, Baker Book House, 96; contribur, Van Geweren, ed, The New International Dictionary of Old Testament Theology and Exegesis, Zondervan, 97. **CONTACT ADDRESS** Lancaster Bible Col, 901 Eden Rd, Lancaster, PA, 17601. **EMAIL** bspender@lbc.edu

SPIEGEL, JAMES S.
PERSONAL Born 07/26/1963, Pontiac, MI, m, 1998 **DISCIPLINE** PHILOSOPHY **EDUCATION** MI State Univ, PhD, 93. **CAREER** Assoc prof, Taylor Univ. **MEMBERSHIPS** APA; Intl Berkeley Soc and Soc of Christian Philosphers. **RESEARCH** Philosophy of Relig; Ethics; George Berkeley. **SELECTED PUBLICATIONS** Auth, Socrates: A Messianic Type for the Gentiles, Philosophia Christi, fall 95; auth, The Theological Orthodoxy of Berkeley's Immaterialism, Faith and Philosophy, April 96; auth, A Berkeleyan Approach to the Problem of Induction, Science and Christian Belief, 98; auth, A New Aesthetic Vision for the Christian Liberal Arts Col, Christian Scholar's Review, Dec 98; auth, Review of A Passion for Wisdom by R.C. Solomon and K.M. Higgins, forthcoming in Teaching Philosophy, Dec 98. **CONTACT ADDRESS** Philosophy Dept, Taylor Univ, Upland, IN, 46989. **EMAIL** jmspiegel@tayloru.edu

SPILLENGER, CLYDE
PERSONAL Born 03/24/1960, New York, NY, s **DISCIPLINE** LAW **EDUCATION** Princeton Univ, AB, 82; Yale Univ, JD, 87; Yale Univ, Mphil, 88. **CAREER** Lectr and res fel, Univ Wisconsin Law School, 90-92; acting prof law, UCLA, 92-98. **MEMBERSHIPS** Am Soc for Legal His; Law & Soc Asn; Org of Am Historians. **RESEARCH** Am legal and constitutional his; law and lang. **SELECTED PUBLICATIONS** Auth, "Reading the Judicial Canon: Alexander Bickel and the Book of Brandeis", Jour of Am Hist 79, 92; auth, "Elusive Advocate: Reconsidering Brandeis as Public Interest Lawyer", Yale Law Jour 105, 96. **CONTACT ADDRESS** School of Law, UCLouisiana, 405 Hilgard Ave., Los Angeles, CA, 90095. **EMAIL** spilleng@mail.law.ucla.edu

SPILSBURY, PAUL
PERSONAL Born 01/29/1966, Port Shepstone, South Africa, m, 1988, 1 child **DISCIPLINE** NEW TESTAMENT STUDIES **EDUCATION** Regent Col, MCS; Univ of Cambridge, PhD. **CAREER** Asst prof bibl stud, Canadian Bible Col, 94-. **MEMBERSHIPS** SBL; Can Soc Bibl Stud. **RESEARCH** Flavius Josephus; Christian origins; ancient use of scripture. **SELECTED PUBLICATIONS** Auth, Contra Apionem and Antiquitates Judaicae: Points of Contact, in Feldman, ed, Josephus' Contra Apionem: Studies in its Character and Context with a Latin Concordance to the Portion Missing In Greek, Brill, 96; auth, God and Israel in Josephus: A Patron-Client Relationship, in Mason, ed, Understanding Josephus, Sheffield, 98; auth, The Image of the Jew in Flavius Josephus' Paraphrase of the Bible, Mohr Siebeck, 98; auth, Josephus' Pattern of Religion, in Carson, ed, Justification and Variegated Nomism: A Fresh Appraisal of Paul and Second Temple Judaism, vol 1, Mohr Siebeck, 99. **CONTACT ADDRESS** 4400 4th Ave, Regina, SK, S4T 0H8. **EMAIL** paul.spilsbury@cbccts.sk.ca

SPINA, FRANK ANTHONY
PERSONAL Born 09/30/1943, Long Beach, CA, m, 1994, 2 children **DISCIPLINE** OLD TESTAMENT STUDIES **EDUCATION** Greenville Col (Ill), BA, 65; Asbury Theological Seminary, MDiv, 68; MA, 70, PhD, 77, Univ Michigan **CAREER** Prof, Seattle Pacific Univ, 73-. **MEMBERSHIPS** Soc of Biblical Lit; Wesleyan Theological Soc; Scholarly Engagement with Anglican Doctrine **RESEARCH** Theological interpretation of Old Testament narrative; canon and hermeneutics **SELECTED PUBLICATIONS** Auth, Eli's Seat: The Transition from Priest to Prophet in Samuel 1-4, Journal for the Study of the Old Testament, 94; Wesleyan Faith Seeking Biblical Understanding, Wesleyan Theological Journal, 95; The Problematic of Faculty Remuneration in the Christian College, Christian Scholars Review, 96; The Face of God: Esau in Canonical Context, The Quest for Context & Meaning: Studies in Biblical Intertextuality in Honor of James A. Sanders, 97; Rahab (the Harlot), Dictionary of Old Testament Theology and Exegesis, 97; Rahab (the Monster), Dictionary of Old Testament Theology and Exegesis, 97. **CONTACT ADDRESS** Dept of Religion, Seattle Pacific Univ, Seattle, WA, 98119. **EMAIL** fspina@spu.edu

SPITZ, ELLEN HANDLER
PERSONAL New York, NY, 3 children **DISCIPLINE** FINE ARTS; PHILOSOPHY **EDUCATION** Barnard Col, BA; Harvard Univ, MAT; Columbia Univ, PhD. **CAREER** Barnard Col; Columbia, CUNY; Hebrew Univ of Jerusalem; Rutgers Univ; Stanford Univ. **HONORS AND AWARDS** Getty scholar, 89-90; Bunting fel, 96-97; fel, Ctr for Adv Study in Behavioral Sci, Stanford Univ, 97-98. **MEMBERSHIPS** Col Art Asn; Amer Soc for Aesthetics; Amer Psychoanalytic Asn. **RESEARCH** Psychological perspectives on art and literature. **SELECTED PUBLICATIONS** Auth, Museum of the Mind, Yale Univ Press, 94; auth, Image and Insight, Columbia Univ Press, 91; auth, Art and Psyche, Yale Univ Press, 85. **CONTACT ADDRESS** Dept. of Art and Art History, Stanford Univ, Stanford, CA, 94305.

SPITZER, MATTHEW L.
DISCIPLINE ADMINISTRATIVE LAW **EDUCATION** Univ Calif, Los Angeles, BA, 73; Univ Southern Calif, JD,77; Calif Inst Technol, PhD, 79. **CAREER** William T. Dalessi Professor of Law,Univ Southern Calif; Director of the Communications Law and Policy Institute; and Director of Law and Economics Programs at the University of Southern California; taught at, Northwestern Univ. **RESEARCH** Administrative Law, Broadcast Regulation, and Economic Analysis of Law. **SELECTED PUBLICATIONS** Auth, Seven Dirty Words and Six Other Stories: Controlling the Content of Print and Broadcast & Experimental Law and Economics; coauth, Public Policy Toward Cable Television. **CONTACT ADDRESS** School of Law, Univ Southern Calif, University Park Campus, Los Angeles, CA, 90089. **EMAIL** mspitzer@usc.edu

SPOHN, WILLIAM C.
PERSONAL Born 06/07/1944, Washington, DC, m, 1996 **DISCIPLINE** CHRISTIAN ETHICS **EDUCATION** Univ Chicago Divinity School, PhD, 78. **CAREER** Asst to assoc prof, Jesuit School of Theol Berkeley, 78-92; Dir Bannan Inst for Jesuit Educ & Christian Values, Santa Clara Univ, 92-. **HONORS AND AWARDS** Presidential Prof Ethics & Common Good, 96-98. **MEMBERSHIPS** Cath Theol Soc Am; Soc Christian Ethics; Am Acad Relig; Highlands Inst Am Relig Thought. **RESEARCH** Scripture and ethics; American religion; spirituality and ethics; moral psychology. **SELECTED PUBLICATIONS** Auth The Magisterium and Morality, Theol Studies, 93; William James on Religious Experience: An Elitist Account?, Am Jour Theol & Philos, 94; Jesus and Ethics, Proceedings of the Cath Theol Soc Am, 94; Jesus and Christian Ethics, Theol Studies, 95; What Are They Saying About Scripture and Ethics, Paulist Press, 95; Morality on the Way of Discipleship: The Use of Scripture in Veritatis Splendor, Veritatis Splendor: American Responses, Sheed and Ward, 95; coauth Knowledge of God and Knowledge of Self: An American Empiricist Approach, Christian Ethics: Problems and Prospects, Pilgrim Press, 96; Finding God in All Things: Jonathan Edwards and Ignatius Loyola, Finding God in All Things: Essays in Honor of Michael J. Buckley, Crossroad Press, 96; Spirituality and Ethics: Exploring the Connections, Theol Studies, 97; coauth, Rights of Passage: The Ethics of Immigration and Refugee Policy, Theol Studies, 98. **CONTACT ADDRESS** Dept of Religious Studies, Santa Clara Univ, Santa Clara, CA, 95053. **EMAIL** wspohn@scu.edu

SPONHEIM, PAUL R.
DISCIPLINE SYSTEMATIC THEOLOGY **EDUCATION** Concordia Col, BA, 52; Luther Sem, BTh, 57; Univ Chicago, MA, 60, PhD, 61. **CAREER** Asst prof, dept ch, Concordia Col; lectr, Univ Chicago, 60-61; vis prof, Lutheran Sem, Gettysburg, Pa, 66-67; vis lectr, 64, 66, 69; assoc prof, 69; prof, 74-; dean acad aff, 74-76. **MEMBERSHIPS** Mem, Amer Acad Rel; Amer Theol Soc; Amer Philos Soc; Assn for the UN; Scandinavian Amer Soc. **SELECTED PUBLICATIONS** Auth, Faith and the Other: A Relational Theology, 93 God: Question and Quest, 85; coauth, Lutherans and the Challenge of Religious Pluralism, 90; Suffering and Redemption: Exploring Christian Witness within a Buddhist Context, 88; coauth, ed, A Primer on Christian Prayer, 88; Christian Dogmatics, 84. **CONTACT ADDRESS** Dept of Systematic Theology, Luther Sem, 2481 Como Ave, St. Paul, MN, 55108. **EMAIL** psponhei@luthersem.edu

SPRAGENS, JANET R.
DISCIPLINE FEDERAL PERSONAL INCOME TAX **EDUCATION** Wellesley Col, BA, 64; George Washington Univ, JD, 68. **CAREER** Prof, Am Univ. **HONORS AND AWARDS** Exec dir, Am Tax Policy Inst; Managing ed, The Tax Lawyer; Chair, Low Income Taxpayer Comt; Consult, U.S. Dept Labor 84-85, Dept Treasury, 84-86; Dept of Juestice, 97, pt. **MEMBERSHIPS** WCL Tax Clinic. Am Law Inst;, ABA Tax Section. Executive Committee, Teaching Tax Comt, ABA; Tax Clinic Modeling Project; depts tax issues;Asn Am Law Sch; Maxwell-Macmillan Fed Taxes Adv Board. **RESEARCH** Tax law **CONTACT ADDRESS** American Univ, 4400 Massachusetts Ave, Washington, DC, 20016.

SPRAGUE, ELMER D., JR.
PERSONAL Born 08/14/1924, Havelock, NE, m, 1948, 4 children **DISCIPLINE** PHILOSOPHY **EDUCATION** Univ NE, Lincoln, BA, 48; Oxford Univ, BA, 50, D Phil, 53. **CAREER** Instr, , 48 Kearney State Tchrs Col; assoc prof, 53, AR Polytechnic Col; prof, 53-97, Brooklyn Col, prof of philos emeritus, Brooklyn Col, CUNY, 97-. **HONORS AND AWARDS** Phi Beta Kappa, NE Alpha, 48; Rhodes Scholar, Oxford Univ, 48-51; fac fel, CUNY, 64, 81; The Paul Robert and Jean Shuman Hanna Prof of Philos, Hamline Univ, 87; vis prof philos, The Col at New Paltz, SUNY, 88; Scholar Incentive Award, CUNY, 93-94. **MEMBERSHIPS** Am Philos Asn; Mind Asn; Hume Soc. **RESEARCH** Metaphysics; philos of mind, Hume. **CONTACT ADDRESS** PO Box 350, Cold Spring, NY, 10516. **EMAIL** sprague@highlands.com

SPRAGUE, ROSAMOND K.
PERSONAL Born 05/16/1922, Brookline, MA, w, 1946 **DISCIPLINE** PHILOSOPHY **EDUCATION** Bryn Mawr Col, BA, 45, MA, 48, PhD, 53. **CAREER** Lectr, Haverford Col, 53-54; pt-time lectr, Bryn Mawr Col, 54-55, 55-56; fel, Am Asoc Univ Women, Cambridge Univ, Princeton Univ, 56-57; vis fel, Princeton Univ, 56-57; instr, Bryn Mawr, 58-61, lectr, 61-62; asst lectr, Univ Birmingham, 64-65; asoc prof, Univ of South Carolina, 65-68, prof, 68-91; vis prof, Univ Toronto, 71-72; vis fel, Wolfson Col, 76; vis prof, Catholic Univ, 92-93. **HONORS AND AWARDS** Founder, Soc for Ancient Greek Philos, pres, 72-74; senior fel, Univ So Carolina, 74; hon Phi Beta Kappa, 75. **SELECTED PUBLICATIONS** Auth, Plato's Use of Fallacy, Routledge, 62; trans, Plato's Euthydemus, Bobbs-Merrill, 65; ed, The Older Sophists, USC, 72; auth, A Matter of Eternity, Eerdmans, 73; trans, Plato's Laches and Charmides, Bobbs-Merrill, 73; auth, Plato's Philosopher-King, USC, 76. **CONTACT ADDRESS** Dept of Philosophy, Univ of South Carolina, Columbia, SC, 29208.

SPRING, RAYMOND LEWIS
PERSONAL Born 08/05/1932, Warsaw, NY, m, 1955, 4 children **DISCIPLINE** LAW **EDUCATION** Washburn Univ Topeka, BA, 57, JD, 59. **CAREER** Atty, Crane, Martin, Claussen & Ashworth, 59-65; from asst prof to assoc prof law, 65-71, asst dean sch, 67-70, actg dean, 70-71, prof & dean sch, 71-78, Distinguished Prof Law, Washburn Univ Topeka, 78-, Vis prof, St Louis Univ, summer, 82. **HONORS AND AWARDS** Prof of Year, 80; Distinguished Serv Award, 87. **MEMBERSHIPS** Am Bar Asn; KS Bar Asn; Topeka Bar Asn. **RESEARCH** Criminal law; law and mental health **SELECTED PUBLICATIONS** Coauth, Vernon's KSA Criminal Code, 71 & Vernon's KSA Code of Criminal Procedure, 73, West Publ; The End of Insanity, Baranski, 82; Patients, Psychiatrist & Lawyers: Law and the Mental Health System, Anderson, 89, 2nd ed, 97. **CONTACT ADDRESS** Washburn Univ of Topeka, Sch of Law, 1700 S W College Ave, Topeka, KS, 66621-0001. **EMAIL** zzspri@washburn.edu

SPROUL, BARBARA CHAMBERLAIN
PERSONAL Born 06/18/1945, New York, NY, 2 children **DISCIPLINE** COMPARATIVE RELIGION, HUMAN RIGHTS **EDUCATION** Sarah Lawrence Col, BA, 66; Columbia Univ, MA, 68, PhD, 72. **CAREER** Asst prof, 72-77, assoc prof, 77-79, prof relig, 79, chmn prog in relig, 73-, Hunter Col; mem exec comt human rights, Amnesty Int USA, 70, gen secy, 78-. **MEMBERSHIPS** Am Acad Relig. **RESEARCH** Creation mythology; human rights. **SELECTED PUBLICATIONS** Ed, Primal Myths, Harper & Row, 79. **CONTACT ADDRESS** Dept of Relig, Hunter Col, CUNY, 695 Park Ave, New York, NY, 10021-5085.

SPROUL, R.C.
DISCIPLINE SYSTEMATIC THEOLOGY **EDUCATION** Westminster Col, BA; Pittsburgh Theol Sem, BD; Free Univ Amsterdam, Drs; Geneva Col, LittD. **CAREER** Adj prof **HONORS AND AWARDS** Founder, ch, bd of Ligonier Ministries; principal spokesman, hist Christian theol; pres, Intl Coun of Bibl Inerrancy. **SELECTED PUBLICATIONS** Gen ed, New Geveva Study Bible. **CONTACT ADDRESS** Dept of Systematic Theology, Reformed Theol Sem, 2101 Carmel Rd, Charlotte, NC, 28226.

SPRUNGER, MARY S.
DISCIPLINE THEOLOGY **EDUCATION** Bethel Col, BA; Univ IL, MA, PhD. **CAREER** Theol Dept, Eastern Mennonite Univ **SELECTED PUBLICATIONS** Articles: Conrad Grebel Rev. **CONTACT ADDRESS** Eastern Mennonite Univ, 1200 Park Road, Harrisonburg, VA, 22802-2462.

SQUADRITO, KATHLEEN MARIE
PERSONAL Born 01/11/1945, San Jose, CA **DISCIPLINE** PHILOSOPHY **EDUCATION** San Jose State Univ, BA, 68; Washington Univ, St Louis, MA, 72, PhD(philos), 73. **CAREER** Asst prof, 73-80, Assoc Prof Philos, Ind-Purdue Univ,

Ft Wayne, 80-. **MEMBERSHIPS** Am Philos Asn. **RESEARCH** John Locke; seventeenth century philosophy; metaphysics. **SELECTED PUBLICATIONS** Auth, Locke, Quine and natural kinds, Mod Schoolman, 72; Locke's view of essence and its relation to racism, 75 & The Essay: 4.4.3, 78, Locke Newslett; Locke's Theory of Sensitive Knowledge, Univ Press Am, 78; John Locke, G K Hall, 79. **CONTACT ADDRESS** Purdue Univ, 2101 Coliseum Blvd E, Fort Wayne, IN, 46805-1445.

SREEDHAR, SUSANNE
PERSONAL Washington, DC **DISCIPLINE** PHILOSOPHY **EDUCATION** Wesleyan Univ, Ba, 97; Univ North Carolina, 98-. **CAREER** Author **RESEARCH** Ethics; political philosophy. **CONTACT ADDRESS** 54 Hwy Bypass, Apt 29D, Chapel Hill, NC, 27516. **EMAIL** sreedhar@email.unc.edu

SREENIVASAN, GOPAL
PERSONAL Born 07/10/1964, Munich, Germany **DISCIPLINE** PHILOSOPHY **EDUCATION** McGill, BA, 86; Oxford, MD, 88; Univ Calif Berkeley, PhD, 93. **CAREER** Asst Prof, Princeton Univ, 93-. **MEMBERSHIPS** Am Philos Asn. **RESEARCH** Moral and Political Philosophy. **SELECTED PUBLICATIONS** Auth, The Limits of Lockor Rights In Property, 95; Interpretation and Reason, Philos and Public Affairs, 98. **CONTACT ADDRESS** Dept of Philosophy, Princeton Univ, 1879 Hall, Princeton, NJ, 08544-1006. **EMAIL** gopal@princeton.edu

ST. CLAIR HARVEY, ARCHER
DISCIPLINE EARLY CHRISTIAN AND BYZANTINE ART **EDUCATION** Princeton Univ, PhD. **CAREER** Assoc prof, Rutgers, The State Univ NJ, Univ Col-Camden; assoc dir, Am Acad in Rome/Soprintendenza Archeologica di Roma Palatine East Excavation. **RESEARCH** Late Antique and early Christian Art; Byzantine influence on Western art. **SELECTED PUBLICATIONS** Auth, A Byzantine Source for the San Paolo Bible, Princeton, 95; coauth, Scavi di un complesso tardo romano sul versante nord ovest dei Palatino (1990), Bolletino di archeologia IX, 91; A Late Roman Domus with Apsidal Hall on the Northeast Slope of the Palatine, Rome Papers (J of Roman Archaeol, suppl ser), 94; coed, The Carvers Art: Medieval Sculpture in Ivory, Bone, and Horn, Jane Voorhees Zimmerli Art Mus, 89. **CONTACT ADDRESS** Dept of Art Hist, Rutgers, The State Univ NJ, Univ Col-Camden, Voorhees Hall, 71 Hamilton St, New Brunswick, NJ, 08903. **EMAIL** astch@rci.rutgers.edu

STACK, GEORGE JOSEPH
PERSONAL Born 11/08/1932, New York, NY, m, 1962, 2 children **DISCIPLINE** PHILOSOPHY **EDUCATION** Pace Col, BA, 60; Pa State Univ, MA, 62, PhD(philos), 64. **CAREER** From instr to asst prof philos, C W Post Col, Long Island Univ, 63-67; from asst prof to assoc prof, 67-70, chmn dept, 70-77, Prof Philos, State Univ NY Col Brockport, 70-, State Univ NY grant-in-aid, 68-70; consult, Ctr Philos Exchange, 70- & Choice, 72- **MEMBERSHIPS** Eastern Div Am Philos Asn. **RESEARCH** History of philosophy; phenomenology and existentialism. **SELECTED PUBLICATIONS** Auth, Nietzsche--The Politics Of Power, Nineteenth Century Prose, Vol 21, 94; Charles Renouvier, Philosopher Of Liberty, Nineteenth Century Prose, Vol 21, 94; Composing The Soul, Reaches Of Nietzsche Psychology, Nineteenth Century Prose, Vol 23, 96; Nietzsche Philosophy Of Science, Nineteenth Century Prose, Vol 23, 96; Nietzsche,Friedrich Philosophy Of Art, Nineteenth Century Prose, Vol 21, 94; Nietzsche Revaluation Of Values--A Study In Strategies, Nineteenth Century Prose, Vol 23, 96. **CONTACT ADDRESS** Dept of Philos, State Univ NY, Brockport, NY, 14420.

STACKHOUSE, JOHN G., JR.
DISCIPLINE THEOLOGY; PHILOSOPHY OF RELIGION; CHURCH HISTORY **EDUCATION** Queen's Univ Kingston, BA, 80; Wheaton Col Grad Sch, 82; Univ Chicago, PhD, 87. **CAREER** Instr, Wheaton Col Grad Sch, 84-86; Asst Prof, NWestern Col, Iowa, 87-90; from Asst Prof to Prof Religion, Univ Manitoba, 90-98; Sangwoo Youtong Chee Prof Theology, Regent Col, Vancouver, 98-. **HONORS AND AWARDS** Prof of the Year (Award for Teaching Excellence), NWestern Col, 89; Rh Found Award for Outstanding Contributions to Schol and Res in the Humanities, Univ Manitoba, 93; Outreach Award for Community Service, Univ Manitoba, 97; First Place for Editorial Writing, Canadian Church Press, 98. **MEMBERSHIPS** Am Acad Relig; Am Soc Church Hist; Canadian Soc Church History; Canadian Evangelical Theol Asn. **RESEARCH** Epistemology; philosophy of religion; religion in North America. **SELECTED PUBLICATIONS** Auth, Canadian Evangelicalism in the Twentieth Century: An Introduction to Its Character, Univ Toronto Press, 93; Can God Be Trusted? Faith and the Challenge of Evil, Oxford Univ Press, 98; author of over 200 journal articles and reviews. **CONTACT ADDRESS** Regent Col, 5800 University Blvd., Vancouver, BC, V6T 2E4. **EMAIL** jgs@regent-college.edu

STACKHOUSE, MAX LYNN
PERSONAL Born 06/29/1935, 3 children **DISCIPLINE** CHRISTIAN ETHICS **EDUCATION** De Pauw Univ, BA, 57; Harvard Univ, BD, 61, PhD, 64. **CAREER** Lectr Christian ethics, Divinity Sch, Harvard Univ, 64-66; from asst prof to assoc prof, 66-72, Prof Christian Ethics, Andover-Newton Theol Sch, 72-93; Stephen Colwell Prof of Christian Ethics, Princeton Theol Sem, 93- ; Vis lectr, Episcopal Theol Sch, Boston Col, Bucknell Univ, Bluffton Col, Northeastern Univ, Tufts Univ, Ohio Wesleyan Univ & Dickinson Col; vis prof, United Theol Col, Bangalore, India, 73. **HONORS AND AWARDS** Winner of Melchor Prize, 76. **MEMBERSHIPS** Fel Soc Relig Higher Educ; fel Soc Europ Cult; Am Acad Social & Polit Philos; Soc Sci Studies Relig (past pres); Am Soc Christian Ethics. **SELECTED PUBLICATIONS** Ed & auth introd, The Righteousness of the Kingdom, Abingdon, 68; coauth, The Death of Dialogue and Beyond, Friendship, 69; auth, The Ethics of Necropolis, 71 & Ethics and the Urban Ethos, 73, Beacon; The Hindu ethos and development, Relig & Soc, fall 73; ed & auth introd, On Being Human Religiously, Beacon, 76; auth, On Moral Business, Eerdmans; auth, Christian Social Ethics in a Global Era, Abingdon; auth, Public Theology and Political Economy, Univ Press of America; auth, Creeds, Society, and Human Rights, Parthenon. **CONTACT ADDRESS** Princeton Theol Sem, PO Box 821, Princeton, NJ, 08542. **EMAIL** max.stackhouse@ptsem.edu

STACY, WAYNE
DISCIPLINE RELIGIOUS STUDIES **EDUCATION** Beach Atlantic Col, BA; Southern Baptist Theol Seminary, PhD. **CAREER** Prof, Midwestern Baptist Theol Seminary, 86-91; prof, 91-. **SELECTED PUBLICATIONS** Auth, pubs on biblical studies. **CONTACT ADDRESS** Dept of Religious Studies and Philosophy, Gardner-Webb Univ, PO Box 997, Boiling Springs, NC, 28017. **EMAIL** rwstacy@shelby.net

STADLER, INGRID
PERSONAL Born 07/06/1930, Vienna, Austria, m, 1952 **DISCIPLINE** PHILOSOPHY **EDUCATION** Vassar Col, BA, 52; Radcliffe Col, MA, 53, PhD, 59. **CAREER** From instr to assoc prof, 58-73, chmn dept, 72-78, Prof Philos, Wellesley Col, 73-, Mem regional selection comt, Woodrow Wilson Fel Found, 62-; Wellesley Col res grant, 63-64; Braitmayer Found fel, 68; consult, WGBH-TV, 72-; res scholar fel, Radcliffe Inst Indedpendent Studies, 72-73; ed, Ethical Issues for our Time, 73; vis scholar philos, Sch Humanities & Soc Sci, Mass Inst Tech & mem bd overseers, Ctr Res Women Higher Educ & Prof, Wellesley Col & Fedn Prof Women's Orgn, 74-; consult, Ed Mgt Serv, Inc, 75-78; mem comt for reaccreditation of Trinity Col, 76 & Smith Col, 77; mem task force on energy, Am Asn Univ Women, 76-77; mem selection comt, Mellon Fac Develop Grants, 76; consult, Project Impact, TV ser, Mass Coun for Arts & Pub Policy & Mt Wachusetts Community Col & panelist, First Ann Conf Business Ethics, Bentley Col, 77; chmn task force for reaccreditation of Wellesley Col & consult-panelist, The Massachusetts Story, Mass Coun for Arts & Pub Policy, 78; prof, Boston Architectural Ctr, 98. **MEMBERSHIPS** Am Philos Asn; Mind Asn; Asn Aesthet. **RESEARCH** Kant; aesthetics; recent and yet outstanding problems in theory of perception; art law, theories of ownership, efficacy of int law and int conventions; cultural policy of Japam and the U.K.; and the trials of war criminals at Nuernberg: causes and consequences. **SELECTED PUBLICATIONS** Auth, Seeing As, Philos Rev, 59; coauth, Kant, Doubleday, 67; auth Contemporary Art and its Philosophical Problems; auth, Treasuring Treasure, forthcoming. **CONTACT ADDRESS** Dept of Philosophy, Wellesley Col, 106 Central St, Wellesley, MA, 02181-8204. **EMAIL** finanz@compuserve.com

STAFFORD, GILBERT W.
PERSONAL Born 12/30/1938, Portageville, MO, m, 1962, 4 children **DISCIPLINE** SYSTEMATIC THEOLOGY **EDUCATION** Anderson Coll, BA, 61; Andover Newton Theol Sch, MDiv, 64; Boston Univ, ThD, 73. **CAREER** Assoc Dean, 80-89 & 98-, Dean of the Chapel, 84-89 & 96-, Prof of Christian Theol, 76-, Dir of the Dr Of Ministry Prog, 98-, Anderson Univ Sch Theol; Commn on Christian Unity of the Church of God, Member, 75-78 & 80-, Chr, 85-90, Member Commn on Faith and Order in the USA, 84; Staley Lectr, 94-. **HONORS AND AWARDS** Christian Ministries Award, Anderson Univ Alumni Assoc; Bethany Heritage Award. **MEMBERSHIPS** AAR, North Amer Acad of Ecumenists. **RESEARCH** Good and Evil; The Kingdom of God and Eschatology. **SELECTED PUBLICATIONS** Auth, Theology for Disciples: Systematic Considerations About the Life of Christian Faith, Anderson, Warner, 96; The Life of Salvation, Anderson, Warner, 79; Beliefs That Guide Us, Anderson, Center for Pastoral Studies, 77; The People of God, Anderson, Center for Pastoral Studies, 77; The Seven Doctrinal Leaders of the Church of God Movement, Anderson, Center for Pastoral Studies, 77; Church of God, Anderson, Indiana, The Renewal of Sunday Worship, vol III in The Complete Library of Christian Worship series, Nashville, Star Song; Booklets, Pub by Mass Communications Board of the Church of God; Gifts Most Precious; Gratitude; Handle With Care, Life's Dreams, Christ Jesus, Our Everything, A Hope for All of Us, 96. **CONTACT ADDRESS** School Theology, Anderson Univ, 1100 E 5th St, Anderson, IN, 46012-3495. **EMAIL** stafford@anderson.edu

STAFFORD, SUE P.
DISCIPLINE PHILOSOPHY **EDUCATION** Wheaton Col, Norton, BA, 67; Univ IL, Chicago Circle, MA, 68; Univ CT, PhD, 72. **CAREER** Assoc prof & dept ch; coach, Simmons Col Debate Club; co-convener, Coun Ch(s), mem, Comt on Tenure and App; work with, Camp Dresser & McKee, an environ consult firm & Mass Corp for Educ Telecommun, MCET; mem, proj team which develop a pollution forecasting comp syst for Mex City. **RESEARCH** Theory of knowledge; philos of mind; tech and ethics. **SELECTED PUBLICATIONS** auth, Taking Philosophy to the Trenches, Philos and Comput, 92; Pattern Detection: Software Answers and the Issues They Raise, Presentation to GTE Laboratories, Waltham, 90; Computers as Partners in Medical Decision Making,invited presentation APPSA, NS, Can, 96; Ethical Implications of Computer-Assisted Decision-Making in Health Care, invited presentation Amer Bar Asn, New Orleans, 94; Knowledge, Ignorance, and Responsibility, invited presentation AAAS, annual meeting, 93; Software for the Detection of Fraudulent Medical Insurance Claims, Proceedings of DIAC-90 Symp, Directions in Advanced Comput, Boston, 90; coauth, When Genetic Information is Not Enough, The Genetic Resource, vol 6, 92. **CONTACT ADDRESS** Dept of Philos, Simmons Col, 300 The Fenway, Boston, MA, 02115. **EMAIL** sstafford@simmons.edu

STAFFORD, WILLIAM SUTHERLAND
DISCIPLINE CHURCH HISTORY **EDUCATION** Stanford Univ, BA, 65-69; Yale Univ, MA, Mphil, 69-74, PhD, 75; Univ de Strasbourg: Fac de theol protestante, 73-74. **CAREER** Tchg fel, Yale Col, 71-73; vis asst prof, Brown Univ, 74-76; asst prof, 76-82; assoc prof, Va Theol Sem, 82-90; David J. Ely prof, 90-; associate dean for Acad Aff, VP. **SELECTED PUBLICATIONS** Auth, Disordered Loves: Healing the Seven Deadly Sins, Cowley Publ, 94; Sexual Norms in the Medieval Church, A Wholesome Example: Sexual Morality in the Episcopal Church, 91; The Eve of the Reformation: Bishop John Fisher, 1509, Hist Mag Protestant Episcopal Church, 85. **CONTACT ADDRESS** Va Theol Sem, 3737 Seminary Rd, Alexandria, VA, 22304. **EMAIL** WSStafford@vts.edu

STAGAMAN, DAVID
PERSONAL Born 07/29/1935, Cincinnati, OH **DISCIPLINE** PHILOSOPHY **EDUCATION** Loyola Univ, BA, 58 MA, 67; West Baden Col, PhL, 60; Bellarmine Sch of Theol, STL, 67; Inst Catholique de Paris, ThD, 75. **CAREER** Vis prof, 72-75, asst prof, 75-83, assoc prof, 84- , acad dean, 87-96,Jesuit School of Theol at Berkeley. **HONORS AND AWARDS** Asn of Theol Sch fel, 78-79; listed, Who's Who in the West; listed, Who's Who in Religion; listed, International Who's Who. **MEMBERSHIPS** Am Acad Relig; Catholic Theol Soc of Am; Pacific Coast Theol Soc. **RESEARCH** Ecclesiology, especially authority in the Church; Wittgenstein and the study of religion. **SELECTED PUBLICATIONS** Auth, Authority in the Church: A Central Issue and Some Other Issues, Tripod, 90; auth, What Authority is Not! Tripod, 90; auth, The Implications for Theology of The Acting Person, in McDermott, ed, The Thought of Pope John Paul II, Gregorain Univ, 93; auth, A Democratic Catholic Church, Christian Century, 93. **CONTACT ADDRESS** Jesuit Sch of Theol, Berkeley, 1735 LeRoy Ave, Berkeley, CA, 94709. **EMAIL** dstagama@jstb.edu

STAINTON, ROBERT J.H.
PERSONAL Born 09/20/1964 **DISCIPLINE** PHILOSOPHY **EDUCATION** York Univ, BA, 87, 88; Mass Inst Tech, PhD, 93; postdoc stud, Ctr for Cognitive Sci, Rutgers Univ, 97; Univ Mass, 96; Inst de Investigaciones Filosoficas, Univ Nacional Autonoma de Mexico, 94. **CAREER** Res coord, York Univ, 88-91; lectr, Salem State Col, 91; assoc prof, 93-. **HONORS AND AWARDS** York Univ Entrance scholar, 84; York Univ In-Course scholarship, 85-87; Glendon Col Philos prize, 88; MIT grad fel, 88; Andrew W Mellon fel, Hum, 88; doc fel, Soc Sci and Hum Res Coun of Can, 90; Andrew W Mellon Dissertation Year fel, 92., Ed, Bulletin of the Can Philos Assn; ch, Vis Speaker Comm, 94-97; Cognitive Sci ORU Distinguished Lectr Series Comm, 94-96; clerk, Fac of Arts and Soc Sci, 97; Chief Acad Proctor, 97; dir, Theoret Ling Org Res Unit, 96-97; adv bd, Col of the Hum, 95-97; planning comm, Doc Prog in Cognitive Sci, 94-96. **RESEARCH** Philosophy of language, pragmatics, philosophy of mind, formal semantics. **SELECTED PUBLICATIONS** Auth, Using Non-Sentences: An Application of Relevance Theory, Pragmatics and Cognition, 94; "Non-Sentential Assertions and Semantic Ellipsis," Ling and Philos, 95; A Note on Pedir and Control in Spanish, ahiers Ling d'Ottawa, 95; Indeterminacy, Opacity and the Identity Theory, Cretica, 95; The Deflation of Belief Contents, Cretica, 96; Philosophical Perspectives on Language, Broadview Press, 96; The Deflation of Belief States, Cretica, 97; "hat Assertion Is Not," Philos Stud, 97; Utterance Meaning and Syntactic Ellipsis, Pragmatics and Cognition, 97; Unembedded Definite Descriptions and Relevance, Revista Alicantina de Estudios Ingleses, 98; "Quantifier Phrases, Meaningfulness 'in Isolation' and Ellipsis," Ling and Philos, 98; co-ed, Philosophy and Linguistic, Westview Press, 98; coauth, "Fodor's New Theory of Computation and Information," Proc of the Eighteenth Conf of the Cognitive Sci Soc, Lawrence Erlbaum Assoc, 96; "Fodor's New Theory of Content and Computation," Mind and Lang, 97; rev(s), Dynamics of Meaning: Anaphora, Presupposition, and the Theory of Grammar, by Gennaro Chierchia, Can Philos

Rev, 95; Connectionism and the Philosophy of Psychology, by T. Horgan and J. Tienson, Can Philos Rev, 96; What Else Can I Tell You? A Pragmatic Study of English Rhetorical Questions as Discursive and Argumentative Acts, by Cornelia Ilie, Lang, 96; Consciousness and the Origins of Thought, by Norton Nelkin, Philos in Rev, 97; Language, Thought and Consciousness, by P. Carruthers, Lang, 97; Syntactic Theory and the Structure of English: A Minimalist Approach, by Andrew Radford, Philos in Rev, 98. **CONTACT ADDRESS** Dept of Philos, Carleton Univ, 1125 Colonel By Dr, Ottawa, ON, K1S 5B6. **EMAIL** Stainton@Ccs.Carleton.Ca

STALEY, JEFFREY L.
PERSONAL Born 12/22/1951, Kansas City, MO, m, 1982, 2 children **DISCIPLINE** THEOLOGY **EDUCATION** Wheaton Col, BA, 73; Fuller Theol Sem, MA, 79; Grad Theol Union, PhD, 85. **CAREER** Univ Portland, 85-92; Univ Notre Dame, 92-93; Seattle Univ, 94-95; Pacific Lutheran Univ, 97- . **MEMBERSHIPS** Am Acad of Relig; Soc of Bibl Lit; Cath Bibl Asn. **RESEARCH** New Testament; literary theory. **SELECTED PUBLICATIONS** Auth, Reading with a Passion: Rhetoric, Autobiography, and the American West in the Gospel of John, Continuum, 95; auth, Narrative Structure (Self Stricture) in Luke 4:14-9:62: The United States of Luke's Story World, Semeia, 95; ed and contribur, Taking It Personally: Autobiographical Biblical Criticism, Semeia, 95; auth, The Politics of Place and the Place of Politics in the Gospel of John, in, More Interpretations than the World Can Contain: Readers and Readings of the Fourth Gospel, Scholars, 98; auth, The Apostle John, in, Freedman, ed, Eerdmans Dictionary of the Bible, Eerdmans, 99; auth, Fathers and Sons: Fragments from an Autobiographical Midrash on the Gospel of John, in, Kitzberger, ed, The Personal Voice in Biblical Interpretation, Routledge, 99; auth, Changing Woman: Postcolonial Reflections on Acts 16:6-40, JSNT, 99. **CONTACT ADDRESS** Dept of Religion, Pacific Lutheran Univ, Tacoma, WA, 98447-0003.

STALLARD, MICHAEL D.
DISCIPLINE THEOLOGY **EDUCATION** Univ Ala, Huntsville, BA, 75; Liberty Baptist Sem, MDiv, 80; Dallas Theol Sem, STM, 84, PhD, 93. **CAREER** Asst prof, 94-95, ASSOC PROF, SYSTEMIC THEOL, BAPTIST BIBLE SEM, 95-; ed, J Ministry & Theol, 98-. **CONTACT ADDRESS** 110 Park St, Clarks Summit, PA, 18411. **EMAIL** mstallard@bbc.edu

STAM, JAMES H.
PERSONAL Born 12/29/1937, Paterson, NJ, m, 1991, 5 children **DISCIPLINE** PHILOSOPHY **EDUCATION** Upsala Col, BA, 58; Univ Vienna, Austria, 58-59; Brandeis Univ, MA, 61, PHD, 64. **CAREER** Prof philos, co-dir, Writing Across the Curriculum, assoc dean Wirths Campus, Upsala Col, 62-95; Millicent Fenwick Prof of Educ and Public Issues, Monmouth Univ, 95- . **HONORS AND AWARDS** Fel, Newberry Libr, 68; NEH Jr Fel, 69; Lindback Award for Distinguished Tchg, 70; NEH summer sem and fel; NYU Assoc and Scholar in Residence, 83-90. **MEMBERSHIPS** Soc for Ancient Greek Philos; Philos of Educ Soc; Hegel Soc of Am; Soc for the Study of African Philos; Nat Asn for Sci, Soc and Technol; Nat Asn for Hum Educ; AAUP. **RESEARCH** History of philosophy; Greek philosophy; German philosophy; philosophy of language; philosophy of education. **SELECTED PUBLICATIONS** Auth, Inquiries into the Origin of Language: The Fate of a Question, in Chomsky, ed, Studies in Language, Harper & Row, 76; auth, Benjamin Lee Whorf, in Encyclopedia of Language and Linguistics, Pergamon, 94; auth, Leadership in the Teaching University, in Sarsar, ed, Education for Leadership and Social Responsibility, Center for the Study of Public Issues, 96; auth, The Courage of One's Words: Characters and Their Arguments in Plato's Laches, in Richardson, ed, Understanding Schleiermacher: From Translation to Interpretation, Edwin Mellen, 98. **CONTACT ADDRESS** Dept of Interdisciplinary Studies, Monmouth Univ, 400 Cedar Ave, West Long Branch, NJ, 07764-1898. **EMAIL** jstam@mondec.monmouth.edu

STAMBAUGH, JOAN
PERSONAL Born 06/10/1932, Pittsburgh, PA **DISCIPLINE** PHILOSOPHY **EDUCATION** Vassar Col, BA, 53; Columbia Univ, MA, 55; Univ Freiburg, PhD(philos), 58. **CAREER** Lectr English, Univ Freiburg, 62-63; from instr to asst prof philos, Vassar Col, 64-69; Asst Prof Philos, Hunter Col, 69-, Ger Res Asn res fel, 60-62; Freiburg Sci Soc fel, 62-63; fel, Arnold Bergstraesser Inst, 63-64; instr, Dutchess Community Col, 66-67; Nat Endowment for Humanities fel, 73-74; co-ed, Heidegger Transl, Harper & Row. **MEMBERSHIPS** Am Philos Asn. **RESEARCH** Nineteenth century and contemporary German thought; problem of time; Buddhism. **SELECTED PUBLICATIONS** Auth, Unterschungen zum Problem der Zeit bei Nietzsche, M Nijhoff, The Hague, 59; Music as a temporal form, J Philos, 64; Das Gleiche in Nietzsches Gedanken der ewigen Wiederkunft des Gleichen, Rev Int Philos, 64; Geist und Welt, Acts XIV Int Cong Philos, 68; Nietzsche's Thought of Eternal Return, Hopkins, 72; A Study Of Dogen--His Philosophy And Religion, Eastern Buddhist, Vol 25, 92; Transcendence, Eastern Buddhist, Vol 28, 95. **CONTACT ADDRESS** Dept of Philos, Hunter Col, CUNY, 695 Park Ave, New York, NY, 10021-5085.

STAMEY, JOSEPH DONALD
PERSONAL Born 01/10/1934, Cisco, TX, m, 1955, 1 child **DISCIPLINE** PHILOSOPHY, RELIGION **EDUCATION** Southern Methodist Univ, BA, 55, BD, 59, MA, 61; Boston Univ PhD(social ethics & sociol of relig), 68. **CAREER** From asst prof to assoc prof, 67-76, prof philos & relig, McMurry Col, 76-. **HONORS AND AWARDS** CASE Prof for TX, 91; Turner Distinguished Prof of Philos and t Mims, AL Rev, 1/76. **CONTACT ADDRESS** Dept Hist, McPherson Col, PO Box 1402, McPherson, KS, 67460-1402. **EMAIL** lengell@mcpherson.edu

STANCELL, DOLORES WILSON PEGRAM
PERSONAL Born 10/26/1936, New York, NY, m **DISCIPLINE** LAW **EDUCATION** Rutgers U, BA 1970; Rutgers Sch of Law, JD 1974; MI State U, Annual Regulatory Studies Prog 1976. **CAREER** NJ Dept of Pub Adv Div of Rate Counsel, asst dep pub adv; Hon David D Furman Superior Ct Chan Div NJ, law sec 1974-75; Rutgers Univ Rutgers Jour of Comptrs & the Law, admin 1973; Jersey Shore Med Ctr, nurse 1972; Middlesex Cty Legal Svcs, legal intern 1970; Rutgers Urban Studies Ctr, rsch asst 1968; Head Start MCEOC, nurse 1967; Head Start, nurse 1966; Beth Israel Hosp, staff nurse 1958-62; Fordham Hosp, staff nurse 1957-58. **HONORS AND AWARDS** Human Rels Awrd Fordham Hosp 1957. **MEMBERSHIPS** Am Bar Assn Sect on Legal Educ & Admissions to the Bar 1977-78; Forum Comm on Hlth Law 1977-78; Gen Practice 1976-77; Natl Bar Assn 1st vp, Women's Div 1977-78; vice pres Civil Trial Advocacy Sect 1977-78; Legislation & Uniform & State Laws Comm 1977-78; nom com Women's Div 1976-77; Fed Bar Assn; Garden State Bar Assn; NJ State Bar Assn; Hlth Leg & Hlth Plng Serv Com 1976-78; Monmouth Bar Assn; Crmnl Pract Com 1976-78; treas Assn Black Women Lawyers NJ 1977-78; Rutgers Law Sch Alumni Assn; Rutgers Univ Alumni Assn; panelist MRC-TV NY Program, Medical Costs, The Breath of Life 1977; Am Nurses Assn; NJ State Nurses Assn; vol Ocean-Monmouth Legal Serv 1972; vol urban agt Rutgers Urban Studies Cen 1967-68; Pub Policy Forum on Civil Disorders & Forum on the Futureof NJ Rutgers Univ 1968; co Rutgers-Douglass Coll Elem Sch Tutorial Prog 1967-68; trustee Unitarian Soc 1970-72; Acad Adv Com 1977-78; bd Parents Assn Rutgers Prep Sch 1970-71; New Brunswick YWCA; Urban League; NAACP. **SELECTED PUBLICATIONS** Articles Wilson, Computerization of Welfare Recipients, Implications for the Individual & The Right to Privacy 4 Rutgers Journal of Computers and The Law 163 (1974); Minoritiy Workers 1 Womens Rights Law Reporter 71 (1972-73). **CONTACT ADDRESS** 10 Commerce Ct, Newark, NJ, 07102.

STANDEN, JEFFERY A.
DISCIPLINE CRIMINAL JUSTICE, CRIMINAL PROCEDURE, JURISPRUDENCE, EVIDENCE **EDUCATION** Georgetown Univ, AB, 82; Univ Va, JD, 86. **CAREER** Clk, Hon Robert F Chapman, US Court of Appeals, 86-87; assoc, Hunton & Williams, Richmond, 86-90; dep gen couns, US Sentencing Comm, 89-90; asst prof, 90-94; assoc prof, 94-97; prof, 97-. **SELECTED PUBLICATIONS** Ed, Va Law Rev. **CONTACT ADDRESS** Sch of Law, Willamette Univ, 900 State St, Salem, OR, 97301. **EMAIL** jstanden@willamette.edu

STANFORD, PRESTON K.
DISCIPLINE PHILOSOPHY **EDUCATION** Univ Calif San Diego, PhD, 97. **CAREER** Asst prof, Univ Calif Irvine, 97-. **MEMBERSHIPS** APA; PSA. **RESEARCH** Philosophy of science; Philosophy of biology; Metaphysics; History of modern philosophy. **SELECTED PUBLICATIONS** Auth, Reference and natural kind terms: The Real Essence of Locke's View, Pac Philos Quart, 98; auth, For Pluralism and Against Realism About Species, Philos Sci, 95. **CONTACT ADDRESS** Dept. of Philosophy, Univ of California, Irvine, CA, 92697-4555. **EMAIL** stanford@uci.edu

STANLEY, JOHN E.
PERSONAL Born 03/24/1943, Connelsville, PA, m, 1970, 2 children **DISCIPLINE** BIBLE **EDUCATION** Anderson Coll, BA, 65; Anderson Sch Theol, MDiv, 69; Lutheran Theol Sem, STM; Univ Denver, Iliff Sch Theol, PhD, 86. **CAREER** Pastor, 69-80; prof, Warner Pacific Coll, 83-95; PROF BIBLICAL & REL STUDIES, MESSIAH COLL, 95-. **HONORS AND AWARDS** Louisville Inst grant, 98; NEH summer grant, 86. **MEMBERSHIPS** Soc Bibl Lit **RESEARCH** Bibl interpretation, psalms. **SELECTED PUBLICATIONS** various **CONTACT ADDRESS** 130 Sholly Dr, Mechanicsburg, PA, 17055. **EMAIL** jstanley@messiah.edu

STANLEY, KATHRYN VELMA
PERSONAL Born 02/09/1967, Detroit, MI, s **DISCIPLINE** LAW **EDUCATION** Spellman College, BA, 1989; Univ of Virginia School of Law, JD, 1992. **CAREER** Children's Defense Fund, student intern, 1988-89; Alabama Capitol Representation Resource Center, staff atty, 1992-. **HONORS AND AWARDS** Black Law Student Assn, Member of the Year, 1992. **MEMBERSHIPS** Sigma Alpha Iota Music Fraternity, vp, 1988-89; Black Law Students Assn, UVA Chapter, pres, 1991-92; Youth Entrepreneurship System, board sec, 1995-. **SELECTED PUBLICATIONS** Essence Magazine, Back Talk, December 1994; Virginia Lawyer (Alumni Magazine), Winter 1995. **CONTACT ADDRESS** Alabama Capital Representation Resource Center, 114 N Hull St, Montgomery, AL, 36105.

STANOVSKY, DEREK
DISCIPLINE PHILOSOPHY **EDUCATION** Univ of Tex Austin, BA, 85, PhD, 94. **CAREER** Appalachian State Univ, lectr, 95-. **RESEARCH** Feminist theory; 20th century continental philosophy. **SELECTED PUBLICATIONS** Auth, Fela and His Wives: The Import of a Postcolonial Masculinity, in: Jouvert: A Jour Postcolonial Stud, vol 2, no 1 98; auth, Speaking As, Speaking For and Speaking With: The Pitfalls and Possibilities of Men Teaching Feminism, Feminist Teacher, vol 11, no 1 97. **CONTACT ADDRESS** Dept of Interdisciplinary Studies, Appalachian State Univ, Boonie, NC, 28608. **EMAIL** stanovskydj@appstate.edu

STANTON VOGELAAR, HAROLD
DISCIPLINE MISSIONS; WORLD RELIGIONS **EDUCATION** New Brunswick Theol Sem; Columbia Univ. **CAREER** Adj prof **HONORS AND AWARDS** Ch, Christian-Muslim Working Group of NCCC's Interfaith Relations; co-ch, Conf for Improved Muslim-Christian Relations of Greater Chicago. **SELECTED PUBLICATIONS** Coauth, Activities of the Immigrant Muslim Communities in Chicago, Muslim Communities in N Am, State U of New York P, 94. **CONTACT ADDRESS** Dept of Missions and World Religions, Lutheran Sch of Theol, 1100 E 55th St, Chicago, IL, 60615. **EMAIL** hvogelaa@lstc.edu

STARBUCK, SCOTT R.
PERSONAL Born 11/12/1963, 2 children **DISCIPLINE** BIBLICAL STUDIES **EDUCATION** Whitworth Col, BA, 85; Princeton Theol Seminary, MDiv, 88, PhD, 95. **CAREER** Res Dir, 83-84, Teaching Asst, 84-85, Co-Dir Resident Chaplain Prog, Whitworth Col, 84-85; Teaching Asst, 87-88, Res Asst, 88-92, Sub-ed and contribr, PTS Int Dead Sea Scrolls Project, 86-87, Actg Dir, Office of Computer Assistance for Textual Res, Princeton Theol Seminary, 88-91; Res Theologian, 91-92, Sr Pastor and Head of Staff, Hopewell Presbyterian Church, 92-97; Sr Pastor and Head of Staff, Wellshire Presbyterian Church, 97-. **HONORS AND AWARDS** National Deans List, 85; Outstanding Philos Student, Whitworth Col, 85; Princeton Doctoral Teaching Fel, 88-91; Princeton Doctoral Fel, 88-91; The George S. Green Doctoral Fel in Old Testament, 88-90; Guest Lectr, Princeton Theol Seminary, 91-92; Vis Lectr in Congregational Ministries, Princeton Theol Seminary, 94-95. **MEMBERSHIPS** Presbytery of Denver; Soc Bibl Lit; Cath Bibl Soc; Am Sch Oriental Res; Samaritan Inst. **SELECTED PUBLICATIONS** Auth, Like Dreamers Lying in Wait, We Lament: A New Reading of Psalm 126, Koinonia, 89; coauth, Graphic Concordance to the Dead Sea Scrolls, Westminster/John Knox, 91; auth, Ministerial Development and Spiritual Support Groups, Testament, Spring 95; And What Had Kings? The Reappropriation of Court Oracles Among the Royal Psalms of the Hebrew Psalter, Univ Mich Press, 96; Engaging the World With Christ: Participating in the Royal Office of Christ, Theol Matters, 98; Court Oracles in the Psalms: A New Examination of the So-Called Royal Psalms in their Ancient Near Eastern Context, Scholars Press (forthcoming). **CONTACT ADDRESS** Wellshire Presbyterian Church, 2999 S. Colorado Blvd., Denver, CO, 80222-6607. **EMAIL** scott_ra_starbuck@juno.com

STARK, HERMAN E.
PERSONAL Born 10/04/1966, Elmhurst, m, 1990 **DISCIPLINE** PHILOSOPHY **EDUCATION** Northern IL Univ, BA, MA; Univ Memphis, PhD. **CAREER** Inst, 92-94, Univ of Memphis; inst, 93-94, Shelby State Comm Col; asst prof, 94-95, Northern Illinios Univ; coordinator of phil, 95-, South Suburban Col. **HONORS AND AWARDS** Magna Cum Laude, Deans Award, Distinction on MA Logic Examinations, The Meritorious Grad Tchng Award, Univ of Memphis; The Amer Phil Assoc Certificate for Tchng Excl. **MEMBERSHIPS** APA **RESEARCH** The nature of rationality **CONTACT ADDRESS** 175 N Harbor Dr, Ste 1604, Chicago, IL, 60601. **EMAIL** hstark@acilan.ssc.cc.il.us

STARK, TRACEY
PERSONAL Born 02/10/1965, Minneapolis, MN, s **DISCIPLINE** PHILOSOPHY **EDUCATION** Boston Col, PhD. **CAREER** Asst prof, Univ Maine Orono; asst prof, St. John's Sem, Boston. **MEMBERSHIPS** APA; Soc for Phenomenol & Existential Philos. **RESEARCH** Phenomenology; critical theory; psychoanalysis. **SELECTED PUBLICATIONS** Auth, "Dignity of the Particular: Adorno on Kant's Aesthetics," Philos & Soc Critisicm; "Arendt & the White Rose," Budhi, forthcoming **CONTACT ADDRESS** 15 Gardner St., Apt. B, Allston, MA, 02134. **EMAIL** starktr@bc.du

STARKEY, LAWRENCE H.
PERSONAL Born 07/10/1919, Minneapolis, MN, 3 children **DISCIPLINE** PHILOSOPHY **EDUCATION** Univ Louisville, BA, 42; Southern Baptist Theol Sem, MDiv, 45; Univ So Calif, MA, 51, PhD, 60. **CAREER** Asst prof Los Angeles Baptist Col and Sem, 47-51; writer, Moody Inst of Sci, 55-57; assoc prof philos, phys sci, Bethel Col, 58-62; assoc prof, philos and relig,

chemn, Linfield Col, 62-63; engg writer, General Dynamics, 63-66; assoc prof philos & hum, Alma Col, 66-68; assoc ed and ed of philos, Encyclopedia Britannica, 68-72; assoc prof philos & hum, chemn, Jamestown Col, 73-75; lectr philos & relig, producer television studies, field coord, N Dakota State Univ, 76-79; mech des Concord Inc, 77-85; instr philos, Moorhead State Univ, 85-86; lectr philos Univ Missouri, 86-87; independent scholar, 88- . **HONORS AND AWARDS** Delegate, citizen ambassador program to Russia and Hungary; J.B. Speed Jr scholar; BA honors in biol. **MEMBERSHIPS** Am Sci Asn; APA; Metaphysical Soc of Am. **RESEARCH** Synoptic thinking; integrating philosophy, religion, science and literature; particle physics; relativity; cosmology; new archaeological findings on the patriarch Joseph. **SELECTED PUBLICATIONS** Auth, A Less Fantastic God: A Biologist Sees Him as Evolving from Matter; auth, The Inherence of Particles in Universe, of Force in Plenum: Leibniz vis-a-vis Relativistic Cosmology and Black-Hole Gravitation; auth, Kant's Cosmological Antinomies and Modern Physics; auth, Necessity and Purposiveness in the Cosmic Setting and History of Life; contribur to People Who Made America: Pictorial Encyclopedia; contribur Encyclopedia Britannica. **CONTACT ADDRESS** 1325 N 63rd St, Wauwatosa, WI, 53213.

STARKS KIERSTEAD, MELANIE

PERSONAL Born 03/20/1960, Potsdam, NY, m, 1984, 2 children **DISCIPLINE** RELIGION **EDUCATION** Houghton Col, BA, 82; Bethany Bible Col, Ba, 83; Wesley Biblical Sem, M. Div, 86; Reformed Theolog Sem, Th.M, 87; Drew Univ, M. Phil, 93, PhD, 96 **CAREER** Tchr, Capital City Chrisitan Acad, 87-88; prof, Phillips Junior Col, 88-89; campus pastor 96-97, prof, 89-90, 92-97, Bartlesville Wesleyan Col; asst prof, Ind Wesleyan Univ, 97-. **HONORS AND AWARDS** Extraordinary People, 97, Houghton Col. **MEMBERSHIPS** Soc Biblical Lit; Am Acad Rel; Wesleyan Theolog Soc. **RESEARCH** 2nd Century Montanism; Luke-Acts; Pastorals. **SELECTED PUBLICATIONS** Auth, art, God of Comfort, 91; auth, art, The Word Inspires Confession, 95; auth, Calling God's people back to Hope, 95; auth, art, The Letter, 96; auth, art, Remembering the One True God's Faithful Love, 97. **CONTACT ADDRESS** 1723 Beechwood Blvd, Marion, IN, 46952. **EMAIL** mkierstead@indwes.edu

STATON, CECIL P., JR.

PERSONAL Born 01/26/1958, Greenville, SC, m, 1986, 2 children **DISCIPLINE** RELIGION **EDUCATION** Furman Univ, BA, 80; Southeastern Baptist Theol Sem, MDiv, 82, MTheol, 85; Univ Oxford, PhD, 88. **CAREER** Publ, Chanticleer Publ, 82-85; Old Test lectr, Regents Pk Col, Univ Oxford, 88; asst prof Chr, Brewton-Parker Col, 89-91; assoc provost & assoc prof, Mercer Univ & Pres. & pres Smyth & Helwys Publ, 91-. **HONORS AND AWARDS** Baggott award for Outstanding Relig maj, Furman Univ, 80; RT Daniel award, 83; G. Henton Davies Prize, 85. **MEMBERSHIPS** Baptist New Ventures Gp, 92-97; AAR; Soc Bibl Lit; Natl Assoc Baptist Prof of Rel; Bd Dir Baptists Today. **RESEARCH** Hebrew and Old Testament. **SELECTED PUBLICATIONS** Auth, Why I am a Baptist, 99; auth, Interpreting Amos for Preaching and Teaching, 95; auth, Interpreting Hosea for Preaching and Teaching, 93; auth, Interpreting Isaiah for Preaching and Teaching, 91. **CONTACT ADDRESS** Smyth & Helwys Publishing, Mercer Univ, 6316 Peake Rd, Macon, GA, 31210-3960. **EMAIL** cps@helwys.com

STAUB, JACOB J.

PERSONAL Born 05/04/1951, New York, NY, m, 1975, 3 children **DISCIPLINE** RELIGION/MEDIEVAL JEWISH PHILOSOPHY, CONTEMPORARY JEWISH THOUGHT **EDUCATION** Reconstructionist Rabbinical College, ordination, 77; Temple Univ, PhD, 80. **CAREER** Asst Prof, Dept Relig, Lafayette Col, 77-83; ACAD DEAN, RECONSTRUCTIONIST RABBINICAL COL, 83-. **HONORS AND AWARDS** Gladstone Prize Fine Teaching; 97; fel, Acad Jewish Philos, 99; Mellow Fel Jewish Philos, **MEMBERSHIPS** Asn Jewish Studies; Am Acad Relig; Reconstructionist Rabbinical Asn. **RESEARCH** Medieval Jewish Philos, Medieval Bible Commentaries. **SELECTED PUBLICATIONS** Coauth, "The Spiritualization of Peoplehood and the Reconstructionist Curriculum of the Future," in Windows on the Jewish Soul: Resources for Teaching the Values of Spiritual Peoplehood, 94, Hauvrot; auth, "Reconstructionism" and "Mordecai M. Kaplan," Encyclopedia Britannica, 99; auth, "Reconstructionist Judaism," The Encyclopedia of Judaism, The Religion, 99, E. J. Brill; auth, "Interpreting Jewish History in Light of Zionism," The Reconstructionist, Spring 98; auth, "How Are We Tested: The Binding of Isaac," Reconstructionism Today, Fall 97; auth, "From Slavery to Freedom," Creating Passover Memories, 97, Making Connections, Community Hebrew Schools; auth, "Mordecai M. Kaplan," "Reconstructionism," "Reconstructionist Rabbinical College," "Milton Steinberg," Oxford Dictionary of the Jewish Religion, 97, Oxford Univ Press; auth, "Evolving Definitions of Evolution," The Reconstructiont, Fall 96; auth, "How Can Reconstructionists Pray?" Reconstructionism Today, Spring 96, and Connecting Prayer and Spirituality: Kol Haneshamah as a Creative Teaching and Learning Text, 96, The Reconstructionist Press; auth, "Flexible Boundaries," The Reconstructionist, Fall 94; auth, "Submission as a Value," Reconstructionism Today, Fall 93; auth, "Theology and Community: A Response," in Imagining the Jewish Future, 92, State Univ NY Press; auth, "Idud Ha-Aliyah MiTzafron Amerika," in Si'ah Mesharim, 92; auth, "Reconstructionism," in Encyclopedia of Jewish-American History and Culture, 92, Garland Publishing; auth, "Reconstructionist Judaism," in Encyclopedia of Religions in the United States: One Hundred Religious Groups Speak for Themselves, 92, Crossroad/Continuum; coauth, "Jewish Philosophy: Medieval and Modern," in The Schocken Guide to Jewish Books, 92, Schocken Books. **CONTACT ADDRESS** Acad Dean, Reconstructionist Rabbinical Col, 1299 Church Rd, Wyncote, PA, 19095. **EMAIL** staub@rrc.edu

STEBENNE, DAVID

PERSONAL Born 07/04/1960, Providence, RI **DISCIPLINE** HISTORY, LAW **EDUCATION** Yale Univ, BA, 82; Columbia Univ, JD, MA, 86, PhD, 91. **CAREER** Lectr, Hist, Yale Univ, 91-93; asst prof, Hist, Ohio State Univ, 93-97; ASSOC PROF, HIST, OHIO STATE UNIV, 97-. **MEMBERSHIPS** Am Hist Asn; Org Am Hist; Bus Hist Conf; DC Bar; Md Bar **RESEARCH** Modern US history; politics, economics, labor & legal history **SELECTED PUBLICATIONS** Arthur J. Goldberg: New Deal Liberal, Oxford Univ Press, 96. **CONTACT ADDRESS** Hist Dept, Ohio State Univ, 106 Dulles Hall, 230 w 17th, Columbus, OH, 43210-1367. **EMAIL** stebenne.1@osu.edu

STECKER, ROBERT

DISCIPLINE PHILOSOPHY **EDUCATION** Mass Inst Tech, PhD, 75. **CAREER** PROF, PHILOS, CENTRAL MICH UNIV. 83-, lectr, Watlow Univ, Singapore, 77-83; asst prof, Univ Houston, 75-76. **CONTACT ADDRESS** 4538 Comanche, Okemos, MI, 40864. **EMAIL** robert.stecker@cmich.edu

STEEGER, WM P.

PERSONAL Born 05/26/1945, Brooklyn, NY, m, 1968, 4 children **DISCIPLINE** OLD TESTAMENT ARCHEOLOGY **EDUCATION** Univ Florida, BA, 67; Southern Baptist Theol Sem, Louisville, Mdiv 70, PhD, 83; Univ of Louisville, KY, MA, 72. **CAREER** Instr, 69-73, Univ of Louisville; Prof, 76-86, Baptist Theol of Southern Africa, Johannesburg, S Africa; Prof, 78-86, Die Theol Sem van die Baptist; Prof, 83-84, Oakland City Coll; Prof, 86-, Ouachita Baptist Univ, Arkadelphia, AR, Chr Div of Rel and Philos. **HONORS AND AWARDS** Phi Kappa Phi; Phi Alpha Theta; Amer Ed, KY, South; Biblical Stud and Archaeol; Man of Achievement; Vis Prof of OT-Southern Baptist Theol Sem, KY. **MEMBERSHIPS** Soc of Biblical Lit; Evangelical Theol Soc; Inst of Biblical Res; Natl Assoc of Baptist Prof of Rel. **RESEARCH** Old Testament; Biblical Archaeology. **SELECTED PUBLICATIONS** Contrib auth, Anchor Bible Dictionary, Doubleday & Co; Contrib auth, Mercer Commentary of the Bible, Mercer Univ Press; auth, Joshua: An Exposition, Baptist Theological College of Southern Africa, Johannesburg, South Africa; Psalms: An Exposition, Old Testament Theology, Old Testament Introduction, Baptist Theo College of S Africa, Johannesburg, S Africa. **CONTACT ADDRESS** Ouachita Baptist Univ, OBU 3720, Arkadelphia, AR, 71998. **EMAIL** steeger@alpha.edu

STEELE, RICHARD B.

PERSONAL Born 11/03/1952, Philadelphia, PA, m, 1978, 3 children **DISCIPLINE** CHRISTIAN THEOLOGY **EDUCATION** Haverford Col, BA, 74; Yale Divinity School, MDiv, 78; Marquette Univ, PhD, 90. **CAREER** Pastor, Trinity-Pilgrim United Methodist Church, Brookfield, WI, 85-95; instr Theol, Marquette Univ, Milwaukee, WI, 93-94; asst prof Theol, Milwaukee Theol Inst, Milwaukee, WI, 90-95; ASSOC PROF THEOL, SEATTLE PACIFIC UNIV, SEATTLE, WA, 95-. **HONORS AND AWARDS** Arthur J. Schmitt fel, Marquette Univ, 86-87; Top Prof Ivy Honorary (Mortarboard), Seattle Pacific Univ, 96. **MEMBERSHIPS** Amer Acad Relig; Hist Soc of the United Methodist Church; Karl Barth Soc; Wesleyan Theol Soc. **RESEARCH** Jonathan Edwards; Eastern Orthodox theology; religion and disability; moral psychology and Christian formation. **SELECTED PUBLICATIONS** Auth, Review of Randy L. Maddox, ed, Aldersgate Reconsidered, Wesleyan Theol J, spring-fall 94; Gracious Affection and True Virtue according to Johnathan Edwards and John Wesley, PhD dissertation, Marquette Univ, 90, rev ed, Wesleyan and Pietist Studies Series, Scarecrow Press, 94; Why Church Growth is a Red Herring, Circuit Rider, March 94; review of Brett Webb-Mitchell, God Plays Piano, Too: The Spiritual Lives of Disabled Children, Medical Col of WI, Bioethics Bull, fall 95; Narrative Theology and the Religious Affections in Theology Without Foundations: Religious Practice and the Future of Theological Truth, ed Stanley Hauerwas, Nancy Murphy, and Mark Nation, Abingdon Press, 94; John Wesley's Synthesis of the Revival Practices of Jonathan Edwards, George Whitefield, and Nicholas von Zinzendorf, Wesleyan Theol J, spring 95; Christ Against Culture--Another Look, Princeton Theol Rev, Feb 97; Response to Charles H. Goodwin, John Wesley: Revival and Revivalism, 1736-1768, Wesleyan Theol J, spring 96; many other articles, and several publications forthcoming. **CONTACT ADDRESS** Seattle Pacific Univ, 3307 Third Ave W, Seattle, WA, 98119-1997. **EMAIL** rsteele@spu.edu

STEEVES, PAUL DAVID

PERSONAL Born 06/20/1941, Attleboro, MA, m, 1962, 2 children **DISCIPLINE** RUSSIAN MODERN & ECCLESIASTICAL HISTORY **EDUCATION** Washington Univ, AB, 62; Univ Kans, MA, 72, PhD(Russ hist), 76. **CAREER** Asst instr Western civilization, Univ Kans, 66-68; vis lectr hist, Kans State Teachers Col, 71-72; asst prof, 72-78, PROF HIST, STETSON UNIV, 78-, DIR RUSS STUDIES, 76-, DIR HONORS PROG, 78-, Ed, Newsletter, Conf Faith & Hist, 79. **HONORS AND AWARDS** O P Backus Award, Univ Kans, 76; W H McInery Award, Stetson Univ, 79. **MEMBERSHIPS** AHA; Conf Faith & Hist; Am Asn Advan Slavic Studies; Soc Study Relig Under Communism; Southern Conf Slavic Studies. **RESEARCH** Evangelical Baptist movement in Russia. **SELECTED PUBLICATIONS** Auth, Baptists as subversives in the contemporary Soviet Union, In: God and Caesar, Conf Faith & Hist, 71; ed, Church and State in USSR, A sourcebook, Stetson Univ, 73; auth, Alexander Karev, evangelical in a Communist land, Fides et Historia, 76; Amendment of Soviet law concerning religious association, J Church & State, 77; Old-Believers In Modern Russia, Russian Rev, Vol 56, 97; A Long Walk To Church--A Contemporary-History Of Russian Orthodoxy, Russian Rev, Vol 56, 97; Out Of The Red Shadows--Anti-Semitism In Stalin Russia, J Of Church And State, Vol 38, 96. **CONTACT ADDRESS** Dept of Hist, Stetson Univ, 421 N Woodland Blvd, Deland, FL, 32720-3761.

STEFANOVIC, RANKO

PERSONAL Born 04/04/1950, Croatia, m, 1972, 2 children **DISCIPLINE** NEW TESTAMENT **EDUCATION** Andrews Univ, PhD **CAREER** Assoc prof, chmn, relig stud, Canadian Univ Col. **MEMBERSHIPS** SBL **RESEARCH** Book of Revelation **SELECTED PUBLICATIONS** Auth, The Background and Meaning of the Sealed Book of Revelation 5, Andrews Univ Press, 96. **CONTACT ADDRESS** 153 College Ave, College Heights, AB, T4L 1Z2. **EMAIL** rstefano@cauc.ab.ca

STEIGERWALD, DIANE

PERSONAL PQ, Canada **DISCIPLINE** PHILOSOPHY **EDUCATION** McGill Univ Montreal, PhD, 94. **CAREER** Author **RESEARCH** Islamic philosophy; dialogue between Abrahamic faiths. **SELECTED PUBLICATIONS** Auth, La pensee philosophique et theologique de Shahrastani, Sainte-Foy: Laval Univ Press, 97; auth, Majlis Discours sur l'Ordre et la creation, Sainte-Foy: Laval Univ Press, 98; auth, L'islam et ses valeurs communes au judeo-christianisme, Laval Univ Press, forthcoming; Le role de la logique dans la reconciliation de la philosophie et de la religion chez Averroes, Laval Theologique et Philosophique, 96; auth, The Divine Word (Kalima) in Shahrastani's Majlis, Studies in Religion and Sciences religieuses, 97. **CONTACT ADDRESS** 161 Rue Saint-Aubin, Chateauguay, PQ, J6K 2S2. **EMAIL** alibaya@minet.ca

STEIKER, CAROL S.

PERSONAL Born 05/31/1961, Philadelphia, PA, m, 1990, 2 children **DISCIPLINE** LAW **EDUCATION** Harvard-Radcliffe Colleges, AB (hist and lit), 82; Harvard Law School, JD, 86. **CAREER** Law clerk to Judge J Skelly Wright, US Court of Appeals for the District of Columbia Circuit, 86-87; law clerk to Justice Thurgood Marshall, US Supreme Court, 87-88; staff attorney, DC Public Defender Service, 88-92. **RESEARCH** Criminal law; criminal procedure; capital punishment; legal ethics. **SELECTED PUBLICATIONS** Auth, Sober Second Thoughts: Reflections on Two Decades of Constitutional Regulation of Capital Punishment, 109 Harvard Law Rev 355, 95; Counter-Revolution in Constitutional Criminal Procedure? Two Audiences, Two Answers, 94 MI Law Rev 2466, 96; Foreword: Punishment and Procedure: Punishment Theory and the Criminal-Civil Procedural Divide, 85 Georgetown Law J 775, 97; with Jordan M Steiker, Judicial Developments in Capital Punishment Law, in America's Experiment with Capital Punishment: Reflections on the Past, Present, and Future of the Ultimate Penal Sanction, Acker, Bohm & Lanier, eds, Carolina Academic Press, 98. **CONTACT ADDRESS** Law School, Harvard Univ, Griswold 409, Cambridge, MA, 02138. **EMAIL** steiker@law.harvard.edu

STEIN, ERIC

PERSONAL Born 07/08/1913, Czechoslovakia, m, 1955 **DISCIPLINE** LAW **EDUCATION** Charles Univ, Czech, Jud, 37; Univ Mich, JD, 42. **CAREER** With US Dept State, 46-55, adv, US Deleg, UN Gen Assembly, 47-55; Prof Law, Law Sch, Univ Mich, Ann Arbor, 55-, Vis prof int orgn, Law Sch, Stanford Univ, 56, 77; Guggenheim fel, 62-63; Soc Sci Res Coun award, 65; mem adv coun, Inst Europ Studies, Free Univ Brussels, 65-; adv panel, Bur Europ Affairs, Dept State & consult dept, 66-69; mem, Atlantic Coun, 66, vchmn comt Atlantic studies, 66-68; vis prof, Inst Advan Legal Studies, Univ London, 75. **HONORS AND AWARDS** Alexander von Humboldt Prize, 82., Dr, Free Univ Brussels, Belgium, 78. **MEMBERSHIPS** Am Bar Asn; Coun Foreign Rels; Am Soc Int Law; Int Acad Comp Law; Brit Inst Int & Comp Law. **RESEARCH** International law and organization; European law; comparative law. **SELECTED PUBLICATIONS** Auth, International-Law In Internal Law--Toward Intization Of Central Eastern-European Constitutions, Am J Of Int Law, Vol 88, 94; Out Of The Ashes Of A Federation, 2 New Constitutions, Am J Of Comparative Law, Vol 45,

97; Peaceful Separation--A New Virus, Columbia J Of Transnational Law, Vol 36, 97. **CONTACT ADDRESS** Law Sch, Univ Mich, Ann Arbor, MI, 48104.

STEIN, HOWARD
PERSONAL Born 01/21/1929, New York, NY, m, 1948, 2 children **DISCIPLINE** PHILOSOPHY OF SCIENCE **EDUCATION** Columbia Univ, AB, 47; Univ Chicago, PhD(philos), 58; Univ MI, Ann Arbor, MS, 59. **CAREER** From asst to asst prof natural sci, Univ Chicago, 49-60; instr math, Brandeis Univ, 59-62; sr mathematician, EDP Div, Honeywell, Inc, 62-66, sr engr, Comp Control Div, 66-67; prof philos, Case Western Reserve Univ, 67-73; prof philos, Columbia Univ, 73-80, prof philos, Univ Chicago, 80-; Nat Sci Found sci fac fel, 58-59 & sr fel, 65-66; mem US nat comt, Int Union Hist & Philos Sci, 72-74; mem sect comt VII of prog comt of 1975, Int Cong Logic, Methodology & Philos Sci, 72-75; Guggenheim fel, 74-75; adv comt hist philos sci, Nat Sci Found, 77-79. **HONORS AND AWARDS** Am Academy of Arts and Sciences, FEL, 89-. **MEMBERSHIPS** Am Philos Asn; Philos Sci Asn; Am Math Soc; AAUP; Fedn Am Sci. **RESEARCH** Foundations of physics; history of physics. **SELECTED PUBLICATIONS** Auth, Newtonian space-time, In: The Annus Mirabilis of Sir Isaac Newton, Maxwell, and Beyond, In: Historical and Philosophical Perspectives of Science, Univ MN, 70; On the Conceptual Structure of Quantum Mechanics, In: Paradigms and Paradoxes, Univ Pittsburgh, 72; Some Philosophical Prehistory of General Relativity, In: Foundations of Space-Time Theories, Univ MN, 77. **CONTACT ADDRESS** Dept of Philos, Univ Chicago, 1010 E 59th St, Chicago, IL, 60637-1512. **EMAIL** h-stein@uchicago.edu

STEIN, ROBERT H.
DISCIPLINE NEW TESTAMENT **EDUCATION** Rutgers Univ, BA; Fuller Theol Sem, BD; Andover Newton Theol Sch, STM; Princeton Theol Sem, PhD; addn stud, Univ Tubingen. **CAREER** Instr, Bethel Theol Sem, 69-97; Mildred and Ernest Hogan prof, 97. **SELECTED PUBLICATIONS** Auth, Luke in Broadman & Holman's New American Commentary; Playing by the Rules; The Method and Message of Jesus' Teachings; Jesus the Messiah. **CONTACT ADDRESS** New Testament Dept, Southern Baptist Theol Sem, 2825 Lexington Rd, Louisville, KY, 40280. **EMAIL** rstein@sbts.edu

STEIN, STEPHEN J.
DISCIPLINE RELIGIOUS STUDIES **EDUCATION** Yale Univ, PhD, 70. **CAREER** Prof. **RESEARCH** History of religions in America; early American history; sectarian studies. **SELECTED PUBLICATIONS** Auth, Transatlantic Extensions: Apocalyptic in Early New England, Manchester, 84; Letters from a Young Shaker: William S. Byrd at Pleasant Hill, Univ Ky, 85; The Shaker Experience in America: A History of the United Society of Believersm, Yale, 92; Jonthan Edwards's Writings: Text, Context, Interpretation, Univ Ind, 96. **CONTACT ADDRESS** Dept of Religious Studies, Indiana Univ, Bloomington, 300 N Jordan Ave, Bloomington, IN, 47405.

STEIN, STEPHEN J.
DISCIPLINE RELIGIOUS STUDIES **EDUCATION** Concordia Sen Col, BA, 62; Concordia Sem, BD, 66; Yale Univ, MA, 68, PhD, 70. **CAREER** Asst prof, 71-73, assoc prof, 73-81, prof, 81-95, CHANCELLOR'S PROF REL STUD, ADJ PROF HIST, 95-,IND UNIV. **RESEARCH** History of religions in America; early American history; sectarian studies. **SELECTED PUBLICATIONS** Auth, Transatlantic Extensions: Apocalyptic in Early New England, Manchester, 84; Letters from a Young Shaker: William S. Byrd at Pleasant Hill, Univ Ky, 85; The Shaker Experience in America: A History of the United Society of Believersm, Yale, 92; Jonthan Edwards's Writings: Text, Context, Interpretation, Univ Ind, 96. **CONTACT ADDRESS** Dept of Religious Studies, Indiana Univ, Bloomington, 300 N Jordan Ave, Bloomington, IN, 47405. **EMAIL** stein@indiana.edu

STEINBOCK, BONNIE
PERSONAL Born 02/06/1947, New York, NY, m, 1977, 3 children **DISCIPLINE** PHILOSOPHY **EDUCATION** Tufts Univ, BA, 68; Univ Calif, Berkeley, PhD(philos), 74. **CAREER** Asst prof philos, Col Wooster, 74-77; asst prof to prof Philos, State Univ NY, Albany, 77-; chair, Philos Dept, 91-94, 98-. **HONORS AND AWARDS** Phi Beta Kappa; Fel, Hastings Center **RESEARCH** Moral philosophy; philosophy of law; bioethics. **SELECTED PUBLICATIONS** Auth, Speciesism and the Idea of Equality, Philos, 4/ 78; ed, Killing and Letting Die, Prentice-Hall, 80, 94; auth, Life Before Birth, Oxford, 92; coauth, Ethical Issues in Modern Medicine, with John Arras, 95. **CONTACT ADDRESS** Dept of Philos, State Univ of NY, 1400 Washington Ave, Albany, NY, 12222-1000. **EMAIL** steinboc@csc.albany.edu

STEINBOCK, DANIEL J.
DISCIPLINE LAW **EDUCATION** Yale Univ, BA, JD. **CAREER** Prof. **SELECTED PUBLICATIONS** Auth, Unaccompanied Refugee Children in Host Country Foster Families, Int J Refugee Law, 96; Refuge and Resistance, Georgetown, 93; The Admission of Unaccompanied Children Into the U.S., Yale Law Policy Rev, 89; co-auth, Unaccompanied Children, 88. **CONTACT ADDRESS** Col Law, Univ of Toledo, Toledo, OH, 43606. **EMAIL** dsteinb@uoft02.utoledo.edu

STEINBUCH, THOMAS A.
PERSONAL Born 10/23/1949, Brooklyn, NY, s **DISCIPLINE** PHILOSOPHY **EDUCATION** Univ Mass Amherst, PhD, philos, 81. **CAREER** Independent scholar. **SELECTED PUBLICATIONS** Auth, A Commentary on Nietzsche's Ecce Homo, Univ Press of Amer, 94. **CONTACT ADDRESS** 501 Brian St., Mt. Horeb, WI, 53572. **EMAIL** steinbuc@mailbag.com

STEINER, VERNON J.
PERSONAL Born 03/25/1950, Wooster, OH, m, 1971, 2 children **DISCIPLINE** THEOLOGICAL STUDIES; OLD TESTAMENT EXEGESIS **EDUCATION** Grace Univ, BA, 72; W Sem, MDiv, 96, ThM, 79; Trinity Evangelical Divinity School, PhD, 92. **CAREER** Sr Pastor, Oak Lake Bible Church Lincoln, NE, 77-86; tchg fel in Hebrew, Trinity Divinity School, 87-90; asst prof Bibl studies, Assc Can Theol School, Langley, BC, 90-95; dir & adj prof, free lance lectr, The Miqra Inst, 95-. **MEMBERSHIPS** SBL; ETS **RESEARCH** Canonical and compositional strategies; Hebrew and Greek exegesis; History of the Hebrew Bible. **CONTACT ADDRESS** 3201 Briarwood Ave, Lincoln, NE, 68516. **EMAIL** VJSTEINER@aol.com

STEINHART, ERIC
DISCIPLINE PHILOSOPHY **EDUCATION** Penn State Univ, BS, 83; Boston Col, MA; SUNY at Stony Brook, PhD, 96. **CAREER** Prof **RESEARCH** Intersection of metaphysics, history of philosophy, and computation; making computational models of metaphysical systems, both historical and of my own invention; 19th century philosophy. **SELECTED PUBLICATIONS** Auth, Digital metaphysics, The Digital Phoenix: How Computers are Changing Philosophy. New York: Basil Blackwell, 98 ; Leibniz's palace of the fates: A 17th century virtual reality system, Presence: Teleoperators and Virtual Environments 6 1, 97; NETMET: A program for generating and interpreting metaphors, Computers and Humanities, 95; Structural idealism, Idealistic Stud, 94; Beyond proportional analogy: A structural model of analogy, Pragmatics and Cognition, 94; Analogical truth-conditions for metaphors, Metaphor and Symbolic Activity, 94; Metaphor, Encycl of Lang and Ling, Oxford: Pergamon Press, 93; coauth, Self-recognition and countermemory, Philos Today, 89; Generating metaphors from networks, Approaches to Metaphor, Synthese Lib, Dordrecht: Kluwer Acad, 94. **CONTACT ADDRESS** Dept of Philosophy, William Paterson Col, 300 Pompton Rd., Atrium 267, Wayne, NJ, 07470.

STEINMAN, JOAN E.
PERSONAL Born 06/19/1947, Brooklyn, NY, 2 children **DISCIPLINE** LAW/PHILOSOPHY **EDUCATION** Univ Rochester, AB, 69; Harvard Law School, JD, 73. **CAREER** Asst prof law, assoc prof law, interim dean, PROF LAW, CHICAGO-KENT COL LAW, ILL INST TECH, 77-. **HONORS AND AWARDS** Ralph L Brill Award, 77; Julia Beveridge Award, 96; Dean's Prize for Excellence in Teaching, 95; served on bench NIU Moot Court Prize Argument, 96. **MEMBERSHIPS** Am Law Inst; Am Asn Univ Women Legal Advocacy Network; Am Bar Asn Chicago Council Lawyers, Fed Courts Comm; Soc Am Law Teachers; Harvard Law School Women's Law Asn; CBA Alliance for Women; Bd, Pro Bono Advocates, 95-; Chicago Lincoln Am Inn of Court; Am Law Inst project, 96-; Am Law Inst Discussion for Fed Judicial Code, 95, and consultative groups for Complex Litigation Project and Restatement of the Law; NASD Board of Arbitrators; Ill Governor's Grievance Panel. **RESEARCH** Fed courts, fed civil procedures, complex litigation, appellate procedure. **SELECTED PUBLICATIONS** Auth, Cross Currents: Supplemental Jurisdication, Removal, and the ALI Revision Project, 74 IND Law Jour, 99; auth, The Scope of Appellate Jurisdiction: Pendent Appellate Jurisdiction Before and After Swint, 49 Hastings Law Jour, 98; auth, The Effects of Case Consolidation on the Procedural Rights of Litigants: What They are, What They Might Be, Part II: Non- Jurisdictional Matters, 42 UCLA Leg Rev, 95; Reverse Removal, 78 Iowa Leg Rev, 93; auth, Supplemental Jurisdiction in 1441 Removed Cases: An Unsurveyed Frontier of Congress's Handiwork, 35 Ariz Leg Rev, 93; auth, Women, Medical Care, and Mass Tort Litigation, 68 Chicago-Ken Leg Rev, excerpted in A Products Liability Anthology, 95. **CONTACT ADDRESS** Chicago Kent Col of Law, Illinois Inst of Tech, 565 W Adams St, Chicago, IL, 60661. **EMAIL** jsteinma@kentlaw.edu

STEINMANN, ANDREW E.
PERSONAL Born 05/29/1954, Cincinnati, OH, m, 1976, 2 children **DISCIPLINE** RELIGIOUS STUDIES **EDUCATION** Univ Mich, PhD, 90. **CAREER** Instr, Concordia Col, 86-90; asst prof, 90-91; adjunct prof, Ashland Univ, 96-. **MEMBERSHIPS** Soc of Bibl Lit; Cath Bibl Asn; Evangelical Theol Soc. **RESEARCH** Near Eastern studies; Biblical studies. **SELECTED PUBLICATIONS** Auth, Are My Prayers Falling on Dear Ears?, 97; ed, God's Word, 95; auth, "Bible (1) Translation," 99; "Response to Leslie Lanier 'On the Public Reading of Scripture'" in Logia: A J of Lutheran Theol, 98; "Communicating the Gospel Without Theological Jargon: Translating the Bible into Reader-Friendly Language" in Concordia Theol Quart, 97; "Jacob's Family Goes to Egypt: Varying Portraits of Unity and Disunity in the Textual Traditions of Exodus 1:1-5" in TC, 97; "When the Translations of Catechetical Proof Texts Don't Communicate" in Concordia J, 96. **CONTACT ADDRESS** 30514 Manhasset Dr, Bay Village, OH, 44140. **EMAIL** asteinmann@aol.com

STEINMETZ, DAVID CURTIS
PERSONAL Born 06/12/1936, Columbus, OH, m, 1959, 2 children **DISCIPLINE** CHURCH HISTORY **EDUCATION** Wheaton Col, Ill, AB, 58; Drew Univ, BD, 61; Harvard Univ, ThD(church hist), 67. **CAREER** From asst prof to assoc prof church hist, Lancaster Theol Sem, 66-71; assoc prof, 71-79, Prof Church Hist & Doctrine, Divinity Sch, Duke Univ, 79-, Am Asn Theol Schs fac fel, Oxford Univ, 70-71; vis prof church hist, Harvard Univ, 77; Guggenheim fel, Cambridge Univ, 77-78. **MEMBERSHIPS** Am Soc Church Hist; Am Soc Reformation Res; Mediaeval Acad Am; Renaissance Soc Am; Soc Bibl Lit. **RESEARCH** History of Christian thought in the late Middle Ages and Reformation. **SELECTED PUBLICATIONS** Auth, The Superiority of Pre-Critical Exegesis, Theol Today, 80; Luther and Staupitz: An Essay in the Intellectual Origins of the Protestant Reformation, Duke, 80; Calvin on Isaiah 6: A Problem in the History of Exegeis, Interpretation, 82; The Theory And Practice Of Exegesis--Proceedings Of The 3rd Int-Colloquium On The Hist Of Biblical Exegesis In The 16th-Century: Geneva, August 31 September 2, 88, Sixteenth Century J, Vol ; An Exploration Of The Human Imagination As An Instrument Of Spiritual Nurture And Theological Reform, Interpretation-A J Of Bible And Theology, Vol 47, 93; Divided By A Common Past--The Reshaping Of The Christian Exegetical Tradition In The 16th-Century, J Of Medieval And Early Modern Studies, Vol 27, 97. **CONTACT ADDRESS** Divinity Sch, Duke Univ, Durham, NC, 27706.

STEMPSEY, WILLIAM EDWARD
PERSONAL Born 01/26/1952, Albany, NY **DISCIPLINE** PHILOSOPHY, BIOETHICS, PATHOLOGY **EDUCATION** Boston Col, BA, Boston Col, 74; SUNY, Buffalo Sch of Med, 78; Loyola Univ, MA, 88; Jesuit Sch of Theol, Berkeley, M Div, 91, STM, 92; Georgetown Univ, PhD, 96. **CAREER** Intern, 78-79, Boston City Hosp, MA; Res, 80-82, Univ Hospital, Boston; tchng fel, 80-82, Pathol, Boston Univ School of Med; res, 84-85, The Children's Hosp, Boston; clin fel in Pathol, 84-85;, Harvard Med Sch clin scholar, 95-96, Ctr for Clin Bioethics, Georgetown Univ Med Ctr; asst prof, 96-, dept of philos, Col Of The Holy Cross **HONORS AND AWARDS** Alpha Epsilon Delta, IL Eta Chapter, 88., Soc of Jesus (Jesuits), 82, ordained priest, 92. **MEMBERSHIPS** The Hastings Center; Kennedy Inst of Ethics; Soc for Health & Human Values; APA; European Soc for Philos of Med & Healthcare, 98-. **RESEARCH** Philos of diagnosis; concepts of health and disease; ethical issues in death and dying; ethics of organ transplantation. **SELECTED PUBLICATIONS** Auth, The Big Blue Van and the Little Children, America 168, no 9, 93; auth, Another Look at Physician-Assisted Suicide, J of Pastoral Care 48, 94; coauth, Incommensurability: Its Implications for the Patient/ Physician Relation, J of Med and Philos 20, 95; auth, Paying People to Give Up Their Organs: The Problem with Commodification of Body Parts, Med Hum Rev, 10, 96; auth, End-of-Life Decisions: Christian Perspectives, Christian Bioethics 3, 97; auth, Laying Down One's Life for Oneself, Christian Bioethics 4, 98; auth, The Battle for Medical Marijuana in the War on Drugs, America 178, no 2, 11, 98. **CONTACT ADDRESS** Dept of Philosophy, Col of the Holy Cross, One College St, Worcester, MA, 01610-2395. **EMAIL** wstempsey@holycross.edu

STENDAHL, KRISTER
PERSONAL Born 04/21/1921, Stockholm, Sweden, m, 1946, 3 children **DISCIPLINE** THEOLOGY **EDUCATION** Univ Uppsala, Teol kand, 44, Teol lic, 49, Teol, dr, 54. **CAREER** Student pastor, Univ Uppsala, 48-50, instr exeg, 51-54, docent, 54; from asst prof to assoc prof New Testament, 54-58, Morrison prof, 58-63, Frothingham prof Bibl studies, 63-68, John Lord prof & dean, 68-79, Andrew W Mellon Prof Divinity, Harvard Divinity Sch, 80- **MEMBERSHIPS** Studiorum Novi Testamenti Soc; Nathan Soederblom Soc; Am Acad Arts & Sci; Soc Bibl Lit. **SELECTED PUBLICATIONS** Auth, The school of St Matthew; ed, The Scrolls and the New Testament; The Bible and the Role of Women, 66, Holy Week, 74 & Paul among Jews and Gentiles, 76, Fortress; Jewish Responses To Early Christians--History And Polemics, 30-150ce, Theology Today, Vol 53, 96. **CONTACT ADDRESS** Divinity Sch, Harvard Univ, Andover Hall, Cambridge, MA, 02138.

STENGER, ROBERT LEO
PERSONAL Born 09/19/1934, St. Paul, MN, m, 1971 **DISCIPLINE** CHRISTIAN ETHICS, LAW **EDUCATION** St Thomas Col, Ill, BA, 56, MA, 57; Cath Univ Am, STD, 63; Univ Iowa, JD, 74. **CAREER** Asst prof philos & theol & head dept, Dominican Col, 63-64; asst prof moral theol, Aquinas Inst Sch Theol, Iowa, 64-68; asst prof Christian ethics, Sch Relig, Univ Iowa, 68-74; asst prof, 74-77, assoc prof, 77-80, Prof Law, Univ Louisville, 80- **MEMBERSHIPS** Cath Theol Soc Am; Am Soc Christian Ethics; Am Bar Asn; Soc Am Law Teachers. **RESEARCH** Constitutional law; mediaeval Canon law; Christian social ethics. **SELECTED PUBLICATIONS** Auth, The episcopacy as an ordo according to the mediaeval Canonists, Medi-

aeval Studies, 67; Repertorium iuris religiosorum: Basel, Universitats bibliothek C V 13, Studies Gratiana, 67; The Supreme Court and illegitimacy, 1968-1977, Family Law Quart, winter 78; Dividing The Child--Social And Legal Dilemmas Of Custody, Univ Of Louisville J Of Family Law, Vol 32, 94. **CONTACT ADDRESS** Sch of Law, Univ of Louisville, Louisville, KY, 40208.

STENSTAD, GAIL
DISCIPLINE PHILOSOPHY **EDUCATION** Vanderbilt Univ, PhD. **CAREER** Assoc prof, E Tenn Stat Univ **MEMBERSHIPS** Heidegger; environmental ethics. **SELECTED PUBLICATIONS** Auth, The Turning in Ereignis and Transformation of Thinking, Heidegger Studies, 96; Thinking what is strange, Heidegger Studies, 94; The last God-A reading, Res Phenomenology, 93; Merleau Ponty's logos: The Sensing of the Flesh, Philos Today, 92; Singing the Earth, Thomas Jefferson Univ, 92; Attuning and Transformation, Heidegger Studies, 91; Thinking (beyond) Being, Heidegger Studies, 90. **CONTACT ADDRESS** Philosophy Dept, East Tennesee State Univ, Box 70717, Johnson City, TN, 37614- 0717. **EMAIL** stenstad@etsu.edu

STENT, MICHELLE DORENE
PERSONAL Born 02/04/1955, New York, NY, s **DISCIPLINE** LAW **EDUCATION** Univ of Puerto Rico, Certificate of Merit 1974; Univ of London, Certificate of Distinction 1975; Tufts Univ, BA 1976; Howard Univ School of Law, JD 1980. **CAREER** Senator Edward W Brooke, intern 1976; Office of Civil Rights, public info consultant 1979; Congressional Black Caucus, graduate student intern 1979; Congressman Charles Rangel, legislative intern 1980; Comm on Educ and Labor US House of Reps, legislative counsel 1980-85; United Negro Coll Fund, dir govt affairs, assoc general counsel, Washington Office, vice pres 1989-. **HONORS AND AWARDS** Articles published Black Issues in Higher Education, Point of View; honorary doctorate, Texas Coll, Tyler, TX, 1987; Title IX Award, Natl Assn for Equal Opportunity in Higher Educ, 1987. **MEMBERSHIPS** Bd dirs Caribbean Action Lobby; consultant Natl Urban League; select comm Congressional Black Caucus Intern Program; mem Delta Theta Phi Law Fraternity, Natl Bar Assn; assn mem Congressional Black Assocs, NAACP, Natl Urban League, Natl Assn of Black Women Attorneys, Coalition of 100 Black Women; bd of dir, Natl Coalition Black Voter Participation 1985-; bd of dir, Capitol City Ballet, 1988-. **SELECTED PUBLICATIONS** Newspaper Articles, NY Voice, Mississippi Memo Digest, Tyler Courier Times, editor/writer, Government Affairs Reports UNCF, 1985-. **CONTACT ADDRESS** United Negro Col Fund Inc, 1025 Vermont Ave, #810 NE, Washington, DC, 20005.

STEPHAN, P.B.
PERSONAL Born 12/29/1950, Somerville, NJ, m, 1976, 3 children **DISCIPLINE** LAW **EDUCATION** Yale Univ, BA 73, MA 74; Univ Virginia, JD 77. **CAREER** Judge L.H. Campbell us Cir App, law clerk, 77-78; Justice LF Powell Supreme Ct US, law clerk 78-79; Univ Virginia, asst prof, assoc prof, prof, Percy Brown Jr Prof, 79 to 90-. **HONORS AND AWARDS** Donahue Lec. **MEMBERSHIPS** ALI; ASIL; ASCL; DC BAR; VA BAR. **RESEARCH** Post Socialist Legal Development, Intl Law, Taxation. **SELECTED PUBLICATIONS** Auth, Constitutional Limitations on Privatization, coauth, Am Jour Comp L, 98; Creative Destruction-Idiosyncratic Claims of International Law and the Helms-Burton Legislation, Stetson L Rev, 98; Accountability and International Law Making: Rules Rents and Legitimacy, NW Jour Intl L & Bus, 97; The Fall-Understanding the Collapse of Soviet Communism, Suffolk U L Rev, 95; Barbarians Inside the Gates: Public Choice Theory and International Economic Law, Am U Jour Intl L & Pol'y, 95; Foreword and Westernization of the European East? In: Law Reform in Post-Communist Europe: The View From Within, coauth, 94; International Business and Economics-Law and Policy, 93, 2nd edition, 96 coauth. **CONTACT ADDRESS** Law School, Virginia Univ, 580 Massie Rd, Charlottesville, VA, 22903-1789. **EMAIL** pbs@virginia.edu

STEPHENS, CYNTHIA DIANE
PERSONAL Born 08/27/1951, Detroit, MI, m **DISCIPLINE** LAW **EDUCATION** Univ of MI, BA 1971; Atlanta Univ, postgraduate 1971-72; Emory Law School, JD 1976. **CAREER** Natl Conf of Black Lawyers, so regional dir 1976-77; Natl League of Cities, coord 1977-78; Pan-African Orthodox Christian Church, genl counsel 1978-82; Michigan Senate, assoc general counsel 1979-82; Wayne County Charter Commn, vice-chmn 1980-81; Law Offices of Cynthia D Stephens, attorney 1981-82; 36th District Ct, judge 1982-85; WAYNE COUNTY COMMUNITY COLL, FACULTY, 1985-; UNIV OF DETROIT LAW SCHOOL, FACULTY, 1988-; WAYNE COUNTY CIRCUIT COURT, JUDGE, 1985-; Detroit Coll of Law, faculty, 1990-95. **HONORS AND AWARDS** Outstanding Woman Awd Woodward Ave Presbyterian Ch 1982; Disting Serv Awd Region 5 Detroit Public Schools 1983; Wolverine Bar Member of the Yr 1984; Little Rock Baptist Ch Golden Heritage Awd for Judicial Excellence 1984; Outstanding Woman in Law Hartford Memorial Bapt Ch 1985; Disting Alumni Awd Cass Tech HS 1987; Susan B Anthony, Natl Organization of Women, 1988; Anita Hill Award, Detroit Human Rights Commission, 1991. **MEMBERSHIPS** Mem Wolverine Bar Assoc 1979; bd mem Wayne Co Neighborhood Legal Serv 1980; mem New Detroit Inc 1981-; bd mem Assoc of Black Judges of MI 1982-89, MI Dist Judges Assoc 1982-85, Greater Detroit Health Care Cncl 1983-85; guest lecturer Southern Univ Women and Leadership Symposium Baton Rouge LA 1983, Western MI Univ Dept of Women Studies Kalamazoo 1983; Univ of MI Symposium series for the Ctr for African and Afro-Amer Studies 1984; mem adv bd African Diaspora Project of the Delta Inst 1984-88; mem City Wide Sch Comm Organization-at-Large 1984-86, Delta Manor LDHA 1984-, YMCA Downtown Detroit 1984; mem Amer Bar Assoc Comm on Judicial Evaluation 1984-85, Delta Sigma Theta Detroit Alumni 1984-85; mem adv bd MI Bar Journal 1985-; Amer Corporate Counsel Pro-Bono Adv Comm 1982-88; bd of commissioners, State Bar of MI 1986-94; mem Natl Conference of Black Lawyers, 1997-; Natl Assoc of Women Judges; MI Judges Assoc. **SELECTED PUBLICATIONS** Auth, "Judicial Selection and Diversity," MI Bar Journal Vol 64 No 6 1985. **CONTACT ADDRESS** 3rd Circuit Court, 1719 City-County Bldg, Detroit, MI, 48226.

STEPHENS, LYNN
DISCIPLINE PHILOSOPHY **EDUCATION** Harvard Univ, MA; Univ Mass, PhD. **CAREER** Prof, Univ Ala Birmingham, 79-. **RESEARCH** Philosophical psychology, history of philosophy. **SELECTED PUBLICATIONS** Coauth, Seven Dilemmas in World Religions, Paragon House, 94; co-ed, Philosophical Psychopathology, MIT Press, 94. **CONTACT ADDRESS** Dept of Philosophy, Univ of Alabama, Birmingham, 1400 University Blvd, Birmingham, AL, 35294-1150.

STERBA, JAMES P.
DISCIPLINE PHILOSOPHY **EDUCATION** LaSalle Col, BA, 66; Univ Pittsburgh, MA, 72, PhD, 73. **CAREER** Prof. **RESEARCH** Political philosophy; environmental ethics; philosophy of peace and justice. **SELECTED PUBLICATIONS** Auth, Feminist Justice and the Pursuit of Peace, Hypatia, 94; Contemporary Social and Political Philosophy, 94; From Liberty to Welfare, Ethics, 94; Justifying Morality and the Challenge of Cognitive Science, Ethics Cognitive Sci, 95; Understanding Evil: American Slavery, the Holocaust and the Conquest of the American Indians, 95; Racism and Sexism: The Common Ground, Comparing Sex Race, 96; Morality in Practice, 96; Is Feminism Good for Men and are Men Good for Feminism?, Men Doing Feminism, 97; Social and Political Philosophy: Classical Western Texts in Feminist and Multicultural Perspectives, 97; Feminist Philosophies, Second Edition, 98; Justice: Alternative Political Perspectives, 98; Justice for Here and Now, 98; Religion and Rawls, 98; A Biocentrist Strikes Back, 98. **CONTACT ADDRESS** Philosophy Dept, Univ of Notre Dame, 336/7 O'Shaughnessy, Notre Dame, IN, 46556. **EMAIL** sterba.1@nd.edu

STERN, DAVID S.
DISCIPLINE PHILOSOPHY **EDUCATION** Louisiana St Univ, BA, 77; Univ CA, San Diego, PhD, 85. **CAREER** Asst prof, 85-89, Louisiana St Univ; vis asst prof, 89-90, Univ of CA, San Diego; asst prof, 90-93, assoc prof, 93-, Univ of Toledo. **MEMBERSHIPS** APA; Hegel Soc of Amer; Metaphysical Soc; Soc for Phenomenology and Existential Phil. **RESEARCH** 19th and 20th Century European phil; social and political phil. **SELECTED PUBLICATIONS** Rev, Michael Inwood, A Hegel Dictionary, Cambridge Blackwell, 92; rev, Thomas Nagel, Equality and Partiality, Oxford Univ Press, 91; rev, Will Kymlicka, Contemporary Political Philosophy An Introduction, Oxford Clarendon Press, 90; auth, Foundationalism Holism or Hegel, GWF Hegel Critical Assessments, Vol III, Routledge, 93; auth, Transcendental Apperception and Subjective Logic Kant and Hegel on the Role of the Subject, Hegel on the Modern World, SUNY Press, 95; auth, The Ties that Bind The Limits of Aesthetic Reflection in Kierkegaards Either/Or, The Intl Kierkegaard Comm Either/Or I, Mercer Univ Press, 95; art, Unending Modernity, Inquiry Vol 38 No 3, 95; auth, Kant and Hegel on the Logic of Being for Self, Proceedings of the Eighth Intl Kant Congress, Vol 1, Marquette Univ Press, 95; auth, State Sovereignty the Politics of Identity and the Place of the Political, Problems Without Borders Persp on the Third World Sov, St. Martins, 96. **CONTACT ADDRESS** Dept of Philosophy, Univ of Toledo, Toledo, OH, 43606. **EMAIL** dstern@utoledo.edu

STERN, LAURENT
PERSONAL Born 03/22/1930, Budapest, Hungary **DISCIPLINE** PHILOSOPHY **EDUCATION** Univ Zurich, PhD, 52. **CAREER** Lectr Philos, City Col NY, 59-61; asst prof, Univ Wash, 61-66; assoc prof, 66-70, chmn dept, 68-71, chmn dept & dir grad prog philos, 76-79, prof Philos, Rutgers Univ, 70-. **MEMBERSHIPS** Am Soc Aesthet; Am Philos Asn; Aristotelian Soc; AAUP. **RESEARCH** Late 19th Century philosophy; Theories of interpretation; Philosophy of literature. **SELECTED PUBLICATIONS** Various articles. **CONTACT ADDRESS** Dept of Philosophy, Rutgers Univ, New Brunswick, NJ, 08903. **EMAIL** lstern@rci.rutgers.edu

STEUSSY, MARTI J.
PERSONAL Born 09/07/1955, Dayton, OH, m, 1978, 2 children **DISCIPLINE** HEBREW BIBLE **EDUCATION** St. Olaf Col, BA, 77; Earlham Sch Relig, MDiv, 82; Vanderbilt, PhD, 92. **CAREER** Vis tchr, Christian Theol Seminary, 88-89, ast prof, 89-96, assoc prof 96-. **HONORS AND AWARDS** Presidential scholar; ATS Sem, Developing Your Role as a Scholar; Nat Relig Leadership Prog. **MEMBERSHIPS** SBL, Asoc of Disciples for Theolog Discussion; Forrest-Moss Inst. **RESEARCH** Narrative criticism; Biblical storytelling; religion and science; environmental ethics. **SELECTED PUBLICATIONS** Auth, Gardens in Babylon, in SBLDS, Scholars Pr, 93; David: Portraits of Power, Studies on Personalities of the Old Testament, Univ S Carolina, 98; "The Ethics of Pet-keeping," Encounter, 98. **CONTACT ADDRESS** Christian Theol Sem, 1000 W 42nd St, Indianapolis, IN, 46208-3301. **EMAIL** MSteussy@cts.edu

STEVENS, GEORGE E.
DISCIPLINE LEGAL DIMENSIONS OF COMMUNICATION **EDUCATION** Univ Minn, PhD, 68. **CAREER** Prof, asst dept hd, Purdue Univ. **SELECTED PUBLICATIONS** Auth, Freedom of Speech in Private Employment: Overcoming the State Action Problem, Am Bus Law J, 82; Legal Protection for a Magazine Article Idea, Jour Quart, 84; Names, Newsworthiness, and the Right to Privacy, Commun and the Law, 91. **CONTACT ADDRESS** Dept of Commun, Purdue Univ, 1080 Schleman Hall, West Lafayette, IN, 47907-1080. **EMAIL** gstevens@sla.purdue.edu

STEVENS, JOHN PAUL
PERSONAL Born 04/20/1920, Chicago, IL, m, 1942, 4 children **DISCIPLINE** LAW **EDUCATION** Univ Chicago, AB, 41; Northwestern Univ, JD, 47. **CAREER** Law clerk, US Supreme Court Justice Wiley Rutledge, 47-48; assoc, Poppenhusen, Johnston, Thompson & Raymond, 48-50; assoc coun, Subcomt Study Monopoly Power, Judiciary Comt US House Rep, 51-52; partner, Rotschild, Hart, Stevens & Barry, 52-70; US circuit judge, Seventh Circuit, Assoc Justice, US Supreme Court, 75-, Mem, Atty General's Nat Comt Study Antitrust Laws, 53-55; The Freedom Of Speech, Yale Law J, Vol 102, 93; Is Justice Irrelevant, Northwestern Univ Law Rev, Vol 87, 93. **CONTACT ADDRESS** US Supreme Court, One First St NE, Washington, DC, 20543.

STEVENS, PAUL W.
DISCIPLINE THEOLOGY **EDUCATION** Miss Col, BA, 60; New Orleans Baptist Theol Sem, BD, 64, PhD, 72. **CAREER** Dir Christian Trng, Southwest Baptist Col, 69-71; serv, New Orleans Baptist Theol Sem, 71-82; dir DMin prog, New Orleans Baptist Theol Sem; dir Cont Edu and Field Edu, New Orleans Baptist Theol Sem; VP Stud Aff, New Orleans Baptist Theol Sem; asst dir Field Mission prog, New Orleans Baptist Theol Sem; dir, Field Edu, 88-; assoc dean for the DMin Degree, 97-. **HONORS AND AWARDS** Pastor, McBee Baptist Church, 56-59; Ctr Hill Baptist Church, 59-62; Buckatunna Baptist Church, 63-65; Coteau Baptist Mission, 66-68; Ridgecrest Baptist Church, 82-88. **MEMBERSHIPS** Assn Theol Filed Edu; In-Service Guidance Dir S Baptist Convention; Nat Coun Bivocational Ministry, SBC; Assn Case Tchg. **SELECTED PUBLICATIONS** Auth, The Supervisory Conference, Chapter in Experiencing Ministry Supervision, Broadman & Holman, 95; pub(s), Encycl S Baptists; Deacon; Jour Suprv and Trng in Ministry. **CONTACT ADDRESS** Sch Theol, Southwestern Baptist Theol Sem, PO Box 22000, Fort Worth, TX, 76122-0418. **EMAIL** pws@swbts.swbts.edu

STEVENS-ARROYO, ANTONIO M.
DISCIPLINE COMPARATIVE RELIGION **EDUCATION** Passionist Monastic Sem, BA, 64; St Michael's Col, MA, 68; NY Univ, MA, 75; Fordham Univ, PhD, 81. **CAREER** Dept Puerto Rican Stud, PROF, 89-, CUNY, BROOKLYN COL; fel, teach, Ctr Stud Am Rel, Woodrow Wilson Ctr, Princeton Univ, Union Theol Sem, Fordham Univ, Rutgers Univ, Ctr Adv Stud Puerto Rico and Caribbean, San Juan, Univ La Laguna, Spain; assoc ed, Encyclopedia Cont Religion, Macmillian Ref Libr; ed bd, Latino Studies Journal. **CONTACT ADDRESS** RISC, Brooklyn Col, CUNY, 2900 Bedford Ave, Brooklyn, NY, 11210. **EMAIL** astevens@brooklyn.cuny.edu

STEVENSON-MOESSNER, JEANNE
PERSONAL Born 03/05/1948, Memphis, TN, m, 1975, 2 children **DISCIPLINE** THEOLOGY **EDUCATION** Vanderbilt Univ, BA, 70; Princeton Theol Sem, MA, Summa cum laude, 75; Univ of Basel, Switz, PhD, 86; Candler School of Theol, Emory Univ, and Columbia Theo Sem, MDiv, 96. **CAREER** Emory Univ, adj; Samford Univ, adj; Columbia Theol Sem, adj asst prof, 84-97; Univ of Dubuque Theol Sem, asst prof, 97-, Presbyterian Minister, ordained, 96-. **MEMBERSHIPS** PCUSA, AAPC, AAR, SPT, PWTE, IAMS, APT, REA, PCAG. **RESEARCH** Pastoral Care of women; multicultural developmental issues; cultural dissolution; maternal bonding. **SELECTED PUBLICATIONS** Mono, Through the Eyes of Women: Insights for Pastoral Care, The Handbook of Women Care, Fortress Press, 96; Women in Travail and Transition: A New Pastoral Care, co-ed, Fortress Press, 91; Theological Dimensions of Maturation in a Missionary Milieu, European Univ

Studies Series 23, P. Lang Verlag, 89; Ephesians: An Idolatry, Pathology, and Theology of the Family, in: Overtures to Biblical Theology, Fortress Press, fc. **CONTACT ADDRESS** Dept of Pastoral Theology, Univ of Dubuque Theological Sem, 2000 University Ave, Dubuque, IA, 52001. **EMAIL** jmoessne@univ.dbq.edu

STEWART, CARLYLE F., III
PERSONAL Born 09/23/1951, Detroit, MI, m, 1988, 3 children **DISCIPLINE** THEOLOGY **EDUCATION** Wilber Force Univ, BA, 73; Univ of Chicago, MA, 74; Chicago Theol Sem, MDiv, 77, DMin, 78; Northwestern Univ, PhD, 82. **CAREER** Garrett-evangelical Theol Sem, asst prof, 82-83; Wayne State Univ, lectr, 87; United Theol Sem, mentor, 95-97; Hope United Methodist Church, sr pastor, 83-. **HONORS AND AWARDS** Hull Univ, Eng, Will Wilber Force Scholar, 71-72; Alpha Kappa Mu Honor Soc, 72; Rockefeller sch, 78-80; Fulbright Fel, 73; Harvard Divinity School, Merrill Fel, 90; Circuit Rider Award, 93 **MEMBERSHIPS** AAR, SBL, ACIL, WTS, BISC **RESEARCH** Ethics, black theology; African American religion; African religion; literature and philosophy. **SELECTED PUBLICATIONS** Auth, Was Abraham Lincoln of African Descent?, in: Transformer News, 95; Recognize Feelings to Help Defuse Anger, Southfield Eccentric, 95; Yes Beethoven Was a Brother!, Transformer News, 95; Justice Theologically Hinges on Justice Socially, Southfield Eccentric, 95; Divine Spirit Colors Your Religious, Scientific Beliefs, Southfield Eccentric, 95; Who's Preaching This Sunday?, Circuit Rider Mag, 97; Street Corner Theology: Indigenous Reflections on the Reality of God in the African American Experience, John Winston Pub, 96; Joy Songs, Trumpet Sounds and Hallelujah Shouts: Sermons in the African - American Preaching Tradition, CSS Pub, 97; How Long Will You Limp?: Sermons on Pentecost, CSS Pub, 97; Sankofa: Celebrations for the African - American Church, United Church Press, 97; Black Spirituality and Black Consciousness: Culture, Soul and Freedom in the African - American Experience, African World Press, 98. **CONTACT ADDRESS** Hope United Methodist Church, 25251 River Dr, Franklin Village, MI, 48025. **EMAIL** dstewarttii@aol.com

STEWART, DANIEL LEWIS
PERSONAL Born 09/25/1937, New York, NY **DISCIPLINE** LAW, ECONOMICS **EDUCATION** Univ Calif, Los Angeles, BA, 58; Harvard Univ, JD, 61; Oxford Univ, MLitt, 63; Univ Wis, PhD(law & econ), 67. **CAREER** Fulbright scholar, Univ Chile, 63-64; proj assoc, Land Tenure Ctr, Univ Wis, 64-65; fel, Int Legal Ctr, Chile, 67-70; assoc atty, Gang, Tyre & Brown, 70; chief, Environ Law Sect, Health Probs Poor, Nat Legal Prog, 70-71; Prof Law, Loyola Law Sch, 71-, Assoc Dean, 81-, Vis prof law & econ; Univ Chile, 67-70; mem hearing bd, South Coast Air Quality Mgt Dist, 77-80, chmn, 78-80; The Law Of Prime-Numbers, Ny Univ Law Rev, Vol 68, 93. **RESEARCH** Theoretical rationale for judicial decisions dealing with natural resource allocation. **SELECTED PUBLICATIONS** Auth, El Derecho de Aguas en Chile, Ed Juridica, Santiago, Chile, 70. **CONTACT ADDRESS** Law Sch, Loyola Marymount Univ, 1441 W Olympic Blvd, Los Angeles, CA, 90015.

STEWART, DAVID
PERSONAL Born 05/16/1938, Savannah, GA, m, 1959, 2 children **DISCIPLINE** PHILOSOPHY **EDUCATION** Abilene Christian Col, BA, 60, MA, 61; Rice Univ, PhD(philos), 65. **CAREER** Lectr philos, Rice Univ, 64-65; asst prof, NTex State Univ, 65-66; exec ed, R B Sweet Publ Co, Austin, Tex, 66-70; from asst prof to assoc prof, 70-78, Prof Philos, Ohio Univ, 78-, Res inst fel, Ohio Univ, 74, assoc provost, 81-93, provost 93-96, trustee prof, Phil, 96-. **MEMBERSHIPS** Am Philos Asn; Am Acad Relig. **SELECTED PUBLICATIONS** coauth, Exploring Phenomenology, Am Libr Asn, 74; co-ed, Social and political essays by Paul Ricoeur, Ohio Univ, 74; The Philosophy of Paul Ricoeur, Beacon, 78; The Meaning of Humanness in a Technological Era, Ohio Univ, 78; auth, Exploring the Philosophy of Religion, Prentice-Hall, 4th ed 98; Fundamentals of Philosophy, Macmillan 4th ed 98; auth, Business Ethics, McGraw Hill, 96. **CONTACT ADDRESS** Dept of Philosophy, Ohio Univ, Athens, OH, 45701-2979. **EMAIL** dstewart1@ohiou.edu

STEWART, MELVILLE Y.
PERSONAL Born 06/19/1935, Boston, MA, m, 1958, 5 children **DISCIPLINE** PHILOSOPHY **EDUCATION** Gordon Col, BA, 58; Westminster Theol Sem, MDiv, 61; Andover Newton Theol Sch, STM, 68; Univ Conn, MA, 72; Univ Minn, PhD, 83. **CAREER** Asst prof, 72-75, assoc prof, 76-86, prof, 87- , Bethel Col; vis prof, St Petersburg State Univ, Russia, 92-93; vis prof, Peking Univ, 96-97. **HONORS AND AWARDS** Greene Prize in Apologetics, 61; dist scholar award, 95-96. **MEMBERSHIPS** MN Philos Assoc; APA. **RESEARCH** Philosophy of religion. **SELECTED PUBLICATIONS** Auth, The Greater-Good Defense, An Essay on the Rationality of Faith; co-ed, Problems in Christian Philosophy; ed, Philosophy of Religion, An Anthology of Contemporary Views; co-ed, East and West Religious Ethics and Other Essays; co-ed, The Symposium of Chinese-American Philosophy and Religious Studies. **CONTACT ADDRESS** Dept of Philosophy, Bethel Col, St Paul, MN, 55112. **EMAIL** stemel@bethel.edu

STEWART, WILLIAM H.
PERSONAL Born 04/18/1935, Greensboro, North Carolina **DISCIPLINE** THEOLOGY **EDUCATION** NC A&T State Univ, BS 1960; Central MI Univ, MA 1973; Blackstone School of Law, JD 1977; Western CO Univ, DBAdm 1980. **CAREER** Coop League of the USA, dir demonstration prog 1966-69; General Elect Co Chicago, training dir 1969-70; City of Ann Arbor, dir model cities prog 1970-71; US Dept of Housing Urban Dev, div dir 1971-75; Exec Seminar Ctr US Civil Serv Commiss, assoc dir 1975-78; TN Valley Authority Div of Energy Use, mgr Community Conserv Proj 1978-86; Mutual Housing Corp, exec dir, 1987-90; Knoxville College, Div of Business & Social Sciences, dir, 1987-91; Mother Love Baptist Church, pastor, 1987-92; US Department of Energy, Southeastern Power Administration, Power Marketing Division, program manager, 1991-94; Macedonia Outreach Ministries, pres, 1994-96; Rochdale Institute, ceo, 1996-. **HONORS AND AWARDS** Youth & Commun Serv Frederick Douglass Chapter Hamilton Co 1981; Serv Award Lane Coll Jackson TN 1981; Distinguished Citizen City of Chattanooga TN 1981; Outstanding Mem Alpha Iota Alpha 1983; Distinguished Serv Sun Belt Assn Ind 1984; Humanitarian Award, Jas B Dudley High School Alumni Assn, 1988; Distinguished Service Award, Southeastern Power Admin, 1994; Doctorate of Divinity, Laurence Univ, 1968; Doctor of Laws, Buckner Univ, 1970. **MEMBERSHIPS** Alpha Phi Alpha Fraternity 1959-; pres bd of dir The Stewart-Candida Co 1978-85; dean Chattanooga Baptist Bible Coll 1981-84; pres bd of dir Chattanooga Area Minority Investment Forum 1981-87; chmn bd of dir Sun Belt Allied Industries 1985-86; chmn Seville-Benz Corp 1986-93; pres, Operation PUSH, Chattanooga, TN, 1986-88. **CONTACT ADDRESS** New Monumental Baptist Church, 715 E 8th Street, Chattanooga, TN, 37403.

STICH, STEPHEN P.
PERSONAL Born 05/09/1943, New York, NY, m, 1971, 2 children **DISCIPLINE** PHILOSOPHY **EDUCATION** Princeton Univ, PhD 68. **CAREER** Univ Michigan, asst prof, assoc prof, 68-78; Univ Maryland, assoc prof, prof, 78-86; UCSD, prof 86-89; Rutgers Univ, Bd of Gov Prof, 89-. **HONORS AND AWARDS** Adv Stud Behav Sci Fel; Erskine Fel. **MEMBERSHIPS** APA; SPP. **RESEARCH** Philosophy of mind, cognitive science, evolutionary psychology. **CONTACT ADDRESS** Dept of Philosophy, Rutgers Univ, New Brunswick, NJ, 08901. **EMAIL** stich@ruccs.rutgers.edu

STICHLER, RICHARD
PERSONAL Born 12/29/1942, Reading, PA, m, 1988 **DISCIPLINE** PHILOSOPHY **EDUCATION** Marlboro Coll, BA, 66; Georgetown Univ, MA, 72, PhD, 78; Drexel Univ, MS, 92 **CAREER** Asst prof/prof, 84-present, Alvernia Coll. **HONORS AND AWARDS** NDEA Title IV Fel:Georgetown Univ; Beta Phi Mu Award: Drexel Univ; Univ Fel: Univ of Maryland; Graduated with Honors: Marlboro Coll **MEMBERSHIPS** Amer Assoc of Univ Profs, member, Committee for Professional Ethics; President, Pennsylvania Division of AAUP (1998-2000); Vice President (96-98); member, Amer Philosophical Assn; Amer Catholic Philosophical Assn **RESEARCH** Ethics; Political Philosophy; Philosophical Psychology; Ancient Philosophy **SELECTED PUBLICATIONS** Auth, Review of Kindly Inquisitors: The New Attacks on Free Thought, by Jonathan Rauch, in Journal of Information Ethics, Spring 95; Review of Only Words, by Catherine A. MacKinnon, in Journal of Information Ethics, Fall 96; Academic Freedom and Faculty Responsibility in Disciplinary Proceedings, Academe, 97; coed, Ethics, Information, and Technology: Readings, Mcfarland and Co., 98. **CONTACT ADDRESS** Dept of Philos, Alvernia Col, Reading, PA, 19607. **EMAIL** stichri@alvernia.edu

STILWELL III, WILLIAM E.
PERSONAL Born 07/28/1936, Cincinnati, OH, m, 1969, 2 children **DISCIPLINE** COUNSELING; PSYCHOLOGY **EDUCATION** Dartmouth, AB, 58; San Jose State Univ, MS, 66; Stanford, PhD, 69. **CAREER** Dept of Mental Hygiene, San Mateo Cty, 66-68; Am Inst of Res, Palo Alto, Calif, 67-69; Prof, Col of Educ, Univ Ky, 69-. **HONORS AND AWARDS** VP, Counseling & Human Dev, 80-82.Coun of Clnical Psychol Prog Outstanding Service, 98. **MEMBERSHIPS** APA; APRA; AAAPP; ROA. **RESEARCH** Human services delivery evaluation; teletherapy; internet in human sci. **SELECTED PUBLICATIONS** Co-auth, Psychology for teachers and students, McGraw-Hill, 81; co-auth, Social work education: Accessible to the handicapped?, J of Educ for Soc Work, 20, 43-50, 84; co-auth, Taming the beast: A comprehensive model for the implementation of microcomputers in education, Educ, 104, 377-384, 84; co-auth, A model for recruitment and retention of minority students in teacher preparation programs, J of Tchr Educ, 39:1, 14-18, 88; co-auth, Internet training programs: A college of education response, Reading Improvement, 34, 106-113, 97. **CONTACT ADDRESS** 1919 Williamsburg Rd, Lexington, KY, 40504-3013. **EMAIL** westil3@pop.uky.edu

STINGL, MICHAEL
DISCIPLINE PHILOSOPHY **EDUCATION** Univ Wis, MA; Univ Toronto, PhD, 86. **RESEARCH** Theoretical ethics; social and political philosophy; philosophy of language; contemporary analytic philosophy; early modern philosophy; formal and informal logic. **SELECTED PUBLICATIONS** Auth, pubs on ethics and feminism. **CONTACT ADDRESS** Dept of Philosophy, Lethbridge Univ, 4401 University Dr W, Lethbridge, AB, T1K 3M4. **EMAIL** stingl@hg.uleth.ca

STITH, K.
PERSONAL Born 03/16/1951, St. Louis, MO, m, 1984, 4 children **DISCIPLINE** ECONOMICS, LAW **EDUCATION** Dartmouth Univ, AB, 73; Harvard Univ Kennedy Sch Govt, MPP, 77; Harvard Law Sch, JD, 77. **CAREER** Assoc prof, 85-91, prof, 91-98, LAFAYETTE S FOSTER PROF LAW, YALE LAW SCH, 98-. **MEMBERSHIPS** Phi Beta Kappa; Am Law Inst; Counc For Relations; Comt Law, Justice, Nat Acad Scis. **RESEARCH** Congress; constitutional law; criminal law. **SELECTED PUBLICATIONS** various **CONTACT ADDRESS** Law Sch, Yale Univ, PO Box 208215, New Haven, CT, 06520-8215.

STITT, ALLAN J.
DISCIPLINE LAW **EDUCATION** Univ Toronto, BC, 84; Windsor Univ, LLB, 88; Univ Detroit, JD, 88; Harvard Univ, LLM, 92. **CAREER** Law clerk, Ontario Court of Appeal; prof. **SELECTED PUBLICATIONS** Co-auth, Understanding the Income Tax Act; co-ed, CCH ADR Practice Manual. **CONTACT ADDRESS** Fac of Law, Univ Toronto, 78 Queen's Park, Toronto, ON.

STIVERS, ROBERT L.
PERSONAL Born 04/25/1940, Cincinnati, OH, m, 1992, 2 children **DISCIPLINE** RELIGION; ETHICS **EDUCATION** Columbia Univ, PhD 73, MPhil 71' Union Theol Sem, MDiv 69; Yale Univ, BA 62. **CAREER** Pacific Lutheran Univ, prof, assoc prof, asst prof, 74 to 97-; Union Theol Sem, grad asst 71-73; US Navy, weapons off 62-66. **MEMBERSHIPS** AAR; SCE; ACT. **RESEARCH** Environmental ethics. **SELECTED PUBLICATIONS** Jour, The Case Method Inst, co-ed vol 5,6,7,8; Christian Ethics: A Case Method Approach, coauth, Orbis Books, 89, 2nd ed, 94; Reformed Faith and Economics, U Press of Amer, 89; The Public Vocation of Christian Ethics, co-ed, Pilgrim Press, 86. **CONTACT ADDRESS** Dept of Religion, Pacific Lutheran Univ, Tacoma, WA, 98447. **EMAIL** stiverrl@plu.edu

STOCKMAN, ROBERT H.
PERSONAL Born 10/06/1953, Meriden, CT, m, 1992, 1 child **DISCIPLINE** HISTORY OF RELIGION **EDUCATION** Wesleyan Univ, BA, 75; Brown Univ, MSc, 77; Harvard Divinity School, MTS, 82, ThD, 90. **CAREER** Grad res asst, Brown Univ, 75-77; instr, Geology and Oceanography, Comm Col of RI, 77-80; instr, Geology, Boston State Col, 80-82; instr, Geology, Univ Lowell, 83-84; instr, Geology and Astronomy, Bentley Col, 83-90; teaching asst, Harvard Univ, 86-89; asst prof relig, DePaul Univ, 95-96; INSTR RELIG, DEPAUL UNIV, 90-95, 96-98. **MEMBERSHIPS** Amer Academy Relig; Middle East Studies Assoc; Soc Iranian Studies; Amer Hist Assoc; Assoc Baha i Studies, member, ex comm, 90-, member and chair, Study of Religions Section, 89-. **RESEARCH** Amer Bahai hist; Amer relig hist. **SELECTED PUBLICATIONS** Auth, The Bahai Faith in America, vol 1, Origins, 1862-1900, Baha i Pub Trust, 85, vol 2, Early Expansion, 1900-1912, George Ronald, 95; The Baha i Faith in America: One Hundred Years, in World Order, vol 25, no 3, spring 94; Paul Johnson's Theosophical Influence in Baha i History: Some Comments, in Theosophical Hist, vol 5, no 4, Oct 94; The Baha i Faith: A Portrait, in Joel Beversluis, ed, A Sourcebook for the Earth's Community of Religions, 2nd ed, CoNexus Press, 95; The Baha i Faith in the 1990's, article in Dr Timothy Miller, ed, America's Alternative Religions, SUNY Press, 95; The Vision of the Baha i Faith, in Martin Forward, Ultimate Visions: Reflections on the Religions We Choose, One World, 95; The Baha i Faith in England and Germany, 1900-1913, in World Order, vol 27, no 3, spring 96; The Baha i Faith section of the Pluralism Project, CD Rom, Columbia Univ Press, 97; many other articles, several forthcoming publications. **CONTACT ADDRESS** 1067 Woodward Ave., South Bend, IN, 46616. **EMAIL** rstockman@usbnc.org

STOEBUCK, WILLIAM BREES
PERSONAL Born 03/18/1929, Wichita, KS, m, 1951, 3 children **DISCIPLINE** LAW **EDUCATION** Wichita State Univ, BA, 51; Ind Univ Bloomington, MA, 53; Univ Wash, JD, 59; Harvard Univ, SJD, 73. **CAREER** Pvt pract law, Seattle, Wash, 59-64; asst prof, Univ Denver, 64-67; Prof Law, Univ Wash, 67-, Ford fel, Law Sch, Harvard Univ, 66-67. **MEMBERSHIPS** Order of the Coif; Am Asn Law Schs. **RESEARCH** Eminent domain; adverse possession; landlord and tenant. **SELECTED PUBLICATIONS** Auth, The property right of access versus the power of eminent domain, Tex Law Rev, 69; Condemnation of rights the condemnee holds in lands of another, Iowa Law Rev, 70; A general theory of eminent domain, Wash Law Rev, 72; Nontrespassory Takings in Eminent Domain, Bobbs, 77; Running covenants: An analytical primer, Wash Law Rev, 77; Police power, takings, and due process, Washington & Lee Law Rev, 80; Back To The Crib, Wash Law Rev, Vol 69, 94. **CONTACT ADDRESS** Sch of Law, Univ Wash, 1100 N E Campus Pky, Seattle, WA, 98105-6605.

STOEFFLER, FRED ERNEST
PERSONAL Born 09/27/1911, Happenbach, West Germany, m, 1941, 2 children **DISCIPLINE** RELIGION, HISTORY OF CHRISTIANITY **EDUCATION** Temple Univ, BS, 38, STM, 45, STD, 48; Yale Univ, BD, 41. **CAREER** Pastor, Methodist Church, 39-51; from asst prof to prof hist Christianity, 51-62, Prof Relig, Temple Univ, 62-, Mem coun, Am Soc Church Hist, 77-79. **MEMBERSHIPS** Am Soc Church Hist; Am Soc Reformation Res; AHA; Acad Polit Sci; Am Acad Relig. **RESEARCH** Reformation; mysticism; pietism. **SELECTED PUBLICATIONS** Auth, Mysticism in the Devotional Literature of Colonial Pennsylvania, Pa Ger Folklore Soc, 49; The Rise of Evangelical Pietism, Brill, Leiden, 65; transl, B Lohse, History of Doctrine, Fortress, 66; auth, German Pietism During the 18th Century, Brill, Leiden, 73; ed & contribr, Continental Pietism and Early American Christianity, Wm B Eerdmans, 76; Anton Wilhelm Bohme: Studies On The Ecumenical Thought And Dealings Of A Pietist From Halle, Church Hist, Vol 61, 92. **CONTACT ADDRESS** Dept of Relig, Temple Univ, Philadelphia, PA, 19122.

STOEHR, KEVIN L.
PERSONAL Born 11/19/1967, Portland, ME **DISCIPLINE** PHILOSOPHY **EDUCATION** Bowdoin Col, BA, 90; Boston Univ, MA, 94, PhD, 96. **CAREER** Asst prof Rhetoric and Hum, Boston Univ. **HONORS AND AWARDS** James Bowdoin Scholar, 90; Fulbright Scholar, 93-94; Junior Fel, Inst of Human Sci, 93, 94. **MEMBERSHIPS** APA. **RESEARCH** Philosophy; literature; politics; religion; film. **CONTACT ADDRESS** 99 Brainerd Rd #2, Allston, MA, 02134. **EMAIL** kstoehr@bu.edu

STOEVER, WILLIAM K.B.
PERSONAL Born 06/20/1941, Riverside, CA, m, 1971 **DISCIPLINE** HISTORY OF RELIGION **EDUCATION** Pomona Col, BA, 63; Yale Univ, MDiv, 66, MPhil, 69, PhD(relig studies), 70. **CAREER** Asst prof, 70-75, assoc prof, 76-80, prof humanities, Western Wash Univ, 80-, Chemn, Dept Lib Studies 78-, Nat Endowment for Humanities res fel, 74-75. **MEMBERSHIPS** AHA; Am Soc Church Hist; Am Acad Relig; Am Studies Asn. **RESEARCH** History and historiography of religion in Amica; 17th century Puritanism; Jonathan Edwards; religion and cultural change. **SELECTED PUBLICATIONS** Auth, Henry Boynton Smith and the German theology of history, Union Sem Quart Rev, fall 69; Nature, grace, and John Cotton: The theological dimension in the New England antinomian controversy, Church Hist, 3/75; A Faire and Easie Way to Heaven: Covenant Theology and Antinomianism in Early Massachusetts, Wesleyan Univ Press, 78; The Godly Will's Discerning: Shepard, Edwards, and the Identification of True Godliness, Jonathan Edwards's Writings: Text, Context, Interpretation, Ind Univ Press, 97. **CONTACT ADDRESS** Dept of Lib Studies, Western Washington Univ, M/S 9084, Bellingham, WA, 98225-5996.

STOKES, LOUIS
PERSONAL Born 02/23/1925, Cleveland, Ohio, m, 1960 **DISCIPLINE** LAW **EDUCATION** Case Western Reserve Univ, 1946-48; Cleveland Marshall Law School, JD, 1953. **CAREER** US House of Representatives, 11th Congressional District, Ohio, rep 1968-98, chairman, House Appropriations Subcommittee on VA-HUD-Independent Agencies, member, Appropriations Subcommittee on the District of Columbia, Subcommittee on Labor-Health and Human Services Education; private practice, attorney; Case Western Univ, visiting scholar, 1998-. **HONORS AND AWARDS** Distinguished Serv Award; Certificate of Appreciation, US Comm on Civil Rights; William L Dawson Award, 1980; honorary degrees: Wilberforce Univ, Shaw Univ, Livingstone College, Ohio College of Podiatric Medicine, Oberlin College, Morehouse College, Meharry Medical College, Atlanta Univ, Howard Univ, Morehouse School of Medicine, Central State Univ, Xavier Univ. **MEMBERSHIPS** Bd of trustees Martin Luther King Jr Ctr for Social Change, Forest City Hosp, Cleveland State Univ; bd dirs Karamu House; vice chmn, trustee bd St Paul AME Zion Church; fellow OH State Bar Assn; mem Cleveland Cuyahoga Cty, Amer Bar Assn, Pythagoras Lodge #9; exec comm Cuyahoga Cty Dem Party; exec comm OH State Dem Party; mem Urban League, Citizens League, John Harlan Law Club, Kappa Alpha Psi, Amer Civil Liberties Union, Plus Club, Amer Legion, African-Amer Inst Intl Adv Council; vice pres NAACP Cleveland Branch 1965-66; vice chmn Cleveland Sub-Com of US Comm on Civil Rights 1966; guest lecturer Cleveland Branch NAACP. **CONTACT ADDRESS** Congressman, US House of Representatives, Rayburn Bldg, Rm 2365, Washington, VT, 20515.

STOKES, MACK B.
PERSONAL Born 12/21/1911, Wonsan, Korea, m, 1942, 3 children **DISCIPLINE** PHILOSOPHICAL THEOLOGY **EDUCATION** Asbury Col, BA, 32; Duke Univ, BD, 35; Boston Univ, PhD, 40. **CAREER** Asst prof, 41, prof, Parker Prof, assoc dean, 43-72, Candler Sch Theol, Emory Univ; Bishop of the United Methodist Church, 72- . **HONORS AND AWARDS** Res fel theol, 36-38, Bowne fel philos, 38-39, Boston Univ; Lambuth Univ, LLS, 63; Millsaps Col, DD, 74. **MEMBERSHIPS** APA. **RESEARCH** Theology and philosophical theology; contemporary issues in these fields. **SELECTED PUBLICATIONS** Auth, The Epic of Revelation, McGraw Hill; auth, Talking with God: A Guide to Prayer, Abingdon, 89; auth, Theology for Preaching, Bristol House, 94; auth, Major United Methodist Beliefs. **CONTACT ADDRESS** 2637 Peachtree Rd NE, Atlanta, GA, 30305.

STOLZENBERG, N.M.
PERSONAL Born 09/06/1961, Boston, MA, m, 1986, 2 children **DISCIPLINE** LAW **EDUCATION** Yale Coll, BA, 84; Harvard Univ Law Sch, JD, 87. **CAREER** Asst prof of law, 88-91, assoc prof, 91-94, prof, 1994 -, USC Law Sch; visiting prof of law, Columbia Univ Law Sch, 95. **RESEARCH** Legal theory; political theory; religion and law; cultural pluralism; law and literature. **SELECTED PUBLICATIONS** Auth, "He Drew a Circle That Shut Me Out: Assimilation, Indoctrination, and the Paradox of a Liberal Education," Harvard Review, v 106, n 581, 93; "Un-covering the Tradition of Jewish 'Dissimilation:' Frankfurter, Bickel, and Cover on Judicial Review," Southern California Interdisciplinary Law Jour, v 809, 94; "A Tale of Two Villages (or Legal Reform Comes to Town)," in NOMOS XXXIX: Ethnicity and Group Rights, 97; "The Puzzling Persistence of Community: The Cases of Airmont and Kiryas Joel," in From Ghetto to Emancipation, Univ Scranton Press, 97; "A Book of Laughter and Forgetting: Kalman's 'Strange Career' and the Marketing of Civic Republicanism," Harvard Law Review, v 111, n 1025, 98; "Jiminy Cricket: A Commentary on Professor Hill's Four Conceptions of Conscience," in NOMOS XL: Integrity and Conscience, NY Univ Press, 98. **CONTACT ADDRESS** Univ of Southern California Law School, Univ Park, Los Angeles, CA, 90089.

STONE, ALAN ABRAHAM
PERSONAL Born 08/15/1929, Boston, MA, m, 1952, 3 children **DISCIPLINE** LAW **EDUCATION** Harvard Univ, AB, 50; Yale Univ, MD, 55. **CAREER** Prof Law & Psychiat, Harvard Univ, 72-, Assoc attending psychiatrist, McLean Hosp, 69-; assoc psychiatirst, 69-77, consult psychiat, Mass Gen Hosp, 77-; fel, Ctr Advan Studies Behav Sci, 80-81; Tanner lectr, 82. **HONORS AND AWARDS** Guttmacher Prize, 76; Guggenheim Award, 78-79; Isaac Ray Award, 82. **MEMBERSHIPS** Fel Am Psychiat Asn (vice-pres, 77-78, pres-elect, 78-79, pres, 79-80); Group Advan Psychiat. **RESEARCH** Psychopathology. **SELECTED PUBLICATIONS** Coauth, Longitudianal Studies of Child Personality, Harvard Univ, 59; The Abnormal Personality Through Literature, Prentice, 66; auth, Legal education on the couch, Harvard Law Rev, 71; Suicide precipitated by psychotherapy, Am J Psychother, 71; Psychiatry kills: a critical evaluation of Dr Thomas Szasz, J Psychiat & Law, 73; ed, Mental Health and Law: A System in Transition, Govt Printing Off, 75; auth, Revisiting The Parable--Truth Without Consequences, Int J Of Law And Psychiatry, Vol 17, 94. **CONTACT ADDRESS** Sch of Law, Harvard Univ, 1525 Massachusetts, Cambridge, MA, 02138-2903.

STONE, CHRISTOPHER D.
DISCIPLINE LAW **EDUCATION** Harvard Univ, AB,59; Yale Univ, JD,62. **CAREER** Roy P. Crocker prof, Univ Southern Calif; US Dept Energy; counseled, US Sentencing Comn on corporate crime; prof, Yale Univ & Univ Mich. **RESEARCH** Business Organizations; International Environmental Law; Property; Law, Language, & Ethics; & Rights of Groups. **SELECTED PUBLICATIONS** Auth, Law, Language, & Ethics; Should Trees Have Standing--Toward Legal Rights for Natural Objects; Where the Law Ends; Earth & Other Ethics; The Gnat is Older than Man: Global Environment & Human Agenda; Should Trees Have Standing. **CONTACT ADDRESS** School of Law, Univ Southern Calif, University Park Campus, Los Angeles, CA, 90089.

STONE, DAVID A.
PERSONAL Born 02/08/1962, Chicago, IL, d **DISCIPLINE** MEDICINE **EDUCATION** Univ professors program, Boston Univ; Forensic Psychiatry, BA/MA, 84; Soc and Technology, PhD, 91. **CAREER** Instr in medicine, Harvard Medical Sch, 95-98; Instr, Harvard Sch of Public Health, 96- ; Asst prof, Tufts Univ Sch of Medicine, 97- . **HONORS AND AWARDS** Phi Beta Kappa; Boston Univ Alumni Award, 84 and 91. **MEMBERSHIPS** APA; **RESEARCH** Philosophy of Human Science **CONTACT ADDRESS** 33 Westbourne Ter, #6, Brookline, MA, 02146-2266. **EMAIL** dstone@hsph.harvard.edu

STONE, JEROME ARTHUR
PERSONAL Born 04/29/1935, Holden, MA, m, 1953, 2 children **DISCIPLINE** PHILOSOPHY, RELIGIOUS STUDIES **EDUCATION** Univ Chicago, BA, 54; Andover Newton Theol Sch, MDiv, 58; Univ Chicago, MA, 64, PhD Philos Relig, 73. **CAREER** Teacher Philos & Relig, Kendall Col, 64-81, chmn, Philos Dept, 68-81, dir, Humanities Div, 74-75; prof Philos, William Rainey Harper Col, 81-, adj assoc prof, Christopher Newport Col, Col William St Mary, 75. **MEMBERSHIPS** Am Philos Asn; Am Acad Relig; NAm Paul Tillich Soc; Asn Develop Philos Teaching (pres, 82-83). **RESEARCH** Environmental Ethics; Cross-cultural philosophy of religion; philosophical hermeneutics; the logic of moral reasoning. **SELECTED PUBLICATIONS** Auth, Tillich and Schelling's later philosophy, In: Kairos and Logos, NAm Paul Tillich Soc, 78; contribr, Samuel Alexander, In: Twentieth-Century Thinkers, Gale Research press; coed, The Chicago School of Theology, 2 Vols, Edwin Mellen, 96. **CONTACT ADDRESS** Dept of Philosophy, William Rainey Harper Col, 1200 W Algonquin, Palatine, IL, 60067-7398. **EMAIL** jstone@harper.cc.il.us

STONE, RONALD HENRY
PERSONAL Born 03/26/1939, Humboldt, IA, 2 children **DISCIPLINE** SOCIAL ETHICS, RELIGION **EDUCATION** Morningside Col, BA, 60; Union Theol Sem, BD, 63; Columbia Univ, PhD(relig, soc), 68. **CAREER** Instr ethics, Union Theol Sem, 67-68; asst prof relig, Columbia Univ, 68-69; assoc prof ethics, 69-72, JOHN WITHERSPOON PROF, CHRISTIAN ETHICS, PITTSBURGH THEOL SEM, 72-; Adj prof relig, Univ Pittsburgh, 72-81; vis scholar, Cambridge Univ, 72 & Harvard Univ, 75. **HONORS AND AWARDS** Am Asn Theol Schs fac grant, 72 & 75. **MEMBERSHIPS** Am Acad Relig; Am Soc Christian Ethics; Soc Relig Higher Educ. **RESEARCH** Political ethics; religion and society; Christian political biography. **SELECTED PUBLICATIONS** Ed, Faith and Politics, Braziller, 68; auth, Reinhold Niebuhr: Prophet to Politicians, Abingdon, 72; Realism and Hope, Univ Press Am, 77; ed, Liberation and Change, 77 & Paul Tillich's Radical Social Thought, 80, John Knox; Profsor Reinhold Niebuhr, Westminster, 92. **CONTACT ADDRESS** 616 N Highland Ave, Pittsburgh, PA, 15206-2525. **EMAIL** rstone@pts.edu

STONE, S.L.
PERSONAL Born 12/01/1952, New York, NY, m, 4 children **DISCIPLINE** RELIGION **EDUCATION** Princeton Univ, BA, 74; Yale Univ, 74-75; Columbia Univ Law Schl, JD, 78. **CAREER** Law clerk, 78-79, Judge John Minor Wisdom, 5th Circuit, US Court of Appeals; atty; 79-83, Paul, Weiss, Rifkind, Wharton & Garrison, NY Litigation Dept; assoc dean, 87-90, Acad Affairs, prof, 83-, Benjamin Cardozo Schl of Law. **HONORS AND AWARDS** Stone Scholar, Columbia Univ; Danforth Fel in Relig & Class Civilization, Yale Univ; BA summa cum laude; Phi Beta Kappa; Univ Scholar George Potts Prize; John Robinson Mem Prize, Princeton. **MEMBERSHIPS** Comm of Profes & Judical Ethics; Comm on Fed Courts; Comm on Legal Ed; Bar Assn of NY; Intl Assn Jewish Lawyers and Jurists. **SELECTED PUBLICATIONS** Art, The Preclusive Effect of State Court Judgments on Subsequent 1983 Actions, 78 Columbia Law Rev, 78; art, Sinaitic and Noahide Law: Legal Pluralism in Jewish Law, 12 Cardozo Law Rev 1157, 91; art, The Transformation of Prophecy, 4 Cardozo Stud in Law & Lit, 167, 92; art, Judaism and Postmodernism, 14 Cardozo Law Rev 98, 93; art, In Pursuit of the Countertext: The Turn to the Jewish Legal Model in Contemporary American Legal Theory, 106 Harvard Law Rev 813, 93; art, The Emergence of Jewish Law In Postmodernist Legal Theory, Harvard Law Schl Occas Paper Ser, 2/94; art, Justice, Mercy, and Gender in Rabbinic Thought, 8 Cardozo Stud in Law & Lit 139, 96; art, What Do American Jews Believe, Symposium, Comm Mag, 96. **CONTACT ADDRESS** Cardozo Sch of Law, 55 5th Ave, New York, NY, 10003. **EMAIL** sstone@mail.yu.edu

STONE, VICTOR J.
PERSONAL Born 03/11/1921, Chicago, IL, m, 3 children **DISCIPLINE** LAW **EDUCATION** Oberlin Col, AB, 42; Columbia Univ, LLB, 48. **CAREER** Assoc law, Sch Law, Columbia Univ, 48-49; res assoc, Sch Law, Univ Chicago, 53-55; from asst prof to assoc prof, 55-59, Prof Law, Col Law, Univ IL, Urbana-Champaign, 59-, Ford Found law fac fel intl legal studies, 62-63; lectr comp law, Int Univ Comp Sci, Luxembourg, 63; vchmn, Ill State Appellate Defender Comn, 73-77 & 78-80; assoc vpres acad affairs, Univ IL, Urbana-Champaign, 75-78; Am Asn Univ Prof, gen coun 78-79, pres 82-84. **HONORS AND AWARDS** LL.D, Oberlin Col, 83. **MEMBERSHIPS** Am Bar Asn; Am Judicature Soc; AAUP (pres, 82-84). **RESEARCH** Judicial administration and procedure; American federalism; conflict of laws. **SELECTED PUBLICATIONS** Coauth, Illinois Pattern Instructions, West Publ, 2nd ed, 71; auth, Original process and appearance, In: Illinois Civil Practice Before Trial, Inst Continuing Educ of Bar, 73; ed, Civil Liberties and Civil Rights: The David C Bawn Memorial Lectures, Univ of IL, 77. **CONTACT ADDRESS** Col of Law, Univ of Illinois, 504 E Pennsylvania, Champaign, IL, 61820-6909. **EMAIL** vstone@law.uiuc.edu

STORCH, STEVEN R.
DISCIPLINE PHILOSOPHY **EDUCATION** SUNY Buffalo, BA, 87; PhD, 97. **CAREER** Vis Prof, 98-, NC St Univ; Vis Prof, NC Weseley Col, 97-. **MEMBERSHIPS** APA; North Amer Sartre Soc. **RESEARCH** Sartre stud; ethics, continental philos. **CONTACT ADDRESS** 2716 Little River Dr, Hillsborough, NC, 27278. **EMAIL** storchs@aol.com

STORTZ, MARTHA ELLEN
DISCIPLINE HISTORICAL THEOLOGY; ETHICS **EDUCATION** Carleton Col, BA; Univ Chicago, MA, PhD. **CAREER** Prof **HONORS AND AWARDS** Mem, convener, GTU Core Dr fac; adv comm, LCA Study on Issues Concerning Homosexuality, 86; bd mem,, Ctr for Women and Rel, GTU; ELCA rep, Intl Consult of Lutheran Women Theologians, Helsinki, 91. **MEMBERSHIPS** Mem, Ctr for Global Edu, Augsburg Col; ELCA Task Force on Theol Edu; ELCA Commn for

Church in Soc Bd. **SELECTED PUBLICATIONS** Auth, PastorPower, Abingdon Press, 93. **CONTACT ADDRESS** Dept of Historical Theology and Ethics, Pacific Lutheran Theol Sem, 2770 Marin Ave, Berkeley, CA, 94708-1597. **EMAIL** mstortz@autobahn.org

STORY, J. LYLE
DISCIPLINE BIBLICAL LANGUAGES; NEW TESTAMENT **EDUCATION** Sterling Col, BA; Fuller Theol Sem, MDiv, PhD. **CAREER** Assoc dean; prof, 84. **SELECTED PUBLICATIONS** Auth, Greek To Me; The Greek Memory System; contrib auth, The Spirit-Filled Life Bible. **CONTACT ADDRESS** Dept of Biblical Languages and New Testament, Regent Univ, 1000 Regent Univ Dr, Virginia Beach, VA, 23464-9831.

STOTT, DEBORAH
DISCIPLINE AESTHETIC STUDIES **EDUCATION** Columbia Univ, Phd, 75. **CAREER** Assoc prof. **RESEARCH** European and Italian art history; history and imagery of early modern women; history of women artists. **SELECTED PUBLICATIONS** Auth, The Sculpture of Andrea and Nino Pisano (rev), 86; Optical Corrections in the Sculpture of Donatello (rev), 87; Style and Theory in Italian Renaissance Reliefs, Cambridge, 83; Fatte a sembianza di pittura: Jacopo Sansovino's Bronze Reliefs in San Marco, Art Bulletin, 82; Jacques Lipchitz and Cubism, Garland, 78; Outsanding Dissertations in the Fine Arts, Garland, 78. **CONTACT ADDRESS** Dept of Aesthetics, Texas Univ, Richardson, TX, 75083-0688. **EMAIL** stott@utdallas.edu

STOWERS, STANLEY KENT
PERSONAL Born 02/24/1948, Munice, IN, m, 1968, 2 children **DISCIPLINE** HISTORY OF EARLY CHRISTIANITY **EDUCATION** Abilene Christian Univ, AB, 70; Princeton Theol Sem, MA, 74; Yale Univ, PhD(relig studies), 79. **CAREER** Asst prof relig studies, Phillips Univ, 79-80; Asst Prof Relig Studies, 81-91, PROF REL STUDIES, BROWN UNIV, 91-. **HONORS AND AWARDS** Sheridan Teaching Award, 97; Woodrow Wilson fel, 92; NEH fel, 91; FIAT fel, 90. **MEMBERSHIPS** Am Acad Relig; Soc Bibl Lit. **RESEARCH** Early Christianity; Hellenistic philosophy; early Christian literature; Greek Religion. **SELECTED PUBLICATIONS** Auth, The Diatribe and Paul's Letter to the Romans, Scholars Press, 81; auth, A Rereading of Romans, Yal Univ Press, 94; auth, Letter Writing in Greco-Roman Anqiquity, Westminster Press, 86. **CONTACT ADDRESS** Dept of Relig Studies, Brown Univ, Box 1927, Providence, RI, 02912-9127. **EMAIL** Stanley_Stowers@brown.edu

STRAMEL, JAMES
PERSONAL Born 04/05/1960, Salina, KS **DISCIPLINE** PHILOSOPHY **EDUCATION** Univ Southern Calif, MA, 85, PhD, 96. **CAREER** Adj fac, Santa Monica Col. **MEMBERSHIPS** APA. **RESEARCH** Ethics, gay studies. **SELECTED PUBLICATIONS** Auth, A New Verdict on the Jury Passage: Theaetetus 201a-c, Ancient Philos, 89; auth, How to Write a Philosophy Paper, Univ Press of Am, 94; auth, Outing, Ethics and Politics: A Reply to Mohr, in Corvino, ed, Same Sex: Debating the Ethics, Culture, and Science of Homosexuality, Rowman & Littlefield, 97. **CONTACT ADDRESS** 201 Ocean Park Blvd, #C, Santa Monica, CA, 90405. **EMAIL** stramel_james@smc.edu

STRANG, J.V.
PERSONAL Born 10/14/1942, Kirtland, OH, s **DISCIPLINE** PHILOSOPHY **EDUCATION** Boston Univ, PhD, 84. **CAREER** Lctr, Plymouth State Col, 90-; Exec dir, Boston Conservative Soc, 87-94. **RESEARCH** Ancient Philosophy; Political Philosophy; Ethics. **CONTACT ADDRESS** Dept of Philosophy, Plymouth State Col, Univ System of New Hampshire, 17 Allston St, Dorchester, MA, 02124. **EMAIL** jstrang@mail.plymouth.edu

STRANGE, JAMES F.
PERSONAL Born 02/02/1938, Pampa, TX, m, 1960, 4 children **DISCIPLINE** BIBLICAL STUDIES, ARCHEOLOGY **EDUCATION** Rice Univ, BA, 59; Yale Univ, MDiv, 64; Drew Univ, PhD, 70. **CAREER** Asst prof, 72-75, assoc prof, 75-80, prof relig studies, Univ S Fla, Tampa, 80-, dean col arts & lett, 81-89, Montgomery fel, William F Albright Inst Archaeol Res, Jerusalem, 70-71; fel Off Judeo-Christian Studies, Duke Univ, 71-72; asoc dir, Joint Exped to Khirbet Shema', Israel, 71-73; assoc dir, Meiron Excavation Proj, Israel, 73-78; vis lectr, Univ of the Orange Free State, Repub S Africa, 79; Nat Endowment for Humanities fel, Jerusalem, 80; dir, Survey in Galilee, 82; dir USF Excavations at Sepphoris, Israel, 83; dir, Excavations Qumran, 96; McMannis Lect, Wheaton Col, 96; Benjamin Meaker vis prof Inst Advan Stud, Univ Bristol, 97. **HONORS AND AWARDS** Samuel Robinson Lect, Wake Forest Univ, 81. **MEMBERSHIPS** Soc Bibl Lit; Israel Explor Soc; Am Schs Orient Res; NY Acad Sci; Soc Sci Explor. **RESEARCH** Archaeology of Israel in Roman to Arab times; Roman and Byzantine ceramics in the Eastern Mediterranean; computer models for Roman-Byzantine archaeology and historical geography. **SELECTED PUBLICATIONS** Coauth, Archaeology and rabbinic tradition at Khirbet Shema, the 1970 and 1971 campaigns, Bibl Archaeologist, 72; Excavations at Meiron in Upper Galilee--1971, 1972, 74 & auth, Late Hellenistic and Herodian ossuary tombs at French Hill, Jerusalem, 75, Bull of Am Schs of Orient Res; coauth, Ancient Synagogue Excavations at Khirbet Shema, Upper Galilee, Israel 1970-1972, Duke Univ, 76; auth, Capernaum, Crucifixion, Methods of, & Magdala, Interpreter's Dictionary of Bible, suppl vol, 76; Excavations at Meiron, in Upper Galilee--1974, 1975: A second preliminary report, 78 & coauth, Excavations at Meiron, 81, Am Schs of Orient Res; Archaeology and the religion of Judaism, Aufstieg und Niedergang der Roemischen Welt, 81; coauth, The Excavations at the Ancient Synagogue of Gush Halav, Israel, 90. **CONTACT ADDRESS** Dept Relig Studies, Univ SFla, 4202 Fowler Ave, CPR 107, Tampa, FL, 33620-9951. **EMAIL** strange@chuma.cas.usf.edu

STRASSER, MARK
PERSONAL Born 06/15/1955, Bridgeport, CT **DISCIPLINE** PHILOSOPHY **EDUCATION** Harvard Col, BA, 77; Univ Chicago, MA, 80, PhD, 84; Stanford Law Schl, JD, 93. **CAREER** Asst prof, phil, 84-87, Univ Texas, Arlington; asst prof, phil, 87-90, Wash Univ, MO; asst prof, 93-96, assoc prof, law, 96-, Capital Univ Law Schl. **HONORS AND AWARDS** NEH sum sem vis fel, ethics & med, Houston TX, 86; NEH sum Inst, Lincoln NE, 84. **RESEARCH** Constitutional law; bioethics & law. **SELECTED PUBLICATIONS** Auth, Francis Hutcheson's Moral Theory: Its Form and Utility, Hollowbrook Commun, 90; auth, The Moral Philosophy of John Stuart Mill: Toward Modifications of Contemporary Utilitarianism, Hollowbrook Commun, 91; auth, Agency, Free Will, and Moral Responsibility, Hollowbrook Pub, 92; auth, Legally Wed: Same-Sex Marriage and the Constitution, Cornell Univ Press, 97; art, Constitutional Limitations and Baehr Possibilities: On Retroactive Legislation, Reasonable Expectations, and Manifest Injustice, 29 Rutgers Law J , 98; auth, Ex Post Facto Laws, Bills of Attainder, and the Definition of Punishment: On DOMA, the Hawaii Amendment, and Federal Constitutional Constraints, 48 Syracuse Law Rev, 98; art, Baker and Some Recipes for Disaster: On DOMA, Covenant Marriages, and Full Faith and Credit Jurisprudence, 64 Brooklyn Law Rev, 98; art, For Whom Bell Tolls: On Subsequent Domiciles' Refusing to Recognize Same-Sex Marriages, 66 Univ Cincinnati Law Rev, 98; art, Natural Law and Same-Sex Marriage, 48 DePaul Law Rev, 98; art, The Futility of Futility?: On Life, Death, and Reasoned Public Policy, 57 Maryland Law Rev, 98. **CONTACT ADDRESS** Law Sch, Capital Univ, 303 East Broad St, Columbus, OH, 43215. **EMAIL** mstrasser@law.capital.edu

STRAUMANIS, JOAN
PERSONAL Born 02/10/1937, New York, NY, w, 1969, 3 children **DISCIPLINE** PHILOSOPHY; MATHEMATICS **EDUCATION** Antioch Col, BA, 57; Univ Col, MA, 59; Univ Maryland, PhD, 74 **CAREER** Tchg asst, Dept of Philos, Univ Maryland, 69-71; Prog Off, Nat Sci Found, 77-78; vis res prof, Dept of Philos, Univ Bristol, 80; from asst prof, 71-76, to assoc prof, 76-82, to prof, 82, Dept of Philos, Denison Univ; prof of Philos, 82-86, Assoc Provost, 82-83, Acad Dean, 83-86, Kenyon Col; prof of Philos & Dean of Fac, 86-92, Rollins Col; Prog Off, 92-95, consult & adj, 95-, Fipse US Dept of Educ; Herbert & Ann Siegel Dean, Col Arts & Sci, 95-97, dean emer & prof of philosophy, 97-, Lehigh Univ. **HONORS AND AWARDS** Univ Col Found Grad fel, 57-58; US Steel Found Grad fel, 67-69; Danforth Assoc, 76; Award Excellence Tchg Univ Maryland, 70; Omicron Delta Kappa, 81; Fac Ldr Award, Denison Univ, 81. **MEMBERSHIPS** Amer Civil Liberties Union; Proj Kalaeidoscope; W Asn Schools & Col; Amer Philos Soc. **RESEARCH** Philosophy of science; Logic; Reform of science education; Womens studies **SELECTED PUBLICATIONS** Auth, The Case Against Human Sociobiology, Amer Philos Asn, 83; Of Sissies and Spinsters: Shifts in Value of Sex-Marked Terms, Amer Philos Asn, Chicago, 83; A Laboratory Manual for the Philosophy of Biology, Philosophy of Biology in the Philosophy Cirriculum, San Fran Univ, 83; auth, Duties to Oneself: An Ethical Basis for Self-Liberation? Jour Soc Philos, 84; Explosive Freedom: Impressions of Glasnost, Rollins Alumni Rec, 88; Struggles with the Maxwell Demon, Rollins Col, 88; Support Issues, The Use of Symbolic Computation in Undergraduate Mathematics, Math Asn Amer, 92; rev, A Deans-Eye View. The Golden Age of Universities on the Make, Change, 92. **CONTACT ADDRESS** Philosophy Dept, Lehigh Univ, 15 University Dr, Bethlehem, PA, 18015. **EMAIL** jcs5@lehigh.edu

STRAUSS, MARCY
DISCIPLINE LAW **EDUCATION** Northwestern Univ, BS, 78; Georgetown Univ, JD, 81. **CAREER** Prof, Loyola Univ 84-; clerk, hon James B. Moran US Dist Ct, Northern Dist Ill, 81-83. **RESEARCH** Writes on, freedom of speech & other Const issues. **CONTACT ADDRESS** Law School, Loyola Marymount Univ, 7900 Loyola Blvd, Burns 403, Los Angeles, CA, 90045. **EMAIL** mstrauss@lmulaw.lmu.edu

STRAUSS, MARK
PERSONAL Born 11/16/1959, Fort Worth, TX, m, 1984, 3 children **DISCIPLINE** NEW TESTAMENT **EDUCATION** Westmont Coll, BA; Talbot School Theol, Mdiv, ThM; Univ Abosdeen, PhD. **CAREER** Prof, Christian Heritage Coll, 92-95; Prof, Bethel Sem San Diego, 93-. **MEMBERSHIPS** Soc of Bibl Lit; Evangel Theol Soc; Inst for Bibl Res. **RESEARCH** New Testament; Bible Translation; Hermeneutics. **CONTACT ADDRESS** 1565 Avenida Ladera, El Cajon, CA, 92020-1303. **EMAIL** m-strauss@Bethel.edu

STRAUSS, PETER L.
PERSONAL Born 02/26/1940, New York, NY, m, 1964, 2 children **DISCIPLINE** ADMINISTRATIVE LAW **EDUCATION** Harvard Univ, AB, 61; Yale Univ, LLB, 64. **CAREER** Law clerk, US Ct Appeals, DC, 64-65 & US Supreme Ct, 65-66; lectr criminal law, Haile Sellassi I Univ, 66-68; asst to solicitor gen, US Dept Justice, 68-71; PROF, ADMIN, CONST & FAMILY LAW, COLUMBIA LAW SCH, 71-; Consult admin law, US Admin conf, 71-74 & 77-80; gen coun, US Nuclear Regulatory Comn, 75-77; consult, ABA Coordr, Group on Regulatory Reform, 80-. **HONORS AND AWARDS** U S Dept of Justice 71; US NRC 77. **MEMBERSHIPS** Am Asn Law Sch; Soc Am Law Teachers; Am Bar Asn. **RESEARCH** Infrastructure of agency rulemaking; presidential participation in agency action; administrative law reform. **SELECTED PUBLICATIONS** Ed, Fetha Nagast, The Law of the Kings, Haile Sellassi I Univ, 68; auth, Administrative Law: Cases and Comments, Gellhorn & Byse, 7th 8th & 9th ed; Administrative Law Problems, Verkuil, 79 & 83. **CONTACT ADDRESS** Law Sch, Columbia Univ, 435 W 116th St, New York, NY, 10027-7201. **EMAIL** strauss@law.columbia.edu

STREETER, JARVIS
PERSONAL Born 07/06/1949, Oakland, CA, m, 1988, 2 children **DISCIPLINE** RELIGIOUS STUDIES **EDUCATION** Univ Southern Calif, Los Angeles BA, 71; Luther Sem St Paul, MD, 82; Yale Univ Divinity School, New Haven, STM, 82; Southern Methodist Univ, Dallas, PhD, 90. **CAREER** Teacher of Math and Sci, Kiriani Harambee High School, Kenya, 71-72; pastoral asst, Ascension Lutheran Church Thousand Oaks, 73-74; vicar and lectr, Gustavus Adolphus Coll, St Peter, 76-77; lec tr, Luther Sem St Paul, 76-77; pastor, St Andrew Lutheran Church and Church of the Christ the Redeemer, 78-79; lectr, Augsburg Coll, Minneapolis, 80; lectr, Southern Methodist Univ Perkins School Theol, 86-87; asst prof, calif Lutheran Univ, 88-93; assoc prof, Calif Lutheran Univ, 93-. **HONORS AND AWARDS** Res Fel, Yale Univ Divinity School, 82-83; Grad Program in Rel Studies Fel, Southern Methodist Univ, 83-88; Outstanding Prof of the Year, Calif Lutheran Univ, 91; Hewlett Foundation Sabbatical Fel, 94. **MEMBERSHIPS** Am Acad of Rel; Evangel Lutheran Church in Am. **RESEARCH** Religion. **SELECTED PUBLICATIONS** Auth, Human nature and Human Sinfulness: Ernest Becker's Anthropology and the Contemporary Western Erbsunde Debate, 90; The Development of Ernest Becker's Anthropology, Soundings: An Interdisciplinary J, forthcoming. **CONTACT ADDRESS** California Lutheran Univ, 60 W Olsen Rd, Thousand Oaks, CA, 91360.

STRIKWERDS, ROBERT A.
DISCIPLINE PHILOSOPHY **EDUCATION** Univ of Notre Dame, PhD, 82. **CAREER** Ind Univ **RESEARCH** Ethics; philosophy of social sciences. **CONTACT ADDRESS** Indiana Univ, Kokomo, 2300 S Washington St, PO Box 9003, Kokomo, IN, 48904-9003.

STROBLE, PAUL E., JR.
PERSONAL Born 01/02/1957, Vandalia, IL, m, 1984, 1 child **DISCIPLINE** RELIGION **EDUCATION** Greenville Col, BA, 79; Yale Divin School, MDiv, 82; Univ of Virginia, PhD, 91. **CAREER** Illinois Dept Conserv, researcher, historic sites, 78-79; Albertus Magnus Coll, ta, 81-82; Univ of Virginia, grad asst, 86-87; N Arizona Univ, p/t instr, 87-91; Linsey Wilson Col, p/t instr, 91; Spalding Univ, p/t instr, 91-95; Presbyterian Theol Sem, 92-, Univ of Louisville, adj instr, 97-99; Indiana Univ S/E, adj instr, 95-. **MEMBERSHIPS** AAR, ISHS, PAS, KBSNA **RESEARCH** Karl Barth and 20th Cent Philo; Antebellum Amer hist; teaching of philo and relig; creative writing. **SELECTED PUBLICATIONS** Auth, Advent Christmas 1997 Study Book: Scriptures for the Church Season, United Methodist Publishing House, 97; Journeys Home: Thoughts and Places, Self pub/illus, 95; The Social Ontology of Karl Barth, Intl Scholars Pub, 94; High on the Okaw's Western Bank: Vandalia, IL, 1819-1839, Univ of Illinois Press, 92; History of Methodism in Louisville and Jefferson County, Kentucky, Encycl of Louisville, f/c; Kentucky Council of Churches, 1947-1997, commis booklet, 97; Ferdinand Ernst and the German Colony at Vandalia, Illinois History Teacher, 97; Systems and Leadership in the Parish, The Quart Rev, 95; Destined in Love: Lectionary Texts By and About Paul, The Quart Rev, 96; Without Running Riot: Kant, Analogical Language and Theological Discourse, Sophia: Jour of Philo, 93. **CONTACT ADDRESS** Dept of Religious Studies, Southeast Indiana Univ, 8919 Bingham Dr, Louisville, KY, 40242-3366. **EMAIL** 103501.466@compuserve.com

STROH, GUY WESTON
PERSONAL Born 03/28/1931, Elizabeth, NJ, m, 1966 **DISCIPLINE** PHILOSOPHY **EDUCATION** Princeton Univ, AB, 53, Am, 55, PhD(Philos), 57. **CAREER** From asst prof to assoc prof, 56-66, prof Philos, Rider Col, 66-, chmn dept, 63-. **HONORS AND AWARDS** Lindback Found Award, 66. **MEM-**

BERSHIPS Am Philos Asn; AAUP; C S Peirce Soc. **RE-SEARCH** American philosophy; ethics; philosophy of mind. **SELECTED PUBLICATIONS** Auth, Plato and Aristotle, An Introduction, Rider Col, 64; American Philosophy from Edwards to Dewey, Van Nostrand, 68; Professor Feibleman's philosophy in relation to currents of the twentieth century, Studium Gen, Heidelberg, 7/71; Mind and spirit in Feibleman's philosophy, Tulane Studies in Philos, 76; American Ethical Thought, Nelson Hall, 79; The Moral Vision of Diana Trilling, Explorations: 20th Century, 92. **CONTACT ADDRESS** Dept of Philosophy, Rider Col, 2083 Lawrenceville, Lawrenceville, NJ, 08648-3099. **EMAIL** philosophy@rider.com

STROHL, JANE E.
DISCIPLINE CHURCH HISTORY **EDUCATION** Vassar Col, BA; Lutheran Theol Sem at Gettysburg, MDiv; Univ Chicago Divinity Sch, MA, PhD. **MEMBERSHIPS** Mem, Intl Lutheran-Orthodox Joint Comm; Amer Acad Rel; Amer Soc of Church Hist; Lutheran Women's Caucus. **RESEARCH** Reformation history. **SELECTED PUBLICATIONS** Auth, God's Life-Giving Promise, Creation Is a Continuing Event, 87; The Call to Ministry of Word and Sacrament, Serving the Word: Lutheran Women Consider Their Calling, Marilyn Preus, 88; Martin Luther, Daily Readings from Spiritual Classics, Paul Ofstedal, 90; Ministry in the Middle Ages and Reformation, Called and Ordained: Lutheran Perspectives on the Office of the Ministry, 90. **CONTACT ADDRESS** Dept of Church History, Pacific Lutheran Theol Sem, 2770 Marin Ave, Berkeley, CA, 94708-1597. **EMAIL** jstrohl@plts.edu

STROKER, WILLIAM DETTWILLER
PERSONAL Born 05/23/1938, Paris, KY, m, 1967, 1 child **DISCIPLINE** NEW TESTAMENT STUDIES, HELLENISTIC RELIGIONS, EARLY CHRISTIANITY **EDUCATION** Transylvania Univ, BA, 60; Yale Univ, BD, 63, MA, 66, PhD, 70. **CAREER** From instr to asst prof, 69-76, assoc prof Relig, 76-82, PROF RELIG, DREW UNIV, 82-. **HONORS AND AWARDS** Scholar-Teacher of the Year, Drew Univ, 89. **MEMBERSHIPS** Soc Bibl Lit. **RESEARCH** Post-Canonical traditions about Jesus; religious thought of the hellenistic period; Pauline theology and influence. **SELECTED PUBLICATIONS** Auth, Postcanonical Sayings of Jesus, 89. **CONTACT ADDRESS** Dept of Relig, Drew Univ, 36 Madison Ave, Madison, NJ, 07940-1493. **EMAIL** WStroker@Drew.edu

STROLL, AVRUM
PERSONAL Born 02/15/1921, Oakland, CA, m, 1955, 2 children **DISCIPLINE** PHILOSOPHY **EDUCATION** Univ Calif, Berkeley, PhD, 51. **CAREER** Univ Oregon, 50-51; Univ British Columbia, 52-63; Univ Calif, San Diego, 63-. **HONORS AND AWARDS** All Univ Calif lectr, 65; Guggenheim fel, 73. **MEMBERSHIPS** APA. **RESEARCH** Philosophy of language; epistemology; history of modern philos. **SELECTED PUBLICATIONS** Auth, That Puzzle We Call the Mind, Grazer Philosophische Studien, 93; auth, Moore and Wittgenstein on Certainty, Oxford Univ, 94; ed, Epistemology: New Essays in the Theory of Knowledge, London, 94; auth, On Following a Rule, in Egidi, ed, Wittgenstein: Mind and Language, Kluwer, 95; auth, The Argument from Possibility, in Skepticism in the History of Philosophy, Kluwer, 96; auth, Ethics Without Principles, Proceedings of the 18th International Wittgenstein Symposium, 96; auth, Sketches of Landscapes: Philosophy by Example, MIT, 98; auth, Twentieth Century Analytic Philosophy, in, A History of Western Philosophy, Columbia, 98; auth, G.E. Moore, in Cambridge Companion to the Philosophers Series, Blackwell, 98; auth, G. E. Moore, in, The Encyclopedia of Empiricism, Greenwood, 98. **CONTACT ADDRESS** Dept of Philosophy, Univ of California, La Jolla, La Jolla, CA, 92093. **EMAIL** astroll@ucsd.edu

STROM, LYLE E.
DISCIPLINE LAW **EDUCATION** Creighton Univ, BA, JD. **CAREER** Clin prof & dir, Robert M. Spire Internship Prog; pvt pract, Omaha, 53-85; from mem US dist Ct dist Nebr, 85 to ch judge, 87-94 and sr judge, 95; ch, Gender Fairness Task Force for the 8th Circuit; co-ch, Fed Practice Comt US dist Ct dist Nebr; adj fac, Creighton Law Sch, tchg Munic Corp, 58-70 and Trial Pract, 74-95. **HONORS AND AWARDS** Highest Triennial Average awd, 53. **MEMBERSHIPS** Eighth Circuit Judicial Conf comt; exec comt and bd trustees, Mid-Am Coun Boy Scouts Am; past pres, Nebr State Bar Asn & Omaha Bar Asn; House Deleg, Nebr State Bar Asn; Nebr Supreme Ct Comt on Practice and Procedure. **SELECTED PUBLICATIONS** Auth, Nebraska Jury Instructions; Nebraska Rules of Evidence; pub(s) in, Creighton Law Rev & Nebr Law Rev. **CONTACT ADDRESS** School of Law, Creighton Univ, 2500 California Plaza, Omaha, NE, 68178.

STROMBERG, JAMES S.
PERSONAL Born 09/06/1926, Chippewa Falls, WI **DISCIPLINE** PHILOSOPHY **EDUCATION** Col St Thomas, BA, 50; Laval Univ, MA, 57, PhL, 59, PhD(philos), 65. **CAREER** From instr to assoc prof, 56-74, Prof Philos, Univ St Thomas, 74-, Chmn Dept, 80-. **MEMBERSHIPS** Am Philos Asn; Am Cath Philos Asn. **RESEARCH** Logic; ethical theory. **SELECTED PUBLICATIONS** Auth, Essay on Experimentum I, Laval Theol et Philos, 67, 68. **CONTACT ADDRESS** Dept of Philosophy, Univ of St. Thomas, 2115 Summit Ave, St. Paul, MN, 55105-1096. **EMAIL** jsstromberg@stthomas.edu

STRONG, DOUGLAS M.
PERSONAL Born 09/27/1956, Buffalo, NY, m, 1986, 2 children **DISCIPLINE** HISTORY OF CHRISTIANITY **EDUCATION** Houghton Col, BA, 78; Princeton Theological Seminary, Mdiv, 81, PhD, 90. **CAREER** PROF OF HIST OF CHRISTIANITY, WESLEY THEOLOGICAL SEMINARY, 89-. **MEMBERSHIPS** Am Acad of Religion; Am Soc of Church Hist; Am Hist Asn; Wesleyan Theological Soc. **RESEARCH** 19th Century American religious history. **SELECTED PUBLICATIONS** Auth, Reading Christian Ethics: A Historical Sourcebook, Westminster John Knox, 96; auth, They Walked in the spirit: Personal Faith and Social Action in America, Westminster John Knox, 97; auth, Perfectionist Politics: Abolitionism and the Religious Tensions of American Democracy. **CONTACT ADDRESS** Wesley Theol Sem, 4500 Massachusetts Ave NW, Washington, DC, 20016.

STRONG, L. THOMAS, III
PERSONAL Born 05/20/1961, Nashville, TN, m, 1984, 2 children **DISCIPLINE** NEW TESTAMENT; GREEK **EDUCATION** New Orleans Baptist Theol Sem, PhD 93, MDiv 87; Union Univ, BA 83. **CAREER** New Orleans Baptist Theol Sem, assoc dean Undergrad stud, ch Theol Dept, assoc prof NT and Greek, 93-. **MEMBERSHIPS** SBL; AAR; ETS; ACS. **RESEARCH** Pauline studies; Textual Criticism; Spiritual Disciplines. **SELECTED PUBLICATIONS** Auth, Contrasts: Luke 18, Theol Educator; An Essential Unity, Theol Edu; Claudius, Biblical Illustrator. **CONTACT ADDRESS** 3939 Gentilly Blvd, New Orleans, LA, 70126. **EMAIL** tstrong@nobts.edu

STRONKS, JULIA K.
DISCIPLINE LAW **EDUCATION** Univ Iowa Col of Law, JD, 85; Univ Maryland-College Park, PhD, 95. **HONORS AND AWARDS** Fulbright, the Netherlands, 92. **RESEARCH** Law and policy; constitutional law; comparative law **CONTACT ADDRESS** Dept of Political Studies, Whitworth Col, Spokane, WA, 99251. **EMAIL** jstronks@whitworth.edu

STROUD, SARAH
DISCIPLINE PHILOSOPHY **EDUCATION** Harvard Univ, BA; Princeton Univ, PhD. **RESEARCH** Contemp analytic moral theory; contemp analytic meta-ethics; hist of moral philos; applied ethics; logic; analytic philos. **SELECTED PUBLICATIONS** Auth, Dworkin and Casey on Abortion, 96; auth, Moral Relativism and Quasi-Absolutism, 98; art, Moral Overridingness and Moral Theory, Pacific Philos Quarterly, 98. **CONTACT ADDRESS** Philosophy Dept, McGill Univ, 845 Sherbrooke St, Montreal, PQ, H3A 2T5.

STRUGNELL, JOHN
PERSONAL Born 05/25/1930, Barnet, England, m, 1957, 5 children **DISCIPLINE** BIBLICAL STUDIES, SEMITICS **EDUCATION** Oxford Univ, BA, 52, MA, 55. **CAREER** Epigraphist, Dead Sea Scrolls, Palestine Archaeol Mus, Jerusalem, 54-56; res, Orient Inst, Chicago, 57; epigraphist, Palestine Archaeol Mus, 57-60; asst prof Old Testament, divinity sch, Duke Univ, 60-66; assoc prof, 66-68, Prof Christian Origins, Divinity Sch, Harvard Univ, 68-, Mem, Brit Sch Archaeol, Jerusalem, 60-; Am Coun Learned Soc fel, 68-69. **RESEARCH** Northwest Semitic epigraphy; Qumran Scrolls; Near-Eastern history. **SELECTED PUBLICATIONS** Auth, Quelques inscriptions Samaritaines, Rev Bibl, 67; Notes en marge, Vol V, Discoveries in the Judean Desert of Jordan, Rev Qumran, 7:163-276; A Critical Note In Evaluation Of The 'Dead Sea Scrolls Uncovered By Robert Eisenman And Michael Wise, J Of Biblical Lit, Vol 112, 93. **CONTACT ADDRESS** Divinity Sch, Harvard Univ, 45 Francis Ave, Cambridge, MA, 02138.

STUART, DOUGLAS KEITH
PERSONAL Born 02/08/1943, Concord, MA, m, 1971, 8 children **DISCIPLINE** OLD TESTAMENT, NEAR EASTERN LANGUAGES **EDUCATION** Harvard Univ, BA, 64, PhD, 71. **CAREER** Instr Near East hist, 68-69, Gordon Col; asst prof, 71-77, assoc prof, 78-81, prof Old Testament, 81-, Gordon-Conwell Theol Sem; pres, 74-, Boston area chap, Huxley Inst Biosocial Res; co-chmn, 75-, Boston Theol Inst; trustee, 80-, Mass Bible Soc; trustee, Boxford Acad, 96-. **MEMBERSHIPS** Am Schs Orient Res; Inst Bibl Res; Evangel Theol Soc; Soc Bibl Lit; Bibl Archeol Soc. **RESEARCH** Hebrew meter; minor prophets; exegesis techniques. **SELECTED PUBLICATIONS** Coauth, How to Read the Bible for All Its Worth, Zondervan Publ House, 82; auth, Hosea-Jonah, Word Biblical Comm, 87; auth, Hosea-Jonah, Word Biblical Themes, 88; auth, Favorite Old Testament Passages, Westminster Press, 89; auth, Malachi, Baker Bk House, 98. **CONTACT ADDRESS** Gordon-Conwell Theol Sem, 130 Essex St, South Hamilton, MA, 01982-2395.

STUART, JAMES DONALD
PERSONAL Born 09/14/1939, Owensboro, KY, m, 1961, 2 children **DISCIPLINE** PHILOSOPHY **EDUCATION** Cincinnati Bible Col, BSL, 62, ThB, 63; Univ Cincinnati, MA, 67, PhD, 70. **CAREER** Instr philos, Univ Cincinnati, 66-68; from Asst Prof to assoc Prof, 68-83, Prof Philos, Bowling Green State Univ, 83. **MEMBERSHIPS** Am Philos Asn. **RESEARCH** Hist of mod philos; Kant; Berkeley; Descartes. **SE-**

LECTED PUBLICATIONS Coauth, Review of G Buchdahl's Metaphysics and the philosophy of science, Philos Sci, 6/72; Kant's two refutations of idealism, 75 & Berkeley's appearance-reality distinction, 77, Southwestern J Philos; Bekeley on Dreaming & Perceiving, Proc Ohio Philos Asn, 76; Asst ed, The Philosopher's Index: A Retrospective Index to US Publications from 1940, 78; Ethical relativism and the teaching of values, Forum, 82; Imposing Values with Respect for Persons, Eastern Ed J, 83; The Role of Dreaming in Descartes' Meditations, Hist Philos Quart, 83; Frankfurt on Descartes Dream Argument, Philos Forum, 85; Descartes' Proof of the External World, Hist Philos Quart, 86; Retributive Justice and Prior Offenses, Philos Forum, 86; Deterrence, Desert, and Drunk Driving, Public Affairs Quart, 89; Logical Thinking, An Introduction to Logic, McGraw Hill, 85, 2nd ed, 97. **CONTACT ADDRESS** Dept of Philos, Bowling Green State Univ, 1001 E Wooster St, Bowling Green, OH, 43403-0001.

STUBENBERG, LEOPOLD
DISCIPLINE PHILOSOPHY **EDUCATION** Univ Graz, BA, 84; Univ Ariz, MA, 88, PhD, 92. **CAREER** Assoc prof. **RESEARCH** Philosophy of mind; epistemology. **SELECTED PUBLICATIONS** Auth, Justifying Basic Belief Forming Processes, Knowledge Tchg Wisdom, 96; The Place of Qualia in the World of Science, 96. **CONTACT ADDRESS** Philosophy Dept, Univ of Notre Dame, 336/7 O'Shaughnessy, Notre Dame, IN, 46556. **EMAIL** stubenberg.1@nd.edu

STUCKEY, PRISCILLA
PERSONAL Born 03/21/1957, OH, s **DISCIPLINE** GENDER AND RELIGIOUS STUDIES **EDUCATION** Grad Theol Union, PhD, 97 **CAREER** Development Editor **HONORS AND AWARDS** Young Scholars Award, 95. **MEMBERSHIPS** Natl Women's Studies Asn **SELECTED PUBLICATIONS** Auth, Light Dispels Darkness: Gender, Ritual and Society in Mozart's The Magic Flute, 95. **CONTACT ADDRESS** 3060 Butters Dr, Oakland, CA, 94602. **EMAIL** pstuckey@california.com

STUDZINSKI, RAYMOND JAMES
PERSONAL Born 04/18/1943, Detroit, MI **DISCIPLINE** RELIGION, PSYCHOLOGY **EDUCATION** St Meinrad Col, BA, 66; IN Univ, MA, 73; Fordham Univ, PhD(theol), 77. **CAREER** Asst prof theol, St Meinrad Sch Theol, 73-77; fel, Menninger Found, 79-81; asst prof relig, 81-85, assoc prof relig, Cath Univ Am, 85-. **MEMBERSHIPS** Soc Sci Study Relig; Relig Res Asn. **RESEARCH** Psychology of religion; contemporary spirituality; spiritual direction. **SELECTED PUBLICATIONS** Spiritual Direction and Midlife Development, Chicago: Loyola Univ Press, 85. **CONTACT ADDRESS** Relig Dept, Catholic Univ of America, 620 Michigan Ave N E, Washington, DC, 20064-0002. **EMAIL** studzinski@cua.edu

STUESSER, LEE
DISCIPLINE LAW **EDUCATION** Winnipeg Univ, BA, 77; Brock Univ, BEd, 79; Guelph Univ, MA, 80; Univ Manitoba, LLB, 84; Harvard Univ, LLM, 86. **CAREER** Asst prof, Univ Ottawa, 86-88; prof, 88-. **RESEARCH** Criminal law; evidence; litigation; remedies. **SELECTED PUBLICATIONS** Auth, An Advocacy Primer, Carswell, 90; Introduction to Advocacy, 93; Essentials of Canadian Law: Evidence, 96. **CONTACT ADDRESS** Fac of Law, Univ Manitoba, Robson Hall, Winnipeg, MB, R3T 2N2. **EMAIL** lstuess@cc.umanitoba.ca

STUHLMUELLER, CARROLL
PERSONAL Born 04/02/1923, Hamilton, OH **DISCIPLINE** SCRIPTURE **EDUCATION** Cath Univ Am, STL, 52; Pontif Bibl Inst, Rome, SSL, 54, SSD, 69. **CAREER** Mem fac, St Meinrad Sch Theol, 65-68; Prof Scripture, Cath Theol Union, 68-, Asst prof, Viatorian Sem, Evanston, Ill, 55-58 & Loretto Jr Col, 59-61, 62-65 & Ursuline Col, 61-63; prof, St John's Univ, NY, 70-75; vis prof, Ecole Biblique & Archaeol, Jerusalem, 73; assoc ed, Cath Bibl Quart, 73-77; ed, The Bible Today, 80-; prof scripture, St John's Univ, NY, fall, 70-74. **HONORS AND AWARDS** DHL, St Benedict Col, 69. **MEMBERSHIPS** Cath Bibl Asn Am (vpres, 77-78, pres, 78-79); Soc Bibl Lit; Col Theol Soc; Theol Soc Am. **RESEARCH** Biblical foundations of mission; prophets Haggai & Zechariah; Biblical spirituality from the Psalms. **SELECTED PUBLICATIONS** Auth, Creative redemption in Deutero-Isaiah, Bibl Inst Press, Rome, 70; Thirsting for the Lord, Alba House, 77; Biblical Meditations for Lent, Paulist Press, 78; ed, Women and Priesthood: Future Directions, Liturgical Press, 78; Biblical Meditations for Easter Season, 79; Biblical Meditations for Advent and Christmas, 80; The Psalms, M Glazier Publ, (2 vols), 82; Biblical foundations of Mission, Orbis Press, 83; Zion Final Destiny--The Development Of The Book Of Isaiah--A Reassessment Of Isaiah-XXXVI-XXXIX, Catholic Biblical Quart, Vol 55, 93; Seeing And Hearing God With The Psalms--The Prophetic Liturgy Of The 2nd-Temple In Jerusalem, J Of Biblical Lit, Vol 112, 93. **CONTACT ADDRESS** Cath Theol Union Chicago, 5401 S Cornell Ave, Chicago, IL, 60615.

STUHR, WALTER MARTIN
DISCIPLINE ETHICS **EDUCATION** Yale Univ, BA; Pacific Lutheran Theol Sem, BD; Univ Chicago, PhD. **CAREER** Acad

dean; prof, 67; dir, MA, MTS, degree prog(s); pres, 78-88. **HONORS AND AWARDS** Co-dir, PLTS Ctr for Lutheran Church Growth and Mission. **MEMBERSHIPS** Mem, Candidacy Comm, ELCA Region I; Richmond Shimada, Japan, Sister City Prog; Soc of Christian Ethics; Bishop's Nuclear Deterrence Planning Comm. **CONTACT ADDRESS** Dept of Ethics, Pacific Lutheran Theol Sem, 2770 Marin Ave, Berkeley, CA, 94708-1597. **EMAIL** wstuhr@plts.edu

STULMAN, LOUIS
PERSONAL Born 08/03/1953, Baltimore, MD, m, 1975, 4 children **DISCIPLINE** RELIGION **EDUCATION** Roberts Wesleyan Col, BA, 78; Drew Univ, MPhil, 81, PhD, 82; Univ Mich, Post Doct, 89. **CAREER** Tchng & res asst, 79-81, Bibl Stud Res fel, 80-81, instr, Hebrew, 81-82, Drew Univ; vis scholar, 88-89, Univ Mich; adj prof, 85-97, prof, 97-,Univ Findlay; asst prof, 82-86, assoc prof, 87-88, prof, 96-97, Gale and Harriette Ritz Prof, 96-97, Dist Scholar, 97-, Winebrenner Theol Sem **HONORS AND AWARDS** Who's Who in Midwest, 94-95; Outstanding Ed, Findlay OH, 89; Outstanding Young Men of Am, 86; Who's Who in Relig and Archaeol, 85-86, 92-93; Hebrew Bible Award, Drew Univ, 81-82; Drew Grad Sch Res Fel, 80-81; Alpha Kappa Sigma Hon Soc, 77-78. **MEMBERSHIPS** Soc of Bibl Lit; Natl Assn of Prof of Hebrew. **SELECTED PUBLICATIONS** Auth, Four Remarkable Women in Matthew 1:1-17, Church Adv 156/7, 91; auth, Sex and Familial Crimes in the D Code: A Witness to Mores in Transition, J for Stud of OT 53, 92; auth, Dynamic Correspondence and Preaching, Homiletic 18/1, 93; rev, Alice Ogden Bellis, The Structure and Composition of Jeremiah 50:2-51:18, Scholar Res & Rev, 95; auth, Insiders and Outsiders in the Book of Jeremiah: Shifts in Symbolic Arrangements, J for Stud of OT 66, 95, reprint, Sheffield Reader: The Prophets, Sheffield Acad Press, 96; auth, Order Amid Chaos: Jeremiah As Symbolic Tapestry, Sheffield Acad Press, 98; auth, Troubling Jeremiah: New Readings of the Book of Jeremiah, Sheffield Acad Press, 99. **CONTACT ADDRESS** Col of Liberal Arts, Univ of Findlay, 1000 N Main St, Findlay, OH, 45840. **EMAIL** stulman@mail.findlay.edu

STUMP, DAVID JAMES
PERSONAL Born 03/21/1955, Santa Monica, CA, m **DISCIPLINE** PHILOSOPHY **EDUCATION** Northwestern Univ, PhD, 88. **CAREER** Assoc prof, Univ San Francisco. **MEMBERSHIPS** APA; PSA; HSS; HOPOS. **RESEARCH** Philosophy of Science. **SELECTED PUBLICATIONS** Auth, Afterword: New Directions in the Philosophy of Science Studies, Disunity of Sci: Boundaries, Contexts and Power, 96; From Epistemology and Metaphysics to Concrete Connections, , Disunity of Sci: Boundaries, Contexts and Power, 96; Poincare's Curious Role in the Formalization of Mathematics, henri Poincare: Sci and Philos, Int Congress Nancy France 94, 96; Reconstructing the Unity of Mathematics circa 1900, Perspectives on Sci, 97; Poincare Jules Henri, Routledge Encycl of Philos, 98; co-ed, The Disunity of Sci: Boundaries, Contexts and Power, 96. **CONTACT ADDRESS** Dept of Philosophy, Univ of San Francisco, San Francisco, CA, 94117-1080. **EMAIL** stumpd@usfca.edu

STURM, DOUGLAS EARL
PERSONAL Born 04/22/1929, Batavia, NY, m, 1953, 2 children **DISCIPLINE** RELIGION, POLITICAL THEORY **EDUCATION** Hiram Col, AB, 50; Univ Chicago, DB, 53, PhD(theol soc ethics), 59. **CAREER** Nat exec secy, Christian Action, 54-56; from asst prof to assoc prof relig, 59-67, assoc prof relig & polit sci, 67-70, actg chmn dept polit sci, 68-69, chmn dept relig, 69-74, 69-74, 89-90, dir univ honors coun, 70-72, presidential prof, 74-80, Prof Relig & Polit Sci, 70-95, PROF EMERITUS, 95-, ADJ PROF, 96-, BUCKNELL UNIV; Am Coun Learned Soc fel, 64-65; Harvard Law Sch fel law & philos, 64-65; Soc Relig Higher Educ fel, 66 & cross-disciplinary studies fel, 67-68; dir, Inst Study Human Values, 66-67; consult ed, Bucknell Press, 71-83; vis prof social ethics, Andover Newton Theol Sch, Newton Centre, 72-73; vis prof ethics & soc, Univ Chicago, 76-77; res fel, Inst Adv Study Rel, Univ Chicago, 83-84; vis res prof, Univ Tenn, 91-92; bd consultants, J Rel, 72-83; edit bd, J Rel Ethics, 74-84; edit bd, J Law and Rel, 82-, edit bd, Soundings. An Interdisc j, 95-. **HONORS AND AWARDS** Lindback Award, 66; Class of 1956 Lect Award, Bucknell, 68; Univ Chicago Div Sch, Alumnus of the Year, 88; Lifetime Achievement, J Law & Rel, 95; Rainey Award, Bucknell Univ, 94; Travis Lectureship Award for Soc Just, 96. **MEMBERSHIPS** Soc Christian Ethics (exec secy, 68-72, vpres, 79-80, pres, 80-81); Soc Values Higher Educ; Am Soc Polit & Legal Philos; European Soc Cult; Am Polit Sci Asn. **RESEARCH** Religious ethics; social and political philosophy; legal philosophy. **SELECTED PUBLICATIONS** Lon Fuller's multidimensional natural law theory, Stanford Law Review, 5/65; Corporations, constitutions, and covenants: On forms of human relations and the problem of legitimacy, J Relig, 9/73; Politics and divinity: Three approaches in American political science, Thought: Am J Cult & Idea, 12/77; On meanings of public good: An exploration, J Relig, 1/78; Process thought and political theory: Implications of principle of internal relations, Rev Politics, 7/79, reprint, Process Thought and Social Theory, 81; American legal realism and the covenantal myth: World-views in the practice of law, Mercer Law Rev, winter 80; The prism of justice: E Pluribus Unum?, The Annual of Soc of Christian Ethics, 81; Praxis and promise: On the ethics of political theology, Ethics, 7/82; auth, Community and alienation: Essays on Process Thought and Public LIfe, Univ Notre Dame, 88; auth, Solidarity and Suffering: Toward a Politics of Rationality, State Univ NY Press, 98. **CONTACT ADDRESS** Col of Arts & Sci, Bucknell Univ, Lewisburg, PA, 17837. **EMAIL** sturm@bucknell.edu

STURM, FRED GILLETTE
PERSONAL Born 10/15/1925, Batavia, NY, m, 1973, 2 children **DISCIPLINE** RELIGION, PHILOSOPHY **EDUCATION** Allegheny Col, AB, 45; Union Theological Seminary, MDiv, 48; Univ of Rochester, AM, 50; Vanderbilt Univ, diploma in Brasilian Studies, 49; Tunghai Univ, certificate in Chinese Culture, 62. **CAREER** Chair of Greek & N.T. Faculdade de Teologia da IMB, 50-52; prof of relig studies, Inst de Porto Alegre, 53; prof of Philos, dir of Intercultural Studies, Western Col for Women, 54-74; adj assoc prof of philos, State Univ of NY at Buffalo, 74-75; PROF OF PHILOS, UNIV OF NMEX, 75-. **HONORS AND AWARDS** Phi Beta Kappa; honorary prof of lang & lit, Shaanxi Teachers Univ. **MEMBERSHIPS** Brasilian Acad of Philos; Am Philos Asn; Soc of Philosophers in Am; Soc for Iberian & Latin Am Thought; Royal Soc for Asian Studies; Int Seminar on Asian Studies. **RESEARCH** Philos of art & aesthetics; East Asian philos; Iberian & Latin American philos. **SELECTED PUBLICATIONS** Auth, Aesthetic Norms in the Philosophy of Xunzi; Korea's Role in the History of East Asian Philosophy; Philosophical Ambiance in Brasilian Independence; Dependence and Originality in Iberoamerican Philosophy; Problems in the Articulation of Tupi-Guarani Welt-und-Lebensanschauung. **CONTACT ADDRESS** Dept of Philos, Univ of New Mexico, Albuquerque, NM, 87131.

STUTTS, DAVID H.
PERSONAL Born 10/28/1949, Orlando, FL, d, 2 children **DISCIPLINE** NEW TESTAMENT STUDIES **EDUCATION** New Orleans Baptist Theol Sem, ThD, 89. **CAREER** Alabama Bd Of Pardons & Paroles, 90-. **MEMBERSHIPS** SBL. **RESEARCH** Textual criticism. **SELECTED PUBLICATIONS** Auth, Textual History of the Gospel of Matthew. **CONTACT ADDRESS** PO Box 611047, Birmingham, AL, 35261-1047. **EMAIL** dwho@aol.com

STYLIANOPOULOS, THEODORE
PERSONAL Born 10/26/1937, Messinia, Greece, m, 1963, 4 children **DISCIPLINE** NEW TESTAMENT STUDIES **EDUCATION** Holy Cross Orthodox Sch of Theology, BA, 62; Boston Univ Sch of Theology, STM, 64; Harvard Divinity Sch, ThD, 72. **CAREER** Prof of New Testament, 67- , Holy Cross. **HONORS AND AWARDS** Lilly Found Fel; Archbishop Iakovos Faculty Prize; Protopresbyter of the Ecumenical Patriarchate of Constantinople. **MEMBERSHIPS** Soc of Biblical Literature; Orthodox Theological Soc in Amer. **RESEARCH** Matthew, John, Paul; Book of Revelation; Hermenentics; Patristics. **SELECTED PUBLICATIONS** Auth, Justin Martyr, Encyclopedia of Early Christianity, 97; auth, The New Testament: An Orthodox Perspective, 97; auth, Orthodox Biblical Interpretation, Dictionary of Biblical Interpretation, 98. **CONTACT ADDRESS** 15 Park Ave, Nutham, MA, 02494. **EMAIL** stylianopoulos@msn.com

SUBER, PETER DAIN
PERSONAL Born 11/08/1951, Evanston, IL **DISCIPLINE** PHILOSOPHY **EDUCATION** Earlham Col, BA, 73; Northwestern Univ, MA, 74, PhD, 78, JD, 82. **CAREER** Lectr philos, Northwestern Univ & Nat Col Educ, 74-79; asst prof, 82-88, assoc prof, 88-95, prof philos, Earlham Col, 95-; Gen ed, Hippias Search Engine. **MEMBERSHIPS** Am Philos Asn; Hegel Soc Am; Nat Lawyers Guild **RESEARCH** Hist of philos; skepticism; reflexivity. **SELECTED PUBLICATIONS** Auth, The place of philosophy in the humanities: A statistical profile, Proc & Address of Am Philos Asn, Vol 55, No 3; The place of philos in the humanities: A statistical profile, In: Proceedings and Addresses of the American Philosophical Association, 2/82; Nomic: A Self-modifying game, In: Metamagical Themas (column), Sci Am, 6/82, and Paradox of Self-Amendment, 90; co-ed, Self-Reference: Reflections on Reflexivity, Martinus Nijhoff, 87; Population changes and Constitutional amendments: Federalism versus democracy, Univ Mich Jour Law Reform, winter 87; Logical Rudeness and A Bibliography of Works on Reflexivity, 87; Analogy exercises for teaching legal reasoning, Jour Law and Educ, winter 88; What is software?, Jour Speculative Philos, 88; The reflexivity of change: The case of language norms, Jour Speculative Philos, 89; Review of Jeff Mason, Philosophical Rhetoric: the Functions of Indirection in Philosophical Writing, Philos and Rhetoric, 90; The paradox of self-amendment in American Constitutional Law, Stanford Lit Rev, spring-fall 90; A case study in Ad Hominem arguments: Fichte's Science of Knowledge, Philos and Rhetoric, 90; The Paradox of Self-Amendment: A Study of Logic, Law, Omnipotence, and Change, Peter Lang Publ, 90; Unsimplifying political correctness, The Earlhamite, spring 92; 50 years later, the questions remain, Ellsworth America, 8/92; The database paradox: Unlimited information and the false blessing of objectivity, Libr Hi Tech, 92; Is philosophy dead?, The Earlhamite, winter 93; A year of teaching with Dialog, Newsletter on Teaching Philos, spring 94; Question-begging under a non-foundational model of argument, Argumentation, 94; Legal reasoning after post-modern critiques of reason, Legal Writing Jour of Legal Writing Inst, 97; Six Exploding Knots; Infinite Reflections, A Crash Course in the Mathematics of Infinite Sets, St John's Rev, 1998; Civil Disobedience, Constitutional Amendment, Paternalism, and Self-Reference in Law, In: Encyclopedia of the Philosophy of Law, Garland Publ, forthcoming; Nine Opinions in the Case of Speluncean Explorers, Routledge. **CONTACT ADDRESS** Dept Philos, Earlham Col, 801 National Rd W, Richmond, IN, 47374-4095. **EMAIL** peters@earlham.edu

SUBOTNIK, DAN
DISCIPLINE LAW **EDUCATION** Columbia Univ, BA, 63; MBA, 66; JD, 66. **CAREER** Corp Fin Off, Birr, Wilson and Comp; lectr, Northwestern Univ; fac mem, Unvi Ill, Chicago; vis assoc prof, Univ Santa Clara; vis assoc prof, Seton Hall Law Schl; lectr Univ Chicago, 80-90; prof Law, Touro Col. **SELECTED PUBLICATIONS** He has written on a wide range of topics including taxation, accounting, and academic research. **CONTACT ADDRESS** Touro Col, Brooklyn, NY, 11230. **EMAIL** DanS@tourolaw.edu

SUGGS, MARION JACK
PERSONAL Born 06/05/1924, Electra, TX, m, 1943, 3 children **DISCIPLINE** BIBLICAL STUDIES **EDUCATION** Univ Tex, BA, 46; Tex Christian Univ, BD, 49; Duke Univ, PhD, 54. **CAREER** Assoc prof, 52-56, Prof New Testament, Brite Divinity Sch, Tex Christian Univ, 56-, Dean, Sch, 77-, Am Coun Learned Soc fel & Am Asn Theol Schs grant, 63-64; chmn patristics sect, Int Greek New Testament Proj, 63- **MEMBERSHIPS** Soc Bibl Lit; Soc New Testament Studies. **RESEARCH** Biblical theology; textual criticism. **SELECTED PUBLICATIONS** Auth, The Layman Reads His Bible, 57 & The Gospel Story, 60, Bethany; co-ed, Studies in the History and Text of the new Testament in Honor & K W Clark, Univ Utah, 67; auth, The world is near you: Romans 10: 6-10 within the purpose of the letter, In: Christian History and Interpretation, Cambridge Univ, 67; Wisdom, Christology and Law in Matthew's Gospel, Harvard Univ, 70; co-ed, Oxford Study Edition, New English Bible, Oxford, 76; The Harper-Collins Study Bible--New-Revised-Standard-Version, With The Apocryphal-Deuterocanonical Books, Interpretation-A J Of Bible And Theology, Vol 49, 95. **CONTACT ADDRESS** 5605 Winifred Dr, Ft Worth, TX, 76133.

SUH, DAE-SUK
PERSONAL Born 11/22/1931, Korea, m, 1960, 2 children **DISCIPLINE** PUBLIC LAW AND GOVERNMENT **EDUCATION** Tex Christian Univ, BA, 56; Ind Univ, MA, 58; Columbia Univ, PhD, 64. **CAREER** Asst prof, Univ Houston, 65-66; assoc prof, 67-71; dir, Ctr for Korean Studies, Univ Hawaii at Manoa, 72-94; prof, 72- . **HONORS AND AWARDS** Honorary prf Yanbian Univ, Yanji, Jilin, China, 91; Korea Found Prof of Policy Studies, Univ Hawaii, 94- . **MEMBERSHIPS** Am Polit Sci Asoc; Asoc for Asian Studies. **RESEARCH** North and South Korea; East Asian security. **SELECTED PUBLICATIONS** Auth, Kim Il Sung: The North Korean Leader, 95; auth, Kin Nichisei to Kin Shonichi, 97; North Korea after Kim Il Sung, 98. **CONTACT ADDRESS** 7122 Niumalu Loop, Honolulu, HI, 96825-1635. **EMAIL** daesook@hawaii.edu

SULLIVAN, JOHN G.
PERSONAL Born 12/12/1936, Newport, RI, m, 1987 **DISCIPLINE** PHILOSOPHY **EDUCATION** Cath Univ of Amer, BA, 58, MA, 59, Basselin fel, 56-59; Lateran Univ, Rome, JCD, 66; Univ NC Chapel Hill, PhD, philos, 82. **CAREER** Exec asst to the Bishop of Providence and asst chancellor for RI diocese, 66-68; admin asst to pres and general mgr of Gallagher Comm, 68-70; mem of fac, dept of philos, Elon Col, 70-; Maude Sharpe Powell prof of philos; co-designer and founding fac mem, SOPHIA, 87-. **HONORS AND AWARDS** Winner, Elon Col Daniel-Danieley award for excellence in teaching, 80; first recipient of Maude Sharpe Powell Professorship, 85; Fac inductee into Phi Kappa Phi, 97. **MEMBERSHIPS** NC Philos Asn; Amer Philos Asn; Omicron Delta Kappa; Phi Kappa Phi. **RESEARCH** Ethics and leadership; Transpersonal developmental psychology; Philosophy of religion; Ancient and medieval philosophy and Eastern philosophy **SELECTED PUBLICATIONS** Auth, Going Down Our Own Well, Meridians, vol 4, 2, 97; auth, Small Mind, Big Mind, Meridians, vol 3, no 2, Spring, 96; auth, On Becoming an Elder, Meridians, vol 2, no 2, Winter, 94; auth, To Come To Life More Fully: An East West Journey, Traditional Acupuncture Inst, 91. **CONTACT ADDRESS** Dept. of Philosophy, Elon Col, Campus box 2102, Elon College, NC, 27244. **EMAIL** sullivan@elon.edu

SULLIVAN, MARY C.
PERSONAL Born 06/15/1931, Rochester, NY **DISCIPLINE** LITERATURE, RELIGION **EDUCATION** Nazareth Col Rochester, BA, 54; Univ Notre Dame, MA, 61, PhD(English), 64; Univ London, MTh, 88. **CAREER** Asst prof English, Catherine McAuley Col, 63-65, pres, 65-68; asst prof, Marymount Col, NY, 67-69; assoc prof lang & lit, 69-81, PROF LANG & LIT, ROCHESTER INST TECHNOL, 81-, dean col liberal arts, 77-87, chair, acad senate, 96-99; Consult & evaluator, Comn Higher Educ, Mid States Asn, 68-90. **MEMBERSHIPS** MLA;

Mercy Higher Ed Colloquium **RESEARCH** Nineteenth and 20th century English and American literature; religion and literature; biography. **SELECTED PUBLICATIONS** Auth, The function of setting in Howells' The Landlord at Lion's Head, Am Lit, 63; Catherine of Dublin, Pageant, 65; Moby Dick, CXXIX: The cabin, Nineteenth Century Fiction, 65; Caroline Gordon: A Reference Guide, G K Hall, 77; Conrad's Paralipsis in the narration of Lord Jim, Conradiana, 78; Catherine McAuley and the Tradition of Mercy, Univ Notre Dame Press, 95; numerous articles in Jour Mercy Asn in Scripture & Theol (MAST). **CONTACT ADDRESS** Col of Lib Arts, Rochester Inst Technol, 1 Lomb Memorial Dr, Rochester, NY, 14623-5603. **EMAIL** mxsgsl@rit.edu

SULLIVAN, RUTH
DISCIPLINE LAW **EDUCATION** Univ Minn, BA; Concord Univ, MA, LLB. **CAREER** Prof. **SELECTED PUBLICATIONS** Auth, pubs on legal drafting, language, law and interpretation. **CONTACT ADDRESS** Fac Common Law, Univ Ottawa, 550 Cumberland St, PO Box 450, Ottawa, ON, K1N 6N5.

SULLIVAN, STEPHEN J.
PERSONAL New York, NY, m, 3 children **DISCIPLINE** PHILOSOPHY **EDUCATION** Cornell Univ, PhD, 90. **CAREER** Asst prof Philos, Univ Southern Ind, 96- . **MEMBERSHIPS** APA; Ind Philos Asn. **RESEARCH** Ethics; epistemology; philosophy of religion. **SELECTED PUBLICATIONS** Auth, Rev of Robert L. Arrington, Rationalism, Realism, and Relativism: Perspectives in Contemporary Moral Epistemology, in Ethics, 91; Harman, Ethical Naturalism, and Token-Token Identity, Philos Papers, 91; Arbitrariness, Divine Commands, and Morality, Intl Jour Philos Rel, 93; Relativism, Evil, and Disagreement: A Reply to Hocutt, Philosophia, 93; Adams's Theistic Argument from the Nature of Morality, Jour Relig Ethics, 93; Why Adam's Needs to Modify His Divine-Command Theory One More Time, Faith and Philos, 94; Goldman's Early Causal Theory of Knowledge, Grazer Philos Stud, 95. **CONTACT ADDRESS** Dept of Philosophy, Southern Ind Univ, Evansville, IN, 47712. **EMAIL** ssulliva.ucs@smtp.usi.edu

SULLIVAN, WILLIAM JOSEPH
PERSONAL Born 05/10/1931, Arlington, MA, m, 1965, 6 children **DISCIPLINE** RELIGIOUS STUDIES **EDUCATION** St Paul's Col, DC, BA, 53, MA, 57; Cath Inst Paris, STL, 63, STD, 67. **CAREER** Asst dir, Newman Ctr, Univ Calif, Berkeley, 57-61; asst dir, Newman Ctr, Mass Inst Technol, 61-62; mem staff, Faith & Order Secretariat, World Coun Churches, Geneva, Switz, 65-66; prog analyst, Off Econ Opportunity, 67-69; asst prof relig studies, 69-75, chmn dept, 70-73, ASSOC PROF RELIG STUDIES, ST JOHN FISHER COL, 75-, Mem adv coun, Off Permanent Diasonate Roman Cath Diocese, Rochester, 78-. **MEMBERSHIPS** Nat Newman Chaplains Asn (treas, 60-62); Col Theol Soc; Cath Theol Soc Am **RESEARCH** Early Christian interpretations of Biblical teachings on poverty and wealth; relationship between Israel and Christianity during the primitive Christian era. **SELECTED PUBLICATIONS** Contribr, The Capuchin Annual, Capuchin, Dublin, 67, Mixed Marriages, an Honest Appraisal, Abbey Press, 67; Why Priests Leave, Hawthorne, 69; coauth, chap, In: Beyond Survival: Bread and Justice in Christian Perspective, Friendship, 77; Crime and Community in Biblical Perspective, 81. **CONTACT ADDRESS** Dept of Relig Studies, St John Fisher Col, 3690 East Ave, Rochester, NY, 14618-3597. **EMAIL** wsullivan@sjfc.edu

SULLIVAN, WINNIFRED F.
PERSONAL Born 04/12/1950, London, England, m, 1975, 2 children **DISCIPLINE** RELIGIOUS STUDIES **EDUCATION** Cornell Univ, BA 71; Univ Chicago, JD 76, PhD 93. **CAREER** Washington & Lee univ, asst prof 94-. **HONORS AND AWARDS** Charlotte Newcombe Diss Fell. **MEMBERSHIPS** AAR; ABA **RESEARCH** Comparative Study of religion and law. **SELECTED PUBLICATIONS** Auth, Paying the Words Extra: Religious Discourse in the Supreme Court of the United States, Cambridge, Harv U Cen for the Stud of World Rel, 94; Religion and the Law, in: Philip Goff and Paul Harvey, eds, Themes in American religion and Culture, UCP, forthcoming; American Religion is Naturally Comparative, in: Kimberly C. Patton and Benjamin C. Ray, eds, A Magic Still Swells: The Case for Comparative Religion in the Post Modern Age, UCP, forthcoming; Judging Religion, Marquette Law Rev, 98; Finding a True Story of American Religion: Comments on L H LaRue's Constitutional Law as Fiction: Narrative in the Rhetoric of Authority, Wash and lee U Law Rev, 96; The Difference Religion Makes: Reflections On Rosenberger, The Christian Century, 96. **CONTACT ADDRESS** Dept of Religion, Washington and Lee Univ, Lexington, VA, 24450. **EMAIL** sullivanw@wlu.edu

SUMLER-EDMOND, JANICE L.
PERSONAL Born 08/10/1948, New York, New York, s **DISCIPLINE** LAW **EDUCATION** UCLA, Los Angeles CA, BA, 1970, MA, 1971; Georgetown Univ, Washington DC, PhD, 1978; UCLA School of Law, Los Angeles CA, JD, 1985. **CAREER** Spelman Coll, Atlanta GA, visiting prof, 1980-81; Reginald Heber Smith Fellowship, legal aid of Los Angeles, 1985-86; Clark Atlanta Univ, Atlanta GA, assoc prof, 1986-; Mack Haygood, McLean, Attorneys, Atlanta, GA, attorney, 1989-95. **HONORS AND AWARDS** Lubic Memorial Law Scholarship, 1983-84; Southern Fellowship Fund Summer Research Award, 1988; Judicine Fellow, US Supreme Court, Washington, DC, 1991-92; Panel of Neutrals, American Arbitration Association. **MEMBERSHIPS** Natl vice dir, Assn of Black Women Historians, 1986-88, natl dir, 1988-90; mem, Georgia Assn of Black Women Attorneys, 1987-; recruiter, Georgetown Univ, 1988-. **SELECTED PUBLICATIONS** "The Forten-Purvis Women and the Antislavery Crusade," Journal of Negro History, 1981; "Personhood and Citizenship: Black Women Litigants, 1867-1890," University of Massachusetts Press, 1997. **CONTACT ADDRESS** History Dept, Clark Atlanta Univ, Brawley Dr & Fair St, Atlanta, GA, 30314.

SUMMERS, CLYDE W.
PERSONAL Born 11/21/1918, Grass Range, MT, m, 1947, 4 children **DISCIPLINE** LAW **EDUCATION** Univ Ill, BS, 39, JD, 42; Columbia Univ, LLM, 46, JSD, 52. **CAREER** From instr to assoc prof law, Univ Toledo, 42-49; assoc prof to prof, Univ Buffalo, 49-57; from vis prof to prof, Yale Univ, 56-75; Prof Law, Univ Pa, 75-, Guggenheim fel, 55; Ford Found fel, 63; Nat Endowment for the Humanities independent study fel, 77-78. **HONORS AND AWARDS** MA, Yale Univ, 57; LLD, Univ Louvain, 66; Dr, Univ Stockholm, 78. **MEMBERSHIPS** Am Bar Asn; Indust Relat Res Asn; Nat Acad Arbitrators; Int Soc Labor Law & Social Legis. **RESEARCH** Labor Law and the Law, 53 & Employment Relations and the Law, 58, Little; Frontiers of Collective Bargaining, Harper, 67; Labor Law: Cases and Materials, Foundation, 68. **SELECTED PUBLICATIONS** Worker Dislocation--Who Bears The Burden--A Comparative-Study of Social Values In 5 Countries, Notre Dame Law Rev, Vol 70, 95; Agenda For Reform--The Future Of Employment Relationships and The Law, Georgetown Law J, Vol 83, 94. **CONTACT ADDRESS** 753 N 26th St, Philadelphia, PA, 19130.

SUMMERS, ROBERT SAMUEL
PERSONAL Born 09/19/1933, Halfway, OR, m, 1955, 5 children **DISCIPLINE** LAW, JURISPRUDENCE **EDUCATION** Univ Ore, BS, 55; Harvard Univ, LLB, 59. **CAREER** Lawyer, Portland, Ore, 59-60; from asst prof to prof, Univ Ore, 60-68; Prof Law, Cornell Univ, 69-, Vis assoc prof law, Stanford Univ, 63-64; consult Coun Legal Educ Opportunity, 68-71; chmn, comt civic educ, Asn Am Law Schs, 72-74. **MEMBERSHIPS** Am Soc Polit & Legal Philos; Asn Am Law Schs. **RESEARCH** Contracts and commercial law. **SELECTED PUBLICATIONS** Gen ed & contribr, Essays in Legal Philosophy & More Essays in Legal Philosophy, Blackwells, Eng, 68 & Univ Calif, 71; coauth, Law, Its Nature, Functions and Limits, Prentice-Hall, 2nd ed, 72; Hornbook on the Uniform Commercial Code, 72 & Teaching Materials on Uniform Commercial Code, 2nd ed, 74, West Publ; auth, The American Legal System, 74 & Justice and Order Through Law, 74, Ginn; Instrumentalism and American Legal Theory, Cornell Univ Press, 82; H.L.A. Hart: The Concept-Of-Law--Estimations, Reflections, And A Personal Memorial, J Of Legal Education, Vol 45, 95. **CONTACT ADDRESS** Law Sch, Cornell Univ, Ithaca, NY, 14850.

SUNDARAM, K.
PERSONAL Born 08/16/1947, Kumbakonam, India, m, 1974, 2 children **DISCIPLINE** PHILOSOPHY **EDUCATION** BS, 66, MA, Mlit, 68, Univ of Madras; SUNY/Buffalo, PhD, 74. **CAREER** Prof and Chr, Lake Mich College, 73-; Adjunct Grad Prof, Siena Heights Univ, 98-99. **HONORS AND AWARDS** Sr Fellow, Ctr for the Study of World Religions, Harvard; NEH grant **MEMBERSHIPS** Amer Phil Assoc; Phil of Science Assoc; Amer Assoc of Phil Teachers **RESEARCH** Philsophy of science; comparative philosophy **SELECTED PUBLICATIONS** Auth, Joseph Priestly and the Sciences in America, Michigan Academian, 99. **CONTACT ADDRESS** Dept of Philosophy, Lake Michigan Col, 2755 E Napier Ave, Benton Harbor, MI, 49022-1899. **EMAIL** sundaram@lmc.cc.mi.us

SUNDBERG, WALTER
DISCIPLINE CHURCH HISTORY **EDUCATION** S.t Olaf Col, BA, 69; Princeton Theol Sem, MDiv, 73, PhD, 81; Univ Tubingen, Ger, 71-72. **CAREER** Instr, Augsburg Col, 81-84; US Army Chaplains prog, 77; Lutheran Theol Sem, Philadelphia, 76; vis prof, Col St. Catherine, 85-86; asst prof, 84; assoc prof, 86; prof, 94-; act ch, hist dept, 87-88. **HONORS AND AWARDS** Rockefeller Theol fel; grad fel; Amer Lutheran Church., Asst minister, Como Park Lutheran Church; ed bd(s), Lutheran Quart; Lutheran Commentator; bd mem, Great Commn Network; Lutheran Bible Ministries; Lutheran Bible Inst; ALC Inter-Church Relations Comm. **MEMBERSHIPS** Mem adv coun, Interpretation. **SELECTED PUBLICATIONS** Contrib, Ministry in 19th Century European Lutheranism, Called and Ordained: Lutheran Perspectives on the Office of Ministry, 90; pub(s), articles in First Things, Lutheran Quart, Lutheran Forum; coauth, The Bible in Modern Culture: Theology and Historical Critical Method from Spinoza to Kasemann, 95. **CONTACT ADDRESS** Dept of Church History, Luther Sem, 2481 Como Ave, St. Paul, MN, 55108. **EMAIL** wsundber@luthersem.edu

SUNSHINE, EDWARD R.
PERSONAL Born 04/28/1939, Tiffin, OH, m, 1977, 1 child **DISCIPLINE** RELIGION, ETHICS **EDUCATION** Loyola Univ, Chicago, BA, 62, MA, 65; Grad Theol Union, PhD, 88. **CAREER** Lect, Theol, 72-76, Loyola Univ; fel, 83-84, Christian Ethics, Pacific Sch of Relig; instr, social ethics, 84, Univ San Fran; instr, moral theol, 84-85, Holy Family Col; instr, theol, 84-86, Roman Cath Diocese, Oakland; lect, relig stud, 86-87, Santa Clara Univ; asst prof, 88-91, assoc prof, 91-, Barry Univ. **HONORS AND AWARDS** Fel, Pacific Sch of Relig, Berkeley, 83-84; Lib travel grant, Ctr for Latin Amer Stud Univ Fla, 91. **MEMBERSHIPS** Cath Theol Soc of Am; AAR; Soc of Christian Ethics; Soc for the Study of Christian Ethics. **RESEARCH** Relation between rhetoric and ethic in Spanish colonial church documents. **SELECTED PUBLICATIONS** Coauth, Catholicism in America: A Moral-Theological Perspective, Chicago Stud, 91; ed, Proceed: First Global Village Conf, Barry Univ Ctr for Applied & Profes Ethics, 92; auth, Sexual Morality from a Social Perspective, Chicago Stud, 92; auth, Prophecy and Persuasion: The Use of Dominican Scholarship by Abolitionist Clerics in Late 17th-Century Cuba, in Human Rights and the Quincentary: Contributions of Dominican Scholars and Missionaries, Rosary Col, 93; auth, Veritatis Splendor et Rhetorica Morum: The Splendor of Truth and the Rhetoric of Morality, in Veritatis Splendor: Amer Responses, Sheed & Ward, 95; coauth, Speaking Morally: The Thirty Year Debate Between Richard A. McCormick and Stanley Hauerwas, Irish Theol Quart, 63:1, 98; auth, Catechisms in the Americas, in Christian Ethics and the New Catechism, Scranton Univ Press, forthcoming. **CONTACT ADDRESS** Dept of Theol and Philos, Barry Univ, 11300 NE Second Ave., Miami Shores, FL, 33161-6695. **EMAIL** sunshine@jeanne.barry.edu

SUPPES, PATRICK
PERSONAL Born 03/17/1922, Tulsa, OK, m, 1979, 5 children **DISCIPLINE** PHILOSOPHY **EDUCATION** Univ Chicago, BS, 43; Columbia Univ, PhD, 50. **CAREER** Instr, 50-52, asst prof, 52-55, assoc prof, 55-59, prof, 59-92, prof emer, 92- , Stanford Univ. **HONORS AND AWARDS** Honory Doctor's degree, Univ Nijmegen, Netherlands, 79; Docteur Honoris Causa, Adacemie de Paris, Univ Rene Descartes, 82. **MEMBERSHIPS** Natl Acad of Sci; AAAS; Norwegian Acad of Sci and Lett; Chilean Acad of Sci; Finnish Acad of Sci and Lett. **RESEARCH** Mathematical psychology; neuropsychology; philosophy of science; educational psychology. **SELECTED PUBLICATIONS** Coauth, Foundations of Measurement, v.2: Geometrical, Threshold, and Probabilistic Representations, Academic, 89; coauth Foundations of Measurement, v.3: Representation, Axiomatization, and Invariance, Academic, 90; auth, Language for Humans and Robots, Blackwell, 91; auth, Models and Methods in the Philosophy of Science: Selected Essays, Kluwer Academic, 93. **CONTACT ADDRESS** 678 Miranda Ave, Stanford, CA, 94306. **EMAIL** suppes@ockham.stanford.edu

SUR, CAROLYN WORMAN
PERSONAL Born 11/21/1942, Effingham, IL, s **DISCIPLINE** SYSTEMATIC THEOLOGY; MATHEMATICS **EDUCATION** Notre Dame Univ, BS, 64; St. Louis Univ, MS, 74, PhD, 92. **CAREER** Teacher, math and biology, Rosary High, St. Louis Archdiocese, 64-66; teacher math, Teutopolis Comm High, Teutopolis, IL, 66-68; teacher math and biology, St. Francis de Sales High, St. Louis, MO, 68-74; teacher, math and biology, St. Paul High School, Highland, IL, 74-80; teacher art, math, and biology, Vincent Gray Alternative High, East St. Louis, IL, 80-83; teacher, math & computers, Aquinas High, Fort Madison, IA, 83-84; teaching asst, depts of math and theol, St. Louis Univ, St. Louis, MO, 84-91; adjunct teacher, math, Washington Univ Col, St. Louis, MO, 89-91; dir of residence, Mount Mary Col, Milwaukee, WI, 91-92; adjunct prof, math, Mount Mary Col, Milwaukee, WI, 94-95; prof, systematic theol, Sacred Heart School of Theol (sem), Hales Corner, WI, 92-94. **HONORS AND AWARDS** Cum laude graduate, 64; 3.805 grade point average, PhD program, 92; Theology: Theta Alpha Kappa National Honor Soc, 85; Mathematics: Pi Mu Epsilon National Honor Soc, 74, Kappa Mu Epsilon, 92; Nat Science Found grant, mathematics, 68-74; Nat Science Found grant, genetics, 77; Bogert Fund-$500 for res on Mysticism (Quaker sponsored), June, 90. **MEMBERSHIPS** Am Academy Relig, 90-; ITEST (Inst for Theol Encounter with Science and Technology, 89-91, 95-98; Int Hildegard of Bingen Soc, 88-94; Am Recorder Soc, 86-87, 92-95. **RESEARCH** Medieval theology, especially writings of Medieval Women Mystics; illuminations; eco-spirituality and cosmology; Am theol issues. **SELECTED PUBLICATIONS** Auth, Feminine Images of God in the Visions of Hildegard of Bingen's Scivias, Edwin Mellon Press, 93; The Post-Abortion Syndrome: A Theological Reflection, America, Sept 28, 96; Unwanted Pregnancies, Abortions are Linked to Low Self-Esteem, Shreveport Times, May 96; The Spirituality of Gardening, Peacework, Jan 97; The Inner City (poetry), in Tracing Shadows, Nat Library of Poetry, 97; Religious Experience and Transcendence in Annie Dillard's Eco-Spirituality, in Wagering on Transcendence, Sheed & Ward, 97. **CONTACT ADDRESS** Greco Inst, Catholic Ctr, 2500 Line Ave., Shreveport, LA, 71104. **EMAIL** csur@dioshpt.org

SUTER, RONALD
PERSONAL Born 11/01/1930, Geneva, Switzerland, m, 1998, 2 children **DISCIPLINE** PHILOSOPHY **EDUCATION** Univ

Chicago, AB, 53; Oxford Univ, BA, 59, MA, 62; Stanford Univ, PhD, 67. **CAREER** Instr, Middlebury Col, VT, 62-63; instr, 63-66, asst prof, 66-69, assoc prof, 69-74, PROF, MI STATE UNIV, 74-. **HONORS AND AWARDS** Pres, Jowett Soc, Oxford, 57; co-chmn, Hume Soc, Stanford, 60-61; dir, 1968 Fall Isenberg Memorial Series on the Philosophy of Ludwig Wittgenstein; Nat Endowment for the Humanities summer stipend, 70; recipient, Col of Arts and Letters Distinguished Fac Res Award, 88-89. **MEMBERSHIPS** APA **RESEARCH** Ethics; philos of art; philos of mind; Wittgenstein. **SELECTED PUBLICATIONS** Auth, The Isenberg Memorial Lecture Series, 1965-1966, ed and auth of the intro, East Lansing: MI State Univ Press, 69; Six Answers to the Problem of Taste, Univ Press Amer, 79; Are You Moral?, Univ Press Amer, 84, revised ed, 91; Interpreting Wittgenstein: A Cloud of Philosophy, a Drop of Grammar, Temple Univ Press, 89, paperback, 91, Korean trans, 98; What is This Thing Called Love?, forthcoming. **CONTACT ADDRESS** Dept of Philos, 955 Lilac Ave., East Lansing, MI, 48823. **EMAIL** suteron@pilot.msu.edu

SUTHERLAND, GAIL HINICH

DISCIPLINE ASIAN RELIGIONS, HINDUISM AND BUDDHISM **EDUCATION** Univ Chicago, PhD, 88. **CAREER** Assoc prof, La State Univ. **RESEARCH** The body, sexuality, food, gender, and ethical reversals in Indian religions; Asian religions in the American South. **SELECTED PUBLICATIONS** Auth, The Disguises of the Demon: The Development of the Yaksa in Hinduism and Buddhism, SUNY, 91; Asvaghosa and Saigyo: A Comparison of Two Buddhist Poets, in Relig and Lit, 91. **CONTACT ADDRESS** Dept of Philos and Relig Stud, Louisiana State Univ, 106 Coates Hall, Baton Rouge, LA, 70803.

SUTTER, LESLIE E.

PERSONAL Born 11/08/1960, Traverse City, MI, m, 1983 **DISCIPLINE** PHILOSOPHY **EDUCATION** CSUDH, MA, 86; Univ Berne, PhD, 91. **CAREER** Adj prof, Edison Col, 94-; prof, 95- , co-chemn Lib Arts, 97- , Int Col. **HONORS AND AWARDS** Dist non-resident scholar, Univ Berne, 93; hon mention, annual philos essay contest, Univ Zurich, 94. **MEMBERSHIPS** Am Hist Asn; APA. **RESEARCH** Existentialism; logical positivism; immigration questions. **SELECTED PUBLICATIONS** Auth, Branches of Philosophy, Hewlitt, 96. **CONTACT ADDRESS** Philosophical Practitioners of Southwest Florida, Key West Professional Center, 1342 Colonial Blvd, Ste K224, Fort Myers, FL, 33907. **EMAIL** leslie@naples.net

SWAIN, CHARLES W.

PERSONAL Born 07/30/1937, Des Moines, IA, m, 1958, 2 children **DISCIPLINE** HISTORY OF RELIGION **EDUCATION** State Univ Iowa, AB, 59; Brown Univ, PhD(relig), 65. **CAREER** Instr relig, Oberlin Col, 63-65; from asst prof to assoc prof, 65-77, Prof Relig, Fla State Univ, 77-, Soc Relig Higher Educ Asian relig fel, 67-68; vis lectr, Ctr Study World Relig, Harvard Univ, 67-68; Helmsley lectr, Brandeis Univ, 68. **MEMBERSHIPS** Am Acad Relig; AAUP; Soc Values Higher Educ. **RESEARCH** History of western religious thought; history of western philosophy; phenomenology of religion. **SELECTED PUBLICATIONS** Auth, The Bible Through the Ages, World Publ, 67; People of the Earth, 76; Hamann and the philosophy of David Hume, J Hist Philos, Vol V, No 4; Doubt in defense of faith, J Am Acad Relig, Vol XXXVI, No 2; Buddhist Spirituality--Indian, Southeast-Asian, Tibetan, And Early Chinese, J Of Ecumenical Studies, Vol 32, 95; Wonhyo And Christianity--Ilshim As A Central Category, J Of Ecumenical Studies, Vol 30, 93; Theology From Asiatic Sources--The Theological Path Of Song,Choan,Seng Prior To The Budding Of Asiatic Ecumenical Discussion, J Of Ecumenical Studies, Vol 33, 96; 7 Dilemmas In World Religions, J Of Ecumenical Studies, Vol 33, 96; A Hist Of Christianity In Asia, Vol 1--Beginnings To 1500, J Of Ecumenical Studies, Vol 31, 94. **CONTACT ADDRESS** Dept of Relig, Florida State Univ, 600 W College Ave, Tallahassee, FL, 32306-1096.

SWAIN, JAMES H.

PERSONAL Born 07/04/1954, Philadelphia, PA, m, 1985 **DISCIPLINE** LAW **EDUCATION** Univ of Bridgeport, BA 1975; Temple Univ School of Law, JD 1978; Univ of Pennsylvania Law School, LLM 1986. **CAREER** US Atty So Dist of NY, summer intern 1977; Third Circuit Ct of Appeals, clerkship intern Hon A Leon Higginbotham 1978; US Dept of Labor, trial atty office of reg solicitor, 1978-88; US Dept of Justice, Eastern PA, asst US atty, 1989-94; US Dept of Justice, Southern FL, 1994-. **HONORS AND AWARDS** Scholar of the Year Award, Omega Psi Phi Frat Inc, Rho Upsilon Chap 1975-76; Distinguished Serv Award, Black Amer Law Students Assn, 1977-78; Certificate of Appreciation, Barristers Assn of Philadelphia, 1978-79, 1979-80; Omega Psi Phi Frat Inc, Mu Omega Chap; US Department of Justice, John Marshall Award, 1992. **MEMBERSHIPS** Barristers Assn of Philadelphia, executive committee, 1979-80, 1986-89, legislation revue committee, 1978-82; mem bd of dir, Community Legal Services, 1988-94; Wynnfield Residents Assn, board of directors, 1988-94, executive vp, 1992-93; mem, Federal Bar Assn Philadelphia Chapter, 1988-; Philadelphia Bar Assn, 1989-; Federal Bar Assn, 1979-; trustee, Mount Pleasant Baptist Church, Philadelphia, PA; Federal Bar Association Miami Chapter, 1996-; Inns of Court University of Miami's Chapter, 1996-; Dade County Black Lawyers Association, 1994-; National Bar Association, Florida State Chapter, 1996-. **SELECTED PUBLICATIONS** Auth, "Protecting Individual Employers: Is it Safe to Complain About Safety?," University of Bridgeport Law Review, 1988. **CONTACT ADDRESS** US Atty's Office, 99 NE 4th St, Miami Beach, FL, 33140.

SWAN, KENNETH P.

DISCIPLINE LAW **EDUCATION** Univ Alberta, LLB, 70. **CAREER** Lectr. **SELECTED PUBLICATIONS** Auth, pubs on various aspects of labour law and labour relations. **CONTACT ADDRESS** Fac of Law, Univ Toronto, 78 Queen's Park, Toronto, ON.

SWANGER, EUGENE R.

DISCIPLINE JAPANESE, CHINESE, BUDDHIST, CONFUCIAN, TAOIST, AND ZEN TRADITIONS **EDUCATION** Capital Univ, BA, BD; Oberlin Col, STM, MA; Univ Iowa, PhD. **CAREER** Prof, 67-; former dept chair. **HONORS AND AWARDS** Alumni Asn Award., Lect, Foreign Service Inst, U. S. State Dept; Distinguished Vis Lect, For Service Inst, 93; NDEA fel, Japan. **RESEARCH** Oriental religions. **SELECTED PUBLICATIONS** Areas: Buddhist Ecumenical Movement, the church-state controversy in Japan, the role of the Shaman in Japan, and omamori story tokens in Japanese culture. **CONTACT ADDRESS** Wittenberg Univ, Post Office Box, Springfield, OH, 45501-0720.

SWANSON, CAROL B.

PERSONAL Born 12/01/1954, Cleveland, OH, m, 1978, 2 children **DISCIPLINE** LAW **EDUCATION** Bowdoin Col, AB, 77; Vanderbilt Univ Sch of Law, JD, 81. **CAREER** Assoc, Sullivan & Cromwell, NY, 81-84; asst US atty, US Atty Office, 84-86; assoc to partner/shareholder, Popham Haik Schnobrich & Kaufman Ltd, 86-89; prof, law, Hamline Univ Sch of Law, 89-. **HONORS AND AWARDS** Phi Beta Kappa, prof of the year award, 90-91. **MEMBERSHIPS** Amer Bar Asn; Minn State Bar Asn; Minn Continuing Legal Educ. **RESEARCH** Business law issues including corporate governance. **SELECTED PUBLICATIONS** Auth, Reinventing Insider Trading: The Supreme Court Misappropriates the Misappropriation Theory, 32, Wake Forest Law Rev, 1157, dec, 97; auth, The Turn in Takeovers: A Study in Public Appeasement and Unstoppable Capitalism, 30, Ga Law Rev, 943, 96; auth, Corporate Governance: Slipping Seamlessly into the Twenty-First Century, 21, J Corp Law, 417, 96; auth, Juggling Shareholder Rights and Strike Suits in Derivative Litigation: The ALI Drops the Ball, 77, Minn Law Rev, 1339, 93; auth, Anticompetitive Practices in Great Britain: Expanded Enforcement Under the Competition Act 1980, 15, V and J Transnational L, 65, 82. **CONTACT ADDRESS** Sch of Law, Hamline Univ, 1536 Hewitt Ave, MS-C2044, St. Paul, MN, 55104-1284. **EMAIL** cswanson@gw.hamline.edu

SWANSON, PAUL L.

PERSONAL Born 10/11/1951, Tokyo, Japan, m, 1977, 4 children **DISCIPLINE** JAPANESE RELIGION **EDUCATION** Univ Wis-Madison, PhD, 85. **CAREER** Fel, Nanzan Inst for Rel and Cult, 90- ; Prof, Fac of Liberal Arts, Nanzan Univ; ed, Japanese Jour of Rel Stud; Intl Advisory Board, the Edinburgh Rev of Theol and Rel, 94- ; Steering Committee, Intl Assn for Asian Philos and Rel, 94- ; Copy and assoc ed, Nanzan Gakuen, for Nanzan Inst, 86-93. **HONORS AND AWARDS** Japan Ministry of Ed Fel, 83-84; Otani Univ Fel, 82-83; Modern Lang and Area Stud Fel, 81-82. **SELECTED PUBLICATIONS** Ed, Tendai Buddhism in Japan, Japanese Jour Rel Stud, 14, 87, 2-3; co-ed, Shugendo and Mountain Religion in Japan, Japanese Jour Rel Stud, 16, 89, 2-3; The Realm of Awakening: A Translation and Study of the Tenth Chapter of Asanga's Mahayanasamgraha, Oxford Univ Press, 89; Foundations of Tien-t'ai Philosophy: The Flowering of the Two Truths, Theory in Chinese Buddhism, Berkeley, Asian Hum Press, 89; Religion and Society in Modern Japan: Selected Reading, Berkeley, Asian Hum Press, 93; The Spirituality of Emptiness in Early Chinese Buddhism, Buddhist Spirituality 1, World Spirituality, an Encyclopedic History of the Religious Quest, 8, 353-375, 93; Tapping the Source Directly: A Japanese Shugendo Apocryphal Text, Japanese Rel, 18, 2, 95-112; Understanding Chih-I Through a Glass, Darkly?, Jour Intl Assn Buddhist Stud, 17, 2, 94, 337-360; Gishin's Collected Teachings of the Tendai Lotus School, Berkeley, Numata Ctr Buddhist Transl Res, 96; What's Going on Here? Chih-I's Use (and Abuse) of Scripture, Jour Intl Assn Buddhist Stud, 20, 1, 97, 1-29; Whay They Say Zen is Not Buddhism, in Pruning the Bodhi Tree, Honolulu: Hawaii UP, 97, 3-29;co-ed, Pilgrimage in Japan, Japanese Jour Rel Stud, 24, 97, 3-4; Pruning the Bodhi Tree: The Storm Over Critical Buddhism, Honolulu: Hawaii UP, 97; **CONTACT ADDRESS** Dept of Arts, Nanzan Univ, 18 Yamazato-cho, Showa-ku, Nagoya, ., 466. **EMAIL** pswanson@ic.nanzan-u.ac.jp

SWARTLEY, WILLARD M.

PERSONAL Born 08/06/1936, Doylestown, PA, m, 1958, 2 children **DISCIPLINE** BIBLICAL STUDIES (NEW TESTAMENT) **EDUCATION** Eastern Mennonite Col, BA, 59; Goshen Bibl Sem, BD, 62; Princeton Theol Sem, PhD, 73. **CAREER** Prof, 78-, Acting Dir , 97, Dir, 79-88, Sum Sch Dir, 90-93, 95, Dean, 95-, Associated Mennonite Biblical Seminary. **HONORS AND AWARDS** Coed, Study of Peace and Scripture Series, 90; Ed, New Testament for Believers Church Bible Commentary Series, Harold Press, 89-. **MEMBERSHIPS** Soc of Bibl Lit; Chicago Soc for Bibl Res; Colloquium on Violence and Religion **RESEARCH** New Testament, hemeneutics. **SELECTED PUBLICATIONS** Slavery, Oxford Companion to the Bible, 93; What Does It Mean to be Ready for the Celebration?, Gospel Herald, 94; Auth, Isreal's Scripture Traditionsand the Synoptic Gospels: Story Shaping Story, Hendrickson, 94; From High-Tech and Triage to Service and Shalom, Mennonite Med Mess, 94; The Anabaptist Use of Scripture: Contemporary Applications and Prospects, Anabaptist Current, 95; War and Peace in the New Testament, Aufstieg und Niedergang der Romischen Welt II, 96; Research Note: Sunday Syllabus Serendipity, Mennonite Quart Rev, 96; CoAuth, Blending Body and Soul: Sociological Study of the New Testament, Conrad Grebel Rev, 96; Auth, War , Encyclopedia of Early Christianity, Garland, 97; The Role of Women in Mark's Gospel: A Narrative Analysis, Bib Theol Bul, 97; A Temple In Time, The Mennonite, 97; Intertextuality in Early Chrisitian Literature, Dict of Later New Test and Its Dev, 97; the Banquet, Persp on the Parables, 97; CoEd Building Communities of Compassion, Harold Press, 98; Mutual Aid Based in Jesus and Early Christianity, Building, 98. **CONTACT ADDRESS** Associated Mennonite Biblical Sem, 3003 Benham Ave, Elkhart, IN, 46517. **EMAIL** wswartley@ambs.edu

SWARTZ, ALICE M.

PERSONAL Born 11/07/1943, Scranton, PA **DISCIPLINE** LITURGICAL STUDIES **EDUCATION** Drew Univ, PhD, 97. **CAREER** Adj asst prof, religious studies, Col St Elizabeth, 98-. **MEMBERSHIPS** Cath Bibl Asn; Amer Acad Relig; Cath Theol Soc Am **RESEARCH** Liturgy; Spirituality **CONTACT ADDRESS** Col of Saint Elizabeth, 2 Convent Rd, Morristown, NJ, 07960.

SWARTZ, BARBARA E.

DISCIPLINE LAW **EDUCATION** Temple Univ, BA, 66; Univ MI, MA, 67; NY Univ, JD, 71; Columbia Univ, MPH, 91. **CAREER** Bruce K Gould Distingished Prof Law, Touro Col; clin assoc prof, NY Univ; lectr, Columbia Univ. **HONORS AND AWARDS** Fulbright scholar, Univ Copenhagen, Denmark, 78-79. **MEMBERSHIPS** Consult, World Health Orgn. **SELECTED PUBLICATIONS** Auth, Responsibility for Drug Induced Injury. **CONTACT ADDRESS** Touro Col, Brooklyn, NY, 11230.

SWAYNE, STEVEN ROBERT

PERSONAL Born 01/25/1957, Los Angeles, CA **DISCIPLINE** THEOLOGY **EDUCATION** Occidental Coll, BA (summa cum laude, phi beta kappa) 1978; Fuller Theological Seminary, MDiv 1983; Univ of CA, Berkeley, CA, PhD candidate, 1990-. **CAREER** Lake Ave Congregational Church, adm Asst to sr pastor 1978-85; Seattle Pacific Univ, dir of campus ministries 1985-90. **HONORS AND AWARDS** recital appearances (piano) on West Coast; first prize, John Wesley Work III Composition Competition 1979; First Prize, Johana Hodges Piano Competition, 1981; Chancellor's Minority Pre-Doctoral Fellowship, Univ of CA-Berkeley, 1990-91. **MEMBERSHIPS** Ordained minister Conservative Congregational Christian Conf 1984-; lay pastor Westminster Chapel 1986-; member, executive committee, Alumni/ae Association, Fuller Theological Seminary 1987-; mem, alumini/ae council, Fuller Theological Seminary, 1989-. **SELECTED PUBLICATIONS** Music published Fred Bock Music Productions; articles published in various Christian periodicals. **CONTACT ADDRESS** Student Ministries, Seattle Pacific Univ, Seattle, WA, 98119.

SWEARER, DONALD K.

PERSONAL Born 08/02/1934, Wichita, KS, m, 1964, 2 children **DISCIPLINE** HISTORY OF RELIGION **EDUCATION** Princeton Univ, BA, cum laude 56, MA, 65, PhD, 67; Yale Univ, BD, 62, STM, 63. **CAREER** Assoc Prof 70-75, Prof 75-, Eugene M Lang Res Prof 87-92, Charles and Harriet Cox McDowell Prof of Religion 92-, Swarthmore College; Instr, Asst Prof 65-70, Oberlin College. **HONORS AND AWARDS** Phi Beta Kappa; Lent Fel; 3 NEH Fels; Fulbright Fel; Guggenheim Fel; 2 Fulbright Fels. **MEMBERSHIPS** AAAS; AAR; ASSR; SBCS; AAUP. **RESEARCH** Buddhism; Comparative Religious Ethics. **SELECTED PUBLICATIONS** Auth, Holism and the Fate of the Earth, Rel and Ecology: Forging an Ethic Across Traditions, forthcoming; Center and Periphery: Buddhism and Politics in Modern Thailand, Buddhism and Politics in Modern Asia, ed, Ian Harris, Cassell's 98; Buddhist Virtue Voluntary Poverty and Extensive Benevolence, J of Rel Ethics, 98; The Worldliness of Buddhism, Wilson Qtly, 97; Bhikkhu Buddhadasa's Interpretation of the Buddha, J of the American Acad of Religion, 96; Hypostasizing the Buddha: Buddha: Image Consecration in Northern Thailand, Hist of Religions, 95; coauth, The Legend of Queen Cama, Camadevivamsa, Albany NY, SUNY Press, 98; auth, The Buddhist World of Southeast Asia, Albany, SUNY Press, 95; Ethics Wealth and Salvation, A Study in Buddhist Social Ethics, coed, Columbia, Univ S Carolina Press, pbk ed, 92. **CONTACT ADDRESS** Dept of Religion, Swarthmore Col, Swarthmore, PA, 19081. **EMAIL** dsweare1@swarthmore.edu

SWEENEY, LEO
PERSONAL Born 09/22/1918, O'Connor, NE **DISCIPLINE** PHILOSOPHY **EDUCATION** St Louis Univ, PhL,-43, MA, 45, STL, 51; Univ Toronto, PhD, 54. **CAREER** From instr to prof philos, St Louis Univ, 54-68; res prof, Creighton Univ, 68-70; vis prof, Cath Univ Am, 70-72; vis prof, 72-74, res prof philos, Loyola Univ, Chicago, 74-, assoc ed, Mod Schoolman, 56-68, corresp ed, 68-. **HONORS AND AWARDS** Am Coun Learned Soc res fel, 63-64; res grant, Creighton Univ, 68-69. **MEMBERSHIPS** Jesuit Philos Asn (secy, 60-63, pres, 65- 66); Am Cath Philos Asn (vpres, 79-80, pres, 80-8 1); Soc Int l'Etude de Philos Medievale; Soc, Ancient Greek Philos; Am Maritain Asn; Fel Cath Schol; Nat Asn Schol; Soc for Medieval/Renaissance Philos; Cardinal Newman Soc; Jesuit Philos Asn. **RESEARCH** Greek philosophy up to Proclus; the problem of divine infinity in Greek, Mediaeval and Renaissance philosophy; metaphysics throughout history of philosophy. **SELECTED PUBLICATIONS** Auth, Metaphysics of Authentic Existentialism, Prentice-Hall, 65; Infinity in the Presocratics: A Bibliographical and Philosophical Study, Nijhoff, The Hague, 72; Bonaventure and Aquinas on Divine Being as Infinite, in Southwestern J Philos, 7/74; Henry Jackson's Interpretation of Plato, in J Hist Philos, 75; Ease in Albert the Great's Texts on Creation, in Albert the Great: Commemorative Essays, Univ Okla Press, 80; Participation and the Structure of Being in Proclus' Elements of Theology, in The Structure of Being: A Neoplatonic Approach, State Univ NY Press, 81; Can Aquinas Speak to the Modern World?, in One Hundred of Thomism: Aeterni Patris and Afterwards, Univ St Thomas Press, 81; ed, Infinity: Proc Am Cath Philos Asn, Vol 55, 81; auth, Greek and Medieval Studies in Honor of Leo Sweeney, SJ, Peter Lang, 94; Authentic Metaphysics in Age of Unreality, Peter Lang, 96; Christian Philosophy, in Greek, Medieval, Contemporary Reflections, Peter Lang, 97; Divine Infinity in Greek and Medieval Thought, Peter Lang, rev ed, 98. **CONTACT ADDRESS** Dept of Philos, Loyola Univ, Chicago, 6525 N Sheridan Rd, Chicago, IL, 60626-5385.

SWEET, JUSTIN
PERSONAL Madison, WI **DISCIPLINE** LAW **EDUCATION** Univ Wis-Madison, BA, 51, LLB, 53. **CAREER** Atty, State of Wis, 53-54; atty pvt pract, 57-58; assoc prof law, 58-63, Prof Law, Univ Calif, Berkeley, 63-, Fulbright prof, Univ Rome, 65-66; vis prof, Hebrew Univ Jerusalem, 70 & Cath Univ Louvain, 73; lectr, Univ Oslo, 73, York Univ, Ont, 76 & Hebrew Univ, Jerusalem, 80; Delay In Construction Contracts--A Comparative-Study Of Legal Issues Under Swiss And Anglo-American Law, Am J Of Comparative Law, Vol 43, 95. **RESEARCH** Architectural and engineering law; basic contract law. **SELECTED PUBLICATIONS** Auth, Legal Aspects of Architectural and Engineering, West Publ, 77. **CONTACT ADDRESS** Sch of Law, Univ of Calif, Berkeley, CA, 94720.

SWEETMAN, BRENDAN M.
PERSONAL Born 08/25/1962, Dublin, Ireland, m, 1984, 2 children **DISCIPLINE** PHILOSOPHY **EDUCATION** Univ Col Dublin, BA, 83, MA, 86; Cambridge Univ, LES, 87; Univ S Cal, MA, 90, PhD, 92. **CAREER** Tutor Philos, Univ Col, 85-86; instr Philos, 90-91, vis lectr, 92, Loyola Marymount Univ; tchg asst, Univ S Cal, 87-91; asst prof, 92-97, Assoc Prof Philos, Rockhurst Col, 97-. **HONORS AND AWARDS** Grad scholar, Univ Col, 84-86; Fulbright Travel Award, Irish Govt, 87; Dean fel, Univ S Cal, 87-91; Pres Res grant, Rockhurst Col, 94 & 96 & 98. **MEMBERSHIPS** Gabriel MarcelSoc; Am Cath Philos Asn; Soc Christian Philos; Am Soc Study Fr Philos; Am Philos Asn; Am Maritain Asn. **RESEARCH** Philosophy of religion; contemporary European philosophy. **SELECTED PUBLICATIONS** Coauth, Comtemporary Perspectives on Religious Epistemology, Oxford Univ Press, 92; Truth and Religious Belief: Conversationson Philosophy of Religion, M. E. Sharpe, 1998;The Pseudo-Problem of Scepticism, Philos Inquiry, 94; Non-conceptual knowledge in Jacques Maritain and Gabriel Marcel, Freedom, Virtue, and the Common Good, Univ Notre Dame, 95; Gabriel Marcel and the Problem of Knowledge, Jour of Am Soc for Study of Fr Philos, 95; The Deconstruction of Western Metaphysics: Derrida and Maritain on Identity, Postmodernism and Christian Philos, 97; Postmodernism, Derrida and Differance: A Critique, Int Philos Quart, 99. **CONTACT ADDRESS** Dept of Philosophy, Rockhurst Col, 1100 Rockhurst Rd., Kansas City, MO, 64110. **EMAIL** Sweetman@Vax1.Rockhurst.Edu

SWENSEN, CLIFFORD HENRIK
PERSONAL Born 11/15/1926, Welch, WV, m, 1948, 5 children **DISCIPLINE** CLINICAL PSYCHOLOGY **EDUCATION** Univ Pitts, BS, 49, MS, 50, PhD, 52. **CAREER** Clin psychol, V A, 52-54; asst to assoc prof, Univ Tenn, 54-62; assoc prof to PROF, PURDUE UNIV, 62-; vis prof, Univ Bergen (Norway), 76-77 & 83-84; vis prof Univ Fla, 68-69; distinguished sci lectr, APA/NSF, 69; Fulbright res/lectr, 76-77. **HONORS AND AWARDS** Gordon A Barrows Mem Award for Distinguished Contrib to Psychol, 90. **MEMBERSHIPS** Am Psychol Asn; Am Psychol Soc; Soc Personality Assessment; Am Asn Appl & Prev Psychol; Midwstrn Psychol Asn; Ind Psychol Asn. **RESEARCH** Clinical psychology; Clinical gerontological psychology; Marriage and family psychology; Interpersonal relations. **SELECTED PUBLICATIONS** coauth Stage of religious faith and reactions to terminal cancer, Jour Psychol & Theol, 93; A guide for adjunctive psychological treatment for cancer pain patients, Innovations in clinical practice: a sourcebook, 93; auth Older individuals in the family, The handbook for developmental family psychology and psychopathology, John Wiley & Sons, 94; coauth Time spent together and relationship quality: long-distance relationships as a test case, Jour of Soc & Personal Relationships, 95; auth Case 3: Janet and Bill, A spiritual strategy for counseling and psychotherapy, Am Psychol Asn, 97. **CONTACT ADDRESS** Dept of Psychol Sci, Purdue Univ, W Lafayette, IN, 47907. **EMAIL** cswensen@psych.purdue.edu

SWETLAND, KENNETH L.
PERSONAL m, 3 children **DISCIPLINE** MINISTRY **EDUCATION** Wheaton Col, AB, 59, MA, 62; Gordon Divinity Sch, MDiv; Andover Newton Theol Sch, Dmin, 76. **CAREER** Chaplain, Penn State Univ; acad dean, prof, Gordon-Conwell Theol Sem, 72-. **HONORS AND AWARDS** Pastor, Pigeon Cove Chapel, 64-72; Calvary Baptist Church, 68-72. **MEMBERSHIPS** Mem, Acad Homiletics; Assn for Case Tchg; Amer Assn of Christian Coun(s); Amer Assn Rel; Soc Biblical Lit. **SELECTED PUBLICATIONS** Auth, The Hidden World of the Pastor: Case Studies on Personal Issues of Real Pastors, Baker Bk House, 95; ed, Jour Case Tchg, 89-91. **CONTACT ADDRESS** Gordon-Conwell Theol Sem, 130 Essex St, South Hamilton, MA, 01982.

SWIDLER, LEONARD
PERSONAL Born 01/06/1929, Sioux City, IA, m, 1957, 2 children **DISCIPLINE** RELIGION; HISTORY **EDUCATION** St Norbert Col, BA, 50; Marquette Univ, MA, 55; Univ Tubingen, STL, 59; Univ Wis, PhD(hist), 61. **CAREER** From asst prof to assoc prof hist, Duquesne Univ, 60-66; Prof Relig, Temple Univ, 66-, Founder & co-ed, J Ecumenical Studies, 64-; mem, Comt Educ for Ecumenism & Presby/ Reformed and Roman Cath Consultation, 65-; fel, Inst Ecumenical & Cult Res, 68-69; Fulbright res grant, Ger, 72-73; guest prof Cath & Protestant theol, Univ Tubingen, 72-73; guest prof Philos, Nankaiv, Tianjin, 87. **HONORS AND AWARDS** LLD, La Salle Col, 77. **MEMBERSHIPS** Am Soc Church Hist; Am Acad Relig; Cath Theol Soc, Am; Church Hist Soc. **RESEARCH** Inter-religious dialogue; modern church history; women in religion and society; global ethics. **SELECTED PUBLICATIONS** Ed, Ecumenism, the Spirit and Worship, 66 & auth, The Ecumenical Vanguard, 66, Duquesne Univ; Freedom in the Church, Pflaum, 69; coauth, Bishops and People, Westminster, 71; Isj en Isjah, 73; auth, Women in Judaism, 76; Blood witness for peace and unity, 77; coauth, Women priests, 77; Yeshua: A Model for Moderns, 87; After the Absolute, 90; Toward a Catholic Constitution, 96; THEORIA, Praxis, 98. **CONTACT ADDRESS** Dept of Religion, Temple Univ, 1114 W Berks St, Philadelphia, PA, 19122-6090. **EMAIL** dialogue@vm.temple.edu

SWINDLER, JAMES KENNETH
PERSONAL Born 09/17/1947, Pratt, KS, m, 1970, 2 children **DISCIPLINE** PHILOSOPHY **EDUCATION** Univ Kans, BA, 73, MA, 73, PhD(philos), 78. **CAREER** Prof and chmn dept of philos, Westminster Col, 77-95; vis assoc prof, Univ of Miami, 83; prof and chmn, dept of philos, Wittenberg Univ, 95-; consultant, Univ of Kansas, 82 NEH, 85, 96-, Baker Univ, 92, Utah State Univ, 93, Arkansas Dept of Higher Ed, 95-6, Davidson Col, 97, Wichita State Univ, 97, Mary Washington Col, 97. **MEMBERSHIPS** Am Philos Asn; Southwestern Philos Soc; AAUP; Cent States Philos Asn;Phi Beta Kappa. **RESEARCH** Metaphysics; history of philosophy; social philosophy. **SELECTED PUBLICATIONS** Auth, Parmenides' Paradox: Negative Reference and Negative Existentials, The Review of Metaphysics, 80; Butchvaror on Existence, Southern Journal of Philosophy, 81; Material Identity and Sameness, Philosophical Topics, 85; MacIntyres' Republic, The Theorist, 90; Davidson';s Razor, Southwest Philosophy Rev, 91; The Permanant Heartland of Subjectivity, Idealistic Studies, 96; Social Intentions: Aggregate, Collective, and General, Philos of the Social Sciences, 96; Weaving: An Analysis of the Constitution of Objects, Construtivist Moral Realism: Intention and Invention in Social Reality, Southwest Philos Rev, 98. **CONTACT ADDRESS** Dept of Philos, Wittenberg Univ, Springfield, OH, 45501-0720. **EMAIL** jswindler@wittenberg.edu

SWINTON, KATHERINE E.
PERSONAL Born 08/14/1950, East York, ON, Canada **DISCIPLINE** LAW/HISTORY **EDUCATION** Univ Alta, BA, 71; Osgoode Hall Law Sch, York Univ, LLB, 75; Yale Univ, LLM, 77. **CAREER** Parliamentary intern, House of Commons, 71-72; law clerk, Supreme Court Can, 75-76; asst prof, Osgoode Hall Law Sch, 77-79; asst prof, 79-82, assoc prof, 82-87, prof fac law, Univ Toronto, 88-97; JUSTICE, ONTARIO COURT (GENERAL DIVISION), 97-. **SELECTED PUBLICATIONS** Auth, The Supreme Court and Canadian Federalism: The Laskin-Dickson Years, 90; co-ed, Studies in Labour Law, 83; co-ed, Competing Constitutional Visions: The Meech Lake Accord, 88; co-ed, Rethinking Federalism, 95. **CONTACT ADDRESS** Ontario Court, 361 University Ave, Toronto, ON, M5G 1T3.

SWITALA, KRISTIN
PERSONAL Born 08/07/1967, Pittsburgh, PA, m, 1996 **DISCIPLINE** PHILOSOPHY **EDUCATION** Villanova Univ, BA, 89; Vanderbilt Univ, PhD, 93. **CAREER** Asst prof, Univ Tenn Chattanooga, 93-. **HONORS AND AWARDS** Outstanding Prof Award, 93; Excellence in Teaching Award, Coll of Art and Sci, 95; Nat Alumni Asn Outstanding Teacher Award 96; Women's Network Best Site Award, 98. **MEMBERSHIPS** APA; SPEP; Phi Betta Kappa, Phi Sigma Tau. **RESEARCH** Continental Philosophy; Feminist Theory. **SELECTED PUBLICATIONS** Auth, Aristotelian History, Dialogue, 91; A Postmodern Musicological Approach to the Authentic Performance Debate, Selected Studies in Phenomenology and Existential Philos, 94; Foucault and the Mutation of Language, Philos Today, 97; Chantal Chawaf Talks About Her New Novel, The Chantal Chawaf Newsletter, 97; Chawaf Discusses Her Influences, The Chantal Chawaf Newsletter, 97; Feminist Theory website, 97; Taking Risks: Teaching Redemption to Freshmen Philosophy Students, The Chantal Chawaf Newsletter, 98. **CONTACT ADDRESS** Dept of Philosophy, Univ Tenn - Chatanooga, Chatanooga, TN, 37403-2598. **EMAIL** Kristin_Switala@utc.edu

SWITALA, KRISTIN
DISCIPLINE PHILOSOPHY **EDUCATION** Villanova Univ, BA, 89; Vanderbilt, PhD, 93. **CAREER** Asst prof. **RESEARCH** Continental philosophy; feminist theory; aesthetics. **SELECTED PUBLICATIONS** Auth, Foucauldian Mutations of Language, Philos Today, 97; Aristotelian History, 91. **CONTACT ADDRESS** Dept of Philosophy, 615 McCallie, Chattanooga, TN, 37403. **EMAIL** Kristin-Switala@utc.edu

SYNAN, EDWARD A.
PERSONAL Born 04/13/1918, Fall River, MA **DISCIPLINE** PHILOSOPHY, MEDIEVAL STUDIES **EDUCATION** Seton Hall Univ, AB, 38; Cath Univ Am, STL, 42; Univ Toronto, MA, 50, PhD, 52; Pontif Inst Medieval Studies, Toronto, LMS, 51. **CAREER** Prof philos & chmn dept, Seton Hall Univ, 52-59; pres, 73-79, Prof Philos, Pontif Inst Medieval Studies, Toronto, 59-, Can Coun grant, 65; PROF, UNIV TORONTO, 59-**HONORS AND AWARDS** LLD, Seton Hall Univ, 73; DLitt, Univ Dallas, 79; ThD, Darlington Sem, 79. **MEMBERSHIPS** Am Cath Philos Asn; Mediaeval Acad Am; Renaissance Soc Am; Am Soc Polit & Legal Philos; Can Philos Asn. **RESEARCH** Medieval philosophy; theology; Christian-Jewish relations. **SELECTED PUBLICATIONS** Auth, The Church and the Jews in the 13th-Century, 1254-1314, Cath Hist Rev, Vol 79, 93; 4 Quodlibets by Pecham,John, Quodlibeta-I-III, Quodlibeta-IV-Romanum, Speculum, Vol 68, 93; Alienated Minority--The Jews of Medieval Latin Europe, Cath Hist Rev, Vol 80, 94; Thomas Aquinas and the Jews, Cath Hist Rev, Vol 82, 96. **CONTACT ADDRESS** Pontifical Inst of Medieval Studies, 59 Queen's Park, Toronto, ON, M5S 2C4.

SYNAN, VINSON
DISCIPLINE CHURCH HISTORY **EDUCATION** Univ Richmond, BA; Univ Ga, MA, PhD. **CAREER** Dean; prof, 94. **SELECTED PUBLICATIONS** Auth, Emmanuel Col:The First Fifty Years, MA thesis, N Wash Press, 68; The Holiness-Pentecostal Movement in the U.S., PhD dissertation, Eerdmans, 71; The Old-Time Power: History of the Pentecostal Holiness Church, Advocate Press, 73; Charismatic Bridges, Word of Life, 74; Aspects of Pencostal/Charismatic Origins, Logos, 75; Azusa Street, Bridge Publ, 80; In the Latter Days, Servant, 85; The Twentieth-Century Pentecostal Explosion, Creation House, 87; Launching the Decade of Evangelization, N Amer Renewal Srv Comm, 90; Under His Banner: A History of the FGBMFI, Gift Publ, 92; The Spirit Said Grow, MARC, World Vision, 92. **CONTACT ADDRESS** Dept of Church History, Regent Univ, 1000 Regent Univ Dr, Virginia Beach, VA, 23464-9831.

SYPNOWICH, CHRISTINE
DISCIPLINE PHILOSOPHY **EDUCATION** Univ Toronto, BA; Oxon Univ, DPhill. **CAREER** Dept Philos, Queen's Univ **RESEARCH** Political philosophy; jurisprudence; Marxist theory; feminist theory. **SELECTED PUBLICATIONS** Auth, The Concept of Socialist Law, Oxford, 90; co-auth, The Social Self, Sage, 95. **CONTACT ADDRESS** Philosophy Dept, Queen's Univ, Kingston, ON, K7L 3N6. **EMAIL** cs4@post.queensu.ca

SYVERUD, K.D.
PERSONAL Born 10/23/1956, Rochester, NY, m, 1982, 3 children **DISCIPLINE** LAW **EDUCATION** Univ Michigan, JD, 81, MA, 83. **CAREER** Dean, Garner Anthony Prof, 97-, Vanderbilt Univ Law Sch; Prof, 87-97, Michigan Law Sch. **HONORS AND AWARDS** J Legal Edu, editor. **MEMBERSHIPS** ALI; ABA; LSA. **RESEARCH** Negotiation; Litigation; Insurance ; Risk; Class Actions; Complex Litigation. **SELECTED PUBLICATIONS** Auth, What Professional Responsibility Scholars Should Know About Insurance, Ct Ins L J, 98; Alternative Dispute Resolution and the Decline of the American Civil Jury, UCLA L Rev, 97; coauth, Why Civil Cases Go to Trial, Dispute Resolution, 97; coauth, Don't Try: Civil Jury Verdicts in a System Geared to Settlement, UCLA L Rev, 96; coauth, The Professional Responsibilities of Insurance Defense Lawyers, Duke L J, 95; On the Demand for Lia-

bility Ins, TX L Rev, 94; Taking Students Seriously: A guide for New Law Teachers, J Legal Edu, 93; coauth, Bargaining Impediments and Settlement Behavior, Ch 3 of Dispute Resolution: Bridging the Settlement Gap, ed, D Anderson, JAI Press 96. **CONTACT ADDRESS** Vanderbilt Univ Law Sch, 21st Ave at Grand, Nashville, TN, 37240. **EMAIL** k.syverud@vanderbilt.edu

SZABADOS, BELA
PERSONAL Born 08/10/1942, Hungary, m, 1966, 1 child **DISCIPLINE** PHILOSOPHY **EDUCATION** Sir George Williams Univ, BA, 66; Univ Calgary, MA, 68, PhD(philos), 72. **CAREER** Lectr philos, Univ Lethbridge, 71-72 & Univ Calgary, 72-73; asst prof, Simon Fraser Univ, 73-74; ASSOC PROF PHILOS, UNIV REGINA, 75-, Can Coun fel, 74-75. **MEMBERSHIPS** Can Philos Asn; Aristotelian Soc; Am Philos Asn. **RESEARCH** Philosophy of mind; philosophy of knowledge; ethics. **SELECTED PUBLICATIONS** Auth, Jews and Gender--Responses to Otto Weininger, Philos Lit, Vol 20, 96. **CONTACT ADDRESS** Dept of Philos, Univ of Regina, Regina, SK, S4S 2A0.

SZASZ, PAUL CHARLES
PERSONAL Born 06/12/1929, Vienna, Austria, m, 1969, 2 children **DISCIPLINE** INTERNATIONAL LAW **EDUCATION** Cornell Univ, BS, 52, LLB, 56. **CAREER** Law clerk, US Court Appeals, 5th Circuit, 56-57; legal officer, Int Atomic Energy Agency, 58-65, nuclear energy control safeguards officer, 65- 66; atty, Int Bank Reconstruct & Develop & Int Centre Settlement Investment Disputes, 66-71; sr legal officer, 71-77, PRIN LEGAL OFF, UN, 77-, Legal coun, Preparatory Comn Int Fund Agr Develop, 76-77, Conf Estab UN Indust Develop Org, 78-79 & Conf Inhumane Conventional Weapons, 78-80. **HONORS AND AWARDS** Ross Essay Prize, Am Bar Asn, 66. **MEMBERSHIPS** Am Soc Int Law; Am Judicature Soc. **RESEARCH** International judicial, administrative and legislative procedures, with special reference to the United Nations system and to the control of nuclear energy. **SELECTED PUBLICATIONS** Auth, The Protection of Human-Rights Through the Dayton/Paris Peace Agreement on Bosnia, Am J Int Law, Vol 90, 96; Peacekeeping in Operation--A Conflict Study of Bosnia, Cornell Int Law J, Vol 28, 95. **CONTACT ADDRESS** New York Univ, 25 Tudor City Pl, Apt 617, New York, NY, 10017.

T

TABBERNEE, WILLIAM
PERSONAL Born 04/21/1944, Rotterdam, Netherlands, m, 3 children **DISCIPLINE** EARLY CHURCH HISTORY **EDUCATION** Coburg Tchrs Col, TPTC, 65; Melbourne Col of Divinity, DipRE, 68, LTh, 68; Univ Melbourne, BA, 72, PhD, 79; Yale Divinity Sch, STM, 73. **CAREER** Lectr, Church history and systematic theol, 73-76, chemn Dept of Christian Thought and Hist, 77-80, Col of the Bible, Melbourne, Australia; dean, Evangelical Theol Asn, Melbourne, Australia, 79-80; prin, Col of the Bible of Churches of Christ in Australia, 81-91; pres, prof of Christian Thought and Hist, 91-94, Stephen J. England prof of Christian Thought and History, 95-, Phillips Grad Sem. **HONORS AND AWARDS** DDiv, Phillips Univ, 93. **MEMBERSHIPS** AAR; NAPS; Australian and New Zealand Soc for Theol Stud. **RESEARCH** Early Christianity; Montanism. **SELECTED PUBLICATIONS** Auth, Montanist Regional Bishops: New Evidence from Ancient Inscriptions, Jour of Early Christian Stud, 93; auth, Evangelism Beyond the Walls, Impact, 95; auth, Lamp-bearing Virgins: An Unusual Episode in the History of Early Christian Worship based on Mt25:1-13, Europ Evangel Soc, 95; auth, Paul of Tarsus: Church Planter Par Excellence, Australian Christian, 96; auth, 25 December, Christmas? Australian Christian, 96; auth, Unfencing the Table: Creeds, Councils, Communion and the Campbells, Mid-Stream, 96; auth, Augustine: Doctor of Love, Australian Christian, 97; auth, Archaeology; Revelation Revelations, Australian Christian, 97; auth, Athanasius: Champion of Orthodoxy, Australian Christian, 97; auth, Eusebius' Theology of Persecution: As Seen in the Various Editions of His Church History, Jour of Early Christian Stud, 97; auth, Ignatius, the Letter- Writing Martyr, Australian Christian, 97; auth, Learning to Handle the Gospel and the Fire Simultaneously: Ministerial Education for the Twenty-First Century, in Exploring Our Destiny, World Convention of Churches of Christ, 97; auth, Montanist Inscriptions and Testimonia: Epigraphic Sources Illustrating the History of Montanism, Patristic Monograph Ser, Mercer Univ, 97; auth, Our Trophies Are Better Than Your Trophies: The Appeal to Tombs and Reliquaries in Montanist- Orthodox Relations, Studia Patristica, 97; auth, Perpetua; The First Woman Journalist, Australian Christian, 97; auth, Eusebius: Chronicler of a Golden Age, Australian Christian, 98; auth, Francis of Assisi: Preacher to the Birds, Australian Christian, 98; auth, Mary Magdalene: A Saint with an Undeserved Reputation, Australian Christian, 98; auth, Restoring Normative Christianity: Episkope and the Christian Church, Mid-Stream, 98. **CONTACT ADDRESS** Phillips Theol Sem, 4242 S Sheridan Rd, Tulsa, OK, 74145. **EMAIL** ptspres@fullnet.net

TABER, JOHN
DISCIPLINE CLASSICAL INDIAN PHILOSOPHY, 19TH CENTURY GERMAN PHILOSOPHY **EDUCATION** Univ Kans, BA, 71; Univ Hamburg, PhD, 79. **CAREER** Assoc prof, Univ NMex. **SELECTED PUBLICATIONS** Auth, Transformative Philosophy: A Study of Sankara, Fichte, and Heidegger, Univ Hawaii Press, 83; contribur, articles on Indian Philos, Routledge Encycl of Philos, 95. **CONTACT ADDRESS** Univ NMex, Albuquerque, NM, 87131.

TAGGART, WALTER JOHN
DISCIPLINE MODERN LAND TRANSACTIONS, SECURED TRANSACTIONS/BANKRUPTCY, FEDERAL COURTS AND THE FEDERAL SYSTEM, NEGOTIABLE INSTRUMENTS AND PAYMENT LAW, REAL ESTATE DOCUMENTATION **EDUCATION** Belmont Abbey Col, AB, 65; Villanova Univ Sch Law, JD, 68. **CAREER** Prof, Villanova Univ. **MEMBERSHIPS** Order of the Coif; Trustee, Amatex Disease Trust and Nat Gypsum Settlement Trust; Trustees' Adv Comt Pacor Settlement Trust; Philadelphia Community Legal serv; Amer Asn Law Sch, Sect on Real Property, Subcomt on Commercial Real Estate, 74-77 & Sect on Creditors' Rights, 80; chp, ABA Sect Corp, Banking, and Bus Law, Comt on Railroad Reorganizations, 76-78; Adv bd, Practical Lawyer, ABA Sect Real Property, Probate and Trust Law, Comt on Creditors' Rights in Real Estate Financing; exec comt, Young Lawyers Sect, Pa Bar Asn. **RESEARCH** Real property, probat, trust law, bankruptcy and business law **SELECTED PUBLICATIONS** Auth, The New Bankruptcy Court System, 59 Bank L.J. 231, 85; The New Bankruptcy Rules, 7 ALI-ABA Course Materials J 7, 84; Collier on Bankruptcy, 15th ed, Vol 5, 1161-74; co-ed and contribur, Practicing Under the Bankruptcy Reform Act, 79 & Moore's Fed Practice, 72 Rev Rule 55, 77 Revision of Conflicts Jurisdiction, Vol 1A, Part 2. **CONTACT ADDRESS** Law School, Villanova Univ, 800 Lancaster Ave, Villanova, PA, 19085-1692. **EMAIL** taggart@law.vill.edu

TAIWO, OLUFEMI
DISCIPLINE PHILOSOPHY **EDUCATION** Univ Ife, Obafemi Awolowo Univ, Ile-Ife, Osun State, Nigeria, BA, 78, MA, 81; Univ Toronto, MA, PhD, 86. **CAREER** Assoc prof, Loyola Univ, 91-; lectr, Obafemi Awolowo Univ, Ile-Ife, Nigeria, 86-90; staff develop fel, Can-Nigeria Linkage Prog Women's Stud Inst Study Women, Mount Saint Vincent Univ & Centre for Int Stud, Dalhousie Univ, Halifax, NS, Can, 88-89; Rockefeller postdr fel, Africana Stud and Res Center, Cornell Univ, Ithaca, NY, 90-91; co-founder, Int Soc African and African Diaspora Philos and Stud, ISAADPS & Int Soc Stud Africa, ISSA; served on, Comt Int Coop Am Philos Asn, 93-96; ed, APA Newsletter on Philos and Int Coop; organized, on behalf Amer Philos Asn, Fulbright 50th Anniversary Distinguished Fel Lect, 96. **RESEARCH** Marxism; philosophy of law; soc and political philosophy; ethics; feminism; African philosophy; nationalism; philosophy of the soc sciences. **SELECTED PUBLICATIONS** Auth,Legal Naturalism: A Marxist Theory of Law, Ithaca: Cornell UP, 96; publ in, The Nigerian J of Philos; Callalloo: J African and African-Amer Arts, Letters and Criticism; Can Rev of Stud in Nationalism; Philos Forum; Int Philos Quart; Tchg Philos; Issue: A J of Opinion. **CONTACT ADDRESS** Dept of Philosophy, Loyola Univ, Chicago, 820 N. Michigan Ave., Chicago, IL, 60611.

TALAR, CHARLES J. T.
PERSONAL Born 12/02/1947, Port Chester, NY, s **DISCIPLINE** SYSTEMATIC THEOLOGY **EDUCATION** St. Mary's Seminary Col, AB, 70; Cath Univ, MA, 73; St. Mary's SOT, STM, 74; Cath Univ, PhD, 80; St. Mary's SOT, STL, 81; New Sch Soc Res, MA, 85; St. Mary's Sem, STD, 87. **CAREER** Assoc pastor, St. Thomas Aquinas Parish, Fairfield, Conn, 79-82; St. Mary's Sem SOT, 84-86; pastor, Church of Our Saviour, English Speaking Int Roman Cath Commun of the Hague, 86-90; vis asst prof, Fordham Univ, 90-91; assoc prof, Alvernia Col, 91-97; prof, St. Mary's Sem and Univ, 97- . **MEMBERSHIPS** Am Acad of Relig; Soc of Bibl Lit; Am Cath Hist Asoc; AIZEN. **RESEARCH** Roman Catholic modernism; nineteenth-century French Catholicism. **SELECTED PUBLICATIONS** Auth, Conspiracy to Commit Heresy: The Anti-Americanist Polemic of Canon Henri Delassus, U.S. Cath Hist, 93; auth, Tropics of Autobiographical Discourse: An Examination of Newman's Apologia, Religions of the Book, 96; auth, Saint of Authority and Saint of the Spirit: Paul Sebatier's Vie de saint Francois d'Assise, Cath Hist Rev, 96; auth, (Anti)hagiography and Mysticism in the Work of J.K. Huysmans, Excavatio, 97; auth, The Effective History of Tradition: Mohler, Le Roy, Schillebeeck, J Hist Modern Theol, 97. **CONTACT ADDRESS** St. Mary's Sem and Univ, 5400 Roland Ave., Baltimore, MD, 21210.

TALBERT, CHARLES H.
PERSONAL Born 03/19/1934, Jackson, MS, m, 1961 **DISCIPLINE** RELIGION **EDUCATION** Samford Univ, BA, 56; Southern Baptist Theol Sem, BD, 59; Vanderbilt Univ, PhD, 63. **CAREER** From asst prof to assoc prof, 63-74, PROF RELIG, WAKE FOREST UNIV, 74-, Lilly Found fel, 59-61; Rockefeller fel, 61-63; Ford Found fel, Duke Univ & Univ NC, 68-69; Soc Relig Higher Educ fel, Rome, 71-72; Reynolds res leave, Wake Forest Univ, 78-79. **MEMBERSHIPS** Soc Bibl Lit; Soc Values Higher Educ; Studiorum Novi Testamenti Soc; Cath Bibl Asn; Nat Asn Baptist Professors of Relig. **RESEARCH** Modern literary criticism and Biblical studies; New Testament; early Christian ethics and spirituality. **SELECTED PUBLICATIONS** Auth, What Are the Gospels--A Comparison with Greco-Roman Biography, J Biblical Lit Vol 0112, 93; Footwashing in John-XIII and the Johannine Community, J Biblical Lit, Vol 0112, 93; Jesus Birth in Luke and the Nature of Religious Language, Heythrop J, Vol 35, 94; The Prayer Texts of Luke-Acts, Interpretation, Vol 48, 94; The Composition of the Gospel According to Luke Against the Background of Ancient Rhetoric, Biblica, Vol 76, 95; The Gifts of God and the Authentication of a Christian--An Exegetical Study of 1-Corinthians-VIII-XI, Cath Biblical Quart, Vol 57, 95. **CONTACT ADDRESS** Wake Forest Univ, Box 7212, Winston-Salem, NC, 27109.

TALBOTT, WILLIAM J.
PERSONAL Born 01/19/1949, Fort Belvoir, VA, d, 2 children **DISCIPLINE** PHILOSOPHY **EDUCATION** Princeton Univ, AB, 70; Harvard Univ, PhD, 76. **CAREER** Asst prof, Dept of Philos, 90-96, assoc prof Dept Pilos, 96-, Univ Wash; NEH fel, 96-97. **MEMBERSHIPS** Am Philos Asn; Soc Philos & Psychol. **RESEARCH** Epistemology; Ethics; Political philosophy; Rational choice theory. **SELECTED PUBLICATIONS** Auth The Reliability of the Cognitive Mechanism: A Mechanist Account of Empirical Justification, Garland Publ, 90; Intentional Self-Deception in a Single, Coherent Self, Philos and Phenomenol Res, 95; rev The Nature of Rationality, The Philos Rev, 95; Rules for Reasoning, in Philos & Psychol, 95; commentary Real Self-Deception, Behavioral and Brain Science, 97; coauth Games Lawyers Play: Legal Discovery and Social Epistemology, Legal Theory, 98. **CONTACT ADDRESS** Dept of Philosophy, Univ Wash, Box 35 3350, Seattle, WA, 98195-3350. **EMAIL** wtalbott@u.washington.edu

TALIAFERRO, CHARLES
PERSONAL Born 08/25/1952, New York, NY, m, 1987 **DISCIPLINE** PHILOSOPHY & LITERATURE **EDUCATION** Univ Rhode Island, MA; Harvard Univ, MTS; Brown, MA & PhD, 94. **CAREER** Instr, Univ Mass, 82-84; instr, Univ Notre Dame, 84-85; vis scholar, Univ Oxford, 91-92; vis fel, Princeton Univ, 98-99; prof, philos, St. Olaf Col, 85-. **HONORS AND AWARDS** NEH fel, 91. **MEMBERSHIPS** Amer Philos Asn. **RESEARCH** Philosophy of mind; Philosophy of religion; Ethics. **SELECTED PUBLICATIONS** Auth, Praying with C. S. Lewis, St. Mary's Press, 98; auth, Contemporary Philosophy of Religion, Blackwell, 98; co-ed, A Companion to Philosophy of Religion, Blackwell, 97; auth, Consciousness and the Mind of God, Cambridge Univ Press, 94. **CONTACT ADDRESS** Dept. of Philosophy, St. Olaf Col, Northfield, MN, 55057. **EMAIL** taliafer@stolaf.edu

TALLEY, ERIC L.
DISCIPLINE LAW **EDUCATION** Univ Calif, San Diego, BA,88; Stanford Univ, JD,95; PhD,95. **CAREER** Assoc prof, Univ Southern Calif; John Olin Foundation fel; prof, Stanford Univ. **MEMBERSHIPS** Phi Beta Kappa. **RESEARCH** Business Organizations; Contracts, Quantitative Methods in the Law, & Law & Strategic Behavior. **SELECTED PUBLICATIONS** Auth, Investment Policy and Exit-Exchange Offers Within Financially Distressed Firms; Contract Renegotiation, Mechanism Design, and the Liquidated Damages Doctrine & Comparable Worth: Its Economic and Political Policy Dimensions. **CONTACT ADDRESS** School of Law, Univ Southern Calif, University Park Campus, Los Angeles, CA, 90089.

TANCREDI, LAURENCE RICHARD
PERSONAL Born 10/15/1940, Hershey, PA **DISCIPLINE** LAW AND MEDICINE; LAW AND PSYCHIATRY; PSYCHIATRIC ETHICS **EDUCATION** Franklin & Marshall Coll, AB, 62; Univ Pa Sch Medicine, MD, 66; Yale Univ Sch Law, JD, 72; Columbia Univ, resid, Psychiatry, 74-75; resid, Yale Univ Sch Med, Psychiatry, 75-77. **CAREER** Sr prof assoc, Inst Medicine, Nat Acad Sci, 72-74; assoc prof, New York Univ Med Sch, Psychiatry, 77-84; adj prof, New York Univ Law Sch, 81-84; med staff, Harris County Psych Center, 89-92; med dir, Regent Hosp, 92-93; CLIN PROF, NEW YORK UNIV MED SCH, 92-; CLIN PROF, UNIV CALIF-SAN DIEGO SCH MED, HEALTH CARE SCI, 93-; MED STAFF, BROOKHAVEN NAT LABS, 96-. **MEMBERSHIPS** Am Coll Psych; AmA cad Psych & Law; Am Psych Asn; Group Advance Psych **RESEARCH** Alternative systems for medical injury compensation; Conceptual foundations of what constitutes scientific fact as that knowledge affects legal decision-making; Implications of discoveries from the use of imaging technologies on understanding how the brain/mind works **SELECTED PUBLICATIONS** Dangerous Diagnostics: The Social Power of Biological Information, Univ Chicago Press, 94; The Anthropology of Medicine, Prager Publ, 97. **CONTACT ADDRESS** 22 Riverside Dr, No 14-A, New York, NY, 10023. **EMAIL** lrt3@juno.com

TANDY, CHARLES
PERSONAL Born 04/04/1947, Princeton, KY, s **DISCIPLINE** PHILOSOPHY **EDUCATION** Univ Louisville, KY South Col, BA, 69; Western Maryland Col, MLA, 85; Univ MS,

PhD, 93. **CAREER** Tchr, physics & math, 71-72, Central City HS KY; caseworker, 72-73, LaGrange Reformatory; caseworker, 73-84, Soc Sec Admin; Dir, 84-88, Life Extension Info Svcs, Tandys Dandys Info Computer & Library Based Res and Info Retrieval; independent consl, 93-, private practice; vis scholar, Philosophy Dept, 94-95, Stanford Univ; vis fac, Intl Programs, 95-97, Purdue Univ; vis fel, Phil & Ed, 97-98, consl asst prof, 98-, Ria Univ Inst for Advanced Study. **HONORS AND AWARDS** First Prize Natl Essay Contest, United Nations Asn of NY; Prof Presentation Travel Fel, Univ of MS; Biographical Listings; Comm Leaders and Noteworthy Amer; Dist of Intl Biography; Intl Who's Who in Com Svc; Intl Who's Who of Intellectuals. **MEMBERSHIPS** Amer Hist Asn; Amer Phil Asn; Intl Asn for Mathematical and Computer Modeling; Phil of Ed Soc. **RESEARCH** Biomedical ethics; English as a foreign language; foundations of education; futuristics; interrelation of the disciplines; metaphysics of personal identity; philosophy of education; philosophy of Kant; philosophy of Kenneth Boulding; world history. **SELECTED PUBLICATIONS** Auth, Educational Implications of the Philosophy of Kenneth Boulding, UMI Inc, 93; auth, A Complete Curriculum For A Quality High School, Cade House, 94; auth, Cryonic-Hibernation in Light of the Biomedical Ethics of Beauchamp and Childress, Amer Cryonics Soc, 95; auth, Curriculum Development of A Graduate Course Philosophy of Education for the Malaysia Univ of Technology at Batu Pahat, Report MUT-1, 95; auth, Curriculum Development of a Graduate Course Introduction to Educational Research For the Malaysia University of Technology at Batu Pahat, Report MUT-2, 95; auth, Establishment of a Graduate Program for the Malaysia University of Technology at Batu Pahat, Vol 1, 2 &3, Midwest Univ Consortium for Intl Activities, Purdue Univ, 95; auth, Philosophy Science and the Advancement of Learning in the 21st Century, Pengajaran Dan Pembelajaran Menuju Ke Abad 21, 96; auth, Curriculum Development of the graduate Course MTT 3113 for the Tun Hussein Onn Institute of Technology, Institut Teknologi Tun Hussein, Report THOIT-1, 96; auth, Curriculum Development of the Graduate Course MTT 1443 for the Tun Hussein Onn Institute of Technology, Institut Teknologi Tun Hussein, Report THOIT-2, 96; auth, Establishment of a Graduate School for Education for the Tun Hussein Onn Institute of Technology, Vol 1, 2&3, Midwest Univ Consortium for Intl Activities, Purdue Univ, 96; auth, Educational Philosophy for the 21st Century, RMIT and VNU Organizing Comm, Higher Ed in the 21st Century Mission and Challenge in Developing Countries Vol 1&2, 96; auth, ITTHO's Graduate Program in Education, Vol 1, 2&3, Midwest Univ Consortium for Intl Activities, Purdue Univ, 96; auth, Educational Philosophy Technical and Vocational Education and Social-Economic Development Toward the Creation and Flourishing of Extraterrestrial Communities, UNESCO UNEVOC, Melbourne Australia, 96; auth, Development of a Graduate Program for the Department of Education and Humanities - Institut Teknologi Tun Hussein Onn, Midwest Univ Consortium for Intl Activities, 97; auth, Simmel Georg 1858-1918, in Global Encycl of Historical Writing Vol 2, Garland Pub, 98; auth, Rickert Heinrich 1863-1936, in Global Encycl of Historical Writing Vol 2, Garland Pub, 98; auth, Oakeshott Michael Joseph 1901-1990, in Global Encycl of Historical Writing Vol 2, Garland Pub, 98; auth, MRQ Analysis of the Ria University Institute, 2nd Intl Conf on Planned Maintenance Reliability and Quality, Oxford England, 98. **CONTACT ADDRESS** Stanford Univ, Palo Alto, CA, 94309. **EMAIL** tandy@ria.edu

TANFORD, J. ALEXANDER

PERSONAL Born 01/23/1950, Iowa City, IA, m, 1992, 2 children **DISCIPLINE** LAW **EDUCATION** Princeton Univ, AB, 72; Duke Univ, JD, 76; Duke Univ, LLM, 79. **CAREER** Instr, Duke Univ School of Law, 77-79; asst prof, Ind Univ School of Law, Bloomington79-83; assoc prof, Ind Univ School of Law, Bloomington 83- 86; vis prof, Washington Univ School of Law, St. Louis, 85; prof, Ind Univ School of Law, Bloomington 86-; vis scholar, Univ of Iowa Col of Law, fall 86 and spring 89. **HONORS AND AWARDS** Teaching Excellence Recognition Award; John S. Hastings Fac Fel; Indiana Supreme Court Rules of Evidence Committee; Harry T. Ice Fac Fel; ICLU Richard Zweig Coopeating Atty Award; Ira C. Batman Fac Fel; Univ Nominee, Lilly Endowment Fac Open Fel; CIC Exchange Scholar; John S. Bradway Fel; Mordecai Soc Award for Teaching. **MEMBERSHIPS** AAUP; Law & Soc Asn; Am Psychology-Law Soc. **RESEARCH** Trial law & procedure, especially interdisciplinary issues in psychology and law. **SELECTED PUBLICATIONS** Auth, "The Law and Psychology of Jury Instructions", in 68 Nebraska Law Review 71, 90; auth, "Racism in the Adversary System: Defense Use of Peremptory Challenges", in 63 Southern Calif Law Review 1015, 90; auth, "The Limits of a Scientific Jurisprudence: The Supreme Court and Psychology", in 66 Indiana Law Journal 137, 90; auth, "Law Reform by Courts, Legislatures and Commissions Following Empirical Research on Jury Instructions", in 25 Law and Soc Review 155, 91; auth, "Novel Scientific Evidence of Intoxication: Acoustic Analysis of Voice Tapes from the Exxon Valdez", in 82 Journal of Criminal Law and Criminology 579, 91; auth, Trial Practice Problems and Case Files 2nd ed, 92; auth, "Thinking About Elephants: Admonitions, Empirical Research and Legal Policy" in 60 UMKC Law Review 645, 92; auth, "Keeping Cross-Examination Under Control", in 18 Am Journal of Trial Advocacy 245, 94; auth, " The Death of Graduation Prayer: the Parrot Sketch Redux", in 24 Journal of Law & Educ 423, 95; auth, "The In/Into Controversy", in 91 Northwestern Univ Law Review 637, 97; auth, The Trial Process: Law, Tactics and Ethics 2nd ed, 93; auth, Indiana Trial Evidence Manual 4th ed, 99. **CONTACT ADDRESS** Sch of Law, Indiana Univ, Bloomington, 211 S. Indiana Ave., Bloomington, IN, 47405. **EMAIL** tanford@ indiana.edu

TANG, PAUL C.L.

PERSONAL Born 01/23/1944, Vancouver, Canada, s **DISCIPLINE** PHILOSOPHY **EDUCATION** Univ Toronto, ARCT, 62; Univ BC Canada, B.Sc, 66; Simon Fraser Univ Canada, MA, 71; Washington Univ, MA, 75, PhD, 82; Georgetown Univ, Kennedy Inst Ethics, Cert, Bioethics, 83; Harvard Univ, NEH Fel, 88. **CAREER** Res asst, biochemist, 68-70, Vancouver General Hosp, Vancouver; lectr, instr, 72-76, Washington Univ; vis lectr, 78-79, res develop officer & asst to grad dean, 80-82, So Illinois Univ; asst prof, 82-85, Grinnell Col; asst prof, assoc, 85-, prof, chmn, phil dept, 88-94, adj prof, Asian & Asian Amer Stud, 94-, prof, Univ Scholars prog, acting chmn, phil dept, 98, grad adv, 98-, Calif St Univ, Long Beach. **HONORS AND AWARDS** Phi Beta Delta; Internationalizing the Curriculum Award, 93; Fac Adv of the Year Award, Asn Students, Inc. CSULB, 88, 89, 91, 95; Cert of Merit, Student Phil Asn (SPA), CSLUB, 88, 89, 90, 93, 94, 96, 97, 98; SPA Fac Mem of the Year Award, 91; Special Award, SPA, 92; Dist Fac Tchng Award, CSULB, 95; Most Valuable Prof Award, Col of Liberal Arts, CSULB, 95; Outstanding Grad Prof Award, SPA, CSULB, 95; APA award for Excel in Tchng, 95, 97; CSULB Outstanding Prof Award, 96-97; CSU System-wide Trustees' Outstanding Prof Award, 96-97; Cert of Recogn, Continued Commitment to Education, CA St Senate, 97; CSULB Scholarly & Creative Act Award, 95, 97; Nobel Laureate in Chem, CSULB, 86; Nobel Laureate in Physics, CSULB, 92. **MEMBERSHIPS** APA; Phil of Science Asn; History of Science Soc; The Hastings Ctr; Amer Soc for Aesthetics; Western Soc Science Asn; NY Acad of Science; Maison Internationale des Intellectuels and of L'Academie MIDI; Paris France & Rain am Lech, Germany. **RESEARCH** Phil of natural science; phil of social science; history & phil of biology; theory of knowledge; phil of lang; logic; Asian phil. **SELECTED PUBLICATIONS** Rev, Introductory Readings in the Philosophy of Science, Isis, Vol 81, 90; rev, The philosophy of Thomas S. Kuhn: Reconstruction and Fundamental Problems, Isis, Vol 82, 91; rev, Laws and Symmetry, Isis, Vol 83; 92; coauth, Urban Violence in Los Angeles: A Philosophical Examination for the Possibility of Social Values, The City of Angels, Kendell/Hunt, 92; coauth, Anti-realism and the Complementarity Model of Mind-Brain, Boston Stud in the Phil of Science, Vol 169, 92, reprinted, Revue Roumaine De Philosophie, Vol 37, 93; rev, Conceptual Revolutions, Isis, Vol 84, 94; auth, Representation and the Complementarity Model of Mind-Brain, Forms of Representations: An Interdisciplinary Theme for Cognitive Science, 96; art, On the Special Logic Thesis in Chinese Philosophy, Metaphilosophy, Vol 28, 97; auth, Ilya Prigogine, Biographical Encycl of Scientists, Marshall Cavendish Corp, 98. **CONTACT ADDRESS** Dept of Philosophy, California State Univ, Long Beach, 1250 Bellflower Blvd, Long Beach, CA, 90840. **EMAIL** pcltang@csulb.edu

TANNEHILL, ROBERT C.

PERSONAL Born 05/06/1934, Clay Center, KS, m, 1955, 3 children **DISCIPLINE** NEW TESTAMENT STUDIES **EDUCATION** Hamline Univ, BA, 56; Yale Divinity Sch, BD, 59; Yale Univ, MA, 60; Yale Univ, PhD, 63. **CAREER** Instr, new testament, Oberlin Grad Sch of Theol, 63-66; asst prof, 66-69, assoc prof, 69-74, prof, 74-, acad dean, 94-, new testament, Meth Theol Sch in Oh. **HONORS AND AWARDS** Danforth fel, 56-63; Tews prize, Yale Divinity Sch, 57; Two Brothers fel, Yale Univ, 60-61; Asn of Theol Sch Facul fel, 69-70; Asn of Theol Sch Basic Theol Scholar and Res Award, 75-76; Asn of Theol Sch Theol Scholar and Res Award, 82; Soc of Bibl Lite, Claremont fel, 82; assoc ed, Soc of Bibl Lite Monogr Series, 79-85; mem, ed board, Jour of Bibl Lit, 88-93; co-chair, lit aspects of the Gospels and Acts grp, Soc of Bibl Lit, 91-96;; Asn of Theol Sch Theol Scholar and Res Award, 94-95. **MEMBERSHIPS** Soc of Bibl Lit; Studiorum Novi Testamenti Soc. **RESEARCH** Luke and Acts; Literary methods in New Testament study. **SELECTED PUBLICATIONS** Auth, Freedom and Responsibility in Scripture Interpretation, with Application to Luke, Literary Studies in Luke-Acts: Essays in Honor of Joseph B. Tyson, 265-78, Mercer Univ Press, 98; auth, Luke, Abingdon New Testament Commentaries, Abingdon Press, 96; auth, Literature, the NT as, The Harper Collins Bible Dictionary, 611-614, Harper San Francisco, 96; auth, The Gospels and Narrative Literature, The New Interpreter's Bible, vol VIII, 56-70, Abingdon Press, 95; auth, Should We Love Simon the Pharisee?, Hermeneutical Reflections on the Pharisees in Luke, Currents in Theol and Mission, 21, 424-433, 94; auth, Cornelius and Tabitha Encounter Luke's Jesus, Interpretation, 48, 347-56, 94. **CONTACT ADDRESS** Methodist Theol School in Ohio, 3081 Columbus Pike, PO Box 8004, Delaware, OH, 43015. **EMAIL** btannehill@mtso.edu

TARALA, JOSEPH J.

PERSONAL m **DISCIPLINE** PHILOSOPHY **EDUCATION** Temple Univ, PhD candidate, 96. **CAREER** Adj Inst, Seton Hall Univ, 2 yrs; Prof, Lincoln Univ, 2 yrs. **MEMBERSHIPS** APA **RESEARCH** Biomedical ethics; practical ethics in general **CONTACT ADDRESS** 1008 Seventh Ave, Toms River, NJ, 08757.

TARLOCK, ANTHONY DAN

PERSONAL Born 06/02/1940, Oakland, CA, m, 1977 **DISCIPLINE** LAW **EDUCATION** Stanford Univ, AB, 62, LLB, 65. **CAREER** Asst prof law, Univ Ky, 66-68; from asst prof to assoc prof, Ind Univ, Bloomington, 68-72, prof, 72-81; PROF LAW, ITT CHICAGO KENT, 81-, Consult pesticide regulation, Nat Acad Sci, 73-75; vis prof law, Univ Pa, 74-75, Univ Chicago, 79 & Univ Mich, 82. **RESEARCH** Water law; land use law; environmental law. **SELECTED PUBLICATIONS** Auth, Local-Government Protection of Biodiversity--What is Its Niche, Univ Chicago Law Rev, Vol 60, 93. **CONTACT ADDRESS** Col of Law, ITT Chicago Kent, Chicago, IL, 60606.

TARR, NINA W.

DISCIPLINE LAW **EDUCATION** Southern Ill Univ, BA; Univ Wash, MA; Univ Iowa, PhD. **CAREER** Prof, Univ Ill Urbana Champaign. **RESEARCH** Family law; legal problems of the elderly poor. **SELECTED PUBLICATIONS** Auth, pubs on clinical education. **CONTACT ADDRESS** Law Dept, Univ Ill Urbana Champaign, 52 E Gregory Dr, Champaign, IL, 61820. **EMAIL** ntarr@law.uiuc.edu

TARTAGLIA, PHILIP

PERSONAL Born 06/02/1935, Albany, NY, m, 1960, 2 children **DISCIPLINE** PHILOSOPHY **EDUCATION** NY Univ, BA, 60, MA, 64, PhD(philos), 66. **CAREER** Asst prof philos, Slippery Rock State Col, 67-68; asst prof, 68-72, assoc prof, 72-85, prof philos, Potsdam Col, 85-. **RESEARCH** Mathematical logic; linguistics; cybernetics; ethics; philos of lang. **SELECTED PUBLICATIONS** Auth, Problems in the Construction of a Theory of Natural Language, Mouton, The Hague, 72. **CONTACT ADDRESS** Dept Philos, Potsdam Col, 44 Pierrepont Ave, Potsdam, NY, 13676-2299.

TASHIRO, PAUL Y.

PERSONAL Born 09/21/1933, Tokyo, Japan, m, 1963, 1 child **DISCIPLINE** BIBLE **EDUCATION** HUC-JIR, Cincinnati, OH, PhD, 89, Bibl & Ancient Near Eastern Stud. **CAREER** Prof, 86-91, Lindsey Wilson Col; prof, 91-, Wesley Theol Sem. **MEMBERSHIPS** Wesleyan Theol Soc; Evangel Theol Soc; Amer Oriental Soc; Inst of Bibl Res; Soc for Bibl Lit; Natl Assn of Prof of Hebrew. **RESEARCH** TNK; Semitic lang; linguistics; comparative linguistics, assyriology. **SELECTED PUBLICATIONS** Auth, Comparative Study on Sumerian Culture and Ancient Japanese Culture; auth, Research Ecology for Ancient Culture and Languages. **CONTACT ADDRESS** Wesley Biblical Sem, 5980 Floral Dr, PO Box 9938, Jackson, MS, 39206-0938. **EMAIL** tashiek@okra.millsaps.edu

TASHJIAN, JIRAIR S.

PERSONAL Born 08/11/1939, Jordan, m, 1966, 2 children **DISCIPLINE** NEW TESTAMENT **EDUCATION** Claremont Grad Univ, PhD, 87. **CAREER** Prof, Southern Nazarene Univ, 83-. **MEMBERSHIPS** Soc of Biblical Lit. **RESEARCH** Gospels, Question of the Historical Jesus. **SELECTED PUBLICATIONS** Auth, Jesus Olivet Discourse in the Second Coming, ed, H. Ray Dunning, Beacon Hill Press, Kansas City, 95. **CONTACT ADDRESS** Southern Nazarene Univ, Bethany, OK, 73008. **EMAIL** jtashjia@snu.edu

TASSI, ALDO

DISCIPLINE PHILOSOPHY **EDUCATION** Fordham Univ, PhD, 70; Marquette Univ, MA, 63; Iona Coll, BA, 55. **CAREER** Prof, 72-present, Loyola Coll MD; Asst Prof, 66-72, Fordham Univ; Asst Prof, 63-66, Duquesne Univ. **HONORS AND AWARDS** Fulbright Scholar to Italy, 61-63. **MEMBERSHIPS** Amer Philos Assoc; Metaphysical Soc of Amer; Amer Catholic Philos Assoc. **RESEARCH** Philosophy and Theatre, Metaphysics, Performance Theory, Philosophy and the Arts, William James, Nietzsche, Aristotle. **SELECTED PUBLICATIONS** Auth, Philosophy and Theatre, International Philosophical Quarterly, 98; Impersonation and Performance, Playing Classical Greek Theatre, eds, S Patsalidis & E Sakellaridou, Univ Studio Press, 98; Philosophy and Theatre: An Essay on Contemplation and Catharsis, International Philosophical Quarterly, 95; Spirituality as a Stage of Being, Divine Representations, ed, A Astell, Paulist Press, 94; Person and the Mask of Being, Philosophy Today, 93. **CONTACT ADDRESS** Dept of Philosophy, Loyola Col, 4501 N Charles St, Baltimore, MD, 21210. **EMAIL** tassi@vax.loyola.edu

TATE, PAUL DEAN

PERSONAL Born 11/22/1945, Fort Worth, TX, m, 1976 **DISCIPLINE** PHILOSOPHY, SANSKRIT **EDUCATION** Univ Tex, Austin, BA, 67; Yale Univ, MPhil, 74, PhD, 76. **CAREER** Dean of Grad Studies, Idaho State Univ **MEMBERSHIPS** Am Philos Assn. **RESEARCH** The philosophy of Martin Heidegger; the nature of language; Indian philosophy. **SELECTED PUBLICATIONS** Auth, His Holiness Gives an Example, Kite Bks, 73; auth, The Agivtic Hotel, Latitude Press, 87. **CONTACT ADDRESS** Idaho State Univ, 921 S 8th Ave, Box 8399, Pocatello, ID, 83209-0001. **EMAIL** tatepaul@isu.edu

TATUM, W. BARNES
PERSONAL Born 04/24/1938, Mobile, AL, m **DISCIPLINE** RELIGIOUS STUDIES **EDUCATION** Birmingham-Southern Col, BA, 60; Duke Univ, BD, 63, PhD, 66; Univ of North Carolina Greensboro, MLS, 91. **CAREER** Relig fac, Huntingdon Col, 66-73; relig fac, Greensboro Col, 73-. **HONORS AND AWARDS** NEH Summer Sem for Col Tchrs, 82, 87. **MEMBERSHIPS** Am Acad of Relig; Soc Bibl Lit; ALA. **RESEARCH** Christian origins; historical Jesus. **SELECTED PUBLICATIONS** Auth, "Did Jesus Heal Simon's Mother-in-Law of a Fever," Dialogue, 94; "The Resurrection & Historical Evidence," Foundations and Facets Forum, 94; John the Baptist and Jesus, Polebridge, 94; Jesus at the Movies, Polebridge, 97; "Jesus' So-Called Triumphal Entry," Foundations and Facets Forum, 98; In Quest of Jesus, rev ed, Abingdon, 99. **CONTACT ADDRESS** Greensboro Col, 815 W Market St, Greensboro, NC, 27401. **EMAIL** tatumb@gborocollege.edu

TATZ, MARK
PERSONAL Born 02/05/1945, New York, NY, d, 2 children **DISCIPLINE** RELIGION **EDUCATION** Univ of Calif Berk, BA, 66; Univ of Wash, MA, 72; Univ British Columbia, PhD, 78. **CAREER** Univ Washington, instr, 74; Naropa Inst Core Faculty, acting chemn, Buddhist Stud, 79-81; Antioch Int, postdoc, instr, 82; Caifl Inst of Integral Stud, prof, 83-91; Inst of Buddhist Stud, adj prof, 91-96; Univ Calif Extension, instr, 92-, Calif Col of Arts & Crafts, sr instr, 96-98. **HONORS AND AWARDS** NDEA fel, Univ British Columbia, Killan fel, Shastri Indo-Can Inst, jr fel, Am Inst Indian Stud, sr fel, Am Acad of Relig, grant. **MEMBERSHIPS** AAR, AOS, AHA, IABS, IATS. **RESEARCH** Indo-Tibetan Buddhism; comparative religions. **SELECTED PUBLICATIONS** Auth, The Skill in Means (Upayakausalya) Sutra. Delhi, Motilal Banarsidass, Tibet House, 94; auth, The Complete Bodhisattva: Asanga's Chapter on Ethics with the Commentary by Tsong-kha-pa, The Basic Path to Awakening, Stud in Asian Thought and Religion, Lewiston NY, Edwin Mellen Press, Philosophic Systems According to Advayavajra and Vajrapani, Jour of Buddhist and Tibetan Studies, 94; auth, Brief Communication (On Thus Have I Heard), in: Indo-Iranian Jour, 93. **CONTACT ADDRESS** 5413 Claremont Ave, Oakland, CA, 94618. **EMAIL** tatz@uclink4.berkeley.edu

TAUBER, ALFRED I.
PERSONAL Born 06/24/1947, Washington, DC, m, 1966, 4 children **DISCIPLINE** PHILOSOPHY; HISTORY OF SCIENCE **EDUCATION** BS, 69, Tufts Univ; MD, 73, Tufts Univ School of Medicine **CAREER** Instr, 78-80, Asst Prof, 80-82, Harvard Medical School; Assoc Prof Medicine, 82-86, Assoc Prof Biochemistry, 82-86; Assoc Prof Pathology, Prof of Medicine, 84-87, Prof of Pathology, 87-, Boston Univ School of Medicine; Prof Philosophy, 92-, College of Arts and Sciences, Boston Univ. **HONORS AND AWARDS** Research Fel in Medicine, Harvard Medical School, 77-78; Clinical Fel in Medicine, Tufts-New England Medical Center Hospital, 75-77. **RESEARCH** Philosophy and the history of science **SELECTED PUBLICATIONS** Coauth, Metchnikoff and the Origins of Immunology: From Metaphor to Theory, 91; Auth, The Immune Self: Theory or Metaphor, 94; Coauth, The Generation of Diversity: Clonal Selection Theory and the Rise of Molecular Immunology, 97; Auth, Confessions of A Medicine Man: An Essay in Popular Philosophy, 99. **CONTACT ADDRESS** Center for Philosophy and History of Science, Boston Univ, Boston, MA, 02115. **EMAIL** atauber@bu.edu

TAVANI, HERMAN
PERSONAL m, 1 child **DISCIPLINE** PHILOSOPHY, PHILOSOPHY AND COMPUTERS **EDUCATION** West Chester Univ, BA, MA; Temple Univ, PhD. **CAREER** Assoc prof, ch, dept Philos, dir, Lib Stud prog, Rivier Col; Vis Sci in Occup Hea, Harvard Univ; vis scholar, assoc fel, Dartmouth Hum Inst; assoc ed, Comput and Soc; bk rev ed, Ethics and Infor Technol; software tech writer, publ supvr, Digital Equip Corp. **MEMBERSHIPS** Pres, Northern New Eng Philos Asn; Am Philos Asn. **SELECTED PUBLICATIONS** Auth, Facts, Opinions, and Value Judgments, InSight, Vol 1, No 2, 94; Teaching Computer Ethics, Comput and Soc, Vol 25, No 2, 95; Ethical Issues for Computer Professionals, Comput and Soc, Vol 25, No 3, 95; Rev of Technology and the Future, 6th ed (ed Albert H. Teich, St Martin's Press, 93). Comput and Soc, Vol 25, No 3, 95; Ethical Issues in the Use of Computers, Comput and Soc, Vol 25, No 4, 95; Computer Matching and Personal Privacy: Can They be Compatible?, in Comput and the Qual of Life (CQL '96): Symp Proc (ed Chuck Huff), ACM Press, 96; CyberEthics and the Future of Computing, Comput and Soc, Vol 26, No 2, 96; Personal Privacy in the Information Age: An Ethical Dilemma, InSight, Vol 3, No 1, 96; The Future of Computing and the Quality of Life, Comput and Soc, Vol 26, No 3, 96; A Bibliography for CPSR and Its Members: Computing, Ethics and Social Responsibility, CPSR Newsl, Vol 14, No 3, 96; Selecting a Computer Ethics Coursebook: A Comparative Study of Five Recent Works, Comput and Soc, Vol 26, N **CONTACT ADDRESS** Rivier Col, Nashua, NH, 03060-5086. **EMAIL** htavani@rivier.edu

TAYLOR, ANGUS
DISCIPLINE PHILOSOPHY **EDUCATION** Queen's Univ, BA; Univ Toronto, MA; Univ Sussex, MSc; York Univ, PhD. **CAREER** Vis asst prof. **RESEARCH** Social and political thought; ethics; and the interrelations of science; nature and society. **SELECTED PUBLICATIONS** Pub(s), Philos of the Soc Sci; Environ Ethics. **CONTACT ADDRESS** Dept of Philosophy, Victoria Univ, PO Box 3045, Victoria, BC, V8W 3P4.

TAYLOR, CHARLES
DISCIPLINE PHILOSOPHY **EDUCATION** Univ Oxford, PhD. **CAREER** Vis prof, Northwestern Univ. **RESEARCH** Ethics, Social and Political Philosophy, Modern European Philosophy. **SELECTED PUBLICATIONS** Auth, Hegel and Modern Society; Philosophical Papers I & II; Sources of the Self. **CONTACT ADDRESS** Dept of Philosophy, Northwestern Univ, 1801 Hinman, Evanston, IL, 60208.

TAYLOR, FELICIA MICHELLE
PERSONAL Born 02/14/1960, Concord, NC, s **DISCIPLINE** CRIMINAL LAW **EDUCATION** Cabarrus Community College, private pilot ground school, 1982; Univ of North Carolina, Chapel Hill, BA, sociology, 1982, Charlotte, MS, criminal justice, 1984; Florida State Univ, PhD, criminology, 1987. **CAREER** Univ of NC at Charlotte, admissions counselor, 1983-84; Barber-Scotia Clg, administrative asst for financial planning and development, 1984-85; Shaw Univ at Raleigh, professor, 1985-87, CAPE Ctr at Wilmington, adjunct professor, 1992; The Florida State Univ, instructor, 1988-91, Academic Support Services, tutor, 1989-91; Florida A&M Univ, adjunct professor, 1990-91; Florida Department of Hlth and Rehabilitative Services, abuse registry counselor, 1991; Univ of NC at Wilmington, guest lecturer, 1992; Federal Bureau of Prisons, research analyst, 1992-; SHAW UNIVERSITY, RALEIGH, NC, PROFESSOR OF CRIMINAL JUSTICE, 1993-. **HONORS AND AWARDS** Honor Court, UNC Chapel Hill, 1980-82; UNC Charlotte, First graduate of Masters of Science Degree in Criminal Justice/Management Program, 1984; Patricia Roberts Harris Fellowship, 1987-. **MEMBERSHIPS** Sweet Carolines 1980-82; Young Democrats 1982-83, Cloud Cappers Ltd Assn 1982-; Delta Sigma Theta, Inc 1984-; CVAN, Volunteer Assn for Battered Women, 1985; intake counselor, Probation & Parole, 1983-84; counselor Mecklenburg Co Charlotte; chmn UNICEF; Hall Rep 1980-81; UNC-Ch sec of dorm 1981-82; UNC Chapel Hill co-chmn 1st UNCF Tennis Tourn in Cabarrus Co; Advisor, Society of Criminal Justice 1985-87; Cooperative Colleges Task Force, 1986; American Criminal Justice Society, 1987-; Criminology Association, 1987-; Academy Criminal Justice Sciences, 1989-90; Guardian Ad Litem, 1988-; mediator, Durham County Mediation Svcs, 1996-; mem, Supreme Court Historical Society, 1994-. **SELECTED PUBLICATIONS** Author, works presented: Conference for Social Problems, "Gender Bias Amongst State Institutional Drug Treatment Programs," April 1990; "Effects of Pornography on Women," April 1988; Assn of Criminal Justice Professionals, "History of Women's Prisons in the State of Florida"; Southern Conference, "Role Play," 1987. **CONTACT ADDRESS** PO Box 51751, Durham, NC, 27717.

TAYLOR, G.H.
PERSONAL Born 06/15/1951, Cambridge, MA, m, 1989, 1 child **DISCIPLINE** LAW **EDUCATION** Boston Univ, AB, 73; Univ Chicago, MA, 76, PhD cand; Harvard Law Sch, JD, 88. **CAREER** Asst prof, 89-95, assoc prof, 95- , Univ Pittsburgh. **HONORS AND AWARDS** Phi Beta Kappa. **MEMBERSHIPS** Am Soc for Pol and Legal Philos. **RESEARCH** Hermeneutics; legal hermeneutics; statutory construction. **SELECTED PUBLICATIONS** Auth, Structural Textualism, BU Law Rev, 95; auth, Textualism at Work, DePaul Law Rev, 95 **CONTACT ADDRESS** School of Law, Univ of Pittsburgh, Pittsburgh, PA, 15260. **EMAIL** taylor@law.pitt.edu

TAYLOR, GENE FRED
PERSONAL Born 07/13/1941, Florence, AL, m, 1964, 1 child **DISCIPLINE** PHILOSOPHY, HUMANITIES **EDUCATION** Florence State Col, BS, 65; FL State Univ, MME, 65, PhD, 69. **CAREER** Assoc prof, 69-76, Prof Philos, Ala A&M Univ, 76-, Evaluator, Comt for Hum in AL. **HONORS AND AWARDS** MA, St John's Col, NM, 75. **MEMBERSHIPS** Am Philos Asn. **RESEARCH** The cognitive status of aesthetic experience. **SELECTED PUBLICATIONS** Auth, The philosophical basis of scientific linguistics, Ala A&M Univ Fac Res J, 8/76. **CONTACT ADDRESS** Dept of Behavioral Sci, Alabama A&M Univ, PO Box 229, Normal, AL, 35762-0285. **EMAIL** gtaylor@asnaam.aamu.edu

TAYLOR, GRACE W.
DISCIPLINE LAW **EDUCATION** Fla State Univ, AB, MA; Univ Fla, JD. **CAREER** Clarence J. TeSelle prof and dir, Legal Inf Ctr, Univ Fla, 62-. **HONORS AND AWARDS** Marian Gould Gallagher Distinguished Service awd, Amer Asn Law Libraries, 97; Marta Lange/Congressional Quart awd, Law and Polit Sci Sect of the Asn Col and Res Libraries, 97. **MEMBERSHIPS** NCAIR bd Trustees, 78-96; AALL; Beta Phi Mu; Phi Beta Kappa, UF chap pres. **RESEARCH** Computers & the law. **CONTACT ADDRESS** School of Law, Univ of Florida, PO Box 117625, Gainesville, FL, 32611-7625. **EMAIL** lawbt@nervm.nerdc.ufl.edu

TAYLOR, JAMES E.
PERSONAL Born 06/28/1956, Portland, OR, m, 1981, 3 children **DISCIPLINE** PHILOSOPHY **EDUCATION** Westmont Col, BA, philos, 78; Fuller Theol Sem, MA, 81; Univ Ariz, MA, 85, PhD, 87. **CAREER** Asst to assoc prof, Bowling Green State Univ, 87-93; assoc prof, Westmont Col, 94-. **HONORS AND AWARDS** Phi Beta Kappa, Univ Ariz, 88; summa cum laude grad, Westmont Col, 78. **MEMBERSHIPS** Amer Philos Asn; Soc of Christ Philos; Phi Sigma Tau philos honor soc; Phi Beta Kappa; Phi Kappa Phi. **RESEARCH** Epistemology; Metaphysics; Philosophy of language; Philosophy of religion. **SELECTED PUBLICATIONS** Rev, The Concept of Faith: A Philosophical Investigation, Philos Books, 96; auth, Plantinga on Epistemic Warrant, Philos and Phenomenol Res, 95; rev, Does God's Existence Need Proof?, Intl Jour for Philos of Relig, 95; rev, Christian Belief in a Postmodern World: The Full Wealth of Conviction, Zygon, 95; rev, The Logic of Rational Theism: Exploratory Essays, Intl Jour for Philos of Relig, 94. **CONTACT ADDRESS** Dept. of Philosophy, Westmont Col, Santa Barbara, CA, 93108. **EMAIL** taylor@westmont.edu

TAYLOR, JON
PERSONAL Born 06/30/1938, Gays Mills, WI, 1938 children **DISCIPLINE** HEBREW SCRIPTURES **EDUCATION** Pontifical Bibl Inst, SSL, 70. **CAREER** Prof Relig, Univ Great Falls, 85-. **MEMBERSHIPS** CBA; AAR; SBL; ASOR; HIART. **RESEARCH** Science and religion. **CONTACT ADDRESS** 1301 20th St S, Great Falls, MT, 59405. **EMAIL** jtaylor01@ugf.edu

TAYLOR, MICHAEL JOSEPH
PERSONAL Born 01/05/1924, Tacoma, WA **DISCIPLINE** THEOLOGY **EDUCATION** Gonzaga Univ, BA, 47, MA, 49; Santa Clara Univ, STM, 55; Woodstock Col, STD, 61. **CAREER** Instr humanities, Bellarmine Prep Sch, 48-51; instr theol, Gonzaga Univ, 56-59; from asst prof to assoc prof, 61-72, Prof Relig Studies, Seattle Univ, 73-94, prof emer, 95-; Lilly fel, 64-65; consult, Idaho Ecumenical Conf, 68; vis prof, Seton Hall Univ, 69-71. **MEMBERSHIPS** Col Theol Soc. **RESEARCH** Sacramental theology; Pauline and Johannine scripture studies. **SELECTED PUBLICATIONS** Auth, Protestant Liturgical Renewal: A Catholic Viewpoint, Newman Press, 63; Liturgy and Christian Unity, with R P Marshall, Prentice-Hall, 65; ed, Liturgical Renewal in the Christian Churches, Helicon, 67; The Sacred and the Secular, Prentice, 68; The Mystery of Sin and Forgiveness, Alba House, 71; Sex: Thoughts for Contemporary Christians, Doubleday, 72; The Mystery of Suffering and Death, 73, A Companion to Paul: Readings in Pauline Theology, 75, A Companion to John: Readings in Johannine Theology, 77 & The Sacraments: Readings in Contemporary Sacramental Theology, 81, Alba House; John, the Different Gospel, Alba House, 83; The Sacraments as Encasement, Liturgical Press, 86; Paul: His Letters, Message and Heritage--A Reflective Commentary, Alba House, 97. **CONTACT ADDRESS** PO Box 80651, Seattle, WA, 98108.

TAYLOR, PATRICIA E.
PERSONAL Born 02/17/1942, New Haven, m **DISCIPLINE** LAW **EDUCATION** IL Inst Tech, BS 1967; Yale Law School, JD, 1971. **CAREER** Commun Prog Inc, commun wrkr 1963-65; Onondaga Lega Svc, law clk 1971-73; Princeton U, vis lctr 1974-. **HONORS AND AWARDS** Reginald Herber Smith Fellow 1971-73; Outst Yng Wmn Am 1974. **MEMBERSHIPS** Mem NJ Bar Assn; US Sup Ct Bar; Allan Guttmacher Institute, bd of dir, 1986-89; assoc Gen Couns Educ Testing Serv Princeton NJ; bd dir ARC 1972-73. **CONTACT ADDRESS** Educ Testing Serv, Rosedale Rd, Princeton, NJ, 08541.

TAYLOR, RAYMOND HARGUS
PERSONAL Born 10/04/1913, Bell County, KY, m, 1954, 2 children **DISCIPLINE** RELIGION **EDUCATION** Cumberland Ky Col, AA, 51; Carson-Newman Col, BA, 53; Southern Baptist Theol Sem, BD, 56, ThD, 61. **CAREER** Pastor, Mt Carmel Baptist Church, Ky, 57-61; Min Christian educ, Temple Baptist Church, NC, 61-63; Chaplain Col, Chowan Col, 63-90; asst pres & dir, Denominational Rel(s), Chowan Col, 90-91; chemn, Dept Rel and Philos, Chowan Col, 91-; deacon, Murfreesboro Baptist Church; bd dir, Hertford County Habitat for Humanity; bd dir, NC Baptist Hist Soc; coord coun, CBF NC. **MEMBERSHIPS** Am Acad Rel; Am Soc of Church Hist; Nat Asn Baptist Prof Rel; NC Baptist Hist Soc; Soc Bibl Lit; Southern Baptist Hist Soc; VA Baptist Hist Soc; William H Whittsitt Baptist Heritage Soc. **RESEARCH** Hist Research & Writing; Drama; Music; Genealogical Research. **SELECTED PUBLICATIONS** Auth, The Baptist Church at Cashie, 1770-1970, 70; A Century and a Quarter of Service: A History of Murfreesboro Church, 1848-1973, 73; Seventy-Five Years of Loving, Sharing, Caring: A History of Winter Park Baptist Church, 1913-1988, 89; Partners in Missions and Ministry: A History of Flat River Baptist Association, 93; The Heritage of a Century: A History of Chadbourn Baptist Church, 1890-1990, 93; Remembering the Past-Renewing the Future: A History of North Rocky Mount Baptist Church, 1895-1995, 96; contrib articles for publ in, Dictionary NC Biog, Encycl Southern Baptists & Mercer Dictionary of the Bible. **CONTACT ADDRESS** Dept of Relig, Chowan Col, 200 Jones Dr, PO Box 1848, Murfreesboro, NC, 27855.

TAYLOR, RICHARD STUART
PERSONAL Born 06/24/1942, Chicago, IL **DISCIPLINE** AMERICAN HISTORY, HISTORY OF RELIGION **EDUCATION** Wheaton Col, Ill, BA, 64; Northern Ill Univ, MA, 70, PhD(hist), 77. **CAREER** Publ ed, 78-80, DIR OFF RES & PUBL, HIST SITES DIV, ILL DEPT CONSERV, 80- **MEMBERSHIPS** AHA; Am Soc Church Hist; Orgn Am Historians; Soc Historians Early Am Repub. **RESEARCH** Evangelicalism in 19th century America; antebellum reform; new thought in the 1920s. **SELECTED PUBLICATIONS** Auth, Preachers--Billy Sunday, and Big-Time American Evangelism, J Am Hist, Vol 80, 93; Between Memory and Reality--Family and Community in Rural Wisconsin, 1870-1970, J Interdisciplinary Hist, Vol 26, 95. **CONTACT ADDRESS** Illinois Historical Preservation Agency, 523 W Monroe Apt 1, Springfield, IL, 62704.

TAYLOR, RODNEY
DISCIPLINE RELIGIOUS STUDIES **EDUCATION** Columbia Univ, PhD. **CAREER** Prof. **SELECTED PUBLICATIONS** Auth, The Religious Dimensions of Confucianism; The Confucian Way of Contemplation; co-auth, They Shall Not Hurt: Human Suffering and Human Caring; pubs on Confucianism as a religious tradition, Neo-Confucian spiritual cultivation, Confucian meditation, and Confucian autobiography. **CONTACT ADDRESS** Religious Studies Dept, Univ of Colorado, Boulder, Boulder, CO, 80309. **EMAIL** Rodney.Taylor@Colorado.edu

TAYLOR, VELANDE P.
PERSONAL Born 09/10/1923, New York, NY, m, 1961 **DISCIPLINE** LITERATURE, PHILOSOPHY **EDUCATION** Hunter Col, BA, 44; Columbia Univ, MA, 45, PhD, 47. **CAREER** Instr, Paul Smiths Col, 46-47; asst prof, East Carolina Univ, 47-59; prof, head hum dept, Colorado Women's Col, 59-66; vis prof. St Mary's Univ, 66-69; prof, Middle Georgia Col, 69-72; prof, writer in residence and ed, Acad J, 74-84, Hong Kong Baptist Col; section ed, URAM J of Int Stud in the Philos of Understanding, 84-89; WordCraft by Lan, 93- ; ed, publ WordCraft Books, 96- . **HONORS AND AWARDS** Int Mark Twain Soc, 47; Freedom Found Order of the Dannebrog, 51, Bronze Medal, 52, Gold Medal, 52. **MEMBERSHIPS** APA; Acad of Am Poets; Int soc of Authors and Artists. **SELECTED PUBLICATIONS** Auth, Homilies in the Marketplace: Parables for Our Rimes, 96; Copper Flowers, 96; Walking Songs, 97; ZBYX: Tokens, 97; Tales from the Archetypal World, 98; Flowing Water, Singing Sand: The Metaphysics of Change, 99; Beside the Still Water, 99; Mode & Muse: Companions on the Journey, forthcoming. **CONTACT ADDRESS** 910 Marion St, #1008, Seattle, WA, 98104-1273.

TAYLOR, WILLIAMSON S.
PERSONAL Born 09/09/1942, m, 1970, 2 children **DISCIPLINE** THEOLOGY **EDUCATION** Boston Univ, School of Theology, ThD, 89. **CAREER** Assoc Dir Ministerial Studies, 86-92, Harvard Divinity School; Sr Pastor, St. Mark's UCC Church, Boston, 84-94; Adjunct Lectr, Florida Intl Univ, 98-. **MEMBERSHIPS** Amer Assoc Religion; Soc Biblical Lit. **RESEARCH** New Testament; comparative religions; personality and culture **CONTACT ADDRESS** 3102 Hollywood Blvd., Hollywood, FL, 33021.

TAYLOR, JR., WALTER F.
DISCIPLINE NEW TESTAMENT **EDUCATION** Midland Lutheran Col, BA, 69; Lutheran Theol Sem, MDiv, 73; Claremont Grad Sch, PhD, 98. **CAREER** Greek instr, S Calif Sch Theol, 73-76; asst prof, 81-84; assoc prof, 84-91; vis prof, Univ Heidelberg, 88-89; prof, Trinity Lutheran Sem, 91-95; Ernest W. and Edith S. Ogram prof, 96-. **SELECTED PUBLICATIONS** Auth, Obligation: Foundation for Paul's Ethics, Trinity Sem Rev, 98, Josephinum Jour Theol, 98; Romans: New Life in Christ Jesus, Inspire, Augsburg, 98; Cultural Anthropology as a Tool for Studying the New Testament: Part II, Trinity Sem Rev, 97; Jesus Within His Social World: Insights from Archaeology, Sociology, and Cultural Anthropology, Word & World, Supplement 3, 97; Cultural Anthropology as a Tool for Studying the New Testament: Part I, Trinity Sem Rev, 96; Captive and Free: Insights From Galatians, Intersections, Augsburg, 95; Reclaiming Revelation, The Lutheran, 93-94. **CONTACT ADDRESS** Bible Dept, Trinity Lutheran Sem, 2199 E Main St, Columbus, OH, 43209-2334. **EMAIL** wtaylor@trinity.capital.edu

TEEHAN, JOHN
PERSONAL Born 03/12/1962, Brooklyn, NY, m, 1987, 2 children **DISCIPLINE** PHILOSOPHY **EDUCATION** Queens Col, MA, 87; Grad Ctr, PHD, 92 **CAREER** Asst Prof of Philos, 89-98, Hofstra Univ; Asst Prof of Philos, 98-pres, Sch for Univ Stud **MEMBERSHIPS** Am Philos Assoc; Am Psych Assoc; Soc of Humanist Philos **RESEARCH** Evolution & Theories of Self & Ethics; Genetic Engineering & Ethics **SELECTED PUBLICATIONS** Auth, "What's a Philosopher to Do," Metaphilosophy, 94; Auth, "In Defense of a Naturalism," Journal of Speculative Philos, 96 **CONTACT ADDRESS** School for Univ Studies, 130 Hofstra Univ, Hempstead, NY, 11549.

TEISER, STEPHEN F.
DISCIPLINE RELIGIOUS STUDIES; EAST ASIAN STUDIES **EDUCATION** Oberlin Col, AB, 78; Princeton Univ, MA, 83; PhD, 86. **CAREER** Vis asst prof, Middlebury Col, 86-87; asst prof, Univ S Ccalif, 87-88; prof dept of religion, Princrton Univ, 88- ; **HONORS AND AWARDS** ACLS Award Best Book Hist Relig, 88; AAS Joseph Levenson Award Best Book Chinese Studies, 94. **MEMBERSHIPS** Asn Asian Studies; Am Acad Relig; Soc Study Chinese Relig; Am Asn Study Relig. **RESEARCH** Chinese Buddhism; manuscripts from Dunhuang. **SELECTED PUBLICATIONS** Auth, The Growth in Purgatory, Religion and Society in T'ang and Sung China, Univ Hawaii Press, 93; The Scripture on the Ten Kings and the Making of Purgatory in Medieval Chinese Buddhism, Univ Hawaii, 94; Popular Religion, Chinese Religion: The State of the Field, Jour Asian Studies, 95; Introduction: The Spirits of Chinese Religion, Religions of China in Practice, Princeton Univ Press, 96; The Ghost Festival in Medieval China, Princeton Univ Press 88. **CONTACT ADDRESS** Dept of Religion, Princeton Univ, Seventy-Nine Hall, Princeton, NJ, 08544-1006. **EMAIL** sfteiser@princeton.edu

TEMPLIN, JOHN ALTON
PERSONAL Born 09/27/1927, Hoehne, CO, m, 1952, 3 children **DISCIPLINE** RELIGION **EDUCATION** Univ Denver, BA, 50; Iliff Sch Theol, ThM, 53, ThD(church hist), 56; Harvard Univ, PhD, 66. **CAREER** Youth dir, assoc minister & minister, Denver, Co!o, 50-54; instr & dir relig life, Southwestern Col, Kans, 54-57; minister to youth, First Congregational Church, Waltham, Mass, 57-61; assoc minister, Wesley Methodist Church, Springfield, Mass, 61-64; minister, W Methodist Church, Fitchburg, Mass, 64-66; asst prof Europ hist, Univ SDak, 66-67; assoc prof, 67-78, PROF CHURCH HIST & HIST THEOL, ILIFF SCH THEOL, 78-, Travel & res grant, Netherlands, 73-74. **MEMBERSHIPS** Am Acad Relig; Am Soc Church Hist; Am Soc Reformation Res; AHA. **RESEARCH** American church history; history of rel:gions; Protestant reformation. **SELECTED PUBLICATIONS** Auth, The 1000 Generation Covenant--Dutch-Reformed Covenant Theology and Group Identity in Colonial South-Africa, 1652-1814, Church Hist, Vol 63, 94; The Piety of Afrikaans Women--Diaries of Guilt, Church Hist, Vol 66, 97; ed, History of the Church of South-Africa--A Document and Source-Book, Church Hist, Vol 62, 93. **CONTACT ADDRESS** Iliff Sch of Theol, 2201 S University Blvd, Denver, CO, 80210.

TENENBAUM, SERGIO
DISCIPLINE ETHICS, HISTORY OF MODERN PHILOSOPHY, PRACTICAL REASON **EDUCATION** Hebrew Univ Jerusalem, BA, 88; Univ Pittsburgh, MA, 93, PhD, 96. **CAREER** Asst prof, Univ NMex. **SELECTED PUBLICATIONS** Auth, Hegel's Critique of Kant in the Philosophy of Right, in Kant Studien; Realists without a Cause: Deflationary Theories of Truth and Ethical Realism, Can J of Philos. **CONTACT ADDRESS** Univ NMex, Albuquerque, NM, 87131.

TEPLY, LARRY L.
DISCIPLINE LAW **EDUCATION** Univ Nebr, BA, 69; Univ Fla, JD, 72; Harvard Univ, LLM, 73. **CAREER** Prof, Creighton Univ; staff atty, US Fed Trade Comn, 76-77. **MEMBERSHIPS** Order of the Coif. **SELECTED PUBLICATIONS** Auth, Legal Research and Citation, 4th ed, West, 92; Legal Writing, Analysis, & Oral Argument, West, 90; Legal Negotiation in a Nutshell, West, 92; coauth, Civil Procedure, Foundation Press, 94; pub(s), Yale Law J; Creighton Law Rev; Tulane Law Rev; Univ Fla Law Rev; Univ Miami Law Rev; J Health Politics; Policy and Law; Hastings Int and Comp Law Rev & Trademark Reporter. **CONTACT ADDRESS** School of Law, Creighton Univ, 2500 California Plaza, Omaha, NE, 68178. **EMAIL** teply@culaw.creighton.edu

TEREZAKIS, KATIE
PERSONAL Born 01/08/1972, CT **DISCIPLINE** PHILOSOPHY **EDUCATION** New School for Social Research, PhD, in progress. **RESEARCH** Political philosophy, Neitzsche, Marx, Hegel, German Idealism. **SELECTED PUBLICATIONS** Auth, Ruthless Criticism/Relentless Creation, Marx, Neitzsche and the End of Modern Society. **CONTACT ADDRESS** Dept of Philosophy, New Sch for Social Research, 65 5th Ave, New York, NY, 10011.

TERMINI, ROSEANN B.
DISCIPLINE LEGAL WRITING AND APPELLATE ADVOCACY **EDUCATION** Drexel Univ, BS, 75; Temple Univ, Med, 79; Temple Univ Sch Law, JD, 85. **CAREER** Instr, Villanova Univ; clerked, Honorable Donald E. Wieand, Superior Ct Pa; past regulatory aff atty, Pa Power and Light; past sr dep atty gen, Off Atty Gen, Commonwealth Pa; taught at, Dickinson Law Sch; past adj prof, Widener Univ Sch Law; **SELECTED PUBLICATIONS** Publ on, consumer contract law, the envt, food pharmaceutical and med device law. **CONTACT ADDRESS** Law School, Villanova Univ, 800 Lancaster Ave, Villanova, PA, 19085-1692. **EMAIL** termini@law.vill.edu

TERNES, HANS
PERSONAL Born 09/10/1937, Kogolniceanu, Romania, m, 1962, 2 children **DISCIPLINE** GERMAN LITERATURE, AESTHETICS **EDUCATION** Univ Il, BA, 61, MA, 63; Univ Pa, PhD, 68. **CAREER** Lectr English, Univ Freiburg, Ger, 65-66; instr Ger, Univ Pa, 66-68; asst prof, 68-75, assoc prof Ger, Lawrence Univ, 76-. **MEMBERSHIPS** Am Asn Teachers Ger; MLA. **RESEARCH** Twentieth century German literature, primarily Thomas Mann, Friedrich Durrenmatt, Franz Kafka; problems in aesthetics, the grotesque; genre studies, nature poetry. **SELECTED PUBLICATIONS** Auth, Das Problem der Gerechtigkeit in Durrenmatts Die Panne, Germanic Notes, 75; Das Groteske in den Werken Thomas Manns, Stuttgarter Arbeiten zur Germanistik, 75; Anmerkungen zur Zeitblomgestalt, Germanic Notes, 76; co-ed, Probleme der Komparatistik & Interpretation, Festschrift for Prof Andre von Gronicka, Bouvier Vlg, Bonn, 78; contribr, Franz Kafka's Hunter Gracchus: an interpretation, Festschrift for Prof Andre von Gronicka, 78; Das Bild des Helden in DDR Roman, Rocky Mtn Rev, 83; The fantastic in the works of Franz Kafha, The Scope of the Fantastic, Greenwood, Inc, 85; Wolfgang Ammon Ein Deutsch-Brasilianischer Schriftsteller, Hans Staden-Jahrbuch, Sao Paulo, 86; Franz Xaver Kroetz, Magill's Critical Survey of Drama: Foreign Languages, Salem Press Ca, 86. **CONTACT ADDRESS** Dept of German, Lawrence Univ, 115 S Drew St, Appleton, WI, 54911-5798. **EMAIL** Hans.Ternes@Lawrence.edu

TERRELL, FRANCIS D'ARCY
PERSONAL Born 05/13/1940, Caledonia, NY, m **DISCIPLINE** LAW **EDUCATION** Univ of Toledo, BS 1970; Columbia Law School, JD 1973. **CAREER** Shearman & Sterling, assoc Attorney 1973-75; Private Practice, LAW 1975-77; Jones & Terrell, partner 1977-82; Bronx Comm Coll, deputy chmn/prof 1982-. **HONORS AND AWARDS** Lt col 20 yrs; Bronze Star; Air Medal; Meritorious Serv Medal; Commendation Medal; Combat Infantry Badge. **MEMBERSHIPS** Mem Amer Business Law Assocs 1984-. **CONTACT ADDRESS** Dept of Business, Bronx Comm Col, CUNY, W 181st & Univ Ave, Bronx, NY, 10453.

TERRELL, HUNTINGTON
PERSONAL Born 10/07/1925, Syracuse, NY, m, 1950, 3 children **DISCIPLINE** PHILOSOPHY, PEACE STUDIES **EDUCATION** Colgate Univ, AB, 44; Harvard Univ, AM, 48, PhD, 56. **CAREER** From instr to assoc prof, 51-67, dir gen educ course in Philos & Relig, 58-63, prof Philos, Colgate Univ, 67-, spec auditor Govt & Philos, Harvard Univ, 68-69; vis fel, Princeton Univ, 64 & 76-77, ret 98. **MEMBERSHIPS** Am Philos Asn; Soc Philos & Pub Affairs. **RESEARCH** Political, international, ecomonic, environmental ethics. **SELECTED PUBLICATIONS** Auth, Moral objectivity and moral freedom, Ethics, 1/65; Are moral considerations always overriding?, Australasian J Philos, 5/69. **CONTACT ADDRESS** Colgate Univ, 13 Oak Dr, Hamilton, NY, 13346 1379.

TERRELL, TIMOTHY PRATER
PERSONAL Born 10/02/1949, Kyoto, Japan, m, 1969, 2 children **DISCIPLINE** LAW, LEGAL PHILOSOPHY **EDUCATION** Univ Md, BA, 71; Yale Univ, JD, 74; Oxford Univ, dipl, 80. **CAREER** Assoc, Kilpatrick & Cody, 74-76; asst prof property trusts & estates, 76-78, ASSOC PROF PROPERTY JURISPRUDENCE, SCH LAW, EMORY UNIV, 78-, Vis prof, Col Law, Univ Iowa, 79. **RESEARCH** Property rights and legal theory; moral philosophy; economic theory and its relation to law and ethics. **SELECTED PUBLICATIONS** Auth, Ethics with an Attitude--Comments on New Directions for Keck Philanthropy, Law Contemp Problems, Vol 58, 95. **CONTACT ADDRESS** Law Sch, Emory Univ, 1364 Clifton Rd N E, Atlanta, GA, 30322-0001.

TERRY, CHARLES T.
DISCIPLINE LAW **EDUCATION** Stanford Univ, BA; SW Univ Sch Law, JD; NY Univ, LLM. **CAREER** Instr, NY Univ; instr, SW Univ Sch Law; assoc dean, prof, Univ Ill, 90-. **SELECTED PUBLICATIONS** Auth, pubs on combining taxation, finance, and economics. **CONTACT ADDRESS** Law Dept, Univ Ill Urbana Champaign, 52 E Gregory Dr, Champaign, IL, 61820. **EMAIL** cterry@law.uiuc.edu

TERRY, J. MARK
DISCIPLINE CHRISTIAN MISSIONS AND EVANGELISM **EDUCATION** John Brown Univ, BS; Southwestern Baptist Theol Sem, MDiv, PhD. **CAREER** Prof, S Baptist Missionary, Philippines; A. P. and Faye Stone assoc prof, 93; assoc dean, Billy Graham Sch Missions, Evangel and Church Growth. **HONORS AND AWARDS** Dir, Globalization Proj. **MEMBERSHIPS** Mem, Evangel Missiological Soc; Amer Soc Missiology; Acad for Evangel in Theol Edu. **SELECTED PUBLICATIONS** Auth, Evangelism: A Concise History, auth, Church Evangelism. **CONTACT ADDRESS** Billy Graham Sch Missions, Evangel and Church Growth, Southern Baptist Theol Sem, 2825 Lexington Rd, Louisville, KY, 40280. **EMAIL** mterry@sbts.edu

TESCHNER, GEORGE A.
DISCIPLINE PHILOSOPHY **EDUCATION** Rutgers Univ, BA; NY Univ, MA; grad fac, New Sch for Soc Res, MA, PhD. **CAREER** Philos, Christopher Newport Univ. **SELECTED PUBLICATIONS** Auth, The Concept of Justice in Computer Managed Telecommunications Featured in Horizons of Justice, Peter Lang Publ, 96. **CONTACT ADDRESS** Dept of Philos, Christopher Newport Univ, 1 University Place Newport News, Newport News, VA, 23606. **EMAIL** teschner@cnu.edu

TESELLE, EUGENE A.
PERSONAL Born 08/08/1931, Ames, IA, m, 1978, 5 children **DISCIPLINE** THEOLOGY **EDUCATION** Univ of Colo, BA, 52; Princeton Theological Seminary, BD, 55; Yale Univ, MA, 60, PhD, 63. **CAREER** Asst minister, First Presbyterian Church of East Orange, 55-58; instr, 62-63; asst prof, Dept of Religious Studies, Yale Univ, 63-69; assoc prof, 69-74, prof, Vanderbilt Divinity School, 74-. **HONORS AND AWARDS** Phi Beta Kappa, 52; Presbyterian Grad Fel, 58; Rockefeller Doctoral Fel, 60; Kent Fel, 61; Thomas Jefferson Award, Vanderbilt Univ, 96. **MEMBERSHIPS** Am Acad of Religion; Am Soc of Church Hist; Soc for Early Christian Studies. **RESEARCH** History of doctrine; theology in the reformed tradition; religion in contemporary society. **SELECTED PUBLICATIONS** Auth, Augustine the Theologian, Herder & Herder, 70; Augustine's Strategy as an Apologist, Villanova Univ Press, 74; Christ in Context: Divine Purpose and Human Possibility, Fortress Press, 75; Thomas Aquinas: Faith and Reason, Graded Press, 88; Living in Two Cities: Augustinian Trajectories in Political Thought, Univ of Scranton Press, forthcoming. **CONTACT ADDRESS** Divinity School, Vanderbilt Univ, Nashville, TN, 37240. **EMAIL** eugene.a.teselle@vanderbilt.edu

TESKE, ROLAND JOHN
PERSONAL Born 10/29/1934, Milwaukee, WI **DISCIPLINE** PHILOSOPHY **EDUCATION** St Louis Univ, BA, 58, MA, 59, PhL, 59, STL, 66; Univ Toronto, PhD(philos), 73. **CAREER** Instr philos, Marquette Univ, 70-73; asst prof, St Louis Univ, 73-74; Asst PROF PHILOS, MARQUETTE UNIV, 74-, Actg dean, Col Philos & Lett, St Louis Univ, 73-74; ed, The Mod Schoolman, 74-76; dir honors prog, Marquette Univ, 78-81. **MEMBERSHIPS** Am Cath Philos Asn; Jesuit Philos Asn. **RESEARCH** Metaphysics; St Augustine; history of philosophy. **SELECTED PUBLICATIONS** Auth, Augustine and the Concepts of Creatio, Conversio, and Formatio--A Systematic Presentation of Augustine Thought, Theol Studies, Vol 53, 92; Augustine and the Limits of Virtue, Theol Studies, Vol 55, 94; Augustine, 'De Doctrina Christiana', J Early Christian Studies, Vol 5, 97; William-Of-Auvergne and the Manichees, Traditio-Studies Ancient Medieval Hist Thought Relig, Vol 48, 93; St-Augustine 'Tractates on the Gospel of John' 112-124, J Early Christian Studies, Vol 5, 97; The Unity of Love for God and Neighbor in Saint Augustine, J Early Christian Studies, Vol 4, 96. **CONTACT ADDRESS** Dept of Philos, Marquette Univ, Milwaukee, WI, 53233.

THAGARD, PAUL
DISCIPLINE PHILOSOPHY **EDUCATION** Univ Toronto, PhD, 77. **RESEARCH** Philos of science; cognitive science; artificial intelligence. **SELECTED PUBLICATIONS** Auth, Conceptual Revolutions, Princeton, 92; Computational Philosophy of Science, MIT, 88; coauth, Induction: Processes of Inference, Learning, and Discovery, MIT, 86; Mental Leaps: Analogy in Creative Thought, MIT, 95. **CONTACT ADDRESS** Dept of Philosophy, Waterloo Univ, 200 University Ave W, Waterloo, ON, N2L 3G1. **EMAIL** pthagard@uwaterloo.ca

THAIN, GERALD JOHN
PERSONAL Born 10/14/1935, Galena, IL, m, 1965, 3 children **DISCIPLINE** LAW **EDUCATION** Univ Iowa, BA, 57, JD, 60. **CAREER** Vis asst prof, Col Human Ecol, Univ Md, 70-74; asst prof law, Univ Wis, 74-76 & Georgetown Univ, 76-77; assoc prof, 77-80, Prof Law, Univ Wis, 80-, Assoc Dean Law, 84-96, Chair, Consumer Law, 92-; Dir, Div Nat Advert Regulation, Fed Trade Comn, 70-73; lectr Food & Drug Law, New York Univ, 73-; co-dir, Ctr Pub Representation, Madison Wis, 77-84, Bd Dir, 98-; scholar in residence, Col Commun, Univ Ill, 80 ; Bd Dir, Consumer Law Litigation Project, 95-; Vis Prof, Giessen Univ (Germany), 95; Vis Prof, Chud Univ (Japan), 97. **HONORS AND AWARDS** N Burkan Copyright Law Contest, Am Soc Composers, Auth & Publ, 60; Distinguished Advert Scholar Award, Univ Ill, 80. **MEMBERSHIPS** Law & Soc Asn. **RESEARCH** Advertising law; administrative law; trade regulation. **SELECTED PUBLICATIONS** Auth, Advertising regulations and new FTC, Fordham Urban Law J, 73; Suffer the Hucksters?, Boston Univ Law Rev, 76; Credit advertising and law, Washington Univ Law Rev, 76; coauth, Public Interest Law, Univ Calif Press, 77; auth, Seven dirty words and FCC, Ky Law J, 79; contribr, White Collar Crime, Free Press, 80; Food Safety Council Final Report, Food Safety Coun, 82; Consumerism in the 1980's, Univ Md Law & Pub Policy Inst, 82; Consumer Law: U.S. & Asia, 96; Cigarette Advertising: Legal vs. Psychological; Constitutional Aspects of Cigarette Regulation, Proceedings of Nat Conf on so-called Tobacco Settlement, Inst for Legal Studies, 97. **CONTACT ADDRESS** Law Sch, Univ of Wis, 975 Bascom Mall, Madison, WI, 53706-1301. **EMAIL** gjthain@law.wisc.edu

THALOS, MARIAM
PERSONAL Born 02/17/1962, Cairo, Egypt, m, 1991, 1 child **DISCIPLINE** PHILOSOPHY **EDUCATION** Univ Ill, PhD, 93. **CAREER** Asst prof, State Univ NY, 93-. **RESEARCH** Philosophy of science; metaphysics; epistemology. **SELECTED PUBLICATIONS** Auth, Naturalism, Philos Educ: An Encyclopedia, 96; auth, Two Dogmas of Naturalized Epistemology, Dialectica, 98; auth, Why We Believe, Jour Gen Philos Sci, Feb, 99; auth, Degrees of Freedom: An Essay on Competitions Between Micro and Macro in Mechanics, Philos & Phenomenol Res, 99; auth, Knowledge in an Age of Individual Economy: A Prolegomenon to Epistemology, Jour Philos Res, 98; auth, The Trouble with Superselection Accounts of Measurement, Philos Sci, 98; auth, A Modest Proposal for Interpreting Structural Explanation, Brit Jour Philos Sci, 98; auth, Conflict and Coordination in the Aftermath of Oracular Statements, Philos Quart, 97; auth, Self-Interest, Autonomy and the Presuppositions of Decision Theory, Am Philos Quart, 97; auth, The Need for Classical Epistemological Foundations: Against a Feminist Alternative, Monist, 94; coauth, Against Conditionalization, Synthese, 90. **CONTACT ADDRESS** Philosophy Dept, SUNY, 607 Baldy Hall, Buffalo, NY, 14260-1010. **EMAIL** thalos@acsu.buffalo.edu

THANDEKA, Null
PERSONAL Born 03/25/1946, Jersey City, NJ **DISCIPLINE** THEOLOGY, PHILOSOPHY OF RELIGION **EDUCATION** Univ Ill, Champaign-Urbana, BS, Journalism, 67; Columbia Univ, MS, Journalism, 68; Univ Calif, Los Angeles, MS, History of Religion, 82; Claremont Grad Sch, PhD, Philosophy of religion and theology, 88. **CAREER** Ast prof, phil/rel, San Francisco State Univ, 87-90; ast prof, William Col, Dept Rel, 91-96; vis sch, Union Theol Sem, 96- 97; Assoc prof theology, culture, Meadville/Lombard Theol Sch, 98-. **HONORS AND AWARDS** Stanford Univ Hum Ctr Fel **MEMBERSHIPS** Am Acad Rel; Unitarian Universalist Ministers Asn; Soc Study Black Rel; Comn on the Status of Women in Academy (AAR). **RESEARCH** Schleiermacher studies; cultural studies; psychoanalytic shame theory. **SELECTED PUBLICATIONS** Auth, I've Known Rivers: Black Theology's Response to Process Theology, Process Studies 18:4, 89; auth, Schleiermacher's Dialektik: The Discovery of the Self that Kant Lost, Harvard Theol Rev, 85:4, 92; auth, The Embodied Self: Friedrich Schleiermacher's Solution to Kant's Problem of the Empirical Self, State Univ of NY Press; auth, The Fate of Black America, Tikkum Mag, Sept/Oct 96; auth, The Self Between Feminist Theory and Theology, in Feminist Thelogy and the Role of Theory, Fortress Press; auth, Learning to be White: Money, Race and God in America, Continuum Pub Co, forthcoming. **CONTACT ADDRESS** Meadville/Lombard Theol Sch, 5701 S Woodlawn Ave, Chicago, IL, 60637. **EMAIL** Thandeka@Meadville.edu

THATCHER, TOM
PERSONAL Born 03/23/1967, m, 1987, 1 child **DISCIPLINE** BIBLICAL LITERATURE **EDUCATION** Cincinnati Bible Col, BA, 89, MA, 92; Cincinnati Bible Sem, MDiv, 92; S Baptist Theol Sem, PhD, 96. **CAREER** Prof, Louisville Bible Col, 92-94; assoc prof, Cincinnati Bible Col & Seminary, 94- . **HONORS AND AWARDS** Salutatorian, Cincinnati Bible Col, 89; Baker Book House Award, Cincinnati Bible Col, 92; Metroversity Graduate Paper Award, 95; Midwest Bible Soc Grad Paper Award, 95. **MEMBERSHIPS** Soc of Biblical Lit; Inst for Biblical Res; Weststar Inst. **RESEARCH** Johannine lit; hist Jesus; Hermenatics; oral tradition. **SELECTED PUBLICATIONS** Auth, Mouth, Temperature, Travel Story, in The Dictionary of Biblical Imagery, IVP 98; Early Christianities and the Synoptic Eclipse: Problems in Situating the Gospel of Thomas, Biblical Inter, 99; John: The Gospel of Ambiguity, Scholars Press, 99; 1 2 3 John, in The Expositor's Bible Commentary, forthcoming; coed, Jesus in Johannine Tradition: New Directions, Fortress, forthcoming. **CONTACT ADDRESS** Cincinnati Bible Col and Sem, 2700 Glenway Ave, Cincinnati, OH, 45204.

THAYER, H.S.
PERSONAL New York, NY, m, 1958, 3 children **DISCIPLINE** PHILOSOPHY **EDUCATION** Bard Col, BA, 45; Columbia Univ, MA, 47, PhD, 49. **CAREER** Instr, 49-54, asst prof, 54-61, philos, Columbia Univ; vis prof, NY Sch of Psychiat, 59-65; asst prof, 61-65, assoc prof & chemn, 65-68, prof, 68-90, philos, CUNY. **HONORS AND AWARDS** Bush Fel, 47, 48; Guggenheim Fel, 70; NEH Fel, 74. **MEMBERSHIPS** APA; Soc for Advanc of Am Philos. **RESEARCH** Ancient Greek philosophy; American philosophy. **SELECTED PUBLICATIONS** Auth, Introduction to Pragmatism & The Meaning of Truth, in, The Works of William James, Harvard, 75; auth, Meaning and Action: A Critical History of Pragmatism, rev ed, Hackett, 81; auth, Objects of Knowledge, in Stuhr, ed, Philosophy and the Reconstruction of Culture, SUNY, 93; auth, Peirce and Truth: Some Reflections, Trans of the C.S. Peirce Soc, 96; auth, Plato's Style: Temporal, Dramatic and Semantic Levels in the Dialogues, in Hart, ed, Plato's Dialogues: The Dialogical Approach, Edwin Mellon, 97. **CONTACT ADDRESS** 4 Salisbury Point, Apt 4B, Nyack, NY, 10960.

THERIAULT, MICHEL
PERSONAL Born 12/02/1942, Toronto, ON, Canada **DISCIPLINE** CANON LAW/HISTORY **EDUCATION** Univ Montreal, Bphil, 62; McGill Univ, MLS, 76; Pontif Univ St Thomas (Rome), JCD, 71. **CAREER** Head acquisitions dept, Univ Montreal Libr, 69-75; chief, Retrospective Nat Biblio Div, Nat Libr Can, 75-85; asst prof, 85-92, ASSOC PROF CANON LAW, ST PAUL UNIV, 92-. **MEMBERSHIPS** Can Canon Law Soc (secy-treas, 88-90, vice-pres, 95-97); Soc Law Eastern Churches (deleg Can, 87-97); Bibliog Soc Can (assoc secy, 81-86). **SELECTED PUBLICATIONS** Auth, Neo-vagin et impuissance, 71; auth, Le livre religieux au Quebec depuis les debuts de l'imprimerie jusqu'a la Confederation 1764-1867, 77; auth, The Institutions of Consecrated Life in Canada from the Beginning of New France up to the Present, 80; ed, Choix et acquisition des documents au Quebec, vol 1, 77; co-ed, Proceedings of the 5th International Congress of Canon Law, 86; co-ed, Code de droit canonique, 90; co-ed, Canonical Studies Presented to Germain Lesage, 91; co-ed, Studia Canonica, Index 1-25 1967-1991, 92; co-ed, Code of Canon Law Annotated, 93; transl, A Manual for Bishops, 94. **CONTACT ADDRESS** Faculty of Canon Law, St Paul Univ, 223 Main St, Ottawa, ON, K1S 1C4.

THIBEAU, MATTHEW J.
PERSONAL Born 12/02/1957, Chicago, IL, m, 1990, 2 children **DISCIPLINE** RELIGION **EDUCATION** Loyola Univ, Chicago, BBA; Univ St Mary of the Lake, Mundelein, IL, M Divinity. **CAREER** Ed consultant, McGraw-Hill; dir, Private/Parochial Marketing, School Div, Macmillan, 89; CA District manager, Macmillan/McGraw-Hill, 90; Dir of Marketing, Wm H. Sadlier, 93; PRESIDENT, BROWN-ROA PUBLISHING CO, 94-. **MEMBERSHIPS** Cath Book Pubs Assoc, brd of dirs; Nat Cath Educational Exhibitors, brd of dirs. **SELECTED PUBLICATIONS** Auth, McGraw-Hill's Reading Teachers Supplement for Faith and Values; coordinated the development of the Integrating Catholic Heritage supplement to The World Around Us (Social Studies prog. **CONTACT ADDRESS** BROWN-ROA, 1665 Embassy West Dr., Suite 200, Dubuque, IA, 52002-2259. **EMAIL** matthew_thibeau@harcourtbrace.com

THIGPEN, CALVIN HERRITAGE
PERSONAL Born 01/07/1924, Greenville, NC, m **DISCIPLINE** MEDICINE, LAW **EDUCATION** VA State Coll, BS 1953; Univ VA, MD 1962, JD 1974. **CAREER** Hopewell, VA, teacher 1953-58; Stuart Prod Co, cosmetics/chem plant mgr 1957-58; Med Coll VA, intern 1962-63; Petersburg General Hosp, staff mem 1963; private practice 1963; VA State Coll, assoc & physician 1964-71; Petersburg Gen Hosp, vice chief/general practice section 1969-70; Office Attorney General VA, intern 1972-73; Univ VA, rsrch asst legal adv 1973-74; Private Practice, Attorney 1975-. **HONORS AND AWARDS** pres, Natl Guardsmen Inc 1967-70; Library Human Resources Amer Bicentennial Rsch Inst 1973; Fellow Amer Coll Legal Med 1976; Mem Bd of Visitors VA State Univ 1978-82; VA Delegate to the White House Conf on Library & Info Serv 1979; Chief of Staff Petersburg Gen Hosp 1980; Diplomate Amer Bd of Legal Med 1982. **MEMBERSHIPS** Mem, Sigma Pi Sigma Natl Physics Hon Soc; Beta Kappa Chi Natl Sci Hon Soc; Phi Delta Phi Legal Fraternity; Dem Com Hopewell 1965-75; bd dir Salvation Army; Hopewell Chamber of Commerce; Old Dominion Med Soc; exec com Old Dominion Med Soc 1965. **CONTACT ADDRESS** 734 South Sycamore St, Petersburg, VA, 23803.

THIRUVENGADAM, RAJ
PERSONAL Born 02/03/1967, Baltimore, MD, s, 1 child **DISCIPLINE** PHILOSOPHY **EDUCATION** Purdue Univ, PhD, 94 **CAREER** Asst Prof, Simmons Col, 94-pres; Assoc Dir, 96-98 **MEMBERSHIPS** Am Philos Assoc; Radical Philos Assoc; Intl Assoc for Philos & Lit; Soc for Asian & Comparative Philos **RESEARCH** Aesthetics; Philosophy of Culture; Asian Philosophy & Religion; Multiculturalism; Social & Political Philosophy **SELECTED PUBLICATIONS** Auth, Getting Tipsy on the Border Between the Banal and the Bizarre: Negotiating Familiarity and Foreignness in Teaching Asian Religions, a presentation to ASIANetwork Conf, Chicago, 96; Democracy as Mass Communicative Action, a presentation to the Philos Dept, Purdue Univ, 94; A Question Before Discourse Ethics: The Problem of the Apostle, a presentation to the Midwest Critical Theory Roundtable, St Louis Univ, 93; How to Read Mass Culture?: A Read-Our-Response Theory, a presentation to the Cultural Studies Collective, Purdue Univ, 93; coauth, What is Enlightened Freedom? An Essay on What Kant Taught Us, in The Long Path to Nearness: A Corporeal Philosophy of Communication, Humanities Press, 97. **CONTACT ADDRESS** Dept of Philos, Simmons Col, 300 The Fenway, Boston, MA, 02115. **EMAIL** rthiruvengad@vmsvax.simmons.edu

THOMAS, CAROLYN
PERSONAL Born 01/29/1936, KY **DISCIPLINE** NEW TESTAMENT **EDUCATION** Union Theol Sem, STM, 81; Fordham Univ, PhD, Bibl stud, 85. **CAREER** Asst prof, NT, 86-89, Gonzaga Univ; prof, 91-, Pontifical Col Josephinum. **HONORS AND AWARDS** Tchng fel, Fordham Univ, 83-85. **MEMBERSHIPS** Cath Bibl Assn; Soc of Bibl Lit. **RE-**

SEARCH Scripture, New Test and evangelization in the church; Philippians **SELECTED PUBLICATIONS** Coauth, You Are Invited, World Lib Pub, 76; auth, Will the Real God Please Stand Up: Healing Our Dysfunctional Images of God, Paulist Press, 91; auth, Gift and Response. A Biblical Spirituality for Contemporary Christians, Paulist Press, 94; art, The Reign of God: The Heart of Mark's Gospel, Josephinum J Theol, 94; art, Economic Issues in Paul, Bible Today 32:5, 94; art, A Mandate for Life: Mark 1:15, Bible Today 33:4, 95; art, Priesthood as Servant-Leadership, Priest 50:11, 94; art, The Priest and Simplicity of Life, Priest 51:10, 95; art, Priesthood and Discipleship, Priest 52:9, 96; art, Every Knee Should Bend, Emmanuel 102:9, 96; auth, Journeys Into John, St Anthony Mes Pres, 98; art, The Millennium: A Time for Reflection, Josephinum J Theol, 98; art, The Priest and the Eucharist, Priest, 98. **CONTACT ADDRESS** 7625 N High St, Columbus, OH, 43235.

THOMAS, CLARENCE
PERSONAL Born 06/23/1948, Pin Point, GA, d **DISCIPLINE** LAW **EDUCATION** Immaculate Conception Seminary, 1967-68; Holy Cross College, BA, 1971; Yale University Law School, JD, 1974. **CAREER** Hill, Jones & Farrington, legal aid, summers, 1971-74; Attorney General John Danforth, State of Missouri, staff member, 1974-77; State of Missouri, asst attorney general, 1974-77; Monsanto Corp, legal counsel, 1977-80; Senator John Danforth, legislative asst, 1979-81; US Federal Govt, Dept of Education, asst secretary for civil rights, 1981-82; Equal Employment Opportunity Commission, chairman, 1982-89; US Court of Appeals for District of Columbia Circuit, appointed circuit judge, 1990-91; UNITED STATES SUPREME COURT JUSTICE, confirmed, 1991-. **MEMBERSHIPS** Black Student Union, Holy Cross College, founder, 1971. **CONTACT ADDRESS** Supreme Court, 1 1st St NE, Washington, DC, 20543-0001.

THOMAS, CLAUDE RODERICK
PERSONAL Born 03/15/1943, Clarksdale, MS, s **DISCIPLINE** LAW **EDUCATION** MI State Univ, BA 1972; Thomas M Cooley Law School, JD 1976. **CAREER** Lansing Police Dept, police officer 1969-75; Ingham Cty Pros Office, asst prosecutor 1976-80; LANSING COMMUNITY COLLEGE, LANSING, MI, ADJUNCT PROF, 1976-; THOMAS M COOLEY LAW SCHOOL, LANDING, MI, ADJUNCT PROF, 1988-; 54A DIST COURT, DISTRICT JUDGE 1981-. **HONORS AND AWARDS** Alumni of the Year Cooley Law School 1981. **MEMBERSHIPS** Mem State Bar Character & Fitness 1977-, Boys Club; bd dir Cooley Credit Union 1980-81; member, Phi Beta Sigma, 1983-. **CONTACT ADDRESS** Lansing City Hall #6, Lansing, MI, 48933.

THOMAS, DAVID
DISCIPLINE RELIGION **EDUCATION** Notre Dame Univ, Doctorate. **CAREER** Instr, Loyola Univ, New Orleans; instr, Saint Louis Univ; instr, St Meinrad Sch Theol; instr, chp, Regis Univ, 81-; adv, Synod on Family Life, Rome; codir, Ctr for Families, Tabor Press. **SELECTED PUBLICATIONS** Auth, The Catholic Catechism: family Style, Tabor Press; We Are Family: Sharing food for the Soul, Tabor Press; In the Midst of Family, and Family Basics: Thriving in the Midst of Threat, Tabor Press. **CONTACT ADDRESS** Regis Univ, Denver, CO, 80221-1099.

THOMAS, DOUGLAS L.
PERSONAL Born 02/28/1945, Jacksonville, Florida, m **DISCIPLINE** LAW **EDUCATION** City Coll NY, BA 1968; Columbia Univ Law Sch, JD 1971. **CAREER** Harvard Law School, teaching fellow faculty; RCA Corp, atty 1973-74; Dewey Ballantine Busby Palmer & Wood, assoc 1971-73; Youth Serv Agy, coord 1971; Youth Serv & Agy, dir 1970; NYC Dept Prob, investigator 1969-71; Harlem Consumer's Union, law asst 1969; Jamaica Comm Corp, dir summer prog 1968; Morningside Comm Center, group leader 1967-68; Prima RE Corp, re salesman 1965-67. **HONORS AND AWARDS** Outstanding achiev awards, goldman scholarship award City Coll Sch Social & Psychol Fndtns; Charles Evan Hughes Fellowship. **MEMBERSHIPS** Mem Assn Bar NYC; NY State Bar Assn Coun Concerned Black Execs; Emerging Black Profl; Intl Law Soc; Black Am Law Students Assn; Omega Psi Phi. **CONTACT ADDRESS** Law Sch, Harvard Univ, Cambridge, MA, 02138.

THOMAS, HERMAN EDWARD
PERSONAL Born 12/12/1941, Bryson City, North Carolina, m **DISCIPLINE** THEOLOGY **EDUCATION** Hartford Sem Fdn, PhD 1978; Duke Univ Divinity Schl, ThM (honors) 1969; Duke Univ Divinity Schl, BD 1966; NCA&T State Univ, BS (cum laude)1963. **CAREER** Berkley HS, Aberdeen, NC, HS teacher 1966-67; Student Affrs, Morris Coll, Sumter, SC, 1968-69; Religion & Phil, Springfield Col, Sprg, MA, instr 1969-74; Black Studies, Springfield Coll, Sprg, MA, coord 1971-74; Rel Stud, asst prof, assoc prof, currently; AAA Studies UNCC, asst dir 1974-86; UTOP, director, 1986-. **HONORS AND AWARDS** Mary Reynolds Babcock Schlrshp Duke Divinity Schl 1963-66; coord-Humanist Afro-Am Hist Project in Charlotte, NC Humanities Comm 1983-83; Religion & Slavery in JWC Pennington Jrnl of ITC 1979. **MEMBERSHIPS** Mem Am Acdmy of Religion 1973-; chair steer commit NC Cncl of Black studies 1975-76; assoc Mnstr First Baptist Church-West 1975-; fdng mem Natl Cncl for Black Studies 1975-; chrmn brd of dir Afro-Amer Cultural Cntr 1979-84; mem Soc for the Study of Black Religion 1980-, recording sec and historian, 1994-97; brd mem Charl-Merk Arts & Science Cncl 1984-. **SELECTED PUBLICATIONS** Author, "A Summary and Critical Analysis of the 'Color of God: the Concept of God in Afro American Thought'," Amez Quarterly, v 102, n 1, pp 38-41, 1990; "Revisioning the American Dream: Individualism and Community in African American Perspective," Star of Zion, v 14, n 21, January 21, 1993; James WC Pennington: African American Churchman and Abolitionist, Garland Publishing, 1995. **CONTACT ADDRESS** UNCC, 121 Garinger Bldg, 9201 University City Blvd, Charlotte, NC, 28223.

THOMAS, JOHN JOSEPH
PERSONAL Born 07/02/1942, Pittsburgh, PA, 2 children **DISCIPLINE** PHILOSOPHY **EDUCATION** La Salle Univ, BA, 65; Univ Miami, MA, 72, PhD(philos), 73. **CAREER** Teaching asst philos, Univ Miami,68-72; instr, Univ Ga, 73-74; Assoc Prof Philos, Columbus Col, 74-77; assoc prof, Columbus Col, 77-93; prof, Colo St Univ, 93-98. **MEMBERSHIPS** Am Philos Asn. **RESEARCH** History of philosophy; physical theories and ontology; social-political philosophy. **CONTACT ADDRESS** Columbus State Univ, 4225 University Ave, Columbus, GA, 31907-5645. **EMAIL** thomas_john@colstate.edu

THOMAS, KENDALL
PERSONAL Born 02/22/1957, East Chicago, Indiana **DISCIPLINE** LAW **EDUCATION** Yale College, New Haven, CT, BA, 1978; Yale Law School, New Haven, CT, JD, 1982. **CAREER** Columbia University in the City of New York, New York, NY, asst/associate professor, 1984-92, prof, 1992-. **CONTACT ADDRESS** School of Law, Columbia Univ, 435 W 116th St, New York, NY, 10027.

THOMAS, MAXINE SUZANNE
PERSONAL Born 01/23/1948, Junction City, Kansas, m **DISCIPLINE** LAW **EDUCATION** Univ of WA, BA 1970, JD 1973. **CAREER** Univ of OR Schl of Law, asst prof 1976-89; Univ of OR, asst dean 1976-79; WA, asst atty gen 1973-76; assoc dean and assoc prof Univ of Georgia l989-. **HONORS AND AWARDS** Nominated OR Outst Young Women 1978, Kellogg Natl Fellow l985-l988, Fulbright lecturer l988. **MEMBERSHIPS** Mem Natl Assc of Clge & Univ Attys 1974-76; standing com on environmental law Amer Bar Assc 1979-; honorary mem Phi Delta Phi 1977-; mem OR Amer Counc on Educ Com to Promote Women to Higher Educ Admin 1978-. **CONTACT ADDRESS** Univ of Georgia School of Law, Athens, GA, 30602.

THOMAS, NIGEL J.T.
PERSONAL Born 02/07/1952, Rochester, United Kingdom, m, 1992, 2 children **DISCIPLINE** HISTORY AND PHILOSOPHY OF SCIENCE **EDUCATION** Leeds Univ, PhD, 87. **CAREER** Instr, Calif Inst Techol, 90-92; instr, Rio Hondo Coll, 96-97; adj asst prof Calif State Univ, 95-. **MEMBERSHIPS** Am Philos Asn; Soc for Philos and Psychol; Cognitive Sci Soc; Hist of Sci Soc; Soc for Machines and Mentality; Cheiron; Am Psychol Asn; Asn for the Scientific Study of Consciousness, Soc for the Multidisciplinary Study of Consciousness. **RESEARCH** Philosophy of Mind; Imagination; Cognitive Science; History of Psychology. **SELECTED PUBLICATIONS** Auth, Imagery and the coherence of Imagination: a Critique of White, J of Philos Res, 97; A Stimulus to the Imagination, Psyche, 97; Mental Imagery, the Stanford Encycl of Philos, 97; entries on Sir Frederick Gowland Hopkins and Marshall W Nirenberg, The Biographical Encycl of Sci, 98; Are Theories of Imagery Theories of Imagination? An Active perception Approach to Conscious Mental Content, Cognitive Sci, forthcoming, rev, The Imagery Debate, 94. **CONTACT ADDRESS** 86 South Sierra Madre Blvd #5, Pasadena, CA, 91107. **EMAIL** nthomas@calstateca.edu

THOMAS, OWEN CLARK
PERSONAL Born 10/11/1922, New York, NY, m, 1981, 3 children **DISCIPLINE** THEOLOGY **EDUCATION** Hamilton Col, AB, 44; Episcopal Theol Sch, BD, 49; Columbia Univ, PhD, 56. **CAREER** Dir col work, Diocese, NY, 51-52; from instr to assoc prof, 52-65, PROF THEOL, EPISCOPAL THEOL SCH, 65-, Vis prof Pontiff Gregorian Univ, 73-74. **HONORS AND AWARDS** DDiv, Hamilton Col, 70. **MEMBERSHIPS** Soc Values Higher Educ; Am Theol Soc; Am Acad Relig. **RESEARCH** Philosophy of religion; systematic theology; history of Christian thought. **SELECTED PUBLICATIONS** Auth, Religious Plurality and Contemporary Philosophy--An Examination of Varieties of Inclusivism and the Myth of Christian Uniqueness--A Critical Survey, Harvard Theol Rev, Vol 87, 94; Public Theology and Counter-Public Spheres--David Tracy, Distinction Between Fundamental and Systematic Christian Theology, a Reconsideration of His Thesis on Religious Pluralism, Harvard Theol Rev, Vol 85, 92. **CONTACT ADDRESS** 10 St John's Rd, Cambridge, MA, 02138.

THOMAS, RANDALL S.
DISCIPLINE LAW, ECONOMICS **EDUCATION** Haverford Col, PA, BA (honors), 77; Univ MI, Ann Arbor, PhD (economics), 83; Univ MI Law School, JD (Order of the Coif, honors), 85. **CAREER** Economist, USAID/Univ MI, Center for Res on Economic Development, Niger, West Africa, and Ann Arbor, MI, 79-82; economist/financial analyst to the World Bank in Malawai, East Africa with Bookers Agriculture Int, Ltd, London, England, Sept to Dec, 82; economic consult to USAID, Somalia, East Africa, May 83; summer law clerk, Piper & Marbury, Baltimore, MD, May-Aug 84; law clerk to the Honorable Charles W Joiner, Fed District Court for the Eastern District of MI, Ann Arbor, MI, 85-86; assoc, Potter Anderson & Corroon, Wilmington, DE, 86-87; Corporate and Securities Law Assoc, Skadden, Arps, Slate, Meagher, & Flom, Wilmington, DE, 87-90; prof, Univ of IA College of Law, Iowa City, 90-95, 96-; vis prof of Law, Univ Washington School of Law, Seattle, March 95, March 96; vis prof of Law, Boston Univ School of Law, 95; vis prof of Law, Univ MI School of Law, 96. **HONORS AND AWARDS** Rackham Grad School fel, Univ MI, Ann Arbor; Nat Health Inst fel, Univ MI, Ann Arbor. **MEMBERSHIPS** DE Bar, 87. **SELECTED PUBLICATIONS** Auth, Improving Shareholder Monitoring of Corporate Management By Expanding Statutory Access to Information, 38 AZ Law Rev, 331, 96, reprinted in Coprorate Practice Commentator 563, 96; Encouraging Relational Investment and Controlling Portfolio Investment in Developing Countries in the Aftermath of the Mexican Financial Crisis, with Entique Carrasco, 34 Columbia J of Transactional Law 539, 96; Using State Inspection Statutes for Discovery in Federal Securities Actions, with Kennneth J Martin, 77 Boston Univ Law Rev 69, 97; reprinted in Corporate Practice Commentator, 523, 97; Reinventing Corporate Governance: Shareholder Activism by Labor Unions, with Stewart Schwab, 96 MI Law Rev 1018, 98; Auctions in Bankruptcy: Theoretical Analysis and Practical Guidance, with Robert G, Hansen, 18 Int Rev of Law and Economics 159, 98; When Should Labor be Allowed to Submit Shareholder Proposals?, with Kenneth J Martin, 73 Washington Law Rev, 41, 98; Firm Committment Underwriting Risk and the Over-Allotment Option: Do We Need Better Legal Regulation?, with James F Cotter, Securities Regulation Law J, fall 98; The Efficiency of Sharing Liability for Hazardous Waste: Effects of Uncertainty Over Damages, with Robert G Hansen, Working Paper, 98; Improving Corporate Bankruptcy Law Through Venue Reform, with Robert Rasmussen, Working Paper, 98; several other publications. **CONTACT ADDRESS** College of Law, Univ of Iowa, Iowa City, IA, 52242.

THOMASMA, DAVID C.
PERSONAL Born 10/31/1939, Chicago, IL, m, 1992, 4 children **DISCIPLINE** PHILOSOPHY, THEOLOGY **RESEARCH** Philosophy of medicine; bioethics; clinical ethics. **CONTACT ADDRESS** Medical Hum, Loyola Univ, Chicago, 2160 S First Ave, Maywood, IL, 60153. **EMAIL** DThomal@luc.edu

THOMASSON, GORDON C.
PERSONAL Born 12/28/1942, Santa Monica, CA, m, 1975, 4 children **DISCIPLINE** HISTORY, RELIGION **EDUCATION** UCLA, AB, 66; UCSB, AM, 72; Cornell Univ, PhD, 87. **CAREER** Asst prof, 80-82, Cuttington Univ; world stud fac, 88-93, Marlboro Col & Schl for Intl Training; asst prof, 93-, Broome Com Col (SUNY); intl stud adj, 96-98, CCNY **RESEARCH** Globval hist, world relig, anthropology of development, Liberia, Southeast Asia, Mormonism. **CONTACT ADDRESS** 280 Academy Dr., Vestal, NY, 13850. **EMAIL** thomasson_g@mail.sunybroome.edu

THOMPSON, ALMOSE ALPHONSE, II
PERSONAL Born 02/12/1942, Shawnee, OK, m **DISCIPLINE** LAW **EDUCATION** UCLA, BS 1962, Teaching Credential 1965, EdD 1972; Cal State Univ Long Beach, MA 1970; Vanderbilt Univ Law School, JD 1988. **CAREER** LA Unified school Dist, secondary teacher 1965-68; CA State Univ, dir project upward bound & asst prof 1968-70; UCLA, part time instructor 1970-71; Holman &Thompson Inc, educ consul 1970-72; Univ of CA Santa Barbara, assoc dean of students; Portland State Univ, asst prof of curriculum & instruction 1972-74; Moorhead State Univ, asst prof of secondary educ 1974-75; CA State Univ, assoc prof & dir; Martin Luther King Jr Genl Hosp & Charles R Drew Post Grad Med School, educ eval specialist 1976-78; City of LA, prog dir 1978-79; Curatron Systems Inc, vice pres & Head of educ div 1978-79; Metropolitan Weekly, staff writer 1980-84; TN State Univ, prof of educ admin; syndicated columnist, Metropolitan Weekly; The Legal Clinic, Nashville, TN, sr partner, 1989-. **HONORS AND AWARDS** Awd for article "Blacks in America before Columbus" Negro History Bulletin 1975; 2 Grad Fellowships UCLA 1964 1970; Awd from The Black Caucus TN Genl Assembly 1982; Awd from the Mayor of Memphis 1982; passed written examination for Tennessee Bar, Tennessee Board of Bar Examiners, 1989. **MEMBERSHIPS** Bd mem Walden Univ Bd of Rsch Advisors & Readers 1984-; rsch fellow selected 3 consecutive yrs Southern Educ Found 1980-83; mem ASPA, Natl Assn of Black, State of TN Pol Sci Assn; State's Media Corp; TN Prof Educational Admin Assn; Natl Assn of Social & Behavorial Scientists. **SELECTED PUBLICATIONS** "Black Studies is Down to This" Black Times 1976; "Albina & Educa-

tional Reform" Portland Observer Special Issue Feb 15 1974; "The Student's Guide to Better Grades" NDS 1983; contributor "On Being Black, An In-Group Analysis" edited by David Pilgrim, published by Wyndham Hall Press 1986. **CONTACT ADDRESS** The Legal Clinic, 939 Jefferson St, Ste 100, Nashville, TN, 37200.

THOMPSON, CYNTHIA L.
PERSONAL Born 06/03/1943, Buffalo, NY **DISCIPLINE** CLASSICS IN GREEK NEW TESTAMENT **EDUCATION** Yale Univ, PhD, 73, MA, 68; Wellesley Coll, BA, 66. **CAREER** Res, 73-75, Harvard Divinity School; Asst Prof of Classics & Religion, 75-80, Denison Univ, Granville, DH; Editor, 80-94, 97-, Westminster John Knox Press; Editor, 94-97, Fortress Press, Minneapolis, Philadelphia, Louisville. **HONORS AND AWARDS** Phi Beta Kappa **MEMBERSHIPS** APA, SBL. **RESEARCH** Women's Adornment in Greek-Roman World; Classical and Biblical Heritage. **SELECTED PUBLICATIONS** Auth, Hairstyles, Head Coverings and St Paul's Portraits From Roman Corinth, Biblical Archaeologist, 88; Rings of Gold-Neither Modest Nor Sensible, Bible Review, 93. **CONTACT ADDRESS** 39 Roslin St, #3, Dorchester, MA, 02124. **EMAIL** cynthom@aol.com

THOMPSON, DAVID L.
PERSONAL Born 05/17/00, Austin, MN, m, 1962, 3 children **DISCIPLINE** BIBLICAL STUDIES **EDUCATION** IN Wesleyan Univ, BA, 62; Asbury Theol Sem, BD, 65, ThM, 67; John Hopkins Univ, PhD, 73. **CAREER** Asbury Theol Sem, 76-82, Prof 86-; Teaching, 73-76, Wesleyan Univ. **HONORS AND AWARDS** Woodrow Wilson Fel. **MEMBERSHIPS** SBL; CBA; IBR; WTS. **RESEARCH** Scriptural Intertexuality; Hermeneutics. **SELECTED PUBLICATIONS** Auth, Holiness for Hurting People: Discipleship as Recovery, Indianapolis IN, Wesleyan Pub House, 98; Bible Study That Works, revised edition, IN, Evangel Press, 94. **CONTACT ADDRESS** Asbury Theol Sem, 204 N Lexington Ave, Wilmore, KY, 40390-1199. **EMAIL** david_thompson@ats.wilmore.ky.us

THOMPSON, GARRETT
DISCIPLINE PHILOSOPHY **EDUCATION** Newcastle on Tyne, Eng, BA, 78; Oxford, Balliol Col, Eng, PhD, 84. **CAREER** Instr, Univ Bogota; National Univ; assoc prof; ch. **SELECTED PUBLICATIONS** Auth, Introduction To Modern Philosophy: Descartes to Kant and Needs. **CONTACT ADDRESS** Dept of Philos, Col of Wooster, Wooster, OH, 44691.

THOMPSON, GEORGE, JR.
PERSONAL Born 10/12/1931, Richmond, VA, w, 1955, 1 child **DISCIPLINE** THEOLOGY **EDUCATION** Va Union Univ, BA, 54; Southern Baptist Theological Seminary, 57; Univ of Chicago, MA, 62, PhD, 74. **CAREER** Assoc prof, Bluefield State Col, 62-62; coord for higher ed rel studies, 65-72, assoc prof, Payne Theological Seminary, 63-72; PROF, E STROUDSBURG UNIV, 72-; vis prof, Harvard Univ, 75-77; VIS PROF, LUTHERAN THEOLOGICAL SEMINARY AT PHILADELPHIA, 81-. **HONORS AND AWARDS** Doctor of Divinity, Martha Vineyard Theological Seminary, 94. **MEMBERSHIPS** Am Acad of Rel; Am Philos Asn; Soc for the Study of Black Philosophy; Soc for the Scientific Study of Rel. **CONTACT ADDRESS** PO Box 945, Glenside, PA, 19038-0945. **EMAIL** gthomp@esu.edu

THOMPSON, KENNETH F.
DISCIPLINE PHILOSOPHY **EDUCATION** Yale Univ, BA; Union Theol Sem, BD; Columbia Univ, PhD. **CAREER** Assoc prof, Loyola Univ,67-; lectr, DePauw Univ, Ind & Loyola's Rome Center; dept chp & dir, grad stud. **RESEARCH** Early modern philosophy, especially Descartes and Hume; Whitehead; philosophy of mind; philosophy of religion. **SELECTED PUBLICATIONS** Auth, Whitehead's Philosophy of Religion; articles on, philos topics. **CONTACT ADDRESS** Dept of Philosophy, Loyola Univ, Chicago, 820 N Michigan Ave, Chicago, IL, 60611.

THOMPSON, LEONARD LEROY
PERSONAL Born 09/24/1934, IN **DISCIPLINE** RELIGIOUS STUDIES **EDUCATION** DePauw Univ, BA, 56; Drew Univ, BD, 60; Univ Chicago, MA, 63, PhD(New Testament), 68. **CAREER** Instr relig, Lawrence Univ, 65-66 & Wright State Univ, 66-68; asst prof, 68-71, assoc prof, 72-80, PROF RELIG, LAWRENCE UNIV, 80-, Nat Endowment for Humanities fel, 81-82. **MEMBERSHIPS** Am Acad Relig; Soc Bibl Lit. **RESEARCH** Biblical studies; Greco-Roman religions. **SELECTED PUBLICATIONS** Auth, Regnum-Caelorum--Patterns of Future Hope in Early Christianity, J Relig, Vol 74, 94; Revelation--Vision of a Just World, Cath Biblical Quart, Vol 55, 93. **CONTACT ADDRESS** Dept of Relig, Lawrence Univ, Appleton, WI, 54911.

THOMPSON, M.T., JR.
PERSONAL Born 04/15/1951, Saginaw, MI, m **DISCIPLINE** LAW **EDUCATION** Oakland Univ, BA 1973; Northeastern Univ Sch of Law, JD 1977. **CAREER** Michigan Bell Telephone Co, mgr 1973-74; Natl Labor Relations Bd, Attorney 1977-79; Lewis White & Clay PC, Attorney 1979-83; MT Thompson Jr PC, Attorney 1983-. **MEMBERSHIPS** Admitted to practice MI Supreme Court 1977, US Sixth Circuit Court of Appeals 1980, US Supreme Court 1984. **SELECTED PUBLICATIONS** Author "Institutional Employment Discrimination as a Legal Concept," 1981. **CONTACT ADDRESS** MT Thompson Jr, PC, 330 South Washington Ave, Saginaw, MI, 48607.

THOMPSON, PAUL B.
PERSONAL Born 07/22/1951, Springfield, MO, m, 1975, 2 children **DISCIPLINE** PHILOSOPHY **EDUCATION** State Univ NY at Stony Brook, PhD. **CAREER** Texas A&M Univ, vis asst prof, asst prof, 81-86; US Agency Intl Devel, vis prof, 86-87; Texas A&M Univ, assoc prof, prof, 87-97; Inst for Biosciences & Tech, A&M Univ, dir, 92-97, Purdue Univ, dist prof, 97-. **HONORS AND AWARDS** Nat Center Food & Agri, res fel, 86-87; Texas A&M, Maria Julia & George R. Jordan, jr prof Award, AAEA Award, 92; AAEA Award, 93; New Mex State Univ, vis dist prof, 93-94; Yale Univ, Post doc Fel, 94-95; Purdue Univ, Joyce & Edward E. Brewer, prof of Appl Ethics, 97-. **MEMBERSHIPS** APA, AAEA, SAFHV, SRA, ISEE, IS for Ecolo & Econ **RESEARCH** Philo of techn; ecolo; econom. **SELECTED PUBLICATIONS** Auth, Agricultural Ethics: Research, Teaching and Public Policy, Iowa State Univ Press, 98; Food Biotechnology in Ethical Perspective, Chapman and Hall, 97; The Spirit of the Soil: Agriculture and Environmental Ethics, Routledge Pub Co, 95; co-ed, Ethics, Public Policy, and Agriculture, Macmillan, 94; Arctic, Sustainability: What It Is and What It Is Not, in: Agro-ecology, 98; Ethics and Food Safety, in: Social Construct of Safe Food: Health, Ethics and Safety in Late Modernity, Workshop Report, 98; Toward a Discourse Ethics for Animal Biotechnology, Biotechnology International, 97; The Cloning Debate, Cent for Sc & Tech Policy Newsletter, 97. **CONTACT ADDRESS** Dept of Philosophy, Purdue Univ, West Lafayette, IN, 47907. **EMAIL** pault@purdue.edu

THOMPSON, WILLIAM J.
PERSONAL Born 01/19/1939, Invercargill, New Zealand **DISCIPLINE** PHYSICS **EDUCATION** Fla State Univ, PhD, 67; Univ Auckland, New Zealand, Dsc, 82. **CAREER** PROF, PHYSICS, UNIV NORTH CAROLINA, 78-. **RESEARCH** Nuclear & quantum physics; Computer physics; Statistics; Applied mathematics. **CONTACT ADDRESS** Dept Physics, Univ North Carolina, Chapel Hill, NC, 27599-3255.

THOMPSON, WILLIAM M.
PERSONAL Born 12/06/1943, Boise, ID, m, 1976, 2 children **DISCIPLINE** PHILOSOPHICAL/SYSTEMATIC THEOLOGY **EDUCATION** St. Thomas Col, BA, 65; M Div, 69; St. Mary's Sem and Univ, STM; Univ of St. Michael's Col, PhD, 73. **CAREER** Asst/assoc prof, Carroll Col, 76-85; assoc prof, Duquesne Univ, 85-87; prof, 87- . **MEMBERSHIPS** Eric Voegelin Soc; Karl Rahner Soc; Cath Theol Soc of Am. **RESEARCH** Theology an philosophy in dialogue; religion and political philosophy; spirituality and theology/religion in dialogue. **SELECTED PUBLICATIONS** Auth, Christology and Spirituality, 91; The Struggle for Theology's Soul, 96. **CONTACT ADDRESS** Dept. of Theology, Duquesne Univ, Pittsburgh, PA, 15282. **EMAIL** thompsonw@duq.edu

THOMSEN, MARK
DISCIPLINE SYSTEMATIC THEOLOGY **EDUCATION** Trinity Theol Sem; Princeton Theol Sem; Northwestern Univ, PhD, Garrett Theol Sem. **CAREER** Instr, Theol Col N Nigeria; Dana Col; Luther Sem; dir, Grad Stud. **HONORS AND AWARDS** Exec dir, Div for Global Mission. **SELECTED PUBLICATIONS** Auth, The Word and the Way of the Cross: Christian Witness among Muslim and Buddhist People, ELCA, 93. **CONTACT ADDRESS** Dept of Systematic Theology, Lutheran Sch of Theol, 1100 E 55th St, Chicago, IL, 60615. **EMAIL** mthomsen@lstc.edu

THOMSON, KATHRYN
DISCIPLINE LAW **EDUCATION** Univ Victoria, BA; Univ British Columbia, LLB; Ottawa Univ, LLM. **CAREER** Law, Univ Victoria. **HONORS AND AWARDS** Dir, Law Found British Columbia. **SELECTED PUBLICATIONS** Auth, pubs on feminist legal theory and equality litigation. **CONTACT ADDRESS** Fac of Law, Univ Victoria, PO Box 2400, Victoria, BC, V8W 3H7. **EMAIL** ket@uvic.ca

THOMSON, WILLIAM
PERSONAL Born 05/24/1927, Ft Worth, TX, m, 1948, 4 children **DISCIPLINE** MUSIC THEORY; PHILOSOPHY **EDUCATION** N Texas State Col, BM, 48, MM, 49; Ind Univ, PhD, 52. **CAREER** SVL Ross State Col, 51-60; prof music theory, Ind Univ, 61-68; scholar in resident, Univ Hawaii, 67-68; Kulas prof music, Case W Res Univ, 68-73; prof music, univ arizona, 73-75; Reigle prof music & dept chr music, SUNY Buffalo, 75-80; Dean School of Music, USC, 80-95. **HONORS AND AWARDS** Outstanding Tchr Awards, Case W Res Univ, 71 & Univ Arizona, 75; Choice Outstanding Acad Book, 92. **MEMBERSHIPS** Soc Mus Theory; Col Mus Soc; Am Musicol Soc. **RESEARCH** Perceptual basis of musical experience. **SELECTED PUBLICATIONS** Coauth, Materials and Structure of Music, 65; auth Introduction to Music as Structure, 69; Music for Listeners, 71; Introduction to Music Reading, 75; Sound, musical, Encycl Britannica, 78; Advanced Music Reading, 81; Schoenbergs Error, 91; trans Consonance and Dissonance in Music, 93; auth, Tonality in Music: A General Theory, 98. **CONTACT ADDRESS** 3333 E California Blvd., Pasadena, CA, 91107. **EMAIL** sansptom@aol.com

THORNBURG, E.G.
PERSONAL Born 05/03/1954, Norwalk, CT, m, 1976, 1 child **DISCIPLINE** LAW **EDUCATION** Col of William and Mary, BA 76; S Methodist Univ, JD 79. **CAREER** SMU, dir, asst prof, assoc prof, prof, 84 to 98-. **HONORS AND AWARDS** Dr. Don M. Smart tchg Awd; Phi Beta Kappa. **MEMBERSHIPS** AALS; ABA; State Bar TX **RESEARCH** Civil proced re; discovery; juries; comparative proced re; judicial discretion. **SELECTED PUBLICATIONS** Auth, Giving the Haves a Little More: Considering the 1998 Discovery Proposals, SMUL, 98; The Power and the Process: Instructions and the Civil Jury, Fordham L Rev, 98; Ch 10&11, 1997 and 1998 Supplements, Dorsano & Crump, TX Civil Proced re: Pretrial Litigation, 89; Metaphors Matter: How Images of Battle, Sports and Sex Shape the Adversary System, Wis Women's L. J., 95; The Costs of Attorney-Client Privilege, Brief, 94. **CONTACT ADDRESS** School of Law, Southern Methodist Univ, PO Box 0116, Dallas, TX, 75275. **EMAIL** ethornbu@mail.smu.edu

THORNELL, RICHARD PAUL
PERSONAL Born 10/19/1936, New York, New York, m **DISCIPLINE** LAW **EDUCATION** Fisk Univ, magna cum laude, 1956; Pomona Coll, 1955; Woodrow Wilson Sch, MPA, 1958; Yale Law Sch, JD, 1971. **CAREER** Howard Univ Sch of Law, prof of Law, currently, vice pres, general counsel, 1984-88, Univ Faculty Senate, immediate past chair; Rosenman Colin Freund Lewis & Cohen NYC, assoc litigation dept 1975-76; US Comm Relations Serv Dept of Justice, chief fed progms staff 1965-66; Africa Reg Ofc US Peace Corps, chief program staff; US Dept of State Agency for Intl Develop, econ & intl rel ofcr 1958-61. **HONORS AND AWARDS** Fisk Univ, Africare Distinguished Serv Awd; Fisk Univ Gen Alumni Assn 1978; Grad Fellowship Princeton U; Fellowship Grant Yale Law Sch; Intl Achievement Awd Willilam S Thompson Intl Law Soc dir com Nat Bd of YMCA'S of USA; exec com m1980. **MEMBERSHIPS** Bars of NY/DC/Fed Cts/US Supreme Ct; bd of advisors, Smithonian Environmental Res Ctr; bd of dir YMCA of Wash DC 1977-83; bd of dir Africare 1977-83; trustee Phelps Stoke Fund 1980-85; lay mem bd of dir, com Nat Bd of YMCA'S of USA; exec com & gen counsel Fisk Univ Gen Alumni Assn 1977-79; Phi Beta Kappa, Delta Chap, Fisk Univ 1956-; elected Council on Foreign Relations. **CONTACT ADDRESS** Howard Univ, 2400 Van Ness St NW, Washington, VT, 20008.

THORP, JOHN
DISCIPLINE PHILOSOPHY **EDUCATION** Trent Univ, BA, 70; Oxford Univ, BPhil, 72; DPhil, 76. **CAREER** Prof **RESEARCH** Ancient Greek culture and philosophy; history of science; philosophy of mind; the status of the human sciences; gay and lesbian studies. **SELECTED PUBLICATIONS** Auth, Le couteau de Delphes: reflexions sur un legs nocif d'Aristote, 96; Aristotle on Probalilistic Reasoning, Can J Rhet Studies, 94; Aristotle's Rehabilitation of Rhetoric, Can Jour Rhet Studies, 93; Asterix et les qualia: la derniere poche de resistance, Dialogue, 93; The Social Construction of Homosexuality (rev), 92; Aristotle's Horror Vacui, Can Jour Philos, 90; La figure d'Achille chez Aristote, 90; Free Will-a defence against neurophysiological determinism, Routledge & Kegan Paul, 80; ed, El libre albedrio, 85. **CONTACT ADDRESS** Dept of Philosophy, Western Ontario Univ, London, ON, N6A 5B8. **EMAIL** jthorp@julian.uwo.ca

THORPE, SAMUEL
DISCIPLINE PHILOSOPHY **EDUCATION** Univ Arkansas, BA, 71; Oral Roberts Univ, MA, 81; Univ Tulsa, PhD, 89. **CAREER** Asst Prof, 91-96, Assoc Prof, 96-, Oral Roberts Univ. **CONTACT ADDRESS** Dept of Theology, Oral Roberts Univ, Tulsa, OK, 74171. **EMAIL** srthorpe@oru.edu

THORSON, NORM
DISCIPLINE LAW **EDUCATION** Univ Nebr, BS; MS; JD; PhD. **CAREER** Prof **HONORS AND AWARDS** Pres, Am Agricultural Law Asn. **RESEARCH** Agricultural law; public lands and natural resources; oil and gas; water law; international environmental law. **SELECTED PUBLICATIONS** Auth, Cases and Materials on Agricultural Law, W; co-auth, Agricultural Law; Nebraska Water Law and Administration. **CONTACT ADDRESS** Law Dept, Univ of Nebraska, Lincoln, 103 Ross McCollum Hall, PO Box 830902, Lincoln, NE, 68588-0420. **EMAIL** nthorson@unlinfo.unl.edu

THRO, LINUS J.
PERSONAL Born 01/15/1913, St. Charles, MO **DISCIPLINE** MEDIEVAL PHILOSOPHY **EDUCATION** St Louis Univ, AB, 34, lic theol, 45; Col Immaculate Conception, lic phil, 38; Univ Montreal, MA, 38; Univ Toronto, PhD, 48. **CAREER** Instr, Regis Col, 38-41; from instr to assoc prof, 49-72, chmn dept, 68-74, PROF MEDIAEVAL PHILOS, ST LOUIS UNIV,

72- **MEMBERSHIPS** Am Philos Asn; Metaphys Soc Am; Am Cath Philos Asn. **RESEARCH** Thought and influence of John Duns Scotus; philosophy and religion in relation to science. **SELECTED PUBLICATIONS** Auth, A Note on Universals, Mod Schoolman: Gilson and Duns Scotus, New Scholasticism; Questions on Aristotle 'Metaphysics X and Xii' by Dymsdale,John in Latin Text and Analysis of 13th-Century Philosophical Work, Manuscripta, Vol 0036, 1992. **CONTACT ADDRESS** Dept of Philos, St Louis Univ, St Louis, MO, 63103.

THRONVEIT, MARK A.
DISCIPLINE OLD TESTAMENT **EDUCATION** St. Olaf Col, BA, 71; Luther Sem, MDiv, GM; Union Theol Sem, PhD, 82. **CAREER** Tchg fel, Union Theol Sem, 979-81; tchg asst, Presbyterian Sch for Christian Educ, 79-80; adj prof, Augsburg Col, 91; St. Thomas Univ, 91; instr, 81; assoc prof, 87-. **HONORS AND AWARDS** AAL scholar; Minnie Bruce awd in New Testament, Luther Sem, 75; James A. Jones Memorial fel., Assoc pastor, First Eng Lutheran Church, 78. **MEMBERSHIPS** Mem, Soc Bibl Lit; member of the steering comm for the Chronicles, Ezra-Nehemiah consultation, 84-86, group, 86-91, section, 91-. **SELECTED PUBLICATIONS** Auth, Ezra-Nehemiah, Interpretation Commentaries, 92; Exploring the Yearly Lectionary Series A, 91; When Kings Speak: Royal Speech and Royal Prayer in Chronicles, 87. **CONTACT ADDRESS** Dept of Old Testament, Luther Sem, 2481 Como Ave, St. Paul, MN, 55108. **EMAIL** mthrontv@luthersem.edu

THURSBY, GENE ROBERT
PERSONAL Born 05/08/1939, Akron, OH, m, 1963 **DISCIPLINE** INDIC RELIGION, HISTORY OF RELIGIONS **EDUCATION** Oberlin Col, BA, 61, BDiv, 64; Duke Univ, PhD(relig), 72. **CAREER** Asst prof, 70-76, ASSOC PROF RELIG, UNIV FLA, 76-, CONSULT, CHOICE: J ASN COL AND RES LIBR, 70-; scholar-diplomat, US Dept State Sem SAsia, 72 and Sem Pop Matters, 73. **MEMBERSHIPS** Am Acad Relig; Am Orient Soc; Royal Asiatic Soc Gt Brit and Ireland; Asn Asian Studies; Soc Asian and Comp Philos. **RESEARCH** Interreligious relations in South Asia; history of Hindu religious and social movements in the 20th century; philosophical analysis for religious uses of language. **SELECTED PUBLICATIONS** Auth, Some Resources for History of Religions, Bull Am Acad Relig, 67; coauth, South Asian Proscribed Publications, 1907-1947, Indian Arch, 69; Hindu-Muslim Relations in British India, Brill, 75; Religious Nationalism in Hindus And Muslims In India, J Asian Hist, Vol 0030, 96. **CONTACT ADDRESS** Dept of Relig, Univ of Fla, P O Box 117410, Gainesville, FL, 32611-7410.

THURSTON, BONNIE BOWMAN
PERSONAL Born 10/05/1952, Bluefield, WV, w, 1980 **DISCIPLINE** ENGLISH, PHILOSOPHY, RELIGION **EDUCATION** Bethany Col, BA, 74; Univ Va, MA, 75, PhD, 79. **CAREER** Grad inst, Eng, 76-79, asst dean, Col Arts and Sci, inst, Eng and Rel stud, 79-80, Univ Va; adj, Eng Theol, Wheeling Jesuit Univ, 80-81; asst prof, Eng, Human, Bethany Col, 81-83; tutor, inst stud Christian Origins, Tuebingen, Ger, 83-85; assoc prof Theol, dir, ch, dept Theol, Wheeling Jesuit Univ, 85-95; prof New Test, Pittsburgh Theol Sem. **HONORS AND AWARDS** Valedictorian, first hon lit, hon soc in Drama, Eng, Jour, Bethany Col , 74; Philip Francis du Pont fel, Univ Va, 76; Who's Who in Bibl studs and Archeol, 87; Who's Who in the World, 87; Who's Who in Rel, 91; schol-in-res, Wheeling Jesuit Univ, 92; Alpha Sigma Nu; Alum achiev awd in Rel. **MEMBERSHIPS** Amer Sch Oriental Res; Catholic Bibl Asn; Intl Thomas Merton Soc; Soc Bibl Lit; Soc Buddhist-Christian Stud. **RESEARCH** New Testament; Christian Origins; Christian Spirituality. **SELECTED PUBLICATIONS** Auth, The Conquered Self: Emptiness and God in Buddhist-Christian Dialogue, Japanese Jour Rel Studs, 12/4, 85; Matt 5:43-45: You, Therefore, must be perfect, Interpretation, 41/2, 87; The Gospel of John and Japanese Buddhism, Japanese Rel, 15/2, 88; Thomas Merton: Pioneer of Buddhist-Christian Dialogue, Cath World, May/June, 89; Wait Here and Watch: A Eucharistic Commentary on Matt 26-28, Chalice, 89; The Windows: A Women's Ministry in the Early Church, Fortress, 89; Language, Gender and Prayer, Lexington Theol Quart, 27/1, 92; Spiritual Life in the Early Church, Fortress, 93; Proclamation 5, Series C: Holy Week, Fortress, 94; Reading Colossians, Ephesians, and II Thessalonians, Crossroad, 95; Women in the New Testament, Crossroad, 98. **CONTACT ADDRESS** Dept of New Testament, Pittsburgh Theol Sem, 616 N Highland Ave, Pittsburgh, PA, 15206. **EMAIL** BThurston@pts.edu

TIBBETTS, PAUL E.
DISCIPLINE PHILOSOPHY **EDUCATION** Univ Ill, PhD, 86. **CAREER** Dept Philos, Univ Dayton **RESEARCH** Epistemology; philosophy of mind; philosophy of science. **SELECTED PUBLICATIONS** Auth, Threading-the-Needle: The Case for and against Common-Sense Realism, Hum Stud 13, 90; Residual Dualism in Computational Theories of Mind, Dialectica, 96; Neurobioloy and the Homoculous Thesis, Man and World, 96. **CONTACT ADDRESS** Dept of Philos, Univ Dayton, 300 Col Park, Dayton, OH, 75062. **EMAIL** tibbetts@checkov.hm.udayton.edu

TIBERIUS, VALERIE
PERSONAL Born 05/28/1967, Toronto, ON, Canada **DISCIPLINE** PHILOSOPHY **EDUCATION** Univ Toronto, BA, 90; MA, 92, PhD, 97, UNC-Chapel Hill. **CAREER** Asst Prof, 97-98, Franklin and Marshall Col; Asst Prof, 98-, Univ Minnesota-Twin Cities. **MEMBERSHIPS** Amer Phil Assoc **RESEARCH** Ethics; practical reason **SELECTED PUBLICATIONS** Auth, Full Information and Ideal Deliberation, Journal of Value Inquiry, 97; Coauth, Arrogance, American Philosophical Quarterly, forthcoming; Auth, Justifying Reasons for Valuing: An Argument Against the Social Account, The Sothern Journal of Philosophy, forthcoming. **CONTACT ADDRESS** Dept of Philosophy, Univ of Minnesota-Twin Cities, 224 Church St. S.E., 355 Ford H, Minneapolis, MN, 55455. **EMAIL** tiber001@tc.umn.edu

TIDMAN, PAUL
DISCIPLINE LOGIC, APPLIED PHILOSOPHY **EDUCATION** Asbury Col, Wilmore, BA, 78; Univ Notre Dame, PhD, 90. **CAREER** Dept Philos, Mt Union Col **RESEARCH** Epistemology/Metaphysics. **SELECTED PUBLICATIONS** Auth, The Justification of A Priori Intuitions, Philos and Phenomenol Res, 56, 96; Logic and Modal Intuitions, The Monist, 77, 94; Conceivability as a Test of Possibility, Amer Philos Quart, 31, 94; Lehrer on a Premise of Epistemic Cogency, Philos Stud, 67, 92 & The Epistemology of Evil Possibilities, Faith and Philos, 10, 93; coauth, Logic and Philosophy, 7th ed, Belmont, Calif: Wadsworth Press, 94;. Instructor's Manual for Logic and Philosophy, 7th ed, Belmont, Calif: Wadsworth Press, 94; contribur, Conceivability, Cambridge Dictionary Philos, Cambridge UP, 95 & Review: Review of Reinhard Grossman's The Fourth Way: A Theory of Knowledge, Mind, 101, 92. **CONTACT ADDRESS** Dept of Philosophy, Mount Union Col, 1972 Clark Ave, Alliance, OH, 44601. **EMAIL** tidmanpa@muc.edu

TIEDE, DAVID L.
DISCIPLINE NEW TESTAMENT **EDUCATION** St. Olaf Col, BA, 62; Luther Sem, BD, 66; Harvard Univ, PhD, 71. **CAREER** Summer instr, Harvard Divinity Sch, 67; tchg fel, Harvard Univ, 69; part time instr, Northeastern Univ, 70; asst prof, Scripps Col; Claremont Col, 70-71; vis prof, Claremont Col, 78-79; vis prof, Yale Divinity Sch, 86-87; prof, 71; pres, 87-. **HONORS AND AWARDS** Assoc pastor, Trinity Lutheran Church, 72-75; bd mem, Tentmakers Ministries; Lutheran Leadership Inst; co-ch, LukeActs Semr of the Soc Bibl Lit; ch of bd of publ, Evangel Lutheran Church Am, ELCA. **SELECTED PUBLICATIONS** Auth, Jesus and the Future, 90; Holy Week: Proclamation 4, 89; Luke: Augsburg Commentary on the New Testament, 88; Search Bible Studies, Units I and II, 83; Prophecy and History, LukeActs, 80. **CONTACT ADDRESS** Dept of New Testament, Luther Sem, 2481 Como Ave, St. Paul, MN, 55108. **EMAIL** dtiede@luthersem.edu

TIERNEY, JAMES E.
DISCIPLINE LAW **EDUCATION** Rutgers Col, BA; Univ NY, JD, LLM. **CAREER** Prof. **SELECTED PUBLICATIONS** Auth, Equitable Recoupment Revised, Ky Law J, 92; Reassessing Sales and Liquidations of Partnership Interests, Fla Tax Rev, 94. **CONTACT ADDRESS** Col Law, Univ of Toledo, Toledo, OH, 43606. **EMAIL** jtierne@uoft02.utoledo.edu

TIERNEY, KEVIN HUGH
PERSONAL Born 09/22/1942, Bristol, United Kingdom, s **DISCIPLINE** HISTORY; LAW **EDUCATION** Cambridge Univ, BA, 64, LLB, 65, MA, 68; Yale Univ, LLM, 67. **CAREER** Lawyer, Donovan Leisure Newton & Irvine, NYC, 68-70; assoc prof to prof, Wayne State Univ Law School, 71-79; vis prof to PROF, HASTINGS COL LAW UNIV CALIF, 79-. McMahon Law Studentship, St John's Col, 65; Lord Mansfield Schol, Lincoln's Inn, 66; Sterling fel Yale Law School, 67; Ransom Ctr fel Univ Texas, 92 & 95. **MEMBERSHIPS** MI State Bar; ALI. **RESEARCH** Conflict of laws; Jurisprudence; Legal history; Biography in general. **SELECTED PUBLICATIONS** Courtroom Testimony: A Policeman's Guide, 71; How to be a Witness, 72; Darrow: A Biography, 79. **CONTACT ADDRESS** 200 McAllister St, Rm 353, San Francisco, CA, 94102. **EMAIL** tierneyk@uchastings.edu

TIERNEY, NATHAN L.
PERSONAL Born 03/16/1953, Swansea, Ukraine, m, 1985, 2 children **DISCIPLINE** PHILOSOPHY **EDUCATION** Columbia Univ, PhD, 89. **CAREER** Calif Lutheran Univ, 90-98; Assoc Prof, Calif Lutheran Univ. **MEMBERSHIPS** Am Philos Asn; Soc for Christian Philos; Nat Asn of Scholars; Asn for Appl and Practical Ethics. **RESEARCH** Ethics; Moral Psychology; Metaphysics of Morals. **SELECTED PUBLICATIONS** Auth, Imagination and Ethical Ideals, 94. **CONTACT ADDRESS** Dept of Philosophy, California Lutheran Univ, Thousand Oaks, CA, 91360. **EMAIL** tierney@clunet.edu

TIERSMA, PETER M.
DISCIPLINE LAW **EDUCATION** Stanford Univ, BA, 74; Univ Calif, San Diego, PhD, 80; Univ Calif, Berkeley, JD, 86. **CAREER** Prof & Joseph Scott fel; Fulbright fel, Neth; lectr, Univ Calif, San Diego & Miami Univ Ohio; clerk, Justice Stanley Mosk, Calif Supreme Ct; private practice, Pettit & Martin, San Francisco & Price, Postel & Parma, Santa Barbara fac, Loyola Law Sch, 90-. **SELECTED PUBLICATIONS** Writes on, relationship between language and the law. **CONTACT ADDRESS** Law School, Loyola Marymount Univ, 7900 Loyola Blvd, Burns 424, Los Angeles, CA, 90045. **EMAIL** ptiersma@lmulaw.lmu.edu

TIESSEN, TERRANCE
PERSONAL Born 02/18/1944, Hamilton, ON, Canada, m, 1965, 4 children **DISCIPLINE** THEOLOGY **EDUCATION** Ontario Bible Col, BTh, 64; Sir Wilfred Laurier Univ, BA, 66; Wheaton Col, MA, 68; Westminster Theol Sem, ThM, 75; Ateneo de Manila Loyola Sch Theol, PhD, 84. **CAREER** Asian Theol Sem Manila, prof, 75-86; Ontario Bible Col, vpres acad & student affairs, 86-89; Providence Col, prof, 93-96; Providence Theol Sem, prof, 93-. **MEMBERSHIPS** AAP, ACT, CETA, CTS, ETS, SCE. **RESEARCH** Divine providence; theology of religion; theology of petitionary prayer. **SELECTED PUBLICATIONS** Auth, Gnosticism as Heresy: The Response of Irenaeus, in: Hellenization Revisited: Shaping a Christian Response within the Greco-Roman World, ed., W.E. Helleman, NY: Univ Press Am, 94; auth, Irenaeus on the Salvation of the Unevangelized, ATLA Monograph Series, Metuchen NJ: Scarecrow Press, 93; auth, Divine Justice and Universal Grace: A Calvinistic Proposal, in: Evangel Rev Theol, 97; auth, Irenaeus and Modern Responses to the Challenge of Religious Pluralism, ATA Jour, 96; auth, Can the Unevangelism Be Saved?: A Review Article, Didaskalia, 93. **CONTACT ADDRESS** Dept of Theology, Providence Theol Sem, Otterburne, MB, R0A 1G0. **EMAIL** ttiessen@providence.mb.ca

TIGAY, JEFFREY HOWARD
PERSONAL Born 12/25/1941, Detroit, MI, m, 1965, 4 children **DISCIPLINE** BIBLICAL STUDIES, ANCIENT NEAR EASTERN LITERATURE **EDUCATION** Columbia Col, BA, 63; Jewish Theol Sem, Am, MHL, 66; Yale Univ, PhD(comp Blbl & Ancient Near East Studies), 71. **CAREER** Jewish Studies Ellis asst prof, 71-77, M Ellis assoc prof to prof Hebrew & Semitic Lang & Lit, Univ Pa, 77-86, Grantee, Nat Sci Found, 72; assoc, Univ Sem on Studies Hebrew Bible, Columbia Univ, 72; Am Coun Learned Soc fel, 75-76; fel, inst Advan Studies, Hebrew Univ, Jerusalem, 78-79; grant, Am Philos Soc, 80 & Am Coun Learned Soc, 80-81; Nat Endowment for Humanties summer res fel, 80; Mem Fedn Jewish Cult fel, 81-82; vis assoc prof, Bible Jewish Theol Sem Am. **HONORS AND AWARDS** Elected fel, Am Acad for Jewish Research, 86; Lindback Award for disting teaching, Univ of Pennsylvania. **MEMBERSHIPS** Am Acad for Jewish Research, Am Schools of Oriental Res; Assoc for Jewish Studies; The Biblical Colloquium; Soc of Biblical Lit. **RESEARCH** Biblical literature; comparative Biblical and ancient Near Eastern studies; ancient Judaism. **SELECTED PUBLICATIONS** Tehilla Le-Moshe Biblical and Judaic Studies in Honor of Moshe Greenberg, Winona Lake, Indiana, Eisenbraun's, coed with M Cogan and B I Eichler. **CONTACT ADDRESS** Dept Orient Studies, Univ of Pennsylvania, 255 S 36th St, Philadelphia, PA, 19104-3805. **EMAIL** jtigay@sas.upenn.edu

TILES, J.E.
PERSONAL Born 01/16/1944, Racine, WI, m, 1969 **DISCIPLINE** PHILOSOPHY **EDUCATION** Carleton Col, BA, 66; Univ Bristol, BA, 68; Univ Bristol, MA, 70; Oxford Univ, PhD, 78 **CAREER** Lectr, Univ Reading, 74-89; prof, Univ Hawaii, 89- **RESEARCH** Ancient Philosophy, Ethics and Social Philosophy **SELECTED PUBLICATIONS** Dewey, Routledge, 88; co-auth, An Introduction to Historical Epistemology, Blackwell, 93; ed, John Dewey: Critical Assessments, Routledge, 92; "Mind, Consciousness and the Social Environment-A Reply to Biesta." Studies Philos Educ, 96; Routledge History of Philosophy, Routledge, 98 **CONTACT ADDRESS** Dept Philos, Univ Hawaii at Manoa, 2530 Dole St., Honolulu, HI, 96822. **EMAIL** jtiles@hawaii.edu

TILLERS, PETER
DISCIPLINE LAW OF EVIDENCE **EDUCATION** Boston Univ, JD, 55; Stanford Univ, AM, 60. **CAREER** Prof, Yeshiva Univ; vcprs, Acad Affairs. **HONORS AND AWARDS** Former chemn, secy,Evidence Secn Asn Am Law Schs; fel Law & Hum, Harvard Univ; Senior Max Rheinstein fel, Univ Munich; legal adv Latvian mission, UN. **RESEARCH** The process of fact investigation, and the logic of inductive inference. **SELECTED PUBLICATIONS** Areas: evidence, inference and investigation. **CONTACT ADDRESS** Yeshiva Univ, 55 Fifth Ave, NY, NY, 10003-4301. **EMAIL** tillers@ymail.yu.edu

TILLES, GERALD EMERSON
PERSONAL Born 07/15/1942, Detroit, MI, m **DISCIPLINE** LAW **EDUCATION** Wayne State U, BSED 1964, MA 1970, JD 1971. **CAREER** Detroit Bd Educ, tchr 1964-70; prv prctc law 1972-75; Cty Wayne, asst corp cnsl 1975-84; Bureau Wrkrs Dsblty Comp State Of MI, admn law judge 1984-, funds administrator 1987, magistrate 1987. **HONORS AND AWARDS** Robbins Awrd Wayne State Law Sch 1971. **MEMBERSHIPS** Pstr/fndr Chapel Savior Ann Arbor, MI 1980-; wrtr MI Chronicle 1971-74; bd review chrmn Superior Twp 1984-; mem Wolverine Bar Assc, State Bar MI; minister United Methodist Church. **CONTACT ADDRESS** State of Michigan, 1200 Sixth St, Detroit, MI, 48226.

TILLEY, JOHN
PERSONAL Born 02/15/1952, Omaha, NE **DISCIPLINE** PHILOSOPHY **EDUCATION** USMA, BS, 75; Univ Ga, MA, 83; Univ Wis, PhD, 88. **CAREER** Asst prof, 88-94, assoc prof, Ind Univ Perdue Univ Indianapolis (IUPUI), 94- . **HONORS AND AWARDS** FACET awd for excellence in tchg, 93; Ind Univ press awd for disting tchg, 97. **MEMBERSHIPS** Amer Philos Assn; S Soc Philos and Phsychol; Soc for Ethics. **RESEARCH** Ethics; Ethical Theory. **SELECTED PUBLICATIONS** Auth, Inner Judgements and Moral Relativism, Philos 18, 88, 171-190; Moral Relativism, Internalism, and the Humean View of Practical Reason, Mod Schoolman 69, 92, 81-109; Accounting for the Tragedy in the Prisoner's Dilemma, synthese 99, 94, 251-276; Two Kinds of Moral Relativism, Jour Value Inquiry 29, 95, 187-192; Motivation and Practical Reasons, Erkenntnis 47, 97, 105-127; Hedonism, in Encycl of Applied Ethics, San Diego, Academic Press Inc, 88, vol 2, 551-559; The Problem for Normative Cultural Relativism, Ratio Juris 11(3), 98, 272-290; Cultural Relativism, Universalism, and the Burden of Proof, Millennium 27(2), 275-297. **CONTACT ADDRESS** Dept of Philosophy, Indiana Univ-Purdue Univ, Indianapolis, 425 University Blvd, Indianapolis, IN, 46202. **EMAIL** jtilley@iupui.edu

TILLEY, TERRENCE W.
PERSONAL Born 04/19/1947, Milwaukee, WI, m, 1969, 2 children **DISCIPLINE** PHILOSOPHY OF RELIGION, SYSTEMATIC THEOLOGY **EDUCATION** Univ San Francisco, AB, 70; Grad Theol Union, Berkeley, PhD, 76. **CAREER** Tchg fel, Theol, The Church Divinity Sch Pacific, 72-74; asst prof Theol, Georgetown Univ, Wash DC, 76-79; asst, assoc prof Rel Stud, St. Michael's Col, Winooski, VT, 79-89; assoc prof to prof Rel, Fla State Univ, 89-94; prof, ch, 94- , Dir grad stud, 94-96, Univ Dayton. **HONORS AND AWARDS** Mackey Lectr, Chaminade Univ, Honolulu, HI, Oct, 96; Tchg Incentive prog awd, Fla State Univ, March 94; vis lectr, Georgetown Univ, Dept Theol, Annual Colloquium, Feb 92; Univ awd excellence tchg, Fla State Univ, 90-91; Col Arts Sci awd for excellence undergrad tchg, Fla State Univ, 90-91; Edmundite Lect in Cath Stud, St. Michael's Col, Vinooski VT, April 89; Bk of the Yr awd for Story Theol, by Col Theol soc, May 31, 86; Gerald E. Dupont awd of the St. Michael's Col Stud Assn for the Outstanding Contributer by a fac mem, to the Col, 83; dir, Natl Endow Human summer sem for sch tchrs, Fla State Univ, Summer 94; Dir, Natl Endow Human summer sem sch tchrs, St. Michael's Col, Summer 90; Fel Col tchrs, NEH, 87-88; Dir, NEH summer sem second tchrs, St. Michael's Col, Summer 87; Participant, NEH summer sem Col tchrs, Duke Univ, Summer, 85; Fel, State Calif, 70-72. **MEMBERSHIPS** Amer Acad Rel; Col Theol Soc; Soc Philos Rel; Cath Theol Soc Am; Karl Rahner Soc; Assn Rel Intellectual Life; Amer Assn Univ Prof. **SELECTED PUBLICATIONS** Auth, Talking of God: An Introduction to Philosophical Analysis of Religious Language, New York, Paulist Press, 78; Hume on God and Evil: Interpreting Dialogues X and IX as a Dramatic Conversation, Jour Am Acad Rel, 56, 4, Dec 88, 703-726; Intratextuality, Incommensurability, and Fideism, Modern Theol, 5, 2, Jan 89, 87-111; The Prudence of Religious Commitment, Horizons, 16, 1, Spring 89, 45-64; God and the Silencing of Job, Modern Theol, 5, 3, April 89, 257-270; Power, Authority and Life in Catholic Cultures, Books & Religion, 16, 3, Fall 89, 5, 26-31; Dying Children and Sacred Space, the Second Annual Edmundite Trust Fund Lecture Pamphlet, Winooski, VT, St Michael's Col, 89; Living Out and Living in The Catholic Tradition, Bk (s) and Rel, 17, 1, Spring 90, 6, 15; Reformed Epistemology and Religious Fundamentalism: How Basic Are Our Basic Beliefs?, Modern Theol, 6, 3, April 90, 237-257; Of Sinners, Saints, Searchers and Sectarians, Bk (s) and Rel, 17, 2, Summer 90, 6, 29, 36; Polemics and Politics in Explaining Religion, The Jour Rel, 71, 2, April 91, 242-254; Lord I Believe: Help My Unbelief: Prayer Without Belief, Modern Theol, 7, 3, April 91, 239-247; From Sea to Shining See, Bk (s) and Rel, 18, 2, Summer 91, 26-27, 38; Author;s Respone to Four Perspectives on The Evils of Theodicy by Alice Laffey, J. Patout Burns, Morny Joy, and Kenneth Surin, Horizons, 18, 2, Fall, 91, 306-312; The Evils of Theodicy, Georgetown UP, 91; Story Theology, Wilmington, Michael Glazier Inc, 85, reprint, Collegeville, Liturgical Press, 91; Extending the Long Black Line, Bk (s) and Rel, 19, 1, Spring 92, 21-22, 32-33; Reformed Epistemology in a Jamesian Perspective, Horizons, 19, 1, Spring 92, 84-98; Story, in New Dictionary of Catholic Spirituality, ed Michael Downey, A Michael Glazier Book, Collegeville, Liturgical Press, 93, 947-948; The Institutional Element in Religious Experience, Modern Theol, 10, 2, April 94, 185-212; Religious Pluralism as a Problem for Practical Religious Epistemology, Rel Stud, 30, 2, June 94, 161-169; The Gift of Walter Ong, Horizons, 21, 1, Spring, 94, 172-178; Evil, God, Existence of God, Knowledge of God, The Modern Catholic Encyclopedia for Faith and Living, Collegeville, Liturgical Press, 94, 299-300, 347-348, 305, 484; In Favor of a Practical Theory, of Religion: Montaigne and Pascal, in Theology Without Foundations, Nashville, Abingdon, 94, 49-74; The Wisdom of Religious Commitment, Georgetown Univ Press, 95; Postmodern Theologies: The Challenge of Religious Diversity, Maryknoll, Orbis, 95; Theodicies in Context, Proceedings of the Fiftieth Annual Convention of the Catholic Theological Society of America, 205-211; Narrative Theology Post Mortem Dei? Paul Ricoeur's Time and Narrative, Ill, and Postmodern Theologies, in Morny Joy, ed, Paul Ricoeur and Narrative: Context and Contestation, Calgary, U of Calgary P, 97, 175-195; Response to My Critics, Philos and Theol, 98, 93-99; co-ed, The Exercise of the Primacy: Continuing the Dialogue, NY, Crossroad Publ Co, 98. **CONTACT ADDRESS** Dept of Religious Studies, Univ of Dayton, Dayton, OH, 45469-1530. **EMAIL** tilley@checkov.hm.udayton.edu

TIMBIE, JANET ANN
PERSONAL Born 10/17/1948, San Francisco, CA, m, 1969, 1 child **DISCIPLINE** HISTORY OF CHRISTIANITY, COPTIC LANGUAGE **EDUCATION** Stanford Univ, AB, 70; Univ Pa, PhD(relig studies), 79. **CAREER** Reader hist and relig, Am Univ, 71-72 and prof lectr relig, 80-81; Dumbarton Oaks Ctr for Byzantine Studies fel, 78-79; Mellon fel, Cath Univ, 79-80; RES AND WRITING, 82-, Ed and transl, US Cath Conf Bishops, 79-82. **MEMBERSHIPS** Cath Bibl Asn; Soc Bibl Lit; Am Acad Relig; Int Asn Coptic Studies. **RESEARCH** Christianity in Egypt through 5th century; development of early Christian monasticism; Coptic language and literature. **SELECTED PUBLICATIONS** Auth, The dating of a Coptic-Sahidic Psalter codex from the University Museum in Philadelphia, Le Museon, 75; Dualism and the Concept of Orthodoxy in the Thought of the Monks of Upper Egypt, Edwin Mellen P; The Status of Women and Gnosticism in Irenaeus and Tertullian, Cath Biblical Quart, Vol 0058, 96; coauth, The Nag Hammadi library in English, Religious Studies Rev, 82; co-ed, The Testament of Job, Scholars Press, 75. **CONTACT ADDRESS** 4608 Merivale Rd, Chevy Chase, MD, 20815.

TIMMERMAN, JOAN H.
PERSONAL Born 11/14/1938, Dickeyville, WI, s **DISCIPLINE** RELIGIOUS STUDIES **EDUCATION** Marquette Univ, PhD. **CAREER** Prof Theol; Prof Leadership Studies, Col St. Catherine.. **HONORS AND AWARDS** Sr. Mona Riley Prof Humanities, 93-96; Ann O'Hare Graff Award, Cath Theol Soc Am, 97. **MEMBERSHIPS** CTSA; SSSS; AAUP **RESEARCH** Sacramental theory; sexuality; Clare Boothe Luce - politics and spirituality. **SELECTED PUBLICATIONS** Auth, Sexuality and Spiritual Growth, Crossroad, 92; co-ed, Walking in Two Worlds. Women's Spiritual Paths, North Star Press, 92; auth, Rethinking Christian Sexuality, The Spiral Path, Yes Int Publ, 93; Religion and Violence. The Persistence of Ambivalence, Transforming a Rape Culture, Milkweed Press, 93; Sex: Sacred or Profane?, Readings in Moral Theology, No. 8. Dialogue About Catholic Sexual Teaching, Paulist, 93; The Sexuality of Jesus and the Human Vocation, Sexuality and the Sacred. Sources for Theological Reflection, Westminster/John Knox, 94. **CONTACT ADDRESS** Col of St. Catherine, 2004 Randolph Ave., #4240, St. Paul, MN, 55105. **EMAIL** JHTimmerman@stkate.edu

TINSLEY, FRED LELAND, JR.
PERSONAL Born 08/30/1944, Detroit, MI, m **DISCIPLINE** LAW **EDUCATION** So U, BA 1969; So U, JD 1972. **CAREER** Champman Tinsley & Reese, prtnr present; Lone Star Gas Co, regulatory atty 1975-77; US Secur & Exchange Commn, trial atty 1973-75; LA Constl Conv, resrch asst 1973; Reginald Heber Smith Fellow Legal Serv 1972. **MEMBERSHIPS** Bd of dir Mental Hlth Assn of Dallas 1976-78; mem adv coun TX Employ Commn 1977-79; bd of dir Dallas Legal Serv Found Inc 1979-; mem exec com Dallas Co Dem Party 1980-; bd of dir Jr Black Acad of Arts & Letters Inc 1980-; asso judge Dallas Muncpl Cts 1978-. **CONTACT ADDRESS** Chapman Tinsley & Reese, One Brookriver Pl, Ste 370, Dallas, TX, 75247.

TIROSH SAMUELSON, HAVA
DISCIPLINE RELIGIOUS STUDIES **EDUCATION** Hebrew Univ Jerusalem, PhD, 78. **CAREER** Prof. **RESEARCH** Medieval and early modern Jewish intellectual history; Jewish philosophy, Kabbalah; medieval European intellectual history. **SELECTED PUBLICATIONS** Auth, Between Worlds-The Life and Thought of Rabbi David ben Judah Messer Leon, SUNY, 91; Continuity and Revision in the Study of Kabbalah, AJS Rev, 91. **CONTACT ADDRESS** Dept of Religious Studies, Indiana Univ, Bloomington, 300 N Jordan Ave, Bloomington, IN, 47405.

TISO, FRANCIS V.
PERSONAL Born 09/19/1950, Mount Vernon, NY **DISCIPLINE** THEOLOGY **EDUCATION** Columbia Univ and Union Theol Seminary, NY, NY, Mphil, 86, PhD, 89; Harvard Univ, Cambridge, MA, Mdiv, 75-78; Cornell Univ Coll of Arts and Sci, Ithaca, NY, AB, 68-72. **CAREER** Docente, 96-97, Univ della Terza Eta, Isernia; Le Rel dell'India Medioevale, 97-98; docente Invitato, Buddhist and Christian Soteriologh, 95-96, Studio Teologico Fiorentino; Direttore to Docente, 86-93, Istituto di Sci Rel, Isernia, Italy; Teaching Asst, 84-85, Columbia Univ; Lectr, Dept of Rel and Philos, 78-83, Mercer Coll; Ed and Admin, 80-83, The Seabury Press, NY. **HONORS AND AWARDS** Amer Philos Soc Res Fellowship, 97-; Amer Acad of Rel Res Fellowship, 97; Pres Fellow, Columbia Univ, 85-87; Field Examinations; Comprehensive Examinations. **MEMBERSHIPS** AOS, AAR. **RESEARCH** Life, songs and teaching of Milanesa, Theology and spirituality of Evagrius Ponticus. **SELECTED PUBLICATIONS** Auth, The Voice of Milarepa: Redaction-critical Research on the Songs and Oral Teachings, The VIIIth Intl Seminar of the IATS, Bloomington, IN, 98; The Sign Beyond All Signs: Christian Monasticism in Dialogue with India, Bangalore Asirvanam Benedictine Monastery, 97; A Catholic Priest Takes a Look at Tibetan Buddhism and Interreligious Dialogue, Lecture at Library of Tibetan Works and Archives, Dharamasala, HP, India, 97; Resurrection and Transformation in Early Christianity and in the Trajectory of Evagrius Ponticus, at the Museum of Science, Brescia, 96. **CONTACT ADDRESS** St Bernard Church, 615 H St., Box 169, Eureka, CA, 95502. **EMAIL** tiso@northcoast.com

TITIEV, ROBERT JAY
PERSONAL Born 07/01/1941, Ann Arbor, MI, m, 1970 **DISCIPLINE** PHILOSOPHY OF SCIENCE **EDUCATION** Harvard Univ, AB, 64; Stanford Univ, MS, 66, PhD(philos), 69. **CAREER** Asst prof, 69-77, assoc prof philos, Wayne State Univ, 77-. **HONORS AND AWARDS** Res grant-in-aid, 72-73. **MEMBERSHIPS** Asn of Symbolic Logic. **RESEARCH** Logic; measurement theory. **SELECTED PUBLICATIONS** Auth, Second Year Algebra, Encycl Britannica Films, 61; Some Model-theoretic Rsults in Measurement Theory, Tech Report, Inst Math Studies Soc, Stanford Univ, 69; Measurement Structures in Classes that are Not Universally Axiomatizable, J Math Psychol, 72; Multidimensional Measurement and Universal Axiomatizability, Theoria, 72; Kripke, Rigid Designators, and Cartesian Dualism, Philos Studies, 74; Computer Presentation of Topics in Measurement Theory, J Educ Data Processing, 74; Sentences, Semantics, Stimuli, and Quine, Theoria, 75; A Locus Problem Involing the Three-dimensional City-block Metric, J Math Psychol, 80; Diagnosis of Ailing Belief Systems, J Philos Res, 93; Causal Trouble, J Philos Res, 95; Arbitrage and the Dutch Book Theorem, J Philos Res, 97; Finiteness, Perception, and the Contrasting Cases of Mathematical Idealization, J Philos Res, 98. **CONTACT ADDRESS** Dept Philos, Wayne State Univ, 51 W Warren Ave, Detroit, MI, 48202-3919.

TM, KING
PERSONAL Born 05/09/1929, Pittsburgh, PA, s **DISCIPLINE** RELIGIOUS STUDIES; THEOLOGY; ENGLISH **EDUCATION** Univ Pitts, BA, 51; Fordham Univ, MA, 59; Univ Strasbourg, DSR, 68. **CAREER** Asst prof, 68-74, assoc prof, 74-89, full prof, 89-, Georgetown Univ. **MEMBERSHIPS** Cosmos & Creation; Univ Fac for Life. **RESEARCH** Science and religion; Psychology and religion; History of spirituality. **SELECTED PUBLICATIONS** Auth, Sartre and the Sacred, Univ Chicago Press, 74; Teilhard's Mysticism of Knowing, Seabury, 81; Teilhard de Chardin, Glazier, 88; Enchantments, Religion and the Power of the Word, Sheed & Ward, 89; Merton: Mystic at the Center of America, Liturgical, 92; Jung's Four & Some Philosophers, Univ Notre Dame Press, 98; coed, Letters of Teilhard de Chardin and Lucile Swan, Georgetown Univ Press, 93. **CONTACT ADDRESS** Dept of Theology, Georgetown Univ, Washington, DC, 20057. **EMAIL** kingt@gunet.georgetown.edu

TOADVINE, TED
PERSONAL Born 03/12/1968, Salisbury, MD, s **DISCIPLINE** PHILOSOPHY **EDUCATION** Salisbury State Univ, BA, philos, 90; Univ Memphis, philos, MA, 95; PhD, 96. **CAREER** William F. Dietrich res fel, Fla Atlantic Univ, 96-97; visiting prof, philos, Kalamazoo Col, 97-98; asst prof, philos, Emporia State Univ, 98-. **MEMBERSHIPS** The Merleau-Ponty Circle; Soc for Phenomenol and Existential Philos; Amer Philos Asn; Southern Soc for Philos & Psychol. **RESEARCH** Phenomenology; Existentialism; Post-structuralism; Environmental philosophy; Aesthetics; Philosophy of nature; History of philosophy. **SELECTED PUBLICATIONS** Auth, The Art of Doubting: Merleau-Ponty and Cezanne, Philos Today, 41, Winter, 97; auth, Absolution of Finitude in Hegel's Phenomenology of Spirit, Southwest Philos Rev, 12, Jul, 96; auth, Hermeneutics and the Principle of Explicability, Auslegung, 20, Summer, 95. **CONTACT ADDRESS** Div. of Social Sciences, Emporia State Univ, Box 4032, Emporia, KS, 66801-5087. **EMAIL** toadvint@emporia.edu

TOBIAS, CARL WILLIAM
DISCIPLINE ADMINISTRATIVE LAW, CONSTITUTIONAL LAW **EDUCATION** Univ Va, LLB. **CAREER** Prof, Univ Montana; vis fac, Georgetown Univ, Temple Univ, Univ NC, Univ Pittsburgh, Rutgers Univ-Camden and Seton Hall; prof, Univ Nev, Las Vegas. **MEMBERSHIPS** Am Law Inst; Dist Ct Local Rules Rev Comt; 9th Circuit Judicial Coun and the Civil Justice Reform Act Adv Gp; US Dist Ct for the Dist of Mont. **SELECTED PUBLICATIONS** Wrote extensively in the areas of federal civil procedure and federal courts, publishing articles in numerous journals, including Cornell Law Rev, Stanford Law Rev, Columbia Law Rev, and Harvard J on Legis. **CONTACT ADDRESS** Univ Nev, Las Vegas, Las Vegas, NV, 89154.

TOBIN, FRANK J.
DISCIPLINE MEDIEVAL LITERATURE AND PHILOSOPHY, GERMAN **EDUCATION** Stanford Univ, PhD. **CAREER** Prof Ger, Univ Nev, Reno; ed bd, Studia Mystica and Mystic Quart. **RESEARCH** Translation of Mechthild von Magdeburg. **SELECTED PUBLICATIONS** Published major books on Meister Eckhart and on Mechthild von Magdeburg, numerous articles on the German Middle Ages, and a co-

authored two-volume anthology of German literature. **CONTACT ADDRESS** Univ Nev, Reno, Reno, NV, 89557. **EMAIL** tobinf@scs.unr.edu

TOBIN, THOMAS HERBERT
PERSONAL Born 11/08/1945, Chicago, IL **DISCIPLINE** NEW TESTAMENT, CHRISTIAN ORIGINS **EDUCATION** Xavier Univ, Ohio, LittB, 67; Loyola Univ Chicago, AM, 73; Harvard Univ, PhD(relig studies), 80. **CAREER** Instr, Xavier Univ, Ohio, 69-70; grad asst, Harvard Univ, 77-80; ASST PROF THEOL, LOYOLA UNIV CHICAGO, 80- **MEMBERSHIPS** Cath Bibl Asn; North Am Patristic Soc; Soc Bibl Lit. **RESEARCH** Ancient philosophy; intertestamental Judaism. **SELECTED PUBLICATIONS** Auth, 4-Ezra--A Commentary on the Book of 4-Ezra, Cath Bibl Quart, Vol 0055, 93; What Shall We Say That Abraham Found in An Analysis of the Relationship Between Jewish Scriptural Interpretation and Traditional Roman Christian Views on Judaism--The Controversy Behind Romans IV, Harvard Theol Rev, Vol 0088, 95; The Self-Perception of the Jewish Diaspora in the Literature of the Hellenistic and Roman Times, Cath Bibl Quart, Vol 0057, 95; The Apocryphon-of-Jannes-and-Jambres-the-Magicians, J Bibl Lit, Vol 0114, 95; Controversy and Continuity in Romans I,18-III, 20 in Observance of the Mosaic Law and Faith in Christ as an Attempt at Appealing to Hellenistic Judaism and 1st-Century Roman Christianity, A Restatement of A Pauline Position, Cath Bibl Quart; The Corinthian Body, Theol Studies, Vol 0057, 96; The Text and Textual Value of Greek Manuscripts of the New-Testament, Pt 3, The Acts of the Apostles, Vol 1, Studies and Supplementary Table, Vol 2, Main Table, Bull Am Soc. **CONTACT ADDRESS** Loyola Univ, Chicago, 1331 W Albion Ave, Chicago, IL, 60626.

TODD, DONALD DAVID
PERSONAL Born 10/26/1930, Pine Bluff, AR, m, 1951, 2 children **DISCIPLINE** PHILOSOPHY **EDUCATION** San Francisco State Col, BA, 58; Univ BC, PhD(philos), 67. **CAREER** Instr philos, Golden State Col, 60-61; lectr, Univ BC, 64-67; asst prof, 67-73, ASSOC PROF PHILOS, SIMON FRASER UNIV, 73- **MEMBERSHIPS** Can Philos Asn. **RESEARCH** Epistemology; history of British Empiricism; aesthetics. **SELECTED PUBLICATIONS** Auth, Reid Redivivus?, Tex Studies Lit Lang 72; Direct Perception, Philos Phenomenol Res, 3/75; Henry James and the Theory of Literary Realism, Philos Lit, fall 76; coauth, Adjusters and Sense Data, Am Philos Quart, 1/72; ed, The Philosophical Orations of Thomas Reid, Philos Res Archives, 6/77. **CONTACT ADDRESS** Dept of Philos, Simon Fraser Univ, Burnaby, BC, V5A 1S6.

TODD, VIRGIL H.
PERSONAL Born 06/22/1921, Davidson Co, TN, m, 1941, 1 child **DISCIPLINE** RELIGION **EDUCATION** Bethel Col, BA, 45; Cumberland Presby Theol Sem, BD, 47; Scarritt Col, MA, 48; Vanderbilt Univ, PhD(Old Testament), 56. **CAREER** Instr, Bethel Col, 46-47, assoc, prof Bible & Relig, 52-54, prof Old Testament, Memphis Theol Sem, 54-, minister, Cumberland Presby Churches, Tenn & Ky, asst moderator, Gen Assembly, 64-65 & 79-80, moderator, Tenn Synod, 67-68; moderator, Gen Assembly, 85-86. **MEMBERSHIPS** Soc Bibl Lit. **RESEARCH** Prophetic Eschatology; the prophecy of Ezekiel. **SELECTED PUBLICATIONS** Auth, The Eschatology of Second Isaiah & Prophet Without Portfolio, Christopher, 72. **CONTACT ADDRESS** Memphis Theol Sem, 168 E Parkway S, Memphis, TN, 38104-4340.

TOENJES, RICHARD H.
DISCIPLINE PHILOSOPHY, BUSINESS ETHICS **EDUCATION** St Louis Univ, BA, 66, MA, 67; Univ Southern CA, PhD, 77. **CAREER** Asst prof, Univ NC, Charlotte. **RESEARCH** Moral motivation in business ethics; existentialist notions of freedom and commitment. **SELECTED PUBLICATIONS** Auth, Toward A Critical Habit of Mind: The Course in Critical Thinking at UNC-Charlotte, APA Newsl on Tchg Philos, 87; coauth, Integrating Liberal Learning into Technical Education, Thought and Action, Vol V, No 2, 89; The Engineer and The Societal Dilemma: A Team Taught Interdisciplinary Approach, 1990 ASEE-SE Sect Proc, Apr, 90. **CONTACT ADDRESS** Univ N. Carolina, Charlotte, Charlotte, NC, 28223-0001. **EMAIL** rhtoenje@email.uncc.edu

TOLLEFSON, CHRIS
DISCIPLINE LAW **EDUCATION** Queen's Univ, BA, 82; Univ Victoria, LLB, 85; Osgoode Hall Law Sch, LLM, 93. **CAREER** Law, Univ Victoria **HONORS AND AWARDS** Exec dir, Univ Victoria Environ Law Centre. **MEMBERSHIPS** Chair, Sierra Legal Defense Fund **SELECTED PUBLICATIONS** Auth, The Wealth of Forests: Markets, Regulation and Sustainable Forestry, Univ British Columbia, 89; pubs on environmental law. **CONTACT ADDRESS** Fac of Law, Univ Victoria, PO Box 2400, Victoria, BC, V8W 3H7. **EMAIL** ctollef@uvic.ca

TOLLIVER, JOEL
PERSONAL Born 02/26/1946, Philadelphia, Pennsylvania, m **DISCIPLINE** THEOLOGY **EDUCATION** Lincoln Univ, BA 1969; Yale Univ, MPH 1971; Colgate Bexler Crozer Theol Sem, MDiv 1985; SUNY at Buffalo, educ admin, PhD 1995. **CAREER** Univ of Rochester, health educator 1971; Empire State Coll, asst prof 1973; Radio Sta WAXI, talk show host 1973-77; City of Rochester, asst to city mgr 1974-82; Monroe Comm Coll, chaplain & administrator; Brockport State Coll, chaplain, admin and inst 1987; Devry Institute of Technology, dean. **HONORS AND AWARDS** Young Man of Am Comm Serv US Jaycees 1977; Comm Serv to Black Ch & Comm United Ch Ministry Inc 1978 & 79; Comm Serv NAACP Elmira State Prison 1980; Church & Comm Serv Award United Ch Ministry, Inc 1983; ed excel awd Black Student Union Monroe Comm Coll 1984; outstanding adult & student awd Rochester Area Coll 1985; leadership dev inst awd SUNY at Brockport 1986; Organization of Students of African Descent Awd for Service to Afro-American Students 1985-89; Nat'l Assoc of Negro Women Awd for Comm Service 1986; United Ch Ministry Awd for Service to Black Family & Community 1986; Community Mediator, Hudson Valley Mohawk Association, 1986; Certificate of Achievement, Martin Luther King Center for Social Change, 1989-90; Conflict/Management Medicator, Center for Dispute Settlement, 1990; New York State Assembly Award for Community Service, 1995. **MEMBERSHIPS** Consult Brockport State Coll 1974; consult Genessee Comm Coll 1974; bd mem United Ch Ministry Inc 1979; bd mem Bridge Vol Inc 1979; mem Urban League 1979; mem Alpha Phi Alpha Frat Inc; mem Alpha Phi Omega Nat Serv Frat; mem Phi Delta Kappa Educational Society, 1989; mem Benevolent Order of Elks; mem Nat'l Sickle Cell Org; mem Martin Luther King Health Center.

TOLLIVER, RICHARD LAMAR
PERSONAL Born 06/26/1945, Springfield, Ohio, d **DISCIPLINE** THEOLOGY **EDUCATION** Miami Univ, Oxford, OH, BA, religion, 1967; Boston Univ, Boston, MA, MA, Afro-American Studies, 1971; Episcopal Divinity School, Cambridge, MA, Master of Divinity, 1971; Howard Univ, Washington, DC, PhD, political science, 1982; Boston Univ, Boston, MA, political science, 1986. **CAREER** St Cyprian's Church, Boston, MA, rector, 1972-77; St Timothy's Church, Washington, DC, rector, 1977-84; US Peace Corps, Kenya, assoc country dir, 1984-86; US Peace Corps, Mauritania, country dir, 1986-88; Howard Univ, Washington, DC, prof, 1988-89; St Edmund's Episcopal Church, Chicago, IL, rector, 1989-. **HONORS AND AWARDS** Fellowship for Doctoral Studies, Natl Science Foundation, 1979-82; Distinguished Service Award, St Augustine's Coll, 1983; Regional Finalist, White House Fellowship, 1983; Distinguished Achievement Medal, Miami University, 1996. **MEMBERSHIPS** Natl Conference of Black Political Scientists, 1982-; Beta Boule, Sigma Pi Phi Fraternity, 1991-; Omega Psi Phi Fraternity, 1968-; pres, St Edmund's Redevt Corp, 1989-; natl bd of dir, Union of Black Episcopalians; vice pres, board of directors, St Edmund's Academy; board of directors of trustees, Bennett College. **CONTACT ADDRESS** Priest, St Edmund's Episcopal Church, 6105 South Michigan Avenue, Chicago, IL, 60637.

TOLTON, CAMERON DAVID EDWARD
PERSONAL Born 08/15/1936, Toronto, ON, Canada **DISCIPLINE** ROMANCE LANGUAGES AND LITERATURES, CINEMA **EDUCATION** Univ Toronto, BA, 58; Harvard Univ, AM, 59, PhD(Romance lang and lit), 65. **CAREER** From lectr to asst prof, 64-69, ASSOC PROF FRENCH, VICTORIA COL, UNIV TORONTO, 69-, MEM, ADV ACAD PANEL, SOC SCI AND HUMANITIES RES COUN OF CAN, 79- **MEMBERSHIPS** MLA; Asn Can Univ Teachers Fr; Can Comp Lit Asn; Film Studies Asn Can. **RESEARCH** Andre Gide; the French novel, 1800-1950; French autobiography. **SELECTED PUBLICATIONS** Auth, Image-Conveying Abstractions in the Works of Andre Gide in Image and Theme: Studies in Modern French Fiction, Harvard Univ, 69; Andre Gide and the Art of Autobiography, Macmillan, Can, 75; The Revirement: A Structural Key to the Novels of Francois Mauriac, Aus J Fr Studies, 1-4/75; Andre Gide and Christopher Isherwood: Two Worlds of Counterfeiters, Comp Lit, spring 78; Le Mottheme Attente et l'Ironie Gidienne, Bull Des Amis D'Andre Gide, 1/82; A Lost Screenplay Unearthed, Mod Lang Rev, Vol 0088, 93; Symbolism And Irony--A New Reading Of Gide 'Traite De Narcisse,' Studi Francesi, Vol 0040, 96. **CONTACT ADDRESS** Dept of French Victoria Col, Univ of Toronto, Toronto, ON, M5S 1K7.

TOMARCHIO, JOHN
PERSONAL Born 08/08/1962, Brooklyn, NY **DISCIPLINE** PHILOSOPHY **EDUCATION** Columbia Univ, BA, 84; MA, 94, PhD, 96, Catholic Univ of Amer. **CAREER** NEH Fel, 96-98, Core Curriculum, Boston Univ; Asst Prof, 98-, Villanova Univ. **HONORS AND AWARDS** Natl Fulbright Fel, Milan-Rome, 94-95. **MEMBERSHIPS** Amer Phil Assoc; Amer Catholic Phil Assoc; Societe Intl Pour L'Etude De la Philosophie Medievale; Soc for Medieval & Renaissance Phil; Soc for Ancient Greek Phil. **RESEARCH** Classical Metaphysics; Thomas Acquinas; history of philosophy **SELECTED PUBLICATIONS** Auth, Four Indices for the Thomistic Axiom: Omne quod recipitur in aliquo recipitur in eo secundum modum recipientis, Medieval Studies, 98; Thomistic Axiomatics in an Age of Computers, History of Philosphy Quarterly, forthcoming. **CONTACT ADDRESS** 150 E. Wynnewood Rd. #236, Wynnewood, PA, 19096. **EMAIL** jtomarch@email.vill.edu

TOMINAGA, THOMAS T.
PERSONAL Pago Pago, American Samoa **DISCIPLINE** PHILOSOPHY **EDUCATION** San Francisco State Univ, BA, 63; Fisk Univ, MA, 65; Georgetown Univ, PhD(philos), 73. **CAREER** Asst prof, 71-79, ASSOC PROF PHILOS, UNIV NEV, LAS VEGAS, 79-, Vis prof East-West comp philos, Univ Orient Studies, Los Angeles, 73-74. **MEMBERSHIPS** Am Philos, Asn; Aristotelian Soc; Asn Asian Studies; Mind Asn; Soc Asian and Comp Philos. **RESEARCH** Analytic philosophy of language, logic, and mind; Wittgenstein-Zen Buddhism; East-West comparative philosophy. **SELECTED PUBLICATIONS** Auth, Wittgensteinian Approach to the Problem of Other Minds, Viewpoint, Winter 69; Auth, Symbols and Referents in Symbolic Logic, Int Logic Rev, 12/76; Reference and Meaning in The Language of Sensation, Lektos, Fall 77; Wittgenstein's Tractatus and Buddhist Four-Fold Logic, Proc Second Int Wittgenstein Symp, 78; Possibility of a Taoist-Like Wittgensteinian Environmental Ethics, J Chinese Philosophy, Vol 21, 94; Coauth, Iris Murdoch and Muriel Spark: A Bibliography, Scarecrow, 76. **CONTACT ADDRESS** Dept of Philos, Univ of Nev, 4505 Maryland Pkwy, Las Vegas, NV, 89154.

TOMLINSON, JOHN G.
DISCIPLINE LAW **EDUCATION** Univ Redlands, BA,66; Univ Calif, Irvine, MA,68; Univ Southern Calif, PhD,74. **CAREER** Assoc dean, Univ Southern Calif. **RESEARCH** Graduate relations, development, and activities central to the "Campaign for the Second Century." **SELECTED PUBLICATIONS** Auth, Surmounting the Prejudices: Four Lives in Legal Education, Community Lawyering, and Philanthropy; Shoulder to Shoulder: Women of the USC Law School During the Early Years & Largely a Student's School -- The Idea of Association. **CONTACT ADDRESS** School of Law, Univ Southern Calif, University Park Campus, Los Angeles, CA, 90089. **EMAIL** ttomlins@usc.edu

TONG, LIK KUEN
PERSONAL Born 10/26/1935, Hong Kong, m, 1969, 3 children **DISCIPLINE** PHILOSOPHY, RELIGION **EDUCATION** NY Univ, BS, 58; New Sch Social Res, PhD, 69. **CAREER** Asst prof, 67-74, assoc prof, 74-80, PROF PHILOS, FAIRFIELD UNIV, 80 -. **HONORS AND AWARDS** Outstanding Educator of America, Outstanding Educrs Am, 75. **MEMBERSHIPS** Am Philos Asn; Soc Asian & comp Philos; Asn Asian Studies; Soc Study Process Philos; Int Soc Chinese Philos; Int Inst for Field-Being. **RESEARCH** Metaphysics; comparative culture and philsophy; history of thought. **SELECTED PUBLICATIONS** Auth, The word and other poems, China Cult Enterprise Co, 69; Confucian jen and platonic eros: A comparative study, 9/73 & Care, wonder, and the polarization of being: An essay on human destiny, 9/74, Chinese Cult, Taipei; The concept of time in Whitehead and the I Ching, 9/74 & The meaning of philosophical silence: Some reflections on the use of language in Chinese thought, 3/76, J Chinese Philos; Context and reality: A critical interpretation of Whitehead's philosophy of organism (Chinese), China Soc Sci Press, 98. **CONTACT ADDRESS** Dept of Philos, Fairfield Univ, 1073 N Benson Rd, Fairfield, CT, 06430-5195. **EMAIL** lktong@fair1.fairfield.edu

TONG, ROSEMARIE
PERSONAL Born 07/19/1947, Chicago, IL, m, 1992, 2 children **DISCIPLINE** PHILOSOPHY **EDUCATION** Marygrove Col, BA, 70; Catholic Univ, MA, 71; Temple Univ, PhD, 78. **CAREER** Asst, assoc prof, philos, Williams Col, 78-88; vis prof, hum, 88-89, prof medical hum and philos, 89- Davidson Col, 89- ; vis prof philos and women's stud, Lafayette Col, 93; prof, liberal arts dept, Univ Miss, 98; dist prof health care ethics, Univ N Carolina, 99. **HONORS AND AWARDS** Teacher of the year, Williams Col, 82; Carnegie Found Prof of the Year, 86; hon DLaws, Marygrove Col, 87; hon DHL, SUNY Oneonta, 93; listed, Who's Who in American Education, Who's Who in the South and Southwest, Who's Who in America. **MEMBERSHIPS** Bioethics Resource Group; North Am Soc for Social Philos; Soc for Health and Human Values; North Am Soc for Social Philos; APA; Am Asn of Bioethics; Am Asn of Philos Tchrs; Am Asn of Univ Women; Am Legal Stud Asn; Am Soc of Law, Medicine, and Ethics; Am Soc for Polit and Legal Philos; Am Soc for Value Inquiry; Asn for Practical and Prof Ethics; Nat Coun for Res on Women; Nat Inst for Healthcare Res; Nat Women Stud Asn; Int Asn of Bioethics; Int Asn for Philos of Law and Social Philos; Int Soc for Value Inquiry. **RESEARCH** Feminist thought; bioethics; healthcare policy; professional and applied ethics. **SELECTED PUBLICATIONS** Auth, Feminine and Feminist Ethics, Wadsworth, 93; coauth, Controlling Our Reproductive Destiny: A Technological and Philosophical Perspective, MIT, 94; co-ed, Feminist Philosophy: Essential Readings in Theory, Reinterpretation, and Application, Westview, 94; auth, Unity in Diversity, Knowledge Products, 95; auth, Feminist Approaches to Bioethics, Westview, 96; co-ed, Feminist Philosophies: Problems, Theories, and Applications, Prentice-Hall, 2d ed, 97; auth, Feminist Thought: A More Comprehensive Introduction, Westview, 98. **CONTACT ADDRESS** Medical Humanities, Davidson Col, PO Box 1719, Davidson, NC, 28036. **EMAIL** rotong@davidson.edu

TOOTE, GLORIA E.A.
PERSONAL Born 11/08/1931, New York, NY **DISCIPLINE** LAW **EDUCATION** Howard Univ School Law, JD 1954; Columbia Univ Graduate School Law, LLM, 1956. **CAREER** Natl Affairs Section Time Magazine, former mem; NYC, Prac law 1954-71; Toote Town Publs Inc, pres; Action Agency Off Volunteer Action Liaison, asst director 1971-73; Dept Housing & Urban Devel, asst sec 1973-75; author & lecturer; NYC, presently engaged in practice of law; Trea Estates & Enter Inc, pres, currently. **HONORS AND AWARDS** Newsmakers Awd, Nat Assn of Black Women Atty, NY Fed of Civil Serv Org, Navajo Tribe, Nat Assn of Real Estate Brokers, Nat Citizens Participation Counc, Nat Bar Assn; YMCA World Serv Awd, Women's Nat Rep Club, New York City Housing Auth, Res Adv Counc MA-CT-NY-NJ, Pol Ldrshp Awd, NNPA. **MEMBERSHIPS** Bd mem, Arbitrator Assn, Consumer Alert, Council of Economic Affairs for the Republic/Natl Black United Fund; cited by the following organizations, Natl Business League, Alpha Kappa Alpha Sorority, US Chamber of Commerce, Natl Newspaper Publication Assn; member, Hoover Institution on War, Revolution and Peace; Fannie Mae, bd of dirs, 1992-. **CONTACT ADDRESS** Trea Estates & Enterprises Ins, 282 W 137th St, New York, NY, 10030-2407.

TOPEL, BERNADETTE
PERSONAL Born 09/16/1947, Minneapolis, MN, s **DISCIPLINE** SYSTEMATIC THEOLOGY **EDUCATION** Univ St. Michael's Col, PhD, 88. **CAREER** Instr, College St. Catherine, 77-78; instr, Fairfield Univ, 86-88; asst prof, Providence Col, 88- . **MEMBERSHIPS** Am Acad of Relig. **RESEARCH** Feminist theology. **CONTACT ADDRESS** 402 Centre Ave., Upper Nyack, NY, 10960.

TORELL, KURT CHARLES
PERSONAL Born 08/04/1962, Stockton, CA, m, 1991, 1 child **DISCIPLINE** PHILOSOPHY **EDUCATION** Boston Univ, BA, 83; Duquesne Univ, MA, 85, PhD, 92; Univ Pitt, MA, 87. **CAREER** Asst Prof, Assoc Prof, Dir, 94-, Lewis Clark State College. **HONORS AND AWARDS** Eugene Baldeck Awd; SAS Awd Teaching Excellence. **MEMBERSHIPS** Hume Soc; APA. **RESEARCH** Modern Philosophy, Native American Philosophy, Environmental Ethics. **SELECTED PUBLICATIONS** Auth, Socrates Meets Two Coyotes, J of Philo Res, 99, forthcoming. **CONTACT ADDRESS** Lewis-Clark State Col, 500 8th Ave, Lewiston, ID, 83501. **EMAIL** ktorell@lcsc.edu

TORIBIO, JOSEFA
PERSONAL Born 10/07/1961, Spain, m, 1991 **DISCIPLINE** PHILOSOPHY **EDUCATION** Complutense Univ, Madrid Spain, BA, 84, Pedagogical Qual, 85, MA, 85, PhD cum laude, 88. **CAREER** GAT, 85-88, asst prof, 89-93, Compultense Univ; asst prof Washington Univ, St. Louis, MO, 93-. **HONORS AND AWARDS** Fellowship DAAD, Dusseldorf, Ger; Fleming Fel, Univ Sussex, Brighton UK **MEMBERSHIPS** APA, SSLMPS **RESEARCH** Philo Mind; Cog Science. **SELECTED PUBLICATIONS** Auth, Meaning and Other Non-Biological Categories, Philo Papers, 88; Pulp Naturalism, Il Cannocchiale Rivista di Studi Filosofici, Twin Pleas: Probing Content and Compositionally Philo and Pheno Research, 97; Ecological Content Prag and Cog, 97; Language in the World, A Philosophical Inquiry Max J. Cresswell, Philo Psychology, 95; Ruritania and Ecology: Reply to Ned Block, Philo Issues, 95. **CONTACT ADDRESS** Dept of Philosophy, Washington Univ, One Brookings Dr, Campus PO Box 1, St. Louis, MO, 63130. **EMAIL** pepa@twinearth.wustl.edu

TORJESEN, KAREN JO
PERSONAL Born 10/10/1945, San Francisco, CA, d **DISCIPLINE** RELIGION **EDUCATION** Claremont Grad Sch, PhD, 82. **CAREER** George August Gottingen Germany, asst prof, 78-82; Mary Washington Col, asst prof, 82-85; Fuller Theol Sem, assoc prof, 85-87; Claremont Grad Univ, prof, 87-. **MEMBERSHIPS** ASCH, AAR. **RESEARCH** Hist Christianity; gender sexuality; women's hist. **SELECTED PUBLICATIONS** Auth, Hermeneutical Procedure and Theological Structure in Origen's Exegesis, Patristische Texte and Untersuchungen, Deutsche Akademie der Wissenschaft, Berlin: de Gruyter, 85; auth, When Women Were Priests: Women's leadership in the Early Church and the Scandal of their Subordination in the Rise of Christianity, Harper/Collins: San Francisco, 93; auth, Als Frauen noch Priesterinnen waren, Frankfurt: Zweitausendeins Verlag, 95; auth, In Praise of Noble Women: Gender and Honor in Ascetic Texts, in: Discursive Formations, Ascetic Piety and the Interpretation of Early Christian Literature, ed., V.Wimbush, Atlanta Press, 92; auth, Martyrs, Ascetics and Gnostics: Gender Crossing in Early Christianity, in: Gender Reversals, ed., S. Ramet, NY: Routledge, forthcoming. **CONTACT ADDRESS** Dept of Religion, Claremont Graduate Sch, Claremont, CA, 91711. **EMAIL** karen.torjesen@cgu.edu

TORNQUIST, LEROY J.
DISCIPLINE CIVIL PROCEDURE, EVIDENCE, NEGOTIATION, TRIAL & APPELLATE PRACTICE **EDUCATION** Northwestern Univ, BS, 62; JD, 65. **CAREER** Assoc, Williams, McCarthy & Kinley, Rockford, Ill, 65-66; partner, King, Robin, Gale & Pillinger, Chicago, 66-71; assoc dean, Loyola Univ, 71-77; vis prof, McGeorge Univ, 77-78; prof, 78-; dean, 78-87. **HONORS AND AWARDS** Ch, Proc & Reg Comm, Park Ridge, Ill, 71; officer, Ore Symphony of Salem, 91- 94. **MEMBERSHIPS** Member & Speakers Comm, Salem City Club, 93-. **SELECTED PUBLICATIONS** Co-auth, Trial Diplomacy. **CONTACT ADDRESS** Sch of Law, Willamette Univ, 900 State St, Salem, OR, 97301. **EMAIL** ltornqui@willamette.edu

TORRAGO, LORETTA
DISCIPLINE PHILOSOPHY **EDUCATION** New York Univ, BA, 89; Cornell Univ, PhD, 96. **CAREER** Asst Prof, 96-, Univ Utah **CONTACT ADDRESS** Dept of Philosophy, Univ of Utah, 341 Orson, Salt Lake City, UT, 84112. **EMAIL** l.torrago@m.cc.utah.edu

TORRES-GREGORY, WANDA
DISCIPLINE PHILOSOPHY **EDUCATION** Univ PR, BA, MA; Boston Univ, PhD. **CAREER** Part-time asst prof; tchr of the Yr Nomination, Suffolk Univ, 96. **RESEARCH** Latin Am philos; philos of lang; logic; 20th century philos. **SELECTED PUBLICATIONS** Auth, Traditional Language and Technological Language, a translations of Uberlieferte Sprache und Technische Sprache, 96; Heidegger y Quine: La posibilidad de un dialogo, in Dialogos 64, 94; Indeterminacy of Translation/ Subdeterminacy of Theory: A Critique, in Dialogos 53, 89; The Question in Latin American Philosophy, a presentation to the Philos Dept, Simmons Col, 96; Martin Heidegger: Language and Technology, a presentation to the Philos Soc, Suffolk Univ, 95. **CONTACT ADDRESS** Dept of Philos, Simmons Col, 300 The Fenway, Boston, MA, 02115.

TOULOUSE, MARK G.
PERSONAL Born 02/01/1952, Des Moines, IA, m, 1976, 3 children **DISCIPLINE** AMERICAN RELIGIOUS HISTORY **EDUCATION** Howard Payne Univ, BA, 74; Southwestern Baptist Theol Sem, MDiv, 77; Univ Chicago, PhD, 84. **CAREER** Instr, relig stud, Ill Benedictine Col, 80-82, asst prof, 82-84; asst prof of hist, Phillips Univ Grad Sem, 84-86; asst prof, Brite Divinity Sch, Texas Chr Univ,86-89, assoc prof, 89-91, assoc dean, 91-94, prof, 94- . **HONORS AND AWARDS** Henry Luce III Fel, 97-98; Who's Who in Relig, 89-90, 92-93; Men of Achievement, 93; Who's Who in Am Educ, 96-97. **MEMBERSHIPS** Am Acad Relig; Am Soc of Church Hist; Disciples of Christ Hist Soc. **RESEARCH** American theology; American religion and culture; history of Christian Church (Disciples of Christ). **SELECTED PUBLICATIONS** Auth, The Christian Century and American Public Life: The Crucial Years,1956-1968, in New Dimensions in Modern American Religious History, 93; auth, A Case Study: Christianity Today and American Public Life, in J of Church and State, 93; auth, W.A. Criswell, in Dictionary of Baptists in America, 94; auth, The Braunschweiger-Bibfeldts: the Metaphysical Incarnation of Wo/Man, in The Unrelieved Paradox, 94; auth, The Christian Church (Disciples of Christ), in Encyclopedia Americana, 94; auth, What is the Role of a Denomination in a Post-Denominational Age, in Lexington Theol Q, 94; auth, Sojourners, in Popular Religious Magazines of the United States, 95; auth, several entries in Encylopedia of Religious Controversies in the United States, 97; auth, The Problem and Promise of Denominational History, in Discipliana, 97; auth, Joined in Discipleship: The Shaping of Contemporary Disciples Identity, Chalice, rev ed, 97; coed, Makers of Christian Theology in America, Abingdon, 97. **CONTACT ADDRESS** Brite Divinity School, Texas Christian Univ, TCU Box 298130, Fort Worth, TX, 76129. **EMAIL** M.Toulouse@tcu.edu

TOWNER, WAYNE SIBLEY
PERSONAL Born 01/10/1933, Scottsbluff, NE, m, 1956, 2 children **DISCIPLINE** RELIGION, PHILOLOGY **EDUCATION** Yale Univ, BA, 54, BD, 60, MA, 61, PhD, 65. **CAREER** Eng tchr, Gerard Inst, Sidon, Lebanon, 54-57; instr Old Testament, Princeton Theol Sem, 63-64; lectr, divinity sch, Yale Univ, 64-65, asst prof 65-69, assoc prof Old Testament, 69-71; prof & dean Theol Sem, Univ Dubuque, 71-75; Prof Old Testament, Union Theol Sem, Richmond, Va, 75-, Dean, 85-88. **HONORS AND AWARDS** First Prize, Theology Category, Harper Collins Annual Best Sermons Award, 87; Second Prize, Christian Ministry, Alfred P Klausner Sermon Award, 97. **MEMBERSHIPS** Soc Bibl Lit. **RESEARCH** Old Testament; rabbinnic lit. **SELECTED PUBLICATIONS** Auth, The Rabbinic Enumeration of Scriptural Examples, Brill, Leiden, 73; How God Deals with Evil, Westminster, 76; Daniel, Westminster John Knox, 84. **CONTACT ADDRESS** 3401 Brook Rd, Richmond, VA, 23227-4514. **EMAIL** stowner@utsva.edu

TOWNES, EMILIE M.
PERSONAL Born 08/01/1955, Durham, NC, s **DISCIPLINE** CHRISTIAN ETHICS **EDUCATION** Univ Chicago, BA, 77; MA, 79; D Min, 82; Northwestern Univ, PhD, 89. **CAREER** Instr, DePaul Univ, 88-89; asst prof, St. Paul Sch Theol, 89-94; assoc prof, 94-98; prof, 98-99; prof, Union Theol Sem, 99- . **HONORS AND AWARDS** ATS Younger Scholars Award. **MEMBERSHIPS** Am Acad of Relig; Soc of Christian Ethics; Soc for the Study of Black Relig; Soc for the Study of Higher Values in Educ. **RESEARCH** Health care; classicism; racism; sexism. **SELECTED PUBLICATIONS** Auth, Womanist Justice, Womanist Hope, 93; auth, A Troubling in My Soul: Womanist Perspectives of Evil and Suffering, 93; auth, In a Blaze of Glory: Womanist Spirituality as Social Witness, 95; ed, Embracing the Spirit: Womanist Perspectives on Hope, Salvation, and Transformation, 97; auth, Breaking the Fine Rain of Death: African American Health Care and a Womanist Ethic of Care, forthcoming. **CONTACT ADDRESS** St. Paul School of Theology, 5123 Truman Rd., Kansas City, MO, 64127. **EMAIL** emtownes@spst.edu

TOWNS, ELMER
PERSONAL Born 10/21/1932, Savannah, GA, m, 1953, 3 children **DISCIPLINE** RELIGION **EDUCATION** Northwestern Col, Minneapolis, Minn, BA; Southern Meth Univ, Dallas, Tex, MA; Dallas Theol Sem, Dallas, Tex, TUM; Garrett Theol Sem, Evanston, Ill, MRE; Fuller Theol Sem, Pasadena, Calif, d min. **CAREER** Prof, Systematic Theol, 71-; dean, Sch of Relig, Liberty Univ, Lynchburg, Va, 71-. **HONORS AND AWARDS** Dr of Divinity, Calif Grad Sch of Theol; Dr. of Litterim, Bapt Bible Col, Springfield, Mo, Gold Medallion, Evang Publ Asn, 95. **MEMBERSHIPS** Evang Theol Soc; N Amer Soc of Church Growth. **RESEARCH** Evangelism; Spirituality. **SELECTED PUBLICATIONS** Auth, Rivers Of Revival, Regal Books, 97; Stories On The Front Porch, Regal Books, 97; Worship Wars, Broadman-Holman, 96; A Journey Through the Old Testament, Harcourt Brace, 96; A Journey Through the New Testament, Harcourt Brace, 96; A Practical Encyclopedia: Evangelism & Church Growth, Regal Books, 95; The Eight Laws of Leadership, Church Growth Inst, 94; Town's Sunday School That Dared to Change, Regal Books, 93; Town's Sunday School Encyclopedia, Tyndale House, 93. **CONTACT ADDRESS** Liberty Univ, 1971 University Blvd., Lynchburg, VA, 24502.

TOWNSEND, DABNEY W., JR.
DISCIPLINE PHILOSOPHY **EDUCATION** Emory Univ, PhD, 70. **CAREER** Asst prof, eng and philos, Catawba Col, 69-73; asst, assoc, prof, philos, Univ Texas, Arlington, 73-97; dean, Col of Arts and Sciences, Armstrong Atlantic State Univ, 97- . **HONORS AND AWARDS** Phi Beta Kappa. **MEMBERSHIPS** Am Soc for Aesthet; Int Aesthet Soc; APA. **RESEARCH** Aesthetics; eighteenth century British philosophy; philosophy of language. **SELECTED PUBLICATIONS** Auth, Hutcheson and Complex Ideas: A Reply to Peter Kivy, J of Aesthet and Art Criticism, 93; auth, The Aesthetics of Joseph Priestley, J of Aesthet and Art Criticism, 93; auth, Metaphor, Hermeneutics, and Situations, in Hahn, ed, Philos of Paul Ricoeur, Open Court, 95; auth, Beauty, in Barbanell, ed, Encyclopedia of Empiricism, Greenwood, 97; auth, The Picturesque, J of Aesthet and Art Criticism, 97; auth, Aesthetics: Classic Readings from the Western Tradition, Wadsworth, 97; auth, An Introduction to Aesthetics, Basil Blackwell, 97; contribur, Kelly, ed, Encyclopedia of Aesthetics, Oxford, 98; contribur, Budd, ed, Routledge Encyclopedia of Philosophy: Aesthetics, Routledge, 98; contribur, Haldane, ed, Routledge Encyclopedia of Philosophy: Modern Philosophers II (Eighteenth Century), Routledge, 98; auth, Eighteenth-Century British Aesthetics, Baywood, 98. **CONTACT ADDRESS** College of Arts and Sciences, Armstrong Atlantic State Univ, Savannah, GA, 31419. **EMAIL** townseda@pirates.armstrong.edu

TRACTENBERG, PAUL L.
PERSONAL Born 06/03/1938, Newark, NJ, m, 1978, 3 children **DISCIPLINE** LAW **EDUCATION** Wesleyan Univ, BA, 60; Univ Mich Law Sch, JD, 63. **CAREER** Atty, Sullivan and Cromwell, NY, 64-65; assoc gen coun, Peace Corps, Washington, DC, 65-67; coun, Governor's Comt Rev Civil Rights Laws, NY, 67-68; atty, Fried, Frank et al, NY, 68-70; assoc prof law, 70-78, Prof Law, Rutgers Law Sch, 78-, Spec coun, New York City Bd Educ, 68-70 and Comn Human Rights, 70-71; dir, Educ Law Ctr Inc, Newark, 73-76; consult official field reader, Nat Inst Educ, 74-79; consult, Chicano Educ Proj 79- and Israeli Ministry Educ and Cult, 81-82; vis prof, Law Fac, Hebrew Univ, Jerusalem, 81-82; CHMN BD, EDUC LAW CTR, 82- **RESEARCH** Impact of courts on educational reform; use of competency testing in public education; education of the handicapped and disadvantaged. **SELECTED PUBLICATIONS** Auth, Current School Problems, Practising Law Inst, 70; Selection of Teachers and Supervisors in Urban School Systems, 72 and Testing the Teacher, 73, Agathon Press; Reforming School Finance Through State Constitutions: Robinson V Cahill Points The Way, Rutgers Law Rev, 27: 365; The Role Of The Courts And Teacher Certification in Legal Issues in Teacher Preparation and Certification, Eric Clearing House Teacher Educ, 6/77; Testing for Minimum Competency: A Legal Analysis in Minimum Competency Achievement Testing: Motives, Models, Measures and Consequences, McCutchan P, 80; Legal Implications of Performance Testing in Vocational Education: An Overview--Performance Testing: Issues Facing Vocational Education, Nat Ctr Res Voc Educ, 80; A Clear and Powerful Voice for Poor Urban Students--Chief-Justice Wilentz, Robert Role, Rutgers Law Rev, Vol 49, 97; coauth, Pupil testing: A legal view, Phi Delta Kappan, 59: 249. **CONTACT ADDRESS** Law Sch, Rutgers Univ, 15 Washington St, Newark, NJ, 07102-3192.

TRAMMELL, RICHARD LOUIS
PERSONAL Born 05/26/1942, Shelbyville, KY, m, 1962, 3 children **DISCIPLINE** AMERICAN PHILOSOPHY, PHI-

LOSOPHY OF RELIGION **EDUCATION** Berea Col, BA, 64; Union theol Sem, NY, BD, 67; Columbia Univ, PhD, 71. **CAREER** Instr philos, Morehead State Univ, 67; asst prof, 71-77, assoc prof, 77-97, Prof Philos, Grove City Col, 97-, Am Philos Soc res grant, 71. **RESEARCH** Charles Peirce. **SELECTED PUBLICATIONS** Auth, Review of Paul Ramsey's Fabricated Man, Union Sem Quart, summer 71; Religion, reason and instinct in the philosophy of C S Peirce, Transactions Charles S Peirce Soc, winter 72; Peirce's final opinion, Transactions XVth World Cong Philos; Saving life and taking time, J Philos, 3/75; Mathematics and the conventionalist assumption, Southwestern J Philos, fall 76; Tooley's moral symmetry principle, Philos Pub Affairs, spring 76; coauth, Fairness, utility and survival, Philosophy, 10/77; auth, Euthanasia and the law, J Soc Philos, 1/78. **CONTACT ADDRESS** Dept of Philos, Grove City Col, 100 Campus Dr, Grove City, PA, 16127-2104.

TRAUB, GEORGE WILLIAM
PERSONAL Born 01/30/1936, Chicago, IL **DISCIPLINE** THEOLOGY & LITERATURE, SPIRITUALITY **EDUCATION** Xavier Univ, BLitt, 58; West Baden Col, PhL, 61; Loyola Univ Chicago, MA, 68; Cornell Univ, PhD, 73. **CAREER** Instr English, Greek & Latin, Loyola Acad, Ill, 61-64; from Asst Prof to Assoc Prof English, 72-87, Jesuit Prof Theology & Dir Ignatian Programs, Xavier Univ, 87-; Dir Formation & Continuing Educ, Chicago Prov Soc of Jesus, 80-85. **MEMBERSHIPS** Coordrs for Mission & Identity, Assoc of Jesuit Cols and Univs. **RESEARCH** Ignatian sprituality; Jesuit history & education; theology and literature. **SELECTED PUBLICATIONS** Coauth, The Desert and the City: An Interpretation of the History of Christian Spirituality, Loyola Univ Press, 84; Do You Speak Ignatian? A Glossary of Terms Used in Ignatian & Jesuit Circles, 3rd ed, Xavier Univ, 98. **CONTACT ADDRESS** Xavier Univ, 3800 Victory Pky, Cincinnati, OH, 45207-5185. **EMAIL** kelleyc@xavier.xu.edu

TRAUTMAN, DONALD T.
PERSONAL Born 06/06/1924, Cleveland, OH, m, 1954, 3 children **DISCIPLINE** LAW **EDUCATION** Harvard Univ, AB and LLB, 51. **CAREER** Law clerk, 52-53; asst prof, 53-56, Prof Law, Harvard Univ, 56-, Adv to reporter, restatement second, Conflict of Laws, 55-71; Guggenheim fel, 69; MEM, US DEPT ADVISORY COMT ON PVT INT LAW, 75- **MEMBERSHIPS** Am Soc Int Law; Am Foreign Law Asn. **RESEARCH** Conflict of laws; admiralty; contracts, federal courts, computers and law. **SELECTED PUBLICATIONS** Auth, 4 Models For International Bankruptcy/, American Journal Of Comparative Law, Vol 41, 93; Some Thoughts on Choice of Law, Judicial Discretion, and the Alis Complex Litigation Project, La Law Rev, Vol 54, 94; coauth, Materials on Accounting, Found, 59; Law of Multistate Problems, Little, 65. **CONTACT ADDRESS** Law Sch, Harvard Univ, Cambridge, MA, 02138.

TRAVERS, ARTHUR HOPKINS
PERSONAL Born 07/29/1936, Gary, IN, m, 1963, 2 children **DISCIPLINE** LAW **EDUCATION** Grinnel Col, BA, 57; Harvard Univ, LLB, 62. **CAREER** Asst prof law, Univ Kans, 65-68, assoc prof, 68-69, prof, 69-71; vis prof, 70-71, prof law, Univ Colo, 71-, actg dean, Law Sch, Univ Colo, 73-74, assoc dean, 74-75; fel law & econ, Law Sch, Univ Colo, 78-79. **MEMBERSHIPS** Am Bar Asn; Am Econ Asn; Selden Soc. **RESEARCH** Antitrust; law and economics; trade regulation, intellectual property. **SELECTED PUBLICATIONS** auth, articles in various law journals, 68-. **CONTACT ADDRESS** Sch of Law, Univ of Colorado, Boulder, PO Box 401, Boulder, CO, 80309-0401. **EMAIL** Arthur.Travers@spot.Colorado.edu

TRAYNOR, MICHAEL
PERSONAL Born 10/25/1934, Oakland, CA, m, 1956, 3 children **DISCIPLINE** ECONOMICS; LAW **EDUCATION** Univ Calif, Berkeley, BA, 55; Harvard Law, JD, 60 **CAREER** Lctr, Univ Calif, 82- **HONORS AND AWARDS** Amer Assoc for the Advance Sci Fel; Amer Bar Found Fel **MEMBERSHIPS** Amer Law Inst; Bar Assoc of San Fran **RESEARCH** Conflict of Laws; Intellectual Property **SELECTED PUBLICATIONS** Auth, "Countering the Excessive Subpoena for Scholarly Research, Law and Contemporary Problems, Law & Contemporary Problems, 97; co-chair, "Unifying Environmental Protection in California," California EPA Unified Environmental Statute Commission, 97; auth, "Clinical Trials: Products Liability and Informed Consent," Ntl L.J., 96 **CONTACT ADDRESS** 1 Maritime Plaza, Ste. 2000, San Francisco, CA, 94111-3580. **EMAIL** traynormt@cooley.com

TREAT, JAMES
PERSONAL Anadarko, OK, m **DISCIPLINE** RELIGIOUS STUDIES **EDUCATION** Grad Theol Union, PhD, 93 **CAREER** Asst prof, Univ Calif Santa Cruz, 92-95; asst prof, Univ New Mex, 95-. **SELECTED PUBLICATIONS** Auth Engaging Students with Native American Community Resources, Am Quart, 93; The Challenges of the Past: A Native American Perspective, The Challenges of the Past, the Challenges of the Future, Church Divinity School Pac, 94; Teaching Tribal/ Reservation History OFF the Reservation, Teaching and Writing Local History--Lac Courte Oreilles, The Newberry Library, 94; ed, Introduction: Native Christian Narrative Discourse, Native and Christian: Indigenous Voices on Religious Identity in the United States and Canada, Routledge, 96; auth, Native People and Interreligious Dialogue in North America: The Indian Ecumenical Conference, Stud in Interreligious Dialogue, 96; coauth, The Indigenous Movement in the Americas: Reflections on Nationalism and Ethnicity, First Nations-Pueblo Originarios, Univ Cal, 96; auth, Native and Christian: Indigenous Voices on Religious Identity in the United States and Canada, Routledge, 96; Religion and American Culture, American Religion Course Outlines, Purdue Univ, 98. **CONTACT ADDRESS** American Studies, Univ New Mex, Ortega Hal, Albuquerque, NM, 87131.

TREDWAY, JOHN THOMAS
PERSONAL Born 09/04/1935, North Tonawanda, NY, m, 1950, 2 children **DISCIPLINE** CHURCH & INTELLECTUAL HISTORY **EDUCATION** Augustana Col, BA, 57; Univ Ill, MA, 58; Garrett Theol Sem, BD, 61; Northwestern Univ, PhD, 64. **CAREER** From asst prof to prof hist, 64-75, dean col, 70-75, pres, 75-, Augustana Col, Ill; vis prof, Waterloo Lutheran Sem, 67-68; chmn, Nat Lutheran-Methodist Theol Dialogs, 77-. **MEMBERSHIPS** Am Soc Church Historians; AHA. **RESEARCH** Nineteenth century American and British church history; modern European intellectual history. **SELECTED PUBLICATIONS** Auth, Newman: Patristics, ecumenics and liberalism, Christian Century, 65; co-ed, The Immigration of Ideas, Augustana Hist Soc, 68. **CONTACT ADDRESS** Augustana Col, Rock Island, IL, 61201.

TRENN, THADDEUS JOSEPH
PERSONAL Born 01/16/1937, Chicago, IL, m, 1969, 1 child **DISCIPLINE** HISTORY AND PHILOSOPHY OF SCIENCE **EDUCATION** St Mary's Col, Minn, BA, 59; Univ Notre Dame, MS, 61 and MA, 62; Univ Wis-Madison, PhD(hist of sci), 72. **CAREER** Instr philos, Univ Santa Clara, Calif, 64-65; asst prof, St Norbert Col, 65-69; tutor hist of sci, Cambridge Univ, 70-71; res assoc, Max-Planck Inst, Ger, 71-73; prof hist sci, Univ Regensburg, West Ger, 73-79; RES ASSOC, MAX PLANCK INST FUR PHYSIK, MUNICH, 79- **HONORS AND AWARDS** American Oxonian, 68; Kurschners Deutscher Gelehrten-Kalender, 77. **MEMBERSHIPS** Sigma Xi; Philos Sci Asn; Am Philos Asn; Hist Sci Soc; NY Acad Sci. **RESEARCH** History of modern experimental physical science; science and public policy; scientific method. **SELECTED PUBLICATIONS** Auth, Brooks,Harriet--Pioneer Nuclear Scientist, Annals Sci, Vol 0050, 1993 **CONTACT ADDRESS** Max-Planck Inst fur Physik, Fohringer Ring 6 8000 Munich 40.

TRESS, DARYL MCGOWAN
PERSONAL New York, NY, m **DISCIPLINE** PHILOSOPHY **EDUCATION** Queens Col, CUNY, BA, 74; SUNY Buffalo, PhD, 83. **CAREER** Asst prof, philos, Fordham Univ, 94- . **HONORS AND AWARDS** Cum Laude, 74. **MEMBERSHIPS** Soc for Ancient Greek Philos; APA. **RESEARCH** Ancient philosophy. **SELECTED PUBLICATIONS** Auth, Relations in Plato's Timaeus, J of Neoplatonic Stud, 94; coauth, Liabilities of the Feminist Use of Narrative: A Study of Sara Ruddick's Story in Maternal Thinking, Public Affairs Q, 95; auth, The Metaphysical Science of Aristotle's Generation of Animals and Its Feminist Critics, in Ward, ed, Feminism and Ancient Philosophy, Routledge, 96; auth, Aristotle's Child: Formation Through Genesis, Oikos and Polis, Ancient Philos, 97; auth, The Philosophical Genesis of Ecology and Environmentalism, in Robinson, ed, The Greeks and the Environment, Rowman & Littlefield, 97; auth, Environmentalism's Relation to the History of Philosophy, Global Bioethics, 98. **CONTACT ADDRESS** Dept of Philosophy, Fordham Univ, Bronx, NY, 10458.

TREUSCH, PAUL E.
PERSONAL Chicago, IL, 1 child **DISCIPLINE** LAW **EDUCATION** Univ Chicago, PhB, 32, JD, 35. **CAREER** Atty, pvt practice, 35-37; law fac legal res & writing, Law Sch, La State Univ, 37-38; asst chief coun, Off Chief Coun, Internal Revenue Serv, 38-70; prof law, 65-73 & 76-79, prof emeritus, 79-, Law Sch, Howard Univ; prof 73-76, prof emeritus, 76-, Sch of Law, Boston Univ; Prof Law, Sch of Law, Southwestern Univ, 79-, Prof lectr law, Law ctr, George Washington Univ, 66-72; prof lectr law, Law Ctr, George Washington, 66-72; nat pres Feb Bar Asn, 69-70; mem, House of Deligates, Am Bar Asn, 70-72; Fed Bar Found Bd, 70-; head, law firm of Winston & Strawn-DC office, 70-72; tax adv comt, Am Law Inst, 79-; special counsel to Sec of US Senate, 70-72. **MEMBERSHIPS** Am Law Inst; Am Judicature Soc; Asn Am Law Sch. **SELECTED PUBLICATIONS** Auth, Tax Exempt Charitable Organizations, Am Law Inst, 88. **CONTACT ADDRESS** 675 S Westmoreland, Los Angeles, CA, 90005-3905. **EMAIL** ptreusch@swlaw.edu

TRIBE, LAURENCE HENRY
PERSONAL Born 10/10/1941, Shanghai, China, m, 1964, 2 children **DISCIPLINE** LAW, PHILOSOPHY **EDUCATION** Harvard Univ, AB, 62, JD, 66. **CAREER** Law clerk, Supreme Court Calif, 66-67 and US Supreme Court, 67-68; exec dir Technol Assessment Panel, Nat Acad Sci, 68-69; asst prof, 69-72, PROF LAW, HARVARD UNIV, 72-, Consult and mem, President's Sci Adv Comt Panel Chemicals and Health, 71-73; mem, Nat Sci Found Adv Comt Computing Activities, 71-74; mem, Nat Sci Found-Nat Endowment Humanities Adv Comt Human Value Implications of Sci and Technol, 73-; consult and mem, US Senate Comt Pub Works, 70-72; mem, Task Force Develop Regulations for Psychosurgery, 73-; chief appellate coun, Calif Energy Comn, Nuclear Moratorium Case, 79-**HONORS AND AWARDS** Coif Award, 78; Scribe Award, 79. **RESEARCH** Legal, constitutional and jurisprudential theory; the role of law in shaping technological development; uses and abuses of mathematical methods in policy and systems analysis. **SELECTED PUBLICATIONS** Auth, Taking Text and Structure Seriously--Reflections on Free-Form Method in Constitutional Interpretation, Harvard Law Rev, Vol 0108, 95; In-Memoriam--Brennan,William,J., Jr, Harvard Law Rev, Vol 0111, 97. **CONTACT ADDRESS** Law Sch, Harvard Univ, 1525 Massachusetts, Cambridge, MA, 02138-2903.

TRIGILIO, JO
DISCIPLINE PHILOSOPHY **EDUCATION** Marietta Col, BA, 83; Univ Oregon, MA, 93, PhD, 96. **CAREER** Vis instr, 97-98, Calif St Univ, Chico; asst prof, 98-, Bentley Col. **HONORS AND AWARDS** Phi Beta Kappa **MEMBERSHIPS** Soc for Women in Phil; Soc for Advan of Amer Phil. **RESEARCH** Feminist theory; feminist epistemology; Amer phil. **CONTACT ADDRESS** 87 Fremont St #1, Somerville, MA, 02145. **EMAIL** jtrigilio@bentley.edu

TRIPLETT, TIM
PERSONAL Born 06/28/1949, OH **DISCIPLINE** EPISTEMOLOGY **EDUCATION** Univ of Massachusetts, Amherst, PhD, 82, MA, 80, Philos; John Hopkins Univ, Baltimore, MD, Grad Courses and Seminars in Philos; Antioch Coll, Yellow Springs, OH, BA, 72; Univ of East Anlia, Norwich, England, Undergrad Philos Curriculum, 69-70. **CAREER** Assoc Prof of Philos, 88-, Lectr, 80-81, Instr, 81-83, Asst Prof, 83-88, Univ of New Hampshire. **HONORS AND AWARDS** Amer Coun of Learned Soc; New Hampshire Coll of Lib Art Faculty Summer Res Stipend; Discretionary Res Support Prog Grant; Sr Faculty Fellowship, Center of Hum, Univ of New Hampshire; Fellowship, Univ of New Hampshire Grad Sch. **MEMBERSHIPS** Amer Philos Assoc. **RESEARCH** Philosophy of Mind; 20th Century Analytic Philosophy; Applied Ethics; Sociology of Knowledge; Formal and Informal Logic; East Asian Philosophy. **SELECTED PUBLICATIONS** Auth, Is There Anthropological Evidence that Logic is Culturally Relative?, British Journal for the Philosophy of Science 45, 94; Review of Knowledge and Evidence, Paul Moser, Cambridge Univ Press, Philosophy and Phenomenological Research 51, pp 945-949, 91; Azande Logic Versus Western Logic? British Journal for the Philosophy of Science 39, pp 361-366, 88; Rescher's Metaphilosophy, in progress; The Viability of Strong Foundationalism, in progress; The Later Sellars: Defender of the Given, in progress; many other pubs. **CONTACT ADDRESS** Dept Philosophy, Univ of New Hampshire, Durham, NH, 03824. **EMAIL** tat@cisunix.unh.edu

TRISCO, ROBERT FREDERICK
PERSONAL Born 11/11/1929, Chicago, IL, s **DISCIPLINE** HISTORY & RELIGION **EDUCATION** St. Mary of the Lake Seminary, BA, 51; Pontifical Gregorian Univ, STL, 55, Hist. Eccl.D, 62. **CAREER** INST, 59-63, ASST PROF, 63-65, ASSOC PROF, 65-75, PROF, 75-96, VICE-RECTOR FOR ACADEMIC AFFAIRS, 66-68, CHEMN, DEPT OF CHURCH HIST, 75-78, PROF, DEPT OF CHURCH HIST, THE CATHOLIC UNIV OF AM, 76-. **HONORS AND AWARDS** Honorary degree, Doctor of Humane Letters, Belmont Abbey Col, 92; Honorary Prelate of His Holiness (Monsignor), 92. **MEMBERSHIPS** Am Catholic Hist Asn; Am Soc of Church Hist; Pontifical Commt for Hist Sci. **RESEARCH** History of the Catholic Church in the United States. **SELECTED PUBLICATIONS** Ed, The Catholic Hist Rev, 63-. **CONTACT ADDRESS** Catholic Univ of America, Curley Hall, Washington, DC, 20064. **EMAIL** TRISCO@cua.edu

TRISTAN, JAYNE A.
PERSONAL Born 06/29/1952, Toronto, ON, Canada, w, 1976, 1 child **DISCIPLINE** PHILOSOPHY **EDUCATION** Univ Oregon, BS, 89, MA, 92; Southern Ill Univ, Carbondale, PhD, 96. **CAREER** Instr, Southern Ill Univ Carbondale, 92-96; instr, Auburn Univ, 97-98; lectr, Univ North Carolina, Charlotte, 98-99. **HONORS AND AWARDS** Doctoral fel 94-95; Morris Eames Scholar Awd, 94-95. **MEMBERSHIPS** APA; Soc for Advancement of Am Philos; Midwest Prgamatist Prog Comm. **RESEARCH** John Dewey's theory of inquiry; history and philosophy of technology; educational practices; inovative, creative and critical thinking technique. **SELECTED PUBLICATIONS** coauth, "Signs Against Trees," Am J of Semiotics, 94; "Warrant and the End of Inquiry," Hester, ed, New Essays on Dewey's Logical Theory, Oxford, 99; "Experiment, Bias, and the Establishment of Standards," Tuana, ed, Feminist Perspectives on John Dewey, Penn State, 99. **CONTACT ADDRESS** Dept of Philosophy, Univ North Carolina Charlotte, 9201 University City Blvd, Charlotte, NC, 28223. **EMAIL** jtristan@newmail.uncc.edu

TROBISCH, DAVID
PERSONAL Born 08/18/1958, Ebolowa, Cameroon, m **DISCIPLINE** THEOLOGY OF NEW TESTAMENT **EDUCATION** Magister theol, 81; Dr theol, 89; Dr theol habil, 95. **CAREER** Hochschulassistent Universitat Heidelberg, GER, 89-

95; vis assoc prof, Yale Divinity School, New Haven, 96-97; assoc prof of New Testament, Bangor Theol Sem, 97-. **MEMBERSHIPS** AAR/SBL. **RESEARCH** Letters of Paul; Biblical manuscripts; Biblical theology; canon. **SELECTED PUBLICATIONS** Ed, with H J Dorn, V. Rosenberger, Zu dem Septuagintapapyrus VBP IV 56, Zeitschrift fur Papyrologie und Epigraphik 61, 85; ed with H J Dorn and V Rosenberger, Nachtrag zu dem Septuagintapapyrus VBP IV 56, Zeitschrift fur Papyrologie und Epigraphik 65, 86; auth, Die Entstehung der Paulusbriefsammlung: Studien zu den Anfangen der christlichen Publizistik, NTOA, 10, Freiburg, Schweiz: Universitatsverlag, Gottingen: Vandenhoeck, 89; ed, Heidelberger Apokryphen, Fetsschrift zum 50, Geburtstag von Prof Klauss Berger, Heidelberg, Wiss-Theoil Sem, 90; ed, In Dubio Pro Dea, Festscrift zum 50, Geburtstag von Prof Gerd Theiben, Heidelberg, Wiss-Theol Sem, 93; auth, Die Verfasserschaft des Hebraerbriefes und die Wiederentdeckung eines echten Paulustextes, In Dubio Deo, 93; Paul's Collection of Letters: Exploring the Origins, Fortress Press, 94, German trans, Kaiser, 94; Die Endredaktion des Neuen Testaments: Eine Untersuchung zur Entstehung der christlichen Bibel, NTOA 31, Vanderhoek, 96; The Formation of the New Testament, and The Formation of the Gospels, in The Good Samaritan (Luke 10:25-37), An American Bible Society Interactive CD-Rom for Windows, Am Bible Soc, 96; Die Mormonen, Konstanz/Neukirchen-Vluyn, 98. **CONTACT ADDRESS** Bangor Theol Sem, 300 Union St, Bangor, ME, 04401. **EMAIL** DTrobisch@BTS.edu

TROTTER, A.H., JR.
PERSONAL Born 10/10/1950, Meriville, TN, m, 1972, 3 children **DISCIPLINE** BIBLICAL STUDIES, FILM AND CULTURE **EDUCATION** Univ Virginia, BA, 72; Gordon-Conwell Theol Sem, MDiv, 75; Univ Cambridge, PhD, 87. **CAREER** Tchr, Westminster Schs, Atlanta, 75-78; exec dir, Elmbrook Christian Study Ctr, 81-87; exec dir, Center for Christian Study, 87- . **RESEARCH** Life of Jesus; Biblical interpretation, New Testament studies; systematic theology; film and culture. **SELECTED PUBLICATIONS** Auth, Interpreting the Epistle to the Hebrews, Baker Book House, 97. **CONTACT ADDRESS** Ctr for Christian Study, 128 Chancellor St, Charlottesville, VA, 22903. **EMAIL** drew@studycenter.net

TROTTER, GARY
DISCIPLINE LAW **EDUCATION** Univ Toronto, LLB, 85; Osgoode Hall Law Sch, LLM, 90; Cambridge Univ, MPhill, 91. **CAREER** Counsel, Crown Law Office-Criminal, Ministry of the Attorney General for Ontario **HONORS AND AWARDS** Ed, Criminal Law Quarterly. **SELECTED PUBLICATIONS** Auth, The Law of Bail in Canada; pubs on criminal law. **CONTACT ADDRESS** Fac of Law, Univ Toronto, 78 Queen's Park, Toronto, ON.

TROTTER, GRIFFIN
PERSONAL Born 12/30/1957, Missoula, MT, m, 1985, 3 children **DISCIPLINE** PHILOSOPHY & MEDICINE **EDUCATION** St Louis Univ, MD, 85; Vanderbilt Univ, PhD, 95. **CAREER** Asst prof Ethics & asst prof Surgery, St Louis Univ. **MEMBERSHIPS** AMA; APA; Soc for the Advan of Am Philos; Asn for Practical and Prof Ethics. **RESEARCH** Healthcare ethics; classical American philosophy. **SELECTED PUBLICATIONS** Auth, The Loyal Physician, Vanderbilt Univ, 97. **CONTACT ADDRESS** 6975 Delmar Blvd, University City, MO, 63130. **EMAIL** trottecg@wpogate.slu.edu

TROUT, J.D.
PERSONAL Born 12/28/1959, Cleveland, OH, m, 1992 **DISCIPLINE** PHILOSOPHY, COGNITIVE SCIENCE AND HISTORY **EDUCATION** Bucknell Univ, philos and history BA, 82; Cornell Univ, MA, 86; Cornell Univ, Philos and cognitive sci PhD, 88. **CAREER** Mellon postdoctoral fel, Bryn Mawr Col, 88-89; visiting asst prof, Va Tech, 91-92; asst prof, 92-, assoc prof, 95-, Loyola Univ. **HONORS AND AWARDS** NSF Predoctoral fel; Mellon postdoctoral fel. **MEMBERSHIPS** Amer Philos Asn; Philos of Sci Asn; Acoustical Soc of Amer; Psychonomic Soc. **RESEARCH** Philosophy of science; Philosophy of mind; Speech perception. **SELECTED PUBLICATIONS** Auth, Measuring the Intentional World: Realism, Naturalism, and Quantitative Methods in the Behavioral Sciences, NY, Oxford Univ Press, 98; coauth, with Paul Mose and Dwayne Mulder, The Theory of Knowledge: A Thematic Introduction, NY, Oxford Univ Press, 98; with Paul Mose, Contemporary Materialism: A Reader, London and NY, Routledge, 95; with Richard Boyd and Philip Gasper, The Philos of Sci, Cambridge, MA, Bradford Books, The MIT Press, 91; articles, Entries on Alchemy and Uniformity of Nature, ed R. Audi, The Cambridge Dict of Philos, Cambridge, Cambridge Univ Press, 95; Diverse Tests on an Independent World, Studies in History and Philosophy of Science, 26, 3, 407-429, 95; Ontological Progress in Science, Can Jour of Philos, 25, 2, 177-201, 95; with P. K. Moser, Physicalism, Supervenience, and Dependence, ed U. D. Yalcin and E. E. Savellos, Supervenience: New Essays, Cambridge, Cambridge Univ Press, 95; Auster Realism and the Worldly Assumptions of Inferential Statistics, ed M. Forbes, D. Hull and R. Burian, PSA 1994, vol 1, Lansing, Mich, Philos of Sci Asn, 190-199, 94; A Realistic Look Backward, Studies in History and Philosophy of Science, 25, 1, 37-64, 94. **CONTACT ADDRESS** Dept. of Philosophy, Loyola Univ, 6525 N Sheridan Rd, Chicago, IL, 60626. **EMAIL** jtrout@orion.it.luc.edu

TROWBRIDGE, JOHN
PERSONAL Born 07/02/1970, Glen Cove, NY, m, 1996, 1 child **DISCIPLINE** PHILOSOPHY **EDUCATION** Washington Univ, AB, 93; MA, Phil, 96, MA, East Asian Lang and Lit, 96, Ohio State Univ; PhD Student, Univ Hawaii at Manoa **CAREER** Grad Teaching Assoc, 94-, Ohio State Univ; **HONORS AND AWARDS** Graduate Degree Fel, East-West Center, 98-; Foreign Lang and Area Studies Fel, 95-96, 96-97. **MEMBERSHIPS** Soc for Asian and Comparative Phil; Amer Phil Assoc; Assoc for Asian Studies **RESEARCH** Classical Chinese and comparative philosophy; epistemology; ancient greek philosophy; asian religions. **SELECTED PUBLICATIONS** The Relationship Between Skepticism and Epistemological Relativism in the Qi Wu Lun, Chapter of the Zhuang 21, 96. **CONTACT ADDRESS** Dept of Philosophy, Univ Hawaii at Manoa, 2530 Dole St., Sakamaki H, Honolulu, HI, 96822-2383. **EMAIL** trowbrid@hawaii.edu

TROYER, JOHN G.
PERSONAL Born 02/12/1943, Detroit, MI, m, 1992, 2 children **DISCIPLINE** PHILOSOPHY **EDUCATION** Swarthmore Col, BA, 65; Harvard Univ, MA, 67, PhD, 71. **CAREER** From instr to asst prof to assoc prof, Univ Conn, 70-. **HONORS AND AWARDS** Frank Knox Mem Fel, 69-70; NEH Younger Humanist Fel, 74. **MEMBERSHIPS** Am Philos Asn; Oxford Bibliog Soc; Int Berkeley Soc; Hume Soc; Soc Philos & Psychol. **RESEARCH** History of modern philosophy; normative theory; epistemology; 17th and 18th century philosophy and science; philosophy of economics; Wittgenstein. **SELECTED PUBLICATIONS** Auth, Locke on the Names of Substances, The Locke Newsl, 75; auth, Rationality and Maximization, Ethics: Found, Problems & Applications, 81; co-ed, Contemporary Readings in Social and Political Ethics, 84; ed, In Defense of Radical Empiricism: Essays and Lectures by Roderick Firth, 97; auth, A Pragmatic Defense of Phenomenalism, Role of Pragmatics in Contemporary Philos, 97. **CONTACT ADDRESS** Dept of Philosophy U-54, Univ of Connecticut, Storrs, CT, 06269-2054.

TRUEMPER, DAVID GEORGE
PERSONAL Born 02/01/1939, Aurora, IL, m, 1963, 2 children **DISCIPLINE** SYSTEMIC THEOLOGY **EDUCATION** Concordia Sr Col, BA, 61; Concordia Sem, MDiv, 65, STM, 69; Lutheran Sch Theol, STD, 74. **CAREER** Instr, 67-72, asst prof, 72-77, assoc prof, Theol, Valparaiso Univ, 77-84, prof Theol, 84-; chmn Theol, 93-; dir coun on Study of Rel, 93-; vis prof, Concordia Sem, 73-74, Concordia Sem-in-Exile, 74 & Univ Notre Dame, 77-78; dir, Study Ctr, Valparaiso Univ, Reutlingen, Germany, 74-76; pastor, St John Lutheran Church, La Crosse, Ind, 79-84. **MEMBERSHIPS** Am Acad Relig; NAm Acad Liturgy; Am Soc Reformation Res; Societas Liturgica; Inst Theol Encounter Sci & Technol. **RESEARCH** Sixteenth-century theological controversy; contemporary Christology; ecumenical theology and interconfessional dialogue. **SELECTED PUBLICATIONS** Coauth, Review essay of A Statement of Scriptural and Confessional Principles, Cresset, 5 & 10/73; ed & contribr, Confession and Congregation, Occasional Paper No 3, Cresset, 78; auth, (Lutheran Churches) Doctrine and theology, nature and function of the church, In: Profiles in Belief, II, Harper & Row, 78; contribr & ed, Promise and Faith, Valparaiso Univ Press, 2nd ed, 80; auth, The myth/truth of Christological arguments, Currents in Theol & Mission, 78; coauth, Keeping the Faith: A Guide to the Christian Message, Fortress Press, 81; auth, The Catholicity of the Augsburg confession, 16th Cent J, 80; man ed, Proceedings of the North American Academy of Liturgy, 86-97. **CONTACT ADDRESS** Dept Theol, Valparaiso Univ, 651 College Ave, Valparaiso, IN, 46383-6493. **EMAIL** david.truemper@valpo.edu

TRULEAR, HAROLD DEAN
DISCIPLINE RELIGION **EDUCATION** Morehouse Col, BA, 75; MPhil, 79, PhD, 83, Drew Univ. **CAREER** Instr, 77-78, Jersey City State Col; Instr, 78-83, Asst Prof, 83-86, Drew Univ, Theol Sch; Dir, Black Church Studies, 87-90, Eastern Baptist Theol Sem; Dean, 90-96, Prof, 96-98, New York Theol Sem; VP, Church Collaborative Initiatives, 98-, Public/Private Ventures. **CONTACT ADDRESS** Public/Private Ventures, One Commerce Sq., 2005 Market St., Philadelphia, PA, 19103. **EMAIL** dtrulear@ppv.org

TRUMBOWER, JEFFREY A.
PERSONAL Born 06/19/1960, Orlando, FL **DISCIPLINE** BIBLICAL STUDIES **EDUCATION** Univ Chicago Divinity Sch, PhD, 89. **CAREER** Asst prof relig stud, 89-96, assoc prof relig stud, 96- , St. Michael's Col. **HONORS AND AWARDS** NEH sem, 93; sr fel, Ctr for the Study of World Relig, Harvard Univ, 98. **MEMBERSHIPS** Soc of Bibl Lit; N Am Patristics Soc. **RESEARCH** Early Christianity; posthumous salvation of non-Christians in early Christianity. **SELECTED PUBLICATIONS** Auth, Born from Above: The Anthropology of the Gospel of John, Mohr, 92; auth, The Historical Jesus and the Speech of Gamaliel, New Testament Stud, 93; auth, The Role of Malachi in the Career of John the Baptist, in Evans, ed, The Gospels and the Scriptures of Israel, JSOT, 94; auth, Traditions Common to the Primary Adam and Eve Books and On the Origin of the World,d J for Stud of Pseudepigrapha, 96; auth, the Acts of Paul and Thecia, in Kiley, ed, Prayer from Alexander to Constantine: A Critical Anthology, Routledge, 97. **CONTACT ADDRESS** 101 Northshore Dr, Burlington, VT, 05401-1269. **EMAIL** jtrumbower@smcvt.edu

TRUNDLE, ROBERT C., JR.
PERSONAL Born 07/07/1943, Washington, DC **DISCIPLINE** PHILOSOPHY **EDUCATION** Ohio St Univ, BA, 72; Univ of Toledo, MA, 74; Univ Colorado Boulder, PhD, 84. **CAREER** Asst, Univ Toledo, 72-74; fel, Rice Univ, 75; instr, Univ Colorado, Colorado Springs, 82-84; asst prof, Regis Col, 82-86; prof, Northern Kentucky Univ, 87- . **HONORS AND AWARDS** Outstanding Jr Prof in Col of Arts & Sciences for Scholar and Teach. **MEMBERSHIPS** Sigma Xi Sci Res Soc; NY Acad of Sci, Phi Kappa Phi; APA; Soc for Medieval and Renaissance Philos. **RESEARCH** Intellectual history; cultural studies. **SELECTED PUBLICATIONS** Auth, with R. Puligandla, Beyond Absurdity, UPA, 86; "Applied Logic," Philos in Sci, 93; "St. Augustine's On Free Choice," Rev of Augustine, 93; Ancient Greek Philosophy, Ashgate, 94; "Thomas' 2nd Way," Logique et Analyse, 94; "St. Augustine's Epistemology," Laval Theologique et Philosophique, 94; "Extraterrestrial Intelligence," method and Sci, 94; "Quantum Fluctuation," Idealistic Stud, 94; "St. Thomas & Modal Logic," Aquinas, 95; "20th Century Despair," Laval Theologique et Philosophique, 96; "Global Ethnic Conflict," Stud in Conflict and Terrorism, 96; "Modalidades aristoelicas de san Agustin," Avgstinvs, 97. **CONTACT ADDRESS** Dept of Social Sciences and Philosophy, No Kentucky Univ, Highland Heights, KY, 41099. **EMAIL** trundle@nku.edu

TSCHEMPLIK, ANDREA
PERSONAL Born 08/16/1961, Darmstadt, Germany, m, 1991 **DISCIPLINE** PHILOSOPHY **EDUCATION** Upsala Col, BA, 82; Bryn mawr Col, MA, 85; CUNY, PhD, 97. **CAREER** Adj prof, Hunter Col, CUNY, 87-91; asst prof philos, Upsala Col, 91-95; adj prof philos, Drew Univ, 95-98; asst prof philos, George Washington Univ, 98- . **HONORS AND AWARDS** Tchr of the year award, 94. **MEMBERSHIPS** APA; Soc for Ancient Greek Philos; Soc for the Stud of Africana Philos; AAUP. **RESEARCH** History of philosophy; Greek philosophy; German philosophy. **SELECTED PUBLICATIONS** Auth, Framing the Question of Knowledge: Beginning Plato's Theaetetus, in press; ed, Plato's Dialogues: New Studies and Interpretations, Rowman & Littlefield, 93. **CONTACT ADDRESS** 17 Deckertown Tpke, Sussex, NJ, 07461. **EMAIL** atschemp@gwu.edu

TSIRPANLIS, CONSTANTINE NICHOLAS
PERSONAL Born 03/18/1935, Cos, Greece **DISCIPLINE** HISTORY, PHILOSOPHY **EDUCATION** Greek Theol Sch Halki, Istanbul, Lic theol, 57; Harvard Univ, STM, 62; Columbia Univ, AM, 66; Fordham Univ, PhD(hist), 73. **CAREER** Instr mod Greek, NY Univ, 64-70; teacher classics and chmn dept, Collegiate Sch, NY, 67-69; instr mod Greek, New Sch Social Res, 68-70; res and writing, 70-72; adj prof world hist, NY Inst Technol, 72-75; ASSOC PROF CHURCH HIST and GREEK STUDIES, UNIFICATION THEOL SEM, 76-, Lectr class philol, Hunter Col, 66-67; lectr medieval and ancient hist, Mercy Col, 72; adj prof Western civilization, Delaware County Community Col, 75, Dutchess County Community Col, 76. **HONORS AND AWARDS** Nat Medal Greek Rebirth, Greek Govt, 72. **MEMBERSHIPS** NAm Acad Ecumenists; Am Soc Neo-Hellenic Studies (exec vpres, 67-69); Am Philol Asn; Medieval Acad Am; NAm Patristic Soc. **RESEARCH** Late Byzantine intellectual history and theology; early Byzantine theology and philosophy; Greek patristics. **SELECTED PUBLICATIONS** Auth, Photian Studies, Church Hist, Vol 0063, 94; Church, Nation and State in Russia and Ukraine, Church Hist, Vol 0066, 97; Heretics, Dissidents, Muslims and Jews in Byzantium, 12th-Century Heresiology-Italian, Church Hist, Vol 0066, 97. **CONTACT ADDRESS** Unification Theol Sem, 10 Dock Rd, Barrytown, NY, 12507.

TU, WEI-MING
PERSONAL Born 02/26/1940, Kunming, China, m, 1963, 1 child **DISCIPLINE** HISTORY, RELIGIOUS PHILOSOPHY **EDUCATION** Tunghai Univ, Taiwan, BA, 61; Harvard Univ, MA, 63, PhD(hist), 68. **CAREER** Vis lectr humanities, Tunghai Univ, Taiwan, 66-67; lectr EAsian studies, Princeton Univ, 67-68, asst prof, 68-71; from asst prof to assoc prof hist, Univ Calif, Berkeley, 71-77, prof, 77-81; PROF CHINESE HIST and PHILOS, HARVARD UNIV, 81-, Consult-panelist, Nat Endowment for Humanities, 75; Am Coun Learned Soc fel, 77; mem bd dirs, Chinese Cult Found San Francisco, 79- **MEMBERSHIPS** Asn Asian Studies; Soc Asian and Comp Philos; Am Acad Polit Sci. **RESEARCH** Chinese intellectual history; Confucianism in East Asia; religious philosophy. **SELECTED PUBLICATIONS** Auth, Introduction--Cultural Perspectives, Daedalus, Vol 0122, 93; Destructive Will and Ideological Holocaust--Maoism as a Source of Social Suffering in China, Daedalus, Vol 0125, 96. **CONTACT ADDRESS** Dept of EAsian Lang and Civilizations, Harvard Univ, Cambridge, MA, 02138.

TUBB, GARY
DISCIPLINE RELIGION **EDUCATION** Harvard Univ, BA, 73, MA, 76, PhD, 79. **CAREER** Prof. **RESEARCH** Sanskrit literary theory. **SELECTED PUBLICATIONS** Auth, pubs on

Sanskrit poetry and poetics. **CONTACT ADDRESS** Dept of Religion, Columbia Col, New York, 2960 Broadway, New York, NY, 10027-6902. **EMAIL** gat4@columbia.edu

TUBBS, JAMES B.
DISCIPLINE RELIGIOUS STUDIES **EDUCATION** Hampden-Sydney Col, BS; Univ Va, MA, PhD. **CAREER** Assoc prof, Univ Detroit Mercy, 86-. **HONORS AND AWARDS** President's awd for Fac Excellence, Col Liberal Arts, 96. **MEMBERSHIPS** Med Ethics Resource Network Mich. **RESEARCH** Christian theology and the moral issues in biomedicine and health care policy. **CONTACT ADDRESS** Dept of Religious Studies, Univ of Detroit Mercy, 4001 W McNichols Rd, PO Box 19900, Detroit, MI, 48219-0900. **EMAIL** TUBBSJB@udmercy.edu

TUCHLER, DENNIS JOHN
PERSONAL Born 12/25/1938, Berlin, Germany, m, 1961, 2 children **DISCIPLINE** LAW **EDUCATION** Reed Col, BA, 60; Univ Chicago, JD, 63. **CAREER** From asst prof to assoc prof law, 65-71, Prof Law, St Louis Univ Sch Law, 71-, Consult, Codification of Ord, City of Dellwood, Mo, 67 & City of Maplewood, Mo, 68-. **RESEARCH** Conflict of laws; legal ethics. **SELECTED PUBLICATIONS** Auth, Boundaries to party autonomy in the UCC: A radical view, St Louis Univ Law J, 67; Oregon conflicts: Toward an analysis of governmental interests?, Ore Law Rev, 68; Some Thoughts about the Rules of Professional Conduct, S Publ Law Forum 25, 86; A Short Summary of American Conflict Law: Choice of Law, St Louis Univ Law J 37, 93. **CONTACT ADDRESS** School of Law, St Louis Univ, 3700 Lindell Blvd, Saint Louis, MO, 63108-3412.

TUCK, DONALD RICHARD
PERSONAL Born 04/24/1935, Albany, NY, m, 1957, 2 children **DISCIPLINE** HISTORY OF RELIGIONS, ASIAN STUDIES **EDUCATION** Nyack Col, BS, 57; Wheaton Col, MA, 65; Univ Iowa, PhD(relig and cult), 70. **CAREER** Minister of youth, Presby Church, Ill, 63-65; interim minister, Methodist Church, Fed Church and United Church of Christ, Iowa, 65-69; teaching and res asst, Sch Relig, Univ Iowa, 67-68; from instr to assoc prof relig, 69-78, PROF RELIG, WESTERN KY UNIV, 78-, Fac res grant, Radhakrishnan and Tagore, 70; fac res grant, Tagore, 72; consult, Choice, 76-, Nat Endowment Humanities, 77- and South Asia in Rev, 78-; fac res grant, Santal Relig, 76 and soc aspects, Bhagavata, Purana, 78. **MEMBERSHIPS** Am Acad Relig; Asn Asian Studies. **RESEARCH** Religion and culture of Modern India; Sarvepalli Radhakrishnan and Rabindranath Tagore; Bengal Vaisnavism-Caitanya. **SELECTED PUBLICATIONS** Auth, Lacuna in Sankara Studies--A Thousand Teachings Upadesasahasri, Asian Philos, Vol 0006, 96. **CONTACT ADDRESS** Dept of Relig and Philos, Western Kentucky Univ, 1 Big Red Way St, Bowling Green, KY, 42101-3576.

TUCKER, GENE M.
PERSONAL Born 01/08/1935, Albany, TX, m, 1957, 2 children **DISCIPLINE** RELIGION; OLD TESTAMENT **EDUCATION** McMurry Col, BA, 57; Yale Divinity School, MD, 60; Yale Univ, MA, 61; PhD, 63. **CAREER** Asst prof Relig, Grad School Relig, Univ S Cal, 63-66; asst prof , Divinity School, Duke Univ, 66-70; assoc prof, 70-77, prof, 77-95, assoc Dean, 78-83, actg dir grad studies relig, 87-88, prof Old Testament, Emer 95- , Candler School Theol, Emory Univ. **MEMBERSHIPS** Soc Bibl Lit (pres 96); Am Schools Oriental Res; Int Orgn Study Old Testament; Colloquium Bibl Res; Am Asn Univ Prof. **SELECTED PUBLICATIONS** Ed, Cultural Anthropology and the Old Testament, Guides to Biblical Scholarship, Fortress Press, 96; coed Marvin A Sweeney, Isaiah 1-39, Forms of the OT Lit, Wm Eerdmans, 96; auth Old Testament, HarperCollins Bible Dictionary, 96; auth Rain on a Land Where No One Lives: Hebrew Bible on the Environ, Jour Bibl Lit, 97; For Everything There is a Season, Reflections on Aging and Spiritual Growth, Abingdon Press, 98; ed The Forms of the Old Testament Literature: A Commentary, Wm Eerdmans, 98; auth of some sixty articles in journals, reference works or volumes of essays including: Jour Bibl Lit, Cath Bibl Quart; Vetus Testamentum; Interpretation; Harpers Dictionary of Bible, Interpreters Dictionary of Bible, Supplementary Volume, Oxford Study Edition: New English Bible. **CONTACT ADDRESS** 234 S Madison, Unit H, Denver, CO, 80209. **EMAIL** gtucker@du.edu

TUCKER, GORDON
PERSONAL m, 3 children **DISCIPLINE** RELIGION **EDUCATION** Harvard Univ, BA; Princeton Univ, PhD. **CAREER** Adj asst prof, Jewish Theol Sem Am. **MEMBERSHIPS** Comt Jewish Law Standards; UJA Fedn NY. **SELECTED PUBLICATIONS** Auth, pubs on Jewish philosophy and law; Jewish affairs. **CONTACT ADDRESS** Dept of Jewish Philos, Jewish Theol Sem of America, 3080 Broadway, PO Box 3080, New York, NY, 10027. **EMAIL** gotucker@jtsa.edu

TUCKER, MARY EVELYN
PERSONAL Born 06/24/1949, New York, NY, m, 1978 **DISCIPLINE** HISTORY, RELIGION **EDUCATION** Trinity Col, BA, 71; SUNY, Fredonia, MA, 72; Fordham Univ, MA, 77; Columbia Univ, PhD, 85. **CAREER** Lectr, Eng, Erie Commun Col, 72; lectr Eng, Notre Dame Seishin Univ, Japan, 73-75; lectr relig, Elizabeth Seton Col, 76-78; preceptor, Columbia Univ, 79-80, 83; asst prof hist, Iona Col, 84-89; assoc prof relig, Bucknell Univ, 89- . **HONORS AND AWARDS** Phi Beta Kappa; HEW fel, 71-72; NEH fel, 77; Columbia Pres fel, 80-81, 81-82; Japan Found fel, 83-84; Mellon fel, 85-86; Columbia Univ postdoctoral res fel, 87-88; Person of the Year Award, Bucknellian, 92; NEH Chair in the Hum, 93-96; sr fel, Center for the Study of World Relig, Harvard Univ, 95-96; Trinity Col Centennial Alumnae Award for Academic Excellence, 97; assoc in res, Reischaur Inst of Japanese Stud, Harvard Univ, 95-99. **MEMBERSHIPS** Neo-Confucian Stud, Columbia Univ. Regional Sem on Japan, Columbia Univ; Am Teilhard Asn; Environ Sabbath, UN Environ Prog; AAR; Asn Asian Stud; Soc for Values in Higher Educ; Asn for Relig and Intellectual Life. **SELECTED PUBLICATIONS** Auth, Moral and Spiritual Cultivation in Japanese Neo-Confucianism: The Life and Thought of Kaibara Ekken (1630-1714), SUNY, 89; coauth, Worldviews and Ecology, Bucknell Univ, 93; co-ed, Buddhism and Ecology: The Interaction of Dharma and Deeds, Harvard Univ, 97; co-ed, Confucianism and Ecology: The Interrelation of Heaven, Earth, and Humans, Harvard Univ, 98. **CONTACT ADDRESS** Dept of Religion, Bucknell Univ, Lewisburg, PA, 17837. **EMAIL** mtucker@bucknell.edu

TUCKER, WILLIAM E.
PERSONAL Born 06/22/1932, Charlotte, NC, m, 1955, 3 children **DISCIPLINE** AMERICAN RELIGIOUS & CHURCH HISTORY **EDUCATION** Atlantic Christian Col, BA, 53, LLD, 78; Tex Christian Univ, BD, 56; Yale Univ, MA, 58, PhD(relig), 60. **CAREER** From assoc prof to prof relig & philos, Atlantic Christian Col, 59-66, chmn dept, 62-66; assoc prof church hist & asst dean, Brite Divinity Sch, Tex Christian Univ, 66-69, prof church hist, 69-76, assoc dean, 69-71, dean, 71-76; pres, Bethany Col, 76-79; chancellor, Tex Christian Univ, 79-98, trustee, Disciples of Christ Hist Soc, 69-; mem bd, Christian Church (Disciples of Christ), 71-, dir bd higher educ, 73-, chmn bd, 75-77; pres, Coun Southwestern Theol Schs, 75-76; vpres, WVa Found Independent Cols, 77-. **HONORS AND AWARDS** LLD, Atlantic Christian Col, 78; DHL, Chapman Col, 81; DHu, Bethany Col, 82. **RESEARCH** American church history since 1865; history and thought of the Christian Church (Disciples of Christ) and related religious groups; Fundamentalism and the Church in America. **SELECTED PUBLICATIONS** Auth, J H Garrison and Disciples of Christ, Bethany, 64; contribr, The Word We Preach, Tex Christian Univ, 70; Westminster Dictionary of Church History, Westminster, 71; Dictionary of American Biography, suppl 3, Scribner's, 73; coauth, Journey in Faith: A History of the Christian Church (Disciples of Christ), Bethany, 75; contribr, Encycl of Southern History, La State Univ Press, 79. **CONTACT ADDRESS** Chancellor Emeritus, Tex Christian Univ, PO Box 297080, Fort Worth, TX, 76129-0002.

TUDY JACKSON, JANICE
PERSONAL Born 09/30/1945, New York, NY **DISCIPLINE** LAW **EDUCATION** City Coll of New York, BA 1977; Univ of MI Labor/Industrial Relations, Certification 1983; Inst of Applied Mgmt & Law, Certification 1985; Cornell Univ/Baruch Coll NY, NY MS-ILR 1989; Columbia University Law School, JD 1992. **CAREER** St Luke's Hosp Sch of Nursing, asst registrar 1970-74; Continental Grain Co, research asst 1975-77, personnel admin 1977-79, EEO officer 1979-80, mgr coll relations 1980-82, regional personnel mgr 1982-84, corp labor relations mgr 1984-86, asst vice pres human resources 1986-88, vice pres labor relations 1988-89; Morgan, Lewis & Bockius, Attorney, 1992-. **HONORS AND AWARDS** Natl Selection for Weinberg Natl Labor Mgmt Certificate; Graphic Art/Design Continental Grain Co Annual Employee Statement 1976-81; International Human Rights Fellowship, Kenya, Columbia Law School, 1990; National YWCA Academy of Woman Achievers, National YWCA, 1989; Barbara Aronstein Black Scholarship, Columbia Law School, 1990; Harlan Fiske Stone Scholar; Charles Evans Hughes Fellow; Jane Marks Murphy Prize, Columbia Law School, 1992; Outstanding Woman Law Graduate, National Assn of Women Lawyers, 1992. **MEMBERSHIPS** Speaker/lecturer Cornell Univ, Purdue Univ, Atlanta Univ, Yale Univ, Howard Univ, Univ of IL 1979-; adv bd mem Atlanta Univ Grad Sch of Business 1979-82; panelist Women Business Owners of NY 1982,83; dir Tutorial Prog Manhattan Ctr for Science & Math 1985-; exec bd mem The EDGES Group Inc 1986-; life mem Delta Sigma Theta Inc 1986; aux mem NY City Commn on the Status of Women 1987-; board of trustees, Manhattan Country School, 1990-. **SELECTED PUBLICATIONS** "ET to Denny - Bossism or Crucifixion," The Esplanade News 1983; editorial "Miscarriage of Justice," NY Amsterdam News 1985. **CONTACT ADDRESS** Morgan, Lewis & Bockius, 101 Park Ave, New York, NY, 10178.

TUELL, STEVEN SHAWN
PERSONAL Born 10/03/1956, Liverpool, OH, m, 1981, 3 children **DISCIPLINE** RELIGIOUS STUDIES AND HEBREW BIBLE **EDUCATION** W VA Wesleyan Col, BA, 78; Princeton Theol Sem, Mdiv, 81; Union Theol Sem, PhD, 89. **CAREER** Pastor, Jacob Albright Meth Chur, WV, 81-85; Asst Prof , Erskine Col, 89-92; Asst Prof, 92-97, Assoc Prof, 97- , Randolph Macon Col. **HONORS AND AWARDS** Who's Who in Bibl Studies & Archeol, 92; Tchr Awrd, United Methodist Brd of Higher Edu and Ministry, 95; Thomas Branch Excel in Tchng, 94 & 96; Who's Who Amer Tchrs, 98; VA Outstndg Prof, 98. **MEMBERSHIPS** Soc Bibl Lit; SE Comm for Stud Religion **RESEARCH** Hebrew Bible, Second Temple Period; Ezekiel; Chronicles; ANE Myth & Religion **SELECTED PUBLICATIONS** Auth, The Law of the Temple in Ezekiel 40-48, Harvard Semitic Monographs Series 49; Atlanta: Scholars, 92; Auth, A Riddle Resolved by an Enigma, Jour of Bibl Lit 112, 93; Acting as a Servant: Luke 22:14-30 and From Death to Life: Luke 23:32-46; 24:33-34, VA United Meth Adv 162, 94. **CONTACT ADDRESS** 100 Slash Drive, Ashland, VA, 23005. **EMAIL** Stuell@rmc.edu

TUERKHEIMER, FRANK M.
PERSONAL Born 07/27/1938, New York, NY, m, 1968, 2 children **DISCIPLINE** LAW **EDUCATION** Columbia Univ, BA, 60; Law Sch Univ NY, LLB, 63. **CAREER** Legal coun to Atty Gen of Switz, 64-65; asst US atty, Southern Dist of NY, 65-70; vis assoc prof, 70-73, Prof Law, Sch of Law, Univ Wis-Madison, 73-, Assoc special prosecutor, Watergate Special Prosecuting Force, 73-75, consult, 75-77; US atty, Western Dist of Wis, 77-81. **HONORS AND AWARDS** Man in the News, NY Times, 4/75; Habush-Bascom Professor of Law, Univ Wis. **SELECTED PUBLICATIONS** Auth, Service of process in New York City: A proposed end to unregulated community, Columbia Law Rev, 72; coauth, Judge Weinfield and the criminal law, NY Univ Law Rev, 75; auth, The executive investigates itself, Calif Law Rev, 77; Prosecution of Criminal Cases: Where Executive and Judicial Power Meet, Am Criminal Law Rev 251, 87; Convictions Through Hearsay in Child Sexual Abuse Cases: A Logical Progression Back to Square One, Marq Law Rev 47, 88; Rape Shield Laws: A Revisit and Proposed Revision, Ohio State Law J 1245, 90; coauth, Clomazone Damage to Off-Site Vegetation: Test Results are Negative But Plants Wither and Die, Whittier Law Rev 749, 93; auth, A More Realistic Approach to Teaching Appellate Advocacy, J Legal Educ 113, 95; United States v. Martinez on Appeal: The Disturbing Anatomy of Harmless Error, Am J Trial Advocacy 269, 97; Evidence: Theory and Practice, Lexis-Nexis, 97 (electronic text). **CONTACT ADDRESS** Law Sch, Univ Wis, 975 Bascom Mall, Madison, WI, 53706-1301. **EMAIL** frankt@cs.wisc.edu

TULL, HERMAN
PERSONAL Born 10/27/1955, Philadelphia, PA, m, 1978, 2 children **DISCIPLINE** HISTORY AND LITERATURE OF RELIGIONS **EDUCATION** Hobart Col, BA, 78; Northwestern Univ, PhD, 85. **CAREER** Asst prof, Rutgers Univ; lectr, Princeton Univ. **HONORS AND AWARDS** Univ fel, Northwestern Univ; Getty Postdoctoral fel. **RESEARCH** Vedic ritual; Gnomic literature in Sanskrit. **SELECTED PUBLICATIONS** Auth, Hinduism, Harper's Dictionary of Religious Education, 90; auth, F. Max Muller and A.B. Keith: 'Twaddle,' the 'Stupid' Myth, and the Disease of Indology, NUMEN, 91; auth, The Tale of 'The Bride and the Monkey': Female Insatiability, Male Impotence, and Simian Virility in Indian Literature, J Hist of Sexuality, 93; auth, The Killing That Is Not Killing: Men, Cattle, and the Origins of Non-Violence (ahimsa) in the Vedic Sacrifice, Indo-Iranian J, 96; auth, The Veduic Origins of Karma: Cosmos as Man in Ancient Indian Myth and Ritual. **CONTACT ADDRESS** 228 Terhune Rd., Princeton, NJ, 08540. **EMAIL** hwtull@msn.com

TULLY, JAMES H.
PERSONAL Born 04/17/1946, Nanaimo, BC, Canada **DISCIPLINE** POLITICAL SCIENCE/PHILOSOPHY **EDUCATION** Univ BC, BA, 74; Univ Cambridge, PhD, 77. **CAREER** Prof, philos & polit sci, McGill Univ, 77-96; adv, Royal Comn Aboriginal Peoples, 92-96; PROF POLITICAL SCIENCE, UNIV VICTORIA, 96-. **SELECTED PUBLICATIONS** Auth, A Discourse on Property, 80; auth, An Approach to Political Philosophy, 93; auth, Strange Multiplicity, 95; ed, John Locke, 83; ed, Meaning and Context, 88; ed, Pufendorf, 91; ed, Philosophy in an Age of Pluralism; ser ed, The Complete Works of John Locke; ser ed, Ideas in Context. **CONTACT ADDRESS** Dept of Political Science, Univ of Victoria, PO Box 3050, Victoria, BC, V8W 3P5.

TUMLIN, JOHN S.
DISCIPLINE PHILOSOPHY **EDUCATION** Emroy Univ; PhD. **CAREER** Tchr lit, Southern Polytech State Univ. **RESEARCH** Sci fiction. **SELECTED PUBLICATIONS** Auth, publ(s) on Herman Melville; ed, to Joel Chandler. **CONTACT ADDRESS** Hum and Tech Commun Dept, Southern Polytech State Univ, S Marietta Pkwy, PO Box 1100, Marietta, GA, 30060.

TUMPKIN, MARY A.
PERSONAL Born 11/13/1949, Detroit, MI, m, 1970, 1 child **DISCIPLINE** BIBLICAL STUDIES **EDUCATION** South FL Center for Theol Studies, Doctor of Ministry, 98. **CAREER** Senior Minister, Universal Truth Center. **RESEARCH** Soc of Biblical Lit; Westar Inst; Am Academy of Relig. **CONTACT ADDRESS** 21310 NW 37th Ave, Carol City, FL, 33056. **EMAIL** mtumpkin@aol.com

TUNICK, DAVID C.
DISCIPLINE LAW **EDUCATION** Univ Calif, Los Angeles, BA, 63; Univ Calif, Los Angeles, JD, 71. **CAREER** Prof & J. Howard Ziemann fel; clerk, hon Malcolm M. Lucas US Dist Ct, Central Dist Calif; practiced, Mori & Katayama, Los Angeles; fac, Loyola Univ, 74-; vis prof, Univ Bridgeport, 83. **SELECTED PUBLICATIONS** Writes on, Computers, the Law & Civil Procedure. **CONTACT ADDRESS** Law School, Loyola Marymount Univ, 7900 Loyola Blvd, Burns 418, Los Angeles, CA, 90045. **EMAIL** dtunick@lmulaw.lmu.edu

TURETZKY, NACHUM
PERSONAL Born 06/04/1961, Israel, m, 1997, 1 child **DISCIPLINE** PHILOSOPHY **EDUCATION** Cuny, BA, 89; CUNY, presently in graduate sch. **CAREER** Adjunct, 98, FH LaGuardia Community Col/CUNY. **MEMBERSHIPS** APA **RESEARCH** Philosophy of sci; Social and political philosophy **CONTACT ADDRESS** 461 Central Park W, 4c, New York, NY, 10025. **EMAIL** turetzky@bway.net

TURKINGTON, RICHARD C.
DISCIPLINE LAW **EDUCATION** Wayne State Univ, BA, 63; Wayne State Univ Sch Law, JD, 66; NY Univ Sch Law, LLM, 67. **CAREER** Prof, Villanova Univ. **MEMBERSHIPS** Interdisciplinary Comt, Health Law Pa Bar Asn; chemn, Amer Asn Law Sch Sect on Defamation and Privacy. **RESEARCH** Privacy; confidentiality; AIDS and HIV related information policy. **SELECTED PUBLICATIONS** Coauth, Privacy: Cases and Materials, 92; contrib ed, AIDS, A Medical-Legal Handbook, 91 & AIDS, Law and Society, Report of the Pennsylvania Bar Association Task Force on Acquired Immune Deficiency Syndrome, 88. **CONTACT ADDRESS** Law School, Villanova Univ, 800 Lancaster Ave, Villanova, PA, 19085-1692. **EMAIL** turk@law.vill.edu

TURNBULL, ROBERT GEORGE
PERSONAL Born 07/01/1918, Scotland, SD, m, 1939, 1 child **DISCIPLINE** PHILOSOPHY **EDUCATION** Univ Minn, BA, 39, PhD(philos), 52; Oberlin Col, BD, 43. **CAREER** Instr humanities, Univ Minn, 48-50; from instr to prof philos, Univ Iowa, 50-64, chmn dept, 53-64; prof, Oberlin Col, 64-65; chmn dept, 68-80, PROF PHILOS, OHIO STATE UNIV, 65-, Mem, Coun Philos Studies, 67-70; ed, Philos Res Archives, 81- **MEMBERSHIPS** Am Philos Asn (exec secy, 66-69, pres, 77-78). **RESEARCH** Ancient and medieval philosophy; ethics; metaphysics. **SELECTED PUBLICATIONS** Auth, The Chain of Change--A Study of Aristotle Physics VII, Philos Sci, Vol 0061, 94. **CONTACT ADDRESS** Dept of Philos, Ohio State Univ, Columbus, OH, 43210.

TURNER, JOHN D.
PERSONAL Born 07/15/1938, Glen Ridge, NJ, m, 1992, 2 children **DISCIPLINE** HISTORY OF RELIGION **EDUCATION** Dartmouth Col, AB, 60; Union Theol Sem, BD, 65, ThM, 66; Duke Univ, PhD, 70. **CAREER** Asst prof, Univ Montana, 71-75; COTNER COL PROF RELIG, 76- , Assoc prof History, 76-83, CHR, PROG RELIG STUD, 78- , PROF CLASSICS & HISTORY, 84- , UNIV NEBRASKA-LINCOLN. **HONORS AND AWARDS** Rockefeller Doctoral fel, 68, Phi Beta Kappa, 69, Duke Univ; Am Soc Learned Soc fel, 76. **MEMBERSHIPS** Soc Bibl Lit; Studiorum Novi Testamenti Soc; Int Soc Neoplatonic Stud; Int Asn Coptic Stud; Corresp Inst Antiq & Christianity. **RESEARCH** Biblical studies; History of Hellenistic/Graeco-Roman Religion and Philosophy; Gnosticism; History of Later Greek Philosophy; Codicology and Papyrology; Greek, Coptic, Egyptian and Hebrew language and literature. **SELECTED PUBLICATIONS** Auth, Typologies of the Sethian Gnostic Treatises from Nag Hammadi, Les textes de Nag Hammadi et le probleme de leur classification: Actes du colloque tenu a Quebec du 15 au 22 Septembre, 1993, Peeters and Univ Laval, 95; ed, The Nag Hammadi Library After Fifty Years: Proceedings of the 1995 Society of Biblical Literature Commemoration, E.J. Brill, 97; auth, To See The Light: A Gnostic Appropriation of Jewish Priestly Practice and Sapiential and Apocalyptic Visionary Lore, Mediators of the Divine: Horizons of Prophecy and Divination on Mediterranean Antiquity, Scholars Press, 98; The Gnostic Seth, Biblical Figures Outside the Bible, Trinity Int Press, 98; Introduction & Commentaire, Zostrien, Presses de l'Universite Laval/Editions Peeters, 99. **CONTACT ADDRESS** Dept of Classics, Univ Nebraska, Lincoln, 238 Andrews Hall, Lincoln, NE, 68588-0337. **EMAIL** jturner@unlinfo.unl.edu

TURNER, ROBERT FOSTER
PERSONAL Born 02/14/1944, Atlanta, GA, m, 1 child **DISCIPLINE** NATIONAL SECURITY LAW, INTERATIONAL LAW, CONSTITUTIONAL LAW, U.S. FOREIGN P **EDUCATION** IN Univ, BA Gov't ,68; Law School, JD 81; SJD, 96; Univ VA, Law School. **CAREER** Co founder and Assoc Dir, Center for Natl Sec Law, Univ of VA, School of Law, 81; Special Asst, Under Sec of Defense for Policy, 81-82; Cousel Pres, Intelligence Oversight Board The White House, 82-84; Principal Deputy Asst, Sec of State for Legislative and Intergovernmental Affair, US Dep of State, 84-85; Pres, US Inst of Peace, Washington DC, 86-87; Assoc Dir, Center for Natl Security Law, Univ VA, School of Law, 87-present. **HONORS AND AWARDS** Distinguished Lectures US Military Academy(West Point); Chm ABA Standing Comm on Executive-Congressional Rlations ABA Section of International Law & Practive, Trustee, Intercollegiate Studies Inst; Dir, Thomas Jefferson Inst for Public Policy; Expert witness before more than a dozen Comm of US Senate and House. **MEMBERSHIPS** Council on Foreign Affairs; Academy of Political Sci; Amer Soc of International Law. **RESEARCH** Natl Security and the Constitution; War Powers; Separation of Powers; Intl Law and the Use of Force; Origins of and Solutions to War; US Foreign Policy and Diplomatic Hist. **SELECTED PUBLICATIONS** Author or editor of: Vietnamese Communism: Its Origins and Development; The Qar Powers Resolution: Its Implementation in Theory and Practice; Nicaragua v. United States: A Look at the Facts; Repealing the War Powers Resolution: Restoring the Rule of Law in US Foreign Policy; National Security Law, Contibutor to major US and foreign newspapers; NT Times, Wall Street Journal ,Washington Post ,Jerusalem Post. **CONTACT ADDRESS** Univ of Virginia, Charlottesville, VA, 22901. **EMAIL** rturner@lawl.law.virginia .edu

TURQUETTE, ATWELL R.
PERSONAL Born 07/14/1914, Texarkana, TX, w, 1937 **DISCIPLINE** PHILOSOPHY **EDUCATION** Univ Arkansas, BA, 36; Duke Univ, MA, 37; Cornell Univ, PhD, 43. **CAREER** Asst prof, 37-38, assoc prof, 39-40, Florida Southern Col; fel, Univ Chicago, 38-39; asst prof, 40-43, instr, 43-45, Cornell Univ; asst prof, 45-48, assoc prof, 48-52, prof, 52-75, prof emer, 75- , Univ Ill, Urbana-Champaign. **HONORS AND AWARDS** Duke Univ scholar; fel, Univ Chicago; fel, Cornell Univ; Rockefeller Gen Educ Board grant; NSF grants. **MEMBERSHIPS** APA; Am Math Soc; Calcutta Math Soc; Symbolic Logic Asn; Charles S Peirce Soc; Bertrand Russell Soc; Soc for Indust and Appl Math; AAAS; NY Acad Sci; IEEE Computer Soc. **RESEARCH** Logic; philosophy of science; history of ideas. **SELECTED PUBLICATIONS** Auth, An Alternative Minimal and Intuitive Exiomatic System for M-Valued Logic, Int Cong of Math, Zurich, 94; auth, Explanation as the Converse of Applications, 10th Int Congress of Logic, Methodology, and Philos of Sci, Florence, 95; auth, A Generalization of Tarski's Moglichkeit, Auckland, 97. **CONTACT ADDRESS** 914 W Clark, Champaign, IL, 61821-3328. **EMAIL** bondturq@novation.net

TUSAN, GAIL S.
PERSONAL Born 08/03/1956, Los Angeles, CA, d **DISCIPLINE** LAW **EDUCATION** University of California, Los Angeles, BA, 1978; George Washington University, JD, 1981; University of Nevada/National Judicial College, 1992. **CAREER** U.S. Department of Justice, intern, 1980-81; Kilpatrick & Cody, associate, 1981-84; Asbill, Porter, associate, 1984-86; Joyner & Joyner, partner, 1986-90; City Court of Atlanta, judge, 1990-92; State Court of Fulton County, judge, 1992-95; Institute of Continuing Judicial Education, faculty member; Georgia State University Law School, faculty member; Superior Court of Fulton County, judge, 1995-. **HONORS AND AWARDS** YWCA of Greater Atlanta's Academy of Women Achievers, Inductee, 1995; Cited by Georgia Informer as one of Georgia's 50 Most Influential Black Women, 1994; Justice Robert Benham, Law Related Supporter of the Year Award, 1992; Martin Luther King Jr Center for Nonviolence and Social Change Community Service Peace and Justice Award, 1991; Ebony, Thirty Leaders of the Future, 1985. **MEMBERSHIPS** Georgia State Bar, 1981-; Georgia Association of Black Women Attorneys, president, 1983, executive committee; Gate City Bar Association; Atlanta Bar Association; Judicial Procedure and Administration Advisory Committee; Committee on Professionalism. **CONTACT ADDRESS** Judge, Superior Court of Fulton County, 185 Central Ave SW, Rm T8955, Atlanta, GA, 30303.

TUSHNET, MARK VICTOR
PERSONAL Born 11/18/1945, Newark, NJ, m, 1969, 2 children **DISCIPLINE** LAW, AMERICAN LEGAL HISTORY **EDUCATION** Harvard Col, BA, 67; Yale Univ JD & MA, 71. **CAREER** Asst prof, 73-76, assoc prof, 76-79, prof law, Univ Wis, 79-; prof law, Georgetown Univ Law Ctr, 81-. **MEMBERSHIPS** Orgn Am Historians; Am Soc Legal Hist; Am Hist Assn; Conf Critical Legal Studies. **RESEARCH** Constitutional law; federal jurisdiction; American legal history. **SELECTED PUBLICATIONS** Auth, The Warren Court in Historical Perspective, ec, University of Press of Virginia, 93; auth, Making Civil Rights Law: Thurgood Marshall and the Supreme Court, 1936-1961, Oxford University Press, 94; auth, Brown v Board of Education, Franklin Watts, 95; coauth, Remnants of Belief: Contemporary Constitutional Issues, Oxford University Press, 96; auth, Making Constitutional Law: Thurgood Marshall and the Supreme Court, 1961-1991, Oxford University Press, 97. **CONTACT ADDRESS** Law Ctr, Georgetown Univ, 600 New Jersey NW, Washington, DC, 20001-2022. **EMAIL** tushnet@law.georgetown.edu

TUTTLE, HOWARD N.
PERSONAL Born 12/15/1935, Salt Lake City, UT, m, 1963, 2 children **DISCIPLINE** PHILOSOPHY **EDUCATION** Univ Utah, BA, 58, MA, 59; Harvard Univ, MA, 63; Brandeis Univ, PhD, 67. **CAREER** Prof philos, Univ New Mexico. **RESEARCH** Philosophy of history; philosophy of life. **SELECTED PUBLICATIONS** Auth, Wilhelm Dilthey's Philosophy of History; auth, The Dawn of Historical Reason; auth, The Crowd is Untruth. **CONTACT ADDRESS** 939 Donner Way, Apt 108, Salt Lake City, UT, 84108.

TWADDELL, GERALD E.
PERSONAL Born 03/23/1943, Dayton, KY, s **DISCIPLINE** PHILOSOPHY **EDUCATION** Sem of St. Pious X, BA, 63; Univ Strasbourg, Diploma d'E F M, 65; Catholic Univ Paris, STB, 67; Univ Cincinnati, MA, 74; Catholic Univ Paris, PhL, 74, D Phil, 77. **CAREER** Prof, Sem of St. Pious X, 67-77, dean, 70-77; asst prof philos, 77-87, assoc prof, 88-92, PROF PHILOS, THOMAS MORE COL, 93-, asst academic dean, 77-81, dir Institutional Res, 81-84, College Marshall, Thomas More Col, Crestview Hills, KY, 85-97. **HONORS AND AWARDS** Mina Shaughnessy Scholar, FIPSE, US Dept of Ed, 83. **MEMBERSHIPS** Am Philos Asn; Am Cath Philos Asn; KY Philos Asn (pres, 82-83); Gabriel Marcel Soc; Am Asn Philos Teachers. **RESEARCH** Theory of value; applied ethics. **CONTACT ADDRESS** Thomas More Col, 333 Thomas More Parkway, Crestview Hills, KY, 41017-3428. **EMAIL** twaddelg@thomasmore.edu

TWEED, THOMAS A.
PERSONAL Born 12/28/1954, Philadelphia, PA, m, 1979, 2 children **DISCIPLINE** RELIGIOUS STUDIES **EDUCATION** Penn State Univ, BS, 77; Harvard Divinity Sch, MTS, 79, Stanford Univ, PhD, 89. **CAREER** Asst prof, Univ Miami, 88-93; asst prof, 93-95, assoc prof, 95- , Univ N Carolina, Chapel Hill. **HONORS AND AWARDS** Award for Excellence, Am Acad Relig, 98. **MEMBERSHIPS** Am Acad Relig; Am Studies Asn; Orgn of Am Historians; Asn of Am Geographers; Am Soc of Church Hist. **RESEARCH** Religion in North America; Catholicism in America; Asian religions in America; immigration and religion. **SELECTED PUBLICATIONS** Auth, American Encounter with Buddhism, Indiand, 92; Our Lady of the Exile, Oxford, 97; ed, Retelling US Religious History, California, 97; co-ed with Prothero, Asian Religions in America, Ocford, 99. **CONTACT ADDRESS** Univ of North Carolina, 101 Saunders Hall, CB #3225, Chapel Hill, NC, 27599-3225. **EMAIL** tatweed@email.unc.edu

TWESIGYE, EMMANUEL
PERSONAL Born 05/25/1948, Rukungiri, Uganda, m, 1976, 4 children **DISCIPLINE** THEOLOGY **EDUCATION** EAU, DipTh, 70; MUK, BA, 73, DipEd, 73; Wheaton Grad Sch, MA, 78; Univ of the South, STM, 79; Vanderbilt Univ, MA, 82, VU, PhD, 83. **CAREER** Chaplain, head, dept of rel stud, Uganda Nat Tchrs Col, 73-77; assoc prof, chemn relig and philos, Fisk Univ, 83-89; prof, dir BWS, Ohio Wesleyan Univ, 89-98. **HONORS AND AWARDS** Honors degrees; listed, Who's Who in the World, Who's Who in the Mid- West, International Who's Who of Intellectuals, 5000 Personalities, Men of Achievement. **MEMBERSHIPS** Am Acad Relig; Soc of Bibl Lit; Am Asn of Philos; Ohio Acad of Relig. **RESEARCH** African theology and philosophy; evolutionary ethics. **SELECTED PUBLICATIONS** Auth, Common Ground: African Religion and Philosophy, 87; auth, The Global Human Problem, 88; Auth, God, Race, Myth and Power, 91; auth, African Religion, Philosophy, and Christianity in Logos-Christ, 96. **CONTACT ADDRESS** Dept of Religion and Philosophy, Ohio Wesleyan Univ, Delaware, OH, 43015. **EMAIL** ektwesig@cc.owu.edu

TWETTEN, DAVID B.
PERSONAL Born 07/06/1957, Spencer, IA, m, 1982, 3 children **DISCIPLINE** PHILOSOPHY **EDUCATION** Univ Toronto, Pontifical Inst of Mediaeval Stud, MSL, 87, PhD, phil and medieval stud, 93. **CAREER** Asst prof, 91-, Marquette Univ. **HONORS AND AWARDS** Dist Scholar Recognition, Marquette Univ, 97; Marquette Univ Sum Fac Fel, 96. **MEMBERSHIPS** APA; ACPA; Soc for Medieval and Renaissance Phil; Soc Intl d'Histoire des Sciences et de la Philosophie Arabes et Islamiques; Soc Intl pour l'Etude de la Philosophie Medievale; Thomas Aquinas Soc, 97; Intl Comm for the History of Medieval and Renaissance Natural Phil. **RESEARCH** Ancient and medieval philosophy **SELECTED PUBLICATIONS** Auth, Why Motion Requires a Cause: The Foundation for a Prime Mover in Aristotle and Aquinas, Phil & the God of Abraham: Essays in Mem of James A Weisheipl, O P, Pontifical Inst of Mediaeval Stud, 91; auth, Averroes on the Prime Mover Proved in the Physics, Viator: Medieval & Renaissance Stud 26, 95; auth, Clearing A Way for Aquinas: How the Proof from Motion Concludes to God, Proc of the Amer Cath Phil Asn 70, 96; auth, Back to Nature in Aquinas, Medieval Phil & Theology 5.2, 96; auth, Albert the Great on Whether Natural Philosophy Proves God's Existence, Archives d'histoire doctrinale et litteraire du moyen age 64, 97. **CONTACT ADDRESS** Dept of Philosophy, Marquette Univ, Coughlin 234, PO Box 1881, Milwaukee, WI, 53201-1881. **EMAIL** twettend@marquette.edu

TWISS, SUMNER BARNES
PERSONAL Born 12/02/1944, Baltimore, MD, m, 1967, 2 children **DISCIPLINE** PHILOSOPHY OF RELIGION, RELIGIOUS ETHICS **EDUCATION** Johns Hopkins Univ, BA, 66; Yale Univ, MA and MPhil, 71, PhD(relig studies), 74. **CAREER** Teaching fel ethics, Divinity Sch, Yale Univ, 69-70, teaching assoc, 70-71; from instr to asst prof relig studies, 71-

76, assoc prof, 76-80, PROF RELIG STUDIES, BROWN UNIV, 80-, Consult ethics, Inst Soc, Ethics and Life Sci, 72, fel, 73; Soc Values Higher Educ fel, 72. **HONORS AND AWARDS** AM, Brown Univ, 77. **MEMBERSHIPS** Am Acad Relig; Soc Sci Study Relig; Soc Values Higher Educ; Inst Soc, Ethics and Life Sci; Am Soc Polit and Legal Philos. **RESEARCH** Logic of religious discourse; comparative religious ethics; ethics and public policy, bioethics. **SELECTED PUBLICATIONS** Auth, Mencius and Aquinas, Jour Rel Ethics, Vol 0021, 93. **CONTACT ADDRESS** Dept of Relig Studies, Brown Univ, 1 Prospect St, Providence, RI, 02912-9127.

TWITCHELL, MARY POE
DISCIPLINE LAW **EDUCATION** Hollins Col, BA; Univ NC, Chapel Hill, MA; Univ Fla, JD; Yale Law Sch, LLM. **CAREER** Prof, Univ Fla, 82-. **MEMBERSHIPS** Civil Justice Reform Adv Gp, US Dist Ct, Middle Dist Fla, 91-93; Fla Bar; Order of the Coif. **RESEARCH** Civil procedure, federal practice. **CONTACT ADDRESS** School of Law, Univ of Florida, PO Box 117625, Gainesville, FL, 32611-7625. **EMAIL** twitchel@law.ufl.edu

TYLENDA, JOSEPH N.
PERSONAL Born 06/26/1928, Dickson City, PA **DISCIPLINE** THEOLOGY **EDUCATION** Univ Scranton, AB, 48; Boston Col, STL, 60; Pontif Gregorian Univ, STD, 64. **CAREER** Asst prof hist theol, Woodstock Col, Md, 64-73, dir libr, 68-70; lectr, Pontif Gregorian Univ, 70-73; assoc prof theol, Loyola Col, Md, 73-74; ASST ED, THEOL STUDIES, 74-. **MEMBERSHIPS** Theol Soc Am; Polish Inst Arts and Sci Am; Am Soc Church Hist. **RESEARCH** John Calvin and reformed theology. **SELECTED PUBLICATIONS** Auth, Later Calvinism--Intl Perspectives, Cath Hist Rev, Vol 0081, 95; Ignatius-Of-Loyola--The Pilgrim Saint, Cath Hist Rev, Vol 0082, 96. **CONTACT ADDRESS** Georgetown Univ, Washington, DC, 20057.

TYLER, RONALD
DISCIPLINE NEW TESTAMENT **EDUCATION** E NM Univ, BA, 61, MA, 64; Baylor Univ, PhD, 73; Vancouver Sch Theol, 77. **CAREER** Instr, Kilgore Col, 62-68; ch, Kilgore Col, 66-68; min, Church of Christ, 68-72; prof, 72-. **HONORS AND AWARDS** Vis fel, Princeton theol sem, 86. **MEMBERSHIPS** Mem, Am Acad Relig; Soc Bibl Lit; Gamma Theta Upsilon; The Cath Bibl Asst Am. **SELECTED PUBLICATIONS** Auth, The Work of the Preacher From the Pastoral Letters,Ventura County Preacher/Elders luncheon, 93; rev(s), Jerry Sumney, Identifying Paul's Opponents: Identifying Paul's Opponents in 2 Corinthians, The Catholic Biblical Quart, 92; Richard Longenecker, Galatians, vol 41, Word Biblical Commentary, Catholic Biblical Quart, 91; Richard Longenecker, Galatians, vol 41, Word Biblical Commentary, Rel Studies Rev, 92. **CONTACT ADDRESS** Dept of Relig, Pepperdine Univ, 24255 Pacific Coast Hwy, Malibu, CA, 90263. **EMAIL** rtyler@pepperdine.edu

TYRRELL, BERNARD JAMES
PERSONAL Born 05/10/1933, Yakima, WA **DISCIPLINE** PHILOSOPHY, RELIGIOUS STUDIES **EDUCATION** Gonzaga Univ, AB, 57, MA, 58; Santa Clara Univ, MA, 66; Fordham Univ, PhD, 72. **CAREER** Asst prof, 72-77, assoc prof, 77-81, PROF TO PROF EMERITUS, PHILOS & RELIG STUDIES, GONZAGA UNIV, 82-. **HONORS AND AWARDS** Phi Beta Kappa, Fordham Univ, 72. **MEMBERSHIPS** Am Acad Relig; Cath Theol Soc; Nat Guild Cath Psychiatrists. **RESEARCH** Religion and psychology. **SELECTED PUBLICATIONS** Auth, The dynamics of conversion, Homiletic & Pastoral Rev, 6/72; Christotherapy, In: Wisdom and Knowledge, Vol II, Abbey Press, 72; New Context of the Philosophy of God, In: Language, Truth and Meaning, Gill & Macmillan, 73; Bernard Lonergan's Philosophy of God, Notre Dame, 74; Christotherapy, Seabury, 75; Christotherapy and the Healing of Communal Consciousness, The Thomist, 10/76; Christotheraphy: A Concrete Instance of a Christian Psychotherapy, Bull Nat Guild Cath Psychiatrists, 77; Christotherapy II: A New Horizon for Counselors, Spiritual Directors and Seekers of Healing and Growth in Christ, Paulist Press, 82; Christointegration, Paulist Press, 89; Affectional Conversation, Method J of Lonergan Studies, Vol 14, No 1, spring 96. **CONTACT ADDRESS** Jesuit House, Gonzaga Univ, 502 E Boone Ave, Spokane, WA, 99258-0001. **EMAIL** btyrrell@gonzaga.edu

TYSON, JOHN R.
DISCIPLINE THEOLOGY **EDUCATION** Grove City Col, AB, 74; Asbury Theol Sem, Mdiv, 77; Grad Sch Drew Univ, MPhil,80, PhD, 83. **CAREER** Prof; Houghton Col, 79; past assoc pastor, First United Methodist Church, Cocoa, Fla. **HONORS AND AWARDS** Founding mem & bd dir, Charles Wesley Soc. **MEMBERSHIPS** Oxford Inst Methodist Theol; Wesleyan Theol Soc, Wesley Stud Sect Amer Acad Rel; Amer Soc Church Historians. **SELECTED PUBLICATIONS** Publ on, theological topics, 3 bk(s). **CONTACT ADDRESS** Dept of Religion and Philosophy, Houghton Col, PO Box 128, Houghton, NY, 14744.

TYSON, JOSEPH B.
PERSONAL Born 08/30/1928, Charlotte, NC, m, 1954, 1 child **DISCIPLINE** RELIGION **EDUCATION** Duke Univ, AB, 50, BD, 53; Union Theol Sem, NY, STM, 55, PhD, 59. **CAREER** From asst prof to assoc prof, 58-74, chmn dept, 65-75, PROF RELIG, SOUTHERN METHODIST UNIV, 74-. **MEMBERSHIPS** Soc Bibl Lit; Am Acad Relig; Studiorum Nova Testamenti Soc. **RESEARCH** New Testament. **SELECTED PUBLICATIONS** Auth, Jews and Judaism in Luke-Acts--An Analysis of the Issue of Anti-Judaism in Early-Christian Literature, New Testament Stud, Vol 0041, 95; The Search for Identity in Syrian Proto-Christianity--Mission, Inculturation and Plurality in Ancient Hellenistic Christianity--German, Jour Biblical Lit, Vol 0115, 96; Jesus Entry Into Jerusalem--In the Context of Lukan Theology and the Politics of His Day, Jour Biblical Lit, Vol 0116, 97. **CONTACT ADDRESS** Dept of Relig Studies, Southern Methodist Univ, P O Box 750001, Dallas, TX, 75275-0001.

U

UDDO, BASILE JOSEPH
PERSONAL Born 04/22/1949, New Orleans, LA, m, 1971, 3 children **DISCIPLINE** CONSTITUTIONAL LAW **EDUCATION** Loyola Univ, New Orleans, BBA, 70; Tulane Univ, JD, 73; Harvard Univ, 74. **CAREER** Instr legal process, Boston Univ, 73-74; asst prof const law, 75-77, assoc prof, 77-81, PROF CONST LAW, LOYOLA UNIV LAW SCH, NEW ORLEANS, 81-, Nat comt, Human Life Found, 79-; consult, Prog Values in Educ, Asn Cath Col and Univ, 80-; Prolife adv comt, US Cath Conf, 80-; adv comt, Am Family Inst, 80- **RESEARCH** Constitutional law--especially relating to issues concerning the right to life; family law--impact of law on families; law and ethics--professional responsibility. **SELECTED PUBLICATIONS** Auth, Federal-Policy on Forgoing Treatment or Care--Contradictions or Consistency, Issues in Law and Medicine, Vol 0008, 92. **CONTACT ADDRESS** Law Sch, Loyola Univ, 6333 Loyola Ave, New Orleans, LA, 70118.

UDOH, FABIAN E.
PERSONAL Born 11/06/1954, Nigeria, m, 1993, 2 children **DISCIPLINE** THEOLOGY **EDUCATION** Duke Univ, PhD, 96. **CAREER** Asst Prof, 96-98, Hobart & William Smith College; Asst Prof, 98-, Humanities, Univ of Notre Dame. **MEMBERSHIPS** AAR/SBL, CBA. **RESEARCH** New Testament interpretation, Second Temple Jewish history, African theology. **CONTACT ADDRESS** Program of Liberal Studies, Univ of Notre Dame, 215 D'shaughnessey, Notre Dame, IN, 46556. **EMAIL** Fabian.E.Udoh.1@nd.edu

UEDA, MAKOTO
PERSONAL Born 05/20/1931, Ono, Japan, m, 1962, 2 children **DISCIPLINE** LITERATURE, AESTHETICS **EDUCATION** Kobe Univ, BLitt, 54; Univ Nebr, MA, 56; Univ Wash, PhD(comp lit), 61. **CAREER** Lectr Japanese, Univ Toronto, 61-62, from asst prof to prof, 62-71; PROF JAPANESE, STANFORD UNIV, 71-. **RESEARCH** Japanese literature, including theatre; comparative literature, especially Japanese and Western; literary theory and criticism. **SELECTED PUBLICATIONS** Auth, Comparative Poetics--An Intercultural Essay on Theories of Literature, Comparative Lit, Vol 0045, 93. **CONTACT ADDRESS** Dept of Asian Languages, Stanford Univ, Stanford, CA, 94305-1926.

UITTI, ROGER W.
PERSONAL Born 10/29/1934, Chicago, IL, m, 1959, 4 children **DISCIPLINE** THEOLOGY **EDUCATION** Northwestern Coll, BA, 56; Wisc Evangel Lutheran Sem, BD, Ordained, 59; Luther Sem St Paul, MTh, 64; Lutheran School of Theo Chicago, PhD, 73. **CAREER** Instr, 62-66, Asst Prof, 66-80, theology, Concordia Coll, River Forest; adj Asst Prof, 77-79, Rosary Coll, River Forest; vis Asst Prof, 79, Mundelein Coll; Assoc Prof, 80-87, Prof, Old Testament, 87-, Dean of stud, 92-98, Lutheran Theo Sem, Saskatoon SK; sessional Lectr, 80-94, Univ of Saskatoon, SK. **HONORS AND AWARDS** LSTC Grad Scholarship, Univ of Chicago, AAL Concordia Coll Fac Scholarship. **MEMBERSHIPS** SBL, EES, AOS. **RESEARCH** Old Testament & the Arts, Old Testament Synoptic study, Old Testament Law/Law Collations. **SELECTED PUBLICATIONS** Auth, The Imagery Behind Luther's Ein feste Burg, in: Church Music, 75; A New Lectionary for a New Church? in: Currents in Theology and Mission, 88; Christian Disunity and Unity, Consensus, 91; Health and Wholeness in the Old Testament, Consensus, 91; co-auth, Duplicate Histories, A New Study Instrument for the Hebrew Bible, in: The Fourth R, 90; co-auth, The Arts and the Church, in: Consensus, 99. **CONTACT ADDRESS** Lutheran Theol Sem, 114 Seminary Cres, Saskatoon, SK, S7N 0X3. **EMAIL** uittir@duke.usask.ca

ULANOV, ANN BELFORD
PERSONAL Born 01/01/1938, Princeton, NJ, m, 1968, 4 children **DISCIPLINE** DEPTH PSYCHOLOGY, CHRISTIAN THEOLOGY **EDUCATION** Radcliffe Col, BA, 59; Union Theol Sem, MDiv, 62, PhD(psychiat and relig), 67. **CAREER** From instr to assoc prof psychiat and relig, Union Theol Sem, 66-74; Psycho-Therapist, 65-; PROF PSYCHIAT AND RELIG, UNION THEOL SEM, 74-, Res psychotherapist, Inst Relig and Health, 62-65; bd mem, C G Jung Training Ctr, 71 **MEMBERSHIPS** Am Asn Pastoral Counr; C G Jung Found Anal Psychol; Int Asn Anal Psychol; Nat Accreditation Asn and Exam Bd Psychoanal; Am Theol Soc. **RESEARCH** Feminine psychology; religion and the unconscious; the witch archetype. **SELECTED PUBLICATIONS** Auth, The Golden Ass of Apuleius--the Liberation of the Feminine in Man, Parabola-Myth Tradition Search for Meaning, Vol 0018, 93; Exploring Sacred Landscapes--Religious and Spiritual Experiences in Psychotherapy, Jour Rel and Health, Vol 0033, 94; The Work of Loewald, Hans, an Introduction and Commentary, Jour Rel and Health, Vol 0033, 94; Leaving My Fathers House-- A Journey to Conscious Femininity, Jour Rel and Health, Vol 0033, 94; A Womans Identity, Jour Rel and Health, Vol 0033, 94; Object Relations Therapy, Jour Rel and Health, Vol 0033, 94; Projective and Introjective Identification and the Use of the Therapists Self, Jour of Rel and Health, Vol 0033, 94; Envy--Further Thoughts, Jour Rel and Health, Vol 0034, 95; Sacred Chaos--Reflections on God Shadow and the Dark Self, Jour Rel and Health, Vol 0034, 95; The Mystery of the Conjunctio--Alchemical Images of Individuation, Jour Rel and Health, Vol 0034, 95; In Gods Shadow--The Collaboration of White, Victor and Jung,C.G., Jour Rel and Health, Vol 0034, 95; Protestantism and Jungian Psychology, Jour of Rel and Health, Vol 0035, 96; A Meeting of Minds--Mutuality in Psychoanalysis, Jour of Rel and Health, Vol 0035, 96; Tillich, Paul First--A Memoir of the Harvard Years, Jour Rel and Health, Vol 0036, 97; Always Becoming--An Autobiography, Jour Rel and Health, Vol 0036, 97; Practicing Wholeness, Jour of Rel and Health, Vol 0036, 97. **CONTACT ADDRESS** 185 E 85th St-35J, New York, NY, 10028.

ULEN, THOMAS S.
DISCIPLINE LAW **EDUCATION** Dartmouth Col, BA; Oxford Univ, MA; Stanford Univ, PhD. **CAREER** Prof, Univ Ill Urban Champaign. **HONORS AND AWARDS** Ed, Int Rev Law Economics. **MEMBERSHIPS** Am Law Economics Asn. **RESEARCH** Law, economics; including quantitative methods of legal decision-making. **SELECTED PUBLICATIONS** Co-auth, Law and Economics. **CONTACT ADDRESS** Law Dept, Univ Ill Urbana Champaign, 52 E Gregory Dr, Champaign, IL, 61820. **EMAIL** tulen@law.uiuc.edu

ULRICH, DOLPH
DISCIPLINE LOGIC, LOGICAL THEORY, PHILOSOPHY OF MATHEMATICS **EDUCATION** Wayne State Univ, PhD. **CAREER** Prof, Purdue Univ. **RESEARCH** Many-valued logics; modal logic. **SELECTED PUBLICATIONS** Coauth, Elementary Symbolic Logic. **CONTACT ADDRESS** Dept of Philos, Purdue Univ, 1080 Schleman Hall, West Lafayette, IN, 47907-1080.

ULRICH, LAWRENCE P.
DISCIPLINE PHILOSOPHY **EDUCATION** Univ Toronto, PhD, 72. **CAREER** Dept Philos, Univ Dayton **RESEARCH** Meidcal ethics; social philosophy; business ethics. **SELECTED PUBLICATIONS** Auth, The Patient Self-Determination Act: A Training Program for Health Care Professionals, Breckenridge Bioethics, 91; The Patient Self-Determination Act and Cultural Diversity, Cambridge Quart of Healthcare Ethics, 94; Ethical Issues in Medical Practice: A Healthcare Education Course for Medical Students, Ohio Univ, 96. **CONTACT ADDRESS** Dept of Philos, Univ Dayton, 300 Col Park, Dayton, OH, 75062. **EMAIL** quinn@checkov.hm.udayton.edu

UMIDI, JOSEPH L.
DISCIPLINE PRACTICAL THEOLOGY **EDUCATION** Kalamazoo Col, BA; Acadia Divinity Col, MDiv; Trinity Evangel Divinity Sch, DMin. **CAREER** Instr, Discipleship Training Sem, YWAM; prof, 85. **HONORS AND AWARDS** Founding bd mem, Hampton Rd(s) United Christians, 90-95; co-founder, consult, Can Christian Commun, Inc; founding bd mem, Leadership Training Intl, 92-96; bd mem, Missions S Am, 94-96; founding bd mem, Operation Breaking Through, 96. **SELECTED PUBLICATIONS** Auth, Avoiding Leadership Snares, Youth Ministries Mag, Sonlife Ministries, Elburn, 95; Leadership Land Mines, Regent Univ Sch of Divinity Rev, vol 1; In the Beginning; Breathe, Canada, Breathe; Ministry By The Book, Living By The Book, Christian Broadcasting Network, Inc, CBN Publ, 93; Surveys of regional prayer strategies, Strategic Intercession for the 90's, Umidi Publ, 94; auth, rel columnist, Can Newspaper. **CONTACT ADDRESS** Dept of Practical Theology, Regent Univ, 1000 Regent Univ Dr, Virginia Beach, VA, 23464-9831.

UNDERWOOD, HARRY
DISCIPLINE LAW **EDUCATION** Oxford Univ, BA, 76; Univ Toronto, LLB, 79. **CAREER** Lawyer, McCarthy Tetrault **RESEARCH** Civil litigation. **SELECTED PUBLICATIONS** Auth, pubs on legal subjects. **CONTACT ADDRESS** Fac of Law, Univ Toronto, 78 Queen's Park, Toronto, ON.

UNDERWOOD, JAMES L.
DISCIPLINE CONST LAW, FEDERAL PRACTICE, AND CIVIL AND POLITICAL RIGHTS **EDUCATION** Emory Univ, AB, 59, JD, 62; Yale Univ, LLM, 66. **CAREER** Strom Thurmond prof, Univ of SC. **SELECTED PUBLICATIONS** Auth, leading treatises on civil litigation in fed courts. **CONTACT ADDRESS** School of Law, Univ of S. Carolina, Law Center, Columbia, SC, 29208-. **EMAIL** JimU@law.law.sc.edu

UNGAR, ANTHONY
DISCIPLINE PHILOSOPHY **EDUCATION** Stanford Univ, PhD. **CAREER** Assoc prof, Univ Albany, State Univ NY. **RESEARCH** Logic, philosophy of logic, philosophy and foundations of mathematics. **SELECTED PUBLICATIONS** Auth, Normalization, Cut-Elimination, and the Theory of Proofs, 92. **CONTACT ADDRESS** Dept of Philosophy, Univ at Albany, SUNY, Albany, NY, 12222. **EMAIL** amu78@cnsunix.albany.edu

UNNO, MARK
DISCIPLINE EAST ASIAN RELIGIONS **EDUCATION** Oberlin, BA, Stanford, MA, PhD. **CAREER** Religion, Carleton Univ. **MEMBERSHIPS** Auth, Japanese Pure Land Buddhism. **CONTACT ADDRESS** Carleton Col, 100 S College St., Northfield, MN, 55057-4016.

UNNO, TAITETSU
PERSONAL Born 02/05/1929, Japan, m, 1958, 1 child **DISCIPLINE** BUDDHIST STUDIES **EDUCATION** Univ Calif, Berkeley, BA, 51; Univ Tokyo, MA, 56, PhD(Buddhist studies), 68. **CAREER** Instr Orient lang, Univ Calif, Los Angeles, 59-61; vis lectr hist, Univ Ill, 68-69, asst prof hist & Asian studies, 69-70, assoc prof, 70-71; Prof World Relig,Smith Col, 71-88, Jill Ker Conway Prof Relig, 88-. **HONORS AND AWARDS** Mellon Fel, 85; Ernest Pon Award for Civil and Human Rights, 88; Japan Found Fel, 94. **MEMBERSHIPS** Asn Asian Studies; Am Acad Relig; Am Orient Soc; NAm Soc Buddhist Studies. **RESEARCH** Buddhist studies; comparative religion; East Asian history. **SELECTED PUBLICATIONS** Auth, The Religious Philosophy of Tanabe Hajime, Asian Humanities Press, 90; The Religious Philosophy of Nishitani Keiji, Asian Humanities Press, 90; Tannisho: A Shin Buddhist Classic, Buddhist Study Ctr, 2nd rev ed, 96; River of Fire, River of Water, Doubleday, 98. **CONTACT ADDRESS** Dept of Relig, Smith Col, 98 Green St, Northampton, MA, 01063-0001. **EMAIL** tunno@sophia.smith.edu

UPTON, THOMAS VERNON
PERSONAL Born 04/27/1948, Antigo, WI, m, 1977 **DISCIPLINE** PHILOSOPHY, THEOLOGY **EDUCATION** Cath Univ Am, BA, 70, MA, 72, PhD, 78. **CAREER** Asst prof, 77-81, assoc prof philos, 81-, Gannon Univ. **HONORS AND AWARDS** NEH, summer sem grant, 80, 83, 86, 88. **MEMBERSHIPS** Am Philos Assn; Ancient Greek Philos; Am Cath Philos Assn. **RESEARCH** Aristotle and Greek philosophy and science; medical ethics. **SELECTED PUBLICATIONS** Auth, Review of Problems In Stoicism, 72; rev, Harold Cherniss: Selected Writings, Rev Metaphysics, 78; art, Imperishable Being And The Role Of Technical Hypotheses In Aristotelian Demonstration, Nature and System, No 2, 80; art, A Note on Aristotelian Epagoge, Phronesis, No 26, 81; art, Aristotle's Moral Epistemology: The Possibility Of Ethical Demonstration, The New Scholasticism, spring 82. **CONTACT ADDRESS** Gannon Univ, University Square, Box 209, Erie, PA, 16541. **EMAIL** t.upton@velocity.net

URBAN WALKER, MARGARET
DISCIPLINE PHILOSOPHY **EDUCATION** Northwestern Univ, PhD. **CAREER** Assoc prof, Fordham Univ. **RESEARCH** Moral theory, moral psych, moral epistemology. **SELECTED PUBLICATIONS** Auth, Partial Consideration, Ethics, 92; Feminism, Ethics, and the Question of theory, Hypatia, 92; Keeping Moral Space Open: New Images of Ethics Consulting, Hastings Ctr Rpt, 93; Where Do Moral Theories Come From? Philos Forum, 95; Feminist Skepticism, Authority, and Transparency, Moral Epistemology, Oxford UP, 95. **CONTACT ADDRESS** Dept of Philos, Fordham Univ, 113 W 60th St, New York, NY, 10023.

URBROCK, WILLIAM JOSEPH
PERSONAL Born 09/14/1938, Chicago, IL, m, 2 children **DISCIPLINE** RELIGION **EDUCATION** Concordia Sr Col, BA, 60; Concordia Sem, MDiv, 64; Harvard Univ, PhD, 75. **CAREER** Asst prof relig, Lycoming Col, 69-71; from Asst Prof to Assoc Prof, 72-80, Prof Relig, Univ Wis-Oshkosh, 80-; ed, Transactions, Wisc Acad Sci, Arts, & Letters, 92-. **MEMBERSHIPS** Soc Bibl Lit; Am Sch Orient Res; Soc Antiquity & Christianity; Cath Bibl Asn Am; Conf Christianity & Lit. **RESEARCH** Biblical studies, Old Testament. **SELECTED PUBLICATIONS** Auth, 'Em Sisera beShirat Devorah, Beit Mikra 131, 92; Blessings and Curses in Anchor Bible Dictionary, 92; The Book of Amos, The Sounds and the Silences, Currents in Theol & Mission, 96; Psalm 90: Moses, Mortality and... the Morning, Currents in Theol & Mission, 98; author of numerous other articles. **CONTACT ADDRESS** Dept of Relig, Univ of Wis, 800 Algoma Blvd, Oshkosh, WI, 54901-8601. **EMAIL** urbrock@uwash.edu

URY, M. WILLIAM
PERSONAL Born 04/05/1956, Cleveland, OH, m, 1984, 4 children **DISCIPLINE** HISTORICAL THEOLOGY **EDUCATION** Asbury Col, BA, 78; Asbury/Theolog Seminary, M.Div, 83; Drew Univ, PhD, 91. **CAREER** Prof, Wesley Theolog Seminary, 89-98. **HONORS AND AWARDS** Tchr of the Year, 94-95; Who's Who in Amer Univ & Col; Phi Alpha Theta; Theta Phi. **MEMBERSHIPS** Amer Acad Relig; Evangel Theolog Seminary; Wesley Theolog Soc. **RESEARCH** Theology; Historical Theology; Philosophy; Languages. **SELECTED PUBLICATIONS** Coauth, Loving Jesus: A Guidebook for Mature Discipleship, Discipleship Manual Vol III, 98; coauth, Following: A Guidebook for Mature Discipleship Vol II, Discipleship Manual, 97; The World is Still Our Parish, Good News Mag, 96. **CONTACT ADDRESS** Wesley Biblical Sem, Box 9928, Jackson, MS, 39286. **EMAIL** 103533,3144@compuserve.com

UTTON, ALBERT E.
PERSONAL Born 07/06/1931, Aztec, NM, m, 1959, 2 children **DISCIPLINE** LAW **EDUCATION** Univ NMex, BA, 53; Oxford Univ, BA, 56, MA, 59. **CAREER** Assoc, John Simms Jr, Law Off, Albuquerque, 59-60; partner, Simms and Robinson, 60-61; from asst prof to assoc prof, 61-68, PROF LAW, UNIV NMEX, 68-, Mem, Inner Temple, Inns of Court, London; mem, Univs Comt Water Resources; mem, Comn Environ Policy, Law and Admin. **MEMBERSHIPS** Int Law Asn; Am Soc Int Law; Int Union Conserv Nature and Natural Resources. **RESEARCH** Law of the continental shelf, planning for the conservation, development and use of natural resources; international resources and environmental law. **SELECTED PUBLICATIONS** Auth, Managing North-American Transboundary Water-Resources .1.--Introduction, Natural Resources Jour, Vol 0033, 93; Assessing North-America Management of Its Transboundary Waters/, Natural Resources Jour, Vol 0033, 93; Water and the Arid Southwest--An International Region Under Stress, Natural Resources Jour, Vol 0034, 94; Which Rule Should Prevail in International Water Disputes--That of Reasonableness or That of No Harm, Natural Resources Jour, Vol 0036, 96; Cuixmala Model Draft Treaty for the Protection of the Environment and the Natural-Resources of North-America, Natural Resources Jour, Vol 0036, 96; Regional Cooperation--The Example of International Waters Systems in the 20th-Century, Natural Resources Jour, Vol 0036, 96. **CONTACT ADDRESS** Sch of Law, Univ of NMex, Albuquerque, NM, 87131.

UVILLER, H. RICHARD
PERSONAL Born 07/03/1929, New York, NY, m, 1964, 1 child **DISCIPLINE** LAW **EDUCATION** Harvard Univ, AB, 51; Yale Law Sch, LLB, 53. **CAREER** Atty, Off Legal Counsel, US Dept Justice, 53-54; asst dist atty, Off Dist Atty, NYC, 54-68; ARTHUR LEVITT PROF LAW, COLUMBIA UNIV, 68-. **MEMBERSHIPS** Am Law Inst; Lawyer's Comt on Violence. **RESEARCH** Criminal process. **SELECTED PUBLICATIONS** Auth, Barker v Wingo: Speedy trial gets a fast shuffle, 12/72, Columbia Law Rev; The virtuous prosecutor in quest of an ethical standard, Mich Law Rev, 5/73; The advocate, the truth & judicial hackles, Univ Pa Law Rev, 5/75; Pleading guilty: A critique of four models, Law & Contemp Prob, winter 77; Zeal and frivolity: The ethical duty of the appellate advocate to tell the truth about the law, Hofstra Rev, spring 78; Processes of Criminal Justice, West, 2nd ed, 79; Evidence of character to prove conduct, Univ Pa Law Rev, 4/82; Trends in search and seizure law, Vand Law Rev, spring 82; The acquisition of evidence for criminal prosecution, Vand Law Rev, 1982; The unworthy victim, Law & Contemp Prob, 84; Seizure by Gunshot, NYU Rev of Law and Soc Change, 86; Evidence from the mind of the criminal suspect, Col Law Rev, 87; Presumed guilty, Univ Pa Law Rev, 88; Tempered Zeal, Contemporary Books, 6/88; Reasonability and the Fourth Amendment, Crim Law Bull, 89; Client taint, Crim J Ethics, 90; Self incrimination by inference, J Crim law & Criminology, 90; Acquitting the guilty, Crim Law Forum, 90; Credence, character, and the rules of evidence, Duke Law J, 93; Unconvinced, unreconstruted & unrepentant, Duke Law J, 94; The lawyer as liar, Crim J Ethics, 94; Virtual Justice: The Flawed Prosecution of Crime in America, Yale Univ Press, 96. **CONTACT ADDRESS** Law Sch, Columbia Univ, 435 W 116th St, New York, NY, 10027-7201. **EMAIL** uviller@law.columbia.edu

UZGALIS, WILLIAM
DISCIPLINE PHILOSOPHIES OF CHINA **EDUCATION** Univ Calif, Irving, BA; Calif State Univ, Long Beach, MA; Stanford Univ, PhD. **CAREER** Philos, Oregon St Univ. **SELECTED PUBLICATIONS** Auth, The Anti-Essential Locke and Natural Kinds; The Same Tyrannical Principle: The Lockean Legacy on Slavery. **CONTACT ADDRESS** Dept Philos, Oregon State Univ, Corvallis, OR, 97331-4501. **EMAIL** wuzgalis@orst.edu

V

VACEK, EDWARD VICTOR
PERSONAL Born 05/12/1942, Omaha, NE **DISCIPLINE** PHILOSOPHY, CHRISTIAN ETHICS **EDUCATION** St Louis Univ, BA, 66, MA, 67, PhL, 68; Weston Sch Theol, MDiv, 73; Northwestern Univ, PhD(philos), 78; Loyola Univ Chicago, STL, 81. **CAREER** Instr math, Campion High Sch, 66-68; instr philos, Creighton Univ, 69-70 & 72-73 & Seattle Univ, 77-78; asst prof ethics, Jesuit Sch Theol, Chicago, 78-81; Prof Ethics, Weston Sch Theol, 81-. **MEMBERSHIPS** Soc Philos Sex & Love; Soc Christian Ethicists; Cath Theol Soc Am. **RESEARCH** Ethics; phenomenology; Max Scheler; love; sexuality. **SELECTED PUBLICATIONS** Auth, Love, Human and Divine: the Heart of Christian Life, Georgetown Univ Press, 94; The Eclipse of Love for God, America, 3/96; Love, Christian and Diverse: A Response to Colin Grant, J Relig Ethics, Spring 96; Love for God -- Is It Obligatory?, The Annual of the Soc Christian Ethics, 96; Divine-Command, Natural-Law, and Mutual-Love Ethics, Theol Studies, 12/96; Religious Life and the Eclipse of Love for God, Rev for Religious, March/April 98; author of numerous other articles. **CONTACT ADDRESS** 3 Phillips Place, Cambridge, MA, 02138-3495. **EMAIL** edvacek@aol.com

VAGTS, DETLEV F.
PERSONAL Born 02/13/1929, Washington, DC, m, 1954, 2 children **DISCIPLINE** LAW **EDUCATION** Harvard Univ, AB, 48, LLB, 51. **CAREER** Asst prof, 59-62, Prof Law, Law Sch, Harvard Univ, 62-, Counr Int Law, US Dept of State, 76-77; assoc reporter, Restatement Foreign Relations Law 79-87. **HONORS AND AWARDS** Max Planck Research Award, 91. **MEMBERSHIPS** Am Bar Asn; Am Soc Int Law; AAAS. **RESEARCH** Corporations and international transactions. **SELECTED PUBLICATIONS** Coauth, Transnational Legal Problems, 68, 2nd ed, 76 & ed, Basic Corporation Law, 73, 2nd ed, 79, Foundation. **CONTACT ADDRESS** Law School, Harvard Univ, 1575 Massachusetts Ave, Cambridge, MA, 02138-2903. **EMAIL** Vagts@law.Harvard.edu

VAILLANCOURT, DANIEL
DISCIPLINE PHILOSOPHY **EDUCATION** St Francis Col, Biddeford, Maine, BA; DePaul Univ Chicago, PhD, 76. **CAREER** Prof; Loyola Univ, 90-; 18 yrs fac, 5 yrs chp Humanities, Mundelein Col; 3 yrs dean, Masters Lib Stud Prog; Fulbright grant, Paris,71-72. **RESEARCH** Philosophy of human nature; contemporary French philosophy; philosophy of religion. **SELECTED PUBLICATIONS** Coauth, Lenin to Gorbachev: Three Generations of Soviet Communists, Harlan-Davidson, 89-rev ed 94; articles in, philos, lit, Marxism & Communism, soc & econ philos; transl several works in, soc philos from Fr to Engl. **CONTACT ADDRESS** Dept of Philosophy, Loyola Univ, Chicago, 820 N Michigan Ave, Chicago, IL, 60611.

VAIRO, GEORGENE M.
DISCIPLINE LAW **EDUCATION** Sweet Briar Col, BA, 72; Univ Va, MEd, 75; Fordham Univ, JD, 79. **CAREER** Prof; clerk, hon Joseph M. McLaughlin, US Dist Ct Eastern Dist NY; assoc spec in Antitrust Law, Skadden, Arps, Slate, Meagher & Flom, NY; fac, Fordham Law Sch, 82-95 & assoc dean, 87-95; ch, Leonard F. Manning Distinguished Ch, 94; chp, Dalkon Shield Claimants Trust; ed bd, Moore's Fed Practice. **MEMBERSHIPS** Amer Law Inst. **RESEARCH** Resolution of mass tort claims. **SELECTED PUBLICATIONS** Publ on, federal procedure and jurisdiction. **CONTACT ADDRESS** Law School, Loyola Marymount Univ, 7900 Loyola Blvd, Burns 317, Los Angeles, CA, 90045. **EMAIL** gvairo@lmulaw.lmu.edu

VALERI, MARK
DISCIPLINE RELIGIOUS STUDIES **EDUCATION** Whitworth, BA, 76; Yale Univ, MDiv, 79; Princeton, PhD, 85. **CAREER** Asst prof Religious Studies, Lewis and Clark; prof Church History, Union Theological Seminary. **HONORS AND AWARDS** Francis Makemie Prize, 95. **RESEARCH** 18th century religion in New England. **SELECTED PUBLICATIONS** Fel Publ, The Economic Thought of Jonathan Edwards, Church Hist 60, 91; auth, The New Divinity and the American Revolution, William and Mary Quart 46, 89; Law and Providence in Joseph Bellamy's New England: The Origins of the New Divinity in Revolutionary America, Oxford Univ, 94; Religious Discipline and the Market: Puritans and the Issue of Usury, William and Mary Quart, 97. **CONTACT ADDRESS** Union Theological Sem, 3401 Brook Rd., Richmond, VA, 23227. **EMAIL** mvaleri@utsva.edu

VALLEGA-NEU, DANIELA
PERSONAL Born 06/13/1966, Vorese, Italy, m, 1998 **DISCIPLINE** PHILOSOPHY **EDUCATION** Albert-Ludwigs-Universitat, Freiburg, GER, MA, 92, PhD, 95. **CAREER** Instr, Friedrich-Schiller-Universitat Jena, GER, summer sem, 97; instr, dept of philos, PA State Univ, spring sem, 98; LECTURER, DEPT OF PHILOS, PA STATE UNIV, FALL SEM, 98. **HONORS AND AWARDS** Fel, Landesgraduierten foerderung von Baden Wuerttemberg, for doctoral these, 93-95; Res fel, DAAD (German Academic Exchange Service), PA State Univ, 97-98. **MEMBERSHIPS** Amer Philos Assoc; Soc for Phenomenology and Existential Philos; Heidegger Circle; Allgemeine Gesellschaft fuer Philosophie in Deutschland; Deutsche Gesellschaft fur Phaenomenologische Forschung; Martin Heidegger Gesellschaft. **RESEARCH** Contemporary continental philos;

phenomenology; hermeneutics; deconstruction. **SELECTED PUBLICATIONS** Auth, Michel Haar, Nietzsche et la metaphysique, Paris: Gallimard, 93, in Philosophischer Literaturanzeiger 47, July-Sept 94; Die Notwendigkeit der Grundung im Zeitalter der Dekonstruktion, Zur Grundung in Heideggers Beitragen zur Philosophie: unter Hinzuziehung der Derridaschen Dekonstruktion, Berlin: Duncker & Humblot, 97; La Questione del Corpo nei Beitrage zur Philosophie, in Giornale di Metafisica, 98; Overcoming the Ontological Difference in Heidigger's Contributions to Philosophy, in Proceedings of the 32nd Annual Heiddegger Conf, Villanova Univ, 98; Gerard Ruff, Am Ursprung der Zeit, Berlin: Duncker & Humblot, 97, in Theologische Literaturzeitung, 98. **CONTACT ADDRESS** Dept of Philos, Pennsylvania State Univ, 240 Sparks Bldg, Univ Park, PA, 16802. **EMAIL** dxn10@psu.edu

VALLENTYNE, PETER
PERSONAL Born 03/25/1952, New Haven, CT, m, 1983 **DISCIPLINE** PHILOSOPHY **EDUCATION** Fellow of the Soc Actuaries, 76; McGill Univ, BA, 78; Univ Pittsburgh, MA, 81; Univ Pittsburgh, PhD, 84. **CAREER** Actuarial Supervisor, Financial Forecasting Dept, Great West Life Assurance Co, Winnipeg, 73-75; admin assoc to the pres, Va Commonwealth Univ, Fall 92; Harvard Mgt Development Prog, 94; ch, Philos Rel stud, Va Commonwealth Univ, 88- ; asst prof, Univ Western Ontario, 84-88; asst prof, Va Commonwealth Univ, 88-90, assoc prof, 90- . **HONORS AND AWARDS** Amer Coun Learned Soc fel, 97; NEH, Ed Div grant, for fac workshops tchg ethics across the curriculum 96-98; Who's Who Among America's Tchrs, 96, and Who's Who in the South and Southwest; Va Found Human pub lect grants, 95-96; Va Commonwealth Univ Res Grant-in-Aid, 90; Res Coun Canada grant for conf on contractarian thought, 87; Canada Coun Doc Fel, 81-83. **MEMBERSHIPS** Amer Philos Assn; Can Philos Assn; S Soc Philos and Psychol; Va Philos Asn. **RESEARCH** Ethical theory; political philosophy. **SELECTED PUBLICATIONS** Auth, Gauthier on Morality and Rationality, Eidos 5, 86, 79-95, reprinted with revisions as Gauthier's Three Projects, in Contractarianism and Rational Choice: Essays on David Gauthier's Morals by Agreement, ed Peter Vallentyne, Cambridge UP, 91, 1-12; The Teleological/Deontological Distinction, The Jour Value Inquiry, 21, 87, 21-32; Utilitarianism and the Outcomes of Action, The Pacific Philosophical Quart, 68, 87, 57-70; Prohibition Dilemmas and Deontic Logic, Logique et Analyse, 18, 87, 113-122; Teleology, Consequentialism, and the Past, The Jour Value Inquiry, 22, 88, 89-101; Rights Based Paretianism, The Canadian Jour Philos, 18, 88, 527-544; Gimmicky Representations of Moral Theories, Metaphilosophy, 19, 88, 253-263; Explicating Lawhood, Philos Sci, 55, 88, 598-613; Critical Review of J. L. Mackie's Persons and Values and Ted Honderich's Morality and Objectivity, The Can Jour Philos, 18, 88, 595-607; Two Types of moral Dilemmas, Erkenntnis, 30, 89, 301-318; how to combine Pareto Optimality with Liberty Considerations, Theory and Decision, 27, 89, 217-240; Equal Opportunity and the Family, Publ Affairs Quart, 3, 89, 29-47, reprinted in Children's Rights Revisioned: Philosophical Readings, ed Rosalind Ladd, Wadsworth Press, 96, 82-97; Contractarianism and the Assumption of Mutual Unconcern, Philos Stud, 56, 89, 187-192, reprinted in Contractarianism and Rational Choice: Essays on David Gauthier's Moral by Agreement, ed Peter Vallentyne, Cambridge UP, 91, 71-75; ed, Contractarianism and Rational Choice: Essays on David Gauthier's Morals by Agreement, Cambridge UPs, 91; The Problem of Unauthorized Welfare, Nous 25, 91, 295-321; Motivational Ties and Doing What One Wants Most, Jour Philos Res, XVI, 91, 437-439; Libertarianism, Autonomy, and Children, Publ Affairs Quart, 5, 91, 333-352; Moral Dilemmas and Comparative Conceptions of Morality, S Jour Philos, XXX, 92, 117-124; Child Liberationism and Legitimate Interference, Jour Soc Philos, 23, 92, 5-15; Utilitarianism and Infinite Utility, Australasian Jour Philos, 71, 93, 212-217; The Connection Between Prudential Goodness and moral Permissibility, Jour Soc Phil, 24, 93, 105-128; Infinite Utility: Anonymity and Person-Centeredness, Australasian jour Philos, 73, 95, 413-420; Taking Justice too Seriously, Utilitas, 7, 95, 207-216; Response-Dependence, Rigidification, and Objectivity, Erkenntnis 44, 95, 101-112; Self-Ownership and Equality: Brute Luck, Gifts, Universal Domination, and Leximin, Ethics 107, 97, 321-343; Infinite Utility and Finitely Additive Value theory, Jour Philos, 94, 97, 5-26; Intrinsic Properties Defined, Philos Stud, 88, 97, 209-219. **CONTACT ADDRESS** Dept of Philosophy, Virginia Commonwealth Univ, Richmond, VA, 23284-2025. **EMAIL** peter.vallentyne@vcu.edu

VALLICELLA, WILLIAM F.
DISCIPLINE PHILOSOPHY **EDUCATION** Boston Coll, PhD, 78. **CAREER** 78-89, Univ of Dayton, OH; 89-91, Case Western Reserve Univ; 91-, independent scholar. **HONORS AND AWARDS** Various NEH Grants **MEMBERSHIPS** APA **RESEARCH** Metaphysics, philosophy of religion, German philosophy. **SELECTED PUBLICATIONS** Auth, God Causation and Occasionalism, in: Religious Stud, 99; Could a Classical Theist be a Physicalist?, in: Faith & Philo, 98; Bundles and Indiscernibility, A Reply to O'Leary-Hawthorne, in: Analysis, 97; On an Insufficient Argument against Sufficient Reason, Ratio, 97; The Hume-Edwards Objection to the Cosmological Argument, J of Philo Research, 97; Concurrentism and Occasionalism, in: Amer Cath Philo Qtly, 96; No Time for Propositions, in: Philosophia, 95; Creation and Existence, in: Intl Philo Qtly, 91. **CONTACT ADDRESS** 1360 E Cindy St, Chandler, AZ, 85225-5433. **EMAIL** billvallicella@compuserve.com

VALOIS, RAYNALD
PERSONAL Born 05/19/1935, Sorel, PQ, Canada, m, 1970, 1 child **DISCIPLINE** AESTHETICS, LOGIC **EDUCATION** Col de St Hyacinthe, Que, BA, 55; Univ du Latran, Rome, BTh, 64; Laval Univ, PhD(philos), 73. **CAREER** Prof philos, Laval Univ, 68-76; secretaire particulier, Ministre Des Richesses Naturelles, Govt Que, 76-78; PROF PHILOS, LAVAL UNIV, 78-. **RESEARCH** Aesthetics of plastic arts. **SELECTED PUBLICATIONS** Auth, Definition and Demonstration in the Logic of Aristotle, Laval Theol et Philos, Vol 0050, 94. **CONTACT ADDRESS** Dept of Philos, Laval Univ, Quebec, PQ, G1K 7P4.

VAN BUREN, JOHN
DISCIPLINE PHILOSOPHY **EDUCATION** McMaster Univ, PhD. **CAREER** Assoc prof, Fordham Univ. **RESEARCH** French poststructuralism, environmental ethics. **SELECTED PUBLICATIONS** Auth, The Young Heidegger: Rumor of the Hidden King, Ind UP, 94; Reading Heidegger From the Start, SUNY Press, 94; Critical Environmental Hermeneutics, Env Ethics, Oxford UP, 95. **CONTACT ADDRESS** Dept of Philos, Fordham Univ, 113 W 60th St, New York, NY, 10023.

VAN CAMP, JULIE C.
PERSONAL Born 06/05/1947, Davenport, IA **DISCIPLINE** PHILOSOPHY **EDUCATION** Mount Holyoke Col MA, 69; Georgetown Univ, JD, 80; Temple Univ, MA, 75, PhD, 82. **CAREER** Temple Univ & Tyler S of A, ta, 70-71; Manor Jr Col, lectr, 71; Black Hawk Col, lectr, 72; Comm Col of Phil, lectr, 72-74; Georgetown Univ Law Cen, law fel, 77-78; G. Mason Univ, lect, 84; Univ of Cal, lectr, 90; Cal State Univ Long Beach, asst prof, assoc prof, 90-. **MEMBERSHIPS** AAUP, APA, ASA, BSA, CHA, CRD, DCA, DC Bar, Cal State Bar. **RESEARCH** Philo probs art law; free speech for artists; philo and dance. **SELECTED PUBLICATIONS** Auth, Non-Verbal Metaphor: A Non-Explanation of Meaning in Dance, in: Brit Jour of Aesthetics, 96; The Colorization Controversy, in: Jour of Value Inquiry, 95; Creating Works of Art From Works of Art: The problem of Derivative Works, Jour of Arts Mgmt, Law and Soc, 94; The Philosophy of Art Law, in: Metaphilo, 94; Indecency on the Internet: Lessons from the Art World, in: Enter, Pub & Arts Handbook, Clark Boardman Callaghan, 96; Judging Aesthetic Value: @ Live Crew, Pretty Woman, and the Supreme Court, in: Enter, Pub & Arts Handbook, 95; Copyright of Choreographic Works, in: Enter, Pub and Arts Handbook, 94. **CONTACT ADDRESS** Dept of Philosophy, California State Univ, Long Beach, 1250 Bellflower Blvd, Long Beach, CA, 90840-2408. **EMAIL** jvancamp@csulb.edu

VAN CLEVE, JAMES
PERSONAL Born 05/19/1948, Mankato, MN, m, 1974, 2 children **DISCIPLINE** PHILOSOPHY **EDUCATION** Univ Iowa, BA, 69; Univ Rochester, MA, 72, PhD, 74. **CAREER** Asst, assoc, prof, philos, Brown Univ, 73- ; Fubright vis prof Jadavpur Univ, Calcutta, 80; vis prof philos, Duke Univ, 93. **HONORS AND AWARDS** Fulbright Award, 80; ACLS fel, 81; Nat Hum Ctr Fel, 90-91. **MEMBERSHIPS** APA; N Am Kant Soc. **RESEARCH** Epistemology; metaphysics; history of modern philosophy. **SELECTED PUBLICATIONS** Auth, Foundationalism, Epistemic Principles, and the Cartesian Circle, Philos Rev, 79; auth, Three Versions of the Bundle Theory, Philos Stud, 85; auth, Right, Left, and the Fourth Dimension, Philos Rev, 87; auth, Semantic Supervenience and Referential Indeterminacy, J of Philos, 92; auth, If Meinong Is Wrong, Is McTaggart Right? Philos Topics, 96; auth, Problems from Kant, Oxford Univ, 99. **CONTACT ADDRESS** Dept of Philosophy, Brown Univ, Providence, RI, 02912. **EMAIL** jvc@brown.edu

VAN DE MORTAL, JOSEPH A.
PERSONAL Born 07/04/1952, Derne, Netherlands, m, 1978, 3 children **DISCIPLINE** PHILOSOPHICAL THEOLOGY **EDUCATION** Univ San Francisco, MA 77. **CAREER** Unitus Col, dept ch, 92-98, prof, 88- . **HONORS AND AWARDS** Templeton Prize Science and Religion, 98 **MEMBERSHIPS** APA, AAR **RESEARCH** Philo of relig; process philo; technology. **SELECTED PUBLICATIONS** Auth, The Thinkers Dictionary: a Handbook for Philosophy, McGraw Hill Press, 95. **CONTACT ADDRESS** Dept of Philosophy, 4642 Hazelbrook Ave, Long Beach, CA, 90808.

VAN DER LINDEN, HARRY
PERSONAL Born 07/03/1950, Eindhoven, Netherlands **DISCIPLINE** PHILOSOPHY **EDUCATION** Univ Utrecht, BS, 72; Univ Groningen, MA, 78; Wash Univ, PhD, 85. **CAREER** Instr, Wash Univ, 81-85; instr, Univ Mo, 84-85; vis asst prof, Colgate Univ, 85-88; vis asst prof, Univ NC Chapel Hill, 88-90; asst prof, 90-93; assoc prof, 93- **HONORS AND AWARDS** Butler Acad grant. **MEMBERSHIPS** Am Philos Asn; Concerned Philos for Peace; North Am Kant Soc; Radical Philos Asn. **RESEARCH** Ethics; Kantian ethics; Political philosophy. **SELECTED PUBLICATIONS** Auth, Kantian Ethics and Socialism, 88; auth, "A Kantian Defense of Enterprise Democracy," 98; "Marx's Political Universalism," in Topoi, 96; "Kant, the Duty to Promote International Peace and Political Intervention," 95. **CONTACT ADDRESS** Dept of Philosophy and Religious Studies, Butler Univ, Indianapolis, IN, 46208. **EMAIL** hvanderl@thomas.butler.edu

VAN DYKE, BRIAN D.
PERSONAL Born 08/19/1962, Auburn, WA, m, 1992, 3 children **DISCIPLINE** THEOLOGY **EDUCATION** Multnomah Bible Col, AA, 87, BSC, 88; Simon Greenleaf Univ, MA, 91; Univ Aberdeen, UK, MTh, 95, PhD, 98. **CAREER** Adj prof, Dominion Col, 97; chaplain, US Army, 98- . **MEMBERSHIPS** APA; British Soc for Phil of Relig. **RESEARCH** Hegel; British idealism;Systematic theology; Philosophy of religion. **SELECTED PUBLICATIONS** Auth, Hegel and Evolution: A Reappraisal, Contemp Philos, 96. rev of A.P.F. Sell's Philosophical Idealism and Christian Belief, Scottish J of Theol. **CONTACT ADDRESS** 3809 Water Oak Dr, Kileen, TX, 76542.

VAN EVRA, JAMES
DISCIPLINE PHILOSOPHY **EDUCATION** Mich State Univ, PhD, 66. **RESEARCH** Logic; philos of science. **SELECTED PUBLICATIONS** Auth, pub(s) on logic and philos of science. **CONTACT ADDRESS** Waterloo Univ, 200 University Ave W, Waterloo, ON, N2L 3G1. **EMAIL** vanevra@uwaterloo.ca

VAN HOOK, JAY M.
PERSONAL Born 01/09/1939, Clifton, NJ, m, 1960, 4 children **DISCIPLINE** PHILOSOPHY **EDUCATION** Calvin Col, BA, 60; Columbia Univ, PhD, 66. **CAREER** From asst prof to assoc prof Philos, Hood Col, 66-74; from assoc prof to prof Philos, Northwestern Col, 74-. **HONORS AND AWARDS** Woodrow Wilson Fel, 60-61. **MEMBERSHIPS** Am Philos Asn; Int Soc African & African Diaspora Philos & Studies; Soc Christian Philos. **RESEARCH** African philosophy; postmodernism; philosophy of religion. **SELECTED PUBLICATIONS** Auth, African Philosophy and the Universalist Thesis, Metaphilosophy, Oct, 97; auth, Kenyan Sage Philosophy: A Review and Critique, The Philos Forum, Fall, 95; auth, African Philosophy: Its Quest for Identity, Quest: Philos Discussions, June, 93; auth, Caves, Canons, and the Ironic Teacher in Richard Rorty's Philosophy of Education, Metaphilosophy, Jan/April, 93; co-ed, Jacques Ellul: Interpretive Essays, 81. **CONTACT ADDRESS** Dept of Philosophy, Northwestern Col, 101 7th St. SW, Orange City, IA, 51041. **EMAIL** vanhook@nwciowa.edu

VAN INWAGEN, PETER
PERSONAL Born 09/21/1942, Rochester, NY, m, 1989, 1 child **DISCIPLINE** PHILOSOPHY **EDUCATION** Rensselner Polytechnic Inst, BS, 65; Univ of Rochester, PhD, 69. **CAREER** Asst Prof to Prof, 71-95, Syracuse Univ; John Cardinal O'Hara Prof of Philo, 95-, Univ of Notre Dame. **HONORS AND AWARDS** NEH, Res Fellowships. **MEMBERSHIPS** APA, Soc of Christian Philos. **RESEARCH** Metaphysics. **SELECTED PUBLICATIONS** Co-ed, Metaphysics, The Big Questions, Oxford, Basil Blackwell, 98; Auth, Material Beings, Ithaca, NY, Cornell Univ Press, 90 and 95; Metaphysics, Boulder; Westview Press and London, Oxford Univ Press, 93; God, Knowledge, and Mystery, Essays in Philosophical Theology, Ithaca, Cornell Univ Press, 95; The Possibility of Resurrection and Other Essays in Christian Apologetics, Boulder, Westview Press, 97; Being, A Study in Ontology, Oxford at the Clarendon Press, forthcoming. **CONTACT ADDRESS** Dept of Philosophy, Univ of Notre Dame, Notre Dame, IN, 46556. **EMAIL** peter.vaninwagen.1@nd.edu

VAN NORDEN, BRYAN W.
DISCIPLINE PHILOSOPHY **EDUCATION** Univ Pa, BA, 85; Stanford Univ, PhD, 91. **CAREER** Asst prof, Vassar Col, 95-; vis asst prof, Univ Northern Iowa, 94-95; Univ Vt, 91-93; lectr, Stanford Univ, 90-91; Chiang Ching-kuo fel, 93; Stanford Center for E Asian Stud For Lang & Area Stud fel, 89; Mellon fel, 85. **RESEARCH** Ethics; Chinese Philosophy. **SELECTED PUBLICATIONS** Auth, Mencius on Courage, in Midwest Stud in Philos, The Philosophy of Religion, Univ Notre Dame Press, 97; Competing Interpretations of the Inner Chapters, Philos East & West, :2, Apr 96; What Should Western Philosophy Learn from Chinese Philosophy, Chinese Language, Thought and Culture: Nivison and His Critics, Open Ct Press, 96; Mencius & Lao Tzu, Cambridge Dictionary of Philosophy, Cambridge Univ Press, 95; ed, The Ways of Confucianism: Investigations in Chinese Philosophy, Open Ct Press, 96; rev(s), Confucian Traditions in East Asian Modernity, Pac Aff, 97; Confucian Moral Self Cultivation, J Asian Stud, 96; A Daoist Theory of Chinese Thought, Ethics, 95; Nature and Heaven in the Xunzi, J Asian Stud, 94; Knowing Words, J Chinese Rel, 93; Tai Chen on Mencius, J Chinese Rel, 93; John Dewey and American Democracy, Philos Eeast & West, 93. **CONTACT ADDRESS** Dept of Philosophy, Vassar Col, 124 Raymond Ave., Poughkeepsie, NY, 12604-0310. **EMAIL** brvannorden@vassar.edu

VAN RHEENEN, GAILYN
DISCIPLINE ANIMISM, EVANGELISM, THEOLOGY OF MISSION **EDUCATION** Harding Univ, BA, 68; ACU, MS, 74; Trinity Evangelical Divinity Sch, Dmiss, 90. **CAREER** Vis missionary, Harding Univ, 77-78, 82-83; prof, 86-. **HONORS AND AWARDS** African mission fel; distinguished alumnus award, Crowley's Ridge Acad, 77; distinguished alumnus in Bible, Harding Univ, 82; grad tchr yr, ACU, 92., VP, Southwest region Evangelical Theol Soc. **MEMBERSHIPS** Mem, Am

Soc Missiology; Evangelical Missiological Soc; Intl Soc Frontier Missiology. **RESEARCH** Anthropology, animism, evangelism, theology of mission. **SELECTED PUBLICATIONS** Auth, Missions Alive! Revitalizing Missions in Churches of Christ, ACU Press, 94; Missions: Biblical Foundations and Contemporary Strategies, Zondervan, 96; Cultural Conceptions of Power in Biblical Perspective, Missiology 21, 93; The Impact of Animistic and Western Perspectives of Illness Upon Medical Missions, Siloam Notes 9, 93; Animism, Secularism, and Theism, Intl Jour Frontier, Missions 10, 93; A Theology of Culture: Desecularizing Anthropology, Intl Bulletin Frontier Missions 14, 97. **CONTACT ADDRESS** Dept of Missions, Abilene Christian Univ, Abilene, TX, 79699-9000. **EMAIL** rheenen@bible.acu.edu

VAN ROOJEN, MARK
DISCIPLINE ETHICS AND SOCIAL-POLITICAL PHILOSOPHY **EDUCATION** Princeton Univ, PhD, 93. **CAREER** Asst prof, Univ Nebr, Lincoln; vis asst prof, Brown Univ, 93-94. **RESEARCH** Metaethics. **SELECTED PUBLICATIONS** Auth, Humean Motivation and Humean Rationality, Philos Stud 79, 95; Moral Functionalism and Moral Reductionism, Philos Quart 46, 96. **CONTACT ADDRESS** Univ Nebr, Lincoln, Lincoln, NE, 68588-0417.

VAN SETERS, JOHN
PERSONAL Born 05/02/1935, Hamilton, ON, Canada, m, 1960, 2 children **DISCIPLINE** OLD TESTAMENT, NEAR EASTERN STUDIES **EDUCATION** Univ Toronto, BA, 58; Yale Univ, MA, 59, PhD(Near Eastern studies), 65; Princeton Theol Sem, BD, 62. **CAREER** Asst prof Near Eastern studies, Waterloo Lutheran Univ, 65-67; assoc prof Old Testament, Andover Newton Theol Sch, 67-70; assoc prof Near Eastern studies, Univ Toronto, 70-76, prof Near Eastern studies, 76-77; James A Gray Prof Bibl Lit, Dept Of Relig, Univ NC, Chapel Hill, 77- & Chmn Dept, 80-88, 93-95. **HONORS AND AWARDS** Woodrow Wilson fel, 58; Princeton fel Old Testament, 62; Obermann fel Yale, 62, 63; Agusta-Hazard Fel, 64; Canada Council res grant, 73; Guggenheim Mem Award; 79-80; NEH sem, 84, 89; NEH res fel, 85-86; ACLS res fel, 91-92; sen res fel, Katholiek Univ Leuven, 97; AHA Breasted Prize, 85; Am Acad Rel bok award, 86; Canadian Hist Asn Ferguson Prize, hon men, 86., Assoc dir Wadi Tumilat archaeol expedition to Tell el Maskhuta, Egypt, 78,81. **MEMBERSHIPS** Am Schs Orient Res; Soc Bibl Lit; Soc Study Egyptian Antiq; Am Orient Soc. **RESEARCH** Book of Genesis; Pentateuch; historical books: Joshua to II Kings. **SELECTED PUBLICATIONS** Auth, The Hyksos: A New Investigation, Yale Univ, 66; The conquest of Sihon's kingdom: A literary examination, J Bibl Lit, 72; The terms Amorite and Hittite in the Old Testament, 72 & Confessional reformulation in the exilic period, 72, Vetus Testamentum; Abraham in History and Tradition, Yale Univ, 75; Recent studies on the Pentateuch: A crisis in method, J Am Orient Soc, 79; The religion of the patriarchs in Genesis, Biblica, 80; Histories and historians of the Ancient Near East: The Israelite, Orientalia, 81; auth, Prologue to History: The Yahwist as Historian in Genesis, Westminster/John Knox Press and Theologischer Verlag (Zurich), 92; auth, The Life of Moses: The Yahwist as Historian in Exodus-Numbers, Westminster/John Knox Press and Kok-Pharos:Lampen, Netherlands, 94; auth, From Faithful Prophet to Villain: Observations on the Tradition History of the Balaam Story, in a Biblical Itinerary: In Search of Method, Form and Content. Essays in Honor of George W. Coats, 97; auth, Solomon's Temple: Fact and Ideology in Biblical and Near Eastern Historiography, Catholic Bibl Q 59, 97; auth, The Deuteronomistic Redaction of the Pentateuch: The CAse Against it. in Deuteronomy and Deuteronomic Literature: Festscrift for C Brekelmans, Leuven Univ Press, 97; auth, The Pentateuch, in The Hebrew Bible Today, Westminster/John Knox Press, 98; scholarly revs in Lutheran World, J Am Oriental Soc, J Bibl Lit, Biblio Orientalis, J Egyptian Archaeol, Orientalistische Literaturzeitung. **CONTACT ADDRESS** Dept of Relig, Univ of North Carolina, Chapel Hill, 101 Saunders Hall, Box 3225, Chapel Hill, NC, 27599. **EMAIL** jvanset@email.unc.edu

VANALLEN, RODGER
PERSONAL Born 04/13/1938, Philadelphia, PA, m, 1963, 3 children **DISCIPLINE** RELIGIOUS STUDIES, THEOLOGY **EDUCATION** Villanova Univ, BS, 59, MA, 64; Temple Univ, PhD(relig), 73. **CAREER** PROF RELIG STUDIES, VILLANOVA UNIV, 64-, Co-ed, Horizons, 73-79, assoc ed, 79-. **MEMBERSHIPS** Col Theol Soc; Am Acad Relig; Cath Theol Soc Am; Am Cath Hist Asn; AAUP. **RESEARCH** American Catholicism; Christian ethics. **SELECTED PUBLICATIONS** Auth, Being Catholic-Commonweal from the 1970s to the 1990s, Horizons, Vol 0021, 94; Exiles from Eden--Religion and the Academic Vocation in America, Horizons, Vol 0021, 94; The Challenge and Promise of a Catholic-University, Horizons, Vol 0022, 95; Shuster, George,N--On the Side of Truth, Cath Hist Rev, Vol 0081, 95; Law and Spirit in the Contemporary Catholic-University--Faith and Culture and American-Catholic Higher-Education Through a Review of Current Literature, Horizons, Vol 0022, 95; From the Heart of the American Church--Catholic Higher-Education and American Culture, Horizons, Vol 0022, 95; Doing the Truth in Love--Conversations About God, Relationships, and Service, Horizons, Vol 0023, 96; Being Right--Conservative Catholics in America, Horizons, Vol 0023, 96; A Showcase of the Future, Opera, Vol 0047, 96; The Frontiers of Catholicism--The Politics of Ideology in a Liberal World, Jour Amer Acad Rel, Vol 0064, 96. **CONTACT ADDRESS** Dept of Relig Studies, Villanova Univ, 845 E Lancaster Ave, Villanova, PA, 19085.

VANCE, DONALD RICHARD
PERSONAL Born 07/18/1957, Mobile, AL, m, 1987 **DISCIPLINE** BIBLICAL INTERPRETATION **EDUCATION** Oral Roberts Univ, BA, 80; Inst Holy Land Stud, Israel, MA, 82; Univ Denver, Iliff Schl Theol, PhD, 87. **CAREER** Adj prof, 86-87, Oral Roberts Univ; adj prof, 89-92, Hebrew & Ugaritic lang, Iliff Schl Theol; adj prof, 90-93, class Hebrew, consort: Colo Christian Univ, Denver Sem, St Thomas Sem, Iliff Schl Theol, Univ of Den, Ctr Judaic Stud; asst prof, 94- Oral Roberts Univ. **HONORS AND AWARDS** Dept Fac Mem of Year, 95-96; Who's Who in Bible Stud & Archaeol; Who's Who Among Amer Col & Univ, 90-92, 91-92, 92-93; Grad Fel, Oral Roberts Schl Theol, 79-80. **RESEARCH** Phoenician lang; NW Semitics; Bibl hermeneutics; Bibl poetry. **SELECTED PUBLICATIONS** Art, The Book of Abraham, Ex-Mormons & Christians Und Newsl 3:4, 92; art, Literary Sources for the History of Palestine and Syria: The Phoenician Inscriptions, Part 2, Bibl Archaeol 57:2, 94; art, Literary Sources for the History of Palestine and Syria: The Phoenician Inscriptions, Part 1, Bibl Archaeol 57:1, 94; art, Toward a Poetics of Biblical Hebrew Poetry: The Question of Meter, PhD Dis, Univ Denver & Iliff Schl Theol, 97. **CONTACT ADDRESS** 7736 S Trenton Ave, Tulsa, OK, 74136-7658. **EMAIL** drvance@oru.edu

VANDALE, ROBERT
DISCIPLINE RELIGION **EDUCATION** Univ Iowa, PhD. **CAREER** Relig, Westminister Col. **RESEARCH** Relig in Am; theol; christian ethics; Mid E rel. **SELECTED PUBLICATIONS** Publ on, relig issues in public edu. **CONTACT ADDRESS** Rel, Hist, Philos, Classics Dept, Westminister Col, New Wilmington, PA, 16172-0001. **EMAIL** vandalrl@westminster.edu

VANDE KEMP, HENDRIKA
PERSONAL Born 12/13/1948, Voorthuizen, Netherlands **DISCIPLINE** CLINICAL PSYCHOLOGY **EDUCATION** Hope College, BA, 71; Univ Mass, MS, 74, PhD, 77. **CAREER** Predoc intnshp, 75-76, Topeka State Hosp; Instr, Asst, Assoc, Prof, 92-, Fuller Theol Sem. **HONORS AND AWARDS** Ntl Honor Soc; Eta Sigma, Phi; Ntl Hon Clas Frat; Psi Chi; Pi Sigma, Alpha; Phi Beta Kappa; Hope College Schshp; NIMH Clin Trnshp; Comm Bldg Awd; Wm Bier Awd; APA Fel; C Davis Weyerhaeuser Awd; John Templeton Foun Awd. **MEMBERSHIPS** CHEIRON; APA; AAMFT; ASD. **RESEARCH** History of Psychology, esp, psychology and religion; Interpersonal Psychology; Family Psychology. **SELECTED PUBLICATIONS** Coauth, Femininity and Shame: Women and men giving voice to the feminine, Lanham MD, U Press of Amer, 97; auth, In Memoriam: Virginia Staudt Sexton, 1916-1997, Intl J for Psycho; of Religion, 98; Psychology and Christian Spirituality: Explorations of the Inner World, J Psychol and Christianity, 96; Religion in college textbooks: Allport's historic 1948 report, Intl J for the Psychol of Religion, 95; Psychol-spiritual dreams in the 19th Century, I, Dreams of death, II Metaphysics and Immortality, J Psychol and Theol, 94; Historical Perspective: Religion and clinical psychology in America, in: Religion and the clinical practice of psychology, E Shafranske, ed, Wash DC, APA, 96. **CONTACT ADDRESS** 180 N Oakland Ave, Pasadena, CA, 91101-1714. **EMAIL** hendrika@fuller.edu

VANDENAKKER, JOHN
PERSONAL Born 11/02/1959, Ottawa, ON, Canada **DISCIPLINE** THEOLOGY **EDUCATION** Gregorian Univ (Rome), ThD, 93. **CAREER** Lectr Theol, Dominican Col, Ottawa. **MEMBERSHIPS** AAR. **SELECTED PUBLICATIONS** Auth Small Christian Communities and the Parish, Sheed & Ward, 94. **CONTACT ADDRESS** 126 Young St, Ottawa, ON, KI4 3P9. **EMAIL** frjohnv@home.com

VANDER KAM, JAMES C.
PERSONAL Born 02/15/1946, Cadillac, MI, m, 1967, 3 children **DISCIPLINE** BIBLICAL STUDIES **EDUCATION** Cal vin Col, BA 68; Calvin Theol Sem, BD 71; Harvard Univ, PhD 76. **CAREER** N Carolina State Univ, asst prof, assoc prof, 76-91; Univ Notre Dame, prof, John A O'Brien Prof, 91 to 98-. **HONORS AND AWARDS** Fulbright Fel; Outstanding Tchg Awd; Outstanding Res Awd; 3 NEH Gnts. **MEMBERSHIPS** SBL; ASOR; CBA. **RESEARCH** Dead Sea Scrolls; Second-Temple Jewish Hist and Lit; Hebrew Bible. **SELECTED PUBLICATIONS** Auth, Calendars in the Dead Sea Scrolls: Measuring Time, London, Routledge, 98; Qumran Cave 4 VI: Poetical and Liturgical Texts, part 1, co-ed, DJD 11, Oxford, Clarendon 98; The Jewish Apocalyptic Heritage in Early Christianity, co-ed, Minneapolis, Fortress Press, 96; Enoch: A Man for All Generations, Columbia, U of S Carolina Press, 95; the Dead Sea Scrolls Today, Grand rapids, Eerdmans, 94, translated into six other lang; The Community of the Renewed Covenant: The Notre Dame Symposium on the Dead Sea Scrolls, Notre Dame, Univ of Notre Dame, 94; Qumran Cave 4, Parabiblical texts, VIII part 1 94, XIV part 2 95, XVII part 3 96, consult ed, Oxford, Clarendon Press. **CONTACT ADDRESS** Dept of Theology, Univ of Notre Dame, 327 O'Shaughnessy Hall, Notre Dame, IN, 46556. **EMAIL** james.c.vanderkam.1@nd.edu

VANDER VLIET, MARVIN J.
PERSONAL Born 12/26/1944, Grand Rapids, MI, m, 1969, 5 children **DISCIPLINE** RELIGION **EDUCATION** Calvin Col, Grand Rapids, BA, 67; Calvin Theol Sem, BD, 72, MTh, 75; Calvin Sem, MDiv, 79, N Amer Bapt Sem, DMin, 93. **CAREER** Christian Reform Church, pastor, 73-. **MEMBERSHIPS** Calvinist Cadet Corps, SBL, Georgetown Deaconal Conference. **RESEARCH** Old Test; Talmud; Qumran. **CONTACT ADDRESS** First Jenison Christian Reformed Church, 8355 Tenth Ave, Jenison, MI, 49428-9232. **EMAIL** mvvliet@aol.com

VANDER WILT, JEFFERY T.
DISCIPLINE THEOLOGY **EDUCATION** Univ Notre Dame, PhD 96. **CAREER** Loyola Marymont Univ, asst prof 98. **MEMBERSHIPS** NAAL; AAR; NAAE. **RESEARCH** Liturgy; Worship; Sacramental Theology; Liturgical Music. **SELECTED PUBLICATIONS** Auth, A Church Without Borders: The Eucharist and the Church in Ecumenical Context, Collegeville, Michael Glazier Books, 98. **CONTACT ADDRESS** Dept of Theology, Loyola Marymount Univ, 7900 Loyola Blvd, Los Angeles, CA, 90045. **EMAIL** jvanderw@lmumail.lmu.edu

VANDERGRIFF, KEN
PERSONAL Born 11/12/1954, Knoxville, TN, m, 1976, 2 children **DISCIPLINE** OLD TESTAMENT **EDUCATION** Fla St Univ, BS, 76; SW Baptist Theol Sem, MA, 81; SW Baptist Theol Sem, PhD, 88 **CAREER** Adj Prof of Relig, 88-95, Wayland Baptist Univ; Adj Prof of Relig, 96-pres, Campbell Univ **HONORS AND AWARDS** Stella Ross Award, 81 **MEMBERSHIPS** Soc of Bibl Equality; Interfaith Alliance; Christians for Bibl Equality **RESEARCH** Intertextuality in the Bible; Use of Bible in Art and Literature **CONTACT ADDRESS** 212 Forest Brook Dr, Apex, NC, 27502. **EMAIL** kenv2@mindspring.com

VANDERPOOL, HAROLD YOUNG
PERSONAL Born 06/28/1936, Port Arthur, Tex, m, 1960, 3 children **DISCIPLINE** AMERICAN HISTORY, ETHICS **EDUCATION** Harding Col, BA, 58; Abilene Christian Univ, MA, 60; Harvard Univ, BD, 63, PhD(relig & hist), 71, ThM, 76. **CAREER** From instr to asst prof relig & Am studies, Wellesey Col, 66-75; Harvard Univ Interfac Prof Med Ethics fel, 75-76; Assoc Prof Hist Med & Med Ethics, Univ Tex Med BR, Galveston, 76- **HONORS AND AWARDS** Kennedy Fnd Fel; Outstand Acad Bk, Assn of Col and Res Lib; Special Govt Emp for the NIH and US FDA **MEMBERSHIPS** Am Asn for Hist Med; AHA; Am Soc Church Hist; Soc Health & Human Values; Am Studies Asn. **RESEARCH** Ethics of reseach with Human Subjects; medical ethics; hisoty of medicine in American society; religion and society. **SELECTED PUBLICATIONS** Auth, The ethics of terminal care, JAMA, 78; auth, Responsibility of Physicians Toward Dying Patients, Medical Complications in Cancer Patients, Raven, 81; auth, Medicine and Religion: How Are They Related? J Relig & Health, 90; auth, Death and Dying: Euthanasia and Sustaining Life: Historical Perspective, Ency of Bioethics, Simon & Schuster MacMillan, 95; coauth, The Ethics of Research Involving Human Subjects, U Pub Group, 96; auth, Doctors and the Dying of Patients in American History, Physician Assisted Suicide, Indiana Univ, 97; auth, Critical Ethical Issues in Clinical Trials with Xenotransplants, The Lancet, 98. **CONTACT ADDRESS** Inst of Med Humanities, Univ of Tex Med Br, 301 University Blvd, Galveston, TX, 77555-1311. **EMAIL** hvanderp@utmb.edu

VANDERVORT, LUCINDA
DISCIPLINE LAW **EDUCATION** Bryn Mawr Col, BA, 68; McGill Univ, MA, 70, PhD, 73; Queen's Univ, LLB, 77; Yale Univ, LLM, 80. **CAREER** Assoc prof, 82- **SELECTED PUBLICATIONS** Auth, Consent and the Criminal Law, 90; Mistake of Law and Sexual Assault: Consent and Mens Rea, 88; Political Control of Independent Administrative Agencies, 80; Blumberg on 'Moral Criticism', 75. **CONTACT ADDRESS** Col of Law, Univ Saskatchewan, 15 Campus Dr, Saskatoon, SK, S7N 5A6.

VANDERWILT, JEFFREY T.
DISCIPLINE RELIGION **EDUCATION** Univ of Notre Dame, PhD, 96. **CAREER** ASST PROF, LOYOLA MARYMOUNT UNIV. **MEMBERSHIPS** N Am Acad of Liturgy. **RESEARCH** Liturgy; church music; hymnology. **SELECTED PUBLICATIONS** Auth, A Church Without Borders: The Church and the Eucharist in Ecumenical Concept, Liturgical Press, 98. **CONTACT ADDRESS** Loyola Marymount Univ, 7900 Loyola Blvd, Los Angeles, CA, 90045-8400. **EMAIL** jvanderw@lmumail.lmu.edu

VANDUZER, ANTHONY J.
DISCIPLINE LAW **EDUCATION** Queen's Univ, BA, LLB; Univ British Columbia, LLM. **CAREER** Assoc prof. **MEM-**

BERSHIPS Can Bar Asn. SELECTED PUBLICATIONS Auth, pubs on corporate law, merger notification under the Canadian Competition Act and business and trade law issues. CONTACT ADDRESS Fac Common Law, Univ Ottawa, 550 Cumberland St, PO Box 450, Ottawa, ON, K1N 6N5. EMAIL mdextras@uottawa.ca

VANNOY, J. ROBERT
PERSONAL Born 03/03/1937, Wilmington, DE, m, 1965, 4 children **DISCIPLINE** OLD TESTAMENT **EDUCATION** Shelton Col, BA, 57; Faith Theol Sem, M Div, STM, 92; Free Univ Amsterdam, The Netherlands, ThD, 77. **CAREER** Instr, Shelton Col, 61-62; instr, Faith Theol Sem, 65-68; asst prof of Old Testament, Faith Theol Sem, 68-71; assoc prof of Old Testament, 71-77, PROF OF OLD TESTAMENT, BIBLICAL THEOLOGICAL SEM, 77-. **MEMBERSHIPS** Evangelical Theol Soc; Soc of Biblical Lit. **RESEARCH** Historical books of the Old Testament; Old Testament Theology. **SELECTED PUBLICATIONS** Contrib, New International Version Study Bible, ed by Kenneth Barker, Zondervan, 85; ed, Interpretation & History: Essays in Honour of Allan A. Macrae, ed by R. Laird Harris, Swee-Hwa Quek, and J. Robert Vannoy, Christian Life Pub, 86; contrib, Baker Encyclopedia of the Bible, ed Walter A. Elwell, Baker Book House, 88; contrib, New Geneva Study Bible, R. C. Sproul, gen ed, Thomas Nelson Pubs, 95; contrib, Evangelical Dictionary of Biblical Theology, ed Walter A. Elwell. Baker, 95; contrib, The New International Dictionary of Old Testament Theology, Willem A. VanGemeren, gen ed, Zondervan, 97. **CONTACT ADDRESS** Biblical Theol Sem, 200 N Main St, Hatfield, PA, 19440. **EMAIL** RVannoy@biblical.edu

VARNADO, DOUGLAS
PERSONAL Born 04/25/1953, Pensacola, FL, m, 1976, 2 children **DISCIPLINE** THEOLOGY; MISSIOLOGY **EDUCATION** Middle Tn St Univ, BS, 76; Tn St Univ, MA Ed, 83; Lipscomb Univ, MAR, 85; Vanderbilt Univ, M.Div, 87; Trinity Evangelical Divinity School, D.Miss, 96. **CAREER** Asst prof of Bible, David Lipscomb Univ, 90-. **HONORS AND AWARDS** Sears Roebuck Tchg Award of Excellence; Tchr of Year, Lipscomb Univ **MEMBERSHIPS** Evangelical Missiological Soc; Soc Bibl Lit; Amer Acad Relig. **RESEARCH** Theology of Spirituality **CONTACT ADDRESS** Dept of Theology, 1013 Battery Ln, Nashville, TN, 37220. **EMAIL** varnadodw@dlu.edu

VARNER, GARY EDWARD
PERSONAL Born 03/10/1957, Newark, OH **DISCIPLINE** PHILOSOPHY **EDUCATION** Ariz State Univ, BA, 80; Univ Ga, MA, 83; Univ Wis, PhD, 88 **CAREER** Asst prof, Tex A&M, 90; assoc prof, Tex A&M, 91- **RESEARCH** Ethical Theory, Political Philosophy, Agricultural Ethics, Logic **SELECTED PUBLICATIONS** Auth, In Nature's Interests? Interests, Animal Rights and Environmental Ethics, Oxford, 98; auth, "Environmental Law and the Eclipse of Land as Private Proper-ty," Ethics and Environmental Policy: Theory Meets Practice, Univ Ga, 94; auth, "What's Wrong with Animal By-products?" Jrnl Agricultural Environ Ethics, 94 **CONTACT ADDRESS** Philosophy Dept, Texas A&M Univ, College Station, TX, 77843. **EMAIL** g-varner@tamu.edu

VARZI, ACHILLE C.
PERSONAL Born 05/08/1958, Italy, m, 1986, 2 children **DISCIPLINE** PHILOSOPHY **EDUCATION** BA, Sociol, Univ Trento, Italy, 82; MA, PhD, Philos, Univ Toronto, Can, 83, 94. **CAREER** Res, Inst for Sci and Tech Res, Trento, Italy, 88-95; asst prof, philos, Columbia Univ, NY, 95-. **MEMBERSHIPS** Amer Philos Asn; Asn for Symbolic Logic; Euro Soc for Analytic Philos. **RESEARCH** Logic; Formal semantics; Metaphysics. **SELECTED PUBLICATIONS** Coauth, with John Nolt and Dennis Rohaytn, Theory and Problems of Logic, 2nd ed, NY, McGraw-Hill, Schaum's series, vii+, 322, 98; with Roberto Casati, Fifty Years of Events: An Annotated Bibliography 1947 to 1997, Bowling Green, Oh, Philos Doc Ctr, 402, 97; co-ed, with Roberto Casati, Events, Aldershot, Dartmouth Publ, The Intl Res Libr of Philos, vol 15, xxxviii+, 519, 96; coauth, with Roberto Casati, Holes and Other Superpcialities, Cambridge, Mass, London, The MIT Press/Bradford Books, x+, 253, 94, paperback, 95; articles, Basic Problems of Mereotopology, ed N. Guarino, Formal Ontology in Informationa Systems, Amsterdam, IOS Press, pp 29-38, 98; Inconsistency Without Contradiction, Notre Dame Jour of Formal Logic, 38, 4, 621-638, 97; with Roberto Casati, Spatial Entities, ed Oliviero Stock, Spatial and Temporal Reasoning, Dordrecht/Boston/London, Kluwer Acad Publ, 73-96, 97; Boundaries, Continuity, and Contact, Nous, 31, 1, 26-58, 97; Reasoning about Space: The Hole Story, Logic and Logical Philos, 4, 3-39, 96; Parts, Wholes, and Part-Whole Relations: The Prospects of Mereotopology, Data and Knowledge Eng, 20, 3, 259-286, 96; with Roberto Casati, The Structure of Spatial Localization, Philos Studies, 82, 2, 205-239, 96; with Fabio Pianesi, Repining Temporal Reference in Event Structures, Notre Dame Jour of Formal Logic, 37, 1, 71-83, 96; with Fabio Pianesi, Events, Topology, and Temporal Relations, The Monist, 78, 1, 89-116, 96; Vagueness, Indiscernibility, and Pragmatics: Comments on Burns', The Southern Jour of Philos, 33, suppl, 49-62, 95; Variable-Binders as Functors, Poznan Studies in the Philosophy of the Sciences and the Humanities, 40, 303-19, 95. **CONTACT ADDRESS** 605 W. 113th St., Apt. 33, New York, NY, 10025. **EMAIL** achille.varzi@columbia.edu

VAUGHAN, FREDERICK
PERSONAL Born 04/19/1935, Dartmouth, NS, Canada, m, 1967, 2 children **DISCIPLINE** CONSTITUTIONAL LAW, POLITICAL PHILOSOPHY **EDUCATION** St Mary's Univ, BA, 56; Gonzaga Univ, MA, 61; Univ Chicago, MA, 64, PhD(polit sci), 67. **CAREER** Lectr polit sci, Royal Mil Col Can, 65-66; from asst prof to assoc prof, 66-76, chmn dept, 71-76, PROF POLIT SCI, UNIV GUELPH, 76-, Vis fel, Wolfson Col, Oxford, 70-71. **MEMBERSHIPS** Can Polit Sci Asn; Am Polit Sci Asn. **RESEARCH** Influence of Epicureanism; judicial biography of Justice E M Hall; Supreme Court of Canada. **SELECTED PUBLICATIONS** Auth, The Rhetoric of Morality and Philosophy, Plato Gorgias and Phaedrus, Philos and Rhet, Vol 0028, 95. **CONTACT ADDRESS** Dept of Polit Studies, Univ of Guelph, Guelph, ON, N1G 2W1.

VAUGHN, BARRY
PERSONAL Born 10/29/1955, Mobile, AL, s **DISCIPLINE** CHURCH HISTORY **EDUCATION** Harvard Univ, BA, 78; Yale Univ, MDiv, 82; Univ of St Andrews, UK, PhD, 90. **CAREER** Asst prof, Samford Univ, 88-90; asst prof, 90-91, adj prof, 93-98, Univ Alabama. **HONORS AND AWARDS** Day fel, 82; Rotary Grad Fel, 84-85. **MEMBERSHIPS** AAR; AHA. **SELECTED PUBLICATIONS** Auth, Benjamin Keach's The Gospel Minister's Maintenance Vindicated and the Status of Ministers among Late Seventeenth Century Baptists, Baptist Rev of Theol, 93; auth, Reluctant Revivalist: Isaac Watts and the Evangelical Revival, Southeastern Comn on the Study of Relig, 93; auth, Resurrection and Grace: The Sermons of Austin Farrer, Preaching, 94; auth, Sermon, Sacrament, and Symbol in the Theology of Karl Rahner, Paradigms, 95; auth, The Glory of a True Church: Benjamin Keach and Church Order among Late Seventeenth Century Particular Baptists, Baptist Hist and Heritage, 95; auth, The Pilgrim Way: A Short History of the Episcopal Church in Alabama, in, Our Church: The Diocese of Alabama in history and Photographs, 96; auth, Gospel Songs and Evangelical Hymnody: Evaluation and Reconsideration, Am Organist, 96; auth, When Men Were Numbered, Anglican Dig, 97; auth, Sermons for Advent and Christmas, Clergy J, forthcoming. **CONTACT ADDRESS** 1600 E 3rd Ave, Apt 3002, San Mateo, CA, 94401-2160. **EMAIL** anglcan@aol.com

VAUGHN, ROBERT GENE
PERSONAL Born 03/10/1944, Chickasha, OK, m, 1969, 2 children **DISCIPLINE** PUBLIC LAW, JUDICIAL PROCESS **EDUCATION** Univ Okla, BA, 66, JD, 69; Harvard Univ, LLM, 70. **CAREER** Assoc attorney, Pub Interest Res Group, 70-72; asst prof, 72-74, assoc prof, 74-77, PROF LAW, THE AM UNIV, 77-, Consult, Nat Ctr Admin Justice, 76-; vchmn, Ethics Comt, Am Bar Asn, 77-79; scholar in residence, Kings Col, Univ London, 79-80; spec adv selection comn on treas and the civil serv, House of Commons, 80. **RESEARCH** Public employment law; government in formation laws and policy. **SELECTED PUBLICATIONS** Auth, Use of Simulations in a First-Year Civil Procedure Class, Jour Legal Edu, Vol 0045, 95. **CONTACT ADDRESS** Sch Law, The American Univ, 4400 Mass Ave N W, Washington, DC, 20016-8200.

VEATCH, ROBERT M.
DISCIPLINE PHILOSOPHY **EDUCATION** Purdue Univ, BA, 61; Univ Ca, MA, 62; Harvard Univ, PhD, 70. **CAREER** Prof. **MEMBERSHIPS** Am Med Asn. **RESEARCH** A Theory of Medical Ethics, Basic Bk, 81; Death, Dying, and the Biological Revolution, Yale, 89. **SELECTED PUBLICATIONS** Auth, **CONTACT ADDRESS** Dept of Philosophy, Georgetown Univ, 37th and O St, Washington, DC, 20057.

VECSEY, CHRISTOPHER
DISCIPLINE RELIGION, NATVE AMERICAN STUDIES **EDUCATION** PhD, 77, Northwestern Univ. **CAREER** Prof, Colgate Univ. **SELECTED PUBLICATIONS** Auth, American Indian Catholics, Padres' Trail, Univ Notre Dame Press, 96; ed, Religion in Native North America, Idaho Press, 90; Handbook of American Indian Religious Freedom, Crossroad/Continuum, 91. **CONTACT ADDRESS** Dept of Philos and Relig, Colgate Univ, 13 Oak Drive, Hamilton, NY, 13346. **EMAIL** wkelly@mail.colgate.edu

VEENKER, RONALD ALLEN
PERSONAL Born 05/13/1937, Huntington Park, CA, m, 1960, 1 child **DISCIPLINE** OLD TESTAMENT; ANCIENT NEAR-EASTERN STUDIES **EDUCATION** Bethel Col, Minn, BA, 59; Bethel Theol Sem, BDiv, 63; Hebrew Union Col, PhD(Ancient NE), 68. **CAREER** Asst prof, Univ Miami, 67-68; assoc prof, 68-76, PROF BIBL STUDIES, WESTERN KY UNIV, 76-, Fel, Hebrew Union Col, Jewish Inst Relig, 77-78. **MEMBERSHIPS** Am Orient Soc; Soc Bibl Lit. **RESEARCH** Old Babylonian economic and legal texts; computer assisted analysis of Old Babylonian economic texts. **SELECTED PUBLICATIONS** Auth, Stages in the Old Babylonical legal process, Hebrew Union Col Annual, 76; contribr, Interpreter's Dictionary of the Bible: Supplement, Abingdon, 76; auth, Gilgamesh and the Magic Plant, Bibl Archaeol, Fall 81; A Response to W.G. Lambert, Bibl Archaeol, Spring 82; Noah, Herald of Righteousness, Proceedings of the Eastern Great Lakes and Midwest Bibl Soc, vol VI, 86; coauth, Me m, the First Ur III Ensi of Ebla, In: Ebla 1975-1985: Dieci anni di studi linguistici e fililogici, Atti del Convegno Internazionale, Napoli, 10/85; auth, Texts and Fragments: The Johnstone Collection, J of Cuneiform Studies, vol 40, no 1, 88; A critical review of Karl van Lerberghe, Old Babylonian Legal and Administrative Texts from Philadelphia, Orientalia Lovaniensia Analecta 21, Uitgeverij Peeters, 86, for the J of the Am Orient Soc, 92; Texts and Fragments: Collection of the Erie Historical Museum, J of Cuneiform Studies, vol 43, no 1, 93. **CONTACT ADDRESS** Dept of Philos & Relig, Western Kentucky Univ, 1 Big Red Way St, Bowling Green, KY, 42101-3576. **EMAIL** ronald.veenker@wku.edu

VEHSE, CHARLES T.
PERSONAL Born 03/07/1961, Huntington, WV, m, 1984, 1 child **DISCIPLINE** HISTORY OF RELIGIONS **EDUCATION** Univ of Chicago, PhD, 98, MA, 85; Brown Univ, AB, 83. **CAREER** Vis Asst Prof, 96-, West VA Univ; lectr, 88-91, Dept of Theo, Loyola Univ Chicago; Tutor for German Lang, 82-83, Brown Univ. **HONORS AND AWARDS** Dean's Prof Travel Grant; Solomon Goldman Lecture; Vis Res Fellow; Fellow, Interuniversity Prog for Jewish Stud; Arie and Ida Crown Mem Res Grant; Lucius N. Littauer Found Res Grant; Bernard H. and Blanche E. Jacobson Found Res Grant; Stipendium des Landes Baden-Wurtemberg. **RESEARCH** Religious and Judaic Studies, German Judaism of the modern era, History and Methods in the History of Religion, Ritual Studies and Comp Liturgy, History and Interpretaion of the Hebrew Bible; Humanities and Social Sciences, German Language and Literature. **SELECTED PUBLICATIONS** Auth, Religious Practice and Consciousness, A Case Study of Time from the 19th century, Consciousness Research Abstracts, Thorverton, UK, J of Consci Stud, 98; Were the Jews of Modern Germany as Emancipated and Assimilated as We Think?, The Solomon Goldman Lectures, 96-97, Spertus Institute of Jewish Studies, Forthcoming; Long Live the King, Historical Fact and Narrative Fiction in 1 Samuel 9-10, The Pitcher Is Broken, Memorial Essays for Gosta WW. Ahlstrom, Sheffield Academic Press, 95. **CONTACT ADDRESS** 742 Ridgeway Ave, Morgantown, WV, 26505-5746. **EMAIL** veh@midway.uchicago.edu

VELEZ, JOSEPH FRANCISCO
PERSONAL Born 01/29/1928, Puebla, Mexico, m, 1969, 6 children **DISCIPLINE** ROMANCE LANGUAGES, THEOLOGY **EDUCATION** Howard Payne Univ, BA, 62; Univ Okla, MA, 68, PhD(romance lang), 69. **CAREER** Instr Span, Univ Okla, 65-68; from asst prof to assoc prof Span and French, Western Ky Univ, 68-71; co-chmn dept Span, 76-77, ASSOC PROF SPAN, BAYLOR UNIV, 71-, DIR LATIN AM STUDIES, 77-, Interim pastor for Span speaking congregation, First Baptist Church, Marlin, Tex, 81. **MEMBERSHIPS** MLA; SCent Mod Lang Asn; Nat Asn Chicano Studies; Am Asn Teachers Span and Port; AAUP. **RESEARCH** Latin American literature. **SELECTED PUBLICATIONS** Auth, Paradise-Lost or Gained, the Literature of Hispanic Exile, Hispania-Jour Devoted Tchg Span and Port, Vol 0076, 93. **CONTACT ADDRESS** Dept of Spanish, Baylor Univ, Waco, TX, 76798.

VELKLEY, RICHARD L.
PERSONAL Born 03/17/1949, Cincinnati, OH, s **DISCIPLINE** PHILOSOPHY **EDUCATION** Cornell Univ, BA, 71; Pa State Univ, 78. **CAREER** Asst & Assoc Prof, Stonehill Col, 87-96; Assoc Prof, Catholic Univ of Am, 97-. **HONORS AND AWARDS** Vis Schol, Harvard Univ, 96; NEH Fellow, Univ Iowa, 92; Bradley Fellow, Univ Toronto, 86-87. **MEMBERSHIPS** Am Catholic Philos Asn; N Am Kant Soc; Hegel Soc. **RESEARCH** European philosophy, 18th century; Kant; Rousseau; German idealism; Heidigger; political philosophy; metaphysics; philosophy of art, culture, education, history. **SELECTED PUBLICATIONS** Auth, Freedom and the End of Reason: On the Moral Foundation of Kant's Critical Philosophy, Univ Chicago Press, 89; ed, The Unity of Reason: Essays on Kant's Phiulosophy, Harvard Univ, Press, 94. **CONTACT ADDRESS** Sch of Philos, Catholic Univ of America, 112A McMahon Hall, Washington, DC, 20064. **EMAIL** velkley@cua.edu

VELTRI, STEPHEN C.
PERSONAL Born 03/29/1955, Pittsburgh, PA, m, 1984, 3 children **DISCIPLINE** LAW **EDUCATION** Univ Pittsburgh, BA, 77; Georgetown Univ, JD, 81; Columbia Univ, LLM, 86. **CAREER** Infor Specialist, Congressional Res Serv, Am Law Div, Libr of Congress, 78-81; assoc atty, Berkman Ruslander Pohl Lieber & Engel, 81-85; prof, Ohio Norhtern Univ Col of Law, 86- . **HONORS AND AWARDS** Fowler v. Harper Award; Teaching Award. **MEMBERSHIPS** ABA; Asoc of Am Law Sch. **RESEARCH** Commerical Paper; Secured Transactions & Property **SELECTED PUBLICATIONS** Auth, Free Speech in Free Universites, Ohio N.U. Law Rev, 93; auth with Ronald S. Gross, Introduction to the Uniform Commercial Code Survey: The Role of the Courts in a Time of Change, Bus Law, 94; auth, Should Foreign Exchange be "Foreign" to Article Two of the Uniform Commercial Code?, 27 Cornell Int Law J 343, 94;

auth, The ABCs of the UCC, Article 3: Negotiable Instruments - Article 4: Bank Deposits and Collection, 97. **CONTACT ADDRESS** Pettit College of Law, Ohio Northern Univ, Ada, OH, 45810. **EMAIL** s-veltri@onu.edu

VENABLE POWELL, BURNELE
DISCIPLINE LAW EDUCATION Univ Mo Kans City, BA; Univ Wis, JD; Harvard Univ, LLM. **CAREER** Prof **RESEARCH** Legal ethics; administrative law. **SELECTED PUBLICATIONS** Auth, The Problem of the Parachuting Practitioner, 92; Open Doors, Open Arms, and Substantially Open Records, Valparaiso Law Rev, 94. **CONTACT ADDRESS** Law Dept, Univ of Missouri, Kansas City, 5100 Rockhill Rd, Kansas City, MO, 64110-2499. **EMAIL** powellb@umkc.edu

VER EECKE, WILFRIED
PERSONAL Born 08/22/1938, Tielt, Belgium, m, 1967, 4 children **DISCIPLINE** PHILOSOPHY **EDUCATION** Leuven, Belgium, Lic Thomistic Philos, 61, Lic Philos in Fac of Arts, 62, PhD, 66; Georgetown Univ, MA, 71. **CAREER** High school tchr, Heule, Belgium, 62-63, Kortrijl, Belgium, 63-65; instr Nursing School, Kortrijl, Belgium, 64-65; res, Nat Sci Found of Belgium, 65-69; asst prof, 67-72, assoc prof, 72-80, chr, 80-83, PROF DEPT OF PHILOS, GEORGETOWN UNIV, 80- . **SELECTED PUBLICATIONS** Auth, Hamlet: Doubting, Wholesomeness, Acting, and Forgiveness, Manuscript, 96; The Law of the Heart and Its Disappointment. Hegel on Law. Lacan on Paranoia, Manuscript, 96; Peirce and Freud: The Tole of Telling the Truth in Therapeutic Speech, 96; The Super-Ego and the Moral Vision of the World, 96; Depletable Resources, Requested Manuscript, 96; The Limits of Both Socialist and Capitalist Economics, Inst for Refromational Studies, Potchefstroomse Univ, 96; A Refundable Tax Credit for Children: Self-Interest-Based and Morally Based Arguments, The Jour of Socio-Economics, 96; The Concept Merit Good, The Ethical Dimension in Economic Theory and the History of Economic Thought, Jour Socio-Economics, 98. **CONTACT ADDRESS** Dept Philos, Georgetown Univ, Washington, DC, 20057. **EMAIL** Vereeckw@Gunet.Georgetown.EDU

VERCHICK, ROBERT R.
PERSONAL Las Vegas, NV **DISCIPLINE** LAW **EDUCATION** Stanford Univ, BA; Harvard Univ, JD. **CAREER** Asst prof **HONORS AND AWARDS** Ed, Harvard Civil Rights-Civil Liberties Law Rev. **RESEARCH** Environmental law. **SELECTED PUBLICATIONS** Auth, pubs on environmental law and land use. **CONTACT ADDRESS** Law Dept, Univ of Missouri, Kansas City, 5100 Rockhill Rd, Kansas City, MO, 64110-2499. **EMAIL** verchickr@umkc.edu

VERHAEGH, MARCUS
PERSONAL Los Angeles, CA **DISCIPLINE** PHILOSOPHY **EDUCATION** Free Univ Amsterdam, Doctorandus, 97. **CAREER** Tchng asst, 97-, Emory Univ. **HONORS AND AWARDS** Natl Merit Scholar, 89. **MEMBERSHIPS** APA. **RESEARCH** Ethics; aesthetics; hist of philos. **SELECTED PUBLICATIONS** Auth, Hypothetical and Psychoanalytic Interpretation, J of Philos Res, 99. **CONTACT ADDRESS** 551 Dorset St, Cambry, CA, 93428. **EMAIL** mverhae@emory.edu

VERHEY, ALLEN DALE
PERSONAL Born 05/14/1945, Grand Rapids, MI, m, 1965, 3 children **DISCIPLINE** CHRISTIAN ETHICS, NEW TESTAMENT STUDIES **EDUCATION** Calvin Col, BA, 66; Calvin Theol Sem, BD, 69; Yale Univ, PhD(relig ethics), 75. **CAREER** Guest lectr christian ethics, Calvin Theol Sem, 72-75; asst prof, 75-80, ASSOC PROF RELIG, HOPE COL, 80-; Ordained minister, Christian Reformed Church, 75-; Lilly Found fel, 77. **MEMBERSHIPS** Soc Ethics, Soc Life Sci; Am Soc Christian Ethics; Soc Bibl Lit. **RESEARCH** The use of scripture in ethics; biblical ethics; the ethics of John Calvin. **SELECTED PUBLICATIONS** Auth, The Holy-Bible and Sanctified Sexuality--An Evangelical Approach to Scripture and Sexual Ethics, Interpretation-Jour Bible and Theol, Vol 0049, 95. **CONTACT ADDRESS** Dept of Philos, Hope Col, 137 E 12th St, Holland, MI, 49423-3698.

VERKAMP, BERNARD
PERSONAL Born 02/20/1938, Huntingburg, IN **DISCIPLINE** HISTORICAL THEOLOGY **EDUCATION** St. Louis Univ, PhD, 72. **CAREER** Prof philos, Vincennes Univ, 72-98. **HONORS AND AWARDS** Phi Beta Kappa, 86. **MEMBERSHIPS** APA; AAUP. **RESEARCH** Philosophy of religion; ethics. **SELECTED PUBLICATIONS** Auth, The Moral Treatment of Returning Warriors, Associated Univ Pr, 93; auth, The Evolution of Religion: A Re-Examination, Univ Scranton, 95; auth, Senses of Mystery: Religious and Nonreligious, Univ Scranton, 97. **CONTACT ADDRESS** 408 N 5th St, Vincennes, IN, 47591. **EMAIL** bverkamp@vunet.vinu.edu

VERMAZEN, BRUCE JAMES
PERSONAL Born 06/06/1940, Cedar Rapids, IA, d **DISCIPLINE** PHILOSOPHY **EDUCATION** Univ Chicago, AB, 61, MA, 62; Stanford Univ, PhD, 67. **CAREER** Instr English, Univ Ky, 62-64; asst prof, 67-76, assoc prof, prof philos, 85-, Univ

Calif, Berkeley, 76-; dept ch, 92-93 & 95-98. **MEMBERSHIPS** Am Philos Asn; Am Soc Aesthet. **RESEARCH** Philosophy of language; ethics; philosophy of mind; American popular music. **SELECTED PUBLICATIONS** Auth, Consistency and underdetermination, Philos & Phenomenol Res, 3/68; auth, Information theory and musical value, J Aesthet & Art Criticism, spring 71; auth, Semantics and semantics, Found Lang, 8/71. **CONTACT ADDRESS** Dept Philos, Univ Calif, 314 Moses Hall, Berkeley, CA, 94720-2391.

VERNEZZE, PETER J.
DISCIPLINE PHILOSOPHY **EDUCATION** Univ Wis, BA, 82, PhD, 88. **CAREER** Assoc prof, Waynesburg Univ. **RESEARCH** Ancient philosophy, history of ideas, critical thinking. **SELECTED PUBLICATIONS** Auth, Reason and the World: A Critical Thinking Textbook, Kendall/Hunt: Dubuque, Iowa, 92, sec ed, 95 **CONTACT ADDRESS** Dept of Political Science, Waynesburg Col, 51 W College St, Waynesburg, PA, 15370. **EMAIL** pvernezze@weber.edu

VERNOFF, CHARLES ELLIOTT
PERSONAL Born 02/11/1942, Miami, FL **DISCIPLINE** COMPARATIVE PHILOSOPHY OF RELIGION **EDUCATION** Univ Chicago, BA, 63; Univ Calif, Santa Barbara, MA, 72, PhD(relig studies), 79. **CAREER** Prof Relig, Cornell Col, 78-. **MEMBERSHIPS** Am Acad Relig; Asn Jewish Studies. **RESEARCH** Theory and method in the study of religion; modern Jewish thought; Holocaust studies. **SELECTED PUBLICATIONS** Auth, Towards a transnatural Judaic theology of Halakhah, In: Jewish Essays and Studies, Vol II, Reconstructionist Rabbinical Col Press, 81. **CONTACT ADDRESS** Dept of Relig, Cornell Col, 600 First St W, Mount Vernon, IA, 52314-1098.

VERTIN, MICHAEL
PERSONAL Born 09/25/1939, Breckenridge, MN **DISCIPLINE** PHILOSOPHY, RELIGION **EDUCATION** St John's Univ, BA, 62; Cath Univ Am, STL, 72; Univ Toronto, PhD(-philos), 73. **CAREER** Spec lectr philos, 70-71, asst prof philos and relig studies, 72-78, ASSOC PROF PHILOS AND RELIG STUDIES, ST MICHAEL'S COL, UNIV TORONTO, 78-, Counr, Coun Scholarly Proj, Bernard Lonergan Trust Dund, 75-82. **MEMBERSHIPS** Am Cath Philos Asn; Can Philos Asn; Cath Theol Soc Am; Metaphys Soc Am. **RESEARCH** The philosophical foundations of interdisciplinary studies; philosophy of theology; God and evil. **SELECTED PUBLICATIONS** Auth, Rational Faith--Catholic Responses to Reformed Epistemology, Stud Rel-Sci Rel, Vol 0024, 95. **CONTACT ADDRESS** St Michael's Col, 81 St Mary St, Toronto, ON, M5S 1J4.

VIDAL, JAIME R.
PERSONAL Born 11/28/1943, Ponce, Puerto Rico **DISCIPLINE** THEOLOGY **EDUCATION** Fordham Univ, PhD, 84. **CAREER** Asst prof rel stud (s), Seton Hall Univ, 85-90; asst dir, Cushwa Ctr Stud Amer Cath, Univ Notre Dame, 90-94; Dir Hispanic Stud (s), Pontifical Col Josephinum, 94-97; Msgr James Supple Ch of Cath Stud (s), Dept Philos/Rel Stud (s), Iowa State Univ, 97- . **MEMBERSHIPS** Medieval Acad Amer; PARAL: Project for the Analysis of Religion Among Latinos; Amer Acad Rel; Am Soc Church Hist; US Cath Hist Soc. **RESEARCH** Medieval Catholicism; Franciscanism; Hispanic Popular Catholicism. **SELECTED PUBLICATIONS** Auth, Citizens, Yet Strangers: The Puerto Rican Experience, in Puerto Rican and Cuban Catholics in the US: 1900-1965 ed Jay P. Dolan and Jaime R. Vidal, vol 2 of Notre Dame History of US Hispanic Catholics, Notre Dame, IN, U of Notre Dame P, 94; Towards an Understanding of Synthesis in Iberian and Hispanic-American Popular Religiosity, in An Enduring Flame: Studies in Latino Popular Religiosity, ed Anthony Stevens Arroyo and Ana Maria Diaz-Stevens. New York, Bildner Ctr W Hemisphere Stud (s), CUNY, 95, 69-95; Christopher Columbus, Bartolome de Las Casas, Santeria, Magic and Voodoo in The Harper Encycl of Catholicism, ed Richard McBrien, San Francisco, 95; Pilgrimage in the Christian Tradition, in Concilium: Rev Intl de Theologie, Aug 96; Hispanic Catholics in America, in The Encycl of US Cath Hist, ed Michael Glazier and Thomas Shelley, Collegeville, MN, The Liturgical Press, Michael Glazier bks, 97. **CONTACT ADDRESS** Dept of Philosophy and Religious Studies, Univ of Iowa, 303 Hayward Ave, Ames, IA, 50014. **EMAIL** jvidal@iastate.edu

VIELKIND, JOHN N.
PERSONAL Born 06/29/1945, Neptune, NJ **DISCIPLINE** PHILOSOPHY **EDUCATION** Duquesne Univ, PhD, 74, MA, 70; St Mary's Sem Univ, BA, 67. **CAREER** Prof, Chr of Philos, 81-, Marshall Univ; Asst Prof Philos, 74-81, Midwestern State Univ, Wichita Falls, TX. **HONORS AND AWARDS** Dean's Merit Award; Sabbatical Leave; Vis Scholar Philos, Vanderbilt Univ; Outstanding Young Men of Amer. **MEMBERSHIPS** APA, WVPS, SPES, North Amer Nietzsche Soc; WV Hum Center. **RESEARCH** Ancient Philosophy, the Platonic Dialogues, Modern Philosophy, Kant and Nietzsche; Continental Philosophy, Heidegger, Derrida and John Sallis. **SELECTED PUBLICATIONS** Auth, The Pathology of a Genealogist, rev of D. Krell's Infectious Nietzsche, in: Research in Phenomenology, 97; A Defense of Philosophical Con-

versation, rec of A. Peperzak's System and History in Philosophy, in: Research in Phenomenology, 88; The Problem of the City in Plato's Republic, Faculty Papers Midwestern State University, 76-77. **CONTACT ADDRESS** 1615 8th Ave, Apt 301, Huntington, WV, 25703. **EMAIL** vielkind@marshall.edu

VILLAFANE, ELDIN
PERSONAL Santa Isabel, Puerto Rico, m, 3 children **DISCIPLINE** CHRISTIAN SOCIAL ETHICS **EDUCATION** Hartwick Col; Cent Bible Col, BA; Wheaton Grad Sch Theol, MA; Boston Univ, PhD. **CAREER** Founding dir, Gordon-Conwell's Ctr for Urban Ministerial Edu, 76-90; prof, Gordon-Conwell Theol Sem, 76-; assoc dean, Urban and Multicult Aff, 90-93; exec dir, Contextualized Urban Theol Edu Enablement Prog. **HONORS AND AWARDS** One of the nation's 10 most influential Hispanic leaders and scholars, Nat Cath Reporter, 92., Pres, Soc Pentecostal Stud; La Communidad of Hisp Amer Scholars of Theol and Rel; co-ch, Greater Boston Develop Coalition; Emmanuel Gospel Center. **SELECTED PUBLICATIONS** Auth, The Liberating Spirit: Toward an Hispanic American Pentecostal Social Ethic, Eerdman's Publ Co, 93; Seek the Peace of the City: Reflections on Urban Ministry, Eerdmans Publ Co. **CONTACT ADDRESS** Gordon-Conwell Theol Sem, 130 Essex St, South Hamilton, MA, 01982.

VIMINITZ, PAUL
DISCIPLINE PHILOSOPHY **EDUCATION** Dalhousie Univ, BA; Univ Regina, MA; Univ Alberta, PhD. **SELECTED PUBLICATIONS** Auth, pubs on ethics and political philosophy. **CONTACT ADDRESS** Dept of Philosophy, Lethbridge Univ, 4401 University Dr W, Lethbridge, AB, T1K 3M4.

VINCENT, DAVID
PERSONAL Born 04/24/1938, Dayton, OH, s **DISCIPLINE** PHILOSOPHY **EDUCATION** OSU, MA, 63; Cath Univ of Am, MA, 60; Cath Univ of Am, BA **CAREER** Tchr of Classics, 64-69, Ath of OH; Tchr of Classics, 69-73, Elder HS, Past Assign, 64-pres, Archdiocese of Cincinnati **CONTACT ADDRESS** St Mary Church, Springfield, OH, 45506-1306. **EMAIL** dvincent@dnaco.net

VINCI, THOMAS
DISCIPLINE PHILOSOPHY **EDUCATION** Univ Toronto, BA, 71; Univ Pittsburgh, PhD, 77. **CAREER** Assoc prof. **RESEARCH** Epistemology, philosophy. of science, history of modern philosophy. **SELECTED PUBLICATIONS** Co-auth, "Novel Confirmation," Brit Jour Phil Sci, 83; auth, Objective Chance, Indicative Conditionals and Decision Theory, Synthese, 88; various entries in the Cambridge Dictionary of Philos, 95; Cartesian Truth, Cambridge UP, 98. **CONTACT ADDRESS** Dept of Philos, Dalhousie Univ, Halifax, NS, B3H 3J5. **EMAIL** thomas.vinci@dal.ca

VINING, JOSEPH
PERSONAL Born 03/03/1938, Fulton, MO, m, 1965, 2 children **DISCIPLINE** LAW AND JURISPRUDENCE **EDUCATION** Yale Univ, BA, 59; Cambridge Univ, MA, 61; Harvard Univ, JD, 64. **CAREER** Atty, Dept Justice, 64-65; asst to exec dir, Nat Crime Comn, 65-66; Prof Law, Univ Mich, Ann Arbor, 69-; Consult, Off Econ Opportunity, 68 & Admin Conf US, 69-72; res assoc, Clare Hall, Cambridge Univ, 73, vis mem, Fac Law, 73. **HONORS AND AWARDS** NEH sr fel, 82-; Rockefeller Found Bellagio Fel, 97. **MEMBERSHIPS** Am Law Inst; Am Acad Arts & Sci. **RESEARCH** Administrative law; legal method and theology; corporate law. **SELECTED PUBLICATIONS** Auth, Legal Identity, Yale Univ Press, 78; The Authoritative and the Authoritarian, Univ Chicago Press, 86; From Newton's Sleep, Princeton Univ Press, 95. **CONTACT ADDRESS** Law Sch, Univ Mich, 625 S State St, Ann Arbor, MI, 48109-1215.

VISION, GERALD
DISCIPLINE PHILOSOPHY **EDUCATION** Univ Mich, PhD, 67. **CAREER** Prof of Philos, Temple Univ **MEMBERSHIPS** Am Philos Asn; Aristotelian Soc; Soc Philos & Psychol. **RESEARCH** Philosophy of language; philosophy of mind; analytic metaphysics; history of philosophy. **SELECTED PUBLICATIONS** Rev RoyBhaskar, Philosophy and the Idea of Freedom, Philos Books, 93; auth, Fictionalism and Fictional Utterance, Pacific Philos Quart, 93; Adimadversions on the Causal Theory of Perception, Philos Quart, 93; The Rule-Following Paradox and Dispositions, Philos and the Cognitive Sci: Papers of the Sixteenth Int Wittgenstein Symp, 93; Problems of Vision: Rethinking the Causal Theory of Perception, Oxford Univ Press, 96; Michael Dummett, The Seas of Language, Philos Books, 95; Disquotational Truth Theories, Proceedings of the Tenth Mtg of Congress for Logic, Method and the Philos Sci, 95; Why Correspondence Truth Will Not Go Away, Notre Dame Jour Formal Logic, 97; Believing Sentences, Philos Studies, 97; Perceptual Content, Philos, 98; Blindsight and Philosophy, Philos Psychol, 98. **CONTACT ADDRESS** Dept of Philosophy, Temple Univ, Philadelphia, PA, 19122. **EMAIL** vision@um.temple.edu

VISOTZKY, BURTON I.
PERSONAL m, 2 children **DISCIPLINE** TALMUD AND RABBINICS **EDUCATION** Univ Ill, BA; Harvard Univ, MA; Jewish Theol Sem Am, MA, PhD. **CAREER** Fac, 77-; assoc and acting dean grad schl, 92-96; Nathan and Janet Appleman Chair Midrash and Interreligious Studies; dir, Louis Finkelstein Inst Relig Soc Studies; adm prof, Union Theol Sem NY. **HONORS AND AWARDS** Vis scholar, Oxford Univ; vis fel and life mem Clare Hall, Univ Cambridge; vis fac, Princeton Theol Sem; vis fac, Russ State Univ Hum; consult and participant in Genesis: A Living Conversation, PBS, 96; consult Prince of Egypt, DreamWorks SKG, 98. **SELECTED PUBLICATIONS** Auth, Reading the Book: Making the Bible a Timeless Text, Doubleday/Anchor, 91; The Genesis of Ethics, Crown; contrib, radio and television programs. **CONTACT ADDRESS** Jewish Theol Sem of America, 3080 Broadway, New York, NY, 10027. **EMAIL** buvisotzky@jtsa.edu

VIVAS, ELISEO
PERSONAL Born 07/13/1901, m, 1925, 1 child **DISCIPLINE** PHILOSOPHY **EDUCATION** Univ Wis, PhD, 35. **CAREER** Asst prof philos, Univ Wis, 36-44; assoc prof, Univ Chicago, 44-47; prof philos and English, Ohio State Univ, 47-51; John Evans prof moral and intellectual philos, 51-69, EMER PROF PHILOS, NORTHWESTERN UNIV, EVANSTON, 69-; Guggenheim Found fel, 39-40; vis distinguished prof philos and English, Rockford Col, 69-71. **MEMBERSHIPS** Am Soc Aesthet; Metaphys Soc Am. **RESEARCH** Value theory. **SELECTED PUBLICATIONS** Auth, Effects of Story Reading on Language, Language Learning, Vol 46, 96. **CONTACT ADDRESS** PO Box 414, Wilmette, IL, 60091.

VIVIAN, CORDY TINDELL
PERSONAL Born 07/30/1924, Howard County, MO, m **DISCIPLINE** THEOLOGY **EDUCATION** Western IL Univ, BA 1948; Amer Baptist Theol Sem, BD 1958; New School for Social Rsch, Doctorate 1984; Western IL Univ, Doctorate 1987. **CAREER** Natl Bapt Conv USA Inc, natl dir 1955-61; 1st Comm Church, pastor 1956-61; Cosmo Comm Church, pastor 1961-63; SCLC, natl dir 1962-67; Shaw Univ, minister 1972-73, natl dir sem without walls 1974-; Black Action Strategies & Info Center Inc (BASIC), bd chmn. **MEMBERSHIPS** Chmn Natl Anti-Klan Network; mem Natl Black Leadership Roundtable; chmn Southern Organizing Comm Educ Fund; bd mem Inst of the Black World; bd mem Intl United Black Fund; co-dir Southern Reg Twentieth Anniversary March on Washington For Jobs Peace & Freedom; bd mem Southern Christian Leadership Conf, Souther Organizing Comm, Natl Council of Black Churchmen, The African Inst for the Study of Human Values; mem Racial Justice Working Group Natl Council Churches; vstg prof Wartburg Theol Sem; intl lecture & consult tours Africa, Tokyo, Isreal, Holland, Manila, Japan. **SELECTED PUBLICATIONS** Auth, Black Power & The Amer Myth, Amer Joseph, Date & Fact Book of Black Amer; editor the Baptist, Layman Mag for Baptist Men; listed in 1000 Successful Blacks, The Ebony Success Library, Odyssey, A Journey Through Black Amer, From Montgomery to Memphis, Clergy in Action Training, Unearthing Seeds of Fire, The Idea of Highlander, The Trouble I've Seen. **CONTACT ADDRESS** BASIC, 595 Parsons St, Atlanta, GA, 30314.

VOELZ, JAMES W.
PERSONAL Born 06/18/1945, Milwaukee, WI, m, 1977, 1 child **DISCIPLINE** EXEGETICAL THEOLOGY **EDUCATION** Concordia Sr Col, BA, 67; Concordia Sem, MDiv, 71; Cambridge Univ, England, PhD, 78. **CAREER** Asst prof, 75-76, Concordia Theol Sem, Ill; asst prof, 76-82, assoc prof, 82-89, Concordia Theol Sem, Ind, 76-82; pastoral asst, Zion Lutheran Church, Ind, 84-88; guest instr, 83, assof prof, 89-93, prof exegetical theol, 93- , dean grad sch, 96- , Concordia Sem. **MEMBERSHIPS** Studiorum Novi Testamenti Soc; Soc of Bibl Lit; Int Org of Septuagint Cognate Stud. **RESEARCH** Greek grammar; hermeneutics; Mark; narrative and parable interpretation. **SELECTED PUBLICATIONS** Auth, Fundamental Greek Grammar, Concordia, 86, 2d ed, 93; auth, Present and Aorist Verbal Aspect: A New Proposal, Neotestamentica, 93; auth, Multiple Signs, Levels of Meaning and Self as Text; Elements of Intertextuality in Intertextuality and the Bible, Semia: An Experimental J for Bibl Criticism, 95; auth, What Does This Mean? Principles of Biblical Interpretation in the Post-Modern World, CPH, 95, 2d ed, 97. **CONTACT ADDRESS** Concordia Sem, 801 DeMun Ave, St. Louis, MO, 63105. **EMAIL** voelzj@csl.edu

VOGEL, MANFRED
PERSONAL Born 09/15/1930, Tel Aviv, Israel, m, 1962 **DISCIPLINE** PHILOSOPHY OF RELIGION **EDUCATION** Wayne State Univ, BA, 53; Columbia Univ, MA, 55, PhD, 64. **CAREER** From asst prof to assoc prof, 63-71, Prof Philos Relig, Northwestern Univ, Evanston, 71, CHMN DEPT, 72-. **MEMBERSHIPS** Am Acad Relig; Am Theol Soc. **SELECTED PUBLICATIONS** Auth, Historicism, the Holocaust and Zionism, Mod Judaism, Vol 14, 94; An Interview with Vogel, Marcia, Wide Angle Quart J Film Hist Theory Criticism Practice, Vol , 97. **CONTACT ADDRESS** Dept Relig, Northwestern Univ, Evanston, IL, 60201.

VOGELS, WALTER A.
PERSONAL Born 10/14/1932, Antwerp, Belgium, s **DISCIPLINE** BIBLICAL STUDIES **EDUCATION** Pontifical Biblical Inst, Rome, LLS, 60; Univ Ottawa, PhD (Th), 68; St Paul Univ, DTh, 70; Gregorian Univ, Rome, LTh, 88. **CAREER** Prof Biblical studies, Int School of Theology of the Missionaries of Africa, Ottawa, 60-68; FULL PROF BIBLICAL STUDIES (HEBREW BIBLE), FACULTY OF THEOLOGY, ST PAUL UNIV, 66-. **MEMBERSHIPS** Assoc Catholique oles studes bibliques en Canada; Cath Biblical Assoc Amer; Cath Biblical Assoc Can; Soc of Biblical Lit; Soc Catholique de la Bible. **RESEARCH** Torah. **SELECTED PUBLICATIONS** Auth, Interpreting Scripture in the Third Millenium, 95; Job: L'homme qui e bien parle de Dieu, 95; Abraham et se legende: Genese 12, 1-25, 11, 96; Moise eux multiples visaper: Der l'Exode eu Deutironome, 97; and 25 articles in the last 5 years. **CONTACT ADDRESS** St Paul Univ, 223 Main St., Ottawa, ON, K1S 1C4. **EMAIL** wvogels@ustpaul.uottawa.ca

VOLKMER, RONALD R.
DISCIPLINE LAW **EDUCATION** Creighton Univ, BA, 66, JD, 68; Univ Ill, LLM, 73. **CAREER** Prof, Creighton Univ, 69-; tchg fel, Univ Ill, 68-69; Cook grad fel, Univ Mich, 75 76. **MEMBERSHIPS** Alpha Sigma Nu; House Deleg, Nebr State Bar Asn; bd dir, Nebr State Bar Found; bd mem, Fam Hous Adv Serv, Inc; ch, Nebr Supreme Ct Adv Coun on Dispute Resolution. **SELECTED PUBLICATIONS** Pub(s), Creighton Law Rev & Iowa Law Rev. **CONTACT ADDRESS** School of Law, Creighton Univ, 2500 California Plaza, Omaha, NE, 68178. **EMAIL** volkmer@culaw.creighton.edu

VOLLMAR, VALERIE J.
DISCIPLINE ESTATE & GIFT TAXATION, ESTATE PLANNING, TRUSTS & ESTATES **EDUCATION** Univ Ore, BA, 68; Willamette Univ, JD, 75. **CAREER** Clk, US District Court, Portland, Ore, 75-77; assoc, clk, Marsh & Lindauer, 77-80; partner, Clark, Marsh, Lindauer, McClinton & Vollmar, Salem, Ore, 81-84; vis prof, 84-85; asst prof, 85-87; assoc prof, 87-93; prof, 93-. **HONORS AND AWARDS** Exec comm, Ore State Bar, 84-90; ch, 88-89; exec comm, Amer Assn Law Sch(s), 88-94; ch, 92. **MEMBERSHIPS** Mem, Phi Beta Kappa; Willamette Valley Estate Planning Coun; Amer Col Trust & Estate Couns. **SELECTED PUBLICATIONS** Comment ed, Willamette Law Jour. **CONTACT ADDRESS** Sch of Law, Willamette Univ, 900 State St, Salem, OR, 97301. **EMAIL** vvollmar@willamette.edu 52

VOLLRATH, JOHN F.
PERSONAL Born 06/22/1941, OH, m, 1971, 1 child **DISCIPLINE** PHILOSOPHY **EDUCATION** Valparaiso Univ, BA, 63; Indiana Univ, PhD, 67. **CAREER** Prof, philos, Univ Wisc Stevens Point, 71-. **HONORS AND AWARDS** Woodrow Wilson fel, 63-64. **MEMBERSHIPS** Philos of Sci Asn; Amer Philos Asn. **RESEARCH** Philosophy of science. **SELECTED PUBLICATIONS** Auth, Science and Moral Values. **CONTACT ADDRESS** Dept of Philosophy, 2100 Main St., Stevens Point, WI, 54481. **EMAIL** jvollrat@uwsp.edu

VOLOKH, EUGENE
PERSONAL Born 02/29/1968, Kiev, USSR **DISCIPLINE** LAW **EDUCATION** UCLA, BS (math-computer science), 83, JD, 92. **CAREER** Law clerk to Judge Alex Kozirski, US Court of Appeals for the Ninth Circuit, 92-93; law clerk to Justice Sandra Day O'Connor, US Supreme Court, 93-94; acting prof, UCLA Law School, 94-. **RESEARCH** Constitutional law; free speech; religion freedom; gun control; equal protection; sexual harassment. **SELECTED PUBLICATIONS** Auth, Computer Media for the Legal Profession, 94 MI Law Rev 2058, 96; Freedom of Speech, Permissible Tailoring and Transcending Strict Scrutiny, 144 Univ PA Law Rev 2417, 96; Material on Free Speech Defense to Sexual Harassmenrt Claims, in Barbara Lindermann & David Kadue, Sexual Harassment in Employment Law, ch 27, BNA Supp 97; The California Civil Rights Initiative: An Interpretive Guide, 44 UCLA Law Rev 1335, 97; What Speech Does "Hostile Work Environment" Harassment law Restrict?, 85 Georgetown Law J, 97, excerpted in Women's Freedom Network, Rethinking Sexual Harassment, Cathy Young, ed, 88; Freedom of Speech, Shielding Children, and Transcending Balancing, 1997 Supreme Court Rev 141; Written Testimony Regarding the Constitutionality of Federal Transportation Contract Set-Asides, Senate Subcommittee on the Constitution, Federalism and Property Rights, Oct 1, 1997; The Commonplace Second Amendment, 73 NYU Law Rev 793, 98; The Amazing Vanishing Second Amendment, 73 NYU Law Rev 831, 98; Freedom of Speech and Independent Judgment Review in Copyright Cases, 107 Yale Law J 2431, 98; Written testimony Regarding the Property of Amending RICO to Exempt Political Protest, House Subcommittee on Crime, July 17, 98; numerous other scholarly articles and other publications. **CONTACT ADDRESS** School of Law, Univ of California, Los Angeles, 405 Hirgard Ave, Los Angeles, CA, 90095. **EMAIL** volokh@law.ucla.edu

VOLZ, CARL A.
DISCIPLINE CHURCH HISTORY **EDUCATION** Concordia Sem, BA, 55, MDiv, 58, STM, 59; Wash Univ, MA, 61; Fordham Univ, PhD, 66; post dr, Cambridge Univ; Trinity Col, Dublin; fel, Univ Chicago, Inst Advan Stud Rel. **CAREER** Instr, Concordia Sem, 64-74; registar, 71-74; guest prof, Martin Luther Sem, Papua, New Guinea, 87; United Theol Col, Bangalore, S India, 88; Luther Sem, Seoul, Korea; Tokyo, Japan, 95; vis prof, Meramec Community Col, 67-71; Concordia Sem, Springfield, 67; Concordia Col, St Paul, 81-83; instr, 74; dept ch, 85-91; dean of stud (s), 75-76; prof, 82-. **HONORS AND AWARDS** Fel(s), John W. Behnken; Lutheran Brotherhood; AAL., Pastor, Christ Lutheran Church, 61-64; ELCA rep, Lutheran-Orthodox Dialogs; bd mem, Ecumenical Inst; dir, Jerusalem House of Studies. **MEMBERSHIPS** Mem, Minn Coun of Churches Comm on Ecumenicity; Comm on Ecumenical Relations of the ELCA Saint Paul Area Synod. **SELECTED PUBLICATIONS** Auth, Pastoral Life and Practice in the Early Church, 90; Faith and Practice in the Early Church, 83; The Church and the Middle Ages, 70; ed, Teaching the Faith, 67. **CONTACT ADDRESS** Dept of Church History, Luther Sem, 2481 Como Ave, St. Paul, MN, 55108. **EMAIL** cvolz@luthersem.edu

VON DEHSEN, CHRISTIAN D.
DISCIPLINE PENTATEUCH, CHRISTOLOGIES OF THE NEW TESTAMENT **EDUCATION** CUNY, BA; Lutheran Theol Sem, MDiv; at Union Theol Sem, MA; PhD. **CAREER** Carthage Col. **MEMBERSHIPS** Phi Beta Kappa **SELECTED PUBLICATIONS** Auth, Policy and Politics: The Genesis and Theology of Social Statements in the Lutheran Church in America. **CONTACT ADDRESS** Carthage Col, 2001 Alford Dr., Kenosha, WI, 53140.

VON ECKARDT, BARBARA
DISCIPLINE PHILOSOPHY OF SCIENCE AND PHILOSOPHY OF PSYCHOLOGY **EDUCATION** Case Western Reserve Univ, PhD, 74. **CAREER** Prof, assoc dean, Col of Arts and Sci, Univ Nebr, Lincoln. **RESEARCH** The foundations of cognitive science. **SELECTED PUBLICATIONS** Auth, Cognitive Psychology and Principled Skepticism, J of Philos 81, 84; What is Cognitive Science?, Cambridge, 93; The Empirical Naivete of the Current Philosophical Conception of Folk Psychology, in P Machamer and M Carrier, eds, Philosophy and the Sciences of Mind, Pittsburgh, 96. **CONTACT ADDRESS** Univ Nebr, Lincoln, Lincoln, NE, 68588-0417.

VON KELLENBACH, KATHARINE
PERSONAL Born 05/18/1960, Stuttgart, Germany, m, 1991, 2 children **DISCIPLINE** FEMINISM AND RELIGION **EDUCATION** Gymnasium Munich, Abitur, 79; Kirchliche Hochschule Berlin, Colloquiuum, 81; Georg August Univ Gottingen, MA, 82; Temple Univ, MA, 84, PhD, 90. **CAREER** Teaching Asst to Instr, Temple Univ, 85-88; Vis Lectr, Lehigh Univ, Spring 89; Vis Asst Prof, Lehigh Univ/Muhlenberg Col/ Moravian Col (joint appointment), 90-91; Asst Prof Religion, St. Mary's Col of Md, 91-. **HONORS AND AWARDS** DAAD Schol, Ger Acad Exchange Service, 83-84; Coolidge Colloquium, Cambridge, Mass, 86; Charlotte W. Newcombe Fel, 89-90; Fac Development Grants, St. Mary's Col, 91-98. **MEMBERSHIPS** Am Acad Relig; Soc Values in Higher Educ; Europ Soc Women Theol Res. **RESEARCH** Jewish and Christian women's ordination; the history and legacy of the Holocaust; German and Christian identity after the Holocaust; Christian and feminist anti-Judaism. **SELECTED PUBLICATIONS** Auth, Anti-Judaism in Feminist Religious Writings, Schol Press, 94; God Does Not Oppress Any Human Being: The Life and Thought of Rabbi Regina Jonas, Leo Baeck Institute: Yearbook XXXIX, 94; Overcoming the Teaching of Contempt, Feminist Companion to the Bible, Sheffield Acad Press, 97; Reproduction and Resistance During the Holocaust, Women and the Holocaust, Univ Am Press (forthcoming); co-ed, Zwischen-Rume: Deutsche Feministische Theologinnen im Ausland (forthcoming); author of numerous articles and other publications. **CONTACT ADDRESS** Dept Philososphy and Religious Studies, St. Mary's Col of Md, St. Mary's City, MD, 20686-0000. **EMAIL** kvonkellenbach@osprey.smcm.edu

VON WYRICK, STEPHEN
PERSONAL Dallas, TX **DISCIPLINE** HEBREW BIBLE **EDUCATION** SW Baptist Theol Sem, M Div, 76, PhD, 81. **CAREER** Prof & Religion Dept Chr, Calif Baptist Col, 86-94; PRrof& Relig Dept Chr, Univ Mary Hardin-Baylor, 94- **HONORS AND AWARDS** NEH; Sr Res fel Wm F Albright Inst. **MEMBERSHIPS** SBL; ASOR; NABPR; NAPH; IES **RESEARCH** Iron I & Late Bronze Age **CONTACT ADDRESS** Univ Mary Hardin-Baylor, 900 College St., UMHB Station Box 8356, Belton, TX, 76513. **EMAIL** swyrick@umhb.edu

VOS, ARVIN G.
PERSONAL Born 07/28/1942, Taintor, IA, m, 1967, 5 children **DISCIPLINE** MEDIEVAL PHILOSOPHY **EDUCATION** Calvin Col, AB, 64; Univ Toronto, MA, 66, PhD(philos), 70. **CAREER** Asst prof, 70-75, assoc prof, 75-80, Prof Philos, Western KY Univ, 81-, Adj prof, Sch Theol, Fuller Theol Sem, 78-79; vis prof philos, Calvin Col, 80-81. **MEMBERSHIPS** Soc Christian Philosophers. **RESEARCH** Thomas Aquinas; Augustine; Dante **SELECTED PUBLICATIONS** Auth, Aquinas, Calvin & Contemporary Protestant Thought, 85. **CONTACT ADDRESS** Dept of Philos & Relig, Western Kentucky Univ, 1 Big Red Way, Bowling Green, KY, 42101-3576. **EMAIL** arvin.vos@wku.edu

VOS, NELVIN LEROY
PERSONAL Born 07/11/1932, Edgerton, MN, m, 1958, 3 children **DISCIPLINE** ENGLISH, THEOLOGY **EDUCATION** Calvin Col, AB, 54; Univ Chicago, AM, 55 PhD(theol & lit), 64. **CAREER** Instr English, Univ Chicago, AM, Unity Christian High Sch, 55-57 & Calvin Col, 57-59; asst prof, Trinity Christian Col, 63-65; assoc prof, 65-70, prof Eng, 70- Head Dept 76-87, VP and Dean, 87-93, Muhlenberg Col. **MEMBERSHIPS** MLA; Conf Christianity & Lit (secy, 65-67, pres, 68-70); Phi Beta Kap; Soc for Arts, Religion, and Contemp Culture. **RESEARCH** Comic theory; contemporary drama; theology and culture. **SELECTED PUBLICATIONS** Auth, The drama of Comedy: Victim and Victor, 66 & For God's Sake Laugh, 67, John Knox; Versions of the Absurd Theater: Ionesco and Albee, Eerdmans, 68; The process of dying in the plays of Edward Albee, Educ Theatre J, 3/73; Monday's Ministries, Fortress, 79; The Great Pendulum of Becoming: Images in Modern drama, Eerdmans, 80. **CONTACT ADDRESS** Dept of English, Muhlenberg Col, 2400 W Chew St, Allentown, PA, 18104-5586. **EMAIL** vos@muhlenberg.edu

VRAME, ANTON C.
PERSONAL Born 04/16/1959, Chicago, IL **DISCIPLINE** RELIGION AND EDUCATION **EDUCATION** Boston College, PhD, 97; Holy Cross Greek Orthodox, MDiv, MA, highest dist, 89; Univ Chicago, MA, 83; DePaul Univ, BA, highest honor, 81. **CAREER** Adj Instr, 95-, Greek Orthodox Sch Theol; managing editor, 96-, Holy Cross Orthodox Press. **MEMBERSHIPS** AAR; APRRE; OTSA. **RESEARCH** Religious Education; Iconography. **SELECTED PUBLICATIONS** Ed, InterMarriage: Orthodox Perspectives, Brookline MA, HCO Press, 97; auth, Forming Orthodox Identity in the Curriculum of the Greek Orthodox Church, in: Personhood: Orthodox Christianity and the Connection Between Mind Body and Soul, ed, John T Chirban, Westport Ct, Bergin and Garvey, 96; An Exegesis of the Epitaphios Threnos, Greek Orth Theol Rev, 94. **CONTACT ADDRESS** 113A Grew Ave, Boston, MA, 4677. **EMAIL** tony_vrame@omaccess.com

VUKOWICH, WILLIAM T.
PERSONAL Born 10/31/1943, East Chicago, IN **DISCIPLINE** LAW **EDUCATION** Ind Univ, AB, 65; Univ Calif, Berkeley, JD, 68; Columbia Univ, JSD, 76. **CAREER** Asst prof law, Willamette Univ, 68-70; assoc prof, 70-73, prof law, Georgetown Univ, 73-; Ford urban law fel, Columbia Univ, 69-70. **MEMBERSHIPS** Order of Coif. **RESEARCH** Commercial law; creditor and debtor rights; life sciences and the law. **SELECTED PUBLICATIONS** Auth, Insurable Interest: When it Must Exist, Willamette Law J, 3/71; art, The Dawning of the Brave New World-Legal, Ethical and Social Issues of Eugenics, Univ Ill Law Forum, 71; art, Debtor's Exemption Rights, Georgetown Law J, 2/74. **CONTACT ADDRESS** Law Ctr, Georgetown Univ, 600 New Jersey NW, Washington, DC, 20001-2022. **EMAIL** vukowich@law.georgetown.edu

VYHMEISTER, NANCY JEAN
PERSONAL Born 08/31/1937, Portland, OR, m, 1959, 2 children **DISCIPLINE** MISSIONS; BIBLICAL STUDIES **EDUCATION** Andrews Univ, EdD, 78. **CAREER** Instr Bibl Lang, River Plate Univ, Argentina, 64-71; asst and assoc prof Mission, 79-84, prof Mission, 91-, Andrews Univ; Prof Bibl Stud (s), Adventist Intl Inst Adv Stud (s), 85-91. **HONORS AND AWARDS** Ed, Andrews Univ Sem Stud (s), 91- . **MEMBERSHIPS** SBL **RESEARCH** Teaching Religion in College; Women in Ministry; Research writing. **SELECTED PUBLICATIONS** Auth, Gramatica Elemental del Griega del Nuevo Testamento, Libertador San Martin, Argentina: Publ SALT, 81; Handbook for Research: Guidelines for Theology Students, Silang, Philippines, AIIAS Publ, 89; transl, ed, Comentario biblico Adventista, vol 7, Boise, Pacific Press, 78-90; Manual de investigacion, Libertador San Martin, Argentina, Publ SALT, 94; The Rich Man in James 2: Does Ancient Patronate Illumine the Text?, Andrews Univ Sem Stud (s), 33, 95, 265-283; Handbook for Research: Guidelines for Theology Students, rev ed, Berrien Springs, MI, SDA Theol Sem, 98; Proper Church Behavior in 1 Timothy 2:8-15, in Women in Ministry: Biblical and Historical Perspectives, ed, Nancy Vyhmeister, 333-354, Berrien Springs, MI, Andrews UP, 98; ed, Women in Ministry: Biblical and Historical Perspectives, Berrien Springs, MI, Andrews UP, 98. **CONTACT ADDRESS** Dept of Mission, Andrews Univ, 4525 Timberland Dr, Berrien Springs, MI, 49103. **EMAIL** vyhmeist@andrews.edu

W

WACHSMUTH, WAYNE R.
PERSONAL Born 06/08/1958, WI, m, 1990, 4 children **DISCIPLINE** ENGLISH GRAMMER; BIBLICAL STUDY **EDUCATION** Bethany Bible Col, BS, 81; Trinity Evangelical Div School, MA, 90. **CAREER** Academic dean, Trinity Col, 96-99 **HONORS AND AWARDS** Joseph Gerhardt Scholar, Registr, dir, student svc **MEMBERSHIPS** Dietrich Bonheoffer Soc **RESEARCH** Contemporary theol **CONTACT ADDRESS** 301 N Emerson, Mt. Prospect, IL, 60056. **EMAIL** WWachs@concentric.net

WADE, JEFFRY
PERSONAL Born 07/30/1950, Jackson, MS, m **DISCIPLINE** LAW **EDUCATION** Univ Fla, JD, 85 **CAREER** Dir, Environmental Div Ctr for Governmental Responsibility, Univ Fla Col of Law, 85-. **RESEARCH** Environmental law; land use planning and regulation; growth management; water law; wetlands protection; coastal zone management; sustainable development; ecosystem management; trade and the environment; international environmental law. **SELECTED PUBLICATIONS** Auth, Hurricane Mitigation and Post-Disaster Redevelopment: Principles and Practices Vols. 1 & 2, Fla Coastal Management Prog, Fla Dept of Community Affairs, 96; auth, Current and Emerging Issues in Florida Water Policy, Fla Ctr for Environmental Studies, Fla Atlantic Univ, 96; auth, "The Brazilian Pantanal and Florida Everglades: A Comparison of Ecosystems, Uses and Management", in Proceedings of the Second Pantanal Symposium, corumba, Mato Graosso do Sul, Brazil, 96; auth, "Minimum Flows and Levels: Analysis of Florida Programs", a report to the Fla Dept of Environmental Protection, Office of Water Policy, 96; co-ed, Protecao de Direitos Ambientais e Sociais: Manual para Operadores Juridicos, United States Information Agency, 98. **CONTACT ADDRESS** Ctr for Governmental Responsibility, 230 Bruton Geer Hall, PO Box 117629, Gainesville, FL, 32611. **EMAIL** wade@law.ufl.edu

WADELL, PAUL J.
PERSONAL Born 03/01/1951, Louisville, KY, s **DISCIPLINE** THEOLOGY **EDUCATION** Univ Notre Dame, PhD, 85. **CAREER** Prof of Theol, Catholic Theol Uniion, 84-87; Vis Prof in Theol, Univ Scranton, 97-98; Assoc Prof in Theol, St Norbert Col, 98. **MEMBERSHIPS** Am Acad of Relig; Soc of Christian Ethics; Catholic Theol Soc of Am. **RESEARCH** Virtues; ethics of St Thomas Aquinas; role of friendship in the Moral Life. **SELECTED PUBLICATIONS** Auth, Taming An Unruly Family Member: Ethics and the Ecological Crisis, The Ecological Challenge: Ethical, Liturgical, and Spiritual Responses, The Liturgical Press, 52-64, 94; auth, Pondering the Anomaly of God's Love: Ethical Reflections on Access to the Sacraments, Developmental Disabilities and Sacramental Access: New Paradigms for Sacramental Encounters, The Liturgical Press, 53-72, 94; auth, The Human Way Out: The Friendship of Charity as a Countercultural Practice, The Merton Annual, vol 8, 38-58, 95; auth, Ethics and the Narrative of Hispanic Americans: Conquest, Community, and the Fragility of Life, Dialogue Rejoined: Theology and Ministry in the United States Hispanic Reality, The Liturgical Press, 125-144, 95; auth, Redeeming the Things We Can Never Undo: The Role of Forgiveness in Anne Tyler's Saint Maybe, New Theol Rev, vol 8, no 2, 34-48, 5/95; auth, Confronting the Sin of Racism: How God's Dream for the World Can Be Redeemed, New Theol Rev, vol 9, no 2, 6-19, 5/96; auth, Morality: A Course on Catholic Living, William H Sadler, Inc, 98. **CONTACT ADDRESS** Relig Stud Dept, St Norbert Col, 100 Grant St, De Pere, WI, 54115-2099.

WADLINGTON, WALTER JAMES
PERSONAL Born 01/17/1931, Biloxi, MS, m, 1955, 4 children **DISCIPLINE** LAW **EDUCATION** Duke Univ, AB, 51; Tulane Univ, LLB, 54. **CAREER** Asst prof law, Tulane Univ, 60-62; assoc prof, 62-64, Prof Law, Univ VA, 64-, James Madison Prof, 69- ; PROF OF LEGAL MEDICINE, UNIV VA SCHOOL MEDICINE, 79- . **RESEARCH** Family breakdown; adoption and child care; state intervention in medical decision making. **SELECTED PUBLICATIONS** Coauth, Cases and Materials on Domestic Relations, 4th ed; & Statutory Materials on Family Law, 71, 74, 2nd ed, 78, Foundation; auth, Divorce without fault without perjury, 52: 32 & The Loving Case: Virginia's anti-miscegenation statute in historical perspective, 52: 1189, Va Law Rev; coauth, Caser and Materials on Law and Medicine, Foundation, 80; Children in the Legal System, 2nd ed, 97. **CONTACT ADDRESS** Law School, Univ Va, Charlottesville, VA, 22903. **EMAIL** wjw@virginia.edu

WAETJEN, HERMAN C.
PERSONAL Born 06/16/1929, Bremen, Germany, m, 1960, 3 children **DISCIPLINE** NEW TESTAMENT **EDUCATION** Concordia Theol Sem, BA, 50, BD, 53; Univ Tubingen, Dr theol(New Testament), 58. **CAREER** Instr philos, Concordia Theol Sem, 57; asst prof New Testament, Univ Southern Calif, 59-62; assoc prof, 62-74, ROBERT S DOLLAR PROF NEW TESTAMENT, SAN FRANCISCO THEOL SEM, 74-; PROF NEW TESTAMENT, GRAD THEOL UNION, 62-; Am Asn Theol Schs res grant, Ger, 65-66; vis prof, Univ Nairobi, 73-74; Am Asn Theol Schs res grant, SAfrica, 79-80; prof, Fed Theol Sem, Pietermaritzburg, SAfrica. **MEMBERSHIPS** Soc Bibl Lit. **RESEARCH** New Testament scholarship; history of religions; Hellenistic culture. **SELECTED PUBLICATIONS** Auth, the Gospel and the Sacred in Poetics of Violence in Mark, Interp J Bible Theol, Vol 50, 96; The Corinthian Body, Theol Today, Vol 53, 97. **CONTACT ADDRESS** San Francisco Theol Sem, San Anselmo, CA, 94960.

WAGGONER, LAWRENCE W.
PERSONAL Born 07/02/1937, Sidney, OH, m, 1963, 2 children **DISCIPLINE** LAW **EDUCATION** Univ Cincinnati, BBA, 60; Univ MI, JD, 63; Oxford Univ, DPhil, 66. **CAREER** Atty, Cravath, Swaine & Moore, 63; prof, Col of Law, Univ IL, 68- 72 & Sch of Law, Univ VA, 72-73; Prof Law, Law Sch, Univ MI, 73. **MEMBERSHIPS** Am Law Inst; Acad fel, Am Col Trust & Estate Coun. **RESEARCH** Property law; federal taxation; estate planning. **SELECTED PUBLICATIONS** Auth, Future Interests in a Nutshell, West Publ Co, 81; coauth, Federal Taxation of Gifts, Trusts, and Estates, West Publ Co, 3rd ed, 97; Family Property Law: Wills, Trusts, and Future Interests, Found Press, 2nd ed, 97. **CONTACT ADDRESS** Law Sch, Univ MI, 625 S State St, Ann Arbor, MI, 48109-1215. **EMAIL** waggoner@umich.edu

WAGNER, ANNICE
DISCIPLINE LAW **EDUCATION** Wayne State Univ, BA, JD. **CAREER** National Capital Housing Authority, general counsel; Superior Court D.C., assoc judge, 1977-90; DC Ct Appeals, assoc judge, beginning 1990; DC SUPREME CT, CHIEF JUDGE, currently; HARVARD UNIV, INSTRUCTOR, currently. **CONTACT ADDRESS** District of Columbia Supreme Court, 500 Indiana Ave NW, Rm 600, Washington, DC, 20001.

WAGNER, MICHAEL FRANK
PERSONAL Born 09/29/1952, Victoria, TX, m, 1974 **DISCIPLINE** MEDIEVAL & ANCIENT PHILOSOPHY **EDUCATION** TX A&M Univ, BA, 74; OH State Univ, MA, 76, PhD(philos), 79. **CAREER** Teaching asst, OH State Univ, 75-79, lectr, 79-80; asst prof Philos, 80-84, assoc prof, 84-88, prof philos, Univ San Diego, 89-; lectr, Capital Univ, 79-80. **MEMBERSHIPS** Am Philos Asn; Int Soc Neoplatonic Studies (US secy, 80-); Soc Medieval & Renaissance Philos; Medieval Asn Pac; Am Cath Philos Asn. **RESEARCH** Medieval neoplatonism and its foundations in ancient thought; history of metaphysics, epistemology and theology and their relation to the development of Western science; informal logic and its relation to formal logic. **SELECTED PUBLICATIONS** Contribr, The Structure of Being: A Neoplatonic Approach, State Univ NY, 82; An Historical Intro to Moral Philos, Prentice-Hall, 90; contrib, Cambridge Companion to Plotinus, 97; misc journals. **CONTACT ADDRESS** Dept Philos, Univ San Diego, 5998 Alcala Park, San Diego, CA, 92110-2492. **EMAIL** mwagner@acusd.edu

WAGNER, PAUL ANTHONY
PERSONAL Born 08/28/1947, Pittsburgh, PA, m, 1970, 3 children **DISCIPLINE** PHILOSOPHY **EDUCATION** Northeast Mo State Univ, BS, 69; Univ Mo-Columbia, MEd, 72, MA, 76, PhD(philos & educ), 78. **CAREER** Instr philos, Moberly Area Jr Col, 74-75; instr philos educ, Univ Mo, 75-79; from asst prof philos & philos educ, Univ Houston, Clear Lake City, 79-87; consult, Dept Corrections, State of Mo, 77-81 & Clear Creek Independent Sch Dist, 79-82; vis scholar, Dept Philos & Inst Math Study Soc Sci, 81; vis scholar, Harvard Univ, 85-86. **MEMBERSHIPS** Am Philos Asn; Philos Sci Asn; Brit Philos Sci Asn; fel, Philos Educ Soc. **RESEARCH** Philosophy of science; ethics; philosophy of education. **SELECTED PUBLICATIONS** Coauth, Philosophic inquiry and the logic of elementary school science education, Sci Educ, fall 77; auth, Punishment and reason in rehabilitating the criminal, Prison J, spring/summer 78; Policy studies, Hobbs and normative prescriptions for organizations, J Thought, 1/81; The Aristotlean notion of nomos and policy studies, Rev J Philos & Soc Sci, 1/81; Rationality, conceptual change and philosophy of education, Scientia, winter 81; A philosophical approach to mathematics education, Proc Philos Educ Soc, 1/81; Philosophy in mathematics education, Metaphilos, 1/82; Moral education, indoctrination and the principle of minimizing substantive moral error, Proc Philos Educ Soc, 3/82; The Ethical Legal and Multicultural Foundations of teaching, Brown/Benchmark Pub, 92. **CONTACT ADDRESS** Dept of Philosophy, Univ of Houston, 2700 Bay Area Blvd, Houston, TX, 77058-1025. **EMAIL** wagner@uhcl.uh.edu

WAGNER, STEVEN
DISCIPLINE PHILOSOPHY **EDUCATION** Princeton Univ, PhD, 78. **CAREER** Assoc prof,Univ Ill Urbana Champaign. **RESEARCH** Metaphysics; philosophy of mind; epistemology; philosophy of mathematics; philosophy of logic; philosophy of language. **SELECTED PUBLICATIONS** Auth, The Rationalist Conception of Logic; Truth, Physicalism and Ultimate Theory; co-ed, Naturalism: A Critical Appraisal. **CONTACT ADDRESS** Philosophy Dept, Univ Ill Urbana Champaign, 52 E Gregory Dr, Champaign, IL, 61820. **EMAIL** shwayder@uiuc.edu

WAGNER, WALTER HERMANN
PERSONAL Born 11/21/1935, Germany, m, 1958, 1 child **DISCIPLINE** CHURCH HISTORY, BIBLICAL STUDIES **EDUCATION** Gettysburg Col, BA, 57; Lutheran Sem, Pa, BD, 60; Drew Univ, PhD (church hist), 68. **CAREER** Asst prof relig and philos, Calif Lutheran Col, 63-65; assoc prof relig and hist, Upsala Col, 65-73; adj prof church hist, Drew Univ, 73-74; Dir Theol Educ, Lutheran Church Am, 77-; Co-pastor, Calvary Lutheran Church, Cranford, NJ, 60-63; adj prof church hist, Lutheran Sem, Pa, 70-71; chmn Div Ecumenical Rels, Lutheran Church Am, NJ Synod, 72-77; pastor, Epiphany Lutheran Church, Warren, NJ, 73-77. **HONORS AND AWARDS** Distinguished Teaching Award, Lindback Found and Upsala Col, 69. **MEMBERSHIPS** Am Soc Church Hist; Soc Bibl Lit; Am

Soc Reformation Hist; Soc Reformation Res. **RESEARCH** New Testament; patristics; Reformation. **SELECTED PUBLICATIONS** Auth, Toward Understanding Justin Martyr, Cithara Essays Judeo-Christian Tradition, Vol 34, 95; Interpretations of Genesis VI, 1-4 in 2nd Century Christianity, J Religious Hist, Vol 20, 96; Clement of Alexandria Self-Understanding and Addressing the Christian Concepts of Theology, Ethics, and Mysticism, Cithara Essays Judeo-Christian Tradition, Vol 36, 96; Scripture and the Church in Selected Essays Sasse, Herman, Church Hist, Vol 66, 97; Journeying to God in Muhammad Isra and Miraj, Cithara Essays Judeo-Christian Tradition, Vol 36, 97. **CONTACT ADDRESS** Div for Prof Leadership, Lutheran Church in America, 2900 Queen Lane, Philadelphia, PA.

WAGNER, WENCESLAS JOSEPH

PERSONAL Born 12/12/1917, Poland, m, 1979, 3 children **DISCIPLINE** LAW, POLITICAL SCIENCES **EDUCATION** Univ Warsaw, LLM, 39; Univ Paris, Dr en Droit, 47; Northwestern Univ, JD, 50, LLM, 53, SJD, 57. **CAREER** Jr judge, Warsaw, Poland, 41-44; res assoc, French Inst Air Transp, 47-48; vis prof Slavic lit, Fordham Univ, 48-49; teaching fel law, Northwestern Univ, 50-53; From instr to prof, Univ Notre Dame, 53-62; prof, Ind Univ, 62-71; PROF LAW, UNIV DETROIT, 71-; Fulbright grant and vis prof, Law Schs, Paris and Rennes, France, 59-60; consult, Law Principles of Civilized Nations Proj, Cornell Univ, 60, vis prof law sch, 61-62; US Dept State lectr, Senegal, Morocco and Algeria, 60, world tour, 62; lectr, Int Fac Comp Law, Luxembourg, 60 and 63; legal coun, Ger Consulate Gen, Ind, 67-68; Fulbright lectr, Latin am, 68; Kosciuszko Found lectr, Poland, 71; vis prof, Univ Clermont-Ferrand, 73; vis prof, Warsaw, 80-81. **MEMBERSHIPS** Am Asn Comp Study Law; Am Foreign Law Asn (vpres, 70-72); Am Soc Legal Hist (treas, 62-64); Polish Inst Arts and Sci Am; Int Asn Cath Jurists (vpres, 73-). **RESEARCH** Comparative law; torts; federalism. **SELECTED PUBLICATIONS** Auth, Supremacy and Integrity in Member State Law as a Limiting Principle in the United States and the European Union, Soundings, Vol 79, 96. **CONTACT ADDRESS** Law Sch, Univ Detroit, Detroit, MI, 48226.

WAHL, RUSSELL

PERSONAL Born 09/02/1952, Oslo, Norway, m, 1984, 2 children **DISCIPLINE** PHILOSOPHY **EDUCATION** Colby Col, BA, 74; Indiana Univ, MA, 77, PhD, 82. **CAREER** Instr, Wabash Col, 80-82; ast prof, 82-85; Ast prof, 85-89, Idaho State Univ, 89-94, asoc prof, 94- , prof. **HONORS AND AWARDS** Phi Beta Kappa, 74; Indiana Univ fel, 75-76; NEH Summer Sem, 83, 86, 91; outstanding research, Idaho State univ, 94. **MEMBERSHIPS** APA. **RESEARCH** Bertrand Russell; Descartes; Arnauld; philosophy of language; logic. **SELECTED PUBLICATIONS** Auth, "Russell's Theory of Meaning and Denotation and On Denoting," J of Hist of Philos, 93; "Impossible Propositions and the Forms of Objections in Wittgenstein's Tractatus," Philos Q, 95; "How Can What I Perceive Be True," Hist of Philos Q, 95; "Antoine Arnauld," Philos of Educ, Garland, 96; "The Port-Royal Logic," Historical Antecedents to Informal Logic, ed Walton and Brinton, Avebury, 97; coauth, "Colour," Philos, 98. **CONTACT ADDRESS** Dept of English and Philosophy, Idaho State Univ, PO Box 8056, Pocatello, ID, 83209. **EMAIL** wahlruss@isu.edu

WAIDA, MANABU

PERSONAL Osaka, Japan **DISCIPLINE** HISTORY OF RELIGION **EDUCATION** Univ Chicago, PhD (hist relig), 74. **CAREER** Asst prof hist relig, St Mary's Univ, Halifax, 70-73; ASSOC PROF HIST RELIG, UNIV ALTA, 74-; Vis asst prof hist relig, Univ Rochester, 74; Can Coun leave fel, 78-79; EXEC, CAN CORP STUDIES IN RELIG, 80-. **MEMBERSHIPS** Can Soc Study Relig (treas, 76-80); Am Acad Relig; Can Asn Asian Studies; Am Asn Asian Studies. **RESEARCH** Myths and symbols; sacrad kingship; religions in Circumpacific Regions. **SELECTED PUBLICATIONS** Auth, Shamanism, History, and the State, Asian Folklore Studies, Vol 54, 95. **CONTACT ADDRESS** Dept of Relig Studies, Univ of Alta, Edmonton, AB, T6G 2E6.

WAINWRIGHT, SUE

PERSONAL Born 01/18/1966, PA, m, 1996 **DISCIPLINE** PHILOSOPHY **EDUCATION** Allentown Col of St. Francis de Sales, BA, 94; Westchester Univ, MA, 95. **CAREER** Adjunct prof, Northampton Community Col. **MEMBERSHIPS** Am Philos Asn. **RESEARCH** Morality; Buddhism. **CONTACT ADDRESS** 4730 Main Rd W, Emmaus, PA, 18049.

WAINWRIGHT, WILLIAM J.

PERSONAL Born 02/14/1935, Kokomo, IN, m, 1958, 2 children **DISCIPLINE** PHILOSOPHY **EDUCATION** Kenyon Coll, BA, 57; Univ of Michigan, MA, 59, PhD, 61. **CAREER** Inst, Asst Prof, 60-62, Univ of Illinois-Urbana; Assoc to Prof, 62-68, Univ of Wisconsin, Milwaukee; Distinguished Prof, 68-. **HONORS AND AWARDS** Woodrow Wilson Fellowship; Horace H. Rackham Fellowship; 3 NEH Summer Fellowship; Distinguished Tchr; Res Award, Univ of Wisconsin; Phi Beta Kappa; Phi Kappa Phi. **MEMBERSHIPS** Amer Philos Assoc; Amer Acad Rel; Soc of Christian Philos; Philos Rel Soc. **RESEARCH** Philosophy of Religion, Ethics, History of Modern Philosophy. **SELECTED PUBLICATIONS** Co-ed, Philosophy of Religion, Selected Readings, William Rowe, Harcourt Brace, 98; auth, Philosophy of Religion, An Annotated Bibliography, Garland Press, 78; Mysticism, Univ of Wisconsin Press. 81; Philosophy of Religion, Wadsworth, 98; Reason and the Heart, Cornell Univ Press, 95; God, Philosophy and Academic Culture, Scholar's Press, 96. **CONTACT ADDRESS** Dept Philosophy, Univ of Wis, Milwaukee, WI, 53201. **EMAIL** wjwain@csd.uwm.edu

WAITS, VA LITA FRANCINE

PERSONAL Born 01/29/1947, Tyler, TX **DISCIPLINE** LAW **EDUCATION** Howard University, BA, 1969; American University, MA, 1974; Texas Southern University, Thurgood Marshall School of Law, JD, 1980. **CAREER** WRC-TV/NBC, producer, 1971-74; Southwestern Bell Telephone Co, manager, 1975; Texas Southern University, instructor, KTSU-FM, manager, 1975-76; U.S. Department of Energy, regional attorney, 1980-81; National Labor Relations Board, field attorney, 1981-82; Law Office of Va Lita Waits, principal, 1982-; City of Tyler, alternate municipal judge, 1984-94. **HONORS AND AWARDS** Austin Metropolitan Business Resource Center, Women of Distinction, 1992; KLTV, Black History Portrait, Leading African-Americans in East Texas, 1991, Top Ladies of Distinction, Top Lady of the Year, 1990; Tyler Independent School District, Distinguished Graduate, 1983; Omega Psi Phi, Public Service in the Area of Law, 1983; service awards from numerous organizations including: Tyler Jaycess, Delta Sigma Theta Sorority, Rosebud Civitan Club, Longview Metropolitan Chamber of Commerce, Texas College, State Bar of Texas Admissions Committee, Bonner Elementary School, District of Columbia Commission on the Status of Women, U.S. Department of Justice, Bureau of Prisons. **MEMBERSHIPS** Founder, Ctr for Non-profit Organization Development, (Houston), 1996; Supreme Court, State of Texas, Bar Admissions Committee, 1983-87; Tyler Metropolitan Chamber of Commerce, founding president, 1989-92; Delta Sigma Theta, Sorority, Tyler Alumnae Chapter, president, 1990-92; Smith County Court Appointed Special Advocates, founding board member, 1989-; Smith County Bar Association, 1982-; Natl Bar Assn, 1984-; National Association of Black Women Lawyers, 1992-; Leadership Texas, 1987-; Texas Assn of African American Chambers of Commerce, secretary, 1993-; Leadership Tyler. **CONTACT ADDRESS** Waits Group, Inc, 9801 Westheimer, Ste 302, Houston, TX, 77042. **EMAIL** waitsgrp@aol.com

WAKIN, MALHAM M.

PERSONAL Born 03/31/1931, Oneonta, NY, m, 1976, 8 children **DISCIPLINE** PHILOSOPHY **EDUCATION** Univ Notre Dame, AB, 52; State Univ NY, Am, 53; Univ Southern Calif, PhD(philos), 59. **CAREER** Res asst, Capitol Area Sch Develop Asn, Albany, NY, 52-53; from instr to prof Philos, 59-64, asst dean Soc Sci & Humanities, 64-65, grad prog, 65-67, head dept Fine Arts & Philos, 67-73, head dept Polit Sci & Philos, 73-77, prof Philos, US Air Force Acad, 67-, head Dept Philos & Fine Arts & assoc dean Acad, 77-; Lyon chmn in Philos, 95-97; prof Emeritus, 97-. **MEMBERSHIPS** Mountain Plains Philos Conf; Am Cath Philos Asn; Inter-Univ Sem Armed Forces & Soc; Joint Services Conf Prof Ethics. **RESEARCH** Ethics; military philosophy; politics and philosophy in Southeast Asia. **SELECTED PUBLICATIONS** Auth, Communities look at their school principals, Capitol Areas Sch Develop Asn, 53; coauth, The vocation of arms, Space Dig, 7/63; auth, Dynamism and discipline, New Scholasticism, Summer 67; The Viet Cong Political Infrastructure, Dept Defense, 68; The American militarytheirs to reason why, Air Force Mag, 3/71; The ethics of leadership, Am Behav Scientist, 5-6/76; ed & contribr, War, Morality, and the Military Profession, Westview Press, 79, 86; coauth, The Teaching of Ethics in the Military, Hastings Ctr, 82. **CONTACT ADDRESS** Dept of Philosophy & Fine Arts, USAF Academy, USAF Academy, CO, 80840.

WALD, PATRICIA M.

PERSONAL Born 09/16/1928, Torrington, CT, m, 1952, 5 children **DISCIPLINE** LAW **EDUCATION** Conn Col for Women, BA, 48; Yale Law Sch, LLB, 51. **CAREER** Law clerk, U.S. Court of Appeals for the Second Circuit, 51-52; assoc, Arnold, Fortas & Porter, 52-53; mem, Nat Conf on Bail & Criminal Justice, 63-64; consult, Nat Conf on Law & Poverty, 65; mem, President's Comn on Crime in the District of Columbia, 65-66; consult, President's Comn on Law Enforcement and Administration of Criminal Justice, 66-67; atty, Office of Criminal Justice, Dept Justice, 67-68; atty, Neighborhood Legal Services Prog, 68-70; consult, Nat Advisory Comt on Civil Disorder, 68; consult, Nat Comn on the Causes & Prevention of Violence, 69; co-Dir, For Found Drug Abuse Res Project, 70; atty, Ctr for Law & Soc Policy, 71-72; dir of Office of Policy & Issues, Sargent Shriver Vice Presidential Campaign, 72; atty, Mental Health Law Project (Litigation Dir 75-77), 72-77; asst atty gen for legislative affairs, 77-79; circuit judge, 79-, chief judge, 86-91, U.S. Court of Appeals for the District of Columbia Circuit. **HONORS AND AWARDS** Distinguished Alumnae Award, Conn Col, 72; August Voelmer Award, Am Soc Criminology, 76; Woman Lawyer of the Year, Women's Bar Asn of D.C., 84; Annual Merit Award, Nat Asn Women Judges (Division 4), 86; Annual Award, NY Women's Bar Asn, 87; Merit Award, Yale Law Sch, 87; Honorary Order of the Coif, Univ Md Law Sch, 91; Sandra Day O'Connor Medal of Honor, Seton Hall Law Sch, 93; Margaret Brent Women Lawyers of Achievement Award, Am Bar Asn Comn on Women in the Professsion, 94; Nat Asn Women Judges Annual Award, 94; Juvenile Ctr Award, 95; Trial Lawyers Asn of Metropolitan Washington Award for Judicial Excellence, 98; The District of Columbia Bar Thurgood Marshall Award, 98; recipient of numerous Doctor Laws. **SELECTED PUBLICATIONS** Auth, Doing Right by Our Kids: A Case Study in the Perils of Making Policy on Television Violence, Univ Minn, 94; auth, Whose Public Interest Is It Anyway?: Advice for Altruistic Young Lawyers, Me. Law Rev 4, 95; auth, Judicial Review - Fiftieth Anniversary of the Administrative Procedure Act, Admin Law Rev 350, 96; auth, Judicial Review in Midpasage: The Uneasy Partnership Between Courts and Agencies Plays On, Tulsa Law J 221, 96; auth, Judicial Review in the Time of Cholera, Admin Law Rev 659, 97; auth, ADR and the Courts: An Update, Duke Law J 1445, 97; author of numerous other articles. **CONTACT ADDRESS** 333 Constitution Ave., NW, Rm. 3832, Washington, DC, 20001. **EMAIL** Patricia_M._Wald@cadc.uscourts.gov

WALDAU, PAUL

PERSONAL Born 01/16/1950, CA **DISCIPLINE** PHILOSOPHY **EDUCATION** Univ Oxford, PhD 98; Harvard Univ, sr fel 97; Claremont Grad Sch, 86-92; Univ Cal LA, JD 78; Stanford Univ, MA 72-74; Univ Chicago, 71-72; Univ Cal Santa Barb, BA summa cum laude, 71. **CAREER** Various Boston-area Univ's, part-time lectr and tutor. **HONORS AND AWARDS** Phi Beta Kappa. **MEMBERSHIPS** APA; AAR; CBA; IIC; ISEE; WCF; Pali Text Soc; L'Chaim Soc; Intl Interfaith Cen; Interdisc Res Netw on the Environ and Soc **RESEARCH** Ethics; philosophical and religious traditions; environ and other animals; environ ethics; applied ethics. **SELECTED PUBLICATIONS** Auth, Buddhism and Ecology: Balancing Convergence Dissonance and the Risk of Anachronism, eds, Mary Evelyn Tucker Duncan Williams, Jour of Bud Ethics, Cambridge MA, Harv Univ Cen for Stud of World Rel, 97; Inclusivist Ethics: Prospects in the Next Millennium, in: Humans and Great Apes at an Ethical Frontier, Smithsonian Inst, 98; Shortcomings in Isolated Traditions of Ethical Discourse: The Case of Andrew Linzey's Animal Theology, Between the Species, 98; Hinduism Buddhism, Judaism and Sacrifice, and Islam, Factory Farming, Specieism, Bushmeat, articles in: The Encycl of Animal Rights and Animal Welfare, eds, Marc Bekoff, Carron A Meany, Greenwood Pub, 97; Buddhism and Animal Rights, in: Buddhism and Contemporary Issues, ed, Damien Keown, Goldsmith Col, Univ London, 97; Farming, Zoos and Specieism, coauth, in: Dict of Ethics Theology and Soc, London, NY, Routledge Press, 96. **CONTACT ADDRESS** 16 Anis Rd, Belmont, MA, 02478. **EMAIL** paulwaldau@aol.com

WALDRON, MARY ANNE

DISCIPLINE LAW **EDUCATION** Brandon Col, BA, 69; Univ Manitoba, LLB, 73; Univ British Columbia, LLM, 75. **CAREER** Asst prof, 72-92; prof, 92-. **RESEARCH** Real estate law; plain language research. **SELECTED PUBLICATIONS** Auth, The Law of Interest in Canada; co-auth, Cases and Materials on Contracts. **CONTACT ADDRESS** Fac of Law, Univ Victoria, PO Box 2400, Victoria, BC, V8W 3H7. **EMAIL** mwaldron@uvic.ca

WALDRON, WILLIAM S.

DISCIPLINE ASIAN RELIGIOUS TRADITIONS **EDUCATION** Univ Wis, BA, PhD. **CAREER** Prof; Middlebury Col, 96-. **RESEARCH** Indigenous psychological systems of Indian Buddhism and their dialogue with modern psychology. **SELECTED PUBLICATIONS** Publ on, res interest. **CONTACT ADDRESS** Dept of Religion, Middlebury Col, Middlebury, VT, 05753.

WALDROP, RICHARD E.

DISCIPLINE MISSIOLOGY **EDUCATION** Northwest Bible Col, BA, 72; Lee Univ, BA, 74; Bethel Theol Sem, MATS, 75; Fuller Theol Sem, MA, 86, DMissiology, 93. **CAREER** Dir, Facultad Teologica Pentecostal, 88-94; ASST PROF WORLD MISSIONS, CHURCH OF GOD THEOL SEM, 94-99. **CONTACT ADDRESS** 90 Walker St NE, Cleveland, TN, 37311. **EMAIL** rewaldrop@aol.com

WALEN, ALEC D.

PERSONAL Born 03/09/1965, Washington, DC, s **DISCIPLINE** LAW & PHILOSOPHY **EDUCATION** Harvard, JD, 98; Univ of Pittsburgh, PhD, 93 **CAREER** Law Clerk, 98-99, Fed Dist Ct of MA, Lect, 97, Kennedy Sch of Gov; Asst Prof, 93-94, Lafayette Col **MEMBERSHIPS** Am Philos Assoc **RESEARCH** Moral, Political, Legal Theory **SELECTED PUBLICATIONS** Auth, Consensual Sex Without Assuming the Risk of Carrying an Unwanted Fetus, Brooklyn Law Review, 97, 1051-1140; Auth, The Defense of marriage Act and Moral Auth, The William & Mary Bill of Rights Journal, 97, 619-642 **CONTACT ADDRESS** 5 Perry St, Cambridge, MA, 02139. **EMAIL** walen@banet.net

WALGREN, KENT

DISCIPLINE LAW **EDUCATION** Brigham Young, BA, 71; Utah Col Law, JD, 74. **CAREER** Asst atty gen, Utah SE-

LECTED PUBLICATIONS Fel Publ, A Bibliography of Pre-1851 Louisiana Scottish Rite Imprints, In: Heredom: Jour Scottish Rite Res Soc 4, 96; auth, A Bibliography of Pre-1851 American Scottish Rite Imprints (non-Louisiana), In: Heredom: J Scottish Rite Res Soc 3, 95; Inside the Salt Lake Temple: Gisbert Bossard's 1911 Photographs, In: Dialogue: A Journal of Mormon Thought 29, No 3, 96. **CONTACT ADDRESS** PO Box 2441, Salt Lake City, UT, 84110.

WALHOUT, DONALD
PERSONAL Born 08/09/1927, Muskegon, MI, m, 1958, 4 children **DISCIPLINE** PHILOSOPHY **EDUCATION** Adrian Col, BA, 49; Yale Univ, MA, 50, PhD, 52. **CAREER** Instr, Yale Univ, 52-53; prof, 53-92, emer prof, philos, 92-, Rockford Col. **HONORS AND AWARDS** Phi Beta Kappa; Adrian Col alumni award, 59; Hackley Distinguished lectr, 88. **MEMBERSHIPS** Amer Philos Asn; Amer Asn of Univ Prof; The Hopkins Soc. **RESEARCH** Ethics and history of philosophy; Philosophy of religion. **SELECTED PUBLICATIONS** Auth, A Comparative Study of Three Aesthetic Philosophies, Hist of Philos Quart, 98; auth, Grading Across a Career, Col Teaching, 97; auth, Hermeneutics and the Teaching of Philosophy, Teaching Philos, 84; auth, Send My Roots Rain, A Study of Religious Experience in the Poetry of Gerard Manley Hopkins, Oh Univ Press, 81; auth, Human Nature and Value Theory, The Thomist, 80; auth, Festival of Aesthetics, Univ Press of Amer, 78; auth, The Good and the Realm of Values, Univ Notre Dame Press, 78. **CONTACT ADDRESS** 320 N. Rockford Av., Rockford, IL, 61107. **EMAIL** donwal@hughestech.net

WALIGORE, JOSEPH
PERSONAL m, 3 children **DISCIPLINE** PHILOSOPHY **EDUCATION** Syracuse Univ, PhD, 95. **CAREER** Lectr;prof, UWSP, 94-. **RESEARCH** New Age Movement and its relationship to other movements in Western cultural history. **SELECTED PUBLICATIONS** Auth, Nagarjuna: Emptiness, Taxes and Tweezers, J Theta Alpha Kappa, 95. **CONTACT ADDRESS** Dept of Philosophy, Univ Wis-SP, Stevens Point, WI, 54481. **EMAIL** jwaligor@uwsp.edu

WALKER, CHARLES EALY, JR.
PERSONAL Born 05/01/1951, Anchorage, AK, m, 1983 **DISCIPLINE** LAW **EDUCATION** University of California Santa Barbara, BA (magna cum laude), 1973; London School of Economics, 1977; Boston College Law School, JD, 1978. **CAREER** Oxnard Union High School District, teacher, 1974-75; U.S. Department of Agriculture Office of the General Counsel, Attorney, 1978-79; Boston Superior Court, law clerk, 1979-80; Suffolk University Law School Council on Legal Education Opportunity, teaching fellow, 1980-82, 1987-89; University of Massachusetts, instructor, 1980-82; Massachusetts Court of Appeals, law clerk, 1980-81; Commonwealth of Massachusetts, assistant Attorney general, 1981-87; New England School of Law, assistant professor, 1987-; Executive of Elder Affairs, general counsel, currently; Massachusetts Commission Against Discrimination, chmn. **HONORS AND AWARDS** Project Commitment Inc, Distinguished Service Award, 1988; New England School of Law, Charles Hamilton Houston Distinguished Service Award, 1990; Governor of Massachusetts, Excellence in Legal Education Citation; Boston College Law School, William Kenneally Alumnus of Year, 1995. **MEMBERSHIPS** Massachusetts Bar Association Committee for Admissions, chair; Roxbury Defenders Committee Inc, acting president, 1982-; Boston College Law School Black Alumni Network, president co-founder, 1981-; Cambridge Economic Opportunity Commission, board of directors, 1982-86; Massachusetts Black Lawyers Association Executive Board, president, 1993-95; NAACP National Urban League, 1985-; Good Shepherd Church of God in Christ Trustee Board, chairman, 1985-; Wheelock College Family Theatre, board of directors; Massachusetts Law Review, editorial board, 1990-. **SELECTED PUBLICATIONS** Author, "Liquor Control Act: Alcoholic Beverages Control Commission," 1986, "Violation of Injunctions: Criminal and Civil Contempt," MBA - Restraining Orders and Injunctions, pages 1-15; Massachusetts Bar Association speaker, "Obedience is Better than Sacrifice," 1988; "The History and Impact of Black Lawyers in Massachusetts," Massachusetts Supreme Judicial Work, Historical Law Society Law Journal. **CONTACT ADDRESS** One Ashburton Place, Boston, MS, 02108.

WALKER, GEORGE KONTZ
PERSONAL Born 07/08/1938, Tuscaloosa, AL, m, 1966, 2 children **DISCIPLINE** LAW, HISTORY **EDUCATION** Univ AL, BA, 59; Vanderbilt Univ, LLB, 66; Duke Univ, MA, 68; Univ VA, LLM, 72. **CAREER** From asst prof to assoc prof, 72-76, Prof Law, Wake Forest Univ, 77-, Woodrow Wilson fel, Duke Univ, 62-63; Sterling fel, Yale Law Sch, 75-76; vis prof law, Marshall-Wythe Sch Law, Col William & Mary, 79-80; vis prof Law, Univ Ala Sch Law, 85; Charles H Stockton Prof Intl Law, Naval War Col, 92-93. **HONORS AND AWARDS** Phi Beta kappa, Order of Barristers (hon), Order of the Coif (hon), Am Law Inst. **MEMBERSHIPS** Virginia, North Carolina Bars; Am Soc Int law; Int law Asn, Am Bar Asn; Maritime Law assoc, VA, NC Bar Asns; admitted to practice in federal courts. **RESEARCH** International law; federal jurisdiction; admiralty; conflict of laws; civil procedure; alternative dispute resolution. **SELECTED PUBLICATIONS** Auth of 10 bks, over 40 bk chpts, articles. **CONTACT ADDRESS** Sch of Law, Wake Forest Univ, PO Box 7206, Winston Salem, NC, 27109-7206.

WALKER, JAMES SILAS
PERSONAL Born 08/21/1933, LaFollette, TN, m, 1954, 4 children **DISCIPLINE** RELIGION, PHILOSOPHY **EDUCATION** Univ Ariz, BA, 54; McCormick Theol Sem, BD, 56; Claremont Grad Sch, PhD (relig), 63. **CAREER** Asst pastor, Cent Presby Church, Denver, Colo, 57-60; assoc prof philos and relig, Huron Col, SDak, 63-66; assoc prof, 66-70, PROF PHILOS AND RELIG AND CHMN DEPT, HASTINGS COL, 70, DEAN, 79-. **MEMBERSHIPS** Am Acad Relig; Soc Bibl Lit; Am Philos Asn; Am Schs Orient Res. **RESEARCH** Contemporary continental theology, especially early Barthian theology; contemporary semantic analysis. **SELECTED PUBLICATIONS** Auth, On the Home Front in the Cold War Legacy of the Hanford Nuclear Site, Revs Am Hist, Vol 21, 93; Romantic Chaos, the Dynamic Paradigm in Novalis Heinrich Von Ofterdingen and Contemporary Science, Ger Quart, Vol 66, 93; The Cold War and American Science in the Military Industrial Academic Complex at Mit and Stanford, Revs Am Hist, Vol 21, 93; Mobilizing against Nuclear Energy in a Comparison of Germany and the United States, Technol Cult, Vol 35, 94; The Atomic Energy Commission and The Politics of Radiation Protection, 67-71, Isis, Vol 85, 94; Cancer Factories in america Tragic Quest For Uranium Self Sufficiency, J Interdisciplinary Hist, Vol 26, 95; The American People in a History, 2nd Edition, J Am Hist, Vol 81, 95; The American People in Creating a Nation and a Society, J Am Hist, Vol 81, 95; History, Collective Memory, and the Decision To Use the Bomb, Dipl Hist, Vol , 95; These United States in the Questions of Our Past, J Am Hist, Vol 81, 95; America in a Narrative History, J Am Hist, Vol 81, 95; Nation of Nations in a Narrative History of the American Republic, J Am Hist, Vol 81, 95; A Short History of the American Nation, J Am Hist, Vol 81, 95; America and Its People, J Am Hist, Vol 81, 95; The Pursuit of Liberty in a History of the American People, J Am Hist, Vol 81, 95; The Great Republic in a History of the American People, J Am Hist, Vol 81, 95; The American Past in a Survey of American History, J Am Hist, Vol 81, 95; The Enduring Vision in a History of the American People, J Am Hist, Vol 81, 95; The National Experience in a History of the United States, J Am Hist, Vol 81, 95; A People and a Nation in a History of the United States, J Am Hist, Vol 81, 95; The American Pageant in a History of the Republic, J Am Hist, Vol 81, 95; American History in a Survey, J Am Hist, Vol 81, 95; Wolf Creek Station in Kansas Gas and Electric Company in the Nuclear Era, Am Hist Rev, Vol 100, 95; The United States, J Am Hist, Vol 81, 95; The Shaping of the American Past, J Am Hist, Vol 81, 95; America in Past and Present, J Am Hist, Vol 81, 95; Wallace, Henry, in His Search For a New World Order, Dipl Hist, Vol 20, 96; Supplying the Nuclear Arsenal in american Production Reactors, 42-92, Pub Historian, Vol , 97; Industrial Policy, Technology, and International Bargaining in Designing Nuclear industries in argentina and Brazil, Isis, Vol 88, 97. **CONTACT ADDRESS** Dept of Philos and Relig, Hastings Col, Hastings, NE, 68901.

WALKER, MARGARET
PERSONAL Born 08/08/1948, Evergreen Park, IL **DISCIPLINE** PHILOSOPHY **EDUCATION** Univ of Illinois at Chicago, BA, 69; Northwestern Univ, MA, 71, PhD, 75. **CAREER** Prof to Full Prof of Philo, 74-, Fordham Univ; Vis Sr Scholar, 97, Univ of South FL, St Petersburg; Vis Assoc Prof, Dept of Philo, 94, Washington Univ; Instr, 91, NEH Simmer Inst, Bethany Coll; Guest Prof, 81, Catholic Univ of Leuven, Belgium. **HONORS AND AWARDS** Frances Elvidge Fellow; Fordham Univ Faculty Fellowships, 82, 86, 92, 96. **MEMBERSHIPS** APA, Society for Women in Philosophy. **RESEARCH** Anglo-American Ethics, Feminist Theory, Wittgenstein. **SELECTED PUBLICATIONS** Auth, Moral Understandings, A Feminist Study in Ethics, NY, Routledge, 98; Ineluctable Feelings and Moral Recognition, Midwest Studies in Philosophy, Vol XXII, eds, PA French, TE Uehling, Jr. and HK Wettstein, Notre Dame, Indiana. Univ of Notre Dame Press, 98; Moral Epistemology in: A Companion to Feminist Philosophy, eds, A Jaggar and I Young, Oxford Blackwell Pub, 98; Geographies of Responsibility, New York, The Hastings Center Report, 97; Picking Up Pieces, Lives, Stories and Integrity, in: Feminists Rethink the Self, ed, DT Meyers, Boulder, Colorado, Westview Press, 97. **CONTACT ADDRESS** Dept of Philosophy, Fordham Univ, 441 E Fordham Road, Bronx, NY, 10458. **EMAIL** mwalker@murray.fordham.edu

WALKER, REBECCA
PERSONAL Born 06/19/1969, Stanford, CA **DISCIPLINE** PHILOSOPHY **EDUCATION** Stanford Univ, AB, 91, PhD, 98. **CAREER** Lectr, Arizona State Univ. **MEMBERSHIPS** Am Philoso Asn. **RESEARCH** Ethical theory and applied ethics. **CONTACT ADDRESS** 2045 E Broadway, #72, Tempe, AZ, 85282. **EMAIL** rwalker@mainex1.asu.edu

WALKER, STANLEY M.
PERSONAL Born 07/15/1942, Chicago, Illinois, m **DISCIPLINE** LAW **EDUCATION** Harvard Coll, AB 1964; Yale Univ Law School, JD, 1967. **CAREER** Judge A Leon Higginbotham US Dist Ct, law clerk, 1967-69; Dechert Price & Rhoads, assoc, 1969-70; Pepper, Hamilton & Scheetz, Assoc, 1970-71; Pennsylvania St Bd of Law Exam's, examiner, 1971-74; Comm Legal Services, staff & mng atty, 1971-72; Greater Philadelphia Comm Devel Corp, exec vice pres, 1972-73; The Rouse Co, sr atty, 1973-79; Univ of Texas School of Law, assoc prof, 1979-89; Exxon Co, USA, counsel, 1989-95; Friendswood Development Company, gen counsel, 1995-. **MEMBERSHIPS** Mem, Amer Bar Assn & Natl Bar Assn; mem, of Bars of US Supreme Court, District of Columbia, Pennsylvania, Maryland, & Texas; mem, Austin Econ Devel Comm, 1985-89; alt mem, City of Austin Bd of Adjustment 1985-86; mem, Action for Metropolitan Govt Comm, 1988-89. **CONTACT ADDRESS** General Counsel, Friendswood Development Company, 17001 Northchase Drive, Ste 140, Houston, TX, 77060-2139.

WALKER, T.B.
PERSONAL Born 05/21/1940, Utica, NY, m, 1988, 5 children **DISCIPLINE** LAW, SOCIOLOGY **EDUCATION** Princeton Univ, BA, 62; Univ Denver, JD, 67, MA, 69. **CAREER** Asst prof of Law, McGeorge Sch Law, Univ of the Pacific, 69-70; vis assoc prof of law, Univ of Toledo, 69-70; assoc prof of law, Indiana Univ, 70-71; Assoc prof to prof of law, Univ Denver, 71- . **HONORS AND AWARDS** Magna Cum Laude, 62, 67; Order of St. Ives; listed Who's Who in Am and Best Lawyers in Am Since 1987., Ed-in-chief, Family Law Q, 83-92. **MEMBERSHIPS** Fel, Am Acad of Matrimonial Lawyers; founding fel, Int Acad of Matrimonial Lawyers; ABA. **RESEARCH** Legal rights of children and the lawyer's role. **SELECTED PUBLICATIONS** Co-auth, Family Law in the Fifty States: An Overview, in Family Law Q, 85-93; auth, Family Law From A to Z: A Primer on Divorce, in Family Advocate, 90. **CONTACT ADDRESS** 6601 S University Blvd, Ste 200, Littleton, CO, 80121. **EMAIL** TBWalker10@aol.com

WALKER, WILLIAM O., JR.
PERSONAL Born 12/06/1930, Sweetwater, TX, d, 3 children **DISCIPLINE** RELIGIOUS STUDIES **EDUCATION** Austin Col, BA, 53; Austin Presbyterian Theol Sem, MDiv, 57; Univ Tex-Austin, MA, 58; Duke Univ, PhD, 62. **CAREER** Inst Greek and Bible, Austin Col, 54-55; inst rel, Duke Univ, 60-62; asst prof, 62-66, assoc prof, 66-75, prof, 75, Rel, Trinity Univ; Dean Div of Hum and Arts, Trinity Univ, 88- . **HONORS AND AWARDS** Alpha Chi Natl Hon Soc, 52; Who's Who among studs in Amer Univ and Col, 52; James Battle Grad fel, Classics, 57; James B. Duke grad fel, 58; Rockefeller Brothers grad fel, 59-60; outstanding ed awd, 83. **MEMBERSHIPS** Studiorum Novi Test Soc; Am Acad Rel; Soc Sci Study Rel; Soc Bibl Lit; Catholic Bibl Asn Amer; Natl Asn Baptist Prof Rel; Col Theol Soc; Amer Asn Univ Prof. **RESEARCH** Interpolations in the Pauline Letts; Relation between Luke-Acts and the Pauline Letts; Son of Man; Synoptic Problems. **SELECTED PUBLICATIONS** Ed, The HarperCollins Bible Pronunciation Guide, San Francisco, Harper San Fran, 94; John 1:43-51 and The Son of Man in the Fourth Gospel, Jour for the Study of the New Test, 56, 94, 31-42; co-ed, The HarperCollins Bible Dictionary, HarperSan Francisco, 96; Kyrios and Epistates as Translations of Rabbi/Rabbouni, The Jour of Higher Crit 4, 1, spring 97, 56-77; Translation and Interpretation fo Ean me in Galatians 2:16, Jour Bibl Lit 116, 3, Fall 97, 515-520; Acts and the Pauline Corpus revisited: Peter's Speech at the Jerusalem Conference, in Literary Studies in Luke-Acts: Essays in Honor of Joseph B. Tyson, Mercer UP, 98, 77-86. **CONTACT ADDRESS** Dept of Humanities and Arts, Trinity Univ, San Antonio, TX, 78212-7200. **EMAIL** wwalker@trinity.edu

WALKER, WYATT TEE
PERSONAL Born 08/16/1929, Brockton, MA, m **DISCIPLINE** THEOLOGY **EDUCATION** VA Union Univ, BS (magna cum laude) 1950, MDiv (summa cum laude) 1953, LHD 1967; Rochester Theological Ctr, Omin 1975; graduate work at the Univ of Ife in Nigeria and Univ of Ghana. **CAREER** Historic Gillfield Baptist Church, Petersburg VA, minister, 1953-60; Dr Martin Luther King Jr, chief of staff; SCLC, Atlanta, vice pres, bd exec dir, 1960-64; Abyssinian Baptist Church, NYC, pulpit minister, 1965-66; Governor NYC, special asst on urban affairs; Cannan Baptist Church of Christ NYC, minister, CEO, 1967-; Church Housing Development Fund Inc, president/CEO, 1975-. **HONORS AND AWARDS** Received numerous human rights awards including the Elks Human Rights Award, 1963; Natl Alpha Awards in Civil Rights, 1965; Shriners Natl Civil Rights Award, 1974; Civil Rights Award, ADA, 1975; Honorary LHD, Virginia Union University, 1967; Honorary DD, Edward Waters College, 1985; Honorary D Litt, Gettysburg College, 1988; Top Fifteen Greatest African American Preacher In the US, Ebony Magazine, 1993; roles in "Mama, I Wanna Sing," & "Malcolm X." **MEMBERSHIPS** mem, World Peace Council, 1971-; Programme to Combat Racism of the World Council of Churches, world commissioner; Consortium for Central Harlem Development, chairman; Religious Action Network of the American Committee on Africa, secretary general, president; Natl Action Network, chairman of the board. **SELECTED PUBLICATIONS** Auth, Black Church Looks at the Bicentennial, Somebody's Calling My Name, Soul of Black Worship, Road to Damascus, The Harvard paper, Soweto Diary, Del World Conf on Religion and Peace, Japan, China Diary, Common Thieves, The Harvard Paper, Soweto Diary, Occasional Papers of a Revolutionary, Spirits that Dwell in Deep Woods. **CONTACT ADDRESS** Ca-

naan Baptist Church, 132 West 116th St, New York, NY, 10026.

WALL, BARBARA E.
DISCIPLINE PHILOSOPHY **EDUCATION** Fordham Univ, BA, 68; Marquette Univ, MA, 70, PhD, 79. **CAREER** Assoc prof & dir, Villanova Univ. **SELECTED PUBLICATIONS** Auth, Love and Death in the Philosophy of Gabriel Marcel, Wash, DC: UP Am, 77; Rerum Novarum and Its Critics on Social and Secual Hierarchies, Four Revolutions: Catholic Social Teaching's Unfinished Agenda, Lanham, MD: UP Am, 93; The Concept of Death in the Philosophy of Gabriel Marcel, Philos Aspects of Thanatol, Vol 2 & Marx's Analysis of the Relationship between Private Property and the State in His Early Writings, Philos Today, 87; co-ed, Journal for Peace and Justice Studies, Vols 1-6. **CONTACT ADDRESS** Dept of Philosophy, Villanova Univ, 800 Lancaster Ave, Villanova, PA, 19085-1692.

WALLACE, B. ALLAN
PERSONAL Born 04/17/1950, Pasadena, CA, m, 1989, 1 child **DISCIPLINE** RELIGIOUS STUDIES **EDUCATION** Amherst Col, BA, 87; Stanford Univ, PhD, 95 **CAREER** Lecu, Univ CA, Santa Barbara **HONORS AND AWARDS** Summa Cum Laude, 87; Phi Beta Kappa, Amherst Col; Jacob Javits Fel, Stanford Univ. **MEMBERSHIPS** Amer Acad of Religion **RESEARCH** Tibetan Buddhism; religion and science interface **SELECTED PUBLICATIONS** Auth, Choosing Reality: A Buddhist View of Physics and the Mind, 96; co-translator, A Guide to the Bodhisattva Way of Life, 97; auth, Dreaming, and Dying: An Exploration of Consciousness with the Dalai Lama, 97; auth, Healing Emotions: Conversations with the Dalai Lama on Mindfulness, Emotions, and Health, 97; auth, translator and ed, Natural Liberation: Padmasambhava's Teaching on the Six Bardos, 98; auth, A Spacious Path to Freedom: Practical Instructions on the Union of Mahamudra and Atiyoga, Karma Chagme, 98; Auth, The Bridge of Quiescence: Experiencing Tibetan Buddhist Meditation, 98; auth, The Buddhist Tradition of Samatha: Methods for Refining and Examing Consciousness, Journal of Consciousness Studies, 99. **CONTACT ADDRESS** Dept of Religious Studies, Univ California, Santa Barbara, CA, 93106. **EMAIL** bwallace@humanitas.ucsb.edu

WALLACE, DANIEL B.
PERSONAL Born 06/05/1952, Pasadena, CA, m, 1974, 4 children **DISCIPLINE** NEW TESTAMENT STUDIES **EDUCATION** Dallas Theol Sem, PhD, 95. **CAREER** Assoc prof, Dallas Theol Sem. **HONORS AND AWARDS** Gold Medallion finalist for Exegetical Syntax; Who's Who in Religion; Int Man of Year. **MEMBERSHIPS** Soc of Bibl Lit; Evangelical Theol Soc; Inst for Bibl Res; Soc of New Testament Studies. **RESEARCH** New Testament. **SELECTED PUBLICATIONS** Auth, Greek Grammar Beyond the Basics: An Exegetical Syntax of the New Testament, 96. **CONTACT ADDRESS** Dallas Theol Sem, 3903 Swiss Ave., Dallas, TX, 75204. **EMAIL** beegleman@aol.com

WALLACE, DEWEY D., JR.
PERSONAL Born 01/08/1936, Chicago, IL, m, 1956, 2 children **DISCIPLINE** RELIGION **EDUCATION** Witworth College, BA 57; Princeton Theol Sem, BD 60; Princeton Univ, MA 62, PhD 65. **CAREER** George Washington Univ, asst prof, assoc prof, prof, 63 to 98-. **HONORS AND AWARDS** Rockefeller Doctoral Fel. **MEMBERSHIPS** AAR; ASCH; PHS. **RESEARCH** English Reformation; religion in 17th century England; Puritanism; religion in the US **SELECTED PUBLICATIONS** Editor, The Pioneer Preacher, by Sherlock Bristol, Urbana, Univ IL Press, 89; editor, The Spirituality of the Later English Puritans: An Anthology , Macon, Mercer Univ Press, 89; Socinianism Justification by Faith and the Sources of John Locke's , The Reasonableness of Christianity, Jour Hist Ideas, 84. **CONTACT ADDRESS** Dept of Religion, George Washington Univ, Washington, DC, 20052. **EMAIL** dwallace@gwis2.circ.gwu.edu

WALLACE, JAMES DONALD
PERSONAL Born 05/21/1937, Troy, NY, m, 1960, 2 children **DISCIPLINE** PHILOSOPHY **EDUCATION** Amherst Col, BA, 59; Cornell Univ, PhD(philos), 63. **CAREER** From instr to assoc prof, 62-70, Prof Philos, Univ Ill, Urbana, 70-. **HONORS AND AWARDS** Am Coun Learned Soc Fel, 83-84; James H. Becker Lectr, Cornell Univ, 90. **MEMBERSHIPS** Am Philos Soc; Am Asn Univ Prof; Asn for Practical and Prof Ethics; Ill Philos Asn. **RESEARCH** Ethical theory, practical ethics, social philosophy. **SELECTED PUBLICATIONS** Auth, Virtues and Vices, Cornell Univ Press, 78; Moral Relevance and Moral Conflict, Cornell Univ Press, 88; Ethical Norms, Particular Cases, Cornell Univ Press, 96. **CONTACT ADDRESS** Dept of Philosophy, Univ of Illinois, Urbana-Champaign, 810 S Wright St, Urbana, IL, 61801-3611. **EMAIL** jwallace@uiuc.edu

WALLACE, JOHN
DISCIPLINE PHILOSOPHY **EDUCATION** Stanford Univ, PhD. **RESEARCH** Philosophy of language; political philosophy; philosophy of education. **SELECTED PUBLICATIONS** Auth, Translation Theories and the Decipherment of Linear B, Theory Decision, Assoc Univ, 84; Positive, Comparative, Superlative, J Philos, 72; On the Frame of Reference, Synthese, 70; Sortal Predicates and Quantification, J Philos, 65; co-auth, Some Thought Experiments about Mind and Meaning, Stanford, 90. **CONTACT ADDRESS** Philosophy Dept, Univ of Minnesota, Twin Cities, 355 Ford Hall, 224 Church St SE, Minneapolis, MN, 55455. **EMAIL** walla003@tc.umn.edu

WALLACE, KATHLEEN
PERSONAL NY **DISCIPLINE** PHILOSOPHY **EDUCATION** SUNY Stony Brook, PhD, 83. **CAREER** Visiting Asst Prof, 84-85, Hunter Coll; Asst Prof, 85-90, Assoc Prof, 90-, Chmn philosophy, Hofstra Univ. **HONORS AND AWARDS** DAAD stipendium, 2 NEH Awds. **MEMBERSHIPS** APA, SWP, SAAP, AAPP, Hume Society. **SELECTED PUBLICATIONS** Co-ed with introduction for, Metaphysics of Natural Complexes, SUNY Press, 89; co-ed, Nature's Perspectives, Prospects for Ordinal Metaphysics, SUNY Press, 90; auth, General Education and the Modern University, in: Liberal Education, 83; Making Categories or Making Worlds II, in: Texas A&M Studies in American Philosophy, 91; Reconstructing Judgement, Emotion and Moral Judgement, in: Hypatia, J of Feminist Philo, 93; Incarnation Difference and Identity, Materialism Self and the Life of Spirit in the Work of George Santayana, in: Metaphysics in Experience, American Philosophy in Transition, ed, D Anderson & R Hart, Fordham Univ Press, 97. **CONTACT ADDRESS** Dept of Philosophy Heger Hall 115, Hofstra Univ, Hempstead, NY, 11549. **EMAIL** phikaw@hofstra.edu

WALLACE, PAUL STARETT, JR.
PERSONAL Born 01/22/1941, Wilmington, NC, m **DISCIPLINE** LAW **EDUCATION** North Carolina Central Univ, BS, 1962, JD, 1966. **CAREER** US Copyright Office Library of Congress, copyright examiner, 1966-71; Congressional Research Serv, Library of Congress, former senior legislative atty, head of the Congress section, amer law div, Washington, DC, 1984-86, coord of multidis programs, 1986-96; Specialist in American Public Law, American Law Division, 1996-. **HONORS AND AWARDS** Mem, Pi Gamma Mu Natl Science Honor Soc; Commendation Award Outstanding Qualities of Leadership & Dedicated Serv, 1980; Distinguished Serv Award, 1984; Fed Bar Assn Longstanding and Dedicated Serv Award, 1986; Omega Psi Phi Fraternity, Alpha Omega Chapter, Scroll of Honor, 1991. **MEMBERSHIPS** Advisory bd, Comm Action for Human Serv Inc, 1983-; Fed Bar Assn News & Jrnl, 1980-81; sec, Cncl of Crct; vice pres, Fed Bar Assn, 1981-82; pres, Capitol Hill Chapter Fed Bar Assn, 1979-80; adv bd mem, Federal Bar News & Journal, 1980-82; natl vice pres, District of Columbia Circuit Fed Bar Assn, 1981-82; chairperson, co-chair, Federal Bar Assn, natl mem committee, 1982-83; Section on the Admin of Justice, Washington, DC, 1984-89; mem, Dist of Columbia Bar Assn, US Supreme Court; continuing educ bd, Fed Bar Assn, 1985-; vice-chairperson, Library of Congress US Savings Bond Campaign, 1985; mem, Omega Psi Phi, US Dist Ct for District of Columbia; mem, US Court of Appeals for the DC Circuit; special editor Fed Bar Assn News & Journal, 1984, 1986; mem US Dist Court for the 8th Circuit, Phiha Delta Law Fraternity Intl; mem, Natl & Amer Bar Assoc; 33 Degree Mason; chairperson continuing educ bd, Fed Bar Assn, 1987-89; bd of trustees, Peoples Congregational Church, Washington, DC, 1985-90; Peoples Congregational Church, church council, 1990-; Foundation of the Federal Bar Association, board of directors, 1991-; Foundation of the Federal Bar Association, advisor, 1991; chairman, Diaconate Board, Peoples Congregational Church, 1993-95; chairman, Church Council, Peoples Congregational Church, 1996-; treasurer, Foundation of the Federal Bar Association, 1993-. **CONTACT ADDRESS** Library of Congress, Independence Ave SE, Washington, DC, 20540.

WALLACE, ROBERT M.
PERSONAL Born 05/15/1947, CA, m, 1990, 4 children **DISCIPLINE** PHILOSOPHY **EDUCATION** Oxford Univ BA 68; Cornell Univ PhD 94. **CAREER** Univ Wisconsin-Milwaukee, assist prof 94-97; Univ Penn, lectr 98-99-. **HONORS AND AWARDS** NEH; ACLS Fel **MEMBERSHIPS** APA; Hegel Soc Amer **RESEARCH** Ethical theory; social and political philo; German philo. **SELECTED PUBLICATIONS** Auth, Hegel on Ethical Life and Social Criticisms, How Hegel Reconciles Private Freedom and Citizenship, forthcoming in Jourl of Philosophical Research; Mutual Recognition and Ethics: A Hegelian Reformulation of the Kantian for the Rationality of Morality, Amer Phil Quart, 95; Blumenberg's Third Way between Habamas and Gadamer, eds T. Flynn and D. Judowitz, SUNY Press, 93. **CONTACT ADDRESS** Dept of Philosophy, Cornell Univ, 1908 East Edgewood Av., Shorewood, WI, 53211. **EMAIL** carol.roberts@mixcom.com

WALLACE, WILLIAM A.
PERSONAL Born 05/11/1918, New York, NY **DISCIPLINE** PHILOSOPHY & HISTORY **EDUCATION** Manhattan Col, BEE, 40; Cath Univ Am, MS, 52; Univ Fribourg, PhD(philos), 59 DrTheol, 61. **CAREER** Lector philos, Dominican House Philos, 54-62; lectr philos & ed, New Cath Encycl, Cath Univ Am, 62-65; prof theol, Dominican House Studies, 67-70; Prof Philos & Hist, Cath Univ Am, 70-88; prof philos, Univ Maryland, College Park, 88- ; Assoc ed, Thomist, 62-; NSF res grants, 65-67, 72-77 & 80-83; trustee, Providence Col, 67-84; mem adv panel, Frog Hist & Philos Sci, NSF, 75-77; mem, Inst Advan Study, Princeton, 76-77; dir gen, Leonine Comn, 76-89; consult, Nat Endowment for Humanities, 76- **HONORS AND AWARDS** DSc, Providence Col, 73; D Litt, Molloy Col, 74; LHD, Manhattan Col, 75; LHD, Fairfield Univ, 86., DSc, Providence Col, 73; DLitt, Molloy Col, 74; LHD, Manhattan Col, 75. **MEMBERSHIPS** Am Cath Philos Asn (vpres, 68, pres, 69); Hist Sci Soc; Philos Sci Asn; Renaissance Soc Am. **RESEARCH** Scientific methodology; medieval and early modern science; Galileo. **SELECTED PUBLICATIONS** Auth, Galileo and His Sources, Princeton, 84; ed, Reinterpreting Galileo, Catholic Univ, 86; ed, Galileo Galilei, Tractactio de demonstratione, Antenore, 88; auth, Galileo, The Jesuits and the Medieval Aristotle, Variorum, 91; auth, Galileo's Logic of Discovery and Proof, Kluwer, 92; ed and transl, Galileo's Logical Treatises, Kluwer, 92; auth, The Modeling of Nature, Catholic Univ, 96. **CONTACT ADDRESS** 3407 Cool Spring Rd, Adelphi, MD, 20983. **EMAIL** wallacew@wam.umd.edu

WALLIS, JAMES
DISCIPLINE PHILOSOPHY, RELIGION **EDUCATION** Claremont Grad Sch, PhD, 93. **CAREER** Prof, 96-, Comm Col So Nev. **HONORS AND AWARDS** Fel, Nat Conf of Christians & Jews, sem in Jerusalem. **MEMBERSHIPS** AAR/SBL; Ctr for Process Stud. **RESEARCH** Jewish-Christian relations; Holocaust studies; Theodicy. **SELECTED PUBLICATIONS** Auth, Post-Holocaust Christianity, Univ Press Am, 97. **CONTACT ADDRESS** 7300 Pirates Cove, # 1057, Las Vegas, NV, 89128. **EMAIL** wallis@nevada.edu

WALSH, CAREY ELLEN
PERSONAL Born 04/03/1960, Troy, NY **DISCIPLINE** HEBREW BIBLE **EDUCATION** Allegeury Col, BA, 82; Yale Divinity Sch, M Div, 85; Univ Chicago, AM, 89; Harvard, ThD, 96. **CAREER** Asst prof, Hebrew Bible, Rhodes Col. **MEMBERSHIPS** CBA; SBL. **RESEARCH** Archaelogy, Social hist of ancient Israel; Ancient Agriculture. **SELECTED PUBLICATIONS** Auth, Fruit of the Vine: Viticulture in Ancient Israel and the Hebrew Bible, HSM, in press; auth, Gods's Vineyard, BR, 98. **CONTACT ADDRESS** Rhodes Col, 2000 N Parkway, Memphis, TN, 38104. **EMAIL** walsh@rhodes.edu

WALSH, DAVID JOHN
PERSONAL Born 07/29/1950, Clonmel, Ireland, m, 1976, 2 children **DISCIPLINE** MODERN AND POLITICAL PHILOSOPHY **EDUCATION** Univ Col Dublin, BA, 72, MA, 74; Univ Va, PhD (govt), 78. **CAREER** Vis asst prof humanities, Univ Fla, 78-79; ASST PROF GOVT AND PHILOS, UNIV SC, SUMTER, 79-. **MEMBERSHIPS** Am Polit Sci Asn; Southern Polit Sci Asn; Hegel Soc Am. **RESEARCH** Relationship between religious experiences and political symbols and movements; Hegel and modern ideological movements; Jacob Boehme and esoteric religious movements of Renaissance. **SELECTED PUBLICATIONS** Auth, State Common Law Wrongful Discharge Doctrines in Update, Refinement, and Rationales, Am Bus Law J, Vol 33, 96; On the Meaning and Pattern of Legal Citations in Evidence from State Wrongful Discharge Precedent Cases, Law Soc Rev, Vol 31, 97. **CONTACT ADDRESS** Dept of Govt and Philos, Univ of SC, Sumter, SC, 29150.

WALSH, JAMES JEROME
PERSONAL Born 05/23/1924, Seattle, WA, m, 1946, 2 children **DISCIPLINE** PHILOSOPHY **EDUCATION** Reed Col, BA, 49; Oxford Univ, AB, 51, MA, 56; Columbia Univ, PhD, 60. **CAREER** From instr to asst prof, 54-62, assoc prof, 63-66, dir grad studies, 63-66, chmn dept, 67-73, Prof Philos, Columbia Univ, 67, DIR GRAD STUDIES, 73-; Am Coun Learned Soc res fel, 62-63; ED, J PHILOS, 64-; Guggenheim fel, 66-67. **MEMBERSHIPS** Am Philos Asn. **RESEARCH** History of philosophy; ethics; mediaeval philosoph. **SELECTED PUBLICATIONS** Auth, Bones of Contention and the Plight of Refugees and Exiles as Determined by the Policies of Rome and the Aetolian League Pharsalus, Phthiotic Thebes, Larisa Cremaste, Echinus, Clas Philol, Vol 88, 93; Flamininus And the Propaganda of Liberation and Rome Relations with Greece at the Beginning of the 2nd Century Bc, Hist Zeitschrift Alte Geschichte, Vol 45, 96. **CONTACT ADDRESS** Dept of Philos, Columbia Univ, New York, NY, 10027.

WALSH, JEROME T.
PERSONAL Born 06/14/1942, Detroit, MI **DISCIPLINE** HEBREW BIBLE **EDUCATION** Pontifical Bible Inst, SSL, 75; Univ Mich, PhD, 82. **CAREER** Assoc prof, 89-95, St John's Univ, NY; prof, 96-, dept head, theol & relig stud, 97-, Univ Botswana. **MEMBERSHIPS** Soc of Biblical Lit; Catholic Biblical Assn Amer. **RESEARCH** Literary analysis of Hebrew Bible. **SELECTED PUBLICATIONS** Auth, 1 Kings, Collegeville, Litur, 96. **CONTACT ADDRESS** 32-23 88th St, Apt 404, Jackson Heights, NY, 11369. **EMAIL** walshjt@noka.ub.bw

WALSH, JOHN H.
PERSONAL Born 09/14/1927, Pittsburgh, PA, m, 1953, 4 children **DISCIPLINE** PHILOSOPHY **EDUCATION** Duquesne Univ, BA, 52, MA, 58; Georgetown Univ, PhD (philos), 68. **CAREER** PROF PHILOS, CALIF STATE COL, PA, 61-. **RESEARCH** Philosophy of play and leisure; philosophical psychology; metaphysics. **SELECTED PUBLICATIONS** Auth, Compliance Inspections and Examinations by the Securities and Exchange Commission, Bus Lawyer, Vol 52, 96. **CONTACT ADDRESS** Dept of Philos, California Univ of Pennsylvania, California, PA, 15419.

WALSH, ROGER
DISCIPLINE PSYCHIATRY **EDUCATION** Univ Queensland, MD 70, PhD 73. **CAREER** Univ Calif Irvine, Prof of Psychiatry, Philosophy, Anthropology. **RESEARCH** Transpersonal Psychology; Comparative Religion; Asian Psychologies and Philosophies; Mediation. **SELECTED PUBLICATIONS** Auth, Paths Beyond Egos: The Transpersonal Vision, co-ed, NY, Tarcher and Putnam. **CONTACT ADDRESS** Dept of Psychiatry, Univ of California, Irvine, Irvine, CA, 92697.

WALSH, THOMAS
PERSONAL Born 11/08/1949, Louisville, KY, m, 1982, 2 children **DISCIPLINE** RELIGION **EDUCATION** Vanderbilt Univ, PhD **CAREER** Exec Dir, 86-pres, Internatl Relig Found **MEMBERSHIPS** AAR; Intl Coalition for Relig Freedom **RESEARCH** Ethics; Interreligious Dialogue **SELECTED PUBLICATIONS** Auth, "Liberalism and Communitarianism: The Global Duel Between the Right and the Good, Sage, 99; Auth, "Ethics in Christianity and Islam," in Muslim Christian Dialogue, Paragon House, 98; **CONTACT ADDRESS** 941 Audubon Pkwy, Louisville, KY, 40213-1109. **EMAIL** tgw@mindspring.com

WALTER, EDWARD F.
PERSONAL Born 10/31/1932, New York, NY, m, 1960, 2 children **DISCIPLINE** PHILOSOPHY **EDUCATION** St John's Univ, NY, BA, 54; NY Univ, MA, 65, PhD, 68. **CAREER** Prof Philos, Univ MO-Kansas City, 66 **MEMBERSHIPS** Western Philos Asn; Am Soc Value Inquiry. **RESEARCH** Soc ethics; polit philos. **SELECTED PUBLICATIONS** Auth, Margolis, the emotive theory, and cognitivism, J Value Inquiry, spring 76; Liberalism and morality and the future, Philos Forum, 76; William James' chance, Midwest J Philos, spring 77; Is libertarianism logically coherent?, Philos & Phenomenol Res, fall 78; Rationality: Minimal and maximal, Reason Papers, winter 78; Personal consent and moral obligation, J Value Inquiry, 15: 19-33; Revising Mill's Utilitarianism, J Social Philos, 5/81; The Immorality of Limiting Growth, State Univ NY, 81. **CONTACT ADDRESS** Dept Philos, Univ MO, 5100 Rockhill Rd, Kansas City, MO, 64110-2499. **EMAIL** ejwalter@unicorn.net

WALTER, JAMES JOSEPH
PERSONAL Born 01/01/1947, Indianapolis, IN, m, 1972, 2 children **DISCIPLINE** CHRISTIAN AND PHILOSOPHICAL ETHICS **EDUCATION** St Meinrad Col, BA, 69; Univ Louvain, Belg, MA and STB, 71, PhD (relig studies), 74. **CAREER** From instr to asst prof moral theol, Cath Univ Am, 72-75; ASSOC PROF MORAL THEOL, ST MEINRAD SCH THEOL, 75-. **MEMBERSHIPS** Soc Christian Ethics; Cath Theol Soc Am; Col Theol Soc. **RESEARCH** Fundamental Christian ethics; social ethics; medical ethics. **SELECTED PUBLICATIONS** Auth, A Theology of Compromise in a Study of Method in the Ethics of Curran, Horizons, Vol 20, 93. **CONTACT ADDRESS** St Meinrad Sch of Theol, St Meinrad, IN, 47577.

WALTERS, GLEN D.
PERSONAL Born 09/21/1954, Trenton, NJ, m, 1976, 2 children **DISCIPLINE** COUNSELING PSYCHOLOGY **EDUCATION** Lebanon Valley Col, BA, psychol, 76; Indiana Univ of Penn, MA, clin psychol, 78; Texas Tech Univ, PhD, coun psychol, 82. **CAREER** Chief, psychol svc, US Disciplinary Barracks, 83-84; adjunct facul, St. Mary Col, 84-85; psychol svc, US Penitentiary, 84-90; psychol cons, Tirrell and Assoc, 85-90; psychol svc, Fed Correctional Inst, 90-92; adjunct facul, Chestnut Hill Col, 95-; adjunct facul, Penn State Schuylkill, 92-; psychol svc, Fed Correctional Inst, 92-. **HONORS AND AWARDS** Anderson-Swenson Scholar Award, Texas Tech Univ, 78-79; Hea Prof Scholar Prog, US Army, 79-81; lic psychol, State of Penn, 90-; Drug Abuse Prog Psychol of the Year, Fed Bur of Prisons, 92; Info, Policy and Pub Affairs Div award for Outstanding contrib to res, Fed Bur of Prisons, 94; assoc ed, Criminal Justice and Behavior, 92-; assoc ed, Intl Jour of Offender Therapy and Comp Criminol, 89-; cons ed, Psychol Assessment: A Jour of Cons and Clin Psychol, 89-; ed adv bd mem, Criminol: An Interdisciplinary Jour, 92-98. **RESEARCH** Genetics of crime; Outcome expectancies for crime, alcohol, and gambling; Effective interventions for crime and addictive behaviors; Development of an integrated theory of human behavior and intervention (Lifestyle Theory). **SELECTED PUBLICATIONS** Auth, The addiction concept: Working hypothesis or self-fulfilling prophesy, Boston, Allyn & Bacon, 99; with J. R. McDonough, The Lifestyle Criminality Screening Form as a predictor of federal parole/probation/supervised release outcome: A three-year follow-up, Legal and Criminol Psychol, 3, 98; with W. N. Elliott & D. Miscoll, Use of the Psychol Inventory of Criminal Thinking Styles in a group of female offenders. Crim Justice and Behavior, 25, 125-134, 98; with W. N. Elliott, Predicting release outcome with the Psychol Inventory of Criminal Thinking Styles: Female date, Legal and Criminol Psychol, 3, 98; Time series and correltaional analyses of inmate-initiated assaultive incidents in a large correctional system, Intl Jour of Offender, Therapy and Comp Criminol, 42, 123-131, 98; Three existential contributions to a theory of lifestyles, Jour of Humanistic Psychol, 38, 4, 25-40, 98; Putting more thought into crime: Nine years later, Intl Jour of Offender Therapy and Comp Criminol, 42, 195-197, 98; Planning for change: An alternative to treatment planning with sexual offenders, Jour of Sex and Marital Therapy, 24, 67-79, 98; The Lifestyle Criminality Screening Form: Psychometric properties and practical utility, Jour of Offender Rehabil, 27, 9-23, 98; Changing lives of crime and drugs: Intervening with the substance abusing criminal offender, Chichester, England, 98. **CONTACT ADDRESS** Psychology Services, Federal Correctional Inst, Schuylkill, PO Box 700, Minersville, PA, 17954.

WALTERS, GWENFAIR
DISCIPLINE CHURCH HISTORY **EDUCATION** Wellesley Col, BA; Gordon-Conwell Theol Sem, MDiv; Cambridge Univ, PhD. **CAREER** Consult, hist archv proj, Cambridge Univ; asst prof, 93-; adv to Women; dir, Edu Tech Develop, Gordon-Conwell Theol Sem, 93-. **RESEARCH** History of worship, spirituality, media, technology, and the arts in the Church. **SELECTED PUBLICATIONS** Ed, Towards Healthy Preaching. **CONTACT ADDRESS** Gordon-Conwell Theol Sem, 130 Essex St, South Hamilton, MA, 01982.

WALTERS, JOHN R.
PERSONAL Born 09/03/1952, Pontiac, MI, m **DISCIPLINE** NEW TESTAMENT **EDUCATION** Univ Mich, BA, 75; Asbury Theol Sem, Mdiv, 79; Univ Oxford, DPhil, 86. **CAREER** Instr, 82-83, Asbury Col; lib, adj prof, 91-, Asbury Theol Sem. **HONORS AND AWARDS** John Wesley Fel, 79-82; Theta Phi, 77. **MEMBERSHIPS** Soc Bibl Lit, 77-; Inst for Bibl Res, 91-. **RESEARCH** Ancient Jewish piety; ancient gnostic piety; ancient Christian piety. **SELECTED PUBLICATIONS** Art, Hebrews, Asbury Bible Comm, 92; auth, Perfection in New Testament Theology, Mellen, 95; art, The Rhetorical Arrangement of Hebrews, Asbury Theol J, 96; auth, Perfection, Purity, Power: Redefining the Spirit-Led Life for the 21st Century, Soc of Pentecostal Stud, 27th annual mtg, 98. **CONTACT ADDRESS** Asbury Theol Sem, 204 N Lexington Ave, Wilmore, KY, 40390-1199. **EMAIL** john_walters@ats.wilmore.ky.us

WALTERS, STANLEY D.
PERSONAL Born 07/30/1937, Lawrence, KS **DISCIPLINE** RELIGION **EDUCATION** Princeton Theol Sem, ThM, 60; Yale Univ, PhD, 62. **CAREER** Greenville Col IL, prof, 61-68; Central Mich Univ, prof, 70-76; Univ Toronto Knox Col, prof, 76-92; Rosedale Presbyterian Church Toronto, minister, 92-. **MEMBERSHIPS** SBL **RESEARCH** Old testament; Hist Biblical Interpretation. **SELECTED PUBLICATIONS** Auth, After Drinking 1 Samuel 1:9, Crossing Boundaries and Linking Horizons: Studies in Honor of Michael C.Astour, 97. **CONTACT ADDRESS** Rosedale Presbyterian Church, 39 Whitney Ave, Toronto, ON, M4W 2A7. **EMAIL** manthano@internet.com

WALTKE, BRUCE K.
DISCIPLINE OLD TESTAMENT **EDUCATION** Dallas Theol Sem, ThD; Harvard Univ, PhD. **CAREER** Instr, Dallas Theol Sem; Regent Col; Westminster Theol Sem; prof-. **HONORS AND AWARDS** Ed, New Geneva Study Bible; co-ed, Theol Wordbook of the Old Testament. **SELECTED PUBLICATIONS** Auth, Intermediate Hebrew Grammar; commentary on Micah. **CONTACT ADDRESS** Dept of Old Testament, RTS Orlando, 1015 Maitland Ctr Commons, Maitland, FL, 32751.

WALTON, CRAIG
PERSONAL Born 12/06/1934, Los Angeles, CA, m, 1980, 6 children **DISCIPLINE** PHILOSOPHY **EDUCATION** Claremont Grad Univ, PhD, 65. **CAREER** Univ S Cal, instr, asst prof, 64-68; N Illinois Univ, asst prof, 68-71; Emory Univ, vis asst prof, 71; N Illinois Univ, assoc prof, 71-72; Univ of Nev, assoc prof, prof, chmn philo, dir/prog coord, Ethics & policy studies, 72-. **HONORS AND AWARDS** Phi Beta Kappa; Barrick Dist Sch; NDEA fell; UNLV Res Sabbatical; 6 eds, Who's Who in the West; Intl Who's Who in Edu; Who's Who in Amer Edu. **MEMBERSHIPS** SSHP, BSHP, APA, Intl Hume Society, Intl Hobbes Society, ISEE, MSA, SSPP, CSPT, SAAP. **RESEARCH** Renaissance and early mod philo: Ramus, Montaigne, Hobbes, Pascal, and Hume; hist of ethics; crit thinking and prac reasoning; moral psycology and edu. **SELECTED PUBLICATIONS** Auth, Treatise on Ethics 1684, by Nicolas Malebranche, in: Intl Archives of the History of Ideas, Kluwer Acad Pub, 93; Hobbes Science of Natural Justice, co-ed, Intl Archives of the Hist of Ideas, Martinus Nijhoff pub, 87; High Level Ethical Risk: Unsound Practices at Yucca Mountain, in: Science Technology and the American West, ed, Stephen Tchudi, Reno, Univ Nev Press, 97. **CONTACT ADDRESS** Inst for Ethics and Policy Studies, Univ Nevada Univ, Las Vegas, NV, 89154-5049. **EMAIL** cwalton@nevada.edu

WALTON, DOUGLAS
DISCIPLINE PHILOSOPHY **EDUCATION** Univ Waterloo, BA, 64; Univ Toronto, PhD, 72. **CAREER** Prof, 69. **HONORS AND AWARDS** Killam res fel, 87-89; fel-in-residence, Netherlands Inst for Advanced Stud in the Hum and Soc Sci, 89-90; ISSA prize, 91. **RESEARCH** Argumentational informal logic. **SELECTED PUBLICATIONS** Coauth, Commitment in Dialogue: Basic Concepts of Interpersonal Reasoning, SUNY Series in Logic and Language, State U of New York P, 95; A Pragmatic Theory of Fallacy, Studies in Rhetoric and Communication Series, U of Alabama P, 95; Arguments from Ignorance, Univ Park, Penn State Press, 96; Argument Structure : A Pragmatic Theory, Toronto Studies in Philosophy, U of Toronto P, 96; Argumentation Schemes for Presumptive Reasoning, Studies in Argumentation Series, N.J. Erlbaum, 96; Fallacies Arising from Ambiguity, Applied Logic Series, Kluwer Acad Publ, 96; Appeal to Pity : Argumentum ad Misericordiam, SUNY Series in Logic and Language, SUNY Press, 97. **CONTACT ADDRESS** Dept of Philosophy, Univ of Winnipeg, 515 Portage Ave, Winnipeg, MB, R3B 2E9. **EMAIL** walton@io.uwinnipeg.ca

WALTON, DOUGLAS NEIL
PERSONAL Born 06/02/1942, Hamilton, ON, Canada, m, 1968 **DISCIPLINE** PHILOSOPHY **EDUCATION** Univ Waterloo, BA, 64; Univ Toronto, PhD (philos), 72. **CAREER** Lectr, 69-71, asst prof, 71-75, ASSOC PROF PHILOS, UNIV WINNEPEG, 76-; Referee, Can J Philos Asn Symbolic Logic; Can Coun fel, Victoria Univ, Wellington, 75-76; adj prof philos, Fac Grad Studies, Univ Manitoba, 77-78; Soc Sci and Humanities Res Coun Can res grant, 77; Soc Sci and Humanities Res Coun fel, Univ Auckland, 80-81. **MEMBERSHIPS** Am Philos Asn; Can Philos Asn; Am Soc Polit and Legal Philos; Hastings Ctr; Am Psychol Asn. **RESEARCH** Philosophy of logic; medical ethics; philosophy of language. **SELECTED PUBLICATIONS** Auth, Alethic, Epistemic, and Dialectical Modes of Argument, Phil Rhet, Vol 26, 93; Begging the Question as a Pragmatic Fallacy, Synthese, Vol 100, 94; Practical Reasoning and the Structure of Fear Appeal Arguments, Phil Rhet, Vol 29, 96. **CONTACT ADDRESS** Dept of Philos, Univ of Winnipeg, Winnipeg, MB, R3B 2E9.

WALTON, KENDALL L.
PERSONAL Born 09/12/1939, m, 1970, 2 children **DISCIPLINE** PHILOSOPHY **EDUCATION** Univ Calif Berkeley, BA, 61; Cornell Univ, PhD, 67. **CAREER** Prof, 95-. **HONORS AND AWARDS** Fel, Am Coun of Learned Soc; Rockefeller Found fel; fel, Am Acad of Arts and Sci. **MEMBERSHIPS** Am Philos Asn; Am Soc for Aesthetics. **RESEARCH** Aesthetics; Philosophy of art; Philosophy of music; Philosophy of the mind. **SELECTED PUBLICATIONS** Auth, "Listening with Imagination: Is Music Representation?," in the J of Aesthetics and Art Criticism, 94; "How Marvelous!: Toward a Theory of Aesthetic Value," in The J of Aesthetics and Art Criticism, 93; "Metaphor and Prop Oriented Make-Believe," in The Europ J of Philos, 93; "Understanding Humour and Understanding Music," in The Interpretation of Music, 93. **CONTACT ADDRESS** Dept of Philosophy, Univ of Michigan, 2215 Angell Hall, Ann Arbor, MI, 48109. **EMAIL** klwalton@umich.edu

WALTON, R. KEITH
PERSONAL Birmingham, AL, m **DISCIPLINE** LAW **EDUCATION** Yale College, BA; Harvard Law School, JD. **CAREER** US District Ct, Northern District of AL, law clerk, 1990-91; King & Spalding, assoc, 1991-93; White House Security Review, deputy dir, 1994-95; US Dept of the Treasury, chief of staff, enforcement, 1993-96; COLUMBIA UNIV, UNIV SCY, 1996-. **MEMBERSHIPS** Enterprise Foundation, NY advisory bd, 1996-; Council on Foreign Relations, NY advisory bd, 1996-; Wilberforce Univ, trustee, 1997-; Alpha Phi Alpha; Sigma Pi Phi. **CONTACT ADDRESS** Columbia Univ, 535 W 116 St, 211 L, New York, NY, 10027.

WALTON, WOODROW E.
PERSONAL Born 11/04/1935, Washington, DC, m, 1959, 2 children **DISCIPLINE** RELIGION **EDUCATION** TX Christn Univ, BA, 57; Duke Univ, BD, Mdiv, 60; Univ of OK, MA, 70; Sch of Theol and Missions-Oral Roberts Univ, Dmin, 93 **CAREER** Pastor, 60-75, Christn Church Disciples of Christ; Evangelist, 81-, Assemblies of Pastoral God **HONORS AND AWARDS** Cert, Inst for Adult Edu, IN Univ, B Honor Roll **MEMBERSHIPS** Am Asn of Christian Counrs **RESEARCH** Biblical studies, US Hist **CONTACT ADDRESS** Norman, OK, 73072-6331.

WAN, ENOCH
DISCIPLINE MISSIONS **EDUCATION** State Univ NY, PhD. **CAREER** Instr, Can Theol Sem; Alan Hayes Belcher prof. **HONORS AND AWARDS** Founder, dir, Ctr for Intercult Stud. **SELECTED PUBLICATIONS** Auth, Mission Resource Manual and A Devotional Commentary on Mark. **CONTACT ADDRESS** Dept of Missions, Reformed Theol Sem, 5422 Clinton Blvd, Jackson, MS, 39209-3099.

WAN, SZE-KAR
PERSONAL Born 04/23/1954, Changsha, China, m, 1996 **DISCIPLINE** RELIGION **EDUCATION** Brandeis Univ, AB, 75; Gordon-Conwell Theol Sem, MDiv, 82; Harvard Univ, ThD, 92. **CAREER** Assoc prof New Testament, Andover Newton Theol Sch, 96-. **HONORS AND AWARDS** Lilly Fac Res Grant, 97-98; Lady Davis Post-Doc Fel, 93-94; Sinclair Kennedy Fel Harvard Univ, 89-90; NWO Fel, 90. **MEMBERSHIPS** SBL/AAR; CBA; Ethnic Chinese Bibl Colloquium. **RESEARCH** Pauline studies; Chinese Christian hermeneutics; New Testament. **SELECTED PUBLICATIONS** Auth, Allegorical Interpretation East and West: A Methodological Enquiry into Comparative Hermeneutics, Text & Experience, 95; auth, Abraham and the Promise of the Spirit: Galatians and the Hellenistic-Jewish Mysticism of Philo, Soc of Bibl Lit 95 Seminar Papers, 95; auth, Charismatic Exegesis: Philo and Paul Compared, Studia Philonica Annual, 94; auth, The Quaestiones et Solutiones in Genesim et in Exodum of Philo Judaeus: A Synoptic Approach, Soc Bibl Lit 93 Seminar Papers, 93. **CONTACT ADDRESS** Dept of New Testament, Andover Newton Theol Sch, 42 Browning Rd, Somerville, MA, 02145. **EMAIL** swan@ants.edu

WANG, HAO
PERSONAL Born 05/20/1931, Tsinan, China, d, 3 children **DISCIPLINE** LOGIC **EDUCATION** Southwestern Asn Univ, China, AB, 43; Tsing Hua Univ, AM, 45; Harvard Univ, PhD, 48. **CAREER** Teacher math, China, 43-46; asst prof philos, Harvard Univ, 51-56; reader in philos math, Oxford Univ, 56-61; PROF, ROCKEFELLER UNIV, 67-; Gordon McKay prof math logic and appl math, Harvard Univ, 61-67; John Locke lectr philos, Univ Oxford, 54-55. **MEMBERSHIPS** Asn Symbolic Logic; Am Acad Arts and Sci; Brit Acad. **RESEARCH** Mathematical logic; general philosophy. **SELECTED PUBLICATIONS** Auth, Time in Philosophy and in Physics in from Kant and Einstein to Godel, Synthese, Vol 102, 95; Tianjin Surveys of 1,000 Urban Households, 1983-1992 in Introduction, Chinese Law and Government, Vol 29, 96. **CONTACT ADDRESS** Rockefeller Univ, New York, NY, 10021.

WANG, ROBIN
PERSONAL Born 08/21/1955, Shanghai, China, 2 children **DISCIPLINE** PHILOSOPHY **EDUCATION** Peking Univ, BA, 80, MA, 83; Univ Notre Dame, MA, 88; Univ Wales, PhD, 98. **CAREER** Asst prof, Peking Univ, 83-85; asst prof, Loyola Marymount Univ. **MEMBERSHIPS** APA; Assoc of Chinese Philos in Am. **RESEARCH** Comparative moral philosophy. **SELECTED PUBLICATIONS** Coauth, Reason and Insight: Western and Eastern Perspectives on the Pursuit of Moral Wisdom. **CONTACT ADDRESS** Dept of Philosophy, Loyola Marymount Univ, 7900 Loyola Blvd, Los Angeles, CA, 90045. **EMAIL** rwang@lmumail.lmu.edu

WANG, WILLIAM KAI-SHENG
PERSONAL Born 02/28/1946, New York, NY, m, 1972, 1 child **DISCIPLINE** LAW, ECONOMICS **EDUCATION** Amherst Col, BA, 67; Yale Univ, JD, 71. **CAREER** Asst to mgr partner risk arbitrage, Gruss & Co, 71-72; from asst prof to assoc prof law, Univ San Diego, 72-77, prof, 77-81; prof law, Law Sch, Hastings Col, 81-, vis prof, Univ Calif, Davis, 75-76 & Law Sch, Hastings Col, spring 80; consult, White House Domestic Policy staff, spring 79. **SELECTED PUBLICATIONS** Auth, Booting the professors, Washington Star, 1/9/78; A tightwad's guide to Las Vegas, New West, 1/29/79 & Moneysworth, 6/79; A chicken in every pot, and forty-one channels for every television set, I Commun & the Law 97, 79; Toilet paper--it's good as gold, San Francisco Chronicle, 4/26/80; The dismantling of higher education, Part 1, 29 Improving Col & Univ Teaching 55 & 29 Improving Col & Univ Teaching 115, 82; Trading on material non-public information on impersonal stock markets: Who is harmed, and who can sue whom under Sec Rule 10b-5?, 54 Southern Calif Law Rev 1217, 81; Reflections on convenience translations: A reply to Professor Brooks, 17 San Diego Law Rev 209, 80 & Corp Coun Annual, 81; Insider Trading, supp, co-auth with Marc Steinberg, Little, Brown, 96, 98. **CONTACT ADDRESS** Law Sch, Hastings Col, 200 Mc Allister St, San Francisco, CA, 94102-4978.

WANGU, MADHU BAZAZ
PERSONAL Born 08/29/1947, Srinagar, India, m, 1971, 2 children **DISCIPLINE** PHENOMENOLOGY OF RELIGION **EDUCATION** Univ Pittsburgh, PA, PhD. **CAREER** Idependent scholar, writer, & teacher. **MEMBERSHIPS** Am Academy of Relig; Asn for Asian Studies. **RESEARCH** Hindu Goddesser; Indian art and aesthetics. **SELECTED PUBLICATIONS** Auth, Hermeneutics of a Kashmiri Mahatmya Text in Context, in Texts in Context: Traditional Hermeneutics in South Asia, ed Jeffrey Timm, SUNY Press, 92; Buddhism: World Religions, Facts on File, 93; Buddha's Meditation Images: Compassion in Stone, and The Temple: Microcosm of Hindu Sel-Understanding, sem papers, Pitt Informal Prof, Univ Pittsburgh, Oct 94; Jain Creativity: Ethics in Art and Indo-Islamic Painting: Portraits of Acculturation, sem papers, Pitt Informal Prog, Univ Pittsburgh, Nov 95; Iconography and Symbology: The Body of the Goddess, sem paper, Pitt Informal Prog, Univ Pittsburgh, Oct 96; Kamala's Final Ascent, unpublished manuscript, 97; A Slice of My Life: A Travelogue, unpublished manuscript, 98; Sacred Femininity: female Images in Indian Art: Past to Present, forthcoming 99. **CONTACT ADDRESS** 301 High Oaks Court, Wexford, PA, 15090. **EMAIL** zoonw@aol.com

WANNER, DIETER
PERSONAL Born 08/08/1942, Bern, Switzerland **DISCIPLINE** ROMANCE AND GENERAL LINGUISTICS **EDUCATION** Univ Zurich, DPhil(Romance ling), 68. **CAREER** Asst pro, 70-75, ASSOC PROF SPAN, ITAL AND LING, UNIV ILL, URBANA-CHAMPAIGN, 75-. **MEMBERSHIPS** Ling Soc Am; MLA. **RESEARCH** Italian linguistics; Romance linguistics; historical linguistics. **SELECTED PUBLICATIONS** Auth, Romance Language Pronouns Which Express Identity, Romance Philol, Vol 46, 93; Motives for Linguistic Change in the Formation of the Spanish Object Pronouns, Hispanic Rev, Vol 62, 94; Grammatical Research on the Characteristics of Rhaeto Romance as Spoken in Graubunden Grisons, Romance Philol, Vol 49, 95; Syntax of Spoken Raeto Romance, Romance Philology, Vol 49, 96. **CONTACT ADDRESS** Dept of Span Ital and Port, Univ of Ill, 4080 FLB, Urbana, IL, 61801.

WANTLAND, BURDETT L.
PERSONAL Born 10/30/1933, Decatur, IL, m, 1956, 3 children **DISCIPLINE** RELIGION AND PHILOSOPHY **EDUCATION** Lincoln Chris College, BA; Christian Theol Sem, MDiv; Butler Univ, MA; Univ Missouri, MA. **CAREER** Asst Prof, 68-, Univ West Georgia. **HONORS AND AWARDS** Honors in Hebrew Greek **MEMBERSHIPS** AAR; SSSR; SBL; WSTSTAR. **RESEARCH** Historical Jews; Nature of Belief. **CONTACT ADDRESS** Dept of Philo and English, State Univ of W Ga, Maple St, Carrollton, GA, 30118. **EMAIL** bwantland@wstga.edu

WARD, ANNALEE R.
PERSONAL Born 09/24/1959, Denver, CO, m, 1982, 2 children **DISCIPLINE** RELIGION **EDUCATION** Calvin Col, BA, 80; Colorado St Univ, MA, 82; Regent Univ, PhD, 97. **CAREER** Assoc prof, Trinity Christian Col, 85-. **HONORS AND AWARDS** Dean's list; Phi Kappa Phi Honor Soc; Faculty Award., Received Relig Commun Assoc Dissertation of the Year; Comprehensive Exams, passed 'With Distinction'. **MEMBERSHIPS** Nat Commun Assoc; Relig Commun Assoc; Popular Culture Assoc. **RESEARCH** Disney animated films; communication ethics. **SELECTED PUBLICATIONS** Auth, Foundational Concepts of Communication Theories, Commun Quarterly, 95; art, The Axiology of The Lion King's Mythic Narrative: Disney as Moral Educator, J of Popular Film & Television, 96; art, The Trouble with Disney Morality, The Banner, 95; art, The Christian Century, Popular Relig Magazines of the United States, 95. **CONTACT ADDRESS** Trinity Christian Col, 6601 W College Dr, Palos Heights, IL, 60463.

WARD, BENJAMIN F.
DISCIPLINE PHILOSOPHY **EDUCATION** Yale Univ; PhD, 72. **CAREER** Prof, 80-, Duke Univ. **RESEARCH** Aesthetics; philos of music; Frankfurt School; process philos; philos of sport. **SELECTED PUBLICATIONS** Auth, publ(s) on metaphysics; comp lit. **CONTACT ADDRESS** Philos Dept, Duke Univ, West Duke Bldg, Durham, NC, 27706.

WARD, BRUCE
DISCIPLINE RELIGIOUS STUDIES **EDUCATION** McMaster Univ, PhD. **RESEARCH** Modern philosophy of religion; religion and literature. **SELECTED PUBLICATIONS** Auth, Dostoevsky and the Hermeneutics of Suspicion, 97; art, The Absent 'Finger of Providence' in The Brothers Karamazov, Lonergan Rev, 96; art, Christianity and the Modern Eclipse of Nature, Jour Am Acad Relig, 95; auth, Prometheus or Cain? Albert Camus's Account of the Western Quest for Justice, 91; auth, The Recovery of Helen: Albert Camus's Attempt to Restore the Greek Idea of Nature, 90. **CONTACT ADDRESS** Religious Studies Dept, Laurentian Univ, 935 Ramsey Lake Rd, Sudbury, ON, P3E 2C6.

WARD, JOHN PRESTON
PERSONAL Born 08/16/1929, Marion, Indiana, d **DISCIPLINE** LAW **EDUCATION** Indiana Univ, AB, 1952; New York Univ School of Law, JD, 1955; Indiana Univ, MA, 1967. **CAREER** Indiana Univ, teaching fellow, 1954-57; self-employed attorney, 1955-85; Indiana Civil Liberties Union, executive dir, 1957-61, general counsel, 1957-62; Indiana Univ, instructor, 1958-62. **MEMBERSHIPS** ACLU; NAACP; American Bar Assn; Indiana State Bar Assn; Indianapolis Bar Assn; National Bar Assn; Marion County Bar Assn; National Urban League; American Assn of University Professors; American Council of the Blind; American Assn of Workers for the Blind, Indianapolis Chapter; Southern Christian Leadership Council.

WARD, JULE D.
PERSONAL Born 09/08/1942, Detroit, MI, m, 1964, 4 children **DISCIPLINE** PRACTICAL THEOLOGY **EDUCATION** Univ of Chicago, Divinity Schl, PhD, theol, 96. **CAREER** Inst, De Paul Univ, 7 yrs. **MEMBERSHIPS** AAR, CTS, SCE, CTSA **RESEARCH** Marriage and family. **CONTACT ADDRESS** Religious Studies, DePaul Univ, 2320 N Kenmore Ave, Chicago, IL, 60614. **EMAIL** juledes@aol.com

WARD, JULIE
DISCIPLINE PHILOSOPHY **EDUCATION** Univ Calif, San Diego, PhD, 84. **CAREER** Assoc prof, Loyola Univ, 90-; former fac, Univ Ore, Mt Holyoke & Stanford; involved in, Women's Stud Comt & its Steering Comt; member, Acad Coun & Core Curric; undergrad adv, philos majors. **RESEARCH** Ancient philosophy, especially Plato, Aristotle; Hellenistic philosophy; feminism. **SELECTED PUBLICATIONS** Auth, Feminism and Ancient Philosophy, Routledge, 96. **CONTACT ADDRESS** Dept of Philosophy, Loyola Univ, Chicago, 820 N Michigan Ave, Chicago, IL, 60611.

WARD, ROY BOWEN
PERSONAL Born 10/10/1934, Jacksonville, FL **DISCIPLINE** RELIGION **EDUCATION** Abilene Christian Col, BA, 56; Harvard Univ, Stb, 59, ThD (New Testament studies), 67. **CAREER** Instr relig, Conn Col, 63-64; From asst prof to assoc prof, 64-77, chmn dept, 71-78, assoc provost, 78-80, PROF RELIG, MIAMI UNIV, 77-; DANFORTH ASSOC, DANFORTH FOUND, 69-; lects, New Testament, Sch Relig, Earlham Col, 70; vis assoc prof relig, Rice Univ, 70-71; admin fel, Am Coun Educ, 76-77. **MEMBERSHIPS** Soc Bible Lit; Am Acad Relig; Studiorum Novi Testamenti Societas. **RESEARCH** New Testament studies; Judaism of the Second Commonwealth; religions of the Hellenistic world. **SELECTED PUBLICATIONS** Auth, the Origins of Christian Faith, Church Hist, Vol 65, 96; Why Unnatural and Exploring the Platonic Account of Bodysoul Dualism in Hellenistic Judaism and Early Christianity in the Tradition Behind Romans I,26-27, Harvard Theol Rev, Vol 90, 97. **CONTACT ADDRESS** Miami Univ, 500 E High St, Oxford, OH, 45056-1602.

WARD, THOMAS M.
DISCIPLINE LAW **EDUCATION** Univ Pa, BA; Notre Dame Univ, LLB; Univ Ill, LLM. **CAREER** Prof; pvt prac, Burlington, Vermont; taught, Univ SC; fac, Louisiana Tech Univ, 76-; past vis prof, Univ Ill, Boston Cole and Northeastern; Jefferson Smurfit vis prof, 84-85; taught, Coun Legal Educ Opportunity Inst prog; past sr fel and adj prof, Franklin Pierce Law Ctr in Concord, NH. **RESEARCH** Intellectual property. **SELECTED PUBLICATIONS** Auth, Intellectual Property in Commerce, 97. **CONTACT ADDRESS** School of Law, Univ of Southern Maine, 96 Falmouth St, PO Box 9300, Portland, ME, 04104-9300.

WARDEN, DUANE
PERSONAL Born 10/16/1942, Franklin, AK, m, 1962, 1 child **DISCIPLINE** RELIGION, NEW TESTAMENT STUDIES **EDUCATION** Harding Univ, BA, 65; Harding Grad School, MA, 78; Duke Univ, PhD, 86. **CAREER** Prof, chair of dept, Ohio Valley Coll, 84-93; prof, asst dean, Harding Univ, 93-. **HONORS AND AWARDS** Teacher of the Year, Ohio valley Coll, 89-90; NEH Grants, 87, 91. **MEMBERSHIPS** Soc of Bibl; Evangel and Theol Soc. **RESEARCH** NT World; I Peter; Hermeneutics. **SELECTED PUBLICATIONS** Auth, Alienation and Communityin 1 Peter, 86; the Forty Thousand Citizens of Ephesus, Classical Philol, 88; Imperail Persecution and the Dating 1 Peter and Revelation, J of the Evangel Theol Soc, 91; The Words of Jesus on Divorce, Restoration Quart, 97. **CONTACT ADDRESS** Harding Univ, Box 2280, Searcy, AR, 72149. **EMAIL** dwarden@harding.edu

WARE, BRUCE A.
DISCIPLINE CHRISTIAN THEOLOGY **CAREER** Asst prof, W Conservative Baptist Sem; asst prof, Bethel Theol Sem; assoc prof, ch dept Biblical and Systematic Theol, Trinity Evangel Divinity Sch; assoc dean, prof, S Baptist Theol Sem. **SELECTED PUBLICATIONS** Co-ed, The Grace of God and the Bondage of the Will. **CONTACT ADDRESS** Christian Theology Dept, Southern Baptist Theol Sem, 2825 Lexington Rd, Louisville, KY, 40280. **EMAIL** bware@sbts.edu

WARFIELD, TED A.
DISCIPLINE PHILOSOPHY **EDUCATION** Univ Ark, BA, 91; Rutgers Univ, PhD, 95. **CAREER** Asst prof. **RESEARCH** Philosophy of mind; epistemology; metaphysics. **SELECTED PUBLICATIONS** Auth, Determinism and Moral Responsibility are Incompatible, Philos Topics, 96; Divine Foreknowledge and Human Freedom are Compatible, Nous, 97; co-ed, Mental Representation: A Reader, 94. **CONTACT ADDRESS** Philosophy Dept, Univ of Notre Dame, 336/7 O'Shaughnessy, Notre Dame, IN, 46556. **EMAIL** warfield.3@nd.edu

WARNKE, GEORGIA
DISCIPLINE SOCIAL AND POLITICAL PHILOSOPHY **EDUCATION** Boston Univ, PhD. **CAREER** PROF, UNIV CALIF, RIVERSIDE. **RESEARCH** Contemporary German philosophy; Feminist philosophy; Ethics. **SELECTED PUBLICATIONS** Auth, "Feminism and Hermeneutics," Hypatia, 93; Justice and Interpretation, MIT Press, 93; "Surrogate Mothering and the Meaning of Family," Dissent, 94; "Communicative Rationality and Cultural Values," Cambridge Companion to Habermas, 95; "Discourse Ethics and Feminist Dilemmas of Difference," Feminists Read Habermas: Gendering the Subject of Discourse, "The One True Sense," The Cardozo Law Rev, 95; "Legitimacy and Consensus: Comments on Part of the Work

of Thomas McCarthy," Philos and Soc Criticism, 96; "Law, Hermeneutics and Public Debate," "Reply to Greenawalt," Yale Jour of Law and the Hum, 97; "Architecture, Reason, and Community Participation," Practices, 97; "Legitimate Prejudices," Laval theologique et philosophique, 97. **CONTACT ADDRESS** Dept of Philos, Univ Calif, 1156 Hinderaker Hall, Riverside, CA, 92521-0209. **EMAIL** warnke@ucrac1.ucr.edu

WARREN, ALVIN C., JR.
PERSONAL Born 05/14/1944, Daytona Beach, FL, m, 1966, 2 children **DISCIPLINE** LAW **EDUCATION** Yale Univ, BA, 66; Univ Chicago, JD, 69. **CAREER** Asst prof, Univ Conn, 69-73; assoc prof, Duke Univ, 73-74; assoc prof and prof, Univ Penn, 74-79; Ropes & Gray Prof Law, Harvard Univ, 79- . **HONORS AND AWARDS** Phi Beta Kappa; Guggenheim Fel. **MEMBERSHIPS** ABA. **RESEARCH** Tax law and policy. **SELECTED PUBLICATIONS** Auth, Integration of Individual and Corporate Income Taxes, American Law Institute, 93; auth, Financial Contract Innovation and Income Tax Policy, Harvard Law Rev, 93; auth, Alternatives for Corporate Tax Reform, in Shapiro, ed, Enterprise Economics and Tax Reform, Progressive Foundation, 94; auth, Alternatives for International Corporate Tax Reform, Tax Law Rev, 94; auth, The Proposal for an Unlimited Savings Allowance, Tax Notes, 95; auth, How Much Capital Income Taxed under an Income Tax is Exempt under a Cash-Flow Tax?, Tax Law Rev, 96; auth, Three Versions of Tax Reform, William and Mary Law Review, 97; coauth, Integration of Corporate and Individual Income Taxes: An Introduction to the Issues, Tax Notes, 98; coauth, Integration of the U.S. Corporate and Individual Income Taxes: The Treasury Department and American Law Institute Reports, Tax Analysts, 98. **CONTACT ADDRESS** Law Sch, Harvard Univ, Cambridge, MA, 02138. **EMAIL** warren@law.harvard.edu

WARREN, ANN KOSSER
PERSONAL Born 04/13/1928, Jersey City, NJ, m, 1949, 5 children **DISCIPLINE** MEDIEVAL AND RELIGIOUS HISTORY **EDUCATION** City Univ New York, BA, 49; Case Western Reserve Univ, MA, 76, PhD (hist), 80. **CAREER** LECTR HIST, CASE WESTERN RESERVE UNIV, 80-; Vis asst prof, Hiram Col, fall, 80. **MEMBERSHIPS** Mediaeval Acad Am; AHA; Soc Church Hist; Midwest Medieval Asn. **RESEARCH** Medieval English recluses: anchorites and hermits; medieval spirituality: pilgrimage phenomena; medieval social history: will studies and family history. **SELECTED PUBLICATIONS** Auth, the Black Death and Pastoral Leadership in the Diocese of Hereford in the 14th Century, Church Hist, Vol 65, 96; A History of Canterbury Cathedral, Albion, Vol 28, 96; Contemplation and Action in the Other Monasticism, Cath Hist Rev, Vol 83, 97. **CONTACT ADDRESS** Dept of Hist, Case Western Reserve Univ, Cleveland, OH, 44106.

WARREN, DONA
PERSONAL Born 03/01/1965, Fargo, ND **DISCIPLINE** PHILOSOPHY **EDUCATION** Univ Minn, PhD, 95. **CAREER** Asst prof philos, Univ Wisc, Stevens Pt, 95- . **HONORS AND AWARDS** Excellence in Tchg Award, 95. **MEMBERSHIPS** APA. **RESEARCH** Philosophy of mind; philosophy of religion. **SELECTED PUBLICATIONS** Auth, Those Who Can, Do: A Response to Sidney Gendin's Am I Wicked? Tchg Philos, 96; auth, How Many Angels Can Dance on the Head of a Pin? The Many Kinds of Questions in Philosophy, Tchg Philos, forthcoming; auth, Externalism and Causality: Simulation and the prospects for a Reconciliation, Mind & Lang, forthcoming. **CONTACT ADDRESS** Philosophy Dept, Univ of Wisconsin, Rm 489 CCC, Stevens Point, WI, 54481-3897. **EMAIL** dwarren@uwsp.edu

WARREN, EDWARD W.
PERSONAL Born 01/20/1929, San Francisco, CA, m, 1955, 3 children **DISCIPLINE** PHILOSOPHY, GREEK **EDUCATION** Stanford Univ, BA, 50; Johns Hopkins Univ, PhD (philos), 61. **CAREER** Asst prof philos, Syracuse Univ, 59-63; From asst prof to prof, 63-70, PROF CLASSICS AND PHILOS, SAN DIEGO STATE UNIV, 70-. **MEMBERSHIPS** Am Philol Asn; Soc Greek Philos; AAUP; Int Soc Neo-Platonic Studies. **RESEARCH** Greek philosophy; Plotinus; metaphysics. **SELECTED PUBLICATIONS** Auth, More Good Than Harm in a First Principle for Environmental Agencies and Reviewing Courts, Ecology Law Quart, Vol 20, 93; Science, Environment, and the Law in Discussion, Ecol Law Quart, Vol 21, 94. **CONTACT ADDRESS** Dept of Class and Orient Lang and Lit, San Diego State Univ, San Diego, CA, 92182.

WARREN, LINDA
PERSONAL Born 05/30/1947, s, 1 child **DISCIPLINE** PHILOSOPHY **EDUCATION** Univ Wash, MSc, 82; SUNY, MA, 95; SUNY, Binghamton, PhD, Candidate **CAREER** SUNY Bing, adj prof, 96-97; Edmonds CC and Seattle Cent CC, Seattle WA, 97-. **HONORS AND AWARDS** TA Award **MEMBERSHIPS** IAPH, SWIP, APA **RESEARCH** Feminist Ethics; Women and Poverty; Global Politics. **SELECTED PUBLICATIONS** Auth, Out of the Class Closet, in: Feminist Teacher. **CONTACT ADDRESS** Dept of Philosophy, Edmonds Comm Col, 9331 244th St S W T-103, Edmonds, WA, 98020.

WARREN, PAUL R.
PERSONAL Born 06/18/1957, Albany, NY, s **DISCIPLINE** PHILOSOPHY **EDUCATION** Alfred Univ, BA, 79; Univ Wisconsin, PhD, 88. **CAREER** TA, 80-85, Univ Wisconsin; instr, 86-88,Rice Univ; asst prof, 88-94, assoc prof, 94- , FL Intl Univ. **RESEARCH** Social political philosophy; Ancient philosophy. **SELECTED PUBLICATIONS** Auth, Should Marxists Be Liberal Egalitarians, Journal of Political Philosophy; auth, Self-Ownership, Reciprocity and Exploration, Canadian Journal of Philosophy. **CONTACT ADDRESS** Dept of Philosophy, Florida Intl Univ, Miami, FL, 33199.

WARREN, SCOTT
DISCIPLINE POLITICAL SCIENCE AND PHILOSOPHY **EDUCATION** Univ VA, BA; Claremont Grad Sch, MA, PhD. **CAREER** Assoc prof, Dean of Stud, Antioch Col. **RESEARCH** Contemp critical theory. **SELECTED PUBLICATIONS** Auth, The Successful College Student and The Emergence of Dialectical Theory, Univ Chicago Press. **CONTACT ADDRESS** Antioch Col, Yellow Springs, OH, 45387.

WARRENER SMITH, SUSAN
PERSONAL Born 08/29/1944, Cincinnati, OH, m, 1982, 3 children **DISCIPLINE** THEOLOGICAL & RELIGIOUS STUDIES **EDUCATION** Boston Univ, BA, 66; Univ Mich, MA, 68; Drew Univ, PhD, 91. **CAREER** Adj Prof, Seton Hall Univ, 90-92; Dir, Christian Educ, 85-95; pastor, 95-. **HONORS AND AWARDS** Mead Hall Circle Study Prize; TA. **MEMBERSHIPS** AAR; Campus Min Asn Columbus **RESEARCH** Cistercian Studies **SELECTED PUBLICATIONS** Auth, Bernard of Clairvaux and the Natural Realm: The Four Elements, Cistercian Stud Quart, 91; rev, The Things of Greater Importance: Bernard of Clairvaux Apologia and the Medieval Attitude Toward Art, Cistercian Stud Quart, 91; auth, Bernard of Clairvaux and the Nature of the Human Being: The Special Senses, Cistercian Stud Quart, 95; Bernard of Clairvaux and the Natural Realm: Images Related to the Elements, Cistercian Stud Quart, 96; The 1996 Institute of Cistercian Studies Conference, Cistercian Stud Quart, 96; The 1997 Institute of Cistercian Studies Conference, Cistercian Stud Quart, 97. **CONTACT ADDRESS** Indianola Presbyterian Church, 1970 Waldeck Ave, Columbus, OH, 43201-1593. **EMAIL** absswss@aol.com

WARTLUFT, DAVID J.
DISCIPLINE AMERICAN LUTHERAN HISTORY **EDUCATION** BA, Muhlenberg Col, 1960; MDiv, LTSP, 1964; MA, Univ Pa, 1964; MS in Library Science, Drexel Univ, 1968; Pastorate in Pa, 1964-65. **CAREER** Dir of the Library; cord, Small Group prog. **HONORS AND AWARDS** Bd of dir(s), treasurer, Lutheran Hist Conf; exec sec, Amer Theol Library Assn. **RESEARCH** Exploring the Lutheran heritage. **SELECTED PUBLICATIONS** Pub(s), on American Lutheranism. **CONTACT ADDRESS** Dept of Practical Theology, Lutheran Theol Sem, 7301 Germantown Ave, Philadelphia, PA, 19119 1794. **EMAIL** Dwartluft@ltsp.edu

WASHINGTON, JAMES MELVIN
PERSONAL Born 04/24/1948, Knoxville, Tennessee, m **DISCIPLINE** THEOLOGY **EDUCATION** Univ of TN Knoxville, BA 1970; Harvard Divinity School, MTS 1970-72; Yale Univ, MPhil 1972-75, PhD 1975-79. **CAREER** Yale Divinity School, instr 1974-76; Union Theol Sem, assoc prof 1976-86, prof, currently; Haverford Coll, vstg assoc prof 1983-84; Columbia Univ, visiting assoc prof 1984-85; Oberlin Coll, vstg assoc prof 1985-86; Union Theol Sem, prof of Modern & American Church History 1986; visiting lecturer Princeton Theological Seminary Princeton, NJ 1989-90; visiting prof Princeton Univ Princeton, NJ 1989-90. **HONORS AND AWARDS** Fellow Woodrow Wilson Found 1970-71; Protestant Fellow Fund for Theol Ed 1971-72; Rockefeller Doctoral Fellow Fund for Theol Ed 1972-74; Teaching Fellow Harvard Univ 1971-72; book Frustrated Fellowship 1985; Christopher Award for editing A Testament of Hope, The Essential Writings of Martin Luther King, Jr 1987. **MEMBERSHIPS** Bd mem Amer Baptist Churches USA 1982-85, Natl Council of Churches 1985-87, Amer Baptist Historical Soc 1977-82; mem, exec comm Faith & Order Commissof the Natl Council of Churches 1985-87; consult Religious Affairs Dept, NAACP; Publications, A Testament of Hope, The Essential Writing of Martin Luther King,Jr (Harper & Row 1986); Frustrated Fellowship, The Black Baptist Quest for Social Power (Mercer Univ Press 1986); assoc editor American Natl Biography 1989-. **CONTACT ADDRESS** Professor Church Hist, Union Theological Seminary, 3041 Broadway, New York, NY, 10027.

WASHINGTON, ROBERT BENJAMIN, JR.
PERSONAL Born 10/11/1942, Blakeley, GA, m, 1969 **DISCIPLINE** LAW **EDUCATION** St Peter's College, BS, econ/political sci, 1967; Howard Law School, JD, 1970; Harvard University Law School, LLM, 1972. **CAREER** Harvard Law School, teaching fellow, 1970-72; US Senate Comm on the District of Columbia, Attorney, 1971-72; Howard Univ Law School, assoc prof of law and director of communication skills, 1972-73; Christopher Columbus College of Law, lecturer, 1972-73; US House of Representatives Comm on the District of Columbia, Attorney, 1973-75; George Washington Univ Law Center, lecturer, 1975, assoc prof of law, 1978; Danzansky, Dickey, Tydings, Quint & Gordon, senior partner, 1975-81; Georgetown Law Center, associate professor, 1978-82; Finley, Kumble, Wagner, senior partner and member of the National Management Committee, 1981-87, managing partner, Washington office, 1986-88; Finley, Kumble, Wagner, Heine, Underberg, Manley, Myerson & Casey, Washington, DC, co-managing partner, 1986-88; Laxalt, Washington, Perito, & Dubuc, managing partner, 1988-91; Washington & Christian, managing partner, 1991-; Washington Strategic Consulting Group, Inc, chairman/chief executive officer, currently. **HONORS AND AWARDS** Cobb Fellowship, Howard Law School, 1969; Harvard Law School, teaching fellowships, 1970-72. **MEMBERSHIPS** District of Columbia Bar Assn; American Bar Assn; Natl Bar Assn; Washington Bar Assn; Federal Bar Assn; American Judicature Society; Supreme Court Historical Society; Phi Alpha Delta Legal Fraternity; board member, Natl Bank of Washington, 1981-89; board member, Medlantic Healthcare Group; board member, Medlantic Management Corp; board member, Healthcare Partners; board member, AVW Electronic Systems Inc; adivsory board, The Home Group (AmBase); board of trustees, Corcoran Gallery of Art; board member, Natl Symphony Orchestra Assn; Metropolitan AME Church. **CONTACT ADDRESS** Washington & Christian, 805 15th St, NW, Washington, DC, 20005.

WATERS, DONOVAN W.M.
DISCIPLINE LAW **EDUCATION** Oxon Univ, BA, 52, BCL, 53, MA, 58, DCL, 90; London Univ, PhD, 63; Univ Victoria, LLD, 95. **CAREER** Prof emer, 96-. **HONORS AND AWARDS** Pres, Int Acad Estate Trust Law. **SELECTED PUBLICATIONS** Auth, The Constructive Trust; The Law of Trusts in Canada. **CONTACT ADDRESS** Fac of Law, Univ Victoria, PO Box 2400, Victoria, BC, V8W 3H7. **EMAIL** dwwaters@uvic.ca

WATERS, JOHN W.
PERSONAL Born 02/05/1936, Atlanta, Georgia, s **DISCIPLINE** THEOLOGY **EDUCATION** Atlanta Univ Summer School, 1955-58; Fisk Univ, BA 1957; Univ of Geneva Switzerland, Cert 1962; GA State Univ, 1964, 1984; Boston Univ, STB 1967, PhD 1970; Univ of Detroit, 1974-75. **CAREER** Army Ed Ctr Ulm W Germany, admin 1960-63; Atlanta Bd of Ed, instr 1957-60, 1963-64; Myrtle Baptist Church W Newton MA, minister 1969; Ctr for Black Studies Univ of Detroit, dir, assoc prof 1970-76; Interdenom Theol Ctr, prof 1976-86; The Gr Solid Rock Baptist Church Riverdale, minister 1981-; senior vice pres 1984-; Primerica Financial Services, College Park, GA, senior vice president, 1984-. **HONORS AND AWARDS** The Natl Fellowship Fund Fellowship in Religion 1968-70; Fellowship The Rockefeller Doctoral Fellowship in Religion 1969-70; Disting Lecturer Inst for Christian Thought John Courtney Murray Newman Ctr MI 1975; first faculty lecturer, Interdenominational Theological Center, 1979. **MEMBERSHIPS** Mem bd dir Habitat for Humanity in Atlanta 1983; mem bd of trustees Interdenom Theol Ctr 1980-84; vice pres Coll Park Ministers Fellowship; chair South Atlanta Joint Urban Ministry 1984-94; Prison Ministries with Women, 1988-96; American Academy of Religion, 1969-; Society of Biblical Literature, 1969-; American Association of University Professors (AAUP), 1971-. **CONTACT ADDRESS** Sr Vice President, Primerica Financial Services, 5480 Old National Hwy, College Park, GA, 30349.

WATERS, KENNETH C.
DISCIPLINE PHILOSOPHY **EDUCATION** Univ Ind, PhD. **RESEARCH** Philosophy of science; evolutionary theories and scientific realiam. **SELECTED PUBLICATIONS** Auth, Genes Made Molecular, Philos Sci, 94; Tempered Realism about the Force of Selection, Philos Sci, 91; Why the Antireductionist Consensus Won't Survive: The Case of Classical Mendelian Genetics, 90; The Conceptual Basis for a Non-Equilibrium Theory of Succession., Trends Ecology Evolution, 90; co-auth, The Illusory Riches of Sober's Monism, J Philos, 90. **CONTACT ADDRESS** Philosophy Dept, Univ of Minnesota, Twin Cities, 355 Ford Hall, 224 Church St SE, Minneapolis, MN, 55455. **EMAIL** ckwaters@maroon.tc.umn.edu

WATERS, RAPHAEL THOMAS
PERSONAL Born 01/16/1924, Sydney, Australia **DISCIPLINE** PHILOSOPHY, PHARMACY **EDUCATION** Univ Sydney, PhC, 45; Univ Montreal, BPh, 59, LPh, 60, DPh, 61. **CAREER** Sr lectr philos, Aquinas Acad, 62-64; lectr, Univ Ottawa, 69-70, asst prof, 70-76; asst prof, 76-81, assoc prof philos, 81-91, prof philos, Niagara Univ, 91-; Intercollegiate Studies Inst Fac Assoc, Niagara Univ; exec dir, Int Mother's Day Walk for Life; Nat Chair, Scholars for Social Justice. **MEMBERSHIPS** Am Cath Philos Asn; Am Maritain Asn; Thomas Aquinas Int Soc NAm. **RESEARCH** Epistemology; social and political philosophy; medical ethics. **SELECTED PUBLICATIONS** Auth, Some Epistemological Questions Concerning the Non-medical Use of Drugs, Rev Univ Ottawa, 10-11/75; The Moral Justification of Capital Punishment: Soc Justice Rev, 82; The Relationship of Moral Philosophy to Moral Theology, Listening, 83; The Nature of Man: A Philosopher's Viewpoint, Linacre Quart, 82, 85; The Two Faces of Capitalism, Soc Justice Rev, July/August 84; Two Ethical Traditions and Their Effects on Human Rights, Proceedings of the Fellow-

ship of Catholic Scholars, 85; Capital Punishment and the Principle of Double Effect, in Philos and Culture, Montreal, ed Montmorency, 5 vols, 86; The Basis for Traditional Rights and Responsibilities Parents, in Parental Rights: The Contemporary Assault on Traditional Liberties, ed Stephen Krason and D'Agostino, Front Royal Christiandom Col Press, 88; Values and Rights in Education, in The Recovery of American Education: Reclaiming a Vision, Lanham, MD, Univ Press Am, 91; Capital Punishment: An Act of Murder, Revenge, or Justice?, Contemp Philos, vol XVI, Nov/Dec 94; Capital Punishment: An Evil Act or An Act of Justice?, Soc Justice Rev, Jan 96; The Structure of the Model Family, Soc Justice Rev, Nov/Dec 96; The Ethics of Eugenics, Soc Justice Rev, Nov/Dec 97; The Common Good: Its Nature and Properties, Soc Justice Rev, July, 98. **CONTACT ADDRESS** Niagara Univ, Niagara Univ, NY, 14109. **EMAIL** rwaters@eagle.niagara.edu

WATSON, ALAN

PERSONAL Born 10/27/1933, Hamilton, Scotland, 2 children **DISCIPLINE** COMPARATIVE LAW, CLASSICAL STUDIES **EDUCATION** Univ Glasgow, MA, 54, LLB, 57; Univ Oxford, DPhil, 60, DCL, 73. **CAREER** Lectr law, Wadham Col, Oxford Univ, 57-59; fel law, Oriel Col, Oxford Univ, 59-65; Douglas prof civil law, Univ Glasgow, 65-68; prof civil law, Univ Edinburgh, 68-79; PROF LAW AND CLASS STUDIES, UNIV PA, 79-; Gen ed, transl Justinian's Digest, Commonwealth Fund, 78. **HONORS AND AWARDS** LLD, Univ Edinburgh, 80. **RESEARCH** Society and legal change; Roman law. **SELECTED PUBLICATIONS** Auth, the Importance of Nutshells, Am J Comp Law, Vol 42, 94; Wilhelm Strad and Bow and the Instrument Dated 1725 and the Tubbs Bow of 1885, Strad, Vol 106, 95; From Legal Transplants to Legal Formants, Am J Comp Law, Vol 43, 95; Introduction to Law For 2nd Year Law Students, J Legal Educ, Vol 46, 96; Aspects of Reception of Law, Am J Comp Law, Vol 44, 96; A History of Private Law in Europe, with Particular Reference to Germany, Am Hist Rev, Vol 102, 97. **CONTACT ADDRESS** Law School, Univ Pa, Philadelphia, PA.

WATSON, CLETUS CLAUDE

PERSONAL Born 11/03/1938, Philadelphia, Pennsylvania, s **DISCIPLINE** THEOLOGY **EDUCATION** St Francis College, Loretto, PA, BA, 1962; St Francis Seminary, Loretto, PA, ordained, 1966; LaSalle University, Philadelphia, PA, MA, 1974; St Charles Seminary, Philadelphia, PA, MDiv, 1976. **CAREER** Bishop Egan High School, Fairless Hills, PA, chairman, teacher, 1966-76; St Francis Prep School, Spring Grove, PA, chairman, dean of students, 1977-81; University of Florida Med School, Gainesville, FL, teacher, med ethics, 1981-85; Holy Faith Catholic Church, Gainesville, FL, assoc pastor, teacher, 1981-85; San Jose Catholic Church, Jacksonville, FL, assoc pastor, teacher, 1985-88; St Joseph Academy, St Augustine, FL, teacher, chairman, 1986-89; Church of the Crucifixion, Jacksonville, FL, pastor, teacher, 1988-. **HONORS AND AWARDS** Black History Month Award, Jacksonville Naval Base, 1987; commissioned in Afro-American ministry, Jacksonville, FL, 1990; One Church/One Child Award, Jacksonville, FL, 1990; Citizens Award, Jacksonville, FL, 1991; Alumni Award in Humanities, St Francis College, 1992; International Biographical Assn Man of the Year Award, 1993; Amer Biographical Inst Man of the Year Award, 1994. **MEMBERSHIPS** Advisory bd member, Presbyteral Council of the Diocese of St Augustine, 1988-95; advisory board member, Afro-American Office (Diocese), 1987-; advisory board member, Catholic Charities Office (Diocese), 1991-97; advisory board member, Ministry Formation Board, 1991-92; member, National Black Catholic Clergy Caucus, 1966-; member, Black Catholic Congress, 1987-. **SELECTED PUBLICATIONS** Author, The Concept of Love: An Ongoing Perspective, Brentwood Christian Press; author, The Concept of God and the Afro-American, Brentwood Christian Press; poems include "A Man Called Black"; "Fifty Plus Five". **CONTACT ADDRESS** Pastor, Church of the Crucifixion Rectory, 3183 W Edgewood Ave, Jacksonville, FL, 32209-1800.

WATSON, D. F.

PERSONAL Born 05/15/1956, Watertown, NY, m, 1984, 1 child **DISCIPLINE** NEW TESTAMENT AND CHRISTIAN ORIGINS **EDUCATION** Houghton Col, BA, 78; Princeton Theol Sem, Master of Divinity, 81; Duke Univ, Dr of Philos, 86. **CAREER** Asst prof of bibl studies, Ashland Theol Sem, 84-86; pastor, Tri-Church Parish United Meth Churches, Steuben, North Western, and Westernville, NY, 87-89; asst prof, 89-92, assoc prof, 92-96, prof, 96-, New Testament studies, chair, dept relig and philos, 93-98, Malone Col, Canton, Oh. **HONORS AND AWARDS** Dict of Intl Bio, 25th ed, 97; 26th ed, 98; 27th ed, 99; Outstanding People of the 20th Cent, 99; Who's Who in Amer Educ, 5th ed, 96-97; Who's Who in the Midwest, 25h ed, 96-97; Who's Who in Bibl Studies and Archaeol, 2nd ed, 93; Malone Col first Distinguished Facul Award for Scholar, 97-98; Malone Col Facul Forum Showcase of Res Award for Res on Ancient Educ: Greek, Roman and Jewish, fall 97; ; Malone Col Facul Forum Showcase of Res Award for Res on The New Testament Tchg on the Antichrist, fall 95; ; Malone Col Facul Forum Showcase of Res Award for Res on A Socio-Rhetorical Commentary on Paul's Epistle to the Philippians, fall 94; Malone Col Facul Forum prize, Developing a Personal Publishing Program, spring, 92; Amer Bible Soc Scholarly Achievement Award for Excellence in Bibl Studies, Houghton, 78; summa cum laude graduate, Houghton, 78; Comprehensive Examination Honors, Houghton, 7; Dean's list, Houghton, 74-78. **MEMBERSHIPS** Studiorum Novi Testamenti Soc, 95-; Soc of Bibl Lit, 81-; Cath Bibl Asn of Amer, 83-; Eastern Great Lakes Bibl Soc, 84-; Inst for Bibl Res, 93-; Intl Soc for the Hist of Rhetoric, 86-; Rhetoric Soc of Amer, 86-; John Wesley Fel, 82-. **RESEARCH** New Testament; Rhetorical criticism; Biblical interpretation **SELECTED PUBLICATIONS** Auth, Rhetorical Criticism of the Bible: A Comprehensive Bibliography with notes on history and method, Bibl Interpretation Series 4, Leiden, E. J. Brill, 94; ed, Persuasive Artistry: Studies in New Testament Rhetoric in Honor of George A. Kennedy, Jour for the Study of the New Testament Supplement series 50, Sheffield, Sheffield Acad Press, 91; articles, ed, Vernon Robbins's Socio-Rhetorical Criticism: A Review, Jour for the Study of the New Testament, 70, 69-115, 98; Rhetorical Criticism of Hebrews and the Catholic Epistles Since 1978, Currents in Res: Bibl Studies 5, 175-207, 97; Rhetorical Criticism of the Pauline Epistles Since 1975, Currents in Res: Bibl Studies 3, 219-48, 95; Building a New Testament Library: James-Revelation, Catalyst: Contemporary Evangelical Perspectives for United Methodist Seminarians 20/4, 3, 94. **CONTACT ADDRESS** Prof. of New Testament Studies, Malone Col, 515 25th St. NW, Canton, OH, 44709. **EMAIL** jwatson@ashland.edu

WATSON, DAIVD LOWES

PERSONAL Born 03/31/1938, Newcastle upon Tyne, England, m, 1961, 2 children **DISCIPLINE** THEOLOGY **EDUCATION** Merton Col. Oxford Univ, BA, 61, MA, 65; Eden Theol Sem, MDiv, 74; Duke Univ, PhD, 78. **CAREER** Asst master, Duke's Sch, 61-64; overseas rep, Am Field Service Int Scholarships, 64-68; West Slough commun dir, 68-71; pastor, Prospect Park United Meth Churches, 71-75; pastor, Holly Springs Un Meth Church, 75-78; McCreless prof evangelism, Perkins Sch Theol, So Meth Univ, 78-84; staff, General Bd Discipleship, Un Meth Church, 84-92; prof theol & congregational life & mission, Wesley Theol Sem, 92-98; Dir, Offic Pastoral Formation, Nashville Episcopal Area, Un Meth Church, 98-. **MEMBERSHIPS** Acad Evangelism in Theol Educ; Am Acad Rel; Am Soc Church Hist; Am Soc Missiology; Asn Profs Missions; Wesleyan Theol Soc; World Meth Hist Soc. **SELECTED PUBLICATIONS** Auth, Accountable Discipleship, Discipleship Resources, 84, 85, 87-90, German ed, 90; auth, Covenant Discipleship: Christian Formation through Mutual Accountability, Discipleship Resources, 91, 95; auth, Forming Christian Disciples: The Role of Covenant Discipleship and Class Leaders in the Congregation, Discipleship Resources, 91, 95; auth, Proclaiming Christ in All His Offices: Priest, Prophet, Potentate, in The Portion of the Poor: Good News to the Poor in the Wesleyan Tradition, Kingswood Books, 95; auth, Response to Creation Theology as a Basis for Global Witness, in Evangelization, The Heart of Mission: A Wesleyan Imperative, General Board of Global Ministries, 95; auth, God's New Household, in The Upper Room 1997 Disciplines, The Upper Room, 96. **CONTACT ADDRESS** Office Pastoral Formation, 149 Smotherman Ct, Murfreesboro, TN, 37129. **EMAIL** DavidLowes@aol.com

WATSON, H. JUSTIN

PERSONAL Born 06/06/1957, VanBuren, AK **DISCIPLINE** RELIGIOUS STUDIES **EDUCATION** Florida State Univ, PhD, 96, MA, 92, Rel; Univ of the South, Polit Sci, BA, 79. **CAREER** Lectr, 97-99, Inst, 96-97, Tchg Asst, 92-95, FSU Dept Rel. **HONORS AND AWARDS** FSU Dissertation Fellowship; FSU Univ Fellowship; Tchg Assoc, FSU Prof for Instr Excellence; Natl Merit Scholar. **MEMBERSHIPS** Amer Acad Rel; Amer Stud Assoc; Amer Soc of Church Hist; Soc for the Sci Stud of Rel; Amer Polit Sci Assoc. **RESEARCH** Contemporary American Social and Political Movements, Christian Right, Evangelicalism and Fundamentalism, New of Alternative Religious Movements; Religious Ethics. **SELECTED PUBLICATIONS** Auth, The Christian Coalition: Dreams of Restoration and Demands for Recognition, NY, St Martin's Press, Scholarly and Reference Division, 97; What the Christian Coalition Really Wants, Louvain Studies, 98. **CONTACT ADDRESS** Dept Religion, Florida State Univ, Tallahassee, FL, 32306-1029. **EMAIL** jwtson@mailer.fsu.edu

WATSON, JAMES R.

PERSONAL Born 07/29/1938, Blue Island, IL, m, 1969 **DISCIPLINE** PHILOSOPHY **EDUCATION** Southern Ill Univ Carbondale, PhD, 73. **CAREER** Prof Philos, Loyola Univ New Orleans, 73-. **HONORS AND AWARDS** Loyola Univ Alumni Teaching Award, 91. **MEMBERSHIPS** APA; Friedrich Nietzsche Soc; Heidegger Conference; IAPL; ISSEI; IPS, SPEP, SPSGH; SPSCVA. **RESEARCH** Continental Philosophy; Visual Imagery; Postmodernism; Holocaust and Genocide; Ethics. **SELECTED PUBLICATIONS** Auth, Between Auschwitz and Tradition: Postmodern Reflections of the task of Thinking, 94; Die Auschwitz Galaxy, 97; Kontinental Philosophie aus Amerika: 22 Photogrammische Portrate, 98; Contemporary Portrayals of Auschwitz and Genocide, 98; Portraits of Continental Philosophers in America, 99. **CONTACT ADDRESS** Dept of Philosophy, Loyola Univ, New Orleans, LA, 70118. **EMAIL** jrwatson@datastar.net

WATSON, JAMES SHAND

PERSONAL Born 07/05/1946, Scotland **DISCIPLINE** INTERNATIONAL LAW **EDUCATION** Edinburgh Univ, LLB, 69; Univ Ill, LLM, 72. **CAREER** Teaching asst, Univ Ill, 70-71; asst prof, 71-74, assoc prof, 74-77, PROF LAW, COL LAW, MERCER UNIV, 77-; Vis prof, Law Sch, Baylor Univ, summer 82. **MEMBERSHIPS** London Inst World Affairs; Am Soc Int Law; Am Soc Polit and Legal Philos. **RESEARCH** Theory of international law and customary legal systems; the law of the sea; human rights. **SELECTED PUBLICATIONS** Auth, Cl 36 Dating and the Bluestones of Stonehenge, Antiquity, Vol 69, 95. **CONTACT ADDRESS** Col Law, Mercer Univ, Macon, GA, 31210.

WATSON, JOANN FORD

DISCIPLINE THEOLOGY **EDUCATION** DePaul Univ, BA, 78; Princeton Theol Sem, M Div, 81; Northwestern Univ, PhD, 84. **CAREER** Prof, theol, Ashland Theol Sem, Ashland, Oh. **HONORS AND AWARDS** Phi Beta Kappa. **MEMBERSHIPS** AAR; SBL. **RESEARCH** Theology; Women's studies. **SELECTED PUBLICATIONS** Auth, Manna for Sisters in Christ; auth, Mutuality in Christ; auth, Meditations in Suffering; auth, Sister to Sister; auth, Karl Barth's Doctrice of Man and Woman. **CONTACT ADDRESS** 910 Center St., Ashland, OH, 44805.

WATSON, MARY ANN

PERSONAL Born 01/27/1944, OH, m, 1978, 2 children **DISCIPLINE** COUNSELING PSYCHOLOGY **EDUCATION** Grove City Coll, BA, Eng & Psychol, 66; Univ Pitts, PhD, Couns Psycol, 69, Johns Hopkins Univ Sch Med, Psych Res Unit, postgrad, 72-73.. **CAREER** PROF, PSYCHOL, METRO STATE COLL DENVER, 74-; vis prof, Psychol, Univ Denver, Sch Soc Work, 86-88; vis prof, St Thom Theol Sem, 93, 95; clinic psychol, priv prac, Marit, sex & rel, 75-. **MEMBERSHIPS** Colo Area Sex Ther; Colo Soc Behav Anal & Ther; Colo Psychol Asn; Am Psychol Asn; Develop Psycho-Biol Res Gp; Educ Comm St Josephs Hosp Psych Dept **SELECTED PUBLICATIONS** "Keeping the Home Fires Burning," Seniro Edition, 92; "Denise, A Transsecual," Patients as Educators: Videocases in Abnormal Psychology, Prentice Hall, 92. **CONTACT ADDRESS** Dept Psychol, Metropolitan State Coll of Denver, 1006 11th St, Denver, CO, 80204. **EMAIL** watsonm@mscd.edu

WATSON, RICHARD ALLAN

PERSONAL Born 02/23/1931, New Market, IA, m, 1955, 1 child **DISCIPLINE** PHILOSOPHY **EDUCATION** Univ Iowa, BA, 53, MA, 57, PhD(philos), 61; Univ Minn, MS, 59. **CAREER** Instr philos, Univ Mich, 61-64; from asst prof to assoc prof, 64-74, Prof Philos, Wash Univ, 74-, Am Coun Learned Soc fel, 67-68; Ctr Advan Study Behav Sci fel, 67-68 & 81-82; pres, Cave Res Found, 65-67; Ctr Int Studies fel, 75-76. **HONORS AND AWARDS** Carmargo Fnd fel, 95; Bogliasco Fnd fel, 98. **MEMBERSHIPS** Am Philos Asn, AAAS. **RESEARCH** History of philosophy; epistemology. **SELECTED PUBLICATIONS** Auth, The Downfall of Cartesianism, 1673-1712, Nijhoff, The Hague, 66; coauth, Man and Nature: An Anthropological Essay in Human Ecology, Harcourt, 69; The Longest Cave, Knopf, 76; Under Plowman's Floor, Zephyrus, 78; The Runner, Copple House, 82; auth, The Philosopher's Joke, Prometheus, 90; auth, The Philosopher's Demise, Univ Mo Press, 95; auth, Niagara, Coffee House Press, 93; auth, The Breakdown of Cartesian Metaphysics, Hum Press Int, 87; auth, Writing Philosophy, S Ill Univ Press, 92; auth, Representational Ideas from Plato to Patricia Churchland, Kluwer Academic, 95; auth, Good Teaching, S Ill Univ Press, 97. **CONTACT ADDRESS** Dept of Philosophy, Wash Univ, Box 1073, St. Louis, MO, 63130-4899.

WATSON, STEPHEN

DISCIPLINE PHILOSOPHY **EDUCATION** Carroll Col, BA, 72; Duquesne Univ, MA, 75, PhD, 79. **CAREER** Prof. **RESEARCH** Contemporary continental thought; 19th century philosophy; aesthetics. **SELECTED PUBLICATIONS** Auth, Between Tradition and Oblivion: Foucault, the Complication of Form, the Literatures of Reason, and the Aesthetics of Existence, Cambridge, 94; Phenomenology, Interpretation, and Community, 95; Interpretation, Dialogue, and Friendship: On the Remainder of Community, Res Phenomenology, 97; Tradition(s): Refiguring Community and Virtue in Classical German Thought, 97; Reinterpreting the Political: Continental Philosophy and Political Theory, 98. **CONTACT ADDRESS** Philosophy Dept, Univ of Notre Dame, 336/7 O'Shaughnessy, Notre Dame, IN, 46556.

WATSON, WALTER

PERSONAL Born 12/31/1925, New York, NY, m, 1953, 2 children **DISCIPLINE** PHILOSOPHY **EDUCATION** Instr to asst prof, Univ Chicago, 51-59; NSF Sci Fac Fel, Cal Inst Technol, 58-59; assoc prof t o prof, 59-92, EMER, 93-, SUNY-Stony Brook; vis app, Univ PR, 63-64 and Univ HI, 82. **MEMBERSHIPS** Am Philos Asn. **RESEARCH** Pluralism. **SELECTED PUBLICATIONS** Auth Principles for Dealing with Disorder, Jour Chinese Philos, 81; The Architectonics of Meaning: Foundations of the New Pluralism, Univ Chicago Pressm 93; Types of Pluralism, The Monist, 90; Systematic Pluralism and The

Foundationalist Controversy, Reason Papers, 91; McKeons Semantic Schema, Philos and Rhetoric, 94; Dogma, Skepticism, and Dialogue, The Third Way: New Directions in Platonic Studies, Rowman and Littlefield, 95; Rembrandts Aristotle, Hypotheses, 96. **CONTACT ADDRESS** 6 Bobs Ln, Setauket, NY, 11733. **EMAIL** Watsonwalt@aol.com

WATTS, JAMES W.
PERSONAL Born 08/24/1960, Zurich, Switzerland, m, 1985, 1 child **DISCIPLINE** HEBREW BIBLE AND THE OLD TESTAMENT **EDUCATION** Pomona Col, BA, 82; Southern Sem, M Div, Th M, 85, 86; Yale Univ, PhD, 90. **CAREER** Visiting asst prof, Stetson Univ, 90-91; asst prof, Hastings Col, 93-98; assoc prof, Hastings Col, 98-. **HONORS AND AWARDS** Phi Beta Kappa, Hastings Col Facul Achievement award. **MEMBERSHIPS** Soc of Bibl Lit; Nat Asn of Prof of Hebrew. **RESEARCH** Biblical Narrative; Mixed genres; Law, ritual and rhetoric in the Hebrew bible. **SELECTED PUBLICATIONS** Auth, Reading Law: The Rhetoricl Shaping of the Pentateuch, Th ebiblical Seminar, Sheffield: Sheffield Academic Press, 99; art, Reader Identification and Alienation in the Legal Rhetoric of the Pentateuch, Bilblical Interpretation 7/1, 99; ed, Forming Prophetic Literature: Essays on Isaiah and the Twelve in Honor of John D. W. Watts, JSOT suppl series 235, Sheffield Acad Press, 96; auth, Psalm and Story: Inset Hymns in Hebrew Narrative, JSOT suppl series 139, JSOT Press, 92; article, The Legal Characterization of Moses in the Rhetoric of the Pentateuch, Jour of Bibl Lit, 117, 415-26, 98; article, The Legal Characterization of God in the Pentateuch, Hebrew Union Col Annual, 67, 1-14, 97; article, Psalmody in Prophecy: Habakkuk 3 in Context, Forming Prophetic Literature, 209-223; article, Public Readings and Pentateuchal Law, Vetus Testamentum, 45, 4, 540-57, 95; article, Rhetorical Strategy in the Composition of the Pentateuch, Jour for the Study of the Old Testament, 68, 3-22, 95; article, Song and the Ancient Reader, Perspectives in Relig Studies, 22, 2, 135-47, 95; article, Leviticus, Mercer Commentary on the Bible, Mercer Univ Press, 157-74, 94; article, This Song: Conspicuous Poetry in Hebrew Prose, Verse in Ancient Near Eastern Prose, Neukirchener Verlag, 345-58, 93. **CONTACT ADDRESS** Hastings Col, Hastings, NE, 68902. **EMAIL** jwatts@hastings.edu

WAUGH, EARLE HOWARD
PERSONAL Born 11/06/1936, Regina, SK, Canada, m, 1970, 3 children **DISCIPLINE** HISTORY OF RELIGION **EDUCATION** McMaster Univ, BA, 59, MA, 65; Univ Chicago, MA, 68, PhD(hist relig), 72. **CAREER** Asst prof relig, Cleveland State Univ, 72-74; Assoc Prof Relig Studies, Univ of Alta, 76-, Chmn Dept, 74-, Mem nat alumni coun, Divinity Sch, Univ Chicago, 73- **MEMBERSHIPS** Am Acad Relig; Mid East Studies Asn; Can Soc Study Relig. **RESEARCH** Islam; Eastern religions; religion in Canada. **SELECTED PUBLICATIONS** Auth, Jealous angels: Aspects of Muslim religious language, Ohio J Relig Studies, Vol 1 No 2; coauth, Religious Encounters with Death, Pa State Univ, 77; auth, Metaphors of death in ecstatic religion, Listening, 78; The Imam in the New World: Models and modification, Festschrift, Univ Chicago, 78; The Other Sides Of Paradise - Explorations Into The Religious Meanings Of Domestic Space In Islam - Campo,Je, History Of Religions, Vol 0033, 1993; The Arab Christian - A History In The Middle-East - Cragg,K, Journal Of Religion, Vol 0073, 1993; The Other Sides Of Paradise - Explorations Into The Religious Meanings Of Domestic Space In Islam - Campo,Je, History Of Religions, Vol 0033, 1993; Muslims, Their Religious Beliefs And Practices, Vols 1-2 - Rippin,A, Studies In Religion-Sciences Religieuses, Vol 0024, 1995; Fundamentalism - Harbinger Of Academic Revisionism/, Journal Of The American Academy Of Religion, Vol 0065, 1997; Sufism, Mystics, And Saints In Modern Egypt - Hoffman,Vj, History Of Religions, Vol 0037, 1997; Sufism, Mystics, And Saints In Modern Egypt - Hoffman,Vj, History Of Religions, Vol 0037, 1997. **CONTACT ADDRESS** Dept of Relig Studies, Univ of Alta, Rm 322 Arts Bldg, Edmonton, AB, T6G 2Ey.

WAUTISCHER, HELMUT
PERSONAL Born 06/15/1954, Klagenfurt, Austria, m, 1990 **DISCIPLINE** PHILOSOPHY, PSYCHOLOGY **EDUCATION** Karl-Franzens Univ, Graz Austria, PhD, 85. **CAREER** Concurrent lectr, San Diego State Univ, 88-91; CSU Long Beach, 89-92; vis asst prof, Humboldt State Univ, 92-94; Universitatslektor, Univ Klagenfurt Austria, 95-97; concurrent lectr, Sonoma State Univ 95-. **HONORS AND AWARDS** Fulbright, 81; Executive Bd SAC, 91-; Executive Bd COPS, 97-. **MEMBERSHIPS** Am Philos Asn; Amer Anthropol Asn; Soc for the A nthropol of Consciousness; Council of Philos Soc; Karl Jasper Soc. **RESEARCH** Consciousness Studies; Philosophical Anthropology. **SELECTED PUBLICATIONS** Auth, Dreaming 'On Love and Awareness' Dialogue and Humanism, 94; ed, Anthropology of Consciousness, 94; Tribal Epistemologies: Essays in the Philosophy of Anthropology, 98. **CONTACT ADDRESS** Dept of Philosophy, Sonoma State Univ, 1801 E Cotati Ave, Rohnert Park, CA, 94928-3609. **EMAIL** wautisch@sonoma.edu

WAY, GARY DARRYL
PERSONAL Born 02/25/1958, Newark, NJ, m, 1987 **DISCIPLINE** LAW **EDUCATION** Rutgers Coll, New Brunswick, NJ, BA 1980; New York Univ School of Law, New York City, JD 1983. **CAREER** Haight, Gardner, Poor & Havens, New York City, associate, 1983-86; National Basketball Assn, New York City, staff Attorney, 1986-88; NBA Properties Inc, New York City, asst general counsel, 1988-. **SELECTED PUBLICATIONS** Author of "Japanese Employers and Title VII," 1983. **CONTACT ADDRESS** NBA Properties Inc, 645 Fifth Ave, New York, NY, 10022.

WAYMACK, MARK H.
DISCIPLINE PHILOSOPHY **EDUCATION** Johns Hopkins Univ, PhD, 87. **CAREER** Assoc prof; co-dir, philos dept's grad prog in Health Care Ethics; Buehler Center on Aging fel; adj asst prof Med, Northwestern Univ Med Sch for its Prog on Med Ethics and Humanities in Med; former fac, Col William and Mary, Univ Md Baltimore County & Univ Md Sch Med. **MEMBERSHIPS** Chicago Clin Ethics Prog; Soc for Health and Human Values & Amer Soc on Aging. **RESEARCH** Health care ethics; ancient Greek ethics, especially Plato; early modern philosophy, especially Hutcheson, Hume; Scottish moral philosophy. **SELECTED PUBLICATIONS** Coauth, Medical Ethics and the Elderly, Health Admin Press, 88; Single-Malt Whiskeys of Scotland, Open Ct, 92; The Book of Classic American Whiskeys, Open Ct, 95. **CONTACT ADDRESS** Dept of Philosophy, Loyola Univ, Chicago, 820 N Michigan Ave, Chicago, IL, 60611.

WAYNE, ANDREW
DISCIPLINE PHILOSOPHY OF SCIENCE **EDUCATION** Univ Toronto, BS, 89; Univ Calif, San Diego, PhD, 94. **CAREER** Ass prof; dir, Sci and Hum Aff Prog. **RESEARCH** History of physics, philosophy of physics. **SELECTED PUBLICATIONS** Auth, "Degrees of Freedom and the Interpretation of Quantum Field Theory," Erkenntnis 46, 97; "Critical Study of Quantum Non-Locality and Relativity by Tim Maudlin," Nous 31, 97; "Theoretical Unity: The Case of the Standard Model," Perspectives on Sci 4, 96; "Bayesianism and Diverse Evidence," Philos of Sci 62, 95. **CONTACT ADDRESS** Dept of Philos, Concordia Univ, Montreal, 1455 de Maisonneuve W, Montreal, PQ, H3G 1M8. **EMAIL** awayne@alcor.concordia.ca

WAYSDORF, SUSAN L.
DISCIPLINE FAMILY LAW AND HEALTH LAW **EDUCATION** Univ Chicago, AB, 72; Univ MD, JD, 91. **CAREER** Assoc prof, tchr & co-dir, HIV-AIDS/Publ Entitlements Clin; Skadden Arps fel & staff atty, Whitman-Walker Legal Serv Dept, Wash DC; adj prof, Howard Univ Sch Law & Am Univ WAsh Col Law; consulted, White House Off of Nat AIDS Policy & Domestic Policy Coun. **HONORS AND AWARDS** Helped to draft legislation affecting women and parents with AIDS, kinship care providers, and prisoners with AIDS. **MEMBERSHIPS** Expert on the issues of women, families and AIDS, and access to health care for the poor; served on the fac for, DC Bar training in family law, child custody, and AIDS advocacy. **SELECTED PUBLICATIONS** Publ on, issues of women, families and AIDS, and access to health care for the poor. **CONTACT ADDRESS** School of Law, Univ of District of Columbia, 4200 Connecticut Ave Northwest, Washington, DC, 20008.

WEATHERFORD, ROY C.
PERSONAL Born 05/30/1943, Middlebrook, AK, m, 1966, 1 child **DISCIPLINE** PHILOSOPHY **EDUCATION** Harvard Univ, PhD, 72. **CAREER** Prof, Univ of South Florida, 72-. **HONORS AND AWARDS** Danforth Grad Fel; Bechtel Prize in Philos. **MEMBERSHIPS** Fla Philos Asn; APA. **RESEARCH** Ethics; Epistemology. **SELECTED PUBLICATIONS** Auth, Philosophical Foundations of Probability Theory; The Implications of Determinism; World Peace and the Human Family. **CONTACT ADDRESS** Dept of Philosophy, Univ of South Florida, Tampa, FL, 33620. **EMAIL** Roy_Weatherford_PhD72@post.harvard.edu

WEATHERLY, JON A.
PERSONAL Born 11/29/1958, Indianapolis, IN, m, 1979, 2 children **DISCIPLINE** THEOLOGY **EDUCATION** Cincinnati Bible Col, BA, 81, MA, 82; Trinity Evangelical Divinity Sch, Mdiv, 84; Univ Aberdeen, PhD, 92. **CAREER** Assoc Min, Southside Christian Church, 84-87; from assoc prof to prof to chemn, 90-, Cincinnati Bible Col and Sem. **HONORS AND AWARDS** Excellence in Tchg Award; Greater Cincinnati Consortium of Colleges and Universities., Valedictorian, 81, Cincinnati Bible Col. **MEMBERSHIPS** Society of Biblical Literature; Evangelical Theological Society; Tyndale Fel. **RESEARCH** Theology of Luke-Acts; early Jewish-Christian relations. **SELECTED PUBLICATIONS** Auth, Monk, Mercenary or Missionary: How Do You Pay Your Preacher, 87; auth, The Jews in Luke-Acts, 89; auth, The Authenticity of 1 Thessalonians 2.13-16: Additional Evidence, 91; auth, Anti-Semitism, 92; rev, History, Literature and Society in the Books of Acts, 98. **CONTACT ADDRESS** Cincinnati Bible Col and Sem, 2700 Glenway Ave, Cincinnati, OH, 45204. **EMAIL** jon.weatherly@cincybible.edu

WEATHERSTON, MARTIN
PERSONAL Born 05/16/1956, Hamilton, ON, Canada, m, 3 children **DISCIPLINE** PHILOSOPHY **EDUCATION** Univ Toronto, BA, 79, MA, 82, PhD, 88. **CAREER** Asst prof, John Carroll Univ, 88-89; asst prof, Univ Toronto, 89-91; from asst prof to assoc prof to chemn, East Stroudsburg Univ, 92-. **MEMBERSHIPS** Heidegger Conf N Am, 97-. **RESEARCH** Heidegger; Kant. **SELECTED PUBLICATIONS** Auth, paper, Heidegger on Assertion and Kantian Institution, 91; auth, paper, The Rigour of Heidegger's Thought, 92; auth, paper, Formal Institutions and the Catergories, 93; auth, paper, Kant's Assessment of Music in the Critique of Judgement, 96. **CONTACT ADDRESS** Dept of Philosophy & Religious Studies, East Stroudsburg Univ of Pennsylvania, East Stroudsburg, PA, 18301. **EMAIL** mweather@esu.edu

WEAVER, DOROTHY JEAN
PERSONAL Born 01/21/1950, Harrisonburg, VA **DISCIPLINE** NEW TESTAMENT **EDUCATION** Union Theological Sem VA, PhD 87; Univ Berne Switzerland Ex Fel 81-82. **CAREER** Eastern Mennonite Seminary, prof 96-; Tantur Ecumenical Inst Jerusalem, vis sch 96; Near East Sch Theology Lebanon, vis prof, 95-96; Eastern Mennonite Sem, asst prof. assoc prof, 87-96; Assoc Biblical Seminaries, vis lect 86-87; Eastern Mennonite Sem, instr 84-86. **HONORS AND AWARDS** Berne Exch fel; union Theo Sem VA; Women's Lectshp; Assoc Menn Bib Sem. **MEMBERSHIPS** CBA; SBL; Matthew Gp mem. **RESEARCH** Gospel of Matthew; Narrative Criticism. **SELECTED PUBLICATIONS** Auth, Matthew's Missionary Discourse: A Literary Critical Analysis, Sheffield Eng, Sheffield Acad Press, 90; Between text and Sermon: John 18:1-19:42, Interpretation, 95; AIDS in the Congregation: Biblical Perspectives, Conrad Grebal Rev, 95; Power and Powerlessness: Matthew's Use of Irony in the Portrayal of Political Leaders, in: Treasures New and Old: Recent Contributions to Matthean Studies, eds, David R. Bauer and Mark Allen Powell, Atl GA, Sch Press, 96; rev, Households and Discipleship: A Study of Matthew, by Warren Carter, Sheffield JSOT Press, 94, and What They are Saying About Matthew's Sermon on the Mount? by Warren Carter, NY/Mahwah NJ, Paulist Press, 94, in: Crit Rev of Books In Religion, 96. **CONTACT ADDRESS** Dept of New Testament, Eastern Mennonite Univ, Harrisonburg, VA, 22802-2462. **EMAIL** weaverdj@emu.edu

WEAVER, J. DENNY
PERSONAL Born 03/20/1941, Kansas City, KS, m, 1965, 3 children **DISCIPLINE** RELIGION **EDUCATION** Goshen Col, BA, 63; Goshen Bibl Sem, MDiv, 70; Duke Univ, PhD, 75. **CAREER** Asst prof, 74-75, asst prof relig, 75-78, assoc prof relig, 78-83, prof relig, 83- , chemn dept of hist and relig, 93- , Goshen College; vis prof of theol, Canadian Mennonite Bible Col, 90-91. **MEMBERSHIPS** Am Soc of Church Hist; Am Acad of Relig; Conf on Faith and Hist; Mennonite Hist Soc. **RESEARCH** Contextual theologies; nonviolent theology; issues in Christology and atonement. **SELECTED PUBLICATIONS** Auth, The Socially Active Community: An Alternative Ecclesiology, in Sawatsky, ed, The Limits of Perfectionism: Conversations with J Lawrence Burkholder, Pandora, 93; auth, Christus Victor, Ecclesiology, and Christology, Mennonite Q Rev, 94; auth, Some Theological Implications of Christus Victor, Mennonite Q Rev, 94; auth, Narrative Theology in an Anabaptist-Mennonite Context, Conrad Grebel Rev, 94; auth, Understandings of Salvation: The Church, Pietistic Experience, and Non-Resistance, in Bowman, ed, Anabaptist Currents: History in Conversation with the Present, Bridgewater Col, 95; auth, The Anabaptist Vision: A Historical or a Theological Future, Conrad Grebel Rev, 95; auth, Amish and Mennonite Soteriology: Revivalism and Free Church Theologizing in the Nineteenth Century, Fides et Historia, 95; auth, Pacifism, in Hillerbrand, ed, The Oxford Encyclopedia of the Reformation, Oxford, 96; auth, Christus Victor, Nonviolence, and Other Religions, in, Weaver, ed, Mennonite Theology in Face of Modernity: Essays in Honor of Gordon D. Kaufman, Bethel Col, 96; auth, Peace-Shaped Theology, Faith and Freedom : A J of Christian Ethics, 96; auth, Keeping Salvation Ethical: Mennonite and Amish Atonement theology in the Late Nineteenth Century, Herald, 97; auth, Teaching for Peace, in Huebner, ed, Mennonite Education in a Post-Christian World: Essays Presented at the Consultation on Higher Education, Winnipeg, June 1997, CMBC Pub, 98; auth, Reading Sixteenth-Century Anabaptism Theologically: Implications for Modern Mennonites as a Peace Church, Conrad Grebel Rev, 98. **CONTACT ADDRESS** Bluffton Col, 280 W College Ave, Bluffton, OH, 45817-1196.

WEAVER, MARY JO
DISCIPLINE RELIGIOUS STUDIES **EDUCATION** Univ Notre Dame, PhD, 73. **CAREER** Prof. **RESEARCH** Roman Catholicism; contemporary Christianity; feminism and Christianity. **SELECTED PUBLICATIONS** Auth, New Catholic Women, 95; Springs of Water in a Dry Land, 92; Introduction to Christianity, 97. **CONTACT ADDRESS** Dept of Religious Studies, Indiana Univ, Bloomington, 300 N Jordan Ave, Bloomington, IN, 47405.

WEAVER, RUSSEL L.
PERSONAL Born 10/24/1952, Kansas City, MS, m, 1995, 2 children **DISCIPLINE** LAW **EDUCATION** Univ Missouri, BA, 74; Univ Missouri, J.D., cum laude, 78 **CAREER** Prof Law, Univ Louisville, 82-; **HONORS AND AWARDS** Order of the Coif; Missouri Law Rev; Judge Roy Harper Prize; Omar E. Robinson & Edward Jayne Scholar; President's Award, Univ Louisville, 93 & 98; Louis D. Brandeis School of Law Awards for scholarship, 92-93; Brown, Todd & Heyburn Fel, 95-97 **RESEARCH** Defamation, Free Speech, Aministrative Law **SELECTED PUBLICATIONS** Coauth, Readings in Criminal Law, Anderson, 98; coauth, Modern Remedies: Cases, Problems & Exercises, West, 97; coauth, Administrative Law and Practice: Problems and Cases, West, 97; coauth, Communications Law: Media, Entertainment & Regulation, Anderson, 97 **CONTACT ADDRESS** Louis Brandeis School of Law, Univ Louisville, Louisville, KY, 40292.

WEBB, EUGENE
PERSONAL Born 11/10/1938, Santa Monica, CA, m, 1964 **DISCIPLINE** COMPARATIVE LITERATURE, RELIGION **EDUCATION** Univ Calif, Los Angeles, BA, 60; Columbia Univ, MA, 26, PhD(comp lit), 65. **CAREER** Asst prof English, Simon Fraser Univ, 65-66; asst prof, 66 76, Prof Comp Relig & Comp Lit, Univ Wash, 76-. **MEMBERSHIPS** Am Acad Relig. **RESEARCH** Twentieth century English, German and French literature; 18th century English; philosophy of history. **SELECTED PUBLICATIONS** Auth, Samuel Beckett: A Study of His Novels, 70 & The Plays of Samuel Beckett, 72 Univ Wash; Peter Owen, London; The New Social-Psychology Of France + Girard,Rene - The Girardian-School, Religion, Vol 0023, 1993; The Dark Dove: The Sacred and Secular in Modern Lit, 75 & Eric Voegelin: Philosopher of History, 81, Univ Wash; Consciousness And Transcendence - The Theology Of Voegelin,Eric - Morrissey,Mp, Journal Of Religion, Vol 0075, 1995; In Search Of The Classic - Reconsidering The Greco-Roman Tradition, Homer To Valery And Beyond - Shankman,S, Comparative Literature, Vol 0048, 1996. **CONTACT ADDRESS** Dept of English, Univ of Washington, Seattle, WA, 98195.

WEBB, GISELA
PERSONAL Born 07/15/1949, San Juan, Puerto Rico, m, 2 children **DISCIPLINE** ISLAMIC STUDIES, COMPARATIVE RELIGION STUDIES, PHILOSOPHY OF MYSTICISM **EDUCATION** Temple Univ, PhD, 89. **CAREER** Assoc prof Dept Relig Stud, Seton Hall Univ, 89-; Phi Beta Kappa; NEH award. **MEMBERSHIPS** AAR; MESA; ACSIS. **RESEARCH** Medieval and contemporary developments of mysticism, esp Sufism womens studies. **SELECTED PUBLICATIONS** Tradition and Innovation in Contemporary American Islamic Spirituality, Muslim Communities in North America, SUNY Press, 94; Islam, Sufism, & Subud, Am Alternative Relig, SUNY Press, 95. **CONTACT ADDRESS** 125 Union Ave, Bala Cynwyd, PA, 19004. **EMAIL** webbgise@shu.edu

WEBBER, GEORGE WILLIAMS
PERSONAL Born 05/02/1920, Des Moines, IA, m, 1943, 5 children **DISCIPLINE** CHRISTIAN ETHICS **EDUCATION** Harvard Col, AB, 42; Union Theol Sem, MDiv, 48; Columbia Univ, PhD, 63. **CAREER** Mem fac, Union Theol Sem, 48-73; Pres, NY Theol Sem, 69-, Group ministry, E Harlem Protestant Parish, 48-65; dir, Metrop Urban Serv Tr, 65-69. **HONORS AND AWARDS** STD, Gen Theol Sem, 69; DD, Yale Univ, 81. **SELECTED PUBLICATIONS** Auth, God's Colony in Man's World, 60, Congregation in Mission, 64 & Today's Church, 79, Abingdon; Led by the Spirit, Pilgrim Books, 90. **CONTACT ADDRESS** New York Theol Sem, 5 W 29th St, New York, NY, 10001-4501.

WEBER, LEONARD J.
DISCIPLINE ETHICS **EDUCATION** Josephinum Col, BA; Marquette Univ, MA; McMaster Univ, PhD. **CAREER** Prof,dir, Univ Detroit Mercy, 72-. **RESEARCH** Practical ethical issues in health care, management, and public service. **CONTACT ADDRESS** Dept of Philosophy, Univ of Detroit Mercy, 4001 W McNichols Rd, PO Box 19900, Detroit, MI, 48219-0900. **EMAIL** WEBERLJ@udmercy.edu

WEBER, MARK E.
PERSONAL Born 09/26/1960, Rapid City, SD, m, 1982, 2 children **DISCIPLINE** PHILOSOPHY **EDUCATION** Whenton Coll, BA, 82; Yale Univ, MA, 85; Boston Univ, PhD, 92. **CAREER** Adj asst prof, Univ Conn; Quinnipiac Coll; Sacred Heart Univ; Univ New Haven. **MEMBERSHIPS** Am Philos Asn; Soc for Philos and Psychol. **RESEARCH** Wittgenstein; Philosophy of Mind. **SELECTED PUBLICATIONS** Wittgenstein on Language: Games of Visual Sensation and Language - Games of Visual Objects, Southern J of Philos, 93; Representation and Intention: Wittgenstein on what makes a picture of a target, Southern J of Philos, 98. **CONTACT ADDRESS** 184 Foster St, New Haven, CT, 06511. **EMAIL** weberme@aol.com

WEBER, MICHAEL
PERSONAL Born 03/27/1965, Toronto, ON, Canada **DISCIPLINE** PHILOSOPHY **EDUCATION** Williams Col, BA, 87; Oxford Univ, BA, 90; Univ Mich, PhD, 98. **CAREER** Asst prof, Yale Univ, 98- . **HONORS AND AWARDS** Mellon Fel, 90. **MEMBERSHIPS** APA. **RESEARCH** Ethics, political philosophy. **SELECTED PUBLICATIONS** Auth, The Resilience of the Atlais Paradox, Ethics, 98. **CONTACT ADDRESS** Dept of Philosophy, Yale Univ, New Haven, CT, 06520. **EMAIL** michael.weber@yale.edu

WEBER, THEODORE R.
PERSONAL Born 06/07/1928, New Orleans, LA, m, 1955, 2 children **DISCIPLINE** THEOLOGY **EDUCATION** Louisana St Univ, BA, 47; Yale Univ, BD, 50, MA, 56, PhD, 58. **CAREER** Pastor, Louisana & Conn, 45-56; prof, soc ethics, 58-97, Candler Schl of Theol, Emory Univ; ministeral staff, 92-93, St Giles Cathedral, Edinburgh; adj prof, 97- Chinese Univ, Hong Kong. **HONORS AND AWARDS** Pres, Soc of Christian Ethics, U.S. & Can, 88; Emory Williams Dist Tchr Award, 87; hon vis scholar, New Col Edinburgh Univ, 92-. **MEMBERSHIPS** Soc of Christian Ehics, Societas Ethica; Soc for the Stud of Christian Ethics. **RESEARCH** Christian political thought; John Wesley's ethics; Reinhold Niebuhr; just war theory. **SELECTED PUBLICATIONS** Auth, Truth & Political Leadership, Pres Address to Soc of Christian Ethics in the U. S. & Can, Ann of Soc of Christian Ethics, 89; auth, Christian Realism, Power, & Peace, Theo Pol & Peace, Orbis Books, 89; auth, Thinking Theologically about International Development, Making of an Economic Vision: John Paul II's On Soc Concern, Univ Press of Amer, 91; art, Political Order in Ordo Sahutis; A Wesleyan Theory of Political Institutions, J of Church & State 3T, 95; auth, Politics in the Order of Salvation: Transforming Wesleyan Pol Ethics, Abingdon Press, 99. **CONTACT ADDRESS** 1641 Ridgewood Dr NE, Atlanta, GA, 30307-1250. **EMAIL** reltrw@emory.edu

WEBER, TIMOTHY P
PERSONAL Born 05/25/1947, Los Angeles, LA, m, 1968, 2 children **DISCIPLINE** THEOLOGY **EDUCATION** UCLA, BA, 69; Fuller Theol Sem, M Div, 72; Univ Chicago, MA, 74, PhD, 76. **CAREER** Asst, assoc, prof, 76-92, Denver Sem; David T Porter Prof, Church hist, 92-96, S Baptist Theol Sem; vice pres, acad affairs, dean of sem, prof, 97-, N Baptist Theol Sem. **RESEARCH** General hist of Christianity; Amer relig hist, evangelicalism, fundamentalism, millennial movements. **CONTACT ADDRESS** Northern Baptist Sem, 660 # Butterfield Rd, Lombard, IL, 60148. **EMAIL** tpweber@northern.seminary.edu

WEBERMAN, DAVID
PERSONAL Born 07/02/1955, Detroit, MI, s **DISCIPLINE** LAW **EDUCATION** Univ of Munich, MA, 82; Columbia Univ, M Phil, 87, PhD, 90. **CAREER** Asst prof, Univ Wisc, 90-98; Fel, Law & Philosophy, Harvard Univ, 98-99. **MEMBERSHIPS** Amer Philos Asn; Soc Phenomenol & Existential Philos. **RESEARCH** 20th Century European philosophy; Philosophy of history; Law interpretation. **SELECTED PUBLICATIONS** Auth, Historische Objektivitat, Peter Lang, 91; Foucault's Reconception of Power, Philos Forum, 95; Heidegger and the Disclosive Character of the Emotions, The S Jour of Philos, 96; Sartre, Emotions and Wallowing, Amer Philos Quart, 96; Liberal Democracy, Autonomy and Ideology Critique, Soc Theory and Practice, 97; The Non-Fixity of the Historical Past, Rev of Metaphysics, 97. **CONTACT ADDRESS** Law Sch, Harvard Univ, ILS 149, Cambridge, MA, 02138. **EMAIL** weberman@law.harvard.edu

WEBSTER, WILLIAM H.
PERSONAL Born 10/26/1946, New York, NY, m **DISCIPLINE** LAW **EDUCATION** New York Univ, BA (cum laude), 1972; Univ of California, Berkeley, School of Law, JD, 1975. **CAREER** Black Law Journal, UCLA & Univ of California at Berkeley, research assoc, 1973; Natl Economic Devel & Law Project, post-grad, 1974-76; Natl Economic Devel & Law Center, Berkeley, CA, atty, 1976-82; Hunter & Anderson, partner, 1983-; Webster & Anderson, managing partner, 1993-. **HONORS AND AWARDS** Martin Luther King Fellowship; New York State Regents Incentive Awards; Howard Memorial Fund Scholarship; Alpha Phi Alpha Scholarship. **MEMBERSHIPS** Past mem bd of dirs, Natl Training Inst for Comm Economic Devel, Artisans Cooperative Inc; past mem, Mayor's Housing Task Force Berkeley; mem, State Bar of California, US Dist Ct No Dist of California, US Tax Ct, Natl Assoc of Bond Lawyers, Natl Bar Assoc, Charles Houston Bar Assn; past mem, City of Berkeley Citizens Comm on Responsible Investments; Kappa Alpha Psi. **SELECTED PUBLICATIONS** "Tax Savings through Intercorporate Billing," Economic Devel Law Center Report, 1980; pub, "Housing, Structuring a Housing Development," Economic Devel Law Center Report, 1978; various other publications. **CONTACT ADDRESS** Webster & Anderson Law Office, 469 Ninth St, Ste 240, Oakland, CA, 94607.

WECHSLER, BURTON D.
DISCIPLINE CONSTITUTIONAL LAW **EDUCATION** Univ Mich, AB, 47; Harvard Law Sch, JD, 49 **CAREER** Prof, Am Univ. **HONORS AND AWARDS** Alumni Distinguished Tchr Award; Outstanding Tchr Award Am Univ, Wash Col Law, 92, 90, 89, 88, 84, 80, 79; Outstanding Tchr Award, 96, 94. Outstanding Fac Award Outstanding Tchg, Am Univ, 95. **RESEARCH** Constitutional Law; Federal Courts; First Amendment. **SELECTED PUBLICATIONS** Auth, Federal Courts, State Criminal Law, and the First Amendment, NY Law Rev; Justice Douglas, A Tribute; Antioch Law Jour; ed, Abortion Law Rep. **CONTACT ADDRESS** American Univ, 4400 Massachusetts Ave, Washington, DC, 20016.

WECKMAN, GEORGE
PERSONAL Born 03/20/1939, Philadelphia, PA **DISCIPLINE** HISTORY OF RELIGION **EDUCATION** Philadelphia Lutheran Sem, BD, 63; Univ Chicago, PhD, 69. **CAREER** Asst prof Philos, 68-72, assoc prof, 72- , Ohio Univ. **MEMBERSHIPS** AAR. **RESEARCH** Monasticism. **SELECTED PUBLICATIONS** Auth, My Brothers' Place: An American Lutheran Monastery, Lawrenceville, VA, Brunswick Publ Corp, 92; Reduction in the Classroom, in Religion and Reductionism: essays on Eliade, Segal, and the Challenge of the Social Sciences for the Study of Religion, ed, Thomas A. Idinopulos and Edward Yonan, Leiden, E.J. Brill, 94, 211-219; Respect of Ohters' Sacreds, in The Sacred and its Scholars, ed Thomas A. Idinopulos and Edward Yonan, Leiden, E.J. Brill, 96. **CONTACT ADDRESS** Dept of Philosophy, Ohio Univ, 19 Park Pl, Athens, OH, 45701. **EMAIL** gweckman@ohiou.edu

WECKSTEIN, DONALD THEODORE
PERSONAL Born 03/15/1932, Newark, NJ, m, 1993, 4 children **DISCIPLINE** LAW **EDUCATION** Univ WI-Madison, BBA, 54; Univ TX, Austin, JD, 58; Yale Univ, LLM, 59. **CAREER** Asst prof law, Sch Law, Univ CT, 59-62; assoc prof, Col Law, Univ TN, 62-67; prof, Sch Law, Univ CT, 67-72; dean, 72-81, Prof Law, Sch Law, Univ San Diego, 72-; consult, Admin Conf US, 69-72; chmn, San Diego County Employee Rels Panel, 73-75; arbitrator labor, Fed Mediation Conciliation Serv, 77. **HONORS AND AWARDS** Phi Delta Phi (Honors) Legal Fraternity, Univ TX, 56-58; First Prize, Nathan Burkan Copyright Competition, Univ TX, 57; Am Jurisprudence Award, Public Utilities, Univ TX, 57. **MEMBERSHIPS** Am Arbit Asn; Indust Rel Res Asn; SPIDR; Nat Acad Arbitrators; Asn Am Law Sch; CA Dispute Resolution Coun; Southern Calif Mediation Asn; Int Soc for Labor Law & Social Security; Dispute Resolution Forum of San Diego; Am Bar Asn; San Diego County Bar Asn; Calif State Bar; TX Bar Asn; served as Ch, mem Bd Dir, Pres, and other numerous positions in many of these and other past orgs. **RESEARCH** Fed court jurisdiction; legal profession and ethics; labor law and arbitration; alternative dispute resolution. **SELECTED PUBLICATIONS** Ed, Education in the Professional Responsibilities of the Lawyer, Univ Va, 70; coauth, Moore's Federal Practice, Matthew Bender, 2nd ed, 64; coauth, Professional Responsibility in a Nutshell, West Publ Co, 80, 2nd ed, 91; author of numerous articles. **CONTACT ADDRESS** Sch of Law, Univ of San Diego, 5998 Alcala Park, San Diego, CA, 92110-2492. **EMAIL** donaldw@acusd.edu

WEDDLE, DAVID L.
PERSONAL Born 01/27/1942, m, 2 children **DISCIPLINE** RELIGION **EDUCATION** Grace Bible Col, Grand Rapids, Mich, BRE, 64; Hope Col, Holland Mich, BA, 66; Harvard Univ, MA, 70, PhD, 73. **CAREER** Asst prof relig stud, Westmont Col, 70-72; lectr relig stud, Univ Calif, 73; asst prof, 73-78, assoc prof, 78-84, prof of religion, 84- , Cornell Col. **HONORS AND AWARDS** Summa Cum Laude, 66; res scholar reading prog of Cedar Rapids Public Lib, funded by US Inst for Peace, 94-95; Norman & Richard Small Senior Faculty Chair, Cornell Col, 98-00. **MEMBERSHIPS** Am Acad Relig; Am Soc of Church Hist; Am Theol Soc; Middle East Stud Asn. **RESEARCH** American religion; Christian theology; Islam. **SELECTED PUBLICATIONS** Auth, Jonathan Edwards on Men and Trees and the Problem of Solidarity, Harvard Theol Rev, 74; auth, The Image of the Self in Jonathan Edwards: A Study of Autobiography and Theology, J of the Am Acad of Relig, 75; auth, The Beauty of Faith in Jonathan Edwards, Ohio J of Relig Stud, 76; auth, The Democracy of Grace: Political Reflections on the Evangelical Theology of Jonathan Edwards, Dialog, 76; auth, The Law and the Revival: A new Divinity for the Settlements, Church Hist, 78; auth, The Liberator as Exorcist: James Cone and the Classic Doctrine of the Atonement, Relig in Life, 80; auth, Christians in Liberal Education, Relig Educ, 85; auth, The Law as Gospel: Revival and Reform in the Theology of Charles G. Finney, Scarecrow, 85; auth, The Melancholy Saint: Jonathan Edwards' Interpretation of David Brainerd as a Model of Evangelical Spirituality, Harvard Theol Rev, 88; auth, The Christian Science Textbook: An Analysis of the Religious Authority of Science and Health by Mary Baker Eddy, Harvard Theol Rev, 91. **CONTACT ADDRESS** 1181 Abbe Creek Rd, Mt Vernon, IA, 52314-9726. **EMAIL** weddle@cornell-iowa.edu

WEDGWOOD, RALPH N.
PERSONAL Born 12/10/1964, Vancouver, BC, Canada, s **DISCIPLINE** PHILOSOPHY **EDUCATION** Oxford Univ, BA, 87; King's Col London, MA, 89; Cornell Univ, PhD, 94. **CAREER** UCLA, vis asst prof, 93-94; Univ of Stirling Scotland, lectr, 94-95; MIT, asst prof, 95-. **HONORS AND AWARDS** NHC fel. **MEMBERSHIPS** APA, BSET. **RESEARCH** Ethics and political philosophy; metaphysics. **SELECTED PUBLICATIONS** Auth, The A Priori Rules of Ra-

tionality, Philosophy and Phenomenological Research, forthcoming; auth, The Fundamental Argument for Same-Sex Marriage, Jour Polit Philos, 98; auth, The Essence of Response-Dependence, Euro Rev Philos, 97; auth, The Fundamental Principle of Practical Reasoning, Intl Jour Philos Stud, 98; auth, Same-Sex Marriage: A Philosophical Defense, Philosophy and Sex, rev ed. 98; auth, Non-Cognitivism, Truth and Logic, Philos Stud, 97; auth, Theories of Content and Theories of Motivation, Euro Jour Philos, 98. **CONTACT ADDRESS** Dept of Philosophy and Linguistics, Massachusetts Inst of Tech, Cambridge, MA, 02139. **EMAIL** wedgwood@mit.edu

WEEKES, MARTIN EDWARD
PERSONAL Born 06/06/1933, New York, NY, m, 1984 **DISCIPLINE** LAW **EDUCATION** Manhattan Coll NY, BS 1954; Univ of So CA, JD 1961. **CAREER** Douglas Aircraft Santa Monica CA, engr draftsman 1956-60; Charles Meram Co Los Angeles, engr 1960-62; Deputy District Atty 1962-63; Div Chief; Co Counsel 1963-. **HONORS AND AWARDS** Rector's Award Episcopal Ch of the Advent 1967; Finished Second in All-Army Talent Contest 1956. **MEMBERSHIPS** First pres Frederick Douglass Child Devel Cntr 1963; mem bd dir Rose Brooks Sch of Performing Arts 1974-; mem Reserve Faculty EPA; Lectured on Environmental Law; guest lecturer USC; **SELECTED PUBLICATIONS** Twenty publications Library of Congress; contrib author CA Adminstr Agency Practice CEB. **CONTACT ADDRESS** County Counsel, LA County, 648 Hall of Administration, Los Angeles, CA, 90012.

WEEMS, VERNON EUGENE, JR.
PERSONAL Born 04/27/1948, Waterloo, IA, s **DISCIPLINE** LAW **EDUCATION** Univ of IA, BA 1970; Univ of Miami Sch of Law, JD 1974. **CAREER** US Small Business Admin, atty/advisor 1977-78, 1979-81; A Nation United Inc, pres/ceo/chmn bd 1982-85; Weems Law Office, Attorney 1978-; Weems Productions and Enterprises, ceo/consultant 1987-. **HONORS AND AWARDS** Recognition of Excellence 1986. **MEMBERSHIPS** Mem Amer Bar Assoc 1977-82, IA State Bar Assoc 1977-82, St Johns Lodge Prince Hall Affil 1977-86, Federal Bar Assoc 1979-82; mem bd of dirs Black Hawk County Iowa Branch NAACP. **SELECTED PUBLICATIONS** Publication "Tax Amnesty Blueprint for Economic Development," 1981; Leadership Awd OIC/Iowa 1982; Service Appreciation Awd Job Service of Iowa 1985; article "Chapter 11 Tax Subsidies," 1986. **CONTACT ADDRESS** Weems Productions/Enterprises, PO Box 72, Waterloo, IA, 50704-0072.

WEIBE, PHILLIP H.
PERSONAL Born 08/23/1945, MB, Canada, m, 1968, 2 children **DISCIPLINE** PHILOSOPHY **EDUCATION** Univ Adelaide (philos), PhD, 73. **CAREER** Asst prof philos, Brandon Univ, Manitoba, 73-78; assoc prof philos, 78-88, FULL PROF, TRINITY WESTERN UNIV, LANGLEY, BC, 88-. **HONORS AND AWARDS** Commonwealth Scholarship to Australia, 70-73. **MEMBERSHIPS** Can Philos Asn; Am Academy Relig. **RESEARCH** Philosophical theology; philosophy of science. **SELECTED PUBLICATIONS** Auth, Hempel and Instantial Confirmation, Philos Res Archives, 2, 76; Criteria of Strengthening Evidence, Philos Res Archives, 4, 78; Theism in an Age of Science, Univ Press Am, 88; Jesus' Divorce Exception, The J of the Evangelical Theol Soc, 32, 89; Existential Assumptions for Aristotelian Logic, The J of Philos Res, 16, 91; Authenticating Biblical Reports of Miracles, The J of Philos Res, 17, 92; Visions of Jesus: Direct Encounters from the New Testament to Today, Oxford Univ Press, 97. **CONTACT ADDRESS** Trinity Western Univ, 7600 Glover Rd., Langley, BC, V3A 6H4. **EMAIL** pweibe@twu.ca

WEIDNER, DONALD JOHN
PERSONAL Born 06/15/1945, Brooklyn, NY, m, 1976, 1 child **DISCIPLINE** LAW **EDUCATION** Fordham Univ, BS, 66; Univ Tex, Austin, JD, 69. **CAREER** Assoc, Willkie, Farr & Gallagher, New York, 69-70; Bigelow fel, Univ Chicago, 70-71; asst prof, Univ SC, 71-74; assoc prof, Cleveland State Univ, 74-76; assoc prof, 76-78, Prof Law, Fla State Univ, 78-, Consult, SC State Housing authorities, 73-74; vis prof law, Univ NMex, 79 & Stanford Univ, 81-82. **MEMBERSHIPS** Am Law Inst. **RESEARCH** Partnership taxation; tax policy; property. **SELECTED PUBLICATIONS** Auth, Yearend sales of losses in real estate partnerships, Univ Ill Law Forum, 74; Realty shelter partnerships in a nutshell, Ind Law Rev, 75; Partnerships allocations and tax reform, Fla State Univ Rev, 77; Pratt and deductions for payments to partners, Real Property, Probate & Trust J, 77; Realty shelters: Nonrecourse financing, tax reform and profit purpose, Southwestern Law J, 78; coauth, Real Estate: Taxation and Bankruptcy, West Publ Co, 79; auth, Transfers of partnership interests and optional adjustments to basis, NMex Law Rev, 80; Partnership allocations and capital accounts analysis, Ohio State Law J, 81; The Revised Uniform Partnership Act - The Reporters Overview, Business Lawyer, Vol 0049, 1993; A Deans Letter To New Law Faculty About Scholarship, Journal Of Legal Education, Vol 0044, 1994; Rupa And Fiduciary Duty - The Texture Of Relationship, Law And Contemporary Problems, Vol 0058, 1995; The Crises Of Legal-Education - A Wake-Up Call For Faculty, Journal Of Legal Education, Vol 0047, 1997. **CONTACT ADDRESS** Col of Law, Florida State Univ, 600 W College Ave, Tallahassee, FL, 32306-1096.

WEIL, LOUIS
DISCIPLINE LITURGICS **EDUCATION** S Methodist Univ, BMus; Harvard Univ, AM; Gen Theol Sem, Peritus Sacrae Liturgiae, Magister Sacrae Liturgiae, STB; Inst Cath de Paris, STD. **CAREER** James F. Hodges prof, Church Divinity Sch Pacific. **SELECTED PUBLICATIONS** Auth, Shape and Focus in Eucharistic Celebration, A Prayer Book for the Twenty-first Century, Church Hymnal Corp, 96; The Place of the Liturgy in Michael Ramsey's Theology, Michael Ramsey as Theologian, Darton, Longman and Todd, 95; The Contribution of the Anglican Theological Review in Recent Liturgical Perspective, Anglican Theol Rev, 94; Reclaiming the Larger Trinitarian Framework of Baptism, Creation and Liturgy, Pastoral Press, 93; Baptism and Mission, Growing in Newness of Life, Anglican Bk Ctr, 93; A Larger Vision of Apostolicity: The End of an Anglo-Catholic Illusion, Fountain of Life, Pastoral Press, 91. **CONTACT ADDRESS** Church Divinity Sch of the Pacific, 2451 Ridge Rd, Berkeley, CA, 94709-1217.

WEILER, JOSEPH
DISCIPLINE LAW **EDUCATION** Univ Toronto, BA, 69; Osgoode Univ, LLB, 72; Univ Calif, LLM, 74. **CAREER** Asst prof, 74-79; assoc prof, 79-87; prof, 87-. **HONORS AND AWARDS** Dir, Pacific Inst Law Pub Policy; dir, Asia Pacific Bus Inst, 85-87. **MEMBERSHIPS** Can Bar Asn. **RESEARCH** Labour law; conflict resolution. **SELECTED PUBLICATIONS** Auth, pubs about labour law, criminal law, and sports and entertainment law. **CONTACT ADDRESS** Fac of Law, Univ British Columbia, 1822 East Mall, Vancouver, BC, V6T 1Z1. **EMAIL** weiler@law.ubc.ca

WEIMA, JEFFREY A.D.
PERSONAL Born 07/16/1960, m, 1983, 5 children **DISCIPLINE** THEOLOGY **EDUCATION** Brock Univ, BA, 83; Calvin Theol Sem, M Div, 86; Th M, 87; St. Michael's Col, Univ Toronto, PhD, 92. **CAREER** Instr, relig & theol, Redeemer Col, 88-92; asst prof, 92-94, assoc prof, 94-, new testament, Calvin Theol Sem. **HONORS AND AWARDS** Grant, Fac Heritage Fund, Calvin Theol Sem, 96, 98; Developing Your Role As A Scholar, 95; grant, Calvin Alumni Asn, 95; doctoral fel, Social Sci and Humanities Res Coun, Canada, 91; Founders' prize, 90; doctoral fel, Wycliffe Col, Univ Toronto, 87-90; Ontario Grad Scholar, Govt of Ontario, 87-90. **MEMBERSHIPS** Soc of Bibl Lit; Chicago Soc of Bibl Res; Inst for Bibl Res; Evangel Theol Soc. **SELECTED PUBLICATIONS** Monogr, co-auth, An Annotated Bibliography of 1 and 2 Thessalonians, New Testament Tools and Studies, 26, Leiden, Brill, 98; monogr, Neglected Endings: The Significance of the Pauline Letter Closings, Jour for the Study of the New Testament suppl series 101, Sheffield, JSOT Press, 94; article, An Apology for the Apologetic Function of 1 Thessalonians 2:1-12, Jour for the Study of the New Testament, 68.4, 73-99, 97; rev, First and Second Thessalonians, Jour of Bibl Lit, 116.4, 761-763, 97; article, The Letter to Diognetus, Dict of the Later New Testament & Its Developments, InterVarsity, 302-304, 97; article, What Does Aristotle Have to Do with Paul? An Evaluation of Rhetorical Criticism, Calvin Theol Jour, 32.2, 458-468, 97; rev, Comfort One Another. Reconstructing the Rhetoric and Audience of 1 Thessaloanians, Jour of the Evangel Theol Soc 39, 482-483, 96; article, How You Must Walk to Please God: Holiness and Discipleship in 1 Thessalonians, Patterns of Discipleship in the New Testament, 98-119, Eerdmans, 96; article, Two Challenges to Our Reformed Heritage, Calvin Sem Forum 3, 1-2, 96; article, 30 Meditations, Today, 45.2, 95; article, The Pauline Letter Closings: Analysis and Hermeneutical Significance, Bull for Bibl Res, 5, 177-198, 95; article, Preaching the Gospel in Rome: A Study of the Epistolary Framework of Romans, Gospel in Paul Studies in Galatians, Corinthians and Romans for Richard N. Longenecker, JSOT Press, 350-380, 94. **CONTACT ADDRESS** Calvin Theol Sem, 3233 Burton St. SE, Grand Rapids, MI, 49546. **EMAIL** weimje@calvin.edu

WEINBERG, HAROLD R.
PERSONAL Born 11/15/1943, Louisville, KY **DISCIPLINE** LAW **EDUCATION** Case Western Reserve Univ, AB, 66, JD, 69; Univ Ill, LLM, 75. **CAREER** Assoc, Ulmer, Berne, Laronge, Glickman & Curtis, 69-71; grad teaching asst, Col Law, Ill, 71-72; asst prof, 72-76, assoc prof, 76-80, Prof Law, Col Law, Univ KY, 80-, Univ Chicago fel law & econ, 78-79; consult, Ky Legis Res Comn, 79-80. **MEMBERSHIPS** Am Soc Legal Hist; Asn Am Law Sch. **RESEARCH** Commercial law; antitrust law; American legal history. **SELECTED PUBLICATIONS** Auth, Tort claims as intangible property: An exploration from an assignee's perspective, 64 Ky Law J 49, 75; Secured party's right to sue third persons for damage to or defects in collateral, 81 Commun Law J 445, 76; Toward maximum facilitation or intent to create enforceable article nine security interests, 18 BC Ind & Commun Law Rev 1, 76; The New law and economics, Rev, 79; Sales law, economics, and the negotiability of goods, 9 J Legis Studies 569, 80; Markets overt, voidable titles, and feckless agents: Judges and efficiency in the antebellum doctrine of good faith purchase, 56 Tulane Law Rev 1, 81; Commercial paper in economic theory and legal history, 70 Ky Law J 1, 81; Legislative-Process And Commercial-Law - Lessons From The Copyright Act Of 1976 And The Uniform-Commercial-Code, Business Lawyer, Vol 0048, 1993. **CONTACT ADDRESS** Sch Law, Temple Univ, Philadelphia, PA, 19122.

WEINBERG, STEVEN
PERSONAL Born 05/03/1933, New York, NY, m, 1 child **DISCIPLINE** THEORETICAL PHYSICS **EDUCATION** AB, Cornell Univ, 54; PhD, Princeton Univ, 57. **CAREER** Josey Regental Prof Sci, Univ TX, 82-; Morris Loeb Vis Prof Physics, Harvard Univ, 83-; Harvard Univ, Higgns Prof Physics, 73-83; Smithsonian Astrophysical Observatory, Sr Sci, 73-83. **HONORS AND AWARDS** Andrew Gemant Award; Natl Medal Of Sci; Nobel Prize in Physics. **MEMBERSHIPS** Matl Acad of Sci; Royal Soc; Am Philos Soc. **RESEARCH** Theoretical Physics. **SELECTED PUBLICATIONS** The Quantum Theory of Fields, Vol 1: Foundations, Cambridge Univ Press, 95; Dreams of a Final Theory, Pantheon, NY, 93; Brazilian ed: Sonhos de uma Teoria Final, 96; Czech ed: Sneni o finalni teorii, 96; Greek ed: (Katoptro; Eyewitness, 67, George, 97: 70; Changing Attitudes and the Standard Model, in the Rise of the Standard Model, L Hoddeson, L Brown, M Rirodan and M Dresden, eds, Cambridge Univ Press, 97; Vor dem Urknall, NZZ Folio Nr 12, 97; Physics and History, Daedalus 127, 98. **CONTACT ADDRESS** Univ Texas, Austin, TX, 78712. **EMAIL** weinberg@physics.utexas.edu

WEINBERGER, LEON JUDAH
PERSONAL Born 08/23/1926, Przemysl, Poland, m, 1954, 3 children **DISCIPLINE** PHILOSOPHY, RELIGION **EDUCATION** Clark Univ, BA, 57; Brandeis Univ, MA, 59, PhD(Near E), 63; Jewish Theol Sem, MHL, 64. **CAREER** From asst prof to assoc prof relig, 64-72, acting head dept relig, 70-71, res grants, 66 & 69, Prof Relig Studies, Univ Ala, 72-, Resource consult teacher educ, Nat Coun Relig & Pub Educ, 72; proj dir, Nat Endowment Humanities grant, 72-73; assoc, Danforth Found, 73; chmn, New Col Rev Bd, Univ Ala, 73-76; gen ed Judaic studies, Univ Ala Press, 74-; Am Acad Jewish Res publ grants, 75 & 78. **HONORS AND AWARDS** Algernon Sydney Sullivan Award, 78. **MEMBERSHIPS** Am Orient Soc; Am Acad Relig. **RESEARCH** Hebrew language and literature; Middle East; comparative religion. **SELECTED PUBLICATIONS** Auth, The Death of Moses in the Synagogue Liturgy, Ann Arbor Publ, 63; Hebrew Poetry in Byzantium, Part I (Hebrew), Hebrew Union Col Annual, 68; On the Provenance of Benjamin B Samuel Qushtani, Jewish Quart Rev, 79; Some beliefs and opinions in the Romaniote liturgy, Hebrew studies, 79; A New Source on the Return to Zion Movement in 13th Century Kastoria (Hebrew), Hadoar, 79; Romaniote Penitential Poetry, Am Acad Jewish Res, 80; Themes in Jewish mysticism in the Romaniote Liturgy (Hebrew), Bitzaron, 80; Mesianic Expectations in Kastoria on the Eve of Sabbatianism, In: Go and Study, Essays and Studies in Honor of Alfred Jospe, Ktav, 80; Karaite Piyyut In Southeastern Europe + Evidence Of Karaite Liturgical Poetic Influence From Rabbanite Neoplatonist Form, Language, And Rhetoric, Jewish Quarterly Review, Vol 0083, 1992; Dari,Moses Moses-Ben-Abraham-Ben-Saadia-Ha-Rofe-Dari, Karaite Poet And Physician + A Study On 13th-Century Medieval Karaism And The Writings Of The Hispanic-Hebrew Rabbanites, Jewish Quarterly Review, Vol 0084, 1994. **CONTACT ADDRESS** Dept of Relig Studies, Univ of Ala, PO Box 6173, University, AL, 35486.

WEINER, NEAL O.
PERSONAL Born 07/24/1942, Baltimore, MD, 2 children **DISCIPLINE** PHILOSOPHY, CLASSICS **EDUCATION** St John's Col, Md, BA, 64; Univ Tex, PhD, 68. **CAREER** Asst prof philos, State Univ NY Col Old Westbury, 68-70; Assoc Prof Philos, Marlboro Col, 70-, Vis assoc prof philos, St Mary's Col, Notre Dame, IN, 77-78; tutor, Grad Inst St John's Col, NM, 78. **HONORS AND AWARDS** Wilson Fellow; Danforth Fellow. **MEMBERSHIPS** Am Philos Asn; Northern New Eng Philos Asn. **RESEARCH** Class philos; psychiatry and ethics. **SELECTED PUBLICATIONS** Auth, The Articulation of Thought, Marlboro Col, 86; The Harmony of the Soul, SUNY, 93 **CONTACT ADDRESS** Dept of Philos, Marlboro Col, General Delivery, Marlboro, VT, 05344-9999.

WEINER, ROBERT
PERSONAL Born 07/30/1950, New Haven, CT, m, 1990, 2 children **DISCIPLINE** PHILOSOPHY, RELIGION, HUMANITIES **EDUCATION** Johns Hopkins Univ, BA, 72; Georgetown Univ, MA, 73; Yale Univ, MA, 75; Univ Cologne, PhD, 81. **CAREER** Editor, Global Digest Intl News Services, 81-84; lect, Calif State Univ, Sonoma, 88-92; lect, coord Lib Stud, Saint Mary's Col, 85-96; chair lib arts, John F. Kennedy Univ, 97-. **MEMBERSHIPS** Am Phil Asn; Asn Integrative Stud; Mod Lang Asn; Nat Coun Teach Eng. **RESEARCH** Creativity, interdisciplinary curricular design, global social change, Leonardo da Vinci. **SELECTED PUBLICATIONS** Auth, "Western & Contemporary Global Conceptions of Creativity in Relief Against Approaches from So-Called 'Traditional' Cultures," in Issues in Integrative Stud, 15, 97; auth, "The Interdisciplinary Tree Exercise," in Developing Adult Learners, 99; auth, Creativity and Beyond, Suny Press, 99. **CONTACT ADDRESS** 5439 Carlton St, Oakland, CA, 94618. **EMAIL** rweiner@jfku.edu

WEINREB, LLOYD L.
PERSONAL Born 10/09/1936, New York, NY, m, 1963, 3 children **DISCIPLINE** LAW, PHILOSOPHY **EDUCATION** Dartmouth Col, BA, 57; Univ Oxford, BA, 59, MA, 63; Har-

vard Law Sch, LLB, 62. **CAREER** Asst prof law, 65-68, prof law, 68-93, dane prof law, Harvard Law Sch 93-. **RESEARCH** Law; political philosophy; legal philosophy. **SELECTED PUBLICATIONS** Auth, Criminal Law, 69, Criminal Process, 69 & ed, Leading Constitutional Cases on Criminal Justice, 73, Found Press; auth, Denial of Justice, Free Press, 77; Law as order, Harvard Law Rev, 78; coauth, Continental Criminal Procedure: Myth and Reality, 78 & auth, Manifest Criminality, Criminal Intent and the Metamorphosis of Larceny, 80, Yale Law J; The Law of Criminal Investigation, Ballinger Publ Co, 82; auth, Natural Law and Justice, Harvard Univ Press, 87; Oedipus at Fenway Park, Harvard Univ Press, 94; Desert, Punishment and Criminial Responsibility, Law and Contemporary Problems, 86; What Are Civil Rights, Social Philos and Policy, 91; Copyright for Functional Expression, Harvard Law Rev, 98. **CONTACT ADDRESS** Law Sch, Harvard Univ, 1545 Massachusetts, Cambridge, MA, 02138-2903.

WEINRIB, ERNEST JOSEPH
PERSONAL Born 04/08/1943, Toronto, ON, Canada, m, 1970 **DISCIPLINE** LAW, ANCIENT HISTORY **EDUCATION** Univ Toronto, BA, 65, LLB, 72; Harvard Univ, PhD(classics), 68. **CAREER** Asst prof classics, 68-70, asst prof law, 72-75, assoc prof, 75-81, Prof Law, Fac Law, Univ Toronto, 81-. **MEMBERSHIPS** Class Can Asn; Asn Can Law Teachers. **RESEARCH** Tort law; Roman law; jurisprudence. **SELECTED PUBLICATIONS** Auth, Judiciary law of M Livius Drusus, Historia, 70; Obnuntiatio: two problems, Z Savigny-Stuftung, 70; A step forward in factual causation, Mod Law Rev, 75; The fiduciary obligation, 75 & Illegality as a tort defense, 76, Univ Toronto; Contribution in a contractual setting, Can Bar Rev, 76; Utilitarianism, Economics, and Legal Theory, Univ Toronto Law J, 80; The Case for a Duty to Rescue, Yale Law J, 80; Obedience to the Law in Plato's Crito, Am J Jurisprudence, 82; The Jurisprudence Of Legal Formalism, Harvard Journal Of Law And Public Policy, Vol 0016, 1993. **CONTACT ADDRESS** Fac of Law, Univ of Toronto, Toronto, ON, M5S 1A1.

WEINSTEIN, JACK B.
PERSONAL Born 08/10/1921, KS, m, 1945, 3 children **DISCIPLINE** LAW **EDUCATION** Brooklyn Col, BA 43; Columbia Univ, LLB 48. **CAREER** George Washington Univ Law, adj prof 92-93; Brooklyn Law Sch, adj prof 87-98; NY Univ Law, adj prof 84-85; NYS Constitutional Conv, advisor 67; NYS Temp Comm, commissioner 66; Columbia Univ Law, 67-98, prof 56-67, assoc prof 52-56; Fed State civil proced, evid, admin, acc, bus law, crim law, advisor, 48-49. **HONORS AND AWARDS** St. Frances Col Hon Doc Degree; Gold Medal NYS Bar; Hon Doc Long Is Univ; Dist Ser Med Awd; Judicial Recognition Awd; Edward J. Devitt Dist Ser Awd; Yale Hon Doc Laws; Hon Wm J Brennan Awd; NLJ Lawyer of the Year; Albany LS Hon Doc Law; Yeshiva U Hon Doc Law; Columbia LS AA Excell Awd; FBC Excell in Jurisp; NY LS Medal of Hon; Allard K. Lowenstein Mem Awd; Charles W Froessel Awd; Brooklyn LS Hon Doc Law; BCAA Alumnus of the Year; Amer Jewish Comm Human Rel Awd. **MEMBERSHIPS** AAAS; AJS; ALI; AAUP; ABA; ABCNY; BANC; IJA; IAJLJ; NLADA; SALT; ISPT; USJC; SCJC. **SELECTED PUBLICATIONS** Auth, United States' Criminal Justice System in: Towards a Procedural Regime for the International Criminal Court, coauth, forthcoming 98; Individual Justice in Mass Torte Litigations, Northwestern Univ Press, 94; Mass Tortes: Cases and Materials, coauth, 94; The Future of Class Actions in Mass Torte Cases: A Roundtable Discussion, Fordham Law Rev, 98; Some Question About Mass Cases and Class Actions, Brooklyn Law Rev, forthcoming; The New York Court of Appeals in the Eyes of a Neophyte, Syracuse Law Rev, forthcoming; The Many Dimensions of Jury Nullification: Jury Nullification is not a Serious Problem it is Important to Understand What it is and Why it Occurs, Judiciature, 98; A trial Judges reflections on Departures from the Federal Sentencing Guidelines, Fed Sentencing Reporter, reprint 97; The Effect of Sentencing on Women Men the Family and the Community, Columbia Jour of Gender and Law, 96; Considering Jury Nullification: When May and Should a Jury Reject the Law to do Justice, Voir Dire Mag, 95; Ethical Dilemmas in Mass Tort Litigation, Northwestern Univ L Rev, 95. **CONTACT ADDRESS** U.S. District Court, Eastern District of NY, 225 Cadman Plaza East, Brooklyn, NY, 11201.

WEINTRAUB, RUSSELL JAY
PERSONAL Born 12/20/1929, New York, NY, m, 1953, 3 children **DISCIPLINE** LAW **EDUCATION** NY Univ, BA, 50; Harvard Univ, LLB, 53. **CAREER** Teaching fel law, Law Sch, Harvard Univ, 55-57; prof, Univ Iowa, 57-65; Prof Law, Law Sch, Univ Tex, Austin, 65-. **RESEARCH** Conflict of laws; commercial law; contracts. **SELECTED PUBLICATIONS** Auth, Commentary on the Conflict of Laws, Found Press, 71, 2nd ed, 80; coauth, Cases and Materials on Conflict of Laws, West, 2nd ed, 72, suppl, 78; Admiralty Choice-Of-Law Rules For Damages, Journal Of Maritime Law And Commerce, Vol 0028, 1997. **CONTACT ADDRESS** Sch of Law, Univ of Tex, 727 E 26th St, Austin, TX, 78705-3224.

WEIR, JOHN P.
DISCIPLINE INSURANCE; TAXATION; CIVIL PROCEDURE; REGULATED INDUSTRIES **EDUCATION** McMaster, BComm; Queen's Univ, LLB; Osgoode, York, LLM. **CAREER** Prof; Osgoode Hall, Barrister-at-Law; past supt, Insurance & asst Dep Minister, Ministry of Financial Institutions, Ont. **RESEARCH** Insurance; taxation; administrative and government regulation; medico-legal; and evidence law. **SELECTED PUBLICATIONS** Auth, Structured Settlements and The Annotated Insurance Act of Ontario; coauth, Norwood on Life Insurance Law in Canada. **CONTACT ADDRESS** Col of Business Administration, Education and Law, Univ of Windsor, 401 Sunset Ave, Windsor, ON, N9B 3P4. **EMAIL** jweir@uwindsor.ca

WEIRICH, PAUL
PERSONAL Born 09/30/1946, Chicago, IL, m, 1968, 2 children **DISCIPLINE** PHILOSOPHY **EDUCATION** Univ Calif, Los Angeles, PhD, 77. **CAREER** Asst prof, Univ Rochester, 78-86; prof, Univ Missouri, 88- . **MEMBERSHIPS** APA. **RESEARCH** Practical reasoning. **SELECTED PUBLICATIONS** Auth, Contractarianism and Bargaining Theory, in Heil, ed, Rationality, Morality, and Self-Interest, Rowman and Littlefield, 93; auth, The Hypothesis of Nash Equilibrium and its Bayesian Justification, in Prawitz, ed, Logic and Philosophy of Science in Uppsala, Kluwer, 94; auth, Comte et Mill sur l'economie politique, Revue Int de Philos, 98; auth, Equilibrium and Rationality: Game Theory Revised by Decision Rules, Cambridge, 98. **CONTACT ADDRESS** Philosophy Dept, Univ of Missouri, Columbia, MO, 65211. **EMAIL** weirichp@missouri.edu

WEISBERG, RICHARD H.
DISCIPLINE CONSTITUTIONAL LAW **EDUCATION** Boston Univ, JD, 55; Stanford Univ, AM, 60. **CAREER** Prof, Yeshiva Univ; **HONORS AND AWARDS** Asso, Cleary, Gottlieb, Steen & Hamilton; Fel, NEH, 72-73, Soc Hum Cornell Univ, 75-76; pres, Law & Hum Inst, 79-86, chair, 87; chair; Law & Hum Sect, Am Asn Law Schs; fel, Am Coun Learned Socs, 89-90. **SELECTED PUBLICATIONS** Auth, The Failure of the Word, Yale, 84, 89, 90; When Lawyers Write, Little, Brown, 87; Poethics: And Other Strategies of Law and Literature, Columbia Univ Press, 92; gen ed, Cardoza Studies in Law and Lit.. **CONTACT ADDRESS** Yeshiva Univ, 55 Fifth Ave, NY, NY, 10003-4301.

WEISBERG, RICHARD HARVEY
PERSONAL Born 05/24/1944, New York, NY, m, 1968, 1 child **DISCIPLINE** LAW **EDUCATION** Brandeis Univ, AB, 65; Cornell Univ, MA, 67, PhD(comp lit), 70; Columbia Univ, JD, 74. **CAREER** Asst prof French & comp lit, Univ Chicago, 71-75; assoc prof, 77-79, Prof Law, Cardozo Law Sch, Yeshiva Univ, 79-, Nat Endowment for Humanities younger humanist fel, 72-73; Cornell Soc for Humanities jr fel, 75-76; vis prof, Sch Law, Minn Univ, fall, 81. **HONORS AND AWARDS** Guggenheim fel, 88-89. **MEMBERSHIPS** Am Comp Lit Asn; MLA; Am Bar Asn. **RESEARCH** Literature and the law; torts; trusts and estates. **SELECTED PUBLICATIONS** Auth, Hamlet and ressentiment, Am Imago, winter 72; Solzhenitsyn's use of the Soviet law in First Circle, Univ Chicago Law Rev, spring 74; An example not to follow: Ressentiment in notes from underground, Mod Fiction Studies, 75-76; Comparative law in comparative literature: Examining magistrate in Dostoyevski and Camus, Rutgers Law Rev, 76; Wigmore's legal novels revisited: New resources for the expansive lawyer, Northwestern Law Rev, 76; Hamlet and un coup de des: Mallarme's emerging constellation, Mod Lang Notes, 77; Law, Literature and Cardozo's Judicial Poetics, Cardozo Law Rev, 79; How Judges Speak: Some Lessons on adjudication in Billy Budd, Sailor with an Application to Justice Rehnquist, New York Univ Law Rev, 82. **CONTACT ADDRESS** Cardozo Law Sch, Yeshiva Univ, 55 Fifth Ave, New York, NY, 10028. **EMAIL** rhweisbg@aol.com

WEISENFELD, JUDITH
DISCIPLINE RELIGION **EDUCATION** Princeton Univ, PhD. **CAREER** Asst prof. **SELECTED PUBLICATIONS** Auth, African American Women and Christian Activism in the New York City YWCA 1905-1945, Harvard, 97; co-ed, This Far by Faith: Readings in African American Women's Religious Biography, Routledge, 96. **CONTACT ADDRESS** Dept of Religion, Columbia Col, New York, 2960 Broadway, New York, NY, 10027-6902. **EMAIL** jweisenfeld@barnard.columbia.edu

WEISS, HEROLD D.
PERSONAL Born 09/05/1934, Montevideo, Uruguay, m, 1962, 2 children **DISCIPLINE** RELIGION **EDUCATION** Andrews Univ, MA, 57, BD, 60; Duke Univ, PhD, 64. **CAREER** Instr relig, Andrews Univ, 61-62, asst prof New Testament, Andrews Univ, 65-69; assoc prof relig studies, 69-72, PROF RELIG STUDIES, ST MARY'S COL, IND, 72-; Adj prof, Univ Notre Dame; McCormick Theol Sem, Chicago & Northern Baptist Theol Sem. **MEMBERSHIPS** Soc Bibl Lit; Am Acad Relig; fel Inst Antiquity & Christianity. **RESEARCH** The religious world of the first century; Biblical studies. **SELECTED PUBLICATIONS** Auth, The pagani among the contemporaries of the first Christians, J Bibl Lit, 86: 42-52; History and a gospel, Novum Testamentum, 10: 81-94; The law in the Epistle to the Colossians, Cath Bibl Quart, 34: 294-314; Footwashing in the Johannine community, Novum Testamentum, 21: 298-325; The Sabbath in the synoptic gospels, JSNT, 90, reprinted, in New Testament Backgrounds: A Sheffield Reader, Sheffield Acad Press, 97; The Sabbath in the fourth Gospel, JBL, 91; Philo on the Sabbath, in Heirs of the Septuagint: Philo, Hellenistic Judaism and Early Christianity, Studia Philonica Annual, 91; The Sabbath among the Samaratins, JSJ, 94; Paul and the judging of days, ZNW, 95; Sabbatismos in the Epistle to the Hebrews, CB!, 96; The Sabbath in the Pauline corpus, in Wisdom and Logos: Studies in Jewish Thought in Honor of David Winston, Studia Philonica Annual, 97; The Sabbath in the writings of Josephus, JSJ, forthcoming. **CONTACT ADDRESS** St Mary's Col, Box 78, Notre Dame, IN, 46556. **EMAIL** hweiss@saintmarys.edu

WEISS, RAYMOND L.
PERSONAL Born 02/12/1930, Cleveland, OH **DISCIPLINE** PHILOSOPHY **EDUCATION** Univ Cincinnati, BA, 51; Hebrew Union Col-Jewish Inst Relig, BHL & MHL, 56; Univ Chicago, PhD, 66. **CAREER** From instr to asst prof, 65-72, assoc prof, 72-80, Prof Philos, Univ Wis-Milwaukee, 80- **MEMBERSHIPS** Am Philos Asn; Am Acad Jewish Res. **RESEARCH** Maimonides; existentialism; ethics. **SELECTED PUBLICATIONS** Auth, Kierkegaard's return to Socrates, New Scholasticism, autumn 71; Language and ethics: Reflections on Maimonides' ethics, J Hist Philos, 10/71; Hermann Cohen's Religion of Reason, Cent Conf Am Rabbis J, winter 74; Historicism and science: Thoughts on Quine, Dialectica, summer 75; coauth, Ethical Writings of Maimonides, NY Univ, 75; Maimonides' Ethics: The Encounter of Philosophic and Religious Morality, Univ Chicago Press, 91. **CONTACT ADDRESS** Dept of Philos, Univ of Wis, PO Box 413, Milwaukee, WI, 53201-0413.

WEISS, ROSLYN
PERSONAL Born 10/21/1952, Brooklyn, NY, m, 1973, 2 children **DISCIPLINE** PHILOSOPHY **EDUCATION** Columbia Univ, PHD, 82 **CAREER** 91-present, Lehigh Univ; 88-91 Univ of Deleware; 81-88, Hood col **HONORS AND AWARDS** Earhart Found Fel; NEH Fel; Center for Hellenic Studies Fel **MEMBERSHIPS** Am Philos Assoc; Int Plato Soc; Assoc for Jewish Studies **RESEARCH** Philosophy **SELECTED PUBLICATIONS** Auth, Socrates Dissatisfied, Oxford Univ Press, 98; Auth, From Freedom to Formalism:Maimonides on Prayer, Journal of the Central Conf of Am Rabbis, Fall 97, 29-43; Auth, Hedonism in the Protagoras and the Sophist's Guarantee, Ancient Philos 10, 1990, 17-39 **CONTACT ADDRESS** Dept of Philosophy, Lehigh Univ, 15 University Dr, Bethlehem, PA, 18015.

WEISSBRODT, DAVID SAMUEL
PERSONAL Born 10/13/1944, Washington, DC, m, 1970, 2 children **DISCIPLINE** LAW **EDUCATION** Univ CA, Berkeley, JD, 69. **CAREER** Assoc prof, 75-78, PROF LAW, SCH OF LAW, UNIV MN, 78-, Co-dir, Univ MN Human Rights Center; co-dir, Univ Mn Human Rights Library (http://www.umn.edu/humanrts); Chair, Int Human Rights Internship Prog, 76-90. **HONORS AND AWARDS** Briggs & Morgan Prof, 89-97; Fredrickson & Byron Prof, 98-; Member, UN Subcommittee on Prevention of Discrimination and Protection of Minorities, 96-99. **MEMBERSHIPS** Am Soc Int Law; Am Law Inst. **RESEARCH** International human rights law; immigration law; administrative law. **SELECTED PUBLICATIONS** Coauth, The Death Penalty Cases, CA Law Rev, 68; The Role of Nongovernmental Organization in the Implementation of Human Rights, Tex Int Law J, 77; Human rights legislation and United States Foreign Policy, Ga J Int & Comp Law, 77; United States Ratification of the Human Rights Covenants, Minn Law Rev, 78; coauth (with McCarthy), Human Rights Fact-finding by Nongovernmental Organizations, Va J Int Law, 81; auth, A New United Nations Mechanism for Encouraging the Ratification of Treaties, Am J Int Law, 82; International Trial Observers, Stanford J Int Law, 82; Strategies for the Selection and Pursuit of International Human Rights Matters, Yale J World Pub Order, 82; coauth, with Parker, Orientation Manual: The UN Commission on Human Rights, its Subcommission, and Related Procedures, 92; co-ed, with Wolfrum, The Right to a Fair Trial, 97; coauth, with Newman, International Human Rights, 2nd ed, 96; auth, Immigration Law and Procedure, 4th ed, 98; and 90 other articles. **CONTACT ADDRESS** Law Sch, Univ of MN, 229 19th Ave S, Minneapolis, MN, 55455-0401. **EMAIL** Weiss001@tc.umn.edu

WEITHMAN, PAUL J.
DISCIPLINE PHILOSOPHY **EDUCATION** Univ Notre Dame, BA, 81; Harvard Univ, MA, 86, PhD, 88. **CAREER** Assoc prof. **RESEARCH** Ethics; contemporary political philosophy; medieval political philosophy. **SELECTED PUBLICATIONS** Auth, Of Assisted Suicide and 'The Philosophers' Brief', Ethics, 98; Equality and Complementarity in the Political Thought of Aquinas, Theological Studies, 98; ed, Religion and Contemporary Liberalism, 97. **CONTACT ADDRESS** Philosophy Dept, Univ of Notre Dame, 336/7 O'Shaughnessy, Notre Dame, IN, 46556. **EMAIL** weithman.1@nd.edu

WELBORN, L.L.
PERSONAL Born 10/04/1954, Memphis, TN, m, 1976, 2 children **DISCIPLINE** RELIGION, NEW TESTAMENT AND EARLY CHRISTIAN LITERATURE **EDUCATION** Harding

Col, BA, 76; Yale Divinity School, MAR, 79; Univ Chicago, MA, 83; Vanderbilt Univ, MA, 84, PhD, 93. **CAREER** Asst prof, McCormick Theol Sem, 85-91; assoc prof, United Theol Sem, 91-98. **HONORS AND AWARDS** National Merit scholarship; Tew Prize; Rotary fel; Harold Stirling Vanderbilt fel. **MEMBERSHIPS** Soc of Biblical Lit. **RESEARCH** Pauline Epistles; Apostolic Fathers; Greco-Roman World. **SELECTED PUBLICATIONS** Auth, Politics and Rhetoric in the Corinthian Epistles, Mercer, 97. **CONTACT ADDRESS** United Theol Sem, 1810 Harvard Blvd, Dayton, OH, 45406.

WELCH, EDWARD L.
PERSONAL Born 03/10/1928, Helena, AR, m **DISCIPLINE** LAW **EDUCATION** St Louis Univ, BS, Commerce, 1957; Washington Univ, St Louis, MO, JD, Order of Coif, 1960. **CAREER** Stockham Roth Buder & Martin, assoc atty; Univ of Wisconsin, Milwaukee, lecturer; Allis-Chalmers Mfg Co, Milwaukee, WI, & Springfield, IL, labor law atty, 1961-67; Natl Labor Relations Bd 14th Region; staff atty, 1967-69; atty. **MEMBERSHIPS** Gen counsel, Natl Alliance of Postal & Fed Employees, Washington, DC, 1971-90; senior litigation specialist 1990-; adj prof, Southern Illinois Univ, Carbondale, 1974-; school bd atty, East St Louis School Dist, 189, 1978-; mem, Amer Bar Assn, Illinois State Bar Assn, Madison City Bar Assn; life mem, NAACP. **CONTACT ADDRESS** PO Box 93, Edwardsville, IL, 62025.

WELCH, ROBERT H.
DISCIPLINE CHURCH ADMINISTRATION **EDUCATION** E Tenn State Univ, BS, 60; Naval Post-Grad Sch, MS, 67; Southwestern Baptist Theol Sem, MARE, 85, PhD, 89. **CAREER** Assoc prof, Univ Okla, 77-82; adj prof, 87-88; asst prof, Liberty Univ Theol Sem, 87-88; assoc prof, Southwestern Baptist Theol Sem, 91-; Hugh Seborn Simpson prof; assoc dean, Advan Stud. **HONORS AND AWARDS** Church bus admin, Trinity Baptist Church, 82-85. **SELECTED PUBLICATIONS** Auth, The Church Organization Manual, NACBA, 96; Leadership Handbook of Practical Theology, Vol III, Leadership and Admin, Baker Bk(s), 94; co-auth, A Maintenance Management Manual for Southern Baptist Churches, Convention Press, 90. **CONTACT ADDRESS** Sch Edu Ministries, Southwestern Baptist Theol Sem, PO Box 22000, Fort Worth, TX, 76122-0418. **EMAIL** bobw@swbts.swbts.edu

WELKER, DAVID DALE
PERSONAL Born 12/18/1938, St. Louis, MO **DISCIPLINE** PHILOSOPHY **EDUCATION** Univ Mich, AB, 60, PhD(philos), 68; Univ Calif, Berkeley, MA, 62. **CAREER** Asst prof, 64-80, ASSOC PROF PHILOS, TEMPLE UNIV, 80-. **RESEARCH** Philosophy of language; metaphysics. **SELECTED PUBLICATIONS** Auth, Existential statements, J Philos, 70; A difficulty in Ziffs theory of meaning, Philos Studies, 70; Locutionary Acts and Meaning, Philos Forum, 73; Subjects, Predicates, and Features, Mind, 79. **CONTACT ADDRESS** Dept of Philos, Temple Univ, 1114 W Berks St, Philadelphia, PA, 19122-6029.

WELLER, ERIC JOHN
PERSONAL Born 01/10/1938, Colchester, England, m, 1959, 4 children **DISCIPLINE** PHILOSOPHY **EDUCATION** Hofstra Univ, BA, 60; Univ Rochester, PhD, 64. **CAREER** From instr to asst prof, 63-69, assoc prof Philos, 69-, Fac Coordr Curric, 67-70, Dean of Studies, 70-76, Acting Dean of Fac, 76-77, Dean Fac, 77-90, CHAIR, DEPT OF PHILOS & RELIG, SKIDMORE COL, 92-. **MEMBERSHIPS** Am Philos Asn. **RESEARCH** Philosophy of the social sciences; philosophical psychology; epistemology. **CONTACT ADDRESS** Dept of Philos, Skidmore Col, 815 N Broadway, Saratoga Springs, NY, 12866-1698. **EMAIL** eweller@skidmore.edu

WELLIVER, KENNETH BRUCE
PERSONAL Born 10/07/1929, Baltimore, Md, m, 1953, 3 children **DISCIPLINE** BIBLE, RELIGION **EDUCATION** DePauw Univ, BA, 51; Yale Univ, BD, 54, MA, 56, PhD(relig), 61. **CAREER** Assoc prof philos & relig, Nat Col, 59-64; instr philos, Jr Col Kansas City, 61-63; assoc prof Bible & relig, 64-68, chmn dept, 65-75, assoc dean, 77-79, Prof Bible & Relig, WVA Wesleyan Col, 68-97, prof emeritus, 97-, Vpres Acad Affairs & Dean Col, 79-87, Vis prof, Grad Sch, Ecumenical Inst, World Coun Churches, 70-71. **MEMBERSHIPS** AAUP; Soc Bibl Lit; Am Acad Relig. **RESEARCH** New Testament history; early Christian Biblical exegesis; Japanese religions. **CONTACT ADDRESS** West Virginia Wesleyan Col, 59 College Ave, Buckhannon, WV, 26201-2699. **EMAIL** welliver@wvwc.edu

WELLMAN, CARL
PERSONAL Born 09/03/1926, Lynn, MA, m, 1953, 4 children **DISCIPLINE** PHILOSOPHY **EDUCATION** Univ Ariz, BA, 49; Harvard Univ, MA, 51, PhD, 54. **CAREER** From instr to prof philos, Lawrence Univ, 53-68; prof philos, 68-, Wash Univ; Am Coun Learned Soc res fel, Univ Mich, 65-66; Nat Endowment Humanities fel, 72-73; Nat Humanities Ctr fel, 82-83. **MEMBERSHIPS** Am Philos Asn; Int Asn Philos Law & Social Philos (secy-gen, 75-79). **RESEARCH** Moral philosophy; philosophy of law; theory of rights. **SELECTED PUBLICATIONS** Auth, Real Rights, Oxford, 95; auth, An Approach to Rights, Kluwer, 97; auth, The Proliferation of Rights, Westview, 98. **CONTACT ADDRESS** Dept of Philosophy, Washington Univ, 1 Brookings Dr, St. Louis, MO, 63130-4899. **EMAIL** wellman@twinearth.wustl.edu

WELLMAN, JAMES K., JR.
PERSONAL Born 08/20/1958, Portland, OR, m, 1985, 2 children **DISCIPLINE** AMERICAN RELIGION **EDUCATION** Univ Wash, BA, 81; Princeton Sem, MDiv, 85; Univ Chicago, PhD, 95. **CAREER** Lectr, Univ Wash, Pacific Lutheran Univ. **HONORS AND AWARDS** Louisville Dis Fel, Louisville Inst Grant; SSR Student Paper Award. **MEMBERSHIPS** AAR; RRA; SSSR. **RESEARCH** Amer relig; 20th cent; business ethics; contemp Amer spirituality. **SELECTED PUBLICATIONS** Auth, The Gold Coast Church and the Ghetto: Christ and Culture in Mainline Protestantism, Univ Ill Press, 99; auth, The Power of Religious Public: Staking Claims in American Society, Praeger Press, 99. **CONTACT ADDRESS** 8527 Hansen Rd., Bainbridge Island, WA, 98110. **EMAIL** jkwamw@sttl.oswest.net

WELLS, DAVID FALCONER
PERSONAL Born 05/11/1939, Bulawayo, Zimbabwe, m, 1965, 2 children **DISCIPLINE** SYSTEMATIC THEOLOGY, CHURCH HISTORY **EDUCATION** Univ London, EngL, BD, 66; Trinity Evangel Divinity Sch, ThM, 67; Univ Manchester, PhD, 69. **CAREER** From asst prof to prof church hist, Trinity Evangel Divinity Sch, 69-77, prof syst theol, 78-79; Prof Syst Theol, Gordon-Conwell Theol Sem, 79-, Acad dean, Gordon-Conwell Theol Sem, Charlotte, 98-; Res fel, Divinity Sch, Yale Univ, 73-74; mem, Int Evangel Roman Cath Dialog Missions, 81-; chmn, Task Force Roman Cath, World Evangel Fel Theol Comn, 81-84. **HONORS AND AWARDS** Distinguished lectr, London Inst for Contemp Christianity, London, 85. **RESEARCH** Contextualization; Christology; Roman Cath modernism. **SELECTED PUBLICATIONS** Ed, Toward a Theology for the Future, Creation House, 71; auth, Revolution in Rome, Inter-Varsity Press, 73; ed, The Evangelicals, Abingdon Press, 75; auth, Search for Salvation, Inter-Varsity Press, 78; The Prophetic Theology of George Tywell, Scholars Press, 81; ed, The Eerdmans Handbook of American Christianity, Eerdmans, 83; auth, The Person of Christ: A Biblical and Historical Analysis of the Incarnation, Crossway, 84; ed, Reformed Theology in America: A History of Its Modern Development, Eerdmans, 85; ed, God the Evangelist: How the Holy Spirit Words to Bring Men and Women to Faith, Eerdmans, 87; ed, Christian Faith and Practice in the Modern World: Theology from an Evangelical Point of View, Eerdmans, 88; ed, Turning to God: Biblical Conversion in the Modern World, Baker, 89; ed, The Gospel in the Modern World: A Tribute to John Stott, InterVarsity, 91; auth, No Place for Truth, Or, Whatever Happened to Evangelical Theology, Eerdmans, 93; auth, God in the Wasteland: The Reality of Truth in a World of Fading Dreams, Eerdmans, 94; auth, Losing Our Virtue: Why the Church Must Recover Its Moral Vision, Eerdmans, 98. **CONTACT ADDRESS** Gordon-Conwell Theol Sem, 130 Essex St, South Hamilton, MA, 01982-2395.

WELLS, DONALD A.
PERSONAL Born 04/17/1917, St. Paul, MN, m, 1940, 2 children **DISCIPLINE** PHILOSOPHY **EDUCATION** Hamline Univ, BA, 40; Boston Univ, STB, 43, PhD, 46. **CAREER** Asst prof, philos, Oregon State Univ, 46-48; asst, assoc, prof, chemn, philos, Washington State Univ, 48-69; prof philos, chemn, Univ Ill, Chicago Cir, 69-71; prof philos, chemn, Univ Hawaii, 71-92. **HONORS AND AWARDS** Sleeper fel, Boston Univ, 44-46; Kent fel, Danforth Found, 42; Ford Found fel, UCLA, 52-53; Rockefeller Found fel, 80., Founder, Int Philos for the Prevention of Nuclear Omnicide. **MEMBERSHIPS** APA; Philos for Peace; Int Philos for the Prevention of Nuclear Omnicide. **RESEARCH** War and moral issues; war crimes; laws of war; just war theory. **SELECTED PUBLICATIONS** Auth, The Law of Land Warfare: A Guide to the US Army Manuals, Greenwood, 92; ed, An Encyclopedia of War and Morality, Greenwood, 96. **CONTACT ADDRESS** 1200 Miramar Ave, #210, Medford, OR, 97504. **EMAIL** donwells@grrtech.com

WELLS, JONATHAN
PERSONAL New York, NY, m, 2 children **DISCIPLINE** BIOLOGY, THEOLOGY **EDUCATION** Yale Univ, PhD , 86; Univ CA, Berkeley, PhD, 94. **CAREER** Post-Doct, res biolog, Univ Calif, Berkeley; sr fel, The Discovery Inst, Seattle, Wash; assoc ed, Origins & Design, Evanston, Ill. **MEMBERSHIPS** AAR; Am Asn for the Advancement of Sci; Am Sci Affil; Am Soc for Cell Biology; Int Soc for the Hist, Philos, and Social Studies of Biology; Soc for Develop Biology. **SELECTED PUBLICATIONS** Auth, Marriage and the Family in Unification Theology, Dialogue & Alliance, 9, 95; auth, Issues in the Creation-Evolution Controversies, The World & I, 96; auth, Confocal Microscopy Analysis of Living Xenopus Eggs and the Mechanism of Cortical Rotation, Development, 122, 96; Microtubule-mediated organelle transport and localization of beta-catenin to the futyre dorsal side of Xenopus eggs, Proc Natl Acad Sci USA, 94, 97; auth, Homology: A Concept in Crisis, Origins and Design 18, 97; auth, Theological Witch-Hunt: The NCC Critique of the Unification Church, J of Unification Stud 1, 97; auth, Evolution by Design, The World & I, 98; auth, Abusing Theology: Howard Van Till's Forgotten Doctrine of Creation's Functional Integrity, Origins & Design 19, 98; Haeckel's Embryos and Evolution: Setting the Record Straight, Amer Biology Tchr, 98. **CONTACT ADDRESS** 20145 Viking's Crest, #3-301, Poulsbo, WA, 98370. **EMAIL** jonwells1@compuserve.com

WELLS, WILLIAM W.
DISCIPLINE LAW **EDUCATION** Eastern Oregon Col, BS; Univ Puget Sound; JD; Univ Wash, MLL. **CAREER** Prof and dir, Garbrecht Law Libr, 86-; past asst dir, Burns Law Libr, George Wash Univ; past sr ref librn, Univ Va Law Sch; assoc provost for Technol, Inf Syst, and Libr, USM, 90; past app to, State Ct Libr Comt. **SELECTED PUBLICATIONS** Auth, Maine's Legal Research Guide. **CONTACT ADDRESS** School of Law, Univ of Southern Maine, 96 Falmouth St, PO Box 9300, Portland, ME, 04104-9300.

WELTON, WILLIAM A.
PERSONAL Born 01/31/1961, Lakewood, OH, s **DISCIPLINE** PHILOSOPHY **EDUCATION** Duquesne Univ, PhD, 93. **CAREER** Instr, philos, Xavier Univ, 97-98. **MEMBERSHIPS** Amer Philos Asn; Soc for Ancient Greek Philos. **RESEARCH** Plato; Aristotle. **SELECTED PUBLICATIONS** Auth, Divine Inspiration and the Origins of the Laws in Plato's Laws, Polis, 14, no 1 and 2, 53-83, 97; co-auth, An Overlooked Motive in Alcibiades' Symposium Speech, Interpretation, 24, 1, 67-84, 96; co-auth, The Viability of Virtue in the Mean, Apeiron, 28, 4, 79-102, 96; auth, Incantation and Expectation in Laws II, Philos and Rhetoric, 29, 3, 211-224, 96. **CONTACT ADDRESS** 4201 Victory Pkwy., Apt. 417, Cincinnati, OH, 45229. **EMAIL** wawel@xv.campus.mci.net

WENDEROTH, CHRISTINE
PERSONAL Born 10/12/1949, Passiaic, NJ, 2 children **DISCIPLINE** THEOLOGICAL STUDIES & LIBRARIANSHIP **EDUCATION** Oberlin Col, BA, 71; Univ NC, MSLS, 73; Emory Univ, MA, 78, PhD, 82. **CAREER** Assoc dir of Library & asst prof of Practical Theology, Columbia Theol Sem, Decatur, GA, 80-93; dir of The Library & asst prof of Ministry, Colgate Rochester Divinity School, 94-. **MEMBERSHIPS** Am Theol Library Asn; AAR/SBL. **RESEARCH** Practical theology; gender studies. **CONTACT ADDRESS** Ambrose Swasey Library, Colgate Rochester Divinity Sch, 1100 S Goodman, Rochester, NY, 14620. **EMAIL** cwenderoth@crds.edu

WENGERT, ROBERT
DISCIPLINE PHILOSOPHY **EDUCATION** Univ Toronto, PhD. **CAREER** Assoc prof, Univ Ill Urbana Champaign. **RESEARCH** Medieval philosophy; history and philosophy of logic; logic programming; applied ethics. **SELECTED PUBLICATIONS** Auth, The Sources of Intuitive Cognition in William of Ockham; The Paradox of the Midwife; Necessity of the Past: What is Ockham's Model?. **CONTACT ADDRESS** Philosophy Dept, Univ Ill Urbana Champaign, 52 E Gregory Dr, Champaign, IL, 61820. **EMAIL** wengert@uiuc.edu

WENINGER, ROBERT
DISCIPLINE PHILOSOPHY **EDUCATION** Frankfurt Univ, PhD. **CAREER** Asst, assoc, Wash Univ, 88-97; PROF, GERM, COMP LIT, CHAIR, DEPT GER, WASH UNIV, 97-. **CONTACT ADDRESS** 703 Harvard Ave, St. Louis, MO, 63130-3135. **EMAIL** rkwening@artsci.wustl.edu

WENNBERG, ROBERT N.
DISCIPLINE PHILOSOPHY **EDUCATION** Univ Calif, Santa Barbara, PhD, 73. **CAREER** Prof philos, 70-. **HONORS AND AWARDS** Tchr yr, 73, 82, 89, 94; fac res award, 86. **RESEARCH** Ethics. **SELECTED PUBLICATIONS** Auth, Terminal Choices: Euthanasia, Suicide and the Right to Die, Eerdmans, 89; Life in the Balance: Exploring the Abortion Controversy, Eerdmans, 85; Animal Suffering and the Problem of Evil, Christian Scholar's Rev, XXI, 91; The Right to Life: Reflections on Three Theories, Christian Scholar's Rev, XIV, 85. **CONTACT ADDRESS** Dept of Philos, Westmont Col, 955 La Paz Rd, Santa Barbara, CA, 93108-1099.

WENNEMYR, SUSAN E.
PERSONAL Born 04/16/1964, Tulsa, OK, m, 1991 **DISCIPLINE** THEOLOGY; CULTURE **EDUCATION** Harvard Univ, BA (Philos), 86; Univ Chicago, PhD (Theol), 95. **CAREER** Asst prof relig, Manchester Col, asst dir of Brethren Colleges Abroad, 93-96; DEAN OF DAVENPORT COL AND INSTR OF RELIG STUDIES, YALE UNIV, 97-. **HONORS AND AWARDS** Mellon fel for graduate study; Mellon dissertation grant. **MEMBERSHIPS** Am Academy Relig; Soc for Values in Higher Ed; Asn on Relig and Intellectual Life. **RESEARCH** Global Christian theology; psychology and relig; deconstructionism and Christian tradition. **SELECTED PUBLICATIONS** Auth, Dancing in the Dark: Deconstructive A/Theology Leaps with Faith, J of the Am Academy of Relig, 66:3, fall 98; Feminist Christian Ethics, in Encyclopedia of Feminism, Routledge, forthcoming. **CONTACT ADDRESS** Box 200018 Yale, New Haven, CT, 06520. **EMAIL** magnus.wennemyr@yale.edu

WERT, NEWELL JOHN
PERSONAL Born 10/10/1926, West Lawn, PA, m, 1947, 3 children **DISCIPLINE** SOCIAL ETHICS **EDUCATION** Albright Col, AB, 47; United Theol Sem, BD, 50; Boston Univ, PhD, 58. **CAREER** Asst prof sociol, Otterbein Col, 54-57; from asst prof to assoc prof, 57-63, prof Christian ethics & dean, United Theol Sem, 63-; mem, study comn on church & state, Nat Coun Churches, 62-64; deleg, World Conf Church & Soc, Geneva, Switz, Aug 66. **HONORS AND AWARDS** Am Assn Theol Schs fac fel studies ecumenical social ethics, Geneva, 66-67. **MEMBERSHIPS** Soc Christian Ethics; Am Acad Relig. **RESEARCH** Sociological writing of Roman Catholic scholars; institutional aspects of Christian churches; professional ethics. **SELECTED PUBLICATIONS** Auth, Dimensions of Decision, Graded Press, 68. **CONTACT ADDRESS** United Theol Sem, 1810 Harvard Blvd, Dayton, OH, 45406-4599.

WERTH, LEE FREDERICK
PERSONAL Born 02/09/1941, York, PA, m, 1967, 2 children **DISCIPLINE** PHILOSOPHY **EDUCATION** Case Western Reserve Univ, BA, 62; Univ Waterloo, PhD, 72. **CAREER** Instr philos, Althouse Col Educ, Univ Western Ont, 69-70; asst prof, 72-78, assoc prof philos, Cleveland State Univ, 79- **MEMBERSHIPS** Philos Sci Asn; Am Philos Asn; Can Philos Asn, Int Soc Study Time. **RESEARCH** Philosophy of space and time; metaphysics; early modern philosophy. **SELECTED PUBLICATIONS** Auth, Annihilating nihilism, 74, Some second thoughts on first principles, 75, A declaration of interdependence 76, Philosophy in Context; Normalizing the paranormal, Am Philos Quart, 1/78; The untenability of Whitehead's theory of extensive connection, Process Studies, spring 78; On again, off again, Philosophers Speak on Science Fiction, Nelson-Hall (in press); Siddhartha and Slaughterhouse Five, The Intersection of Science Fiction & Philosophy, Greenwood (in press); ed, Science fiction & philosophy, Philos Context, Vol 11, 81; Clarifying Concrecence in Whitehead's Process Philosophy, Chap 12-The Study of Time VII: Time and Process, Int Univ, 93; Evolutionary Epistemology and Pragmatism, in Living Doubt (Essays concerning the epistemology of Charles Sanders Peirce), Kluwer Acad Publ, 94; The Anthropocentric Predicaments and the Search for Extraterrestrial Intelligence, J Appl Philos, 98. **CONTACT ADDRESS** Dept of Philos, Cleveland State Univ, 1983 E 24th St, Cleveland, OH, 44115-2440.

WERTHEIMER, ELLEN
DISCIPLINE CONTRACTS, PRODUCTS LIABILITY, MEDICAL MALPRACTICE, THE SUPREME COURT **EDUCATION** Yale Univ, BA, 75; Yale Law Sch, JD, 79. **CAREER** Prof, Villanova Univ; clerked to, Honorable Frank A. Kaufman, US Dist Judge, US Dist Ct Dist Md & to Honorable James Hunter III, US Circuit Judge, US Ct Appeals Third Circuit;past assoc, Pepper, Hamilton & Scheetz; past ch, Villanova Curric Comt and Clerkship Comt. **MEMBERSHIPS** Order Coif; Phi Beta Kappa. **RESEARCH** Products liability; medical malpract, law and medicine, torts. **SELECTED PUBLICATIONS** Auth, Unavoidably Unsafe Products: A Modest Proposal, Chi- Kent L Rev, 96; The Third Restatement of Torts: An Unreasonably Dangerous Doctrine, Suffolk U L. Rev, 95; The Smoke Gets in Their Eyes: Product Category Liability and Alternative Feasible Designs in the Third Restatement, Tenn L Rev, 94; Azzarello Agonistes: Bucking the Strict Products Liability Tide, Temple L Rev, 93 & Unknowable Dangers and The Death of Strict Products Liability: The Empire Strikes Back, Cinc L Rev, 92. **CONTACT ADDRESS** Law School, Villanova Univ, 800 Lancaster Ave, Villanova, PA, 19085-1692. **EMAIL** wertheim@law.vill.edu

WERTHEIMER, ROGER
PERSONAL Born 04/10/1942, Buffalo, NY, d **DISCIPLINE** PHILOSOPHY **EDUCATION** Brandeis Univ, BA, 63; Harvard Univ, MA, 67; Harvard Univ, 69; Portland Metro Police Acad, OPOC, 70; Boston Univ, Psych Coun Train, 76. **CAREER** AGREE Co, Pres, 84-98; Cal State Univ, lectr, 95; L B State Univ, CA, assoc prof, 89-94; Univ Houston, vis assoc prof, 83-84; Carnegie Mell Univ, assoc prof, 77-83; Univ Houston, vis assoc prof, 77; Univ Cincinnati, v assoc prof, 76; Boston State Hosp, researcher; therapist, 75-77; Tuffs Univ, vis assoc prof, 74-75; Guggenheim Fel 73-74. **HONORS AND AWARDS** Harvard Univ Grad Scholarships, 64 - 65; NYS Regents Fel, 66; Kent Fel, 67; Harvard Univ, CAR Prize, 69; Guggenheim Fel, 73; Mellon Gnt, 78; CSULB Inter Edu Award, 91; NEH Grant, 94; APA Rockefeller Prize, 98 **MEMBERSHIPS** MPPS, APA, AAAE **RESEARCH** Ethics; philosophy; epistemology. **SELECTED PUBLICATIONS** Auth, The Significance of Sense: Meaning, Modality and Morality, Cornell UP, 72; Socratic Skepticism, in: Metaphilosophy, 93; Synonymy Without Analyticity, in: Inter Philo Pre Exchange, 94; Constraining Condemning, in: Ethics, 98; Identity: Logic, Ontology, Epistemology, in: Philo 98. **CONTACT ADDRESS** 1327 North Olive Dr #A, North Hollywood, CA, 90069. **EMAIL** rwertheim@juno.com

WERTZ, S.K.
PERSONAL Born 10/27/1941, Amarillo, TX, M, 1967 **DISCIPLINE** PHILOSOPHY **EDUCATION** Univ OK, PhD, 70; Univ Kent at Canterbury, post grad, 65; Rice Univ, post grad, 88. **CAREER** Texas Christian Univ, Ft Worth, inst, asst prof, assoc prof, prof, 30 yr. **HONORS AND AWARDS** Fel Amer Acad of Kinesi and Phys Edu, 95-, Phi Beta Delta (NHSIS), Alumni mem Phi Beta Kappa, TCU Chap **MEMBERSHIPS** APA, ASA, PSSS, Hume Society, Collingwood Society, SPS, AAKPE **RESEARCH** Hist mod philo; philo of hist; aesth and sport. **SELECTED PUBLICATIONS** Auth, Talking a Good Game: Inquiries into the Principles of Sport, S Meth Univ Press, 91; Sports Inside Out: Readings in Literature and Philosophy, Tex Christ Univ Press, 85, Human Nature and Art: From Descartes and Hume to Tolstoy, Jour Aesth Edu, 98; Mill on Mathematics: The Ayer-Quinton Interpretations, SW Philo Rev, 97; Moral Judgements in History: Humes Position, Hume Studies, 96; Sport Conundrum (Its Massive Appeal): Bernard Jeu's Semiotic Solution, Aethlon: Jour of Sport Lit, 96; Is Sport Unique? A Question of Definability, Jour Philo of Sport, 95; The Role of Practice in Collingwood's Theory of Art, SW Philo Review, 95; Hume and the Historiography of Science, Jour Hist of Ideas, 93. **CONTACT ADDRESS** Dept of Philosophy, Texas Christian Univ, PO Box 297250, Fort Worth, TX, 76219. **EMAIL** swertz@gamma.is.tuc.edu

WESS, ROBERT C.
DISCIPLINE PHILOSOPHY **EDUCATION** Scotus Col, BA, 62; Xavier Univ, MA, 66; Univ Notre Dame; PhD, 70. **CAREER** Tchr, OH Dominican Col, 72-79; tchr, Pembroke State Univ, 79-84; tchr, S Polytech State Univ, 84-. **MEMBERSHIPS** MLA; GA SC Col Asn. **RESEARCH** Compos studies. **SELECTED PUBLICATIONS** Auth, publ(s) on Puritan lit; work of Washington Irving; res and tchg compos. **CONTACT ADDRESS** Hum and Tech Commun Dept, Southern Polytech State Univ, S Marietta Pkwy, PO Box 1100, Marietta, GA, 30060.

WESSELSCHMIDT, QUENTIN F.
PERSONAL Born 02/03/1937, Washington, MD, m, 1963 **DISCIPLINE** THEOLOGY, CLASSICS (GREEK AND LATIN) **EDUCATION** St Paul's Jr Coll, Concordia, MO, 57; Concordia Sr Coll, BA, 59; Concordia Sem, BD, 63; Marquette Univ, MA, 69, Univ Iowa, PhD, 79. **CAREER** Pastor, Our Savior Lutheran Church, IL, 63-65; prof, Concordia Coll, WI, 65-73; instr, Milwaukee Lutheran High Schhol, WI, 74-77; prof, Concordia Sem, Mo, 77-. **MEMBERSHIPS** North Am Patristic Soc; Am Philol Asn; Class Asn of the Mid w and s. **RESEARCH** Patristics. **SELECTED PUBLICATIONS** Auth, chapter, Heritage, Motion; Chapter, Light from Above; articles, Concordia J. **CONTACT ADDRESS** 801 De Mun Ave, St. Louis, MO, 63105.

WEST, CHARLES CONVERSE
PERSONAL Born 02/03/1921, Plainfield, NJ, m, 1944, 3 children **DISCIPLINE** THEOLOGY, ETHICS **EDUCATION** Columbia Univ, BA, 42; Union Theol Sem, NY, BD, 45; Yale Univ, PhD, 55. **CAREER** Instr hist, Peking Nat Univ, 48; soc sci, Cheeloo Univ, 48-49; Christian ethics, Nanking Theol Sem, 49-50; dozent, Kirchliche Hochsch, Berlin, Ger, 51-53; assoc dir, Ecumenical Inst, Bessey World Council Churches, 56-61; charge de cours theol, Inst Hautes Etudes Oecumeniques, Univ Geneva, 56-61; assoc prof, 61-63, Prof Christian Ethics, Princeton Theol Sem, 63-91, Acad Dean, 79-84, EMERITUS, 91-, Mem comt on confession of 1967, United Presby Church USA, 61-67; chmn, US Asn Christian Peace Conf, 65-72; mem int affairs comn, Nat Coun Churches, 67-69; working comt, dept church & soc, World Coun Churches, 68-83; John Courtney Murray fel, Woodstock Theol Ctr, 76-77. **MEMBERSHIPS** Am Soc Christian Ethics (vpres, 72-73, pres, 73-74); Am Theol Soc (vpres, 82-83, pres, 83-84). **RESEARCH** Christian theology and action in an East Asian environment; Christianity and Marxism; theology and ethics of politics. **SELECTED PUBLICATIONS** Auth, Communism and The Theologians, SCM Press, London, 58, Westminster & McMillan, 63; Outside the Camp, Doubleday, 59; coauth, The Sufficiency of God: Essays in Honor of Dr W A Visser 't Hooft, SCM Press & Westminster, 63; Community, Christian and secular, In: Man in Community, Asn Press, 66; Act and being in Christian and Marxist perspective, In: Openings for Marxist-Christian Dialogue, Abingdon, 69; auth, Ethics, Violence and Revolution, Coun Relig & Int Affairs, 70; The Power to be Human, Macmillan, 71; Facts, morals and the bomb, In: To Avoid Catastrophe, Eerdmans, 79. **CONTACT ADDRESS** Princeton Theol Sem, PO Box 821, Princeton, NJ, 08542. **EMAIL** ccwrcw@bellatlantic.net

WEST, DELNO C.
PERSONAL Born 04/08/1936, IA, m, 1959, 3 children **DISCIPLINE** MEDIEVAL & CHURCH HISTORY **EDUCATION** Northeast MO State Univ, BS, 60; Univ Denver, MA, 61; Univ Calif, Los Angeles, PhD(medieval hist), 70. **CAREER** Asst prof, 69-75, assoc prof, 75-78, asst to acad vpres, 76-80, Prof Medieval Hist, Northern Ariz Univ, 78-, Chmn Dept Hist, 80-, Mem, Ariz-Mex Comn, 76- & Flagstaff Airport Comn, 77-; chmn, Ariz Medieval & Renaissance Ctr, 81. **MEMBERSHIPS** AHA; Mediaeval Acad Am; Rocky Mountain Medieval & Renaissance Asn (pres, 81-82). **RESEARCH** Franciscans; Joachimism; 13th century Italy. **SELECTED PUBLICATIONS** Auth, The Reformed Church and the Friars Minor: The moderate Joachite position of Fra Salimbene, Archivum Franciscanum Historicum, 71; The present state of Salimbene studies with a bibliographic appendix of the major works, Franciscan Studies, 72; ed, Joachim of Fiore in Christian Thought, B Franklin, 74; co-ed, On Pre-Modern Technology and Science, Undene, 76; auth, Between flesh and spirit: Joachite themes in the cronics of Fra Salimbene, J Medieval Hist, 77; The Education of a Joachite-Franciscan, In: Prophecy and Millenarianism: Essays in Honour of Marjorie Reeves, Longman's Press, 80; A note on the date of the expositio super regulum by Hugh J Degue, Rocky Mountain Medieval & Renaissance J, 80; Columbus And The Ends Of The Earth - Europe Prophetic Rhetoric As Conquering Ideology - Kadir,D, Cithara-Essays In The Judeo-Christian Tradition, Vol 0032, 1993; The Portuguese Columbus - Secret-Agent Of King-John-Ii - Barreto,M, American Historical Review, Vol 0098, 1993; Reading Columbus - Zamora,M, Americas, Vol 0051, 1994; The Apocalypse In The Middle-Ages - Emmerson,Rk, Mcginn,B, Catholic Historical Review, Vol 0080, 1994; The Classical-Tradition And The America, Vol 1 - European Images Of The America And The Classical-Tradition, Pt 1 - Haase,W, Reinhold,M, Journal Of American History, Vol 0082, 1995. **CONTACT ADDRESS** Dept of Hist, No Arizona Univ, Flagstaff, AZ, 86001.

WEST, FREDERICK S.
PERSONAL Born 11/10/1944, St. Paul, MN, m, 1973, 4 children **DISCIPLINE** THEOLOGY **EDUCATION** Grinnell Col, BA, 67; Chicago Theol Sem, MDiv, 74; Univ Notre Dame, PhD, 88. **CAREER** Adjunct instr, United Theol Sem, 99-. **MEMBERSHIPS** Am Acad of Relig; North Am Acad of Liturgy; Mercersburg Soc. **RESEARCH** Liturgical methodology. **SELECTED PUBLICATIONS** Auth, Scripture and Memory: The Ecumenical Hermeneutic of the Three-Year Lectionaries, 97; The Comparative Liturgy of Anton Baumstark, 95; "An Annotated Bibliography of the Three-Year Lectionaries," 93; "Models of Renewing Worship: United Church of Christ Worship," 93. **CONTACT ADDRESS** 200 Oak Knoll Dr, Marine on St. Croix, MN, 55047.

WEST, GEORGE FERDINAND, JR.
PERSONAL Born 10/25/1940, Adams Co, MS, m **DISCIPLINE** LAW **EDUCATION** Tougaloo Coll, BA 1962; So Univ Sch of Law, JD 1966; Univ MS, JD 1968. **CAREER** Natchez Adams Co Sch Bd, appt/co-atty 1967-95; State Adv Bd for Voc Edn, appt 1968; Natchez-Adams Co C of C, appt/dir 1974; Jeff Co Sch Sys, atty 1974; MS Sch Bd Assn, dir/atty; Radio Pgm "FACT-FINDING", modrtr; Copiah-Lincoln Jr Coll Natchez Br, bus law prof; Natchez News Leader, mg edtr;Private Practice Natchez, MS, **HONORS AND AWARDS** Outstand Yng Men in Am 1967-; Comm Ldr of Am 1972; Lifetime Rosco Pound Fellow 1972; Most Distinguished Black Attorney Travelers Coalition, 1988; Doctor of Humane Letters, Natchez Coll, 1989; Man of the Year, Natchez, MS, NAACP, 1990; Man of the Year, Natchez Business & Civic League, 1991; Most Outstanding Attorney, NAACP, 1992; Recorded first music album entitled "Ole Time Way," 1993; Outstanding Attorney for the African Methodist Episcopal Southern District & Man of the Year, Zion Chapel AME Church, 1995; recognized by the Magnolia Bar Assn and recipint of the "Pioneer and Leadership Award" 1997-98. **MEMBERSHIPS** Mem MS Bar Assn 1968; rsrchr/procter MS State Univ 1973; NAACP; Natchez Bus & Civ Lgue; vice pres Gov Com Hire the Hndcp; trust/sunday sch tchr Zion Chap AME Ch; contributing editor, Bluff City Post, 1978-; chmn, Natchez-Adams School Bd, 1988-. **CONTACT ADDRESS** PO Box 1202, Natchez, MS, 39120.

WEST, HENRY ROBISON
PERSONAL Born 12/16/1933, Athens, GA, m, 1955, 2 children **DISCIPLINE** PHILOSOPHY **EDUCATION** Emory Univ, AB, 54; Duke Univ, MA, 58; Union Theol Sem, MDiv, 59; Harvard Univ, PhD(philos), 65. **CAREER** Instr hist philos & sociol, Spelman Col, 57-60; instr humanities, Mass Inst Technol, 61- 65; from asst prof to assoc prof, 65-76, prof philos, Macalester Col, 76-, Old Dominion fel, 65; vis asst prof, Univ Minn, 68; Ford Found grant, Oxford, 70-71; vis prof, Univ Chicago, 78-79. **MEMBERSHIPS** Soc Philos & Pub Affairs; Am Philos Asn; Am Soc Polit & Legal Philos; Southern Soc Philos & Psychol. **RESEARCH** Utilitarian ethics; the philosphy of John Stuart Mill; political philosophy. **SELECTED PUBLICATIONS** Auth, Reconstructing Mill's proof of the principle of utility, Mind, 4/72; Utilitarianism, Encyclopedia Britannica, 15th ed, Encycl Brit, 74; Mill's naturalism, J Value Inquiry, 75; Mill's qualitative hedonism, Philos, 76; Comparing utilitarianism, Philos Res Arch, 76; Mill's moral conservatism, Midwest Studies Philos, 76; co-ed, Moral Philosophy: Classic Texts and Contemporary Problems, Dickenson, 77; Mill's proof of the principle of utility, In: The Limits of Utilitarianism, Univ Minn Press, 81. **CONTACT ADDRESS** Dept of Philosophy, Macalester Col, 1600 Grand Ave, St. Paul, MN, 55105-1899. **EMAIL** west@macalester.edu

WEST, JAMES E.
PERSONAL Born 08/29/1960, Oceanside, CA, m, 1983, 1 child **DISCIPLINE** THEOLOGY **EDUCATION** Carson-Newman Col, BA, 85; Southern Baptist Theol Sem, MDiv, 88, ThM, 91; Andersonville Baptist Sem, ThD, 94. **CAREER** Browns Baptist Church, Norlina NC, pastor, 86-90; Vance-Granville Comm Col, inst, 87-91; Tabbs Creek Baptist Church,

pastor, 90-93; First Baptist Church Petros TN, pastor, 93-, Quartz Hill Sch of Theol, adj prof, 96-. **HONORS AND AWARDS** Ordained Baptist Minister. **MEMBERSHIPS** SBL, DPV, ASOR, CBAA, IOTS, FJS. **RESEARCH** New testament; Hebrew literature; historical Jesus. **SELECTED PUBLICATIONS** Auth, The Eerdman's Dictionary of the Bible, entries; Abaddon, Apollyon, Hades, Sheol, Eerdman's Pub, 99; auth, Biblical Studies, A Beginner's Guide, Quartz Hill Pub, 98; auth, essays, Quartz Hill Jour of Theol; abstracts in: Old Testament Abstracts. **CONTACT ADDRESS** First Baptist Church, 321 Main St, Petros, TN, 37845-0300. **EMAIL** Jwest@highland.net

WEST, MARTHA S.

PERSONAL Born 02/05/1946, Pomona, CA, 3 children **DISCIPLINE** HISTORY; LAW **EDUCATION** Brandeis Univ, BA, 67; Indiana Univ, JD, 74. **CAREER** Atty, 74-82; asst prof, Univ Calif Davis Law Sch, 82-88; prof and assoc dean, 88-92; prof, 92- . **HONORS AND AWARDS** The 1981 Redding Scholar, Indianapolis Chamber of Com, Lacy Exec Leadership Series, 81-82; The Ruth E. Anderson Award from Women's Res and Resources Ctr and Women's Studies Prog, UC Davis, for outstanding service on behalf of campus women, 90; Sacramento YWCA Outstanding Woman of the Year in Educ, 91; The Deanna Falge Award for diversity and affirmative action, UC Davis, 96; The William & Sally Rutte Distinguished Teaching Award, UCD Law Sch, 97. **MEMBERSHIPS** AAUP; NLG; ABA. **RESEARCH** Women's legal rights; sex discrimination in higher education. **SELECTED PUBLICATIONS** Auth, Women Faculty: Frozen in Time, Academe, 95; auth, History Lessons: Affirmative Action, The Women's Rev of Books, 96; auth, The Hictorical Roots of Affirmative Action, La Raza Law J, 96; co-auth with H.H. Kay, Sex-Based Discrimination: Text, Cases, and Materials, 96; auth, Equitable Funding of Public Schools under State Constitutional Law, J Gender, Race, and Justice, 98. **CONTACT ADDRESS** School of Law, Univ of Calif.-Davis, Davis, CA, 95616. **EMAIL** mswest@ucdavis.edu

WESTACOTT, EMRYS

PERSONAL Born 10/22/1956, Nottingham, England, m, 1986, 2 children **DISCIPLINE** PHILOSOPHY **EDUCATION** Sheffield, BA, 79; McGill, MA, 84; Univ Texas, PhD, 95. **CAREER** Vis asst prof, Southwestern Univ, 95-96; asst prof, Alfred Univ, 96- . **MEMBERSHIPS** APA. **RESEARCH** Relativism; ethics; continental philosophy. **SELECTED PUBLICATIONS** Auth, On the Motivations for Relativism, Cogito; auth, Relativism: An Allegorical Elucidation, Philos Now; auth, Relativism and Autonomy, The Philos Forum; auth, Teaching Mills On Liberty, Tchg Philos. **CONTACT ADDRESS** Division of Human Studies, Alfred Univ, Alfred, NY, 14802. **EMAIL** westacott@bigvax.alfred.edu

WESTBLADE, DONALD

DISCIPLINE NEW TESTAMENT **EDUCATION** Williams Col, BA, 74; Fuller Sem, MDiv, 78; Yale Univ, 83, MPhil, 87. **CAREER** ASST PROF REL, 89-98, HILLSDALE COL. **MEMBERSHIPS** SBL, AAR, IBR, ETS **RESEARCH** New Testament ethics and rhetoric; New Testament theology. **SELECTED PUBLICATIONS** Auth, Divine Election in the Pauline Literature, in The Grace of God, The Bondage of the Will, vol 1, Balar, 95. **CONTACT ADDRESS** Hillsdale Col, 33 E College, Hillsdale, MI, 49242. **EMAIL** westblade@ac.hillsdale.edu

WESTLEY, RICHARD J.

DISCIPLINE PHILOSOPHY **EDUCATION** Marquette University, BA; Univ Toronto, MA; LMS Bontifical Inst Mediaeval Stud, Toronto;Univ Toronto, PhD, 54. **CAREER** Prof; Loyola Univ, part-time 57 & full-time 68-; lectr, Loyola's Inst Pastoral Stud, Chicago & Barat Col, Lake Forest, Ill. **RESEARCH** Aristotle's ethics; medieval philosophy, especially Aquinas; Kant's ethics; Kierkegaard; Feuerbach; Marx; philosophy of religion; ethical theory; Christian ethics; health care ethics. **SELECTED PUBLICATIONS** Auth, When It's Right to Die: Conflicting Voices, Difficult Choices, 94; Good Things Happen: Experiencing Community in Small Groups, 92; Life, Death and Science, 59; A Theology of Presence, 88; Morality and Its Beyond, 84; Redemptive Intimacy, 81; The Right to Die, 80; What a Modern Catholic Believes About the Right to Life, 73 & I Believe - You Believe, 73. **CONTACT ADDRESS** Dept of Philosophy, Loyola Univ, Chicago, 820 N Michigan Ave, Chicago, IL, 60611.

WESTMORELAND, ROBERT B.

DISCIPLINE ETHICS, POLITICAL PHILOSOPHY, PHILOSOPHY OF LAW **EDUCATION** Davidson Col, BA; Univ NC, Chapel Hill, MA, PhD. **CAREER** Asst prof, Univ MS, 89-. **RESEARCH** The problem of moral objectivity. **SELECTED PUBLICATIONS** Auth, Liberalism and the AIDS Crisis, Clin Res and Regulatory Aff, 95. **CONTACT ADDRESS** Univ MS, Oxford, MS, 38677. **EMAIL** prrbw@vm.cc.olemiss.edu

WESTON, BURNS H.

PERSONAL Born 11/05/1933, Cleveland, OH, d, 2 children **DISCIPLINE** INTERNATIONAL LAW, JURISPRUDENCE. **EDUCATION** Oberlin Col, BA, 56; Yale Univ, LLB, 61, JSD, 70. **CAREER** Assoc atty, Paul, Weiss, Rifkind, Wharton & Garrison, NY, 61-64; from asst prof to assoc prof law, 66-69, dir, Ctr World Order Studies, 72-76, prof Law, Univ Iowa, 69-, res fel, Procedural Aspects of Int Law Inst, 67-; consult Naval War Col, 68-69; vis lectr, Grinnell Col, 74-; Inst for World Order sr fel, 76-78, mem exec comt, Consortium on Peace Res, Educ & Develop, 76-; consult, Club Rome Proj on Global Learning, 77-; mem bd trustees, Global Educ Assocs, 78-**MEMBERSHIPS** Am Soc Int Law; Int Studies Asn; Consortium on Peace Res, Educ & Develop; Int Peace Res Asn; World Future Studies Fedn. **RESEARCH** Third World development; international claims; peace and world order education. **SELECTED PUBLICATIONS** Auth, International Law and the Deprivation of Foreign Wealth: a Framework for Future Inquiry, in: The Future of the International Legal Order--Wealth and Resources, 70; coauth, Valuation upon the Deprivation of Foreign Enterprise: A Policy-Oriented Approach to the Problem of Compensation Under International Law, In: The Valuation of Nationalized Property in International Law, 71; auth, International Claims: Postwar French Practice, Syracuse Univ, 71; coauth, International Claims: Their Settlement by Lump Sum Agreements, Univ Va, 75; auth, Constructive Takings Under International Law: A Modest Foray into the Problem of Creeping Expropriation, Va J Int Law, 75; contribr & co-ed, Toward World Order and Human Dignity: Essays in Honor Myres S McDougal, Free Press, 76; auth, Contending with a Planet in Peril and Change: The Rationale and Meaning of World Order Education, Inst for World Order, 78. **CONTACT ADDRESS** Col of Law, Univ of Iowa, 464 Boyd Law Bldg, Iowa City, IA, 52242-1113. **EMAIL** burns-weston@uiowa.edu

WESTON, THOMAS SPENGLER

PERSONAL Born 03/14/1944, Abilene, TX, m, 1977, 5 children **DISCIPLINE** PHILOSOPHY OF SCIENCE, LOGIC **EDUCATION** Mass Inst Tech, BS, 66, PhD(philos), 74. **CAREER** Instr philos, Mass Inst Tech, 69-70; from instr to asst prof, Univ Southern Calif, 70-74; asst prof to prof philos, San Diego State Univ, 74-. **MEMBERSHIPS** Asn Symbolic Logic. **RESEARCH** Philosophy of science; logic. **SELECTED PUBLICATIONS** Auth, Theories whose quantification cannot be substitutional, Nous, 11/74; Kreisel, the continuum hypothesis and second-order set theory, J Philos Logic, 76; The continuum hypothesis is independent of second-order set theory, Notre Dame J Formal Logic, 77; Approximate Truth, J of Philos Logic, vol 16, 87; Approximate Truth and Scientific Realism, Philos of Sci, vol 59, 92. **CONTACT ADDRESS** Dept of Philos, San Diego State Univ, 5500 Campanile Dr, San Diego, CA, 92182-8142. **EMAIL** tweston@mail.sdsu.edu

WESTPHAL, JONATHAN

DISCIPLINE PHILOSOPHY **EDUCATION** Univ London, PhD, 81. **CAREER** Assoc prof. **SELECTED PUBLICATIONS** Auth, Colour: A Philosophical Introduction; Colour: Some Philosophical Problems From Wittgenstein; Philosophical Propositions; ed, Certainty and of Justice; co-ed, Reality of Time and of Life and Death. **CONTACT ADDRESS** Dept of English and Philosophy, Idaho State Univ, Pocatello, ID, 83209. **EMAIL** westjona@isu.edu

WESTPHAL, KENNETH R.

PERSONAL Born 12/20/1955, Evanston, IL, m, 1987, 2 children **DISCIPLINE** PHILOSOPHY **EDUCATION** Univ of Ill, BA, 77; Univ of Wis, MA, 81, PhD 86. **CAREER** Vis asst prof, Purdue Univ, 86-88; asst prof, 88-94; assoc prof, 94-. **HONORS AND AWARDS** Gustafson Fel, Univ of NH, 91; NEH fel, 92; Alexander von Humboldt-Stiftung res grant, 95. **MEMBERSHIPS** Am Philos Asn; Int Kant-Gesellschaft; North Am Kant Soc; Hegel Soc of Am; Hegel Soc of Great Britain; North Am Nietzsche Soc; North Am Fichte Soc. **RESEARCH** Kant; Hegel; Nietzsche; Contemporary epistemology. **SELECTED PUBLICATIONS** Auth, Hegel's Epistemological Realism: A Study of the Aim and Method of Hegel's Phenomenology of Spirit; "Kant on the Sublime," 98; "Hegel, Formalism, and Robert Turner's Ceramic Art," 97. **CONTACT ADDRESS** Dept of Philosophy, Univ of New Hampshire, Hamilton Smith Hall, Durham, NH, 03824. **EMAIL** krwestphal@aol.com

WESTPHAL, MEROLD

DISCIPLINE PHILOSOPHY **EDUCATION** Yale Univ, PhD. **CAREER** Distinguished prof, Fordham Univ. **RESEARCH** Philos of relig and polit theology. **SELECTED PUBLICATIONS** Auth, History and Truth in Hegel's Phenomenology, Hum Press, 79, 90; God, Guilt, and Death: An Existential Phenomenology of Religion, Ind UP, 87; Kierkegaard's Critique of Reason and Society, Mercer UP, 87, Penn State UP, 91; Suspicion and Faith: The Religious Uses of Modern Atheism, Eerdmans Press, 1993; Becoming a Self: A Reading of Kierkegaard's Concluding Unscientific Postscript, Purdue UP, 96. **CONTACT ADDRESS** Dept of Philos, Fordham Univ, 113 W 60th St, New York, NY, 10023.

WETTSTEIN, HOWARD K.

PERSONAL Born 08/11/1943, Richmond, VA, m, 1969, 2 children **DISCIPLINE** PHILOSOPHY **EDUCATION** Yeshiva Col, BA, 65; CUNY, PhD, 76. **CAREER** Asst prof, Univ Minn, Morris, 74-81; vis assoc prof, Stanford Univ, 81-83; assoc prof, Univ Notre Dame, 83-89; prof, chemn dept 92-98, philos, Univ Calif, Riverside, 89- . **HONORS AND AWARDS** NEH, 81-82; ACLS, 81-82. **MEMBERSHIPS** APA. **RESEARCH** Philosophy of language; philosophy of religion. **SELECTED PUBLICATIONS** Co-ed, Midwest Stud in Philos, 75- ; auth, Has Semantics Rested Upon A Mistake: And Other Essays, Stanford, 91; auth, Terra Firma: Wittgenstein's Naturalism, The Monist, 95; auth, Doctrine, Faith and Philos, 97; auth, Awe and the Religious Life: A Naturalistic Perspective, in Wettstein, ed, Midwest Studies in Philosophy: The Philosophy of Religion, 98; auth, Against Theodicy, in Dawson, ed, Proceedings of the 20th World Congress of Philosophy, Philosophy Documentation Center, forthcoming. **CONTACT ADDRESS** Dept of Philosophy, Univ of California, Riverside, Riverside, CA, 92521. **EMAIL** Howard.Wettstein@ucr.edu

WETZEL, JAMES

DISCIPLINE PHILOSOPHY OF RELIGION **EDUCATION** Columbia Univ, PhD, 90. **CAREER** Assoc prof, Colgate Univ. **SELECTED PUBLICATIONS** Auth, Time After Augustine, Religious Studies; Moral Personality, Perversity, and Original Sin, Jour Rel Ethics; Some Thoughts in the Anachronism in Forgiveness. **CONTACT ADDRESS** Dept of Philos and Relig, Colgate Univ, 13 Oak Drive, Hamilton, NY, 13346. **EMAIL** jwetzel@mail.colgate.edu

WETZEL, JAMES RICHARED

PERSONAL Born 12/02/1959, Baltimore, MD **DISCIPLINE** RELIGION **EDUCATION** Princeton Univ, BA, 82; Columbia Univ, MA, 84, PhD, 90. **CAREER** ASSOC PROF OF PHILOS RELIG, COLGATE UNIV, 88-. **HONORS AND AWARDS** Charlotte Newcombe, 87; postdoctoral fel, Center for Philos of Rel, Notre Dame, 91-92; Phi Eta Sigma Prof of the Year, 97. **RESEARCH** Medieval philosophy; philosophy of religion; Augustine; mysticism. **SELECTED PUBLICATIONS** Auth, Augustine and the Limits of Virtue, Cambridge Univ Press, 92; Infinite Return: Two Ways of Wagering with Pascal, Relig Studies, 93; auth, Moral Personality, Perversity, and Original Sin, J of Relig Ethics, 95; auth, The Missing Adam: A Reply to Gilbert Meilander, J of Relig Ethics, 95; auth, Time After Augustine, Relig Studies, 95. **CONTACT ADDRESS** Dept of Philos & Relig, Colgate Univ, 13 Oak Dr, Hamilton, NY, 13346-1398. **EMAIL** jwetzel@mail.colgate.edu

WEXLER, DAVID BARRY

PERSONAL Born 04/04/1941, Brooklyn, NY, m, 1963, 2 children **DISCIPLINE** LAW **EDUCATION** State Univ NY, BA, 61; NY Univ, JD, 64. **CAREER** Assoc prof, 67-70, Prof Law, Col Law, Univ Ariz, 70-, Lectr, Law Ctr, Georgetown Univ, 66-67; consult, President's Comn Law Enforcement and Admin Justice, 67, Nat Comn Marihuana & Drug Abuse, 72 & Courts Task Force, Nat Adv Comt Criminal Justice Standards & Goals, 72; assoc ed, Criminology. **HONORS AND AWARDS** Manfred S Guttmacher Forensic Phychiat Award, Am Psychiat Asn, 72. **RESEARCH** Criminal law and procedure; law and psychiatric justice; law and psychiatry. **SELECTED PUBLICATIONS** Coauth, The administration of psychiatric justice: Theory and practice in Arizona, Ariz Law Rev, 71; auth, Therapeutic justice, Minn Law Rev, 12/72; Token and taboo: Behavior modification, Token economies and the law, Calif Law Rev, 1/73; Therapeutic Jurisprudence And Changing Conceptions Of Legal Scholarship, Behavioral Sciences & The Law, Vol 0011, 1993; Reflections On The Scope Of Therapeutic Jurisprudence, Psychology Public Policy And Law, Vol 0001, 1995; What Works - Reducing Reoffending - Mcguire,J, Behavioral Sciences & The Law, Vol 0015, 1997. **CONTACT ADDRESS** Col of Law, Univ of Ariz, University of AZ, Tucson, AZ, 85721-0001.

WEXLER, STEPHEN

DISCIPLINE LAW **EDUCATION** Columbia Univ, BA, 64; Univ NY, LLB, 67; LLM, 68. **CAREER** Prof. **HONORS AND AWARDS** Grad, Professional Baseball Umpires School **RESEARCH** Legal philosophy; consumer protection. **SELECTED PUBLICATIONS** Auth, pubs about burden of proof. **CONTACT ADDRESS** Fac of Law, Univ British Columbia, 1822 East Mall, Vancouver, BC, V6T 1Z1. **EMAIL** wexler@law.ubc.ca

WEYRAUCH, WALTER OTTO

PERSONAL Born 08/27/1919, Lindau, Germany, m, 1952, 3 children **DISCIPLINE** LAW **EDUCATION** Univ Frankfurt, Dr jur, 51; Georgetown Univ, Llb, 55; Harvard Univ, Llm, 56; Yale Univ, JSD, 62. **CAREER** Asst instr law, Yale Univ Law Sch, 56-57; from Assoc Prof to Prof, 57-98, Distinguished Prof Law, Col Law, Univ Fla, 98-; Mem, Ger Bar, Frankfurt, 49-52; US Court of Appeals, Allied High Comn, 51; vis consult soc sci, Space Sci Lab, Univ Calif, Berkeley, 65-66; chmn, comt studies beyond first degree in law, Asn Am Law Sch, 65-67; vis prof law, Rutgers Univ Sch Law, 68; polit sci, Univ Calif, Berkeley, 68-69; consult, Comn Experts Problems Succession of Hague Conf Pvt Int Law, US State Dept, 69-72; vis prof law, Univ

Frankfurt, Ger, 75; Stephen C. O'Connell Chair; Honorary Prof of Law, Johann Wolfgang Goethe Univ, Frankfurt Main, Ger, 80-. **MEMBERSHIPS** Int Soc of Family Law; Law and Soc Asn. **RESEARCH** Law and the social sciences; family law; comparative law. **SELECTED PUBLICATIONS** Auth, The Personality of Lawyers, Yale Univ, 64; Dual systems of family law, Calif Law Rev, 5/66; Zum Gesellschaftsbild des Juristen, Luchterhand, Neuwied, Ger, 70; The basic law or constitution of a small group, J Social Issues, 71; Taboo and magic in law, Stanford Law Rev, 73; coauth, Autonomous Lawmaking: The Case of the Gypsies, Yale Law J 103, 93; auth, Romaniya: An Introduction to Gypsy Law, Am J of Comparative Law 45, 97; Oral Legal Traditions of Gypsies and Some American Equivalents, Am J Comparative Law 45, 97; ed, Gypsy Law Symposium, Am J Comparative Law, Spring 97. **CONTACT ADDRESS** Col of Law, Univ of Florida, Gainesville, FL, 32611-9500.

WHALEY, DOUGLAS JOHN
PERSONAL Born 09/25/1943, Huntingburg, IN, d, 1 child **DISCIPLINE** LAW **EDUCATION** Univ Md, BA, 65; Univ Tex, JD, 68. **CAREER** Assoc law firm, Chapman & Culter, 68-70; from asst prof to prof law, Law Sch, Ind Univ, Indianapolis, 70-76; PROF LAW, COL LAW, OHIO STATE UNIV, 76-; Vis prof, Sch Law, Univ NC, 73-74 & Univ Calif, Hastings, 82-83. **RESEARCH** Commercial law; consumer problems. **SELECTED PUBLICATIONS** Auth, Warranties & the Practitioner, Practicing Law Inst, 81; contribr, Couse's Ohio Legal Forms, Anderson Publ Co, 82; Problems & Materials on Commercial Law, Aspen, 97; Problems & Materials on Consumer Law, Aspen, 98. **CONTACT ADDRESS** Law Sch, Ohio State Univ, 55 W 12th Ave, Columbus, OH, 43210-1306. **EMAIL** dglswhaley@aol.com

WHARTON, A.C., JR.
PERSONAL Born 08/17/1944, Lebanon, Tennessee, m **DISCIPLINE** LAW **EDUCATION** TSU, BA 1966; Univ MS, JD 1971. **CAREER** EEOC, decision drafter 1967-68; trial attorney, 1971-73; Lawyers Com for Civil Rights Under Law, proj dir 1973; Univ MS, adj prof; Shelby Co TN, pub defender 1980; Private Practice, Wharton & Wharton. **HONORS AND AWARDS** US Atty Gen Honor Law Grad Prog 1971. **MEMBERSHIPS** Past exec dir Memphis Area Leagl Serv Inc; mem Amer Bar Assn; Natl Legal Aid & Defender Assn; Natl Bar Assn; TN Bar Assn; NAACP; pres Leadership Memphis Alumni Assn 1979; Operation PUSH; Urban League. **CONTACT ADDRESS** 161 Jefferson Ave, Ste 402, Memphis, TN, 38103.

WHEELER, ARTHUR M.
PERSONAL Born 11/20/1928, Toledo, OH, d, 3 children **DISCIPLINE** PHILOSOPHY; ENGLISH **EDUCATION** Bowling Green State Univ, BA, 51; Univ Chicago, MA, 53; Univ WI, Madison, PhD, 58. **CAREER** Instr, 58-62, asst prof, 62-66, assoc prof, 66-70, prof, 70-91, Kent State Univ, Ohio; RETIRED. **HONORS AND AWARDS** Summer res grants, 66, 79; Sigma Tau Delta (English). **MEMBERSHIPS** AAUP; Amer Philos Assoc; Ohio Philos Assoc; Tri-State Philos Assoc; Soc for the Philos Study of Relig; Southern Soc for Philos and Psychol; Ohio Academy of Relig. **RESEARCH** Ethics; philos of relig; free will. **SELECTED PUBLICATIONS** Auth, On Lewis' Imperatives of Right, Phil Studies, 61; God and Myth, Hibbert Journal, 64; Are Theological Utterances Assertions?, Sophia, 69; Bliks as Assertions and as Attackable, Phil Studies, 74; Prima Facie and Actual Duty, Analysis, 77; On Moral Nose, Phil Quart, 77; Fiat Justitia, ruat Caelum, Ethics, 86. **CONTACT ADDRESS** 7686 Diagonal Rd., Kent, OH, 44240.

WHEELER, DAVID L.
PERSONAL Born 12/08/1946, Louisville, KY, m, 1990, 2 children **DISCIPLINE** THEOLOGY **EDUCATION** Georgetown Col, BA, 68; Yale Divinity Sch, MDiv, 71, Grad Theol Union, ThD, 84. **CAREER** Adj prof, Montclair St Univ, 84-85; prof, Cent Baptist Theol Sem, 85- . **HONORS AND AWARDS** Luther Wesley Smith Citation, Amer Baptist Churches, 89 **MEMBERSHIPS** Amer Acad of Relig; Amer Philos Assoc; Baptist Assoc of Philos Teachers; Nat Assoc of Baptist Prof of Relig; Soc of Christian Philos. **RESEARCH** Evangelical faith & process; relational thought; atonement; religious lang. **SELECTED PUBLICATIONS** Auth, Renewal Through the Classics, Christian Ministry, 96; Renewal Ecclesiology, Renew, 96; The Cosmic Christ and the Man of Sorrows, Explorations: J for Adventurous Thought, 96; Quine and the Religious Uses of Language, Perspectives in Relig Stud, 97; Central Thoughts for Ministry in the Twenty-First Century, Smyth & Helwys, 98. **CONTACT ADDRESS** Central Baptist Theol Sem, 741 N 31 St, Kansas City, KS, 66102. **EMAIL** wheels@cbts.edu

WHEELER, SAMUEL C., III
DISCIPLINE PHILOSOPHY **EDUCATION** Carleton Col, BA, 66; Princeton Univ, PhD, 70. **CAREER** ASST PROF TO PROF, UNIV CONN, 70-. **MEMBERSHIPS** APA; Scholars for the Second Amendment. **RESEARCH** Metaphysics, ethics, ancient philosophy, deconstruction. **SELECTED PUBLICATIONS** Auth, "Plato's Enlightenment," in Hist of Phil Quart, vol 14, 2, 97; auth, "Reparations Reconstructed," in Am Phil Quart, vol 34, 3, 97; auth, "Self-Defense and Coerced Risk-Acceptance," in Pub Aff Quart, vol 11, 4, 97; auth, "Arms as Insurance," Pub Aff Quart, 99. **CONTACT ADDRESS** Univ of Connecticut, U-54, 103 Manchester Hall, 344 Mansfield Rd, Storrs, CT, 06269. **EMAIL** swheeler@uconnvm.uconn.edu

WHEELER III, SAMUEL C.
DISCIPLINE PHILOSOPHY **EDUCATION** Carleton Col, BA, 66; Princeton Univ, PhD, 70. **CAREER** Dept Philos, Univ Conn **SELECTED PUBLICATIONS** Auth, A Deconstructive Wittgenstein?, Annals of Scholar, 87; Wong's Moral Relativity, Philos and Phenomenol Res, 87; Wittgenstein as Conservative Deconstructor, New Lit Hist, , 88; Luddism Reappraised: A Philosophy for the Nineties, Changing Work, 88; Derrida for Dancy and Sosa's Companion to Epistemology, Blackwells, 92; Davidson on Metaphor, Encycl of Aesthetics, Garland, 95. **CONTACT ADDRESS** Dept of Philos, Univ Conn, 344 Mansfield Rd, Storrs, CT, 06269.

WHELAN, STEPHEN T.
PERSONAL Born 07/28/1947, Philadelphia, PA, m, 1971, 1 child **DISCIPLINE** LAW/HISTORY **EDUCATION** Princeton Univ, BA, 68; Harvard Univ, JD, 71. **CAREER** Atty, 75-, partner, 78, Thacher Proffitt & Wood, Mudge Rose Guthrie & Alexander. **HONORS AND AWARDS** Magna cum laude, Princeton Univ; Outstanding Sr, student pol org, Princeton Univ. **MEMBERSHIPS** Amer Bar Asn; Fel, Amer Col of Investment Counsel; The Economic Club, NY. **RESEARCH** Financial law; econ history **SELECTED PUBLICATIONS** Auth, New York's Uniform Commercial Code New Article 2A, Matthew Bender & Co., 94; art, American Bar Association Annual Survey: Leases, Bus Lawyer, Vol 49, 94 & Vol 50, 95 & Vol 51, 96 & Vol 52, 97; art, Securitization of Medical Equipment Finance Contracts, Med Finance & Tech Yearbook, Euromoney Pub, 95; art, Securitization of Medical Equipment Finance Contracts, World Leasing Yearbook, Euromoney Pub, 96; coauth, The ABC's of the UCC: Article 2A (Leases), Amer Bar Asn, 97; art, Asset Securitization, Comm Finance Guide, Matthew Bender, 98. **CONTACT ADDRESS** Thacher Proffitt & Wood, 2 World Trade Ctr, New York, NY, 10048. **EMAIL** swhelan@thacherproffitt.com

WHELAN, WINIFRED
PERSONAL Chicago, IL **DISCIPLINE** THEOLOGY **EDUCATION** Marquette, MA, 68; Northwestern Univ, PhD, 85. **CAREER** Prof, St Bonaventure Univ. **MEMBERSHIPS** Am Acad Rel; Asn Prof Res Rel Educ. **RESEARCH** Religious education; epistemology. **SELECTED PUBLICATIONS** Auth, art, 1209: Founding of the Franciscans, 97; auth, art, 1009: The Church of the Holy Sepulchre is Destroyed, 97; auth, art, Theologians and Women's Theology, 97; auth, art, Roman Catholic Church, 98; auth, art, Chicago, 98. **CONTACT ADDRESS** St. Bonaventure Univ, Box 144, St. Bonaventure, NY, 14778-0144. **EMAIL** whelan@sbu.edu

WHIDDEN, WOODROW W., II
PERSONAL Born 10/15/1944, Orlando, FL, m, 1969, 3 children **DISCIPLINE** THEOLOGY **EDUCATION** Southern Adventist Univ, BA, 67; Seventh-day Adventist Theol Sem, BDiv, 69; Drew Univ, MA, 87, PhD, 89. **CAREER** Prof, 90-. **MEMBERSHIPS** Adventist Soc for Relig Studies; Wesleyan Theol Soc; Am Acad of Relig. **RESEARCH** Adventism; Theology; American religion and culture. **SELECTED PUBLICATIONS** Auth, Ellen White on the Humanity of Christ, 97; Ellen G. White on Salvation, 95; auth, "Salvation Pilgrimage: The Adventist Journey into Justification by Faith and Trinitarianism," in Ministry, 98; "Ellen White and the Basics of Salvation," in Ministry, 97; "Wesleyan on Imputation: A Truly Reckoned Reality or Antinomian Polemical Wreckage?", in The Asbury Theol J, 97; "Adventist Soteriology: The Wesleyan Connection," in Wesleyan Theol J, 95; "The Vindication of God and the Harvest Principle," in Ministry, 94; "Eschatology, Soteriology, and Social Activism in Four Mid-Nineteenth Century Holiness Methodists," in Wesleyan Theol J, 1994; "Essential Adventism or Historic Adventism?", in Ministry, 93. **CONTACT ADDRESS** Religion Dept, Andrews Univ, 208 Griggs Hall, Berrien Springs, MI, 49104. **EMAIL** whiddenw@andrews.edu

WHIPPS, JUDY
PERSONAL Born 10/12/1951, Muskegon, MI, m, 1987 **DISCIPLINE** PHILOSOPHY **EDUCATION** Grand Valley State Univ, BA, 92; Univ Chicago, MA, 95; The Union Inst, PhD, 98. **CAREER** Vis prof, Philos, Grand Valley State Univ, 95- . **HONORS AND AWARDS** Outstanding stud awd, Mich Asn Gov Boards of State Univ, 92; Liberal stud (s) dept Outstanding stud awd, 92. **MEMBERSHIPS** Amer Philos Asn; Soc Advance Amer Philos. **RESEARCH** Pragmatism; social and political philosophy; feminism. **SELECTED PUBLICATIONS** Auth, Rev, Needleman, Money and the Meaning of Life, Grand Rapids Press, Oct 92. **CONTACT ADDRESS** Dept of Philosophy, Grand Valley State Univ, 3154 Pine Meadow, Grandville, MI, 49418. **EMAIL** judywhipps@aol.com; Whippsj.@gvsu.edu

WHITACRE, RODNEY A.
PERSONAL Born 12/28/1949, Des Moines, IA, m, 1972, 2 children **DISCIPLINE** BIBLICAL STUDIES **EDUCATION** Gordon Col, AB, 73; Gordon-Conwell Theol Seminary, MATS, 76; Univ Cambridge, PhD, 81. **CAREER** Dir Greek Prog, Gordon-Conwell Theol Seminary, 81-83; Prof Bibl Studies, Trinity Episcopal Sch Ministry, 83-. **MEMBERSHIPS** Soc Bibl Studies; Inst Bibl Res. **RESEARCH** New Testament; Hellenistic Greek. **SELECTED PUBLICATIONS** Auth, Johannine Polemic: The Role of Tradition and Theology, Schol Press, 82; The Moon of Our Darkness ¤: Unity and Diversity in Scripturel, Mission & Ministry, 91; The Biblical Vision ¤Regarding Women's Ordinationl, The Evangelical Cath, 94; Studying the Scriptures, The Evangelical Cath, 94; John, IVP New Testament Commentary, InterVarsity Press (forthcoming 99). **CONTACT ADDRESS** Trinity Episcopal Sch for Ministry, 311 Eleventh St., Ambridge, PA, 15003. **EMAIL** RodWhitacre@TESM.edu

WHITBECK, CAROLINE
DISCIPLINE PHILOSOPHY **EDUCATION** Wellesley Col, BA, 62; Boston Univ, MA, 65; Massachusetts Inst Technology, PhD, 70. **CAREER** Teach asst, math, 63-65, The Mitre Corp; Lectr, 68-70, asst prof, 70-71, res assoc in psychiatry, 71-73, Yale Univ; asst prof, 73-78, SUNY Albany, post dr fel, 77-78, The Hastings Center; assoc prof, 78-82, Dept of Preventative Med and Comm Health, Univ of TX Med School Galveston; res fel, Center for Policy Alt, 9/82-8/83, vis assoc prof, School of Engineering, 9/83-8/86, lectr, mech eng & res scholar, 9/86-1/88, sr lectr in mech eng, 1/88-6/97, Mass Inst of Tech; prof, Dept of Mech and Aerospace Eng & Philosophy & Elmer G. Beamer-Hubert H Schneider Prof in Ethics, 97-, Case Western Reserve Univ. **HONORS AND AWARDS** Hastings Center Fel, 77-78; NSF Vis Professorship of Women, 83-85; Amer Asn for the Advancement of Science Fel, 89; Phi Beta Kappa; Vis Scholar, 94-95. **MEMBERSHIPS** Amer Asn of Bioethics; Amer Asn for the Advancement of Univ Prof; Amer Phil Asn; Asn for Practical and Prof Ethics; Asn of MIT Alumnae; Hastings Center; Inst of Electrical and Electronic Eng; Phil of Science Asn; Sigma Xi; Soc for Women in Phil; Soc of Women Eng. **RESEARCH** Practical ethics; professional ethics in eng, science, health care and education; research ethics; bioethics (incl ethical issues in genetics; phil of science, technology, & med; the education development of women and minorities in eng and other scientific professions; feminist phil. **SELECTED PUBLICATIONS** Auth, Imaging Technologies, Encycl of Childbearing, Oryx Press, 93; auth, Virtual Environments: Ethical issues and Significant Confusions, Presence: Teleoperators and Virtual Environments, 93; auth, Ought We Blame Technology for the Failings of Medical Ethics? A Response to Daniel Callahan's How Technology Seduced the Sanctity of Life, First Things, 94; auth, Teaching Ethics to Scientist and Engineers: Moral Agents and Moral Problems, Science & Engineering Ethics, 95; auth, Biomedical Engineering, 2nd Ed of Encycl of Bioethics, Macmillan, 95; auth, Trust, 2nd Ed of Encycl of Bioethics, Macmillan, 95; auth, Trustworthy Research, and Editorial Introduction, Science & Eng Ethics, 95; auth, Ethics as Design: Doing Justice to Moral Problems, Hastings Center Report, 96; art, Problems and Cases: New Directions in Ethics 1980-1996, Jour of Prof Ethics, 97; coauth, Science, Scientist and Human Rights Education, Human Rights Education in the 21st Century: Conceptual and Practical Challenges, Univ of PA Press, 97; auth, Using Problems and Cases in Teaching Professional Ethics: Theory and Practice, Tchng Criminal Justice Ethics: Strategic Issues, Anderson Pub Co, 97; auth, Research Ethics, Encycl of Applied Ethics, Academic Press, 98; auth, Ethics in Engineering Practice and Research, Cambridge Univ Press, 98. **CONTACT ADDRESS** Philosophy Dept, Case Western Reserve Univ, 10900 Euclid Ave, Cleveland, OH, 44106-7199.

WHITE, ALFRED LOE
PERSONAL Born 10/19/1957, Framingham, MA, m, 1993, 2 children **DISCIPLINE** PHILOSOPHY **EDUCATION** Catholic Univ of Amer, PhD, 97. **CAREER** Asst Prof, 98-, Univ of Baltimore. **HONORS AND AWARDS** Full Fel at Catholic Univ. **MEMBERSHIPS** ACPA **RESEARCH** Philosophy of mind, Thomas Aquinas, Phenomenology. **SELECTED PUBLICATIONS** Auth, Why the Cognitive Power?, Proceedings of the 1998 Amer Cath Philo Assoc, 98. **CONTACT ADDRESS** 10092 Hatbrim Terrace, Columbia, MD, 21046. **EMAIL** awhite@ubmail.ubalt.edu

WHITE, CHARLES SIDNEY JOHN
PERSONAL Born 09/25/1929, New Richmond, WI **DISCIPLINE** HIST OF RELIGIONS, HINDUISM & MEDIEVAL & MODERN HINDI POETRY **EDUCATION** Univ WI, BA, 51; Univ of the Am, MA, 57; Univ Chicago, MA, 62, PhD, 64. **CAREER** Asst prof Indian studies, Univ WI, 65-66; asst prof, relig thought & S Asian studies, Univ PA, 66-71; coordr, ctr Asian Studies, 73-76, assoc prof, Am Univ, 71-78, Dir Ctr Asian Studies, 76-78, Prof Philos & Relig, Am Univ 78-94, Prof Emer Philos & Relig, 95-, chmn dept philos & relig, 84-87 & 88-94, Dir Inst Vaishnava Studies, 71-; Vis lectr Hist Relig, Princeton Univ, 68; Vis prof world relig, Lakehead Univ, Thunder Bay, Ontario, 74, 77, 80, 82, 84 & 88 (summers); Vis prof, Wesley Sem, Fall 85; Jr fel, Am Inst Indian Studies, Poona, India, 64-65 & res fel, Agra, 68-69, trustee, 73-; Kern Found Fel, 72. **HONORS AND AWARDS** Inst Int Educ graduate award, Span lang and lit, Universidad nacional de Mexico; Rockefeller Doctoral fel, relig, hon, Univ Chicago, 61; NDEA fel, Hindu-Urdu, Univ Chicago 61-64; Am Philos Soc fel, 66-67; Summer res grant,

Univ PA, India, 70; Col Arts & Sci travel res grant, summer 74; Am Univ travel grant, India, summer 76; Center for Asian Studies, Am Univ, summer grant, 78; Smithsonian Grant, prin investigator, India, 82-83; Am Univ Col Arts & Sci Award fro Outstanding Scholar, 84; Am Univ Senate Comt Res, India, summer 87; CAS Mellon Award; Am Inst Indian Studies fac res fel, India, 95, spring 97. **MEMBERSHIPS** Am Asn Asian Studies; Am Acad Relig; Am Orient Soc; Soc Sci Study Relig. **RESEARCH** Hist of relig methodology; Hindu lit; Islam. **SELECTED PUBLICATIONS** Auth, Sufism in Hindi literature, 64 & Krishna as divine child, 70, Hist Relig; Heaven, In: The Encyclopedia Britannica, 65; Resources for the study of Medieval Hindu devotional religion,, Am Philos Soc Yearbk 67; A Note Toward Understanding in Field Method, In: Understanding in History of Relition, Univ Chicago Press, 67; Bhakti, In: The Encyclopedia Britannica, 68; Devi, Dharma, Dayanand Saraswati, Durga, Diwali, The Encyclopedia Americana, 68; Krsna as divine child, Hist Relig, 70; The Sai Baba movement, J Asian Studies, 72; Henry S Olcott: A Buddhist apostle, Theosophist, 4/73; co-auth, Responses to Jay J Bim on Bernard Meland, Jour Relig, 4/73; Swami Muktananda, Hist Relig, 74; Caurasi Pad of Sri Hit Harivams (transl), Univ Hawaii, 77; Structure in history of religions, Hist Relig, 78; Ramayana, Ramanuja, Ram Mohan Roy, Ramakrishna, Encyclopedia Americana, 79; Ramakrishna's Americans, Yugantar Prakashan, 79; Madhva, Mahavira, Mantra, Mandala, Manu, Encyclopedia Americana, 79; Mother Guru: Jnanananda of Madras, India, In: Unspoken Worlds: Women's Religious Lives, Harper and Row, 80, 2nd ed, Wadsworth, 88; The Hindu Holy Person, Ramakrishna, Satya Sai Baba, J Krishnamurti, Ramana Maharshi, Sadhu, Guru, Rsi, Acarya, Meher Baba, In: Abingdon Dictionary of Living Religions, 81, Perennial Dictionary of World Religions, Harper and Row, 89; Untouchables, Parsis, Encyclopedia Americana, 81; Kuan Yin, Juggernaut, Kali, Kama Sutra, Karma, Kautilya, Krishna, Jiddu Krishnamurti, Kshatriya, Kumbha Mela, Lakshmi, In: Encyclopedia Americana, 82; co-auth, The Religious Quest, Univ Md. 83, 2nd ed, 85; Religion in Asia, In: Funk and Wagnall's Yearbook, 85-93, and Collier's International Yearbook; Almsgiving, Gift Giving, Jiddu Krishnamurti: A Biograhy, In: Encyclopedia of Religion, Macmillan Co, 86; Inwardness and privacy: Last bastions of religious life, Theosophis, 86 & Holistic Human Concern for World Welfare, 87; Indian developments: Sainthood in Hinduism, In: Sainthood: Its Manifestations in World Religions, Univ Calif Press, 88, paperbk, 8/90; co-auth, Joseph Campbell: Transformations of Myth Through Time, and An Anthology of Readings, Harcourt Brace Jovanovich, 89; co-ath (with David Haberman), rev, Sonic Theology: Hinduism and Sacred Sound by Guy L Beck, Jour Vaisnava Studies, spring 94; Nimbarka Sampradaya, Anandamayi Ma, Ramana Marsi, Sadhu, Swami, svamin, In: HarperCollins Dictionary of Religion, 95; The remaining Hindi works of Sri Hit Harivams, Jour Vaisnava Studies, fall 96; Mircea Eliade, Bengal Nights ... Maitreyi Devi, It Does Not Die, rev, Love and Politics for Eliade, Annals of Scholarship, summer 97; Muhammad as Spiritual Master, In: The Quest, 8/98. **CONTACT ADDRESS** Dept of Philos & Relig, American Univ, 4400 Massachusetts Ave NW, Washington, DC, 20016-8200.

WHITE, DAVID A.

PERSONAL Born 03/23/1942, South Bend, IN, m, 1973, 2 children **DISCIPLINE** PHILOSOPHY **EDUCATION** Univ Toronto, PhD, 73. **CAREER** Instr, Christian Bros Univ, 66-67; Marian Col, 67-68, 69-70, 72-73; asst prof, Mankato State Univ, 73-75; mem fac, New School for Soc Res, 78; adj asoc prof, DePaul Univ, 82- ; instr, Northwestern Univ, 93- . **HONORS AND AWARDS** NEH Summer Stipend, Case Western Reserve Univ, 74; ACLS Fel, 85-86. **MEMBERSHIPS** Amer Philos Assoc **RESEARCH** Ancient philosophy; philosophy and literature; aesthetics; philosophy and children. **SELECTED PUBLICATIONS** Auth, The Turning Wheel, Susquehanna, 88; Myth and Metaphysics in Plato's Phaedo, Susquehanna, 89; Rhetoric and Reality in Plato's Phaedrus, SUNY, 93. **CONTACT ADDRESS** 6608 N Bosworth, Chicago, IL, 60626-4224. **EMAIL** dwhite6886@aol.com

WHITE, DAVID BENJAMIN

PERSONAL Born 03/06/1917, Macon, MO, m, 1945 **DISCIPLINE** PHILOSOPHY **EDUCATION** Northeastern State Col, BS, 37; Okla State Univ, MA, 39; Univ of the Pac, PhD(Asian studies), 59. **CAREER** Prof English, Friends Univ, 46-48; from instr to asst prof English & philos, 48-67, prof philos, 67-74, Elizabeth Sarah Bloedel Prof Philos, Macalester Col, 74-. **RESEARCH** Contemporary Indian philosophies; Mohandas K Gandhi; inductive studies of religions. **CONTACT ADDRESS** Dept of Philosophy, Macalester Col, 1600 Grand Ave, St. Paul, MN, 55105-1899. **EMAIL** wellshowe@macalester.edu

WHITE, FRANKIE WALTON

PERSONAL Born 09/08/1945, Yazoo City, MS **DISCIPLINE** LAW **EDUCATION** Wellesley College, 1964-65; Tougaloo Coll, BA (magna cum laude) 1966; Univ of CA at Los Angeles, MA 1967; Syracuse University, Syracuse, NY, 1972-73; Univ of MS, JD 1975. **CAREER** Fisk Univ, instructor of English 1967-69; Wellesley Coll, lecturer in English 1969-70; Tougaloo Coll, asst prof of English 1970-71; Syracuse Univ, asst dir of financial aid 1971-72; Central MS Legal Svcs, staff atty 1975-77; State of MS, spec asst atty general 1977; TX Southern Univ, student legal counselor 1977-79; State of MS, asst atty general 1979-. **HONORS AND AWARDS** Woodrow Wilson Fellow; Reginald Heber Smith Comm Lawyer Fellow; Women of Achievement Awd in Law & Govt Women for Progress of Mississippi Inc 1981; Distinguished Alumni Citation NAFEO 1986. **MEMBERSHIPS** Alpha Kappa Alpha Sor Inc 1964-; mem Magnolia, Mississippi Bar Assn 1975-; The Links Inc 1977-; Commission of Colleges Southern Assn of Colls & Schools 1982-; bd of trustees, Southern Assn of Colleges & Schools, 1988-91; Leadership Jackson, 1989-; chairman, Council of State Education Attorneys, 1990-91; bd of dirs, Natl Assn of State Boards of Education, 1991. **CONTACT ADDRESS** State of Mississippi, P O Box 220, Jackson, MS, 39205.

WHITE, FREDERIC PAUL, JR.

PERSONAL Born 02/12/1948, Cleveland, Ohio, m **DISCIPLINE** LAW **EDUCATION** Columbia Coll New York, BA, 1970; Columbia Law School New York, JD, 1973. **CAREER** Squire Sanders & Dempsey, assoc attny, 1973-78; Cleveland State Univ, asst professor, 1978-81, assoc prof, 1981-86, prof, 1986-, assoc dean, 1994-. **MEMBERSHIPS** Mem, bd of trustees, Cleveland Legal Aid Soc, 1981-84, Trinity Cathedral Comm Devel Fund, 1981-89; pres, Norman S Minor Bar Assn, 1984; acting judge & referee, Shaker Heights Municipal Court, 1984-90; mem, Omega Psi Phi Fraternity Inc, Zeta Omega Chapter; host, CSU City Focus radio show, 1981-85; bd of advisors, African-Amer Museum, 1986-90. **SELECTED PUBLICATIONS** Book, "Ohio Landlord Tenant Law," Banks-Baldwin Law Publ Co, 1984, 2nd ed, 1990, 3rd ed, 1995; 2 law review articles, "Cleveland Housing Ct," "Ohio Open Meeting Law"; Contrib Author Antieau's Local Govt Law; co-author chapts "Criminal Procedure Rules for Cleveland Housing Ct"; Frequent guest on local TV/radio landlord-tenant law subjects; contributing editor, Powell on Real Property; Thompson on Real Property. **CONTACT ADDRESS** Cleveland State Univ, 1801 Euclid Ave, Cleveland, OH, 44115.

WHITE, G. EDWARD

PERSONAL Born 03/19/1941, Northampton, MA, m, 1966, 2 children **DISCIPLINE** AMERICAN STUDIES; LAW **EDUCATION** Amherst Col, BA, 63; MA, 64, PhD, 67, Yale Univ; Harvard Law School, JD, 70. **CAREER** Univ Va, Sch Law **RESEARCH** American constitutional and legal history **CONTACT ADDRESS** Univ of Virginia School of Law, 580 Massie Rd., Charlottesville, VA, 22903-1789. **EMAIL** gewhite@law1.virginia.edu

WHITE, HOWARD A.

PERSONAL Born 10/06/1927, New York, New York, m, 1968 **DISCIPLINE** LAW **EDUCATION** City College (CCNY), BEE, 1949; St Johns Univ, JD, 1954; New York Univ, MPA, 1959. **CAREER** Powsner, Katz & Powsner, associate, 1953-62; Federal Communications Comm, general atty, (public utilities), 1962-66; Communications Satellite Corp, general atty, 1966-68; ITT Communications, general counsel & exec vp, 1968-87; St Johns Univ School of Law, prof of law, 1988-. **MEMBERSHIPS** Federal Communications Bar Assn; American Bar Assn; NY State Bar Assn. **SELECTED PUBLICATIONS** "Five Tuning The Federal Govt Role in Public Broadcasting," 46 Fed Comm LJ 491, 1994. **CONTACT ADDRESS** Professor of Law, St. Johns Univ, 8000 Utopia Parkway, Jamaica, NY, 11439.

WHITE, HUGH

PERSONAL Born 12/02/1936, Columbus, GA, m, 1960, 2 children **DISCIPLINE** HEBREW BIBLE **EDUCATION** Asbury Col, AB, 58; Candl Sch of Theol, BA, 61; Drew Univ, Phd, 67 **CAREER** Assoc Prof, 65-70 TN Wesleyan Col; Prof, 70-pres, Rutgers Univ **HONORS AND AWARDS** Outst Tch Award, 70; RJ Dept of Higher Educ Award, 85 **MEMBERSHIPS** Am Acad of Relig; Soc of Bibl Lit; Soc for Study of Narrative; Walker Percy Soc **RESEARCH** Ancient Narrative **SELECTED PUBLICATIONS** Auth, Narration & Discourse in the Book of Genesis, Cambridge, 91 **CONTACT ADDRESS** 47 Truman Ave, Haddonfield, NJ, 08033. **EMAIL** hwhite@crab.rutgers.edu

WHITE, JAMES JUSTESEN

PERSONAL Born 02/19/1934, Omaha, NE, m, 1956, 3 children **DISCIPLINE** LAW **EDUCATION** Amherst Col, BA, 56; Univ Mich, JD, 62. **CAREER** From asst prof to assoc prof, 64-70, Prof Law, Univ Mich, Ann Arbor, 70-. **RESEARCH** Commercial law; consumer credit. **SELECTED PUBLICATIONS** Coauth, Teaching Materials on Commercial Transactions, 69 & Handbook on the Uniform Commercial Code, 72, West; Letter To Edwards,Harry, Michigan Law Review, Vol 0091, 1993; Harveys Silence - Comment, American Bankruptcy Law Journal, Vol 0069, 1995; Reforming Article-9 Priorities In Light Of Old Ignorance And New Filing Rules, Minnesota Law Review, Vol 0079, 1995. **CONTACT ADDRESS** Law Sch, Univ of Mich, Ann Arbor, MI, 48104.

WHITE, JANICE G.

PERSONAL Born 08/21/1938, Cincinnati, OH, m, 1962 **DISCIPLINE** LAW **EDUCATION** Western Reserve University, BA, 1963; Capital University Law School, JD, 1977. **CAREER** Legal Aid Society of Columbus, Reginald Heber Smith Community, Law Fellow, 1977-79; Franklin County Public Defender, juvenile unit, public defender, 1979-80; Ohio State Legal Services Association, legislative counsel, 1980-84; State Employment Relations Board, labor relations specialist, 1984, administrative law judge, 1984-88; CAPITAL UNIVERSITY LAW & GRADUATE CENTER, ALUMNI RELATIONS & MULTI-CULTURAL AFFAIRS DIRECTOR, 1988-. **HONORS AND AWARDS** United Church of Christ, Outstanding Woman in the Ohio Conference, 1985; Columbus Alumnae Chapter, Outstanding Delta, 1986; United Negro College Fund Inc, Meritorious Service Award, 1989. Reginald Heber Smith, Community Law Fellow, 1977-79; assisted in the negotiations for release of hostages from Teheran, 1980. **MEMBERSHIPS** American Bar Association; Ohio Bar Association; Central Community House; Links Inc; National Conference of Black Lawyers; Women Lawyers of Franklin County Inc; Columbus Commission on Community Relations; Delta Sigma Theta Sorority Inc; United Negro College Fund. **CONTACT ADDRESS** Alumni Relations & Minority Affairs, Capital Univ, 303 E Broad St, Columbus, OH, 43215-3200.

WHITE, JOHN D.

PERSONAL Born 07/23/1948, Benham, KY **DISCIPLINE** MUSIC; PHILOSOPHY **EDUCATION** Univ Ky, BM, 70; Univ Idaho, MM, 72; Univ Iowa, PhD, 77. **CAREER** Sabbatical replacement, Willamette Univ, spring, 74; asst prof, 76-78, interim chair, 78-79, assoc prof, 78-80, dept chair, fall, 80, Western Wy Community Col, driver, Webb's Trucking, spring, 81; assoc prof, Benedict Col, 81-82; assoc prof, Chattahoochee Valley State Community Col, 82-83; grad study in philos, Univ Ky, spring, 84; lectr, Okla State Univ, 84-85; grad asst, Univ Tex Austin, 85-86; grad study in philos, Univ Iowa, spring, 87; assoc prof, Col of the Ozarks, 87-88; pianist, Univ Iowa, 88-89; prof, philos/humanities, Talladega Col, 89-. **SELECTED PUBLICATIONS** Auth, The Pythagorean Derivation and Theories of Truth, 96; auth, The Substance Argument, 95; auth, The Confluence of Deism, African Creation Myth, and Thomas Hobbes, 94; auth, Philosophy of Law, 94; auth, The Origin of Number, 93; auth, The Antigone Effect, 92; auth, Belief System Internal Inconsistency, 91; auth, The Maker's Mind Model in Aesthetics, 91; auth, The Analysis of Law and the Nesting of the Philosophy of History in the History of Empiricism, 88; auth, Some Remarks on Some Remarks on Logical Form, 87; auth, Considerations on Infinity Derived from Spinozist Theory, 87; auth, Empiricism, Hume, Quantum Mechanics, and Universe Models, 86. **CONTACT ADDRESS** Dept. of Philosophy, Talladega Col, Campus Box 165, Talladega, AL, 35160.

WHITE, JOHN L.

PERSONAL Born 05/31/1940, Washington, MO, m, 1961, 3 children **DISCIPLINE** NEW TESTAMENT, CHRISTIAN ORIGINS **EDUCATION** William Jewell Coll, BA, 62; Vanderbilt Univ, MA, 68; PhD, 70. **CAREER** Asst prof, Mo School Rel, 69-75; assoc prof, 76-81; assoc prof, Loyola Univ Chicago, 81-87; prof, Loyola Univ Chicago, 87-. **HONORS AND AWARDS** Chairman of Soc of Bibl Lit Ancient Epistography Group, 74-79; Assoc in Council Soc of Bibl Lit, 79-81; bd of Dir of Polebridge Puss, 87-; Pres, Chicago Soc of Bibl Res. **MEMBERSHIPS** Am Soc of Papyrology; cath Bibl Asn; Chicago Soc of Bibl Res; Soc of Bibl Lit. **RESEARCH** Ancient letterwriting; First generation Christianity; St Paul; Influence of Greco-Roman culture on Christianity. **SELECTED PUBLICATIONS** Auth, Apostolic Mission and Apostolic Message, Origins and Method, 93. **CONTACT ADDRESS** 6545 N Bosworth, Chicago, IL, 60626. **EMAIL** Jwhite@luc.edu

WHITE, KEVIN

DISCIPLINE AQUINAS, MEDIEVAL PHILOSOPHY **EDUCATION** Univ Ottawa, PhD. **CAREER** Philos, Catholic Univ Am. **RESEARCH** Thomistic psychology; Aquinas; Augustine. **SELECTED PUBLICATIONS** Auth, The Meaning of Phantasia in Aristotle's De anima, III, 3-8, Dialogue 24, 85; St Thomas Aquinas and the Prologue to Peter of Auvergne's Quaestiones super De sensu et sensato, Documenti e studi sulla tradizione filosofica medievale 1, 90; three previously unpublished chapters from St Thomas Aquinas's Commentary on Aristotle's Meteora: Sentencia super Meteora 2;13-15, Mediaeval Studies 54 , 92; The Virtues of Man the Animal sociale: Affabilitas and Veritas in Aquinas, The Thomist 57, 93; Individuation in Aquinas's Super Boetium De Trinitate, Q;4, American Catholic Philosophical Quarterly 69, 95; Aquinas on the Immediacy of the Union of Soul and Body, in Paul Lockey, ed;, Studies in Thomistic Theology, Houston: Center for Thomistic Studies, 96; Ed, Hispanic Philosophy in the Age of Discovery, Catholic Univ Am Press, 97; Coed, Jean Capreolus et son temps, Cerf, 97. **CONTACT ADDRESS** Catholic Univ of America, 620 Michigan Ave Northeast, Washington, DC, 20064. **EMAIL** whitek@cua.edu

WHITE, LELAND J.

PERSONAL Charleston, SC **DISCIPLINE** RELIGION **EDUCATION** St Mary's Sem & Univ, BA, 62; Pontif Univ Gregoriana, Rome, STL, 66; Univ Mich, Ann Arbor, MA, 72; Duke Univ, PhD(relig), 74, Seton Hall Univ Law Sch, JD, 92. **CAREER** Instr theol, Sulpician Sem of the Northwest, 68-69 & St

John Provincial Sem, 69-70; asst prof relig studies, Nazareth Col, Kalamazoo, 74-76; asst prof, Siena Col, 76-82, chmn relig studies dept, 79-82; Prof Theol, St John's Univ, Jamaica NY, 82-, Nat Endowment for Humanities fel relig, Yale Univ, 76; dir, Reinhold Niebuhr Inst Relig & Cult, 77-79; mem, bd of assoc ed, Bibl Theol Bull, 80-; Nat Endowment for Humanities fel, Princeton Univ, 81; Leo John Dehon fel theol, 82. **MEMBERSHIPS** Am Bar Assoc, SC Bar Assoc, AM Acad Relig; Cath Theol Soc Am; Col Theol Soc; AAUP. **RESEARCH** Theology; religion and culture; political theology. **SELECTED PUBLICATIONS** Auth, Religion and Law in America, 98; auth, Bible, Church and Culture, 97; auth, Jesus the Christ: A Bibliography, 88; auth, Christ and the Christian Movement: Jesus in the New Testament, the Creeds and Modern Theology, 85; auth, Theology and Authority: A Cross-Cultural Analysis of Theological Scripts, Theology and Authority **CONTACT ADDRESS** Dept of Theol and Relig Stu, St John's Univ, 8000 Utopia Pky, Jamaica, NY, 11439-0001. **EMAIL** whitelel@shu.edu

WHITE, M. CHRIS
PERSONAL Born 10/16/1943, SC, m, 1965, 2 children **DISCIPLINE** RELIGION **EDUCATION** Emory Univ, PhD, 72. **CAREER** Prof relig, 72-80, Exec Vice-Pres, Elon Col, 80-86; pres, Gardner-Webb Univ, 86- . **HONORS AND AWARDS** Woodrow Wilson Fel. **MEMBERSHIPS** AAR; SBL. **RESEARCH** New Testament studies. **CONTACT ADDRESS** Gardner-Webb Univ, PO Box 897, Boiling Springs, NC, 28017. **EMAIL** mcwhite@gardner-webb.edu

WHITE, MARSHA
PERSONAL Born 04/02/1950, Boston, MA **DISCIPLINE** HEBREW BIBLE **EDUCATION** Harvard Univ, PhD, 94. **CAREER** Instr, Phillips Exeter Academy, 84-85; teaching fel, Harvard Col, 88, 90, 91; instr, Harvard Divinity School, fall 91; lect, Col of the Holy Cross, 93-94; instr, Hebrew Col, Brookline, MA, 94-95; lect, Univ MA, spring 95; instr, Classical Asn of New England Summer Inst, 94-98; instr, Temple Bethel, 95-96; vis asst prof, Wesleyan Univ, fall 96; lect, Andover Newton Theol School, 95-97; vis lect in Judaic Studies, Brown Univ, fall 97; instr, Havurat Shalom, Sommerville, MA, 97-98. **HONORS AND AWARDS** Listed in Who's Who in Biblical Studies and Archaeology, 2nd ed (1992-93), Washington, DC: Biblical Archaeology Soc, 93; Soc Biblical Literature Regional Scholar. **MEMBERSHIPS** Soc Biblical Lit; Asn for Jewish Studies. **RESEARCH** Ancient Israelite historiography. **SELECTED PUBLICATIONS** Auth, The Elohistic Depiction of Aaron: A Study in the Levite-Zadokite Controversy, in Studies in the Pentateuch, ed, J. A. Emerton, supplemental to Vetus Testamentum 41, Leiden: Brill, 90; Jonah, in The Women's Bible Commentary, eds Carol Newsom and Sharon Ringe, Louisville: Westminster/John Knox, 92; Naboth's Vineyard and Jehu's Coup: The Legitimation, of a Dynastic Extermination, Vetus Testamentum 44, 94; The Elijah Legends and Jehu's Coup, Brown Judaic Studies 311, Atlanta: Scholars, 97; Review of Diversity in Pre-Exilic Hebrew by Ian Young, JBL 116, 97; Bathsheba, Elisha, Nathan, Uriah, in Eerdmans Dictionary of the Bible, eds, David Noel Freedman, Allen C. Myers, Astrid B. Beck, Grand Rapids: Eerdmans, forthcoming. **CONTACT ADDRESS** 16 Mountain Ave., Somerville, MA, 02143-1309. **EMAIL** mesh33@aol.com

WHITE, MORTON G.
PERSONAL Born 04/29/1917, New York, NY, m, 1940, 2 children **DISCIPLINE** PHILOSOPHY **EDUCATION** City Col New York, BS, 36; Columbia Univ, AM, 38, PhD, 42. **CAREER** Instr physics, City Col New York, 43; instr philos, Columbia Univ, 42-46; asst prof, Univ Pa, 46-48, Harvard Univ, 48-50, assoc prof, 50-53, prof, 53-70, chmn dept, 54-57, acting chmn dept, 67-69; Prof Philos, Sch Hist Studies, Inst Advan Study, 70-87, PROF EMERITUS, 87-, Woodbridge prize, Columbia Univ, 42; Guggenheim fel, 50-51; vis prof, Univ Tokyo, Summers 52 & 60 & spring 66; mem, Inst Advan Study, 53-54, 62-63, 67-68 & 68-69; fel, Ctr Advan Studies Behav Sci, 59-60; Am Coun Learned Socs, 62-63; vis prof, City Univ New York, 68-69. **HONORS AND AWARDS** Butler Medal, Columbia Univ 61., LHD, City Univ New York, 75. **MEMBERSHIPS** Fel Am Acad Arts & Sci; Am Philos Soc; Am Antiquarian Soc; Am Philos Asn. **RESEARCH** Epistemology; philosophy of history; history of American thought. **SELECTED PUBLICATIONS** Auth, The Origin of Dewey's Instrumentalism, 43, Columbia Univ; auth, Social Thought in Ameica, 49, Viking; ed, The Age of Analysis, 55, Houghton Mifflin; auth, Toward Reunion in Philosophy, 56, Harvard Univ; auth, Religion, Politics and The Higher Learning, 59 & coauth, The Intellectual Versus The City, 62, Harvard Univ; auth, Foundations of Historical Knowledge, Harper, 65; Science and Sentiment in America, 72 ed, Documents in The History of American Philosophy, 72, auth, Pragmatism and the American Mind, 73, Philosophy of the American Revolution, 78 & What Is and What Ought to Be Done, 81, Oxford Univ; co-auth, Journeys to the Japanese, Univ British Columbia, 86; auth, Philosophy, The Federalist, and the Constitution, Oxford Univ, 87; auth, The Question of Free Will, Princeton Univ, 93. **CONTACT ADDRESS** Inst for Advanced Studies, Princeton, NJ, 08540.

WHITE, NICHOLAS P.
PERSONAL Born 07/17/1942, New York, NY, d, 3 children **DISCIPLINE** PHILOSOPHY **EDUCATION** Harvard, BA, 63, MA, 65, PhD, 70. **CAREER** Univ of Mich, asst prof, assoc prof, prof, 68-94; Univ of Utah, Pres prof, 94-. **HONORS AND AWARDS** ACLS, NEH, Guggenheim Fel. **RESEARCH** Greek philo; Metaphysics; ethics. **CONTACT ADDRESS** Dept of Philosophy, Utah Univ, Salt Lake City, UT, 84112.

WHITE, R. FOWLER
DISCIPLINE NEW TESTAMENT AND BIBLICAL LANGUAGES **EDUCATION** Vanderbilt Univ, BA, MA; Dallas Theol Sem, ThM; Westminster Theol Sem, PhD. **CAREER** Dean, Knox Theol Sem. **RESEARCH** Biblical theology and hermeneutics. **CONTACT ADDRESS** Knox Theol Sem, 5554 N Federal Hwy, Ft. Lauderdale, FL, 33308.

WHITE, STEPHEN W.
PERSONAL Born 11/01/1941, Atlanta, GA, m, 1963, 2 children **DISCIPLINE** PHILOSOPHY **EDUCATION** Oglethorpe Univ, BA, 66; Univ Ga, Ma, 69, PhD, 71. **CAREER** From asst prof to assoc prof to prof, 70-85, E Tenn State Univ; assoc prof, Auburn Univ, 85-98; ed, Natl Forum, 78-93; ed, Child & Adolescent Newsletter, 93-94. **HONORS AND AWARDS** Phi Kappa Phi; Phi Beta Kappa. **MEMBERSHIPS** Amintaphil; Southern Society Philos Psychol; Am Philos Asn; Society Scholar Publ. **RESEARCH** Social-political philosophy; applied ethics. **CONTACT ADDRESS** 2664 Bent Creek Rd, Auburn, AZ, 36830. **EMAIL** whitesw@mail.auburn.edu

WHITE, V. ALAN
PERSONAL Born 04/05/1953, Florence, AL **DISCIPLINE** PHILOSOPHY **EDUCATION** Univ of Tennessee, PhD, 82. **CAREER** Asst Prof, Assoc Prof to Prof Philos, 81-, Univ of Wisconsin-Manitowoc. **HONORS AND AWARDS** Carnegie CASE, Wisconsin Prof Yr, 96-97. **MEMBERSHIPS** APA, Aratotelum Soc. **RESEARCH** Metaphysics; Philosophy of Science. **SELECTED PUBLICATIONS** Auth, Frankfurt, Failure and Finding Fault, Sorites, 98; co-auth, Introductory Philosophy-A Restricted Tipic Approach, In The Socratic Tradition, Essays on Teaching Philosophy, ed, Tziporah Kasachkoff, pub by Rowman and Littlefield, 98; Ray on the Twin Paradox, Metaphysical Review: Essays on the Foundations of Physics, 97; Picturing Einstein's Train of Thought, Philosophy, 96; Single-Topic Introductory Philosophy-An Update, Teaching Philosophy, 96. **CONTACT ADDRESS** Dept Philosophy, Univ of Wis Center Manitowoc, Manitowoc, WI, 54220. **EMAIL** awhite@uwc.edu

WHITE CRAWFORD, SIDNIE
DISCIPLINE HEBREW BIBLE, HISTORY AND LITERATURE OF SECOND TEMPLE JUDAISM **EDUCATION** Trinity Col, BA, 81; Harvard Divinity Sch, MTS, 84; Harvard Univ, PhD, 88. **CAREER** Instr, Harvard Divinity Sch, 87-88; asst prof, St Olaf Col, 88-89; asst prof, 89-96, Chp of the Fac, 95-96, assoc prof Relig Stud, Albright Col, 96-; assoc prof, ch, Classics, Univ Nebr, Lincoln, 96-; ed bd, TC: An Electronic J for Textual Criticism; ed bd, J for Stud of Pseudepigrapha. **HONORS AND AWARDS** Abraham Joshua Heschel Prize for Relig Stud, 81; Cert of Distinction in Tchg, Harvard Univ, 87; Postdoctoral fel, NEH/Am Sch of Orient Res, 89-90; Dorot fel, WF Albright Inst for Archaeol Res, 90; NEH summer sem, Yeshiva Univ; Grant-in-Aid, Am Coun of Lrnd Soc, 91; Jacob Albright Award, 91; Fac Mem of Yr, 91; NEH Travel-to-Collections grant, 91; fel, Annenberg Inst for Jewish Stud, 92; sr assoc mem, Am Sch of Class Stud, Athens, 93; travel grant, Am Coun of Lrnd Soc, 94; United Methodist Church Award for Exemplary Tchg, Albright Col, 95. **MEMBERSHIPS** Past pres, exec bd, Am Acad of Relig, 92.93; Am Sch of Orient Res; Int Orgn for Stud of Qumran; Soc of Bibl Lit; secy, Bd of Trustees, ch, Long-Range Planning Comt, WF Albright Inst for Archaeol Res. **RESEARCH** Critical editions of unpublished biblical and non-biblical manuscripts from Cave 4, Qumran. **SELECTED PUBLICATIONS** Auth, Three Fragments from Qumran Cave 4 and their Relationship to the Temple Scroll, Jewish Quart Rev 85, 94; "Amram, Testament of," "Angelic Liturgy," and 18 other entries in Dictionary of Biblical Judaism, Macmillan, 95; 4QDeuteronomya, c, d, f, g, i, n, o, p, Discoveries in the Judaean Desert XIV, Oxford Univ, 95; Has Every Book of the Bible Been Found Among the Dead Sea Scrolls?, Bible Rev XII, 96; coauth, 4QReworked Pentateuch: 4Q364-367, with an appendix on 4Q365a, Discoveries in the Judaean Desert XIII, Oxford Univ, 94. **CONTACT ADDRESS** Univ Nebr, Lincoln, Lincoln, NE, 68588-0417. **EMAIL** rgorman@unlinfo.unl.edu

WHITEBOOK, JOEL
DISCIPLINE PHILOSOPHY **EDUCATION** New Sch Soc Res, PhD, 78; CUNY, PhD, 84. **CAREER** Adj prof, Eugene Lang Col. **RESEARCH** Psychoanalysis and psychotherapy; Foucault. **SELECTED PUBLICATIONS** Auth, articles on psych, philos, and economics; Perversion and Utopia: A Study in Psychoanalysis and Critical Theory, 95. **CONTACT ADDRESS** Eugene Lang Col, New Sch for Social Research, 66 West 12th St, New York, NY, 10011.

WHITEBREAD, CHARLES H.
PERSONAL Born 04/02/1943, Washington, DC **DISCIPLINE** CRIMINAL PROCEDURE, JUVENILE LAW **EDUCATION** Princeton Univ, BA, 65; Yale Univ, LLB, 68. **CAREER** Prof Law, Univ Va Law Sch, 68-81; George T Pfleger prof Law, Univ Southern Calif Law Sch, 81-, Legal staff mem, Forensic Psychiat Clinic, Univ Va Hospital, 68-81; consult, Nat Comn Causes & Prev Violence, 68-69 & Nat Comn Marijuana & Drug Abuse, 71-72; fac mem, Fed Bur Invest Nat Acad, 72-; lectr, Am Acad Judicial Educ Conf, 72- & Nat Asn Dist Attys, 81-. **HONORS AND AWARDS** Israel Peres Prize, Yale Univ Law Sch, 68. **MEMBERSHIPS** Am Bar Asn. **RESEARCH** Criminal procedure; juvenile law and procedure. **SELECTED PUBLICATIONS** Auth, Interrogations in New Haven: The impact of Miranda, Yale Law J, 76: 1519; ed, Mass Production Justice and the Constitutional Ideal, Univ Va Press, 69; auth, 2 chaps in Educational Perspectives in the Drug Abuse Crisis, 71; coauth, The Marijuana Conviction, Univ Va Press, 74; Juvenile Law & Procedure, Nat Coun Juvenile Ct Judges, 74; auth, Constitutional Criminal Procedure, Am Acad Judicial Educ, 78; coauth, Criminal Procedure, 3 rd ed, 93; coauth, Cases & Materials on Children in the Legal System 2nd ed, Found Press, 97. **CONTACT ADDRESS** Law Sch, Univ of Southern California, 699 Exposition Blvd, Los Angeles, CA, 90089-0071. **EMAIL** cwhitebr@law.usc.edu

WHITEHEAD JR, BRADY
DISCIPLINE NEW TESTAMENT **EDUCATION** Rhodes Col, BA, 52; Candler Sch of Theol, MDiv, 55; Grad Sch of Arts & Sci, MA, 57; Boston Univ Sch of Theol, ThD, 72 **CAREER** Prof, 67-98, Lambuth Univ **MEMBERSHIPS** Soc of Bibl Lit **SELECTED PUBLICATIONS** Auth, What Goes Around Comes Around: An Essay on the Unity of the Book of Isaiah; How Methodists Interpret the Bible **CONTACT ADDRESS** 4600 Bells Hwy, Jackson, TN, 38305.

WHITEHOUSE, GEORGE
DISCIPLINE COMMUNICATIONS LAW **EDUCATION** Univ Southern MS, BS, 71, MS, 72, PhD, 74; Cath Univ Am, WA, JD, 85. **CAREER** Prof & dir, Grad Study, Dept Mass Commun; Legal asst to Comnr, Fed Commun Comn, WA, 84-85; legal asst to ch counsel & VP for Congressional-Govt Relations of the Nat Asn of Broadcasters, WA, 83-84; asst prof & dir, Div Broadcasting & Jour, Mass Commun Dept, Univ Tex, 80-82; assoc prof & dir, Div Mass Commun, Univ N Ala, 78-80; prof, Stephens Col; Columbia, 74-78; commun adv, governments Saudi Arabia & Iran, US State Dept in Jeddah, SA & Teheran; Supt, US Air Force Sch Commun Adminr & Sch Commun, US Air Force Tehn Training Command; res & develop engineer. **MEMBERSHIPS** Fed Commun Bar Asn; Am Bar Asn; ABA Forum Comt on Commun Law; DC Bar Asn; DC Ct of Appeals Bar; Pa Bar Asn; Asn Educ in Jour and Mass Commun; Broadcast Educ Asn; Radio-TV News Directors Asn; Soc Prof Jour; Broadcast Educ Asn; Sioux City, IA Press Club; Soc Motion Picture and TV Engineers; Soc Broadcast Engineers; Am Consult League. **RESEARCH** Effects of the newly legislated Telecommunications Act of 96. **SELECTED PUBLICATIONS** Auth, High Definition Television (HDTV): A Primer, Commun Lawyer, 89; The Professionalization of Journalists, keynote address to Sioux City Press Club, 89; The Professionalization of Journalism, for Commun Lawyer, 86; Understanding the New Technologies of the Mass Media, textbk, Prentice-Hall, 86; The Berwick Doctrine: Suburban Community Policy, Fed Commun Comn, Wash, 84; coauth, Broadcasting and Government, contributing author, Nat Asn Broadcasters, Wash, 84; reviewer-consult, For Houghton Mifflin, prepubl manuscript of textbk, Introd to Telecommun, McGregor, 96; For McGraw-Hill, prepubl manuscript of textbk, Media Law, 3rd ed, Holsinger, 95; For Focal Press, prepubl manuscript of textbk, Winning The Global TV News Game, Johnston, 95; For Focal Press, prepubl manuscript of workbk, Cases and Exercises in Electronic Media Mgt, 94; For McGraw-Hill, prepubl manuscript for textbk, The Int World of Electronic Media, 93 & For Prentice-Hall, prepubl manuscript for Mng the Electronic Media, 91. **CONTACT ADDRESS** Dept of Mass Commun, Univ SD, 414 E Clark St, Vermillion, SD, 57069. **EMAIL** gwhiteho@sundance.usd.edu

WHITFORD, WILLIAM C.
PERSONAL Born 01/16/1940, Madison, WI, m, 1965, 4 children **DISCIPLINE** LAW **EDUCATION** Univ Wis, BA, 61; Yale Univ, LLB, 64. **CAREER** Law clerk, US Ct Appeals, Washington, DC circuit, 64-65; asst prof, 65-69, assoc prof, 69-71, PROF LAW, UNIV WIS, MADISON, 71-; Young-Bascom Prof Bus Law, 86-; Vis sr lectr, Univ Col, Dar es Salaam, Tanzania, 67-69; vis prof law, Stanford Univ, 72-73; Fulbright vis prof, Univ Nairobi, 75-76; vis prof, Boston Univ Sch Law, 87. **MEMBERSHIPS** Law & Soc Asn; Conf Critical Legal Studies. **RESEARCH** Consumer law; taxation. **SELECTED PUBLICATIONS** Auth, Strict products liability and the auto industry, Vol 1968, 68, Law and the consumer transaction: A case study of the auto warranty, Vol 1968, 69, The functions of disclosure regulation of consumer transactions, Vol 1973, 73, coauth, Why process consumer complaints, Vol 1974, 74, The impact of denying self-help repossession of automobiles, Vol 1975, 75, auth, A critique of the consumer credit collection system, Vol 1979, 79 & Structuring consumer protection legislation to maximize effectiveness, Vol 1981, 82, Wis Law Rev;

Comment on a theory of consumer product warranty, Yale Law J, Vol 91, 82; The small case procedure of the United States Tax Court: A successful small claims court, ABFRJ, 85; Ian Macneil's contribution to contracts scholarship, Wis Law Rev, 85; The appropriate role of security interests in consumer transactions, Cardozo Law Rev, 86; Lowered horizons: Implementation research in a post-CLS world, Wis Law Rev, 86; Has the time come to repeal chapter 13, Ind Law J, 89; co-auth, Bargaining over equity's share in the bankruptcy reorganization of large, publicly held companies, Univ Pa Law Rev, 90; co-auth, Venue choice and forum shopping in the bankruptcy reorganization of large publicly held companies, Wis Law Rev, 91; co-auth, Preemptive cramdown, Am Bank Law J, 91; Corporate governance in the bankruptcy reorganization of large publicly held companies, Univ Pa Law Rev, 93; Patterns in the bankruptcy reorganization of large, publicly held companies, Cornell Law Rev, 93; co-auth, Compensating unsecured creditors for extraordinary bankruptcy reorganization risks, Wash Univ Law Rev, 94; What's right about chapter 11, Wash Univ Law Rev, 94; The ideal of individualized justice: Consumer bankruptcy as consumer protection, and consumer protection in consumer bankruptcy, Am Bank Law J, 94; What's right about chapter 11?, Wash Univ Law Rev, 94; co-auth, Compensating unsecured creditors for extraordinary bankruptcy reorganization risks, Wash Univ Law Rev, 94; Contract law and the control of standardized terms in consumer contracts: An American report, European Rev of Private Law, 95; co-auth, Contracts: Law in Action, Michie, 95; co-auth, A black critique of the Internal Revenue Code, Wis Law Rev, 96; Changing definitions of fresh start in American bankruptcy law, J Consumer Policy, 97; Remarkable, NC Law Rev, 98 (forthcoming). **CONTACT ADDRESS** Law Sch, Univ of Wis, 975 Bascom Mall, Madison, WI, 53706-1301. **EMAIL** whitford@macc.wisc.edu

WHITLOCK, LUDER
PERSONAL m, 3 children **DISCIPLINE** PASTORAL MINISTRY **EDUCATION** Univ Fla; Westminster Theol Sem; Vanderbilt Univ, PhD. **CAREER** Prof, 75; actg pres, 78; pres, 79-. **HONORS AND AWARDS** Actg pres, Found for Reformation; dir, Key Life Network, Inc; VP, Exec Comm of the Assoc Theol Sch(s), USA, Can; dir, Nat Assn of Evangel; co-pres, Intl Reformed fel; dir, Natl Commn on Higher Educ; adv bd(s), Found for Thought and Ethics; Amer Acad of Ministry; Ed Adv Bd of Leadership; Intl Inst for Christian Stud; ed adv bd, Reformed Mind: A Jour for the Spiritual and Intellectual Develop of Church Leaders; Christian Assn of PrimeTimers; Bibl Manhood and Womanhood; Christian Coun; New Heritage USA; Mission Amer Nat Comm; Outstanding Young Men of Am. He is also on the Board of Reference, Patkai Ministries, India and Belhaven Col. **MEMBERSHIPS** Mem, Fel of Evangel Sem Pres(s); Mission Am Natl Comm. **SELECTED PUBLICATIONS** Contrib, The Evangel Dictionary of Theol; Baker Encycl of the Bible; Reformed Theol in Am; The Changing of the Evangel Mind; The Dictionary of Twentieth Century Christian Biography. **CONTACT ADDRESS** Dept of Pastoral Ministry, Reformed Theol Sem, 5422 Clinton Blvd, Jackson, MS, 39209-3099.

WHITMAN, JEFFREY P.
PERSONAL Born 04/25/1955, Scanton, PA, m, 1978, 2 children **DISCIPLINE** PHILOSOPHY **EDUCATION** US Military Acad, BS, 77; Brown Univ, PhD, 91. **CAREER** Commissioned Officer, US Army, 77-95; asst and assoc prof, US Military Acad, West Point, NY, 87-95; asst prof Philos, Susquehanna Univ, PA, 95- . **MEMBERSHIPS** Amer Philos asn; Asn Practical prof Ethics; Amer Asn Philos tchrs. **RESEARCH** Applied Ethics; Ethics; Epistemology; Just War Theory. **SELECTED PUBLICATIONS** Auth, Utilitarianism and the Laws of Land Warfare, Publ Affairs Quart, July 93; The Many Guises of the Slippery Slope Argument, Soc Theory and Practice, Spring 94; Citizens and Soldiers: Teaching Just War Theory at the US Military Academy, Tchg Philos, March 94; The Soldier as Conscientous Objector, Publ Affairs Quart, Jan 95; Reclaiming the Medical Profession, Prof Ethics, Spring 95; An End to Sovereignty?, The Jour of Soc Philos, Fall 96; auth, The Power and Value of Philosophical Skepticism, Lanham, MD, Rowman and Littlefield, 96; Exploring Moral Character in the Philosophy Class, Tchg Philos, June 98. **CONTACT ADDRESS** Dept of Philosophy, Susquehanna Univ, Selingsgrove, PA, 17870. **EMAIL** whitman@susqu.edu

WHITMAN HOFF, JOAN
DISCIPLINE PHILOSOPHY **EDUCATION** Roger Williams Col, AS, 73, BA, 74; Univ RI, MA, 77; Am Univ, PhD, 82. **CAREER** Assoc prof, Lock Haven Univ, 90-. **HONORS AND AWARDS** NEH, summer sem for College Teachers, 83; fac summer fel, Northern Ky Univ, 85; fac summer res grant, Bentley Col, 87; Adele Mellen Prize, Edwin Mellen Press, 86-87; NEH, summer sem for col tchr, 88; summer grant, Bentley Col, 89; Can stud fac res grant, Can Embassy, 89-90; Can stud fac enrichment grant, Can Embassy, 90-91. **SELECTED PUBLICATIONS** Auth, The Texaco Incident, J of Bus Ethics, 87; Theoretical Frameworks for Worker-Management Cooperation, Int Asn of Quality Circles State of The Art Conf Proc, 89; Child Custody, Children's Rights and Education, The Midwest Philos of Educ Soc Proc, 1989; Students, Ethics and the Surveys, A Commentary, J of Bus Ethics, 89; The Exxon Valdez Crisis, in The Corporation, Ethics And The Environment, ed W. Hoffman et al, Quorum Bks, 90; Selected Comments on Crocker's 'Functioning and Capability: The Foundation of Sen's Development Ethic', Montclair State Univ's Inst for Critical Thinking Working Paper ser, 91. **CONTACT ADDRESS** Dept of Philos, Lock Haven Univ, Pennsylvania, Lock Haven, PA, 17745.

WHITNEY, BARRY L.
PERSONAL Born 12/10/1947, Cornwall, ON, Canada, 3 children **DISCIPLINE** PHILOSOPHY **EDUCATION** McMaster Univ, BA, 71, PhD, 77. **CAREER** Prof, 76-. **MEMBERSHIPS** AAR; Am Philos Asn. **RESEARCH** Process philosophy; Philosophy of religion and theodicy. **SELECTED PUBLICATIONS** Auth, Theodicy: An Annotated Bibliography, 1960-1991, 98; Theodicy, 93; What Are They Saying About God and Evil?, 89; Evil and the Process God, 85. **CONTACT ADDRESS** Dept of Classics, Univ of Windsor, PO Box 33830, Detroit, MI, 48232. **EMAIL** whitney@uwindsor.com

WHITNEY, RUTH
PERSONAL Born 03/08/1938, Quincy, IL, d **DISCIPLINE** RELIGION **EDUCATION** Marquette Univ, BS; Catholic Univ Am, MA, PhD. **CAREER** Asst prof, relig, Rutgers Univ, 73-79; Adj fac, Women's Studies, Univ So Fla, 89- . **HONORS AND AWARDS** Alpha Sigma Nu. **MEMBERSHIPS** Am Acad Relig; Natl Women's Stud Asn. **RESEARCH** Women; religion; spirituality; psychology; politics. **SELECTED PUBLICATIONS** Auth, Feminism and Love: Transforming Ourselves and Our World, Cross Cultural, 98. **CONTACT ADDRESS** 700 14th Ave N, St. Petersburg, FL, 33701-1018. **EMAIL** WhitneyRA@aol.com

WHITT, L.A.
PERSONAL Born 08/03/1952, San Diego, CA, m, 1994 **DISCIPLINE** PHILOSOPHY **EDUCATION** The Col of William and Mary, BA, 75; Queen's Univ , MA, 76; Univ Western Ontario, PhD, 85. **CAREER** Vis lectr, 83-84, Univ IL-Urbana; asst prof, 84-86, Southern Methodist Univ; vis assoc prof, 93-94, Cornell Univ; vis fel, 96, Australian Natl Univ; asst prof, 86-92, assoc prof, 92- , MI Technological Univ. **HONORS AND AWARDS** Vis Fel at The Humanities Research Ctr of the Australian Natl Univ, 96. **MEMBERSHIPS** APA; Radical Philosophy Assn; Philosophy of Science Assn; Soc for the Social Studies of Science; Soc for Women in Philosophy; Australia and New Zealand and Law and History Soc; Amer Indian Sci and Engineering Soc. **RESEARCH** Science Studies; Indigenous Studies; Legal Studies. **SELECTED PUBLICATIONS** Auth, Cultural Imperialism and the Marketing of Native America, The American Indian Culture and Research Journal, 95; auth, Resisting Value-Bifurcation: Indigenist Critiques of the Human Genome Diversity Project, Daring To Be Good: Feminist Essays in Ethico-Politics, 98; auth, Biocolonialism and the Commodification of Knowledge, Science as Culture, 98. **CONTACT ADDRESS** Humanities Dept, Michigan Tech Univ, Houghton, MI, 49931. **EMAIL** lawhitt@mtu.edu

WHITTAKER, JOHN
DISCIPLINE PSYCHOLOGY OF RELIGION, THEORIES OF RELIGION, PHILOSOPHY OF RELIGION, AND P **EDUCATION** Yale Univ, PhD, 74. **CAREER** Prof Relig Stud, dir, Relig Stud prog, La State Univ. **RESEARCH** The philosophy of religion; the philosophy of D.Z. Phillips. **SELECTED PUBLICATIONS** Auth, Matters of Faith and Matters of Principle, Trinity UP, 81; The Logic of Religious Persuasion, Peter Lang, 91. **CONTACT ADDRESS** Dept of Philos and Relig Stud, Louisiana State Univ, 106 Coates Hall, Baton Rouge, LA, 70803.

WHITTEN, RALPH U.
DISCIPLINE LAW **EDUCATION** Univ Texas, BBA, 66, JD, 69; Harvard Univ, LLM, 72. **CAREER** Prof, Creighton Univ; law clerk, US Ct Appeals 4th Circuit, 69-70; tchg fel, Harvard Law Sch, 70-72; prof, Univ SC Sch Law, 72-77. **MEMBERSHIPS** Order of the Coif. **SELECTED PUBLICATIONS** Coauth, The Constitution and the Common Law, DC Health, 77; Cases and Problems on Civil Procedure: Basic and Advanced, Rothman, 97; Civil Procedure, Found Press, 94; pub(s), Amer J Comp Law; Maine Law Rev; Hastings Constitutional Law Quart; Memphis State Law Rev; Creighton Law Rev; NC Law Rev; Duke Law J. **CONTACT ADDRESS** School of Law, Creighton Univ, 2500 California Plaza, Omaha, NE, 68178. **EMAIL** rwhitten@culaw.creighton.edu B1284. University of Southern California URL: http://www.usc.edu/ Univ of Southern California University Park Campus Los Angeles California 90089 (213) 740-2311 Email: admitusc@usc.edu

WHITTIER, DUANE HAPGOOD
PERSONAL Born 09/15/1928, Hanover, NH, m, 1960 **DISCIPLINE** PHILOSOPHY **EDUCATION** Univ NH, BA, 50; Univ IL, MA, 52, PhD, 61. **CAREER** From instr to asst prof philos, PA State Univ, 61-67; assoc prof, 67-78, Prof Philos, Univ NH, 78-, Vis prof, Univ IL, 63-64. **RESEARCH** Aesthetics; hist Am philos; metaphysics. **SELECTED PUBLICATIONS** Auth, Basic assumption and argument in philosophy, 10/64 & Causality and the self, 4/65, Monist; contribr, Studies in Philosophy and the History of Science, Coronado, 70; auth, Metaphor as aesthetic meaning, New Scholasticism, 78; The Frankenstein axiom, Int Philos Quart, 79; Akrasia: The Absence of Which Virtue?, Logos, 87. **CONTACT ADDRESS** Dept of Philos, Univ of NH, 125 Technology Dr, Durham, NH, 03824-4724.

WICCLAIR, MARK ROBERT
PERSONAL Born 01/06/1944, Los Angeles, CA, m, 1973, 1 child **DISCIPLINE** PHILOSOPHY **EDUCATION** Reed Col, BA, 66; Columbia Univ, MPhil, 74, PhD, 76. **CAREER** Fulbright fel, 66-67; rom instr to asst prof philos, Lafayette Col, 75-78; from asst prof to prof phil, adjunct prof med, 90-, WVa Univ, 78-, Consult, WVa Public Radio, 79-81 adjunct prof med, Univ Pittsburgh, 91-. **HONORS AND AWARDS** Phi Beta Kappa, 66; Woodrow Wilson fel, 67-68; Hum Found WVA Fel, 80 & 87; NEH fel, 88; Outstanding Teacher Award, WVA Univ, 87-88, 88-89; Outstanding Res Award WVA Univ, 94-95; Benedum Distinguished Schol Award WVA Univ, 96-97; Outstanding Pub Serv Award, 96-97. **MEMBERSHIPS** Am Philos Asn; Am Soc Bioethics Hum. **RESEARCH** Ethics; medical ethics; ethics and aging. **SELECTED PUBLICATIONS** Auth, Film and mental processes, 3/77 & The principle of nonintervention: A critical examination of a contractarian justification, 2/78, Proc & Add Am Philos Asn; Film theory and Hugo Muensterberg's The Film: A Psychological Study, J Aesthet Ed, 7/78; Human rights and intervention, Human Rights and United States Foreign Policy: Principles and Applications, Lexington Books, 79; Rawls and the principle of nonintervention, John Rawls' Theory of Social Justice, Ohio Univ, 80; The abortion controversy and the claim that this body is mine, Social Theory & Prac, fall 81; Is prostitution morally wrong?, Philos Res Archives, 81; Ethics and the Elderly, Oxford Univ, 93; Medical ethics in the United States, Marmara Med J, 95; Mandatory Retirement: An ethical analysis, SW J on Aging, 95; Futility: A conceptual and ethical analysis, McGraw-Hill, 96. **CONTACT ADDRESS** Dept of Philos, West Virginia Univ, PO Box 6312, Morgantown, WV, 26506-6312. **EMAIL** mrw@med.pitt.edu

WICKER, KATHLEEN O'BRIEN
PERSONAL Born 05/24/1937, Buffalo, NY **DISCIPLINE** NEW TESTAMENT, CLASSICAL LANGUAGES **EDUCATION** Mundelein Col, BA, 59; Loyola Univ, Chicago, PhD(hist western origins), 66. **CAREER** From instr to asst prof hist & classics, Mundelein Col, 65-71; asst prof, 71-77, assoc prof, 76-84, prof, 84- , New Testament, Mary W Johnson and J Stanley Johnson prof in Hum, 96- , Scripps Col. **HONORS AND AWARDS** Lectr classics, Loyola Univ Chicago, 70-71; partic, Corpus Hellenisticum Novi Testamenti Proj, 71-77; actg dean fac, Scripps Col, 79-81. **MEMBERSHIPS** Soc Bibl Lit. **RESEARCH** Plutarch; Hellenistic philosophy and religion. **SELECTED PUBLICATIONS** Auth, De Defectu Oraculorum, In: Plutarch's Theological Writings and the Early Christian Literature, E J Brill, Leiden, 74; First Century Marriage Ethics, In: No Famine in the Land, Scholars, 75; Plutarch: Mulierum Virtutes, In: Plutarch's Ethical Writings and the Early Christian Literature, E J Brill, Leiden, 78. **CONTACT ADDRESS** Dept of Religion, Scripps Col, 1030 Columbia Ave, Claremont, CA, 91711-3948.

WIDER, KATHLEEN V.
DISCIPLINE PHILOSOPHY **EDUCATION** Wayne State Univ, PhD, 78. **CAREER** Assoc to Asst Prof, 88-, Univ of Michigan-Dearborn; Adjunct Assoc Prof Philo, 87-88, Hunter Coll, CUNY; Adj Prof Philo and Eng, 80-87, Center for Creative Stud. **MEMBERSHIPS** APA, SPEP, SSP&P, Sartre Soc of North Amer. **RESEARCH** Philosophy of mind, Sartre, Existential Philosophy, bridges between continental and analytic Philosophy. **SELECTED PUBLICATIONS** Auth, The Bodily Nature of Consciousness, Sartre and Contemporary Philosophy of Mind, Ithaca, NY, Cornell Univ Press, 97; The Failure of self-consciousness in Sartre's Being and Nothingness, reprint permission requested by Garland Press, 96; Truth and Existence, The Idealism in Sartre's Theory of Truth, International Journal of Philosophical Studies, 95; Sartre and the Long-Distance Truck Driver, The Journal of the British Society for Phenomenology, 93. **CONTACT ADDRESS** Humanities Dept, Univ of Mich-Dearborn, Dearborn, MI, 48128. **EMAIL** kwider@umich.edu

WIDISS, ALAN I.
PERSONAL Born 09/28/1938, Los Angeles, CA, m, 1964, 3 children **DISCIPLINE** LAW **EDUCATION** Univ Southern Calif, BS, 60, LLB, 63; Harvard Univ, LLM, 64. **CAREER** From asst prof to assoc prof, 65-69, prof, 69-78, Josephine R Witte Distinguished Prof Law, Univ Iowa, 78-, Dir, Mass No-Fault Study, 71-76; chmn sect on teaching methods, Asn Am Law Schs, 72-78; mem, Bd Fellows, Univ Iowa Sch Relig, 76-. **MEMBERSHIPS** Am Bar Asn; Am Law Inst; Order of Coif. **RESEARCH** Insurance and insurance regulation; dispute resolution techniques and processes; contract law and remedies. **SELECTED PUBLICATIONS** Auth, Perspectives on uninsured motorist coverage, Northwestern Law Rev, 67; A Guide to Uninsured Motorist Coverage, W H Anderson, 69; coauth, Legal assistance for the rural poor: An Iowa study, Iowa Law Rev, 70; ed, Materials on the Techniques and Processes for the Resolution of Disputes (3 vols), Multilith Ed, 71; coauth, No-Fault Au-

tomobile Insurance in Action: The Experiences in Massachusetts, Florida, Delaware and Michigan, Oceana, 77; ed & coauth, Arbitration: Commercial Disputes, Insurance and Tort Claims, Practicing Law Inst, 79; auth, The enforceability of arbitration terms in uninsured motorist coverages and other form contracts, Iowa Law Rev, 66: 241-271; Contracts: Problems, Judicial Decisions, Legislation and Commentaries on the Law Governing Commercial Transactions and Other Agreements, Multilith Ed, 81; To Insure Or Not To Insure Persons Infected With The Virus That Causes Aids, Iowa Law Review, Vol 0077, 1992. **CONTACT ADDRESS** Col of Law, Univ of Iowa, 290 Boyd Law Buildng, Iowa City, IA, 52242.

WIEBE, DONALD
PERSONAL Born 04/29/1943, Niagara Falls, ON, Canada, m, 1965, 1 child **DISCIPLINE** PHILOSOPHY/RELIGION **EDUCATION** Univ Lancaster, UK, PhD, 74. **CAREER** Asst prof, 75-77, Canadian Nazarene Col; asst prof, 80-82, assoc prof, 82-87, prof, 87-, Trinity Col, Univ Toronto. **MEMBERSHIPS** AAR; N Amer Assn for Stud of Relig; Intl Assn for Hist of Relig. **RESEARCH** Method & theory in the stud of relig; phil of the soc sci. **SELECTED PUBLICATIONS** Art, Religion and the Scientific Impulse in the Nineteenth Century: Friedrich Max Muller and the Birth of the Science of Religion, Intl J Comp Relig 1, 95; art, Toward Founding a Science of Religion: The Contribution of C. P. Tiele, The Sum of Our Choices: Essays in Honor of Eric J. Sharpe, Scholars Press, 96; art, Theology and the Academic Study of Religion in the United States, India & Beyond: Aspects of Lit, Meaning, Ritual & Thought, Essays in Honour of Frits Staal, Kegan Paul Intl, 97; art, On Theological Resistance to the Scientific Study of Religion: Values and the Value-Free Study of Religion, Krakow: Wydawnictwo Naukowe WSP, 97; art, A Religious Agenda Continued: a Review of the Presidential Addresses to the AAR, Method & Theory in the Stud of Relig 9, 97; art, Dissolving Rationality: The Anti-Science Phenomenon and Its Implications for the Study of Religion, Rationality in Stud of Relig, Univ Aarhus Press, 97. **CONTACT ADDRESS** Trinity Col, 6 Hoskin Ave, Toronto, ON, M5S 1H8. **EMAIL** dweibe@trinity.utoronto.ca

WIEDMANN, SALLY N.
PERSONAL Born 10/27/1949, Fargo, ND, m, 1971, 1 child **DISCIPLINE** PHILOSOPHY **EDUCATION** Univ N Iowa, BA, 90, MPhil, 92; Univ Miami, PhD, 96. **CAREER** Vis instr, 96-97, adj inst, 97-98, Univ Central Florida; ast prof, North Georgia Col, 98-. **HONORS AND AWARDS** Summa Cum Laude, 90. **MEMBERSHIPS** APA. **RESEARCH** Environmental ethics; environmental justice; environment and public policy. **CONTACT ADDRESS** 499 Cosen's Ln, Dahlonega, GA, 30533. **EMAIL** snwiedmann@nugget.ngc.peachnet.edu

WIEGERS, WANDA
DISCIPLINE LAW **EDUCATION** Univ Saskatchewan, LLB, 78, BA, 83; Univ Toronto, LLM, 87. **CAREER** Assoc prof, 87-. **MEMBERSHIPS** Law Soc Saskatchewan. **RESEARCH** Economic analysis of law; feminist and critical legal theory; women and the welfare state; poverty law. **SELECTED PUBLICATIONS** Auth, Compensation for Wife Abuse: Empowering Victims?, Law Rev, 94; Economic Analysis of Law and 'Private Ordering': A Feminist Critique, 92; The Use of Age, Sex, and Marital Status as Rating Variables in Automobile Insurance, 89. **CONTACT ADDRESS** Col of Law, Univ Saskatchewan, 15 Campus Dr, Saskatoon, SK, S7N 5A6. **EMAIL** Wiegers@law.usask.ca

WIERENGA, EDWARD RAY
PERSONAL Born 10/14/1947, Chicago, IL, m, 1971, 2 children **DISCIPLINE** PHILOSOPHY & RELIGIOUS STUDIES **EDUCATION** Calvin Col, AB, 69; Univ Mass, Amherst, MA & PhD, 74. **CAREER** Asst prof philos, IL State Univ, 74-75 & Calvin Col, 75-77; Asst Prof Philos Relig, Univ Rochester, 77-94, prof relig, univ rochester, 94. **MEMBERSHIPS** Am Philos Asn. **RESEARCH** Philos of relig; metaphysics; epistemology. **SELECTED PUBLICATIONS** Auth, The Nature of God, cornell, 89. **CONTACT ADDRESS** Prog of Relig Studies, Univ of Rochester, 500 Joseph C Wilson, Rochester, NY, 14627-9000. **EMAIL** edwd@troi.cc.rochester.edu

WIGAL, GRACE J.
DISCIPLINE LEGAL RESEARCH AND WRITING **EDUCATION** Marshall Univ, BA, 72, MA, 76; W Va Univ Col Law, JD, 89. **CAREER** Instr, Col Law, 90; dir, Legal Res and Wrtg Prog, 92; dir, Acad Support Prog, 93; dir, Appellate Advocacy Prog; act dir, -. **HONORS AND AWARDS** W Va Law Rev Lit award, 89. **MEMBERSHIPS** Order of the Coif. **SELECTED PUBLICATIONS** Ed, W V Law Rev; Auth, bk(s), articles, on legal issues that arise in the medical and construction settings. **CONTACT ADDRESS** Law Sch, W Va Univ, PO Box 6009, Morgantown, WV, 26506-6009.

WIGALL, STEVE R.
PERSONAL Born 04/15/1951, Lindsay, CA, m, 1973, 1 child **DISCIPLINE** SPIRITUAL DIRECTIONAL THEOLOGY **EDUCATION** Boston Univ School Theol, ThD, 98. **MEMBERSHIPS** Presby N N England **RESEARCH** Spiritual direction - Protestant and Reformed. **SELECTED PUBLICA-**

TIONS Auth What is a Spiritual Directors Authority, Rev for Relig, 97; Historys Role in Defining Spiritual Direction, Rev for Relig, 98; A Sacramental Paradigm Employing the Lords Supper in Calvin as a Theological Rationale for Spiritual Direction, Boston School Theol, 98. **CONTACT ADDRESS** 296 Lowell St, Lawrence, MA, 01841. **EMAIL** uncwig@aol.com

WIGGINS, JAMES BRYAN
PERSONAL Born 08/24/1935, Mexia, TX, m, 1956, 2 children **DISCIPLINE** RELIGION; HISTORY **EDUCATION** Tex Wesleyan Col, BA, 57; Southern Methodist Univ, BD, 59; Drew Univ, PhD(hist theol), 63. **CAREER** Instr English, Union Jr Col, 60-63; from asst prof to assoc prof relig, 63-75, Prof Relig, Syracuse Univ, 75-, Chmn, 81-, Soc Relig Higher Educ fel; Found Arts, Relig & Cult fel. **MEMBERSHIPS** Am Acad Relig; Am Soc Church Hist. **RESEARCH** Interaction of theology with other strands of intellectual history, particularly since Reformation; Narrative language in religious discourse; religion and Culture studies. **SELECTED PUBLICATIONS** Auth, The Methodist episcopacy: 1784-1900, Drew Gateway, 63; John Fletcher: The embattled saint, Wesleyan Col, 65; coauth, The foundations of Christianity, Ronald, 69; auth, Theological reflections on reflecting on the future, Crosscurrents, winter 71; Story, In: Echoes of the Wordless Word, Am Acad Relig, fall 73; ed, Religion as Story, Harper & Row, 75; auth, Re-visioning psycho-history, Theology Today, 76; contribr, Death and Eschatology, In: Introduction to Study of Religion, Harper & Row, 78; Christianity: A Cultural Perspective, Prentice Hall, 84; In Praise of Religion Diversity, Routledge, 96. **CONTACT ADDRESS** Dept of Religion, Syracuse Univ, 501 HL, Syracuse, NY, 13244.

WIGGINS, WILLIAM H., JR.
PERSONAL Born 05/30/1934, Port Allen, Louisiana, m **DISCIPLINE** THEOLOGY **EDUCATION** OH Wesleyan U, BA 1956; Phillip's Sch of Theol, BD 1961; Louisville Prebyn Theol Sem, MTh 1965; IN U, PhD 1974. **CAREER** IN Univ, asso prof 1980-, asst prof 1974-79, grad teaching asst & lecturer 1969-73; TX Coll, dir rel life 1965-69; Freeman Chapel CME Church, pastor 1962-65; Lane Coll, prof 1961-62. **HONORS AND AWARDS** Num grants & flwhps; num publ; doc film "In the Rapture" anthologized wks appear in num publ & jour. **MEMBERSHIPS** Fellow of the Folklore Inst IN U; founder dir Afro-Am Folk Archive IN U; so reg dir IN Chap Assn for the Study of Afro-Am Life & History; mem Smithsonian Inst African Diaspora Adv Gr Com; exec bd Hoosier Folklore Soc; ed bd The Jour of the Folklore Inst; prestr Am Folklife Fest 1975-76; field wk Smithsonian Inst 1975-76; pres Assn of African-Am Folklorists Minister Christian Meth Epis Ch; mem Am Folklore Soc; Nat Cncl for Blk Studies; Assn for the Study of Afro-Am Life & History; Assn of African & African-Am Folklorists; Hoosier Folklore Soc; Pop Cult Assn;Num Grants **CONTACT ADDRESS** Dept of Folklore, Indiana Univ, Bloomington, Bloomington, IN, 47401.

WIGGINS JR., OSBORNE P.
DISCIPLINE PHILOSOPHY **EDUCATION** New Sch for Soc Res, PhD. **CAREER** Dept Philos, Univ Louisville **HONORS AND AWARDS** Egner prize, Univ Zurich. **RESEARCH** Philos of psychiatry. **SELECTED PUBLICATIONS** Auth, articles on Husserl and other phenomenological figures; ed, Philos Perspectives on Psychiatric Diagnostic Classification, The Johns Hopkins UP, 94. **CONTACT ADDRESS** Dept of Philos, Univ Louisville, 2301 S 3rd St, Louisville, KY, 40292. **EMAIL** opwigg01@ulkyvm.louisville.edu

WIKE, VICTORIA S.
DISCIPLINE PHILOSOPHY **EDUCATION** MacMurray Col, BA ; Univ de Paris Sorbonne, LL; Pa State Univ, MA, PhD. **CAREER** Prof, Loyola Univ Chicago, 79-; 1 yr lectr, Univ Rome Campus. **RESEARCH** Early modern philosophy, especially Descartes, Spinoza, Kant; Kant's moral philosophy; health care ethics. **SELECTED PUBLICATIONS** Auth, Kant on Happiness in Ethics, 94; Kant's Antinomies of Reason, 82; articles in, J Value Inquiry, Idealistic Stud, The Southern J Philos. **CONTACT ADDRESS** Dept of Philosophy, Loyola Univ, Chicago, 820 N Michigan Ave, Chicago, IL, 60611.

WILCOX, JOEL
PERSONAL Born 03/22/1951, Grand rapids, MI, m, 1984 **DISCIPLINE** PHILOSOPHY **EDUCATION** Univ Minnesota, PhD 90; John Hopkins Univ, MA 84. **CAREER** Providence College, dir, assoc prof, asst prof, 93 to 97-; Xavier Univ LA, asst prof 90-93. **MEMBERSHIPS** APA, IAGP; RIPS; SAGP; SIPR **RESEARCH** Greek Philos and Asian Philos. **SELECTED PUBLICATIONS** Auth, Whole-Natured Forms in Empedocles' Cosmic Cycle, Stud in Ancient Greek Philos, SUNY Press, 98; Empedocles, Dictionary of Literary Biography: Greek Authors, Gale Research Co, 95; The Origins of Epistemology in Early Greek Thought, Edwin Mellen Press, 94, anthologized in: The Philosophical Yearbook, Inst for Philos, 95; Invted rev of K. H. Volkman-Schluck, Die Philosophie der Vorsokratiker: Der Anfang der abendlandischen Metaphysik, Ancient Philos, 94; On the Distinction Between Thought and Perception in Heraclitus, Apeiron, 93. **CONTACT ADDRESS** Dept of Philosophy, Providence Col, Providence, RI, 02918. **EMAIL** wilcoxjs@providence.edu

WILCOX, JOHN R.
DISCIPLINE RELIGION **EDUCATION** Marist Col, BA, 61; Fordham Univ, MA, 66; Union Theological Seminary, PhD, 77. **CAREER** High Sch Teacher, Marist high Schs, 62-67; instr, Marist Col, 67-68; adjunct instr, Fordham Univ, 70-74; prof, Manhattan Col, 74-. **MEMBERSHIPS** Collegium; Am Asn of Univ Admin; Asn for Practical and Prof Ethics; Col Theology Society; Hastings Ctr; Society for Bus Ethics; Society of Christian Ethics; Society for the Values in Higher Educ. **SELECTED PUBLICATIONS** Coauth, Promoting an Ethical Campus Culture: The Values Audit, NASPA Jour, Vol 29 No 4, 92; auth, The Leadership Compass: Values and Ethics in Higher Education, Higher Educ Repot, No 1, 92; ed, The Internationalization of American Business: Ethical Issues and Cases, McGraw-Hill, 92; auth, A Report on the Mandate: Ethics Training in the Futures Industry, Ethikos: Examining Ethical Issues in Bus, Vol 9 No 1, 95. **CONTACT ADDRESS** Religious Studies Dept, Manhattan Col, Bronx, NY, 10471. **EMAIL** jwilcox@manhattan.edu

WILD, ROBERT ANTHONY
PERSONAL Born 03/30/1940, Chicago, IL **DISCIPLINE** NEW TESTAMENT, HISTORY OF RELIGION **EDUCATION** Loyola Univ Chicago, BA, 62, MA, 67; Jesuit Sch Theol, STL, 70; Harvard Univ, PhD(Study relig), 77. **CAREER** Teacher Latin & Greek, St Xavier High Sch, Cincinnati, 64-67; instr New Testament, 75-77, asst prof, 77-82, Assoc Prof New Testament, Marquette Univ, 82-. **MEMBERSHIPS** Cath Bibl Asn; Soc Bibl Lit. **RESEARCH** Graeco-Roman mystery cults, the Pauline writings and gnosticism; the development of the traditions about Jesus. **SELECTED PUBLICATIONS** Auth, The Serapeum at Soli, Cyprus, Numina Aegaea 2, 75; Diversification in Roman Period Isis worship: The Nile water pitcher, Soc Bibl Lit 1977 Sem Papers, 77; The known Isis-Sarapis sanctuaries of the Roman period, In: Aufstieg und Niedergang der Romischen Welt, Religion, Principat; The Isis-Sarapis Cult, Relig & Ethics Inst, 78; Water in the Cultic Worship of Isis and Sarapis, E J Brill, Leiden, 81; The Sentences of Sextus, Scholars Press, 81; And Sarapis In The Roman World - Takacs,Sa, Catholic Biblical Quarterly, Vol 0059, 1997. **CONTACT ADDRESS** Dept of Theol, Marquette Univ, Milwaukee, WI, 53233.

WILDER, ROBERT JAY
PERSONAL Born 03/09/1960, Baltimore, MD, m, 1993, 2 children **DISCIPLINE** ENVIRONMENTAL SCIENCE **EDUCATION** Univ Calif, Santa Barbara, BA, 82, MA, 88, PhD, 91; Univ San Diego Sch of Law, JD, 85. **CAREER** Lectr, environ stud, polit sci, Univ Calif, Santa Barbara, 91, 92; vis Fulbright lectr, Univ So Pacific, 92-93; asst prof, polit sci, Univ Mass, 93-96; lectr, Environ Stud, & Sch of Environ Sci and Mgt, Univ Calif, Santa Barbara, 96-. **HONORS AND AWARDS** Nat Acad Sci Young Investigator in Coastal Ecol & in Biodiversity; AAAS/EPA Fel; Fulbright Fel; Sea Grant Fel. **MEMBERSHIPS** Am Polit Sci Asn; AAAS; Marine Aff and Policy Asn; Asn of Polit and Life Sci. **RESEARCH** Marine policy; environmental politics, policy and law. **SELECTED PUBLICATIONS** Auth, Prevention Rather than Cure, Nature, 94; auth, Building an Environmental Regime Based on Precaution, Pollution Prevention and Industrial Ecology, in, Environmental Science & Engineering, AAAS, 95; auth, The Law of the Sea Convention as Stimulus for Robust Environmental Policy, in Mann-Borgese, ed, Ocean Yearbook 12, Univ Chicago, 96; auth, Listening to the Sea: The Politics of Improving Environmental Protection, Pittsburgh, 98. **CONTACT ADDRESS** Environmental Studies, Univ California, Santa Barbara, Santa Barbara, CA, 93106. **EMAIL** robw@msi.ucsb.edu

WILEY, GEORGE
PERSONAL Born 11/26/1946, Jackson, TN, m, 1993, 3 children **DISCIPLINE** RELIGION **EDUCATION** Univ NC Chapel Hill, BA, 68; Emory Univ, MD, 71; PhD, 78. **CAREER** Prof, Baker Univ, 77-. **HONORS AND AWARDS** Morehead Scholar; Phi Betta Kappa; Osborne Chair of Rel. **MEMBERSHIPS** Am Acad of Rel. **RESEARCH** Early Christianity; Christian Ethics. **CONTACT ADDRESS** Baker Univ, Box 65, Baldwin City, KS, 66006-0065. **EMAIL** wiley@harvey.bakeru.edu

WILIAMS, RON G.
DISCIPLINE PHILOSOPHY **EDUCATION** Stanford Univ, PhD, 75. **CAREER** Prof. **RESEARCH** Logic philosophy of language; philosophy of science; aesthetics. **SELECTED PUBLICATIONS** Co-auth, Philosophical Analysis, 65; Ritual Art and Knowledge, 93. **CONTACT ADDRESS** Philosophy Dept, Colorado State Univ, Fort Collins, CO, 80523.

WILKINS, DAVID BRIAN
DISCIPLINE LAW **EDUCATION** Harvard University; Harvard Law School, JD. **CAREER** US Supreme Court Justice Thurgood Marshall, clerk; Harvard Law School, professor, currently. **SELECTED PUBLICATIONS** Fourth African-American tenured professor at Harvard University. **CONTACT ADDRESS** Law Sch, Harvard Univ, 1545 Massachusetts Ave1545 Massachusetts Ave, Cambridge, MA, 02138.

WILKS, ANDREW C.
PERSONAL Born 09/19/1963, Oak Ridge, TN, m, 1987, 2 children **DISCIPLINE** RELIGIOUS ETHICS **EDUCATION** Univ Tenn Knoxville, BA, 86; Univ Va, MA, 89; Univ Va, PhD, 92. **CAREER** Asst ed, Ctr for Biomedical Ethics, Univ Va, Charlottesville, Va, 90-92; trainee consult, Ethics Consult Svc, Univ Va Health Sci Ctr, Charlottesville, Va, 91-92; adjunct facul, Germanna Comm Col, Locust Grove, Va, 89; tchg asst, dept of relig studies and health sci ctr, Univ Va, Charlottesville, Va, Basic Clinical Ethics and Helth Care Law, 89-92, Amer Relig Hist, 1850-Present, 90, theol, ethics, and med, 87-89, relig ethics and moral prob, 87-89; visg prof, Pacific Coast Banking Sch, Seattle, Wash, 8/96, 8/97; visg prof, Helsinki Sch of Econ and Bus Admin, Helsinki, Finland, 9/96, 9/97; Asst prof, Univ Wash, grad bus sch, 92-. **HONORS AND AWARDS** Phi Beta Kappa; Omicron Delta Kappa; Phi Kappa Phi. **MEMBERSHIPS** Soc for Bus Ethics; Acad of Mgt. **RESEARCH** Business ethics. **SELECTED PUBLICATIONS** Coauth, with R. Edward Freeman, Organization Studies and the New Pragmatism, Orgn Sci, 123-140, Mar-Apr, 98; auth, In Search of Experts: A Conception of Expertise for Business Ethics, Bus Ethics Quart, vol 8, 105-126, jan 98; Health Care Ethics/Business Ethics, entry in Dict of Bus Ethics, Oxford Univ Press, 97; On Macintrye, Modernity and the Virtues: A Response to Dobson, Bus Ethics Quart, vol 7, 133-135, oct 97; Reflections on The Practical Relevance of Feminist Thought to Business, Bus Ethics Quart, vol 6, 523-532, oct 96; coauth, An Evaluation of Journal Quality: The Perspective of Business Ethics Researchers, with Robbin Derry, Bus Ethics Quart, vol 6, 359-372, jul 96; coauth, Integrating Strategic Decision-Making and Business Ethics: A Cognitive Approach, with Anne Ilinitch, Acad of Mgt Best Paper Proceed for 1996; auth, Overcoming the Separation Thesis: The Need for Reconsideration of SIM Research, Bus and Soc, 89-118, mar 96; coauth, Is Pharmacy a Profession?, Ethical Issues in Pharmacy, with William E. Fassett, ed Bruce D. Weinstein, Vancouver, Wash, Applied Therapeutics, 1-28, 96; auth, The Business Ethics Movement: Where are We Headed and What Can We Learn From Our Colleagues in Bioethics?, Bus Ethics Quart, vol 5, 603-20, jul 95; Albert Schweitzer or Ivan Boeksy? Whey We Should Reject the Dichotomy Between Medicine and Business, Jour of Bus Ethics, vol 14, 339-51, may 95; A Note on Sexual Harassment and A Note on Sexual Harassment Policy, Case Studies in Bus Ethics, 4th ed, ed Thomas Donaldson and Al Gini, Upper Saddle River, NJ, Prentice Hall, 198-204, 96; coauth, with Daniel R. Gilbert, Jr. and R. Edward Freeman, A Feminist Re-Interpretation of the Stakeholder Concept, Bus Ethics Quart, vol 4, 475-98, oct 94. **CONTACT ADDRESS** Graduate School of Business, Univ of Washington, Box 353200, Seattle, WA, 98195. **EMAIL** acwckw@u.washington.edu

WILL, JAMES EDWARD
PERSONAL Born 01/18/1928, Palatine, IL, m, 1949, 5 children **DISCIPLINE** SYSTEMATIC THEOLOGY **EDUCATION** NCent Col, BA, 49; Evangel Theol Sem, BD, 52; Columbia Univ & Union Theol Sem, PhD, 62. **CAREER** Asst prof relig, NCent Col, 55-59; from assoc prof to prof philos theol, Evangel Theol Sent, 59-73; Prof Syst Theol, Garrett Theol Sem, 73-98 (retired), Fac adv, Nat Intersem Coun Intersem Movement, 66-67 & 68-69; Am Asn Theol Schs fac studies fel, Free Univ Berlin, 67-68; mem comn faith & order, Nat Coun Churches, 70-78; deleg, Democratic Nat Convention, 72; dir, Peace Inst, Garrett Evangel Theol Sem, 75-85 & Univ Vienna, 74-75; mem, Interunit Comt on Int Concerns, Nat Coun Churches, 79-85, Working Comt Churches' Human Rights Prog, 79 & Continuation Comt Warsaw Europ Christian Forum, 79-; chmn, Corsortium for Int Theol Educ, 79-81; Ecumenical Inst, Tantua, 86, Univ Zimbabwe, 89. **MEMBERSHIPS** Am Theol Soc; Am Soc Christian Ethics; Am Acad of Relig. **RESEARCH** Marxist-Christian dialogue; philosophical theol; peace and justice; Inter-relig dialogue. **SELECTED PUBLICATIONS** Auth, Understanding the impact of world-wide inequities, Christian Century, 5/75; Local congregations: Reluctant peacemakers, Explor, fall 77; The place of ideology in theology, J Ecumenical Studies, winter 77; Must Walls Divide?, Friendship Press, 81; Philosophy and Social Thought, Congregatio Sanctissimi Redemptoris, 81; Christian-Marxist ethical dialogue from a process perspective, Encounter, autumn 81; Promise and Peril in Poland, 1/81 & European peace and American churches, 3/82, The Christian Century; Christology of Peace, Westminster/John Knox, 89; The Universal God, Westminster/John Knox, 94. **CONTACT ADDRESS** 1010 Lake Ave, Wilmette, IL, 60091. **EMAIL** j-will@nwu.edu

WILLACY, HAZEL M.
PERSONAL Born 04/20/1946, MS, m **DISCIPLINE** LAW **EDUCATION** Smith Clg, BA 1967; Case Western Reserve U, JD 1976. **CAREER** Bureau of Labor Stats, lbr ecnmst 1967-72; Baker Hostetter, atty 1976-80; Sherwin Williams, labor rel atty 1980-82, asst dir labor relations, 1983-87, dir Labor Relations, 1987-93; dir, Empl Policies/Labor Relations, 1993-. **HONORS AND AWARDS** Order of Coif 1976. **MEMBERSHIPS** Mem ABA OH St Bar Asso 1976-; mem, board of directors, Northeast Chapter, Industrial Relations Research Assn; mem, bd of trustees, Meridia Physician Network, 1995-. **SELECTED PUBLICATIONS** articles publ 1970, 76, 80. **CONTACT ADDRESS** Sherwin Williams Co, 101 Prospect Ave, Cleveland, OH, 44115.

WILLEMS, ELIZABETH
PERSONAL Born 05/22/1937, Cologne, MN **DISCIPLINE** MORAL THEOLOGY; PSYCHOLOGY **EDUCATION** Univ Chicago, MA, 81; Marquette Univ, PhD, 86. **CAREER** Prof, Moral Theology & Dir MA Prog, 94-, Notre Dame Sem, 85-. **HONORS AND AWARDS** Ats fel; Nat Cath Press Asn Award **MEMBERSHIPS** CTSA; CTS; SCE **RESEARCH** Moral theology: Social ethics, principles, sexual ethics. **SELECTED PUBLICATIONS** Auth, Understanding Catholic Morality, Crossroad, 97. **CONTACT ADDRESS** 2901 S Carrollton, New Orleans, LA, 70118. **EMAIL** EWILL74623@aol.com

WILLETT, CYNTHIA
DISCIPLINE CONTEMPORARY CONTINENTAL PHILOSOPHY **EDUCATION** PA State Univ, PhD, 88. **CAREER** Philos, Emory Univ. **SELECTED PUBLICATIONS** Auth, Maternal Ethics and Other Slave Moralities. **CONTACT ADDRESS** Emory Univ, Atlanta, GA, 30322-1950.

WILLIAMS, CHRISTOPHER
PERSONAL Born 09/23/1960, Oak Hill, OH **DISCIPLINE** PHILOSOPHY **EDUCATION** Furman Univ, BA, 82; Univ Pitts, MA, 88, PhD, 93. **CAREER** Vis asst prof, 90-91, asst prof, 91-98, assoc prof, 98- Univ Nevada, Reno. **HONORS AND AWARDS** Fel, Soc for Hum, Cornell Univ, 98-99. **MEMBERSHIPS** APA; Amer Soc for Aesthetics; British Soc for Aesthetics; Hume Soc. **RESEARCH** Aesthetics; ethics; philosophy of mind. **SELECTED PUBLICATIONS** Art, Is Tragedy Paradoxical?, British J of Aesthetics 38, 98; art, Modern Art Theories, J of Aesthetics & Art Criticism 56, 98; auth, A Cultivated Reason, Univ Park, PA, Penn St Univ Press, 98. **CONTACT ADDRESS** Dept of Philosophy, Univ of Nevada, Reno, NV, 89557. **EMAIL** ctw@unv.edu

WILLIAMS, CLIFFORD
PERSONAL Born 12/07/1943, Chicago, IL, m, 1965, 1 child **DISCIPLINE** PHILOSOPHY **EDUCATION** Wheaton Col, BA, 67; Ind Univ, PhD, 72. **CAREER** Instr to asst prof to assoc prof, St. John Fisher Col, Rochester, NY, 68-82; vis assoc prof, Houghton Col, Houghton, NY, 80; assoc prof to prof, Trinity Col, 82- ; vis prof, Wheaton Col, 98-99. **HONORS AND AWARDS** Teaching Excellence & Campus Leadership Award, 89. **MEMBERSHIPS** Soc of Christian Philos; Philos of Time Soc. **RESEARCH** Philos of time; Kierkegaard. **SELECTED PUBLICATIONS** Auth, Singleness of Heart: Restoring the Divided Soul, Eerdmans Publ Co, 94, Regent Col Publ, 98; Christian Materialism and the Parity Thesis, Int J for Philos of Relig, 96; The Metaphysics of A- and B- Time, The Philos quart, 96; A Bergsonian Approach to A- and B- Time, Philos, 98; B- Time Transition, Philos Inquiry, 98. **CONTACT ADDRESS** Dept of Philosophy, Trinity Col, Deerfield, IL, 60015. **EMAIL** cwilliam@trin.edu

WILLIAMS, CYNTHIA A.
DISCIPLINE LAW **EDUCATION** Univ Calif Berkeley, BA; Univ NY, JD. **CAREER** Law clerk, Judge Milton L. Schwartz, US District Court; asst prof, Univ Ill Urbana Champaign. **HONORS AND AWARDS** Am Jurisprudence Awd., Ed, NY Univ Law rev. **RESEARCH** Torts; business organizations; securities regulation; and a seminar on corporate social responsibility. **SELECTED PUBLICATIONS** Auth, pubs on voter registration. **CONTACT ADDRESS** Law Dept, Univ Ill Urbana Champaign, 52 E Gregory Dr, Champaign, IL, 61820. **EMAIL** cwilliam@law.uiuc.edu

WILLIAMS, DENNIS E.
DISCIPLINE CHRISTIAN EDUCATION **EDUCATION** Bob Jones Univ, BS, MA; N Ariz Univ, MA; Southwestern Baptist Theol Sem, MRE, PhD. **CAREER** Exec dir, Christian Ministries Convention, 84-94; prof, ch dept Edu Ministries and Admin, Denver Sem, 71-94; instr, King of Kings Col, Tel Aviv; Providence Theol Sem, Can; Caribbean Grad Sch Theol; Asian Grad Sch Theol; Asian Theol Sem, Philippines; dean, Sch Christian Edu and Leadership, prof, S Baptist Theol Sem, 94-. **HONORS AND AWARDS** Distinguished Educator award, Southwestern Baptist Rel Edu Assn. **SELECTED PUBLICATIONS** Auth, Volunteers For Today's Church: How To Recruit and Retain Workers; contrib, Leadership Handbook of Practical Theol; Christian Edu:Foundations For The Future; pub(s), Christian Edu Today; Christian Edu Jour; Key To Christian Edu; Leader Idea Bank; Small Gp Letter; Super Sunday Sch Sourcebook. **CONTACT ADDRESS** Sch Christian Edu and Leadership, Southern Baptist Theol Sem, 2825 Lexington Rd, Louisville, KY, 40280. **EMAIL** dwilliams@sbts.edu

WILLIAMS, DONALD T.
PERSONAL Born 01/10/1951, Norfolk, VA, m, 1972, 2 children **DISCIPLINE** THEOLOGY **EDUCATION** Taylor Univ, BA, 73; Trinity Evangel Div School, MDiv, 76; Univ Georgia, PhD, 85. **CAREER** Pastor, First Evangel Free Church, Marietta, GA, 82-87; vis lectr and tutor, Centre for Medieval and Renaissance Stud of Keble Col, Oxford Univ, 94, 97; pastor, Trinity Fel, Toccoa, GA, 92- ; assoc prof English, Toccoa Falls Col, 87- . **HONORS AND AWARDS** Faculty Scholar of the Year, Toccoa Falls Col, 97. **MEMBERSHIPS** Ministerial Asn, Evangel Free Church of Am; Evangel Theol Soc; Evangel Philos Soc; Southeastern Renaissance Conf; Mythopoeic Soc. **RESEARCH** Theology; Medieval and Renaissance literature; philosophy; theology and literature. **SELECTED PUBLICATIONS** Auth, The Person and the Work of the Holy Spirit, Broadman & Holman, 94; auth, The Candle Rekindled: Hugh Latimer on the Temporal Order, in Bauman, ed, Evangelical Renderings: To God and Caesar, Christian Publ, 94; auth, Christian Poetics, Past and Present, in, Barratt, ed, The Discerning Reader: Christian Perspectives on Literature and Theory, Baker, 95; auth, John Foxe, in, Bauman, ed, Historians of the Christian Tradition: Their Methodology and Influence on Western Thought, Broadman & Holman, 95; auth, Apologetic Responses to Post-Modernism: Panel Discussion, Philosophia Christi, 96; auth, Apologetic Responses to Post-Modernism: A Symposium, in, Bauman, ed, Evangelical Apologetics: Selected Essays from the 1995 Evangelical Theological Society Convention, Christian Publ, 96; auth, Inklings of Reality: Essays Toward A Christian Philosophy of Letters, Toccoa Falls Press, 96; auth, Reflections from Plato's Cave: Musings on the History of Philosophy, Philosophia Christi, 97; auth, The Disciple's Prayer, Christian Publ, 99. **CONTACT ADDRESS** PO Box 800807, Toccoa Falls, GA, 30598. **EMAIL** dtw@toccoafalls.edu

WILLIAMS, GARY C.
PERSONAL Born 01/07/1952, Santa Monica, California, m, 1980 **DISCIPLINE** LAW **EDUCATION** UCLA, BA, 1973; Stanford Law School, JD, 1976. **CAREER** California Agricultural Labor Relations Board, staff attorney; ACLU Foundation of Southern California, asst legal dir, staff attorney; Loyola University School of Law, professor, currently. **MEMBERSHIPS** Southern Christian Leadership Conference/LA, bd of dir; ACLU of Southern California, bd of dir; Mount Hebron Baptist Church, chairman; Stanford Law School Board of Visitors. **SELECTED PUBLICATIONS** Hastings Constitutional Law Quarterly, "The Wrong Side of the Tracks," p 845, 1992; Southwestern University Law Review, "Can Government Limit Tenant Blacklisting?," vol 24, p 1077, 1995. **CONTACT ADDRESS** Professor, Loyola Univ School of Law, 1441 W. Olympic Blvd., Los Angeles, CA, 90043.

WILLIAMS, GARY G. COHEN
DISCIPLINE RELIGION **EDUCATION** Temple Univ, BSed, 56; Faith Theol Sem, Mdiv, 61, STM, 64; Grace Theol Sem, ThD, 66. **SELECTED PUBLICATIONS** Contib ed, Kirban Prophecy Bible; Red Letter Bible; Christian Life Bible. **CONTACT ADDRESS** Trinity Int Univ, 500 NE 1st Ave, PO Box 109674, Miami, FL, 33101-9674.

WILLIAMS, GREGORY HOWARD
PERSONAL Born 11/12/1943, Muncie, Indiana, m **DISCIPLINE** LAW **EDUCATION** Ball St U, BA 1966; Univ of MD, MA 1969; George Washington U, JD 1971, MPhil 1977, PhD 1982. **CAREER** Delaware Co, IN, deputy sheriff 1963-66; US Senate, legal aide 1971-73; GW Washington Project Washington DC, coord 1973-77; Univ of IA, assoc dean law prof 1977-87, professor of law, 1987-93; Ohio State University, College of Law, dean and Carter C Kissell prof of law, 1993- **MEMBERSHIPS** Consultant Foreign Lawyer Training Prog Wash DC 1975-77; consultant Natl Inst (Minority Mental Health Prog) 1975; mem IA Adv Comm US Civil Rights Commn 1978-88; mem IA Law Enforcement Academy Council 1979-85; pres-elect, Assn of American Law Schools, 1998. **SELECTED PUBLICATIONS** Book, Law and Politics of Police Discretion 1984; article "Police Rulemaking Revisited" Journal Laws & Cont Problems 1984; article "Police Discretion" IA Law Review 1983; book The Iowa Guide to Search & Seizure 1986; Author, Life on the Color Line, The True Story of a White Boy Who Discovered He Was Black, 1995. **CONTACT ADDRESS** Dean, Ohio State Univ, Col of Law, 55 W 12th Avenue, Columbus, OH, 43210.

WILLIAMS, J. RODMAN
PERSONAL m, 3 children **DISCIPLINE** SYSTEMATIC THEOLOGY **EDUCATION** Davidson Col, AB; Union Theol Sem, BD, ThM, Columbia Univ, PhD **CAREER** Instr, Austin Presbyterian Sem; pres, prof, Melodyland Sch Theol; prof, Regent Univ. **HONORS AND AWARDS** Chaplain, US Marine Corps; pastor, First Presbyterian Church; pres, Intl Presbyterian Charismatic Communion; organizer, leader, first Europ Charismatic Leaders Conf(s); pres, Soc Pentecostal Stud. **SELECTED PUBLICATIONS** Auth, Contemporary Existentialism and Christian Faith, 65; The Era of the Spirit, 71; The Pentecostal Reality, 72; Ten Teachings, 74; The Gift of the Holy Spirit Today, 80; Renewal Theology, vol 1, God, the World, and Redemption, Zondervan, 88; Renewal Theology, vol 2, Salvation, the Holy Spirit, and Christian Living, Zondervan, 90; The Gifts of the Holy Spirit, Charisma, 92; Biblical Truth and Experience: A Reply to Charismatic Chaos by John F. MacArthur, Jr, Paraclete 27/3, 93; What Catholics Should Know about Protestants, Charisma, 95; Renewal Theology, vol 3, The Church, the Kingdom, and Last Things, Zondervan, 92; Renewal Theology, Zondervan, 96. **CONTACT ADDRESS** Dept of Systematic Theology, Regent Univ, 1000 Regent Univ Dr, Virginia Beach, VA, 23464-9831.

WILLIAMS, JAY G.
PERSONAL Born 12/18/1932, Rome, NY, m, 1956, 4 children **DISCIPLINE** RELIGION **EDUCATION** Hamilton Col, BA, 54; Union Theol Semi NY, M(Div), 57; Columbia Univ, PhD(philos relig), 64. **CAREER** Assoc dir, A Christian Ministry in Nat Parks, Nat Coun Churches, 57-60; from instr to prof relig, 60-76, Walcott-Barlett Prof Ethics & Christian Evidences, Hamilton Col, 76-. **HONORS AND AWARDS** Ford humanities grants, 70-72. **MEMBERSHIPS** Am Acad Relig; Hermetic Studies; Buddhist-Christian Studies. **RESEARCH** Philos rel. East and West. **SELECTED PUBLICATIONS** Auth, Ten Words of Freedom, Fortress, 71; Understanding the Old Testament, Barron's, 73; Yeshua Buddha, Quest, 78; Judaism, Quest, 80; Spiritual Approach to Male/Female Relations, Quest, 84; Riddle of the Sphyx, UPA, 90; Angels and Mortals, Quest, 90; Along the Silk Route, GSP, 91; Matters of Life and Death, GSP, 93; Dark Trees and Empty Sky, GSP, 94; A Reassessment of Absolute Skepticism and Religious Faith, Mellen, 96; Education of Edward Robinson, UTS, 97. **CONTACT ADDRESS** Dept of Relig Studies, Hamilton Col, 198 College Hill Rd., Clinton, NY, 13323-1292. **EMAIL** jwilliam@Hamilton.edu

WILLIAMS, JUNIUS W.
PERSONAL Born 12/23/1943, Suffolk, VI **DISCIPLINE** LAW **EDUCATION** Amherst Coll, BA 1965; Yale Law Sch, JD 1968; Inst of Pol Kennedy Sch of Gov Harvard Univ, fellow 1980. **CAREER** Newark Comm Devel Admin & Model Cities Prog, dir 1970-73; Essex Newark Legal Svcs, exec dir 1983-85; City of Newark, candidate for mayor 1982; Private Practice, Attorney 1973-83, 1985-; "Return to the Source," New Jersey, business manager, vocalist, instrumentalist, 1985-; real estate developer, Newark, NJ, 1987-; Town of Irvington, Irvington, NJ, legislative counsel, 1990-94, town Attorney, 1994-. **HONORS AND AWARDS** Distinguished Service Awd Newark Jaycees 1974; Concerned Citizens Awd Bd of Concerned Citizens Coll of Med & Dentistry of NJ; Fellow MARC 1967-68, 1973. **MEMBERSHIPS** 3rd vice pres Natl Bar Assn; 2nd vice pres 1976; pres Natl Bar Assn 1978-79; mem bd of dirs Agricultural Missions Inc; mem Natl, Amer, NJ, Essex Co Bar Assn; mem Critical Minorities Problems Comm; Natl Assn Housing & Redevel Officials; mem Equal Oppor Fund Bd 1980; Essex Co Ethics Comm 1980; fndr & dir Newark Area Planning Assn 1967-70; co-chmn Comm Negotiating Team NJ Coll Med & Dentistry Controversey 1967; guest spkr/lecturer Yale Univ, Harvard Law Sch, Rutgers Univ, Cornell Univ, Univ NC; pres Yale Law Sch Assoc of NJ 1981-82; fndr/pres Leadership Development Group 1980-; consultant Council of Higher Educ in Newark; bd of trustees Essex Co Coll 1980-84; mem & former sec Newark Collaboration Group; founder/first chmn Ad Hoc Comm of Univ Heights 1984-86; UniversityHeights Neighborhood Develent Corp., consultant, developer, 1986-93. **CONTACT ADDRESS** 132 Harper Ave, Irvington, NJ, 07111.

WILLIAMS, KAREN HASTIE
PERSONAL Born 09/30/1944, Washington, DC, m **DISCIPLINE** LAW **EDUCATION** Univ of Neuchatel Switzerland, Cert 1965; Bates Coll, BA 1966; Fletcher School of Law & Diplomacy Tufts Univ, MA 1967; Columbus Law School Catholic Univ of Amer, JD 1973. **CAREER** Fried Frank Harris Shriver & Kampelman, assoc atty 1975-77; US Senate Comm on Budget, chief counsel 1977-80; Office of Fed Procurement Policy Office of Mgmt & Budget, admin 1980-81; Crowell & Moring, of counsel 1982, sr partner. **HONORS AND AWARDS** Director's Choice Award, 1993; National Women's Economic Alliance; Breast Cancer Awareness Award, Columbia Hospital for Women, 1994; Judge Learned Hand Award, 1995, American Jewish Committee. **MEMBERSHIPS** Past chmn, Amer Bar Assoc Publ Contract Law Sect; bd of dir Crestar Bank Washington DC; Lawyers Comm for Civil Rights Under Law; board of directors Federal National Mortgage Association; board of directors Washington Gas Light Co; chair Black Student Fund; bd of dir exec comm DC Chap Amer Red Cross; chair, bd of dir Greater Washington Rsch Ctr; bd of dir NAACP Legal Defense Fund; former mem Trilateral Commission; Continental Airlines Inc, bd of directors; bd of directors, Sun America Inc. **CONTACT ADDRESS** Crowell and Moring, 1001 Pennsylvania Ave, NW, Washington, DC, 20004.

WILLIAMS, KYLE
PERSONAL Born 01/25/1963, Denver, CO **DISCIPLINE** RELIGION **EDUCATION** Hunter Coll, BA; SUNY Albany, MA. **CAREER** Admin, Lincoln Center/Institute; admin, New York Open Center; Prof religion, Hunter Coll. **MEMBERSHIPS** AAR **RESEARCH** Religion & the Arts **CONTACT ADDRESS** 611 W 158th St, #6E, New York, NY, 10032.

WILLIAMS, MARCUS DOYLE
PERSONAL Born 10/24/1952, Nashville, TN, m **DISCIPLINE** LAW **EDUCATION** Fisk Univ, BA, 1973 (university honors); Catholic Univ of Amer, School of Law, JD, 1977. **CAREER** Office of the Commonwealth Atty, asst commonwealth atty, 1978-80; George Mason Univ, lecturer in business legal studies, 1980-95; Office of the County Atty, asst county atty, 1980-87; Gen Dist Court, judge, 1987-90; CIRCUIT COURT, JUDGE, 1990-; National Judicial College, faculty, 1992. **HONORS AND AWARDS** Beta Kappa Chi, Scientific Honor Soc, Fisk Univ Chapter, 1973; Distinguished Youth Award, Office of the Army, Judge Advocate Gen, 1976; Thomas J Watson Fellow, 1977-78; Fairfax County Bd of Supvr, Serv Commendation, 1987; Serv Appreciation Award, Burke-Fairfax Jack & Jill, 1989; Service Appreciation Award, Black Law Students Assn of Catholic University, 1990; Otis Smith Alumnus Award, 1997; American Participant Program Lectures, Liberia, Zambia, Botswana, sponsored by USIA, 1990; **MEMBERSHIPS** Bd mem, Fairfax-Falls Church, Criminal Justice Adv Bd, 1980-81; freelance writer and reviewer, 1981-; mem, Amer Business Law Assn, 1984-; bd of assocs, St Paul's Coll, 1986-87; vice chmn, Continuing Legal Educ Comm, Fairfax Bar Assn, 1986-87; Virginia delegate, National Conference of Special Court Judges, 1990; Omega Psi Phi Fraternity, 1971. **SELECTED PUBLICATIONS** Articles: "Arbitration of Intl Commercial Contracts: Securities and Antitrust Claims," Virginia Lawyer, 1989, "European Antitrust Law and its Application to Amer Corp," Whittier Law Review, 1987, "Judicial Review: The Guardian of Civil Liberties and Civil Rights," George Mason University Civil Rights Law Journ 1991, "Lawyer, Judge, Solicitor, General Education: A Tribute to Wade H McCree, Jr," National Black Law Journal, 1990. **CONTACT ADDRESS** Circuit Court, 4110 Chain Bridge Rd, Fairfax, VA, 22030.

WILLIAMS, MEREDITH
PERSONAL Born 07/29/1947, Anniston, AL, m, 1973, 1 child **DISCIPLINE** PHILOSOPHY **EDUCATION** New York Univ, PhD, 74. **CAREER** Asst, Assoc Prof, Wesleyan Univ, 74-85; Assoc Prof, Northwestern Univ, 85-. **MEMBERSHIPS** AAUP; Soc for Phil & Psychology; Amer Phil Assoc. **RESEARCH** Philosophy of the mind & psychology **SELECTED PUBLICATIONS** Auth, Wittgenstein, Kant, and the Metaphysics of Experience, Kant-Studien, 90; Narrow Content, Norms and the Individual, Midwest Studies in Philosophy, 90; Externalism and the Philosophy of the Mind, Philosophical Quarterly, 90; Rules, Community and the Individual, Meaning-Scepticism, 91; Private States, Public Places, International Philosophical Quarterly, 94; The Philosophical Significance of Learning in the Later Wittgenstein, Canadian Journal of Philosophy, 94; The Implicit Intricacy of Thought and Action, Making Sense with Words and Concepts, 97; The Etiology of the Obvious, Wittgenstein in America, forthcoming; Auth, Wittgenstein, Mind and Meaning: Toward a Social Conception of Mind, 98. **CONTACT ADDRESS** Dept of Philosophy, Northwestern Univ, 1818 Hinman, Evanston, IL, 60208.

WILLIAMS, MICHAEL J.
DISCIPLINE PHILOSOPHY **EDUCATION** Princeton Univ, PhD. **CAREER** Charles and Emma Morrison prof Humanities, Northwestern Univ. **RESEARCH** Epistemology, history of modern philosophy. **SELECTED PUBLICATIONS** Auth, Groundless Belief; Unnatural Doubts. **CONTACT ADDRESS** Dept of Philosophy, Northwestern Univ, 1801 Hinman, Evanston, IL, 60208.

WILLIAMS, PAUL R.
DISCIPLINE LAW AND INTERNATIONAL RELATIONS **EDUCATION** Univ Calif Davis, BA, Stanford Univ, JD. **CAREER** Asst prof, Am Univ. **HONORS AND AWARDS** Exec dir, Public Int Law & Policy Gp; dir, Public Inst Law Policy Prog, Carnegie Endowment. **RESEARCH** International communication policy and law. **SELECTED PUBLICATIONS** Auth, Treatment of Detainees **CONTACT ADDRESS** American Univ, 4400 Massachusetts Ave, Washington, DC, 20016.

WILLIAMS, PETER W.
PERSONAL Born 08/08/1944, Hollywood, FL, m, 1980, 2 children **DISCIPLINE** RELIGIOUS STUDIES **EDUCATION** Harvard Univ, AB, 65; Yale Univ, AM, 67, MPhil, 68, PhD, 70. **CAREER** DISTINGUISHED PROF OF RELIG AND AM STUDIES, MIAMI UNIV, 70-. **HONORS AND AWARDS** Pres, Amer Soc of Church Hist. **MEMBERSHIPS** Amer Studies Assoc; Amer Academy Relig; Hist Soc of the Episcopal Church; Soc of Architectural Historians; Vernacular Architecture Forum. **RESEARCH** Amer religious architecture. **SELECTED PUBLICATIONS** Auth, Houses of God: Region, Religion and Architecture in the United States, Univ IL Press, 97. **CONTACT ADDRESS** Dept of Relig, Miami Univ, Oxford, OH, 45056. **EMAIL** williapw@muohio.edu

WILLIAMS, PRESTON N.
PERSONAL Born 05/23/1926, Alcolu, South Carolina, m **DISCIPLINE** THEOLOGY **EDUCATION** Washington & Jefferson Coll, AB 1947, MA 1948; Johnson C Smith Univ, BD 1950; Yale Univ, STM 1954; Harvard Univ, PhD 1967. **CAREER** Boston Univ School Theol, Martin Luther King Jr prof social ethics 1970-71; Harvard Div School, acting dean 1974-75, Houghton prof theol & contemporary change 1971-. **HONORS AND AWARDS** Ordained to ministry Presb Church 1950. **MEMBERSHIPS** Acting dir WEB DuBois Inst 1975-77; editor-at-large Christian Century 1972-; mem, pres Amer Acad Religion 1975-; dir, pres Amer Soc Christian Ethics 1974-75; mem Phi Beta Kappa. **SELECTED PUBLICATIONS** Contrib articles to professional jrnls. **CONTACT ADDRESS** Divinity Sch, Harvard Univ, 45 Francis Ave, Cambridge, MA, 02138.

WILLIAMS, SAMUEL KEEL
PERSONAL Born 03/18/1940, Rocky Mount, NC, m, 1962, 3 children **DISCIPLINE** RELIGION **EDUCATION** Wake Forest Univ, BA, 62; Southeastern Baptist Theol Sem, BD, 66; Harvard Univ, PhD(relig), 72. **CAREER** Instr relig, Wake Forest Univ, 69-70; instr relig & actg chaplain, 71-72, asst prof to prof Relig, Colo Col, 73-. **HONORS AND AWARDS** Fulbright Schol, 62-63; Woodrow Wilson Fel, 66-67; Sears-Roebuck Found Award for Excellence in Teaching, 90. **MEMBERSHIPS** Soc Bibl Lit; Catholic Bibl Asn. **RESEARCH** Early Christian soteriology; Pauline theology. **SELECTED PUBLICATIONS** Auth, Jesus' Death as Saving Event: The Background and Origin of a Concept, Scholars, 75; Galatians, Abingdon, 97. **CONTACT ADDRESS** Dept of Relig, Colorado Col, 14 E Cache La Poudre, Colorado Springs, CO, 80903-3294. **EMAIL** swilliams@ColoradoCollege.edu

WILLIAMS, WILBERT LEE
PERSONAL Born 08/25/1938, Corsicana, Texas, m, 1961 **DISCIPLINE** LAW **EDUCATION** Prairie View A&M Coll, BS 1960; Howard Univ School of Law, JD 1971; Inst for New Govt Attys 1971; Howard Univ School of Divinity, 1987-90 M Div. **CAREER** US Dept of Agr, farm mgmt supr 1965-68; United Planning Org Wash DC, exec ofcr 1968-71; US Dept of Agr Office of Gen Counsel Wash DC, atty 1971-84; US Dept of Agr, equal opportunity officer; pastor, The First New Horizon Baptist Church, currently. **HONORS AND AWARDS** Recip 1st Annual Achievement Award OEO Natl Advisory Comm for Legal Serv Program 1968. **MEMBERSHIPS** Past vice pres & founding mem CHASE Inc; former mem DC Neighborhood Reinvestment Commission; past mem bd dir Neighborhood Legal Serv Program Washington DC; past mem bd trustee United Planning Org Washington DC. **SELECTED PUBLICATIONS** President and founder, The First New Horizon Community Development Corp. **CONTACT ADDRESS** Pastor, The First New Horizon Baptist Church, PO Box 176, Clinton, MD, 20735.

WILLIAMS, WILLIAM C.
PERSONAL Born 07/12/1937, Wilkes-Barre, PA, m, 1959, 1 child **DISCIPLINE** BIBLICAL STUDIES **EDUCATION** Central Bible Col, BA, 63, MA, 64; New York Univ, MA, 66, PhD, 75. **CAREER** Reference Librarian, Hebraic Section, Library of Congress, Washington, DC, 67-69; PROF OF OLD TESTAMENT, SOUTHERN CA COL, COSTA MESA, 69-; vis prof: Singapore, Malaysia, Belgium, Great Britain, 85; Israel, 86; Regent Univ, Virginia Beach, VA, 92. **HONORS AND AWARDS** Nat Defense Educ Act Title VI fel, NYU, 64-67; NEH Scholar, summer 92; Marquis' Who's Who in America, 94-; Delta Sigma, 96; Delta Alpha, Distinguished Educator Award, 97; Sigma Chi Pi, 97; Distinguished Educator Award, Assemblies of God, 98., Postdoctoral Study: Hebrew Univ, Jerusalem, Israel, Semitic Langs, 77-78; Inst of Holyland Studies, Jerusalem, Israel, Archaeology and Geography of Israel, spring 86. **MEMBERSHIPS** Soc of Biblical Lit; Am Academy of Relig; Evangelical Theol Soc; Inst of Biblical Res; Am Asn of Profs of Hebrew. **RESEARCH** Hebrew lang and related Biblical theology. **SELECTED PUBLICATIONS** Auth, Greek word studies for The Complete Biblical Library, The New Testament Greek-English Dictionary, The Complete Biblical Library, 90; Hebrew I: A Study Guide, 80, 86, & Hebrew II: A Study Guide, 86, Int Correspondence Inst; articles for Evangelical Dictionary of Biblical Theology, ed Walter Elwell, Baker, 96; Commentary on Hosea for Pentecostal Commentary Series, Sheffield Academic Press, forthcoming; They Spoke From God, a textbook for Old Testament Survey, Logion, forthcoming; articles for the New International Dictionary of Old Testament Theology, Zondervan, forthcoming; numerous other articles and publications; translation and revision consultant for several publications. **CONTACT ADDRESS** Southern California Col, 55 Fair Dr., Costa Mesa, CA, 92627. **EMAIL** wwilliams@sccu.edu

WILLIAMS, WINTON E.
DISCIPLINE LAW **EDUCATION** Tulane Univ, BBA; Univ Miss, LLB; Yale Univ, LLM. **CAREER** Prof, Univ Fla, 69-. **MEMBERSHIPS** Miss Bar; Phi Delta Phi; Omicron Delta Kappa; Phi Kappa Phi. **RESEARCH** Creditors' remedies and bankruptcy, secured transactions in personal property, sales. **SELECTED PUBLICATIONS** Auth, Games Creditors Play: Collecting from Overextended Consumers. **CONTACT ADDRESS** School of Law, Univ of Florida, PO Box 117625, Gainesville, FL, 32611-7625. **EMAIL** williams.win@law.ufl.edu

WILLIAMS, YVONNE LAVERNE
PERSONAL Born 01/07/1938, Washington, DC, s **DISCIPLINE** LAW **EDUCATION** Barnard Coll, BA, 1959; Boston Univ, MA, 1961; Georgetown Univ, JD, 1977. **CAREER** US Info Agency, foreign serv officer, 1961-65; African-Amer Inst New York, dir womens Africa comm, 1966-68; Benedict Coll, Columbia, SC, assc prof African American studies, 1968-70; US Congress Washington, DC, press sec Hon Walter Fauntroy, 1970-72; African-Amer Scholars Council Washington, DC, dir 1972-73; Leva Hawes Symington Martin, Washington, DC, assoc atty, 1977-79; Brimmer & Co Washington, DC, asst vice pres, 1980-82; Tuskegee University, vice pres for Fed & Intl

Rel & Legal Counsel 1983-1996; Academy for Educational Development Public Policy & Intl Affairs Fellowship Program, natl dir, 1996-. **HONORS AND AWARDS** Boston University, African Research & Studies Program Fellowship, 1959-60. **MEMBERSHIPS** Mem Oper Crossroads Africa, 1960-, Barnard-in-Washington, 1960-; mem Amer Bar Assoc, 1980-, Natl Bar Assoc, 1980-, Dist of Columbia Bar, 1980-; alumnae trustee, Barnard Coll, New York, NY, 1988-92; mem, Overseas Devel Council, Washington, DC, 1988-; bd of dir, Golden Rule Apartments, Inc, Washington, DC, 1986-. **SELECTED PUBLICATIONS** Author, "William Monroe Trotter, (1872-1934)"; in Reid "The Black Prism," New York, 1969. **CONTACT ADDRESS** Public Policy and Intl Affairs Fellowship Prog, 1875 Conn Ave NW, Washington, DC, 20009.

WILLIAMSON, CLARK M.
PERSONAL Born 11/03/1935, Memphis, TN, m, 1960, 1 child **DISCIPLINE** THEOLOGY **EDUCATION** Transylvania Univ, BA, Univ Chicago, BD, MA, PhD, 69. **CAREER** Christian Theol Sem, prof; Sch of Theol Claremont, vis prof; Chateau de Bossey Ecumenical Inst, vis prof. **MEMBERSHIPS** CSGJ, ATS, AAR, ADTD, TCCC. **SELECTED PUBLICATIONS** Auth, A Mutual Witness: Toward Critical Solidarity Between Jews and Christians, ed. St. Louis: Chalice Press, 92; auth, The Church and the Jewish People, ed., St Louis: Chalice Press, 94; auth, A Guest in the House of Israel, Louisville: Westminister/ John Knox Press, 93; auth, Mark, Mahwah NJ: Paulist Press, forthcoming; Adventures of the Spirit: A Guide to Worship from the Perspective of Process Theology, coauth, Lanham MD: Univ Press Am, 97; The Vital Church, coauth, St Louis MO: Chalis Press, 98. **CONTACT ADDRESS** Christian Theol Sem, PO Box 88267, Indianapolis, IN, 46208.

WILLIAMSON, LAMAR
PERSONAL Born 07/24/1926, Monticello, AZ, m, 1949, 4 children **DISCIPLINE** BIBLICAL THEOLOGY **EDUCATION** Davidson Col, BA, 47; Union Theol Seminary, BD, 51; Fac Theol Protestante, Montpellier, France, BTheol, 52; Yale Univ, PhD, 63. **CAREER** Pastor, Harveyton and Hall Memorial Presbyterian Churches, 52-56; Prof New Testament, Inst Superieur de Theol, Kanduga, Zaire, 57-66; Vis Prof New Testament, Union Theol Seminary, 66-68; Prof Bibl Studies, Presbyterian Sch Christian Educ, 69-91; Prof New Testament, Fac Theol Reformee au Kasai, Zaire/Congo, 92-94. **HONORS AND AWARDS** Phi Beta Kappa; Omega Delta Kappa. **MEMBERSHIPS** Soc Bibl Lit. **RESEARCH** Fourth gospel. **SELECTED PUBLICATIONS** Auth, Mark, Interpretation: A Bible Commentary for Teaching and Preaching, John Knox Press, 83; Ishaku: An African Christian Between Two Worlds, Fairway Press, 92; transl, Prayers for My Village, Upper Room Bks, 94; co-ed, A Book of Reformed Prayers, Westminster John Knox Press, 98. **CONTACT ADDRESS** PO Box 224, Montreat, NC, 28757. **EMAIL** lamar@buncombe.main.nc.us

WILLIAMSON, WILLIAM B.
PERSONAL Born 01/27/1918, Amsterdam, NY, m, 1941, 2 children **DISCIPLINE** PHILOSOPHY **EDUCATION** Temple Univ, BS, 40, STB, 42, EdD, 66; Lutheran Theo Sem, STM, 45; Lehigh Univ, MA, 50. **CAREER** Instructor Chaplin School, WW II, US Army; Asst Prof, 45-50, Lehigh Univ; Assoc Prof, Cheyney State Coll; Prof, Ursinus Coll. **HONORS AND AWARDS** Episcopal Church Fel, Hon DD, National Univ; Hon Fel, Oriel College Oxford Univ; Hon DHL, Lindbeck Awd for Distinguished Teaching, Ursinus Coll. **RESEARCH** The question of the historical Jesus, who wrote the New Testament? **SELECTED PUBLICATIONS** Auth, A Handbook for Episcopalians, Morehouse-Barlow, 60; Ian Ramsey, Hendrickson Pub, 92; An Encyclopedia of Religions in the United States, Crossroads, 91; Night Thoughts About God, in: The Unitarian Universalist Christian, 91; Is the USA a Christian Nation? in: Free Inquiry, 93; Evangelism for Today, in: The Living Church, 93; A New Look at Primary Focus, in: Episcopal Life, The Penn Episcopalian, 94. **CONTACT ADDRESS** Pine Run Community, 12 Golden Rain Cluster, Doylestown, PA, 18901.

WILLIMON, WILLIAM HENRY
PERSONAL Born 05/15/1946, Greenville, SC, m, 1969, 2 children **DISCIPLINE** PASTORAL THEOLOGY **EDUCATION** Wofford Col, BA, 68; Yale Univ, MDiv, 71; Emory Univ, STD, 73. **CAREER** ASSOC PROF LITURGY & WORSHIP, DUKE UNIV, 76-, Pastor, Northside United Methodist Church, 80. **MEMBERSHIPS** NAm Acad Liturgy; Am Acad Relig. **RESEARCH** Liturgy and ethics; Christian worship. **SELECTED PUBLICATIONS** Auth, A Peculiarly Christian Account of Sin, Theol Today, Vol 0050, 93; Why a Pastor Should not be a Person, Theol Today, Vol 0050, 94; Blasphemy, Theol Today, Vol 0051, 94; Christian Ethics + Finding a Place for a Private Religion Under the Social Public Guarantee of the American Constitution--When the Personal is Public is Cosmic, Theol Today, Vol 0052, 95; Theological Table Talk, Theol Today, Vol 0052, 95; Luck--A Secular Faith, Theol Today, Vol 0053, 96; Why We All Cant Just Get Along, Theol Today, Vol 0053, 97. **CONTACT ADDRESS** Sch Divin, Duke Univ, Durham, NC, 27706.

WILLIS, ROBERT E.
PERSONAL Scottsbluff, NE, m, 1950, 4 children **DISCIPLINE** CHRISTIAN ETHICS, MODERN RELIGIOUS THOUGHT **EDUCATION** Occidental Col, AB, 55; San Francisco Theol Sem, BD, 58, ThD(ethics & theol), 66. **CAREER** Asst prof relig, Col Emporia, 60-62; ASSOC PROF RELIG, HAMLINE UNIV, 62-, Vis asst prof, Macalester Col, 68-69. **MEMBERSHIPS** Am Acad Relig; Am Soc Christian Ethics; AAUP; fel Soc Values Higher Educ. **RESEARCH** Jewish-Christian relations. **SELECTED PUBLICATIONS** Auth, Auschwitz and the Good + National-Socialism and Morality, a Radical Challenge Towards a Reconfiguring of the Nazi Ethic, Holocaust and Genocide Stud, Vol 0008, 94. **CONTACT ADDRESS** Dept of Relig, Hamline Univ, 1536 Hewitt Ave, St Paul, MN, 55104.

WILLIS, STEVEN J.
DISCIPLINE LAW **EDUCATION** La State Univ, BS, JD; NY Univ, LLM. **CAREER** Prof, Univ Fla, 81-.. **MEMBERSHIPS** La Bar; Fla Bar; La Soc Certified Public Accountants; Order of the Coif. **RESEARCH** Partnership taxation, tax exempt organizations and income taxation. **CONTACT ADDRESS** School of Law, Univ of Florida, PO Box 117625, Gainesville, FL, 32611-7625. **EMAIL** willis@law.ufl.edu

WILLIS, TIM
PERSONAL Born 11/03/1959, Nashville, TN, m, 1982, 3 children **DISCIPLINE** RELIGION **EDUCATION** Abilene Christian Univ, BA, 81, MA, Mdiv, 84; Harvard Univ, 84-90. **CAREER** Vis instr, Abilene Christian Univ , 87; tchg asst, Abilene Christian Univ 87-88; vis prof, 89-90; asst prof, 90-94; assoc prof, 94-. **HONORS AND AWARDS** Hon Bible Student, 81; grants, Christian Scholar Found, 86-88; tchg fel, Harvard Univ, 81-84. **SELECTED PUBLICATIONS** Auth, Mate, Mother, and Metaphor: Gomer and Israel in Hosea 1-3, Essays on Women in Earliest Christianity, Vol Two, MO: Col Press, 95; His Steadfast Love Endures Forever: General Remarks on the Book of Psalms, Leaven, 96; The Nature of Jephthah's Authority, Catholic Biblical Quart 57, 96; rev, Review of Charisma and Authority in Israelite Society, by Rodney R. Hutton, Restoration Quart 38, 96. **CONTACT ADDRESS** Dept of Relig, Pepperdine Univ, 24255 Pacific Coast Hwy, Malibu, CA, 90263.

WILLS, DAVID WOOD
PERSONAL Born 01/25/1942, Portland, IN, m, 1964, 3 children **DISCIPLINE** RELIGION **EDUCATION** Yale Univ, BA, 62; Princeton Theol Sem, BD, 66; Harvard Univ, PhD(relig & soc), 75. **CAREER** Asst prof, Univ Southern Calif, 70-72; from Asst Prof to Prof Relig, 72-94, Winthop H. Smith Prof Relig, Amherst Col, 94-. **MEMBERSHIPS** Soc Values Higher Educ; Am Acad Relig; Am Soc Church Hist; Soc Christian Ethics; Am Studies Asn. **RESEARCH** African-American religious history; religious history of the Atlantic world; American religious history. **SELECTED PUBLICATIONS** Contribr, Black Apostles: Afro-American Churchmen Confront the Twentieth Century, 78 & co-ed (with Richard Newman) & contribr, Black Apostles at Home and Abroad: Afro-Americans and the Christian Mission from the Revolution to Reconstruction, 82, G.K. Hall; contribr, Between the Times: The Travail of the Protestant Establishment in America, 1900-1960, 89; Religion and American Politics: From the Colonial Period to the 1980's, 90; Dictionary of Christianity in America, 90; Blackwell Dictionary of Evangelical Biography: 1730-1860, 95; Minority Faiths and the Protestant Mainstream, 97. **CONTACT ADDRESS** Dept of Relig, Amherst Col, Amherst, MA, 01002-5003. **EMAIL** dwwills@amherst.edu

WILLS, GREGORY A.
DISCIPLINE CHURCH HISTORY **EDUCATION** Duke Univ, BS; Gordon-Conwell Theol Sem, MDiv; Duke Univ, ThM; Emory Univ, PhD. **CAREER** Archives and spec coll(s) libn, Boyce Centennial Lib, asst prof, S Baptist Theol Sem. **SELECTED PUBLICATIONS** Auth, dissertation, Democratic Religion: Freedom, Authority, and Church Discipline in the Baptist South, 1785-1900, Oxford UP; entries on Basil Manly, Jr. and Jesse Mercer, Amer Nat Biography. **CONTACT ADDRESS** Dept of Church History, Southern Baptist Theol Sem, 2825 Lexington Rd, Louisville, KY, 40280. **EMAIL** gwills@sbts.edu

WILLS, LAWRENCE M.
PERSONAL Born 04/10/1954, Calhoun, KY, m, 1982, 2 children **DISCIPLINE** NEW TESTAMENT **EDUCATION** Harvard Col, BA, 76; Harvard Divinity Schl, MTS, 80, ThD, 87. **CAREER** Dir, lang stud, 85-93, asst prof, N Test, 93-94, Harvard Divinity Schl; assoc prof, bibl stud, 94- Episcopal Divinity Schl. **HONORS AND AWARDS** Jewish Novel in the Ancient World, awarded Outstanding Acad Bk 1995, Choice Mag. **MEMBERSHIPS** Soc of Biblical Lit; Assn for Jewish Stud. **RESEARCH** Ancient Judaism; New Testament; Hebrew Bible **SELECTED PUBLICATIONS** Auth, Quest of the Historical Gospel, Routledge, 97; auth, Jewish Novel in the Ancient World, Cornell, 95. **CONTACT ADDRESS** Episcopal Divinity Sch, 99 Brattle St, Cambridge, MA, 02138. **EMAIL** lwills@episdivschool.org

WILMOT, DAVID WINSTON
PERSONAL Born 04/26/1944, Panama, m **DISCIPLINE** LAW **EDUCATION** Univ of AR, BA 1970; Georgetown Univ Law Ctr, JD 1973. **CAREER** Little Rock, asst city mgr 1968-70; Dolphin Branton Stafford & Webber, legal asst 1970-72; Georgetown Univ Law Ctr, rsch asst; OEO Legal Svcs, intern; DC Proj on Comm Legal Asst, dep dir 1972-73; DC Convention Ctr Bd of Dirs, general counsel; Hotel Assoc Washington DC, general counsel; Georgetown Univ, asst dean, dir 1973-92; Harmon & Wilmot, partner, 1992-. **HONORS AND AWARDS** Dean's List 1967-70; Dean's Counselor Awd Univ of AR 1969; Outstanding Serv Awd Georgetown Univ Stud Bar Assoc 1971; Cert of Merit DC Citz for Better Ed 1972; Jeffrey Crandall Awd 1972; WA Law Reptr Prize 1973; Robert D L'Heureux Scholarship. **MEMBERSHIPS** Pres Stud for Equality 1967-68; vice pres GULC Legal Aid Soc 1972-73; pres Black Amer Law Stud Assoc 1972-73; adv bd DC Bds & Comms Adv Bd Georgetown Today 1973-76; mem DC Bar, PA Bar;, US Supreme Court of Appeals, DC Ct of Appeals, Supreme Ct of PA, Assoc of Amer Law Schools, Law School Admin Council, Amer Bar Assoc, Trial Lawyers Assoc, Natl Bar Assoc, Natl Conf of Black Lawyers, Alpha Kappa Psi, Lawyers Study Group, Potomac Fiscal Soc; public employees relations bd Wash DC; mem Firemens & Policement Retirement Bd; mem bd of dirs Federal City Natl Bank, Washington Waterfront Restaurant Corp; mem bd of governors Georgetown Univ Alumni Assoc; mem bd of dirs District Cablevision Inc. **CONTACT ADDRESS** Harmon & Wilmot, LLP, 1010 Vermont Ave NW, Washington, DC, 20005.

WILSHIRE, BRUCE W.
PERSONAL Born 02/08/1932, Los Angeles, CA, m, 1959, 2 children **DISCIPLINE** PHILOSOPHY **EDUCATION** USC, BA, 53, NYU, MA, 60, PhD, 66. **CAREER** Rutgers Univ New Brunswick, NJ, prof, 69-. **SELECTED PUBLICATIONS** Auth, William James and Phenomenology: A Study of the Principles of Psychology, 78; auth, Role Playing & Identity: The Limits of Theater as Metaphor, 91; auth, The Moral Collapse of the University: Professionalism, Purity, Alienation, 90; auth, Wild Hunger: The Primal Roots of Modern Addiction, 98; auth, Looking Forward to the First Day: American Philosophy: Primed and Pragmatic, forthcoming. **CONTACT ADDRESS** Dept of Philosophy, Rutgers New Brunswick Univ, 1360 Marlborough Ave, Plainfield, NJ, 07060. **EMAIL** Donnaww@juno.com

WILSON, BRADLEY E.
PERSONAL Born 07/01/1961, Detroit, MI, m, 1997 **DISCIPLINE** PHILOSOPHY **EDUCATION** Purdue Univ, BA, 82; Univ of N Carolina, 85, PhD, 91. **CAREER** Univ of Pittsburgh, vis asst prof, 91-96; Slippery Rock Univ, asst prof, 97-. **HONORS AND AWARDS** Phi Beta Kappa **MEMBERSHIPS** APA, PSA **RESEARCH** Hist and philo of biology; med ethics; philo of med. **SELECTED PUBLICATIONS** Auth, Changing Conceptions of Species, in: Bio & Philo, 96; Futility and the Obligations of Physicians, in: Bioethics, 97; Fitting the Picture to the Frame: Comments for Ruth Millikan, in: Mindscapes: Philo, Sc and the Mind, Univ of Pitt Press, 97; A (Not-So-Radical) Solution to the Species Problem, in Bio & Philo, 95; Comments on Ruse's The Species Problem, in: Concepts, Theol 7 Rationality in the Bio Sc, Univ of Pitt Press, 95; Are Species Sets?, in: Bio & Philo, 91. **CONTACT ADDRESS** Dept of Philosophy, Slippery Rock Univ, Slippery Rock, PA, 16057. **EMAIL** Bradley.Wilson@sru.edu

WILSON, CHARLES REAGAN
PERSONAL Born 02/02/1948, Nashville, TN **DISCIPLINE** AMERICAN HISTORY, RELIGION **EDUCATION** Univ Tex, El Paso, BA, 70, MA, 72; Univ Tex, Austin, PhD(hist), 77. **CAREER** Vis prof Am studies, Univ Wuerzburg, West Ger, 77-78; lectr, Univ Tex, El Paso, 78-80; vis prof, Tex Tech Univ, 80-81; ASST PROF AM HIST, UNIV MISS, 81-, Co-ed, Encycl Southern Cult, 81- **RESEARCH** Southern culture; American religion; popular culture. **SELECTED PUBLICATIONS** Auth, Bishop Thomas Frank Gailor: Celebrant of Southern tradition, Tenn Hist Quart, fall 79; The religion of the lost cause: Southern civil religion, J Southern Hist, 5/80; Baptized in Blood: The Religion of the Lost Cause, 1865-1920, Univ Ga Press, 80; Robert Lewis Dabney: Religion and the Southern holocaust, Va Mag Hist & Biog, 1/81; Southern funerals, cemeteries, the lost cause, Thomas Frank Gailor and Charles Todd Quintard, Encycl Southern Relig (in prep). **CONTACT ADDRESS** Univ of Miss, Box 6640, University, MS, 38655.

WILSON, CLARENCE S., JR.
PERSONAL Born 10/22/1945, Brooklyn, NY, m, 1972 **DISCIPLINE** LAW **EDUCATION** Williams College, BA, 1967; Foreign Service Institute of the United States, 1969; Northwestern University, School of Law, JD, 1974. **CAREER** US Department of State, Caracas, Venezuela, third secretary, vice counsel, 1969-71; Friedman and Koven, associate Attorney, 1974-76; United States Gypsum Company, legal department, 1976-79; sole practitioner, 1979-81; Law Offices of Jewel S Lafontant, partner, 1981-83; Chicago-Kent College of Law, adjunct professor, 1981-94; Boodell, Sears, Sugrue, Giambalvo and Crowley, associate Attorney, 1983-84; sole practitioner and counsel, 1984-; Columbia College, adjunct professor, 1996-97.

MEMBERSHIPS Trustee, Chicago Symphony Orchestra, 1987-96; Art Institute of Chicago, bd mbr, Cmte on Twentieth Century Painting, Sculpture, Development, 1989-, trustee, 1990-; director, 1974-83, advisory board member, 1983-, Citizens Information Service of Illinois; bd mbr, The Harold Washington Foundation, 1989-92; bd mbr, Implementation Cmsn of The Lawyers Trust Fund of Illinois, 1983-85; bd mbr, Northwestern Univ School of Law Alumni Assn, 1979-84; project manager, Dept of Justice Task Force, The President's Private Sector Survey on Cost Control in the Federal Government, "The Grace Commission," 1982-84; governing bd, Illinois Arts Cncl, 1984-89, panel, Established Regional Organizations, 1998-; Illinois representative, Arts Midwest, 1985-89; Chicago and Cook County Bar Associations; trustee, Merit Music Program, 1991-96; Chicago Department of Cultural Affairs, Mayor's Advsry Bd, 1988-97; School of the Art Institute of Chicago, mem bd of governors, 1994-; Dept of Music at the Univ of Chicago, visiting committee mem, 1992-; Ministry of Culture, Republic of Venezuela, special counsel, 1989-90; DuSable Museum of African American History Inc, outside counsel, 1988-; Jazz Museum of Chicago, vice chair, 1994-97. **SELECTED PUBLICATIONS** Author, "Visual Arts and the Law," in Law and the Arts--Art and the Law, 1979; author of several copyright/art law articles. **CONTACT ADDRESS** 25 E Washington St, Ste 1515, Chicago, IL, 60602-1804. **EMAIL** hcwilson@ix.netcom.com

WILSON, DANNY K.
PERSONAL Born 03/24/1959, Corinth, MS, m, 1987, 2 children **DISCIPLINE** THEOLOGY; NEW TESTAMENT STUDIES **EDUCATION** Union Univ, BA, 80; Mdiv, 84, PhD, 95, Southwest Theological Seminary **CAREER** Minister of Youth Activities, First Baptist Church, AR, 85-88; Minister of Youth Activities, Eastern Hills Baptist Church, AL, 88-90; Teaching Fel, Southwestern Baptist Theological Seminary, TX, 92-95. **HONORS AND AWARDS** Faculty of the Year, 97 and 98. **MEMBERSHIPS** AAR/SBL; Inst for Biblical Research; In Service Guidance Assoc. **RESEARCH** Messianic Secrecy **CONTACT ADDRESS** California Baptist Col, 8432 Magnolia Ave, Riverside, CA, 92504. **EMAIL** dwilson@calbaptist.edu

WILSON, HOLLY
DISCIPLINE PHILOSOPHY **EDUCATION** Vanderbilt Univ, BA, 79; Pa State Univ, MA, 84; PhD, 89. **CAREER** Asst prof, Marquette Univ, 88-96; adj prof, Mundelein Sem, 96-97; asst prof, Northeast LA Univ, 97-. **HONORS AND AWARDS** PBK. **MEMBERSHIPS** Am Philos Asn; N Am Kant Soc; Soc for Women in Philos; Soc for Phenomenol and Existential Philos. **RESEARCH** Kant; Hermeneutics; Feminist Philosophy; Ethics. **SELECTED PUBLICATIONS** Auth, Gadamer's Alleged Conservatism, Selected Studies in Phenomenol and Existential Philos, 96; Kant's Integration and Morality, Kantstudien, 97; Kant and Ecofeminism, Ecofeminism: Women, Culture, Nature, 97; Rethinking Kant from the Perspective of Ecofeminism, Feminist Interpretation of Kant, 97; Kant's Evolutionary Theory of Marriage, Autonomy and Community: readings in Contemporary Kantian Soc Philos, forthcoming. **CONTACT ADDRESS** History and Government, Northeast Louisiana Univ, Monroe, LA, 71209. **EMAIL** hwilson@alpha.nlu.edu

WILSON, JACK HOWARD
PERSONAL Born 02/11/1935, Lenoir City, TN **DISCIPLINE** NEW TESTAMENT **EDUCATION** Univ Tenn, BA, 56; Emory Univ, BD, 58, PhD, 62. **CAREER** ASSOC PROF RELIG, TENN WESLEYAN COL, 62-65, PROF, 65-80. **MEMBERSHIPS** Soc Bibl Lit; Am Acad Relig. **SELECTED PUBLICATIONS** Auth, The Corinthians who say there is no resurrection of the dead, Z Neutestamentliche Wiss, 68. **CONTACT ADDRESS** Virtue Rd, Lenoir City, TN, 37771.

WILSON, JOHN ELBERT
PERSONAL m **DISCIPLINE** CHURCH HISTORY **EDUCATION** Emory Univ, BA, 64; Drew Univ, MDiv, 67; Claremont Grad Univ, PhD, 75. **CAREER** PD, church hist, Univ of Basel, Switzerland, 83-84; PROF OF CHURCH HIST, PITTSBURGH THEOLOGICAL SEMINARY, 84-. **MEMBERSHIPS** Am Acad of Relig; Am Soc of Church Hist; Int Schelling Soc. **SELECTED PUBLICATIONS** Auth, Schellings Mythologie. Zur Auslegung der Philosophie der Mythologie und der Offenbarung, Frommann-Holzboog, 93; auth, Schelling und Nietzsche. Zur Auslegung der freuhen Werke Friedrich Nietzsches, W. de Gruyter, 96. **CONTACT ADDRESS** Pittsburgh Theol Sem, 616 N Highland Ave, Pittsburgh, PA, 15206-2596. **EMAIL** jewilson@pts.edu

WILSON, JOHN FREDERICK
PERSONAL Born 04/01/1933, Ipswich, MA, m, 1954, 4 children **DISCIPLINE** AMERICAN RELIGIOUS HISTORY **EDUCATION** Harvard Col, AB, 54; Union Theol Sem, NY, MDiv, 57, PhD, 62. **CAREER** Lectr relig, Barnard Col, 57-58; from instrto prof, 60-77,asst dean, 65-72, chmn dept, 74-81, COLLORD PROF RELIG, PRINCETON UNIV, 77-, Mem bd dirs, Union Theol Sem, NY, 77-. **MEMBERSHIPS** AHA; Am Soc Church Hist (pres, 76); Soc Values Higher Educ; Asn Document Editing; Am Studies Asn. **RESEARCH** Puritan studies; religion in American history; Jonathan Edwards. **SELECTED PUBLICATIONS** Auth, The Churching of America, 1776-1990, J Church and State, Vol 0035, 93; When Time Shall be no More, J Interdisciplinary Hist, Vol 0024, 94; A New Denominational Historiography + The Importance of Continuing Study of Denominations for American Religious History, Relig and Amer Culture J of Int, Vol 0005, 95; Cosmos in the Chaos, Theol Today, Vol 0053, 96; Religious Melancholy and Protestant Experience in America, J Interdisciplinary Hist, Vol 0026, 96; The Politics of Revelation and Reason, J Interdisciplinary Hist, Vol 0028, 97. **CONTACT ADDRESS** Dept of Relig, Princeton Univ, 13 1879 Hall, Princeton, NJ, 08544.

WILSON, JONATAN R.
DISCIPLINE BIBLICAL AND CONTEMPORARY THEOLOGY **EDUCATION** Duke Univ, PhD, 89. **CAREER** Sr pastor, Edmonds Baptist Church, 80-86; lectr, Duke Univ, 87; adj asst, Fuller Theol Sem Extension, 91, 94; assoc prof, Westmont Col, 89-. **HONORS AND AWARDS** Tchr yr, 93. **RESEARCH** Ethics. **SELECTED PUBLICATIONS** Auth, Living Faithfully in a Fragmented World. Trinity Press International, 97; Theology as Cultural Critique: The Achievement of Julian Hartt, Mercer UP, 96; Toward a Trinitarian Rule of Worship, CRUX 29/2, 93. **CONTACT ADDRESS** Dept of Rel, Westmont Col, 955 La Paz Rd, Santa Barbara, CA, 93108-1099.

WILSON, KENT
DISCIPLINE PHILOSOPHY **EDUCATION** Univ Pittsburgh, PhD, 69. **CAREER** Assoc prof, Univ IL at Chicago . **RESEARCH** Philos of lang; metaphysics; lang and mind; linguistic theory; philosophical logic; epistemology. **SELECTED PUBLICATIONS** Auth, Some Reflections on the Prosentential Theory of Truth, D. Reidel, 90; Comment on Jim Mackenzie, Peter of Spain, and Begging the Question, Jour Philos Logic, 92; co-auth, The Intentional Fallacy: Defending Beardsley, Jour Aesthet Art Criticism, 95; co-ed, Philosophical Logic, D. Reidel, 69. **CONTACT ADDRESS** Philos Dept, Univ Illinois Chicago, S Halsted St, PO Box 705, Chicago, IL, 60607. **EMAIL** kentw@uic.edu

WILSON, KIM ADAIR
PERSONAL Born 09/04/1956, New York, NY, s **DISCIPLINE** LAW **EDUCATION** Boston College, BA cum laude, 1978; Hofstra University School of Law, JD, 1982. **CAREER** New York City Department of Investigation, investigative attorney, 1986-89; NEW YORK STATE SUPREME COURT, COURT ATTORNEY, 1989-. **HONORS AND AWARDS** New York Association of Black Psychologists, The Nelson Mandela International Citizen of the Year Award, 1994; National Bar Association, Outstanding Bar Association Affiliate Chapter Award, 1995; The Judicial Friends, The Jane Matilda Bolin Award, 1996; Consortium of Doctors, Inductee, 1998. **MEMBERSHIPS** National Bar Association, bd of governors, 1995-; New York State Bar Association, house of delegates, 1994-; Metropolitan Black Bar Association, president, 1994-96; NY State Bar Assoc, house of delegates, 1994-97. **SELECTED PUBLICATIONS** Co-author: "Affirmative Action Can Help Create Tradition of Excellence," New York Law Journal, May 1995; "US Constitution and its Meaning to the African-American Community," National Bar Association Magazine, Volume 10, No 4, pp 3 & 30; Author of book review, Affirmative Action, Race & American Values, published my book review, New York Law Journal, Jan 10, 1997. **CONTACT ADDRESS** New York State Supreme Court, Bronx County, 851 Grand Concourse, Ste 217, Bronx, NY, 10451.

WILSON, ROBERT
DISCIPLINE PHILOSOPHY **EDUCATION** Cornell Univ, PhD, 92. **CAREER** Assoc prof, Univ Ill Urbana Champaign. **RESEARCH** Philosophy of mind; philosophy of science; cognitive science. **SELECTED PUBLICATIONS** Auth, Cartesian Psychology and Physical Minds, Cambridge, 95; Wide Computationalism; Promiscuous Realism. **CONTACT ADDRESS** Philosophy Dept, Univ Ill Urbana Champaign, 52 E Gregory Dr, Champaign, IL, 61820. **EMAIL** rwilson@uiuc.edu

WILSON, SAMUEL S.
PERSONAL Born 08/11/1924, Cincinnati, OH, 4 children **DISCIPLINE** LAW **EDUCATION** Princeton Univ, AB, 47; Univ Cincinnati, JD, 61. **CAREER** Reporter, Cincinnati Times-Star, 47-52, Washington corresp, 52-56, asst city ed, 56-57, assoc ed, 57-58; atty, Nieman, Aug, Elder & Jacobs, Ohio, 61-65; assoc prof law, 65-68, actg dean col law, 69-70, PROF LAW, UNIV CINCINNATI, 68, DEAN, COL LAW, 74-, CONSULT, NIEMMA, AUG, ELDER & JACOBS, OHIO, 65, COHEN, TODD, KITE & SPIEGEL, 69-70 & WAITE, SCHINDEL, BAYLESS & SCHNEIDER, 73-. **MEMBERSHIPS** Am Bar Asn. **RESEARCH** Constitutional law; civil procedure; real property. **SELECTED PUBLICATIONS** Auth, Rutter, Irvin, C.--in Memoriam, Univ Cincinnati Law Rev, Vol 0061, 93. **CONTACT ADDRESS** Col of Law, Univ of Cincinnati, Cincinnati, OH, 45221.

WILSON, VICTOR M.
PERSONAL Born 07/27/1946, Padhlam, England, m, 1973, 2 children **DISCIPLINE** BIBLICAL STUDIES AND RHETORICAL CRITICISM **EDUCATION** Barton Col, BA (summa cum laude), 76; Princeton Theological Seminary, MDiv, 79; Emory Univ, DMin, 92. **CAREER** Adjunct prof, Barton Col, 82-83; lectr, Eastern Theological Seminary, 93-94; PASTOR, ST. JOHN'S PRESBYTERIAN CHURCH, 92-. **HONORS AND AWARDS** Friar Alumni Award, Princeton Seminary; Nat Acad Honor Soc; Who's Who in Am Col and Univ; Nat Soc Sci Honor Soc; Am Bible Soc Award. **MEMBERSHIPS** Soc of Biblical Lit; Catholic Biblical Asn. **RESEARCH** Rhetorical Criticism of Biblical and Ancient Classical Literature. **SELECTED PUBLICATIONS** Auth, Divine Symmetries: The Art of Biblical Literature, 97. **CONTACT ADDRESS** St John's Presbyterian Church, PO Box 399, Devon, PA, 19333-0399. **EMAIL** vmwswd@aol.com

WILSON, WILLIE FREDERICK
PERSONAL Born 03/08/1944, Newport News, Virginia, m, 1973 **DISCIPLINE** THEOLOGY **EDUCATION** Ohio Univ, BS, 1966; Howard Univ, Divinity School, MDiv, 1969; Doctoral Studies, 1969-71. **CAREER** Union Temple Baptist Church, pastor, 1973-. **HONORS AND AWARDS** USA Today, Top 10 Most Valuable People in USA, 1985; US Presidential Svc Awd, 1997; Natl Congress of Black Churchmen, One of 100 Model African American Churches in America. **SELECTED PUBLICATIONS** Publication, "The African American Wedding Manual"; Ordained as WOLOF priest in Gambia, West Africa, 1980; enstated as Ashanti subchief in Ghana, 1993. **CONTACT ADDRESS** Pastor, Union Temple Baptist Church, 1225 W Street SE, Washington, VT, 20020.

WIMBERLY, EDWARD P.
PERSONAL Born 10/22/1943, THE, Pennsylvania, m, 1966 **DISCIPLINE** THEOLOGY **EDUCATION** Univ of Arizona, BA, 1965; Boston Univ, School of Theology, STB, 1968, STM, 1971; Boston Univ Graduate School, PhD, 1976. **CAREER** Emmanuel Church, pastor, 1966-68; St Andrews United Methodist Church, pastor, 1968-74; Worcester Council of Churches, urban minister, 1969-72; Solomon Carter Fuller Mental Health Center, pastoral consultant, 1973-75; Interdenominational Theological Center, Atlanta, assoc professor, 1975-83; Oral Roberts Univ, School of Theology, Tulsa, assoc professor, assoc dean, doctoral studies, 1983-85; Garrett Evangelical Theological Seminary, Evanston, IL, assoc professor, pastoral care, 1985-. **HONORS AND AWARDS** Serv award, United Methodist Children's Home, 1983. **MEMBERSHIPS** Bd of dirs, United Methodist Children's Home, 1977-83, Interdenominational Theological Center, 1982-83; mem, Amer Assn of Pastoral Counselors, 1976-, Amer Assn of Marriage & Family Therapists, 1976-, Friends of Wesley Comm Center, 1983-; mem & bd of dirs, Destination Discovery, 1983-. **SELECTED PUBLICATIONS** Auth, "Pastoral Counseling and Spiritual Values," 1982; co-author with Anne Wimberly, "Liberation and Human Wholeness," 1986; co-author with wife, "One House One Hope," 1989. **CONTACT ADDRESS** Garrett-Evangelical Theol Sem, 2121 Sheridan Rd, Evanston, IL, 60201.

WIMBUSH, VINCENT L.
DISCIPLINE RELIGION **EDUCATION** Harvard Univ, MA, PhD. **CAREER** Prof. **SELECTED PUBLICATIONS** Ed, Ascetic Behavior in Greco-Roman Antiquity: A Sourcebook, 90; Discursive Formations, Ascetic Piety, and the Interpretation of Early Christian Literature, 92; co-ed, Asceticism. **CONTACT ADDRESS** Dept of Religion, Columbia Col, New York, 2960 Broadway, New York, NY, 10027-6902. **EMAIL** vw7@columbia.edu

WINDLEY, SUSAN M.
DISCIPLINE RELIGION **EDUCATION** MA, 91, PhD, 98, Vanderbilt Univ. **CAREER** Asst Prof, Theology, Univ of St. Thomas **CONTACT ADDRESS** Univ St. Thomas, 2115 Summit Ave., St. Paul, MN, 55105. **EMAIL** smwindley@stthomas.edu

WINFREY, CHARLES EVERETT
PERSONAL Born 03/06/1935, Brighton, Tennessee, m **DISCIPLINE** THEOLOGY **EDUCATION** Lane Coll, BA 1961; Vanderbilt U, MDiv 1964; Univ of TN, MS 1974. **CAREER** Metro Public School Nashville, english teacher 1966-; CME Church Nashville, minister Capers Mem 1965-; Phillips Chapel CME Church Nashville, minister 1964-65; W Jackson Circuit CME, 1961-64; Graham Chapel CME Church Savannah, 1958-61. **HONORS AND AWARDS** Rel Man of Yr, Kappa Alpha Psi 1971; Good Conduct Award, USMC 1954; chaplain St Sen 1973; Hon Sgt-at-Arms, St Leg 1974. **MEMBERSHIPS** Mem Ad Hoc Com; Kappa Alpha Psi; life mem NEA; mem Met Act Commn; TE MNEA; dean of ldrshp training Nashville-Clarksville Dist CME Ch. **CONTACT ADDRESS** 319 15 Ave N, Nashville, TN.

WING, ADRIEN KATHERINE
PERSONAL Born 08/07/1956, Oceanside, California, d **DISCIPLINE** LAW **EDUCATION** Newark Academy, HS, 1974; Princeton, AB, 1978; UCLA, MA, 1979; Stanford Law School, JD, 1982. **CAREER** Upward Bound, UCLA, teacher/counselor, 1979; Rosenfeld, Meyer & Susman, law clerk, 1980; United Nations, intern, 1981; Curtis, Mallet, et al, lawyer, 1982-

86; Rabinowitz, Boudin, et al, lawyer, 1986-87; University of Iowa Law School, professor of law, 1987-. **HONORS AND AWARDS** Haywood Burns-Shanara Gilbert Award, 1997; National Conference of Black Lawyers, Hope Stevens Award, 1988; numerous others. **MEMBERSHIPS** Natl Conf of Black Lawyers, intl chair, 1985-95; Transafrica Forum Scholars Council, 1993-95; Assn of Black Princeton Alumni Bd, 1982-87; Stanford Law School , bd of visitors, 1993-96; American Soc of Intl Law, Southern Africa interest group chair, 1994-95; Council on Foreign Relations, life member, 1993-; Natl Black Law Students Assn, bd of directors, 1981-82, American Friends Service Comm, Middle East Programs Bd 1998-2000; American Assn of Law Schools Minority Section Executive Comm 1997-; Intl Third World Legal Studies Assn Bd 1996-, Princeton Comm to Nominate Trustees 1997-00, Princeton Alumni Council 1996-2000, Iowa Peace Institute Bd 1993-95; Iowa City Foreign Relations Council Bd 1989-94; Palestine Human Rights Campaigns Bd 1986-91; American Soc of Intl Law Executive Council 1986-89, 1996-99, Executive Comm 1998-99; American Bar Assn, American Branch Intl Law Assn, Natl Bar Assn, Soc of American Law Teachers; Bd of editors' American Journal of Comparative Law. **SELECTED PUBLICATIONS** Over 40 publications including: Democracy, Constitutionalism & Future State of Palestine, Jerusalem, 1994; "Rape, Ethnicity, Culture", Critical Race Theory Reader, Temple Univ, 1995; "Weep Not Little Ones", in African Americans & the Living Constitution, Smithsonian, 1995; Editor of Critical Race Feminism: A Reader, NYU, 1997; Languages: French, Swahili, Portuguese. **CONTACT ADDRESS** Professor, Univ of Iowa Law School, Iowa City, IA, 52242. **EMAIL** adrien-wing@wiowa.edu

WININGER, KATHLEEN
DISCIPLINE PHILOSOPHY **EDUCATION** Temple Univ, PhD, 88. **CAREER** Assoc prof and dept ch; taught at, Univ Nairobi; past lect, East Africa. **RESEARCH** Aesthetics; film theory; African philosophy; philosophy of culture in the 20th and late 19th centuries. **SELECTED PUBLICATIONS** Auth, Friedrich Nietzsche's Reclamation of Philosophy, Rodopi, 97; co-ed, Philosophy and Sex, Prometheus, 98. **CONTACT ADDRESS** Dept of Philosophy, Univ of Southern Maine, 96 Falmouth St, PO Box 9300, Portland, ME, 04104-9300.

WININGS, KATHY
PERSONAL Born 04/04/1953, Indianapolis, IN, s **DISCIPLINE** RELIGION & EDUCATION **EDUCATION** Fordham Univ, BA, 86; Unification Theol Seminary, MRE/MDiv, 87; Teachers Col, EdD, 96. **CAREER** Asst Prof. Unification Theol Seminary, 90-, Dir DMin Prog, 97-; Exec Dir, Int Relief Friendship Found, 94-; Dir, Nat Youth Ministry, 97-. **HONORS AND AWARDS** Kappa Delta Pi. **MEMBERSHIPS** APRRE; REA; Natl Asn Ecumenical Staff; AAUW. **RESEARCH** Education - curriculum & teaching; ministry; service learning. **SELECTED PUBLICATIONS** Ed, contrib, Understanding the Church of the Latter-Day Saints, Christian Traditions in America; The Role on Religion in Promoting World Peace, World Univ Times; Mind and Body: The Role of Service Learning in the Curriculum (forthcoming). **CONTACT ADDRESS** 117 White Plains Rd., Tarrytown, NY, 10591. **EMAIL** IRFFint@aol.com

WINK, WALTER
PERSONAL Born 05/21/1935, Dallas, TX, m, 1979, 3 children **DISCIPLINE** NEW TESTAMENT STUDIES **EDUCATION** Southern Methodist Univ, BA, 56; Union Theol Sem, MDiv, 59, PhD, 63. **CAREER** Pastor, United Methodist Church, Hitchcock, Tex, 62-67; asst prof New Testament, 67-70, assoc prof New Testament, 70-76, Union Theol Sem, NYC; prof bibl interpretation, Auburn Theol Sem, 76- . **HONORS AND AWARDS** Magna Cum Laude, 56; Peace fel, US Inst of Peace, 89. **MEMBERSHIPS** Am Acad Relig; Soc for Bibl Lit; Studiorum Novi Testamenti Societas. **SELECTED PUBLICATIONS** Auth, Cracking the Gnostic Code: The Powers in Gnosticism, Scholars, 93; auth, Proclamation 5: Holy Week, Year B, Fortress, 93; auth, Healing a Nation's Wounds: Reconciliation on the Road to Democracy, Sweden, Life and Peace Inst, 97; auth, The Third Way: Reclaiming Jesus' Nonviolent Alternative, Netherlands, Int Fel of Reconciliation, 97; auth, The Powers That Be, Doubleday, 98; auth, When the Powers Fall: Reconciliation on the Road to Democracy, Fortress, 98. **CONTACT ADDRESS** Auburn Theol Sem, 3041 Broadway, New York, NY, 10027. **EMAIL** wwink@bcn.net

WINKLER, KENNETH
PERSONAL Born 10/25/1950, Rockville Center, NY, m, 1997, 2 children **DISCIPLINE** PHILOSOPHY **EDUCATION** Trinity Col, BA, 71; Univ Texas, PhD, 77. **CAREER** Prof Philos, Wellesley Col, 78-; vis prof Philos, Harvard Summer School, 92, 95, 96; vis lctr, MIT, 94; vis prof, Brandeis Univ, 92; lctr, Harvard Univ, 91-92; lctr, UCLA, 80; vis asst prof, UCLA, 78; asst prof, Kalamazoo Col, 77-78. **HONORS AND AWARDS** NEH Fel, 94-95; ACLS Fel, 89-90; Andrew W. Mellon Fac Fel, Harvard Univ, 82-83; Phi Beta Kappa, 71. **MEMBERSHIPS** Amer Philos Assoc **RESEARCH** Early Modern Philosophy **SELECTED PUBLICATIONS** Ed & auth, John Locke, An Essay Concerning Human Understanding, Hackett, 96; Lock on Personal Identity, Jour History of Philos, 91; Berkeley: An Interpretation, Oxford Pr, 89. **CONTACT ADDRESS** Dept of Philosophy, Wellesley Col, Wellesley, MA, 02481. **EMAIL** kwinkler@wellesley.edu

WINSTON, DIANE
DISCIPLINE RELIGION **EDUCATION** Princeton Univ, PhD, 96. **CAREER** Relig, New York Univ. **MEMBERSHIPS** AAR; SSSR; ASCH; OAH; ASA **RESEARCH** Amer relig hist; relig and media; relig and higher educ **CONTACT ADDRESS** Center for Media, Culture and History, New York Univ, 25 Waverly, New York, NY, 10012. **EMAIL** dwinston@princeton.edu

WINSTON, KENNETH IRWIN
PERSONAL Born 06/17/1940, Boston, MA **DISCIPLINE** LEGAL PHILOSOPHY **EDUCATION** Harvard Univ, BA, 62; Columbia Univ, MA, 68, PhD(philos), 70. **CAREER** Instr philos, Columbia Univ, 68-69; asst prof, 69-76, assoc prof, 76-82, prof Philos, Wheaton Col, MA, 82-98; LECTURER IN ETHICS, HARVARD UNIV, 98-; Am Coun Learned Soc study fel & res fel, Ctr Study Law & Soc, Berkeley, CA, 72-73; vis asst prof, Brown Univ, 75; lectr educ, Harvard Univ, 78-79; Nat Endowment for Humanities fel & vis scholar, Harvard Law Sch, 80-81. **HONORS AND AWARDS** John Dewey Sr Fel, 84-85; A. Howard Meneely Prof, Wheaton Col, 96-98. **MEMBERSHIPS** Eastern Div Am Philos Asn; Conf Study Polit Thought; Soc Philos & Pub Affairs; Am Soc Polit & Legal Philos. **RESEARCH** Philosophy of law; practical ethics. **SELECTED PUBLICATIONS** Auth, Justice and rules: A Criticism, Proc Int Cong Legal & Social Philos, 71; On Treating Like Cases Alike, CA Law Rev, 1/74; Self-incrimination in Context, Southern CA Law Rev, 3/75; Visions of the Law, summer 75 & Forms of Tyranny, spring 77, Working Papers for a New Soc; Taking Dworkin Seriously, Harvard Civil Rights/Civil Lib Law Rev, 4/78; ed, The Principles of Social Order: Selected Essays of Lon L Fuller, Duke Univ, 81; auth, Toward a Liberal Conception of Legislation, In: Liberal Democracy, New York Univ Press, 82; ed, The Responsible Judge: Readings in Judicial Ethics, with John T. Noonan, Jr, Praeger, 93; ed, Gender and Public Policy: Cases and Comments, with Mary Jo Bane, Westview, 93; auth, Teaching With Cases, in Teaching Criminal Justice Ethics, ed, J. Kleinig and M. L. Smith, Anderson, 97; Moral Opportunism: A Case Study, in Integrity and Conscience, ed, I. Shapiro and R. M. Adams, NYU, 98. **CONTACT ADDRESS** Kennedy School of Government, Harvard Univ, 79 J. F. K. Street, Cambridge, MA, 02138. **EMAIL** kenneth_winston@harvard.edu

WINSTON, MORTON
DISCIPLINE BIOMEDICAL ETHICS **EDUCATION** Univ IL, MA,72; PhD, 78. **CAREER** Philos, Col NJ. **HONORS AND AWARDS** Co-dir, Core Course: Soc, Ethics, Tech; Adv, TCNJ Amnesty Int; Former Ch, Fac Res Leave Comt; Dept Philos & Relig; Ch, Board dir, Amnesty Intl USA; Fulbright Fel S Africa. **SELECTED PUBLICATIONS** Auth, Philosophy of Human Rights, Wadsworth Publ Company, 89. **CONTACT ADDRESS** Col of New Jersey, PO Box 7718, Ewing, NJ, 08628-0718.

WINSTON, MORTON E.
PERSONAL Born 01/16/1949, Philadelphia, PA, m, 1971, 3 children **DISCIPLINE** PHILOSOPHY, BIOMEDICAL ETHICS **EDUCATION** Univ IL, Urbana-Champaign, PhD, 78. **CAREER** Adjunct prof philos, Master of Liberal Arts Prog, Johns Hopkins Univ, 86-98; PROF PHILOS, THE COL OF NEW JERSEY, 79-98. **HONORS AND AWARDS** Fulbright Scholar, South Africa, 92; Phi Beta Kappa; Phi Kappa Phi. **MEMBERSHIPS** Amer Philos Assoc. **RESEARCH** Human rights theory; biomedical ethics; cognitive science. **SELECTED PUBLICATIONS** Auth, Prospects for a Revaluation of Academic Values, in Joseph Moxley, ed, The Processes and Politics of Scholarly Publication, NY: Greenwood Press, 95; An Emergency Response System for the International Community: Commentary on The Politics of Rescue, Ethics and International Affairs, vol 11, 97; The Prevention of Institutionalized Intergroup Violence, Health and Human Rights, vol 2, no 3, July 97; ed, with Ralph Edelbach, Society, Ethics, and Technology, Belmont, CA: Wadsworth Pub Co, 99. **CONTACT ADDRESS** Dept of Philos and Relig, The Col of New Jersey, Ewing, NJ, 08628-7718.

WINSTON SUTER, DAVID
DISCIPLINE NEW TESTAMENT **EDUCATION** Davidson Col, BA, 64; Univ Chicago, BD, 67; MA, 70, PhD, 77.. **CAREER** Asst prof, Wichita State Univ, 74-81; Vis Asst prof, Pacific Lutheran Univ, 81-83; Assoc prof, Saint Martin's Col, 83-89; Prof, Saint Martin's Col, 89-. **HONORS AND AWARDS** Burlington Northern Found Award , 90-91; The Commander's Certificate, 94; Nat Endowment Hum Summer Sem Col Tchrs: The Adam and Eve Narrative in Christian and Jewish Tradition, 96., Dean, Hum dept. **SELECTED PUBLICATIONS** Auth, The Drama of Christian Theology in the Gospel of John, Jour Relig, 69; Apocalyptic Patterns in the Similitudes of Enoch, Scholars Press, 78; Fallen Angel, Fallen Priest: The Problem of Family Purity in 1 Enoch 6-16, Hebrew Union Col Annual, 79; Tradition and Composition, Scholars Press, 79; Masal in the Similitudes of Enoch, Jour Biblical Lit, 81; Weighed in the Balance: The Similitudes of Enoch in Recent Discussion, Relig Studies Rev, 81; The Measure of Redemption: The Similitudes of Enoch, Nonviolence, and National Integrity, Scholars Press, 83; Apocrypha, Old Testament, Baruch, the Book of, Bel and the Dragon, Daniel, the Additions to, Ecclesiasticus, Esdras, the First Book of, Esdras, the Second Book of, Esther, the Rest of the Book of, Gentile, Judith, The Letter of Jeremiah, Maccabees, the First Book of the, Maccabees, the Second Book of the, The Prayer of Manasseh, Pseudonym, The Song of the Three Children, Susanna, Theophany, Tobit, Vengeance, and The Wisdom of Solomon, Harper & Row, 85; Atmosphere as Antagonist: The Symbolism of Evil in Mark, Explorations: Jour Adventurous Thought, 89; Of the Devil's Party: The Marriage of Heaven and Hell in Satanic Verses, S Asian Rev, 92; Apocrypha, Old Testament, Baruch, the Book of, Bel and the Dragon, Daniel, the Additions to, Ecclesiasticus, Esdras, the First Book of, Esdras, the Second Book of, Esther, the Rest of the Book of, Gentile, Judith, The Letter of Jeremiah, Maccabees, the First Book of the, Maccabees, the Second Book of the, Maccabees, the Third Book of the, Maccabees, the Fourth Book of the, The Prayer of Manasseh, Psalm 151, Pseudonym, The Song of the Three Children, Susanna, Theophany, Tobit, Vengeance, and The Wisdom of Solomon, Harper San Francisco, 96. **CONTACT ADDRESS** Saint Martin's Col, 5300 Pacific Ave, Lacey, WA, 98503-1297.

WINTER, DOUGLAS E.
PERSONAL Born 10/30/1950, St. Louis, MO, m, 1977, 2 children **DISCIPLINE** LAW **EDUCATION** Univ Ill, BS, 71, MS, 72; Harvard Law Sch, JD, 75; US Army Judge Advocate General's Sch, Honor Grad, 77. **CAREER** Lieutenant, Military Intelligence, US Army, 73-76; Law Clerk, US Court Appeals 8th Circuit, 75-76; Assoc Atty, Covington & Burling, 76-77, 78-80, 81-84; Captain, Judge Advocate General Corps, US Army, 77; Vis Prof, Univ Iowa Col Law, 80-81; Assoc Atty, Bryan Cave McPheeters & McRoberts, 85-86; Partner Atty, 87-97, Retired Partner Atty (Of Counsel), Bryan Cave LLP, 98-; Self-employed professional writer, 76-. **HONORS AND AWARDS** Nothern Va Festival of the Lit Arts Prize, 79; World Fantasy Award winner, 86; Int Horror Award winner, 95, Loop, 96; Whitman-Walker Clinic Public Service Award, 97. **MEMBERSHIPS** Am Bar Asn; member of bar associations of Mo, Ill, and DC; Nat Bk Critics Circle; Horror Writers Asn. **SELECTED PUBLICATIONS** Auth, Stephen King, Starmont House, 82; Shadowings: The Reader's Guide to Horror Fiction, Starmont House, 83; Stephen King: The Art of Darkness, New Am Libr, 84; Faces of Fear, Berkeley, 85; ed, Black Wine, Dark Harvest, 86; auth, Splatter: A Cautionary Tale, Footsteps Press, 87; ed, Prime Evil, New Am Libr, 88; auth, Darkness Absolute, Pulphouse Press, 91; Black Sun, One Eyed Dog, 94; ed, Revelations, HarperCollins, 97; auth, American Zombie, Borderlands Press (forthcoming 98); Clive Barker: The Dark Fantastic. HarperCollins (forthcoming 99); James Herbert: Horror, Harper Collins (forthcoming 99); author of numerous articles and short fiction. **CONTACT ADDRESS** Bryan Cave LLP, 700 13th St. NW, Washington, DC, 20005.

WINTER, JOHN ELLSWORTH
PERSONAL Born 10/26/1926, York, PA, m, 1982 **DISCIPLINE** PHILOSOPHY AND SOCIOLOGY **EDUCATION** Juniata col, BA, 50; Villanova Univ, MA, 63; Temple Univ, 69. **CAREER** York Coll, PA, 58-63; Clarion Univ, PA, 63-64; Millersville Univ, PA, 64-77, 78-94; Univ of Vienna, Austria, 77-78 . **HONORS AND AWARDS** Coleman Award; Outstanding Tchr of Amer. **MEMBERSHIPS** AAUP; Foundation of Thanatology; APSCUF; PA Phil Assn; Am Phil Assn; Hobbes Assn; Kierkegaard Soc **RESEARCH** Philosophical anthropology; humor; political theory. **SELECTED PUBLICATIONS** The New American Scholar, Oregon St Univ, 63; A New Theory of Election to Public Office in America, Chicago, 98. **CONTACT ADDRESS** 1447 Casey Key Dr, Punta Gord, Punta Gorda, FL, 33950. **EMAIL** ejwinter@peganet.com

WINTER, RALPH A.
DISCIPLINE LAW **EDUCATION** Univ British Columbia, BA, 74; Univ Ca, MA, PhD, 79. **CAREER** Prof **SELECTED PUBLICATIONS** Auth, pubs on economics of competition policy, the theory of contracts, industrial organization and the interaction between the tort system and liability insurance markets; co-auth, Competition Policy and Vertical Exchange. **CONTACT ADDRESS** Fac of Law, Univ Toronto, 78 Queen's Park, Toronto, ON.

WINTERS, FRANCIS XAVIER
PERSONAL Born 10/12/1933, Roaring Spring, PA **DISCIPLINE** POLITICAL ETHICS, THEOLOGY **EDUCATION** Fordham Univ, AB, 58, MAT, 59, PhD, 73; Woodstock Col, PhL, 58, STB, 63, STL, 65. **CAREER** Instr Latin, English & Fr, Loyola High Sch, Baltimore, 58-61; instr philos, Loyola Col, Md, 66-67; instr Christian ethics, 70, asst prof & dean fac, 71-72, asst prof theol, 72-77, Woodstock Col; assoc prof theol, Sch Foreign Serv, Georgetown Univ, 77-, prof, 98; Trustee, Coun Relig & Int Affairs, 71-; mem bd dir, Wheeling Col, 72; trustee, Gonzaga High Sch, Washington, DC, 72-; consult ethics, Comn Orgn Govt Conduct Foreign Policy, 75-76; lectr ethics, Army War Col, Carlisle, Penn, 76-78, Foreign Serv Inst, US Dept State, 77. **HONORS AND AWARDS** Teacher of Year Award, Sch Foreign Serv, Georgetown Univ, 78 & 82. **RESEARCH** Ethics and international relations; ethical theory; religion in America. **SELECTED PUBLICATIONS** Auth, Nuclear Deterrence Morality: Atlantic Community Bishops in

Tension, Theol Studies, 9/82; auth, The Year of the Hare: America in Vietnam, 1/63-2/64, University of Georgia Press, 97. **CONTACT ADDRESS** Sch of Foreign Serv, Georgetown Univ, Washington, DC, 20057-0001. **EMAIL** wintersf@gunet.georgetown.edu

WINTLE, THOMAS
DISCIPLINE CHURCH HISTORY **EDUCATION** Chicago Theol Sem, DMN, 75 **CAREER** Par Minist, 75-95, Par Minist, 95-pres **MEMBERSHIPS** AAR; ASCH **RESEARCH** New England Church Hist **SELECTED PUBLICATIONS** Auth, A New England Village Church, 85 **CONTACT ADDRESS** 3 Conant Rd, Weston, MA, 02193-1625.

WIPPEL, JOHN FRANCIS
PERSONAL Born 08/21/1933, Pomeroy, OH **DISCIPLINE** PHILOSOPHY **EDUCATION** Cath Univ Am, BA, 55, MA, 56, STL, 60; Cath Univ Louvain, PhD(philos), 65; Maitre-Agrege, Louvain-la-Neuve, 81. **CAREER** Instr, 60-61, 63-65, from asst prof to assoc prof, 65-72, prof Philos, 72- , acad vice pres, 89-96, Cath Univ Am, 72- . **HONORS AND AWARDS** Nat Endowment for Humanities younger humanist fel, 71; Cardinal Mercier Prize, Louvain-la-Neuve, 81; NEH fel, 84-85. **MEMBERSHIPS** Metaphys Soc Am; Am Cath Philos Asn, pres 86-87; Int Soc Study Mediaeval Philos; Am Philos Asn; Mediaeval Acad Am; Soc Medieval & Renaissance Philos (pres, 82-84). **RESEARCH** History of medieval philosophy; metaphysics. **SELECTED PUBLICATIONS** Auth, The Metaphysical Thought of Godrey of Foutaines, Cath Univ Am, 81; auth, Boethus of Dacia: On the Supreme Good, On the Eternity of the World, On Dreams, Toronto, 87; auth, Metaphysical Themes in Thomas Aquinas, Catholic Univ America, 84; auth, Mediaeval Reactions to the Encounter Between Faith and Reason, Marquette, 95; coauth, Medieval Philosophy from St. Augustine to Nicholas of Cusa, Free Press, 69; auth, Studies in Medieval Philosophy, Catholic Univ America, 87. **CONTACT ADDRESS** Sch of Philosophy, Catholic Univ of America, Washington, DC, 20064.

WIRTH, JASON M.
PERSONAL Born 02/03/1963, San Francisco, CA **DISCIPLINE** PHILOSOPHY **EDUCATION** Holy Cross, Worcester, MA, BA, 85; Villanova Univ, MA, 90; Binghamton Univ, PhD, 94. **CAREER** Asst Prof of Philo, 94-, Oglethorpe Univ, Atlanta. **HONORS AND AWARDS** Fellowship of Amer Assoc of Coll and Univ; Polished Apple Award; Fulbright Fellowship; Univ Fellowship; Edge Awd; DAAD Fellowship; John Tich Award; Phi Beta Kappa; Alpha Sigma Nu; Phi Sigma Tau. **MEMBERSHIPS** GCPC, GPS, SPEP, APA, IAPL. **RESEARCH** German Philosophers from Kant to present; Contemporary French Philosophy. **SELECTED PUBLICATIONS** Auth, It Has, Like you, No Name, Paul Celan and the Question of Address, in: Encountering the Other, Studies in Literature, History and Culture, ed, G Brinker-Gabler, Albany: The State Univ of NY Press, 95; Translation of Martin Heidegger's Letters on His Political Involvement, The Graduate Journal Of Philosophy: Special Issue: Heidegger and Politics, 91; Thoughts on Cynthia Willett's Maternal Ethics and Other Slave Moralities, The Fifth Meeting of the Georgia Continental Philosophy Circle, Oglethorpe Univ, 97; On The Margins o f Eros: Plato, Bataille and Deleuze, the 21st Annual Meeting of the International Association for Philosophy and Literature, Univ of South Alabama, 97. **CONTACT ADDRESS** Dept of Philosophy, Oglethorpe Univ, 4484 Peachtree Road NE, Atlanta, GA, 30319. **EMAIL** jsirth@oglethorpe.edu

WIRZBA, NORMAN
PERSONAL Born 02/07/1964, AB, Canada **DISCIPLINE** PHILOSOPHY **EDUCATION** Univ Lethbridge, BA, 86; Yale Univ Div School, MA, 88; Loyola Univ Chicago, MA, 91, PhD, 93. **CAREER** Univ Sask, St. Thomas, asst prof, 93-95; Georgetown Col, asst prof, 95-. **MEMBERSHIPS** APA, SCPT **RESEARCH** Continental philosophy; philosophy of religion; environmental philosophy; theology. **SELECTED PUBLICATIONS** Auth, Love's Reason: From Heideggerian to Christian Charity, in: Postmod Philo and Christ Thought, forthcoming; The Needs of Thought and the Affirmation of Life, in: Intl Philo Quart, 97; Teaching as Propaedeutic to Religion, in; Intl Jour for Philo of Relig, 96. **CONTACT ADDRESS** Dept of Philosophy, Georgetown Col, Georgetown, KY, 40324. **EMAIL** nwirzba@georgetowncollege.edu

WISE, EDWARD MARTIN
PERSONAL Born 08/08/1938, New York, NY, 2 children **DISCIPLINE** LAW, LEGAL HISTORY **EDUCATION** Univ Chicago, BA, 56; Cornell Univ, LLB, 59; NY Univ, LLM, 60. **CAREER** Res assoc, Comparative Criminal Law Proj, 63-64; res fel, Inst Judicial Admin, 64-65; assoc prof, 65-68, PROF LAW, WAYNE STATE UNIV, 68-, Vis prof, NY Univ Sch Law, 68; gen coun, Am Civil Liberties Union Mich, 77-; vis prof, Univ Utrecht, 79. **MEMBERSHIPS** Am Soc Legal Hist; Int Asn Penal Law (secy-treas, 68-72); Am Soc Int Law; Selden Soc. **RESEARCH** International and comparative criminal law; legal history. **SELECTED PUBLICATIONS** Auth, The Law of the Other--The Mixed Jury and Changing Concepts of Citizenship, Law, and Knowledge, Amer J Legal Hist, Vol 0040, 96. **CONTACT ADDRESS** Law Sch, Wayne State Univ, 468 Ferry Mall, Detroit, MI, 48202-3698.

WISE, PHILIP D.
PERSONAL Born 01/03/1949, Andalusia, AL, m, 1968, 3 children **DISCIPLINE** THEOLOGY **EDUCATION** Samford Univ, BA, 70; MA, 73, PhD, 80, New Orleans Baptist Theological Seminary. **CAREER** Lctr, Culham Col, Abingdon, England, 74-76; Lectr, United National Baptist Theology Seminary, New Orleans, 70-71; Guest Lctr, Baptist Seminary, Ogbomosho, Nigeria, 84; Guest Lctr, Intl Baptist Seminary, Singapore, 90; Guest Lctr, Cetown Baptist Col, South Africa, 92; Lectr, 77-78, Adjunct Lctr, 97, New Orleans Baptist Theological Seminary; Pastor, First Baptist Church, Dothan, Alabama, 89-. **HONORS AND AWARDS** Recipient Samford Univ Alabama Minister of the Year, 94; Paul Harris Fel, 97. **MEMBERSHIPS** Selma Ministers Assoc; Blue-Gray Football Assoc; Central Alabama Fellowship of Christian Athletes; Amer Cancer Soc of Montgomery; Dothan Ministerial Union; Dothan Area Chamber of Commerce; Dothan Area United Way; Brd Trustees, Samford Univ. **RESEARCH** Baptist World Alliance Commission on Doctrine and Interchurch Cooperation **SELECTED PUBLICATIONS** Coauth, A Dictionary of Doctrinal Terms, 83; Auth, Theology and the Pastorate, Proclaim, 84; Biblical Inerrancy: Pro or Con, Theological Educator, 88; Is Anyone for Divorce, Alabama Baptist Ethics Commission Magazine, 98. **CONTACT ADDRESS** 116 Pine Tree Dr., Dothan, AL, 36303. **EMAIL** philipwise@aol.com

WISEMAN, JAMES A.
PERSONAL Born 02/19/1942, Louisville, KY, s **DISCIPLINE** THEOLOGY **EDUCATION** Georgetown Univ, BA 63; Cath Univ Amer, MA 70, STD 79. **CAREER** Cath Univ Amer, asst prof, assoc prof, ch, 95 to 98-. **MEMBERSHIPS** CTSA; SSCS. **RESEARCH** Christian Spirituality; Interreligious Dialogue; Science and Religion. **SELECTED PUBLICATIONS** Auth, Mystical Literature and Modern Unbelief, Christian Spirituality and the Culture of Modernity: The Thought of Louis Dupre, Peter J. Casarella, George P. Schner, eds, Grand Rapids, Eerdmans, 98; The Spirituality of St. Therese of Lisieux as Seen in Her Poetry, Comm: Intl Catholic Rev, 97; The Kingdom of God in Monastic Interreligious Dialogue, Stud Missionalia, 97; The Interfaith Conf of Metro Washington, Jour of Ecumen Stud, 97; Emptiness: A Christian Perspective, Dialogue and Alliance: A Jour of Interfaith Understanding, 93. **CONTACT ADDRESS** Dept of Theology, The Catholic Univ of America, Washington, DC, 20064. **EMAIL** wiseman@cua.edu

WISEMAN, MARY BITTNER
PERSONAL Born 08/21/1936, Philadelphia, PA, m, 1989, 1 child **DISCIPLINE** AESTHETICS; FEMINISM **EDUCATION** St John's Col, Md, AB, 59; Harvard Univ, AM, 63; Columbia Univ, PhD, 74. **CAREER** From Instr to Prof Philos, Brooklyn Col of the City of New York, 72-, Prof of Philos and Comparative Lit, Grad Sch of the City Univ of New York; Dep exec officer, Humanities Inst, Brooklyn Col, 81-. **MEMBERSHIPS** Am Philos Asn; Am Soc Aesthet; Soc Women Philos; Col Art Asn. **RESEARCH** Philosophy of art; interpretation; theory of criticism. **SELECTED PUBLICATIONS** Auth, The Ecstasies of Roland Bartles, Routledge, 89; numerous articles in Am Philos Quart, Brit J of Aesthetics, J Aesthetics & Art Criticism, and others. **CONTACT ADDRESS** Dept of Philos, Brooklyn Col, CUNY, 2901 Bedford Ave, Brooklyn, NY, 11210-2813. **EMAIL** hagold@aol.com

WISHART, LYNN
DISCIPLINE LEGAL RESEARCH **EDUCATION** W Va Univ, BA, 69; Univ Mich, AMLS, 71; Wash Univ, JD, 77. **CAREER** Assoc dir, law libraries, Georgetown Univ, 81-84, Washington Univ, 78-81, Lee Univ, 78-81; Prof, Yeshiva Univ; Dir Law Library, Yeshiva Univ. **HONORS AND AWARDS** West Excellence Acad Law Librarianship Award, 96. **MEMBERSHIPS** Am Library Asn; Am Asn Law Libraries. **SELECTED PUBLICATIONS** Area: library literature. **CONTACT ADDRESS** Yeshiva Univ, 55 Fifth Ave, NY, NY, 10003-4301. **EMAIL** wishart@ymail.yu.edu

WISSLER, ROBERT W.
PERSONAL Born 03/01/1917, Richmond, IN, m, 4 children **DISCIPLINE** PATHOLOGY, IMMUNOPATHOLOGY, NUTRITIONAL PATHOLOGY **EDUCATION** Earlham Coll, AB, 39; Univ Chicago, MS, 43, PhD, 46, MD, 48. **CAREER** Instr, 43-48, asst prof, 49-54, assoc prof, 55-60, prof, 61-, pathology, Donald N. Pritzker Distinguished Service Prof of Pathology, Univ Chicago, currently. **HONORS AND AWARDS** Keynote speaker, 27th Hugh Lofland Conf, 94; Donald S. Frederickson Career Achievement Award, Xth Intl. Atherosclerosis Symposium, Montreal, Canada, 94; election to AAAS fellowship, 95; Emperor's Rising Sun award and medal from Japanese colleagues, 95; co-organizer, 29th Hugh Lofland Conf, 97. **MEMBERSHIPS** Amer Heart Assn, Coun on Arteriosclerosis, 55-; Intl Soc Cardiology, 67-; Lankenau Hospital, Scientific Advisory Bd, Div of Research, 70- ; Intl Cardiology Found, 72-; Amer Medical Assn, sr mem, 95-. **RESEARCH** Immune reaction to neoplasia; pathogenesis of atherosclerosis. **SELECTED PUBLICATIONS** Coauth, "A Study of the Development of Atherosclerosis in Childhood and Young Adults: Risk Factors and the Prevention of Progression in Japan and the USA," Path Intl, vol 46, 96; coauth, "Pathomorphological Findings of Lp(a) Deposition in Arterial Intima," Current Therapy (Japan), suppl, 96; coauth, "Microscopic Findings Associated with Blood Pressure Indices in Postmortem Human Aorta Samples from Young People (Ages 15-34)," Cardiovasc Path, vol 5, 96; coauth, "Effects of Serum Lipoproteins and Smoking on Atherosclerosis in Young Men and Women," Arterioscler Thromb Vasc Biol, vol 17, 97; auth, comments on the article, "Lipids and Atherosclerosis: An Impossible Causal Relationship," Am Clin Lab, vol 17, 98. **CONTACT ADDRESS** 5550 S. Shore Dr., No. 515, Chicago, IL, 60637-1904.

WITHERINGTON, BEN
PERSONAL Born 12/30/1951, High Point, NC, m, 1977, 2 children **DISCIPLINE** RELIGION **EDUCATION** Univ N Carolina, BA, 74; Gordon-Conwell Theol Sem, MDiv, 77; Univ Durham, England, PhD, 81. **CAREER** Ashland Theo Sem, prof NT, 84-95; Asbury Theol Sem, prof NT, 95-. **MEMBERSHIPS** SBL, SNTS **RESEARCH** New testament **SELECTED PUBLICATIONS** Auth, The Jesus Quest: The Third Search for the Jew of Nazareth, Intervarsity Press, 95; Conflict and Community in Corinth: A Socio-Rhetorical Commentary on I and II Corinthians, Will B. Eerdmans, 95; John's Wisdom: A Commentary on the Fourth Gospel, Westmin/John Knox Press, 95; The Many Faces of Christ: The Christologies of the New Testament and Beyond, Crossroads, 98; Grace in Galatia: A Commentary on Paul's Letter to the Galatians, T&T Clark, 98; Paul Quest: The Search for the Jew from Tarsus, Intervar Press, 98. **CONTACT ADDRESS** Dept of New Testament, Asbury Theol Sem, 2004 Lampton Circle, Lexington, KY, 40514. **EMAIL** ben_witherington@wilmore.ky.us

WITHERSPOON, EDWARD, JR.
DISCIPLINE RELIGION; PHILOSOPHY **EDUCATION** Vanderbilt Univ, BS, 85; Univ Pittsburgh, PhD, 96. **CAREER** Vis asst prof, Univ Il Urbana-Champaign, 97-98; asst prof, Colgate Univ, 98- . **MEMBERSHIPS** Amer Philos Assoc **CONTACT ADDRESS** Dept of Philos & Relig, Colgate Univ, Hamilton, NY, 13346. **EMAIL** ewitherspoon@mail.colgate.edu

WITMAN, EDWARD PAUL
PERSONAL Born 01/27/1945, Baldwin, NY, m, 1969, 2 children **DISCIPLINE** PHILOSOPHY **EDUCATION** Georgetown Univ, AB, 67; Fordham Univ, MA, 69, PhD(philos), 78; Cert in Bioethics and Medical Humanities, Columbia Univ Col of Physicians and Surgeons and Albert Einstein Col of Medicine-Mountefiore Medical Center, 97. **CAREER** Teaching fel philos, Fordham Univ, 69-71; vis lectr, Cathedral Col, NY, 71-72, 72-73; from instr to asst prof, 72-78, assoc prof Philos, 78-86, FULL PROF, GEORGIAN COURT COL, 87-, chairman, dept of philos, 86, elected CEO of Faculty Assembly, 95-96. **MEMBERSHIPS** Soc Adv Process Studies; Am Philos Asn; Am Cath Philos Asn; Am Soc for Bioethics and the Humanities. **RESEARCH** Alfred N Whitehead; process philosophy; social & political philosophy; medical ethics. **CONTACT ADDRESS** Dept of Philos, Georgian Court Col, 900 Lakewood Ave, Lakewood, NJ, 08701-2697. **EMAIL** witman@georgian.edu

WITMER, DONALD G.
PERSONAL PA **DISCIPLINE** PHILOSOPHY **EDUCATION** New Col of the Univ of So Fla, BA, 90; Rutgers Univ, PhD, 97. **CAREER** Asst prof, 97-, Univ of Fla. **MEMBERSHIPS** APA. **RESEARCH** Metaphysics; philos of mind; language; ethics. **SELECTED PUBLICATIONS** Auth, Is Natural Kindness a Natural Kind?, co-auth, Philos Stud, 98; auth, What is Wrong with the Manifestability Argument for Supervenience, Australian J of Philos, 98; auth, Sufficiency Claims and Physicalism: A Formulation, Physicalism and Its Discontents, Cambridge Univ Press, forthcoming; auth, Supervenience Physicalism and the Problem of Extras, The So J of Philos, forthcoming; auth, Ontology, 98, dict entry, online Dict of Philos of Mind; auth, Identity Theories, 98, dict entry, online Dict of Philos of Mind. **CONTACT ADDRESS** Philos Dept, Univ of Florida, Gainesville, FL, 32611-8545. **EMAIL** gwitmer@phil.ufl.edu

WITT, CHARLOTTE
DISCIPLINE PHILOSOPHY **EDUCATION** Georgetown Univ, PhD, 80. **CAREER** Assoc prof. **RESEARCH** Ancient philosophy; feminism; metaphysics. **SELECTED PUBLICATIONS** Auth, Substance and Essence in Aristotle, Cornell, 89; co-ed, A Mind of One's Own: Feminist Essays on Reason and Objectivity, Westview, 92. **CONTACT ADDRESS** Philosophy Dept, Univ of New Hampshire, Hamilton Smith Hall, Durham, NH, 03824.

WITTE, JOHN
PERSONAL Born 08/14/1959, St. Catherines, ON, Canada, m, 1995, 2 children **DISCIPLINE** LAW; LEGAL HISTORY **EDUCATION** Harvard Law Sch, JD, 85. **CAREER** Asst prof, Emory Univ, 89-91; assoc, 91-93; prof, 93; Jonas Robitscher prof, 93- . **HONORS AND AWARDS** Most Outstanding Prof, SBA, 92-93, 94-94, 97-98; Most Outstanding Educator Award, United Methodist Found for Christian Higher Educ, 94; Max Rheinstein Fel, Alexander von Humboldt-Stiftung, Bonn, 95;

Prof of the Year, Black Law Students Asoc, 97-98; Abraham Kuyper Prize for Excellence in Theology and Public Life, Princeton Theol Sem, 99. **MEMBERSHIPS** ABA; State Bar of Georgia; Soc of Christian Ethics. **RESEARCH** European legal history; American legal history; church-state relations; religious liberty; law and religion; religion and human rights; Protestant Reformation; Canon law. **SELECTED PUBLICATIONS** Co-ed with Johan D. Van der Vyver, Religious Human Rights in Global Perspective: Religious Perspectives, 96; auth, From Sacrament to Contract: Marriage, Religion and Law in the Western Tradition, 97; Co-ed with Michael Bourdeaux, Orthodoxy and Proselytism in Russia: The War for New Souls, 99; auth, Essentia Liberty: The American Experiment in Religious Freedom, 99. **CONTACT ADDRESS** School of Law, Emory Univ, 1301 Clifton Rd., Atlanta, GA, 30322-2770. **EMAIL** jwitte@law.emory.edu

WITTRUP, ELEANOR
DISCIPLINE PHILOSOPHY **EDUCATION** Harvard Div Sch, MTS, 89; Univ Calif, San Diego, PhD, 92. **CAREER** Univ Mass, Lowell, 92-95; Univ of the Pacific, 95- . **MEMBERSHIPS** APA; Hume Soc; Concerned Philos for Peace. **RESEARCH** Ethics; philosophy of mind; Hume; Kant. **CONTACT ADDRESS** Philosophy Dept, Univ of the Pacific, 3601 Pacific Ave, Stockton, CA, 95211. **EMAIL** ewittrup@uop.edu

WOGAMAN, JOHN PHILIP
PERSONAL Born 03/18/1932, Toledo, OH, m, 1956, 4 children **DISCIPLINE** SOCIAL ETHICS **EDUCATION** Col of the Pac, BA, 54; Boston Univ, STB, 57, PhD(social ethics), 60. **CAREER** From asst prof to assoc prof Bible & social ethics, Univ of the Pac, 61-66, dir Pac ctr student social issues, 61-66; assoc prof, 66-69, PROF CHRISTIAN SOCIAL ETHICS, WESLEY THEOL SEM, 69- DEAN, 72-, Fac res fel, Asn Theol Schs US & Can, 75. **MEMBERSHIPS** Am Soc Christian ethics (pres, 76-77); Am Acad Relig; Am Theol Soc. **RESEARCH** Church-state relations; theological ethics; economic ethics. **SELECTED PUBLICATIONS** Auth, With Liberty and Justice for Whom, J Church and State, Vol 0034, 92. **CONTACT ADDRESS** Wesley Theol Sem, 4400 Massachusetts Ave NW, Washington, DC, 20016.

WOLF, ARNOLD J.
PERSONAL Born 03/19/1924, Chicago, IL, m, 1987, 6 children **DISCIPLINE** JEWISH THEOLOGY; SOCIAL RESPONSIBILITY **EDUCATION** Univ CA, AA, 42; HUC-JIR, MHL, 48, DD, 73. **CAREER** USNR (decorated), 51-53; cong s.., 57-72; Yale Univ, 72-80; HAM ISAMM ISRAEL, 80-. **HONORS AND AWARDS** Ed, Judaism; First Jewish delegate to WCC, Nairobi, 75. **MEMBERSHIPS** CCAR; JCUA; JPF; Chair of Breira, 76-78. **RESEARCH** Modern Jewish thought. **SELECTED PUBLICATIONS** Auth, with L. Huffman, Jewish Spiritual Journeys; Unfinished Rabbi; Challenge to Confirmands; What is Man?; Rediscovering Judaism. **CONTACT ADDRESS** 1100 East Hyde Park Blvd., Chicago, IL, 60615.

WOLF, HERBERT CHRISTIAN
PERSONAL Born 04/06/1923, Baltimore, MD, m, 1947, 5 children **DISCIPLINE** RELIGION **EDUCATION** Johns Hopkins Univ, AB, 43; Capital Univ, BD, 47; Univ Chicago, MA, 59; Harvard Univ, ThD, 68. **CAREER** Instr relig, Capital Univ, 45-47; lectr & Nat Lutheran Coun campus pastor, Mich State Univ, 48-57; from asst prof to assoc prof relig, 57-69, chmn dept, 69-79, PROF RELIG, WITTENBERG UNIV, 69-, Vis prof relig, Hood Col, 71-72, United Theol Col, Bangalore, India, 74. **MEMBERSHIPS** Am Acad Relig; Am Theol Asn; AAUP; Conf Relig SIndia. **RESEARCH** Lingayat movement in South India; the quest of the historical Jesus; concept of God as person. **SELECTED PUBLICATIONS** Auth, The responsibility of the church in higher education, 2/51 & Kierkegaard and the quest of the historical Jesus, 2/64, Lutheran Quart; An introduction to the idea of God as person, J Bibl & Relig, 1/64; Kierkegaard and Bultmann: The Quest of the Historical Jesus, Augsburg, 64. **CONTACT ADDRESS** Dept of Relig, Wittenberg Univ, Springfield, OH, 45501.

WOLF, KENNETH BAXTER
PERSONAL Born 06/01/1957, Santa Barbara, CA, 2 children **DISCIPLINE** HISTORY, RELIGIOUS STUDIES **EDUCATION** Stanford, BA (Religious Studies), 79, PhD (History), 85. **CAREER** Asst prof, 85-92, ASSOC PROF, POMONA COL, 92-, chair, Hist Dept, 95-98. **HONORS AND AWARDS** Phi Beta Kappa; Inst for Advanced Study, member 89-91; Wig Distinguished Prof, Pomona Col, 88, 93, 98. **MEMBERSHIPS** Medieval Academy; Medieval Asn of the Pacific; Assoc Members of the Inst for Advanced Study. **RESEARCH** Medieval Mediterranean hist; late antique/medieval Christianity; saints. **SELECTED PUBLICATIONS** Auth, The Earliest Spanish Christian Views of Islam, Church Hist 55, 86; Conquerors and Chroniclers of Early Medieval Spain, Liverpool Univ Press, 90, revised ed, forthcoming; The Earliest Latin Lives of Muhammad, in Michael Gervers and Ramzi Jibran Bikhazi, eds, Conversion and Continuity: Indigenous Christian Communities in Islamic Lands, Eighth to Eighteenth Centuries, Pontifical Inst of Mediaeval Studies, 90; Crusade and Narrative: Bohemond and the Gesta Francorum, J of Medieval Hist, 17, 91; The 'Moors' of West Africa and the Beginnings of the Portuguese Slave Trade, J of Medieval and Renaissance Studies 24, 94; Making History: The Normans and Their Historians in Eleventh-century Italy, Univ PA Press, 95; Christian Views of Islam in Early Medieval Spain, in John Tolan, ed, Medieval Christian Perspectives of Islam: A Collection of Essays, Garland, 96; Christian Martyrs in Muslim Spain, Cambridge Univ Press, 88, Japanese ed, K. Hayashi, trans, Tosui Shobou Press, 98; Muhammad as Antichrist in Ninth-century Cordoba, in Mark Meyerson, ed, Christians, Muslims and Jews in Medieval and Early Modern Spain: Interaction and Cultural Change, Univ Notre Dame Press, forthcoming. **CONTACT ADDRESS** 551 N. College Ave., Claremont, CA, 91711. **EMAIL** kwolf@pomona.edu

WOLF, SUSAN R.
PERSONAL Born 07/23/1952, Chicago, IL, m, 1978, 2 children **DISCIPLINE** MATH AND PHILOSOPHY; PHILOSOPHY **EDUCATION** Yale Univ, BA, 74; Princeton Univ, PhD, 78. **CAREER** Asst prof, 78-81, Harvard Univ; asst prof, 81-86, Univ of Maryland; assoc prof, 86-90, prof, 90-98, Duane Peterson prof of ethics, 98, Johns Hopkins Univ. **HONORS AND AWARDS** Amer Council of Learned Societies fel, 81-82; Amer Assn of Univ Women Postdoctoral fel, 81-82; John Simon Guggenheim Memorial fel, 93-94. **MEMBERSHIPS** Amer Philosophical Assn; Amer Soc for Political and Legal Philosophy; AAUP. **RESEARCH** Ethics; Philosophy of Mind. **SELECTED PUBLICATIONS** Auth, Freedom Within Reason, 90; auth, Two Levels of Pluralism, Ethics, July 92; auth, Morality and Partiality, Philosophical Perspectives, 92; auth, Meaning and Morality, Proceedings of the Aristotelian Society, 97; auth, Happiness and Meaning: Tow Aspect of the Good Life, Social Philosphy & Policy, 97. **CONTACT ADDRESS** Dept of Philosophy, Johns Hopkins Univ, Baltimore, MD, 21218. **EMAIL** swolf@jhv.edu

WOLFE, DAVID L.
PERSONAL Born 03/07/1939, Lock Haven, PA, m, 1962, 3 children **DISCIPLINE** ANTHROPOLOGY, THEOLOGY, PHILOSOPHY, PHILOSOPHY OF EDUCATION **EDUCATION** Wheaton Col, BA, 61, MA, 64; NY Univ, PhD, 69. **CAREER** Inst to assoc prof of Philos, The Kings Col, NY, 63-70; asst to assoc prof of Philos, Wheaton Col, 70-74; assoc to prof of Philos, Gordon Col, 74-87; pastor, The Tunbridge Church, Tunbridge, VT, 87-. **MEMBERSHIPS** Am Philos Asn **RESEARCH** Religious epistemology' Philosophy of education; Philosophy of science. **SELECTED PUBLICATIONS** Auth Epistemology: The Justification of Belief, InterVarsity Press, 82; coed The Reality of Christian Learning, Christian Univ Press, 87; coed Slogans or Distinctives: Reforming Christian Education, Univ Press Am, 93. **CONTACT ADDRESS** Rivendell, 6 Wolfe Dr, Tunbridge, VT, 05077. **EMAIL** rivendell5@juno.com

WOLFE, DEBORAH CANNON PARTRIDGE
PERSONAL Born 1222, Cranford, New Jersey, d **DISCIPLINE** THEOLOGY **EDUCATION** Columbia Univ, EdD, MA; Jersey City State Coll, BS; Postdoctoral Study, Vassar Coll, Union Theological Seminary, Jewish Theological Seminary of Amer. **CAREER** Tuskegee Univ, prof & dir grad work 1938-50; Queens College of CUNY, prof of education, 1950-86; vstg prof, NY Univ 1951-54, Univ of MI 1952, Fordham Univ 1952-53, Columbia Univ 1953-54, TX Coll 1955, Univ of IL 1956-57, Wayne State Univ 1961, Grambling Univ; US House of Reps, ed chief comm on ed & labor 1962-65; Macmillan Publ Co, ed consult 1964; NSF, consult 1967-70; City Univ Ctr for African & Afro-Amer Studies and African Study Abroad, dir 1968-77; Natl Leadership Training Inst US Ofc of Ed, cons, vocational & tech ed 1968-71; First Baptist Church Cranford NJ, assoc minister, 1975; Queens Coll, prof ed 1950-86; New Jersey State Board of Education, 1963-93. **HONORS AND AWARDS** Bldgs named in honor of Deborah Wolfe: Trenton State Coll 1970, Macon County, AL ; Award Hon Mem, Natl Soc for Prevention of Juvenile Delinquency; Women of Courage Radcliffe Coll; Special Honors Natl Alliance of Black School Educators, Northeastern Region Natl Assn of Colored Women's Clubs, Shrewsbury AME Zion Church; Citizen of the Year B'nai B'rith 1986; Citation Serv Omega Psi Phi Fraternity; Sojourner Truth Award Natl Ann of Business & Professional Women; Top Ladies of Distinction Hon Mem, 1986; Medal for Comm Serv Queens Coll of CUNY, 1986; Distinguished Service Award, Univ of Medicine & Dentistry of New Jersey and Seton Hall Univ; Honorary Doctorates: Stockton State Coll, Kean Coll of New Jersey, Jersey City State Coll Monmouth Coll, Centenary Coll, Bloomfield Coll, William Pater Coll, and numerous other educational institutions, 26 in all; Medal of Honor, Daughters of American Revolution; Women of Achievement, National YMCA; visiting scholar, Princeton Theological Seminary. **MEMBERSHIPS** Chair NJ State Bd of Higher Educ 1988-93; chmn admiss comm Queens Coll CUNY, UN Rep for Ch Women United 1971-; chmn AAUW Legis Prog Comm 1973-77; Commn on Fed Rel Amer Council on Ed 1972-77; trustee bd science serv AAAS; mem trustee bd Seton Hall Univ; adv comm Bd of Educ Cranford NJ; grand basileus, Zeta Phi Beta Sorority, 1954-65, chair, 1975-, Zeta Pi Beta Educ Found; sec Kappa Delta Pi Educ Foundation; vice pres, Natl Council of Negro Women; bd of dirs, Home Mission Council, Progressive Natl Baptist Convention; Resolutions Comm, Natl Assn of State Boards of Education; board of trustees: Science Service; Education Development Center; former pres, National Alliance of Black School Educators; chair, Monroe Human Relations Commission; pres, Rossmoor Interfaith Council. **CONTACT ADDRESS** First Baptist Church, 100 High St, Cranford, NJ, 07016.

WOLFE, ROBERT F.
PERSONAL Independence, MO **DISCIPLINE** THEOLOGY **EDUCATION** Calvin Col, BA, 78; Westminster Sem, MA, 81; Calvin Sem, MDiv, 87; Southwestern Theol Sem, PhD, 96. **CAREER** Hosp chap, 87-88, Parkland Mem Hospital; tchng fel, res asst, 90-91; pastor/intern, pastor, 85-87. **HONORS AND AWARDS** Grad with honors, Westminster Sem & Calvin Sem. **MEMBERSHIPS** AAR; Soc of Bibl Lit; Inst for Bibl Res. **RESEARCH** The historical Jesus; early Christianity; phil of relig. **SELECTED PUBLICATIONS** Art, Rhetorical Elements in the Speeches of Acts 7 and 17, J Transl & Test-Ling, vol 6 no 3, 93 **CONTACT ADDRESS** 102 Blackfoot Trail N, Lake Kiowa, TX, 76240. **EMAIL** bwolfe@safeweb.net

WOLFF, ROBERT PAUL
PERSONAL Born 12/27/1933, New York, NY, m, 1962 **DISCIPLINE** PHILOSOPHY **EDUCATION** Harvard Univ, AB, 53, AM, 54, PhD(philos), 57. **CAREER** Instr philos, Harvard Univ, 58-61; asst prof philos & soc sci, Univ Chicago, 61-64; from assoc prof to prof philos, Columbia Univ, 64-71; prof Philos, 71-91, PROF AFRO-AM STUDIES, UNIV MA, 92-; Soc Sci Res Coun fel, 57-58. **MEMBERSHIPS** Am Soc Polit & Legal Philos; Am Philos Asn. **RESEARCH** History of modern philosophy; social and political philosophy; philosophy of education. **SELECTED PUBLICATIONS** Ed, The Essential Hume, New Am Libr, 69; In Defense of Anarchism, Harper, 70; Philosophy: A Modern Encounter, Prentice-Hall, 71; The Rule of Law, Simon & Schuster, 71; Styles of Political Action in America, Random, 72;The Autonomy of Reason, Harper, 73; auth, About Philosophy, Prentice-Hall, 76; Understanding Rawls, Princeton Univ, 77. **CONTACT ADDRESS** Dept of Afro-Am Studies, Univ of Massachusetts, Amherst, MA, 01002. **EMAIL** rwolff@afroam.umass.edu

WOLFMAN, BERNARD
PERSONAL Born 07/08/1924, Philadelphia, PA, 3 children **DISCIPLINE** LAW **EDUCATION** Univ Pa, AB, 46, JD, 48. **CAREER** Part-time instr polit sci, Univ Pa, 46-49, part-time lectr, Law Sch, 59-62, part-time prof, 62-63, prof law, 63-76, chmn univ senate & chmn task force on univ governance 69-70, dean, 70-75; Gemmill prof tax law & tax policy, Univ Pa Law Sch, 73-76; Fessenden Prof Law Taxation, Harvard Univ Law Sch, 76-, Consult, US Treasury Dept, 63-68, 77-80; vis prof, Harvard Law Sch, 64-65; Adv Group Comnr Internal Revenue 66-67; gen counsel, AAUP, 66-68; consult, Am Law Inst-Income Tax Proj, 74-; exec comt, Fed Tax Inst New England, 76-. **HONORS AND AWARDS** Fel, Cent Adv Study Behav Sci, 75-76; Irvine lectr, Law Sch, Cornell Univ, 80; Fel, Am Col of Tax Counsel, Regent for 1st Circuit., LLD, Jewish Theol Sem, 71. **MEMBERSHIPS** Am Bar Asn; Am Law Inst; Order Coif. **RESEARCH** Tax law. **SELECTED PUBLICATIONS** Auth, Professors and the ordinary and necessary business expense, Univ Pa Law Rev, 64; Federal tax policy and the support of science, In: Law and the Social Role of Science, Rockefeller Univ, 66; Bosch, its implications and aftermath: The effect of state court adjudications on federal tax litigation, Univ Miami Ann Inst Estate Planning 69; Federal Income Taxation of Corporate Enterprise, Aspen Law & Bus, 3rd ed, 90; The Behavior of Justice Douglas in Federal Tax Cases, Univ Pa Law Rev, 12/73; sr auth, Dissent Without Opinion: The Behavior of Justice William O Douglas in Federal Tax Cases, Univ Pa, 75; The supreme court in the Lyon's den: A failure of judicial process, Cornell Law Rev, 81; coauth, Ethical problems in federal tax practice, Aspen Law & Bus, 3d ed, 85; coauth, Standards of Tax Practice, Aspen Law & Bus, 4th ed, 97. **CONTACT ADDRESS** Law Sch, Harvard Univ, 1545 Massachusetts Ave, Cambridge, MA, 02138-4623. **EMAIL** wolfman@law.harvard.edu

WOLFRAM, CHARLES W.
PERSONAL Born 02/28/1937, Cleveland, OH, m, 1965, 2 children **DISCIPLINE** CIVIL PROCEDURE, LEGAL ETHICS **EDUCATION** Univ Notre Dame, AB, 59; Univ Tex Law Sch, LLB, 62. **CAREER** Asst prof law, Univ Minn Law Sch, 65-67, assoc prof, 67-70, prof, 70-82; PROF LAW, CORNELL LAW SCH, 82-, Vis prof law, Southern Calif Law Ctr, 76-77 & Cornell Law Sch, 81-82. **MEMBERSHIPS** Am Law Inst. **RESEARCH** American civil procedure; legal ethics; federal jurisdiction. **SELECTED PUBLICATIONS** Auth, Mass Torts--Messy Ethics, Cornell Law Rev, Vol 0080, 95. **CONTACT ADDRESS** Law Sch, Cornell Univ, Myron Taylor Hall, Ithaca, NY, 14853-4901.

WOLGAST, ELIZ H.
PERSONAL Born 02/27/1929, NJ, m, 1949, 2 children **DISCIPLINE** ENGLISH; PHILOSOPHY **EDUCATION** Cornell Univ, BA, 50, MA, 52; Univ Wash, PhD, 55. **CAREER** Univ Calif Davis, 66-67; Calif State Hayward, 68-97; visiting prof, Dartmouth Col, 75-76; Univ Wales, Lampeter, 95, 96. **HONORS AND AWARDS** NEH fel, 78, 88; Finnish Acad fel, 92; Rockefeller Bellagio fel, 88. **MEMBERSHIPS** APA. **RE-**

SEARCH Wittgenstein; Ethics; Epistemology. **SELECTED PUBLICATIONS** Auth, Democracy: The Message from Athens, Consequences of Modernity in Contemporary Legal Theory, Dunker & Humbolt, 98; auth, Mental Causes and the Will, Philos Investigations, Winter, 97; auth, Moral Paradigms, Philos, Spring, 95; auth, Individualism and Democratic Citizenship, Democrazia e Diritto, Summer, 94; auth, The Demands of Public Reason, Columbia Law Rev, Oct, 94; auth, Primitive Reactions, Philos Investigations, Oct, 94; auth, Ethics of an Artificial Person: Lost Responsibility in Professions and Organizations, Stanford Univ Press, 92; auth, La Grammatica della Giustizia, Riuniti, Italy, 91; auth, The Grammar of Justice, Cornell Univ Press, 87; auth, Equality and the Rights of Women, Cornell Univ Press, 80; auth, Paradoxes of Knowledge, Cornell Univ Press, 77. **CONTACT ADDRESS** 1536 Olympus Av., Berkeley, CA, 94708. **EMAIL** ewolgast@csuhayward.edu

WOLLENBERG, BRUCE
PERSONAL Born 10/12/1943, IN, m, 1969, 1 child **DISCIPLINE** RELIGIOUS STUDIES **EDUCATION** Univ Cal SB, PhD 86. **CAREER** St. Mark Lutheran Church, pastor, 98-. **MEMBERSHIPS** AAR **RESEARCH** American Religion; Post Modern Theology. **SELECTED PUBLICATIONS** Auth, Christian Social Thought in Great Britain Between the Wars, Univ Press of Amer, 97. **CONTACT ADDRESS** St Mark Lutheran Church, 100 Alderman Rd, Charlottesville, VA, 22903-1782. **EMAIL** brucew@stmarklutheran.org

WOOD, BRYANT G.
PERSONAL Born 10/07/1936, Endicott, NY, m, 1958, 4 children **DISCIPLINE** NEAR EASTERN STUDIES, BIBLICAL HISTORY, AND SYRO-PALESTINIAN ARCHAEOLOGY **EDUCATION** Univ Mich, MA, 74; Univ Toronto, PhD, 85. **CAREER** Visitng Prof, Dept of Near Eastern Studies, Univ Toronto, 89-90; Res Analysit, 90-94, DIR, ASSOC FOR BIBLICAL RES, 95-. **HONORS AND AWARDS** Endowment for Biblical Res Grant, 81; Travel Grant, 81, Summer Stipend, Nat Endowment for the Humanities, 92. **MEMBERSHIPS** Near East Archaeol Soc; Inst for Biblical Res. **RESEARCH** Archaeology of the Bronze Age and Iron Age Periods in Palestine. **SELECTED PUBLICATIONS** Auth, Pottery Making in Bible Times, By the Sweat of Thy Brow: Labor and Laborers in the Biblical World, Sheffield Academic Press, forthcoming; Cisterns and Reservoirs, Encyclo of the Dead Sea Scrolls, Oxford Univ Press, forthcoming; Water Systems, Encyclo of the Dead Sea Scrolls, Oxford Univ Press, forthcoming; The Role of Shechem in the Conquest of Canaan, To Understand the Scriptures: Essays in Honor of William H. Shea, Inst of Archeaol/Siegfried H. Horn Archaeol Museum, Andrews Univ, 97; Kh. Nisya, 94, Israel Exploration J, 95; Biblical Archaeology's Greatest Achievement, Failure and Challenge, Biblical Archaeol Rev, 95; Rev of Excavations at Tell Deir Alla, Bullet of the Am Schools of Oriental Res, 94; coauth, Kh. Nisya, 93, Israel Exploration J, 94. **CONTACT ADDRESS** Associates for Biblical Res, 4328 Crestview Rd., Harrisburg, PA, 17112-2005.

WOOD, CHARLES M.
PERSONAL Born 11/22/1944, Salida, CO, m, 1966, 1 child **DISCIPLINE** THEOLOGY **EDUCATION** Univ Denver, BA, 66; Boston Univ Sch of Theology, ThM, 69; Yale Univ, Mphilo, 71, PhD, 72. **CAREER** Unit Meth Chrch, Rocky Mtn Ann Con, Pastoral Minis, 72-76; Perkins School of Theology, SO Meth Univ, Asst Prof to Prof, theol, 76-92, Assoc Dean for Acad Affs, 90-93, Lehman Prof, Christ Doct, 92-. **HONORS AND AWARDS** Phi Beta Kappa; Omicron Delta Kappa. **MEMBERSHIPS** Am Acad Rel; Am Theo Soc. **RESEARCH** Philos and Systema Theolo. **SELECTED PUBLICATIONS** Scripture Authenticity and Truth, J Rel, 96; The Question of the Doctrine of Providence, Theology Today, 92; Vision and Discernment, Scholars Press, 85; The Formation of Christian Understanding, Westminster Press, 81, 2d ed, Trinity Press, 93; Theory and Religious Understanding, Scholars Press, 75. **CONTACT ADDRESS** Perkins School of Theology, Southern Methodist Univ, Dallas, TX, 75275-0133. **EMAIL** cwood@mail.smu.edu

WOOD, FORREST E., JR.
DISCIPLINE PHILOSOPHY **EDUCATION** Baylor Univ, BA, 58; Southwestern Baptist Theol Sem, ThD, 64; Southwestern Baptist Theol Sem, PhD, 74. **CAREER** Instr philos, Texas Wesleyan Col, 63-64; asst prof philos, Louisiana Col, 64-66; assoc prof philos, 66-86, prof, 87- , chemn Philos and Relig Dept, Univ So Mississippi. **HONORS AND AWARDS** Mem, Assoc of Philos of Relig, 85- ; evaluator, NEH; ed review board, Philos in the Contemporary World, 94- ; evaluator, Miss Humanities Coun; pres, Soc for Philos of Relig, 77-78; Danforth Assoc, 79-86. **MEMBERSHIPS** Soc for Philos of Relig; Miss Philos Soc; APA; Southern Soc for Philos and Psychol; Southwestern Philos Soc; Metaphysical Soc; Center for Process Stud. **SELECTED PUBLICATIONS** Auth, Whiteheadian Thought As A Basis for A Philosophy of Religion, University Press of Am, 86; auth, Henry David Thoreau: Vegetarian Hunter and Fisherman, Southwest Philos Rev, 93; auth, A Natural Philosophy of Our Time, Contemporary Philosophy, 95; auth, The Delights and Dilemmas of Hunting: The Hunting Versus Anti-Hunting Debate, University Press of America, 97. **CONTACT ADDRESS** Univ of Southern Mississippi, Southern Sta, PO Box 5015, Hattiesburg, MS, 39408.

WOOD, JOHN A.
DISCIPLINE CHRISTIAN ETHICS **EDUCATION** Columbia Bible Col, BA, 60; Southwestern Baptist Theol Sem, BD, 66; Baylor Univ, PhD, 75. **CAREER** PROF RELIG, BAYLOR UNIV, 81-. **MEMBERSHIPS** Amer Academy Relig; Soc of Christian Ethics. **RESEARCH** Peace issues; business ethics; analysis of films from an ethical perspective. **CONTACT ADDRESS** Dept of Relig, Baylor Univ, Waco, TX, 76798. **EMAIL** John_Wood@Baylor.edu

WOOD, REGA
PERSONAL Born 12/08/1944, Pasadena, CA, m, 1965, 2 children **DISCIPLINE** PHILOSOPHY **EDUCATION** Reed Col, BA, 68; Cornell Univ, MA, 71, PhD, 75. **CAREER** Asst prof, St. Bonaventure Univ, 76-87, assoc prof, 87-89, full prof, 89-96; adjunct prof, Yale Divinity Sch; vis lect, Univ Calif San Diego, 86; senior res scholar, Yale Univ, 96-. **HONORS AND AWARDS** Am Philos Soc res grant, 97; Nat Endow for the Humanities fel, 97, archival res grant, 93; Alexander von Humboldt res fel, 91-92 & 83-84. **MEMBERSHIPS** Soc for Medieval and Renaissance Philos. **RESEARCH** Philosophy; History. **SELECTED PUBLICATIONS** Auth, Ockham on the Virtues, 97; "Richard Rufus and the Classical Tradition," 97; "Causality and Demonstration: An Early Scholastic Posterior Analytics Commentary," 96; "Individual Forms: Richard Rufus and John Duns Scotus," 96; "Richard Rufus and English Scholastic Discussion of Individuation," 96; "Angelic Individuation: According to Richard Rufus, St. Bonaventure and St. Thomas Aquinas," 96. **CONTACT ADDRESS** Philosophy Dept, Yale Univ, New Haven, CT, 06520-8306. **EMAIL** Rufus@Pantheon.Yale.edu

WOOD, ROBERT
DISCIPLINE PHILOSOPHY **EDUCATION** Marquette Univ, BA, MA, PhD. **CAREER** Dept Philos, Univ Dallas **SELECTED PUBLICATIONS** Auth, Plato's Line Revisited: The Pedagogy of Complete Reflection, Rev of Metaphysics, 91; Six Heideggerian Figures, Amer Cath Philos Quart, 95; Being and Manifestness, Intl Philos Quart, 95; Recovery of the Aesthetic Center, Proc of the Amer Cath Philos Assn, 95. **CONTACT ADDRESS** Dept of Philos, Univ Dallas, 1845 E Northgate Dr, Irving, TX, 75062. **EMAIL** rwood@acad.udallas.edu

WOOD, WILLIAM L., JR.
PERSONAL Born 12/04/1940, Cleveland, OH, m **DISCIPLINE** LAW **EDUCATION** Brown U, BA 1962; Yale Law Sch, JD 1965. **CAREER** Untd Ch of Christ, 1964; Mandell & Wright Houston TX, assoc 1965-68; Intl Nickel Co N Y & Pfizer Inc NY atty 1968-71; Union Carbide Corp NY atty 1971-74; City of N Y, gen cnsl & controller 1974-79; NY S Atty Gen, chief ed bureau 1979-81; NY St Office of Prof Disc, exec dir 1981-85; Wood & Scher, Attys, partner 1985-. **HONORS AND AWARDS** Black Achvrs in Industry Awd 1974 (Nom by Union Carbine Corp). **MEMBERSHIPS** Contributing editor, Discipline, natl journla covering prof discipline, 1982-84; Information Please Almanac, editor, 1981-82; NY St Dental Journal, What Every Dentist Should know about Prof Misconduct, June/July 1982 (vol 48 no 6 pp 378-380); NY St Dental Journal, an interview on prof dicipline Oct 1982 (vol 48 no 8 p 538); NY St Pharmacist, recent changes in prof dicipline (vol 57 no 1, Fall 1982, p v); NY St Dental Journal, Record retentiona professional responsibility even after the patient has gone, Feb 1984 (vol 50, no 2, p 98); NY St Pharmacist, To the new Supvr Pharmacist Congratulations & a word of Warning, summer 1983, vol 57, no 4; NY St Pharmacist, The violations comm vol 58, no 3, Spring 1984; Veterinary News, Legal Remedies for Unpaid Fees, May 1984; admtd to TX 1965, NY Bar 1969; NY St Bar Asso, Am Arbitration Asso, One Hundred Black Men Inc, Am Pub Hlth Asso, Natl Clearinghouse on Licensure, Enfrcmnt & Regulation. **CONTACT ADDRESS** Wood & Scher Attys at Law, One Chase Rd, Scarsdale, NY, 10583.

WOODHOUSE, MARK B.
DISCIPLINE METAPHYSICS, PHILOSOPHY OF TIME, PHILOSOPHY OF MIND, EASTERN PHILOSOPHY AND **EDUCATION** Univ Miami, PhD, 70. **CAREER** Assoc prof, Ga State Univ. **SELECTED PUBLICATIONS** Auth, A Preface to Philosophy, 5th ed. **CONTACT ADDRESS** Georgia State Univ, Atlanta, GA, 30303. **EMAIL** phlmbw@panther.gsu.edu

WOODRING, ANDREW N.
PERSONAL Born 04/10/1954, Defiance, OH, m, 1976, 3 children **DISCIPLINE** THEOLOGY **EDUCATION** Harvard Univ, BA, 76; Gordon-Conwell Theol Sem, M.Div, 80; Trinity Int Univ, PhD, 99. **CAREER** Pastor, Hope Evangelical Free Church, 84-92; adj prof, John Brown Univ, 92-93, 96-97; asst prof, LeTourneau Univ, 98-. **MEMBERSHIPS** Evangelical Theol Soc; Soc Biblical Lit; Am Asn Relig. **RESEARCH** Church history; 18th century Evangelical revivals. **CONTACT ADDRESS** PO Box 7001, Longview, TX, 75607-7001. **EMAIL** woodrina@letu.edu

WOODRUFF, PAUL
PERSONAL Born 08/28/1943, Summit, NJ, m, 1973, 2 children **DISCIPLINE** PHILOSOPHY **EDUCATION** Princeton Univ, PhD, 73. **CAREER** Prof, Univ Tex Austin, 73-. **MEMBERSHIPS** Am Philos Asn. **RESEARCH** Ancient Greek Philosophy. **SELECTED PUBLICATIONS** Auth, articles on philosophical topics; coauth, Plato: Phaedrus, 95; Early Greek Political Thought from Homer to the Sophists, 95. **CONTACT ADDRESS** Dept of Philosophy, Univ of Tex, Austin, TX, 78712. **EMAIL** pbw@mail.utexas.edu

WOODWARD, J.
PERSONAL Born 09/17/1946, Chicago, IL, m, 1978, 1 child **DISCIPLINE** PHILOSOPHY **EDUCATION** Carelton Col, BA, 68; Univ Texas, PhD, 77. **CAREER** Prof, phil, 92-, Calif Inst Tech. **RESEARCH** Philosophy of science **SELECTED PUBLICATIONS** Auth, Supervenience and Singular Causal Claims, Explan & Its Limits, Cambridge Univ Press, 90; auth, Liberalism and Migration, Free Movement: Ethical Issues in the Transnational Migration of People and Money, Harvester-Wheatsheaf, 92; art, Realism About Laws, Erkenntnis 36, 92; auth, Capacities and Invariance, Phil Problems of the Internal & External Worlds: Essays Concerning the Phil of Adolph Grunbaum, Univ Pitts Press, 93; auth, Causality and Explanation in Econometrics, On the Reliability of Economic Models: Essays in the Phil of Economics, Kluwer, 95; coauth, Conduct, Misconduct and the Structure of Science, Amer Scientist, 96; art, Explanation, Invariance and Intervention, PSA 96; auth, Causal Modeling, Probabilities and Invariance, Causality in Crisis? Statistical Methods and the Search for Causal Knowledge in the Social Sciences, Univ Notre Dame Press, 97. **CONTACT ADDRESS** Div of Humanities and Social Sciences, California Polytech State Univ, Pasadena, CA, 91175. **EMAIL** jfw@hss.caltech.edu

WOODYARD, DAVID O.
PERSONAL Born 04/27/1932, Oak Park, IL, m, 1955, 2 children **DISCIPLINE** RELIGION **EDUCATION** Denison Univ, BA, 54; Union Theol Sem, NY, MDiv, 58; Oberlin Col, DMin, 65. **CAREER** Dir univ Christian fel, Univ Conn, 58-60; asst prof relig & dean chapel, 60-77, assoc prof, 78-81, Prof Relig & Chmn Dept, Denison Univ, 81-, Danforth Intern Prog, 56-57. **MEMBERSHIPS** Nat asn Col & Univ Chaplains; Am Acad Religion. **RESEARCH** The doctrine of God; liberation theology; social ethics. **SELECTED PUBLICATIONS** Auth, Happenings in higher education, Foundations: J Baptist Hist & Theol, 7/67; Living Without God--Before God, 68, To Be Human Now!, 69, The Opaqueness of God, 70, Beyond Cynicism: The Practice of Hope, 73 & Strangers and Exiles: Living by Promises, 74, Westminster; coauth, Journey Toward Freedom: Economic Structures and Theological Perspectives, Fairleigh Dickinson Univ Press, 82; Risking Liberation: Middle Class Powerlessness and Social Heroism, John Knox Press, 88; Liberating Nature: Theology and Economics in the New Order, Pilgrim Press, 99. **CONTACT ADDRESS** Dept of Relig, Denison Univ, 1 Denison University, Granville, OH, 43023-1359. **EMAIL** MAX:woodyard@denison.edu

WORKS, ROBERT G.
DISCIPLINE LAW **EDUCATION** Kans State Univ, BA; St Louis Univ, JD. **CAREER** Prof **RESEARCH** Contracts; insurance. **SELECTED PUBLICATIONS** Auth, Nebraska Property and Liability Insurance Law, 85. **CONTACT ADDRESS** Law Dept, Univ of Nebraska, Lincoln, 103 Ross McCollum Hall, PO Box 830902, Lincoln, NE, 68588-0420. **EMAIL** rworks@unlinfo.unl.edu

WORTH, SARAH ELIZABETH
PERSONAL Born 03/12/1970, Ann Arbor, MI **DISCIPLINE** PHILOSOPHY, AESTHETICS, ANCIENT PHILOSOPHY, BIOMEDICAL ETHICS **EDUCATION** Furman Univ, BA, 92; Univ of Louisville, MA, 94; SUNY Buffalo, PhD, 97. **CAREER** Asst prof, Allegheny Col, 97-98; asst prof, Miami Univ, 98-99. **RESEARCH** Aesthetics; ancient philosophy. **SELECTED PUBLICATIONS** "Wittgenstein's Musical Understanding," British J of Aesthet, v 37, no 2. **CONTACT ADDRESS** Dept of Philosophy, Miami Univ, 212 Hall Auditorium, Oxford, OH, 45056. **EMAIL** worthse@muohio.edu

WREN, THOMAS
PERSONAL Kansas City, MO, m, 2 children **DISCIPLINE** PHILOSOPHY **EDUCATION** Northwstrn Univ, PhD, 69; Loyola Univ Chicago, MA, 65; St. Marys Col, MED, 65; DePaul Univ, MA, 62; St. Marys Col, BA, 59 **CAREER** Prof, 66-pres, Loyola Univ Chicago **SELECTED PUBLICATIONS** Auth, Caring about Morality; Philosophy of Development; The Moral Domain; The Moral Self, The Personal Universe **CONTACT ADDRESS** 1036 Judson Ave, Evanston, IL, 60202.

WREN, THOMAS E.
DISCIPLINE PHILOSOPHY **EDUCATION** Northwestern Univ, PhD. **CAREER** Prof, Loyola Univ, 66-; vis prof, Calif; fac, Loyola Univ Rome Center; VP, Asn for the Philos of Educ. **RESEARCH** Aristotle's ethics; normative ethics; metaethics; moral psychology; moral education; social philosophy; action theory. **SELECTED PUBLICATIONS** Auth, Caring About Morality, Routledge & MIT Press, 91; coauth, Promise-Giving and Treaty-Making, Brill, 92; Philosophy of Development, Kluwer; articles on, philos of hist & cross-cultural understanding. **CONTACT ADDRESS** Dept of Philosophy, Loyola Univ, Chicago, 820 N Michigan Ave, Chicago, IL, 60611.

WRIGGINS, JENNIFER
DISCIPLINE LAW **EDUCATION** Yale Univ, AB; Harvard Univ, JD. **CAREER** Prof; taught in, Trial Advocacy Workshop, Harvard Law Sch, 94, 95; clerked, Hon Edward T. Gignoux, US Dist Judge, Portland, Maine; past asst atty gen, Civil Rights Div Mass Atty Generals' Off in Boston; past Articles and Exec Ed, Harvard Women's Law J; past partner, Pressman, Kruskal & Wriggins in Cambridge, Mass. **MEMBERSHIPS** Bd Cambridge-Somerville Legal Serv; bd, Maine Civil Liberties Union and Civil Liberties Union Mass. **SELECTED PUBLICATIONS** Auth, Rape, Racism and the Law; Genetics, IQ, Determinism, and Torts: The Example of Discovery in Lead Exposure Litigation, Boston Univ Law Rev, 97; sect on Rape, in The Reader's Companion to US Women's Hist, 97; coauth, Supreme Ct amicus brief in the case of UAW v. Johnson Controls. **CONTACT ADDRESS** School of Law, Univ of Southern Maine, 96 Falmouth St, PO Box 9300, Portland, ME, 04104-9300.

WRIGHT, CHARLES ALAN
PERSONAL Born 09/03/1927, Philadelphia, PA, m, 1950, 5 children **DISCIPLINE** LAW **EDUCATION** Wesleyan Univ, AB, 47; Yale Univ, LLB, 49. **CAREER** From asst prof to assoc prof law, Univ Minn, 50-55; from assoc prof to prof, 55-65, Charles T McCormick Prof Law, 65-80, WILLIAM B BATES CHAIR FOR THE ADMIN OF JUSTICE, UNIV TEX, AUSTIN, 80-97, Vinson & Elkins Chair in Law, 95, Hayden W Head Regents Chair for Fac Excellence, 91; Consult, Ala Comn Procedural Reform, 56-57; vis prof, Univ Pa, 59-60; mem adv comt rules of civil procedure, Judicial Conf US, 61-64, standing comt rules practice & procedure, 64-76; reporter, Am Law Inst Studies Div Jurisdiction Between State & Fed Courts, 63-69; vis prof, Univ Pa Law School, 59-60, vis prof, Harvard Univ, 64-65, law, Yale Univ, 68-69, vis fel, Wolfson Col, Cambridge, Engl, 84; Arthur Goodhart vis prof, Legal Sci, Univ Cambridge, Cambridge, Engl, 90-91, vis scholar, Victoria Univ Wellington, New Zealand, 93; consult to counsel for President of US, 73-74; mem, Permanent Comt Oliver Wendell Holmes Devise, 75-. **HONORS AND AWARDS** Student Bar Asn Teaching Excellence Award, 80; fel, Am Acad Arts & Sci, 84; Fel Res Award, Fel of Am Bar Found, 89; Doctor of Humane Letters, honoris causa, Episcopal Theol Sem of Southwest, Austin, Tex, 92; Leon Green Award, Tex Law Rev, 93; Distinguished Alum Award, Wesleyan Univ, Middletown, CT, 93; Robert B McKay Prof Award, Tort & Insurance Sect, Am Bar Asn, 95; Clarity Award for Clear Legal Writing, Plain English Comt, State Bar Mich, 97; Fordham-Stein Prize, Fordham Univ, 97; Learned Hand Medal, Fed Bar Counc, 98. **MEMBERSHIPS** Am Bar Asn; Am Law Inst; Am Judicature Soc; Inst Judicial Admin. **RESEARCH** Federal courts; judicial procedure; constitutional law. **SELECTED PUBLICATIONS** Auth, Wright's Minnesota Rules, 54; Cases on Remedies, 55; ed, Barron & Holtzoff, Federal Practice & Procedure, 58-61; co-auth, Cases on Federal Courts, 4th-9th ed, 62-92; Wright on Federal Courts, 1st-5th ed, 63-94; co-auth, Procedure -- The Handmaid of Justice, 65; co-auth, The American Law Institute Study of the Division of Jurisdiction between State and Federal Courts, 69; Federal Practice and Procedure, Criminal, Civil, Evidence, Jurisdiction and Related Matters, 69-97. **CONTACT ADDRESS** Law Sch, Univ Tex, Austin, 727 E Dean Keeton, Austin, TX, 78705-3224.

WRIGHT, DANAYA C.
DISCIPLINE LAW **EDUCATION** Cornell Univ, BA; Univ Ariz, MA; Cornell Univ, JD; Johns Hopkins Univ, PhD. **CAREER** Asst prof, Univ Fla, 98-; past adj prof, Ind Univ; past vis assoc prof, Ariz State Univ. **MEMBERSHIPS** Law and Soc Asn; Amer Soc for Legal Hist. **RESEARCH** Estates &trusts, feminist theory, franchise law, jurisprudence, legal history, and property. **CONTACT ADDRESS** School of Law, Univ of Florida, PO Box 117625, Gainesville, FL, 32611-7625. **EMAIL** wrightdc@law.ufl.edu

WRIGHT, JOHN
PERSONAL Born 05/03/1942, Toronto, ON, Canada, m, 1997, 2 children **DISCIPLINE** PHILOSOPHY **EDUCATION** Univ Toronto, BA, 64, MA, 67; York Univ, PhD. **CAREER** Asst prof, 83 87, assoc prof, 87-90, full prof, 90, Univ Windsor; vis prof, Univ Bologna, 94; Hannah vis prof, Univ W Ontario, 92-93; Prof, Central Mich Univ, 98-. **HONORS AND AWARDS** Can Counc Killam Postdoctoral fel. **MEMBERSHIPS** Am Philos Asn; Am Soc Eighteenth Century Studies; Hume Soc. **RESEARCH** 17th & 18th Century philosophy; Descartes; Locke; Hume. **SELECTED PUBLICATIONS** Auth, Hume and Hume's Connexions, Edinburgh Univ Press & Penn State Univ Press, 94; art on Cartesianism, Determinism, Dualism, Hume, Hutcheson, Leibniz, Locke, Malebranche, Mind-Body Relationship, Rationalism, Reason, Scepticism, A Dictionary of Eighteenth Century World Hist, Oxford, 94; Butler and Hume on Habit and Moral Character, Hume and Humes Connexions, Edinburgh Univ Press & Penn State Univ Press, 94; Lo schiavo delle passioni: Morale e religione in Hume, Revista di Filosofia, 95; Humes Academia Scepticism: A Reappraisal of his Philosophy of Human Understanding, David Hume: Critical Assessments, Routledge, 95; rev, Humes Theory of Consciousness, Hume Studies, 95; auth, Hume, Descartes and the Materiality of the Soul, The Philosophical Canon in the 17th and 18th Centuries, Univ Rochester Press, 96. **CONTACT ADDRESS** Dept of Philososphy and Religion, Central Michigan Univ, Mt Pleasant, MI, 48859.

WRIGHT, JOHN H.
PERSONAL Born 02/13/1922, San Francisco, CA **DISCIPLINE** THEOLOGY **EDUCATION** Mt St Michael's Sem, PhL, 46; Gonzaga Univ, MA, 46; Alma Col, STL, 53; Gregorian Univ, STD, 57. **CAREER** Instr philos, Gonzaga Univ, 46-49; prof extraordinarius theol, Gregorian Univ, 56-60; PROF THEOL, JESUIT SCH THEOL, BERKELEY, 60-; Prof Syst Theol, Grad Theol Union, 66-, Am Asn Theol Schs grant, 71-72; Bernard Hanley theol, Santa Clara Univ, 79-80. **MEMBERSHIPS** Cath Theol Soc Am (vpres, 71-72, pres, 72-73). **RESEARCH** Divine providence; theological method; ecumenism. **SELECTED PUBLICATIONS** Auth, Haight,Roger Spirit Christology--A Roman-Catholic Contention of the Divinity of Jesus-Christ as Being Fully Integrated in Humanity, Theol Stud, Vol 0053, 92; Biblical Faith and Natural Theology--The Gifford-Lectures for 1991, Theol Stud, Vol 0054, 93; Science, Theology and the Transcendental Horizon--Einstein, Kant and Tillich, Theol Stud, Vol 0057, 96; The Human Factor--Evolution, Culture, and Religion, Theol Stud, Vol 0056, 95; She Who Is--The Mystery of God in Feminist Theological Discourse, Theol Stud, Vol 0054, 93. **CONTACT ADDRESS** Jesuit Sch of Theol, Berkeley, 1735 LeRoy Ave, Berkeley, CA, 94709.

WRIGHT, JOHN ROBERT
PERSONAL Born 10/20/1936, Carbondale, IL **DISCIPLINE** PATRISTIC & MEDIEVAL CHURCH HISTORY **EDUCATION** Univ of the South, BA, 58; Emory Univ, MA, 59; Gen Theol Sem, MDiv, 63; Oxford Univ, DPhil, 67. **CAREER** Instr church hist, Episcopal Theol Sch, MA, 66-68; asst prof ecclesiastical hist, 68-72, prof church hist, Gen Theol Sem, 72-, res assoc, Pontifical Inst Mediaeval Studies, Toronto, 76 & 81; mem, Comn Faith & Order, World Coun Churches & Standing Ecumenical Comn of Episcopal Church, 77-; mem, Anglican/Roman Cath Consult in US, 70-; res scholar, Huntington Libr, 77. **MEMBERSHIPS** AHA; Mediaeval Acad Am; Am Soc Church Hist; Church Hist Soc. **RESEARCH** Fourteenth century church-state and Anglo-Papal relations; Walter Reynolds, Archbishop of Canterbury 1314-1327; Lambert of Auxerre, mid-thirteenth century Dominican commentator on Aristotle. **SELECTED PUBLICATIONS** Ed, Handbook of American Orthodoxy, Forward Movement, 72; co-ed, Episcopalians and Roman Catholics: Can They Ever Get Together?, Dimension, 72; coauth, A Pope for All Christians?, Paulist, 76 & SPCK, 77; auth, A Communion of Communions: One Eucharistic Fellowship, Seabury, 79; The Church and The English Crown 1305-1334, Pontifical Inst Mediaeval Studies, Toronto, 80; The Canterbury Statement and the Five Priesthoods, One in Christ, Vol 11: 3 & Anglican Theol Rev, Vol 57: 4; Anglicans and the Papacy, J Ecumenical Studies, Vol 13: 3; The Accounts of the Constables of Bordeaux 1381-1390, with Particular Notes on their Ecclesiastical and Liturgical Significance, Mediaeval Studies, 42: 238-307; An Anglican Commentary on Selected Documents of Vatican II, Ecumenical Trends, Vol 9: 8 & 9. **CONTACT ADDRESS** General Theol Sem, 175 9th Ave, New York, NY, 10011-4924. **EMAIL** wright@gts.edu

WRIGHT, LARRY
DISCIPLINE PHILOSOPHY OF SCIENCE **EDUCATION** Ind Univ, PhD. **CAREER** PROF, UNIV CALIF, RIVERSIDE. **RESEARCH** Basic reasoning; Wittgenstein; Philosophy of science. **SELECTED PUBLICATIONS** Auth, Teleological Explanation, Univ Calif Press, 76; Practical Reasoning, Harcourt Brace Jovanovich, 88; Argument and Deliberation: A Plea for understanding, The Jour of Philos, Vol 92, No 11, 95. **CONTACT ADDRESS** Dept of Philos, Univ Calif, 1156 Hinderaker Hall, Riverside, CA, 92521-0209. **EMAIL** lwright@citrus.ucr.edu

WRIGHT, NICHOLAS THOMAS
PERSONAL Born 12/01/1948, Morpeth, England, m, 1971, 4 children **DISCIPLINE** NEW TESTAMENT **EDUCATION** Oxford Univ, BA, 71, BA, 73, MA, 75, DPhil, 81; Cambridge Univ, PhD(theol), 81. **CAREER** Res fel theol, Merton Col, Oxford, 75-78; fel & chaplain, Downing Col, Cambridge, 78-81; ASST PROF NEW TESTAMENT, MCGILL UNIV, 81- **RESEARCH** Pauline theology; christology, New Testament and modern; hermeneutics. **SELECTED PUBLICATIONS** Auth, Beyond New-Testament Theology--A Story and a Program, Jour Theol Stud, Vol 0043, 92; Paul, Jour Theol Stud, Vol 0043, 92; The Pagan Apostle--Heretical Double Meaning Within the Works of the Apostle Paul with a Brief Survey of Greek Mythology--German, Jour Theol Stud, Vol 0043, 92. **CONTACT ADDRESS** Fac of Relig Studies, 3520 University St, Montreal, PQ, H3A 2A7.

WRIGHT, ROBERTA V. HUGHES
PERSONAL Detroit, MI, m, 1989 **DISCIPLINE** LAW **EDUCATION** Univ of MI, PhD 1973; Wayne State Univ Law Sch, JD; Wayne State U, MEd. **CAREER** Detroit Pub Sch, past sch social worker; Detroit Comm on Children & Youth, past dir; Shaw Coll, past vice pres for Academic Affairs; County Public Admin, practicing lawyer Michigan Courts & admitted to practice bar, District of Columbia and Supreme Court of USA; Lawrence, former prof; First Independence Nat Bank, inst organizer & dir; Charro Book Co, Inc, vice pres, currently. **HONORS AND AWARDS** Recipient NAACP Freedom Award; MI Chronicle Newspaper Cit of Yr; Harriet Tubman Award; Alpha Kappa Alpha Sorority Recognition Award; Quality Quintet Award Detroit Skyliner Mag. **MEMBERSHIPS** Mem Am Bar Assn; mem MI Bar Assn; past mem Am & MI Trial Lawyers Assn; mem Oakland Co Bar Assn; mem Detroit Bar Assn; Wayne State Univ Law Alumni; Univ of MI Alumni Assn; AKA Sorority; life mem NAACP; mem Renaissance Club; million dollar mem Museum of African American History. **CONTACT ADDRESS** Charro Book Co Inc, 29777 Telegraph Rd #2500, Southfield, MI, 48034.

WRIGHT, TERRENCE C.
DISCIPLINE PHENOMENOLOGY AND CONTEMPORARY PHILOSOPHIES OF LITERATURE AND AESTHETICS **EDUCATION** St Vincent Col, BA; Villanova Univ, MA; Bryn Mawr Col, PhD. **CAREER** Fac, Mt Saint Mary's Col, 89-. **RESEARCH** Theories of interpretation in art and literature and the nature of poetic expression. **SELECTED PUBLICATIONS** Publ on, relationship between poetry and philos. **CONTACT ADDRESS** Dept of Philosophy, Mount Saint Mary's Col, 16300 Old Emmitsburg Rd, Emmitsburg, MD, 21727-7799. **EMAIL** wright@msmary.edu

WRIGHT-BOTCHWEY, ROBERTA YVONNE
PERSONAL Born 10/09/1946, York, South Carolina **DISCIPLINE** LAW **EDUCATION** Fisk U, BA 1967; Yale U, ISSP cert 1966; Univ MI Sch of Andrew Iii, JD. **CAREER** Private Practice; NC Central Univ School of Law, asst prof corp counsel Tanzania Legal Corp Dar es Salaam Tanzania; Zambia Ltd Lusaka Zambia, sr legal asst rural devel corp. **HONORS AND AWARDS** Outstdg Young Women of Am 1976; Sydney P Raymond lectr Jackson State Univ 1977. **MEMBERSHIPS** Mem NC Assn of Blck Lawyers; Nat Bar Assn; Nat Conf of Black Lawyers; SC & DC Bar Assn; hon mem Delta Theta Phi; consult EPA 1976; lectr Sci Jury Sel & Evidence Workshop; legal adv Zambian Corp Del to Tel Aviv, Israel 1971; Atty Gen of Zambia Select Com to Investigate Railways 1972; Delta Sigma Theta Sor; consult Women's Prison Group 1975; consult EPA Environmental Litigation Workshop 1976; NCBL Commn to Invest Discrim Prac in Law Schs 1977; dir Councon Legal Educ Oppor Summer Inst 1977; Phi Beta Kappa 1967. **CONTACT ADDRESS** 339 E Main, PO Box 10646, Rock Hill, SC, 29730.

WU, JOSEPH SEN
PERSONAL Born 09/10/1934, Canton, China, m, 1982, 3 children **DISCIPLINE** PHILOSOPHY, CHINESE CLASSICS **EDUCATION** Taiwan Norm Univ, BA, 59; Wash Univ, MA, 62; Southern Ill Univ, PhD(philos), 67. **CAREER** From instr to asst prof philos Univ Mo-St Louis, 63-67; asst prof, Northern Ill Univ, 67-70; assoc prof, 70-73, prof philos, Calif State Univ Sacramento 73-, vis prof, Loyola Univ, Ill, 69-70 & Nat Taiwan Univ, 76-77. **MEMBERSHIPS** Am Philos Asn; Soc Comp & Asian Philos. **RESEARCH** American philosophy; Far Eastern philosophy; philosophy of culture. **SELECTED PUBLICATIONS** Auth, Contemporary Western Philosophy from an Eastern viewpoint, Int Philos Quart, 68; The Paradoxical Situation of Western Philosophy and the Search for Chinese Wisdom, Inquiry, 71; Understanding Maoism, Studies Soviet Thought, 74; Comparative Philosophy and Culture (in Chinese), Tung Ta, Taiwan, 78; Clarification and Enlightenment: Essays in Comparative Philosophy, Univ Am, 78; many articles in contemporary philosophy and comparative philosophy in 1980's and 1990's. **CONTACT ADDRESS** Dept of Philos, California State Univ, Sacramento, 6000 J St, Sacramento, CA, 95819-6033.

WU, JULIE L.
PERSONAL Born 08/20/1949, Hong Kong, m, 1983 **DISCIPLINE** NEW TESTAMENT **EDUCATION** Fuller Theol Sem, PhD, 92. **CAREER** Assoc Prof of New Testament, Dir of Masters Degree Prog, 93-, Logos Evangelical Sem. **MEMBERSHIPS** Soc of Biblical Lit. **RESEARCH** Pauline Lit and Theol. **SELECTED PUBLICATIONS** Auth, Liturgical Elements, in: Dictionary of Paul and his Letters, IVP, 93; Hymns, Liturgical Elements, Mary in: Dictionary of the Later New Testament and Its Development, IVP, 97. **CONTACT ADDRESS** 9358 Telstar Ave, El Monte, CA, 91731. **EMAIL** jleewu@yahoo.com

WU, KUANG-MING
PERSONAL Born 07/24/1933, Tainan, China, m, 1961, 4 children **DISCIPLINE** PHILOSOPHY, RELIGION **EDUCATION** Yale Univ, BD, 62, STM, 63, PhD(philos), 65. **CAREER** Instr philos, Yale Univ, 65-68; asst prof, 68-71, assoc prof, 71-80, PROF PHILOS, UNIV WIS-OSHKOSH, 80-, Vis prof philos, Univ Tex, El Paso, 81-82. **MEMBERSHIPS** Int Soc Chinese Philos. **RESEARCH** Oriental studies; existentialism and phenomenology. **SELECTED PUBLICATIONS** Auth, 2 Visions of the Way--A Study of the Wang-Pi Commentary and the Ho-Shang-Kung Commentary on the Lao Tzu, Philos E and W, Vol 0043, 93; The Tao of the Tao Te Ching--A Translation and Commentary, Philos E and W, Vol 0043, 93; Tao Te Ching, The Classic Book of Integrity and the Way--A

New Translation Based on the Recently Discovered Ma-Wang-Tui Manuscripts, Philos E and W, Vol 0043, 93. **CONTACT ADDRESS** Dept of Philos, Univ of Wis, Oshkosh, WI, 54901.

WUBNIG, JUDY
PERSONAL Brooklyn, NY **DISCIPLINE** PHILOSOPHY **EDUCATION** Swathmore Col, BA, 55; Yale Univ, MA, 58, PhD, 63. **CAREER** Instr, hum, Col Basic Studs, Boston Univ, 60-62; instr, dept philos, Tufts Univ, 62-63; lectr, Univ Col, Northern Univ, 63-66; ASST PROF PHILOSOPHY, UNIV WATERLOO, 65-. **MEMBERSHIPS** Nat Asn Scholars; Am Philos Asn; Can Asn Univ Tchrs; Kant Ges; Metaphysical Soc N Am; Univ Ctrs Rational Alternatives. **SELECTED PUBLICATIONS** Auth, The Merit Criterion of Employment: An Examination of some Current Arguments Against Its Use, 76; auth, What Happened to Merit?, in Kitchener-Waterloo Record, 85; auth, The Rule of Ignorance in the United States and Canada, in Measure, 91. **CONTACT ADDRESS** Dept of Philosophy, Univ Waterloo, Waterloo, ON, N2L 3G1. **EMAIL** jwubnig@uwaterloo.ca

WURZBURGER, WALTER S.
PERSONAL Born 03/09/1920, Munich, Germany, m, 1947, 3 children **DISCIPLINE** PHILOSOPHY **EDUCATION** Yeshiva Col, BA, 43; Harvard Univ, MA, 46, PhD, 51. **CAREER** Adjunct prof, Yeshiva Univ, 67-. **MEMBERSHIPS** Am Philol Asn; Am Acad of Relig. **RESEARCH** Ethics; Philosophy of religion. **SELECTED PUBLICATIONS** Auth, Ethics of Responsibility, 94. **CONTACT ADDRESS** 138 Hards Ln, Lawrence, NY, 11559. **EMAIL** WURZBUR@ymail.yu.edu

WYDRZYNSKI, CHRISTOPHER J.
DISCIPLINE CONSTITUTIONAL; JUDICIAL REVIEW; ADMINISTRATIVE LAW; CONSTITUTIONAL LITIGATION AND IMMIGRATION LAW **EDUCATION** Univ Windsor, BA, LLB; Osgoode, LLM. **CAREER** Prof; Osgoode Hall, Barrister-at-Law; res dir, Legal Prof Res Prog. **SELECTED PUBLICATIONS** Auth, Immigration Law & Procedure. **CONTACT ADDRESS** Col of Business Administration, Education and Law, Univ of Windsor, 401 Sunset Ave, Windsor, ON, N9B 3P4. **EMAIL** cwydrzy@uwindsor.ca

WYLIE, ALISON
PERSONAL Swindon, England **DISCIPLINE** PHILOSOPHY **EDUCATION** Mt Allison Univ, BA, 76; State Univ NY, Binghamton, MA, 78, PhD, 82. **CAREER** Vis postdoc fel, Calgary Inst Hum, 81-82; Mellon postdoc fel & instr, dept phil, Washington Univ, St. Louis, 83-84; instr, Univ Calgary, 84-85; asst prof, 85-89, fac arts res prof, 87-88, assoc prof, 89-93, PROF PHILOSOPHY, UNIV WESTERN ONT, 93-. **MEMBERSHIPS** Ctr Archaeol Public Interest; Am Philos Asn; Philos Sci Asn; Can Soc Hist Philos Sci; Can Soc Women Philos; Can Philos Asn. **SELECTED PUBLICATIONS** Auth, The Disunity of Science, 96; co-ed, Ethics in American Archaeology: Challenge for the 1990s, 95; co-ed, Equity Issues for Women in Archaeology, 94; co-ed, Critical Traditions in Contemporary Archaeology: Essays in the Philosophy, History and Socio-Politics of Archaeology, 89. **CONTACT ADDRESS** Dept of Philosophy, Univ Western Ont, London, ON, N6A 3K7. **EMAIL** awyllie@julian.uwo.ca

WYMA, KEITH D.
PERSONAL Born 09/24/1967, Beaver Falls, PA, m, 1991 **DISCIPLINE** PHILOSOPHY **EDUCATION** Calvin Col, BA, 90; Notre Dame, MA, 94, PhD, 97. **CAREER** Adj asst prof, 97-98, Notre Dame; adj instr, 97-98, Indiana Univ; asst prof, 98-, Whitworth Col. **RESEARCH** Moral responsibility, weakness of will, moral rational, justification. **CONTACT ADDRESS** Religion/Philosophy Dept, Whitworth Col, 300 W Hawthorne, Spokane, WA, 99251. **EMAIL** kwyma@whitworth.edu

WYRE, STANLEY MARCEL
PERSONAL Born 03/31/1953, Detroit, MI, m, 1988 **DISCIPLINE** LAW **EDUCATION** Lawrence Institute of Technology, BS, 1976; Detroit College of Law, JD, 1984. **CAREER** Walbridge Aldinger Co, project estimator, 1976-78; Palmer Smith Co., senior construction estimator/director, 1979-83; Charfoos, Christensen & Archer PC, attorney-at-law, 1984; Barton-Malow Co, construction manager, 1984-87; professional photographer; Detroit College of Law, adjunct professor, 1985-; Lawrence Institute of Technology, assistant professor, 1985-; Detroit Public Schools, assistant superintendent, 1992-. **MEMBERSHIPS** American Arbitrator Association, arbitrator. **CONTACT ADDRESS** Assistant Superintendent, Physical Plant, Detroit Public Schools, 5057 Woodward Ave, School Center Bldg, Ste 520, Detroit, MI, 48202.

WYRICK, STEPHEN V.
PERSONAL Born 03/01/1952, Dallas, TX, m, 1974, 2 children **DISCIPLINE** RELIGION **EDUCATION** SW Theol Sem, PhD, 91, Mdiv, 76; Dallas Bapt Univ, BA, 73 **CAREER** Prof, 94-, Univ of Mary Hardin-Baylor; Prof, 86-94, CA Bapt Col **HONORS AND AWARDS** Sr Res Fel **MEMBERSHIPS** Am Asn of Univ Prof **RESEARCH** Bibl Archaeol **CONTACT ADDRESS** Belton, TX, 76513.

WYSCHOGROD, MICHAEL
PERSONAL Born 09/28/1928, Berlin, Germany, m, 1955, 2 children **DISCIPLINE** PHILOSOPHY **EDUCATION** City Col New York, BSS, 49; Columbia Univ, PhD, 53. **CAREER** Asst prof philos, City Col New York, 56-63, from asst prof to assoc prof, 63-68; assoc prof, 68-71, prof Philos, Baruch Col, 71, chmn dept, 76-92; PROF RELIGIOUS STUDIES, UNIV HOUSTON, 92-; Ed, Tradition, 60-; vis lectr, Jewish Theol Sem, NY, 67-68; vis assoc prof, Dropsie Univ, 68-70; vis prof, Heidelberg Col, 80. **MEMBERSHIPS** Asn Jewish Studies; Am Philos Asn. **RESEARCH** Philosophical psychology; philosophy of religion; Jewish thought. **SELECTED PUBLICATIONS** Auth, Kierkegaard and Heidegger--the Ontology of Existence; Faith and the Holocaust, Judaism, summer 71; The Law, Jews and Gentiles--a Jewish Perspective, Lutheran Quart, Vol 21, No 4; coauth (with David Berger), Jews and Jewish Christianity, 78; The Body of Faith: God and the People Israel. **CONTACT ADDRESS** Religious Studies, Univ of Houston, Houston, TX, 77204-3784.

Y

YADAV, BIBHUTI S
PERSONAL Born 07/10/1943, Ghazipur Uttar Pradesh, India **DISCIPLINE** INDIAN PHILOSOPHY AND RELIGION **EDUCATION** Benaras Hindu Univ, BA, 62, MA, 64, PhD(philos, Buddhism & Vedanta), 70. **CAREER** Asst prof, 72-80, ASSOC PROF INDIAN PHILOS & RELIG, TEMPLE UNIV, 80- **MEMBERSHIPS** Asn Asian Studies. **RESEARCH** Buddhism and Vedanta; Bhartrhar and Indian philosophy of language; Kashmir saivism. **SELECTED PUBLICATIONS** Auth, Between Vasubandhu and Kumarila, Jour Dharma, Vol 0020, 95; Vallabha Positive Response to Buddhism, Jour Dharma, Vol 0019, 94. **CONTACT ADDRESS** Dept of Relig, Temple Univ, 1114 W Berks St, Philadelphia, PA, 19122-6029.

YAFFE, MARTIN DAVID
PERSONAL Born 02/19/1942, Hamilton, ON, Canada, m, 1963, 2 children **DISCIPLINE** PHILOSOPHY **EDUCATION** Univ Toronto, BA, 63; Claremont Grad Sch, PhD(philos), 68 **CAREER** PROF PHILOS, N TEX STATE UNIV, 68-, Lectr philos, Tel-Aviv Univ, 71-72; vis prof relig studies, Southern Methodist Univ, 78-. **HONORS AND AWARDS** Nat Endowment for Humanities transl grant, 81-82; Bradley fel, 91. **MEMBERSHIPS** Acad Jewish Philos; Am Acad Relig; Am Polit Sci Asn; Nat Asn Scholars; North Am Spinoza Soc **RESEARCH** Classical political philosophy; Jewish philosophy. **SELECTED PUBLICATIONS** Auth, Saint Thomas Aquinas, The Literal Expostion on the Book of Job: A Scriptural Commentary Concerning Providence; Scholars Press, 88; On Leo Strauss's Philosophy and Law: A Review Essay, Modern Judaism, 89; Autonomy, Community, Authority: Hermann Cohen, Carl Schmitt, Leo Strauss, In: Autonomy and Community, SUNY Press, 91; Leo Strauss as Judaic Thinker: Some First Notions, Relig Studies Rev, 1/91; One-Sided Platonism: Hermann Cohen on the Social Ideal in Plato and the Prophets, Il cannocchiale, 91; The Case Against the Great books--And Its Refutation, In: The Core and the Canon: A National Debate, Univ North Tex Press, 93; Two Recent Treatments of Spinoza's Theologico-Politico Treatise: A Review Essay, Modern Judaism, 93; Biblical Religion and Liberal Democracy: Comments on Spinoza's Theologico-Political Treatise and Sack's Commentary on the Book of Genesis, Polit Sci Rev, 94; On Beginning to Translate Spinoza's Tractatus Theologico-Politicus, Il cannocchiale, Rome, 94; The Histories and Successes of the Hebrews: The Demise of the Biblical Polity in Spinoza's Theologico-Political Treatise, Jewish Polit Studies Rev, 95; An Unsung Appreciation of the Musical-Erotic in Mozart's Don Giovanni: Hermann Cohen's Nod Toward Kierkegaard's Either/Or, In: International Kierkegaard Commentary on Either/Or I, Mercer Univ Press, 95; Spinoza's Theologico-Political Treatise--A First Inside Look, In: Piety and Humanity: Essays on Religion and Early Modern Political Philosophy, Rowman & Littlefield, 97; Shylock and the Jewish Question, Johns Hopkins Univ Press, 97. **CONTACT ADDRESS** Dept of Philos, Univ North Tex, PO Box 310920, Denton, TX, 76203-0920. **EMAIL** yaffe@unt.edu

YAGISAWA, TAKASHI
PERSONAL Born 12/11-1953, Nagano, Japan, m, 1987 **DISCIPLINE** PHILOSOPHY **EDUCATION** Princeton Univ, PhD, 81; Univ London, BA, 77. **CAREER** Asst Prof, Assoc Prof, Prof, 87 to 94-, Cal State Univ Northridge; vis Asst Prof, 86-87, Univ NC Chapel Hill; vis Prof, 85-86, NYU; vis Prof, 84-85, Univ Minn. **MEMBERSHIPS** APA **RESEARCH** Philosophy of Language; Metaphysics; Philosophy of Mind. **SELECTED PUBLICATIONS** Auth, five entries: Essentialism, Saul Kripke, Modal Logic, Montague Grammar, Naming and Necessity, in: Iwanamii Dictionary of Philosophy, K Mishima, ed et al, in Japanese, Tokyo, Iwanami Shoten, 97; Knocked Out Senseless: Naturalism and Analyticity, The Maribor Papers: Essays on Semantic Naturalism, Dunja Jutric, ed, Maribor Slovenia, Univ Maribor Press, 97; Reference Ex Machina, Karlovy Vary Studies in Reference and Meaning, J Hill, P Kotatko, eds, Prague, Filosophia Pub, 905; five entries: Definiendum, Definition, Intensionalisty, Logical Syntax, Rational Reconstruction, in: Cambridge Dictionary of Philosophy, Robert Audi, ed, Cambridge, Cambridge Univ Press, 95; Thinking in Neurons: Comments on Schiffer, Philo Stud, 94; Logic Purified Nous 27, 93. **CONTACT ADDRESS** Philosophy Dept, California State Univ, Northridge, Northridge, CA, 91330-8253. **EMAIL** takashi.yagisawa@csun.edu

YALDEN, ROBERT
DISCIPLINE LAW **EDUCATION** Queen's Univ, BA, 84; Oxon Univ, MA, 86; Univ Toronto, LLM, 88. **CAREER** Law clerk, Madame Justice Wilson, Supreme Court Can, 89-90. **RESEARCH** Corporate and securities law. **SELECTED PUBLICATIONS** Auth, pubs on issues in corporate, administrative and constitutional law; co-auth, Corporations: Principles and Policies. **CONTACT ADDRESS** Fac of Law, Univ Toronto, 78 Queen's Park, Toronto, ON.

YALOWITZ, STEVEN
DISCIPLINE PHILOSOPHY **EDUCATION** Columbia Univ,PhD, 91. **CAREER** PROF, PHILOS, UNIV CALIF, SAN DIEGO. **RESEARCH** Intersection of semantics and psychology. **SELECTED PUBLICATIONS** Auth, Rationality and the Argument for Anomalous Monism, Philos Stud. **CONTACT ADDRESS** Dept of Philos, Univ Calif, San Diego, 9500 Gilman Dr, La Jolla, CA, 92093.

YAMASHITA, TADANORI
PERSONAL Born 12/23/1929, Tokyo, Japan, m, 1954 **DISCIPLINE** RELIGION **EDUCATION** Yale Univ, BD, 59, PhD(-Near East lang & lit), 64. **CAREER** From instr to asst prof, 63-73, assoc prof, 73-80, prof relig, Mt Holyoke Col, 80-. **MEMBERSHIPS** Am Orient Soc; Asn Asian Studies; Soc Bibl Lit. **RESEARCH** Mythology of ancient Near East; myths and legends in Mahayana Buddhist Scriptures. **CONTACT ADDRESS** Dept Relig, Mount Holyoke Col, 50 College St, South Hadley, MA, 01075-1461. **EMAIL** tyamashi@mtholyoke.edu

YANAL, ROBERT JOHN
PERSONAL Born 02/03/1948, Shenandoah, PA **DISCIPLINE** PHILOSOPHY **EDUCATION** Univ Pittsburgh, BA, 69; Univ Ill, Chicago Circle, MA, 70, PhD(philos), 75. **CAREER** From Asst Prof to Assoc Prof, 74-90, Prof Philos, Wayne State Univ, 90-. **MEMBERSHIPS** Am Philos Asn; Am Soc Aesthet. **RESEARCH** Philosophy of art; philosophy of law; ethics. **SELECTED PUBLICATIONS** Auth, Denotation and the aesthetic appreciation of literature, J Aesthet & Art Criticism, 78; Words and music, J Philos, 81; Aristotle's definition of poetry, Nous, 82; Hart, Dworkin, judges, and new law, Monist, 85; The unimportance of being worthless, Am Philos Quart, 86; Self-esteem, Nous, 87; Hume and others on the paradox of tragedy, J Aesthet & Art Criticism, 91; The paradox of emotion and fiction, Pacific Philos Quart, 94; The Danto-Wollheim meaning theory of art, Ratio, 96; The paradox of suspense, British J Aesthet, 96; Paradoxes of Emotion and Fiction, Penn State Press, 98. **CONTACT ADDRESS** Dept of Philos, Wayne State Univ, 51 West Warren, Detroit, MI, 48202-3919. **EMAIL** Robert.Yanal@wayne.edu

YANDELL, K. DAVID
DISCIPLINE PHILOSOPHY **EDUCATION** Univ Wis, Madison, PhD. **CAREER** Asst prof & asst chp, dept Philos at Loyola Univ Chicago, 93-. **RESEARCH** Early modern philosophy, especially Descartes; metaphysics; social and political philosophy. **SELECTED PUBLICATIONS** Articles in, Hist Philos Quart & Brit J Hist Philos. **CONTACT ADDRESS** Dept of Philosophy, Loyola Univ, Chicago, 820 N. Michigan Ave., Chicago, IL, 60611.

YANDELL, KEITH E.
PERSONAL Born 07/16/1938, Davenport, IA, m, 1959, 4 children **DISCIPLINE** PHILOSOPHY **EDUCATION** Wayne State Univ, BA & MA, 60; Ohio State Univ, PhD(philos), 66. **CAREER** Instr philos, Ohio State Univ, 65-66; from asst prof to prof, Univ Wis-Madison, 66-77, PROF SOUTH ASIAN STUDIES, 78-80. Nat Endowment for Humanities younger humanist grant, 72-73. **MEMBERSHIPS** Am Philos Asn; Hume Soc. **RESEARCH** Philosophy of religion; history of philosophy; metaphysics. **SELECTED PUBLICATIONS** Auth, Hell--The Logic of Damnation, Rel Stud, Vol 0031, 95; The Most Brutal and Inexcusable Error in Counting--Trinity and Consistency, Rel Stud, Vol 0030, 94; Tragedy and Evil, Intl Jour Philos Rel, Vol 0036, 94; The Concept of Faith--A Philosophical Investigation, Intl Jour Philos Rel, Vol 0041, 97. **CONTACT ADDRESS** Univ Wis, 414 S Segoe Rd, Madison, WI, 53711.

YANG, XIAOSI
PERSONAL Born 03/31/1953, Shuzhou, China, m, 2 children **DISCIPLINE** PHILOSOPHY **EDUCATION** Johns Hopkins Univ, PhD, 98. **CAREER** Instr, Univ of Chicago, 98- . **MEMBERSHIPS** APA. **RESEARCH** Philosophy of family; epistemology. **CONTACT ADDRESS** 5547 S Dorchester, Apt 2, Chicago, IL, 60637.

YAQUB, ALADDIN M.
DISCIPLINE LOGIC **EDUCATION** Univ Baghdad, BS, 78; Univ Wis, MA, 88, 90, PhD, 91. **CAREER** Asst prof, Univ NMex. **SELECTED PUBLICATIONS** Auth, The Liar Speaks the Truth: A Defense of the Revision Theory of Truth, Oxford, 93. **CONTACT ADDRESS** Univ NMex, Albuquerque, NM, 87131.

YARBROUGH, MARILYN VIRGINIA
PERSONAL Born 08/31/1945, Bowling Green, KY, m, 1987 **DISCIPLINE** LAW **EDUCATION** Virginia State Univ, BA 1966; UCLA, JD 1973. **CAREER** IBM, systms eng 1966-68; Westinghouse, systms eng 1969-70; Catonsville Community College, instr data proc 1970; Boston College Law School, teaching fellow 1975-76; Duke Law School, visting prof 1983-84; Univ of Kansas, law prof, 1976-87 & assoc vice chancellor 1983-87; Univ of Tennessee-Knoxville, law dean 1987-91; University of North Carolina Law School, professor of law, 1992-. **HONORS AND AWARDS** Kansas Univ Women's Hall of Fame; Doctor of Laws, Univ of Puget Sound School of Law 1989; Frank D Reeves Award, Natl Conference of Black Lawyers 1988; Society of American Law Teachers Award, 1991; YWCA Tribute to Women Award for Education, 1989; Distinguished Alumni Award, Virginia State University, 1988; ABA, Women Lawyers of Achievement Award, 1991. **MEMBERSHIPS** Pres bd cmt wrk Law Sch Admsn Cncl 1976-89; bd mem Accrediting Cncl Ed Journalism Mass Communications 1976-83; chmn KS Crime Victims Reparations Bd, 1980-83; Lawrence Housing Auth 1984-86; council member Am Bar Assc Sect Legal Ed Admsn to the Bar 1984-85; pres United Way of Lawrence, KS, 1985; KS Commission on Civil Rights, 1986-; NCAA Conf on Infractions, 1986-88, chairman, 1986-87; Rotary International, 1988-90; Pulitzer Prize board, 1990-; Poynter Institute for Media Studies, board of directors, 1990-92; First American Bank of Knoxville, board of directors, 1987-; United Way of Knoxville, board of directors, 1990-91. **CONTACT ADDRESS** Law Sch, Univ of No Carolina, Chapel Hill, NC, 27599.

YARBROUGH, O. LARRY
DISCIPLINE BIBLICAL STUDIES (BOTH JEWISH AND CHRISTIAN SCRIPTURES), THE ORIGINS OF CHR **EDUCATION** Birmingham-Southern Col, AB; Cambridge Univ, MA; Emory Univ, MDiv; Yale Univ, PhD. **CAREER** Prof; Middlebury Col, 83-. **SELECTED PUBLICATIONS** Auth, Not Like the Gentiles: Marriage Rules in the Letters of Paul; co-ed, The Social World of the Earliest Christians. **CONTACT ADDRESS** Dept of Religion, Middlebury Col, Middlebury, VT, 05753.

YARTZ, FRANK J.
DISCIPLINE PHILOSOPHY **EDUCATION** St Louis Univ, MA, PhD. **CAREER** Assoc prof. **RESEARCH** Ancient philosophy; presocratics, Plato, Aristotle; medieval philosophy, especially Aquinas; early modern philosophy. **SELECTED PUBLICATIONS** Auth, Ancient Greek Philosophy, 84 & Modern Philosophy, 95; articles in, Mediaeval Stud. **CONTACT ADDRESS** Dept of Philosophy, Loyola Univ, Chicago, 820 N. Michigan Ave., Chicago, IL, 60611.

YATES, JENNY
PERSONAL Born 10/19/1943, Greenville, SC **DISCIPLINE** PHILOSOPHY **EDUCATION** Furman Univ, BA, 65; Yale Div School, MAR, 67; Syracuse Univ, PhD, 73; C. G. Jung Inst, PG Dipl, 92. **CAREER** Calif tchr, vis assoc prof, 84; Yale Univ, res fel, 96-97; Wells Col, asst prof, assoc prof, prof, chemn, 75-. **HONORS AND AWARDS** Wells Col, Tchg excellence Award. **MEMBERSHIPS** AAR, APA, Intl. AAP, IRSJA. **RESEARCH** Archetypical Psychology and the Female Self. **SELECTED PUBLICATIONS** Auth, forthcoming, Encountering Jung on Death and Immortality, Princeton Univ Press, 99; coauth, The Near Death Experience, Routledge Press, 96; auth, Psyche and the Split-Brain, Univ Press of Am, 94. **CONTACT ADDRESS** Dept of Religion and Philosophy, Wells Col, Aurora, NY, 13026. **EMAIL** jyates@wells.edu

YATES, WILSON
PERSONAL Born 03/09/1937, Matthews, MO, m, 1961, 2 children **DISCIPLINE** SOCIAL ETHICS, RELIGION **EDUCATION** Southeast Mo State Univ, AB, 60; Vanderbilt Divinity Sch MDiv, 62; Harvard Univ, PhD(relig & sociol), 68. **CAREER** Asst prof, 67-70, assoc prof, 71-78, prof church & soc, United Theol Sem Twin Cities, 77-; prof rel, soc, & arts, 88; Dean of Sem, 88; Pres of Sem, 96. **MEMBERSHIPS** Soc Christian Ethics; Soc Sci Studies Relig; Europ Cult Soc; Soc Relig Higher Educ. **RESEARCH** Social ethics and the social sciences; ethics and the family; religion and art. **SELECTED PUBLICATIONS** Art, The Future of the Arts in Theological Education, British Journal of Theological Education, Winter 91-92; contributing ed, Theological Education, Sacred Imagination: The Arts and Theological Education, ATS Vol XXXI, No 1, Autumn, 94; co-ed, Theological Reflection on the Grotesque in Art and Literature, Eerdmans Publishing Co, 97. **CONTACT ADDRESS** United Theol Sem of the Twin Cities, 3000 5th St NW, New Brighton, MN, 55112-2598.

YEE, GALE A.
PERSONAL Born 04/09/1949, OH, s **DISCIPLINE** HEBREW BIBLE; OLD TESTAMENT **EDUCATION** Univ St Michael's Col, PhD, 85. **CAREER** Prof, Univ St Thomas, 84-98; interim dir, Feminist Liberation Theol Prog, Episcopal Divinity School, 98-; **HONORS AND AWARDS** Aquinas Found Fel; Cath Bibl Asn Your Scholars Fel. **MEMBERSHIPS** Cath Bibl Asn; Soc Bibl Lit; Ethnic Chinese Bibl Conoquiun **RESEARCH** Hebrew Bible; Feminist Theory; Literary Theory. **SELECTED PUBLICATIONS** Auth, Composition & Tradition in the Book of Moses; Judges and Method; Jewish Feasts and the Gospel of John; Moses, New Interpreters Bible. **CONTACT ADDRESS** Episcopal Divinity Sch, 99 Brattle St, Cambridge, MA, 02138. **EMAIL** gyee@episdivschool.org

YEGGE, ROBERT BERNARD
PERSONAL Born 06/17/1934, Denver, CO **DISCIPLINE** LAW **EDUCATION** Princeton Univ, AB, 56; Univ Denver, MA, 58, JD, 59. **CAREER** Instr law, 59-63, adj assoc prof, 63-65, actg dean col, 65, dean col, 66-77, PROF LAW, COL LAW, UNIV DENVER, 66, EMER DEAN COL, 77-, Assoc, Yegge, Hall & Evans, Attorneys-at-Law, 59-62, partner, 62-78; chmn adv comt, dept sociol, Princeton Univ, 62-69; chmn, Colo Coun Migrant & Seasonal Agr Workers & Families, 65-70; chmn, Colo Coun Arts St Humanities, 68-79; asst to pres, Denver Post, 71-73, managing trustee, Denver Ctr Performing Arts, 72-76; chmn law, sci & techol comt, Nat Sci Found, 77-; partner, Nelson & Harding, 78-; dean & prof law, Univ San Francisco, 80. **HONORS AND AWARDS** Educ Award, Latin Am Educ Found, 76. **MEMBERSHIPS** Law & Soc Asn (pres, 65-70); Am Bar Asn; Am Sociol Asn; Am Acad Polit & Soc Sci; Am Law Inst. **RESEARCH** Relationships of law to society; legal change; legal relationships within the university. **SELECTED PUBLICATIONS** Auth, Divorce Litigants Without Lawyers, Family Law Quart, Vol 0028, 94. **CONTACT ADDRESS** Col of Law, Univ of Denver, Denver, CO, 80204.

YEO, KHIOK-KHNG
PERSONAL Born 06/01/1960, Malaysia, m, 1984, 3 children **DISCIPLINE** RELIGION **EDUCATION** St. Paul Bibl Col, BA, 87; Garrett-Evangel Theol Sem, MDiv, 90; Northwestern Univ, PhD, 92. **CAREER** Prof, Alliance Sem, Hong Kong, 93-96; prof New Testament Interpretation, Garrett-Evangel Sem, 96-. **HONORS AND AWARDS** Alliance Ward Fel, 96-97; Dempster Fel, 90-92; John Wesley Fel, 90-92. **MEMBERSHIPS** Am Acad Relig; Soc Bibl Lit; Cath Bibl Lit. **RESEARCH** New Testament; Hermeneutics; cross-cultural studies. **SELECTED PUBLICATIONS** Auth, Rhetorical Interaction in 1 Corinthians 8 and 10: A Formal Analysis with Implications for a Cross-Cultural, Chinese Hermeneutic, 95; auth, Cross-Cultural Rhetorical Hermeneutics, 95; auth, Truth and Life, 95; auth, Lucan Wisdom: A Literary and Theological Reading of Luke, 95; auth, Between Female and Male: Feminist Theology and Hermeneutic, 95; auth, Ancestor Worship: Rhetorical and Cross-Cultural Hermeneutical Response, 96; auth, Spirituality, 96; auth, What Has Jerusalem to Do with Beijing? Biblical Interpretation from a Chinese Perspective, 98; auth, A Rhetorical Study of Acts 17:22-31: What Has Jerusalem to Do with Athens and Beijing?, Jian Dao: Jour Bibl Theol, 94; auth, Revelation 5 in the Light of Pannenberg's Christology: Christ the End of History and the Hope of the Suffering, Asian Jour Theol, Oct, 94; auth, Isiah 5:1-7 and 27:2-6: Let's Hear the Whole Song of Rejection and Restoration, Jian Dao: Jour Bibl Theol, 95; auth, The Yin and Yang of God (Exodus 3:14) and Humanity (Genesis 1:27), Zeitschrift fur Religions und Geistesgeschichte, 94; auth, The Rhetorical Hermeneutic of 1 Corinthians 8 and Chinese Ancestor Worship, Bibl Interpretation, 94; auth, A Relational Theology of Worship: Wholeness from Creation of God to Recreation in Christ, Asia Jour Theol, 95; auth, A Confucian Reading of Romans 7:14-25: Nomos (Law) and Li (Propriety), Jian Dao: Jour Bibl Theol, 96; auth, The Christocentricness of Multi-Cultural Hermeneutics, Jian Dao: Jour Bibl Theol, 96. **CONTACT ADDRESS** Dept of New Testament Interp, Garrett-Evangelical Theol Sem, 2121 Sheridan Rd., Evanston, IL, 60201. **EMAIL** kkyeo@nwu.edu

YEZZI, RONALD D.
PERSONAL Born 04/26/1938, Erie, PA, m, 1960, 2 children **DISCIPLINE** PHILOSOPHY **EDUCATION** Univ Chicago, SB, 60; S Ill Univ, MA, 63, PhD, 68. **CAREER** Instr to asst prof Philos, Univ Tenn, 65-69; asst prof, 69-71, assoc prof, 71-79, prof Philosophy, 79-, Mankato State Univ. **MEMBERSHIPS** Am Philos Asn; Minn Philos Soc. **RESEARCH** Social and political philosophy; Business ethics; Medical ethics; Ethics; Philosophy of science. **SELECTED PUBLICATIONS** Auth Practical Ethics, G Bruno & Co, 93; Philosophical Problems: God, Free Will, and Determinism, G Bruno & Co, 93; Philosophical Problems: The Good Life, G Bruno & Co, 94; PhilosophyFirst Business Ethics: An Internet Course, 98. **CONTACT ADDRESS** 201 Chancery Ln, Mankato, MN, 56001. **EMAIL** yezzi@mankato.msus.edu

YIANNOPOULOS, A.N.
PERSONAL Born 03/13/1928, Thessaloniki, Greece, m, 1967, 2 children **DISCIPLINE** LAW **EDUCATION** Univ Thessaloniki, LLB, 50; Univ Chicago, MCL, 54; Univ Calif, Berkeley, LLM, 55, JSD, 56; Univ Cologne, JD, 61. **CAREER** Prof law, La State Univ, Baton Rouge, 58-79; W R IRBY PROF LAW, TULANE UNIV, NEW ORLEANS, 79-, Reporter, La State Law Inst, 62- **RESEARCH** Civil law; comparative law; admirality. **SELECTED PUBLICATIONS** Auth, Civil Liability for Abuse of Right--Something Old, Something New, La Law Rev, Vol 0054, 94. **CONTACT ADDRESS** Tulane Univ, 662 Sunset Blvd, Baton Rouge, LA, 70808.

YIZAR, MARVIN
PERSONAL Born 09/06/1950, Atlanta, GA, d, 4 children **DISCIPLINE** CRIMINAL JUSTICE AND PHILOSOPHY **EDUCATION** GA State Univ, BS, 77; CA State Univ, MA, 91; Univ SAfrica, PhD, 98. **CAREER** Res consul & tchr, 72-80, Fulton County; City of Atlanta, 80-88; State Of Ga, 88-98. **HONORS AND AWARDS** Who's Who in Am; Key to City of Atlanta; Lt Colonel GA Natl Guard. **MEMBERSHIPS** APA; Ancient and Accepted Free Masons Scottish Rite. **RESEARCH** Artificial intelligence; logic programming; metaphysics; philos of mind; epistemology; phenomenology; theory of knowledge. **SELECTED PUBLICATIONS** Auth, What Black Muslims Under Farakhan Believe, 96; auth, Goedel's Incompleteness versus the Skolem-Lowenheim Theory, 97; auth, An Analysis of the Religious Philosophy of Free Masonry, 98. **CONTACT ADDRESS** HCO1-EF302048, Reidsville, GA, 30453-9802.

YOCUM, GLENN E.
PERSONAL Born 07/14/1943, Hershey, PA, m, 1979, 3 children **DISCIPLINE** RELIGIOUS STUDIES **EDUCATION** Franklin & Marshall Col, BA, 65; Univ Oxford, DTh, 67; Union Theol Sem, MDiv, 69; Univ Penn, PhD, 76. **CAREER** C milo connick prof, religious studies, Whittier Col, 83-; ed. jour of amer acad relig, 94-. **HONORS AND AWARDS** Phi Beta Kappa; Amer Inst Indian Studies sr res fel, 81-82 & 89-90; Fulbright-Hays res fel, 89-90. **MEMBERSHIPS** Amer Acad Relig; Amer Oriental Soc; Asn Asian Studies; Mid E Studies Asn. **RESEARCH** Religion in South India; Religion in Turkey. **SELECTED PUBLICATIONS** Auth, The Ripening of Tamil Bhakti, Jour of Am Acad Relig, 94; Burning Widows, Sacred Prostitutes, and Perfect Wives: Recent Studies of Hindu Women, Relig Studies Rev, 94; Islam and Gender in Turkey, Relig Studies Rev, 95; auth,Techniques for Teaching the Advanced Religious Studies Course on Islam, CCHA Rev, 97. **CONTACT ADDRESS** Dept of Religious Studies, Whittier Col, Whittier, CA, 90608. **EMAIL** gyocum@whittier.edu

YOCUM, SANDRA MIZE
DISCIPLINE RELIGIOUS STUDIES **EDUCATION** Marquette Univ, PhD. **CAREER** Asst prof; dir, Grad Stud, Univ Dayton. **RESEARCH** American catholicism. **SELECTED PUBLICATIONS** Pubs, co-ed, American Catholic Traditions: Resources for Renewal, 97. **CONTACT ADDRESS** Dept of Religious Studies, Univ of Dayton, 300 College Park, 347 Humanities, Dayton, OH, 45469-1679. **EMAIL** mize@checkov.hm.udayton.edu

YODER, JOHN C.
PERSONAL Born 02/12/1942, Iowa City, IA, m, 1966, 2 children **DISCIPLINE** THEOLOGY **EDUCATION** Goshen Col, BA, 64; Mennonite Biblical Sem, MDiv, 70; Northwestern Univ, PhD. **CAREER** Prof, polit sci, 77-80, North Park Col; prof, hist of polit, 80-, Whitworth Col. **RESEARCH** Liberian civil values **CONTACT ADDRESS** Dept of History & Politics, Whitworth Col, Spokane, WA, 99251. **EMAIL** johnyoder@whitworth.edu

YOLTON, JOHN W.
PERSONAL Born 11/10/1921, Birmingham, AL, m, 1945, 2 children **DISCIPLINE** PHILOSOPHY **EDUCATION** McMaster Univ, D Litt, 76; York Univ, LLD, 74; Oxford Univ, Dphil, 52; Univ Cincinnati, BA, 45. MA, 46. **CAREER** Prof Emeritus, Rutgers Univ, 92; John Locke Prof of History of Philos, Rutgers Univ, 89-92; prof Philos, Rutgers Univ, 78-92; chair Philos Dept, Rutgers Univ, 87-88; Dean Rutgers Col, Rutgers Univ, 78-85; prof Philos, York Univ, 63-78; chair Philos Dept, York Univ, 63-73; prof Philos, Univ Maryland, 61-63. **HONORS AND AWARDS** Fulbright Grantee, Balliol Col, 50-52; Univ Fel, Univ Calif Berkeley, 49-50; Ntl Endowment Humanities Fel, 88-89; dir of seminar, Space and Time, Matter and Mind, Folger Shakespeare Libr, 81; FCS Schiller Essay Prize, Univ Calif Berkeley, 48; AS Eddington Essay First Prize, Institut International des Sciences Theoriques, Brussels, 56. **MEMBERSHIPS** Amer Philos Quart Ed Brd, 64-83; History of Philos Quart Ed Brd, 84-90; Studies in History of Philos & Sci Ed Brd; Jour History of Philos Ed Brd; Philos of Soc Sci Ed Brd; Jour of History of Ideas Ed Brd; Studi Internazionali di Felosofia Ed Brd; Eighteenth Century Studies Ed Brd, 82-85; Brit Jour History of Philos Ed Brd. **SELECTED PUBLICATIONS** Perception and Reality: A History from Descartes to Kant, Cornell Univ Pr, 96; A Locke Dictionary, Blackwell, 93; The Blackwell Companion to the Enlightenment, Blackwell Reference, 92; Ed, Philosophy, Religion and Science in the 17th and 18th Centuries, Univ Rochester Pr, 90. **CONTACT ADDRESS** Dept of Philosophy, Rutgers Univ, 39 Wakefield Ln, Piscataway, NJ, 08854.

YORK, ANTHONY DELANO
PERSONAL Born 08/23/1934, Winston-Salem, NC, m, 1957, 4 children **DISCIPLINE** BIBLICAL LITERATURE, SEMITIC LANGUAGES **EDUCATION** Cornell Univ, PhD(Semitic lang), 73. **CAREER** Fel Hebrew, Oxford Ctr for Post-Grad Hebrew, 73-75; lectr Hebrew, Leeds Univ, 75-78; asst prof, 78-81, ASSOC PROF BIBLE, UNIV CINCINNATI, 81-. **MEMBERSHIPS** Soc Old Testament Study. **RESEARCH** Targum; Book of Job; ancient versions of the bible. **SELECTED PUBLICATIONS** Auth, Approaches to Teaching the Hebrew Bible as Literature in Translation, Jour Amer Oriental Soc, Vol 0116, 96. **CONTACT ADDRESS** Univ Cincinnati, 3343 Sherlock Ave, Cincinnati, OH, 45220.

YOUNG, DAVID
PERSONAL Born 12/29/1960, Nashville, TN, m, 1983, 2 children **DISCIPLINE** RELIGION; NEW TESTAMENT **EDUCATION** Harding Graduate Sch of Relig, MA, 87; Vanderbilt Univ, MA, 91, PhD, 94. **CAREER** Minister, North Boulevard Church of Christ. **MEMBERSHIPS** AAR; SBL. **RESEARCH** New Testament **CONTACT ADDRESS** 1112 N Rutherford Blvd, Murfreesboro, TN, 37130-1372.

YOUNG, ERNEST A.
DISCIPLINE CONSTITUTIONAL LAW **EDUCATION** Dartmouth Col, BA, 90; Harvard Law Sch, JD, 93. **CAREER** Vis asst prof, Villanova Univ; past res asst to, prof Laurence Tribe; clerked, Judge Michael Boudin US Ct Appeals First Circuit & US Supreme Ct Justice David Souter; assoc, Cohan, Simpson, Cowlishaw & Wulff in Dallas, Texas, and Covington & Burling in Wash, DC; adj prof, Georgetown Univ Law Ctr. **HONORS AND AWARDS** Sears prize; best brief award; **RESEARCH** Administrative law, admiralty law, constitutional law, fed courts. **SELECTED PUBLICATIONS** Auth, Rediscovering Conservatism: Burkean Political Theory & Constitutional Interpretation, 72 NC L. Rev 619, 94; The Supreme Court, 1991 Term--Leading Cases, 106 Harv L. Rev 163, 92; Recent Developments: Regulation of Racist Speech: In re: Welfare of RAV, 14 Harv J. Law Pub Pol'y 903, 91. **CONTACT ADDRESS** Law School, Villanova Univ, 800 Lancaster Ave, Villanova, PA, 19085-1692. **EMAIL** young@law.vill.edu

YOUNG, JAMES O.
DISCIPLINE PHILOSOPHY **EDUCATION** Simon Fraser Univ, BA; Univ Waterloo, MA; Univ Boston, PhD. **CAREER** Instr, Univ Calgary; res fel, Melbourne Univ; assoc prof, 85. **RESEARCH** Philosophy of language; epistemology; metaphysics and aesthetics. **SELECTED PUBLICATIONS** Auth, Global Anti-realism, 95; pub(s), Brit Jour of Aesthet; Can Jour of Philos; Erkenntnis; Jour Aesthet and Art Critcism; Metaphilosophy; Philos and Phenomen Res; Synthese. **CONTACT ADDRESS** Dept of Philosophy, Victoria Univ, PO Box 3045, Victoria, BC, V8W 3P4. **EMAIL** joyoung@uvvm.uvic.ca

YOUNG, JOHN TERRY
PERSONAL Born 09/22/1929, Houston, TX, m, 1954, 2 children **DISCIPLINE** THEOLOGY **EDUCATION** Baylor Univ, BA, 51; Southwestern Baptist Theol Sem, BD, 55, ThD, 62. **CAREER** Pastor, First Southern Baptist Church, Chula Vista, Calif, 57-62, Village Baptist Church, San Lorenzo, 62-63; ed, Calif Southern Baptist, 63-71; Prof Theol, New Orleans Baptist Theol Sem, 71-98, Mem, Baptist Joint Comt Pub Affairs, 65-72; Resolutions Count of Southern Baptist Convention, 70 & 72. **MEMBERSHIPS** Am Acad Relig **SELECTED PUBLICATIONS** Auth, The Spirit Within You, 77 & The Church-Alive and Growing, 78, Broadman; A living church in a dying world, Theol Educ, 78; Compelled By The Cross, Broadman, 80. **CONTACT ADDRESS** 14839 N 22nd Ln, Phoenix, AZ, 85023.

YOUNG, KATHERINE K
PERSONAL Washington, DC **DISCIPLINE** HISTORY OF RELIGIONS **EDUCATION** Univ Vt, BA, 66; Univ Chicago, MA, 70; McGill Univ, PhD(hist relig), 78. **CAREER** ASSOC PROF HINDUISM, MCGILL UNIV, 75-. **MEMBERSHIPS** Am Acad Relig; Am Oriental Soc; Am Asian Studies Asn; Int Asn Buddhist Studies. **RESEARCH** Religion in South India, especially Srivaisnavism; pilgrimage in the Hindu tradition; women in the Hindu and Buddhist traditions of India. **SELECTED PUBLICATIONS** Auth, Response to Andersen, Ruth Review of the Annual Review of Women in World Religions, a Philosophy East and West Feature Review, Philos E and W, Vol 0047, 97. **CONTACT ADDRESS** Fac of Relig Studies, McGill Univ, Montreal, PQ, H3A 2A7.

YOUNG, MICHAEL KENT
PERSONAL Born 11/04/1949, Sacramento, CA, m, 1972, 3 children **DISCIPLINE** JAPANESE LAW & LEGAL INSTITUTIONS **EDUCATION** Brigham Young Univ, BA, 73; Harvard Univ, JD, 76. **CAREER** Law clerk, Supreme Judicial Court Mass, 76-77 & Supreme Court US, 77-78; Assoc Prof, Sch Law, Columbia Univ, 78-, Dir, Ctr Japanese Legal Studies, 80-, Vis Scholar, Fac Law, Univ Tokyo, 78-80; Japan Found fel, Fac Law, Univ Tokyo, 79-80. **MEMBERSHIPS** Soc Japanese Am Legal Studies; Asn Asian Studies. **RESEARCH** Japanese administrative practices, especially administrative guidance; Japanese commercial practices, especially related to international commercial transactions; Japanese legal consciousness, especially alternative modes of dispute resolution and use of contractual devices for private ordering of legal affairs. **SELECTED PUBLICATIONS** Auth, Trilateral Perspectives on International Legal Issues: Relavance of Domestic Law & Policy, ed, 96; An Overview of the Fundamentals of US Trade Law and Policy, 98; International Environmental Law with J Charney, T Schoenbaum & P Sands; Michie Publishing, Inc, 98. **CONTACT ADDRESS** Sch of Law, George Washington Univ, 20005 H St, NW, Washington, DC, 20052.

YOUNG, PAMELA DICKEY
PERSONAL Born 12/16/1955, NS, Canada **DISCIPLINE** RELIGIOUS STUDIES **EDUCATION** Southern Methodist Univ, PhD, 83. **CAREER** Asst prof, assoc prof, prof, Queen's Univ Dept of Relig Stud, 85- ; chemn, 96- . **MEMBERSHIPS** Am Acad Relig; Am Theol Soc; Canadian Soc for Stud of Relig; Canadian Theol Soc. **RESEARCH** Women and religion; feminine and theology; twentieth century theology; religion and culture. **SELECTED PUBLICATIONS** Ed, Theological Reflections on Ministry and Sexual Orientation, Trinity, 90; auth, Feminist Theology/Christian Theology: In Search of Method, Fortress, 90; auth, Teologia Feminista--Teologia Christiana: En Gusqueda de un Metodo, Demac, 93; auth, Theology and Commitment, Toronto J of Theol, 93; auth, Ubi Christus Ibi Ecclesia: Some Christological Themes Relevant in Formulating New Ecclesiologies, in Wilson, ed, New Wine: The Challenge of the Emerging Ecclesiologies to Church Renewal, World Alliance of Reformed Churches, 94; auth, Christ in a Post-Christian World: How Can We Believe in Jesus Christ When Those Around Us Believe Differently or Not at All? Fortress, 95; auth, Feminist Theology: From Past to Future, in Joy, ed, Gender, Genre and Religion: Feminist Reflections, Wilfrid Laurier, 95; auth, Beyond Moral Influence to an Atoning Life, Theol Today, 95; auth, Experience, and, Norm, in Isherwood, ed, An A to Z of Feminist Theology, Sheffield Acad, 96; auth, Encountering Jesus Through the Earliest Witnesses, Theol Stud, 96; auth, Theme and Variation: The Social Gospel in a New Key, Toronto J of Theol, 96; auth, The Resurrection of Whose Body: A Feminist Look at the Question of Transcendence, in Downing, ed, Psychoanalysis, Feminism and Religion, forthcoming; **CONTACT ADDRESS** Dept of Religious Studies, Queen's Univ, Kingston, ON, K7L 3N6. **EMAIL** youngpd@post.queensu.ca

YOUNGBLOOD, RONALD F.
PERSONAL Born 08/10/1931, Chicago, IL, m, 1952, 2 children **DISCIPLINE** OLD TESTAMENT **EDUCATION** Valparaiso Univ, BA, 52; Fuller Theol Sem, BD, 55; Dropsie Col, PhD, 61. **CAREER** Asst hist, Valparaiso Univ, 51-52; student instr Hebrew, Fuller Theol Sem, 54-55; Semitic lang, Dropsie Col, 58-61; asst prof Old Testament lang, Bethel Theol Sem, 61-65; assoc prof Old Testament interpretation, 65-70, prof Old Testament, 70-78; prof Old Testament & assoc dean, Wheaton Col Grad Sch, 78-80, dean, grad sch, 80-81; prof Old Testament & Semitic lang, Trinity Evangel Divinity Sch, 81-82; PROF OLD TESTAMENT & HEBRREW, BETHEL SEM SAN DIEGO, 82-; Grant, Land of Bible Workshop, NY Univ, 66; fel archaeol, Hebrew Union Col, Jerusalem, 67-68; ed, Evangel Theol Soc, 76-98; mem exec comt on Bible transl, New Int Version, 78-. **MEMBERSHIPS** Evangel Theol Soc; Near E Archaeol Soc. **RESEARCH** Old Testament literature; Hebrew; Amarna correspondence. **SELECTED PUBLICATIONS** Auth, Amorite influence in a Canaanite Amarna letter, Bull Am Schs Orient Res, 12/62; Lqr't in Amos 4:12, J Bibl Lit, 3/71; The Heart of the Old Testament, 71, 2nd ed, 98 & Special Day Sermons, 73, Baker Bk; Faith of Our Fathers, Regal, 76; How It All Began, Regal, 80; Exodus, Moody, 83; Themes from Isaiah, Regal, 83; assoc ed, NIV Study Bible, Zonderwan, 85; ed, The Genesis Debate, Thomas Nelson, 86; Nelson's Quick Reference Bible Concordance, Thomas Nelson, 93; gen ed, Nelson's New Illustrated Bible Dictionary, 95; exec ed, New International Reader's Version, Zonderwan, 98. **CONTACT ADDRESS** Bethel Sem, San Diego, 6116 Arosa St, San Diego, CA, 92115-3999.

YOVEL, YIRMIYAHU
DISCIPLINE PHILOSOPHY **EDUCATION** Hebrew University, PhD, 68. **CAREER** Hans Jonas Prof Philos. **RESEARCH** Hist of mod philos; ethics; Spinoza; Kant; Hegel; Nietzsche; existential thought; Jewish rationalists. **SELECTED PUBLICATIONS** Auth, Commentary to Hegel's Preface to the Phenomenology of Spirit, 96; Spinoza and Other Heretics, 89; Kant and the Philosophy of History, 80; Kant and the Renewal of Metaphysics, 73; ed, God and Nature: Spinoza's Metaphysics, 91; Nietzsche as Affirmative Thinker, 86 and 88; Philosophy of Action and History, 78. **CONTACT ADDRESS** Eugene Lang Col, New Sch for Social Research, 66 West 12th St, New York, NY, 10011.

YU, ANTHONY C.
PERSONAL Born 10/06/1938, Hong Kong, m, 1963, 1 child **DISCIPLINE** RELIGION, WESTERN & CHINESE LITERATURE **EDUCATION** Houghton Col, BA, 60; Fuller Theol Sem, STB, 63; Univ Chicago, PhD(relig & lit), 69. **CAREER** Instr English, Univ Ill Chicago Circle, 67-68; from instr to asst prof relig & lit, 68-74, assoc prof, 74-78, Prof Relig & Lit, Divinity Sch & Prof Dept Far Eastern Lang & Civilizations, Comt Social Thought, English & Comp Lit, Univ Chicago, 78-90, Asst ed, J Asian Studies, 75-77, co-ed, Monogr Ser, 77-; Guggenheim Mem Found fel Chinese Lit, 76-77; Nat Endowment for Humanities special grant, 77-80 & 81-82; co-ed, J Relig, 80-90; Carl Darling Buck Distinguished Service Prof Humanities, 90; Sr Fel, Am Coun of Learned Soc, 86-87; Master Texts Study Grant, Seminar for Public Sch Teachers, NEH, 92; **HONORS AND AWARDS** Gordon J Laing Prize, Univ of Chicago Press, 83. **MEMBERSHIPS** Asn Asian Studies, Elec Mem, China & Inner Asia Coun, 79-82; Am Acad Relig; Milton Soc of Am, Life Mem; MLA, Elec Mem, Exec Council, 98-01; Mem, Board of Dir, Illinois Hum Coun, 95-98. **RESEARCH** Religious approaches to classical literatures, western and nonwestern; comparative literature; translation. **SELECTED PUBLICATIONS** Auth, New Gods and old order: Tragic theology in the Prometheus Bound, J Am Acad Relig, 71; ed, Parnasus Revisited: Modern Criticism and The Epic Tradition, Am Libr Asn, 73; auth, Problems and prospects in Chinese-Western literary relations, In: Yearbook of General and Comparative Literature, 74; Chapter nine and the problem of narrative structure, J Asian Studies, 75; On translating the Hsi-yu chi, In: The Art and Profession of Translation, Hong Kong Transl Soc, 76; translr & ed, The Journey to the West, Vol I, Univ Chicago, 77; Self and family in the Hung-lou meng, Chinese Lit: Essays, Articles, Rev, 80; Life in the garden: Freedom and the image of God in Paradise Lost, J Relig, 80; Order of Temptations in Paradis Regained, in Perspectives on Christology, ed, Marguerite Shuster & Richard Muller, Zondervan, 91; Rereading the Stone: Desire and the Making of Fiction in Hongloumeng, Princeton, 97. **CONTACT ADDRESS** Divinity Sch, Univ of Chicago, 1025-35 E 58th St, Chicago, IL, 60637-1577. **EMAIL** acyu@midway.uchicago.edu

YUN, SAMUEL
PERSONAL Born 06/19/1958, Seoul, Korea, m, 1984, 4 children **DISCIPLINE** BIBLICAL STUDIES **EDUCATION** Univ of Dubuque Theol Sch, MAR, 85; Harvard Divinity Sch, ThM, 87. **CAREER** Assoc prof, Presbyterian Theol Sem in Am, 85- ; adj prof, New Brunswick Theol Sem, 94- ; pastor, Princeton Korean Presbyterian Church, 93- . **MEMBERSHIPS** SBL; AAR. **RESEARCH** Biblical spirituality. **SELECTED PUBLICATIONS** Auth, Living the Word, 90; auth, Living the Prayer, 94; auth, Living the Faith, 97. **CONTACT ADDRESS** 9 Sayre Dr, Princeton, NJ, 08540. **EMAIL** samuelyun@hotmail.com

YUSA, M.
DISCIPLINE PHILOSOPHY OF RELIGION; HISTORY OF IDEAS; BUDDHIST-CHRISTIAN DIALOGUE, NISH **EDUCATION** Univ CA at Santa Barbara, PhD, 83. **CAREER** Asst Prof, Assoc Prof, Prof, Western Washington Univ, 93-present. **HONORS AND AWARDS** Japan Found Research Fel, 93-94. **MEMBERSHIPS** Amer Acad Rel; Assoc for Asian Studies; Amer Oriental Soc **RESEARCH** Cross-cultural hist of ideas **SELECTED PUBLICATIONS** Intl Encyclopedia of Philosophy, Zeami, 98; Monumenta Nipponica, Philosophy and Inflation, Miki Kiyoshi in Weimar Germany 1922-24, 98, Nishida and Hearn, 96; A Companion to World Philosophies, Contemporary Buddhist Philosophy, Blackwell Publishers, Oxford, 97; Eastern Buddhist, Nishida Kitaro Mem Issue, Reflections on Nishida Studies, 95; Shiso No. 857 special issue commemorating 50th aniv of death of Nishida Kitaro, A Reflection on the Study of Nishida Philosophy in America, 95; Rude Awakenings: The Kyoto School, Zen, and the Question of Nationalism, Nishida and Totalitarianism: A Philosopher's Resistance, Univ of Hawaii Press, Honolulu, 95; Religion and Women, Women in Shinto: Images Remembered, State Univ of NY Press, Albany, 94. **CONTACT ADDRESS** Dept of Modern and Classical Languages, Western Washington Univ, Bellingham, WA, 98225.

Z

ZAAS, PETER S.
DISCIPLINE RELIGIOUS STUDIES **EDUCATION** Oberlin Col, AB, 74; Univ Chicago, MA, 77, PhD, 82. **CAREER** Vis scholar, Duke Univ, 78-79; instr, Hamilton Col, 79-81; asst prof, Hamilton Col, 81-82 and Siena College, 82-89 & 89-95; prof, Siena Col, 95; ch, Dept Rel Stud, Siena Col, 92-95; serv to other inst(s), St Bernard's Inst, Empire State Col, Yale Divinity Sch, Skidmore Col & New Brunswick Theol Sem; mem, SBL Pauline Ethics Sem, 79-81; charter bd mem, Siena Inst Jewish Christian Stud & coordr, 89-92; actg dir, Siena Ins Jewish-Christian Stud, 91-92 & dir, 92-; ch, dept Rel Stud, Siena Col, 92-95; Convener, SBL Bibl Ethics and Exegesis Consultation, 85-86 & SBL Exegesis of Texts on Bibl Ethics Gp, 87-93; instr, Chautauqua Inst, 91-93; Siena Comt(s), Col Conduct, Long Range Plan, on Admis, Acad Comp Adv, Fac & ch Comparability. **MEMBERSHIPS** SBL, AAR, NAm Patristics Soc. **RESEARCH** Moral thought in Jewish and early Christian lit; The Church Fathers as Evidence for Jewish Life in Late Antiquity Hist and lit of Hellenistic Judaism; Christian origins; Histo-

riography of early Christianity. **SELECTED PUBLICATIONS** Auth, Prophecy in Contemporary Jewish Religious Thought, Original essays on critical concepts, movements, and beliefs, NY, Scribner's Press, 87, paperback ed, Free Press, 89; Catalogues and Context: I Corinthians 5 and 6, New Testament Stud 34, 88; John Boswell and Pauline Sexual Ethics, Voices, 87; Protology and Eschatology in the Jewish-Christian Dialogue, in Torah and Revelation, Lewiston, NY, The Edwin Mellen Press, 92; Forward to J O Holloway, III, Peripetew as a Thematic Marker for Pauline Ethics, San Francisco: Mellen Res UP, 92; Paul and the hklh: Dietary Laws for Gentiles in I Corinthians 8-10, Jewish Law Asn Stud VII, Paris Conf Vol, Atlanta, Scholars Press, 94; What Comes out of a Person is What Makes a Person Impure: Jesus as Sadducee, Jewish Law Asn Stud VIII, Jerusalem 94 Conf Vol, Atlanta: Scholars Press, 96; rev(s), A Hidden Revolution, Bibl Archeol, 81; The Lord's Table: Eucharist and Passover in Early Christianity, 2nd Century, 82. **CONTACT ADDRESS** Dept of Relig Studies, Siena Col, 515 Loudon Rd., Loudonville, NY, 12211-1462. **EMAIL** ZAAS@SIENA.EDU

ZABLOTSKY, PETER A.
DISCIPLINE LAW **EDUCATION** PA State Univ, BA, summa cum laude, 77; Columbia Univ, JD, 80. **CAREER** Assoc prof, Touro Col; writing and res ed, Columbia J of Law and Soc Prob; coordr, legal writing and Res prog, NY Law Schl. **HONORS AND AWARDS** Harlan Fiske Stone scholar. **SELECTED PUBLICATIONS** Publ in the areas of products liability, torts, civil rights, criminal procedure, and domestic rel(s). **CONTACT ADDRESS** Touro Col, Brooklyn, NY, 11230.

ZACHARIAS, RAVI
DISCIPLINE CULTURE AND RELIGION **EDUCATION** Univ New Delhi, BA; Ontario Bible Col, BTh; Trinity Evangel Theol Sem, MDiv; Houghton Col, DD; Asbury Col, LLD; post grad stud, Ridley Hall, Cambridge Univ. **CAREER** Distinguished vis prof. **SELECTED PUBLICATIONS** Auth, Can Man Live Without God; A Shattered Visage: The Real Face of Atheism; Deliver Us From Evil; Cries of the Heart. **CONTACT ADDRESS** Southern Evangel Sem, 4298 McKee Rd, Charlotte, NC, 28270.

ZACHARY, STEVEN W.
PERSONAL Born 04/24/1958, St Paul, MN, d **DISCIPLINE** LAW **EDUCATION** Mankato State University, BS, 1981; University of Minnesota School of Law, JD, 1984. **CAREER** City of St Paul, human rights specialist, 1984-92; William Mitchell College of Law, adjunct professor, 1989-92; State of Minnesota, diversity and equal opportunity director, 1992-97. **HONORS AND AWARDS** William Mitchell College of Law, Haines Distinguished Service Award, 1992. **MEMBERSHIPS** NAACP St Paul Branch, president, 1990-93; MCLU, board member, 1990-93; MN Minority Lawyer's Association, 1987-93; JRLC, criminal justice taskforce chairperson, 1991-92; St Peter Claver School, school board president, 1987-88. **SELECTED PUBLICATIONS** What's In Store for Civil Rights in 1990. **CONTACT ADDRESS** Diversity & Equal Opportunity Director, State of Minnesota, Department of Employee Relations, 200 Centennial Office Bldg, 658 Cedar St, St Paul, MN, 55155.

ZACK, NAOMI
PERSONAL Born 07/21/1944, Brooklyn, NY, d, 2 children **DISCIPLINE** PHILOSOPHY **EDUCATION** NY Univ, BA, 66; Columbia Univ, PhD, 70. **CAREER** Assoc Prof, 90-, SUNY at Albany. **HONORS AND AWARDS** Woodrow Wilson Fel, NEH Fel, Woodrow Wilson Dissertation Fel, Pres ASVI 98. **MEMBERSHIPS** APA, CCSWP, ISVI. **RESEARCH** Racial theory, 17th century Philosophy. **SELECTED PUBLICATIONS** Auth, Bachelors of Science, Seventeenth Century Identity, Then and Now, Temple Univ Press, 96; Race and Mixed Race, Temple Univ Press, 93; Thinking About Race, Wadsworth Pub Co, 98; ed intro & art, The American Sexualization of Race, in: Race/Sex, Their Sameness, Difference and Interplay, Routledge, 97; auth, Life After Race, in: American Mixed Race, Constructing Microdiversity, Rowman & Littlefield, 95. **CONTACT ADDRESS** Dept of Philosophy, SUNY Albany, Albany, NY, 12222. **EMAIL** nzack@cnsunix.albany.edu

ZAFERSON, WILLIAM S.
PERSONAL Born 02/10/1925, Greece, m, 1955 **DISCIPLINE** PHILOSOPHY **EDUCATION** Univ Athens, BA, 52, PhD, 76; Univ Chicago, MA, 65. **CAREER** Asst prof, philos, Univ Upper Iowa, Fayette, 66-68; prof philos, marymount Col, 68-70; prof philos, St Mary's Univ, 70-72. **HONORS AND AWARDS** Magna Cum Laude, 76; A. Daniel Shovey fel, Univ Chicago. **MEMBERSHIPS** Am Asn Learned Soc; APA; AAUP; NRTA. **RESEARCH** Ancient Greek mythology; original Greek texts of Hesiod, Homer, Pindar; the Greek tragedians; Plato; Aristotle; Plotines; the Bible; Epictetus; Heraclitus. **SELECTED PUBLICATIONS** Auth, The Meaning of Metempsychosis, 65; auth, The Universe, Its Elements and Justice, 74; auth, A Hymn to Health, 75; auth, The Platonic View of Moral Law and the Influence of the Tragedians on Plato's Thoughts, 76; auth, The Songs of the Muses for Gods and Men, 97. **CONTACT ADDRESS** PO Box 1551, Chicago, IL, 60690.

ZAGANO, PHYLLIS
DISCIPLINE RELIGION; LITERATURE **EDUCATION** Marymount Col, BA, 69; Boston Univ, MS, 70; C.W. Post Center of Long Island Univ, MA, 72; St. John's Univ, MA, 90; State Univ New York Stony Brook, PhD **CAREER** Boston Univ, 88- **MEMBERSHIPS** Amer Acad Rel; Amer Cath Philos Assoc; Amer Jour Historians Assoc; Col Theol Soc; Soc Study Christian Spirituality; Spiritual Directors Int **SELECTED PUBLICATIONS** Co-ed, Twentieth Century Apostles, Liturgical, 99; co-ed, The Exercise of the Primacy: Continuing the Dialogue, Crossroad/Herder, 98; auth, "The Language of Prayer," Handbook of Spirituality for Ministers, Vol.2, Paulist Press, 99 **CONTACT ADDRESS** 250 E 63rd St, New York, NY, 10021. **EMAIL** pzagano@su.edu

ZAHAVY, TZVEE
PERSONAL Born 11/23/1949, New York, NY, m, 1974, 2 children **DISCIPLINE** JEWISH AND RELIGIOUS STUDIES **EDUCATION** Yeshiva Univ, BA, 70, MS, 73; Brown Univ, PhD(relig studies), 76. **CAREER** Teaching asst relig studies, Brown Univ, 74-76; asst prof, 76-80, Assoc PROF JEWISH STUDIES & GRAD FAC RELIG STUDIES & ANCIENT STUDIES, UNIV MINN, 80-, Vis assoc prof Near East Studies, Univ Calif, Berkeley, 80; Am Coun Learned Soc fel, 82-83. **MEMBERSHIPS** Asn Jewish Studies; Soc Bibl; Lit; Am Acad Relig. **RESEARCH** Judaism in late antiquity; Rabbinics; Jewish prayer. **SELECTED PUBLICATIONS** Auth, Parables in Midrash--Narrative and Exegesis in Rabbinic Literature, Jour Amer Acad Rel, Vol 0061, 93. **CONTACT ADDRESS** Univ of Minn, 176 Kaleber Court, Minneapolis, MN, 55455.

ZALLEN, DORIS T.
PERSONAL Born 03/07/1941, Brooklyn, NY, m, 1964, 2 children **DISCIPLINE** BIOLOGY **EDUCATION** Harvard Univ, AM, 63; Brooklyn Coll, BS, 61; Harvard Univ, PhD, 66. **CAREER** Res Fel, Univ Rochester NY, 77-83; asst prof, Nazareth Coll, Rochester, 79-83; assoc prof Va Tech, 83-96; prof, VA Tech, 96-. **HONORS AND AWARDS** Phi Beta Kappa; Sigma Xi; NIH postdoctoral Fel; NUCEA award; Welcome Trust Travel awards; Certificated Service, Nat Inst of Health. **MEMBERSHIPS** AAAS; Hist of Sci Soc; Am Soc of Human Genetics; British Soc for the Hist of Sci. **RESEARCH** Social, ethical and policy issues related to genetics and the reproductive technologies; History of genetics. **SELECTED PUBLICATIONS** Auth, Does It Run in the Family? A Consumer's Guide to DNA Testing for Genetic Disorders, 97. **CONTACT ADDRESS** Virginia Tech, 233 Lane Hall, Blacksburg, VA, 24061-0227. **EMAIL** dtzallen@vt.edu

ZANER, RICHARD
PERSONAL Born 09/20/1933, Duncan, AZ, m, 1956, 2 children **DISCIPLINE** PHILOSOPHY & BIOETHICS **EDUCATION** Univ Houston, BS, 57; New Sch for Social Res, Grad Facul of Social and Polit Sci, PhD, 61. **CAREER** Instr, The New Sch, 60; Asst prof, Lamar State Col, 61-63; assoc prof, chair, Trinity Univ, 64-67; assoc prof, chair, Univ Tex Austin, 67-71; dir & prof, social sci and humanities in med, State Univ NY Stony Brook, 71-73; Easterwood prof & chair, Southern Methodist Univ, 73-81; A. G. Stahlman prof, med ethics, med, prof philos, prof ethics relig studies, Vanderbilt Univ. **HONORS AND AWARDS** Schutz mem award, PhD dissertation, 61; univ scholar, Univ Ctr of Ga, 75; Dotterer lectr, Pa State Univ, 81; prin speaker, 200th anniv celeb, Georgetown Univ, 89; Kegley lectr, Calif State Univ Bakersfield, 91; Leys lectr, Southern Ill Univ, 95; Inaugural Christine Martin lectr, Aust Bioethics Asn, 97; Inaugural lectr, Univ Melbourne Ctr for Bioethics, 97; Alfred Schutz mem lectr, Univ Ky, 97. **MEMBERSHIPS** Amer Philos Asn; Soc Phenomenol & Existential Philos; Soc Health & Human Values; Amer Soc Law & Ethics; Inst Soc, Ethics & Life Sci; Amer Psychol Asn; Amer Asn Univ Prof. **RESEARCH** Ethics in health care; Research ethics; Philosophy of medicine; Philosophical anthropology; Bioethics; Professional ethics. **SELECTED PUBLICATIONS** Auth, Ethical Issues in Cancer Pain Management, Cancer Pain Mgt: Principles and Practice, Butterworth-Heineman Publ, 97; auth, Phenomenology of Medicine, Encycl of Phenomenol, Kluwer Acad Publ, 97; foreward, Nursing Ethics: Therapeutic Caring Presence, Jones & Bartlett Publ, 95, auth, Reflection on Pain and Embodiment, Politics and the Human Body: Assault on Dignity, Vanderbilt Univ Press, 95; auth, Interpretation and Dialogue: Medicine as a Moral Discipline, Essays in Honor of Maurice Natanson, The Prism of Self, Kluwer Acad Publ, 95; auth, Phenomenology and the Clinical Event, Phenomenol of the Cultural Disciplines, Kluwer Acad Publ, vol 16, contrib to phenomenol, 94; auth, Experience and Moral Life: A Phenomenological Approach to Bioethics, A Matter of Principles? Ferment in U.S. Bioethics, The Park Ridge Ctr for the Study of Health, Faith and Ethics, Trinity Press Intl, 94; auth, Encountering the Other, Duties in Others, Theol and Med Series, Kluwer Acad Publ, 94; auth, Body: Embodiment: The Phenomenological Tradition, Encycl of Bioethics, The Kennedy Inst of Bioethics, new ed, 94; auth, Illness and the Other, Theol Analyses of the Clinical Encounter, Theol and Med Series, Kluwer Acad Publ, 94. **CONTACT ADDRESS** Center for Clinical and Research Ethics, Vanderbilt Univ Medical Center, 319 Oxford House, Nashville, TN, 37232-4350. **EMAIL** richard.zaner@mcmail.vanderbilt.edu

ZAVODNY, JOHN
DISCIPLINE PHILOSOPHY **EDUCATION** Univ Tennessee, PhD. **CAREER** Adj prof, E Tenn State Univ. **SELECTED PUBLICATIONS** Auth, This Isn't About Shoes, Is It? A Response to Heidegger, Derrida and Shoes; The Therapeutic Philosophy of Richard Rorty. **CONTACT ADDRESS** Philosophy Dept, East Tennesee State Univ, Box 70717, Johnson City, TN, 37614- 0717. **EMAIL** zavodnyj@etsu.edu

ZELLNER, HAROLD MARCELLARS
PERSONAL Born 05/06/1943, Macon, GA **DISCIPLINE** PHILOSOPHY **EDUCATION** Univ Miami, BA, 64, PhD(-philos), 71. **CAREER** Asst prof, 72-80, ASSOC PROF PHILOS, KENT STATE UNIV, 80- **MEMBERSHIPS** Am Philos Asn. **RESEARCH** Metaphysics; epistemology. **SELECTED PUBLICATIONS** Auth, Skepticism in Homer, Class Quart, Vol 0044, 1994; Antigone and the Wife of Intaphrenes--Sophocles, Class World, Vol 0090, 97. **CONTACT ADDRESS** Dept of Philos, Kent State Univ, Kent, OH, 44240.

ZEMAN, JAROLD K.
PERSONAL Born 02/27/1926, Czechoslovakia **DISCIPLINE** CHURCH HISTORY **EDUCATION** Knox Col, Univ Toronto, BD, 52; Univ Zurich, DTheol, 66; McMaster Univ, DD, 85; Acadia Univ, DD, 94. **CAREER** Dir, Cont Theol Educ, 70-81, 85-91, dir confs, 81-85, PROF CHURCH HISTORY, ACADIA UNIV & ACADIA DIVINITY COL, 68-91; dir, Acadia Ctr Baptist Anabaptist Stud, Acadia Univ, 91-97. **MEMBERSHIPS** Pres, Baptist Fed Can, 79-82; mem, Rel Adv Comt CBC, 79-84; mem, Can Soc Ch Hist; Am Soc Ch Hist; Am Acad Relig. **SELECTED PUBLICATIONS** Auth, God's Mission and Ours, 63; auth, The Whole World at Our Door, 64; auth, Historical Topography of Moravian Anabaptism, 67; auth, The Anabaptists and the Czech Brethren, 69; auth, Baptists in Canada and Co-operative Christianity, 72; auth, The Hussite Movement and the Reformation, 77; auth, Baptist Roots and Identity, 78; auth, Renewal of Church and Society in the Hussite Reformation, 84; coauth, Baptists in Canada 1760-1990: A Bibliography, 89; ed, Baptists in Canada, 80. **CONTACT ADDRESS** PO Box 164, Wolfville, NS, BOP 1XO.

ZEMAN, VLADIMIR
DISCIPLINE PHILOSOPHY **EDUCATION** Charles Univ, dipl in philos, 60; Charles Univ, Prague, PhD, 67; add stud and res, Austria and Ger. **CAREER** Dept Philos, Concordia Univ **RESEARCH** German idealism. **SELECTED PUBLICATIONS** Auth, Can Eco- and Techno-Philosophies replace Humanism?, Advances in Ecosystems Research; co-ed, coauth, Transcendental Philosophy and Everyday Experience, Hermann Cohen's Concept of Transcendental Method, Hum Press, 97. **CONTACT ADDRESS** Dept of Philos, Concordia Univ, Montreal, 1455 de Maisonneuve W, Montreal, PQ, H3G 1M8. **EMAIL** zemvlad@alcor.concordia.ca

ZHENG, YIWEI
PERSONAL Born 08/16/1972, Shanghai, China, m, 1998 **DISCIPLINE** PHILOSOPHY **EDUCATION** Shanghai Jiao Tong Univ, BS, 87; Cleveland State Univ, MA, 93; Indiana Univ, PhD, 98. **CAREER** Dept Philos, Indiana Univ. **HONORS AND AWARDS** Fel, Univ Iowa, 94-95; Larry Taylor Essay Prize, New Mexico and West Texas Philos Soc, 96; grad acad excellence awd, Indiana Univ, 97; Oscar R. Ewing Essay Prize, Indiana Univ, 98; APA grad stud travel stipend, APA, 98. **MEMBERSHIPS** APA; Radical Philos Asn; Southwestern Philos Soc. **RESEARCH** History of analytical philosophy; phenomenology and existentialism; history of philosophy. **SELECTED PUBLICATIONS** Auth, "On Hume's Theory of Self," Southwest Philos Stud, 97; "On the Self-destructive Nature of Consciousness," Philos, 97; "Ontology and Ethics in Sartre's Being and Nothingness," Southern J of Philos, 97; "On the Picture Theory in Wittgenstein's Tractatus," Kampits, ed, "Applied Ethics," Kirchberg, 98; "Metaphysical Simplicity and Semantical Complexity of Connotative Terms in ockham's Mental Language," Modern Schoolman, forthcoming; "Ockham's Connotation Theory and Ontological Elimination," J of Philos Res, forthcoming; "Configurations and Properties of Objects in Wittgenstein's Tractatus," Philos Investigations, forthcoming. **CONTACT ADDRESS** Dept of Philosophy, Indiana Univ, Bloomington, Sycamore Hall 026, Bloomington, IN, 47405. **EMAIL** yiwzheng@indiana.edu

ZIETLOW, REBECCA
DISCIPLINE LAW **EDUCATION** Barnard Col, BA; Yale Law Sch, JD. **CAREER** Asst prof. **SELECTED PUBLICATIONS** Auth, Two Wrongs Don't Add Up to Rights: The Importance of Preserving due Process in Light of Recent Welfare Reform Measures, Am Univ Law Rev, 96. **CONTACT ADDRESS** Col Law, Univ of Toledo, Toledo, OH, 43606. **EMAIL** rzietlo@uoft02.utoledo.edu

ZILE, ZIGURDS LAIMONS
PERSONAL Born 07/24/1927, Riga, Latvia **DISCIPLINE** LAW **EDUCATION** Univ Wis-Madison, BA, 56, LLB, 58, LLM, 59; Harvard Univ, SJD, 67. **CAREER** From asst prof to assoc prof, 61-66, PROF LAW, UNIV WIS-MADISON, 66-, Vis prof law, Univ Helsinki, Finland, 77-78. **MEMBERSHIPS**

Am Asn Advan Slavic Studies; Asn Advan Baltic Studies. **RESEARCH** Soviet, environmental and international law. **SELECTED PUBLICATIONS** Auth, Toward the Rule of Law in Russia--Political and Legal Reform in the Transition Period, Slavic Rev, Vol 0053, 94. **CONTACT ADDRESS** Law Sch, Univ of Wis, Madison, WI, 53706.

ZILLMAN, DONALD N.
DISCIPLINE LAW **EDUCATION** Univ Wis, BS, JD; Univ Va, LLM. **CAREER** Godfrey prof; Maine's first Godfrey prof Law; dean Law Sch, 91-98; past distinguished vis prof, US Mil Acad at West Point; prof, Univ Utah and dir, University's Energy Law Ctr, 79-86; dir, Univ Utah Col Law's Grad Stud, 86; past mem, US Army Judge Advocate General's Corps; past spec asst atty gen, Ariz; past vis prof, Univ Southampton, Engl. **MEMBERSHIPS** Acad Adv Gp, Int Bar Asn on energy and natural resources law; ed bd, J Energy and Natural Resources Law. **RESEARCH** Government tort liability; military law and natural resources law. **SELECTED PUBLICATIONS** Auth or coauth, Foundation Press text on Energy Law; Maine Tort Law; Constitutional Law for the Citizen Soldier. **CONTACT ADDRESS** School of Law, Univ of Southern Maine, 96 Falmouth St, PO Box 9300, Portland, ME, 04104-9300.

ZIMANY, ROLAND DANIEL
PERSONAL Born 08/05/1936, East Orange, NJ, m, 1976 **DISCIPLINE** CHRISTIAN THEOLOGY, MODERN PHILOSOPHY **EDUCATION** Princeton Univ, AB, 58; NY Univ, MBA, 65; Union Theol Sem, NY, MDiv, 74; Duke Univ, PhD(relig), 80. **CAREER** ASST PROF PHILOS & RELIG, BLACKBURN COL, 80- **MEMBERSHIPS** Am Acad Relig. **RESEARCH** Hermeneutics; theology; Heidegger. **SELECTED PUBLICATIONS** Auth, Not Every Spirit--A Dogmatics of Christian Disbelief, Jour Amer Acad Rel, Vol 0064, 96. **CONTACT ADDRESS** 413 Morgan St, Carlinville, IL, 62626.

ZIMMERMAN, DEAN
DISCIPLINE PHILOSOPHY **EDUCATION** Mankato State Univ, BA, 86; Brown Univ, MA, 90, PhD, 92. **CAREER** Assoc prof. **RESEARCH** Metaphysics; epistemology. **SELECTED PUBLICATIONS** Auth, Immanent Causation, Philos Perspectives, 97; Coincident Objects: Could a 'Stuff Ontology' Help?, Analysis, 97; Distinct Indiscernibles and the Bundle Theory, Mind, 97; Temporal Parts and Supervenient Causation: The Incompatibility of Two Humean Doctrines, Australasian J Philos, 98; co-ed, Metaphysics: The Big Questions, 98. **CONTACT ADDRESS** Philosophy Dept, Univ of Notre Dame, 336/7 O'Shaughnessy, Notre Dame, IN, 46556. **EMAIL** zimmerman.4@nd.edu

ZIMMERMAN, JOYCE ANN
PERSONAL Born 04/13/1945, Dayton, OH **DISCIPLINE** THEOLOGY **EDUCATION** Univ Dayton, BS, 68; Athenaeum Ohio, MA, 73; St. John's Univ, MA, 81; Univ Ottawa, MA, 82, PhD, 87; St. Paul Univ, STL, 83, STD, 87. **CAREER** Ed, CPPS Newsl, 97-; adv, Nat Conf Cath Bishops Comm Liturgy, 95-; adj prof, Athenaeum Ohio, 94-; prof liturgy & dir sem liturgy, Conception Sem Col, 93-96; ed, liturgical ministry, 92-; dir, Inst Liturgical Ministry, 91-, fac, Summer Inst Pastoral Liturgy, St. Paul Univ, 90-92. **MEMBERSHIPS** N Am Acad Liturgy; Am Acad Relig. **RESEARCH** Liturgical theology; hermeneutics; methodology. **SELECTED PUBLICATIONS** Auth, Liturgy and Hermeneutics, 99; auth, Liturgy and Music: Lifetime Learning, 98; auth, Pray without Ceasing: Prayer for Morning and Evening, 93; auth, Liturgy as Living Faith: A Liturgical Spirituality, 93; auth, Theology of Liturgical Assembly: Saints, Relics & Rites, Liturgy, 98; coauth, Penance: Some Critical Issues, liturgical ministry, 95; auth, Liturgical Assembly: Who is the Subject of Liturgy?, liturgical ministry, 94; auth, A Blessing in Disguise? On Adoration of the Blessed Sacrament, Nat Bull Liturgy, Summer, 97; auth, When Do We Pray What? On the Relationship of Liturgical and Devotional Prayer, Nat Bull Liturgy, Summer, 97; auth, Making Sense of Time, Assembly, Nov, 96; coauth, Morning and Evening: Order of Service for Presider, Cantor, and Accompanist, 96; auth, A New Commandment: Eucharist as Loving, Eating and Drinking, and Serving, The Wine Cellar, Feb, 95; auth, Stop Decorating and Start Enhancing Your Worship, Today's Parish, Oct, 94; auth, Your Worship Space and the Liturgical Year, Today's Parish, Oct, 94. **CONTACT ADDRESS** 721 Hallworth Pl, Dayton, OH, 45426-4817. **EMAIL** ilm@vandcom.com

ZIMMERMAN, MICHAEL E.
PERSONAL Born 07/07/1946, Akron, OH, m, 1986, 1 child **DISCIPLINE** PHILOSOPHY **EDUCATION** La State Univ, BA, 68; Tulane Univ, MA, 71, PhD, 74. **CAREER** Asst prof, Denison Univ, 74-75; ASSOC PROF, 75-83, PROF, TULANE UNIV, 83-. **HONORS AND AWARDS** NEH Fel, 88-89 **MEMBERSHIPS** AAR; APA; SPEP; ISEE; ISEP. **RESEARCH** Heidegger; environ philos; Buddhism; philos & gender; transpersonal philos. **SELECTED PUBLICATIONS** Auth, Contesting Earth's Future: Radical Ecology and Postmodernity, Univ of Calif Press, 94; Deep Ecology's Approach to the Environmental Crisis, Philosophy, Humanity and Ecology, African Center for Tech Studies Press, 94; Martin heidegger: Anti-Naturalistic Critic of Technological Modernity, Ecological Thinkers, Guilford, 95; The Threat of Ecofascism, Soc Theory and Practice, 95; A Transpersonal Diagnosis of the Ecological Crisis, ReVision, 96; ed, The Thought of Martin Heidegger, Tulane Studies in Philos, New Orleans, 84; Environmental Philosophy: From Animal Rights to Radical Ecology, Prentice-Hall, 93 & 97; **CONTACT ADDRESS** Dept of Philos, Tulane Univ, New Orleans, LA, 70118. **EMAIL** michaelz@mailhost.tcs.tulane.edu

ZINKIN, MELISSA R.
PERSONAL Born 10/13/1967, New York, NY, s **DISCIPLINE** PHILOSOPHY **EDUCATION** Northwestern Univ, PhD, 99. **CAREER** BIRMINGHAM UNIV, 9/98-. **HONORS AND AWARDS** DAAD fel; Humanities teaching fel, Northwestern Univ. **MEMBERSHIPS** APA **RESEARCH** Kant; modern philos; philos of science; political philos; feminist theory. **SELECTED PUBLICATIONS** Auth, Habermas on Intelligibility, Southern J of Philos, fall 98; review of Women, Property and Politics, by Donna Dickenson, Ethics, forthcoming. **CONTACT ADDRESS** Philos, SUNY, Binghamton, PO Box 600, Binghamton, NY, 13902-6000. **EMAIL** mzinkin@birmingham.edu

ZIOLKOWSKI, ERIC JOZEF
PERSONAL Born 12/28/1958 **DISCIPLINE** RELIGION; LITERATURE **EDUCATION** Dartmouth Col, BA, 80; Univ Chicago, MA, 81; Univ Chicago, PhD, 87 **CAREER** Asst prof Comparative Literature, Univ Wisconsin Madison, 87-88; asst prof Religion, Lafayette Col, 88-94; assoc prof Religion, Lafayette Col, 94- **HONORS AND AWARDS** Fel, Soc Arts Relig Cult, 97-; Thomas Roy and Lura Forrest Jones Award for Superior Teaching, 98 **MEMBERSHIPS** Amer Acad Relig; Amer Assoc Univ Prof; Amnesty Int **RESEARCH** Religion and Literature, History of Religion, Philosophy of Religion **SELECTED PUBLICATIONS** A Museum of Faiths: Histories and Legacies of the 1893 World's Parliament of Religions, Scholars Press, 93; The Sanctification of Don Quixote: From Hidalgo to Priest, Penn St Univ, 91; "Religion and Literature and the History of Religions: Grounds for Alliance." Jour Lit Theol, 98; "Sancho Panza and Nemi's Priest: Reflections on Myth and Literature." Myth and Method, 96 **CONTACT ADDRESS** Dept Relig, Lafayette Col, Easton, PA, 18042. **EMAIL** ziolkowski@lafayette.edu

ZIRKEL, PATRICIA MCCORMICK
PERSONAL Born 11/02/1943, m, 1968, 1 child **DISCIPLINE** HISTORICAL THEOLOGY **EDUCATION** St Thomas Aquinas Col, Sparkill, NY, BS Ed, 66; St John's Univ, MA, 78; Fordham Univ, PhD, 89. **CAREER** Assoc prof, St Vincent's Col, St John's Univ, 90-. **HONORS AND AWARDS** Faculty Merit award, 97, 98. **MEMBERSHIPS** Am Academy of Relig; Am Asn of Univ Profs; Col Theol Soc; Medieval Academy of America. **RESEARCH** Christian theol-Medieval Europe; Christian Liturgy; Theodicy-Holocaust Studies. **SELECTED PUBLICATIONS** Auth, The Ninth Century Eucharistic Controversy: A Context for the Beginnnings of Eucharistic Doctrine in the West, Worship, vol 68, no 1, Jan 94; Why Should It Be Neccessary That Christ Be Immolated Daily?, Paschasius Radbertus on Daily Eucharist, Am Benedictine Rev, Sept 96; The Body of Christ and the Future of Liturgy, Anglican Theol Rev, forthcoming. **CONTACT ADDRESS** 6 Brancatelli Ct, West Islip, NY, 11795-2502. **EMAIL** zirkelp@stjohns.edu

ZITO, ANGELA
DISCIPLINE RELIGION **EDUCATION** Univ Chicago, PhD, 89. **CAREER** Asst prof. **RESEARCH** History of Chinese religion and philosophy; history of ritual in China; history of the Chinese monarchy. **SELECTED PUBLICATIONS** Auth, Body, Subject and Power in China, Univ Chicago, 94; Of Body and Bush: Grand Sacrifice as Text Performance in 18th Century China, Univ Chicago, 97. **CONTACT ADDRESS** Dept of Religion, Columbia Col, New York, 2960 Broadway, New York, NY, 10027-6902. **EMAIL** azito@barnard.columbia.edu

ZLOTKIN, NORMAN
DISCIPLINE LAW **EDUCATION** Univ Toronto, LLB, 69; London Univ, LLM, 70. **CAREER** Assoc prof, 81-; assoc dean, 96-97. **HONORS AND AWARDS** Res dir, Native Law Centre, 82-86. **MEMBERSHIPS** Law Soc Saskatchewan; Law Soc Upper Can. **SELECTED PUBLICATIONS** Auth, Judicial Recognition of Aboriginal Customary Law in Canada, 84; coauth, Affirming Aboriginal Title: A New Basis for Comprehensive Negotiations, 96. **CONTACT ADDRESS** Col of Law, Univ Saskatchewan, 15 Campus Dr, Saskatoon, SK, S7N 5A6. **EMAIL** Zlotkin@law.usask.ca

ZONG, DESHENG
PERSONAL Born 05/11/1961, Dali, China, m, 1989, 1 child **DISCIPLINE** PHILOSOPHY **EDUCATION** Tulane Univ, PhD, 98. **MEMBERSHIPS** APA. **RESEARCH** Ethics; Chinese philos. **SELECTED PUBLICATIONS** Auth, Epistemic Logic in Mohist Works, Philosphy East and West 50:2 (Epistemic). **CONTACT ADDRESS** 83 Hudson St, Somerville, MA, 02143. **EMAIL** dzong@msn.edu

ZUCK, LOWELL H.
PERSONAL Born 06/24/1926, Ephrata, PA, m, 1950, 1 child **DISCIPLINE** CHURCH HISTORY **EDUCATION** Elizabethtown Col, BA, 47; Bethany Bibl Sem, BD, 50; Yale Univ, STM, 51, MA, 52, PhD(Reformation church hist), 55. **CAREER** Vis prof philos & relig, Col Idaho, 54-55; from asst prof to assoc prof, 55-62, PROF CHURCH HIST, EDEN THEOL SEM, 62-, Teacher univ col, Washington Univ, 57-; Am Asn Theol Schs grants, 64-65 & 75-76; Am Philos Soc grant, 80; Nat Endowment for Humanities summer seminar, Johns Hopkins Univ, 82. **MEMBERSHIPS** AHA; Am Soc Church Hist; Am Soc Reformation Res (treas, 69-78); 16th Century Studies Conf (treas, 69-71, pres, 71-72). **RESEARCH** Anabaptist research; Reformation church history; Puritan church history. **SELECTED PUBLICATIONS** Auth, From Reformation Orthodoxy to the Enlightenment--Geneva 1670-1737--French, Church Hist, Vol 0063, 94; Ingdoms--The Church and Culture Through the Ages, Sixteenth Century Jour, Vol 0025, 94; Sin and the Calvinists--Morals Control and the Consistory in the Reformed Tradition, Church Hist, Vol 0065, 96; Hochstift and Reformation--Studies in the History of the Imperial Church Between 1517 and 1648--German, Sixteenth Century Jour, Vol 0027, 96; Calvinism in Europe, 1540-1620, Church Hist, Vol 0065, 96; Adultery and Divorce in Calvin, John Geneva, Church Hist, Vol 0065, 96; Poverty and Deviance in Early-Modern Europe, Sixteenth Century Jour, Vol 0027, 96; A Short History of Renaissance and Reformation Europe--Dances Over Fire and Water, Sixteenth Century Jour, Vol 0027, 96; The Oxford Encyclopedia of the Reformation, 4 Vols, Sixteenth Century Jour, Vol 0028, 97; Documents on the Continental Reformation, Sixteenth Century Jour, Vol 0028, 97. **CONTACT ADDRESS** Eden Theol Sem, 475 E Lockwood Ave, St Louis, MO, 63119.

ZUKOWSKI, EDWARD, JR.
PERSONAL Born 12/25/1946, South River, NJ, m, 1991, 1 child **DISCIPLINE** THEOLOGY **EDUCATION** Fordham, PhD, 84. **CAREER** Assoc prof and chair, Religious Studies, Col of Mount St Vincent, Riverdale, NY, 87-. **HONORS AND AWARDS** Teacher of the Year, 89, 96; Science and Religion Course Competition Award, Templeton Found, 98. **MEMBERSHIPS** Cath Theol Soc of Am; Col Theol Soc; Soc of Christian Ethics; Karl Rahner Soc; Am Academy of Relig; Am Soc for Psychol Res. **RESEARCH** Conscience; theology. **SELECTED PUBLICATIONS** Auth, Dimensions of Faith in History, Acton, MA: Cogley Press, 92; The Good Conscience of Nazi Doctors, Annal of Soc of Christian Ethics, 94. **CONTACT ADDRESS** Col of Mount Saint Vincent, 6301 Riverdale Ave, Riverdale, NY, 10471. **EMAIL** MeZukowski@aol.com

ZUPKO, JACK
DISCIPLINE MEDIEVAL PHILOSOPHY **EDUCATION** Cornell Univ, PhD, 89. **CAREER** Philos, Emory Univ. **SELECTED PUBLICATIONS** Articles, Jour His Philos, Medieval Philos & Theol, Mediaeval Studies, Rev Metaphysics. **CONTACT ADDRESS** Emory Univ, Atlanta, GA, 30322-1950.

ZVI, EHUD BEN
PERSONAL Born 03/12/1951, Argentina, m, 3 children **DISCIPLINE** BIBLICAL STUDIES **EDUCATION** The Hebrew Univ, BS, 74; Open Univ Israel, BS, 87; Tel Aviv Univ, MA, 84; Emory Univ, PhD, 90. **CAREER** Prof, Univ Alberta, 94-.. **MEMBERSHIPS** SBL; ASOR; CBA; CSBS; AAR. **RESEARCH** Hebrew Bible and its historical context. **SELECTED PUBLICATIONS** Auth, A Historical-Critical Study of the Book of Zephaniah, de Gruyter, 91; coauth, Readings in Biblical Hebrew, an Intermediate Textbook, Yale Univ Press, 93; auth, A Gateway to the Chronicler's Teaching: The Account of the Reign of Ahaz in 2nd Chronicles 28:1-27, 93; auth, History and Prophetic Texts, History and Interpretation: Essays in Honor of John H. Hayes, JSOT Press, 93; auth, Understanding the Message of the Tripartite Prophetic Books, 93; auth, A Sense of Proportion: An Aspect of the Theology of the Chronicler, 95; auth, Inclusion In and Exclusion From Israel as Conveyed by the Use of the Term 'Israel' Postmonarch Biblical Texts, The Pitcher is Broken: Memorial Essays for Gosta, JSOT Press, 95; auth, Prelude to a Reconstruction of the Historical Manassic Judah, 96; auth, Studying Prophetic Texts Against Their Original Backgrounds: Pre-ordained Scripts and Alternative Horizons of Research, Prophets and Paradigms: Essays in Honor of Gene M. Tucker, Sheffield Academic Press, 96; auth, Twelve Prophetic Books or 'The Twelve.' A Few Preliminary Considerations, Forming Prophetic Literature: Essays on Isaiah and the Twelve in Honor of John D.W. Watts, Sheffield Academic Press, 96; auth, A Historical-Critical Study of the Book of Obadiah, de Gruyter, 96; auth, The Chronicler as a Historian: building Texts, The Chronicler as Historian, Sheffield Academic Press, 97; auth, The Urban Center of Jerusalem and the Development of the Literature of the Hebrew Bible, in Aspects of Urbanism in Antiquity, Sheffield Academic Press, 97; auth, Micah 1.2-16: Observations and Possible Implications, 98; auth, Looking at the Primary (Hi)story and the Prophetic Books as Literary/Theological Units within the Frame of the Early Second Temple Period: Some Considerations, SJOT 12, 98. **CONTACT ADDRESS** Religious Studies Dept, Univ of Alberta, Edmonton, AB, T6G 2E6. **EMAIL** ehud.ben.zvi@ualberta.ca

ZWEIBEL, ELLEN
DISCIPLINE LAW **EDUCATION** Univ NY, BA; Brooklyn Law Sch, JD; Denver Univ, LLM. **CAREER** Prof. **SELECTED PUBLICATIONS** Auth, pubs on income tax policy issues relating to women and children, and alternative dispute resolution and mediation training. **CONTACT ADDRESS** Fac Common Law, Univ Ottawa, 550 Cumberland St, PO Box 450, Ottawa, ON, K1N 6N5. **EMAIL** mdextras@uottawa.ca

ZWEIG, ARNULF
PERSONAL Born 11/11/1930, Essen, Germany, m, 1957, 2 children **DISCIPLINE** PHILOSOPHY **EDUCATION** Univ of Rochester, BA, 52; Stanford Univ, PhD, 60. **CAREER** Univ of Oregon, asst prof, assoc prof, prof, prof emeritus, assoc dean, Dept head; MIT vis prof, 64-65; Harvard, vis prof, 67-68; Tufts, vis prof, 70. **HONORS AND AWARDS** Yale Univ Fel, ACLS Fel, NEH grants, Stanford Hum Prog Fel. **MEMBERSHIPS** APA, NAKS, IAP **RESEARCH** Kant; ethics; philo of law; aesthetics. **SELECTED PUBLICATIONS** Auth, trans & ed, Kant: Correspondence, Cambridge; auth, The Essential Kant; Wittgensteins Silence; Kant's Children. **CONTACT ADDRESS** 20 East 9th St, Apt 10-D, NYC, NY, 10003-5944. **EMAIL** zweig@oregon.uoregon.edu

ZWICKY, JAN
PERSONAL AB, Canada **DISCIPLINE** PHILOSOPHY **EDUCATION** Univ Calgary, BA, 76; Univ Toronto, MA, 77, PhD, 81. **CAREER** Prof, Univ Waterloo, 81-82, 85-86; prof, Princeton Univ, 82-83; prof, Univ Western Ont, 89-90; prof, Univ Alta, 92-93; prof, Univ NB, 94-96; PROF, UNIV VICTORIA 96-. **RESEARCH** History of ideas; metaphilosophy; and ancient Greek philosophy. **SELECTED PUBLICATIONS** Auth, Wittgenstein Elegies, 86; auth, The New Room, 89; auth, Lyric Philosophy, 92; auth, Songs for Relinquishing the Earth, 96. **CONTACT ADDRESS** PO Box 1149, Mayerthorpe, AB, T0E 1N0.

Geographic Index

Davis
Bruch, C.S.
Byrd, James David, Jr.
Dundon, Stanislaus
Imwinkelried, Edward
Johnson, Kevin R.
Juenger, Friedrich K.
Merlino, Scott A.
Oakley, John Bilyeu
Schaeffer, Peter Moritz-Friedrich
West, Martha S.

El Cajon
Strauss, Mark

El Monte
Hwang, Tzu-Yang
Wu, Julie L.

Elk Court
Peitz-Hillenbrand, Darlene

Eureka
Tiso, Francis V.

Fairfax
Leighton, Taigen Daniel

Fremont
Nakasone, Ronald

Fresno
Benko, Stephen
Boyd, Robert
Martens, Elmer Arthur
Pitt, Jack
Pressman, H. Mark

Fullerton
Brattstrom, Bayard H.
Brown, Daniel Aloysius
Frazee, Charles Aaron
Hanson, Bruce
Reich, Louis John

Gilroy
Hargis, Jeffrey W.

Glendora
Dingilian, Der Stepanos

Gold River
Loewy, Roberta S.

Goleta
Dell'Agostino, David
Nogales, Patti

Hayward
Sapontzis, Steve Frederic

Hollywood
Shaw, Curtis Mitchell

Huntington Beach
Mason, Jeffrey A.

Inglewood
Reid, Benjamin F.

Irvine
Antonelli, Gian Aldo
Ayala, Francisco J.
Johnson, Ben
Maddy, Penelope
Munevar, Gonzalo
Santas, Gerasimos
Skyrms, Brian
Stanford, Preston K.
Walsh, Roger

Kensington
Kohn, Richard
Sinclair, Scott G.

La Crescenta
O'Sullivan, Michael

La Jolla
Arneson, Richard J.
Brink, David O.
Churchland, Paul M.
Doppelt, Gerald D.
Friedman, Richard Elliott
Glymour, Clark
Hardimon, Michael O.

Jolley, Nicholas
Kitcher, Patricia
Kitcher, Philip
Martin, Wayne M.
Mitchell, Sandra D.
Morris, Paul
Neuhouser, Frederick
Reynolds, Edward
Sher, Gila
Stroll, Avrum
Yalowitz, Steven

La Mesa
Ruja, Harry

La Mirada
Bloom, John A.
Finley, Thomas John

Laguna Hills
Levesque, Paul J.

Lancaster
Sharkey, Paul

Livermore
Grill, T.R.
Porter, Andrew P.

Long Beach
Battenfield, James R.
Burke, Albie
Tang, Paul C.L.
Van Camp, Julie C.
Van De Mortal, Joseph A.

Los Alamitos
Piar, Carlos R.

Los Altos Hills
Roth, Jean

Los Angeles
Altman, Scott A.
Araiza, William
Arlen, Jennifer H.
Armour, Jody D.
Barnes, Willie R.
Benson, Robert W.
Berenbaum, Michael
Bernstein, Jerry
Bice, Scott H.
Blumberg, Grace Ganz
Borsch, Frederick Houk
Brecht, Albert O.
Campbell, Lee W.
Chang, Howard F.
Chapple, C.K.
Chemerinsky, Erwin
Christol, Carl Quimby
Cody, Martin Leonard
Cohen, Stephen Marshall
Collins, Kenneth L.
Crossley, John
Cruz, David B.
Darden, Christopher A.
Dudziak, Mary L.
Dukeminier, Jesse
Ellwood, Robert S.
Estrich, Susan
Finegan, Edward J.
Fletcher, George Philip
Franklin, Carl M.
Franklin, Floyd
Friedman, Philip Allan
Fry, Michael G.
Garet, Ronald R.
Garry, Ann
Gordon, Walter Lear, III
Griffith, Thomas D.
Harris, Jimmie
Hill, Jacqueline R.
Hossein, Ziai
Johnson, Chas Floyd
Just, Felix
Karst, Kenneth L.
Keating, Gregory C.
Klein, William A.
Klerman, Daniel M.
Knoll, Michael S.
Knopoff, L.
Krier, James Edward
Krupp, E.C.
Kushner, James Alan
Lancaster, Herman Burtram
Lawrence, Lary
Lazaroff, Daniel E.
Lefcoe, George

Levine, Martin L.
Lovett, Leonard
Lowenstein, D.H.
Lyon, Thomas D.
Marder, Nancy S.
Matovina, Timothy M.
May, Christopher N.
Maynard, Therese H.
McCaffery, Edward J.
McCann, Edwin
Mead, Lisa M.
Miller, Donald
Munzer, Stephen Roger
Myers, Charles Edward
Naim, Elissa Ben
Passameck, Stephen Maurice
Peters, Aulana Louise
Pillsbury, Samuel H.
Popiden, John Robert
Pugsley, Robert Adrian
Rausch, Thomas P.
Resnik, Judith
Ryan, Herbert Joseph
Saks, Elyn R.
Saltzman, Robert M.
Shapiro, Michael H.
Simon, Larry G.
Slawson, W. David
Smith, Edwin M.
Sobel, Lionel S.
Solum, Lawrence B.
Spillenger, Clyde
Spitzer, Matthew L.
Stewart, Daniel Lewis
Stolzenberg, N.M.
Stone, Christopher D.
Strauss, Marcy
Talley, Eric L.
Tiersma, Peter M.
Tomlinson, John G.
Treusch, Paul E.
Tunick, David C.
Vairo, Georgene M.
Vander Wilt, Jeffery T.
Vanderwilt, Jeffery T.
Volokh, Eugene
Wang, Robin
Weekes, Martin Edward
Whitebread, Charles H.
Williams, Gary C.

Los Gatos
Freeman, Eugene

Malibu
Caldwell, Harry M.
Carver, Marc
Chesnutt, Randall D.
Clark, W. Royce
Cochran, Robert F., Jr.
Colson, Darrel D.
Dunaway, Baxter
Durham, Ken R.
Gough, Russell W.
Henslee, William D.
Highfield, Ronald Curtis
Hughes, Richard T.
James, Bernard
Lynn, Richardson R.
Marrs, Riock R.
McDowell, Markus
Mendosa, Antonio
Miller, Anthony
Ogden, Gregory L.
Paniccia, Patricia L.
Smith, F. Lagard
Tyler, Ronald
Willis, Tim

Marina del Rey
Moore, Max

Menlo Park
Holleran, John Warren
Patzia, Arthur G.

Merced
Hallman, Max

Mill Valley
Arbino, Gary P.
Harrop, Clayton Keith
Honeycutt, Dwight A.
Hornecker, Ronald L.
Martin, D. Michael
Nelson, Stanley A.
Schweer, G. William

Moorpark
Daurio, Janice

Moraga
Lu, Matthias

Mount View
Brennan, Mary Alethea

Newhall
Halstead, Thomas

North Hollywood
Wertheimer, Roger

Northridge
Crittenden, Charles
Goss, James
Kellenberger, Bertram James
McIntyre, Ronald Treadwell
Saunders, Kurt M.
Shofner, Robert Dancey
Sicha, Jeffrey Franklin
Yagisawa, Takashi

Oak Park
Smith, Kathryn

Oakland
Baker-Kelly, Beverly
Benham, Priscilla
Braungardt, Jurgen
Burris, John L.
Clegg, Jerry Stephen
Ford, Judith Donna
Giurlanda, Paul
Giurlanda, Paul
Hopkins, Donald Ray
Moody, Linda A.
Patten, Priscilla C.
Pavesich, Vida
Roberts, Wendy Hunter
Skaggs, Rebecca
Stuckey, Priscilla
Tatz, Mark
Webster, William H.
Weiner, Robert

Orange
Deck, Allan F.
Hennessy, Anne
Martin, Mike W.

Pacific Palisades
Popkin, Richard
Reichenbach, Maria

Palo Alto
Forbes, A. Dean
Goldworth, Amnon
Scoledes, Aristotle
Tandy, Charles

Pasadena
Bricker, Daniel P.
Brown, Colin
Goldingay, John
Gooden, Winston Earl
Hagner, Donald A.
McClendon, James Em., Jr.
Murphy, Nancey
Scholer, David M.
Thomas, Nigel J.T.
Thomson, William
Vande Kemp, Hendrika
Woodward, J.

Pomona
Ross, Peter W.

Redding
Brown, Stephen G.

Redlands
Hester, James D.

Redondo Beach
Heim, Michael R.

Ripon
Radic, Randall

Riverside
Cranor, Carl
Fischer, John Martin
Gaustad, Edwin Scott
Glidden, David

Hoefer, Carl
Hoffman, Paul
Keller, Pierre
Kim, Wonil
Magnus, Bernd
Marti, Genoveva
O'Connor, June Elizabeth
Reath, Andrews
Reck, Erich H.
Schwitzgebel, Eric
Warnke, Georgia
Wettstein, Howard K.
Wilson, Danny K.
Wright, Larry

Rohnert Park
Clayton, Philip
Wautischer, Helmut

Sacramento
Cooper, Joseph
Harris, Stephen Leroy
Loewy, Erich H.
Raye, Vance Wallace
Smith, Heman Bernard
Wu, Joseph Sen

San Anselmo
Liebert, Elizabeth
Park, Eung Chun
Waetjen, Herman C.

San Bernardino
Kallenberg, Brad J.

San Clemente
Goodman-Delahunty, Jane

San Diego
Alexander, Larry
Aquino, Maria Pilar
Atterton, Peter C.
Baber, Harriet Erica
Barbone, Steven
Carver, Frank G.
Coates, Robert Crawford
Corlett, J. Angelo
Donnelly, John
Eaton, Kent A.
Fisher, Robert Thaddeus
Gillman, Florence Morgan
Johnson, Willard
Macy, Gary A.
McKinney, George Dallas, Jr.
Nelson, Lance E.
Powell, Sam
Rigali, Norbert Jerome
Rohatyn, Dennis Anthony
Rosenstein, Leon
Scorgie, Glen G.
Wagner, Michael Frank
Warren, Edward W.
Weckstein, Donald Theodore
Weston, Thomas Spengler
Youngblood, Ronald F.

San Francisco
Arnelle, Hugh Jesse
Bach, Kent
Bassett, William W.
Beasley, Alice Margaret
Brandt, Eric A.
Brown, Amos Cleophilus
Buckley, Francis J.
Burneko, Guy
Cavanaugh, Thomas A.
Coleman, Arthur H.
Davis, Morris E.
Davis, Morris E.
Elliott, John Hall
Fitzgerald, Desmond J.
FitzGerald, Desmond J.
Forrester, William Ray
Hajdin, Mane
Jeffers, Clifton R.
Mattie, U.
McCarthy, J. Thomas
Mendieta, Eduardo
Needleman, Jacob
Silvers, Anita
Stump, David James
Tierney, Kevin Hugh
Traynor, Michael
Wang, William Kai-Sheng

San Gabriel
Chen, John C.

Fisher, Eugene J.
Fitzmyer, Joseph Augustine
Ford, John Thomas
Fuller, Alfredia Y.
Gallagher, David M.
Galston, M.
Garvey, John Leo
Gavil, Andrew I.
Gellhorn, Gay
Gerber, William
Gignac, Francis Thomas
Gillis, Chester
Golden, Donald Leon
Goldfarb, Ronald L.
Gomez Lobo, Alfonso
Gostin, Lo
Greenberg, Gershon
Gros, Jeffrey
Guttman, Egon
Haines, Diana
Hamilton, Eugene Nolan
Happel, Stephen P.
Harre, Rom
Hart, Christopher Alvin
Hassing, Richard F.
Hayden, John Carleton
Hayes, Diana L.
Heelan, Patrick Aidan
Henry, Brent Lee
Hicks, H. Beecher, Jr.
Hunter, Jerry L.
Johnson, Johnnie L., Jr.
Jollimore, Troy
Jones, Charles B.
Jordan, Emma Coleman
Jordan, Emma Coleman
Kellogg, Frederic R.
King, Patricia Ann
Kotz, Samuel
Kramer, Robert
Krattenmaker, Thomas George
Kress, Robert Lee
Kuhn, Steve
Kuhn, Steven Thomas
Kurland, Adam H.
Lamaute, Denise
Lamm, Julia A.
Lance, Mark
Langan, John P.
Latham, Weldon Hurd
Lee, K. Samuel
Lee, Milton C., Jr.
Leonard, Walter J.
Lewis, Neil
Lewis, William A., Jr.
Loewe, William Patrick
Ludwinowski, Rett R.
Marcin, Raymond B.
Marthaler, Berard Lawrence
McEleney, Neil Joseph
McIntosh, Simeon Charles
McLean, George Francis
McManus, Frederick Richard
Minnich, Nelson H.
Mitchell, Alan C.
Mohan, Robert Paul
Morris, Calvin S.
Murphy, Mark Christopher
Newsome, Clarence Geno
Norton, Eleanor Holmes
Orlans, F. Barbara
Orr, Janice
Page, Joseph Anthony
Parker, Vernon B.
Patterson, Elizabeth Hayes
Payne, Steven
Pellegrino, Edmund Daniel
Pinkard, Terry
Pitofsky, Robert
Powers, Madison
Pozzo, Riccardo
Pritzl, Kurt
Quander, Rohulamin
Queen, Evelyn E. Crawford
Quitslund, Sonya Antoinette
Raskin, Jamin
Raven-Hansen, Pete
Rehnquist, William Hubbs
Reich, Warren T.
Reid, Inez Smith
Reuscher, John
Rice, Paul R.
Richardson, Henry
Robbins, Ira Paul
Rossi, Christopher
Rothstein, Paul Frederick
Salla, Michael
Salzman, Jim
Sanders, Cheryl J.

Sargentich, Thomas O.
Schall, James Vincent
Schlagel, Richard H.
Schmidt, Frederick W.
Schwartz, Herman
Seidman, Louis Michael
Shalleck, Ann
Shanks, Hershel
Sherman, Nancy
Smith, George P.
Smith, J. Clay, Jr.
Sokolowski, Robert S.
Spragens, Janet R.
Stent, Michelle Dorene
Stevens, John Paul
Strong, Douglas M.
Studzinski, Raymond James
Thomas, Clarence
Tm, King
Trisco, Robert Frederick
Tushnet, Mark Victor
Tylenda, Joseph N.
Vaughn, Robert Gene
Veatch, Robert M.
Velkley, Richard L.
Ver Eecke, Wilfried
Vukovich, William T.
Wagner, Annice
Wald, Patricia M.
Wallace, Dewey D., Jr.
Wallace, Paul Starett, Jr.
Washington, Robert Benjamin, Jr.
Waysdorf, Susan L.
Wechsler, Burton D.
White, Charles Sidney John
White, Kevin
Williams, Karen Hastie
Williams, Paul R.
Williams, Yvonne LaVerne
Wilmot, David Winston
Winter, Douglas E.
Winters, Francis Xavier
Wippel, John Francis
Wiseman, James A.
Wogaman, John Philip
Young, Michael Kent

FLORIDA

Archer
Sarver, Vernon T.

Aripeka
Harley, Gail M.

Boca Raton
Banchetti-Robino, Marina P.
Berger, Alan L.
Fiore, Robin N.
Glynn, Simon

Bonita Springs
James, Robert N.

Carol City
Tumpkin, Mary A.

Coral Gables
Alexandrakis, Aphrodite
Coscullsia, Victor
Fitzgerald, John Thomas, Jr.
Goldman, Alan H.
Haack, Susan
Lemos, Ramon M.
Pospesel, Howard

Daytona Beach
Golden, Evelyn Davis
Hamlin, Ernest Lee
Perkins, Moreland

DeLand
Reddish, Mitchell Glenn
Steeves, Paul David

Delray Beach
Marietta, Don E.

Fort Lauderdale
Mulvey, Ben
Reymond, Robert L.
Robertson, O. Palmer
White, R. Fowler

Fort Myers
Sutter, Leslie E.

Fort Pierce
Cohen, Elliot

Gainesville
Alexander, Laurence Benedict
Ankersen, Thomas T.
Baldwin, Fletcher N., Jr.
Barnett Lidsky, Lyrissa C.
Baum, Robert J.
Bennett, Gerald T.
Calfee, Dennis A.
Chamberlin, Bill F.
Cohn, Stuart R.
Collier, Charles W.
Cotter, Thomas F.
Craig-Taylor, Phyliss
D'Amico, Robert
Davis, Jeffrey
Dawson, George L.
Dilley, Patricia E.
Dowd, Nancy E.
Flournoy, Alyson Craig
Friel, Michael K.
Gordon, Michael W.
Hackett, David H.
Harrison, Jeffrey L.
Hiers, Richard H.
Hudson, Davis M.
Hurst, Thomas R.
Isenberg, Sheldon Robert
Israel, Jerold H.
Jacobs, Michelle S.
Juergensmeyer, Julian C.
Lear, Elizabeth T.
Lewis, Jeffrey E.
Little, Joseph W.
Lokken, Lawrence
Ludwig, Kirk
Malavet, Pedro A.
Mashburn, Amy R.
Matasar, Richard
Mazur, Diane H.
McCoy, Francis T.
McCulloch, Elizabeth
McMahon, Martin J., Jr.
Millender, Michael J.
Miller, C. Douglas
Mills, Jon L.
Moberly, Robert B.
Moffat, Robert C.L.
Nagan, Winston P.
Nicholas, James C.
Noah, Lars
Nunn, Kenneth B.
Oberst, Michael A.
Ray, Greg
Richardson, David M.
Rush, Sharon E.
Seigel, Michael L.
Slobogin, Christopher
Smillov, Marin S.
Smith, David T.
Taylor, Grace W.
Thursby, Gene Robert
Twitchell, Mary Poe
Wade, Jeffry
Weyrauch, Walter Otto
Williams, Winton E.
Willis, Steven J.
Witmer, Donald G.
Wright, Danaya C.

Hollywood
Taylor, Williamson S.

Jacksonville
Bowen, David H.
Koegler, Hans-Herbert
Watson, Cletus Claude

Lakeland
Silber, Daniel
Smith, W. Alan

Maitland
Farrell, Frank
Gamble, Richard C.
Hill, Charles
James, Frank
Kistemaker, Simon
McReynolds Kidd, Reggie
Nash, Ronald
Nicole, Roger
Pratt, Richard L., Jr.
Waltke, Bruce K.

Melbourne
Ritson, G. Joy

Miami
Casebier, Allan
Chung, Bongkil
Gudorf, Christine E.
Hawkins, Benjamin Sanford, Jr.
Heine, Steven
Katz, Nathan
Kling, David
Knox, George F.
Koperski, Veronica
Krebs, Victor J.
Madden, Daniel Patrick
Northup, Lesley A.
Ross, Ralph M.
Skjoldal, Neil O.
Smith, Harold Teliaferro, Jr.
Warren, Paul R.
Williams, Gary G. Cohen

Miami Beach
Swain, James H.

Miami Shores
Iozzio, Mary Jo
Sunshine, Edward R.

Pensacola
Arnold, Barry
Howe, Lawrence W.

Pompano Beach
Gauss, Charles E.

Punta Gorda
Winter, John Ellsworth

Sanibel
Ennis, Robert H.

Sarasota
Herdt, Jennifer A.
Snyder, Lee Daniel

Spring Hill
Raskin, Jay

St. Augustine
Klein, Ellen R.

St. Augustine Beach
Goldthwait, John T.

St. Petersburg
Beal, Timothy K.
Beane, Dorothea Annette
Brown, James J.
Bryant, David J.
DesAutels, Peggy
Foltz, Bruce
Goetsch, James R.
Jacob, Bruce Robert
Neusner, Jacob
Rhodes Bailly, Constantina
Whitney, Ruth

Tallahassee
Bedell, George Chester
Dalton, Peter C.
Dickson, David Franklin
Felder, David W.
Griffith, Elwin Jabez
Gruender, Carl David
Hatchett, Joseph Woodrow
Hodges, Donald Clark
Jacobs, Ennis Leon, Jr.
Jung, Darryl
Kaelin, Eugene Francis
Kleck, Gary
Lyon, Gordon W.
Mabe, Alan R.
Matthews, Patricia
Morales, Maria H.
Ravenell, William Hudson
Rickless, Samuel
Smith, Jeraldine Williams
Swain, Charles W.
Watson, H. Justin
Weidner, Donald John

Tampa
Anton, John P.
Argen, Ralph J., III
DeChant, Dell
French, Peter A.
Jorgensen, Danny L.
McAlister, Linda L.
Miller, John F., III

Polythress, N.G.
Schonfeld, Martin
Strange, James F.
Weatherford, Roy C.

West Palm Beach
Nolan, Richard T.

Winter Park
Cook, J. Thomas
Edge, Hoyt Littleton
Rubarth, Scott M.

GEORGIA

Athens
Bennett-Alexander, Dawn DeJuana
Clarke, Bowman Lafayette
Gordon, Walter Martin
Halper, Edward Charles
Harrison, Frank Russell
Hellerstein, Walter
Heslep, Robert Durham
Kleiner, Scott Alter
Power, William L.
Rice, Berry
Rosenberg, Alexander
Thomas, Maxine Suzanne

Atlanta
Almeder, Robert F.
Arrington, Robert Lee
Bailey, Randall Charles
Barlow, Brian C.
Bell, Linda A.
Berman, Harold J.
Bianchi, Eugene Carl
Blumenfeld, David
Blumenthal, David Reuben
Borowski, Oded
Brady, Michelle E.
Buss, Martin John
Carney, William J.
Carr, David
Carr, Davis
Carter, Lawrence E., Sr.
Chopp, Rebeca S.
Clark, J. Michael
Conwill, Giles
Cooper, Clarence
Costen, Melva Wilson
Culpepper, R. Alan
Darden, George Harry
Eiesland, Nancy L.
Ellingsen, Mark
Ferguson, William Dean
Flynn, Thomas R.
Fotion, Nicholas
Franklin, Robert Michael
Gerkin, Charles Vincent
Ghosh, Shuba
Gouinlock, James
Grant, Jacquelyn
Grant Luckhardt, C.
Hall, Pamela M.
Hallen, Barry
Hartle, Ann
Harwood, Robin
Hawk, Charles Nathaniel, III
Helminiak, Daniel A.
Herman, Jonathan
Holifield, E. Brooks
Holladay, Carl R.
Holler, Clyde
Hooker, Paul K.
Humber, James Michael
Hunter, Rodney J.
Jacobson, Stephen
Johnson, Ronald W.
Kasfir, Sidney L.
Kiersky, James H.
Knight, Caroly Ann
Kuntz, Paul G.
Livingston, Donald W.
Luckhardt, C. Grant
Machado, Daisy L.
Makkreel, Rudolf A.
Martinez, Roy
McCauley, Robert N.
Miller, J. Maxwell
Mohanty, Jitendra N.
Neujahr, Philip Joseph
Norton, Bryan G.
Overbeck, James A.
Parchment, Steven
Persons, W. Ray
Pollard, Alton Brooks, III

Wren, Thomas
Yeo, Khiok-Khng

Flossmoor
Collins, John J.

Galesburg
Factor, Ralph Lance

Glen Ellyn
Maller, Mark P.

Godfrey
Mozur, Gerald E.

Gurnee
Schnabel, Eckhard j.

Homewood
Gerrish, Brian Albert

Jacksonville
Goulding, James Allan
Koss, David Henry
Palmer, Richard E.

Kaneville
Lee, Sungho

La Grange
Atkins, Robert A., Jr.

Lake Forest
Benton, Catherine
Miller, Ronald H.

Lebanon
Neale, Philip Whitby

Lombard
Borchert, Gerald Leo
Dayton, Donald Wilber
Weber, Timothy P

Macomb
Bracey, Willie Earl
Davenport, Harbert William
Helm, Thomas Eugene
Keeling, Lytle Bryant
Morelli, Mario Frank

Maywood
Thomasma, David C.

Monmouth
Johnson, J. Prescott
Li, Chenyang

Mount Prospect
Pankey, William J.
Wachsmuth, Wayne R.

Mundelein
Davis, Kenneth G.
Lefebure, Leo D.
Lodge, John G.

Murphysboro
Lyons, Robin R.

Naperville
Mueller, Howard Ernest

Normal
Anderson, David Leech
Bailey, Alison
Baldwin, John R.
Machina, Kenton F.

Oak Brook
Brown, Dale W.
Durnbaugh, Donald F.

Orland Hills
Merwin, Peter Matthew

Palatine
Stone, Jerome Arthur

Palos Heights
Ward, Annalee R.

Peoria
Fuller, Robert Charles

Quincy
Biallas, Leonard John

Ridge
Doherty, Barbara

River Forest
Froehlich, Charles Donald
Heider, George C.
McElwain, Hugh Thomas

Riverside
Martin, Marty

Rock Island
Tredway, John Thomas

Rockford
Hicks, Stephen R.C.
Walhout, Donald

Romeoville
McVann, Mark
Nissim-Sabat, Marilyn

Springfield
Boltuc, Piotr
Kitching, Benita
Taylor, Richard Stuart

St. Anne
Capriotti, Emile

Urbana
Baron, Marcie
Hoffman, Valerie J.
McMahan, Jefferson
Schmitt, Frederick Francis
Schoedel, William Richard
Wallace, James Donald
Wanner, Dieter

Wauconda
Bolchazy, Ladislaus J.

Wheaton
Callahan, James
Elwell, Walter Alexander
Ericson, Norman R.
Fletcher, David B.
Hawthorne, Gerald F.
Hein, Rolland Neal
Lewis, James F.
McRay, John Robert
Noll, Mark Allan

Wilmette
Vivas, Eliseo
Will, James Edward

Woodridge
Rapple, Eva Marie

INDIANA

Anderson
Burnett, Fredrick Wayne
Massey, James Earl
Stafford, Gilbert W.

Bloomington
Ackerman, James S.
Alexander, Scott C.
Aman, Alfred C., Jr.
Bokenkamp, Stephen R.
Bradley, Craig M.
Brakke, David
Campany, Robert F.
Cocchiarella, Nino Barnabas
Dauschmidt, Kenneth G.
Dickson, Michael
Dunn, Jon Michael
Dworkin, Roger Barnett
Eisenberg, Paul D.
Friedman, Michael
Gaetke, Eugene Roger
Gupta, Anil K.
Haberman, David L.
Hart, James G.
Hofstadter, Douglas Richard
Johnson, Luke Timothy
Kleinbauer, W. Eugene
Koertge, Noretta
Larson, Gerald J.
Lloyd, Elisabeth A.

Lopez-Morillas, Consuelo
Marks, Herbert J.
McRae, John R.
Miller, Richard B.
Mongoven, Ann
Nakhnikion, George
Orsi, Robert A.
Pietsch, Paul Andrew
Preus, J. Samuel
Smith, David H.
Sorrenson, Richard J.
Stein, Stephen J.
Stein, Stephen J.
Tanford, J. Alexander
Tirosh Samuelson, Hava
Weaver, Mary Jo
Wiggins, William H., Jr.
Zheng, Yiwei

Crawfordsville
Peebles, I.Hall
Placher, William C.

Elkhart
Bender, Ross Thomas
Dyck, Cornelius John
Koontz, Gayle Gerber
Lind, Millard C.
Swartley, Willard M.

Evansville
Sullivan, Stephen J.

Floyds Knobs
Shields, George W.

Fort Wayne
Butler, Clark Wade
Collins, Robert H.
Gerig, Wesley Lee
Kumfer, Earl T.
Maier, Walter A.
Scaer, David P.
Squadrito, Kathleen Marie

Gary
Grimes, Douglas M.

Goshen
Boys, Samuel A.
Graber-Miller, Keith A.

Greencastle
Allen, O. Wesley, Jr.
Chandler, Marthe Atwater
Holm, Tawny
Shannon, Daniel E.

Greenwood
Clapper, Gregory

Hagerstown
Lambert, Byron C.

Hammond
Koenig, Thomas Roy
Rowan, John R.

Hanover
Barlow, Philip L.
Campbell, Joseph Gordon
Cassel, J. David

Huntington
Fairchild, Mark R.
Sanders, John

Indianapolis
Allen, Ronald J.
Ashanin, Charles B.
Bepko, Gerald L.
Burke, Michael B.
Byrne, Edmund F.
Funk, David A.
Heise, Michael
Houser, Nathan
Jackson, William Joseph
Janzen, John Gerald
Johnston, Carol F.
Kinney, E.D.
Miller, James Blair
Nagy, Paul
Planeaux, Christopher
Reidy, David
Saatkamp, Herman J.
Saffire, Paula Reiner
Smurl, James Frederick

Steussy, Marti J.
Tilley, John
van der Linden, Harry
Williamson, Clark M.

Jeffersonville
Besson, Paul Smith

Kokomo
Lopes, Dominic McIver
Strikwerds, Robert A.

Marion
Bence, Clarence
Drury, Keith
Kierstead, Melanie Starks
Lennox, Stephen J.
Lo, Jim
Starks Kierstead, Melanie

Mishawaka
Blowers, LaVerne P.
Erdel, Timothy Paul

Muncie
Mertens, Thomas R.

New Albany
Bowden, James Henry

New Castle
Schubert, E.

Newburgh
Martin, Edward N.

North Manchester
Brown, Kenneth Lee
Deeter, Allen C

Notre Dame
Ameriks, Karl
Ashley, James Matthew
Attridge, Harold William
Blanchette, Patricia
Blenkinsopp, Joseph
Bobik, Joseph
Burrell, David
Burtchaell, James T.
Cavadini, John C.
Crosson, Frederick J.
Dallmayr, Fred Reinhard
David, Marian
Delaney, Cornelius F.
DePaul, Michael R.
Detlefsen, Michael
Dolan, Jay P.
Dunne, John Scribner
Fiorenza, Elizabeth Schussler
Flint, Thomas P.
Fox, Christopher B.
Freddoso, Alfred J.
Gutting, Gary Michael
Howard, Don A.
Jenkins, John
Jordan, Mark D.
Klima, Gyula
Kmiec, Douglas William
Kremer, Michael
Krieg, Robert A.
Leyerle, Blake
Loux, Michael
Malloy, Edward A.
Manier, A. Edward
Marsden, G.M.
McBrien, Richard Peter
McCormick, R.A.
McInerny, Ralph M.
McKim, Vaughn R.
McMullin, Ernan
Mirowski, Philip E.
Murphy, Edward Joseph
Neyrey, Jerome H.
O'Connor, David
Phelps, Teresa Godwin
Plantinga, Alvin
Quinn, Philip L.
Ramsey, William M.
Rice, Charles E.
Ripple, Kenneth Francis
Robinson, John H.
Rodes, Robert Emmet
Sayre, Kenneth Malcolm
Sayre, Patricia
Sent, Esther Mirjam
Shin, Sun Joo
Shrader-Frechette, Kristin
Smith, Randall Brian

Smithburn, John Eric
Solomon, William David
Sterba, James P.
Stubenberg, Leopold
Udoh, Fabian E.
van Inwagen, Peter
Vander Kam, James C.
Warfield, Ted A.
Watson, Stephen
Weiss, Herold D.
Weithman, Paul J.
Zimmerman, Dean

Richmond
Barbour, Hugh
Suber, Peter Dain

South Bend
Devenish, Philip Edward
Meier, John P.
Naylor, Andrew
Stockman, Robert H.

St. Meinrad
Cody, Aelred
Walter, James Joseph

Terre Haute
Barad, Judith
Gennaro, Rocco J.
Grcic, Joseph M.
Johnson, David Lawrence

Upland
Charles, J. Daryl
Corduan, Winfried
Harbin, Michael A.
Helyer, Larry R.
Spiegel, James S.

Valparaiso
Bachman, James V.
Bass, Dorothy C.
Brant, Dale
Brietzke, Paul H.
Geiman, Kevin
Hatcher, Richard Gordon
Klein, Kenneth
Krodel, Gottfried G.
Ludwig, Theodore Mark
Meilaender, Gilbert
Niedner, Frederick A.
Rast, Walter Emil
Truemper, David George

Valparaiso
Kennedy, Thomas

Vincennes
Rinderle, Walter
Verkamp, Bernard

West Lafayette
Bergmann, Michael
Bertolet, Rod
Cover, Jan
Curd, Martin
Curd, Martin Vincent
Gill, Michael
Gustason, William
Kuehn, Manfred
Marina, Jacqueline
Martinez, Jacqueline M.
Matustik, Martin J. Beck
McBride, William Leon
Mitchell, Donald
Mumby, Dennis K.
Rowe, William L.
Russow, Lilly-Marlene
Scerri, Eric R.
Schrag, Calvin
Schrag, Calvin Orville
Scott, Kermit
Seigfried, Charlene
Stevens, George E.
Swensen, Clifford Henrik
Thompson, Paul B.
Ulrich, Dolph

Winona Lake
Bateman, Herbert W.

IOWA

Ames
Bishop, Michael
Donaghy, John A.
Hollenbach, Paul William
Klemke, Elmer Daniel
Robinson, William Spencer
Rudge, David W.
Soroka, Jacek
Vidal, Jaime R.

Burlington
Benjamin, Paul

Cedar Falls
Crownfield, David R.
Holland, Margaret G.
Robinson, James Burnell

Cedar Rapids
Martin, Charlotte Joy
Robinson, Mary Elizabeth
Sessions, Robert

Davenport
Jacobson, Paul Kenneth
Johnson, Geraldine Ross

Decorah
Bailey, Storm M.
Bunge, Wilfred F.
Hanson, Bradley
Sieber, John Harold

Des Moines
Baker, Thomas Eugene
Kniker, Charles R.
Patrick, Dale
Sisk, G.C.

Dubuque
Albin, Thomas R.
Ashley, Benedict M
Bailey, James L.
Bloesch, Donald G.
Colyer, Elmer M.
Freund, Norm
Healey, Robert Mathieu
Jung, L. Shannon
Kang, Wi Jo
Kang, Wi Jo
Martin, Raymond Albert
McDermott, John J.
Platt, Elizabeth Ellan
Priebe, Duane A.
Quere, Ralph Walter
Skiba, Paulette
Stevenson-Moessner, Jeanne
Thibeau, Matthew J.

Forest City
Hamre, James S.

Grinnell
Burkle, Howard R.
Cummins, W. Joseph
Goldberg, Sanford C.
Meehan, M. Johanna
Rosenthal, Michael A.
Schrift, Alan D.

Iowa City
Adamek, Wendi
Addis, Laird Clark
Andreasen, Nancy C.
Baird, Robert Dahlen
Beaudoin, John M.
Bergmann, Gustav
Boyle, John Phillips
Bozeman, Theodore Dwight
Butchvarov, Panayot K.
Clinton, Robert N.
Duerlinger, James
Fales, Evan Michael
Forell, George Wolfgang
Fumerton, Richard A.
Kuntz, J. Kenneth
Landini, Gregory
McPherson, James Alan
Nickelsburg, George William Elmer
Pachow, Wang
Spalding, James Colwell
Thomas, Randall S.
Weston, Burns H.
Widiss, Alan I.

Wing, Adrien Katherine

Janesville
Hallberg, Fred William

Mount Vernon
Ihlan, Amy
Vernoff, Charles Elliott
Weddle, David L.

Orange City
Rohrer, James
Van Hook, Jay M.

Sioux City
Cooney, William
Lawrence, John Shelton

Waterloo
Weems, Vernon Eugene, Jr.

KANSAS

Atchison
Macierowski, E.M.
Meade, Denis
Nowell, Irene

Baldwin City
Hatcher, Donald L.
Wiley, George

Emporia
Roark, Dallas Morgan
Toadvine, Ted

Hillsboro
Miller, Douglas B.

Hutchinson
Chalfant, William Y.

Kansas City
Keeney, Donald E.
May, David M.
Wheeler, David L.

Lawrence
Coggins, George Cameron
Cole, Richard
Cudd, Ann E.
Genova, Anthony Charles
Head, John W.
Marquis, Donald Bagley
Martin, Rex
Miller, Timothy Alan
Minor, Robert Neil
Mirecki, Paul A.
Shafer-Landau, Russell

Manhattan
Linder, Robert Dean

McPherson
Stamey, Joseph Donald

North Newton
Friesen, Duane K.

Ottawa
Discher, Mark R.

Overland Park
Olson, Richard P.

Roeland Park
Knight, Henry H.

Sterling
MacArthur, Steven D.

Topeka
Concannon, James M.
Elrod, Linda Diane Henry
Griffin, Ronald Charles
Henry Elrod, Linda
Rabouin, E. Michelle
Ryan, David L.
Spring, Raymond Lewis

Wichita
Dooley, Patricia
Keel, Vernon
Mandt, Almer J., III

Pyles, John E.

Winfield
Gray, Wallace

KENTUCKY

Barbourville
Sisson, Russell

Berea
Pearson, Eric

Bowling Green
Casey, Kenneth
Curtis-Howe, E. Margaret
Long, John Edward
Schoen, Edward Lloyd
Tuck, Donald Richard
Veenker, Ronald Allen
Vos, Arvin G.

Burgin
Huddleston, Tobianna W.

Covington
Blair, George Alfred

Crestview Hills
Twaddell, Gerald E.

Danville
Cooney, Brian Patrick
Glazier-McDonald, Beth
McCollough, C. Thomas
Mount, Charles Eric, Jr.
Mount, Eric, Jr.
Scarborough, Milton R.

Georgetown
Lunceford, Joseph E.
Redditt, Paul L.
Wirzba, Norman

Grayson
Fiensy, David A.
Pickens, George F.

Highland Heights
Bell, Sheila Trice
Richards, Jerald H.
Trundle, Robert C., Jr.

Lexington
Daniel, E. Randolph
Dowd, Sharyn
Dunnavant, Anthony L.
Fakhrid-Deen, Nashid Abdullah
Faupel, William
Frank, Daniel H.
High, Dallas Milton
Jones, Paul Henry
Manns, James William
McAvoy, Jane
Meinke, William B.
Moseley, James G.
Nugent, Donald Christopher
Olshewsky, Thomas Mack
Perreiah, Alan Richard
Pickens, Rupert Tarpley
Smaw, Eric
Stilwell, William E., III
Witherington, Ben

Louisville
Akin, Daniel L.
Alperson, Philip A.
Anderson, Marvin W.
Barnette, Henlee Hulix
Beougher, Timothy K.
Blaising, Craig A.
Blevins, James Lowell
Cabal, Ted
Chancellor, James D.
Conver, Leigh E.
Cook, E. David
Cooper, Burton
Cruz, Virgil
Cunningham, Jack R.
Drinkard, Joel F., Jr.
Ellis Smith, Marsha A.
Fuller, Russell T.
Hausman, Carl A.
House, Paul R.
Hoyt-O'Connor, Paul E.

Hughes, Robert Don
John, Eileen
Kimball, Robert
Lawless, Charles E.
Maloney, Thomas
March, Wallace Eugene
Martin, Janice R.
Martos, Joseph
Masolo, D.A.
Mitchell, C. Ben
Mohler, R. Albert, Jr.
Mueller, David L.
Pelletier, Samuel R.
Poethig, Eunice Blanchard
Polhill, John B.
Potter, Nancy
Rainer, Thom S.
Richardson, Brian C.
Schreiner, Thomas R.
Simpson, Mark E.
Stein, Robert H.
Stenger, Robert Leo
Stroble, Paul E., Jr.
Terry, J. Mark
Walsh, Thomas
Ware, Bruce A.
Weaver, Russel L.
Wiggins, Osborne P., Jr.
Williams, Dennis E.
Wills, Gregory A.

Morehead
Mangrum, Franklin M.

Murray
Foreman, Terry Hancock

Owensboro
Fager, Jeff

Richmond
Fox, James Walker
Gray, Bonnie Jean
Harris, Bond

Williamsburg
Ramey, George

Wilmore
Anderson, Neil D.
Arnold, Bill T.
Green, Joel B.
Hamilton, Victor Paul
Kinghorn, Kenneth Cain
Layman, Fred Dale
Lyon, Robert William
Madden, Edward
Peterson, Michael Lynn
Thompson, David L.
Walters, John R.

LOUISIANA

Baton Rouge
Baker, John R.
Bennett, Philip W.
Blakesley, Christopher L.
Bowers, J.W.
Buehler, Arthur F.
Burkett, Delbert Royce
Crawford, William Edward
Day, Louis A.
Dubois, Sylvie
Fitzgerald, Patrick
Harned, David D.
Henderson, Edward H.
Henderson, John B.
Irvine, Stuart
Isadore, Harold W.
Johnson, Ernest L.
Jones, Carolyn
Jones, Carolyn M.
Knight, Gary
Korwar, Arati
May, John R.
McMahon, Robert
Payne, Rodger M.
Schufreider, Gregory
Seynaeve, Jaak
Shirley, Edward S.
Sirridge, Mary
Sutherland, Gail Hinich
Whittaker, John
Yiannopoulos, A.N.

Lake Charles
Sennett, James

Marrero
Gumms, Emmanuel George, Sr.

Monroe
Hingle, Norwood N., III
Madden, Patrick
Wilson, Holly

New Orleans
Bogdan, Radu J.
Bourgeois, Patrick Lyall
Brower, Bruce W.
Bruns, James Edgar
Burger, Ronna C.
Doll, Mary A.
Duffy, Stephen Joseph
Folse, Henry J., Jr.
Forbes, Graeme
Glenn, John Deavenport, Jr.
Gnuse, Robert
Golluber, Michael
Green, O. Harvey
Hanks, Donald
Herbert, Gary
Holloway, Alvin J.
Howard, David M., Jr.
Johnson, Edward
Jordan, Eddie J., Jr.
Klebba, James Marshall
Lee, Donald S.
Lee, Donald Soule
Lodge, Paul A.
Mack, Eric M.
Mazoue, Jim
Phillips, Clarence Mark
Reck, Andrew Joseph
Schalow, Frank
Soble, Alan
Strong, L. Thomas, III
Uddo, Basile Joseph
Watson, James R.
Willems, Elizabeth
Zimmerman, Michael E.

Shreveport
Otto, David
Rigby, Kenneth
Sur, Carolyn Worman

MAINE

Bangor
Trobisch, David

Brunswick
Gelwick, Richard
Long, Burke O'Connor
Pols, Edward

Lewiston
Kolb, David Alan

Orono
Acampora, Christa Davis
Cunningham, Sarah B.
Howard, Michael W.

Portland
Caffentzis, C. George
Cluchey, David P.
Delogu, Orlando E.
Gavin, William
Grange, Joseph
Gregory, David D.
Lang, Michael B.
Louden, Robert B.
Murphy, Julien
Rieser, Alison
Schwanauer, Francis
Ward, Thomas M.
Wells, William W.
Wininger, Kathleen
Wriggins, Jennifer
Zillman, Donald N.

Presque Isle
Blackstone, Thomas L.

South Berwick
Olbricht, Thomas H.

Steep Falls
Keay, Robert

Waterville
Geller, David A.
Hudson, Yeager
Longstaff, Thomas R.W.
McArthur, Robert L.

MARYLAND

Adelphi
Wallace, William A.

Annapolis
O'Donovan-Anderson, Michael

Babson Park
Seitz, Brian

Baltimore
Achinstein, Peter
Barker, Evelyn M.
Bauerschmidt, Frederick Christian
Bett, Richard
Bittner, Thomas
Bowman, Leonard Joseph
Brumbaugh, John Maynard
Carter, Charles Edward
Chiu, Hungdah
Fee, Elizabeth
Fitts, Leroy
Geiger, Mary Virginia
Gorman, Michael J.
Hillers, Delbert Roy
Ike, Alice Denise
Kahane, Howard
Lasson, Kenneth L.
Leder, Drew L.
Makarushka, Irena
McKinney, Richard I.
Neander, K.
Power, Garrett
Roca, Robert Paul
Scherer, Imgard S.
Schneewind, Jerome B.
Sellers, Mortimer
Talar, Charles J. T.
Tassi, Aldo
Wolf, Susan R.

Bethesda
Devos, Jean
Geyer, Alan
Godsey, John Drew

Cantonsville
Pilch, John J.

Catonsville
Field, Thomas Tilden

Chevy Chase
Miller, Franklin
Ricciardelli, Angela R.
Timbie, Janet Ann

Clinton
Williams, Wilbert Lee

College Park
Brown, Peter G.
Claude, Richard P.
Darden, Lindley
Darden, Lindley
Devitt, Michael
Gaines, Robert N.
Levinson, Jerrold
Martin, Raymond Frederick
Moss, Alfred A., Jr.
Pasch, Alan
Penner, Merrilynn J.
Sagoff, Mark

Columbia
Keeton, Morris Teuton
White, Alfred Loe

Edgewater
Hammer, Jane R.

Emmitsburg
Collinge, William Joseph
Conway, Gertrude D.
Donovan, John F.

Drummond, John J.
McDonald, Patricia M.
Portier, William L.
Selner-Wright, Susan C.
Wright, Terrence C.

Frederick
Hein, David
Moreland, Raymond T., Jr.

Frostburg
Bramann, Jorn Karl

Germantown
Gabriele, Edward

Hyattsville
Komonchak, Joseph Andrew

La Plata
Bilsker, Richard L.

Largo
Cloud, W. Eric

Lexington Park
McNeill, Susan Patricia

Lutherville
Muuss, Rolf Eduard Helmut

Rockville
Haffner, Marlene Elisabeth
McDonald, Peter J.T.

Salisbury
Clement, Grace
Kane, Francis
Miller, Jerome A.

Silver Spring
Howze, Karen Aileen
Hunt, Mary Elizabeth
Morse, Oliver
Rodriguez, Angel Manuel
Smith, David R.

St. Mary's City
Krondorfer, Bjoern
Paskow, Alan
Rosemont, Henry
Von Kellenbach, Katharine

Stevenson
Penczek, Alan

MASSACHUSETTS

Allston
D'Agostino, Peter R.
Stark, Tracey
Stoehr, Kevin L.

Amherst
Aune, Bruce Arthur
Baker, Lynne R.
Chappell, Vere Claiborne
Elias, Jamal J.
Gyatso, J.
Hodder, Alan
Kennick, William Elmer
Matthews, Gareth Blanc
Mazor, Lester Jay
Mills, Patricia J.
Moore, Joseph G.
Niditch, Susan
Sleigh, Robert Collins
Wills, David Wood
Wolff, Robert Paul

Belmont
Waldau, Paul

Beverly
Jerin, Robert A.
McCarthy, Thomas

Boston
Andresen, Jensine
Ashe, Marie
Barash, Carol Isaacson
Beauchesne, Richard J.
Blum, Karen M.
Blum, Lawrence A.
Blumenson, Eric D.

Brinkmann, Klaus
Brown, Barry
Burch, Sharon Peebles
Carty-Bennia, Denise S.
Cass, Ronald Andrew
Cavallaro, Rosanna
Clark, Gerard J.
Day, Kate N.
Dodd, Victoria J.
Eisenstat, Steven M.
Epps, Valerie C.
Feld, Alan L.
Ferrarin, Alfredo
Floyd, Juliet
Foster, Lawrence
Fredriksen, P.
Friedland, B.
Garrett, Gerald R.
Gilkes, Cheryl Townsend
Givelber, Daniel James
Glannon, Joseph William
Gregory, Wanda Torres
Haakonssen, Knud
Hall, David
Harvey, Mark S.
Harvey, William Burnett
Hecht, Neil S.
Hines, Mary E.
Hintikka, Jaakko
Horne, Ralph Albert
Ireland, Roderick Louis
Kaye, Lawrence J.
Kee, Howard Clark
Klare, Karl E.
Kopaczynski, Germain
Krakauer, Eric
Levine, Julius B.
Lidz, Joel W.
Lindberg, Carter Harry
Lyons, David
Mason, Herbert Warren
Nathanson, Stephen Lewis
Neville, Robert C.
Nolan, John Joseph
Oliver, Harold Hunter
Park, William Wynnewood
Partan, Daniel Gordon
Perlin, Marc G.
Perlmutter, Richard Mark
Pruett, Gordon Earl
Radden, Jennifer
Raymond, Diane
Roberts, Wesley A.
Silbaugh, Katherine
Silber, John Robert
Stafford, Sue P.
Tauber, Alfred I.
Thiruvengadam, Raj
Torres-Gregory, Wanda
Vrame, Anton C.

Brockton
Caranfa, Angelo

Brookline
Chryssavgis, John
Fox, Sanford J.
Marangos, Frank
Stone, David A.

Cambridge
Abe, Nobuhiko
Appel, Frederick
Appiah, Kwame Anthony
Bartholet, Elizabeth
Benhabib, Seyla
Bok, Derek Curtis
Bovon, Francois
Clifford, Richard J.
Cox, Archibald
Daley, Brian Edward
Dershowitz, Alan Morton
Dyck, Arthur James
Fideler, Paul Arthur
Fisher, Roger
Foerst, Anne
Fried, Charles
Frug, Gerald Ellison
Graham, William A.
Haar, Charles Monroe
Hanson, Paul David
Harrington, Daniel Joseph
Harris, Errol E.
Heck, Richard
Henrich, Dieter
Herwitz, David Richard
Horovitz, Amir
Hullett, James N.
Jasanoff, Sheila S.

Jolls, C.
Kane, Thomas Anthony
Kaplow, Louis
Katz, Milton
Kaufman, Gordon Dester
Keenan, J.F.
Keeton, Robert Ernest
Keller, Evelyn Fox
Koester, Helmut
Korsgaard, Christine M.
Kuhn, Thomas Samuel
Kujawa, Sheryl A.
LaMothe, Kimerer L.
Marrow, Stanley Behjet
Martin, Jane Roland
Martin, Joan M.
Martin, Michael Lou
Minow, Martha
Moran, Richard
Nesson, Charles Rothwell
Nozick, Robert
Ogletree, Charles J., Jr.
Parsons, Charles D.
Putnam, Hilary
Rawls, John
Reibetanz, S. Sophia
Robana, Abderrahman
Rorty, Amelie Oksenberg
Roush, Sherrilyn
Sachs, John R.
Sander, Frank E A
Scanlon, T.M.
Scheffler, Israel
Shapiro, David Louis
Singer, Irving
Sohn, Louis Bruno
Steiker, Carol S.
Stendahl, Krister
Stone, Alan Abraham
Strugnell, John
Thomas, Douglas L.
Thomas, Owen Clark
Trautman, Donald T.
Tribe, Laurence Henry
Tu, Wei-Ming
Vacek, Edward Victor
Vagts, Detlev F.
Walen, Alec D.
Warren, Alvin C., Jr.
Weberman, David
Wedgwood, Ralph N.
Weinreb, Lloyd L.
Wilkins, David Brian
Williams, Preston N.
Wills, Lawrence M.
Winston, Kenneth Irwin
Wolfman, Bernard
Yee, Gale A.

Carlisle
Russell, C. Allyn

Charlestown
Schiavona, Christopher F.

Chestnut Hill
Blanchette, Oliva
Braude, Benjamin
Byrne, Patrick Hugh
Cahill, Lisa Sowle
Cleary, John J.
Deleeuw, Patricia Allwin
Egan, Harvey Daniel
Groome, Thomas H.
Gurtler, Gary M.
Haskin, Dayton
Himes, Michael J.
Monan, James Donald
Morrill, Bruce T.
Pope, Stephen J.

Dorchester
Strang, J.V.
Thompson, Cynthia L.

Essex
Buckley, Thomas W.

Fall River
Kaufman, William E.

Framingham
Joseph, Stephen

Jamaica Plain
Abrahamsen, Valerie
Denby, David A.
Sands, Kathleen M.

Serequeberhan, Tsenay

Lawrence
Wigall, Steve R.

Lynn
Cahoone, Lawrence
Fox, Samuel

Marlborough
Burris, John, Jr.

Medford
Bauer, Nancy
Bedau, Hugo Adam
Cartwright, Helen Morris
Dennett, Daniel C.
Krimsky, Sheldon
Mcconnell, Jeff
Meagher, Robert Francis
Rubin, Alfred P.

Newton
Baron, Charles Hillel
Fontaine, Carole R.
Holladay, William Lee
John, P.M.
Katz, Sanford Noah

Newton Centre
Carlston, Charles E.
Everett, William J.
Fackre, Gabriel Joseph
Howe, Ruth-Arlene W.
Pazmino, Robert W.

North Adams
Silliman, Matthew R.

North Andover
Kitts, Margo
Ledoux, Arthur

Northampton
Connolly, John M.
Derr, Thomas Sieger
Donfried, Karl P.
Lazerowitz, Alice Ambrose
Moulton, Janice
Unno, Taitetsu

Norton
Ekman Ladd, Rosalind
Ladd, Rosalind Ekman

Nutham
Stylianopoulos, Theodore

Paxton
Bilodeau, Lorraine

Quincy
Braaten, Laurie

Sherborn
Chung, Chai-sik

Somerville
Trigilio, Jo
Wan, Sze-Kar
White, Marsha
Zong, Desheng

South Hadley
Berkey, Robert Fred
Crosthwaite, Jane Freeman
Ferm, Deane William
Yamashita, Tadanori

South Hamilton
Beale, Gregory
Besancon Spencer, Aida
Clark Kroeger, Catherine
Davis, John Jefferson
Gibson, Scott M.
Gruenler, Royce Gordon
Isaac, Gordon L.
Kaiser, Walter C., Jr.
Kline, Meredith George
Lints, Richard
Mounce, William D.
Niehaus, Jeffrey J.
Padilla, Alvin
Polischuk, Pablo
Pratico, Gary D.
Richardson, Kurt A.
Robinson, Haddon W.

Henrich, Sarah
Hillmer, Mark
Hopper, David Henry
Huffman, Douglas S.
Hultgren, Arland
Hultgren, Arthur J.
Jacobson, Diane L.
Keifert, Patrick
Kimble, Melvin
Kittelson, James
Koester, Craig R.
Kolb, Robert
Kolden, Marc
Laine, James W.
Laumakis, Stephen J.
Limburg, James
Martinson, Paul V.
Martinson, Roland
Miller, Roland
Nestingen, James A.
Nichol, Todd W.
Nysse, Richard W.
O'Hara, Mary L.
Olson, Roger E.
Patton, Corrine
Paul, Garrett E.
Paulson, Steven
Penchansky, David
Pinn, Anthony B.
Polk, Timothy H.
Ramshaw, Elaine Julian
Reiter, David Dean
Schweigert, Francis J.
Simpson, Gary M.
Simundson, Daniel J.
Snook, Lee E.
Sponheim, Paul R.
Stewart, Melville Y.
Stromberg, James S.
Sundberg, Walter
Swanson, Carol B.
Thronveit, Mark A.
Tiede, David L.
Timmerman, Joan H.
Volz, Carl A.
West, Henry Robison
White, David Benjamin
Willis, Robert E.
Windley, Susan M.
Zachary, Steven W.

St. Peter
Clark, Jack Lowell

Winona
Byman, Seymour David

MISSISSIPPI

Boston
Davis, Willie J.
Sherwood, Wallace Walter
Soden, Richard Allan
Walker, Charles Ealy, Jr.

Clinton
Fant, Gene C., Jr.

Hattiesburg
Browning, Daniel C.
Holley, David M.
Paprzycka, Katarzyna
Wood, Forrest E., Jr.

Jackson
Ammon, Theodore G.
Bennett, Patricia W.
Brown, Kristen M.
Curry, Allen
Davis, Ralph
Deterding, Paul E.
Easley, Ray
Harvey, James Cardwell
Hoffecker, W. Andrew
Long, Paul
Mitias, Michael Hanna
Rankin, Duncan
Smith, Steven G.
Tashiro, Paul Y.
Ury, M. William
Wan, Enoch
White, Frankie Walton
Whitlock, Luder

Kosciusko
Cox, Howard A.

Lorman
Bristow, Clinton, Jr.

Natchez
West, George Ferdinand, Jr.

Oxford
Harrington, Michael L.
Lawhead, William F.
Lynch, Michael P.
Westmoreland, Robert B.

University
Davis, Robert N.
Harrington, Michael Louis
Wilson, Charles Reagan

MISSOURI

Canton
Gossai, Hemchand

Colombia
Bien, Joseph J.

Columbia
Bondeson, William B.
Crowley, Sue Mitchell
Fischer, David Arnold
Kultgen, John
McBain, James F., Jr.
Raitt, Jill
Santos, Sherod
Weirich, Paul

Columbus
Rueda, Ana

Fayette
Burres, Kenneth Lee

Fulton
Mattingly, Richard Edward

Hannibal
Bergen, Robert D.

Jefferson City
Mattingly, Susan Shotliff

Kansas City
Bangs, Carl
Berger, Mark
Berman, Jeffrey B.
Brady, Jules M.
Bredeck, Martin James
Carter, Warren
Cooper, Corinne
Dunlap, Elden Dale
Feagin, Susan Louise
Ferguson, Kenneth D.
Hood, Edwin T.
Howell, John C.
Hoyt, Christopher R.
Jones, William Paul
Kobach, Kris W.
Lambert, Jean Christine
Levit, Nancy
Matthaei, Sondra
McCarty, Doran Chester
Miles, Delos
Moenssens, Andre A.
Popper, Robert
Raser, Harold E.
Reitz, Charles
Richards, Edward P.
Schultz, Joseph P.
Sweetman, Brendan M.
Townes, Emilie M.
Venable Powell, Burnele
Verchick, Robert R.
Walter, Edward F.

Kirksville
Hsieh, Dinghwa Evelyn

Lees Summit
Nanos, Mark D.

Liberty
Chance, J. Bradley
David, Keith R.
Horne, Milton P.

Louis
Jones, David Clyde

Nevada
Byer, Inez

Parkville
Gall, Robert S.

Springfield
Browning, Peter
Burgess, Stanley M.
Cotton, Roger D.
Ess, Charles
Hedrick, Charles Webster
Luckert, Karl Wilhelm
Moran, Jon S.
Moyer, James Carroll
Shields, Mary
Shields, Mary E.

St. Louis
Anderson, Vinton Randolph
Arand, Charles P.
Bartelt, Andrew H.
Bayer, Hans F.
Bechtel, Will
Berman, Scott
Berquist, Jon L.
Blackwell, Richard Joseph
Bourke, Vernon Joseph
Brauer, James L.
Brown, Eric
Burns, J. Patout, Jr.
Cargas, Harry James
Charron, William C.
Clarke, Anne-Marie
Danker, Frederick W.
Davis, Lawrence H.
Dorsey, Elbert
Doyle, James F.
DuBois, James M.
Feuerhahn, Ronald R.
Finney, Paul Corby
Friedman, Marilyn A.
Fuss, Peter L.
Gaffney, John Patrick
Gass, William Howard
Gerard, Jules Bernard
Gibbs, Jeffrey A.
Goergen, Donald J.
Gordon, Robert M.
Gordon, Robert Morris
Greenfield, Michael M.
Greenhaward, David M.
Heil, John P.
Jackson, Carol E.
Joy, Peter
Karamustafa, Ahmet T.
Klass, Dennis
Kleingeld, Pauline
Levie, Howard Sidney
Levin, Ronald Mark
Magill, Gerard
Mandelker, Daniel Robert
McGlone, Mary M.
Munson, Ronald
Nagel, Norman E.
Nelson, Lynn Hankinson
Norwood, Kimberly Jade
Ordower, Henry M.
Parr, Chris
Paulson, Stanley Lowell
Raabe, Paul R.
Raj, Victor A.R.
Rawling, J. Piers
Rosin, Robert L.
Ross, Stephanie A.
Roth, Paul A.
Rowold, Henry
Sale, Mary
Schuchard, Bruce G.
Searls, Eileen H.
Shapiro, Henry L.
Thro, Linus J.
Toribio, Josefa
Tuchler, Dennis John
Voelz, James W.
Watson, Richard Allan
Wellman, Carl
Weninger, Robert
Wesselschmidt, Quentin F.
Zuck, Lowell H.

University City
Trotter, Griffin

Warrensburg
Cust, Kenneth F.T.
Selvidge, Marla J.

MONTANA

Bozeman
Shaw, Marvin C.

Great Falls
Taylor, Jon

Helena
Ferst, Barry Joel
Hart, John
Lambert, Richard Thomas

Missoula
Elliott, Deni
Harrington, Henry R

NEBRASKA

Blair
Madsen, Charles Clifford

College Park
Bub, Jeffrey

Fremont
Hansen, Carl L.

Hastings
Walker, James Silas
Watts, James W.

Kearney
Glazier, Stephen D.
Martin, Thomas

Lincoln
Audi, Robert
Becker, Edward
Berger, Lawrence
Cahan, Jean
Casullo, Albert
Crawford, Dan
Crump, Arthel Eugene
Denicola, Robert C.
Eskridge, Chris W.
Heckman, Peter
Hoffman, Peter Toll
Hugly, Philip
Lepard, Brian
Mendola, Joseph
Newman, Lex
Penrod, Steven D.
Perlman, Harvey
Pitt, David
Potter, Nelson
Potuto, Josephine R.
Sayward, Charles
Steiner, Vernon J.
Thorson, Norm
Turner, John D.
van Roojen, Mark
Von Eckardt, Barbara
White Crawford, Sidnie
Works, Robert G.

Norfolk
Donaldson, Daniel J.
Dykstra, Wayne A.
Huddleston, Mark

Omaha
Andrus, Kay L.
Blizek, William L.
Brooks, Catherine M.
Burke, Ronald R.
Cederblom, Jerry
Conces, Rory J.
Edler, Frank H. W.
Fenner, G. Michael
Freund, Richard A.
Green, Barbara S.
Green, J. Patrick
Hamm, Michael Dennis
Hauser, Richard Joseph
Jensen, Tim
Kuo, Lenore
Larson, David A.
Lawson Mack, Raneta

Mahern, Catherine
Mangrum, R. Collin
Newman, Andrew
Okhamafe, Imafedia
Palmer, Russ
Palmer, Russell W
Pieck, Manfred
Roddy, Nicole
Santoni, Roland J.
Schultenover, David
Shaffer, Nancy E.
Shanahan, Thomas Joseph
Shkolnick, Rodney
Shugrue, Richard E.
Strom, Lyle E.
Teply, Larry L.
Volkmer, Ronald R.
Whitten, Ralph U.

NEVADA

Las Vegas
Appell, Annette Ruth
Bybee, Jay S.
Finocchiaro, Maurice A.
McAffee, Thomas B.
Shanab, Robert
Tobias, Carl William
Tominaga, Thomas T.
Wallis, James
Walton, Craig

Reno
Achtenberg, Deborah
Axtell, G.S.
Hoffman, Piotr
Lucash, Frank S.
Marschall, John Peter
Nickles, Thomas
Tobin, Frank J.
Williams, Christopher

NEW HAMPSHIRE

Canaan
Spalding, Christopher J.

Durham
Brockelman, Paul
Christie, Drew
De Vries, Willem
deVries, Willem
Dusek, Rudolph Valentine
Dusek, Val
Frankfurter, David
McNamara, Paul
Sample, Ruth
Triplett, Tim
Westphal, Kenneth R.
Whittier, Duane Hapgood
Witt, Charlotte

Hanover
Breeden, James Pleasant
Doney, Willis
Gert, Bernard
Green, Ronald Michael
Moor, James H.
Penner, Hans Henry

Keene
Lee, Sander H.
Lee, Sander H.

Manchester
Berthold, George Charles
Huff, Peter A.

Nashua
Tavani, Herman

Peterborough
Donelan, James

Plymouth
Leibowitz, Constance

Delmar
Baskin, Judith R.

Dobbs Ferry
Ephraim, Charlesworth W.
Foster, James Hadlei

Douglaston
Lauder, Robert Edward

East Aurora
Kubicki, Judith M.

Eden
Dumain, Harold

Elmhurst
Dude, Carl K.

Farmingdale
Friel, James P.

Floral Park
Callender, Carl O.

Flushing
Altman, Ira
Fontinell, Eugene
McManus, Edgar J.
Pecorino, Philip Anthony

Fly Creek
Kuzminski, Adrian

Fredonia
Belliotti, Raymond A.
Kohl, Marvin

Garden City
Lasky, Geoffery
Lewis, Lloyd Alexander, Jr.

Garrison
Sharpe, Virginia A.

Geneseo
Cook, William Robert
Edgar, William John
Soffer, Walter

Geneva
Baer, Eugen Silas
Daise, Benjamin
Gerhart, Mary
Lee, Steven Peyton

Greenvale
Berleant, Arnold
Brier, Bob

Hamilton
Buehler, Arthur
Carter, John Ross
Glazebrook, Patricia
Irwin, Joyce Louise
Jacobs, Jonathan
McCabe, David
McIntyre, Lee C.
Plata, Fernando
Rubenstein, Eric M.
Terrell, Huntington
Vecsey, Christopher
Wetzel, James
Wetzel, James Richard
Witherspoon, Edward, Jr.

Hammondsport
Gilmour, John C.

Harrison
Pepper, George B.

Hastings on Hudson
Forman, Robert

Hemlock
Eberle, Rolf A.

Hempstead
Holland, Robert A.
Pearl, Leon
Teehan, John
Wallace, Kathleen

Houghton
Schultz, Carl
Tyson, John R.

Huntington
Klein, Richard

Ithaca
Bailey, Lee
Benson, LeGrace
Carmichael, Calum Macneill
Clermont, Kevin Michael
Cramton, Roger C.
Hodes, Harold T.
Hutcheson, Richard E.
Kates, Carol A.
Kingsbury, John Merriam
McKenna, Michael S.
Palmer, Larry Isaac
Pinch, Trevor J.
Powers, David Stephen
Rachlinski, J.J.
Rendsburg, G.A.
Schwab, Stewart J.
Sherry, John E.H.
Simson, Rosalind S.
Smith, Daniel L.
Summers, Robert Samuel
Wolfram, Charles W.

Jackson Heights
Walsh, Jerome T.

Jamaica
Gregory, David L.
Satterfield, Patricia Polson
Slattery, Kenneth F.
White, Howard A.
White, Leland J.

Katonah
Nnoruka, Sylvanus I.

Lawrence
Wurzburger, Walter S.

Loudonville
Boisvert, Raymond
Dick, Michael B.
Meany, Mary Walsh
Zaas, Peter S.

Louisville
Burkey, John

Lynbrook
Langiulli, Nino Francis

Mount Vernon
Shaw, Susan J.

New Paltz
Heath, Eugene

New Rochelle
Deignan, Kathleen P.
Jonas, Hans
O'Neill, William George
Pilant, Craig Wesley

New York
Addams, Robert David
Alexakis, Alexander
Arkway, Angela
Awn, Peter
Babich, Babette E.
Balmer, Randall
Barnes, Joseph Nathan
Baumbach, Gerard
Baumrin, Bernard Herbert
Bell, Derrick Albert, Jr.
Bernstein, Richard J.
Berofsky, Bernard A.
Bleich, J. David
Boghossian, Paul
Borg, Dorothy
Borradori, Giovanna
Boyle, Ashby D., II
Braxton, Edward Kenneth
Brickman, Lester
Capra, Daniel J.
Carman, Taylor
Carpenter, James Anderson
Castelli, Elizabeth
Christopher, Russell L.
Cohen, Burton I.
Cohen, Martin Aaron

Cone, James H.
Cunningham, L.A.
Cunningham, Sarah Gardner
Davies, Brian
de Grazia, Edward
de Vries, Paul
Deutsch, Celia
Diller, Matthew
Dinkins, David N.
Donohue, John Waldron
Dorsen, Norman
Dougherty, Ray Cordell
Driver, Tom Faw
Farnsworth, Edward Allan
Feerick, John David
Feingold, Henry L.
Felsenfeld, Carl
Field, Hartry
Fine, Kit
Fletcher, Robert E.
Fogelman, Martin
Foti, Veronique Marion
Fox, Eleanor M.
Fox, Eleanor M.
Franck, Thomas M.
Freeman, James B.
Fritsche, Johannes
Ganz, David L.
Gardner, Richard Newton
Garfinkel, Stephen Paul
Garro, A.M.
Gillman, Neil
Gluck, Andrew L.
Gottwald, Norman Karol
Gourevitch, Victor
Govan, Reginald C.
Gowans, Christorher W.
Grad, Frank P.
Graham, William C.
Gray, Ronald A.
Greco, John
Green, Judith
Greenawalt, Robert Kent
Gurinder, Singh Mann
Gyug, Richard F.
Halberstam, Malvina
Halberstam (Guggenheim), Malvina
Halivni, David
Hamilton, Charles Vernon
Han, Jin Hee
Hardy, Michael A.
Hasker, R. William
Hauser, Thomas
Hawley, John Stratton
Haywoode, M. Douglas
Heidt, Sarah L.
Heller, Agnes
Henkin, Louis
Hoeflin, Ronald K.
Iannuzzi, John N.
Irvine, Dale T.
Isasi-Diaz, Ada Maria
Johnson, John W.
Johnson, Patricia L.
Jones, Judith A.
Jones, William K.
Kamm, Frances Myrna
Katsoris, Constantine N.
Kaufmann, Frank
Kelbley, Charles A.
Kennedy-Day, Kiki
Kenny, Alfreida B.
Korn, Harold Leon
Kraemer, David
Kristeller, Paul Oskar
Kuhns, Richard
Lackey, Douglas Paul
Lamm, Norman
Landes, George Miller
Landesman, Charles
Lapidus Lerner, Anne
Lawergren, Bo
Levi, Isaac
Lieberman, Jethro K.
Lienhard, Joseph T.
Lindt, Gillian
Lowenfeld, Andreas F
Lusky, Louis
Mann, Gurinder Singh
Marcus, David
Marsh, James L.
Martinez, H. Salvador
Martyn, James Louis
McGowen Tress, Daryl
McLaughlin, Joseph M.
Menke, Christoph
Meron, Theodor
Miller, Danna R.

Millstein, Ira M.
Mothersill, Mary
Muller, Ralf
Mullin, Robert Bruce
Myers, David
Nagel, Thomas
Nelkin, Dorothy
Nikulin, Dmitri
Olitzky, Kerry M.
Ostertag, Gary
Parker, Kellis E.
Parker, Kellis E.
Patry, William F.
Patterson, Mark R.
Pearce, Russell G.
Perillo, Joseph M.
Price, Monroe E.
Proudfoot, Wayne
Quigley, Timothy R.
Quinn, Thomas Michael
Rabinowitz, Mayer E.
Reese, Thomas
Reichberg, Gregory M.
Reid, John Phillip
Reidenberg, Joel R.
Riggins, Thomas
Rosenfeld, Michel
Rosenthal, David M.
Roth, Joel
Rubin Schwartz, Shuly
Rubinstein, Ernest
Rudenstine, David
Sanders, John E.
Santa Maria, Dario Atehortua
Schneider, Samuel
Schroeder, Jeanne L.
Schwartz, William
Scott, Gregory L.
Segal, Alal Franklin
Segal, Alan
Seiple, David I.
Shaw, Theodore Michael
Sherwood, O. Peter
Shriver, Donald W.
Simmelkjaer, Robert T.
Slater, Peter
Smit, Hans
Smith, Terry
Soffer, Gail
Somerville, Robert
Sorensen, Roy
Sovern, Michael I.
Sovern, Michael I.
Sproul, Barbara Chamberlain
Stambaugh, Joan
Stone, S.L.
Strauss, Peter L.
Szasz, Paul Charles
Tancredi, Laurence Richard
Terezakis, Katie
Thomas, Kendall
Tillers, Peter
Toote, Gloria E.A.
Tubb, Gary
Tucker, Gordon
Tudy Jackson, Janice
Turetzky, Nachum
Ulanov, Ann Belford
Urban Walker, Margaret
Uviller, H. Richard
van Buren, John
Varzi, Achille C.
Visotzky, Burton I.
Walker, Wyatt Tee
Walsh, James Jerome
Walton, R. Keith
Wang, Hao
Washington, James Melvin
Way, Gary Darryl
Webber, George Williams
Weisberg, Richard H.
Weisberg, Richard Harvey
Weisenfeld, Judith
Westphal, Merold
Whelan, Stephen T.
Whitebook, Joel
Williams, Kyle
Wimbush, Vincent L.
Wink, Walter
Winston, Diane
Wishart, Lynn
Wright, John Robert
Yovel, Yirmiyahu
Zagano, Phyllis
Zito, Angela
Zweig, Arnulf

Newburgh
Cotter, James Finn

Niagara University
Bonnette, Dennis
Waters, Raphael Thomas

Nyack
Crockett, William
Nilsson, Donal E.
Thayer, H.S.

Ogdensburg
Rocker, Stephen

Oneonta
Burrington, Dale E.
Green, Michael
Koch, Michael
Koddermann, Achim
Malhotra, Ashok Kumar
Roda, Anthony
Shrader, Douglas Wall, Jr.

Orangeburg
Lounibos, John

Ossining
deVries, Paul

Oswego
Echelbarger, Charles G.

Peekskill
Kaebnick, Gregory E.

Pomona
Kolak, Daniel

Port Jefferson
Schievella, P.S.

Potsdam
Tartaglia, Philip

Poughkeepsie
Amaru-Halpern, Betsy
Brakas, Jurgis
Cladis, Mark S.
Fortna, Robert Tomson
Jarow, E.H.
Lott, John Bertrand
Neill, Warren
Van Norden, Bryan W.

Purchase
Clark, Mary T.

Queensbury
Muscari, Paul G.

Riverdale
Meyers, Michael
Rubsys, Anthony L.
Zukowski, Edward, Jr.

Rochester
Beck, Lewis White
Cadorette, Curt R.
Couture, Pamela D.
Curren, Randall R.
Doolittle, James
Engerman, Stanley Lewis
Feldman, Richard Harold
Gordon, Dane R.
Holmes, Robert Lawrence
Homerin, T. Emil
Karaban, Roslyn A.
Kollar, Nathan Rudolph
Laidlaw, E.A.
Lemke, Werner Erich
May, Melanie A.
Meerbote, Ralf
Sanders, John T.
Sullivan, Mary C.
Sullivan, William Joseph
Wenderoth, Christine
Wierenga, Edward Ray

Rockville Centre
Foster, Matthew

Rye
Bernstein-Nahar, Avi K.

Saratoga Springs
Denzey, Nicola
Weller, Eric John

Root, Michael
Sager, Allan Henry
Scanlan, James P.
Stebenne, David
Strasser, Mark
Taylor, Walter F., Jr.
Thomas, Carolyn
Turnbull, Robert George
Warrener Smith, Susan
Whaley, Douglas John
White, Janice G.
Williams, Gregory Howard

Dayton
Anderson, William P.
Barnes, Michael H.
Barr, David Lawrence
Benson, Paul H.
Branick, Vincent P.
Chinchar, Gerald T.
Doyle, Dennis M.
Fischer, Marilyn R.
Fouke, Daniel C.
Gorrell, Donald Kenneth
Griffin, Paul R.
Heft, James L.
Herbenick, Raymond M.
Hertig, Paul
Hertig, Young Lee
Inbody, Tyron Lee
Inglis, John
Jablonski, Leanne M.
Johnson, Patricia Altenbernd
Kim, Ai Ra
Kozar, Joseph F.
Kunkel, Joseph C.
Luke, Brian A.
Lysaught, M. Therese
Martin, Judith G.
Monasterio, Xavier O.
Moore, Cecilia
Mosher Lockwood, Kimberly
Mosser, Kurt
Nelson, James David
Quinn, John F.
Richards, William M.
Tibbetts, Paul E.
Tilley, Terrence W.
Ulrich, Lawrence P.
Welborn, L.L.
Wert, Newell John
Yocum, Sandra Mize
Zimmerman, Joyce Ann

Delaware
Easton, Loyd D.
Mercadante, Linda A.
Michael, Randall Blake
Tannehill, Robert C.
Twesigye, Emmanuel

Findlay
Cecire, Robert C.
Draper, David E.
Kern, Gilbert Richard
Resseguie, James L.
Shilling, Burnette P.
Stulman, Louis

Gambier
Adler, Joseph
Alder, Joseph A.
DePascuale, Juan E.

Granville
Cort, John E.
Lisska, Anthony Joseph
Martin, James Luther
Santoni, Ronald Ernest
Santoni, Ronald Ernest
Woodyard, David O.

Hiram
Slingerland, Dixon

Huber Heights
Puckett, Pauline N.

Kent
Barnbaum, Deborah
Culbertson, Diana
Fischer, Norman Arthuf
Ryan, Frank X.
Wheeler, Arthur M.
Zellner, Harold Marcellars

Marietta
Machaffie, Barbara J.

Milford
Oppenheim, Frank M.

Mount Vernon
Cubie, David Livingston

Munroe Falls
DiPucci, William

New Concord
Barrett, J. Edward
McClelland, William Lester

Newark
Shapiro, Stewart
Shiels, Richard Douglas

Oberlin
Krassen, Miles
McInerney, Peter K.
Merrill, Daniel Davy
Richman, Paula

Oxford
Forshey, Harold Odes
Kane, Stanley
Kelly, Jim Kelly
McKenna, Bill
Momeyer, Rick
Pappu, Rama Rao
Seidel, Asher M.
Sommer, John D.
Ward, Roy Bowen
Williams, Peter W.
Worth, Sarah Elizabeth

Painesville
Miller, Benjamin

Pepper Pike
Gromada, Conrad T.

Reynoldsburg
Rolwing, Richard J.

Shaker Heights
Giannelli, Paul Clark

Springfield
Copeland, Warren R.
Levy, Robert J.
Millen, R.L.
Nelson, Paul T.
Swanger, Eugene R.
Swindler, James Kenneth
Vincent, David
Wolf, Herbert Christian

Steubenville
Miletic, Stephen F.

Stow
Ophardt, Michael

Toledo
Andersen, Roger William
Barrett, John A.
Bourguignon, Henry J.
Bullock, Joan R.
Chapman, Douglas K.
Closius, Phillip J.
Edwards, Richard W.
Eisler, Beth A.
Friedman, Howard M.
Harris, David A.
Hopperton, Robert J.
Jackman, Henry
Kadens, Michael G.
Kennedy, Bruce
Kennedy, Robin M.
Kirtland, Robert
Martyn, Susan
Merritt, Frank S.
Moran, Gerald P.
Mostaghel, Deborah M.
Puligandla, Ramakrishna
Quick, Albert T.
Raitt, Ronald D.
Ray, Douglas E.
Richman, William M.
Steinbock, Daniel J.
Stern, David S.
Tierney, James E.
Zietlow, Rebecca

University Heights
McGinn, Sheila E.

Warren
Eminhizer, Earl Eugene

Wickliffe
Hunter, Frederick Douglas
Latcovich, Mark A.

Wilberforce
Garland, John William

Wilmington
Jones, Thomas Canby

Wooster
Bell, Richard H.
Bucher, Glenn R.
Grillo, Laura
Harris, Ishwar C.
Hustwit, Ronald E.
Scholz, Susanne
Smith, Robert Houston
Thompson, Garrett

Worthington
Handwerk-Noragon, Patricia
Josephson, Goodman
Meier, Samuel

Yellow Springs
Patel, Ramesh
Warren, Scott

Youngstown
Bache, Christopher Martin
Leck, Glorianne Mae
Minogue, Brendan Patrick
Shipka, Thomas A.

OKLAHOMA

Bethany
Tashjian, Jirair S.

Broken Arrow
Lederle, Henry

Norman
Barker, Peter
Boyd, Tom Wesley
De Bolt, Darian C.
Doty, Ralph
Foreman, Jonathan Barry
Hambrick, A. Fred
Merrill, Kenneth Rogers
Scaperlanda, Michael
Walton, Woodrow E.

Oklahoma City
Arrow, Dennis Wayne
Coulson, Richard
Emler, Donald
Gigger, Helen C.

Shawnee
Roberts, Victor William

Stillwater
Cain, James
Converse, Hyla Stuntz
Lawry, Edward George
Luebke, Neil Robert
Scott, Walter Gaylord

Tulsa
Blankemeyer, Kenneth Joseph
Brown, Paul Llewellyn
Goodwin, James Osby
Mansfield, Mecklin Robert
Smith, Dennis E.
Tabbernee, William
Thorpe, Samuel
Vance, Donald Richard

OREGON

Corvallis
Campbell, Courtney S.
Dean Moore, Kathleen
Hosoi, Y. Tim
Leibowitz, Flora L.
List, Peter C.
Moore, Kathleen Dean
Ramsey, Jeff

Roberts, Lani
Scanlan, Michael
Uzgalis, William

Eugene
Forell, Caroline
Hildreth, Richard George
Porter, Samuel C.
Sanders, Jack Thomas
Sheets-Johnstone, Maxine

Forest Grove
Marenco, Marc

Gresham
Alexander, Ralph H.

Hammond
Lambert, J. Karel

Medford
Wells, Donald A.

Monmouth
Cannon, Dale W.
Perlman, Mark

Newberg
Newell, Roger
Oropeza, B.J.

Portland
Balcomb, Raymond
Bernstine, Daniel O.
Blumm, Micahel C.
Borg, Marcus J.
Cook, Jonathan A.
Cox, Chana B.
Danner, Dan Gordon
Dempsey, Carol J.
Donkel, Douglas L.
Duboff, Leonard David
Faller, Thompson Mason
Foulk, Gary J.
Garland, Michael John
Gauthier, Jeff
Havas, Randall E.
Johnnson, Thomas F.
Jones, Shawn
Lass, Tris
Lubeck, Ray
Martin, Ernest L.
Mayr, Franz Karl
Mazur, Dennis J.
Passell, Dan
Peck, William Dayton
Robertson, Teresa
Rohrbaugh, Richard L.
Ross, Jamie
Rottschaefer, William Andrew

Salem
Ackerman, Robert M.
Bartlett, Steven J.
Cameron, David L.
Griffith, Gwendolyn
Hagedorn, Richard B.
Isom, Dallas W.
Misner, Robert L.
Nafziger, James A.R.
Richardson, Dean M.
Runkel, Ross R.
Standen, Jeffery A.
Tornquist, Leroy J.
Vollmar, Valerie J.

St. Benedict
McHatten, Mary Timothy

PENNSYLVANIA

Allentown
Meade, E.M.
Vos, Nelvin Leroy

Ambridge
Whitacre, Rodney A.

Annville
Heffner, John Howard

Ardmore
Kline, George Louis

Bala-Cynwyd
Webb, Gisela

Bethlehem
Baehr, Amy R.
Girardot, Norman J.
Lindgren, John Ralph
Straumanis, Joan
Weiss, Roslyn

Bloomsburg
Hales, Steven

Bryn Mawr
Dostal, Robert J.
Duska, Ronald F.
Krausz, Michael
Lassek, Yun Ja
Prialkowski, Kristoff

California
Walsh, John H.

Carlisle
Pulcini, Theodore

Chambersburg
Buck, Harry Merwyn
Platt, David S.

Clarion
Bartkowiak, Julia

Clarks Summit
Lawlor, John I.
Stallard, Michael D.

Coopersburg
Eckardt, Alice Lyons

Cranberry Twp
Cayard, W.W.

Dallas
Painter, Mark A.

Devon
Wilson, Victor M.

Doylestown
Bittner Wiseman, Mary
Williamson, William B.

Du Bois
Evans, Dale Wilt

East Stroudsburg
Ayers, James R.
Weatherston, Martin

Easton
Bechtel, Lyn
Ziolkowski, Eric Jozef

Edinboro
Drane, James Francis

Elkins Park
Melchionne, Kevin
Murphy, Laurence Lyons

Emmaus
Wainwright, Sue

Erie
Frankforter, Albertus Daniel
Upton, Thomas Vernon

Fleetwood
Lucas, Raymond E.

Gettysburg
Gritsch, Eric W.

Glenside
Thompson, George, Jr.

Greensburg
Grammer, Michael B.

Greenville
Peterson, Greg

Grove City
Bowne, Dale Russell
Trammell, Richard Louis

Halberstam, Michael
Harvey, John D.
Hoppman, R.A.
Hubbard, F. Patrick
Johanson, Herbert A.
Jones, Donald L.
Khushf, George
Lacy, Philip T.
Long, Eugene T., III
Mather, Henry S.
McAninch, William S.
McCullough, Ralph C., II
Medlin, S. Alan
Montgomery, John E.
Nolan, Dennis R.
Owen, David G.
Patterson, Elizabeth G.
Peterson, Brian
Quirk, William J.
Skrupskelis, Ignas Kestutis
Smalls, O'Neal
Sprague, Rosamond K.
Underwood, James L.

Conway
DeWitt, Franklin Roosevelt

Due West
Farley, Benjamin Wirt

Florence
Hall, Ronald L.

Greenville
Beale, David Otis
Block, John Martin
Buford, Thomas O.
McKnight, Edgar Vernon

Greenwood
Archie, Lee C.

Hartsville
Doubles, Malcolm Carroll

Inman
Combes, Richard E.

Myrtle Beach
Rauhut, Nils

Okatie
Fitzgerald, John Joseph

Orangeburg
Gore, Blinzy L.

Pawleys Island
Comfort, Philip W.

Rock Hill
Craighead, Houston Archer
Wright-Botchwey, Roberta Yvonne

Spartanburg
Bullard, John Moore
Keller, James Albert

Sumter
Coyne, Anthony M.
Walsh, David John

SOUTH DAKOTA

Sioux Falls
Leslie, Benjamin C.

Vermillion
Meyer, Leroy N.
Whitehouse, George

Yankton
Frigge, S. Marielle
Kessler, Ann Verona
Kessler, S. Ann

TENNESSEE

Blountville
Charlton, Charles Hayes

Bristol
Fulop, Timothy E.

Chattanooga
Hall, Thor
Jacobs, David C.
Lippy, Charles
Resnick, Irven M.
Stewart, William H.
Switala, Kristin
Switala, Kristin

Clarksville
Gildric, Richard P.

Cleveland
Bowdle, Donald N.
McMahan, Oliver
Moore, Rickie D.
Simmons, William A.
Waldrop, Richard E.

Germantown
Cox, Steven L.
Miller, Stephen R.

Jackson
Chambers, Alex A.
Davenport, Gene Looney
Dockery, David S.
Gushee, David P.
Whitehead, Brady, Jr.

Jefferson City
Hawkins, Merrill M.

Johnson City
Fesmire, Steven A.
Gold, Jeff
Hardwig, John R.
Keith, Heather
LaFollette, Hugh
Rogers, Kim W.
Shanks, Niall
Shields, Bruce E.
Stenstad, Gail
Zavodny, John

Knoxville
Alexakos, Panos D.
Aquila, Richard E.
Bennett, James O.
Cohen, Sheldon M.
Edwards, Rem B.
Freeman, Edward C.
Nelson, James L.
Perhac., Ralph M.
Speidell, Todd

Lenoir City
Wilson, Jack Howard

Memphis
Batey, Richard A.
Bensman, Marvin Robert
Bufford, Edward Eugene
Chambliss, Prince C., Jr.
Dekar, Paul R.
Favazza, Joseph A.
Lacy, William Larry
Lewis, Jack Pearl
Limper, Peter Frederick
McKim, Donald K.
Muesse, Mark William
Nenon, Thomas J.
Prince, Arthur
Reed, Ross Channing
Robinson, Hoke
Shoemaker, David W.
Simco, Nancy Davis
Todd, Virgil H.
Walsh, Carey Ellen
Wharton, A.C., Jr.

Milligan College
Farmer, Craig S.
Kenneson, Philip D.

Murfreesboro
Bombardi, Ronald Jude
Watson, Daivd Lowes
Young, David

Nashville
Baldwin, Lewis V.
Belton, Robert
Birch, Adolpho A., Jr.

Blumstein, James Franklin
Brown, R.L.
Butler, Trent C.
Charney, Jonathan Isa
Compton, John J.
Cooper, Almeta E.
DeHart, Paul
Fields, Milton
Fisher, Eli D.
Graham, George Jackson
Haas, Peter J.
Hambrick, Charles Hilton
Handy, William Talbot, Jr.
Harrelson, Walter
Harrod, Howard L.
Haynes, William J., Jr.
Hester, D. Micah
Hodges, Michael P.
Hodgson, Peter C.
Hooks, Benjamin Lawson
Johnson, Dale Arthur
Lachs, John
Maier, Harold Geistweit
McCoy, Thomas Raymond
McFague, Sallie
Miller-McLemore, Bonnie Jean
Millgram, Elijah
Moss, C. Michael
Nancarrow, Paul S.
Owens, Dorothy M.
Patte, Daniel
Picirilli, Robert Eugene
Reid, Garnett
Schrag, Oswald O.
Syverud, K.D.
Teselle, Eugene A.
Thompson, Almose Alphonse, II
Varnado, Douglas
Winfrey, Charles Everett
Zaner, Richard

Petros
West, James E.

Sewanee
Armentrout, Donal Smith
Battle, Michael
Hawkins, Ralph K.
Rhys, J Howard W.

Sewanne
Conn, Christopher

TEXAS

Abilene
Ellis, Robert
Ferguson, Everett
Foster, Douglas A.
Guild, Sonny
Osburn, Carroll D.
Shuler, Philip L.
Slate, Philip
Van Rheenen, Gailyn

Arlington
Bing, Robert
Bradshaw, Denny
del Carmen, Alex
Polk, Elmer

Austin
Angelelli, Ignazio Alfredo
Baade, Hans Wolfgang
Bauder, Mark
Bonevac, Daniel Albert
Braybrooke, David
Causey, Robert Louis
Colvin, Christopher
Dearman, John Andrew
Floyd, Michael H.
Graglia, L.A.
Hamilton, Robert W.
Higgins, Kathleen Marie
Hildebrand, David
Hull, Richard T.
Kane, Robert
Lewis, Randy Lynn
MacKey, Louis Henry
Martinich, Aloysius Patrick
Mersky, Roy Martin
Moore, T.J.
Mourelatos, Alexander Phoebus Dionysiou
Parker, Joseph Caiaphas, Jr.
Pennock, Robert T.

Ratner, Steven Richard
Roberts, Kathryn L.
Seung, Thomas Kaehao
Solomon, Robert Charles
Weinberg, Steven
Weintraub, Russell Jay
Woodruff, Paul
Wright, Charles Alan

Belton
Reynolds, J. Alvin
Von Wyrick, Stephen
Wyrick, Stephen V.

Bryan
Botham, Thad M.

Canyon
Githiga, John Gatungu

College Station
Allen, Colin
Aune, James Arnt
Burch, Robert W.
Davenport, Manuel Manson
Gert, Heather
Hand, Michael
Harris, Charles Edwin
McCann, Hugh Joseph
McDermott, John J.
Menzel, Christopher
Pappas, Gregory F.
Radzik, Linda
Smith, Robin
Varner, Gary Edward

Conroe
Matheny, Paul Duane

Corpus Christi
Sencerz, Stefan

Dallas
Babcock, William Summer
Bock, Darrell L.
Burns, J. Lanier
Deschner, John
Furnish, Victor Paul
Howe, Leroy T.
James, H. Rhett
Mabery, Lucy
McCullagh, Mark
McKnight, Joseph Webb
Merrill, Eugene H.
Nobles, Patricia Joyce
Ogden, Schubert Miles
Ortiz, Victor
Rollins, Richard Albert
Santillana, Fernando
Shuman, Daniel Wayne
Thornburg, E.G.
Tinsley, Fred Leland, Jr.
Tyson, Joseph B.
Wallace, Daniel B.
Wood, Charles M.

Denton
Barnhart, Joe Edward
Emery, Sarah W.
Gunter, Pete A.Y.
Sibley, Jack Raymond
Yaffe, Martin David

El Paso
Best, Steven
Hall, David
Hall, David Lynn
Simon, Julius J.

Fort Worth
Babler, John
Brehm, H. Alan
Brisco, Thomas V.
Brister, C.W.
Dale Lea, Thomas
Flowers, Ronald Bruce
Garrett, James Leo
Garrett, Robert I., Jr.
Gouwens, David J.
Johnson, Rick L.
Kent, Dan Gentry
Kirkpatrick, W. David
Lea, Thomas Dale
Lovejoy, Grant I.
Lyon, Steve
Mathis, Robert
McBeth, Harry Leon
Middleton, Darren J. N.

Schmidt, Daryl Dean
Stevens, Paul W.
Suggs, Marion Jack
Toulouse, Mark G.
Tucker, William E.
Welch, Robert H.
Wertz, S.K.

Galveston
Carter, Michele A.
Vanderpool, Harold Young

Georgetown
Gottschalk, Peter
Hobgood-Oster, Laura
Spellman, Norman Woods

Houston
Barksdale, Leonard N., III
Beard, James William, Jr.
Bongmba, Elias Kifon
Brody, Boruch Alter
Bullock, James
Carroll, Beverlee Jill
Crowell, Steven G.
Douglas, James Matthew
Engelhardt, Hugo Tristram, Jr.
Foreman, Peggy E.
Gilmore, Robert McKinley, Sr.
Gilmore, Vanessa D.
Grandy, Richard E.
Hall, Benjamin Lewis, III
Hillar, Marian
Jefferson, Overton C.
Johnson, Caliph
Kitchel, Mary Jean
Klein, Anne
Kulstad, Mark Alan
Lanning, Bill L.
Lobel, Diana
McCullough, Laurence B.
McMullen, Mike
Nelson, William N.
Parsons, Keith M.
Schiefen, Richard John
Shelp, Earl E.
Wagner, Paul Anthony
Waits, Va Lita Francine
Walker, Stanley M.
Wyschogrod, Michael

Huntsville
Fair, Frank Kenneth
Harnsberger, R. Scott
Patrick, Darryl L.

Irving
Balas, David L.
Boomer, Dennis
Frank, William A.
Lehrberger, James
Lowery, Mark
Norris, John Martin
Pacwa, Mitch
Parens, Joshua
Rosemann, Philipp W.
Sepper, Dennis L.
Simmons, Lance
Smith, Janet E.
Wood, Robert

Kileen
Van Dyke, Brian D.

Lake Kiowa
Wolfe, Robert F.

Longview
Farrell, Hobert K.
Hummel, Bradford Scott
Woodring, Andrew N.

Lubbock
Averill, Edward W.
Bubany, Charles Phillip
Curzer, Howard J.
Ketner, Kenneth Laine
Lewis, Peter J.
Nathan, Daniel O.
Patty, Stacy L.
Ransdell, Joseph M.
Schaller, Walter E.

Marshall
Miller, Telly Hugh
Potts, Donald R.

Spokane
Baird, Forrest
Bynagle, Hans Edward
Cook, Michael L.
Dallen, James
Doohan, Helen
Edwards, James R.
Edwards, James R.
Graham, J. Michele
Hartin, Patrick John Christopher
Mohrlang, Roger L.
Pomerleau, Wayne Paul
Sittger, Gerald L.
Sittser, Gerald
Stronks, Julia K.
Tyrrell, Bernard James
Wyma, Keith D.
Yoder, John C.

Steilacoom
Pilgrim, Walter E.

Tacoma
Alward, Lori L.
Arbaugh, George E.
Edwards, Douglas R.
Eklund, Emmet Elvin
Govig, Stewart D.
Ives, Christopher
Kay, Judith Webb
Nordby, Jon Jorgen
O'Connell Killen, Patricia
Oakman, Douglas
Pinzino, Jane M.
Skover, David
Staley, Jeffrey L.
Stivers, Robert L.

Vancouver
Dawn, Marva J.

Vashon Island
Lone, Jana M.

Yakima
Matsen, Herbert S.

WEST VIRGINIA

Buckhannon
Welliver, Kenneth Bruce

Elkins
Phipps, William Eugene

Huntington
Henderson, Herbert H.
Vielkind, John N.

Morgantown
Basu, Ananyo
Cohen, Debra R.
Drange, Theodore Michael
Eichorn, Lisa
Elkins, James R.
Jokic, Aleksander
Maxey, B. Ann
Meitzen, Manfred Otto
Morris, William O.
Potesta, Woodrow A.
Selinger, Carl Marvin
Shapiro, Daniel
Vehse, Charles T.
Wicclair, Mark Robert
Wigal, Grace J.

Parkersburg
Allen, Bernard Lee

West Liberty
Gold, Jonathan

WISCONSIN

Appleton
Boardman, William Smith
Dreher, John Paul
Ternes, Hans
Thompson, Leonard Leroy

De Pere
Abel, Donald C.
Kersten, Frederick Irving

Wadell, Paul J.

Eau Claire
Gross, Rita M.
Picart, Caroline Joan Kay S.

Germantown
Beck, John A.

Kenosha
Cress, Donald Alan
Hauck, Allan
Lochtefeld, James G.
Maczka, Romwald
Magurshak, Daniel J.
von Dehsen, Christian D.

La Crosse
Barmore, Frank E.

Lake Geneva
Slocum, Robert B.

Madison
Baldwin, Gordon Brewster
Brighouse, M.H.
Buhnemann, Guldrun
Card, Claudia F.
Dickey, Walter J.
Eells, Ellery T.
Enc, Berent
Fain, Haskell
Fox, Michael
Galanter, Marc
Harris, Max R.
Hausman, Daniel M.
Jones, James Edward, Jr.
Kamtekar, Rachana
Knipe, David Maclay
Levine, Andrew
MacAulay, Stewart
Melli, Marygold Shire
Miller, Barbara Butler
Schoville, Keith Norman
Singer, Marcus G.
Skloot, Robert
Sober, Elliott Reuben
Thain, Gerald John
Tuerkheimer, Frank M.
Whitford, William C.
Yandell, Keith E.
Zile, Zigurds Laimons

Manitowoc
White, V. Alan

Megrion
Garcia, Albert L.

Mequon
Maschke, Timothy

Milwaukee
Barbee, Lloyd Augustus
Bieganowski, Ronald
Carey, Patrick W.
Conlon, James J.
Copeland, M. Shawn
Del Colle, Ralph
Edwards, Richard Alan
Goldin, Owen Michael
Hockenbery, Jennifer D.
Kolasny, Judette M.
Kurz, William Stephen
Levy, Ian Christopher
Luce, David R.
Maguire, Daniel C.
Misner, Paul
Nardin, Terry
Schaefer, Jame
Spence, Joseph Samuel, Sr.
Teske, Roland John
Twetten, David B.
Wainwright, William J.
Weiss, Raymond L.
Wild, Robert Anthony

Mount Horeb
Steinbuch, Thomas A.

Oshkosh
Burr, John Roy
Cordero, Ronald Anthony
Linenthal, Edward Tabor
Missner, Marshall Howard
Urbrock, William Joseph
Wu, Kuang-Ming

Platteville
Drefcinski, Shane

Ripon
Doss, Seale

River Falls
Gilson, Greg

Shorewood
Nerenberg, Bruce Edward
Wallace, Robert M.

Stevens Point
Bailiff, John
Billings, John R.
Cohen, Andrew I.
Fadner, Donald E.
Herman, Arthur L.
Keefe, Alice Ann
Nelson, Michael P.
Overholt, Thomas William
Vollrath, John F.
Waligore, Joseph
Warren, Dona

Two Rivers
Abele, Robert P.

Watertown
Henry, Carl F.H.

Waukesha
Hemmer, Joseph

Wauwatosa
Scholz, Daniel J.
Starkey, Lawrence H.

Whitewater
Shibles, Warren Alton

WYOMING

Laramie
Dwyer, James G.
Martin, James August
Porterfield, Amanda
Seckinger, Donald Sherman
Sherline, Ed

PUERTO RICO

Bayamon
Pagan, Carmen J.

San Juan
Martinez, Felipe
Pagan, Samuel
Ramos-Gonzalez, Carlos
Ramos-Mattei, Carlos J.

Trujillo Alto
Garcia, Aurelio A.

VIRGIN ISLANDS

St. Thomas
Ballentine, Krim M.

CANADA

ALBERTA

Armena
Jensen, Gordon A.

Calgary
Baker, John Arthur
Hexham, Irving
Jensen, Debra J.
Macintosh, John James
Martin, Charles Burton
Neale, David
Osler, Margaret Jo
Penelhum, Terence M.

Cochrane
Peacock, Kevin

College Heights
Heer, Larry G.
Stefanovic, Ranko

Edmonton
Bowker, Wilbur F.
Cahill, P. Joseph
Frederick, G. Marcille
Ingles, Ernie B.
Kambeitz, Teresita
Krispin, Gerald
Leske, Adrian M.
Oosterhuis, Tom
Page, Sydney
Schouls, Peter A.
Scott, Timothy
Shiner, Roger Alfred
Waida, Manabu
Waugh, Earle Howard
Zvi, Ehud Ben

Lethbridge
Brown, Bryson
O'Dea, Jane
Peacock, Kent
Rodrigues, Hillary
Stingl, Michael
Viminitz, Paul

Mayerthorpe
Zwicky, Jan

BRITISH COLUMBIA

Abbotsford
Abegg G., Martin

Burnaby
Todd, Donald David

Langley
Chamberlain, Paul
Weibe, Phillip H.

New Westminster
Leschert, Dale

Qualicum Beach
Sly, Dorothy

Vancouver
Bakan, Joel
Blom, Joost
Borrows, John
Boyle, Christine
Brunnee, Jutta
Bryden, Philip
Cairns, Hugh A.C.
Edinger, Elizabeth
Egleston, Don
Elliot, Robin
Ericson, Richard
Farquhar, Keith
Franson, Robert T.
Gaston, Lloyd
Grant, Isabel
Grenz, Stanley J.
Head, Ivan
Iyer, Nitya
Kline, Marlee
MacCrimmon, Marilyn
MacDougall, Bruce
MacIntyre, James
McClean, Albert
Mosoff, Judith
Neufeld, Dietmar
Paterson, Robert
Pavlich, Dennis
Potter, Pitman
Pue, Wesley W.
Salzberg, Stephan
Sanders, Douglas
Sheppard, Anthony
Smith, Lynn C.
Stackhouse, John G., Jr.
Weiler, Joseph
Wexler, Stephen

Victoria
Bates, Jennifer
Cassels, Jamie

Casswell, Donald G.
Cohen, David
Coward, Harold G.
Daniels, Charles B.
Ferguson, Gerry
Foss, Jeffrey E.
Foster, Hamar
Galloway, J. Donald C.
Gillen, Mark R.
Heyd, Thomas
Kilcoyne, John R.
Kluge, Eike-Henner W.
Langer, Monika
Lapprand, Marc
Lessard, Hester A.
M'Gonigle, R. Michael
Macleod, Colin
Maloney, Maureen A.
McCartney, Sharon
McDorman, Ted L.
McLaren, John P.S.
Morgan, Charles G.
Morgan, Gerald
Neilson, William A.W.
Petter, Andrew J.
Rae Baxter, Laurie
Robinson, Lyman R.
Taylor, Angus
Thomson, Kathryn
Tollefson, Chris
Tully, James H.
Waldron, Mary Anne
Waters, Donovan W.M.
Young, James O.

MANITOBA

Brandon
Florida, Robert E.

Otterburne
Perry, Tim
Tiessen, Terrance

Winnipeg
Busby, Karen
Creamer, David G.
Day, Peggy
Day, Terence Patrick
Desmond, Lawrence Arthur
Esau, Alvin
Fainstein, Lisa
Harvey, Cameron
Jeal, Roy R.
Klassen, William
Klostermaier, Klaus Konrad
McGillivray, Anne
Penner, Roland
Schwartz, Bryan
Shillington, V. George
Sneiderman, Barney
Stuesser, Lee
Walton, Douglas
Walton, Douglas Neil

NEWFOUNDLAND

St. John's
Langford, Michael J.

NOVA SCOTIA

Antigonish
Berridge, John Maclennan
English, Leona
MacDonald, Burton
Mensch, James

Canning
Parent, Mark

Halifax
Abdul-Masih, Marguerite
Baylis, Francoise
Brett, Nathan C.
Burns, Steven A.M.
Campbell, Richmond M.
Campbell, Susan
Hogan, Melinda
Hymers, Michael
MacIntosh, Duncan
Maitzen, Stephen